Goldmine PRICE GUIDE TO 45 rpm records

3rd EDITION

by Tim Neely

Published by

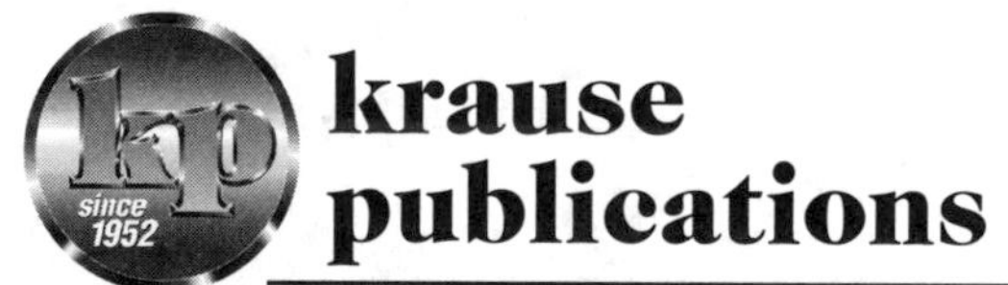

700 E. State Street • Iola, WI 54990-0001
Telephone: 715/445-2214

Please call or write for our free catalog of music publications.
Our toll-free number to place an order or obtain a free catalog is 800-258-0929
or please use our regular business telephone 715-445-2214
for editorial comment and further information.

Library of Congress Catalog Number: 96-76685

ISBN: 0-87349-245-5

Printed in the United States of America

Contents

Introduction to the 3rd Edition

First, I want to thank you for picking up this book. Many of you have read and/or purchased the first two editions of the *Goldmine Price Guide to 45 RPM Records*, for which I also thank you.

With approximately 60,000 7-inch singles of all kinds - regular 45s, extended play singles, even records that play at 33 1/3 rpm but are the size of 45s - the second edition was by far the most comprehensive price guide on singles ever published. Many of you were moved to write us with suggestions, additions and corrections to the listings. Some of those have been incorporated into this third edition, which is the most complete book of 45 rpm singles and values issued in the United States.

Of course, future editions can be even better, and we tell you how to make that possible later in this introduction. But for now, let's fill you in on what to expect in this third edition.

What's new

The *Goldmine Price Guide to 45 RPM Records* continues to evolve. Many of the changes are in response to suggestions from readers. Here are some we've made for the third edition:

- ♦ We've added more than 100 pages to the book. This has enabled us to add many artists with long discographies, mostly in the pop and country realms, that we simply did not have space for in the past.
- ♦ We've made a start on a record label identifying guide. We've listed about 100 different labels, both major and independent, including some you won't find anywhere else, and how to identify when a particular American 45 was pressed. Label variations for singles are quite often different than with LPs.
- ♦ For the first time, we have an eight-page color insert. Here you'll get a rare opportunity to see some obscure and interesting picture sleeves in color, most for the first time in a price guide. Also, we've put in some colored vinyl 45s from the 1940s to the present. Finally, we've included color documentation of variations for a prominent label. We hope to do at least one significant label in each future edition. Who knows, maybe this will be such a popular feature that an entire record label identifying book would be warranted.
- ♦ We've begun to "break up" the listings of multiple performers with the same name. Many of you didn't like that we put every group that used the same name under one common listing. The same name, in some cases, can refer to over a dozen different acts! Often, the music can range from doo-wop to garage rock to smooth R&B to country. When we've been able to verify it with reasonable certainty, we've created separate listings for each of these artists.
- ♦ We continue to add listings for 7-inch extended play singles. They are becoming more popular in the collector's market as they are better documented. We can still use more information, but you'll see that the listings are more complete than ever.
- ♦ Finally, we've got a short feature on the most valuable U.S. 45 - and it's not what you might think it is, unless you're a fan of really obscure music from the 1960s.

What's the same

If you've missed prior editions of this book, where've you been? Seriously, though, there are certain features that our readers have come to expect, and you will be hard pressed to find them anywhere else. These include:

- ■ More individual listings for 45s and picture sleeves than any other book, including soul, rhythm & blues, rockabilly, rock and pop.
- ■ An easy way to track your collection. Every listing is preceded by a check box, so you can use the book to note which records you have.
- ■ The most accurate listings in the hobby. We have tried not to list anything that we could not confirm. This, alas, is not always possible, but there are fewer "phantom" listings in here than in any other price guide.
- ■ Photos you won't find in any other price guide. Among these are a previously undocumented Mamas and the Papas picture sleeve, some rare promotional sleeves, and a few other surprises.

Market trends

45 rpm records remain the most avidly collected music format in the world, despite the best efforts of major record companies to kill them off. This has been true since at least the early 1970s, and it's likely to remain true for quite some time.

That is why, in a world where the pervasive (and sometimes pernicious) influence of online auctions has had a negative effect on albums, the market for 45s remains strong.

You won't find as many, or as dramatic, price increases as we saw between the first and second editions of this book. But there are some general trends:

♦ There has been an increase in interest in hit singles from the 1970s. That's in part because of the renewed interest in 1970s music as a whole. The "common" 1970s single that used to fetch $3 for a near-mint copy now tends toward the $4-$5 mark, and sometimes more.

♦ The Rolling Stones can now safely be put right behind Elvis Presley and the Beatles in worldwide collecting interest. We've added their promotional singles to this edition because of the often vast difference in value between Stones promos and stock copies. Also, their 1978 "Beast of Burden" picture

sleeves had one of the biggest gains in value since the last edition.

♦ Elvis Presley 45s on Sun remain hot. Curiously, unlike most other records, much of the upward action is in lesser-condition copies. People are starting to pay prices for VG or even VG-minus copies of these singles that they would not have paid for near-mint copies a few years ago.

♦ Otherwise, the market has stabilized somewhat from the dizzying ride it was on in the late 1990s. A lot of rare records changed hands in that time. What has happened is that many of those choice items are now in possession of people who want to keep them for a while. Thus, their availability on the open market is drying up. This could create another "boom" in the future if demand stays high.

Grading your records

The maxim to remember when buying (and selling) 45s is this:

Condition is (almost) everything!

If an item is unusually rare or desirable, it may be acceptable in any condition, as you might never see it again. But even with those items with a three- and four-figure value, the better condition a record (or sleeve), the more money it will fetch.

The grading system established by Goldmine magazine many years ago, with the occasional refinement, has become the most widely accepted in record collecting.

Visual or Play Grading?

In an ideal world, every record would be played before it is graded. But the time involved makes it impractical for most dealers, and anyway, it's rare that you get a chance to hear a record before you buy through the mail. Some advertisers play-grade everything and say so. But unless otherwise noted, records are visually graded.

How to Grade

Look at everything about a record - its playing surface, its label, its edges - under a strong light. Then, based on your overall impression, give it a grade based on the following criteria:

Mint (M): Absolutely perfect in every way - certainly never played. Should be used sparingly as a grade, if at all.

Near Mint (NM or M-): A nearly perfect record. Many dealers won't give a grade higher than this, implying (perhaps correctly) that no record is ever truly perfect.

The record should show no obvious signs of wear. A 45 rpm or EP sleeve should have no more than the most minor defects, such as almost invisible ring wear or other signs of slight handling.

Near Mint is the highest price listed in this price guide. Anything that exceeds this, in the opinion of both buyer and seller, is worth significantly more than the highest value in here.

Very Good Plus (VG+): Generally worth 50 percent of the Near Mint value.

A Very Good Plus record will show some signs that it was played and otherwise handled by a previous owner who took good care of it.

Record surfaces may show some slight signs of wear and may have slight scuffs or very light scratches that don't affect one's listening experience. Slight warps that do not affect the sound are OK.

The label may have some ring wear or discoloration, but it should be barely noticeable. The center hole will not have been misshapen by repeated play.

Picture sleeves will have some slight ring wear, lightly turned-up corners, or a slight seam split.

In general, if not for a couple minor things wrong with it, this would be Near Mint. All but the most mint-crazy collectors will find a Very Good Plus record highly acceptable.

This grade is sometimes called Excellent.

Very Good (VG): Generally worth 25 percent of the Near Mint value.

Many of the defects found in a VG+ record will be more pronounced in a VG disc.

Surface noise will be evident upon playing, especially in soft passages and during a song's intro and fade, but will not overpower the music otherwise. Groove wear will start to be noticeable, as will light scratches (deep enough to feel with a fingernail) that will affect the sound.

Labels may be marred by writing, or have tape or stickers (or their residue) attached. The same will be true of picture sleeves. However, it will not have all of these problems at the same time, only two or three of them.

Very Good is the lowest value we list in here. This, not the Near Mint price, should be your guide when determining how much a record is worth, as a dealer will rarely pay you more than 25 percent of its Near Mint value. (He/she has to make a profit, after all.)

Good (G), Good Plus (G+): Generally worth 10-15 percent of the Near Mint value.

Good does not mean Bad! A record in Good or Good Plus condition can be put onto a turntable and will play through without skipping. But it will have significant surface noise and scratches and visible groove wear (on a styrene record, the groove will be starting to turn white).

A sleeve will have seam splits, especially at the bottom or on the spine. Tape, writing, ring wear or other defects will start to overwhelm the object.

If it's a common item, you'll probably find another copy in better shape eventually. Pass it up. But if it's something you have been seeking for years, and the price is right, get it...and keep looking to upgrade.

Poor (P), Fair (F): Generally worth 0-5 percent of the Near Mint price.

The record is cracked, badly warped, and won't play through without skipping or repeating. The picture sleeve is water damaged, split on all three seams and heavily marred by wear and/or writing.

Except for impossibly rare records otherwise unattainable, records in this condition should be bought or sold for no more than a few cents each.

Common collecting abbreviations

In addition to the letters used to designate a record's grade, it's not uncommon to see other abbreviations used in dealer advertisements. Knowing the more common ones helps to prevent confusion. Here are some:

boot: bootleg (illegal pressing)
cc: cut corner
co: cutout
coh: cut-out hole
cov, cv, cvr: cover
demo: demonstration record (synonym for promo, this is the more common term overseas)
dh: drill hole
dj: disc jockey (promotional) record
ep: extended play (can be used for both 45s and LPs)
gf: gatefold (cover)
imp: import
ins: insert
lbl: label
m, mo: monaural (mono)
m/s: mono/stereo (usually used to describe a promo single that has the same song on both sides, with the only difference in the type of sound)
nap: (does) not affect play
noc: number on cover
nol: number on label
obi: not actually an abbreviation, "obi" is the Japanese word for "sash" and is used to describe the strip of paper usually wrapped around Japanese (and occasional US) pressings of LPs.
orig: original
pr, pro, promo: promotional record
ps: picture sleeve (the cover that appears with some 45s and most 7-inch extended play singles).
q: quadraphonic
re: reissue
rec: record
repro: reproduction
ri: reissue
rw: ring wear
s: stereo
sl: slight
sm: saw mark
soc: sticker on cover
sol: sticker on label
ss: still sealed
s/t: self-titled
st: stereo
sw: shrink wrap
toc: tape on cover
tol: tape on label
ts: taped seam
w/: with
wlp: white label promo
wobc: writing on back cover
woc: writing on cover
wofc: writing on front cover
wol: writing on label
wr: wear
wrp: warp
xol: "x" on label

Some notes on the pricing

The prices listed in this book were determined from many sources.

The more common items reflect a consensus of used record shops and collectors, plus prices in ads over the past few months. In some ways, these items are more difficult to get a handle on; they sell without much publicity because of their low value, thus they aren't reported as often.

The rarer items are often the matter of conjecture because they so rarely come up for public sale. A high auction price for a truly rare piece can be the only way such an item's "worth" can be gauged, no matter what someone says about the value being inflated. Records, as with all collectibles, are only worth what someone will pay for them.

Because of the inexact nature of this undertaking, that's why we always urge you to use a book such as this as a guide and not as the final word on pricing.

We, too, can always use more input on the subject. See the **How you can help** section for more information.

And by the way, the publisher of the book does not engage in the buying and selling of records. So the prices listed in here should not be construed as "offers to buy" or "offers to sell" from Krause Publications.

Some notes on promotional records

I am often asked about promotional 45s (other terms for the same thing include, but are not limited to, "promo" or "demonstration" or "audition copy" or "record prevue" or "D.J. copy"). "I have such-and-such a record, but it's a promo. How do I determine the value?"

First, I can't see us ever attempting to list every promotional counterpart to every record listed in this book. To do so would be a consumption of space better used for unique listings. It would come close to doubling the length of the book. Some selected promos are listed, either because they are unique — in other words, the only version of the record is promotional, or the promo came on colored vinyl — or because there is a significant, verifiable price difference between the promo and stock copies. In other words, most unlisted promo 45s go for a price range not too far removed from the stock copy equivalent. (The biggest exception here is Elvis Presley.) There is also usually a verifiable premium attached to Columbia, Epic and related labels' "Demonstration Only - Not For Sale" picture sleeves of the 1980s. They usually bring from 50 to 100 percent more than the listed values, unless a different value is listed separately.

Another rule of thumb when it comes to promos: In most cases, the more valuable a stock copy is, the less valuable the promo is. That's because in these instances, there are fewer stock copies known to exist than the promos.

Finally, in this book, we treat the vast majority of post-1990 singles — including so-called "For Jukeboxes Only!" releases on the Capitol family of labels — as regular stock copies, unless marked otherwise on the label.

Making sense of the listings

We've told you about most of the features in the book. Let's break down a listing to see what a line means.

The artist's name is in bold, all capital letters. They are mostly alphabetized the way our computer did, so blame any things that seem out of order on it.

Underneath some artists are cross-references or other information we feel is helpful. Cross-references to other artists in the book are in all capital letters. In some cases, we know that the artist name actually was used by several different acts. When we haven't been able to ascertain with certainty which ones are which, they are left together.

When we have separated the artists, the most famous (usually, but not always, the most collectible) will be listed first, usually with the number (1) in parentheses after it. (The exceptions are artists whose fame or number of records overshadows all others with the same name, or those who rarely used "The" before their name, such as Eagles, Outlaws and Pretenders.) The rest will be arranged alphabetically by record label and will be followed by the appropriate parenthetical number, (2), (3) and so on. This way, you'll know if there is more than one entry for the same artist name; only those names listed more than once will have the supplementary number. If a number is skipped, it's because in our database we have only albums but no singles listed by that act. Any that we don't know where they go will be listed last with a (U) for Unknown after it.

Then we have grouped the discographies by record label. Under each record label are individual listings in numerical order, ignoring prefixes. The exception is the RCA Victor label. We first list the APBO series numerically, then the PB/GB series numerically (ignoring the letters), then finally the 1949-73 records in order of prefix.

Each line starts with a check box, which you can use to keep track of what you have. Then comes the record number. You'll also find both sides of each record listed (using chart data or double-sided promo copies to try to list the A-side first), separated by a slash (or a double slash in some cases); the year of release; and the value in Very Good, Very Good-Plus and Near Mint condition.

For many listings, you'll see a letter or two in brackets after the record number. These designate something special about the listing as follows:

DJ: some sort of promotional copy, usually for radio stations, and not meant for public sale

M: mono record (for late-1950s and early-1960s records that came out in both mono and stereo)

PS: picture sleeve (this is the value for the sleeve alone; combine the record and sleeve value to get an estimated worth for the two together)

S: stereo record (again, when the record was pressed both in mono and stereo)

(x) where x is a number: the number of records in a set

In some cases, the VG and/or the VG+ columns have no listed price. That indicates that the item in question goes for under $2 in that condition. All items should have at least a Near Mint value. For those that have no value in any column, an explanation usually follows.

Finally, some items have lines in italics following them. That defines something about the item listed above, such as who also is on the record, or a color of label or vinyl.

With extended play singles, the songs on each are listed in the order they appear on the record where known, separated by slashes. A double slash indicates the end of Side 1 and the start of Side 2. Some contents listings are preceded by an asterisk (*). This indicates that the songs that follow are the contents of the EP, but we're not 100 percent sure that this is the exact order. Help on clarifying these is appreciated.

Selling your records

At some point, perhaps after looking through this book, you may decide that you want to sell your collection. Good for you! And you want to take them to your local used record store with the idea that you'll get the prices you see in this book. Bad for you!

What the values in here reflect are *retail* prices - what a collector might pay for the item from a dealer, and not what a dealer will pay a collector for resale. Too many non-collectors (and even some collectors) don't understand that.

I know one dealer who has told me that he won't buy records from someone who tells him they consulted a price guide first. While that is extreme, it shows the distrust some dealers have for books like this and how the public uses (and abuses) them.

Just as importantly, the highest values are for records in the best condition (re-read the section on "Grading your records"). And there is a reason for that: Truly pristine records are very difficult to find! This is especially true for the hits and other sought-after discs of the 1950s and 1960s. Many collectors are willing to pay handsomely for them - but for many of the records in this book, Near Mint examples aren't even known to exist!

One reason we've expanded the price listing to three grades of condition is to reflect that. There's a tendency to look at the highest price listed for something and assume that's what your record is worth. More realistically, though, such a small percentage of records are truly Near Mint - especially from the 1950s and 1960s and earlier - that your own records, if you were a typical accumulator and not a collector, are considerably less than Near Mint.

Even if you do end up trying to sell to a dealer, choose him or her carefully. It's always best to find someone who has a customer base for your kind of records.

There is only one way you'll be able to get anything close to the prices listed for most items, and that's to sell them direct to the collector.

The "old-fashioned" way is through record collecting magazines. The oldest and most widely read remains *Goldmine*, which was founded in 1974. Published every two weeks, the magazine is loaded with ads from people selling records of all kinds and from all eras. *Goldmine* has advertising salespeople who will help you put your ad together for maximum impact. To see what *Goldmine* is about, pick up a copy. It is available at all Tower Records stores in the U.S., most Barnes and Noble and Borders bookstores and hundreds of independent record dealers. If you still can't find a copy, call 1-800-258-0929.

The "new" way to sell records and other memorabilia is over the Internet. The most popular method is through the online auction, and the most popular of these sites is eBay (www.ebay.com).

Online selling seems to draw two widely different audiences. One is very much the same audience as a stand-alone record store, except on a global scale rather than a regional one. Browsers who know next to nothing about record collecting and the relative scarcity of the listed pieces are common. These are people who can sometimes be fooled into paying too much for a common piece, especially certain million-selling compact discs, because of three magic letters: "OOP," short for "out of print." Just because something's out of print doesn't mean it has vanished off the face of the earth!

The other audience drawn to online sales are the hyper-specialists, and this is often where items can justifiably go for much larger sums than in a retail store. Thanks to search engines on most of the better sites, a fan of, say, the Beach Boys can type in the words "Beach Boys" and find nothing but the Beach Boys-related material. People who specialize in one artist will usually pay more - sometimes a lot more - than someone who collects a more broad range of artists. But because they are specialists, they also know which items are common, so they don't get taken on the easy stuff.

I have bought records over the web, and have yet to have significant problems. It's faster than "snail mail" and less expensive than a long-distance telephone call. But it's not perfect. Just as in real life, it pays to be wary.

As a seller, you are reaching a larger audience than you would in a record collecting magazine, but also a much less targeted one. The Internet seems to be a good place to sell lower-priced items that might take up valuable space in an expensive print ad. But many more valuable pieces sit or fetch less than they might through more traditional means.

Also, many sellers have found that eBay overreacts if you say you are selling a promo. Promos are an accepted part of record collecting; there's even an entire book on collecting promotional records and CDs, and it's from the same publisher as this book. Despite that, eBay can, and does, remove these items, almost at random, for no good reason. (It's one thing if you're selling an advance copy of a CD that hasn't been issued to the general public yet. It's another to try to sell a 25-year-old vinyl promo.) So if you're selling promos, be aware of this.

Finally, we've found that some sellers, especially those who also sell by more "traditional" means such as stores or mail-order catalogs, are souring on the online auction because of the number of bidders who fail to follow through on their winning bids.

As a buyer, you have to watch out for overgraded, under-described items. Photos of the items help. Also, buying from someone who deals in records as a primary area rather than as an obvious sideline to his/her Beanie Baby business is recommended. Look for dealers with strong feedback ratings; that is a sign of satisfied customers. Also, check for use of something resembling the Goldmine grading system. People who say their albums are in "good condition" don't know record collecting, because "good" is a low grade in the world of records (as it is in some other collecting areas, such as coins).

Also as a buyer, don't be afraid to e-mail the seller if you have any questions about the item. If you don't get a satisfactory answer, or get no answer at all, don't bid.

Finally, if you have the winning bid - by all means, honor it!

We feel the online world will continue to grow in importance over time. At some point it may become the biggest market for collectible records. So we'll continue to keep an eye on it. But even with its growth, it's still far from eclipsed other proven selling methods.

The Most Valuable American 45? Not What You Might Think

Over the years, several different American 45s have held the unofficial title of "most valuable." Most recently, the first U.S. single by the Beatles, "My Bonnie" by Tony Sheridan and the Beat Brothers on Decca, held that crown. But for the third edition of the *Goldmine Price Guide to 45 RPM Records*, we introduce a new MVP (most valuable platter). It's a record that most Americans probably have never heard of, much less heard!

According to Pete Smith, a British dealer in so-called "Northern Soul" music, the American 45 of "Do I Love You (Indeed I Do)" by Frank Wilson, on Soul S-35019, sold for 15,000 pounds (roughly $24,000 U.S.) to a disc jockey in Scotland in late 1998. That price dwarfs the $17,000-plus paid for a mint copy of Elvis Presley's "That's All Right" on Sun in October 1998. In this book, we list the near-mint value of the Wilson disc at $20,000, but should the Wilson disc ever come up for auction again, that could be very conservative.

Unlike Elvis' Sun debut, which is relatively common for a four- or five-figure disc, the Wilson record is truly rare.

Only two legitimate copies of "Do I Love You" are known to exist, both promos. In 1993, the better of the two copies, a near-mint example, sold for $12,500 to a British collector, which is about where we listed the value in the last edition of this book. It's on the want lists of hundreds, if not thousands, of Northern Soul collectors; its availability on a legitimate British Motown CD has not diminished the demand for the original. Nor has the fact that the UK issue of this song on 45 (Tamla Motown TMG 1170), released in 1979 because of the demand for the original, can be found for about 20 pounds.

This record is little known outside the world of Northern Soul, a catch-all term coined in the early 1970s to describe the kind of soul music played in the clubs of Northern England and Scotland. (Combine the "Carolina beach music" club scene with the collecting fanaticism of many vocal group fans, and add in a dash of the competitiveness of hip-hop DJs, and you get an idea what Northern Soul is about.) "Do I Love You" by Frank Wilson has long been the Holy Grail to these collectors, who are as fanatic as they come. Songs that Americans ignore completely become treasured rarities overseas.

Wilson, not to be confused with J. Frank Wilson of "Last Kiss" fame, was a staff arranger and composer at Motown. Not as well known as such giants as Holland-Dozier-Holland and Whitfield-Strong, he still had his share of involvement with hits. Among the songs he co-wrote were "Love Child" and "Up The Ladder To The Roof," both hits for the Supremes; he was the co-producer of "Keep On Truckin'" by Eddie Kendricks.

But it's his one and only single release that sets Northern Soul fans' hearts on fire.

In the fall of 1998 the following ad appeared on a UK web site dedicated to Northern Soul: "FOR SALE BY AUCTION. ULTRA RARE northern soul 45's including Frank Wilson Soul 35019 - mint, original copy. All material is in the $1,000.00 minimum bid range. SERIOUS enquiries (sic) ONLY." It then gave a mailing address for bidders to use.

An Edinburgh, Scotland club DJ named Kenny Burrell (no known relation to the jazz artist of the same name) was the high bidder on the ultimate Northern Soul collectible. Since then, Burrell has been known to actually play his $24,000 record in a club. From another Northern Soul web site comes this eyewitness report from a club in Edinburgh called the Spiders Web from February of 1999: "Kenny Burrell closed down the night and played a piece of vinyl I did not have to ask to identify and ... had to leave the toilet to ensure that it was being played from the vinyl. I could not get too close to the decks due to the number of people on the dance floor but I can confirm I saw a Stanton 500 cutting through the grooves of Frank Wilson's 'Do I Love You'."

How you can help

This book has approximately 70,000 listings by thousands of artists. All of this information is housed in a growing database of records, which will make both future price guides and *Goldmine* magazine better products.

As you look through this third edition of the *Goldmine Price Guide to 45 RPM Records*, you'll see we've filled in some holes, but we've created some new ones in the process. And as before, we ask your help in the process to make this the most complete and accurate book of its kind.

While any information is helpful, here are some of the areas where we rely heavily on your input to improve:

Picture sleeves, both real and imaginary. Previously unknown sleeves are popping up all the time. Do you have a picture sleeve for a record that none is listed as being available? First, make sure it's a United States sleeve (it will usually say "Printed in U.S.A." somewhere on it, and it won't refer to any other nation), then let us know. We'll probably ask for photocopies or scans of both sides to confirm its authenticity.

Also, we've pointed out some sleeves that, based on all available evidence, we don't believe really exist, even though others have claimed that they do. Some of these "phantom" sleeves have been deleted; others remain in the book, ready to be removed. Any information on these sleeves, too, is appreciated.

Jukebox singles and EPs. From the early 1960s to the middle 1970s, many record labels made special 7-inch, usually stereo, 33 1/3 discs with small holes. These were made for special jukeboxes. Early on, these singles were like regular 45s, with one song per side. But for the most part, they were "mini-LPs" or, as one brand was called, "Little LPs." Most of these EPs had three songs per side and came with shrunken, two-tone renderings of the LP cover and a strip of jukebox title strips. We've begun documenting these, but more information is needed.

Regular EPs and "contents unknown" listings. Thanks to help from readers like you, we've filled in hundreds, if not thousands, of these extended-play listings. But there are still many gaps. If you can help us with them, we appreciate it. But if you can be accurate, we appreciate it even more.

Anywhere you see the words "(contents unknown)," we'd like to know exactly what's on the record. What we need is side 1 and side 2, plus sleeve variations. As the titles of extended plays are often not listed on the records, we feel that actually listing the songs will be of greater help to the collector.

For the best results, follow these guidelines:

- Use the *record*, not the jacket, to determine the exact order of songs. Often, the titles on the sleeve are arranged to look better and don't necessarily correspond to the playing order.
- Not all EPs list Side 1 and Side 2 explicitly. So how do you tell? Look for the master numbers, which are usually found below the main number. On most EPs, the master number for Side 1 is one smaller than the master number for Side 2. For example, one of the Conway Twitty EPs listed in these pages has a Side 1 master number of "59-EP-33" and a Side 2 number of "59-EP-34." Another example: One of the Elvis Presley EPs has a Side 1 master number of "G2WH-7209" and a Side 2 number of "G2WH-7210." You get the idea.

Also, on those EP listings with an asterisk before the contents, we need confirmation of the exact order of tracks.

So if you're an EP collector, you can play a big role in helping us.

Basically, we'd like to know about anything you know about an artist's U.S. records that isn't in the book.

We receive many letters, phone calls and e-mails, so we can't acknowledge all of them. But rest assured that your correction or addition, whether it be one item or hundreds, helps in the long run.

You can contact the author by mail:

Tim Neely
Goldmine Price Guide to 45 RPM Records, 3rd Edition
700 E. State St.
Iola, WI 54990

or by phone:

(715) 445-2214 or 4612, ext. 782 (I am available most weekdays from 8 a.m.-5 p.m. Central Time)

or by e-mail:
neelyt@krause.com

Please include a *daytime* telephone number with all correspondence so I can reply in case I have questions.

Acknowledgments

Once again, I'd like to thank everyone who bought either the first or second edition, or both, of the *Goldmine Price Guide to 45 RPM Records*. I'd especially like to thank all those who sent me feedback, both positive and negative. Many were inspired to correct errors, both of omission and commission. In addition to the U.S. and Canada, I received letters and other correspondence from England, Germany, Belgium, Italy and Israel, among others. It's gratifying to know that we reach a worldwide record collecting community that cares about getting it right.

I'd also like to thank the many people who have written in response to another book, the *Goldmine Standard Catalog of American Records 1950-1975.* As there is some overlap in material, many people who send corrections for that book have their material appear here first. As recently as the second edition came out, some people sent me information that I've already been able to incorporate into this volume. Many of you (over 150 names!) I thanked in the second edition of the Standard Catalog; I thank you all again.

I especially want to thank Alan Lowell of Beverly, Mass., for his help. He has contributed many of the rare and interesting picture sleeves you see, both in the color section and throughout the book. A big help as always was Thomas Grosh of Very English and Rolling Stone in Lancaster, Pa. Joel Whitburn of Record Research in Memomonie Falls, Wis., and Greg Berry of Fast Hits Music in Merideth, N.H., helped fill in gaps, sometimes where I didn't know there even was one. Thanks, too, to British record dealer Pete Smith for the heads-up on the new "most valuable 45." And also, I wish to thank Good Rockin' Tonight, the auction house in California, for its continued help. Some of the rarities pictured in this book are from their quarterly auctions of rare and desirable records. For more information, visit their web site located at www.goodrockintonight.com or call (949) 833-1899 or (800) 531-1899.

At Krause Publications, I wish to thank Bill Krause, the head of the books division, and Debbie Bradley, managing editor, for their ideas. Thanks, too, to Greg Loescher, *Goldmine* magazine editor, and Cathy Bernardy, associate editor, for their continued support. Also, thanks to Jeff Kenton and Bonnie Tetzlaff for their computer help, and to the Krause proofreading, art and production staff members for their contributions.

Finally, at home I wish to thank my mother, Judith Neely, and my siblings, Sue Turchick, Mary Woerner, Eileen Neely and Nancy Beard, for always being there. And God, without whom none of this would be possible.

Tim Neely
March 2001

Record Label Identifier

For the most part, the most collectible records are original pressings. Those are the ones that presumably were available when the 45 was first pressed.

The biggest exceptions are in the catalogs of those artists who transcend almost all the rules — The Beatles and Elvis Presley. Some late-1960s Capitol pressings of Beatles 45s go for several times the originals because they are so outrageously rare. And the same is true of orange-label RCA Victor Presley EPs.

That said, though, most collectors who aren't out to get every variety of every 45 prefer an original edition. If not for this, there would be even more of a difference between these scarce repressings and the originals.

Most hit 45s, after a time, were deleted from record company catalogs. In their place, companies created reissue series with various names, such as "Gold Standard Series" (RCA Victor), "Hall of Fame Series" (Columbia), "Starline" (Capitol), "Back to Back Hits" (Warner Bros.), and my two favorite names, "Revival of the Fittest" (Island) and "Amnesia Series" (I.R.S.). Sometimes, entire labels dedicated to almost nothing but reissues sprang up; the most frequently encountered of these are Lost-Nite, Lana, Eric and Collectables. These reissues are almost always worth a small fraction of the originals that are listed in this book.

Not all labels had oldies series, though. Decca, for example, never had a formal reissue series. (The 25500 series, sometimes considered to be a reissue line, had as many new titles as reissues in it.) Thus the label kept the same pairings and number in print for decades in some cases, changing only the label design. For example, Bing Crosby's "White Christmas," first issued on 45 in 1950, exists on three different Decca labels, all with the same catalog number. Even on labels with a reissue series, some titles remained in print with their original numbers for years. Capitol seemed to do this most often, as not only did Beatles 45s keep their original catalog numbers until 1981, but so did some Beach Boys singles, Nat King Cole's "The Christmas Song" and, of all things, Robert Mitchum's "The Ballad of Thunder Road"!

Thus this rough guide to help you date 45s.

One big warning before we go into the list: There can be significant overlap between label designs. This usually happens for one of two reasons. First is that, at the major labels, the order of release may not exactly coincide with the order the numbers were assigned. Sometimes, a single release will be delayed or accelerated, which means that some singles with earlier numbers may be "original" on a later label variation than later ones. Second, most of the independent labels farmed out their manufacturing to independent pressing plants. If a record was in high demand, a plant sometimes used whatever label was available, even if it was the wrong color or an older design. (Thus the numerous variations of Beatles 45s on Vee Jay.) This rarely happened with the majors.

And another thing: This identifier only deals with regular 45s. 78s and EPs are not covered.

Eventually, with your help, we'd like this to be even more thorough. Instead of listing label variations by approximate year of changeover, we'd like to nail down exact numbers (or at least as close as possible) where a label changed from one to another. Sometimes, because of printing plant overlap, this will not be possible. But the closer we get, the better the guide gets.

We'd also like information on labels we chose to omit this time around, either because we don't know or because the information we do have is confusing.

By the way, this guide does not attempt to delve into the various promotional labels record companies used. The most common variant is a white version of the label that was in use at the time. But not always; some labels used pink, blue, lime green or cream labels (just to name a few shades of the rainbow); some used the same labels as stock copies and added promotional wording to the typesetting or a star to the A-side; still others didn't do promos at all.

Enough ado, let's go:

A&M

1962: Light brown label with brown print.

1962-late 1973: Brown label, A&M trumpet logo in white box at left.

Late 1973-early 1981: Silver gray label with fading A&M logo.

Early 1981-mid 1986: Red label, black ring along outer edge.

Mid 1986-late 1986: White label with black strip through center hole and A&M logo at right.

Late 1986-late 1989: Black label with white strip through center hole and A&M logo at right.

Late 1989-late 1990: Dark blue label.

Late 1990-1995: Red label.

1996-1999: Tan label, new A&M logo at upper left.

2000: White label.

ABC/ABC-PARAMOUNT

1955-65: "ABC-Paramount" along top of label with rainbow design underneath.

1966: Label becomes simply "ABC." First issues had black labels with "ABC RECORDS" in two lines in silver print at top.

1966-67: Black label, "abc" in white circle at top, no box around outside.

1967-72: Black label, "abc" in white circle at top with multi-color box around outside.

1973: Very short-lived label; black with white triangle at top and "ABC" in children's blocks inside.

This label was gone by mid-1973 and replaced by the 1967-72 design until a new label could be created.

1974-77: Multi-colored (yellow, orange, purple) "target" label with "abc Records" at top of label between two lines.

1977-79: Multi-colored (yellow, orange, purple) "target" label with "abc" in an eighth note at top of label.

In 1979, the label was bought by MCA, which quickly replaced current ABC singles with tan-label MCA issues with the same number.

ABC DUNHILL

See DUNHILL.

ABKCO

Allan Klein's reissue label, singles have light blue labels with a darker blue logo above the center hole.

ACE

1955 (500-504): Black label.

1955 (505-511): Yellow label.

1955 (512): Blue label.

1955-57 (513-527): Yellow label.

1957-58 (528-553): White label, catalog number at bottom.

1958-62 (554-600s): White label, catalog number at right.

1962-63 (8000s): Yellow label.

Some records in the 570s also exist on purple labels.

ALADDIN

1950-54 (3000s through 3259): Blue label.

1954-57 (3260-3399): Maroon label.

1957-end (3400-end): Black label.

ARISTA

1975-mid 1976: White label, blue "Arista" logo at top.

Mid 1976: Light blue label, black "Arista" logo at top.

Late 1976-early 1977: Light blue label, white "Arista" at top.

Early 1977-1978: Black label, blue "Arista" logo at top.

1979-1983: Fading blue label.

1984-1990: Black label, "ARISTA" above multicolor mountain skyline.

1991-97: Black label, "ARISTA" above white mountain skyline.

Late 1990s country issues: White and green label.

APPLE

1968-75: Green "Granny Smith" apple label on one side, sliced apple on the other. Some, though not all, singles from 1968-70 had a line of small white print on the sliced side with "A Subsidiary of Capitol Industries, Inc." along the bottom and a tiny Capitol logo. The small print appears only to have been used at one Capitol pressing plant, so two 45s could both be originals, yet one will have the "Capitol logo" and the other won't.

1975: "All Rights Reserved" disclaimer added to the label print.

Some 45s have unsliced apples on both sides; others have custom apples; others have custom labels that don't include an apple.

ARGO

1956-57: Black label, silver print, ship at top.

1957-60: Black label, silver print, "ARGO" vertically at left.

1960-65: Tan label. There is some overlap with the 1957-60 label.

ASYLUM

1972-73 (11000 series): White label, "door-in-a-circle" logo at top of label.

1973-74: "Clouds" label, door at top, "ASYLUM" to left of door, "RECORDS" to the right.

1974-84: "Clouds" label, door at top, "ASYLUM RECORDS" above door. Around 1975, a small "W" (Warner Communications) logo was added to the label print.

1976: Some 45s in this era were issued with a solid blue label with a small "a" at the top. All of these also exist with the clouds label.

1985-89: Split black and yellow label.

1992-95 (reactivated label): Light blue label.

1996: White label.

ATCO

1955-57: Maroon label.

1957-77: White and yellow label.

1978-mid 1980s: Gray label

Mid 1980s-end: White label, "ATCO" in multi-colored letters at top.

ATLANTIC (pop)

1951-56: Yellow and black label, no "fan" logo at lower left. (In the 1970s, some Atlantic singles were reissued with the yellow and black labels and the original catalog numbers, but these all have the "fan" logo on them and are not as collectible as the originals.)

1956-62: Red and black label, no "fan" logo at lower left.

1963-90: Red and black label with "fan" logo at lower left. Most of the changes to this label were subtle.

1990-present: Purple and black label.

Some 45s were issued with custom labels.

BANG

1966-73 (500 series, early 700s): Yellow label with "BANG records" gun logo at top.

1974-78 (711?-740): Sky blue label with clouds and stylized "BANG" curving around the top.

1979-82 (Columbia distribution): Light brown label, red logo on top.

BARNABY

1970-73 (CBS distribution): Light blue label, treble clef logo at left.

1973 (MGM distribution): White label with line drawing.

1974-79 (distributed by GRT/Janus): Multicolor label, yellow rim, vinyl record hanging limply from tree. Early pressings of 601 have white labels with no graphic elements.

BELL

1954-early 1960s: Bell was a budget label. Three distinct label designs are known, which may or may not overlap. Some have yellow and black labels; some have white and black labels; some have blue labels with silver print and "BELL RECORD" along top outer edge and a bell underneath.

1965-69: Blue label, silver print.

1970-74: Silver label, black print.

BIG TOP

All have pink labels.

BIG TREE

1970-71: Red and yellow label.

1971-74: Red and white label.

1974-76: Light blue and red label.

1976-80: Multicolor label.

BRUNSWICK

1950-53 (80000 and 84000 series): Black label, silver print.

1957-60 (reactivated label, 55000-55166): Maroon label, silver print.

1960-63: (55167-55250): Orange label, black print.

1963-1970s (55251-up): Black label, arrow-shaped color bars.

BUDDAH

1967 (1-no later than 22): Green label, black print. This label also exists on Buddah 31.

1967-72 (no later than 23-low 300s?): Multi-color kaleidoscope label with black drawing of Buddha at bottom and "BUDDAH RECORDS" on either side of drawing.

1972-77: Maroon label with smiling Buddha figure, "BUDDAH RECORDS" in white at top.

1978-end: Black label, new logo at top, Arista logo added at bottom.

CADENCE

1953-54 (1230-1237): Maroon or red label with silver "JULIUS LA ROSA" at top of label with his image. (Yes, all these were by Mr. LaRosa.)

1954-61 (1238?-1402?): Maroon lower two-thirds of label; upper third is silver with "cadence" in lowercase and a metronome logo.

1961-64 (1403?-1447): Red label, black rim with "CADENCE RECORDS" inside in white.

CADET

Cadet replaced the Argo label in 1965. Several Argo titles were reissued with Cadet labels (most notably "Book of Love" by the Monotones).

The first label was an all light blue label with "CADET" across the top in black.

The second label was a fading blue label with "CADET" across the top in fading red, white and blue letters.

1971-end (GRT distribution): Yellow label, red rim, horizontal red stripe through center hole, "CADET" at left.

CAMEO

1956: Some very early numbers may exist on dark blue labels.

1957-60 (no later than 105-175?): Orange label, black print, cameo at top.

1960-67: (176?-no earlier than 441): Red and black label, white cameo in yellow border at left.

1967-68 (mid 400s-497; 2000 series): Red and tan label, new logo at top.

CANADIAN-AMERICAN

1959-61 (101-127?): Black label, silver print.

1961-65 (128?-200 series): Black label, five color bars across top of label.

CAPITOL

1949: Purple label, number has a "54-" prefix. Some early Capitol singles also were pressed on red (country), maroon (classical) or yellow (children's) labels.

1950-55: Purple label, "F" prefix before number, large Capitol logo at top.

1956-59: Purple label, "F" prefix before number, much smaller Capitol logo at top.

1959-61: Purple label, Capitol logo at left, title of song at top, artist at bottom.

1961-68: Orange and yellow "swirl" label, Capitol logo at left, title of song at top, artist at bottom. Most singles of this era exist with two different typefaces. The "eastern" editions have taller, lighter title and artist print; the "western" editions have shorter, bolder title and artist print.

Mid 1968-early 1969: Orange and yellow "swirl" label, Capitol logo at left, much smaller title and artist print than either 1961-68 version. They also add the words "A Subsidiary of Capitol Industries" to the perimeter print at the bottom, and almost all of these have a reeded edge around the outside of the label.

Early to mid 1969: Red and orange "target" label with "old" Capitol logo in an oval at left.

Mid 1969-late 1972: Red and orange "target" label with "new" round Capitol logo at left. The black circle above the word "Capitol" will have a white dot in the middle; some may or may not have a thin white circle in the middle of the black circle.

Late 1972-mid 1978: Orange label, olive green "Capitol" at bottom of label. Records by R&B-oriented artists have a red label with a black "Capitol" at bottom.

Mid 1978-mid 1983: Matte-finish purple label. Most of these have a reeded edge around the outside of the label, or have space for one.

Mid 1983-mid 1988: Black label, rainbow ring around outer edge, black print in colorband.

Mid 1988-1991: Glossy purple label, much larger than 1978-83 label with no reeded edge (nor space for one).

1992-present: Glossy purple label, "FOR JUKEBOXES ONLY!" at left. Capitol Nashville and a few non-country Capitol 45s in this series have white labels.

Some Capitol 45s from the 1970s forward were issued with custom labels or "retro" labels.

CASABLANCA

1974 (0000 series): Dark blue label with Bogart mug and "Manufactured and Distributed by Warner Bros. Records Inc." in white along the bottom.

1974-76 (801-856?): Dark blue label with Bogart mug, "Manufactured and Distributed by Casablanca Records Inc." in white along the bottom.

1976-77 (857?-884?): Tan label, desert scene at top, "Casablanca" at top.

1977-81 (885?-2300s): Tan label, desert scene at top, "Casablanca Record and FilmWorks" at top.

1981-end (2300s into six-digit numbers): "Manufactured and Distributed by Polygram" at bottom.

CHANCELLOR

1958-59 (1001-1036?): Pink label, black print.

1959-63 (1037?-end): Black label, silver print, "Chancellor" in red across top of label.

CHECKER

1952-54 (750s to ca. 800): Maroon label with checkerboard (sometimes erroneously called a "web") at top, no "Record Co." under the word "Checker."

1954-57 (801?-876?): As above, except with the words "Record Co." added under "Checker."

1957-63: Maroon label, silver print, "CHECKER" vertically at left.

1963-65: Blue label with black and red checkers. There is plenty of overlap with this label and the above one, though sometimes the old label is more red than maroon.

1965-end: Fading blue label, no checkers on top.

CHESS

1951-57: Blue and silver label, chess pieces on top.

1957-61: Blue label, silver print, "CHESS" vertically at left.

1961-63: Orange, yellow and black label with small "CHESS" horizontally at right. There is some overlap with the above blue label.

1963-66: Black label, "CHESS" in white across top. Again, there is overlap with the above two labels.

1966-72: Fading blue label, "CHESS" across top.

1972-mid 1970s: Orange and blue label.

CHRYSALIS

1972-77: Green label, red butterfly at lower left, "Chrysalis" in red along bottom.

1977-87: White label fading to blue at bottom, white butterfly at lower left, "Chrysalis" in white along bottom.

1987-89: White label, colored butterfly at left.

1989-91: Off-white label, different butterfly logo.

1992-95: White label, "FOR JUKEBOXES ONLY!" at left.

COLUMBIA (pop)

1950-57: Maroon label, gold print.

1957-58: Yellow label, black print.

1959-62: Bright red label, black print.

1962-63: Orange label, title and artist both at bottom.

1963-64: Transitional period; many different color labels (orange, yellow, green, pink, red, possibly others), with artist's name at left and song title at bottom.

1965-70: Red label, black print, artist's name at left (sometimes on its side), song title at bottom.

1970-71: Another transitional period with at least four different labels in use simultaneously: the 1965-70 red label; a new red label with "COLUMBIA" around the outside perimeter in white; an orange label with "Columbia" (mixed case letters) repeated in the background; and an orange label with "COLUMBIA" (upper case letters) repeated in the background.

Mid 1971-mid 1972: Orange label with "COLUMBIA" (upper case letters) repeated in the background.

Mid 1972-early 1973: Gray label.

Early 1973-present: Orange label, "COLUMBIA" in white across the top. Only minor modifications have been made to this label in the almost 30 years since, most notably the addition of a bar code at left in the mid 1980s.

A small number of Columbia 45s since 1973 were issued with custom labels.

CORAL

1950-early 1960s: Orange label. Some scattered records have maroon labels.

Early 1960s-1969: Black label with color bars and "CORAL" logo at left.

COTILLION

1969-72: Red label, "Cotillion" in box at top.

1976-80s: Reactivated label; purple with a round "C" logo at top.

DECCA (pop)

1950-54: Black label, "DECCA" curving at top with lines on either side of the label name.

1955-60: Black label, "DECCA" curving at top, star underneath the first "C" with lines on either side of the star. Mysteriously, some U.S. pressings exist with the 1950-54 label well after this label became predominant.

1960-73: Black label, "DECCA" in five colors of print at left on its side, a rainbow color bar at right.

NOTE: Almost all Decca 45s have the numbers machine stamped in the dead wax, not scrawled in.

Decca was reactivated as a country label in the 1990s. Early 45s from this series have black labels; later ones have purple labels.

DELUXE

1950-52: Black label with "AA" after number.

1953-54: Black label without "AA" after number; "High Fidelity" is NOT on the label.

1955-59: Black label, with "High Fidelity" on label.

1960-end: Yellow label, black print.

DOOTONE/DOOTO

1951-57: Most originals have non-glossy maroon Dootone labels, though some also exist with black or blue labels, and no address on the label.

1957 (412-416): Maroon Dooto label, silver print.

1957-58 (417-440): Yellow label, Dooto logo in red oval.

1958-59 (441-450s, 700s): Yellow label, Dooto logo in blue oval.

1959-61 (450s-465?): Black label, multi-colored print.

1961 (466-471): Brief return of "Dootone" label, red label with multi-color print.

1962 on (472-end): Maroon Dooto label, multi-colored print.

DOT

1950-52: Maroon label, gold print.

1952-53: Yellow label, black print.

1953-56: Maroon label, silver print, "Gallatin, Tenn." address on label.

Mid 1956: Maroon label, silver print, "Hollywood, Calif." address on label. A very short-lived variation.

1956-68: Black label, script "Dot" in multi-color letters at top.

1968-69: Black label, "DOT" in white box at top.

1969-74: Purple and orange label, "DOT" in box at top of label.

1974-75: Multi-colored (yellow, orange, purple) "target" label with "abc Dot Records" at top of label between two lines.

1976-77: Multi-colored (yellow, orange, purple) "target" label with "abc Dot" at top of label between two lines.

DUNHILL

1965-68: Black label, "DUNHILL" in white with gold border at top.

1968-72: Black label, "DUNHILL" and "abc" in multi-colored boxes at top.

1973: "DUNHILL" in a white rectangle spelled out in children's blocks. Very short-lived label. Quickly replaced by 1968-72 label again until another new label was created.

1974-75: Multi-colored (yellow, orange, purple) "target" label with "abc Dunhill" at top of label between two lines.

ELEKTRA

Early 1960s-1966: Gold label.

1966-67 (45601-45615): Yellow and black label, "ELEKTRA" in gold across top, "idol head" and white line above label name.

1967-69: White, black and red label with red and white stylized "E"s on upper half of label.

1969-70: Yellow and black label, single stylized "E" at top, white "X" through entire label. There is some overlap with the above and below labels.

1970-74: Grayish label, caterpillar at top.

1975-79: Green label, butterfly at left. There is some overlap with the 1970-74 label.

1976: Red label, white stylized "E" at top. This was used for only a short time, mostly in late 1976, and all of these also exist with the "butterfly" label.

1979-83: Red label, white stylized "E" at top. This time the label stuck.

1984: White label with new, small Elektra logo at top; a very short-lived label.

1980-89: Red and black label, "ELEKTRA" across top.

1989-91: Gray label.

1991-present: Tan label.

EMBER

1956-58: Red or red-orange label.

1958-60: Pale blue and white label with other colors mixed in, "EMBER" spelled out with flaming logs at top.

1960-end: Black label.

EMI AMERICA/EMI MANHATTAN/EMI

1978-80: Green label.

1980-87: Gray label.

1987-88: (EMI Manhattan) White label, yellow and black design elements.

1989-92: (EMI) Blue label. The 1992 issues have "FOR JUKEBOXES ONLY!" on the label.

1993-97: (EMI) White label, "FOR JUKEBOXES ONLY!" at left.

END

1957: Black label.

1957-59: White label (sometimes appears gray) with two halves of dog at top.

1959-end: Multi-color label with two halves of dog at top.

EPIC

1953-62: Yellow label, black lines around outside of label.

1962-73: Yellow label, black lines around outside of "EPIC" at top of label.

1973-79: Orange label, with white concentric circular lines.

1979-present: Dark blue label, script "Epic" logo.

FRATERNITY

1956-58: Light blue label.

1959-early 1960s: Dark blue label.

Early 1960s: Red label, black print.

Mid to late 1960s and beyond: Maroon label, silver print.

GEFFEN

1980 (only known to exist on early pressings of 49563): Warner Bros. label with "GEFFEN RECORDS" in a box just above the center hole.

1980-85: White label with horizontal pinstripes.

1985-1990s: Black label.

GONE

1957: Black label, "GONE" in "shadow print" at top.

1957-59: Black label, head and open mouth logo inside the letter "O."

1959-end: Multicolor label.

GORDY

1962-67: Purple label, "Gordy" in cursive yellow letters at top superimposed over an oval with the slogan "IT'S WHAT'S IN THE GROOVES THAT COUNT."

1968-1980s: Purple label, "GORDY" in purple to left of center hole, yellow wedge going through center hole from left to right. There is some overlap in 1967 between label designs.

HICKORY

The earliest labels are tan with brown print. No later than the early 1960s, this was replaced with a red label with silver print.

1963-73: Black label, rainbow at upper left.

1973-75: Brown label, rainbow at upper left, "MGM Records" lion at right of center hole.

1976-77: Multi-colored (yellow, orange, purple) "target" label with "abc Records" at top of label between two lines and the "Hickory" logo at left of center hole.

1977-79: Multi-colored (yellow, orange, purple) "target" label with "abc" in an eighth note at top of label, and "Hickory" logo to the right of the note.

IMPERIAL

1952-54: Blue label, script "IMPERIAL" at top.

1954-55: Red label, script "IMPERIAL" at top.

1955-57: Red label, block "IMPERIAL" at top.

1957-63: Black label, white block "IMPERIAL" at top. There is significant overlap with the red label; some red label pressings are known as late as 1959.

1964-66: Black label, pink and white color blocks at upper and lower left, "IR" logo in box at center left.

1966-70: Black label, green color blocks at upper and lower left, "IR" logo in box at center left.

INFINITY (pop)

In business for just over a year (late 1978 to late 1979), it lasted long enough to have two label variations. The earliest 45s have a primarily white label with "optical illusion" logo at the top. Later 45s have a primarily brown label with a slightly different rendering of the optical illusion logo.

ISLAND

Since the label was first set up as a U.S. entity in 1972, it's been distributed by Capitol, independently, by Warner Bros. and Atco (at the same time for different artists!) and PolyGram. The labels have changed even more often than the distribution, and it's possible we missed a variation or two.

1972-74: Sunray label, "ISLAND" along bottom of label in stylized letters.

1974-75: Yellow background on label, "water skier" offshore, "island" along top.

1975-77: Black label with "I" logo at bottom and "Island Records" underneath.

1977-82: Orange and blue label.

1982-83: Dark purple label with skyscraper at left and "Island" slanting upward.

1983-84: Light blue label, "Island" in red across top.

1985-90: Black label, logo at bottom.

1990s: Some have white labels; others have black labels with Island logo at top.

JAMIE

1956-58: Black label.

1958-59: Yellow label, "JAMIE" at top.

1959-early 1970s: White and yellow label, "jamie" vertically at left.

1970s: Orange and black label.

JANUS

1970: White label, gold and black print.

1970-77: Brownish gold label.

1977-78: Red label.

JOSIE

1954-57: Light brown label, "Joz" logo at top, brown print.

1957-59: Light brown label, "Joz" logo at top, red print.

1959-1970s: Peach label, yellow "josie" logo in black oval, multi-color lines emanating from bottom of oval.

JUBILEE

1951-52: Dark blue label, "Jubilee" in script print, no line under "Jubilee."

1952-59: Dark blue label, "Jubilee" in script print, with line under "Jubilee."

1959-1970s: Black label.

KAMA SUTRA

1965: Almost all the label is taken up by a red sunburst with black print. Some yellow is also visible.

Early 1966: Yellow label, red sunburst around outside of label, "Kama Sutra" in red.

Mid 1966-1969: Yellow label, "Kama Sutra" in black.

1970-72: Pink label.

1972-74: Light blue label, Garden of Eden scene at top.

KEEN

1957: Black label, silver print.

1958-59: Colored vertical stripes with letters of "KEEN" in individual gray circles.

1959: Silver label, black print.

1959-60: Black label, "KEEN" to left of center hole, five-color vertical stripe next to it.

KING

1951-55: Maroon label, gold print on country series (3-digit and numbers in the 1000 series through ca. 1470).

1951-55: Blue label, silver print, the words "High Fidelity" are absent (4000 series to ca. 4830).

1955-59: Both series are the same, with blue labels and the words "High Fideilty" in relatively small print.

1959-69: Blue label, "High Fidelity" in even larger print.

1969-71: Orange and brown label. James Brown 45s had his photo on them.

KIRSHNER

Successor to Calendar Records.

1969-mid 1970s: Orange label, "KIRSHNER" in individual boxes across the top.

Mid 1970s-early 1980s (CBS distribution): White label with multi-color top.

LAURIE

1957-58 (3013-3019?): Light blue or gray labels, "Laurie Records" at top. This label also exists on some pressings of 3366 (from 1966)!

1958-1970s: White, red and black labels. Through approximately 3215, the record number stood alone. After this, the letters "LR" were added before the record number. Earlier numbers with "LR" before them are reissues.

LIBERTY

1955-60: Green label, silver print. Some are known to exist with all-black labels with silver print and also with blue labels with silver print. All of these have the "LIBERTY" logo across the top of the label.

1961-66: Black label, rainbow colored area left of center hole, "LIBERTY" in rectangle at 9 o'clock.

1966-69: Black label, rainbow colored area left of center hole, "LIBERTY" in black inside a rounded white box with Statue of Liberty graphic.

1970-71: Black label, rainbow colored area left of center hole, "LIBERTY" in black inside a squared-off white box with Statue of Liberty graphic.

1980-86 (reactivated label): Gray label, "Liberty" in multi-colored letters across top.

1992-95 (re-reactivated label): White label, "FOR JUKEBOXES ONLY!" at left.

LONDON

1949-55: Blue label, gold print.

1956-61: Blue label, silver or white print.

1962-mid 1965: White label, deep blue inserts, two egg-shaped purple areas at 3 and 9 o'clock, "LONDON RECORDS" encircles the entire label.

Mid 1965-1976: "Blue swirl" label, with alternating triangles of three shades of blue and "LONDON" in stylized letters across top. In mid 1974, the prefix on London 45s changed from "45" to "5E."

1977-82: Multi-colored "sunrise" label.

1983-95: White label, upside-down triangle logo at top.

London 45s on black labels are imports.

MCA

Late 1972: Black label, white print.

1973-late 1978: Black label, silver print, rainbow at upper left.

Late 1978-early 1980: Tan label, darker tan circle around outside.

Early 1980-1998: Light blue label, rainbow at upper left.

1998-present (pop): White label.

1998-present (country): Gray label.

Some 45s were issued with custom labels.

MERCURY

1950-52 (numbers in 4-digit series, mostly 5000s and 8000s): Maroon label, "Mercury" stands alone at top.

1952-57: Some maroon, some black labels, "Mercury" stands alone at top. Also known to exist are pink and green labels in this series.

1957-late 1964: A few early maroon labels, but mostly black labels, "Mercury" in an oval at top. Blue labels are also known to exist on some 45s around 1959.

Late 1964-1967: Red label, "MERCURY" stands alone in white letters across top.

1967-mid 1968: Tan and orange "swirl" label, "Mercury" in oval at top. (There is some overlap with the above label.)

Mid 1968-mid 1974: Red label, white "mercury" in white oval at top. (Again, there is some overlap with the above label.)

Mid 1974-early 1983: Chicago skyline label.

Early 1983-1996: Black label, "mercury" in neon-effect letters across top.

1996-present: Black label, "Mercury" in red diamond at top.

Some Mercury singles were pressed with custom labels or "retro" labels.

MGM

1949-58: Yellow label.

1959: Yellow label with "12th Anniversary" under logo at top in red letters.

1960-68: Black label.

1968-76: Blue and gold label.

MONUMENT

1958-59: Black label.

1959-60: White label, vertical gold pinstripes.

1960-63: White label with copper swirl.

1963: White label with multicolor swirl.

1964-71: Yellow label with light green swirl.

1971-76: Dark orange, almost brown, label.

1977-81: Black label, "MONUMENT" spelled out in simulated stone-carved letters across top.

1982-83: Silver label.

1999-2000: Reactivated; white label.

MOTOWN

1960-61 (1000-1010): Pink label, diagonal lines at top, "MOTOWN" vertically at upper left.

1961-early 1990s: Blue label with Detroit-area map at top.

Early 1990s-present: White label.

ODE

1967-70: Yellow label, "Ode" logo in black print left of the center hole.

1970-71: White and silver label, "Ode 70" at upper right.

1971-75: White and silver label, "Ode Records Inc." at upper right.

1975-78: Tan label with both Ode and Epic logos.

PARKWAY

1958 (801): Blue label.

1958-60 (802-811): White label, blue print.

1960-61 (812-829?): Orange label, black print.

1961-1967 (830?-end): Orange and yellow label, white "PARKWAY" at top.

PHILIPS

1962-Mid 1967: Black label.

Mid 1967-Mid 1972: Light blue label. (Some 1968 singles exist on the black label.)

Mid 1972-1976: Dark blue label with white and silver print.

PHILLES

1961-62 (101-106): Orange label.

1962-63 (104-115): Blue and black label. (Notice that there is overlap with the orange label.)

1963-66 (116-136): Yellow and red label.

POLYDOR

Polydor began issuing 45s in America in 1969. All have red labels. (Orange label Polydor 45s are imports.)

PORTRAIT

1976-early 80s: Gray label.

1980s: Black label.

Custom labels were used on some releases.

RARE EARTH

1969: The lower half of the label is white. The upper half has an orange background, a drawing of a tree and the words "RARE EARTH" in white. This label was later used as the promo label, but for the first editions of early 45s, it also was the stock label.

1970-76 (511-550): All-orange label with a drawing of a tree and the words "RARE EARTH" in white.

RCA VICTOR (pop)

1949: Aqua label, "RCA VICTOR" in a semicircle on the upper half of the label, outline of Nipper logo at right with circular "RCA" logo to its upper left, gold print.

1950-52: Aqua label, same design as above, but with silver print (RCA found that the original gold print faded very easily).

1952-54: Black label, same design as above.

1954-65: Usually called "black label, dog on top." A smaller "RCA VICTOR" is in white at top, with a full-bodied Nipper logo underneath it. Through 1957, some editions have a white horizontal line at roughly 10 and 2 o'clock; this simply indicates that the 45 was pressed in Rockaway, N.J. Also, some editions are missing the dog on top; this is most likely a factory error.

1965-68: Usually called "black label, dog at left." "RCA VICTOR" is on two lines at right of label; full-bodied Nipper logo is at left, title of song is at top, artist is at bottom.

1968-76: Orange label, no dog; "RCA" outline at left turned on its side, "Victor" at 3 o'clock, both in white.

1974-75: Gray label starting with PB-10001; this label overlapped with the orange label. Gray labels were used in the east, orange in the west.

1975-76: Brown label. There is some overlap with gray labels, and even more with orange labels. Again, brown labels dominate in the east, orange in the west.

1976-88: Usually called "black label, dog near top." "RCA" outline at 12 o'clock, Nipper logo at 1 o'clock, no "Victor" on label.

1988-90s: Various, including same label as 1976-88 style (country only); red label, circular RCA logo at top; silver label, red circular RCA logo at top; silver label, Nipper logo at top; various combinations of white, red and silver. Most pop singles starting in the late 1990s have white labels with circular RCA logo at top.

RED BIRD

All have yellow labels with black print. A red bird is above the center hole, and the words "Red" and "Bird" are on either side of it in black.

REPRISE

1961 (possibly only on 20,001): Light blue label.

1961-late 1964: Peach label.

Late 1964-late 1967: Orange and brown label.

Late 1967-early 1970: Lighter orange (tan) label with steamboat and both "W7" and "r:" logos.

Early 1970-early 1980s: Lighter orange (tan) label with steamboat, but with only the "r:" logo.

1986-87 (reactivated label): Black label.

1988-present: Light blue and maize label.

Mid 1990s-present: Some issues have a peach, green and pink label with steamboat logo in right corner. Some others have a white label with a reproduction of the early 1970s-early 1980s design.

ROULETTE

1957 (4001-4004?): Maroon label, silver print, or red label, black print, "Roulette" in script at top, with roulette numbers along outside of the label.

1957 (after the above): Red label, black print, "ROULETTE" in capital letters, roulette wheel along top half of label only.

1957-58 (still later): Red label, black print, "Roulette" at top, no roulette wheel around edge.

1958-62 (4050?-4400?): White label with six colored "spokes."

1962-63: Pink label.

1963-67: Orange and yellow label.

1967-76: Orange and yellow label with gray circle added between outer and inner parts of label design.

SCEPTER

1958-60 (1201-1208?): White label, blue print.

1960-61 (1209?-1216?): Red label, "Scepter" in black script and a silver outline.

1961-71: Red label, black wedge through center hole, "SCEPTER RECORDS" in white in two lines at the left of the center hole.

1967-1973: Kaleidoscopic label, "SCEPTER RECORDS" in black inside white oval at top of label. Before mid-1971, this seems to have been a custom label for records by Dionne Warwick, but by late 1971 this was used for all Scepter singles.

1974-76: Dark blue label, "SCEPTER" in white.

SHELTER

1971-72 (8900-8910?): Red label with an upside-down Superman logo at left.

1972-73: Red label with blacked-out upside-down Superman logo on top.

1974-76 (MCA distribution): Yellow label.

1977-78 (ABC distribution): Orange label.

SPECIALTY

1951-57: White, yellow and black label, black bars at left and right have a wavy line through the center.

1957-1980s: Same as above, except the two black bars do NOT have a wavy line through the center.

SUN

1953-67: Mustard yellow label, chocolate brown print. Musical notes ring the outer edge of the label. Alternating brown and yellow rays emanate from the center hole area. The letters "SUN" are in yellow over the rays. At the bottom of the label, in yellow print with brown background, are the words "Memphis, Tennessee." NOTE: Any Sun single on the above label with black print is a reproduction or counterfeit.

1968-86: Yellow label, brown print. Four "targets" are visible in the lower half of the label. The music notes only go around half the label instead of nearly all of it, and at the bottom is "Sun International Corp., A Division of the Shelby Singleton Corp., Nashville, U.S.A."

SWAN

1958 (4001 only?): White label, red print, "SWAN" in block letters at top.

1958-63: White label, red print, "Swan" in script.

1963-66: Black label, silver print, "Swan" in script. The black label adds the words "DON'T DROP OUT" at 10 o'clock. There is some overlap with the white label, and some of the overlapping white labels have "DON'T DROP OUT" on them.

TAMLA

1959-61 (101-102, 54024-54040s): Yellow label, horizontal lines at top of label, "TAMLA" vertically at upper left.

1961-67 (54040s-54175?): Yellow label, globe and record at top of label. Most of these have the record at the top left and globe at top right, but some early records have the globe and record overlapping.

1967-mid 1980s: Yellow label, "TAMLA" logo in a box at top of label.

TOLLIE

1964 (9001-9010s): Yellow label. 9001 and 9008 also exist on black labels.

1964-65 (9010s-end): White label with olive, yellow, red, blue and purple color bars.

TOWER

1965-68: Orange label.

1968-69: Multi-colored, striped label.

UNITED ARTISTS

1959-60: Red and black label, "UNITED" at left of center hole, "ARTISTS" at right.

1960-62?" Black label, "UA" at top, multi-colored lines along outside of label.

1962?-63?: Black label, United Artists logo in white rounded square box, other colors on label.

1963?-64?: Black label, United Artists logo in white rounded square box, vertical lines tangential to center hole.

1964?-1968: Black label, United Artists logo in white rounded square box, no other lines.

1968-70: Pink and orange label.

1970-71: Black label, orange at upper and lower left, United Artists logo at center left.

1971-77: Tan label, "UA" at top.

1978-80: "Sunrise" label.

UNIVERSAL

A country label that lasted for exactly one year (1989). The earliest 45s had black and pale yellow labels; later ones have black and red labels.

VEE JAY

1953-56: Maroon label with neither "Made in U.S.A." nor "Trade Mark Reg." on label.

1956-58: Maroon label, "Made in U.S.A." on label.

1958-60: Maroon label, "Trade Mark Reg." on label.

1960-63: Black label, rainbow ring around outside rim, oval logo at top. At least one record exists with a red ring around the outside rim rather than a rainbow rim.

Mid 1963-early 1964: Black label, rainbow ring around outside rim, large "VJ" and smaller "VEE JAY RECORDS" in brackets at top.

Early 1964-mid 1965: Numerous different labels.

VIK

A 1950s RCA subsidiary, its issues were black with a multi-color "Vik" logo across the top.

VIRGIN

Virgin's American history is spotty at times; for some years there was no Virgin Records in America, but material that came out on Virgin U.K. was leased to other labels.

1973-75: White label, "two virgins" painting at top of label, distributed by Atlantic.

1976-78: Unknown label design, distributed by CBS.

1979-80: White label, "Virgin" in red letters, again distributed by Atlantic.

1981: Unknown design, distributed by RSO.

1983-86: Black label, "Virgin" and "Epic" logos on label. (All of these were Culture Club singles.)

1987-89: Black label, blue upside-down triangle logo at top of label.

1989-90: Orange label.

1990-92: Purple label.

1993-present: White label, "FOR JUKEBOXES ONLY!" at left.

WARNER BROS.

1958-60: Pink label.

1960-64: Red label with colored arrows around the inside of the label.

1964-68: Orange label with lines around the outside of the label.

1968-70: Olive green label with "W7" in a box at the top and "Warner Bros.-Seven Arts Records" along the top outer edge.

1970-73: Olive green label with "WB" in a shield at the top and "Warner Bros. Records" along the top outer edge.

1973-78: So-called "Burbank" label; color palm-tree street scene with "Burbank, Home of Warner Bros. Records" along top edge.

1978-early 1980s: Gray or white label with horizontal pinstripes.

Early 1980s-present: White label.

Some Warner Bros. singles have custom labels.

"X"

This subsidiary of RCA Victor released 45s from 1954 through 1956. The label is white with red print and a big red "X" at the top of the label.

A

ABBA

Also see BJORN AND BENNY.

ATLANTIC

Number	Title (A Side/B Side)	Yr	VG	VG+	NM
❑ PR 380 [DJ]	Happy New Year (mono/stereo)	1980	3.00	6.00	12.00
❑ PR 390 [DJ]	Happy New Year	1980	3.00	6.00	12.00
—One-sided promo					
❑ 3035	Waterloo/Watch Out	1974	—	2.50	5.00
❑ 3035 [PS]	Waterloo	1974	3.75	7.50	15.00
—Sleeve is promo only					
❑ 3209	Honey Honey/Dance (While the Music Still Goes On)	1974	—	2.50	5.00
❑ 3240	Hasta Manana/Ring Ring	1975	—	2.50	5.00
❑ 3265	SOS/Man in the Middle	1975	—	2.50	5.00
❑ 3310	I Do, I Do, I Do, I Do, I Do/Bang-a-Boomerang	1975	—	2.50	5.00
❑ 3315	Mamma Mia/Tropical Loveland	1976	—	2.50	5.00
❑ 3346	Fernando/Rock Me	1976	—	2.00	4.00
❑ 3346	Fernando/Tropical Loveland	1976	—	2.00	4.00
❑ 3372	Dancing Queen/That's Me	1976	—	2.00	4.00
❑ 3387	Knowing Me, Knowing You/Happy Hawaii	1977	—	2.00	4.00
❑ 3387 [PS]	Knowing Me, Knowing You/Happy Hawaii	1977	—	2.50	5.00
❑ 3434	Money, Money, Money/Crazy World	1977	—	2.00	4.00
❑ 3434 [PS]	Money, Money, Money/Crazy World	1977	—	3.00	6.00
❑ 3449	The Name of the Game/I Wonder (Departure)	1977	—	2.00	4.00
❑ 3457	Take a Chance on Me/I'm a Marionette	1978	—	2.00	4.00
❑ 3457 [PS]	Take a Chance on Me/I'm a Marionette	1978	—	3.00	6.00
❑ 3574	Does Your Mother Know/Kisses of Fire	1979	—	2.00	4.00
❑ 3574 [PS]	Does Your Mother Know/Kisses of Fire	1979	—	2.50	5.00
❑ 3609	Voulez-Vous/Angeleyes	1979	—	2.00	4.00
❑ 3609 [PS]	Voulez-Vous/Angeleyes	1979	—	2.50	5.00
❑ 3629	Chiquitita/Lovelight	1979	—	2.00	4.00
❑ 3630	Chiquitita (Spanish Version)/I Have a Dream (Spanish Version)	1979	—	2.50	5.00
❑ 3652	Gimme! Gimme! Gimme! (A Man After Midnight)/ The King Has Lost His Crown	1980	—	2.00	4.00
❑ 3776	The Winner Takes It All/Elaine	1980	—	2.00	4.00
❑ 3806	Super Trouper/The Piper	1981	—	2.00	4.00
❑ 3806 [PS]	Super Trouper/The Piper	1981	—	2.00	4.00
❑ 3826	On and On and On/Lay All Your Love on Me	1981	—	2.00	4.00
❑ 3889	When All Is Said and Done/Should I Laugh or Cry	1982	—	—	3.00
❑ 3889 [PS]	When All Is Said and Done/Should I Laugh or Cry	1982	—	—	3.00
❑ 4031	The Visitors/Head Over Heels	1982	—	—	3.00
❑ 4031 [PS]	The Visitors/Head Over Heels	1982	—	—	3.00
❑ 89881	One of Us/Should I Laugh or Cry	1983	—	—	3.00
❑ 89881 [PS]	One of Us/Should I Laugh or Cry	1983	—	2.00	4.00
❑ 89948	The Day Before You Came/Cassandra	1982	—	—	3.00

ABDUL, PAULA

VIRGIN

Number	Title (A Side/B Side)	Yr	VG	VG+	NM
❑ S7-18850	Crazy Cool/The Choice Is Yours	1995	—	—	3.00
❑ S7-18877	Forever Your Girl/(It's Just) The Way That You Love Me	1995	—	—	3.00
❑ 38493	My Love Is for Real/Didn't I Say I Love You	1995	—	—	2.00
❑ 38493 [PS]	My Love Is for Real/Didn't I Say I Love You	1995	—	—	2.00
❑ 98584	Will You Marry Me/Goodnight, My Love	1992	—	2.00	4.00
❑ 98683	Blowing Kisses in the Wind/Spellbound	1991	—	2.00	4.00
❑ 98737	Vibeology/Vibeology (House Mix)	1991	—	2.00	4.00
❑ 98752	The Promise of a New Day/The Promise of a New Day (West Coast 12")	1991	—	2.00	4.00
❑ 98828	Rush, Rush/Rush, Rush (Dub Mix)	1991	—	2.00	4.00
❑ 99158	Opposites Attract/One or the Other	1989	—	—	2.00
❑ 99158 [PS]	Opposites Attract/One or the Other	1989	—	—	2.00
❑ 99196	Cold Hearted/One or the Other	1989	—	—	2.00
❑ 99196 [PS]	Cold Hearted/One or the Other	1989	—	—	2.00
❑ 99230	Forever Your Girl/Next to You	1989	—	—	2.00
❑ 99230 [PS]	Forever Your Girl/Next to You	1989	—	—	2.00
❑ 99256	Straight Up/Straight Up (Power Mix)	1988	—	—	3.00
❑ 99256	Straight Up/Cold Hearted	1988	—	2.00	4.00
❑ 99282	(It's Just) The Way That You Love Me/(It's Just) The Way That You Love Me (Dub)	1988	—	2.00	4.00
—Originals on black labels					
❑ 99282	(It's Just) The Way That You Love Me/(It's Just) The Way That You Love Me (Dub)	1988	—	—	3.00
—Second pressing on orange labels					
❑ 99282 [PS]	(It's Just) The Way That You Love Me/(It's Just) The Way That You Love Me (Dub)	1988	—	2.00	4.00
❑ 99329	Knocked Out/(Instrumental)	1988	—	—	3.00
❑ 99329 [PS]	Knocked Out/(Instrumental)	1988	—	—	3.00

ABSTRACK REALITY

SPORT

Number	Title (A Side/B Side)	Yr	VG	VG+	NM
❑ 104	Love Burns Like a Fire/(Instrumental)	1967	50.00	100.00	200.00

AC/DC

ATCO

Number	Title (A Side/B Side)	Yr	VG	VG+	NM
❑ 7068	High Voltage/It's a Long Way to the Top	1976	2.00	4.00	8.00
❑ 7086	Problem Child/Let There Be Rock	1977	2.00	4.00	8.00
❑ 98881	Moneytalks/Borrowed Time	1990	—	2.00	4.00

ATLANTIC

Number	Title (A Side/B Side)	Yr	VG	VG+	NM
❑ 3499	Rock 'N' Roll Damnation/Kick in the Teeth	1978	—	2.50	5.00
❑ 3553	Whole Lotta Rosie/Hell Ain't a Bad Place to Be	1979	—	2.50	5.00
❑ 3617	Highway to Hell/Night Prowler	1979	—	2.50	5.00
❑ 3644	Touch Too Much/Walk All Over You	1980	—	2.50	5.00
❑ 3761	You Shook Me All Night Long/Have a Drink on Me	1980	—	2.50	5.00
❑ 3787	Back in Black/What Do You Do for Money Honey	1980	—	2.50	5.00
❑ 3894	Let's Get It Up/Snowballed	1982	—	2.00	4.00
❑ 3894 [PS]	Let's Get It Up/Snowballed	1982	—	3.00	6.00
❑ 4029	For Those About to Rock We Salute You/T.N.T.	1982	—	2.00	4.00
❑ 4029 [PS]	For Those About to Rock We Salute You/T.N.T.	1982	2.00	4.00	8.00
❑ 89098	The Way I Wanna Rock 'N' Roll/Kissin' Dynamite	1988	—	—	3.00
❑ 89136	Heatseeker/Go Zone	1988	—	—	3.00
❑ 89136 [PS]	Heatseeker/Go Zone	1988	—	2.00	4.00
❑ 89377	You Shook Me All Night Long/She's Got Balls	1986	—	2.00	4.00
❑ 89425	Who Made Who/Guns for Hire (Live)	1986	—	—	3.00
❑ 89425 [PS]	Who Made Who/Guns for Hire (Live)	1986	—	2.00	4.00
❑ 89532	Danger/Back in Business	1985	—	—	3.00
❑ 89532 [PS]	Danger/Back in Business	1985	—	2.00	4.00
❑ 89614	Jailbreak/Show Business	1984	—	—	3.00
❑ 89614 [PS]	Jailbreak/Show Business	1984	—	2.00	4.00
❑ 89722	Flick of the Switch/Badlands	1983	—	—	3.00
❑ 89774	Guns for Hire/Landslide	1983	—	2.00	4.00
❑ 89774 [PS]	Guns for Hire/Landslide	1983	—	3.00	6.00

ACCENTS, THE

Several different groups.

Number	Title (A Side/B Side)	Yr	VG	VG+	NM
ACCENT					
❑ 1036	Voice of the Boyous/Where Will You Be	1956	7.50	15.00	30.00
❑ 1037	The Name Song/This Ole Body	1956	7.50	15.00	30.00
BANGAR					
❑ 605	Wherever There's a Will/Howlin' for My Baby	1964	3.75	7.50	15.00
❑ 629	Searchin'/You Don't Love Me	1964	3.75	7.50	15.00
❑ 648	Road Runner/Why	1965	3.75	7.50	15.00
BRUNSWICK					
❑ 55100	Wiggle Waggle/Dreamin' and Schemin'	1958	3.75	7.50	15.00
❑ 55123	I Give My Heart to You/Ching-a-Ling	1959	3.75	7.50	15.00
C-R-C					
❑ 1017	I've Got Better Things to Do/Then He Starts to Cry	1964	5.00	10.00	20.00
—Featuring Sandi					
CHALLENGE					
❑ 59254	Tell Me/Better Watch Out Boy	1964	3.75	7.50	15.00
❑ 59294	Sweet Talk/Tell Me	1965	3.00	6.00	12.00
CHARTER					
❑ 1017	I've Got Better Things to Do/Then He Starts to Cry	1964	3.75	7.50	15.00
—Featuring Sandi					
COMMERCE					
❑ 5012	Tell Me/Better Watch Out Boy	1964	5.00	10.00	20.00
CORAL					
❑ 62151	Autumn Leaves/Anything You Want Me to Be	1959	3.75	7.50	15.00
GARRETT					
❑ 4008	Wherever There's a Will/Howlin' for My Baby	1964	5.00	10.00	20.00
❑ 4014	Road Runner/Why	1965	5.00	10.00	20.00
JERDEN					
❑ 728	Linda Lou/Stickey	1964	3.00	6.00	12.00
—Featuring Ron Peterson					
JUBILEE					
❑ 5353	Red Light/22 Del Rio Ave.	1958	3.75	7.50	15.00
KARATE					
❑ 529	He's the One/On the Run	1966	3.75	7.50	15.00
LIBERTY					
❑ 55813	I Really Love You/What Do You Want to Do (Little Darlin')	1965	3.00	6.00	12.00
M-PAC!					
❑ 7216	New Girl/Do You Need a Good Man	1964	5.00	10.00	20.00
MERCURY					
❑ 72154	Enchanted Garden/Tell Me Now	1963	2.50	5.00	10.00
ONE-DERFUL					
❑ 4833	You Better Think Again/Who You Gonna Love	1965	5.00	10.00	20.00
RCA VICTOR					
❑ 74-0127	Love Is a Many-Splendored Thing/Yours Until Tomorrow	1969	—	3.00	6.00
SULTAN					
❑ 5500	Rags to Riches/Where Can I Go?	1961	15.00	30.00	60.00
VEE JAY					
❑ 484	Our Wonderful Love/A Hundred Walkin' Cats	1963	2.00	4.00	8.00

ACE, JOHNNY

Number	Title (A Side/B Side)	Yr	VG	VG+	NM
DUKE					
❑ 102	My Song/Follow the Rule	1952	20.00	40.00	80.00
❑ 107	Cross My Heart/Angel	1953	15.00	30.00	60.00
❑ 112	The Clock/Ace's Wild	1953	15.00	30.00	60.00
❑ 118	Saving My Love for You/Yes Baby	1953	10.00	20.00	40.00
❑ 128	Please Forgive Me/You've Been Gone So Long	1954	10.00	20.00	40.00
❑ 132	Never Let Me Go/Burley Cutie	1954	10.00	20.00	40.00
❑ 136	Pledging My Love/No Money	1954	10.00	20.00	40.00
❑ 136	Pledging My Love/Anymore	1954	10.00	20.00	40.00
❑ 144	Anymore/How Can You Be So Mean	1955	10.00	20.00	40.00
❑ 148	So Lonely/I'm Crazy	1956	7.50	15.00	30.00
❑ 154	Still Love You So/Don't You Know	1956	7.50	15.00	30.00
FLAIR					
❑ 1015	Midnight Hours Journey/Trouble and Me	1953	37.50	75.00	150.00
—B-side by Earl Forrest					

7-Inch Extended Plays

DUKE

Number	Title (A Side/B Side)	Yr	VG	VG+	NM
❑ 80	(contents unknown)	1955	37.50	75.00	150.00
❑ 80 [PS]	Memorial Album	1955	37.50	75.00	150.00
❑ 81	(contents unknown)	1955	37.50	75.00	150.00
❑ 81 [PS]	Tribute to Johnny Ace	1955	37.50	75.00	150.00

ACE, SONNY

ATLANTIC

Number	Title (A Side/B Side)	Yr	VG	VG+	NM
❑ 2364	Wooleh Booleh/Chili Peppers	1966	2.50	5.00	10.00

ACE IN THE HOLE BAND

Also see GEORGE STRAIT.

D

Number	Title (A Side/B Side)	Yr	VG	VG+	NM
❑ 1309	I Just Can't Go On Dying Like This/Honky Tonk Downstairs	1978	12.50	25.00	50.00
❑ 1313	The Way I Feel About You/Lonesome Rodeo Cowboy	1978	10.00	20.00	40.00

Number	Title (A Side/B Side)	Yr	VG	VG+	NM
❑ 1316	I Don't Want to Talk It Over Anymore/Loneliest Singer in Town	1979	7.50	15.00	30.00

ACKLIN, BARBARA

Number	Title (A Side/B Side)	Yr	VG	VG+	NM
BRUNSWICK					
❑ 55319	Fool, Fool, Fool (Look in the Mirror)/Your Sweet Loving	1967	2.00	4.00	8.00
❑ 55355	I've Got You Baby/Old Matchmaker	1967	2.00	4.00	8.00
❑ 55379	Love Makes a Woman/Come and See My Baby	1968	2.00	4.00	8.00
❑ 55388	Just Ain't No Love/Please Sunrise Please	1968	2.00	4.00	8.00
❑ 55388 [PS]	Just Ain't No Love/Please Sunrise Please	1968	3.75	7.50	15.00
❑ 55399	Am I the Same Girl/Be By My Side	1969	2.00	4.00	8.00
❑ 55412	Seven Days of Night/Raggedy Ride	1969	2.00	4.00	8.00
❑ 55421	After You/More Ways Than One	1969	2.00	4.00	8.00
❑ 55433	Is It Me/Someone Else's Arms	1970	2.00	4.00	8.00
❑ 55440	I Did It/I'm Living with a Memory	1970	2.00	4.00	8.00
❑ 55447	I Can't Do My Thing/Make the Man Love You	1971	2.00	4.00	8.00
❑ 55465	Lady, Lady, Lady/Stop, Look and Listen	1971	2.00	4.00	8.00
❑ 55486	I Call It Trouble/Love You Are Mine Today	1972	2.00	4.00	8.00
❑ 55501	I'm Gonna Bake a Man/I Call It Trouble	1973	—	3.00	6.00
CAPITOL					
❑ 3892	Raindrops/Here You Come Again	1974	—	2.50	5.00
❑ 4013	Special Loving/You Gave Him Everything, But I Gave Him Love	1974	—	2.50	5.00
❑ 4061	Give Me Some of Your Sweet Love/Fire Love	1975	—	2.50	5.00

ACORNS, THE

Number	Title (A Side/B Side)	Yr	VG	VG+	NM
UNART					
❑ 2006	Angel/I'm Gonna Stick to You	1958	5.00	10.00	20.00
❑ 2015	Please Come Back/Your Name and Mine	1959	5.00	10.00	20.00

AD LIBS, THE

Probably all the same group.

Number	Title (A Side/B Side)	Yr	VG	VG+	NM
AGP					
❑ 101	New York in the Dark/Human	1968	25.00	50.00	100.00
BLUE CAT					
❑ 102	The Boy from New York City/Kicked Around	1965	3.75	7.50	15.00
❑ 114	Ask Anybody/He Ain't No Angel	1965	2.50	5.00	10.00
❑ 119	On the Corner/Oo-Wee Oh Me Oh My	1965	2.50	5.00	10.00
❑ 123	Just a Down Home Girl/Johnny My Boy	1966	2.50	5.00	10.00
CAPITOL					
❑ 2944	Love Me/Know All About You	1970	—	3.00	6.00
JOHNNIE BOY					
❑ 01	Santa's On His Way/I Stayed Home (New Year's Eve)	19??	2.00	4.00	8.00
KAREN					
❑ 1527	Think of Me/Every Boy and Girl	1966	5.00	10.00	20.00
PHILIPS					
❑ 40461	Don't Ever Leave Me/You're in Love	1967	2.00	4.00	8.00
SHARE					
❑ 101	You're Just a Rolling Stone/Show a Little Appreciation	1969	2.00	4.00	8.00
❑ 104	Giving Up/Appreciation	1969	2.00	4.00	8.00
❑ 106	The Boy from New York City/Nothing Worse Than Being Alone	1969	2.00	4.00	8.00

ADAM'S APPLES

Number	Title (A Side/B Side)	Yr	VG	VG+	NM
BRUNSWICK					
❑ 55330	Don't Take It Out on This World/Don't You Want Me Home	1967	25.00	50.00	100.00
❑ 55367	You Are the One I Love/Stop Along the Way	1968	12.50	25.00	50.00

ADAMS, ART

Number	Title (A Side/B Side)	Yr	VG	VG+	NM
CHERRY					
❑ 1004	Rock Crazy Baby/Indian Joe	1960	25.00	50.00	100.00
❑ 1018	Dancing Doll/She Don't Live Here Anymore	1960	25.00	50.00	100.00

ADAMS, BILLY

Number	Title (A Side/B Side)	Yr	VG	VG+	NM
AMY					
❑ 893	You and Me/Go (Go On, Get Out of Here Now)	1963	3.00	6.00	12.00
APT					
❑ 25072	My Happiness/Big M	1962	3.00	6.00	12.00
CAPITOL					
❑ 4308	Count Every Star/Peggy's Party	1959	6.25	12.50	25.00
❑ 4373	Can't Get Enough/The Gods Were Angry With Me	1960	6.25	12.50	25.00
DECCA					
❑ 30724	Baby I'm Bugged/Short Hair and Turtle Neck Sweater	1958	7.50	15.00	30.00
DOT					
❑ 15689	You Heard Me Knocking/True Love Will Come Your Way	1958	7.50	15.00	30.00
FERN					
❑ 807	Darling Take My Hand/Tender Years	1961	6.25	12.50	25.00
❑ 808	Tattle Tale/Born to Be a Loser	1961	6.25	12.50	25.00
❑ 812	Rip Van Winkle/Sleep Baby Sleep	1961	6.25	12.50	25.00
❑ 813	Comic Strip/Call Me	1961	6.25	12.50	25.00
HOME OF THE BLUES					
❑ 239	Looking for My Baby/Had the Blues	1962	2.50	5.00	10.00
❑ 242	My Happiness/Big M	1962	5.00	10.00	20.00
NAU VOO					
❑ 802	You've Gotta Have a Duck Tail/Walking Star	1959	25.00	50.00	100.00
❑ 805	Return of the All American Boy/That's My Baby	1959	18.75	37.50	75.00
❑ 808	Blue Eyed Ella/Fun House	1959	18.75	37.50	75.00
QUINCY					
❑ 932	Rock Pretty Mama/(B-side unknown)	195?	500.00	1000.	1500.
SUN					
❑ 389	Got My Mojo Workin'/Betty and Dupree	1964	5.00	10.00	20.00
❑ 391	Trouble in My Mind/Lookin' for Mary Ann	1964	5.00	10.00	20.00
❑ 394	Reconsider Baby/Ruby Jane	1964	5.00	10.00	20.00
❑ 401	Open the Door, Richard/Rock Me Baby	1966	5.00	10.00	20.00

ADAMS, FAYE

Number	Title (A Side/B Side)	Yr	VG	VG+	NM
ATLANTIC					
❑ 1007	Sweet Talk/Watch Out, I Told You	1953	12.50	25.00	50.00
HERALD					
❑ 416 *—Black vinyl*	Shake a Hand/I've Got to Leave You	1953	7.50	15.00	30.00
❑ 416 *—Red vinyl*	Shake a Hand/I've Got to Leave You	1953	25.00	50.00	100.00
❑ 419	I'll Be True/Happiness to My Soul	1953	6.25	12.50	25.00
❑ 423	Say a Prayer/Every Day	1954	6.25	12.50	25.00
❑ 429	Somebody, Somewhere, Someday/Crazy Mixed-Up World	1954	6.25	12.50	25.00
❑ 434	Hurts Me to My Heart/Ain't Gonna Tell	1954	6.25	12.50	25.00
❑ 439	I Owe My Heart to You/Love Ain't Nothin' to Play With	1954	6.25	12.50	25.00
❑ 444	Anything for a Friend/Your Love Has My Heart Burning	1955	6.25	12.50	25.00
❑ 450	You Ain't Been True/My Greatest Desire	1955	6.25	12.50	25.00
❑ 457	Angels Tell Me/Tag Along	1955	6.25	12.50	25.00
❑ 462	No Way Out/Same Old Me	1955	6.25	12.50	25.00
❑ 470	Teen-Age Heart/Witness to the Crime	1956	6.25	12.50	25.00
❑ 480	Takin' You Back/Don't Forget to Smile	1956	6.25	12.50	25.00
❑ 489	Anytime, Anyplace, Anywhere/The Hammer Keeps Knockin'	1956	6.25	12.50	25.00
❑ 512	Shake a Hand/I'll Be True	1958	5.00	10.00	20.00
IMPERIAL					
❑ 5443	Keeper of My Heart/So Much	1957	5.00	10.00	20.00
❑ 5456	Johnny Lee/You're Crazy	1957	5.00	10.00	20.00
❑ 5471	I Have a Twinkle in My Eye/Someone Like You	1957	5.00	10.00	20.00
❑ 5525	When We Kiss/Everything	1958	5.00	10.00	20.00
LIDO					
❑ 603	That's All Right/It Made Me Cry	1960	3.00	6.00	12.00
❑ 606	It Can't Be Wrong/I Waited So Long	1960	3.00	6.00	12.00
SAVOY					
❑ 1606	Cry, You Crazy Heart/Step Up and Rescue Me	1960	3.00	6.00	12.00
❑ 4357	Sinner Man/God	197?	—	2.50	5.00
WARWICK					
❑ 590	Shake a Hand/It Hurts to My Heart	1960	3.00	6.00	12.00
❑ 620	Johnny, Don't/Obey My Rules	1961	3.00	6.00	12.00
❑ 638	It Can't Be Wrong/It's Nice to Know	1961	3.00	6.00	12.00

ADAMS, RICHIE

Number	Title (A Side/B Side)	Yr	VG	VG+	NM
BELTONE					
❑ 1001	No Mistakin' It/The Right Way	1961	3.75	7.50	15.00
❑ 1011	Two Initials (In a Heart)/What Took You So Long	1961	3.75	7.50	15.00
CONGRESS					
❑ 217	I Understand/Lookin' for the Blues	1964	3.75	7.50	15.00
❑ 226	Are You Changing/The King	1964	3.75	7.50	15.00
❑ 232	Slippin' Away/What Am I	1965	3.75	7.50	15.00
❑ 248	Every Window in the City/I Ain't Gonna Make It Without You	1965	3.75	7.50	15.00
❑ 256	Road to Nowhere/I Can't Escape from You	1965	15.00	30.00	60.00
IMPERIAL					
❑ 5806	Something Inside of Me Died/I Got Eyes	1962	3.75	7.50	15.00
❑ 5838	My Prayer of Love/Pakistan	1962	3.75	7.50	15.00
❑ 5856	It's Worth It/Test of Love	1962	3.75	7.50	15.00
MCA					
❑ 41182	The Best of the Rest of Our Lives/Warm	1980	—	2.00	4.00
MGM					
❑ 13629	You Were Mine/Better Off Without You	1966	2.50	5.00	10.00
P.I.P.					
❑ 6519	Mamacita/Lisa Lisa	1976	—	2.00	4.00
RIBBON					
❑ 6910	Lonely One/Tell Me Baby Did You Wait	1960	3.00	6.00	12.00
❑ 6913	Back to School/Don't Go, My Love, Don't Go	1960	3.00	6.00	12.00

ADDEO, NICKY

Number	Title (A Side/B Side)	Yr	VG	VG+	NM
EARLS					
❑ 1533	Gloria/Bring Back Your Heart	19??	2.50	5.00	10.00
MELODY					
❑ 1417	Where There Is Love/You Can Depend on Me	1964	6.25	12.50	25.00
REVELATION					
❑ 7-101	Danny Boy/A Lovely Way to Spend An Evening	1964	125.00	250.00	500.00
SAVOY					
❑ 200 *—Black vinyl*	Gloria/Bring Back Your Heart	1963	50.00	100.00	200.00
❑ 200 *—Red vinyl*	Gloria/Bring Back Your Heart	1963	100.00	200.00	400.00
❑ 200 *—Green vinyl*	Gloria/Bring Back Your Heart	1963	75.00	150.00	300.00
SELSOM					
❑ 104	Over the Rainbow/Fool #2	1965	50.00	100.00	200.00

ADDRISI, DICK

Also see THE ADDRISI BROTHERS.

Number	Title (A Side/B Side)	Yr	VG	VG+	NM
VALIANT					
❑ 742	You're Bad/Excuse Me	1966	3.00	6.00	12.00

ADDRISI BROTHERS, THE

Also see DICK ADDRISI.

Number	Title (A Side/B Side)	Yr	VG	VG+	NM
BELL					
❑ 45434	Somebody Found Her/Who Do You Think I Am	1974	—	2.00	4.00
BRAD					
❑ 003	I'll Be True/Everybody's Happy	1958	8.75	17.50	35.00
BUDDAH					
❑ 566	Slow Dancin' Don't Turn Me On (Short)/Slow Dancin' Don't Turn Me On (Long)	1977	—	2.50	5.00
❑ 579	Does She Do It Like She Dances/Baby, Love Is a Two-Way Street	1977	—	2.00	4.00
❑ 587	Never My Love/Emergency	1977	—	2.00	4.00

Number	Title (A Side/B Side)	Yr	VG	VG+	NM
COLUMBIA					
❑ 45521	We've Got to Get It On Again/You Make It All Worthwhile	1972	—	2.50	5.00
❑ 45610	One Last Time/I Can Feel You	1972	—	2.50	5.00
❑ 45705	Lifetime/I Can Count on You	1972	—	2.50	5.00
DEL-FI					
❑ 4116	Cherrystone/Lilies Grow High	1959	7.50	15.00	30.00
❑ 4120	Saving My Kisses/Un Jarro	1959	7.50	15.00	30.00
❑ 4125	It's Love/Back to the Old Salt Mine	1959	7.50	15.00	30.00
❑ 4130	Gonna See My Baby/Ven Ami	1959	6.25	12.50	25.00
ELEKTRA					
❑ 47203	Honey Come Home/Red-Eye Flight	1981	—	2.00	4.00
IMPERIAL					
❑ 5715	What a Night for Love/Poor Little Girls	1960	5.00	10.00	20.00
POM POM					
❑ 4160	The Dance Is Over/Socialite	1962	6.25	12.50	25.00
PRIVATE STOCK					
❑ 45012	Wait for Me/You Made All the Difference	1975	—	2.00	4.00
SCOTTI BROTHERS					
❑ 500	Ghost Dancer/Ghost Dancer	1979	—	2.00	4.00
❑ 500 [PS]	Ghost Dancer/Ghost Dancer	1979	—	3.00	6.00
—Promo-only title sleeve					
❑ 506	As Long As the Music Keeps Playing/(B-side unknown)	1979	—	2.00	4.00
VALIANT					
❑ 720	Mr. Love/Side by Side	1965	3.00	6.00	12.00
❑ 6047	Love Me Baby/The Way You Look at Him	1964	3.00	6.00	12.00
❑ 6058	C'mon Home Baby/Little Miss Sad	1964	3.75	7.50	15.00
WARNER BROS.					
❑ 5268	The Dance Is Over (Dance with Me)/Sleeping Beauty	1962	3.75	7.50	15.00
❑ 7249	Time to Love/Good News	1968	2.50	5.00	10.00

ADELPHIS, THE

Number	Title (A Side/B Side)	Yr	VG	VG+	NM
RIM					
❑ 2020	Darlin' It's You/Kathleen	1958	37.50	75.00	150.00
—Artist's name listed as "Adelphies"					
❑ 2020	Darlin' It's You/Kathleen	1958	25.00	50.00	100.00
—Artist's name spelled correctly as "Adelphis"					

ADLIBS, THE

Not to be confused with THE AD LIBS, this is a British group.

Number	Title (A Side/B Side)	Yr	VG	VG+	NM
INTERPHON					
❑ 7717	Neighbour, Neighbour/Lovely Ladies	1965	2.50	5.00	10.00

ADMIRALS, THE

Number	Title (A Side/B Side)	Yr	VG	VG+	NM
KING					
❑ 4772	Oh Yes/Left with a Broken Heart	1955	62.50	125.00	250.00
❑ 4782	Close Your Eyes/Give Me Love	1955	62.50	125.00	250.00
❑ 4792	It's a Sad, Sad Feeling/Ow	1955	12.50	25.00	50.00
—With Lucky Millinder					

ADMIRATIONS, THE

More than one group.

Number	Title (A Side/B Side)	Yr	VG	VG+	NM
ATOMIC					
❑ 12871	Dear Lady/Memories Are Here to Stay	195?	50.00	100.00	200.00
BRUNSWICK					
❑ 55332	Hey Mama/Lonely Street	1967	5.00	10.00	20.00
HULL					
❑ 1202	Moonlight/Ain't It Funny	1965	50.00	100.00	200.00
KELLWAY					
❑ 108	Over the Rainbow/In My Younger Days	196?	2.50	5.00	10.00
MERCURY					
❑ 71521	The Bells of Roja Rita/Little Bo Poop	1959	10.00	20.00	40.00
❑ 71883	To the Aisle/Hey Senorita	1962	50.00	100.00	200.00
ONE-DERFUL					
❑ 4849	Wait Till I Get to Know You/(Instrumental)	1967	6.25	12.50	25.00
❑ 4851	Don't Leave Me/All for You	1967	6.25	12.50	25.00

ADORABLES, THE

Number	Title (A Side/B Side)	Yr	VG	VG+	NM
GOLDEN WORLD					
❑ 4	Daddy Please/Deep Freeze	1964	6.25	12.50	25.00
❑ 10	School's All Over/Be	1964	6.25	12.50	25.00
❑ 25	Ooh Boy!/Devil in His Eyes	1965	10.00	20.00	40.00
PEACOCK					
❑ 1924	The Drive/Baby, Come and Get It	1963	3.00	6.00	12.00

ADRIAN AND THE SUNSETS

Number	Title (A Side/B Side)	Yr	VG	VG+	NM
SUNSET					
❑ 602	Breakthrough/Cherry Pie	1963	10.00	20.00	40.00
❑ 602 [PS]	Breakthrough/Cherry Pie	1963	30.00	60.00	120.00

ADVENTURERS, THE (1)

Number	Title (A Side/B Side)	Yr	VG	VG+	NM
COLUMBIA					
❑ 42227	Rock and Roll Uprising/My Mama Done Told Me	1961	10.00	20.00	40.00

ADVENTURERS, THE (U)

Number	Title (A Side/B Side)	Yr	VG	VG+	NM
BLUE ROCK					
❑ 4071	Something Bad (Is Happening)/Nobody Can Save Me	1968	2.00	4.00	8.00
CAPITOL					
❑ F-4292	Rip Van Winkle/Trail Blazer	1959	3.75	7.50	15.00
COMPASS					
❑ 7010	Easy Baby/(These Days) A Good Girl Is So Hard to Find	1967	2.00	4.00	8.00
MECCA					
❑ A-11	2 O'Clock Express/Shaggin'	1960	10.00	20.00	40.00
MIRACLE					
❑ 1	2 O'Clock Express/October Days	1960	5.00	10.00	20.00

AEROSMITH

Also see JOE PERRY PROJECT; WHITFORD-ST. HOLMES BAND.

Number	Title (A Side/B Side)	Yr	VG	VG+	NM
COLUMBIA					
❑ 08536	Chip Away the Stone/S.O.S.	1989	—	2.00	4.00
❑ 10034	Train Kept a-Rollin'/Spaced	1974	—	3.00	6.00
❑ 10105	S.O.S. (Too Bad)/Lord of the Thighs	1975	—	3.00	6.00
❑ 10155	Sweet Emotion/Pandora's Box	1975	—	2.50	5.00
❑ 10206	Walk This Way/Round and Round	1975	—	3.00	6.00
❑ 10253	Toys in the Attic/You See Me Crying	1975	—	3.00	6.00
❑ 10278	Dream On/Somebody	1975	—	2.50	5.00
—Contains the full-length version of A-side					
❑ 10359	Last Child/Combination	1976	—	2.50	5.00
❑ 10407	Home Tonight/Pandora's Box	1976	—	2.50	5.00
❑ 10449	Walk This Way/Uncle Salty	1976	—	2.50	5.00
❑ 10516	Back in the Saddle/Nobody's Fault	1977	—	2.50	5.00
❑ 10637	Draw the Line/Bright, Light, Fright	1977	—	2.50	5.00
❑ 10699	Kings and Queens/Critical Mass	1978	—	2.50	5.00
❑ 10727	Get It Up/Milk Cow Blues	1978	—	2.50	5.00
❑ 10802	Come Together/Kings and Queens	1978	—	2.50	5.00
❑ 10880	Chip Away the Stone (Studio)//S.O.S./Chip Away the Stone (Live)	1979	—	3.00	6.00
❑ 11181	Remember (Walking in the Sand)/Bone to Bone (Coney Island White Fish Boy)	1980	—	2.50	5.00
❑ 45894	Dream On/Somebody	1973	—	3.00	6.00
—Contains a remixed, edited version of A-side					
❑ 46029	Pandora's Box/Same Old Song and Dance	1974	—	3.00	6.00
❑ 78499	Falling in Love (Is Hard on the Knees)/Fall Together	1997	—	—	2.00
—Small hole					
❑ 78499 [PS]	Falling in Love (Is Hard on the Knees)/Fall Together	1997	—	—	2.00
❑ 78569	Hole in My Soul/Falling Off	1997	—	—	2.00
❑ 78569 [PS]	Hole in My Soul/Falling Off	1997	—	—	2.00
❑ 78592	I Don't Want to Miss a Thing/Animal Crackers// Taste of India (Rock Remix)	1998	—	—	2.00
❑ 78592 [PS]	I Don't Want to Miss a Thing/Animal Crackers// Taste of India (Rock Remix)	1998	—	—	2.00
GEFFEN					
❑ 19143	Livin' on the Edge/Don't Stop	1993	—	—	3.00
❑ 19256	Cryin'/Walk On Down	1993	—	—	3.00
❑ 19264	Amazing/Fever	1993	—	—	3.00
❑ 19267	Crazy/Gotta Love It	1994	—	—	3.00
❑ 19377	Blind Man/Head First	1994	—	—	3.00
❑ 19927	The Other Side/My Girl	1990	—	—	3.00
❑ 19946	What It Takes/Monkey on My Back	1990	—	—	3.00
❑ 22845	Love in an Elevator/Young Lust	1989	—	—	3.00
❑ 22845 [PS]	Love in an Elevator/Young Lust	1989	—	—	3.00
❑ 27915	Rag Doll/St. John	1988	—	—	3.00
❑ 27915 [PS]	Rag Doll/St. John	1988	—	—	3.00
❑ 28240	Dude (Looks Like a Lady)/Simoriah	1987	—	—	3.00
❑ 28240 [PS]	Dude (Looks Like a Lady)/Simoriah	1987	—	—	3.00
❑ 28249	Angel/Girl Keeps Coming Apart	1987	—	—	3.00
❑ 28249 [PS]	Angel/Girl Keeps Coming Apart	1987	—	—	3.00
❑ 28814	Shela/Gypsy Boots	1986	—	2.00	4.00

AKENS, JEWEL

Number	Title (A Side/B Side)	Yr	VG	VG+	NM
AMERICAN INT'L					
❑ 110	When Something Is Wrong with My Baby/I Just Can't Turn My Habit into Love	196?	—	3.00	6.00
CAPEHART					
❑ 5007	(Dancing) The Mashed Potatoes/Wee Bit More of Your Lovin'	1962	3.00	6.00	12.00
COLGEMS					
❑ 66-1025	It's a Sin to Tell a Lie/You Better Move On	1968	2.00	4.00	8.00
CREST					
❑ 1098	(Dancing) The Mashed Potatoes/Wee Bit More of Your Lovin'	1962	2.50	5.00	10.00
ERA					
❑ 104	Buenos Aires/Mississippi Syrup Sopper	1969	—	3.00	6.00
❑ 3141	The Birds and the Bees/Tic Tac Toe	1964	3.75	7.50	15.00
❑ 3142	Georgie Porgie/Around the Corner	1965	2.50	5.00	10.00
❑ 3147	You Sure Know How to Hurt a Guy/It's the Only Way to Fly	1965	2.50	5.00	10.00
❑ 3154	You Don't Need a Crowd/I've Arrived	1965	2.50	5.00	10.00
❑ 3156	A Slice of the Pie/You Better Believe It	1965	2.50	5.00	10.00
❑ 3164	My First Lonely Night/Mama Take Your Daughter Back	1966	2.50	5.00	10.00
❑ 3207	A Slice of the Pie/A Land Where Animals Are People	1969	2.00	4.00	8.00
MDM					
❑ 191	Christine/Please God	1988	—	2.00	4.00
—As "Jewel Akens, Mr. Birds and Bees"					

ALADDINS, THE

The group on Witch is probably not the same as the others.

Number	Title (A Side/B Side)	Yr	VG	VG+	NM
ALADDIN					
❑ 3275	Remember/Cry Baby Cry	1955	50.00	100.00	200.00
❑ 3298	I Had a Dream Last Night/Get Off My Feet	1955	50.00	100.00	200.00
❑ 3314	All My Life/So Long, Farewell, Bye Bye	1956	50.00	100.00	200.00
❑ 3358	Help Me/Lord, Show Me	1957	50.00	100.00	200.00
FRANKIE					
❑ 6	Dot, My Love/My Charlene	1958	100.00	200.00	400.00
WITCH					
❑ 109	Please Love Me/Munch	1962	12.50	25.00	50.00
❑ 111	Our Love Will Be/Simple Simon	1962	12.50	25.00	50.00

ALAIMO, STEVE

Also see THE REDCOATS; THE UNKNOWNS.

Number	Title (A Side/B Side)	Yr	VG	VG+	NM
ABC					
❑ 10805	So Much Love/Truer Than True	1966	3.00	6.00	12.00
❑ 10833	Happy/On the Beach	1966	3.00	6.00	12.00

Number	Title (A Side/B Side)	Yr	VG	VG+	NM
❑ 10873	Pardon Me (It's My First Day Alone)/Savin' All My Love	1966	3.00	6.00	12.00
❑ 10917	You Don't Love Me/You Don't Know Like I Know	1967	2.50	5.00	10.00

ABC-PARAMOUNT

Number	Title (A Side/B Side)	Yr	VG	VG+	NM
❑ 10540	Love's Gonna Live Here/Let Her Go	1964	3.00	6.00	12.00
❑ 10553	Love Is a Many Splendored Thing/Fade Out	1964	3.00	6.00	12.00
❑ 10580	I Don't Know/That's What Love Will Do	1964	3.00	6.00	12.00
❑ 10605	Happy/Everybody Knows But Her	1964	3.00	6.00	12.00
❑ 10620	Real Live Girl/Need You	1965	3.00	6.00	12.00
❑ 10643	Laughing on the Outside/Tomorrow Is Another Day	1965	3.00	6.00	12.00
❑ 10680	Cast Your Fate to the Wind/Mais Oui	1965	3.00	6.00	12.00
❑ 10712	Blowin' in the Wind/Lady of the House	1965	3.00	6.00	12.00
❑ 10764	Bright Lights Big City/Once a Day	1966	3.00	6.00	12.00

ATCO

Number	Title (A Side/B Side)	Yr	VG	VG+	NM
❑ 6512	New Orleans/Ooh Poo Pah Doo	1967	2.00	4.00	8.00
❑ 6560	Cuando Yo Vuelvo Ami Tierra/Todavia	1968	2.50	5.00	10.00
❑ 6561	Denver/I Do	1968	2.00	4.00	8.00
❑ 6589	1 x 1 Ain't 2/My Friend	1968	2.00	4.00	8.00
❑ 6620	Thank You for the Sunshine Days/Watching the Trains Go	1968	2.00	4.00	8.00
❑ 6659	I'm Thankful/Afetr the Smoke Is Gone	1969	2.00	4.00	8.00

—With Betty Wright

Number	Title (A Side/B Side)	Yr	VG	VG+	NM
❑ 6710	One Woman/And Then I Tripped Over Your Goodbye	1969	2.00	4.00	8.00
❑ 6732	Melissa/Smilin' in My Sleep	1970	—	3.00	6.00
❑ 6797	Can't You See/(On the) Wild Side of Life	1971	—	3.00	6.00

CHECKER

Number	Title (A Side/B Side)	Yr	VG	VG+	NM
❑ 981	Big Bad Beulah/I Cried All the Way Home	1961	3.00	6.00	12.00
❑ 989	All Night Long/I'm Thankful	1961	3.00	6.00	12.00
❑ 998	The Waiting's So Hard/You Got Me Whistling	1961	3.00	6.00	12.00
❑ 1006	Mashed Potatoes/Mashed Potatoes (Part 2)	1962	3.00	6.00	12.00
❑ 1018	My Friend/Going Back to Mary	1962	3.00	6.00	12.00
❑ 1024	Cry Myself to Sleep/One Good Reason	1962	3.00	6.00	12.00
❑ 1032	Every Day I Have to Cry/Little Girl	1962	3.00	6.00	12.00
❑ 1042	A Lifetime of Loneliness/It's a Long, Long Way to Happiness	1963	3.00	6.00	12.00
❑ 1047	Don't Let the Sun Catch You Cryin'/I Told You So	1963	3.00	6.00	12.00
❑ 1054	Michael — Pt. 1/Michael — Pt. 2	1963	3.00	6.00	12.00

DADE

Number	Title (A Side/B Side)	Yr	VG	VG+	NM
❑ 1800	Home by Eleven/I Wanna Kiss You	1959	12.50	25.00	50.00
❑ 1805	Love Letters/You Can Fall in Love	1959	12.50	25.00	50.00

DICKSON

Number	Title (A Side/B Side)	Yr	VG	VG+	NM
❑ 6444/5	Blue Fire/My Heart Never Said Goodbye	1960	5.00	10.00	20.00

ENTRANCE

Number	Title (A Side/B Side)	Yr	VG	VG+	NM
❑ 7501	When My Little Girl Is Smiling/Gemini	1971	—	2.50	5.00
❑ 7503	Thorn in Our Roses/Nobody's Fool	1971	—	2.50	5.00
❑ 7507	Amerikan Music/Nobody's Fool	1972	—	2.50	5.00
❑ 7513	Sand in My Pocket/Gemini	1972	—	2.50	5.00

IMPERIAL

Number	Title (A Side/B Side)	Yr	VG	VG+	NM
❑ 5699	My Heart Never Said Goodbye/Blue Fire	1960	3.75	7.50	15.00
❑ 5717	Unchained Melody/It Happens Ev'ry Time	1961	3.75	7.50	15.00
❑ 66003	Gotta Lotta Love/Happy Pappy	1963	3.00	6.00	12.00

LIFETIME

Number	Title (A Side/B Side)	Yr	VG	VG+	NM
❑ 6112/3	Jelly/The Girl Can't Help It	1957	20.00	40.00	80.00

MARLIN

Number	Title (A Side/B Side)	Yr	VG	VG+	NM
❑ 6064	I Want You to Love Me/Blue Skies	1959	7.50	15.00	30.00
❑ 6065	The Weekend's Over/Girls! Girls! Girls!	1959	6.25	12.50	25.00
❑ 6067	She's My Baby/Should I Care?	1959	6.25	12.50	25.00
❑ 6103	Spooky/The Redcoats Are Coming	1961	7.50	15.00	30.00

—As "Count Stephen"

TONE LATINO

Number	Title (A Side/B Side)	Yr	VG	VG+	NM
❑ 5051	Yo No Se Que Voy A Hacer Sin Ti/No Quiero Dejaria Ya	1970	2.00	4.00	8.00

7-Inch Extended Plays

CHECKER

Number	Title (A Side/B Side)	Yr	VG	VG+	NM
❑ EP-5135	Don't Cry/I Wake Up Crying//Cry/Don't Let the Sun Catch You Crying	1963	20.00	40.00	80.00
❑ EP-5135 [PS]	(title unknown)	1963	20.00	40.00	80.00

ALAMO, TONY

MGM

Number	Title (A Side/B Side)	Yr	VG	VG+	NM
❑ 11390	Merry Christmas Darling/It's Christmas Time	1952	5.00	10.00	20.00

ALAN, LEE

LEE ALAN PRESENTS

Number	Title (A Side/B Side)	Yr	VG	VG+	NM
❑ (no #)	A Trip to Miami	1964	125.00	250.00	500.00

—Interviews with the Beatles; a giveaway with Lee Alan's two-page story of his trip ($200 NM)

ALDA, ALEX

Actually Nick Massi of THE FOUR SEASONS.

ONE WAY

Number	Title (A Side/B Side)	Yr	VG	VG+	NM
❑ 224	The Ballad of Mr. Nixon/Little Pony	1976	—	2.50	5.00

TOPIX

Number	Title (A Side/B Side)	Yr	VG	VG+	NM
❑ 6007 [DJ]	Little Pony (one-sided)	1961	25.00	50.00	100.00

ALEXANDER, ARTHUR

BUDDAH

Number	Title (A Side/B Side)	Yr	VG	VG+	NM
❑ 492	Every Day I Have to Cry Some/Everybody Needs Somebody to Love	1975	—	2.50	5.00
❑ 522	Sharing the Night Together/She'll Throw Stones at You	1976	—	2.50	5.00
❑ 602	Sharing the Night Together/She'll Throw Stones at You	1978	—	2.00	4.00

DOT

Number	Title (A Side/B Side)	Yr	VG	VG+	NM
❑ 16309	You Better Move On/A Shot of Rhythm and Blues	1962	5.00	10.00	20.00
❑ 16357	Soldier of Love/Where Have You Been	1962	5.00	10.00	20.00
❑ 16387	Anna/I Hang My Head and Cry	1962	5.00	10.00	20.00
❑ 16425	You're the Reason/Go Home Girl	1963	3.75	7.50	15.00
❑ 16454	I Wonder Where You Are Tonight/Dream Girl	1963	3.75	7.50	15.00
❑ 16509	Pretty Girls Everywhere/Baby Baby	1963	3.75	7.50	15.00
❑ 16554	Where Did Sally Go/Keep Her Guessin'	1963	3.75	7.50	15.00
❑ 16616	Black Knight/Ole John Amos	1964	3.00	6.00	12.00
❑ 16737	Detroit City/You Don't Care	1965	3.00	6.00	12.00

JUDD

Number	Title (A Side/B Side)	Yr	VG	VG+	NM
❑ 1020	Sally Sue Brown/The Girl That Radiates That Charm	1960	12.50	25.00	50.00

—As "June Alexander"

MONUMENT

Number	Title (A Side/B Side)	Yr	VG	VG+	NM
❑ 1060	I Need You Baby/Spanish Harlem	1968	2.00	4.00	8.00

SOUND STAGE 7

Number	Title (A Side/B Side)	Yr	VG	VG+	NM
❑ 2556	The Other Woman/(Baby) For You	1965	2.50	5.00	10.00
❑ 2572	Turn Around (And Try Me)/Show Me the Road	1966	2.50	5.00	10.00
❑ 2619	Set Me Free/Love's Where Life Begins	1968	2.00	4.00	8.00
❑ 2626	Bye Bye Love/Another	1969	2.00	4.00	8.00
❑ 2652	Glory Road/Cry Like a Baby	1970	2.00	4.00	8.00

WARNER BROS.

Number	Title (A Side/B Side)	Yr	VG	VG+	NM
❑ 7571	I'm Comin' Home/It Hurts to Want It So Bad	1972	—	3.00	6.00
❑ 7633	Mr. John/You Got Me Knockin'	1972	—	3.00	6.00
❑ 7658	Burning Love/It Hurts to Want It So Bad	1972	—	3.00	6.00

ALEXANDER, JOE, AND THE CUBANS

With a pre-Chess CHUCK BERRY in the band.

BALLAD

Number	Title (A Side/B Side)	Yr	VG	VG+	NM
❑ 1008	Oh Maria/I Hope These Words Will FInd You Well	1954	500.00	1000.	1500.

ALEXANDER, JUNE

See ARTHUR ALEXANDER.

ALEXANDER, MAX

CAPROCK

Number	Title (A Side/B Side)	Yr	VG	VG+	NM
❑ 116	Little Rome/Rock, Rock, Rock Everybody	1959	50.00	100.00	200.00

ALEXANDER AND THE GREATS

ARVEE

Number	Title (A Side/B Side)	Yr	VG	VG+	NM
❑ 5064	Swanee Stomp/Waterlogged	1963	10.00	20.00	40.00

LIMELIGHT

Number	Title (A Side/B Side)	Yr	VG	VG+	NM
❑ 3040	Do the Mustang/Hot Dang Mustang	1964	10.00	20.00	40.00

ALEXANDER'S TIMELESS BLOOZBAND

KAPP

Number	Title (A Side/B Side)	Yr	VG	VG+	NM
❑ 967	Maybe Baby/Power of Your Love	1969	3.00	6.00	12.00

MATAMAT

Number	Title (A Side/B Side)	Yr	VG	VG+	NM
❑ 101	Love So Strong/Horn Song	1967	5.00	10.00	20.00

UNI

Number	Title (A Side/B Side)	Yr	VG	VG+	NM
❑ 55044	Love So Strong/Horn Song	1967	3.75	7.50	15.00

ALFI AND HARRY

LIBERTY

Number	Title (A Side/B Side)	Yr	VG	VG+	NM
❑ 55008	The Trouble with Harry/Little Beauty	1955	6.25	12.50	25.00
❑ 55016	The Word Game Song/Persian on Excursion	1956	6.25	12.50	25.00
❑ 55066	Safari/Cloding Time	1957	6.25	12.50	25.00

ALICE IN CHAINS

COLUMBIA

Number	Title (A Side/B Side)	Yr	VG	VG+	NM
❑ 78176	Grind/Nutshell	1995	—	2.50	5.00

—Deleted on day of issue

(COLUMBIA)

Number	Title (A Side/B Side)	Yr	VG	VG+	NM
❑ CS7-04013 [DJ]	Bleed the Freak/Put You Down	1991	6.25	12.50	25.00

—White label with no label name

ALICE JEAN AND THE MONDELLOS

See THE MONDELLOS.

ALIOTTA-HAYNES-JEREMIAH

AMPEX

Number	Title (A Side/B Side)	Yr	VG	VG+	NM
❑ 11012	Pitter Patter/(B-side unknown)	1970	2.00	4.00	8.00

—As "Aliotta Haynes"

Number	Title (A Side/B Side)	Yr	VG	VG+	NM
❑ 11026	Tomorrow's Another Day/One Night Stand	1971	2.00	4.00	8.00

—As "Aliotta Haynes"

SNOW QUEEN

Number	Title (A Side/B Side)	Yr	VG	VG+	NM
❑ 1000	Lake Shore Drive/(B-side unknown)	1973	5.00	10.00	20.00

ALIVE AND KICKING

ROULETTE

Number	Title (A Side/B Side)	Yr	VG	VG+	NM
❑ 7078	Tighter, Tighter/Sunday Morning	1970	—	2.50	5.00
❑ 7087	Just Let It Come/Mother Carey's Chicken	1970	—	2.50	5.00
❑ 7094	London Bridge/You Gave Me Something	1971	—	2.50	5.00
❑ 7113	Good Ole Lovin' Back Home/Jordan	1971	—	2.50	5.00

ALLAN, CHAD

Member of the early GUESS WHO.

MALA

Number	Title (A Side/B Side)	Yr	VG	VG+	NM
❑ 12033	Thru the Looking Glass/Ramon's Hourglass	1968	—	3.00	6.00

REPRISE

Number	Title (A Side/B Side)	Yr	VG	VG+	NM
❑ 1003	On the Back Step/West Coast Girl	1971	—	3.00	6.00

ALLAN, DAVIE, AND THE ARROWS

CUDE

Number	Title (A Side/B Side)	Yr	VG	VG+	NM
❑ 101	War Path/Beyond the Blue	1963	25.00	50.00	100.00

GET HIP

Number	Title (A Side/B Side)	Yr	VG	VG+	NM
❑ GH-209	The Born Losers Theme/The Glory Stompers	1997	—	—	2.00
❑ GH-209 [PS]	The Born Losers Theme/The Glory Stompers	1997	—	—	2.00

MARC

Number	Title (A Side/B Side)	Yr	VG	VG+	NM
❑ 3223	War Path/Beyond the Blue	1963	12.50	25.00	50.00

MGM

Number	Title (A Side/B Side)	Yr	VG	VG+	NM
❑ 14299	It's the Little Things You Do/Haven't You Heard	1971	2.00	4.00	8.00
❑ 14374	Head Over Heels/Here It Comes	1972	2.00	4.00	8.00
❑ 14432	Dawn of the 7th Cavalry/Little Big Horn	1972	2.00	4.00	8.00
❑ 14560	And Evil Did Too/Pleasure Girl	1973	2.00	4.00	8.00
❑ 14650	Apache '73/Run of the Arrow	1973	2.00	4.00	8.00

MRC

Number	Title (A Side/B Side)	Yr	VG	VG+	NM
❑ 0901	Stoked on Surf/Flashback	1984	—	2.50	5.00

Number	Title (A Side/B Side)	Yr	VG	VG+	NM
PRIVATE STOCK					
❑ 45001	Touch Too Much/We Can Make It Together	1974	—	3.00	6.00
SIDEWALK					
❑ 1	Apache '65/Blue Guitar	1965	5.00	10.00	20.00
TOWER					
❑ 116	Apache '65/Blue Guitar	1965	3.75	7.50	15.00
❑ 133	Moon Dawg '65/Dance the Freddie	1965	3.00	6.00	12.00
❑ 142	Baby Ruth/I'm Looking Over a Four Leaf Clover	1965	3.00	6.00	12.00
❑ 158	Space Hop/Granny Goose	1965	3.00	6.00	12.00
❑ 267	Wild Angels Theme/UFO	1966	3.00	6.00	12.00
❑ 295	Blue's Theme/Bongo Party	1966	3.00	6.00	12.00
❑ 341	Devil's Angels/Cody's Theme	1967	3.00	6.00	12.00
❑ 381	Cycle-Delic/Blue Rides Again	1967	3.00	6.00	12.00
❑ 446	Wild in the Streets/Shape of Things to Come	1968	3.00	6.00	12.00
ALLEN, BARRY					
DOT					
❑ 16799	Pretty Paper/Hurry, Santa, Hurry	1965	5.00	10.00	20.00
ALLEN, BILLY					
EL DORADO					
❑ 505	Butterfly/Oo Wee Baby	1957	5.00	10.00	20.00
—As "Bill Allen"					
IMPERIAL					
❑ 5500	Please Give Me Something/Since I Have You	1958	25.00	50.00	100.00
ALLEN, JESSE					
ALADDIN					
❑ 3129	Rock This Morning/Gonna Move Away from Town	1953	50.00	100.00	200.00
BAYOU					
❑ 011	Dragnet/Take It Easy	1953	25.00	50.00	100.00
CORAL					
❑ 65078	My Suffering/Let's Party	1952	50.00	100.00	200.00
IMPERIAL					
❑ 5256	Gotta Call That Number/Gonna Tell My Mama	1953	50.00	100.00	200.00
—With Audrey Walker					
❑ 5285	Sittin' and Wonderin'/I Wonder What's the Matter	1954	62.50	125.00	250.00
❑ 5303	What a Party/The Things I'm Gonna Do	1954	50.00	100.00	200.00
❑ 5315	Rockin' and Rollin'/I Love You So	1954	50.00	100.00	200.00
ALLEN, LEE					
ALADDIN					
❑ 3334	Shimmy/Rockin' at Cosmos	1956	6.25	12.50	25.00
EMBER					
❑ 1027	Walkin' with Mr. Lee/Promenade	1957	6.25	12.50	25.00
❑ 1031	Strollin' with Mr. Lee/Boppin' at the Hop	1958	5.00	10.00	20.00
❑ 1039	Tic Toc/Chuggin'	1958	5.00	10.00	20.00
❑ 1047	Jim Jam/Short Circuit	1958	5.00	10.00	20.00
❑ 1057	Cat Walk/Creole Alley	1959	5.00	10.00	20.00
❑ 1082	Twistin' with Mr. Lee/Twist Around the Clock	1962	3.75	7.50	15.00
7-Inch Extended Plays					
EMBER					
❑ 103	(contents unknown)	1958	50.00	100.00	200.00
❑ 103 [PS]	Walkin' with Mr. Lee	1958	50.00	100.00	200.00
ALLEN, MILTON					
RCA VICTOR					
❑ 47-6994	Love A Love A Lover/Just Look, Don't Touch, She's Mine	1957	7.50	15.00	30.00
❑ 47-7116	Don't Bug Me Baby/Jamboree	1957	12.50	25.00	50.00
ALLEN, RICHIE					
ERA					
❑ 3058	Blue Holiday/Goochie Bamba	1961	5.00	10.00	20.00
IMPERIAL					
❑ 5683	Stranger from Durango/Redskin	1960	5.00	10.00	20.00
❑ 5701	Sally Ann/Why Did It End	1960	3.75	7.50	15.00
—As "Dickie Allen"					
❑ 5720	Haunted Guitar/In a Persian Market	1961	5.00	10.00	20.00
❑ 5846	Mr. Hobbs (Theme)/Comin' Back to You	1962	3.75	7.50	15.00
❑ 5865	Not So Quiet/A Touch of Blue	1962	3.75	7.50	15.00
❑ 5872	Cave Man/Room 304	1962	5.00	10.00	20.00
❑ 5885	Kick Off/Undercurrent	1962	5.00	10.00	20.00
❑ 5917	Butterscotch/Sunday Picnic	1963	3.75	7.50	15.00
❑ 5929	Foot Stomp U.S.A./Skag Along Pete	1963	5.00	10.00	20.00
❑ 5941	Surf Beater/The Rising Surf	1963	3.75	7.50	15.00
❑ 5984	The Quiet Surf/Ballad of the Surf	1963	3.75	7.50	15.00
TOWER					
❑ 273	Stranger from Durango/Nothing Good	1966	3.00	6.00	12.00
ALLEN, TONY					
ALADDIN					
❑ 3403	Time Won't Wait on You/Holy Smoke, Baby	1957	5.00	10.00	20.00
BETHLEHEM					
❑ 3002	Come-A, Come-A Baby/Just Like Before	1961	3.00	6.00	12.00
❑ 3004	It Hurts Me So/The Trakey-Doo	1962	3.00	6.00	12.00
DIG					
❑ 104	It Hurts Me So/Check Yourself	1955	5.00	10.00	20.00
❑ 109	I Found An Angel/I'm Dreaming	1956	12.50	25.00	50.00
EBB					
❑ 115	Come Back/Why in the World	1957	5.00	10.00	20.00
IMPERIAL					
❑ 5523	Strange Talk/Call My Name	1958	3.75	7.50	15.00
❑ 5547	Forgive Me/Rockin' Shoes	1958	3.75	7.50	15.00
JAMIE					
❑ 1143	Train of Love/God Gave Me You	1959	3.75	7.50	15.00
KENT					
❑ 364	Dreaming/Be My Love, Be My Love	1961	3.00	6.00	12.00
SPECIALTY					
❑ 560	Nite Owl/I	1955	12.50	25.00	50.00

Number	Title (A Side/B Side)	Yr	VG	VG+	NM
❑ 570	Check Yourself Baby/Especially	1956	7.50	15.00	30.00
TAMPA					
❑ 157	Be My Love, Be My Love/Tell Me	195?	7.50	15.00	30.00
—As "The Wonders"					
ULTRA					
❑ 104	It Hurts Me So/Check Yourself	1955	7.50	15.00	30.00
UNITED ARTISTS					
❑ 50190	Now Is Forever/Triple Cross	1967	2.00	4.00	8.00
ALLENS, ARVEE					
See RITCHIE VALENS.					
ALLEY CATS, THE					
EPIC					
❑ 9778	Lily of the West/I Should Have Stayed at Home Tonight	1965	3.00	6.00	12.00
PHILLES					
❑ 108	Puddin N' Tain (Ask Me Again, I'll Tell You the Same)/Feel So Good	1962	6.25	12.50	25.00
PHILLES/COLLECTABLES					
❑ 3201	Puddin' and Tain/Then He Kissed Me	1985	—	3.00	6.00
—Red vinyl; part of box set "Phil Spector Wall of Sound Series Vol. 2"; B-side by the Crystals					
❑ 3201	Puddin' and Tain/Then He Kissed Me	1986	—	2.50	5.00
—Black vinyl; B-side by the Crystals					
WHIPPET					
❑ 202	This Thing Called Love/Spang-a-Lang	1957	5.00	10.00	20.00
❑ 209	Snap, Crackle and Pop/Last Night	1958	5.00	10.00	20.00
ALLIES, THE					
REPRISE					
❑ 674	I Would Love You/The Sound of Children	1968	5.00	10.00	20.00
VALIANT					
❑ 748	I'll Sell My Soul/Burning Glass	1966	10.00	20.00	40.00
ALLISON, GENE					
CHAMPION					
❑ 1008	Goodbye My Love/If Things Don't Change	196?	3.00	6.00	12.00
❑ 1019	Now We're Together/Understand	196?	3.00	6.00	12.00
❑ 1022	You're Gonna Be Sorry/I Know We Can Make It	196?	3.00	6.00	12.00
DECCA					
❑ 30185	You're My Baby/Somebody Somewhere	1957	3.75	7.50	15.00
MONUMENT					
❑ 876	Ev'rybody's Got a Little Problem/Now Hear This	1965	2.00	4.00	8.00
REF-O-REE					
❑ 703	Having a Party/Almost Sundown	196?	2.50	5.00	10.00
❑ 709	I Understand/Somebody Somewhere	196?	2.50	5.00	10.00
❑ 727	How Long's the Train Been Gone/You Can Make It If You Try & Have Faith	196?	2.50	5.00	10.00
❑ 729	I Understand/Almost Sundown	196?	2.50	5.00	10.00
VEE JAY					
❑ 256	You Can Make It If You Try/Hey, Hey, I Love You	1957	5.00	10.00	20.00
❑ 273	Have Faith/My Heart Remembers	1958	3.75	7.50	15.00
❑ 286	I Don't Know Why/Let's Sit and Talk	1958	3.75	7.50	15.00
❑ 299	Everything Will Be Alright/I'm a Fool Wanting You	1958	3.75	7.50	15.00
❑ 305	Tell Me the Truth/Reap What You Sow	1959	3.75	7.50	15.00
❑ 317	Everybody But Me/I Believe in Myself	1959	3.75	7.50	15.00
❑ 329	I'll Be Waiting for You/Let There Be Women	1959	3.75	7.50	15.00
❑ 341	Why Do You Treat Me So Cold/Oh Yeah I'm in Love	1960	3.75	7.50	15.00
❑ 365	Ask/Tell Me Sugar Baby	1960	3.75	7.50	15.00
ALLISON, KEITH					
AMY					
❑ 11024	Who Do You Love/Don't Want Nobody But You	1968	3.00	6.00	12.00
COLUMBIA					
❑ 43619	Look at Me/I Ain't Blaming You	1966	3.00	6.00	12.00
❑ 43619 [PS]	Look at Me/I Ain't Blaming You	1966	6.25	12.50	25.00
❑ 43900	Action/Glitter and Gold	1966	3.00	6.00	12.00
❑ 44028	Louise/Freeborn Man	1967	3.00	6.00	12.00
❑ 44028 [PS]	Louise/Freeborn Man	1967	6.25	12.50	25.00
❑ 44853	Birds of a Feather/To Know Her Is to Love Her	1969	2.50	5.00	10.00
❑ 45115	Everybody/Wednesday's Child	1970	2.50	5.00	10.00
WARNER BROS.					
❑ 5681	Sweet Little Rock and Roller/The Girl Can't Help It	1965	3.00	6.00	12.00
❑ 5681 [PS]	Sweet Little Rock and Roller/The Girl Can't Help It	1965	6.25	12.50	25.00
ALLISONS, THE					
COLUMBIA					
❑ 42034	Words/Blue Tears	1961	2.50	5.00	10.00
LONDON					
❑ 1977	Are You Sure/There's One Thing More	1961	2.50	5.00	10.00
❑ 1977 [PS]	Are You Sure/There's One Thing More	1961	6.25	12.50	25.00
SMASH					
❑ 1749	Lessons in Love/Oh My Love	1962	2.50	5.00	10.00
ALLMAN, DUANE AND GREGG					
Of THE ALLMAN BROTHERS BAND and THE ALLMAN JOYS.					
BOLD					
❑ 200	Morning Dew/Morning Dew	1973	2.50	5.00	10.00
❑ 200 [DJ]	Morning Dew/Morning Dew	1973	5.00	10.00	20.00
—Promo on red vinyl					
ALLMAN, GREGG					
Of THE ALLMAN BROTHERS BAND and THE ALLMAN JOYS. Also see ALLMAN AND WOMAN.					
CAPRICORN					
❑ 0035	Midnight Rider/Multi-Colored Lady	1973	—	2.50	5.00
❑ 0042	Don't Mess Up a Good Thing/Please Call Home	1974	—	2.00	4.00
❑ 0053	Midnight Rider/Don't Mess Up a Good Thing	1975	—	2.00	4.00
—Back to Back Hits series					
❑ 0279	Cryin' Shame/One More Try	1977	—	2.00	4.00
EPIC					
❑ 06998	I'm No Angel/Lead Me On	1987	—	2.00	4.00

Number	Title (A Side/B Side)	Yr	VG	VG+	NM
❑ 07215	Can't Keep Running/Anything Goes	1987	—	—	3.00
❑ 07430	Evidence of Love/Anything Goes	1987	—	—	3.00
❑ 08041	Slip Away/Every Hungry Woman	1988	—	—	3.00

ALLMAN AND WOMAN
GREGG ALLMAN and CHER.

WARNER BROS.

Number	Title (A Side/B Side)	Yr	VG	VG+	NM
❑ 8504	Love Me/Move Me	1977	—	2.50	5.00

ALLMAN BROTHERS BAND, THE
Also see ALLMAN AND WOMAN; THE ALLMAN JOYS; DUANE AND GREGG ALLMAN; GREGG ALLMAN; DICKIE BETTS; THE HOUR GLASS.

ARISTA

Number	Title (A Side/B Side)	Yr	VG	VG+	NM
❑ 0555	Angeline/So Long	1980	—	2.00	4.00
❑ 0584	Mystery Woman/Hell and High Water	1981	—	2.00	4.00
❑ 0618	Straight from the Heart/Leavin'	1981	—	2.00	4.00
❑ 0618 [PS]	Straight from the Heart/Leavin'	1981	—	2.00	4.00
❑ 0643	Two Rights/Never Knew How Much	1981	—	2.00	4.00

CAPRICORN

Number	Title (A Side/B Side)	Yr	VG	VG+	NM
❑ 0003	Ain't Wastin' Time No More/Melissa	1972	—	2.50	5.00
❑ 0007	Melissa/Blue Sky	1972	—	2.50	5.00
❑ 0014	One Way Out/Standback	1972	—	2.50	5.00
❑ 0027	Ramblin Man/Pony Boy	1973	—	2.50	5.00
❑ 0036	Jessica/Come and Go Blues	1973	—	2.50	5.00
❑ 0050	Ain't Wastin' Time No More/Blue Sky	1974	—	2.00	4.00
—Back to Back Hits series					
❑ 0051	Ramblin Man/Jessica	1974	—	2.00	4.00
—Back to Back Hits series					
❑ 0246	Nevertheless/Louisiana Lou and Three Card Monty John	1975	—	2.00	4.00
❑ 0320	Crazy Love/Just Ain't Easy	1979	—	2.00	4.00
❑ 0326	Can't Take It With You/Sail Away	1979	—	2.00	4.00
❑ 8003	Black Hearted Woman/Every Hungry Woman	1970	—	3.00	6.00
❑ 8011	Revival (Love Is Everywhere)/Leave My Blues at Home	1971	—	2.50	5.00
❑ 8014	Whipping Post/Midnight Rider	1971	—	2.50	5.00

EPIC

Number	Title (A Side/B Side)	Yr	VG	VG+	NM
❑ 73504	Good Clean Fun/Seven Turns	1990	—	2.00	4.00

ALLMAN JOYS, THE
Early ALLMAN BROTHERS BAND.

DIAL

Number	Title (A Side/B Side)	Yr	VG	VG+	NM
❑ 4046	Spoonful/You Deserve Each Other	1966	10.00	20.00	40.00

ALMA-KEYS, THE
KISKI

Number	Title (A Side/B Side)	Yr	VG	VG+	NM
❑ 2056	Please Come Back to Me/Jumpin' Twist	1962	75.00	150.00	300.00

ALTAIRS, THE
GEORGE BENSON was a member.

AMY

Number	Title (A Side/B Side)	Yr	VG	VG+	NM
❑ 803	If You Love Me/Groove Time	1960	5.00	10.00	20.00

ALTON AND JIMMY
SUN

Number	Title (A Side/B Side)	Yr	VG	VG+	NM
❑ 323	Have Faith in My Love/No More Crying the Blues	1959	6.25	12.50	25.00

ALVIN AND BILL
FERNWOOD

Number	Title (A Side/B Side)	Yr	VG	VG+	NM
❑ 124	Typing Jive/How Long	1960	15.00	30.00	60.00

ALVIN AND THE CHIPMUNKS
See THE CHIPMUNKS.

AMBASSADORS, THE (1)
Male vocal group from Philadelphia.

ARCTIC

Number	Title (A Side/B Side)	Yr	VG	VG+	NM
❑ 150	Ain't Got the Love of One Girl/Music Makes You Wanna Dance	1969	2.50	5.00	10.00
❑ 153	Storm Warning/I Dig You Baby	1969	2.50	5.00	10.00
❑ 156	Can't Take My Eyes Off You/A.W.O.L.	1969	2.50	5.00	10.00

ATLANTIC

Number	Title (A Side/B Side)	Yr	VG	VG+	NM
❑ 2442	(I've Got to Find) Happiness)/I'm So Proud of My Baby	1967	2.50	5.00	10.00
❑ 2491	Good Love Gone Bad/Happiness	1968	2.50	5.00	10.00
❑ 2547	We Got Love/Never Get Tired of Loving You	1968	2.50	5.00	10.00

AMBASSADORS, THE (2)
British band known as The Saints in the U.K.

DOT

Number	Title (A Side/B Side)	Yr	VG	VG+	NM
❑ 16528	Surfin' John Brown/Big Breaker	1963	7.50	15.00	30.00

AMBASSADORS, THE (U)
CUCA

Number	Title (A Side/B Side)	Yr	VG	VG+	NM
❑ 1022	Christmas Polka/Little Drummer Boy	1960	3.00	6.00	12.00

SOUND STAGE 7

Number	Title (A Side/B Side)	Yr	VG	VG+	NM
❑ 2588	If You Don't Know (You Better Ask Somebody)/ There's Something on My Baby's Mind	1967	2.50	5.00	10.00

TIMELY

Number	Title (A Side/B Side)	Yr	VG	VG+	NM
❑ 1001	Darling I'm Sorry/Willa-Bea	1954	100.00	200.00	400.00

UPTOWN

Number	Title (A Side/B Side)	Yr	VG	VG+	NM
❑ 734	I Need Someone/Bear With Me	1965	6.25	12.50	25.00

AMBOY DUKES, THE
Also see TED NUGENT.

DISCREET

Number	Title (A Side/B Side)	Yr	VG	VG+	NM
❑ 1199	Sweet Revenge/Ain't It the Truth	1974	—	3.00	6.00
—As "Ted Nugent and the Amboy Dukes"					

MAINSTREAM

Number	Title (A Side/B Side)	Yr	VG	VG+	NM
❑ 676	Baby Please Don't Go/Psalms of Aftermath	1968	3.00	6.00	12.00
❑ 684	Journey to the Center of the Mind/Mississippi Murderer	1968	3.75	7.50	15.00
❑ 693	You Talk Sunshine, I Breathe Fire/Scottish Tea	1968	3.00	6.00	12.00
❑ 700	Prodigal Man/Good Natured Emma	1969	3.00	6.00	12.00
❑ 704	For His Namesake/Loaded for Bear	1969	3.00	6.00	12.00
❑ 711	Flight of the Byrd/Ivory Castles	1969	3.00	6.00	12.00

AMELIO, JOHNNY
BLUE MOON

Number	Title (A Side/B Side)	Yr	VG	VG+	NM
❑ 405	Jugue/Downbeat	1957	37.50	75.00	150.00
❑ 408	Jo-Ann, Jo-Ann/I'll Forever Love You	1958	25.00	50.00	100.00
❑ 410	Jugue/Jo-Ann, Jo-Ann	1958	20.00	40.00	80.00

AMERICAN BEATLES, THE
BYP

Number	Title (A Side/B Side)	Yr	VG	VG+	NM
❑ 1001	She's Mine/Theme of the American Beetles	1964	5.00	10.00	20.00
—As "The American Beetles"					

ROULETTE

Number	Title (A Side/B Side)	Yr	VG	VG+	NM
❑ 4550	You Did It to Me/Don't Be Unkind	1964	3.75	7.50	15.00
❑ 4559	School Days/Hey Hey Girl	1964	3.75	7.50	15.00

AMERICAN BLUES, THE
Early incarnation of ZZ TOP.

AMY

Number	Title (A Side/B Side)	Yr	VG	VG+	NM
❑ 997	Your Love Is True/Say So	1967	6.25	12.50	25.00

KARMA

Number	Title (A Side/B Side)	Yr	VG	VG+	NM
❑ 1001	If I Were a Carpenter/(B-side unknown)	1967	10.00	20.00	40.00

AMERICAN BREED, THE
Members of this band later formed RUFUS.

ACTA

Number	Title (A Side/B Side)	Yr	VG	VG+	NM
❑ 802	I Don't Think You Know/Give Two Young Lovers a Chance	1967	2.00	4.00	8.00
❑ 804	Step Out of Your Mind/Same Old Thing	1967	2.50	5.00	10.00
❑ 808	Don't Forget About Me/Short Skirts	1967	2.00	4.00	8.00
❑ 811	Bend Me, Shape Me/Mindrocker	1967	3.00	6.00	12.00
❑ 821	Green Light/Don't It Make You Cry	1968	2.00	4.00	8.00
❑ 821 [PS]	Green Light/Don't It Make You Cry	1968	5.00	10.00	20.00
❑ 824	Ready, Willing and Able/Take Me If You Want Me	1968	2.00	4.00	8.00
❑ 827	Anyway You Want Me/Master of My Fate	1968	2.00	4.00	8.00
❑ 830	Private Zoo/Keep the Faith	1968	2.00	4.00	8.00
❑ 833	Hunky Funky/Enter Her Majesty	1969	2.00	4.00	8.00
❑ 836	Room at the Top/Walls	1969	2.00	4.00	8.00
❑ 837	Cool It/The Brain	1969	2.00	4.00	8.00

PARAMOUNT

Number	Title (A Side/B Side)	Yr	VG	VG+	NM
❑ 0040	When I'm With You/Can't Make It Without You	1970	—	3.00	6.00

AMERICAN FOUR, THE
With Arthur Lee, future leader of LOVE.

SELMA

Number	Title (A Side/B Side)	Yr	VG	VG+	NM
❑ 2001	Luci Baines/Soul Food	1964	12.50	25.00	50.00

AMERICAN SPRING
Formed by ex-members of THE HONEYS. Also see SPRING.

COLUMBIA

Number	Title (A Side/B Side)	Yr	VG	VG+	NM
❑ 45834	Fallin' in Love/Shyin' Away	1973	7.50	15.00	30.00
❑ 45834 [PS]	Fallin' in Love/Shyin' Away	1973	15.00	30.00	60.00

AMOS, TORI
Also see Y KANT TORI READ.

ATLANTIC

Number	Title (A Side/B Side)	Yr	VG	VG+	NM
❑ 84104	Spark/Purple People	1998	—	—	3.00
❑ 84412	Cruel (Shady Feline Mix)/Raspberry Swirl (Lip Gloss Version)	1998	—	—	3.00
❑ 84532	Bliss/Hey Jupiter (Live)	1999	—	—	3.00
❑ 84534	1000 Oceans/Baker Baker (Live)	1999	—	—	3.00

MEA

Number	Title (A Side/B Side)	Yr	VG	VG+	NM
❑ 5290	Baltimore/Walking with You	1980	150.00	300.00	600.00
—As "Ellen Amos"					

ANASTASIA
LAURIE

Number	Title (A Side/B Side)	Yr	VG	VG+	NM
❑ 3066	Time Bomb/That's My Kind of Love	1960	6.25	12.50	25.00

STASI

Number	Title (A Side/B Side)	Yr	VG	VG+	NM
❑ 1000	Every Road I Walk Along/Bicycle Hop	196?	50.00	100.00	200.00
❑ 1001	Seven Days a Week/Nothing Beats My Girl	196?	37.50	75.00	150.00

ANDANTES, THE
DOT

Number	Title (A Side/B Side)	Yr	VG	VG+	NM
❑ 16495	My Baby's Gone/No Yo Ru	1963	6.25	12.50	25.00

V.I.P.

Number	Title (A Side/B Side)	Yr	VG	VG+	NM
❑ 25006	If You Were Mine/(Like a) Nightmare	1964	625.00	1250.	2500.
—One of the rarest of all Motown-related 45s					

ANDERS, BERNIE
KING

Number	Title (A Side/B Side)	Yr	VG	VG+	NM
❑ 4833	My Heart Believes/Too Late I Learned	1955	12.50	25.00	50.00

ANDERS & PONCIA
Also see THE MULBERRY FRUIT BAND; THE TRADEWINDS.

KAMA SUTRA

Number	Title (A Side/B Side)	Yr	VG	VG+	NM
❑ 240	So It Goes/Virgin of the Night	1967	3.00	6.00	12.00

WARNER BROS.

Number	Title (A Side/B Side)	Yr	VG	VG+	NM
❑ 7271	Take His Love/I'm Beginning to Touch You	1969	2.00	4.00	8.00
❑ 7294	Make a Change (To Something Better)/Lucky	1969	2.00	4.00	8.00

ANDERSON, BROTHER JAMES
SUN

Number	Title (A Side/B Side)	Yr	VG	VG+	NM
❑ 406	I'm Gonna Move in the Room with the Lord/My Soul Needs Resting	1967	12.50	25.00	50.00

ANDERSON, SONNY
IMPERIAL

Number	Title (A Side/B Side)	Yr	VG	VG+	NM
❑ 5634	Yes, I'm Gonna Love You/Lonely, Lonely Train	1959	12.50	25.00	50.00
❑ 5689	Our Love Could Never Be/Fool	1960	12.50	25.00	50.00

ANDERSON, VICKI

Also see JAMES BROWN.

Number	Title (A Side/B Side)	Yr	VG	VG+	NM
BROWNSTONE					
❑ 4202	I'm Too Tough for Mr. Big Stuff/Sound Funky	1971	—	3.00	6.00
❑ 4204	I'll Work It Out/In the Land of Milk and Honey	1971	—	3.00	6.00
❑ 4307	Don't Throw Your Love in the Garbage Can/In the Land of Milk and Honey	1972	—	3.00	6.00
DELUXE					
❑ 6201	Wide Awake in a Dream/Nobody Cares	1966	2.00	4.00	8.00
FONTANA					
❑ 1527	Never, Never Let You Go (Part 1)/Never, Never Let You Go (Part 2)	1965	3.00	6.00	12.00
KING					
❑ 6066	You Send Me/Unchain My Heart	1967	2.00	4.00	8.00
❑ 6091	Think/Nobody Cares	1967	2.50	5.00	10.00
—A-side: With James Brown					
❑ 6109	Tears of Joy/If You Don't Give Me	1967	2.00	4.00	8.00
❑ 6138	That Feelin' Is Real/Baby Don't You Know	1967	2.00	4.00	8.00
❑ 6152	You've Got the Power/What the World Needs Now Is Love	1968	2.50	5.00	10.00
—A-side: With James Brown					
❑ 6221	What the World Needs Now Is Love/I'll Work It Out	1969	2.00	4.00	8.00
❑ 6251	The Answer to Mother Popcorn (I Got a Mother for You)/I'll Work It Out	1969	2.00	4.00	8.00
❑ 6274	Wide Awake in a Dream/I Want to Be in the Land of Milk and Honey	1969	2.00	4.00	8.00
❑ 6293	Let It Be Me/No More Heartaches, No More Pain	1970	2.50	5.00	10.00
—A-side: With James Brown					
❑ 6314	Never Find a Love Like Mine/No More Heartaches, No More Pain	1970	2.00	4.00	8.00
❑ 6377	Message from the Soul Sisters Part 1/Yesterday	1971	2.00	4.00	8.00
SMASH					
❑ 1985	I Love You/Nobody Cares	1965	2.50	5.00	10.00
TUFF					
❑ 420	I Can't Stop Loving You/I Lost a Good Man	1964	2.50	5.00	10.00

ANDREWS, LEE, AND THE HEARTS

Number	Title (A Side/B Side)	Yr	VG	VG+	NM
ARGO					
❑ 1000	Tear Drops/The Girl Around the Corner	1957	12.50	25.00	50.00
CASINO					
❑ 110	Baby, Come Back/I Wonder	1958	7.50	15.00	30.00
❑ 452	Try the Impossible/Nobody's Home	1958	200.00	400.00	600.00
—With playing cards on label					
❑ 452	Try the Impossible/Nobody's Home	1958	50.00	100.00	200.00
—All-black label					
CHESS					
❑ 1665	Long Lonely Nights/The Clock	1957	10.00	20.00	40.00
—Sliver-top "chess pieces" label					
❑ 1665	Long Lonely Nights/The Clock	1957	3.75	7.50	15.00
—All-blue label					
❑ 1675	Tear Drops/The Girl Around the Corner	1957	5.00	10.00	20.00
—All-blue label (if a "chess pieces" label exists, we aren't aware of it)					
CRIMSON					
❑ 1002	Oh My Love/'Island of Love	1967	2.00	4.00	8.00
❑ 1009	Nevertheless/Island of Love	1967	2.00	4.00	8.00
❑ 1015	I've Had It/Little Bird	1968	2.00	4.00	8.00
GOTHAM					
❑ 318	Bluebird of Happiness/Show Me the Meringue	1956	50.00	100.00	200.00
❑ 320	Lonely Room/Leona	1956	75.00	150.00	300.00
❑ 321	Just Suppose/It's Me!	1956	75.00	150.00	300.00
GRAND					
❑ 156	Teardrops/The Girl Around the Corner	1962	3.00	6.00	12.00
❑ 157	Long Lonely Nights/The Clock	1962	3.00	6.00	12.00
LANA					
❑ 110	Long Lonely Nights/The Clock	196?	—	3.00	6.00
❑ 111	Try the Impossible/Nobody's Home	196?	—	3.00	6.00
❑ 112	Teardrops/The Girl Around the Corner	196?	—	3.00	6.00
—Lana records are reissues					
LOST-NITE					
❑ 104	The Fairest/Much Too Much	196?	—	3.00	6.00
❑ 106	The Bells of St. Mary/Much Too Much	196?	—	3.00	6.00
❑ 108	The White Cliffs of Dover/Much Too Much	196?	—	3.00	6.00
❑ 110	Maybe You'll Be There/Baby Come Back	196?	—	3.00	6.00
❑ 135	The Bluebird of Happiness/Show Me the Meringue	196?	—	3.00	6.00
❑ 136	Lonely Room/Leona	196?	—	3.00	6.00
❑ 137	Just Suppose/It's Me	196?	—	3.00	6.00
❑ 176	Teardrops/The Girl Around the Corner	196?	—	3.00	6.00
❑ 190	Long Lonely Nights/The Clock	196?	—	3.00	6.00
❑ 193	Try the Impossible/Nobody's Home	196?	—	3.00	6.00
❑ 216	All I Ask Is Love/Maybe You'll Be There	196?	—	3.00	6.00
❑ 234	Glad to Be Here/Why Do I	196?	—	3.00	6.00
—All the above Lost-Nite records (three-digit numbers) are reissues					
❑ 1001	Cold Gray Dawn/All You Can Do	1968	2.00	4.00	8.00
❑ 1004	Oh My Love/Can't Do Without You	1968	2.00	4.00	8.00
❑ 1005	Quiet As It's Kept/Island of Love	1968	2.00	4.00	8.00
—The above three are NOT reissues					
MAIN LINE					
❑ 102	Long Lonely Nights/The Clock	1957	100.00	200.00	400.00
—Green label, no address					
❑ 102	Long Lonely Nights/The Clock	1957	50.00	100.00	200.00
—Black label, Philadelphia address on label					
❑ 102	Long Lonely Nights/The Clock	1962	7.50	15.00	30.00
—Black label, no address					
❑ 105	Teardrops/The Girl Around the Corner	1962	3.00	6.00	12.00
PARKWAY					
❑ 860	I'm Sorry, Pillow/Gee, But I'm Lonesome	1962	3.75	7.50	15.00
❑ 866	Looking Back/Operator	1963	3.75	7.50	15.00
RAINBOW					
❑ 252	Maybe You'll Be There/Baby Come Back	1954	100.00	200.00	400.00
—Black vinyl					
❑ 252	Maybe You'll Be There/Baby Come Back	1954	200.00	400.00	800.00
—Red vinyl					
❑ 252	Maybe You'll Be There/Baby Come Back	1962	2.50	5.00	10.00
—Reissue with large print					
❑ 256	White Cliffs of Dover/Much Too Much	1954	375.00	750.00	1500.
—Yellow label original					
❑ 256	White Cliffs of Dover/Much Too Much	1962	2.50	5.00	10.00
—Blue label reissue					
❑ 259	The Bells of St. Mary's/The Fairest	1954	150.00	300.00	600.00
—Yellow label original					
❑ 259	The Bells of St. Mary's/The Fairest	1962	2.50	5.00	10.00
—Blue label reissue					
RCA VICTOR					
❑ 47-8929	Quiet As It's Kept/You're Taking a Long Time Coming Back	1966	2.50	5.00	10.00
SWAN					
❑ 4065	I Miss You So/I've Got to Cry	1960	25.00	50.00	100.00
❑ 4076	A Night Like This/You Gave to Me	1961	37.50	75.00	150.00
❑ 4087	P.S. I Love You/I Cried	1961	50.00	100.00	200.00
UNITED ARTISTS					
❑ 123	Try the Impossible/Nobody's Home	1958	6.25	12.50	25.00
❑ 136	Why Do I/Glad to Be Here	1958	5.00	10.00	20.00
❑ 151	Maybe You'll Be There/All I Ask Is Love	1958	5.00	10.00	20.00
❑ 162	Boom/Just Suppose	1959	5.00	10.00	20.00
❑ 592	Try the Impossible/Nobody's Home	1963	3.75	7.50	15.00

ANGEL, JOHNNY

Number	Title (A Side/B Side)	Yr	VG	VG+	NM
EXCELLO					
❑ 2077	I Realize/Baby I'm Confessin'	1956	6.25	12.50	25.00
FELSTED					
❑ 8633	Lady of Spain/Without Her Heart	1961	5.00	10.00	20.00
❑ 8646	Mashed Potatoe Stomp/One More Tomorrow	1962	5.00	10.00	20.00
❑ 8659	Looking for a Fool/Roller Motion	1962	5.00	10.00	20.00
GARDENA					
❑ 117	All Night Party/Baby, You've Got Soul	1961	3.75	7.50	15.00
IMPERIAL					
❑ 5673	Falling Teardrops/Doubt	1960	10.00	20.00	40.00
JAF					
❑ 2024	Lonely Nights/Seven Words	1961	3.75	7.50	15.00
LIBERTY					
❑ 55895	Summertime Blues/Biggest Part of Me	1966	2.00	4.00	8.00
POWER					
❑ 250	Starlight/The Story of Love	1959	30.00	60.00	120.00
SWAN					
❑ 4263	This Is the Night for Love/You've Been Wrong	1966	10.00	20.00	40.00
VIN					
❑ 1004	Teenage Wedding/Baby, It's Love	1958	6.25	12.50	25.00

ANGEL, JOHNNY T.

Number	Title (A Side/B Side)	Yr	VG	VG+	NM
BELL					
❑ 45472	Tell Laura I Love Her/The Way I Feel Tonight	1974	—	2.00	4.00
YORKSVILLE					
❑ 45090	Tell Laura I Love Her/The Way I Feel Tonight	1974	—	3.00	6.00

ANGELS, THE (1)

Female vocal group.

Number	Title (A Side/B Side)	Yr	VG	VG+	NM
CAPRICE					
❑ 107	'Til/A Moment Ago	1961	7.50	15.00	30.00
—With horizontal "Caprice" logo; B-side listed as "A Moment Ago" but plays "Cotton Fields"					
❑ 107	'Til/A Moment Ago	1961	5.00	10.00	20.00
—With semicircular "Caprice" logo					
❑ 112	Cry Baby Cry/That's All I Ask of You	1962	5.00	10.00	20.00
❑ 116	Everybody Loves a Lover/Blow Joe	1962	3.75	7.50	15.00
❑ 118	You Should Have Told Me/I'd Be Good for You	1962	3.75	7.50	15.00
❑ 121	Cotton Fields/A Moment Ago	1963	3.75	7.50	15.00
POLYDOR					
❑ 14222	You're All I Need to Get By/Poppa's Side of the Bed	1974	—	2.50	5.00
RCA VICTOR					
❑ 47-9129	I Had a Dream I Lost You/What to Do	1967	2.50	5.00	10.00
❑ 47-9246	Go Out and Play/You'll Never Get to Heaven (If You Break My Heart)	1967	2.50	5.00	10.00
❑ 47-9404	You're the Cause of It/With Love	1967	2.50	5.00	10.00
❑ 47-9541	The Medley: Moments to Remember-Theme from A Summer Place-One Summer Night/If I Didn't Love You	1968	2.50	5.00	10.00
❑ 47-9612	But for Love/The Man with the Green Eyes	1968	2.50	5.00	10.00
❑ 47-9681	Merry Go Round/So Nice (Samba De Verao)	1968	2.50	5.00	10.00
SMASH					
❑ 1834	My Boyfriend's Back/(Love Me) Now	1963	4.00	8.00	16.00
❑ 1854	I Adore Him/Thank You and Goodnight	1963	3.75	7.50	15.00
❑ 1854 [PS]	I Adore Him/Thank You and Goodnight	1963	15.00	30.00	60.00
❑ 1870	Wow Wow Wee (He's the Boy for Me)/Snowflakes and Teardrops	1964	3.75	7.50	15.00
❑ 1885	Little Beatle Boy/Java	1964	5.00	10.00	20.00
❑ 1915	Jamaica Joe/Dream Boy	1964	3.75	7.50	15.00
❑ 1915 [PS]	Jamaica Joe/Dream Boy	1964	15.00	30.00	60.00
❑ 1931	World Without Love/The Boy from Crosstown	1964	3.75	7.50	15.00
❑ 1931 [PS]	World Without Love/The Boy from Crosstown	1964	20.00	40.00	80.00
—The existence of this sleeve has been confirmed!					

ANGELS, THE (2)

Male vocal group.

Number	Title (A Side/B Side)	Yr	VG	VG+	NM
GEE					
❑ 1024	Glory of Love/It's You I Love Best	1956	15.00	30.00	60.00

Number	Title (A Side/B Side)	Yr	VG	VG+	NM
GRAND					
❑ 115	Wedding Bells/Times Have Changed	1954	100.00	200.00	400.00
—With no address on label					
❑ 115	Wedding Bells/Times Have Changed	1954	12.50	25.00	50.00
—With address on label					
❑ 121	A Lovely Way to Spend An Evening/You're Still My Baby	1954	125.00	250.00	500.00
—With no address on label					
❑ 121	A Lovely Way to Spend An Evening/You're Still My Baby	1954	12.50	25.00	50.00
—With address on label					

ANGELS, THE (3)

Different male vocal group than (2). Also see THE SAFARIS.

Number	Title (A Side/B Side)	Yr	VG	VG+	NM
TAWNY					
❑ 101	A Lover's Poem (To Him)/A Lover's Poem (To Her)	1959	10.00	20.00	40.00

ANGELS, THE (U)

Number	Title (A Side/B Side)	Yr	VG	VG+	NM
ASCOT					
❑ 2139	Irresistible/Cotton Fields	1963	3.00	6.00	12.00
CAMEO					
❑ 250	You Turn Me On/Raining Teardrops	1963	3.75	7.50	15.00

ANGIE AND THE CHICKLETTES

Number	Title (A Side/B Side)	Yr	VG	VG+	NM
APT					
❑ 25080	Treat Him Tender Maureen (Now That Ringo Belongs to You)/Tommy	1965	7.50	15.00	30.00

ANGLO-AMERICANS, THE

Number	Title (A Side/B Side)	Yr	VG	VG+	NM
CHATTAHOOCHIE					
❑ 705	The Music Never Stops/Are You Ready for This?	1966	7.50	15.00	30.00

ANGLOS, THE

Two different groups?

Number	Title (A Side/B Side)	Yr	VG	VG+	NM
ORBIT					
❑ 201	Incense/You're Fooling Me	1965	12.50	25.00	50.00
—Steve Winwood is on this record, his first					
SCEPTER					
❑ 12204	Since You've Been Gone/A Small Town Boy	1967	5.00	10.00	20.00

ANIMALS, THE

Includes "Eric Burdon and the Animals." Also see ERIC BURDON; ERIC BURDON AND WAR; ALAN PRICE.

Number	Title (A Side/B Side)	Yr	VG	VG+	NM
ABKCO					
❑ 4025	House of the Rising Sun/Bring It On Home to Me	1973	—	2.50	5.00
—Contains the full-length version of A-side					
❑ 4026	We Gotta Get Out of This Place/It's My Life	1973	—	2.00	4.00
❑ 4037	Don't Let Me Be Misunderstood/Talkin' About You	1973	—	2.00	4.00
❑ 4038	I'm Cryin'/Boom Boom	1973	—	2.00	4.00
I.R.S.					
❑ 9920	The Night/No John No	1983	—	2.50	5.00
❑ 9923	Love Is For All Time/It's Too Late	1983	—	2.50	5.00
JET					
❑ XW-1070	Fire on the Sun/Riverside County	1977	—	3.00	6.00
MGM					
❑ CS 11 5	Celebrity Scene: The Animals	1967	20.00	40.00	80.00
—Box set of five singles (13791-13795). Price includes box, all 5 singles, jukebox title strips, bio. Records are sometimes found by themselves, so they are also listed separately.					
❑ KGC 178	Gonna Take You Back to Walker/Baby Let Me Take You Home	196?	2.00	4.00	8.00
—Reissue label					
❑ KGC 179	The House of the Rising Sun/I'm Crying	196?	2.50	5.00	10.00
—Reissue label; A-side, despite being labeled 2:58, actually plays 4:29					
❑ KGC 180	Don't Let Me Be Misunderstood/Boom Boom	196?	2.00	4.00	8.00
—Reissue label					
❑ KGC 181	We Gotta Get Out of This Place/Don't Bring Me Down	196?	2.00	4.00	8.00
—Reissue label					
❑ KGC 182	It's My Life/Inside Looking Out	196?	2.00	4.00	8.00
—Reissue label					
❑ 13242	Gonna Send You Back to Walker (Gonna Send You Back to Georgia)/Baby, Let Me Take You Home	1964	3.75	7.50	15.00
❑ 13264	The House of the Rising Sun/Talkin' About You	1964	3.75	7.50	15.00
❑ 13264 [PS]	The House of the Rising Sun/Talkin' About You	1964	7.50	15.00	30.00
❑ 13274	I'm Crying/Take It Easy Baby	1964	3.75	7.50	15.00
❑ 13274 [PS]	I'm Crying/Take It Easy Baby	1964	6.25	12.50	25.00
❑ 13298	Boom Boom/Blue Feeling	1964	3.75	7.50	15.00
❑ 13298 [PS]	Boom Boom/Blue Feeling	1964	6.25	12.50	25.00
❑ 13311	Don't Let Me Be Misunderstood/Club A-Go-Go	1964	3.75	7.50	15.00
❑ 13339	Bring It On Home to Me/For Miss Caulker	1965	3.00	6.00	12.00
❑ 13339 [PS]	Bring It On Home to Me/For Miss Caulker	1965	6.25	12.50	25.00
❑ 13382	We Gotta Get Out of This Place/I Can't Believe It	1965	3.00	6.00	12.00
❑ 13414	It's My Life/I'm Going to Change the World	1965	3.00	6.00	12.00
❑ 13468	Inside-Looking Out/You're On My Mind	1966	3.00	6.00	12.00
❑ 13514	Don't Bring Me Down/Cheating	1966	3.00	6.00	12.00
❑ 13582	See See Rider/She'll Return It	1966	2.50	5.00	10.00
—Starting here, records are by "Eric Burdon and the Animals"					
❑ 13636	Help Me Girl/That Ain't Where It's At	1966	2.50	5.00	10.00
❑ 13721	When I Was Young/A Girl Called Sandoz	1967	2.50	5.00	10.00
❑ 13769	San Franciscan Nights/Good Times	1967	2.50	5.00	10.00
❑ 13769 [PS]	San Franciscan Nights/Good Times	1967	6.25	12.50	25.00
❑ 13791	Don't Bring Me Down/When I Was Young	1967	3.00	6.00	12.00
❑ 13792	See See Rider/Hey Gyp	1967	3.00	6.00	12.00
❑ 13793	Inside-Looking Out/Help Me Girl	1967	3.00	6.00	12.00
❑ 13794	San Franciscan Nights/Good Times	1967	3.00	6.00	12.00
❑ 13795	It's All Meat/The Other Side of This Life	1967	3.00	6.00	12.00
❑ 13868	Monterey/Ain't That So	1967	2.50	5.00	10.00
❑ 13868 [PS]	Monterey/Ain't That So	1967	6.25	12.50	25.00
❑ 13917	Anything/It's All Meat	1968	2.50	5.00	10.00
❑ 13939	Sky Pilot (Part 1)/Sky Pilot (Part 2)	1968	2.50	5.00	10.00
—First pressings have black labels					
❑ 13939	Sky Pilot (Part 1)/Sky Pilot (Part 2)	1968	2.00	4.00	8.00
—Second pressings have blue and gold labels					
❑ 14013	River Deep, Mountain High/White Houses	1968	2.00	4.00	8.00

ANKA, PAUL

Also see PAUL ANKA/GEORGE HAMILTON IV/JOHNNY NASH.

Number	Title (A Side/B Side)	Yr	VG	VG+	NM
ABC-PARAMOUNT					
❑ 45-PRO-104	(You Can) Share Your Love/I Talk to You (On the Telephone)	1958	7.50	15.00	30.00
—Evidently a custom pressing for Paul Anka's fan club					
❑ S 296-1 [S]	(All of a Sudden) My Heart Sings/(B-side unknown)	1959	10.00	20.00	40.00
❑ S 296-2 [S]	(titles unknown)	1959	10.00	20.00	40.00
❑ S 296-3 [S]	C'est Si Bon/Comme Ci, Comme Ca	1959	10.00	20.00	40.00
❑ S 296-4 [S]	Melodie D'Amour/I Miss You So	1959	10.00	20.00	40.00
❑ S 296-5 [S]	I Love Paris/If You Love Me, Really Love Me	1959	10.00	20.00	40.00
—The above five are jukebox singles excerpting the LP "My Heart Sings"					
❑ 9831	Diana/Don't Gamble with Love	1957	5.00	10.00	20.00
❑ 9855	I Love You, Baby/Tell Me That You Love Me	1957	7.50	15.00	30.00
❑ 9880	You Are My Destiny/When I Stop Loving You	1958	5.00	10.00	20.00
❑ 9907	Crazy Love/Let the Bells Keep Ringing	1958	5.00	10.00	20.00
❑ 9937	Midnight/Verboten!	1958	5.00	10.00	20.00
❑ 9956	Just Young/So It's Goodbye	1958	5.00	10.00	20.00
❑ 9987 [M]	(All of a Sudden) My Heart Sings/That's Love	1958	5.00	10.00	20.00
❑ S-9987 [S]	(All of a Sudden) My Heart Sings/That's Love	1958	12.50	25.00	50.00
❑ 10011 [M]	I Miss You So/Late Last Night	1959	3.75	7.50	15.00
❑ 10011 [PS]	I Miss You So/Late Last Night	1959	6.25	12.50	25.00
❑ S-10011 [S]	I Miss You So/Late Last Night	1959	12.50	25.00	50.00
❑ 10022 [M]	Lonely Boy/Your Love	1959	3.75	7.50	15.00
❑ S-10022 [S]	Lonely Boy/Your Love	1959	12.50	25.00	50.00
❑ 10040 [M]	Put Your Head on My Shoulder/Don't Ever Leave Me	1959	3.75	7.50	15.00
❑ 10040 [PS]	Put Your Head on My Shoulder/Don't Ever Leave Me	1959	6.25	12.50	25.00
❑ S-10040 [S]	Put Your Head on My Shoulder/Don't Ever Leave Me	1959	12.50	25.00	50.00
❑ 10064 [M]	It's Time to Cry/Something Has Changed Me	1959	3.75	7.50	15.00
❑ 10064 [PS]	It's Time to Cry/Something Has Changed Me	1959	6.25	12.50	25.00
❑ S-10064 [S]	It's Time to Cry/Something Has Changed Me	1959	12.50	25.00	50.00
❑ 10082 [M]	Puppy Love/Adam and Eve	1960	3.75	7.50	15.00
❑ 10082 [PS]	Puppy Love/Adam and Eve	1960	6.25	12.50	25.00
❑ S-10082 [S]	Puppy Love/Adam and Eve	1960	12.50	25.00	50.00
❑ 10106 [M]	My Home Town/Something Happened	1960	3.75	7.50	15.00
❑ 10106 [PS]	My Home Town/Something Happened	1960	6.25	12.50	25.00
❑ S-10106 [S]	My Home Town/Something Happened	1960	12.50	25.00	50.00
❑ 10132 [M]	Hello Young Lovers/I Love You in the Same Old Way	1960	3.75	7.50	15.00
❑ 10132 [PS]	Hello Young Lovers/I Love You in the Same Old Way	1960	6.25	12.50	25.00
❑ S-10132 [S]	Hello Young Lovers/I Love You in the Same Old Way	1960	12.50	25.00	50.00
❑ 10147 [M]	Summer's Gone/I'd Have to Share	1960	3.75	7.50	15.00
❑ 10147 [PS]	Summer's Gone/I'd Have to Share	1960	5.00	10.00	20.00
❑ S-10147 [S]	Summer's Gone/I'd Have to Share	1960	12.50	25.00	50.00
❑ 10163	Rudolph, the Red-Nosed Reindeer/I Saw Mommy Kissing Santa Claus	1960	6.25	12.50	25.00
❑ 10168 [M]	The Story of My Love/Don't Say You're Sorry	1960	3.75	7.50	15.00
❑ 10168 [PS]	The Story of My Love/Don't Say You're Sorry	1960	6.25	12.50	25.00
❑ S-10168 [S]	The Story of My Love/Don't Say You're Sorry	1960	12.50	25.00	50.00
❑ 10169	It's Christmas Everywhere/Rudolph, the Red-Nosed Reindeer	1960	4.00	8.00	16.00
❑ 10169 [PS]	It's Christmas Everywhere/Rudolph, the Red-Nosed Reindeer	1960	6.25	12.50	25.00
❑ 10194	Tonight My Love, Tonight/I'm Just a Fool Anyway	1961	3.00	6.00	12.00
❑ 10194 [PS]	Tonight My Love, Tonight/I'm Just a Fool Anyway	1961	6.25	12.50	25.00
❑ 10220	Dance On Little Girl/I Talk to You	1961	3.00	6.00	12.00
❑ 10220 [PS]	Dance On Little Girl/I Talk to You	1961	6.25	12.50	25.00
❑ 10239	Kissin' on the Phone/Cinderella	1961	3.00	6.00	12.00
❑ 10239 [PS]	Kissin' on the Phone/Cinderella	1961	6.25	12.50	25.00
❑ 10279	Loveland/The Bells at My Wedding	1961	3.00	6.00	12.00
❑ 10282	The Fools Hall of Fame/Far from the Lights of Town	1961	3.00	6.00	12.00
❑ 10311	I'll Never Find Another You/Uh Huh	1962	2.50	5.00	10.00
❑ 10338	I'm Coming Home/Why	1962	2.50	5.00	10.00
BARNABY					
❑ 2027	You're Some Kind of Friend/Why Are You Leaning on Me, Sir	1971	—	3.00	6.00
BUDDAH					
❑ 252	Do I Love You/So Long City	1971	—	2.50	5.00
❑ 294	Everything's Been Changed/Jubilation	1972	—	2.50	5.00
❑ 314	Something Good Is Coming/Life Song	1972	—	2.50	5.00
❑ 337	While We're Still Young/This Is Your Song	1973	—	2.50	5.00
❑ 349	Hey Girl/You and Me Today	1973	—	2.50	5.00
COLUMBIA					
❑ 03897	Hold Me 'Til the Mornin' Comes/This Is the First Time	1983	—	—	3.00
❑ 03897 [PS]	Hold Me 'Til the Mornin' Comes/This Is the First Time	1983	—	2.00	4.00
❑ 04187	Gimme the Word/No Way Out	1983	—	—	3.00
—A-side: With Karla DeVito					
❑ 04407	Second Chance/Walk a Fine Line	1984	—	—	3.00
❑ 07358	No Way Out/Just for Once	1987	—	—	3.00
—A-side: Paul Anka and Julia Migenas; B-side: Migenas solo					
EPIC					
❑ 50298	You/Make It Up to Me in Love	1976	—	2.00	4.00
—With Odia Coates					
ERIC					
❑ 200	Diana/Don't Gamble with Love	197?	—	2.00	4.00
❑ 200 [PS]	Diana/Don't Gamble with Love	197?	—	2.50	5.00

Number	Title (A Side/B Side)	Yr	VG	VG+	NM
FAME					
❑ XW-345	Flashback/Let Me Get to Know You	1973	—	2.00	4.00
RCA					
❑ PB-11351	Lovely Lady/Brought Up in New York	1978	—	2.00	4.00
❑ PB-11351 [PS]	Lovely Lady/Brought Up in New York	1978	—	2.50	5.00
❑ PB-11395	This Is Love/I'm By Myself Again	1978	—	2.00	4.00
❑ PB-11662	As Long As We Keep Believing/Headlines	1979	—	2.00	4.00
❑ PB-11957	Rainbow/After All	1980	—	—	—
—Unreleased					
❑ PB-12184	We Love Each Other/Think I'm in Love Again	1981	—	—	3.00
❑ PB-12225	I've Been Waiting for You All My Life/Think I'm in Love Again	1981	—	—	3.00
❑ PB-12262	Lady Lay Down/You're Still a Part of Me	1981	—	—	3.00
RCA VICTOR					
❑ VP1-2502 [S]	Young, Alive and In Love/Young and Foolish	1962	10.00	20.00	40.00
❑ VP2-2502 [S]	Younger Than Springtime/You Make Me Feel So Young	1962	10.00	20.00	40.00
❑ VP3-2502 [S]	This Life of Mine/Life Is Just a Bowl of Cherries	1962	10.00	20.00	40.00
❑ VP4-2502 [S]	I Love Life/Aren't You Glad You're You?	1962	10.00	20.00	40.00
❑ VP5-2502 [S]	Falling in Love with You/You're Just in Love	1962	10.00	20.00	40.00
—The above five are 33 1/3 rpm, small hole jukebox singles excerpting the LP "Young, Alive and In Love"					
❑ GB-10180	Diana/Put Your Head on My Shoulders	1975	—	2.00	4.00
—Gold Standard Series					
❑ GB-10181	Puppy Love/Lonely Boy	1975	—	2.00	4.00
—Gold Standard Series					
❑ GB-10182	You Are My Destiny/Tonight, My Love, Tonight	1975	—	2.00	4.00
—Gold Standard Series					
❑ 37-7977	Love Me Warm and Tender/I'd Like to Know	1962	6.25	12.50	25.00
—"Compact Single 33" (small hole, plays at LP speed)					
❑ 47-7977	Love Me Warm and Tender/I'd Like to Know	1962	2.50	5.00	10.00
❑ 47-7977 [PS]	Love Me Warm and Tender/I'd Like to Know	1962	5.00	10.00	20.00
❑ 47-8030	A Steel Guitar and a Glass of Wine/I Never Knew Your Name	1962	2.50	5.00	10.00
❑ 47-8030 [PS]	A Steel Guitar and a Glass of Wine/I Never Knew Your Name	1962	5.00	10.00	20.00
❑ 47-8068	Every Night (Without You)/There You Go	1962	2.50	5.00	10.00
❑ 47-8068 [PS]	Every Night (Without You)/There You Go	1962	5.00	10.00	20.00
❑ 47-8097	Eso Beso (That Kiss!)/Give Me Back My Heart	1962	2.50	5.00	10.00
❑ 47-8097 [PS]	Eso Beso (That Kiss!)/Give Me Back My Heart	1962	5.00	10.00	20.00
❑ 47-8115	Love (Makes the World Go 'Round)/Crying in the Wind	1962	2.50	5.00	10.00
❑ 47-8115 [PS]	Love (Makes the World Go 'Round)/Crying in the Wind	1962	5.00	10.00	20.00
❑ 47-8158	Think About It/At Night	1963	—	—	—
—Unreleased					
❑ 47-8170	Remember Diana/At Night	1963	2.50	5.00	10.00
❑ 47-8170 [PS]	Remember Diana/At Night	1963	5.00	10.00	20.00
❑ 47-8195	Hello Jim/You've Got the Nerve to Call This Love	1963	2.50	5.00	10.00
❑ 47-8195 [PS]	Hello Jim/You've Got the Nerve to Call This Love	1963	5.00	10.00	20.00
❑ 47-8237	Wondrous Are the Ways of Love/Hurry Up and Tell Me	1963	2.50	5.00	10.00
❑ 47-8237 [PS]	Wondrous Are the Ways of Love/Hurry Up and Tell Me	1963	5.00	10.00	20.00
❑ 47-8272	Did You Have a Happy Birthday/For No Good Reason at All	1963	2.50	5.00	10.00
❑ 47-8272 [PS]	Did You Have a Happy Birthday/For No Good Reason at All	1963	5.00	10.00	20.00
❑ 47-8311	From Rocking Horse to Rocking Chair/Cheer Up	1964	2.00	4.00	8.00
❑ 47-8311 [PS]	From Rocking Horse to Rocking Chair/Cheer Up	1964	3.75	7.50	15.00
❑ 47-8349	My Baby's Comin' Home/No, No	1964	2.00	4.00	8.00
❑ 47-8349 [PS]	My Baby's Comin' Home/No, No	1964	3.75	7.50	15.00
❑ 47-8396	In My Imagination/It's Easy to Say	1964	2.00	4.00	8.00
❑ 47-8396 [PS]	In My Imagination/It's Easy to Say	1964	3.75	7.50	15.00
❑ 47-8441	Cindy Go Home/Ogni Volta	1964	2.00	4.00	8.00
❑ 47-8441 [PS]	Cindy Go Home/Ogni Volta	1964	3.75	7.50	15.00
❑ 47-8493	Sylvia/Behind My Smile	1965	2.00	4.00	8.00
❑ 47-8595	Dream Me Happy/The Loneliest Boy in the World	1965	2.00	4.00	8.00
❑ 47-8662	Every Day a Heart Is Broken/As If There Were No Tomorrow	1965	2.00	4.00	8.00
❑ 47-8764	Truly Yours/Oh, Such a Stranger	1965	2.00	4.00	8.00
❑ 47-8839	I Wish/I Went to Your Wedding	1966	2.00	4.00	8.00
❑ 47-8893	I Can't Help Loving You/Can't Get Along Very Well Without Her	1966	2.00	4.00	8.00
❑ 47-9032	Poor Old World/I'd Rather Be a Stranger	1966	2.00	4.00	8.00
❑ 47-9128	Until It's Time for You to Go/Would You Still Be My Baby	1967	2.00	4.00	8.00
❑ 47-9228	A Woman Is a Sentimental Thing/That's How Love Goes	1967	2.00	4.00	8.00
❑ 47-9457	Can't Get You Out of My Mind/When We Get There	1968	2.00	4.00	8.00
❑ 47-9648	Goodnight My Love/This Crazy World	1968	2.00	4.00	8.00
❑ 47-9767	Happy/Can't Get You Out of My Mind	1969	2.00	4.00	8.00
❑ 47-9846	Midnight Mistress/Before It's Too Late-This Land Is Your Land	1970	2.00	4.00	8.00
❑ 74-0126	In the Still of the Night/Pickin' Up the Pieces	1969	2.00	4.00	8.00
❑ 74-0164	Sincerely/Next Year	1969	2.00	4.00	8.00
RPM					
❑ 472	I Confess/Blau-Wile Deveest Fontaine	1956	20.00	40.00	80.00
❑ 499	I Confess/Blau-Wile Deveest Fontaine	1957	7.50	15.00	30.00
UNITED ARTISTS					
❑ XW-454	(You're) Having My Baby/Papa	1974	—	2.00	4.00
❑ XW-569	One Man Woman/One Woman Man//Let Me Get to Know You	1974	—	2.00	4.00
—A-side: With Odia Coates					
❑ XW-615	I Don't Like to Sleep Alone/How Can Anything Be Beautiful After You	1975	—	2.00	4.00
❑ XW-615 [PS]	I Don't Like to Sleep Alone/How Can Anything Be Beautiful After You	1975	—	2.00	4.00
❑ XW-682	(I Believe) There's Nothing Stronger Than Our Love/Today I Became a Fool	1975	—	3.00	6.00
—Canada-only release					
❑ XW-685	(I Believe) There's Nothing Stronger Than Our Love/Today I Became a Fool	1975	—	2.00	4.00
❑ XW-737	Times of Your Life/Water Runs Deep	1975	—	2.00	4.00
❑ XW-737 [PS]	Times of Your Life/Water Runs Deep	1975	—	2.00	4.00
❑ XW-789	Anytime (I'll Be There)/Something About You	1976	—	2.00	4.00
❑ XW-896	Happier/Closing Doors	1976	—	3.00	6.00
—Canada-only release					
❑ XW-911	Happier/Closing Doors	1976	—	2.00	4.00
❑ XW-945	I'll Help You/Never Gonna Fall in Love Like I Fell in Love with You	1977	—	2.00	4.00
❑ XW-972	My Best Friend's Wife/Never Gonna Fall in Love Like I Fell in Love with You	1977	—	2.00	4.00
❑ XW-1018	Tonight/Everybody Ought to Be in Love	1977	—	2.00	4.00
❑ XW-1157	(You're) Having My Baby//One Man Woman/One Woman Man	1978	—	—	3.00
—Reissue					
❑ XW-1158	I Don't Like to Sleep Alone/Times of Your Life	1978	—	—	3.00
—Reissue					

ANKA, PAUL/GEORGE HAMILTON IV/JOHNNY NASH

Also see each artist's individual listings.

Number	Title (A Side/B Side)	Yr	VG	VG+	NM
ABC-PARAMOUNT					
❑ 9974	The Teen Commandments/If You Learn to Pray	1958	6.25	12.50	25.00

ANN-MARGRET

Number	Title (A Side/B Side)	Yr	VG	VG+	NM
ARIOLA					
❑ 7511	Love Rush/For You	1979	—	3.00	6.00
AVCO EMBASSY					
❑ 4547	Today/Today	1970	3.75	7.50	15.00
—B-side by Lenny Stack					
LHI					
❑ 1	It's a Nice World to Visit/You Turned My Head Around	1969	—	3.00	6.00
❑ 2	Chico/Sleep in the Grass	1969	—	3.00	6.00
—With Lee Hazlewood					
❑ 5	The Dark End of the Street/Victims of the Night	1969	—	3.00	6.00
—With Lee Hazlewood					
❑ 11	Walk Out of My Mind/Hangin' In	1970	—	3.00	6.00
—With Lee Hazlewood					
MCA					
❑ 41186	Love Rush/For You	1980	—	2.50	5.00
❑ 41223	Midnight Message/For You	1980	—	2.50	5.00
RCA VICTOR					
❑ VP1-2551 [S]	Jim Dandy/Thirteen Men	1962	10.00	20.00	40.00
❑ VP2-2551 [S]	Rock and Roll Waltz/There'll Be Some Changes Made	1962	10.00	20.00	40.00
❑ VP3-2551 [S]	Make Love to Me/Tell Me, Tell Me	1962	10.00	20.00	40.00
❑ VP4-2551 [S]	C'est Si Bon/Please Don't Talk About Me When I'm Gone	1962	10.00	20.00	40.00
❑ VP5-2551 [S]	Inka Dinka Doo/Begin the Beguine	1962	10.00	20.00	40.00
—The above five are 33 1/3 rpm, small hole jukebox singles excerpting the LP "The Vivacious One"					
❑ 37-7857	I Ain't Got Nobody/Lost Love	1961	6.25	12.50	25.00
—"Compact Single 33" (small hole, plays at LP speed)					
❑ 37-7894	I Just Don't Understand/I Don't Hurt Anymore	1961	6.25	12.50	25.00
—"Compact Single 33" (small hole, plays at LP speed)					
❑ 37-7952	It Do Me So Good/Gimme Love	1961	6.25	12.50	25.00
—"Compact Single 33" (small hole, plays at LP speed)					
❑ 47-7857	I Ain't Got Nobody/Lost Love	1961	3.00	6.00	12.00
❑ 47-7894	I Just Don't Understand/I Don't Hurt Anymore	1961	3.75	7.50	15.00
❑ 47-7894 [PS]	I Just Don't Understand/I Don't Hurt Anymore	1961	6.25	12.50	25.00
❑ 47-7952	It Do Me So Good/Gimme Love	1961	2.50	5.00	10.00
❑ 47-7952 [PS]	It Do Me So Good/Gimme Love	1961	6.25	12.50	25.00
❑ 47-7986	What Am I Supposed to Do/Let's Stop Kidding Each Other	1962	2.50	5.00	10.00
❑ 47-7986 [PS]	What Am I Supposed to Do/Let's Stop Kidding Each Other	1962	6.25	12.50	25.00
❑ 47-8061	Jim Dandy/I Was Only Kidding	1962	2.50	5.00	10.00
❑ 47-8061 [PS]	Jim Dandy/I Was Only Kidding	1962	6.25	12.50	25.00
❑ 47-8130	No More/So Did I	1963	2.50	5.00	10.00
❑ 47-8130 [PS]	No More/So Did I	1963	6.25	12.52	25.00
❑ 47-8168	Bye Bye Birdie/Take All the Kisses	1963	2.50	5.00	10.00
❑ 47-8168 [PS]	Bye Bye Birdie/Take All the Kisses	1963	6.25	12.50	25.00
❑ 47-8295	Hey Little Star/Man's Favorite Sport	1963	2.50	5.00	10.00
❑ 47-8446	He's My Man/Someday Soon	1964	2.50	5.00	10.00
❑ 47-8446 [PS]	He's My Man/Someday Soon	1964	7.50	15.00	30.00
❑ 47-8734	Mister Kiss Kiss Bang Bang/What Did I Have That I Don't Have Now	1965	2.50	5.00	10.00
❑ 47-9013	The Swinger/You've Come a Long Way from St. Louis	1966	2.50	5.00	10.00

ANNETTE

Also see FRANKIE AVALON AND ANNETTE FUNICELLO.

Number	Title (A Side/B Side)	Yr	VG	VG+	NM
BUENA VISTA					
❑ 336	Jo Jo the Dog Faced Boy/Lonely Guitar	1959	5.00	10.00	20.00
❑ 336	Jo Jo the Dog Faced Boy/Love Me Forever	1959	3.75	7.50	15.00
❑ 339	Wild Willie/Lonely Guitar	1959	3.75	7.50	15.00
❑ 339 [PS]	Wild Willie/Lonely Guitar	1959	7.50	15.00	30.00
❑ 344	Especially for You/My Heart Became of Age	1959	3.75	7.50	15.00
❑ 349	First Name Initial/My Heart Became of Age	1959	3.75	7.50	15.00
❑ 349 [PS]	First Name Initial/My Heart Became of Age	1959	7.50	15.00	30.00
❑ 354	O Dio Mio/It Took Dreams	1960	3.75	7.50	15.00
❑ 354 [PS]	O Dio Mio/It Took Dreams	1960	7.50	15.00	30.00
❑ 359	Train of Love/Tell Me Who's the Girl	1960	3.75	7.50	15.00
❑ 359 [PS]	Train of Love/Tell Me Who's the Girl	1960	10.00	20.00	40.00
❑ 362	Pineapple Princess/Luau Cha Cha Cha	1960	3.75	7.50	15.00
❑ 362 [PS]	Pineapple Princess/Luau Cha Cha Cha	1960	7.50	15.00	30.00
❑ 369	Talk to Me Baby/I Love You Baby	1960	3.75	7.50	15.00
❑ 369 [PS]	Talk to Me Baby/I Love You Baby	1960	7.50	15.00	30.00
❑ 374	Dream Boy/Please, Please Signore	1961	3.75	7.50	15.00
❑ 374 [PS]	Dream Boy/Please, Please Signore	1961	7.50	15.00	30.00
❑ 375	Indian Giver/Mama, Mama Rosa (Where's the Spumoni)	1961	3.75	7.50	15.00

Number	Title (A Side/B Side)	Yr	VG	VG+	NM
❑ 375 [PS]	Indian Giver/Mama, Mama Rosa (Where's the Spumoni)	1961	7.50	15.00	30.00
❑ 384	Hawaiian Love Talk/Blue Muu Muu	1961	3.75	7.50	15.00
❑ 384 [PS]	Hawaiian Love Talk/Blue Muu Muu	1961	12.50	25.00	50.00
❑ 388	Dreamin' About You/Strummin' Song	1961	3.75	7.50	15.00
❑ 388 [PS]	Dreamin' About You/Strummin' Song	1961	7.50	15.00	30.00
❑ 392	That Crazy Place From Outer Space/Seven Moons (Of Batalayre)	1962	3.75	7.50	15.00

—B-side by Danny Saval and Tom Tryon

Number	Title (A Side/B Side)	Yr	VG	VG+	NM
❑ 392 [PS]	That Crazy Place From Outer Space/Seven Moons (Of Batalayre)	1962	10.00	20.00	40.00
❑ 394	The Truth About Youth/I Can't Do the Sum	1962	3.75	7.50	15.00
❑ 394 [PS]	The Truth About Youth/I Can't Do the Sum	1962	10.00	20.00	40.00
❑ 400	My Little Grass Shack/Hukilau	1962	3.75	7.50	15.00
❑ 405	He's My Ideal/Mr. Piano Man	1962	3.75	7.50	15.00
❑ 405 [PS]	He's My Ideal/Mr. Piano Man	1962	7.50	15.00	30.00
❑ 407	Bella Bella Florence/Canzone d'Amoure	1962	3.75	7.50	15.00

—With Marcochi

Number	Title (A Side/B Side)	Yr	VG	VG+	NM
❑ 407 [PS]	Bella Bella Florence/Canzone d'Amoure	1962	37.50	75.00	150.00
❑ 414	Teenage Wedding/Walkin' and Talkin'	1962	5.00	10.00	20.00
❑ 414 [PS]	Teenage Wedding/Walkin' and Talkin'	1962	150.00	300.00	600.00
❑ 427	Treat Him Nicely/Promise Me Anything	1963	3.75	7.50	15.00
❑ 427 [PS]	Treat Him Nicely/Promise Me Anything	1963	15.00	30.00	60.00
❑ 431	Merlin Jones/The Scrambled Egghead	1964	3.00	6.00	12.00

—With Tommy Kirk

Number	Title (A Side/B Side)	Yr	VG	VG+	NM
❑ 431 [PS]	Merlin Jones/The Scrambled Egghead	1964	7.50	15.00	30.00
❑ 432	Custom City/Rebel Rider	1964	5.00	10.00	20.00
❑ 432 [PS]	Custom City/Rebel Rider	1964	20.00	40.00	60.00
❑ 433	Muscle Beach Party/I Dream About Frankie	1964	3.75	7.50	15.00
❑ 433 [PS]	Muscle Beach Party/I Dream About Frankie	1964	7.50	15.00	30.00
❑ 436	Bikini Beach Party/The Clyde	1964	3.75	7.50	15.00
❑ 436 [PS]	Bikini Beach Party/The Clyde	1964	10.00	20.00	40.00
❑ 437	The Wah-Watusi/The Clyde	1964	3.00	6.00	12.00
❑ 438	Something Borrowed, Something Blue/How Will I Know My Love	1965	3.75	7.50	15.00
❑ 438 [PS]	Something Borrowed, Something Blue/How Will I Know My Love	1965	20.00	40.00	80.00
❑ 440	The Monkey's Uncle/How Will I Know My Love	1965	3.00	6.00	12.00

—With the Beach Boys backing up

Number	Title (A Side/B Side)	Yr	VG	VG+	NM
❑ 440 [PS]	The Monkey's Uncle/How Will I Know My Love	1965	5.00	10.00	20.00
❑ 442	The Boy to Love/No One Else Could Be Prouder	1965	3.00	6.00	12.00
❑ 450	No Way to Go But Up/Crystal Ball	1966	3.00	6.00	12.00
❑ 475	The Computer Wore Tennis Shoes/Merlin Jones	1970	2.00	4.00	8.00

DISNEYLAND

Number	Title (A Side/B Side)	Yr	VG	VG+	NM
❑ 102	How Will I Know My Love/Don't Jump to Conclusions	1958	6.25	15.00	30.00
❑ 102 [PS]	How Will I Know My Love/Don't Jump to Conclusions	1958	12.50	25.00	50.00
❑ 114	That Crazy Place in Outer Space/Gold Doubloons and Pieces of Eight	1958	10.00	20.00	40.00

—B-side: "Theme from the Hardy Boys"

Number	Title (A Side/B Side)	Yr	VG	VG+	NM
❑ 118	Tall Paul/Ma, He's Making Eyes at Me	1959	5.00	10.00	20.00
❑ 786	That Crazy Place From Outer Space/Happy Glow	196?	2.50	5.00	10.00

—No artist credit on label, but A-side is the same recording as Disneyland 114

EPIC

Number	Title (A Side/B Side)	Yr	VG	VG+	NM
❑ 9829	Baby Needs Me Now/Moment of Silence	1965	6.25	12.50	25.00

—With Cecil Null

STARVIEW

Number	Title (A Side/B Side)	Yr	VG	VG+	NM
❑ 3001	The Promised Land/In Between and Out of Love	1983	2.50	5.00	10.00
❑ 3001 [PS]	The Promised Land/In Between and Out of Love	1983	2.50	5.00	10.00

TOWER

Number	Title (A Side/B Side)	Yr	VG	VG+	NM
❑ 326	What's a Girl to Do/When You Get What You Want	1967	7.50	15.00	30.00

ANNIE AND THE ORPHANS

CAPITOL

Number	Title (A Side/B Side)	Yr	VG	VG+	NM
❑ 5144	My Girl's Been Bitten by the Beatle Bug/A Place Called Happiness	1964	5.00	10.00	20.00
❑ 5144 [PS]	My Girl's Been Bitten by the Beatle Bug/A Place Called Happiness	1964	6.25	12.50	25.00

ANTELL, PETE

BOUNTY

Number	Title (A Side/B Side)	Yr	VG	VG+	NM
❑ 103	The Times They Are a-Changin'/Yesterrday and Tomorrow	1965	3.75	7.50	15.00

CAMEO

Number	Title (A Side/B Side)	Yr	VG	VG+	NM
❑ 234	Night Time/Something About You	1962	5.00	10.00	20.00
❑ 264	You in Disguise/Keep It Up	1963	3.75	7.50	15.00

NEW VOICE

Number	Title (A Side/B Side)	Yr	VG	VG+	NM
❑ 818	Wanting/Warm Smoke	1967	2.50	5.00	10.00

ANTHONY, LAMONT

See LAMONT DOZIER.

ANTHONY, NICK

ABC-PARAMOUNT

Number	Title (A Side/B Side)	Yr	VG	VG+	NM
❑ 9919	More Than Ever/You're Real Keen, Jelly Bean	1958	5.00	10.00	20.00
❑ 9985	Forbidden Love/My Baby's Gone	1958	5.00	10.00	20.00

ANTHONY, RAYBURN

AUDIOGRAPH

Number	Title (A Side/B Side)	Yr	VG	VG+	NM
❑ 444	Tennessee Whiskey, Texas Women/(B-side unknown)	1983	—	3.00	6.00
❑ 459	Dance for a Crystal Ball/(B-side unknown)	1983	—	3.00	6.00

MEGA

Number	Title (A Side/B Side)	Yr	VG	VG+	NM
❑ 0048	Binoculars/Wild Flowers	1971	—	3.50	7.00

MERCURY

Number	Title (A Side/B Side)	Yr	VG	VG+	NM
❑ 55042	I Thought You Were Easy/This One's for You	1978	—	2.00	4.00
❑ 55053	Shadows of Love/Fire in the Night	1979	—	2.00	4.00
❑ 55063	It Won't Go Away/Baby Take It from Me	1979	—	2.00	4.00
❑ 57006	The Wild Side of Life/I Don't Believe I'll Fall in Love Today	1979	—	2.00	4.00

—A-side with Kitty Wells

Number	Title (A Side/B Side)	Yr	VG	VG+	NM
❑ 57024	Married Women/Cheatin' Fire	1980	—	2.00	4.00
❑ 57040	What Do You Need with Another Man/(B-side unknown)	1980	—	2.00	4.00

MILLION

Number	Title (A Side/B Side)	Yr	VG	VG+	NM
❑ 19	Memphis Morning/(B-side unknown)	1972	2.00	4.00	8.00

MONUMENT

Number	Title (A Side/B Side)	Yr	VG	VG+	NM
❑ 1004	I've Worn Out My Welcome Home/Walkin' on My Heart in High Heel Sneakers	1967	2.50	5.00	10.00
❑ 1023	There'll Be Many Tomorrows (Before I Forget Yesterday)/A Woman Whose Love Is Hard to Keep	1967	2.50	5.00	10.00

MUSICOR

Number	Title (A Side/B Side)	Yr	VG	VG+	NM
❑ 1073	You're Driving You Out of My Mind/Big Foot Again	1965	2.50	5.00	10.00

POLYDOR

Number	Title (A Side/B Side)	Yr	VG	VG+	NM
❑ 14346	Crazy Again/Mother Country Music	1976	—	2.50	5.00
❑ 14367	If You Don't Like Hank Williams/This Time Marie	1976	—	3.00	6.00
❑ 14380	Lonely Eyes/Walkin'	1977	—	2.50	5.00
❑ 14398	Hold Me/Don't Fall in Love	1977	—	2.50	5.00
❑ 14423	She Keeps Hangin' On/Talk About a Feeling	1977	—	2.50	5.00
❑ 14457	Maybe I Should've Been Listenin'/This Time Marie	1978	—	2.50	5.00
❑ 14482	Ain't No California/Talk About a Feeling	1978	—	2.50	5.00

STOP

Number	Title (A Side/B Side)	Yr	VG	VG+	NM
❑ 240	You Still Turn Me On/Bag Is You	1969	2.00	4.00	8.00

SUN

Number	Title (A Side/B Side)	Yr	VG	VG+	NM
❑ 333	Alice Blue Gown/St. Louis Blues	1959	5.00	10.00	20.00
❑ 339	There's No Tomorrow/Who's Gonna Shoe Your Pretty Foot	1960	5.00	10.00	20.00
❑ 373	Big Dream/How Well I Know	1962	5.00	10.00	20.00

ANTHONY AND THE SOPHOMORES

Also see THE DYNAMICS (3).

ABC

Number	Title (A Side/B Side)	Yr	VG	VG+	NM
❑ 10844	Heartbreak/I'll Go Through Life Loving You	1966	5.00	10.00	20.00

ABC-PARAMOUNT

Number	Title (A Side/B Side)	Yr	VG	VG+	NM
❑ 10737	Gee (But I'd Give the World)/It Depends On You	1965	5.00	10.00	20.00
❑ 10770	Get Back to You/Wild for Her	1966	5.00	10.00	20.00

GRAND

Number	Title (A Side/B Side)	Yr	VG	VG+	NM
❑ 163	Embraceable You/Beautiful Dreamer	1963	15.00	30.00	60.00

JAMIE

Number	Title (A Side/B Side)	Yr	VG	VG+	NM
❑ 1330	Serenade (From The Student Prince)/Work Out	1967	3.75	7.50	15.00
❑ 1340	One Summer Night/Work Out	1967	3.75	7.50	15.00

JASON SCOTT

Number	Title (A Side/B Side)	Yr	VG	VG+	NM
❑ 18	Embraceable You/Beautiful Dreamer	1978	—	2.00	4.00

MERCURY

Number	Title (A Side/B Side)	Yr	VG	VG+	NM
❑ 72103	Play Those Oldies Mr. D.J./Clap Your Hands	1963	15.00	30.00	60.00
❑ 72168	Swingin' at the Chariot/Better Late Than Never	1963	7.50	15.00	30.00

ANTWINETTES, THE

RCA VICTOR

Number	Title (A Side/B Side)	Yr	VG	VG+	NM
❑ 47-7398	Johnny/Kill It	1958	10.00	20.00	40.00

AORTA

ATLANTIC

Number	Title (A Side/B Side)	Yr	VG	VG+	NM
❑ 2545	Strange/Shape of Things to Come	1968	5.00	10.00	20.00

COLUMBIA

Number	Title (A Side/B Side)	Yr	VG	VG+	NM
❑ 44870	Strange/Ode to Missy Mztsfpklk	1969	2.50	5.00	10.00

HAPPY TIGER

Number	Title (A Side/B Side)	Yr	VG	VG+	NM
❑ 567	Sandcastles/Willie Jean	1970	3.75	7.50	15.00

APHRODITE'S CHILD

PHILIPS

Number	Title (A Side/B Side)	Yr	VG	VG+	NM
❑ 40536	Other People/Plastics Nevermore	1968	5.00	10.00	20.00
❑ 40587	End of the World/You Always Stand in My Way	1969	5.00	10.00	20.00

POLYDOR

Number	Title (A Side/B Side)	Yr	VG	VG+	NM
❑ 15005	Magic Mirror/I Want to Live	1969	2.00	4.00	8.00

VERTIGO

Number	Title (A Side/B Side)	Yr	VG	VG+	NM
❑ 107	Babylon/Break	1973	—	3.00	6.00

APPLE, FIONA

CLEAN SLATE/WORK

Number	Title (A Side/B Side)	Yr	VG	VG+	NM
❑ 78595	Criminal/Sleep to Dream (Live)	1998	—	2.00	4.00

APPLEJACKS, THE (1)

Essentially Dave Appell. The below includes his "solo" records.

B.T. PUPPY

Number	Title (A Side/B Side)	Yr	VG	VG+	NM
❑ 554	The Son of a Preacher Man/Girl of the Skies	1970	2.00	4.00	8.00

—As "Dave Appell"

CAMEO

Number	Title (A Side/B Side)	Yr	VG	VG+	NM
❑ 110	Love in the Jungle/Chitter Chatter Baby	1957	5.00	10.00	20.00
❑ 132	Dinner with Drac/No Name Theme	1958	6.25	12.50	25.00
❑ 138	Moonlight Serenade/Walk On	1958	5.00	10.00	20.00
❑ 149	Mexican Hat Rock/Sophisticated Swing	1958	5.00	10.00	20.00
❑ 149	Mexican Hat Rock/Stop! Red Light	1958	4.00	8.00	16.00
❑ 155	Rocka-Tonga/Am I Blue	1958	5.00	10.00	20.00

—First pressing contains a typographical error on A-side

Number	Title (A Side/B Side)	Yr	VG	VG+	NM
❑ 155	Rocka-Conga/Am I Blue	1958	4.00	8.00	16.00

—Later pressings have correct A-side title

Number	Title (A Side/B Side)	Yr	VG	VG+	NM
❑ 158	Bunny Hop/Night Train Stroll	1959	4.00	8.00	16.00
❑ 170	Circle Dance/Love Scene	1959	4.00	8.00	16.00
❑ 177	The Untouchables/Memories Are Made of This	1960	4.00	8.00	16.00
❑ 184	Theme from The Young Ones/September Song	1960	3.75	7.50	15.00

—As "Dave Appell and His Orchestra"

Number	Title (A Side/B Side)	Yr	VG	VG+	NM
❑ 203	Mexican Hat Twist/Let's Continental	1961	3.75	7.50	15.00
❑ 207	Happy Jose/Noivous	1961	3.75	7.50	15.00

—As "Dave Appell and His Orchestra"

Number	Title (A Side/B Side)	Yr	VG	VG+	NM
❑ 222	Struttin' in the Summertime/Any Time	1962	3.75	7.50	15.00
❑ 248	Hippies Waltz/Back in 60 Seconds	1963	3.75	7.50	15.00
❑ 283	Hot Toddy/Dance of the Hours	1963	3.75	7.50	15.00
❑ 321	She Loves You/Bongo Beach	1964	3.75	7.50	15.00

—As "Dave Appell and His Orchestra"

APPLEJACKS, THE (2)

British band.

LONDON

Number	Title (A Side/B Side)	Yr	VG	VG+	NM
❑ 9658	Baby Jane/Tell Me When	1964	3.00	6.00	12.00
❑ 9681	Like Dreamers Do/Everybody Fall Down	1964	3.75	7.50	15.00
❑ 9709	You're the One for Me/Three Little Words	1964	3.00	6.00	12.00
❑ 9709	You're the One for Me/Send Me Love	1964	3.00	6.00	12.00

APPLEJACKS, THE (U)

Number	Title (A Side/B Side)	Yr	VG	VG+	NM
DECCA					
❑ 9-29218	Smarter/My Heart Will Wait for You	1954	5.00	10.00	20.00
❑ 9-29330	Sweet Patootie Pie/Reunion	1954	5.00	10.00	20.00
PRESIDENT					
❑ 1005	Ring Around My Baby/Love Express	1956	5.00	10.00	20.00
❑ 1006	Teenage Meeting/Ooh Baby Ooh	1956	5.00	10.00	20.00
❑ 1011	Rock and Roll Story/Rainbow of Love	1956	5.00	10.00	20.00

APPRECIATIONS, THE

Number	Title (A Side/B Side)	Yr	VG	VG+	NM
JUBILEE					
❑ 5525	Afraid of Love/Far from Your Love	1966	3.00	6.00	12.00
SPORT					
❑ 108	There's a Place in My Heart/She Never Really Believed Me	1967	25.00	50.00	100.00
❑ 112	It's Better to Cry/Gimme Back My Soul	1967	50.00	100.00	200.00

AQUATONES, THE

Number	Title (A Side/B Side)	Yr	VG	VG+	NM
FARGO					
❑ 1001	You/She's the One for Me	1958	6.25	12.50	25.00
❑ 1002	Say You'll Be Mine/So Fine	1958	6.25	12.50	25.00
❑ 1003	Our First Kiss/The Drive-In	1958	6.25	12.50	25.00
❑ 1005	My Treasure/My One Desire	1959	6.25	12.50	25.00
❑ 1015	Every Time/There's a Long, Long Trail	1960	6.25	12.50	25.00
❑ 1016	Wanted/Crazy for You	1961	6.25	12.50	25.00
❑ 1022	My Treasure/Say You'll Be Mine	1961	6.25	12.50	25.00
❑ 1111	My Darling/For You, For You	196?	5.00	10.00	20.00

ARBORS, THE

Number	Title (A Side/B Side)	Yr	VG	VG+	NM
CARNEY					
❑ 1011	A Symphony for Susan/Love Is the Light	1966	6.25	12.50	25.00
DATE					
❑ 1529	A Symphony for Susan/Love Is the Light	1966	2.50	5.00	10.00
❑ 1546	Dreamer Girl/Just Let It Happen	1967	2.50	5.00	10.00
❑ 1561	Graduation Day/I Win the Whole Wide World	1967	2.50	5.00	10.00
❑ 1570	Love for All Seasons/With You Girl	1967	2.50	5.00	10.00
❑ 1581	Valley of the Dolls/You Are the Music	1967	2.50	5.00	10.00
❑ 1601	That's the Way It Is/Graduation Day	1968	2.50	5.00	10.00
❑ 1638	The Letter/Most of All	1969	3.00	6.00	12.00
❑ 1645	I Can't Quit Her/Lovin' Tonight (Maybe Tonight)	1969	2.50	5.00	10.00
❑ 1651	Touch Me/Motet	1969	2.50	5.00	10.00
❑ 1672	Julie I Tried/Okalona River Bottom Band	1970	2.50	5.00	10.00
MERCURY					
❑ 72456	Anybody Here for Love/The Girl with the Heather Green Eyes	1965	3.00	6.00	12.00

ARCADIA

Splinter group from DURAN DURAN.

Number	Title (A Side/B Side)	Yr	VG	VG+	NM
ATLANTIC					
❑ 89370	Say the Word/(Instrumental)	1986	—	2.00	4.00
❑ 89370 [PS]	Say the Word/(Instrumental)	1986	—	2.00	4.00
CAPITOL					
❑ 5501	Election Day/She's Moody and Grey; She's Mean and She's Restless	1985	—	—	3.00
	—A-side: Guest vocal by Grace Jones				
❑ 5501 [PS]	Election Day/She's Moody and Grey; She's Mean and She's Restless	1985	—	—	3.00
❑ 5542	Goodbye Is Forever/Missing	1985	—	—	3.00
❑ 5542 [PS]	Goodbye Is Forever/Missing	1985	—	2.00	4.00
❑ 5570	The Flame/Flame Game	1986	—	—	3.00
❑ 5570 [PS]	The Flame/Flame Game	1986	—	2.50	5.00

ARCHERS, THE

Number	Title (A Side/B Side)	Yr	VG	VG+	NM
LAURIE					
❑ 3207	Hey Rube/Unwind It	1963	3.75	7.50	15.00
SUMMER					
❑ 502	Motorcycle Michael/Golden Girl	196?	7.50	15.00	30.00

ARCHIBALD

Number	Title (A Side/B Side)	Yr	VG	VG+	NM
IMPERIAL					
❑ 5212	Early Morning Blues/Great Big Eyes	1953	750.00	1125.	1500.
❑ 5358	Stack-O-Lee (Part 1)/Stack-O-Lee (Part 2)	1955	25.00	50.00	100.00

ARCHIES, THE

Also see RON DANTE.

Number	Title (A Side/B Side)	Yr	VG	VG+	NM
CALENDAR					
❑ 63-1006	Bang-Shang-a-Lang/Truck Driver	1968	2.00	4.00	8.00
❑ 63-1006 [PS]	Bang-Shang-a-Lang/Truck Driver	1968	4.00	8.00	16.00
❑ 63-1007	Feelin' So Good (S.K.O.O.B.Y.-D.O.O.)/Love Light	1968	2.00	4.00	8.00
❑ 63-1007 [PS]	Feelin' So Good (S.K.O.O.B.Y.-D.O.O.)/Love Light	1968	4.00	8.00	16.00
❑ 63-1008	Sugar Sugar/Melody Hill	1969	2.50	5.00	10.00
KIRSHNER					
❑ 63-1009	Sunshine/Over and Over	1970	2.00	4.00	8.00
❑ 63-5002	Jingle Jangle/Justine	1969	2.00	4.00	8.00
❑ 63-5003	Who's Your Baby/Senorita Rita	1970	2.00	4.00	8.00
❑ 63-5009	Everything's Alright/Together We Two	1970	2.00	4.00	8.00
❑ 63-5011	Throw a Little Love My Way/This Is Love	1971	2.00	4.00	8.00
❑ 63-5014	A Summer Prayer for Peace/Maybe I'm Wrong	1971	2.00	4.00	8.00
❑ 63-5014 [PS]	A Summer Prayer for Peace/Maybe I'm Wrong	1971	4.00	8.00	16.00
❑ 63-5018	Love Is Living in You/Hold On to Lovin'	1972	2.00	4.00	8.00
❑ 63-5021	Strangers in the Morning/Plum Crazy	1972	2.00	4.00	8.00

ARDELLS, THE

Number	Title (A Side/B Side)	Yr	VG	VG+	NM
EPIC					
❑ 9621	Eefananny/Lonely Valley	1963	3.75	7.50	15.00
MARCO					
❑ 102	Every Day of the Week/Roll On	1961	7.50	15.00	30.00
SELMA					
❑ 4001	Seven Lonely Nights/You Can Fall in Love	1963	6.25	12.50	25.00

ARGENT

Rod Argent's group after THE ZOMBIES broke up.

Number	Title (A Side/B Side)	Yr	VG	VG+	NM
DATE					
❑ 1659	Liar/Schoolgirl	1970	2.50	5.00	10.00
EPIC					
❑ 10718	Rejoice/Sweet Mary	1971	—	3.00	6.00
❑ 10746	Celebration/Kingdom	1971	—	3.00	6.00
❑ 10852	Hold Your Head Up/Closer to Heaven	1972	2.00	4.00	8.00
❑ 10919	Tragedy/He's a Dynamo	1972	—	2.50	5.00
❑ 10972	God Gave Rock and Roll To You/Christmas for the Free	1973	—	2.50	5.00
❑ 11019	It's Only Money, Part 2/Losing Hold	1973	—	2.50	5.00
❑ 11137	Man for All Seasons/Music from the Spheres	1974	—	2.50	5.00
❑ 50025	The Coming of Kohoutek/Thunder and Lightning	1974	—	2.50	5.00

ARGYLES, THE (1)

See THE HOLLYWOOD ARGYLES.

ARGYLES, THE (2)

Number	Title (A Side/B Side)	Yr	VG	VG+	NM
BALLY					
❑ 1030	Moonbeam/Every Time You Smile	1957	10.00	20.00	40.00

ARIELS, THE

Number	Title (A Side/B Side)	Yr	VG	VG+	NM
BRENT					
❑ 7060	Feels Like I'm Cryin'/I Love You	1967	15.00	30.00	60.00

ARISTOCRATS, THE

May be two different groups.

Number	Title (A Side/B Side)	Yr	VG	VG+	NM
ARGO					
❑ 5275	Maid of the Mist/Vagabonds	1957	6.25	12.50	25.00
ESSEX					
❑ 366	Believe Me/I'm Waiting for Ships	1954	15.00	30.00	60.00

ARLINGTON, BRUCE

Number	Title (A Side/B Side)	Yr	VG	VG+	NM
KING					
❑ 5918	You Made Me Cry/How Could You Know	1964	7.50	15.00	30.00

ARNOLD, BILLY BOY

See BILLY BOY.

ARNOLD, EDDY

Number	Title (A Side/B Side)	Yr	VG	VG+	NM
CURB					
❑ 73088	Cattle Call (with LeAnn Rimes)/I Walk Alone	1999	—	—	3.00
MGM					
❑ 14478	So Many Ways/Once in a While	1972	—	2.50	5.00
❑ 14535	If the Whole World Stopped Lovin'/My Son, I Wish You Everything	1973	—	2.00	4.00
❑ 14600	Oh, Oh, I'm Falling in Love Again/Anyway You Want Me	1973	—	2.00	4.00
❑ 14672	She's Got Everything I Need/I'm Glad You Happened to Me	1973	—	2.00	4.00
❑ 14711	Just for Old Times Sake/I Got This Thing About You	1974	—	2.00	4.00
❑ 14734	I Wish That I Had Loved You Better/Let It Be Love	1974	—	2.00	4.00
❑ 14769	Butterfly/If You Could Only Love Me Now	1974	—	2.00	4.00
❑ 14780	Red Roses for a Blue Lady/I Will	1975	—	2.00	4.00
❑ 14827	Middle of a Memoryl Just Had You on My Mind	1975	—	2.00	4.00
RCA					
❑ 2750-7-R	You Don't Miss a Thing/Just One Time	1990	—	2.00	4.00
❑ PB-10794	Put Me Back Into Your World/Goodnight Irene	1976	—	2.00	4.00
❑ PB-10899	(I Need You) All the Time/I've Never Loved Anyone More	1977	—	2.00	4.00
❑ PB-11031	Freedom Ain't the Same as Being Free/Till You Can Make It On Your Own	1977	—	2.00	4.00
❑ PB-11133	Where Lonely People Go/Penny Arcade	1977	—	2.00	4.00
❑ PB-11257	Country Lovin'/I've So Much to Be Thankful For	1978	—	2.00	4.00
❑ PB-11319	I'm the South/You Are My Sunshine	1978	—	2.00	4.00
❑ PB-11422	If Everyone Had Someone Like You/You're a Beautiful Place to Be	1978	—	2.00	4.00
❑ PB-11537	What In Her World Did I Do/Love of My Life	1979	—	2.00	4.00
❑ PB-11668	Goodbye/You're So Good At Lovin' Me	1979	—	2.00	4.00
❑ PB-11752	If I Ever Had to Say Goodbye to You/Love of My Life	1979	—	2.00	4.00
❑ PB-11918	Let's Get It While the Gettin's Good/You Cared Enough (To Give Your Very Best)	1980	—	2.00	4.00
❑ PB-12039	That's What I Get for Loving You/Undivided Love	1980	—	2.00	4.00
❑ PB-12136	Don't Look Now (But We Just Fell in Love)/There's Women (Then There's My Woman)	1980	—	2.00	4.00
❑ PB-12226	Bally-Hoo Days/Two Hearts Beat Better Than One	1981	—	2.00	4.00
❑ PB-13000	All I'm Missing Is You/Don't It Break Your Heart	1981	—	2.00	4.00
❑ PB-13094	Don't Give Up on Me/In Love with Loving You	1982	—	2.00	4.00
❑ PB-13339	The Valley Below/Make the World Go Away	1982	—	2.00	4.00
❑ PB-13452	The Blues Don't Care Who's Got 'Em/Wooden Heart	1983	—	2.00	4.00
❑ 62598	Out of the Blue/On a Night Like This	1993	—	2.00	4.00
RCA VICTOR					
❑ PB-10701	Cowboy/Don't Let the Good Times Roll Away	1976	—	2.00	4.00
❑ 47-2729	Anytime/What a Fool I Was	1949	7.50	15.00	30.00
❑ 47-2730	Bouquet of Roses/Texarkana Baby	1949	7.50	15.00	30.00
❑ 47-2776	I'm Thinking Tonight of My Blue Eyes/Rockin' Alone	1949	7.50	15.00	30.00
❑ 47-2777	It Makes No Difference Now/Molly Darling	1949	7.50	15.00	30.00
❑ 47-2778	The Prisoner's Song/Seven Years with the Wrong Woman	1949	7.50	15.00	30.00

Number	Title (A Side/B Side)	Yr	VG	VG+	NM
❑ 47-3310	That's How Much I Love You/Chained to a Memory	1949	6.25	12.50	25.00
❑ 47-3311	Will the Circle Be Unbroken/Who, At My Door, Is Standing	1949	6.25	12.50	25.00
❑ 47-4243	When My Blue Moon Turns to Gold Again/White Azaleas	1951	5.00	10.00	20.00
❑ 47-4244	When You and I Were Young, Maggie/Roll Along Kentucky Moon	1951	5.00	10.00	20.00
❑ 47-4245	That Little Boy of Mine/Sinner's Prayer	1951	5.00	10.00	20.00
❑ 47-4273	Somebody's Been Beating My Time/Heart Strings	1951	5.00	10.00	20.00
❑ 47-4413	Bundle of Southern Sunshine/Call Her Your Sweetheart	1951	5.00	10.00	20.00
❑ 47-4490	Take My Hand, Precious Lord/Open Thy Merciful Arms	1952	5.00	10.00	20.00
❑ 47-4569	Easy on the Eyes/Anything That's Part of You	1952	5.00	10.00	20.00
❑ 47-4597	Bouquet of Roses/Texarkana Baby	1952	5.00	10.00	20.00
❑ 47-4598	It's a Sin/Anytime	1952	5.00	10.00	20.00
❑ 47-4599	That's How Much I Love You/A Heart Full of Love	1952	5.00	10.00	20.00
❑ 47-4600	I'll Hold You in My Heart (Till I Can Hold You in My Arms)/Don't Rob Another Man's Castle	1952	5.00	10.00	20.00
❑ 47-4787	A Full Time Job/Shephard of My Heart	1952	5.00	10.00	20.00
❑ 47-4954	Older and Bolder/I'd Trade All My Tomorrows (For Just One Yesterday)	1952	5.00	10.00	20.00
❑ 47-5020	My Desire/I Want to Thank You Lord	1952	5.00	10.00	20.00
❑ 47-5108	Eddy's Song/Condemned Without a Trial	1952	5.00	10.00	20.00
❑ 47-5189	When Your Hair Has Turned to Silver/Angry	1953	5.00	10.00	20.00
❑ 47-5192	Moonlight and Roses/Missouri Waltz	1953	5.00	10.00	20.00
❑ 47-5193	You Always Hurt the One You Love/I'm Gonna Lock My Heart	1953	5.00	10.00	20.00
❑ 47-5196	The Old Rugged Cross/Have Thine Own Way, Lord	1953	5.00	10.00	20.00
❑ 47-5197	Someday Somewhere/When I've Done My Best	1953	5.00	10.00	20.00
❑ 47-5305	Free Home Demonstration/How's the World Treating You	1953	5.00	10.00	20.00
❑ 47-5415	Mama, Come Get Your Baby Boy/If I Never Get to Heaven	1953	5.00	10.00	20.00
❑ 47-5525	I Really Don't Want to Know/I'll Never Get Over You	1953	5.00	10.00	20.00
❑ 47-5601	Rose of Calvary/Prayer	1954	5.00	10.00	20.00
❑ 47-5634	My Everything/Second Fling	1954	5.00	10.00	20.00
❑ 47-5753	Chapel on the Hill/A Touch of God's Hand	1954	5.00	10.00	20.00
❑ 47-5805	This Is the Thanks I Get (For Loving You)/Hep Cat Baby	1954	5.00	10.00	20.00
❑ 47-5905	Christmas Can't Be Far Away/I'm Your Private Santa Claus	1954	5.00	10.00	20.00
❑ 47-6000	I've Been Thinking/Don't Forget	1955	3.75	7.50	15.00
❑ 47-6001	It Took a Miracle/I Always Have Someone to Turn To	1955	3.75	7.50	15.00
❑ 47-6069	Two Kinds of Love/In Time	1955	3.75	7.50	15.00
❑ 47-6139	The Cattle Call/The Kentuckian Song	1955	5.00	10.00	20.00
❑ 47-6198	Just Call Me Lonesome/That Do Make It Nice	1955	3.75	7.50	15.00
❑ 47-6290	The Richest Man/I Walked Alone Last Night	1955	3.75	7.50	15.00
❑ 47-6365	Trouble in Mind/When You Say Goodbye	1955	3.75	7.50	15.00
❑ 47-6407	Bayou Baby/Do You Know Where God Lives	1956	3.75	7.50	15.00
❑ 47-6502	You Don't Know Me/The Rockin' Mockin' Bird	1956	3.75	7.50	15.00
❑ 47-6601	Casey Jones (The Brave Engineer)/You Were Mine for Awhile	1956	3.75	7.50	15.00
❑ 47-6699	The Ballad of Wes Tancred/I Wouldn't Know Where to Begin	1956	3.75	7.50	15.00
❑ 47-6708	Mutual Admiration Society/If'n	1956	3.75	7.50	15.00
—With Jaye P. Morgan					
❑ 47-6773	A Dozen Hearts/A Good Lookin' Blonde	1956	3.75	7.50	15.00
❑ 47-6842	One/Do You Love Me	1957	3.00	6.00	12.00
—With Jaye P. Morgan					
❑ 47-6905	Gonna Find Me a Bluebird/Little Bit	1957	3.00	6.00	12.00
❑ 47-6975	Crazy Dream/Open Your Heart	1957	3.00	6.00	12.00
❑ 47-7040	Little Miss Sunbeam/When He Was Young	1957	3.00	6.00	12.00
❑ 47-7089	Wagon Wheels/You're Made Up for Everything	1957	3.00	6.00	12.00
❑ 47-7143	Too Soon to Know/I Need Somebody	1958	3.00	6.00	12.00
❑ 47-7221	Peck a Cheek/Before You Know It	1958	3.00	6.00	12.00
❑ 47-7292	The Day You Left Me/Real Love	1958	3.00	6.00	12.00
❑ 47-7340	Till You Come Back Again/I'm a Good Boy	1958	3.00	6.00	12.00
❑ 47-7435	Chip Off the Old Block/I'll Hold You in My Heart (Till I Can Hold You in My Arms)	1959	2.50	5.00	10.00
❑ 47-7542	Tennessee Stud/What's the Good (Of All This Love)	1959	2.50	5.00	10.00
❑ 47-7619	Did It Rain/Sittin' By Sittin' Bull	1959	2.50	5.00	10.00
❑ 47-7661	Boot Hill/Johnny Reb, That's Me	1959	2.50	5.00	10.00
❑ 47-7727	Little Sparrow/My Arms Are a House	1960	2.50	5.00	10.00
❑ 47-7794	Before This Day Ends/Just Out of Reach	1960	2.50	5.00	10.00
❑ 47-7861	(Jim) I Wore a Tie Today/Just Call Me Lonesome	1961	2.50	5.00	10.00
❑ 47-7926	One Grain of Sand/The Worst Night of My Life	1961	2.50	5.00	10.00
❑ 47-7984	Tears Broke Out on Me/I'll Do As Much for You Someday	1962	2.00	4.00	8.00
❑ 47-8048	A Little Heartache/After Loving You	1962	2.00	4.00	8.00
❑ 47-8102	Does He Mean That Much to You/Tender Touch	1962	2.00	4.00	8.00
❑ 47-8160	Yesterday's Memories/Lonely Balladeer	1963	2.00	4.00	8.00
❑ 47-8160 [PS]	Yesterday's Memories/Lonely Balladeer	1963	3.75	7.50	15.00
❑ 47-8207	A Million Years or So/Just a Ribbon	1963	2.00	4.00	8.00
❑ 47-8253	Jealous Hearted Me/I Met Her Today	1963	2.00	4.00	8.00
❑ 47-8296	Molly/The Song of the Coo Coo	1963	2.00	4.00	8.00
❑ 47-8363	Sweet Adorable You/Why	1964	—	3.00	6.00
❑ 47-8445	I Thank My Lucky Stars/I Don't Cry No More	1964	—	3.00	6.00
❑ 47-8516	What's He Doing in My World/Laura Lee	1965	—	3.00	6.00
❑ 47-8632	I'm Letting You Go/The Days Gone By	1965	—	3.00	6.00
❑ 47-8679	Make the World Go Away/The Easy Way	1965	2.00	4.00	8.00
❑ 47-8679 [PS]	Make the World Go Away/The Easy Way	1965	3.75	7.50	15.00
❑ 47-8749	I Want to Go With You/Better Stop Tellin' Lies (About Me)	1965	2.00	4.00	8.00
❑ 47-8749 [PS]	I Want to Go With You/Better Stop Tellin' Lies (About Me)	1965	3.75	7.50	15.00

Number	Title (A Side/B Side)	Yr	VG	VG+	NM
❑ 47-8818	The Last Word in Lonesome Is Me/Mary Claire Melvina Rebecca Jane	1966	—	3.00	6.00
❑ 47-8818 [PS]	The Last Word in Lonesome Is Me/Mary Claire Melvina Rebecca Jane	1966	3.00	6.00	12.00
❑ 47-8869	The Tip of My Fingers/Long, Long Friendship	1966	—	3.00	6.00
❑ 47-8869 [PS]	The Tip of My Fingers/Long, Long Friendship	1966	3.00	6.00	12.00
❑ 47-8965	Somebody Like Me/Taking Chances	1966	—	3.00	6.00
❑ 47-8965 [PS]	Somebody Like Me/Taking Chances	1966	3.00	6.00	12.00
❑ 47-9027	The Angel and the Stranger/The First Word	1966	—	3.00	6.00
❑ 47-9080	Lonely Again/Love on My Mind	1967	—	3.00	6.00
❑ 47-9182	Misty Blue/Calling Mary Names	1967	—	3.00	6.00
❑ 47-9265	Turn the World Around/The Long Ride Home	1967	—	3.00	6.00
❑ 47-9368	Here Comes Heaven/Baby That's Loving	1967	—	3.00	6.00
❑ 47-9387	Jolly Old St. Nicholas/This World of Ours	1967	2.00	4.00	8.00
❑ 47-9437	Here Comes the Rain, Baby/The World I Used to Know	1968	—	3.00	6.00
❑ 47-9525	It's Over/No Matter Whose Baby You Are	1968	—	3.00	6.00
❑ 47-9606	Then You Can Tell Me Goodbye/Apples, Raisins and Roses	1968	—	3.00	6.00
❑ 47-9667	They Don't Make Love Like They Used To/What a Wonderful World	1968	—	3.00	6.00
❑ 47-9801	Soul Deep/(Today) I Started Loving You Again	1969	—	3.00	6.00
❑ 47-9848	A Man's Kind of Woman/Living Under Pressure	1970	—	2.50	5.00
❑ 47-9889	From Heaven to Heartache/Ten Times Forever More	1970	—	2.50	5.00
❑ 47-9935	Portrait of My Woman/I Really Don't Want to Know	1970	—	2.50	5.00
❑ 47-9968	A Part of America Died/Call Me	1971	—	2.50	5.00
❑ 47-9993	Welcome to My World/It Ain't No Big Thing	1971	—	2.50	5.00
❑ 48-0001	Bouquet of Roses/Texarkana Baby	1949	12.50	25.00	50.00
—Originals on green vinyl					
❑ 48-0001	Bouquet of Roses/Texarkana Baby	1949	6.25	12.50	25.00
—Second pressings: Green label, black vinyl					
❑ 48-0001 [PS]	Bouquet of Roses/Texarkana Baby	1949	20.00	40.00	80.00
—Brown and dark brown title sleeve					
❑ 48-0002	Anytime/What a Fool I Was	1949	12.50	25.00	50.00
—Originals on green vinyl					
❑ 48-0002	Anytime/What a Fool I Was	195?	6.25	12.50	25.00
—Second pressings: Green label, black vinyl					
❑ 48-0016	I'm Thinking Tonight of My Blue Eyes/Rockin' Alone	1949	12.50	25.00	50.00
—Originals on green vinyl					
❑ 48-0016	I'm Thinking Tonight of My Blue Eyes/Rockin' Alone	1949	6.25	12.50	25.00
—Second pressings: Green label, black vinyl					
❑ 48-0017	It Makes No Difference Now/Molly Darling	1949	12.50	25.00	50.00
—Originals on green vinyl					
❑ 48-0017	It Makes No Difference Now/Molly Darling	195?	6.25	12.50	25.00
—Second pressings: Green label, black vinyl					
❑ 48-0018	The Prisoner's Song/Seven Years with the Wrong Woman	1949	12.50	25.00	50.00
—Originals on green vinyl					
❑ 48-0018	The Prisoner's Song/Seven Years with the Wrong Woman	1949	6.25	12.50	25.00
—Second pressings: Green label, black vinyl					
❑ 48-0019	Will the Circle Be Unbroken/Who at My Door Is Standing	1949	12.50	25.00	50.00
—Originals on green vinyl					
❑ 48-0019	Will the Circle Be Unbroken/Who at My Door Is Standing	195?	6.25	12.50	25.00
—Second pressings: Green label, black vinyl					
❑ 48-0025	A Heart Full of Love (For a Handful of Kisses)/Then I Turned and Walked Slowly Away	1949	12.50	25.00	50.00
—Originals on green vinyl					
❑ 48-0025	A Heart Full of Love (For a Handful of Kisses)/Then I Turned and Walked Slowly Away	1949	6.25	12.50	25.00
—Second pressings: Green label, black vinyl					
❑ 48-0026	Just a Little Lovin' (Will Go a Long, Long Way)/My Daddy Is Only a Picture	1949	12.50	25.00	50.00
—Originals on green vinyl					
❑ 48-0026	Just a Little Lovin' (Will Go a Long, Long Way)/My Daddy Is Only a Picture	1949	6.25	12.50	25.00
—Second pressings: Green label, black vinyl					
❑ 48-0030	I'll Hold You in My Heart (Till I Can Hold You in My Arms)/Don't Bother to Cry	1949	12.50	25.00	50.00
—Originals on green vinyl					
❑ 48-0030	I'll Hold You in My Heart (Till I Can Hold You in My Arms)/Don't Bother to Cry	1949	6.25	12.50	25.00
—Second pressings: Green label, black vinyl					
❑ 48-0042	There's Not a Thing (I Wouldn't Do for You)/Don't Rob Another Man's Castle	1949	12.50	25.00	50.00
—Originals on green vinyl					
❑ 48-0042	There's Not a Thing (I Wouldn't Do for You)/Don't Rob Another Man's Castle	1949	6.25	12.50	25.00
—Second pressings: Green label, black vinyl					
❑ 48-0080	I'm Throwing Rice (At the Girl That I Love)/Show Me the Way Back to Your Heart	1949	12.50	25.00	50.00
—Originals on green vinyl					
❑ 48-0080	I'm Throwing Rice (At the Girl That I Love)/Show Me the Way Back to Your Heart	1949	6.25	12.50	25.00
—Second pressings: Green label, black vinyl					
❑ 48-0083	One Kiss Too Many/The Echo of Your Footsteps	1949	12.50	25.00	50.00
—Originals on green vinyl					
❑ 48-0083	One Kiss Too Many/The Echo of Your Footsteps	1950	6.25	12.50	25.00
—Second pressings: Green label, black vinyl					
❑ 48-0127	C-H-R-I-S-T-M-A-S/Will Santa Come to Shanty Town	1949	12.50	25.00	50.00
—Originals on green vinyl					
❑ 48-0127	C-H-R-I-S-T-M-A-S/Will Santa Come to Shanty Town	1949	6.25	12.50	25.00
—Second pressings: Green label, black vinyl					

Number	Title (A Side/B Side)	Yr	VG	VG+	NM
❑ 48-0136	The Nearest Thing to Heaven/The Cattle Call	1949	12.50	25.00	50.00
—Originals on green vinyl					
❑ 48-0136	The Nearest Thing to Heaven/The Cattle Call	1949	6.25	12.50	25.00
—Second pressings: Green label, black vinyl					
❑ 48-0137	There's No Wings on My Angel/You Know How Talk Gets Around	1949	12.50	25.00	50.00
—Originals on green vinyl					
❑ 48-0137	There's No Wings on My Angel/You Know How Talk Gets Around	1949	6.25	12.50	25.00
—Second pressings: Green label, black vinyl					
❑ 48-0138	Just a Little Lovin' (Will Go a Long, Long Way)/ I'm Throwing Rice (At the Girl That I Love)	1949	12.50	25.00	50.00
—Originals on green vinyl					
❑ 48-0138	Just a Little Lovin' (Will Go a Long, Long Way)/ I'm Throwing Rice (At the Girl That I Love)	1949	6.25	12.50	25.00
—Second pressings: Green label, black vinyl					
❑ 48-0150	Take Me in Your Arms and Hold Me/Mama and Daddy Broke My Heart	1949	12.50	25.00	50.00
—Originals on green vinyl					
❑ 48-0150	Take Me in Your Arms and Hold Me/Mama and Daddy Broke My Heart	1949	6.25	12.50	25.00
—Second pressings: Green label, black vinyl					
❑ 48-0165	The Lily of the Valley/Evil, Tempt Me Not	1950	12.50	25.00	50.00
—Originals on green vinyl					
❑ 48-0165	The Lily of the Valley/Evil, Tempt Me Not	1950	6.25	12.50	25.00
—Second pressings: Green label, black vinyl					
❑ 48-0166	When Jesus Beckons Me Home/Beautiful Isle	1950	12.50	25.00	50.00
—Originals on green vinyl					
❑ 48-0166	When Jesus Beckons Me Home/Beautiful Isle	1950	6.25	12.50	25.00
—Second pressings: Green label, black vinyl					
❑ 48-0167	Hills of Tomorrow/Softly and Tenderly	1950	12.50	25.00	50.00
—Originals on green vinyl					
❑ 48-0167	Hills of Tomorrow/Softly and Tenderly	1950	6.25	12.50	25.00
—Second pressings: Green label, black vinyl					
❑ 48-0174	That Wonderful Mother of Mine/Mother	1950	12.50	25.00	50.00
—Originals on green vinyl					
❑ 48-0174	That Wonderful Mother of Mine/Mother	1950	6.25	12.50	25.00
—Second pressings: Green label, black vinyl					
❑ 48-0175	Bring Roses to Her Now/I Wish I Had a Girl	1950	12.50	25.00	50.00
—Originals on green vinyl					
❑ 48-0175	Bring Roses to Her Now/I Wish I Had a Girl	1950	6.25	12.50	25.00
—Second pressings: Green label, black vinyl					
❑ 48-0176	My Mother's Sweet Voice/I Wouldn't Trade the Silver	1950	12.50	25.00	50.00
—Originals on green vinyl					
❑ 48-0176	My Mother's Sweet Voice/I Wouldn't Trade the Silver	1950	6.25	12.50	25.00
—Second pressings: Green label, black vinyl					
❑ 48-0197	To My Sorrow/Easy Rockin' Chair	1950	12.50	25.00	50.00
—Originals on green vinyl					
❑ 48-0197	To My Sorrow/Easy Rockin' Chair	1950	6.25	12.50	25.00
—Second pressings: Green label, black vinyl					
❑ 48-0198	It's a Sin/I Couldn't Believe It Was True	1950	12.50	25.00	50.00
—Originals on green vinyl					
❑ 48-0198	It's a Sin/I Couldn't Believe It Was True	1950	6.25	12.50	25.00
—Second pressings: Green label, black vinyl					
❑ 48-0199	What Is Life Without Love/Be Sure There's No Mistake	1950	12.50	25.00	50.00
—Originals on green vinyl					
❑ 48-0199	What Is Life Without Love/Be Sure There's No Mistake	1950	6.25	12.50	25.00
—Second pressings: Green label, black vinyl					
❑ 48-0300	Little Angel with the Dirty Face/Why Should I Cry?	1950	12.50	25.00	50.00
—Originals on green vinyl					
❑ 48-0300	Little Angel with the Dirty Face/Why Should I Cry?	1950	6.25	12.50	25.00
—Second pressings: Green label, black vinyl					
❑ 48-0342	Cuddle Buggin' Baby/Enclosed, One Broken Heart	1950	12.50	25.00	50.00
—Originals on green vinyl					
❑ 48-0342	Cuddle Buggin' Baby/Enclosed, One Broken Heart	1950	6.25	12.50	25.00
—Second pressings: Green label, black vinyl					
❑ 48-0382	The Lovebug Itch/A Prison Without Walls	1950	12.50	25.00	50.00
—Originals on green vinyl					
❑ 48-0382	The Lovebug Itch/A Prison Without Walls	1950	6.25	12.50	25.00
—Second pressings: Green label, black vinyl					
❑ 48-0390	White Christmas/Santa Claus Is Comin' to Town	1950	12.50	25.00	50.00
—Originals on green vinyl					
❑ 48-0390	White Christmas/Santa Claus Is Comin' to Town	1950	6.25	12.50	25.00
—Second pressings: Green label, black vinyl					
❑ 48-0412	There's Been a Change in Me/Tie Me to Your Apron Strings Again	1950	12.50	25.00	50.00
—Originals on green vinyl					
❑ 48-0412	There's Been a Change in Me/Tie Me to Your Apron Strings Again	1950	6.25	12.50	25.00
—Second pressings: Green label, black vinyl					
❑ 48-0425	May the Good Lord Bless and Keep You/I'm Writing a Letter to the Lord	1951	12.50	25.00	50.00
—Originals on green vinyl					
❑ 48-0425	May the Good Lord Bless and Keep You/I'm Writing a Letter to the Lord	1951	5.00	10.00	20.00
—Second pressings: Green label, black vinyl					
❑ 48-0444	Kentucky Waltz/A Million Miles from Your Heart	1951	12.50	25.00	50.00
—Originals on green vinyl					
❑ 48-0444	Kentucky Waltz/A Million Miles from Your Heart	1951	5.00	10.00	20.00
—Second pressings: Green label, black vinyl					
❑ 48-0476	I Wanna Play House with You/Something Old, Something New	1951	6.25	12.50	25.00
❑ 48-0495	Jesus and the Atheist/He Knows	1951	6.25	12.50	25.00
❑ 74-0120	Please Don't Go/Heaven Below	1969	—	2.50	5.00
❑ 74-0175	But For Love/My Lady of Love	1969	—	2.50	5.00
❑ 74-0226	You Fool/You Don't Need Me Anymore	1969	—	2.50	5.00
❑ 74-0282	Since December/Morning of Our Mind	1969	—	2.50	5.00
❑ 74-0559	I Love You Dear/Long Life, Lots of Happiness	1971	—	2.50	5.00
❑ 74-0641	Lonely People/If It's Alright with You	1972	—	2.50	5.00
❑ 74-0705	Poison Red Berries/Just Out of Reach	1972	—	2.50	5.00
❑ 74-0747	Lucy/The Last Letter	1972	—	2.50	5.00
❑ 74-0842	An Angel Sleeps Beside Me/Sweet Bunch of Daisies	1972	—	—	—
—Unreleased					

7-Inch Extended Plays

RCA VICTOR

Number	Title (A Side/B Side)	Yr	VG	VG+	NM
❑ 547-0100	I'll Hold You in My Heart (Till I Can Hold You in My Arms)/A Heart Full of Love (For a Handful of Kisses)//Anytime/Texarkana Baby	1952	5.00	10.00	20.00
—Part of 2-EP set EPB-3027					
❑ EPA 260	The Cattle Call/The Nearest Thing to Heaven// I'm Throwing Rice (At the Girl That I Love)/Just a Little Lovin' (Will Go a Long, Long Way)	195?	5.00	10.00	20.00
❑ EPA 260 [PS]	Eddy Arnold Sings	195?	5.00	10.00	20.00
❑ EPA 261	Beautiful Isle of Somewhere/When Jesus Beckons Me Home//(In the) Hills of Tomorrow/ Softly and Tenderly	195?	5.00	10.00	20.00
❑ EPA 261 [PS]	Eddy Arnold's Favorite Sacred Songs	195?	5.00	10.00	20.00
❑ EPA 473	C-H-R-I-S-T-M-A-S/Will Santy Come to Shanty Town//White Christmas/Santa Claus Is Comin' to Town	1953	5.00	10.00	20.00
❑ EPA 473 [PS]	(title unknown)	1953	5.00	10.00	20.00
❑ EPA 500	*Open Thy Merciful Arms/Take My Hand, Precious Lord/My Desire/I Want to Thank You, Lord	195?	5.00	10.00	20.00
❑ EPA 500 [PS]	Open Thy Merciful Arms	195?	5.00	10.00	20.00
❑ EPB 3027 [PS]	Anytime (Country Classics)	1952	5.00	10.00	20.00
—Two-pocket jacket for two-EP set					

ARNOLD, VANCE, AND THE AVENGERS

See JOE COCKER.

ARRIBIANS, THE

J.O.B.

Number	Title (A Side/B Side)	Yr	VG	VG+	NM
❑ 1116	To Look at a Star/Working and Gambling	1958	200.00	400.00	800.00

ARTISTICS, THE

BRUNSWICK

Number	Title (A Side/B Side)	Yr	VG	VG+	NM
❑ 55301	I'm Gonna Miss You/Hope We Have	1966	2.00	4.00	8.00
❑ 55315	Girl I Need You/Glad I Met You	1967	2.00	4.00	8.00
❑ 55326	Love Song/I'll Always Love You	1967	2.00	4.00	8.00
❑ 55342	The Chase Is On/One Last Chance	1967	2.00	4.00	8.00
❑ 55353	You Make Me Happy/Nothing But Heartaches	1967	2.00	4.00	8.00
❑ 55370	Hard to Carry On/Trouble, Heartaches and Pain	1968	2.00	4.00	8.00
❑ 55384	Lonely Old World/You Left Me	1968	2.00	4.00	8.00
❑ 55404	Walking Tall/What Happened	1969	2.00	4.00	8.00
❑ 55416	Price of Love/Yesterday's Girl	1969	2.00	4.00	8.00
❑ 55431	Just Another Heartache/Ain't It Strange	1970	2.00	4.00	8.00
❑ 55444	(I Want You To) Make My Life Over/Sugar Cane	1971	2.00	4.00	8.00
❑ 55477	Being in Love/It's Those Little Things That Count	1972	2.00	4.00	8.00
❑ 55493	She's Heaven/Look Out I'm Gonna Get You	1973	2.00	4.00	8.00

OKEH

Number	Title (A Side/B Side)	Yr	VG	VG+	NM
❑ 7177	I Need Your Love/What'll I Do	1963	2.50	5.00	10.00
❑ 7193	Get My Hands on Some Lovin'/I'll Leave It Up to You	1964	2.50	5.00	10.00
❑ 7217	In Another Man's Arms/Patty Cake	1965	2.50	5.00	10.00
❑ 7232	This Heart of Mine/I'll Come Running	1965	2.50	5.00	10.00
❑ 7243	Loveland/So Much Love in My Heart	1966	2.50	5.00	10.00

ARTISTS UNITED AGAINST APARTHEID

MANHATTAN

Number	Title (A Side/B Side)	Yr	VG	VG+	NM
❑ 50017	Sun City/Not So Far Away (Dub)	1985	—	—	3.00
❑ 50017	Sun City/Not So Far Away (Dub)	1985	—	—	3.00
❑ 50026	Let Me See Your I.D. (Street Mix)/Let Me See Your I.D. (Album Mix)	1986	—	2.00	4.00

ASCOTS, THE

More than one group.

Number	Title (A Side/B Side)	Yr	VG	VG+	NM
ACE					
❑ 650	I'm Touched/Perfect Love	1962	6.25	12.50	25.00
ARROW					
❑ 736	Easier Said Than Done/Is It Really You	1958	7.50	15.00	30.00
BETHLEHEM					
❑ 3046	Hip Talk/She Did	1962	3.75	7.50	15.00
DUAL-TONE					
❑ 1120	Acapulco Run/The Gladiator	1963	15.00	30.00	60.00
J&S					
❑ 1628/9	What Love Can Do/Everything Will Be Alright	1958	7.50	15.00	30.00
KING					
❑ 5679	I Don't Care One Bit/Tonight	1962	7.50	15.00	30.00
SUPER					
❑ 102	Monkey See, Monkey Do/You Can't Do That	1966	5.00	10.00	20.00
❑ 103	Midnight Hour/Midnight Hour (Part 2)	1966	5.00	10.00	20.00
❑ 104	Put Your Arms Around Me/Sookie Sookie	1966	5.00	10.00	20.00

ASHLEY, DEL

See DAVID GATES.

ASHLEY, JOHN

Number	Title (A Side/B Side)	Yr	VG	VG+	NM
CAPEHART					
❑ 5006	Little Lou/I Need Your Lovin'	1961	12.50	25.00	50.00
DOT					
❑ 15775	Born to Rock/Pickin' on the Wrong Chicken	1958	12.50	25.00	50.00
❑ 15878	My Story/Let the Good Times Roll	1958	3.75	7.50	15.00
INTRO					
❑ 6097	Bermuda/Let Yourself Go Go Go	196?	7.50	15.00	30.00
SILVER					
❑ 1002	I Want to Hear It from You/Seriously in Love	1959	6.25	12.50	25.00

Number	Title (A Side/B Side)	Yr	VG	VG+	NM
❑ 1005	Cry of the Wild Goose/One Love	1960	6.25	12.50	25.00
ASHLEY, ROBERT					
MERCURY					
❑ 71365	Comic Strip Rock and Roll/The Baby	1957	12.50	25.00	50.00
ASHLEY, TONY					
DECCA					
❑ 32240	I'll Never Be Satisfied/All Along I've Loved You	1967	5.00	10.00	20.00
❑ 32342	We Must Have Love/I Can't Put You Down	1968	5.00	10.00	20.00
❑ 32520	I'll Go Crazy/Just a Taste	1969	15.00	30.00	60.00
ASHTON, GARDNER AND DYKE					
CAPITOL					
❑ 2981	Hymn to Everyone/Mister Freako	1970	—	2.50	5.00
❑ 3060	Resurrection Shuffle/I'm Your Spiritual Breadman	1971	—	3.00	6.00
❑ 3206	Can You Get It/Oh Lord	1971	—	2.50	5.00
❑ 3288	Delirium/Still Got a Long Way to Go	1972	—	2.50	5.00
ASSEMBLED MULTITUDE, THE					
ATLANTIC					
❑ 2737	Overture from Tommy (A Rock Opera)/Mud	1970	—	2.00	4.00
❑ 2764	Woodstock/Mr. Peppercorn	1970	—	2.00	4.00
❑ 2780	Medley from "Superstar" (A Rock Opera)/Where the Wood Bine Twineth	1971	—	2.00	4.00
❑ 2870	Godfather Waltz/Mac Arthur Park	1972	—	2.00	4.00
ASSOCIATION, THE					
COLUMBIA					
❑ 45602	Indian Wells Woman/Darling Be Home Soon	1972	—	2.50	5.00
❑ 45654	Come the Fall/Kicking the Gong Around	1972	—	2.50	5.00
ELEKTRA					
❑ 47094	Dreamer/You Turn the Light On	1980	—	2.00	4.00
❑ 47146	Small Town Lovers/Across the Persian Gulf	1981	—	2.00	4.00
JUBILEE					
❑ 5505	Babe I'm Gonna Leave You/Baby Can't You Hear Me Call Your Name	1965	6.25	12.50	25.00
MUMS					
❑ 6016	Names, Tags, Numbers & Labels/Rainbows Bent	1973	—	2.00	4.00
RCA VICTOR					
❑ PB-10217	One Sunday Morning/Life Is a Carnival	1975	—	2.00	4.00
VALIANT					
❑ 730	Too Many Mornings/Forty Times	1965	3.75	7.50	15.00
❑ 741	Along Comes Mary/Your Own Love	1966	3.00	6.00	12.00
❑ 747	Cherish/Don't Blame It On Me	1966	3.00	6.00	12.00
❑ 755	Pandora's Golden Heebie Jeebies/Standing Still	1966	2.50	5.00	10.00
❑ 755 [PS]	Pandora's Golden Heebie Jeebies/Standing Still	1966	5.00	10.00	20.00
❑ 758	No Fair at All/Looking Glass	1967	2.50	5.00	10.00
WARNER BROS.					
❑ 7040	Pandora's Golden Heebie Jeebies/Standing Still	1967	2.00	4.00	8.00
❑ 7041	Windy/Sometime	1967	2.50	5.00	10.00
❑ 7074	Never My Love/Requiem for the Masses	1967	2.50	5.00	10.00
—A picture sleeve is rumored to exist					
❑ 7105	Along Comes Mary/Cherish	1968	2.00	4.00	8.00
—"Back to Back Hits" series on "W7" label					
❑ 7119	Windy/Never My Love	1968	2.00	4.00	8.00
—"Back to Back Hits" series on "W7" label					
❑ 7163	Everything That Touches You/We Love Us	1968	2.00	4.00	8.00
—Orange "WB" label					
❑ 7195	Time for Livin'/Birthday Morning	1968	2.00	4.00	8.00
❑ 7229	Six Man Band/Like Always	1968	2.00	4.00	8.00
❑ 7267	Goodbye Columbus/The Time It Is Today	1969	2.00	4.00	8.00
❑ 7277	Under Branches/Hear in Here	1969	2.00	4.00	8.00
❑ 7305	Yes, I Will/I Am Up for Europe	1969	2.00	4.00	8.00
❑ 7349	Are You Ready/Dubuque Blues	1969	2.00	4.00	8.00
❑ 7372	Just About the Same/Look at Me, Look at You	1970	—	3.00	6.00
❑ 7429	Along the Way/Traveler's Guide	1970	—	3.00	6.00
❑ 7471	P.F. Sloan/Traveler's Guide	1971	—	3.00	6.00
❑ 7515	Bring Yourself Home/It's Gotta Be Real	1971	—	3.00	6.00
❑ 7524	That's Racin'/Makes Me Cry (Funny Kind of Song)	1971	—	3.00	6.00
ASTORS, THE					
STAX					
❑ 139	What Can It Be/Just Enough to Hurt Me	1963	20.00	40.00	80.00
❑ 170	Candy/I Found Out	1965	6.25	12.50	25.00
❑ 179	Mystery Woman/In the Twilight Zone	1965	6.25	12.50	25.00
❑ 232	Daddy Didn't Tell You/More Power to You	1967	3.00	6.00	12.00
ASTRO JETS, THE					
IMPERIAL					
❑ 5760	Hide and Seek/Boom-A-Lay	1961	5.00	10.00	20.00
ASTRONAUTS, THE (1)					
Best known as a surf-instrumental group.					
RCA VICTOR					
❑ 47-8194	Baja/Kuk	1963	5.00	10.00	20.00
❑ 47-8224	Hot Doggin'/Everyone But Me	1963	5.00	10.00	20.00
❑ 47-8224 [PS]	Hot Doggin'/Everyone But Me	1963	15.00	30.00	60.00
❑ 47-8298	Competition Coupe/Surf Party	1963	5.00	10.00	20.00
❑ 47-8364	Go Fight for Her/Swim Little Mermaid	1964	5.00	10.00	20.00
❑ 47-8419	Main Title from Ride the Wild Surf/Around and Around	1964	5.00	10.00	20.00
❑ 47-8463	I'm a Fool/Can't You See I Do	1964	5.00	10.00	20.00
❑ 47-8499	Almost Grown/My Sin Is Pride	1965	5.00	10.00	20.00
❑ 47-8545	Tomorrow's Gonna Be Another Day/Razza Matazz	1965	5.00	10.00	20.00
❑ 47-8628	It Doesn't Matter Anymore/The La La La Song	1965	5.00	10.00	20.00
❑ 47-8885	In My Car/Main Street	1966	3.75	7.50	15.00
❑ 47-9109	I Know You Rider/Better Things	1967	3.75	7.50	15.00
ASTRONAUTS, THE (U)					
JAN ELL					
❑ 459	Geneva Twist/Take 17	1962	7.50	15.00	30.00
LUNEY					
❑ 100	Ridge Route/Blast Off	1962	7.50	15.00	30.00
MERCURY					
❑ 71675	Alabama Jubilee/Gadabout	1960	3.00	6.00	12.00
PALLADIUM					
❑ 610	Come Along Baby/Trying to Get to You	1962	25.00	50.00	100.00
TRIAL					
❑ 3521	Farewell/Chili Charlene	1960	50.00	100.00	200.00
VANRUS					
❑ 1000	Ski Lift/Blues Beat	1962	7.50	15.00	30.00
ATLANTICS, THE					
COLUMBIA					
❑ 42877	Greensleeves/Bombera	1963	5.00	10.00	20.00
❑ 43023	War of the World/Bow Man	1964	5.00	10.00	20.00
LINDA					
❑ 103	Boo-Hoo-Hoo/Everything Is Gonna Be All Right	1961	6.25	12.50	25.00
❑ 107	Remember the Night/Flame of Love	1962	20.00	40.00	80.00
RAMPART					
❑ 614	Let Me Call You Sweetheart/Home on the Range	1964	3.00	6.00	12.00
❑ 643	Beaver Shot/Fine, Fine, Fine	1965	2.50	5.00	10.00
❑ 647	Slopp Dance/Sonny and Cher	1965	2.50	5.00	10.00
ATTITUDES					
DARK HORSE					
❑ 8404	Sweet Summer Music/If We Want To	1977	—	2.00	4.00
❑ 8452	Good News/In a Stranger's Arms	1977	—	2.00	4.00
❑ 10004	Ain't Love Enough/The Whole World's Crazy	1975	—	2.50	5.00
❑ 10008	Lend a Hand/Honey Don't Leave L.A.	1976	—	2.50	5.00
❑ 10011	Sweet Summer Music/If We Want To	1976	—	2.50	5.00
ATTRACTIONS, THE					
BELL					
❑ 659	Destination You/Find Me	1967	5.00	10.00	20.00
❑ 674	New Girl in the Neighborhood/That Girl Is Mine	1967	5.00	10.00	20.00
❑ 690	Why Shouldn't a Man Cry/Some of Your Time	1967	5.00	10.00	20.00
JUNE BUG					
❑ 697/8	You Don't Know, Boy/Think Back	1966	6.25	12.50	25.00
ATWOOD THE ELECTRIC ICEMAN					
Actually the SIR DOUGLAS QUINTET with Atwood Allen.					
UNI					
❑ 55216	Bossier City/Michoacan	1970	—	3.00	6.00
AUDREY					
PLUS					
❑ 104	Dear Elvis/Dear Elvis (Part 2)	1956	20.00	40.00	80.00
—Black vinyl; a red vinyl pressing has been reported but is unconfirmed					
AUGUST AND DENEEN					
ABC					
❑ 11082	We Go Together/Can't Get You Out of My Head	1968	15.00	30.00	60.00
AUSTIN, PATTI					
ABC					
❑ 11104	Music to My Heart/Love 'Em and Leave 'Em Kind of Love	1968	3.75	7.50	15.00
COLUMBIA					
❑ 45337	Are We Ready for Love/Now That I Know What Loneliness Is	1971	—	2.50	5.00
❑ 45410	Black California/All Good Gifts-Day by Day	1971	—	2.50	5.00
❑ 45499	God Only Knows/Can't Forget the One I Love	1971	—	2.50	5.00
❑ 45592	Day by Day/Didn't Say a Word	1972	—	2.50	5.00
❑ 45785	Come to Him/Turn On the Music	1973	—	2.50	5.00
❑ 45906	Being with You/Take a Closer Look	1973	—	2.50	5.00
CORAL					
❑ 62455	He's Good Enough for Me/Earl	1965	5.00	10.00	20.00
❑ 62471	I Wanna Be Loved/A Most Unusual Boy	1965	5.00	10.00	20.00
❑ 62478	Someone's Gonna Cry/You'd Better Know What You're Getting	1966	25.00	50.00	100.00
❑ 62491	Take Your Time/Take Away the Pain Stain	1966	5.00	10.00	20.00
❑ 62500	Leave a Little Love/My Lovelight Ain't Gonna Shine	1966	5.00	10.00	20.00
❑ 62511	Got to Check You Out/What a Difference a Day Makes	1967	5.00	10.00	20.00
❑ 62518	Only All the Time/Oh How I Need You Joe	1967	5.00	10.00	20.00
❑ 62541	I'll Keep Loving You/You're Too Much a Part of Me	1967	5.00	10.00	20.00
❑ 62548	(I've Given) All My Love/Why Can't We Try It Again	1968	5.00	10.00	20.00
CTI					
❑ 7	In My Life (Part 1)/In My Life (Part 2)	1973	—	2.50	5.00
—With Jerry Butler					
❑ 33	Say You Love Me/In My Life	1976	—	2.00	4.00
❑ 41	We're in Love/Golden Oldies	1977	—	2.00	4.00
❑ 51	Love Me by Name/You Fooled Me	1978	—	2.00	4.00
❑ 59	What's at the End of the Rainbow/In My Life	1978	—	2.00	4.00
❑ 9600	Body Language/People in Love	1980	—	2.00	4.00
❑ 9601	I Want You Tonight/Love Me Again	1980	—	2.00	4.00
QWEST					
❑ 27718	Smoke Gets In Your Eyes/How Long Has This Been Goin' On?	1988	—	—	3.00
❑ 27718 [PS]	Smoke Gets In Your Eyes/How Long Has This Been Goin' On?	1988	—	—	3.00
❑ 28573	Only a Breath Away/Summer Is the Coldest Time of Year	1986	—	—	3.00
❑ 28659	Gettin' Away with Murder/Anything Can Happen Here	1986	—	—	3.00
❑ 28788	The Heat of Heat/Hot in the Flames of Love	1986	—	—	3.00
❑ 28935	Honey for the Bees/Hot in the Flames of Love	1985	—	—	3.00

Number	Title (A Side/B Side)	Yr	VG	VG+	NM
❑ 29136	All Behind Us Now/Fine Fine Fella (Got to Have You)	1984	—	2.00	4.00
❑ 29234	Shoot the Moon/Change Your Attitude	1984	—	2.00	4.00
❑ 29305	Rhythm of the Street/Solero	1984	—	2.00	4.00
❑ 29373	It's Gonna Be Special/Solero	1984	—	2.00	4.00
❑ 29618	How Do You Keep the Music Playing/same (Long Version)	1983	—	2.00	4.00
❑ 29727	Every Home Should Have One/Solero	1983	—	2.00	4.00
❑ 49754	Do You Love Me/Solero	1981	—	2.00	4.00
❑ 49854	Every Home Should Have One/Solero	1981	—	2.50	5.00
❑ 50036	Baby, Come to Me/Solero	1982	—	2.00	4.00
—With James Ingram					

UNITED ARTISTS

Number	Title (A Side/B Side)	Yr	VG	VG+	NM
❑ 50520	The Family Tree/Magical Boy	1969	2.00	4.00	8.00
❑ 50588	I Will Wait for You/Big Mouth	1969	2.00	4.00	8.00
❑ 50640	Your Love Made a Difference in Me/It's Easier to Laugh Than Cry	1970	2.00	4.00	8.00

AUTOSALVAGE

RCA VICTOR

Number	Title (A Side/B Side)	Yr	VG	VG+	NM
❑ 47-9506	Parahighway/Rampant Generalities	1968	3.00	6.00	12.00

AUTRY, GENE

CHALLENGE

Number	Title (A Side/B Side)	Yr	VG	VG+	NM
❑ 1009	No Back Door to Heaven/You're the Only Good Thing	1957	3.00	6.00	12.00
❑ 1010	Rudolph the Red-Nosed Reindeer/Here Come Santa Claus	1957	3.00	6.00	12.00
—Re-recordings of originals on Columbia					
❑ 59030	Rudolph, the Red-Nosed Reindeer/Here Come Santa Claus	1958	3.00	6.00	12.00
❑ 59030 [PS]	Rudolph, the Red-Nosed Reindeer/Here Come Santa Claus	1958	5.00	10.00	20.00

COLUMBIA

Number	Title (A Side/B Side)	Yr	VG	VG+	NM
❑ 4-56	Rudolph, the Red-Nosed Reindeer/If It Doesn't Snow on Christmas	1951	5.00	10.00	20.00
—Yellow label, red print; second number on label is 90049					
❑ 4-56 [PS]	Rudolph, the Red-Nosed Reindeer/If It Doesn't Snow on Christmas	1951	6.25	12.50	25.00
—Sleeve was manufactured with a hole in the middle					
❑ 4-68	Peter Cottontail/Funny Little Bunny	1950	5.00	10.00	20.00
—Yellow label, red print; second number on label is unknown					
❑ 4-68 [PS]	Peter Cottontail/Funny Little Bunny	1950	6.25	12.50	25.00
—Sleeve was manufactured with a hole in the middle					
❑ 4-75	Frosty the Snow Man/When Santa Claus Gets Your Letter	1951	5.00	10.00	20.00
—Yellow label, red print; second number on label is 90072					
❑ 4-75 [PS]	Frosty the Snow Man/When Santa Claus Gets Your Letter	1951	6.25	12.50	25.00
—Sleeve was manufactured with a hole in the middle					
❑ 4-84	Here Comes Santa Claus/He's a Chubby Little Fellow	1951	5.00	10.00	20.00
—Yellow label, red print; second number on label is 90088					
❑ 4-84 [PS]	Here Comes Santa Claus/He's a Chubby Little Fellow	1951	6.25	12.50	25.00
—Sleeve was manufactured with a hole in the middle					
❑ 4-121	Thirty-Two Feet — Eight Little Tails/(Hedrock, Coco and Joe) The Three Little Dwarfs	1952	5.00	10.00	20.00
—Yellow label, red print; second number on label is 90135					
❑ 4-121 [PS]	Thirty-Two Feet — Eight Little Tails/(Hedrock, Coco and Joe) The Three Little Dwarfs	1952	6.25	12.50	25.00
—Sleeve was manufactured with a hole in the middle					
❑ 4-122	Poppy the Puppy/He'll Be Coming Down the Chimney (Like He Always Did Before)	1952	5.00	10.00	20.00
—Yellow label, red print; second number on label is 90136					
❑ 4-122 [PS]	Poppy the Puppy/He'll Be Coming Down the Chimney (Like He Always Did Before)	1952	6.25	12.50	25.00
—Sleeve was manufactured with a hole in the middle					
❑ 4-150	Merry Texas Christmas, You All!/The Night Before Christmas (In Texas, That Is)	1953	3.75	7.50	15.00
—Yellow label, red print; second number on label is 90172					
❑ 4-150 [PS]	Merry Texas Christmas, You All!/The Night Before Christmas (In Texas, That Is)	1953	5.00	10.00	20.00
—Sleeve was manufactured with a hole in the middle					
❑ 4-176	Santa Claus Is Comin' to Town/Up on the Housetop (Ho! Ho! Ho!)	1954	3.75	7.50	15.00
—Yellow label, red print					
❑ 4-176 [PS]	Santa Claus Is Comin' to Town/Up on the Housetop (Ho! Ho! Ho!)	1954	5.00	10.00	20.00
❑ 2-210 (?)	Ellie Mae/Sun Flower	1949	10.00	20.00	40.00
—Microgroove 33 1/3 rpm single					
❑ 2-270 (?)	My Empty Heart/I Wish I Had Stayed Over Yonder	1949	10.00	20.00	40.00
—Microgroove 33 1/3 rpm single					
❑ 2-320 (?)	Santa, Santa, Santa/He's a Chubby Little Fellow	1949	10.00	20.00	40.00
—Microgroove 33 1/3 rpm single					
❑ 2-340 (?)	When the Silver Colorado Turns to Gold/Whirlwinds	1949	10.00	20.00	40.00
—Microgroove 33 1/3 rpm single					
❑ 2-370 (?)	Riders in the Sky/Cowboy Trademarks	1949	10.00	20.00	40.00
—Microgroove 33 1/3 rpm single					
❑ 1-375	Rudolph, the Red-Nosed Reindeer/If It Doesn't Snow on Christmas	1949	10.00	20.00	40.00
—Microgroove 33 1/3 rpm single					
❑ 6-375	Rudolph, the Red-Nosed Reindeer/If It Doesn't Snow on Christmas	1950	6.25	12.50	25.00
—Reissue on 45 of a single originally on 33 1/3 Microgroove single					
❑ 2-430 (?)	Mule Train/Cowboy Serenade	1950	10.00	20.00	40.00
—Microgroove 33 1/3 rpm single					
❑ 2-480 (?)	Poison Ivy/A New Star Is Shining	1950	10.00	20.00	40.00
—Microgroove 33 1/3 rpm single					
❑ 2-550 (?)	Take Me Back to My Boots and Saddle/Dust	1950	10.00	20.00	40.00
—Microgroove 33 1/3 rpm single					
❑ 1-575	Peter Cottontail/Funny Little Bunny	1950	10.00	20.00	40.00
—Microgroove 33 1/3 rpm single					
❑ 1-630 (?)	Roses/The Roses I Picked for Our Wedding	1950	10.00	20.00	40.00
—Microgroove 33 1/3 rpm single					
❑ 1-741 (?)	Blue Canadian Rockies/Onteora	1950	10.00	20.00	40.00
—Microgroove 33 1/3 rpm single					
❑ 6-741 (?)	Blue Canadian Rockies/Onteora	1950	6.25	12.50	25.00
❑ 1-742	Frosty the Snow Man/When Santa Claus Gets Your Letter	1950	10.00	20.00	40.00
—Microgroove 33 1/3 rpm single					
❑ 6-742	Frosty the Snow Man/When Santa Claus Gets Your Letter	1950	5.00	10.00	20.00
❑ 1-765 (?)	Goodnight Irene/Texans Never Cry	1950	10.00	20.00	40.00
—Microgroove 33 1/3 rpm single					
❑ 6-765 (?)	Goodnight Irene/Texans Never Cry	1950	6.25	12.50	25.00
❑ 1-810 (?)	Little Johnny Pilgrim/Guffy the Goofy Gobbler	1950	10.00	20.00	40.00
—Microgroove 33 1/3 rpm single					
❑ 6-810 (?)	Little Johnny Pilgrim/Guffy the Goofy Gobbler	1950	6.25	12.50	25.00
❑ 38-06189	The Statue in the Bay/God Bless America	1986	—	2.00	4.00
❑ 4-20377	Here Comes Santa Claus (Down Santa Claus Lane)/An Old-Fashioned Tree	1950	5.00	10.00	20.00
—Reissue on 45 of a single originally on 78					
❑ 20709	I Love You Because/The Last Straw	1950	6.25	12.50	25.00
❑ 20727	Silver Haired Daddy/Mississippi Valley Blues	1950	6.25	12.50	25.00
❑ 20763	Rose Colored Memories/Let Me Cry on Your Shoulder	1950	6.25	12.50	25.00
❑ 20775	The Statue in the Bay/The Place Where I Worship	1951	5.00	10.00	20.00
❑ 20814	At Mail Call Today/I'll Be Back	1951	5.00	10.00	20.00
❑ 20865	When It's Springtime in the Rockies/I Don't Want to Set the World on Fire	1951	5.00	10.00	20.00
❑ 20899	Heartsick Soldier/I'm Learning to Live	1952	3.75	7.50	15.00
❑ 20904	Am I a Pastime/I Was Just Walkin'	1952	3.75	7.50	15.00
❑ 20929	Diesel Smoke/Stop Your Gambling	1952	3.75	7.50	15.00
❑ 21035	I've Lived a Lifetime for You/Story Book of Love	1952	3.75	7.50	15.00
❑ 21144	Love Is So Misleadin'/Don't Send Your Love	1953	3.75	7.50	15.00
❑ 21207	Bimbo/Roly Poly	1954	3.75	7.50	15.00
❑ 21229	Angels in the Sky/A Voice in the Choir	1954	3.75	7.50	15.00
❑ 21252	Closing the Book/My Lazy Day	1954	3.75	7.50	15.00
❑ 21269	20-20 Vision/You're the Only Good Thing	1954	3.75	7.50	15.00
❑ 21280	I'm a Fool to Care/A Broken Promise Means a Broken Heart	1954	3.75	7.50	15.00
❑ 21304	When He Grows Tired of You/It Just Don't Seem Like Home	1954	3.75	7.50	15.00
❑ 21329	Barney the Bashful Bullfrog/Little Peter Pumpkin Eater	1954	3.75	7.50	15.00
❑ 21358	I'm Innocent/You're an Angel	1955	3.75	7.50	15.00
❑ 21481	You've Got to Take the Bitter with the Sweet/Two Cheaters in Love	1956	3.75	7.50	15.00
❑ 21527	God's in the Saddle/If Today Were the End of the World	1956	3.75	7.50	15.00
❑ 33023	Back in the Saddle Again/Tumbling Tumbleweeds	196?	2.00	4.00	8.00
—"Hall of Fame" reissue; red and black label					
❑ 33165	Rudolph, the Red-Nosed Reindeer/Here Comes Santa Claus (Down Santa Claus Lane)	1970	—	2.50	5.00
—"Hall of Fame" reissue; red and black label					
❑ 33165	Rudolph, the Red-Nosed Reindeer/Here Comes Santa Claus (Down Santa Claus Lane)	198?	—	—	3.00
—"Hall of Fame" reissue; gray label					
❑ 38610	Rudolph, the Red-Nosed Reindeer/If It Doesn't Snow On Christmas	1951	3.75	7.50	15.00
—Second 45 issue of this song					
❑ 38907	Frosty The Snowman/When Santa Claus Gets Your Letter	1951	3.75	7.50	15.00
—Second 45 issue of this song					
❑ 3-39086	My Heart Cries for You/Teardrops from My Eyes	1950	7.50	15.00	30.00
—Microgroove 33 1/3 rpm single					
❑ 4-39086	My Heart Cries for You/Teardrops from My Eyes	1950	5.00	10.00	20.00
❑ 39217	Sonny the Bunny/Bunny Roundup Time	1951	5.00	10.00	20.00
❑ 39347	Crime Will Never Pay/Gold Can Buy Anything	1951	3.75	7.50	15.00
❑ 39371	Mr. and Mississippi/How Long Is Forever	1951	3.75	7.50	15.00
❑ 39405	Old Soldiers Never Die/God Bless America	1951	3.75	7.50	15.00
❑ 39461	Frosty the Snow Man/An Old-Fashioned Tree	1951	3.00	6.00	12.00
❑ 39462	When Santa Claus Gets Your Letter/He's a Chubby Little Fellow	1951	3.00	6.00	12.00
❑ 39463	Rudolph, the Red-Nosed Reindeer/Here Comes Santa Claus (Down Santa Claus Lane)	1951	3.00	6.00	12.00
❑ 39464	Santa, Santa, Santa/If It Doesn't Snow on Christmas	1951	3.00	6.00	12.00
❑ 39542	Poppy the Puppy/He'll Be Coming Down the Chimney (Like He Always Did Before)	1951	3.75	7.50	15.00
❑ 39543	Thirty-Two Feet — Eight Little Tails/(Hedrock, Coco and Joe) The Three Little Dwarfs	1951	3.75	7.50	15.00
❑ 39808	Don't Believe a Word They Say/God's Little Candles	1952	3.75	7.50	15.00
❑ 39876	The Night Before Christmas Song/Look Out the Window	1952	3.75	7.50	15.00
—With Rosemary Clooney					
❑ 40092	Where Did My Snowman Go?/Freddie the Little Fir Tree	1953	3.75	7.50	15.00
❑ 40135	I Wish My Mom Would Marry Santa Claus/Sleigh Bells	1953	3.75	7.50	15.00
❑ 40167	Easter Morning/The Horse with the Easter Bonnet	1954	3.75	7.50	15.00
❑ 40589	Round, Round the Christmas Tree/Merry Christmas Tree	1955	3.75	7.50	15.00
❑ 40790	Everyone's a Child at Christmas/You Can See Old Santa Claus	1956	3.75	7.50	15.00
❑ 40931	Johnny Reb and Billy Yank/Happy Little Island	1957	3.00	6.00	12.00
❑ 40960	Half Your Heart/Darlin' What More Can I Do	1957	3.00	6.00	12.00
❑ 44632	Back in the Saddle Again/Home on the Range	1968	2.00	4.00	8.00

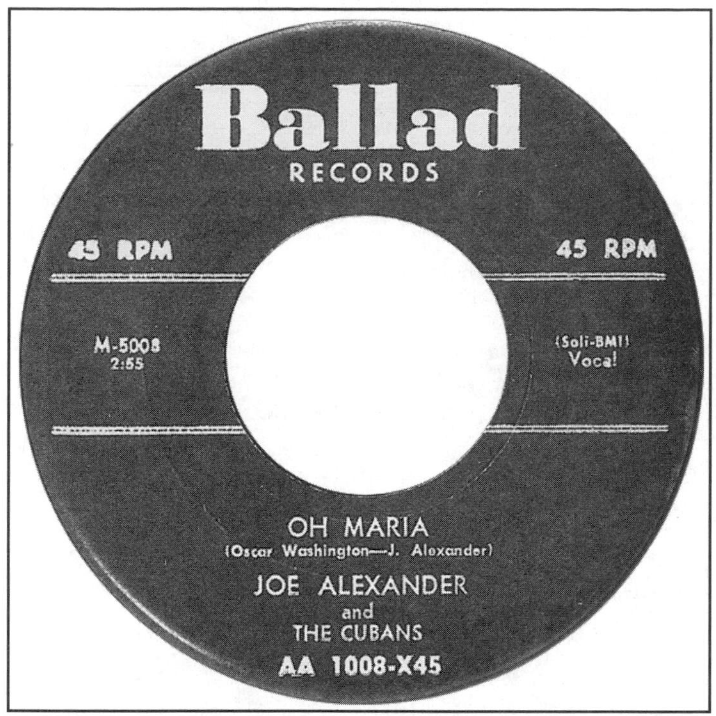

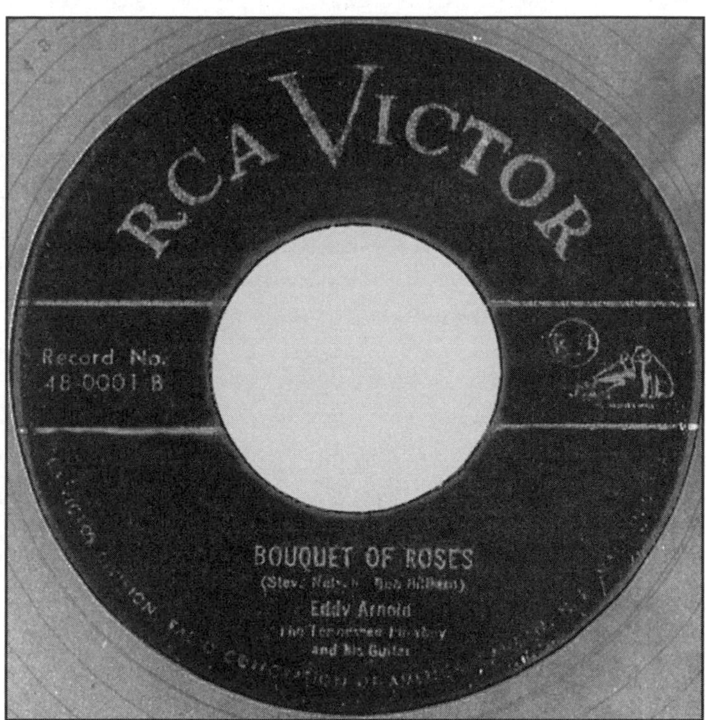

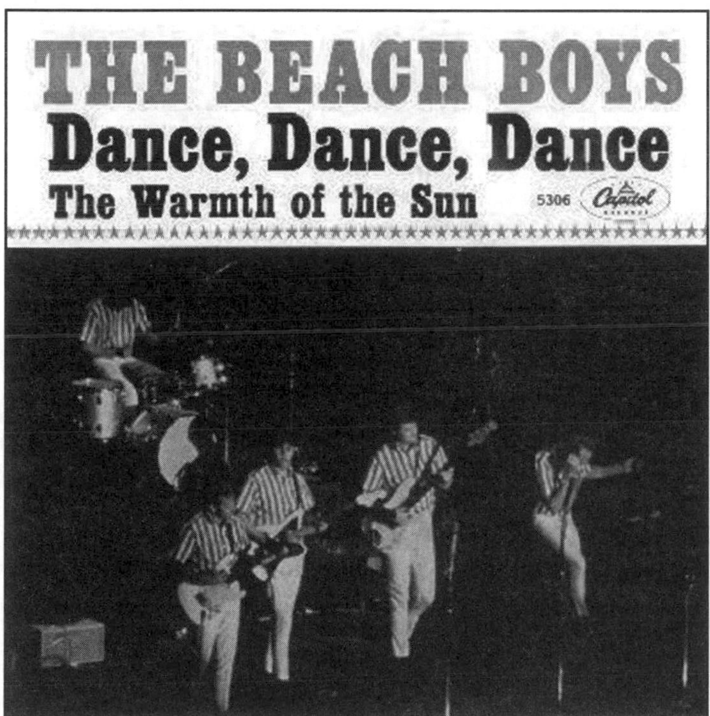

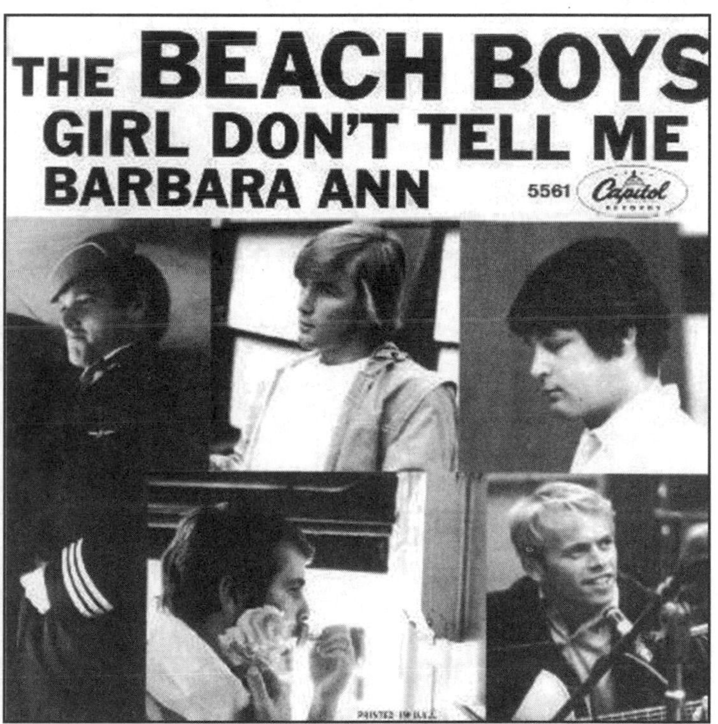

(Top left) Listening to this record, it's hard to believe that "Oh Maria" by Joe Alexander and the Cubans marked the first appearance on disc by Chuck Berry. (Top right) In the late 1940s, no country artist sold more records and was played more frequently on radio and jukeboxes than Eddy Arnold. In tribute, when RCA Victor introduced the 45 rpm single in March of 1949, the first numbered country single was Arnold's huge crossover hit, "Bouquet of Roses." (Bottom left) "Barbara Ann," "Ten Little Indians" and the Capitol version of "Heroes and Villains" are well-known as hard-to-find Beach Boys picture sleeves. Also at three figures in near-mint condition is "Dance, Dance, Dance." (Bottom right) Speaking of the "Barbara Ann" picture sleeve, here's the less frequently seen B-side of the same sleeve, "Girl Don't Tell Me."

Number	Title (A Side/B Side)	Yr	VG	VG+	NM
CRICKET					
❑ CX-6	Rudolph, the Red-Nosed Reindeer/Tinker Town Santa Claus	196?	3.00	6.00	12.00
—B-side by the Cricketones					
MISTLETOE					
❑ 801	Rudolph, The Red-Nosed Reindeer/Up On The House Top	196?	2.00	4.00	8.00
REPUBLIC					
❑ 001	Back in the Saddle Again/The Last Round-Up	1977	—	2.50	5.00
❑ 326	Rudolph the Red-Nosed Reindeer/Here Comes Santa Claus	1976	—	2.00	4.00
❑ 1405	Rudolph the Red-Nosed Reindeer/Here Comes Santa Claus	1969	2.00	4.00	8.00
❑ 2001	Nine Little Reindeer/Buon Natale (Means Merry Christmas)	1959	3.00	6.00	12.00
❑ 2001 [PS]	Nine Little Reindeer/Buon Natale (Means Merry Christmas)	1959	3.00	6.00	12.00
❑ 2002	Santa's Comin' in a Whirlybird/Jingle Bells	1959	3.00	6.00	12.00

AVALON, FRANKIE

Number	Title (A Side/B Side)	Yr	VG	VG+	NM
AMOS					
❑ 127	The Star/Woman Cryin'	1969	—	2.50	5.00
BOBCAT					
❑ 4103	Such a Miracle/You're the Miracle	1983	—	2.00	4.00
CHANCELLOR					
❑ 11FX 1	Christmas Holiday/Dear Gesu Bambino	196?	5.00	10.00	20.00
❑ G-1 [DJ]	Shy Guy/Too Young	1959	10.00	20.00	40.00
—Promo-only record made for "Acnecare"					
❑ 1004	Cupid/Jivin' with the Saints	1957	5.00	10.00	20.00
❑ 1006	Shy Guy/Teacher's Pet	1957	5.00	10.00	20.00
❑ 1011	Dede Dinah/Ooh La La	1958	3.75	7.50	15.00
❑ 1016	You Excite Me/Darlin'	1958	3.75	7.50	15.00
❑ 1021	Ginger Bread/Blue Betty	1958	3.75	7.50	15.00
❑ 1021 [PS]	Ginger Bread/Blue Betty	1958	10.00	20.00	40.00
❑ 1026	I'll Wait for You/What Little Girl	1958	3.75	7.50	15.00
❑ 1026 [PS]	I'll Wait for You/What Little Girl	1958	10.00	20.00	40.00
❑ 1031 [M]	Venus/I'm Broke	1959	5.00	10.00	20.00
❑ 1031 [PS]	Venus/I'm Broke	1959	10.00	20.00	40.00
❑ S-1031 [S]	Venus/I'm Broke	1959	10.00	20.00	40.00
❑ 1036 [M]	Bobby Sox to Stockings/A Boy Without a Girl	1959	5.00	10.00	20.00
—Originals have pink labels					
❑ 1036 [M]	Bobby Sox to Stockings/A Boy Without a Girl	1959	3.00	6.00	12.00
—Reissues have black labels					
❑ 1036 [PS]	Bobby Sox to Stockings/A Boy Without a Girl	1959	10.00	20.00	40.00
❑ S-1036 [S]	Bobby Sox to Stockings/A Boy Without a Girl	1959	10.00	20.00	40.00
❑ 1040 [M]	Just Ask Your Heart/Two Fools	1959	3.75	7.50	15.00
❑ 1040 [PS]	Just Ask Your Heart/Two Fools	1959	7.50	15.00	30.00
❑ S-1040 [S]	Just Ask Your Heart/Two Fools	1959	10.00	20.00	40.00
❑ 1045 [M]	Why/Swingin' on a Rainbow	1959	3.75	7.50	15.00
❑ 1045 [PS]	Why/Swingin' on a Rainbow	1959	7.50	15.00	30.00
❑ S-1045 [S]	Why/Swingin' on a Rainbow	1959	10.00	20.00	40.00
❑ 1048	Don't Throw Away All Those Teardrops/Talk, Talk, Talk	1960	3.75	7.50	15.00
❑ 1048 [PS]	Don't Throw Away All Those Teardrops/Talk, Talk, Talk	1960	7.50	15.00	30.00
❑ 1052	Where Are You/Tuxedo Junction	1960	3.75	7.50	15.00
❑ 1052 [PS]	Where Are You/Tuxedo Junction	1960	7.50	15.00	30.00
❑ 1056	Togetherness/Don't Let Love Pass You By	1960	3.75	7.50	15.00
❑ 1056 [PS]	Togetherness/Don't Let Love Pass You By	1960	7.50	15.00	30.00
❑ 1065	A Perfect Love/The Puppet Song	1960	3.75	7.50	15.00
❑ 1065 [PS]	A Perfect Love/The Puppet Song	1960	7.50	15.00	30.00
❑ 1071	All of Everything/Call Me Anytime	1961	3.00	6.00	12.00
❑ 1071 [PS]	All of Everything/Call Me Anytime	1961	6.25	12.50	25.00
❑ 1077	Who Else But You/Gotta Get a Girl	1961	3.00	6.00	12.00
❑ 1081	Voyage to the Bottom of the Sea/Summer of '61	1961	3.00	6.00	12.00
❑ 1081 [PS]	Voyage to the Bottom of the Sea/Summer of '61	1961	6.25	12.50	25.00
❑ 1087	True, True Love/Married	1961	2.50	5.00	10.00
❑ 1087 [PS]	True, True Love/Married	1961	5.00	10.00	20.00
❑ 1095	Sleeping Beauty/The Lonely Bit	1961	2.50	5.00	10.00
❑ 1095 [PS]	Sleeping Beauty/The Lonely Bit	1961	5.00	10.00	20.00
❑ 1101	After You've Gone/If You Don't Think I'm Leaving	1962	2.50	5.00	10.00
❑ 1101 [PS]	After You've Gone/If You Don't Think I'm Leaving	1962	5.00	10.00	20.00
❑ 1107	You Are Mine/Ponchinello	1962	2.50	5.00	10.00
❑ 1107	You Are Mine/Italiano	1962	3.00	6.00	12.00
❑ 1107 [PS]	You Are Mine/Ponchinello	1962	5.00	10.00	20.00
❑ 1114	Venus/I'm Broke	1962	2.50	5.00	10.00
❑ 1115	A Miracle/Don't Let Me Stand in Your Way	1962	2.50	5.00	10.00
❑ 1115 [PS]	A Miracle/Don't Let Me Stand in Your Way	1962	5.00	10.00	20.00
❑ 1125	Dance the Bossa Nova/Welcome Home	1962	2.50	5.00	10.00
❑ 1125 [PS]	Dance the Bossa Nova/Welcome Home	1962	5.00	10.00	20.00
❑ 1131	My Ex-Best Friend/First Love Never Dies	1963	2.50	5.00	10.00
❑ 1134	Come Fly with Me/Girl Back Home	1963	2.50	5.00	10.00
❑ 1135	Cleopatra/Heartbeats	1963	2.50	5.00	10.00
❑ 1139	Beach Party/Don't Stop Now	1963	3.75	7.50	15.00
DE-LITE					
❑ 907	Beauty School Dropout/Midnight Lady	1978	—	2.00	4.00
❑ 907 [PS]	Beauty School Dropout/Midnight Lady	1978	—	2.50	5.00
❑ 1578	Venus/Venus (Disco Version)	1976	—	2.00	4.00
❑ 1578 [PS]	Venus/Venus (Disco Version)	1976	2.00	4.00	8.00
❑ 1582	Thank You for That Extra Sunrise/It's His Game	1976	—	2.00	4.00
❑ 1584	It's Never Too Late/Where ILeave Off (And You Begin)	1976	—	2.00	4.00
❑ 1589	Midnight Lady/Does She Wonder Where I Am	1977	—	2.00	4.00
❑ 1591	Splish Splash/When I Said I Love You	1977	—	2.00	4.00
❑ 1595	Roses Grow Beyond the Wall/Midnight Lady	1977	—	2.00	4.00
METROMEDIA					
❑ 181	Come On Back to Me Baby/Empty	1970	—	2.50	5.00
❑ 192	Heart of Everything/I Want You Near Me	1970	—	2.50	5.00
REGALIA					
❑ 5508	I'm in the Mood for Love/It's the Same Old Dream	1972	—	2.50	5.00
REPRISE					
❑ 0697	Dancing on the Stars/But I Do	1968	2.00	4.00	8.00
❑ 0796	Don't You Do It/It's Over	1968	2.00	4.00	8.00
❑ 0826	For Your Love/Why Don't They Understand	1969	2.00	4.00	8.00
UNITED ARTISTS					
❑ 728	Again/Don't Make Fun of Me	1964	2.50	5.00	10.00
❑ 748	My Love Is Here to Stay/New-Fangled, Jingle-Jangle, Swimming Suit from Paris	1964	2.50	5.00	10.00
❑ 748 [PS]	My Love Is Here to Stay/New-Fangled, Jingle-Jangle, Swimming Suit from Paris	1964	5.00	10.00	20.00
❑ 800	Moon River/Every Girl Should Get Married	1964	2.50	5.00	10.00
❑ 895	There'll Be Rainbows Again/I'll Take Sweden	1965	2.50	5.00	10.00
"X"					
❑ 0006	Trumpet Sorrento/The Rock	1954	12.50	25.00	50.00
❑ 0026	Trumpet Tarantella/Dormi, Dormi	1954	12.50	25.00	50.00
7-Inch Extended Plays					
CHANCELLOR					
❑ B-5000	Shy Guy/The One I Love//Trumpet Instrumental/Undecided	1959	12.50	25.00	50.00
❑ B-5000 [PS]	The Young Frankie Avalon	1959	12.50	25.00	50.00

AVALON, FRANKIE, AND ANNETTE FUNICELLO

Also see each artist's individual listings.

Number	Title (A Side/B Side)	Yr	VG	VG+	NM
PACIFIC STAR					
❑ 569	(Together We Can Make a) Merry Christmas/The Night Before Christmas	1981	—	2.50	5.00
—Red vinyl					
❑ 569 [PS]	(Together We Can Make a) Merry Christmas/The Night Before Christmas	1981	—	2.50	5.00

AVALONS, THE

More than one group.

Number	Title (A Side/B Side)	Yr	VG	VG+	NM
ALADDIN					
❑ 3336	I Miss You/Love Me	1956	7.50	15.00	30.00
CASINO					
❑ 108	You Do Something to Me/You Can Count on Me	1959	50.00	100.00	200.00
DICE					
❑ 90/91	Louella/You Broke Our Hearts	1958	37.50	75.00	150.00
GROOVE					
❑ 0141	Chains Around My Heart/Och! She Flew	1956	37.50	75.00	150.00
—Black vinyl					
❑ 0141	Chains Around My Heart/Och! She Flew	1956	125.00	250.00	500.00
—Green vinyl					
❑ 0174	It's Funny But It's True/Sugar Sugar	1956	37.50	75.00	150.00
NPC					
❑ 302	Begin the Beguine/Malanese	1964	6.25	12.50	25.00
ROULETTE					
❑ 4568	Is It the End/Many Things from Your Window	1964	3.00	6.00	12.00
UNART					
❑ 2007	Hearts Desire/Ebbtide	1958	30.00	60.00	120.00

AVANT-GARDE, THE

Game-show host CHUCK WOOLERY was in this group.

Number	Title (A Side/B Side)	Yr	VG	VG+	NM
COLUMBIA					
❑ 44388	Yellow Beads/Honey and Gall	1967	2.00	4.00	8.00
❑ 44590	Naturally Stoned/Honey and Gall	1968	2.00	4.00	8.00
❑ 44701	Fly with Me/Revelations Revelations	1968	2.00	4.00	8.00
—While not issued with a picture sleeve, some stock copies came with a lyric insert. Triple the value if this is included.					

AVANTIS, THE

Probably more than one group.

Number	Title (A Side/B Side)	Yr	VG	VG+	NM
ARGO					
❑ 5436	Keep On Dancing/I Want to Dance	1963	3.75	7.50	15.00
ASTRA					
❑ 1006	Gypsy Surfer/Wax 'Em Down	1963	10.00	20.00	40.00
CHANCELLOR					
❑ 1144	Gypsy Surfer/Wax 'Em Down	1963	6.25	12.50	25.00
IKON					
❑ 115	Too Much/Mid-Night Blues	196?	6.25	12.50	25.00
PEPPER					
❑ 435	You Got a Funny Way/One Man's Poison	196?	3.00	6.00	12.00
REGENCY					
❑ 108	Do the Surfin' Granny/Surfin' Granny	1964	10.00	20.00	40.00
❑ 110	Phantom Surfer/Lucille	1964	10.00	20.00	40.00

AVERAGE WHITE BAND

Number	Title (A Side/B Side)	Yr	VG	VG+	NM
ARISTA					
❑ 0515	Let's Go Round Again/Shine	1980	—	2.00	4.00
❑ 0553	For You, For Love/Whatcha 'Gonna Do for Me	1980	—	2.00	4.00
❑ 0580	Into the Night/(B-side unknown)	1980	—	2.00	4.00
❑ 0679	Easier Said Than Done/(B-side unknown)	1982	—	2.00	4.00
❑ 1022	Cupid's in Fashion/(B-side unknown)	1982	—	2.00	4.00
ATLANTIC					
❑ 3044	Nothing You Can Do/I Just Can't Give You Up	1974	—	2.00	4.00
❑ 3229	Pick Up the Pieces/Work to Do	1974	—	2.50	5.00
❑ 3261	Cut the Cake/Person to Person	1975	—	2.00	4.00
❑ 3285	If I Ever Lose This Heaven/High Flyin' Woman	1975	—	2.00	4.00
❑ 3304	School Boy Crush/Groovin' the Night Away	1975	—	2.00	4.00
❑ 3354	Queen of My Soul/Would You Stay	1976	—	2.00	4.00
❑ 3363	Soul Searching/Love of Your Own	1976	—	2.00	4.00
❑ 3388	Cloudy/Love Your Life	1977	—	2.00	4.00
❑ 3402	Get It Up/Keepin' It To Myself	1977	—	2.00	4.00
—With Ben E. King					
❑ 3427	A Star in the Ghetto/What Is Soul?	1977	—	2.00	4.00
—With Ben E. King					
❑ 3444	Fool for You Anyway/The Message	1977	—	2.00	4.00
—With Ben E. King					
❑ 3481	Your Love Is a Miracle/One Look	1978	—	2.00	4.00
❑ 3500	Big City Lights/She's a Dream	1978	—	2.00	4.00

Number	Title (A Side/B Side)	Yr	VG	VG+	NM
❑ 3563	Walk On By/Too Late to Cry	1979	—	2.00	4.00
❑ 3581	Feel No Fret/Fire Burning	1979	—	2.00	4.00
❑ 3614 [DJ]	When Will You Be Mine (same on both sides)	1979	—	2.00	4.00
—May be promo only					
MCA					
❑ 40168	This World Has Music/The Jugglers	1973	—	2.50	5.00
❑ 40196	Twilight Zone/How Can You Go Home	1974	—	2.50	5.00

AVONS, THE (1)

Male vocal group.

Number	Title (A Side/B Side)	Yr	VG	VG+	NM
ASTRA					
❑ 1023	Baby/Whisper (Softly)	1966	7.50	15.00	30.00
—Reissue of Hull material					
HULL					
❑ 717	Our Love Will Never End/I'm Sending S.O.S.	1956	50.00	100.00	200.00
—Black label					
❑ 717	Our Love Will Never End/I'm Sending S.O.S.	1956	12.50	25.00	50.00
—Red label					
❑ 722	Baby/Bonnie	1957	37.50	75.00	150.00
❑ 726	You Are So Close to Me/Gonna Catch You Nappin'	1958	30.00	60.00	120.00
❑ 728	What Will I Do/Please Come Back to Me	1958	30.00	60.00	120.00
❑ 731	What Love Can Do/On the Island	1958	30.00	60.00	120.00
❑ 744	Whisper (Softly)/If I Just (Had My Way)	1961	25.00	50.00	100.00
—White label					
❑ 744	Whisper (Softly)/If I Just (Had My Way)	1961	25.00	50.00	100.00
—Pink label					
❑ 744	Whisper (Softly)/If I Just (Had My Way)	196?	20.00	40.00	80.00
—Brown label					
❑ 754	A Girl to Call My Own/The Grass Is Greener on the Other Side	1962	37.50	75.00	150.00
—White label					
❑ 754	A Girl to Call My Own/The Grass Is Greener on the Other Side	1962	20.00	40.00	80.00
—Brown label					

AVONS, THE (U)

Number	Title (A Side/B Side)	Yr	VG	VG+	NM
ABET					
❑ 9419	Talk to Me/Got to Get Used to You	1967	2.00	4.00	8.00
EXCELLO					
❑ 2296	Since I Met You Baby/He's My Hero	1968	2.00	4.00	8.00
GROOVE					
❑ 58-0022	Oh, Gee Baby/Push a Little Harder	1963	3.75	7.50	15.00
❑ 58-0022 [PS]	Oh, Gee Baby/Push a Little Harder	1963	7.50	15.00	30.00
❑ 58-0033	Words Written on Water/Rolling Stone	1964	3.00	6.00	12.00
❑ 58-0039	Whatever Happened to Our Love/Tonight Kiss Your Baby Goodbye	1964	3.00	6.00	12.00
MERCURY					
❑ 71618	We Fell in Love/Pickin' Petals	1960	3.75	7.50	15.00
REF-O-REE					
❑ 700	Tell Me Baby/A Sample of My Love	196?	5.00	10.00	20.00
SOUND STAGE 7					
❑ 2561	Be Good to Your Baby/Just As Long As I Live	1966	2.50	5.00	10.00

AXTON, HOYT

Number	Title (A Side/B Side)	Yr	VG	VG+	NM
20TH FOX					
❑ 6648	Five Dollar Bill/Smoky	1966	2.50	5.00	10.00
A&M					
❑ 1437	Sweet Misery/Less Than the Song	1973	—	2.50	5.00
❑ 1497	When the Morning Comes/Billie's Theme	1974	—	2.50	5.00
❑ 1607	Boney Fingers/Life Machine	1974	—	2.50	5.00
❑ 1657	Nashville/Speed Trap	1974	—	2.50	5.00
❑ 1683	Lion in the Winter/No No Song	1975	—	2.50	5.00
❑ 1713	In a Young Girl's Mind/Southbound	1975	—	2.50	5.00
❑ 1811	Flash of Fire/Paid in Advance	1976	—	2.00	4.00
BRIAR					
❑ 100	Georgia Hoss Soldier/Drinking Gourd	1961	3.75	7.50	15.00
CAPITOL					
❑ 3121	Alice in Wonderland/Have a Nice Day	1971	—	3.00	6.00
❑ 3167	California Women/Ease Your Pain	1971	—	3.00	6.00
❑ 3259	Speed Traps/Hey, Mr. Pilot Man	1972	—	3.00	6.00
COLGEMS					
❑ 66-1005	San Fernando/Ten Thousand Sunsets	1967	2.50	5.00	10.00
COLUMBIA					
❑ 44810	Snowblind Friend/It's All Right Now	1969	—	3.50	7.00
❑ 44850	Way Before the Time of Towns/It's All Right Now	1969	—	3.50	7.00
ELEKTRA					
❑ 47133	Flo's Yellow Rose/Lion in the Winter	1981	—	2.00	4.00
HORIZON					
❑ 2	Grizzly Bear/Gypsy Woman	1963	2.50	5.00	10.00
❑ 6	The Happy Song/We'll Sing in the Sunshine	1963	2.50	5.00	10.00
❑ 351	Greenback Dollar/Crawdad Song	1962	3.75	7.50	15.00
❑ 360	Grizzly Bear/Gypsy Woman	1963	3.00	6.00	12.00
❑ 361	This Little Light/Thunder 'N' Lightnin'	1963	3.00	6.00	12.00
❑ 362	One More Round/Greenback Dollar	1963	3.00	6.00	12.00
JEREMIAH					
❑ 1000	Della and the Dealer/A Young Girl's Mind	1979	—	2.00	4.00
❑ 1001	A Rusty Old Halo/Keep Hollin'	1979	—	2.00	4.00
❑ 1003	Wild Bull Rider/Torpedo	1979	—	2.00	4.00
❑ 1005	Evangelina/So Hard to Give It All Up	1980	—	2.00	4.00
❑ 1006	Boozers Are Losers (When the Benders Don't End)/Politicians	1980	—	2.00	4.00
❑ 1008	Where Did the Money Go/Smile As You Go By	1980	—	2.00	4.00
❑ 1011	The Devil/Jealous Man	1981	—	2.00	4.00
❑ 1012	Win This One/Ease Your Pain	1981	—	2.00	4.00
❑ 1014	She's Too Lazy to Be Crazy/You Do Not Tango	1982	—	2.00	4.00
❑ 1015	There Stands the Glass/James Dean and the Junkman	1982	—	2.00	4.00
❑ 1016	Pistol Packin' Mama/Fearless the Wonderdog	1982	—	2.00	4.00
❑ 1017	Warm Storms and Wild Flowers/Don't Fence Me In	1983	—	2.00	4.00
❑ 1018	If You're a Cowboy/I Collect Hearts	1983	—	2.00	4.00
MCA					
❑ 40711	You're the Hangnail in My Life/Never Been to Spain	1977	—	2.00	4.00
❑ 40731	Little White Moon/Funeral of the King	1977	—	2.50	5.00
VEE JAY					
❑ 604	L.A. Town/Double Double Dare	1964	3.00	6.00	12.00
❑ 619	Bring Your Lovin'/Tiger in the Closet	1964	3.00	6.00	12.00
❑ 659	Hush Hush Sweet Charlotte/After You've Gone	1965	2.50	5.00	10.00

AZALEAS, THE

Number	Title (A Side/B Side)	Yr	VG	VG+	NM
ROMULUS					
❑ 3001	Hands Off/One Drummer Can't Keep Time	1963	7.50	15.00	30.00

AZTEX

Number	Title (A Side/B Side)	Yr	VG	VG+	NM
STAFF					
❑ (# unknown)	I Said Move/(B-side unknown)	196?	625.00	1250.	2500.

B

B. BUMBLE AND THE STINGERS

Number	Title (A Side/B Side)	Yr	VG	VG+	NM
DYMO					
❑ 13	Pollywog/Slumber Party	196?	2.50	5.00	10.00
ERA BACK TO BACK HITS					
❑ 038	Bumble Boogie/Angel Baby	197?	—	3.00	6.00
—B-side by Rosie and the Originals					
ERIC					
❑ 297	Nut Rocker/Bumble Boogie	197?	—	2.00	4.00
GOLDIES 45					
❑ 2465	Bumble Boogie/School Day Blues	1973	—	2.50	5.00
❑ 2466	Nut Rocker/Nautilus	1973	—	2.50	5.00
GOLDISC					
❑ 3106	Nut Rocker/Bumble Boogie	198?	—	2.00	4.00
HI OLDIES					
❑ 409	Nut Rocker/Nautilus	197?	—	2.50	5.00
HIGHLAND					
❑ 2001	Bumble Boogie/School Day Blues	196?	2.50	5.00	10.00
MERCURY					
❑ 72614	Green Hornet Theme/Flight of the Hornet	1966	2.50	5.00	10.00
❑ 72665	Silent Movies/Twelfth Street Rag	1967	2.50	5.00	10.00
OLDIES 45					
❑ 37	Nut Rocker/Nautilus	1964	2.00	4.00	8.00
❑ 065	Nut Rocker/Baby I Love You	197?	—	2.50	5.00
—B-side by Joe Weaver and the Don Juans					
RENDEZVOUS					
❑ 140	Bumble Boogie/School Day Blues	1961	5.00	10.00	20.00
❑ 151	Boogie Woogie/Near You	1961	3.75	7.50	15.00
❑ 160	Bee Hive/Caravan	1961	3.75	7.50	15.00
❑ 166	Nut Rocker/Nautilus	1962	3.75	7.50	15.00
❑ 174	Rockin-On-And-Off/Mashed #5	1962	3.00	6.00	12.00
❑ 179	Apple Knocker/The Moon and the Sea	1962	3.00	6.00	12.00
❑ 182	Dawn Cracker/Scales	1962	3.00	6.00	12.00
❑ 186	12th Street Rag/Canadian Sunset	1962	3.00	6.00	12.00
❑ 192	Baby Mash/Night Time Madness	1962	3.00	6.00	12.00
❑ 210	In the Mood/Chicken Chow Mein	1963	3.00	6.00	12.00
TRIAD					
❑ 778	Chariots from the Stars/Funky Mud	197?	—	3.00	6.00
WAX					
❑ 13	Pollywog/Slumber Party	196?	2.50	5.00	10.00
—"Wax" in small vertical print					
❑ 13	Pollywog/Slumber Party	196?	2.00	4.00	8.00
—"Wax" in large sideways print					

B.R.A.T.T.S., THE

Number	Title (A Side/B Side)	Yr	VG	VG+	NM
TOLLIE					
❑ 9024	Secret Weapon (The British Are Coming)/Jealous Kinda Woman	1964	5.00	10.00	20.00

BABIES, THE

Number	Title (A Side/B Side)	Yr	VG	VG+	NM
ABC DUNHILL					
❑ 4148	I Wanna Testify/Party Time	1968	3.00	6.00	12.00
DUNHILL					
❑ 4085	You Make Me Feel Like Someone/The Hand of Fate	1967	4.00	8.00	16.00
❑ 4085 [PS]	You Make Me Feel Like Someone/The Hand of Fate	1967	7.50	15.00	30.00
❑ 4101	I'm Not Asking for the World/Goodbye My Love, Goodbye	1967	3.75	7.50	15.00

BABY BUGS, THE

Number	Title (A Side/B Side)	Yr	VG	VG+	NM
VEE JAY					
❑ 594	Bingo/Bingo's Bongo Bingo Party	1964	6.25	12.50	25.00
❑ 594 [PS]	Bingo/Bingo's Bongo Bingo Party	1964	18.75	37.50	75.00

BABY DOLLS, THE

Number	Title (A Side/B Side)	Yr	VG	VG+	NM
BOOM					
❑ 60002	I Will Do It ('Cause He Wants Me To)/Now That I've Lost You	1966	2.50	5.00	10.00
GAMBLE					
❑ 213	Please Don't Rush Me/There You Are	1968	2.00	4.00	8.00
HOLLYWOOD					
❑ 1111	Got to Get You Into My Life/Why Can't I Make Him Like You	1960	10.00	20.00	40.00
MASKE					
❑ 103	Go Away Baby/I'm Lonely	1960	12.50	25.00	50.00
❑ 701	Thanks, Mr. DJ/What a Wonderful Love	1961	30.00	60.00	120.00

RCA VICTOR

Number	Title (A Side/B Side)	Yr	VG	VG+	NM
❑ 47-7296	Tutti Frutti/Cause I'm in Love	1958	3.75	7.50	15.00

WARNER BROS.

Number	Title (A Side/B Side)	Yr	VG	VG+	NM
❑ 5086	Hey Baby/Quiet	1959	3.00	6.00	12.00

BABY GRAND

Featuring Rob Hyman and Eric Bazilian, future members of the HOOTERS.

ARISTA

Number	Title (A Side/B Side)	Yr	VG	VG+	NM
❑ 0293	Bring Me Your Broken Heart/Lady of My Dreams	1977	—	2.50	5.00
❑ 0312	Never Enough/Lady of My Dreams	1978	—	2.50	5.00
❑ 0374	Walk Away Renee/Much Too Much	1978	—	2.50	5.00
❑ 0394 [DJ]	All Night Long (same on both sides)	1979	—	2.50	5.00

—May be promo only

BABY RAY

IMPERIAL

Number	Title (A Side/B Side)	Yr	VG	VG+	NM
❑ 66216	There's Something On Your Mind/House on Soul Hill	1966	3.75	7.50	15.00
❑ 66232	Elvira/Just Because	1967	3.75	7.50	15.00
❑ 66256	Your Sweet Love/Yours Until Tomorrow	1967	3.75	7.50	15.00

BABY RAY AND THE FERNS

An early production of FRANK ZAPPA.

DONNA

Number	Title (A Side/B Side)	Yr	VG	VG+	NM
❑ 1378	How's Your Bird/The World's Greatest Sinner	1963	50.00	100.00	200.00

BACHELORS, THE (1)

British Invasion male vocal group.

LONDON

Number	Title (A Side/B Side)	Yr	VG	VG+	NM
❑ 9584	Charmaine/Old Bill	1963	3.00	6.00	12.00
❑ 9623	Faraway Places/Is There a Chance	1964	3.00	6.00	12.00
❑ 9632	Whispering/No Light in the Window	1964	3.00	6.00	12.00
❑ 9639	Diane/Happy Land	1964	3.00	6.00	12.00
❑ 9639	Diane/I Believe	1964	3.75	7.50	15.00
❑ 9672	I Believe/Sweet Lullaby	1964	3.00	6.00	12.00
❑ 9672 [PS]	I Believe/Sweet Lullaby	1964	6.25	12.50	25.00
❑ 9693	I Wouldn't Trade You for the World/Beneath the Willow Tree	1964	3.00	6.00	12.00
❑ 9693 [PS]	I Wouldn't Trade You for the World/Beneath the Willow Tree	1964	6.25	12.50	25.00
❑ 9724	No Arms Can Ever Hold You/Oh Samuel, Don't Die	1964	3.00	6.00	12.00
❑ 9762	Marie/You Can Tell	1965	2.50	5.00	10.00
❑ 9793	Chapel in the Moonlight/The Old Wishing Well	1965	2.50	5.00	10.00
❑ 9793 [PS]	Chapel in the Moonlight/The Old Wishing Well	1965	5.00	10.00	20.00
❑ 9828	Love Me with All of Your Heart/There's No Room in My Heart	1966	2.50	5.00	10.00
❑ 20010	Can I Trust You/My Girl	1966	2.50	5.00	10.00
❑ 20018	Walk with Faith in Your Heart/Queen Molly Malone of Ireland	1966	2.50	5.00	10.00
❑ 20027	Marta/Oh How I Miss You	1967	2.00	4.00	8.00
❑ 20033	Learn to Live Without You/3 O'Clock Flamingo Street	1967	2.00	4.00	8.00
❑ 20051	Punky's Dilemma/It's a Beautiful Day	1968	2.00	4.00	8.00
❑ 20063	Love Is All/The Colours of Love	1970	—	3.00	6.00
❑ 20071	Diamonds Are Forever/Where There's a Heartache	1971	—	3.00	6.00

BACHELORS, THE (2)

American male vocal group.

ALADDIN

Number	Title (A Side/B Side)	Yr	VG	VG+	NM
❑ 3210	Pretty Baby/Can't Help Loving You	1953	625.00	1250.	2500.

ROYAL ROOST

Number	Title (A Side/B Side)	Yr	VG	VG+	NM
❑ 620	I Found Love/You've Lied	1952	75.00	150.00	300.00

BACHELORS, THE (U)

None of these are group (1), though some could be group (2).

EPIC

Number	Title (A Side/B Side)	Yr	VG	VG+	NM
❑ 9369	Do the Madison/Bachelor's Club	1960	3.00	6.00	12.00

MERCURY

Number	Title (A Side/B Side)	Yr	VG	VG+	NM
❑ 8159	Yesterday's Roses/Hereafter	1949	75.00	150.00	300.00

MGM

Number	Title (A Side/B Side)	Yr	VG	VG+	NM
❑ 12668	Sometimes/Teenage Memory	1958	5.00	10.00	20.00

NATIONAL

Number	Title (A Side/B Side)	Yr	VG	VG+	NM
❑ 104	From Your Heart/A Million Teardrops	1957	6.25	12.50	25.00
❑ 115	Today, Tomorrow, Forever/I Want a Girl	1957	6.25	12.50	25.00

POPLAR

Number	Title (A Side/B Side)	Yr	VG	VG+	NM
❑ 101	After/You Know, I Know (I Love You)	1957	12.50	25.00	50.00

SMASH

Number	Title (A Side/B Side)	Yr	VG	VG+	NM
❑ 1723	The Day I Met You/Hey Little Girl	1961	3.00	6.00	12.00

BACHMAN, RANDY

Also see BACHMAN-TURNER OVERDRIVE; THE GUESS WHO.

POLYDOR

Number	Title (A Side/B Side)	Yr	VG	VG+	NM
❑ 14478	Is the Night Too Cold for Dancing/Maybe Again	1978	—	2.00	4.00

BACHMAN-TURNER OVERDRIVE

Also see RANDY BACHMAN; BRAVE BELT.

COMPLEAT

Number	Title (A Side/B Side)	Yr	VG	VG+	NM
❑ 127	For the Weekend/Just Look at Me Now	1984	—	2.00	4.00
❑ 133	My Sugaree/Service with a Smile	1984	—	2.00	4.00
❑ 137	My Sugaree/(B-side unknown)	1985	—	2.00	4.00

MERCURY

Number	Title (A Side/B Side)	Yr	VG	VG+	NM
❑ 73383	Gimmie Your Money Please/Little Gandy Dancer	1973	—	2.50	5.00
❑ 73417	Blue Collar/Hold Back the Water	1973	—	2.50	5.00
❑ 73457	Let It Ride/Tramp	1974	—	2.00	4.00
❑ 73487	Takin' Care of Business/Stonegates	1974	—	2.00	4.00
❑ 73622	You Ain't Seen Nothin' Yet/Free Wheelin'	1974	—	2.00	4.00
❑ 73656	Roll On Down the Highway/Sledgehammer	1975	—	2.00	4.00
❑ 73683	Hey You/Flat Broke Love	1975	—	2.00	4.00
❑ 73724	Down to the Line/She's a Devil	1975	—	2.00	4.00
❑ 73724 [PS]	Down to the Line/She's a Devil	1975	2.00	4.00	8.00
❑ 73766	Take It Like a Man/Woncha Take Me for a While	1976	—	2.00	4.00
❑ 73784	Looking Out for #1/Find Out About Love	1976	—	2.00	4.00
❑ 73843	Gimme Your Money Please/Four Wheel Drive	1976	—	2.00	4.00
❑ 73903	Freeways/My Wheels Won't Turn	1977	—	2.00	4.00
❑ 73926	Shotgun Rider/Down, Down	1977	—	2.00	4.00
❑ 73951	Life Still Goes On (I'm Lonely)/Just for You	1977	—	2.00	4.00
❑ 73987	Down the Road/A Long Time for a Little While	1978	—	2.00	4.00
❑ 74046	Heaven Tonight/Heartaches	1979	—	2.00	4.00
❑ 74062	End of the Line/Jamaica	1979	—	2.00	4.00

BACK BEAT

LAURIE

Number	Title (A Side/B Side)	Yr	VG	VG+	NM
❑ 3092	Rock and Roll Symphony, 1st and 2nd Movements	1961	5.00	10.00	20.00

BACKBEAT BAND

Band members: Greg Dulli, Don Fleming, Thurston Moore, Mike Mills, Dave Grohl.

DRY HUMP

Number	Title (A Side/B Side)	Yr	VG	VG+	NM
❑ 010	Money/Dizzy Miss Lizzy	1994	—	2.50	5.00
❑ 010 [PS]	Money/Dizzy Miss Lizzy	1994	—	2.50	5.00

—With insert advertising other Dry Hump releases

VIRGIN

Number	Title (A Side/B Side)	Yr	VG	VG+	NM
❑ S7-17912	Money/Dizzy Miss Lizzy//He's Wearing My Bathrobe	1994	—	2.00	4.00

—As "Backbeat"

BACKSTREET BOYS

JIVE

Number	Title (A Side/B Side)	Yr	VG	VG+	NM
❑ 42453	Quit Playing Games (With My Heart)/Lay Down Beside Me	1997	—	—	3.00
❑ 42510	Everybody (Backstreet's Back)/As Long As You Love Me	1998	—	—	3.00
❑ 42562	All I Have to Give (Album Version)/All I Have to Give (Part II, The Conversation Mix)	1999	—	—	3.00
❑ 42595	I Want It That Way (same on both sides)	1999	—	—	3.00
❑ 42624	Larger Than Life (The Video Mix) (same on both sides)	1999	—	—	3.00
❑ 42758	Shape of My Heart (same on both sides)	2000	—	2.00	4.00

BACKUS, JIM

DICO

Number	Title (A Side/B Side)	Yr	VG	VG+	NM
❑ 101	I Was a Teenage Reindeer/The Office Party	1959	5.00	10.00	20.00

DORE

Number	Title (A Side/B Side)	Yr	VG	VG+	NM
❑ 899	Dirty Old Man/Frigid	1974	—	2.50	5.00

JUBILEE

Number	Title (A Side/B Side)	Yr	VG	VG+	NM
❑ 5330	Delicious!/I Need a Vacation	1958	3.75	7.50	15.00

—As "Jim Bakus and Friend"

Number	Title (A Side/B Side)	Yr	VG	VG+	NM
❑ 5351	Cave Man/Why Don't You Go Home for Christmas	1958	3.00	6.00	12.00
❑ 5361	Cave Man/Rock on the Roof	1959	3.00	6.00	12.00

BACON, GAR

BATON

Number	Title (A Side/B Side)	Yr	VG	VG+	NM
❑ 248	There's Gonna Be Rockin' Tonight/Y-I-O-U	1957	15.00	30.00	60.00
❑ 250	Justice/Pucker Up	1958	10.00	20.00	40.00

DALE

Number	Title (A Side/B Side)	Yr	VG	VG+	NM
❑ 105	Chains of Love/Mary Jane	1957	6.25	12.50	25.00
❑ 108	Dutch Treat/I'll Never Fail You	1958	7.50	15.00	30.00

OKEH

Number	Title (A Side/B Side)	Yr	VG	VG+	NM
❑ 7115	Marshall, Marshall/Too Young to Love	1959	5.00	10.00	20.00

RKO UNIQUE

Number	Title (A Side/B Side)	Yr	VG	VG+	NM
❑ 395	Lonesome Wail/You and Your Love	1957	5.00	10.00	20.00

BAD BOYS, THE

WARNER BROS.

Number	Title (A Side/B Side)	Yr	VG	VG+	NM
❑ 5605	The Owl and the Pussycat/That's What I'll Do	1965	3.00	6.00	12.00

BADD BOYS, THE

EPIC

Number	Title (A Side/B Side)	Yr	VG	VG+	NM
❑ 10119	Never Going Back to Georgia/River Deep Mountain High	1967	12.50	25.00	50.00
❑ 10165	Folks in a Hurry/I Told You So	1967	15.00	30.00	60.00

BADFINGER

APPLE

Number	Title (A Side/B Side)	Yr	VG	VG+	NM
❑ 1803	Maybe Tomorrow/And Her Daddy's a Millionaire	1969	7.50	15.00	30.00

—By "The Iveys"; with star on label

Number	Title (A Side/B Side)	Yr	VG	VG+	NM
❑ 1803	Maybe Tomorrow/And Her Daddy's a Millionaire	1969	5.00	10.00	20.00

—By "The Iveys"; without star on label

Number	Title (A Side/B Side)	Yr	VG	VG+	NM
❑ 1815	Come and Get It/Rock of All Ages	1969	—	3.00	6.00
❑ 1815	Come and Get It/Rock of All Ages	1969	2.00	4.00	8.00

—With Capitol logo on B-side bottom

Number	Title (A Side/B Side)	Yr	VG	VG+	NM
❑ 1822	No Matter What/Carry On Till Tomorrow	1970	—	3.00	6.00
❑ 1822	No Matter What/Carry On Till Tomorrow	1970	5.00	10.00	20.00

—With star on A-side label

Number	Title (A Side/B Side)	Yr	VG	VG+	NM
❑ 1841	Day After Day/Money	1971	5.00	10.00	20.00

—With star on A-side label

Number	Title (A Side/B Side)	Yr	VG	VG+	NM
❑ 1841	Day After Day/Money	1971	—	3.00	6.00
❑ 1841 [DJ]	Day After Day/Money	1971	30.00	60.00	120.00

—White label

Number	Title (A Side/B Side)	Yr	VG	VG+	NM
❑ 1844	Baby Blue/Flying	1972	—	3.00	6.00
❑ 1844 [DJ]	Baby Blue/Flying	1972	30.00	60.00	120.00

—White label

Number	Title (A Side/B Side)	Yr	VG	VG+	NM
❑ 1844 [PS]	Baby Blue/Flying	1972	3.75	7.50	15.00
❑ 1864	Apple of My Eye/Blind Owl	1973	—	3.00	6.00
❑ P-1864 [DJ]	Apple of My Eye (mono/stereo)	1973	6.25	12.50	25.00

APPLE/AMERICOM

Number	Title (A Side/B Side)	Yr	VG	VG+	NM
❑ 1803P/M-300	Maybe Tomorrow/And Her Daddy's a Millionaire	1969	150.00	300.00	600.00

—By "The Iveys"; four-inch flexidisc sold from vending machines

CAPITOL

Number	Title (A Side/B Side)	Yr	VG	VG+	NM
❑ S7-17487	Baby Blue/Day After Day	1993	—	—	3.00

—Blue vinyl

Number	Title (A Side/B Side)	Yr	VG	VG+	NM
❑ S7-17487	Baby Blue/Day After Day	1993	—	2.50	5.00
—Black vinyl					
ELEKTRA					
❑ 46022	Lost Inside Your Love/Come Down Hard	1979	—	2.50	5.00
❑ 46025	Love Is Gonna Come At Last/Sail Away	1979	—	2.50	5.00
RADIO					
❑ 3793	Hold On/Passin' Time	1981	—	2.50	5.00
❑ 3815	I Got You/Rock and Roll Contract	1981	—	2.50	5.00
❑ 3833	Because I Love You/Too Hung Up on You	1981	—	2.50	5.00
WARNER BROS.					
❑ 7801	I Miss You/Shine On	1974	—	3.00	6.00
BADU, ERYKAH					
UNIVERSAL/KEDAR					
❑ US7-56189	Tyrone/On & On	1998	—	2.00	4.00
BAEZ, JOAN					
A&M					
❑ 1334	Song of Bangladesh/Prison Trilogy (Billy Rose)	1972	—	2.50	5.00
❑ 1334 [PS]	Song of Bangladesh/Prison Trilogy (Billy Rose)	1972	2.50	5.00	10.00
❑ 1362	In the Quiet Morning/To Bobby	1972	—	2.00	4.00
❑ 1362 [PS]	In the Quiet Morning/To Bobby	1972	2.00	4.00	8.00
❑ 1393	Love Song to a Stranger/Tumbleweed	1972	—	2.00	4.00
❑ 1454	The Best of Friends/Mary Call	1973	—	2.00	4.00
❑ 1472	Less Than the Song/Windrose	1973	—	2.00	4.00
❑ 1516	Forever Young/Guantanamera	1974	—	2.00	4.00
❑ 1703	Blue Sky/Dida	1975	—	2.00	4.00
❑ 1737	Diamonds and Rust/Winds of the Old Days	1975	—	2.50	5.00
❑ 1802	Please Come to Boston/Love Song to a Stranger	1976	—	2.00	4.00
❑ 1820	Never Dreamed You'd Leave in Summer/ Children and All That Jazz	1976	—	2.00	4.00
❑ 1884	Caruso/Time Is Passing Us By	1976	—	2.00	4.00
❑ 1906	O Brother/Still Waters at Night	1977	—	2.00	4.00
DECCA					
❑ 32890	Silent Running/Rejoice in the Sun	1971	—	3.00	6.00
GUARDIAN					
❑ S7-19727	No Mermaid/Diamonds and Rust	1997	—	—	3.00
PHILCO-FORD					
❑ HP-36	There But For Fortune/Pack Up Your Sorrows	1969	5.00	10.00	20.00
—4-inch plastic "Hip Pocket Record" with color sleeve					
PORTRAIT					
❑ 70006	I'm Blowing Away/The Altar Boy and the Sheep	1977	—	2.00	4.00
❑ 70009	Time Rag/Miracles	1977	—	2.00	4.00
❑ 70032	Light a Light/Michael	1979	—	2.00	4.00
RCA VICTOR					
❑ 74-0568	The Ballad of Sacco and Vanzetti/Here's to You	1971	—	3.00	6.00
VANGUARD					
❑ 35012	Banks of the Ohio/Old Blue	1962	2.00	4.00	8.00
❑ 35013	Lonesome Road/Pal of Mine	1962	2.00	4.00	8.00
❑ 35018	What Have They Done to the Rain/Danger Waters	1963	2.00	4.00	8.00
❑ 35023	We Shall Overcome/What Have They Done to the Rain	1963	2.00	4.00	8.00
❑ 35026	Medley: With God on Our Side/Railroad Bill// Rambler Gambler	1964	2.00	4.00	8.00
❑ 35031	There But for Fortune/Daddy You Been On My Mind	1965	2.00	4.00	8.00
❑ 35031 [PS]	There But for Fortune/Daddy You Been On My Mind	1965	7.50	15.00	30.00
❑ 35040	Pack Up Your Sorrows/Swallow Song	1966	2.00	4.00	8.00
❑ 35046	Little Drummer Boy/Cantique de Noel	1966	2.50	5.00	10.00
❑ 35055	Be Not Too Hard/The North	1967	2.00	4.00	8.00
❑ 35088	Love Is Just a Four-Letter Word/Love Minus Zero-No Limit	1969	2.00	4.00	8.00
❑ 35092	If I Knew/Rock Salt and Nails	1969	2.00	4.00	8.00
❑ 35098	Four Days Gone/Hickory Wind	1969	2.00	4.00	8.00
❑ 35103	No Expectations/One Day at a Time	1970	—	3.00	6.00
❑ 35106	Sweet Sir Galahad/The Ghetto	1970	—	3.00	6.00
❑ 35114	Carry It On/Rock Salt and Nails	1970	—	3.00	6.00
❑ 35138	The Night They Drove Old Dixie Down/When Time Is Stolen	1971	2.00	4.00	8.00
❑ 35145	Let It Be/Poor Wayfaring Stranger	1971	—	3.00	6.00
❑ 35148	Will the Circle Be Unbroken/Just a Closer Walk with Thee	1972	—	2.50	5.00
❑ 35158	Blessed Are/The Brand New Tennessee Waltz	1972	—	2.50	5.00
BAGDASARIAN, ROSS					
Real name of DAVID SEVILLE, who also invented THE CHIPMUNKS.					
CORAL					
❑ 60544	Come On-a My House/Oh Beauty	1951	7.50	15.00	30.00
❑ 60597	The Girl with the Tambourine/He Says Mu-Humm	1951	6.25	12.50	25.00
IMPERIAL					
❑ 66379	Jone-Cone-Phone/Spanish Pizza	1969	2.50	5.00	10.00
❑ 66414	You've Got Me on a Merry-Go-Round/You Better Open Your Eyes	1969	2.50	5.00	10.00
LIBERTY					
❑ 55013	The Bold and the Brave/See a Teardrop Fall	1956	5.00	10.00	20.00
❑ 55193	Judy/Maria from Madrid	1959	4.00	8.00	16.00
❑ 55239	Lotta Bull/(B-side unknown)	1959	4.00	8.00	16.00
❑ 55275	Lazy Lovers/One Finger Waltz	1960	4.00	8.00	16.00
❑ 55462	Armen's Theme/Russian Roulette	1962	3.75	7.50	15.00
❑ 55557	Cecelia/Gotta Get to Your House	1963	3.75	7.50	15.00
❑ 55619	Lucy, Lucy/Scalliwags and Sinners	1963	3.75	7.50	15.00
❑ 55810	La Noche/Naval Maneuver	1965	3.00	6.00	12.00
❑ 55837	Come On-a My House/Gotta Get to Your House	1965	3.00	6.00	12.00
❑ 56004	Walking Birds of Carnaby/Red Wine	1967	3.00	6.00	12.00
❑ 56043	Yallah/Naval Maneuver	1968	—	—	—
—Unreleased					
❑ 56048	When I Look in Your Eyes/Sands of Time	1968	3.00	6.00	12.00
❑ 56165	I Treasure Thee/Lie Lie	1969	3.00	6.00	12.00

Number	Title (A Side/B Side)	Yr	VG	VG+	NM
MERCURY					
❑ 70254	Let's Have a Merry, Merry Christmas/Hey Brother, Pour the Wine	1953	6.25	12.50	25.00
BAGELS, THE					
WARNER BROS.					
❑ 5420	I Wanna Hold Your Hair/Yeah, Yeah, Yeah, Yeah	1964	3.75	7.50	15.00
BAGGYS, THE					
PIPELINE					
❑ 501	El Surfer/El Seagull	1963	10.00	20.00	40.00
BAILEY, THOMAS					
FEDERAL					
❑ 12559	Fran/Just Won't Move	1969	3.00	6.00	12.00
❑ 12567	Wish I Was Back/Percy's Place	1970	25.00	50.00	100.00
BAINES, VICKI					
LOMA					
❑ 2078	We Can Find True Love/Sweeter Than Sweet Things	1967	3.00	6.00	12.00
PARKWAY					
❑ 957	Losing You/Got to Run	1965	6.25	12.50	25.00
❑ 966	Country Girl/Are You Kidding	1966	25.00	50.00	100.00
BAKER, BOBBY					
SWAN					
❑ 4037	Baby Blue Eyes/Hush Our Secret	1959	3.75	7.50	15.00
BAKER, CHARLIE					
LIBERTY					
❑ 55226	Star of Wonder/You Crack Me Up	1959	6.25	12.50	25.00
MUNRAB					
❑ 106	Star of Wonder/You Crack Me Up	1959	37.50	75.00	150.00
BAKER, DONNIE, AND THE DEMENSIONALS					
RAINBOW					
❑ 219	Drinkin' Pop Sodee-Odee (Pop Pop)/Sleepy Time Gal	1953	15.00	30.00	60.00
—Black vinyl					
❑ 219	Drinkin' Pop Sodee-Odee (Pop Pop)/Sleepy Time Gal	1953	37.50	75.00	150.00
—Red vinyl					
BAKER, GEORGE, SELECTION					
COLOSSUS					
❑ 112	Little Gren Bag/Pretty Little Dreamer	1970	—	2.50	5.00
❑ 117	Dear Ann/Fly	1970	—	2.00	4.00
❑ 124	I Wanna Love You/Impressions	1970	—	2.00	4.00
WARNER BROS.					
❑ 8115	Paloma Blanca/Dreamboat	1975	—	2.00	4.00
❑ 8207	Baby Blue/Morning Sky	1976	—	2.00	4.00
BAKER, GINGER, 'S AIR FORCE					
Also see BLIND FAITH; CREAM.					
ATCO					
❑ 6750	Man of Constant Sorrow/Doin' It	1970	—	2.50	5.00
❑ 6816	Atunde! (We Are Here) Part 1/Atunde! (We Are Here) Part 2	1971	—	2.50	5.00
BAKER, LAVERN					
ATLANTIC					
❑ 1004	How Can You Leave a Man Like This/Soul on Fire	1953	12.50	25.00	50.00
❑ 1030	I Can't Hold Out Any Longer/I'm Living My Life for You	1954	10.00	20.00	40.00
❑ 1047	Tweedlee Dee/Tomorrow Night	1954	10.00	20.00	40.00
❑ 1057	Bop-Ting-a-Ling/That's All I Need	1955	10.00	20.00	40.00
❑ 1075	Play It Fair/That Lucky Old Sun	1955	10.00	20.00	40.00
❑ 1087	Get Up Get Up (You Sleepyhead)/My Happiness Forever	1956	6.25	12.50	25.00
❑ 1093	Fee Fee Fi Fo Fum/I'll Do the Same for You	1956	6.25	12.50	25.00
❑ 1104	I Can't Love You Enough/Still	1956	6.25	12.50	25.00
❑ 1116	Jim Dandy/Tra La La	1956	6.25	12.50	25.00
❑ 1136	Jim Dandy Got Married/The Game of Love	1957	6.25	12.50	25.00
❑ 1150	Humpty Dumpty Heart/Love Me Right	1957	6.25	12.50	25.00
❑ 1163	St.Louis Blues/Miracles	1957	6.25	12.50	25.00
❑ 1176	Substitute/Learning to Love	1958	6.25	12.50	25.00
❑ 1189	Harbor Lights/Whipper Snapper	1958	6.25	12.50	25.00
❑ 2001	It's So Fine/Why Baby Why	1958	6.25	12.50	25.00
❑ 2007	I Cried a Tear/Dix-A-Billy	1958	6.25	12.50	25.00
❑ 2021	I Waited Too Long/You're Teasing Me	1959	5.00	10.00	20.00
❑ 2033	So High So Low/If You Love Me	1959	5.00	10.00	20.00
❑ 2041	Tiny Tim/For the Love of You	1959	5.00	10.00	20.00
❑ 2048	Shake a Hand/Manana	1960	5.00	10.00	20.00
❑ 2059	Wheel of Fortune/Shadows of Love	1960	3.75	7.50	15.00
❑ 2067	A Help-Each-Other Romance/How Often	1960	3.75	7.50	15.00
—With Ben E. King					
❑ 2077	Bumble Bee/My Time Will Come	1960	3.75	7.50	15.00
❑ 2090	You're the Boss/I'll Never Be Free	1961	3.75	7.50	15.00
—With Jimmy Ricks					
❑ 2099	Saved/Don Juan	1961	3.75	7.50	15.00
❑ 2109	I Didn't Know I Was Crying/Hurtin' Inside	1961	3.75	7.50	15.00
❑ 2119	Hey, Memphis/Voodoo Voodoo	1961	3.75	7.50	15.00
❑ 2137	Must I Cry Again/No Love So True	1962	3.00	6.00	12.00
❑ 2167	See See Rider/The Story of My Love	1962	3.00	6.00	12.00
❑ 2186	Trouble in Mind/Half of Your Love	1963	3.00	6.00	12.00
❑ 2203	Itty Bitty Girl/Oh, Johnny Oh, Johnny	1963	3.00	6.00	12.00
❑ 2234	You'd Better Find Yourself Another Fool/Go Away	1964	2.50	5.00	10.00
❑ 2267	Fly Me to the Moon/Ain't Gonna Cry No More	1965	2.50	5.00	10.00
BRUNSWICK					
❑ 55285	Let Me Belong to You/Pledging My Love	1965	2.00	4.00	8.00
❑ 55287	Think Twice/Please Don't Hurt Me	1965	2.00	4.00	8.00
—With Jackie Wilson					
❑ 55291	One Monkey (Don't Stop the Show)/Baby	1966	2.00	4.00	8.00

Number	Title (A Side/B Side)	Yr	VG	VG+	NM
❑ 55297	Batman to the Rescue/Call Me Darling	1966	2.50	5.00	10.00
❑ 55311	Nothing Like Being in Love/Wrapped, Tied and Tangled	1967	2.00	4.00	8.00
❑ 55341	Born to Lose/I Need You So	1967	2.00	4.00	8.00
❑ 55408	I'm the One to Do It/Baby	1969	—	3.00	6.00
KING					
❑ 4556	Trying/Snuff Dipper	1952	12.50	25.00	50.00
—B-side by Todd Rhodes					
❑ 4583	Must I Cry Again/Hog Maw and Cabbage Slaw	1952	12.50	25.00	50.00
—B-side by Todd Rhodes					
❑ 4601	Lost Child/Thunderball Boogie	1953	12.50	25.00	50.00
—B-side by Todd Rhodes					

7-Inch Extended Plays

Number	Title (A Side/B Side)	Yr	VG	VG+	NM
ATLANTIC					
❑ 566	(contents unknown)	1956	50.00	100.00	200.00
❑ 566 [PS]	LaVern Baker: Tweedle Dee	1956	25.00	50.00	100.00
❑ 588	*Jim Dandy/Still/Play It Fair/Tra La La	1957	20.00	40.00	80.00
❑ 588 [PS]	LaVern Baker: Jim Dandy	1957	37.50	75.00	150.00
❑ 617	(contents unknown)	1958	20.00	40.00	80.00
❑ 617 [PS]	LaVern Baker: I Cried a Tear	1958	37.50	75.00	150.00

BAKER, MICKEY "GUITAR"

Also see MICKEY AND SYLVIA.

Number	Title (A Side/B Side)	Yr	VG	VG+	NM
ATLANTIC					
❑ 2042	Third Man Theme/Baia	1959	3.00	6.00	12.00
KING					
❑ 5951	Side Show/Steam Roller	1964	2.50	5.00	10.00
❑ 5979	Do What You Do/Night Blue	1965	2.50	5.00	10.00
MGM					
❑ 12418	Spinnin' Rock Boogie/Tricky	1957	5.00	10.00	20.00
RAINBOW					
❑ 288	Shake Walkin'/Greasy Spoon	1955	7.50	15.00	30.00
❑ 299	Bandstand Stomp/Rock with a Sock	1955	7.50	15.00	30.00
❑ 303	Old Devil Moon/Guitarambo	1955	7.50	15.00	30.00
SAVOY					
❑ 867	Guitar Mambo/Riverboat	1952	12.50	25.00	50.00
❑ 874	Love Me Baby/Oh Happy Day	1953	12.50	25.00	50.00

BAKER, PENNY, AND THE PILLOWS

Number	Title (A Side/B Side)	Yr	VG	VG+	NM
WITCH					
❑ 123	Bring Back the Beatles/Gonna Win Him	1964	5.00	10.00	20.00
❑ 123 [PS]	Bring Back the Beatles/Gonna Win Him	1964	5.00	10.00	20.00

BAKER, RONNIE

Number	Title (A Side/B Side)	Yr	VG	VG+	NM
LAURIE					
❑ 3128	My Story/I Want to Be Loved	1962	15.00	30.00	60.00
❑ 3164	Land of Love/Time Told Me	1963	5.00	10.00	20.00
❑ 3250	See You in September/Young at Heart	1964	5.00	10.00	20.00

BAKER, YVONNE

Also see THE SENSATIONS.

Number	Title (A Side/B Side)	Yr	VG	VG+	NM
JAMIE					
❑ 1290	What a Difference Love Makes/Funny What Time Can Do	1965	3.00	6.00	12.00
MODERN					
❑ 1055	A Woman Needs a Man/My Baby Needs Me	196?	2.50	5.00	10.00
PARKWAY					
❑ 140	You Didn't Say a Word/To Prove My Love Is True	1967	25.00	50.00	100.00

BAKER SISTERS, THE

Number	Title (A Side/B Side)	Yr	VG	VG+	NM
MERCURY					
❑ 70839	Too Many Teardrops/Break the String	1956	5.00	10.00	20.00
❑ 70980	Little Monster/One By One	1956	5.00	10.00	20.00
❑ 71074	Trinidaddy/Careless Love	1957	5.00	10.00	20.00
UNIQUE					
❑ 324	Last Bus Home/If You're Ever Gonna Leave Me	1956	3.75	7.50	15.00

BALIN, MARTY

Also see JEFFERSON AIRPLANE; JEFFERSON STARSHIP.

Number	Title (A Side/B Side)	Yr	VG	VG+	NM
CHALLENGE					
❑ 9146	Nobody But You/You Made Me Fall	1962	12.50	25.00	50.00
❑ 9156	I Specialize in Love/You're Alive with Love	1962	12.50	25.00	50.00
EMI AMERICA					
❑ 8084	Hearts/Freeway	1981	—	2.00	4.00
❑ 8084 [PS]	Hearts/Freeway	1981	—	2.50	5.00
❑ 8093	Atlanta Lady (Something About Your Love)/Lydia	1981	—	2.00	4.00
❑ 8153	What Love Is/Will You Forever	1983	—	2.00	4.00
❑ 8153 [PS]	What Love Is/Will You Forever	1983	—	2.50	5.00
❑ 8160	Do It for Love/Heart of Stone	1983	—	2.00	4.00
❑ 8160 [PS]	Do It for Love/Heart of Stone	1983	—	2.50	5.00

BALLARD, FLORENCE

Former member of THE SUPREMES.

Number	Title (A Side/B Side)	Yr	VG	VG+	NM
ABC					
❑ 11074	Goin' Out of My Head/It Doesn't Matter How I Say It	1968	7.50	15.00	30.00
❑ 11144	Love Ain't Love/Forever Faithful	1968	7.50	15.00	30.00

BALLARD, HANK, AND THE MIDNIGHTERS

Includes records credited only to Hank Ballard. Also see THE MIDNIGHTERS; THE ROYALS (1).

Number	Title (A Side/B Side)	Yr	VG	VG+	NM
CHESS					
❑ 2111	Love, Why Is It Taking You So Long/I'm a Junkie for My Baby's Love	1971	—	3.00	6.00
KING					
❑ 5171	Teardrops on Your Letter/The Twist	1959	7.50	15.00	30.00
❑ 5195 [M]	Kansas City/I'll Keep You Happy	1959	6.25	12.50	25.00
❑ S-5195 [S]	Kansas City/I'll Keep You Happy	1959	12.50	25.00	50.00
❑ 5215 [M]	Sugaree/Rain Down Tears	1959	6.25	12.50	25.00
❑ S-5215 [S]	Sugaree/Rain Down Tears	1959	12.50	25.00	50.00
❑ 5245	Cute Little Ways/A House with No Windows	1959	6.25	12.50	25.00
❑ 5275	I Could Love You/Never Knew	1959	6.25	12.50	25.00
❑ 5289	Look at Little Sister/I Said I Wouldn't Beg You	1959	6.25	12.50	25.00
❑ 5312	The Coffee Grind/Waiting	1960	6.25	12.50	25.00
❑ 5341	Finger Poppin' Time/I Love You, I Love You So-o-o	1960	6.25	12.50	25.00
❑ 5400	Let's Go, Let's Go, Let's Go/If You'd Forgive Me	1960	6.25	12.50	25.00
❑ 5430	The Hoochi Coochi Coo/I'm Thinking of You	1960	5.00	10.00	20.00
❑ 5459	Let's Go Again (Where We Went Last Night)/Deep Blue Sea	1961	5.00	10.00	20.00
❑ 5491	The Continental Walk/What Is This I See	1961	5.00	10.00	20.00
❑ 5491 [PS]	The Continental Walk/What Is This I See	1961	20.00	40.00	80.00
❑ 5510	The Switch-A-Roo/The Float	1961	3.75	7.50	15.00
❑ 5513	The Big Frog/Doin' Everything	1961	3.75	7.50	15.00
—B-side by Henry Moore					
❑ 5535	Nothing But Good/Keep On Dancing	1961	3.75	7.50	15.00
❑ 5550	Big Red Sunset/Can't You See — I Need a Friend	1961	3.75	7.50	15.00
❑ 5578	Do You Remember/I'm Gonna Miss You	1961	3.75	7.50	15.00
❑ 5593	Do You Know How to Twist/Broadway	1962	3.75	7.50	15.00
❑ 5601	It's Twistin' Time/Autumn Breeze	1962	3.75	7.50	15.00
❑ 5635	Good Twistin' Tonight/I'm Young	1962	3.75	7.50	15.00
❑ 5655	I Want to Thank You/Excuse Me	1962	3.75	7.50	15.00
❑ 5677	Dream World/When I Need You	1962	3.75	7.50	15.00
❑ 5693	Shaky Mae/I Love and Care for You	1962	3.75	7.50	15.00
❑ 5703	Bring Me Your Love/She's the One	1962	3.75	7.50	15.00
❑ 5713	All the Things in Life That Please You/The Rising Tide	1963	3.75	7.50	15.00
❑ 5719	The House on the Hill/That Low-Down Move	1963	3.75	7.50	15.00
❑ 5729	Christmas Time for Everyone But Me/Santa Claus Is Coming	1963	3.75	7.50	15.00
❑ 5746	How Could You Leave Your Man Alone/Walkin' and Talkin'	1963	3.75	7.50	15.00
❑ 5798	Those Lonely, Lonely Feelings/It's Love, Baby	1963	3.75	7.50	15.00
❑ 5821	Buttin' In/I'm Leavin'	1963	3.75	7.50	15.00
❑ 5835	Don't Let Temptation Turn You Around/Have Mercy, Have a Little Pity	1964	3.75	7.50	15.00
❑ 5860	Don't Fall in Love with Me/I'm So Mad with You	1964	3.75	7.50	15.00
❑ 5884	I Don't Know How to Do But One Thing/These Young Girls	1964	3.75	7.50	15.00
❑ 5901	Stay Away from My Baby/She's Got a Whole Lot of Soul	1964	3.75	7.50	15.00
❑ 5931	Daddy Rolling Stone/What's Your Name	1964	3.75	7.50	15.00
❑ 5954	Let's Get the Show on the Road/A Winner Never Quits	1964	3.75	7.50	15.00
❑ 5963	One Monkey Don't Stop No Show/What Can I Tell You	1964	3.75	7.50	15.00
❑ 5974	The Handwriting on the Wall/I Done It	1964	3.75	7.50	15.00
❑ 5996	Poppin' the Whip/You, Just You	1965	3.00	6.00	12.00
❑ 6001	I'm Just a Fool and Everybody Knows/Do It Zulu Style	1965	3.00	6.00	12.00
❑ 6018	Sloop and Slide/My Sun Is Going Down	1966	3.00	6.00	12.00
❑ 6031	I'm Ready/Togetherness	1966	3.00	6.00	12.00
❑ 6055	I Was Born to Move/He Came Alone	1966	3.00	6.00	12.00
❑ 6092	Here Comes the Hurt/Dance Till It Hurt Cha	1967	3.00	6.00	12.00
❑ 6119	You're in Real Good Hands/Unwind Yourself	1967	3.00	6.00	12.00
❑ 6131	Funky's Soul Train/Which Way Should I Turn	1967	3.00	6.00	12.00
❑ 6177	I'm Back to Stay/Come On Wit' It	1968	3.00	6.00	12.00
❑ 6196	How You Gonna Get Respect (When You Haven't Cut Your Process Yet)/Teardrops on Your Letter	1968	2.50	5.00	10.00
—As "Hank Ballard Along With The Dapps"					
❑ 6215	You're So Sexy/Thrill on the Hill	1969	2.50	5.00	10.00
—As "Hank Ballard Along With The Dapps"					
❑ 6228	Are You Lonely for Me Baby/With Our Sweet Lovin' Self	1969	2.50	5.00	10.00
❑ 6244	Butter Your Popcorn/Funky Soul Train	1969	3.75	7.50	15.00
❑ 6246	Come On with It/Blackenized	1969	3.75	7.50	15.00
❑ 6332	Work With Me Annie/Sexy Ways	1970	2.50	5.00	10.00
PEOPLE					
❑ 604	Teardrops on Your Letter/Annie Had a Baby	1972	—	2.50	5.00
❑ 606	With Your Sweet Lovin' Self/Finger Poppin' Time	1972	—	2.50	5.00
POLYDOR					
❑ 14128	Finger Poppin' Time/From the Love Side	1972	—	2.50	5.00
❑ 14166	Going to Get a Thrill/(B-side unknown)	1973	—	2.50	5.00
SILVER FOX					
❑ 23	Sunday Morning Coming Down/Love Made a Fool of Me	1970	—	3.00	6.00
STANG					
❑ 5053	Let's Go Streaking/Let's Go Streaking (Part 2)	1974	—	2.50	5.00
❑ 5058	Hey There Sexy Lady/(Instrumental)	1975	—	2.50	5.00
❑ 5061	Let's Go Skinny Dipping/Love On Love	1975	—	2.50	5.00

7-Inch Extended Plays

Number	Title (A Side/B Side)	Yr	VG	VG+	NM
KING					
❑ 435	Teardrops on Your Letter/The Twist//Cute Little Ways/House with No Windows	1959	30.00	60.00	120.00
❑ 435 [PS]	Singin' and Swingin', Vol. 1	1959	30.00	60.00	120.00
❑ 436	(contents unknown)	1959	30.00	60.00	120.00
❑ 436 [PS]	Singin' and Swingin', Vol. 2	1959	30.00	60.00	120.00

BALLARD, KENNY

Number	Title (A Side/B Side)	Yr	VG	VG+	NM
GENIE					
❑ 101	Lady of Stone/(B-side unknown)	196?	7.50	15.00	30.00
KAPP					
❑ 602	Mr. Magic/Oh How I Cried	1964	6.25	12.50	25.00
ROULETTE					
❑ 4716	Your Letter/I'm Losing You	1966	3.75	7.50	15.00

BALLOON FARM, THE

Number	Title (A Side/B Side)	Yr	VG	VG+	NM
LAURIE					
❑ 3405	A Question of Tempature/Hurtin' for Your Lovin'	1967	5.00	10.00	20.00
—First pressing has misspelled A-side					
❑ 3405	A Question of Temperature/Hurtin' for Your Lovin'	1967	2.50	5.00	10.00
—Second pressing corrects A-side spelling					
❑ 3445	Hurry Up Sundown/Farmer Brown	1968	2.50	5.00	10.00

BALTINEERS, THE

TEENAGE

Number	Title (A Side/B Side)	Yr	VG	VG+	NM
❑ 1000	Moments Like This/New Love	1956	75.00	150.00	300.00
❑ 1002	Tears in My Eyes/Joe's Calypso	1956	75.00	150.00	300.00

BAN-LONS, THE

FIDELITY

Number	Title (A Side/B Side)	Yr	VG	VG+	NM
❑ 4051	Highest Mountain/Hey Baby	1959	50.00	100.00	200.00
❑ 4056	I Like It/Hey Good Lookin'	1959	50.00	100.00	200.00

BANANA SPLITS, THE

DECCA

Number	Title (A Side/B Side)	Yr	VG	VG+	NM
❑ 32391	We're the Banana Splits/Wait Til Tomorrow	1968	3.00	6.00	12.00
❑ 32429	The Tra-La-La Song (One Banana, Two Banana)/ Toy Piano Melody	1968	3.00	6.00	12.00
❑ 32429 [PS]	The Tra-La-La Song (One Banana, Two Banana)/ Toy Piano Melody	1968	6.25	12.50	25.00
❑ 32536	Pretty Painted Carousel/Long Live Love	1969	3.00	6.00	12.00
❑ 32536 [PS]	Pretty Painted Carousel/Long Live Love	1969	6.25	12.50	25.00

7-Inch Extended Plays

KELLOGG'S/HANNA-BARBERA

Number	Title (A Side/B Side)	Yr	VG	VG+	NM
❑ 34578	The Tra La La Song/That's the Pretty Part of You/ /It's a Good Day for a Parade/The Very First Kid on My Block	1969	5.00	10.00	20.00
❑ 34578 [PS]	Kellogg's Presents The Banana Splits, Vol. 1	1969	5.00	10.00	20.00
❑ 34579	Doin' the Banana Split/I Enjoy Being a Boy (In Love with You)//The Beautiful Calliopa/Let Me Remember You Smiling	1969	5.00	10.00	20.00
❑ 34579 [PS]	Kellogg's Presents The Banana Splits, Vol. 2	1969	5.00	10.00	20.00

BAND, THE

CAPITOL

Number	Title (A Side/B Side)	Yr	VG	VG+	NM
❑ 2269	The Weight/I Shall Be Released	1968	2.00	4.00	8.00

—First pressing credits "Jaime Robbie Robertson, Rick Danko, Richard Manuel, Garth Hudson, Levon Helm"

Number	Title (A Side/B Side)	Yr	VG	VG+	NM
❑ 2635	Up on Cripple Creek/The Night They Drove Old Dixie Down	1969	—	3.00	6.00
❑ 2705	Rag Mama Rag/The Unfaithful Servant	1969	—	3.00	6.00
❑ 2705 [PS]	Rag Mama Rag/The Unfaithful Servant	1969	—	3.00	6.00
❑ 2870	Time to Kill/The Shape I'm In	1970	—	3.00	6.00
❑ 3199	Life Is a Carnival/The Moon Struck One	1971	—	3.00	6.00
❑ 3249	When I Paint My Masterpiece/Where Do We Go from Here	1971	—	—	—

—Unreleased?

Number	Title (A Side/B Side)	Yr	VG	VG+	NM
❑ 3433	Don't Do It/Rag Mama Rag	1972	—	2.50	5.00
❑ 3500	Hang Up My Rock & Roll Shoes/Caledonia Mission	1972	—	2.50	5.00
❑ 3758	Ain't Got No Home/Get Up Jake	1973	—	2.50	5.00
❑ 3828	Third Man Theme/W.S. Walcott Medicine Show	1974	—	2.50	5.00
❑ 4230	Ophelia/Hobo Jungle	1976	—	2.00	4.00
❑ 4316	Twilight/Acadian Driftwood	1976	—	2.00	4.00
❑ 4361	Georgia on My Mind/The Night They Drove Old Dixie Down	1976	—	2.00	4.00
❑ 58876	The Shape I'm In/Life Is a Carnival	2000	—	2.00	4.00

WARNER BROS.

Number	Title (A Side/B Side)	Yr	VG	VG+	NM
❑ 8592	Out of the Blue/The Well	1978	—	2.00	4.00

BAND AID

COLUMBIA

Number	Title (A Side/B Side)	Yr	VG	VG+	NM
❑ 04749	Do They Know It's Christmas?/Feed the World	1984	—	2.50	5.00
❑ 04749 [PS]	Do They Know It's Christmas?/Feed the World	1984	—	2.50	5.00

BAND WITHOUT A NAME, THE

SIDEWALK

Number	Title (A Side/B Side)	Yr	VG	VG+	NM
❑ 913	Theme from "Thunder Alley"/Time After Time	1967	5.00	10.00	20.00

TOWER

Number	Title (A Side/B Side)	Yr	VG	VG+	NM
❑ 246	Turn On Your Love Light/Perfect Girl	1966	3.75	7.50	15.00
❑ 246 [PS]	Turn On Your Love Light/Perfect Girl	1966	7.50	15.00	30.00

BANDS OF GOLD

SMASH

Number	Title (A Side/B Side)	Yr	VG	VG+	NM
❑ 2058	It's Over/You Won't Change Me	1966	6.25	12.50	25.00

BANGLES

Also see THE BANGS.

COLUMBIA

Number	Title (A Side/B Side)	Yr	VG	VG+	NM
❑ 04479	Hero Takes a Fall/Where Were You When I Needed You	1984	—	—	3.00
❑ 04479 [PS]	Hero Takes a Fall/Where Were You When I Needed You	1984	—	3.00	6.00
❑ 04634	Going Down to Liverpool/Dover Beach	1984	—	2.00	4.00
❑ 04770	Hero Takes a Fall (Remix)/Tell Me	1985	2.50	5.00	10.00
❑ 04770 [PS]	Hero Takes a Fall (Remix)/Tell Me	1985	2.50	5.00	10.00
❑ 05757	Manic Monday/In a Different Light	1986	—	—	3.00

—A-side written by Prince under pseudonym "Christopher"

Number	Title (A Side/B Side)	Yr	VG	VG+	NM
❑ 05757 [PS]	Manic Monday/In a Different Light	1986	—	—	3.00
❑ 05886	If She Knew What She Wants/Not Like You	1986	—	—	3.00
❑ 05886 [PS]	If She Knew What She Wants/Not Like You	1986	—	—	3.00
❑ 06257	Walk Like an Egyptian/Angels Don't Fall in Love	1986	—	—	3.00

—No picture sleeve issued in U.S.

Number	Title (A Side/B Side)	Yr	VG	VG+	NM
❑ 06674	Walking Down Your Street/Let It Go	1987	—	—	3.00
❑ 06674 [PS]	Walking Down Your Street/Let It Go	1987	—	—	3.00
❑ 08090	In Your Room/Bell Jar	1988	—	—	3.00
❑ 08090 [PS]	In Your Room/Bell Jar	1988	—	—	3.00
❑ 08385	Manic Monday/Hazy Shade of Winter	1988	—	—	3.00

—Gray label "Golden Oldies" reissue

Number	Title (A Side/B Side)	Yr	VG	VG+	NM
❑ 08386	Walk Like an Egyptian/Walking Down Your Street	1988	—	—	3.00

—Gray label "Golden Oldies" reissue

Number	Title (A Side/B Side)	Yr	VG	VG+	NM
❑ 68533	Eternal Flame/What I Meant to Say	1989	—	—	3.00
❑ 68744	Be with You/Let It Go	1989	—	—	3.00
❑ 73791	Eternal Flame/What I Meant to Say	1991	—	—	3.00

—Reissue

DEF JAM

Number	Title (A Side/B Side)	Yr	VG	VG+	NM
❑ 07630	Hazy Shade of Winter/She's Lost You	1987	—	—	3.00

—B-side by Joan Jett and the Blackhearts

Number	Title (A Side/B Side)	Yr	VG	VG+	NM
❑ 07630 [PS]	Hazy Shade of Winter/She's Lost You	1987	—	—	3.00

BANGS, THE

Early incarnation of the BANGLES.

DOWNKIDDIE

Number	Title (A Side/B Side)	Yr	VG	VG+	NM
❑ 001	Getting Out of Hand/Call On Me	1981	12.50	25.00	50.00

—Yellow label (original)

Number	Title (A Side/B Side)	Yr	VG	VG+	NM
❑ 001	Getting Out of Hand/Call On Me	1981	10.00	20.00	40.00

—Blue label

Number	Title (A Side/B Side)	Yr	VG	VG+	NM
❑ 001	Getting Out of Hand/Call On Me	1981	10.00	20.00	40.00

—Green label

Number	Title (A Side/B Side)	Yr	VG	VG+	NM
❑ 001 [PS]	Getting Out of Hand/Call On Me	1981	15.00	30.00	60.00

BANKS, BESSIE

Number	Title (A Side/B Side)	Yr	VG	VG+	NM
BLUE CAT					
❑ 106	Go Now/It Sounds Like My Baby	1965	2.50	5.00	10.00
SPOKANE					
❑ 4009	Do It Now/(You Should Have Been a) Doctor	1963	3.75	7.50	15.00
TIGER					
❑ 102	Go Now/It Sounds Like My Baby	1964	5.00	10.00	20.00
VERVE					
❑ 10519	I Can't Make It (Without You Baby)/Need You	1967	2.00	4.00	8.00
VOLT					
❑ 4112	Ain't No Easy Way/Try to Leave Me If You Can	1974	—	3.00	6.00
WAND					
❑ 163	Do It Now/(You Should Have Been a) Doctor	1964	3.00	6.00	12.00

BANKS, DARRELL

Number	Title (A Side/B Side)	Yr	VG	VG+	NM
ATCO					
❑ 6471	Here Come the Tears/I've Got That Feeling	1967	6.25	12.50	25.00
❑ 6484	Angel Baby Don't You Leave Me/Look Into the Eyes of a Fool	1967	6.25	12.50	25.00
COTILLION					
❑ 44006	I Wanna Go Home/Love of My Woman	1968	2.50	5.00	10.00
REVILOT					
❑ 201	Open the Door to Your Heart/Our Love Is In the Pocket	1966	3.75	7.50	15.00
❑ 203	Somebody (Somewhere) Needs You/Baby Whatcha Got (For Me)	1966	3.75	7.50	15.00
VOLT					
❑ 4014	Just Because Your Love Has Gone/I'm the One Who Loves You	1969	2.50	5.00	10.00
❑ 4026	Beautiful Feeling/No One Blinder	1969	2.50	5.00	10.00

BANKS, DOUG

Number	Title (A Side/B Side)	Yr	VG	VG+	NM
ARGO					
❑ 5483	I Just Keep Dancing/Baby Since You Went Away	1964	15.00	30.00	60.00
GUYDEN					
❑ 2082	Ain't That Just Like a Woman/Never Say Goodbye	1963	15.00	30.00	60.00

BANKS, EDDIE

Number	Title (A Side/B Side)	Yr	VG	VG+	NM
JOSIE					
❑ 804	Sugar Diabetes/Rock-a-Bye Blues	1956	10.00	20.00	40.00

BANKS, HOMER

Number	Title (A Side/B Side)	Yr	VG	VG+	NM
GENIE					
❑ 1000	Hooked by Love/Lady of Stone	1966	12.50	25.00	50.00
MINIT					
❑ 32008	Do You Know What/60 Minutes of Your Love	1966	6.25	12.50	25.00
❑ 32020	Hooked by Love/Lady of Stone	1967	6.25	12.50	25.00

BANNED, THE

Number	Title (A Side/B Side)	Yr	VG	VG+	NM
FONTANA					
❑ 1604	My Life Is My Own/Nothing Matters But You	1967	2.50	5.00	10.00
❑ 1616	It Couldn't Happen Here/Annie Went to Ohio	1968	2.50	5.00	10.00
❑ 1616 [PS]	It Couldn't Happen Here/Annie Went to Ohio	1968	5.00	10.00	20.00
❑ 1621	Goodbye, Groovy, Goodbye/A Blanket of Sound	1968	2.50	5.00	10.00

BAR-KAYS, THE

HIGH STACKS

Number	Title (A Side/B Side)	Yr	VG	VG+	NM
❑ 9801	Body Fine/Hey Rufus!	1999	—	—	3.00

—B-side by Rufus Thomas; artist listed as "The Barkays"

MERCURY

Number	Title (A Side/B Side)	Yr	VG	VG+	NM
❑ 73833	Shake Your Rump to the Funk/Summer of Our Love	1976	—	2.00	4.00
❑ 73888	Too Hot to Stop (Pt. 1)/Bang Bang (Stick 'Em Up)	1977	—	2.00	4.00
❑ 73915	Spellbound/You're So Sexy	1977	—	2.00	4.00
❑ 73971	Let's Have Some Fun/Cozy	1977	—	2.00	4.00
❑ 73994	Attitudes/Can't Keep My Hands Off You	1978	—	2.00	4.00
❑ 74039	I'll Dance/Angel Eyes	1978	—	2.00	4.00
❑ 74048	Shine/Are You Being Real	1979	—	2.00	4.00
❑ 76015	Move Your Boogie Body/Love's What It's All About	1979	—	2.00	4.00
❑ 76036	Today is the Day/Loving You Is My Occupation	1980	—	2.00	4.00
❑ 76088	Boogie Body Land/Running In and Out of My Life	1980	—	2.00	4.00
❑ 76097	Body Fever/Deliver Us	1981	—	2.00	4.00
❑ 76123	Hit and Run/Say It Through Love	1981	—	2.00	4.00
❑ 76143	Freaky Behavior/Backseat Driver	1982	—	2.00	4.00
❑ 76187	Do It (Let Me See You Shake)/Feels Like I'm Falling in Love	1982	—	2.00	4.00
❑ 810435-7	She Talks to Me with Her Body/Anticipation	1983	—	2.00	4.00
❑ 818631-7	Freakshow on the Dance Floor/Lovers Should Never Fall in Love	1984	—	2.00	4.00
❑ 870018-7	Don't Hang Up/Contagious	1988	—	—	3.00
❑ 870018-7 [PS]	Don't Hang Up/Contagious	1988	—	—	3.00
❑ 870214-7	Many Mistakes/Contagious	1988	—	—	3.00
❑ 872102-7	Struck by You/Your Place or Mine	1989	—	—	3.00
❑ 872102-7 [PS]	Struck by You/Your Place or Mine	1989	—	—	3.00

Number	Title (A Side/B Side)	Yr	VG	VG+	NM
❑ 872954-7	Animal/Time Out	1989	—	—	3.00
❑ 872954-7 [PS]	Animal/Time Out	1989	—	—	3.00
❑ 880045-7	Dirty Dancer/Dirty Dancer	1984	—	—	3.00
❑ 880255-7	Sexomatic/(B-side unknown)	1984	—	—	3.00
❑ 880966-7	Your Place or Mine/(B-side unknown)	1985	—	—	3.00
❑ 884232-7	Banging the Walls/Gina	1985	—	—	3.00
❑ 888837-7	Certified True/It Be That Way Sometimes	1987	—	—	3.00
STAX					
❑ 3216	Holy Ghost/Monster	1978	—	2.50	5.00
VOLT					
❑ 148	Soul Finger/Knucklehead	1967	2.00	4.00	8.00
❑ 154	Give Everybody Some/Don't Do That	1967	—	3.00	6.00
❑ 158	A Hard Day's Night/I Want Someone	1968	—	3.00	6.00
❑ 4007	Copy Cat/In the Middle	1968	—	3.00	6.00
❑ 4011	Don't Stop Dancing/Don't Stop Dancing (Part 2)	1969	—	3.00	6.00
❑ 4019	Midnight Cowboy/A.J. The Housefly	1969	—	3.00	6.00
❑ 4033	Song and Dance/I Thank You	1970	—	3.00	6.00
❑ 4050	Montego Bay/Humpin'	1971	—	2.50	5.00
❑ 4073	Son of Shaft/Song and Dance	1972	—	2.50	5.00
❑ 4081	Dance, Dance, Dance/Memphis at Sunrise	1972	—	2.50	5.00
❑ 4092	You're the Best Thing That Ever Happened to Me/You're Still My Brother	1973	—	2.50	5.00
❑ 4097	God Is Watching/It Ain't Easy	1973	—	2.50	5.00

BARBARA AND THE BELIEVERS

Number	Title (A Side/B Side)	Yr	VG	VG+	NM
CAPITOL					
❑ 5866	When You Wish Upon a Star/What Can Happen to Me Now	1967	4.00	8.00	16.00

BARBARA AND THE BOYS

Number	Title (A Side/B Side)	Yr	VG	VG+	NM
DOT					
❑ 15794	Hooty Sapperticker/Cobra	1958	3.75	7.50	15.00

BARBARA AND THE BROWNS

Number	Title (A Side/B Side)	Yr	VG	VG+	NM
STAX					
❑ 150	Big Party/You Belong to Her	1964	5.00	10.00	20.00
❑ 158	Please Be Honest with Me/In My Heart	1964	3.75	7.50	15.00
❑ 164	I Don't Want Trouble/My Lover	1965	3.75	7.50	15.00

BARBARIANS, THE

Number	Title (A Side/B Side)	Yr	VG	VG+	NM
JOY					
❑ 290	Hey Little Bird/You've Got to Understand	1964	12.50	25.00	50.00
LAURIE					
❑ 3308	Are You a Boy or Are You a Girl/Take It or Leave It	1965	5.00	10.00	20.00
❑ 3321	Susie Q/What the New Breed Say	1965	5.00	10.00	20.00
❑ 3326	Moulty/I'll Keep On Seeing You	1965	5.00	10.00	20.00

BARBEES, THE

Early version of THE VELVELETTES.

Number	Title (A Side/B Side)	Yr	VG	VG+	NM
STEPP					
❑ 236	The Wind/Que Pasa	1963	50.00	100.00	200.00

BARBER, CHRIS

Number	Title (A Side/B Side)	Yr	VG	VG+	NM
ATLANTIC					
❑ 2016	Hush-a-Bye/You Don't Understand	1959	3.00	6.00	12.00
LAURIE					
❑ 3022	Petite Fleur/Wild Cat Blues	1958	3.75	7.50	15.00
❑ 3022 [PS]	Petite Fleur/Wild Cat Blues	1958	6.25	12.50	25.00
❑ 3026	Rugged Cross/Thriller Rag	1959	3.00	6.00	12.00
❑ 3057	Swanee River/ Lonesome	1960	3.00	6.00	12.00
❑ 3154	It Looks Like a Big Night Tonight/King Kong	1963	3.00	6.00	12.00
LONDON					
❑ 9571V	The Loneliness of the Long Distance Runner/Valley of Roses	1963	3.00	6.00	12.00

BARBRA AND NEIL

BARBRA STREISAND and NEIL DIAMOND.

Number	Title (A Side/B Side)	Yr	VG	VG+	NM
COLUMBIA					
❑ 3-10840	You Don't Bring Me Flowers/(Instrumental)	1978	—	2.50	5.00

BARD, ANNETTE

One of THE TEDDY BEARS.

Number	Title (A Side/B Side)	Yr	VG	VG+	NM
IMPERIAL					
❑ 5643	What Difference Does It Make/Alibi	1960	12.50	25.00	50.00

BARDS, THE (1)

Number	Title (A Side/B Side)	Yr	VG	VG+	NM
BURDETTE					
❑ 103	I Want You/Freedom Catcher	1971	2.00	4.00	8.00
CAPITOL					
❑ 2041	The Jabberwocky/Never Too Much Love	1967	2.50	5.00	10.00
❑ 2148	The Owl and the Pussycat/The Light of Love	1968	2.50	5.00	10.00
❑ 2148 [PS]	The Owl and the Pussycat/The Light of Love	1968	5.00	10.00	20.00
JERDEN					
❑ 907	Good Time Charlie's Got the Blues/Tunesmith	1969	3.00	6.00	12.00
PARROT					
❑ 337	Good Time Charlie's Got the Blues/Tunesmith	1969	2.50	5.00	10.00
❑ 344	Our Love/Jubilation	1970	2.50	5.00	10.00
❑ 351	Day by Day/Wadda Wadda	1970	2.50	5.00	10.00
PICCADILLY					
❑ 224	The Owl and the Pussycat/The Light of Love	1966	5.00	10.00	20.00
❑ 232	The Jabberwocky/My Generation	1966	3.00	6.00	12.00
❑ 242	Our Love/Jubilation	1967	3.00	6.00	12.00

BARDS, THE (2)

Number	Title (A Side/B Side)	Yr	VG	VG+	NM
DAWN					
❑ 208	I'm a Wine Drinker/Easy Going Baby	1954	62.50	125.00	250.00
❑ 209	Gravy/Avalon	1954	62.50	125.00	250.00

BARE, BOBBY

Also see BILL PARSONS.

Number	Title (A Side/B Side)	Yr	VG	VG+	NM
AMI					
❑ 1328	America's Missing Children/(B-side unknown)	198?	—	2.50	5.00
CAPITOL					
❑ F3557	Down on the Corner of Love/Another Love Has Ended	1956	7.50	15.00	30.00
❑ F3686	Darling Don't/Life of a Fool	1957	7.50	15.00	30.00
❑ F3771	The Livin' End/Beggar	1957	7.50	15.00	30.00
COLUMBIA					
❑ 02038	Learning to Live Again/Appaloosa Rider	1981	—	2.00	4.00
❑ 0 2414	Take Me As I Am (Or Let Me Go)/White Freight Liner Blues	1981	—	2.00	4.00
❑ 02577	Dropping Out of Sight/She Is Gone	1981	—	2.00	4.00
❑ 02690	New Cut Road/Let Him Roll	1982	—	2.00	4.00
❑ 02895	If You Ain't Got Nothing (You've Got Nothing To Lose)/Golden Memories	1982	—	2.00	4.00
❑ 03135	New Cut Road/Numbers	1982	—	—	3.00
—Reissue					
❑ 03149	(I'm Not) A Candle in the Wind/Cold Day in Hell	1982	—	2.00	4.00
❑ 03334	Praise the Lord and Send Me the Money/I've Been Rained On Too	1982	—	2.00	4.00
❑ 03628	It's a Dirty Job/Caught in the Spotlight	1983	—	2.00	4.00
—A-side with Lacy J. Dalton					
❑ 03809	The Jogger/Gravy Train	1983	—	2.00	4.00
❑ 04092	Diet Song/Stacy Brown Got Two	1983	—	2.00	4.00
❑ 10690	Too Many Nights Alone/A Yard Full of Rusty Cars	1978	—	2.50	5.00
❑ 10831	Sleep Tight, Good Night Man/Hot Afternoon	1978	—	2.50	5.00
❑ 10891	Healin'/Love Is a Cold Wind	1979	—	2.00	4.00
❑ 10998	Till I Gain Control Again/I'll Feel a Whole Lot Better	1979	—	2.00	4.00
❑ 11045	No Memories Hangin' Round/This Has Happened Before	1979	—	2.00	4.00
—With Roseanne Cash					
❑ 11170	Numbers/When Hippies Get Older	1980	—	2.00	4.00
❑ 11259	Tequila Sheila/Quaaludes Again	1980	—	2.00	4.00
❑ 11365	Food Blues/Used Cars	1980	—	2.00	4.00
❑ 11408	Willie Jones/If That Ain't Love	1980	—	2.00	4.00
EMI AMERICA					
❑ 8279	When I Get Home/Party of the First Part	1985	—	—	3.00
❑ 8296	Reno and Me/Party of the First Part	1985	—	—	3.00
❑ 8317	Better Not Look Down/Wait Until Tomorrow	1986	—	—	3.00
❑ 8333	Real Good/Wait Until Tomorrow	1986	—	—	3.00
EPIC					
❑ 10652	My God and I/In the Quiet of Your Love	1970	—	3.00	6.00
—B-side by Keith Barbour					
FRATERNITY					
❑ 861	I'm Hanging Up My Rifle/That's Where I Wanna Be	1959	10.00	20.00	40.00
❑ 867	Sweet Singing Sam/More Than a Poor Boy Could Give	1960	7.50	15.00	30.00
❑ 871	No Letter from My Baby/Lynchin' Party	1960	5.00	10.00	20.00
❑ 878	Book of Love/Lorena	1961	5.00	10.00	20.00
❑ 885	Sailor Man/Island of Love	1961	5.00	10.00	20.00
❑ 890	Zigzag Twist/Brooklyn Bridge	1961	5.00	10.00	20.00
❑ 892	The Day My Rainbow Fell/That Mean Old Clock	1961	5.00	10.00	20.00
MERCURY					
❑ 73097	How I Got to Memphis/It's Freezing in El Paso	1970	—	3.00	6.00
❑ 73148	Come Sundown/Woman You Have Been a Friend to Me	1970	—	3.00	6.00
❑ 73203	Please Don't Tell Me How the Story Ends/Where Have All the Seasons Gone	1971	—	3.00	6.00
❑ 73236	Short and Sweet/A Million Miles to the City	1971	—	3.00	6.00
❑ 73279	What Am I Gonna Do/Love Forever	1972	—	3.00	6.00
❑ 73317	Sylvia's Mother/Music City U.S.A.	1972	—	3.00	6.00
RCA					
❑ PB-10718	Put a Little Lovin' on Me/Those City Lights	1976	—	2.50	5.00
❑ PB-10790	Drop Kick Me, Jesus/Baby Wants to Boogie	1976	—	3.00	6.00
❑ PB-10852	Vegas/The Shelter of Your Eyes	1976	—	2.50	5.00
—A-side by Bobby and Jeannie Bare					
❑ PB-10902	Look Who I'm Cheatin' On Tonight/If You Think I'm Crazy Now (You Should Have Seen Me When I Was a Kid)	1977	—	2.50	5.00
❑ PB-11037	Red Neck Hippie Romance/Bottom Dollar	1977	—	2.50	5.00
❑ PB-11673	Hurricane Shirley/Crazy Arms	1979	—	2.50	5.00
—B-side by Willie Nelson					
RCA VICTOR					
❑ APBO-0063	You Know Who/Send Tomorrow to the Moon	1973	—	2.50	5.00
❑ AMAO-0119	Shame on Me/Above and Beyond	1973	—	2.50	5.00
❑ APBO-0197	Daddy What If/Restless Wind	1973	—	2.50	5.00
❑ APBO-0261	Marie Laveau/Mermaid	1974	—	2.50	5.00
❑ PB-10037	Where'd I Come From/Scarlet Ribbons	1974	—	2.50	5.00
—By "Bobby Bare, Jr., and Mommy"					
❑ PB-10096	Singin' in the Kitchen/You Are	1974	—	2.50	5.00
—As "Bobby Bare and the Family"					
❑ GB-10166	Daddy What If/Ride Me Down Easy	1975	—	—	3.00
—Gold Standard Series issue					
❑ PB-10223	Back in Huntsville Again/Warm and Free	1975	—	2.50	5.00
❑ PB-10318	Alimony/Daddy's Been Around the House Too Long	1975	—	2.50	5.00
❑ PB-10409	Cowboys and Daddys/High Plains Jamboree	1975	—	2.50	5.00
❑ GB-10495	Singin' in the Kitchen/You Are	1975	—	—	3.00
—Gold Standard Series issue					
❑ GB-10496	Marie Laveau/Mermaid	1975	—	—	3.00
—Gold Standard Series issue					
❑ GB-10497	Where'd I Come From/Scarlet Ribbons	1975	—	—	3.00
—Gold Standard Series issue					
❑ PB-10556	The Winner/Up Against the Wall Redneck Mother	1976	—	2.50	5.00
❑ 47-8032	Shame on Me/Above and Beyond	1962	3.00	6.00	12.00
❑ 47-8083	I Don't Believe I'll Fall in Love Today/To Whom It May Concern	1962	3.00	6.00	12.00
❑ 47-8083 [PS]	I Don't Believe I'll Fall in Love Today/To Whom It May Concern	1962	6.25	12.50	25.00
❑ 47-8146	Dear Waste Basket/I'd Fight the World	1963	3.00	6.00	12.00
❑ 47-8183	Detroit City/Heart of Ice	1963	3.75	7.50	15.00

Number	Title (A Side/B Side)	Yr	VG	VG+	NM
❑ 47-8183 [PS]	Detroit City/Heart of Ice	1963	6.25	12.50	25.00
❑ 47-8238	500 Miles Away from Home/It All Depends On Linda	1963	3.75	7.50	15.00
❑ 47-8294	Miller's Cave/Jeannie's Last Kiss	1963	3.00	6.00	12.00
❑ 47-8358	Have I Stayed Away Too Long/More Than a Poor Boy Can Give	1964	3.00	6.00	12.00
❑ 47-8395	He Was a Friend of Mine/When I'm Gone	1964	3.00	6.00	12.00
❑ 47-8443	Four Strong Winds/Take Me Home	1964	3.00	6.00	12.00
❑ 47-8509	Times Are Gettin' Hard/One Day at a Time	1965	2.50	5.00	10.00
❑ 47-8571	It's Alright/She Picked a Perfect Day	1965	2.50	5.00	10.00
❑ 47-8654	Just to Satisfy You/Memories	1965	2.50	5.00	10.00
❑ 47-8699	Talk Me Some Sense/Delia's Gone	1965	2.50	5.00	10.00
❑ 47-8758	In the Same Old Way/Long Black Veil	1965	2.50	5.00	10.00
❑ 47-8851	The Streets of Baltimore/She Took My Sunshine Away	1966	2.50	5.00	10.00
❑ 47-8988	Homesick/Guess I'll Move On Down the Line	1966	2.50	5.00	10.00
❑ 47-9098	Charleston Railroad Tavern/Vincennes	1967	2.00	4.00	8.00
❑ 47-9191	Come Kiss Me Love/Sandy's Crying Again	1967	2.00	4.00	8.00
❑ 47-9314	The Piney Wood Hills/They Covered Up the Old Swimmin' Hole	1967	2.00	4.00	8.00
❑ 47-9450	Find Out What's Happening/When Am I Ever Gonna Settle Down	1968	2.00	4.00	8.00
❑ 47-9568	A Little Bit Later On Down the Line/Don't Do Like I Done, Son (Do What I Say)	1968	2.00	4.00	8.00
❑ 47-9643	The Town That Broke My Heart/My Baby	1968	2.00	4.00	8.00
❑ 74-0110	(Margie's At) The Lincoln Park Inn/Rainy Day in Richmond	1969	—	3.00	6.00
❑ 74-0202	Which One Will It Be/My Frame of Mind	1969	—	3.00	6.00
❑ 74-0264	God Bless America Again/Baby, What Else Can I Do	1969	—	3.00	6.00
❑ 74-0866	I Hate Goodbyes/Fallin' Apart	1973	—	3.00	6.00
❑ 74-0918	Ride Me Down Easy/A Train That Never Runs	1973	—	3.00	6.00
RICE					
❑ 5057	Christian Soldier/Dropping Out of Sight	1973	—	2.50	5.00
❑ 5060	Love Forever/A Million Miles to the City	1973	—	2.50	5.00
❑ 5066	I Took a Memory to Lunch/It's Freezing in St. Paul	1974	—	2.50	5.00

BARE, BOBBY, AND SKEETER DAVIS

Also see each artist's individual listings.

Number	Title (A Side/B Side)	Yr	VG	VG+	NM
RCA VICTOR					
❑ 47-8496	A Dear John Letter/Too Used to Being with You	1965	2.50	5.00	10.00
❑ 47-9789	Your Husband, My Wife/Before the Sunshine	1969	—	3.00	6.00

BARE, BOBBY, NORMA JEAN, & LIZ ANDERSON

Number	Title (A Side/B Side)	Yr	VG	VG+	NM
RCA VICTOR					
❑ 47-8963	The Game of Triangles/Bye Bye Bye	1966	2.50	5.00	10.00

BARENAKED LADIES

Number	Title (A Side/B Side)	Yr	VG	VG+	NM
REPRISE					
❑ 16827	Pinch Me/Falling for the First Time	2000	—	—	3.00
❑ 16936	Call and Answer/It's All Been Done	1999	—	—	3.00
❑ 17174	One Week/When You Dream	1998	—	—	3.00
❑ 17290	Brian Wilson/Break Your Heart	1997	—	—	3.00
❑ 17499	The Old Apartment/Lovers in a Dangerous Time	1997	—	—	3.00

BARGE, GENE

Number	Title (A Side/B Side)	Yr	VG	VG+	NM
CHECKER					
❑ 839	Way Down Home/Country	1954	7.50	15.00	30.00
❑ 1110	Fine Twine/The "In" Crowd	1965	2.50	5.00	10.00
LEGRAND					
❑ 1006	Thinking of You/Autumn Leaves	1961	10.00	20.00	40.00
PARAMOUNT					
❑ 0160	Love Theme from "The Godfather"/Gina	1972	—	2.50	5.00

BARIN, PETE

Number	Title (A Side/B Side)	Yr	VG	VG+	NM
SABINA					
❑ 504	So Wrong/Broken Heart	1962	12.50	25.00	50.00
❑ 512	Loneliest Guy in the World/Look Out for Cindy	1962	7.50	15.00	30.00

BARITONES, THE

Number	Title (A Side/B Side)	Yr	VG	VG+	NM
DORE					
❑ 501	After School Rock/Sentimental Baby	1958	10.00	20.00	40.00

BARKER, DELBERT

Number	Title (A Side/B Side)	Yr	VG	VG+	NM
KING					
❑ 4951	That's a Sin/No Good, Robin Hood	1956	7.50	15.00	30.00
❑ 5008	Wild Heart/There Must Be a Way	1957	7.50	15.00	30.00
❑ 5031	Amanda/Broken Heart	1957	7.50	15.00	30.00
❑ 6042	It Can't Last Long/Color Me Gone	1966	2.50	5.00	10.00

BARNES, BENNY

Number	Title (A Side/B Side)	Yr	VG	VG+	NM
D					
❑ 1052	Gold Records in the Snow/Happy Little Blue Bird	1959	15.00	30.00	60.00
HALL-WAY					
❑ 1203	A Bar with No Beer/Headed for Heartbreak	1964	2.50	5.00	10.00
❑ 1207	It's Good to Be Home/For a Minute There	1965	2.50	5.00	10.00
KAPP					
❑ 859	A Bar with No Beer/Headed for Heartbreak	1967	2.00	4.00	8.00
❑ 912	Sweet Suzannah/It's My Mind That's Broken	1968	2.00	4.00	8.00
MEGA					
❑ 0071	Woman, Leave My Mind Alone/I'm Just Here to Get My Baby Off My Mind	1972	—	2.50	5.00
MERCURY					
❑ 71048	Poor Man's Riches/Those Who Know	1957	5.00	10.00	20.00
❑ 71057	Poor Old Me/Penalty	1957	5.00	10.00	20.00
❑ 71119	Nickels Worth of Dreams/Mine All Mine	1957	5.00	10.00	20.00
❑ 71188	King for a Day/Your Old Stand By	1957	5.00	10.00	20.00
❑ 71284	Moon Over My Shoulder/Lonely Street	1958	6.25	12.50	25.00
❑ 71552	Beggar to a King/The Fastest Gun Alive	1959	5.00	10.00	20.00
❑ 71600	That-a Boy Willie/Token of Love	1960	5.00	10.00	20.00
❑ 71637	Pretty Little Girl/Message in the Wind	1960	5.00	10.00	20.00
❑ 71717	You're Still on My Mind/I Think I'll Take a Walk and Disappear	1960	5.00	10.00	20.00
❑ 71806	Yearning/Go On, Go On	1961	5.00	10.00	20.00
❑ 71896	The World's Worst Loser/I Changed My Mind	1961	5.00	10.00	20.00
MUSICOR					
❑ 1100	Let Me Live As Long As I Can/Tea Leaves Don't Lie	1965	2.00	4.00	8.00
❑ 1127	Have We Really Tried/Heartache's Comin'	1965	2.00	4.00	8.00
❑ 1169	Diesel Smoke/That's How I Need You	1966	2.00	4.00	8.00
❑ 1194	Stand By Your Window/You're Not There	1966	2.00	4.00	8.00
❑ 1223	What's the Matter with Me/Third Time Down	1966	2.00	4.00	8.00
❑ 1247	I'm Her Lover/Same Old Boat	1967	2.00	4.00	8.00
❑ 1277	Let One Call Do It All/Rosanna Martin	1967	2.00	4.00	8.00
PLAYBOY					
❑ 5808	I've Got Some Gettin' Over You to Do/I'll Drink to That	1977	2.00	4.00	8.00
❑ 6084	Little Brown Paper Bag Blues/(B-side unknown)	1976	2.00	4.00	8.00
RCA VICTOR					
❑ 47-9830	An Old Memory Got in My Eye/You're Everywhere	1970	—	3.00	6.00
❑ 74-0271	Pressure Cooker/To the Ones I Love	1969	—	3.00	6.00
STARDAY					
❑ 236	Once Again/No Fault of Mine	1956	7.50	15.00	30.00
❑ 262	Poor Man's Riches/Those Who Know	1956	7.50	15.00	30.00
❑ 401	You Gotta Pay/Heads You Win	1958	6.25	12.50	25.00

BARNES, BILLY

Number	Title (A Side/B Side)	Yr	VG	VG+	NM
LIBERTY					
❑ 55421	Until/To Prove My Love	1962	6.25	12.50	25.00
UNITED ARTISTS					
❑ 148	You'd Have to Fall in Love/If You But Knew	1958	5.00	10.00	20.00
❑ 157	I'm Coming to See You/What Am I Supposed to Do	1959	5.00	10.00	20.00
❑ 218	Home Again/I Wish I Didn't Love You So	1960	5.00	10.00	20.00
❑ 311	C.C. Rider/Here Am I	1961	5.00	10.00	20.00

BARNES, GEORGE

Number	Title (A Side/B Side)	Yr	VG	VG+	NM
DECCA					
❑ 30398	Tammy/Around the World	1957	5.00	10.00	20.00
MERCURY					
❑ 71968	Transville/Spooky	1962	7.50	15.00	30.00

BARNES, J.J.

Number	Title (A Side/B Side)	Yr	VG	VG+	NM
BUDDAH					
❑ 120	Evidence/I'll Keep Coming Back	1969	3.75	7.50	15.00
CONTEMPO					
❑ 7003	How Long/The Erroll Flynn	1977	—	2.50	5.00
GROOVESVILLE					
❑ 1006	Baby Please Come Back Home/Chains of Love	1967	3.75	7.50	15.00
❑ 1008	Now That I Got You Back/Forgive Me	1967	3.75	7.50	15.00
❑ 1009	Easy Living/(B-side unknown)	1967	4.00	8.00	16.00
INVASION					
❑ 1001	My Baby/(You Still) My Baby	1970	2.50	5.00	10.00
KABLE					
❑ 437	Won't You Let Me Know/My Love Came Tumbling Down	1960	12.50	25.00	50.00
MAGIC TOUCH					
❑ 1000	To An Early Grave/Cloudy Days	1970	2.50	5.00	10.00
MICKAY'S					
❑ 3004	Just One More Time/Hey Child, I Love You	1963	20.00	40.00	80.00
❑ 4472	Get a Hold of Yourself/Lonely No More	1964	20.00	40.00	80.00
PERCEPTION					
❑ 546	Just a Living Doll/Touching You	1974	—	3.00	6.00
REVILOT					
❑ 216	Hold On to It/Now She's Gone	1968	3.75	7.50	15.00
❑ 218	I'll Keep Coming Back/Sad Day a-Comin'	1968	3.75	7.50	15.00
❑ 222	Our Love Is in the Pocket/All Your Goodies Are Gone	1968	20.00	40.00	80.00
❑ 225	So-Called Friends/Now She's Gone	1968	3.75	7.50	15.00
RIC-TIC					
❑ 106	Please Let Me In/I Think I Found a Love	1965	3.75	7.50	15.00
❑ 110	Real Humdinger/I Ain't Gonna Do It	1966	3.75	7.50	15.00
❑ 115	Day Tripper/Don't Bring Me Bad News	1966	3.75	7.50	15.00
❑ 117	Deeper in Love/Say It	1966	3.75	7.50	15.00
RICH					
❑ 1005	Won't You Let Me Know/My Love Came Tumbling Down	1960	25.00	50.00	100.00
❑ 1737	Won't You Let Me Know/My Love Came Tumbling Down	1962	6.25	12.50	25.00
RING					
❑ 101	She Ain't Ready/Poor-Unfortunate Me	1964	6.25	12.50	25.00
SCEPTER					
❑ 1266	Just One More Time/Hey Child, I Love You	1964	7.50	15.00	30.00
VOLT					
❑ 4027	Got to Get Rid of You/Snowflakes	1969	3.75	7.50	15.00

BARNES, SIDNEY

Number	Title (A Side/B Side)	Yr	VG	VG+	NM
BLUE CAT					
❑ 125	I Hurt on the Other Side/Switchy Walk	1966	37.50	75.00	150.00
CHESS					
❑ 2094	Baloney/Old Times	1970	2.50	5.00	10.00
PARACHUTE					
❑ 521	Hold On I'm Coming/Your Love Is So Good to Me	1978	—	2.00	4.00
RED BIRD					
❑ 10-039	You'll Always Be in Style/I'm So Glad	1965	10.00	20.00	40.00
❑ 10-054	I Hurt on the Other Side/Switchy Walk	1966	10.00	20.00	40.00

BARNUM, H.B.

Number	Title (A Side/B Side)	Yr	VG	VG+	NM
CAPITOL					
❑ 2036	Baby, Love Me/The Bad Luck's on Me	1967	3.00	6.00	12.00
❑ 2139	Vaya Con Dios/What Did Sister Do	1968	2.50	5.00	10.00
❑ 2317	Happiness/It's Just a Game, Love	1968	2.50	5.00	10.00

Number	Title (A Side/B Side)	Yr	VG	VG+	NM
❑ 5391	I'm a Man/The Record	1965	3.00	6.00	12.00
❑ 5440	Gimme Some/Don't Forget 127th Street	1965	3.00	6.00	12.00
❑ 5477	I Can't Help It/Dance with Me	1965	3.00	6.00	12.00
❑ 5748	Gotta Go/Nobody Wants to Hear Nobody's Trouble	1966	3.00	6.00	12.00
❑ 5932	Heartbreaker/Searchin' for My Soul	1967	5.00	10.00	20.00
DECCA					
❑ 32892	Run to Daylight/Howard Hardsell	1971	—	2.50	5.00
—B-side by Tom Patchett and Jay Tarses					
ELDO					
❑ 111	Lost Love/Hallelujah	1960	3.75	7.50	15.00
IMPERIAL					
❑ 5530	Blue Moon/Tia-Juana	1958	10.00	20.00	40.00
❑ 66011	Backstage/Rented Tuxedo	1964	3.00	6.00	12.00
❑ 66046	Skakiaan (Skokiaan)/Ska Drums	1964	3.00	6.00	12.00
❑ 66063	Calpyso Blues/Three Room Flat	1964	3.00	6.00	12.00
❑ 66074	Eternal Love/So What	1964	3.00	6.00	12.00
RCA VICTOR					
❑ 47-7960	Baby Baby Baby (All the Time)/How Many More Times	1961	3.75	7.50	15.00
❑ 47-8014	Call On Me/Oh My Achin' Back	1962	3.75	7.50	15.00
❑ 47-8112	Lonely Hearts/It Hurts Too Much to Cry	1962	15.00	30.00	60.00
UNITED ARTISTS					
❑ XW338	Theme from "5 on the Back Hand Side"/Keep It Comin'	1973	—	2.50	5.00

BARONS, THE

Several different groups.

Number	Title (A Side/B Side)	Yr	VG	VG+	NM
BELLAIRE					
❑ 103	The Bandit/Wanderin'	1963	5.00	10.00	20.00
BROWNFIELD					
❑ 1035	Hope I Please You/Don't Burn It	196?	12.50	25.00	50.00
DART					
❑ 126	Lonely Loretta/Lula Mae	1959	6.25	12.50	25.00
❑ 134	Perfect Love/Until the Thirteenth Chime	1960	6.25	12.50	25.00
DECCA					
❑ 29293	Exactly Like You/Forget About Me	1954	30.00	60.00	120.00
❑ 48323	A Year and a Day/My Baby's Gone	1954	30.00	60.00	120.00
DEMON					
❑ 1520	Gravel Gert/The Fight	1959	3.75	7.50	15.00
EPIC					
❑ 9586	Don't Go Away (Pretty Little Girl)/Pledge of a Fool	1963	7.50	15.00	30.00
❑ 9747	Lucky Star/Remember Rita	1964	37.50	75.00	150.00
❑ 10093	Don't Go Away (Pretty Little Girl)/Pledge of a Fool	1966	3.75	7.50	15.00
IMPERIAL					
❑ 5343	Eternally Yours/Boom Boom	1955	30.00	60.00	120.00
❑ 5343	Eternally Yours/Boom Boom	1955	75.00	150.00	300.00
—Red vinyl, probably promo only					
❑ 5359	I Know I Was Wrong/My Dream, My Love	1955	30.00	60.00	120.00
❑ 5370	Cold Kisses/Searching for You	1955	30.00	60.00	120.00
❑ 5383	So Long My Darling/Crying for You Baby	1956	30.00	60.00	120.00
❑ 5397	Don't Walk Out/Once in a Lifetime	1956	20.00	40.00	80.00
❑ 66057	Silence/I Just Go Wild Inside	1964	3.75	7.50	15.00
RCA VICTOR					
❑ 47-9034	Since You're Gone/My Smile Is Bigger (Than Your Smile)	1966	6.25	12.50	25.00
SPARTAN					
❑ 400	I've Been Hurt/Willow Weep for Me	196?	3.75	7.50	15.00
TENDER					
❑ 511	Drawbridge/(B-side unknown)	1958	3.75	7.50	15.00

BAROQUE ENSEMBLE OF THE MERSEYSIDE KAMMERMUSIKGESELLSCHAFT, THE

Number	Title (A Side/B Side)	Yr	VG	VG+	NM
ELEKTRA					
❑ 45602	You've Got to Hide Your Love Away/Ticket to Ride	1966	3.00	6.00	12.00

BARRACUDA

Number	Title (A Side/B Side)	Yr	VG	VG+	NM
RCA VICTOR					
❑ 47-9660	The Dance of St. Francis/Lady Fingers	1968	5.00	10.00	20.00
❑ 47-9660 [PS]	The Dance of St. Francis/Lady Fingers	1968	10.00	20.00	40.00
❑ 47-9743	Julie (The Song I Sing Is To You)/Sleeping Out the Storm	1969	3.00	6.00	12.00

BARRAN, BOB

Number	Title (A Side/B Side)	Yr	VG	VG+	NM
SILVER STREAK					
❑ 311	Tom Tom Rock/Mother Goose Hop	1960	37.50	75.00	150.00

BARRETT, RICHARD

Number	Title (A Side/B Side)	Yr	VG	VG+	NM
20TH FOX					
❑ 150	Lovely One/The Snake and the Bookworm	1959	3.75	7.50	15.00
ATLANTIC					
❑ 2142	Some Other Guy/Tricky Dicky	1962	3.75	7.50	15.00
—As "Richie Barrett"					
CRACKERJACK					
❑ 4012	Summer's Love/Let Me Down Easy	1963	3.75	7.50	15.00
GONE					
❑ 5056	Come Softly to Me/Walking Through Dreamland	1959	7.50	15.00	30.00
—With the Chantels					
❑ 5060	Summer's Love/All Is Forgiven	1959	7.50	15.00	30.00
—With the Chantels					
METRO					
❑ 20006	Lovable/Only One Way	1959	3.75	7.50	15.00
MGM					
❑ 12616	Smoke Gets In Your Eyes/Remember Me	1958	7.50	15.00	30.00
❑ 12659	Body and Soul/The Party	1958	7.50	15.00	30.00
SEVILLE					
❑ 104	Dream On/I Am Yours	1960	3.75	7.50	15.00

BARRETT, SYD

Member of the earliest incarnation of PINK FLOYD.

7-Inch Extended Plays

Number	Title (A Side/B Side)	Yr	VG	VG+	NM
CAPITOL					
❑ NR-58186	Terrapin/Octopus//Baby Lemonade/Effervescent Elephant	1994	—	3.00	6.00
—Pink vinyl					
❑ NR-58186 [PS]	Crazy Diamond	1994	—	3.00	6.00

BARRI, STEVE

Cohort of P.F. SLOAN. Also see THE FANTASTIC BAGGYS; THE GRASS ROOTS; THE IMAGINATIONS (2); THE INNER CIRCLE; THE LIFEGUARDS (2); PHILIP AND STEPHAN; THE RALLY PACKS; THE STREET CLEANERS; THEMES INC.; WILLIE AND THE WHEELS.

Number	Title (A Side/B Side)	Yr	VG	VG+	NM
RONA					
❑ 1003	Down Around the Corner/Please Let It Be You	1961	10.00	20.00	40.00
❑ 1004	I Want Your Love/Story of the Ring	1961	10.00	20.00	40.00
❑ 1005	Two Different Worlds/Don't Run Away from Love	1962	10.00	20.00	40.00
❑ 1006	Never Before/Whenever You Kiss Me	1962	10.00	20.00	40.00

BARRIX, BILLY

Number	Title (A Side/B Side)	Yr	VG	VG+	NM
CHESS					
❑ 1662	Cool Off Baby/Almost	1958	5000.	7500.	10000.
—Outrageously rare rockabilly record					

BARRY, JEFF

Also see THE RAINDROPS.

Number	Title (A Side/B Side)	Yr	VG	VG+	NM
A&M					
❑ 1422	Walkin' in the Sun/Whatcha Wanna Do	1973	—	2.50	5.00
BELL					
❑ 45140	Sweet Saviour/Love Has Never Let Me Down	1971	—	3.00	6.00
DECCA					
❑ 31037	Never Never/It Won't Hurt	1959	5.00	10.00	20.00
❑ 31089	Lenore/Why Does the Feeling Go Away	1960	5.00	10.00	20.00
RCA VICTOR					
❑ 47-7477	It's Called Rock & Roll/Hip Couples	1959	6.25	12.50	25.00
❑ 47-7797	The Face from Outer Space/Lovely Lips	1960	6.25	12.50	25.00
❑ 47-7821	All You Need Is a Quarter/Teen Quartet	1960	6.25	12.50	25.00
RED BIRD					
❑ 10-026	I'll Still Love You/Our Love Can Still Be Saved	1965	4.00	8.00	16.00
UNITED ARTISTS					
❑ 440	We Got Love Money Can't Buy/Welcome Home	1962	4.00	8.00	16.00
❑ 50529	Much Too Young/Where It's At	1969	2.00	4.00	8.00

BARRY, JOE

Number	Title (A Side/B Side)	Yr	VG	VG+	NM
ABC DOT					
❑ 17724	If You Really Want Me To, I'll Go/You're Why I'm So Lonely	1977	—	2.00	4.00
JIN					
❑ 132	Greatest Moment of My Life/Heartbroken Love	1961	3.75	7.50	15.00
❑ 144	I'm a Fool to Care/I Got a Feeling	1961	6.25	12.50	25.00
❑ 150	Je Suis Bet Pour T'Amer/Oh Teet Fille	1961	3.75	7.50	15.00
❑ 157	Till the End of the World/You Don't Have to Be a Baby to Cry	1962	3.75	7.50	15.00
NUGGET					
❑ 1023	Today I Started Loving You Again/California Sun	196?	2.50	5.00	10.00
❑ 1027	Chantilly Lace/Ode to a Woman	196?	2.50	5.00	10.00
❑ 1034	Always/I'm Feelin' Blue Again	196?	2.50	5.00	10.00
SMASH					
❑ 1702	I'm a Fool to Care/I Got a Feeling	1961	3.00	6.00	12.00
❑ 1710	Teardrops in My Heart/For You Sunshine	1961	2.50	5.00	10.00
❑ 1727	You Don't Have to Be a Baby to Cry/Till the End of the World	1961	2.50	5.00	10.00
❑ 1745	Little Papoose/Why Did You Say Goodbye	1962	2.50	5.00	10.00
❑ 1762	Just Because/Little Jewel of the Veaux Carre	1962	2.50	5.00	10.00

BARRY, JOHN

Number	Title (A Side/B Side)	Yr	VG	VG+	NM
20TH FOX					
❑ 472	Theme from "Man in the Middle"/Barney's Blues	1964	3.00	6.00	12.00
CAPITOL					
❑ F4212	Snap 'N Whistle/Long Long	1959	3.75	7.50	15.00
COLUMBIA					
❑ 43320	A Man Alone/Barbara's Theme	1965	2.00	4.00	8.00
❑ 43360	The Knack (And How to Get It)/The Knack (And How to Get It)	1965	2.50	5.00	10.00
—B-side by Johnny DeLittle					
❑ 43544	The Chase/Saturday Night Philosopher	1966	2.50	5.00	10.00
❑ 43801	Theme from Born Free/Goldfinger	1966	2.50	5.00	10.00
❑ 43951	Wednesday's Child/Sleep Well, My Darling	1966	2.50	5.00	10.00
❑ 44167	You Only Live Twice/The Girl with the Sun in Her Hair	1967	2.00	4.00	8.00
❑ 44721	The Lion in Winter/To Rome	1968	2.00	4.00	8.00
❑ 44891	Midnight Cowboy/Fun City	1969	—	3.00	6.00
❑ 45062	On Her Majesty's Secret Service/We Have All the Time in the World	1970	—	3.00	6.00
❑ 45140	Theme from "The Appointment"/The More Things Change	1970	—	3.00	6.00
DECCA					
❑ 31815	A Man Alone (Jazz Version)/A Man Alone (Latin Version)	1965	2.50	5.00	10.00
EPIC					
❑ 10865	The Persuaders/The Girl with the Sun in Her Hair	1972	—	3.00	6.00
KING					
❑ 5495	Black Stockings/Get Lost Jack Frost	1961	3.75	7.50	15.00
MERCURY					
❑ 72261	From Russia with Love/007	1964	3.00	6.00	12.00
MGM					
❑ 13591	Born Free/Elsa at Play	1966	2.00	4.00	8.00
UNITED ARTISTS					
❑ 581	James Bond Theme/March of the Mandarins	1963	3.75	7.50	15.00
❑ 743	Big Shield/Zulu Stomp	1964	2.50	5.00	10.00

Number	Title (A Side/B Side)	Yr	VG	VG+	NM
❑ 791	Goldfinger/Troubadour	1964	2.50	5.00	10.00
❑ 863	From Russia with Love/James Bond Theme	1965	2.50	5.00	10.00
WARNER BROS.					
❑ 7230	Highway 101/Petula	1968	—	3.00	6.00

BARRY, LEN

Former member of THE DOVELLS.

Number	Title (A Side/B Side)	Yr	VG	VG+	NM
AMY					
❑ 11026	4-5-6 (Now I'm Alone)/Funky Night	1968	—	3.00	6.00
❑ 11037	You're My Picasso, Baby/Christopher Columbus	1968	—	3.00	6.00
❑ 11047	The Child Is Born/Wouldn't It Be Beautiful	1968	—	3.00	6.00
BUDDAH					
❑ 284	Just the Two of Us/Diggin' Life	1972	—	2.50	5.00
❑ 284 [PS]	Just the Two of Us/Diggin' Life	1972	—	3.00	6.00
CAMEO					
❑ 303	Jim Dandy/Don't Come Back	1964	3.00	6.00	12.00
❑ 318	Little White House/Hearts Are Trump	1964	3.00	6.00	12.00
DECCA					
❑ 31788	Lip Sync (To the Tongue Twisters)/At the Hop '65	1965	2.50	5.00	10.00
❑ 31827	1-2-3/Bullseye	1965	3.75	7.50	15.00
❑ 31889	Like a Baby/Happiness (Is a Girl Like You)	1966	2.50	5.00	10.00
❑ 31923	Somewhere/It's a Crying Shame	1966	2.50	5.00	10.00
❑ 31969	It's That Time of the Year/Happily Ever After	1966	2.50	5.00	10.00
❑ 32011	I Struck It Rich/Love Is	1966	2.50	5.00	10.00
❑ 32054	Would I Love You/You Baby	1966	2.50	5.00	10.00
MERCURY					
❑ 72299	Let's Do It Again/Happy Days	1964	3.00	6.00	12.00
PARAMOUNT					
❑ 0206	Heaven Plus Earth/I'm Marching to the Music	1973	—	2.50	5.00
PARKWAY					
❑ 969	Little White House/Hearts Are Trump	1966	2.00	4.00	8.00
RCA VICTOR					
❑ 47-9150	Our Song/The Moving Finger Writes	1967	2.00	4.00	8.00
❑ 47-9275	All Those Memories/Rainy Side of the Street	1967	2.00	4.00	8.00
❑ 47-9348	The ABC's of Love/Come Rain or Shine	1967	2.00	4.00	8.00
❑ 47-9464	Sweet and Funny/I Like the Way	1968	2.00	4.00	8.00
SCEPTER					
❑ 12251	Put Out the Fire/Spread It On Like Butter	1969	2.00	4.00	8.00
❑ 12263	Keem-O-Sabe/This Old World	1969	2.00	4.00	8.00
❑ 12284	Bob & Carol & Ted & Alice/In My Present State of Mind	1970	—	3.00	6.00

BARRY AND THE TAMERLANES

Also see BARRY DeVORZON.

Number	Title (A Side/B Side)	Yr	VG	VG+	NM
VALIANT					
❑ 703	I Wonder What She's Doing Tonight/Roberta	1965	3.00	6.00	12.00
❑ 6034	I Wonder What She's Doing Tonight/Don't Go	1963	5.00	10.00	20.00
❑ 6040	Roberta/Butterfly	1964	3.75	7.50	15.00
❑ 6046	Lucky Guy/I Don't Want to Be Your Clown	1964	3.75	7.50	15.00
❑ 6050	A Date with Judy/Pretty Things	1964	3.75	7.50	15.00
❑ 6059	Gee/Don't Cry Cindy	1964	3.75	7.50	15.00

BARTEL, LOU

Number	Title (A Side/B Side)	Yr	VG	VG+	NM
ABC-PARAMOUNT					
❑ 9801	Natural, Natural Baby/My Idea of Heaven	1957	6.25	12.50	25.00
❑ 9877	Blue Moon/I'm Gonna Kiss My Baby Goodnight	1957	6.25	12.50	25.00
APOLLO					
❑ 473	I Pray/(Zoom) Give Me Your Tonight	1954	37.50	75.00	150.00

BARTHOLOMEW, DAVE

Number	Title (A Side/B Side)	Yr	VG	VG+	NM
DECCA					
❑ 48216	Tra La La/Teejim	1951	30.00	60.00	120.00
IMPERIAL					
❑ 5210	Who Drank the Beer While I Was in the Rear/The Rest of My Life	1952	30.00	60.00	120.00
—Dave Bartholomew records on Imperial before 5210 are unconfirmed on 45 rpm					
❑ 5249	No More Black Nights/Air Tight	1953	30.00	60.00	120.00
❑ 5273	Texas Hop/When the Saints Go Marchin' In Boogie	1954	37.50	75.00	150.00
❑ 5308	Cat Music/Jump Children	1954	30.00	60.00	120.00
❑ 5322	Another Mule/I Want to Be with Her	1955	12.50	25.00	50.00
❑ 5350	Every Night, Every Day/Four Winds	1955	12.50	25.00	50.00
❑ 5373	Shrimp and Gumbo/An Old Cowhand from a Blues Band	1956	10.00	20.00	40.00
❑ 5390	Would You/Turn Your Lamp Down Low	1956	10.00	20.00	40.00
❑ 5408	Lovin' You/Three Time Loser	1956	7.50	15.00	30.00
❑ 5438	The Monkey/The Shuffling	1957	6.25	12.50	25.00
❑ 5460	How Could You/Barrel House	1957	6.25	12.50	25.00
❑ 5481	Hard Times (The Slop)/Cinderella	1957	6.25	12.50	25.00
❑ 5560	Button Blues/Short Subjects	1959	5.00	10.00	20.00
❑ 5702	I Cried/Somebody New	1960	5.00	10.00	20.00
❑ 5714	People Are Talking/Yeah, Yeah	1961	5.00	10.00	20.00
❑ 5803	I'm Walkin'/Going to the River	1962	3.75	7.50	15.00
❑ 5835	A Sunday Kind of Love/Honky Tonk Trumpet	1962	3.75	7.50	15.00
KING					
❑ 4482	Sweet Home Blues/Twins	1951	37.50	75.00	150.00
❑ 4508	In the Alley/I'll Never Be the Same	1952	50.00	100.00	200.00
❑ 4523	Lawdy, Lawdy, Lawd (Part 1)/Lawdy, Lawdy, Lawd (Part 2)	1952	37.50	75.00	150.00
❑ 4544	My Ding-a-Ling/Bad Habit	1952	62.50	125.00	250.00
❑ 4559	The Golden Rule/Mother Knows Best	1952	25.00	50.00	100.00
❑ 4585	High Flying Woman/Stormy Weather	1953	25.00	50.00	100.00

BARTON, ERNIE

Number	Title (A Side/B Side)	Yr	VG	VG+	NM
PHILLIPS INTERNATIONAL					
❑ 3528	Stairway of Love/Raining the Blues	1958	5.00	10.00	20.00
❑ 3541	Open the Door Richard/Shut Your Mouth	1959	37.50	75.00	150.00

BASIL, TONI

Number	Title (A Side/B Side)	Yr	VG	VG+	NM
A&M					
❑ 791	Breakaway/I'm 28	1966	50.00	100.00	200.00
CHRYSALIS					
❑ 2638	Mickey/Thief on the Loose	1982	—	—	3.00
❑ 2638 [PS]	Mickey/Thief on the Loose	1982	—	—	3.00
❑ 2665	Mickey (Spanish)/Thief on the Loose	1982	—	2.00	4.00
❑ 2665 [PS]	Mickey (Spanish)/Thief on the Loose	1982	—	2.00	4.00
❑ 03537	Shoppin' from A to Z/Time After Time	1983	—	—	3.00
❑ 03537 [PS]	Shoppin' from A to Z/Time After Time	1983	—	—	3.00
❑ 03539	Mickey/Thief on the Loose	1983	—	—	3.00
—Reissue					
❑ 42711	Street Beat/(B-side unknown)	1983	—	—	3.00
❑ 42753	Over My Head/Best Performance	1983	—	—	3.00
❑ 42753 [PS]	Over My Head/Best Performance	1983	—	—	3.00
RAZOR & TIE					
❑ 93018-07507	Mickey (Radio Remix)/Mickey ("Killa Klub" Edit)	1999	—	—	3.00

BASKERVILLE HOUNDS, THE

Number	Title (A Side/B Side)	Yr	VG	VG+	NM
AVCO EMBASSY					
❑ 4504	Hold Me/Here I Come, Miami	1968	2.50	5.00	10.00
BUDDAH					
❑ 17	Caroline/Last Night on the Back Porch	1967	2.50	5.00	10.00
DOT					
❑ 17004	Space Rock, Part 1/Space Rock, Part 2	1967	2.50	5.00	10.00
❑ 17017	Debbie/Jackie's Theme	1967	2.50	5.00	10.00
❑ 17037	Baby, Am I Losing/Never on Sunday	1967	2.50	5.00	10.00
TEMA					
❑ 125	Debbie/Jackie's Theme	1966	3.75	7.50	15.00
❑ 128	Space Rock, Part 1/Space Rock, Part 2	1966	3.75	7.50	15.00
❑ 131	Christmas Is Here (But Not For Long)/Make Me Your Man	1966	3.75	7.50	15.00
❑ 131 [PS]	Christmas Is Here (But Not For Long)/Make Me Your Man	1966	12.50	25.00	50.00
❑ 132	All You Had to Do Was Ask/Who Does She Love	1967	3.75	7.50	15.00
❑ 135	Hold Me/Here I Come, Miami	1967	3.75	7.50	15.00

BASS, FONTELLA

Number	Title (A Side/B Side)	Yr	VG	VG+	NM
BOBBIN					
❑ 134	I Don't Hurt Anymore/Brand New Love	1962	3.75	7.50	15.00
❑ 140	Honey Bee/Bad Boy	1963	3.75	7.50	15.00
CHECKER					
❑ 1097	Don't Mess Up a Good Thing/Baby, What You Want Me to Do	1965	2.50	5.00	10.00
—With Bobby McClure					
❑ 1111	You'll Miss Me (When I'm Gone)/Don't Jump	1965	2.50	5.00	10.00
—With Bobby McClure					
❑ 1120	Rescue Me/Soul of the Man	1965	5.00	10.00	20.00
—Red label with "Checker" vertically on left					
❑ 1120	Rescue Me/Soul of the Man	1965	3.75	7.50	15.00
—Light blue label with red and black checkers					
❑ 1131	Recovery/Leave It in the Hands of Love	1965	2.50	5.00	10.00
❑ 1137	I Surrender/I Can't Rest	1966	2.50	5.00	10.00
❑ 1147	Safe and Sound/You'll Never Ever Know	1966	2.50	5.00	10.00
❑ 1183	Lucky in Love/Sweet Lovin' Daddy	1967	2.50	5.00	10.00
EPIC					
❑ 50341	Soon as I Touched Him/You Can Betcha in Love	1977	—	2.00	4.00
PAULA					
❑ 360	Who You Gonna Blame/Hold On This Time	1972	—	2.50	5.00
❑ 367	I Need to Be Loved/I Want Everyone to Know	1972	—	2.50	5.00
❑ 376	It Sure Is Good/I'm Leaving the Choice to You	1973	—	2.50	5.00
❑ 389	Home Wrecker/Now That I've Found a Good Thing	1973	—	2.50	5.00
❑ 393	Talking About Freedom/It's Hard to Get Back In	1974	—	2.50	5.00

BASS, FONTELLA, AND TINA TURNER

Number	Title (A Side/B Side)	Yr	VG	VG+	NM
VESUVIUS					
❑ 1002	This Would Make Me Happy/Poor Little Fool	1963	6.25	12.50	25.00

BASTILLES, THE

Number	Title (A Side/B Side)	Yr	VG	VG+	NM
PHILIPS					
❑ 40453	Tenderly/Vengeance	1967	5.00	10.00	20.00

BATS, THE (1)

British group.

Number	Title (A Side/B Side)	Yr	VG	VG+	NM
HBR					
❑ 445	Big Bright Eyes/Nothing at All	1965	2.50	5.00	10.00
PARROT					
❑ 40013	Listen to My Heart/You Look Good Together	1967	2.50	5.00	10.00

BATS, THE (U)

Number	Title (A Side/B Side)	Yr	VG	VG+	NM
FLAME					
❑ 5155	Batmobile/Batusi	1966	10.00	20.00	40.00

BATTIN, SKIP

Member of later versions of THE BYRDS.

Number	Title (A Side/B Side)	Yr	VG	VG+	NM
AURORA					
❑ 159	The Dating Game Theme/Night Time Girl	1966	3.75	7.50	15.00
GROOVE					
❑ 58-0055	Searchin'/She Acts Like We Never Have Met	1965	10.00	20.00	40.00
❑ 58-0065	Ten Feet Tall/What's Mine Is Mine	1965	10.00	20.00	40.00
SIGNPOST					
❑ 70010 [DJ]	Ballad of Dick Clark (mono/stereo)	1973	—	3.00	6.00
—May be promo only					

BAUHAUS

Number	Title (A Side/B Side)	Yr	VG	VG+	NM
A&M					
❑ 2524	Ziggy Stardust/Lagartija-Nick/Third Uncle	1983	6.25	12.50	25.00
❑ 2524 [PS]	Ziggy Stardust/Lagartija-Nick/Third Uncle	1983	6.25	12.50	25.00

BAUM, ALLEN

Number	Title (A Side/B Side)	Yr	VG	VG+	NM
RED ROBIN					
❑ 124	My Kinda Woman/Too Much Competition	1954	100.00	200.00	400.00

BAXTER, RONNIE

ATCO

Number	Title (A Side/B Side)	Yr	VG	VG+	NM
❑ 6093	Drivin' Me Out of My Mind/Afraid of Love	1957	10.00	20.00	40.00

GONE

Number	Title (A Side/B Side)	Yr	VG	VG+	NM
❑ 5036	Someone to Love Me/Gates of Heaven	1958	7.50	15.00	30.00
❑ 5041	Gates of Heaven/Prisoner of Love	1958	7.50	15.00	30.00
❑ 5050	Is It Because/I Finally Found You	1958	7.50	15.00	30.00
❑ 5058	Is It Because/I Finally Found You	1959	7.50	15.00	30.00
❑ 5084	It's Magic/If You Let Me	1960	6.25	12.50	25.00

MARK-X

Number	Title (A Side/B Side)	Yr	VG	VG+	NM
❑ 8001	It's Magic/If You Let Me	1959	3.00	6.00	12.00

BAY CITY 5

See LUIGI MARTINI AND THE BAY CITY 5.

BAY CITY ROLLERS

ARISTA

Number	Title (A Side/B Side)	Yr	VG	VG+	NM
❑ 0120	Bye Bye Baby/It's for You	1975	—	2.50	5.00
❑ 0149	Saturday Night/Marlina	1975	—	2.00	4.00
❑ 0149 [PS]	Saturday Night/Marlina	1975	—	3.00	6.00
❑ 0170	Money Honey/Maryanne	1976	—	2.00	4.00
❑ 0170 [PS]	Money Honey/Maryanne	1976	—	3.00	6.00
❑ 0185	Rock and Roll Love Letter/Shanghai'd in Love	1976	—	2.00	4.00
❑ 0193	Don't Stop the Music (Long)/Don't Stop the Music (Short)	1976	—	2.50	5.00
❑ 0205	I Only Want to Be with You/Write a Letter	1976	—	2.00	4.00
❑ 0216	Yesterday's Hero/My Lisa	1976	—	2.00	4.00
❑ 0233	Dedication/Rock N' Roller	1977	—	2.00	4.00
❑ 0233 [PS]	Dedication/Rock N' Roller	1977	—	2.50	5.00
❑ 0256	You Made Me Believe in Magic/Dance Dance Dance	1977	—	2.00	4.00
❑ 0272	The Way I Feel Tonight/Love Power	1977	—	2.50	5.00
❑ 0272	The Way I Feel Tonight/Sweet Virginia	1977	—	2.50	5.00
❑ 0363	Where Will I Be Now/If You Were My Woman	1978	—	2.00	4.00
❑ 0476	Turn On the Radio/Hello and Welcome Home	1979	—	2.00	4.00

—As "The Rollers"

BELL

Number	Title (A Side/B Side)	Yr	VG	VG+	NM
❑ 45169	Keep On Dancing/Alright	1972	—	3.00	6.00
❑ 45274	Manana/I Heard You Singing Your Song	1972	—	3.00	6.00
❑ 45481	Shang-a-Lang/(B-side unknown)	1974	—	3.00	6.00
❑ 45607	Summerlove Sensation/(B-side unknown)	1974	—	3.00	6.00
❑ 45618	All of Me Loves All of You/(B-side unknown)	1974	—	3.00	6.00

BAYOU BOYS, THE

CHECKER

Number	Title (A Side/B Side)	Yr	VG	VG+	NM
❑ 765	Dinah/Bambalays	1952	37.50	75.00	150.00

BEACH, BILL

KING

Number	Title (A Side/B Side)	Yr	VG	VG+	NM
❑ 4940	Peg Pants/You're Gonna Like My Baby	1956	37.50	75.00	150.00

BEACH BOYS, THE

Also see GLEN CAMPBELL; DAVE AND THE MARKSMEN; BRUCE JOHNSTON; MIKE LOVE; BRIAN WILSON; BRIAN WILSON AND MIKE LOVE; CARL WILSON; DENNIS WILSON.

BROTHER

Number	Title (A Side/B Side)	Yr	VG	VG+	NM
❑ 1001	Heroes and Villains/You're Welcome	1967	3.00	6.00	12.00
❑ 1001 [PS]	Heroes and Villains/You're Welcome	1967	25.00	50.00	100.00

—Not to be confused with Capitol 5826, which is a completely different sleeve

BROTHER/REPRISE

Number	Title (A Side/B Side)	Yr	VG	VG+	NM
❑ 0101	Wouldn't It Be Nice/Sloop John B	1973	—	2.50	5.00
—"Back to Back Hits" series					
❑ 0102	God Only Knows/Caroline, No	1973	—	2.50	5.00
—"Back to Back Hits" series					
❑ 0103	Good Vibrations/Heroes and Villains	1973	—	2.50	5.00
—"Back to Back Hits" series					
❑ 0104	Darlin'/Wild Honey	1973	—	2.50	5.00
—"Back to Back Hits" series					
❑ 0105	Friends/Be Here in the Morning	1973	—	2.50	5.00
—"Back to Back Hits" series					
❑ 0106	Do It Again/Cottonfields	1973	—	2.50	5.00
—"Back to Back Hits" series					
❑ 0107	I Can Hear Music/Bluebirds Over the Mountain	1973	—	2.50	5.00
—"Back to Back Hits" series					
❑ 0118	Rock and Roll Music/It's O.K.	1977	—	2.00	4.00
—"Back to Back Hits" series					
❑ 0894	Add Some Music to Your Day/Susie Cincinnati	1970	2.00	4.00	8.00
❑ 0929	Slip On Through/This Whole World	1970	2.50	5.00	10.00
❑ 0957	It's About Time/Tears in the Morning	1970	5.00	10.00	20.00
❑ 0998	Cool, Cool Water/Forever	1971	20.00	40.00	80.00
❑ 1015	Long Promised Road/Deirdre	1971	5.00	10.00	20.00
❑ 1047	Long Promised Road/Til I Die	1971	5.00	10.00	20.00
❑ 1058	Surf's Up/Don't Go Near the Water	1971	12.50	25.00	50.00
❑ 1091	You Need a Mess of Help to Stand Alone/Cuddle Up	1972	7.50	15.00	30.00
❑ 1101	Marcella/Hold On Dear Brother	1972	7.50	15.00	30.00
❑ 1138	Sail On Sailor/Only With You	1972	2.50	5.00	10.00
❑ 1156	California Saga (On My Way to Sunny Californ-I-A)/Funky Pretty	1973	2.50	5.00	10.00
❑ 1310	I Can Hear Music/Let the Wind Blow	1974	2.50	5.00	10.00
❑ 1321	Child of Winter (Christmas Song)/Susie Cincinnati	1974	12.50	25.00	50.00
❑ 1321 [DJ]	Child of Winter (Christmas Song) (mono/stereo)	1974	6.25	12.50	25.00
❑ 1325	Sail On Sailor/Only With You	1975	2.00	4.00	8.00
❑ 1336	Wouldn't It Be Nice/Caroline, No	1975	3.00	6.00	12.00
❑ 1354	Rock and Roll Music/The T M Song	1976	—	2.00	4.00
❑ 1368	It's O.K./Had to Phone Ya	1976	—	2.00	4.00
❑ 1375	Everyone's In Love with You/Susie Cincinnati	1976	—	2.00	4.00
❑ 1389	Honkin' Down the Highway/Solar System	1977	—	2.00	4.00
❑ 1394	Peggy Sue/Hey Little Tomboy	1978	—	2.00	4.00

CANDIX

Number	Title (A Side/B Side)	Yr	VG	VG+	NM
❑ 301	Surfin'/Luau	1961	50.00	100.00	200.00
—Label says "Distributed by Era Records Sales, Inc."					
❑ 301	Surfin'/Luau	1961	75.00	150.00	300.00
—No mention of Era Records on label					
❑ 331	Surfin'/Luau	1962	50.00	100.00	200.00

CAPITOL

Number	Title (A Side/B Side)	Yr	VG	VG+	NM
❑ 2028	Wild Honey/Wind Chimes	1967	3.00	6.00	12.00
❑ 2068	Darlin'/Here Today	1967	3.00	6.00	12.00
❑ 2068 [PS]	Darlin'/Here Today	1967	5.00	10.00	20.00
❑ 2160	Friends/Little Bird	1968	3.00	6.00	12.00
❑ 2239	Do It Again/Wake the World	1968	3.00	6.00	12.00
❑ 2360	Bluebirds Over the Mountain/Never Learn Not to Love	1968	3.00	6.00	12.00
❑ 2432	I Can Hear Music/All I Want to Do	1969	3.00	6.00	12.00
❑ 2530	Break Away/Celebrate the News	1969	3.00	6.00	12.00
❑ 2765	Cottonfields/The Nearest Faraway Place	1970	5.00	10.00	20.00
❑ 3924	Surfin' U.S.A./The Warmth of the Sun	1974	—	2.50	5.00
❑ 4093	Little Honda/Hawaii	1975	—	2.50	5.00
❑ 4110	Barbara Ann/Little Honda	1975	—	2.50	5.00
❑ 4334	Be True to Your School/Graduation Day	1976	—	2.50	5.00
❑ 4777	Surfin' Safari/409	1962	6.25	12.50	25.00
❑ 4777 [PS]	Surfin' Safari/409	1962	20.00	40.00	80.00
❑ 4880	Ten Little Indians/County Fair	1962	7.50	15.00	30.00
❑ 4880 [PS]	Ten Little Indians/County Fair	1962	50.00	100.00	200.00
❑ 4932	Surfin' U.S.A./Shut Down	1963	6.25	12.50	25.00
—Version 1: Brian Wilson listed as composer of "Surfin' U.S.A."					
❑ 4932	Surfin' U.S.A./Shut Down	1963	6.25	12.50	25.00
—Version 2: Chuck Berry listed as composer of "Surfin' U.S.A."					
❑ 5009	Surfer Girl/Little Deuce Coupe	1963	6.25	12.50	25.00
❑ A-5030	The Beach Boys Medley/God Only Knows	1981	—	2.50	5.00
❑ 5069	Be True to Your School/In My Room	1963	6.25	12.50	25.00
❑ 5096	Little Saint Nick/The Lord's Prayer	1963	7.50	15.00	30.00
—Orange and yellow swirl label					
❑ 5096	Little Saint Nick/The Lord's Prayer	1969	4.50	9.00	18.00
—Red and orange "target" label					
❑ 5096	Little Saint Nick/The Lord's Prayer	1972	3.75	7.50	15.00
—Orange label with "Capitol" at bottom of label					
❑ 5096	Little Saint Nick/The Lord's Prayer	1978	—	2.50	5.00
—Purple label					
❑ 5096	Little Saint Nick/The Lord's Prayer	1982	—	2.50	5.00
—Black label with colorband					
❑ 5118	Fun, Fun, Fun/Why Do Fools Fall in Love	1964	6.25	12.50	25.00
—A-side songwriter listed as "Brian Wilson"					
❑ 5118	Fun, Fun, Fun/Why Do Fools Fall in Love	1964	5.00	10.00	20.00
—A-side songwriter listed as "Brian Wilson-Mike Love"					
❑ 5118 [PS]	Fun, Fun, Fun/Why Do Fools Fall in Love	1964	10.00	20.00	40.00
❑ 5174	I Get Around/Don't Worry Baby	1964	6.25	12.50	25.00
—Orange and yellow swirl label					
❑ 5174	I Get Around/Don't Worry Baby	1969	3.00	6.00	12.00
—Red and orange "target" label					
❑ 5174	I Get Around/Don't Worry Baby	1972	2.00	4.00	8.00
—Orange label with "Capitol" at bottom					
❑ 5174	I Get Around/Don't Worry Baby	1978	—	2.50	5.00
—Purple label					
❑ 5174	I Get Around/Don't Worry Baby	1982	—	2.50	5.00
—Black label with colorband					
❑ 5174 [PS]	I Get Around/Don't Worry Baby	1964	10.00	20.00	40.00
❑ 5245	When I Grow Up (To Be a Man)/She Knows Me Too Well	1964	6.25	12.50	25.00
❑ 5245 [PS]	When I Grow Up (To Be a Man)/She Knows Me Too Well	1964	12.50	25.00	50.00
—With green border					
❑ 5245 [PS]	When I Grow Up (To Be a Man)/She Knows Me Too Well	1964	10.00	20.00	40.00
—With blue border					
❑ 5306	Dance, Dance, Dance/The Warmth of the Sun	1964	6.25	12.50	25.00
❑ 5306 [PS]	Dance, Dance, Dance/The Warmth of the Sun	1964	30.00	60.00	120.00
❑ 5312	The Man with All the Toys/Blue Christmas	1964	7.50	15.00	30.00
❑ 5372	Do You Wanna Dance/Please Let Me Wonder	1965	5.00	10.00	20.00
❑ 5372 [PS]	Do You Wanna Dance/Please Let Me Wonder	1965	10.00	20.00	40.00
❑ 5395	Help Me, Rhonda/Kiss Me, Baby	1965	6.25	12.50	25.00
❑ 5395 [PS]	Help Me, Rhonda/Kiss Me, Baby	1965	10.00	20.00	40.00
❑ 5464	California Girls/Let Him Run Wild	1965	6.25	12.50	25.00
—Orange and yellow swirl label					
❑ 5464	California Girls/Let Him Run Wild	1969	2.50	5.00	10.00
—Red and orange "target" label					
❑ 5464	California Girls/Let Him Run Wild	1973	2.00	4.00	8.00
—Orange label with "Capitol" at bottom of label					
❑ 5464	California Girls/Let Him Run Wild	1978	—	2.50	5.00
—Purple label					
❑ 5464 [PS]	California Girls/Let Him Run Wild	1965	10.00	20.00	40.00
❑ 5540	The Little Girl I Once Knew/There's No Other (Like My Baby)	1965	5.00	10.00	20.00
❑ 5540 [PS]	The Little Girl I Once Knew/There's No Other (Like My Baby)	1965	10.00	20.00	40.00
❑ 5561	Barbara Ann/Girl Don't Tell Me	1965	5.00	10.00	20.00
❑ 5561 [PS]	Barbara Ann/Girl Don't Tell Me	1965	37.50	75.00	150.00
—Glossy finish					
❑ 5561 [PS]	Barbara Ann/Girl Don't Tell Me	1965	50.00	100.00	200.00
—Non-glossy finish					
❑ B-5595	Rock and Roll to the Rescue/Good Vibrations (Live in London)	1986	—	—	3.00
❑ B-5595 [PS]	Rock and Roll to the Rescue/Good Vibrations (Live in London)	1986	—	2.00	4.00
❑ 5602	Sloop John B/You're So Good to Me	1966	5.00	10.00	20.00
—Orange and yellow swirl label					
❑ 5602	Sloop John B/You're So Good to Me	1969	2.50	5.00	10.00
—Red and orange "target" label					
❑ 5602	Sloop John B/You're So Good to Me	1973	2.00	4.00	8.00
—Orange label with "Capitol" at bottom of label					
❑ 5602	Sloop John B/You're So Good to Me	1978	—	2.50	5.00
—Purple label					
❑ 5602 [PS]	Sloop John B/You're So Good to Me	1966	7.50	15.00	30.00

Number	Title (A Side/B Side)	Yr	VG	VG+	NM
❑ B-5630	California Dreamin'/Lady Liberty	1986	—	—	3.00
❑ 5676	Good Vibrations/Let's Go Away for Awhile	1966	5.00	10.00	20.00
❑ 5676 [PS]	Good Vibrations/Let's Go Away for Awhile	1966	7.50	15.00	30.00
❑ 5706	Wouldn't It Be Nice/God Only Knows	1966	5.00	10.00	20.00
—Even though it has a higher number, this single was released before "Good Vibrations."					
❑ 5826 [PS]	Heroes and Villains	1967	100.00	200.00	400.00
—U.S. picture sleeve for unreleased record. This sleeve, however, was exported and used in other countries.					
❑ S7-17521	409/Punchline	1993	—	2.00	4.00
❑ S7-17522	Be True to Your School/Things We Did Last Summer	1993	—	2.00	4.00
❑ S7-17523	Do You Wanna Dance/Ruby Baby	1993	—	2.00	4.00
❑ S7-18205	Merry Christmas, Baby/Santa's Beard	1994	—	2.00	4.00
—Green vinyl					
❑ S7-19765	The Man with All the Toys/We Three Kings of Orient Are	1997	—	—	3.00
❑ B-44297	Don't Worry Baby/Tequila Dreams	1989	—	2.00	4.00
—A-side: With the Everly Brothers; B-side by Dave Grusin					
❑ B-44297 [PS]	Don't Worry Baby/Tequila Dreams	1989	2.50	5.00	10.00
❑ S7-57886	Frosty the Snowman/Little Saint Nick	1992	—	2.50	5.00
—Originals on black vinyl					
❑ S7-57886	Frosty the Snowman/Little Saint Nick	1993	—	2.00	4.00
—Second pressing on green vinyl					
❑ 58745	Child of Winter (Christmas Song)/Winter Symphony	1998	—	2.00	4.00
❑ 58746	Christmas Is Here Again/Auld Lang Syne	1998	—	2.00	4.00
❑ 58747	I'll Be Home for Christmas/Little Saint Nick (Alternate Version)	1998	—	2.00	4.00
❑ 7PRO-79789 [DJ]	Still Cruisin' (same on both sides)	1989	15.00	30.00	60.00
—Vinyl is promo only					
❑ 7PRO-79841 [DJ]	Somewhere Near Japan (same on both sides)	1989	15.00	30.00	60.00
—Vinyl is promo only					
CAPITOL CUSTOM					
❑ (no #)	Spirit of America/Boogie Woodie	1963	50.00	100.00	200.00
❑ (no #) [PS]	Spirit of America/Boogie Woodie	1963	150.00	300.00	600.00
—Promo for KFWB and opening day of Wallich's Music City South Bay store					
❑ 2936/7	Salt Lake City/Amusemant Parks U.S.A.	1965	50.00	100.00	200.00
CAPITOL STARLINE					
❑ 6059	Be True to Your School/In My Room	1965	3.75	7.50	15.00
—Originals have green swirl labels					
❑ 6060	Ten Little Indians/She Knows Me Too Well	1965	3.75	7.50	15.00
—Originals have green swirl labels					
❑ 6081	Help Me, Rhonda/Do You Wanna Dance?	1966	3.75	7.50	15.00
—Originals have green swirl labels					
❑ 6094	Surfin' U.S.A./Shut Down	1966	3.75	7.50	15.00
—Originals have green swirl labels					
❑ 6095	Surfin' Safari/409	1966	3.75	7.50	15.00
—Originals have green swirl labels					
❑ 6105	Dance, Dance, Dance/The Warmth of the Sun	1967	3.00	6.00	12.00
—Originals have red and white "target" labels					
❑ 6106	Fun, Fun, Fun/Why Do Fools Fall in Love	1967	3.00	6.00	12.00
—Originals have red and white "target" labels					
❑ 6107	Surfer Girl/Little Deuce Coupe	1967	3.00	6.00	12.00
—Originals have red and white "target" labels					
❑ 6132	Good Vibrations/Barbara Ann	1968	3.00	6.00	12.00
—Originals have red and white "target" labels					
❑ 6204	When I Grow Up (To Be a Man)/She Knows Me Too Well	197?	—	2.50	5.00
—Originals have grayish labels					
❑ 6205	Wendy/Little Honda	197?	—	2.50	5.00
—Originals have grayish labels					
❑ 6259	Barbara Ann/Little Honda	1978	—	2.00	4.00
—Originals have grayish labels					
❑ 6277	Little Saint Nick/The Lord's Prayer	1981	—	—	3.00
—Originals have blue labels					
❑ 6280	I Get Around/Don't Worry Baby	1981	—	—	3.00
—Originals have blue labels					
❑ 6289	California Girls/Let Him Run Wild	1981	—	—	3.00
—Originals have blue labels					
❑ 6295	Sloop John B/You're So Good to Me	1981	—	—	3.00
—Originals have blue labels					
CARIBOU					
❑ 02633	Come Go with Me/Don't Go Near the Water	1981	—	—	3.00
❑ 04913	Getcha Back/Male Ego	1985	—	—	3.00
❑ 04913 [PS]	Getcha Back/Male Ego	1985	—	—	3.00
❑ 05433	It's Gettin' Late/It's OK	1985	—	—	3.00
❑ 05433 [PS]	It's Gettin' Late/It's OK	1985	—	—	3.00
❑ 05624	She Believes in Love Again/It's Just a Matter of Time	1985	—	—	3.00
❑ 05624 [PS]	She Believes in Love Again/It's Just a Matter of Time	1985	—	—	3.00
❑ 9026	Here Comes the Night/Baby Blue	1979	—	2.00	4.00
❑ 9029	Good Timin'/Love Surrounds Me	1979	—	2.00	4.00
❑ 9030	Lady Lynda/Full Sail	1979	—	2.00	4.00
❑ 9031	It's a Beautiful Day/Sumahama	1979	—	2.00	4.00
❑ 9032	Goin' On/Endless Harmony	1980	—	2.00	4.00
❑ 9033	Livin' with a Heartache/Santa Ana Winds	1980	—	2.00	4.00
❑ 9034	School Day (Ring! Ring! Goes the Bell)/When Girls Get Together	1980	—	—	—
—Not known to exist					
❑ 9034 [DJ]	School Day (Ring! Ring! Goes the Bell) (same on both sides)	1980	50.00	125.00	250.00
CRITIQUE					
❑ 99392	Happy Endings/California Girls	1987	—	—	3.00
—A-side: With Little Richard					
ELEKTRA					
❑ 69385	Kokomo/Tutti-Frutti	1988	—	—	3.00
—B-side by Little Richard					
ERA BACK TO BACK HITS					
❑ 042	Surfer Girl/The Freeze	197?	2.00	4.00	8.00
—A-side is from the Hite Morgan sessions; B-side by Tony & Jo					
❑ 043	Surfin'/Surfin' Safari	197?	2.00	4.00	8.00
—Both sides from the Hite Morgan sessions					
FBI					
❑ 7701	East Meets West/Rhapsody	1986	5.00	10.00	20.00
—With Frankie Valli and the Four Seasons					
ODE					
❑ 66016	Wouldn't It Be Nice/The Times They Are a-Changing	1971	7.50	15.00	30.00
—B-side by Merry Clayton					
SUB POP					
❑ 363	I Just Wasn't Made for These Times/Wouldn't It Be Nice//Here Today	1996	—	2.50	5.00
—Newly released versions from the Pet Sounds box set					
❑ 363 [PS]	I Just Wasn't Made for These Times/Wouldn't It Be Nice//Here Today	1996	—	2.50	5.00
—Not seam sealed (folded piece of cardboard)					
X					
❑ 301	Surfin'/Luau	1961	250.00	500.00	1000.
7-Inch Extended Plays					
CAPITOL					
❑ SXA-1981 [DJ]	Your Summer Dream/Our Car Club/Surfer Girl//Catch a Wave/In My Room/Hawaii	1963	37.50	75.00	150.00
—Small hole, 33 1/3 rpm jukebox EP					
❑ SXA-1981 [PS]	Surfer Girl	1963	37.50	75.00	150.00
❑ R-5267	Wendy/Don't Back Down//Little Honda/Hushabye	1964	15.00	30.00	60.00
❑ R-5267 [PS]	4-By the Beach Boys	1964	15.00	30.00	60.00

BEACH BOYS, THE (2)

No relation to the group that became famous.

Number	Title (A Side/B Side)	Yr	VG	VG+	NM
KAPP					
❑ 289	Bathing Beauty/On the Beach at Sunset	1959	6.25	12.50	25.00

BEACH BUMS, THE

Early BOB SEGER.

Number	Title (A Side/B Side)	Yr	VG	VG+	NM
ARE YOU KIDDING ME?					
❑ 1010	Florida Time/The Ballad of the Yellow Beret	1966	15.00	30.00	60.00
—B-side credited to "D. Dodger"					

BEACH GIRLS, THE

Number	Title (A Side/B Side)	Yr	VG	VG+	NM
DYNO-VOX					
❑ 202	Goin' Places/Skiing in the Snow	1965	6.25	12.50	25.00
VAULT					
❑ 905	He's My Surfin' Guy/Bobby's the Boy	1963	7.50	15.00	30.00

BEACH NUTS, THE

Number	Title (A Side/B Side)	Yr	VG	VG+	NM
BANG					
❑ 504	Out in the Sun (Hey-O)/Someday Soon	1965	12.50	25.00	50.00
CORONADO					
❑ 131	Surf Ride '65/The Last Ride	1965	12.50	25.00	50.00
❑ 131 [PS]	Surf Ride '65/The Last Ride	1965	15.00	30.00	60.00

BEACHNUTS, THE

Number	Title (A Side/B Side)	Yr	VG	VG+	NM
BANG					
❑ 504	Out in the Sun (Hey-O)/Someday So On	1965	7.50	15.00	30.00

BEAGLES, THE

Number	Title (A Side/B Side)	Yr	VG	VG+	NM
ERA					
❑ 3132	Let's All Sing Like the Birdies Sing/Deep in the Heart of Texas	1964	3.75	7.50	15.00
❑ 3132 [PS]	Let's All Sing Like the Birdies Sing/Deep in the Heart of Texas	1964	6.25	12.50	25.00
HIT					
❑ 113	Can't Buy Me Love/White on White	1964	3.00	6.00	12.00
—B-side by Fred York					

BEAN, YOUNG BILLY

See BILLY BURNETTE.

BEARD, DEAN

Number	Title (A Side/B Side)	Yr	VG	VG+	NM
ATLANTIC					
❑ 1137	On My Mind Again/Rakin' and Scrapin'	1957	10.00	20.00	40.00
❑ 1162	Party Party/Stand By Me	1957	10.00	20.00	40.00
❑ 1182	Take Time to Love Me/Hold Me Close	1958	7.50	15.00	30.00
CANDIX					
❑ 341	The Day That I Lost You/Villa Acuna	1962	3.00	6.00	12.00
CHALLENGE					
❑ 59033	Egad, Charlie Brown/Keeper of the Key	1958	6.25	12.50	25.00
❑ 59048	Holding On to a Memory/Little Lover	1959	6.25	12.50	25.00
EDMORAL					
❑ 1011	On My Mind Again/Rakin' and Scrapin'	1956	37.50	75.00	150.00
JOED					
❑ 715	Coffee Break/Tropical Nights	1962	6.25	12.50	25.00
SIMS					
❑ 299	(Are There) Honkytonks in Heaven/Pocketful of Stardust	1966	2.50	5.00	10.00
WINSTON					
❑ 1063	I Don't Know How/The Red Rose	1962	3.00	6.00	12.00
❑ 1073	Don't Let the Stars Get In Your Eyes/That's How It Gets Sun Up	1963	3.00	6.00	12.00
❑ 1075	Smile Pretty for Me Temper/To Me	1963	3.00	6.00	12.00
—With Bill Graham					

BEASTIE BOYS

Number	Title (A Side/B Side)	Yr	VG	VG+	NM
CAPITOL					
❑ S7-18042	Get It Together/Futterman's Rule	1994	—	—	3.00
—White vinyl					

Number	Title (A Side/B Side)	Yr	VG	VG+	NM
❑ S7-18125	Sure Shot (Clean Version)/Sabotage (Clean Version)	1994	—	—	3.00
—Blue vinyl					
❑ S7-18578	Root Down/Ricky's Theme	1995	—	—	3.00
❑ S7-19973	Intergalactic/Peanut Butter & Jelly	1998	—	2.00	4.00
❑ B-44454	Hey Ladies/Shake Your Rump	1989	—	2.00	4.00
❑ B-44472	Shadrach/And What You Give Is What You Get	1989	—	2.50	5.00
❑ 58816	Alive/Big Shot (Live)	1999	—	—	3.00

DEF JAM

Number	Title (A Side/B Side)	Yr	VG	VG+	NM
❑ 05683	She's On It/Slow and Low	1985	—	2.50	5.00
❑ 05683 [PS]	She's On It/Slow and Low	1985	—	2.50	5.00
❑ 05864	Hold It Now, Hit It/Hold It Now, Hit It (Acapella)	1986	—	3.00	6.00
❑ 06341	Paul Revere/It's the New Style	1986	—	3.00	6.00
❑ 06595	(You Gotta) Fight for Your Right (To Party!)/Paul Revere	1987	—	3.00	6.00
❑ 06675	She's Crafty/No Sleep Till Brooklyn	1987	—	2.00	4.00
❑ 07020	Brass Monkey/Posse in Effect	1987	—	2.00	4.00
❑ 08388	(You Gotta) Fight for Your Right (To Party!)/She's On It	1988	—	—	3.00
—"Golden Oldies" reissue					

7-Inch Extended Plays

RAT CAGE

Number	Title (A Side/B Side)	Yr	VG	VG+	NM
❑ MOTR 21	(contents unknown)	1982	5.00	10.00	20.00
❑ MOTR 21 [PS]	Polly Wog Stew	1982	5.00	10.00	20.00

BEAT BROTHERS, THE

MGM

Number	Title (A Side/B Side)	Yr	VG	VG+	NM
❑ 13201	Nick Nack Hully Gully/Lantern Hully Gully	1963	4.00	8.00	16.00

BEATIN' PATH, THE

FONTANA

Number	Title (A Side/B Side)	Yr	VG	VG+	NM
❑ 1583	The Original Nothing People/I Waited So Long	1967	5.00	10.00	20.00

BEATLE-ETTES, THE

ASSAULT

Number	Title (A Side/B Side)	Yr	VG	VG+	NM
❑ 1893	Yes, You Can Hold My Hand/Yes, You Can Hold My Hand (Part 2)	1964	5.00	10.00	20.00

JAMIE

Number	Title (A Side/B Side)	Yr	VG	VG+	NM
❑ 1270	Dance, Beatle, Dance/We Were Meant to Be Married	1964	5.00	10.00	20.00

JUBILEE

Number	Title (A Side/B Side)	Yr	VG	VG+	NM
❑ 5472	Only Seventeen/Now We're Together	1964	5.00	10.00	20.00

BEATLES, THE

Also see PETE BEST; GEORGE HARRISON; JOHN LENNON; PAUL McCARTNEY; RINGO STARR.

APPLE

Number	Title (A Side/B Side)	Yr	VG	VG+	NM
❑ Promo-1970 [DJ]	Dialogue from the Beatles' Motion Picture "Let It Be"	1970	15.00	30.00	60.00
❑ 2056	Hello Goodbye/I Am the Walrus	1971	7.50	15.00	30.00
—With star on A-side label					
❑ 2056	Hello Goodbye/I Am the Walrus	1971	2.50	5.00	10.00
—Without star on A-side label					
❑ 2056	Hello Goodbye/I Am the Walrus	1975	5.00	10.00	20.00
—With "All Rights Reserved" disclaimer					
❑ 2138	Lady Madonna/The Inner Light	1971	7.50	15.00	30.00
—With star on A-side label					
❑ 2138	Lady Madonna/The Inner Light	1971	2.50	5.00	10.00
—Without star on A-side label					
❑ 2138	Lady Madonna/The Inner Light	1975	5.00	10.00	20.00
—With "All Rights Reserved" disclaimer					
❑ 2276	Hey Jude/Revolution	1968	3.75	7.50	15.00
—Original: With small Capitol logo on bottom of B-side label					
❑ 2276	Hey Jude/Revolution	1968	2.50	5.00	10.00
—With "Mfd. by Apple" on label					
❑ 2276	Hey Jude/Revolution	1975	5.00	10.00	20.00
—With "All Rights Reserved" disclaimer					
❑ 2490	Get Back/Don't Let Me Down	1969	2.50	5.00	10.00
—Original: With small Capitol logo on bottom of B-side label					
❑ 2490	Get Back/Don't Let Me Down	1969	2.50	5.00	10.00
—With "Mfd. by Apple" on label					
❑ 2490	Get Back/Don't Let Me Down	1975	5.00	10.00	20.00
—With "All Rights Reserved" disclaimer					
❑ 2531	The Ballad of John and Yoko/Old Brown Shoe	1969	2.50	5.00	10.00
—Original: With small Capitol logo on bottom of B-side label					
❑ 2531	The Ballad of John and Yoko/Old Brown Shoe	1969	2.50	5.00	10.00
—With "Mfd. by Apple" on label					
❑ 2531	The Ballad of John and Yoko/Old Brown Shoe	1975	5.00	10.00	20.00
—With "All Rights Reserved" disclaimer					
❑ 2531 [PS]	The Ballad of John and Yoko/Old Brown Shoe	1969	25.00	50.00	100.00
❑ 2654	Something/Come Together	1969	25.00	50.00	100.00
—Original: With small Capitol logo on bottom of B-side label					
❑ 2654	Something/Come Together	1969	2.50	5.00	10.00
—With "Mfd. by Apple" on label					
❑ 2654	Something/Come Together	1975	5.00	10.00	20.00
—With "All Rights Reserved" disclaimer					
❑ 2764	Let It Be/You Know My Name (Look Up My Number)	1970	3.00	6.00	12.00
—Original: With small Capitol logo on bottom of B-side label					
❑ 2764	Let It Be/You Know My Name (Look Up My Number)	1970	2.50	5.00	10.00
—With "Mfd. by Apple" on label					
❑ 2764	Let It Be/You Know My Name (Look Up My Number)	1975	5.00	10.00	20.00
—With "All Rights Reserved" disclaimer					
❑ 2764 [PS]	Let It Be/You Know My Name (Look Up the Number)	1970	25.00	50.00	100.00
❑ 2832	The Long and Winding Road/For You Blue	1970	5.00	10.00	20.00
—Original: With small Capitol logo on bottom of B-side label					
❑ 2832	The Long and Winding Road/For You Blue	1970	2.50	5.00	10.00
—With "Mfd. by Apple" on label					
❑ 2832	The Long and Winding Road/For You Blue	1975	5.00	10.00	20.00
—With "All Rights Reserved" disclaimer					
❑ 2832 [PS]	The Long and Winding Road/For You Blue	1970	25.00	50.00	100.00
❑ 5112	I Want to Hold Your Hand/I Saw Her Standing There	1971	7.50	15.00	30.00
—With star on label					
❑ 5112	I Want to Hold Your Hand/I Saw Her Standing There	1971	2.50	5.00	10.00
—Without star on label					
❑ 5112	I Want to Hold Your Hand/I Saw Her Standing There	1975	5.00	10.00	20.00
—With "All Rights Reserved" disclaimer on label					
❑ 5150	Can't Buy Me Love/You Can't Do That	1971	7.50	15.00	30.00
—With star on A-side label					
❑ 5150	Can't Buy Me Love/You Can't Do That	1971	2.50	5.00	10.00
—Without star on A-side label					
❑ 5150	Can't Buy Me Love/You Can't Do That	1975	3.75	7.50	15.00
—With "All Rights Reserved" disclaimer on label					
❑ 5222	A Hard Day's Night/I Should Have Known Better	1971	7.50	15.00	30.00
—With star on A-side label					
❑ 5222	A Hard Day's Night/I Should Have Known Better	1971	2.50	5.00	10.00
—Without star on A-side label					
❑ 5222	A Hard Day's Night/I Should Have Known Better	1975	3.75	7.50	15.00
—With "All Rights Reserved" disclaimer					
❑ 5234	I'll Cry Instead/I'm Happy Just to Dance with You	1971	7.50	15.00	30.00
—With star on A-side label					
❑ 5234	I'll Cry Instead/I'm Happy Just to Dance with You	1971	2.50	5.00	10.00
—Without star on A-side label					
❑ 5234	I'll Cry Instead/I'm Happy Just to Dance with You	1975	3.75	7.50	15.00
—With "All Rights Reserved" disclaimer					
❑ 5235	And I Love Her/If I Fell	1971	7.50	15.00	30.00
—With star on A-side label					
❑ 5235	And I Love Her/If I Fell	1971	2.50	5.00	10.00
—Without star on A-side label					
❑ 5235	And I Love Her/If I Fell	1975	3.75	7.50	15.00
—With "All Rights Reserved" disclaimer					
❑ 5255	Matchbox/Slow Down	1971	7.50	15.00	30.00
—With star on A-side label					
❑ 5255	Matchbox/Slow Down	1971	2.50	5.00	10.00
—Without star on A-side label					
❑ 5255	Matchbox/Slow Down	1975	3.75	7.50	15.00
—With "All Rights Reserved" disclaimer					
❑ 5327	I Feel Fine/She's a Woman	1971	7.50	15.00	30.00
—With star on A-side label					
❑ 5327	I Feel Fine/She's a Woman	1971	2.50	5.00	10.00
—Without star on A-side label					
❑ 5327	I Feel Fine/She's a Woman	1975	3.75	7.50	15.00
—With "All Rights Reserved" disclaimer					
❑ 5371	Eight Days a Week/I Don't Want to Spoil the Party	1971	7.50	15.00	30.00
—With star on A-side label					
❑ 5371	Eight Days a Week/I Don't Want to Spoil the Party	1971	2.50	5.00	10.00
—Without star on A-side label					
❑ 5371	Eight Days a Week/I Don't Want to Spoil the Party	1975	3.75	7.50	15.00
—With "All Rights Reserved" disclaimer					
❑ 5407	Ticket to Ride/Yes It Is	1971	7.50	15.00	30.00
—With star on A-side label					
❑ 5407	Ticket to Ride/Yes It Is	1971	2.50	5.00	10.00
—Without star on A-side label					
❑ 5407	Ticket to Ride/Yes It Is	1975	3.75	7.50	15.00
—With "All Rights Reserved" disclaimer					
❑ 5476	Help!/I'm Down	1971	7.50	15.00	30.00
—With star on A-side label					
❑ 5476	Help!/I'm Down	1971	2.50	5.00	10.00
—Without star on A-side label					
❑ 5476	Help!/I'm Down	1975	3.75	7.50	15.00
—With "All Rights Reserved" disclaimer					
❑ 5498	Yesterday/Act Naturally	1971	7.50	15.00	30.00
—With star on A-side label					
❑ 5498	Yesterday/Act Naturally	1971	2.50	5.00	10.00
—Without star on A-side label					
❑ 5498	Yesterday/Act Naturally	1975	3.75	7.50	15.00
—With "All Rights Reserved" disclaimer					
❑ 5555	We Can Work It Out/Day Tripper	1971	7.50	15.00	30.00
—With star on A-side label					
❑ 5555	We Can Work It Out/Day Tripper	1971	2.50	5.00	10.00
—Without star on A-side label					
❑ 5555	We Can Work It Out/Day Tripper	1975	3.75	7.50	15.00
—With "All Rights Reserved" disclaimer					
❑ 5587	Nowhere Man/What Goes On	1971	7.50	15.00	30.00
—With star on A-side label					
❑ 5587	Nowhere Man/What Goes On	1971	2.50	5.00	10.00
—Without star on A-side label					
❑ 5587	Nowhere Man/What Goes On	1975	3.75	7.50	15.00
—With "All Rights Reserved" disclaimer					
❑ 5651	Paperback Writer/Rain	1971	7.50	15.00	30.00
—With star on A-side label					
❑ 5651	Paperback Writer/Rain	1971	2.50	5.00	10.00
—Without star on A-side label					
❑ 5651	Paperback Writer/Rain	1975	3.75	7.50	15.00
—With "All Rights Reserved" disclaimer					
❑ 5715	Yellow Submarine/Eleanor Rigby	1971	7.50	15.00	30.00
—With star on A-side label					
❑ 5715	Yellow Submarine/Eleanor Rigby	1971	2.50	5.00	10.00
—Without star on A-side label					
❑ 5715	Yellow Submarine/Eleanor Rigby	1975	3.75	7.50	15.00
—With "All Rights Reserved" disclaimer					
❑ 5810	Penny Lane/Strawberry Fields Forever	1971	7.50	15.00	30.00
—With star on A-side label					
❑ 5810	Penny Lane/Strawberry Fields Forever	1971	2.50	5.00	10.00
—Without star on A-side label					

Number	Title (A Side/B Side)	Yr	VG	VG+	NM
❑ 5810	Penny Lane/Strawberry Fields Forever	1975	3.75	7.50	15.00
—With "All Rights Reserved" disclaimer					
❑ 5964	All You Need Is Love/Baby, You're a Rich Man	1971	7.50	15.00	30.00
—With star on A-side label					
❑ 5964	All You Need Is Love/Baby, You're a Rich Man	1971	2.50	5.00	10.00
—Without star on A-side label					
❑ 5964	All You Need Is Love/Baby, You're a Rich Man	1975	3.75	7.50	15.00
—With "All Rights Reserved" disclaimer					
❑ 58348	Baby It's You/I'll Follow the Sun//Devil in Her Heart/Boys	1995	—	2.00	4.00
—All 4 tracks from BBC sessions					
❑ 58348 [PS]	Baby It's You/I'll Follow the Sun//Devil in Her Heart/Boys	1995	—	2.00	4.00
❑ 58497	Free as a Bird/Christmas Time (Is Here Again)	1995	—	2.00	4.00
—Small center hole; all with large hole were "dinked" somewhere other than when manufactured and have little, if any, value					
❑ 58497 [PS]	Free as a Bird/Christmas Time (Is Here Again)	1995	—	2.00	4.00
❑ 58544	Real Love/Baby's in Black (Live)	1996	—	—	3.00
—Small center hole; all with large hole were "dinked" somewhere other than when manufactured and have little, if any, value					
❑ 58544 [PS]	Real Love/Baby's in Black (Live)	1996	—	—	3.00
APPLE/AMERICOM					
❑ 2276/M-221	Hey Jude/Revolution	1969	75.00	150.00	300.00
—Four-inch flexi-disc sold in vending machines; "Hey Jude" is edited to 3:25					
❑ 2490/M-335	Get Back/Don't Let Me Down	1969	250.00	500.00	1000.
—Four-inch flexi-disc sold in vending machines					
❑ 2531/M-382	The Ballad of John and Yoko/Old Brown Shoe	1969	200.00	400.00	800.00
—Four-inch flexi-disc sold in vending machines					
❑ 5715	Yellow Submarine/Eleanor Rigby	1969	1000.	1500.	2000.
—Four-inch flexi-disc sold in vending machines					
ATCO					
❑ 6302	Sweet Georgia Brown/Take Out Some Insurance On Me Baby	1964	50.00	100.00	200.00
❑ 6308	Ain't She Sweet/Nobody's Child	1964	12.50	25.00	50.00
—With "Vocal by John Lennon" on left of label					
❑ 6308	Ain't She Sweet/Nobody's Child	1964	15.00	30.00	60.00
—With "Vocal by John Lennon" under "The Beatles"					
❑ 6308 [PS]	Ain't She Sweet/Nobody's Child	1964	125.00	250.00	500.00
—Sleeves with black and green print are reproductions					
ATLANTIC					
❑ OS-13243	Ain't She Sweet/Sweet Georgia Brown	1983	2.50	5.00	10.00
—"Oldies Series"					
BACKSTAGE					
❑ 1112 [DJ]	Like Dreamers Do/Love of the Loved	1982	6.25	12.50	25.00
—Promotional 45 from "Oui" magazine					
❑ 1122 [DJ]	Love of the Loved/Memphis	1983	6.25	12.50	25.00
—Promotional picture disc					
❑ 1133 [DJ]	Like Dreamers Do/Three Cool Cats	1983	6.25	12.50	25.00
—Promotional picture disc					
❑ 1155 [DJ]	Crying, Waiting, Hoping/Take Good Care of My Baby	1983	6.25	12.50	25.00
BEATLES FAN CLUB					
❑ (1964)	Season's Greetings from the Beatles	1964	75.00	150.00	300.00
—Tri-fold soundcard					
❑ (1965)	The Beatles Third Christmas Record	1965	20.00	40.00	80.00
—Flexi-disc					
❑ (1965) [PS]	The Beatles Third Christmas Record	1965	25.00	50.00	100.00
❑ (1966)	Everywhere It's Christmas	1966	37.50	75.00	150.00
—Postcard					
❑ (1967)	Christmastime Is Here Again	1967	37.50	75.00	150.00
—Postcard					
❑ (1968) H-2041	The Beatles 1968 Christmas Record	1968	15.00	30.00	60.00
—Flexi-disc					
❑ (1968) H-2041 [PS]	The Beatles 1968 Christmas Record	1968	17.50	35.00	70.00
❑ (1969) H-2565	Happy Christmas 1969	1969	10.00	20.00	40.00
—Flexi-disc					
❑ (1969) H-2565 [PS]	Happy Christmas 1969	1969	15.00	30.00	60.00
CAPITOL					
❑ 2056	Hello Goodbye/I Am the Walrus	1967	7.50	15.00	30.00
—Original: Orange and yellow swirl, without "A Subsidiary Of"... in perimeter label print; publishing credited to "Maclen" (we're not sure which came first)					
❑ 2056	Hello Goodbye/I Am the Walrus	1967	7.50	15.00	30.00
—Original: Orange and yellow swirl, without "A Subsidiary Of"... in perimeter label print; publishing credited to "Comet" (we're not sure which came first)					
❑ 2056	Hello Goodbye/I Am the Walrus	1968	12.50	25.00	50.00
—Orange and yellow swirl label with "A Subsidiary Of" in perimeter print					
❑ 2056	Hello Goodbye/I Am the Walrus	1969	15.00	30.00	60.00
—Red and orange "target" label with Capitol dome logo					
❑ 2056	Hello Goodbye/I Am the Walrus	1969	5.00	10.00	20.00
—Red and orange "target" label with Capitol round logo					
❑ 2056	Hello Goodbye/I Am the Walrus	1976	—	3.00	6.00
—Orange label with "Capitol" at bottom					
❑ 2056	Hello Goodbye/I Am the Walrus	1978	2.00	4.00	8.00
—Purple label; label has reeded edge					
❑ 2056	Hello Goodbye/I Am the Walrus	1983	—	3.00	6.00
—Black label with colorband					
❑ 2056	Hello Goodbye/I Am the Walrus	1988	—	2.50	5.00
—Purple label; label has smooth edge					
❑ 2056 [PS]	Hello Goodbye/I Am the Walrus	1967	25.00	50.00	100.00
❑ P 2056 [DJ]	Hello Goodbye/I Am the Walrus	1967	62.50	125.00	250.00
—Light green label promo					
❑ 2138	Lady Madonna/The Inner Light	1968	7.50	15.00	30.00
—Original: Orange and yellow swirl, without "A Subsidiary Of"... in perimeter label print					
❑ 2138	Lady Madonna/The Inner Light	1968	12.50	25.00	50.00
—Orange and yellow swirl label with "A Subsidiary Of" in perimeter print					
❑ 2138	Lady Madonna/The Inner Light	1969	15.00	30.00	60.00
—Red and orange "target" label with Capitol dome logo					
❑ 2138	Lady Madonna/The Inner Light	1969	5.00	10.00	20.00
—Red and orange "target" label with Capitol round logo					

Number	Title (A Side/B Side)	Yr	VG	VG+	NM
❑ 2138	Lady Madonna/The Inner Light	1976	—	3.00	6.00
—Orange label with "Capitol" at bottom					
❑ 2138	Lady Madonna/The Inner Light	1978	2.00	4.00	8.00
—Purple label; label has reeded edge					
❑ 2138	Lady Madonna/The Inner Light	1983	—	3.00	6.00
—Black label with colorband					
❑ 2138	Lady Madonna/The Inner Light	1988	—	2.50	5.00
—Purple label; label has smooth edge					
❑ 2138 [PS]	Lady Madonna/The Inner Light	1968	25.00	50.00	100.00
❑ 2138 [PS]	Lady Madonna/The Inner Light	1968	5.00	10.00	20.00
—"Beatles Fan Club" insert that was issued with above sleeve. Originals are glossy.					
❑ P 2138 [DJ]	Lady Madonna/The Inner Light	1968	50.00	100.00	200.00
—Light green label promo					
❑ 2276	Hey Jude/Revolution	1976	—	3.00	6.00
—Orange label with "Capitol" at bottom					
❑ 2276	Hey Jude/Revolution	1978	2.00	4.00	8.00
—Purple label; label has reeded edge					
❑ 2276	Hey Jude/Revolution	1983	—	3.00	6.00
—Black label with colorband					
❑ 2276	Hey Jude/Revolution	1988	—	2.50	5.00
—Purple label; label has smooth edge					
❑ 2490	Get Back/Don't Let Me Down	1976	—	3.00	6.00
—Orange label with "Capitol" at bottom					
❑ 2490	Get Back/Don't Let Me Down	1978	2.00	4.00	8.00
—Purple label; label has reeded edge					
❑ 2490	Get Back/Don't Let Me Down	1983	—	3.00	6.00
—Black label with colorband; "Get Back" replaced by LP version as on Let It Be					
❑ 2490	Get Back/Don't Let Me Down	1988	—	2.50	5.00
—Purple label; label has smooth edge; "Get Back" replaced by LP version as on Let It Be					
❑ 2531	The Ballad of John and Yoko/Old Brown Shoe	1976	—	—	—
—Orange label with "Capitol" at bottom; should exist, but not known to exist					
❑ 2531	The Ballad of John and Yoko/Old Brown Shoe	1978	—	3.00	6.00
—Purple label; label has reeded edge					
❑ 2531	The Ballad of John and Yoko/Old Brown Shoe	1983	—	3.50	7.00
—Black label with colorband					
❑ 2531	The Ballad of John and Yoko/Old Brown Shoe	1988	—	3.00	6.00
—Purple label; label has smooth edge					
❑ 2654	Something/Come Together	1976	—	3.00	6.00
—Orange label with "Capitol" at bottom					
❑ 2654	Something/Come Together	1978	—	3.00	6.00
—Purple label; label has reeded edge					
❑ 2654	Something/Come Together	1983	—	3.00	6.00
—Black label with colorband					
❑ 2654	Something/Come Together	1988	—	2.50	5.00
—Purple label; label has smooth edge					
❑ 2764	Let It Be/You Know My Name (Look Up My Number)	1976	—	3.00	6.00
—Orange label with "Capitol" at bottom					
❑ 2764	Let It Be/You Know My Name (Look Up My Number)	1978	2.00	4.00	8.00
—Purple label; label has reeded edge					
❑ 2764	Let It Be/You Know My Name (Look Up My Number)	1983	—	3.00	6.00
—Black label with colorband					
❑ 2764	Let It Be/You Know My Name (Look Up My Number)	1988	—	2.50	5.00
—Purple label; label has smooth edge					
❑ 2832	The Long and Winding Road/For You Blue	1976	—	3.00	6.00
—Orange label with "Capitol" at bottom					
❑ 2832	The Long and Winding Road/For You Blue	1978	2.00	4.00	8.00
—Purple label; label has reeded edge					
❑ 2832	The Long and Winding Road/For You Blue	1983	—	3.00	6.00
—Black label with colorband					
❑ 2832	The Long and Winding Road/For You Blue	1988	—	2.50	5.00
—Purple label; label has smooth edge					
❑ 4274	Got to Get You Into My Life/Helter Skelter	1976	—	3.00	6.00
—Original: Orange label with "Capitol" at bottom, George Martin's name not on label					
❑ 4274	Got to Get You Into My Life/Helter Skelter	1976	2.50	5.00	10.00
—Orange label with "Capitol" at bottom, George Martin's name is on label					
❑ 4274	Got to Get You Into My Life/Helter Skelter	1978	—	3.00	6.00
—Purple label; label has reeded edge					
❑ 4274	Got to Get You Into My Life/Helter Skelter	1983	—	3.00	6.00
—Black label with colorband					
❑ 4274	Got to Get You Into My Life/Helter Skelter	1988	—	2.50	5.00
—Purple label; label has smooth edge					
❑ 4274 [PS]	Got to Get You Into My Life/Helter Skelter	1976	—	2.50	5.00
❑ P-4274 [DJ]	Got to Get You Into My Life (mono/stereo)	1976	10.00	20.00	40.00
❑ P-4274 [DJ]	Helter Skelter (mono/stereo)	1976	10.00	20.00	40.00
❑ 4347	Ob-La-Di, Ob-La-Da/Julia	1976	2.00	4.00	8.00
—Original: Orange label with "Capitol" at bottom					
❑ 4347	Ob-La-Di, Ob-La-Da/Julia	1978	2.00	4.00	8.00
—Purple label; label has reeded edge					
❑ 4347	Ob-La-Di, Ob-La-Da/Julia	1983	—	3.00	6.00
—Black label with colorband					
❑ 4347	Ob-La-Di, Ob-La-Da/Julia	1988	—	2.50	5.00
—Purple label; label has smooth edge					
❑ 4347 [PS]	Ob-La-Di, Ob-La-Da/Julia	1976	2.00	4.00	8.00
—Sleeves are individually numbered; very low numbers (under 1000) can fetch premium prices					
❑ P-4347 [DJ]	Ob-La-Di, Ob-La-Da (mono/stereo)	1976	10.00	20.00	40.00
❑ 4506 [PS]	Girl/You're Going to Lose That Girl	1977	3.75	7.50	15.00
—Sleeve for a single that was never pressed					
❑ P-4506 [DJ]	Girl (mono/stereo)	1977	50.00	100.00	200.00
—Promo only; all colored vinyl versions are counterfeits					
❑ 4612	Sgt. Pepper's Lonely Hearts Club Band-With a Little Help from My Friends/A Day in the Life	1978	2.00	4.00	8.00
—Original: Purple label; label has reeded edge					
❑ 4612	Sgt. Pepper's Lonely Hearts Club Band-With a Little Help from My Friends/A Day in the Life	1983	—	3.00	6.00
—Black label with colorband					

Number	Title (A Side/B Side)	Yr	VG	VG+	NM
❑ 4612	Sgt. Pepper's Lonely Hearts Club Band-With a Little Help from My Friends/A Day in the Life	1988	—	2.50	5.00
—Purple label; label has smooth edge					
❑ 4612 [PS]	Sgt. Pepper's Lonely Hearts Club Band-With a Little Help from My Friends/A Day in the Life	1978	5.00	10.00	20.00
❑ P-4612 [DJ]	Sgt. Pepper's Lonely Hearts Club Band-With a Little Help from My Friends (mono/stereo)	1978	10.00	20.00	40.00
❑ B-5100	The Beatles' Movie Medley/Fab Four on Film	1982	12.50	25.00	50.00
—Stock copy; not officially released, but some got out by mistake					
❑ B-5100 [PS]	The Beatles' Movie Medley/Fab Four on Film	1982	5.00	10.00	20.00
❑ PB-5100 [DJ]	The Beatles' Movie Medley/Fab Four on Film	1982	6.25	12.50	25.00
❑ B-5107	The Beatles' Movie Medley/I'm Happy Just to Dance with You	1982	—	2.50	5.00
❑ B-5107 [PS]	The Beatles' Movie Medley/I'm Happy Just to Dance with You	1982	—	2.50	5.00
❑ 5112	I Want to Hold Your Hand/I Saw Her Standing There	1964	10.00	20.00	40.00
—First pressing credits "Walter Hofer" as B-side publisher					
❑ 5112	I Want to Hold Your Hand/I Saw Her Standing There	1964	8.75	17.50	35.00
—Second pressing credits "George Pincus and Sons" as B-side publisher					
❑ 5112	I Want to Hold Your Hand/I Saw Her Standing There	1964	7.50	15.00	30.00
—Third (and all later) pressings credit "Gil Music" as B-side publisher					
❑ 5112	I Want to Hold Your Hand/I Saw Her Standing There	1968	15.00	30.00	60.00
—Orange and yellow swirl label with "A Subsidiary Of" in perimeter print					
❑ 5112	I Want to Hold Your Hand/I Saw Her Standing There	1969	6.25	12.50	25.00
—Red and orange "target" label, round logo					
❑ 5112	I Want to Hold Your Hand/I Saw Her Standing There	1969	15.00	30.00	60.00
—Red and orange "target" label, dome logo					
❑ 5112	I Want to Hold Your Hand/I Saw Her Standing There	1976	2.50	5.00	10.00
—Orange label, "Capitol" logo on bottom					
❑ 5112	I Want to Hold Your Hand/I Saw Her Standing There	1978	3.75	7.50	15.00
—Purple label					
❑ 5112	I Want to Hold Your Hand/I Saw Her Standing There	1984	—	2.50	5.00
—20th anniversary reissue; black print on perimeter of label (1964 pressings are white)					
❑ 5112	I Want to Hold Your Hand/I Saw Her Standing There	1994	—	2.50	5.00
—30th anniversary reissue; has "NR-58123" engraved in record's trail-off area					
❑ 5112 [PS]	I Want to Hold Your Hand/I Saw Her Standing There	1964	25.00	50.00	100.00
—Die-cut, crops George Harrison's head in photo					
❑ 5112 [PS]	I Want to Hold Your Hand/I Saw Her Standing There	1964	25.00	50.00	100.00
—Straight cut, shows all of George Harrison's head					
❑ 5112 [PS]	I Want to Hold Your Hand/WMCA Good Guys	1964	500.00	1000.	2000.
—Giveaway from New York radio station with photo of WMCA DJs on rear					
❑ 5112 [PS]	I Want to Hold Your Hand/I Saw Her Standing There	1984	—	3.00	6.00
—Same as 1964 sleeve except has "1984" in small print, and Paul McCartney's cigarette is airbrushed out					
❑ 5112 [PS]	I Want to Hold Your Hand/I Saw Her Standing There	1994	—	2.00	4.00
—Same as 1964 sleeve except "Reg. U.S. Pat. Off." has periods (1964s do not). Also came with a plastic sleeve with a "30th Anniversary" and UPC stickers (add 25%)					
❑ 5150	Can't Buy Me Love/You Can't Do That	1964	7.50	15.00	30.00
—Original: Orange and yellow swirl, without "A Subsidiary Of"... in perimeter label print					
❑ 5150	Can't Buy Me Love/You Can't Do That	1964	2000.	3000.	4000.
—Yellow vinyl (unauthorized); value is conjecture					
❑ 5150	Can't Buy Me Love/You Can't Do That	1964	1000.	1500.	2000.
—Yellow and black vinyl (unauthorized); value is conjecture					
❑ 5150	Can't Buy Me Love/You Can't Do That	1968	12.50	25.00	50.00
—Orange and yellow swirl label with "A Subsidiary Of" in perimeter print					
❑ 5150	Can't Buy Me Love/You Can't Do That	1969	6.25	12.50	25.00
—Red and orange "target" label, dome logo					
❑ 5150	Can't Buy Me Love/You Can't Do That	1969	15.00	30.00	60.00
—Red and orange "target" label, round logo					
❑ 5150	Can't Buy Me Love/You Can't Do That	1976	—	3.00	6.00
—Orange label with "Capitol" at bottom					
❑ 5150	Can't Buy Me Love/You Can't Do That	1978	3.75	7.50	15.00
—Purple label					
❑ 5150 [PS]	Can't Buy Me Love/You Can't Do That	1964	200.00	400.00	800.00
—One of the rarest Beatles picture sleeves. Numerous counterfeits exist; if in doubt, see an expert.					
❑ B-5189	Love Me Do/P.S. I Love You	1982	—	2.50	5.00
—Original: Orange and yellow swirl label, black print					
❑ B-5189	Love Me Do/P.S. I Love You	1983	—	3.00	6.00
—Black label with colorband					
❑ B-5189	Love Me Do/P.S. I Love You	1988	—	2.00	4.00
—Purple label; label has smooth edge					
❑ B-5189 [PS]	Love Me Do/P.S. I Love You	1982	—	2.50	5.00
❑ PB-5189 [DJ]	Love Me Do (same on both sides)	1982	3.75	7.50	15.00
❑ 5222	A Hard Day's Night/I Should Have Known Better	1964	7.50	15.00	30.00
—Original: Orange and yellow swirl, without "A Subsidiary Of"... in perimeter label print; first version credited both "Unart" and "Maclen" as publishers					
❑ 5222	A Hard Day's Night/I Should Have Known Better	1964	7.50	15.00	30.00
—Orange and yellow swirl, without "A Subsidiary Of"... in perimeter label print; second version credited only "Maclen" as publishers					
❑ 5222	A Hard Day's Night/I Should Have Known Better	1968	12.50	25.00	50.00
—Orange and yellow swirl with "A Subsidiary Of"... on perimeter print in white					
❑ 5222	A Hard Day's Night/I Should Have Known Better	1968	25.00	50.00	100.00
—Orange and yellow swirl with "A Subsidiary Of"... on perimeter print in black					
❑ 5222	A Hard Day's Night/I Should Have Known Better	1969	15.00	30.00	60.00
—Red and orange "target" label with Capitol dome logo					
❑ 5222	A Hard Day's Night/I Should Have Known Better	1969	5.00	10.00	20.00
—Red and orange "target" label with Capitol round logo					

Number	Title (A Side/B Side)	Yr	VG	VG+	NM
❑ 5222	A Hard Day's Night/I Should Have Known Better	1976	—	3.00	6.00
—Orange label with "Capitol" at bottom					
❑ 5222	A Hard Day's Night/I Should Have Known Better	1978	3.75	7.50	15.00
—Purple label					
❑ 5222 [PS]	A Hard Day's Night/I Should Have Known Better	1964	25.00	50.00	100.00
❑ 5234	I'll Cry Instead/I'm Happy Just to Dance with You	1964	10.00	20.00	40.00
—Original: Orange and yellow swirl, without "A Subsidiary Of"... in perimeter label print					
❑ 5234	I'll Cry Instead/I'm Happy Just to Dance with You	1968	15.00	30.00	60.00
—Orange and yellow swirl label with "A Subsidiary Of" in perimeter print					
❑ 5234	I'll Cry Instead/I'm Happy Just to Dance with You	1969	17.50	35.00	70.00
—Red and orange "target" label with Capitol dome logo					
❑ 5234	I'll Cry Instead/I'm Happy Just to Dance with You	1969	5.00	10.00	20.00
—Red and orange "target" label with Capitol round logo					
❑ 5234	I'll Cry Instead/I'm Happy Just to Dance with You	1976	—	3.00	6.00
—Orange label with "Capitol" at bottom					
❑ 5234	I'll Cry Instead/I'm Happy Just to Dance with You	1978	3.75	7.50	15.00
—Purple label					
❑ 5234 [PS]	I'll Cry Instead/I'm Happy Just to Dance with You	1964	37.50	75.00	150.00
❑ 5235	And I Love Her/If I Fell	1964	7.50	15.00	30.00
—Original: Orange and yellow swirl, without "A Subsidiary Of"... in perimeter label print; publishers listed as "Unart" and "Maclen"					
❑ 5235	And I Love Her/If I Fell	1964	7.50	15.00	30.00
—Original: Orange and yellow swirl, without "A Subsidiary Of"... in perimeter label print; publishers listed as "Maclen" only					
❑ 5235	And I Love Her/If I Fell	1968	12.50	25.00	50.00
—Orange and yellow swirl with "A Subsidiary Of"... on perimeter print in white					
❑ 5235	And I Love Her/If I Fell	1968	18.75	37.50	75.00
—Orange and yellow swirl with "A Subsidiary Of"... on perimeter print in black					
❑ 5235	And I Love Her/If I Fell	1969	5.00	10.00	20.00
—Red and orange "target" label with Capitol dome logo					
❑ 5235	And I Love Her/If I Fell	1969	15.00	30.00	60.00
—Red and orange "target" label with Capitol round logo					
❑ 5235	And I Love Her/If I Fell	1976	—	3.00	6.00
—Orange label with "Capitol" at bottom					
❑ 5235	And I Love Her/If I Fell	1978	3.75	7.50	15.00
—Purple label					
❑ 5235 [PS]	And I Love Her/If I Fell	1964	30.00	60.00	120.00
❑ 5255	Matchbox/Slow Down	1964	7.50	15.00	30.00
—Original: Orange and yellow swirl, without "A Subsidiary Of"... in perimeter label print					
❑ 5255	Matchbox/Slow Down	1968	12.50	25.00	50.00
—Orange and yellow swirl label with "A Subsidiary Of" in perimeter print					
❑ 5255	Matchbox/Slow Down	1969	15.00	30.00	60.00
—Red and orange "target" label with Capitol dome logo					
❑ 5255	Matchbox/Slow Down	1969	5.00	10.00	20.00
—Red and orange "target" label with Capitol round logo					
❑ 5255	Matchbox/Slow Down	1976	—	3.00	6.00
—Orange label with "Capitol" at bottom					
❑ 5255	Matchbox/Slow Down	1978	3.75	7.50	15.00
—Purple label					
❑ 5255 [PS]	Matchbox/Slow Down	1964	37.50	75.00	150.00
❑ 5327	I Feel Fine/She's a Woman	1964	7.50	15.00	30.00
—Original: Orange and yellow swirl, without "A Subsidiary Of"... in perimeter label print					
❑ 5327	I Feel Fine/She's a Woman	1968	12.50	25.00	50.00
—Orange and yellow swirl label with "A Subsidiary Of" in perimeter print					
❑ 5327	I Feel Fine/She's a Woman	1969	5.00	10.00	20.00
—Red and orange "target" label with Capitol dome logo					
❑ 5327	I Feel Fine/She's a Woman	1969	15.00	30.00	60.00
—Red and orange "target" label with Capitol round logo					
❑ 5327	I Feel Fine/She's a Woman	1976	—	3.00	6.00
—Orange label with "Capitol" at bottom					
❑ 5327	I Feel Fine/She's a Woman	1978	3.75	7.50	15.00
—Purple label					
❑ 5327 [PS]	I Feel Fine/She's a Woman	1964	20.00	40.00	80.00
❑ 5371	Eight Days a Week/I Don't Want to Spoil the Party	1965	7.50	15.00	30.00
—Original: Orange and yellow swirl, without "A Subsidiary Of"... in perimeter label print					
❑ 5371	Eight Days a Week/I Don't Want to Spoil the Party	1968	12.50	25.00	50.00
—Orange and yellow swirl label with "A Subsidiary Of" in perimeter print					
❑ 5371	Eight Days a Week/I Don't Want to Spoil the Party	1969	15.00	30.00	60.00
—Red and orange "target" label with Capitol dome logo					
❑ 5371	Eight Days a Week/I Don't Want to Spoil the Party	1969	5.00	10.00	20.00
—Red and orange "target" label with Capitol round logo					
❑ 5371	Eight Days a Week/I Don't Want to Spoil the Party	1976	—	3.00	6.00
—Orange label with "Capitol" at bottom					
❑ 5371	Eight Days a Week/I Don't Want to Spoil the Party	1978	3.75	7.50	15.00
—Purple label					
❑ 5371 [PS]	Eight Days a Week/I Don't Want to Spoil the Party	1965	6.25	12.50	25.00
—Die-cut sleeve					
❑ 5371 [PS]	Eight Days a Week/I Don't Want to Spoil the Party	1965	18.75	37.50	75.00
—Straight-cut sleeve					
❑ 5407	Ticket to Ride/Yes It Is	1965	7.50	15.00	30.00
—Original: Orange and yellow swirl, without "A Subsidiary Of"... in perimeter label print					
❑ 5407	Ticket to Ride/Yes It Is	1968	12.50	25.00	50.00
—Orange and yellow swirl with "A Subsidiary Of"... on perimeter print in white					
❑ 5407	Ticket to Ride/Yes It Is	1968	25.00	50.00	100.00
—Orange and yellow swirl with "A Subsidiary Of"... on perimeter print in black					
❑ 5407	Ticket to Ride/Yes It Is	1969	15.00	30.00	60.00
—Red and orange "target" label with Capitol dome logo					
❑ 5407	Ticket to Ride/Yes It Is	1969	5.00	10.00	20.00
—Red and orange "target" label with Capitol round logo					
❑ 5407	Ticket to Ride/Yes It Is	1976	—	3.00	6.00
—Orange label with "Capitol" at bottom					
❑ 5407	Ticket to Ride/Yes It Is	1978	3.75	7.50	15.00
—Purple label					
❑ 5407 [PS]	Ticket to Ride/Yes It Is	1965	25.00	50.00	100.00
❑ B-5439 [PS]	Leave My Kitten Alone/Ob-La-Di, Ob-La-Da	1985	12.50	25.00	50.00
—Sleeve for a record that was never released, not even as a promo					
❑ 5476	Help!/I'm Down	1965	7.50	15.00	30.00
—Original: Orange and yellow swirl, without "A Subsidiary Of"... in perimeter label print					
❑ 5476	Help!/I'm Down	1968	12.50	25.00	50.00
—Orange and yellow swirl with "A Subsidiary Of"... on perimeter print in white					

Number	Title (A Side/B Side)	Yr	VG	VG+	NM
❑ 5476	Help!/I'm Down	1968	25.00	50.00	100.00
—Orange and yellow swirl with "A Subsidiary Of"... on perimeter print in black					
❑ 5476	Help!/I'm Down	1969	15.00	30.00	60.00
—Red and orange "target" label with Capitol dome logo					
❑ 5476	Help!/I'm Down	1969	5.00	10.00	20.00
—Red and orange "target" label with Capitol round logo					
❑ 5476	Help!/I'm Down	1976	—	3.00	6.00
—Orange label with "Capitol" at bottom					
❑ 5476	Help!/I'm Down	1978	3.75	7.50	15.00
—Purple label					
❑ 5476 [PS]	Help!/I'm Down	1965	18.75	37.50	75.00
❑ 5498	Yesterday/Act Naturally	1965	7.50	15.00	30.00
—Original: Orange and yellow swirl, without "A Subsidiary Of"... in perimeter label print					
❑ 5498	Yesterday/Act Naturally	1968	12.50	25.00	50.00
—Orange and yellow swirl with "A Subsidiary Of"... on perimeter print in white					
❑ 5498	Yesterday/Act Naturally	1968	25.00	50.00	100.00
—Orange and yellow swirl with "A Subsidiary Of"... on perimeter print in black					
❑ 5498	Yesterday/Act Naturally	1969	15.00	30.00	60.00
—Red and orange "target" label with Capitol dome logo					
❑ 5498	Yesterday/Act Naturally	1969	5.00	10.00	20.00
—Red and orange "target" label with Capitol round logo					
❑ 5498	Yesterday/Act Naturally	1976	—	3.00	6.00
—Orange label with "Capitol" at bottom					
❑ 5498	Yesterday/Act Naturally	1978	3.75	7.50	15.00
—Purple label					
❑ 5498 [PS]	Yesterday/Act Naturally	1965	25.00	50.00	100.00
❑ 5555	We Can Work It Out/Day Tripper	1965	7.50	15.00	30.00
—Original: Orange and yellow swirl, without "A Subsidiary Of"... in perimeter label print					
❑ 5555	We Can Work It Out/Day Tripper	1968	12.50	25.00	50.00
—Orange and yellow swirl label with "A Subsidiary Of" in perimeter print					
❑ 5555	We Can Work It Out/Day Tripper	1969	15.00	30.00	60.00
—Red and orange "target" label with Capitol dome logo					
❑ 5555	We Can Work It Out/Day Tripper	1969	5.00	10.00	20.00
—Red and orange "target" label with Capitol round logo					
❑ 5555	We Can Work It Out/Day Tripper	1969	500.00	1000.	1500.
—Red and white "Starline" label (mispress)					
❑ 5555	We Can Work It Out/Day Tripper	1976	—	3.00	6.00
—Orange label with "Capitol" at bottom					
❑ 5555	We Can Work It Out/Day Tripper	1978	3.75	7.50	15.00
—Purple label					
❑ 5555 [PS]	We Can Work It Out/Day Tripper	1978	15.00	30.00	60.00
❑ 5587	Nowhere Man/What Goes On	1966	6.25	12.50	25.00
—Original: Orange and yellow swirl, without "A Subsidiary Of"... in perimeter label print; composers of B-side listed as "John Lennon-Paul McCartney"					
❑ 5587	Nowhere Man/What Goes On	1966	12.50	25.00	50.00
—Orange and yellow swirl, without "A Subsidiary Of"... in perimeter label print; B-side composers listed as "Lennon-McCartney-Starkey"					
❑ 5587	Nowhere Man/What Goes On	1968	12.50	25.00	50.00
—Orange and yellow swirl label with "A Subsidiary Of" in perimeter print					
❑ 5587	Nowhere Man/What Goes On	1969	15.00	30.00	60.00
—Red and orange "target" label with Capitol dome logo					
❑ 5587	Nowhere Man/What Goes On	1969	5.00	10.00	20.00
—Red and orange "target" label with Capitol round logo					
❑ 5587	Nowhere Man/What Goes On	1976	—	3.00	6.00
—Orange label with "Capitol" at bottom					
❑ 5587	Nowhere Man/What Goes On	1978	3.75	7.50	15.00
—Purple label					
❑ 5587 [PS]	Nowhere Man/What Goes On	1966	10.00	20.00	40.00
❑ B-5624	Twist and Shout/There's a Place	1986	—	2.50	5.00
—Black label with colorband					
❑ B-5624	Twist and Shout/There's a Place	1988	—	2.50	5.00
—Purple label; label has smooth edge					
❑ P-B-5624 [DJ]	Twist and Shout (same on both sides)	1986	3.75	7.50	15.00
❑ 5651	Paperback Writer/Rain	1966	6.25	12.50	25.00
—Original: Orange and yellow swirl, without "A Subsidiary Of"... in perimeter label print					
❑ 5651	Paperback Writer/Rain	1968	12.50	25.00	50.00
—Orange and yellow swirl with "A Subsidiary Of"... on perimeter print in white					
❑ 5651	Paperback Writer/Rain	1968	25.00	50.00	100.00
—Orange and yellow swirl with "A Subsidiary Of"... on perimeter print in black					
❑ 5651	Paperback Writer/Rain	1969	15.00	30.00	60.00
—Red and orange "target" label with Capitol dome logo					
❑ 5651	Paperback Writer/Rain	1969	5.00	10.00	20.00
—Red and orange "target" label with Capitol round logo					
❑ 5651	Paperback Writer/Rain	1976	—	3.00	6.00
—Orange label with "Capitol" at bottom					
❑ 5651	Paperback Writer/Rain	1978	3.75	7.50	15.00
—Purple label					
❑ 5651 [PS]	Paperback Writer/Rain	1966	18.75	37.50	75.00
❑ 5715	Yellow Submarine/Eleanor Rigby	1966	6.25	12.50	25.00
—Original: Orange and yellow swirl, without "A Subsidiary Of"... in perimeter label print; print on perimeter is white					
❑ 5715	Yellow Submarine/Eleanor Rigby	1966	12.50	25.00	50.00
—Orange and yellow swirl, without "A Subsidiary Of"... in perimeter label print; print on perimeter is yellow (mispress)					
❑ 5715	Yellow Submarine/Eleanor Rigby	1968	12.50	25.00	50.00
—Orange and yellow swirl label with "A Subsidiary Of" in perimeter print					
❑ 5715	Yellow Submarine/Eleanor Rigby	1969	5.00	10.00	20.00
—Red and orange "target" label with Capitol dome logo					
❑ 5715	Yellow Submarine/Eleanor Rigby	1969	15.00	30.00	60.00
—Red and orange "target" label with Capitol round logo					
❑ 5715	Yellow Submarine/Eleanor Rigby	1976	—	3.00	6.00
—Orange label with "Capitol" at bottom					
❑ 5715	Yellow Submarine/Eleanor Rigby	1978	3.75	7.50	15.00
—Purple label					
❑ 5715 [PS]	Yellow Submarine/Eleanor Rigby	1966	25.00	50.00	100.00
❑ 5810	Penny Lane/Strawberry Fields Forever	1967	6.25	12.50	25.00
—Original: Orange and yellow swirl, without "A Subsidiary Of"... in perimeter label print; "Penny Lane" time listed as 3:00					

Number	Title (A Side/B Side)	Yr	VG	VG+	NM
❑ 5810	Penny Lane/Strawberry Fields Forever	1967	7.50	15.00	30.00
—Orange and yellow swirl, without "A Subsidiary Of"... in perimeter label print; "Penny Lane" time listed as 2:57					
❑ 5810	Penny Lane/Strawberry Fields Forever	1968	12.50	25.00	50.00
—Orange and yellow swirl label with "A Subsidiary Of" in perimeter print					
❑ 5810	Penny Lane/Strawberry Fields Forever	1969	15.00	30.00	60.00
—Red and orange "target" label with Capitol dome logo					
❑ 5810	Penny Lane/Strawberry Fields Forever	1969	5.00	10.00	20.00
—Red and orange "target" label with Capitol round logo					
❑ 5810	Penny Lane/Strawberry Fields Forever	1976	—	3.00	6.00
—Orange label with "Capitol" at bottom					
❑ 5810	Penny Lane/Strawberry Fields Forever	1978	3.75	7.50	15.00
—Purple label					
❑ 5810 [PS]	Penny Lane/Strawberry Fields Forever	1967	25.00	50.00	100.00
❑ P 5810 [DJ]	Penny Lane/Strawberry Fields Forever	1967	75.00	150.00	300.00
—Light green promo; most copies have an extra trumpet solo at the end of "Penny Lane"					
❑ P 5810 [DJ]	Penny Lane/Strawberry Fields Forever	1967	150.00	300.00	600.00
—Light green promo; a few copies have no trumpet solo at the end of "Penny Lane"					
❑ 5964	All You Need Is Love/Baby, You're a Rich Man	1967	6.25	12.50	25.00
—Original: Orange and yellow swirl, without "A Subsidiary Of"... in perimeter label print					
❑ 5964	All You Need Is Love/Baby, You're a Rich Man	1968	12.50	25.00	50.00
—Orange and yellow swirl label with "A Subsidiary Of" in perimeter print					
❑ 5964	All You Need Is Love/Baby, You're a Rich Man	1969	18.75	37.50	75.00
—Red and orange "target" label with Capitol dome logo					
❑ 5964	All You Need Is Love/Baby, You're a Rich Man	1969	5.00	10.00	20.00
—Red and orange "target" label with Capitol round logo					
❑ 5964	All You Need Is Love/Baby, You're a Rich Man	1976	—	3.00	6.00
—Orange label with "Capitol" at bottom					
❑ 5964	All You Need Is Love/Baby, You're a Rich Man	1978	3.75	7.50	15.00
—Purple label					
❑ 5964 [PS]	All You Need Is Love/Baby, You're a Rich Man	1967	10.00	20.00	40.00
❑ P 5964 [DJ]	All You Need Is Love/Baby, You're a Rich Man	1967	62.50	125.00	250.00
—Light green label promo					
❑ S7-17488	Birthday/Taxman	1994	12.50	25.00	50.00
—Black vinyl "error" pressing					
❑ S7-17488	Birthday/Taxman	1994	—	2.00	4.00
—Green vinyl					
❑ S7-17688	She Loves You/I'll Get You	1994	—	2.00	4.00
—Red vinyl					
❑ S7-17689	I Want to Hold Your Hand/This Boy	1994	—	2.00	4.00
—Clear vinyl					
❑ S7-17690	Can't Buy Me Love/You Can't Do That	1994	—	2.00	4.00
—Gren vinyl					
❑ S7-17691	Help!/I'm Down	1994	—	2.00	4.00
—White vinyl					
❑ S7-17692	A Hard Day's Night/Things We Said Today	1994	—	2.00	4.00
—White vinyl					
❑ S7-17693	All You Need Is Love/Baby You're a Rich Man	1994	—	2.00	4.00
—Pink vinyl					
❑ S7-17694	Hey Jude/Revolution	1994	—	2.00	4.00
—Blue vinyl					
❑ S7-17695	Let It Be/You Know My Name (Look Up My Number)	1994	—	2.00	4.00
—Yellow vinyl					
❑ S7-17696	Yellow Submarine/Eleanor Rigby	1994	—	2.00	4.00
—Yellow vinyl					
❑ S7-17697	Strawberry Fields Forever/Penny Lane	1994	—	2.00	4.00
—Red vinyl					
❑ S7-17698	Something/Come Together	1994	—	2.00	4.00
—Blue vinyl					
❑ S7-17699	Twist and Shout/There's a Place	1994	—	2.00	4.00
—Pink vinyl					
❑ S7-17700	Here Comes the Sun/Octopus's Garden	1994	—	2.00	4.00
—Gold/orange vinyl					
❑ S7-17701	Sgt. Pepper's Lonely Hearts Club Band-With a Little Help from My Friends/A Day in the Life	1994	—	2.00	4.00
—Clear vinyl					
❑ S7-18888	Norwegian Wood/If I Needed Someone	1995	12.50	25.00	50.00
—Green vinyl; 1,000 pressed, given by Collectors' Choice Music to buyers of Beatles reissue LPs					
❑ S7-18889	You've Got to Hide Your Love Away/I've Just Seen a Face	1996	—	2.00	4.00
—Gold/orange vinyl					
❑ S7-18890	Magical Mystery Tour/The Fool on the Hill	1996	—	2.00	4.00
—Yellow vinyl					
❑ S7-18891	Across the Universe/Two of Us	1996	—	2.00	4.00
—Clear vinyl					
❑ S7-18892	While My Guitar Gently Weeps/Blackbird	1996	—	2.00	4.00
—Blue vinyl					
❑ S7-18893	It's All Too Much/Only a Northern Song	1996	—	2.00	4.00
—Blue vinyl					
❑ S7-18894	Nowhere Man/What Goes On	1996	—	2.00	4.00
—Green vinyl					
❑ S7-18895	We Can Work It Out/Day Tripper	1996	—	2.00	4.00
—Pink vinyl					
❑ S7-18896	Lucy in the Sky with Diamonds/When I'm 64	1996	—	2.00	4.00
—Red vinyl					
❑ S7-18897	Here, There and Everywhere/Good Day Sunshine	1996	—	2.00	4.00
—Yellow vinyl					
❑ S7-18898	The Long and Winding Road/For You Blue	1996	—	2.00	4.00
—Blue vinyl					
❑ S7-18899	Got to Get You Into My Life/Helter Skelter	1996	—	2.00	4.00
—Gold/orange vinyl					
❑ S7-18900	Ob-La-Di, Ob-La-Da/Julia	1996	—	2.00	4.00
—Clear vinyl					
❑ S7-18901	Yesterday/Act Naturally	1996	—	2.00	4.00
—Pink vinyl					
❑ S7-18902	Paperback Writer/Rain	1996	—	2.00	4.00
—Red vinyl					
❑ S7-19341	Norwegian Wood (This Bird Has Flown)/If I Needed Someone	1996	—	—	3.00

Number	Title (A Side/B Side)	Yr	VG	VG+	NM
❑ S7-56785	Love Me Do/P.S. I Love You	1992	—	2.00	4.00
❑ S7-56785	Love Me Do/P.S. I Love You	1992	7.50	15.00	30.00
—Small pressing on red vinyl "by mistake"					
❑ 72133	Roll Over Beethoven/Please Mister Postman	1964	12.50	25.00	50.00
—Orange and yellow swirl; Canadian release that was heavily imported to the U.S.					
❑ 72144	All My Loving/This Boy	1964	12.50	25.00	50.00
—Orange and yellow swirl; Canadian release that was heavily imported to the U.S.					
❑ 72144	All My Loving/This Boy	1971	25.00	50.00	100.00
—Canadian number with U.S. labels (red and orange "target" label)					
❑ 7PRO-79551/2 [DJ]	Love Me Do/P.S. I Love You	1992	6.25	12.50	25.00
❑ 7PRO-79551/2 [PS]	Love Me Do/P.S. I Love You	1992	6.25	12.50	25.00
CAPITOL STARLINE					
❑ 6061	Twist and Shout/There's a Place	1965	30.00	60.00	120.00
—Green swirl label					
❑ 6062	Love Me Do/P.S. I Love You	1965	30.00	60.00	120.00
—Green swirl label					
❑ 6063	Please Please Me/From Me to You	1965	30.00	60.00	120.00
—Green swirl label					
❑ 6064	Do You Want to Know a Secret/Thank You Girl	1965	30.00	60.00	120.00
—Green swirl label					
❑ 6065	Roll Over Beethoven/Misery	1965	30.00	60.00	120.00
—Green swirl label					
❑ 6065	Roll Over Beethoven/Misery	1971	7.50	15.00	30.00
—Red and orange "target" label					
❑ 6066	Boys/Kansas City	1965	20.00	40.00	80.00
—Green swirl label					
❑ 6066	Boys/Kansas City	1971	7.50	15.00	30.00
—Red and orange "target" label					
❑ 6278	I Want to Hold Your Hand/I Saw Her Standing There	1981	5.00	10.00	20.00
—Originals have blue labels					
❑ 6279	Can't Buy Me Love/You Can't Do That	1981	2.00	4.00	8.00
—Originals have blue labels					
❑ 6281	A Hard Day's Night/I Should Have Known Better	1981	2.00	4.00	8.00
—Originals have blue labels					
❑ 6282	I'll Cry Instead/I'm Happy Just to Dance with You	1981	2.00	4.00	8.00
—Originals have blue labels					
❑ 6283	And I Love Her/If I Fell	1981	2.00	4.00	8.00
—Originals have blue labels					
❑ 6284	Matchbox/Slow Down	1981	2.00	4.00	8.00
—Originals have blue labels					
❑ 6286	I Feel Fine/She's a Woman	1981	2.00	4.00	8.00
—Originals have blue labels					
❑ 6287	Eight Days a Week/I Don't Want to Spoil the Party	1981	2.00	4.00	8.00
—Originals have blue labels					
❑ 6288	Ticket to Ride/Yes It Is	1981	2.00	4.00	8.00
—Originals have blue labels					
❑ 6290	Help!/I'm Down	1981	2.00	4.00	8.00
—Originals have blue labels					
❑ 6291	Yesterday/Act Naturally	1981	2.00	4.00	8.00
—Originals have blue labels					
❑ 6293	We Can Work It Out/Day Tripper	1981	2.00	4.00	8.00
—Originals have blue labels					
❑ 6294	Nowhere Man/What Goes On	1981	2.00	4.00	8.00
—Originals have blue labels					
❑ 6296	Paperback Writer/Rain	1981	2.00	4.00	8.00
—Originals have blue labels					
❑ 6297	Yellow Submarine/Eleanor Rigby	1981	2.00	4.00	8.00
—Originals have blue labels					
❑ 6299	Penny Lane/Strawberry Fields Forever	1981	2.00	4.00	8.00
—Originals have blue labels					
❑ 6300	All You Need Is Love/Baby You're a Rich Man	1981	2.00	4.00	8.00
—Originals have blue labels					
CAPITOL/EVATONE					
❑ 420826cs	All My Loving/You've Got to Hide Your Love Away	1982	2.50	5.00	10.00
—Flexi-disc issued as giveaway by The Musicland Group; "Musicland" version					
❑ 420826cs	All My Loving/You've Got to Hide Your Love Away	1982	5.00	10.00	20.00
—Flexi-disc issued as giveaway by The Musicland Group; "Discount" version					
❑ 420826cs	All My Loving/You've Got to Hide Your Love Away	1982	6.25	12.50	25.00
—Flexi-disc issued as giveaway by The Musicland Group; "Sam Goody" version					
❑ 420827cs	Magical Mystery Tour/Here Comes the Sun	1982	2.50	5.00	10.00
—Flexi-disc issued as giveaway by The Musicland Group; "Musicland" version					
❑ 420827cs	Magical Mystery Tour/Here Comes the Sun	1982	5.00	10.00	20.00
—Flexi-disc issued as giveaway by The Musicland Group; "Discount" version					
❑ 420827cs	Magical Mystery Tour/Here Comes the Sun	1982	6.25	12.50	25.00
—Flexi-disc issued as giveaway by The Musicland Group; "Sam Goody" version					
❑ 420828cs	Rocky Raccoon/Why Don't We Do It in the Road?	1982	2.50	5.00	10.00
—Flexi-disc issued as giveaway by The Musicland Group; "Musicland" version					
❑ 420828cs	Rocky Raccoon/Why Don't We Do It in the Road?	1982	5.00	10.00	20.00
—Flexi-disc issued as giveaway by The Musicland Group; "Discount" version					
❑ 420828cs	Rocky Raccoon/Why Don't We Do It in the Road?	1982	6.25	12.50	25.00
—Flexi-disc issued as giveaway by The Musicland Group; "Sam Goody" version					
❑ 830771 X	Till There Was You/Three Cool Cats	1983	—	3.00	6.00
—Flexi-disc issued as giveaway with a book					
❑ 1214825cs	German Medley	1983	15.00	30.00	60.00
—Flexi-disc given away by House of Guitars in New York					
CICADELIC/BIODISC					
❑ 001	A Hard Day's Night Open End Interview	1990	3.75	7.50	15.00
—Limited edition of 700; lower numbers increase value substantially					
❑ 001	A Hard Day's Night Open End Interview	1990	7.50	15.00	30.00
—"Records Etc." pressing					
❑ 002	Help! Open End Interview	1990	—	2.50	5.00
❑ 002 [PS]	Help! Open End Interview	1990	—	2.50	5.00
COLLECTABLES					
❑ 1501	I'm Gonna Sit Right Down and Cry Over You/Roll Over Beethoven	1982	—	—	3.00
❑ 1501 [PS]	I'm Gonna Sit Right Down and Cry Over You/Roll Over Beethoven	1982	—	—	3.00
❑ 1502	Hippy Hippy Shake/Sweet Little Sixteen	1982	—	—	3.00
❑ 1502 [PS]	Hippy Hippy Shake/Sweet Little Sixteen	1982	—	—	3.00
❑ 1503	Lend Me Your Comb/Your Feets Too Big	1982	—	—	3.00
❑ 1503 [PS]	Lend Me Your Comb/Your Feets Too Big	1982	—	—	3.00
❑ 1504	Where Have You Been All My Life/Mr. Moonlight	1982	—	—	3.00
❑ 1504 [PS]	Where Have You Been All My Life/Mr. Moonlight	1982	—	—	3.00
❑ 1505	A Taste of Honey/Besame Mucho	1982	—	—	3.00
❑ 1505 [PS]	A Taste of Honey/Besame Mucho	1982	—	—	3.00
❑ 1506	Till There Was You/Everybody's Trying to Be My Baby	1982	—	—	3.00
❑ 1506 [PS]	Till There Was You/Everybody's Trying to Be My Baby	1982	—	—	3.00
❑ 1507	Kansas City-Hey Hey Hey Hey/Ain't Nothing Shakin Like the Leaves on a Tree	1982	—	—	3.00
❑ 1507 [PS]	Kansas City-Hey Hey Hey Hey/Ain't Nothing Shakin Like the Leaves on a Tree	1982	—	—	3.00
❑ 1508	To Know Her Is To Love Her/Little Queenie	1982	—	—	3.00
❑ 1508 [PS]	To Know Her Is To Love Her/Little Queenie	1982	—	—	3.00
❑ 1509	Falling in Love Again/Sheila	1982	—	—	3.00
❑ 1509 [PS]	Falling in Love Again/Sheila	1982	—	—	3.00
❑ 1510	Be-Bop-a-Lula/Hallelujah I Love Her So	1982	—	—	3.00
❑ 1510 [PS]	Be-Bop-a-Lula/Hallelujah I Love Her So	1982	—	—	3.00
❑ 1511	Red Sails in the Sunset/Matchbox	1982	—	—	3.00
❑ 1511 [PS]	Red Sails in the Sunset/Matchbox	1982	—	—	3.00
❑ 1512	Talkin' Bout You/Shimmy Shake	1982	—	—	3.00
❑ 1512 [PS]	Talkin' Bout You/Shimmy Shake	1982	—	—	3.00
❑ 1513	Long Tall Sally/I Remember You	1982	—	—	3.00
❑ 1513 [PS]	Long Tall Sally/I Remember You	1982	—	—	3.00
❑ 1514	Ask Me Why/Twist and Shout	1982	—	—	3.00
❑ 1514 [PS]	Ask Me Why/Twist and Shout	1982	—	—	3.00
❑ 1515	I Saw Her Standing There/Can't Help It "Blue Angel"	1982	—	—	3.00
—B-side is actually "Reminiscing"					
❑ 1515 [PS]	I Saw Her Standing There/Can't Help It "Blue Angel"	1982	—	—	3.00
❑ 1516	I'll Try Anyway/I Don't Know Why I Do (I Just Do)	1987	2.50	5.00	10.00
—Despite label credit to The Beatles, both are Peter Best recordings					
❑ 1517	She's Not the Only Girl in Town/More Than I Need Myself	1987	2.50	5.00	10.00
—Despite label credit to The Beatles, both are Peter Best recordings					
❑ 1518	I'll Have Everything Too/I'm Checking Out Now Baby	1987	2.50	5.00	10.00
—Despite label credit to The Beatles, both are Peter Best recordings					
❑ 1519	How'd You Get to Know Her Name/If You Can't Get Her	1987	2.50	5.00	10.00
—Despite label credit to The Beatles, both are Peter Best recordings					
❑ 1520	Cry for a Shadow/Rock and Roll Music	1987	—	2.50	5.00
—Despite label credit to The Beatles, B-side is a Peter Best recording					
❑ 1521	Let's Dance/If You Love Me Baby	1987	—	3.00	6.00
—Despite label credit to The Beatles, A-side is a Tony Sheridan solo recording					
❑ 1522	What'd I Say/Sweet Georgia Brown	1987	—	3.00	6.00
—Despite label credit to The Beatles, A-side is a Tony Sheridan solo recording					
❑ 1523	Ruby Baby/Ya Ya	1987	—	3.00	6.00
—Despite label credit to The Beatles, both are by Tony Sheridan without the Fab Four					
❑ 1524	Why/I'll Try Anyway	1987	—	3.00	6.00
—Despite label credit to The Beatles, B-side is a Peter Best recording					
DECCA					
❑ 31382	My Bonnie/The Saints	1962	7500.	11250.	15000.
—By "Tony Sheridan and the Beat Brothers"; black label with color bars (all-black label with star under "Decca" should be a counterfeit)					
❑ 31382 [DJ]	My Bonnie/The Saints	1962	1000.	2000.	3000.
—By "Tony Sheridan and the Beat Brothers"; pink label, star on label under "Decca"					
EVA-TONE					
❑ 830771X [DJ]	Til There Was You/Three Cool Cats (both on same side)	1983	—	3.00	6.00
—Red plastic flexidisc; issued as giveaway with a Beatles price guide					
MGM					
❑ 13213	My Bonnie (My Bonnie Lies Over the Ocean)/The Saints (When the Saints Go Marching In)	1964	10.00	20.00	40.00
—The Beatles with Tony Sheridan; no reference to LP on label					
❑ 13213	My Bonnie (My Bonnie Lies Over the Ocean)/The Saints (When the Saints Go Marching In)	1964	12.50	25.00	50.00
—The Beatles with Tony Sheridan; LP number on label					
❑ 13213 [DJ]	My Bonnie (My Bonnie Lies Over the Ocean)/The Saints (When the Saints Go Marching In)	1964	75.00	150.00	300.00
—The Beatles with Tony Sheridan					
❑ 13213 [PS]	My Bonnie (My Bonnie Lies Over the Ocean)/The Saints (When the Saints Go Marching In)	1964	30.00	60.00	120.00
—The Beatles with Tony Sheridan					
❑ 13227	Why/Cry for a Shadow	1964	37.50	75.00	150.00
—The Beatles with Tony Sheridan					
❑ 13227 [DJ]	Why/Cry for a Shadow	1964	62.50	125.00	250.00
—The Beatles with Tony Sheridan					
❑ 13227 [PS]	Why/Cry for a Shadow	1964	100.00	200.00	400.00
—The Beatles with Tony Sheridan					
OLDIES 45					
❑ #149	Do You Want to Know a Secret/Thank You Girl	1965	3.75	7.50	15.00
❑ #150	Please Please Me/From Me to You	1965	3.75	7.50	15.00
❑ #151	Love Me Do/P.S. I Love You	1965	3.75	7.50	15.00
❑ #152	Twist and Shout/There's a Place	1965	3.75	7.50	15.00
SWAN					
❑ 4152	She Loves You/I'll Get You	1963	150.00	300.00	600.00
—Semi-glossy white label/red print; "Don't Drop Out" not on label					
❑ 4152	She Loves You/I'll Get You	1963	162.50	325.00	650.00
—Flat white label/red print, "Don't Drop Out" not on label					
❑ 4152	She Loves You/I'll Get You	1963	162.50	325.00	650.00
—Semi-glossy white label/red print, "Don't Drop Out" on label					
❑ 4152	She Loves You/I'll Get You	1963	150.00	300.00	600.00
—Semi-glossy white label/blue printing					
❑ 4152	She Loves You/I'll Get You	1964	10.00	20.00	40.00
—Black label, silver print, "Don't Drop Out" not on label					
❑ 4152	She Loves You/I'll Get You	1964	7.50	15.00	30.00
—Black label, silver print, "Don't Drop Out" on label					

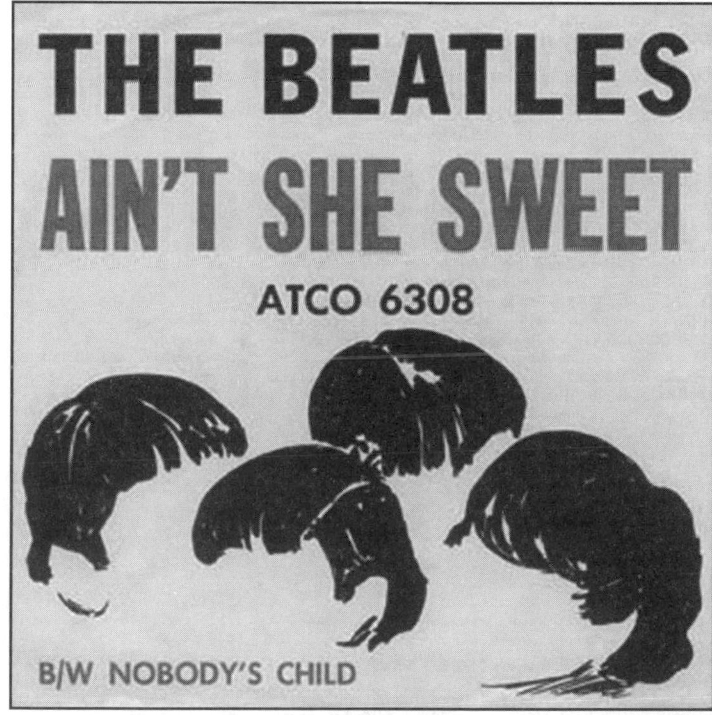

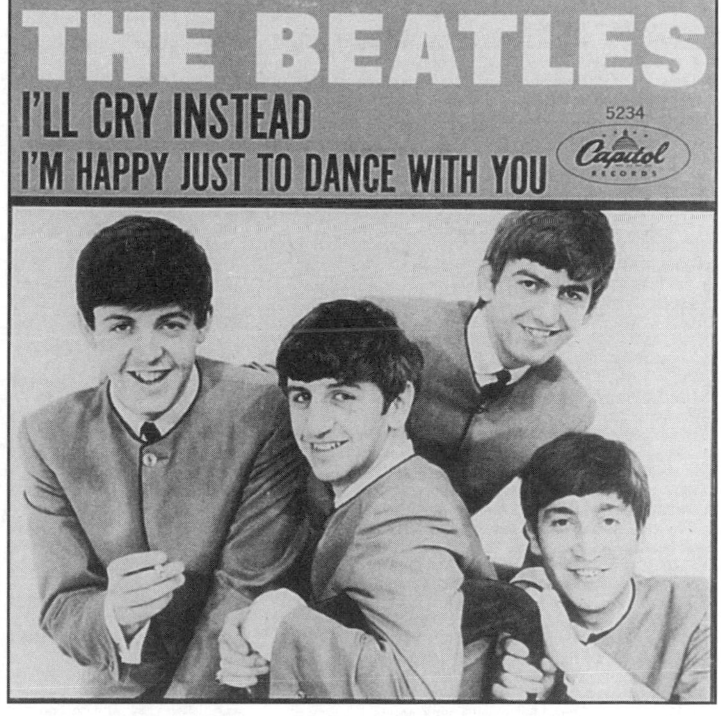

As the success of *The Beatles 1* indicates, the Fab Four continues to fascinate, even today. And their original records and sleeves are as collectible as ever. (Top left) The very first U.S. record to include the Beatles was this Decca single of "My Bonnie," which was credited to Tony Sheridan and the Beat Brothers. Copies in VG to VG-plus condition have been known to fetch $10,000 or more. (Top right) One of the rarest of all Beatles records is this mysterious promo for "Anna." Issued during Vee Jay's Beatle frenzy of 1964, it may have been meant to see if radio would pick it up as a hit for single release. Or it may have been serviced to make "Anna," which was on the Vee Jay EP, easier to play. Whatever, it's so rare that it almost never comes up for sale, so the $10,000 we list for a near-mint copy is probably conservative. (Bottom left) Authentic copies of "Ain't She Sweet," one of the Beatles' rarest picture sleeves, have bluish letters on the title words. They also have a straight cut across the top - curved cut "Ain't She Sweet" sleeves are fakes. (Bottom right) One of the rarest Capitol picture sleeves, from "I'll Cry Instead," is yet another recycling of the same photo used on "I Want to Hold Your Hand" and "Can't Buy Me Love."

Number	Title (A Side/B Side)	Yr	VG	VG+	NM
❑ 4152	She Loves You/I'll Get You	1964	12.50	25.00	50.00
—Black label, silver print, "Produced by George Martin" on both labels					
❑ 4152	She Loves You/I'll Get You	1964	12.50	25.00	50.00
—Black label, silver print, "Produced by George Martin" on only one label					
❑ 4152	She Loves You/I'll Get You	196?	5.00	10.00	20.00
—Black label, silver print, "Don't Drop Out" not on label, smaller numbers in trailoff area					
❑ 4152	She Loves You/I'll Get You	196?	12.50	25.00	50.00
—White label, red or maroon print, same as above					
❑ 4152 [DJ]	She Loves You/I'll Get You	1963	125.00	250.00	500.00
—Thick print, no "Don't Drop Out" on label					
❑ 4152 [DJ]	She Loves You/I'll Get You	1963	112.50	225.00	450.00
—Thin print, "Don't Drop Out" on label					
❑ 4152 [DJ]	She Loves You/I'll Get You	1963	125.00	250.00	500.00
—Flat white label, no "Don't Drop Out" on label					
❑ 4152 [DJ]	I'll Get You (one-sided)	1964	200.00	400.00	600.00
❑ 4152 [PS]	She Loves You/I'll Get You	1964	30.00	60.00	120.00
❑ 4182	Sie Liebt Dich (She Loves You)/I'll Get You	1964	37.50	75.00	150.00
—White label, "Sie Liebt Dich (She Loves You)" on one line					
❑ 4182	Sie Liebt Dich (She Loves You)/I'll Get You	1964	37.50	75.00	150.00
—White label, "(She Loves You)" under "Sie Liebt Dich," narrow print					
❑ 4182	Sie Liebt Dich (She Loves You)/I'll Get You	1964	37.50	75.00	150.00
—White label, "(She Loves You)" under "Sie Liebt Dich," wide red print					
❑ 4182	Sie Liebt Dich (She Loves You)/I'll Get You	1964	43.75	87.50	175.00
—White label, "(She Loves You)" under "Sie Liebt Dich," wide orange print					
❑ 4182 [DJ]	Sie Liebt Dich (She Loves You)/I'll Get You	1964	100.00	200.00	400.00
—White label, "(She Loves You)" under "Sie Liebt Dich"					
❑ 4182 [DJ]	Sie Liebt Dich (She Loves You)/I'll Get You	1964	112.50	225.00	450.00
—White label, "Sie Liebt Dich (She Loves You)" on one line					

TOLLIE

Number	Title (A Side/B Side)	Yr	VG	VG+	NM
❑ 9001	Twist and Shout/There's a Place	1964	12.50	25.00	50.00
—Yellow label, green print, "tollie" lowercase					
❑ 9001	Twist and Shout/There's a Place	1964	12.50	25.00	50.00
—Yellow label, black print, "TOLLIE" stands alone					
❑ 9001	Twist and Shout/There's a Place	1964	12.50	25.00	50.00
—Yellow label, black print, black "tollie" in box					
❑ 9001	Twist and Shout/There's a Place	1964	15.00	30.00	60.00
—Yellow label, black print, purple "tollie" in box					
❑ 9001	Twist and Shout/There's a Place	1964	12.50	25.00	50.00
—Yellow label, black print, black "TOLLIE" in thin box					
❑ 9001	Twist and Shout/There's a Place	1964	18.75	37.50	75.00
—Yellow label, black print, "TOLLIE" in brackets					
❑ 9001	Twist and Shout/There's a Place	1964	15.00	30.00	60.00
—Yellow label, blue print					
❑ 9001	Twist and Shout/There's a Place	1964	20.00	40.00	80.00
—Yellow label, purple print					
❑ 9001	Twist and Shout/There's a Place	1964	20.00	40.00	80.00
—Yellow label, green print, "TOLLIE" uppercase					
❑ 9001	Twist and Shout/There's a Place	1964	15.00	30.00	60.00
—Black label, silver print					
❑ 9008	Love Me Do/P.S. I Love You	1964	12.50	25.00	50.00
—Yellow label, black print (any logo or print variation)					
❑ 9008	Love Me Do/P.S. I Love You	1964	12.50	25.00	50.00
—Yellow label, blue/green print					
❑ 9008	Love Me Do/P.S. I Love You	1964	15.00	30.00	60.00
—Black label, silver print					
❑ 9008 [DJ]	Love Me Do/P.S. I Love You	1964	100.00	200.00	400.00
❑ 9008 [PS]	Love Me Do/P.S. I Love You	1964	37.50	75.00	150.00

UNITED ARTISTS

Number	Title (A Side/B Side)	Yr	VG	VG+	NM
❑ SP-2357 [DJ]	A Hard Day's Night Theatre Lobby Spot	1964	500.00	1000.	1500.
❑ UAEP 10029 [DJ]	A Hard Day's Night Open End Interview	1964	500.00	1000.	1500.
❑ ULP-42370	Let It Be Radio Spots	1970	400.00	800.00	1200.

VEE JAY

Number	Title (A Side/B Side)	Yr	VG	VG+	NM
❑ (no #) [PS]	We Wish You a Merry Christmas and a Happy New Year	1964	20.00	40.00	80.00
—Used with any Vee Jay or Tollie Beatles single in 1964-65 holiday season					
❑ Spec. DJ No. 8	Ask Me Why/Anna	1964?	5000.	7500.	10000.
—One of the more controversial items in Beatles collecting, but it is nonetheless authentic					
❑ 498	Please Please Me/Ask Me Why	1963	800.00	1200.	1600.
—Misspelled "The Beattles"; number is "#498"					
❑ 498	Please Please Me/Ask Me Why	1963	750.00	1125.	1500.
—Misspelled "The Beattles"; number is "VJ 498"					
❑ 498	Please Please Me/Ask Me Why	1963	800.00	1200.	1600.
—Correct spelling; number is "#498"					
❑ 498	Please Please Me/Ask Me Why	1963	300.00	600.00	900.00
—Correct spelling; number is "VJ 498"; thick print					
❑ 498	Please Please Me/Ask Me Why	1963	1000.	1500.	2000.
—Correct spelling; number is "VJ 498"; brackets label					
❑ 498 [DJ]	Please Please Me/Ask Me Why	1963	550.00	825.00	1100.
—Misspelled "The Beattles"					
❑ 522	From Me to You/Thank You Girl	1963	150.00	300.00	600.00
—Black rainbow label; "Vee Jay" in oval					
❑ 522	From Me to You/Thank You Girl	1963	300.00	600.00	900.00
—Black rainbow label; "VJ" in brackets					
❑ 522	From Me to You/Thank You Girl	1963	200.00	400.00	800.00
—Plain black label					
❑ 522 [DJ]	From Me to You/Thank You Girl	1963	125.00	250.00	500.00
❑ 581	Please Please Me/From Me to You	1964	12.50	25.00	50.00
—Black rainbow label, oval logo					
❑ 581	Please Please Me/From Me to You	1964	11.25	22.50	45.00
—Plain black label with two horizontal lines					
❑ 581	Please Please Me/From Me to You	1964	18.75	37.50	75.00
—Plain black label, brackets logo					
❑ 581	Please Please Me/From Me to You	1964	18.75	37.50	75.00
—Yellow label					
❑ 581	Please Please Me/From Me to You	1964	40.00	80.00	160.00
—White label					
❑ 581	Please Please Me/From Me to You	1964	62.50	125.00	250.00
—Purple label					
❑ 581	Please Please Me/From Me to You	1964	15.00	30.00	60.00
—Plain black label, "VEE JAY" stands alone					
❑ 581	Please Please Me/From Me to You	1964	16.25	32.50	65.00
—Plain black label, "VJ" stands alone					
❑ 581	Please Please Me/From Me to You	1964	15.00	30.00	60.00
—Black rainbow label, brackets logo					
❑ 581	Please Please Me/From Me to You	1964	15.00	30.00	60.00
—Plain black label, oval logo					
❑ 581 [DJ]	Please Please Me/From Me to You	1964	200.00	400.00	600.00
—White label, blue print; "Promotional Copy" on label					
❑ 581 [DJ]	Please Please Me/From Me to You	1964	300.00	600.00	900.00
—White label, blue print; no "Promotional Copy" on label					
❑ 581 [PS]	Please Please Me/From Me to You	1964	1250.	1875.	2500.
—Special "The Record That Started Beatlemania" promo-only sleeve					
❑ 581 [PS]	Please Please Me/From Me to You	1964	125.00	250.00	500.00
❑ 587	Do You Want to Know a Secret/Thank You Girl	1964	12.50	25.00	50.00
—Black rainbow label, oval logo					
❑ 587	Do You Want to Know a Secret/Thank You Girl	1964	16.25	32.50	65.00
—Plain black label; "Vee Jay" in oval					
❑ 587	Do You Want to Know a Secret/Thank You Girl	1964	16.25	32.50	65.00
—Plain black label; "VJ" in brackets					
❑ 587	Do You Want to Know a Secret/Thank You Girl	1964	16.25	32.50	65.00
—Plain black label; "VJ" stands alone					
❑ 587	Do You Want to Know a Secret/Thank You Girl	1964	12.50	25.00	50.00
—Plain black label; "VEE JAY" stands alone					
❑ 587	Do You Want to Know a Secret/Thank You Girl	1964	11.25	22.50	45.00
—Plain black label with two horizontal lines; "VJ" in brackets					
❑ 587	Do You Want to Know a Secret/Thank You Girl	1964	16.25	32.50	65.00
—Yellow label					
❑ 587	Do You Want to Know a Secret/Thank You Girl	1964	10.00	20.00	40.00
—Black rainbow label, brackets logo					
❑ 587 [DJ]	Do You Want to Know a Secret/Thank You Girl	1964	150.00	300.00	600.00
❑ 587 [PS]	Do You Want to Know a Secret/Thank You Girl	1964	30.00	60.00	120.00

(NO LABEL)

Number	Title (A Side/B Side)	Yr	VG	VG+	NM
❑ MBRF-55551	Decade	1974	—	—	—
—A clever bootleg of radio spots for the Beatles' back catalog, compiled without authorization by two former Capitol employees.					

7-Inch Extended Plays

CAPITOL

Number	Title (A Side/B Side)	Yr	VG	VG+	NM
❑ SXA-2047 [PS]	Meet the Beatles	1964	150.00	300.00	600.00
—With all jukebox title strips intact (deduct 33 percent if missing, deduct less if material is there but not intact)					
❑ SXA-2047 [S]	(contents unknown)	1964	100.00	200.00	400.00
—33 1/3 rpm, small hole jukebox edition					
❑ SXA-2080 [PS]	The Beatles' Second Album	1964	150.00	300.00	600.00
—With all jukebox title strips intact (deduct 33 percent if missing, deduct less if material is there but not intact)					
❑ SXA-2080 [S]	(contents unknown)	1964	100.00	200.00	400.00
—33 1/3 rpm, small hole jukebox edition					
❑ SXA-2108 [PS]	Something New	1964	150.00	300.00	600.00
—With all jukebox title strips intact (deduct 33 percent if missing, deduct less if material is there but not intact)					
❑ SXA-2108 [S]	(contents unknown)	1964	100.00	200.00	400.00
—33 1/3 rpm, small hole jukebox edition					
❑ EAP 1-2121	Roll Over Beethoven/This Boy//All My Loving/ Please Mr. Postman	1964	25.00	50.00	100.00
❑ EAP 1-2121 [PS]	Four by the Beatles	1964	75.00	150.00	300.00
❑ PRO-2548/9 [DJ]	Open End Interview with the Beatles	1964	200.00	400.00	800.00
—33 1/3 rpm, small hole. Authentic copies have colorband along outside of label.					
❑ PRO-2548/9 [PS]	Open End Interview with the Beatles	1964	250.00	500.00	1000.
—Contains script for interview. Authentic copies are glossy and have a die-cut thumb tab.					
❑ PRO-2598/9 [DJ]	The Beatles Second Album Open End Interview	1964	200.00	400.00	800.00
—33 1/3 rpm, small hole; interview plus three songs from the LP					
❑ PRO-2598/9 [PS]	The Beatles Second Album Open End Interview	1964	250.00	500.00	1000.
—Contains script for interview					
❑ R-5365	Honey Don't/I'm a Loser//Mr. Moonlight/ Everybody's Trying to Be My Baby	1965	20.00	40.00	80.00
❑ R-5365 [PS]	4-By the Beatles	1965	50.00	100.00	200.00

POLYDOR

Number	Title (A Side/B Side)	Yr	VG	VG+	NM
❑ PRO 1113-7 [DJ]	Ain't She Sweet/Cry for a Shadow//My Bonnie/ The Saints	1994	6.25	12.50	25.00
❑ PRO 1113-7 [PS]	Backbeat	1994	6.25	12.50	25.00
—Picture sleeve for above sampler					

VEE JAY

Number	Title (A Side/B Side)	Yr	VG	VG+	NM
❑ 1-903	Misery/Taste of Honey//Ask Me Why/Anna	1964	10.00	20.00	40.00
—Black rainbow label, oval logo					
❑ 1-903	Misery/Taste of Honey//Ask Me Why/Anna	1964	31.25	62.50	125.00
—Plain black label, oval logo					
❑ 1-903	Misery/Taste of Honey//Ask Me Why/Anna	1964	31.25	62.50	125.00
—Black rainbow label, brackets logo, "Ask Me Why" in much larger print					
❑ 1-903	Misery/Taste of Honey//Ask Me Why/Anna	1964	22.50	45.00	90.00
—Black rainbow label, brackets logo, all titles the same size					
❑ 1-903	Misery/Taste of Honey//Ask Me Why/Anna	1964	50.00	100.00	200.00
—Plain black label, brackets logo					
❑ 1-903	Misery/Taste of Honey//Ask Me Why/Anna	1964	37.50	75.00	150.00
—Plain black label, "VEE JAY" stands alone					
❑ 1-903 [DJ]	Misery/Taste of Honey//Ask Me Why/Anna	1964	100.00	200.00	400.00
—White and blue label, all titles the same size					
❑ 1-903 [DJ]	Misery/Taste of Honey//Ask Me Why/Anna	1964	75.00	150.00	300.00
—White and blue label, "Ask Me Why" in much larger print					
❑ 1-903 [PS]	Souvenir of Their Visit to America	1964	15.00	30.00	60.00
—Cardboard sleeve					
❑ 1-903 [PS]	Souvenir of Their Visit to America	1964	4000.	6000.	8000.
—"Ask Me Why/The Beatles" plugged on promo-only sleeve					

BEATSTALKERS, THE

PRESS

Number	Title (A Side/B Side)	Yr	VG	VG+	NM
❑ 5001	Left, Right, Left/Get a Better Hold On	1966	3.75	7.50	15.00

BEAU, BILLY

DOT

Number	Title (A Side/B Side)	Yr	VG	VG+	NM
❑ 16281	Hey Daddy (I'm Gonna Tell Santa On You)/ Santa's Coffee	1961	10.00	20.00	40.00

BEAU BRUMMELS, THE

Also see SAL VALENTINO.

AUTUMN

Number	Title (A Side/B Side)	Yr	VG	VG+	NM
❑ 8	Laugh, Laugh/Still in Love with You Baby	1965	3.75	7.50	15.00
—White label					
❑ 8	Laugh, Laugh/Still in Love with You Baby	1965	3.00	6.00	12.00
—Tan label					
❑ 10	Just a Little/They'll Make You Cry	1965	3.75	7.50	15.00
❑ 16	You Tell Me Why/I Want You	1965	2.00	4.00	8.00
❑ 20	Don't Talk to Strangers/In Good Time	1965	2.00	4.00	8.00
❑ 24	Good Time Music/Sad Little Girl	1965	2.00	4.00	8.00

RHINO

Number	Title (A Side/B Side)	Yr	VG	VG+	NM
❑ RNOR 4506	Laugh, Laugh/Just a Little	1984	—	2.00	4.00
❑ RNOR 4506 [PS]	Laugh, Laugh/Just a Little	1984	—	2.00	4.00

WARNER BROS.

Number	Title (A Side/B Side)	Yr	VG	VG+	NM
❑ 5813	One Too Many Mornings/She Reigns	1966	2.00	4.00	8.00
❑ 5848	Fine with Me/Here We Are Again	1966	2.00	4.00	8.00
❑ 7014	Don't Make Promises/Two Days 'Til Tomorrow	1967	2.00	4.00	8.00
❑ 7079	Magic Hollow/Lower Level	1967	2.00	4.00	8.00
❑ 7204	Are You Happy/Lift Me	1968	—	3.00	6.00
❑ 7218	I'm a Sleeper/Long Walking Down to Misery	1968	—	3.00	6.00
❑ 7260	Cherokee Girl/Deep Water	1969	—	3.00	6.00
❑ 8119	You Tell Me Why/Down to the Bottom	1975	—	2.50	5.00

BEAU-MARKS, THE

Probably more than one group.

MAINSTREAM

Number	Title (A Side/B Side)	Yr	VG	VG+	NM
❑ 688	Clap Your Hands/Daddy Said	1968	2.50	5.00	10.00

PORT

Number	Title (A Side/B Side)	Yr	VG	VG+	NM
❑ 70029	Little Miss Twist/Lovely Little Lady	1962	3.75	7.50	15.00

RUST

Number	Title (A Side/B Side)	Yr	VG	VG+	NM
❑ 5035	School Is Out/Classmates	1961	5.00	10.00	20.00
❑ 5050	I'll Never Be the Same/Tender Years	1962	5.00	10.00	20.00

SHAD

Number	Title (A Side/B Side)	Yr	VG	VG+	NM
❑ 5017	Clap Your Hands/Daddy Said	1960	5.00	10.00	20.00
❑ 5021	Cause We're in Love/Billy Went a-Walkin'	1960	5.00	10.00	20.00

TIME

Number	Title (A Side/B Side)	Yr	VG	VG+	NM
❑ 1032	Oh Joan/Rockin' Blues	1961	7.50	15.00	30.00

BEAUMONT, JIMMY

Of THE SKYLINERS.

BANG

Number	Title (A Side/B Side)	Yr	VG	VG+	NM
❑ 510	Tell Me/I Feel Like I'm Falling in Love	1965	5.00	10.00	20.00
❑ 525	I Never Loved Her Anyway/You Got Too Much Going for You	1966	7.50	15.00	30.00

COLPIX

Number	Title (A Side/B Side)	Yr	VG	VG+	NM
❑ 607	The End of a Story/Baion Rhythms	1961	7.50	15.00	30.00

GALLANT

Number	Title (A Side/B Side)	Yr	VG	VG+	NM
❑ 3007	Please Send Me Someone to Love/There Is No Other Love	196?	5.00	10.00	20.00
❑ 3012	Love Is a Dangerous Game/Just a Little Closer	196?	3.00	6.00	12.00

MAY

Number	Title (A Side/B Side)	Yr	VG	VG+	NM
❑ 112	Ev'rybody's Cryin'/Camera	1961	6.25	12.50	25.00
❑ 115	I Should Have Listened to Mama/Juarez	1962	6.25	12.50	25.00
❑ 120	Never Say Goodbye/I'm Gonna Try My Wings	1962	6.25	12.50	25.00
❑ 136	I'll Always Be in Love with You/Give Her My Best	1963	6.25	12.50	25.00

BEAVERS, THE

CAPITOL

Number	Title (A Side/B Side)	Yr	VG	VG+	NM
❑ F3956	Sack Dress/Rockin' at the Drive-In	1958	6.25	12.50	25.00
❑ F4015	The Road to Happiness/Low As I Can Be	1958	5.00	10.00	20.00

BECK

BONGLOAD

Number	Title (A Side/B Side)	Yr	VG	VG+	NM
❑ 11	Steve Threw Up/Mutherfucker	1994	—	3.00	6.00
❑ 11 [PS]	Steve Threw Up/Mutherfucker	1994	—	3.00	6.00

DGC

Number	Title (A Side/B Side)	Yr	VG	VG+	NM
❑ 19270	Loser/Alcohol	1994	—	3.00	6.00

K

Number	Title (A Side/B Side)	Yr	VG	VG+	NM
❑ 45	It's All in Your Mind//Feather in Your Cap/Whiskey Can Can	1994	—	2.00	4.00
❑ 45 [PS]	It's All in Your Mind//Feather in Your Cap/Whiskey Can Can	1994	—	2.00	4.00

BECK, JEFF

Includes the Jeff Beck Group, of whom ROD STEWART was lead singer. Also see BECK, BOGERT AND APPICE; THE YARDBIRDS.

EPIC

Number	Title (A Side/B Side)	Yr	VG	VG+	NM
❑ 05595	Gets Us All in the End/You Know We Know	1985	—	—	3.00
❑ 10157	Beck's Bolero/Hi-Ho Silver Lining	1967	4.00	8.00	16.00
❑ 10218	Rock My Plimsoul/Tally Man	1967	4.00	8.00	16.00
❑ 10390	Blues De Luxe/Ol' Man River	1968	3.00	6.00	12.00
❑ 10484	Jailhouse Rock/Plynth (Water Down the Drain)	1969	3.00	6.00	12.00
❑ 10814	Got the Feeling/Situation	1971	2.50	5.00	10.00
❑ 10938	Definitely Maybe/Hi Ho Silver Lining	1973	2.50	5.00	10.00
❑ 50112	Constipated Duck/You Know What I Mean	1975	—	3.00	6.00
❑ 50276	Come Dancing/Head for Backstage Pass	1976	—	2.00	4.00
❑ 50914	Too Much to Lose/The Final Peace	1980	—	2.00	4.00

BECK, JEFF, AND ROD STEWART

Also see each artist's individual listings.

EPIC

Number	Title (A Side/B Side)	Yr	VG	VG+	NM
❑ 05416	People Get Ready/Back on the Street	1985	—	—	3.00
❑ 05416 [PS]	People Get Ready/Back on the Street	1985	—	—	3.00

BECK, BOGERT & APPICE

Also see JEFF BECK; VANILLA FUDGE.

EPIC

Number	Title (A Side/B Side)	Yr	VG	VG+	NM
❑ 10998	I'm So Proud/Oh to Love You	1973	2.00	4.00	8.00
❑ 11027	Lady/Oh to Love You	1973	2.00	4.00	8.00

BED BUGS, THE

LIBERTY

Number	Title (A Side/B Side)	Yr	VG	VG+	NM
❑ 55679	Yeah Yeah/Lucy Lucy	1964	6.25	12.50	25.00

BEE GEES

Also see THE BUNBURYS; BARRY GIBB; MAURICE GIBB; ROBIN GIBB; JIMMY HANNAN.

ATCO

Number	Title (A Side/B Side)	Yr	VG	VG+	NM
❑ 6487	New York Mining Disaster 1941/I Can't See Nobody	1967	3.00	6.00	12.00
❑ 6487	New York Mining Disaster 1941 Have You Seen My Wife, Mr. Jones/I Can't See Nobody	1967	2.50	5.00	10.00
❑ 6487 [DJ]	New York Mining Disaster 1941/I Can't See Nobody	1967	6.25	12.50	25.00
—Artist not listed on label.					
❑ 6503	To Love Somebody/Close Another Door	1967	2.50	5.00	10.00
❑ 6521	Holiday/Every Christian Lion Hearted Man Will Show You	1967	2.50	5.00	10.00
❑ 6532	(The Lights Went Out in) Massachusetts/Sir Geoffrey Saved the World	1967	2.50	5.00	10.00
❑ 6548	Words/Sinking Ships	1968	2.50	5.00	10.00
❑ 6570	Jumbo/The Singer Sang His Song	1968	2.00	4.00	8.00
❑ 6603	I've Gotta Get a Message to You/Kitty Can	1968	2.00	4.00	8.00
❑ 6639	I Started a Joke/Kilburn Towers	1969	2.00	4.00	8.00
❑ 6657	First of May/Lamplight	1969	2.00	4.00	8.00
❑ 6682	Tomorrow Tomorrow/Sun in My Morning	1969	2.00	4.00	8.00
❑ 6702	Don't Forget to Remember/The Lord	1969	2.50	5.00	10.00
❑ 6702	Don't Forget to Remember/I Lay Down and Die	1969	2.00	4.00	8.00
❑ 6741	If Only I Had My Mind on Something Else/ Sweetheart	1970	2.00	4.00	8.00
❑ 6752	I.O.I.O./Then You Left Me	1970	2.00	4.00	8.00
❑ 6795	Lonely Days/Man for All Seasons	1971	—	3.00	6.00
❑ 6824	How Can You Mend a Broken Heart/Country Woman	1971	—	3.00	6.00
❑ 6847	Don't Wanna Live Inside Myself/Walking Back to Waterloo	1971	—	3.00	6.00
❑ 6871	My World/On Time	1972	—	2.50	5.00
❑ 6896	Run to Me/Road to Alaska	1972	—	2.50	5.00
❑ 6909	Alive/Paper Mache, Cabbages and Kings	1972	—	2.50	5.00

EMMC

Number	Title (A Side/B Side)	Yr	VG	VG+	NM
❑ (no #)	A Personal Message from the Bee Gees/The Rescue of Bonnie Prince Wally	1979	2.50	5.00	10.00
—Official Bee Gees Fan Club record; small hole, plays at 33 1/3 rpm					

POLYDOR

Number	Title (A Side/B Side)	Yr	VG	VG+	NM
❑ 31457 1006 7	Alone/How Deep Is Your Love	1997	—		3.00

RSO

Number	Title (A Side/B Side)	Yr	VG	VG+	NM
❑ 401	Saw a New Morning/My Life Has Been a Song	1973	—	3.00	6.00
❑ 404	Wouldn't I Be Someone/Elisa	1973	—	3.00	6.00
❑ 408	Mr. Natural/It Doesn't Matter Much Anymore	1974	—	3.00	6.00
❑ 410	Throw a Penny/I Can't Let Go	1974	—	3.00	6.00
❑ 501	Charade/Heavy Breathing	1974	—	3.00	6.00
❑ 510	Jive Talkin'/Wind of Change	1975	—	2.00	4.00
❑ 515	Nights on Broadway/Edge of the Universe	1975	—	2.00	4.00
❑ 519	Fanny (Be Tender With My Love)/Country Lanes	1975	—	2.00	4.00
❑ 853	You Should Be Dancing/Subway	1976	—	2.00	4.00
❑ 859	Love So Right/You Stepped Into My Life	1976	—	2.00	4.00
❑ 867	Boogie Child/Lovers	1976	—	2.00	4.00
❑ 880	Edge of the Universe/Words	1977	—	2.00	4.00
❑ 882	How Deep Is Your Love/Can't Keep a Good Man Down	1977	—	2.00	4.00
❑ 885	Stayin' Alive/If I Can't Have You	1977	—	2.00	4.00
❑ 889	Night Fever/Down the Road	1978	—	2.00	4.00
❑ 907	She's Leaving Home/Oh! Darling	1978	—	2.00	4.00
—B-side by Robin Gibb solo					
❑ 913	Too Much Heaven/Rest Your Love on Me	1978	—	2.00	4.00
❑ 918	Tragedy/Until	1979	—	2.00	4.00
❑ 925	Love You Inside Out/I'm Satisfied	1979	—	2.00	4.00
❑ 1066	He's a Liar/(Instrumental)	1981	—	—	3.00
❑ 1067	Living Eyes/I Still Love You	1981	—	—	3.00
❑ 8001	Come On Over/Jive Talkin'	1980	—	2.00	4.00
—Reissue series; first time on 45 for A-side					
❑ 8019	More Than a Woman/Night Fever	1980	—	2.00	4.00
—Reissue series; first time on 45 for A-side					
❑ 813373-7	The Woman in You/Stayin' Alive	1983	—	—	3.00
❑ 813373-7 [PS]	The Woman in You/Stayin' Alive	1983	—	3.00	6.00
❑ 815235-7	Someone Belonging to Someone/I Love You Too Much	1983	—	—	3.00
❑ 815235-7 [PS]	Someone Belonging to Someone/I Love You Too Much	1983	—	3.00	6.00

WARNER BROS.

Number	Title (A Side/B Side)	Yr	VG	VG+	NM
❑ 22733	You Win Again/Will You Ever Let Me	1989	—	2.50	5.00
❑ 22889	One/Wing and a Prayer	1989	—	—	3.00
❑ 22889 [PS]	One/Wing and a Prayer	1989	—	—	3.00
❑ 28139	E.S.P./Overnight	1987	—	—	3.00
❑ 28139 [PS]	E.S.P./Overnight	1987	—	2.00	4.00
❑ 28351	You Win Again/Backtafunk	1987	—	—	3.00
❑ 28351 [PS]	You Win Again/Backtafunk	1987	—	—	3.00

BEEFEATERS, THE

Early version of THE BYRDS.

ELEKTRA

Number	Title (A Side/B Side)	Yr	VG	VG+	NM
❑ 45013	Please Let Me Love You/It Won't Be Long	1964	125.00	250.00	500.00
❑ 45013 [DJ]	Please Let Me Love You/It Won't Be Long	1964	62.50	125.00	250.00

BEEHIVES, THE

KING

Number	Title (A Side/B Side)	Yr	VG	VG+	NM
❑ 5881	I Want to Hold Your Hand/She Loves You	1964	3.75	7.50	15.00

BEES, THE

At least two different groups.

Number	Title (A Side/B Side)	Yr	VG	VG+	NM
FINCH					
❑ 506	So Jealous/(B-side unknown)	196?	18.75	37.50	75.00
IMPERIAL					
❑ 5314	Toy Bell/Snatchin' Back	1954	50.00	100.00	200.00
❑ 5320	I Want to Be Loved/Get Away Baby	1954	75.00	150.00	300.00
LIVERPOOL					
❑ 62225	Voices Green and Purple/(B-side unknown)	1966	20.00	40.00	80.00
❑ 62225 [PS]	Voices Green and Purple/(B-side unknown)	1966	25.00	50.00	100.00
MIRWOOD					
❑ 5503	She's An Artist/Leave Me Be	1965	6.25	12.50	25.00

BEETLES, THE

Number	Title (A Side/B Side)	Yr	VG	VG+	NM
BLUE CAT					
❑ 115	Ain't That Love/Welcome to My Heart	1965	3.75	7.50	15.00
—Also issued as "The Bouquets"					

BEGA, LOU

Number	Title (A Side/B Side)	Yr	VG	VG+	NM
RCA					
❑ 65851	Mambo No. 5 (A Little Bit of...)/Beauty on the TV-Screen	1999	—	2.00	4.00

BEL-AIRES, THE (1)

Number	Title (A Side/B Side)	Yr	VG	VG+	NM
CROWN					
❑ 126	Cherry Pie/Tick Tock	1954	12.50	25.00	50.00
FLIP					
❑ 303	This Paradise/Let's Party Awhile	1954	25.00	50.00	100.00
—Maroon label					
❑ 303	This Paradise/Let's Party Awhile	1954	12.50	25.00	50.00
—Blue label					
❑ 304	White Port and Lemon Juice/This Is Goodbye	1955	25.00	50.00	100.00

BEL-AIRES, THE (U)

We don't know what, if any, relation these are to group (1).

Number	Title (A Side/B Side)	Yr	VG	VG+	NM
DECCA					
❑ 30631	My Yearbook/Rockin' An' Strollin'	1958	7.50	15.00	30.00
MERCURY					
❑ 71763	Knock Knock Knock (Knocking on My Door)/Wear My Class Ring on a Ribbon	1961	3.00	6.00	12.00
NU SOUND					
❑ 1022	Palmeras/Pony Rock	1962	3.00	6.00	12.00

BEL-LARKS, THE

Number	Title (A Side/B Side)	Yr	VG	VG+	NM
RANSOM					
❑ 5001	A Million and One Dreams/(B-side unknown)	1963	125.00	250.00	500.00

BELAIRS, THE

Number	Title (A Side/B Side)	Yr	VG	VG+	NM
ARVEE					
❑ A-5034	Mr. Moto/Little Brown Jug	1961	10.00	20.00	40.00
❑ A-5054	Volcanic Action/Runaway	1962	7.50	15.00	30.00

BELFAST GYPSIES, THE

Also see THEM.

Number	Title (A Side/B Side)	Yr	VG	VG+	NM
LOMA					
❑ 2051	Gloria's Dream/Secret Police	1966	3.75	7.50	15.00
❑ 2060	Portland Town/People, Let's Freak Out	1966	3.75	7.50	15.00

BELL, ARCHIE, AND THE DRELLS

Number	Title (A Side/B Side)	Yr	VG	VG+	NM
ATLANTIC					
❑ 2478	Tighten Up/Tighten Up — Part 2	1968	2.00	4.00	8.00
❑ 2478	Tighten Up/Dog Eat Dog	1968	3.00	6.00	12.00
❑ 2534	I Can't Stop Dancing/You're Such a Beautiful Child	1968	—	3.50	7.00
❑ 2559	Do the Choo Choo/Love Will Rain on You	1968	—	3.50	7.00
❑ 2583	(There's Gonna Be A) Showdown/Go for What You Know	1968	—	3.50	7.00
❑ 2612	I Love My Baby/Just a Little Closer	1969	—	3.50	7.00
❑ 2644	Girl You're Too Young/Do the Hand Jive	1969	—	3.50	7.00
❑ 2663	My Balloon's Going Up/Giving Up Dancing	1969	—	3.50	7.00
❑ 2693	A World Without Music/Here I Go Again	1969	—	3.50	7.00
❑ 2721	Don't Let the Music Slip Away/Houston, Texas	1970	—	3.50	7.00
❑ 2744	I Wish/Get from the Bottom	1970	—	3.50	7.00
❑ 2769	Wrap It Up/Deal with Him	1970	—	3.50	7.00
❑ 2793	I Just Want to Fall in Love/Love at First Sight	1971	—	3.00	6.00
❑ 2829	Let the World Know/Archie's in Love	1971	—	3.00	6.00
❑ 2855	Green Power/I Can't Face You Baby	1972	—	3.00	6.00
BECKET					
❑ 45-4	Any Time Is Right/(B-side unknown)	1981	—	2.00	4.00
EAST WEST					
❑ 2048	She's My Woman/The Yankee Dance	1968	—	3.50	7.00
GLADES					
❑ 1707	Dancing to Your Music/Count the Ways	1973	—	3.00	6.00
❑ 1711	Ain't Nothing for a Man in Love/You Never Know What's On a Woman's Mind	1973	—	3.00	6.00
❑ 1718	Girls Grow Up Faster Than Boys/Love's Gonna Rain on You	1973	—	3.00	6.00
OVIDE					
❑ 228	Tighten Up/Dog Eat Dog	1967	7.50	15.00	30.00
PHILADELPHIA INT'L					
❑ 3605	Nothing Comes Easy/Right Here Is Where I Want to Be	1976	—	2.50	5.00
❑ 3615	Everybody Have a Good Time/I Bet I Can Do That Dance You're Doin'	1977	—	2.50	5.00
❑ 3632	Glad You Can Make It/There's No Other Like You	1977	—	2.50	5.00
❑ 3637	I've Been Missing You/It's Hard Not to Love You	1977	—	2.50	5.00
❑ 3651	Old People/On the Radio	1978	—	2.50	5.00
TSOP					
❑ 4767	I Could Dance All Night/King of the Castle	1975	—	2.50	5.00
❑ 4774	The Soul City Walk/King of the Castle	1975	—	2.50	5.00
❑ 4775	Let's Groove (Part 1)/Let's Groove (Part 2)	1976	—	2.50	5.00
WMOT					
❑ 03057	Touchin' You/(Instrumental)	1982	—	2.50	5.00

BELL, CARL, AND THE NORVAIRS

Number	Title (A Side/B Side)	Yr	VG	VG+	NM
LAURIE					
❑ 3014	Birth of the Beat/Open House in Your Heart	1958	6.25	12.50	25.00

BELL, FREDDIE, AND THE BELL BOYS

Number	Title (A Side/B Side)	Yr	VG	VG+	NM
MERCURY					
❑ 70919	Stay Loose, Mother Goose/All Right, OK, You Win	1956	5.00	10.00	20.00
❑ 71075	Take the First Train Out of Town/Hey There You	1957	5.00	10.00	20.00
❑ 71105	Rockin' Is My Business/You're Gonna Be Sorry	1957	10.00	20.00	40.00
TEEN					
❑ 101	Hound Dog/Move Me Baby	1955	12.50	25.00	50.00
❑ 103	Old Town Hall/5-10-15 Hours	1955	7.50	15.00	30.00
WING					
❑ 90066	Giddy Up a Ding Dong/I Said It and I'm Glad	1956	10.00	20.00	40.00
❑ 90082	The Hucklebuck/Rompin' and Stompin'	1956	10.00	20.00	40.00

BELL, MADELINE

Number	Title (A Side/B Side)	Yr	VG	VG+	NM
ASCOT					
❑ 2156	You Don't Love Me No More/Don't Cross Over to My Side of the Street	1964	2.50	5.00	10.00
❑ 2180	Don't Cry My Heart/Daytime	1965	2.50	5.00	10.00
BRUT					
❑ 808	All That Love Went to Waste/A Touch of Class	1973	—	2.50	5.00
MOD					
❑ 1007	I'm Gonna Make You Love Me/Picture Me Gone	1967	3.00	6.00	12.00
PHILIPS					
❑ 40517	I'm Gonna Make You Love Me/Picture Me Gone	1968	2.00	4.00	8.00
❑ 40539	Finding You, Loving You/Doing Things Together with You	1968	—	3.00	6.00
❑ 40582	Step Inside Love/What I'm Supposed to Do	1969	—	3.00	6.00
PYE					
❑ 71061	I Always Seem to Wind Up Loving You/Your Smile	1976	—	2.00	4.00

BELL, WILLIAM

Number	Title (A Side/B Side)	Yr	VG	VG+	NM
ATLANTIC					
❑ 13154	Everyday Will Be Like A Holiday/Winner	197?	—	2.00	4.00
—Oldies Series reissue					
KAT FAMILY					
❑ 03502	Bad Time to Break Off/The Truth in Your Eyes	1983	—	2.00	4.00
❑ 03995	Playing Hard to Get/The Truth in Your Eyes	1983	—	2.00	4.00
MERCURY					
❑ 73839	Tryin' to Love Two/If Sex Was All We Had	1976	—	2.50	5.00
❑ 73922	Coming Back for More/You I Absolutely Positively Love	1977	—	2.00	4.00
❑ 73961	Your Love Keeps Me Goin'/Easy Comin' Out	1977	—	2.00	4.00
STAX					
❑ 0005	Private Number/Love-Eye-Tis	1968	—	2.50	5.00
—With Judy Clay					
❑ 0015	I Forgot to Be Your Lover/Bring the Curtains Down	1968	—	3.00	6.00
❑ 0017	Left-Over Love/My Baby Specializes	1968	—	2.50	5.00
—With Judy Clay					
❑ 0032	My Whole World Is Falling Down/All God's Children Got Soul	1969	—	2.50	5.00
❑ 0038	My Kind of Girl/Happy	1969	—	2.50	5.00
❑ 0043	Love's Sweet Sensation/Strung Out	1969	—	2.50	5.00
—With Mavis Staples					
❑ 0044	I Can't Stop/I Need You Woman	1969	—	2.50	5.00
—With Carla Thomas					
❑ 0054	Born Under a Bad Sign/A Smile Can't Hide a Broken Heart	1969	—	2.50	5.00
❑ 0067	All I Have to Do Is Dream/Leave the Girl Alone	1970	—	2.50	5.00
—With Carla Thomas					
❑ 0070	Lonely Soldier/Let Me Ride	1970	—	2.50	5.00
❑ 0092	A Penny for Your Thoughts/Till My Back Ain't Got No Bone	1971	—	2.50	5.00
❑ 0106	All for the Love of a Woman/I'll Be Home	1971	—	2.50	5.00
❑ 116	You Don't Miss Your Water/Formula of Love	1961	5.00	10.00	20.00
❑ 128	Any Other Way/Please Help Me I'm Falling	1962	5.00	10.00	20.00
❑ 0128	If You Really Love Him/Save Us	1972	—	2.50	5.00
❑ 132	I Told You So/What'Cha Gonna Do	1963	3.75	7.50	15.00
❑ 135	Just As I Thought/I'm Waiting on You	1963	3.75	7.50	15.00
❑ 138	Somebody Mentioned Your Name/What Can I Do to Forget	1963	3.75	7.50	15.00
❑ 141	I'll Show You/Monkeying Around	1963	3.75	7.50	15.00
❑ 146	Don't Make Something Out of Nothing/Who Will It Be Tomorrow	1964	3.00	6.00	12.00
❑ 0157	Livin' on Borrowed Time/The Man in the Street	1973	—	2.50	5.00
❑ 174	Crying All By Myself/Don't Stop Now	1965	3.00	6.00	12.00
❑ 0175	You've Got the Kind of Love I Need/I've Got to Go On Without You	1973	—	2.50	5.00
❑ 191	Share What You Got/Marching Off to War	1966	2.50	5.00	10.00
❑ 0198	All I Need Is Your Love/Gettin' What You Want	1974	—	2.50	5.00
❑ 199	Soldier's Goodbye/Never Like This Before	1966	2.50	5.00	10.00
❑ 212	Everybody Loves a Winner/You're Such a Sweet Thing	1967	2.00	4.00	8.00
❑ 0221	Get It While It's Hot/Nobody Walks Away from Love Unhurt	1974	—	2.50	5.00
❑ 227	One Plus One/Eloise (Hang On In There)	1967	2.00	4.00	8.00
❑ 237	Everyday Will Be Like a Holiday/Ain't Got No Girl	1967	2.00	4.00	8.00
❑ 248	A Tribute to a King (Otis Redding)/Every Man Oughta Have a Woman	1968	—	3.00	6.00
WRC					
❑ 202	I Don't Want to Wake Up (Feelin' Guilty)/(B-side unknown)	1986	—	2.50	5.00
—With Janice Bullock					
❑ 204	Headline News/(B-side unknown)	1986	—	2.50	5.00

BELL HOPS, THE

Probably two different groups.

Number	Title (A Side/B Side)	Yr	VG	VG+	NM
BARB					
❑ 100	Angela/Ring Dang Doo Ting-a-Ling	1958	6.25	12.50	25.00
❑ 101/2	Teenage Years/Carmella	1958	6.25	12.50	25.00
DECCA					
❑ 48208	For the Rest of My Life/It Would Take a Million Years	1951	25.00	50.00	100.00
❑ 48239	I'm All Yours/Where Is Love	1951	25.00	50.00	100.00
TIN PAN ALLEY					
❑ 153	Please Don't Say No to Me/Merchant Street Blues	1956	37.50	75.00	150.00

BELL NOTES, THE

Number	Title (A Side/B Side)	Yr	VG	VG+	NM
AUTOGRAPH					
❑ 204	Little Girl in Blue/Too Young or Too Old	1960	6.25	12.50	25.00
CLOCK					
❑ 71889	There She Goes/My Pledge to You	1961	5.00	10.00	20.00
MADISON					
❑ 136	Shortnin' Bread/To Each His Own	1960	5.00	10.00	20.00
❑ 141	Real Wild Child/Friendly Star	1960	5.00	10.00	20.00
TIME					
❑ 1004	I've Had It/Be Mine	1958	7.50	15.00	30.00
—First pressing on blue labels					
❑ 1004	I've Had It/Be Mine	1959	6.25	12.50	25.00
—Later pressings on red labels					
❑ 1010	Old Spanish Town/She Went Thataway	1959	6.25	12.50	25.00
❑ 1013	That's Right/Betty Dear	1959	6.25	12.50	25.00
❑ 1015	You're a Big Girl Now/Don't Ask Me Why	1959	6.25	12.50	25.00
❑ 1017	White Buckskin Sneakers and Checkerboard Socks/No Dice	1959	6.25	12.50	25.00

7-Inch Extended Plays

Number	Title (A Side/B Side)	Yr	VG	VG+	NM
TIME					
❑ TEP-100	I've Had It/Be Mine//Dream Street/A Sad Guitar	1959	25.00	50.00	100.00
❑ TEP-100 [PS]	I've Had It	1959	25.00	50.00	100.00

BELL TONES, THE

Number	Title (A Side/B Side)	Yr	VG	VG+	NM
RAMA					
❑ 170	Heart to Heart/The Wedding	1955	50.00	100.00	200.00

BELLE AND SEBASTIAN

Number	Title (A Side/B Side)	Yr	VG	VG+	NM
MATADOR					
❑ OLE 448-7	Legal Man/Winter Wooskie	2000	—	—	3.00
—Small center hole					
❑ OLE 448-7 [PS]	Legal Man/Winter Wooskie	2000	—	—	3.00

BELLS, THE (1)

Canadian band with male and female lead singers.

Number	Title (A Side/B Side)	Yr	VG	VG+	NM
MGM					
❑ 14533	Child of Mine/He Was Me, He Was You	1973	—	2.00	4.00
❑ 14624	Love Once Removed/The Singer	1973	—	2.00	4.00
POLYDOR					
❑ 15016	Fly Little White Dove, Fly/Follow the Sun	1970	—	2.00	4.00
❑ 15023	Stay Awhile/Sing a Song of Freedom	1971	—	2.50	5.00
❑ 15025	Je Vais Rester/Blanc Petit Ois Eau Blanc	1970	—	2.00	4.00
❑ 15027	I Love You Lady Dawn/Rain	1971	—	2.00	4.00
❑ 15029	She's a Lady/Sweet Sounds of Music	1971	—	2.00	4.00
❑ 15031	To Know You Is To Love You/For Better For Worse	1971	—	2.00	4.00
❑ 15036	Oh My Love/You You You	1972	—	2.00	4.00
❑ 15039	Lord, Don't You Think It's Time/Easier Said Than Done	1972	—	2.00	4.00
❑ 15063	Kris Collection/Simple Song of Freedom	1973	—	2.00	4.00

BELLS, THE (2)

Male vocal group.

Number	Title (A Side/B Side)	Yr	VG	VG+	NM
RAMA					
❑ 166	What Can I Tell Her Now/Let Me Love You, Love You	1955	125.00	250.00	500.00

BELLTONES, THE

Number	Title (A Side/B Side)	Yr	VG	VG+	NM
GRAND					
❑ 102	Estelle/Promise Love	1954	2000.	3000.	4000.

BELLUS, TONY

Number	Title (A Side/B Side)	Yr	VG	VG+	NM
ERA BACK TO BACK HITS					
❑ 048	Robbin' the Cradle/Rockin' Little Angel	197?	—	2.50	5.00
—B-side by Ray Smith					
KING					
❑ 5973	Mustang/Goodbye Baby, Goodbye	1964	3.00	6.00	12.00
NRC					
❑ 023	Robbin' the Cradle/Valentine Girl	1959	5.00	10.00	20.00
—Available with the letters "NRC" with no background, with the title of the song in either orange or blue letters; also with each letter of "NRC" in a background box. No difference in value.					
❑ 035	Hey Little Darlin'/Only Your Heart	1959	5.00	10.00	20.00
❑ 040	Little Dreams/Young Girls	1959	5.00	10.00	20.00
❑ 045	Hey Little Darlin'/Young Girls	1959	5.00	10.00	20.00
❑ 051	The End of My Love/The Echo of An Old Song	1960	5.00	10.00	20.00
—Available on both white and tan labels, no difference in value					
❑ 058	The Great Pretender/Give Me a Heart	1960	5.00	10.00	20.00

BELMONTS, THE

Also see DION AND THE BELMONTS; BUDDY SHEPPARD AND THE HOLIDAYS.

Number	Title (A Side/B Side)	Yr	VG	VG+	NM
DOT					
❑ 17173	Reminiscing/She Only Wants to Do Her Thing	1968	3.75	7.50	15.00
❑ 17257	Have You Heard-The Worst That Could Happen/Answer Me My Love	1969	3.75	7.50	15.00
LAURIE					
❑ 3080	We Belong Together/Such a Long Way	1961	7.50	15.00	30.00
❑ 3631	A Brand New Song/Story Teller	1975	—	2.50	5.00
❑ 3698	Medley/You're the Only Girl for Me	198?	—	2.50	5.00
—B-side by Ernie Maresca					
SABINA					
❑ 502	I Need Some One/That American Dance	1961	6.25	12.50	25.00
❑ 503	Hombre/I Confess	1962	6.25	12.50	25.00
❑ 505	Come On Little Angel/How About Me	1962	6.25	12.50	25.00
—Black label					
❑ 505	Come On Little Angel/How About Me	1962	5.00	10.00	20.00
—Greenish label					
❑ 507	Diddle-Dee-Dum (What Happens When Your Love Has Gone)/Farewell	1962	5.00	10.00	20.00
❑ 509	Ann Marie/Ac-Cent-Tchu-Ate the Positive	1963	5.00	10.00	20.00
❑ 513	Let's Call It a Day/Walk On Boy	1963	5.00	10.00	20.00
❑ 517	More Important Things to Do/Walk On Boy	1963	5.00	10.00	20.00
❑ 519	C'mon Everybody/Why	1964	5.00	10.00	20.00
❑ 521	Summertime/Nothing in Return	1964	5.00	10.00	20.00
SABRINA					
❑ 500	Tell Me Why/Smoke from Your Cigarette	1961	6.25	12.50	25.00
❑ 501	Searching for a New Love/Don't Get Around Much Anymore	1961	6.25	12.50	25.00
STRAWBERRY					
❑ 106	Cheek to Cheek/Voyager	1976	—	2.50	5.00
SURPRISE					
❑ 1000	Tell Me Why/Smoke from Your Cigarette	1961	25.00	50.00	100.00
UNITED ARTISTS					
❑ 809	Wintertime/I Don't Know Why, I Just Do	1965	5.00	10.00	20.00
❑ 904	(Then) I Walked Away/Today My Love Has Gone Away	1965	5.00	10.00	20.00
❑ 966	I Got a Feeling/To Be with You	1965	5.00	10.00	20.00
❑ S7-19769	Wintertime/Please Come Home for Christmas	1997	—	2.00	4.00
—B-side by Dion on The Right Stuff					
❑ 50007	Come with Me/You're Like a Mystery	1966	6.25	12.50	25.00

BELUSHI, JOHN

Number	Title (A Side/B Side)	Yr	VG	VG+	NM
MCA					
❑ 40950	Louie Louie/Money	1978	—	2.50	5.00

BELVIN, ANDY

Number	Title (A Side/B Side)	Yr	VG	VG+	NM
ATCO					
❑ 6289	Travelin' Mood/Flip Flip	1964	3.00	6.00	12.00
CANDIX					
❑ 338	Walking the Blues/Prettiest Girl	1962	5.00	10.00	20.00
VAULT					
❑ 908	Travelin' Mood/Flip Flop	1964	3.75	7.50	15.00

BELVIN, JESSE

Also see THE CLIQUES; JESSE AND MARVIN.

Number	Title (A Side/B Side)	Yr	VG	VG+	NM
ALADDIN					
❑ 3431	Let Me Dream/Sugar Doll	1958	10.00	20.00	40.00
CASH					
❑ 1056	Dry Your Tears/Beware	1957	25.00	50.00	100.00
—Black and silver label					
❑ 1056	Dry Your Tears/Beware	1957	6.25	12.50	25.00
—Orange and black label					
CLASS					
❑ 267	I'm Confessin'/Deep in My Heart	1960	6.25	12.50	25.00
HOLLYWOOD					
❑ 1059	Betty My Darling/Dear Heart	1956	100.00	200.00	400.00
IMPACT					
❑ 23	Tonight My Love/Looking for Love	1962	3.75	7.50	15.00
JAMIE					
❑ 1145	Goodnight My Love (Pleasant Dreams)/My Desire	1959	5.00	10.00	20.00
KENT					
❑ 326	Sentimental Reasons/Senorita	1959	6.25	12.50	25.00
KNIGHT					
❑ 2012	Little Darling/Deacon Dan Tucker	1959	10.00	20.00	40.00
MODERN					
❑ 1005	Goodnight My Love (Pleasant Dreams)/Let Me Love You Tonight	1956	10.00	20.00	40.00
❑ 1005	Goodnight My Love (Pleasant Dreams)/I Want You With Me Xmas	1956	10.00	20.00	40.00
❑ 1013	I Need You So/Senorita	1957	7.50	15.00	30.00
❑ 1015	By My Side/Don't Close the Door	1957	7.50	15.00	30.00
❑ 1020	Sad and Lonesome/I'm Not Free	1957	7.50	15.00	30.00
❑ 1025	You Send Me/Summertime	1957	7.50	15.00	30.00
❑ 1027	My Satellite/Just to Say Hello	1957	7.50	15.00	30.00
MONEY					
❑ 208	I'm Only a Fool/Trouble and Misery	1955	15.00	30.00	60.00
RCA VICTOR					
❑ 47-7310	Volare/Ever Since We Met	1958	5.00	10.00	20.00
❑ 47-7387	Funny/Pledging My Love	1958	5.00	10.00	20.00
❑ 47-7469	Guess Who/My Girl Is Just Enough Woman for Me	1959	5.00	10.00	20.00
❑ 47-7543	Here's a Heart/It Could've Been Worse	1959	5.00	10.00	20.00
❑ 47-7596	Give Me Love/I'll Never Be Lonely Again	1959	5.00	10.00	20.00
❑ 47-7675	Something Happens to Me/The Door Is Always Open	1960	5.00	10.00	20.00
❑ 47-8040	Guess Who/Funny	1962	3.75	7.50	15.00
❑ 61-7469	Guess Who/My Girl Is Just Enough Woman for Me	1959	12.50	25.00	50.00
—"Living Stereo" (large hole, plays at 45 rpm)					
RECORDED IN HOLLYWOOD					
❑ 120	Dream Girl/Hang Your Tears Out to Dry	1951	150.00	300.00	600.00
❑ 412	Love Comes Tumbling Down/(B-side unknown)	1953	100.00	200.00	400.00
SPECIALTY					
❑ 435	Confusin' Blues/Baby Don't Go	1952	20.00	40.00	80.00
❑ 550	Gone/One Little Blessing	1955	12.50	25.00	50.00
❑ 559	Where's My Girl/Love, Love of My Life	1955	12.50	25.00	50.00

BEN, LA BRENDA

GORDY

Number	Title (A Side/B Side)	Yr	VG	VG+	NM
❑ 7009	Camel Walk/The Chaperone	1962	12.50	25.00	50.00
❑ 7021	I Can't Help It, I Gotta Dance/Just Be Yourself	1963	12.50	25.00	50.00

MOTOWN

Number	Title (A Side/B Side)	Yr	VG	VG+	NM
❑ 1033	Camel Walk/Chaperone	1962	100.00	200.00	400.00

BENATAR, PAT

CHRYSALIS

Number	Title (A Side/B Side)	Yr	VG	VG+	NM
❑ 2373	If You Think You Know How to Love Me/(B-side unknown)	1979	2.00	4.00	8.00
❑ 2395	Heartbreaker/My Clone Sleeps Alone	1979	—	2.00	4.00
❑ 2395 [PS]	Heartbreaker/My Clone Sleeps Alone	1979	—	3.00	6.00
❑ 2419	We Live for Love/So Sincere	1980	—	2.00	4.00
❑ 2419 [PS]	We Live for Love/So Sincere	1980	—	3.00	6.00
❑ 2450	You Better Run/Out-A Touch	1980	—	2.00	4.00
❑ 2464	Hit Me with Your Best Shot/Prisoner of Love	1980	—	2.00	4.00
❑ 2464 [PS]	Hit Me with Your Best Shot/Prisoner of Love	1980	—	2.00	4.00
❑ 2487	Treat Me Right/Never Wana Leave You	1981	—	2.00	4.00
❑ 2487 [PS]	Treat Me Right/Never Wana Leave You	1981	—	2.00	4.00
❑ 2529	Fire and Ice/Hard to Believe	1981	—	2.00	4.00
❑ 2529 [PS]	Fire and Ice/Hard to Believe	1981	—	2.00	4.00
❑ 2555	Promises in the Dark/Evil Genius	1981	—	2.00	4.00
❑ 2555 [PS]	Promises in the Dark/Evil Genius	1981	—	2.00	4.00
❑ 2647	Shadows of the Night/The Victim	1982	—	2.00	4.00
❑ 2647 [PS]	Shadows of the Night/The Victim	1982	—	2.00	4.00
❑ 03536	Little Too Late/Fight It Out	1983	—	—	3.00
❑ 03536 [PS]	Little Too Late/Fight It Out	1983	—	—	3.00
❑ 03541	Shadows of the Night/The Victim	1983	—	2.00	4.00
❑ S7-17490	Somebody's Baby/Crying	1993	—	—	3.00
❑ S7-17592	Everybody Lay Down/Promises in the Dark (Live)	1993	—	—	3.00
❑ S7-18301	Hit Me with Your Best Shot/Heartbreaker	1995	—	—	3.00
❑ S7-18302	Shadows of the Night/Little Too Late	1995	—	—	3.00
❑ S7-18913	Please Come Home for Christmas/True Love	1995	—	—	3.00
❑ 42688	Looking for a Stranger/I'll Do It	1983	—	—	3.00
❑ 42688 [PS]	Looking for a Stranger/I'll Do It	1983	—	—	3.00
❑ 42732	Love Is a Battlefield/Hell Is For Children	1983	—	—	3.00
❑ 42732 [PS]	Love Is a Battlefield/Hell Is For Children	1983	—	—	3.00
❑ 42826	We Belong/Suburban King	1984	—	—	3.00
❑ 42826 [PS]	We Belong/Suburban King	1984	—	—	3.00
❑ 42843	Ooh Ooh Song/La Cancion Ooh Ooh	1984	—	—	3.00
❑ 42843 [PS]	Ooh Ooh Song/La Cancion Ooh Ooh	1984	—	—	3.00
❑ 42877	Invincible (Theme from Legend of Billie Jean)/(Instrumental)	1985	—	2.00	4.00
❑ 42877	Invincible (Theme from The Legend of Billie Jean)/(Instrumental)	1985	—	—	3.00

—Note slightly altered subtitle

Number	Title (A Side/B Side)	Yr	VG	VG+	NM
❑ 42877 [PS]	Invincible (Theme from The Legend of Billie Jean)/(Instrumental)	1985	—	—	3.00
❑ 42927	Sex as a Weapon/Red Vision	1985	—	—	3.00
❑ 42927 [PS]	Sex as a Weapon/Red Vision	1985	—	—	3.00
❑ 42968	Le Bel Age/Walking in the Underground	1986	—	—	3.00
❑ 43268	All Fired Up/Cool Zero	1988	—	—	3.00
❑ 43268 [PS]	All Fired Up/Cool Zero	1988	—	—	3.00
❑ 43301	Don't Walk Away/Lift 'Em On Up	1988	—	—	3.00
❑ 43314	Let's Stay Together/Wide Awake in Dreamland	1988	—	—	3.00
❑ 43314 [PS]	Let's Stay Together/Wide Awake in Dreamland	1988	—	—	3.00

TRACE

Number	Title (A Side/B Side)	Yr	VG	VG+	NM
❑ 5293	Day Gig/Last Saturday	1976	10.00	20.00	40.00

BENNETT, BOYD

KING

Number	Title (A Side/B Side)	Yr	VG	VG+	NM
❑ 1413	Waterloo/I've Had Enough	1954	8.75	17.50	35.00
❑ 1432	Poison Ivy/You Upset Me Baby	1955	8.75	17.50	35.00
❑ 1443	Everlovin'/Boogie at Midnight	1955	8.75	17.50	35.00
❑ 1470	Seventeen/Little Old You-All	1955	8.75	17.50	35.00

—Maroon label

Number	Title (A Side/B Side)	Yr	VG	VG+	NM
❑ 1470	Seventeen/Little Old You-All	1955	6.25	12.50	25.00

—Blue label

Number	Title (A Side/B Side)	Yr	VG	VG+	NM
❑ 1475	Tennessee Rock and Roll/Oo, Oo, Oo	1955	6.25	12.50	25.00
❑ 1494	My Boy-Flat Top/Banjo Rock and Roll	1955	6.25	12.50	25.00
❑ 4853	Desperately/The Most	1955	6.25	12.50	25.00
❑ 4874	Right Around the Corner/Partners for Life	1956	6.25	12.50	25.00
❑ 4903	Blue Suede Shoes/Mumbles Blues	1956	6.25	12.50	25.00
❑ 4925	Let Me Love You/Groovy Age	1956	6.25	12.50	25.00
❑ 4953	Hit That Jive, Jack/Rabbit-Eye Pink and Charcoal Black	1956	6.25	12.50	25.00
❑ 4985	Rockin' Up a Storm/A Lock of Your Hair	1956	6.25	12.50	25.00
❑ 5021	I'm Moving On/Big Jay Shuffle	1957	6.25	12.50	25.00
❑ 5049	Big Boy/Put the Chain on the Door	1957	6.25	12.50	25.00
❑ 5097	Sentimental Journey/Boy Meets Girl	1957	6.25	12.50	25.00
❑ 5113	Signed, Sealed and Delivered/Her Momma Doesn't Think It's Right	1958	6.25	12.50	25.00
❑ 5115	Click Clack/Move	1958	6.25	12.50	25.00
❑ 5282	High School Hop/Cool Disc Jockey	1959	6.25	12.50	25.00
❑ 5374	Seventeen/My Boy Flat Top	1960	6.25	12.50	25.00
❑ 5738	Teenage Years/Hear Me Talking	1963	3.75	7.50	15.00

MERCURY

Number	Title (A Side/B Side)	Yr	VG	VG+	NM
❑ 71409	Tight Tights/Tear It Up	1959	5.00	10.00	20.00
❑ 71479	Boogie Bear/A Boy Can Tell	1959	5.00	10.00	20.00
❑ 71537	Naughty Rock and Roll/Lover's Night	1959	5.00	10.00	20.00
❑ 71605	It's Wonderful/Amo, Amas, Amat	1960	5.00	10.00	20.00
❑ 71648	Seventeen/Sarasota	1960	5.00	10.00	20.00
❑ 71724	Hershey Bar/Big Junior	1960	5.00	10.00	20.00
❑ 71813	Coffee Break/The Brain	1961	5.00	10.00	20.00

7-Inch Extended Plays

KING

Number	Title (A Side/B Side)	Yr	VG	VG+	NM
❑ 377	(contents unknown)	1956	50.00	100.00	200.00
❑ 377 [PS]	Boyd Bennett	1956	75.00	150.00	300.00
❑ 383	(contents unknown)	1956	50.00	100.00	200.00
❑ 383 [PS]	Rock & Roll with Boyd Bennett & the Rockets	1956	75.00	150.00	300.00

BENNETT, CLIFF, AND THE REBEL ROUSERS

ABC

Number	Title (A Side/B Side)	Yr	VG	VG+	NM
❑ 10842	Got to Get You Into My Life/Baby Each Day	1966	3.75	7.50	15.00

AMY

Number	Title (A Side/B Side)	Yr	VG	VG+	NM
❑ 930	If Only You'd Reply/Three Rooms with Running Water	1965	3.75	7.50	15.00

ASCOT

Number	Title (A Side/B Side)	Yr	VG	VG+	NM
❑ 2146	Everybody Loves a Lover/My Old Stand By	1964	3.75	7.50	15.00

CAPITOL

Number	Title (A Side/B Side)	Yr	VG	VG+	NM
❑ 4621	I'm in Love with You/You've Got What I Like	1961	12.50	25.00	50.00
❑ 5309	One Way Love/I'm in Love with You	1964	3.75	7.50	15.00

BENNETT, JOE, AND THE SPARKLETONES

ABC-PARAMOUNT

Number	Title (A Side/B Side)	Yr	VG	VG+	NM
❑ 9837	Black Slacks/Boppin' Rock Boogie	1957	7.50	15.00	30.00
❑ 9867	Penny Loafers and Bobby Socks/Rocket	1957	7.50	15.00	30.00
❑ 9885	Cotton Pickin' Rocker/I Dig You Baby	1958	7.50	15.00	30.00
❑ 9929	Little Turtle/We've Had It	1958	7.50	15.00	30.00
❑ 9959	Do the Stop/Late Again	1958	7.50	15.00	30.00

PARIS

Number	Title (A Side/B Side)	Yr	VG	VG+	NM
❑ 530	Bayou Rock/Beautiful One	1959	7.50	15.00	30.00
❑ 537	Boys Do Cry/What the Heck	1959	6.25	12.50	25.00
❑ 546	Softly/What the Heck	1960	6.25	12.50	25.00

BENNETT, TONY

COLUMBIA

Number	Title (A Side/B Side)	Yr	VG	VG+	NM
❑ AE 28 [DJ]	My Favorite Things/I Love the Winter Weather	1970	2.00	4.00	8.00
❑ AE 28 [PS]	My Favorite Things/I Love the Winter Weather	1970	3.00	6.00	12.00

—Theme Song for 1970 Christmas Seals Campaign

Number	Title (A Side/B Side)	Yr	VG	VG+	NM
❑ 1-640 (?)	The Boulevard of Broken Dreams/I Wanna Be Loved	1950	6.25	12.50	25.00

—Microgroove 7-inch 33 1/3 rpm single

Number	Title (A Side/B Side)	Yr	VG	VG+	NM
❑ 1-670 (?)	Let's Make Love/I Can't Give You Anything But Love, Baby	1950	6.25	12.50	25.00

—Microgroove 7-inch 33 1/3 rpm single

Number	Title (A Side/B Side)	Yr	VG	VG+	NM
❑ 1-800 (?)	Sing You Sinners/Kiss You	1950	6.25	12.50	25.00

—Microgroove 7-inch 33 1/3 rpm single

Number	Title (A Side/B Side)	Yr	VG	VG+	NM
❑ 6-800 (?)	Sing You Sinners/Kiss You	1950	5.00	10.00	20.00
❑ 06138	Why Do People Fall in Love/Moments Like This	1986	—	—	3.00
❑ 07658	White Christmas/All of My Life	1987	—	—	3.00
❑ 07658 [PS]	White Christmas/All of My Life	1987	—	—	3.00
❑ 31272 [S]	(contents unknown)	1961	3.00	6.00	12.00
❑ 31273 [S]	(contents unknown)	1961	3.00	6.00	12.00
❑ 31274 [S]	(contents unknown)	1961	3.00	6.00	12.00
❑ 31275 [S]	(contents unknown)	1961	3.00	6.00	12.00
❑ 31276 [S]	(contents unknown)	1961	3.00	6.00	12.00
❑ 31563 [S]	(contents unknown)	1962	3.00	6.00	12.00
❑ 31564 [S]	(contents unknown)	1962	3.00	6.00	12.00
❑ 31565 [S]	(contents unknown)	1962	3.00	6.00	12.00
❑ 31566 [S]	(contents unknown)	1962	3.00	6.00	12.00
❑ 31567 [S]	(contents unknown)	1962	3.00	6.00	12.00

—Anyone who can fill in these gaps -- the above 10 all are Columbia "Stereo 7" singles -- please let us know.

Number	Title (A Side/B Side)	Yr	VG	VG+	NM
❑ 39187	Once There Lived a Fool/I Can't Give You Anything But Love, Baby	1951	3.75	7.50	15.00
❑ 39209	Beautiful Madness/Valentino Tango	1951	3.75	7.50	15.00
❑ 3-39209	Beautiful Madness/Valentino Tango	1951	6.25	12.50	25.00

—Microgroove 7-inch 33 1/3 rpm single

Number	Title (A Side/B Side)	Yr	VG	VG+	NM
❑ 39362	Because of You/I Won't Cry Anymore	1951	3.00	6.00	12.00
❑ 39449	Cold, Cold Heart/While We're Young	1951	3.00	6.00	12.00
❑ 39555	Blue Velvet/Solitaire	1951	3.00	6.00	12.00
❑ 39635	Silly Dreamer/Since My Love Has Gone	1952	3.00	6.00	12.00
❑ 39745	Here in My Heart/I'm Lost Again	1952	3.00	6.00	12.00
❑ 39764	Have a Good Time/Please My Love	1952	3.00	6.00	12.00
❑ 39815	You Could Make Me Smile Again/Roses of Yesterday	1952	3.00	6.00	12.00
❑ 39824	Because of You/I Won't Cry Anymore	1952	2.50	5.00	10.00
❑ 39825	The Boulevard of Broken Dreams/I Wanna Be Loved	1952	2.50	5.00	10.00
❑ 39826	Once There Lived a Fool/The Valentine Tango	1952	2.50	5.00	10.00
❑ 39827	Cold, Cold Heart/While We're Young	1952	2.50	5.00	10.00
❑ 39910	Congratulations to Someone/Take Me	1953	3.00	6.00	12.00
❑ 39964	I'm the King of Broken Hearts/No One Will Ever Know	1953	3.00	6.00	12.00
❑ 40004	Someone Turned the Moon Upside Down/I'll Go	1953	3.00	6.00	12.00
❑ 40048	Rags to Riches/Here Comes That Heartache Again	1953	3.00	6.00	12.00
❑ 40121	Stranger in Paradise/Why Does It Have to Be Me	1953	3.00	6.00	12.00
❑ 40169	There'll Be No Teardrops Tonight/My Heart Won't Say Goodbye	1954	3.00	6.00	12.00
❑ 40213	Until Yesterday/Please Driver, Once Around the Park Again	1954	3.00	6.00	12.00
❑ 40272	Cinnamon Sinner/Take Me Back Again	1954	3.00	6.00	12.00
❑ 40376	Funny Thing/My Pretty Shoo-Gah	1954	3.00	6.00	12.00
❑ 40427	It's Too Soon to Know/Close Your Eyes	1955	2.50	5.00	10.00
❑ 40491	What Will I Tell My Heart/Punch and Judy Love	1955	2.50	5.00	10.00
❑ 40523	May I Never Love Again/Don't Tell Me Why	1955	2.50	5.00	10.00
❑ 40567	How Can I Replace You/Tell Me That You Love Me	1955	2.50	5.00	10.00
❑ 40598	Come Next Spring/Afraid of the Dark	1955	2.50	5.00	10.00
❑ 40632	Sing You Sinners/Capri in May	1956	2.50	5.00	10.00
❑ 40667	Can You Find It in Your Heart/Forget Her	1956	2.50	5.00	10.00
❑ 40726	From the Candy Store on the Corner to the Chapel on the Hill/Happiness Street (Corner Sunshine Square)	1956	2.50	5.00	10.00
❑ 40770	The Autumn Waltz/Just in Time	1956	2.50	5.00	10.00
❑ 40849	One Kiss Away from Heaven/Sold to the Man with the Broken Heart	1957	2.50	5.00	10.00
❑ 40907	One for My Baby (And One More for the Road)/No Hard Feelings	1957	2.50	5.00	10.00
❑ 40965	In the Middle of An Island/I Am	1957	2.50	5.00	10.00

Number	Title (A Side/B Side)	Yr	VG	VG+	NM
❑ 41032	Ca, C'est L'amour/I Never Felt More Like Falling in Love	1957	2.50	5.00	10.00
❑ 41086	Love Song from Beauty and the Beast/Weary Blues From Waitin'	1957	2.50	5.00	10.00
❑ 41127	You're So Right for Me/Alone at Last	1958	2.50	5.00	10.00
❑ 41157	Crazy Rhythm/The Beat of My Heart	1958	2.50	5.00	10.00
❑ 41172	Young and Warm and Wonderful/Now I Lay Me Down to Sleep	1958	2.50	5.00	10.00
❑ 41237	Firefly/The Night That Heaven Fell	1958	2.50	5.00	10.00
❑ 41237 [PS]	Firefly/The Night That Heaven Fell	1958	5.00	10.00	20.00
❑ 41298	Love, Look Away/Blue Moon	1958	2.50	5.00	10.00
❑ 41341	It's So Peaceful in the Country/Being True to One Another	1959	2.50	5.00	10.00
❑ 41381	The Cool School/You'll Never Get Away from Me	1959	2.50	5.00	10.00
❑ 41434	Smile/You Can't Love 'Em All	1959	2.50	5.00	10.00
❑ 41520	Climb Ev'ry Mountain/Ask Anyone in Love	1959	2.50	5.00	10.00
❑ 41595	I'll Bring You a Rainbow/Ask Me (I Know)	1960	2.00	4.00	8.00
❑ 41691	Put On a Happy Face/Baby, Talk to Me	1960	2.00	4.00	8.00
❑ 41770	Till/I Am	1960	2.00	4.00	8.00
❑ 41860	Marriage-Go-Round/Somebody	1960	2.00	4.00	8.00
❑ 41874	Ramona/Follow Me	1960	2.00	4.00	8.00
❑ 41965	The Best Is Yet to Come/Marry Young	1961	2.00	4.00	8.00
❑ 42003	Toot Toot Tootsie (Goodbye)/I'm Coming Virginia	1961	2.00	4.00	8.00
❑ 42135	Close Your Eyes/Rules of the Road	1961	2.00	4.00	8.00
❑ 42219	Tender Is the Night/Comes Once in a Lifetime	1961	2.00	4.00	8.00
❑ 42332	I Left My Heart In San Francisco/Once Upon a Time	1962	2.00	4.00	8.00
❑ 42332 [PS]	I Left My Heart In San Francisco/Once Upon a Time	1962	3.75	7.50	15.00
❑ 42395	Candy Kisses/Have I Told You Lately That I Love You	1962	2.00	4.00	8.00
❑ 42634	I Wanna Be Around/I Will Live My Life for You	1962	2.00	4.00	8.00
❑ 42779	The Good Life/Spring in Manhattan	1963	2.00	4.00	8.00
❑ 42820	This Is All I Ask/True Blue Lou	1963	2.00	4.00	8.00
❑ 42886	Don't Wait Too Long/Limehouse Blues	1963	2.00	4.00	8.00
❑ 42931	The Little Boy/The Moment of Truth	1963	2.00	4.00	8.00
❑ 42996	When Joanna Loved Me/The Kid's a Dreamer	1964	2.00	4.00	8.00
❑ 43073	It's a Sin to Tell a Lie/A Taste of Honey	1964	2.00	4.00	8.00
❑ 43141	Who Can I Turn To (When Nobody Needs Me)/Waltz for Debby	1964	2.00	4.00	8.00
❑ 43202	The Best Thing to Be Is a Person/The Brightest Smile in Town	1964	2.00	4.00	8.00
❑ 43220	If I Ruled the World/Take the Moment	1965	—	3.00	6.00
❑ 43331	Fly Me to the Moon (In Other Words)/How Insensitive	1965	—	3.00	6.00
❑ 43431	The Shadow of Your Smile/I'll Only Miss Her When I Think of Her	1965	—	3.00	6.00
❑ 43508	Song from The Oscar/Baby Dream Your Dream	1966	—	3.00	6.00
❑ 43508 [PS]	Song from The Oscar/Baby Dream Your Dream	1966	2.50	5.00	10.00
❑ 43715	Georgia Rose/The Very Thought	1966	—	3.00	6.00
❑ 43768	A Time for Love/Touch the Earth	1966	—	3.00	6.00
❑ 43954	What Makes It Happen/Country Girl	1966	—	3.00	6.00
❑ 43954 [DJ]	What Makes It Happen/Country Girl	1966	3.75	7.50	15.00

—Orange-vinyl promo issue

Number	Title (A Side/B Side)	Yr	VG	VG+	NM
❑ 44154	Keep Smiling at Trouble/Days of Love	1967	—	2.50	5.00
❑ 44258	For Once in My Life/How Do You Say Auf Wiedersehn	1967	—	3.00	6.00
❑ 44443	The Glory of Love/A Fool of Fools	1968	—	2.50	5.00
❑ 44510	Yesterday I Heard the Rain/Sweet Georgie Fame	1968	—	2.50	5.00
❑ 44584	Hushabye Mountain/Hi-Ho	1968	—	2.50	5.00
❑ 44688	Where Is Love/My Favorite Things	1968	—	2.50	5.00
❑ 44755	People/They All Laughed	1969	—	2.50	5.00
❑ 44824	Whoever You Are, I Love You/A Place Over the Sun	1969	—	2.50	5.00
❑ 44855	What the World Needs Now Is Love/Play It Again Sam	1969	—	2.50	5.00
❑ 44947	I've Gotta Be Me/A Lonely Place	1969	—	2.50	5.00
❑ 45032	MacArthur Park/Before We Say Goodbye	1969	—	2.50	5.00
❑ 45073	Little Green Apples/Coco	1970	—	2.50	5.00
❑ 45109	Something/Eleanor Rigby	1970	—	2.50	5.00
❑ 45157	Everybody's Talkin'/Think How It's Gonna Be	1970	—	2.50	5.00
❑ 45205	Something/Think How It's Gonna Be	1970	—	2.50	5.00
❑ 45255	I'll Begin Again/I Do Not Know a Day I Did Not Love You	1970	—	2.50	5.00
❑ 45316	(Where Do I Begin) Love Story/I'll Begin Again	1971	—	2.50	5.00
❑ 45376	I Want to Be Happy/Tea for Two	1971	—	2.50	5.00
❑ 45411	More and More/I'm Losing My Mind	1971	—	2.50	5.00
❑ 45449	Walkabout/How Beautiful Is Night	1971	—	2.50	5.00
❑ 45493	Remind Me/The Riviera	1971	—	2.50	5.00
❑ 45523	Somewhere Along the Line/The Summer Knows	1972	—	2.50	5.00
❑ 45573	Twilight World/Easy Come, Easy Go	1972	—	2.50	5.00
❑ 45613	Love/Maybe This Time	1972	—	2.50	5.00
❑ JZSP 112321 [DJ]	Love Theme from "The Sandpiper" (The Shadow of Your Smile) (same on both sides)	1965	2.00	4.00	8.00

—Black vinyl promo

MGM

Number	Title (A Side/B Side)	Yr	VG	VG+	NM
❑ 14607	My Love/(B-side unknown)	1973	—	2.00	4.00

VERVE

Number	Title (A Side/B Side)	Yr	VG	VG+	NM
❑ 10690	Living Together, Growing Together/The Good Things in Life	1972	—	2.00	4.00
❑ 10702	O Solo Mio/The Good Things in Life	1973	—	2.00	4.00
❑ 10714	Tell Her It's Snowing/If I Could Go Back	1973	—	2.00	4.00

7-Inch Extended Plays

COLUMBIA

Number	Title (A Side/B Side)	Yr	VG	VG+	NM
❑ B-2582	*One for My Baby/I Can't Give You Anything But Love/Solitaire/Once There Lived a Fool	1959	2.50	5.00	10.00
❑ B-2582	Tony Bennett (Hall of Fame Series)	1959	2.50	5.00	10.00
❑ 7-9173 [PS]	Tony Bennett's Greatest Hits Volume III	1964	3.00	6.00	12.00
❑ 7-9173 [S]	I Left My Heart in San Francisco/I Wanna Be Around/Quiet Nights of Quiet Stars//The Good Life/A Taste of Honey/The Best Is Yet to Come	1964	2.50	5.00	10.00

—33 1/3 rpm, small hole, "Special Coin Operator Release"

Number	Title (A Side/B Side)	Yr	VG	VG+	NM
❑ B-9382	*These Foolish Things/I Can't Give You Anything But Love/Boulevard of Broken Dreams/I'll Be Seeing You	1957	2.50	5.00	10.00
❑ B-9382 [PS]	Tony	1957	2.50	5.00	10.00
❑ ZTEP 26851/2	Because of You/In the Middle of an Island/Cold, Cold Heart//From Rags to Riches/Come Next Spring/Can You Find It in Your Heart	1957	6.25	12.50	25.00

—Coca-Cola promotional item

Number	Title (A Side/B Side)	Yr	VG	VG+	NM
❑ ZTEP 26851/2 [PS]	Tony Bennett Autographed Edition of Hits	1957	6.25	12.50	25.00

—Coca-Cola promotional item

BENNY AND THE BEDBUGS

DCP

Number	Title (A Side/B Side)	Yr	VG	VG+	NM
❑ 1008	The Beatle Beat/Roll Over Beethoven	1964	3.75	7.50	15.00
❑ 1008 [PS]	The Beatle Beat/Roll Over Beethoven	1964	6.25	12.50	25.00

BENSON, GEORGE

Also see THE ALTAIRS.

ARISTA

Number	Title (A Side/B Side)	Yr	VG	VG+	NM
❑ 0251	The Greatest Love of All/Ali's Theme	1977	—	2.00	4.00

—B-side by Michael Masser

Number	Title (A Side/B Side)	Yr	VG	VG+	NM
❑ 0251 [PS]	The Greatest Love of All/Ali's Theme	1977	—	3.00	6.00

A&M

Number	Title (A Side/B Side)	Yr	VG	VG+	NM
❑ 1003	Chattanooga Choo Choo/The Shape of Things to Come	1968	—	3.00	6.00
❑ 1057	Don't Let Me Lose This Dream Part 1/Part 2	1969	—	3.00	6.00
❑ 1076	Jackie All/My Woman's Good to Me	1969	—	3.00	6.00
❑ 1124	My Cherie Amour/Tell It Like It Is	1969	—	3.00	6.00
❑ 1128	I Got a Woman Part 1/I Got a Woman Part 2	1969	—	3.00	6.00
❑ 8395	Golden Slumbers-You Never Give Me Your Money (Medley)/(B-side unknown)	1971	—	3.00	6.00

—May be promo only

COLUMBIA

Number	Title (A Side/B Side)	Yr	VG	VG+	NM
❑ 43684	Summertime/Ain't That Peculiar	1966	2.50	5.00	10.00
❑ 43998	The Man from Toledo/Georgia Stick	1967	2.50	5.00	10.00

CTI

Number	Title (A Side/B Side)	Yr	VG	VG+	NM
❑ 25	Supership/My Latin Brother	1975	—	3.00	6.00
❑ 30	Summertime & 2001 (Part 1)/Summertime & 2001 (Part 2)	1977	—	2.50	5.00
❑ 47	Hold On, I'm Comin'/Gone	1978	—	2.50	5.00

GROOVE

Number	Title (A Side/B Side)	Yr	VG	VG+	NM
❑ 0024	It Should Have Been Me #2/She Makes Me Mad	1954	10.00	20.00	40.00

PRESTIGE

Number	Title (A Side/B Side)	Yr	VG	VG+	NM
❑ 317	Just Another Sunday/Shadow Dancers	1964	3.00	6.00	12.00

WARNER BROS.

Number	Title (A Side/B Side)	Yr	VG	VG+	NM
❑ 8209	This Masquerade/Lady	1976	—	2.50	5.00
❑ 8268	Breezin'/Six to Four	1976	—	2.00	4.00
❑ 8360	Everything Must Change/The Wind and I	1977	—	2.00	4.00
❑ 8377	Gonna Love You More/Valdez in the Country	1977	—	2.00	4.00
❑ 8542	On Broadway/We As Love	1978	—	2.00	4.00
❑ 8542 [PS]	On Broadway/We As Love	1978	—	2.50	5.00
❑ 8604	Lady Blue/California P.M.	1978	—	2.00	4.00
❑ 8759	Love Ballad/You're Never Too Far from Me	1979	—	2.00	4.00
❑ 8759 [PS]	Love Ballad/You're Never Too Far from Me	1979	—	2.50	5.00
❑ 8843	Unchained Melody/Before You Go	1979	—	2.00	4.00
❑ 27537	Good Habit/Stephanie	1989	—	—	3.00
❑ 27658	Twice the Love/(Instrumental)	1989	—	—	3.00
❑ 27658 [PS]	Twice the Love/(Instrumental)	1989	—	—	3.00
❑ 27780	Let's Do It Again/Let Go	1988	—	—	3.00
❑ 27780 [PS]	Let's Do It Again/Let Go	1988	—	—	3.00
❑ 28410	Did You Hear Thunder/Teaser	1987	—	—	3.00
❑ 28523	Shiver/Love Is Here Tonight	1986	—	—	3.00
❑ 28640	Kisses in the Moonlight/Open Your Eyes (Instrumental)	1986	—	—	3.00
❑ 28640 [PS]	Kisses in the Moonlight/Open Your Eyes (Instrumental)	1986	—	—	3.00
❑ 28969	New Day/No One Emotion	1985	—	—	3.00
❑ 29042	I Just Wanna Hang Around You/Beyond the Sea (La Mer)	1985	—	—	3.00
❑ 29120	20-20/Shark Bite	1984	—	2.00	4.00
❑ 29120 [PS]	20-20/Shark Bite	1984	—	2.00	4.00
❑ 29442	In Your Eyes/Never Too Far to Fall	1983	—	2.00	4.00
❑ 29563	Lady Love Me (One More Time)/Being with You	1983	—	2.00	4.00
❑ 29649	Inside Love (So Personal)/In Search of a Dream	1983	—	2.00	4.00
❑ 29649 [PS]	Inside Love (So Personal)/In Search of a Dream	1983	—	2.00	4.00
❑ 49051	Hey Girl/Welcome Into My World	1979	—	2.00	4.00
❑ 49505	Give Me the Night/Dinorah, Dinorah	1980	—	2.00	4.00
❑ 49505 [PS]	Give Me the Night/Dinorah, Dinorah	1980	—	2.50	5.00
❑ 49570	Love Dance/Love X Love	1980	—	2.00	4.00
❑ 49637	Midnight Love Affair/Turn Off the Lamplight	1980	—	2.00	4.00
❑ 49846	Turn Your Love Around/Nature Boy	1981	—	2.00	4.00
❑ 49846 [PS]	Turn Your Love Around/Nature Boy	1981	—	2.00	4.00
❑ 50005	Never Give Up on a Good Thing/Livin' Inside Your Love	1982	—	2.00	4.00
❑ 50005 [PS]	Never Give Up on a Good Thing/Livin' Inside Your Love	1982	—	2.00	4.00

BENSON, GEORGE, AND EARL KLUGH

WARNER BROS.

Number	Title (A Side/B Side)	Yr	VG	VG+	NM
❑ 27975	Since You're Gone/Love Theme from "Romeo and Juliet"	1988	—	—	3.00
❑ 28244	Dreamin'/Love Theme from "Romeo and Juliet"	1987	—	—	3.00

BENTLEYS, THE

SMASH

Number	Title (A Side/B Side)	Yr	VG	VG+	NM
❑ 1967	She's My Hot Rod Queen/Why Does Everybody Want to Hold My Baby	1965	6.25	12.50	25.00
❑ 1988	Did Anybody Lose a Tear/Why Didn't I Listen to Mother	1965	6.25	12.50	25.00

BENTON, BROOK

Also see THE SANDMEN (2); DINAH WASHINGTON AND BROOK BENTON.

Number	Title (A Side/B Side)	Yr	VG	VG+	NM
ALL PLATINUM					
❑ 2364	Can't Take My Eyes Off You/Weekend with Feathers	1976	—	2.50	5.00
BRUT					
❑ 810	Lay Lady Lay/A Touch of Class	1973	—	2.50	5.00
❑ 816	South Carolina/(B-side unknown)	1973	—	2.50	5.00
COTILLION					
❑ 44007	I Just Don't Know What to Do with Myself/Do Your Own Thing	1968	2.00	4.00	8.00
❑ 44031	She Knows What to Do with 'Em/Touch 'Em with Love	1969	2.00	4.00	8.00
❑ 44034	Nothing Can Take the Place of You/Woman Without Love	1969	2.00	4.00	8.00
❑ 44057	Rainy Night in Georgia/Where Do You Go from Here	1969	2.50	5.00	10.00
❑ 44072	My Way/A Little Bit of Soap	1970	—	3.00	6.00
❑ 44078	Don't It Make You Want to Go Home/I've Gotta Be Me	1970	—	3.00	6.00
❑ 44093	Shoes/Let Me Fix It	1970	—	3.00	6.00
❑ 44110	Whoever Finds This, I Love You/Heaven Help Us All	1971	—	3.00	6.00
❑ 44119	Take a Look at Your Hands/If You Think God Is Dead	1971	—	3.00	6.00
❑ 44130	Please Send Me Someone to Love/She Even Woke Me Up to Say Goodbye	1971	—	3.00	6.00
❑ 44138	A Black Child Can't Smile/If You Think God Is Dead	1971	—	3.00	6.00
❑ 44141	Soul Santa/Let Us All Get Together with the Lord	1971	2.00	4.00	8.00
❑ 44152	Movin' Day/Poor Make Believer	1972	—	3.00	6.00
EPIC					
❑ 9177	Love Made Me Your Fool/Give Me a Sign	1956	6.25	12.50	25.00
❑ 9199	The Wall/All My Love Belongs to You	1957	6.25	12.50	25.00
MERCURY					
❑ 30101	Merry Christmas, Happy New Year/This Time Of The Year	196?	2.00	4.00	8.00
—Reissue					
❑ 71394	It's Just a Matter of Time/Hurtin' Inside	1959	3.75	7.50	15.00
❑ 71443	Endlessly/So Close	1959	3.75	7.50	15.00
❑ 71478	Thank You Pretty Baby/With All of My Heart	1959	3.75	7.50	15.00
❑ 71512	So Many Ways/I Want You Forever	1959	3.75	7.50	15.00
❑ 71554	This Time of the Year/Nothing in the World	1959	3.75	7.50	15.00
❑ 71558	This Time of the Year/How Many Times	1959	3.75	7.50	15.00
❑ 71566	The Ties That Bind/Hither, Thither and Yon	1960	3.00	6.00	12.00
❑ 71566 [PS]	The Ties That Bind/Hither, Thither and Yon	1960	5.00	10.00	20.00
❑ 71652	Kiddio/The Same One	1960	3.00	6.00	12.00
❑ 71652 [PS]	Kiddio/The Same One	1960	5.00	10.00	20.00
❑ 71722	Fools Rush In (Where Angels Fear to Tread)/ Someday You'll Want Me to Want You	1960	3.00	6.00	12.00
❑ 71722 [PS]	Fools Rush In (Where Angels Fear to Tread)/ Someday You'll Want Me to Want You	1960	5.00	10.00	20.00
❑ 71730	This Time of the Year/Merry Christmas, Happy New Year	1960	3.00	6.00	12.00
❑ 71774	Think Twice/For My Baby	1961	3.00	6.00	12.00
❑ 71774 [PS]	Think Twice/For My Baby	1961	5.00	10.00	20.00
❑ 71820	The Boll Weevil Song/Your Eyes	1961	3.00	6.00	12.00
❑ 71820 [PS]	The Boll Weevil Song/Your Eyes	1961	5.00	10.00	20.00
❑ 71859	Frankie and Johnny/It's Just a House Without You	1961	3.00	6.00	12.00
❑ 71859 [PS]	Frankie and Johnny/It's Just a House Without You	1961	5.00	10.00	20.00
❑ 71903	Revenge/Really Really	1961	3.00	6.00	12.00
❑ 71903 [PS]	Revenge/Really Really	1961	5.00	10.00	20.00
❑ 71912	Shadrack/The Lost Penny	1961	3.00	6.00	12.00
❑ 71912 [PS]	Shadrack/The Lost Penny	1961	5.00	10.00	20.00
❑ 71925	Walk on the Wild Side/Somewhere in the Used to Be	1962	2.50	5.00	10.00
❑ 71925 [PS]	Walk on the Wild Side/Somewhere in the Used to Be	1962	5.00	10.00	20.00
❑ 71962	Hit Record/Thanks to the Fool	1962	2.50	5.00	10.00
❑ 71962 [PS]	Hit Record/Thanks to the Fool	1962	5.00	10.00	20.00
❑ 72009	Two Tickets to Paradise/It's Alright	1962	—	—	—
—Unreleased					
❑ 72024	Lie to Me/With the Touch of Your Hand	1962	2.50	5.00	10.00
❑ 72024 [PS]	Lie to Me/With the Touch of Your Hand	1962	5.00	10.00	20.00
❑ 72055	Hotel Happiness/Still Waters Run Deep	1962	2.50	5.00	10.00
❑ 72055 [PS]	Hotel Happiness/Still Waters Run Deep	1962	5.00	10.00	20.00
❑ 72099	I Got What I Wanted/Dearer Than Life	1963	2.50	5.00	10.00
❑ 72099 [PS]	I Got What I Wanted/Dearer Than Life	1963	5.00	10.00	20.00
❑ 72135	My True Confession/Tender Years	1963	2.50	5.00	10.00
❑ 72135 [PS]	My True Confession/Tender Years	1963	5.00	10.00	20.00
❑ 72177	Two Tickets to Paradise/Don't Hate Me	1963	2.50	5.00	10.00
❑ 72177 [PS]	Two Tickets to Paradise/Don't Hate Me	1963	5.00	10.00	20.00
❑ 72214	This Time of the Year/You're All I Want for Christmas	1963	2.50	5.00	10.00
❑ 72214 [DJ]	You're All I Want For Christmas/This Time Of The Year	1963	2.50	5.00	10.00
❑ 72230	Going, Going, Gone/After Midnight	1963	2.50	5.00	10.00
❑ 72230 [PS]	Going, Going, Gone/After Midnight	1963	5.00	10.00	20.00
❑ 72266	Too Late to Turn Back Now/Another Cup of Coffee	1964	2.50	5.00	10.00
❑ 72266 [PS]	Too Late to Turn Back Now/Another Cup of Coffee	1964	5.00	10.00	20.00
❑ 72303	A House Is Not a Home/Come On Back	1964	2.50	5.00	10.00
❑ 72303 [PS]	A House Is Not a Home/Come On Back	1964	5.00	10.00	20.00
❑ 72333	Lumberjack/Don't Do What I Did (Do What I Say)	1964	2.50	5.00	10.00
❑ 72333 [PS]	Lumberjack/Don't Do What I Did (Do What I Say)	1964	5.00	10.00	20.00
❑ 72365	Do It Right/Please, Please Make It Easy	1964	2.50	5.00	10.00
❑ 72365 [PS]	Do It Right/Please, Please Make It Easy	1964	5.00	10.00	20.00
❑ 72398	Special Years/Where There's a Will (There's a Way)	1965	2.50	5.00	10.00
❑ 72446	Love Me Now/A-Sleepin' at the End of the Bed	1965	2.50	5.00	10.00
❑ 872796-7	It's Just a Matter of Time/Hurtin' Inside	1989	—	2.00	4.00
❑ 872798-7	Endlessly/So Many Ways	1989	—	2.00	4.00
MGM					
❑ 14440	If You've Got the Time/You Take Me Home Honey	1972	—	2.50	5.00
OKEH					
❑ 7058	The Kentuckian Song/Ooh	1955	6.25	12.50	25.00
❑ 7065	Bring Me Love/Some of My Best Friends	1956	6.25	12.50	25.00
OLDE WORLD					
❑ 1100	Makin' Love Is Good for You/Better Times	1977	—	2.50	5.00
❑ 1107	Soft/Glow Love	1978	—	2.50	5.00
POLYDOR					
❑ 2015	I Cried for You/Love Me a Little	1979	—	2.00	4.00
RCA VICTOR					
❑ 47-7489	Only Your Love/(B-side unknown)	1959	—	—	—
—Unreleased?					
❑ 47-8693	Mother Nature, Father Time/You're Mine	1965	2.50	5.00	10.00
❑ 47-8693 [PS]	Mother Nature, Father Time/You're Mine	1965	5.00	10.00	20.00
❑ 47-8768	Where There's Life/Only a Girl Like You	1965	2.50	5.00	10.00
❑ 47-8830	Too Much Good Lovin'/A Sailor Boy's Love Song	1966	2.50	5.00	10.00
❑ 47-8879	Break Her Heart/In the Evening in the Moonlight	1966	2.50	5.00	10.00
❑ 47-8944	Where Does a Man Go to Cry/The Roach Song	1966	2.50	5.00	10.00
❑ 47-8995	So True in Life, So True in Love/If You Only Knew	1966	2.50	5.00	10.00
❑ 47-9031	Our First Christmas Together/Silent Night	1966	3.00	6.00	12.00
❑ 47-9096	Wake Up/All My Love Belongs to You	1967	2.00	4.00	8.00
❑ 47-9105	Keep the Faith Baby/Going to Soulsville	1967	2.00	4.00	8.00
REPRISE					
❑ 0611	You're the Reason I'm Living/Laura (Tell Me What He's Got That I Ain't Got)	1967	2.00	4.00	8.00
❑ 0649	Glory of Love/Weakness in a Man	1967	2.00	4.00	8.00
❑ 0676	Instead (Of Loving You)/Lonely Street	1968	2.00	4.00	8.00
STAX					
❑ 0231	Winds of Change/I Keep Thinking to Myself	1974	—	2.50	5.00
VIK					
❑ 0285	I Wanna Do Everything for You/Come On Be Nice	1957	5.00	10.00	20.00
❑ 0311	A Million Miles from Nowhere/Devoted	1957	5.00	10.00	20.00
❑ 0325	Because You Love Me/Crinoline Skirt	1958	5.00	10.00	20.00
❑ 0336	Crazy in Love with You/I'm Coming Back to You	1958	5.00	10.00	20.00

BENTON, BROOK, AND DAMITA JO

Also see each artist's individual listings.

Number	Title (A Side/B Side)	Yr	VG	VG+	NM
MERCURY					
❑ 72196	Yaba-Taba-Do/Almost Persuaded	1963	—	—	—
—Unreleased					
❑ 72207	Baby You Got It Made/Stop Foolin'	1963	2.50	5.00	10.00

BERMUDAS, THE

Number	Title (A Side/B Side)	Yr	VG	VG+	NM
ERA					
❑ 3125	Donnie/Chu Sen Ling	1964	3.00	6.00	12.00

BERNA-DEAN

Number	Title (A Side/B Side)	Yr	VG	VG+	NM
IMPERIAL					
❑ 5792	I Walk in My Sleep/Little Willie	1961	5.00	10.00	20.00
❑ 5840	He's Mine/One Gal in Town, Five Men Hagin' Around	1962	5.00	10.00	20.00
❑ 5877	Morning, Noon and Night/The World Keeps Changing	1962	5.00	10.00	20.00
❑ 5950	The President Says Walk/I Wonder	1963	5.00	10.00	20.00
❑ 5978	Hello/Sleepless Nights	1963	5.00	10.00	20.00

BERNARD, ROD

Number	Title (A Side/B Side)	Yr	VG	VG+	NM
ARBEE					
❑ 101	Recorded in England/Somebody Wrote That Song for My Baby	1965	2.50	5.00	10.00
❑ 104	Gimme Back My Cadillac/Don't You Think I've Paid Enough	1965	2.50	5.00	10.00
❑ 105	Those Were Our Songs/Just Another Lie	1966	2.50	5.00	10.00
ARGO					
❑ 5327	This Should Go On Forever/Pardon Mr. Gordon	1959	5.00	10.00	20.00
❑ 5338	You're On My Mind/My Life Is a Mystery	1959	5.00	10.00	20.00
CARL					
❑ (# unknown)	Linda Gail/Little Bitta Mama	1957	6.25	12.50	25.00
CRAZY CAJUN					
❑ 9020	Papa Thibodeaux/My Little Jollie Blonde	1978	—	2.50	5.00
HALLWAY					
❑ 1806	I Had a Girl/Wedding Bells	1963	3.75	7.50	15.00
❑ 1902	Who's Gonna Rock My Baby/Colinda	1962	3.75	7.50	15.00
❑ 1906	New Orleans Jail/Fais Do-Do	1962	3.75	7.50	15.00
❑ 1915	Forgive/I Want Somebody	1963	3.75	7.50	15.00
❑ 1917	Diggy Liggy Lo/The Clock	1963	3.75	7.50	15.00
❑ 1919	Loneliness/Boss Man's Son	1964	3.75	7.50	15.00
❑ 1922	My Own Mother-in-Law/I Might As Well	1964	3.75	7.50	15.00
JIN					
❑ 105	This Should Go On Forever/Pardon, Mr. Gordon	1958	10.00	20.00	40.00
❑ 232	Congratulations to You Darling/You're the Reason I'm in Love	1968	2.00	4.00	8.00
❑ 237	To Have and Hold/Cajun Honey	1968	2.00	4.00	8.00
❑ 240	Big Mamou/New Orleans Jail	1969	2.00	4.00	8.00
❑ 307	Don't You Think I've Paid Enough/Somebody Wrote That Song for Me	1974	—	2.50	5.00
❑ 325	Breaking Up Is Hard to Do/Sometimes I Walk in My Sleep	1975	—	2.50	5.00
❑ 338	This Should Go On Forever/I Spent a Week There Last Night	1975	—	2.50	5.00
❑ 350	A Winner in Love/I Forgot I Had These Memories of You	1975	—	2.50	5.00
❑ 373	Mardi Gras in New Orleans/Oh Mother Dear	1976	—	2.50	5.00
❑ 376	Go On, Go On/I Naver Had the One I Wanted	1976	—	2.50	5.00
MERCURY					
❑ 71507	Shedding Teardrops Over You/One More Chance	1959	5.00	10.00	20.00
❑ 71592	One of These Days/Let's Get Together Tonight	1960	5.00	10.00	20.00
❑ 71654	Two Young Fools in Love/Dance Fool Dance	1960	5.00	10.00	20.00

Number	Title (A Side/B Side)	Yr	VG	VG+	NM
❑ 71689	Sttrange Kisses/Just a Memory	1960	5.00	10.00	20.00
❑ 71767	Lonely Hearts Club/Who Knows	1961	4.00	8.00	16.00
❑ 71842	(Tell Me) Sometime/I'm Not Lonely Anymore	1961	4.00	8.00	16.00
SCEPTER					
❑ 12195	Those Were Our Songs/Recorded in England	1967	4.00	8.00	16.00
TEAR DROP					
❑ 3044	Our Teenage Love/Doing the Oo-Wa-Woo	1966	2.50	5.00	10.00
❑ 3052	You're the Reason I'm in Love/My Jole Blon	1966	2.50	5.00	10.00
❑ 3060	No Money Down/Little Green Man	1967	2.50	5.00	10.00
❑ 3117	This Should Go On Forever/Recorded in England	1969	2.00	4.00	8.00

BERRY, CHUCK

Also see JOE ALEXANDER AND THE CUBANS.

Number	Title (A Side/B Side)	Yr	VG	VG+	NM
ATCO					
❑ 7203	Oh What a Thrill/California	1979	—	2.00	4.00
CHESS					
❑ 1604	Maybellene/Wee Wee Hours	1955	12.50	25.00	50.00
❑ 1610	Thirty Days (To Come Back Home)/Together	1955	12.50	25.00	50.00
❑ 1615	No Money Down/Down Bound Train	1956	12.50	25.00	50.00
❑ 1626	Roll Over Beethoven/Drifting Heart	1956	12.50	25.00	50.00
❑ 1635	Too Much Monkey Business/Brown Eyed Handsome Man	1956	12.50	25.00	50.00
❑ 1645	You Can't Catch Me/Havana Moon	1956	12.50	25.00	50.00
❑ 1653	School Day (Ring! Ring! Goes the Bell)/Deep Feeling	1957	12.50	25.00	50.00
❑ 1664	Oh Baby Doll/La Jaunda	1957	12.50	25.00	50.00
❑ 1671	Rock & Roll Music/Blue Feeling	1957	7.50	15.00	30.00
❑ 1683	Sweet Little Sixteen/Reelin' and Rockin'	1958	7.50	15.00	30.00
❑ 1691	Johnny B. Goode/Around and Around	1958	7.50	15.00	30.00
❑ 1697	Beautiful Delilah/Vacation Time	1958	7.50	15.00	30.00
❑ 1700	Carol/Hey Pedro	1958	7.50	15.00	30.00
❑ 1709	Sweet Little Rock and Roll/Joe Joe Gun	1958	7.50	15.00	30.00
❑ 1714	Run Rudolph Run/Merry Christmas Baby	1958	10.00	20.00	40.00
❑ 1716	Anthony Boy/That's My Desire	1959	7.50	15.00	30.00
❑ 1722	Almost Grown/Little Queenie	1959	7.50	15.00	30.00
❑ 1729	Back in the U.S.A./Memphis Tennessee	1959	7.50	15.00	30.00
❑ 1737	Broken Arrow/Childhood Sweetheart	1959	10.00	20.00	40.00
❑ 1747	Too Pooped to Pop ("Casey")/Let It Rock	1960	6.25	12.50	25.00
❑ 1754	Bye Bye Johnny/Worried Life Blues	1960	6.25	12.50	25.00
❑ 1763	I Got to Find My Baby/Mad Lad	1960	6.25	12.50	25.00
❑ 1767	Our Little Rendezvous/Jaguar and Thunderbird	1960	6.25	12.50	25.00
❑ 1779	I'm Talking About You/Little Star	1961	6.25	12.50	25.00
❑ 1799	Come On/Go-Go-Go	1961	5.00	10.00	20.00
❑ 1853	I'm Talking About You/Diploma for Two	1963	5.00	10.00	20.00
❑ 1866	Memphis/Sweet Little Sixteen	1963	5.00	10.00	20.00
❑ 1883	Nadine (Is It You?)/O Rangutang	1964	5.00	10.00	20.00
❑ 1898	No Particular Place to Go/You Two	1964	5.00	10.00	20.00
❑ 1898 [PS]	No Particular Place to Go/You Two	1964	12.50	25.00	50.00
❑ 1906	You Never Can Tell/Brenda Lee	1964	5.00	10.00	20.00
❑ 1906 [PS]	You Never Can Tell/Brenda Lee	1964	10.00	20.00	40.00
❑ 1912	Little Marie/Go Bobby Soxer	1964	3.75	7.50	15.00
❑ 1912 [PS]	Little Marie/Go Bobby Soxer	1964	10.00	20.00	40.00
❑ 1916	Promised Land/Things I Used to Do	1964	3.75	7.50	15.00
❑ 1916 [PS]	Promised Land/Things I Used to Do	1964	12.50	25.00	50.00
❑ 1926	Dear Dad/Lonely School Days	1965	3.75	7.50	15.00
❑ 1943	It Wasn't Me/Welcome Back Pretty Girl	1965	3.75	7.50	15.00
❑ 1943 [PS]	It Wasn't Me/Welcome Back Pretty Girl	1965	7.50	15.00	30.00
❑ 1960	Ramona Say Yes/Lonely School Days	1966	3.75	7.50	15.00
❑ 1963	Ramona Say Yes/Havana Moon	1966	3.75	7.50	15.00
❑ 2090	Tulane/Have Mercy Judge	1970	—	3.00	6.00
❑ 2131	My Ding-a-Ling/Johnny B. Goode	1972	—	3.00	6.00
—All-blue label					
❑ 2131	My Ding-a-Ling/Johnny B. Goode	1972	—	2.00	4.00
—Orange and blue label					
❑ 2136	Reelin' & Rockin'/Let's Boogie	1972	—	2.00	4.00
❑ 2140	Roll 'Em Pete/Bio	1973	—	2.00	4.00
❑ 2169	Baby What You Want Me to Do/Shake, Rattle and Roll	1975	—	2.00	4.00
COLLECTABLES					
❑ 3437	Run Rudolph Run/Merry Christmas Baby	199?	—	—	3.00
MERCURY					
❑ 30143	Maybellene/Sweet Little Sixteen	196?	—	3.00	6.00
❑ 30144	Memphis/School Day (Ring, Ring Goes the Bell)	196?	—	3.00	6.00
❑ 30145	Back in the U.S.A./Roll Over Beethoven	196?	—	3.00	6.00
❑ 30146	Johnny B. Goode/Rock and Roll Music	196?	—	3.00	6.00
—The Mercury 30000 series are re-recordings of the Chess hits					
❑ 72643	Club Nitty Gritty/Laugh and Cry	1966	2.50	5.00	10.00
❑ 72680	Back to Memphis/I Do Really Love You	1967	2.50	5.00	10.00
❑ 72748	It Hurts Me Too/Feelin' It	1967	2.50	5.00	10.00
❑ 72840	Louie to Frisco/Ma Dear	1968	2.50	5.00	10.00
❑ 72963	It's Too Dark in There/Good Looking Woman	1969	5.00	10.00	20.00
❑ 72963 [PS]	It's Too Dark in There/Good Looking Woman	1969	7.50	15.00	30.00
PHILCO-FORD					
❑ HP-34	Maybellene/Roll Over Beethoven	1969	5.00	10.00	20.00
—4-inch plastic "Hip Pocket Record" with color sleeve					

7-Inch Extended Plays

Number	Title (A Side/B Side)	Yr	VG	VG+	NM
CHESS					
❑ CH-5118	School Day (Ring, Ring Goes the Bell)/Wee Wee Hours//Brown Eyed Handsome Man/Too Much Monkey Business	1957	30.00	60.00	120.00
❑ CH-5118 [PS]	Head Over Heels	1957	50.00	100.00	200.00
❑ CH-5119	Rock & Roll Music/Blue Feeling//Oh Baby Doll/ La Jaunda (Espanol)	1957	25.00	50.00	100.00
❑ CH-5119 [PS]	Rock and Roll Music	1957	50.00	100.00	200.00
❑ CH-5121	Sweet Little Sixteen/Rockin' at the Philharmonic/ /Reelin' and Rockin'/Guitar Boogie	1958	25.00	50.00	100.00
❑ CH-5121 [PS]	Sweet Little Sixteen	1958	50.00	100.00	200.00
❑ CH-5124	(contents unknown)	1958	25.00	50.00	100.00
❑ CH-5124 [PS]	Pickin' Berries	1958	50.00	100.00	200.00
❑ EP-5126	Jo Jo Gun/Sweet Little Rock and Roller//Johnny B. Goode/Around and Around	1958	25.00	50.00	100.00
❑ EP-5126 [PS]	Sweet Little Rock and Roller	1958	50.00	100.00	200.00

BERRY, DAVE

Number	Title (A Side/B Side)	Yr	VG	VG+	NM
LONDON					
❑ 9666	Memphis Tennessee/My Baby Left Me	1964	3.75	7.50	15.00
❑ 9698	The Crying Game/Don't Gimme No Lip Child	1964	4.00	8.00	16.00
❑ 9781	This Strange Effect/Now	1965	3.75	7.50	15.00
❑ 20038	Do I Still Figure in Your Life/Latisha	1968	2.00	4.00	8.00
PARROT					
❑ 40010	Picture Me Gone/Baby's Gone	1967	2.50	5.00	10.00

BERRY, JAN

Includes records as "Jan Barry" and "I Jan I." Also see JAN AND DEAN.

Number	Title (A Side/B Side)	Yr	VG	VG+	NM
A&M					
❑ 1957	Little Queenie/That's the Way It Is	1977	3.75	7.50	15.00
❑ 2020	Skateboard Surfin' U.S.A. (Sidewalk Surfin' with Me)/How How I Love You	1978	3.75	7.50	15.00
LIBERTY					
❑ 55845	The Universal Coward/I Can't Wait to Love You	1965	5.00	10.00	20.00
❑ 55845 [PS]	The Universal Coward/I Can't Wait to Love You	1965	75.00	150.00	300.00
ODE					
❑ 66023	Mother Earth/Blue Moon Shuffle	1972	5.00	10.00	20.00
❑ 66034	Don't You Just Know It/Blue Moon Shuffle	1973	10.00	20.00	40.00
—With Brian Wilson on co-lead vocals on A-side					
❑ 66050	Tinsel Town/Blow Up Music	1974	5.00	10.00	20.00
—As "I Jan I"					
❑ 66120	Sing Sang a Song/Sing Sang a Song (Singalong Version)	1976	5.00	10.00	20.00
RIPPLE					
❑ 6101	Tomorrow's Teardrops/My Midsummer Night's Dream	1961	25.00	50.00	100.00
—As "Jan Barry"					

BERRY, MIKE

Number	Title (A Side/B Side)	Yr	VG	VG+	NM
CORAL					
❑ 62341	A Tribute to Buddy Holly/Every Little Kiss	1962	15.00	30.00	60.00
❑ 62357	Don't You Think It's Time/Loneliness	1963	7.50	15.00	30.00
❑ 62483	Gonna Fall in Love/It Comes and Goes	1966	4.00	8.00	16.00
EPIC					
❑ 50748	I Am a Rocker/Boogaloo Dues	1979	—	2.00	4.00
❑ 50913	Stay Close to Me/One by One	1980	—	2.00	4.00
MCA					
❑ 40432	Don't Be Cruel/It's All Over	1975	—	2.50	5.00

BERRY, RICHARD

Number	Title (A Side/B Side)	Yr	VG	VG+	NM
FLAIR					
❑ 1016	I'm Still in Love with You/One Little Prayer	1953	20.00	40.00	80.00
❑ 1052	Bye Bye/At Last	1954	15.00	30.00	60.00
—With the Dreamers					
❑ 1055	What You Do to Me/The Big Break	1954	15.00	30.00	60.00
❑ 1058	Daddy Daddy/Baby Darling	1954	15.00	30.00	60.00
—With the Dreamers					
❑ 1064	Please Tell Me/Oh Oh Get Out of the Car	1955	12.50	25.00	50.00
❑ 1068	God Gave Me You/Doncha Go	1955	12.50	25.00	50.00
❑ 1071	Next Time/Crazy Lover	1955	12.50	25.00	50.00
❑ 1075	Together/Jelly Roll	1955	12.50	25.00	50.00
FLIP					
❑ 318	Take the Key/No Kissin' and Huggin'	1956	10.00	20.00	40.00
❑ 321	Louie, Louie/You Are My Sunshine	1957	15.00	30.00	60.00
❑ 321	Louie, Louie/Rock, Rock, Rock	1957	10.00	20.00	40.00
❑ 327	Sweet Sugar You/Rock, Rock, Rock	1957	10.00	20.00	40.00
❑ 331	You're the Girl/You Look So Good	1958	10.00	20.00	40.00
❑ 336	Heaven on Wheels/The Mess Around	1958	10.00	20.00	40.00
❑ 339	Besame Mucho/Do I, Do I	1958	7.50	15.00	30.00
❑ 349	Have Love, Will Travel/No Room	1960	7.50	15.00	30.00
❑ 352	I'll Never Ever Love Again/Somewhere There's a Rainbow	1961	7.50	15.00	30.00
❑ 360	You Look So Good/You Are My Sunshine	1962	7.50	15.00	30.00
HAPPY TIGER					
❑ 5063	Louie Louie/Rock Rock Rock	1972	2.00	4.00	8.00
K&G					
❑ 9001	I'm Your Fool/In a Really Big Way	1961	7.50	15.00	30.00
RPM					
❑ 448	Rockin' Man/Big John	1955	25.00	50.00	100.00
❑ 452	Pretty Brown Eyes/I Am Bewildered	1956	7.50	15.00	30.00
❑ 465	Angel of My Life/Yama Yama Pretty Mama	1956	25.00	50.00	100.00
❑ 477	Wait for Me/Good Love	1956	7.50	15.00	30.00
SMASH					
❑ 1789	What Good Is a Heart/Everybody's Got a Lover But Me	1963	3.00	6.00	12.00
❑ 1811	I'm Learning/Empty Chair	1963	3.00	6.00	12.00
WARNER BROS.					
❑ 5164	Walk Right In/It's All Right	1960	12.50	25.00	50.00

BERRY KIDS, THE

Number	Title (A Side/B Side)	Yr	VG	VG+	NM
MGM					
❑ 12379	Go, Go, Go, Right Into Town/Love Me, Love	1956	20.00	40.00	80.00
❑ 12496	Rootie Tootie/Yo're My Teenage Baby	1957	20.00	40.00	80.00

BEST, PETER (1)

Former drummer with THE BEATLES.

Number	Title (A Side/B Side)	Yr	VG	VG+	NM
CAMEO					
❑ 391	Boys/Kansas City	1965	20.00	40.00	80.00
❑ 391 [PS]	Boys/Kansas City	1965	25.00	50.00	100.00
HAPPENING					
❑ 405	If You Can't Get Her/Don't Play with Me	1964	45.00	90.00	180.00
❑ 1117/8	If You Can't Get Her/The Way I Feel About You	1966	37.50	75.00	150.00
—Label credit: "Best of the Beatles (Peter Best)"					
MR. MAESTRO					
❑ 711	I Can't Do Without You Now/Keys to My Heart	1965	50.00	100.00	200.00
—Label credit: "Best of the Beatles"; black vinyl					

Number	Title (A Side/B Side)	Yr	VG	VG+	NM
❑ 711	I Can't Do Without You Now/Keys to My Heart	1965	37.50	75.00	150.00
	—Label credit: "Best of the Beatles"; blue vinyl				
❑ 712	Casting My Spell/I'm Blue	1965	37.50	75.00	150.00
	—Black vinyl				
❑ 712	Casting My Spell/I'm Blue	1965	50.00	100.00	200.00
	—Blue vinyl				

ORIGINAL BEATLES DRUMMER

Number	Title (A Side/B Side)	Yr	VG	VG+	NM
❑ 800	(I'll Try) Anyway/I Wanna Be There	1964	45.00	90.00	180.00

BEST, PETER (2)

This Peter Best is from Australia.

CAPITOL

Number	Title (A Side/B Side)	Yr	VG	VG+	NM
❑ 2092	Carousel of Love/Want You	1968	7.50	15.00	30.00

BETTS, DICKEY

Also see THE ALLMAN BROTHERS BAND.

ARISTA

Number	Title (A Side/B Side)	Yr	VG	VG+	NM
❑ 0255	Nothing You Can Do	1977	—	2.00	4.00
❑ 0269	Bougainvilla/Sweet Virginia	1977	—	2.00	4.00
❑ 0333	Atlanta's Burning Down/Mr. Blues Man	1978	—	2.00	4.00

CAPRICORN

Number	Title (A Side/B Side)	Yr	VG	VG+	NM
❑ 0213	Kissimmee Kid/Long Time Gone	1974	—	2.50	5.00
❑ 0221	Highway Call/Rain	1975	—	2.50	5.00

BIG BAD VOODOO DADDY

COOLSVILLE

Number	Title (A Side/B Side)	Yr	VG	VG+	NM
❑ S7-19895	You & Me & the Bottle Makes 3 Tonight (Baby)/Jumpin' Jack	1998	—	2.00	4.00

BIG BEATS, THE

Also see TRINI LOPEZ.

COLUMBIA

Number	Title (A Side/B Side)	Yr	VG	VG+	NM
❑ 41072	Clark's Expedition/Big Boy	1958	6.25	12.50	25.00
❑ 41179	Rush Me/Sentimental Journey	1958	6.25	12.50	25.00

BIG BOPPER

D

Number	Title (A Side/B Side)	Yr	VG	VG+	NM
❑ 1008	Chantilly Lace/The Purple People Eater Meets the Witch Doctor	1958	62.50	125.00	250.00

MERCURY

Number	Title (A Side/B Side)	Yr	VG	VG+	NM
❑ 71219	Beggar to a King/Crazy Blue	1957	15.00	30.00	60.00
	—As "Jape Richardson"				
❑ 71312	A Teenage Mom/Monkey Song	1958	15.00	30.00	60.00
	—As "Jape Richardson"				
❑ 71343	Chantilly Lace/The Purple People Eater Meets the Witch Doctor	1958	5.00	10.00	20.00
❑ 71375	Big Bopper's Wedding/Little Red Riding Hood	1958	3.75	7.50	15.00
❑ 71416	Someone's Watching Over You/Walking Through My Dreams	1959	3.75	7.50	15.00
❑ 71451	It's the Truth, Ruth/That's What I'm Talkin' About	1959	3.75	7.50	15.00
❑ 71482	Pink Petticoats/Time Clock	1959	3.75	7.50	15.00

BIG BROTHER

ALL AMERICAN

Number	Title (A Side/B Side)	Yr	VG	VG+	NM
❑ 5718	E.S.P./Brother, Where Are You	1970	10.00	20.00	40.00

BIG BROTHER AND THE HOLDING COMPANY

Also see JANIS JOPLIN.

COLUMBIA

Number	Title (A Side/B Side)	Yr	VG	VG+	NM
❑ 44626	Piece of My Heart/Turtle Blues	1968	2.50	5.00	10.00
❑ 45284	Keep On/Home on the Strange	1970	—	3.00	6.00
❑ 45502	Black Widow Spider/Nu Boogaloo Jam	1971	—	3.00	6.00

MAINSTREAM

Number	Title (A Side/B Side)	Yr	VG	VG+	NM
❑ 657	All Is Loneliness/Blindman	1967	3.00	6.00	12.00
❑ 662	Down on Me/Call On Me	1967	3.00	6.00	12.00
❑ 666	Bye Bye Baby/Intruder	1968	3.00	6.00	12.00
❑ 675	Women Is Losers/Caterpillar	1968	3.00	6.00	12.00
❑ 675	Women Is Losers/Light Is Faster Than Sound	1968	3.00	6.00	12.00
❑ 678	Coo Coo/The Last Time	1968	3.00	6.00	12.00

BIG ED AND HIS COMBO

See EDDIE BURNS.

BIG FRANK AND THE ESSENCES

BLUE ROCK

Number	Title (A Side/B Side)	Yr	VG	VG+	NM
❑ 4012	Secret/I Won't Let Her See Me Cry	1965	50.00	100.00	200.00

PHILIPS

Number	Title (A Side/B Side)	Yr	VG	VG+	NM
❑ 40283	Secret/I Won't Let Her See Me Cry	1965	25.00	50.00	100.00

BIG GUYS, THE

Probably two different groups.

PALETTE

Number	Title (A Side/B Side)	Yr	VG	VG+	NM
❑ 5110	Walkin' the Board/Faith 7	1963	6.25	12.50	25.00
❑ 5114	Propulsion/(B-side unknown)	1964	6.25	12.50	25.00

WARNER BROS.

Number	Title (A Side/B Side)	Yr	VG	VG+	NM
❑ 7047	Hang My Head and Cry/Mr. Cupid (Don't You Call on Me)	1967	12.50	25.00	50.00

BIG MAYBELLE

BRUNSWICK

Number	Title (A Side/B Side)	Yr	VG	VG+	NM
❑ 55234	Candy/Cry	1962	3.00	6.00	12.00
❑ 55242	Cold, Cold Heart/Why Was I Born	1963	3.00	6.00	12.00
❑ 55256	Everybody's Got a Home But Me/How Deep Is the Ocean	1963	3.00	6.00	12.00

CHESS

Number	Title (A Side/B Side)	Yr	VG	VG+	NM
❑ 1967	It's a Man's Man's Man's World/Big Maybelle Sings the Blues	1966	2.50	5.00	10.00

OKEH

Number	Title (A Side/B Side)	Yr	VG	VG+	NM
❑ 6931	Gabbin' Blues/Rain Down Rain	1953	10.00	20.00	40.00
❑ 6955	Way Back Home/Just Want Your Love	1953	10.00	20.00	40.00
❑ 6998	Send for Me/Jimmy Mule	1953	10.00	20.00	40.00
❑ 7009	My Country Man/Maybelle's Blues	1953	10.00	20.00	40.00
❑ 7026	I've Got a Feelin'/You'll Never Know	1954	7.50	15.00	30.00
❑ 7042	My Big Mistake/I'm Gettin' 'Long Alright	1954	7.50	15.00	30.00
❑ 7053	Ain't No Use/Don't Leave Poor Me	1955	7.50	15.00	30.00
❑ 7060	Whole Lotta Shakin' Goin' On/One Monkey Don't Stop No Show	1955	7.50	15.00	30.00
❑ 7066	Such a Cutie/The Other Night	1956	7.50	15.00	30.00
❑ 7069	Gabbin' Blues/New Kind of Mambo	1956	7.50	15.00	30.00

PARAMOUNT

Number	Title (A Side/B Side)	Yr	VG	VG+	NM
❑ 0237	Blame It on Your Love/See See Rider	1973	—	3.00	6.00

PORT

Number	Title (A Side/B Side)	Yr	VG	VG+	NM
❑ 3002	Let Me Go/No Better for You	1965	3.00	6.00	12.00

ROJAC

Number	Title (A Side/B Side)	Yr	VG	VG+	NM
❑ 112	96 Tears/That's Life	1966	2.50	5.00	10.00
❑ 115	I Can't Wait Any Longer/Turn the World Around the Other Way	1967	2.00	4.00	8.00
❑ 116	Mama (He Treats Your Daughter Mean)/Keep That Man	1967	2.00	4.00	8.00
❑ 118	Quittin' Time/I Can't Wait Any Longer	1967	2.00	4.00	8.00
❑ 121	Heaven Will Welcome You, Dr. King/Eleanor Rigby	1968	2.50	5.00	10.00
❑ 124	How It Lies/Old Love Never Dies	1968	2.00	4.00	8.00
❑ 1003	Careless Love/My Mother's Eyes	196?	2.00	4.00	8.00
❑ 1969	Don't Pass Me By/It's Been Raining	1966	2.50	5.00	10.00

SAVOY

Number	Title (A Side/B Side)	Yr	VG	VG+	NM
❑ 1195	Candy/That's a Pretty Good Love	1956	5.00	10.00	20.00
❑ 1500	Mean to Me/Tell Me Who	1956	3.75	7.50	15.00
❑ 1512	I Don't Want to Cry/All of Me	1957	3.75	7.50	15.00
❑ 1519	Rock House/Jim	1957	3.75	7.50	15.00
❑ 1527	So Long/Ring Dang Dilly	1957	3.75	7.50	15.00
❑ 1536	Blues Early, Early (Part 1)/Blues Early, Early (Part 2)	1958	3.75	7.50	15.00
❑ 1541	White Christmas/Silent Night	1958	3.75	7.50	15.00
❑ 1558	Baby Won't You Please Come Home/Say It Isn't Do	1959	3.75	7.50	15.00
❑ 1572	A Good Man Is Hard to Find/Pitiful	1959	3.75	7.50	15.00
❑ 1576	Some of These Days/I Understand	1959	3.75	7.50	15.00
❑ 1583	I Got It Bad and That Ain't Good/Ramblin' Blues	1960	3.75	7.50	15.00
❑ 1583	I Got It Bad and That Ain't Good/Until the Real Thing Comes Along	1960	3.75	7.50	15.00
❑ 1595	I Ain't Got Nobody/Going Home Baby	1961	3.75	7.50	15.00

SCEPTER

Number	Title (A Side/B Side)	Yr	VG	VG+	NM
❑ 1288	I Don't Want to Cry/Yesterday's Kisses	1965	3.00	6.00	12.00

BIG STAR

Alex Chilton, formerly of THE BOX TOPS, was lead singer.

ARDENT

Number	Title (A Side/B Side)	Yr	VG	VG+	NM
❑ 2902	When My Baby's Beside Me/In the Street	1972	6.25	12.50	25.00
❑ 2904	Watch the Sunrise/Don't Lie to Me	1972	6.25	12.50	25.00
	—With correct song on B-side. Label has the number "AS-01180" on it.				
❑ 2904	Watch the Sunrise/Don't Lie to Me	1972	12.50	25.00	50.00
	—B-side plays the song "Thirteen" in error. Label has the number "AS-01127" on it.				
❑ 2909	O My Soul/Morphatoo—I'm in Love with a Girl	1974	5.00	10.00	20.00
❑ 2912	September Gurls/(B-side unknown)	1974	5.00	10.00	20.00

BIKINIS, THE

DOT

Number	Title (A Side/B Side)	Yr	VG	VG+	NM
❑ 15808	Fatima the Dreamer/Kitchy Koo	1958	6.25	12.50	25.00
❑ 15872	Chop Stick Rock/A'Right, A'Ready	1958	10.00	20.00	40.00

ROULETTE

Number	Title (A Side/B Side)	Yr	VG	VG+	NM
❑ 4073	Bikini/Boogie Rock 'n' Roll	1958	6.25	12.50	25.00

TOP RANK

Number	Title (A Side/B Side)	Yr	VG	VG+	NM
❑ 2032	Crazy Vibrations/Spunky	1959	6.25	12.50	25.00

BILLY AND LILLIE

Also see BILLY FORD.

ABC-PARAMOUNT

Number	Title (A Side/B Side)	Yr	VG	VG+	NM
❑ 10421	Love Me Sincerely/Whip It To Me Baby	1963	7.50	15.00	30.00
❑ 10489	Carry Me Across the Threshold/Why I Love Billy (Lillie)	1963	7.50	15.00	30.00

CAMEO

Number	Title (A Side/B Side)	Yr	VG	VG+	NM
❑ 412	Nothing Moves (Without a Little Push)/The Two of Us	1966	2.50	5.00	10.00
❑ 435	You Got Me by the Heart/Hear You Better Hear	1966	2.50	5.00	10.00

SWAN

Number	Title (A Side/B Side)	Yr	VG	VG+	NM
❑ 4002	La Dee Dah/The Monster	1957	7.50	15.00	30.00
	—"SWAN" in all capital letters; B-side by Billy Ford and the Thunderbirds				
❑ 4002	La Dee Dah/The Monster	1958	5.00	10.00	20.00
	—Only the S in "Swan" is capitalized; B-side by Billy Ford and the Thunderbirds				
❑ 4005	Happiness/Creepin' Crawlin' Cryin'	1958	5.00	10.00	20.00
❑ 4011	The Greasy Spoon/Hanging On to You	1958	5.00	10.00	20.00
❑ 4020	Lucky Ladybug/I Promise You	1958	6.25	12.50	25.00
❑ 4030	Tumbled Down/A.H. Thomas the Cat	1959	3.75	7.50	15.00
❑ 4036	Bells, Bells, Bells/Honeymoonin'	1959	3.75	7.50	15.00
❑ 4042	Terrific Together/Swampy	1959	3.75	7.50	15.00
❑ 4051	Free for All/The Ins and Outs of Love	1960	3.75	7.50	15.00
❑ 4058	That's the Way the Cookie Crumbles (Ah-So)/Over the Mountain, Across the Sea	1960	3.75	7.50	15.00
❑ 4069	Ain't Comin' Back (To You)/Bananas	1961	3.75	7.50	15.00

BILLY AND THE BEATERS

See BILLY VERA.

BILLY AND THE ESSENTIALS

CAMEO

Number	Title (A Side/B Side)	Yr	VG	VG+	NM
❑ 344	Remember Me Baby/The Actor	1965	100.00	200.00	400.00

JAMIE

Number	Title (A Side/B Side)	Yr	VG	VG+	NM
❑ 1229	The Dance Is Over/Steady Girl	1962	7.50	15.00	30.00
❑ 1239	Over the Weekend/Maybe You'll Be There	1962	7.50	15.00	30.00

LANDA

Number	Title (A Side/B Side)	Yr	VG	VG+	NM
❑ 691	The Dance Is Over/Steady Girl	1962	12.50	25.00	50.00

MERCURY

Number	Title (A Side/B Side)	Yr	VG	VG+	NM
❑ 72127	Young at Heart/Lonely Weekend	1963	6.25	12.50	25.00
❑ 72210	Last Dance/Yes Sir, That's My Baby	1963	6.25	12.50	25.00

Number	Title (A Side/B Side)	Yr	VG	VG+	NM
SMASH					
❑ 2045	Babalu's Wedding Day/My Way of Saying	1966	3.75	7.50	15.00
❑ 2071	Don't Cry (Sing Along with the Music)/Baby Go Away	1966	3.00	6.00	12.00
SSS INTERNATIONAL					
❑ 706	I Wrote a Song/Oh What a Feeling	1967	3.00	6.00	12.00
BILLY BOY					
VEE JAY					
❑ 146	I Wish You the World/I Was Fooled	1955	20.00	40.00	80.00
❑ 171	I Ain't Got You/Don't Stay Out All Night	1956	20.00	40.00	80.00
—Label lists artist as "Billy Boy Arnold"					
❑ 192	Here's My Picture/You've Got Me Wrong	1956	10.00	20.00	40.00
❑ 238	Kissing at Midnight/My Heart Is Crying	1957	10.00	20.00	40.00
❑ 260	Rockinitis/Prisoner's Plea	1957	10.00	20.00	40.00
BILLY JOE AND THE CHECKMATES					
DORE					
❑ 620	Percolator (Twist)/Round & Round & Round & Round	1961	3.75	7.50	15.00
❑ 636	Rocky's Theme/Twist That Thing	1962	3.00	6.00	12.00
❑ 643	The Chester Drag/Laughing Machine Gunner	1962	3.00	6.00	12.00
❑ 652	Chalypso Dancer/My Friend, the Rain	1962	3.00	6.00	12.00
❑ 664	Solid Gold Hubcaps/Laughing Woodpecker	1963	3.00	6.00	12.00
❑ 668	Bossville/One More Cup	1963	3.00	6.00	12.00
❑ 680	Shake, Shake, Shake/Summertime in Venice	1963	3.00	6.00	12.00
❑ 685	Last Dance/My Friend the Rain	1963	3.00	6.00	12.00
❑ 694	The Drifter/Nashville West (One More Time)	1963	3.00	6.00	12.00
❑ 697	Forbidden Planet/Slauson, Baby, Slauson	1964	3.00	6.00	12.00
❑ 703	Spotlight Dance/Zip Code	1964	3.00	6.00	12.00
❑ 720	C'mopn Everybody (Part 1)/C'mon Everybody (Part 2)	1964	3.00	6.00	12.00
❑ 728	Bells of Rome/Shadows	1965	2.50	5.00	10.00
❑ 747	Clair de Looney/Holding Hands	1966	2.50	5.00	10.00
❑ 756	Voyage to the Bottom of the Sea/Nutty Dance Instructor	1966	2.50	5.00	10.00
❑ 791	A Man and a Woman/Floatin'	1967	2.50	5.00	10.00
❑ 857	Ambrosia/Newport Beach Concerto	1971	—	3.00	6.00
❑ 871	Try It, You'll Like It/Topless Dancer	1972	—	2.50	5.00
❑ 884	Aphrodisiac (Part 1)/Aphrodisiac (Part 2)	1973	—	2.50	5.00
❑ 892	Flaky (same on both sides)	1974	—	2.50	5.00
❑ 982	Raindrops, Mem'ries, and Tears/Liuvio, Memorias, y Lagramas	1985	—	2.00	4.00
BINKLEY, JIMMY					
ALADDIN					
❑ 3193	Night Life/Hot Smoke	1953	30.00	60.00	120.00
CHANCE					
❑ 1134	Hey, Hey Sugar Ray/Midnite Wail	1953	50.00	100.00	200.00
CHECKER					
❑ 789	Wine, Wine, Wine/Boogie On the Hour	1954	50.00	100.00	200.00
❑ 835	Messin' Around/You Made a Boo-Boo	1956	25.00	50.00	100.00
NOTE					
❑ 10002	Why Oh Why/Blue Moon	1957	75.00	150.00	300.00
BIRD WATCHERS, THE					
LAURIE					
❑ 3399	Turn Around Girl/You Got It	1967	3.00	6.00	12.00
MALA					
❑ 527	Girl I've Got News for You/Eddie's Tune	1966	7.50	15.00	30.00
❑ 536	I'm Gonna Love You Anyway/A Little Bit of Lovin'	1966	7.50	15.00	30.00
❑ 548	I'm Gonna Do It to You/I Have No Worried Mind	1966	7.50	15.00	30.00
❑ 555	Mary Mary (It's to You That I Belong)/Cry a Little Bit	1967	7.50	15.00	30.00
BIRKIN, JANE, AND SERGE GAINSBOURG					
FONTANA					
❑ 1665	Je T'Aime...Moi Non Plus/Jane B	1969	2.00	4.00	8.00
❑ 1684	La Decadanse/Les Langues de Chat	1969	—	2.50	5.00
BISCAYNES, THE					
NORTHRIDGE					
❑ 1001	Church Key/Moment of Truth	1963	15.00	30.00	60.00
—B-side by the Surfaris					
REPRISE					
❑ 20180	Church Key/Moment of Truth	1963	7.50	15.00	30.00
—B-side by the Surfaris					
BISHOP, EDDIE					
ABC					
❑ 10858	Candy Man/What You're Doing to Me	1966	6.25	12.50	25.00
ABC-PARAMOUNT					
❑ 10799	What Did He Say?/Call Me	1966	15.00	30.00	60.00
BJORN AND BENNY					
Early ABBA.					
PLAYBOY					
❑ 50014	Merry-Go-Round/People Need Love	1972	7.50	15.00	30.00
❑ 50018	Another Town, Another Train/I Am Just a Girl	1973	7.50	15.00	30.00
❑ 50025	Rock 'N Roll Band/Another Town, Another Train	1973	7.50	15.00	30.00
BLACK, BILL, 'S COMBO					
COLUMBIA					
❑ 44867	But It's Alright/Slow Action	1969	—	2.50	5.00
❑ 44983	California Dreamin'/Funky Train	1969	—	2.50	5.00
❑ 45092	Heaven Knows/One Five One Eight Chelsea	1970	—	2.50	5.00
❑ 45162	Keep the Customer Satisfied/One Five One Eight Chelsea	1970	—	2.50	5.00
HI					
❑ 2018	Smokie (Part 2)/Smokie (Part 1)	1959	5.00	10.00	20.00
❑ 2021	White Silver Sands/The Wheel	1960	5.00	10.00	20.00
❑ 2022	Josephine/Dry Bones	1960	3.75	7.50	15.00
❑ 2022 [PS]	Josephine/Dry Bones	1960	6.25	12.50	25.00

Number	Title (A Side/B Side)	Yr	VG	VG+	NM
❑ 2026	Don't Be Cruel/Rollin'	1960	3.75	7.50	15.00
❑ 2026 [PS]	Don't Be Cruel/Rollin'	1960	6.25	12.50	25.00
❑ 2027	Blue Tango/Willie	1960	3.75	7.50	15.00
❑ 2027 [PS]	Blue Tango/Willie	1960	6.25	12.50	25.00
❑ 2028	Hearts of Stone/Royal Blue	1961	3.00	6.00	12.00
❑ 2029	Old Time Religion/He's Got the Whole World in His Hands	1961	10.00	20.00	40.00
—Stereo single, small hole, plays at 33 1/3 rpm					
❑ 2030	Do Lord/When the Roll Is Called Up Yonder	1961	10.00	20.00	40.00
—Stereo single, small hole, plays at 33 1/3 rpm					
❑ 2031	Down by the Riverside/It Is No Secret (What God Can Do)	1961	10.00	20.00	40.00
—Stereo single, small hole, plays at 33 1/3 rpm					
❑ 2032	When the Saints Go Marching In/(B-side unknown)	1961	10.00	20.00	40.00
—Stereo single, small hole, plays at 33 1/3 rpm					
❑ 2033	Just a Closer Walk with Thee/This Old House	1961	10.00	20.00	40.00
—Stereo single, small hole, plays at 33 1/3 rpm					
❑ 2036	Ole Buttermilk Sky/Yogi	1961	3.00	6.00	12.00
❑ 2036 [PS]	Ole Buttermilk Sky/Yogi	1961	6.25	12.50	25.00
❑ 2038	Movin'/Honky Train	1961	3.00	6.00	12.00
❑ 2042	Twist-Her/My Girl Josephine	1961	3.00	6.00	12.00
❑ 2045	Twist-Her/Night Train	1962	10.00	20.00	40.00
—Stereo single, small hole, plays at 33 1/3 rpm					
❑ 2046	The Hucklebuck/Corrina, Corrina	1962	10.00	20.00	40.00
—Stereo single, small hole, plays at 33 1/3 rpm					
❑ 2047	Johnny B. Goode/(B-side unknown)	1962	10.00	20.00	40.00
—Stereo single, small hole, plays at 33 1/3 rpm					
❑ 2048	Josephine/My Girl Josephine	1962	10.00	20.00	40.00
—Stereo single, small hole, plays at 33 1/3 rpm					
❑ 2049	Slippin' and Slidin'/Twist with Me, Baby	1962	10.00	20.00	40.00
—Stereo single, small hole, plays at 33 1/3 rpm					
❑ 2052	Twistin' — White Silver Sands/My Babe	1962	3.00	6.00	12.00
❑ 2052 [PS]	Twistin' — White Silver Sands/My Babe	1962	6.25	12.50	25.00
❑ 2055	So What/Blues for the Red Boy	1962	3.00	6.00	12.00
❑ 2059	Joey's Song/Hot Taco	1962	3.00	6.00	12.00
❑ 2064	Do It — Rat Now/Little Jasper	1963	3.00	6.00	12.00
❑ 2069	Monkey-Shine/Love Gone	1963	3.00	6.00	12.00
❑ 2072	Comin' On/Soft Winds	1964	3.00	6.00	12.00
❑ 2077	Tequila/Raunchy	1964	3.00	6.00	12.00
❑ 2079	Little Queenie/Boo Ray	1964	3.00	6.00	12.00
❑ 2085	Come On Home/He'll Have to Go	1964	2.50	5.00	10.00
❑ 2094	Spootin'/Crazy Feeling	1965	2.50	5.00	10.00
❑ 2106	Hey, Good Lookin'/Mountain of Love	1966	2.50	5.00	10.00
❑ 2115	Rambler/You Call Everybody Darling	1966	2.50	5.00	10.00
❑ 2124	Son of Smokie/Peg Leg	1967	2.00	4.00	8.00
❑ 2145	Turn On Your Love Life/Ribbon of Darkness	1968	—	3.00	6.00
❑ 2153	Red Light/Bright Lights, Big City	1968	—	3.00	6.00
❑ 2168	Creepin' Around/The Son of Hickory Holler's Tramp	1969	—	3.00	6.00
❑ 2185	No More/Closin' Time	1971	—	2.50	5.00
❑ 2208	Daylite/Four A.M.	1972	—	2.50	5.00
❑ 2234	Smokey Bourbon Street/Mighty Fine	1973	—	2.50	5.00
❑ 2277	Soul Serenade/Pickin'	1974	—	2.00	4.00
❑ 2283	Truck Stop/Boilin' Cabbage	1975	—	2.00	4.00
❑ 2291	Almost Persuaded/Back Up and Push	1975	—	2.00	4.00
❑ 2301	Fire on the Bayou/Memphis Soul	1976	—	2.00	4.00
❑ 2311	I Can Help/Jump Back Joe	1976	—	2.00	4.00
❑ 2317	Redneck Rock/Yakety Sax	1976	—	2.00	4.00
❑ 78508	Cashin' In (A Tribute to Luther Perkins)/L.A. Blues	1978	—	2.00	4.00
MEGA					
❑ 0036	Rings/Cotton Carnival	1971	—	2.50	5.00
❑ 0052	Oh Happy Day/Sugar Cured	1971	—	2.50	5.00
❑ 0070	Harlem Nocturne/Sassy Parts	1972	—	2.50	5.00
❑ 0086	Night Train/Bluff City	1972	—	2.50	5.00
❑ 0113	Listen to the Music/Memphis Shuffle	1973	—	2.50	5.00
❑ 0117	Satin Sheets/Memphis Shuffle	1973	—	2.50	5.00
❑ 201	Smokie Part 2/Tequila	1973	—	2.50	5.00
❑ 207	Oh Happy Day/Listen to the Music	1974	—	2.00	4.00
7-Inch Extended Plays					
HI					
❑ HSP 2 [PS]	(title unknown)	1962	3.75	7.50	15.00
❑ HSP 2 [S]	My Babe/40 Miles of Bad Road/Ain't That Lovin' You Baby//What'd I Say/The Walk/Witchcraft	1962	3.75	7.50	15.00
—33 1/3 rpm jukebox single, small hole					
❑ SBG 26 [PS]	Bill Black's Combo Goes Big Band	196?	2.50	5.00	10.00
❑ SBG 26 [S]	T.D.'s Boogie Woogie/Tuxedo Junction/ Canadian Sunset//Leap Frog/In the Mood/So Rare	196?	2.50	5.00	10.00
—33 1/3 rpm jukebox single, small hole					
❑ HE 22002	Honky Tonk/Cherry Pink//Singing the Blues/You Win Again	1961	10.00	20.00	40.00
❑ HE 22002 [PS]	Solid and Raunchy	1961	10.00	20.00	40.00
BLACK, CILLA					
BELL					
❑ 726	Step Inside Love/I Couldn't Take My Eyes Off You	1968	5.00	10.00	20.00
CAPITOL					
❑ 5196	You're My World/Suffer Now I Must	1964	3.75	7.50	15.00
❑ 5258	It's for You/He Won't Ask Me	1964	3.00	6.00	12.00
❑ 5373	One Little Voice/Is It Love	1965	3.00	6.00	12.00
❑ 5414	I've Been Wrong Before/My Love Came Home	1965	3.00	6.00	12.00
❑ 5595	Love's Just a Broken Heart/Yesterday	1966	3.00	6.00	12.00
❑ 5595 [PS]	Love's Just a Broken Heart/Yesterday	1966	7.50	15.00	30.00
❑ 5674	Alfie/Night Time Is Here	1966	3.00	6.00	12.00
❑ 5763	Don't Answer Me/The Right One Is Left	1966	3.00	6.00	12.00
❑ 5782	A Fool Am I/For No One	1966	3.00	6.00	12.00
DJM					
❑ 70007	What the World Needs Now Is Love/Only Forever Will Do	1969	2.00	4.00	8.00
❑ 70011	Without Him/It'll Never Happen Again	1969	2.00	4.00	8.00

Number	Title (A Side/B Side)	Yr	VG	VG+	NM
❑ 70012	Surround Yourself with Sorrow/It'll Never Happen Again	1969	2.00	4.00	8.00
❑ 70014	Conversations/London Bridge	1969	2.00	4.00	8.00
❑ 70015	If I Thought You'd Ever Change Your Mind/It Feels So Good	1970	2.00	4.00	8.00
❑ 70016	If I Thought You'd Ever Change Your Mind/ Conversations	1970	2.00	4.00	8.00
❑ 70018 [DJ]	Across the Universe (mono/stereo)	1970	3.00	6.00	12.00
EMI					
❑ 4003	He Was a Writer/I'll Never Run Out of You	1974	—	3.00	6.00
PRIVATE STOCK					
❑ 45040	I'll Take a Tango/To Know Him Is To Love Him	1975	—	2.50	5.00
❑ 45077	Fantasy/It's Now	1976	—	2.50	5.00

BLACK, JAY
The second "Jay" of JAY AND THE AMERICANS.

Number	Title (A Side/B Side)	Yr	VG	VG+	NM
ATLANTIC					
❑ 3273	Dolphins/Running Scared	1975	—	2.50	5.00
MIDSONG INT'L					
❑ 72012	The Part of Me That Needs You Most/You Stole the Music	1980	—	2.00	4.00
MILLENNIUM					
❑ 618	Love Is In the Air/Please Stay	1978	—	2.50	5.00
PRIVATE STOCK					
❑ 45058	Every Time You Walk in the Room/I'd Build a Bridge	1975	—	2.50	5.00
ROULETTE					
❑ 7198	One Night Affair/Between Two Worlds	1976	—	3.00	6.00
UNITED ARTISTS					
❑ 50116	What Will My Mary Say/Return to Me	1967	3.00	6.00	12.00
❑ 50116 [PS]	What Will My Mary Say/Return to Me	1967	6.25	12.50	25.00

BLACK, OSCAR

Number	Title (A Side/B Side)	Yr	VG	VG+	NM
ATLANTIC					
❑ 956	Love, Love, Love/Troubled Man Blues	1952	37.50	75.00	150.00
GROOVE					
❑ 0012	I'll Get By/Hold Me Baby	1954	15.00	30.00	60.00
—With Sue Allen					
❑ 0102	Be My Baby/Ain't Nobody Home But Me	1955	15.00	30.00	60.00
—With Sue Allen					
❑ 0115	Baby, Please Don't Go/I'll Live My Life Alone	1955	15.00	30.00	60.00
—With Sue Allen					
❑ 0130	Think of Tomorrow/Set a Wedding Day	1955	15.00	30.00	60.00
—With Sue Allen and the Four Students					
❑ 0168	Into Each Heart (Some Tears Must Fall)/If I Cry Tomorrow	1956	12.50	25.00	50.00
—With Sue Allen					
SAVOY					
❑ 1600	I Got a Feeling/I'm a Fool to Care	1961	3.75	7.50	15.00

BLACK, TERRY

Number	Title (A Side/B Side)	Yr	VG	VG+	NM
DUNHILL					
❑ 4005	How Many Guys/Only Sixteen	1965	2.50	5.00	10.00
❑ 4046	Ordinary Girl/Baby's Gone	1966	2.50	5.00	10.00
TOLLIE					
❑ 9026	Unless You Care/Can't We Go Somewhere	1964	3.00	6.00	12.00
❑ 9041	Say It Again/Everyone Can Tell	1965	3.00	6.00	12.00
❑ 9041 [PS]	Say It Again/Everyone Can Tell	1965	5.00	10.00	20.00

BLACK, TERRY, AND LAUREL WARD

Number	Title (A Side/B Side)	Yr	VG	VG+	NM
KAMA SUTRA					
❑ 540	Oh Babe/Goin' Down	1972	—	2.50	5.00

BLACK OAK ARKANSAS

Number	Title (A Side/B Side)	Yr	VG	VG+	NM
ATCO					
❑ 6829	Lord Have Mercy on My Soul/Uncle Lijah	1971	—	2.50	5.00
❑ 6849	Singing the Blues/Hot and Nasty	1971	—	2.50	5.00
❑ 6878	Keep the Faith/The Big One's Still Coming	1972	—	2.00	4.00
❑ 6893	Full Moon Ride/We Help Each Other	1972	—	2.00	4.00
❑ 6925	Hot and Nasty/Hot Rod	1973	—	2.00	4.00
❑ 6948	Jim Dandy/Red Hot Lovin'	1973	—	2.50	5.00
❑ 7003	Hey Y'all/Sting Me	1974	—	2.00	4.00
❑ 7015	Taxman/Dixie	1975	—	2.00	4.00
❑ 7019	Back Door Man/Good Stuff	1975	—	2.00	4.00
CAPRICORN					
❑ 0284	Not Fade Away/Feels So Good	1978	—	2.00	4.00
—Label lists artist as "Black Oak"					
❑ 0305	Ride with Me/Wind in Our Sails	1978	—	2.00	4.00
—Label lists artist as "Black Oak"					
ENTERPRISE					
❑ 9010	King's Row/Older Than Grandpa	1970	2.50	5.00	10.00
MCA					
❑ 40496	Ace in the Hole/Strong Enough to Be Gentle	1975	—	2.00	4.00
❑ 40536	Great Balls of Fire/Highway Pirate	1976	—	2.00	4.00
❑ 40586	A Fistful of Love/Storm of Passion	1976	—	2.00	4.00
❑ 40621	When the Band Was Singin' "Shakin' All Over"/ Bad Boy's Back in School	1976	—	2.00	4.00

BLACK SABBATH
Also see OZZY OSBOURNE.

Number	Title (A Side/B Side)	Yr	VG	VG+	NM
WARNER BROS.					
❑ 7437	Paranoid/Wizard	1970	2.50	5.00	10.00
❑ 7530	Iron Man/Electric Funeral	1971	2.00	4.00	8.00
❑ 7625	Laguna Sunrise/Tomorrow's Dream	1972	2.00	4.00	8.00
❑ 7764	Sabbath, Bloody Sabbath/Changes	1973	2.00	4.00	8.00
❑ 7802	Iron Man/Electric Funeral	1974	2.00	4.00	8.00
❑ 8315	Rock 'N' Roll Doctor/It's Alright	1976	—	3.00	6.00
❑ 29434	Stonehenge/Trashed	1983	—	3.00	6.00
❑ 49549	Lady Evil/Children of the Sea	1980	—	3.00	6.00

BLACK SATIN
See THE FIVE SATINS.

BLACKBURN, LOU

Number	Title (A Side/B Side)	Yr	VG	VG+	NM
IMPERIAL					
❑ 5943	Grand Prix/Jazz-a-Nova	1963	7.50	15.00	30.00
❑ 5998	Two Note Samba/17 Richmond Park	1963	5.00	10.00	20.00

BLACKJACK
With Bruce Kulick (later of KISS) and Michael Bolotin (better known as MICHAEL BOLTON). The group on 20th Century may be a different band.

Number	Title (A Side/B Side)	Yr	VG	VG+	NM
20TH CENTURY					
❑ 2279	Inland Sea/Joyride	1976	2.00	4.00	8.00
POLYDOR					
❑ 2026	For You/Fallin'	1979	2.50	5.00	10.00
❑ 2046	Southern Ballad (If This Means Losing You)/ Without Your Love	1979	2.50	5.00	10.00
❑ 2123	My World Is Empty Without You/Airwaves	1980	2.50	5.00	10.00
❑ 14572	Heart of Mine/Love Me Tonight	1979	2.50	5.00	10.00

BLACKWELL, OTIS

Number	Title (A Side/B Side)	Yr	VG	VG+	NM
ATLANTIC					
❑ 1165	Make Ready for Love/When You're Around	1957	10.00	20.00	40.00
❑ 1178	Turtle Dove/What a Coincidence	1958	10.00	20.00	40.00
CUB					
❑ 9092	Jeannie's Wedding/I'd Rather Kiss You Than Eat	1961	5.00	10.00	20.00
❑ 9107	Sister Twister/Ga Ga	1962	5.00	10.00	20.00
DATE					
❑ 1006	Don't Run Away/Handle with Care	1958	7.50	15.00	30.00
EPIC					
❑ 10654	Just Keep It Up/It's All Over Me	1970	6.25	12.50	25.00
GROOVE					
❑ 0034	Oh, What a Babe/Here I Am	1954	10.00	20.00	40.00
JAY-DEE					
❑ 784	Daddy Rolling Stone/Tears! Tears! Tears!	1953	12.50	25.00	50.00
❑ 787	You're My Love/Bartender Fill It Up Again	1954	12.50	25.00	50.00
❑ 791	On That Power Line/Don't You Know How I Love You	1954	12.50	25.00	50.00
❑ 792	I'm Standing at the Doorway/Nobody Met the Train	1954	12.50	25.00	50.00
❑ 794	My Josephine/Ain't Got No Time	1954	12.50	25.00	50.00
❑ 798	Go Away Mr. Blues/I'm Comin' Back Baby	1955	12.50	25.00	50.00
❑ 802	You Move Me Baby/My Poor Broken Heart	1955	12.50	25.00	50.00
❑ 808	Oh What a Wonderful Time/Let the Daddy Hold You	1955	12.50	25.00	50.00
MGM					
❑ 13090	Kiss Away/Grandaddy of Them All	1962	5.00	10.00	20.00
RCA VICTOR					
❑ 47-5069	Wake You Fool/Please Help Me Find	1952	12.50	25.00	50.00
❑ 47-5225	The Fool That I Be/Number 000	1953	12.50	25.00	50.00

BLADES, CAROL

Number	Title (A Side/B Side)	Yr	VG	VG+	NM
GEE					
❑ 1029	When Will I Know/What Did I Do Wrong	1957	50.00	100.00	200.00

BLADES OF GRASS, THE

Number	Title (A Side/B Side)	Yr	VG	VG+	NM
JUBILEE					
❑ 5582	Happy/That's What a Boy Likes	1967	2.00	4.00	8.00
❑ 5590	Just Another Face/Baby You're a Real Good Friend of Mine	1967	2.00	4.00	8.00
❑ 5605	Help/Justah	1967	2.00	4.00	8.00
❑ 5616	You Won't Find That Girl/Charlie and Fred	1968	2.00	4.00	8.00
❑ 5622	The Way You'll Never Be/You Turned Off the Sun	1968	2.00	4.00	8.00
❑ 5635	I Love You, Alice B. Toklas/That's What a Boy Likes	1968	2.00	4.00	8.00
❑ 5662	Love Her and Cherish Her/Pageant	1969	2.00	4.00	8.00

BLAINE, HAL

Number	Title (A Side/B Side)	Yr	VG	VG+	NM
ABC DUNHILL					
❑ 4181	Beverly Drive/Midnight at Fink's	1969	3.00	6.00	12.00
DUNHILL					
❑ 4006	La Bamba/Topsy '65	1965	3.75	7.50	15.00
❑ 4021	Secret Agent Man/Midnight at Pink's	1966	3.75	7.50	15.00
❑ 4049	Bang Bang Rhythm/Drums A-Go-Go	1966	3.75	7.50	15.00
❑ 4074	The Swinger/Drums A-Go-Go	1967	3.75	7.50	15.00
❑ 4091	Love-In (December)/Wiggy (November)	1967	3.75	7.50	15.00
❑ 4102	The Invaders/Secret Agent Man	1967	3.75	7.50	15.00
❑ 4142	Allegro from "Mac Arthur Park"/Drums A-Go-Go	1968	3.75	7.50	15.00
MELODY HOUSE					
❑ 100	Slow Gate/South of Shreveport	1962	10.00	20.00	40.00
RCA VICTOR					
❑ 47-8147	Hawaii 1963/East Side Story	1963	6.25	12.50	25.00
❑ 47-8223	Dance with the Surfin' Band/The Drummer Plays for Me	1963	6.25	12.50	25.00
❑ 47-8282	Challenger II/Gear Stripper	1963	6.25	12.50	25.00
ROCK-IT					
❑ 1000	Alamo Rock/Alamo Rock (Part 2)	1959	12.50	25.00	50.00

BLAKE, TOMMY

Number	Title (A Side/B Side)	Yr	VG	VG+	NM
BUDDY					
❑ 107	I'm a Fool/Kool It	1958	7.50	15.00	30.00
CHANCELLOR					
❑ 101	I Gotta Be Somewhere/Three Cheers for the Red, White and Blue	19??	2.50	5.00	10.00
RCA VICTOR					
❑ 47-6925	Freedom/Mr. Hoody	1957	12.50	25.00	50.00
SUN					
❑ 278	Flatfoot Sam/Lordy Hoody	1957	25.00	50.00	100.00
❑ 300	Sweetie Pie/I Dig You	1958	75.00	150.00	300.00

BLAND, BILLY

OLD TOWN

Number	Title (A Side/B Side)	Yr	VG	VG+	NM
❑ 1016	Chicken in the Basket/The Fat Man	1956	5.00	10.00	20.00
❑ 1022	Chicken Hop/Oh You for Me	1956	5.00	10.00	20.00
❑ 1035	If I Could Be Your Man/I Had a Dream	1957	5.00	10.00	20.00
❑ 1076	Let the Little Girl Dance/Sweet Thing	1960	6.25	12.50	25.00
❑ 1082	You Were Born to Be Loved/Pardon Me	1960	3.75	7.50	15.00
❑ 1088	Make Believe Lover/Harmonys	1960	3.75	7.50	15.00
❑ 1093	Everything That Shines Ain't Gold/Keep Talkin' That Sweet Talk	1960	3.75	7.50	15.00
❑ 1098	I Cross My Heart/Steady Kind	1961	3.75	7.50	15.00
❑ 1105	My Heart's On Fire/Can't Stop Her from Dancing	1961	3.75	7.50	15.00
❑ 1109	Do the Bug with Me/Uncle Bud	1962	3.75	7.50	15.00
❑ 1114	Busy Little Boy/All I Want to Do Is Cry	1961	3.75	7.50	15.00
❑ 1124	Mama Stole the Chicken/I Spent My Life Loving You	1962	3.75	7.50	15.00
❑ 1128	Darling Won't You Think of Me/How Many Hearts	1962	3.75	7.50	15.00
❑ 1143	Doing the Mule/Farmer in the Dell	1963	3.75	7.50	15.00
❑ 1151	A Little Touch of Your Love/Little Boy Blue	1963	3.75	7.50	15.00

ST. LAWRENCE

Number	Title (A Side/B Side)	Yr	VG	VG+	NM
❑ 1005	She's Already Married/My Divorce	1965	3.00	6.00	12.00

TIP TOP

Number	Title (A Side/B Side)	Yr	VG	VG+	NM
❑ 708	Chicken in the Basket/Chicken Hop	1958	5.00	10.00	20.00

BLAND, BOBBY

Includes records by "Bobby 'Blue' Bland."

ABC

Number	Title (A Side/B Side)	Yr	VG	VG+	NM
❑ 12105	Yolanda/When You Come to the End of Your Road	1975	—	2.00	4.00
❑ 12134	I Take It On Home/You've Never Been This Far Before	1975	—	2.00	4.00
❑ 12156	Today I Started Loving You Again/Too Far Gone	1976	—	2.00	4.00
❑ 12189	It Ain't the Real Thing/Who's Foolin' Who	1976	—	2.00	4.00
❑ 12280	The Soul of a Man/If I Weren't a Gambler	1977	—	2.00	4.00
❑ 12330	Sittin' on a Poor Man's Throne/I Intend to Take Your Place	1978	—	2.00	4.00
❑ 12360	Love to See You Smile/I'm Just Your Man	1978	—	2.00	4.00
❑ 12405	Come Fly with Me/Ain't God Something	1978	—	2.00	4.00

ABC DUNHILL

Number	Title (A Side/B Side)	Yr	VG	VG+	NM
❑ 4369	This Time I'm Gone for Good/Where Baby Went	1973	—	2.50	5.00
❑ 4379	Goin' Down Slow/Up and Down World	1974	—	2.50	5.00
❑ 15003	Ain't No Love in the Heart of the City/Twenty-Four Hour Blues	1974	—	2.50	5.00
❑ 15015	I Wouldn't Treat a Dog (The Way You Treated Me)/I Ain't Gonna Be the First to Cry	1974	—	2.50	5.00

DUKE

Number	Title (A Side/B Side)	Yr	VG	VG+	NM
❑ 105	Lovin' Blues/I.O.U. Blues	1952	75.00	150.00	300.00
❑ 115	Army Blues/No Blow, No Show	1953	50.00	100.00	200.00
❑ 141	Time Out/It's My Life Baby	1955	15.00	30.00	60.00
❑ 146	You or None/Woke Up Screaming	1955	15.00	30.00	60.00
❑ 153	I Can't Put You Down/You've Got Bad Intentions	1956	12.50	25.00	50.00
❑ 160	I Learned My Lesson/I Don't Believe	1956	10.00	20.00	40.00
❑ 160	I Learned My Lesson/Lead Us On	1956	10.00	20.00	40.00
❑ 167	Don't Want No Woman/I Smell Trouble	1957	7.50	15.00	30.00
❑ 170	Farther Up the Road/Sometime Tomorrow	1957	7.50	15.00	30.00
❑ 182	Teach Me/Bobby's Blues	1957	6.25	12.50	25.00
❑ 185	You Got Me Where You Want Me/Loan a Helping Hand	1958	6.25	12.50	25.00
❑ 196	Little Boy Blue/Last Night	1958	6.25	12.50	25.00
❑ 300	You Did Me Wrong/I Lost Sight of the World	1959	6.25	12.50	25.00
❑ 303	Wishing Well/I'm Not Ashamed	1959	6.25	12.50	25.00
❑ 310	Is It Real/Someday	1959	6.25	12.50	25.00
❑ 314	I'll Take Care of You/That's Why	1959	6.25	12.50	25.00
❑ 318	Lead Me On/Hold Me Tenderly	1960	6.25	12.50	25.00
❑ 327	Cry Cry Cry/I've Been Wrong So Long	1960	6.25	12.50	25.00
❑ 332	I Pity the Fool/Close to You	1961	5.00	10.00	20.00
❑ 336	Don't Cry No More/How Does a Cheating Woman Feel	1961	5.00	10.00	20.00
❑ 338	Ain't That Loving You/Jelly, Jelly, Jelly	1961	5.00	10.00	20.00
❑ 340	Don't Cry No More/Saint James Infirmary	1961	5.00	10.00	20.00
❑ 344	Turn On Your Love Light/You're the One (That I Need)	1961	5.00	10.00	20.00
❑ 347	Who Will the Next Fool Be/Blue Moon	1962	5.00	10.00	20.00
❑ 352	Yield Not to Temptation/How Does a Cheating Woman Feel	1962	5.00	10.00	20.00
❑ 355	Stormy Monday Blues/Your Friends	1962	5.00	10.00	20.00
❑ 360	That's the Way Love Is/Call On Me	1962	5.00	10.00	20.00
❑ 366	Sometimes You Gotta Cry a Little/You're Worth It All	1963	3.75	7.50	15.00
❑ 369	Ain't It a Good Thing/Queen for a Day	1963	3.75	7.50	15.00
❑ 370	The Feeling Is Gone/I Can't Stop Singing	1963	3.75	7.50	15.00
❑ 375	Ain't Nothing You Can Do/Honey Child	1964	3.75	7.50	15.00
❑ 377	Share Your Love with Me/After It's Too Late	1964	2.50	5.00	10.00
❑ 383	Ain't Doing Too Bad (Part 1)/Ain't Doing Too Bad (Part 2)	1964	2.50	5.00	10.00
❑ 385	These Hands (Small But Mighty)/Today	1965	2.50	5.00	10.00
❑ 386	Blind Man/Black Night	1965	2.50	5.00	10.00
❑ 390	Dust Got in Daddy's Eyes/Ain't No Telling	1965	2.50	5.00	10.00
❑ 393	I'm Too Far Gone (To Turn Around)/If You Could Read My Mind	1965	2.50	5.00	10.00
❑ 402	Good Time Charlie/Good Time Charlie (Part 2)	1966	2.00	4.00	8.00
❑ 407	Poverty/Building a Fire with Hair	1966	2.00	4.00	8.00
❑ 412	Back in the Same Old Bag Again/I Ain't Myself Anymore	1966	2.00	4.00	8.00
❑ 416	You're All I Need/Deep in My Soul	1967	2.00	4.00	8.00
❑ 421	That Did It/Getting Used to the Blues	1967	2.00	4.00	8.00
❑ 426	A Touch of the Blues/Shoes	1967	2.00	4.00	8.00
❑ 432	Driftin' Blues/You Could Read My Mind	1968	2.00	4.00	8.00
❑ 433	Honey Child/A Piece of Gold	1968	2.00	4.00	8.00
❑ 435	Save Your Love for Me/Share Your Love with Me	1968	2.00	4.00	8.00
❑ 440	Rockin' in the Same Old Boat/Wouldn't You Rather Have Me	1968	2.00	4.00	8.00
❑ 447	Gotta Get to Know You/Baby I'm On My Way	1969	2.00	4.00	8.00
❑ 449	Chains of Love/Ask Me 'Bout Nothing (But the Blues)	1969	2.00	4.00	8.00
❑ 458	If You've Got a Heart/Sad Feeling	1970	2.00	4.00	8.00
❑ 460	Lover with a Reputation/If Love Ruled the World	1970	2.00	4.00	8.00
❑ 464	Keep On Loving Me (You'll See the Change)/I Just Got to Forget About You	1970	2.00	4.00	8.00
❑ 466	I'm Sorry/Yum Yum Tree	1971	2.00	4.00	8.00
❑ 471	Shape Up or Ship Out/The Love That We Share (Is True)	1971	2.00	4.00	8.00
❑ 472	Do What You Set Out to Do/Ain't Nothing You Can Do	1972	2.00	4.00	8.00
❑ 477	I'm So Tired/If You Could Read My Mind	1972	2.00	4.00	8.00
❑ 480	That's All There Is/I Don't Want Another Mountain to Climb	1973	2.00	4.00	8.00

KENT

Number	Title (A Side/B Side)	Yr	VG	VG+	NM
❑ 378	Love You Baby/Drifting	1962	2.50	5.00	10.00

—With Ike Turner

MALACO

Number	Title (A Side/B Side)	Yr	VG	VG+	NM
❑ 2122	Members Only/I Just Got to Know	1985	—	—	3.00
❑ 2126	Can We Make Love Tonight/In the Ghetto	1986	—	—	3.00
❑ 2133	Angel/I Hear You Thinkin'	1986	—	—	3.00

MCA

Number	Title (A Side/B Side)	Yr	VG	VG+	NM
❑ 41140	Tit for Tat/Come Fly with Me	1979	—	2.00	4.00
❑ 41197	Soon as the Weather Breaks/To Be Friends	1980	—	2.00	4.00
❑ 51068	You'd Be a Millionaire/Swat Vibrator	1981	—	—	3.00
❑ 51181	What a Difference A Day Makes/Givin' Up the Streets for Love	1982	—	—	3.00
❑ 52085	Recess in Heaven/Exactly, Where It's At	1982	—	—	3.00
❑ 52136	Here We Go Again/You're About to Win	1982	—	—	3.00
❑ 52180	Is This the Blues/You're About to Win	1983	—	—	3.00
❑ 52270	If It Ain't One Thing/Tell Mr. Bland	1983	—	—	3.00
❑ 52436	Looking Back/You Got Me Loving You	1984	—	—	3.00
❑ 52482	Get Real Clean/It's Too Bad	1984	—	—	3.00
❑ 52508	You Are My Christmas/New Merry Christmas Baby	1984	—	—	3.00

WAND

Number	Title (A Side/B Side)	Yr	VG	VG+	NM
❑ 1102	Honey, You've Been On My Mind/You've Got Time	1965	3.75	7.50	15.00

BLAND, BOBBY, AND B.B. KING

Also see each artist's individual listings.

ABC IMPULSE

Number	Title (A Side/B Side)	Yr	VG	VG+	NM
❑ 31006	Let the Good Times Roll/Strange Things	1976	—	2.00	4.00
❑ 31009	Everyday I Have the Blues/The Thrill Is Gone	1976	—	2.00	4.00

BLANDERS, THE

SMASH

Number	Title (A Side/B Side)	Yr	VG	VG+	NM
❑ 2005	Jitterbug/Desert Sands	1965	12.50	25.00	50.00

BLANE, MARCIE

SEVILLE

Number	Title (A Side/B Side)	Yr	VG	VG+	NM
❑ 120	Bobby's Girl/Time to Dream	1962	5.00	10.00	20.00

—Exists with "Seville" logo straight across the top of the label, and with the "Seville" logo curving around the top of the label. No difference in value has yet been noted.

Number	Title (A Side/B Side)	Yr	VG	VG+	NM
❑ 123	What Does a Girl Do?/How Can I Tell Him	1963	4.00	8.00	16.00
❑ 126	Little Miss Fool/Rag Time Sound	1963	4.00	8.00	16.00
❑ 128	You Gave My Number to Billy/Told You So	1963	4.00	8.00	16.00
❑ 130	Why Can't I Get a Guy/Who's Going to Take My Daddy's Place	1963	4.00	8.00	16.00
❑ 133	Bobby Did/After the Laughter	1964	4.00	8.00	16.00
❑ 137	The Hurtin' Kind/She'll Break the String	1965	4.00	8.00	16.00

BLAVAT, JERRY

CAMEO

Number	Title (A Side/B Side)	Yr	VG	VG+	NM
❑ 393	Discophonic Walk/Back to School One More Time	1965	3.00	6.00	12.00

EPIC

Number	Title (A Side/B Side)	Yr	VG	VG+	NM
❑ 10193	Jerry's Theme/Let's Love Again	1967	3.00	6.00	12.00

FAVOR

Number	Title (A Side/B Side)	Yr	VG	VG+	NM
❑ 100	Discophonic Walk/Back to School One More Time	1965	3.75	7.50	15.00

ROULETTE

Number	Title (A Side/B Side)	Yr	VG	VG+	NM
❑ 7085	Tasty (To Me)/Oh Be Joyous	1970	2.00	4.00	8.00

—With the Geatorettes

BLAZER BOY

IMPERIAL

Number	Title (A Side/B Side)	Yr	VG	VG+	NM
❑ 5199	Mornin'Train/Joe's Kid Sister	1952	25.00	50.00	100.00
❑ 5244	Surprise Blues/Waiting for My Baby	1953	25.00	50.00	100.00
❑ 5801	New Orleans Twist/That's Where It's At	1962	5.00	10.00	20.00

BLENDELLS, THE

COTILLION

Number	Title (A Side/B Side)	Yr	VG	VG+	NM
❑ 44020	Night After Night/The Love That I Needed	1968	2.50	5.00	10.00

ERA BACK TO BACK HITS

Number	Title (A Side/B Side)	Yr	VG	VG+	NM
❑ 023	Dance with Me/Land of 1000 Dances	197?	—	2.50	5.00

—B-side by Cannibal and the Headhunters

RAMPART

Number	Title (A Side/B Side)	Yr	VG	VG+	NM
❑ 641	La La La La La/Huggies Bunnies	1964	6.25	12.50	25.00

REPRISE

Number	Title (A Side/B Side)	Yr	VG	VG+	NM
❑ 0291	La La La La La/Huggies Bunnies	1964	5.00	10.00	20.00
❑ 0340	Dance with Me/Get Your Baby	1965	5.00	10.00	20.00

BLENDERS, THE

Several different groups.

AFO

Number	Title (A Side/B Side)	Yr	VG	VG+	NM
❑ 305	Graveyard/It Takes Time	1962	75.00	150.00	300.00

ALADDIN

Number	Title (A Side/B Side)	Yr	VG	VG+	NM
❑ 3449	Two Loves/Soda Shop	1959	250.00	500.00	1000.

CLASS

Number	Title (A Side/B Side)	Yr	VG	VG+	NM
❑ 236	My Heart's Desire/Little Rose	1958	10.00	20.00	40.00

Number	Title (A Side/B Side)	Yr	VG	VG+	NM
CORTLAND					
❑ 102	Love Is a Treasure/Fisherman	1962	3.00	6.00	12.00
❑ 103	Everybody's Got a Right/What Have You Got	1962	3.00	6.00	12.00
DECCA					
❑ 27403	The Masquerade Is Over/Little Small Town Girl	1951	100.00	200.00	400.00
❑ 27587	All I Gotta Do Is Think of You/The Busiest Corner	1951	75.00	150.00	300.00
❑ 28092	Just a Little Walk with Me/I'd Be a Fool Again	1952	75.00	150.00	300.00
❑ 28241	Never in a Million Years/Memories of You	1952	75.00	150.00	300.00
❑ 48156	Gone/Honeysuckle Rose	1950	75.00	150.00	300.00
❑ 48158	Count Every Star/Would I Still Be the One in Your Heart	1950	75.00	150.00	300.00
❑ 48183	I'm So Crazy for Love/What About Tonight	1950	75.00	150.00	300.00
❑ 48244	My Heart Will Never Forget/You Do the Dreaming	1951	75.00	150.00	300.00
JAY DEE					
❑ 780	Don't Play Around with You/You'll Never Smile Again	1953	50.00	100.00	200.00
MAR-V-LUS					
❑ 6010	Your Love Has Got Me Down/Love Is a Good Thing Going	1966	50.00	100.00	200.00
MGM					
❑ 11488	I Don't Miss You Anymore/If That's the Way You Want It Baby	1953	100.00	200.00	400.00
❑ 11531	Please Take Me Back/Isn't It a Shame	1953	100.00	200.00	400.00
RCA VICTOR					
❑ 47-6591	I've Told Every Little Star/Cecilia	1956	15.00	30.00	60.00
❑ 47-6712	Wake Up to Music/New Sensations in Sound	1956	12.50	25.00	50.00
❑ 47-7009	I'm Following You/Since I Kissed My Baby Goodbye	1957	12.50	25.00	50.00
WANGER					
❑ 189	Angel/Old MacDonald	1959	6.25	12.50	25.00
WITCH					
❑ 114	Daughter/Everybody's Got a Right	1963	4.00	8.00	16.00
❑ 117	Boys Think/Squat and Squirm	1963	3.75	7.50	15.00
❑ 123	One Time/(B-side unknown)	1964	3.75	7.50	15.00

BLESSING, MICHAEL

See MICHAEL NESMITH.

BLEU LIGHTS, THE

Number	Title (A Side/B Side)	Yr	VG	VG+	NM
BAYSOUND					
❑ 67003	Forever/They Don't Know My Heart	1968	10.00	20.00	40.00
❑ 67007	Bony Moronie/Lonely Man's Prayer	1968	7.50	15.00	30.00
❑ 67010	Yes I Do/The End of My Dreams	1969	7.50	15.00	30.00

BLIND FAITH

Also see GINGER BAKER'S AIR FORCE; ERIC CLAPTON; STEVE WINWOOD.

Number	Title (A Side/B Side)	Yr	VG	VG+	NM
POLYDOR					
❑ 871798-7	Presence of the Lord/Can't Find My Way Home	1989	—	2.00	4.00
RSO					
❑ 873	Presence of the Lord/Can't Find My Way Home	1977	2.00	4.00	8.00
—First single release from 1969 self-titled album					

BLINKY

Number	Title (A Side/B Side)	Yr	VG	VG+	NM
MOTOWN					
❑ 1134	I Wouldn't Change the Man He Is/I'll Always Love You	1968	2.00	4.00	8.00
❑ 1168	How You Gonna Keep It/This Time Last Summer	1970	25.00	50.00	100.00
❑ 1233	You Get a Tangle in Your Life Line/This Man of Mine	1973	—	3.00	6.00
MOWEST					
❑ 5019	For Your Precious Love/So Tired	1972	—	3.00	6.00
❑ 5033	T'Ain't Nobody's Bizness If I Do/What More Can I Do	1973	—	2.50	5.00
SOUL					
❑ 35089	How You Gonna Keep It/This Time Last Summer	1971	—	3.00	6.00

BLISTERS, THE

Number	Title (A Side/B Side)	Yr	VG	VG+	NM
LIBERTY					
❑ 55577	Shortnin' Bread/Cookie Rockin' in Her Stockings	1963	3.00	6.00	12.00
❑ 55647	Rich in My Pocket, Poor in My Heart/Friendly Loans	1963	3.00	6.00	12.00
TITANIC					
❑ 5005	Fifty Mile Hike/Recitation	1963	5.00	10.00	20.00

BLODWYN PIG

Number	Title (A Side/B Side)	Yr	VG	VG+	NM
A&M					
❑ 1158	Dear Jill/Summer Day	1969	—	3.00	6.00

BLOND

Number	Title (A Side/B Side)	Yr	VG	VG+	NM
FONTANA					
❑ 1673	Deep Inside My Heart/I Will Bring You Flowers in the Morning	1969	3.00	6.00	12.00
❑ 1673 [PS]	Deep Inside My Heart/I Will Bring You Flowers in the Morning	1969	4.00	8.00	16.00

BLONDIE

Number	Title (A Side/B Side)	Yr	VG	VG+	NM
CHRYSALIS					
❑ 2220	Denis/I'm On E	1977	—	2.50	5.00
❑ 2251	I'm Gonna Love You Too/Just Go Away	1978	—	2.50	5.00
❑ 2271	Hanging on the Telephone/Fade Away and Radiate	1978	—	2.50	5.00
❑ 2271 [PS]	Hanging on the Telephone/Fade Away and Radiate	1978	—	2.50	5.00
❑ 2295	Heart of Glass/11:59	1979	—	2.00	4.00
❑ 2295 [PS]	Heart of Glass/11:59	1979	—	2.00	4.00
❑ 2336	One Way or Another/Just Go Away	1979	—	2.00	4.00
❑ 2379	Dreaming/Living in the Real World	1979	—	2.00	4.00
❑ 2408	The Hardest Part/Sound Asleep	1980	—	2.00	4.00
❑ 2408 [PS]	The Hardest Part/Sound Asleep	1980	—	2.00	4.00
❑ 2410	Atomic/Die Young Stay Pretty	1980	—	2.00	4.00
❑ 2410 [PS]	Atomic/Die Young Stay Pretty	1980	—	2.00	4.00
❑ 2414	Call Me/Call Me (instrumental)	1980	—	—	3.00
❑ 2414 [PS]	Call Me/Call Me (instrumental)	1980	—	2.50	5.00
—Photo of Richard Gere on sleeve.					
❑ 2414 [PS]	Call Me/Call Me (instrumental)	1980	—	—	3.00
—Photo of Deborah Harry on sleeve.					
❑ 2465	The Tide Is High/Suzy and Jeffrey	1980	—	—	3.00
❑ 2465 [PS]	The Tide Is High/Suzy and Jeffrey	1980	—	—	3.00
❑ 2485	Rapture/Walk Like Me	1981	—	—	3.00
❑ 2485 [PS]	Rapture/Walk Like Me	1981	—	—	3.00
❑ 2603	Island of Lost Souls/Dragonfly	1982	—	—	3.00
❑ 2603 [PS]	Island of Lost Souls/Dragonfly	1982	—	—	3.00
❑ S7-18303	Rapture/One Way or Another	1995	—	—	3.00
❑ S7-18304	Heart of Glass/Call Me	1995	—	—	3.00
❑ S7-18396	Atomic/Atomic (Diddy Remix)	1995	—	—	3.00
❑ S7-18848	Union City Blue (Diddy's Remix Edit)/Union City Blue	1995	—	—	3.00
❑ 42944	Heart of Glass/Hanging on the Telephone	1985	—	—	3.00
—Silver label reissue					
❑ 42945	One Way or Another/Dreaming	1985	—	—	3.00
—Silver label reissue					
❑ 42946	Call Me/Atomic	1985	—	—	3.00
—Silver label reissue					
PRIVATE STOCK					
❑ 45097	X Offender/In the Sun	1976	7.50	15.00	30.00
❑ 45097 [DJ]	X Offender (mono)/X Offender (stereo)	1976	2.50	5.00	10.00
❑ 45141	In the Flesh/Man Overboard	1977	5.00	10.00	20.00
❑ 45141 [DJ]	In the Flesh (mono/stereo)	1977	2.50	5.00	10.00

BLOOD, SWEAT AND TEARS

Also see DAVID CLAYTON-THOMAS; AL KOOPER.

Number	Title (A Side/B Side)	Yr	VG	VG+	NM
ABC					
❑ 12310	Blue Street/Somebody I Trusted	1977	—	2.00	4.00
COLUMBIA					
❑ 10151	Got to Get You Into My Life/Naked Man	1975	—	2.50	5.00
❑ 10189	No Show/Yesterday's Music	1975	—	2.50	5.00
❑ 10400	You're the One/Heavy Blue	1976	—	2.50	5.00
❑ 44559	I Can't Quit Her/House in the Country	1968	2.00	4.00	8.00
❑ 44776	You've Made Me So Very Happy/Blues — Part 2	1969	—	3.00	6.00
❑ 44871	Spinning Wheel/More and More	1969	—	3.00	6.00
❑ 45008	And When I Die/Sometimes in Winter	1969	—	3.00	6.00
❑ 45204	Hi-De-Ho/The Battle	1970	—	2.50	5.00
❑ 45235	Lucretia Mac Evil/Lucretia's Reprise	1970	—	2.50	5.00
❑ 45427	Go Down Gamblin'/Valentine's Day	1971	—	2.50	5.00
❑ 45427 [PS]	Go Down Gamblin'/Valentine's Day	1971	2.00	4.00	8.00
❑ 45477	Lisa, Listen to Me/Cowboys and Indians	1971	—	2.50	5.00
❑ 45661	So Long Dixie/Alone	1972	—	2.50	5.00
❑ 45661 [PS]	So Long Dixie/Alone	1972	2.00	4.00	8.00
❑ 45755	Velvet/I Can't Move No Mountains	1973	—	2.50	5.00
❑ 45937	Roller Coaster/Inner Crisis	1973	—	2.50	5.00
❑ 45965	Save Our Ship/Song for John	1973	—	2.50	5.00
❑ 46059	Tell Me That I'm Wrong/Rock Reprise	1974	—	2.50	5.00
MCA					
❑ 41198	Nuclear Blues/Agitato	1980	—	2.00	4.00

7-Inch Extended Plays

Number	Title (A Side/B Side)	Yr	VG	VG+	NM
COLUMBIA					
❑ 7-30590 [PS]	Blood, Sweat and Tears 4	1971	3.00	6.00	12.00
❑ 7-30590 [S]	*Redemption/Lisa, Listen to Me/A Look to My Heart (duet)/A Look to My Heart (inst.)/For My Lady/Mama Gets High	1971	2.50	5.00	10.00
—33 1/3 rpm, small hole jukebox release					

BLOODROCK

Number	Title (A Side/B Side)	Yr	VG	VG+	NM
CAPITOL					
❑ 2736	Fatback/Gotta Find a Way	1970	—	3.00	6.00
❑ 3009	D.O.A./Children's Heritage	1971	2.00	4.00	8.00
❑ 3089	You Gotta Roll/A Certain Kind	1971	—	3.00	6.00
❑ 3161	Jessica/You Gotta Roll	1971	—	3.00	6.00
❑ 3227	Rock and Roll Candy Man/Don't Eat the Children	1971	—	3.00	6.00
❑ 3320	Erosion/Castle of Thoughts	1972	—	2.50	5.00
❑ 3399	Castle of Thoughts/D.O.A.	1972	—	2.50	5.00
❑ 3451	Help Is On the Way/Thank You Daniel Ellsburg	1972	—	2.50	5.00
❑ 3770	Voices/Thank You Daniel Ellsburg	1973	—	2.50	5.00

BLOOM, BOBBY

Number	Title (A Side/B Side)	Yr	VG	VG+	NM
KAMA SUTRA					
❑ 210	Heart of Town/Make the Radio a Little Louder	1966	3.00	6.00	12.00
—As "Bobby Mann"					
❑ 223	Love, Don't Let Me Down/Where Is the Woman	1967	2.50	5.00	10.00
❑ 229	Count on Me/Was I Dreamin'	1967	2.50	5.00	10.00
KAPP					
❑ 710	I Still Remember/Rough and Tough	1965	3.00	6.00	12.00
L&R					
❑ 157	Montego Bay/Try a Little Harder	1970	—	3.00	6.00
MAP CITY					
❑ 306	Emergency/Again 'N' Again	1970	—	3.00	6.00
MGM					
❑ 14212	Make Me Happy/This Thing I've Gotten Into	1970	—	2.50	5.00
❑ 14246	We're All Goin' Home/Careful Not to Break the Spell	1971	—	2.50	5.00
❑ 14292	We Need Each Other/You Touch Me	1971	—	2.50	5.00
❑ 14343	I Really Got It Bad for You/Until They Say Mercy	1972	—	2.50	5.00
❑ 14437	Stay on Top/Sha La Boom Boom	1972	—	2.50	5.00
❑ 14614	The Island/Oh, I Wish I Knew	1973	—	2.50	5.00
ROULETTE					
❑ 7095	Oh Yesterday/Where Are We Going	1971	—	2.50	5.00
WHITE WHALE					
❑ 285	All I Wanna Do Is Dance/Taggin' Along	1968	2.00	4.00	8.00

BLOSSOMS, THE
Probably all the same group.

Number	Title (A Side/B Side)	Yr	VG	VG+	NM
BELL					
❑ 780	You've Lost That Lovin' Feeling/Something So Wrong	1969	2.00	4.00	8.00
❑ 797	(You're My) Soul and Inspiration/Stand By	1969	2.00	4.00	8.00
❑ 857	I Ain't Got to Love Nobody Else/Don't Take Your Love	1970	2.00	4.00	8.00
❑ 937	One Step Away/Break Your Promise	1970	2.00	4.00	8.00
CAPITOL					
❑ F3822	Move On/He Promised Me	1957	7.50	15.00	30.00
❑ F3878	Little Louie/Have Faith in Me	1958	6.25	12.50	25.00
❑ F4072	Baby Daddy-O/No Other Love	1958	6.25	12.50	25.00
CHALLENGE					
❑ 9109	Son-In-Law/I'll Wait	1961	5.00	10.00	20.00
—B-side by the Coeds					
❑ 9122	Hard to Get/Write Me a Letter	1961	5.00	10.00	20.00
❑ 9138	The Search Is Over/Big Talking Jim	1962	5.00	10.00	20.00
EEOC					
❑ 8172	Things Are Changing (same on both sides)	1965	37.50	75.00	150.00
❑ 8172 [PS]	Things Are Changing (same on both sides)	1965	37.50	75.00	150.00
—Promotional item for the Equal Employment Opportunity Commission					
EPIC					
❑ 50434	There's No Greater Love (Than Mine for You My Love)/Walking on Air	1977	—	2.50	5.00
LION					
❑ 108	Touchdown/It's All Up to You	1972	—	3.00	6.00
❑ 125	Grandma's Hands/Cherish What Is Dear to You	1972	—	3.00	6.00
MGM					
❑ 13964	Tweedlee Dee/You Got Me Hummin'	1968	2.50	5.00	10.00
ODE					
❑ 101	Stoney End/Wonderful	1967	3.00	6.00	12.00
❑ 106	Cry Like a Baby/Wonderful	1968	3.00	6.00	12.00
❑ 125	Stoney End/Wonderful	1969	3.00	6.00	12.00
OKEH					
❑ 7162	I'm in Love/What Makes Love	1963	5.00	10.00	20.00
REPRISE					
❑ 0436	Good, Good Lovin'/That's When the Tears Start	1965	3.75	7.50	15.00
❑ 0475	Lover Boy/My Love, Come Home	1966	3.75	7.50	15.00
❑ 0522	Let Your Love Shine on Me/Deep Into My Heart	1966	3.75	7.50	15.00
❑ 0639	Deep Into My Heart/Good, Good Lovin'	1967	3.75	7.50	15.00

BLUE, JAY

Number	Title (A Side/B Side)	Yr	VG	VG+	NM
IMPERIAL					
❑ 5587	Get Off My Back/The Coolest	1959	20.00	40.00	80.00

BLUE ANGEL
Features CYNDI LAUPER.

Number	Title (A Side/B Side)	Yr	VG	VG+	NM
POLYDOR					
❑ 2149	I Had a Love/Take a Chance	1980	2.50	5.00	10.00

BLUE BELLES, THE
Also see PATTI LaBELLE AND THE BLUE BELLES.

Number	Title (A Side/B Side)	Yr	VG	VG+	NM
ATLANTIC					
❑ 987	The Story of a Fool/Cancel the Call	1953	37.50	75.00	150.00

BLUE CHEER

Number	Title (A Side/B Side)	Yr	VG	VG+	NM
MERCURY					
❑ 872804-7	Summertime Blues/Just a Little Bit	1989	—	2.00	4.00
—Reissue					
PHILIPS					
❑ 40516	Summertime Blues/Out of Focus	1968	3.00	6.00	12.00
❑ 40516 [PS]	Summertime Blues/Out of Focus	1968	6.25	12.50	25.00
❑ 40541	Just a Little Bit/Gypsy Ball	1968	2.50	5.00	10.00
❑ 40561	Sun Cycle/Albert's Shuffle	1968	2.50	5.00	10.00
❑ 40561	Sun Cycle/Feathers from Our Tree	1968	2.50	5.00	10.00
❑ 40602	West Coast Child of Sunshine/When It All Gets Old	1969	2.00	4.00	8.00
❑ 40651	All Night Long/Fortunes	1969	2.00	4.00	8.00
❑ 40664	Hello L.A., Bye-Bye Birmingham/Natural Man	1970	2.00	4.00	8.00
❑ 40682	Ain't That the Way/Fool	1970	2.00	4.00	8.00
❑ 40691	Babji (Twilight Raga)/Pilot	1971	2.00	4.00	8.00
❑ 40691	Babji (Twilight Raga)/Fool	1971	2.50	5.00	10.00

BLUE CHRISTIE

Number	Title (A Side/B Side)	Yr	VG	VG+	NM
SUN					
❑ 1143	Making Love in the Summertime/The Feeling's Good	1979	—	2.00	4.00

BLUE DIAMONDS, THE
With Ernie Kador (later ERNIE K-DOE)

Number	Title (A Side/B Side)	Yr	VG	VG+	NM
SAVOY					
❑ 1134	Honey Baby/No Money	1954	15.00	30.00	60.00

BLUE JAYS, THE (1)
Los Angeles-based male vocal group.

Number	Title (A Side/B Side)	Yr	VG	VG+	NM
MILESTONE					
❑ 2008	Lover's Island/You're Gonna Cry	1961	10.00	20.00	40.00
—Dark blue label					
❑ 2008	Lover's Island/You're Gonna Cry	1961	7.50	15.00	30.00
—Light blue and white label					
❑ 2008	Lover's Island/You're Gonna Cry	1961	7.50	15.00	30.00
—Green label					
❑ 2009	Tears Are Falling/Tree Tall Men	1961	7.50	15.00	30.00
❑ 2010	Let's Make Love/Rock, Rock, Rock	1962	5.00	10.00	20.00
❑ 2012	The Right to Love/Rock, Rock, Rock	1962	5.00	10.00	20.00
❑ 2014	Venus, My Love/Tall Len	1962	15.00	30.00	60.00

BLUE JAYS, THE (2)
Chicago-based (probably) male vocal group.

Number	Title (A Side/B Side)	Yr	VG	VG+	NM
CHECKER					
❑ 782	White Cliffs of Dover/Hey Poppa	1953	1000.	1500.	2000.

BLUE JAYS, THE (U)

Number	Title (A Side/B Side)	Yr	VG	VG+	NM
LAURIE					
❑ 3037	Sweet Georgia Brown/J.J.'s Blues	1959	6.25	12.50	25.00
MAP CITY					
❑ 300	Hang On/Hard Thing to Accept	1969	—	3.00	6.00
❑ 307	Freedom (Where Have You Gone)/(B-side unknown)	1971	—	3.00	6.00
❑ 311	Jackson/Wacka Wacka	1971	—	3.00	6.00
PHILIPS					
❑ 40186	Who (Will I Be Today)?/Come On Baby	1964	3.75	7.50	15.00
ROULETTE					
❑ 4169	Practical Joker/Barbara	1959	5.00	10.00	20.00
❑ 4264	Kum Ba Yah/Cave Man Love	1960	5.00	10.00	20.00
WARNER BROS.					
❑ 7299	Edgy/I'm Only Dreaming	1969	—	3.00	6.00

BLUE MAGIC

Number	Title (A Side/B Side)	Yr	VG	VG+	NM
ATCO					
❑ 6910	Spell/Guess Who	1972	—	3.00	6.00
❑ 6930	Look Me Up/What's Come Over Me	1973	—	3.00	6.00
❑ 6949	Stop to Start/Where Have You Been	1973	—	3.00	6.00
❑ 6961	Sideshow/Just Don't Want to Be Lonely	1974	—	3.00	6.00
❑ 7004	Three Ring Circus/Welcome to the Club	1974	—	3.00	6.00
❑ 7014	Love Has Found Its Way to Me/When Ya Coming Home	1975	—	3.00	6.00
❑ 7031	Chasing Rainbows/You Won't Have to Tell Me Goodbye	1975	—	2.50	5.00
❑ 7046	Grateful Part 1/Grateful Part 2	1976	—	2.50	5.00
❑ 7052	Freak-N-Stein/Stop and Get a Hold of Yourself	1976	—	2.50	5.00
❑ 7061	Teach Me (It's Something About Love)/Spark of Love	1976	—	2.50	5.00
❑ 7090	I Waited/Can't Get You Out of My Mind	1978	—	2.00	4.00
CAPITOL					
❑ 4977	Land of Make Believe/Remember November	1981	—	2.00	4.00
DEF JAM					
❑ 68566	Romeo and Juliet/Couldn't Get to Sleep Last Night	1989	—	2.00	4.00
LIBERTY					
❑ 56146	Can I Say I Love You/One, Two, Three	1969	2.50	5.00	10.00
MIRAGE					
❑ 99843	See Through/(B-side unknown)	1983	—	2.00	4.00
❑ 99869	Since You Been Gone/If You Move You Lose	1983	—	2.00	4.00
OBR					
❑ 68900	It's Like Magic/Couldn't Get to Sleep Last Night	1989	—	2.00	4.00
❑ 69016	You Are My Everything/Feels So Good	1989	—	2.00	4.00
WMOT					
❑ 4003	Summer Snow/(B-side unknown)	1976	—	2.50	5.00

BLUE NOTES, THE (1)
This group evolved into HAROLD MELVIN AND THE BLUE NOTES.

Number	Title (A Side/B Side)	Yr	VG	VG+	NM
3 SONS					
❑ 103	WPLJ/While I'm Away	1962	7.50	15.00	30.00
COLLECTABLES					
❑ 1113	Winter Wonderland/O Holy Night	198?	—	2.00	4.00
—Reissue					
JOSIE					
❑ 800	If You Love Me/There's Something in Your Eyes, Eloise	1956	50.00	100.00	200.00
❑ 814	Letters/With This Pen	1957	30.00	60.00	120.00
—As "Todd Randall and the Blue Notes"					
❑ 823	The Retribution Blues/Wagon Wheels	1957	37.50	75.00	150.00
PORT					
❑ 70021	If You Love Me/There's Something in Your Eyes, Eloise	1958	15.00	30.00	60.00
RED TOP					
❑ 135	My Hero/A Good Woman	1963	7.50	15.00	30.00
UNI					
❑ 55132	Got Chills and Cold Thrills/Never Gonna Leave You	1969	3.00	6.00	12.00
❑ 55201	This Time Will Be Different/Lucky Me	1970	3.00	6.00	12.00
VAL-UE					
❑ 213	My Hero/A Good Woman	1960	20.00	40.00	80.00
❑ 215	Winter Wonderland/O Holy Night	1960	20.00	40.00	80.00

BLUE NOTES, THE (2)
Earlier male vocal group, no relation to (1).

Number	Title (A Side/B Side)	Yr	VG	VG+	NM
RAMA					
❑ 25	If You'll Be Mine/Too Hot to Handle	1953	50.00	100.00	200.00

BLUE NOTES, THE (U)
None of these appear to be by (1) or (2), but we don't know how many different groups are represented below.

Number	Title (A Side/B Side)	Yr	VG	VG+	NM
20TH CENTURY					
❑ 1213	Blue Star/(B-side unknown)	1961	3.75	7.50	15.00
DOT					
❑ 15692	My Steady Girl/Mighty Lou	1958	6.25	12.50	25.00
—B-side by Henry Wilson					
❑ 15720	Darling of Mine/I Love Her So	1958	6.25	12.50	25.00
TNT					
❑ 150	Darling of Mine/I Love Her So	1958	7.50	15.00	30.00

BLUE ORCHIDS, THE

Number	Title (A Side/B Side)	Yr	VG	VG+	NM
LONDON					
❑ 9637	Love Hit Me/Don't Make Me Mad	1964	2.50	5.00	10.00
❑ 9669	Oo-Chang-a-Lang/I've Got That Feeling	1964	2.50	5.00	10.00

BLUE OYSTER CULT

Number	Title (A Side/B Side)	Yr	VG	VG+	NM
COLUMBIA					
❑ 02415	Burnin' for You/Vengeance (The Fact)	1981	—	2.00	4.00
❑ 02415 [PS]	Burnin' for You/Vengeance (The Fact)	1981	—	2.50	5.00

Number	Title (A Side/B Side)	Yr	VG	VG+	NM
❑ 03137	(Don't Fear) The Reaper/Burnin' for You	1982	—	2.00	4.00
—Reissue					
❑ 04298	Shooting Shark/Dragon Lady	1984	—	—	3.00
❑ 04435	Take Me Away/Let Go	1984	—	—	3.00
❑ 05845	Dancin' in the Ruins/Shadow Warrior	1986	—	—	3.00
❑ 06199	Perfect Water/Spy in the House of Knight	1986	—	—	3.00
❑ 10046	Dominance and Submission/Career of Evil	1974	—	3.00	6.00
❑ 10169	Born to Be Wild/Born to Be Wild	1975	—	3.00	6.00
❑ 10384	(Don't Fear) The Reaper/Tattoo Vampire	1976	—	3.00	6.00
❑ 10560	Debby Denise/This Ain't the Summer of Love	1977	—	2.50	5.00
❑ 10659	Goin' Through the Motions/Searchin' for Celine	1977	—	2.50	5.00
❑ 10697	Godzilla/Nosferatu	1978	—	2.50	5.00
❑ 10725	Godzilla (Live)/Godzilla	1978	—	2.50	5.00
❑ 10841	We Gotta Get Out of This Place/E.T.I. (Extra Terrestrial Intelligence)	1978	—	2.50	5.00
❑ 11055	In There/Lonely Teardrops	1979	—	2.00	4.00
❑ 11145	You're Not the One (I Was Looking For)/Moon Crazy	1979	—	2.00	4.00
❑ 11401	Here's Johnny (The Marshall Plan)/Divine Wind	1980	—	2.00	4.00
❑ 45598	Cities on Flame with Rock and Roll/Before the Kiss, A Redcap	1972	2.50	5.00	10.00
❑ 45879	Hot Rods to Hell/Seven Screaming Diz Busters	1973	—	3.00	6.00
❑ 45879 [PS]	Hot Rods to Hell/Seven Screaming Diz Busters	1973	3.00	6.00	12.00
❑ 74716	(Don't Fear) The Reaper/Burnin' for You	1992	—	—	3.00
—Reissue					

BLUE RIDGE RANGERS, THE
See JOHN FOGERTY.

BLUE RONDOS, THE
PARKWAY

Number	Title (A Side/B Side)	Yr	VG	VG+	NM
❑ 937	Little Baby/Baby I Go for You	1964	3.00	6.00	12.00

BLUE THINGS, THE
RCA VICTOR

Number	Title (A Side/B Side)	Yr	VG	VG+	NM
❑ 47-8692	La Do Da Da/I Must Be Doing Something Wrong	1965	6.25	12.50	25.00
❑ 47-8860	Doll House/Man on the Street	1966	6.25	12.50	25.00
❑ 47-8998	Orange Rooftop of Your Mind/One Hour Cleaners	1966	6.25	12.50	25.00
❑ 47-9203	Twist and Shout/You Can Live in Our Tree	1967	6.25	12.50	25.00
❑ 47-9308	Yes, My Friend/Somebody Help Me	1967	6.25	12.50	25.00
RUFF					
❑ 1000	Mary Lou/Your Turn to Cry	1965	10.00	20.00	40.00
❑ 1002	Pretty Thing/Just Two Days Ago	1965	10.00	20.00	40.00

BLUE TONES, THE
BLUE JAY

Number	Title (A Side/B Side)	Yr	VG	VG+	NM
❑ 101	I'll Love You Till the End of Time/(Instrumental)	1965	37.50	75.00	150.00
—Reissued on Swan 4200 by "The Royal Teens"					

BLUENOTES, THE
Probably not related to any of the groups called THE BLUE NOTES, they were a white male vocal group from North Carolina.

BROOKE

Number	Title (A Side/B Side)	Yr	VG	VG+	NM
❑ 111	I Don't Know What It Is/You Can't Get Away from Love	1959	4.00	8.00	16.00
❑ 116	Forever on My Mind/I'm Gonna Find Out	1960	3.75	7.50	15.00
❑ 119	It Had to be You/Summer Love	1960	3.75	7.50	15.00

BLUES MAGOOS
ABC

Number	Title (A Side/B Side)	Yr	VG	VG+	NM
❑ 11226	Heartbreak Hotel/I Can Feel It (Feelin' Time)	1969	2.00	4.00	8.00
❑ 11250	Never Goin' Back to Georgia/Feelin' Time	1969	2.00	4.00	8.00
❑ 11283	Gulf Coast Bound/Sea Breeze Express	1970	2.00	4.00	8.00
GANIM					
❑ 1000	Who Do You Love/Let Your Love Ride	1968	10.00	20.00	40.00
MERCURY					
❑ 72590	Tobacco Road/Sometimes I Think About You	1966	3.75	7.50	15.00
❑ 72622	(We Ain't Got) Nothin' Yet/Gotta Get Away	1966	5.00	10.00	20.00
❑ 72660	Pipe Dream/There's a Chance We Can Make It	1967	3.75	7.50	15.00
❑ 72660 [PS]	Pipe Dream/There's a Chance We Can Make It	1967	7.50	15.00	30.00
❑ 72692	One by One/Dante's Inferno	1967	3.75	7.50	15.00
❑ 72692 [PS]	One by One/Dante's Inferno	1967	7.50	15.00	30.00
❑ 72707	I Wanna Be There/Summer Is the Man	1967	2.50	5.00	10.00
❑ 72729	Life Is Just a Cher O'Bowlies/There She Goes	1967	2.50	5.00	10.00
❑ 72762	Jingle Bells/Santa Claus Is Coming to Town	1967	2.50	5.00	10.00
❑ 72838	I Can Hear the Grass Grow/Yellow Rose	1968	2.50	5.00	10.00
❑ 872806-7	(We Ain't Got) Nothin' Yet/Pipedream	1989	—	—	3.00
—Reissue					
VERVE FOLKWAYS					
❑ 5006	People Had No Faces/So I'm Wrong and You Are Right	1966	5.00	10.00	20.00
—As "The Bloos Magoos"					
❑ 5006	People Had No Faces/So I'm Wrong and You Are Right	1966	3.75	7.50	15.00
❑ 5044	People Had No Faces/So I'm Wrong and You Are Right	1967	3.75	7.50	15.00

BLUES PROJECT, THE
CAPITOL

Number	Title (A Side/B Side)	Yr	VG	VG+	NM
❑ 3374	Crazy Girl/Easy Lady	1972	2.00	4.00	8.00
MCA					
❑ 40154	Fly Away/Louisiana Blues	1973	—	2.50	5.00
VERVE FOLKWAYS					
❑ 5004	Back Door Man/Violets of Dawn	1966	3.75	7.50	15.00
❑ 5013	Catch the Wind/I Want to Be Your Driver	1966	3.75	7.50	15.00
❑ 5019	Where There's Smoke There's Fire/Goin' Down Louisiana	1966	3.75	7.50	15.00
❑ 5019 [PS]	Where There's Smoke There's Fire/Goin' Down Louisiana	1966	6.25	12.50	25.00
❑ 5032	I Can't Keep from Crying Sometimes/The Way My Baby Walks	1966	3.75	7.50	15.00
❑ 5040	No Time Like the Right Time/Steve's Song	1967	3.00	6.00	12.00
VERVE FORECAST					
❑ 5063	Gentle Dreams/Lost in the Shuffle	1967	3.00	6.00	12.00

BLUNSTONE, COLIN
Also see THE ZOMBIES.

EPIC

Number	Title (A Side/B Side)	Yr	VG	VG+	NM
❑ 10826	Caroline Goodbye/Misty Roses	1972	—	2.50	5.00
❑ 10868	Say You Don't Mind/Though You Are Far Away	1972	—	2.50	5.00
❑ 10948	I Don't Believe in Miracles/I've Always Had You	1973	—	2.50	5.00
❑ 10981	Pay Me Later/I Want Some More	1973	—	2.50	5.00
❑ 11004	Andorra/Carolina Goodbye	1973	—	2.50	5.00
ROCKET					
❑ PB-11356	I'll Never Forget You/You Are the Way for Me	1978	—	2.00	4.00
❑ PB-11412	Photograph/Touch and Go	1978	—	2.00	4.00

BLUR
VIRGIN

Number	Title (A Side/B Side)	Yr	VG	VG+	NM
❑ S7-19581	Song 2/Get Out of Cities	1997	—	2.00	4.00
❑ S7-19650	M.O.R./Look Inside America	1997	—	2.00	4.00
❑ 58792	Tender (Radio Edit)/Coffee & T.V.	1999	—	—	3.00

BO PETE
See NILSSON.

BOB AND EARL
CHENE

Number	Title (A Side/B Side)	Yr	VG	VG+	NM
❑ 103	The Sissy/(B-side unknown)	1964	2.50	5.00	10.00
CLASS					
❑ 213	That's My Desire/You Made a Boo-Boo	1957	10.00	20.00	40.00
❑ 231	Gee Whiz/When She Walks	1958	7.50	15.00	30.00
❑ 232	Chains of Love/Sweet Pea	1958	7.50	15.00	30.00
❑ 247	That's My Desire/You Made a Boo-Boo	1959	6.25	12.50	25.00
LOMA					
❑ 2004	Everybody Jerk/Just One Look in Your Eyes	1964	2.50	5.00	10.00
MARC					
❑ 104	Harlem Shuffle/I'll Come Running	1963	5.00	10.00	20.00
MIRWOOD					
❑ 5517	Baby It's Over/Dancin' Everywhere	1966	2.00	4.00	8.00
❑ 5526	I'll Keep Running Back/Baby, Your Time Is My Time	1966	2.00	4.00	8.00
TEMPE					
❑ 102	Don't Ever Leave Me/Oh Baby Doll	1962	3.75	7.50	15.00
UNI					
❑ 55196	Uh Uh No No/(Pickin' Up) Love's Vibrations	1970	—	3.00	6.00
❑ 55248	Get Ready for the New Day/Honey, Sugar, My Sweet Thing	1970	—	3.00	6.00
WHITE WHALE					
❑ 310	Harlem Shuffle/I'll Come Running	1969	3.00	6.00	12.00

BOB AND JERRY
Bob Feldman and Jerry Goldstein, later of THE STRANGELOVES.

COLUMBIA

Number	Title (A Side/B Side)	Yr	VG	VG+	NM
❑ 42162	We're the Guys (Who Drove Your Baby Wild)/Dreamy Eyes	1961	3.00	6.00	12.00
MUSICOR					
❑ 1018	Chubby Isn't Chubby Anymore/Nursery Rhym Floks	1962	3.00	6.00	12.00
RENDEZVOUS					
❑ 100	Ghost Satellite/Who's Gonna Cry for Me	1958	3.75	7.50	15.00

BOB AND LUCILLE
DITTO

Number	Title (A Side/B Side)	Yr	VG	VG+	NM
❑ 121	What's the Password/Demon Lover	1962	20.00	40.00	80.00
❑ 126	Eeny-Meeny-Miney-Moe/The Big Kiss	1962	20.00	40.00	80.00
DOT					
❑ 17327	Dream Baby/Southbound Plane	1969	2.00	4.00	8.00
—As "Bob Regan and Lucille Starr"					
KING					
❑ 5631	Eeny-Meeny-Miney-Moe/The Big Kiss	1962	7.50	15.00	30.00

BOB AND SHERI
SAFARI

Number	Title (A Side/B Side)	Yr	VG	VG+	NM
❑ 101	The Surfer Moon/Humpty Dumpty	1962	2000.	3000.	4000.
—Light blue label (other colors and colored vinyl are reproductions or counterfeits)					
❑ 101 [DJ]	The Surfer Moon/Humpty Dumpty	1962	250.00	500.00	1000.
—White label					

BOB B. SOXX AND THE BLUE JEANS
PHILLES

Number	Title (A Side/B Side)	Yr	VG	VG+	NM
❑ 107	Zip-a-Dee-Doo-Dah/Flip and Nitty	1962	5.00	10.00	20.00
❑ 110	Why Do Lovers Brak Each Other's Heart?/Dr. Kaplan's Office	1963	5.00	10.00	20.00
❑ 113	Not Too Young to Get Married/Annette	1963	5.00	10.00	20.00
PHILLES/COLLECTABLES					
❑ 3207	Not Too Young to Get Married/There's No Other (Like My Baby)	1985	—	3.00	6.00
—Gold vinyl; part of box set "Phil Spector Wall of Sound Series Vol. 1"; B-side by the Crystals					
❑ 3207	Not Too Young to Get Married/There's No Other (Like My Baby)	1986	—	2.50	5.00
—Black vinyl; B-side by the Crystals					

BOBBETTES, THE
ATLANTIC

Number	Title (A Side/B Side)	Yr	VG	VG+	NM
❑ 1144	Mr. Lee/Look at the Stars	1957	6.25	12.50	25.00
❑ 1159	Speedy/Come-a Come-a	1957	5.00	10.00	20.00
❑ 1181	Zoomy/Rock and Ree-Ah-Zole	1958	5.00	10.00	20.00
❑ 1194	The Dream/Um Bow Bow	1958	5.00	10.00	20.00
❑ 2027	Don't Say Goodnight/You Are My Sweetheart	1959	5.00	10.00	20.00
❑ 2069	I Shot Mr. Lee/Untrue Love	1960	7.50	15.00	30.00
DIAMOND					
❑ 133	Row, Row, Row/Teddy	1963	3.00	6.00	12.00

Number	Title (A Side/B Side)	Yr	VG	VG+	NM
❑ 142	Close Your Eyes/Somebody Bad Stole De Wedding Bell	1963	3.00	6.00	12.00
❑ 156	My Mamma Said/Sandman	1964	3.00	6.00	12.00
❑ 166	I'm Climbing a Mountain/In Paradise	1964	3.00	6.00	12.00
❑ 181	You Ain't Seen Nothing Yet/I'm Climbing a Mountain	1965	3.00	6.00	12.00
❑ 189	Love Is Blind/Teddy	1965	3.00	6.00	12.00
END					
❑ 1093	Mr. Johnny Q/Teach Me Tonight	1961	5.00	10.00	20.00
❑ 1095	I Don't Like It Like That (Part 1)/I Don't Like It Like That (Part 2)	1961	5.00	10.00	20.00
GALLANT					
❑ 1006	Oh, My Papa/I Cried	1960	5.00	10.00	20.00
GONE					
❑ 5112	I Don't Like It Like That (Part 1)/Mr. Johnny Q	1961	3.75	7.50	15.00
JUBILEE					
❑ 5427	Over There/Loneliness	1962	3.00	6.00	12.00
❑ 5442	The Broken Heart/Mama, Papa	1962	3.00	6.00	12.00
KING					
❑ 5490	Oh My Papa/Dance With Me Georgie	1961	3.75	7.50	15.00
❑ 5551	Are You Satisfied/Looking for a Lover	1961	3.75	7.50	15.00
❑ 5623	I'm Stepping Out Tonight/My Dearest	1962	3.75	7.50	15.00
RCA VICTOR					
❑ 47-8832	I've Gotta Face the World/Having Fun	1966	3.75	7.50	15.00
❑ 47-8983	It's All Over/Happy-Go-Lucky Me	1966	3.75	7.50	15.00
TRIPLE-X					
❑ 104	I Shot Mr. Lee/Billy	1960	5.00	10.00	20.00
❑ 106	Have Mercy Baby/Dance with Me Georgie	1960	5.00	10.00	20.00

BOBBIE & BOOBIE

Number	Title (A Side/B Side)	Yr	VG	VG+	NM
DICE					
❑ 480	Cool, Cool Christmas/Teenage Party	195?	50.00	100.00	200.00

BOBBIE JEAN

Number	Title (A Side/B Side)	Yr	VG	VG+	NM
SUN					
❑ 342	You Burned the Bridges/Cheaters Never Win	1960	5.00	10.00	20.00

BOBBY AND HIS ORBITS

Number	Title (A Side/B Side)	Yr	VG	VG+	NM
GONE					
❑ 5126	Your Cheatin' Heart/I Don't Stand a Chance	1962	6.25	12.50	25.00
SEECO					
❑ 6005	Felicia/Bandstand Dancing	1959	20.00	40.00	80.00
❑ 6030	Teen Age Love/What Do I Say (When I'm Close to You)	1960	12.50	25.00	50.00

BOBBY AND THE DUKES

Number	Title (A Side/B Side)	Yr	VG	VG+	NM
PHILIPS					
❑ 40293	Ah, Ah, Ah/Come Go with Me	1965	5.00	10.00	20.00

BOBBY THE POET

See SENATOR BOBBY.

BOCEPHUS

See HANK WILLIAMS, JR.

BOCKY AND THE VISIONS

Number	Title (A Side/B Side)	Yr	VG	VG+	NM
PHILIPS					
❑ 40224	Mojo Hanna/Spirit of '64	1964	6.25	12.50	25.00
❑ 40242	I'm Pickin' Petals/I'm Not Worth It	1964	6.25	12.50	25.00

BOENZEE CRYQUE

With Rusty Young, later of POCO.

Number	Title (A Side/B Side)	Yr	VG	VG+	NM
CHICORY					
❑ 406	Sky Gone Gray/Still in Love with You Baby	1966	7.50	15.00	30.00
UNI					
❑ 55012	Sky Gone Gray/Still in Love with You Baby	1967	5.00	10.00	20.00
❑ 55022	Watch the Time/You Won't Believe It's True	1967	5.00	10.00	20.00

BOLIN, TOMMY

Also see THE JAMES GANG; ZEPHYR.

Number	Title (A Side/B Side)	Yr	VG	VG+	NM
NEMPEROR					
❑ 004	The Grind/Homeward Strut	1976	2.00	4.00	8.00
❑ 005	Savannah Woman/Marching Power	1976	2.00	4.00	8.00

BOLTON, MICHAEL

Includes records as "Michael Bolotin." Also see BLACKJACK.

Number	Title (A Side/B Side)	Yr	VG	VG+	NM
COLUMBIA					
❑ 03800	Fighting for My Life/Fool's Game	1983	—	2.00	4.00
❑ 04154	I Almost Believed You/She Did the Same Thing	1983	—	2.00	4.00
❑ 04823	Everybody's Crazy/She Did the Same Thing	1985	—	—	3.00
❑ 07322	That's What Love Is All About/Take a Look at My Face	1987	—	—	3.00
❑ 07680	(Sittin' On) The Dock of the Bay/Call My Name	1988	—	—	3.00
❑ 07680 [PS]	(Sittin' On) The Dock of the Bay/Call My Name	1988	—	—	3.00
❑ 07794	Wait on Love/I Almost Believed You	1988	—	—	3.00
❑ 07794 [PS]	Wait on Love/I Almost Believed You	1988	—	—	3.00
❑ 07983	Walk Away/The Hunger	1988	—	—	3.00
❑ 68909	Soul Provider/The Hunger	1989	—	—	3.00
❑ 73017	How Am I Supposed to Live Without You/Forever Eyes	1989	—	—	3.00
❑ 73257	How Can We Be Lovers/That's What Love Is All About	1990	—	—	3.00
❑ 73342	When I'm Back on My Feet Again/Walk Away	1990	—	—	3.00
❑ 73490	Georgia on My Mind/Take a Look at My Face	1990	—	—	3.00
❑ 73719	Love Is a Wonderful Thing/Soul Provider	1991	—	—	3.00
❑ 73889	Time, Love and Tenderness/That's What Love Is All About	1991	—	—	3.00
❑ 74020	When a Man Loves a Woman/Save Me	1991	—	—	3.00
❑ 74184	Missing You Now/It's Only My Heart	1992	—	—	3.00
❑ 74798	Reach Out I'll Be There/White Christmas	1992	—	2.00	4.00
❑ 77260	Said I Loved You...But I Lied/Soul Provider	1993	—	—	3.00
❑ 77376	Completely/That's What Love Is All About	1994	—	—	3.00
❑ 77941	Can I Touch You...There?/Ain't Got Nothing If You Ain't Got Love	1995	—	—	3.00
RCA					
❑ PB-10650	You Make Me Feel Like Lovin' You/If I Had Your Lovin'	1976	2.50	5.00	10.00
—As "Michael Bolotin"					
RCA VICTOR					
❑ PB-10283	Your Love/Dream While You Can	1975	2.50	5.00	10.00
—As "Michael Bolotin"					

BON-AIRS, THE

Number	Title (A Side/B Side)	Yr	VG	VG+	NM
KING					
❑ 4975	Stop the World/Bermuda	1956	7.50	15.00	30.00

BON BONS, THE

Number	Title (A Side/B Side)	Yr	VG	VG+	NM
CORAL					
❑ 62402	What's Wrong with Ringo/Come On Baby	1964	15.00	30.00	60.00
❑ 62435	Everybody Wants My Boyfriend/Each Time	1964	12.50	25.00	50.00

BON JOVI

Number	Title (A Side/B Side)	Yr	VG	VG+	NM
ISLAND					
❑ 314-562801-7	It's My Life/Next 100 Years	2000	—	2.00	4.00
❑ 314-572770-7	Thank You for Loving Me/Bed of Roses	2001	—	2.00	4.00
—Red vinyl					
JAMBCO					
❑ 862088-7	In These Arms/Say a Prayer	1993	—	—	3.00
❑ 862428-7	I'll Sleep When I'm Dead/Never Say Goodbye	1993	—	—	3.00
❑ 864432-7	Keep the Faith/I Wish Everyday Could Be Like Christmas	1992	—	—	3.00
—A-side is not a Christmas song					
❑ 864852-7	Bed of Roses/Lay Your Hands on Me	1993	—	—	3.00
MERCURY					
❑ 818309-7	Runaway/Love Lies	1984	—	2.00	4.00
❑ 818309-7 [PS]	Runaway/Love Lies	1984	—	3.00	6.00
❑ 818958-7	She Don't Know Me/Burning for Love	1984	—	2.00	4.00
❑ 818958-7 [PS]	She Don't Know Me/Burning for Love	1984	—	3.00	6.00
❑ 852296-7	Something for the Pain/Lie to Me	1995	—	—	3.00
❑ 856226-7	Always/Living in Sin	1994	—	—	3.00
❑ 856824-7	This Ain't a Love Song/Always (Live at A&M Studios)	1995	—	—	3.00
❑ 870657-7	Bad Medicine/99 in the Shade	1988	—	—	3.00
❑ 870657-7 [PS]	Bad Medicine/99 in the Shade	1988	—	—	3.00
❑ 872156-7	Born to Be My Baby/Love for Sale	1988	—	—	3.00
❑ 872156-7 [PS]	Born to Be My Baby/Love for Sale	1988	—	—	3.00
❑ 872564-7	I'll Be There for You/Homebound Train	1989	—	—	3.00
❑ 872564-7 [PS]	I'll Be There for You/Homebound Train	1989	—	—	3.00
❑ 874452-7	Lay Your Hands on Me/Runaway (Live)	1989	—	—	3.00
❑ 874452-7 [PS]	Lay Your Hands on Me/Runaway (Live)	1989	—	—	3.00
❑ 876070-7	Living in Sin/Love Is War	1989	—	—	3.00
❑ 876070-7 [PS]	Living in Sin/Love Is War	1989	—	—	3.00
❑ 880736-7	Only Lonely/Always Run to You	1985	—	2.00	4.00
❑ 880736-7 [PS]	Only Lonely/Always Run to You	1985	—	3.00	6.00
❑ 880951-7	In and Out of Love/Breakout	1985	—	2.00	4.00
❑ 883396-7	Never Say Goodbye/Social Disease	1986	—	2.00	4.00
❑ 884299-7	Price of Love/Silent Night	1986	—	2.00	4.00
❑ 884660-7	Runaway/She Don't Know Me	1986	—	—	3.00
—Reissue					
❑ 884953-7	You Give Love a Bad Name/Raise Your Hands	1986	—	—	3.00
❑ 884953-7 [PS]	You Give Love a Bad Name/Raise Your Hands	1986	—	—	3.00
❑ 888184-7	Livin' on a Prayer/Wild in the Streets	1986	—	—	3.00
❑ 888184-7 [PS]	Livin' on a Prayer/Wild in the Streets	1986	—	—	3.00
❑ 888467-7	Wanted Dead or Alive/I'd Die for You	1987	—	—	3.00
❑ 888467-7 [PS]	Wanted Dead or Alive/I'd Die for You	1987	—	—	3.00

BON JOVI, JON

Number	Title (A Side/B Side)	Yr	VG	VG+	NM
MERCURY					
❑ 875896-7	Blaze of Glory/You Really Got Me Now	1990	—	—	3.00
❑ 878392-7	Miracle/Blood Money	1990	—	—	3.00

BONADUCE, DANNY

One of the stars of the TV series "The Partridge Family," but he doesn't appear on any of the records.

Number	Title (A Side/B Side)	Yr	VG	VG+	NM
LION					
❑ 145	Blueberry You/Dreamland	1973	2.50	5.00	10.00
❑ 145 [PS]	Blueberry You/Dreamland	1973	6.25	12.50	25.00

BONAIRS, THE

Number	Title (A Side/B Side)	Yr	VG	VG+	NM
DOOTONE					
❑ 325	It's Christmas/I'm Alone Tonight	1953	37.50	75.00	150.00
—B-side by Ernie Tavares Trio					

BONDS, GARY U.S.

Number	Title (A Side/B Side)	Yr	VG	VG+	NM
ATCO					
❑ 6689	The Star/You Need a Personal Manager	1969	—	3.00	6.00
BLUFF CITY					
❑ 221	My Love Song/Blue Grass	1974	—	2.50	5.00
BOTANIC					
❑ 1002	I'm Glad You're Back/Funky Lies	1968	2.00	4.00	8.00
EMI AMERICA					
❑ 8079	This Little Girl/Way Back When	1981	—	2.00	4.00
❑ 8079 [PS]	This Little Girl/Way Back When	1981	—	2.50	5.00
❑ 8089	Jole Blon/Just Like a Child	1981	—	2.00	4.00
❑ 8099	Your Love/Just Like a Child	1981	—	2.00	4.00
❑ 8117	Out of Work/Bring Her Back	1982	—	2.00	4.00
❑ 8117 [PS]	Out of Work/Bring Her Back	1982	—	2.50	5.00
❑ 8133	Love's on the Line/Way Back When	1982	—	2.00	4.00
❑ 8145	Turn the Music Down/Way Back When	1982	—	2.00	4.00
LEGRAND					
❑ 1003	New Orleans/Please Forgive Me	1960	5.00	10.00	20.00
—Original lists artist as "By-U.S. Bonds"; purple label					
❑ 1003	New Orleans/Please Forgive Me	1960	3.75	7.50	15.00
—Gold and red label					
❑ 1005	Not Me/Give Me One More Chance	1961	5.00	10.00	20.00
—Artist listed as "U.S. Bonds"; purple label					

Number	Title (A Side/B Side)	Yr	VG	VG+	NM
❑ 1005	Not Me/Give Me One More Chance	1961	3.75	7.50	15.00
—Gold and red label					
❑ 1008	Quarter to Three/Time Ole Story	1961	10.00	20.00	40.00
—Artist listed as "U.S. Bonds"; purple label					
❑ 1008	Quarter to Three/Time Ole Story	1961	3.75	7.50	15.00
—Artist listed as "U.S. Bonds"; gold and red label					
❑ 1008 [PS]	Quarter to Three/Time Ole Story	1961	10.00	20.00	40.00
❑ 1009	School Is Out/One Million Years	1961	5.00	10.00	20.00
—Artist listed as "U.S. Bonds"					
❑ 1009	School Is Out/One Million Years	1961	3.75	7.50	15.00
—Artist listed as "Gary (U.S.) Bonds" as are all later Legrand singles					
❑ 1009 [PS]	School Is Out/One Million Years	1961	10.00	20.00	40.00
❑ 1012	School Is In/Trip to the Moon	1961	3.75	7.50	15.00
❑ 1015	Dear Lady/Havin' So Much Fun	1961	5.00	10.00	20.00
—Original title of A-side					
❑ 1015	Dear Lady Twist/Havin' So Much Fun	1962	3.75	7.50	15.00
❑ 1018	Twist, Twist Senora/Food of Love	1962	3.75	7.50	15.00
❑ 1019	Seven Day Weekend/Gettin' a Groove	1962	3.75	7.50	15.00
❑ 1020	Copy Cat/I'll Change That Too	1962	3.75	7.50	15.00
❑ 1022	Mixed Up Faculty/I Dig This Station	1962	3.75	7.50	15.00
❑ 1025	Do the Limbo with Me/Where Did That Naughty Little Girl Go	1962	3.75	7.50	15.00
❑ 1027	I Don't Wanta Wait/What a Dream	1963	3.00	6.00	12.00
❑ 1029	No More Homework/She's Alright	1963	3.00	6.00	12.00
❑ 1030	Perdido Part 1/Perdido Part 2	1963	3.00	6.00	12.00
❑ 1031	King Kong's Monkey/My Sweet Ruby Rose	1964	3.00	6.00	12.00
❑ 1032	The Music Goes Round and Round/Ella Is Yella	1964	3.00	6.00	12.00
❑ 1034	You Little Angel You/My Little Miss America	1964	3.00	6.00	12.00
❑ 1035	Oh Yeah, Oh Yeah/Let ❑ Oh Yeah, Oh Yeah/ Let Me Go Lover	1965	2.50	5.00	10.00
❑ 1039	Beaches U.S.A./Do the Bumpsie	1965	2.50	5.00	10.00
❑ 1040	Take Me Back to New Orleans/I'm That Kind of Guy	1966	2.50	5.00	10.00
❑ 1041	Due to Circumstances Under My Control/Slow Motion	1966	2.50	5.00	10.00
❑ 1043	Send Her Back to Me/Workin' for My Baby	1967	2.50	5.00	10.00
❑ 1045	Call Me for Christmas/Mixed Up Faculty	1967	3.00	6.00	12.00
❑ 1046	Sarah Jane/What a Crazy World	1967	2.50	5.00	10.00

MCA

Number	Title (A Side/B Side)	Yr	VG	VG+	NM
❑ 52335	One More Time Around the Block, Ophelia/ Deadline U.S.A.	1984	—	2.00	4.00
—B-side by Shalamar					
❑ 52400	New Orleans/Rhythm of the Rain	1984	—	2.00	4.00
—With Neil Sedaka					

PRODIGAL

Number	Title (A Side/B Side)	Yr	VG	VG+	NM
❑ 0612	Grandma's Washboard/Believing You	1975	—	2.50	5.00

SUE

Number	Title (A Side/B Side)	Yr	VG	VG+	NM
❑ 17	One Broken Heart/Can't Use You in My Business	1970	—	3.00	6.00

BONFIRE, MARS

Real name: Dennis McCrohan. Also see SPARROW; STEPPENWOLF.

COLUMBIA

Number	Title (A Side/B Side)	Yr	VG	VG+	NM
❑ 44772	Faster Than the Speed of Life/She	1969	2.50	5.00	10.00
❑ 44888	In Christina's Arms/Lady Moon Walker	1969	2.50	5.00	10.00

BONNEVILLES, THE

More than one group.

BARRY

Number	Title (A Side/B Side)	Yr	VG	VG+	NM
❑ 104	Lorraine/Zu Zu	1962	12.50	25.00	50.00

CAPRI

Number	Title (A Side/B Side)	Yr	VG	VG+	NM
❑ 102	Give Me Your Love/Until You Say We're Through	1959	12.50	25.00	50.00

CORAL

Number	Title (A Side/B Side)	Yr	VG	VG+	NM
❑ 62273	Johnny/Freeway U.S.A.	1961	5.00	10.00	20.00

MUNICH

Number	Title (A Side/B Side)	Yr	VG	VG+	NM
❑ 103	Lorraine/Zu Zu	1960	75.00	150.00	300.00
—Red label					
❑ 103	Lorraine/Zu Zu	1960	25.00	50.00	100.00
—Black label					

WHITEHALL

Number	Title (A Side/B Side)	Yr	VG	VG+	NM
❑ 30002	I Do/Make Believe Lovin'	1959	7.50	15.00	30.00

BONNIE AND BUDDY

See BONNIE GUITAR.

BONNIE AND THE TREASURES

PABLO

Number	Title (A Side/B Side)	Yr	VG	VG+	NM
❑ 7014	Davey, I'm So Glad It Rained/The Lonely Surfer	1964	10.00	20.00	40.00
—B-side by the Mid-Americans					

PHI-DAN

Number	Title (A Side/B Side)	Yr	VG	VG+	NM
❑ 5005	Home of the Brave/Our Song	1965	10.00	20.00	40.00

BONNIWELL, T.S.

Sean Bonniwell of THE MUSIC MACHINE.

CAPITOL

Number	Title (A Side/B Side)	Yr	VG	VG+	NM
❑ 2551	Sleep/Where Am I to Go	1969	2.50	5.00	10.00

BONNIWELL'S MUSIC MACHINE

See THE MUSIC MACHINE.

BONO, SONNY

See SONNY; SONNY AND CHER.

BONZO DOG BAND, THE

IMPERIAL

Number	Title (A Side/B Side)	Yr	VG	VG+	NM
❑ 66345	I'm the Urban Spaceman/Canyons of Your Mind	1969	3.75	7.50	15.00
—As "The Bonzo Dog Doo-Dah Band"					
❑ 66373	Mr. Apollo/Ready Made	1969	3.75	7.50	15.00
—As "The Bonzo Dog Doo-Dah Band"					

UNITED ARTISTS

Number	Title (A Side/B Side)	Yr	VG	VG+	NM
❑ 50809	I'm the Urban Spaceman/Canyons of Your Mind	1971	2.50	5.00	10.00
❑ 50943	Slush/King of Scurf	1972	3.75	7.50	15.00

BOOKER, JOHN LEE

See JOHN LEE HOOKER.

BOOKER T. AND PRISCILLA

Also see BOOKER T. AND THE MG'S.

A&M

Number	Title (A Side/B Side)	Yr	VG	VG+	NM
❑ 1298	The Wedding Song/She	1971	—	2.50	5.00
❑ 1487	Crippled Crow/Wild Fox	1973	—	2.50	5.00

BOOKER T. AND THE MG'S

Also see BOOKER T. AND PRISCILLA.

ASYLUM

Number	Title (A Side/B Side)	Yr	VG	VG+	NM
❑ 45392	Sticky Stuff/The Stick	1977	—	2.00	4.00
❑ 45424	Grab Bag/Reincarnation	1977	—	2.00	4.00

A&M

Number	Title (A Side/B Side)	Yr	VG	VG+	NM
❑ 2100	Knockin' on Heaven's Door/Let's Go Dancin'	1978	—	2.00	4.00
—As "Booker T. Jones"					
❑ 2234	The Best of You/Let's Go Dancin'	1980	—	2.00	4.00
—As "Booker T. Jones"					
❑ 2279	Will You Be the One/Cookie	1980	—	2.00	4.00
—As "Booker T. Jones"					
❑ 2374	I Want You/You're the Best	1981	—	2.00	4.00
❑ 2394	Don't Stop Your Love/I Came to Love You	1982	—	2.00	4.00

COLUMBIA

Number	Title (A Side/B Side)	Yr	VG	VG+	NM
❑ 77526	Cruisin'/Just My Imagination	1994	—	2.00	4.00

EPIC

Number	Title (A Side/B Side)	Yr	VG	VG+	NM
❑ 50031	Evergreen/Song for Casey	1974	—	2.00	4.00
❑ 50078	Front Street Rag/Mama Stewart	1975	—	2.00	4.00
❑ 50149	Life Is Funny/Tennessee Voodoo	1975	—	2.00	4.00

STAX

Number	Title (A Side/B Side)	Yr	VG	VG+	NM
❑ 0001	Soul-Limbo/Heads Or Tails	1968	2.00	4.00	8.00
❑ 0013	Hang 'Em High/Over Easy	1968	2.00	4.00	8.00
❑ 0028	Time Is Tight/Johnny I Love You	1969	2.00	4.00	8.00
❑ 0037	Mrs. Robinson/Soul Clap '69	1969	2.00	4.00	8.00
❑ 0049	Slum Baby/Meditation	1969	2.00	4.00	8.00
❑ 0073	Something/Sunday Sermon	1970	—	3.00	6.00
❑ 0082	Melting Pot/Kinda Easy Like	1970	—	3.00	6.00
❑ 127	Green Onions/Behave Yourself	1962	5.00	10.00	20.00
—Gray label					
❑ 127	Green Onions/Behave Yourself	1962	4.00	8.00	16.00
—Blue label					
❑ 131	Jellybread/Aw' Mercy	1963	3.00	6.00	12.00
❑ 134	Big Train/Home Grown	1963	3.00	6.00	12.00
❑ 134	Big Train/Burnt Biscuits	1963	3.00	6.00	12.00
❑ 137	Chinese Checkers/Plum Nellie	1963	3.00	6.00	12.00
❑ 142	Mo' Onions/Tic Tac Toe	1963	3.00	6.00	12.00
❑ 142	Mo' Onions/Fannie Mae	1963	3.00	6.00	12.00
❑ 153	Soul Dressing/MG Party	1964	2.50	5.00	10.00
❑ 161	Can't Be Still/Terrible Thing	1964	2.50	5.00	10.00
❑ 169	Boot-Leg/Outrage	1965	2.50	5.00	10.00
❑ 0169	Sugarcane/Blackride	1973	—	2.50	5.00
—As "The MG's"					
❑ 182	Red Beans and Rice/Be My Lady	1965	2.50	5.00	10.00
❑ 196	Booker-Loo/My Sweet Potato	1966	2.50	5.00	10.00
❑ 0200	Breezy/Neckbone	1974	—	2.50	5.00
—As "The MG's"					
❑ 203	Jingle Bells/Winter Wonderland	1966	3.00	6.00	12.00
❑ 211	Hip-Hug-Her/Summertime	1967	2.50	5.00	10.00
❑ 224	Groovin'/Slim Jenkin's Place	1967	2.50	5.00	10.00
❑ 236	Silver Bells/Winter Snow	1967	3.00	6.00	12.00

VOLT

Number	Title (A Side/B Side)	Yr	VG	VG+	NM
❑ 102	Green Onions/Behave Yourself	1962	7.50	15.00	30.00

BOONE, PAT

BUENA VISTA

Number	Title (A Side/B Side)	Yr	VG	VG+	NM
❑ 487	Little Green Tree/The Sounds of Christmas	1973	—	3.50	7.00

CAPITOL

Number	Title (A Side/B Side)	Yr	VG	VG+	NM
❑ 2763	What Are You Doing the Rest of Your Life/Now I'm Saved	1970	—	2.50	5.00
❑ 2860	Picking Up Pebbles/Oh My God	1970	—	2.50	5.00

DOT

Number	Title (A Side/B Side)	Yr	VG	VG+	NM
❑ S-200 [S]	With the Wind and the Rain in Your Hair/Good Rockin' Tonight	1959	10.00	20.00	40.00
❑ S-203 [S]	For a Penny/The Wang Dang Taffy Apple Tango	1959	10.00	20.00	40.00
❑ S-207 [S]	Twixt Twlve and Twenty/Rock Boll Weevil	1959	10.00	20.00	40.00
❑ S-211 [S]	Fools Hall of Fame/The Brightest Wishing Star	1959	10.00	20.00	40.00
❑ S-218 [S]	Beyond the Sunset/My Faithful Heart	1959	10.00	20.00	40.00
❑ S-220 [S]	(Welcome) New Lovers/Words	1960	10.00	20.00	40.00
❑ S-221 [S]	Walking the Floor Over You/Spring Rain	1960	10.00	20.00	40.00
❑ S-228 [S]	Delia Gone/Candy Street	1960	10.00	20.00	40.00
❑ 15338	Two Hearts/Tra La La	1955	5.00	10.00	20.00
❑ 15377	Ain't That a Shame/Tennessee Saturday Night	1955	5.00	10.00	20.00
❑ 15422	At My Front Door/No Other Arms	1955	5.00	10.00	20.00
❑ 15435	Gee Whittakers!/Take the Time	1955	5.00	10.00	20.00
❑ 15443	Tutti Frutti/I'll Be Home	1956	5.00	10.00	20.00
❑ 15457	Long Tall Sally/Just As Long As I'm with You	1956	5.00	10.00	20.00
❑ 15472	I Almost Lost My Mind/I'm in Love with You	1956	5.00	10.00	20.00
❑ 15490	Friendly Persuasion (Thee I Love)/Chains of Love	1956	5.00	10.00	20.00
—Original on maroon label					
❑ 15490	Friendly Persuasion (Thee I Love)/Chains of Love	1956	3.75	7.50	15.00
—Second pressing on black label					
❑ 15521	Don't Forbid Me/Anastasia	1956	3.75	7.50	15.00
❑ 15545	Why Baby Why/I'm Waiting Just for You	1957	3.75	7.50	15.00
❑ 15570	Love Letters in the Sand/Bernardine	1957	3.75	7.50	15.00
❑ 15570 [PS]	Love Letters in the Sand/Bernardine	1957	7.50	15.00	30.00
❑ 15602	Remember You're Mine/There's a Gold Mine in the Sky	1957	3.75	7.50	15.00
❑ 15660	April Love/When the Swallows Come Back to Capistrano	1957	3.75	7.50	15.00
❑ 15690	It's Too Soon to Know/A Wonderful Time Up There	1958	3.75	7.50	15.00

Number	Title (A Side/B Side)	Yr	VG	VG+	NM
❑ 15750	Sugar Moon/Cherie, I Love You	1958	3.75	7.50	15.00
❑ 15750 [PS]	Sugar Moon/Cherie, I Love You	1958	7.50	15.00	30.00
❑ 15785	If Dreams Came True/That's How Much I Love You	1958	3.75	7.50	15.00
❑ 15825	Gee, But It's Lonely/For My Good Fortune	1958	3.75	7.50	15.00
❑ 15840	I'll Remember Tonight/The Mardi Gras March	1958	3.75	7.50	15.00
❑ 15840 [PS]	I'll Remember Tonight/The Mardi Gras March	1958	7.50	15.00	30.00
❑ 15888 [M]	With the Wind and the Rain in Your Hair/Good Rockin' Tonight	1959	3.75	7.50	15.00
❑ 15914 [M]	For a Penny/The Wang Dang Taffy Apple Tango	1959	3.75	7.50	15.00
❑ 15955 [M]	Twixt Twlve and Twenty/Rock Boll Weevil	1959	3.75	7.50	15.00
❑ 15955 [PS]	Twixt Twlve and Twenty/Rock Boll Weevil	1959	7.50	15.00	30.00
❑ 15982 [M]	Fools Hall of Fame/The Brightest Wishing Star	1959	3.75	7.50	15.00
❑ 15982 [PS]	Fools Hall of Fame/The Brightest Wishing Star	1959	7.50	15.00	30.00
❑ 16006 [M]	Beyond the Sunset/My Faithful Heart	1959	3.75	7.50	15.00
❑ 16015	To the Center of the Earth Part 1/Part 2	1959	5.00	10.00	20.00
❑ 16028	Ain't That a Shame/I'll Be Home	1960	2.50	5.00	10.00
❑ 16033	I Almost Lost My Mind/Friendly Persuasion	1960	2.50	5.00	10.00
❑ 16034	Don't Forbid Me/April Love	1960	2.50	5.00	10.00
❑ 16035	Love Letters in the Sand/A Wonderful Time Up There	1960	2.50	5.00	10.00
❑ 16048	(Welcome) New Lovers/Words	1960	3.00	6.00	12.00
❑ 16048 [PS]	(Welcome) New Lovers/Words	1960	5.00	10.00	20.00
❑ 16073	Walking the Floor Over You/Spring Rain	1960	3.00	6.00	12.00
❑ 16073 [PS]	Walking the Floor Over You/Spring Rain	1960	5.00	10.00	20.00
❑ 16122	Delia Gone/Candy Street	1960	3.00	6.00	12.00
❑ 16152	Dear John/Alabam	1960	3.00	6.00	12.00
❑ 16176	The Exodus Song (This Land Is Mine)/There's a Moon Out Tonight	1961	3.00	6.00	12.00
❑ 16190	Cherry Pink and Apple Blossom White/On Both Sides	1961	3.00	6.00	12.00
❑ 16209	Moody River/A Thousand Years	1961	3.75	7.50	15.00
❑ 16244	Big Cold Wind/That's My Desire	1961	3.00	6.00	12.00
❑ 16278	Louella/(B-side unknown)	1961	—	—	—
—Unreleased?					
❑ 16284	Johnny Will/Just Let Me Dream	1961	3.00	6.00	12.00
❑ 16312	I'll See You in My Dreams/Pictures in the Fire	1961	3.00	6.00	12.00
❑ 16349	Quando, Quando, Quando (Tell Me When)/Willing and Eager	1962	2.50	5.00	10.00
❑ 16368	Speedy Gonzales/The Locket	1962	3.00	6.00	12.00
❑ 16391	Ten Lonely Guys/Lover's Lane	1962	2.50	5.00	10.00
❑ 16416	In the Room/Mexican Joe	1963	2.50	5.00	10.00
❑ 16439	Days of Wine and Roses/Meditation	1963	2.50	5.00	10.00
❑ 16474	Always You and Me/Main Attraction	1963	2.50	5.00	10.00
❑ 16494	Tie Me Kangaroo Down Sport/I Feel Like Crying	1963	2.50	5.00	10.00
❑ 16498	Amore Baciami/Gondoli Gondola	1963	2.50	5.00	10.00
❑ 16498	Main Attraction/Si Si Si	1963	2.50	5.00	10.00
❑ 16525	Love Me/Mr. Moon	1963	2.50	5.00	10.00
❑ 16547	Santa's Coming in a Whirleybird/Oh Holy Night	1963	2.50	5.00	10.00
❑ 16559	Some Enchanted Evening/That's Me	1963	2.50	5.00	10.00
❑ 16576	I Like What You Do/Never Put It in Writing	1964	2.00	4.00	8.00
❑ 16598	I Understand (Just How You Feel)/Rosemarie	1964	2.00	4.00	8.00
❑ 16626	Side by Side/I'll Never Be Free	1964	2.00	4.00	8.00
—By "Pat and Shirley Boone"					
❑ 16641	Sincerely/Don't You Just Know It	1964	2.00	4.00	8.00
❑ 16658	Beach Girl/Little Honda	1964	7.50	15.00	30.00
❑ 16668	Goodbye, Charlie/Love, Who Needs It	1964	2.00	4.00	8.00
❑ 16684	I'd Rather Die Young/I Want It That Way	1964	2.00	4.00	8.00
❑ 16699	Blueberry Hill/Heartaches	1965	2.00	4.00	8.00
❑ 16707	Baby Elephant Walk/Say Goodbye	1965	2.00	4.00	8.00
❑ 16728	Pearly Shells/Crazy Arms	1965	2.00	4.00	8.00
❑ 16738	Mickey Mouse/Time Marches On	1965	2.00	4.00	8.00
❑ 16738	Mickey Mouse/(Welcome) New Lovers	1965	2.00	4.00	8.00
❑ 16754	Rainy Days/With My Eyes Wide Open I'm Dreaming	1965	2.00	4.00	8.00
❑ 16785	I Love You So Much It Hurts/Meet Me Tonight in Dreamland	1965	2.00	4.00	8.00
❑ 16808	A Man Alone/Run to Me, Baby	1966	2.00	4.00	8.00
❑ 16825	As Tears Go By/Judith	1966	2.00	4.00	8.00
❑ 16836	It Seems Like Yesterday/Well Remembered, Highly Thought Of Love Affair	1966	2.00	4.00	8.00
❑ 16871	Five Miles from Home/Don't Put Your Feet in the Lemonade	1966	2.00	4.00	8.00
❑ 16903	Wrath of Grapes/You Don't Need Me Anymore	1966	2.00	4.00	8.00
❑ 16933	Wish You Were Here, Buddy/Love for You	1966	2.00	4.00	8.00
❑ 16998	Hurry Sundown/What If They Gave a War and Nobody Came	1967	—	3.00	6.00
❑ 17018	Have You Heard (It's All Over)/Me	1967	—	3.00	6.00
❑ 17027	In the Mirror of Your Mind/Swanee Is a River	1967	—	3.00	6.00
❑ 17045	By the Time I Get to Phoenix/Ride Ride Ride	1967	—	3.00	6.00
❑ 17056	The Green Kentucky Hills of Home/You Mean All the World to Me	1967	—	3.00	6.00
❑ 17076	It's a Happening World/Emily	1968	—	3.00	6.00
❑ 17098	500 Miles/I Had a Dream	1968	—	3.00	6.00
❑ 17122	Gonna Find Me a Bluebird/Deafening Roar of Silence	1968	—	3.00	6.00
❑ 17156	Beyond One Memory/September Blues	1968	—	3.00	6.00
HITSVILLE					
❑ 6037	Texas Woman/It's Gone	1976	—	2.50	5.00
❑ 6042	Oklahoma Sunshine/Won't Be Home Tonight	1976	—	2.50	5.00
❑ 6047	Country Days and Country Nights/Lovelight Comes a Shining	1976	—	2.50	5.00
❑ 6054	Colorado Country Morning/Don't Want to Fall Away from You	1977	—	2.50	5.00
LAMB & LION					
❑ 818	It's OK to Be a Kid at Christmas/Don't Let the Season Pass You By	1979	—	2.50	5.00
LION					
❑ 106	Mr. Blue/Song of the Children of Israel (Exodus)	1972	—	2.50	5.00
—With the Boone Girls					
❑ 119	I Believe in Music/Children Learn What They Live	1972	—	2.50	5.00
—With the Boone Family					
❑ 126	Empty Chairs/If You're Gonna Make a Fool of Somebody	1972	—	2.50	5.00
MC					
❑ 5001	Whatever Happened to the Good Old Honky Tonk/Ain't Going Down in the Ground Before My Time	1977	—	2.50	5.00
MELODYLAND					
❑ 6001	Candy Lips/Young Girl	1974	—	2.50	5.00
❑ 6005	Indiana Girl/Young Girl	1975	—	2.50	5.00
❑ 6018	I'd Do It with You/Yester-Me, Yester-You, Yesterday	1975	—	2.50	5.00
—A-side with Shirley Boone					
❑ 6029	Glory Train/U.F.O.	1976	—	2.50	5.00
MGM					
❑ 14242	All for the Love of Sunshine/M.I.A-P.O.W.	1971	—	2.50	5.00
❑ 14282	C'mon, Give a Hand/Where There's a Heartache	1971	—	2.50	5.00
❑ 14470	I Saw the Light/Great Speckled Bird	1972	—	2.50	5.00
❑ 14521	Tying the Pieces Together/Hayden Carter	1973	—	2.00	4.00
❑ 14521 [PS]	Tying the Pieces Together/Hayden Carter	1973	—	2.50	5.00
❑ 14601	Everything Begins and Ends with You/Golden Rocket	1973	—	2.00	4.00
REPUBLIC					
❑ 7049	My Heart Belongs to You/Until You Tell Me So	1953	6.25	12.50	25.00
❑ 7062	Remember to Be Mine/Half Way Chance with You	1953	6.25	12.50	25.00
❑ 7084	I Need Someone/Loving You Madly	1954	6.25	12.50	25.00
❑ 7119	My Heart Belongs to You/I Need Someone	1955	5.00	10.00	20.00
TETRAGRAMMATON					
❑ 1516	July, You're a Woman/Break My Mind	1969	—	2.50	5.00
❑ 1529	Never Goin' Back/What's Gnawing at Me	1969	—	2.50	5.00
❑ 1540	You Win Again/Good Morning, Dear	1969	—	2.50	5.00
WARNER BROS.					
❑ 49097	Midnight/Can You Feel the Love	1979	—	2.00	4.00
—By "Pat and Shirley Boone"					
❑ 49255	Hostage Prayer/Love's Got a Way of Hanging On	1980	—	2.00	4.00
❑ 49596	Colorado Country Morning/Whatever Happened to the Good Old Honky Tonk	1980	—	2.00	4.00
❑ 49691	Won't Be Home Tonight/Throw It Away	1981	—	2.00	4.00

7-Inch Extended Plays

Number	Title (A Side/B Side)	Yr	VG	VG+	NM
DOT					
❑ DEP-1049	At My Front Door/Tennessee Saturday Night//Ain't That a Shame/Two Hearts	1956	5.00	10.00	20.00
❑ DEP-1049 [PS]	Pat Boone	1956	5.00	10.00	20.00
❑ DEP-1053	Treasure of Love/B-I-N-G-O//Hoboken Baby/Am I Seeing Angels	1956	5.00	10.00	20.00
❑ DEP-1053 [PS]	Pat On Mike	1956	5.00	10.00	20.00
❑ DEP-1054	Coax Me A Little/The Mocking Bird In The Willow Tree//Indiana Holiday/Marry Me, Marry Me	1956	5.00	10.00	20.00
❑ DEP-1054 [PS]	Pat Boone Sings Songs from Friendly Persuasion	1956	5.00	10.00	20.00
❑ DEP-1055	Don't Forbid Me/Why Did I Choose You?//Rock Me Baby/The Fat Man	1957	5.00	10.00	20.00
❑ DEP-1055 [PS]	A Date with Pat Boone	1957	5.00	10.00	20.00
❑ DEP-1056	Just a Closer Walk with Thee/Peace in the Valley//He'll Understand/Steal Away	1957	5.00	10.00	20.00
❑ DEP-1056 [PS]	A Closer Walk with Thee	1957	5.00	10.00	20.00
❑ DEP-1057	Technique/Cathedral in the Pines//Louella/Without My Love	1957	5.00	10.00	20.00
❑ DEP-1057 [PS]	Four by Pat	1957	5.00	10.00	20.00
❑ DEP-1062	White Christmas/Silent Night//Jingle Bells/Santa Claus Is Comin' to Town	1957	7.50	15.00	30.00
❑ DEP-1062 [PS]	... And a Very Merry Christmas	1957	7.50	15.00	30.00
❑ DEP-1064	Chattanooga Shoe Shine Boy/Harbor Lights//Tutti Frutti/I'll Be Home	195?	3.75	7.50	15.00
❑ DEP-1064 [PS]	Tutti Frutti	195?	3.75	7.50	15.00
❑ DEP-1068	The Lord's Prayer/I Believe//Ave Maria/He	195?	3.75	7.50	15.00
❑ DEP-1068 [PS]	The Lord's Prayer	195?	3.75	7.50	15.00
❑ DEP-1069	Autumn Leaves/Blueberry Hill//Cold, Cold Heart/St. Louis Blues	1958	5.00	10.00	20.00
❑ DEP-1069 [PS]	Star Dust	1958	5.00	10.00	20.00
❑ DEP-1075	Loyalty/Bourbon Street Blues//Bigger Than Texas/A Fiddle, A Rifle, An Axe and a Bible	1958	3.75	7.50	15.00
❑ DEP-1075 [PS]	Mardi Gras	1958	3.75	7.50	15.00
❑ DEP-1076	*You Can't Be True, Dear/My Happiness//Now Is the Hour/Side by Side	1959	3.75	7.50	15.00
❑ DEP-1076 [PS]	Side by Side	1959	3.75	7.50	15.00
—By "Pat & Shirley Boone"					
❑ DEP-1081	Beyond The Sunset/It Is No Secret//My God Is Real (Yes, God Is Real)/Yield Not To Temptation	195?	3.75	7.50	15.00
❑ DEP-1081 [PS]	Hymns We Love	195?	3.75	7.50	15.00
❑ DEP-1082	*Tenderly/Fascination/True Love/Maybe You'll Be There	196?	3.75	7.50	15.00
❑ DEP-1082 [PS]	Tenderly	196?	3.75	7.50	15.00
❑ DEP-1083	(contents unknown)	196?	3.75	7.50	15.00
❑ DEP-1083 [PS]	Pat's Great Hits	196?	3.75	7.50	15.00
❑ DEP-1086	(contents unknown)	196?	3.75	7.50	15.00
❑ DEP-1086 [PS]	I'm In the Mood for Love	196?	3.75	7.50	15.00
❑ DEP-1090	(contents unknown)	196?	3.75	7.50	15.00
❑ DEP-1090 [PS]	Beyond the Sunset	196?	3.75	7.50	15.00
❑ DEP-1091	(contents unknown)	196?	3.75	7.50	15.00
❑ DEP-1091 [PS]	Journey to the Center of the Earth	196?	3.75	7.50	15.00
❑ DEP-1098	(contents unknown)	196?	3.75	7.50	15.00
❑ DEP-1098 [PS]	All Hands On Deck	196?	3.75	7.50	15.00

BOOTLES, THE

Number	Title (A Side/B Side)	Yr	VG	VG+	NM
GNP CRESCENDO					
❑ 311	I'll Let You Hold My Hand/Never Till Now	1964	3.75	7.50	15.00

BOP-A-LOOS, THE

Number	Title (A Side/B Side)	Yr	VG	VG+	NM
MERCURY					
❑ 70552	Teach Me Tonight/South Parkway Mambo	1955	5.00	10.00	20.00
❑ 70553	Tweedle Dee/Bongo Mambo	1955	5.00	10.00	20.00
❑ 70568	Hearts of Stone/Miracle Mambo	1955	5.00	10.00	20.00

Number	Title (A Side/B Side)	Yr	VG	VG+	NM
❑ 70569	Sincerely/Cuban Carnival	1955	5.00	10.00	20.00

BOP-CHORDS, THE

HOLIDAY

Number	Title (A Side/B Side)	Yr	VG	VG+	NM
❑ 2601	Castle in the Sky/My Darling to You	1957	50.00	100.00	200.00
—*Black label*					
❑ 2601	Castle in the Sky/My Darling to You	196?	12.50	25.00	50.00
—*Red label, double lines*					
❑ 2601	Castle in the Sky/My Darling to You	196?	6.25	12.50	25.00
—*Red label, single line*					
❑ 2603	When I Woke Up This Morning/I Really Love You	1957	50.00	100.00	200.00
—*Black label*					
❑ 2603	When I Woke Up This Morning/I Really Love You	196?	12.50	25.00	50.00
—*Red label*					
❑ 2608	Baby/So Why	1957	75.00	150.00	300.00
—*Red label*					

BORDERSONG

With Ann and Nancy Wilson, later of HEART.

GREAT NORTHWEST

Number	Title (A Side/B Side)	Yr	VG	VG+	NM
❑ 704	She's a Good Woman/Morning	1976	6.25	12.50	25.00

BOSTIC, EARL

KING

Number	Title (A Side/B Side)	Yr	VG	VG+	NM
❑ 4444	Sleep/September Song	1951	7.50	15.00	30.00
❑ 4454	Always/How Could It Have Been You and I	1951	7.50	15.00	30.00
❑ 4475	Flamingo/I'm Getting Sentimental Over You	1951	7.50	15.00	30.00
❑ 4491	I Got Loaded/Chains of Love	1951	10.00	20.00	40.00
❑ 4511	The Moon Is Low/Lover Come Back to Me	1952	6.25	12.50	25.00
❑ 4536	Linger Awhile/Velvet Sunset	1952	6.25	12.50	25.00
❑ 4550	Moonglow/Ain't Misbehavin'	1952	6.25	12.50	25.00
❑ 4570	For You/Smoke Gets In Your Eyes	1952	6.25	12.50	25.00
❑ 4586	You Go to My Head/Hour of Parting	1953	6.25	12.50	25.00
❑ 4603	The Sheik of Araby/Steamwhistle Jump	1953	6.25	12.50	25.00
❑ 4623	Cherokee/The Song Is Ended	1953	6.25	12.50	25.00
❑ 4644	Melancholy Serenade/What, No Pearls?	1953	6.25	12.50	25.00
❑ 4653	The Very Thought of You/Memories	1953	6.25	12.50	25.00
❑ 4674	Deep Purple/Smoke Rings	1953	6.25	12.50	25.00
❑ 4683	Off Shore/Don't You Do It	1953	6.25	12.50	25.00
❑ 4699	My Heart at Thy Sweet Voice/Cracked Ice	1954	5.00	10.00	20.00
❑ 4708	Jungle Drums/Danube Waves	1954	5.00	10.00	20.00
❑ 4723	Blue Skies/Mambolino	1954	5.00	10.00	20.00
❑ 4730	These Foolish Things/Mambostic	1954	5.00	10.00	20.00
❑ 4741	Ubangi Stomp/Time on My Hands	1954	5.00	10.00	20.00
❑ 4754	Song of the Islands/Liebestraum	1954	5.00	10.00	20.00
❑ 4765	Embraceable You/Night and Day	1955	5.00	10.00	20.00
❑ 4776	Melody of Love/Sweet Lorraine	1955	5.00	10.00	20.00
❑ 4790	Cocktails for Two/When Your Lover Has Gone	1955	5.00	10.00	20.00
❑ 4799	Remember/Cherry Bean	1955	5.00	10.00	20.00
❑ 4815	East of the Sun/Dream	1955	5.00	10.00	20.00
❑ 4829	For All We Know/Beyond the Blue Horizon	1955	5.00	10.00	20.00
❑ 4845	O Solo Mio/Poeme	1955	5.00	10.00	20.00
❑ 4883	I Love You Truly/'Cause You're My Lover	1956	3.75	7.50	15.00
❑ 4905	Bugle Call Rag/I'll String Along with You	1956	3.75	7.50	15.00
❑ 4943	Roses of Picardy/Where or When	1956	3.75	7.50	15.00
❑ 4978	Harlem Nocturne/I Hear a Rhapsody	1956	3.75	7.50	15.00
❑ 5025	Too Fine for Crying/Avalon	1957	3.75	7.50	15.00
❑ 5041	Temptation/September Song	1957	3.75	7.50	15.00
❑ 5056	She's Funny That Way/Exercise	1957	3.75	7.50	15.00
❑ 5071	Vienna, City of My Dreams/Just Too Shy	1957	3.75	7.50	15.00
❑ 5081	A Gay Day/Answer Me	1957	3.75	7.50	15.00
❑ 5092	Josephine/Jeannie I Dream of Lilac Time	1957	3.75	7.50	15.00
❑ 5106	Southern Fried/No Name Jive	1958	3.75	7.50	15.00
❑ 5120	Lester Leaps In/Pompton Turnpike	1958	3.75	7.50	15.00
❑ 5127	Honeysuckle Rose/Back Beat	1958	3.75	7.50	15.00
❑ 5133	Woodchopper's Ball/John's Idea	1958	3.75	7.50	15.00
❑ 5136	Twilight Time/Over Waves Rock	1958	3.75	7.50	15.00
❑ 5144	Pinkie/Home Sweet Home Rock	1958	3.75	7.50	15.00
❑ 5152	Goodnight Sweetheart/Indian Boogie Woogie	1958	3.75	7.50	15.00
❑ 5161	Red Skin Cha Cha/Rockin' with Richard	1958	3.75	7.50	15.00
❑ 5175	My Reverie Cha Cha/Barcarole	1959	3.00	6.00	12.00
❑ 5190	Up There in Orbit/Sweet Pea	1959	3.00	6.00	12.00
❑ 5203	Up There in Orbit (Part 1)/Up There in Orbit (Part 2)	1959	3.00	6.00	12.00
❑ 5209	La Cucaracha Cha Cha/Dancing in the Dark	1959	3.00	6.00	12.00
❑ 5229	Who Cares/Feeling Cool	1959	3.00	6.00	12.00
❑ 5252	White Horse/Dark Eyes	1959	3.00	6.00	12.00
❑ 5263	Gondola/Once in a While	1959	3.00	6.00	12.00
❑ 5290	Tut-Strut/All the Things You Are	1959	3.00	6.00	12.00
❑ 5301	Ebb Tide/Hildegarde	1959	3.00	6.00	12.00
❑ 5309	Let's Move Out/I Burned Your Letter	1960	3.00	6.00	12.00
❑ 5314	Off Shore/Hello '60	1960	3.00	6.00	12.00
❑ 5317	Elegie/Out of Nowhere	1960	3.00	6.00	12.00
❑ 5345	Make Believe/A Gay Day	1960	3.00	6.00	12.00
❑ 5362	Tuxedo Junction/Polonaise	1960	3.00	6.00	12.00
❑ 5402	720 in the Books/Just in Time	1960	3.00	6.00	12.00
❑ 5454	That Old Black Magic/Full Moon and Empty Arms	1961	2.50	5.00	10.00
❑ 5477	Jersey Bounce/Because of You	1961	2.50	5.00	10.00
❑ 5564	The Thrill Is Gone/April in Portugal	1961	2.50	5.00	10.00
❑ 5600	How Deep Is the Ocean/Wrap It	1962	2.50	5.00	10.00
❑ 5636	Dark Eyes/People Will Say We're in Love	1962	2.50	5.00	10.00
❑ 5661	More Than You Know/Don't Blame Me	1962	2.50	5.00	10.00
❑ 5683	Ducky/Deep in My Heart	1962	2.50	5.00	10.00
❑ 5699	Autumn Leaves/Anita's Theme	1962	2.50	5.00	10.00
❑ 5711	El Choclo Bossa Nova/My Reverie	1963	2.50	5.00	10.00
❑ 5742	Cherry Pink (And Apple Blossom White)/Your Cheatin' Heart	1963	2.50	5.00	10.00
❑ 5776	Love Letters in the Sand/Tammy	1963	2.50	5.00	10.00
❑ 5819	Apple Cake/Don't Do It Please	1963	2.50	5.00	10.00
❑ 5839	Telstar Drive/Fast Track	1964	2.00	4.00	8.00
❑ 5861	Let's Dance Little Girl/Summertime	1964	2.00	4.00	8.00
❑ 5900	Make Believe/Star Gazer	1964	2.00	4.00	8.00
❑ 5925	The Pink Panther/Lawrence of Arabia	1964	2.00	4.00	8.00
❑ 5944	From Russia with Love/My Special Dream	1964	2.00	4.00	8.00
❑ 5955	Theme from The Unforgiven/Dominique	1964	2.00	4.00	8.00
❑ 5961	Hello Dolly/Walk on the Wild Side	1964	2.00	4.00	8.00
❑ 5977	More/Charade	1965	2.00	4.00	8.00
❑ 6254	September Song/Harlem Nocturne	1969	—	2.50	5.00

7-Inch Extended Plays

KING

Number	Title (A Side/B Side)	Yr	VG	VG+	NM
❑ EP-200	Flamingo/Swing Low Sweet Boogie//I Can't Give You Anything But Love/The Moon Is Low	195?	6.25	12.50	25.00
❑ EP-200 [PS]	Earl Bostic and His Alto Sax, Vol. 1	195?	6.25	12.50	25.00
❑ EP 201	*Sleep/Earl's Imagination/Lover Come Back to Me/I'm Gettin' Sentimental Over You	1953	6.25	12.50	25.00
❑ EP 201 [PS]	Earl Bostic and His Alto Sax, Vol. 2	1953	6.25	12.50	25.00
❑ EP 202	*Always/Linger Awhile/Merry Widow/Earl Blows a Fuse	1953	6.25	12.50	25.00
❑ EP 202 [PS]	Earl Bostic and His Alto Sax, Vol. 3	1953	6.25	12.50	25.00
❑ EP 203	*Deep Purple/Velvet Sunset/Choppin' It Down/You Go to My Head	1953	6.25	12.50	25.00
❑ EP 203 [PS]	Earl Bostic and His Alto Sax, Vol. 4	1953	6.25	12.50	25.00
❑ EP 204	*Cherokee/Seven Steps/No Name Blues/Don't You Do It	1953	6.25	12.50	25.00
❑ EP 204 [PS]	Earl Bostic and His Alto Sax, Vol. 5	1953	6.25	12.50	25.00
❑ EP 205	*Moonglow/For You/Blip Boogie/Wrap It Up	1953	6.25	12.50	25.00
❑ EP 205 [PS]	Earl Bostic and His Alto Sax, Vol. 6	1953	6.25	12.50	25.00
❑ EP 206	*Filibuster/The Sheik of Araby/Smoke Gets in Your Eyes/The Hour of Parting	1953	6.25	12.50	25.00
❑ EP 206 [PS]	Earl Bostic and His Alto Sax, Vol. 7	1953	6.25	12.50	25.00
❑ EP 207	*Serenade/Ain't Misbehavin'/Smoke Rings/Steamwhistle Jump	1953	6.25	12.50	25.00
❑ EP 207 [PS]	Earl Bostic and His Alto Sax, Vol. 8	1953	6.25	12.50	25.00
❑ EP 245	Melancholy Serenade/What! No Pearls//The Very Thought of You/Memories	1954	5.00	10.00	20.00
❑ EP 245 [PS]	Earl Bostic and His Alto Sax, Vol. 9	1954	5.00	10.00	20.00
❑ EP 284	*Jungle Drums/The Song Is Ended/Off Shore/Cracked Ice	1954	5.00	10.00	20.00
❑ EP 284 [PS]	Earl Bostic and His Alto Sax, Vol. 10	1954	5.00	10.00	20.00
❑ EP 285	*Danube Waves/My Heart at Thy Sweet Voice/Poeme/O Sole Mio	1954	5.00	10.00	20.00
❑ EP 285 [PS]	Earl Bostic and His Alto Sax, Vol. 11	1954	5.00	10.00	20.00
❑ EP 347	*Mambostic/Time on My Hands/Mambolino/Ven-A-Mi	1955	5.00	10.00	20.00
❑ EP 347 [PS]	Earl Bostic and His Alto Sax, Vol. 12	1955	5.00	10.00	20.00
❑ EP 350	*Blue Skies/These Foolish Things/Song of the Islands/Ubangi Stomp	1955	5.00	10.00	20.00
❑ EP 350 [PS]	Earl Bostic and His Alto Sax, Vol. 13	1955	5.00	10.00	20.00
❑ EP 355	*Cherry Bean/Liebestraum/Night and Day/Embraceable You	1955	5.00	10.00	20.00
❑ EP 355 [PS]	Earl Bostic and His Alto Sax, Vol. 14	1955	5.00	10.00	20.00
❑ EP 363	*Melody of Love/Cocktails for Two/Blue Moon/Remember	1955	5.00	10.00	20.00
❑ EP 363 [PS]	Earl Bostic and His Alto Sax, Vol. 15	1955	5.00	10.00	20.00
❑ EP 375	*Dream/Beyond the Blue Horizon/East of the Sun/For All We Know	1956	5.00	10.00	20.00
❑ EP 375 [PS]	Earl Bostic with Strings, Vol. 16	1956	5.00	10.00	20.00
❑ EP 381	*Bugle Call Rag/I'll String Along with You/I Love You Truly/'Cause You're My Lover	1956	5.00	10.00	20.00
❑ EP 381 [PS]	Bostic Blows, Vol. 17	1956	5.00	10.00	20.00
❑ KEP 398	Harlem Nocturne/I Hear a Rhapsody//Roses of Picardy/Where or When	1957	5.00	10.00	20.00
❑ KEP 398 [PS]	Earl Bostic, Vol. 18	1957	5.00	10.00	20.00
❑ EP-417	(contents unknown)	1958	5.00	10.00	20.00
❑ EP-417 [PS]	Showcase of Swinging Dance Hits, Vol. 1	1958	5.00	10.00	20.00
❑ EP-418	Two O'Clock Jump/Back Beat//John's Idea/Royal Garden Blues	1958	5.00	10.00	20.00
❑ EP-418 [PS]	Showcase of Swinging Dance Hits, Vol. 2	1958	5.00	10.00	20.00
❑ EP-420	Twilight Time/Stairway to the Stars//Rockin' with Richard/Be My Love	1958	5.00	10.00	20.00
❑ EP-420 [PS]	Alto Magic in Hi Fi, Vol. 1	1958	5.00	10.00	20.00
❑ EP-421	(contents unknown)	1958	5.00	10.00	20.00
❑ EP-421 [PS]	Alto Magic in Hi Fi, Vol. 2	1958	5.00	10.00	20.00
❑ EP-422	C Jam Blues/Wee-Gee Board//The Wrecking Rock/Home Sweet Home Rock	1958	5.00	10.00	20.00
❑ EP-422 [PS]	Alto Magic in Hi Fi, Vol. 3	1958	5.00	10.00	20.00

ROYALE

Number	Title (A Side/B Side)	Yr	VG	VG+	NM
❑ EP 367	The Man I Love/All On//Hurricane Blues/The Major and the Minor	195?	3.75	7.50	15.00
❑ EP 367 [PS]	His Saxophone and Orchestra	195?	3.75	7.50	15.00

BOSTIC, EARL, AND BILL DOGGETT

Also see each artist's individual listings.

KING

Number	Title (A Side/B Side)	Yr	VG	VG+	NM
❑ 4930	Mean to Me/Bo-Do Rock	1956	3.75	7.50	15.00
❑ 4954	Indiana/Bubbins Rock	1956	3.75	7.50	15.00
❑ 5427	Special Delivery Stomp/Earl's Dog	1960	2.50	5.00	10.00

BOSTICK, CALVIN

CHESS

Number	Title (A Side/B Side)	Yr	VG	VG+	NM
❑ 1530	Christmas Won't Be Christmas Without You/Four-Eleven Boogie	1952	37.50	75.00	150.00

BOSTON CRABS, THE

CAPITOL

Number	Title (A Side/B Side)	Yr	VG	VG+	NM
❑ 5493	Down in Mexico/Who?	1965	2.50	5.00	10.00

TOWER

Number	Title (A Side/B Side)	Yr	VG	VG+	NM
❑ 368	Gin House/Leave My Woman Alone	1967	2.50	5.00	10.00

BOTKIN, PERRY, JR.

Also see BARRY DeVORZON.

A&M

Number	Title (A Side/B Side)	Yr	VG	VG+	NM
❑ 1856	Nadia's Theme (The Young and the Restless)/Down the Line	1976	2.50	5.00	10.00
—*Original issue; Barry DeVorzon's name was added after he threatened legal action*					

Number	Title (A Side/B Side)	Yr	VG	VG+	NM
❑ 1856 [PS]	Nadia's Theme (The Young and the Restless)/ Down the Line	1976	2.50	5.00	10.00
—Sleeve with only Perry Botkin Jr.'s name on it (see above listing)					
❑ 1967	Looking for Home/Lovers	1977	—	2.00	4.00
❑ 1990	Bridges/Love Theme from Aspen	1977	—	2.00	4.00
DECCA					
❑ 30912	The Execution Theme/Waltz of the Hunter	1959	3.00	6.00	12.00
MGM					
❑ 14357	Soley Soley/(B-side unknown)	1972	—	2.50	5.00
—As "Perry Botkin, Inc."					
❑ 14379	Bless the Beasts and Children/Lost	1972	—	2.50	5.00
PRIDE					
❑ 1005	Journey to Moscow/Ellie's Theme	1972	—	2.50	5.00
VALIANT					
❑ 719	Where Does Love Go (Instrumental)/Where Does Love Go (Vocal)	1965	2.00	4.00	8.00
—B-side by Charles Boyer					
❑ 6025	Careless Love/Wabash Cannonball	1962	2.50	5.00	10.00

BOUQUETS

Number	Title (A Side/B Side)	Yr	VG	VG+	NM
BLUE CAT					
❑ 115	Welcome to My Heart/Ain't That Love	1965	7.50	15.00	30.00
MALA					
❑ 472	I Love Him So/No Love at All	1964	3.75	7.50	15.00
VEST					
❑ 8000	Yeah Babe/Girls, Girls	1963	3.75	7.50	15.00

BOWEN, JIMMY

Number	Title (A Side/B Side)	Yr	VG	VG+	NM
CAPEHART					
❑ 5005	Teenage Dreamworld/It's Against the Law	1962	5.00	10.00	20.00
❑ 5005 [PS]	Teenage Dreamworld/It's Against the Law	1962	12.50	25.00	50.00
CREST					
❑ 1085	Don't Drop It/Somebody to Love	1961	5.00	10.00	20.00
REPRISE					
❑ 0264	The Biggest Lover in Town/The Big Bus	1964	2.50	5.00	10.00
❑ 0358	The Golden Eagle/Spanish Cricket	1965	2.50	5.00	10.00
❑ 0450	Wonder Mother/Captain Gorgeous	1966	2.50	5.00	10.00
❑ 0592	Raunchy/It's Such a Pretty World Today	1967	2.50	5.00	10.00
ROULETTE					
❑ 4001	I'm Stickin' With You/Ever Lovin' Fingers	1957	5.00	10.00	20.00
—With the Rhythm Orchids					
❑ 4010	Warm Up to Me Baby/I Trusted You	1957	5.00	10.00	20.00
❑ 4017	Ever Since That Night/Don't Tell Me Your Troubles	1957	5.00	10.00	20.00
❑ 4023	Cross Over/It's Shameful	1957	5.00	10.00	20.00
❑ 4057	Can She Kiss/Keeping You	1958	5.00	10.00	20.00
❑ 4083	By the Light of the Silvery Moon/The Two Step	1958	5.00	10.00	20.00
❑ 4102	My Kind of Woman/Blue Moon	1958	5.00	10.00	20.00
❑ 4122	Always Faithful/Wish I Were Tied to You	1958	5.00	10.00	20.00
❑ 4175	You're Just Wasting Your Time/Walkin' on Air	1959	5.00	10.00	20.00
❑ 4224	Oh Yeah! Oh Yeah! Mm Mm/Your Loving Arms	1960	5.00	10.00	20.00
TRIPLE D					
❑ 798	I'm Stickin' With You/Party Doll	1956	250.00	500.00	1000.
—B-side by Buddy Knox					

7-Inch Extended Plays

Number	Title (A Side/B Side)	Yr	VG	VG+	NM
ROULETTE					
❑ 302	(contents unknown)	1957	50.00	100.00	200.00
❑ 302 [PS]	Jimmy Bowen	1957	50.00	100.00	200.00

BOWIE, DAVID

Number	Title (A Side/B Side)	Yr	VG	VG+	NM
BACKSTREET					
❑ 52024	Cat People/Paul's Theme	1982	—	—	3.00
—B-side by Georgio Moroder					
❑ 52024 [PS]	Cat People/Paul's Theme	1982	—	—	3.00
DERAM					
❑ 85009	Rubber Band/There Is a Happy Land	1967	25.00	50.00	100.00
❑ 85016	Love You Till Tuesday/Did You Ever Have a Dream	1967	25.00	50.00	100.00
EMI AMERICA					
❑ 8158	Let's Dance/Cat People (Putting Out Fire)	1983	—	—	3.00
❑ 8158 [PS]	Let's Dance/Cat People (Putting Out Fire)	1983	—	—	3.00
❑ 8165	China Girl/Shake It	1983	—	—	3.00
❑ 8165 [PS]	China Girl/Shake It	1983	—	2.50	5.00
❑ 8177	Modern Love/Modern Love (Live)	1983	—	—	3.00
❑ 8177 [PS]	Modern Love/Modern Love (Live)	1983	—	—	3.00
❑ 8190	Without You/Criminal Law	1984	—	—	3.00
❑ 8190 [PS]	Without You/Criminal Law	1984	—	—	3.00
❑ 8231	Blue Jean/Dancin' with the Big Boys	1984	2.00	4.00	8.00
—First pressing on blue vinyl					
❑ 8231	Blue Jean/Dancin' with the Big Boys	1984	—	—	2.00
❑ 8231 [PS]	Blue Jean/Dancin' with the Big Boys	1984	—	—	2.00
—Both colors of vinyl have the same picture sleeve					
❑ 8246	Tonight/Tumble and Twirl	1984	—	—	3.00
❑ 8246 [PS]	Tonight/Tumble and Twirl	1984	—	2.50	5.00
—Fold-out poster sleeve					
❑ 8251	This Is Not America/(Instrumental)	1984	—	—	3.00
❑ 8251 [PS]	This Is Not America/(Instrumental)	1984	—	—	3.00
—With the Pat Metheny Group					
❑ 8271	Loving the Alien/Don't Look Down	1985	—	—	3.00
❑ 8271 [PS]	Loving the Alien/Don't Look Down	1985	—	—	3.00
❑ 8308	Absolute Beginners/Absolute Beginnners (Dub Mix)	1986	—	—	3.00
❑ 8308 [PS]	Absolute Beginners/Absolute Beginnners (Dub Mix)	1986	—	—	3.00
❑ 8323	Underground/(instrumental)	1986	—	—	3.00
❑ 8323 [PS]	Underground/(instrumental)	1986	—	—	3.00
❑ 8380	Day In Day Out/Day In Day Out	1987	—	—	3.00
❑ 8380 [PS]	Day In Day Out/Day In Day Out	1987	—	—	3.00
❑ 43020	Time Will Crawl/Time Will Crawl	1987	—	—	3.00
❑ 43020 [PS]	Time Will Crawl/Time Will Crawl	1987	2.50	5.00	10.00
❑ 43031	Never Let Me Down/Never Let Me Down	1987	—	—	3.00
❑ 43031 [PS]	Never Let Me Down/Never Let Me Down	1987	—	—	3.00
LONDON					
❑ 20079	The Laughing Gnome/The Gospel According to Tony Day	1973	12.50	25.00	50.00
MERCURY					
❑ 72949	Space Oddity/Wild-Eyed Boy from Freecloud	1969	12.50	25.00	50.00
❑ 73075	Memory of a Free Festival Part 1/Part 2	1970	50.00	100.00	200.00
❑ 73173 [DJ]	All the Madmen (mono/stereo)	1971	37.50	75.00	150.00
—May be promo only					
RCA					
❑ PB-10664	TVC 15/We Are the Dead	1976	—	2.50	5.00
❑ PB-10736	Stay/Word on a Wing	1976	—	2.50	5.00
❑ PB-10905	Sound and Vision/A New Career in a New Town	1977	—	2.50	5.00
❑ GB-10938	Fame/Golden Years	1977	—	—	3.00
—Gold Standard Series issue					
❑ GB-10938	Fame/Golden Years	1977	—	—	3.00
—Gold Standard Series issue					
❑ PB-11017	Be My Wife/The Speed of Life	1977	—	2.50	5.00
❑ PB-11121	Heroes/V-2 Schneider	1977	—	2.50	5.00
❑ PB-11190	Beauty and the Beast/Sense of Doubt	1978	—	2.50	5.00
❑ PB-11585	Boys Keep Swinging/Fantastic Voyage	1979	—	2.50	5.00
❑ PB-11661	D.J./Fantastic Voyage	1979	—	2.50	5.00
❑ PB-11724	Look Back in Anger/Repetition	1979	—	2.50	5.00
❑ PB-11887	John I'm Only Dancing 1972/Joe the Lion	1980	—	2.50	5.00
❑ JH-12078 [PS]	Ashes to Ashes/It's No Game	1980	3.75	7.50	15.00
—Promo-only sleeve of Bowie holding a shoe and looking down at it					
❑ PB-12078	Ashes to Ashes/It's No Game	1980	—	2.50	5.00
❑ PB-12078 [PS]	Ashes to Ashes/It's No Game	1980	—	2.50	5.00
❑ JE-12087 [DJ]	Fashion/It's No Game/Teenage Wildlife	1980	100.00	200.00	400.00
❑ PB-12134	Fashion/Scream Like a Baby	1980	—	2.50	5.00
❑ PB-12134 [PS]	Fashion/Scream Like a Baby	1980	—	2.50	5.00
❑ PH-13400	Peace on Earth-Little Drummer Boy/Fantastic Voyage	1982	—	2.50	5.00
—A-side with Bing Crosby					
❑ PH-13400 [PS]	Peace on Earth-Little Drummer Boy/Fantastic Voyage	1982	2.50	5.00	10.00
—A-side with Bing Crosby					
❑ PB-13660	White Light-White Heat/Cracked Actor	1983	—	2.50	5.00
❑ PB-13660 [PS]	White Light-White Heat/Cracked Actor	1983	—	2.50	5.00
❑ PB-13769	1984/TVC 15	1984	—	2.50	5.00
❑ PB-13769 [PS]	1984/TVC 15	1984	—	2.50	5.00
RCA VICTOR					
❑ APBO-0001	Time/The Prettiest Star	1973	—	3.00	6.00
❑ APBO-0001 [PS]	Time/The Prettiest Star	1973	200.00	400.00	800.00
❑ APBO-0028	Let's Spend the Night Together/Lady Grinning Soul	1973	—	3.00	6.00
❑ APBO-0160	Sorrow/Amsterdam	1973	—	3.00	6.00
❑ APBO-0287	Rebel Rebel/Lady Grinning Soul	1974	2.50	5.00	10.00
—All copies contain an alternate mix of "Rebel, Rebel"					
❑ APBO-0293	Diamond Dogs/Holy Holy	1974	2.50	5.00	10.00
—Part of U.S. numbering system, but released only outside the U.S.					
❑ PB-10026	1984/Queen Bitch	1974	—	3.00	6.00
❑ PB-10105	Rock and Roll with Me/Panic in Detroit	1974	—	3.00	6.00
❑ PB-10152	Young Americans/Knock on Wood	1975	—	3.00	6.00
—Tan label (Indianapolis pressing)					
❑ PB-10152	Young Americans/Knock on Wood	1975	—	3.00	6.00
—Orange label (West Coast pressing)					
❑ PB-10320	Fame/Right	1975	—	3.00	6.00
—Tan label (Indianapolis pressing)					
❑ PB-10320	Fame/Right	1975	—	3.00	6.00
—Orange label (West Coast pressing)					
❑ PB-10441	Golden Years/Can You Hear Me	1975	—	3.00	6.00
❑ GB-10468	Changes/Andy Warhol	1975	—	2.00	4.00
—Gold Standard Series issue					
❑ GB-10469	Young Americans/Knock on Wood	1975	—	2.00	4.00
—Gold Standard Series issue					
❑ GB-10470	Space Oddity/The Man Who Sold the World	1975	—	2.00	4.00
—Gold Standard Series issue					
❑ 74-0605	Changes/Andy Warhol	1971	2.50	5.00	10.00
—Orange label (original)					
❑ 74-0605	Changes/Andy Warhol	1974	—	3.00	6.00
—Tan or gray label					
❑ 74-0719	Starman/Suffragette City	1972	—	3.00	6.00
❑ 74-0719 [PS]	Starman/Suffragette City	1972	7.50	15.00	30.00
❑ 74-0838	The Jean Genie/Hang On to Yourself	1972	—	3.00	6.00
❑ 74-0876	Space Oddity/The Man Who Sold the World	1973	—	3.00	6.00
❑ 74-0876 [PS]	Space Oddity/The Man Who Sold the World	1973	5.00	10.00	20.00
VIRGIN					
❑ S7-19517	Dead Man Walking/Little Wonder	1997	—	2.00	4.00
❑ 58833	Changes/Rebel Rebel	2000	—	2.00	4.00
❑ 58834	Fame/Golden Years	2000	—	2.00	4.00
—Both are full-length versions, not the single edits					
❑ 58835	Let's Dance (single edit)/Modern Love	2000	—	2.00	4.00
WARNER BROS.					
❑ 5815	Can't Stop Thinking About Me/And I Say to Myself	1966	100.00	200.00	400.00
—As "David Bowie and the Lower Third"					

7-Inch Extended Plays

Number	Title (A Side/B Side)	Yr	VG	VG+	NM
RCA VICTOR					
❑ 45-103 [DJ]	Space Oddity/Moonage Daydream//(B-side unknown)	1972	5.00	10.00	20.00
❑ 45-103 [PS]	David Bowie	1972	5.00	10.00	20.00

BOWIE, DAVID, AND MICK JAGGER

Also see each artist's individual listings.

Number	Title (A Side/B Side)	Yr	VG	VG+	NM
EMI AMERICA					
❑ 8288	Dancing in the Street/(instrumental)	1985	—	—	3.00
❑ 8288 [PS]	Dancing in the Street/(instrumental)	1985	—	—	3.00

BOX OF FROGS

Featuring ex-members of THE YARDBIRDS.

Number	Title (A Side/B Side)	Yr	VG	VG+	NM
EPIC					
❑ 04593	The Edge/Two Steps Ahead	1984	—	2.50	5.00

BOX TOPS, THE

Lead singer Alex Chilton was later in BIG STAR.

Number	Title (A Side/B Side)	Yr	VG	VG+	NM
ARISTA					
❑ 9488	Sweet Cream Ladies/Neon Rainbow	1986	—	—	3.00
—"Flashback" oldies series					
BELL					
❑ 865	Come On Honey/You Keep Tightening Up on Me	1970	2.00	4.00	8.00
❑ 923	Let Me Go/Got to Hold On to You	1970	2.00	4.00	8.00
❑ 981	King's Highway/Since I've Been Gone	1971	2.00	4.00	8.00
GUSTO					
❑ 2112	The Letter/Cry Like a Baby	1981	—	2.00	4.00
—Re-recordings					
HI					
❑ 2228	It's All Over/Sugar Creek Woman	1972	—	3.00	6.00
❑ 2242	Hold On Girl/Angel	1973	—	3.00	6.00
MALA					
❑ 565	The Letter/Happy Times	1967	3.00	6.00	12.00
❑ 580	Neon Rainbow/Everything I Am	1967	2.50	5.00	10.00
❑ 593	Cry Like a Baby/The Door You Closed to Me	1968	3.00	6.00	12.00
❑ 12005	Choo Choo Train/Fields of Clover	1968	2.50	5.00	10.00
❑ 12017	I Met Her in Church/People Gonna Talk	1968	2.50	5.00	10.00
❑ 12035	Sweet Cream Ladies, Forward March/I See Only Sunshine	1968	2.50	5.00	10.00
❑ 12038	I Shall Be Released/I Must Be the Devil	1969	2.50	5.00	10.00
❑ 12040	Soul Deep/The Happy Song	1969	2.50	5.00	10.00
❑ 12042	Turn On a Dream/Together	1969	2.50	5.00	10.00
PHILCO-FORD					
❑ HP-27	The Letter/Happy Times	1968	5.00	10.00	20.00
—4-inch plastic "Hip Pocket Record" with color sleeve					
SPHERE SOUND					
❑ 77001	The Letter/Happy Times	1969	2.50	5.00	10.00
—Blue label; reissue					
❑ 77001	The Letter/Happy Times	1970	2.00	4.00	8.00
—Silver label; reissue					
❑ 77002	Cry Like a Baby/The Door You Closed to Me	1970	2.00	4.00	8.00
—Silver label; reissue					
STAX					
❑ 0199	It's Gonna Be O.K./Willobee and Dale	1974	—	3.00	6.00

BOXER, KARL

Number	Title (A Side/B Side)	Yr	VG	VG+	NM
DOT					
❑ 16853	Hava Nagila/A Piece of the Action	1966	5.00	10.00	20.00

BOYCE, TOMMY

Also see TOMMY BOYCE AND BOBBY HART.

Number	Title (A Side/B Side)	Yr	VG	VG+	NM
A&M					
❑ 809	Sunday, The Day Before Monday/The Green Grass (Is Turning Brown)	1966	3.75	7.50	15.00
❑ 826	In Case the Wind Should Blow/Simon Smith and the Amazing Dancing Bear	1966	6.25	12.50	25.00
CAPITOL					
❑ 3136	Alice My Sweet/Eve Laurain	1971	—	2.50	5.00
CHELSEA					
❑ BCBO-0101	Thank God for Rock and Roll/Krush on Kris	1973	—	2.50	5.00
—As "Christopher Cloud"					
❑ 78-0118	Zip-a-Dee-Doo-Dah/Interpretation of War	1973	—	2.50	5.00
—As "Christopher Cloud"					
COLPIX					
❑ 794	Let's Go Where the Action Is/(Instrumental)	1966	5.00	10.00	20.00
DOT					
❑ 16117	The Gypsy Song/Give Me the Clue	1960	5.00	10.00	20.00
MGM					
❑ 13400	Pretty Thing (You Look Out of Sight Tonight)/I Don't Have to Worry 'Bout You	1965	3.75	7.50	15.00
❑ 13429	Little Suzy Somethin'/Pee's N' Que's	1965	3.75	7.50	15.00
R-DELL					
❑ 111	Betty Jean/I'm Not Sure	1960	6.25	12.50	25.00
RCA VICTOR					
❑ 47-7975	Along Came Linda/You Look So Lonely	1961	5.00	10.00	20.00
❑ 47-8025	Come Here Joanne/The Way I Used to Do	1962	5.00	10.00	20.00
❑ 47-8074	I'll Remember Carol/Too Late for Tears	1962	5.00	10.00	20.00
❑ 47-8126	Have You Had a Change of Heart/Sweet Little Baby, I Care	1963	5.00	10.00	20.00
❑ 47-8208	Don't Be Afraid/A Million Things to Say	1963	5.00	10.00	20.00
WOW					
❑ 345	Is It True/Little One	1961	5.00	10.00	20.00

BOYCE, TOMMY, AND BOBBY HART

Also see each artist's individual listings.

Number	Title (A Side/B Side)	Yr	VG	VG+	NM
AQUARIAN					
❑ 380	I'll Blow You a Kiss in the Wind/Smilin'	1970	—	2.00	4.00
❑ 380 [PS]	I'll Blow You a Kiss in the Wind/Smilin'	1970	—	3.00	6.00
A&M					
❑ 858	Out and About/My Little Chickadee	1967	2.50	5.00	10.00
❑ 858 [PS]	Out and About/My Little Chickadee	1967	5.00	10.00	20.00
❑ 874	Sometimes She's a Little Girl/Love Every Day	1967	2.50	5.00	10.00
❑ 874 [PS]	Sometimes She's a Little Girl/Love Every Day	1967	5.00	10.00	20.00
❑ 893	I Wonder What She's Doing Tonight/The Ambushers	1967	3.00	6.00	12.00
❑ 893 [PS]	I Wonder What She's Doing Tonight/The Ambushers	1967	5.00	10.00	20.00
❑ 919	Goodbye Baby (I Don't Want to See You Cry)/Where Angels Go, Trouble Follows	1968	2.50	5.00	10.00
❑ 919 [PS]	Goodbye Baby (I Don't Want to See You Cry)/Where Angels Go, Trouble Follows	1968	5.00	10.00	20.00
❑ 948	Alice Long (You're Still My Favorite Girlfriend)/P.O. Box 9847	1968	2.50	5.00	10.00
❑ 948 [PS]	Alice Long (You're Still My Favorite Girlfriend)/P.O. Box 9847	1968	5.00	10.00	20.00
❑ 993	We're All Going to the Same Place/6 + 6	1968	2.50	5.00	10.00
❑ 993 [PS]	We're All Going to the Same Place/6 + 6	1968	2.50	5.00	10.00
❑ 1017	Maybe Somebody Heard/It's All Happening on the Inside	1969	2.00	4.00	8.00
❑ 1031	L.U.V. (Let Us Vote)/I Wanna Be Free	1969	2.00	4.00	8.00
❑ 1031 [PS]	L.U.V. (Let Us Vote)/I Wanna Be Free	1969	3.75	7.50	15.00

BOYD, EDDIE

Number	Title (A Side/B Side)	Yr	VG	VG+	NM
ART TONE					
❑ 832	I'm Comin' Home/Operator	1962	3.75	7.50	15.00
BEA & BABY					
❑ 101	I'm Comin' Home/Thank You Baby	1959	3.75	7.50	15.00
❑ 107	Blue Monday Blues/The Blues Is Here to Stay	1959	3.75	7.50	15.00
❑ 108	Come Home/You've Got to Reap What You Sow	1959	3.75	7.50	15.00
CHESS					
❑ 1523	Cool Kind Treatment/Rosa Lee Swing	1952	25.00	50.00	100.00
❑ 1533	24 Hours/The Tickler	1953	25.00	50.00	100.00
—Black vinyl					
❑ 1533	24 Hours/The Tickler	1953	100.00	200.00	400.00
—Red vinyl					
❑ 1541	Third Degree/Back Beat	1953	50.00	100.00	200.00
—Black vinyl					
❑ 1541	Third Degree/Back Beat	1953	125.00	250.00	500.00
—Red vinyl					
❑ 1552	That's When I Miss You So/Tortured Soul	1953	20.00	40.00	80.00
❑ 1561	Nothing But Trouble/Picture in the Frame	1954	15.00	30.00	60.00
❑ 1573	Hush Baby, Don't You Cry/Came Home This Morning	1954	15.00	30.00	60.00
❑ 1576	Driftin'/Rattin' and Runnin' Around	1954	15.00	30.00	60.00
❑ 1582	The Story of Bill/Please Help Me	1954	15.00	30.00	60.00
❑ 1595	The Nightmare Is Over/Real Good Feeling	1955	12.50	25.00	50.00
❑ 1606	I'm a Prisoner/I've Been Deceived	1955	12.50	25.00	50.00
❑ 1621	Don't/Life Gets to Be a Burden	1956	10.00	20.00	40.00
❑ 1634	Just a Fool/Four Leaf Clover	1956	10.00	20.00	40.00
❑ 1660	I Got a Woman/Hotel Blues	1957	10.00	20.00	40.00
❑ 1674	I Got the Blues/She's the One	1957	10.00	20.00	40.00
HERALD					
❑ 406	Lonesome for My Baby/I'm Goin' Downtown	1953	100.00	200.00	400.00
J.O.B.					
❑ 1007	Five Long Years/Blue Coat Man	1952	37.50	75.00	150.00
—Black vinyl					
❑ 1007	Five Long Years/Blue Coat Man	1952	75.00	150.00	300.00
—Red vinyl					
❑ 1009	It's Miserable to Be Alone/I'm Pleading	1953	75.00	150.00	300.00
❑ 1114	I Love You/Save Her Doctor	1957	15.00	30.00	60.00
RCA VICTOR					
❑ 50-0006	What Makes These Things Happen/Chicago Is Just That Way	1950	30.00	60.00	120.00
—Gray label, orange vinyl					

BOYD, MICKEY, AND THE PLAIN VIEWERS

See THE STRING-A-LONGS.

BOYFRIENDS, THE

Also known as THE FIVE DISCS.

Number	Title (A Side/B Side)	Yr	VG	VG+	NM
KAPP					
❑ 569	Let's Fall in Love/Oh Lana	1964	25.00	50.00	100.00

BOYZ II MEN

Number	Title (A Side/B Side)	Yr	VG	VG+	NM
MOTOWN					
❑ 2090	Motownphilly/Under Pressure	1991	—	2.50	5.00
❑ 2162	Please Don't Go/Uhh Ahh	1992	—	—	3.00
❑ 2168	It's So Hard to Say Goodbye to Yesterday/Sympin'	1992	—	—	3.00
❑ 2178	End of the Road/1-4-All-4-1	1992	—	2.00	4.00
—B-side by East Coast All-Stars					
❑ 2193	In the Still of the Night (I'll Remember)/Who's Lovin' You	1992	—	2.00	4.00
—B-side by The Jackson Five					
❑ 2218	Let It Snow/Silent Night	1993	—	—	3.00
❑ 2257	I'll Make Love to You/Thank You	1994	—	—	3.00
❑ 860284-7	On Bended Knee/I'll Make Love to You (Sexy Version)	1994	—	—	3.00
❑ 860422-7	Water Runs Dry/Vibin'	1995	—	—	3.00
❑ 860714-7	4 Seasons of Loneliness (LP Version)/same (B II M Version)	1997	—	—	3.00
❑ 860744-7	A Song for Mama/(Instrumental)	1997	—	—	3.00
UNIVERSAL					
❑ 012 158183-7	Pass You By (same on both sides)	2000	—	—	3.00

BOZE, CALVIN

Number	Title (A Side/B Side)	Yr	VG	VG+	NM
ALADDIN					
❑ 3045	Waiting and Drinking/If You Ever Had the Blues	1950	37.50	75.00	150.00
❑ 3055	Safronia Blues/Angel City Blues	1950	37.50	75.00	150.00
❑ 3065	Lizzie Lou/Lizzie Lou (Part 2)	1950	37.50	75.00	150.00
❑ 3072	Stinkin' from Drinkin'/Look Out for Tomorrow Today	1950	25.00	50.00	100.00
❑ 3079	Beat Street on Saturday Night/Choo Choo Ch'Boogieing My Baby Back Home	1951	25.00	50.00	100.00
❑ 3086	Slippin' and Slidin'/Baby, You're Tops with Me	1951	25.00	50.00	100.00
❑ 3100	I've Got News for You/I Can't Stop Crying	1951	20.00	40.00	80.00
❑ 3110	I'm Gonna Steam Off the Stamp/Fish Tail	1952	20.00	40.00	80.00
❑ 3122	Hey, Lawdy Miss Clawdy/My Friend Told Me	1952	20.00	40.00	80.00
❑ 3132	Good Time Sue/Keep Your Nose Out of My Business	1952	15.00	30.00	60.00
❑ 3142	The Blue Tango/The Glory of Love	1952	15.00	30.00	60.00
❑ 3143	Blue Shuffle/Popside	1952	15.00	30.00	60.00
❑ 3147	Looped/Blow Man Blow	1952	15.00	30.00	60.00
❑ 3160	Havin' a Time/Shamrock	1953	12.50	25.00	50.00

Number	Title (A Side/B Side)	Yr	VG	VG+	NM
❑ 3181	That Other Woman/Shoot De Pistol	1953	12.50	25.00	50.00
IMPERIAL					
❑ 5844	Shamrock/Safronia B	1962	3.00	6.00	12.00

BRADLEY, JAN

Number	Title (A Side/B Side)	Yr	VG	VG+	NM
CHESS					
❑ 1845	Mama Didn't Lie/Lovers Like Me	1962	2.50	5.00	10.00
❑ 1851	These Tears/Baby What Can I Do	1963	2.00	4.00	8.00
❑ 1884	Curfew Blues/Pack My Things	1964	2.00	4.00	8.00
❑ 1897	Please Mr. D.J./Two of a Kind	1964	2.00	4.00	8.00
❑ 1919	I'm Over You/The Brush-Off	1964	2.00	4.00	8.00
❑ 1975	Just a Summer Memory/He'll Wait for Me	1966	—	3.00	6.00
❑ 1996	Trust Me/Things a Woman Needs	1967	—	3.00	6.00
❑ 2023	Your Kind of Love/It's Just Your Way	1967	—	3.00	6.00
❑ 2043	You Have Me What's Missing/Nights in New York City	1968	—	3.00	6.00
FORMAL					
❑ 1044	Mama Didn't Lie/Lovers Like Me	1962	50.00	100.00	200.00
❑ 1048	Dear Sears and Roebuck/(B-side unknown)	1963	3.00	6.00	12.00
HOOTENANNY					
❑ 1	Christmas Time (Part 1)/Christmas Time (Part 2)	1962	3.00	6.00	12.00

BRADSHAW, JACK

Number	Title (A Side/B Side)	Yr	VG	VG+	NM
DECCA					
❑ 29654	My Heart, My Heart/Flirting with You	1955	6.25	12.50	25.00
GLENN					
❑ 754	No, No/Welcome Heart	1955	15.00	30.00	60.00
❑ 755	I Got What You Need/You Hurt Me	195?	15.00	30.00	60.00
MAR-VEL					
❑ 750	Don't Tease Me/Don't Cause Me to Hate You	1954	25.00	50.00	100.00
❑ 751	Searchin'/My Heart, My Heart	1955	15.00	30.00	60.00
❑ 752	It Just Ain't Right/Naughty Girls	1955	15.00	30.00	60.00
❑ 753	Jo Jo/Men Are Weak	1955	25.00	50.00	100.00
❑ 756	Saturday Night Special/Out of the Picture	195?	15.00	30.00	60.00

BRADSHAW, TINY

Number	Title (A Side/B Side)	Yr	VG	VG+	NM
KING					
❑ 4357	I Hate You/Well Oh Well	1950	15.00	30.00	60.00
❑ 4376	After You've Gone/Boogie Green	1950	15.00	30.00	60.00
❑ 4397	Butterfly/I'm Going to Have Myself a Ball	1950	15.00	30.00	60.00
❑ 4417	Breaking Up the House/If You Don't Love Me, Tell Me So	1950	15.00	30.00	60.00
❑ 4427	Walk That Mess/One, Two, Three, Kick Blues	1951	15.00	30.00	60.00
❑ 4447	Brad's Blues/Two Dry Bones on the Pantry Shelf	1951	15.00	30.00	60.00
❑ 4457	Bradshaw Boogie/Walkin' the Chalk Line	1951	15.00	30.00	60.00
❑ 4467	I'm a High Ballin' Daddy/You Came By	1951	15.00	30.00	60.00
❑ 4487	T-99/Long Time Baby	1951	50.00	100.00	200.00
❑ 4497	The Train Kept a-Rollin'/Knockin' Blues	1951	50.00	100.00	200.00
❑ 4537	Mailman's Sack/Newspaper Boy Blues	1952	50.00	100.00	200.00
❑ 4547	Rippin' and Runnin'/Lay It on the Line	1952	50.00	100.00	200.00
❑ 4577	Strange/Soft	1952	12.50	25.00	50.00
❑ 4713	Don't Worry 'Bout Me/Overflow	1954	10.00	20.00	40.00
❑ 4727	Spider Web/The Gypsey	1954	10.00	20.00	40.00
❑ 4747	A Stack of Dollars/Cat Fruit	1954	10.00	20.00	40.00
❑ 4757	Light/Choice	1954	10.00	20.00	40.00
❑ 4777	Cat Nap/Stomping Room Only	1955	10.00	20.00	40.00
❑ 4787	Phantom Turnpike/Come On	1955	10.00	20.00	40.00
❑ 5114	Short Shorts/Bushes	1958	6.25	12.50	25.00

7-Inch Extended Plays

Number	Title (A Side/B Side)	Yr	VG	VG+	NM
KING					
❑ EP 248	Off and On/Free for All//South of the Orient/Later	195?	10.00	20.00	40.00
❑ EP 248 [PS]	Tiny Bradshaw, Vol. 2	195?	10.00	20.00	40.00

BRADY BUNCH, THE

Also see CHRIS KNIGHT; MIKE LOOKINLAND; MAUREEN McCORMICK; EVE PLUMB; BARRY WILLIAMS.

Number	Title (A Side/B Side)	Yr	VG	VG+	NM
PARAMOUNT					
❑ 0062	Frosty the Snowman/Silver Bells	1970	3.00	6.00	12.00
❑ 0062 [PS]	Frosty the Snowman/Silver Bells	1970	7.50	15.00	30.00
❑ 0141	We Can Make the World a Whole Lot Brighter/Time to Change	1972	3.00	6.00	12.00
❑ 0167	Time to Change/We'll Always Be Friends	1972	3.00	6.00	12.00
❑ 0205	Zuckerman's Famous Pig/Charlotte's Web	1973	3.00	6.00	12.00
❑ 0205 [PS]	Zuckerman's Famous Pig/Charlotte's Web	1973	5.00	10.00	20.00
❑ 0229	I'd Love You to Want Me/Everything I Do	1973	3.00	6.00	12.00
—As "The Brady Bunch Kids"					

BRAMLETT, BONNIE

Half of DELANEY AND BONNIE.

Number	Title (A Side/B Side)	Yr	VG	VG+	NM
CAPRICORN					
❑ 0229	Higher and Higher/It's Time	1975	—	2.00	4.00
❑ 0262	Let's Go, Let's Go, Let's Go/Never Gonna Give You Up	1976	—	2.00	4.00
❑ 0306	Except for Real/I've Just Seen a Face	1978	—	2.00	4.00
COLUMBIA					
❑ 45897	Good Vibrations/How Glad I Am	1973	—	2.50	5.00

BRAMLETT, DELANEY

Half of DELANEY AND BONNIE.

Number	Title (A Side/B Side)	Yr	VG	VG+	NM
COLUMBIA					
❑ 45696	I'm Not Your Lover, I'm Your Lover/Over and Over	1972	—	2.50	5.00
❑ 45781	We Can't Be Seen Together/Thank God	1973	—	2.50	5.00
❑ 45950	Are You a Beatle or a Rolling Stone/California Rain	1973	2.50	5.00	10.00
CREAM					
❑ 8147	What's a Little Love/I Love to Love You	1981	—	2.00	4.00
—By "Delaney and Bekka Bramlett"					
GNP CRESCENDO					
❑ 328	Heartbreak Hotel/You Never Looked Sweeter	1964	3.75	7.50	15.00
❑ 339	Liverpool Lou/You Have No Choice	1965	3.75	7.50	15.00
❑ 363	Without Your Love/A Better Man Than Me	1965	3.75	7.50	15.00
INDEPENDENCE					
❑ 76	Guess I Must Be Dreaming/Don't Let It	1967	3.75	7.50	15.00

BRASS RING, THE

Number	Title (A Side/B Side)	Yr	VG	VG+	NM
ABC DUNHILL					
❑ 4164	For the Love of Ivy/The Theme from The Odd Couple	1968	—	3.00	6.00
DUNHILL					
❑ 4023	The Phoenix Love Theme (Sensa Fine)/Lightning Bug	1966	—	3.00	6.00
❑ 4036	Lara's Theme/Secret Love	1966	—	3.00	6.00
❑ 4047	California Dreamin'/Samba de Orfeu	1966	—	3.00	6.00
❑ 4059	Lapland/Patricia	1966	—	3.00	6.00
❑ 4065	The Dis-Advantages of You/The Dating Game	1967	—	3.00	6.00
❑ 4090	Love in the Open Air/Wait for Me	1967	5.00	10.00	20.00
❑ 4090 [PS]	Love in the Open Air/Wait for Me	1967	7.50	15.00	30.00
—Sleeve says this is "Paul McCartney's first non-Beatles song"					
❑ 4108	Monday, Monday/Flower Ring	1967	—	3.00	6.00
❑ 4132	Cherry Pink & Apple Blossom White/Adoro (Don't Tempt Me)	1968	—	3.00	6.00

7-Inch Extended Plays

Number	Title (A Side/B Side)	Yr	VG	VG+	NM
ABC DUNHILL					
❑ LP-DS-50044 [DJ]	Mrs. Robinson/This Guy's in Love with You/For Love of Ivy//Do You Know the Way to San Jose/Love Is Blue/Honey	1969	3.00	6.00	12.00
—Small hole, 33 1/3 rpm jukebox EP					
❑ LP-DS-50044 [PS]	Only Love	1969	3.00	6.00	12.00

BRAVE BELT

Also see RANDY BACHMAN.

Number	Title (A Side/B Side)	Yr	VG	VG+	NM
REPRISE					
❑ 1039	Holy Train/Crazy Arms-Crazy Eyes	1971	—	2.50	5.00
❑ 1061	Never Comin' Home/Can You Feel It	1971	—	2.50	5.00
❑ 1083	Another Way Out/Dunrobin's Gone	1972	—	2.50	5.00

BRAVE NEW WORLD

Number	Title (A Side/B Side)	Yr	VG	VG+	NM
EPIC					
❑ 10123	It's Tomorrow/Cried	1967	5.00	10.00	20.00

BREAD

Also see DAVID GATES; JIMMY GRIFFIN.

Number	Title (A Side/B Side)	Yr	VG	VG+	NM
ELEKTRA					
❑ 45365	Lost Without Your Love/Change of Heart	1976	—	2.00	4.00
❑ 45389	Hooked on You/Our Lady of Sorrow	1977	—	2.00	4.00
❑ 45666	Dismal Day/Anyway You Want Me	1969	2.00	4.00	8.00
❑ 45668	Could I/You Can't Measure the Cost	1969	—	3.00	6.00
❑ 45686	Make It With You/Why Do You Keep Me Waiting	1970	—	2.00	4.00
—Red, black and white label					
❑ 45686	Make It With You/Why Do You Keep Me Waiting	1970	—	2.00	4.00
—Yellow and black label					
❑ 45701	It Don't Matter to Me/Call on Me	1970	—	2.00	4.00
❑ 45701 [PS]	It Don't Matter to Me/Call on Me	1970	2.00	4.00	8.00
❑ 45711	Let Your Love Go/Too Much Love	1971	—	2.00	4.00
❑ 45720	If/Take Comfort	1971	—	2.00	4.00
❑ 45720 [PS]	If/Take Comfort	1971	2.00	4.00	8.00
❑ 45740	Mother Freedom/Life in Your Love	1971	—	2.00	4.00
❑ 45751	Baby I'm-a Want You/Truckin'	1971	—	2.00	4.00
❑ 45765	Everything I Own/I Don't Love You	1972	—	2.00	4.00
❑ 45784	Diary/Down on My Knees	1972	—	2.00	4.00
❑ 45803	The Guitar Man/Just Like Yesterday	1972	—	2.00	4.00
❑ 45818	Sweet Surrender/Make It By Yourself	1972	—	2.00	4.00
❑ 45832	Aubrey/Didn't Even Know Her Name	1973	—	2.00	4.00

BREAKAWAYS, THE

Number	Title (A Side/B Side)	Yr	VG	VG+	NM
CAMEO					
❑ 323	That's How It Goes/He Doesn't Love Me	1964	3.75	7.50	15.00
LONDON INT'L.					
❑ 10526	That Boy of Mine/Here She Comes	1963	3.00	6.00	12.00
MELBOURNE					
❑ 1805	Granada/The Flipper	1964	3.00	6.00	12.00

BREAKERS, THE

Number	Title (A Side/B Side)	Yr	VG	VG+	NM
AMY					
❑ 938	Don't Send Me No Flowers (I Ain't Dead Yet)/Love of My Life	1965	3.75	7.50	15.00
BRANA					
❑ 1001/2	Kama-Kaze/Surf Breaker	1963	15.00	30.00	60.00
DJB					
❑ 116	Jet Stream/Beach Head	1964	12.50	25.00	50.00
❑ 116	Super Jet Rumble/Beach Head	1964	12.50	25.00	50.00
—Revised A-side title					
IMPACT					
❑ 14	Surfin' Tragedy/Surf Bird	1963	6.25	12.50	25.00
—Black vinyl					
❑ 14	Surfin' Tragedy/Surf Bird	1963	20.00	40.00	80.00
—Gold vinyl					
JERDEN					
❑ 789	All My Nights, All My Days/Better for the Both of Us	1966	5.00	10.00	20.00
MARSH					
❑ 206	Balboa Memories/Long Way Home	1963	12.50	25.00	50.00
RIVERTON					
❑ 102	All My Nights, All My Days/Better for the Both of Us	1966	10.00	20.00	40.00

BREEDLOVE, JIMMY

Number	Title (A Side/B Side)	Yr	VG	VG+	NM
ATCO					
❑ 6094	That's My Baby/Over Somebody Else's Shoulder	1957	6.25	12.50	25.00
❑ 6105	I Can Still Hear You Say You Love Me/I Wish I Were Twins	1957	6.25	12.50	25.00
DIAMOND					
❑ 144	Jealous Fool/Lil' Ol' Me	1963	7.50	15.00	30.00

Number	Title (A Side/B Side)	Yr	VG	VG+	NM
EPIC					
❑ 9270	Could This Be Love/This Too Shall Pass Away	1958	5.00	10.00	20.00
❑ 9283	Love Is All We Need/Lovable	1958	5.00	10.00	20.00
❑ 9289	Love Is All We Need/Oo-Wee Good Gosh A-Mighty	1958	5.00	10.00	20.00
❑ 9319	All Is Forgiven/I Say Hello	1959	5.00	10.00	20.00
❑ 9360	To Belong/Waiting for You	1960	5.00	10.00	20.00
JUBILEE					
❑ 5551	Jealous Fool/The Greatest Love (Nothing Less, Nothing More)	1966	2.50	5.00	10.00
OKEH					
❑ 7145	Anytime You Want Me/My Guardian Angel	1962	3.00	6.00	12.00
❑ 7152	Don't Let It Happen/Queen Bee	1962	3.00	6.00	12.00
ROULETTE					
❑ 7010	I Can't Help Lovin' You/I Saw You	1968	2.00	4.00	8.00
7-Inch Extended Plays					
RCA CAMDEN					
❑ CEP-447	(contents unknown)	1958	6.25	12.50	25.00
❑ CEP-447 [PS]	Rock 'N' Roll Music	1958	6.25	12.50	25.00

BREEN, BOBBY

Number	Title (A Side/B Side)	Yr	VG	VG+	NM
CHIC					
❑ 1003	If the Night Could Tell You/Wait	1956	3.75	7.50	15.00
❑ 1013	We Will Make Love/Rainbow	1957	3.75	7.50	15.00
LYRIC					
❑ 105	It's a Sin/Valley of Romance	196?	5.00	10.00	20.00
MOTOWN					
❑ 1053	How Can We Tell Him/Better Late Than Never	1964	6.25	12.50	25.00
❑ 1059	You're Just Like You/Here Comes That Heartache	1964	6.25	12.50	25.00
❑ 1059 [PS]	You're Just Like You/Here Comes That Heartache	1964	10.00	20.00	40.00
NRC					
❑ 055	Hawaii Calls/Theme from A Summer Place	1960	2.50	5.00	10.00

BRENDA AND THE TABULATIONS

Number	Title (A Side/B Side)	Yr	VG	VG+	NM
CHOCOLATE CITY					
❑ 004	Home to Myself/Leave Me Alone	1976	—	2.00	4.00
❑ 009	(I'm a) Superstar/Take It or Leave It	1977	—	2.00	4.00
❑ 012	Let's Go All the Way (Down)/I Keep Coming Back for More	1977	—	2.00	4.00
DIONN					
❑ 500	Dry Your Eyes/The Wash	1967	2.50	5.00	10.00
❑ 501	Who's Lovin' You/Stay Together Young Lovers	1967	2.50	5.00	10.00
❑ 503	Just Once in a Lifetime/Hey Boy	1967	2.50	5.00	10.00
❑ 504	When You're Gone/Hey Boy	1967	2.50	5.00	10.00
❑ 507	To the One I Love/Baby You're So Right	1968	2.50	5.00	10.00
❑ 509	I Can't Get Over You/That's in the Past	1968	2.50	5.00	10.00
❑ 511	Reason to Live/Hey Boy	1968	2.50	5.00	10.00
❑ 512	That's the Price You Have to Pay/I Wish I Hadn't Done What I Did	1969	2.50	5.00	10.00
EPIC					
❑ 10898	Little Bit of Love/Let Me Be Happy	1972	—	3.00	6.00
❑ 10954	One Girl Too Late/The Magic of Your Love	1973	—	3.00	6.00
❑ 11000	Key to My Heart/Love Is Just a Carnival	1973	—	3.00	6.00
❑ 11059	I'm in Love/Walk On In	1973	—	3.00	6.00
❑ 50081	Let Me Be Happy/Little Bit of Love	1975	—	2.00	4.00
PHILCO-FORD					
❑ HP-40	Dry Your Eyes/When You're Gone	1969	5.00	10.00	20.00
—4-inch plastic "Hip Pocket Record" with color sleeve					
TOP & BOTTOM					
❑ 401	The Touch of You/Stop Sneaking Around	1969	2.00	4.00	8.00
❑ 403	And My Heart Sang (Tra La La)/Lies, Lies, Lies	1970	2.00	4.00	8.00
❑ 404	Don't Make Me Over/You've Changed	1970	2.00	4.00	8.00
❑ 406	A Child No One Wanted/Scuse Us All	1970	2.00	4.00	8.00
❑ 407	Right on the Tip of My Tongue/Always and Forever	1971	2.00	4.00	8.00
❑ 408	A Part of You/Where There's a Will	1971	2.00	4.00	8.00
❑ 411	Why Didn't I Think of That/A Love You Can Depend On	1971	2.00	4.00	8.00

BRENSTON, JACKIE

Number	Title (A Side/B Side)	Yr	VG	VG+	NM
CHESS					
❑ 1458	Rocket "88"/Come Back Where You Belong	1951	5000.	7500.	10000.
—Early rockabilly classic; obscenely rare, even though the 45s were pressed later					
❑ 1469	In My Real Gone Rocket/Tuckered Out	1951	500.00	750.00	1000.
❑ 1472	Juiced/Independent Woman	1951	500.00	750.00	1000.
❑ 1496	Leo the Louse/Hi-Ho Baby	1952	125.00	250.00	500.00
❑ 1532	Blues Got Me Again/Starvation	1953	62.50	125.00	250.00
FEDERAL					
❑ 12283	What Can It Be/Gonna Wait for My Chance	1956	12.50	25.00	50.00
❑ 12291	Much Later/The Mistreater	1957	12.50	25.00	50.00
SUE					
❑ 736	Trouble Up the Road/You Ain't the One	1961	5.00	10.00	20.00

BRENT, RONNIE

Number	Title (A Side/B Side)	Yr	VG	VG+	NM
COLT 45					
❑ 101	Crazy Feeling/Shirley Ann	1959	6.25	12.50	25.00
❑ 109	Cowboys and Indians/Flow Gently	1959	6.25	12.50	25.00
UNITED ARTISTS					
❑ 108	My Sweet Verlene/Love	1958	10.00	20.00	40.00

BRENT, TONY

Number	Title (A Side/B Side)	Yr	VG	VG+	NM
ROULETTE					
❑ 4113	Girl of My Dreams/Don't Play That Melody	1958	3.00	6.00	12.00

BREWER AND SHIPLEY

Number	Title (A Side/B Side)	Yr	VG	VG+	NM
A&M					
❑ 905	The Keeper of the Keys/I Can't See Her	1968	2.00	4.00	8.00
—Artist reads "Michael Brewer and Tom Shipley"					
❑ 938	Green Bamboo/Truly Right	1968	2.00	4.00	8.00
—Artist reads "Michael Brewer and Tom Shipley"					
❑ 996	Dreamin' in the Shade/Tame and Changes	1968	2.00	4.00	8.00
BUDDAH					
❑ 154	Rise Up Easy Rider/Boomerang	1970	—	2.00	4.00
CAPITOL					
❑ 3933	Fair Play/How Are You	1974	—	2.00	4.00
❑ 4105	Brain Damage/Rock and Roll Hostage	1975	—	2.00	4.00
KAMA SUTRA					
❑ 512	People Love Each Other/Witchi-Tai-To	1970	—	2.00	4.00
❑ 516	One Toke Over the Line/Oh Mommy	1970	—	2.50	5.00
❑ 524	Tarkio Road/Seems Like a Long Time	1971	—	2.00	4.00
❑ 539	Shake Off the Demon/Indian Summer	1972	—	2.00	4.00
❑ 547	Natural Child/Yankee Lady	1972	—	2.00	4.00
❑ 567	Black Sky/Fly, Fly Fly	1972	—	2.00	4.00

BRIDGE, THE

See THE BROOKLYN BRIDGE.

BRIGATI

With Eddie Brigati, ex-RASCALS.

Number	Title (A Side/B Side)	Yr	VG	VG+	NM
ASYLUM					
❑ 45328	Groovin'/Lost in the Wilderness	1976	—	2.50	5.00
❑ 45349	Gotta Get Next to Somebody/Made in Spain (Bambu)	1976	—	2.50	5.00

BRIGGS, LILLIAN

Number	Title (A Side/B Side)	Yr	VG	VG+	NM
ABC-PARAMOUNT					
❑ 10253	I Want You to Be My Baby/I'm Burning for You	1961	2.50	5.00	10.00
CORAL					
❑ 62108	Rag Mop/Smile for the People	1959	2.50	5.00	10.00
❑ 62136	Blues in the Night/Is There a Man in the House	1959	2.50	5.00	10.00
❑ 62156	Hooray for the Rock/Diddy Boppers	1959	2.50	5.00	10.00
❑ 62193	Be Mine/Not a Soul	1960	2.50	5.00	10.00
❑ 62223	I Care for You/That's What It's Like to Be Lonesome	1960	2.50	5.00	10.00
EPIC					
❑ 9115	I Want You to Be My Baby/Don't Stay Away Too Long	1955	7.50	15.00	30.00
❑ 9120	Give Me a Band and My Baby/It Could've Been Me	1955	7.50	15.00	30.00
❑ 9138	Rock and Roll-y Poly Santa Claus/Can't Stop	1955	7.50	15.00	30.00
❑ 9141	Follow the Leader/That's the Only Way to Live	1956	5.00	10.00	20.00
❑ 9151	Eddie, My Love/Teens in Jeans from New Orleans	1956	5.00	10.00	20.00
❑ 9166	The Gypsy Goofed/Too Close for Comfort	1956	5.00	10.00	20.00
❑ 9190	I'll Be Gone/Mean Words	1956	5.00	10.00	20.00
❑ 9214	Sugar Blues/Boogie Blues	1957	3.75	7.50	15.00
❑ 9249	She Sells Sea Shells/I	1957	3.75	7.50	15.00
SUNBEAM					
❑ 104	Come Home/Till We Meet Again	1958	3.00	6.00	12.00
❑ 114	Hey Ba Ba Re Bop/I've Got Your Heart	1958	3.00	6.00	12.00
7-Inch Extended Plays					
EPIC					
❑ B-7163	(contents unknown)	1956	10.00	20.00	40.00
❑ B-7163 [PS]	High Priestess of Rock 'n' Roll	1956	10.00	20.00	40.00

BRIKS, THE

Number	Title (A Side/B Side)	Yr	VG	VG+	NM
BISMARK					
❑ 1013	Foolish Baby/Can You See Me	1966	50.00	100.00	200.00
DOT					
❑ 16876	Foolish Baby/Can You See Me	1966	6.25	12.50	25.00

BRIM, JOHN

Number	Title (A Side/B Side)	Yr	VG	VG+	NM
CHESS					
❑ 1588	Go Away/That Ain't Right	1955	50.00	100.00	200.00
❑ 1624	I Would Hate to See You Go/You Got Me Where You Want Me	1956	50.00	100.00	200.00
PARROT					
❑ 799	Tough Times/Gary Stomp	1954	175.00	350.00	700.00
—Black vinyl					
❑ 799	Tough Times/Gary Stomp	1954	400.00	800.00	1200.
—Red vinyl					

BRIMSTONES, THE

Number	Title (A Side/B Side)	Yr	VG	VG+	NM
MGM					
❑ 13653	It's All Over But the Crying/What Is This Life	1966	5.00	10.00	20.00
WORLD PACIFIC					
❑ 77834	Cold Hearted Woman/I'm in Misery	1966	7.50	15.00	30.00

BRINSLEY SCHWARZ

Also see NICK LOWE.

Number	Title (A Side/B Side)	Yr	VG	VG+	NM
CAPITOL					
❑ 3004	Rock and Roll Women/Hymn to Be	1970	2.00	4.00	8.00
UNITED ARTISTS					
❑ 50915	Nightingale/Silver Pistol	1972	—	3.00	6.00
❑ 50976	Nervous on the Road/Happy Doing What We're Doing	1972	—	3.00	6.00

BRISTOL, JOHNNY

Also see JOHNNY AND JACKIE.

Number	Title (A Side/B Side)	Yr	VG	VG+	NM
ATLANTIC					
❑ 3360	Do It to My Mind/Love to Take a Chance to Taste the Wine	1976	—	2.00	4.00
❑ 3391	I Sho Like Groovin' with You/You Turn Me On to Love	1977	—	2.00	4.00
❑ 3421	Waiting on Love/She's So Amazing	1977	—	2.00	4.00
❑ 3501	When He Comes (You Will Know)/Strangers in the Dark Corners	1978	—	2.00	4.00
❑ 3526	Why Stop Now/When He Comes (You Will Know)	1978	—	2.00	4.00
HANDSHAKE					
❑ 02594	Take Me Down/Loving and Free	1981	—	2.00	4.00

(Top left) Before it became a big hit on the Mercury label, the Big Bopper's "Chantilly Lace" was issued on the Texas country-oriented label called "D." Many well-known country artists made records for the label, including Willie Nelson and George Strait (under the name Ace In The Hole Band). (Top right) Not generally known to exist until a few years ago, the No. 1 hit "Quarter to Three" by U.S. Bonds was issued with the original Legrand purple label in addition to the gold and red label that appears on most copies. (Bottom left) How hard a time did Mercury have trying to make David Bowie a success in the States? His third Mercury single, "All the Madmen," apparently never got past the promotional stage. The label dropped him, RCA picked him up — and the rest is history. (Bottom right) Who would have thought, when his debut single, "Much Too You (To Feel This Damn Old)" came out in the spring of 1989, that its singer, Garth Brooks, would become the most popular artist of the 1990s? He's also one of the most collectible artists of the 1990s.

Number	Title (A Side/B Side)	Yr	VG	VG+	NM
❑ 5300	My Guy/My Girl//(B-side unknown)	1980	—	2.00	4.00
—With Amii Stewart					
❑ 5304	Love No Longer Has a Hold on Me/(B-side unknown)	1981	—	2.00	4.00
MGM					
❑ 14715	Hang On In There Baby/Take Care of You for Me	1974	—	2.50	5.00
❑ 14762	You and I/It Don't Hurt No More	1974	—	2.50	5.00
❑ 14792	Leave My World/All Goodbyes Aren't Good	1975	—	2.50	5.00
❑ 14814	Love Takes Tears/Go On and Dream	1975	—	2.50	5.00
POLYDOR					
❑ 813982-7	Hang On In There Baby/Stand By Me	1983	—	—	3.00
—Reissue					

BRITISH CASUALS, THE

See THE CASUALS (3).

BROGUES, THE

Two members became part of QUICKSILVER MESSENGER SERVICE.

Number	Title (A Side/B Side)	Yr	VG	VG+	NM
CHALLENGE					
❑ 59311	But Now I'm Fine/Someday	1965	7.50	15.00	30.00
❑ 59316	I Ain't No Miracle Worker/Don't Shoot Me Down	1965	7.50	15.00	30.00
TWILIGHT					
❑ 408	But Now I'm Fine/Someday	1965	10.00	20.00	40.00
❑ 408	But Now I'm Fine/Early Bird	1965	10.00	20.00	40.00

BRONZETTES, THE

Number	Title (A Side/B Side)	Yr	VG	VG+	NM
PARKWAY					
❑ 929	Hot Spot/Run, Run, You Little Fool	1964	3.00	6.00	12.00

BROOKLYN BRIDGE, THE

Also see JOHNNY MAESTRO.

Number	Title (A Side/B Side)	Yr	VG	VG+	NM
BUDDAH					
❑ 60	Little Red Boat by the River/From My Window	1968	—	3.00	6.00
❑ 75	Worst That Could Happen/Your Kite, My Kite	1968	2.00	4.00	8.00
❑ 95	Welcome Me Love/Blessed Is the Rain	1969	—	3.00	6.00
❑ 126	Your Husband, My Wife/Upside Down	1969	—	3.00	6.00
❑ 139	You'll Never Walk Alone/Minstrel Sunday	1969	—	3.00	6.00
❑ 162	Free as the Wind/He's Not a Happy Man	1970	—	3.00	6.00
❑ 179	Down by the River/Look Again	1970	—	3.00	6.00
❑ 193	Day Is Done/Opposites	1970	—	3.00	6.00
❑ 193	Day Is Done/Easy Way	1970	—	3.00	6.00
❑ 199	Nights in White Satin/Cynthia	1971	2.00	4.00	8.00
❑ 230	Wednesday in Your Garden (mono/stereo)	1971	2.00	4.00	8.00
—Stock copy unknown					
❑ 293	Man in a Band/Bruno's Place	1972	2.00	4.00	8.00
❑ 317	I Feel Free (mono/stereo)	1972	2.50	5.00	10.00
—As "The Bridge"; stock copy unknown					
COLLECTABLES					
❑ 3997	Have Yourself A Merry Little Christmas/A Christmas Long Ago (Jingle Jingle)	199?	—	—	3.00
—As "Johnny Maestro and the Brooklyn Bridge"; B-side by the Echelons					

BROOKS, CHUCK, AND THE SHARPIES

Number	Title (A Side/B Side)	Yr	VG	VG+	NM
DUB					
❑ 2844	Spinning My Wheels/You Make Me Feel Mean	1958	75.00	150.00	300.00

BROOKS, DONNIE

Number	Title (A Side/B Side)	Yr	VG	VG+	NM
CHALLENGE					
❑ 59331	I Call Your Name/Be Fair	1966	2.00	4.00	8.00
❑ 59344	Pink Carousel/Mission Man	1966	2.00	4.00	8.00
ERA					
❑ 3004	Lil' Sweetheart/If You're Lookin'	1959	5.00	10.00	20.00
❑ 3007	White Orchid/Sway and Move with the Beat	1959	5.00	10.00	20.00
❑ 3014	The Devil Ain't a Man/How Long	1960	5.00	10.00	20.00
❑ 3018	Mission Bell/Do It for Me	1960	5.00	10.00	20.00
❑ 3028	Doll House/Round Robin	1960	3.75	7.50	15.00
❑ 3028 [PS]	Doll House/Round Robin	1960	6.25	12.50	25.00
❑ 3042	Memphis/That's Why	1961	3.75	7.50	15.00
❑ 3042 [PS]	Memphis/That's Why	1961	6.25	12.50	25.00
❑ 3049	All I Can Give/Wishbone	1961	3.75	7.50	15.00
❑ 3052	Boomerang/How Long	1961	3.75	7.50	15.00
❑ 3059	Sweet Lorraine/Up to My Ears in Tears	1961	3.75	7.50	15.00
❑ 3063	Goodnight Judy/Your Little Boy's Gone Home	1961	3.75	7.50	15.00
❑ 3071	My Favorite Kind of Face/He Stole Flo	1962	3.75	7.50	15.00
❑ 3077	Oh You Beautiful Doll/Just a Bystander	1962	3.75	7.50	15.00
❑ 3095	Cries My Heart/It's Not That Easy	1962	3.75	7.50	15.00
❑ 3194	Blue Soldier/Love Is Funny That Way	1968	2.00	4.00	8.00
HAPPY TIGER					
❑ 526	Abracadabra/I Know You as a Woman	1970	—	2.50	5.00
❑ 544	Hush/I Know You as a Woman	1970	—	2.50	5.00
❑ 551	My God and I/Pink Carousel	1970	—	2.50	5.00
❑ 566	(I Wanna) Have You for Myself/Rub-a-Dub-Dub	1971	—	2.50	5.00
❑ 579	I'm Gonna Make You Love Me/Pink Carousel	1971	—	2.50	5.00
MIDSONG INT'L.					
❑ 1007	Big John/Get Fame, Son	1978	—	2.00	4.00
OAK					
❑ 1019	The Song That I Sing Is For You/Country Dude	1971	—	2.50	5.00
REPRISE					
❑ 0261	Gone/Girl Machine	1964	2.50	5.00	10.00
❑ 0311	Can't Help Lovin' You/Pickin' Up the Pieces	1964	2.50	5.00	10.00
❑ 0363	Hey, Little Girl/I Never Get to Love You	1965	2.50	5.00	10.00
YARDBIRD					
❑ 8006	Sunglasses on the Sand/Sunshine, Summertime and Love	1968	—	3.00	6.00
❑ 8008	Hush/Sunshine, Summertime and Love	1968	—	3.00	6.00
❑ 8010	Tree Trimming Time/(Instrumental)	1968	—	3.00	6.00

BROOKS, DUSTY, AND HIS TONES WITH JUANITA BROWN

Number	Title (A Side/B Side)	Yr	VG	VG+	NM
SUN					
❑ 182	Heaven or Fire/Tears and Wine	1953	1500.	2250.	3000.

BROOKS, GARTH

Also see TRISHA YEARWOOD.

Number	Title (A Side/B Side)	Yr	VG	VG+	NM
CAPITOL					
❑ S7-19851	Longneck Bottle/Rollin'	1998	—	2.00	4.00
❑ B-44342	Much Too Young (To Feel This Damn Old)/Alabama Clay	1989	2.00	4.00	8.00
❑ B-44430	If Tomorrow Never Comes/Nobody Gets Off in This Town	1989	2.50	5.00	10.00
❑ B-44492	Not Counting You/Cowboy Bill	1989	—	3.00	6.00
❑ 58788	Lost in You/It Don't Matter to the Sun	1999	—	2.00	4.00
—"Garth Brooks as Chris Gaines"					
❑ 7PRO-79024	The Dance (same on both sides)	1990	3.00	6.00	12.00
—Promo-only issue; later released as stock copy on 44629					
CAPITOL NASHVILLE					
❑ S7-18842	She's Every Woman/The Cowboy Song	1995	—	3.00	6.00
❑ S7-18948	The Fever/The Night Will Only Know	1995	—	3.00	6.00
❑ S7-19022	The Beaches of Cheyenne/Ireland	1996	—	3.00	6.00
❑ NR-44629	The Dance (same on both sides)	1990	2.00	4.00	8.00
❑ NR-44647	Friends in Low Places/Nobody Gets Off in This Town	1990	2.50	5.00	10.00
❑ NR-44650	Unanswered Prayers/Alabama Clay	1990	2.00	4.00	8.00
❑ NR-44701	Two of a Kind, Workin' on a Full House/The Dance	1991	—	3.00	6.00
❑ NR-44727	The Thunder Rolls/Victim of the Game	1991	2.00	4.00	8.00
❑ NR-44771	Rodeo/New Way to Fly	1991	2.00	4.00	8.00
❑ NR-44800	Shameless/Against the Grain	1991	2.00	4.00	8.00
❑ 58845	Do What You Gotta Do/A Friend to Me	2000	—	2.00	4.00
❑ 58899	It's the Most Wonderful Time of the Year/Sleigh Ride	2000	—	2.00	4.00
❑ 7PRO-79216/39	Friends in Low Places (Edited Version)/Friends in Low Places (LP Version)	1990	3.00	6.00	12.00
—Promo-only issue; the two versions were later released on 44647 (edit) and Liberty 57733 (LP version)					
LIBERTY					
❑ S7-17324	That Summer/Dixie Chicken	1993	—	2.50	5.00
❑ S7-17440	Every Now and Then/Face to Face	1993	—	2.50	5.00
❑ S7-17441	The Dance/If Tomorrow Never Comes	1993	—	2.50	5.00
❑ S7-17496	Ain't Going Down (Til the Sun Comes Up)/Kickin' and Screamin'	1993	2.00	4.00	8.00
❑ S7-17639	American Honky-Tonk Bar Association/Everytime That It Rains	1993	—	3.00	6.00
❑ S7-17649	Silent Night/White Christmas	1993	2.00	4.00	8.00
—Red vinyl					
❑ S7-17802	Standing Outside the Fire/Cold Shoulder	1994	—	3.00	6.00
❑ S7-17972	One Night a Day/Mr. Blue	1994	—	2.50	5.00
❑ S7-18136	Callin' Baton Rouge/Same Old Story	1994	—	3.00	6.00
—Red vinyl					
❑ S7-18399	Much Too Young (To Feel This Damn Old)/Rodeo	1995	—	3.00	6.00
—Green vinyl					
❑ S7-18400	Two of a Kind, Workin' On a Full House/Unanswered Prayers	1995	—	2.00	4.00
❑ S7-18554	The Red Strokes/Burning Bridges	1995	—	2.50	5.00
❑ S7-56824	Somewhere Other Than the Night/Mr. Right	1992	—	3.00	6.00
❑ S7-56973	Learning to Live Again/Walking After Midnight	1993	2.50	5.00	10.00
—Red vinyl					
❑ S7-56973	Learning to Live Again/Walking After Midnight	1993	—	2.50	5.00
—Black vinyl					
❑ S7-57733	What She's Doing Now/Friends in Low Places	1992	—	3.00	6.00
❑ S7-57734	Papa Loved Mama/New Way to Fly	1992	—	3.00	6.00
❑ S7-57744	The Thunder Rolls/Shameless	1992	—	3.00	6.00
❑ S7-57765	The River/We Bury the Hatchet	1992	—	3.00	6.00
❑ S7-57883	Friends in Low Places (Live Version)/Thunder Rolls (Live Version)	1992	—	3.00	6.00
❑ S7-57892	God Rest Ye Merry Gentlemen/White Christmas	1992	—	2.50	5.00
❑ S7-57893	The Old Man's Back in Town/Santa Looked a Lot Like Daddy	1992	—	2.50	5.00
❑ S7-57894	Go Tell It on the Mountain/The Friendly Beast	1992	—	2.50	5.00
❑ S7-57994	We Shall Be Free/Night Rider's Lament	1992	—	3.00	6.00

BROOKS BROTHERS, THE

Number	Title (A Side/B Side)	Yr	VG	VG+	NM
LONDON					
❑ 1987	Warpaint/Sometimes	1961	3.75	7.50	15.00
❑ 9668	Once in Awhile/Poor Plan	1964	2.50	5.00	10.00
—As "The Brooks"					
LONDON INT'L.					
❑ 10501	Ain't Gonna Wash for a Week/One Last Kiss	1962	3.00	6.00	12.00
❑ 10515	Too Scared/Tell Tale	1962	3.00	6.00	12.00

BROONZY, BIG BILL

Number	Title (A Side/B Side)	Yr	VG	VG+	NM
CHESS					
❑ 1546	Little City Woman/Lonesome	1953	100.00	200.00	400.00
MERCURY					
❑ 8160	You've Been Mistreating Me/I Stay Blue All the Time	1951	7.50	15.00	30.00
—Released on 78 in 1949					
❑ 8261	Willie Mae Blues/Hollerin' the Blues	1951	7.50	15.00	30.00
❑ 8271	Hey Hey/Walkin' the Lonesome Road	1952	7.50	15.00	30.00
❑ 8284	Mopper's Blues/I Know She Will	1952	7.50	15.00	30.00
❑ 70039	South Bound Train/Leavin' Day	1953	6.25	12.50	25.00
❑ 71352	Tomorrow/Hey Hey	1958	5.00	10.00	20.00

BROTHERHOOD OF MAN, THE

Number	Title (A Side/B Side)	Yr	VG	VG+	NM
BELL					
❑ 45456	When Love Catches Up on You/(B-side unknown)	1974	—	2.00	4.00
DERAM					
❑ 85056	Love One Another/A Little Bit of Heaven	1970	—	3.00	6.00
❑ 85059	United We Stand/Say a Prayer	1970	—	3.00	6.00
❑ 85065	Where Are You Going To My Love/Living in the Land of Love	1970	—	2.50	5.00
❑ 85070	This Boy/You Can Depend on Me	1971	—	2.50	5.00
❑ 85073	Reach Out Your Hand/A Better Tomorrow	1971	—	2.50	5.00
❑ 85077	Sing in the Sunshine/You and I	1971	—	2.50	5.00

Number	Title (A Side/B Side)	Yr	VG	VG+	NM
❑ 85078	California Sunday Morning/Do Your Thing	1972	—	2.50	5.00
❑ 85081	Say a Prayer/Follow Me	1972	—	2.50	5.00
MERCURY					
❑ 882118-7	United We Stand/My Baby Loves Lovin'	1986	—	2.00	4.00
—Reissue; B-side by White Plains					
PRIVATE STOCK					
❑ 45148	Oh Boy (The Mood I'm In)	1977	—	2.00	4.00
❑ 45165	Angelo/All Night	1977	—	2.00	4.00
PYE					
❑ 70176	Sweet Lady from Georgia/Sugar Honey Love	1976	—	2.00	4.00
❑ 71043	Spring of 1912/(B-side unknown)	1976	—	2.00	4.00
❑ 71066	Save Your Kisses for Me/Let's Love Together	1976	—	2.00	4.00

BROTHERS, THE

Number	Title (A Side/B Side)	Yr	VG	VG+	NM
ARGO					
❑ 5318	Lazy Susan/Deep Sleep	1958	5.00	10.00	20.00
❑ 5329	Sioux City Sue/Deep Sleep	1959	5.00	10.00	20.00
CHECKER					
❑ 995	My True Love/One Lonely Heart	1961	3.75	7.50	15.00

BROTHERS CAIN, THE

Number	Title (A Side/B Side)	Yr	VG	VG+	NM
ACTA					
❑ 810	Better Times/Pupil Alexander	1967	6.25	12.50	25.00
❑ 820	It Sure Is Groovy/Anyway You Like It	1968	6.25	12.50	25.00
MERCURY					
❑ 72437	In Love with One/Two Wrongs	1965	6.25	12.50	25.00

BROWN, ARTHUR, THE CRAZY WORLD OF

Number	Title (A Side/B Side)	Yr	VG	VG+	NM
ATLANTIC					
❑ 2556	Fire/Rest Cure	1968	2.50	5.00	10.00
MERCURY					
❑ 873504-7	Fire/Rest Cure	1990	—	—	3.00
—Reissue					
TRACK					
❑ 2582	I Put a Spell on You/Nightmare	1968	2.00	4.00	8.00

BROWN, BUSTER

Number	Title (A Side/B Side)	Yr	VG	VG+	NM
FIRE					
❑ 507	Sugar Babe/I'm Going — But I'll Be Back	1962	5.00	10.00	20.00
❑ 516	Raise a Rucks Tonight/Gonna Love My Baby	1962	5.00	10.00	20.00
❑ 1008	Fannie Mae/Lost in a Dream	1959	6.25	12.50	25.00
❑ 1020	The Madison Shuffle/John Henry	1960	5.00	10.00	20.00
❑ 1023	Is You Is or Is You Ain't My Baby/Don't Dog Your Woman	1960	5.00	10.00	20.00
❑ 1032	Sincerely/Doctor Brown	1960	5.00	10.00	20.00
❑ 1040	Blues When It Rains/Good News	1961	5.00	10.00	20.00
❑ 2021	Sugar Babe/Don't Dog Your Woman	1962	3.75	7.50	15.00
RCA VICTOR					
❑ PB-10023	Eloise/Fallin' Out of Love	1974	—	2.50	5.00
WHITE WHALE					
❑ 316	The Proud One/I've Got It Made	1969	2.50	5.00	10.00

BROWN, CHARLES

Number	Title (A Side/B Side)	Yr	VG	VG+	NM
ACE					
❑ 561	Educated Fool/I Want to Go Back Home	1959	3.00	6.00	12.00
—With Amos Milburn					
❑ 599	Love's Like a River/Boys Will Be Boys	1960	3.00	6.00	12.00
❑ 599	Love's Like a River/Sing My Blues Tonight	1960	3.00	6.00	12.00
ALADDIN					
❑ 3076	Black Night/Once There Was a Fool	1951	37.50	75.00	150.00
—Charles Brown records on Aladdin prior to 3076 are unconfirmed on 45 rpm					
❑ 3091	I'll Always Be in Love with You/The Message	1951	20.00	40.00	80.00
❑ 3092	Seven Long Days/Don't Fool with My Heart	1951	20.00	40.00	80.00
❑ 3116	Hard Times/Tender Heart	1952	20.00	40.00	80.00
❑ 3120	Still Water/My Last Affair	1952	20.00	40.00	80.00
❑ 3138	See/Without Your Love	1952	20.00	40.00	80.00
❑ 3157	Rollin' Like a Pebble in the Sand/Alley Batting	1952	20.00	40.00	80.00
❑ 3163	Evening Shadows/Moonrise	1953	15.00	30.00	60.00
❑ 3176	Take Me/Rising Sun	1953	15.00	30.00	60.00
❑ 3191	Lonesome Feeling/I Lost Everything	1953	15.00	30.00	60.00
❑ 3200	All My Life/Don't Leave Me Poor	1953	15.00	30.00	60.00
❑ 3209	P.S. I Love You/Cryin' and Driftin' Blues	1953	15.00	30.00	60.00
❑ 3220	Everybody's Got Trouble/I Fool Around with You	1954	10.00	20.00	40.00
❑ 3235	Let's Walk/Crying Mercy	1954	10.00	20.00	40.00
❑ 3254	My Silent Love/Foolish	1954	10.00	20.00	40.00
❑ 3272	By the Bend of the River/Honey Slipper	1955	7.50	15.00	30.00
❑ 3284	Night After Night/Walk with Me	1955	7.50	15.00	30.00
❑ 3290	Hot Lips and Seven Kisses/Fools' Paradise	1955	7.50	15.00	30.00
❑ 3296	My Heart Is Mended/Trees, Trees	1955	7.50	15.00	30.00
❑ 3316	Please Don't Drive Me Away/One Minute to One	1956	6.25	12.50	25.00
❑ 3342	Soothe Me/I'll Always Be in Love with You	1956	6.25	12.50	25.00
❑ 3348	Merry Christmas, Baby/Black Night	1956	6.25	12.50	25.00
❑ 3366	Please Believe Me/It's a Sin to Tell a Lie	1957	5.00	10.00	20.00
❑ 3423	Hard Times/Ooh, Ooh Sugar	1958	5.00	10.00	20.00
BLUES SPECTRUM					
❑ 17	Merry Christmas, Baby/Rockin' Blues	197?	—	3.00	6.00
BLUESWAY					
❑ 61031	Merry Christmas, Baby/Rainy, Rainy Day	1969	—	3.00	6.00
CASH					
❑ 1052	Lost in the Night/I Sold My Heart to the Junkman	1957	7.50	15.00	30.00
—B-side by the Basin Street Boys					
CHARLENA					
❑ 001	Please Come Home For Christmas/Santa Claus Santa Claus	197?	—	2.00	4.00
❑ 001 [PS]	Please Come Home For Christmas/Santa Claus Santa Claus	197?	—	2.50	5.00
EASTWEST					
❑ 106	When Did You Leave Heaven/We've Got a Lot in Common	1958	5.00	10.00	20.00
EMI					
❑ S7-18213	Please Come Home for Christmas/Merry Christmas Baby	1994	—	2.00	4.00
—Green vinyl					
GALAXY					
❑ 762	I'm Gonna Push On/Cry No More	1968	2.50	5.00	10.00
❑ 766	Abraham, Martin, and John/(B-side unknown)	1968	2.50	5.00	10.00
HOLLYWOOD					
❑ 1006	Pleading for Your Love/The Best I Can Do	1954	10.00	20.00	40.00
❑ 1021	Merry Christmas Baby/Sleigh Ride	1954	5.00	10.00	20.00
—Charles Brown's first recording of the A-side, released on 78 on Exclusive 254 (1946); B-side by Lloyd Glenn; maroon label					
❑ 1021	Merry Christmas Baby/Sleigh Ride	196?	2.00	4.00	8.00
—B-side by Lloyd Glenn; color label					
❑ 1021	Merry Christmas Baby/Sleigh Ride	197?	—	2.50	5.00
—B-side by Lloyd Glenn; black label					
IMPERIAL					
❑ 5830	Fool's Paradise/Lonesome Feeling	1962	2.50	5.00	10.00
❑ 5902	Merry Christmas Baby/I Lost Everything	1962	2.50	5.00	10.00
❑ 5905	Black Night/Drifting Blues	1963	2.50	5.00	10.00
❑ 5961	I'm Savin' My Love for You/Please Don't Drive Me Away	1963	2.50	5.00	10.00
JEWEL					
❑ 814	Christmas in Heaven/Just a Blessing	1970	—	3.00	6.00
❑ 815	Merry Christmas Baby/Please Come Home for Christmas	1970	—	3.00	6.00
❑ 830	I Don't Know/For You	1972	—	2.50	5.00
❑ 838	I've Got Your Love/I Just Can't Get Over You	1973	—	2.50	5.00
❑ 847	Please Come Home for Christmas/Christmas in Heaven	1974	—	2.50	5.00
KENT					
❑ 501	Merry Christmas Baby/3 O'Clock Blues	1968	2.50	5.00	10.00
KING					
❑ 5405	Please Come Home for Christmas/Christmas (Comes But Once a Year)	1960	3.00	6.00	12.00
—B-side by Amos Milburn; original blue label					
❑ 5405	Please Come Home for Christmas/Christmas (Comes But Once a Year)	1970	—	3.00	6.00
—B-side by Amos Milburn; black label					
❑ 5439	Angel Baby/Baby Oh Baby	1961	3.00	6.00	12.00
❑ 5464	I Wanna Go Back Home/My Little Baby	1961	3.00	6.00	12.00
—With Amos Milburn					
❑ 5523	Butterfly/This Fool Has Learned	1961	3.00	6.00	12.00
❑ 5530	Christmas in Heaven/It's Christmas All Year 'Round	1961	3.00	6.00	12.00
❑ 5570	Without a Friend/If You Play with Cats	1961	3.00	6.00	12.00
❑ 5722	I'm Just a Drifter/I Don't Want Your Rambling Letters	1963	2.50	5.00	10.00
❑ 5726	It's Christmas Time/Christmas Finds Me Lonely	1963	2.50	5.00	10.00
❑ 5731	Christmas Questions/Wrap Yourself in a Christmas Package	1963	2.50	5.00	10.00
❑ 5802	If You Don't Believe I'm Crying/I Wanna Be Close	1963	2.50	5.00	10.00
❑ 5825	Lucky Dreamer/Too Fine for Crying	1963	2.50	5.00	10.00
❑ 5852	Blow Out All the Candles/Come Home	1964	2.50	5.00	10.00
❑ 5946	Christmas Blues/My Most Miserable Christmas	1964	2.50	5.00	10.00
❑ 5947	Christmas Comes (But Once a Year)/Bringin' In a Brand New Year	1964	2.50	5.00	10.00
❑ 6094	Regardless/The Plan	1967	2.00	4.00	8.00
❑ 6192	Hang On a Little Longer/Black Night	1968	2.00	4.00	8.00
❑ 6194	Merry Christmas, Baby/Let's Make Every Day Christmas	1968	2.00	4.00	8.00
❑ 6420	For the Good Times/Lonesome and Driftin'	1973	—	2.50	5.00
LIBERTY					
❑ 1393	Merry Christmas, Baby/Silent Night	1980	—	2.50	5.00
—B-side by Baby Washington					
❑ 5902	Merry Christmas, Baby/I Lost Everything	196?	2.00	4.00	8.00
—Reissue of Imperial 5902					
LILLY					
❑ 506	Bon Voyage/Bye and Bye	1962	2.50	5.00	10.00
MAINSTREAM					
❑ 607	Pledging My Love/Tomorrow Night	1965	2.00	4.00	8.00
NOLA					
❑ 702	Standing on the Outside/I'll Love You (If You Let Me)	1965	2.00	4.00	8.00
SWING TIME					
❑ 238	Merry Christmas, Baby/Lost In The Night	195?	25.00	50.00	100.00
—Originally released on 78, but a 45 does exist					
❑ 253	I'll Miss You/New Orleans Blues	1952	30.00	60.00	120.00
❑ 259	Be Fair with Me/Sunny Road	1952	30.00	60.00	120.00
TEEM					
❑ 1008	Merry Christmas Baby/Christmas Finds Me Oh So Sad	19??	—	3.00	6.00
UNITED ARTISTS					
❑ 0085	Drifting Blues/Black Night	1973	—	2.00	4.00
—Silver Spotlight Series issue					
❑ 0086	I Lost Everything/Lonesome Feeling	1973	—	2.00	4.00
—Silver Spotlight Series issue					
❑ XW582	Merry Christmas Baby/(B-side unknown)	1974	—	2.50	5.00
UPSIDE					
❑ PRO 002	Santa Claus Boogie (one-sided)	1986	—	2.00	4.00
—Flexidisc					
❑ PRO 002 [PS]	Santa Claus Boogie	1986	—	2.00	4.00

BROWN, CLARENCE "GATEMOUTH"

Number	Title (A Side/B Side)	Yr	VG	VG+	NM
PEACOCK					
❑ 1600	Baby Take It Easy/Just Got Lucky	1952	100.00	200.00	400.00
❑ 1607	Dirty Work at the Crossroads/You Got Money	1952	62.50	125.00	250.00
❑ 1617	Boogie Uproar/Hurry Back Good News	1953	50.00	100.00	200.00
❑ 1619	Please Tell Me Baby/Gate Walks to Board	1953	50.00	100.00	200.00
❑ 1633	Midnight Hour/For Now So Long	1954	37.50	75.00	150.00

Number	Title (A Side/B Side)	Yr	VG	VG+	NM
❑ 1637	Okie Dokie Stomp/Depression Blues	1954	37.50	75.00	150.00
❑ 1653	Gate's Salty Blues/Rock My Blues Away	1955	25.00	50.00	100.00
❑ 1662	Ain't That Dandy/September Song	1956	20.00	40.00	80.00
❑ 1692	Just Before Dawn/Swinging the Gate	1958	10.00	20.00	40.00

BROWN, GEORGE WASHINGTON

See VAN DYKE PARKS.

BROWN, JAMES

AUGUSTA SOUND

Number	Title (A Side/B Side)	Yr	VG	VG+	NM
❑ 94023	Bring It On ... Bring It On/The Night Time Is the Right Time (To Be With the One That You Love)	1983	—	2.00	4.00

A&M

Number	Title (A Side/B Side)	Yr	VG	VG+	NM
❑ 3022	I Got You (I Feel Good)/Nowhere to Run	1988	—	2.00	4.00
—B-side by Martha and the Vandellas					
❑ 3022 [PS]	I Got You (I Feel Good)/Nowhere to Run	1988	—	2.00	4.00
—"Good Morning Vietnam" sleeve					

BACKSTREET

Number	Title (A Side/B Side)	Yr	VG	VG+	NM
❑ 52215	King of Soul/Theme from Doctor Detroit	1983	—	—	3.00
—B-side by Devo					

BETHLEHEM

Number	Title (A Side/B Side)	Yr	VG	VG+	NM
❑ 3089	I Loves You Porgy/Yours and Mine	1969	3.75	7.50	15.00
❑ 3098	A Man Has to Go Back to the Crossroads/The Drunk	1969	3.75	7.50	15.00

FEDERAL

Number	Title (A Side/B Side)	Yr	VG	VG+	NM
❑ 12258	Please, Please, Please/Why Do You Do Me?	1956	10.00	20.00	40.00
❑ 12264	I Don't Know/I Feel That Old Feeling Coming On	1956	6.25	12.50	25.00
❑ 12277	No, No, No, No/Hold My Baby's Hand	1956	6.25	12.50	25.00
❑ 12289	Just Won't Do Right/Let's Make It	1957	6.25	12.50	25.00
❑ 12290	I Won't Plead No More/Chonnie On Chon	1957	6.25	12.50	25.00
❑ 12292	Gonna Try/Can't Be the Same	1957	6.25	12.50	25.00
❑ 12295	Love or a Game/Messing with the Blues	1957	6.25	12.50	25.00
❑ 12300	I Walked Alone/You're Mine, You're Mine	1957	6.25	12.50	25.00
❑ 12311	Baby Cries Over the Ocean/That Dood It	1957	6.25	12.50	25.00
❑ 12316	Begging, Begging/That's When I Lost My Heart	1958	6.25	12.50	25.00
❑ 12337	Try Me/Tell Me What I Did Wrong	1958	7.50	15.00	30.00
❑ 12348	I Want You So Bad/There Must Be a Reason	1959	5.00	10.00	20.00
❑ 12352 [M]	I've Got to Change/It Hurts to Tell You	1959	5.00	10.00	20.00
❑ S-12352 [S]	I've Got to Change/It Hurts to Tell You	1959	12.50	25.00	50.00
❑ 12361 [M]	Don't Let It Happen to Me/Good Good Lovin'	1959	5.00	10.00	20.00
❑ S-12361 [S]	Don't Let It Happen to Me/Good Good Lovin'	1959	12.50	25.00	50.00
❑ 12364	It Was You/Got to Cry	1959	5.00	10.00	20.00
❑ 12369	I'll Go Crazy/I Know It's True	1960	5.00	10.00	20.00
❑ 12370	Think/You've Got the Power	1960	5.00	10.00	20.00
❑ 12378	This Old Heart/I Wonder When You're Coming Home	1960	5.00	10.00	20.00

KING

Number	Title (A Side/B Side)	Yr	VG	VG+	NM
❑ 5423	The Bells/And I Do Just What I Want	1960	3.75	7.50	15.00
❑ 5438	The Scratch/Hold It	1961	3.75	7.50	15.00
❑ 5442	Bewildered/If You Want Me	1961	3.75	7.50	15.00
❑ 5466	I Don't Mind/Love Don't Love Nobody	1961	3.75	7.50	15.00
❑ 5485	Sticky/Suds	1961	3.75	7.50	15.00
❑ 5519	Night Flying/Cross Firing	1961	3.75	7.50	15.00
❑ 5524	Baby You're Right/I'll Never, Never Let You Go	1961	3.75	7.50	15.00
❑ 5547	Just You and Me, Darling/I Love You, Yes I Do	1961	3.75	7.50	15.00
❑ 5573	Lost Someone/Cross Firing	1961	3.75	7.50	15.00
❑ 5614	Night Train/Why Does Everything Happen to Me	1962	3.75	7.50	15.00
❑ 5654	Tell Me Why/Say So Long	1962	3.75	7.50	15.00
—With Yvonne Fair					
❑ 5657	Shout and Shimmy/Come Over Here	1962	3.75	7.50	15.00
❑ 5672	Mashed Potatoes U.S.A./You Don't Have to Go	1962	3.75	7.50	15.00
❑ 5687	It Hurts to Be in Love/You Can Make It If You Try	1962	3.75	7.50	15.00
—With Yvonne Fair					
❑ 5698	(Can You) Feel It Part 1/(Can You) Feel It Part 2	1962	3.75	7.50	15.00
❑ 5701	Three Hearts in a Tangle/I've Got Money	1962	3.75	7.50	15.00
❑ 5710	Like a Baby/Every Beat of My Heart	1963	3.75	7.50	15.00
❑ 5739	Prisoner of Love/Choo Choo	1963	3.75	7.50	15.00
❑ 5767	These Foolish Things/Can You Feel It — Part 1	1963	3.75	7.50	15.00
❑ 5803	Signed, Sealed and Delivered/Waiting in Vain	1963	3.75	7.50	15.00
❑ 5829	The Bells/I've Got to Change	1963	3.75	7.50	15.00
❑ 5842	Oh Baby Don't You Weep (Part 1)/Oh Baby Don't You Weep (Part 2)	1964	3.75	7.50	15.00
❑ 5842 [PS]	Oh Baby Don't You Weep (Part 1)/Oh Baby Don't You Weep (Part 2)	1964	6.25	12.50	25.00
❑ 5853	Please, Please, Please/In the Wee Wee Hours	1964	3.75	7.50	15.00
❑ 5876	How Long Darling/Again	1964	3.75	7.50	15.00
❑ 5899	So Long/Dancin' Little Thing	1964	3.75	7.50	15.00
❑ 5922	Tell Me What You're Gonna Do/I Don't Care	1964	3.75	7.50	15.00
❑ 5952	Think/Try Me	1964	3.75	7.50	15.00
❑ 5956	Fine Old Foxy Self/Medley	1964	3.75	7.50	15.00
❑ 5968	Have Mercy Baby/Just Won't Do Right	1964	3.75	7.50	15.00
❑ 5995	This Old Heart/It Was You	1965	3.00	6.00	12.00
❑ 5999	Papa's Got a Brand New Bag Part I/Papa's Got a Brand New Bag Part II	1965	3.75	7.50	15.00
❑ 6015	I Got You (I Feel Good)/I Can't Help It (I Just Do, Do, Do)	1965	3.75	7.50	15.00
❑ 6020	I'll Go Crazy/Lost Someone	1966	3.00	6.00	12.00
❑ 6025	Ain't That a Groove Part I/Ain't That a Groove Part II	1966	3.00	6.00	12.00
❑ 6029	Prisoner of Love/I've Got to Change	1966	3.00	6.00	12.00
❑ 6033	Come Over Here/Tell Me What You're Gonna Do	1966	3.00	6.00	12.00
❑ 6035	It's a Man's Man's Man's World/Is It Yes Or Is It No?	1966	3.00	6.00	12.00
❑ 6037	I've Got Money/Just Won't Do Right	1966	3.00	6.00	12.00
❑ 6040	I Don't Care/It Was You	1966	3.00	6.00	12.00
❑ 6044	This Old Heart/How Long Darling	1966	3.00	6.00	12.00
❑ 6048	Money Won't Change You Part 1/Money Won't Change You Part 2	1966	3.00	6.00	12.00
❑ 6056	Don't Be a Drop-Out/Tell Me That You Love Me	1966	3.00	6.00	12.00
❑ 6064	The Christmas Song (Version 1)/The Christmas Song (Version 2)	1966	3.75	7.50	15.00
❑ 6065	Sweet Little Baby Boy (Part 1)/Sweet Little Baby Boy (Part 2)	1966	3.00	6.00	12.00
❑ 6071	Bring It Up/Nobody Knows	1967	3.00	6.00	12.00
❑ 6072	Let's Make Christmas Mean Something This Year (Part 1)/Let's Make Christmas Mean Something This Year (Part 2)	1967	3.00	6.00	12.00
❑ 6086	Kansas City/Stone Fox	1967	3.00	6.00	12.00
❑ 6091	Think/Nobody Cares	1967	3.00	6.00	12.00
—A-side: With Vicki Anderson; B-side: Vicki Anderson solo					
❑ 6100	Let Yourself Go/Good Rockin' Tonight	1967	3.00	6.00	12.00
❑ 6110	Cold Sweat — Part 1/Cold Sweat — Part 2	1967	3.00	6.00	12.00
❑ 6111	Mona Lisa/It Won't Be Me	1967	15.00	30.00	60.00
—Evidently not released or pulled shortly after release					
❑ 6112	America Is My Home — Part 1/America Is My Home — Part 2	1967	3.00	6.00	12.00
❑ 6122	Get It Together (Part 1)/Get It Together (Part 2)	1967	3.00	6.00	12.00
❑ 6133	The Soul of J.B./Funky Soul #1	1967	3.00	6.00	12.00
❑ 6141	I Guess I'll Have to Cry, Cry, Cry/Just Plain Funk	1967	3.00	6.00	12.00
❑ 6144	I Can't Stand Myself (When You Touch Me)/There Was a Time	1967	3.00	6.00	12.00
❑ 6151	You've Got to Change Your Mind/I'll Lose My Mind	1968	3.00	6.00	12.00
—A-side: With Bobby Byrd; B-side: Bobby Byrd solo					
❑ 6152	You've Got the Power/What the World Needs Now Is Love	1968	3.00	6.00	12.00
—A-side: With Vicki Anderson; B-side: Vicki Anderson solo					
❑ 6155	I Got the Feelin'/If I Ruled the World	1968	3.00	6.00	12.00
❑ 6164	Here I Go/Shhhh	1968	3.00	6.00	12.00
❑ 6166	Licking Stick — Licking Stick (Part 1)/Licking Stick — Licking Stick (Part 2)	1968	3.00	6.00	12.00
❑ 6187	Say It Loud — I'm Black and I'm Proud (Part 1)/Say It Loud — I'm Black and I'm Proud (Part 2)	1968	2.50	5.00	10.00
❑ 6187	Say It Loud — I'm Black But I'm Proud (Part 1)/Say It Loud — I'm Black But I'm Proud (Part 2)	1968	6.25	12.50	25.00
—Some copies have the above erroneous title on both sides					
❑ 6198	Goodbye My Love/Shades of Brown	1968	2.50	5.00	10.00
❑ 6203	Santa Claus Go Straight to the Ghetto/You Know It	1968	2.50	5.00	10.00
❑ 6204	Believers Shall Enjoy/Tit for Tat (Ain't No Turning Back)	1968	2.50	5.00	10.00
❑ 6205	Let's Unite the World at Christmas/In the Middle (Part 1)	1968	2.50	5.00	10.00
❑ 6206	In the Middle (Part 2)/Tit for Tat (Ain't No Turning Back)	1969	2.50	5.00	10.00
—A-side: With Marva Whitney					
❑ 6213	Give It Up or Turnit A Loose/I'll Lose My Mind	1969	2.50	5.00	10.00
❑ 6216	Shades of Brown (Part 2)/A Talk with the News	1969	2.50	5.00	10.00
—B-side by Steve Soul					
❑ 6218	You Got to Have a Job/I'm Tired, I'm Tired, I'm Tired	1969	2.50	5.00	10.00
—A-side with Marva Whitney; B-side: Marva Whitney solo					
❑ 6222	Soul Pride (Part 1)/Soul Pride (Part 2)	1969	2.50	5.00	10.00
❑ 6223	You've Got to Have a Mother for Me (Part 1)/You've Got to Have a Mother for Me (Part 2)	1969	2.50	5.00	10.00
❑ 6224	I Don't Want Nobody to Give Me Nothing (Open Up the Door, I'll Get It Myself) Part 1/Part 2	1969	2.50	5.00	10.00
❑ 6235	Little Groove Maker (Part 1)/Any Day Now	1969	2.50	5.00	10.00
❑ 6235	Little Groove Maker (Part 1)/I'm Shook	1969	2.50	5.00	10.00
❑ 6240	The Popcorn/The Chicken	1969	2.50	5.00	10.00
❑ 6245	Mother Popcorn (You Got to Have a Mother for Me) Part 1/Mother Popcorn (You Got to Have a Mother for Me) Part 2	1969	2.50	5.00	10.00
❑ 6250	Lowdown Popcorn/Top of the Stack	1969	2.50	5.00	10.00
❑ 6255	Let a Man Come In and Do the Popcorn Part One/Sometime	1969	2.50	5.00	10.00
❑ 6258	World (Part 1)/World (Part 2)	1969	2.50	5.00	10.00
❑ 6273	I'm Not Demanding (Part 1)/I'm Not Demanding (Part 2)	1969	2.50	5.00	10.00
❑ 6275	Part Two (Let a Man Come In and Do the Popcorn)/Get a Little Hipper	1969	2.50	5.00	10.00
❑ 6277	It's Christmas Time (Part 1)/It's Christmas Time (Part 2)	1969	2.50	5.00	10.00
❑ 6280	Ain't It Funky Now (Part 1)/Ain't It Funky Now (Part 2)	1970	2.00	4.00	8.00
❑ 6290	Funky Drummer (Part 1)/Funky Drummer (Part 2)	1970	2.00	4.00	8.00
❑ 6292	It's a New Day (Part 1)/It's a New Day (Part 2)	1970	2.00	4.00	8.00
❑ 6293	Let It Be Me/No More Heartaches, No More Pain	1970	2.00	4.00	8.00
—A-side: With Vicki Anderson; B-side: Vicki Anderson solo					
❑ 6300	Talkin' Loud and Sayin' Nothing (Part 1)/Talkin' Loud and Sayin' Nothing (Part 2)	1970	2.00	4.00	8.00
❑ 6310	Brother Rapp (Part 1)/Brother Rapp (Part 2)	1970	2.00	4.00	8.00
❑ 6318	Get Up (I Feel Like Being A) Sex Machine (Part 1)/Get Up (I Feel Like Being A) Sex Machine (Part 2)	1970	2.00	4.00	8.00
❑ 6322	I'm Not Demanding (Part 1)/I'm Not Demanding (Part 2)	1970	2.00	4.00	8.00
❑ 6329	Call Me Super Bad (Part 1 & Part 2)/Bewitched	1970	5.00	10.00	20.00
—First pressing: Note longer title					
❑ 6329	Super Bad (Part 1 & Part 2)/Bewitched	1970	2.00	4.00	8.00
❑ 6339	Hey America/(Instrumental)	1970	2.00	4.00	8.00
❑ 6339 [PS]	Hey America/(Instrumental)	1970	3.75	7.50	15.00
❑ 6340	Santa Claus Is Definitely Here to Stay/(Instrumental)	1970	2.00	4.00	8.00
❑ 6340 [PS]	Santa Claus Is Definitely Here to Stay/(Instrumental)	1970	7.50	15.00	30.00
❑ 6347	Get Up, Get Into It, Get Involved Pt. 1/Get Up, Get Into It, Get Involved Pt. 2	1971	2.00	4.00	8.00
❑ 6359	Talking Loud and Saying Nothing — Part 1/Talking Loud and Saying Nothing — Part 2	1971	2.00	4.00	8.00
❑ 6363	I Cried/World (Part 2)	1971	2.00	4.00	8.00
❑ 6366	Spinning Wheel (Part 1)/Spinning Wheel (Part 2)	1971	2.00	4.00	8.00
❑ 6368	Soul Power Pt. 1/Soul Power Pt 2 & Pt. 3	1971	2.00	4.00	8.00

Number	Title (A Side/B Side)	Yr	VG	VG+	NM
MERCURY					
❑ 885190-7	Prisoner of Love/Please, Please, Please	1986	—	2.00	4.00
—Reissue					
❑ 885194-7	Get on the Good Foot/Give It Up or Turnit A Loose	1986	—	2.00	4.00
—Reissue					
PEOPLE					
❑ 664	Everybody Wanna Be Funky One More Time Pt. 1/Everybody Wanna Be Funky One More Time Pt. 2	1976	—	2.50	5.00
❑ 2500	Escape-ism (Part 1)/Escape-ism (Parts 2 & 3)	1971	—	3.00	6.00
❑ 2501	Hot Pants Pt. 1 (She Got to Use What She Got to Get What She Wants)/Hot Pants Pt. 2	1971	—	3.00	6.00
POLYDOR					
❑ 2005	Star Generation/Women Are Something Else	1979	—	2.50	5.00
❑ 2034	The Original Disco Man/Let the Boogie Do the Rest	1979	—	2.50	5.00
❑ 2054	Regrets/Stone Cold Drag	1979	—	2.50	5.00
❑ 2078	Let the Funk Flow/Sometimes That's All There Is	1980	—	2.50	5.00
❑ 2129	Get Up Offa That Thing/It's Too Funky in Here	1980	—	2.50	5.00
❑ 2167	Give the Bass Player Some Part 1/Part 2	1981	—	2.50	5.00
❑ 14088	Make It Funky Part 1/Make It Funky Part 2	1971	—	3.00	6.00
❑ 14098	My Part/Make It Funky, Part 3//Make It Funky, Part 4	1971	—	3.00	6.00
❑ 14100	I'm a Greedy Man Part 1/I'm a Greedy Man Part 2	1971	—	3.00	6.00
❑ 14109	Talking Loud and Saying Nothing Part 1/Part 2	1972	—	3.00	6.00
❑ 14110	Nothing Beats a Try But a Fail/Hot Pants Road	1972	—	—	—
—Unreleased					
❑ 14116	King Heroin/Theme from King Heroin	1972	—	3.00	6.00
❑ 14116 [PS]	King Heroin/Theme from King Heroin	1972	2.50	5.00	10.00
❑ 14125	There It Is Part 1/There It Is Part 2	1972	—	3.00	6.00
❑ 14129	Honky Tonk Part 1/Honky Tonk Part 2	1972	—	3.00	6.00
—Artist credit: "James Brown Soul Train"					
❑ 14139	Get On the Good Foot Part 1/Get On the Good Foot Part 2	1972	—	3.00	6.00
❑ 14153	I Got a Bag of My Own/Public Enemy #1	1972	—	3.00	6.00
❑ 14155	I Got a Bag of My Own/I Know It's True	1972	7.50	15.00	30.00
—Manufactured in U.S. for export					
❑ 14157	What My Baby Needs Now Is a Little More Lovin'/This Guy-This Girl's in Love	1972	—	3.00	6.00
—With Lyn Collins					
❑ 14161	Santa Claus Goes Straight to the Ghetto/Sweet Little Baby Boy	1972	—	3.00	6.00
❑ 14162	I Got Ants in My Pants (and I want to dance) Part 1/Part 2	1973	—	2.50	5.00
❑ 14168	Down and Out in New York City/Mama's Dead	1973	—	2.50	5.00
❑ 14169	The Boss/Like It Is, Like It Was	1973	—	2.50	5.00
❑ 14177	Think/Something	1973	—	2.50	5.00
❑ 14185	Think/Something	1973	—	2.50	5.00
❑ 14193	Woman Part 1/Woman Part 2	1973	—	2.50	5.00
❑ 14194	Sexy, Sexy, Sexy/Slaughter Theme	1973	—	2.50	5.00
❑ 14199	Let It Be Me/It's All Right	1973	—	2.50	5.00
—With Lyn Collins					
❑ 14206	I Got a Good Thing Part 1/I Got a Good Thing Part 2	1973	—	2.50	5.00
❑ 14210	Stoned to the Bone Part 1/Stoned to the Bone Part 2	1973	—	2.50	5.00
—Notice corrected title					
❑ 14210	Stone to the Bone Part 1/Stone to the Bone Part 2	1973	2.50	5.00	10.00
❑ 14223	The Payback Part 1/The Payback Part 2	1974	—	2.50	5.00
❑ 14223 [PS]	The Payback Part 1/The Payback Part 2	1974	2.50	5.00	10.00
❑ 14244	My Thang/Public Enemy No. 1	1974	—	2.50	5.00
❑ 14255	Papa Don't Take No Mess Part 1/Part 2	1974	—	2.50	5.00
❑ 14258	Funky President (People It's Bad)/Coldblooded	1974	—	2.50	5.00
❑ 14268	Reality/I Need Your Love So Bad	1975	—	2.50	5.00
❑ 14270	Sex Machine Part 1/Sex Machine Part 2	1975	—	2.50	5.00
❑ 14274	Thank You For Letting Me Be Myself And... Part 1/Part 2	1975	—	2.50	5.00
❑ 14279	Dead On It Part 1/Dead On It Part 2	1975	—	—	—
—Unreleased					
❑ 14281	Hustle (Dead On It) Part 1/Hustle (Dead On It) Part 2	1975	—	2.50	5.00
❑ 14295	Superbad, Superslick Part 1/Superbad, Superslick Part 2	1975	—	2.50	5.00
❑ 14301	Hot (I Need to Be Loved, Loved, Loved, Loved)/Superbad, Superslick	1975	—	2.50	5.00
❑ 14302	Dooley's Junkyard Dogs Part 1/Part 2	1975	—	2.50	5.00
❑ 14303	(I Love You) For Sentimental Reasons/Goodnight My Love	1975	—	2.50	5.00
❑ 14326	Get Up Offa That Thing/Release the Pressure	1976	—	2.50	5.00
❑ 14354	I Refuse to Lose/Home Again	1976	—	2.50	5.00
❑ 14360	Bodyheat Part 1/Bodyheat Part 2	1976	—	2.50	5.00
❑ 14388	Kiss in 77/Woman	1977	—	2.50	5.00
❑ 14409	Give Me Some Skin/People Wake Up and Live	1977	—	2.50	5.00
—With the J.B.'s					
❑ 14433	Take Me Higher and Groove Me/Summertime	1977	—	2.50	5.00
—B-side by Martha and James					
❑ 14438	If You Don't Give a Doggone About It/People Who Criticize	1977	—	2.50	5.00
—With the New J.B.'s					
❑ 14460	Love Me Tender/Have a Happy Day	1978	—	2.50	5.00
—With the New J.B.'s					
❑ 14465	Eyesight/I Never Never Never Will Forget	1978	—	2.50	5.00
❑ 14487	The Spank/Love Me Tender	1978	—	2.50	5.00
❑ 14512	Nature Part 1/Nature Part 2	1978	—	2.50	5.00
❑ 14522	For Goodness Sakes, Look at Those Cakes Part 1/Part 2	1979	—	2.50	5.00
❑ 14540	Someone to Talk To Part 1/Someone to Talk To Part 2	1979	—	2.50	5.00
❑ 14557	It's Too Funky in Here/Are We Really Dancing	1979	—	2.50	5.00
❑ 871804-7	Think/Lost Someone	1989	—	—	3.00
—Reissue					
❑ 871808-7	Out of Sight/Maybe the Last Time	1989	—	—	3.00
—Reissue					
❑ 871810-7	I Got You (I Feel Good)/Papa's Got a Brand New Bag	1989	—	—	3.00
—Reissue					
❑ 887500-7	(Get Up I Feel Like Being a) Sex Machine/Vincent's Theme	1988	—	—	3.00
—B-side by Ethan James					
❑ 887500-7 [PS]	(Get Up I Feel Like Being a) Sex Machine/Vincent's Theme	1988	—	2.00	4.00
—B-side by Ethan James					
SCOTTI BROS.					
❑ 05682	Living in America/Farewell	1985	—	—	3.00
—B-side by Vince Di Cola					
❑ 05682 [PS]	Living in America/Farewell	1985	—	—	3.00
❑ 06275	Gravity/Gravity (Dub Mix)	1986	—	—	3.00
❑ 06275 [PS]	Gravity/Gravity (Dub Mix)	1986	—	—	3.00
❑ 06568	How Do You Stop/House of Rock	1987	—	—	3.00
❑ 06568 [PS]	How Do You Stop/House of Rock	1987	—	—	3.00
❑ 07090	Let's Get Personal/Repeat the Bat	1987	—	—	3.00
❑ 07783	I'm Real/Gravity	1988	—	—	3.00
❑ 07783 [PS]	I'm Real/Gravity	1988	—	—	3.00
❑ 07975	Static/Godfather Runnin' the Joint	1988	—	—	3.00
❑ 08088	Time to Get Busy/Busy J.B.	1988	—	—	3.00
❑ 68559	It's Your Money $/You and Me	1989	—	—	3.00
❑ 75286	(So Tired of Standing Still We Got to) Move On/You Are My Everything	1991	—	2.00	4.00
SMASH					
❑ 1898	Caledonia/Evil	1964	3.00	6.00	12.00
❑ 1898	Caldonia/Evil	1964	3.00	6.00	12.00
❑ 1898 [PS]	Caledonia/Evil	1964	6.25	12.50	25.00
❑ 1908	The Things That I Used to Do/Out of the Blue	1964	3.00	6.00	12.00
❑ 1908 [PS]	The Things That I Used to Do/Out of the Blue	1964	10.00	20.00	40.00
❑ 1919	Out of Sight/Maybe the Last Time	1964	3.00	6.00	12.00
❑ 1919 [PS]	Out of Sight/Maybe the Last Time	1964	10.00	20.00	40.00
❑ 1949	Who's Afraid of Virginia Woolf? Part 1/Part 2	1964	—	—	—
—Unreleased					
❑ 1975	Devil's Hideaway/Who's Afraid of Virginia Woolf?	1965	2.50	5.00	10.00
❑ 1989	I Got You/Only You	1965	12.50	25.00	50.00
—Withdrawn					
❑ 2008	Try Me/Papa's Got a Brand New Bag	1965	2.50	5.00	10.00
❑ 2028	New Breed Part 1/New Breed Part 2	1966	2.50	5.00	10.00
❑ 2042	James Brown's Boo-Ga-Loo/Lost in the Mood of Changes	1966	2.50	5.00	10.00
❑ 2064	Let's Go Get Stoned/Our Day Will Come	1966	2.50	5.00	10.00
❑ 2093	Jimmy Mack/What Do You Like	1967	2.50	5.00	10.00
T.K.					
❑ 1039	Rapp Payback (Where Iz Moses) Part 1/Part 2	1980	—	2.00	4.00
❑ 1042	Stay with Me/Smokin' and Drinkin'	1981	—	2.00	4.00
7-Inch Extended Plays					
KING					
❑ 430	(contents unknown)	1959	50.00	100.00	200.00
❑ 430 [PS]	Please, Please, Please	1959	100.00	200.00	400.00
❑ 826	(contents unknown)	1963	20.00	40.00	80.00
❑ 826 [PS]	Live at the Apollo	1963	30.00	60.00	120.00

BROWN, JAMES (2)

Number	Title (A Side/B Side)	Yr	VG	VG+	NM
MGM					
❑ 11987	The Berry Tree/I Lost When I Found You	1955	3.00	6.00	12.00
❑ 12011	The Kentuckian Song/The Man from Laramie	1955	3.00	6.00	12.00
❑ 12080	The White Buffalo/It's Lonesome Out Tonight	1955	3.00	6.00	12.00

BROWN, JOE, AND THE BRUVVERS

Number	Title (A Side/B Side)	Yr	VG	VG+	NM
BELL					
❑ 45364 [DJ]	Hey Mama (mono/stereo)	1973	—	3.00	6.00
—May be promo only					
CAMEO					
❑ 241	It Only Took a Minute/All Things Bright and Beautiful	1963	3.00	6.00	12.00
DOT					
❑ 16508	Hava Nagila/That's What Love Will Do	1963	3.00	6.00	12.00
HICKORY					
❑ 1329	Sally Ann/Little Ukulele	1965	2.50	5.00	10.00
JAMIE					
❑ 1298	Lonely Circus/Teardrops in the Rain	1965	2.50	5.00	10.00
❑ 1327	Sea of Heartbreak/Mrs. O's Theme	1966	2.50	5.00	10.00
KAPP					
❑ 2068	Adieu, Monsieur Le Professeur/Diamonds of Dew	1969	—	3.00	6.00
LONDON INT'L.					
❑ 10507	What a Crazy World We're Living In/Popcorn	1962	3.75	7.50	15.00
❑ 10517	A Picture of You/A Lay-About's Lament	1962	3.75	7.50	15.00
❑ 10522	Your Tender Look/The Other Side of Town	1962	3.75	7.50	15.00
STELLAR					
❑ 1504	Hava Nagila/That's What Love Will Do	1963	3.75	7.50	15.00
VERTIGO					
❑ 201	I Was Lost/Cincinnati Floor	1974	—	2.50	5.00
—As "Brown's Home Brew"					
WARNER BROS.					
❑ 7055	With a Little Help from My Friends/Won't You Show Me Around	1967	2.00	4.00	8.00

BROWN, MAXINE

Also see CHUCK JACKSON AND MAXINE BROWN.

Number	Title (A Side/B Side)	Yr	VG	VG+	NM
ABC-PARAMOUNT					
❑ 10235	I Don't Need You No More/Think of Me	1961	3.00	6.00	12.00
❑ 10255	After All We've Been Through Together/My Life	1961	3.00	6.00	12.00
❑ 10290	I Got a Funny Kind of Feeling/What I Don't Know	1962	3.00	6.00	12.00
❑ 10315	Forget Him/A Man	1962	3.00	6.00	12.00
❑ 10327	No Time for Cryin'/Wanting You	1962	3.00	6.00	12.00
❑ 10343	I Kneel at Your Throne/If I Knew Then	1962	3.00	6.00	12.00
❑ 10370	Promise Me Anything/Am I Falling in Love	1962	3.00	6.00	12.00

Number	Title (A Side/B Side)	Yr	VG	VG+	NM
❑ 10388	Life Goes On Just the Same/If You Have No Real Objections	1962	3.00	6.00	12.00
AVCO					
❑ 4585	Always and Forever/Make Love to Me	1971	—	2.50	5.00
❑ 4604	Treat Me Like a Lady/I.O.U.	1972	—	2.50	5.00
❑ 4612	Picked Up, Packed and Went Away/(B-side unknown)	1972	—	2.50	5.00
COMMONWEALTH UNITED					
❑ 3001	We'll Cry Together/Darling Be Home Soon	1969	—	3.00	6.00
❑ 3008	I Can't Get Along Without You/Reason to Believe	1970	—	3.00	6.00
EPIC					
❑ 10334	Seems You've Forsaken My Love/Plum Outa Sight	1968	2.50	5.00	10.00
❑ 10424	Love in Them There Hills/From Loving You	1968	2.50	5.00	10.00
NOMAR					
❑ 103	All in My Mind/Harry, Let's Marry	1960	3.75	7.50	15.00
❑ 106	Funny/Now That You've Gone	1961	3.75	7.50	15.00
❑ 107	Heaven in Your Arms/Maxine's Place	1961	3.75	7.50	15.00
—B-side by Frankie and the Flips					
WAND					
❑ 135	Ask Me/Yesterday's Kisses	1963	2.50	5.00	10.00
❑ 135 [PS]	Ask Me/Yesterday's Kisses	1963	12.50	25.00	50.00
❑ 142	Coming Back to You/Since I Found You	1963	2.50	5.00	10.00
❑ 152	Little Girl Lost/You Upset My Soul	1964	2.00	4.00	8.00
❑ 158	I Cry Alone/Put Yourself in My Place	1964	2.00	4.00	8.00
❑ 162	Oh No Not My Baby/You Upset My Soul	1964	3.00	6.00	12.00
❑ 173	It's Gonna Be Alright/You Do Something to Me	1965	2.00	4.00	8.00
❑ 185	Anything for a Laugh/One Step at a Time	1965	2.00	4.00	8.00
❑ 1104	If You Gotta Make a Fool of Somebody/You're in Love	1965	2.00	4.00	8.00
❑ 1117	One in a Million/Anything You Do Is Alright	1966	2.00	4.00	8.00
❑ 1128	We Can Work It Out/Let Me Give You My Lovin'	1966	2.00	4.00	8.00
❑ 1145	I Don't Need Anything/The Secret of Livin'	1967	2.00	4.00	8.00
❑ 1179	Soul Serenade/He's the Only Guy I'll Ever Love	1968	2.00	4.00	8.00

BROWN, MICHAEL

Also see THE LEFT BANKE; STORIES.

Number	Title (A Side/B Side)	Yr	VG	VG+	NM
ESTATE					
❑ 04075	Dancing to Your Music/(Instrumental)	1983	—	2.00	4.00
KAMA SUTRA					
❑ 563	Circles/Premonitions	1972	2.50	5.00	10.00
PORTRAIT					
❑ 01047	Love Talk/Love You Back to Me	1981	—	2.00	4.00
—With Janice Dempsey					

BROWN, NAPPY

Number	Title (A Side/B Side)	Yr	VG	VG+	NM
ICHIBAN					
❑ 206	Lemon Squeezin' Daddy/Small Red Apples	1989	—	2.50	5.00
SAVOY					
❑ 1129	That Man/I Wonder	1954	7.50	15.00	30.00
❑ 1135	Is It True, Is It True/Two-Faced Woman	1954	7.50	15.00	30.00
❑ 1155	Don't Be Angry/It's Really You	1955	6.25	12.50	25.00
❑ 1162	Piddly Patter Patter/There'll Come a Day	1955	6.25	12.50	25.00
❑ 1176	Doodle I Love You/Sittin' in the Dark	1955	6.25	12.50	25.00
❑ 1187	Open Up That Door/Pleasing You	1956	6.25	12.50	25.00
❑ 1196	Am I/Love Baby	1956	6.25	12.50	25.00
❑ 1506	Little by Little/I'm Getting Lonesome	1956	5.00	10.00	20.00
❑ 1511	Pretty Girl (Yea Yea Yea)/I'm Gonna Get You	1957	5.00	10.00	20.00
❑ 1514	Goody Goody Gum Drops/Bye Bye Baby	1957	5.00	10.00	20.00
❑ 1525	The Right Time/Oh You Don't Know	1957	5.00	10.00	20.00
❑ 1530	If You Need Some Lovin'/I'm in the Mood	1958	5.00	10.00	20.00
❑ 1547	Skidy Wo/I Cried Like a Baby	1958	5.00	10.00	20.00
❑ 1551	It Don't Hurt No More/My Baby	1958	5.00	10.00	20.00
❑ 1555	You're Going to Need Someone/Skiddy Woe	1958	5.00	10.00	20.00
❑ 1562	A Long Time/All Right Now	1959	5.00	10.00	20.00
❑ 1569	This Is My Confession/For Those Who Love	1959	5.00	10.00	20.00
❑ 1575	I Cried Like a Baby/So Deep	1959	5.00	10.00	20.00
❑ 1579	Give Me Your Love/Too Shy	1959	5.00	10.00	20.00
❑ 1582	Down in the Alley/My Baby Knows	1960	3.75	7.50	15.00
❑ 1587	Baby, Cry, Cry, Cry, Baby/What's Come Over You	1960	3.75	7.50	15.00
❑ 1588	Apple of My Eye/Baby I Got News for You	1960	3.75	7.50	15.00
❑ 1592	The Hole I'm In/Nobody Can Say	1960	3.75	7.50	15.00
❑ 1594	Coal Miner/Honnie-Bonnie	1961	3.75	7.50	15.00
❑ 1598	Don't Be Angry/Any Time Is the Right Time	1961	3.75	7.50	15.00
❑ 1616	Didn't You Know/I've Had My Fun	1962	3.75	7.50	15.00
❑ 1621	Lock on the Door/So Glad I Don't Have to Cry No More	1963	3.75	7.50	15.00

BROWN, ROY

Number	Title (A Side/B Side)	Yr	VG	VG+	NM
BLUESWAY					
❑ 61002	New Orleans Women/Standing on Broadway (Watching the Girls)	1967	2.00	4.00	8.00
DELUXE					
❑ 3318	Big Town/Train Time Blues	1951	50.00	100.00	200.00
—Roy Brown singles on DeLuxe before 3318 are unconfirmed on 45 rpm					
❑ 3318	Big Town/Train Time Blues	1951	100.00	200.00	400.00
—Blue vinyl					
❑ 3319	Bar Room Blues/Good Rockin' Man	1951	50.00	100.00	200.00
—Black vinyl					
❑ 3319	Bar Room Blues/Good Rockin' Man	1951	100.00	200.00	400.00
—Blue vinyl					
❑ 3323	I've Got the Last Laugh Now/Brown Angel	1951	50.00	100.00	200.00
—Black vinyl					
❑ 3323	I've Got the Last Laugh Now/Brown Angel	1951	100.00	200.00	400.00
—Blue vinyl					
HOME OF THE BLUES					
❑ 107	Don't Break My Heart/A Man with the Blues	1960	6.25	12.50	25.00
❑ 110	Tired of Being Alone/Rocking All the Time	1960	6.25	12.50	25.00
❑ 115	Oh So Wonderful/Sugar Baby	1961	6.25	12.50	25.00
❑ 122	Rock and Roll Jamboree/I Need a Friend	1961	6.25	12.50	25.00
IMPERIAL					
❑ 5422	Everybody/Saturday Night	1957	7.50	15.00	30.00
❑ 5427	Party Doll/I'm Sticking with You	1957	7.50	15.00	30.00
❑ 5439	Let the Four Winds Blow/Diddy-Y-Diddy-O	1957	7.50	15.00	30.00
❑ 5455	I'm Convicted of Love/I'm Ready to Play	1957	7.50	15.00	30.00
❑ 5469	Tick of the Clock/Slow Down Little Eva	1957	7.50	15.00	30.00
❑ 5489	Ain't Gonna Do It/Sail On Little Girl	1958	7.50	15.00	30.00
❑ 5510	Hip Shakin' Baby/Be My Love Tonight	1958	7.50	15.00	30.00
❑ 5969	Let the Four Winds Blow/Diddy-Yi-Diddy-Yo	1963	5.00	10.00	20.00
KING					
❑ 4602	Travelin' Man/Hurry, Hurry Baby	1953	15.00	30.00	60.00
❑ 4609	Grandpa Stole My Baby/Money Can't Buy Love	1953	15.00	30.00	60.00
❑ 4704	Trouble at Midnight/Bootlegging Baby	1954	15.00	30.00	60.00
❑ 4715	Up Jumped the Devil/This Is My Last Goodbye	1954	15.00	30.00	60.00
❑ 4722	No Love at All/Don't Let It Rain	1954	15.00	30.00	60.00
❑ 4731	Ain't It a Shame/Gal from Kokomo	1954	15.00	30.00	60.00
❑ 4743	Worried Life Blues/Black Diamond	1954	15.00	30.00	60.00
❑ 4761	Fannie Brown Got Married/Queen of Diamonds	1955	12.50	25.00	50.00
❑ 4816	Shake 'Em Up Baby/Letter to Baby	1955	12.50	25.00	50.00
❑ 4834	My Little Angel Child/She's Gone Too Long	1955	12.50	25.00	50.00
❑ 5178	La-Dee-Dah-Dee/Melinda	1959	5.00	10.00	20.00
❑ 5207	I Never Had It So Good/Rinky Dinky Doo	1959	5.00	10.00	20.00
❑ 5218	Hard Luck Blues/Good Looking and Forty	1959	5.00	10.00	20.00
❑ 5247	School Bell Rock/Ain't No Rocking No More	1959	5.00	10.00	20.00
❑ 5333	Ain't Got No Blues Today/Adorable One	1960	5.00	10.00	20.00
❑ 5521	Mighty Mighty Man/Good Man Blues	1961	5.00	10.00	20.00
MERCURY					
❑ 73166	It's My Fault Darling/Love for Sale	1970	—	3.00	6.00
❑ 73219	Mail Man Blues/Hunky Funky Woman	1971	—	3.00	6.00

BROWN, RUTH

Number	Title (A Side/B Side)	Yr	VG	VG+	NM
ATLANTIC					
❑ 919	Teardrops from My Eyes/Am I Making the Same Mistake	1950	100.00	200.00	400.00
—This and Atlantic 914 were the label's first two 45s.					
❑ 948	Shine On—Big Bright Moon Shine On/Without My Love	1951	15.00	30.00	60.00
—Ruth Brown records on Atlantic before 948 (except 919) are unconfirmed on 45 rpm					
❑ 962	5-10-15 Hours/Be Anything But Be Mine	1952	12.50	25.00	50.00
❑ 973	Daddy Daddy/Have a Good Time	1952	12.50	25.00	50.00
❑ 978	Three Letters/Good for Nothing Joe	1952	12.50	25.00	50.00
❑ 986	(Mama) He Treats Your Daughter Mean/R.B. Blues	1953	15.00	30.00	60.00
❑ 993	Wild Wild Young Men/Mend Your Ways	1953	10.00	20.00	40.00
❑ 1005	The Tears Keep Tumblin' Down/I Would If I Could	1953	7.50	15.00	30.00
❑ 1018	Love Contest/If You Don't Want Me	1954	7.50	15.00	30.00
❑ 1023	Sentimental Journey/It's All in Your Mind	1954	7.50	15.00	30.00
❑ 1027	If I Had Any Sense/Hello Little Boy	1954	7.50	15.00	30.00
❑ 1036	Oh What a Dream/Please Don't Freeze	1954	7.50	15.00	30.00
❑ 1044	Somebody Touch Me/Mambo Baby	1954	7.50	15.00	30.00
❑ 1051	Ever Since My Baby's Been Gone/Bye Bye Young Men	1955	7.50	15.00	30.00
❑ 1059	I Can See Everybody's Baby/As Long As I'm Moving	1955	7.50	15.00	30.00
❑ 1072	What'd I Say/It's Love Baby (24 Hours of the Day)	1955	7.50	15.00	30.00
❑ 1077	Love Has Joined Us Together/I Gotta Have You	1955	7.50	15.00	30.00
—With Clyde McPhatter					
❑ 1082	Old Man River/I Want to Do More	1956	6.25	12.50	25.00
❑ 1091	Sweet Baby of Mine/I'm Getting Right	1956	6.25	12.50	25.00
❑ 1102	I Want to Be Loved/Mom, Oh Mom	1956	6.25	12.50	25.00
❑ 1113	Smooth Operator/I Still Love You	1956	6.25	12.50	25.00
❑ 1125	Lucky Lips/My Heart Is Breaking Over You	1957	6.25	12.50	25.00
❑ 1140	When I Get You Baby/One More Time	1957	6.25	12.50	25.00
❑ 1153	Show Me/I Hope We Meet	1957	6.25	12.50	25.00
❑ 1166	A New Love/Look Me Up	1957	6.25	12.50	25.00
❑ 1177	Book of Lies/Just Too Much	1958	6.25	12.50	25.00
❑ 1197	This Little Girl's Gone/Why Me	1958	6.25	12.50	25.00
❑ 2008	Mama, He Treats Your Daughter Mean/I'll Step Aside	1958	5.00	10.00	20.00
❑ 2015	5-10-15 Hours/Itty Bitty Girl	1959	5.00	10.00	20.00
❑ 2026	Jack O'Diamonds/I Can't Hear a Word You Say	1959	5.00	10.00	20.00
❑ 2035	I Don't Know/Papa Daddy	1959	5.00	10.00	20.00
❑ 2052	Don't Deceive Me/I Burned Your Letter	1960	5.00	10.00	20.00
❑ 2064	The Door Is Still Open/What I Wouldn't Give	1960	5.00	10.00	20.00
❑ 2075	Taking Care of Business/Honey Boy	1960	5.00	10.00	20.00
❑ 2088	Sure 'Nuff/Here He Comes	1961	3.75	7.50	15.00
❑ 2104	It Tears Me All to Pieces/Anyone But You	1961	3.75	7.50	15.00
DECCA					
❑ 31598	What Happened to You/Yes Sir That's My Baby	1964	2.50	5.00	10.00
❑ 31640	Come a Little Closer/I Love Him and I Know It	1964	2.50	5.00	10.00
MAINSTREAM					
❑ 611	On the Good Ship Lollipop/Hurry On Down	1965	2.50	5.00	10.00
PHILIPS					
❑ 40028	Shake a Hand/Say It Again	1962	3.00	6.00	12.00
❑ 40056	Mama He Treats Your Daughter Mean/Hold My Hand	1962	3.00	6.00	12.00
❑ 40086	He Tells Me with His Eyes/If You Don't Tell Nobody	1963	3.00	6.00	12.00
❑ 40119	Satisfied/If You Don't Tell Nobody	1963	3.00	6.00	12.00

7-Inch Extended Plays

Number	Title (A Side/B Side)	Yr	VG	VG+	NM
ATLANTIC					
❑ 505	Teardrops from My Eyes/5-10-15//Mama He Treats Your Daughter Mean/So Long	1953	25.00	50.00	100.00
❑ 505 [PS]	Ruth Brown Sings	1953	37.50	75.00	150.00
❑ 585	*Lucky Lips/Mambo Baby/Smooth Operator/Oh What a Dream	1957	15.00	30.00	60.00
❑ 585 [PS]	Ruth Brown	1957	30.00	60.00	120.00

BROWN, SKIPPY

Number	Title (A Side/B Side)	Yr	VG	VG+	NM
CHANCE					
❑ 1129	So Many Days/Tale of Woe	1953	62.50	125.00	250.00

BROWN, TOMMY

Number	Title (A Side/B Side)	Yr	VG	VG+	NM
ABC-PARAMOUNT					
❑ 10632	Ain't So/Well, There Goes My Heart	1965	3.00	6.00	12.00
DOT					
❑ 16130	Tra-La-La/Weepin' and Cryin'	1960	3.75	7.50	15.00
GROOVE					
❑ 0132	Don't Leave Me/Won't You Forgive Me	1955	7.50	15.00	30.00
❑ 0143	The Thrill Is Gone/Gambler's Prayer	1956	7.50	15.00	30.00
IMPERIAL					
❑ 5476	Rock Away My Blues/Someday, Somewhere	1957	12.50	25.00	50.00
❑ 5533	Just for You/A Heart with No Feeling	1958	7.50	15.00	30.00
KING					
❑ 4658	How Much Do You Think I Can Stand/Fore Day Train	1953	37.50	75.00	150.00
❑ 4679	Goodbye, I'm Gone/Since You Left Me Dear	1953	15.00	30.00	60.00
UNITED					
❑ 183	Remember Me/Southern Woman	1956	37.50	75.00	150.00

BROWN, WINI

Number	Title (A Side/B Side)	Yr	VG	VG+	NM
COLUMBIA					
❑ 1-872	A Good Man Is Hard to Find/This Is the Last Time	1950	10.00	20.00	40.00
—Microgroove 7-inch, 33 1/3 rpm single					
❑ 6-872	A Good Man Is Hard to Find/This Is the Last Time	1950	7.50	15.00	30.00
JARO					
❑ 77018	Gone Again/Johnny with the Gentle Hand	1960	5.00	10.00	20.00
MERCURY					
❑ 5870	Here in My Heart/Your Happiness Is Mine	1952	50.00	100.00	200.00
❑ 8270	Be Anything — Be Mine/Heaven Knows Why	1952	50.00	100.00	200.00
❑ 70062	Tear Down the Sky/Can't Stand No More	1953	25.00	50.00	100.00
RCA VICTOR					
❑ 47-6970	Available Lover/It's All in Your Mind	1957	5.00	10.00	20.00

BROWN'S HOME BREW

See JOE BROWN AND THE BRUVVERS.

BROWNE, JACKSON

Number	Title (A Side/B Side)	Yr	VG	VG+	NM
ASYLUM					
❑ 11004	Doctor My Eyes/Looking Into You	1972	—	2.50	5.00
❑ 11006	Rock Me on the Water/Something Fine	1972	—	2.00	4.00
❑ 11023	Redneck Friend/Those Times You've Come	1973	—	2.00	4.00
❑ 11030	Ready or Not/Take It Easy	1974	—	2.00	4.00
❑ 45227	Walking Slow/Before the Deluge	1975	—	2.00	4.00
❑ 45242	Fountains of Sorrow/The Late Show	1975	—	2.00	4.00
❑ 45379	Here Come Those Tears Again/Linda Paloma	1976	—	2.00	4.00
❑ 45399	The Pretender/Daddy's Tune	1977	—	2.00	4.00
❑ 45460	Running on Empty/Nothing But Time	1978	—	2.00	4.00
❑ 45460 [PS]	Running on Empty/Nothing But Time	1978	—	2.50	5.00
❑ 45485 A/B	Stay/Rosie	1978	—	2.50	5.00
❑ 45485 A/B [PS]	Stay/Rosie	1978	—	2.50	5.00
❑ 45485 A/C	Stay/The Load-Out	1978	—	2.00	4.00
❑ 45543	You Love the Thunder/The Road	1978	—	2.00	4.00
❑ 45543 [PS]	You Love the Thunder/The Road	1978	—	2.50	5.00
❑ 47003	Boulevard/Call It a Loan	1980	—	2.00	4.00
❑ 47003 [PS]	Boulevard/Call It a Loan	1980	—	2.50	5.00
❑ 47036	That Girl Could Sing/Of Missing Persons	1980	—	2.00	4.00
❑ 69543	In the Shape of a Heart/Voice of America	1986	—	—	3.00
❑ 69566	For America/Till I Go Down	1986	—	—	3.00
❑ 69566 [PS]	For America/Till I Go Down	1986	—	—	3.00
❑ 69764	For a Rocker/Downtown	1984	—	—	3.00
❑ 69764 [PS]	For a Rocker/Downtown	1984	—	—	3.00
❑ 69791	Tender Is the Night/On the Day	1983	—	—	3.00
❑ 69791 [PS]	Tender Is the Night/On the Day	1983	—	—	3.00
❑ 69826	Lawyers in Love/Say It Isn't True	1983	—	—	3.00
❑ 69826 [PS]	Lawyers in Love/Say It Isn't True	1983	—	—	3.00
❑ 69982	Somebody's Baby/The Crow on the Cradle [w/ Graham Nash & David Lindley]	1982	—	2.00	4.00
❑ 69982 [PS]	Somebody's Baby/The Crow on the Cradle [w/ Graham Nash & David Lindley]	1982	—	2.00	4.00
ELEKTRA					
❑ 69292	World in Motion/My Personal Revenge	1989	—	2.00	4.00

BROWNETTES, THE

Number	Title (A Side/B Side)	Yr	VG	VG+	NM
KING					
❑ 6153	Baby, Don't You Know/Never Find a Love Like Mine	1968	5.00	10.00	20.00

BROWNSVILLE STATION

Number	Title (A Side/B Side)	Yr	VG	VG+	NM
BIG TREE					
❑ 144	Rock with the Music/(B-side unknown)	1972	—	2.50	5.00
❑ 156	The Red Back Spider/Rock with the Music	1972	—	2.50	5.00
❑ 161	Let Your Yeah Be Yeah/Mister Robert	1973	—	2.50	5.00
❑ 15005	I'm the Leader of the Gang/Meet Me on the Fourth Floor	1974	—	2.00	4.00
❑ 15005	I'm the Leader of the Gang/Fast Phyllis	1974	—	2.00	4.00
❑ 16001	Kings of the Party/Ostrich	1974	—	2.00	4.00
❑ 16011	Smokin' in the Boy's Room/Barefootin'	1973	—	2.50	5.00
❑ 16029	I Got It Bad for You/Mama Don't Allow No Parkin'	1974	—	2.00	4.00
EPIC					
❑ 50695	Love Stealer/Fever	1979	—	2.00	4.00
—As "Brownsville"					
HIDEOUT					
❑ 1957	Rock and Roll Holiday/Jailhouse Rock	1969	3.00	6.00	12.00
POLYDOR					
❑ 14017	Rock and Roll Holiday/Jailhouse Rock	1969	—	2.50	5.00
PRIVATE STOCK					
❑ 45149	Lady (Put the Light on Me)/Rockers and Rollers	1977	—	2.00	4.00
❑ 45167	The Martian Boogie/Mr. Johnson Sez	1977	—	2.00	4.00
WARNER BROS.					
❑ 7441	Be-Bop Confidential/City Life	1970	2.00	4.00	8.00
❑ 7456	Roadrunner/Do the Bosco	1971	2.00	4.00	8.00
❑ 7501	That's Fine/Tell Me All About It	1971	2.00	4.00	8.00

BRUCE, ED

Number	Title (A Side/B Side)	Yr	VG	VG+	NM
EPIC					
❑ 50424	When I Die, Just Let Me Go to Texas/I've Not Forgotten Marie	1977	—	2.00	4.00
❑ 50475	Star Studded Nights/Wedding Dress	1977	—	2.00	4.00
❑ 50503	Love Somebody to Death/I Can't Seem to Get the Hang of Telling Her Goodbye	1977	—	2.00	4.00
❑ 50544	Man Made of Glass/Never Take Candy from a Stranger	1978	—	2.00	4.00
❑ 50613	The Man That Turned My Mama On/Give My Old Memory a Call	1978	—	2.00	4.00
❑ 50645	Angeline/Give My Old Memory a Call	1978	—	2.00	4.00
MCA					
❑ 41201	Diane/Blue Umbrella	1980	—	—	3.00
❑ 41273	The Last Cowboy Song/The Outlaw and the Stranger	1980	—	—	3.00
❑ 51018	Girls, Women & Ladies/The Last Thing She Said	1980	—	—	3.00
❑ 51076	Evil Angel/Easy Temptations	1981	—	—	3.00
❑ 51139	(When You Fall in Love) Everything's a Waltz/Thirty-Nine and Holding	1982	—	—	3.00
❑ 51210	You're the Best Break This Old Heart Ever Had/It Just Makes Me Want You More	1982	—	—	3.00
❑ 52036	Love's Found You and Me/I Take the Chance	1982	—	—	3.00
❑ 52109	Ever, Never Lovin' You/Theme from "Bret Maverick"	1982	—	—	3.00
❑ 52156	My First Taste of Texas/One More Shot of "Old Back Home Again"	1983	—	—	3.00
❑ 52210	You're Not Leaving Here Tonight/I Think I'm in Love	1983	—	—	3.00
❑ 52251	If It Was Easy/You've Got Her Eyes	1983	—	—	3.00
❑ 52295	After All/It Would Take a Fool	1983	—	—	3.00
❑ 52433	Tell 'Em I've Gone Crazy/Birds of Paradise	1984	—	—	3.00
MONUMENT					
❑ 1118	Song for Jenny/Puzzles	1968	—	3.00	6.00
❑ 1138	Everybody Wants to Get to Heaven/When a Man Becomes a Man	1969	—	3.00	6.00
❑ 1155	Hey Porter/The Love of My Heart	1969	—	3.00	6.00
RCA					
❑ 5005-7-R	Fools for Each Other/Memphis Roots	1986	—	—	3.00
—A-side with Lynn Anderson					
❑ 5077-7-R	Quietly Crazy/Memphis Routes	1986	—	—	3.00
❑ PB-13937	You Turn Me On Like a Radio/If It Ain't Love	1984	—	—	3.00
❑ PB-14037	When Givin' Up Was Easy/Texas Girl, I'm Closing In on You	1985	—	—	3.00
❑ PB-14150	If It Ain't Love/The Migrant	1985	—	—	3.00
❑ PB-14305	Nights/Fifteen to Forty-Three (Man In the Middle)	1986	—	—	3.00
RCA VICTOR					
❑ 47-7842	Flight 303/Spun Gold	1961	3.75	7.50	15.00
❑ 47-9044	Walker's Woods/Lonesome Is Me	1966	2.00	4.00	8.00
❑ 47-9155	Last Train to Clarksville/I'm Getting Better	1967	2.00	4.00	8.00
❑ 47-9315	The Price I Pay to Stay/If I Could Just Go Home	1967	2.00	4.00	8.00
❑ 47-9394	Shadows of Her Mind/Her Sweet Love and the Baby	1967	2.00	4.00	8.00
❑ 47-9475	I'll Take You Away/Give More Than You Take	1968	2.00	4.00	8.00
❑ 47-9553	Painted Girls and Wine/Ninety-Seven More to Go	1968	2.00	4.00	8.00
❑ 61-7842 [S]	Flight 303/Spun Gold	1961	7.50	15.00	30.00
—"Living Stereo" (large hole, plays at 45 rpm)					
SUN					
❑ 276	Rock Boppin' Baby/More Than Yesterday	1957	7.50	15.00	30.00
—As "Edwin Bruce"					
❑ 292	Sweet Woman/Part of My Life	1958	10.00	20.00	40.00
—As "Edwin Bruce"					
UNITED ARTISTS					
❑ XW204	A House in New Orleans/Good Jelly Jones	1973	—	2.00	4.00
❑ XW353	July, You're a Woman/The Rain in Baby's Life	1973	—	2.00	4.00
❑ XW403	It's Not What She Done/The Devil Ain't a Lonely Woman's Friend	1974	—	2.00	4.00
❑ XW732	Mammas Don't Let Your Babies Grow Up to Be Cowboys/It's Not What She's Done (It's What You Didn't Do)	1975	—	2.50	5.00
❑ XW774	The Littlest Cowboy Rides Again/The Feel of Being Gone	1976	—	2.00	4.00
❑ XW811	Sleep All Mornin'/Working Man's Prayer	1976	—	2.00	4.00
❑ XW862	For Love's Own Sake/When Wide Open Spaces and Cowboys Are Gone	1976	—	2.00	4.00
WAND					
❑ 136	It's Coming to Me/The Greatest Man	1963	3.00	6.00	12.00
❑ 156	I'm Gonna Have a Party/Half a Love	1964	3.00	6.00	12.00

BRUCE, JACK

Ex-member of CREAM.

Number	Title (A Side/B Side)	Yr	VG	VG+	NM
RSO					
❑ 507	Keep It Down/Keep On Wondering	1975	—	2.50	5.00

BRUCE AND TERRY

BRUCE JOHNSTON and TERRY MELCHER.

Number	Title (A Side/B Side)	Yr	VG	VG+	NM
COLUMBIA					
❑ 42956	Custom Machine/Makaha at Midnight	1964	5.00	10.00	20.00
❑ 43055	Summer Means Fun/Yeah!	1964	5.00	10.00	20.00
❑ 43238	I Love You Model T/Carmen	1965	5.00	10.00	20.00
❑ 43378	Raining in My Heart/Four Strong Winds	1965	4.00	8.00	16.00
❑ 43479	Thank You Baby/Come Love	1965	4.00	8.00	16.00
❑ 43582	Don't Run Away/Girl It's All Right Now	1966	4.00	8.00	16.00
EQUINOX					
❑ PB-10238	Rebecca/Take It to Mexico	1975	2.50	5.00	10.00
—As "Bruce Johnston and Terry Melcher"					

BRUINS, THE

Number	Title (A Side/B Side)	Yr	VG	VG+	NM
COMET					
❑ 2167	Nobody But You/One More Try	1964	6.25	12.50	25.00

GENERAL AMERICAN

Number	Title (A Side/B Side)	Yr	VG	VG+	NM
❑ 721	Go On and Cry/Can't Believe That You've Grown Up	1965	10.00	20.00	40.00

ROULETTE

Number	Title (A Side/B Side)	Yr	VG	VG+	NM
❑ 4566	Believe Me/The Slide	1964	5.00	10.00	20.00

BRUNO, BRUCE

ROULETTE

Number	Title (A Side/B Side)	Yr	VG	VG+	NM
❑ 4386	Hey Little One/Some Time, Some Place	1961	5.00	10.00	20.00
❑ 4427	Venus in Blue Jeans/Dear Joanne	1962	5.00	10.00	20.00

BRYAN, BILLY

See GENE PITNEY.

BRYAN, WES

CLOCK

Number	Title (A Side/B Side)	Yr	VG	VG+	NM
❑ 1013	Honey Baby/So Blue Over You	1959	5.00	10.00	20.00

ROULETTE

Number	Title (A Side/B Side)	Yr	VG	VG+	NM
❑ 4289	I Guess I'll Never Know/Melodie D'Amour	1960	3.75	7.50	15.00

UNITED ARTISTS

Number	Title (A Side/B Side)	Yr	VG	VG+	NM
❑ 102	Tiny Spacemen/Lonesome Love	1957	7.50	15.00	30.00
❑ 122	Wait for Me Baby/Freeze!	1958	6.25	12.50	25.00

BUBBLE PUPPY, THE

INTERNATIONAL ARTISTS

Number	Title (A Side/B Side)	Yr	VG	VG+	NM
❑ 128	Hot Smoke and Sasafrass/Lonely	1969	5.00	10.00	20.00
❑ 133	Beginning/If I Had a Reason	1969	6.25	12.50	25.00
❑ 136	Days of Our Time/Thinkin' About Thinkin'	1969	6.25	12.50	25.00
❑ 138	What Do You See/Hurry Sundown	1970	6.25	12.50	25.00
❑ 138 [DJ]	What Do You See/Hurry Sundown	1970	12.50	25.00	50.00

—Green vinyl promo

BUBI AND BOB

SPHINX

Number	Title (A Side/B Side)	Yr	VG	VG+	NM
❑ 1201	The Mummy/Biscayne Beat	1959	7.50	15.00	30.00

BUCCANEERS, THE

RAINBOW

Number	Title (A Side/B Side)	Yr	VG	VG+	NM
❑ 211	Dear Ruth/Fine Brown Flame	1953	200.00	400.00	800.00

RAMA

Number	Title (A Side/B Side)	Yr	VG	VG+	NM
❑ 21	The Stars Will Remember/Come Back My Love	1954	500.00	1000.	2000.
❑ 24	In the Mission of St. Augustine/You Did Me Wrong	1954	500.00	1000.	2000.

SOUTHERN

Number	Title (A Side/B Side)	Yr	VG	VG+	NM
❑ 101	Dear Ruth/Fine Brown Flame	1953	2000.	3000.	4000.

—All copies are on red vinyl

BUCHANAN, BILL

Also see BUCHANAN AND ANCELL; BUCHANAN AND CELLA; BUCHANAN AND GOODMAN; BUCHANAN AND GREENFIELD.

GONE

Number	Title (A Side/B Side)	Yr	VG	VG+	NM
❑ 5032	The Thing/Happy Day	1958	7.50	15.00	30.00

UNITED ARTISTS

Number	Title (A Side/B Side)	Yr	VG	VG+	NM
❑ 531	The Night Before Halloween/Beware	1962	3.75	7.50	15.00

BUCHANAN AND ANCELL

Also see BILL BUCHANAN.

FLYING SAUCER

Number	Title (A Side/B Side)	Yr	VG	VG+	NM
❑ 501	The Creature/Meet the Creature	1957	10.00	20.00	40.00

BUCHANAN AND CELLA

Also see BILL BUCHANAN.

ABC-PARAMOUNT

Number	Title (A Side/B Side)	Yr	VG	VG+	NM
❑ 10033	String Along with Pal-O-Mine/More and More String Along with Pal-O-Mine	1959	6.25	12.50	25.00

BUCHANAN AND GOODMAN

Also see BILL BUCHANAN; DICKIE GOODMAN.

COMIC

Number	Title (A Side/B Side)	Yr	VG	VG+	NM
❑ 500	Flying Saucer the Third/The Cha Cha Lesson	1959	10.00	20.00	40.00

LUNIVERSE

Number	Title (A Side/B Side)	Yr	VG	VG+	NM
❑ 101X	Back to Earth Part 1/Back to Earth Part 2	1956	50.00	100.00	200.00
❑ 101	The Flying Saucer Part 1/The Flying Saucer Part 2	1956	12.50	25.00	50.00

—Most labels have the entire word "Luniverse" typeset

Number	Title (A Side/B Side)	Yr	VG	VG+	NM
❑ 101	The Flying Saucer Part 1/The Flying Saucer Part 2	1956	25.00	50.00	100.00

—Original labels have a handwritten "L" at the beginning of the printed word "Universe"

Number	Title (A Side/B Side)	Yr	VG	VG+	NM
❑ 102X	Public Opinion Part 1/Public Opinion Part 2	1956	—	—	—

—Not known to exist

Number	Title (A Side/B Side)	Yr	VG	VG+	NM
❑ 102	Buchanan and Goodman On Trial/Crazy	1956	10.00	20.00	40.00
❑ 103	The Banana Boat Story/The Mystery (In Slow Motion)	1957	10.00	20.00	40.00
❑ 105	Flying Saucer The 2nd/Martian Melody	1957	10.00	20.00	40.00
❑ 107	Santa and the Satellite Part 1/Santa and the Satellite Part 2	1957	10.00	20.00	40.00
❑ 108	The Flying Saucer Goes West/Saucer Serenade	1958	10.00	20.00	40.00

NOVELTY

Number	Title (A Side/B Side)	Yr	VG	VG+	NM
❑ 301	Frankenstein of '59/Frankenstein Returns	1959	10.00	20.00	40.00

BUCHANAN AND GREENFIELD

Also see BILL BUCHANAN.

NOVEL

Number	Title (A Side/B Side)	Yr	VG	VG+	NM
❑ 711	The Invasion/What a Lovely Party	1964	7.50	15.00	30.00

—Originals have all-red labels

Number	Title (A Side/B Side)	Yr	VG	VG+	NM
❑ 711	The Invasion/What a Lovely Party	1972	2.00	4.00	8.00

—Red and white label reissue

BUCKEYES, THE

DELUXE

Number	Title (A Side/B Side)	Yr	VG	VG+	NM
❑ 6110	Since I Fell for You/My Only You	1957	75.00	150.00	300.00
❑ 6126	Dottie Baby/Begging You Please	1957	100.00	200.00	400.00

BUCKINGHAM, LINDSEY

Also see BUCKINGHAM NICKS; FLEETWOOD MAC.

ASYLUM

Number	Title (A Side/B Side)	Yr	VG	VG+	NM
❑ 47223	Trouble/Mary Lee Jones	1981	—	2.00	4.00
❑ 47223 [PS]	Trouble/Mary Lee Jones	1981	—	2.00	4.00
❑ 47408	It Was I/Love from Here, Love from There	1982	—	2.00	4.00

ELEKTRA

Number	Title (A Side/B Side)	Yr	VG	VG+	NM
❑ 69675	Slow Dancing/D.W. Suite	1984	—	—	3.00
❑ 69714	Go Insane/Play in the Rain	1984	—	—	3.00
❑ 69714 [PS]	Go Insane/Play in the Rain	1984	—	2.00	4.00

WARNER BROS.

Number	Title (A Side/B Side)	Yr	VG	VG+	NM
❑ 29570	Holiday Road/The Trip (Theme from Vacation)	1983	—	2.00	4.00

—B-side by Ralph Burns

BUCKINGHAM NICKS

Also see LINDSEY BUCKINGHAM; FLEETWOOD MAC; STEVIE NICKS.

POLYDOR

Number	Title (A Side/B Side)	Yr	VG	VG+	NM
❑ 14209	Don't Let Me Down Again/The Races Are Run	1973	12.50	25.00	50.00
❑ 14229	Crying in the Night/Without a Leg to Stand On	1974	12.50	25.00	50.00
❑ 14335	Don't Let Me Down Again/Crystal	1976	7.50	15.00	30.00
❑ 14428	Crying in the Night/Stephanie	1977	7.50	15.00	30.00
❑ 14428 [PS]	Crying in the Night/Stephanie	1977	15.00	30.00	60.00

BUCKINGHAMS, THE (1)

Chicago band. Also see THE FALLING PEBBLES.

COLUMBIA

Number	Title (A Side/B Side)	Yr	VG	VG+	NM
❑ 44053	Don't You Care/Why Don't You Love Me	1967	2.00	4.00	8.00
❑ 44053 [PS]	Don't You Care/Why Don't You Love Me	1967	3.00	6.00	12.00
❑ 44182	Mercy, Mercy, Mercy/You Are Gone	1967	2.00	4.00	8.00
❑ 44182 [PS]	Mercy, Mercy, Mercy/You Are Gone	1967	3.00	6.00	12.00
❑ 44254	Hey Baby (They're Playing Our Song)/And Our Love	1967	2.00	4.00	8.00
❑ 44254 [PS]	Hey Baby (They're Playing Our Song)/And Our Love	1967	3.00	6.00	12.00
❑ 44378	Susan/Foreign Policy	1967	2.00	4.00	8.00
❑ 44378 [PS]	Susan/Foreign Policy	1967	3.00	6.00	12.00
❑ 44533	Back in Love Again/You Misunderstand Me	1968	2.00	4.00	8.00
❑ 44533 [PS]	Back in Love Again/You Misunderstand Me	1968	3.00	6.00	12.00
❑ 44672	Where Did You Come From/Song of the Breeze	1968	2.00	4.00	8.00
❑ 44672 [PS]	Where Did You Come From/Song of the Breeze	1968	3.00	6.00	12.00
❑ 44790	This Is How Much I Love You/Can't You Find the Words	1969	2.00	4.00	8.00
❑ 44790 [PS]	This Is How Much I Love You/Can't You Find the Words	1969	3.00	6.00	12.00
❑ 44923	It's a Beautiful Day/Difference of Opinion	1969	2.00	4.00	8.00
❑ 45066	It Took Forever/I Got a Feelin'	1970	2.00	4.00	8.00

PHILCO-FORD

Number	Title (A Side/B Side)	Yr	VG	VG+	NM
❑ HP-14	Kind of a Drag/Lawdy Miss Clawdy	1968	5.00	10.00	20.00

—4-inch plastic "Hip Pocket Record" with color sleeve

RED LABEL

Number	Title (A Side/B Side)	Yr	VG	VG+	NM
❑ 71001	Veronica/Can We Talk About It	1985	—	2.00	4.00
❑ 71001 [PS]	Veronica/Can We Talk About It	1985	—	2.50	5.00

SPECTRASOUND

Number	Title (A Side/B Side)	Yr	VG	VG+	NM
❑ 4618	Sweets for My Sweet/Beginner's Love	1967	5.00	10.00	20.00

U.S.A.

Number	Title (A Side/B Side)	Yr	VG	VG+	NM
❑ 844	I'll Go Crazy/I Don't Wanna Cry	1966	3.00	6.00	12.00
❑ 848	I Call Your Name/Makin' Up and Breakin' Up	1966	3.00	6.00	12.00
❑ 853	I've Been Wrong/Love Ain't Enough	1966	3.00	6.00	12.00
❑ 860	Kind of a Drag/You Make Me Feel So Good	1966	3.75	7.50	15.00

—Light blue label with all dark blue printing

Number	Title (A Side/B Side)	Yr	VG	VG+	NM
❑ 860	Kind of a Drag/You Make Me Feel So Good	1966	3.75	7.50	15.00

—Light blue label with red, white, blue and black printing

Number	Title (A Side/B Side)	Yr	VG	VG+	NM
❑ 869	Lawdy Miss Clawdy/I Call Your Name	1967	3.00	6.00	12.00
❑ 869	Lawdy Miss Clawdy/Making Up and Breaking Up	1967	3.00	6.00	12.00
❑ 873	Summertime/Don't Want to Cry	1967	3.00	6.00	12.00

BUCKINGHAMS, THE (2)

These two records are not by group (1).

LAURIE

Number	Title (A Side/B Side)	Yr	VG	VG+	NM
❑ 3258	Gonna Say Goodbye/Many Times	1964	2.50	5.00	10.00

SEG-WAY

Number	Title (A Side/B Side)	Yr	VG	VG+	NM
❑ 1004	Lobo Lobo/Rockin' Piper	1962	2.50	5.00	10.00

BUDDIES, THE

COMET

Number	Title (A Side/B Side)	Yr	VG	VG+	NM
❑ 2143	Hully Gully Baby/Must Be True Love	1961	6.25	12.50	25.00

DECCA

Number	Title (A Side/B Side)	Yr	VG	VG+	NM
❑ 29840	The Most Happy Fella/Two Skeletons on a Tin Roof	1956	3.75	7.50	15.00
❑ 29953	Bag of Bones/Every Time the Phone Rings	1956	3.75	7.50	15.00
❑ 30355	A Prom and a Promise/The Lottery	1957	3.75	7.50	15.00
❑ 31920	Duckman Part 1/Duckman Part 2	1966	2.00	4.00	8.00

GLORY

Number	Title (A Side/B Side)	Yr	VG	VG+	NM
❑ 230	I Stole Your Heart/I Waited	1955	37.50	75.00	150.00

OKEH

Number	Title (A Side/B Side)	Yr	VG	VG+	NM
❑ 7123	Castle of Love/Give Me Your Love	1959	3.75	7.50	15.00

SWAN

Number	Title (A Side/B Side)	Yr	VG	VG+	NM
❑ 4073	Spooky Spider/Lebone Delada	1961	3.75	7.50	15.00
❑ 4170	The Beatle/Pulsebeat	1964	6.25	12.50	25.00

TIARA

Number	Title (A Side/B Side)	Yr	VG	VG+	NM
❑ 6121	She's a Loser/Heartless	1959	6.25	12.50	25.00

BUFFALO SPRINGFIELD

Also see DEWEY MARTIN AND MEDICINE BALL; JIM MESSINA; STEPHEN STILLS; NEIL YOUNG.

ATCO

Number	Title (A Side/B Side)	Yr	VG	VG+	NM
❑ 6428	Nowadays Clancy Can't Even Sing/Go And Say Goodbye	1966	5.00	10.00	20.00
❑ 6452	Everybody's Wrong/Burned	1966	5.00	10.00	20.00
❑ 6459	For What It's Worth/Do I Have to Come Right Out and Say It	1967	3.75	7.50	15.00

Number	Title (A Side/B Side)	Yr	VG	VG+	NM
❑ 6459	For What It's Worth (Stop, Hey, What's That Sound)/Do I Have to Come Right Out and Say It	1967	3.00	6.00	12.00
❑ 6499	Bluebird/Mr. Soul	1967	5.00	10.00	20.00
❑ 6519	Rock 'N' Roll Woman/A Child's Claim to Fame	1967	2.50	5.00	10.00
❑ 6545	Expecting to Fly/Everydays	1968	2.50	5.00	10.00
❑ 6572	Uno Mundo/Merry-Go-Round	1968	2.50	5.00	10.00
❑ 6602	Special Care/Kind Woman	1968	2.50	5.00	10.00
❑ 6615	Four Days Gone/On the Way Home	1968	2.50	5.00	10.00

BUFFETT, JIMMY

ABC

Number	Title (A Side/B Side)	Yr	VG	VG+	NM
❑ 11399	You Went to Paris/Peanut Butter Conspiracy	1973	—	—	—
—Unreleased? (Assigned by mistake?)					
❑ 12113	Door Number Three/Dallas	1975	—	2.50	5.00
❑ 12143	Big Red/Havana Daydreamin'	1975	—	2.50	5.00
❑ 12175	The Captain and the Kid/Cliches	1976	—	2.50	5.00
❑ 12200	Something So Feminine About a Mandolin/Woman Goin' Crazy on Caroline Street	1976	—	2.50	5.00
❑ 12254	Margaritaville/Miss You So Badly	1977	—	2.00	4.00
❑ 12305	Changes in Latitudes, Changes in Attitudes/Landfall	1977	—	2.00	4.00
❑ 12305 [PS]	Changes in Latitudes, Changes in Attitudes/Landfall	1977	—	3.00	6.00
❑ 12358	Cheeseburger in Paradise/African Friend	1978	—	2.00	4.00
❑ 12391	Livingston Saturday Night/Cowboy in the Jungle	1978	—	2.00	4.00
❑ 12428	Manana/The Coast of Marsailles	1978	—	2.00	4.00

ABC DUNHILL

Number	Title (A Side/B Side)	Yr	VG	VG+	NM
❑ 4348	The Great Filling Station Hold Up/Why Don't We Get Drunk	1973	2.00	4.00	8.00
❑ 4353	The Great Filling Station Hold Up/They Can't Dance Like Carmen No More	1973	—	2.00	4.00
❑ 4359	Grapefruit-Juicy Fruit/I Found Me a Home	1973	—	2.00	4.00
❑ 4372	You Went to Paris/Peanut Butter Conspiracy	1973	—	2.00	4.00
❑ 4378	Ringling: Ringling/Saxophones	1974	—	2.00	4.00
❑ 4385	Come Monday/The Wino and I Know	1974	—	2.50	5.00
❑ 15008	Come Monday/The Wino and I Know	1974	—	2.00	4.00
❑ 15011	Brand New Country Star/Pencil Thin Moustache	1974	—	2.00	4.00
❑ 15029	Presents to Send You/A Pirate Looks at Forty	1975	—	2.00	4.00

ASYLUM

Number	Title (A Side/B Side)	Yr	VG	VG+	NM
❑ 69890	I Don't Know (Spicoli's Theme)/She's My Baby (And She's Out of Control)	1982	—	2.00	4.00
—B-side by Palmer & Jost					

BARNABY

Number	Title (A Side/B Side)	Yr	VG	VG+	NM
❑ 2013	The Christian/Richard Frost	1970	2.50	5.00	10.00
❑ 2019	He Ain't Free/There Ain't Nothing Soft About Hard Times	1970	2.50	5.00	10.00
❑ 2023	Captain America/Truckstop Salvation	1970	2.50	5.00	10.00

FULL MOON

Number	Title (A Side/B Side)	Yr	VG	VG+	NM
❑ 49659	Survive/Send Me Somebody to Love	1981	—	2.00	4.00
—B-side by Kathy Walker					

FULL MOON/ASYLUM

Number	Title (A Side/B Side)	Yr	VG	VG+	NM
❑ 47073	Hello Texas/Lyin' Eyes [by the Eagles]	1980	—	2.50	5.00

ISLAND

Number	Title (A Side/B Side)	Yr	VG	VG+	NM
❑ 562144-7	Pacing the Cage/I Will Play for Gumbo	1999	—	—	3.00

MCA

Number	Title (A Side/B Side)	Yr	VG	VG+	NM
❑ S45-17084 [DJ]	Christmas In The Caribbean (same on both sides)	1985	—	2.50	5.00
❑ 41109	Fins/Dreamsicle	1979	—	2.00	4.00
❑ 41161	Volcano/Stranded on a Sandbar	1979	—	2.00	4.00
❑ 41199	Boat Drinks/Survive	1980	—	2.00	4.00
❑ 51061	It's My Job/Little Miss Magic	1981	—	2.00	4.00
❑ 51105	Stars Fell on Alabama/Growing Older But Not Up	1981	—	2.00	4.00
❑ 52013	It's Midnight And I'm Not Famous Yet/When Salome Plays the Drum	1982	—	2.00	4.00
❑ 52050	If I Could Just Get It on Paper/Where's the Party	1982	—	2.00	4.00
❑ 52298	One Particular Harbour/Distantly in Love	1983	—	2.00	4.00
❑ 52333	Brown Eyed Girl/Twelve Volt Man	1984	—	2.00	4.00
❑ 52438	When the Wild Life Betrays Me/Ragtop Day	1984	—	2.00	4.00
❑ 52499	Come to the Moon/Bigger Than the Both of Us	1984	—	2.00	4.00
❑ 52550	Who's the Blond Stranger/She's Going Out of My Mind	1985	—	—	3.00
❑ 52607	Gypies in the Palace/Jolly Mon Sing	1985	—	—	3.00
❑ 52664	If the Phone Doesn't Ring, It's Me/Frank and Lola	1985	—	—	3.00
❑ 52752	Please Bypass This Heart/Beyond the End	1986	—	—	3.00
❑ 52849	I Love the Now/No Plane on Sunday	1986	—	—	3.00
❑ 52932	Creola/You'll Never Work in Dis Bidness Again	1986	—	—	3.00
❑ 53035	Take It Back/Floridays	1987	—	—	3.00
❑ 53360	Homemade Music/L'air de la Louisiane	1988	—	—	3.00
❑ 53396	Bring Back the Magic/That's What Living Is to Me	1988	—	—	3.00
❑ 53675	Take Another Road/Off to See the Lizard	1989	—	—	3.00
❑ 54680	Another Saturday Night/Souvenirs	1993	—	—	3.00

BUG COLLECTORS, THE

CATCH

Number	Title (A Side/B Side)	Yr	VG	VG+	NM
❑ 103	The Beatle Bug/Thief in the Night	1964	5.00	10.00	20.00

BUG MEN, THE

See THE STRING-A-LONGS.

BUGALOOS, THE

CAPITOL

Number	Title (A Side/B Side)	Yr	VG	VG+	NM
❑ 2946	Senses of Our World/For a Friend	1970	3.00	6.00	12.00

BUGGS, THE

SOMA

Number	Title (A Side/B Side)	Yr	VG	VG+	NM
❑ 1413	The Buggs vs. The Beatles/She Loves You	1964	6.25	12.50	25.00

BUGS, THE

ASTOR

Number	Title (A Side/B Side)	Yr	VG	VG+	NM
❑ 001	Albert Albert/Strangler in the Night	1966	3.75	7.50	15.00
❑ 001 [PS]	Albert Albert/Strangler in the Night	1966	3.75	7.50	15.00

HIT

Number	Title (A Side/B Side)	Yr	VG	VG+	NM
❑ 106	She Loves You/Dawn (Go Away)	1964	3.00	6.00	12.00
—B-side by the Chellows					
❑ 111	Twist and Shout/Stay	1964	3.00	6.00	12.00
—B-side by the Chellows					

BUNBURYS, THE

ERIC CLAPTON and THE BEE GEES in disguise.

ARISTA

Number	Title (A Side/B Side)	Yr	VG	VG+	NM
❑ 9760	Fight (No Matter How Long)/(Instrumental)	1988	—	2.00	4.00
❑ 9760 [PS]	Fight (No Matter How Long)/(Instrumental)	1988	—	2.00	4.00

BUOYS, THE

POLYDOR

Number	Title (A Side/B Side)	Yr	VG	VG+	NM
❑ 14201	Liza's Last Ride/Downtown Singer	1973	—	3.00	6.00

SCEPTER

Number	Title (A Side/B Side)	Yr	VG	VG+	NM
❑ 12254	These Days/Don't You Know It's Over	1969	2.00	4.00	8.00
❑ 12275	Timothy/It Feels Good	1970	2.50	5.00	10.00
❑ 12275 [PS]	Timothy/It Feels Good	1970	5.00	10.00	20.00
❑ 12318	Give Up Your Guns/Prince of Thieves	1971	2.00	4.00	8.00
❑ 12331	Tell Me Heaven Is Here/Bloodknot	1971	2.00	4.00	8.00

BURDON, ERIC

Also see THE ANIMALS; ERIC BURDON AND WAR.

CAPITOL

Number	Title (A Side/B Side)	Yr	VG	VG+	NM
❑ 3997	The Real Me/Letter from the County Farm	1974	—	2.50	5.00
❑ 4007	Ring of Fire/The Real Me	1974	—	2.50	5.00

MGM

Number	Title (A Side/B Side)	Yr	VG	VG+	NM
❑ 14296	Headin' for Home/Soledad	1971	—	2.50	5.00
—With Jimmy Witherspoon					

UNITED ARTISTS

Number	Title (A Side/B Side)	Yr	VG	VG+	NM
❑ 50842	Headin' for Home/Soledad	1971	—	—	—
—With Jimmy Witherspoon; assigned to MGM					

BURDON, ERIC, AND THE ANIMALS

See THE ANIMALS.

BURDON, ERIC, AND WAR

Also see ERIC BURDON; WAR.

ABC

Number	Title (A Side/B Side)	Yr	VG	VG+	NM
❑ 12244	Magic Mountain/Home Dream	1977	—	2.50	5.00

MGM

Number	Title (A Side/B Side)	Yr	VG	VG+	NM
❑ 14118	Spill the Wine/Magic Mountain	1970	—	3.00	6.00
❑ 14118 [PS]	Spill the Wine/Magic Mountain	1970	3.00	6.00	12.00
❑ 14196	They Can't Take Away Our Music/Home Cookin'	1970	—	2.50	5.00

BURGESS, DAVE

Also see THE CHAMPS.

CHALLENGE

Number	Title (A Side/B Side)	Yr	VG	VG+	NM
❑ 1001	Don't Cry. For You I Love/Fire in the Eyes	1957	6.25	12.50	25.00
—As "Dave Dupree"					
❑ 1002	Flame of Love/Well, It Isn't Fair	1957	6.25	12.50	25.00
—As "Dave Dupree"					
❑ 1005	A Job Well Done/Our Tomorrow	1957	6.25	12.50	25.00
—As "Dave Dupree"					
❑ 1008	I'm Available/Who's Gonna Cry	1957	6.25	12.50	25.00
❑ 1018	Take This Love/Maybelle	1958	5.00	10.00	20.00
—As "Dave Burgess and the Champs"					
❑ 59032	Lovey Dovey Baby/I Hang My Head and Cry	1958	5.00	10.00	20.00
❑ 59037	I Don't Want to Know/Lulu	1959	5.00	10.00	20.00
❑ 59045	Everlovin'/Just for Me	1959	5.00	10.00	20.00
❑ 59101	Without You/Are You Teasing Me	1961	5.00	10.00	20.00

OKEH

Number	Title (A Side/B Side)	Yr	VG	VG+	NM
❑ 7002	Don't Put a Dent in My Heart/Judalina	1953	6.25	12.50	25.00
❑ 7044	Gratefully Yours/Too Late for Tears	1954	6.25	12.50	25.00

TAMPA

Number	Title (A Side/B Side)	Yr	VG	VG+	NM
❑ 104	Down, Down/Don't Turn Your Back on Love	1955	6.25	12.50	25.00
❑ 105	I Love Paris/Five Foot Two, Eyes of Blue	1955	6.25	12.50	25.00

BURGESS, FRANK

TRUE

Number	Title (A Side/B Side)	Yr	VG	VG+	NM
❑ 94	American Man/(B-side unknown)	1988	—	3.00	6.00
❑ 96	What It Boils Down To/(B-side unknown)	1989	—	3.00	6.00

BURGESS, SONNY

PHILLIPS INT'L.

Number	Title (A Side/B Side)	Yr	VG	VG+	NM
❑ 3551	Sadie's Back in Town/Kiss Goodnight	1960	7.50	15.00	30.00

SUN

Number	Title (A Side/B Side)	Yr	VG	VG+	NM
❑ 247	Red Headed Woman/We Wanna Boogie	1956	37.50	75.00	150.00
❑ 263	Ain't Got a Thing/Restless	1957	20.00	40.00	80.00
❑ 285	My Bucket's Got a Hole in It/Sweet Misery	1958	12.50	25.00	50.00
❑ 304	Thunderbird/Itchy	1958	7.50	15.00	30.00

BURKE, BUDDY

BULLSEYE

Number	Title (A Side/B Side)	Yr	VG	VG+	NM
❑ 1002	That Big Old Moon/Street of Sorrows	195?	37.50	75.00	150.00

BURKE, SOLOMON

ABC DUNHILL

Number	Title (A Side/B Side)	Yr	VG	VG+	NM
❑ 4388	Midnight and You/I Have a Dream	1974	—	2.50	5.00
❑ 15009	Midnight and You/I Have a Dream	1974	—	2.00	4.00

AMHERST

Number	Title (A Side/B Side)	Yr	VG	VG+	NM
❑ 736	Please Don't You Say Goodbye to Me/See That Girl	1978	—	2.00	4.00

APOLLO

Number	Title (A Side/B Side)	Yr	VG	VG+	NM
❑ 485	Christmas Presents/When I'm All Alone	1955	7.50	15.00	30.00
❑ 487	I'm in Love/Why Do Me That Way	1956	6.25	12.50	25.00
❑ 491	I'm All Alone/To Thee	1956	6.25	12.50	25.00
❑ 500	No Man Walks Alone/Walking in a Dream	1956	6.25	12.50	25.00
❑ 505	A Picture of You/You Can Run But You Can't Hide	1957	6.25	12.50	25.00
❑ 511	I Need You Tonight/This Is It	1957	6.25	12.50	25.00
❑ 512	For You and You Alone/You Are My One Love	1957	6.25	12.50	25.00
❑ 522	They Always Say/Don't Cry	1958	6.25	12.50	25.00

Number	Title (A Side/B Side)	Yr	VG	VG+	NM
❑ 527	My Heart Is a Chapel/This Is It	1958	6.25	12.50	25.00
ATLANTIC					
❑ 2089	Keep the Magic Working/How Many Times	1961	5.00	10.00	20.00
❑ 2114	Just Out of Reach (Of My Two Open Arms)/Be-Bop Grandma	1961	5.00	10.00	20.00
❑ 2131	Cry to Me/I Almost Lost My Mind	1962	5.00	10.00	20.00
❑ 2147	Down in the Valley/I'm Hanging Up My Heart for You	1962	3.75	7.50	15.00
❑ 2157	I Really Don't Want to Know/Tonight My Heart She Is Crying (Love Is a Bird)	1962	3.75	7.50	15.00
❑ 2170	Go On Back to Him/I Said I Was Sorry	1962	3.75	7.50	15.00
❑ 2180	Words/Home in Your Heart	1963	3.75	7.50	15.00
❑ 2185	If You Need Me/You Can Make It If You Try	1963	3.75	7.50	15.00
❑ 2196	Can't Nobody Love You/Stupidity	1963	3.75	7.50	15.00
❑ 2205	You're Good for Me/Beautiful Brown Eyes	1963	3.75	7.50	15.00
❑ 2218	He'll Have to Go/Rockin' Soul	1964	3.75	7.50	15.00
❑ 2226	Goodbye Baby (Baby Goodbye)/Someone to Love Me	1964	3.75	7.50	15.00
❑ 2241	Everybody Needs Somebody to Love/Looking for My Baby	1964	3.75	7.50	15.00
❑ 2254	Yes I Do/Won't You Give Him (One More Chance)	1964	3.75	7.50	15.00
❑ 2259	The Price/More Rockin' Soul	1964	3.75	7.50	15.00
❑ 2276	Got to Get You Off My Mind/Peepin'	1965	3.75	7.50	15.00
❑ 2288	Tonight's the Night/Maggie's Farm	1965	3.75	7.50	15.00
❑ 2299	Someone Is Watching/Dance, Dance, Dance	1965	3.00	6.00	12.00
❑ 2308	Only Love (Can Save Me Now)/A Little Girl That Loves Me	1965	3.00	6.00	12.00
❑ 2314	Baby Come On Home/(No, No, No) Can't Stop Lovin' You Now	1965	3.00	6.00	12.00
❑ 2327	I Feel a Sin Coming On/Mountain of Pride	1966	2.50	5.00	10.00
❑ 2345	Lawdy Miss Clawdy/Suddenly	1966	2.50	5.00	10.00
❑ 2349	Keep Looking/Don't Want You No More	1966	2.50	5.00	10.00
❑ 2359	When She Touches Me/Woman How Do You Make Me Love You Like I Do	1966	2.50	5.00	10.00
❑ 2369	Presents for Christmas/A Tear Fell	1966	3.00	6.00	12.00
❑ 2378	Keep a Light in the Window Till I Come Home/Time Is a Thief	1967	2.50	5.00	10.00
❑ 2416	Take Me (Just As I Am)/Stayed Away Too Long	1967	2.50	5.00	10.00
❑ 2459	It's Been a Change/Detroit City	1967	2.50	5.00	10.00
❑ 2483	Party People/Need Your Love So Bad	1968	2.50	5.00	10.00
❑ 2507	I Wish I Knew (How It Would Feel to Be Free)/It's Just a Matter of Time Baby	1968	2.50	5.00	10.00
❑ 2527	Save it/Meet Me in Church	1968	2.50	5.00	10.00
❑ 2566	Get Out of My Life Woman/What'd I Say	1968	2.50	5.00	10.00
BELL					
❑ 759	Up Tight Good Woman/I Can't Stop	1969	2.00	4.00	8.00
❑ 783	Proud Mary/What Am I Living For	1969	2.00	4.00	8.00
❑ 806	That Lucky Old Sun/How Big a Fool	1969	2.00	4.00	8.00
❑ 829	I'm Gonna Stay Right Here/Generation of Revelations	1969	2.00	4.00	8.00
❑ 891	God Knows I Love You/In the Ghetto	1970	—	3.00	6.00
CHESS					
❑ 2159	You and Your Baby Blues/I'm Leaving on That Late, Late Train	1975	—	2.00	4.00
❑ 2172	Let Me Wrap My Arms Around You/Everlasting Love	1975	—	2.00	4.00
INFINITY					
❑ 50046	Sidewalks, Fences and Walls/Boo-Hoo-Hoo (Cra-Cra-Craya)	1979	—	2.50	5.00
MALA					
❑ 420	This Little Ring/I'm Not Afraid	1960	5.00	10.00	20.00
MCI					
❑ 712842	You're All I Want For Christmas/No Place Like Home	19??	2.00	4.00	8.00
—B-side by Rayne					
MGM					
❑ 14185	Lookin' Out My Back Door/All for the Love of Sunshine	1970	—	3.00	6.00
❑ 14221	The Electronic Magnetism (That's Heavy, Baby)/Bridge of Life	1971	—	3.00	6.00
❑ 14279	J.C. I Know Who You Are/The Things Love Will Make You Do	1971	—	3.00	6.00
❑ 14302	The Night They Drove Old Dixie Down/PSR 1983	1971	—	3.00	6.00
❑ 14353	Love's Street and Fool's Road/I Got to Tell It	1972	—	3.00	6.00
❑ 14402	We're Almost Home/Fight Back	1972	—	3.00	6.00
❑ 14425	Get Up and Do Something for Yourself/We're Almost Home	1972	—	3.00	6.00
❑ 14571	Shambala/Love Thy Neighbor	1973	—	3.00	6.00
❑ 14651	Georgia Up North/Here Comes the Train	1973	—	3.00	6.00
POINTBLANK					
❑ S7-19520	Ooooooyou/Today Is Your Birthday	1997	—	2.00	4.00
PRIDE					
❑ 1017	I Can't Stop Loving You (Part 1)/I Can't Stop Loving You (Part 2)	1972	—	3.00	6.00
❑ 1022	All I Want for Christmas/I Can't Stop Loving You (Part 1)	1972	—	3.00	6.00
❑ 1028	My Prayer/Ookie Bookie Man	1973	—	3.00	6.00
❑ 1038	Sentimental Journey/Vaya Con Dios	1973	—	3.00	6.00
—With Lady Lee					

BURLAND, SASCHA & THE SKIPJACK CHOIR

Number	Title (A Side/B Side)	Yr	VG	VG+	NM
COLUMBIA					
❑ 42009	Gorilla Walk/Hole in My Soul	1960	5.00	10.00	20.00
RCA VICTOR					
❑ 47-8277	Have Yourself a Merry Little Christmas/The Chickens Are in the Chimes	1963	7.50	15.00	30.00
❑ 47-8277 [PS]	Have Yourself a Merry Little Christmas/The Chickens Are in the Chimes	1963	10.00	20.00	40.00

BURNETT, FRANCES

Number	Title (A Side/B Side)	Yr	VG	VG+	NM
CORAL					
❑ 62092	Come to Me/So Many Tears	1959	25.00	50.00	100.00
❑ 62127	Please Remember Me/How I Miss You So	1959	25.00	50.00	100.00
❑ 62164	I Love Him So/Too Proud	1960	25.00	50.00	100.00
❑ 62214	She Was Taking My Baby/Sweetie	1960	25.00	50.00	100.00
DECCA					
❑ 30571	Spin the Wheel/A Promise Made a Fool of Me	1958	30.00	60.00	120.00

BURNETTE, BILLY

Also see FLEETWOOD MAC.

Number	Title (A Side/B Side)	Yr	VG	VG+	NM
A&M					
❑ 743	Just Because We're Kids/Little Girl, Big Love	1964	6.25	12.50	25.00
—As "Young Billy Bean"; A-side written by Dr. Seuss!					
❑ 1794	Baby/Just Another Love Song	1976	—	2.50	5.00
CAPRICORN					
❑ 18525	I Still Remember (How to Miss You)/I Recovered, I Survived	1993	—	—	3.00
❑ 18751	Tangled Up in Texas/Into the Storm	1992	—	—	3.00
COLUMBIA					
❑ 02527	Let the New Love Begin/I Don't Know Why	1981	—	2.00	4.00
❑ 02699	The Bigger the Love/I Don't Know Why	1982	—	2.00	4.00
❑ 11380	Don't Say No/Rockin' L.A.	1980	—	2.00	4.00
❑ 11432	Oh Susan/Sittin' On Ready	1981	—	2.00	4.00
ENTRANCE					
❑ 7515	Broken Hearted/I'm Always Wondering	1972	—	2.50	5.00
MCA CURB					
❑ 52626	Ain't It Just Like Love/Guitar Bug	1985	—	—	3.00
❑ 52710	Who's Using Your Heart Tonight/It Ain't Over	1985	—	—	3.00
❑ 52749	It's Not Easy/Try Me	1985	—	—	3.00
❑ 52852	Soldier of Love/Guitar Bug	1986	—	—	3.00
POLYDOR					
❑ 2024	What's a Little Love Between Friends/Precious Times	1979	—	2.00	4.00
❑ 14530	Dreamin' My Way Back to You/Shoo-Be-Doo	1979	—	2.00	4.00
❑ 14549	Believe What You Say/Mississippi Line	1979	—	2.00	4.00
WARNER BROS.					
❑ 7327	Frog Prince/One Extreme to the Other	1969	2.00	4.00	8.00
❑ 19042	Nothin' to Do (And All Night to Do It)/Can't Get Over You	1992	—	—	3.00

BURNETTE, DORSEY

Also see DORSEY AND JOHNNY BURNETTE.

Number	Title (A Side/B Side)	Yr	VG	VG+	NM
ABBOTT					
❑ 188	Let's Fall in Love/The Devil's Queen	1956	12.50	25.00	50.00
❑ 190	At a Distance/Jungle Magic	1957	12.50	25.00	50.00
CALLIOPE					
❑ 8004	Things I Treasure/One Mornin'	1977	—	3.00	6.00
❑ 8012	Soon As I Touched Her/Dear Hearted Children	1977	—	3.00	6.00
CAPITOL					
❑ 3073	New Orleans Woman/After the Long Drive Home	1971	—	2.50	5.00
❑ 3190	Shelby County Penal Farm/Children of the Universe	1971	—	2.50	5.00
❑ 3307	In the Spring (The Roses Always Turn Red)/The Same Old You, The Same Old Me	1972	—	2.50	5.00
❑ 3404	I Just Couldn't Let Her Walk Away/Church Bells	1972	—	2.50	5.00
❑ 3463	Cry Mama/Lonely to Be Alone	1972	—	2.50	5.00
❑ 3529	I Let Another Good One Get Away/Take Your Weapons, Lay 'Em Down	1973	—	2.50	5.00
❑ 3588	Keep Out of My Dreams/Mama, Mama	1973	—	2.50	5.00
❑ 3678	Darlin' (Don't Come Back)/Sweet Lovin' Woman	1973	—	2.50	5.00
❑ 3796	It Happens Every Time/Mr. Jukebox, Sing a Lullaby	1973	—	2.50	5.00
❑ 3829	Bob, All the Playboys, and Me/The Bootleggers	1974	—	2.50	5.00
❑ 3887	Daddy Loves You Honey/True Love Means Forgiving	1974	—	2.50	5.00
❑ 3963	What Ladies Can Do (When They Want To)/Tangerine	1974	—	2.50	5.00
CEE-JAM					
❑ 16	Bertha Lou/'Til the Law Says Stop	1957	20.00	40.00	80.00
DOT					
❑ 16230	Rainin' in My Heart/A Full House	1961	4.00	8.00	16.00
❑ 16265	The Feminine Touch/Sad Boy	1961	4.00	8.00	16.00
❑ 16305	A Country Boy in the Army/A Dying Ember	1961	4.00	8.00	16.00
ELEKTRA					
❑ 46513	Here I Go Again/What Would It Profit Me	1979	—	2.00	4.00
❑ 46586	B.J. Kick-a-Beaux/What Would It Profit Me	1980	—	2.00	4.00
ERA					
❑ 3012	(There Was a)Tall Oak Tree/Juarez Town	1960	5.00	10.00	20.00
❑ 3019	Hey Little One/Big Rock Candy Mountain	1960	4.00	8.00	16.00
❑ 3025	The Ghost of Billy Malloo/Red Roses	1960	4.00	8.00	16.00
❑ 3033	The River and the Mountain/This Hotel	1960	4.00	8.00	16.00
❑ 3033 [PS]	The River and the Mountain/This Hotel	1960	10.00	20.00	40.00
❑ 3041	Hard Rock Mine/(It's No) Sin	1961	4.00	8.00	16.00
❑ 3045	Great Shakin' Fever/That's Me Without You	1961	4.00	8.00	16.00
HAPPY TIGER					
❑ 546	To Be a Man/Fly Away and Hurry Home	1970	—	3.00	6.00
❑ 563	One Lump Sum/Call Me Lowdown	1970	—	3.00	6.00
HICKORY					
❑ 1458	The House That Jack Built/Ain't That Fine	1967	2.00	4.00	8.00
IMPERIAL					
❑ 5561	Try/You Came as a Miracle	1959	6.25	12.50	25.00
❑ 5597	Lonely Train/Misery	1959	6.25	12.50	25.00
❑ 5668	Way in the Middle of the Night/Your Love	1960	6.25	12.50	25.00
❑ 5756	House with a Tin Roof Top/Circle Rock	1961	6.25	12.50	25.00
❑ 5987	House with a Tin Roof Top/Circle Rock	1963	3.75	7.50	15.00
LIBERTY					
❑ 56087	The Greatest Love/Thin Little Simple Little Plain Little Girl	1969	—	3.00	6.00
MEL-O-DY					
❑ 113	Little Acorn/Cold As Usual	1964	3.75	7.50	15.00
❑ 116	Jimmy Brown/Everybody's Angel	1964	3.75	7.50	15.00
❑ 118	Long Long Time Ago/Ever Since the World Began	1964	3.75	7.50	15.00

Number	Title (A Side/B Side)	Yr	VG	VG+	NM
MELODYLAND					
❑ 6007	Molly (I Ain't Gettin' Any Younger)/She's Feeling Low	1975	—	2.50	5.00
❑ 6019	Lyin' in Her Arms Again/Doggone the Dogs	1975	—	2.50	5.00
❑ 6031	Ain't No Heartbreak/I Dreamed I Saw	1976	—	2.50	5.00
MERCURY					
❑ 72546	To Remember/In the Morning	1966	—	—	—
—Unreleased?					
MUSIC FACTORY					
❑ 417	I'll Walk Away/Son, You've Got to Make It Alone	1968	2.00	4.00	8.00
REPRISE					
❑ 0246	Four for Texas/Foolish Pride	1963	3.75	7.50	15.00
❑ 0246 [PS]	Four for Texas/Foolish Pride	1963	10.00	20.00	40.00
❑ 20093	Castle in the Sky/Boys Keep Hanging Around	1962	3.75	7.50	15.00
❑ 20121	Darling Jane/I'm a Waitin' For Ya Baby	1962	3.75	7.50	15.00
❑ 20177	Invisible Chains/Pebbles	1963	3.75	7.50	15.00
❑ 20208	One of the Lonely/Where's the Girl	1963	3.75	7.50	15.00
SMASH					
❑ 2029	To Remember/In the Morning	1966	2.50	5.00	10.00
❑ 2039	If You Want to Love Somebody/Teach Me Little Children	1966	2.50	5.00	10.00
❑ 2062	Tall Oak Tree/I Just Can't Be Tamed	1966	2.50	5.00	10.00
U.S. NAVY					
❑ (# unknown)	Be a Navy Man	196?	10.00	20.00	40.00
❑ (# unknown) [PS]	Be a Navy Man	196?	5.00	10.00	20.00

BURNETTE, DORSEY AND JOHNNY

Also see each artist's individual listings.

Number	Title (A Side/B Side)	Yr	VG	VG+	NM
CORAL					
❑ 62190	Blues Stay Away from Me/Midnight Train	1960	50.00	100.00	200.00
—As "Johnny and Dorsey Burnette"					
IMPERIAL					
❑ 5509	Warm Love/My Honey	1958	25.00	50.00	100.00
—As "Burnette Brothers"					
REPRISE					
❑ 20153	It Don't Take Much/Hey Sue	1963	5.00	10.00	20.00

BURNETTE, JOHNNY

Includes the Rock 'N' Roll Trio. Also see DORSEY AND JOHNNY BURNETTE.

Number	Title (A Side/B Side)	Yr	VG	VG+	NM
CAPITOL					
❑ 5023	All Week Long/It Isn't There	1963	3.75	7.50	15.00
❑ 5114	You Taught Me the Way to Love You/The Opposite	1964	3.75	7.50	15.00
❑ 5176	Walkin' Talkin' Doll/Sweet Suzie	1964	3.75	7.50	15.00
CHANCELLOR					
❑ 1116	I Wanna Thank Your Folks/The Giant	1962	3.75	7.50	15.00
❑ 1123	Party Girl/Tag Along	1962	3.75	7.50	15.00
❑ 1129	Remember Me/Time Is Not Enough	1962	3.75	7.50	15.00
CORAL					
❑ 61651	Tear It Up/You're Undecided	1956	75.00	150.00	300.00
❑ 61675	Midnight Train/Oh Baby Babe	1956	75.00	150.00	300.00
❑ 61719	The Train Kept a-Rollin'/Honey Hush	1956	62.50	125.00	250.00
❑ 61758	Lonesome Train/I Just Found Out	1956	75.00	150.00	300.00
❑ 61829	Eager Beaver Baby/Touch Me	1957	75.00	150.00	300.00
❑ 61869	Drinkin' Wine Spo-Dee-O-Dee/Butterfingers	1957	75.00	150.00	300.00
❑ 61918	Rock Billy Boogie/If You Want It Enough	1957	75.00	150.00	300.00
FREEDOM					
❑ 44001	I'm Restless/Kiss Me	1958	20.00	40.00	80.00
❑ 44011	Gumbo/Me and the Bear	1959	20.00	40.00	80.00
❑ 44017	Sweet Baby Doll/I'll Never Love Again	1959	20.00	40.00	80.00
LIBERTY					
❑ 55222	Settin' the Woods on Fire/Kentucky Waltz	1959	5.00	10.00	20.00
❑ 55243	Don't Do It/Patrick Henry	1959	5.00	10.00	20.00
❑ 55258	Dreamin'/Cincinnati Fireball	1960	5.00	10.00	20.00
❑ 55285	You're Sixteen/I Beg Your Pardon	1960	5.00	10.00	20.00
❑ 55285 [PS]	You're Sixteen/I Beg Your Pardon	1960	12.50	25.00	50.00
❑ 55298	Little Boy Sad/(I Go) Down to the River	1961	3.75	7.50	15.00
❑ 55298 [PS]	Little Boy Sad/(I Go) Down to the River	1961	10.00	20.00	40.00
❑ 55318	Big Big World/Ballad of the One Eyed Jacks	1961	3.75	7.50	15.00
❑ 55318 [PS]	Big Big World/Ballad of the One Eyed Jacks	1961	10.00	20.00	40.00
❑ 55345	Girls/I've Got a Lot of Things to Do	1961	3.75	7.50	15.00
❑ 55377	Honestly I Do/Fools Like Me	1961	3.75	7.50	15.00
❑ 55379	God, Country and My Baby/Honestly I Do	1961	3.75	7.50	15.00
❑ 55416	Clown Shoes/The Way I Am	1962	3.75	7.50	15.00
❑ 55448	The Fool of the Year/The Poorest Boy in Town	1962	3.75	7.50	15.00
❑ 55489	Damn the Defiant/Lonesome Waters	1962	3.75	7.50	15.00
MAGIC LAMP					
❑ 515	Bigger Man/Less Than a Heartache	1964	12.50	25.00	50.00
❑ 515 [PS]	Bigger Man/Less Than a Heartache	1964	75.00	150.00	300.00
SAHARA					
❑ 512	Fountain of Love/What a Summer Day	1964	3.75	7.50	15.00
UNITED ARTISTS					
❑ 0018	Dreamin'/Little Boy Sad	1973	—	2.00	4.00
—Silver Spotlight Series issue					
❑ 0019	You're Sixteen/God, Country and My Baby	1973	—	2.00	4.00
—Silver Spotlight Series issue					
VON					
❑ 1006	You're Undecided/Go, Mule, Go	1954	1500.	2250.	3000.

7-Inch Extended Plays

Number	Title (A Side/B Side)	Yr	VG	VG+	NM
LIBERTY					
❑ LSX-1004	(contents unknown)	1960	25.00	50.00	100.00
❑ LSX-1004 [PS]	Dreamin'	1960	37.50	75.00	150.00
❑ LSX-1011	Little Boy Sad/Don't Do It//You're Sixteen/I Go Down to the River	1961	25.00	50.00	100.00
❑ LSX-1011 [PS]	Johnny Burnette's Hits	1961	37.50	75.00	150.00

BURNETTE, ROCKY

Number	Title (A Side/B Side)	Yr	VG	VG+	NM
EMI AMERICA					
❑ 8043	Tired of Toein' the Line/Boogie Down in Mobile, Alabama	1980	—	2.50	5.00
❑ 8050	Baby Tonight/Because of You	1980	—	2.00	4.00
❑ 8060	Fallin' in Love (Bein' Friends)/Roll Like a Wheel	1980	—	2.00	4.00

BURNETTE BROTHERS

See DORSEY AND JOHNNY BURNETTE.

BURNS, EDDIE

Number	Title (A Side/B Side)	Yr	VG	VG+	NM
CHECKER					
❑ 790	Biscuit Baking Mama/Superstition	1954	75.00	150.00	300.00
—As "Big Ed and His Combo"					
CHESS					
❑ 1672	Treat Me Like I Treat You/Don't Cha Leave Me Baby	1957	10.00	20.00	40.00
DELUXE					
❑ 6024	Hello Miss Jessie Lee/Dealing with the Devil	1953	50.00	100.00	200.00
HARVEY					
❑ 111	Orange Driver/Hard Hearted Woman	1962	25.00	50.00	100.00
❑ 115	The Thing to Do/Mean and Evil (Baby)	1962	7.50	15.00	30.00
❑ 118	Orange Driver/Messin' with My Bread	1962	7.50	15.00	30.00
JVB					
❑ 82	Treat Me Like I Treat You/Don't Cha Leave Me Baby	1957	25.00	50.00	100.00

BURRITO BROTHERS, THE

See THE FLYING BURRITO BROTHERS.

BURTON, JAMES

Number	Title (A Side/B Side)	Yr	VG	VG+	NM
PHILIPS					
❑ 40137	Swamp Surfer/Everybody Listen to the Dobro	1963	10.00	20.00	40.00
—As "Jimmy Dobro"					

BUSH, KATE

Number	Title (A Side/B Side)	Yr	VG	VG+	NM
EMI AMERICA					
❑ 8003	Wuthering Heights/Kite	1978	—	3.00	6.00
❑ 8003 [PS]	Wuthering Heights/Kite	1978	2.50	5.00	10.00
❑ 8006	The Man with the Child in His Eyes/Moving	1978	—	3.00	6.00
❑ 8285	Running Up That Hill/Under the Ivy	1985	—	2.00	4.00
❑ 8285 [PS]	Running Up That Hill/Under the Ivy	1985	—	2.50	5.00
❑ 8302	Hounds of Love/Burning Bridge	1985	—	2.00	4.00
❑ 8302 [PS]	Hounds of Love/Burning Bridge	1985	—	2.50	5.00
❑ 8327	The Big Sky/Not This Time	1986	—	2.00	4.00
❑ 8327 [PS]	The Big Sky/Not This Time	1986	—	2.50	5.00
❑ 8363	Experiment IV/Wuthering Heights (New Vocal)	1986	—	2.00	4.00
❑ 8363 [PS]	Experiment IV/Wuthering Heights (New Vocal)	1986	—	2.50	5.00
❑ 8386	Cloudbursting/The Man with the Child in His Eyes	1986	—	2.50	5.00
❑ 8386 [PS]	Cloudbursting/The Man with the Child in His Eyes	1986	—	3.00	6.00

BUSTERS, THE

Number	Title (A Side/B Side)	Yr	VG	VG+	NM
ARLEN					
❑ 735	Bust Out/Astronaut's	1963	5.00	10.00	20.00
❑ 740	All American Surfer/Pine Tree Hop	1963	5.00	10.00	20.00
❑ 745	Heartaches/Torrid Zone	1964	5.00	10.00	20.00
UNITED ARTISTS					
❑ 0145	Bust Out/The Green Mosquito	1973	—	2.50	5.00
—Silver Spotlight Series issue; B-side by the Tune Rockers					

BUTLER, JERRY

Also see GENE CHANDLER; BETTY EVERETT; THE IMPRESSIONS.

Number	Title (A Side/B Side)	Yr	VG	VG+	NM
ABNER					
❑ 1024	Lost/One by One	1959	7.50	15.00	30.00
❑ 1028	Hold Me Darling/Rainbow Valley	1959	7.50	15.00	30.00
❑ 1030	I Was Wrong/Couldn't Go to Sleep	1959	7.50	15.00	30.00
❑ 1035	A Lonely Soldier/I Found a Love	1960	7.50	15.00	30.00
FOUNTAIN					
❑ 400	No Love Without Changes/All the Way	1982	—	3.00	6.00
ICHIBAN					
❑ 269	Angel Flying Too Close to the Ground/You're the Only One	1992	—	—	3.00
❑ 290	Need to Belong/Sure Feels Good	1993	—	—	3.00
MCA					
❑ 52177	Let's Talk It Over/Especially You	1983	—	2.00	4.00
—With Stix Hooper; B-side by Stix Hooper solo					
MERCURY					
❑ 72592	Love (Oh How Sweet It Is)/Loneliness	1966	2.50	5.00	10.00
❑ 72625	You Make Me Feel Like Someone/For What You Made of Me	1966	2.50	5.00	10.00
❑ 72648	I Dig You Baby/Some Kinda Magic	1966	2.50	5.00	10.00
❑ 72676	Why Do I Lose You/You Walked Into My Life	1967	2.50	5.00	10.00
❑ 72698	You Don't Know What You've Got Until You Lose It/The Way I Love You	1967	2.50	5.00	10.00
❑ 72721	Mr. Dream Merchant/'Cause I Love You So	1967	2.50	5.00	10.00
❑ 72764	Lost/You Don't Know What You've Got Until You Lose It	1968	2.00	4.00	8.00
❑ 72798	Never Give You Up/Beside You	1968	2.00	4.00	8.00
❑ 72850	Hey, Western Union Man/Just Can't Forget About You	1968	2.00	4.00	8.00
❑ 72876	Are You Happy/I Still Love You	1968	2.00	4.00	8.00
❑ 72898	Only the Strong Survive/Just Because I Really Love You	1969	2.00	4.00	8.00
❑ 72929	Moody Woman/Go Away — Find Yourself	1969	2.00	4.00	8.00
❑ 72960	What's the Use of Breaking Up/Brand New Me	1969	2.00	4.00	8.00
❑ 72991	Don't Let Love Hang You Up/Walking Around in Teardrops	1969	2.00	4.00	8.00
❑ 73015	Got to See If I Can't Get Mommy (To Come Back Home)/I Forgot to Remember	1970	2.00	4.00	8.00
❑ 73045	I Could Write a Book/Since I Lost You, Baby	1970	2.00	4.00	8.00
❑ 73101	Where Are You Going/You Can Fly	1970	2.00	4.00	8.00
❑ 73131	How Does It Feel/Special Memory	1970	2.00	4.00	8.00
❑ 73169	If It's Real What I Feel/Why Are You Leaving Me	1971	—	3.00	6.00
❑ 73210	How Did We Lose It baby/Do You Finally Need a Friend	1971	—	3.00	6.00
❑ 73241	Walk Easy My Son/Let Me Be	1971	—	3.00	6.00
❑ 73290	I Only Have Eyes for You/A Prayer	1972	—	3.00	6.00

Number	Title (A Side/B Side)	Yr	VG	VG+	NM
❑ 73335	One Night Affair/Life's Unfortunate Song	1972	—	3.00	6.00
❑ 73443	Power of Love/What Do You Do on a Sunday Afternoon	1973	—	3.00	6.00
❑ 73459	That's How Heartaches Are Made/Too Many Danger Signs	1974	—	3.00	6.00
❑ 73495	Take the Time to Tell Her/High Stepper	1974	—	3.00	6.00
❑ 73629	You and Me Against the World/Playing on You	1974	—	3.00	6.00
❑ 872914-7	Only the Strong Survive/Lost	1989	—	—	3.00
—Reissue					
❑ 872916-7	Never Give You Up/Hey, Western Union Man	1989	—	—	3.00
—Reissue					
MISTLETOE					
❑ 803	Silent Night/O Holy Night	1974	—	2.50	5.00
MOTOWN					
❑ 1403	The Devil in Mrs. Jones/Don't Wanna Be Reminded	1976	—	2.50	5.00
❑ 1403 [PS]	The Devil in Mrs. Jones/Don't Wanna Be Reminded	1976	2.50	5.00	10.00
❑ 1414	I Wanna Do It to You/I Don't Wanna Be Reminded	1977	—	2.50	5.00
❑ 1421	Chalk It Up/I Don't Want Nobody to Know	1977	—	2.50	5.00
❑ 1422	It's a Lifetime Thing/Kiss Me Now	1977	—	2.50	5.00
—With Thelma Houston					
PHILADELPHIA INT'L					
❑ 3113	Don't Be Ashamed/Best Love I Ever Had	1980	—	2.00	4.00
❑ 3117	Tell Me Girl (Why It Has to End)/We've Got This Feeling Again	1980	—	2.00	4.00
❑ 3656	(I'm Just Thinking About) Cooling Out/Are You Lonely Tonight	1978	—	2.00	4.00
❑ 3664	(I'm Just Thinking About) Cooling Out/Are You Lonely Tonight	1978	—	2.00	4.00
❑ 3673	I'm Glad to Be Back/Nothing Says I Love You Like I Love You	1979	—	2.00	4.00
❑ 3683	Let's Make Love/Dream World	1979	—	2.00	4.00
VEE JAY					
❑ 354	He Will Break Your Heart/Thanks to You	1960	5.00	10.00	20.00
❑ 371	Silent Night/O Holy Night	1960	5.00	10.00	20.00
❑ 375	Find Another Girl/When Trouble Calls	1961	3.75	7.50	15.00
❑ 390	I See a Fool/I'm a Telling You	1961	3.75	7.50	15.00
❑ 396	For Your Precious Love/Sweet Was the Wine	1961	3.75	7.50	15.00
❑ 405	Moon River/Aware of Love	1961	3.75	7.50	15.00
❑ 426	Isle of Sirens/Chi Town	1962	3.75	7.50	15.00
❑ 451	Make It Easy on Yourself/It's Too Late	1962	3.75	7.50	15.00
❑ 463	You Can Run/I'm the One	1962	3.75	7.50	15.00
❑ 475	Theme from Taras Bulba (Wishing Star)/You Go Right Through Me	1963	3.00	6.00	12.00
❑ 475 [PS]	Theme from Taras Bulba (Wishing Star)/You Go Right Through Me	1963	10.00	20.00	40.00
❑ 486	You Won't Be Sorry/Whatever You Want	1963	3.00	6.00	12.00
❑ 526	Strawberries/I Almost Lost My Head	1963	3.00	6.00	12.00
❑ 534	Where's the Girl?/How Beautifully You Lie	1963	3.00	6.00	12.00
❑ 556	Just a Little Bit/A Woman with Soul	1963	3.00	6.00	12.00
❑ 567	Need to Belong/Give Me Your Love	1963	3.00	6.00	12.00
❑ 588	Giving Up on Love/I've Been Trying	1964	3.00	6.00	12.00
❑ 598	I Stand Accused/I Don't Want to Hear Anymore	1964	3.00	6.00	12.00
❑ 598 [PS]	I Stand Accused/I Don't Want to Hear Anymore	1964	7.50	15.00	30.00
❑ 651	Good Times/I've Grown Accustomed to Her Face	1965	3.00	6.00	12.00
❑ 696	I Can't Stand to See You Cry/Nobody Needs Your Love	1965	3.00	6.00	12.00
❑ 707	Believe in Me/Just for You	1965	3.00	6.00	12.00
❑ 711	Moon River/Make It Easy on Yourself	1966	3.00	6.00	12.00
❑ 715	For Your Precious Love/Give It Up	1966	3.00	6.00	12.00

BUTLER, JERRY, AND BRENDA LEE EAGER

Also see each artist's individual listings.

Number	Title (A Side/B Side)	Yr	VG	VG+	NM
MERCURY					
❑ 73255	Ain't Understading Mellow/Windy City Soul	1971	—	3.00	6.00
❑ 73301	(They Long to Be) Close to You/You Can't Always Tell	1972	—	3.00	6.00
❑ 73395	Can't Understand It/How Long Will It Last	1973	—	3.00	6.00
❑ 73422	We Were Lovers, We Were Friends/The Love We Had Stays On My Mind	1973	—	3.00	6.00

BUTLER, JERRY, AND THE IMPRESSIONS

See THE IMPRESSIONS.

BUTLER, JIMMY

Number	Title (A Side/B Side)	Yr	VG	VG+	NM
GEM					
❑ 222	Trim Your Tree/Cruelty For Kindness	1954	12.50	25.00	50.00

BUTTERFLYS, THE

ELLIE GREENWICH as a girl group.

Number	Title (A Side/B Side)	Yr	VG	VG+	NM
RED BIRD					
❑ 10-009	Goodnight Baby/The Swim	1964	6.25	12.50	25.00
❑ 10-016	I Wonder/Gee, Baby, Gee	1964	6.25	12.50	25.00

BUTTS BAND

With Robbie Krieger and John Densmore of THE DOORS.

Number	Title (A Side/B Side)	Yr	VG	VG+	NM
BLUE THUMB					
❑ 242	Pop a Top/Baja Bus	1973	2.00	4.00	8.00
❑ 252	I Won't Be Alone Anymore/Kansas City	1974	2.00	4.00	8.00
❑ 263	Get Up, Stand Up/Mike's Blues	1975	2.00	4.00	8.00

BYRD, CURTIS

Number	Title (A Side/B Side)	Yr	VG	VG+	NM
CANDIX					
❑ 340	Pretty Woman/Turn Some More Lights On	1962	6.25	12.50	25.00

BYRDS, THE

Also see SKIP BATTIN; THE BEEFEATERS; GENE CLARK; DAVID CROSBY; ROGER McGUINN; GRAM PARSONS.

Number	Title (A Side/B Side)	Yr	VG	VG+	NM
ASYLUM					
❑ 11016	Full Circle/Long Live the King	1973	—	2.50	5.00
❑ 11019	Cowgirl in the Sand/Long Live the King	1973	—	2.50	5.00
COLUMBIA					
❑ 43271	Mr. Tambourine Man/I Knew I'd Want You	1965	3.75	7.50	15.00
❑ 43271 [DJ]	Mr. Tambourine Man (same on both sides)	1965	37.50	75.00	150.00
—Red vinyl promo					
❑ 43271 [PS]	Mr. Tambourine Man	1965	75.00	150.00	300.00
—Promo-only sleeve promoting the Byrds' appeance on the TV show Hullabaloo					
❑ 43332	All I Really Want to Do/I'll Feel a Whole Lot Better	1965	3.75	7.50	15.00
❑ 43332 [DJ]	All I Really Want to Do (same on both sides)	1965	25.00	50.00	100.00
—Red vinyl promo					
❑ 43332 [DJ]	I'll Feel a Whole Lot Better (same on both sides)	1965	30.00	60.00	120.00
—Red vinyl promo					
❑ 43424	Turn! Turn! Turn! (To Everything There Is a Season)/She Don't Care About Time	1965	3.75	7.50	15.00
❑ 43424 [DJ]	Turn! Turn! Turn! (To Everything There Is a Season) (same on both sides)	1965	25.00	50.00	100.00
—Red vinyl promo					
❑ 43501	It Won't Be Wrong/Set You Free This Time	1965	3.00	6.00	12.00
❑ 43578	Eight Miles High/Why	1966	3.00	6.00	12.00
❑ 43578 [PS]	Eight Miles High/Why	1966	15.00	30.00	60.00
❑ 43702	5 D (Fifth Dimension)/Captain Soul	1966	3.00	6.00	12.00
❑ 43766	Mr. Spaceman/What's Happening	1966	3.00	6.00	12.00
❑ 43987	So You Want to Be a Rock 'N' Roll Star/Everybody's Been Burned	1967	3.00	6.00	12.00
❑ 44054	My Back Pages/Renaissance Fair	1967	3.00	6.00	12.00
❑ 44157	Have You Seen Her Face/Don't Make Waves	1967	2.50	5.00	10.00
❑ 44157 [PS]	Have You Seen Her Face/Don't Make Waves	1967	10.00	20.00	40.00
❑ 44230	Lady Friend/Old John Robertson	1967	2.50	5.00	10.00
❑ 44362	Goin' Back/Change Is Now	1967	2.00	4.00	8.00
❑ 44499	Artificial Energy/You Ain't Going Nowhere	1968	2.00	4.00	8.00
❑ 44643	Pretty Boy Floyd/I Am a Pilgrim	1968	2.00	4.00	8.00
❑ 44746	Drug Store Truck Drivin' Man/Bad Night at the Whiskey	1969	2.00	4.00	8.00
❑ 44868	Lay Lady Lay/Old Blue	1969	2.00	4.00	8.00
❑ 44990	Ballad of Easy Rider/Oil in My Lamp	1969	2.50	5.00	10.00
❑ 44990	Wasn't Born to Follow/Ballad of Easy Rider	1969	2.00	4.00	8.00
❑ 45071	Jesus Is Just Alright/It's All Over Now, Baby Blue	1970	2.00	4.00	8.00
❑ 45259	Chestnut Mare/Just a Season	1970	—	3.00	6.00
❑ 45440	Glory Glory/Citizen Kane	1971	—	3.00	6.00
❑ 45514	America's Great National Pastime/Farther Along	1971	—	3.00	6.00
❑ 45761	Jesus Is Just Alright/Mr. Spaceman	1973	2.50	5.00	10.00
❑ JZSP 116476 [DJ]	He Was a Friend of Mine (same on both sides)	1966	10.00	20.00	40.00

7-Inch Extended Plays

Number	Title (A Side/B Side)	Yr	VG	VG+	NM
COLUMBIA/SCHOLASTIC					
❑ CV 10287	Lover of the Bayou/So You Want to Be a Rock and Roll Star//Chimes of Freedom/Goin' Back	1971	7.50	15.00	30.00
❑ CV 10287 [PS]	The Byrds	1971	7.50	15.00	30.00

BYRNES, EDD

Number	Title (A Side/B Side)	Yr	VG	VG+	NM
WARNER BROS.					
❑ 5047 [M]	Kookie, Kookie (Lend Me Your Comb)/You're the Top	1959	5.00	10.00	20.00
—A-side by Edward Byrnes and Connie Stevens; B-side by Edward Byrnes					
❑ 5047 [PS]	Kookie, Kookie (Lend Me Your Comb)/You're the Top	1959	10.00	20.00	40.00
—A-side by Edward Byrnes and Connie Stevens; B-side by Edward Byrnes					
❑ S-5047 [S]	Kookie, Kookie (Lend Me Your Comb)/You're the Top	1959	12.50	25.00	50.00
❑ 5087	Like I Love You/Kookie's Mad Pad	1959	4.00	8.00	16.00
—Artist credit: "Edd Byrnes and Friend"					
❑ 5087 [PS]	Like I Love You/Kookie's Mad Pad	1959	10.00	20.00	40.00
—Artist credit: "Edd Byrnes and Friend"					
❑ 5114	Kookie's Love Song Part 1/Kookie's Love Song Part 2	1959	4.00	8.00	16.00
—With the Mary Kay Trio					
❑ 5114 [PS]	Kookie's Love Song Part 1/Kookie's Love Song Part 2	1959	10.00	20.00	40.00
—With the Mary Kay Trio					
❑ 5121	Yulesville/Lonely Christmas	1959	4.00	8.00	16.00
❑ 5121 [PS]	Yulesville/Lonely Christmas	1959	10.00	20.00	40.00

7-Inch Extended Plays

Number	Title (A Side/B Side)	Yr	VG	VG+	NM
WARNER BROS.					
❑ EA 1309	Hot Broad Rock/I Don't Dig You, Kookie//Saturday Night on Sunset Strip/The Kookie Cha-Cha-Cha	1959	12.50	25.00	50.00
❑ EA 1309 [PS]	Kookie	1959	12.50	25.00	50.00

BYRON, LORD DOUGLAS

Number	Title (A Side/B Side)	Yr	VG	VG+	NM
DOT					
❑ 16685	Surfin' Santa/The Drink That Makes You Shrink	1964	7.50	15.00	30.00
UNION					
❑ 505	Big Bad Ho-Dad/Coffee House	1962	10.00	20.00	40.00
—B-side by the Continentals					

BYSTANDERS, THE

Number	Title (A Side/B Side)	Yr	VG	VG+	NM
CHESS					
❑ 2007	Royal Blue Summer Sunshine Day/Make Up Your Mind	1967	3.75	7.50	15.00

C

C.A. QUINTET, THE

Number	Title (A Side/B Side)	Yr	VG	VG+	NM
CANDY FLOSS					
❑ 102	Smooth as Silk/Dr. of Philosophy	1968	20.00	40.00	80.00
FALCON					
❑ 70	Mickey's Monkey/I Want You to Love Me Girl	1967	25.00	50.00	100.00
❑ 71	Blow to My Soul/She's Got to Be True	1967	25.00	50.00	100.00

C.L. AND THE PICTURES

Also see CURTIS LEE.

Number	Title (A Side/B Side)	Yr	VG	VG+	NM
DUNES					
❑ 2010	I'm Asking Forgiveness/Let's Take a Ride	1962	6.25	12.50	25.00
❑ 2017	Afraid/Mary Go 'Round	1962	6.25	12.50	25.00
❑ 2023	I'm Sorry/That's What's Happening	1963	6.25	12.50	25.00
JAMIE					
❑ 1398	You Really Slipped One By Me/The Same People (That You Meet Going Up, You Meet Coming Down)	1971	3.75	7.50	15.00
—As "C.L. Weldon and the Pictures"					
MONUMENT					
❑ 854	He'll Only Hurt You/Talking About My Baby	1964	5.00	10.00	20.00
❑ 888	Could This Be Magic/Yolanda	1965	5.00	10.00	20.00
❑ 958	Baby, Not Now/Jigsaw Puzzle	1966	5.00	10.00	20.00

C-NOTES, THE

Number	Title (A Side/B Side)	Yr	VG	VG+	NM
EVERLAST					
❑ 5005	On Your Mark/From Now On	1957	12.50	25.00	50.00

C.O.D.'S, THE

Number	Title (A Side/B Side)	Yr	VG	VG+	NM
KELLMAC					
❑ 1003	Michael/Cry No More	1965	3.00	6.00	12.00
❑ 1005	Pretty Baby/I'm a Good Guy	1965	5.00	10.00	20.00
❑ 1012	Coming Back Girl/It Must Be Love	1966	25.00	50.00	100.00

C-QUENTS, THE

Number	Title (A Side/B Side)	Yr	VG	VG+	NM
CAPETOWN					
❑ 4027	All I Want For Christmas Is You/Merry Christmas, Baby	1962	75.00	150.00	300.00
ESSICA					
❑ 4	Dearest One/It's You and Me	196?	7.50	15.00	30.00

CABOT, SEBASTIAN

Number	Title (A Side/B Side)	Yr	VG	VG+	NM
MGM					
❑ 13650	It Ain't Me Babe/And Mostly They Sing	1966	3.75	7.50	15.00

CADETS, THE

Also see THE JACKS.

Number	Title (A Side/B Side)	Yr	VG	VG+	NM
JAN-LAR					
❑ 102	Don't/Car Crash	1960	15.00	30.00	00.00
MODERN					
❑ 956	Don't Be Angry/I Cried	1955	12.50	25.00	50.00
❑ 960	Rollin' Stone/Fine Lookin' Baby	1955	12.50	25.00	50.00
❑ 963	I Cried/Fine Lookin' Baby	1955	10.00	20.00	40.00
❑ 969	Annie Met Henry/So Will I	1955	10.00	20.00	40.00
❑ 971	Do You Wanna Rock/If It Is Wrong	1956	25.00	50.00	100.00
❑ 985	Church Bells May Ring/Heartbreak Hotel	1956	10.00	20.00	40.00
❑ 994	Stranded in the Jungle/I Want You	1956	10.00	20.00	40.00
❑ 1000	I Got Loaded/Dancin' Dan	1956	10.00	20.00	40.00
❑ 1006	Fools Rush In/I'll Be Spinning	1956	10.00	20.00	40.00
❑ 1012	Heaven Help Me/Love Bandit	1957	10.00	20.00	40.00
❑ 1017	Wiggle Waggle Woo/You Belong to Me	1957	10.00	20.00	40.00
❑ 1019	Pretty Evey/Rum, Jamaica Rum	1957	12.50	25.00	50.00
—As "Aaron Collins and the Cadets"					
❑ 1024	Hands Across the Table/Love Can Do Most Anything	1957	10.00	20.00	40.00
—As "Will Jones and the Cadets"					
❑ 1026	Ring Chimes/Baby Ya Know	1957	10.00	20.00	40.00
SHERWOOD					
❑ 211	One More Chance/I'm Looking for a Job	1960	12.50	25.00	50.00

CADILLACS, THE

Number	Title (A Side/B Side)	Yr	VG	VG+	NM
ARTIC					
❑ 101	Fool/The Right Kind of Lovin'	1964	25.00	50.00	100.00
CAPITOL					
❑ 4825	Groovy, Groovy Love/White Gardenia	1962	5.00	10.00	20.00
❑ 4935	La Bomba/I Saw You	1963	5.00	10.00	20.00
—As "Bobby Ray and the Cadillacs"					
JOSIE					
❑ 765	Gloria/I Wonder Why	1954	175.00	350.00	700.00
❑ 765	Gloria/I Wonder Why	196?	6.25	12.50	25.00
—Reissue with 1960s label					
❑ 769	Wishing Well/I Want to Know About Love	1954	125.00	250.00	500.00
❑ 773	Sympathy/No Chance	1955	25.00	50.00	100.00
❑ 778	Widow Lady/Down the Road	1955	50.00	100.00	200.00
❑ 785	Speedo/Let Me Explain	1955	15.00	30.00	60.00
❑ 792	Zoom/You Are	1956	12.50	25.00	50.00
❑ 798	Woe Is Me/Betty My Love	1956	12.50	25.00	50.00
❑ 805	The Girl I Love/That's All I Need	1956	25.00	50.00	100.00
❑ 807	Rudolph the Red-Nosed Reindeer/Shack-a Doo	1956	10.00	20.00	40.00
❑ 812	Sugar Sugar/About That Girl Named Lou	1957	10.00	20.00	40.00
❑ 820	My Girl Friend/Broken Heart	1957	12.50	25.00	50.00
❑ 821	Lucy/Hurry Home	1957	10.00	20.00	40.00
—As "The Original Cadillacs"					
❑ 829	Buzz-Buzz-Buzz/Yes, Yes Baby	1957	10.00	20.00	40.00
—As "The Original Cadillacs"					
❑ 836	Speedo Is Back/A' Looka Here	1958	7.50	15.00	30.00
❑ 842	Holy Smoke Baby/I Want to Know	1958	7.50	15.00	30.00
❑ 846	Peek-a-Book/Oh, Oh Lolita	1958	7.50	15.00	30.00
❑ 857	Copy Cat/Jay Walker	1959	7.50	15.00	30.00
❑ 861	Cool It Fool/Please Mr. Johnson	1959	7.50	15.00	30.00
❑ 866 [M]	Romeo/Always My Darling	1959	7.50	15.00	30.00
❑ 870	Dumbell/Bad Dan McGoon	1959	7.50	15.00	30.00
❑ 876	Tell Me Today/It's Love	1960	7.50	15.00	30.00
❑ 883	That's Why/The Boogie Man	1960	7.50	15.00	30.00
❑ 915	Wayward Wanderer/I'll Never Let You Go	1963	5.00	10.00	20.00
—As "The Original Cadillacs"					
JUBILEE					
❑ 8010 [S]	Romeo/Always My Darling	1959	15.00	30.00	60.00
LANA					
❑ 118	Speedo/Baby It's All Right	196?	—	3.00	6.00
—Reissue					
❑ 119	Gloria/Hey Bob E Re Bob	196?	—	3.00	6.00
—Reissue					
MERCURY					
❑ 71738	I'm Willing/Thrill Me So	1961	25.00	50.00	100.00
POLYDOR					
❑ 14031	Deep in the Heart of the Ghetto (Part 1)/Deep in the Heart of the Ghetto (Part 2)	1969	3.75	7.50	15.00
—As "The Original Cadillacs"					
ROULETTE					
❑ 4654	Let's Get Together/She's My Connection	1965	5.00	10.00	20.00
SMASH					
❑ 1712	You Are to Blame/What to Bet	1961	6.25	12.50	25.00

CAESAR AND CLEO

See SONNY AND CHER.

CAGLE, WADE

Number	Title (A Side/B Side)	Yr	VG	VG+	NM
SUN					
❑ 360	Groovy Train/Highland Rock	1961	6.25	12.50	25.00

CAHPERONES, THE

See THE CHAPERONES.

CAKE, THE

Number	Title (A Side/B Side)	Yr	VG	VG+	NM
DECCA					
❑ 32179	Mockingbird/Baby That's Me	1967	2.50	5.00	10.00
❑ 32212	You Can Have Him/I Know	1967	2.50	5.00	10.00
❑ 32235	Fire Fly/Rainbow Wood	1967	2.50	5.00	10.00
❑ 32347	PT 280/Have You Heard the News 'Bout Miss Molly	1968	2.50	5.00	10.00

CALE, J.J.

Number	Title (A Side/B Side)	Yr	VG	VG+	NM
LIBERTY					
❑ 55840	Dick Tracy/It's a Go-Go Place	1965	3.75	7.50	15.00
❑ 55881	Outside Lookin' In/In Our Time	1966	3.75	7.50	15.00
❑ 55931	After Midnight/Slow Motion	1966	3.75	7.50	15.00
MCA					
❑ 51095	Carry On/Deep Dark Dungeon	1981	—	2.00	4.00
MERCURY					
❑ 76145	Devil in Disguise/Drifter's Wife	1982	—	—	3.00
❑ 814497-7	Losers/Reality	1983	—	—	3.00
SHELTER					
❑ 7306	Magnolia/Crazy Mama	1971	2.00	4.00	8.00
❑ 7314	Crazy Mama/Don't Go to Strangers	1971	—	3.00	6.00
❑ 7321	After Midnight/Crying Eyes	1972	—	3.00	6.00
❑ 7326	Lies/Riding Home	1972	—	3.00	6.00
❑ 7332	Going Down/Louisiana Women	1973	—	3.00	6.00
❑ 40238	Cajun Moon/Starbound	1974	—	2.50	5.00
❑ 40290	I'll Be There/Precious Memories	1974	—	2.50	5.00
❑ 40366	I Got the Same Old Blues/Rock and Roll Records	1975	—	2.50	5.00
❑ 62002	Hey Baby/Cocaine	1976	—	3.00	6.00

CALIFORNIA

Number	Title (A Side/B Side)	Yr	VG	VG+	NM
LAURIE					
❑ 3612	See You in September/Ivy Ivy	1974	—	2.00	4.00
❑ 3639	Song of a Thousand Voices/Abraham, Martin and John	1976	—	2.00	4.00
❑ 3647	Jeans On/Doo-Wop Music	1976	—	2.00	4.00
❑ 3651	I'm Just Thinking of You/Doo-Wop Music	1977	—	2.00	4.00
❑ 3695	Summer Fun Medley/Paris	1981	—	2.00	4.00
RCA					
❑ PB-11769	Everybody Needs a Little Help/I'm a Poet	1979	2.50	5.00	10.00
RSO					
❑ 901	I Can Hear Music/Love's Supposed to Be That Way	1978	2.50	5.00	10.00
WARNER BROS.					
❑ 8253	Happy in Hollywood/Music, Music, Music	1976	2.50	5.00	10.00
❑ 8307	(Just to Let You Know) I Love You So/Happy in Hollywood	1977	2.50	5.00	10.00

CALIFORNIA, RANDY

Also see SPIRIT.

Number	Title (A Side/B Side)	Yr	VG	VG+	NM
EPIC					
❑ 10927	Walkin' the Dog/Live for the Day	1972	2.00	4.00	8.00

CALIFORNIA MUSIC

Number	Title (A Side/B Side)	Yr	VG	VG+	NM
EQUINOX					
❑ PB-10120	Don't Worry Baby/Ten Years' Harmony	1974	3.75	7.50	15.00
❑ PB-10363	Why Do Fools Fall in Love/Don't Worry Baby	1975	3.75	7.50	15.00
❑ PB-10572	Jamaica Farewell/California Music	1976	3.75	7.50	15.00

CALIFORNIANS, THE (1)

Number	Title (A Side/B Side)	Yr	VG	VG+	NM
CRAZY HORSE					
❑ 1318	Nausea Beast/Glass Disguise	1969	2.50	5.00	10.00

CALIFORNIANS, THE (2)

JESSE BELVIN appears on this record.

Number	Title (A Side/B Side)	Yr	VG	VG+	NM
FEDERAL					
❑ 12231	My Angel/Heavenly Ruby	1955	75.00	150.00	300.00

CALVANES, THE

DECK

Number	Title (A Side/B Side)	Yr	VG	VG+	NM
❑ 579	Dreamworld/5, 7 or 9	1958	25.00	50.00	100.00
❑ 580	My Love Song/Horror Pictures	1958	25.00	50.00	100.00

DOOTONE

Number	Title (A Side/B Side)	Yr	VG	VG+	NM
❑ 371	Crazy Over You/Don't Take Your Love from Me	1956	50.00	100.00	200.00
❑ 380	One More Kiss/Florabelle	1956	50.00	100.00	200.00

7-Inch Extended Plays

DOOTONE

Number	Title (A Side/B Side)	Yr	VG	VG+	NM
❑ 205	(contents unknown)	1956	100.00	200.00	400.00
❑ 205 [PS]	Voices for Lovers	1956	150.00	300.00	600.00

CAMELOTS, THE

AANKO

Number	Title (A Side/B Side)	Yr	VG	VG+	NM
❑ 1001	Your Way/Don't Leave Me Baby	1963	20.00	40.00	80.00
❑ 1004	Sunday Kind of Love/My Imagination	1963	20.00	40.00	80.00

CAMEO

Number	Title (A Side/B Side)	Yr	VG	VG+	NM
❑ 334	Don't Leave Me Baby/Love Call	1964	7.50	15.00	30.00

—B-side by the Ebonaires

COMET

Number	Title (A Side/B Side)	Yr	VG	VG+	NM
❑ 930	Scratch/Charge	1962	3.75	7.50	15.00

CRIMSON

Number	Title (A Side/B Side)	Yr	VG	VG+	NM
❑ 1001	Don't Leave Me Baby/The Letter	1963	7.50	15.00	30.00

DREAM

Number	Title (A Side/B Side)	Yr	VG	VG+	NM
❑ 1001	Your Way/I Wonder	1967	2.00	4.00	8.00

EMBER

Number	Title (A Side/B Side)	Yr	VG	VG+	NM
❑ 1108	Pocahontas/Searching for My Baby	1964	5.00	10.00	20.00

LAURIE

Number	Title (A Side/B Side)	Yr	VG	VG+	NM
❑ 3239	Marie/Daddy's Going Away Again	1964	5.00	10.00	20.00

—As "The Harps"

NIX

Number	Title (A Side/B Side)	Yr	VG	VG+	NM
❑ 101	Lulu/Never Been in Love Before	1961	5.00	10.00	20.00

RELIC

Number	Title (A Side/B Side)	Yr	VG	VG+	NM
❑ 530	Chain of Broken Hearts/Rat Race	196?	2.00	4.00	8.00

—B-side by the Bootleggers

Number	Title (A Side/B Side)	Yr	VG	VG+	NM
❑ 541	Dance Girl/That's My Baby	1965	2.00	4.00	8.00

—B-side by the Suns

TIMES SQUARE

Number	Title (A Side/B Side)	Yr	VG	VG+	NM
❑ 32	Dance Girl/That's My Baby	1964	2.50	5.00	10.00

—B-side by the Suns

7-Inch Extended Plays

CLIFTON/UGHA

Number	Title (A Side/B Side)	Yr	VG	VG+	NM
❑ EP 507/1	Music to My Ears/Daddy's Going Away// Pocahontas/Don't Leave Me Baby	1981	—	2.50	5.00
❑ EP 507/1 [PS]	(title unknown)	1981	—	2.50	5.00

CAMEOS, THE

CAMEO

Number	Title (A Side/B Side)	Yr	VG	VG+	NM
❑ 123	Merry Christmas/New Year's Eve	1957	37.50	75.00	150.00
❑ 123	Merry Christmas/New Year's Eve	197?	2.50	5.00	10.00

—Reproduction of the original 1957 release

CAMERON, JIMMY AND VELLA

REPRISE

Number	Title (A Side/B Side)	Yr	VG	VG+	NM
❑ 0483	Lovin' You Is Such a Groove/I Know a Place	1966	7.50	15.00	30.00

UNLIMITED GOLD

Number	Title (A Side/B Side)	Yr	VG	VG+	NM
❑ 1422	Mornin' Time/There Is No Other Love	1980	—	2.00	4.00

CAMP, THE

SCEPTER

Number	Title (A Side/B Side)	Yr	VG	VG+	NM
❑ 12159	Marching/Long Long Trail	1966	20.00	40.00	80.00

CAMPBELL, CHOKER

APT

Number	Title (A Side/B Side)	Yr	VG	VG+	NM
❑ 25011	Walk Awhile/Walking on Thin-Soled Shoes	1958	15.00	30.00	60.00

ATLANTIC

Number	Title (A Side/B Side)	Yr	VG	VG+	NM
❑ 1014	Last Call for Whiskey/How Could You Do This	1953	10.00	20.00	40.00
❑ 1038	Have You Seen My Baby/Jackie Mambo	1954	10.00	20.00	40.00

FORTUNE

Number	Title (A Side/B Side)	Yr	VG	VG+	NM
❑ 808	Frankie and Johnny/Rocking and Jumping	1953	15.00	30.00	60.00

MOTOWN

Number	Title (A Side/B Side)	Yr	VG	VG+	NM
❑ 1072	Come See About Me/Pride and Joy	1964	6.25	12.50	25.00

CAMPBELL, GLEN

Also see THE BEACH BOYS; THE CHAMPS; GEE CEES.

ATLANTIC AMERICA

Number	Title (A Side/B Side)	Yr	VG	VG+	NM
❑ 99525	Call Home/Sweet 16	1986	—	—	3.00
❑ 99559	Cowpoke/Rag Doll	1986	—	—	3.00
❑ 99600	It's Just a Matter of Time/Gene Autry, My Hero	1985	—	—	3.00
❑ 99600 [PS]	It's Just a Matter of Time/Gene Autry, My Hero	1985	—	2.00	4.00
❑ 99647	(Love Always) Letter to Home/An American Trilogy	1985	—	—	3.00
❑ 99691	A Lady Like You/Tennessee	1984	—	—	3.00
❑ 99768	Faithless Love/Scene of the Crime	1984	—	—	3.00
❑ 99893	On the Wings of My Victory/A Few Good Men	1983	—	—	3.00
❑ 99930	I Love How You Love Me/Hang On Baby (Ease My Mind)	1983	—	—	3.00
❑ 99967	Old Home Town/Heartache #3	1982	—	2.00	4.00
❑ 99967 [PS]	Old Home Town/Heartache #3	1982	—	2.00	4.00

CAPEHART

Number	Title (A Side/B Side)	Yr	VG	VG+	NM
❑ 5008	Death Valley/Nothin' Better Than a Pretty Woman	1961	6.25	12.50	25.00

CAPITOL

Number	Title (A Side/B Side)	Yr	VG	VG+	NM
❑ 2015	By the Time I Get to Phoenix/You've Still Got a Place in My Heart	1967	—	3.50	7.00
❑ 2076	Hey Little One/My Baby's Gone	1968	—	3.50	7.00
❑ 2076 [PS]	Hey Little One/My Baby's Gone	1968	3.00	6.00	12.00
❑ 2146	I Wanna Live/That's All That Matters	1968	—	3.50	7.00
❑ 2224	Dreams of the Everyday Housewife/Kelli Ho-Down	1968	—	3.50	7.00
❑ 2302	Wichita Lineman/Fate of Man	1968	—	3.00	6.00
❑ 2336	Christmas Is for Children/There's No Place Like Home	1968	2.00	4.00	8.00
❑ 2428	Galveston/How Come Every Time I Itch I Wind Up Scratchin' You	1969	—	3.00	6.00
❑ 2494	Where's the Playground Susie/Arkansas	1969	—	3.00	6.00
❑ 2573	True Grit/Hava Nagila	1969	—	3.00	6.00
❑ 2659	Try a Little Kindness/Lonely My Lonely Friend	1969	—	3.00	6.00
❑ 2718	Honey Come Back/Where Do You Go	1970	—	3.00	6.00
❑ 2787	Oh Happy Day/Someone Above	1970	—	3.00	6.00
❑ 2843	Everything a Man Could Ever Need/Norwood (Me and My Guitar)	1970	—	3.00	6.00
❑ 2905	It's Only Make Believe/Pave Your Way Into Tomorrow	1970	—	3.00	6.00
❑ 3062	Dream Baby (How Long Must I Dream)/Here and Now	1971	—	3.00	6.00
❑ 3123	The Last Time I Saw Her/Bach Talk	1971	—	3.00	6.00
❑ 3254	Oklahoma Sunday Morning/Everybody's Got to Go There Sometime	1972	—	3.00	6.00
❑ 3305	Manhattan, Kansas/Wayfaring Stranger	1972	—	3.00	6.00
❑ 3382	We All Pull the Load/Wherefore and Why	1972	—	3.50	7.00
❑ 3411	I Will Never Pass This Way Again/We All Pull the Load	1972	—	3.00	6.00
❑ 3483	One Last Time/All My Tomorrows	1972	—	3.00	6.00
❑ 3509	I Believe in Christmas/New Snow on the Roof	1972	—	3.00	6.00
❑ 3548	I Knew Jesus (Before He Was a Star)/On This Road	1973	—	2.50	5.00
❑ 3669	Bring Back My Yesterday/Beautiful Love Song	1973	—	2.50	5.00
❑ 3735	Wherefore and Why/Give Me Back That Old Familiar Feeling	1973	—	2.50	5.00
❑ 3808	Houston (I'm Coming to See You)/Honestly Love	1973	—	2.50	5.00
❑ 3926	Bonaparte's Retreat/Too Many Mornings	1974	—	2.50	5.00
❑ 3988	It's a Sin When You Love Somebody/If I Were Loving You	1974	—	2.50	5.00
❑ 4095	Rhinestone Cowboy/Lovelight	1975	—	2.00	4.00
❑ 4155	Country Boy (You Got Your Feet in L.A.)/Record Collector's Dream	1975	—	2.00	4.00
❑ 4245	Then You Can Tell Me Goodbye-Don't Pull Your Love/I Miss You Tonight	1976	—	2.00	4.00
❑ 4288	See You on Sunday/Bloodline	1976	—	2.00	4.00
❑ 4376	Southern Nights/William Tell Overture	1976	—	2.00	4.00
❑ 4445	Sunflower/How High Did We Go	1977	—	2.00	4.00
❑ 4515	God Must Have Blessed America/Amazing Grace	1977	—	2.00	4.00
❑ 4584	Another Fine Mess/Can You Fool	1978	—	2.00	4.00
❑ 4638	Can You Fool/Let's All Sing a Song About It	1978	—	2.00	4.00
❑ 4682	I'm Gonna Love You/Love Takes You Higher	1979	—	2.00	4.00
❑ 4715	California/Never Tell You No Lies	1979	—	2.00	4.00
❑ 4769	Hound Dog Man/Tennessee Home	1979	—	2.00	4.00
❑ 4783	Too Late to Worry — Too Blue to Cry/How Do I Tell My Heart Not to Break	1962	3.75	7.50	15.00
❑ 4799	My Prayer/Don't Lose Me in the Confusion	1979	—	2.00	4.00
❑ 4856	Long Black Limousine/Here I Am	1962	2.50	5.00	10.00
❑ 4856 [PS]	Long Black Limousine/Here I Am	1962	5.00	10.00	20.00
❑ 4865	Somethin' 'Bout You Baby I Like/Late Night Confession	1980	—	2.00	4.00

—With Rita Coolidge

Number	Title (A Side/B Side)	Yr	VG	VG+	NM
❑ 4867	Kentucky Means Paradise/Truck Driving Man	1962	3.75	7.50	15.00

—As "The Green River Boys Featuring Glen Campbell"

Number	Title (A Side/B Side)	Yr	VG	VG+	NM
❑ 4909	Hollywood Smiles/Hooked on Love	1980	—	2.00	4.00
❑ 4925	Oh My Darling/Prima Donna	1963	3.00	6.00	12.00
❑ 4959	I Don't Want to Know Your Name/Daisy a Day	1981	—	2.00	4.00
❑ 4986	Why Don't We Just Sleep on It Tonight/It's Your World	1981	—	2.00	4.00

—With Tanya Tucker

Number	Title (A Side/B Side)	Yr	VG	VG+	NM
❑ 4990	Divorce Me C.O.D./Dark As a Dungeon	1963	3.00	6.00	12.00
❑ 5037	As Far As I'm Concerned/Same Old Places	1963	3.00	6.00	12.00
❑ 5172	Let Me Tell You About Mary/Through the Eyes of a Child	1964	3.00	6.00	12.00
❑ 5279	Summer, Winter, Spring and Fall/Heartaches Can Be Fun	1964	3.00	6.00	12.00
❑ 5279 [PS]	Summer, Winter, Spring and Fall/Heartaches Can Be Fun	1964	6.25	12.50	25.00
❑ 5360	It's a Woman's World/Tomorrow Never Comes	1965	3.00	6.00	12.00
❑ 5441	Guess I'm Dumb/That's All Right	1965	30.00	60.00	120.00

—A Brian Wilson "Pet Sounds"-like production

Number	Title (A Side/B Side)	Yr	VG	VG+	NM
❑ 5504	The Universal Soldier/Spanish Shades	1965	2.50	5.00	10.00
❑ 5545	Less of Me/Private John Q	1965	2.50	5.00	10.00
❑ 5638	Can't You See I'm Tryin'/Satisfied Mind	1966	2.50	5.00	10.00
❑ 5773	Burning Bridges/Only the Lonely	1966	2.50	5.00	10.00
❑ 5854	I Gotta Have My Baby Back/Just to Satisfy You	1967	2.50	5.00	10.00
❑ 5939	Gentle on My Mind/Just Another Man	1967	2.00	4.00	8.00

—Orange and yellow swirl, without "A Subsidiary Of"... in perimeter label print

Number	Title (A Side/B Side)	Yr	VG	VG+	NM
❑ 5939	Gentle on My Mind/Just Another Man	1968	—	3.00	6.00

—Orange and yellow swirl label with "A Subsidiary Of" in perimeter print

Number	Title (A Side/B Side)	Yr	VG	VG+	NM
❑ 7PRO-79107	On a Good Night (same on both sides)	1990	—	3.00	6.00

—Vinyl is promo only

Number	Title (A Side/B Side)	Yr	VG	VG+	NM
❑ 7PRO-79279	Somebody's Leavin' (same on both sides)	1990	—	3.00	6.00

—Vinyl is promo only

Number	Title (A Side/B Side)	Yr	VG	VG+	NM
❑ 7PRO-79966	Walkin' in the Sun (same on both sides)	1990	—	3.00	6.00

—Vinyl is promo only

CENECO

Number	Title (A Side/B Side)	Yr	VG	VG+	NM
❑ 1324	Dreams for Sale/I've Got to Win	1961	6.25	12.50	25.00
❑ 1356	I Wonder/You, You, You	1961	5.00	10.00	20.00

COMPLEAT

Number	Title (A Side/B Side)	Yr	VG	VG+	NM
❑ 113	Letting Go/(Instrumental)	1983	—	2.00	4.00

CREST

Number	Title (A Side/B Side)	Yr	VG	VG+	NM
❑ 1087	Turn Around, Look at Me/Brenda	1961	5.00	10.00	20.00
❑ 1096	The Miracle of Love/Once More	1962	3.75	7.50	15.00

EVEREST

Number	Title (A Side/B Side)	Yr	VG	VG+	NM
❑ 2500	Delight, Arkansas/Walk Right In	1969	—	3.00	6.00

LIBERTY

Number	Title (A Side/B Side)	Yr	VG	VG+	NM
❑ S7-18214	Blue Christmas/Feliz Navidad	1994	—	2.50	5.00

—B-side on EMI Latin by Jose Feliciano; red vinyl

Number	Title (A Side/B Side)	Yr	VG	VG+	NM
MCA					
❑ 41323	Dream Lover/Bronco	1980	—	2.00	4.00
—A-side with Tanya Tucker					
❑ 53108	The Hand That Rocks the Cradle/Arkansas	1987	—	—	3.00
—A-side with Steve Wariner					
❑ 53172	Still Within the Sound of My Voice/In My Life	1987	—	—	3.00
❑ 53218	I Have You/I'm a One Woman Man	1987	—	—	3.00
❑ 53245	I Remember You/For Sure, For Certain, Forever, For Always	1988	—	—	3.00
❑ 53426	Heart of the Matter/Light Years	1988	—	—	3.00
❑ 53493	More Than Enough/Our Movie	1989	—	—	3.00
MIRAGE					
❑ 3845	I Love My Truck/Melody's Melody	1981	—	2.00	4.00
STARDAY					
❑ 853	For the Love of a Woman/Smokey Blue Eyes	1968	2.00	4.00	8.00
UNIVERSAL					
❑ UVL-66024	She's Gone, Gone, Gone/William Tell Overture	1989	—	2.00	4.00
WARNER BROS.					
❑ 49609	Any Which Way You Can/Medley from Any Which Way You Can	1980	—	2.00	4.00
—B-side by Texas Opera Company					

CAMPBELL, GLEN, AND BOBBIE GENTRY
Also see each artist's individual listings.

Number	Title (A Side/B Side)	Yr	VG	VG+	NM
CAPITOL					
❑ 2314	Less of Me/Morning Glory	1968	—	3.00	6.00
❑ 2387	Let It Be Me/Little Green Apples	1969	—	3.00	6.00
❑ 2745	All I Have to Do Is Dream/Less of Me	1970	—	3.00	6.00

CAMPBELL, JO ANN
Also see JO ANN AND TROY.

Number	Title (A Side/B Side)	Yr	VG	VG+	NM
ABC-PARAMOUNT					
❑ 10134 [M]	A Kookie Little Paradise/Bobby, Bobby, Bobby	1960	6.25	12.50	25.00
❑ S-10134 [S]	A Kookie Little Paradise/Bobby, Bobby, Bobby	1960	12.50	25.00	50.00
❑ 10172	But Maybe This Year/Crazy Daisy	1960	5.00	10.00	20.00
❑ 10200	Motorcycle Michael/Puka Puka Pants	1961	5.00	10.00	20.00
❑ 10224	Eddie My Love/It Wasn't Right	1961	5.00	10.00	20.00
❑ 10258	Mama Don't Wait/Duane	1961	5.00	10.00	20.00
❑ 10300	I Changed My Mind Jack/You Made Me Love You	1962	5.00	10.00	20.00
❑ 10335	Amateur Night/I Wish It Would Rain All Summer	1962	5.00	10.00	20.00
CAMEO					
❑ 223	I'm the Girl from Wolverton Mountain/Sloppy Joe	1962	5.00	10.00	20.00
❑ 237	Let Me Do It My Way/Mr. Fix-It Man	1962	5.00	10.00	20.00
❑ 249	Mother Please/Waitin' for Love	1963	5.00	10.00	20.00
EL DORADO					
❑ 504	Forever Young/Come On Baby	1957	10.00	20.00	40.00
❑ 509	Funny Thing/I Can't Give You Anything But Love	1957	10.00	20.00	40.00
GONE					
❑ 5014	Wait a Minute/It's True	1957	10.00	20.00	40.00
❑ 5014	Wait a Minute/I'm in Love with You	1957	7.50	15.00	30.00
❑ 5021	You're Driving Me Mad/Rock and Roll Love	1958	7.50	15.00	30.00
❑ 5027	Whassa Matter with You/You-Oo	1958	7.50	15.00	30.00
❑ 5037	I Really, Really Love You/I'm Nobody's Baby Now	1958	7.50	15.00	30.00
❑ 5049	Happy New Year Baby/Tall Boy	1958	7.50	15.00	30.00
❑ 5055	Mama/Nervous	1959	7.50	15.00	30.00
❑ 5068	Beach Comber/I Ain't Got No Steady Date	1959	7.50	15.00	30.00
POINT					
❑ 4	I'm Coming Home Late Tonight/Wherever You Go	1956	10.00	20.00	40.00
RORI					
❑ 711	Jim Dandy/Five Minutes More	1962	5.00	10.00	20.00

CAMPERS, THE
Includes SONNY CURTIS and THE CRICKETS (1).

Number	Title (A Side/B Side)	Yr	VG	VG+	NM
PARKWAY					
❑ 974	The Ballad of Batman/The Batmobile	1966	7.50	15.00	30.00
❑ 974	The Ballad of Batman/The Batmobile	1966	8.75	17.50	35.00
—Original label credit: "The Camps"					

CAMPI, RAY

Number	Title (A Side/B Side)	Yr	VG	VG+	NM
COLPIX					
❑ 166	French Fries/Hear What I Wanna Hear	1960	3.75	7.50	15.00
D					
❑ 1047	The Ballad of Donna and Peggy Sue/A Man I Met (Tribute to The Big Bopper)	1959	10.00	20.00	40.00
DOMINO					
❑ 700	My Screamin' Screamin' Meemie/With You	1958	7.50	15.00	30.00
DOT					
❑ 15617	It Ain't Me/Give That Love to Me	1957	15.00	30.00	60.00
ROLLIN' ROCK					
❑ 006	Eager Boy/Dobroggie	1978	—	2.50	5.00
❑ 008	Tore Up/If It's All the Same to You	1978	—	2.50	5.00
❑ 014	Sixteen Chicks/Pan American Boogie	1979	—	2.50	5.00
❑ 019	My Baby Left Me/A Li'l Bit of Heartache	1979	—	2.50	5.00
❑ 027	Wrong, Wrong, Wrong/Booze It	1980	—	2.00	4.00
❑ 029	Scrumptious Baby/I Didn't Mean to Be Mean	1980	—	2.00	4.00
❑ 031	Merle's Boogie-Woogie-Missouri/Sweet Temptation Guitar Rag	1980	—	2.00	4.00
—With Merle Travis					
❑ 038	Rockin' at the Ritz/Quit Your Triplin'	1981	—	2.00	4.00
❑ 044	Rattlin' Daddy/Wild One	1981	—	2.00	4.00
❑ 046	Texas Sands/How Long Can You Feel	1982	—	2.00	4.00
❑ 047	Sweet Woman Blues/The Newest Wave	1982	—	2.00	4.00
❑ 052	Rockabilly Man/Hollywood Cats	1983	—	2.00	4.00
TNT					
❑ 145	Caterpillar/Play It Cool	1958	75.00	150.00	300.00
WINSOR					
❑ 6401	Billie Jean/Shenandoah	1964	7.50	15.00	30.00

CAMPS, THE
See THE CAMPERS.

CANADIAN BEADLES, THE

Number	Title (A Side/B Side)	Yr	VG	VG+	NM
TIDE					
❑ 2203	I Think I'm Gonna Cry/I'll Show You the Way	1964	3.75	7.50	15.00
❑ 2206	I'm Coming Home/Love Walk Away	1964	3.75	7.50	15.00
—As "Vic, Paul and Bruce"					

CANDY AND THE KISSES

Number	Title (A Side/B Side)	Yr	VG	VG+	NM
CAMEO					
❑ 336	The 81/Two Happy People	1964	5.00	10.00	20.00
❑ 355	Soldier Boy (Of Mine)/Shakin' Time	1964	5.00	10.00	20.00
DECCA					
❑ 32415	Chains of Love/Someone Out There	1968	—	3.00	6.00
SCEPTER					
❑ 12106	Keep On Searchin'/Together	1965	3.75	7.50	15.00
❑ 12125	Sweet and Lovely/Out in the Streets Again	1965	3.75	7.50	15.00
❑ 12136	Tonight's the Night/The Last Time	1966	3.00	6.00	12.00

CANDYMEN, THE

Number	Title (A Side/B Side)	Yr	VG	VG+	NM
ABC					
❑ 10995	Georgia Pines/Movies in My Mind	1967	2.00	4.00	8.00
❑ 11023	Deep in the Night/Stone Blues Man	1967	2.00	4.00	8.00
❑ 11048	Sentimental Lady/Ways	1968	2.00	4.00	8.00
❑ 11077	Candy Man/Crowded Room	1968	2.00	4.00	8.00
❑ 11141	Go and Tell the People/It's Gonna Get Good in a Minute	1968	2.00	4.00	8.00
❑ 11175	I'll Never Forget/Lonely Eyes	1969	2.00	4.00	8.00
LIBERTY					
❑ 56172	Happy Tonight/Papers	1970	2.00	4.00	8.00

CANNED HEAT

Number	Title (A Side/B Side)	Yr	VG	VG+	NM
ALA					
❑ 1996	C.C. Shooter/Harley Davidson Blues	1984	—	2.50	5.00
—As "Heat Brothers '84"					
ATLANTIC					
❑ 3010	One More River to Cross/Highway 401	1974	—	2.00	4.00
❑ 3236	The Harder They Come/Rock 'N' Roll Show	1975	—	2.00	4.00
CAPITOL					
❑ S7-57890	Christmas Blues/Christmas Is the Time to Say "I Love You"	1992	—	2.00	4.00
—B-side by Billy Squier					
LIBERTY					
❑ 55979	Rolin' and Tumblin'/Bullfrog Blues	1967	2.00	4.00	8.00
❑ 56005	Evil Woman/The World Is a Jug	1967	2.00	4.00	8.00
❑ 56038	On the Road Again/Boogie Music	1968	—	3.00	6.00
❑ 56077	Going Up the Country/One Kind Favor	1968	—	3.00	6.00
❑ 56077 [PS]	Going Up the Country/One Kind Favor	1968	3.75	7.50	15.00
❑ 56079	Christmas Blues/The Chipmunk Song	1968	6.25	12.50	25.00
—B-side with the Chipmunks					
❑ 56097	Time Was/Low Down	1969	—	3.00	6.00
❑ 56127	Sic 'Em Pigs/Poor Man	1969	—	3.00	6.00
❑ 56140	Change My Ways/Get Off My Back	1969	—	3.00	6.00
❑ 56151	Let's Work Together/I'm Her Man	1970	—	3.00	6.00
❑ 56180	Future Blues/Going Up the Country	1970	—	3.00	6.00
❑ 56217	My Time Ain't Long/Wooly Bully	1970	—	3.00	6.00
UNITED ARTISTS					
❑ 0058	On the Road Again/This Was	1973	—	2.00	4.00
—"Silver Spotlight Series" reissue					
❑ 0059	Going Up the Country/Let's Work Together	1973	—	2.00	4.00
—"Silver Spotlight Series" reissue					
❑ XW167	Rock and Roll Music/Lookin' for My Rainbow	1973	—	2.50	5.00
❑ XW243 [DJ]	Harley Davidson Blues (mono/stereo)	1973	—	3.00	6.00
—Stock copy apparently does not exist					
❑ 50831	Long Way from L.A./Hill's Stomp	1971	—	2.50	5.00
❑ 50892	Rockin' with the King/I Don't Care What You Tell Me	1972	—	2.50	5.00
❑ 50927	Sneakin' Around/Cherokee Dance	1972	—	2.50	5.00

CANNIBAL AND THE HEADHUNTERS

Number	Title (A Side/B Side)	Yr	VG	VG+	NM
AIRES					
❑ 1001	Mean So Much/Dance By the Light	1968	3.75	7.50	15.00
CAPITOL					
❑ 2393	Get It On Up (Get Up the Courage)/Mean So Much	1969	3.75	7.50	15.00
DATE					
❑ 1516	La Bamba/Zulu King	1966	3.75	7.50	15.00
❑ 1525	Land of 1,000 Dances/Love Bird	1966	3.75	7.50	15.00
ERA BACK TO BACK HITS					
❑ 023	Land of 1,000 Dances/Dance with Me	197?	—	2.50	5.00
—B-side by the Blendells					
RAMPART					
❑ 642	Land of 1,000 Dances/I'll Show You How to Love Me	1964	5.00	10.00	20.00
❑ 644	Here Comes Love/Nau Ninny Nau	1965	3.75	7.50	15.00
❑ 646	I Need Your Loving/Follow the Music	1965	3.75	7.50	15.00
❑ 654	Out of Sight/Please Baby Please	1965	3.75	7.50	15.00

CANNON, FREDDIE

Number	Title (A Side/B Side)	Yr	VG	VG+	NM
AMHERST					
❑ 201	Dance to the Bop/(She's a) Mean Rebel Rouser	1983	—	2.00	4.00
❑ 327	Rockin' in My Socks/Rockin' in My Socks	1988	—	3.00	6.00
BUDDAH					
❑ 242	Rockin' Robin/Red Valley	1971	2.50	5.00	10.00
CLARIDGE					
❑ 401	Palisades Park/Way Down Yonder in New Orleans	1975	—	3.00	6.00
❑ 416	Sugar/Sugar (Part 2)	1976	—	3.00	6.00
HQ					
❑ (no #) [DJ]	Kennywood Park/With a Little Love	1987	—	3.00	6.00

Number	Title (A Side/B Side)	Yr	VG	VG+	NM
❑ (no #) [PS]	Kennywood Park/With a Little Love	1987	2.00	4.00	8.00
—Promotional item for KDKA Radio, Pittsburgh, Pa.					
MCA					
❑ 40269	Rock and Roll ABC's/Superman	1974	3.75	7.50	15.00
METROMEDIA					
❑ 262	If You've Got the Time/Take Me Back	1972	2.50	5.00	10.00
MIASOUND					
❑ 1002	Let's Put the Fun Back in Rock and Roll/Your Mama Ain't Always Right	1981	—	2.50	5.00
—With the Belmonts					
RADIO ACTIVE GOLD					
❑ 64	Rockin' Robin/Red Valley	197?	—	2.50	5.00
ROYAL AMERICAN					
❑ 2	Charged-Up, Turned-On Rock-N-Roll Singer/I Ain't Much, But I'm Yours	1970	2.50	5.00	10.00
❑ 11	Nite Time Lady/I Ain't Much, But I'm Yours	1970	2.50	5.00	10.00
❑ 288	Strawberry Wine/Blossom Dear	1969	2.50	5.00	10.00
SIRE					
❑ 4103	Beautiful Downtown Burbank/If You Give Me a Title	1969	2.50	5.00	10.00
SWAN					
❑ 4031	Tallahassee Lassie/You Know	1959	5.00	10.00	20.00
❑ 4038	Okefenokee/Kookie Hat	1959	5.00	10.00	20.00
❑ 4043	Way Down Yonder in New Orleans/Fractured	1959	5.00	10.00	20.00
❑ 4043 [PS]	Way Down Yonder in New Orleans/Fractured	1959	7.50	15.00	30.00
❑ 4050	Chattanooga Shoe Shine Boy/Boston "My Home Town"	1960	3.75	7.50	15.00
❑ 4050 [PS]	Chattanooga Shoe Shine Boy/Boston "My Home Town"	1960	7.50	15.00	30.00
❑ 4053	Jump Over/The Urge	1960	3.75	7.50	15.00
❑ 4053 [PS]	Jump Over/The Urge	1960	7.50	15.00	30.00
❑ 4057	Happy Shades of Blue/Chattanooga Choo Choo	1960	3.75	7.50	15.00
❑ 4057 [PS]	Happy Shades of Blue/Chattanooga Choo Choo	1960	7.50	15.00	30.00
❑ 4061	Humdinger/My Blue Heaven	1960	3.75	7.50	15.00
❑ 4061 [PS]	Humdinger/My Blue Heaven	1960	7.50	15.00	30.00
❑ 4066	Muskrat Ramble/Two Thousand-88	1961	3.75	7.50	15.00
❑ 4066 [PS]	Muskrat Ramble/Two Thousand-88	1961	7.50	15.00	30.00
❑ 4071	Buzz Buzz A-Diddle It/Opportunity	1961	3.75	7.50	15.00
❑ 4078	Transistor Sister/Walk to the Moon	1961	3.75	7.50	15.00
❑ 4078 [PS]	Transistor Sister/Walk to the Moon	1961	7.50	15.00	30.00
❑ 4083	For Me and My Gal/Blue Plate Special	1961	3.75	7.50	15.00
❑ 4096	Teen Queen of the Week/Wild Guy	1962	3.75	7.50	15.00
❑ 4106	Palisades Park/June, July and August	1962	4.00	8.00	16.00
❑ 4117	What's Gonna Happen When Summer's Done/Broadway	1962	3.75	7.50	15.00
❑ 4122	If You Were a Rock and Roll Record/The Truth, Ruth	1962	3.75	7.50	15.00
❑ 4132	Come On and Love Me/Four Letter Man	1963	3.00	6.00	12.00
❑ 4139	Patty Baby/Betty Jean	1963	3.00	6.00	12.00
❑ 4149	Everybody Monkey/Oh Gloria	1963	6.25	12.50	25.00
❑ 4155	Do What the Hippies Do/That's the Way Girls Are	1963	3.00	6.00	12.00
❑ 4168	What a Party/Sweet Georgia Brown	1964	3.00	6.00	12.00
❑ 4178	The Ups and Downs of Love/It's Been Nice	1964	6.25	12.50	25.00
WARNER BROS.					
❑ 5409	Abigail Beecher/All American Girl	1964	3.00	6.00	12.00
❑ 5434	OK Wheeler, The Used Car Dealer/Odie Cologne	1964	3.00	6.00	12.00
❑ 5448	Summertime U.S.A./Gotta Good Thing Goin'	1964	3.00	6.00	12.00
❑ 5487	Little Autograph Seeker/Too Much Monkey Business	1964	3.00	6.00	12.00
❑ 5615	Little Miss A-Go-Go/In the Night	1965	3.00	6.00	12.00
❑ 5615 [PS]	Little Miss A-Go-Go/In the Night	1965	6.25	12.50	25.00
❑ 5645	Action/Beachwood City	1965	3.75	7.50	15.00
❑ 5666	Let Me Show You Where It's At/The Old Rag Man	1965	3.00	6.00	12.00
❑ 5673	She's Something Else/Little Bitty Corrine	1965	3.00	6.00	12.00
❑ 5693	The Dedication Song/Come On, Come On	1966	3.00	6.00	12.00
❑ 5810	The Greatest Show on Earth/Hokie Pokie Girl	1966	3.00	6.00	12.00
❑ 5832	The Laughing Song/Natalie	1966	3.00	6.00	12.00
❑ 5859	Run for the Sun/Use Your Imagination	1966	3.00	6.00	12.00
❑ 5876	A Happy Clown/In My Wildest Dreams	1966	6.25	12.50	25.00
❑ 7019	Maverick's Flat/Run to the Poet Man	1967	6.25	12.50	25.00
❑ 7075	20th Century Fox/Cincinnati Woman	1967	6.25	12.50	25.00
WE MAKE ROCK & ROLL					
❑ 1601	Rock Around the Clock/Sock It to the Judge	1968	—	3.00	6.00
❑ 1604	Sea Cruise/She's a Friday Night Fox	1968	—	3.00	6.00

CANTINA BAND, THE

LOU CHRISTIE was a member.

Number	Title (A Side/B Side)	Yr	VG	VG+	NM
MILLENIUM					
❑ YB-11818	Summer '81 Medley/Out in California	1981	2.00	4.00	8.00

CAP-TANS, THE

The group on Anna is different than the others, but the others may not all be the same.

Number	Title (A Side/B Side)	Yr	VG	VG+	NM
ANNA					
❑ 1122	I'm Afraid/Tight Skirts and Crazy Sweaters	1960	75.00	15.00	30.00
CORAL					
❑ 65071	Asking/Who Can I Turn To	1951	75.00	150.00	300.00
DOT					
❑ 15114	I'm So Crazy for Love/With All My Love	1953	25.00	50.00	100.00
GOTHAM					
❑ 233	My, My, My, Ain't She Pretty/Never Be Lonely	1950	100.00	200.00	400.00
❑ 268	I Thought I Could Forget You/Waiting at the Station	1951	75.00	150.00	300.00

CAPALDI, JIM

Also see TRAFFIC.

Number	Title (A Side/B Side)	Yr	VG	VG+	NM
ATLANTIC					
❑ 89625	I'll Keep Holding On/Tales of Power	1984	—	2.00	4.00
❑ 89783 [DJ]	Tonight You're Mine (same on both sides)	1983	—	2.00	4.00
—May be promo only					
❑ 89799	Living on the Edge/Gifts of Unknown Things	1983	—	—	3.00
❑ 89849	That's Love/Runaway	1983	—	—	3.00
❑ 89849 [PS]	That's Love/Runaway	1983	—	2.00	4.00
ISLAND					
❑ 003	It's All Right/Whale Meat Again	1974	—	2.50	5.00
❑ 025	It's All Up to You/I've Got So Much Lovin'	1975	—	2.50	5.00
❑ 045	Love Hurts/Sugar Honey	1976	—	2.00	4.00
❑ 055	Goodbye Love/(B-side unknown)	1976	—	2.00	4.00
❑ 067	Goodnight and Good Morning/Short Cut Draw Blood	1976	—	2.00	4.00
❑ 1204	Eve/Going Down Slow All the Way	1972	—	3.00	6.00
❑ 1205	Oh How We Danced/Open Your Heart	1972	—	3.00	6.00
❑ 1216	Tricky Dicky Rides Again/Love Is All You Can Try	1973	—	2.50	5.00
❑ 99220	Some Came Running/Favela Music	1989	—	—	3.00
❑ 99220 [PS]	Some Came Running/Favela Music	1989	—	—	3.00
❑ 99266	Something So Strong/Child in the Storm	1988	—	—	3.00
❑ 99266 [PS]	Something So Strong/Child in the Storm	1988	—	—	3.00
RSO					
❑ 912	Daughter of the Night/I'm Gonna Do It	1978	—	2.00	4.00

CAPEHART, JERRY

Number	Title (A Side/B Side)	Yr	VG	VG+	NM
CASH					
❑ 1021	Walkin' Stick Boogie/Rollin'	1956	50.00	100.00	200.00
—With Eddie and Hank Cochran					
CREST					
❑ 1101	Song of New Orleans/The Young and Blue (Theme)	1962	12.50	25.00	50.00

CAPERS, THE

Number	Title (A Side/B Side)	Yr	VG	VG+	NM
DORE					
❑ 587	Rockin' Round the Mountain/What Is This Thing Called Love	1961	3.00	6.00	12.00
VEE JAY					
❑ 297	Miss You My Dear/Early One Morning	1958	6.25	12.50	25.00
❑ 315	Candy Store Blues/High School Diploma	1959	6.25	12.50	25.00

CAPITAL CITY ROCKETS

Number	Title (A Side/B Side)	Yr	VG	VG+	NM
ELEKTRA					
❑ 45855	Breakfast in Bed/Grab Your Honey	1973	2.00	4.00	8.00
❑ 45872	Little Bit O' Fun/Ten Hole Dollars	1973	2.00	4.00	8.00

CAPITOLS, THE (1)

Detroit-based R&B vocal group.

Number	Title (A Side/B Side)	Yr	VG	VG+	NM
KAREN					
❑ 1524	Cool Jerk/Hello Stranger	1966	3.75	7.50	15.00
❑ 1525	I Got to Handle It/Zig Zagging	1966	2.50	5.00	10.00
❑ 1526	We Got a Thing That's In the Groove/Tired Running from You	1966	2.50	5.00	10.00
❑ 1534	Patty Cake/Take a Chance on Me Baby	1967	2.50	5.00	10.00
❑ 1536	Cool Pearl/Don't Say Maybe Baby	1967	2.50	5.00	10.00
❑ 1537	Cool Jerk '68/Afro Twist	1968	2.50	5.00	10.00
❑ 1543	Soul Brother, Soul Sister/Ain't That Terrible	1968	2.50	5.00	10.00
❑ 1546	Soul Soul/When You're in Trouble	1969	2.50	5.00	10.00
❑ 1549	I Thought She Loved Me/When You're in Trouble	1969	2.50	5.00	10.00

CAPITOLS, THE (2)

Not group (1).

Number	Title (A Side/B Side)	Yr	VG	VG+	NM
CARLTON					
❑ 461	I Let Her Go/I've Got a Girl	1958	150.00	300.00	600.00

CAPITOLS, THE (U)

None of these is by group (1), though it's possible that one or more is by group (2).

Number	Title (A Side/B Side)	Yr	VG	VG+	NM
CINDY					
❑ 3002	Rosemary/Millie	1957	50.00	100.00	200.00
GATEWAY					
❑ 721	Day By Day/Little Things	1964	75.00	150.00	300.00
PET					
❑ 807	Angel of Love/'Cause I Love You	1958	50.00	100.00	200.00
TRIUMPH					
❑ 601	Three O'Clock Rock/Write Me a Love Letter	1959	7.50	15.00	30.00

CAPONE, SUSAN

Number	Title (A Side/B Side)	Yr	VG	VG+	NM
PILGRIM					
❑ 704	I'll Be Dancing/Four or Five Hundred Kisses	1956	6.25	12.50	25.00
❑ 718	Click-I-Dee, Click-I-Dee/Maybe Someday	1956	6.25	12.50	25.00

CAPRIS, THE (1)

Italian male vocal group from New York.

Number	Title (A Side/B Side)	Yr	VG	VG+	NM
20TH CENTURY					
❑ 1201	My Weakness/Yes, My Baby, Please!	1957	15.00	30.00	60.00
AMBIENT SOUND					
❑ 02697	There's a Moon Out Again/Morse Code of Love	1982	—	3.00	6.00
CANDLELITE					
❑ 422	Oh, My Darling/Rock Pretty Baby	196?	3.00	6.00	12.00
LIFETIME					
❑ 1001/2	Oh My Darling/Rock Pretty Baby	1961	25.00	50.00	100.00
LOST-NITE					
❑ 101	There's a Moon Out Tonight/Indian Girl	1961	17.50	35.00	70.00
—Pink label original					
❑ 101	There's a Moon Out Tonight/Indian Girl	196?	2.00	4.00	8.00
—Yellow label reissue					
❑ 148	Little Girl/When	196?	2.00	4.00	8.00
MR. PEEKE					
❑ 118	Limbo/From the Vine Came the Grape	1963	5.00	10.00	20.00
OLD TOWN					
❑ 1094	There's a Moon Out Tonight/Indian Girl	1961	7.50	15.00	30.00
—Light blue label					
❑ 1094	There's a Moon Out Tonight/Indian Girl	1962	5.00	10.00	20.00
—Mostly black label					
❑ 1099	Where I Fell in Love/Some People Think	1961	7.50	15.00	30.00
❑ 1103	Tears in My Eyes/Why Do I Cry	1961	7.50	15.00	30.00
❑ 1107	Girl in My Dreams/My Island in the Sun	1961	7.50	15.00	30.00
PLANET					
❑ 1010	There's a Moon Out Tonight/Indian Girl	1958	400.00	800.00	1200.

Number	Title (A Side/B Side)	Yr	VG	VG+	NM
SABRE					
❑ 201/2	My Promise to You/Bop! Bop! Bop!	1959	37.50	75.00	150.00
TROMMERS					
❑ 101	There's a Moon Out Tonight/Indian Girl	1961	6.25	12.50	25.00
—Red label					
❑ 101	There's a Moon Out Tonight/Indian Girl	1961	6.25	12.50	25.00
—White label (not a promo)					

CAPRIS, THE (2)

Different male vocal group than (1).

Number	Title (A Side/B Side)	Yr	VG	VG+	NM
GOTHAM					
❑ 304	God Only Knows/That's What You're Doing to Me	1954	150.00	300.00	600.00
—Blue label					
❑ 304	God Only Knows/That's What You're Doing to Me	1954	30.00	60.00	120.00
—Red label					
❑ 304	God Only Knows/That's What You're Doing to Me	1956	20.00	40.00	80.00
—Yellow label					
❑ 306	It Was Moonglow/Too Poor to Love	1955	50.00	100.00	200.00
❑ 308	It's a Miracle/Let's Linger Awhile	1956	30.00	60.00	120.00

CAPTAIN AND TENNILLE

Number	Title (A Side/B Side)	Yr	VG	VG+	NM
A&M					
❑ 1624	The Way I Want to Touch You/Disney Girls	1974	—	3.00	6.00
❑ 1672	Love Will Keep Us Together/Gentle Stranger	1975	—	2.00	4.00
❑ 1672 [PS]	Love Will Keep Us Together/Gentle Stranger	1975	—	3.00	6.00
❑ 1715	Por Amor Vivremos (Love Will Keep Us Together)/Broddy Bounce	1975	—	2.50	5.00
❑ 1725	The Way I Want to Touch You/Broddy Bounce	1975	—	2.00	4.00
❑ 1725 [PS]	The Way I Want to Touch You/Broddy Bounce	1975	—	3.00	6.00
❑ 1774	Como Yo Quiero Sentorte (The Way I Want to Touch You)/El Rebote de Broddy	1975	—	2.50	5.00
❑ 1782	Lonely Night (Angel Face)/Smile for Me One More Time	1976	—	2.00	4.00
❑ 1782 [PS]	Lonely Night (Angel Face)/Smile for Me One More Time	1976	—	3.00	6.00
❑ 1817	Shop Around/Butterscotch Castle	1976	—	2.00	4.00
❑ 1817 [PS]	Shop Around/Butterscotch Castle	1976	—	3.00	6.00
❑ 1870	Muskrat Love/Honey Come Love Me	1976	—	2.00	4.00
❑ 1870 [PS]	Muskrat Love/Honey Come Love Me	1976	—	3.00	6.00
❑ 1894	Song of Joy/Wedding Song (There Is Love)	1976	—	—	—
—Unreleased					
❑ 1912	Can't Stop Dancin'/Mis Canciones (The Good Songs)	1977	—	2.00	4.00
❑ 1912 [PS]	Can't Stop Dancin'/Mis Canciones (The Good Songs)	1977	—	3.00	6.00
❑ 1944	Come In from the Rain/We Never Really Said Goodbye	1977	—	2.00	4.00
❑ 1944 [PS]	Come In from the Rain/We Never Really Said Goodbye	1977	—	3.00	6.00
❑ 1970	Circles/1954 Boogie Blues	1977	—	2.00	4.00
❑ 2027	I'm On My Way/We Never Really Said Goodbye	1978	—	2.00	4.00
❑ 2027 [PS]	I'm On My Way/We Never Really Said Goodbye	1978	—	3.00	6.00
❑ 2063	You Never Done It Like That/"D" Keyboard Blues	1978	—	2.00	4.00
❑ 2063 [PS]	You Never Done It Like That/"D" Keyboard Blues	1978	—	3.00	6.00
❑ 2106	You Need a Woman Tonight/Love Me Like a Baby	1978	—	2.00	4.00
❑ 2106 [PS]	You Need a Woman Tonight/Love Me Like a Baby	1978	—	3.00	6.00
❑ 8600	Lonely Night (Angel Face)/Shop Around	1977	—	2.00	4.00
—Originals on green and yellow labels (later issues $3 NM)					
❑ 8600 [PS]	Lonely Night (Angel Face)/Shop Around	1977	—	3.00	6.00
❑ 8601	Song of Joy/Wedding Song (There Is Love)	1977	—	2.00	4.00
—Originals on green and yellow labels (later issues $3 NM)					
❑ 8601 [PS]	Song of Joy/Wedding Song (There Is Love)	1977	—	3.00	6.00
BUTTERSCOTCH CASTLE					
❑ 001	The Way I Want to Tocuh You/Disney Girls	1974	20.00	40.00	80.00
CASABLANCA					
❑ 2215	Do That To Me One More Time/Deep in the Dark	1979	—	2.00	4.00
❑ 2243	Love on a Shoestring/How Can You Be So Cold	1980	—	2.00	4.00
❑ 2247	Amame Una Vez Mas (Do That To Me One More Time)/Deep in the Dark	1980	—	2.00	4.00
❑ 2264	Baby You Still Got It/Happy Together (A Fantasy)	1980	—	2.00	4.00
❑ 2320	This Is Not the First Time/Gentle Stranger	1980	—	2.00	4.00
❑ 2328	Don't Forget Me/Keep Our Love Warm	1981	—	2.00	4.00
JOYCE					
❑ 101	The Way I Want to Tocuh You/Disney Girls	1974	10.00	20.00	40.00
PUREBRED					
❑ 0001	Tahoe Snow/Here Comes Santa Claus	198?	—	2.50	5.00
❑ 0001 [PS]	Tahoe Snow/Here Comes Santa Claus	198?	—	3.00	5.00

CAPTAIN BEEFHEART

Also see FRANK ZAPPA.

Number	Title (A Side/B Side)	Yr	VG	VG+	NM
A&M					
❑ 794	Diddy Wah Diddy/Who Do You Think You're Fooling	1966	10.00	20.00	40.00
❑ 818	Moonchild/Here I Am, Here I Always Am	1966	12.50	25.00	50.00
BUDDAH					
❑ 9	Yellow Brick Road/Abba Zaba	1967	3.75	7.50	15.00
❑ 108	Plastic Factory/Where There's Woman	1969	3.75	7.50	15.00
EPIC					
❑ 03190	Ice Cream for Crow/Light Reflected Off the Oceans of the Moon	1982	—	2.50	5.00
❑ 03190 [PS]	Ice Cream for Crow/Light Reflected Off the Oceans of the Moon	1982	—	3.00	6.00
MERCURY					
❑ 73494	I Got Love on My Mind/Upon the My-O-My	1974	2.00	4.00	8.00
REPRISE					
❑ 1068	Click Clack/I'm Gonna Boogalize You Baby	1972	3.75	7.50	15.00
❑ 1133	Too Much Time/My Head Is My Only House Unless It Rains	1972	3.75	7.50	15.00

CAPTAIN ZAP AND THE MOTORTOWN CUT-UPS

Number	Title (A Side/B Side)	Yr	VG	VG+	NM
MOTOWN					
❑ 1151	The Luney Landing/The Luney Take-Off	1969	5.00	10.00	20.00

CAPTIVATIONS, THE

Number	Title (A Side/B Side)	Yr	VG	VG+	NM
GARPAX					
❑ 44179	Red Hot Scrambler-Go/Speed Shift	1964	7.50	15.00	30.00
PENTACLE					
❑ 1635	Red Hot Scramblers-Go/Speed Shift	1964	15.00	30.00	60.00

CARAVELLES, THE (1)

British female vocal group.

Number	Title (A Side/B Side)	Yr	VG	VG+	NM
SMASH					
❑ 1852	You Don't Have to Be a Baby to Cry/The Last One to Know	1963	3.75	7.50	15.00
❑ 1869	Have You Ever Been Lonely/Don't Blow Your Cool	1964	3.00	6.00	12.00
❑ 1901	You Are Here/How Can I Be Sure	1964	3.00	6.00	12.00
❑ 1958	I Don't Care If the Sun Don't Shine/I Like a Man	1964	3.00	6.00	12.00

CARAVELLES, THE (U)

These may or may not be the same group, but they are definitely not group (1).

Number	Title (A Side/B Side)	Yr	VG	VG+	NM
JOEY					
❑ 301	Falling for You/Shake Baby	1963	37.50	75.00	150.00
❑ 6208	One Little Kiss/Twistin' Marie	1962	25.00	50.00	100.00
STARMAKER					
❑ 1925	Pink Lips/Angry Angel	1961	6.25	12.50	25.00

CARBO, CHUCK

Also see THE SPIDERS (1).

Number	Title (A Side/B Side)	Yr	VG	VG+	NM
ACE					
❑ 631	Tears, Tears and More Tears/I Shouldn't, But I Do	1961	3.00	6.00	12.00
❑ 666	Out on a Limb/Getting Out	1962	3.00	6.00	12.00
IMPERIAL					
❑ 5405	That's the Way to Win My Heart/Goodbye	1956	6.25	12.50	25.00
❑ 5423	Honey Bee/That's My Desire	1957	7.50	15.00	30.00
❑ 5452	The Bells Are Ringing/Poor Boy	1957	5.00	10.00	20.00
❑ 5479	I Miss You/The Times	1957	5.00	10.00	20.00
INSTANT					
❑ 3240	In the Night/Run. Henry	1962	3.00	6.00	12.00
❑ 3254	Two Tables Away/What Does It Take	1962	3.00	6.00	12.00
REX					
❑ 1003	Promises/Be My Girl	1959	3.75	7.50	15.00
❑ 1011	Lucy Brown/A Picture of You	1960	3.75	7.50	15.00
❑ 1012	Blue Velvet/It's You	1960	3.75	7.50	15.00

CARDBOARD ZEPPELIN

Supposedly a pseudonym for THE REGENTS.

Number	Title (A Side/B Side)	Yr	VG	VG+	NM
LAURIE					
❑ 3433	City Lights/Ten Story Building	1968	6.25	12.50	25.00

CARDINALS, THE (1)

Baltimore-based male vocal group.

Number	Title (A Side/B Side)	Yr	VG	VG+	NM
ATLANTIC					
❑ 952	I'll Always Love You/Pretty Baby Blues	1952	100.00	200.00	400.00
—Cardinals records on Atlantic before 952 are unconfirmed on 45 rpm					
❑ 958	Wheel of Fortune/Kiss Me Baby	1952	150.00	300.00	600.00
❑ 972	The Bump/She Rocks	1952	75.00	150.00	300.00
❑ 995	You Are My Only Love/Lovie Darling	1953	100.00	200.00	400.00
❑ 1025	Please Baby/Under a Blanket of Blue	1954	50.00	100.00	200.00
❑ 1054	The Door Is Still Open/Misirlou	1955	20.00	40.00	80.00
❑ 1067	Come Back My Love/Two Things I Love	1955	25.00	50.00	100.00
❑ 1079	Lovely Girl/There Goes My Heart to You	1955	25.00	50.00	100.00
❑ 1090	Choo Choo/Off Shore	1956	12.50	25.00	50.00
❑ 1103	The End of the Story/I Won't Make You Cry Anymore	1956	12.50	25.00	50.00
❑ 1126	Near You/One Love	1957	10.00	20.00	40.00

CARDINALS, THE (2)

Number	Title (A Side/B Side)	Yr	VG	VG+	NM
CHA CHA					
❑ 740	I Want You/Tomato Juice	1966	7.50	15.00	30.00
❑ 740 [PS]	I Want You/Tomato Juice	1966	12.50	25.00	50.00
❑ 741	Go Go Baby/Hatchet Face	1966	6.25	12.50	25.00
❑ 742	Saturday Night/I'm Gonna Tell on You	1966	6.25	12.50	25.00
❑ 748	When You're Away/I'm Gonna Tell on You	1966	6.25	12.50	25.00

CAREFREES, THE

Number	Title (A Side/B Side)	Yr	VG	VG+	NM
LONDON INT'L.					
❑ 10614	We Love You Beatles/Hot Blooded Lover	1964	5.00	10.00	20.00
—Red label					
❑ 10614	We Love You Beatles/Hot Blooded Lover	1964	5.00	10.00	20.00
—Gold label					
❑ 10614 [PS]	We Love You Beatles/Hot Blooded Lover	1964	10.00	20.00	40.00
❑ 10615	Paddy Whack/Aren't You Glad You're You	1964	3.75	7.50	15.00

CAREY, MARIAH

Number	Title (A Side/B Side)	Yr	VG	VG+	NM
COLUMBIA					
❑ 73348	Vision of Love//Prisoner/All In Your Mind/Someday (album snippets)	1990	—	—	3.00
❑ 73455	Love Takes Time/Sent from Up Above	1990	—	—	3.00
❑ 73561	Someday (Album Version)/Alone in Love	1990	—	2.50	5.00
❑ 73561	Someday (New 7" Jackswing)/Alone in Love	1991	—	—	3.00
❑ 73743	I Don't Wanna Cry/You Need Me	1991	—	—	3.00
❑ 73977	Emotions/Vanishing	1991	—	—	3.00
❑ 74088	Can't Let Go/To Be Around You	1991	—	—	3.00
❑ 74239	Make It Happen/Emotions (Special Motion Edit)	1992	—	—	3.00
❑ 74330	I'll Be There/So Blessed	1992	—	—	3.00
❑ 77080	Dreamlover/Do You Think of Me	1993	—	—	3.00
❑ 77224	Hero/Everything Fades Away	1993	—	—	3.00
❑ 77358	Without You/Never Forget You	1994	—	—	3.00
❑ 77499	Anytime You Need a Friend/Music Box	1994	—	—	3.00
❑ 77629	Endless Love/(Instrumental)	1994	—	—	3.00
—With Luther Vandross					
❑ 78043	Fantasy/Fantasy (Bad Boy with O.D.B.)	1995	—	—	3.00
❑ 78072	One Sweet Day/I Am Free	1995	2.00	4.00	8.00
—With Boyz II Men; deleted on day of issue					

Number	Title (A Side/B Side)	Yr	VG	VG+	NM
❑ 78270	Always Be My Baby/Long Ago	1996	—	—	2.00
❑ 78270 [PS]	Always Be My Baby/Long Ago	1996	—	—	2.00
❑ 78648	Honey (LP Version)/Honey (Bad Boy Remix)	1997	—	—	2.00
❑ 78648 [PS]	Honey (LP Version)/Honey (Bad Boy Remix)	1997	—	—	2.00
❑ 78821	My All/Breakdown	1998	—	—	2.00
❑ 78821 [PS]	My All/Breakdown	1998	—	—	2.00
❑ 79093	I Still Believe-Pure Imagination/I Still Believe	1999	—	—	2.00
❑ 79093 [PS]	I Still Believe-Pure Imagination/I Still Believe	1999	—	—	2.00
❑ 79260	Heartbreaker (Featuring Jay-Z)/Heartbreaker (Featuring Da Brat and Missy Elliott)	1999	—	—	3.00
❑ 79338	Thank God I Found You (album version)/Thank God I Found You (celebratory mix)	2000	—	—	3.00
❑ 79348	Can't Take That Away (Mariah's Theme)/Crybaby	2000	—	—	3.00

CARIANS, THE
Also see THE CORDIALS.

Number	Title (A Side/B Side)	Yr	VG	VG+	NM
INDIGO					
❑ 136	She's Gone/Snooty Friends	1961	25.00	50.00	100.00
MAGENTA					
❑ 04	Only a Dream/Girls	1961	12.50	25.00	50.00

CARLISLE, BELINDA
Also see GO-GO'S.

Number	Title (A Side/B Side)	Yr	VG	VG+	NM
ARK 21					
❑ S7-19941	In Too Deep/California	1998	—	—	3.00
I.R.S.					
❑ S45-17262 [DJ]	Since You've Gone (same on both sides)	1987	—	2.50	5.00
❑ S45-17262 [PS]	Since You've Gone	1987	—	2.50	5.00
❑ 52815	Mad About You/I Never Wanted a Rich Man	1986	—	—	3.00
❑ 52815 [PS]	Mad About You/I Never Wanted a Rich Man	1986	—	—	3.00
❑ 52889	I Feel the Magic/From the Heart	1986	—	—	3.00
❑ 52889 [PS]	I Feel the Magic/From the Heart	1986	—	—	3.00
MCA					
❑ 53181	Heaven Is a Place on Earth/We Can Change	1987	—	—	3.00
❑ 53181 [PS]	Heaven Is a Place on Earth/We Can Change	1987	—	—	3.00
❑ 53242	I Get Weak/Should I Let You In?	1987	—	—	3.00
❑ 53242 [PS]	I Get Weak/Should I Let You In?	1987	—	—	3.00
❑ 53308	Circle in the Sand/We Can Change	1988	—	—	3.00
❑ 53308 [PS]	Circle in the Sand/We Can Change	1988	—	—	3.00
❑ 53377	I Feel Free/Should I Let You In?	1988	—	—	3.00
❑ 53377 [PS]	I Feel Free/Should I Let You In?	1988	—	—	3.00
❑ 53706	Leave a Light On/Shades of Michelangelo	1989	—	3.00	6.00
—A-side features a guitar solo by George Harrison.					
❑ 53783	Summer Rain/Shades of Michelangelo	1989	—	—	3.00
VIRGIN					
❑ S7-17598	It's Too Real (Big Hairy Animal)/Window of the World	1993	—	2.00	4.00

CARLISLE, BOB

Number	Title (A Side/B Side)	Yr	VG	VG+	NM
JIVE/DIADEM					
❑ 42456	Butterfly Kisses (Album Version)/Butterfly Kisses (The Country Remix)	1997	—	2.50	5.00

CARLO

Number	Title (A Side/B Side)	Yr	VG	VG+	NM
LAURIE					
❑ 3063	Happy Time/Rockin' Rocket	1960	5.00	10.00	20.00
—As "Carlo and Jimmy"					
❑ 3151	Baby Doll/Write Me a Letter	1962	7.50	15.00	30.00
❑ 3157	Little Orphan Girl/Mairzy Doats	1963	7.50	15.00	30.00
❑ 3175	Five Minutes More/The Story of Love	1963	7.50	15.00	30.00
❑ 3227	Ring-a-Ling/Stranger in My Arms	1964	12.50	25.00	50.00
RAFTIS					
❑ 110	Claudine/Fever	1970	3.00	6.00	12.00

CARLTON, CARL

Number	Title (A Side/B Side)	Yr	VG	VG+	NM
20TH CENTURY					
❑ 2459	This Feeling's Rated X-Tra/Fighting in the Name of Love	1980	—	2.00	4.00
❑ 2488	She's a Bad Mama Jama (She's Built, She's Stacked)/This Feeling's Rated X-Tra	1981	—	2.00	4.00
❑ 2513	Let Me Love You Till the Morning Comes/Sexy Lady	1982	—	2.00	4.00
❑ 2601	I Think It's Gonna Be Alright/Let Me Love You Till the Morning Comes	1982	—	2.00	4.00
ABC					
❑ 11378	You Can't Stop a Man in Love/You Times Me Plus Love	1973	—	2.50	5.00
❑ 12059	Smokin' Room/Signed, Sealed, Delivered, I'm Yours	1974	—	2.50	5.00
❑ 12089	Morning, Noon and Nightime/Our Day Will Come	1975	—	2.50	5.00
❑ 12166	Ain't Gonna Tell Nobody (About You)/Live for Today, Not for Tomorrow	1976	—	2.50	5.00
❑ 12226	Let's Groove/Live for Today, Not for Tomorrow	1976	—	2.50	5.00
BACK BEAT					
❑ 588	Competition Ain't Nothin'/Three Way Love	1968	—	3.00	6.00
—As "Little Carl Carlton"					
❑ 598	46 Drums — 1 Guitar/Why Don't They Leave Us Alone	1968	—	3.00	6.00
—As "Little Carl Carlton"					
❑ 603	Look at Mary Wonder (How I Got Over)/Bad for Each Other	1969	—	3.00	6.00
—As "Little Carl Carlton"					
❑ 610	Don't Walk Away/Hold On a Little Longer	1969	—	3.00	6.00
❑ 613	Drop By My Place/Two Timer	1970	—	3.00	6.00
—As "Little Carl Carlton"					
❑ 617	I Can Feel It/You've Got So Much (To Learn About Love)	1970	—	3.00	6.00
❑ 619	Sure Miss Loving You/Wild Child	1970	—	3.00	6.00
❑ 621	Wild Child/Look at Mary Wonder (How I Got Over)	1971	—	3.00	6.00
❑ 624	The Generation Gap/Where Have You Been	1972	—	3.00	6.00
❑ 627	I Won't Let That Chump Break Your Heart/Why Don't They Leave Us Alone	1972	—	3.00	6.00
❑ 629	It Ain't Been Easy/I Wanna Be Your Main Squeeze	1973	—	3.00	6.00
❑ 630	Everlasting Love/I Wanna Be Your Main Squeeze	1974	2.00	4.00	8.00
❑ 27001	Everlasting Love/I Wanna Be Your Main Squeeze	1974	—	2.50	5.00
CASABLANCA					
❑ 880949-7	Private Property/Mama's Boy	1985	—	—	3.00
❑ 884274-7	Slipped, Tripped (Fooled Around and Fell in Love)/Hot	1986	—	—	3.00
GOLDEN WORLD					
❑ 23	Nothin' No Sweeter Than Love/I Love True Love	1965	6.25	12.50	25.00
LANDO					
❑ 8527	So What/(B-side unknown)	1965	12.50	25.00	50.00
MERCURY					
❑ 73969	Something's Wrong/You, You	1977	—	2.00	4.00
RCA					
❑ PB-13313	Baby I Need Your Loving/Everyone Can Be a Star	1982	—	2.00	4.00
❑ PB-13406	Swing That Sexy Thang/Just One Kiss	1982	—	2.00	4.00

CARMEL SISTERS, THE

Number	Title (A Side/B Side)	Yr	VG	VG+	NM
COLPIX					
❑ 767	Go, Go, G.T.O./Sunny Winter	1965	75.00	150.00	300.00
—As "Carol and Cheryl"					
JUBILEE					
❑ 5464	Joey's Comin' Home/The Rumor	1963	5.00	10.00	20.00

CARMEN, ERIC
Also see CYRUS ERIE; THE QUICK; RASPBERRIES.

Number	Title (A Side/B Side)	Yr	VG	VG+	NM
ARISTA					
❑ 0165	All By Myself/Everything	1975	—	2.00	4.00
❑ 0184	Never Gonna Fall in Love Again/No Hard Feelings	1976	—	2.00	4.00
❑ 0200	Sunrise/My Girl	1976	—	2.00	4.00
❑ 0266	She Did It/Someday	1977	—	2.00	4.00
❑ 0266 [PS]	She Did It/Someday	1977	—	3.00	6.00
❑ 0295	Boats Against the Current/Take It or Leave It	1977	—	2.00	4.00
❑ 0319	Marathon Man/I Think I Found Myself	1978	—	2.00	4.00
❑ 0354	Change of Heart/Hey Deanie	1978	—	2.00	4.00
❑ 0384	Baby I Need Your Lovin'/Heaven Can Wait	1979	—	2.00	4.00
❑ 0435	Haven't We Come a Long Way/End of the World	1979	—	2.00	4.00
❑ 0506	It Hurts Too Much/You Need Some Lovin'	1980	—	2.00	4.00
❑ 0550	All for Love/Tonight You're Mine	1980	—	2.00	4.00
❑ 9686	Make Me Lose Control/That's Rock 'N' Roll	1988	—	—	3.00
❑ 9686 [PS]	Make Me Lose Control/That's Rock 'N' Roll	1988	—	—	3.00
❑ 9736	Boats Against the Current/No Hard Feelings	1988	—	—	3.00
❑ 9746	Reason to Try/Sunrise	1988	—	—	3.00
❑ 9746 [PS]	Reason to Try/Sunrise	1988	—	—	3.00
COOL					
❑ 101	The Rock Stops Here/(Instrumental)	1988	—	—	3.00
❑ 101 [PS]	The Rock Stops Here/(Instrumental)	1988	—	—	3.00
EPIC					
❑ 10669	I'll Hold Out My Hand/It Won't Be the Same Without You	1970	—	—	—
—Not known to exist					
GEFFEN					
❑ 29032	I'm Through with Love/Maybe My Baby	1985	—	—	3.00
❑ 29032 [PS]	I'm Through with Love/Maybe My Baby	1985	—	—	3.00
❑ 29118	I Wanna Hear It from Your Lips/Spotlight	1985	—	—	3.00
❑ 29118 [PS]	I Wanna Hear It from Your Lips/Spotlight	1985	—	—	3.00
RCA					
❑ 5315-7-R	Hungry Eyes/Where Are You Tonight	1987	—	—	3.00

CARNATIONS, THE
Several different groups.

Number	Title (A Side/B Side)	Yr	VG	VG+	NM
DERBY					
❑ 789	Tree in the Meadow/Clown of the Masquerade	1952	100.00	200.00	400.00
ENRICA					
❑ 1001	Gimme, Gimme, Gimme/Love, Open My Heart	1959	6.25	12.50	25.00
FRATERNITY					
❑ 863	Red Wing/Casual	1960	6.25	12.50	25.00
LAURIE					
❑ 3163	Punctuation/Funny Time	1963	6.25	12.50	25.00
LESCAY					
❑ 3002	Long Tall Girl/Is There Such a World	1961	25.00	50.00	100.00
SAVOY					
❑ 1172	Angels Sent You to Me/Night Time Is the Right Time	1955	15.00	30.00	60.00
TERRY-TONE					
❑ 199	Barbary Coast/Sleepy Hollow	1960	10.00	20.00	40.00
UNIVERSITY					
❑ 606	Leap Year/A Wing and a Prayer	1960	6.25	12.50	25.00

CARO, NYDIA

Number	Title (A Side/B Side)	Yr	VG	VG+	NM
ROULETTE					
❑ 4588	Ask Me What I Want for Christmas/Hey Johnny What	1964	3.00	6.00	12.00
❑ 4588 [PS]	Ask Me What I Want for Christmas/Hey Johnny What	1964	5.00	10.00	20.00

CAROL AND CHERYL
See THE CARMEL SISTERS.

CAROL AND GERRI

Number	Title (A Side/B Side)	Yr	VG	VG+	NM
MGM					
❑ 13568	How Can I Ever Find the Way/On You, Heartache Looks Good	1966	10.00	20.00	40.00

CAROLS, THE (1)
Female group.

Number	Title (A Side/B Side)	Yr	VG	VG+	NM
LAMP					
❑ 2001	My Search Is Over/Keko	1957	12.50	25.00	50.00

CAROLS, THE (2)

Male group.

Number	Title (A Side/B Side)	Yr	VG	VG+	NM
SAVOY					
❑ 896	Fifty Million Women/I Got a Feelin'	1953	37.50	75.00	150.00

CAROUSEL, THE

Number	Title (A Side/B Side)	Yr	VG	VG+	NM
ABC					
❑ 10953	One Mistake/Only One for Me	1967	3.00	6.00	12.00
TEEN TOWN					
❑ 108	I've Been with You/What Will You Do for Me	1969	3.75	7.50	15.00
❑ 116	To Say Goodbye/I Get Along Indefinitely	1969	3.75	7.50	15.00

CAROUSELS, THE

Possibly more than one group.

Number	Title (A Side/B Side)	Yr	VG	VG+	NM
ABC-PARAMOUNT					
❑ 10233	Symptoms of Love/The Hush of Love	1961	6.25	12.50	25.00
AUTUMN					
❑ 13	Beneath the Willow/Sail Away	1965	2.50	5.00	10.00
GONE					
❑ 5118	You Can Come If You Want To/Pretty Little Thing	1961	12.50	25.00	50.00
❑ 5118	If You Want To/Pretty Little Thing	1961	7.50	15.00	30.00
❑ 5131	Never Let Him Go/Dirty Tricks	1962	6.25	12.50	25.00
GUYDEN					
❑ 2102	I Wanna Fly/Something Else	1964	3.00	6.00	12.00
JAGUAR					
❑ 3029	Drive-In Movie/Rendezvous	1959	15.00	30.00	60.00
SPRY					
❑ 116	I've Cried Enough/Did I Cry Enough	1962	37.50	75.00	150.00

CARPENTERS

Number	Title (A Side/B Side)	Yr	VG	VG+	NM
A&M					
❑ 1142	Ticket to Ride/Your Wonderful Parade	1969	2.50	5.00	10.00
❑ 1183	(They Long to Be) Close to You/I Kept On Loving You	1970	—	2.50	5.00
❑ 1217	We've Only Just Begun/All of My Life	1970	—	2.50	5.00
❑ 1217 [PS]	We've Only Just Begun/All of My Life	1970	—	3.00	6.00
❑ 1236	Merry Christmas Darling/Mr. Guder	1970	—	3.00	6.00
—A-side vocal is different than later releases of this song					
❑ 1236 [PS]	Merry Christmas Darling/Mr. Guder	1970	2.00	4.00	8.00
❑ 1243	For All We Know/Don't Be Afraid	1971	—	2.00	4.00
❑ 1243 [PS]	For All We Know/Don't Be Afraid	1971	—	3.00	6.00
❑ 1260	Rainy Days and Mondays/Saturday	1971	—	2.00	4.00
❑ 1260 [PS]	Rainy Days and Mondays/Saturday	1971	—	3.00	6.00
❑ 1289	Superstar/Bless the Beasts and Children	1971	—	2.00	4.00
❑ 1289 [PS]	Superstar/Bless the Beasts and Children	1971	—	3.00	6.00
❑ 1322	Hurting Each Other/Maybe It's You	1972	—	2.00	4.00
❑ 1322 [PS]	Hurting Each Other/Maybe It's You	1972	—	3.00	6.00
❑ 1351	It's Going to Take Some Time/Flat Baroque	1972	—	2.00	4.00
❑ 1351 [PS]	It's Going to Take Some Time/Flat Baroque	1972	—	3.00	6.00
❑ 1367	Goodbye to Love/Crystal Lullaby	1972	—	2.00	4.00
❑ 1367 [PS]	Goodbye to Love/Crystal Lullaby	1972	—	3.00	6.00
❑ 1391	Top of the World/Druscilla Penny	1972	—	—	—
—Unreleased					
❑ 1413	Sing/Druscilla Penny	1973	—	2.00	4.00
❑ 1413 [PS]	Sing/Druscilla Penny	1973	—	3.00	6.00
❑ 1446	Yesterday Once More/Road Ode	1973	—	2.00	4.00
❑ 1446 [PS]	Yesterday Once More/Road Ode	1973		3.00	0.00
❑ 1468	Top of the World/Heather	1973	—	2.00	4.00
—Originals have brown labels					
❑ 1468	Top of the World/Heather	1973	—	—	3.00
—Second pressings have silvery labels					
❑ 1468 [PS]	Top of the World/Heather	1973	—	3.00	6.00
❑ 1521	I Won't Last a Day Without You/One Love	1974	—	2.00	4.00
❑ 1521 [PS]	I Won't Last a Day Without You/One Love	1974	—	3.00	6.00
❑ 1646	Please Mister Postman/This Masquerade	1974	—	2.00	4.00
❑ 1646 [PS]	Please Mister Postman/This Masquerade	1974	—	3.00	6.00
❑ 1648	Santa Claus Is Coming to Town/Merry Christmas Darling	1974	—	2.50	5.00
❑ 1648 [PS]	Santa Claus Is Coming to Town/Merry Christmas Darling	1974	2.50	5.00	10.00
❑ 1677	Only Yesterday/Happy	1975	—	2.00	4.00
❑ 1677 [PS]	Only Yesterday/Happy	1975	—	3.00	6.00
❑ 1721	Solitaire/Love Me for What I Am	1975	—	2.00	4.00
❑ 1721 [PS]	Solitaire/Love Me for What I Am	1975	—	3.00	6.00
❑ 1800	There's a Kind of Hush (All Over the World)/(I'm Caught Between) Goodbye and I Love You	1976	—	2.00	4.00
❑ 1800 [PS]	There's a Kind of Hush (All Over the World)/(I'm Caught Between) Goodbye and I Love You	1976	—	3.00	6.00
❑ 1828	I Need to Be in Love/Sandy	1976	—	2.00	4.00
❑ 1859	Goofus/Boat to Sail	1976	—	2.00	4.00
❑ 1940	All You Get from Love Is a Love Song/I Have You	1977	—	2.00	4.00
❑ 1978	Calling Occupants of Interplanetary Craft/Can't Smile Without You	1977	—	2.00	4.00
❑ 1978 [PS]	Calling Occupants of Interplanetary Craft/Can't Smile Without You	1977	—	3.00	6.00
❑ 1991	The Christmas Song/Merry Christmas Darling	1977	—	2.50	5.00
❑ 1991 [PS]	The Christmas Song/Merry Christmas Darling	1977	2.00	4.00	8.00
❑ 2008	Sweet, Sweet Smile/I Have You	1978	—	2.00	4.00
❑ 2097	I Believe You/B'wana She No Home	1978	—	2.00	4.00
❑ 2344	Touch Me When We're Dancing/Because We Are In Love (The Wedding Song)	1981	—	2.00	4.00
❑ 2344 [PS]	Touch Me When We're Dancing/Because We Are in Love (The Wedding Song)	1981	—	2.00	4.00
❑ 2370	(Want You) Back in My Life Again/Somebody's Been Lyin'	1981	—	2.00	4.00
❑ 2386	Those Good Old Dreams/When It's Gone	1981	—	2.00	4.00
❑ 2405	Beechwood 4-5789/Two Sides	1982	—	2.00	4.00
❑ 2585	Make Believe It's Your First Time/Look to Your Dreams	1983	—	2.00	4.00
❑ 2585 [PS]	Make Believe It's Your First Time/Look to Your Dreams	1983	—	2.50	5.00
❑ 2620	Sailing on the Tide/Your Baby Doesn't Love You Anymore	1984	—	2.00	4.00
❑ 2700	Do You Hear What I Hear/Little Altar Boy	1984	2.50	5.00	10.00
❑ 2735	Yesterday Once More/(They Long to Be) Close to You-We've Only Just Begun	1985	5.00	10.00	20.00
❑ 2735 [PS]	Yesterday Once More/(They Long to Be) Close to You-We've Only Just Begun	1985	5.00	10.00	20.00
❑ 8620	The Christmas Song/Merry Christmas Darling	1982	—	2.50	5.00
❑ 8620 [PS]	The Christmas Song/Merry Christmas Darling	1982	2.50	5.00	10.00
MAGIC LAMP					
❑ 704	I'll Be Yours/Looking for Love	1967	500.00	1000.	2000.
—As "Karen Carpenter", but Richard also was on this record					

CARPETS, THE

Number	Title (A Side/B Side)	Yr	VG	VG+	NM
FEDERAL					
❑ 12257	Why Do I/Let Her Go	1956	50.00	100.00	200.00
❑ 12269	Lonely Me/Chicken Backs	1956	50.00	100.00	200.00

CARR, CATHY

Number	Title (A Side/B Side)	Yr	VG	VG+	NM
CORAL					
❑ 60907	Heartbroken/Half Pink Boogie	1953	3.00	6.00	12.00
❑ 60988	I Just Can't Get That Melody Out of My Mind/Somebody Told You a Lie	1953	3.00	6.00	12.00
❑ 61092	I'll Cry at Your Wedding/Cryin' for the Caroline's	1953	3.00	6.00	12.00
❑ 61646	I'll Cry at Your Wedding/Heartbroken	1956	2.50	5.00	10.00
FRATERNITY					
❑ 718	Morning, Noon and Night/Toward Evening	1955	5.00	10.00	20.00
❑ 734	Ivory Tower/Please Please Believe Me	1956	3.75	7.50	15.00
❑ 743	Heart Hideaway/The Boy on Page 35	1956	3.75	7.50	15.00
❑ 750	Oh Baby/Waltzing to the Blues	1956	3.75	7.50	15.00
❑ 757	It Looks Like Love/Una Momenta	1957	3.00	6.00	12.00
❑ 765	Wild Honey/Speak for Yourself John	1957	3.00	6.00	12.00
❑ 782	House of Heartache/Presents from the Past	1957	3.00	6.00	12.00
❑ 793	Doll Baby/Don't Come to My Party	1958	3.00	6.00	12.00
LAURIE					
❑ 3133	Ivory Tower/Should I Believe Him	1962	2.50	5.00	10.00
❑ 3147	Sailorboy/Next Time a Band Plays a Waltz	1962	2.50	5.00	10.00
❑ 3161	I Waded in the Water/In Place of You	1963	2.50	5.00	10.00
❑ 3206	My Favorite Song/The Ghost of a Broken Heart	1963	2.50	5.00	10.00
❑ 3378	When You Come Home Again/The Ghost of a Broken Heart	1967	—	3.00	6.00
ROULETTE					
❑ 4107	To Know Him Is to Love Him/Put Away the Invitation	1958	3.00	6.00	12.00
❑ 4125	First Anniversary/With Love	1959	3.00	6.00	12.00
❑ 4152 [M]	I'm Gonna Change Him/The Little Things You Do	1959	3.00	6.00	12.00
❑ SSR-4152 [S]	I'm Gonna Change Him/The Little Things You Do	1959	7.50	15.00	30.00
❑ 4187	Shy/Personal Secret	1959	3.00	6.00	12.00
❑ 4219	Little Sister/Dark River	1960	3.00	6.00	12.00
❑ 4248	A Little Time/What Do I Do Now	1960	3.00	6.00	12.00
❑ 4296	I Want to Be Your Pet/Golden Locket	1960	3.00	6.00	12.00
❑ 4323	Johnny's Song/Someone Told You a Lie	1961	3.00	6.00	12.00
❑ 4367	Yearning/Baseball He Loves	1961	3.00	6.00	12.00
❑ 4383	I Can't Begin to Tell You/You're Breaking My Heart	1961	3.00	6.00	12.00
SMASH					
❑ 1726	Footprints in the Snow/Nein, Nein, Fraulein	1961	3.00	6.00	12.00

CARR, JAMES

Number	Title (A Side/B Side)	Yr	VG	VG+	NM
ATLANTIC					
❑ 2803	Hold On/I'll Put It to You	1971	3.00	6.00	12.00
GOLDWAX					
❑ 108	You Don't Want Me/Only Fools Run Away	1965	7.50	15.00	30.00
❑ 112	I Can't Make It/Lovers' Competition	1965	7.50	15.00	30.00
❑ 119	He's Better Than You/Talk Talk	1965	7.50	15.00	30.00
❑ 302	You've Got My Mind Messed Up/That's What I Want to Know	1966	5.00	10.00	20.00
❑ 309	Love Attack/Come Back to Me Baby	1966	3.75	7.50	15.00
❑ 311	Pouring Water on a Drowning Man/Forgetting You	1966	3.75	7.50	15.00
❑ 317	The Dark End of the Street/Lovable Girl	1967	4.00	8.00	16.00
❑ 323	Let It Happen/A Losing Game	1967	3.75	7.50	15.00
❑ 328	I'm a Fool for You/Gonna Send You Back to Georgia	1967	3.75	7.50	15.00
❑ 332	A Man Needs a Woman/Stronger Than Love	1968	3.75	7.50	15.00
❑ 335	Life Turned Her That Way/A Message to Young Lovers	1968	3.75	7.50	15.00
❑ 338	Freedom Train/That's the Way Love Turned Out for Me	1968	3.75	7.50	15.00
❑ 340	To Love Somebody/These Ain't Teardrops	1969	3.75	7.50	15.00
❑ 343	Everybody Needs Somebody/Row, Row Your Boat	1969	3.75	7.50	15.00

CARROLL, ANDREA

Number	Title (A Side/B Side)	Yr	VG	VG+	NM
BIG TOP					
❑ 515	The Doolang/This Time Tomorrow	1964	10.00	20.00	40.00
❑ 3156	It Hurts to Be Sixteen/Why Am I So Shy	1963	5.00	10.00	20.00
EPIC					
❑ 9438	I've Got a Date with Frankie/Young and Lonely	1961	25.00	50.00	100.00
❑ 9450	Please Don't Talk to the Lifeguard/Room of Memories	1961	5.00	10.00	20.00
❑ 9471	Gee Dad/The Charm on My Arm	1961	5.00	10.00	20.00
❑ 9471 [PS]	Gee Dad/The Charm on My Arm	1961	10.00	20.00	40.00
❑ 9523	Miss Happiness/Fifteen Shades of Pink	1962	5.00	10.00	20.00
RCA VICTOR					
❑ 47-8618	Mr. Music Man/Sally Fool	1965	5.00	10.00	20.00
UNITED ARTISTS					
❑ 982	The World Isn't Big Enough/She Gets Everything She Wants	1966	5.00	10.00	20.00
❑ 50039	Hey, Beach Boy/Why Should We Take the Easy Way Out	1966	7.50	15.00	30.00

CARROLL, BERNADETTE

Number	Title (A Side/B Side)	Yr	VG	VG+	NM
JULIA					
❑ 1106	My Heart Stood Still/Sweet Sugar Sweet	1962	3.75	7.50	15.00
LAURIE					
❑ 3217	Nicky/All the Way Home I Cried	1964	3.75	7.50	15.00
—The Four Seasons sing backup on this record					
❑ 3238	Party Girl/I Don't Wanna Know	1964	3.75	7.50	15.00
❑ 3268	Happy Birthday/Homecoming Party	1964	3.75	7.50	15.00
❑ 3278	The Hero/One Little Lie	1964	3.75	7.50	15.00
❑ 3311	Circus Girl/Don't Hurt Me	1965	3.75	7.50	15.00
❑ 3320	He's Just a Playboy/Try Your Luck	1965	3.75	7.50	15.00

CARROLL, WAYNE

Number	Title (A Side/B Side)	Yr	VG	VG+	NM
KING					
❑ 5123	Chicken Out/Cindy Lee	1958	12.50	25.00	50.00
❑ 5134	Rockin' Chair Momma/There's Been a Change in Me	1958	12.50	25.00	50.00
❑ 5146	He Cheated/Wall Around Your Heart	1958	12.50	25.00	50.00

CARROLL BROTHERS, THE

Number	Title (A Side/B Side)	Yr	VG	VG+	NM
CAMEO					
❑ 140	(My Gal Is) Red Hot/Dearly Beloved	1959	20.00	40.00	80.00
❑ 213	Don't Knock the Twist/Bo Diddley	1962	5.00	10.00	20.00
❑ 221	Sweet Georgia Brown/Boot It	1962	5.00	10.00	20.00
FELSTED					
❑ 8550	Movin' Day/I Found You	1959	5.00	10.00	20.00

CARTER, CLARENCE

Number	Title (A Side/B Side)	Yr	VG	VG+	NM
ABC					
❑ 12058	Warning/On Your Way Down	1974	—	2.00	4.00
❑ 12094	Everything Comes Up Roses/A Very Special Love Song	1975	—	2.00	4.00
❑ 12130	I Got Caught/Take It All Off	1975	—	2.00	4.00
❑ 12162	Dear Abby/Love Ain't Here No More	1976	—	2.00	4.00
❑ 12224	Heart Full of Song/All Messed Up	1976	—	2.00	4.00
ATLANTIC					
❑ 2461	I Can't See Myself/Looking for a Fox	1967	—	3.00	6.00
❑ 2508	Slip Away/Funky Fever	1968	2.00	4.00	8.00
❑ 2569	Too Weak to Fight/Let Me Comfort You	1968	—	3.00	6.00
❑ 2576	Back Door Santa/That Old Time Feeling	1968	2.00	4.00	8.00
❑ 2605	Snatching It Back/Making Love	1969	—	3.00	6.00
❑ 2642	The Feeling Is Right/You Can't Miss What You Can't Measure	1969	—	3.00	6.00
❑ 2660	Doin' Our Thing/I Smell a Rat	1969	—	3.00	6.00
❑ 2702	Take It Off Him and Put It On Me/A Few Troubles I've Had	1970	—	3.00	6.00
❑ 2726	I Can't Leave Your Love Alone/Devil Woman	1970	—	3.00	6.00
❑ 2748	Patches/Say It One More Time	1970	—	3.00	6.00
❑ 2774	It's All in Your Mind/Till I Can't Take It Anymore	1970	—	3.00	6.00
❑ 2801	The Court Room/Getting the Bills	1971	—	3.00	6.00
❑ 2818	Slipped, Tripped, and Fell in Love/I Hate to Love and Run	1971	—	3.00	6.00
❑ 2842	I'm the One/Scratch My Back	1971	—	3.00	6.00
❑ 2875	If You Can't Beat 'Em/Lonesomest Lonesome	1972	—	3.00	6.00
—With Candi Carter					
FAME					
❑ XW179	Put On Your Shoes and Walk/I Found Somebody New	1973	—	2.50	5.00
❑ XW250	Sixty Minute Man/Mother-in-Law	1973	—	2.50	5.00
❑ XW330	I'm the Midnight Special/I Got Another Woman	1973	—	2.50	5.00
❑ XW415	Love's Trying to Come to You/Heartbreak Woman	1974	—	2.50	5.00
❑ 1010	Tell Daddy/I Stayed Away Too Long	1966	3.00	6.00	12.00
❑ 1013	Thread the Needle/Don't Make My Baby Cry	1967	3.00	6.00	12.00
❑ 1016	Road of Love/She Ain't Gonna Do Right	1967	3.00	6.00	12.00
❑ 91006	Back in Your Arms/Holdin' Out	1972	—	2.50	5.00
ICHIBAN					
❑ 101	Messin' with My Mind/I Was in the Neighborhood	1986	—	—	3.00
❑ 106	If You Let Me Take You Home/So You're Leaving Me	1986	—	—	3.00
❑ 108	Strokin'/Love Me with Feelin'	1987	2.00	4.00	8.00
❑ 116	Doctor C.C./I Stayed Away Too Long	1987	—	—	3.00
❑ 131	Grandpa Can't Find His Kate/What'd I Say	1988	—	—	3.00
❑ 135	Trying to Sleep Tonight/(B-side unknown)	1988	—	—	3.00
❑ 158	I'm Just Not Good/I'm the Best	1989	—	—	3.00
❑ 164	Why Do I Stay Here and Take This Shit fro You/It's a Man Down There	1989	—	—	3.00
❑ 213	In Between a Rock and a Hard Place/Dance to the Blues	1990	—	—	3.00
❑ 222	Things Ain't Like They Used to Be/Pickin' 'Em Up, Layin' 'Em Down	1990	—	—	3.00
❑ 238	I Ain't Leaving, Girl/If You See My Lady	1991	—	—	3.00
❑ 262	"G" Spot/Hot Dog	1992	—	—	3.00
❑ 275	Hand Me Down Love/Let's Get a Quickie	1992	—	—	3.00
RONN					
❑ 90	I Couldn't Refuse Your Love/What Was I Supposed to Do?	1977	—	2.50	5.00
VENTURE					
❑ 130	Jimmy's Disco/Searching	1980	—	2.00	4.00
❑ 141	Let's Burn/If I Stay	1980	—	2.00	4.00
❑ 145	It's a Monster Thang/If I Were Yours	1981	—	2.00	4.00
❑ 147	Can We Slip Away Again/If I Were Yours	1981	—	2.00	4.00

CARTER, MEL

Number	Title (A Side/B Side)	Yr	VG	VG+	NM
AMOS					
❑ 132	Everything Stops for a Little While/This Is My Life	1970	—	3.00	6.00
❑ 139	Kiss Tomorrow Goodbye/This Is My Life	1970	—	3.00	6.00
ARWIN					
❑ 123	Sugar/I'm Coming Home	1960	3.75	7.50	15.00
BELL					
❑ 743	Didn't We/I Pretend	1968	—	3.00	6.00
❑ 775	Another Saturday Night/Coming From You	1969	—	3.00	6.00
CREAM					
❑ 8041	You Changed My Life Again/(B-side unknown)	1980	—	2.00	4.00
❑ 8143	Who's Right, Who's Wrong/I Don't Wanna Get Over You	1981	—	2.00	4.00
DERBY					
❑ 1003	When a Boy Falls in Love/So Wonderful	1963	3.00	6.00	12.00
❑ 1005	Time of Young Love/Wonderful Love	1963	3.00	6.00	12.00
❑ 1008	Why I Call Her Mine/After the Party, the Meeting Is Sweeter	1964	3.00	6.00	12.00
IMPERIAL					
❑ 66052	'Deed I Do/What's On Your Mind	1964	2.00	4.00	8.00
❑ 66078	I'll Never Be Free/The Richest Man Alive	1964	2.00	4.00	8.00
❑ 66101	High Noon/I Just Can't Imagine	1965	2.00	4.00	8.00
❑ 66113	Hold Me, Thrill Me, Kiss Me/Sweet Little Girl	1965	2.50	5.00	10.00
❑ 66138	(All of a Sudden) My Heart Sings/When I Hold the Hand of the One I Love	1965	2.00	4.00	8.00
❑ 66148	Love Is All We Need/I Wish I Didn't Love You So	1965	2.00	4.00	8.00
❑ 66165	Band of Gold/Detour	1966	2.00	4.00	8.00
❑ 66183	You You You/If You Lose Her	1966	2.00	4.00	8.00
❑ 66208	Take Good Care of Her/Tar and Cement	1966	2.00	4.00	8.00
❑ 66228	As Time Goes By/Look to the Rainbow	1966	2.00	4.00	8.00
LIBERTY					
❑ MLC-1 [DJ]	The Star Spangled Banner (same on both sides)	196?	3.00	6.00	12.00
—Promo only; "This record is issued by Liberty Records as a Public Service" on label					
❑ 55970	Edelweiss/For Once in My Life	1968	—	3.00	6.00
❑ 55987	Star Dust/Enter Laughing	1967	—	3.00	6.00
❑ 56000	Be My Love/Look Into My Love	1967	—	3.00	6.00
❑ 56015	Excuse Me/The Other Woman	1968	—	3.00	6.00
PRIVATE STOCK					
❑ 45057	Put a Little Love Away/Dancing for Dimes	1975	—	2.00	4.00
❑ 45087	My Coloring Book	1976	—	2.00	4.00
ROMAR					
❑ 711	She Is Me/Do Me Wrong, But Do Me	1973	—	2.00	4.00
❑ 714	Treasure of Love/Do Me Wrong, But Do Me	1973	—	2.00	4.00
❑ 716	I Only Have Eyes for You/Treasure of Love	1974	—	2.00	4.00

CARTER, SONNY

Number	Title (A Side/B Side)	Yr	VG	VG+	NM
CARLTON					
❑ 481	Crying Over You/My Lonely Life	1959	—	—	—
—Unreleased?					
DOT					
❑ 15921	Crying Over You/My Lonely Life	1959	7.50	15.00	30.00
KING					
❑ 4739	There Is No Greater Love/Oh Baby	1954	12.50	25.00	50.00
❑ 4756	It's Strange but True/I Solemnly Swear	1954	12.50	25.00	50.00

CARTEY, RIC

Number	Title (A Side/B Side)	Yr	VG	VG+	NM
ABC-PARAMOUNT					
❑ 10415	Poor Me/Something in My Eye	1963	3.00	6.00	12.00
NRC					
❑ 503	My Heart Belongs to You/Scratching on the Screen	1959	12.50	25.00	50.00
RCA VICTOR					
❑ 47-6751	Young Love/Oooh-Eee	1956	20.00	40.00	80.00
❑ 47-6828	Heart Throb/I Wancha to Know	1957	20.00	40.00	80.00
❑ 47-6920	Let Me Tell You About Love/Born to Love One Woman	1957	30.00	60.00	120.00
❑ 47-7011	My Babe/Hello Down Easy	1957	30.00	60.00	120.00
STARS					
❑ 539	Young Love/Oooh-Eee	1956	37.50	75.00	150.00

CASANOVAS, THE

Number	Title (A Side/B Side)	Yr	VG	VG+	NM
APOLLO					
❑ 471	That's All/Are You for Real	1955	25.00	50.00	100.00
❑ 474	It's Been a Long Time/Hush-a-Mecca	1955	37.50	75.00	150.00
❑ 477	I Don't Want You to Go/Please Be My Love	1955	37.50	75.00	150.00
❑ 483	My Baby's Love/Sleepy Head Mama	1956	37.50	75.00	150.00
❑ 519	Please Be Mine/For You and You Alone	1957	25.00	50.00	100.00
❑ 523	(I Got a) Good Lookin' Baby/You Are My Queen	1957	25.00	50.00	100.00

CASCADES, THE

Probably all the same group.

Number	Title (A Side/B Side)	Yr	VG	VG+	NM
ARWIN					
❑ 132	Cheryl's Going Home/Truly Julie's Blues	1966	2.00	4.00	8.00
❑ 134	Midnight Lace/All's Fair in Love and War	1966	2.00	4.00	8.00
CANBASE					
❑ 714	I Started a Joke/Sweet America	1972	—	2.50	5.00
CHARTER					
❑ 1018	She Was Never Really Mine (To Lose)/My Best Girl	1964	5.00	10.00	20.00
❑ 1018	She Was Never Mine (To Really Lose)/My Best Girl	1964	3.75	7.50	15.00
ERA BACK TO BACK HITS					
❑ 027	Rhythm of the Rain/Harlem Shuffle	197?	—	2.50	5.00
—A-side is a re-recording; B-side by Bob and Earl					
LIBERTY					
❑ 55822	She'll Love Again/I Bet You Won't Stay	1965	2.50	5.00	10.00
LONDON					
❑ 177	Two-Sided Man/The Woman's A Girl	1972	—	2.50	5.00
PROBE					
❑ 453	Two-Sided Man/Everyone Is Blossoming	1968	2.00	4.00	8.00
❑ 453 [PS]	Two-Sided Man/Everyone Is Blossoming	1968	3.75	7.50	15.00
RCA VICTOR					
❑ 47-8206	Cinderella/A Little Like Lovin'	1963	3.75	7.50	15.00
❑ 47-8268	For Your Sweet Love/Jeannie	1963	3.00	6.00	12.00
❑ 47-8321	Little Betty Falling Star/Those Were the Good Old Days	1964	3.75	7.50	15.00
❑ 47-8402	I Dare You to Cry/Awake	1964	3.00	6.00	12.00
RENEE					
❑ 105	Pains in My Heart/One That I Can Spare	19??	5.00	10.00	20.00

Number	Title (A Side/B Side)	Yr	VG	VG+	NM
SMASH					
❑ 2083	Hey Little Girl of Mine/Blue Hours	1967	2.00	4.00	8.00
❑ 2101	Flying on the Ground/Main Street	1967	2.00	4.00	8.00
UNI					
❑ 55152	Maybe the Rain Will Fall/Naggin' Cries	1969	2.00	4.00	8.00
❑ 55169	Indian River/Big City Country Boy	1969	2.00	4.00	8.00
❑ 55200	But For Love/Hazel Autumn Cocoa Brown	1970	2.00	4.00	8.00
❑ 55231	April, May, June and July/Big Ugly Sky	1970	2.00	4.00	8.00
VALIANT					
❑ 6021	There's a Reason/Second Chance	1962	6.25	12.50	25.00
❑ 6026	Rhythm of the Rain/Let Me Be	1962	5.00	10.00	20.00
❑ 6028	Shy Girl/The Last Leaf	1963	3.75	7.50	15.00
❑ 6032	I Wanna Be Your Lover/My First Day Alone	1963	3.75	7.50	15.00
WARNER BROS.					
❑ 7114	Rhythm of the Rain/The Last Leaf	1968	—	2.50	5.00
—"Back to Back Hits" series; originals on green "W7" label					

CASEY, AL

Also see DUANE EDDY.

Number	Title (A Side/B Side)	Yr	VG	VG+	NM
BLUE HORIZON					
❑ 925	Cookin'/Hot Foot	1962	6.25	12.50	25.00
DOT					
❑ 15524	A Fool's Blues/Juice	1956	7.50	15.00	30.00
❑ 15563	Guitar Man/Come What May	1957	10.00	20.00	40.00
HIGHLAND					
❑ 1002	Got the Teenage Blues/(B-side unknown)	1959	10.00	20.00	40.00
❑ 1004	Night Beat/The Stinger	1960	6.25	12.50	25.00
LIBERTY					
❑ 55117	Willa Mae/She Gotta Shake	1957	5.00	10.00	20.00
MCI					
❑ 1005	Pink Panther/If I Told You	1965	3.75	7.50	15.00
STACY					
❑ 925	Cookin'/Hot Foot	1962	3.75	7.50	15.00
❑ 936	Jivin' Around/Doin' the Shotish	1962	3.75	7.50	15.00
❑ 950	Laughin'/Chicken Feathers	1962	3.75	7.50	15.00
❑ 956	Doin' It/Monte Carlo	1963	3.75	7.50	15.00
❑ 961	Full House/Indian Love Call	1963	3.75	7.50	15.00
❑ 962	Surfin' Hootenanny/Easy Pickin'	1963	5.00	10.00	20.00
—Black vinyl					
❑ 962	Surfin' Hootenanny/Easy Pickin'	1963	10.00	20.00	40.00
—Red vinyl					
❑ 964	Surfin' Blues/Guitars, Guitars, Guitars	1963	3.75	7.50	15.00
❑ 971	Cookin'/What Are We Gonna Do in '64	1964	3.75	7.50	15.00
UNITED ARTISTS					
❑ 158	The Stinger/Keep Talking	1959	6.25	12.50	25.00
❑ 494	Jivin' Around/Doin' the Shotish	1962	6.25	12.50	25.00

CASH, ALVIN

Number	Title (A Side/B Side)	Yr	VG	VG+	NM
CHESS					
❑ 2098	Getaway/Saddle Up	1970	2.00	4.00	8.00
DAKAR					
❑ 4559	Doin' the Ali Shuffle/The Feeling	1976	—	2.50	5.00
MAR-V-LUS					
❑ 6002	Twine Time/The Bump	1964	3.75	7.50	15.00
❑ 6005	The Barracuda/Do It One More Time	1965	2.50	5.00	10.00
❑ 6006	Un Wind the Twine/The Penguin	1965	2.50	5.00	10.00
❑ 6009	Boston Monkey/Unwind the Twine	1965	2.50	5.00	10.00
❑ 6012	The Philly Freeze/No Deposit No Return	1966	2.50	5.00	10.00
❑ 6014	Alvin's Boo-Ga-Loo/Let's Do Some Good Timing	1966	2.50	5.00	10.00
❑ 6015	Doin' the Ali Shuffle/Feel So Good	1967	2.50	5.00	10.00
❑ 6019	Different Strokes for Different Folks/The Change	1967	2.50	5.00	10.00
SEVENTY-7					
❑ 112	Alvin's Doing His Thing/It's a Party	1972	—	3.00	6.00
❑ 118	Doin' the Creep/Party Time	1972	—	3.00	6.00
SOUND STAGE 7					
❑ 1509	Funky Washing Machine/I Don't Want It	1973	—	3.00	6.00
TODDLIN' TOWN					
❑ 104	Alvin's Bag/Whip It On Me	1968	2.00	4.00	8.00
❑ 111	Keep On Dancing/(Instrumental)	1968	2.00	4.00	8.00
❑ 119	Funky '69/Moaning and Groaning	1969	2.00	4.00	8.00
❑ 124	Poppin' Popcorn/(Instrumental)	1969	2.00	4.00	8.00
WESTBOUND					
❑ 159	Stone Thing (Part 1)/Stone Thing (Part 2)	1970	2.00	4.00	8.00

CASH, BOBBY

Number	Title (A Side/B Side)	Yr	VG	VG+	NM
KING					
❑ 5844	Mona Lisa/Teen Love	1964	7.50	15.00	30.00
❑ 5864	Only Make Believe/Run, Fool, Run	1964	7.50	15.00	30.00
❑ 5894	The Answer to My Dreams/I Don't Need Your Love and Kisses	1964	7.50	15.00	30.00

CASH, JOHNNY

Number	Title (A Side/B Side)	Yr	VG	VG+	NM
AMERICAN					
❑ 18091	Drive On/Delia's Gone	1994	—	2.00	4.00
A&M					
❑ 2291	The Death of Me/One More Shot	1980	—	2.00	4.00
—With Levon Helm					
CACHET					
❑ 4504	Wings in the Morning/What on Earth	1980	—	2.50	5.00
❑ 4504 [PS]	Wings in the Morning/What on Earth	1980	—	2.50	5.00
COLUMBIA					
❑ 02189	Mobile Bay/The Hard Way	1981	—	2.00	4.00
❑ 02669	The Reverend Mr. Black/Chattanooga City Limit Sign	1982	—	2.00	4.00
❑ 03058	Georgia on a Fast Train/Sing a Song	1982	—	2.00	4.00
❑ 03317	Fair Weather Friends/Ain't Gonna Hobo No More	1982	—	2.00	4.00
❑ 03524	I'll Cross Over Jordan Some Day/We Must Believe in Magic	1983	—	2.00	4.00
❑ 04060	I'm Ragged, But I'm Right/Brand New Dance	1983	—	2.00	4.00
❑ 04227	Johnny 99/New Cut Road	1983	—	—	3.00
❑ 04428	That's the Truth/Joshua Gone Barbados	1984	—	—	3.00
❑ 04513	The Chicken in Black/The Battle of Nashville	1984	—	—	3.00
❑ 04740	They Killed Him/The Three Bells	1985	—	—	3.00
—With the Carter Family					
❑ 04860	Crazy Old Soldier/It Ain't Gonna Worry My Mind	1985	—	—	3.00
—A-side: Ray Charles and Johnny Cash; B-side: Ray Charles and Mickey Gilley					
❑ 04881	Highwayman/The Human Condition	1985	—	—	3.00
—A-side: Willie Nelson/Waylon Jennings/Johnny Cash/Kris Kristofferson; B-side: Nelson, Cash					
❑ 04881 [PS]	Highwayman/The Human Condition	1985	—	2.50	5.00
—A-side: Willie Nelson/Waylon Jennings/Johnny Cash/Kris Kristofferson; B-side: Nelson, Cash					
❑ 05594	Desperadoes Waiting for a Train/The Twentieth Century Is Almost Over	1985	—	—	3.00
—A-side: Willie Nelson/Waylon Jennings/Johnny Cash/Kris Kristofferson; B-side: Nelson, Cash					
❑ 05672	I'm Leaving Now/Easy Street	1985	—	—	3.00
❑ 08406	Highwayman/Desperadoes Waiting for a Train	1988	—	—	3.00
—Waylon Jennings/Willie Nelson/Johnny Cash/Kris Kristofferson; reissue					
❑ 10011	The Junkie and the Juicehead/Crystal Chandeliers and Burgundy	1974	—	2.50	5.00
❑ 10048	Father and Daughter, Father and Son/Don't Take Your Love to Town	1974	—	2.50	5.00
—With Rosey Nix					
❑ 10066	The Lady Came from Baltimore/Lonesome to the Bone	1974	—	2.50	5.00
❑ 10116	My Old Kentucky Home (Turpentine and Dandelion Wine)/Hard Times Comin'	1975	—	2.50	5.00
❑ 10177	Look at Them Beans/All Around Cowboy	1975	—	2.50	5.00
❑ 10237	Texas — 1947/I Hardly Ever Sing Beer Drinking Songs	1975	—	2.50	5.00
❑ 10279	Strawberry Cake/I Got Stripes	1975	—	2.50	5.00
❑ 10321	One Piece at a Time/Go On Blues	1976	—	2.50	5.00
❑ 10381	Sold Out of Flagpoles/Mountain Lady	1976	—	2.50	5.00
❑ 10424	It's All Over/Ridin' on the Cotton Belt	1976	—	2.50	5.00
❑ 10483	The Last Gunfighter Ballad/City Jail	1977	—	2.50	5.00
❑ 10587	Lady/Hit the Road and Go	1977	—	2.50	5.00
❑ 10623	After the Ball/Calilou	1977	—	2.50	5.00
❑ 10681	I Would Like to See You Again/Lately	1978	—	2.50	5.00
❑ 10817	Gone Girl/I'm Alright Now	1978	—	2.50	5.00
❑ 10855	It'll Be Her/It Comes and Goes	1978	—	2.50	5.00
❑ 10888	I Will Rock and Roll with You/A Song for the Life	1979	—	2.50	5.00
❑ 10961	(Ghost) Riders in the Sky/I'm Gonna Sit on the Porch and Pick on My Guitar	1979	—	2.50	5.00
❑ 10961 [PS]	(Ghost) Riders in the Sky/I'm Gonna Sit on the Porch and Pick on My Guitar	1979	—	3.00	6.00
❑ 11103	I'll Say It's True/Cocaine Blues	1979	—	2.50	5.00
❑ 11237	Bull Rider/Lonesome to the Bone	1980	—	2.00	4.00
❑ 11283	Song of a Patriot/She's a Go-er	1980	—	2.00	4.00
❑ 11340	Cold Lonesome Morning/The Cowboy Who Started the Fight	1980	—	2.00	4.00
❑ 11399	The Last Time/Rockabilly Blues (Texas 1965)	1980	—	2.00	4.00
❑ 11424	Without Love/It Ain't Nothing New Babe	1981	—	2.00	4.00
❑ 30843 [S]	Loading Coal/Slow Rider	1960	7.50	15.00	30.00
❑ 30844 [S]	Lumberjack/Dorrance of Ponchartrain	1960	7.50	15.00	30.00
❑ 30845 [S]	When Papa Played the Dobro/Going to Memphis	1960	7.50	15.00	30.00
❑ 30846 [S]	Old Doc Brown/Boss Jack	1960	7.50	15.00	30.00
—The above four are "Stereo Seven" 33 1/3 rpm jukebox singles from "JS 7-12" and the album "Ride This Train"					
❑ 30847 [S]	One More Ride/Run Softly, Blue River	1960	7.50	15.00	30.00
—"Stereo Seven" 33 1/3 rpm jukebox single from "JS 7-12," but from the album "The Fabulous Johnny Cash"					
❑ 31109 [S]	Seasons of My Heart/I Couldn't Keep from Crying	1961	7.50	15.00	30.00
❑ 31110 [S]	My Shoes Keep Walking Back to You/Time Changes Everything	1961	7.50	15.00	30.00
❑ 31111 [S]	Transfusion Blues/I'd Just Be Fool Enough (To Fall)	1961	7.50	15.00	30.00
❑ 31112 [S]	I'm So Lonesome I Could Cry/I Will Miss You When You Go	1961	7.50	15.00	30.00
❑ 31113 [S]	Just One More/Honky Tonk Girl	1961	7.50	15.00	30.00
—The above five are "Stereo Seven" 33 1/3 rpm jukebox singles from "JS 7-29" and the album "Now There Was a Song"					
❑ 3-38990	Hey Porter/Big River	1964	7.50	15.00	30.00
—Stereo jukebox single, plays at 33 1/3 rpm; rather than the usual rainbow "target" label of Columbia "Stereo Seven" singles, this one has green labels					
❑ 41251	All Over Again/What Do I Care	1958	3.75	7.50	15.00
❑ 41251 [PS]	All Over Again/What Do I Care	1958	10.00	20.00	40.00
❑ 41313	Don't Take Your Guns to Town/I Still Miss Someone	1959	3.75	7.50	15.00
❑ 41313 [PS]	Don't Take Your Guns to Town/I Still Miss Someone	1959	10.00	20.00	40.00
❑ 41371	Frankie's Man, Johnny/You, Dreamer, You	1959	3.75	7.50	15.00
❑ 41427	I Got Stripes/Five Feet High and Rising	1959	3.75	7.50	15.00
❑ 41481	The Little Drummer Boy/I'll Remember You	1959	3.75	7.50	15.00
❑ 41481 [PS]	The Little Drummer Boy/I'll Remember You	1959	10.00	20.00	40.00
❑ 41618	Seasons of My Heart/Smiling Bill McCall	1960	3.75	7.50	15.00
❑ 41707	Second Honemoon/Honky Tonk Girl	1960	3.75	7.50	15.00
❑ 41804	Going to Memphis/Loading Coal	1960	3.75	7.50	15.00
❑ 41920	Girl in Saskatoon/Locomotive Man	1960	3.75	7.50	15.00
❑ 41995	The Rebel-Johnny Yuma/Forty Shades of Green	1961	3.00	6.00	12.00
❑ 41995 [PS]	The Rebel-Johnny Yuma/Forty Shades of Green	1961	6.25	12.50	25.00
❑ 42147	Tennessee Flat Top Box/Tall Men	1961	3.00	6.00	12.00
❑ 42147 [PS]	Tennessee Flat Top Box/Tall Men	1961	6.25	12.50	25.00
❑ 42301	The Big Battle/What I've Learned	1962	3.00	6.00	12.00
❑ 42301 [PS]	The Big Battle/What I've Learned	1962	6.25	12.50	25.00
❑ 42425	In the Jailhouse Now/A Little at a Time	1962	3.00	6.00	12.00
❑ 42425 [PS]	In the Jailhouse Now/A Little at a Time	1962	6.25	12.50	25.00
❑ 42512	Bonanza!/Pick a Bale o' Cotton	1962	3.00	6.00	12.00
❑ 42615	Peace in the Valley/Were You There	1962	3.00	6.00	12.00
—With the Carter Family					
❑ 42665	Busted/Send a Picture of Mother	1963	2.50	5.00	10.00
❑ 42665 [PS]	Busted/Send a Picture of Mother	1963	6.25	12.50	25.00
❑ 42788	Ring of Fire/I'd Still Be There	1963	2.50	5.00	10.00
❑ 42788 [DJ]	Ring of Fire (same on both sides)	1963	10.00	20.00	40.00
—Red vinyl promo					

Number	Title (A Side/B Side)	Yr	VG	VG+	NM
❑ 42788 [PS]	Ring of Fire/I'd Still Be There	1963	7.50	15.00	30.00
❑ 42880	The Matador/Still in Town	1963	2.50	5.00	10.00
❑ 42880 [PS]	The Matador/Still in Town	1963	5.00	10.00	20.00
❑ 42964	Understand Your Man/Dark as a Dungeon	1964	2.50	5.00	10.00
❑ 43058	The Ballad of Ira Hayes/Bad News	1964	2.50	5.00	10.00
❑ 43145	It Ain't Me, Babe/Time and Time Again	1964	2.50	5.00	10.00
❑ 43206	Orange Blossom Special/All of God's Children Ain't Free	1965	2.00	4.00	8.00
❑ 43313	Mister Garfield/Streets or Laredo	1965	2.00	4.00	8.00
❑ 43342	The Sons of Katie Elder/A Certain Kinda Hurtin'	1965	2.00	4.00	8.00
❑ 43420	Happy to Be with You/Pickin' Time	1965	2.00	4.00	8.00
❑ 43496	The One on the Right Is On the Left/Cotton Pickin' Hands	1965	2.00	4.00	8.00
❑ 43673	Everybody Loves a Nut/Austin Prison	1966	—	3.00	6.00
❑ 43763	Boa Constrictor/Bottom of a Mountain	1966	—	3.00	6.00
❑ 43921	You Beat All I Ever Saw/Put the Sugar to Bill	1966	—	3.00	6.00
❑ 44288	The Wind Changes/Red Velvet	1967	—	3.00	6.00
❑ 44373	Rosanna's Going Wild/Roll Call	1967	—	3.00	6.00
❑ 44373 [PS]	Rosanna's Going Wild/Roll Call	1967	2.50	5.00	10.00
❑ 44513	Folsom Prison Blues/The Folk Singer	1968	—	3.00	6.00
❑ 44513 [PS]	Folsom Prison Blues/The Folk Singer	1968	2.50	5.00	10.00
❑ 44689	Daddy Sang Bass/He Turned the Water Into Wine	1968	—	3.00	6.00
❑ 44944	A Boy Named Sue/San Quentin	1969	—	3.00	6.00
❑ 45020	Blistered/See Ruby Fall	1969	—	3.00	6.00
❑ 45134	What Is Truth/Sing a Traveling Song	1970	—	2.50	5.00
❑ 45211	Sonday Morning Coming Down/I'm Gonna Try to Be That Way	1970	—	2.50	5.00
❑ 45269	Flesh and Blood/This Side of the Law	1970	—	2.50	5.00
❑ 45339	Man in Black/Little Bit of Yesterday	1971	—	2.50	5.00
❑ 45393	Singing in Viet Nam Talking Blues/You've Got a New Light Shining	1971	—	2.50	5.00
❑ 45460	Papa Was a Good Man/I Promise You	1971	—	2.50	5.00
❑ 45534	A Thing Called Love/Daddy	1972	—	2.50	5.00
❑ 45590	Kate/Miracle Man	1972	—	2.50	5.00
❑ 45660	Oney/Country Trash	1972	—	2.50	5.00
❑ 45740	Any Old Wind That Blows/Kentucky Straight	1972	—	2.50	5.00
❑ 45786	Children/Last Summer	1973	—	2.50	5.00
❑ 45938	Pick the Wildwood Flower/Diamonds in the Rough	1973	—	2.50	5.00

—With Mother Maybelle and the Carter Family

Number	Title (A Side/B Side)	Yr	VG	VG+	NM
❑ 45979	Christmas As I Knew It/That Christmasy Feeling	1973	—	2.50	5.00

—With Tommy Cash

Number	Title (A Side/B Side)	Yr	VG	VG+	NM
❑ 45997	Orleans Parish Prison/Jacob Green	1974	—	2.50	5.00
❑ 46028	Ragged Old Flag/Don't Go Near the Water	1974	—	2.50	5.00
❑ 60516	The Baron/I Will Dance with You	1981	—	2.00	4.00
❑ 69067	Ragged Old Flag/I'm Leaving Now	1989	—	—	3.00
❑ 73233	America Remains/Silver Stallion	1990	—	—	3.00

—Waylon Jennings/Willie Nelson/Johnny Cash/Kris Kristofferson

Number	Title (A Side/B Side)	Yr	VG	VG+	NM
❑ 73381	Born and Raised in Black and White/Texas	1990	—	—	3.00

—The Highwaymen (Waylon Jennings/Willie Nelson/Johnny Cash/Kris Kristofferson)

Number	Title (A Side/B Side)	Yr	VG	VG+	NM
❑ 73572	American Remains/Texas	1990	—	—	3.00

—The Highwaymen (Waylon Jennings/Willie Nelson/Johnny Cash/Kris Kristofferson)

EPIC

Number	Title (A Side/B Side)	Yr	VG	VG+	NM
❑ 50778	There Ain't No Good Chain Gang/I Wish I Was Crazy Again	1979	—	2.50	5.00

—Johnny Cash/Waylon Jennings

LIBERTY

Number	Title (A Side/B Side)	Yr	VG	VG+	NM
❑ S7-18486	It Is What It Is/The Devil's Right Hand	1995	—	—	3.00

—By The Highwaymen

MERCURY

Number	Title (A Side/B Side)	Yr	VG	VG+	NM
❑ 870010-7	W. Lee O'Daniel (And the Light Crust Dough Boys)/Letters from Homes	1987	—	—	3.00
❑ 870237-7	Cry, Cry, Cry/Get Rhythm	1988	—	—	3.00
❑ 870688-7	Tennessee Flat Top Box/That Old Wheel	1988	—	—	3.00

—A-side with Hank Williams, Jr.

Number	Title (A Side/B Side)	Yr	VG	VG+	NM
❑ 872420-7	Ballad of a Teenage Queen/Get Rhythm	1988	—	—	3.00

—With Roseanne Cash and the Everly Brothers

Number	Title (A Side/B Side)	Yr	VG	VG+	NM
❑ 874562-7	The Last of the Drifters/(B-side unknown)	1989	—	—	3.00

—With Tom T. Hall

Number	Title (A Side/B Side)	Yr	VG	VG+	NM
❑ 875626-7	Cat's in the Cradle/I Love You, Love You	1990	—	—	3.00
❑ 878292-7	Goin' By the Book/Beans for Breakfast	1990	—	—	3.00
❑ 878710-7	The Greatest Cowboy of Them All/Hey Porter	1990	—	—	3.00
❑ 878968-7	The Mystery of Life/I'm an Easy Rider	1990	—	—	3.00
❑ 888459-7	The Night Hank Williams Came to Town/I'd Rather Have You	1987	—	—	3.00
❑ 888719-7	Sixteen Tons/The Ballad of Barbara	1987	—	—	3.00
❑ 888838-7	Let Him Roll/My Ship Will Sail	1987	—	—	3.00

SCOTTI BROS.

Number	Title (A Side/B Side)	Yr	VG	VG+	NM
❑ 02803	The General Lee/Duelin' Dukes	1982	—	2.00	4.00

—Narration on B-side: Sorrell Booke

SMASH

Number	Title (A Side/B Side)	Yr	VG	VG+	NM
❑ 884934-7	Sixteen Candles/Rock & Roll (Fais-Do-Do)	1986	—	2.00	4.00

—With Jerry Lee Lewis, Roy Orbison and Carl Perkins

Number	Title (A Side/B Side)	Yr	VG	VG+	NM
❑ 888142-7	We Remember the King/Class of '55	1987	—	2.00	4.00

—With Jerry Lee Lewis, Roy Orbison and Carl Perkins; B-side by Carl Perkins solo

SUN

Number	Title (A Side/B Side)	Yr	VG	VG+	NM
❑ 221	Hey Porter/Cry, Cry, Cry	1955	10.00	20.00	40.00
❑ 232	Folsom Prison Blues/So Doggone Lonesome	1956	7.50	15.00	30.00
❑ 241	I Walk the Line/Get Rhythm	1956	10.00	20.00	40.00
❑ 258	Train of Love/There You Go	1956	7.50	15.00	30.00
❑ 266	Next in Line/Don't Make Me Go	1957	7.50	15.00	30.00
❑ 279	Home of the Blues/Give My Love to Rose	1957	7.50	15.00	30.00
❑ 283	Ballad of a Teenage Queen/Big River	1958	6.25	12.50	25.00
❑ 295	Guess Things Happen That Way/Come In Stranger	1958	6.25	12.50	25.00
❑ 295 [PS]	Guess Things Happen That Way/Come In Stranger	1958	10.00	20.00	40.00
❑ 302	The Ways of a Woman in Love/The Nearest Thing to Heaven	1958	6.25	12.50	25.00
❑ 309	It's Just About Time/Just Thought You'd Like to Know	1958	6.25	12.50	25.00
❑ 316	Luther Played the Boogie/Thanks a Lot	1959	5.00	10.00	20.00
❑ 321	Katy Too/I Forgot to Remember to Forget	1959	5.00	10.00	20.00
❑ 331	Goodbye Little Darlin'/You Tell Me	1959	5.00	10.00	20.00
❑ 334	Straight A's in Love/I Love You Because	1960	5.00	10.00	20.00
❑ 343	Story of a Broken Heart/Down the Street to 301	1960	5.00	10.00	20.00
❑ 347	Mean Eyed Cat/Port of Lonely Hearts	1960	5.00	10.00	20.00
❑ 355	Oh Lonesome Me/Life Goes On	1961	5.00	10.00	20.00
❑ 363	Sugartime/My Treasurer	1961	5.00	10.00	20.00
❑ 376	Born to Lose/Blue Train	1962	5.00	10.00	20.00
❑ 392	Wide Open Road/Belshazar	1964	5.00	10.00	20.00
❑ 1103	Get Rhythm/Hey Porter	1969	—	3.00	6.00
❑ 1111	Rock Island Line/Next in Line	1970	—	3.00	6.00
❑ 1121	Big River/Come In Stranger	1971	—	2.50	5.00

7-Inch Extended Plays

COLUMBIA

Number	Title (A Side/B Side)	Yr	VG	VG+	NM
❑ B-2155	The Rebel — Johnny Yuma/Remember the Alamo//The Ballad of Boot Hill/Lorena	1961	3.75	7.50	15.00
❑ B-2155 [PS]	The Rebel — Johnny Yuma	1961	3.75	7.50	15.00
❑ B-12531	Run Softly, Blue River/That's All Over//I Still Miss Someone/Supper-Time	1958	3.00	6.00	12.00
❑ B-12531 [PS]	The Fabulous Johnny Cash, Vol. I	1958	3.00	6.00	12.00
❑ B-12532	Frankie's Man, Johnny/The Troubadour//Don't Take Your Guns to Town/That's Enough	1958	3.00	6.00	12.00
❑ B-12532 [PS]	The Fabulous Johnny Cash, Vol. II	1958	3.00	6.00	12.00
❑ B-12533	(A-side unknown)//Pickin' Time/Shepherd of My Heart	1958	3.00	6.00	12.00
❑ B-12533 [PS]	The Fabulous Johnny Cash, Vol. III	1958	3.00	6.00	12.00
❑ B-12841	It Was Jesus/I Saw a Man//Are All the Children In?/The Old Account	1959	3.00	6.00	12.00
❑ B-12841 [PS]	Hymns by Johnny Cash, Vol. I	1959	3.00	6.00	12.00
❑ B-12842	Lead Me Gently Home/Swing Low, Sweet Chariot//Snow in His Hair/Lead Me Father	1959	3.00	6.00	12.00
❑ B-12842 [PS]	Hymns by Johnny Cash, Vol. II	1959	3.00	6.00	12.00
❑ B-12843	I Call Him/These Things Shall Pass//He'll Be a Friend/God Will	1959	3.00	6.00	12.00
❑ B-12843 [PS]	Hymns by Johnny Cash, Vol. III	1959	3.00	6.00	12.00
❑ B-13391	(contents unknown)	1959	3.00	6.00	12.00
❑ B-13391 [PS]	Songs of Our Soil, Vol. I	1959	3.00	6.00	12.00
❑ B-13392	(contents unknown)	1959	3.00	6.00	12.00
❑ B-13392 [PS]	Songs of Our Soil, Vol. II	1959	3.00	6.00	12.00
❑ B-13393	Old Apache Squaw/Don't Step on Mother's Roses//My Grandfather's Clock/It Could Be You	1959	3.00	6.00	12.00
❑ B-13393 [PS]	Songs of Our Soil, Vol. III	1959	3.00	6.00	12.00
❑ B-14631	Seasons of My Heart/I Feel Better All Over//I Couldn't Keep from Crying/Time Changes Everything	1960	3.00	6.00	12.00
❑ B-14631 [PS]	Now, There Was a Song, Vol. I	1960	3.00	6.00	12.00
❑ B-14632	My Shoes Just Keep Walking Back to You/I'd Just Be Fool Enough (To Fall)//Transfusion Blues/Why Do You Punish Me	1960	3.00	6.00	12.00
❑ B-14632 [PS]	Now, There Was a Song, Vol. II	1960	3.00	6.00	12.00
❑ B-14633	I Will Miss You When You Go/I'm So Lonesome I Could Cry//Just One More/Honky Tonk Girl	1960	3.00	6.00	12.00
❑ B-14633 [PS]	Now, There Was a Song, Vol. III	1960	3.00	6.00	12.00

SUN

Number	Title (A Side/B Side)	Yr	VG	VG+	NM
❑ EPA-111	I Can't Help It/You Win Again//Hey Good Lookin'/I Could Never Be Ashamed	1956	10.00	20.00	40.00
❑ EPA-111 [PS]	Johnny Cash Sings Hank Williams	1956	15.00	30.00	60.00
❑ EPA-112	Rock Island Line/I Heard That Lonesome Whistle//Country Boy/If the Good Lord's Willin'	1956	7.50	15.00	30.00
❑ EPA-112 [PS]	Country Boy	1956	12.50	25.00	50.00
❑ EPA-113	I Walk the Line/The Wreck of the Old '97//Folsom Prison Blues/Doin' My Time	1958	7.50	15.00	30.00
❑ EPA-113 [PS]	I Walk the Line	1958	12.50	25.00	50.00
❑ EPA-114	The Ways of a Woman in Love/Next in Line//Guess Things Happen That Way/Train of Love	1958	7.50	15.00	30.00
❑ EPA-114 [PS]	His Top Hits	1958	12.50	25.00	50.00
❑ SEP-116	Home of the Blues/Big River//You're the Nearest Thing to Heaven/I Can't Help It	1959	7.50	15.00	30.00
❑ SEP-116 [PS]	Home of the Blues	1959	12.50	25.00	50.00
❑ SEP-117	So Doggone Lonesome/I Was There When It Happened//Cry, Cry, Cry/Remember Me	1958	7.50	15.00	30.00
❑ SEP-117 [PS]	Johnny Cash	1958	12.50	25.00	50.00

CASH, JOHNNY, AND JUNE CARTER

COLUMBIA

Number	Title (A Side/B Side)	Yr	VG	VG+	NM
❑ 10436	Old Time Feeling/Far Side Banks of Jordan	1976	—	2.50	5.00
❑ 44011	Jackson/Pack Up Your Sorrows	1967	—	3.00	6.00
❑ 44158	Long-Legged Guitar Pickin' Man/You'll Be All Right	1967	—	3.00	6.00
❑ 45064	If I Were a Carpenter/'Cause I Love You	1970	—	2.50	5.00
❑ 45431	No Need to Worry/I'll Be Loving You	1971	—	2.50	5.00
❑ 45631	If I Had a Hammer/I Gotta Go	1972	—	2.50	5.00
❑ 45758	The Loving Gift/Help Me Make It Through the Night	1973	—	2.50	5.00
❑ 45890	Praise the Lord and Pass the Soup/The Ballad of Barbara	1973	—	2.50	5.00
❑ 45929	Allegheny/We're for Love	1973	—	2.50	5.00

CASH, JOHNNY, AND WAYLON JENNINGS

Also see each artist's individual listings.

COLUMBIA

Number	Title (A Side/B Side)	Yr	VG	VG+	NM
❑ 05896	Even Cowgirls Get the Blues/American by Birth	1986	—	—	3.00
❑ 06287	The Ballad of $40/Field of Diamonds	1986	—	—	3.00
❑ 10742	There Ain't No Good Chain Gang/I Wish I Was Crazy Again	1978	—	2.50	5.00

CASHMERES, THE

Possibly more than one group.

HERALD

Number	Title (A Side/B Side)	Yr	VG	VG+	NM
❑ 474	Little Dream Girl/Do I Upset You	1956	20.00	40.00	80.00

JOSIE

Number	Title (A Side/B Side)	Yr	VG	VG+	NM
❑ 894	Life Line/Where Have You Been	1961	3.00	6.00	12.00

Number	Title (A Side/B Side)	Yr	VG	VG+	NM
LAKE					
❑ 703	Everything's Gonna Be Alright/Four Lonely Nights	1960	7.50	15.00	30.00
❑ 705	Satisfied/Satisfied (Part 2)	1961	6.25	12.50	25.00
LAURIE					
❑ 3078	I Believe in St. Nick/A Very Special Birthday	1960	10.00	20.00	40.00
❑ 3088	I Gotta Go/Singing Waters	1961	6.25	12.50	25.00
❑ 3105	Poppa Said/Bobby Come On Home	1961	6.25	12.50	25.00
MERCURY					
❑ 70501	My Sentimental Heart/Yes, Yes, Yes	1954	20.00	40.00	80.00
❑ 70617	Don't Let It Happen Again/Boom Mag-Azeno-Vip Vay	1955	20.00	40.00	80.00
❑ 70679	There's a Rumor/Second Hand Heart	1955	20.00	40.00	80.00
RELIC					
❑ 1005	Satisfied/Satisfied (Part 2)	1970	—	3.00	6.00

CASINOS, THE (1)

Male vocal group from Cincinnati.

Number	Title (A Side/B Side)	Yr	VG	VG+	NM
BUCCANEER					
❑ 3000	Then You Can Tell Me Goodbye/I Still Love You	196?	2.00	4.00	8.00
—Reissue of Fraternity release					
FRATERNITY					
❑ 944	She's Out of Sight/The Gallop	1965	2.50	5.00	10.00
❑ 949	Right There Beside You/The Gallop	1965	2.50	5.00	10.00
❑ 977	Then You Can Tell Me Goodbye/I Still Love You	1967	3.00	6.00	12.00
❑ 985	It's All Over Now/Tailor Made	1967	2.50	5.00	10.00
❑ 987	Forever and a Night/How Long Has It Been	1967	2.50	5.00	10.00
❑ 995	When I Stop Dreaming/Please Love	1967	2.50	5.00	10.00
❑ 997	Bye Bye Love/Walk Through This World with Me	1967	2.50	5.00	10.00
❑ 1020	These Are the Things We'll Share/Casinos Having Fun	1969	2.50	5.00	10.00
❑ 1028	I Wish I Were Anyone But Me/I Just Want to Stay Here	1969	2.50	5.00	10.00
❑ 1200	Father John/The Old Saloon	1970	2.50	5.00	10.00
❑ 1201	Wisdom of Love/My House	1970	2.50	5.00	10.00
❑ 1250	Loving Her Was Easier/A Restless Wind	1971	2.50	5.00	10.00
MILLION					
❑ 13	I'm Walking Behind You/Angels Were All Asleep	1972	2.50	5.00	10.00
—As "Gene Hughes and the Casinos"					
UNITED ARTISTS					
❑ 50255	Here I Am/Peggy	1968	2.50	5.00	10.00
—As "Gene Hughes and the Casinos"					
❑ 50313	Nobody's Child/Leaving Makes the Rain Come Down	1968	2.50	5.00	10.00
—As "Gene Hughes and the Casinos"					

CASINOS, THE (U)

Some of these no doubt are group (1), but not all of them are, and we're not sure which is which.

Number	Title (A Side/B Side)	Yr	VG	VG+	NM
AIRTOWN					
❑ 002	That's the Way/Too Good to Be True	1967	3.75	7.50	15.00
ALTO					
❑ 2002	I Like It Like That/Baby Don't Do It	1961	7.50	15.00	30.00
CASINO					
❑ 111	My Love for You/Why Am I a Fool	1960	10.00	20.00	40.00
CERTRON					
❑ 10015	Coal River/(B-side unknown)	1970	—	3.00	6.00
ITZY					
❑ 2	Do You Recall?/The Swim	1964	12.50	25.00	50.00
NAME					
❑ 7739	Do You Recall?/The Swim	1962	62.50	125.00	250.00
OLIMPIC					
❑ 251	Do You Recall?/The Swim	1963	37.50	75.00	150.00
SIMS					
❑ 306	Moon River/Soul Serenade	1966	3.00	6.00	12.00
TERRY					
❑ 115	Gee Whiz/Lovely One	1964	15.00	30.00	60.00
❑ 116	That's the Way/Too Good to Be True	1964	12.50	25.00	50.00

CASSIDY, DAVID

Also see THE PARTRIDGE FAMILY.

Number	Title (A Side/B Side)	Yr	VG	VG+	NM
BELL					
❑ 45150	Cherish/All I Want to Do Is Touch You	1971	—	2.50	5.00
❑ 45150 [PS]	Cherish/All I Want to Do Is Touch You	1971	—	3.00	6.00
❑ 45187	Could It Be Forever/Blind Hope	1972	—	2.00	4.00
❑ 45187 [PS]	Could It Be Forever/Blind Hope	1972	—	3.00	6.00
❑ 45220	How Can I Be Sure/Ricky's Tune	1972	—	2.00	4.00
❑ 45260	Rock Me Baby/Two Time Loser	1972	—	2.00	4.00
❑ 45386	Daydream/Can't Go Home Again	1973	—	2.00	4.00
❑ 45413	Daydreamer/The Puppy Song	1973	—	2.00	4.00
❑ 45605	Breaking Up Is Hard to Do/Please Please Me	1974	—	2.00	4.00
MCA					
❑ 41101	Hurt So Bad/Once a Fool	1979	—	2.00	4.00
RCA					
❑ PB-10788	I'll Have to Go Away (Saying Goodbye)/Gettin' It in the Streets	1976	2.00	4.00	8.00
❑ PB-10921	Saying Goodbye Ain't Easy (We'll Have to Go Away)/Rosa's Cantina	1977	2.00	4.00	8.00
RCA VICTOR					
❑ PB-10321	Get It Up for Love/Love In Bloom	1975	2.50	5.00	10.00
❑ PB-10405	This Could Be the Night/Darlin'	1975	2.50	5.00	10.00
❑ PB-10585	Tomorrow/Bedtime	1976	2.50	5.00	10.00
❑ PB-10647	Breakin' Down Again/On Fire	1976	2.50	5.00	10.00

CASTALEERS, THE

Number	Title (A Side/B Side)	Yr	VG	VG+	NM
DONNA					
❑ 1349	That's Why I Cry/My Baby's All Right	1961	6.25	12.50	25.00
FELSTED					
❑ 8504	Come Back/Hi-Fi Baby	1958	12.50	25.00	50.00
❑ 8512	Lonely Boy/My Bull Fightin' Baby	1958	10.00	20.00	40.00
❑ 8585	You're My Dream/I'll Be Around	1959	15.00	30.00	60.00
PLANET					
❑ 44	That's Why I Cry/My Baby's All Right	1961	10.00	20.00	40.00

CASTANETS, THE

Number	Title (A Side/B Side)	Yr	VG	VG+	NM
TCF					
❑ 1	I Love Him/Funky Wunky Piano	1963	2.50	5.00	10.00

CASTAWAYS, THE (1)

Garage rock band from Minnesota.

Number	Title (A Side/B Side)	Yr	VG	VG+	NM
BEAR					
❑ 2000	I Feel So Fine/Hit the Road Jack	1967	10.00	20.00	40.00
ERA BACK TO BACK HITS					
❑ 016	Liar, Liar/Surfin' Bird	197?	—	2.50	5.00
—B-side by the Trashmen					
ERIC					
❑ 247	Liar, Liar/Surfin' Bird	197?	—	2.50	5.00
—B-side by the Trashmen; reissue					
FONTANA					
❑ 1615	Walking in Different Circles/Just On High	1968	3.75	7.50	15.00
❑ 1626	Lavender Popcorn/What Kind of Face	1968	3.75	7.50	15.00
LANA					
❑ 151	Liar, Liar/Sam	196?	2.00	4.00	8.00
—Reissue					
SOMA					
❑ 1433	Liar, Liar/Sam	1965	3.75	7.50	15.00
❑ 1442	Goodbye Babe/A Man's Gotta Be a Man	1965	3.00	6.00	12.00
❑ 1461	Girl in Love/Should Happen to Me	1966	3.00	6.00	12.00
❑ 1469	Liar, Liar/Surfin' Bird	1966	3.00	6.00	12.00
—B-side by the Trashmen					
TAUNAH					
❑ 7745	(I) Feel So Fine/Hit the Road Jack	1967	3.00	6.00	12.00

CASTAWAYS, THE (2)

Not sure who they are, but they are not (1), (3) or (4).

Number	Title (A Side/B Side)	Yr	VG	VG+	NM
CAPITOL					
❑ 4340	The Twitch/Vibrations	1960	3.00	6.00	12.00

CASTAWAYS, THE (3)

Not sure who they are, but they are not (1), (2) or (4).

Number	Title (A Side/B Side)	Yr	VG	VG+	NM
EXCELLO					
❑ 2038	I Wish/Teasin'	1954	10.00	20.00	40.00

CASTAWAYS, THE (4)

Different group, probably from California.

Number	Title (A Side/B Side)	Yr	VG	VG+	NM
GNP CRESCENDO					
❑ 302	Tarzan/Wild Boy	1963	2.50	5.00	10.00
❑ 310	Moritat/Pass It Around	1964	2.50	5.00	10.00

CASTAWAYS, THE (U)

May go with (4) above, or possibly not.

Number	Title (A Side/B Side)	Yr	VG	VG+	NM
WITCH					
❑ 124	Don't You Just Know It/I Go Ape	1964	7.50	15.00	30.00

CASTELLES, THE

Number	Title (A Side/B Side)	Yr	VG	VG+	NM
ATCO					
❑ 6069	Happy and Gay/Hey Baby Baby	1956	25.00	50.00	100.00
CLASSIC ARTISTS					
❑ 114	At Christmas Time/One Little Teardrop	1989	—	2.00	4.00
GRAND					
❑ 101	My Girl Awaits Me/Sweetness	1954	500.00	1000.	2000.
—Blue label original					
❑ 103	This Silver Ring/Wonder Why	1954	500.00	1000.	2000.
—Glossy yellow label original					
❑ 105	Do You Remember/If You Were the Only Girl	1954	375.00	750.00	1500.
—Glossy yellow label original					
❑ 109	Baby Can't You See/Over a Cup of Coffee	1954	500.00	1000.	2000.
—Blue label original					
❑ 114	Marcella/I'm a Fool to Care	1955	400.00	800.00	1200.
—Cream label original					
❑ 122	My Wedding Day/Heavenly Father	1955	1750.	3500.	7000.
—Cream label original					

CASTELLS, THE

Number	Title (A Side/B Side)	Yr	VG	VG+	NM
BLACK GOLD					
❑ 306	Save a Chance/Children Who Dream	196?	2.00	4.00	8.00
DECCA					
❑ 31834	Just Walk Away/An Angel Cried	1965	3.75	7.50	15.00
❑ 31967	Life Goes On/I Thought You'd Like That	1966	3.75	7.50	15.00
ERA					
❑ 3038	Little Sad Eyes/Romeo	1961	6.25	12.50	25.00
❑ 3048	Sacred/I Get Dreamy	1961	6.25	12.50	25.00
❑ 3057	My Miracle/Make Believe Wedding	1961	5.00	10.00	20.00
❑ 3064	The Vision of You/Stiki De Boom Boom	1961	5.00	10.00	20.00
❑ 3073	So This Is Love/On the Streets of Tears	1962	5.00	10.00	20.00
❑ 3083	Oh, What It Seemed to Be/Stand There, Mountain	1962	5.00	10.00	20.00
❑ 3089	Echoes in the Night/The Only One	1962	5.00	10.00	20.00
❑ 3098	Clown Prince/Eternal Spring, Eternal Love	1962	5.00	10.00	20.00
❑ 3102	Little Sad Eyes/Initials	1963	5.00	10.00	20.00
❑ 3107	Some Enchanted Evening/What Do Little Girls Dream Of	1963	5.00	10.00	20.00
LAURIE					
❑ 3444	I'd Like to Know/Rocky Ridges	1968	2.50	5.00	10.00
UNITED ARTISTS					
❑ 50324	Two Lovers/Jerusalem	1968	2.50	5.00	10.00
WARNER BROS.					
❑ 5421	I Do/Teardrops	1964	20.00	40.00	80.00
—A-side written and produced by Brian Wilson					
❑ 5445	Could This Be Magic/Shinny Up Your Own Side	1964	7.50	15.00	30.00
❑ 5486	Love Finds a Way/Tell Her If I Could	1964	5.00	10.00	20.00

CASTLE, JOEY

Number	Title (A Side/B Side)	Yr	VG	VG+	NM
HEADLINE					
❑ 1008	Rock and Roll Daddy-O/Wild Love	1959	100.00	200.00	400.00
RCA VICTOR					
❑ 47-7283	That Ain't Nothin' But Right/Come A Little Closer Baby	1958	15.00	30.00	60.00

CASTLE, TONY

Number	Title (A Side/B Side)	Yr	VG	VG+	NM
EASTWEST					
❑ 107	Terry/Young and In Love	1958	7.50	15.00	30.00
GONE					
❑ 5099	Salty/Salty, Part 2	1961	5.00	10.00	20.00
❑ 5099	Salty/Hi Lili, Hi Lo	1961	6.25	12.50	25.00
❑ 5105	Sincerely/Tara's Themes	1961	5.00	10.00	20.00
❑ 5107	Seems Like Old Times/The Loneliest Girl in the World	1961	5.00	10.00	20.00
TREY					
❑ 3002	Kiss Me Goodnight/The Fool	1960	6.25	12.50	25.00

CASTLE KINGS, THE

Number	Title (A Side/B Side)	Yr	VG	VG+	NM
ATLANTIC					
❑ 2107	You Can Get Him Frankenstein/Loch Lomond	1961	7.50	15.00	30.00
—Produced by Phil Spector					
❑ 2158	Jeanette/The Caissons Go Rolling Along	1962	3.75	7.50	15.00

CASTON, BOBBY

Number	Title (A Side/B Side)	Yr	VG	VG+	NM
ATLAS					
❑ 1103	Call Me Darling/Why Wasn't I Told	1958	25.00	50.00	100.00

CASTOR, JIMMY, BUNCH

Also see THE CLINTONIAN CUBS.

Number	Title (A Side/B Side)	Yr	VG	VG+	NM
ATLANTIC					
❑ 3011	Maggie (Part 1)/Maggie (Part 2)	1974	—	2.50	5.00
❑ 3045	Everything Man (E-Man)/Heaven Kissed	1974	—	2.50	5.00
❑ 3232	The Bertha Butt Boogie (Part 1)/The Bertha Butt Boogie (Part 2)	1975	—	2.50	5.00
❑ 3270	Potential/Daniel	1975	—	2.50	5.00
❑ 3295	King Kong (Part 1)/King Kong (Part 2)	1975	—	2.50	5.00
❑ 3302	The Christmas Song (Chestnuts Roasting on an Open Fire)/Merry Christmas	1975	—	3.50	7.00
❑ 3316	Supersound/Drifting	1976	—	2.00	4.00
❑ 3331	Bom Bom/What's Best	1976	—	2.00	4.00
❑ 3362	Everything Is Beautiful to Me/The Magic Is in the Music	1976	—	2.00	4.00
❑ 3369 [DJ]	I Don't Wanna Lose You (mono/stereo)	1976	—	2.50	5.00
—May be promo-only					
❑ 3375	Space Age/Dracula	1976	—	2.00	4.00
❑ 3396	I Love a Mellow Groove/I Don't Want to Lose You	1977	—	2.00	4.00
❑ 3424	The Return of Leroy (Part 1)/The Return of Leroy (Part 2)	1977	—	2.00	4.00
❑ 3451	Magnolia/TR-7	1978	—	2.00	4.00
❑ 3455	Maximum Stimulation/It Was You	1978	—	2.00	4.00
ATOMIC					
❑ 100	Somebody Mentioned Your Name/This Girl of Mine	1957	125.00	250.00	500.00
CAPITOL					
❑ 2358	Hey Shorty (Part 1)/Hey Shorty (Part 2)	1968	2.00	4.00	8.00
❑ 2487	Psycho Man/The Real McCoy	1969	2.00	4.00	8.00
❑ 2634	Helpless/Make Me	1969	2.00	4.00	8.00
CATAWBA					
❑ 05676	Godzilla/(Instrumental)	1985	—	—	3.00
COMPASS					
❑ 7019	Soul Sister/Rattlesnake	1968	2.00	4.00	8.00
COTILLION					
❑ 44253	Don't Do That!/Don't Do That! (Part 2)	1979	—	2.00	4.00
❑ 45004	Party People/I Just Wanna Stop	1979	—	2.00	4.00
DECCA					
❑ 31963	In a Boogaloo Bag (Part 1)/In a Boogaloo Bag (Part 2)	1966	2.50	5.00	10.00
DRIVE					
❑ 6271	Bertha Butt Encounters Vadar/(B-side unknown)	1978	—	2.00	4.00
❑ 6276	You Light Up My Life/Let It Out	1978	—	2.00	4.00
HULL					
❑ 758	Poor Loser/Oh Suzzana	1963	5.00	10.00	20.00
LONG DISTANCE					
❑ 702	Can't Help Falling in Love/Stay with Me (Spend the Night)	1980	—	2.50	5.00
RCA VICTOR					
❑ APBO-0047	How Beautiful You Are/I'm Not a Child Anymore	1973	—	2.50	5.00
❑ AMBO-0120	Troglodyte (Cave Man)/Luther the Anthropod	1973	—	2.00	4.00
—Gold Standard Series					
❑ 48-1024	Say Leroy (The Creature from the Black Lagoon Is Your Father) (Parts 1 & 2)	1972	—	2.50	5.00
❑ 48-1029	Troglodyte (Cave Man)/I Promise to Remember	1972	—	3.00	6.00
❑ 74-0583	My Brightest Day/You Better Be Good	1971	—	2.50	5.00
❑ 74-0763	Luther the Anthropod/Party Life	1972	—	2.50	5.00
❑ 74-0836	Paradise/The First Time Ever I Saw Your Face	1972	—	2.50	5.00
❑ 74-0953	Soul Serenade/Purple Haze-Foxey Lady (Tribute to Jimi Hendrix)	1973	—	2.50	5.00
SALSOUL					
❑ 7018	E-Man Boogie '82/Any Way, Any Where, Any Time	1982	—	2.00	4.00
❑ 7058	E-Man Boogie '83/It's Just Begun	1983	—	2.00	4.00
SMASH					
❑ 2069	Hey, Leroy, Your Mama's Calling You/Ham Hocks Espanol	1966	2.00	4.00	8.00
❑ 2085	Just You Girl/Magic Saxophone	1967	2.00	4.00	8.00
❑ 2099	Leroy Is In the Army/Dry	1967	2.00	4.00	8.00
❑ 2120	Jamaica Farewell/Mini-Sonata	1967	2.00	4.00	8.00
WING					
❑ 90078	I Promise/I Know the Meaning of Love	1956	30.00	60.00	120.00

CASUALAIRS, THE

Number	Title (A Side/B Side)	Yr	VG	VG+	NM
AUTUMN					
❑ 21	Just For You/This Is a Mean World	1965	6.25	12.50	25.00
CRAIG					
❑ 5001	Bossa Nova Twist/Cruising	1962	10.00	20.00	40.00
MONA-LEE					
❑ 136	At the Dance/Satsfied	1959	10.00	20.00	40.00

CASUALS, THE (1)

See THE ORIGINAL CASUALS.

CASUALS, THE (2)

Number	Title (A Side/B Side)	Yr	VG	VG+	NM
DOT					
❑ 15557	Somebody Help Me/My Love Song for You	1957	6.25	12.50	25.00
❑ 15671	Hello Love/Till You Come Back to Me	1957	6.25	12.50	25.00

CASUALS, THE (3)

British group.

Number	Title (A Side/B Side)	Yr	VG	VG+	NM
MAINSTREAM					
❑ 692	I've Got Something Too/Jesamine (A Butterfly Child)	1968	2.50	5.00	10.00
❑ 697	Touched/Toy	1968	2.50	5.00	10.00
—As "The British Casuals"					

CASUALS, THE (4)

Number	Title (A Side/B Side)	Yr	VG	VG+	NM
MINARET					
❑ 109	Money/Big Hammer	1963	3.75	7.50	15.00
MONUMENT					
❑ 905	Promise Her Anything (But Give Her Love)/Walk	1965	3.00	6.00	12.00
❑ 937	Walk Away/If You Don't	1966	3.00	6.00	12.00
SOUND STAGE 7					
❑ 2534	Mustang 2 + 2/Play Me a Sad Song	1964	3.75	7.50	15.00

CAT MOTHER AND THE ALL NIGHT NEWS BOYS

Number	Title (A Side/B Side)	Yr	VG	VG+	NM
POLYDOR					
❑ 14002	Good Old Rock 'N Roll/Bad News	1969	2.00	4.00	8.00
❑ 14007	Can You Dance to It/Marie	1969	—	3.00	6.00
—Both of the above were produced by Jimi Hendrix					
❑ 14029	Last Go-Round/I Must Be Dreaming	1970	—	3.00	6.00
❑ 14126	Letter to the President/Ode to Oregon	1972	—	3.00	6.00
❑ 14138	She Came from a Different World/Three and Me	1972	—	3.00	6.00

CATALINAS, THE (1)

Studio band of Los Angeles session pros.

Number	Title (A Side/B Side)	Yr	VG	VG+	NM
RIC					
❑ 113	Banzai Wipeout/Beach Walkin'	1964	6.25	12.50	25.00
❑ 164	Boss Barracuda/Surfer Boy	1965	6.25	12.50	25.00
SIMS					
❑ 134	Bail Out/Bulletin	1963	3.75	7.50	15.00

CATALINAS, THE (2)

Five-man vocal group.

Number	Title (A Side/B Side)	Yr	VG	VG+	NM
LITTLE					
❑ 811/2	Give Me Your Love/Castle of Love	1957	50.00	100.00	200.00

CATALINAS, THE (U)

Number	Title (A Side/B Side)	Yr	VG	VG+	NM
20TH FOX					
❑ 286	Sweetheart/Unchained Melody	1962	7.50	15.00	30.00
❑ 299	Safari/Pretty Little Nashville Girl	1962	7.50	15.00	30.00
BACK BEAT					
❑ 513	Speechless/Flying Formation with You	1958	7.50	15.00	30.00
DEE JAY					
❑ 1010	Bail Out/Bulletin	1963	10.00	20.00	40.00
DIAL					
❑ 3008	Cha Cha Joe/Echo One	1963	3.00	6.00	12.00
GLORY					
❑ 285	Marlene/With Your Girl — Yeah!	1958	5.00	10.00	20.00
ORIGINAL SOUND					
❑ 48	Your Tender Lips/Gonna Tell	1964	3.00	6.00	12.00
RITA					
❑ 1006	Ring of Stars/Wooly Wooly Willie	1960	5.00	10.00	20.00
SCEPTER					
❑ 12188	Tick Tock/You Haven't the Right	1967	3.75	7.50	15.00

CATES, RONNIE

Number	Title (A Side/B Side)	Yr	VG	VG+	NM
TERRACE					
❑ 7501	Ol' Man River/Long Time	1961	12.50	25.00	50.00
❑ 7508	For My Very Own/Long Time	1962	12.50	25.00	50.00

CATHY JEAN AND THE ROOMATES

Also see THE ROOMATES.

Number	Title (A Side/B Side)	Yr	VG	VG+	NM
PHILIPS					
❑ 40106	My Hert Belongs to Only You/I Only Want You	1963	5.00	10.00	20.00
—As "Cathy Jean"					
❑ 40143	Double Trouble/Believe Me	1963	5.00	10.00	20.00
—As "Cathy Jean"					
VALMOR					
❑ 007	Please Love Me Forever/Canadian Sunset	1961	6.25	12.50	25.00
—Sleeve is promo only					
❑ 007	Please Love Me Forever/Canadian Sunset	1961	3.75	7.50	15.00
—Black label					
❑ 007 [PS]	Please Love Me Forever/Canadian Sunset	1961	17.50	35.00	70.00
—Sleeve is promo only					
❑ 009	Make Me Smile Again/Sugar Cake	1961	6.25	12.50	25.00
❑ 011	I Only Want You/One Love	1961	5.00	10.00	20.00
❑ 016	Please Tell Me/Sugar Cake	1962	5.00	10.00	20.00

CAVALIERE, FELIX

Also see FELIX AND THE ESCORTS; THE RASCALS.

Number	Title (A Side/B Side)	Yr	VG	VG+	NM
BEARSVILLE					
❑ 0300	High Price to Pay/Mountain Men	1974	—	2.50	5.00
❑ 0302	Everlasting Love/Future Train	1975	—	2.50	5.00

Number	Title (A Side/B Side)	Yr	VG	VG+	NM
❑ 0305	Never Felt Love Before/Love Came	1975	—	2.50	5.00
EPIC					
❑ 50785	Castles in the Air/Outside Your Window	1979	—	2.00	4.00
❑ 50829	Only a Lonely Heart Sees/You Turned Me Around	1980	—	2.00	4.00
❑ 50880	Dancin' the Night Away/Good to Have Love Back	1980	—	2.00	4.00

CAVALIERS, THE
Probably several different groups.

Number	Title (A Side/B Side)	Yr	VG	VG+	NM
APT					
❑ 25004	Dance, Dance, Dance/Play By the Rules of Love	1958	10.00	20.00	40.00
CORAL					
❑ 62245	Teen Fever/Funky	1961	3.00	6.00	12.00
DECCA					
❑ 29556	Somewhere, Sometime, Someday/Honor Bright	1955	3.75	7.50	15.00
GALENA					
❑ 1277	Blowin' Smoke/Ten More Miles	1962	5.00	10.00	20.00
MUSIC WORLD					
❑ 101	The Magic Age of Sixteen/So Young, So Warm, So Beautiful	1963	7.50	15.00	30.00
NRC					
❑ 028	Dreamy Bikini/Charm Bracelet	1959	3.75	7.50	15.00
RCA VICTOR					
❑ 47-9054	Dance Little Girl/Hold On to My Baby	1966	7.50	15.00	30.00
❑ 47-9321	I Really Love You/I've Gotta Find Her	1967	5.00	10.00	20.00

CAVE DWELLERS, THE

Number	Title (A Side/B Side)	Yr	VG	VG+	NM
ABC-PARAMOUNT					
❑ 10735	Sinking Feeling/Sling My Rock	1965	5.00	10.00	20.00

CELEBRATION FEATURING MIKE LOVE
Also see THE BEACH BOYS.

Number	Title (A Side/B Side)	Yr	VG	VG+	NM
MCA					
❑ S45-1986 [DJ]	Almost Summer/Almost Summer (KRTH Version)	1978	2.50	5.00	10.00
—Special promo for Los Angeles radio station					
❑ 40891	Almost Summer/Lookin' Good	1978	—	2.50	5.00
❑ 40930	Summer in the City/Island Girl	1978	—	2.00	4.00
PACIFIC ARTS					
❑ 105	Gettin' Hungry/Star Baby	1979	2.50	5.00	10.00

CELEBRITYS, THE

Number	Title (A Side/B Side)	Yr	VG	VG+	NM
CAROLINE					
❑ 2301	Juanita/(B-side unknown)	1956	150.00	300.00	600.00
❑ 2302	Absent Minded/We Made Romance	1956	150.00	300.00	600.00

CELLOS, THE

Number	Title (A Side/B Side)	Yr	VG	VG+	NM
APOLLO					
❑ 510	Rang Tang Ding Dong/You Took My Love	1957	20.00	40.00	80.00
❑ 510	Rang Tang Ding Dong (I Am the Japanese Sandman)/You Took My Love	1957	6.25	12.50	25.00
❑ 515	Under Your Spell/The Juicy Crocodile	1957	12.50	25.00	50.00
❑ 516	The Be-Bop Mouse/Girlie That I Love	1957	12.50	25.00	50.00
❑ 524	I Beg for Your Love/What's the Matter with You	1958	15.00	30.00	60.00

CELTICS, THE

Number	Title (A Side/B Side)	Yr	VG	VG+	NM
AL-JACK'S					
❑ 0002	Can You Remember/Send Me Someone to Love	1958	2500.	3750.	5000.
WAR CONN					
❑ 2216	Darline, Darling/Only the Lonely	1962	100.00	200.00	400.00

CETERA, PETER
Also see CHICAGO; THE EXCEPTION.

Number	Title (A Side/B Side)	Yr	VG	VG+	NM
ATLANTIC					
❑ 89145	I Wasn't the One (Who Said Goodbye)/If You Need Someone Tonight	1988	—	—	3.00
—With Agnetha Faltskog					
❑ 89145 [PS]	I Wasn't the One (Who Said Goodbye)/If You Need Someone Tonight	1988	—	—	3.00
FULL MOON					
❑ 49885	How Many Times/Livin' in the Limelight	1981	—	2.00	4.00
❑ 50052	I Can Feel It/On the Line	1982	—	2.00	4.00
WARNER BROS.					
❑ 18651	Feels Like Heaven/World Falling Down	1993	—	—	3.00
—With Chaka Khan					
❑ 27563	Holding Out/Scheherazade	1989	—	—	3.00
❑ 27563 [PS]	Holding Out/Scheherazade	1989	—	—	3.00
❑ 27712	Best of Times/Only Love Knows Why	1988	—	—	3.00
❑ 27712 [PS]	Best of Times/Only Love Knows Why	1988	—	—	3.00
❑ 27824	One Good Woman/One More Story	1988	—	—	3.00
❑ 27824 [PS]	One Good Woman/One More Story	1988	—	—	3.00
❑ 28383	Only Love Knows Why/Evil Eye	1987	—	—	3.00
❑ 28383 [PS]	Only Love Knows Why/Evil Eye	1987	—	—	3.00
❑ 28507	Big Mistake/Livin' in the Limelight	1986	—	—	3.00
❑ 28507 [PS]	Big Mistake/Livin' in the Limelight	1986	—	—	3.00
❑ 28597	The Next Time I Fall/Holy Holy	1986	—	—	3.00
—A-side with Amy Grant					
❑ 28597 [PS]	The Next Time I Fall/Holy Holy	1986	—	—	3.00
❑ 28662	Glory of Love/On the Line	1986	—	—	3.00
❑ 28662 [PS]	Glory of Love/On the Line	1986	—	2.00	4.00
—Peter Cetera's name in pale green letters					
❑ 28662 [PS]	Glory of Love/On the Line	1986	—	—	3.00
—Peter Cetera's name in red letters					

CEYLEIB PEOPLE, THE

Number	Title (A Side/B Side)	Yr	VG	VG+	NM
VAULT					
❑ 940	Changes/Ceyladd Seyta	1968	5.00	10.00	20.00

CHAD AND JEREMY
Also see CHAD AND JILL STUART.

Number	Title (A Side/B Side)	Yr	VG	VG+	NM
CAPITOL STARLINE					
❑ 6087	A Summer Song/Willow Weep for Me	1966	2.00	4.00	8.00
—Green and white swirl label					
COLUMBIA					
❑ 43277	Before and After/Fare Thee Well	1965	2.50	5.00	10.00
❑ 43277 [DJ]	Before and After/Fare Thee Well	1965	10.00	20.00	40.00
—Red vinyl					
❑ 43339	I Don't Wanna Lose You Baby/Pennies	1965	2.00	4.00	8.00
❑ 43339 [PS]	I Don't Wanna Lose You Baby/Pennies	1965	5.00	10.00	20.00
❑ 43414	I Have Dreamed/Should I?	1966	2.00	4.00	8.00
❑ 43490	Teenage Failure/Early Morning Rain	1965	2.00	4.00	8.00
❑ 43490 [PS]	Teenage Failure/Early Morning Rain	1965	5.00	10.00	20.00
❑ 43682	Distant Shores/Last Night	1966	2.00	4.00	8.00
❑ 43682 [PS]	Distant Shores/Last Night	1966	5.00	10.00	20.00
❑ 43807	You Are She/I Won't Cry	1966	2.00	4.00	8.00
❑ 43807 [PS]	You Are She/I Won't Cry	1966	5.00	10.00	20.00
❑ 44131	Rest in Peace/Family Way	1967	2.00	4.00	8.00
❑ 44379	Painted Dayglow Smile/Editorial	1967	2.00	4.00	8.00
❑ 44525	Sister Marie/Rest in Peace	1968	2.00	4.00	8.00
❑ 44660	Paxton Quigley's Had the Course/You Need Feet	1968	2.00	4.00	8.00
❑ 44660 [PS]	Paxton Quigley's Had the Course/You Need Feet	1968	4.00	8.00	16.00
—Promo-only sleeve of a Nazi military rally					
ROCSHIRE					
❑ 95046	Bite the Bullet/How Many Trains	1983	—	2.00	4.00
❑ 95050 [DJ]	Bite the Bullet/Interview	1983	3.00	6.00	12.00
❑ 95061	Dreams/Zanzibar Sunset	1983	—	2.00	4.00
WORLD ARTISTS					
❑ 1021	Yesterday's Gone/Lemon Tree	1964	2.50	5.00	10.00
—As "Chad Stuart and Jeremy Clyde"					
❑ 1027	A Summer Song/No Tears for Johnny	1964	2.50	5.00	10.00
—As "Chad Stuart and Jeremy Clyde"					
❑ 1034	Willow Weep for Me/If She Was Mine	1964	2.50	5.00	10.00
❑ 1034 [PS]	Willow Weep for Me/If She Was Mine	1964	5.00	10.00	20.00
❑ 1041	If I Loved You/Donna, Donna	1965	2.50	5.00	10.00
❑ 1041 [PS]	If I Loved You/Donna, Donna	1965	5.00	10.00	20.00
❑ 1052	What Do You Want from Me/A Very Good Year	1965	2.50	5.00	10.00
—As "Chad Stuart and Jeremy Clyde"					
❑ 1056	From a Window/My Coloring Book	1965	2.50	5.00	10.00
❑ 1060	September in the Rain/Only for the Young	1965	2.50	5.00	10.00

CHAFFIN, ERNIE

Number	Title (A Side/B Side)	Yr	VG	VG+	NM
SUN					
❑ 262	Feelin' Low/Lonesome for My Baby	1957	7.50	15.00	30.00
❑ 275	Laughin' and Jokin'/I'm Lonesome	1957	7.50	15.00	30.00
❑ 307	Nothing Can Change My Love for You/Born to Lose	1958	6.25	12.50	25.00
❑ 320	Don't Ever Leave Me/Miracle of You	1959	6.25	12.50	25.00

CHAIN REACTION
This Chain Reaction includes Steve Tallarico, later known as Steve Tyler of AEROSMITH.

Number	Title (A Side/B Side)	Yr	VG	VG+	NM
DATE					
❑ 1538	When I Needed You/The Sun	1966	7.50	15.00	30.00

CHAIRMEN OF THE BOARD

Number	Title (A Side/B Side)	Yr	VG	VG+	NM
INVICTUS					
❑ 1251	Finder's Keepers/Finder's Keepers (Part 2)	1973	—	2.50	5.00
❑ 1263	Life & Death/Love with Me, Love with Me	1974	—	2.50	5.00
❑ 1268	Everybody Party All Night/Morning Glory	1974	—	2.50	5.00
❑ 1271	Let's Have Some Fun/Love at First Sight	1974	—	2.50	5.00
❑ 1276	The Skin I'm In/Love at First Sight	1975	—	2.50	5.00
❑ 1278	You've Got Extra Added Power in Your Love/Someone Just Like You	1975	—	2.50	5.00
❑ 9074	Give Me Just a Little More Time/Since the Days of Pigtails	1970	—	3.00	6.00
❑ 9078	(You've Got Me) Dangling on a String/I'll Come Crawling	1970	—	2.50	5.00
❑ 9079	Everything's Tuesday/Patches	1970	—	2.50	5.00
❑ 9081	Pay to the Piper/Bless You	1970	—	2.50	5.00
❑ 9081 [PS]	Pay to the Piper/Bless You	1970	2.50	5.00	10.00
❑ 9086	Chairman of the Board/When Will She Tell Me She Needs Me	1971	—	2.50	5.00
❑ 9089	Hanging On (To) A Memory/Tracked and Trapped	1971	—	2.50	5.00
❑ 9099	Try On My Love for Size/Working on a Building of Love	1971	—	2.50	5.00
❑ 9103	Men Are Getting Scarce/Bravo! Hurray!	1971	—	2.50	5.00
❑ 9106	Bittersweet/Elmo James	1972	—	2.50	5.00
❑ 9122	Everybody's Got a Song to Sing/Working on a Building of Love	1972	—	2.50	5.00
❑ 9126	Let Me Down Easy/I Can't Find Myself	1972	—	2.50	5.00

CHALETS, THE

Number	Title (A Side/B Side)	Yr	VG	VG+	NM
DART					
❑ 1026	Who's Laughing-Who's Crying/Fat Fat Fat! Mom-Mi-O	1961	6.25	12.50	25.00
LAURIE					
❑ 3348	She's Not the Marrying Type/(Theme from) She's Not the Marrying Type	1966	3.00	6.00	12.00
MUSICNOTE					
❑ 1001	Who's Laughing-Who's Crying/Fat Fat Fat! Mom-Mi-O	1962	5.00	10.00	20.00
TRU-LITE					
❑ 1001	Who's Laughing-Who's Crying/Mom-Mia	1961	12.50	25.00	50.00

CHALLENGERS, THE (1)
California surf and instrumental group.

Number	Title (A Side/B Side)	Yr	VG	VG+	NM
GNP CRESCENDO					
❑ 362	The Man from U.N.C.L.E./The Streets of London	1965	2.50	5.00	10.00
❑ 362	The Man from U.N.C.L.E./Summer Nights	1965	2.50	5.00	10.00
❑ 368	Walk with Me/How Could It	1966	2.50	5.00	10.00
❑ 376	Wipe Out/North Beach	1966	2.50	5.00	10.00
❑ 380	Milord/What If It Should Rain	1966	2.50	5.00	10.00
❑ 396	The Water Country/Everything to Me	1967	2.50	5.00	10.00
❑ 400	Color Me In/Before You	1968	2.50	5.00	10.00
❑ 412	Chitty Chitty Bang Bang/Lonely Little Girl	1968	2.50	5.00	10.00

Number	Title (A Side/B Side)	Yr	VG	VG+	NM
TRIUMPH					
❑ 112	Pipeline/Asphalt Spinner	1966	7.50	15.00	30.00
VAULT					
❑ 900	Bull Dog/Torquay	1963	5.00	10.00	20.00
❑ 902	Moondawg/Tidal Wave	1963	5.00	10.00	20.00
❑ 904	Foot Tapper/On the Move	1963	5.00	10.00	20.00
❑ 910	Hot Rod Hootenanny/Maybellene	1964	7.50	15.00	30.00
❑ 913	Hot Rod Show/K-39	1964	7.50	15.00	30.00
❑ 918	Channel Nine/Can't Seem to Make You Mine	1965	5.00	10.00	20.00

CHALLENGERS, THE (2)
Mid-1960s R&B group.

Number	Title (A Side/B Side)	Yr	VG	VG+	NM
CHESS					
❑ 1957	Tossin' and Turnin'/Don;t You Know It	1966	2.50	5.00	10.00

CHALLENGERS, THE (3)
Members of this group later recorded as THE OLYMPICS.

Number	Title (A Side/B Side)	Yr	VG	VG+	NM
MELATONE					
❑ 1002	I Can Tell/The Mambo Beat	1956	75.00	150.00	300.00

CHALLENGERS, THE (4)
Members of this group later recorded as UNDERGROUND SUNSHINE.

Number	Title (A Side/B Side)	Yr	VG	VG+	NM
NIGHT OWL					
❑ 6794	I Wanna Hold You/The Challengers Take a Ride on the Jefferson Airplane	1967	7.50	15.00	30.00

CHALLENGERS, THE (5)
British group.

Number	Title (A Side/B Side)	Yr	VG	VG+	NM
TRIODEX					
❑ 102	Goofus/Lazy Twist	1960	5.00	10.00	20.00
❑ 107	Deadline/Cry of the Wild Goose	1961	5.00	10.00	20.00

CHALLENGERS, THE (U)
May be another record by group (2), but we're not sure.

Number	Title (A Side/B Side)	Yr	VG	VG+	NM
CUCA					
❑ 1500	Hear My Message/I Wanna Hold You	1968	2.00	4.00	8.00

CHALLENGERS III, THE

Number	Title (A Side/B Side)	Yr	VG	VG+	NM
TRI-PHI					
❑ 1012	Stay/Honey, Honey, Honey	1962	12.50	25.00	50.00
—As "The Challengers III"					
❑ 1012	Stay/Honey, Honey, Honey	1962	7.50	15.00	30.00
—As "The Challengers"					
❑ 1020	Every Day/I Hear an Echo	1963	12.50	25.00	50.00

CHAMAELEON CHURCH
Chevy Chase was in this group.

Number	Title (A Side/B Side)	Yr	VG	VG+	NM
MGM					
❑ 13929	Your Golden Love/Camillia I Changing	1968	3.00	6.00	12.00

CHAMBERLAIN, RICHARD

Number	Title (A Side/B Side)	Yr	VG	VG+	NM
MCA					
❑ 40691	Secret Kingdom/The Slipper and the Rose Waltz	1977	—	2.00	4.00
MGM					
❑ 13075	Theme from Dr. Kildare (Three Stars Will Shine Tonight)/A Kiss to Build a Dream On	1962	2.50	5.00	10.00
❑ 13075 [PS]	Theme from Dr. Kildare (Three Stars Will Shine Tonight)/A Kiss to Build a Dream On	1962	5.00	10.00	20.00
❑ 13097	Love Me Tender/All I Do Is Dream of You	1962	2.50	5.00	10.00
❑ 13097 [PS]	Love Me Tender/All I Do Is Dream of You	1962	5.00	10.00	20.00
❑ 13121	All I Have to Do Is Dream/Hi-Lili, Hi-Lo	1963	2.50	5.00	10.00
❑ 13121 [PS]	All I Have to Do Is Dream/Hi-Lili, Hi-Lo	1963	5.00	10.00	20.00
❑ 13148	I Will Love You/True Love	1963	2.50	5.00	10.00
❑ 13148 [PS]	I Will Love You/True Love	1963	5.00	10.00	20.00
❑ 13170	Blue Guitar/They Long to Be Close to You	1963	2.50	5.00	10.00
❑ 13170 [PS]	Blue Guitar/They Long to Be Close to You	1963	5.00	10.00	20.00
❑ 13205	Stella By Starlight/Georgia on My Mind	1964	2.00	4.00	8.00
❑ 13285	Rome Will Never Leave You/You Always Hurt the One You Love	1964	2.00	4.00	8.00
❑ 13285 [PS]	Rome Will Never Leave You/You Always Hurt the One You Love	1964	3.75	7.50	15.00
❑ 13340	Joy in the Morning/April Love	1965	2.00	4.00	8.00
❑ 13340 [PS]	Joy in the Morning/April Love	1965	5.00	10.00	20.00

CHAMBERLAIN, WILT "THE STILT"

Number	Title (A Side/B Side)	Yr	VG	VG+	NM
END					
❑ 1066	By the River/That's Easy to Say	1960	6.25	12.50	25.00

CHAMBERS BROTHERS, THE

Number	Title (A Side/B Side)	Yr	VG	VG+	NM
AVCO					
❑ 4632	Let's Go, Let's Go, Let's Go/Do You Believe in Magic	1974	—	2.00	4.00
❑ 4638	1-2-3/Looking Back	1974	—	2.00	4.00
❑ 4657	Miss Lady Brown/Stealin' Watermelons	1975	—	2.00	4.00
COLUMBIA					
❑ 43816	Time Has Come Today/Dinah	1966	3.00	6.00	12.00
❑ 43957	All Strung Out Over You/Falling in Love	1967	—	3.00	6.00
❑ 44080	Please Don't Leave Me/I Can't Stand It	1967	—	3.00	6.00
❑ 44296	Uptown/Love Me Like the Rain	1967	—	3.00	6.00
❑ 44414	Time Has Come Today/People Get Ready	1968	2.00	4.00	8.00
❑ 44679	I Can't Turn You Loose/Do Your Thing	1968	—	3.00	6.00
❑ 44679 [PS]	I Can't Turn You Loose/Do Your Thing	1968	2.50	5.00	10.00
❑ 44779	Are You Ready/You Got the Power to Turn Me On	1969	—	3.00	6.00
❑ 44890	Wake Up/Everybody Needs Someone	1969	—	3.00	6.00
❑ 44986	Have a Little Faith/Baby Takes Care of Business	1969	—	2.50	5.00
❑ 45055	Merry Christmas, Happy New Year/Did You Stop to Pray This Morning	1969	—	3.00	6.00
❑ 45088	Love, Peace and Happiness/If You Want Me To	1970	—	2.50	5.00
❑ 45146	To Love Somebody/Let's Do It	1970	—	2.50	5.00
❑ 45277	Love, Peace and Happiness/Funky	1970	—	2.50	5.00
❑ 45394	When the Evening Comes/New Generation	1971	—	2.50	5.00
❑ 45488	Heaven/(By the Hair on) My Chinny Chin Chin	1971	—	3.00	6.00
❑ 45518	Merry Christmas, Happy New Year/Did You Stop to Pray This Morning	1971	—	3.00	6.00
❑ 45837	Boogie Children/You Make the Magic	1973	—	3.00	6.00
ROXBURY					
❑ 2034	Bring It On Down Front Pretty Mama/Midnight Blue	1976	—	2.50	5.00
VAULT					
❑ 920	Call Me/Seventeen	1965	3.75	7.50	15.00
❑ 923	Pretty Girls Everywhere/Love Me Like the Rain	1966	3.00	6.00	12.00
❑ 945	Shout Part 1/Shout Part 2	1968	2.00	4.00	8.00
❑ 955	Just a Closer Walk with Thee/Girls We Love You	1969	—	3.00	6.00
❑ 967	House of the Rising Sun/Blues Get Off My Shoulder	1970	—	3.00	6.00

CHAMP, BILLY

Number	Title (A Side/B Side)	Yr	VG	VG+	NM
ABC-PARAMOUNT					
❑ 10518	Believe Me/Hush-A-Bye	1964	7.50	15.00	30.00

CHAMPLAINS, THE
FRED PARRIS of THE FIVE SATINS is the lead voice.

Number	Title (A Side/B Side)	Yr	VG	VG+	NM
UNITED ARTISTS					
❑ 346	Ding Dong/Have You Changed Your Mind	1961	10.00	20.00	40.00

CHAMPLIN, BILL
Formerly with THE SONS OF CHAMPLIN; later with CHICAGO.

Number	Title (A Side/B Side)	Yr	VG	VG+	NM
ELEKTRA					
❑ 47240	Tonight Tonight/Without You	1981	—	2.00	4.00
❑ 47429	Take it Uptown/The Fool Is All	1982	—	2.00	4.00
❑ 47456	Sara/One Way Ticket	1982	—	2.00	4.00
EPIC					
❑ 50589	What Good Is Love/Yo' Mama	1978	—	2.50	5.00

CHAMPS, THE
Also see DAVE BURGESS; GLEN CAMPBELL; CHUCK RIO; SEALS AND CROFTS.

Number	Title (A Side/B Side)	Yr	VG	VG+	NM
CHALLENGE					
❑ 1016	Tequila/Train to Nowhere	1958	6.25	12.50	25.00
❑ 1016	Tequila/Train to Nowhere	1958	150.00	300.00	600.00
—Blue vinyl (one known to exist)					
❑ 9113	The Shoddy Shoddy/Sombrero	1961	5.00	10.00	20.00
❑ 9116	Cantina/Panic Button	1961	5.00	10.00	20.00
❑ 9131	Tequila Twist/Limbo Rock	1961	5.00	10.00	20.00
❑ 9140	Experiment in Terror/La Cucaracha	1962	3.75	7.50	15.00
❑ 9143	What a Country/I've Just Seen Her	1962	3.75	7.50	15.00
❑ 9162	Limbo Dance/Latin Limbo	1962	3.75	7.50	15.00
❑ 9174	Varsity Rock/That Did It	1962	3.75	7.50	15.00
❑ 9180	Mr. Cool//3/4 Mash	1963	3.75	7.50	15.00
❑ 9189	Nik Nak/Shades	1963	3.75	7.50	15.00
❑ 9199	Cactus Juice/Roots	1963	3.75	7.50	15.00
❑ 59007	El Rancho Rock/Midnighter	1958	5.00	10.00	20.00
❑ 59018	Chariot Rock/Subway	1958	5.00	10.00	20.00
❑ 59026	Turnpike/Rockin' Mary	1958	5.00	10.00	20.00
❑ 59035	Gone Train/Beatnik	1958	5.00	10.00	20.00
❑ 59043	Moonlight Bay/Caramba	1959	5.00	10.00	20.00
❑ 59049	Night Train/The Rattler	1959	5.00	10.00	20.00
❑ 59053	Sky High/Double Eagle Rock	1959	5.00	10.00	20.00
❑ 59063	Too Much Tequila/Twenty Thousand Leagues	1960	5.00	10.00	20.00
❑ 59076	Red Eye/The Little Matador	1960	5.00	10.00	20.00
❑ 59086	Alley Cat/Coconut Grove	1960	5.00	10.00	20.00
❑ 59097	The Face/Tough Train	1960	5.00	10.00	20.00
❑ 59103	Hokey Pokey/Jumping Bean	1961	5.00	10.00	20.00
❑ 59219	San Juan/Jalisco	1963	3.75	7.50	15.00
❑ 59236	Switzerland/Only the Young	1964	3.75	7.50	15.00
❑ 59263	Fraternity Waltz/Kahlua	1964	3.75	7.50	15.00
❑ 59276	French 75/Bright Lights, Big City	1965	3.75	7.50	15.00
❑ 59314	The Man from Durango/Red Pepper	1965	3.75	7.50	15.00
❑ 59322	Anna/Buckaroo	1965	3.75	7.50	15.00
REPUBLIC					
❑ 246	Tequila '76 (Long)/Tequila '76 (Short)	1976	2.00	4.00	8.00
❑ 246 [PS]	Tequila '76 (Long)/Tequila '76 (Short)	1976	2.00	4.00	8.00
WE'RE BACK					
❑ 1	Tequila '77/From Me to You	1977	2.00	4.00	8.00
7-Inch Extended Plays					
CHALLENGE					
❑ EP-7100	Tequila/I'll Be There//Train to Nowhere/Lollipop	1958	37.50	75.00	150.00
❑ EP-7100 [PS]	Tequila	1958	37.50	75.00	150.00

CHANCE, NOLAN

Number	Title (A Side/B Side)	Yr	VG	VG+	NM
CONSTELLATION					
❑ 144	She's Gone/If He Makes You	1965	6.25	12.50	25.00
❑ 161	Don't Use Me/Just Like the Weather	1965	30.00	60.00	120.00

CHANCERS, THE

Number	Title (A Side/B Side)	Yr	VG	VG+	NM
DOT					
❑ 15870	Shirley Ann/My One	1958	7.50	15.00	30.00

CHANDELIERS, THE

Number	Title (A Side/B Side)	Yr	VG	VG+	NM
ANGLE TONE					
❑ 521	Blueberry Sweet/(B-side unknown)	1958	62.50	125.00	250.00
—As "Chandeliers Quintet"					
❑ 521	Blueberry Sweet/(B-side unknown)	1958	50.00	100.00	200.00
—As "Chandeliers"; black vinyl					
❑ 521	Blueberry Sweet/(B-side unknown)	1958	100.00	200.00	400.00
—As "Chandeliers"; colored vinyl					

CHANDELLES, THE

Number	Title (A Side/B Side)	Yr	VG	VG+	NM
DOT					
❑ 16553	El Gato/Jetster	1963	6.25	12.50	25.00

CHANDLER, DENIECE
See DENIECE WILLIAMS.

CHANDLER, GENE
Includes records as "The Duke of Earl." Also see THE DUKAYS.

Number	Title (A Side/B Side)	Yr	VG	VG+	NM
20TH CENTURY					
❑ 2411	When You're #1/I'll Remember You	1979	—	2.00	4.00

Number	Title (A Side/B Side)	Yr	VG	VG+	NM
❑ 2428	Do What Comes So Natural/That Funky Disco Rhythm	1979	—	2.00	4.00
BRUNSWICK					
❑ 55312	Girl Don't Care/My Love	1967	2.00	4.00	8.00
❑ 55339	There Goes the Lover/Tell Me What I Can Do	1967	2.00	4.00	8.00
❑ 55383	There Was a Time/Those Were the Good Old Days	1968	2.00	4.00	8.00
❑ 55394	Teacher, Teacher/Pit of Loneliness	1968	2.00	4.00	8.00
❑ 55413	Eleanor Rigby/Familiar Footsteps	1969	2.00	4.00	8.00
❑ 55425	This Bitter Earth/Suicide	1969	2.00	4.00	8.00
CHECKER					
❑ 1155	I Fooled You This Time/Such a Pretty Thing	1966	2.00	4.00	8.00
❑ 1165	To Be a Lover/After the Laughter	1967	2.00	4.00	8.00
❑ 1190	I Won't Need You/No Peace, No Satisfaction	1967	2.00	4.00	8.00
❑ 1199	River of Tears/It's Time to Settle Down	1968	2.00	4.00	8.00
❑ 1220	Go Back Home/In My Baby's House	1969	2.00	4.00	8.00
CHI-SOUND					
❑ 1001	I'll Make the Living If You Make the Loving Worthwhile/(B-side unknown)	1982	—	2.50	5.00
❑ 1168	Give Me the Cue/Tomorrow We May Not Feel the Same	1978	—	2.00	4.00
❑ 2386	Get Down/I'm the Traveling Kind	1978	—	2.00	4.00
❑ 2404	Please Sunrise/Greatest Love Ever Known	1979	—	2.00	4.00
❑ 2411	When You're #1/I'll Remember You	1979	—	2.50	5.00
❑ 2451	Does She Have a Friend?/Let Me Make Love to You	1980	—	2.00	4.00
❑ 2468	Lay Me Gently/You've Been So Good to Me	1980	—	2.00	4.00
❑ 2480	Rainbow '80/I'll Be There	1980	—	2.00	4.00
❑ 2494	I'm Attracted to You/I've Got to Meet You	1981	—	2.00	4.00
❑ 2507	Love Is the Answer/Godsend	1981	—	2.00	4.00
CONSTELLATION					
❑ 104	From Day to Day/It's No Good for Me	1963	2.50	5.00	10.00
❑ 110	Pretty Little Girl/A Little Like Lovin'	1963	2.50	5.00	10.00
❑ 112	Think Nothing About It/Wish You Were Here	1964	2.50	5.00	10.00
❑ 114	Soul Hootenanny (Part 1)/Soul Hootenanny (Part 2)	1964	2.50	5.00	10.00
❑ 124	A Song Called Soul/You Left Me	1964	2.50	5.00	10.00
❑ 130	Just Be True/A Song Called Soul	1964	2.50	5.00	10.00
❑ 136	Bless Our Love/London Town	1964	2.50	5.00	10.00
❑ 141	What Now/If You Can't Be True	1964	2.50	5.00	10.00
❑ 146	You Can't Hurt Me No More/Everybody Let's Dance	1965	2.00	4.00	8.00
❑ 149	Nothing Can Stop Me/The Big Lie	1965	2.00	4.00	8.00
❑ 158	Rainbow '65 (Part 1)/Rainbow '65 (Part 2)	1965	2.00	4.00	8.00
❑ 160	Good Times/No One Can Love You	1965	2.00	4.00	8.00
❑ 164	Here Come the Tears/Soul Hootenanny (Part 2)	1965	2.00	4.00	8.00
❑ 166	Baby That's Love/Bet You Never Thought	1966	2.00	4.00	8.00
❑ 167	(I'm Just a) Fool for You/Buddy Ain't It a Shame	1966	2.00	4.00	8.00
❑ 169	I Can Take Care of Myself/If I Can't Save It	1966	2.00	4.00	8.00
❑ 172	Mr. Big Shot/I Hate to Be the One to Say	1966	2.00	4.00	8.00
CURTOM					
❑ 1979	Don't Have to Be Lyin' Babe (Part 1)/Don't Have to Be Lyin' Babe (Part 2)	1973	—	2.50	5.00
❑ 1986	Baby I Still Love You/I Understand	1973	—	2.50	5.00
❑ 1992	Without You Here/Just Be There	1973	—	2.50	5.00
FASTFIRE					
❑ 7003	Haven't Heard That Line Before/(B-side unknown)	1985	—	2.00	4.00
❑ 7005	Lucy/(B-side unknown)	1986	—	2.00	4.00
MERCURY					
❑ 73083	Groovy Situation/Not the Marrying Kind	1970	—	3.00	6.00
❑ 73121	Simply Call It Love/Give Me a Chance	1970	—	3.00	6.00
❑ 73206	You're a Lady/Stone Cold Feeling	1971	—	3.00	6.00
❑ 73258	Yes I'm Ready (If I Don't Get to Go)/Pillars of Glass	1971	—	3.00	6.00
SALSOUL					
❑ 7051	You're the One/I Keep Comin' Back for More	1983	—	2.00	4.00
—With Jaime Lynn					
VEE JAY					
❑ 416	Duke of Earl/Kissin' in the Kitchen	1961	6.25	12.50	25.00
❑ 416	Duke of Earl/Kissin' in the Kitchen	1962	5.00	10.00	20.00
—Some later pressings as "The Duke of Earl"					
❑ 440	Walk On with the Duke/London Town	1962	3.75	7.50	15.00
—As "The Duke of Earl"					
❑ 450	Daddy's Home/The Big Lie	1962	3.75	7.50	15.00
—As "The Duke of Earl"					
❑ 455	I'll Follow You/You Left Me	1962	3.75	7.50	15.00
—As "The Duke of Earl"					
❑ 461	Tear for Tear/Miracle After Miracle	1962	3.75	7.50	15.00
❑ 468	You Threw a Lucky Punch/Rainbow	1962	3.75	7.50	15.00
❑ 511	Check Yourself/Forgive Me	1963	3.75	7.50	15.00
❑ 536	Baby, That's Love/Man's Temptation	1963	3.75	7.50	15.00

CHANDLER, GENE, AND BARBARA ACKLIN

Also see each artist's individual listings.

Number	Title (A Side/B Side)	Yr	VG	VG+	NM
BRUNSWICK					
❑ 55366	Love Won't Start/Show Me the Way to Go	1968	2.00	4.00	8.00
❑ 55387	From the Teacher to the Preacher/Anywhere But Nowhere	1968	2.00	4.00	8.00
❑ 55405	Little Green Apples/Will I Find You	1969	2.00	4.00	8.00

CHANDLER, GENE, AND JERRY BUTLER

Also see each artist's individual listings.

Number	Title (A Side/B Side)	Yr	VG	VG+	NM
MERCURY					
❑ 73163	You Just Can't Win (By Making the Same Mistake)/The Show Is Grooving	1971	—	3.00	6.00
❑ 73195	Two and Two (Take This Woman Off the Corner)/Everybody Is Waiting	1971	—	3.00	6.00

CHANEY, LON

Number	Title (A Side/B Side)	Yr	VG	VG+	NM
TOWER					
❑ 114	Monster's Holiday/Yuletide Jerk	1964	6.25	12.50	25.00

CHANGIN' TIMES, THE

Number	Title (A Side/B Side)	Yr	VG	VG+	NM
BELL					
❑ 675	Free Spirit/You Just Seem to Know	1967	5.00	10.00	20.00
❑ 711	Show Me the Way to Go Home/When the Good Sun Shines	1968	5.00	10.00	20.00
PHILIPS					
❑ 40320	Pied Piper/Thank You Babe	1965	5.00	10.00	20.00
❑ 40341	How Is the Air Up There/Young and Innocent Girl	1965	5.00	10.00	20.00
❑ 40368	Goin' Lovin' with You/I Should Have Brought Her Home	1966	3.75	7.50	15.00
❑ 40401	Aladdin/All in the Mind of a Young Girl	1966	3.75	7.50	15.00

CHANGING SCENE, THE

Number	Title (A Side/B Side)	Yr	VG	VG+	NM
FONTANA					
❑ 1669	Is It Really Worth It/Sing Me Something Pretty	1969	3.00	6.00	12.00

CHANNEL, BRUCE

Number	Title (A Side/B Side)	Yr	VG	VG+	NM
ELEKTRA					
❑ 46587	One More Last Chance/That's the Truth, Ruth	1980	—	2.00	4.00
KING					
❑ 5294	Will I Ever Love Again/Blow Down Baby	1959	7.50	15.00	30.00
❑ 5331	Now or Never/Boy, This Stuff Kills Me	1960	7.50	15.00	30.00
❑ 5620	Now or Never/Will I Ever Love Again	1962	5.00	10.00	20.00
LE CAM					
❑ 122	Going Back to Louisiana/Forget Me Not	1964	2.50	5.00	10.00
❑ 125	My Baby/Blue Monday	1964	2.50	5.00	10.00
❑ 953	Hey! Baby/Dream Girl	1961	10.00	20.00	40.00
❑ 1117	A Presley Medley/A Man Without a Woman	1977	—	2.50	5.00
❑ 7277	The King Is Free (Love Me)/Funky Dude (Andy and the Dude)	1977	—	2.50	5.00
MALA					
❑ 579	Mr. Bus Driver/It's Me	1967	2.50	5.00	10.00
❑ 592	Keep On/Barbara Allen	1968	2.50	5.00	10.00
❑ 12011	California/Water the Family Tree	1968	2.50	5.00	10.00
❑ 12027	Try Me/Nobody	1968	2.50	5.00	10.00
❑ 12041	The Web/Mrs. P	1969	2.50	5.00	10.00
MANCO					
❑ 1035	Run Romance, Run/Don't Leave Me	1962	5.00	10.00	20.00
MEL-O-DY					
❑ 112	That's What's Happenin'/Satisfied Mind	1964	3.75	7.50	15.00
❑ 114	You Make Me Happy/You Never Looked Better	1964	3.75	7.50	15.00
SMASH					
❑ 1731	Hey! Baby/Dream Girl	1962	5.00	10.00	20.00
❑ 1752	Number One Man/If Only I Had Known	1962	3.75	7.50	15.00
❑ 1769	Come On Baby/Mine Exclusively	1962	3.75	7.50	15.00
❑ 1780	Stand Tough/Somewhere in This Town	1962	3.75	7.50	15.00
❑ 1780 [PS]	Stand Tough/Somewhere in This Town	1962	7.50	15.00	30.00
❑ 1792	Oh Baby/Let's Hurt Together	1962	3.75	7.50	15.00
❑ 1826	No Other Baby/Night People	1963	3.75	7.50	15.00
❑ 1826 [PS]	No Other Baby/Night People	1963	7.50	15.00	30.00
❑ 1838	The Dipsy Doodle/Send Her Home	1963	3.75	7.50	15.00
❑ 1838 [PS]	The Dipsy Doodle/Send Her Home	1963	7.50	15.00	30.00
TEENAGER					
❑ 601	Run Romance, Run/Don't Leave Me	1960	7.50	15.00	30.00

CHANNELLS, THE

See THE CHANNELS (2).

CHANNELS, THE (1)

Group led by Earl Lewis.

Number	Title (A Side/B Side)	Yr	VG	VG+	NM
CHANNEL					
❑ 1000	Gloria/You Said You Loved Me	1971	2.50	5.00	10.00
❑ 1001	We Belong Together/Hey Girl, I'm in Love with You	1972	2.50	5.00	10.00
❑ 1002	You Got What It Takes/Crazy Mixed-Up World	1972	2.50	5.00	10.00
❑ 1003	Close Your Eyes/Work with Me Annie	1973	2.50	5.00	10.00
❑ 1004	Over Again/In My Arms to Stay	1973	2.50	5.00	10.00
❑ 1006	A Thousand Miles Away/Don't Let the Green Grass Fool You	1974	2.50	5.00	10.00
FIRE					
❑ 1001	My Heart Is Sad/The Girl Next Door	1959	12.50	25.00	50.00
—As "Earl Lewis and the Channels"					
FURY					
❑ 1021	Bye Bye Baby/My Love Will Never Die	1959	12.50	25.00	50.00
❑ 1071	Bye Bye Baby/My Love Will Never Die	1963	10.00	20.00	40.00
GONE					
❑ 5012	That's My Desire/Stay As You Are	1957	15.00	30.00	60.00
❑ 5019	Altar of Love/All Alone	1957	15.00	30.00	60.00
PORT					
❑ 70014	The Closer You Are/Now You Know	1960	6.25	12.50	25.00
—Reissue of Whirlin' Disc 100					
❑ 70017	The Gleam in Your Eyes/Stars in the Sky	1960	6.25	12.50	25.00
—Reissue of Whirlin' Disc 102					
❑ 70022	Flames in My Heart/My Lovin' Baby	1961	6.25	12.50	25.00
—Reissue of Whirlin' Disc 109					
❑ 70023	I Really Love You/What Do You Do	1961	6.25	12.50	25.00
—Reissue of Whirlin' Disc 107					
RARE BIRD					
❑ 5017	She Blew My Mind/Breaking Up Is Hard to Do	1971	2.50	5.00	10.00
WHIRLIN' DISC					
❑ 100	The Closer You Are/Now You Know	1956	62.50	125.00	250.00
—Block-letter label name; publisher listed as "Bob-Dan Music"					
❑ 100	The Closer You Are/Now You Know	1956	50.00	100.00	200.00
—Block-letter label name; publisher listed as "Spinning Wheel Music"					
❑ 100	The Closer You Are/Now You Know	1956	25.00	50.00	100.00
—Label name is all caps, but not in block letters					
❑ 102	The Gleam in Your Eyes/Stars in the Sky	1956	50.00	100.00	200.00
❑ 107	I Really Love You/What Do You Do	1957	50.00	100.00	200.00
❑ 109	Flames in My Heart/My Lovin' Baby	1957	50.00	100.00	200.00

CHANNELS, THE (2)

Group led by Tony and Gene Williams.

Number	Title (A Side/B Side)	Yr	VG	VG+	NM
ENJOY					
❑ 2001	Sad Song/My Love	1963	6.25	12.50	25.00
GROOVE					
❑ 58-0046	Anything You Do/I've Got My Eyes on You	1964	6.25	12.50	25.00
❑ 58-0061	Old Chinatown/You Can Count on Me	1965	6.25	12.50	25.00
HIT RECORD					
❑ 700	In My Arms to Stay/You Hurt Me	1963	10.00	20.00	40.00
—As "The Channells"					

CHANNELS, THE (3)

Neither of the above.

Number	Title (A Side/B Side)	Yr	VG	VG+	NM
MERCURY					
❑ 71501	Earthquake/Jungle Lights	1959	3.00	6.00	12.00

CHANTAY'S

Number	Title (A Side/B Side)	Yr	VG	VG+	NM
DOT					
❑ 145	Pipeline/Move It	1966	2.00	4.00	8.00
—Reissue; black label					
❑ 145	Pipeline/Move It	1969	—	3.00	6.00
—Reissue; orange-red label					
❑ 16440	Pipeline/Move It	1963	6.25	12.50	25.00
❑ 16492	Monsoon/Scotch Highs	1963	5.00	10.00	20.00
DOWNEY					
❑ 104	Pipeline/Move It	1963	15.00	30.00	60.00
❑ 108	Monsoon/Scotch Highs	1963	7.50	15.00	30.00
❑ 116	Space Probe/Continental Missile	1964	5.00	10.00	20.00
❑ 120	Only If You Care/Love Can Be Cruel	1964	5.00	10.00	20.00
❑ 126	Beyond/I'll Be Back Someday	1964	5.00	10.00	20.00
❑ 130	Three Coins in the Fountain/Greens	1965	5.00	10.00	20.00

CHANTECLAIRS, THE

Number	Title (A Side/B Side)	Yr	VG	VG+	NM
DOT					
❑ 1227	Baby Please/Someday Love Will Come My Way	1954	18.75	37.50	75.00
❑ 15404	Believe Me, Beloved/I've Never Been There	1955	15.00	30.00	60.00

CHANTELS, THE

Also see ARLENE SMITH; THE VENEERS.

Number	Title (A Side/B Side)	Yr	VG	VG+	NM
CARLTON					
❑ 555	Look in My Eyes/Glad to Be Back	1961	5.00	10.00	20.00
❑ 564	Still/Well, I Told You	1961	5.00	10.00	20.00
❑ 569	Summertime/Here It Comes Again	1962	5.00	10.00	20.00
END					
❑ 1001	He's Gone/The Plea	1957	20.00	40.00	80.00
—Black label					
❑ 1005	Maybe/Come My Little Baby	1957	20.00	40.00	80.00
—Black label					
❑ 1005	Maybe/Come My Little Baby	1958	10.00	20.00	40.00
—Gray (white) label					
❑ 1005	Maybe/Come My Little Baby	1959	5.00	10.00	20.00
—Multi-color label					
❑ 1015	Every Night/Whoever You Are	1958	7.50	15.00	30.00
—Gray (white) label					
❑ 1015	Every Night/Whoever You Are	1959	5.00	10.00	20.00
—Multi-color label					
❑ 1020	I Love You So/How Could You Call It Off	1958	10.00	20.00	40.00
❑ 1026	Prayer/Sure of Love	1958	6.25	12.50	25.00
❑ 1030	If You Try/Congratulations	1958	6.25	12.50	25.00
❑ 1037	Never Let Go/I Can't Take It	1959	6.25	12.50	25.00
❑ 1048	I'm Confessin'/Goodbye to Love	1959	6.25	12.50	25.00
❑ 1069	Whoever You Are/How Could You Call It Off	1960	6.25	12.50	25.00
❑ 1103	Believe Me (My Angel)/I	1961	15.00	30.00	60.00
—Originally released on Princeton 102 as "The Veneers"					
❑ 1105	There's Our Song Again/I'm the Girl	1961	6.25	12.50	25.00
LUDIX					
❑ 101	Eternally/Swamp Water	1963	5.00	10.00	20.00
❑ 106	That's Why I'm Happy/Some Tears Fall Dry	1963	5.00	10.00	20.00
RCA VICTOR					
❑ 74-0347	I'm Gonna Win Him Back/Love Makes All the Difference in the World	1970	2.50	5.00	10.00
ROULETTE					
❑ 7064	Maybe/He's Gone	1969	2.50	5.00	10.00
TCF HALL					
❑ 123	Take Me As I Am/There's No Forgetting Me	1965	3.75	7.50	15.00
VERVE					
❑ 10387	You're Welcome to My Heart/Soul of a Soldier	1966	3.75	7.50	15.00
❑ 10435	Indian Giver/It's Just Me	1966	3.75	7.50	15.00
7-Inch Extended Plays					
END					
❑ 201	(contents unknown)	1958	37.50	75.00	150.00
❑ 201 [PS]	I Love You So	1958	62.50	125.00	250.00
❑ 202	(contents unknown)	1958	25.00	50.00	100.00
❑ 202 [PS]	C'est Si Bon	1958	50.00	100.00	200.00

CHANTERS, THE (1)

Number	Title (A Side/B Side)	Yr	VG	VG+	NM
COMBO					
❑ 78	Why/Watts	1954	125.00	250.00	500.00
❑ 92	I Love You/Hot Mamma	1955	100.00	200.00	400.00
DELUXE					
❑ 6162	My My Darling/I Need Your Tenderness (I Love You Darling)	1958	12.50	25.00	50.00
❑ 6166	Row Your Boat/Stars in the Skies	1958	10.00	20.00	40.00
—Black label					
❑ 6166	Row Your Boat/Stars in the Skies	1958	5.00	10.00	20.00
—Yellow label					
❑ 6172	Angel Darling/Five Little Kisses	1958	12.50	25.00	50.00
❑ 6177	No, No, No/Over the Rainbow	1958	10.00	20.00	40.00
❑ 6191	No, No, No/I Make This Pledge (To You)	1961	7.50	15.00	30.00
❑ 6194	My My Darling/At My Door	1961	10.00	20.00	40.00
❑ 6200	Row Your Boat/No, No, No	1963	7.50	15.00	30.00
KEM					
❑ 2740	Lonesome Me/Golden Apple	1955	75.00	150.00	300.00
RPM					
❑ 415	Tell Me, Thrill Me/She Wants to Mambo	1954	75.00	150.00	300.00

CHANTERS, THE (2)

Number	Title (A Side/B Side)	Yr	VG	VG+	NM
MGM					
❑ 13750	Free As A Bird/Bongo, Bongo	1967	—	3.00	6.00

CHANTEURS, THE

With Eugene Record, later of THE CHI-LITES.

Number	Title (A Side/B Side)	Yr	VG	VG+	NM
VEE JAY					
❑ 519	You've Got a Great Love/The Grizzly Bear	1963	5.00	10.00	20.00

CHANTONES, THE

Number	Title (A Side/B Side)	Yr	VG	VG+	NM
CAPITOL					
❑ 4661	Stormy Weather/Sweet Georgia Brown	1961	6.25	12.50	25.00
CARLTON					
❑ 485	Five Little Numbers/It's Just a Summer Love	1958	7.50	15.00	30.00
TOP RANK					
❑ 2066	Don't Open That Door/Tangerock	1960	6.25	12.50	25.00

CHANTS, THE (1)

British soul group.

Number	Title (A Side/B Side)	Yr	VG	VG+	NM
CAMEO					
❑ 277	I Don't Care/Come Go with Me	1963	5.00	10.00	20.00
❑ 297	I Could Write a Book/A Thousand Stars	1964	5.00	10.00	20.00
INTERPHON					
❑ 7703	She's Mine/Then I'll Be Home	1964	3.75	7.50	15.00

CHANTS, THE (U)

None of these are by group (1), but we doubt all of them are by the same group.

Number	Title (A Side/B Side)	Yr	VG	VG+	NM
CAPITOL					
❑ F3949	Lost and Found/Close Friends	1958	5.00	10.00	20.00
CHECKER					
❑ 1209	Surfside/Chicken 'N' Gravy	1968	2.00	4.00	8.00
EKO					
❑ 3567/77	Respectable/Kiss Me Goodbye	1961	7.50	15.00	30.00
MGM					
❑ 13008	Respectable/Kiss Me Goodbye	1961	5.00	10.00	20.00
NITE OWL					
❑ 40	Heaven and Paradise/When I'm With You	1960	75.00	150.00	300.00
—Maroon label original					
❑ 40	Heaven and Paradise/When I'm With You	1960	10.00	20.00	40.00
—Black label, black vinyl					
❑ 40	Heaven and Paradise/When I'm With You	196?	5.00	10.00	20.00
—Red vinyl					
❑ 40	Heaven and Paradise/When I'm With You	196?	5.00	10.00	20.00
—Blue vinyl					
❑ 40	Heaven and Paradise/When I'm With You	196?	5.00	10.00	20.00
—Yellow vinyl					
U.W.R.					
❑ 4243	Rockin' Santa/Respectable	1962	6.25	12.50	25.00
VERVE					
❑ 10244	Dick Tracy/Choo Choo	1961	5.00	10.00	20.00

CHAPEL, JEAN

Number	Title (A Side/B Side)	Yr	VG	VG+	NM
CHALLENGE					
❑ 59350	Tell It Like It Is/I'm Your Woman	1966	2.00	4.00	8.00
❑ 59362	You Can Take Me/Stamp Out Loneliness	1967	2.00	4.00	8.00
❑ 59370	In the Reach of Your Arms/This Waltz Is Mine	1967	2.00	4.00	8.00
❑ 59376	Hungry Eyes/Green Paper	1967	2.00	4.00	8.00
❑ 59381	Dino's TV Door/If I Never Get You	1967	2.00	4.00	8.00
❑ 59386	See and Ye Shall Find/I Really Go for You	1968	2.00	4.00	8.00
KAPP					
❑ 2034	Bluebird Ridge/I Started Loving You Again	1969	—	3.00	6.00
❑ 2082	I'm Your Woman/The Roll Call	1970	—	3.00	6.00
RCA VICTOR					
❑ 47-6681	I Won't Be Rockin' Tonight/Welcome to the Club	1956	10.00	20.00	40.00
❑ 47-6892	Oo-Ba La Baby/I Had a Dream	1957	6.25	12.50	25.00
SMASH					
❑ 1829	Don't Let Go/Your Tender Love	1963	3.00	6.00	12.00
SUN					
❑ 244	I Won't Be Rockin' Tonight/Welcome to the Club	1956	12.50	25.00	50.00

CHAPERONES, THE

Number	Title (A Side/B Side)	Yr	VG	VG+	NM
JOSIE					
❑ 880	Dance with Me/Cruise to the Moon	1960	37.50	75.00	150.00
—With typographical error listing group as "The Cahperones"					
❑ 880	Dance with Me/Cruise to the Moon	1960	6.25	12.50	25.00
—With correct group name on label					
❑ 885	Shining Star/My Shadow and Me	1960	6.25	12.50	25.00
❑ 891	Man from the Moon/Blueberry Sweet	1961	12.50	25.00	50.00

CHAPINS, THE

Harry, Steve and Tom Chapin.

Number	Title (A Side/B Side)	Yr	VG	VG+	NM
EPIC					
❑ 10761	Workin' On My Life/The Only Thing (You Ever Really Have to Do Is Die)	1971	3.00	6.00	12.00
ROCK-LAND					
❑ 664	Old Time Movies/Not Your Kind	1966	3.75	7.50	15.00
❑ 664 [PS]	Old Time Movies/Not Your Kind	1966	6.25	12.50	25.00

CHAPMAN, GRADY

Number	Title (A Side/B Side)	Yr	VG	VG+	NM
IMPERIAL					
❑ 5591	Garden of Memories/Tell Me That You Care	1959	3.00	6.00	12.00
❑ 5611	Come Away/Let's Talk About Us	1959	3.00	6.00	12.00
KNIGHT					
❑ 2003	Say You Will Be Mine/Starlight, Starbright	1958	7.50	15.00	30.00

Number	Title (A Side/B Side)	Yr	VG	VG+	NM
MERCURY					
❑ 71632	Sweet Thing/I Know What I Want	1960	3.00	6.00	12.00
❑ 71698	Ambush/My Life Would Be Worth Living	1960	12.50	25.00	50.00
❑ 71771	I'll Never Question Your Love/This, That, 'N the Other	1961	3.00	6.00	12.00
MONEY					
❑ 204	I Need You So/Don't Blooper	1955	75.00	150.00	300.00
ZEPHYR					
❑ 016	My Love Will Never Change/Smiling	1957	7.50	15.00	30.00

CHARGERS, THE

Also see JESSE BELVIN.

Number	Title (A Side/B Side)	Yr	VG	VG+	NM
RCA VICTOR					
❑ 47-7301	Old MacDonald/Dandelion	1958	7.50	15.00	30.00

CHARIOTEERS, THE

Number	Title (A Side/B Side)	Yr	VG	VG+	NM
COLUMBIA					
❑ 1-168	A Kiss and a Rose/A Cottage in Old Donegal	1949	150.00	300.00	600.00
—Microgroove 7-inch, 33 1/3 rpm single					
❑ 1-363	This Side of Heaven/Hawaiian Sunset	1949	150.00	300.00	600.00
—Microgroove 7-inch, 33 1/3 rpm single					
JOSIE					
❑ 787	I've Got My Heart on My Sleeve/Don't Play No Mambo	1955	20.00	40.00	80.00
MGM					
❑ 12569	The Candles/I Didn't Mean to Be Mean to You	1957	20.00	40.00	80.00
RCA VICTOR					
❑ 47-6098	Easy Does It/Tremble, Tremble, Tremble	1955	20.00	40.00	80.00

CHARIOTS, THE

Number	Title (A Side/B Side)	Yr	VG	VG+	NM
TIME					
❑ 1006	Gloria/(B-side unknown)	1959	10.00	20.00	40.00

CHARLATANS, THE

Number	Title (A Side/B Side)	Yr	VG	VG+	NM
KAPP					
❑ 779	The Shadow Knows/32-20	1967	12.50	25.00	50.00
❑ 779 [PS]	The Shadow Knows/32-20	1967	20.00	40.00	80.00
PHILIPS					
❑ 40610	High Coin/When I Go Sailin' By	1969	10.00	20.00	40.00
❑ 40610 [PS]	High Coin/When I Go Sailin' By	1969	20.00	40.00	80.00
—Sleeve is promo only					
❑ 44824 [DJ]	Date: May 19, 1969	1969	15.00	30.00	60.00
—One-sided, promo only					

CHARLES, BOBBY

Number	Title (A Side/B Side)	Yr	VG	VG+	NM
BEARSVILLE					
❑ 0010	Small Town Talk/Save Me Jesus	1973	—	2.00	4.00
CHESS					
❑ 1609	Later Alligator/On Bended Knee	1955	12.50	25.00	50.00
❑ 1617	Why Did You Leave/Don't You Know I Love You	1956	12.50	25.00	50.00
❑ 1628	Only Time Will Tell/Take It Easy, Greasy	1956	12.50	25.00	50.00
❑ 1638	Laura Lee/No Use Knocking	1956	12.50	25.00	50.00
❑ 1647	Put Your Arms Around Me/Why Can't You, Honey	1957	10.00	20.00	40.00
❑ 1658	No More/You Can Suit Yourself	1957	10.00	20.00	40.00
❑ 1670	One Eyed Jack/Yea Yea Baby	1957	10.00	20.00	40.00
IMPERIAL					
❑ 5542	Since She's Gone/At the Jamboree	1958	5.00	10.00	20.00
❑ 5557	Oh Yeah/Since I Lost You	1958	5.00	10.00	20.00
❑ 5579	The Town Is Talking/What Can I Do	1959	5.00	10.00	20.00
❑ 5642	Bye Bye Baby/Those Eyes	1960	5.00	10.00	20.00
❑ 5681	What a Party/I Just Want You	1960	5.00	10.00	20.00
❑ 5691	Four Winds/Nothing Sweet As You	1960	5.00	10.00	20.00
JEWEL					
❑ 728	Everybody's Laughing/Everybody Knows	1964	2.50	5.00	10.00
❑ 729	Goodnight Irene/I Hope	1964	2.50	5.00	10.00
❑ 735	Ain't Misbehavin'/Preacher's Daughter	1964	2.50	5.00	10.00
❑ 740	Oh Lonesome Me/One More Glass of Wine	1964	2.50	5.00	10.00
PAULA					
❑ 226	The Walk/Worrying Over You	1965	2.50	5.00	10.00

CHARLES, DON

Number	Title (A Side/B Side)	Yr	VG	VG+	NM
WORLD ARTISTS					
❑ 1031	She's Mine/Big Talk from a Little Man	1964	2.50	5.00	10.00

CHARLES, JIMMY

Number	Title (A Side/B Side)	Yr	VG	VG+	NM
PROMO					
❑ 1002	A Million to One/Hop Scotch Hop	1960	3.75	7.50	15.00
❑ 1003	The Age for Love/Follow the Swallow	1960	3.75	7.50	15.00
❑ 1003 [PS]	The Age for Love/Follow the Swallow	1960	5.00	10.00	20.00
❑ 1004	Santa Won't Be Blue This Christmas/I Saw Mommy Kissing Santa Claus	1960	3.75	7.50	15.00
❑ 1004 [PS]	Santa Won't Be Blue This Christmas/I Saw Mommy Kissing Santa Claus	1960	5.00	10.00	20.00
❑ 1005	Christmasville U.S.A./A Little White Mouse Called Steve	1960	3.75	7.50	15.00
❑ 1005 [PS]	Christmasville U.S.A./A Little White Mouse Called Steve	1960	5.00	10.00	20.00

CHARLES, RAY

Also see BILLY JOEL.

Number	Title (A Side/B Side)	Yr	VG	VG+	NM
ABC					
❑ 10808	Let's Go Get Stoned/At the Train	1966	2.00	4.00	8.00
❑ 10840	I Chose to Sing the Blues/Hopelessly	1966	2.00	4.00	8.00
❑ 10865	Please Say You're Fooling/I Don't Need No Doctor	1966	2.00	4.00	8.00
❑ 10901	I Want to Talk About You/Something Inside Me	1967	2.00	4.00	8.00
❑ 10938	Here We Go Again/Somebody Ought to Write a Book About It	1967	2.00	4.00	8.00
❑ 10970	In the Heat of the Night/Somebody's Got to Change	1967	2.00	4.00	8.00
❑ 11009	Yesterday/Never Had Enough of Nothing Yet	1967	2.00	4.00	8.00
❑ 11045	That's a Lie/Go On Home	1968	2.00	4.00	8.00
❑ 11045 [PS]	That's a Lie/Go On Home	1968	3.75	7.50	15.00
❑ 11090	Eleanor Rigby/Understanding	1968	2.00	4.00	8.00
❑ 11133	Sweet Young Thing Like You/Listen, They're Playing Our Song	1968	2.00	4.00	8.00
❑ 11170	If It Wasn't for Bad Luck/When I Stop Dreaming	1969	2.00	4.00	8.00
—With Jimmy Lewis					
❑ 11193	I'll Be Your Servant/I Don't Know What Time It Was	1969	2.00	4.00	8.00
❑ 11213	Let Me Love You/I'm Satisfied	1969	2.00	4.00	8.00
❑ 11239	We Can Make It/I Can't Stop Loving You Baby	1969	2.00	4.00	8.00
❑ 11251	Someone to Watch Over Me/Claudie Mae	1969	2.00	4.00	8.00
❑ 11259	Laughin' and Clownin'/That Thing Called Love	1970	2.00	4.00	8.00
❑ 11271	If You Were Mine/Till I Can't Take It Anymore	1970	2.00	4.00	8.00
❑ 11291	Don't Change on Me/Sweet Memories	1971	2.00	4.00	8.00
❑ 11308	Feel So Bad/Your Love Is So Doggone Good	1971	—	3.00	6.00
❑ 11317	What Am I Living For/Tired of My Tears	1971	—	3.00	6.00
❑ 11329	Look What They've Done to My Song, Ma/America the Beautiful	1972	—	3.00	6.00
❑ 11337	Hey Mister/There'll Be No Peace Without All Men as One	1972	—	3.00	6.00
❑ 11344	Every Saturday Night/Take Me Home, Country Roads	1973	—	3.00	6.00
❑ 11351	I Can Make It Through the Days (But Oh Those Lonely Nights)/Ring of Fire	1973	—	3.00	6.00
ABC-PARAMOUNT					
❑ 4801 [S]	Don't Cry Baby/Teardrops from My Eyes	1964	5.00	10.00	20.00
❑ 4802 [S]	Baby, Don't You Cry/Cry Me a River	1964	5.00	10.00	20.00
❑ 4803 [S]	I Cried for You/Cry	1964	5.00	10.00	20.00
❑ 4804 [S]	A Tear Fell/No One to Cry To	1964	5.00	10.00	20.00
❑ 4805 [S]	You've Got Me Crying Again/After My Laughter Came Tears	1964	5.00	10.00	20.00
—The above five are 33 1/3 rpm, small hole jukebox singles excerpted from the LP "Sweet and Sour Tears"					
❑ 10081	My Baby/Who You Gonna Love	1960	3.75	7.50	15.00
❑ 10118	Sticks and Stones/Worried Life Blues	1960	3.00	6.00	12.00
❑ 10135	Georgia on My Mind/Carry Me Back to Old Virginny	1960	3.75	7.50	15.00
❑ 10141	Them That Got/I Wonder	1960	3.00	6.00	12.00
❑ 10164	Ruby/Heard Hearted Woman	1960	3.00	6.00	12.00
❑ 10244	Hit the Road Jack/The Danger Zone	1961	3.75	7.50	15.00
❑ 10266	Unchain My Heart/But on the Other Hand, Baby	1961	3.75	7.50	15.00
❑ 10314	Hide 'Nor Hair/At the Club	1962	3.00	6.00	12.00
❑ 10330	I Can't Stop Loving You/Born to Lose	1962	3.75	7.50	15.00
❑ 10345	You Don't Know Me/Careless Love	1962	3.75	7.50	15.00
❑ 10375	You Are My Sunshine/Your Cheating Heart	1962	3.00	6.00	12.00
❑ 10405	Don't Set Me Free/The Brightest Smile in Town	1963	3.00	6.00	12.00
❑ 10435	Take These Chains from My Heart/No Letter Today	1963	3.75	7.50	15.00
❑ 10453	No One/Without Love (There Is Nothing)	1963	3.00	6.00	12.00
❑ 10481	Busted/Making Believe	1963	3.75	7.50	15.00
❑ 10509	That Lucky Old Sun/Old Man Time	1963	2.50	5.00	12.00
❑ 10530	Baby Don't You Cry/My Heart Cries for You	1964	3.00	6.00	12.00
❑ 10557	My Baby Don't Dig Me/Something's Wrong	1964	3.00	6.00	12.00
❑ 10571	No One to Cry To/A Tear Fell	1964	3.00	6.00	12.00
❑ 10588	Smack Dab in the Middle/I Wake Up Crying	1964	3.00	6.00	12.00
❑ 10609	Makin' Whoopee/(Instrumental)	1964	3.00	6.00	12.00
❑ 10615	Cry/Teardrops from My Eyes	1965	3.00	6.00	12.00
❑ 10649	I Gotta Woman (Part 1)/I Gotta Woman (Part 2)	1965	3.00	6.00	12.00
❑ 10663	Without a Song (Part 1)/Without a Song (Part 2)	1965	3.00	6.00	12.00
❑ 10700	I'm a Fool to Care/Love's Gonna Live Here	1965	3.00	6.00	12.00
❑ 10720	The Cincinnati Kid/That's All I Am to You	1965	3.00	6.00	12.00
❑ 10739	Crying Time/When My Dreamboat Comes Home	1965	3.75	7.50	15.00
❑ 10785	Together Again/You're Just About to Lose Your Clown	1966	3.00	6.00	12.00
ATLANTIC					
❑ 976	Roll with Me Baby/The Midnight Hour	1952	125.00	250.00	500.00
❑ 984	The Sun's Gonna Shine Again/Jumpin' in the Morning	1953	100.00	200.00	400.00
❑ 999	Mess Around/Funny (But I Still Love You)	1953	50.00	100.00	200.00
❑ 1008	Feelin' Sad/Heartbreaker	1953	25.00	50.00	100.00
❑ 1021	It Should've Been Me/Sinner's Prayer	1954	12.50	25.00	50.00
❑ 1037	Don't You Know/Losing Hand	1954	7.50	15.00	30.00
❑ 1050	I've Got a Woman/Come Back	1954	12.50	25.00	50.00
❑ 1063	This Little Girl of Mine/A Fool for You	1955	7.50	15.00	30.00
❑ 1076	Blackjack/Greenbacks	1955	7.50	15.00	30.00
❑ 1085	Drown in My Own Tears/Mary Ann	1956	6.25	12.50	25.00
❑ 1096	Hallelujah, I Love Her So/What Would I Do Without You	1956	5.00	10.00	20.00
❑ 1108	Lonely Avenue/Leave My Woman Alone	1956	5.00	10.00	20.00
❑ 1124	I Want to Know/Ain't That Love	1957	5.00	10.00	20.00
❑ 1143	It's All Right/Get On the Right Track Baby	1957	5.00	10.00	20.00
❑ 1154	Swanee River Rock (Talkin' 'Bout That River)/I Want a Little Girl	1957	5.00	10.00	20.00
❑ 1172	Talkin' 'Bout You/What Kind of a Man Are You	1958	3.75	7.50	15.00
❑ 1180	Yes Indeed/I Had a Dream	1958	3.75	7.50	15.00
—With the Cookies					
❑ 1196	My Bonnie/You Be My Baby	1958	3.75	7.50	15.00
❑ 2006	Rockhouse (Part 1)/Rockhouse (Part 2)	1958	3.75	7.50	15.00
❑ 2010	(Night Time Is) The Right Time/Tell All the World About You	1959	3.75	7.50	15.00
❑ 2022	Tell Me How Do You Feel/That's Enough	1959	3.75	7.50	15.00
❑ 2031	What'd I Say (Part I)/What'd I Say (Part II)	1959	5.00	10.00	20.00
❑ 2043	I'm Movin' On/I Believe to My Soul	1959	3.00	6.00	12.00
❑ 2047	Let the Good Times Roll/Don't Let the Sun Catch You Cryin'	1960	3.00	6.00	12.00
❑ 2055	Heartbreaker/Just for a Thrill	1960	3.00	6.00	12.00
❑ 2068	Tell the Truth/Sweet Sixteen Bars	1960	3.00	6.00	12.00
❑ 2084	Come Rain or Come Shine/Tell Me You'll Wait for Me	1960	3.00	6.00	12.00
❑ 2094	Early in the Morning/A Bit of Soul	1961	3.00	6.00	12.00
❑ 2106	Am I Blue/It Should've Been Me	1961	3.00	6.00	12.00

Number	Title (A Side/B Side)	Yr	VG	VG+	NM
❑ 2118	I Wonder Who/Hard Times (No One Knows Better Than I)	1961	3.00	6.00	12.00
❑ 2174	Carryin' That Load/Feelin' Sad	1963	2.50	5.00	10.00
❑ 2239	Talkin' 'Bout You/In a Little Spanish Town	1964	2.50	5.00	10.00
❑ 2470	Come Rain or Come Shine/Tell Me You'll Wait for Me	1968	2.50	5.00	10.00
❑ 3443	I Can See Clearly Now/Anonymous Love	1977	—	2.50	5.00
❑ 3473	A Peace That We Never Could Enjoy/Game Number Nine	1978	—	2.50	5.00
❑ 3527	Riding Thumb/You Forgot Your Memories	1978	—	2.50	5.00
❑ 3549 [DJ]	Christmas Time (same on both sides)	1978	—	3.00	6.00
—May be promo-only					
❑ 3611	Some Enchanted Evening/20th Century Fox	1979	—	2.50	5.00
❑ 3634	Just Because/Love Me or Set Me Free	1979	—	2.50	5.00
❑ 3762	Compared To What/Now That We've Found Each Other	1980	—	2.50	5.00
❑ 5005	Doodlin' (Part 1)/Doodlin' (Part 2)	1960	3.75	7.50	15.00
BARONET					
❑ 7111	See See Rider/I Used to be So Happy	1960	3.00	6.00	12.00
❑ 7111 [PS]	See See Rider/I Used to be So Happy	1960	6.25	12.50	25.00
COLUMBIA					
❑ 03429	String Bean/Born to Love Me	1982	—	2.00	4.00
❑ 03810	You Feel Good All Over/ 3/4 Time	1983	—	—	3.00
❑ 04083	Ain't Your Memory Got No Pride at All/I Don't Want No Strangers Sleeping in My Bed	1983	—	—	3.00
❑ 04297	We Didn't See a Thing/I Wish You Were Here Tonight	1983	—	—	3.00
—A-side with George Jones and Chet Atkins					
❑ 04420	Do I Ever Cross Your Mind/They Call It Love	1984	—	—	3.00
❑ 04500	Woman (Sensuous Woman)/I Was On Georgia Time	1984	—	—	3.00
❑ 04531	Rock and Roll Shoes/Then I'll Be Over You	1984	—	—	3.00
—Ray Charles and B.J. Thomas					
❑ 04715	Seven Spanish Angels/Who Cares	1984	—	—	3.00
—A-side with Willie Nelson; B-side with Janie Frickie					
❑ 04860	It Ain't Gonna Worry My Mind/Crazy Old Soldier	1985	—	—	3.00
—A-side with Mickey Gilley; B-side with Johnny Cash					
❑ 05575	Two Old Cats Like Us/Little Hotel Room	1985	—	—	3.00
—A-side with Hank Williams, Jr.					
❑ 06172	Pages of My Mind/Slip Away	1986	—	—	3.00
❑ 06370	Dixie Moon/A Little Bit of Heaven	1986	—	—	3.00
❑ 08393	Seven Spanish Angels/It Ain't Gonna Worry My Mind	1988	—	—	3.00
—Reissue; A-side with Willie Nelson, B-side with Mickey Gilley					
CROSSOVER					
❑ 973	Come Live with Me/Everybody Sing	1973	—	2.50	5.00
❑ 974	Louise/Somebody	1974	—	2.50	5.00
❑ 981	Living for the City/Then We'll Be Home	1975	—	2.50	5.00
❑ 985	America the Beautiful/Sunshine	1976	—	3.00	6.00
—A-side is a different recording than that on the B-side of ABC 11329					
IMPULSE!					
❑ 200	One Mint Julep/Let's Go	1961	2.50	5.00	10.00
❑ 202	I've Got News for You/I'm Gonna Move to the Outskirts of Town	1961	2.50	5.00	10.00
RCA					
❑ PB-10800	Oh Lawd, I'm On My Way/Oh Bess, Where's My Bess	1976	—	2.50	5.00
ROCKIN'					
❑ 504	Walkin' and Talkin' (To Myself)/I'm Wonderin' and Wonderin'	1952	75.00	150.00	300.00
SITTIN' IN WITH					
❑ 641	Baby Let Me Hear You Call My Name/Guitar Blues	1952	75.00	150.00	300.00
❑ 651	I Can't Do No More/Roly Poly	1952	—	—	—
—Unconfirmed on 45 rpm					
SWING TIME					
❑ 250	Baby, Let Me Hold Your Hand/Lonely Boy	1951	125.00	250.00	500.00
—Ray Charles records on Swing Time before 250 are unconfirmed on 45 rpm					
❑ 274	Kissa Me Baby/I'm Glad for Your Sake	1952	125.00	250.00	500.00
❑ 297	Baby Won't You Please Come Home/Hey Now	1952	—	—	—
—Unconfirmed on 45 rpm					
❑ 300	Baby Let Me Hear You Call My Name/Guitar Blues	1952	125.00	250.00	500.00
❑ 326	The Snow Is Falling/Misery in My Heart	1953	125.00	250.00	500.00
TANGERINE					
❑ 1015	Booty Butt/Sidewinder	1971	—	3.00	6.00
TIME					
❑ 1026	I Found My Baby/Guitar Blues	1960	3.75	7.50	15.00
❑ 1054	Why Did You Go/Back Home	1962	3.00	6.00	12.00
WARNER BROS.					
❑ 18611	A Song for You/I Can't Get Enough	1993	—	—	3.00
❑ 49608	Beers to You/Cotton-Eyed Clint	1980	—	2.50	5.00
—A-side with Clint Eastwood; B-side by Texas Opera Company					
7-Inch Extended Plays					
ATLANTIC					
❑ EP 587	*Ain't That Love/Greenbacks/Drown in My Own Tears/Hallelujah I Love Her So	1956	25.00	50.00	100.00
❑ EP 587 [PS]	Ray Charles	1956	25.00	50.00	100.00
❑ EP 597	(contents unknown)	1957	25.00	50.00	100.00
❑ EP 597 [PS]	The Great Ray Charles	1957	25.00	50.00	100.00
❑ EP 607	(contents unknown)	1958	25.00	50.00	100.00
❑ EP 607 [PS]	Rock with Ray Charles	1958	25.00	50.00	100.00
❑ EP 619	*Let the Good Times Roll/Come Rain or Come Shine/Don't Let the Sun Catch You Cryin'/Alexander's Ragtime Band	1959	25.00	50.00	100.00
❑ EP 619 [PS]	The Genius of Ray Charles	1959	25.00	50.00	100.00

CHARLES, RAY, AND BETTY CARTER

Number	Title (A Side/B Side)	Yr	VG	VG+	NM
ABC-PARAMOUNT					
❑ 10298	Baby It's Cold Outside/We'll Be Together Again	1962	2.50	5.00	10.00

CHARLES, SONNY

Also see THE CHECKMATES LTD.

Number	Title (A Side/B Side)	Yr	VG	VG+	NM
FRATERNITY					
❑ 935	Speechless/These Two Feet	1964	4.00	8.00	12.00
HIGHRISE					
❑ 2001	Put It in a Magazine/Week-End Father Song	1982	—	2.00	4.00
❑ 2006	Always on My Mind/One-Eyed Jacks	1983	—	2.00	4.00
RCA VICTOR					
❑ 74-0645	It's Alright in the City/Nicasio	1972	—	3.00	6.00

CHARLES AND CARL

Number	Title (A Side/B Side)	Yr	VG	VG+	NM
RED ROBIN					
❑ 137	Lucky Star/One More Chance	1955	25.00	50.00	100.00

CHARLES RIVER VALLEY BOYS, THE

Number	Title (A Side/B Side)	Yr	VG	VG+	NM
ELEKTRA					
❑ 45642	I've Just Seen a Face/Ticket to Ride	1968	2.50	5.00	10.00

CHARLETTES, THE

Number	Title (A Side/B Side)	Yr	VG	VG+	NM
ANGIE					
❑ 1002	The Fight's Not Over/Whatever Happened to Our Love	1963	6.25	12.50	25.00

CHARMAINES, THE

Number	Title (A Side/B Side)	Yr	VG	VG+	NM
DOT					
❑ 16351	Where Is the Boy Tonight/On the Wagon	1961	5.00	10.00	20.00

CHARMERS, THE (1)

Female group.

Number	Title (A Side/B Side)	Yr	VG	VG+	NM
ALADDIN					
❑ 3337	All Alone/Johnny My Dear	1956	15.00	30.00	60.00
❑ 3341	He's Gone/Oh! Yes	1956	15.00	30.00	60.00
IMPERIAL					
❑ 5957	All Alone/Johnny My Dear	1963	3.00	6.00	12.00
—Reissue of Aladdin 3337					

CHARMERS, THE (2)

Another female group, not the same as group (1).

Number	Title (A Side/B Side)	Yr	VG	VG+	NM
CENTRAL					
❑ 1002	The Beating of My Heart/Why Does It Have to Be Me	1954	200.00	400.00	800.00
❑ 1006	Tony, My Darling/In the Rain	1954	250.00	500.00	1000.
TIMELY					
❑ 1009	I Was Wrong/The Mambo	1955	250.00	500.00	1000.
❑ 1011	The Church on the Hill/Battle Axe	1955	250.00	500.00	1000.

CHARMERS, THE (U)

Probably none of these are group (1) or (2), but which ones go together, we don't yet know.

Number	Title (A Side/B Side)	Yr	VG	VG+	NM
CO-REC					
❑ 101	The Letter/Watch What You Do	1963	5.00	10.00	20.00
JAF					
❑ 2021	Little Fool/Hard to Get	1961	6.25	12.50	25.00
LAURIE					
❑ 3142	My Kind of Love/Johnny	1962	5.00	10.00	20.00
❑ 3173	Shy Guy/I Cried	1963	5.00	10.00	20.00
❑ 3203	Work It Out/Sweet Talk	1963	5.00	10.00	20.00
LOUIS					
❑ 6806	It's a Funny Way We Met/Where's the Boy	1965	3.00	6.00	12.00
PIP					
❑ 8000	Looking for Trouble/After You Walk Me Home	1964	3.00	6.00	12.00
SILHOUETTE					
❑ 522	Rock, Rhythm and Blues/Letters Don't Have Arms	1957	15.00	30.00	60.00
SURE SHOT					
❑ 104	Lessons from the Stars/My Love	1963	75.00	150.00	300.00
TERRACE					
❑ 7512	Visiting Day/Whatever Happened to Baby Jane	1962	6.25	12.50	25.00

CHARMETTES, THE

Number	Title (A Side/B Side)	Yr	VG	VG+	NM
FEDERAL					
❑ 12345	Johnny, Johnny/School Letter	1959	10.00	20.00	40.00
HI					
❑ 2003	My Love with All My Heart/Skating in Blue Light	1958	5.00	10.00	20.00
KAPP					
❑ 547	Please Don't Kiss Me Again/What Is a Tear	1963	7.50	15.00	30.00
❑ 570	Oozi-Oozi-Ooh/He's a Wise Guy	1964	6.25	12.50	25.00
MALA					
❑ 491	My Lover Is a Boy Scout/Mailbox	1964	3.00	6.00	12.00
TRI-DISC					
❑ 103	Why Oh Why/On a Night Like Tonight	1962	6.25	12.50	25.00
WORLD ARTISTS					
❑ 1053	Stop the Wedding (Preacher Man)/Sugar Boy	1965	6.25	12.50	25.00

CHARMS, THE

Also see OTIS WILLIAMS AND THE CHARMS.

Number	Title (A Side/B Side)	Yr	VG	VG+	NM
CHART					
❑ 608	Love's Our Inspiration/Love, Love Stick Stov	1956	10.00	20.00	40.00
❑ 613	Heart of a Rose/I Offer You	1956	10.00	20.00	40.00
❑ 623	I'll Be True/Boom Diddy Boom Boom	1956	10.00	20.00	40.00
DELUXE					
❑ 6000	Heaven Only Knows/Loving Baby	1953	125.00	250.00	500.00
❑ 6014	Happy Are We/What Do You Know About That	1953	100.00	200.00	400.00
❑ 6034	Bye Bye Baby/Please Believe in Me	1954	100.00	200.00	400.00
❑ 6050	Quiet Please/55 Seconds	1954	100.00	200.00	400.00
❑ 6056	Come to Me Baby/My Baby, Dearest Darling	1954	50.00	100.00	200.00
❑ 6062	Hearts of Stone/Who Knows	1954	12.50	25.00	50.00
❑ 6065	Two Hearts/The First Time We Met	1954	12.50	25.00	50.00
❑ 6072	Crazy, Crazy Love/Mambo Sh-Mambo	1955	12.50	25.00	50.00
❑ 6076	Ling, Ting, Tong/Bazoom (I Need Your Lovin')	1955	12.50	25.00	50.00
❑ 6080	Ko Ko Mo (I Love You So)/Whadya Want?	1955	12.50	25.00	50.00
❑ 6082	Whadya Want?/Crazy, Crazy Love	1955	10.00	20.00	40.00

Number	Title (A Side/B Side)	Yr	VG	VG+	NM
❑ 6087	When We Get Married/Let the Happenings Happen	1955	10.00	20.00	40.00
❑ 6089	One Fine Day/It's You, You, You	1955	10.00	20.00	40.00
ROCKIN'					
❑ 516	Heaven Only Knows/Loving Baby	1953	200.00	400.00	800.00
CHARTERS, THE					
May all be the same group.					
ALVA					
❑ 1001	I Lost You/My Little Girl	1963	75.00	150.00	300.00
MEL-O-DY					
❑ 104	Trouble Lover/Show Me Some Sign	1962	500.00	1000.	2000.
MERRY-GO-ROUND					
❑ 103	Lost in a Dream/This Makes Me Mad	1963	15.00	30.00	60.00
TARX					
❑ 1003	My Rose/El Merengue	1962	25.00	50.00	100.00
CHARTS, THE					
EVERLAST					
❑ 5001	Deserie/Zoop	1957	20.00	40.00	80.00
❑ 5002	Dance Girl/Why Do You Cry	1957	20.00	40.00	80.00
❑ 5006	You're the Reason (I'm in Love)/I've Been Wondering	1958	15.00	30.00	60.00
❑ 5008	I Told You So/All Because of Love	1958	15.00	30.00	60.00
❑ 5010	My Diane/All Because of You	1958	17.50	35.00	70.00
❑ 5026	Deserie/Zoop	1963	6.25	12.50	25.00
GUYDEN					
❑ 2021	For the Birds/Ooba-Gooba	1959	5.00	10.00	20.00
WAND					
❑ 1112	Deserie/Fell in Love with Your Baby	1966	6.25	12.50	25.00
❑ 1124	Livin' the Night Life/Nobody Made You Love Me	1966	15.00	30.00	60.00
CHAVELLES, THE					
VITA					
❑ 127	Valley of Love/Red Tape	1956	37.50	75.00	150.00
CHAVIS BROTHERS, THE					
ASCOT					
❑ 2177	Torture Me/Humpty Dumpty Time	1965	3.00	6.00	12.00
CLOCK					
❑ 1025	I Love You/So Tired	1960	6.25	12.50	25.00
CORAL					
❑ 62270	Old Time Rock and Roll/Baby, Don't Leave Me	1961	7.50	15.00	30.00
—As "The Five Chavis Brothers"					
PARKWAY					
❑ 851	Slippin' and Slidin'/Good Old Mountain Dew	1962	3.75	7.50	15.00
CHEAP TRICK					
ASYLUM					
❑ 47187	I Must Be Dreamin'/Reach Out	1981	—	2.00	4.00
❑ 47187 [PS]	I Must Be Dreamin'/Reach Out	1981	—	2.00	4.00
COLUMBIA					
❑ 06137	Mighty Wings/Dog Fight #3	1986	—	—	3.00
—B-side by Harold Faltermeyer					
❑ 06137 [PS]	Mighty Wings/Dog Fight #3	1986	—	—	3.00
EPIC					
❑ 02968	If You Want My Love/Four Letter Word	1982	—	2.00	4.00
❑ 03233	She's Tight/All I Really Want to Do	1982	—	2.00	4.00
❑ 03233 [PS]	She's Tight/All I Really Want to Do	1982	—	2.50	5.00
❑ 03741	One on One/Saturday at Midnight	1983	—	2.00	4.00
❑ 03845	If You Want My Love/She's Tight	1983	—	2.00	4.00
—Reissue					
❑ 04078	Dancing the Night Away/Don't Make Our Love a Crime	1983	—	2.00	4.00
❑ 04078 [PS]	Dancing the Night Away/Don't Make Our Love a Crime	1983	—	2.00	4.00
❑ 04216	I Can't Take It/You Talk Too Much	1983	—	2.00	4.00
❑ 05431	Tonight It's You/Wild, Wild Women	1985	—	2.00	4.00
❑ 05431 [PS]	Tonight It's You/Wild, Wild Women	1985	—	2.50	5.00
❑ 06540	It's Only Love/Name of the Game	1987	—	2.00	4.00
❑ 07745	The Flame/Through the Night	1988	—	—	3.00
—Custom label					
❑ 07745 [PS]	The Flame/Through the Night	1988	—	—	3.00
❑ 07965	Don't Be Cruel/I Know What I Want	1988	—	—	3.00
❑ 07965 [PS]	Don't Be Cruel/I Know What I Want	1988	—	—	3.00
❑ 08097	Ghost Town/Wrong Side of Love	1988	—	—	3.00
❑ 08097 [PS]	Ghost Town/Wrong Side of Love	1988	—	—	3.00
❑ 50375	Oh, Candy/Daddy Should Have Stayed in High School	1977	2.50	5.00	10.00
❑ 50435	I Want You to Want Me/Oh Boy	1977	2.50	5.00	10.00
❑ 50485	Southern Girls/You're All Talk	1977	2.50	5.00	10.00
❑ 50570	Surrender/Auf Wiedersehn	1978	2.50	5.00	10.00
❑ 50625	California Man/I Want You to Want Me	1978	2.50	5.00	10.00
—B-side was first American issue of version that became a hit on Epic 50680					
❑ 50680	I Want You to Want Me/Clock Strikes Ten	1979	—	2.00	4.00
❑ 50680 [PS]	I Want You to Want Me/Clock Strikes Ten	1979	2.50	5.00	10.00
❑ 50743	Ain't That a Shame/Old Kiddies	1979	—	2.00	4.00
❑ 50774	Dream Police/Heaven Tonight	1979	—	2.00	4.00
❑ 50774 [PS]	Dream Police/Heaven Tonight	1979	2.50	5.00	10.00
❑ 50814	Voices/The House Is Rockin' (With Domestic Problems)	1979	—	2.00	4.00
❑ 50814 [PS]	Voices/The House Is Rockin' (With Domestic Problems)	1979	2.50	5.00	10.00
❑ 50887	Everything Works If You Let It/Way of the World	1980	—	2.00	4.00
❑ 50942	Stop This Game/Who D'King	1980	—	2.00	4.00
❑ 50970	The World's Greatest Lover/High Priest of Rhythmic Noise	1981	—	2.00	4.00
❑ 68543	Never Had a Lot to Lose/All He Needs Is a Dream	1989	—	—	3.00
❑ 73444	Can't Stop Fallin' Into Love/You Drive, I'll Steer	1990	—	—	3.00
❑ 73580	Wherever Would I Be/Busted	1990	—	—	3.00
❑ 73792	The Flame/Through the Night	1991	—	—	3.00
—Reissue					

Number	Title (A Side/B Side)	Yr	VG	VG+	NM
EPIC LEGACY					
❑ ES7 8290 [DJ]	I Want You to Want Me (Alternate Version)//Waitin' for the Man/Heroin (Live)	1996	—	2.50	5.00
❑ ES7 8290 [PS]	I Want You to Want Me (Alternate Version)//Waitin' for the Man/Heroin (Live)	1996	—	2.50	5.00
PASHA					
❑ 04392	Up the Creek/Passion in the Dark (One Track Heart)	1984	—	2.00	4.00
—B-side by Danny Spanos					
SUB POP					
❑ 393	Baby Talk/Brontosaurus	1997	—	—	2.00
❑ 393 [PS]	Baby Talk/Brontosaurus	1997	—	—	2.00
WARNER BROS.					
❑ 29723	Spring Break/Get Ready	1983	—	2.00	4.00
CHECKER, CHUBBY					
Also see BOBBY RYDELL; DEE DEE SHARP.					
20TH CENTURY					
❑ 2040	Reggae My Way/Gypsy	1973	—	2.50	5.00
❑ 2075	She's a Bad Woman/Happiness Is a Girl Like You	1974	—	2.50	5.00
ABKCO					
❑ 4001	The Twist/Loddy Lo	1972	—	2.50	5.00
❑ 4002	The Hucklebuck/Pony Time	1972	—	2.50	5.00
❑ 4003	Limbo Rock/Let's Limbo Some More	1972	—	2.50	5.00
❑ 4004	Hey Bobba Needle/Hooka Tooka	1972	—	2.50	5.00
❑ 4027	Slow Twistin'/Birdland	1973	—	2.50	5.00
AMHERST					
❑ 716	The Rub/Move It	1976	—	2.00	4.00
BUDDAH					
❑ 100	Back in the U.S.S.R./Windy Cream	1969	3.00	6.00	12.00
MCA					
❑ 51233	Running/Is Tonight the Night	1982	—	2.50	5.00
❑ 52015	Running/Is Tonight the Night	1982	—	2.00	4.00
❑ 52043	Harder Than Diamond/Your Love	1982	—	2.00	4.00
PARKWAY					
❑ 003 [DJ]	Never on Sunday/Alouette	1962	10.00	20.00	40.00
—Yellow label, black print, promo only					
❑ 004 [DJ]	Love Is Like a Twist/Peppermint Twist	1962	10.00	20.00	40.00
—Yellow label, black print, promo only					
❑ 005 [DJ]	Your Lips and Mine/Dear Lady Twist	1962	10.00	20.00	40.00
—Yellow label, black print, promo only					
❑ 006 [DJ]	The Jet/The Ray Charles-ton	1962	7.50	15.00	30.00
❑ 105	You Got the Power/Looking at Tomorrow	1966	3.75	7.50	15.00
❑ 112	Karate Monkey/Her Heart	1966	3.75	7.50	15.00
❑ 804	The Class/Schooldays, Oh Schooldays	1959	7.50	15.00	30.00
❑ 808	Samson and Delilah/Whole Lotta Laughin'	1959	6.25	12.50	25.00
❑ 810	Dancing Dinosaur/Those Private Eyes (Keep Watchin' Me)	1960	6.25	12.50	25.00
—The existence of both 808 and 810 has been confirmed since the last edition					
❑ 811	The Twist/Toot	1960	7.50	15.00	30.00
—First pressings have white label with blue print					
❑ 811	The Twist/Toot	1960	5.00	10.00	20.00
—Second pressings have orange label with black print					
❑ 811	The Twist/Twistin' U.S.A.	1961	3.75	7.50	15.00
❑ 811 [DJ]	The Twist/Twistin' U.S.A.	1961	50.00	100.00	200.00
—Promo copy on red vinyl					
❑ 811 [DJ]	The Twist/Twistin' U.S.A.	1961	37.50	75.00	150.00
—Promo copy on yellow vinyl					
❑ 811 [PS]	The Twist/Twistin' U.S.A.	1961	6.25	12.50	25.00
❑ 813	The Hucklebuck/Whole Lotta Shakin' Goin' On	1960	3.75	7.50	15.00
❑ 818	Pony Time/Oh, Susannah	1960	3.75	7.50	15.00
❑ 822	Dance the Mess Around/Good, Good Lovin'	1961	3.75	7.50	15.00
❑ 824	Let's Twist Again/Everything's Gonna Be Alright	1961	3.75	7.50	15.00
❑ 824 [PS]	Let's Twist Again/Everything's Gonna Be Alright	1961	6.25	12.50	25.00
❑ 830	The Fly/That's the Way It Goes	1961	3.75	7.50	15.00
❑ 830 [PS]	The Fly/That's the Way It Goes	1961	6.25	12.50	25.00
❑ 835	Slow Twistin'/La Paloma Twist	1962	3.75	7.50	15.00
—Features female vocal by Dee Dee Sharp					
❑ 835 [PS]	Slow Twistin'/La Paloma Twist	1962	6.25	12.50	25.00
❑ 842	Dancin' Party/Gotta Get Myself Together	1962	3.75	7.50	15.00
❑ 842 [PS]	Dancin' Party/Gotta Get Myself Together	1962	6.25	12.50	25.00
❑ 849	Limbo Rock/Popeye The Hitch-Hiker	1962	3.75	7.50	15.00
❑ 849 [PS]	Limbo Rock/Popeye The Hitch-Hiker	1962	6.25	12.50	25.00
❑ 862	Twenty Miles/Let's Limbo Some More	1963	3.75	7.50	15.00
❑ 862 [PS]	Twenty Miles/Let's Limbo Some More	1963	6.25	12.50	25.00
❑ 873	Birdland/Black Cloud	1963	3.75	7.50	15.00
❑ 873 [PS]	Birdland/Black Cloud	1963	6.25	12.50	25.00
❑ 879	Surf Party/Twist It Up	1963	3.75	7.50	15.00
❑ 879 [PS]	Surf Party/Twist It Up	1963	6.25	12.50	25.00
❑ 890	Loddy Lo/Everything's Gonna Be Alright	1963	4.00	8.00	16.00
❑ 890	Loddy Lo/Hooka Tooka	1963	3.75	7.50	15.00
❑ 890 [PS]	Loddy Lo/Everything's Gonna Be Alright	1963	7.00	14.00	28.00
❑ 890 [PS]	Loddy Lo/Hooka Tooka	1963	6.25	12.50	25.00
❑ 907	Hey Bobba Needle/Spread Joy	1964	3.75	7.50	15.00
❑ 907 [PS]	Hey Bobba Needle/Spread Joy	1964	6.25	12.50	25.00
❑ 920	Lazy Elsie Molly/Rosie	1964	3.75	7.50	15.00
❑ 920 [PS]	Lazy Elsie Molly/Rosie	1964	6.25	12.50	25.00
❑ 922	She Wants T'Swim/You Better Believe It, Baby	1964	3.00	6.00	12.00
❑ 922 [PS]	She Wants T'Swim/You Better Believe It, Baby	1964	6.25	12.50	25.00
❑ 936	Lovely, Lovely (Loverly, Loverly)/The Weekend's Here	1964	3.00	6.00	12.00
❑ 936 [PS]	Lovely, Lovely (Loverly, Loverly)/The Weekend's Here	1964	6.25	12.50	25.00
❑ 949	Let's Do the Freddie/(At the) Discoteque	1965	3.00	6.00	12.00
❑ 959	Everything's Wrong/Cu Me La Be-Stay	1965	3.00	6.00	12.00
❑ 965	You Just Don't Know/Two Hearts Make One Love	1965	50.00	100.00	200.00
❑ 989	Hey You! Little Boo-Ga-Loo/Pussy Cat	1966	3.00	6.00	12.00
SEA BRIGHT					
❑ 5128	Read You Like a Book/(B-side unknown)	1986	—	2.00	4.00

Number	Title (A Side/B Side)	Yr	VG	VG+	NM
TIN PAN APPLE					
❑ 887571-7	The Twist (Yo, Twist!)/The Twist (Buffapella)	1988	—	—	3.00
—"Stupid def vocals" on a Fat Boys record					
❑ 887571-7 [PS]	The Twist (Yo, Twist!)/The Twist (Buffapella)	1988	—	—	3.00
7-Inch Extended Plays					
PARKWAY					
❑ 5001	The Ray Charles-ton/The Mess Around//The Jet/The Continental Walk	1961	15.00	30.00	60.00
—Small hole, plays at 33 1/3 rpm					
❑ 5001 [PS]	Chubby Checker	1961	15.00	30.00	60.00
—Paper die-cut sleeve					

CHECKERLADS, THE

Number	Title (A Side/B Side)	Yr	VG	VG+	NM
RCA VICTOR					
❑ 47-8986	Shake Yourself Down/Baby Send for Me	1966	6.25	12.50	25.00

CHECKERS, THE (1)

Number	Title (A Side/B Side)	Yr	VG	VG+	NM
FEDERAL					
❑ 12355	So Fine/Sentimental Heart	1959	12.50	25.00	50.00
❑ 12375	White Cliffs of Dover/Let Me Come Back	1960	12.50	25.00	50.00
KING					
❑ 4558	Flame in My Heart/Oh, Oh, Oh Baby	1952	250.00	500.00	1000.
❑ 4581	Night's Curtains/Let Me Come Back	1952	250.00	500.00	1000.
❑ 4596	My Prayer Tonight/Love Wasn't There	1953	250.00	500.00	1000.
❑ 4626	Ghost of My Baby/I Wanna Know	1953	200.00	400.00	800.00
❑ 4673	I Promise You/You Never Had It So Good	1953	125.00	250.00	500.00
❑ 4675	White Cliffs of Dover/Without a Song	1953	125.00	250.00	500.00
❑ 4710	House with No Windows/Don't Stop Dan	1954	125.00	250.00	500.00
❑ 4719	Over the Rainbow/You've Been Fooling Around	1954	100.00	200.00	400.00
❑ 4751	I Wasn't Thinking, I Was Drinking/Mama's Daughter	1954	125.00	250.00	500.00
❑ 4764	Trying to Hold My Girl/Can't Find My Sadie	1955	125.00	250.00	500.00
❑ 5156	Heaven Only Knows/Nine More Miles	1958	100.00	200.00	400.00
❑ 5592	Over the Rainbow/Love Wasn't There	1962	5.00	10.00	20.00
—As "The Original Checkers"					

CHECKERS, THE (2)

Different group than (1).

Number	Title (A Side/B Side)	Yr	VG	VG+	NM
ARVEE					
❑ 5035	Skooby Doo (Part 1)/Skooby Doo (Part 2)	1961	5.00	10.00	20.00
❑ 5037	Swingin' Summer/Skooby Doo	1961	5.00	10.00	20.00

CHECKERS, THE (3)

Not the same group as (1) though on the same label. Also see THE FIVE WINGS.

Number	Title (A Side/B Side)	Yr	VG	VG+	NM
KING					
❑ 5199	Teardrops Are Falling/Rock-A-Locka	1959	15.00	30.00	60.00
—Originally released as King 4781 by The Five Wings					

CHECKERS, THE (U)

Some of these may be the same group as (2), but not all of them.

Number	Title (A Side/B Side)	Yr	VG	VG+	NM
DOTTIE					
❑ 1001	Big Car/Buzz	196?	5.00	10.00	20.00
JERDEN					
❑ 710	Black Cat/Soft Blue	1963	5.00	10.00	20.00
MERCURY					
❑ 72354	Red Ball Express/Come Back Home	1964	3.00	6.00	12.00
SKYLA					
❑ 1120	Blue Saturday/Cascade	1961	5.00	10.00	20.00

CHECKMATES LTD., THE

Also see SONNY CHARLES.

Number	Title (A Side/B Side)	Yr	VG	VG+	NM
A&M					
❑ 1006	Spanish Harlem/Baby Don't You Get Crazy	1968	2.00	4.00	8.00
❑ 1040	Love Is All I Have to Give/Never Should Have Lied	1969	2.00	4.00	8.00
❑ 1053	Black Pearl/Lazy Susan	1969	2.50	5.00	10.00
—As "Sonny Charles and the Checkmates Ltd."					
❑ 1127	Spanish Harlem/Proud Mary	1969	2.00	4.00	8.00
—As "Sonny Charles and the Checkmates Ltd."					
❑ 1130	Proud Mary/Do You Love Your Baby	1969	2.00	4.00	8.00
—As "Sonny Charles and the Checkmates Ltd."					
CAPITOL					
❑ 5603	Do the Walk/Glad for You	1966	5.00	10.00	20.00
❑ 5753	I Can Hear the Rain/Kissin' Her and Cryin' for You	1966	7.50	15.00	30.00
❑ 5814	Please Don't Take My World Away/Mastered the Art of Love	1966	5.00	10.00	20.00
❑ 5922	Walk in the Sunlight/A & I	1967	5.00	10.00	20.00
FANTASY					
❑ 800	Let's Do It/Take All the Time You Need	1977	—	2.50	5.00
❑ 823	Greedy for Your Love/That's How It Feels (When Two People Fall in Love)	1978	—	2.50	5.00
GREEDY					
❑ 111	I'm Laying My Heart on the Line/Make Love to Your Mind	1977	—	2.50	5.00
POLYDOR					
❑ 14313	All Alone by the Telephone/Body Language	1976	—	2.50	5.00

CHEERIOS, THE

Number	Title (A Side/B Side)	Yr	VG	VG+	NM
GOLDEN OLDIES					
❑ 1	Ding Dong Honeymoon/Where Are You Tonight	196?	5.00	10.00	20.00
INFINITY					
❑ 011	Ding Dong Honeymoon/Where Are You Tonight	1961	100.00	200.00	400.00

CHEERS, THE

1970s game-show host Bert Convy was a member.

Number	Title (A Side/B Side)	Yr	VG	VG+	NM
CAPITOL					
❑ F2921	Bazoom (I Need Your Lovin')/Arrivederci	1954	6.25	12.50	25.00
❑ F3019	Whadaya Want/Bernie's Tune	1955	6.25	12.50	25.00
❑ F3075	Can't We Be More Than Friends/Blueberries	1955	6.25	12.50	25.00
❑ F3146	I Must Be Dreaming/Fancy Meeting You Here	1955	6.25	12.50	25.00
❑ F3219	Black Denim Trousers and Motorcycle Boots/Some Night in Alaska	1955	6.25	12.50	25.00
❑ F3353	The Chicken/Don't Do Anything	1956	5.00	10.00	20.00
❑ F3409	Heaven on Earth/Que Pasa Muchacha	1956	5.00	10.00	20.00
MERCURY					
❑ 71083	Chug Chug Toot Toot/Big Feet	1957	3.75	7.50	15.00
❑ 71100	Two Hearts/You Never Have the Time	1957	3.75	7.50	15.00
—As "Bert Convy and the Cheers"					
NRC					
❑ 5003	Hold That Line/Blue Serenade	1958	3.75	7.50	15.00

CHEETAHS, THE

Number	Title (A Side/B Side)	Yr	VG	VG+	NM
PHILIPS					
❑ 40239	Mecca/That Goodnight Kiss	1964	2.50	5.00	10.00

CHEMICAL BROTHERS, THE

Number	Title (A Side/B Side)	Yr	VG	VG+	NM
ASTRALWERKS					
❑ 38669	Let Forever Be/Hey Boy Hey Girl	1999	—	—	3.00

CHER

Also see ALLMAN AND WOMAN; SONNY AND CHER.

Number	Title (A Side/B Side)	Yr	VG	VG+	NM
ANNETTE					
❑ 1000	Ringo I Love You/Beatles Blues	1964	175.00	350.00	700.00
—As "Bonnie Jo Mason"; a Phil Spector production					
ATCO					
❑ 6658	Yours Until Tomorrow/Thought of Loving You	1969	—	3.00	6.00
❑ 6684	Chastity's Song/I Walk on Gilded Splinters	1969	—	3.00	6.00
❑ 6704	For What It's Worth/Hangin' On	1969	—	3.00	6.00
❑ 6713	You've Made Me So Very Happy/First Time	1969	—	3.00	6.00
❑ 6793	Superstar/First Time	1971	—	3.00	6.00
❑ 6868	Lay Baby Lay/(Just Enough to Keep Me) Hangin' On	1972	—	2.50	5.00
CASABLANCA					
❑ 965	Take Me Home/My Song (Too Far Gone)	1979	—	2.00	4.00
❑ 987	It's Too Late to Love Me Now/Wasn't It Good	1979	—	2.00	4.00
❑ 2208	Hell on Wheels/Git Down (Guitar Groupie)	1979	—	2.00	4.00
❑ 2228	Boys and Girls/Holdin' Out for Love	1979	—	2.00	4.00
COLUMBIA					
❑ 02850	Rudy/Do I Ever Cross Your Mind	1982	—	2.00	4.00
❑ 02850 [PS]	Rudy/Do I Ever Cross Your Mind	1982	—	2.50	5.00
❑ 03150	Walk With Me/I Paralyze	1982	—	2.00	4.00
GEFFEN					
❑ 19023	Love and Understanding/Trail of Broken Hearts	1991	—	2.00	4.00
❑ 19105	Save Up All Your Tears/A World Without Heroes	1991	—	—	3.00
❑ 19659	The Shoop Shoop Song (It's In His Kiss)/Love on a Rooftop	1990	—	—	3.00
❑ 19953	Heart of Stone/All Because of You	1990	—	—	3.00
❑ 22844	Just Like Jesse James/Starting Over	1989	—	—	3.00
❑ 22886	If I Could Turn Back Time/Some Guys	1989	—	—	3.00
❑ 22886 [PS]	If I Could Turn Back Time/Some Guys	1989	—	—	3.00
❑ 27529	After All (Love Theme from "Chances Are")/Dangerous Times	1989	—	—	3.00
—With Peter Cetera					
❑ 27529 [PS]	After All (Love Theme from "Chances Are")/Dangerous Times	1989	—	2.50	5.00
❑ 27742	Main Man/(It's Been Hard Enough) Gettin' Over You	1988	—	—	3.00
❑ 27742 [PS]	Main Man/(It's Been Hard Enough) Gettin' Over You	1988	—	—	3.00
❑ 27894	Skin Deep/Perfection	1988	—	—	3.00
❑ 27894 [PS]	Skin Deep/Perfection	1988	—	—	3.00
❑ 27986	We All Sleep Alone/Working Girl	1988	—	—	3.00
❑ 27986 [PS]	We All Sleep Alone/Working Girl	1988	—	—	3.00
❑ 28191	I Found Someone/Dangerous Times	1987	—	—	3.00
❑ 28191 [PS]	I Found Someone/Dangerous Times	1987	—	—	3.00
IMPERIAL					
❑ 66081	Dream Baby/Stan Quetzal	1964	10.00	20.00	40.00
—By "Cherilyn"					
❑ 66114	All I Really Want to Do/I'm Gonna Love You	1965	3.00	6.00	12.00
❑ 66136	See See Blues/Where Do You Go	1965	3.00	6.00	12.00
❑ 66160	Bang Bang (My Baby Shot Me Down)/Needles and Pins	1966	3.00	6.00	12.00
❑ 66160	Bang Bang (My Baby Shot Me Down)/Our Day Will Come	1966	3.00	6.00	12.00
❑ 66192	Alfie/She's No Better Than Me	1966	2.50	5.00	10.00
❑ 66217	Behind the Door/Magic in the Air	1966	2.50	5.00	10.00
❑ 66223	Dream Baby/Mama (When My Dollies Have Babies)	1966	2.50	5.00	10.00
❑ 66252	Hey Joe/Our Day Will Come	1967	2.50	5.00	10.00
❑ 66261	You Better Sit Down Kids/Elusive Butterfly	1967	3.00	6.00	12.00
❑ 66261	You Better Sit Down Kids/Mama (When My Dollies Have Babies)	1967	2.50	5.00	10.00
❑ 66282	But I Can't Love You More/Click Song Number One	1968	2.00	4.00	8.00
❑ 66307	Take Me for a Little While/A Song Called Children	1968	2.00	4.00	8.00
KAPP					
❑ 2134	Classified 1-A/Don't Put It on Me	1971	—	3.00	6.00
❑ 2146	Gypsys, Tramps and Thieves/He'll Never Know	1971	—	3.00	6.00
—Black label					
❑ 2146	Gypsys, Tramps and Thieves/He'll Never Know	1971	—	2.00	4.00
—Multi-color label					
❑ 2158	The Way of Love/Don't Put It on Me	1972	—	2.00	4.00
❑ 2171	Living in a House Divided/One Honest Man	1972	—	2.00	4.00
❑ 2184	Don't Hide Your Love/First Time	1972	—	2.00	4.00
MCA					
❑ 40039	Am I Blue/How Long Has This Been Going On	1973	—	2.00	4.00
❑ 40102	Half-Breed/Melody	1973	—	2.00	4.00
❑ 40161	Dark Lady/Two People Clinging to a Thread	1973	—	2.00	4.00
❑ 40245	Train of Thought/Dixie Girl	1974	—	2.00	4.00
❑ 40273	I Saw a Man and He Danced With His Wife/I Hate to Sleep Alone	1974	—	2.00	4.00
❑ 40324	Carousel Man/When You Find Out Where You're Going Let Me Know	1974	—	2.00	4.00
❑ 40375	Rescue Me/Dixie Girl	1975	—	2.00	4.00

Number	Title (A Side/B Side)	Yr	VG	VG+	NM
REPRISE					
❑ 17695	One by One/I Wouldn't Treat a Dog (The Way You Treated Me)	1996	—	—	3.00
UNITED ARTISTS					
❑ 0106	All I Really Want to Do/Where Do You Go	1973	—	2.00	4.00
—"Silver Spotlight Series" reissue					
❑ 0107	Bang Bang (My Baby Shot Me Down)/You Better Sit Down Kids	1973	—	2.00	4.00
—"Silver Spotlight Series" reissue					
❑ XW511	Sunny/Alfie	1974	—	2.00	4.00
❑ 50864	Reason to Believe/Will You Still Love Me Tomorrow	1971	—	2.00	4.00
❑ 50974	Old Man River/Our Day Will Come	1972	—	2.00	4.00
WARNER BROS.					
❑ 8096	Geronimo's Cadillac/These Days	1975	—	2.00	4.00
❑ 8263	Borrowed Time/Long Distance Love Affair	1976	—	2.00	4.00
❑ 8311	Pirate/Send the Man Over	1976	—	2.00	4.00
❑ 8366	War Paint and Soft Feathers/Sand the Man Over	1977	—	2.00	4.00
❑ 17119	Believe (Album Version)/Believe (Xenomania Mix)	1998	—	—	3.00
WARNER/SPECTOR					
❑ 0400	Baby, I Love You/A Woman's Story	1974	2.50	5.00	10.00
❑ 0402	Just Enough to Keep Me Hangin' On/A Love Like Yours	1975	2.50	5.00	10.00
—With Nilsson					

CHEROKEES, THE (1)

Number	Title (A Side/B Side)	Yr	VG	VG+	NM
CHALLENGE					
❑ 9135	Cherokee Stomp/Uprisin'	1961	5.00	10.00	20.00

CHEROKEES, THE (2)

Male vocal group.

Number	Title (A Side/B Side)	Yr	VG	VG+	NM
GRAND					
❑ 106	Rainbow of Love/I Had a Thrill	1954	250.00	500.00	1000.
❑ 110	Please Tell Me So/Remember When	1954	250.00	500.00	1000.
PEACOCK					
❑ 1656	Drip Drip/Is She Real	1955	50.00	100.00	200.00

CHEROKEES, THE (3)

Number	Title (A Side/B Side)	Yr	VG	VG+	NM
GUYDEN					
❑ 2044	Cherokee/Harlem Nocturne	1960	3.75	7.50	15.00
❑ 2044 [PS]	Cherokee/Harlem Nocturne	1960	7.50	15.00	30.00

CHEROKEES, THE (4)

British band.

Number	Title (A Side/B Side)	Yr	VG	VG+	NM
MGM					
❑ 13334	Seven Daffodils/Wondrous Place	1964	3.75	7.50	15.00
❑ 13433	Dig a Little Deeper/I Will Never Turn My Back on You	1965	5.00	10.00	20.00

CHEROKEES, THE (5)

FRED PARRIS of THE FIVE SATINS was a member.

Number	Title (A Side/B Side)	Yr	VG	VG+	NM
UNITED ARTISTS					
❑ 367	My Heavenly Angel/Bed Bug	1961	25.00	50.00	100.00

CHERRY SLUSH

Number	Title (A Side/B Side)	Yr	VG	VG+	NM
U.S.A.					
❑ 895	I Cannot Stop You/Don't Walk Away	1968	5.00	10.00	20.00
❑ 004	Gotta Take It Easy/Day Don't Come	1968	5.00	10.00	20.00

CHESTERFIELDS, THE (1)

Number	Title (A Side/B Side)	Yr	VG	VG+	NM
A&M					
❑ 2041	That Is Rock and Roll/Why Do Fools Fall in Love	1978	—	2.50	5.00

CHESTERFIELDS, THE (2)

Number	Title (A Side/B Side)	Yr	VG	VG+	NM
CHESS					
❑ 1559	I'm in Heaven/All Messed Up	1954	100.00	200.00	400.00

CHESTERFIELDS, THE (3)

Number	Title (A Side/B Side)	Yr	VG	VG+	NM
CUB					
❑ 9008	I Got Fired/Meet Me at the Candy Store	1958	6.25	12.50	25.00

CHESTERFIELDS, THE (4)

Number	Title (A Side/B Side)	Yr	VG	VG+	NM
PHILIPS					
❑ 40060	A Dream Is But a Dream/You Walked Away	1962	50.00	100.00	200.00

CHESTERS, THE

See LITTLE ANTHONY AND THE IMPERIALS.

CHEVRONS, THE

Number	Title (A Side/B Side)	Yr	VG	VG+	NM
BRENT					
❑ 7000	That Comes With Love/Don't Be Heartless	1959	12.50	25.00	50.00
❑ 7007	Lullabye/The Day After Forever	1959	12.50	25.00	50.00
❑ 7015	Little Darlin'/Little Star	1960	12.50	25.00	50.00
TIME					
❑ 1	Come Go with Me/I'm in Love Again	1960	10.00	20.00	40.00

CHI-LITES, THE

Number	Title (A Side/B Side)	Yr	VG	VG+	NM
BLUE ROCK					
❑ 4007	I'm So Jealous/The Mix-Mix Song	1965	6.25	12.50	25.00
❑ 4020	Doing the Snatch/Bassology	1965	6.25	12.50	25.00
❑ 4037	Never No More/She's Mine	1965	12.50	25.00	50.00
BRUNSWICK					
❑ 55398	Give It Away/What Do I Wish For	1969	2.00	4.00	8.00
❑ 55414	Let Me Be the Man My Daddy Was/The Twelfth of Never	1969	2.00	4.00	8.00
❑ 55422	I'm Gonna Make You Love Me/To Change My Love	1969	2.00	4.00	8.00
❑ 55426	24 Hours of Sadness/You're No Longer Part of My Heart	1970	2.00	4.00	8.00
❑ 55438	I Like Your Lovin' (Do You Like Mine)/You're No Longer Part of My Heart	1970	2.00	4.00	8.00
❑ 55442	Are You My Woman (Tell Me So)/Troubles A-Comin'	1970	2.00	4.00	8.00
❑ 55450	(For God's Sake) Give More Power to the People/Troubles A-Comin'	1971	2.00	4.00	8.00
❑ 55455	We Are Neighbors/What Do I Wish For	1971	2.00	4.00	8.00
❑ 55458	I Want to Pay You back (For Loving Me)/Love Uprising	1971	2.00	4.00	8.00
❑ 55462	Have You Seen Her/Yes I'm Ready	1971	—	3.00	6.00
❑ 55471	Oh Girl/Being in Love	1972	—	3.00	6.00
❑ 55478	The Coldest Days of My Life (Part 1)/The Coldest Days of My Life (Part 2)	1972	—	3.00	6.00
❑ 55483	A Lonely Man/The Man and the Woman (The Boy and the Girl)	1972	—	3.00	6.00
❑ 55489	We Need Order/Living in the Footsteps of Another Man	1972	—	3.00	6.00
❑ 55491	A Letter to Myself/Sally	1973	—	3.00	6.00
❑ 55496	My Heart Just Keeps On Breakin'/Just Two Teenage Kids	1973	—	3.00	6.00
❑ 55500	Stoned Out of My Mind/Someone Else's Arms	1973	—	3.00	6.00
❑ 55502	I Found Someone/Marriage License	1973	—	3.00	6.00
❑ 55505	Homely Girl/Never Had It So Good and Felt So Bad	1974	—	3.00	6.00
❑ 55512	There Will Never Be Any Peace (Until God Is Seated at the Conference Table)/Too Good	1974	—	3.00	6.00
❑ 55514	You Got to Be the One/Happiness Is Your Middle Name	1974	—	3.00	6.00
❑ 55515	Toby/That's How Long	1974	—	3.00	6.00
❑ 55520	It's Time for Love/Here I Am	1975	—	3.00	6.00
❑ 55522	Don't Burn No Bridges/(Instrumental)	1975	—	3.00	6.00
—With Jackie Wilson					
❑ 55525	The Devil Is Doing His Work/I'm Not a Gambler	1976	—	3.00	6.00
❑ 55528	You Don't Have to Go/(Instrumental)	1976	—	3.00	6.00
❑ 55546	First Time/Marriage License	1978	—	2.50	5.00
CHI-SOUND					
❑ 2472	Heavenly Body/Strung Out	1980	—	2.00	4.00
❑ 2481	Have You Seen Her/Supermad (About You Baby)	1981	—	2.00	4.00
❑ 2495	All I Wanna Do Is Make Love to You/Round and Round	1981	—	2.00	4.00
❑ 2503	Me and You/Tell Me Where It Hurts	1981	—	2.00	4.00
❑ 2600	Hot on a Thing (Called Love)/Whole Lot of Good Lovin'	1982	—	2.00	4.00
❑ 2604	Try My Side (Of Love)/Get Down with Me	1982	—	2.00	4.00
DAKAR					
❑ 600	Baby It's Time/Price of Love	1968	3.00	6.00	12.00
—As "Marshall and the Chi-Lites"					
DARAN					
❑ 011	One by One/You Did That to Me	1964	25.00	50.00	100.00
—As "The Hi-Lites"					
❑ 0111	Pretty Girl/Love Bandit	1966	12.50	25.00	50.00
—As "Marshall and the Chi-Lites"					
❑ 222	I'm So Jealous/The Mix-Mix Song	1964	25.00	50.00	100.00
—As "The Hi-Lites"					
INPHASION					
❑ 7205	Stay a Little Longer/Higher	1979	—	2.50	5.00
❑ 7208	The Only One for Me (One in a Million)/You Won't Be Lonely Too Long	1979	—	2.50	5.00
JA-WES					
❑ 0888	You Did That to Me/I Won't Care About You	1966	3.75	7.50	15.00
LARC					
❑ 81015	Bottom's Up/Bottom's Up Groove	1983	—	2.00	4.00
❑ 81023	Bad Motor Scooter/I Just Wanna Hold You	1983	—	2.00	4.00
MERCURY					
❑ 73844	Happy Being Lonely/Love Can Be Dangerous	1976	—	2.50	5.00
❑ 73886	Vanishing Love/I Turn Away	1977	—	2.50	5.00
❑ 73934	My First Mistake/Stop Still	1977	—	2.50	5.00
❑ 73954	If I Had a Girl/I've Got Love on My Mind	1977	—	2.50	5.00
PRIVATE I					
❑ 04365	Stop What You're Doin'/Little Girl	1984	—	—	3.00
❑ 04484	Let Today Come Back Tomorrow/Gimme Whatcha Got	1984	—	—	3.00
REVUE					
❑ 11005	Love Is Gone/Love Me	1967	3.00	6.00	12.00
❑ 11018	(Um, Um) My Baby Loves Me/That's My Baby for You	1968	3.00	6.00	12.00

CHIC

Number	Title (A Side/B Side)	Yr	VG	VG+	NM
ATLANTIC					
❑ 3435	Dance, Dance, Dance (Yowsah, Yowsah, Yowsah)/Sao Paulo	1977	—	2.00	4.00
❑ 3469	Everybody Dance/You Can Get By	1978	—	2.00	4.00
❑ 3519	Le Freak/Savoir Faire	1978	—	2.00	4.00
❑ 3519 [PS]	Le Freak/Savoir Faire	1978	—	2.50	5.00
❑ 3557	I Want Your Love/(Funny) Bone	1979	—	2.00	4.00
❑ 3557 [PS]	I Want Your Love/(Funny) Bone	1979	—	2.50	5.00
❑ 3584	Good Times/A Warm Summer Night	1979	—	2.00	4.00
❑ 3584 [PS]	Good Times/A Warm Summer Night	1979	—	2.50	5.00
❑ 3620	My Forbidden Lover/What About Me	1979	—	2.00	4.00
❑ 3638	My Feet Keep Dancing/Will You Cry (When You Hear This Song)	1979	—	2.00	4.00
❑ 3665	Rebels Are We/Open Up	1980	—	2.00	4.00
❑ 3768	Real People/Chip Off the Old Block	1980	—	2.00	4.00
❑ 3887	Stage Fright/So Fine	1982	—	2.00	4.00
❑ 89725	Give Me the Lovin'/You Got Some Love for Me	1983	—	—	3.00
❑ 89954	Hangin'/Chic (Everybody Say)	1982	—	—	3.00
BUDDAH					
❑ 583	Dance, Dance, Dance (Yowsah, Yowsah, Yowsah)/Sao Paulo	1977	5.00	10.00	20.00
MIRAGE					
❑ 4032	Soup for One/Burn Hard	1982	—	2.00	4.00
❑ 4051	Why/Why	1982	—	2.00	4.00
—B-side by Carly Simon					

CHIC-LETS, THE

JOSIE

Number	Title (A Side/B Side)	Yr	VG	VG+	NM
❑ 919	I Want You to Be My Boyfriend/Don't Goof on Me	1964	3.75	7.50	15.00

CHICAGO

Also see PETER CETERA; BILL CHAMPLIN; ROBERT LAMM.

COLUMBIA

Number	Title (A Side/B Side)	Yr	VG	VG+	NM
❑ 10049	Wishing You Were Here/Life Saver	1974	—	2.50	5.00
❑ 10092	Harry Truman/Till We Meet Again	1975	—	2.50	5.00
❑ 10092 [PS]	Harry Truman/Till We Meet Again	1975	—	3.00	6.00
❑ 10131	Old Days/Hideaway	1975	—	2.50	5.00
❑ 10200	Brand New Love Affair/Hideaway	1975	—	2.50	5.00
❑ 10360	Another Rainy Day in New York City/Hope for Love	1976	—	2.50	5.00
❑ 10390	If You Leave Me Now/Together Again	1976	—	2.50	5.00
❑ 10523	You Are On My Mind/Gently I'll Wake You	1977	—	2.50	5.00
❑ 10620	Baby, What a Big Surprise/Takin' It On Uptown	1977	—	2.50	5.00
❑ 10620 [PS]	Baby, What a Big Surprise/Takin' It On Uptown	1977	2.50	5.00	10.00

—Sleeve appears to be promo only

Number	Title (A Side/B Side)	Yr	VG	VG+	NM
❑ 10683	Little One/Till the End of Time	1978	—	2.50	5.00
❑ 10737	Take Me Back to Chicago/Policeman	1978	—	2.50	5.00
❑ 10845	Alive Again/Love Was New	1978	—	2.50	5.00
❑ 10879	No Tell Lover/Take a Chance	1979	—	2.50	5.00
❑ 10935	Gone Long Gone/The Greatest Love on Earth	1979	—	2.00	4.00
❑ 11061	Must Have Been Crazy/Closer to You	1979	—	2.00	4.00
❑ 11124	Street Player/Window Dreamin'	1979	—	2.00	4.00
❑ 11341	Song for You/I'd Rather Be Rich	1980	—	—	—

—Unreleased?

Number	Title (A Side/B Side)	Yr	VG	VG+	NM
❑ 11345	Thunder and Lightning/I'd Rather Be Rich	1980	—	2.00	4.00
❑ 11376	The American Dream/Song for You	1980	—	2.00	4.00
❑ 44909	Questions 67 and 68/Listen	1969	—	3.00	6.00
❑ 44909 [PS]	Questions 67 and 68/Listen	1969	2.50	5.00	10.00
❑ 45011	Beginnings/Poem 58	1969	—	3.00	6.00
❑ 45127	Make Me Smile/Colour My World	1970	—	2.50	5.00
❑ 45127 [PS]	Make Me Smile/Colour My World	1970	2.00	4.00	8.00
❑ 45194	25 or 6 to 4/Where Do We Go from Here	1970	—	2.50	5.00
❑ 45264	Does Anybody Really Know What Time It Is?/Listen	1970	—	2.50	5.00
❑ 45264 [PS]	Does Anybody Really Know What Time It Is?/Listen	1970	2.00	4.00	8.00
❑ 45331	Free/Free Country	1971	—	2.50	5.00
❑ 45331 [PS]	Free/Free Country	1971	2.00	4.00	8.00
❑ 45370	Lowdown/Loneliness Is Just a Word	1971	—	2.50	5.00
❑ 45370 [PS]	Lowdown/Loneliness Is Just a Word	1971	2.00	4.00	8.00
❑ 45417	Beginnings/Colour My World	1971	—	2.50	5.00
❑ 45417 [PS]	Beginnings/Colour My World	1971	2.00	4.00	8.00
❑ 45467	Questions 67 and 68/I'm a Man	1971	—	2.50	5.00
❑ 45657	Saturday in the Park/Alma Mater	1972	—	2.50	5.00
❑ 45717	Dialogue (Parts 1 and 2)/Now That You've Gone	1972	—	2.50	5.00
❑ 45717 [PS]	Dialogue (Parts 1 and 2)/Now That You've Gone	1972	—	3.00	6.00
❑ 45880	Feelin' Stronger Every Day/Jenny	1973	—	2.50	5.00
❑ 45933	Just You 'N' Me/Critic's Choice	1973	—	2.50	5.00
❑ 46020	(I've Been) Searchin' So Long/Byblos	1974	—	2.50	5.00
❑ 46062	Call On Me/Prelude to Aire	1974	—	2.50	5.00

FULL MOON

Number	Title (A Side/B Side)	Yr	VG	VG+	NM
❑ 29798	What You're Missing/Rescue You	1983	—	2.00	4.00
❑ 29911	Love Me Tomorrow/Bad Advice	1982	—	2.00	4.00
❑ 29979	Hard to Say I'm Sorry/Sonny Think Twice	1982	—	2.00	4.00

REPRISE

Number	Title (A Side/B Side)	Yr	VG	VG+	NM
❑ 19466	Chasin' the Wind/Only Time Can Heal the Wounded	1991	—	—	3.00
❑ 22741	What Kind of Man Would I Be?/25 or 6 to 4	1990	—	—	3.00
❑ 22741 [PS]	What Kind of Man Would I Be?/25 or 6 to 4	1990	—	2.50	5.00
❑ 22985	We Can Last Forever/One More Day	1989	—	—	3.00
❑ 27757	You're Not Alone/It's Alright	1988	—	—	3.00
❑ 27757 [PS]	You're Not Alone/It's Alright	1988	—	—	3.00
❑ 27766	Look Away/Come In from the Night	1988	—	—	3.00
❑ 27766 [PS]	Look Away/Come In from the Night	1988	—	—	3.00
❑ 27855	I Don't Wanna Live Without Your Love/I Stand Up	1988	—	—	3.00
❑ 27855 [PS]	I Don't Wanna Live Without Your Love/I Stand Up	1988	—	—	3.00

WARNER BROS.

Number	Title (A Side/B Side)	Yr	VG	VG+	NM
❑ 28283	Niagara Falls/I Believe	1987	—	—	3.00
❑ 28283 [PS]	Niagara Falls/I Believe	1987	—	2.50	5.00
❑ 28424	If She Would Have Been Faithful.../Forever	1987	—	—	3.00
❑ 28424 [PS]	If She Would Have Been Faithful.../Forever	1987	—	—	3.00
❑ 28512	Will You Still Love Me/25 or 6 to 4	1986	—	—	3.00
❑ 28628	25 or 6 to 4/One More Day	1986	—	—	3.00
❑ 28628 [PS]	25 or 6 to 4/One More Day	1986	—	—	3.00
❑ 29082	Along Comes a Woman/We Can't Stop the Hurtin'	1985	—	—	3.00
❑ 29126	You're the Inspiration/Once in a Lifetime	1984	—	—	3.00
❑ 29214	Hard Habit to Break/Remember the Feeling	1984	—	—	3.00
❑ 29214 [PS]	Hard Habit to Break/Remember the Feeling	1984	—	—	3.00
❑ 29306	Stay the Night/Only You	1984	—	—	3.00
❑ 29306 [PS]	Stay the Night/Only You	1984	—	—	3.00

CHICKEN SHACK

Also see CHRISTINE McVIE.

BLUE HORIZON

Number	Title (A Side/B Side)	Yr	VG	VG+	NM
❑ 100	Tears in the Wind/The Things You Put Me Through	1970	—	3.00	6.00
❑ 302	Maudie/Diary of Your Life	1972	—	3.00	6.00

DERAM

Number	Title (A Side/B Side)	Yr	VG	VG+	NM
❑ 7537	As Time Goes Passing By/(B-side unknown)	1972	—	2.50	5.00

EPIC

Number	Title (A Side/B Side)	Yr	VG	VG+	NM
❑ 10414	Six Nights in Seven/Worried About My Woman	1968	2.50	5.00	10.00

CHIFFONS, THE

BIG DEAL

Number	Title (A Side/B Side)	Yr	VG	VG+	NM
❑ 6003	Tonight's the Night/Do You Know	1960	20.00	40.00	80.00

BUDDAH

Number	Title (A Side/B Side)	Yr	VG	VG+	NM
❑ 171	So Much in Love/Strange, Strange Feeling	1970	2.50	5.00	10.00

B.T. PUPPY

Number	Title (A Side/B Side)	Yr	VG	VG+	NM
❑ 558	Secret Love/Strange, Strange Feeling	1970	2.50	5.00	10.00

LAURIE

Number	Title (A Side/B Side)	Yr	VG	VG+	NM
❑ 3152	He's So Fine/Oh My Lover	1963	5.00	10.00	20.00
❑ 3166	Lucky Me/Why Am I So Shy?	1963	3.75	7.50	15.00
❑ 3179	One Fine Day/Why Am I So Shy	1963	5.00	10.00	20.00
❑ 3195	A Love So Fine/Only My Friend	1963	3.00	6.00	12.00
❑ 3212	I Have a Boyfriend/I'm Gonna Dry My Eyes	1963	3.00	6.00	12.00
❑ 3224	Tonight I Met an Angel/Easy to Love	1964	3.00	6.00	12.00
❑ 3262	Sailor Boy/When the Summer Is Through	1964	3.00	6.00	12.00
❑ 3275	What Am I Gonna Do with You/Strange, Strange Feeling	1964	3.00	6.00	12.00
❑ 3301	Nobody Knows What's Going On (In My Mind But Me)/Did You Ever Go Steady	1965	3.00	6.00	12.00
❑ 3301	Nobody Knows What's Going On (In My Mind But Me)/The Real Thing	1965	3.00	6.00	12.00
❑ 3318	Tonight I'm Gonna Dream/Heavenly Place	1965	3.00	6.00	12.00
❑ 3340	Sweet Talkin' Guy/Did You Ever Go Steady	1966	3.75	7.50	15.00
❑ 3350	Out of This World/Just a Boy	1966	2.50	5.00	10.00
❑ 3357	Stop, Look, Listen/March	1966	2.50	5.00	10.00
❑ 3364	My Boyfriend's Back/I Got Plenty of Nuttin'	1966	2.50	5.00	10.00
❑ 3377	If I Knew Then/Keep the Boy Happy	1967	2.50	5.00	10.00
❑ 3423	Just for Tonight/Teach Me How	1968	2.50	5.00	10.00
❑ 3423	Just for Tonight/Keep the Boy Happy	1968	2.50	5.00	10.00
❑ 3460	Up on the Bridge/March	1968	2.50	5.00	10.00
❑ 3497	Love Me Like You're Gonna Lose Me/Three Dips of Ice Cream	1969	2.50	5.00	10.00
❑ 3630	My Sweet Lord/Main Nerve	1975	2.50	5.00	10.00
❑ 3648	Dream, Dream, Dream/Oh My Lover	1976	2.50	5.00	10.00

REPRISE

Number	Title (A Side/B Side)	Yr	VG	VG+	NM
❑ 20103	After Last Night/Doctor of Hearts	1962	5.00	10.00	20.00

RUST

Number	Title (A Side/B Side)	Yr	VG	VG+	NM
❑ 5070	When the Boy's Happy (The Girl's Happy Too)/Hockaday, Part 1	1963	6.25	12.50	25.00

—As "The Four Pennies"

Number	Title (A Side/B Side)	Yr	VG	VG+	NM
❑ 5071	Dry Your Eyes/My Block	1963	6.25	12.50	25.00

—As "The Four Pennies"

WILDCAT

Number	Title (A Side/B Side)	Yr	VG	VG+	NM
❑ 601	Never Never/No More Tomorrows	1961	6.25	12.50	25.00

CHILDREN, THE

ATCO

Number	Title (A Side/B Side)	Yr	VG	VG+	NM
❑ 6633	Maypole/I'll Be Your Sunshine	1968	5.00	10.00	20.00

CINEMA

Number	Title (A Side/B Side)	Yr	VG	VG+	NM
❑ 025	Pills/(B-side unknown)	1968	7.50	15.00	30.00

LARAMIE

Number	Title (A Side/B Side)	Yr	VG	VG+	NM
❑ 666	Picture Me/(B-side unknown)	1967	10.00	20.00	40.00

MAP CITY

Number	Title (A Side/B Side)	Yr	VG	VG+	NM
❑ 304	What If I/Evil Woman	1970	3.00	6.00	12.00

ODE

Number	Title (A Side/B Side)	Yr	VG	VG+	NM
❑ 66005	From the Very Start/Such a Fine Night	1970	5.00	10.00	20.00
❑ 66013	Fire King/Hand of a Lady	1971	5.00	10.00	20.00

CHILLIWACK

Also see THE COLLECTORS.

A&M

Number	Title (A Side/B Side)	Yr	VG	VG+	NM
❑ 1310	Lonesome Mary/Ridin'	1971	—	3.00	6.00
❑ 1395	Ground Hog/Nothin' to Do	1972	—	3.00	6.00

MILLENNIUM

Number	Title (A Side/B Side)	Yr	VG	VG+	NM
❑ YB-11813	My Girl (Gone, Gone, Gone)/Sign Here	1981	—	2.00	4.00
❑ YB-13102	I Believe/Living in Stereo	1981	—	2.00	4.00
❑ YB-13110	Whatcha Gonna Do/I Really Don't Mind	1982	—	2.00	4.00
❑ YB-13117	Secret Information/I Really Don't Mind	1982	—	2.00	4.00
❑ YB-13123	Lean On Me/Night Time	1983	—	—	—

—Canceled

MUSHROOM

Number	Title (A Side/B Side)	Yr	VG	VG+	NM
❑ 7022	California Girl/Reach	1976	—	2.50	5.00
❑ 7024	Fly By Night/Mary Lo & Me	1977	—	2.50	5.00
❑ 7025	Something Better/Rain-O	1977	—	2.50	5.00
❑ 7028	Baby Blue/Something Better	1977	—	2.50	5.00
❑ 7033	Arms of Mary/I Wanna Be the One	1978	—	2.50	5.00
❑ 7038	Never Be the Same/I Wanna Be the One	1978	—	2.50	5.00
❑ 7046	Communication Breakdown/Are You With Me	1979	—	2.50	5.00

PARROT

Number	Title (A Side/B Side)	Yr	VG	VG+	NM
❑ 350	I Must Have Been Blind/Chain Train	1970	2.00	4.00	8.00
❑ 357	Everyday/Sundown	1970	2.00	4.00	8.00

SIRE

Number	Title (A Side/B Side)	Yr	VG	VG+	NM
❑ 716	Crazy Talk/In and Out	1974	—	2.50	5.00
❑ 718	Come On Over/Time Don't Mean a Thing to You	1975	—	2.50	5.00
❑ 720	If You Want My Love/Train's a-Comin' Back	1975	—	2.50	5.00
❑ 723	Last Day of December/Magnolia	1976	—	2.50	5.00

CHIMES, THE (1)

LAURIE

Number	Title (A Side/B Side)	Yr	VG	VG+	NM
❑ 3211	Whose Heart Are You Breaking Now/Baby's Coming Home	1963	3.75	7.50	15.00

METRO

Number	Title (A Side/B Side)	Yr	VG	VG+	NM
❑ 1	Whose Heart Are You Breaking Now/Baby's Coming Home	1963	10.00	20.00	40.00

TAG

Number	Title (A Side/B Side)	Yr	VG	VG+	NM
❑ 444	Once in Awhile/Summer Night	1960	10.00	20.00	40.00

—Maroon label

Number	Title (A Side/B Side)	Yr	VG	VG+	NM
❑ 444	Once in Awhile/Summer Night	1960	10.00	20.00	40.00

—Light blue label

Number	Title (A Side/B Side)	Yr	VG	VG+	NM
❑ 444	Once in Awhile/Oh, How I Love You So	1960	12.50	25.00	50.00

—B-side is actually by a group called the Bi-Tones, though credited to the Chimes

Number	Title (A Side/B Side)	Yr	VG	VG+	NM
❑ 445	I'm in the Mood for Love/Only Love	1961	7.50	15.00	30.00
❑ 447	Let's Fall in Love/Dream Girl	1961	6.25	12.50	25.00
❑ 450	Paradise/My Love	1961	7.50	15.00	30.00

Number	Title (A Side/B Side)	Yr	VG	VG+	NM

CHIMES, THE (2)
On the Arrow label, see FREDDIE SCOTT.

CHIMES, THE (3)
On the Flair label, see THE FLAIRS.

CHIMES, THE (U)
Some of these may be group (1).

HOUSE OF BEAUTY

Number	Title (A Side/B Side)	Yr	VG	VG+	NM
❑ 3	Tears from An Angel's Eyes/(B-side unknown)	1959	20.00	40.00	80.00

LIMELIGHT

Number	Title (A Side/B Side)	Yr	VG	VG+	NM
❑ 3000	Cry, Baby, Cry/Angel Child	1963	6.25	12.50	25.00
❑ 3002	Du Wap/Stop, Look and Listen	1963	6.25	12.50	25.00

RESERVE

Number	Title (A Side/B Side)	Yr	VG	VG+	NM
❑ 120	When School Starts Again/Nervous Heart	1957	10.00	20.00	40.00

ROYAL ROOST

Number	Title (A Side/B Side)	Yr	VG	VG+	NM
❑ 577	Dearest Darling/A Fool Was I	1955	175.00	350.00	700.00

SPECIALTY

Number	Title (A Side/B Side)	Yr	VG	VG+	NM
❑ 555	Tears on My Pillow/Cindy Lou	1955	15.00	30.00	60.00
❑ 574	Chop Chop/Pretty Little Girl	1956	15.00	30.00	60.00

CHIPMUNKS, THE
The later incarnation produced by Ross Bagdasarian, Jr.

EPIC

Number	Title (A Side/B Side)	Yr	VG	VG+	NM
❑ 74776	Achy Breaky Heart/I Ain't No Dang Cartoon	1992	—	2.00	4.00
—As "Alvin and the Chipmunks"; with Billy Ray Cyrus on A-side					
❑ 77768	Rockin' Around the Christmas Tree/Rudolph the Red-Nosed Reindeer	1994	—	2.00	4.00
—As "Alvin and the Chipmunks"					

EXCELSIOR

Number	Title (A Side/B Side)	Yr	VG	VG+	NM
❑ SIS 1001	You May Be Right/Crazy Little Thing Called Love	1980	—	2.50	5.00
❑ SIS 1002	Call Me/Refugee	1980	—	2.50	5.00
❑ SIS 1002 [PS]	Call Me/Refugee	1980	—	3.00	6.00

RCA

Number	Title (A Side/B Side)	Yr	VG	VG+	NM
❑ PB-12247	On the Road Again/Coward of the County	1981	—	2.00	4.00
❑ PB-12301	Mamas Don't Let Your Babies Grow Up to Be Chipmunks/Lunchbox	1981	—	2.00	4.00
—With Jerry Reed					
❑ PB-12354	The Chipmunk Song/Sleigh Ride	1981	—	2.00	4.00
❑ PB-12354 [PS]	The Chipmunk Song/Sleigh Ride	1981	—	2.50	5.00
❑ PB-13098	Bette Davis Eyes/Heartbreaker	1982	—	2.00	4.00
❑ PB-13098 [PS]	Bette Davis Eyes/Heartbreaker	1982	—	2.00	4.00
❑ PB-13374	E.T. and Me/Tomorrow (Theme from "Annie")	1982	—	2.00	4.00
❑ PB-13374 [PS]	E.T. and Me/Tomorrow (Theme from "Annie")	1982	—	2.00	4.00

CHIPMUNKS, THE, DAVID SEVILLE AND
The original incarnation. Also see ROSS BAGDASARIAN; DAVID SEVILLE.

DOT

Number	Title (A Side/B Side)	Yr	VG	VG+	NM
❑ 16997	Apple Picker/Sorry About That, Herb	1967	3.00	6.00	12.00

EMI

Number	Title (A Side/B Side)	Yr	VG	VG+	NM
❑ S7-17645	The Chipmunk Song/Frosty the Snowman	1993	—	2.00	4.00
—Green vinyl					

LIBERTY

Number	Title (A Side/B Side)	Yr	VG	VG+	NM
❑ 55168	The Chipmunk Song/Almost Good	1958	6.25	12.50	25.00
—Blue-green label					
❑ 55168	The Chipmunk Song/Almost Good	1958	7.50	15.00	30.00
—Black label					
❑ 55179	Alvin's Harmonica/Mediocre	1959	5.00	10.00	20.00
❑ 55200	Ragtime Cowboy Joe/Flip Side	1959	5.00	10.00	20.00
❑ 55200 [PS]	Ragtime Cowboy Joe/Flip Side	1959	10.00	20.00	40.00
❑ 55233	Alvin's Orchestra/Copyright 1960	1960	3.75	7.50	15.00
❑ 55233 [PS]	Alvin's Orchestra/Copyright 1960	1960	10.00	20.00	40.00
❑ 55246	Coming 'Round the Mountain/Sing a Goofy Song	1960	3.75	7.50	15.00
❑ 55246 [PS]	Coming 'Round the Mountain/Sing a Goofy Song	1960	10.00	20.00	40.00
❑ 55250	The Chipmunk Song/Alvin's Harmonica	1959	3.75	7.50	15.00
—Blue-green label, no horizontal lines					
❑ 55250	The Chipmunk Song/Alvin's Harmonica	1961	3.00	6.00	12.00
—Blue-green label with horizontal lines					
❑ 55250 [PS]	The Chipmunk Song/Alvin's Harmonica	1959	10.00	20.00	40.00
—Sleeve has Chipmunks depicted somewhat like real chipmunks					
❑ 55250 [PS]	The Chipmunk Song/Alvin's Harmonica	1961	7.50	15.00	30.00
—Sleeve has Chipmunks depicted as the familiar cartoon characters					
❑ 55277	Alvin for President/Sack Time	1960	3.75	7.50	15.00
❑ 55277 [PS]	Alvin for President/Sack Time	1960	10.00	20.00	40.00
❑ 55289	Rudolph, the Red-Nosed Reindeer/Spain	1960	3.75	7.50	15.00
❑ 55289 [PS]	Rudolph, the Red-Nosed Reindeer/Spain	1960	10.00	20.00	40.00
❑ 55424	The Alvin Twist/I Wish I Could Speak French	1962	3.75	7.50	15.00
❑ 55452	America the Beautiful/My Wild Irish Rose	1962	3.75	7.50	15.00
❑ 55544	Alvin's All Star Chipmunk Band/Old MacDonald Cha Cha Cha	1963	3.75	7.50	15.00
❑ 55544 [PS]	Alvin's All Star Chipmunk Band/Old MacDonald Cha Cha Cha	1963	10.00	20.00	40.00
❑ 55632	Eefin' Alvin/Flip Side	1963	3.75	7.50	15.00
❑ 55635	The Night Before Christmas/Wonderful Day	1963	3.75	7.50	15.00
❑ 55635 [PS]	The Night Before Christmas/Wonderful Day	1963	7.50	15.00	30.00
❑ 55734	All My Lovin'/Do You Want to Know a Secret	1964	3.75	7.50	15.00
❑ 55773	Do-Re-Mi/Supercalifragilisticexpialidocious	1965	3.00	6.00	12.00
❑ 55832	I'm Henry VIII, I Am/What's New Pussycat	1965	3.00	6.00	12.00
❑ 56079	The Chipmunk Song/Christmas Blues	1968	4.00	8.00	16.00
—With Canned Heat					

SUNSET

Number	Title (A Side/B Side)	Yr	VG	VG+	NM
❑ 61002	Talk to the Animals/My Friend the Doctor	1968	2.50	5.00	10.00
❑ 61002 [PS]	Talk to the Animals/My Friend the Doctor	1968	3.75	7.50	15.00
❑ 61003	Chitty Chitty Bang Bang/Hushabye Mountain	1968	2.50	5.00	10.00
❑ 61003 [PS]	Chitty Chitty Bang Bang/Hushabye Mountain	1968	3.75	7.50	15.00

UNITED ARTISTS

Number	Title (A Side/B Side)	Yr	VG	VG+	NM
❑ 0056	The Chipmunk Song/Ragtime Cowboy Joe	1973	2.00	4.00	8.00
—"Silver Spotlight Series" reissue					
❑ 0057	Alvin's Harmonica/Rudolph, the Red-Nosed Reindeer	1973	2.00	4.00	8.00
—"Silver Spotlight Series" reissue					
❑ XW576	The Chipmunk Song/Rudolph, the Red-Nosed Reindeer	1974	—	3.00	6.00

7-Inch Extended Plays

LIBERTY

Number	Title (A Side/B Side)	Yr	VG	VG+	NM
❑ LSX-1007	The Chipmunk Song/Ragtime Cowboy Joe//Alvin's Harmonica/If You Love Me	1960	7.50	15.00	30.00
❑ LSX-1007 [PS]	Let's All Sing with the Chipmunks	1960	12.50	25.00	50.00
❑ LSX-1017	Wonderful Day/Christmas Time//Deck The Halls/The Night Before Christmas	1963	5.00	10.00	20.00
❑ LSX-1017 [PS]	Christmas with the Chipmunks, Volume 2	1963	12.50	25.00	50.00

CHIPS, THE (1)
Male vocal group.

JOSIE

Number	Title (A Side/B Side)	Yr	VG	VG+	NM
❑ 803	Rubber Biscuit/Oh My Darlin'	1956	25.00	50.00	100.00

CHIPS, THE (2)
PHILIPS

Number	Title (A Side/B Side)	Yr	VG	VG+	NM
❑ 40520	Mixed Up Shook Up Girl/Break It Gently	1968	2.50	5.00	10.00

CHIPS, THE (3)
Memphis group.

SATELLITE

Number	Title (A Side/B Side)	Yr	VG	VG+	NM
❑ 105	As You can See/You Make Me Feel So Good	1961	30.00	60.00	120.00

CHIPS, THE (4)
STRAND

Number	Title (A Side/B Side)	Yr	VG	VG+	NM
❑ 25027	Darling (I Need Your Love)/You're On My Side	1961	10.00	20.00	40.00

VENICE

Number	Title (A Side/B Side)	Yr	VG	VG+	NM
❑ 101	Darling (I Need Your Love)/You're On My Side	1961	30.00	60.00	120.00

CHIPS, THE (5)
Lead singer: JOE SOUTH.

TOLLIE

Number	Title (A Side/B Side)	Yr	VG	VG+	NM
❑ 9042	Party People/Long Lonely Winter	1965	2.50	5.00	10.00

CHIPS, THE (U)
EMBER

Number	Title (A Side/B Side)	Yr	VG	VG+	NM
❑ 1077	What a Lie/Bye, Bye, My Love	1961	5.00	10.00	20.00

CHOCOLATE WATCH BAND, THE
TOWER

Number	Title (A Side/B Side)	Yr	VG	VG+	NM
❑ 373	Are You Gonna Be There (At the Love-In)/No Way Out	1967	12.50	25.00	50.00

UPTOWN

Number	Title (A Side/B Side)	Yr	VG	VG+	NM
❑ 740	Baby Blue/Sweet Young Thing	1967	75.00	150.00	300.00
❑ 749	Misty Lane/She Weaves a Tender Trap	1967	12.50	25.00	50.00

CHOIR, THE
Two members went on to form the RASPBERRIES.

CANADIAN AMERICAN

Number	Title (A Side/B Side)	Yr	VG	VG+	NM
❑ 203	It's Cold Outside/I'm Goin' Home	1967	10.00	20.00	40.00

INTREPID

Number	Title (A Side/B Side)	Yr	VG	VG+	NM
❑ 75020	Gonna Have a Good Time Tonight/So Much Love	1970	5.00	10.00	20.00

ROULETTE

Number	Title (A Side/B Side)	Yr	VG	VG+	NM
❑ 4738	It's Cold Outside/I'm Goin' Home	1967	3.75	7.50	15.00
❑ 4760	No One Here to Play With/Don't You Feel a Little Sorry for Me	1967	3.75	7.50	15.00
❑ 7005	Changin' My Mind/When You Were With Me	1968	3.75	7.50	15.00

CHORALS, THE
DECCA

Number	Title (A Side/B Side)	Yr	VG	VG+	NM
❑ 29914	In My Dreams/Rock and Roll Baby	1956	20.00	40.00	80.00

CHORDCATS, THE
See THE CHORDS.

CHORDETTES, THE
ATLANTIC

Number	Title (A Side/B Side)	Yr	VG	VG+	NM
❑ 89310	Lollipop/Never on Sunday	1986	—	—	3.00
❑ 89310 [PS]	Lollipop/Never on Sunday	1986	—	—	3.00

CADENCE

Number	Title (A Side/B Side)	Yr	VG	VG+	NM
❑ 1239	It's You, It's You I Love/True Love Goes On and On	1954	3.75	7.50	15.00
❑ 1247	Mr. Sandman/I Don't Wanna See You Cryin'	1954	3.75	7.50	15.00
❑ 1259	Lonely Lips/The Dudelsack Song	1955	3.00	6.00	12.00
❑ 1267	Hummingbird/I Told a Lie	1955	3.00	6.00	12.00
❑ 1273	The Wedding/I Don't Know, I Don't Care	1955	3.00	6.00	12.00
❑ 1284	Eddie My Love/Whispering Willie	1956	3.00	6.00	12.00
❑ 1291	Born to Be with You/Love Never Changes	1956	3.00	6.00	12.00
❑ 1299	Lay Down Your Arms/Teenage Goodnight	1956	3.00	6.00	12.00
❑ 1307	Come Home to My Arms/(Fifi's) Walking the Poodle	1957	3.00	6.00	12.00
❑ 1319	Echo of Love/Like a Baby	1957	3.00	6.00	12.00
❑ 1330	Just Between You and Me/Soft Sands	1957	3.00	6.00	12.00
❑ 1341	Photographs/Baby of Mine	1957	3.00	6.00	12.00
❑ 1345	Lollipop/Baby Come-a Back-a	1958	3.75	7.50	15.00
❑ 1349	Zorro/Love Is a Two-Way Street	1958	3.00	6.00	12.00
❑ 1349 [PS]	Zorro/Love Is a Two-Way Street	1958	6.25	12.50	25.00
❑ 1361	No Other Arms, No Other Lips/We Should Be Together	1959	2.50	5.00	10.00
❑ 1366	A Girl's Work Is Never Done/No Wheels	1959	2.50	5.00	10.00
❑ 1366 [PS]	A Girl's Work Is Never Done/No Wheels	1959	6.25	12.50	25.00
❑ 1367	Forever/Ho Hum	1959	2.50	5.00	10.00
❑ 1382	All My Sorrows/A Broken Vow	1960	2.50	5.00	10.00
❑ 1402	Never on Sunday/A Faraway Star	1961	2.50	5.00	10.00
❑ 1412	The Exodus Song/Theme from Goodbye Again (Say No More-It's Goodbye)	1961	2.50	5.00	10.00
❑ 1417	Adios/White Rose of Athens	1962	2.50	5.00	10.00
❑ 1425	In the Deep Blue Sea/All My Sorrows	1962	2.50	5.00	10.00
❑ 1442	True Love Goes On and On/All My Sorrows	1963	2.50	5.00	10.00

COLUMBIA

Number	Title (A Side/B Side)	Yr	VG	VG+	NM
❑ 38756	When You Were Sweet Sixteen/Moonlight Bay	1950	3.75	7.50	15.00
❑ 38757	Carry Me Back to Old Virginny/Ballin' the Jack	1950	3.75	7.50	15.00

Number	Title (A Side/B Side)	Yr	VG	VG+	NM
❑ 38758	Tell Me Why/Shine On Harvest Moon	1950	3.75	7.50	15.00
❑ 38759	I'd Love to Live in Loveland (With a Love Like You)/When Day Is Done	1950	3.75	7.50	15.00

—The above four comprise box set B-201

Number	Title (A Side/B Side)	Yr	VG	VG+	NM
❑ 39251	Runnin' Wild/Alice Blue Gown	1951	3.75	7.50	15.00
❑ 39252	Love Me and the World Is Mine/Lonesome That's All	1951	3.75	7.50	15.00
❑ 39253	Moonlight on the Ganges/Let the Rest of the World Go By	1951	3.75	7.50	15.00
❑ 39254	The World Is Waiting for the Sunrise/Love's Old Sweet Song	1951	3.75	7.50	15.00
❑ 39793	Carolina Moon//The Anniversary Waltz/ Sentimental Journey	1952	3.75	7.50	15.00
❑ 39794	A Little Street Where Old Friends Meet//Basin Street Blues + 1	1952	3.75	7.50	15.00
❑ 39795	Drifting and Dreaming + 1//I'm Drifting Back to Dreamland/Angry	1952	3.75	7.50	15.00
❑ 39796	S'posin'/The Sweetheart of Sigma Chi//Kentucky Babe/In the Sweet Long Ago	1952	3.75	7.50	15.00

7-Inch Extended Plays

CADENCE

Number	Title (A Side/B Side)	Yr	VG	VG+	NM
❑ CEP 101	Mr. Sandman/Hummingbird//Born to Be with You/ Soft Sands	1956	3.75	7.50	15.00
❑ CEP 101 [PS]	The Chordettes	1956	3.75	7.50	15.00

COLUMBIA

Number	Title (A Side/B Side)	Yr	VG	VG+	NM
❑ B-401 [PS]	The Chordettes Sing Your Requests	195?	3.00	6.00	12.00

—Double-pocket sleeve for 1878 and 1879

Number	Title (A Side/B Side)	Yr	VG	VG+	NM
❑ 5-1878	Wait Till the Sun Shines Nellie/They Say It's Wonderful//Wonderful One/Darkness on the Delta	195?	3.00	6.00	12.00
❑ 5-1879	I Wonder Who's Kissing Her Now?/For Me and My Gal//I Believe/Down Among the Sheltering Pines	195?	3.00	6.00	12.00

CHORDS, THE

ATCO

Number	Title (A Side/B Side)	Yr	VG	VG+	NM
❑ 6213	Sh-Boom/Little Maiden	1961	3.75	7.50	15.00

—As "The Sh-Booms"

ATLANTIC

Number	Title (A Side/B Side)	Yr	VG	VG+	NM
❑ 2074	Blue Moon/Short Skirts	1960	5.00	10.00	20.00

—As "The Sh-Booms"

CASINO

Number	Title (A Side/B Side)	Yr	VG	VG+	NM
❑ 451	Tears in Your Eyes/Don't Be a Jumpin' Jack	1958	7.50	15.00	30.00

CAT

Number	Title (A Side/B Side)	Yr	VG	VG+	NM
❑ 104	Sh-Boom/Cross Over the Bridge	1954	30.00	60.00	120.00
❑ 104	Sh-Boom/Little Maiden	1954	15.00	30.00	60.00
❑ 109	Zippety Zum (I'm in Love)/Bless You (For Being an Angel)	1954	10.00	20.00	40.00
❑ 112	A Girl to Love/Hold Me Baby	1955	10.00	20.00	40.00

—As "The Chordcats"

Number	Title (A Side/B Side)	Yr	VG	VG+	NM
❑ 117	Could It Be/Pretty Wild	1955	10.00	20.00	40.00

—As "The Sh-Booms"

METRO

Number	Title (A Side/B Side)	Yr	VG	VG+	NM
❑ 20015	Elephant Walk/Pretty Face	1959	5.00	10.00	20.00

VIK

Number	Title (A Side/B Side)	Yr	VG	VG+	NM
❑ 0295	I Don't Want to Set the World on Fire/Lu Lu	1957	7.50	15.00	30.00

—As "The Sh-Booms"

CHOSEN FEW, THE

Many different groups.

AUTUMN

Number	Title (A Side/B Side)	Yr	VG	VG+	NM
❑ 17	Nobody But Me/I Think It's Time	1965	2.50	5.00	10.00

CANADIAN AMERICAN

Number	Title (A Side/B Side)	Yr	VG	VG+	NM
❑ 202	Cute Thing/One of Those Songs	1967	3.00	6.00	12.00

CANUSA

Number	Title (A Side/B Side)	Yr	VG	VG+	NM
❑ 504	Summer's Love/Hey Joe	1967	3.75	7.50	15.00

CANYON

Number	Title (A Side/B Side)	Yr	VG	VG+	NM
❑ 1000	Talking All the Love I Can/Birth of a Playboy	196?	2.50	5.00	10.00

CO-OP

Number	Title (A Side/B Side)	Yr	VG	VG+	NM
❑ 510	Why Can't I Love You/La La La La La	1966	3.00	6.00	12.00
❑ 511	Summer's Love/(Instrumental)	1967	3.00	6.00	12.00

CRYSTAL

Number	Title (A Side/B Side)	Yr	VG	VG+	NM
❑ 1107	You're a Big Girl Now/(B-side unknown)	196?	2.50	5.00	10.00

DART

Number	Title (A Side/B Side)	Yr	VG	VG+	NM
❑ 1080	Foolin' Around with Me/We Walk Together	1967	2.00	4.00	8.00

DENIM

Number	Title (A Side/B Side)	Yr	VG	VG+	NM
❑ 1092	Pink Clouds and Lemonade/Stop in the Name of Love	196?	2.00	4.00	8.00

LIBERTY

Number	Title (A Side/B Side)	Yr	VG	VG+	NM
❑ 55919	Synthetic Man/The Last Man Alive	1966	2.50	5.00	10.00
❑ 55962	Asian Chrome/Earth Above, Sky Below	1967	2.50	5.00	10.00

NORTH BEACH

Number	Title (A Side/B Side)	Yr	VG	VG+	NM
❑ 1003	Nobody But Me/I Think It's Time	1965	3.75	7.50	15.00

PLAYBOY

Number	Title (A Side/B Side)	Yr	VG	VG+	NM
❑ 106	I've Had It/Ask Me Baby	196?	2.50	5.00	10.00

POWER INTERNATIONAL

Number	Title (A Side/B Side)	Yr	VG	VG+	NM
❑ 872	Another Goodbye/Forget About the Past	1966	10.00	20.00	40.00

RCA VICTOR

Number	Title (A Side/B Side)	Yr	VG	VG+	NM
❑ 74-0217	Maybe the Rain Will Fall/Deeper In	1969	2.00	4.00	8.00
❑ 74-0254	I'll Never Change You/Talk with Me	1969	2.00	4.00	8.00

ROULETTE

Number	Title (A Side/B Side)	Yr	VG	VG+	NM
❑ 7015	Footsee/You Can Never Be Wrong	1968	2.00	4.00	8.00

CHRISTIAN, DIANE

BELL

Number	Title (A Side/B Side)	Yr	VG	VG+	NM
❑ 610	It Happened One Night/Wonderful Guy	1965	2.50	5.00	10.00
❑ 617	Little Boy/Why Don't the Boy Leave Me Alone	1965	2.50	5.00	10.00

SMASH

Number	Title (A Side/B Side)	Yr	VG	VG+	NM
❑ 1862	Has Anybody Seen My Boyfriend/There's So Much About My Baby	1963	2.50	5.00	10.00

CHRISTIAN, ROGER

RENDEZVOUS

Number	Title (A Side/B Side)	Yr	VG	VG+	NM
❑ 195	The Meaning of Merry Christmas/Little Mary Christmas	1962	6.25	12.50	25.00

CHRISTIE

EPIC

Number	Title (A Side/B Side)	Yr	VG	VG+	NM
❑ 10626	Yellow River/Down the Mississippi Line	1970	—	2.50	5.00
❑ 10695	San Bernadino/Here I Am	1971	—	2.00	4.00
❑ 10732	Man of Many Faces/Country Sam	1971	—	2.00	4.00

CHRISTIE, LOU

Also see THE CANTINA BAND; THE CLASSICS (2); THE CLAMS.

ALCAR

Number	Title (A Side/B Side)	Yr	VG	VG+	NM
❑ 207	Close Your Eyes/Funny Thing	1963	6.25	12.50	25.00
❑ 208	You're With It/Tomorrow Will Come	1963	6.25	12.50	25.00

AMERICAN MUSIC MAKERS

Number	Title (A Side/B Side)	Yr	VG	VG+	NM
❑ 006	The Jury/Little Did I Know	1963	7.50	15.00	30.00

BUDDAH

Number	Title (A Side/B Side)	Yr	VG	VG+	NM
❑ 65	Genesis and the Third Verse/Rake Up the Leaves	1968	2.00	4.00	8.00
❑ 76	Canterbury Road/Saints of Aquarius	1969	2.00	4.00	8.00
❑ 116	I'm Gonna Make You Mine/I'm Gonna Get Married	1969	—	3.00	6.00
❑ 149	Are You Getting Any Sunshine/It'll Take Time	1970	—	2.50	5.00
❑ 163	Love Is Over/She Sold Me Magic	1970	—	2.50	5.00
❑ 192	Indian Lady/Glory River	1970	—	2.50	5.00
❑ 231 [DJ]	Waco (same on both sides)	1971	—	3.00	6.00

—Stock copy does not exist

Number	Title (A Side/B Side)	Yr	VG	VG+	NM
❑ 235	Waco/Lighthouse	1971	—	2.50	5.00
❑ 257	Mickey's Monkey/She Sold Me Magic	1971	6.25	12.50	25.00
❑ 285	Sing Me, Sing Me/Paper Song	1972	—	2.50	5.00
❑ 285 [PS]	Sing Me, Sing Me/Paper Song	1972	2.50	5.00	10.00

—Sleeve appears to be promo only

Number	Title (A Side/B Side)	Yr	VG	VG+	NM
❑ 312	Shuffle On Down to Pittsburgh/I'm Gonna Get Married	1972	5.00	10.00	20.00

CO & CE

Number	Title (A Side/B Side)	Yr	VG	VG+	NM
❑ 235	Outside the Gates of Heaven/All That Glitters Isn't Gold	1966	2.50	5.00	10.00

COLPIX

Number	Title (A Side/B Side)	Yr	VG	VG+	NM
❑ 735	Merry-Go-Round/Guitars and Bongos	1964	3.00	6.00	12.00
❑ 753	Pot of Gold/Have I Sinned	1964	3.00	6.00	12.00
❑ 770	Make Summer Last Forever/Why Did You Do It Baby	1965	3.00	6.00	12.00
❑ 778	A Teenager in Love/Back Track	1965	3.00	6.00	12.00
❑ 799	Cryin' on My Knees/Big Time	1966	3.00	6.00	12.00
❑ 799 [PS]	Cryin' on My Knees/Big Time	1966	6.25	12.50	25.00

COLUMBIA

Number	Title (A Side/B Side)	Yr	VG	VG+	NM
❑ 44062	Shake Hands and Walk Away Cryin'/Escape	1967	3.75	7.50	15.00
❑ 44177	Self Expression/Back to the Days of the Romans	1967	3.75	7.50	15.00
❑ 44240	(I Remember) Gina/Escape	1967	3.75	7.50	15.00
❑ 44338	Back to the Days of the Romans/Don't Stop Me	1967	3.75	7.50	15.00

C&C

Number	Title (A Side/B Side)	Yr	VG	VG+	NM
❑ 102	The Gypsy Cried/Red Sails in the Sunset	1962	50.00	100.00	200.00

EPIC

Number	Title (A Side/B Side)	Yr	VG	VG+	NM
❑ 50244	Summer in Malibu/Ridin' in My Van	1976	3.75	7.50	15.00

LIFESONG

Number	Title (A Side/B Side)	Yr	VG	VG+	NM
❑ 1775	Theme from "People" (Part 1)/Theme from "People" (Part 2)	1978	12.50	25.00	50.00

—As "Sacco"

MGM

Number	Title (A Side/B Side)	Yr	VG	VG+	NM
❑ 13412	Lightnin' Strikes/Cryin' in the Streets	1965	3.75	7.50	15.00
❑ 13473	Rhapsody in the Rain/Trapeze	1966	5.00	10.00	20.00

—Original version of A-side had racy (by 1966 standards) lyrics: "We were makin' out in the rain/And in this car, our love went much too far." Matrix number in dead wax is "66-XY-308"

Number	Title (A Side/B Side)	Yr	VG	VG+	NM
❑ 13473	Rhapsody in the Rain/Trapeze	1966	3.75	7.50	15.00

—Revised A-side has altered lyrics: "We fell in love in the rain/And in this car, love came like a falling star." Matrix number in dead wax is "66-XY-308 D.J."

Number	Title (A Side/B Side)	Yr	VG	VG+	NM
❑ 13473 [PS]	Rhapsody in the Rain/Trapeze	1966	5.00	10.00	20.00
❑ 13533	Painter/Du Ronda	1966	2.50	5.00	10.00
❑ 13533 [PS]	Painter/Du Ronda	1966	5.00	10.00	20.00
❑ 13576	If My Car Could Only Talk/Song of Lita	1966	2.50	5.00	10.00
❑ 13623	Since I Don't Have You/Wild Life's in Season	1966	2.50	5.00	10.00

MIDLAND INT'L.

Number	Title (A Side/B Side)	Yr	VG	VG+	NM
❑ MB-10848	You're Gonna Make Love to Me/Fantasies	1976	3.75	7.50	15.00
❑ MB-10959	Spanish Wine/Dancing in the Sand	1977	3.75	7.50	15.00

MIDSONG INT'L.

Number	Title (A Side/B Side)	Yr	VG	VG+	NM
❑ 72013	Don't Knock My Love (Short)/Don't Knock My Love (Long)	1980	2.50	5.00	10.00

—With Pia Zadora

PLATEAU

Number	Title (A Side/B Side)	Yr	VG	VG+	NM
❑ 4551	Guardian Angels/(B-side unknown)	1981	10.00	20.00	40.00

RHINO

Number	Title (A Side/B Side)	Yr	VG	VG+	NM
❑ 90105	O Holy Night (same on both sides)	1991	—	3.00	6.00

—With the University of Pittsburgh Men's Glee Club

ROULETTE

Number	Title (A Side/B Side)	Yr	VG	VG+	NM
❑ 4457	The Gypsy Cried/Red Sails in the Sunset	1963	5.00	10.00	20.00

—White label with spokes

Number	Title (A Side/B Side)	Yr	VG	VG+	NM
❑ 4457	The Gypsy Cried/Red Sails in the Sunset	1963	3.75	7.50	15.00

—Pink label

Number	Title (A Side/B Side)	Yr	VG	VG+	NM
❑ 4457	The Gypsy Cried/Red Sails in the Sunset	1964	2.50	5.00	10.00

—Orange and yellow label

Number	Title (A Side/B Side)	Yr	VG	VG+	NM
❑ 4481	Two Faces Have I/All That Glitters Isn't Gold	1963	3.75	7.50	15.00
❑ 4504	How Many Teardrops/You and I (Have a Right to Cry)	1963	3.00	6.00	12.00
❑ 4527	Shy Boy/It Can Happen	1963	3.00	6.00	12.00
❑ 4545	Stay/There They Go	1964	3.75	7.50	15.00
❑ 4554	When You Dance/Maybe You'll Be There	1964	6.25	12.50	25.00

SLIPPED DISC

Number	Title (A Side/B Side)	Yr	VG	VG+	NM
❑ 45270	Summer Days/The One and Only Original Sunshine Kid	1976	3.75	7.50	15.00

Number	Title (A Side/B Side)	Yr	VG	VG+	NM
THREE BROTHERS					
❑ 400	Blue Canadian Rocky Dream/Wilma Lee and Stoney	1973	2.00	4.00	8.00
❑ 402	Beyond the Blue Horizon/Saddle the Wind	1974	—	2.50	5.00
❑ 403	You Were the One/Good Morning	1974	2.00	4.00	8.00
❑ 405	Hey You Cajun/Sunbeam	1974	2.50	5.00	10.00
WORLD					
❑ 1002	The Jury/Little Did I Know	1963	7.50	15.00	30.00

CHRISTIE, SUSAN

Number	Title (A Side/B Side)	Yr	VG	VG+	NM
COLUMBIA					
❑ 43595	I Love Onions/Take Me As You Find Me	1966	2.50	5.00	10.00
❑ 44117	Tonight You Belong to Me/Toy Balloon	1967	—	3.00	6.00
❑ 44327	All I Have to Do Is Dream/Anywhere You Are	1967	—	3.00	6.00

CHRISTMAS SPIRIT, THE (1)

William B. Williams, narrator.

Number	Title (A Side/B Side)	Yr	VG	VG+	NM
DUEL					
❑ 503	It's Christmas/A World to Grow Up In	1961	3.00	6.00	12.00

CHRISTMAS SPIRIT, THE (2)

Members of THE TURTLES with LINDA RONSTADT.

Number	Title (A Side/B Side)	Yr	VG	VG+	NM
WHITE WHALE					
❑ 290	Christmas Is My Time of Year/Will You Still Believe	1968	20.00	40.00	80.00

CHRISTOPHER (1)

Number	Title (A Side/B Side)	Yr	VG	VG+	NM
BELL					
❑ 679	Hey Girl/Every Boy in the World	1967	3.75	7.50	15.00
DATE					
❑ 1664	Santa Ana Winds/Spring	1970	3.00	6.00	12.00

CHRISTOPHER (U)

Number	Title (A Side/B Side)	Yr	VG	VG+	NM
DOT					
❑ 17133	Valerie/Sunday Life	1968	3.75	7.50	15.00

CHRISTY, DON

See SONNY.

CHUBBY AND THE TURNPIKES

Some members later were in TAVARES.

Number	Title (A Side/B Side)	Yr	VG	VG+	NM
CAPITOL					
❑ 5840	I Didn't Try/I Know the Inside Story	1967	7.50	15.00	30.00

CHUCK-A-LUCKS, THE

Number	Title (A Side/B Side)	Yr	VG	VG+	NM
BOW					
❑ 305	Heaven Knows/Chuck-a-Luck	1957	12.50	25.00	50.00
CANDLELITE					
❑ 424	Heaven Knows/Chuck-a-Luck	196?	3.00	6.00	12.00
JUBILEE					
❑ 5415	Tarzan's Date/Unconditional Surrender	1961	5.00	10.00	20.00
LIN					
❑ 5010	Who Am I?/The Devil's Train	1958	6.25	12.50	25.00
❑ 5014	The Magic of First Love/Disc Jockey Fever	1958	12.50	25.00	50.00
MEL-O-DY					
❑ 106	Sugar Cane Curtain/Dingbat Diller	1963	6.25	12.50	25.00
WARNER BROS.					
❑ 5198	Long John/Pick Up and Deliver	1961	5.00	10.00	20.00
❑ 5234	Cotton Pickin' Love/I'm Hospitalized Over You	1961	5.00	10.00	20.00

CHUCKLES, THE

Also see THE THREE CHUCKLES.

Number	Title (A Side/B Side)	Yr	VG	VG+	NM
ABC-PARAMOUNT					
❑ 10276	Runaround/Lonely Traveler	1961	3.75	7.50	15.00

CHUMBAWAMBA

Number	Title (A Side/B Side)	Yr	VG	VG+	NM
UNIVERSAL/REPUBLIC					
❑ US7-56191	Tubthumping/Amnesia	1998	—	2.00	4.00

CHURCH, EUGENE

Number	Title (A Side/B Side)	Yr	VG	VG+	NM
CLASS					
❑ 235	Pretty Girls Everywhere/For the Rest of My Life	1958	6.25	12.50	25.00
❑ 254	Miami/I Ain't Goin' for That	1959	3.00	6.00	12.00
❑ 261	Jack of All Trades/Without Soul	1959	3.00	6.00	12.00
❑ 266	The Struttin' Kind/That's What's Happenin'	1960	3.00	6.00	12.00
KING					
❑ 5545	Mind Your Own Business/You Got the Right Idea	1961	3.00	6.00	12.00
❑ 5589	That's All I Need/Geneva	1962	2.50	5.00	10.00
❑ 5610	Light of the Moon/I'm Your Taboo Man	1962	2.50	5.00	10.00
❑ 5659	The Right Girl, the Right Time/Pretty Baby Won't You Come On Home	1962	2.50	5.00	10.00
❑ 5715	Sixteen Tons/Time Has Brought About a Change	1963	2.50	5.00	10.00
RENDEZVOUS					
❑ 132	Good News/Polly	1960	3.00	6.00	12.00
SPECIALTY					
❑ 604	How Long/Open Up Your Heart	1957	5.00	10.00	20.00
WORLD PACIFIC					
❑ 77866	Dollar Bill/U Maka Hanna	1967	3.75	7.50	15.00

CHURCH STREET FIVE, THE

Number	Title (A Side/B Side)	Yr	VG	VG+	NM
LEGRAND					
❑ 1004	A Night with Daddy G (Part 1)/A Night with Daddy G (Part 2)	1961	6.25	12.50	25.00
—Purple label original					
❑ 1004	A Night with Daddy G (Part 1)/A Night with Daddy G (Part 2)	1961	3.75	7.50	15.00
—Red, gold and white "shield" label					
❑ 1010	Fallen Arches/Everybody's Happy	1961	5.00	10.00	20.00
❑ 1014	Church Street Walk/I'm Gonna Sue	1961	5.00	10.00	20.00
❑ 1021	Daddy G Rides Again/Hey Now	1962	5.00	10.00	20.00
❑ 1026	Moonlight in Vermont/Sing a Song Children	1963	5.00	10.00	20.00

CICCONE YOUTH

SONIC YOUTH in disguise.

Number	Title (A Side/B Side)	Yr	VG	VG+	NM
NEW ALLIANCE					
❑ 030	Burnin' Up/Tuff Titty Rap/Into the Groovey	1986	2.50	5.00	10.00
❑ 030 [PS]	Burnin' Up/Tuff Titty Rap/Into the Groovey	1986	2.50	5.00	10.00

CINDERELLAS, THE (1)

Female vocal group.

Number	Title (A Side/B Side)	Yr	VG	VG+	NM
COLUMBIA					
❑ 41540	The Trouble with Boys/Puppy Dog	1959	3.75	7.50	15.00
DECCA					
❑ 30830	Mr. Dee Jay/Yum Yum Yum	1959	6.25	12.50	25.00
❑ 30925	I Was Only 15/You Never Shoulda Gone Away	1959	6.25	12.50	25.00

CINDERELLAS, THE (2)

Another female vocal group.

Number	Title (A Side/B Side)	Yr	VG	VG+	NM
DIMENSION					
❑ 1026	Baby, Baby, I Still Love You/Please Don't Wake Me	1964	10.00	20.00	40.00
MERCURY					
❑ 72394	Fairy Tale/Mr. Happy Love	1965	2.50	5.00	10.00

CINDY AND LINDY

Number	Title (A Side/B Side)	Yr	VG	VG+	NM
ABC-PARAMOUNT					
❑ 9847	The Language of Love/Brigette's Song	1957	6.25	12.50	25.00
❑ 9886	Shakin'/Sittin' It Out	1958	6.25	12.50	25.00
CORAL					
❑ 62008	The Wonder That Is You/I'll String Along with You	1958	5.00	10.00	20.00
❑ 62072	Saturday Night in Tia-Juana/You Can't Mail an Elephant	1959	5.00	10.00	20.00
❑ 62119	Before and After/Big Bells and Bongo Drummers	1959	5.00	10.00	20.00
❑ 62165	Let's Go Steady/There Are Such Things	1960	5.00	10.00	20.00
PILGRIM					
❑ 702	Let's Go Steady/The Wedding Is Over	1956	3.75	7.50	15.00
❑ 705	Hungry Heart/Livin' and Bein' Loved	1956	3.75	7.50	15.00

CINNAMON ANGELS

May be the same group as THE CINNAMONS.

Number	Title (A Side/B Side)	Yr	VG	VG+	NM
B.T. PUPPY					
❑ 559	Calypso Girl/Let's Be Sweethearts	1970	2.00	4.00	8.00

CINNAMONS, THE

Number	Title (A Side/B Side)	Yr	VG	VG+	NM
B.T. PUPPY					
❑ 503	I'm Not Gonna Worry/Strange, Strange Feeling	1964	2.00	4.00	8.00
❑ 508	Mr. Cupid '65/Dance to the Music	1965	2.00	4.00	8.00

CIRCUS MAXIMUS

Group features JERRY JEFF WALKER.

Number	Title (A Side/B Side)	Yr	VG	VG+	NM
VANGUARD					
❑ 35063	Lonely Man/Negative Dreamer Girl	1968	5.00	10.00	20.00

CITATIONS, THE

More than one group.

Number	Title (A Side/B Side)	Yr	VG	VG+	NM
BALLAD					
❑ 101	I Will Stand By You/To Win the Race	1967	25.00	50.00	100.00
CANADIAN AMERICAN					
❑ 136	Mystery of Love/Magic Eyes	1962	7.50	15.00	30.00
—As "Nicki North and the Citations"					
DON-EL					
❑ 113	It Hurts Me/Kiss in the Night	1961	10.00	20.00	40.00
EPIC					
❑ 9603	Moon Race/Slippin' and Slidin'	1963	6.25	12.50	25.00
FRATERNITY					
❑ 910	The Girl Next Door/Ten Miles from Nowhere	1963	5.00	10.00	20.00
❑ 992	The Girl Next Door/Ten Miles from Nowhere	1967	3.00	6.00	12.00
MERCURY					
❑ 72286	Chicago/The Stomp	1964	3.75	7.50	15.00
MGM					
❑ 13373	That Girl of Mine/Down Went the Curtain	1965	5.00	10.00	20.00
PRINCESS					
❑ 54	Carmen P./Everybody Philly	1965	7.50	15.00	30.00
ROULETTE					
❑ 4623	Carmen P./Everybody Philly	1965	3.75	7.50	15.00
SARA					
❑ 3301	Moon Race/Slippin' and Slidin'	1963	12.50	25.00	50.00
SWAN					
❑ 4062	Fiddlin' Around/Fire Ritual	1960	10.00	20.00	40.00
VANGEE					
❑ 301	The Girl Next Door/Ten Miles from Nowhere	1963	10.00	20.00	40.00

CITIZEN KING

Number	Title (A Side/B Side)	Yr	VG	VG+	NM
WARNER BROS.					
❑ 16965	Better Days (And the Bottom Drops Out)/Basement Show	1999	—	—	3.00

CITY, THE

CAROLE KING was a member.

Number	Title (A Side/B Side)	Yr	VG	VG+	NM
ODE					
❑ 113	Snow Queen/Paradise Alley	1968	3.00	6.00	12.00
❑ 117	That Old Sweet Rule/Why Are You Leaving	1968	3.00	6.00	12.00
❑ 119	(Hi-De-Ho) That Old Sweet Roll/Why Are You Leaving	1969	3.00	6.00	12.00

CITY SURFERS, THE

Number	Title (A Side/B Side)	Yr	VG	VG+	NM
CAPITOL					
❑ 5002	Beach Ball/Sun Tan Baby	1963	6.25	12.50	25.00
❑ 5052	Powder Puff/Fifty Miles to Go	1963	6.25	12.50	25.00

CLANTON, JIMMY

Number	Title (A Side/B Side)	Yr	VG	VG+	NM
ACE					
❑ 537	I Trusted You/That's You Baby	1958	5.00	10.00	20.00
❑ 546	Just a Dream/You Aim to Please	1958	5.00	10.00	20.00

Number	Title (A Side/B Side)	Yr	VG	VG+	NM
❑ 551	A Letter to An Angel/A Part of Me	1958	5.00	10.00	20.00
❑ 560	My Love Is Strong/Ship on a Stormy Sea	1959	3.75	7.50	15.00
❑ 567 [M]	My Own True Love/Little Boy in Love	1959	3.75	7.50	15.00
❑ 567 [PS]	My Own True Love/Little Boy in Love	1959	7.50	15.00	30.00
❑ 567 [S]	My Own True Love/Little Boy in Love	1959	7.50	15.00	30.00
❑ 575	Go, Jimmy, Go/I Trusted You	1959	5.00	10.00	20.00
—Normal white label					
❑ 575	Go, Jimmy, Go/I Trusted You	1959	6.25	12.50	25.00
—Purple label					
❑ 575 [PS]	Go, Jimmy, Go/I Trusted You	1959	7.50	15.00	30.00
❑ 585	Another Sleepless Night/I'm Gonna Try	1960	3.75	7.50	15.00
❑ 585 [PS]	Another Sleepless Night/I'm Gonna Try	1960	7.50	15.00	30.00
❑ 600	Come Back/Wait	1960	3.75	7.50	15.00
❑ 600 [PS]	Come Back/Wait	1960	7.50	15.00	30.00
❑ 607	What Am I Gonna Do/If I	1961	3.75	7.50	15.00
❑ 607 [PS]	What Am I Gonna Do/If I	1961	7.50	15.00	30.00
❑ 616	Down the Aisle/No Longer Blue	1961	3.75	7.50	15.00
❑ 616 [PS]	Down the Aisle/No Longer Blue	1961	7.50	15.00	30.00
—With Mary Ann Mobley					
❑ 622	I Just Wanna Make Love/Don't Look at Me	1961	3.75	7.50	15.00
❑ 622 [PS]	I Just Wanna Make Love/Don't Look at Me	1961	7.50	15.00	30.00
❑ 634	Lucky in Love with You/Not Like a Brother	1961	3.75	7.50	15.00
❑ 634 [PS]	Lucky in Love with You/Not Like a Brother	1961	7.50	15.00	30.00
❑ 641	Twist On Little Girl/Wayward Love	1962	3.75	7.50	15.00
❑ 641 [PS]	Twist On Little Girl/Wayward Love	1962	7.50	15.00	30.00
❑ 642	Twist On Little Girl/Wayward Love//Green Light/Happy Times	1962	12.50	25.00	50.00
❑ 642 [PS]	Teenage Millionaire	1962	12.50	25.00	50.00
❑ 655	Just a Moment/Because I Do	1962	3.75	7.50	15.00
❑ 655 [PS]	Just a Moment/Because I Do	1962	7.50	15.00	30.00
❑ 664 [DJ]	Venus in Blue Jeans/Highway Bound	1962	6.25	12.50	25.00
—No stock copies exist with this catalog number					
❑ 668	Heart Hotel/Many Dreams	1963	3.00	6.00	12.00
❑ 8001	Venus in Blue Jeans/Highway Bound	1962	3.75	7.50	15.00
❑ 8005	Darkest Street in Town/Dreams of a Fool	1962	2.50	5.00	10.00
❑ 8006	Endless Nights/Another Day, Another Heartache	1963	2.50	5.00	10.00
❑ 8006 [PS]	Endless Nights/Another Day, Another Heartache	1963	5.00	10.00	20.00
❑ 8007	Cindy/I Care Enough (To Give the Very Best)	1963	2.50	5.00	10.00
IMPERIAL					
❑ 66242	Absence of Lisa/C'mon Jim	1967	2.00	4.00	8.00
❑ 66274	Calico Junction/I'll Be Loving You	1968	2.00	4.00	8.00
LAURIE					
❑ 3508	Curly/The Girl Who Cried Love (Once Too Often)	1969	2.00	4.00	8.00
❑ 3508	Curly/I'll Never Forget Your Love	1969	2.50	5.00	10.00
❑ 3534	Tell Me/I'll Never Forget Your Love	1969	2.00	4.00	8.00
MALA					
❑ 500	Hurting Each Other/Don't Keep Your Friends Away	1965	2.50	5.00	10.00
❑ 516	Everything I Touch Turns to Tears/That Special Way	1965	2.50	5.00	10.00
PHILIPS					
❑ 40161	Red Don't Go with Blue/All the Words in the World	1963	2.50	5.00	10.00
❑ 40181	I'll Step Aside/I Won't Cry Anymore	1964	2.50	5.00	10.00
❑ 40208	If I'm a Fool for Loving You/A Million Drums	1964	2.50	5.00	10.00
❑ 40219	Follow the Sun/Lock the Windows	1964	2.50	5.00	10.00
SPIRAL					
❑ 3406	The Coolest Hot Pants/(Instrumental)	1971	—	2.50	5.00
STARCREST					
❑ 078 [DJ]	Old Rock 'N Roller (mono/stereo)	1978	—	2.50	5.00
—May be promo only					
STARFIRE					
❑ 104	I Wanna Go Home/You Kissed a Fool Goodbye	1976	—	2.50	5.00
VIN					
❑ 1028	What Am I Living For/Wedding Blues	1962	2.50	5.00	10.00

7-Inch Extended Plays

Number	Title (A Side/B Side)	Yr	VG	VG+	NM
ACE					
❑ 101	(contents unknown)	1959	25.00	50.00	100.00
❑ 101 [PS]	Jimmy Clanton	1959	25.00	50.00	100.00
❑ 102	(contents unknown)	1959	37.50	75.00	150.00
❑ 102 [PS]	Thinking of You	1959	37.50	75.00	150.00

CLAPTON, ERIC

Also see BLIND FAITH; CREAM; DEREK AND THE DOMINOS; B.B. KING; THE YARDBIRDS.

Number	Title (A Side/B Side)	Yr	VG	VG+	NM
ATCO					
❑ 6784	After Midnight/Easy Now	1970	—	3.00	6.00
DUCK					
❑ 28279	Tearing Us Apart/Hold On	1987	—	—	3.00
—With Tina Turner					
❑ 28279 [PS]	Tearing Us Apart/Hold On	1987	—	—	3.00
—With Tina Turner					
❑ 28391	Behind the Sun/Grand Illusion	1987	—	—	3.00
❑ 28514	It's in the Way That You Use It/Grand Illusion	1986	—	—	3.00
❑ 28514 [PS]	It's in the Way That You Use It/Grand Illusion	1986	—	—	3.00
❑ 28986	See What Love Can Do/She's Waiting	1985	—	—	3.00
❑ 29081	Forever Man/Too Bad	1985	—	—	3.00
❑ 29081 [PS]	Forever Man/Too Bad	1985	—	—	3.00
❑ 29647	Pretty Girl/The Shape You're In	1983	—	2.00	4.00
❑ 29780	I've Got a Rock 'n' Roll Heart/Man in Love	1983	—	2.00	4.00
—Custom silver label with Duck logo					
POLYDOR					
❑ 15049	Let It Rain/Easy Now	1972	—	2.50	5.00
❑ 15056	Bell Bottom Blues/Little Wing	1973	—	2.50	5.00
—Reissue of Derek and the Dominos recordings, but under Clapton's name					
❑ 887403-7	After Midnight/I Can't Stand It	1988	—	—	3.00
❑ 887403-7 [PS]	After Midnight/I Can't Stand It	1988	—	—	3.00
REPRISE					
❑ 17621	Change the World/Danny Boy	1996	—	—	3.00
❑ 18044	Motherless Child/Driftin'	1994	—	—	3.00
❑ 18787	Layla/Signe	1992	—	—	3.00
❑ 19038	Tears in Heaven/Tracks and Lines	1992	—	—	3.00
❑ 22732	Pretending/Before You Accuse Me	1989	—	—	3.00
❑ 22732 [PS]	Pretending/Before You Accuse Me	1989	—	—	3.00
RSO					
❑ 409	I Shot the Sheriff/Give Me Strength	1974	—	2.50	5.00
❑ 500	I Shot the Sheriff/Give Me Strength	1974	—	2.00	4.00
❑ 503	Willie and the Hand Jive/Main Line Florida	1975	—	2.00	4.00
❑ 509	Swing Low Sweet Chariot/Pretty Blue Eyes	1975	—	2.00	4.00
❑ 513	Knockin' on Heaven's Door/Someone Like You	1975	—	2.00	4.00
❑ 861	Hello Old Friend/All Our Pastimes	1976	—	2.00	4.00
❑ 868	Carnival/Hungry	1976	—	2.00	4.00
❑ 886	Lay Down Sally/Next Time You See Her	1978	—	2.00	4.00
❑ 895	Wonderful Tonight/Peaches and Diesel	1978	—	2.00	4.00
❑ 910	Promises/Watch Out for Lucy	1978	—	2.00	4.00
❑ 928	Tulsa Time/Cocaine	1979	—	2.50	5.00
—Studio versions of the two songs					
❑ 1039	Tulsa Time/Cocaine	1980	—	2.00	4.00
—Live versions of the two songs					
❑ 1051	Early in the Morning/Blues Power	1980	—	2.00	4.00
❑ 1060	I Can't Stand It/Black Rose	1981	—	2.00	4.00
❑ 1064	Another Ticket/Rita Mae	1981	—	2.00	4.00
❑ 1064 [PS]	Another Ticket/Rita Mae	1981	—	2.50	5.00
WARNER BROS.					
❑ 29780	I've Got a Rock 'n' Roll Heart/Man in Love	1983	—	2.50	5.00
—Original pressing on white WB label					

CLAREMONTS, THE

Number	Title (A Side/B Side)	Yr	VG	VG+	NM
APOLLO					
❑ 517	Why Keep Me Dreaming/Angel of Romance	1957	15.00	30.00	60.00
❑ 751	Why Keep Me Dreaming/Angel of Romance	1963	6.25	12.50	25.00

CLARK, CHRIS

Number	Title (A Side/B Side)	Yr	VG	VG+	NM
MOTOWN					
❑ 1114	From Head to Toe/The Beginning of the End	1967	3.75	7.50	15.00
❑ 1121	Whisper You Love Me Boy/The Beginning of the End	1968	3.75	7.50	15.00
V.I.P.					
❑ 25031	Do Right, Baby, Do Right/Don't Be Too Long	1965	3.75	7.50	15.00
❑ 25038	Love's Gone Mad/Put Yourself in My Place	1965	15.00	30.00	60.00
❑ 25038	Love's Gone Bad/Put Yourself in My Place	1965	5.00	10.00	20.00
—Same song as above A-side, but with corrected title					
❑ 25041	I Love You/I Want to Go Back There Again	1966	3.75	7.50	15.00

CLARK, CLAUDINE

Number	Title (A Side/B Side)	Yr	VG	VG+	NM
CHANCELLOR					
❑ 1113	Party Lights/Disappointed	1962	5.00	10.00	20.00
—exists on two different labels					
❑ 1124	Telephone Game/Walkin' Through a Cemetery	1962	3.00	6.00	12.00
❑ 1130	Walk Me Home/Who Will You Hurt	1963	3.00	6.00	12.00
HERALD					
❑ 523	Teenage Blues/Angel of Happiness	1958	10.00	20.00	40.00
JAMIE					
❑ 1279	Moon Madness/(The Strength) To Be Strong	1964	2.50	5.00	10.00
❑ 1291	Buttered Popcorn/A Sometimes Thing	1964	2.50	5.00	10.00
TCF HALL					
❑ 18	Foxy/Standin' on Tip Toes	196?	2.50	5.00	10.00

CLARK, DAVE, FIVE

Number	Title (A Side/B Side)	Yr	VG	VG+	NM
CONGRESS					
❑ 212	I Knew It All the Time/That's What I Said	1964	5.00	10.00	20.00
❑ 212 [PS]	I Knew It All the Time/That's What I Said	1964	10.00	20.00	40.00
EPIC					
❑ 9656	Glad All Over/I Know You	1964	3.75	7.50	15.00
❑ 9656 [PS]	Glad All Over/I Know You	1964	5.00	10.00	20.00
❑ 9671	Bits and Pieces/All of the Time	1964	3.00	6.00	12.00
❑ 9678	Do You Love Me/Chaquita	1964	3.00	6.00	12.00
❑ 9692	Can't You See That She's Mine/No TIme to Lose	1964	3.00	6.00	12.00
❑ 9692 [PS]	Can't You See That She's Mine/No TIme to Lose	1964	5.00	10.00	20.00
❑ 9704	Because/Theme Without a Name	1964	3.00	6.00	12.00
❑ 9704 [PS]	Because/Theme Without a Name	1964	5.00	10.00	20.00
❑ 9722	Everybody Knows (I Still Love You)/Ol' Sol	1964	3.00	6.00	12.00
❑ 9722 [PS]	Everybody Knows (I Still Love You)/Ol' Sol	1964	5.00	10.00	20.00
❑ 9739	Any Way You Want It/Crying Over You	1964	3.00	6.00	12.00
❑ 9763	Come Home/Your Turn to Cry	1965	3.00	6.00	12.00
❑ 9763 [PS]	Come Home/Your Turn to Cry	1965	5.00	10.00	20.00
❑ 9786	Reelin' and Rockin'/I'm Thinking	1965	3.00	6.00	12.00
❑ 9811	I Like It Like That/Hurting Inside	1965	3.00	6.00	12.00
❑ 9811 [PS]	I Like It Like That/Hurting Inside	1965	5.00	10.00	20.00
❑ 9833	Catch Us If You Can/On the Move	1965	3.00	6.00	12.00
❑ 9833 [PS]	Catch Us If You Can/On the Move	1965	5.00	10.00	20.00
❑ 9863	Over and Over/I'll Be Yours (My Love)	1965	3.00	6.00	12.00
❑ 9863 [DJ]	Over and Over (same on both sides)	1965	10.00	20.00	40.00
—Promo only on red vinyl					
❑ 9863 [PS]	Over and Over/I'll Be Yours (My Love)	1965	5.00	10.00	20.00
❑ 9863 [PS]	Over and Over	1965	100.00	200.00	400.00
—Promo-only black and white sleeve					
❑ 9882	At the Scene/I Miss You	1966	3.00	6.00	12.00
❑ 9882 [PS]	At the Scene/I Miss You	1966	5.00	10.00	20.00
❑ 10004	Try Too Hard/All Night Long	1966	3.00	6.00	12.00
❑ 10004 [PS]	Try Too Hard/All Night Long	1966	5.00	10.00	20.00
❑ 10031	Please Tell Me Why/Look Before You Leap	1966	3.00	6.00	12.00
❑ 10031 [PS]	Please Tell Me Why/Look Before You Leap	1966	5.00	10.00	20.00
❑ 10053	Satisfied with You/Don't Let Me Down	1966	3.00	6.00	12.00
❑ 10053 [PS]	Satisfied with You/Don't Let Me Down	1966	5.00	10.00	20.00
❑ 10076	Nineteen Days/Sitting Here Baby	1966	3.00	6.00	12.00
❑ 10076 [DJ]	Nineteen Days (same on both sides)	1966	10.00	20.00	40.00
—Promo only on red vinyl					
❑ 10076 [PS]	Nineteen Days/Sitting Here Baby	1966	5.00	10.00	20.00
❑ 10114	I've Got to Have a Reason/Good Time Woman	1966	3.00	6.00	12.00
❑ 10114 [PS]	I've Got to Have a Reason/Good Time Woman	1966	5.00	10.00	20.00
❑ 10144	You Got What It Takes/Doctor Rhythm	1967	3.00	6.00	12.00
❑ 10144 [PS]	You Got What It Takes/Doctor Rhythm	1967	5.00	10.00	20.00

Number	Title (A Side/B Side)	Yr	VG	VG+	NM
❑ 10179	You Must Have Been a Beautiful Baby/Man in the Pin Stripe Suit	1967	3.00	6.00	12.00
❑ 10179 [PS]	You Must Have Been a Beautiful Baby/Man in the Pin Stripe Suit	1967	6.25	12.50	25.00
❑ 10209	A Little Bit Now/You Don't Play Me Around	1967	3.75	7.50	15.00
❑ 10209 [PS]	A Little Bit Now/You Don't Play Me Around	1967	5.00	10.00	20.00
❑ 10244	Red and Blue/Concentration Baby	1967	3.75	7.50	15.00
❑ 10265/60 [DJ]	Everybody Knows/Best of Both Worlds	1968	6.25	12.50	25.00
—B-side by Lulu; odd promo					
❑ 10265	Everybody Knows/Inside and Out	1967	3.75	7.50	15.00
❑ 10265 [PS]	Everybody Knows/Inside and Out	1967	7.50	15.00	30.00
❑ 10325	Please Stay/Forget	1968	3.75	7.50	15.00
❑ 10375	Red Balloon/Maze of Love	1968	3.75	7.50	15.00
❑ 10375 [PS]	Red Balloon/Maze of Love	1968	6.25	12.50	25.00
❑ 10476	Paradise (Is Half As Nice)/34-06	1969	3.75	7.50	15.00
❑ 10476 [PS]	Paradise (Is Half As Nice)/34-06	1969	7.50	15.00	30.00
❑ 10509	If Somebody Loves You/Best Day's Work	1969	3.75	7.50	15.00
❑ 10547	Bring It On Home to Me/Darling, I Love You	1969	3.75	7.50	15.00
❑ 10547 [PS]	Bring It On Home to Me/Darling, I Love You	1969	5.00	10.00	20.00
❑ 10635	Here Comes Summer/Five by Five	1970	3.75	7.50	15.00
❑ 10684	Good Old Rock and Roll (Medley)/One Night	1970	5.00	10.00	20.00
❑ 10684 [PS]	Good Old Rock and Roll (Medley)/One Night	1970	7.50	15.00	30.00
❑ 10704	Southern Man/If You Wanna See Me Cry	1971	10.00	20.00	40.00
❑ 10768	Won't You Be My Lady/Into Your Life	1971	5.00	10.00	20.00
❑ 10894	Rub It In/I'm Sorry Baby	1972	5.00	10.00	20.00
EPIC MEMORY LANE					
❑ 2225	Glad All Over/Bits and Pieces	1972	—	2.00	4.00
❑ 2230	Because/Do You Love Me	1972	—	2.00	4.00
❑ 2234	Any Way You Want It/Can't You See That She's Mine	1972	—	2.00	4.00
❑ 2239	I Like It Like That/Everybody Knows (I Still Love You)	1972	—	2.00	4.00
❑ 2248	Over and Over/Catch Us If You Can	1972	—	2.00	4.00
❑ 2294	Bring It On Home to Me/If Somebody Loves You	1972	—	2.00	4.00
❑ 2313	I Like It Like That/Can't You See That She's Mine	1972	—	2.00	4.00
❑ 2316	Come Home/You Got What It Takes	1972	—	2.00	4.00
HOLLYWOOD					
❑ 65909	Over and Over/You Got What It Takes	1993	—	2.00	4.00
❑ 65909 [PS]	Over and Over/You Got What It Takes	1993	—	3.00	6.00
❑ 65910	I Like It Like That/Reelin' and Rockin'	1993	—	2.00	4.00
❑ 65910 [PS]	I Like It Like That/Reelin' and Rockin'	1993	—	3.00	6.00
❑ 65911	Glad All Over/Bits and Pieces	1993	—	2.00	4.00
❑ 65911 [PS]	Glad All Over/Bits and Pieces	1993	—	3.00	6.00
❑ 65912	Do You Love Me/Can't You See That She's Mine	1993	—	2.00	4.00
❑ 65912 [PS]	Do You Love Me/Can't You See That She's Mine	1993	—	3.00	6.00
❑ 65913	Catch Us If You Can/Try Too Hard	1993	—	2.00	4.00
❑ 65913 [PS]	Catch Us If You Can/Try Too Hard	1993	—	3.00	6.00
❑ 65914	Because/Everybody Knows (I Still Love You)	1993	—	2.00	4.00
❑ 65914 [PS]	Because/Everybody Knows (I Still Love You)	1993	—	3.00	6.00
❑ 65915	Any Way You Want It/Come Home	1993	—	2.00	4.00
❑ 65915 [PS]	Any Way You Want It/Come Home	1993		3.00	6.00
JUBILEE					
❑ 5476	Chaquita/In Your Heart	1964	7.50	15.00	30.00
LAURIE					
❑ 3188	I Walk the Line/First Love	1963	12.50	25.00	50.00
RUST					
❑ 5078	I Walk the Line/First Love	1964	10.00	20.00	40.00

7-Inch Extended Plays

Number	Title (A Side/B Side)	Yr	VG	VG+	NM
EPIC					
❑ E 26185 [PS]	The Dave Clark Five's Greatest Hits	1966	17.50	35.00	70.00
❑ E 26185 [R]	Over and Over/Can't You See That She's Mine/I Like It Like That//Catch Us If You Can/Because/Glad All Over	1966	17.50	35.00	70.00
—33 1/3 rpm, small hole, jukebox edition					
❑ E 26221 [PS]	More Greatest Hits	1966	17.50	35.00	70.00
❑ E 26221 [R]	Try Too Hard/Please Tell Me Why/Reelin' and Rockin'//Satisfied with You/At the Scene/All Night Long	1966	17.50	35.00	70.00
—33 1/3 rpm, small hole, jukebox edition					

CLARK, DEE

Also see THE DELEGATES (3); KOOL GENTS.

Number	Title (A Side/B Side)	Yr	VG	VG+	NM
ABNER					
❑ (no #) [DJ]	Blues Get Off My Shoulder (B-side blank)	1959	25.00	50.00	100.00
—White label; noted as "Special D.J. Release from Latest E.P."					
❑ 1019	Nobody But You/When I Call on You	1958	6.25	12.50	25.00
❑ 1026	Just Keep It Up/Whispering Grass	1959	6.25	12.50	25.00
❑ 1029	Hey Little Girl/If It Wasn't for Love	1959	6.25	12.50	25.00
❑ 1029 [PS]	Hey Little Girl/If It Wasn't for Love	1959	10.00	20.00	40.00
❑ 1032	How About That/Blues Get Off My Shoulder	1959	6.25	12.50	25.00
❑ 1037	At My Front Door/Cling-a-Ling	1960	6.25	12.50	25.00
CHELSEA					
❑ 3025	Ride a Wild Horse/(Instrumental)	1975	—	2.50	5.00
COLUMBIA					
❑ 44200	In These Very Tender Moments/Lost Girl	1967	2.00	4.00	8.00
CONSTELLATION					
❑ 108	Crossfire Time/I'm Going Home	1963	3.00	6.00	12.00
❑ 113	It's Raining/That's My Girl	1964	3.00	6.00	12.00
❑ 120	Come Closer/That's My Girl	1964	3.00	6.00	12.00
❑ 132	Warm Summer Breeze/Heartbreak	1964	3.00	6.00	12.00
❑ 142	Ain't Gonna Be Your Fool/In My Apartment	1964	3.00	6.00	12.00
❑ 147	T.C.B./It's Impossible	1965	3.00	6.00	12.00
❑ 155	I Can't Run Away/She's My Baby	1965	3.00	6.00	12.00
❑ 165	I Don't Need (Nobody Like You)/Hot Potatoe	1966	3.00	6.00	12.00
❑ 173	Old Fashion Love/I'm Goin' Home	1966	3.00	6.00	12.00
FALCON					
❑ 1002	Gloria/Kangaroo Hop	1957	7.50	15.00	30.00
❑ 1005	Seven Nights/24 Boy Friends	1957	10.00	20.00	40.00
❑ 1009	Oh Little Girl/Wondering	1958	10.00	20.00	40.00
LIBERTY					
❑ 56152	24 Hours of Loneliness/Where Did All the Good Times Go	1970	—	2.50	5.00
UNITED ARTISTS					
❑ 50759	You Can Make Me Feel So Good/Old Time Religion	1971	—	2.50	5.00
VEE JAY					
❑ 355	You're Looking Good/Gloria	1960	3.75	7.50	15.00
❑ 372	Your Friends/Because I Love You	1961	3.75	7.50	15.00
❑ 383	Raindrops/I Want to Love You	1961	5.00	10.00	20.00
❑ 394	Gotos Delluvia (Raindrops)/Livin' with Vivian	1961	3.75	7.50	15.00
—B-side by Al Smith					
❑ 409	Don't Walk Away from Me/You're Telling Our Secrets	1961	3.75	7.50	15.00
❑ 428	You Are Like the Wind/Drums in My Heart	1962	3.75	7.50	15.00
❑ 443	Dance On Little Girl/Fever	1962	3.75	7.50	15.00
❑ 462	I'm Going Back to School/Nobody But You	1962	3.75	7.50	15.00
❑ 487	I'm a Soldier Boy/Shook Up Over You	1963	3.75	7.50	15.00
❑ 532	How Is He Treating You/The Jones Boy	1963	3.75	7.50	15.00
❑ 548	Walking My Dog/Nobody But Me	1963	3.75	7.50	15.00
WAND					
❑ 1177	Nobody But You (Part 1)/Nobody But You (Part 2)	1968	2.00	4.00	8.00
WARNER BROS.					
❑ 7720	Raindrops '73/I'm a Happy Man	1973	—	2.50	5.00

7-Inch Extended Plays

Number	Title (A Side/B Side)	Yr	VG	VG+	NM
ABNER					
❑ 900	(contents unknown)	1959	30.00	60.00	120.00
❑ 900 [PS]	Dee Clark	1959	30.00	60.00	120.00

CLARK, DOUG, AND THE HOT NUTS

Number	Title (A Side/B Side)	Yr	VG	VG+	NM
JUBILEE					
❑ 5536	Baby Let Me Bang Your Box Part 1/Baby Let Me Bang Your Box Part 2	1966	5.00	10.00	20.00
❑ 5546	Milk the Cow/Go, Doug, Go	1966	3.75	7.50	15.00

CLARK, GENE

Also see THE BYRDS.

Number	Title (A Side/B Side)	Yr	VG	VG+	NM
ASYLUM					
❑ 45222	Life's Greatest Fool/From a Silver Petal	1974	—	2.50	5.00
COLUMBIA					
❑ 43903	Echoes/I Found You	1966	3.75	7.50	15.00
❑ 43903 [PS]	Echoes/I Found You	1966	75.00	150.00	300.00
❑ 44088	Is Yours Mine/So You Say You Lost Your Baby	1967	3.75	7.50	15.00
RSO					
❑ 876	Home Run King/Lonely Saturday	1977	—	2.50	5.00

CLARK, PETULA

Number	Title (A Side/B Side)	Yr	VG	VG+	NM
ABC DUNHILL					
❑ 15007	Never Been a Horse That Couldn't Be Rode/I'm the Woman You Need	1974	—	2.50	5.00
❑ 15019	Loving Arms/I'm the Woman You Need	1974	—	2.50	5.00
CORAL					
❑ 60971	Song of the Mermaid/Tell Me Truly	1953	6.25	12.50	25.00
❑ 61077	Where Did My Snowman Go/Three Little Kittens	1953	6.25	12.50	25.00
ESSEX					
❑ (# unknown)	Majorca/Fascinating Rhythm	1955	—	—	—
—We have not been able to confirm this record's existence. Readers?					
IMPERIAL					
❑ 5582	The Little Blue Man/Baby Lover	1959	5.00	10.00	20.00
❑ 5600	Where Do I Go from Here/Mama's Talkin' Soft	1959	5.00	10.00	20.00
❑ 5655	Now That I Need You/I Love a Violin	1960	5.00	10.00	20.00
KING					
❑ 1371	The Little Shoemaker/Helpless	1954	6.25	12.50	25.00
LAURIE					
❑ 3143	Jumble Sale/The Road	1962	3.75	7.50	15.00
❑ 3156	I Will Follow Him/Darling Cheri	1963	3.75	7.50	15.00
❑ 3236	Elle Est Finie/J'ai Tout Oublie	1964	3.75	7.50	15.00
❑ 3259	In Love/The Road	1964	3.75	7.50	15.00
❑ 3316	In Love/Darling Cheri	1965	3.00	6.00	12.00
❑ 3573	Jumble Sale/The Road	1971	—	3.00	6.00
LONDON INT'L.					
❑ 10504	My Friend the Sea/With All My Love	1962	3.75	7.50	15.00
❑ 10510	I'm Counting on You/Some Other World	1962	3.75	7.50	15.00
❑ 10516	Tender Love/Whistlin' for the Moon	1962	3.75	7.50	15.00
MGM					
❑ 12049	The Pendulum Song/Romance in Rome	1955	6.25	12.50	25.00
❑ 14392	My Guy/Little Bit of Lovin'	1972	—	2.50	5.00
❑ 14431	Wedding Song (There Is Love)/Song Without End	1972	—	2.50	5.00
❑ 14511	Serenade of Love/I Can't Remember	1973	—	2.50	5.00
❑ 14577	Gratification/I Can't Remember	1973	—	2.50	5.00
❑ 14673	Silver Spoon/Fixing to Live	1973	—	2.50	5.00
❑ 14708	Come On Home/The Old Fashioned Way	1974	—	2.50	5.00
SCOTTI BROS.					
❑ 02676	Natural Love/Because I Love Him	1982	—	2.00	4.00
❑ 02979	Blue Eyes Crying in the Rain/Love Won't Always Pass You By	1982	—	2.00	4.00
❑ 03171	Dreamin' with My Eyes Wide Open/Afterglow	1982	—	2.00	4.00
WARNER BROS.					
❑ 5494	Downtown/You'd Better Love Me	1964	3.75	7.50	15.00
—Originals have red labels with arrows					
❑ 5494	Downtown/You'd Better Love Me	1964	2.50	5.00	10.00
—Later pressings have orange labels					
❑ 5612	I Know a Place/Jack and John	1965	2.50	5.00	10.00
❑ 5643	You'd Better Come Home/Heart	1965	2.50	5.00	10.00
❑ 5661	Round Every Corner/Two Rivers	1965	2.50	5.00	10.00
❑ 5684	My Love/Where Am I Going	1965	2.50	5.00	10.00
❑ 5802	A Sign of the Times/Time for Love	1966	2.50	5.00	10.00
❑ 5835	I Couldn't Live Without Your Love/Your Way of Life	1966	2.50	5.00	10.00
❑ 5863	Who Am I/Love Is a Long Journey	1966	2.50	5.00	10.00

Number	Title (A Side/B Side)	Yr	VG	VG+	NM
❑ 5882	Color My World/Take Me Home Again	1966	2.50	5.00	10.00
❑ 7002	This Is My Song/High	1967	2.50	5.00	10.00
❑ 7049	Don't Sleep in the Subway/Here Comes the Morning	1967	2.50	5.00	10.00
❑ 7073	The Cat in the Window (The Bird in the Sky)/ Fancy Dancin' Man	1967	2.50	5.00	10.00
❑ 7097	The Other Man's Grass Is Always Greener/At the Crossroads	1967	2.50	5.00	10.00
❑ 7170	Kiss Me Goodbye/I've Got Love Going for Me	1968	2.50	5.00	10.00
—Originals have orange labels					
❑ 7170	Kiss Me Goodbye/I've Got Love Going for Me	1968	2.00	4.00	8.00
—Later pressings have green labels with "W7" logo					
❑ 7216	Don't Give Up/Every Time I See a Rainbow	1968	2.00	4.00	8.00
❑ 7244	American Boys/Look to the Sky	1968	2.00	4.00	8.00
❑ 7275	Happy Heart/Love Is the Only Thing	1969	2.00	4.00	8.00
❑ 7310	Look at Mine/If Somebody Loves You	1969	2.00	4.00	8.00
❑ 7343	No One Better Than You/Things Bringht and Beautiful	1969	2.00	4.00	8.00
❑ 7422	Beautiful Sounds/The Song Is Love	1970	2.00	4.00	8.00
❑ 7467	The Song of My Life/Couldn't Sleep	1971	2.00	4.00	8.00
❑ 7484	I Don't Know How to Love Him (Superstar)/Maybe	1971	2.00	4.00	8.00
WARWICK					
❑ 652	Romeo/Isn't It a Lovely Day	1961	5.00	10.00	20.00

CLARK, ROY

Number	Title (A Side/B Side)	Yr	VG	VG+	NM
ABC					
❑ 12328	Must You Throw Dirt in My Face/Lazy River	1978	—	2.00	4.00
❑ 12365	Where Have You Been All of My Life/Near You	1978	—	2.00	4.00
❑ 12402	The Happy Days/Shoulder to Shoulder (Arm and Arm)	1978	—	2.00	4.00
❑ 12437	Is It Hot in Here (Or Is It Me)/Jolly Ho (Happy Hour)	1978	—	2.00	4.00
—With Buck Trent					
ABC DOT					
❑ 17530	Dear God/Take Good Care of Her	1974	—	2.00	4.00
❑ 17545	You're Gonna Love Yourself in the Morning/ Banjoy	1975	—	2.00	4.00
❑ 17565	Heart to Heart/Someone Cares for You	1975	—	2.00	4.00
❑ 17605	If I Had to Do It All Over Again/It Sure Looks Good on You	1976	—	2.00	4.00
❑ 17626	Think Summer/Whatever Happened to Gauze	1976	—	2.00	4.00
❑ 17647	I Have a Dream, I Have a Love/Half a Love	1976	—	2.00	4.00
❑ 17712	We Can't Build a Fire in the Rain/I'm So Lonesome I Could Cry	1977	—	2.00	4.00
CAPITOL					
❑ 4595	Under the Double Eagle/Black Sapphire	1961	3.00	6.00	12.00
❑ 4670	Texas Twist/Wildwood Twist	1961	3.00	6.00	12.00
❑ 4794	Talk About a Party/As Long As I'm Movin'	1962	3.00	6.00	12.00
❑ 4956	Tips of My Fingers/Spooky Movies	1963	2.50	5.00	10.00
❑ 5047	Good Time Charlie/Application for Love	1963	2.50	5.00	10.00
❑ 5099	Through the Eyes of a Fool/Sweet Violets	1964	2.50	5.00	10.00
❑ 5163	Take Me As I Am/If You'll Pardon Me	1964	2.50	5.00	10.00
❑ 5233	It's My Way/I'm Forgetting Now	1964	2.50	5.00	10.00
❑ 5300	Alabama Jubilee/Down Yonder	1964	2.50	5.00	10.00
❑ 5350	When the Wind Blows In Chicago/Live Fast Love Hard	1965	2.50	5.00	10.00
❑ 5445	The Color of Her Love Is Blue/Too Pooped to Pop	1965	2.50	5.00	10.00
❑ 5512	So Much to Remember/Turn Around and Look Again	1965	2.50	5.00	10.00
❑ 5565	Malaguena/Overdue Blues	1965	2.50	5.00	10.00
❑ 5619	Rose Colored Glasses/Everybody Watches Me	1966	2.50	5.00	10.00
❑ 5664	Hey Sweet Thing/If You Want It, Come and Get It	1966	2.50	5.00	10.00
—With Mary Taylor					
❑ 5770	St. Louis Blues/Just a Closer Walk with Thee	1966	2.50	5.00	10.00
CHURCHILL					
❑ 52469	Another Lonely Night With You/(Instrumental)	1984	—	2.00	4.00
❑ 94002	Paradise Knife and Gun Club/I Don't Care	1982	—	2.50	5.00
❑ 94007	Tennessee Saturday Night/Tumbling Tumbleweeds	1982	—	2.50	5.00
❑ 94007 [PS]	Tennessee Saturday Night/Tumbling Tumbleweeds	1982	—	3.00	6.00
❑ 94011	Here We Go Again/Early in the Morning	1982	—	2.50	5.00
❑ 94016	Christmas Wouldn't Be Christmas Without You/ A Way Without Words	1982	—	3.00	6.00
❑ 94017	I'm a Booger/A Way Without Words	1983	—	2.50	5.00
❑ 94025	Wildwood Flower/Southern Nights	1983	—	2.50	5.00
DOT					
❑ 17117	Do You Believe This Town/It Just Happened That Way	1968	—	3.00	6.00
❑ 17187	Love Is Just a State of Mind/Look to the Sky	1968	—	3.00	6.00
❑ 17246	Yesterday, When I Was Young/Just Another Man	1969	—	2.50	5.00
❑ 17299	September Song/For the Life of Me	1969	—	2.50	5.00
❑ 17324	Right or Left at Oak Street/I Need to Be Needed	1969	—	2.50	5.00
❑ 17335	Then She's a Lover/Say Amen	1969	—	2.50	5.00
❑ 17349	I Never Picked Cotton/Lonesome Too Long	1970	—	2.50	5.00
❑ 17355	Thank God and Greyhound/Strangers	1970	—	2.50	5.00
❑ 17368	A Simple Thing As Love/I'd Fight the World	1971	—	2.50	5.00
❑ 17370	(Where Do I Begin) Love Story/Theme from "Love Story"	1971	—	2.50	5.00
❑ 17386	She Cried/Back in the Race	1971	—	2.50	5.00
❑ 17395	Magnificent Sanctuary Bird/Be Ready	1971	—	2.50	5.00
❑ 17413	I'll Take the Time/Ode to a Critter	1972	—	2.50	5.00
❑ 17426	The Lawrence Welk—Hee Haw Counter-Revolution Polka/When the Wind Blows	1972	—	2.50	5.00
❑ 17449	Come Live with Me/Darby's Castle	1973	—	2.50	5.00
❑ 17458	Riders in the Sky/Roy's Guitar Boogie	1973	—	2.50	5.00
❑ 17480	Somewhere Between Love and Tomorrow/I'll Paint You a Song	1973	—	2.50	5.00
❑ 17498	Honeymoon Feelin'/I Really Don't Want to Know	1974	—	2.50	5.00
❑ 17518	The Great Divide/Chomp'n	1974	—	2.50	5.00
HALLMARK					
❑ 0001	What a Wonderful World/(Instrumental)	1989	—	2.50	5.00
❑ 0004	But, She Loves Me/(B-side unknown)	1989	—	2.50	5.00
MCA					
❑ 41122	Caldonia/Four O'Clock in the Morning	1979	—	2.00	4.00
❑ 41153	Chain Gang of Love/Why Don't We Go Somewhere and Love	1979	—	2.00	4.00
❑ 41208	If There Were Only Time for Love/Then I'll Be Over You	1980	—	2.00	4.00
❑ 41288	For Love's Own Sake/They'll Never Take Her Love from Me	1980	—	2.00	4.00
❑ 51031	I Ain't Got Nobody/Play Me a Little Traveling Music	1980	—	2.00	4.00
❑ 51079	She Can't Give It Away/Dig a Little Deeper in the Well	1981	—	2.00	4.00
❑ 51111	Love Takes Two/Come Sundown	1981	—	2.00	4.00
SILVER DOLLAR					
❑ 0001	Tobacco Road/Black Sapphire	1986	—	2.50	5.00
❑ 0001 [PS]	Tobacco Road/Black Sapphire	1986	2.00	4.00	8.00
❑ 0004	Juke Box Saturday Night/Night Life	1986	—	2.50	5.00
SONGBIRD					
❑ 51167	The Last Word in Jesus Is Us/Shinin' Face	1981	—	2.00	4.00
TOWER					
❑ 331	Orange Blossom Special/The Great Pretender	1967	2.00	4.00	8.00

CLARK, SANFORD

Number	Title (A Side/B Side)	Yr	VG	VG+	NM
DOT					
❑ 15481	The Fool/Lonesome for a Letter	1956	12.50	25.00	50.00
—Originals have maroon labels					
❑ 15481	The Fool/Lonesome for a Letter	1956	6.25	12.50	25.00
—Second pressings have black labels					
❑ 15516	A Cheat/Usta Be My Baby	1956	6.25	12.50	25.00
❑ 15534	Oooo Baby/9 Lb. Hammer	1957	6.25	12.50	25.00
❑ 15556	The Glory of Love/Darling Dear	1957	6.25	12.50	25.00
❑ 15585	Love Charms/Loo-Be-Doo	1957	6.25	12.50	25.00
❑ 15646	Swanee River Rock/The Man Who Made an Angel Cry	1957	6.25	12.50	25.00
❑ 15738	Modern Romance/Travelin' Man	1958	37.50	75.00	150.00
JAMIE					
❑ 1107	Sing 'Em Some Blues/Still as the Night	1958	5.00	10.00	20.00
❑ 1120	Bad Luck/My Jealousy	1959	5.00	10.00	20.00
❑ 1129	Run Boy Run/New Kind of Fool	1959	5.00	10.00	20.00
❑ 1153	Go On Home/Pledging My Love	1960	5.00	10.00	20.00
LHI					
❑ 1203	The Son of Hickory Holler's Tramp/Black Widow Spider	1968	2.00	4.00	8.00
❑ 1213	Love Me Till Then/Farm Labor Camp No. 2	1968	2.00	4.00	8.00
MCI					
❑ 1003	The Fool/Lonesome for a Letter	1956	50.00	100.00	200.00
RAMCO					
❑ 1972	The Fool '66/Step Aside	1966	3.75	7.50	15.00
❑ 1976	Shades/Once Upon a Time	1966	3.00	6.00	12.00
❑ 1979	They Call Me Country/Climbin' the Walls	1967	3.00	6.00	12.00
❑ 1987	It's Nothing to Me/Calling All Hearts	1967	3.00	6.00	12.00
❑ 1992	The Big Lie/Where's the Floor	1967	3.00	6.00	12.00
TREY					
❑ 3016	It Hurts Me Too/Guess It's Love	1961	5.00	10.00	20.00
WARNER BROS.					
❑ 5473	She Taught Me/Just Blessin'	1964	3.75	7.50	15.00
❑ 5624	Houston/Hard Feelings	1965	3.75	7.50	15.00

CLARKE, ALLAN

Also see THE HOLLIES.

Number	Title (A Side/B Side)	Yr	VG	VG+	NM
ASYLUM					
❑ 45313	Light a Light/If You Think You Know How to Love Me	1976	—	2.00	4.00
ATLANTIC					
❑ 3459	(I Will Be Your) Shadow in the Street/The Passenger	1978	—	2.00	4.00
❑ 3497	I Wasn't Born Yesterday/The Man Who Manufactured Daydreams	1978	—	2.00	4.00
❑ 3522	I'm Betting My Life on You/Who's Goin' Out the Back Door	1978	—	2.00	4.00
ELEKTRA					
❑ 46617	Slipstream/Imagination's Child	1979	—	2.00	4.00
❑ 47019	The Only Ones/Driving the Doomsday Cars	1980	—	2.00	4.00
EPIC					
❑ 10914	Baby It's Alright with Me/Ruby	1972	—	2.00	4.00

CLASS-AIRES, THE

Number	Title (A Side/B Side)	Yr	VG	VG+	NM
HONEY BEE					
❑ (# unknown)	Too Old to Cry/My Tears Start to Fall	195?	500.00	1000.	2000.

CLASS-NOTES, THE

Number	Title (A Side/B Side)	Yr	VG	VG+	NM
DOT					
❑ 15786	You Inspire Me/Goodness Gracious	1958	7.50	15.00	30.00
HAMILTON					
❑ 50011	Take It Back/Bessie's House	1959	15.00	30.00	60.00

CLASSIC IV, THE

Number	Title (A Side/B Side)	Yr	VG	VG+	NM
ALGONQUIN					
❑ 1650	Limbo Under The Christmas Tree/Early Christmas	1962	7.50	15.00	30.00
TWIST					
❑ 1001	Island of Paradise/Heavenly Bliss	1962	25.00	50.00	100.00

CLASSICS, THE (1)

Brooklyn vocal group led by Emil Stucchio.

Number	Title (A Side/B Side)	Yr	VG	VG+	NM
BED-STUY					
❑ 222	Again/The Way You Look Tonight	196?	2.50	5.00	10.00
DART					
❑ 1015	So in Love/Cinderella	1960	7.50	15.00	30.00
❑ 1024	Life Is But a Dream, Sweetheart/That's the Way	1961	50.00	100.00	200.00
❑ 1032	Angel Angela/Eenie Minie Mo	1961	12.50	25.00	50.00

Number	Title (A Side/B Side)	Yr	VG	VG+	NM
MERCURY					
❑ 71829	Life Is But a Dream, Sweetheart/That's the Way	1961	6.25	12.50	25.00
MUSICNOTE					
❑ 118	P.S. I Love You/Wrap Your Troubles in Dreams	1963	6.25	12.50	25.00
❑ 1116	Till Then/Eenie Minie Mo	1963	6.25	12.50	25.00
—Black vinyl, blue label					
❑ 1116	Till Then/Eenie Minie Mo	1963	25.00	50.00	100.00
—Gold vinyl					
❑ 1116	Till Then/Eenie Minie Mo	1963	37.50	75.00	150.00
—Multi-color vinyl					
❑ 1116	Till Then/Eenie Minie Mo	1963	7.50	15.00	30.00
—Black vinyl, yellow label					
MUSICTONE					
❑ 1114	So in Love/Cinderella	1963	5.00	10.00	20.00
❑ 6131	Too Young/Who's Laughing, Who's Crying	1964	5.00	10.00	20.00
PICCOLO					
❑ 500	I Apologize/Love for Today	1965	6.25	12.50	25.00
STORK					
❑ 2	You'll Never Know/Dancing with You	1964	6.25	12.50	25.00
STREAM LINE					
❑ 1028	Life Is But a Dream, Sweetheart/Nuttin' in the Noggin	1961	6.25	12.50	25.00

CLASSICS, THE (2)

With LOU CHRISTIE.

Number	Title (A Side/B Side)	Yr	VG	VG+	NM
STARR					
❑ 508	Close Your Eyes/Funny Things	1960	50.00	100.00	200.00
—Reissued on Alcar with Lou Christie's name prominently mentioned					

CLASSICS, THE (3)

Canadian group.

Number	Title (A Side/B Side)	Yr	VG	VG+	NM
JERDEN					
❑ 742	Till I Met You/It Didn't Take Much	1964	7.50	15.00	30.00

CLASSICS, THE (U)

Some of these could be group (1); none of them are group (2); probably none of these are group (3).

Number	Title (A Side/B Side)	Yr	VG	VG+	NM
CLASS					
❑ 219	If Only the Sky Was a Mirror/Gosh, But This Is Love	1958	17.50	35.00	70.00
CREST					
❑ 1063	Let Me Dream/You're the Prettiest One	1959	20.00	40.00	80.00
MV					
❑ 1000	Christmas Is Here/(B-side unknown)	19??	2.50	5.00	10.00
PROMO					
❑ 1010	Blue Moon/Little Boy Lost	1961	7.50	15.00	30.00
—As "Herb Lance and the Classics"					
RO-ANN					
❑ 1002	Je Vous Aime/Burning Desire	1959	250.00	500.00	1000.
SHELTER					
❑ 7318	Mr. Fire Coal-Man/Flashing My Whip	1972	—	2.50	5.00
—B-side by Hugh Roy					
TOP RANK					
❑ 2061	You're Everything/Burning Love	1960	6.25	12.50	25.00

CLASSICS IV

Number	Title (A Side/B Side)	Yr	VG	VG+	NM
ARLEN					
❑ 746	Don't Make Me Wait/It's Too Late	1964	5.00	10.00	20.00
CAPITOL					
❑ 5710	Cry Baby/Pollyanna	1966	3.75	7.50	15.00
—As "The Classics"					
❑ 5816	Little Darlin'/Nothing to Lose	1966	3.75	7.50	15.00
IMPERIAL					
❑ 66259	Spooky/Poor People	1967	2.00	4.00	8.00
❑ 66293	Soul Train/Strange Changes	1968	2.00	4.00	8.00
❑ 66304	Mama's and Papa's/Waves	1968	2.00	4.00	8.00
❑ 66328	Stormy/Ladies' Man	1968	5.00	10.00	20.00
❑ 66328	Stormy/24 Hours of Loneliness	1968	2.00	4.00	8.00
❑ 66352	Traces/Mary, Mary Row Your Boat	1969	2.00	4.00	8.00
❑ 66378	Everyday With You Girl/Sentimental Lady	1969	2.00	4.00	8.00
❑ 66393	Change of Heart/Rainy Day	1969	—	3.00	6.00
—Starting here, "Dennis Yost and the Classics IV"					
❑ 66424	Midnight/The Comic	1969	—	3.00	6.00
❑ 66439	The Funniest Thing/Nobody Loves You But Me	1970	—	3.00	6.00
LIBERTY					
❑ 56182	God Knows I Loved Her/We Miss You	1970	—	3.00	6.00
❑ 56200	Where Did All the Good Times Go/Ain't It the Truth	1970	—	3.00	6.00
MGM					
❑ 14785	My First Day Without You/Lovin' Each Other	1975	—	2.00	4.00
MGM SOUTH					
❑ 7002	What Am I Crying For/All in Your Mind	1972	—	2.50	5.00
❑ 7012	Rosanna/One Man Show	1973	—	2.50	5.00
❑ 7016	Save the Sunlight/Make Me Believe It	1973	—	2.50	5.00
❑ 7020	I Knew It Would Happen/Love Me or Leave Me Alone	1973	—	2.50	5.00
❑ 7027	It's Now Winter's Day/Losing My Mind	1974	—	2.50	5.00
UNITED ARTISTS					
❑ 0125	Stormy/Spooky	1973	—	2.00	4.00
—"Silver Spotlight Series" reissue					
❑ 0126	Traces/Everyday with You Girl	1973	—	2.00	4.00
—"Silver Spotlight Series" reissue					
❑ 50777	Most of All/It's Time for Love	1971	—	2.50	5.00
❑ 50805	Cherry Hill Park/Pick Up the Pieces	1971	—	2.50	5.00

CLAY, CASSIUS

Number	Title (A Side/B Side)	Yr	VG	VG+	NM
COLUMBIA					
❑ 43007	Stand By Me/I Am the Greatest	1964	6.25	12.50	25.00
❑ 43007 [PS]	Stand By Me/I Am the Greatest	1964	12.50	25.00	50.00
❑ ZSP 75717/77185 [DJ]	The Prediction/Will the Real Sonny Liston Please Fall Down	1964	10.00	20.00	40.00
❑ ZSP 75717/77185 [PS]	The Prediction/Will the Real Sonny Liston Please Fall Down	1964	20.00	40.00	80.00

CLAY, CHRIS

Number	Title (A Side/B Side)	Yr	VG	VG+	NM
VELTONE					
❑ 111	Santa Under Analysis Part 1/Santa Under Analysis Part 2	1960	6.25	12.50	25.00

CLAY, JOE

Number	Title (A Side/B Side)	Yr	VG	VG+	NM
VIK					
❑ 0211	Duck Tail/Sixteen Chicks	1956	25.00	50.00	100.00
❑ 0218	Get On the Right Track/Cracker Jack	1956	25.00	50.00	100.00

CLAY, OTIS

Number	Title (A Side/B Side)	Yr	VG	VG+	NM
COTILLION					
❑ 44001	She's About a Mover/You Don't Miss Your Water	1968	2.00	4.00	8.00
❑ 44009	Do Right Woman, Do Right Man/That Kind of Lovin'	1968	—	3.50	7.00
❑ 44068	Pouring Water on a Drowning Man/Hard Working Women	1970	—	3.50	7.00
❑ 44101	Is It Over/I'm Qualified	1970	—	3.50	7.00
DAKAR					
❑ 610	Baby Jane/You Hurt Me for the Last Time	1969	—	3.50	7.00
ECHO					
❑ 2002	Check It Out/(B-side unknown)	1975	2.50	5.00	10.00
GLADES					
❑ 1736	All I Need Is You/Special Kind of Soul	1976	2.50	5.00	10.00
HI					
❑ 2206	Home Is Where the Heart Is/Brand New Thing	1972	—	3.00	6.00
❑ 2214	Precious Precious/Too Many Hands	1972	—	3.00	6.00
❑ 2226	Trying to Live My Life Without You/Let Me Be the One	1972	—	3.50	7.00
❑ 2239	I Can't Make It Alone/I Didn't Know the Meaning of Pain	1973	—	3.00	6.00
❑ 2252	If I Could Reach Out/I Die a Little Bit Each Day	1973	—	3.00	6.00
❑ 2266	Woman Don't Live Here No More/You Can't Escape the Hands of Love	1974	—	3.00	6.00
❑ 2270	You Did Something to Me/I Was Jealous	1974	—	3.00	6.00
KAYVETTE					
❑ 5130	All Because of Your Love/Today My World Fell	1977	—	2.50	5.00
❑ 5133	Let Me In/Sweet Woman's Love	1977	—	2.50	5.00
ONE-DERFUL!					
❑ 4834	Three Is a Crowd/Flame in Your Heart	1965	2.50	5.00	10.00
❑ 4837	I Paid the Price/Tired of Falling In (And Out of) Love	1966	2.50	5.00	10.00
❑ 4841	I Testify/I'm Satisfied	1966	2.50	5.00	10.00
❑ 4846	Flame in Your Heart/It's Easier Said, Than Done	1967	2.00	4.00	8.00
❑ 4848	That's How It Is (When You're in Love)/Show Place	1967	2.00	4.00	8.00
❑ 4850	A Lasting Love/Got to Find a Way	1967	2.00	4.00	8.00
❑ 4852	Don't Pass Me By/That'll Get You What You Want	1968	2.00	4.00	8.00

CLAY, TOM

Number	Title (A Side/B Side)	Yr	VG	VG+	NM
BIG TOP					
❑ 3055	The Little Boy/That's All	1960	5.00	10.00	20.00
CHANT					
❑ 103	Marry Me/(B-side unknown)	1959	25.00	50.00	100.00
IBBB					
❑ ZTSC 97436/7	Remember, We Don't Like Them, We Love Them: Official IBBB Interview	1964	37.50	75.00	150.00
—Interviews with the Beatles					
MOWEST					
❑ 5002	What the World Needs Now Is Love/Abraham, Martin and John//The Victors	1971	—	3.00	6.00
—Mostly orange label					
❑ 5002	What the World Needs Now Is Love/Abraham, Martin and John//The Victors	1971	—	2.50	5.00
—Blue and yellow label					
❑ 5007	Whatever Happened to Love/Baby I Need Your Loving	1971	—	2.00	4.00

CLAYTON-THOMAS, DAVID

Also see BLOOD, SWEAT AND TEARS.

Number	Title (A Side/B Side)	Yr	VG	VG+	NM
ATCO					
❑ 6347	Hey Hey Hey Hey/Walk That Walk	1965	3.75	7.50	15.00
COLUMBIA					
❑ 45569	Sing a Song/We're All Meat from the Same Bone	1972	—	2.50	5.00
❑ 45603	North Beach Racetrack/Magnificent Sanctuary Band	1972	—	2.50	5.00
❑ 45675	Yesterday's Music/Falling by Degrees	1972	—	2.50	5.00
DECCA					
❑ 32556	Say Boss Man/Done Somebody Wrong	1969	2.50	5.00	10.00
EPIC					
❑ 03792	I Can't Blame a Broken Heart/Some Hearts Get All the Breaks	1983	—	2.00	4.00
RCA VICTOR					
❑ APBO-0078	Workin' on the Railroad/Prof. Longhair	1973	—	2.00	4.00
❑ APBO-0216	Yolanda/Workin' on the Railroad	1974	—	2.00	4.00
❑ APBO-0296	Take the Money and Run/Anytime... Babe	1974	—	2.00	4.00
❑ 74-0966	Hernando's Hideaway/Harmony Junction	1973	—	2.00	4.00
ROULETTE					
❑ 7048	No, No, No/Monopoly	1969	2.50	5.00	10.00
TOWER					
❑ 206	Take Me Back/Out of the Sunshine	1966	3.00	6.00	12.00
❑ 263	Born with the Blues/Brainwashed	1966	3.00	6.00	12.00

CLEAR LIGHT

Also see CLIFF DeYOUNG.

Number	Title (A Side/B Side)	Yr	VG	VG+	NM
ELEKTRA					
❑ 45622	She's Ready to Be Free/Black Roses	1967	3.00	6.00	12.00
❑ 45626	They Who Have Nothing/Ballad of Freddie and Larry	1968	3.00	6.00	12.00

CLEE-SHAYS, THE

Number	Title (A Side/B Side)	Yr	VG	VG+	NM
TRIUMPH					
❑ 65	The Man from U.N.C.L.E./Dynamite	1966	5.00	10.00	20.00

CLEFS, THE

Number	Title (A Side/B Side)	Yr	VG	VG+	NM
CHESS					
❑ 1521	We Three/(B-side unknown)	1952	100.00	200.00	400.00

CLEFS OF LAVENDER HILL, THE

Number	Title (A Side/B Side)	Yr	VG	VG+	NM
DATE					
❑ 1510	Stop! — Get a Ticket/First Tell Me Why	1966	5.00	10.00	20.00
❑ 1530	One More Time/So I'll Try	1966	5.00	10.00	20.00
❑ 1533	Play with Fire/It Won't Be Long	1966	5.00	10.00	20.00
❑ 1567	Gimme One Good Reason/Oh, Say My Love	1967	5.00	10.00	20.00
THAMES					
❑ 100	Stop! — Get a Ticket/First Tell Me Why	1966	10.00	20.00	40.00

CLEFTONES, THE

Number	Title (A Side/B Side)	Yr	VG	VG+	NM
CLASSIC ARTISTS					
❑ 121	She's So Fine/Trudy	1990	—	2.00	4.00
GEE					
❑ 1000	You Baby You/I Was Dreaming	1955	15.00	30.00	60.00
❑ 1011	Little Girl of Mine/You're Driving Me Mad	1956	10.00	20.00	40.00
❑ 1016	Can't We Be Sweethearts/Niki-Hoeky	1956	10.00	20.00	40.00
❑ 1025	String Around My Heart/Happy Memories	1956	10.00	20.00	40.00
❑ 1031	Why Do You Do Me Like You Do/I Like Your Style of Making Love	1957	10.00	20.00	40.00
❑ 1038	See You Next Year/Ten Pairs of Shoes	1957	10.00	20.00	40.00
❑ 1041	Hey Babe/What Did I Do That Was Wrong	1957	10.00	20.00	40.00
❑ 1048	Lover Boy/Beginners in Love	1958	7.50	15.00	30.00
❑ 1064	Heart and Soul/How Do You Feel	1961	6.25	12.50	25.00
❑ 1067	(I Love You) For Sentimental Reasons/'Deed I Do	1961	5.00	10.00	20.00
❑ 1074	Earth Angel/Blues in the Night	1961	5.00	10.00	20.00
❑ 1077	Again/Do You	1961	5.00	10.00	20.00
❑ 1079	Lover Come Back to Me/There She Goes	1962	5.00	10.00	20.00
❑ 1080	How Deep Is the Ocean/Some Kinda Blue	1962	5.00	10.00	20.00
OLD TOWN					
❑ 1011	The Masquerade Is Over/My Dearest Darling	1955	125.00	250.00	500.00
ROULETTE					
❑ 4094	Trudy/She's So Fine	1958	6.25	12.50	25.00
❑ 4161	Mish Mash Baby/Cuzin Casanova	1959	6.25	12.50	25.00
❑ 4302	She's Gone/Shadows on the Very Last Row	1960	6.25	12.50	25.00
WARE					
❑ 6001	She's Forgotten You/Right from the Git Go	1964	3.75	7.50	15.00

CLEMENT, JACK

Number	Title (A Side/B Side)	Yr	VG	VG+	NM
ELEKTRA					
❑ 45397	Just Because You Ask Me To/When I Dream	1977	—	2.00	4.00
❑ 45474	We Must Believe in Magic/When I Dream	1978	—	2.00	4.00
❑ 45518	All I Want to Do in Life/It'll Be Her	1978	—	2.00	4.00
❑ 45547	Gone Girl/There She Goes	1978	—	2.00	4.00
HALLWAY					
❑ 1796	Time After Time After Time/My Voice Is Changing	1963	3.75	7.50	15.00
JMI					
❑ 10	The One on the Right Is the One on the Left/The Child That's in the Manger	1972	—	3.00	6.00
❑ 14	She Thinks I Still Care/Never Give a Heartache a Place to Go	1973	—	3.00	6.00
❑ 20	Steal Away/(B-side unknown)	1973	—	3.00	6.00
❑ 43	The One on the Right Is on the Left/Feet	1974	—	3.00	6.00
RCA VICTOR					
❑ 47-7602	Whole Lotta Lookin'/Edge of Town	1959	3.75	7.50	15.00
SUN					
❑ 291	Ten Years/Your Lover Boy	1958	6.25	12.50	25.00
❑ 311	The Black Haired Man/Wrong	1958	6.25	12.50	25.00

CLICKETTES, THE

Number	Title (A Side/B Side)	Yr	VG	VG+	NM
CHECKER					
❑ 1060	I Just Can't Help It/(Instrumental)	1963	5.00	10.00	20.00
DICE					
❑ 83/84	Jive Time Turkey/A Teenager's First Love	1959	37.50	75.00	150.00
❑ 92/93	To Be a Part of You/Because of My Best Friend	1959	30.00	60.00	120.00
❑ 94/95	Warm, Soft and Lovely/Why Oh Why	1959	30.00	60.00	120.00
❑ 96/97	Lover's Prayer/Grateful	1959	37.50	75.00	150.00
—With distribution by Memo Record Corp.					
❑ 96/97	Lover's Prayer/Grateful	1959	17.50	35.00	70.00
❑ 100	But Not for Me/I Love You I Swear	1960	30.00	60.00	120.00
GUYDEN					
❑ 2043	Where Is He/The Lone Lover	1960	7.50	15.00	30.00
TUFF					
❑ 373	I Just Can't Help It/(Instrumental)	1964	5.00	10.00	20.00

CLICKS, THE

Number	Title (A Side/B Side)	Yr	VG	VG+	NM
JOSIE					
❑ 780	Come Back to Me/Peace and Commitment	1955	75.00	150.00	300.00

CLIFF, BENNY

Number	Title (A Side/B Side)	Yr	VG	VG+	NM
DRIFT					
❑ 1441	Shake Um Um Rock/The Breaking Point	1959	1000.	2000.	3000.

CLIFF, JIMMY

Number	Title (A Side/B Side)	Yr	VG	VG+	NM
A&M					
❑ 1146	Wonderful World, Beautiful People/Waterfall	1969	2.00	4.00	8.00
❑ 1146 [PS]	Wonderful World, Beautiful People/Waterfall	1969	3.00	6.00	12.00
❑ 1167	Come Into My Life/Viet Nam	1970	2.00	4.00	8.00
❑ 1201	You Can Get It If You Really Want/Be Aware	1970	2.00	4.00	8.00
❑ 1270	Goodbye Yesterday/Let's Seize the Time	1971	2.00	4.00	8.00
COLUMBIA					
❑ 03216	Special/Peace Officer	1982	—	2.00	4.00
❑ 04141	Reggae Night/Love Heights	1983	—	2.00	4.00
❑ 04335	We All Are One/Roots Woman	1984	—	2.00	4.00
❑ 05396	Hot Shot/Modern World	1985	—	2.00	4.00
❑ 05716	American Sweet/Reggae Movement	1985	—	2.00	4.00
❑ 06235	Club Paradise/Third World People	1986	—	—	3.00
❑ 06235 [PS]	Club Paradise/Third World People	1986	—	—	3.00
❑ 07692	Love Me, Love Me/Sunshine in the Music	1988	—	—	3.00
MCA					
❑ 51043	I Am the Living/Love Again	1981	—	2.00	4.00
❑ 51094	Another Summer/It's the Beginning of the End	1981	—	2.00	4.00
❑ 51211	My Philosophy/Shelter of Your Love	1981	—	2.00	4.00
REPRISE					
❑ 1177	Black Queen/Born to Win	1973	—	3.00	6.00
❑ 1315	You Can't Be Wrong and Get Right/Music Maker	1974	—	3.00	6.00
❑ 1383	The Harder They Come/Viet Nam	1977	—	3.00	6.00
VEEP					
❑ 1265	Aim and Ambition/Give and Take	1967	3.75	7.50	15.00
❑ 1276	That's the Way Life Goes/Thank You	1968	3.75	7.50	15.00

CLIFFORD, BUZZ

Number	Title (A Side/B Side)	Yr	VG	VG+	NM
A&M					
❑ 878	Just Can't Wait/On My Way	1967	2.50	5.00	10.00
CAPITOL					
❑ 5880	Bored to Tears/Swing in My Back Yard	1967	2.50	5.00	10.00
COLUMBIA					
❑ 41774	Hello, Mr. Moonlight/Blue Lagoon	1960	5.00	10.00	20.00
❑ 41876	Baby Sitter Boogie/Driftwood	1960	6.25	12.50	25.00
❑ 41876	Baby Sittin' Boogie/Driftwood	1960	5.00	10.00	20.00
❑ 41876 [PS]	Baby Sittin' Boogie/Driftwood	1960	12.50	25.00	50.00
❑ 41979	Three Little Fishes/Just Because	1961	5.00	10.00	20.00
❑ 41979 [PS]	Three Little Fishes/Just Because	1961	12.50	25.00	50.00
❑ 42019	I'll Never Forget/The Awakening	1961	12.50	25.00	50.00
❑ 42019 [PS]	I'll Never Forget/The Awakening	1961	20.00	40.00	80.00
❑ 42177	Moving Day/Loneliness	1961	5.00	10.00	20.00
❑ 42177 [PS]	Moving Day/Loneliness	1961	12.50	25.00	50.00
❑ 42290	Forever/Magic Circle	1962	6.25	12.50	25.00
❑ 42290 [PS]	Forever/Magic Circle	1962	12.50	25.00	50.00
DOT					
❑ 17329	(Baby I Could Be) So Good At Loving You/ Children Are Crying Aloud	1970	—	3.00	6.00
❑ 17344	Procter and Gunther/I Am the River	1971	—	3.00	6.00
RCA VICTOR					
❑ 47-8935	Until Then/Let Her Go (It's All Right)	1966	3.00	6.00	12.00
ROULETTE					
❑ 4451	No One Loves Me Like You Do/More Dead Than Alive	1962	3.75	7.50	15.00

CLIFFORD, DOUG

Of CREEDENCE CLEARWATER REVIVAL.

Number	Title (A Side/B Side)	Yr	VG	VG+	NM
FANTASY					
❑ 686	Latin Music/Take a Train	1972	—	2.50	5.00
❑ 686 [PS]	Latin Music/Take a Train	1972	—	3.00	6.00

CLIFFORD, MIKE

Number	Title (A Side/B Side)	Yr	VG	VG+	NM
AMERICAN INT'L.					
❑ 138	Broken Hearted Man/When Cindy When	1970	—	2.50	5.00
❑ 158	Do Your Own Thing/You Better Start Singing Soon	1971	—	2.50	5.00
❑ 171	You Say Love/It's a Dream Way	1970	—	2.00	4.00
CAMEO					
❑ 381	Before I Loved Her/Shirl Girl	1965	2.50	5.00	10.00
❑ 395	Out in the Country/Courtin'	1966	2.50	5.00	10.00
COLUMBIA					
❑ 41862	Stranger/Poor Little Girl	1960	3.00	6.00	12.00
❑ 41964	Look in Any Window/Uh Huh	1961	3.00	6.00	12.00
❑ 42029	Pretty Little Girl in the Yellow Dress/At Last	1961	3.00	6.00	12.00
❑ 42226	When We Marry/Bombay	1961	3.00	6.00	12.00
❑ 42226 [PS]	When We Marry/Bombay	1961	6.25	12.50	25.00
❑ 42335	Joanna/Mary, Mary	1962	3.00	6.00	12.00
LIBERTY					
❑ 55207	Should I/Whisper Whisper	1959	3.75	7.50	15.00
—With Patience and Prudence					
❑ 55219	I Don't Know Why/I'm Afraid to Say I Love You	1959	3.00	6.00	12.00
SIDEWALK					
❑ 917	Send Her Flowers/This Time, Time May Be Wrong	1967	2.00	4.00	8.00
❑ 939	Gas Hassle/Mary Jane	1968	2.00	4.00	8.00
UNITED ARTISTS					
❑ 489	Close to Cathy/She's Just Another Girl	1962	3.00	6.00	12.00
❑ 557	What to Do with Laurie/That's What They Said	1963	2.50	5.00	10.00
❑ 588	Danny's Dream/One Boy Too Late	1963	2.50	5.00	10.00
❑ 614	Gee, I Don't Remember/Cotton Dresses	1963	2.50	5.00	10.00
❑ 713	It Had Better Be Tonight/All the Colors of the Rainbow	1964	2.50	5.00	10.00
❑ 763	See You in September/One By One, The Roses Died	1964	2.50	5.00	10.00
❑ 794	Don't Make Her Cry/Barbara's Theme	1964	2.50	5.00	10.00
❑ 823	How to Murder Your Wife/Here's To My Lover	1965	2.50	5.00	10.00

CLIMATES, THE

Number	Title (A Side/B Side)	Yr	VG	VG+	NM
HOLIDAY INN					
❑ 2206	Don't Be Cruel/Tell Him Tonite	1967	3.00	6.00	12.00
SUN					
❑ 404	No You for Me/Breaking Up Again	1967	6.25	12.50	25.00

CLIMAX

With Sonny Geraci, formerly of THE OUTSIDERS.

Number	Title (A Side/B Side)	Yr	VG	VG+	NM
CAROUSEL					
❑ 30050	Hard Rock Group/(B-side unknown)	1971	—	2.50	5.00
❑ 30055	Precious and Few/Park Preserve	1971	—	2.50	5.00
PARAMOUNT					
❑ 0023	You've Gotta Try/Friendship	1970	—	3.00	6.00

ROCKY ROAD

Number	Title (A Side/B Side)	Yr	VG	VG+	NM
❑ 30055	Precious and Few/Park Preserve	1972	—	2.00	4.00
—Reissue of Carousel 30055					
❑ 30061	Life and Breath/If It Feels Good, Do It	1972	—	2.00	4.00
❑ 30064	Caroline This Time/Rainbow Rides Are Free	1972	—	2.00	4.00
❑ 30072	Rock and Roll Heaven/Face the Music	1973	—	2.50	5.00
❑ 30074	Walking in the Georgia Rain/(B-side unknown)	1973	—	2.00	4.00
❑ 30077	It's Gonna Get Better/(B-side unknown)	1974	—	2.00	4.00

CLIMAX BLUES BAND

Includes records as "Climax Chicago Blues Band."

SIRE

Number	Title (A Side/B Side)	Yr	VG	VG+	NM
❑ 351	Reap What I've Sowed	1971	—	3.00	6.00
❑ 358	Hey Mama/That's All	1972	—	3.00	6.00
❑ 705	Shake Your Love/Mule on the Dole	1973	—	3.00	6.00
❑ 712	Goin' to New York/I Am Constant	1974	—	2.50	5.00
❑ 713	Sense of Direction/Losin' the Humbles	1974	—	2.50	5.00
❑ 715	Reaching Out/Milwaukee Truckin' Blues	1974	—	2.50	5.00
❑ 721	Running Out of Time/Using the Power	1975	—	2.50	5.00
❑ 736	Couldn't Get It Right/Sav'ry Gravy	1977	—	2.50	5.00
❑ 747	Berlin Blues/Together and Free	1977	—	2.00	4.00
❑ 1026	Makin' Love/Gospel Singer	1978	—	2.00	4.00
❑ 1031	Mistress Moonshine/Teardrops	1978	—	2.00	4.00
❑ 49012	Long Distance Love/Children of the Nightime	1979	—	2.00	4.00
❑ 49098	Money in Your Pocket/Summer Rain	1979	—	2.00	4.00

WARNER BROS.

Number	Title (A Side/B Side)	Yr	VG	VG+	NM
❑ 49605	One for Me and You/Gotta Have More Love	1980	—	2.00	4.00
❑ 49669	I Love You/Horizontalized	1981	—	2.50	5.00
❑ 49850	Darlin'/This Time You're the Singer	1981	—	2.00	4.00
❑ 50018	Breakdown/Shake It Lucy	1982	—	2.00	4.00

CLIMBERS, THE

J&S

Number	Title (A Side/B Side)	Yr	VG	VG+	NM
❑ 1652/3	My Darlin' Dear/Angels in Heaven Know I Love You	1957	25.00	50.00	100.00
❑ 1658	I Love You/Train, Car, Boat or Plane	1957	200.00	400.00	800.00

CLINE, PATSY

4 STAR

Number	Title (A Side/B Side)	Yr	VG	VG+	NM
❑ 1033	Life's Railway to Heaven/If I Could See the World	1978	—	2.50	5.00

CORAL

Number	Title (A Side/B Side)	Yr	VG	VG+	NM
❑ 61464	A Church, a Courtroom, Then Goodbye/Honky Tonk Merry-Go-Round	1955	7.50	15.00	30.00
❑ 61523	Turn the Cards Slowly/Hidin' Out	1955	7.50	15.00	30.00
❑ 61583	I Love You Honey/Come Right In	1956	6.25	12.50	25.00

DECCA

Number	Title (A Side/B Side)	Yr	VG	VG+	NM
❑ 29963	Stop, Look and Listen/I've Loved and Lost Again	1956	5.00	10.00	20.00
❑ 30221	Walkin' After Midnight/A Poor Man's Roses (Or a Rich Man's Gold)	1957	5.00	10.00	20.00
❑ 30221 [PS]	Walkin' After Midnight/A Poor Man's Roses (Or a Rich Man's Gold)	1957	20.00	40.00	80.00
❑ 30339	Try Again/Today, Tomorrow and Forever	1957	3.75	7.50	15.00
❑ 30406	Three Cigarettes in an Ashtray/A Stranger in My Arms	1957	3.75	7.50	15.00
❑ 30504	I Don't Wanta/Then You'll Know	1957	3.75	7.50	15.00
❑ 30542	Stop the World/Walking Dream	1958	3.75	7.50	15.00
❑ 30659	Come On In/Let the Teardrops Fall	1958	3.75	7.50	15.00
❑ 30706	Never No More/I Can See an Angel	1958	3.75	7.50	15.00
❑ 30746	Just Out of Reach (Of My Two Open Arms)/If I Could See The World	1958	3.75	7.50	15.00
❑ 30794	Dear God/He Will Do for You	1958	3.75	7.50	15.00
❑ 30846	Yes, I Understand/Cry Not for Me	1959	3.75	7.50	15.00
❑ 30929	Got a Lot of Rhythm in My Soul/I'm Blue Again	1959	5.00	10.00	20.00
❑ 31061	Lovesick Blues/How Can I Face Tomorrow	1960	3.00	6.00	12.00
❑ 31128	There He Goes/Crazy Dream	1960	3.00	6.00	12.00
❑ 31205	I Fall to Pieces/Lovin' in Vain	1961	3.00	6.00	12.00
❑ 31317	Crazy/Who Can I Count On	1961	3.00	6.00	12.00
❑ 31354	She's Got You/Strange	1962	3.00	6.00	12.00
❑ 31377	When I Get Thru with You (You'll Love Me Too)/Imagine That	1962	3.00	6.00	12.00
❑ 31377 [PS]	When I Get Thru with You (You'll Love Me Too)/Imagine That	1962	6.25	12.50	25.00
❑ 31406	So Wrong/You're Stronger Than Me	1962	3.00	6.00	12.00
❑ 31429	Heartaches/Why Can't He Be You	1962	3.00	6.00	12.00
❑ 31455	Leavin' On Your Mind/Tra Le La Le La Triangle	1963	2.50	5.00	10.00
❑ 31455 [PS]	Leavin' On Your Mind/Tra Le La Le La Triangle	1963	6.25	12.50	25.00
❑ 31483	Sweet Dreams (Of You)/Back in Baby's Arms	1963	2.50	5.00	10.00
❑ 31522	Faded Love/Blue Moon of Kentucky	1963	2.50	5.00	10.00
❑ 31552	When You Need a Laugh/I'll Sail My Ship Alone	1963	2.50	5.00	10.00
❑ 31588	Your Kinda Love/Someday You'll Want Me to Love You	1964	2.50	5.00	10.00
❑ 31616	Love Letters in the Sand/That's How a Heartache Begins	1964	2.50	5.00	10.00
❑ 31671	He Called Me Baby/Bill Bailey Won't You Please Come Home	1964	2.50	5.00	10.00
❑ 31754	Your Cheatin' Heart/I Can't Help It (If I'm Still in Love with You)	1965	2.50	5.00	10.00
❑ 34130 [S]	Foolin' 'Round/The Wayward Wind	1962	5.00	10.00	20.00
❑ 34131 [S]	South of the Border (Down Mexico Way)/I Love You So Much It Hurts	1962	5.00	10.00	20.00
❑ 34132 [S]	Crazy/Seven Lonely Days	1962	6.25	12.50	25.00
❑ 34133 [S]	San Antonio Rose/True Love	1962	5.00	10.00	20.00
—The above four are 33 1/3, small hole jukebox singles					

EVEREST

Number	Title (A Side/B Side)	Yr	VG	VG+	NM
❑ 2011	Then You'll Know/Hungry for Love	1963	3.00	6.00	12.00
❑ 2020	Walking After Midnight/That Wonderful Someone	1963	3.00	6.00	12.00
❑ 2031	I Can See an Angel/Just Out of Reach	1963	3.00	6.00	12.00
❑ 2039	I've Loved and Lost Again/I Love You Honey	1964	2.50	5.00	10.00
❑ 2045	In Care of the Blues/If I Could See the World (Through the Eyes of a Child)	1964	2.50	5.00	10.00
❑ 2052	Got a Lot of Rhythm (In My Soul)/Love Me, Love Me, Honey Do	1964	2.50	5.00	10.00
❑ 2060	Crazy Dream/There He Goes	1965	2.50	5.00	10.00
❑ 20005	I Don't Wanta/I Can't Forget	1962	3.75	7.50	15.00

KAPP

Number	Title (A Side/B Side)	Yr	VG	VG+	NM
❑ 659	Just a Closer Walk with Thee	1965	3.75	7.50	15.00
—One-sided release, possibly promo only					

MCA

Number	Title (A Side/B Side)	Yr	VG	VG+	NM
❑ 41303	Always/I Sail My Ship Alone	1980	—	2.00	4.00
❑ 51038	I Fall to Pieces/True Love	1980	—	2.00	4.00
❑ 52052	So Wrong/I Fall to Pieces	1982	—	—	3.00
—A-side: With Jim Reeves (electronically created duet)					
❑ 52684	Sweet Dreams/Blue Moon of Kentucky	1985	—	—	3.00

RCA

Number	Title (A Side/B Side)	Yr	VG	VG+	NM
❑ PB-12346	Have You Ever Been Lonely (Have You Ever Been Blue)/Welcome to My World	1981	—	—	3.00
—With Jim Reeves (electronically created duet)					

STARDAY

Number	Title (A Side/B Side)	Yr	VG	VG+	NM
❑ 7030	Walking After Midnight/Lovesick Blues	1965	2.50	5.00	10.00
❑ 8024	Walking After Midnight/Lovesick Blues	1971	—	3.00	6.00

7-Inch Extended Plays

CORAL

Number	Title (A Side/B Side)	Yr	VG	VG+	NM
❑ EC 81159	*Honky Tonk Merry-Go-Round/A Church, a Courtroom, and Then Goodbye/Turn the Cards Slowly/Hidin' Out	1958	6.25	12.50	25.00
❑ EC 81159 [PS]	Songs by Patsy Cline	1958	7.50	15.00	30.00

DECCA

Number	Title (A Side/B Side)	Yr	VG	VG+	NM
❑ ED 2542	*That Wonderful Someone/Three Cigarettes in an Ashtray/Hungry for Love/Fingerprints	1958	5.00	10.00	20.00
❑ ED 2542 [PS]	Patsy Cline	1958	5.00	10.00	20.00
❑ ED 2703	*I Fall to Pieces/Lovin' in Vain/Lovesick Blues/There He Goes	1961	3.75	7.50	15.00
❑ ED 2703 [PS]	Patsy Cline	1961	3.75	7.50	15.00
❑ ED 2707	*Crazy/Foolin' 'Round/Who Can I Count On/South of the Border	1961	3.75	7.50	15.00
❑ ED 2707 [PS]	Patsy Cline	1961	3.75	7.50	15.00
❑ ED 2719	*She's Got You/Strange/The Wayward Wind/I Love You So Much It Hurts	1962	3.75	7.50	15.00
❑ ED 2719 [PS]	She's Got You	1962	3.75	7.50	15.00
❑ ED 2729	So Wrong/You're Stronger Than Me//Heartaches/Your Cheatin' Heart	1962	3.75	7.50	15.00
❑ ED 2729 [PS]	Patsy Cline	1962	3.75	7.50	15.00
❑ ED 2757	*Leavin' on Your Mind/Tra Le La Le La Triangle/Half As Much/Lonely Street	1963	3.75	7.50	15.00
❑ ED 2757 [PS]	Leavin' on Your Mind	1963	3.75	7.50	15.00
❑ ED 2759	Just a Closer Walk with Thee/Life's Railroad to Heaven//Dear God/He Will Do for You	1963	3.75	7.50	15.00
❑ ED 2759 [PS]	Dear God	1963	3.75	7.50	15.00
❑ ED 2768	I'm Blue Again/How Can I Face Tomorrow//I'm Moving Along/Love Love Love Me Honey Do	1964	3.75	7.50	15.00
❑ ED 2768 [PS]	How Can I Face Tomorrow	1964	3.75	7.50	15.00
❑ ED 2770	Someday You'll Want Me to Want You/Faded Love//When You Need a Laugh/I'll Sail My Ship Alone	1964	3.75	7.50	15.00
❑ ED 2770 [PS]	Someday You'll Want Me to Want You	1964	3.75	7.50	15.00
❑ ED 2794	(contents unknown)	1965	3.75	7.50	15.00
❑ ED 2794 [PS]	Portrait of Patsy Cline	1965	3.75	7.50	15.00
❑ ED 2802	(contents unknown)	1965	3.75	7.50	15.00
❑ ED 2802 [PS]	Love Letters in the Sand	1965	3.75	7.50	15.00

PATSY CLINE

Number	Title (A Side/B Side)	Yr	VG	VG+	NM
❑ EPF-16	Try Again/Turn the Cards Slowly//Come On In/Stop Look and Listen	195?	10.00	20.00	40.00
❑ EPF-16 [PS]	(title unknown)	195?	10.00	20.00	40.00
❑ EP-21	Three Cigarettes/Hungry for Love//Fingerprints/That Wonderful Someone	195?	10.00	20.00	40.00
❑ EP-21 [PS]	(title unknown)	195?	10.00	20.00	40.00

CLINTON, GEORGE

Also see PARLIAMENT; FUNKADELIC; THE PARLIAMENTS.

ABC

Number	Title (A Side/B Side)	Yr	VG	VG+	NM
❑ 12040	Hold On to Your Lady/Nothing in This Whole World	1974	—	3.00	6.00

CAPITOL

Number	Title (A Side/B Side)	Yr	VG	VG+	NM
❑ B-5160	Loopzilla/Pot Sharing Tots	1982	—	2.00	4.00
❑ B-5201	Atomic Dog/Atomic Dog (Instrumental)	1983	—	2.00	4.00
❑ B-5201 [PS]	Atomic Dog/Atomic Dog (Instrumental)	1983	—	3.00	6.00
❑ B-5222	Get Dressed/Free Alterations	1983	—	2.00	4.00
❑ B-5222 [PS]	Get Dressed/Free Alterations	1983	—	2.00	4.00
❑ B-5296	Nubian Nut/Free Alterations	1983	—	2.00	4.00
❑ B-5296 [PS]	Nubian Nut/Free Alterations	1983	—	2.00	4.00
❑ B-5324	Quickie/Last Dance	1984	—	2.00	4.00
❑ B-5324 [PS]	Quickie/Last Dance	1984	—	2.00	4.00
❑ B-5332	Last Dance/Get Dressed	1984	—	2.00	4.00
❑ B-5332 [PS]	Last Dance/Get Dressed	1984	—	2.00	4.00
❑ B-5473	Double Oh-Oh/Bangladesh	1985	—	2.00	4.00
❑ B-5473 [PS]	Double Oh-Oh/Bangladesh	1985	—	2.00	4.00
❑ B-5504	Bullet Proof/Silly Millimeter	1985	—	2.00	4.00
❑ B-5558	Do Fries Go With That Shake/Pleasure of Exhaustion (Do It Till I Drop)	1986	—	2.00	4.00
❑ B-5602	Hey Good Lookin' (Remix)/Hey Good Lookin' (Mirror Mix)	1986	—	2.00	4.00
❑ B-5642	R&B Skeletons (In the Closet)/Nubian Nut	1986	—	2.00	4.00

PAISLEY PARK

Number	Title (A Side/B Side)	Yr	VG	VG+	NM
❑ 22790	Tweakin'/French Kiss	1989	—	—	3.00
❑ 27557	Why Should I Dog U Out?/(Instrumental)	1989	—	—	3.00
❑ 27557 [PS]	Why Should I Dog U Out?/(Instrumental)	1989	—	—	3.00

CLINTONIAN CUBS, THE

JIMMY CASTOR was a member.

MY BROTHERS

Number	Title (A Side/B Side)	Yr	VG	VG+	NM
❑ 508	She's Just My Size/Confusion	1960	75.00	150.00	300.00

CLIQUE, THE (1)
Texas band.

WHITE WHALE

Number	Title (A Side/B Side)	Yr	VG	VG+	NM
❑ 312	Superman/Shadow of Your Love	1969	3.00	6.00	12.00
❑ 323	Sugar on Sunday/Superman	1969	3.75	7.50	15.00
❑ 333	Soul Mate/I'll Hold Out My Hand	1969	2.50	5.00	10.00
❑ 338	I'm Alive/Sparkle and Shine	1970	2.50	5.00	10.00
❑ 361	Memphis/Southbound Wind	1970	2.50	5.00	10.00
❑ 367 [DJ]	Judy, Judy, Judy (same on both sides)	1970	3.00	6.00	12.00

—May be promo only

CLIQUE, THE (2)
British band.

ABC-PARAMOUNT

Number	Title (A Side/B Side)	Yr	VG	VG+	NM
❑ 10655	She Ain't No Good/Time, Time, Time	1965	2.50	5.00	10.00

CLIQUE, THE (U)
Some of these may be early records by group (1) or later records by group (2).

Number	Title (A Side/B Side)	Yr	VG	VG+	NM
CINEMA					
❑ 001	Stay By Me/Splash One	1967	7.50	15.00	30.00
LAURIE					
❑ 3365	Sun Come Up/Drifter's Melody	1966	2.50	5.00	10.00
SCEPTER					
❑ 12202	Stay By Me/Splash One	1967	5.00	10.00	20.00
❑ 12212	Gotta Get Away/Love Ain't Easy	1967	5.00	10.00	20.00

CLIQUES, THE
Also see JESSE BELVIN; EUGENE CHURCH.

MODERN

Number	Title (A Side/B Side)	Yr	VG	VG+	NM
❑ 987	Girl in My Dreams/I Wanna Know Why	1956	12.50	25.00	50.00
—Blue label					
❑ 987	Girl in My Dreams/I Wanna Know Why	1956	7.50	15.00	30.00
—Black label					
❑ 995	My Desire/I'm in Love with a Gal	1956	7.50	15.00	30.00

CLOUD, CHRISTOPHER
See TOMMY BOYCE.

CLOVERS, THE

Number	Title (A Side/B Side)	Yr	VG	VG+	NM
ATLANTIC					
❑ 934	Don't You Know I Love You/Skylark	1951	250.00	500.00	1000.
❑ 944	Fool, Fool, Fool/Needless	1951	62.50	125.00	250.00
❑ 963	One Mint Julep/Middle of the Night	1952	25.00	50.00	100.00
❑ 969	Ting-A-Ling/Wonder Where My Baby's Gone	1952	25.00	50.00	100.00
❑ 977	I Played the Fool/Hey, Miss Fannie	1952	62.50	125.00	250.00
❑ 989	Yes, It's You/Crawlin'	1953	15.00	30.00	60.00
❑ 1000	Good Lovin'/Here Goes a Fool	1953	20.00	40.00	80.00
❑ 1010	Comin' On/The Feeling Is So Good	1953	37.50	75.00	150.00
❑ 1022	Lovey Dovey/Little Mama	1954	12.50	25.00	50.00
❑ 1035	Your Cash Ain't Nothin' But Trash/I've Got My Eyes on You	1954	12.50	25.00	50.00
❑ 1046	I Confess/Alrighty, Oh Sweetie	1954	12.50	25.00	50.00
❑ 1052	Blue Velvet/If You Love Me (Why Don't You Tell Me So)	1955	15.00	30.00	60.00
❑ 1060	Love Big/In the Morning Time	1955	12.50	25.00	50.00
❑ 1073	Nip Sip/If I Could Be Loved By You	1955	12.50	25.00	50.00
❑ 1083	Devil or Angel/Hey, Doll Baby	1956	50.00	100.00	200.00
—Yellow label, no spinner					
❑ 1083	Devil or Angel/Hey, Doll Baby	1956	10.00	20.00	40.00
—Red label, no spinner					
❑ 1083	Devil or Angel/Hey, Doll Baby	1956	2000.	3000.	4000.
—Red label, no spinner; red vinyl; value is conjecture					
❑ 1094	Love, Love, Love/Your Tender Lips	1956	10.00	20.00	40.00
❑ 1107	From the Bottom of My Heart/Bring Me Love	1956	7.50	15.00	30.00
❑ 1118	A Lonely Fool/Baby, Baby, Oh My Darling	1956	7.50	15.00	30.00
❑ 1129	Here Comes Romance/You Good-Looking Woman	1957	7.50	15.00	30.00
❑ 1139	I-I-I Love You/So Young	1957	7.50	15.00	30.00
❑ 1152	There's No Tomorrow/Down in the Alley	1957	7.50	15.00	30.00
❑ 1175	Wishing for Your Love/All About You	1958	7.50	15.00	30.00
❑ 2129	Drive It Home/The Bootie Green	1961	5.00	10.00	20.00
BRUNSWICK					
❑ 55249	Love! Love! Love!/The Kickapoo	1963	3.00	6.00	12.00
JOSIE					
❑ 992	For Days/Too Long Without Some Loving	1968	2.50	5.00	10.00
❑ 997	Try My Lovin' On You/Sweet Side of a Soulful Woman	1968	2.50	5.00	10.00
POPLAR					
❑ 110	The Gossip Wheel/Please Come On to Me	1958	6.25	12.50	25.00
❑ 111	The Good Old Summertime/Idaho	1958	6.25	12.50	25.00
PORT					
❑ 3004	Poor Baby/He Sure Could Hypnotize	1965	2.50	5.00	10.00
PORWIN					
❑ 1001/2	Stop Pretending/One More Time	1963	3.75	7.50	15.00
—As "Buddy Baliey and the Clovers"					
❑ 1004	It's All in the Game/That's What I Will Be	1963	3.75	7.50	15.00
—As "Buddy Baliey and the Clovers"					
STENTON					
❑ 7001	Please Mr. Sun/Gimme, Gimme, Gimme	1961	20.00	40.00	80.00
—As "Tippie and the Clovermen"					
TIGER					
❑ 201	Bossa Nova Baby/The Bossa Nova (My Heart Said)	1962	3.75	7.50	15.00
—As "Tippie and the Clovers"					
UNITED ARTISTS					
❑ 0133	Love Potion #9/Stay Awhile	1973	—	2.00	4.00
—"Silver Spotlight Series" reissue					
❑ 174	Rock and Roll Tango/That Old Black Magic	1959	6.25	12.50	25.00
❑ 180	Love Potion #9/Stay Awhile	1959	6.25	12.50	25.00
❑ 209	One Mint Julep/Lovey	1960	6.25	12.50	25.00
❑ 227	Easy Lovin'/I'm Confessin' That I Love You	1960	6.25	12.50	25.00
❑ 263	Yes It's You/Burning Fire	1960	6.25	12.50	25.00
❑ 307	The Honeydripper/Have Gun	1961	6.25	12.50	25.00
WINLEY					
❑ 255	Let Me Hold You/Wrapped Up in a Dream	1961	3.75	7.50	15.00
❑ 265	I Need You Now/Gotta Quit You	1962	3.75	7.50	15.00
❑ 265	They're Rockin' Down the Street/Be My Baby	1962	3.75	7.50	15.00
—As "The Fabulous Clovers"					
7-Inch Extended Plays					
ATLANTIC					
❑ 504	One Mint Julep/Fool, Fool, Fool//Hey, Miss Fannie/I Played the Fool	1953	50.00	100.00	200.00
❑ 504 [PS]	The Clovers Sing	1953	50.00	100.00	200.00
❑ 537	(contents unknown)	1954	37.50	75.00	150.00
❑ 537 [PS]	The Clovers Sing	1954	50.00	100.00	200.00
❑ 590	*Love, Love, Love/Devil or Angel/Blue Velvet/From the Bottom of My Heart	1955	37.50	75.00	150.00
❑ 590 [PS]	The Clovers	1955	50.00	100.00	200.00

CLOWNEY, DAVID
See DAVE "BABY" CORTEZ.

CLUSTERS, THE

Number	Title (A Side/B Side)	Yr	VG	VG+	NM
END					
❑ 1115	Pardon My Heart/Darling Can't You Tell	1962	10.00	20.00	40.00
EPIC					
❑ 9330	Forecast of Our Love/Long Legged Maggie	1959	20.00	40.00	80.00
TEE GEE					
❑ 102	Pardon My Heart/Darling Can't You Tell	1958	75.00	150.00	300.00
—No mention of Gone distribution					
❑ 102	Pardon My Heart/Darling Can't You Tell	1958	75.00	150.00	300.00
—With Gone distribution mentioned; publishing by Emkay Music					
❑ 102	Pardon My Heart/Darling Can't You Tell	1958	30.00	60.00	120.00
—With Gone distribution mentioned; publishing by Real Gone Music					

COASTERS, THE
Also see THE ROBINS.

Number	Title (A Side/B Side)	Yr	VG	VG+	NM
AMERICAN INT'L.					
❑ 1122	If I Had a Hammer/If I Had a Hammer (Disco Version)	1976	—	2.50	5.00
—As "The World Famous Coasters"					
ATCO					
❑ 6064	Down in Mexico/Turtle Dovin'	1956	20.00	40.00	80.00
❑ 6073	One Kiss Led to Another/Brazil	1956	15.00	30.00	60.00
❑ 6087	Searchin'/Young Blood	1957	17.50	35.00	70.00
—Maroon label (first pressing)					
❑ 6087	Searchin'/Young Blood	1957	6.25	12.50	25.00
—White and yellow label					
❑ 6098	Idol with the Golden Head/(When She Wants Good Lovin') My Baby Comes to Me	1957	10.00	20.00	40.00
❑ 6104	Sweet Georgia Brown/What Is the Secret of Your Success	1957	10.00	20.00	40.00
❑ 6111	Dance!/Gee, Golly	1958	10.00	20.00	40.00
❑ 6116	Yakety Yak/Zing Went the Strings of My Heart	1958	6.25	12.50	25.00
❑ 6126	The Shadow Knows/Sorry But I'm Gonna Have to Pass	1958	6.25	12.50	25.00
❑ 6132	Charlie Brown/Three Cool Cats	1959	6.25	12.50	25.00
❑ 6141	Along Came Jones/That Is Rock and Roll	1959	5.00	10.00	20.00
❑ 6146	Poison Ivy/I'm a Hog for You	1959	5.00	10.00	20.00
❑ 6153	Run Red Run/What About Us	1959	5.00	10.00	20.00
❑ 6163	Besame Mucho (Part 1)/Besame Mucho (Part 2)	1960	6.25	12.50	25.00
❑ 6168	Wake Me, Shake Me/Stewball	1960	6.25	12.50	25.00
❑ 6178	Shoppin' for Clothes/The Snake and the Book Worm	1960	6.25	12.50	25.00
❑ 6186	Thumbin' a Ride/Wait a Minute	1961	5.00	10.00	20.00
❑ 6192	Little Egypt (Ying-Yang)/Keep On Rolling	1961	5.00	10.00	20.00
❑ 6204	Girls, Girls, Girls (Part 1)/Girls, Girls, Girls (Part 2)	1961	5.00	10.00	20.00
❑ 6210	Bad Blood/(Ain't That) Just Like Me	1961	5.00	10.00	20.00
❑ 6219	Teach Me How to Shimmy/Ridin' Hood	1962	5.00	10.00	20.00
❑ 6234	The Climb/(Instrumental)	1962	5.00	10.00	20.00
❑ 6251	The P.T.A./Bull Tick Waltz	1962	5.00	10.00	20.00
❑ 6287	Speedo's Back in Town/T'Ain't Nothin' to Me	1964	3.75	7.50	15.00
❑ 6300	Lovey Dovey/Bad Detective	1964	3.75	7.50	15.00
❑ 6321	Wild One/I Must Be Dreaming	1964	3.75	7.50	15.00
❑ 6341	Hungry/Lady Like	1965	3.75	7.50	15.00
❑ 6356	Money Honey/Let's Go Get Stoned	1965	3.75	7.50	15.00
❑ 6379	Bell Bottom Slacks and a Chinese Kimono (She's My Little Spodee-O)/Crazy Baby	1965	6.25	12.50	25.00
❑ 6407	Saturday Night Fish Fry/She's a Yum Yum	1966	3.75	7.50	15.00
ATLANTIC					
❑ 89361	Yakety Yak/Stand By Me	1986	—	—	3.00
❑ 89361 [PS]	Yakety Yak/Stand By Me	1986	—	—	3.00
—B-side by Ben E. King. See listing of this record under "King, Ben E." for more information.					
CHELAN					
❑ 2000	Searchin' '75/Young BLood	1975	—	2.50	5.00
—As "The Coasters 2+2"					
DATE					
❑ 1552	Soul Pad/Down Home Girl	1967	5.00	10.00	20.00
❑ 1607	Everybody's Woman/She Can	1968	5.00	10.00	20.00
❑ 1617	D.W. Washburn/Everybody's Woman	1968	5.00	10.00	20.00
KING					
❑ 6385	Love Potion #9/D.W. Washburn	1972	—	3.00	6.00
❑ 6389	Cool Jerk/Talkin' 'Bout a Woman	1972	—	3.00	6.00
❑ 6404	Soul Pad/D.W. Washburn	1972	—	3.00	6.00
SAL WA					
❑ 1001	Take It Easy, Greasy/You Move Me	1975	—	2.50	5.00
TURNTABLE					
❑ 504	Act Right/The World Is Changing	1969	2.50	5.00	10.00

7-Inch Extended Plays

ATCO

Number	Title (A Side/B Side)	Yr	VG	VG+	NM
❑ 4501	Searchin'/Young Blood//(When She Wants Good Lovin') My Baby Comes to Me/Idol with the Golden Head	1958	37.50	75.00	150.00
❑ 4501 [PS]	Rock and Roll	1958	50.00	100.00	200.00
❑ 4503	*Yakety Yak/Framed/Loop De Loop Mambo/Riot in Cell Block Number Nine	1959	50.00	100.00	200.00
❑ 4503 [PS]	Keep Rockin' with the Coasters	1959	50.00	100.00	200.00
❑ 4506	*Charlie Brown/Three Cool Cats/The Shadow Knows/Sorry But I'm Gonna Have to Pass	1959	37.50	75.00	150.00
❑ 4506 [PS]	The Coasters	1959	37.50	75.00	150.00
❑ 4507	Along Came Jones/That Is Rock & Roll//Dance!/Gee, Golly	1959	37.50	75.00	150.00
❑ 4507 [PS]	The Coasters' Top Hits	1959	37.50	75.00	150.00

COBRAS, THE (1)

STEVIE RAY VAUGHAN was a member of this Cobras.

ARMADILLO

Number	Title (A Side/B Side)	Yr	VG	VG+	NM
❑ 79-1	Blow Joe Blow (Crazy 'Bout a Saxophone)/Sugaree	1980	25.00	50.00	100.00

COBRAS, THE (2)

CASINO

Number	Title (A Side/B Side)	Yr	VG	VG+	NM
❑ 1309	La La/Goodbye Molly	1963	20.00	40.00	80.00

SWAN

Number	Title (A Side/B Side)	Yr	VG	VG+	NM
❑ 4176	La La/Goodbye Molly	1964	6.25	12.50	25.00

COBRAS, THE (3)

MODERN

Number	Title (A Side/B Side)	Yr	VG	VG+	NM
❑ 964	Sindy/I Will Return	1955	75.00	150.00	300.00
—Original spelling of A-side					
❑ 964	Cindy/I Will Return	1955	37.50	75.00	150.00
—Revised spelling of A-side					

COBRAS, THE (U)

These may be by group (2), but we're not sure.

MONOGRAM

Number	Title (A Side/B Side)	Yr	VG	VG+	NM
❑ 519	Thumpin'/Don't Even Know Your Name	1964	3.00	6.00	12.00

STAX

Number	Title (A Side/B Side)	Yr	VG	VG+	NM
❑ 148	Shake Up/Restless	1964	3.75	7.50	15.00

COCHRAN, EDDIE

Also see COCHRAN BROTHERS; JEWEL AND EDDIE.

CAPEHART

Number	Title (A Side/B Side)	Yr	VG	VG+	NM
❑ 5003	Rough Stuff/Our Love	1960	6.25	12.50	25.00
❑ 5003 [PS]	Rough Stuff/Our Love	1960	50.00	100.00	200.00

CREST

Number	Title (A Side/B Side)	Yr	VG	VG+	NM
❑ 1026	Skinny Jim/Half Loved	1956	75.00	150.00	300.00

LIBERTY

Number	Title (A Side/B Side)	Yr	VG	VG+	NM
❑ 55056	Sittin' in the Balcony/Dark Lonely Street	1957	7.50	15.00	30.00
❑ 55070	Mean When I'm Mad/One Kiss	1957	7.50	15.00	30.00
❑ 55070 [PS]	Mean When I'm Mad/One Kiss	1957	500.00	1000.	1500.
❑ 55087	Drive In Show/Am I Blue	1957	7.50	15.00	30.00
❑ 55112	Twenty Flight Rock/Cradle Baby	1957	37.50	75.00	150.00
❑ 55123	Jeannie, Jeannie, Jeannie/Pocketful of Hearts	1958	7.50	15.00	30.00
❑ 55138	Pretty Girl/Theresa	1958	8.75	17.50	35.00
❑ 55144	Summertime Blues/Love Again	1958	7.50	15.00	30.00
❑ 55166	C'mon Everybody/Don't Ever Let Me Go	1958	7.50	15.00	30.00
❑ 55177	Teen Age Heaven/I Remember	1959	7.50	15.00	30.00
❑ 55177	Teenage Heaven/I Remember	1959	10.00	20.00	40.00
—Note difference in title					
❑ 55203	The Boll Weevil Song/Somethin' Else	1959	7.50	15.00	30.00
❑ 55217	Hallelujah I Love Her So/Little Angel	1959	7.50	15.00	30.00
❑ 55242	Three Steps to Heaven/Cut Across Shorty	1960	10.00	20.00	40.00
❑ 55278	Lonely/Sweetie Pie	1960	6.25	12.50	25.00
❑ 55389	Weekend/Lonely	1961	7.50	15.00	30.00

UNITED ARTISTS

Number	Title (A Side/B Side)	Yr	VG	VG+	NM
❑ 0014	Summertime Blues/Cut Across Shorty	1973	—	2.00	4.00
❑ 0015	C'mon Everybody/Twenty Flight Rock	1973	—	2.00	4.00
❑ 0016	Sittin' in the Balcony/Somethin' Else	1973	—	2.00	4.00
—0014, 0015, 0016 are "Silver Spotlight Series" reissues					

7-Inch Extended Plays

LIBERTY

Number	Title (A Side/B Side)	Yr	VG	VG+	NM
❑ 3061-1	(contents unknown)	1958	50.00	100.00	200.00
❑ 3061-1 [PS]	Singin' to My Baby, Part 1	1958	50.00	100.00	200.00
❑ 3061-2	(contents unknown)	1958	50.00	100.00	200.00
❑ 3061-2 [PS]	Singin' to My Baby, Part 2	1958	50.00	100.00	200.00
❑ 3061-3	(contents unknown)	1958	50.00	100.00	200.00
❑ 3061-3 [PS]	Singin' to My Baby, Part 3	1958	50.00	100.00	200.00

COCHRAN, HANK

Also see COCHRAN BROTHERS.

CAPITOL

Number	Title (A Side/B Side)	Yr	VG	VG+	NM
❑ 4585	Willie/Uphill All the Way	1978	—	2.00	4.00

DOT

Number	Title (A Side/B Side)	Yr	VG	VG+	NM
❑ 17361	One Night for Willie/Back to His	1970	—	3.00	6.00

ELEKTRA

Number	Title (A Side/B Side)	Yr	VG	VG+	NM
❑ 46596	Make the World Go Away/I Don't Do Windows	1980	—	2.00	4.00
❑ 47062	A Little Bitty Tear/He's Got You	1980	—	2.00	4.00

GAYLORD

Number	Title (A Side/B Side)	Yr	VG	VG+	NM
❑ 6426	Yesterday's Memories/When You Gotta Go	1963	3.00	6.00	12.00
❑ 6431	A Good Country Song/Same Old Hurt	1963	3.00	6.00	12.00

LIBERTY

Number	Title (A Side/B Side)	Yr	VG	VG+	NM
❑ 55402	Lonely Little Mansion/Has Anybody Seen Me Lately	1962	3.00	6.00	12.00
❑ 55461	Sally Was a Good Old Girl/The Picture Behind the Picture	1962	3.00	6.00	12.00
❑ 55498	I'd Fight the World/Lucy, Let Your Lovelight Shine	1962	3.00	6.00	12.00
❑ 55520	I Remember/Private John Q	1963	2.50	5.00	10.00
❑ 55644	Tootsie's Orchid Lounge/Go On Home	1963	2.50	5.00	10.00

MONUMENT

Number	Title (A Side/B Side)	Yr	VG	VG+	NM
❑ 994	All of Me Belongs to You/I Just Burned a Dream	1967	—	3.00	6.00
❑ 1012	It Couldn't Happen to a Nicer Guy/Tootsie's Orchid Lounge	1967	—	3.00	6.00
❑ 1033	A Happy Goodbye/Speak Well of Me to the Kids	1967	—	3.00	6.00
❑ 1051	Has Anybody Seen Me Lately/I Woke Up	1968	—	3.00	6.00

RCA VICTOR

Number	Title (A Side/B Side)	Yr	VG	VG+	NM
❑ 47-8329	My Baby's His Baby Now/What Kind of Bird Is That	1964	2.50	5.00	10.00
❑ 47-8375	She Always Comes Back to Me/Your Country Boy	1964	2.50	5.00	10.00
❑ 47-8457	I Want to Go with You/Sad Songs and Waltzes	1964	2.50	5.00	10.00
❑ 47-8528	Somewhere in My Dreams/Going in Training	1965	2.50	5.00	10.00
❑ 47-8616	Who's Gonna/Let's Be Different	1965	2.50	5.00	10.00
❑ 47-8694	Hank Today and Him Tomorrow/I'm Alone	1965	2.50	5.00	10.00
❑ 47-8827	The Crying Section/Only You Can Make Me Well	1966	2.00	4.00	8.00
❑ 47-8955	That's What I'll Say/I Lie a Lot	1966	2.00	4.00	8.00

COCHRAN, HANK, AND WILLIE NELSON

Also see each artist's individual listings.

CAPITOL

Number	Title (A Side/B Side)	Yr	VG	VG+	NM
❑ 4635	Ain't Life Hell/I'm Going With You This Time	1978	—	2.50	5.00

COCHRAN, JACKIE LEE

ABC-PARAMOUNT

Number	Title (A Side/B Side)	Yr	VG	VG+	NM
❑ 9930	Buy a Car/I Want You	1958	20.00	40.00	80.00

DECCA

Number	Title (A Side/B Side)	Yr	VG	VG+	NM
❑ 30206	Ruby Pearl/Mama Don't You Think I Know	1957	30.00	60.00	120.00

JAGUAR

Number	Title (A Side/B Side)	Yr	VG	VG+	NM
❑ 3031	Georgia Lee Brown/I Wanna See You	1959	30.00	60.00	120.00

SIMS

Number	Title (A Side/B Side)	Yr	VG	VG+	NM
❑ 107	Hip Shakin' Mama/Riverside Jump	1956	50.00	100.00	200.00

SPRY

Number	Title (A Side/B Side)	Yr	VG	VG+	NM
❑ 120	Pity Me/Endless Love	1959	62.50	125.00	250.00

VIV

Number	Title (A Side/B Side)	Yr	VG	VG+	NM
❑ 988	I Want You/Buy a Car	1958	37.50	75.00	150.00

COCHRAN BROTHERS

EDDIE COCHRAN and HANK COCHRAN, who are not brothers.

EKKO

Number	Title (A Side/B Side)	Yr	VG	VG+	NM
❑ 1003	Mr. Fiddle/Two Blue Singing Stars	1955	62.50	125.00	250.00
❑ 1005	Guilty Conscience/Your Tomorrow Never Comes	1955	62.50	125.00	250.00
❑ 3001	Tired and Sleepy/Fool's Paradise	1956	75.00	150.00	300.00

COCKER, JOE

ASYLUM

Number	Title (A Side/B Side)	Yr	VG	VG+	NM
❑ 45540	Fun Time/Watching the River Flow	1978	—	2.00	4.00
❑ 46001	Lady Put the Light Out/Wasted Years	1978	—	2.00	4.00

A&M

Number	Title (A Side/B Side)	Yr	VG	VG+	NM
❑ 928	Marjorine/New Age of the Lily	1968	2.50	5.00	10.00
❑ 991	With a Little Help from My Friends/Something's Coming On	1968	2.50	5.00	10.00
❑ 1063	Feeling Alright/Sandpaper Cadillac	1969	—	3.00	6.00
—Reissued in 1971 with the same number					
❑ 1112	Delta Lady/She's So Good to Me	1969	—	2.50	5.00
❑ 1147	She Came In Through the Bathroom Window/Change in Louise	1969	—	2.50	5.00
❑ 1147 [PS]	She Came In Through the Bathroom Window/Change in Louise	1969	—	3.00	6.00
❑ 1174	The Letter/Space Captain	1970	—	2.50	5.00
❑ 1174 [PS]	The Letter/Space Captain	1970	—	3.00	6.00
❑ 1200	Cry Me a River/Give Peace a Chance	1970	—	2.50	5.00
❑ 1200	Cry Me a River/Please Give Peace a Chance	1970	—	2.50	5.00
❑ 1200 [PS]	Cry Me a River/Give Peace a Chance	1970	—	3.00	6.00
❑ 1258	High Time We Went/Black-Eyed Blues	1971	—	2.00	4.00
❑ 1258 [PS]	High Time We Went/Black-Eyed Blues	1971	—	3.00	6.00
❑ 1370	Midnight Rider/Woman to Woman	1972	—	2.00	4.00
❑ 1370 [PS]	Midnight Rider/Woman to Woman	1972	—	3.00	6.00
❑ 1407	Pardon Me Sir/St. James Infirmary Blues	1973	—	2.00	4.00
❑ 1407 [PS]	Pardon Me Sir/St. James Infirmary Blues	1973	—	3.00	6.00
❑ 1539	Put Out the Light/If I Love You	1974	—	2.00	4.00
❑ 1539 [PS]	Put Out the Light/If I Love You	1974	—	3.00	6.00
❑ 1626	I Can Stand a Little Rain/I Get Mad	1974	—	2.00	4.00
❑ 1641	You Are So Beautiful/It's a Sin When You Love Somebody	1974	—	2.00	4.00
❑ 1749	I Think It's Going to Rain Today/Oh Mama	1975	—	2.00	4.00
❑ 1758	Jamaica Say You Will/It's All Over But the Shoutin'	1975	—	2.00	4.00
❑ 1805	The Man in Me (Part 1)/The Man in Me (Part 2)	1976	—	2.00	4.00
❑ 1830	Jealous Kind/You Came Along	1976	—	2.00	4.00
❑ 1855	I Broke Down/You Came Along	1976	—	2.00	4.00
❑ 2019	Feeling Alright/Cry Me a River	1978	—	2.00	4.00

CAPITOL

Number	Title (A Side/B Side)	Yr	VG	VG+	NM
❑ B-5338	Civilized Man/A Girl Like You	1984	—	—	3.00
❑ B-5338 [PS]	Civilized Man/A Girl Like You	1984	—	2.00	4.00
❑ B-5390	Crazy in Love/Come On In	1984	—	—	3.00
❑ B-5412	Edge of a Dream/Tempted	1984	—	—	3.00
❑ B-5412 [PS]	Edge of a Dream/Tempted	1984	—	2.00	4.00
❑ B-5557	Shelter Me/Tell Me There's a Way	1986	—	—	3.00
❑ B-5589	You Can Leave Your Hat On/Long Drag of the Cigarette	1986	—	2.50	5.00
❑ B-5589 [PS]	You Can Leave Your Hat On/Long Drag of the Cigarette	1986	—	3.00	6.00
❑ B-5626	Don't Drink the Water/Don't You Love Me Anymore	1986	—	—	3.00
❑ S7-18124	The Simple Things/Unchain My Heart (90's Version)	1994	—	—	3.00
—White vinyl					
❑ B-44072	Unchain My Heart/Satisfied	1987	—	—	3.00
❑ B-44072 [PS]	Unchain My Heart/Satisfied	1987	—	—	3.00
❑ B-44101	Two Wrongs (Don't Make a Right)/Isolation	1987	—	—	3.00
❑ B-44182	A Woman Loves a Man/La Vie En Rose	1988	—	—	3.00
—B-side by Edith Piaf					

Number	Title (A Side/B Side)	Yr	VG	VG+	NM
❑ B-44182 [PS]	A Woman Loves a Man/La Vie En Rose	1988	—	—	3.00
❑ 44590	Living in the Promiseland/She Came In Through the Bathroom Window (Live)	1990	—	2.00	4.00
❑ NR-44590	Living in the Promiseland/She Came In Through the Bathroom Window (Live)	1990	—	2.00	4.00
❑ S7-57988	Feels Like Forever/When the Night Comes	1992	—	—	3.00
❑ 7PRO-79025	[DJ]What Are You Doing with a Fool Like Me (same on both sides)	1990	—	2.50	5.00
—Vinyl is promo only					
❑ 7PRO-79711	[DJ]When the Night Comes (same on both sides)	1989	—	2.50	5.00
—Vinyl is promo only					
ISLAND					
❑ 99875	Throw It Away/Easy Rider	1983	—	2.00	4.00
MCA					
❑ 51177	I'm So Glad I'm Standing Here Today/Standing Tall	1981	—	2.00	4.00
—With the Crusaders					
❑ 51222	This Old World's Too Funky for Me/Standing Tall	1981	—	2.00	4.00
—With the Crusaders					
❑ 53077	Love Lives On/On My Way to You	1987	—	2.00	4.00
❑ 53077 [PS]	Love Lives On/On My Way to You	1987	—	2.00	4.00
PHILIPS					
❑ 40255	I'll Cry Instead/Precious Words	1965	10.00	20.00	40.00
—Originally by "Vance Arnold and the Avengers"					
❑ 40255	I'll Cry Instead/Precious Words	1965	10.00	20.00	40.00
—Artist listed as "Joe Cocker"					
THE RIGHT STUFF					
❑ S7-19857	Human Touch/One Step Up	1998	—	—	3.00
—B-side by Paul Cebar					

COCKER, JOE, AND JENNIFER WARNES

Also see each artist's individual listings.

Number	Title (A Side/B Side)	Yr	VG	VG+	NM
ISLAND					
❑ 99996	Up Where We Belong/Sweet Li'l Woman	1982	—	2.00	4.00
❑ 99996 [PS]	Up Where We Belong/Sweet Li'l Woman	1982	—	2.00	4.00

COE, JAMIE

Number	Title (A Side/B Side)	Yr	VG	VG+	NM
ABC-PARAMOUNT					
❑ 10120	Goodbye, My Love, Goodbye/There's Never Been a Night	1960	5.00	10.00	20.00
❑ 10149	The Story of Jesse James/Say You	1960	5.00	10.00	20.00
❑ 10203	I'm Gettin' Married/Two Dozen and a Half	1961	5.00	10.00	20.00
❑ 10267	How Low Is Low/Little Darling, Little Darling	1961	5.00	10.00	20.00
ADDISON					
❑ 15001	Summertime Symphony/There's Gonna Be a Day	1959	5.00	10.00	20.00
❑ 15003	I'll Go On Loving You/School Day Blues	1959	5.00	10.00	20.00
BIG TOP					
❑ 3107	Cleopatra/But Yesterday	1962	5.00	10.00	20.00
❑ 3139	The Fool/I've Got That Feeling Again	1963	5.00	10.00	20.00
CAMEO					
❑ 424	Greenback Dollar/But Yesterday	1966	3.75	7.50	15.00
ENTERPRISE					
❑ 5005	The Dealer/Close Your Eyes	1964	3.00	6.00	12.00
❑ 5050	My Girl/I Cried on My Pillow	1964	3.00	6.00	12.00
❑ 5055	Good Enough for a King/I Was the One	1965	3.00	6.00	12.00
❑ 5070	The One Who Really Loves You/A Long Time Ago	1965	3.00	6.00	12.00
❑ 5080	Greenback Dollar/But Yesterday	1965	5.00	10.00	20.00
❑ 5095	First Girl/Very Few	1966	3.75	7.50	15.00
REPRISE					
❑ 295	Close Your Eyes/The Dealer	1964	3.00	6.00	12.00

COEDS, THE

Number	Title (A Side/B Side)	Yr	VG	VG+	NM
SWING					
❑ 101	You're My First Love/Mark My Words	1964	6.25	12.50	25.00
—THE TOKENS sing backup on this record					

COGAN, ALMA

Number	Title (A Side/B Side)	Yr	VG	VG+	NM
AMERICAN ARTS					
❑ 4	I Love You Much Too Much/Tennessee Waltz	1964	2.50	5.00	10.00
CAPITOL					
❑ F4170	Mama Says/Last Night on the Back Porch	1959	3.00	6.00	12.00
❑ 4547	Cowboy Jimmy Joe/Just Couldn't Resist Her with Her Pocket Transistor	1961	3.00	6.00	12.00
LAURIE					
❑ TL 18	Snakes Snails and Puppy Dog Tails/How Many Days How Many Nights	1965	2.50	5.00	10.00
RCA VICTOR					
❑ 47-6063	Blue Again/Paper Kisses	1955	3.75	7.50	15.00
❑ 47-6236	Got N' Idea/Give a Fool a Chance	1955	3.75	7.50	15.00
❑ 47-6405	Twenty Tiny Fingers/Never Do a Tango with an Eskimo	1956	3.00	6.00	12.00
❑ 47-6573	Willie Can/Pickin' a Chicken	1956	3.00	6.00	12.00

COINS, THE

Number	Title (A Side/B Side)	Yr	VG	VG+	NM
GEE					
❑ 10	Cheatin' Baby/Blue, Can't Get No Place with You	1954	500.00	1000.	2000.
❑ 11	Look at Me Girl/S.R. Blues	1954	500.00	1000.	2000.
❑ 1007	Look at Me Girl/Two Loves Have I	1956	150.00	300.00	600.00
—B-side by the Colonials					
MODEL					
❑ 2001	Loretta/Please	1955	500.00	1000.	2000.

COLDER, BEN

See SHEB WOOLEY.

COLE, COZY

Number	Title (A Side/B Side)	Yr	VG	VG+	NM
BETHLEHEM					
❑ 3067	Big Boss/Cozy and Bossa	1963	2.00	4.00	8.00
COLUMBIA					
❑ 43657	Whole Lotta Shakin' Goin' On/Watch It	1966	2.00	4.00	8.00
CORAL					
❑ 62339	Big Noise from Winnetka (Part 1)/Big Noise from Winnetka (Part 2)	1962	2.00	4.00	8.00
❑ 62379	Rockin' Drummer/Sing, Sing, Sing (With a Swing)	1963	2.00	4.00	8.00
—With Gary Chester					
❑ 62395	Ol' Man Moses/Christopher Columbus	1964	2.00	4.00	8.00
❑ 62417	Cozy Beat/Night Beach	1964	2.00	4.00	8.00
FELSTED					
❑ 8546	Caravan Part 1/Caravan Part 2	1959	2.50	5.00	10.00
GRAND AWARD					
❑ 1023	Caravan Part 1/Caravan Part 2	1959	3.00	6.00	12.00
KING					
❑ 5222	Blow-Up/Flop-Down	1959	2.50	5.00	10.00
❑ 5242	Strange/D Natural Rock	1959	2.50	5.00	10.00
❑ 5254	Melody of a Dreamer/Soft	1959	2.50	5.00	10.00
❑ 5265	Boy Meets Girl/Playtime Blues	1959	2.50	5.00	10.00
—With Lee Parker					
❑ 5287	Stain Glass/D'Mitri	1959	2.50	5.00	10.00
❑ 5303	Play, Cozy, Play/Cozy's Mambo	1960	2.50	5.00	10.00
❑ 5316	Blockhead/Teen-Age Ideas	1960	2.50	5.00	10.00
❑ 5337	Drum Fever/Bag of Tricks	1960	2.50	5.00	10.00
❑ 5363	Cozy's Corner/Red Ball	1960	2.50	5.00	10.00
❑ 5390	Ha Ha Cha-Cha/The Pogo Hop	1960	2.50	5.00	10.00
LOVE					
❑ 5003/4	Topsy I/Topsy II	1958	3.75	7.50	15.00
❑ 5014	Turvy I/Turvy II	1958	3.00	6.00	12.00
MERCURY					
❑ 71385	St. Louis Blues/Father Cooperates	1958	3.00	6.00	12.00
MGM					
❑ 11794	Hound Dog Special/Terrible Sight	1954	3.00	6.00	12.00

COLE, DON

Number	Title (A Side/B Side)	Yr	VG	VG+	NM
COED					
❑ 548	Free Flight/Squad Car	1961	5.00	10.00	20.00
GUYDEN					
❑ 2059	Lie Detector Machine/Born to Be with You	1961	25.00	50.00	100.00
KENT					
❑ 305	Saturday Night Party Time/Sweet Lovin' Honey	1958	20.00	40.00	80.00
RPM					
❑ 502	Snake Eyed Mama/Kiss of Love	1957	50.00	100.00	200.00
—With Al Casey					

COLE, NAT KING

Includes reissues of material by the King Cole Trio.

Number	Title (A Side/B Side)	Yr	VG	VG+	NM
AMERICAN PIE					
❑ 9067	The Christmas Song/Ramblin' Rose	198?	—	2.50	5.00
—Reissue					
CAPITOL					
❑ 54-530	Three Little Words/I'll Never Be the Same	1949	5.00	10.00	20.00
—Part of "CCF-156"					
❑ F606	Lillian/Lush Life	1949	3.75	7.50	15.00
—Add 1/3 if "O.C." (optional center) is still in the center of the record					
❑ F889	I Almost Lost My Mind/Baby Won't You Say You Love Me	1950	3.75	7.50	15.00
—Nat King Cole records on Capitol before F889 are unconfirmed on 45 rpm, except as listed					
❑ F1010	Mona Lisa/The Greatest Inventor (Of Them All)	1950	3.75	7.50	15.00
❑ F1030	I Don't Know Why/You're the Cream in My Coffee	1950	3.75	7.50	15.00
❑ F1032	I'm in the Mood for Love/Don't Blame Me	1950	3.75	7.50	15.00
❑ F1033	(I Love You) For Sentimental Reasons/I Can't See for Lookin'	1950	3.75	7.50	15.00
❑ F1034	Little Girl/What Can I Say	1950	3.75	7.50	15.00
❑ F1035	Portrait of Jenny/Lost April	1950	3.75	7.50	15.00
❑ F1036	Exactly Like You/That's What	1950	3.75	7.50	15.00
❑ F1037	Sweet Georgia Brown/I Know That You Know	1950	3.75	7.50	15.00
❑ F1038	This Way Out/Rex Rhumba	1950	3.75	7.50	15.00
❑ F1133	Home (When Shadows Fall)/Tunnel of Love	1950	3.75	7.50	15.00
❑ F1176	Get Out and Get Under/Hey, Not Now	1950	3.75	7.50	15.00
❑ F1184	Orange Colored Sky/Jambo	1950	3.75	7.50	15.00
❑ F1203	Frosty the Snow Man/A Little Christmas Tree	1950	7.50	15.00	30.00
❑ F1270	Time Out for Tears/Get to Gettin'	1951	3.00	6.00	12.00
❑ F1365	Jet/Magic Tree	1951	3.00	6.00	12.00
❑ F1401	Always You/Destination Moon	1951	3.00	6.00	12.00
❑ F1449	Too Young/That's My Girl	1951	3.00	6.00	12.00
❑ F1468	Red Sails in the Sunset/Little Child	1951	3.00	6.00	12.00
❑ F1501	Because of Rain/Song of Delilah	1951	3.00	6.00	12.00
❑ F1565	Early American/My Brother	1951	3.00	6.00	12.00
❑ F1613	Sweet Lorraine/Kee-Mo Ky-Mo	1951	3.00	6.00	12.00
❑ F1627	Lost April/Calypso Blues	1951	3.00	6.00	12.00
❑ F1650	Embraceable You/It's Only a Paper Moon	1951	2.50	5.00	10.00
—As "The King Cole Trio"					
❑ F1663	Nature Boy/For All We Know	1951	2.50	5.00	10.00
❑ F1669	Makin' Whoopee/This Is My Night to Dream	1951	2.50	5.00	10.00
❑ F1672	Lush Life/I Miss You So	1951	2.50	5.00	10.00
❑ F1673	Mona Lisa/No Moon at All	1951	2.50	5.00	10.00
❑ F1674	Too Young/(I Love You) For Sentimental Reasons	1952	2.50	5.00	10.00
❑ F1689	Pretend/Unforgettable	1954	2.50	5.00	10.00
—Most of the Capitol 1600 series were reissues, some of material from 78s					
❑ F1747	Make Believe Land/I'll Always Remember You	1951	3.00	6.00	12.00
❑ F1808	Unforgettable/My First, My Last Love	1951	3.00	6.00	12.00
❑ F1815	I Still See Elisa/You're OK for TV	1951	3.00	6.00	12.00
❑ F1863	Walkin'/I'm Hurtin'	1951	3.00	6.00	12.00
❑ F1893	Here's to My Lady/Miss Me	1951	3.00	6.00	12.00
❑ F1925	Wine, Women and Song/A Weaver of My Dreams	1952	3.00	6.00	12.00
❑ F1968	You Weren't There/You Will Never Grow Old	1952	2.50	5.00	10.00
❑ F1994	Easter Sunday Morning/Summer Is a Comin' On	1952	2.50	5.00	10.00
❑ F2069	Somewhere Along the Way/What Does It Take to Make You Take Me	1952	2.50	5.00	10.00
❑ 2088	Thank You, Pretty Baby/Brazilian Love Song	1968	—	3.00	6.00
❑ F2130	Walking My Baby Back Home/Funny (Not Much)	1952	2.50	5.00	10.00
❑ F2212	Because You're Mine/I'm Never Satisfied	1952	2.50	5.00	10.00

Number	Title (A Side/B Side)	Yr	VG	VG+	NM
❑ F2230	Faith Can Move Mountains/The Ruby and the Pearl	1952	2.50	5.00	10.00
❑ F2309	Strange/How (Do I Go About It)	1952	2.50	5.00	10.00
❑ F2346	Pretend/Don't Let Your Eyes Go Shopping	1953	2.50	5.00	10.00
❑ F2389	Can't I/Blue Gardenia	1953	2.50	5.00	10.00
❑ 2451	I'm Gonna Laugh You Right Out of My Life/People	1969	—	3.00	6.00
❑ F2459	I Am in Love/My Flaming Heart	1953	2.50	5.00	10.00
❑ F2498	Return to Paradise/Angel Eyes	1953	2.50	5.00	10.00
❑ F2540	A Fool Was I/If Love Is Good to Me	1953	2.50	5.00	10.00
❑ F2610	Lover Come Back to Me/That's All	1953	2.50	5.00	10.00
❑ F2616	Mrs. Santa Claus/The Little Boy That Santa Claus Forgot	1953	5.00	10.00	20.00
❑ F2687	Answer Me, My Love/Why	1953	2.50	5.00	10.00
❑ F2734	It Happens to Be Me/Alone Too Long	1954	2.50	5.00	10.00
❑ F2803	Make Her Mine/I Envy	1954	2.50	5.00	10.00
❑ F2897	Smile/It's Crazy	1954	2.50	5.00	10.00
❑ F2949	Hajji Baba (Persian Lament)/Unbelievable	1954	2.50	5.00	10.00
❑ F2955	The Christmas Song (Merry Christmas to You)/ My Two Front Teeth (All I Want for Christmas)	1954	5.00	10.00	20.00
❑ F2985	Open Up the Doghouse/Long, Long Ago	1954	3.75	7.50	15.00
—With Dean Martin					
❑ F3027	Darling Je Vous Aime Beaucoup/The Sand and the Sea	1955	2.50	5.00	10.00
❑ F3095	A Blossom Fell/If I May	1955	3.75	7.50	15.00
—B-side: With the Four Knights					
❑ F3136	My One Sin/Blues from Kiss Me Deadly	1955	2.50	5.00	10.00
❑ F3234	Forgive My Heart/Someone You Love	1955	2.50	5.00	10.00
❑ F3305	Take Me Back to Toyland/I'm Gonna Laugh You Right Out of My Life	1955	5.00	10.00	20.00
❑ F3328	Ask Me/Nothing Ever Changes My Love for You	1956	2.50	5.00	10.00
❑ F3390	Too Young to Go Steady/Never Let Me Go	1956	2.50	5.00	10.00
❑ F3456	That's All There Is to That/My Dream Sonata	1956	2.50	5.00	10.00
❑ F3551	Night Lights/To the Ends of the Earth	1956	2.50	5.00	10.00
❑ F3560	Mrs. Santa Claus/Take Me Back to Toyland	1956	3.75	7.50	15.00
❑ 3561	The Christmas Song (Merry Christmas to You)/ The Little Boy That Santa Claus Forgot	1960	2.00	4.00	8.00
—Purple label, Capitol logo on side					
❑ 3561	The Christmas Song (Merry Christmas to You)/ The Little Boy That Santa Claus Forgot	1962	—	3.00	6.00
—Orange and yellow swirl label					
❑ 3561	The Christmas Song (Merry Christmas to You)/ The Little Boy That Santa Claus Forgot	1973	—	2.00	4.00
—Orange label with "Capitol" at bottom					
❑ F3561	The Christmas Song (Merry Christmas to You)/ The Little Boy That Santa Claus Forgot	1956	3.75	7.50	15.00
—Original with "F" prefix, Capitol logo on top					
❑ F3619	Ballerina/You Are My First Love	1957	2.50	5.00	10.00
❑ F3702	When Rock and Roll Come to Trinidad/China Gate	1957	3.75	7.50	15.00
❑ F3737	Send for Me/My Personal Possession	1957	3.75	7.50	15.00
—B-side: With the Four Knights					
❑ F3782	With You on My Mind/The Song of Raintree County	1957	2.50	5.00	10.00
❑ F3860	Angel Smile/Back in My Arms	1957	2.50	5.00	10.00
❑ F3939	Looking Back/Do I Like It	1958	2.50	5.00	10.00
❑ F4004	Come Closer to Me/Nothing in the World	1958	2.50	5.00	10.00
❑ F4056	Non Dimenticar (Don't Forget)/Bend a Little My Way	1958	2.50	5.00	10.00
❑ F4125	Madrid/Give Me Your Love	1959	2.50	5.00	10.00
❑ F4184	You Made Me Love You/I Must Be Dreaming	1959	2.50	5.00	10.00
❑ F4248	Sweet Bird of Youth/Midnight Flyer	1959	2.50	5.00	10.00
❑ F4248 [PS]	Sweet Bird of Youth/Midnight Flyer	1959	7.50	15.00	30.00
❑ 4301	The Happiest Christmas Tree/Buon Natale	1959	3.00	6.00	12.00
❑ 4325	What'cha Gonna Do/Time and the River	1960	2.00	4.00	8.00
❑ 4369	Is It Better to Have Loved and Lost/That's You	1960	2.00	4.00	8.00
❑ 4393	My Love/Steady	1960	2.00	4.00	8.00
❑ 4481	If I Knew/World in My Arms	1960	2.00	4.00	8.00
❑ 4519	Illusion/When It's Summer	1961	2.00	4.00	8.00
❑ 4555	Goodnight, Little Leaguer/The First Baseball Game	1961	2.00	4.00	8.00
❑ 4582	Take a Fool's Advice/Make It Last	1961	2.00	4.00	8.00
❑ 4623	Let True Love Begin/Cappuccina	1961	2.00	4.00	8.00
❑ 4672	Magic Moment/Step Right Up	1961	2.00	4.00	8.00
❑ 4714	Look No Further/The Right Thing to Say	1962	2.00	4.00	8.00
❑ 4804	Ramblin' Rose/Good Times	1962	3.00	6.00	12.00
❑ 4804 [PS]	Ramblin' Rose/Good Times	1962	5.00	10.00	20.00
❑ 4870	Dear Lonely Hearts/Who's Next in Line	1962	3.00	6.00	12.00
❑ 4870 [PS]	Dear Lonely Hearts/Who's Next in Line	1962	5.00	10.00	20.00
❑ 4919	All Over the World/Nothing Goes Up (Without Coming Down)	1963	2.00	4.00	8.00
❑ 4965	Those Lazy-Hazy-Crazy Days of Summer/In the Cool of Day	1963	3.00	6.00	12.00
❑ 4965 [PS]	Those Lazy-Hazy-Crazy Days of Summer/In the Cool of Day	1963	5.00	10.00	20.00
❑ 5027	That Sunday, That Summer/Mr. Wishing Well	1963	3.00	6.00	12.00
❑ 5125	My True Carrie, Love/A Rag a Bone, A Hank of Hair	1964	2.00	4.00	8.00
❑ 5155	I Don't Want to Be Hurt Anymore/People	1964	2.00	4.00	8.00
❑ 5219	Marnie/More and More of the Amore	1964	2.00	4.00	8.00
❑ 5261	L-O-V-E/I Don't Want to See Tomorrow	1964	2.00	4.00	8.00
❑ 5412	The Ballad of Cat Ballou/They Can't Make Her Cry	1965	2.00	4.00	8.00
—With Stubby Kay					
❑ 5412 [PS]	The Ballad of Cat Ballou/They Can't Make Her Cry	1965	3.75	7.50	15.00
❑ 5486	Wanderlust/You'll See	1965	2.00	4.00	8.00
❑ 5549	One Sun/Looking Back	1965	2.00	4.00	8.00
❑ 5683	Let Me Tell You, Babe/For the Want of a Kiss	1966	2.00	4.00	8.00
❑ F15509	Straighten Up and Fly Right/Nature Boy	1950	3.75	7.50	15.00
—All the Capitol 15000 series on 45s are from multi-disc box sets					
❑ F15510	You Call It Madness/The Frim Fram Sauce	1950	3.75	7.50	15.00
❑ F15511	(Get Your Kicks on) Route 66/Gee Baby Ain't I Been Good to You	1950	3.75	7.50	15.00
❑ F15552	Yes Sir That's My Baby/I Used to Love You	1950	3.75	7.50	15.00
❑ F15553	For All We Know/'Tis Autumn	1950	3.75	7.50	15.00
❑ F15554	Bop Kick/Laugh Cool Clown	1950	3.75	7.50	15.00
❑ F15564	Sweet Lorraine/It's Only a Paper Moon	1950	3.75	7.50	15.00
❑ F15565	The Man I Love/Body and Soul	1950	3.75	7.50	15.00
❑ F15566	Embraceable You/What Is This Thing Called Love	1950	3.75	7.50	15.00
❑ F15643	Jumpin' at Capitol/Love for Sale	1950	3.75	7.50	15.00
—B-side by Benny Carter Orchestra					
❑ F15728	Makin' Whoopee/Honeysuckle Rose	1951	3.00	6.00	12.00
❑ F15729	I'll String Along with You/Too Marvelous for Words	1951	3.00	6.00	12.00
❑ F15730	This Is My Night to Dream/Rhumba Azul	1951	3.00	6.00	12.00
❑ F15843	Return Trip/St. Louis Blues	1952	3.00	6.00	12.00
—B-side by Freddie Slack					
❑ F15868	Penthouse Serenade/If I Should Lose You	1952	3.00	6.00	12.00
❑ F15869	Somebody Loves Me/Down by the Old Mill Stream	1952	3.00	6.00	12.00
❑ F15870	Laura/Polka Dots and Moonbeams	1952	3.00	6.00	12.00
❑ F15922	Walkin' My Baby Back Home/Kay's Lament	1952	3.00	6.00	12.00
—B-side by Kay Starr					
❑ S7-19764	Mrs. Santa Claus/Take Me Back to Toyland	1997	—	—	3.00
❑ S7-57887	The Christmas Song/O Holy Night	1992	—	2.00	4.00
—Originals on black vinyl					
❑ S7-57887	The Christmas Song/O Holy Night	1993	—	2.00	4.00
—Second pressing on red vinyl					
❑ F-90036	(All I Want for Christmas Is) My Two Front Teeth/ The Christmas Song (Merry Christmas To You)	1949	5.00	10.00	20.00
—B-side is the original King Cole Trio hit version, possibly its only U.S. release on 45					

TAMPA

Number	Title (A Side/B Side)	Yr	VG	VG+	NM
❑ 134	Vom-Vim-Veedle/All for You	1957	3.00	6.00	12.00
❑ 134 [PS]	Vom-Vim-Veedle/All for You	1957	6.25	12.50	25.00

7-Inch Extended Plays

CAPITOL

Number	Title (A Side/B Side)	Yr	VG	VG+	NM
❑ EAP 1-332	(contents unknown)	195?	3.00	6.00	12.00
❑ EAP 1-332 [PS]	Penthouse Serenade, Part 1	195?	3.00	6.00	12.00
❑ EAP 2-332	(contents unknown)	195?	3.00	6.00	12.00
❑ EAP 2-332 [PS]	Penthouse Serenade, Part 2	195?	3.00	6.00	12.00
❑ EAP 1-420	*Love Is Here to Stay/A Handful of Stars/Almost Like Being in Love/Tenderly	1954	3.00	6.00	12.00
❑ EAP 1-420 [PS]	Two in Love, Part 1	1954	3.00	6.00	12.00
❑ EAP 2-420	*A Little Street Where Old Friends Meet/This Can't Be Love/Dinner for One Please, James/ There Goes My Heart	1954	3.00	6.00	12.00
❑ EAP 2-420 [PS]	Two in Love, Part 2	1954	3.00	6.00	12.00
❑ EPA 1-500	*Lover Come Back/Pretend/A Fool Was I/I'm Hurtin'	1954	3.00	6.00	12.00
❑ EPA 1-500 [PS]	Songs by Nat King Cole	1954	3.00	6.00	12.00
❑ EAP 1-514	(contents unknown)	1954	3.00	6.00	12.00
❑ EAP 1-514 [PS]	Tenth Anniversary Album, Part 1	1954	3.00	6.00	12.00
❑ EAP 2-514	(contents unknown)	1954	3.00	6.00	12.00
❑ EAP 2-514 [PS]	Tenth Anniversary Album, Part 2	1954	3.00	6.00	12.00
❑ EAP 3-514	The Love Nest/But All I've Got Is Me//Lovelight/ Where Were You	1954	3.00	6.00	12.00
❑ EAP 3-514 [PS]	Tenth Anniversary Album, Part 3	1954	3.00	6.00	12.00
❑ EAP 4-514	Peaches/I Can't Be Bothered//Mother Nature and Father Time/Wish I Were Somebody Else	1954	3.00	6.00	12.00
❑ EAP 4-514 [PS]	Tenth Anniversary Album, Part 4	1954	3.00	6.00	12.00
❑ EBF 1-514 [PS]	Tenth Anniversary Album, Parts 1 and 2	1954	5.00	10.00	20.00
—Gatefold sleeve for some editions of EAP 1-514 and 2-514					
❑ EBF 2-514 [PS]	Tenth Anniversary Album, Parts 3 and 4	1954	5.00	10.00	20.00
—Gatefold sleeve for some editions of EAP 3-514 and 4-514					
❑ EAP 1-782	Sometimes I'm Happy//Just You, Just Me/When I Grow Too Old to Dream	1956	2.50	5.00	10.00
❑ EAP 1-782 [PS]	After Midnight, Part 1	1956	2.50	5.00	10.00
❑ EAP 2-782	Lonely One/I Know That You Know//Sweet Lorraine	1956	2.50	5.00	10.00
❑ EAP 2-782 [PS]	After Midnight, Part 2	1956	2.50	5.00	10.00
❑ EAP 3-782	(contents unknown)	1956	2.50	5.00	10.00
❑ EAP 3-782 [PS]	After Midnight, Part 3	1956	2.50	5.00	10.00
❑ EAP 4-782	(contents unknown)	1956	2.50	5.00	10.00
❑ EAP 4-782 [PS]	After Midnight, Part 4	1956	2.50	5.00	10.00
❑ EBF 1-782 [PS]	After Midnight, Parts 1 & 2	1956	5.00	10.00	20.00
—Gatefold sleeve for some editions of EAP 1-782 and 2-782					
❑ EAP 1-813	*Around the World/Fascination/An Affair to Remember/There's a Gold Mine in the Sky	1957	3.00	6.00	12.00
❑ EAP 1-813 [PS]	Around the World	1957	3.00	6.00	12.00
❑ EAP 1-824	*Love Is the Thing/Stay as Sweet as You Are/ When I Fall in Love/Where Can I Go Without You?	1957	3.00	6.00	12.00
❑ EAP 1-824 [PS]	Love Is the Thing, Part 1	1957	3.00	6.00	12.00
❑ EAP 2-824	Maybe It's Because I Love You Too Much/It's All in the Game//Stardust/When Sunny Gets Blue	1957	3.00	6.00	12.00
❑ EAP 2-824 [PS]	Love Is the Thing, Part 2	1957	3.00	6.00	12.00
❑ EAP 3-824	(contents unknown)	1957	3.00	6.00	12.00
❑ EAP 3-824 [PS]	Love Is the Thing, Part 3	1957	3.00	6.00	12.00
❑ EAP 1-903	(contents unknown)	195?	3.00	6.00	12.00
❑ EAP 1-903 [PS]	Just One of Those Things, Part 1	195?	3.00	6.00	12.00
❑ EAP 2-903	Don't Get Around Much Anymore/The Party's Over//Once in a While/Just for the Fun of It	195?	3.00	6.00	12.00
❑ EAP 2-903 [PS]	Just One of Those Things, Part 2	195?	3.00	6.00	12.00
❑ EAP 3-903	(contents unknown)	195?	3.00	6.00	12.00
❑ EAP 3-903 [PS]	Just One of Those Things, Part 3	195?	3.00	6.00	12.00
❑ EAP-960	(contents unknown)	1958	2.50	5.00	10.00
❑ EAP-960 [PS]	Looking Back	1958	2.50	5.00	10.00
❑ EAP 1-993	*Overture (Introducing "Love Theme" and "Hesitating Blues")/Harlem Blues/Yellow Dog Blues/St. Louis Blues	1958	3.00	6.00	12.00
❑ EAP 1-993 [PS]	St. Louis Blues, Part 1	1958	3.00	6.00	12.00
❑ EAP 2-993	(contents unknown)	1958	3.00	6.00	12.00
❑ EAP 2-993 [PS]	St. Louis Blues, Part 2	1958	3.00	6.00	12.00
❑ EAP 3-993	(contents unknown)	1958	3.00	6.00	12.00
❑ EAP 3-993 [PS]	St. Louis Blues, Part 3	1958	3.00	6.00	12.00

Number	Title (A Side/B Side)	Yr	VG	VG+	NM
❑ EAP 1-1031	*Cachito/Maria Elena/Las Mananitas/Quizas, Quizas, Quizas	1958	3.00	6.00	12.00
❑ EAP 1-1031 [PS]	Cole Espanol, Part 1	1958	3.00	6.00	12.00
❑ EAP 2-1031	(contents unknown)	1958	3.00	6.00	12.00
❑ EAP 2-1031 [PS]	Cole Espanol, Part 2	1958	3.00	6.00	12.00
❑ EAP 3-1031	(contents unknown)	1958	3.00	6.00	12.00
❑ EAP 3-1031 [PS]	Cole Espanol, Part 3	1958	3.00	6.00	12.00
❑ EAP 1-1084	Paradise/Cherchez La Femme//Impossible/ Found A Million Dollar Baby (In A Five And Ten Cent Store)	195?	2.50	5.00	10.00
❑ EAP 1-1084 [PS]	The Very Thought of You, Part 1	195?	2.50	5.00	10.00
❑ EAP 2-1084	(contents unknown)	195?	2.50	5.00	10.00
❑ EAP 2-1084 [PS]	The Very Thought of You, Part 2	195?	2.50	5.00	10.00
❑ EAP-1138	(contents unknown)	195?	2.50	5.00	10.00
❑ EAP-1138 [PS]	Non Dimenticar	195?	2.50	5.00	10.00
❑ EAP 1346	(contents unknown)	195?	2.50	5.00	10.00
❑ EAP 1346 [PS]	The Happiest Christmas Tree	195?	2.50	5.00	10.00
❑ EAP-1500	(contents unknown)	196?	2.50	5.00	10.00
❑ EAP-1500 [PS]	Songs by Nat King Cole	196?	2.50	5.00	10.00
❑ EAP-1535	(contents unknown)	195?	2.50	5.00	10.00
❑ EAP-1535 [PS]	By the Beautiful Sea	195?	2.50	5.00	10.00
❑ EAP-1696	(contents unknown)	196?	2.50	5.00	10.00
❑ EAP-1696 [PS]	Love Songs by Nat King Cole	196?	2.50	5.00	10.00
❑ EAP-1709	(contents unknown)	196?	2.50	5.00	10.00
❑ EAP-1709 [PS]	Strip for Action	196?	2.50	5.00	10.00
❑ SXA-2195 [PS]	L-O-V-E	1965	2.50	5.00	10.00
❑ SXA-2195 [S]	Your Love/My Kind of Girl/Three Little Words//L-O-V-E/Coquette/More	1965	2.50	5.00	10.00

—33 1/3 rpm, small hole

Number	Title (A Side/B Side)	Yr	VG	VG+	NM
❑ EAP 1-9026	The Christmas Song/Mrs. Santa Claus//Frosty The Snowman/Little Christmas Tree	195?	3.00	6.00	12.00
❑ EAP 1-9026 [PS]	The Christmas Song	195?	3.00	6.00	12.00
❑ EAP 1-9120	If I Give My Heart To You/Hold My Hand//Pappa Loves Mambo/Teach Me Tonight	1954	3.00	6.00	12.00
❑ EAP 1-9120 [PS]	Nat King Cole Sings	1954	3.00	6.00	12.00

COLE, NATALIE

CAPITOL

Number	Title (A Side/B Side)	Yr	VG	VG+	NM
❑ 4109	This Will Be/Joey	1975	—	2.50	5.00
❑ 4193	Inseparable/How Come You Won't Stay Here	1975	—	2.00	4.00
❑ 4259	Sophisticated Lady (She's a Different Lady)/ Good Morning Heartache	1976	—	2.00	4.00
❑ 4328	Mr. Melody/Not Like Mine	1976	—	2.00	4.00
❑ 4360	I've Got Love on My Mind/Unpredictable You	1976	—	2.00	4.00
❑ 4439	Party Lights/Peaceful Living	1977	—	2.00	4.00
❑ 4509	Our Love/La Costa	1977	—	2.00	4.00
❑ 4572	Annie Mae/Just Can't Stay Away	1978	—	2.00	4.00
❑ 4623	Lucy in the Sky with Diamonds/Lovers	1978	—	2.00	4.00
❑ 4690	Stand By/Who Will Carry On	1979	—	2.00	4.00
❑ 4722	Sorry/You're So Good	1979	—	2.00	4.00
❑ 4767	Your Lonely Heart/The Winner	1979	—	2.00	4.00
❑ 4869	Someone That I Used to Love/Don't Look Back	1980	—	2.00	4.00
❑ 4924	Hold On/Paradise	1980	—	2.00	4.00
❑ A-5021	You Were Right Girl/Across the Nation	1981	—	2.00	4.00
❑ A-5045	Nothin' But a Fool/The Joke Is On You	1981	—	2.00	4.00

ELEKTRA

Number	Title (A Side/B Side)	Yr	VG	VG+	NM
❑ 64816	The Christmas Song (Chestnuts Roasting on an Open Fire)/Nature Boy	1991	—	2.00	4.00
❑ 64875	Unforgettable/Cottage for Sale	1991	—	2.00	4.00

EMI

Number	Title (A Side/B Side)	Yr	VG	VG+	NM
❑ 50185	Miss You Like Crazy/Good to Be Back	1989	—	—	3.00
❑ 50185 [PS]	Miss You Like Crazy/Good to Be Back	1989	—	2.50	5.00
❑ 50213	I Do/Miss You Like Crazy	1989	—	—	3.00
❑ 50231	As a Matter of Fact/(B-side unknown)	1989	—	—	3.00

EMI MANHATTAN

Number	Title (A Side/B Side)	Yr	VG	VG+	NM
❑ 50117	Pink Cadillac/I Wanna Be That Woman	1988	—	—	3.00
❑ 50138	When I Fall in Love/Pink Cadillac	1988	—	—	3.00
❑ 50138 [PS]	When I Fall in Love/Pink Cadillac	1988	—	2.00	4.00

EPIC

Number	Title (A Side/B Side)	Yr	VG	VG+	NM
❑ 04000	Too Much Mister/Where's Your Angel	1983	—	2.00	4.00
❑ 04147	Keep 'Em on the Outside/I Won't Deny You	1983	—	2.00	4.00

GEFFEN

Number	Title (A Side/B Side)	Yr	VG	VG+	NM
❑ 28152	Over You/After Midnite	1987	—	—	3.00

—With Ray Parker Jr.

MANHATTAN

Number	Title (A Side/B Side)	Yr	VG	VG+	NM
❑ 50073	Jump Start/More Than the Stars	1987	—	—	3.00
❑ 50073 [PS]	Jump Start/More Than the Stars	1987	—	2.00	4.00
❑ 50094	I Live for Your Love/More Than the Stars	1987	—	—	3.00
❑ 50094 [PS]	I Live for Your Love/More Than the Stars	1987	—	2.00	4.00

MODERN

Number	Title (A Side/B Side)	Yr	VG	VG+	NM
❑ 99589	Secrets/Nobody's Soldier	1985	—	—	3.00
❑ 99630	A Little Bit of Heaven/When I Need It Bad, You Got It Good	1985	—	—	3.00
❑ 99648	Dangerous/Love Is On the Way	1985	—	—	3.00
❑ 99648 [PS]	Dangerous/Love Is On the Way	1985	—	—	3.00

COLE, NATALIE, AND PEABO BRYSON

CAPITOL

Number	Title (A Side/B Side)	Yr	VG	VG+	NM
❑ 4804	Gimme Some Time/Love Will Find You	1979	—	2.00	4.00
❑ 4826	What You Won't Do for Love/You're a Lonely Heart	1980	—	2.00	4.00

COLE, PAULA

WARNER BROS.

Number	Title (A Side/B Side)	Yr	VG	VG+	NM
❑ 16910	I Believe in Love/Night	1999	—	—	3.00

WARNER BROS./IMAGO

Number	Title (A Side/B Side)	Yr	VG	VG+	NM
❑ 17318	I Don't Want to Wait/Hitler's Brothers	1997	—	2.00	4.00
❑ 17373	Where Have All the Cowboys Gone?/Hush, Hush, Hush	1997	—	2.50	5.00

COLLECTIVE SOUL

ATLANTIC

Number	Title (A Side/B Side)	Yr	VG	VG+	NM
❑ 83003	Precious Declaration (Remix)/Link	1997	—	—	3.00
❑ 84006	Listen/Precious Declaration	1997	—	—	3.00
❑ 87088	The World I Know/Smashing Young Man	1995	—	—	3.00
❑ 87157	December/Gel	1995	—	—	3.00
❑ 87237	Shine/Breathe	1994	—	—	3.00

COLLECTORS, THE

Early incarnation of CHILLIWACK.

VALIANT

Number	Title (A Side/B Side)	Yr	VG	VG+	NM
❑ 760	Old Man/Looking at a Baby	1967	7.50	15.00	30.00

WARNER BROS.

Number	Title (A Side/B Side)	Yr	VG	VG+	NM
❑ 7059	Listen to the Words/Fisherwoman	1967	5.00	10.00	20.00
❑ 7159	Make It Easy/Fat Bird	1968	5.00	10.00	20.00
❑ 7194	Lydia Purple/She (Will O' the Wind)	1968	3.75	7.50	15.00
❑ 7194	Lydia Purple/I Ain't No Rich Man	1968	3.00	6.00	12.00
❑ 7300	Early Morning/My Love Delights Me	1969	3.00	6.00	12.00

COLLEGIANS, THE (1)

WINLEY

Number	Title (A Side/B Side)	Yr	VG	VG+	NM
❑ 224	Zoom, Zoom, Zoom/On Your Merry Way	1958	12.50	25.00	50.00
❑ 261	Oh I Need Your Love/Tonite, Oh Tonite	1962	7.50	15.00	30.00
❑ 263	Right Around the Corner/Teenie Weenie Little Bit	1962	7.50	15.00	30.00

X-TRA

Number	Title (A Side/B Side)	Yr	VG	VG+	NM
❑ 108	Let's Go for a Ride/Heavenly Night	1958	75.00	150.00	300.00

—Small print label (title and artist about 1/8-inch high)

Number	Title (A Side/B Side)	Yr	VG	VG+	NM
❑ 108	Let's Go for a Ride/Heavenly Night	1961	15.00	30.00	60.00

—Large print label (title and artist about 1/4-inch high)

COLLEGIANS, THE (U)

Some of these may be by group (1), but others are not.

CAT

Number	Title (A Side/B Side)	Yr	VG	VG+	NM
❑ 110	Rickety Tickety Melody/The Sackbut, the Psaltery and the Dulcimer	1954	6.25	12.50	25.00

GROOVE

Number	Title (A Side/B Side)	Yr	VG	VG+	NM
❑ 0163	Blue Solitude/Please Let Me Be the One	1956	10.00	20.00	40.00

HILLTOP

Number	Title (A Side/B Side)	Yr	VG	VG+	NM
❑ 1866	Nomad/Fred's Boogie	1960	5.00	10.00	20.00
❑ 1867	The Saints (Part 1)/The Saints (Part 2)	1960	5.00	10.00	20.00
❑ 1868	Cookin'/Happy Parakeet	1961	5.00	10.00	20.00

HUDCO

Number	Title (A Side/B Side)	Yr	VG	VG+	NM
❑ STAR-1/2	Ooh Poo Pah Doo/Silver Dollar	196?	3.00	6.00	12.00

POST

Number	Title (A Side/B Side)	Yr	VG	VG+	NM
❑ 10002	I'm Ready/Grandma Told Me So	1962	5.00	10.00	20.00

COLLINS, ALBERT

20TH FOX

Number	Title (A Side/B Side)	Yr	VG	VG+	NM
❑ 6708	Cookin' Catfish/Taking My Time	1968	2.00	4.00	8.00

GREAT SCOTT

Number	Title (A Side/B Side)	Yr	VG	VG+	NM
❑ 007	Albert's Alley/Defrost	1963	7.50	15.00	30.00

HALLWAY

Number	Title (A Side/B Side)	Yr	VG	VG+	NM
❑ 1913	Albert's Alley/Defrost	1963	5.00	10.00	20.00
❑ 1920	Frosty/Tremble	1964	7.50	15.00	30.00
❑ 1925	Backstroke/Thaw Out	1964	5.00	10.00	20.00

IMPERIAL

Number	Title (A Side/B Side)	Yr	VG	VG+	NM
❑ 66351	Ain't Got Time/Got a Good Thing Goin'	1969	2.00	4.00	8.00
❑ 66391	Do the Sissy/Turnin' On	1969	2.00	4.00	8.00
❑ 66412	Conversation for Collins/And Then It Started Raining	1969	2.00	4.00	8.00

KANGAROO

Number	Title (A Side/B Side)	Yr	VG	VG+	NM
❑ 103	Freeze/(B-side unknown)	1958	15.00	30.00	60.00
❑ 104	Collins Shuffle/(B-side unknown)	1958	15.00	30.00	60.00

LIBERTY

Number	Title (A Side/B Side)	Yr	VG	VG+	NM
❑ 56184	Coon 'n Collards/Do What You Want to Do	1970	2.00	4.00	8.00

TCF HALL

Number	Title (A Side/B Side)	Yr	VG	VG+	NM
❑ 104	Sno Cone (Part 1)/Sno Cone (Part 2)	1965	2.50	5.00	10.00
❑ 116	Dyin' Flu/Hot 'N' Cold	1966	2.50	5.00	10.00
❑ 127	Frost Bite/Don't Lose Your Cool	1966	2.50	5.00	10.00

COLLINS, BIG TOM

KING

Number	Title (A Side/B Side)	Yr	VG	VG+	NM
❑ 4483	Heartache Blues/Real Good Feeling	1951	25.00	50.00	100.00
❑ 4568	Heart Breaking Woman/Watchin' My Stuff	1952	25.00	50.00	100.00

COLLINS, JUDY

ELEKTRA

Number	Title (A Side/B Side)	Yr	VG	VG+	NM
❑ 45008	Turn, Turn, Turn/Farewell	1963	2.50	5.00	10.00
❑ 45253	Send In the Clowns/Houses	1975	—	2.50	5.00

—Large print label (original)

Number	Title (A Side/B Side)	Yr	VG	VG+	NM
❑ 45253	Send In the Clowns/Houses	1977	—	2.00	4.00

—Small print label (reissue)

Number	Title (A Side/B Side)	Yr	VG	VG+	NM
❑ 45289	Angel, Spread Your Wings/The Moon Is a Harsh Mistress	1975	—	2.00	4.00
❑ 45355	Bread and Roses/Out of Control	1976	—	2.00	4.00
❑ 45372	Everything Must Change/Special Delivery	1976	—	2.00	4.00
❑ 45415	Born to the Breed/Special Delivery	1977	—	2.00	4.00
❑ 45601	I'll Keep It With Mine/Thirsty Boots	1965	2.00	4.00	8.00
❑ 45610	I Think It's Going to Rain Today/Hard Lovin' Losers	1966	2.00	4.00	8.00
❑ 45639	Both Sides Now/Who Knows Where the Time Goes	1968	2.00	4.00	8.00

—Red, white and black label

Number	Title (A Side/B Side)	Yr	VG	VG+	NM
❑ 45639	Both Sides Now/Who Knows Where the Time Goes	1968	—	3.00	6.00

—Yellow and black label

Number	Title (A Side/B Side)	Yr	VG	VG+	NM
❑ 45649	Someday Soon/My Father	1969	—	3.00	6.00
❑ 45657	Chelsea Morning/Pretty Polly	1969	—	3.00	6.00
❑ 45657 [PS]	Chelsea Morning/Pretty Polly	1969	3.75	7.50	15.00
❑ 45680	Pack Up Your Sorrows/Turn, Turn, Turn	1970	—	2.50	5.00
❑ 45709	Amazing Grace/Nightingale II	1971	—	2.50	5.00

Number	Title (A Side/B Side)	Yr	VG	VG+	NM
❑ 45755	Open the Door/Innisfree	1971	—	2.50	5.00
❑ 45813	In My Life/Sunny Goodge Street	1972	—	2.00	4.00
❑ 45831	Cook with Honey/So Begins the Task	1973	—	2.00	4.00
❑ 45849	The Hostage/Secret Gardens	1973	—	2.00	4.00
❑ 46020	Hard Times for Lovers/Happy End	1979	—	2.00	4.00
❑ 46020 [PS]	Hard Times for Lovers/Happy End	1979	—	3.00	6.00
❑ 46050	Where or When/Dorothy	1979	—	2.00	4.00
❑ 46623	Bright Morning Star/Almost Free	1980	—	2.00	4.00
❑ 46651	The Rainbow Connection/Running for My Life	1980	—	2.00	4.00
❑ 47243	Memory/The Life You Dream	1981	—	2.00	4.00
❑ 47434	It's Gonna Be One of Those Nights/Mama Mama	1982	—	2.00	4.00
❑ 69662	Only You/Dream On	1985	—	—	3.00
❑ 69697	Home Again/Dream On	1984	—	2.00	4.00

—A-side with T.G. Sheppard

COLLINS, LARRY
Also see THE COLLINS KIDS.

COLUMBIA

Number	Title (A Side/B Side)	Yr	VG	VG+	NM
❑ 4-41727	The Rebel — Johnny Yuma/Spur of the Moment	1960	3.75	7.50	15.00
❑ 4-41953	Get Along Home Cindy/What About Tomorrow	1960	3.75	7.50	15.00
❑ 4-42131	One Step Down/There She Stands, The One	1961	3.75	7.50	15.00
❑ 4-42394	T-Bone/Wild and Wicked Love	1962	3.75	7.50	15.00
❑ 4-42534	Hey Mama Boom-a-Lacka/More Than a Friend	1962	3.75	7.50	15.00

MONUMENT

Number	Title (A Side/B Side)	Yr	VG	VG+	NM
❑ 1148	New York City, R.F.D./Say Goodbye	1969	2.00	4.00	8.00
❑ 1196	The Outcast/Shake Hands with the Devil	1970	2.00	4.00	8.00

COLLINS, LORRIE
Also see THE COLLINS KIDS.

COLUMBIA

Number	Title (A Side/B Side)	Yr	VG	VG+	NM
❑ 4-41541	The Lonesome Road/Another Man Done Gone	1959	5.00	10.00	20.00
❑ 4-41673	Blues in the Night/That's Your Affair	1960	5.00	10.00	20.00
❑ 4-42242	Home of the Blues/Waitin' and Watchin'	1961	3.75	7.50	15.00

COLLINS, LYN
Also see JAMES BROWN.

KING

Number	Title (A Side/B Side)	Yr	VG	VG+	NM
❑ 6373	Wheels of Life/Just Won't Do Right	1971	2.00	4.00	8.00

PEOPLE

Number	Title (A Side/B Side)	Yr	VG	VG+	NM
❑ 608	Think (About It)/Ain't No Sunshine	1972	2.50	5.00	10.00
❑ 615	Me and My Baby Got a Good Thing Goin'/I'll Never Let You Break My Heart Again	1972	—	3.00	6.00
❑ 618	Mama Feel Good/Fly Me to the Moon	1973	—	3.00	6.00
❑ 623	How Long Can I Keep It Up (Part 1)/How Long Can I Keep It Up (Part 2)	1973	—	3.00	6.00
❑ 626	Take Me As I Am/Make the World a Better Place	1973	—	3.00	6.00
❑ 630	We Wanted to Parrty, Parrty, Parrty/You Can't Beat Two People in Love	1973	—	3.00	6.00
❑ 633	Take Me Just As I Am/Don't Make Me Over	1973	—	3.00	6.00
❑ 636	Give It Up or Turnit A Loose/What the World Needs Now Is Love	1974	—	3.00	6.00
❑ 641	Wide Awake in a Dream/Rock Me Again & Again & Again & Again & Again & Again	1974	—	3.00	6.00
❑ 650	Rock Me Again & Again & Again & Again & Again & Again/You Can't Love Me If You Don't Respect Me	1974	—	3.00	6.00
❑ 657	Baby Don't Do It/How Long Can I Keep It Up	1975	—	3.00	6.00
❑ 659	If You Don't Know Me By Now/Baby Don't Do It	1975	—	3.00	6.00
❑ 662	Mr. Big Stuff/Rock Me Again & Again & Again & Again & Again & Again	1975	—	3.00	6.00

COLLINS, PHIL
Also see GENESIS.

ATLANTIC

Number	Title (A Side/B Side)	Yr	VG	VG+	NM
❑ 3790	I Missed Again/I'm Not Moving	1981	—	—	3.00
❑ 3790 [PS]	I Missed Again/I'm Not Moving	1981	—	3.00	6.00
❑ 3824	In the Air Tonight/The Roof Is Leaking	1981	—	—	3.00
❑ 3824 [PS]	In the Air Tonight/The Roof Is Leaking	1981	—	3.00	6.00
❑ 87360	Hero/Coverage	1993	—	2.00	4.00

—A-side: David Crosby and Phil Collins; B-side: David Crosby solo

Number	Title (A Side/B Side)	Yr	VG	VG+	NM
❑ 87800	Hang In Long Enough/Separate Lives	1990	—	—	3.00
❑ 87885	Something Happened on the Way to Heaven/Lionel	1990	—	—	3.00
❑ 87955	Do You Remember?/I Wish It Would Rain Down (Live)	1990	—	—	3.00
❑ 88738	I Wish It Would Rain Down/You've Been in Love (That Little Bit)	1989	—	—	3.00
❑ 88738 [PS]	I Wish It Would Rain Down/You've Been in Love (That Little Bit)	1989	—	—	3.00
❑ 88774	Another Day in Paradise/Heat on the Street	1989	—	—	3.00
❑ 88774 [PS]	Another Day in Paradise/Heat on the Street	1989	—	—	3.00
❑ 88980	Two Hearts/The Robbery	1989	—	—	3.00
❑ 88980 [PS]	Two Hearts/The Robbery	1989	—	2.00	4.00
❑ 89017	Groovy Kind of Love/Big Noise	1988	—	—	3.00
❑ 89017 [PS]	Groovy Kind of Love/Big Noise	1988	—	2.00	4.00
❑ 89472	Take Me Home/Only You Know and I Know	1985	—	—	3.00
❑ 89472 [PS]	Take Me Home/Only You Know and I Know	1985	—	2.00	4.00
❑ 89498	Separate Lives (Love Theme from White Nights)/(Instrumental)	1985	—	—	3.00

—With Marilyn Martin

Number	Title (A Side/B Side)	Yr	VG	VG+	NM
❑ 89498 [PS]	Separate Lives (Love Theme from White Nights)/(Instrumental)	1985	—	2.50	5.00

—With promo shot from the movie on front of sleeve

Number	Title (A Side/B Side)	Yr	VG	VG+	NM
❑ 89498 [PS]	Separate Lives (Love Theme from White Nights)/(Instrumental)	1985	—	2.00	4.00

—With photo of Phil and Marilyn on front of sleeve

Number	Title (A Side/B Side)	Yr	VG	VG+	NM
❑ 89536	Don't Lose My Number/We Said Hello Goodbye	1985	—	—	3.00
❑ 89536 [PS]	Don't Lose My Number/We Said Hello Goodbye	1985	—	—	3.00
❑ 89560	Sussudio/I Like the Way	1985	—	—	3.00
❑ 89560 [PS]	Sussudio/I Like the Way	1985	—	—	3.00
❑ 89588	One More Night/The Man with the Horn	1985	—	—	3.00
❑ 89588 [PS]	One More Night/The Man with the Horn	1985	—	—	3.00
❑ 89700	Against All Odds (Take a Look at Me Now)/The Search	1984	—	—	3.00

—B-side by Larry Carlton

Number	Title (A Side/B Side)	Yr	VG	VG+	NM
❑ 89700 [PS]	Against All Odds (Take a Look at Me Now)/The Search	1984	—	—	3.00
❑ 89864	I Cannot Believe It's True/Thru These Walls	1983	—	—	3.00
❑ 89877	I Don't Care Anymore/The West Side	1983	—	—	3.00
❑ 89877 [PS]	I Don't Care Anymore/The West Side	1983	—	—	3.00
❑ 89933	You Can't Hurry Love/Do You Know	1982	—	—	3.00
❑ 89933 [PS]	You Can't Hurry Love/Do You Know	1982	—	—	3.00

COLLINS KIDS, THE
Also see LARRY COLLINS; LORRIE COLLINS.

COLUMBIA

Number	Title (A Side/B Side)	Yr	VG	VG+	NM
❑ 4-21470	Beetle Bug Bop/Hush Money	1955	7.50	15.00	30.00
❑ 4-21514	The Rockaway/Make Him Behave	1956	7.50	15.00	30.00
❑ 4-21543	I'm in My Teens/They're Still in Love	1956	7.50	15.00	30.00
❑ 4-21560	Rock and Roll Polka/My First Love	1956	7.50	15.00	30.00
❑ 4-40760	You Are My Sunshine/Nobody's Darling But Mine	1956	5.00	10.00	20.00

—With Carl Smith, Rosemary Clooney and Gene Autry

Number	Title (A Side/B Side)	Yr	VG	VG+	NM
❑ 4-40824	Move a Little Closer/Go Away, Don't Bother Me	1957	7.50	15.00	30.00
❑ 4-40921	Hop, Skip and Jump/Young Heart	1957	7.50	15.00	30.00
❑ 4-41012	Party/Heartbeat	1957	20.00	40.00	80.00
❑ 4-41087	Hoy Hoy/Mama Worries	1958	12.50	25.00	50.00
❑ 4-41149	Mercy/Sweet Talk	1958	12.50	25.00	50.00
❑ 4-41225	Rock Boppin' Baby/Whistle Bait	1958	15.00	30.00	60.00

—As "Lorrie and Larry Collins"

Number	Title (A Side/B Side)	Yr	VG	VG+	NM
❑ 4-41329	Sugar Plum/Kinda Like Love	1959	6.25	12.50	25.00

COLOGNES, THE
LUMMTONE

Number	Title (A Side/B Side)	Yr	VG	VG+	NM
❑ 102	A River Flows/A Bird and a Bee	1960	37.50	75.00	150.00

COLORADO
With members of THE FIREBALLS.

UNI

Number	Title (A Side/B Side)	Yr	VG	VG+	NM
❑ 55280	My Babe/Country Comfort	1971	—	3.00	6.00
❑ 55302	Dogwood/Moonshine	1971	—	3.00	6.00

COLTS, THE
ANTLER

Number	Title (A Side/B Side)	Yr	VG	VG+	NM
❑ 4003	Never No More/The Shiek of Araby	1959	10.00	20.00	40.00
❑ 4007	Guiding Angel/The Shiek of Araby	1959	10.00	20.00	40.00

MAMBO

Number	Title (A Side/B Side)	Yr	VG	VG+	NM
❑ 112	Adorable/Lips Red as Wine	1955	100.00	200.00	400.00

PLAZA

Number	Title (A Side/B Side)	Yr	VG	VG+	NM
❑ 505	Hey, Pretty Baby/Sweet Sixteen	1962	5.00	10.00	20.00

VITA

Number	Title (A Side/B Side)	Yr	VG	VG+	NM
❑ 112	Adorable/Lips Red as Wine	1955	37.50	75.00	150.00
❑ 121	Honey Bun/Sweet Sixteen	1955	30.00	60.00	120.00
❑ 130	Never No More/Hey You Shoo-Bee-Ooh Bee	1956	30.00	60.00	120.00

COLYER, KEN
LONDON

Number	Title (A Side/B Side)	Yr	VG	VG+	NM
❑ 1655	Down by the Riverside/Take This Hammer	1956	3.00	6.00	12.00
❑ 1674	Casey Jones/Streamline Train	1956	3.00	6.00	12.00

COMFORTABLE CHAIR, THE
ODE

Number	Title (A Side/B Side)	Yr	VG	VG+	NM
❑ 109	Be Me/Some Soon, Some Day	1968	2.50	5.00	10.00
❑ 112	I'll See You/Now	1968	2.50	5.00	10.00

COMMANDER CODY AND HIS LOST PLANET AIRMEN
ARISTA

Number	Title (A Side/B Side)	Yr	VG	VG+	NM
❑ 0271	Seven-Eleven/You Snooze You Lose	1977	—	2.00	4.00
❑ 0344	Thank You Lone Ranger/My Day	1978	—	2.00	4.00

DOT

Number	Title (A Side/B Side)	Yr	VG	VG+	NM
❑ 17487	Daddy's Drinking Up Our Christmas/Honeysuckle Honey	1973	—	3.00	6.00
❑ 17500	Diggy Liggy Lo/Outgoing Person	1974	—	2.50	5.00

PARAMOUNT

Number	Title (A Side/B Side)	Yr	VG	VG+	NM
❑ 0130	Lost in the Ozone/Midnight Shift	1971	—	3.00	6.00
❑ 0146	Hot Rod Lincoln/My Home in My Hand	1972	—	3.00	6.00
❑ 0169	Beat Me Daddy, Eight to the Bar/Daddy's Gonna Treat You Right	1972	—	3.00	6.00
❑ 0178	Truck Stop Rock/Mama Hated Diesels	1972	—	3.00	6.00
❑ 0193	Semi-Truck/Watch My .38	1973	—	3.00	6.00
❑ 0216	Smoke! Smoke! Smoke! (That Cigarette)/Rock That Boogie	1973	—	3.00	6.00
❑ 0216 [PS]	Smoke! Smoke! Smoke! (That Cigarette)/Rock That Boogie	1973	2.50	5.00	10.00
❑ 0278	Riot in Cell Block No. 9/Oh, Momma Momma	1974	—	3.00	6.00

WARNER BROS.

Number	Title (A Side/B Side)	Yr	VG	VG+	NM
❑ 8073	Don't Let Go/Keep On Lovin' Her	1975	—	2.00	4.00
❑ 8164	It's Gonna Be One of Those Nights/Roll Your Own	1975	—	2.00	4.00

COMMITMENTS, THE
MCA

Number	Title (A Side/B Side)	Yr	VG	VG+	NM
❑ 54257	Mustang Sally/Take Me to the River	1991	—	2.50	5.00
❑ 54258	Chain of Fools/The Dark End of the Street	1991	—	2.50	5.00
❑ 54259	Destination Anywhere/I Can't Stand the Rain	1991	—	2.50	5.00
❑ 54260	Try a Little Tenderness/Do Right Woman, Do Right Man	1991	—	2.50	5.00
❑ 54261	Treat Her Right/Mr. Pitiful	1991	—	2.50	5.00
❑ 54262	I Never Loved a Man/In the Midnight Hour	1991	—	2.50	5.00
❑ 54263	Bye Bye Baby/Slip Away	1991	—	2.50	5.00

—These seven singles, which comprise the movie soundtrack of "The Commitments," were usually sold in a set (though not boxed) with custom jukebox strips (add $10)

COMMODORES
Also see LIONEL RICHIE.

MOTOWN

Number	Title (A Side/B Side)	Yr	VG	VG+	NM
❑ 1268	Are You Happy/There's a Song in My Heart	1973	—	3.00	6.00

Number	Title (A Side/B Side)	Yr	VG	VG+	NM
❑ 1307	Machine Gun/There's a Song in My Heart	1974	—	2.50	5.00
❑ 1319	I Feel Sanctified/It Is As Good As You Make It	1974	—	2.50	5.00
❑ 1338	Slippery When Wet/The Bump	1975	—	2.50	5.00
❑ 1361	This Is Your Life/Look What You've Done to Me	1975	—	2.50	5.00
❑ 1366	Wide Open/(B-side unassigned)	1975	—	—	—
—Unreleased					
❑ 1381	Sweet Love/Better Never Than Forever	1976	—	2.00	4.00
❑ 1394	Come Inside/Time	1976	—	—	—
—Unreleased					
❑ 1399	High on Sunshine/Thumpin' Music	1976	—	—	—
—Unreleased					
❑ 1402	Just to Be Close to You/Thumpin' Music	1976	—	2.00	4.00
❑ 1408	Fancy Dancer/Cebu	1977	—	2.00	4.00
❑ 1418	Easy/Can't Let You Tease Me	1977	—	2.00	4.00
❑ 1425	Brick House/Captain Quickdraw	1977	—	2.00	4.00
❑ 1432	Too Hot Ta Trot/Funky Situation	1977	—	2.00	4.00
❑ 1443	Three Times a Lady/Look What You've Done to Me	1978	—	2.00	4.00
❑ 1452	Flying High/X-Rated Movie	1978	—	2.00	4.00
❑ 1457	Say Yeah/(B-side unassigned)	1978	—	—	—
—Unreleased					
❑ 1466	Sail On/Thumpin' Music	1979	—	2.00	4.00
❑ 1474	Still/Such a Woman	1979	—	2.00	4.00
❑ 1479	Wonderland/Lovin' You	1979	—	2.00	4.00
❑ 1489	Old Fashion Love/Sexy Lady	1980	—	2.00	4.00
❑ 1495	Heroes/Funky Situation	1980	—	2.00	4.00
❑ 1502	Jesus Is Love/Mighty Spirit	1980	—	3.00	6.00
❑ 1514	Lady (You Bring Me Up)/Gettin' It	1981	—	2.00	4.00
❑ 1527	Oh No/Lovin' You	1981	—	2.00	4.00
❑ 1604	Why You Wanna Try Me/X-Rated Movie	1982	—	2.00	4.00
❑ 1651	Painted Pictures/Reach High	1982	—	—	3.00
❑ 1661	Sexy Lady/Reach High	1983	—	—	3.00
❑ 1694	Only You/Cebu	1983	—	—	3.00
❑ 1719	Been Lovin' You/Turn Off the Lights	1984	—	—	3.00
❑ 1773	Nightshift/I Keep Running	1985	—	—	3.00
❑ 1773 [PS]	Nightshift/I Keep Running	1985	—	3.00	6.00
❑ 1788	Animal Instinct/Lightin' Up the Sky	1985	—	—	3.00
❑ 1802	Janet/I'm in Love	1985	—	—	3.00

MOWEST

Number	Title (A Side/B Side)	Yr	VG	VG+	NM
❑ 5009	I'm Looking for Love/At the Zoo	1972	2.00	4.00	8.00
❑ 5038	Determination/Don't You Be Worried	1973	2.00	4.00	8.00

POLYDOR

Number	Title (A Side/B Side)	Yr	VG	VG+	NM
❑ 871370-7	Ain't Giving Up/Grrip	1989	—	—	3.00
❑ 885358-7	Goin' to the Bank/Serious Love	1986	—	—	3.00
❑ 885358-7 [PS]	Goin' to the Bank/Serious Love	1986	—	—	3.00
❑ 885538-7	Take It from Me/I Wanna Rock You	1987	—	—	3.00
❑ 885538-7 [PS]	Take It from Me/I Wanna Rock You	1987	—	—	3.00
❑ 885760-7	United in Love/Talk to Me	1987	—	—	3.00
❑ 885760-7 [PS]	United in Love/Talk to Me	1987	—	—	3.00
❑ 887939-7	Solitaire/Stretchhh	1988	—	—	3.00
❑ 887939-7 [PS]	Solitaire/Stretchhh	1988	—	—	3.00

COMMODORES, THE

None of the below are the popular 1970s-1980s group, but they aren't all the same group, either.

ATLANTIC

Number	Title (A Side/B Side)	Yr	VG	VG+	NM
❑ 2633	Keep On Dancing/Rise Up	1969	2.00	4.00	8.00

BRUNSWICK

Number	Title (A Side/B Side)	Yr	VG	VG+	NM
❑ 55126	Laughing with Tears/Who Dat	1959	5.00	10.00	20.00

CHALLENGE

Number	Title (A Side/B Side)	Yr	VG	VG+	NM
❑ 1004	Sweet Angel/Not a Day Goes By	1957	5.00	10.00	20.00
❑ 1007	Faith/I'll Be There	1957	5.00	10.00	20.00

DOT

Number	Title (A Side/B Side)	Yr	VG	VG+	NM
❑ 15372	Uranium/Riding on a Train	1955	6.25	12.50	25.00
❑ 15425	Cream Puff/Close to My Heart	1955	6.25	12.50	25.00
❑ 15439	Speedoo/Whole Lotta Shakin' Goin' On	1956	6.25	12.50	25.00
❑ 15461	Two Loves Have I/Who Said I Said That	1956	6.25	12.50	25.00

COMO, PERRY

RCA

Number	Title (A Side/B Side)	Yr	VG	VG+	NM
❑ 9096-7-R [DJ]	I May Never Pass This Way Again (same on both sides)	1989	—	2.50	5.00
—Promotional record for Christmas Seals					
❑ PB-10122	Christmas Dream/Christ Is Born	1976	—	—	3.00
—Reissue; black label, dog near top					
❑ PB-11185	Girl You Made It Happen/Where You're Concerned	1977	—	—	3.00
❑ PB-11434	When I Wanted You/Forever	1978	—	—	3.00
❑ PB-12028	Colors of My Life/Someone Is Waiting	1980	—	—	3.00
❑ PB-12088	Not While I'm Around/When	1980	—	—	3.00
❑ PB-12146	You Are My World/Regrets	1981	—	—	3.00
❑ PB-13069	Goodbye for Now (Theme from "Reds")/Jason	1982	—	—	3.00
❑ PB-13307	I Wish It Could Be Christmas Forever/Toyland	1982	—	2.00	4.00
❑ PB-13453	So It Goes/Fancy Dancer	1983	—	—	3.00
❑ PB-13613	As My Love for You/The Second Time	1983	—	—	3.00
❑ PB-13690	The Best of Times/Son on the Sand	1983	—	—	3.00

RCA VICTOR

Number	Title (A Side/B Side)	Yr	VG	VG+	NM
❑ APBO-0096	Love Don't Care/Walk Right Back	1973	—	2.00	4.00
❑ SP-45-119 [DJ]	(There's No Place Like) Home For The Holidays/I'll Be Home For Christmas	1962	3.00	6.00	12.00
❑ APBO-0225	Beyond Tomorrow/It All Seems to Fall Into Line	1974	—	2.00	4.00
❑ APBO-0274	Weave Me the Sunshine/I Don't Know What He Told You	1974	—	2.00	4.00
❑ E3VW 1339/F7OW 9047 [DJ]	Rudolph the Red-Nosed Reindeer/Rudolph the Red-Nosed Reindeer	1955	3.75	7.50	15.00
—B-side by the Three Suns					
❑ K2NW 6096/7 [DJ]	(Intro) I May Never Pass This Way Again/(Alternate Intro) I May Never Pass This Way Again	1959	3.00	6.00	12.00
—Promotional record for Christmas Seals					
❑ PB-10045	In These Crazy Times/Temptation	1974	—	—	3.00
❑ PB-10122	Christmas Dream/Christ Is Born	1974	—	2.00	4.00
—Gray label					
❑ GB-10174	Catch a Falling Star/Dream Along with Me	1975	—	—	3.00
—Gold Standard Series					
❑ GB-10175	Hot Diggity (Dog Ziggity Boom)/Don't Let the Stars Get In Your Eyes	1975	—	—	3.00
—Gold Standard Series					
❑ GB-10176	Prisoner of Love/Magic Moments	1975	—	—	3.00
—Gold Standard Series					
❑ GB-10177	Round and Round/Wanted	1975	—	—	3.00
—Gold Standard Series					
❑ PB-10257	Wonderful Baby/World of Dreams	1975	—	—	3.00
❑ PB-10402	Just Out of Reach/Love Put a Song in My Heart	1975	—	2.00	4.00
❑ GB-10471	And I Love You So/Love Looks So Good on You	1975	—	—	3.00
—Gold Standard Series					
❑ PB-10604	Then You Can Tell Me Goodbye/The Grass Keeps Right On Growing	1976	—	—	3.00
❑ 47-2728	Because/If You Had All the World and All the Gold	1949	3.75	7.50	15.00
❑ 47-2747	What'll I Do?/Love Me or Leave Me	1949	3.75	7.50	15.00
❑ 47-2843	When Your Hair Has Turned to Silver/When Day Is Done	1949	3.75	7.50	15.00
❑ 47-2844	Carolina Moon/Body and Soul	1949	3.75	7.50	15.00
❑ 47-2845	I'm Always Chasing Rainbows/If We Can't Be the Same Old Sweethearts, We'll Just Be the Same Old Friends	1949	3.75	7.50	15.00
—The above three comprise box set WP 187, "A Sentimental Date with Perry"					
❑ 47-2886	Prisoner of Love/Temptation	1949	3.75	7.50	15.00
❑ 47-2887	Till the End of Time/Because	1949	3.75	7.50	15.00
❑ 47-2888	When You Were Sweet Sixteen/Song of Songs	1949	3.75	7.50	15.00
❑ 47-2892	Forever and Ever/I Don't See Me in Your Eyes Anymore	1949	3.75	7.50	15.00
❑ 47-2896	Bali Ha'i/Some Enchanted Evening	1949	3.75	7.50	15.00
❑ 47-2899	"A" You're Adorable/When Is Sometime?	1949	3.75	7.50	15.00
❑ 47-2919	Every Time I Meet You/Two Little, New Little, Blue Little Eyes	1949	3.75	7.50	15.00
❑ 47-2931	Let's Take an Old-Fashioned Walk/Just One Way to Say I Love You	1949	3.75	7.50	15.00
❑ 47-2969	That Christmas Feeling/Winter Wonderland	1949	5.00	10.00	20.00
❑ 47-2970	I'll Be Home for Christmas/Santa Claus Is Coming to Town	1949	5.00	10.00	20.00
❑ 47-2971	Silent Night/White Christmas	1949	5.00	10.00	20.00
❑ 47-2972	Jingle Bells/O Come All Ye Faithful	1949	5.00	10.00	20.00
❑ 47-2997	Give Me Your Hand/I Wish I Had a Record	1949	3.75	7.50	15.00
❑ 47-3036	A Dreamer's Holiday/The Meadows of Heaven	1949	3.75	7.50	15.00
❑ 47-3211	Please Believe Me/Did Anyone Ever Tell You, Mrs. Murphy	1949	3.75	7.50	15.00
❑ 47-3226	Easter Parade/Song of Songs	1949	3.75	7.50	15.00
❑ 47-3229	With a Song in My Heart/Blue Room	1949	3.75	7.50	15.00
❑ 47-3267	Far Away Places/Missouri Waltz	1949	3.75	7.50	15.00
❑ 47-3763	If You Were Only Mine/Let's Go to the Church	1950	3.00	6.00	12.00
❑ 47-3850	Bless This House/The Rosary	1950	3.00	6.00	12.00
❑ 47-3851	Mother Dear O Pray For Me/Hoy God, We Praise Thy Name	1950	3.00	6.00	12.00
❑ 47-3852	Rock of Ages/Prayer of Thanksgiving	1950	3.00	6.00	12.00
❑ 47-3905	Patricia/Watchin' the Trains Go By	1950	3.00	6.00	12.00
❑ 47-3922	The Best Thing for You/Marrying for Love	1950	3.00	6.00	12.00
❑ 47-3930	A Bushel and a Peck/She's a Lady	1950	3.00	6.00	12.00
—With Betty Hutton					
❑ 47-3931	Marchita/So Long Sally	1950	3.00	6.00	12.00
❑ 47-3933	The Christmas Symphony/There Is No Christmas Like a Home Christmas	1950	3.75	7.50	15.00
❑ 47-3997	If/Zing, Zing, Zoom, Zoom	1950	3.00	6.00	12.00
❑ 47-4033	Without a Song/More Than You Know	1951	3.00	6.00	12.00
❑ 47-4034	It's Only a Paper Moon/Me and My Shadow	1951	3.00	6.00	12.00
❑ 47-4035	That Old Gang of Mine/I Found a Million Dollar Baby	1951	3.00	6.00	12.00
❑ 47-4081	Tumbling Tumbleweeds/You Don't Know What Lonesome Is	1951	3.00	6.00	12.00
—With the Sons of the Pioneers					
❑ 47-4112	Hello Young Lovers/We Kissed in a Shadow	1951	3.00	6.00	12.00
❑ 47-4158	There's No Boat Like a Rowboat/There's a Big Blue Cloud (Next to Heaven)	1951	3.00	6.00	12.00
❑ 47-4203	Surprising/Cara Cara Bella Bella	1951	3.00	6.00	12.00
❑ 47-4314	It's Beginning to Look Like Christmas/There Is No Christmas Like a Home Christmas	1951	3.75	7.50	15.00
❑ 47-4445	Garden in the Rain/Oh, How I Miss You Tonight	1952	3.00	6.00	12.00
❑ 47-4453	Please Mr. Sun/Tulips and Heather	1952	3.00	6.00	12.00
❑ 47-4527	You'll Never Walk Alone/Over the Rainbow	1952	3.00	6.00	12.00
❑ 47-4528	Black Moonlight/I Concentrate on You	1952	3.00	6.00	12.00
❑ 47-4529	My Heart Stood Still/If There's Someone	1952	3.00	6.00	12.00
❑ 47-4530	Summertime/While We're Young	1952	3.00	6.00	12.00
❑ 47-4631	One Little Candle/It's Easter Time	1952	3.00	6.00	12.00
❑ 47-4687	Why Did You Leave Me/Lonesome, That's All	1952	3.00	6.00	12.00
❑ 47-4707	Childhood Is a Meadow/One Little Candle	1952	3.00	6.00	12.00
❑ 47-4744	Maybe/Watermelon Weather	1952	3.00	6.00	12.00
—With Eddie Fisher					
❑ 47-4877	My Love and Devotion/Sweethearts' Holiday	1952	3.00	6.00	12.00
❑ 47-5064	Don't Let the Stars Get In Your Eyes/Lies	1952	3.00	6.00	12.00
❑ 47-5152	Wild Horses/I Confess	1953	3.00	6.00	12.00
❑ 47-5277	Say You're Mine Again/My One and Only Heart	1953	3.00	6.00	12.00
❑ 47-5317	No Other Love/Keep It Gay	1953	3.00	6.00	12.00
❑ 47-5317 [PS]	No Other Love/Keep It Gay	1953	5.00	10.00	20.00
❑ 47-5447	You Alone (Solo Tu)/Pa-Paya Mama	1953	3.00	6.00	12.00
❑ 47-5571	I Believe/Onward Christian Soldiers	1953	3.00	6.00	12.00
❑ 47-5572	Act of Contrition/Good Night Sweet Jesus	1953	3.00	6.00	12.00
❑ 47-5573	Abide with Me/Nearer, My God, To Thee	1953	3.00	6.00	12.00
❑ 47-5574	Eli, Eli/Kol Niore	1953	3.00	6.00	12.00
❑ 47-5647	Wanted/Look Out the Window	1954	3.00	6.00	12.00
❑ 47-5749	Hit and Run Affair/There Never Was a Night So Beautiful	1954	3.00	6.00	12.00
❑ 47-5857	Papa Loves Mambo/The Things I Didn't Do	1954	3.00	6.00	12.00
❑ 47-5950	(There's No Place Like) Home for the Holidays/Silk Stockings	1954	3.00	6.00	12.00

Number	Title (A Side/B Side)	Yr	VG	VG+	NM
❑ 47-5994	Ko Ko Mo (I Love You So)/You'll Always Be My Lifetime Sweetheart	1955	2.50	5.00	10.00
❑ 47-6059	Door of Dreams/Nobody	1955	2.50	5.00	10.00
❑ 47-6137	Chee Chee O-Chee (Sang the Little Bird)/Two Lost Souls	1955	2.50	5.00	10.00
—With Jaye P. Morgan					
❑ 47-6192	Tina Marie/Fooled	1955	2.50	5.00	10.00
❑ 47-6294	All at Once You Love Her/The Rose Tattoo	1955	2.50	5.00	10.00
❑ 47-6321	Home for the Holidays/God Rest Ye Merry Gentlemen	1955	3.00	6.00	12.00
❑ 47-6427	Hot Diggity (Dog Ziggity Boom)/Juke Box Baby	1956	2.50	5.00	10.00
❑ 47-6554	More/Glendora	1956	2.50	5.00	10.00
❑ 47-6590	Somebody Up There Likes Me/Dream Along with Me	1956	2.50	5.00	10.00
❑ 47-6590 [PS]	Somebody Up There Likes Me/Dream Along with Me	1956	7.50	15.00	30.00
❑ 47-6670	Moonlight Love/Chincherinchee	1956	2.50	5.00	10.00
❑ 47-6815	Round and Round/Mi Casa, Su Casa (My House Is Your House)	1957	2.50	5.00	10.00
❑ 47-6904	The Girl with the Golden Braids/My Little Baby	1957	2.50	5.00	10.00
❑ 47-6991	Dancin'/Marchin' Along to the Blues	1957	2.50	5.00	10.00
❑ 47-7050	Just Born (To Be Your Baby)/Ivy Rose	1957	2.50	5.00	10.00
❑ 47-7128	Catch a Falling Star/Magic Moments	1957	3.00	6.00	12.00
❑ 47-7202	Kewpie Doll/Dance Only with Me	1958	2.50	5.00	10.00
❑ 47-7274	Moon Talk/Beats There a Heart So True	1958	2.50	5.00	10.00
❑ 47-7353	Love Makes the World Go 'Round/Mandolins in the Moonlight	1958	2.50	5.00	10.00
❑ 47-7464	Tomboy/Kiss Me and Kiss Me and Kiss Me	1959	2.50	5.00	10.00
❑ 47-7541	I Know/You Are in Love	1959	2.50	5.00	10.00
❑ 47-7541 [PS]	I Know/You Are in Love	1959	6.25	12.50	25.00
❑ 47-7628	I May Never Pass This Way Again/A Still Small Voice	1959	2.50	5.00	10.00
❑ 47-7650	Ave Maria/The Lord's Prayer	1959	2.50	5.00	10.00
❑ 47-7670	Delaware/I Know What God Is	1960	2.00	4.00	8.00
❑ 47-7812	Make Someone Happy/Gone Is My Love	1960	2.00	4.00	8.00
❑ 47-7962	You're Following Me/Especially for the Young	1961	2.00	4.00	8.00
❑ 47-8004	Caterina/The Island of Forgotten Lovers	1962	2.00	4.00	8.00
❑ 47-8004 [PS]	Caterina/The Island of Forgotten Lovers	1962	5.00	10.00	20.00
❑ 47-8186	(I Love You) Don't You Forget It/One More Mountain	1963	2.00	4.00	8.00
❑ 47-8186 [PS]	(I Love You) Don't You Forget It/One More Mountain	1963	5.00	10.00	20.00
❑ 47-8533	Dream On Little Dreamer/My Own Peculiar Way	1965	2.00	4.00	8.00
❑ 47-8533 [PS]	Dream On Little Dreamer/My Own Peculiar Way	1965	5.00	10.00	20.00
❑ 47-8636	Oowee, Oowee/Summer Wind	1965	2.00	4.00	8.00
❑ 47-8722	Meet Me at the Altar/Bye, Bye, Little Girl	1965	2.00	4.00	8.00
❑ 47-8823	Stay with Me/Coo Coo Roo Coo Coo Paloma	1966	2.00	4.00	8.00
❑ 47-8945	Forget Domani/One Day Is Like Another	1966	2.00	4.00	8.00
❑ 47-9165	Stop! And Think It Over/How Beautiful the World Can Be	1967	—	3.00	6.00
❑ 47-9262	I Looked Back/A World of Love (That I Found)	1967	—	3.00	6.00
❑ 47-9356	What Love Is Made Of/You Made It That Way	1967	—	3.00	6.00
❑ 47-9367	Christmas Bells/Love Is a Christmas Rose	1967	2.00	4.00	8.00
❑ 47-9367 [PS]	Christmas Bells/Love Is A Christmas Rose	1967	2.50	5.00	10.00
❑ 47-9448	The Father of Girls/Somebody Makes It So	1968	—	2.50	5.00
❑ 47-9533	Happy Man/Another Go-Round	1968	—	2.50	5.00
❑ 47-9683	There Is No Christmas Like a Home Christmas/Christmas Eve	1968	—	3.00	6.00
❑ 47-9722	Seattle/Sunshine Wine	1969	—	2.50	5.00
❑ 52-0071	Ave Maria/The Lord's Prayer	1949	6.25	12.50	25.00
—Blue vinyl original					
❑ 52-0071	Ave Maria/The Lord's Prayer	1949	3.00	6.00	12.00
—Black vinyl reissue					
❑ 74-0193	Happiness Comes, Happiness Goes/That's All This Old World Needs	1969	—	2.00	4.00
❑ 74-0356	Don't Leave Me/Love Is Spreading All Over the World	1970	—	2.00	4.00
❑ 74-0387	It's Impossible/Long Life. Lots of Happiness	1970	—	2.50	5.00
❑ 74-0436	Don't Leave Me/Love Is Spreading All Over the World	1971	—	2.00	4.00
❑ 74-0444	El Condor Pasa/I Think of You	1971	—	2.00	4.00
❑ 74-0518	My Days of Loving You/Yesterday I Heard the Rain	1971	—	2.00	4.00
❑ 74-0906	And I Love Her So/Love Looks So Good on You	1973	—	2.00	4.00
❑ 447-0110	Ave Maria/The Lord's Prayer	1955	3.00	6.00	12.00
❑ 447-0810	Silent Night/O Come, All Ye Faithful	196?	—	2.50	5.00
❑ 447-0811	That Christmas Feeling/I'll Be Home For Christmas	196?	—	2.50	5.00
❑ 447-0812	Home for the Holidays/God Rest Ye Merry Gentlemen	196?	—	2.50	5.00

USAF

Number	Title (A Side/B Side)	Yr	VG	VG+	NM
❑ 85/86 [DJ]	"Special Christmas Show" Home For The Holidays/Merry Merry Christmas To You	195?	3.75	7.50	15.00
—B-side by Art Mooney					

7-Inch Extended Plays

RCA CAMDEN

Number	Title (A Side/B Side)	Yr	VG	VG+	NM
❑ CAE-410	Without a Song/More Than You Know//Me and My Shadow/Dream Along with Me	195?	2.00	4.00	8.00
❑ CAE-410 [PS]	Dream Along with Me	195?	2.00	4.00	8.00

RCA VICTOR

Number	Title (A Side/B Side)	Yr	VG	VG+	NM
❑ EYA-19	The Story of the First Christmas//Santa Claus Is Coming to Town/Jingle Bells	195?	3.75	7.50	15.00
—"Little Nipper" Children's Series issue					
❑ SPD-27 [PS]	Perry Como	195?	3.75	7.50	15.00
—Box for 10-EP set plus booklet					
❑ SPD-28	South of the Border/Because/Bless This House//Breezin' Along with the Breeze/Lies/You'll Never Walk Alone	1957	5.00	10.00	20.00
❑ SPD-28 [PS]	Kleenex Presents Perry Como Highlighter	1957	5.00	10.00	20.00
❑ 547-0033	When Day Is Done/Carolina Moon//What'll I Do/If We Can't Be the Same Old Sweethearts We'll Just Be the Same Old Friends	1952	2.50	5.00	10.00
—Part of 2-EP set EPB 3035					
❑ 547-0034	I'm Always Chasing Rainbows/Love Me or Leave Me//Body and Soul/When Your Hair Has Turned to Silver (I Will Love You Just the Same)	1952	2.50	5.00	10.00
—Part of 2-EP set EPB 3035					
❑ SP-45-55	Hot Diggity/Patricia/Lazy Bones//Dream Along with Me/Land of Dreams/Bewitched	1958	5.00	10.00	20.00
❑ SP-45-55 [PS]	Kleenex Tissues Presents RCA Victor's '59 Highlighter: Perry Como and His Friends	1958	5.00	10.00	20.00
❑ 547-0059	Prisoner of Love/Because//When You Were Sweet Sixteen/Far Away Places	1952	2.50	5.00	10.00
—Part of 2-EP set EPB 3044					
❑ EPA-293	(contents unknown)	195?	3.00	6.00	12.00
❑ EPA-293 [PS]	Perry Como Sings His Favorite Songs of Worship	195?	3.00	6.00	12.00
❑ EPA-409	(contents unknown)	195?	3.00	6.00	12.00
❑ EPA-409 [PS]	Perry Como Sings the Hits from Broadway Shows	195?	3.00	6.00	12.00
❑ EPA-410	(contents unknown)	195?	3.00	6.00	12.00
❑ EPA-410 [PS]	Songs of Faith	195?	3.00	6.00	12.00
❑ EPA-451	(contents unknown)	195?	3.00	6.00	12.00
❑ EPA-451 [PS]	Perry Como Sings the Hits from Broadway Shows	195?	3.00	6.00	12.00
❑ 547-0454	(contents unknown)	1954	2.50	5.00	10.00
—Record 1 of 2-EP set EPB 3224					
❑ 547-0455	Temptation/Prisoner of Love//When You Were Sweet Sixteen/Because	1954	2.50	5.00	10.00
—Record 2 of 2-EP set EPB 3224					
❑ EPA-496	The Night Before Christmas/God Rest Ye Merry, Gentlemen//The 12 Days of Christmas/C-H-R-I-S-T-M-A-S	195?	3.00	6.00	12.00
❑ EPA-496 [PS]	Around The Christmas Tree	195?	3.00	6.00	12.00
❑ EPA-497	(contents unknown)	195?	3.00	6.00	12.00
❑ EPA-497 [PS]	Around the Christmas Tree	195?	3.00	6.00	12.00
❑ EPA-563	(contents unknown)	1954	3.00	6.00	12.00
❑ EPA-563 [PS]	Wanted	1954	3.00	6.00	12.00
❑ EPA-642	For Me and My Gal/My Funny Valentine//It Happened in Monterey/It's the Talk of the Town	1955	3.00	6.00	12.00
❑ EPA-642 [PS]	P.C.	1955	3.00	6.00	12.00
❑ EPA-728	(contents unknown)	1955	3.00	6.00	12.00
❑ EPA-728 [PS]	Perry Como Sings Hits from Broadway Shows	1955	3.00	6.00	12.00
❑ EPA-738	(contents unknown)	1955	3.00	6.00	12.00
❑ EPA-738 [PS]	Relaxing with Perry Como	1955	3.00	6.00	12.00
❑ EPA-739	(contents unknown)	1955	3.00	6.00	12.00
❑ EPA-739 [PS]	A Sentimental Date with Perry Como	1955	3.00	6.00	12.00
❑ EPA-903	(contents unknown)	1956	3.00	6.00	12.00
❑ EPA-903 [PS]	Perry Como Sings	1956	3.00	6.00	12.00
❑ EPA-920	*Santa Claus Is Comin' to Town/Frosty the Snow Man/Winter Wonderland/Rudolph, the Red-Nosed Reindeer/Jingle Bells	1956	3.00	6.00	12.00
❑ EPA-920 [PS]	Perry Como Sings Merry Christmas Music	1956	3.00	6.00	12.00
❑ 547-1049	Joy to the World/White Christmas//God Rest Ye Merry, Gentlemen/The Christmas Song	1955	2.50	5.00	10.00
—Part of 2-EP set EPB 1243					
❑ EPB 1243 [PS]	Merry Christmas Music	1955	5.00	10.00	20.00
—Cover for 2-EP set					
❑ EPA 1-1463	Swinging Down the Lane/South of the Border//Honey, Honey (Bless Your Heart)/Angry	1957	2.50	5.00	10.00
❑ EPA 1-1463 [PS]	We Get Letters, Vol. 1	1957	2.50	5.00	10.00
❑ EPB 3035 [PS]	A Sentimental Date with Perry	1952	2.50	5.00	10.00
—Double-pocket cover for 547-0033 and 547-0034					
❑ EPB 3044 [PS]	Supper Club Favorites	1952	2.50	5.00	10.00
—Two-pocket jacket for two-EP set					
❑ EPB 3224 [PS]	Como's Golden Records	1954	2.50	5.00	10.00
—Double-pocket cover for 547-0454 and 547-0455					
❑ EPA-4285 [M]	Accentuate the Positive/Red Sails in the Sunset//Birth of the Blues/It Had to Be You	1958	2.50	5.00	10.00
❑ EPA-4285 [PS]	(title unknown)	1958	2.50	5.00	10.00
❑ ESP-4285 [PS]	(title unknown)	1958	5.00	10.00	20.00
❑ ESP-4285 [S]	Accentuate the Positive/Red Sails in the Sunset//Birth of the Blues/It Had to Be You	1958	5.00	10.00	20.00
❑ EPA-4326	A Still Small Voice/I May Never Pass This Way Again//He's Got the Whole World in His Hands/When You Come to the End of the Day	1958	2.50	5.00	10.00
❑ EPA-4326 [PS]	(title unknown)	1958	2.50	5.00	10.00
❑ EPA-5012	*Don't Let the Stars Get In Your Eyes/Wanted/Papa Loves Mambo/Hot Diggity (Dog Ziggity Boom)	1958	2.50	5.00	10.00
❑ EPA-5012 [PS]	Como's Golden Records	1958	2.50	5.00	10.00
❑ EPA-5029	Round and Round/When You Were Sweet Sixteen//Till the End of Time/A Hubba Hubba Hubba	1958	2.50	5.00	10.00
❑ EPA-5029 [PS]	Como's Golden Records, Volume 2	1958	2.50	5.00	10.00
❑ EPA-5030	*Temptation/Mi Casa, Su Casa/Prisoner of Love/Because	1958	2.50	5.00	10.00
❑ EPA-5030 [PS]	Como's Golden Records, Volume 3	1958	2.50	5.00	10.00
❑ EPA-5109	Juke Box Baby/Catch a Falling Star//Tina Marie/Magic Moments	1959	2.50	5.00	10.00
❑ EPA-5109 [PS]	(title unknown)	1959	2.50	5.00	10.00
❑ 599-9156	For Me and My Gal/As Time Goes By//I Believe/When Day Is Done	1957	2.00	4.00	8.00
—Side 1 and 20 of 10-EP set SPD-27					
❑ 599-9157	Far Away Places/Till the End of Time//Don't Let the Stars Get In Your Eyes/Bali Ha'I	1957	2.00	4.00	8.00
—Side 2 and 19 of 10-EP set SPD 27					
❑ 599-9158	It's a Good Day/My Funny Valentine//You'll Never Walk Alone/Hello Young Lovers	1957	2.00	4.00	8.00
—Side 3 and 18 of 10-EP set SPD 27					
❑ 599-9159	If There Is Someone Lovelier Than You/Over the Rainbow//Body and Soul/Lies	1957	2.00	4.00	8.00
—Side 4 and 17 of 10-EP set SPD 27					

Number	Title (A Side/B Side)	Yr	VG	VG+	NM
❑ 599-9160	Temptation/Black Moonlight//All at Once You Love Her/Look Out the Window	1957	2.00	4.00	8.00
—Side 5 and 16 of 10-EP set SPD 27					
❑ 599-9161	If/When You Were Sweet Sixteen//I've Got the World on a String/You Do Something To Me	1957	2.00	4.00	8.00
—Side 6 and 15 of 10-EP set SPD 27					
❑ 599-9162	Prisoner of Love/Carolina Moon//One for My Baby/In the Still of the Night	1957	2.00	4.00	8.00
—Side 7 and 14 of 10-EP set SPD 27					
❑ 599-9163	What'll I Do/Blue Moon//Hot Diggity (Dog Ziggity Boom)/It Happened in Monterey	1957	2.00	4.00	8.00
—Side 8 and 13 of 10-EP set SPD 27					
❑ 599-9164	With a Song in My Heart/No Other Love//Breezin' Along with the Breeze/It's the Talk of the Town	1957	2.00	4.00	8.00
—Side 9 and 12 of 10-EP set SPD 27					
❑ 599-9165	Wanted/Love Me or Leave Me//Pa-Paya Mama/I Gotta Right to Sing the Blues	1957	2.00	4.00	8.00
—Side 10 and 11 of 10-EP set SPD 27					

COMO, PERRY, AND THE FONTANE SISTERS
Also see each artist's individual listings.

Number	Title (A Side/B Side)	Yr	VG	VG+	NM
RCA VICTOR					
❑ 47-3082	I Wanna Go Home (With You)/Hush Little Darlin'	1949	3.75	7.50	15.00
❑ 47-3113	Bibbidi-Bobbidi-Boo/A Dream Is a Wish Your Heart Makes	1949	3.75	7.50	15.00
❑ 47-3747	Hoop-Dee-Doo/On the Outgoing Tide	1950	3.00	6.00	12.00
❑ 47-3846	I Cross My Fingers/If You Were My Girl	1950	3.00	6.00	12.00
❑ 47-3945	You're Just in Love/It's a Lovely Day Today	1950	3.00	6.00	12.00
❑ 47-4269	Rollin' Stone/With All My Heart and Soul	1951	3.00	6.00	12.00
❑ 47-4344	Here's to My Lady/If Wishes Were Kisses	1951	3.00	6.00	12.00
❑ 47-4542	Noodlin' Rag/Play Me a Hurtin' Tune	1952	3.00	6.00	12.00
❑ 47-4959	To Know You (Is to Love You)/My Lady Loves to Dance	1952	3.00	6.00	12.00
❑ 47-5524	Silver Bells/Kissing Bridge	1953	3.00	6.00	12.00

COMPANIONS, THE
More than one group.

Number	Title (A Side/B Side)	Yr	VG	VG+	NM
AMY					
❑ 852	No Fool Am I/How Could You	1962	25.00	50.00	100.00
ARLEN					
❑ 722	These Foolish Things/It's Too Late	1963	20.00	40.00	80.00
BROOK'S					
❑ 100	Why, Oh Why Baby/I Didn't Know (You Got Married)	1959	15.00	30.00	60.00
COLUMBIA					
❑ 42279	I'll Always Love You/A Little Bit of Blue	1962	7.50	15.00	30.00
DOVE					
❑ 240	Falling/Oh, What a Feeling!	1958	30.00	60.00	120.00
FEDERAL					
❑ 12397	Why, Oh Why Baby/I Didn't Know (You Got Married)	1960	7.50	15.00	30.00
GENERAL AMERICAN					
❑ 711	Be Yourself/Help a Lonely Guy	1962	5.00	10.00	20.00
GINA					
❑ 722	These Foolish Things/It's Too Late	1963	12.50	25.00	50.00

COMPETITORS, THE

Number	Title (A Side/B Side)	Yr	VG	VG+	NM
DOT					
❑ 16560	Power Shift/Little Stick Nomad	1963	10.00	20.00	40.00

COMPLIMENTS, THE

Number	Title (A Side/B Side)	Yr	VG	VG+	NM
CONGRESS					
❑ 243	Shake It Up, Shake It Down/You Are My Sunshine	1965	12.50	25.00	50.00
❑ 252	The Time of Her Life/Everybody Loves a Lover	1965	12.50	25.00	50.00
MIDAS					
❑ 304	Borrow 'Til Morning/Beware, Beware	1968	7.50	15.00	30.00

COMPOSERS, THE

Number	Title (A Side/B Side)	Yr	VG	VG+	NM
AMPEN					
❑ 221	Woe Is Me/Elephant Drag	196?	75.00	150.00	300.00
ERA					
❑ 3118	I Had a Dream/You and Yours	1963	5.00	10.00	20.00

COMSTOCK, BOBBY

Number	Title (A Side/B Side)	Yr	VG	VG+	NM
ASCOT					
❑ 2164	Right Hand Man/Always	1964	3.75	7.50	15.00
❑ 2175	I'm a Man/I'll Make You Glad	1965	3.00	6.00	12.00
❑ 2193	This Magic Moment/Shotgun Sally	1965	3.00	6.00	12.00
❑ 2216	Can't Judge a Book/Out of Sight	1966	3.00	6.00	12.00
ATLANTIC					
❑ 2051	Jambalaya/Let's Talk It Over	1960	5.00	10.00	20.00
BLAZE					
❑ 349	Tennessee Waltz/Sweet Talk	1959	6.25	12.50	25.00
FESTIVAL					
❑ 25000	Garden of Eden/Piece of Paper	1961	5.00	10.00	20.00
JUBILEE					
❑ 5392	Bony Maronie/Do That Little Thing	1960	5.00	10.00	20.00
❑ 5396	Jezebel/Your Big Brown Eyes	1961	5.00	10.00	20.00
LAWN					
❑ 202	Let's Stomp/I Want to Do It	1963	3.75	7.50	15.00
❑ 210	Susie Baby/Take a Walk	1963	3.75	7.50	15.00
❑ 217	The Chicken Back/Sunny	1963	3.75	7.50	15.00
❑ 219	Your Boyfriend's Back/This Little Love of Mine	1963	5.00	10.00	20.00
❑ 224	I Can't Help Myself/Run My Heart	1963	3.75	7.50	15.00
❑ 229	The Beatle Bounce/Since You Been Gone	1964	5.00	10.00	20.00
❑ 232	Can It Be True/Ain't That Just Like Me	1964	3.75	7.50	15.00
❑ 255	I Wanna Do It/This Little Love of Mine	1965	3.00	6.00	12.00
MOHAWK					
❑ 124	The Wayward Wind/Everyday Blues	1960	5.00	10.00	20.00
TRIUMPH					
❑ 602	Jealous Fool/Zig Zag	1959	6.25	12.50	25.00

CONCORDS, THE (1)

Number	Title (A Side/B Side)	Yr	VG	VG+	NM
BOOM					
❑ 60021	Down the Aisle of Love/I Feel Love Comin'	1966	10.00	20.00	40.00
EPIC					
❑ 9697	Should I Cry/It's Our Wedding Day	1964	15.00	30.00	60.00
GRAMERCY					
❑ 304	Cross My Heart/Our Last Goodbye	1961	12.50	25.00	50.00
—No candy canes on label					
❑ 304	Cross My Heart/Our Last Goodbye	1961	50.00	100.00	200.00
—With candy canes on label					
❑ 305	My Dreams/Scarlet Ribbons	1961	10.00	20.00	40.00
HERALD					
❑ 576	Marlene/Our Love Wasn't Meant to Be	1962	6.25	12.50	25.00
❑ 578	Cold and Frosty Morning/Don't Go Now	1963	7.50	15.00	30.00
POLYDOR					
❑ 14036	Down the Aisle of Love/I Feel a Love Comin' On	1970	3.00	6.00	12.00
RCA VICTOR					
❑ 47-7911	Again/The Boy Most Likely	1961	7.50	15.00	30.00
RUST					
❑ 5048	One Step from Heaven/Away	1962	7.50	15.00	30.00

CONCORDS, THE (2)

Number	Title (A Side/B Side)	Yr	VG	VG+	NM
EMBER					
❑ 1007	I'm Satisfied with Rock 'N' Roll/I'll Always Say Please	1956	15.00	30.00	60.00
HARLEM					
❑ 2328	Candlelight/Monticello	1954	150.00	300.00	600.00

CONDORS, THE

Number	Title (A Side/B Side)	Yr	VG	VG+	NM
HUNTER					
❑ 2503/4	Swetest Angel/Little Curly Top	1960	250.00	500.00	1000.

CONFESSIONS, THE

Number	Title (A Side/B Side)	Yr	VG	VG+	NM
EPIC					
❑ 9474	Be-Bop Baby/Before You Change Your Mind	1961	6.25	12.50	25.00

CONLEY, ARTHUR

Number	Title (A Side/B Side)	Yr	VG	VG+	NM
ATCO					
❑ 6463	Sweet Soul Music/Let's Go Steady	1967	2.50	5.00	10.00
❑ 6494	Shake, Rattle and Roll/You Don't Have to See Me	1967	2.00	4.00	8.00
❑ 6529	Whole Lot of Woman/Love Comes and Goes	1967	2.00	4.00	8.00
❑ 6563	Funky Street/Put Our Love Together	1968	2.00	4.00	8.00
❑ 6588	People Sure Act Funny/Burning Fire	1968	2.00	4.00	8.00
❑ 6622	Is That You Love/Aunt Dora's Love Soul Shack	1968	2.00	4.00	8.00
❑ 6640	Ob-La-Di, Ob-La-Da/Otis Sleep On	1968	2.00	4.00	8.00
❑ 6661	Speak Her Name/Run On	1969	—	3.00	6.00
❑ 6706	Star Review/Love Sure Is a Powerful Thing	1969	—	3.00	6.00
❑ 6733	Hurt/They Call the Wind Maria	1970	—	3.00	6.00
❑ 6747	God Bless/(Your Love Has Brought Me A) Mighty Long Way	1970	—	3.00	6.00
❑ 6790	Nobody's Fault But Mine/Day-O	1970	—	3.00	6.00
CAPRICORN					
❑ 0001	More Sweet Soul Music/Walking on Eggs	1972	2.50	5.00	10.00
❑ 0006	Rita/More Sweet Soul Music	1972	2.00	4.00	8.00
❑ 0047	Bless You/It's So Nice	1973	2.00	4.00	8.00
❑ 8017	I'm Living Good/I'm So Glad You're Here	1971	2.50	5.00	10.00
FAME					
❑ 1007	I Can't Stop/In the Same Old Way	1966	3.75	7.50	15.00
❑ 1009	Take Me (Just As I Am)/I'm Gonna Forget About You	1966	3.75	7.50	15.00
JOTIS					
❑ 470	I'm a Lonely Stranger/Where Lead Me	1965	5.00	10.00	20.00
❑ 472	Who's Fooling Who/There's a Place for Us	1966	5.00	10.00	20.00
PHILCO-FORD					
❑ HP-15	Sweet Soul Music/You Don't Have to See Me	1968	3.75	7.50	15.00
—4-inch plastic "Hip Pocket Record" with color sleeve					

CONNORS, CAROL
Also see THE CARMEL SISTERS; THE TEDDY BEARS.

Number	Title (A Side/B Side)	Yr	VG	VG+	NM
CAPITOL					
❑ 5152	Never/Angel, My Angel	1964	6.25	12.50	25.00
COLUMBIA					
❑ 41976	You Are My Answer/My Diary	1961	6.25	12.50	25.00
❑ 42155	Listen to the Beat/My Special Boy	1961	6.25	12.50	25.00
❑ 42337	That's All It Takes/What Do You See in Him	1962	6.25	12.50	25.00
ERA					
❑ 3084	Two Rivers/Big, Big Love	1962	7.50	15.00	30.00
❑ 3096	Tommy Go Away/I Wanna Know	1962	7.50	15.00	30.00
MIRA					
❑ 219	Lonely Little Beach Girl/My Baby Looks, But He Don't Touch	1965	6.25	12.50	25.00
❑ 219 [PS]	Lonely Little Beach Girl/My Baby Looks, But He Don't Touch	1965	12.50	25.00	50.00
N.T.C.					
❑ 3131	Yum Yum Yamaha	1964	12.50	25.00	50.00
—One-sided single					
❑ 3131 [PS]	Yum Yum Yamaha	1964	25.00	50.00	100.00

CONRAD, JESS

Number	Title (A Side/B Side)	Yr	VG	VG+	NM
LONDON					
❑ 1967	Mystery Girl/Just the Two of Us	1961	3.00	6.00	12.00
❑ 2005	Little Ship/Walk Away	1961	3.00	6.00	12.00

CONSORTS, THE

Number	Title (A Side/B Side)	Yr	VG	VG+	NM
APT					
❑ 25066	Please Be Mine/Time After Time	1962	30.00	60.00	120.00
COUSINS					
❑ 1004	Please Be Mine/Time After Time	1961	100.00	200.00	400.00

CONTENDERS, THE

More than one group.

Number	Title (A Side/B Side)	Yr	VG	VG+	NM
BETH					
❑ 1001	I'll Show You How to Love/(B-side unknown)	195?	5.00	10.00	20.00
BLUE SKY					
❑ 105	Mr. Dee Jay/Yes I Do	1959	150.00	300.00	600.00
CHATTAHOOCHIE					
❑ 644	The Dune Bugy/Go Ahead	1964	6.25	12.50	25.00
❑ 656	Johnny B. Goode/Rise 'N' Shine	1964	6.25	12.50	25.00
JACKPOT					
❑ 48002	Tequila Song/Wild Man	1959	10.00	20.00	40.00
JAVA					
❑ 101	The Clock/Look at Me	196?	25.00	50.00	100.00
—Gold label					
❑ 101	The Clock/Look at Me	196?	6.25	12.50	25.00
—Red label					

CONTINENTAL GEMS, THE

Number	Title (A Side/B Side)	Yr	VG	VG+	NM
GUYDEN					
❑ 2091	My Love Will Follow You/Everywhere	1963	100.00	200.00	400.00

CONTINENTALS, THE (1)

Number	Title (A Side/B Side)	Yr	VG	VG+	NM
ERA					
❑ 3003	Cool Penguin/Soap Sudz	1959	5.00	10.00	20.00
PENGUIN					
❑ 1002	Cool Penguin/Soap Sudz	1959	10.00	20.00	40.00

CONTINENTALS, THE (2)

Number	Title (A Side/B Side)	Yr	VG	VG+	NM
PORT					
❑ 70018	Dear Lord/Fine Fine Frame	1960	7.50	15.00	30.00
❑ 70024	Picture of Love/Soft and Sweet	1961	7.50	15.00	30.00
WHIRLIN' DISC					
❑ 101	Dear Lord/Fine Fine Frame	1956	50.00	100.00	200.00
❑ 105	Picture of Love/Soft and Sweet	1957	50.00	100.00	200.00

CONTINENTALS, THE (3)

Number	Title (A Side/B Side)	Yr	VG	VG+	NM
RAMA					
❑ 190	You Are An Angel/Giddy Up a Ding Dong	1956	375.00	750.00	1500.
—Blue label					
❑ 190	You Are An Angel/Giddy Up a Ding Dong	1956	37.50	75.00	150.00
—Red label					

CONTINENTALS, THE (U)

Some of these may be groups (1), (2) or (3); many are not.

Number	Title (A Side/B Side)	Yr	VG	VG+	NM
AOK					
❑ 1025	Take Me/She Wants You	1966	6.25	12.50	25.00
BOLO					
❑ 720	I'm Coming Home/The Turnaround	1960	7.50	15.00	30.00
CUCA					
❑ 1063	Tic-Toc/Sue	1961	7.50	15.00	30.00
DAVIS					
❑ 466	Don't Do It, Baby/Tongue Twister	1959	10.00	20.00	40.00
HUNTER					
❑ 3503	It Doesn't Matter/Whisper It	1960	300.00	600.00	1200.
KEY					
❑ 517	Take a Gamble on Me/Meanwhile Back at the Ranch	1956	25.00	50.00	100.00
LIFETIME					
❑ 1019	Cathy's Clown/Maybe Baby	1966	2.50	5.00	10.00
VANDAN					
❑ 8067	No Money No Luck Blues/Pink Champagne	196?	5.00	10.00	20.00

CONTOURS, THE

Number	Title (A Side/B Side)	Yr	VG	VG+	NM
GORDY					
❑ 7005	Do You Love Me/Move Mr. Man	1962	5.00	10.00	20.00
❑ 7012	Shake Sherry/You Better Get in Line	1963	3.75	7.50	15.00
❑ 7016	Don't Let Her Be Your Baby/It Must Be Love	1963	3.00	6.00	12.00
❑ 7019	Pa I Need a Car/You Get Ugly	1963	3.00	6.00	12.00
❑ 7029	Can You Do It/I'll Stand By You	1964	3.00	6.00	12.00
❑ 7037	Can You Jerk Like Me/That Day When She Needed Me	1964	3.00	6.00	12.00
❑ 7044	First I Look at the Purse/Searching for a Girl	1965	3.00	6.00	12.00
❑ 7052	Just a Little Misunderstanding/Determination	1966	3.00	6.00	12.00
❑ 7059	It's So Hard Being a Loser/Your Love Grows More Precious Every Day	1967	3.00	6.00	12.00
HOB					
❑ 116	I'm So Glad/Yours Is My Heart Alone	1961	30.00	60.00	120.00
MOTOWN					
❑ 1008	Whole Lotta Woman/Come On and Be Mine	1961	125.00	250.00	500.00
❑ 1012	The Stretch/Funny	1962	200.00	400.00	800.00
MOTOWN YESTERYEAR					
❑ 448	Do You Love Me/Shake Sherry	1972	—	2.00	4.00
❑ 448 [PS]	Do You Love Me/Shake Sherry	1988	—	2.50	5.00
—"Dirty Dancing" sleeve; without cut-out hole					
ROCKET					
❑ 41192	I'm a Winner/Makes Me Wanna Come Back	1980	—	2.00	4.00
TAMLA					
❑ 7012	Shake Sherry/You Better Get in Line	1963	37.50	75.00	150.00
—Tamla label used in error for a Gordy release					

CONVINCERS, THE

Number	Title (A Side/B Side)	Yr	VG	VG+	NM
MOVIN'					
❑ 100	Rejected Love/Go Back Baby	1962	100.00	200.00	400.00

COODER, RY

Number	Title (A Side/B Side)	Yr	VG	VG+	NM
MUSICOR					
❑ 1148	Life Game/1983	1966	2.50	5.00	10.00
REPRISE					
❑ 0910	Goin' to Brownsville/Available Space	1970	—	3.00	6.00
❑ 0940	Alimony/Pigmeat	1970	—	3.00	6.00
❑ 1009	Dark Is the Night/On a Monday	1971	—	3.00	6.00
❑ 1071	Billy the Kid/Money Honey	1972	—	3.00	6.00
❑ 1167	Billy the Kid/Boomer's Story	1973	—	3.00	6.00
WARNER BROS.					
❑ 8384	School Is Out/Jesus on the Mainline	1977	—	2.50	5.00
❑ 27945	Get Rhythm/Get Back to Okinawa	1988	—	2.00	4.00
❑ 28158	All Shook Up/Get Your Lies Straight	1987	—	2.00	4.00
❑ 28158 [PS]	All Shook Up/Get Your Lies Straight	1987	—	2.00	4.00
❑ 28723	Crossroads/Feel It (Bad Blues)	1986	—	2.00	4.00
❑ 28725	Tell Me Something Slick/Billy and Annie	1986	—	2.00	4.00
❑ 49055	Down in Hollywood/Little Sister	1979	—	2.50	5.00
❑ 49081	The Very Thing That Makes You Rich/Little Sister	1979	—	2.50	5.00
❑ 49677	Girls from Texas/Borderline	1981	—	2.00	4.00
❑ 49704	Crazy 'Bout an Automobile/Borderline	1981	—	2.00	4.00

COOK, KEN

Number	Title (A Side/B Side)	Yr	VG	VG+	NM
PHILLIPS INT'L.					
❑ 3534	I Was a Fool/Crazy Baby	1959	12.50	25.00	50.00
—Roy Orbison appears on this record (uncredited)					

COOKE, SAM

Number	Title (A Side/B Side)	Yr	VG	VG+	NM
CHERIE					
❑ 4501	Darling I Need You Now/Win Your Love for Me	1971	2.00	4.00	8.00
KEEN					
❑ 2005	Stealing Kisses/All of My Life	1958	6.25	12.50	25.00
❑ 2006 [M]	Win Your Love for Me/Almost in Your Arms	1958	6.25	12.50	25.00
—Blue vinyl					
❑ 5-2006 [S]	Win Your Love for Me/Love Song from Houseboat	1959	25.00	50.00	100.00
—Blue vinyl					
❑ 3-2008	Love You Most of All/Blue Moon	1958	6.25	12.50	25.00
❑ 3-2018 [M]	Everybody Likes to Cha Cha Cha/Little Things You Do	1959	6.25	12.50	25.00
❑ 5-2018 [S]	Everybody Likes to Cha Cha Cha/Little Things You Do	1959	10.00	20.00	40.00
❑ 2022 [M]	Only Sixteen/Let's Go Steady Again	1959	6.25	12.50	25.00
❑ 5-2022 [S]	Only Sixteen/Let's Go Steady Again	1959	12.50	25.00	50.00
❑ 2101	Summertime/Summertime (Part 2)	1959	6.25	12.50	25.00
❑ 2105	There! I've Said It Again/One Hour Ahead of the Possee	1959	6.25	12.50	25.00
❑ 2111	'T'ain't Nobody's Bizness (If I Do)/No One	1960	6.25	12.50	25.00
❑ 2112	Wonderful World/Along the Navajo Trail	1960	5.00	10.00	20.00
❑ 2117	With You/I Thank God	1960	5.00	10.00	20.00
❑ 2118	Steal Away/So Glamorous	1960	5.00	10.00	20.00
❑ 2122	Mary, Mary Lou/Eee-Yi-Ee-Yi-Oh	1960	5.00	10.00	20.00
❑ 4002	(I Love You) For Sentimental Reasons/Desire Me	1958	6.25	12.50	25.00
❑ 4009	You Were Made for Me/Lonely Island	1958	6.25	12.50	25.00
❑ 34013	You Send Me/Summertime	1957	6.25	12.50	25.00
RCA					
❑ PB-14146	Bring It On Home to Me/Nothing Can Change This Love	1985	2.00	4.00	8.00
RCA VICTOR					
❑ 37-7053	That's It-I Quit-I'm Movin' On/What Do You Say	1961	15.00	30.00	60.00
—"Compact Single 33" (small hole, plays at LP speed)					
❑ 47-7701	Teenage Sonata/If You Were the Only Girl	1960	5.00	10.00	20.00
❑ 47-7730	You Understand Me/I Belong to Your Heart	1960	3.75	7.50	15.00
❑ 47-7730 [PS]	You Understand Me/I Belong to Your Heart	1960	6.25	12.50	25.00
❑ 47-7783	Chain Gang/I Fall in Love Every Day	1960	3.75	7.50	15.00
❑ 47-7783 [PS]	Chain Gang/I Fall in Love Every Day	1960	6.25	12.50	25.00
❑ 47-7816	Sad Mood/Love Me	1960	3.75	7.50	15.00
❑ 47-7853	That's It-I Quit-I'm Movin' On/What Do You Say	1961	3.75	7.50	15.00
❑ 47-7883	Cupid/Farewell, My Darling	1961	3.75	7.50	15.00
❑ 47-7883 [PS]	Cupid/Farewell, My Darling	1961	6.25	12.50	25.00
❑ 47-7927	Feel It/It's All Right	1961	3.75	7.50	15.00
❑ 47-7927 [PS]	Feel It/It's All Right	1961	6.25	12.50	25.00
❑ 47-7983	Twistin' the Night Away/One More Time	1962	3.75	7.50	15.00
❑ 47-8036	Bring It On Home to Me/Having a Party	1962	3.75	7.50	15.00
❑ 47-8088	Nothing Can Change This Love/Somebody Have Mercy	1962	3.75	7.50	15.00
❑ 47-8088 [PS]	Nothing Can Change This Love/Somebody Have Mercy	1962	6.25	12.50	25.00
❑ 47-8129	Send Me Some Lovin'/Baby, Baby, Baby	1963	3.75	7.50	15.00
❑ 47-8129 [PS]	Send Me Some Lovin'/Baby, Baby, Baby	1963	6.25	12.50	25.00
❑ 47-8164	Another Saturday Night/Love Will Find a Way	1963	3.75	7.50	15.00
❑ 47-8164 [PS]	Another Saturday Night/Love Will Find a Way	1963	6.25	12.50	25.00
❑ 47-8215	Frankie and Johnny/Cool Train	1963	3.00	6.00	12.00
❑ 47-8215 [PS]	Frankie and Johnny/Cool Train	1963	6.25	12.50	25.00
❑ 47-8247	Little Red Rooster/You Gotta Move	1963	3.00	6.00	12.00
❑ 47-8247 [PS]	Little Red Rooster/You Gotta Move	1963	6.25	12.50	25.00
❑ 47-8299	Good News/Basin Street Blues	1963	3.00	6.00	12.00
❑ 47-8299	Ain't That Good News/Basin Street Blues	1963	5.00	10.00	20.00
—Original A-side title (or a scarce reissue)					
❑ 47-8368	Good Times/Tennessee Waltz	1964	3.00	6.00	12.00
❑ 47-8426	Cousin of Mine/That's Where It's At	1964	3.00	6.00	12.00
❑ 47-8486	Shake/A Change Is Gonna Come	1964	3.00	6.00	12.00
❑ 47-8539	It's Got the Whole World Shakin'/Ease My Troublin' Mind	1965	2.50	5.00	10.00
❑ 47-8586	When a Boy Falls in Love/The Piper	1965	2.50	5.00	10.00
❑ 47-8631	Sugar Dumpling/Bridge of Tears	1965	2.50	5.00	10.00
❑ 47-8631 [PS]	Sugar Dumpling/Bridge of Tears	1965	6.25	12.50	25.00
❑ 47-8751	Feel It/That's All	1965	2.50	5.00	10.00
❑ 47-8803	Let's Go Steady Again/Trouble Blues	1966	2.50	5.00	10.00
❑ 47-8934	Meet Me at Mary's Place/If I Had a Hammer	1966	2.50	5.00	10.00
SAR					
❑ 122 [DJ]	Just for You/Made for Me	1961	25.00	50.00	100.00
—Promo only ("Audition" on label); possibly made as leverage during contract renegotiation at RCA Victor, one source claims only five (5) copies were made					
SPECIALTY					
❑ 596	Forever/Lovable	1957	7.50	15.00	30.00
—As "Dale Cook"					
❑ 619	I'll Come Running Back to You/Forever	1957	7.50	15.00	30.00
❑ 627	That's All I Need to Know/I Don't Want to Cry	1958	7.50	15.00	30.00
❑ 667	Happy in Love/I Need You Now	1959	7.50	15.00	30.00

Number	Title (A Side/B Side)	Yr	VG	VG+	NM
❑ 921	Must Jesus Bear the Cross Alone/The Last Mile of the Way	1970	2.50	5.00	10.00
—With the Soul Stirrers					
❑ 928	Just Another Day/Christ Is All	1973	2.50	5.00	10.00
—With the Soul Stirrers					
❑ 930	That's Heaven to Me/Lord, Remember Me	1974	2.50	5.00	10.00
—With the Soul Stirrers					

7-Inch Extended Plays

KEEN

Number	Title (A Side/B Side)	Yr	VG	VG+	NM
❑ B-2001	(contents unknown)	1958	20.00	40.00	80.00
❑ B-2001 [PS]	Songs by Sam Cooke, Volume 1	1958	20.00	40.00	80.00
❑ B-2002	*You Send Me/The Lonesome Road/That Lucky Old Sun/Canadian Sunset	1958	20.00	40.00	80.00
❑ B-2002 [PS]	Songs by Sam Cooke, Volume 2	1958	20.00	40.00	80.00
❑ B-2003	Summertime/Danny Boy//Around the World/Ol' Man River	1958	20.00	40.00	80.00
❑ B-2003 [PS]	Songs by Sam Cooke, Volume 3	1958	20.00	40.00	80.00
❑ B-2006	(contents unknown)	1958	20.00	40.00	80.00
❑ B-2006 [PS]	Encore, Volume 1	1958	20.00	40.00	80.00
❑ B-2007	*When I Fall in Love/I Cover the Waterfront/ Running Wild/Today I Sing the Blues	1958	20.00	40.00	80.00
❑ B-2007 [PS]	Encore, Volume 2	1958	20.00	40.00	80.00
❑ B-2008	(contents unknown)	1958	20.00	40.00	80.00
❑ B-2008 [PS]	Encore, Volume 3	1958	20.00	40.00	80.00
❑ B-2010	Love Song from Houseboat/Lonely Island//Win Your Love for Me/All of My Life	1959	20.00	40.00	80.00
❑ B-2010 [PS]	Sam Cooke Sings His Hits	1959	20.00	40.00	80.00
❑ B-2012	Let's Call the Whole Thing Off/God Bless the Child//Comes Love/Lover Girl	1959	20.00	40.00	80.00
❑ B-2012 [PS]	Tribute to the Lady, Volume 1	1959	20.00	40.00	80.00
❑ B-2013	(contents unknown)	1959	20.00	40.00	80.00
❑ B-2013 [PS]	Tribute to the Lady, Volume 2	1959	20.00	40.00	80.00
❑ B-2014	(contents unknown)	1959	20.00	40.00	80.00
❑ B-2014 [PS]	Tribute to the Lady, Volume 3	1959	20.00	40.00	80.00

RCA VICTOR

Number	Title (A Side/B Side)	Yr	VG	VG+	NM
❑ LPC-126	Chain Gang/If You Were the Only Girl//Teenage Sonata/You Understand Me	1961	5.00	10.00	20.00
❑ LPC-126 [PS]	Sam Cooke Sings	1961	5.00	10.00	20.00
❑ EPA-4375	Another Saturday Night/You Send Me//Only Sixteen/Bring It On Home to Me	1963	5.00	10.00	20.00
❑ EPA-4375 [PS]	Another Saturday Night	1963	5.00	10.00	20.00

COOKER, JOHN LEE

See JOHN LEE HOOKER.

COOKIE AND HIS CUPCAKES

CHESS

Number	Title (A Side/B Side)	Yr	VG	VG+	NM
❑ 1848	Got You On My Mind/I've Been So Lonely	1963	3.75	7.50	15.00

JUDD

Number	Title (A Side/B Side)	Yr	VG	VG+	NM
❑ 1002	Mathilda/Married Life	1958	12.50	25.00	50.00
—With "h" in A-side title					
❑ 1002	Matilda/Married Life	1958	7.50	15.00	30.00
—Without "h" in A-side title					
❑ 1015	Until Then/Close Up the Back Door	1959	10.00	20.00	40.00

KHOURY'S

Number	Title (A Side/B Side)	Yr	VG	VG+	NM
❑ 703	Mathilda/Married Life	1958	15.00	30.00	60.00

LYRIC

Number	Title (A Side/B Side)	Yr	VG	VG+	NM
❑ 1003	Mathilda/I'm Twisted	1963	5.00	10.00	20.00
❑ 1004	Got You On My Mind/I've Been So Lonely	1963	5.00	10.00	20.00

MERCURY

Number	Title (A Side/B Side)	Yr	VG	VG+	NM
❑ 71748	Matilda Has Finally Come Back/As Part of Everything	1961	5.00	10.00	20.00

PAULA

Number	Title (A Side/B Side)	Yr	VG	VG+	NM
❑ 221	Mathilda/I'm Twisted	1965	3.00	6.00	12.00
❑ 230	Belinda/Trouble in My Life	1965	2.50	5.00	10.00

COOKIES, THE

ATLANTIC

Number	Title (A Side/B Side)	Yr	VG	VG+	NM
❑ 1061	Precious Love/Later, Later	1955	7.50	15.00	30.00
❑ 1084	In Paradise/Passing Time	1956	7.50	15.00	30.00
❑ 1110	Down By the River/My Lover	1956	6.25	12.50	25.00
❑ 2079	Passing Time/In Paradise	1960	5.00	10.00	20.00

DIMENSION

Number	Title (A Side/B Side)	Yr	VG	VG+	NM
❑ 1002	Chains/Stranger in My Arms	1962	5.00	10.00	20.00
❑ 1008	Don't Say Nothin' Bad/Softly in the Night	1963	5.00	10.00	20.00
❑ 1008	Don't Say Nothin' Bad (About My Baby)/Softly in the Night	1963	3.75	7.50	15.00
❑ 1012	I Want a Boy for My Birthday/Will Power	1963	3.75	7.50	15.00
❑ 1020	Girls Grow Up Faster Than Boys/Only to Other People	1963	3.75	7.50	15.00
❑ 1032	I Never Dreamed/The Old Crowd	1964	3.75	7.50	15.00

JOSIE

Number	Title (A Side/B Side)	Yr	VG	VG+	NM
❑ 822	King of Hearts/Hippy-Dippy-Daddy	1957	7.50	15.00	30.00

LAMP

Number	Title (A Side/B Side)	Yr	VG	VG+	NM
❑ 8008	Don't Let Go/All Night Mambo	1954	10.00	20.00	40.00

WARNER BROS.

Number	Title (A Side/B Side)	Yr	VG	VG+	NM
❑ 7025	All My Trials/Wounded	1967	2.50	5.00	10.00
❑ 7047	Mr. Cupid (Don't You Call on Me)/Hang My Head and Cry	1967	2.50	5.00	10.00
—B-side by the Big Guys					

COOL, CALVIN, AND THE SURF KNOBS

CHARTER

Number	Title (A Side/B Side)	Yr	VG	VG+	NM
❑ 7	Beach Bash/El Tocolote	1963	10.00	20.00	40.00

COOL HEAT

See WIND.

COOL SOUNDS, THE

PULSAR

Number	Title (A Side/B Side)	Yr	VG	VG+	NM
❑ 2421	Comin' Home (Free)/Rag Doll	1969	12.50	25.00	50.00

WARNER BROS.

Number	Title (A Side/B Side)	Yr	VG	VG+	NM
❑ 7538	I'll Take You Back/Where Do We Go from Here	1971	7.50	15.00	30.00
❑ 7575	A Love Like Ours Could Last a Million Years or More/Who Can I Turn To	1972	7.50	15.00	30.00
❑ 7615	Boy Wonder/Free	1972	7.50	15.00	30.00

COOLBREEZERS, THE

ABC-PARAMOUNT

Number	Title (A Side/B Side)	Yr	VG	VG+	NM
❑ 9865	You Know I Go for You/My Brother	1957	25.00	50.00	100.00

BALE

Number	Title (A Side/B Side)	Yr	VG	VG+	NM
❑ 100/101	The Greatest Love of All/Eda Weda Bug	1958	15.00	30.00	60.00
❑ 102/103	Let Christmas Ring/Hello, Mister New Year	1958	50.00	100.00	200.00

EBONY

Number	Title (A Side/B Side)	Yr	VG	VG+	NM
❑ 1015	Won't You Come In/Pack Your Bags and Go	1956	125.00	250.00	500.00
—As "The Little Coolbreezers"					

COOPER, ALICE

Also see NAZZ (2); THE SPIDERS (2).

ATLANTIC

Number	Title (A Side/B Side)	Yr	VG	VG+	NM
❑ 3254	Only Women/Cold Ethyl	1975	—	2.50	5.00
❑ 3280	Department of Youth/Some Folks	1975	—	2.50	5.00
❑ 3298	Welcome to My Nightmare/Cold Ethyl	1975	—	2.50	5.00

EPIC

Number	Title (A Side/B Side)	Yr	VG	VG+	NM
❑ 08114	I Got a Line on You/Livin' on the Edge	1988	—	—	3.00
—B-side by Britney Fox					
❑ 68958	Poison/Trash	1989	—	—	3.00
❑ 73085	House of Fire/Ballad of Dwight Fry	1989	—	—	3.00
❑ 73845	Hey Stoopid/It Rained All Night	1991	—	—	3.00
❑ 73983	Love's a Loaded Gun/Fire	1991	—	—	3.00

MCA

Number	Title (A Side/B Side)	Yr	VG	VG+	NM
❑ 52904	He's Back (The Man Behind the Mask)/Billion Dollar Baby	1986	—	—	3.00
❑ 52904 [PS]	He's Back (The Man Behind the Mask)/Billion Dollar Baby	1986	—	—	3.00
❑ 53212	Freedom/Time to Kill	1987	—	—	3.00
❑ 53212 [PS]	Freedom/Time to Kill	1987	—	—	3.00

STRAIGHT

Number	Title (A Side/B Side)	Yr	VG	VG+	NM
❑ 101	Reflected/Living	1969	75.00	150.00	300.00
—Promos worth about 10% of this value					

WARNER BROS.

Number	Title (A Side/B Side)	Yr	VG	VG+	NM
❑ 7141	Eighteen/Caught in a Dream	1972	—	2.00	4.00
—"Back to Back Hits" series (originals have green labels)					
❑ 7398	Shoe Salesman/Return of the Spiders	1970	5.00	10.00	20.00
❑ 7449	Eighteen/Body	1971	—	2.50	5.00
❑ 7490	Caught in a Dream/Hallowed Be My Name	1971	—	2.50	5.00
❑ 7529	Under My Wheels/Desperado	1971	—	2.50	5.00
❑ 7568	Be My Lover/Yeah, Yeah, Yeah	1972	—	2.50	5.00
❑ 7596	School's Out/Gutter Cat	1972	—	2.50	5.00
❑ 7596 [PS]	School's Out/Gutter Cat	1972	2.50	5.00	10.00
❑ 7631	Elected/Luney Tune	1972	—	2.50	5.00
❑ 7631 [PS]	Elected/Luney Tune	1972	2.50	5.00	10.00
❑ 7673	Hello Hurray/Generation Landslide	1972	—	2.50	5.00
❑ 7691	No More Mr. Nice Guy/Raped and Freezin'	1973	—	2.50	5.00
❑ 7724	Billion Dollar Babies/Mary Ann	1973	—	2.50	5.00
❑ 7762	Teenage Lament '74/Hard Hearted Alice	1973	—	2.50	5.00
❑ 7783	Muscle of Love/Crazy Little Child	1974	—	2.50	5.00
❑ 8023	I'm Eighteen/Muscle of Love	1974	—	2.50	5.00
❑ 8228	I Never Cry/Go to Hell	1976	—	2.00	4.00
❑ 8349	You and Me/It's Hot Tonight	1977	—	2.00	4.00
❑ 8349 [PS]	You and Me/It's Hot Tonight	1977	2.00	4.00	8.00
❑ 8448	(No More) Love at Your Convenience/I Never Wrote Those Songs	1977	—	2.50	5.00
❑ 8607	School's Out/Eighteen	1978	2.00	4.00	8.00
❑ 8695	How You Gonna See Me Now/No Tricks	1978	—	2.50	5.00
❑ 8760	From the Inside/Nurse Rosetta	1979	—	2.00	4.00
❑ 29828	I Am the Future/Tag, You're It	1982	—	2.00	4.00
❑ 29928	I Like Girls/Zorro's Ascent	1982	—	2.00	4.00
❑ 49204	Clones (We're All)/Model Citizen	1980	—	2.00	4.00
❑ 49204 [PS]	Clones (We're All)/Model Citizen	1980	—	2.50	5.00
❑ 49526	Dance Yourself to Death/Talk Talk	1980	—	2.00	4.00
❑ 49780	You Want It, You Got It/Who Do You Think We Are	1981	—	2.00	4.00
❑ 49848	Generation Landslide '81/Seven and Seven Is	1981	—	2.00	4.00

COOPER, BO

See RON DANTE.

COOPER, CHRISTINE

PARKWAY

Number	Title (A Side/B Side)	Yr	VG	VG+	NM
❑ 122	I Must Have You (Or No One)/Good Looks (They Don't Count)	1966	3.75	7.50	15.00
❑ 971	S.O.S./Say What You Feel	1966	6.25	12.50	25.00
❑ 983	(They Call Him) A Bad Boy/Heartaches Away My Boy	1966	10.00	20.00	40.00

COOPER, DOLLY

DOT

Number	Title (A Side/B Side)	Yr	VG	VG+	NM
❑ 15495	Big Rock Inn/I'm Looking Through Your Window	1956	3.00	6.00	12.00
❑ 15535	The Confession of a Fool/Tell Me, Tell Me	1957	3.00	6.00	12.00

EBB

Number	Title (A Side/B Side)	Yr	VG	VG+	NM
❑ 109	Wild Love/Time Brings About a Change	1957	3.00	6.00	12.00

MODERN

Number	Title (A Side/B Side)	Yr	VG	VG+	NM
❑ 965	My Man/Ay La Bas	1955	10.00	20.00	40.00
❑ 977	Teenage Prayer/Down So Long	1956	12.50	25.00	50.00
❑ 986	Teenage Wedding Bells/Every Day and Every Night	1956	12.50	25.00	50.00

SAVOY

Number	Title (A Side/B Side)	Yr	VG	VG+	NM
❑ 1121	You Gotta Be Good to Yourself/Love Can't Be Blind	1954	5.00	10.00	20.00

COOPER, JOHNNY

ERMINE

Number	Title (A Side/B Side)	Yr	VG	VG+	NM
❑ 37	Rivalry/I Found Love with You	1961	5.00	10.00	20.00

Number	Title (A Side/B Side)	Yr	VG	VG+	NM
❑ 38	Little Bride/Dumb Dumb Bunny	1962	7.50	15.00	30.00
❑ 40	While You're Young/Diggity Doggity	1962	5.00	10.00	20.00
❑ 44	Oreo/Flame of Love	1962	5.00	10.00	20.00

COOPER, LES, AND THE SOUL ROCKERS

Also see THE EMPIRES (1).

Number	Title (A Side/B Side)	Yr	VG	VG+	NM
ARRAWAK					
❑ 1008	I Can Do the Soul Jerk/At the World's Fair	1965	3.00	6.00	12.00
ATCO					
❑ 6644	Gonna Have a Lotta Fun/Thank God for You	1969	2.00	4.00	8.00
DIMENSION					
❑ 1023	Motor City/Swobblin'	1963	5.00	10.00	20.00
ENJOY					
❑ 2024	Owee Baby/Let's Do the Boston Monkey	1965	2.50	5.00	10.00
EVERLAST					
❑ 5016	Twistin'/Dig Yourself	1963	3.00	6.00	12.00
❑ 5019	Wiggle Wobble/Dig Yourself	1963	3.75	7.50	15.00
❑ 5023	Garbage Can/Bossa Nova Dance	1963	3.00	6.00	12.00

COOPERETTES, THE

Number	Title (A Side/B Side)	Yr	VG	VG+	NM
ABC					
❑ 11156	Peace Maker/Trouble	1968	3.00	6.00	12.00
❑ 11197	Spiral Road/Trouble	1969	3.00	6.00	12.00
BRUNSWICK					
❑ 55296	Goodbye School/Goodbye School (Part 2)	1966	3.75	7.50	15.00
❑ 55307	Don't Trust Him/Everything's Wrong	1966	3.75	7.50	15.00
❑ 55329	(Life Has) No Meaning Now/Shing-a-Ling	1967	6.25	12.50	25.00

COPAS, COWBOY

Number	Title (A Side/B Side)	Yr	VG	VG+	NM
DOT					
❑ 15668	Blue Kimono/Breeze	1957	5.00	10.00	20.00
❑ 15735	Circle Rock/My Little Red Wagon	1958	15.00	30.00	60.00
❑ 15847	A World That's Real/Looking for an Angel	1958	5.00	10.00	20.00
KING					
❑ 951	The Strange Little Girl/You'll Never See Me Cry	1951	10.00	20.00	40.00
❑ 964	Tennessee Flat Guitar/I Love You	1951	7.50	15.00	30.00
❑ 980	I'm Glad I'm On the Inside/Four Books in the Bible	1951	7.50	15.00	30.00
❑ 1000	'Tis Sweet to Be Remembered/Because of You	1951	7.50	15.00	30.00
❑ 1003	O Little Town of Bethlehem/It Came Upon the Midnight Clear	1951	7.50	15.00	30.00
❑ 1004	White Christmas/Jingle Bells	1951	7.50	15.00	30.00
❑ 1034	Copy Cat/Those Gone and Left Me Blues	1952	7.50	15.00	30.00
❑ 1040	I'll Pay the Price/'Tis Sweet to Be Remembered	1951	7.50	15.00	30.00
❑ 1046	Four Bare Walls and a Ceiling/I Can't Stop Loving You	1952	7.50	15.00	30.00
❑ 1064	Boomerang/It's Enough to Make Anyone Cry	1952	7.50	15.00	30.00
❑ 1080	Golden Moon/I Can't Remember to Forget	1952	7.50	15.00	30.00
❑ 1136	I've Grown So Used to You/It's No Sin to Love You	1952	7.50	15.00	30.00
❑ 1139	Purple Rose/Some Fine Morning	1952	7.50	15.00	30.00
❑ 1151	Feelin' Low/Love Me Now	1952	7.50	15.00	30.00
❑ 1166	Doll of Clay/If Wishes Were Horses	1953	6.25	12.50	25.00
❑ 1200	I Can't Go On/A Wreath at the Door of My Heart	1953	6.25	12.50	25.00
❑ 1234	Tennessee Senorita/If You Will Let Me Be Your Love	1953	6.25	12.50	25.00
❑ 1253	Look What I Got/Will You Forget	1953	6.25	12.50	25.00
❑ 1274	Blue Waltz/A Heartache Ago	1953	6.25	12.50	25.00
❑ 1306	He Stands By His Window/The Man Upstairs	1954	6.25	12.50	25.00
❑ 1313	Unwanted Alone/Sorry	1954	6.25	12.50	25.00
❑ 1329	I'll Be There/I'm a Stranger in My Home	1954	6.25	12.50	25.00
❑ 1359	Return to Sender/I'll Waltz with You	1954	6.25	12.50	25.00
❑ 1386	Carbon Copy/I'm Glad for Your Sake	1954	6.25	12.50	25.00
❑ 1407	When I Lost You/Why Should I Want Her	1954	6.25	12.50	25.00
❑ 1424	Hello Darling/The Talking Mule	1955	6.25	12.50	25.00
❑ 1444	The Stone Was Rolled Away/The Silver That Nailed Him to the Cross	1955	6.25	12.50	25.00
❑ 1456	Pledging My Love/Shamed of Myself	1955	6.25	12.50	25.00
❑ 1464	The Party's Over/Summer Kisses	1955	6.25	12.50	25.00
❑ 1486	Tragic Romance/Listen to My Heart	1955	6.25	12.50	25.00
❑ 1507	Blue Yesterday/Tell Me More	1955	6.25	12.50	25.00
❑ 4865	Any Old Time/Don't Shake Hands with the Devil	1956	5.00	10.00	20.00
❑ 5270	Tennessee Waltz/Signed, Sealed and Delivered	1959	3.75	7.50	15.00
—As "Lloyd Copas"					
❑ 5392	Carolina Sunshine Girl/Rose of Tennessee	1960	3.75	7.50	15.00
❑ 5437	A Stranger in My Home/Old Faithful and True Love	1960	3.75	7.50	15.00
❑ 5479	It's a Shame/You Walked Right Out of My Dreams	1961	3.75	7.50	15.00
❑ 5544	It's a Lonely World/Don't Let Them Change Your Mind	1961	3.75	7.50	15.00
❑ 5571	Sweet Thing/Signed, Sealed, Then Forgotten	1961	3.75	7.50	15.00
❑ 5638	I Built a Fence Around My Heart/My Blues Are Gone	1962	3.75	7.50	15.00
❑ 5676	When Jesus Beckons Me Home/I Saw the Light	1962	3.75	7.50	15.00
❑ 5733	Signed, Sealed and Delivered/The Hopes of a Broken Heart	1963	3.00	6.00	12.00
❑ 5734	Breeze/The Road of Broken Hearts	1963	3.00	6.00	12.00
STARDAY					
❑ 476	Mom and Dad's Affair/Black Cloud Risin'	1959	3.75	7.50	15.00
❑ 493	South Pacific Shore/That's All I Can Remember	1960	3.75	7.50	15.00
❑ 501	Alabam/I Can	1960	5.00	10.00	20.00
❑ 524	I Have a Friend/The Hem of His Garment	1960	3.75	7.50	15.00
❑ 528	Sittin' Flat on Ready/Midnight In Heaven	1960	3.75	7.50	15.00
❑ 542	Flat Top/True Love (Is the Greatest Thing)	1961	3.75	7.50	15.00
❑ 552	Sunny Tennessee/Dreaming	1961	3.75	7.50	15.00
❑ 559	Signed, Sealed and Delivered/New Filipino Baby	1961	3.75	7.50	15.00
❑ 573	Sal/A Thousand Miles of Ocean	1961	3.75	7.50	15.00
❑ 585	There'll Come a Time Someday/Seven Seas from You	1962	3.75	7.50	15.00
❑ 595	Sold the Farm/Table in the Corner	1962	3.75	7.50	15.00
❑ 606	Bury Me Face Down/Heart on the Run	1962	3.75	7.50	15.00
❑ 612	Family Reunion/Smoke on the Water	1962	3.75	7.50	15.00
❑ 621	Goodbye Kisses/The Gypsy Girl	1963	3.00	6.00	12.00
❑ 641	Louisiana/Break Away, Break Away	1963	3.00	6.00	12.00
❑ 658	Autobiography/The Rainbow and the Rose	1963	3.00	6.00	12.00
❑ 685	Old Man's Story/Pretty Diamonds	1964	3.00	6.00	12.00
❑ 708	Ride in My Little Red Wagon/Black Eyed Susie	1965	2.50	5.00	10.00
❑ 729	Waltzing with Sin/Blue Kimono	1965	2.50	5.00	10.00
❑ 750	Cowboy's Deck of Cards/Beyond the Sunset	1966	2.50	5.00	10.00
❑ 7000	Alabam/Goodbye Kisses	197?	—	2.50	5.00
❑ 7001	Signed, Sealed and Delivered/New Filipino Baby	197?	—	2.50	5.00
❑ 7015	I Dreamed of a Hillbilly Heaven/Tragic Romance	197?	—	2.50	5.00
❑ 8006	Signed, Sealed and Delivered/Hillbilly Heaven	197?	—	2.50	5.00
❑ 8029	Alabam/Filipino Baby	197?	—	2.50	5.00

COPASETICS, THE

Number	Title (A Side/B Side)	Yr	VG	VG+	NM
PREMIUM					
❑ 409	Believe in Me/Collegian	1956	50.00	100.00	200.00

COPELAND, KEN

Number	Title (A Side/B Side)	Yr	VG	VG+	NM
DOT					
❑ 15686	Where the Rio Rosa Flows/Locked in the Arms of Love	1958	3.75	7.50	15.00
IMPERIAL					
❑ 5432	Pledge of Love/Night Air	1957	5.00	10.00	20.00
—B-side by The Mints					
❑ 5453	Teenage/Bed of Lies	1957	5.00	10.00	20.00
❑ 5466	I Want to Go Steady/I Would Give My Heart	1957	5.00	10.00	20.00
LIN					
❑ 5007	Pledge of Love/Night Air	1957	10.00	20.00	40.00
—B-side by The Mints					
❑ 5017	Fanny Brown/Chaser of Hearts	1957	10.00	20.00	40.00

CORDEL, PAT

Also see THE ELEGANTS.

Number	Title (A Side/B Side)	Yr	VG	VG+	NM
CLUB					
❑ 1011	Darling, Come Back/My My Tears	1956	500.00	1000.	1500.
—And the Crescents					
MICHELLE					
❑ 503	Darling, Come Back/My My Tears	1959	37.50	75.00	150.00
—And the Elegants					
VICTORY					
❑ 1001	Darling, Come Back/My My Tears	1963	20.00	40.00	80.00
—And the Elegants					

CORDELLS, THE

Number	Title (A Side/B Side)	Yr	VG	VG+	NM
BARGAIN					
❑ 5004	The Beat of My Heart/Laid Off	1962	12.50	25.00	50.00
BULLSEYE					
❑ 1017	Believe in Me/Please Don't Go	1958	25.00	50.00	100.00

CORDIALS, THE

Several different groups.

Number	Title (A Side/B Side)	Yr	VG	VG+	NM
7 ARTS					
❑ 707	Dawn Is Almost Here/Keep An Eye	1961	25.00	50.00	100.00
BETHLEHEM					
❑ 3019	What's the Matter with Me/I'm Not Crying Anymore	1961	6.25	12.50	25.00
CORDIAL					
❑ 1001	I'm Ashamed/Sentimental Jorney	1960	25.00	50.00	100.00
FELSTED					
❑ 8653	Once in a Lifetime/What Kind of Fool Am I	1962	7.50	15.00	30.00
LIBERTY					
❑ 55784	Oh, How I Love Her/You Can't Believe in Love	1965	6.25	12.50	25.00
REVEILLE					
❑ 106	Eternal Love/The International Twist	1962	75.00	150.00	300.00
WHIP					
❑ 276	Listen My Heart/My Heart's Desire	1961	62.50	125.00	250.00

COREY, JOHN

Number	Title (A Side/B Side)	Yr	VG	VG+	NM
VEE JAY					
❑ 466	Pollyanna/I'll Forget	1962	7.50	15.00	30.00
—Backing group: The Four Seasons					
❑ 514	Hey Little Runaround/The Prettiest Girl I've Kissed Today	1963	2.50	5.00	10.00

CORNELIUS BROTHERS AND SISTER ROSE

Number	Title (A Side/B Side)	Yr	VG	VG+	NM
PLATINUM					
❑ 105/6	Treat Her Like a Lady/Over at My Place	1970	3.00	6.00	12.00
UNITED ARTISTS					
❑ 0131	Treat Her Like a Lady/Over at My Place	1973	—	2.00	4.00
—"Silver Spotlight Series" reissue					
❑ XW208	Let Me Down Easy/Gonna Be Sweet for You	1973	—	2.50	5.00
❑ XW313	I Just Can't Stop Loving You/These Lonely Nights	1973	—	2.50	5.00
❑ XW377	Big Time Lover/Wonderful Tune	1974	—	2.50	5.00
❑ XW512	Too Late to Turn Back Now/Don't Ever Be Lonely (A Poor Little Fool Like Me)	1974	—	2.00	4.00
—Reissue					
❑ XW533	Trouble Child/Got to Testify	1974	—	2.50	5.00
❑ XW534	Since I Found My Baby/I Love Music	1974	—	2.50	5.00
❑ 50721	Treat Her Like a Lady/Over at My Place	1970	—	2.50	5.00
❑ 50910	Too Late to Turn Back Now/Lift Your Love Higher	1972	—	2.50	5.00
❑ 50954	Don't Ever Be Lonely (A Poor Little Fool Like Me)/I'm So Glad to Be Loved by You	1972	—	2.50	5.00
❑ 50996	I'm Never Gonna Be Alone Anymore/Let's Stay Together	1972	—	2.50	5.00

CORNELLS, THE

Number	Title (A Side/B Side)	Yr	VG	VG+	NM
GAREX					
❑ 100	Mama's Little Baby/Wak-A-Cha	1962	7.50	15.00	30.00
❑ 102	Malibu Surf/Agua Caliente	1963	7.50	15.00	30.00
❑ 201	Beach Bound/Lone Star Stomp	1963	7.50	15.00	30.00
❑ 206	Surf Fever/Do the Slauson	1963	7.50	15.00	30.00

CORNERSHOP

Number	Title (A Side/B Side)	Yr	VG	VG+	NM
LUAKA BOP/WARNER BROS.					
❑ PRO-S-8869 [DJ]	Brimful of Asha/It's Indian Tobacco My Friend	1997	—	2.50	5.00
—Red vinyl					
❑ PRO-S-8869 [PS]	Brimful of Asha/It's Indian Tobacco My Friend	1997	—	2.50	5.00
—Picture sleeve and vinyl outer sleeve					

CORNISH, GENE

Also see THE RASCALS.

Number	Title (A Side/B Side)	Yr	VG	VG+	NM
DAWN					
❑ 550	Let's Do the Capri/Lonely I Will Say	1964	7.50	15.00	30.00
❑ 551	I Wanna Be a Beatle/Oh Misery	1964	10.00	20.00	40.00
VASSAR					
❑ 319	Since I Lost You/Winner Take All	1962	5.00	10.00	20.00
❑ 321	My Baby Ran Away from Me/(B-side unknown)	1962	6.25	12.50	25.00

CORONETS, THE

Number	Title (A Side/B Side)	Yr	VG	VG+	NM
CHESS					
❑ 1549	Nadine/I'm All Alone	1953	50.00	100.00	200.00
—Silver top label					
❑ 1549	Nadine/I'm All Alone	1958	3.00	6.00	12.00
—All-blue label					
❑ 1553	It Would Be Heavenly/Baby's Coming Home	1953	100.00	200.00	400.00
—Black vinyl					
❑ 1553	It Would Be Heavenly/Baby's Coming Home	1953	200.00	400.00	800.00
—Red vinyl					
GROOVE					
❑ 0114	I Love You More/Crime Doesn't Pay	1955	25.00	50.00	100.00
❑ 0116	The Bible Tells Me So/Hush	1955	37.50	75.00	150.00
STERLING					
❑ 903	Don't Deprive Me/Little Boy	1955	62.50	125.00	250.00

CORSAIRS, THE

Number	Title (A Side/B Side)	Yr	VG	VG+	NM
HY-TONE					
❑ 110	Goodbye Darling/Rock Lilly Rock	1957	375.00	750.00	1500.
SMASH					
❑ 1715	Time Waits/It Won't Be a Sin	1961	3.75	7.50	15.00
TUFF					
❑ 375	Save a Little Monkey/(Instrumental)	1963	2.50	5.00	10.00
❑ 402	On the Spanish Side/The Change in You	1964	2.50	5.00	10.00
TUFF/CHESS					
❑ 1808	Smoky Places/Thinkin'	1961	6.25	12.50	25.00
❑ 1818	I'll Take You HJome/Sittin' on Your Doorstep	1962	3.00	6.00	12.00
❑ 1830	Dancing Shadows/While	1962	3.00	6.00	12.00
❑ 1840	At the Stroke of Midnight/Listen to My Little Heart	1962	3.00	6.00	12.00
❑ 1847	Stormy/It's Almost Sunday Morning	1963	3.00	6.00	12.00

CORT, BOB

Number	Title (A Side/B Side)	Yr	VG	VG+	NM
LONDON					
❑ 1713	Don't You Rock Me Daddy-O/It Takes a Worried Man to Sing a Worried Blues	1957	3.75	7.50	15.00
❑ 1742	Freight Train/Roll Jen Jenkins	1957	3.00	6.00	12.00
❑ 1748	Maggie Mae/Jessamine	1957	3.00	6.00	12.00
—With Liz Winters					

CORTEZ, DAVE "BABY"

Number	Title (A Side/B Side)	Yr	VG	VG+	NM
ALL PLATINUM					
❑ 2339	Funky Robot (Part 1)/Funky Robot (Part 2)	1972	—	2.50	5.00
❑ 2342	Unaddressed Letter/Funky Robot (Part 1)	1972	—	2.50	5.00
❑ 2343	Someone Has Taken Your Place/Born Funky	1973	—	2.50	5.00
❑ 2345	Hell Street Junction/(Instrumental)	1973	—	2.50	5.00
❑ 2347	Soul Walkin'/(B-side unknown)	1974	—	2.50	5.00
ARGO					
❑ 5462	Let It Be You/I'm Gonna Stay	1964	2.50	5.00	10.00
CHESS					
❑ 1829	Rinky Dink/Getting Right	1962	2.50	5.00	10.00
❑ 1834	Happy Weekend/Fiddle Sticks	1962	2.50	5.00	10.00
❑ 1842	Tweedle Dee/Gift of Love	1962	2.50	5.00	10.00
❑ 1850	Hot Cakes! 1st Serving/Hot Cakes! 2nd Serving	1963	2.00	4.00	8.00
❑ 1861	Organ Shout/Precious You	1963	2.00	4.00	8.00
❑ 1874	Happy Feet/Gettin' to the Point	1963	2.00	4.00	8.00
CLOCK					
❑ 1006	You're the Girl/Eeny Meeny Minie Mo	1958	5.00	10.00	20.00
❑ 1009	The Happy Organ/Love Me As I Love You	1959	5.00	10.00	20.00
❑ 1012	The Whistling Organ/I'm Happy	1959	3.00	6.00	12.00
❑ 1014	Piano Shuffle/It's a Sin to Tell a Lie	1959	3.00	6.00	12.00
❑ 1016	Dave's Special/Whispers	1959	3.00	6.00	12.00
❑ 1020	You're Just Right/Deep in the Heart of Texas	1960	3.00	6.00	12.00
❑ 1021	You're the Girl/I'm Happy	1960	3.00	6.00	12.00
❑ 1024	Cat Nip/Talk Is Cheap	1960	3.00	6.00	12.00
❑ 1031	Hurricane/The Shift	1960	3.00	6.00	12.00
❑ 1034	Summertime/Walking with You	1961	3.00	6.00	12.00
❑ 1036	Tootsie/Second Chance	1961	3.00	6.00	12.00
❑ 71824	Tootsie/Second Chance	1961	2.50	5.00	10.00
❑ 71851	The Happy Organ/Piano Shuffle	1961	2.50	5.00	10.00
❑ 71875	C'mon and Stomp/Calypso Love Song	1961	2.50	5.00	10.00
EMBER					
❑ 1011	Soft Lights/Movin' and Groovin'	1956	10.00	20.00	40.00
—As "David Clowney"					
EMIT					
❑ 301	Fiesta/(B-side unknown)	1962	2.50	5.00	10.00
EPIC					
❑ 9732	Poppin' Popcorn/The Question	1964	2.50	5.00	10.00
JULIA					
❑ 1829	Rinky Dink/Getting Right	1962	6.25	12.50	25.00
OKEH					
❑ 7102	You Give Me Heebie Jeebies/Honey Baby	1958	5.00	10.00	20.00
❑ 7208	Popping Popcorn/The Question (Do You Love Me)	1964	2.00	4.00	8.00
PARIS					
❑ 513	Shakin'/Hoot Owl	1958	7.50	15.00	30.00
—As "Dave Clowney"					
ROULETTE					
❑ 4628	Tweetie Pie/Things Ain't What They Used to Be	1965	2.00	4.00	8.00
❑ 4679	Count Down/Summertime	1966	2.00	4.00	8.00
❑ 4693	Sticks and Stones/Do Any Dance	1966	2.00	4.00	8.00
❑ 4717	Belly Rub (Part 1)/Belly Rub (Part 2)	1967	2.00	4.00	8.00
❑ 4759	Hula Hoop/Come Back	1967	2.00	4.00	8.00
❑ 4783	Hot Chocolate/Soul Groovin'	1967	2.00	4.00	8.00
T-NECK					
❑ 907	I Turned You On/I Know Who You Been Socking It To	1969	—	3.00	6.00
❑ 913	Save Me/My Little Girl	1969	—	3.00	6.00
WINLEY					
❑ 259	Jamin' (Part 1)/Jamin' (Part 2)	1961	2.50	5.00	10.00
❑ 262	Skins and Sounds/Little Paris Melody	1962	2.50	5.00	10.00
❑ 267	Scotty (Part 1)/Scotty (Part 2)	1962	2.50	5.00	10.00
7-Inch Extended Plays					
CLOCK					
❑ EP 1-4039-C	The Happy Organ/The Whistling Organ//Catnip/Deep in the Heart of Texas	1959	6.25	12.50	25.00
❑ EP 1-4039-C [PS]	Dave "Baby" Cortez and His Happy Organ	1959	6.25	12.50	25.00
RCA VICTOR					
❑ EPA-4342 [M]	*The Happy Organ/Love Me As I Love You/Dave's Special/You're the Girl	1959	3.00	6.00	12.00
❑ EPA-4342 [PS]	The Happy Organ	1959	3.00	6.00	12.00
❑ ESP-4342 [PS]	The Happy Organ	1959	5.00	10.00	20.00
❑ ESP-4342 [S]	(contents unknown)	1959	5.00	10.00	20.00

CORVELLS, THE

Number	Title (A Side/B Side)	Yr	VG	VG+	NM
ABC-PARAMOUNT					
❑ 10324	Take My Love/Daisy	1962	50.00	100.00	200.00
BLAST					
❑ 203	The Bells/Don't Forget	1961	37.50	75.00	150.00
CUB					
❑ 9122	One (Is Such a Lonely Number)/The Joke's On Me	1963	5.00	10.00	20.00
LIDO					
❑ 509	We Made a Vow/Miss Jones	1957	50.00	100.00	200.00
LUPINE					
❑ 104	He's So Fine/Baby Sitting	1962	6.25	12.50	25.00
TIP TOP					
❑ 509	We Made a Vow/Miss Jones	1957	75.00	150.00	300.00

COSMIC RAYS, THE

Number	Title (A Side/B Side)	Yr	VG	VG+	NM
SATURN					
❑ 222	Bye Bye/Someone's in Love	1960	750.00	1500.	3000.
❑ 401	Daddy's Gonna Tell You No Lies/Dreaming	1960	500.00	1000.	2000.

COSTELLO, ELVIS

Number	Title (A Side/B Side)	Yr	VG	VG+	NM
COLUMBIA					
❑ AE7 1171 [DJ]	Accidents Will Happen/Alison/Watching the Detectives	1979	—	—	3.00
—Extra record included in first editions of LP "Armed Forces"					
❑ AE7 1171 [PS]	Live at Hollywood High	1979	—	2.50	5.00
❑ AE7 1172 [DJ]	My Funny Valentine/(What's So Funny 'Bout) Peace, Love and Undestanding	1980	3.00	6.00	12.00
—Promo only on red vinyl					
❑ 02629	A Good Year for the Roses/The Angel Steps Out of Heaven	1981	—	2.00	4.00
❑ 03202	Man Out of Time/(B-side unknown)	1982	—	—	3.00
❑ 03269	Man Out of Time	1982	—	2.50	5.00
—One-sided budget release					
❑ 04045	Everyday I Write the Book/Heathen Town	1983	—	—	3.00
❑ 04045 [PS]	Everyday I Write the Book/Heathen Town	1983	—	—	3.00
❑ 04266	Let Them All Talk/Shipbiulding	1983	—	—	3.00
❑ 04502	The Only Flame in Town/Turning the Town Red	1984	—	—	3.00
❑ 04502 [PS]	The Only Flame in Town/Turning the Town Red	1984	—	—	3.00
❑ 04625	I Wanna Be Loved/Love Field	1984	—	—	3.00
❑ 05809	Don't Let Me Be Misunderstood/Brand New Hairdo	1986	—	—	3.00
—By "The Costello Show Featuring Elvis Costello"					
❑ 06059	Lovable/Get Yourself Another Fool	1986	—	—	3.00
—By "The Costello Show Featuring Elvis Costello"					
❑ 06326	Tokyo Storm Warning/Tokyo Storm Warning	1986	—	—	3.00
❑ 10641	Alison/Miracle Man	1977	2.50	5.00	10.00
—Contains a remix of "Alison" otherwise unavailable on U.S. vinyl					
❑ 10696	Watching the Detectives/Blame It on Cain-Mystery Dance	1978	2.50	5.00	10.00
❑ 10705	Alison/Watching the Detectives	1978	2.50	5.00	10.00
—Contains the same remix of "Alison" as above					
❑ 10762	This Year's Girl/Big Tears	1978	—	3.00	6.00
❑ 10919	Accidents Will Happen/Sunday's Best	1979	—	3.00	6.00
❑ 11194	I Can't Stand Up for Falling Down/Girls Talk	1980	—	3.00	6.00
❑ 11251	I Can't Stand Up for Falling Down/Girls Talk//Secondary Modern/King Horse	1980	—	3.00	6.00
❑ 11251 [PS]	I Can't Stand Up for Falling Down/Girls Talk//Secondary Modern/King Horse	1980	—	3.00	6.00
❑ 11284	New Amsterdam/Wednesday Week	1980	—	2.00	4.00
❑ 11389	Gettin' Mighty Crowded/Radio Sweetheart	1980	—	2.00	4.00
❑ 33401	Accidents Will Happen/Alison	198?	—	2.00	4.00
—"Hall of Fame" reissue					
❑ 60519	Watch Your Step/Luxembourg	1981	—	2.00	4.00
❑ 60519 [PS]	Watch Your Step/Luxembourg	1981	—	2.00	4.00
WARNER BROS.					
❑ 22981	Veronica/You're No Good	1989	—	—	3.00
❑ 22981 [PS]	Veronica/You're No Good	1989	—	—	3.00

COTTON, JAMES

BUDDAH

Number	Title (A Side/B Side)	Yr	VG	VG+	NM
❑ 461	Boogie Thing/Fever	1975	—	2.50	5.00
❑ 468	Rocket 88/One More Mile	1975	—	2.50	5.00

LOMA

Number	Title (A Side/B Side)	Yr	VG	VG+	NM
❑ 2042	Laying in the Weeds/Complete This Order	1966	3.00	6.00	12.00

SUN

Number	Title (A Side/B Side)	Yr	VG	VG+	NM
❑ 199	My Baby/Straighten Up, Baby	1954	375.00	750.00	1500.
❑ 206	Cotton Crop Blues/Hold Me in Your Arms	1954	450.00	900.00	1800.

VERVE FORECAST

Number	Title (A Side/B Side)	Yr	VG	VG+	NM
❑ 5053	Good Time Charlie/Off the Wall	1967	2.50	5.00	10.00
❑ 5066	Feelin' Good/Don't Start Me Talkin'	1967	2.50	5.00	10.00
❑ 5107	The Coach's Better Days/(B-side unknown)	1969	2.00	4.00	8.00

COUGAR, JOHN(NY)

See JOHN MELLENCAMP.

COUNT FIVE, THE

DOUBLE SHOT

Number	Title (A Side/B Side)	Yr	VG	VG+	NM
❑ 104	Psychotic Reaction/They're Gonna Get You	1966	3.75	7.50	15.00
—First pressing, with label logo at top					
❑ 104	Psychotic Reaction/They're Gonna Get You	1966	3.00	6.00	12.00
—Later pressings, with label logo at side					
❑ 106	Peace of Mind/The Morning After	1966	3.00	6.00	12.00
❑ 110	You Must Believe Me/Teeny Bopper, Teeny Bopper	1967	3.00	6.00	12.00
❑ 115	Merry-Go-Round/Contrast	1967	3.00	6.00	12.00
❑ 125	Declaration of Independence/Revelation in Slow Motion	1968	3.00	6.00	12.00
❑ 141	Mailman/Pretty Big Mouth	1969	3.00	6.00	12.00

COUNT ROCKIN' SIDNEY

See ROCKIN' SIDNEY.

COUNT STEPHEN

See STEVE ALAIMO.

COUNTING CROWS

DGC

Number	Title (A Side/B Side)	Yr	VG	VG+	NM
❑ 069-497216-7	Hanginaround/A Long December	1999	—	—	3.00
❑ 069-497411-7	Mrs. Potter's Lullaby/All My Friends	2000	—	—	3.00

COUNTRY BOYS, THE

Also see DAVID GATES.

DEL-FI

Number	Title (A Side/B Side)	Yr	VG	VG+	NM
❑ 4245	The Okie Surfer/Blue Surf	1964	10.00	20.00	40.00

COUNTRY HAMS, THE

See PAUL McCARTNEY.

COUNTRY JOE AND THE FISH

Includes releases by "Country Joe McDonald."

FANTASY

Number	Title (A Side/B Side)	Yr	VG	VG+	NM
❑ 758	Breakfast for Two/Lost My Connection	1976	—	2.00	4.00
❑ 765	Save the Whales/Oh Jamaica	1976	—	2.00	4.00
❑ 780	Love Is a Fire/I Need You	1976	—	2.00	4.00
❑ 814	Southern Cross/Coyote	1978	—	2.00	4.00
❑ 822	Bring Back the Sixties, Man/Sunshine Through My Window	1978	—	2.00	4.00
❑ 876	Private Parts/Take Time Out	1979	—	2.00	4.00

PHILCO-FORD

Number	Title (A Side/B Side)	Yr	VG	VG+	NM
❑ HP-35	Not So Sweet Martha Lorraine/Masked Marauder	1969	6.25	12.50	25.00
—4-inch plastic "Hip Pocket Record" with color sleeve					

VANGUARD

Number	Title (A Side/B Side)	Yr	VG	VG+	NM
❑ 35052	Not So Sweet Martha Lorraine/The Masked Marauder	1967	2.50	5.00	10.00
❑ 35059	Janis (Part 1)/Janis (Part 2)	1967	2.50	5.00	10.00
❑ 35061	Who Am I/Thursday	1968	2.50	5.00	10.00
❑ 35061 [PS]	Who Am I/Thursday	1968	5.00	10.00	20.00
❑ 35068	Rock and Soul (Part 1)/Rock and Soul (Part 2)	1968	2.50	5.00	10.00
❑ 35090	Here I Go Again/Baby, You're Driving Me Crazy	1969	2.00	4.00	8.00
❑ 35112	I-Feel-Like-I'm-Fixin'-to-Die Rag/Janis	1970	2.00	4.00	8.00
❑ 35133	Hold On, It's Coming/Playing with Fire	1971	—	2.50	5.00
—Starting here, as "Country Joe McDonald"					
❑ 35150	Hang On/Hand of Man	1972	—	2.50	5.00
❑ 35161	Fantasy/I Seen a Rocket	1972	—	2.50	5.00
❑ 35181	Doctor Hip/Satisfactorily	1973	—	2.00	4.00
❑ 35184	Chloe/Jesse James	1974	—	2.00	4.00

7-Inch Extended Plays

RAG BABY

Number	Title (A Side/B Side)	Yr	VG	VG+	NM
❑ 1001	(contents unknown)	1966	25.00	50.00	100.00
❑ 1001 [PS]	Rag Baby	1966	50.00	100.00	200.00
—Actually an envelope in which the record came					

COUNTS, THE (1)

Male vocal group from Indianapolis.

DOT

Number	Title (A Side/B Side)	Yr	VG	VG+	NM
❑ 1188	Darling Dear/I Need You Always	1954	15.00	30.00	60.00
❑ 1199	Hot Tamales/Baby Don't You Know	1954	12.50	25.00	50.00
❑ 1210	My Dear, My Darling/She Won't Say Yes	1954	10.00	20.00	40.00
❑ 1226	Baby I Want You/Waitin' Around for You	1954	10.00	20.00	40.00
❑ 1235	Wailin' Little Mama/Let Me Go	1955	7.50	15.00	30.00
❑ 1243	From This Day On/Love and Understanding	1955	7.50	15.00	30.00
❑ 1265	I Need You Tonight/Sally Walker	1955	7.50	15.00	30.00
❑ 1275	To Our Love/Heartbreaker	1956	6.25	12.50	25.00
❑ 16105	Darling Dear/I Need You Always	1960	5.00	10.00	20.00

NOTE

Number	Title (A Side/B Side)	Yr	VG	VG+	NM
❑ 20000	Sweet Names/I Guess I Brought It All on Myself	1956	50.00	100.00	200.00

COUNTS, THE (2)

Detroit-based funk group.

AWARE

Number	Title (A Side/B Side)	Yr	VG	VG+	NM
❑ 038	Funk/Too Bad	1974	—	2.50	5.00
❑ 046	Sacrifice/Funk Pump	1974	—	2.50	5.00
❑ 049	All the Fair/On the Music	1975	—	2.50	5.00
❑ 054	Magic Ride/Short Cut	1975	—	2.50	5.00

WESTBOUND

Number	Title (A Side/B Side)	Yr	VG	VG+	NM
❑ 191	Thinking Single/Why Not Start All Over Again	1972	—	2.50	5.00

COUNTS, THE (U)

It appears as if none of these are by group (1) or (2), and they aren't all by the same group.

COUNT

Number	Title (A Side/B Side)	Yr	VG	VG+	NM
❑ 5	The Beat/After Beat	196?	5.00	10.00	20.00

MANCO

Number	Title (A Side/B Side)	Yr	VG	VG+	NM
❑ 1060	Surfer's Paradise/Chug-a-Lug	1964	10.00	20.00	40.00

MERCURY

Number	Title (A Side/B Side)	Yr	VG	VG+	NM
❑ 71318	Shake the Town/Teenage Guy and Girl	1958	3.75	7.50	15.00

PANORAMA

Number	Title (A Side/B Side)	Yr	VG	VG+	NM
❑ 9	Chitlins, Etc./Clyde, Clyde, The Cow's Outside	1965	2.50	5.00	10.00
❑ 33	Come Now/Since I Fell for You	1966	2.50	5.00	10.00

SEA CREST

Number	Title (A Side/B Side)	Yr	VG	VG+	NM
❑ 6003	Turn On Song/Enchanted Sea	1964	5.00	10.00	20.00
❑ 6004	Doggin'/And Then I Cried	1964	3.75	7.50	15.00

SMASH

Number	Title (A Side/B Side)	Yr	VG	VG+	NM
❑ 1821	Stormy Weather/True Love's Gone	1963	2.50	5.00	10.00

COURTNEY, LOU

BUDDAH

Number	Title (A Side/B Side)	Yr	VG	VG+	NM
❑ 121	Let Me Turn You On/Tryin' to Find My Woman	1969	2.00	4.00	8.00

EPIC

Number	Title (A Side/B Side)	Yr	VG	VG+	NM
❑ 11062	What Do You Want Me to Do/Beware	1973	—	2.50	5.00
❑ 11088	I Don't Need Nobody Else/Why	1974	—	2.50	5.00
❑ 50046	The Best Thing a Man Can Do for His Woman/I'm Serious About Lovin' You	1974	—	2.50	5.00
❑ 50070	Just to Let Him Break Your Heart/Somebody New Is Lovin' You	1975	—	2.50	5.00

IMPERIAL

Number	Title (A Side/B Side)	Yr	VG	VG+	NM
❑ 66006	Come On Home/The Man with the Cigar	1963	3.00	6.00	12.00
❑ 66043	Little Old Love Maker/Professional Lover	1964	3.00	6.00	12.00

PHILIPS

Number	Title (A Side/B Side)	Yr	VG	VG+	NM
❑ 40287	I Watched You Slowly Slip Away/I'll Cry If I Want To	1965	25.00	50.00	100.00

POP-SIDE

Number	Title (A Side/B Side)	Yr	VG	VG+	NM
❑ 4594	Hey Joyce/I'm Mad About You	1967	2.50	5.00	10.00
❑ 4596	If the Shoe Fits/It's Love Now	1968	2.50	5.00	10.00

RIVERSIDE

Number	Title (A Side/B Side)	Yr	VG	VG+	NM
❑ 4588	Skate Now/I Can Always Tell	1966	2.50	5.00	10.00
❑ 4589	Do the Thing/Man Is Lonely	1967	2.50	5.00	10.00
❑ 4591	You Ain't Ready/I've Got Just the Thing	1967	2.50	5.00	10.00

VERVE

Number	Title (A Side/B Side)	Yr	VG	VG+	NM
❑ 10602	Do the Horse/Rubber Neckin'	1968	2.00	4.00	8.00
❑ 10631	Please Stay/You Can Give Your Love to Me	1968	2.00	4.00	8.00

COURVALE, KEITH

DOT

Number	Title (A Side/B Side)	Yr	VG	VG+	NM
❑ 15844	Trapped Love/Steelworker Blues	1958	25.00	50.00	100.00

COUSINS, THE (1)

DECCA

Number	Title (A Side/B Side)	Yr	VG	VG+	NM
❑ 30609	I'm in Love with You/Be Nice to Me	1958	5.00	10.00	20.00

FIDELITY

Number	Title (A Side/B Side)	Yr	VG	VG+	NM
❑ 3010	Love Is Blind/How We'll Love	1959	7.50	15.00	30.00

COUSINS, THE (2)

PARKWAY

Number	Title (A Side/B Side)	Yr	VG	VG+	NM
❑ 823	St. Louis Blues/No One Knows	1961	3.75	7.50	15.00
❑ 848	When My Baby Smiles at Me/Some of These Days	1962	3.00	6.00	12.00
❑ 870	Sweet Georgia Brown/Outside the Wall	1963	3.00	6.00	12.00

COUSINS, THE (U)

Neither group (1) nor group (2).

VERSATILE

Number	Title (A Side/B Side)	Yr	VG	VG+	NM
❑ 105	Down That Lonely Road/(B-side unknown)	1960	20.00	40.00	80.00

WYNNE

Number	Title (A Side/B Side)	Yr	VG	VG+	NM
❑ 132	Guilty/(B-side unknown)	1959	125.00	250.00	500.00

COVAY, DON

Also see THE SOLDIER BOYS.

ARNOLD

Number	Title (A Side/B Side)	Yr	VG	VG+	NM
❑ 1002	Pony Time/Love Boat	1961	6.25	12.50	25.00
—As "The Goodtimers"					
❑ 1002	Pony Time/Love Boat	1961	3.00	6.00	12.00
—As "Don Covay and the Goodtimers"					

ATLANTIC

Number	Title (A Side/B Side)	Yr	VG	VG+	NM
❑ 1147	Bip Bop Bip/Silver Dollar	1957	20.00	40.00	80.00
—As "Pretty Boy"					
❑ 2280	The Boomerang/Daddy Loves Baby	1965	2.50	5.00	10.00
❑ 2286	Please Do Something/A Woman's Love	1965	2.50	5.00	10.00
❑ 2301	See Saw/I Never Get Enough of Your Love	1965	2.50	5.00	10.00
❑ 2323	Sookie Sookie/Watching the Late Late Shoe	1966	2.50	5.00	10.00
❑ 2340	You Put Something On Me/Iron Out the Rough Spots	1966	2.50	5.00	10.00
❑ 2357	Somebody's Got to Love You/Temptation Was Too Strong	1966	2.50	5.00	10.00
❑ 2375	Shing-Aling '67/I Was There	1967	2.50	5.00	10.00
❑ 2407	40 Days — 40 Nights/The Usual Place	1967	2.50	5.00	10.00
❑ 2440	You've Got Me on the Critical List/Never Had No Love	1967	2.50	5.00	10.00
❑ 2481	Chain of Fools/Prove It	1968	2.50	5.00	10.00
❑ 2494	Don't Let Go/It's In the Wind	1968	2.50	5.00	10.00
❑ 2521	Gonna Send You Back to Your Mama/House on the Corner	1968	2.50	5.00	10.00
❑ 2565	I Stole Some Love/Snake in the Grass	1968	2.50	5.00	10.00
❑ 2609	Sweet Pea/C.C. Rider Blues	1969	2.50	5.00	10.00

Number	Title (A Side/B Side)	Yr	VG	VG+	NM
❑ 2666	Ice Cream Man (The Gimmie Game)/Black Woman	1969	2.50	5.00	10.00
❑ 2725	Everything I Do Goin' Be Funky/Key to the Kighway	1970	2.00	4.00	8.00
❑ 2742	Soul Stirrer/Sookie Sookie	1970	2.00	4.00	8.00
BIG					
❑ 617	Switchin' in the Kitchen/Rockin' the Mule	1958	20.00	40.00	80.00
—As "Pretty Boy"					
BIG TOP					
❑ 3060	Hey There/I'm Coming Down with the Blues	1960	3.75	7.50	15.00
BLAZE					
❑ 350	Standing in the Doorway/(B-side unknown)	1958	7.50	15.00	30.00
CAMEO					
❑ 239	The Popeye Waddle/One Little Bot Had Money	1962	3.00	6.00	12.00
❑ 251	Wiggle Wobble/Do the Bug	1963	3.00	6.00	12.00
COLUMBIA					
❑ 41981	Shake Wid the Snake/Every Which-a Way	1961	5.00	10.00	20.00
❑ 42058	Hand Jive Workout/See About Me	1961	5.00	10.00	20.00
❑ 42197	Now That I Need You/Teen Life Swag	1961	25.00	50.00	100.00
EPIC					
❑ 9484	It's Twistin' Time/Twistin' Train	1961	3.75	7.50	15.00
—As "The Goodtimers"					
JANUS					
❑ 164	Sweet Thang/Standing in the Grits Line	1971	—	3.00	6.00
❑ 181	Daddy Please Don't Go Out/Shoes Under My Bed	1972	—	3.00	6.00
LANDA					
❑ 704	You're Good for Me/Truth of the Lite	1965	2.50	5.00	10.00
MERCURY					
❑ 71385	I Was Checkin' Out She Was Checkin' In/Money	1973	—	3.00	6.00
❑ 71430	Somebody's Been Enjoying My Home/Bad Mouthing	1973	—	3.00	6.00
❑ 71469	It's Better to Have (And Don't Need)/Leave Him (Part 1)	1974	—	3.00	6.00
❑ 73311	Overtime Man/Dungeon #3	1972	—	3.00	6.00
❑ 73648	Rumble in the Jungle/We Can't Make It No More	1975	—	3.00	6.00
NEWMAN					
❑ 500	Badd Boy/(Instrumental)	1980	—	2.50	5.00
PARKWAY					
❑ 894	Ain't That Silly/Turn It On	1964	3.00	6.00	12.00
❑ 910	The Froog/One Little Boy Had Money	1964	3.00	6.00	12.00
PHILADELPHIA INT'L.					
❑ 3594	Right Time for Love/No Tell Motel	1976	—	2.50	5.00
❑ 3602	Travelin' in Heavy Traffic/Once You Have It	1976	—	2.50	5.00
ROSEMART					
❑ 801	Mercy Mercy/Can't Stay Away	1964	3.75	7.50	15.00
❑ 802	Take This Hurt Off Me/Please Don't Let Me Know	1964	3.00	6.00	12.00
SUE					
❑ 709	Betty Jean/Believe It or Not	1958	7.50	15.00	30.00
U-VON					
❑ 102	Back to the Roots (Part 1)/Back to the Roots (Part 2)	1977	—	2.50	5.00

COWBOY JUNKIES

Number	Title (A Side/B Side)	Yr	VG	VG+	NM
RCA					
❑ 8879-7-R	Sweet Jane/200 More Miles	1989	—	2.50	5.00
❑ 8879-7-R [PS]	Sweet Jane/200 More Miles	1989	—	2.50	5.00
❑ 8997-7-R	Misguided Angel/Postcard Blues	1989	—	2.50	5.00

COWSILL, BILL

Also see THE COWSILLS.

Number	Title (A Side/B Side)	Yr	VG	VG+	NM
MGM					
❑ 14166	When Everybody's Here/I Wish I Could Say the Same About You	1970	—	3.00	6.00

COWSILL, JOHN

Also see THE COWSILLS.

Number	Title (A Side/B Side)	Yr	VG	VG+	NM
MGM					
❑ 14003	Path of Love/Captain Sad and His Ship of Fools	1968	2.00	4.00	8.00

COWSILL, SUSAN

Also see THE COWSILLS.

Number	Title (A Side/B Side)	Yr	VG	VG+	NM
WARNER BROS.					
❑ 8232	It Might As Well Rain Until September/Mohammad's Radio	1976	—	2.50	5.00
❑ 8333	The Next Time That I See You/I Think of You	1977	—	2.50	5.00

COWSILLS, THE

Also see BILL COWSILL; JOHN COWSILL; SUSAN COWSILL.

Number	Title (A Side/B Side)	Yr	VG	VG+	NM
GASATANKA/ROCKVILLE					
❑ 6139	Christmastime (Song for Marissa)/Some Good Years	1993	—	—	3.00
—Green vinyl					
❑ 6139	Christmastime (Song For Marisa)/Some Good Years	1993	—	2.00	4.00
—Clear vinyl					
❑ 6139 [PS]	Christmastime (Song for Marissa)/Some Good Years	1993	—	—	3.00
JODA					
❑ 103	All I Really Wanta Be Is Me/And the Next Day, Too	1965	7.50	15.00	30.00
LONDON					
❑ 149	On My Side/There Is No Child	1971	2.00	4.00	8.00
❑ 153	You/Crystal Claps	1971	2.00	4.00	8.00
❑ 170	Blue Road/Covered Wagon	1972	2.00	4.00	8.00
MGM					
❑ 13810	The Rain, the Park and Other Things/River Blue	1967	2.50	5.00	10.00
❑ 13810 [PS]	The Rain, the Park and Other Things/River Blue	1967	3.00	6.00	12.00
❑ 13886	We Can Fly/A Time for Remembrance	1967	2.00	4.00	8.00
❑ 13886 [PS]	We Can Fly/A Time for Remembrance	1967	3.00	6.00	12.00
❑ 13909	In Need of a Friend/Mister Flynn	1968	2.00	4.00	8.00
❑ 13909 [PS]	In Need of a Friend/Mister Flynn	1968	3.00	6.00	12.00
❑ 13944	Indian Lake/Newspaper Blanket	1968	2.50	5.00	10.00
—First pressings have black labels					
❑ 13944	Indian Lake/Newspaper Blanket	1968	2.00	4.00	8.00
—Second pressings have blue and gold labels					
❑ 13944 [PS]	Indian Lake/Newspaper Blanket	1968	3.00	6.00	12.00
❑ 13981	Poor Baby/Meet Me at the Wishing Well	1968	2.00	4.00	8.00
❑ 14011	The Impossible Years/Candy Kid	1968	2.00	4.00	8.00
❑ 14026	Hair/What Is Happy	1969	3.00	6.00	12.00
❑ 14063	The Prophecy of Daniel and John the Divine (Six-Six-Six)/Gotta Get Away from It All	1969	2.00	4.00	8.00
❑ 14084	Silver Threads and Golden Needles/Love, American Style	1969	2.50	5.00	10.00
❑ 14084 [PS]	Silver Threads and Golden Needles/Love, American Style	1969	3.00	6.00	12.00
❑ 14106	Start to Love/Two by Two	1970	2.00	4.00	8.00
PHILIPS					
❑ 40382	Most of All/Siamese Cat	1966	2.50	5.00	10.00
❑ 40382 [PS]	Most of All/Siamese Cat	1966	3.75	7.50	15.00
❑ 40406	Party Girl/What's It Gonna Be Like	1966	2.50	5.00	10.00
❑ 40437	A Most Peculiar Man/Could It Be, Let Me Know	1967	2.50	5.00	10.00

7-Inch Extended Plays

Number	Title (A Side/B Side)	Yr	VG	VG+	NM
MGM					
❑ EP1	*All My Days/Nothing to Do/The Milk Song/The Fun Song	1969	2.50	5.00	10.00
—American Dairy Association promotional item					
❑ EP1 [PS]	The Cowsills Collector's Record	1969	6.25	12.50	25.00
—American Dairy Association promotional item					

CRADDOCK, BILLY "CRASH"

Also recorded as "Bill Craddock" and "Crash Craddock," both included below.

Number	Title (A Side/B Side)	Yr	VG	VG+	NM
ABC					
❑ 11342	Afraid I'll Want to Love Her One More Time/Treat Her Right	1972	—	3.00	6.00
❑ 11349	Don't Be Angry/I'm a White Boy	1973	—	3.00	6.00
❑ 11364	Slippin' and Slidin'/Living Example	1973	—	3.00	6.00
❑ 11379	'Till the Water Stops Runnin'/What Does a Loser Say	1973	—	3.00	6.00
❑ 11412	Sweet Magnolia Blossom/Home Is Such a Lonely Place to Go	1973	—	3.00	6.00
❑ 11437	Rub It In/It's Hard to Love a Hungry, Worried Man	1974	—	3.00	6.00
❑ 12013	Rub It In/It's Hard to Love a Hungry, Worried Man	1974	—	2.00	4.00
❑ 12036	Ruby, Baby/Walk When Love Walks	1974	—	2.50	5.00
❑ 12068	Still Thinkin' 'Bout You/Stay a Little Longer in Your Bed	1975	—	2.50	5.00
❑ 12104	I Love the Blues and the Boogie Woogie/No Deposit, No Return	1975	—	2.50	5.00
❑ 12335	Another Woman/The Words Still Rhyme	1978	—	2.00	4.00
❑ 12357	Think I'll Go Somewhere (And Cry Myself to Sleep)/It All Came Back	1978	—	2.00	4.00
❑ 12384	Don Juan/Things Are Mostly Fine	1978	—	2.00	4.00
ABC DOT					
❑ 17584	Easy As Pie/She's Mine	1975	—	2.50	5.00
❑ 17619	Walk Softly/She's About a Mover	1976	—	2.50	5.00
❑ 17635	You Rubbed It In All Wrong/I Need Somebody to Love Me	1976	—	2.50	5.00
❑ 17659	Broken Down in Tiny Pieces/Shake It Easy	1976	—	2.50	5.00
❑ 17682	Just a Little Thing/The First Time	1977	—	2.50	5.00
❑ 17701	A Tear Fell/A Piece of the Rock	1977	—	2.50	5.00
❑ 17723	The First Time/Walk When Love Walks	1977	—	2.50	5.00
ATLANTIC					
❑ 88851	Just Another Miserable Day (Here in Paradise)/Softly Diana	1989	—	—	3.00
❑ 88851 [PS]	Just Another Miserable Day (Here in Paradise)/Softly Diana	1989	—	2.00	4.00
CAPITOL					
❑ 4545	I Cheated on a Good Woman's Love/Not a Day Goes By	1978	—	2.00	4.00
❑ 4575	I've Been Too Long Lonely Baby/Jailhouse Rock	1978	—	2.00	4.00
❑ 4624	Hubba Hubba/Let's Go Back to the Beginning	1978	—	2.00	4.00
❑ 4672	If I Could Write a Song As Beautiful As You/Never Ending	1978	—	2.00	4.00
❑ 4707	My Mama Never Heard Me Sing/As Long As I Live	1979	—	2.00	4.00
❑ 4753	Robinhood/We Never Made It to Chicago	1979	—	2.00	4.00
❑ 4792	Till I Stop Shaking/Sneak Out of Love with You	1979	—	2.00	4.00
❑ 4838	I Just Had You on My Mind/You Just Wanta Be Mine	1980	—	2.00	4.00
❑ 4875	Sea Cruise/She's Got Legs	1980	—	2.00	4.00
❑ 4935	A Real Cowboy (You Say You're)/One Dream Coming, One Dream Going	1980	—	2.00	4.00
❑ 4972	It Was You/Betty Ruth	1981	—	2.00	4.00
❑ 5011	I Just Need You For Tonight/Leave Your Love A-Smokin'	1981	—	2.00	4.00
❑ 5051	Now That the Feeling's Gone/She's Good to Me	1981	—	2.00	4.00
❑ 5139	Love Busted/Darlin' Take Care of Yourself	1982	—	2.00	4.00
❑ 5170	The New Will Never Wear Off on You/Hold Me Tight	1982	—	2.00	4.00
CARTWHEEL					
❑ 193	Knock Three Times/The Best I Ever Had	1971	—	3.50	7.00
❑ 196	Dream Lover/I Ran Out of Time	1971	—	3.50	7.00
❑ 201	You Better Move On/Confidence and Common Sense	1971	—	3.50	7.00
❑ 210	Ain't Nothin' Shakin' (But the Leaves on the Trees)/She's My Angel	1972	—	3.50	7.00
❑ 216	I'm Gonna Knock on Your Door/What He Don't Know	1972	—	3.50	7.00
❑ 222	Afraid I'll Want to Love Her One More Time/Treat Her Right	1972	3.00	6.00	12.00
CEE CEE					
❑ 5400	Tell Me When I'm Hot/When the Feeling Is Right	1983	—	2.50	5.00
CHART					
❑ 1004	Go On Home Girl/Learning to Live Without You	1967	2.00	4.00	8.00
❑ 1025	Your Love Is What Is/Anything That's Part of You	1968	2.00	4.00	8.00

Number	Title (A Side/B Side)	Yr	VG	VG+	NM
❑ 1415	There Ought to Be a Law/Two Arms Full of Lonely	1966	2.50	5.00	10.00
❑ 1450	Whipping Boy/The Love We Live Without	1967	2.50	5.00	10.00
❑ 5126	Go On Home Girl/Whipping Boy	1971	2.00	4.00	8.00
❑ 5154	Your Love Is What Is/Whipping Boy	1972	2.00	4.00	8.00
COLONIAL					
❑ 721	Bird Doggin'/Millionaire	1958	10.00	20.00	40.00
COLUMBIA					
❑ 41316	Am I to Be the One/I Miss You So Much	1959	6.25	12.50	25.00
❑ 41367	Sweetie Pie/Blabbermouth	1959	7.50	15.00	30.00
❑ 41470	Don't Destroy Me/Boom Boom Baby	1959	6.25	12.50	25.00
❑ 41470 [PS]	Don't Destroy Me/Boom Boom Baby	1959	12.50	25.00	50.00
❑ 41536	I Want That/Since She Turned Seventeen	1960	7.50	15.00	30.00
❑ 41619	All I Want Is You/Letter of Love	1960	6.25	12.50	25.00
❑ 41619 [PS]	All I Want Is You/Letter of Love	1960	12.50	25.00	50.00
❑ 41677	One Last Kiss/Is It True or False	1960	5.00	10.00	20.00
❑ 41822	Heavenly Love/Good Time Billy	1961	5.00	10.00	20.00
DATE					
❑ 1007	Lulu Lee/Ah, Poor Little Baby	1958	10.00	20.00	40.00
KING					
❑ 5912	Betty, Betty/Right Around the Corner	1964	6.25	12.50	25.00
❑ 5924	My Baby's Got Flat Feet/One Heartache Too Many	1964	6.25	12.50	25.00
❑ 5964	Teardrops on Your Letter/Love You More Everyday	1964	5.00	10.00	20.00
MERCURY					
❑ 71811	Truly True/How Lonely He Must Be	1961	5.00	10.00	20.00
❑ 71862	A Diamond Is Forever/Old King Cole	1962	6.25	12.50	25.00

CRAIG, JIMMY

Number	Title (A Side/B Side)	Yr	VG	VG+	NM
BRILL					
❑ 1	All for You/Gonna Love My Baby	1959	20.00	40.00	80.00
IMPERIAL					
❑ 5592	Walking in Darkness/Oh Little Girl	1959	3.75	7.50	15.00
WARWICK					
❑ 542	Drifter/Let Me Stay	1960	3.75	7.50	15.00

CRAIG, THE

Number	Title (A Side/B Side)	Yr	VG	VG+	NM
FONTANA					
❑ 1579	I Must Be Mad/Suspense	1967	6.25	12.50	25.00

CRAMPS, THE

Number	Title (A Side/B Side)	Yr	VG	VG+	NM
I.R.S.					
❑ 9014	Garbage Man/Drug Train	1980	2.50	5.00	10.00
❑ 9014 [PS]	Garbage Man/Drug Train	1980	2.50	5.00	10.00
❑ 9021	Goo Goo Muck/She Said	1981	2.50	5.00	10.00
❑ 9021 [PS]	Goo Goo Muck/She Said	1981	2.50	5.00	10.00
MEDICINE LABEL					
❑ 17932	Naked Girl Falling Down the Stairs/Confessions of a Psycho Cat	1995	—	2.00	4.00
❑ 17976	Ultra Twist/No Club Low Wolf	1995	—	2.00	4.00
❑ 18045	Let's Get F*cked Up/How Come You Do Me	1994	—	2.00	4.00
VENGEANCE					
❑ 666	Surfin' Bird/The Way I Walk	1978	12.50	25.00	50.00
❑ 666 [PS]	Surfin' Bird/The Way I Walk	1978	15.00	30.00	60.00
❑ 668	Human Fly/Domino	1978	12.50	25.00	50.00
❑ 668 [PS]	Human Fly/Domino	1978	15.00	30.00	60.00

CRANBERRIES, THE

Number	Title (A Side/B Side)	Yr	VG	VG+	NM
ISLAND					
❑ 854206-7	Zombie/Ode to My Family	1995	—	—	3.00
❑ 854802-7	When You're Gone/Free to Decide	1996	—	—	3.00
❑ 858172-7	Linger/Dreams	1994	—	—	3.00

CRANE, SHERRY

Number	Title (A Side/B Side)	Yr	VG	VG+	NM
SUN					
❑ 328	Willie Willie/Winnie the Parakeet	1959	6.25	12.50	25.00

CRAWFORD, BOBBY

Also see THE CRAWFORD BROTHERS.

Number	Title (A Side/B Side)	Yr	VG	VG+	NM
DEL-FI					
❑ 4211	Mrs. Smith, Please Wake Up/That Little Old Lovemaker Me	1963	3.75	7.50	15.00
❑ 4236	I Want to Be a Good Guy/(B-side unknown)	1964	3.75	7.50	15.00

CRAWFORD, CAROLYN

Number	Title (A Side/B Side)	Yr	VG	VG+	NM
MERCURY					
❑ 74036	Coming On Strong/Love Song for You	1978	—	2.50	5.00
—Mercury titles as "Caroline Crawford"					
❑ 74054	You'll Wait/Breakdown	1979	—	2.50	5.00
❑ 76013	The Strut/I'll Be Here for You	1979	—	2.50	5.00
MOTOWN					
❑ 1050	Forget About Me/Devil in His Heart	1963	10.00	20.00	40.00
❑ 1064	My Smile Is Just a Frown Turned Upside Down/I'll Come Running	1964	12.50	25.00	50.00
—Original version of A-side title					
❑ 1064	My Smile Is Just a Frown (Turned Upside Down)/I'll Come Running	1964	5.00	10.00	20.00
—Revised version of A-side title					
❑ 1070	My Heart/When Someone's Good to You	1964	10.00	20.00	40.00
PHILADELPHIA INT'L.					
❑ 3553	Just Got to Be More Careful/Saving All the Love I Got for You	1974	—	2.50	5.00
❑ 3570	It Takes Two to Make One/No Matter How Bad Things Are, I Still Love You	1975	—	2.50	5.00
❑ 3580	Good & Plenty/If You Move, You Lose	1975	—	2.50	5.00

CRAWFORD, JOHNNY

Also see THE CRAWFORD BROTHERS.

Number	Title (A Side/B Side)	Yr	VG	VG+	NM
DEL-FI					
❑ 4162	Daydreams/So Goes the Story	1961	3.75	7.50	15.00
❑ 4162 [PS]	Daydreams/So Goes the Story	1961	6.25	12.50	25.00
❑ 4165	Your Love Is Growing Cold/Treasure	1961	3.75	7.50	15.00
❑ 4165 [PS]	Your Love Is Growing Cold/Treasure	1961	6.25	12.50	25.00
❑ 4172	Patti Ann/Donna	1962	3.75	7.50	15.00
❑ 4178	Cindy's Birthday/Something Special	1962	3.75	7.50	15.00
❑ 4178 [PS]	Cindy's Birthday/Something Special	1962	6.25	12.50	25.00
❑ 4181	Your Nose Is Gonna Grow/Mr. Blue	1962	3.75	7.50	15.00
❑ 4181 [PS]	Your Nose Is Gonna Grow/Mr. Blue	1962	6.25	12.50	25.00
❑ 4188	Rumors/No One Really Loves a Clown	1962	3.75	7.50	15.00
❑ 4188 [PS]	Rumors/No One Really Loves a Clown	1962	6.25	12.50	25.00
❑ 4193	Proud/Lonesome Town	1963	3.75	7.50	15.00
❑ 4203	Cry on My Shoulder/When I Fall in Love	1963	3.75	7.50	15.00
❑ 4215	What Happened to Janie/Petite Chanson	1963	3.75	7.50	15.00
❑ 4221	Cindy's Gonna Cry/Debbie	1963	3.75	7.50	15.00
❑ 4229	Sandy/Ol' Shorty	1963	3.75	7.50	15.00
❑ 4231	Judy Loves Me/Living in the Past	1963	3.75	7.50	15.00
❑ 4242	The Girl Next Door (Once Upon a Time)/Sittin' and Watchin'	1964	3.75	7.50	15.00
❑ 4305	Am I Too Young/Janie Please Believe It	1965	3.75	7.50	15.00
SIDEWALK					
❑ 932	Angelica/Everybody Has Their Day	1968	3.00	6.00	12.00
❑ 941	Good Guys Finish Last/Everyone Should Own a Dream	1968	3.00	6.00	12.00
WYNNE					
❑ 124	Dance with the Dolly (With the Hole in Her Stocking)/Ask	1958	5.00	10.00	20.00

CRAWFORD BROTHERS, THE

Number	Title (A Side/B Side)	Yr	VG	VG+	NM
DEL-FI					
❑ 4191	Good Buddies/You Gotta Wear Shoes	1963	3.75	7.50	15.00
❑ 4191 [PS]	Good Buddies/You Gotta Wear Shoes	1963	6.25	12.50	25.00

CRAYONS, THE

Number	Title (A Side/B Side)	Yr	VG	VG+	NM
COUNSEL					
❑ 122	Love at First Sight/I Saw You	1963	7.50	15.00	30.00

CRAYTON, PEE WEE

Number	Title (A Side/B Side)	Yr	VG	VG+	NM
ALADDIN					
❑ 3112	When It Rains It Pours/Daybreak	1952	25.00	50.00	100.00
❑ 3112	When It Rains It Pours/Daybreak	1952	500.00	1000.	1500.
—Green vinyl					
EDCO					
❑ 1009	Ev'ry Night About This Time/(B-side unknown)	196?	6.25	12.50	25.00
❑ 1010	Money Tree/When Darkness Falls	196?	6.25	12.50	25.00
FOX					
❑ 10069	Give Me One More Chance/(B-side unknown)	196?	7.50	15.00	30.00
GUYDEN					
❑ 2048	I'm Still in Love with You/Time on My Hands	1961	3.75	7.50	15.00
IMPERIAL					
❑ 5288	Do Unto Others/Every Dog Has a Day	1954	50.00	100.00	200.00
❑ 5297	Wine-O/Hurry Hurry	1954	125.00	250.00	500.00
❑ 5321	I Need Your Love/You Know — Yeah	1955	12.50	25.00	50.00
❑ 5338	My Idea About You/I Got News for You	1955	12.50	25.00	50.00
❑ 5345	Eyes Full of Tears/Runnin' Wild	1955	12.50	25.00	50.00
❑ 5353	Yours Truly/Be Faithful	1955	12.50	25.00	50.00
JAMIE					
❑ 1190	'Tain't Nobody's Business If I Do/Little Bitty Things	1961	3.75	7.50	15.00
MODERN					
❑ 892	Cool Evening/Have You Lost Your Love for Me	1951	25.00	50.00	100.00
POST					
❑ 2007	Don't Go/I Must Go On	1955	10.00	20.00	40.00
❑ 2007	I Must Go On/(B-side unknown)	1955	7.50	15.00	30.00
RECORDED IN HOLLYWOOD					
❑ 408	Pappy's Blues/Crying and Walking	1954	25.00	50.00	100.00
❑ 426	Baby Pat the Floor/I'm Your Prisoner	1954	25.00	50.00	100.00
SMASH					
❑ 1774	Sabre Twist/Hillbilly Blues	1962	3.00	6.00	12.00
VEE JAY					
❑ 214	A Frosty Night/The Telephone Is Ringing	1956	10.00	20.00	40.00
❑ 252	I Don't Care/I Found My Peace of Mind	1957	10.00	20.00	40.00
❑ 266	Fiddle Dee Dee/Is This the Price I Pay	1957	10.00	20.00	40.00

CRAZY ELEPHANT

Number	Title (A Side/B Side)	Yr	VG	VG+	NM
BELL					
❑ 763	Gimme Gimme Good Lovin'/Dark Part of My Mind	1969	2.00	4.00	8.00
❑ 804	Pam/Sunshine, Red Wine	1969	—	3.00	6.00
❑ 817	Gimme Some More/My Babe (Honey Pie)	1969	—	3.00	6.00
❑ 846	There's a Better Day a-Comin' (Na, Na, Na, Na)/Space Buggy	1969	—	3.00	6.00
❑ 875	Land Rover/There Ain't No Umbopo	1970	—	3.00	6.00

CRAZY HORSE

Also see THE ROCKETS (4); NEIL YOUNG.

Number	Title (A Side/B Side)	Yr	VG	VG+	NM
EPIC					
❑ 10925	Rock and Roll Band/Outside Lookin' In	1972	—	2.50	5.00
M.O.C.					
❑ 671	Love/High on Lovin'	1967	3.00	6.00	12.00
REPRISE					
❑ 1007	Downtown/Crow Jane Lady	1971	—	2.50	5.00
❑ 1025	Dance, Dance, Dance/Carolay	1971	—	2.50	5.00
❑ 1046	Beggars Day/Dirty, Dirty	1971	—	2.50	5.00
❑ 1075	All Alone Now/One Thing I Love	1972	—	2.50	5.00

CRAZY JOE AND THE VARIABLE SPEED BAND

Number	Title (A Side/B Side)	Yr	VG	VG+	NM
CASABLANCA					
❑ 2298	Eugene/Madam Palm	1980	—	2.50	5.00
—Produced by Ace Frehley of Kiss					
❑ 2334	Ice Cream/Ugga Ugga Boo	1981	—	2.00	4.00

CREACH, PAPA JOHN

Also see HOT TUNA; JEFFERSON AIRPLANE; JEFFERSON STARSHIP.

Number	Title (A Side/B Side)	Yr	VG	VG+	NM
BUDDAH					
❑ 509	I'm the Fiddle Man/Joyce	1975	—	2.00	4.00

Number	Title (A Side/B Side)	Yr	VG	VG+	NM
DJM					
❑ 1102	All the World Loves a Winner/Southern Strut	1979	—	2.00	4.00
GRUNT					
❑ 65-0501	Over the Rainbow/The Janitor Drives a Cadillac	1971	—	2.50	5.00
❑ 65-0505	Papa John's Down Home Blues/String Jet Rock	1971	—	2.50	5.00
❑ 65-0508	Filthy Funky (Part 1)/Filthy Funky (Part 2)	1972	—	2.50	5.00

CREAM

Also see GINGER BAKER'S AIR FORCE; JACK BRUCE; ERIC CLAPTON.

Number	Title (A Side/B Side)	Yr	VG	VG+	NM
ATCO					
❑ 6462	I Feel Free/N.S.U.	1967	3.75	7.50	15.00
❑ 6488	Strange Brew/Tales of Brave Ulysses	1967	3.75	7.50	15.00
❑ 6522	Spoonful/Spoonful (Part 2)	1967	3.75	7.50	15.00
❑ 6544	Sunshine of Your Love/SWLABR	1968	2.00	4.00	8.00
❑ 6575	Anyone for Tennis/Pressed Rat and Warthog	1968	2.00	4.00	8.00
❑ 6617	White Room/Those Were the Days	1968	2.00	4.00	8.00
❑ 6646	Crossroads/Passing the Time	1969	2.00	4.00	8.00
❑ 6668	Badge/What a Bringdown	1969	2.00	4.00	8.00
❑ 6708	Sweet Wine/Lawdy Mama	1969	2.50	5.00	10.00

CREATION, THE

Number	Title (A Side/B Side)	Yr	VG	VG+	NM
DECCA					
❑ 32155	If I Stay Too Long/Nightmares	1967	3.00	6.00	12.00
❑ 32227	How Does It Feel to Feel/Life Is Just Beginning	1967	3.00	6.00	12.00
PLANET					
❑ 116	Making Time/Try and Stop Me	1966	3.75	7.50	15.00
❑ 119	Painter Man/Biff Bang Pow	1966	3.75	7.50	15.00

CREATIONS, THE

Many different groups.

Number	Title (A Side/B Side)	Yr	VG	VG+	NM
GLOBE					
❑ 102	Just Remember Me/Times Are Changing	1967	5.00	10.00	20.00
❑ 103	I've Got to Find Her/Times Are Changing	1967	5.00	10.00	20.00
❑ 1000	Oh Baby/Plenty of Love	1967	5.00	10.00	20.00
JAMIE					
❑ 1197	The Bells/Shang Shang	1961	6.25	12.50	25.00
LIDO					
❑ 501	You Are My Darling/There Goes the Girl I Love	1956	75.00	150.00	300.00
MEL-O-DY					
❑ 101	This Is Our Night/You're My Inspiration	1962	—	—	—
MERIDIAN					
❑ 7550	The Wedding/I've Got a Feeling	1962	25.00	50.00	100.00
PATTI-JO					
❑ 1703	Seventeen/You'll Always Be Mine	1962	50.00	100.00	200.00
PENNY					
❑ 9022	Lady Luck/We're in Love	1962	15.00	30.00	60.00
PINE CREST					
❑ 101	Woke Up in the Morning/Strolling Through the Park	1961	100.00	200.00	400.00
RADIANT					
❑ 103	Don't Listen to What Others Say/Don't Listen to What Others Say, Part 2	1964	6.25	12.50	25.00
TAKE TEN					
❑ 1501	Lady Luck/We're in Love	1963	7.50	15.00	30.00
TIP TOP					
❑ 400	Every Night I Pray/Mommy and Daddy	1956	50.00	100.00	200.00
❑ 501	You Are My Darling/There Goes the Girl I Love	1956	50.00	100.00	200.00
—At least one source claims this is a bootleg.					
TOP HAT					
❑ 1003	Crash/Chickie Darling	1964	10.00	20.00	40.00
❑ 1003 [PS]	Crash/Chickie Darling	1964	20.00	40.00	80.00
❑ 1004	Don't Be Mean/(B-side unknown)	1965	12.50	235.00	50.00
❑ 1004 [PS]	Don't Be Mean/(B-side unknown)	1965	25.00	50.00	100.00
VIRTUE					
❑ 2517	I'm So in Love with You/Save the People	1971	—	3.00	6.00
❑ 2518	Don't Let Me Down/The Price I Have to Pay	1971	—	3.00	6.00
❑ 2520	Nothing Too Good for You/You Mean So Much	1972	—	3.00	6.00
❑ 2521	You Make Me Feel So Good/That's How Strong My Love Is	1972	—	3.00	6.00
❑ 2522	How Sweetly Simple/Lovin' Simple	1973	—	3.00	6.00
ZODIAC					
❑ 1005	A Dream/Foot Steps	1967	2.00	4.00	8.00

CREATORS, THE (1)

Number	Title (A Side/B Side)	Yr	VG	VG+	NM
DOOTO					
❑ 463	I've Had You/Drafted, Volunteered, Enlisted	1961	6.25	12.50	25.00
DORE					
❑ 635	Too Far to Turn Around/Hello There, Mister Grave Digger	1962	15.00	30.00	60.00

CREATORS, THE (2)

Number	Title (A Side/B Side)	Yr	VG	VG+	NM
EPIC					
❑ 9605	Crazy Love/Cross Fire	1963	3.75	7.50	15.00
HI-Q					
❑ 5021	Wear My Ring/Booga Bear	1961	20.00	40.00	80.00
—Normal print label					
❑ 5021	Wear My Ring/Booga Bear	1961	6.25	12.50	25.00
—Bold print label					
TIME					
❑ 1038	Do You Remember/There's Going to Be an Angel	1961	6.25	12.50	25.00

CREATORS, THE (3)

Number	Title (A Side/B Side)	Yr	VG	VG+	NM
PHILIPS					
❑ 40058	Boy, He's Got It/Yeah, He's Got It	1962	6.25	12.50	25.00
❑ 40083	I'll Stay Home (New Year's Eve)/Shoom Ba Boom	1962	75.00	150.00	300.00
T-KAY					
❑ 110	I'll Never, Never Do It Again/Boy, He's Got It!	1962	20.00	40.00	80.00

CREEDENCE CLEARWATER REVIVAL

Also see DOUG CLIFFORD; JOHN FOGERTY; TOM FOGERTY; TOMMY FOGERTY AND THE BLUE VELVETS; THE GOLLIWOGS.

Number	Title (A Side/B Side)	Yr	VG	VG+	NM
FANTASY					
❑ 616	Suzie Q (Part One)/Suzie Q (Part Two)	1968	—	3.00	6.00
❑ 617	I Put a Spell on You/Walk on the Water	1968	2.00	4.00	8.00
❑ 619	Proud Mary/Born on the Bayou	1969	—	3.00	6.00
❑ 622	Bad Moon Rising/Lodi	1969	—	3.00	6.00
❑ 625	Green River/Commotion	1969	—	3.00	6.00
❑ 634	Down on the Corner/Fortunate Son	1969	—	3.00	6.00
❑ 634 [PS]	Down on the Corner/Fortunate Son	1969	3.00	6.00	12.00
❑ 637	Travelin' Band/Who'll Stop the Rain	1970	—	3.00	6.00
❑ 637 [PS]	Travelin' Band/Who'll Stop the Rain	1970	3.00	6.00	12.00
❑ 641	Up Around the Bend/Run Through the Jungle	1970	—	3.00	6.00
❑ 641 [PS]	Up Around the Bend/Run Through the Jungle	1970	3.00	6.00	12.00
❑ 645	Lookin' Out My Back Door/Long As I Can See the Light	1970	—	3.00	6.00
❑ 645 [PS]	Lookin' Out My Back Door/Long As I Can See the Light	1970	3.00	6.00	12.00
❑ 655	Have You Ever Seen the Rain/Hey Tonight	1971	—	3.00	6.00
❑ 665	Sweet Hitch-Hiker/Door to Door	1971	—	3.00	6.00
❑ 665 [PS]	Sweet Hitch-Hiker/Door to Door	1971	3.00	6.00	12.00
❑ 676	Someday Never Comes/Tearin' Up the Country	1972	—	3.00	6.00
❑ 759	I Heard It Through the Grapevine/Good Golly Miss Molly	1976	—	2.00	4.00
❑ 759 [PS]	I Heard It Through the Grapevine/Good Golly Miss Molly	1976	—	2.50	5.00
❑ 908	Tombstone Shadow/Commotion	1981	—	2.00	4.00
❑ 917	Medley U.S.A./Bad Moon Rising	1981	—	2.00	4.00
❑ 920	Cotton Fields/Lodi	1981	—	2.00	4.00
❑ 957	Medley (from "I Heard It Through the Grapevine" to "Up Around the Bend")/Medley (from "Proud Mary" to "Lodi")	1985	2.50	5.00	10.00
❑ 2832/3 [DJ]	45 Revolutions Per Minute (Part 1)/45 Revolutions Per Minute (Part 2)	1970	10.00	20.00	40.00
❑ 2832/3 [PS]	45 Revolutions Per Minute (Part 1)/45 Revolutions Per Minute (Part 2)	1970	15.00	30.00	60.00
SCORPIO					
❑ 412	Porterville/Call It Pretending	1968	20.00	40.00	80.00

CRESCENDOS, THE (1)

Nashville-based vocal group.

Number	Title (A Side/B Side)	Yr	VG	VG+	NM
NASCO					
❑ 6005	Oh Julie/My Little Girl	1957	6.25	12.50	25.00
❑ 6009	School Girl/Crazy Hop	1958	6.25	12.50	25.00
❑ 6009 [PS]	School Girl/Crazy Hop	1958	12.50	25.00	50.00
❑ 6021	Rainy Sunday/Young and In Love	1958	6.25	12.50	25.00
❑ 6021 [PS]	Rainy Sunday/Young and In Love	1958	12.50	25.00	50.00
NASHBORO					
❑ (no #)	The Crescendos	1957	12.50	25.00	50.00
—Large-hole omnibus sleeve, often found with "Oh Julie," but may have been used on other Nasco singles					
TAP					
❑ 7027	Oh Julie/Angel Face	1962	3.75	7.50	15.00
❑ 7027 [PS]	Oh Julie/Angel Face	1962	6.25	12.50	25.00

CRESCENDOS, THE (2)

Number	Title (A Side/B Side)	Yr	VG	VG+	NM
ATLANTIC					
❑ 1109	Sweet Dreams/Finders Keepers	1956	7.50	15.00	30.00
❑ 2014	I'll Be Seeing You/Sweet Dreams	1959	3.75	7.50	15.00

CRESCENDOS, THE (U)

Some of these may be group (1); it's unlikely that any are group (2).

Number	Title (A Side/B Side)	Yr	VG	VG+	NM
DOMAIN					
❑ 1025	A Fellow Needs a Girl/Black Cat	1964	3.75	7.50	15.00
IMPRO					
❑ 5006	Tidal Wave/Crescendo Special	1962	10.00	20.00	40.00
NU SOUND					
❑ 1007	Count Down/Hawk Walk	1961	7.50	15.00	30.00
❑ 1014	Sweet Talk/Movin' Wild	1961	7.50	15.00	30.00
SCARLET					
❑ 4007	Strange Love/Let's Take a Walk	1960	7.50	15.00	30.00
❑ 4009	Angel Face/I'm So Ashamed	1961	12.50	25.00	50.00

CRESCHENDOS, THE

Number	Title (A Side/B Side)	Yr	VG	VG+	NM
GONE					
❑ 5100	My Heart's Desire/Take My Heart	1961	7.50	15.00	30.00
MUSIC CITY					
❑ 831	My Heart's Desire/Take My Heart	1960	100.00	200.00	400.00
—Green label					
❑ 831	My Heart's Desire/Take My Heart	1960	50.00	100.00	200.00
—Maroon label					
❑ 831	My Heart's Desire/Take My Heart	1961	12.50	25.00	50.00
—Black label					
❑ 839	Teenage Prayer/I Don't Mind	1961	62.50	125.00	250.00
SATURN					
❑ 404	Surfing Strip/Hanging Ten	1963	12.50	25.00	50.00

CRESENTS, THE

Number	Title (A Side/B Side)	Yr	VG	VG+	NM
JOYCE					
❑ 102	Everybody Knew But Me/Rosemarie	1957	62.50	125.00	250.00

CRESTONES, THE

Number	Title (A Side/B Side)	Yr	VG	VG+	NM
MARKIE					
❑ 117	She's a Bad Motorcycle/Grasshopper Dance	1963	12.50	25.00	50.00
U.S.A.					
❑ 835	My Girl/The Chopper	1965	3.00	6.00	12.00

CRESTS, THE

Also see JOHNNY MAESTRO.

Number	Title (A Side/B Side)	Yr	VG	VG+	NM
COED					
❑ 501	Pretty Little Angel/I Thank the Moon	1958	37.50	75.00	150.00
—"Coed" in red print					
❑ 501	Pretty Little Angel/I Thank the Moon	1958	10.00	20.00	40.00
—"Coed" in red and black print					
❑ 506	16 Candles/Beside You	1958	7.50	15.00	30.00
❑ 509	Six Nights a Week/I Do	1959	6.25	12.50	25.00
❑ 511	Flower of Love/Molly Mae	1959	6.25	12.50	25.00
❑ 515	The Angels Listened In/I Thank the Moon	1959	7.56	15.00	30.00
❑ 521	A Year Ago Tonight/Paper Clown	1959	6.25	12.50	25.00
❑ 525	Step by Step/Gee (But I'd Give the World)	1960	6.25	12.50	25.00
❑ 531	Trouble in Paradise/Always You	1960	6.25	12.50	25.00
❑ 535	Journey of Love/If My Heart Could Write a Letter	1960	5.00	10.00	20.00
❑ 537	Isn't It Amazing/Molly Mae	1960	5.00	10.00	20.00
❑ 543	I Remember (In the Still of the Night)/Good Golly Miss Molly	1961	6.25	12.50	25.00
❑ 561	Little Miracles/Baby I Gotta Know	1962	7.50	15.00	30.00
CORAL					
❑ 62403	You Blew Out the Candles/A Love to Last a Lifetime	1964	7.50	15.00	30.00
HARVEY					
❑ 5002	Sixteen Candles/My Juanita	1981	2.50	5.00	10.00
—Red vinyl					
JOYCE					
❑ 103	My Juanita/Sweetest One	1957	75.00	150.00	300.00
—Label name: "JoYce"					
❑ 103	My Juanita/Sweetest One	1959	12.50	25.00	50.00
—Label name: "Joyce"					
❑ 105	No One to Love/Wish She Was Mine	1957	75.00	150.00	300.00
KING TUT					
❑ 172	Earth Angel/Tweedlee Dee	197?	2.00	4.00	8.00
LANA					
❑ 101	16 Candles/(B-side unknown)	196?	2.00	4.00	8.00
—Oldies reissue					
❑ 102	Trouble in Paradise/I Thank the Moon	196?	2.00	4.00	8.00
—Oldies reissue					
❑ 103	Step by Step/Gee (But I'd Give the World)	196?	2.00	4.00	8.00
—Oldies reissue					
MUSICTONE					
❑ 1106	My Juanita/Sweetest One	1961	5.00	10.00	20.00
SCEPTER					
❑ 12112	I'm Stepping Out of the Picture/Afraid of Love	1965	3.75	7.50	15.00
SELMA					
❑ 311	Guilty/Number One with Me	1962	18.75	37.50	75.00
—A-side has spoken intro					
❑ 311	Guilty/Number One with Me	1962	6.25	12.50	25.00
—A-side does not have spoken intro					
❑ 4000	Did I Remember/Tears Will Fall	1963	7.50	15.00	30.00
TIMES SQUARE					
❑ 2	No One to Love/Wish She Was Mine	1962	5.00	10.00	20.00
—Red vinyl					
❑ 6	Baby/I Love You So	1964	3.75	7.50	15.00
❑ 97	Baby/I Love You So	1964	3.00	6.00	12.00
TRANS ATLAS					
❑ 696	The Actor/Three Tears in a Bucket	1962	7.50	15.00	30.00
7-Inch Extended Plays					
COED					
❑ 101	(contents unknown)	1960	100.00	200.00	400.00
❑ 101 [PS]	The Angels Listened In	1960	100.00	200.00	400.00

CREW CUTS, THE

Number	Title (A Side/B Side)	Yr	VG	VG+	NM
4 CORNERS OF THE WORLD					
❑ 120	Don't Be Angry/Earth Angel	1962	2.50	5.00	10.00
ABC-PARAMOUNT					
❑ 10450	Hip-Huggers/You're a Star, Donna, Donna	1963	3.00	6.00	12.00
CHESS					
❑ 1892	Ain't That Nice/Yeah, Yeah, She Wants Me	1964	2.50	5.00	10.00
FIREBIRD					
❑ 1805	My Heart Belongs to Only You/You've Been In	1970	—	2.50	5.00
MERCURY					
❑ 70341	Crazy 'Bout You Baby/Angela Mia	1954	5.00	10.00	20.00
❑ 70404	Sh-Boom/I Spoke Too Soon	1954	6.25	12.50	25.00
❑ 70404	Sh-Boom/I Spoke Too Soon	1954	12.50	25.00	50.00
—7-inch 78 rpm on vinyl					
❑ 70404 [PS]	Sh-Boom/I Spoke Too Soon	1954	25.00	50.00	100.00
—Sleeve accompanying the 78: "PopSi Hit Record of the Month"					
❑ 70443	Oop-Shoop/Do Me Good Baby	1954	3.75	7.50	15.00
❑ 70490	All I Wanna Do/The Barking Dog	1954	3.75	7.50	15.00
❑ 70491	Dance, Mr. Snowman, Dance/Twinkle Toes	1954	3.75	7.50	15.00
❑ 70494	The Whippenpoof Song/Varsity Drag	1954	3.75	7.50	15.00
❑ 70529	Ko Ko Mo (I Love You So)/Earth Angel	1955	3.75	7.50	15.00
❑ 70597	Don't Be Angry/Chop Chop Boom	1955	3.75	7.50	15.00
❑ 70598	Unchained Melody/Two Hearts, Two Kisses	1955	3.75	7.50	15.00
❑ 70634	A Story Untold/Carmen's Boogie	1955	3.75	7.50	15.00
❑ 70668	Gum Drop/Present Arms	1955	3.75	7.50	15.00
❑ 70710	Slam! Bam!/Are You Having Any Fun	1955	3.75	7.50	15.00
❑ 70741	Angels In the Sky/Mostly Martha	1955	3.75	7.50	15.00
❑ 70782	Seven Days/That's Your Mistake	1956	3.75	7.50	15.00
❑ 70840	Out of the Picture/Honey Hair, Sugar Lips, Eyes of Blue	1956	3.75	7.50	15.00
❑ 70890	Tell Me Why/Rebel in Town	1956	3.75	7.50	15.00
❑ 70922	Bei Mir Bist Du Schoen/Thirteen Going on Fourteen	1956	3.75	7.50	15.00
❑ 70977	Love in a Home/Keeper of the Flame	1956	3.75	7.50	15.00
❑ 70988	The Varsity Drag/Halls of Ivy	1956	3.75	7.50	15.00
❑ 71022	Young Love/Little by Little	1956	3.75	7.50	15.00
❑ 71076	The Angels/Whatever, Whenever. Whoever	1957	3.75	7.50	15.00
❑ 71125	Suzie Q/Such a Shame	1957	3.75	7.50	15.00
❑ 71168	I Sit in My Window/Hey, You Face	1957	3.75	7.50	15.00
❑ 71223	I Like It Like That/Be My Only Love	1957	3.75	7.50	15.00
RCA VICTOR					
❑ 47-7320	Forever My Darling/Hey Stella	1958	3.00	6.00	12.00
❑ 47-7359	That's My Desire/Baby Be Mine	1958	3.00	6.00	12.00
❑ 47-7446	Fraternity Pin/Can You Hear Me	1959	3.00	6.00	12.00
❑ 47-7509	Gone, Gone, Gone/Someone in Heaven	1959	3.00	6.00	12.00
❑ 47-7577	Bermuda/Kin-Ni-Ki-Nic	1959	3.00	6.00	12.00
❑ 47-7667	It Is No Secret/No, No, Nevermore	1960	3.00	6.00	12.00
❑ 47-7734	American Beauty Rose/The Shrine on Top of the Hill	1960	3.00	6.00	12.00
❑ 47-7759	Aura Lee/Going to Church on Sunday	1960	3.00	6.00	12.00
VEE JAY					
❑ 569	The Three Bells/Spanish Is the Loving Tongue	1963	3.00	6.00	12.00
WARWICK					
❑ 558	Over the Mountain/Searchin'	1960	3.00	6.00	12.00
❑ 585	You and the Angels/I Care for You	1960	3.00	6.00	12.00
❑ 595	Malaguena/Why Not	1960	3.00	6.00	12.00
❑ 623	The Legend of Gunga Din/Number One with Me	1961	3.00	6.00	12.00
WHALE					
❑ 507	Twistin' All the World/Electric Chair	1962	3.00	6.00	12.00
❑ 508	Laura Love/Little Donkey	1962	3.00	6.00	12.00
❑ 509	Hush Little Baby/Ti-Pi-Tum	1962	3.00	6.00	12.00
7-Inch Extended Plays					
MERCURY					
❑ EP-1-3274	Down the Old Ox Road/The Whiffenpoof Song//We're Working Our Way Through College/Varsity Drag	1956	3.00	6.00	12.00
❑ EP-1-3274 [PS]	The Crew Cuts On Campus	1956	3.00	6.00	12.00

CREWE, BOB

Includes records as "The Bob Crewe Generation" and similar names.

Number	Title (A Side/B Side)	Yr	VG	VG+	NM
20TH CENTURY					
❑ 2271	Street Talk/Street Talk (Part 2)	1976	—	2.00	4.00
ABC-PARAMOUNT					
❑ 10204	Swingin' Family Tree/La La Loretta	1961	3.00	6.00	12.00
❑ 10246	One More Lie/I'm Goin' Home (On My Way)	1961	3.00	6.00	12.00
❑ 10273	Another Day/Come to Me	1961	3.00	6.00	12.00
BRUNSWICK					
❑ 55021	I Can't Shake the Blues/Torn and Tattered Heart	1957	3.75	7.50	15.00
CORAL					
❑ 61688	Melody for Lovers/Can't Get Away from It	1956	3.75	7.50	15.00
CREWE					
❑ 605	Dandylion/Day By Day & Prepare Ye	1971	—	2.50	5.00
DYNO VOICE					
❑ 229	Music to Watch Girls By/Girls on the Rocks	1966	2.00	4.00	8.00
❑ 231	After the Ball/One More Year	1967	—	3.00	6.00
❑ 233	Miniskirts/Theme for a Lazy Girl	1967	—	3.00	6.00
❑ 237	A Lover's Concerto/You Only Live Twice	1967	—	3.00	6.00
❑ 902	Birds of Britain/I Will Wait for You	1968	—	3.00	6.00
❑ 906	Winter Warm/Song from Moulin Rouge	1968	—	3.00	6.00
❑ 915	To Give (The Reason I Live)/Battle Hymn of the Republic	1968	—	3.00	6.00
❑ 928	Angel Is Love/Black Queen's Beads	1968	—	3.00	6.00
ELEKTRA					
❑ 45346	Time for You and Me/Free (Medley)	1976	—	2.00	4.00
❑ 45380	Menage a Trois/I Am Free-Keep Walkin'	1976	—	2.00	4.00
❑ 45404	It Took a Long Time (For the First Time In My Life)/In Another Life	1977	—	2.00	4.00
❑ 45425	Marriage Made in Heaven/In Another Life	1977	—	2.00	4.00
JUBILEE					
❑ 5148	Cash Register Heart/Change of Heart	1954	5.00	10.00	20.00
❑ 5164	Punch/It's All Over	1954	5.00	10.00	20.00
MELBA					
❑ 119	Guessin' Games/Don't Call Me Chicken	1957	3.75	7.50	15.00
METROMEDIA					
❑ 229	Mammy Blue/Better Be Gone	1972	—	2.50	5.00
❑ 243	Takin' Care of Each Other/(B-side unknown)	1972	—	2.50	5.00
PHILIPS					
❑ 40241	Rag Doll/Ronnie	1964	2.00	4.00	8.00
❑ 40241 [PS]	Rag Doll/Ronnie	1964	3.75	7.50	15.00
—Has photo of the Four Seasons on it; the sleeve even looks as if it belongs to a Four Seasons record until you read a bit more closely!					
SPOTLIGHT					
❑ 393	Penny Nickel Dime Quarter (On a Teenage Date)/How Long	1956	5.00	10.00	20.00
VIK					
❑ 0307	Charm Bracelet/Do Be Do Be Do	1957	6.25	12.50	25.00
❑ 0333	Of Sun, the Sea and the Sand/Sweet Talk	1958	5.00	10.00	20.00
WARWICK					
❑ 519	The Whippenpoof Song/Let's Pretend	1959	3.00	6.00	12.00
❑ 534	Cool Time/Quite a Picture	1960	3.00	6.00	12.00
❑ 553	Silhouettes/Let's Get Serious	1960	3.00	6.00	12.00
❑ 579	Little Girl of Mine/To Ev'ry Girl, To Ev'ry Boy	1960	3.00	6.00	12.00
❑ 601	Oh, How I Miss You Tonight/Ev'rytime	1960	3.00	6.00	12.00
❑ 616	She's Only Wonderful/On the Street Where You Live	1961	3.00	6.00	12.00

CRIBBINS, BERNARD

Number	Title (A Side/B Side)	Yr	VG	VG+	NM
UNITED ARTISTS					
❑ 907	Right Said Fred/Quietly Bonkers	1965	2.50	5.00	10.00

CRICKETS, THE (1)

BUDDY HOLLY's group. Includes records credited to "The Crickets" both during and after Holly's life. Also see SONNY CURTIS; IVAN; NIKI SULLIVAN.

Number	Title (A Side/B Side)	Yr	VG	VG+	NM
BARNABY					
❑ 2061	Rockin' 50's Rock 'N' Roll/True Love Ways	1972	5.00	10.00	20.00

Number	Title (A Side/B Side)	Yr	VG	VG+	NM
BRUNSWICK					
❑ 55009	That'll Be the Day/I'm Lookin' for Someone to Love	1957	12.50	25.00	50.00
❑ 55035	Oh, Boy!/Not Fade Away	1957	12.50	25.00	50.00
❑ 55053	Maybe Baby/Tell Me How	1958	12.50	25.00	50.00
❑ 55072	Think It Over/Fool's Paradise	1958	12.50	25.00	50.00
❑ 55094	It's So Easy/Lonesome Tears	1958	12.50	25.00	50.00
❑ 55124	Love's Made a Fool of You/Someone, Someone	1959	10.00	20.00	40.00
❑ 55153	When You Ask About Love/Deborah	1959	10.00	20.00	40.00
CORAL					
❑ 62198	More Than I Can Say/Baby, My Heart	1960	10.00	20.00	40.00
❑ 62238	Peggy Sue Got Married/Don't Cha Know	1960	10.00	20.00	40.00
❑ 62407	Maybe Baby/Not Fade Away	1964	7.50	15.00	30.00
EPIC					
❑ 34-08028	T-Shirt/Hollywould	1988	—	2.50	5.00
❑ 34-08028 [PS]	T-Shirt/Hollywould	1988	—	2.50	5.00
LIBERTY					
❑ 55392	He's Old Enough to Know Better/I'm Feeling Better	1961	6.25	12.50	25.00
❑ 55441	Don't Ever Change/I'm Not a Bad Boy	1962	6.25	12.50	25.00
❑ 55492	I Believe in You/Parisian Girl	1962	6.25	12.50	25.00
❑ 55495	Little Hollywood Girl/Parisian Girl	1962	6.25	12.50	25.00
❑ 55540	My Little Girl/Teardrops Fall Like Rain	1963	6.25	12.50	25.00
❑ 55603	Don't Say You Love Me/April Avenue	1963	6.25	12.50	25.00
❑ 55660	Lonely Avenue/You Can't Be In-Between	1964	6.25	12.50	25.00
❑ 55668	Please, Please Me/From Me to You	1964	12.50	25.00	50.00
❑ 55696	(They Call Her) La Bomba/All Over You	1964	6.25	12.50	25.00
❑ 55742	We Gotta Get Together/I Think I've Caught the Blues	1964	6.25	12.50	25.00
❑ 55767	Everybody's Got a Little Problem/Now Hear This	1965	6.25	12.50	25.00
MGM					
❑ 14541	Hayride/Wasn't It Nice	1973	3.75	7.50	15.00
MUSIC FACTORY					
❑ 415	Million Dollar Movie/A Million Miles Apart	1968	5.00	10.00	20.00
7-Inch Extended Plays					
BRUNSWICK					
❑ EB 71036	*I'm Looking for Someone to Love/That'll Be the Day/Not Fade Away/Oh! Boy	1957	75.00	150.00	300.00
❑ EB 71036 [PS]	The Chirping Crickets	1957	75.00	150.00	300.00
❑ EB 71038	*Maybe Baby/Rock Me My Baby/Send Me Some Lovin'/Tell Me How	1958	62.50	125.00	250.00
❑ EB 71038 [PS]	The Sound of the Crickets	1958	62.50	125.00	250.00

CRICKETS, THE (2)

Black vocal group featuring Dean Barlow.

Number	Title (A Side/B Side)	Yr	VG	VG+	NM
DAVIS					
❑ 459	I'm Going to Live My Life Alone/Man from the Moon	1958	15.00	30.00	60.00
JAY DEE					
❑ 777	Dreams and Wishes/When I Met You	1953	50.00	100.00	200.00
❑ 781	Fine As Wine/I'm Not the Same One You Love	1953	50.00	100.00	200.00
❑ 785	Changing Partners/Your Love	1954	37.50	75.00	150.00
❑ 786	Just You/My Little Baby's Shoes	1954	37.50	75.00	150.00
❑ 789	Are You Looking for a Sweetheart/Never Give Up Hope	1954	37.50	75.00	150.00
❑ 795	I'm Going to Live My Life Alone/Man from the Moon	1954	37.50	75.00	150.00
MGM					
❑ 11428	You're Mine/Milk and Gin	1953	62.50	125.00	250.00
❑ 11507	I'll Cry No More/For You I Have Eyes	1953	50.00	100.00	200.00

CRISS, PETER

Also see KISS.

Number	Title (A Side/B Side)	Yr	VG	VG+	NM
CASABLANCA					
❑ 952	Don't You Let Me Down/Hooked on Rock and Roll	1978	—	3.00	6.00
❑ 961	You Still Matter to Me/Hooked on Rock and Roll	1979	—	3.00	6.00
❑ 2311	I Found Love/By Myself	1980	—	2.50	5.00

CRITTERS, THE

Number	Title (A Side/B Side)	Yr	VG	VG+	NM
KAPP					
❑ 727	He'll Make You Cry/Children & Flowers	1965	2.50	5.00	10.00
❑ 752	Younger Girl/Gone for a While	1966	3.00	6.00	12.00
❑ 769	Mr. Dieingly Sad/It Won't Be That Way	1966	3.00	6.00	12.00
❑ 769 [PS]	Mr. Dieingly Sad/It Won't Be That Way	1966	5.00	10.00	20.00
❑ 793	Bad Misunderstanding/Forever or No More	1966	2.50	5.00	10.00
❑ 805	Marryin' Kind of Love/New York Bound	1967	2.50	5.00	10.00
❑ 838	Don't Let the Rain Fall Down on Me/Walk Like a Man Again	1967	2.50	5.00	10.00
❑ 858	Little Girl/Dancing in the Streets	1967	2.50	5.00	10.00
MUSICOR					
❑ 1044	I'm Gonna Give/Georgianna	1964	5.00	10.00	20.00
PRANCER					
❑ 6001	No One But You/I'm Telling Everyone	1969	2.00	4.00	8.00
PROJECT 3					
❑ 1326	Good Morning Sunshine/A Moment of Being with You	1968	2.00	4.00	8.00
❑ 1332	Touch 'N' Go/Younger Generation	1968	2.00	4.00	8.00
❑ 1349	Cool Sunday Morning/Lisa, But Not the Same	1969	2.00	4.00	8.00
❑ 1363	She Said She Loved Him/I Just Want to Sit Right Here and Look at You	1969	2.00	4.00	8.00

CROCE, A.J.

Number	Title (A Side/B Side)	Yr	VG	VG+	NM
OMTOWN					
❑ 88639	Maybe/Summer Can't Come Too Soon	2000	—	—	3.00

CROCE, JIM

Number	Title (A Side/B Side)	Yr	VG	VG+	NM
21 RECORDS					
❑ 94969	Workin' at the Car Wash Blues/Rapid Roy (The Stock Car Boy)	1987	—	—	3.00
❑ 94970	It Doesn't Have to Be That Way/Time in a Bottle	1987	—	—	3.00
❑ 94971	I'll Have to Say I Love You in a Song/I Got a Name	1987	—	—	3.00
❑ 94972	You Don't Mess Around with Jim/Photographs and Memories	1987	—	—	3.00
❑ 94973	Bad, Bad Leroy Brown/Operator (That's Not the Way It Feels)	1987	—	—	3.00
ABC					
❑ 11328	You Don't Mess Around with Jim/Photographs and Memories	1972	—	2.00	4.00
❑ 11335	Operator (That's Not the Way It Feels)/Rapid Roy (The Stock Car Boy)	1972	—	2.00	4.00
❑ 11346	One Less Set of Footsteps/It Doesn't Have to Be That Way	1973	—	2.00	4.00
❑ 11359	Bad, Bad Leroy Brown/A Good Time Man Like Me Ain't Got No Business (Singin' the Blues)	1973	—	2.50	5.00
—ABC logo in children's building blocks					
❑ 11359	Bad, Bad Leroy Brown/A Good Time Man Like Me Ain't Got No Business (Singin' the Blues)	1973	—	2.00	4.00
—Regular ABC logo					
❑ 11389	I Got a Name/Alabama Rain	1973	—	2.00	4.00
❑ 11405	Time in a Bottle/Hard Time Losin' Man	1973	—	2.00	4.00
❑ 11413	It Doesn't Have to Be That Way/Roller Derby Queen	1973	—	2.00	4.00
❑ 11413 [PS]	It Doesn't Have to Be That Way/Roller Derby Queen	1973	—	2.50	5.00
❑ 11424	I'll Have to Say I Love You in a Song/Salon and Saloon	1974	—	2.00	4.00
❑ 11447	Workin' at the Car Wash Blues/Thursday	1974	—	2.00	4.00
❑ 12015	Workin' at the Car Wash Blues/Thursday	1974	—	2.50	5.00
LIFESONG					
❑ 45001	Chain Gang Medley/Stone Walls	1975	—	2.00	4.00
❑ 45005	Maybe Tomorrow/Mississippi Lady	1976	—	2.00	4.00
❑ 45018 [DJ]	It Doesn't Have to Be That Way (mono/stereo)	1976	—	2.50	5.00
—Promo-only release; Lifesong sleeve has custom sticker (add $4)					

CROCKETT, G.L.

Number	Title (A Side/B Side)	Yr	VG	VG+	NM
CHECKER					
❑ 1121	Look Out Mabel/Did You Ever Love Somebody	1965	10.00	20.00	40.00
CHIEF					
❑ 7010	Look Out Mabel/Did You Ever Love Somebody	1958	25.00	50.00	100.00
—As "G. Davy Crockett"					

CROCKETT, HOWARD

Number	Title (A Side/B Side)	Yr	VG	VG+	NM
DOT					
❑ 15593	If You'll Let Me/You've Got Me Lyin'	1957	12.50	25.00	50.00
❑ 15701	The Night Rider/Branded	1958	10.00	20.00	40.00
❑ 17457	The House Where Momma Lived/Last Will and Testament (Of a Drinking Man)	1973	—	3.00	6.00
❑ 17482	I Feel More Like Myself Than I Did a While Ago/I'd Like to Be Everybody for Just One Day	1973	—	3.00	6.00
❑ 17509	The Calling/Pictures and Memories	1974	—	3.00	6.00
MANCO					
❑ 1002	Sluefoot the Bear/Polly Ann	1960	12.50	25.00	50.00
❑ 1012	That Old Juke Box/Steamboat Bill	1961	7.50	15.00	30.00
❑ 1023	Just a Poor Man/I've Got You Worried Too	1961	7.50	15.00	30.00
MEL-O-DY					
❑ 109	The Big Wheel/That Silver-Haired Daddy of Mine	1963	6.25	12.50	25.00
❑ 111	Bringing In the Gold/I've Been a Long Time Leaving	1963	6.25	12.50	25.00
❑ 115	My Lil's Run Off/Spanish Lace and Memories	1964	6.25	12.50	25.00
❑ 119	Put Me in Your Pocket/The Miles	1964	6.25	12.50	25.00
❑ 121	All the Good Times Are Gone/The Great Titanic	1965	6.25	12.50	25.00
SMASH					
❑ 1721	Deep Elm Dave/Going Down to Soldiers	1961	10.00	20.00	40.00
❑ 1750	Break Away Billy Boy/Out of Bounds Again	1962	10.00	20.00	40.00
❑ 1782	Jessie and the Glendale Train/Trail of Tears	1962	20.00	40.00	80.00
STOP					
❑ 136	The Big Cat/You're Messin' Up My Mind	1968	2.00	4.00	8.00
❑ 172	The Big Day/You Can't Get to All of 'Em Jack	1968	2.00	4.00	8.00
❑ 210	Soap and Water/A Man with No Face	1969	2.00	4.00	8.00
❑ 238	Where Were You/The Story of Bango	1969	2.00	4.00	8.00
❑ 250	The Law Says/Ask Little Brother	1969	2.00	4.00	8.00

CROSBY, BING

Number	Title (A Side/B Side)	Yr	VG	VG+	NM
AMOS					
❑ 111	Hey Jude/Lonely Street	1969	—	3.00	6.00
❑ 116	It's All in the Game/More and More	1969	—	2.50	5.00
BING CROSBY					
❑ (no #) [DJ]	How Lovely Is Christmas/Never Be Afraid	195?	5.00	10.00	20.00
—Crowley's Milk promotional item					
CAPITOL					
❑ F-3695	Man on Fire/Seven Nights a Week	1957	3.00	6.00	12.00
❑ 4548	Simple Love Affair/That's How I Met Your Mother	1978	—	2.00	4.00
❑ 5088	Do You Hear What I Hear/Christmas Dinner Country Style	1963	2.00	4.00	8.00
❑ S7-19766	Do You Hear What I Hear?/I Wish You a Merry Christmas	1997	—	—	3.00
COLUMBIA					
❑ 41104	Straight Down the Middle/Tomorrow's My Lucky Day	1958	3.00	6.00	12.00
❑ 41387	Say One for Me/I Couldn't Care Less	1959	3.00	6.00	12.00
❑ 41496	The Secret of Christmas/Just What I Wanted for Christmas	1959	3.75	7.50	15.00
DAYBREAK					
❑ 1001	A Time to Be Jolly/And the Bells Rang	1971	—	3.00	6.00
—Black label					
❑ 1001	A Time to Be Jolly/And the Bells Rang	1971	—	2.50	5.00
—Yellow label					
❑ 1001 [PS]	A Time to Be Jolly/And the Bells Rang	1971	—	2.50	5.00
DECCA					
❑ 1-256 [PS]	Jingle Bells/Santa's Coming	19??	3.75	7.50	15.00
—With the Andrews Sisters; alternate number is 23281					

Number	Title (A Side/B Side)	Yr	VG	VG+	NM
23281	Jingle Bells/Santa Claus Is Comin' to Town	1950	3.00	6.00	12.00
—With the Andrews Sisters; lines label; Sides 1 and 2 of "Album No. 9-65"					
23495	McNamara's Band/Dear Old Donegal	1950	3.00	6.00	12.00
—Reissue of 78; part of "Album No. 9-31"					
23777	Silent Night/Adeste Fideles (O Come All Ye Faithful)	1950	3.00	6.00	12.00
—Lines label; Sides 3 and 4 of "Album No. 9-65"					
23777	Silent Night/Adeste Fideles (O Come All Ye Faithful)	1955	2.50	5.00	10.00
—Star on label					
23777	Silent Night/Adeste Fideles (O Come All Ye Faithful)	1960	2.00	4.00	8.00
—Color bars on label					
23777 [PS]	Silent Night/Adeste Fideles (O Come All Ye Faithful)	1960	3.75	7.50	15.00
—Sleeve came with early 1960s pressings					
23778	White Christmas/God Rest Ye Merry Gentlemen	1950	3.00	6.00	12.00
—Lines label; Sides 5 and 6 of "Album No. 9-65"					
23778	White Christmas/God Rest Ye Merry Gentlemen	1955	2.50	5.00	10.00
—Star on label					
23778	White Christmas/God Rest Ye Merry Gentlemen	1960	2.00	4.00	8.00
—Color bars on label					
23778 [PS]	White Christmas/God Rest Ye Merry Gentlemen	1960	3.75	7.50	15.00
—Sleeve came with early 1960s pressings					
23779	I'll Be Home for Christmas (If Only in My Dreams)/Faith of Our Fathers	1950	3.00	6.00	12.00
—Lines label; Sides 7 and 8 of "Album No. 9-65"					
23786	Who Threw the Overalls in Mrs. Murphy's Chowder?/It's the Same Old Overalls	1950	3.00	6.00	12.00
—Reissue of 78; part of "Album No. 9-31"					
23787	Did Your Mother Come from Ireland?/Where the River Shannon Flows	1950	3.00	6.00	12.00
—Reissue of 78; part of "Album No. 9-31"					
23789	Too-Ra-Loo-Ra-Loo-Ral/I'll Take You Home Again Kathleen	1950	3.00	6.00	12.00
—Reissue of 78; part of "Album No. 9-31"					
24658	Here Comes Santa Claus/The Twelve Days of Christmas	1949	—	—	—
—Unknown on 45 rpm					
24659	You're All I Want for Christmas/The First Noel	1949	—	—	—
—Unknown on 45 rpm					
24670	Christmas Carols (Part 1)/Christmas Carols (Part 2)	1949	—	—	—
—Unknown on 45 rpm					
25003	Take Me Back to My Boots and Saddle/My Little Buckaroo	1950	3.00	6.00	12.00
—Reissue of 78; part of "Album No. 9-145"					
25020	Clementine/The Old Oaken Bucket	1950	3.00	6.00	12.00
—Reissue of 78; part of "Album No. 9-145"					
25497	Sierra Sue/Along the Santa Fe Trail	1950	3.00	6.00	12.00
—Reissue of 78; part of "Album No. 9-145"					
25520	Memories Are Made of This/My Blue Heaven	1961	—	3.00	6.00
25540	Moments to Remember/Vaya Con Dios	1961	—	3.00	6.00
25643	Avalon/On the Alamo	1964	—	3.00	6.00
25661	Chinatown, My Chinatown/I'm Confessin' (That I Love You)	1965	—	3.00	6.00
25665	Between the Devil and the Deep Blue Sea/Georgia on My Mind	1965	—	3.00	6.00
27013	Jamboree Jones/Dixieland Band	1950	3.00	6.00	12.00
27018	I Didn't Slip, I Wasn't Pushed, I Fell/So Tall a Tree	1950	3.00	6.00	12.00
27019	Home Cookin'/When the Sun Goes Down	1950	3.00	6.00	12.00
27111	La Vie En Rose/I Cross My Fingers	1950	3.00	6.00	12.00
27112	Play a Simple Melody/Sam's Song	1950	3.00	6.00	12.00
—By "Gary Crosby and Friend" (guess who the friend is)					
27117	All My Love/The Friendly Islands	1950	3.00	6.00	12.00
27143	This Could Be Forever/Helpless	1950	3.00	6.00	12.00
—With Louanne Hogan					
27158	Ave Maria/Home Sweet Home	1950	3.00	6.00	12.00
27159/30126 [DJ]	Rudolph The Red-Nosed Reindeer/I Heard the Bells on Christmas Day	1956	5.00	10.00	20.00
—Green label promo with two different numbers on the record!					
27159	Rudolph, the Red-Nosed Reindeer/The Teddy Bear's Picnic	1950	3.00	6.00	12.00
27173	Life Is So Peculiar/High on the List	1950	3.00	6.00	12.00
—With the Andrews Sisters					
27219	Harbor Lights/Beyond the Reef	1950	3.00	6.00	12.00
27228	Mele Kalikimaka/Poppa Santa Claus	1950	3.00	6.00	12.00
—With the Andrews Sisters					
27229	Silver Bells/That Christmas Feeling	1950	3.00	6.00	12.00
—A-side with Carol Richards					
27230	A Marshmallow World/Looks Like a Cold, Cold Winter	1950	3.00	6.00	12.00
27231	Autumn Leaves/This Is the Time	1950	3.00	6.00	12.00
27232	If I Were a Bell/I've Never Been in Love Before	1950	3.00	6.00	12.00
—A-side with Patti Andrews					
27241	And You'll Be Mine/Accidents Will Happen	1950	3.00	6.00	12.00
27249	A Crosby Christmas (Part 1)/A Crosby Christmas (Part 2)	1950	—	—	—
—As "Gary, Phillip, Dennis, Lindsay and Bing Crosby"; unreleased on this number?					
27250	The Best Thing for You/Marrying for Love	1950	3.00	6.00	12.00
27263	Wouldn't It Be Funny/One More for the Blue and White	1950	3.00	6.00	12.00
27264	Accidents Will Happen/Milady	1950	3.00	6.00	12.00
—With Dorothy Kirsten					
27275	Oh! What a Beautiful Morning/People Will Say We're in Love	1950	2.50	5.00	10.00
27276	If I Loved You/Close As Pages in a Book	1950	2.50	5.00	10.00
27277	They Say It's Wonderful/I Love You	1950	2.50	5.00	10.00
27278	Evalina/The Eagle and Me	1950	2.50	5.00	10.00
27404	May the Good Lord Bless and Keep You/A Perfect Day	1951	2.50	5.00	10.00
27441	An Early American/My Own Bit of Land	1951	2.50	5.00	10.00
27443	The Meadows of Heaven/The Last Mile Home	1951	2.50	5.00	10.00
27461	Then You've Never Been Blue/You Gotta Show Me	1951	2.50	5.00	10.00
27477	Sparrow in the Tree Top/Forsaking All Others	1951	2.50	5.00	10.00
—With the Andrews Sisters					
27478	St. Patrick's Day Parade/With My Shillelagh Under My Arm	1951	2.50	5.00	10.00
27483	Sentimental Music/Any Town Is Paris When You're Young	1951	2.50	5.00	10.00
27500	Feudin' and Fightin'/Goodbye, My Lovers, Goodbye	1951	2.50	5.00	10.00
27505	When My Dreamboat Comes Home/Walking the Floor Over You	1951	2.50	5.00	10.00
27508	Silver Moon/More I Cannot Wish You	1951	2.50	5.00	10.00
27536	Maria Bonita/Quizas, Quizas, Quizas	1951	2.50	5.00	10.00
27549	Yours Is My Heart Alone/Beautiful Love	1951	2.50	5.00	10.00
27550	I Kiss Your Hand, Madame/The Kiss in Your Eyes	1951	2.50	5.00	10.00
27551	Girl of My Dreams/I'll Remember April	1951	2.50	5.00	10.00
27553	Country Style/Home Cookin'	1951	2.50	5.00	10.00
27554	I Only Want a Buddy — Not a Sweetheart/When the White Azaleas Start Blooming	1951	2.50	5.00	10.00
27555	Weddin' Day/(B-side unknown)	1951	2.50	5.00	10.00
—With the Andrews Sisters					
27577	Moonlight Bay/When You and I Were Young Maggie Blues	1951	2.50	5.00	10.00
—As "Gary and Bing Crosby"					
27588	Hello Young Lovers/Something Wonderful	1951	2.50	5.00	10.00
27589	Getting to Know You/I Whistle a Happy Tune	1951	2.50	5.00	10.00
27595	With This Ring I Thee Wed/Here Ends the Rainbow	1951	2.50	5.00	10.00
27605	Going My Way/Swinging on a Star	1951	2.50	5.00	10.00
27606	Old Soldiers Never Die/My Own Bit of Land	1951	2.50	5.00	10.00
27631	Black Ball Ferry Line/The Yodeling Ghost	1951	2.50	5.00	10.00
—With the Andrews Sisters					
27643	I Might Be Your Once in a While/Indian Summer	1951	2.50	5.00	10.00
27653	(Why Did I Twll You I Was Going to) Shanghai/I've Got to Fall in Love Again	1951	2.50	5.00	10.00
27667	Row, Row, Row/Love Me or Leave Me	1951	2.50	5.00	10.00
27678	In the Cool, Cool, Cool of the Evening/Misto Christophe Columbo	1951	2.50	5.00	10.00
—With Jane Wyman					
27679	Your Own Little House/Bonne Nuit	1951	2.50	5.00	10.00
27768	I Will Remember You/The Loneliness of Evening	1951	2.50	5.00	10.00
27830	Domino/When the World Was Young	1951	2.50	5.00	10.00
27831	Christmas in Killarney/It's Beginning to Look Like Christmas	1951	3.75	7.50	15.00
27852	A Weaver of Dreams/I Still See Alisa	1951	2.50	5.00	10.00
27934	At Last, At Last!/The Isle of Innisfree	1952	2.50	5.00	10.00
27951	Copacabana/Granada	1952	2.50	5.00	10.00
28048	2 Shillelagh O'Sullivan/That Tumbledown Shack in Athlone	1952	2.50	5.00	10.00
28061	Don't Ever Be Afraid to Go Home/Rosaleen	1952	2.50	5.00	10.00
28195	Galway Bay/The Isle of Innisfree	1952	2.50	5.00	10.00
28210	Mine/You've Got Me Where You Want Me	1952	3.00	6.00	12.00
—With Judy Garland					
28217	Just for You/A Flight of Fancy	1952	2.50	5.00	10.00
28254	On the 10:10 from Ten-Ten-Tennessee/Just for You	1952	2.50	5.00	10.00
28255	Zing a Little Zong/The Maiden of Guadaloupe	1952	2.50	5.00	10.00
—With Jane Wyman					
28256	The Live Oak Tree/I'll Si-Si You in Bahia	1952	2.50	5.00	10.00
—With the Andrews Sisters					
28261	The Bells of St. Mary's/Kathleen	1952	2.50	5.00	10.00
28265	Till the End of the World/Just a Little Lovin'	1952	2.50	5.00	10.00
—With Grady Martin					
28303	Poinciana/Symphony	1952	2.50	5.00	10.00
28319	Deep in the Heart of Texas/Do You Care	1952	2.50	5.00	10.00
28419	Cool Water/South Rampart Street Parade	1952	2.50	5.00	10.00
—With the Andrews Sisters					
28463	Sleigh Ride/Little Jack Frost Get Lost	1952	3.75	7.50	15.00
28470	Open Up Your Heart/You Don't Know What Lonesome Is	1952	2.50	5.00	10.00
28511	Sleigh Bell Serenade/Keep It a Secret	1952	3.75	7.50	15.00
28513	The Road to Bali/Chicago Style	1952	2.50	5.00	10.00
—With Bob Hope					
28514	Merry Go Run Around/Hoot Mon	1952	2.50	5.00	10.00
—With Peggy Lee and Bob Hope					
28515	To See You/Moonflowers	1952	2.50	5.00	10.00
—B-side by Peggy Lee					
28581	Hush-a-Bye/Mother Darlin'	1953	2.50	5.00	10.00
28610	A Quiet Girl/Ohio	1953	2.50	5.00	10.00
28683	I Love My Baby (My Baby Loves Me)/There's Music in You	1953	2.50	5.00	10.00
28733	Tenderfoot/Walk Me By the River	1953	2.50	5.00	10.00
28743	It Had to Be You/Granada	1953	2.50	5.00	10.00
28805	Magic Window/Cela Mi Est Egal	1953	2.50	5.00	10.00
28814	Mademoiselle de Paris/Embrasse — Moi Bien	1953	2.50	5.00	10.00
28955	Down By the Riverside/What a Little Moonlight Can Do	1953	2.50	5.00	10.00
—As "Bing and Gary Crosby"					
28963	Ida! Sweet as Apple Cider/I Can't Believe ThatYou're in Love	1953	2.50	5.00	10.00
28969	Y'All Come/Changing Partners	1954	2.50	5.00	10.00
29024	Secret Love/My Love, My Love	1954	2.50	5.00	10.00
29054	Young at Heart/I Get So Lonely	1954	2.50	5.00	10.00
29144	If You Love Me (Really Love Me)/Liebchen	1954	2.50	5.00	10.00
29147	Call of the South/Cornbelt Symphony	1954	2.50	5.00	10.00
—As "Bing and Gary Crosby"					
29212	In the Good Old Summertime/Oh Tell Me Why (The Stars Do Shine)	1954	2.50	5.00	10.00
29251	Count Your Blessings Instead of Sheep/What Can You Do with a General	1954	2.50	5.00	10.00

Number	Title (A Side/B Side)	Yr	VG	VG+	NM
❑ 29341	Old Man-Mandy/Gee, I Wish I Was Back in the Army	1954	2.50	5.00	10.00
❑ 29342	White Christmas/Snow	1954	3.75	7.50	15.00
—A-side with Danny Kaye; B-side by Peggy Lee and Trudi Stevens					
❑ 29357	The Song from Desiree/Who Gave You the Roses	1954	2.50	5.00	10.00
❑ 29376	River/Tobermory Bay	1954	2.50	5.00	10.00
❑ 29409	Dissertation on State of Bliss/It's Mine, It's Yours	1955	2.50	5.00	10.00
❑ 29410	The Land Around Us/The Search Is Through	1955	2.50	5.00	10.00
❑ 29483	Farewell/Jim, Johnny & Jonah	1955	2.50	5.00	10.00
❑ 29493	Silver Moon/Nobody	1955	2.50	5.00	10.00
❑ 29568	She Is the Sunshine of Virginia/(All She'd Say Was) Uh-Huh	1955	2.50	5.00	10.00
❑ 29634	You Are My Sunshine/Nobody's Darling But Mine	1955	2.50	5.00	10.00
❑ 29636	Angel Bells/Let's Harmonize	1955	2.50	5.00	10.00
❑ 29777	The First Snowfall/The Next Time It Happens	1956	2.00	4.00	8.00
❑ 29790	Christmas Is A-Comin'/Is Christmas Only a Tree	1955	3.00	6.00	12.00
❑ 29817	John Barleycorn/When You're in Love	1956	2.00	4.00	8.00
❑ 29850	In a Little Spanish Town ('Twas On a Night Like This)/Ol' Man River	1956	2.00	4.00	8.00
❑ 29981	Honeysucle Rose/Swanee	1956	2.00	4.00	8.00
❑ 30023	When My Baby Smiles at Me/April Showers	1956	2.00	4.00	8.00
❑ 30082	Now Is the Hour/Tumbling Tumbleweeds	1956	2.00	4.00	8.00
❑ 30120	Around the World/Love in a Home	1956	2.50	5.00	10.00
❑ 30126	I Heard the Bells on Christmas Day/Christmas Is a-Comin'	1956	3.00	6.00	12.00
❑ 30126 [DJ]	I Heard the Bells on Christmas Day/Christmas Is a-Comin'	1956	3.00	6.00	12.00
—Pink label, black type					
❑ 30262	Around the World/Around the World	1957	2.00	4.00	8.00
—B-side by Victor Young					
❑ 30262 [PS]	Around the World/Around the World	1957	3.75	7.50	15.00
❑ 30488	Chinatown My Chinatown/Alabamy Bound	1957	2.00	4.00	8.00
❑ 30555	Gigi/Trust Your Destiny to Your Star	1958	2.00	4.00	8.00
❑ 30828	Rain/Church Bells	1959	2.00	4.00	8.00
❑ 38031 [DJ]	Around the World/Mississippi Mud	1957	2.50	5.00	10.00
—Green label					
❑ 38031 [PS]	Around the World/Mississippi Mud	1957	5.00	10.00	20.00
❑ 40181	A Crosby Christmas (Part 1)/A Crosby Christmas (Part 2)	1950	7.50	15.00	30.00
—As "Gary, Phillip, Dennis, Lindsay and Bing Crosby"					
KAPP					
❑ 196	How Lovely Is Christmas/My Own Individual Star	1957	3.00	6.00	12.00
❑ 196 [PS]	How Lovely Is Christmas/My Own Individual Star	1957	5.00	10.00	20.00
LITTLE GOLDEN					
❑ EP407	Boy At A Window/How Lovely Is Christmas	195?	2.50	5.00	10.00
❑ EP407 [PS]	Boy At A Window/How Lovely Is Christmas	195?	3.00	6.00	12.00
LONDON					
❑ 20095	There's Nothing I Haven't Sung About/The Way We Were	1977	—	2.00	4.00
MCA					
❑ 38056	Rudolph The Red-Nosed Reindeer/I Heard The Bells On Christmas Day	198?	—	2.00	4.00
❑ 40830	White Christmas/When the Blue of the Night Meets the Gold of the Day	1977	—	2.50	5.00
❑ 40830 [PS]	White Christmas/When the Blue of the Night Meets the Gold of the Day	1977	—	2.50	5.00
❑ 65019	Jingle Bells/Santa Claus Is Comin' to Town	1973	—	2.00	4.00
—With the Andrews Sisters; black label with rainbow					
❑ 65019	Jingle Bells/Santa Claus Is Comin' to Town	1980	—	—	3.00
—With the Andrews Sisters; blue label with rainbow					
❑ 65021	Silent Night/Adeste Fideles (O Come All Ye Faithful)	1973	—	2.00	4.00
—Black label with rainbow					
❑ 65021	Silent Night/Adeste Fideles (O Come All Ye Faithful)	1980	—	—	3.00
—Blue label with rainbow					
❑ 65022	White Christmas/God Rest Ye Merry Gentlemen	1973	—	2.00	4.00
—Black label with rainbow					
❑ 65022	White Christmas/God Rest Ye Merry Gentlemen	1980	—	—	3.00
—Blue label with rainbow					
MGM					
❑ 12946	The Second Time Around/Incurably Romantic	1960	2.00	4.00	8.00
POLYDOR					
❑ 14452	Yesterday, When I Was Young/June in January	1978	—	2.00	4.00
P.I.P.					
❑ 8903	Where the Rainbow Ends/What's More American	197?	—	2.50	5.00
RCA VICTOR					
❑ 47-7695	It's a Good Day/The Music of Home	1960	2.00	4.00	8.00
REPRISE					
❑ 0283	Don't Be a Do-Badder/The Hukilau Song	1964	—	3.00	6.00
❑ 0315	It's Christmas Time Again/Christmas Candles	1964	3.00	6.00	12.00
—With Fred Waring and the Pennsylvanians					
❑ 0315 [PS]	It's Christmas Time Again/Christmas Candles	1964	3.75	7.50	15.00
❑ 0424	The White World of Winter/The Secret of Christmas	1965	2.00	4.00	8.00
❑ 0478	How Green Was My Valley/Far from Home	1966	—	2.50	5.00
❑ 0645	Step to the Rear/What Do We Do with the World	1967	—	2.50	5.00
UNITED ARTISTS					
❑ XW700	Send In the Clowns/That's What Life Is All About	1975	—	2.00	4.00
VERVE					
❑ 2025	I've Got Five Dollars/Mountain Greenery	1956	2.50	5.00	10.00
WARNER BROS.					
❑ PRO 146 [DJ]	I Wish You a Merry Christmas/Winter Wonderland//The Littlest Angel	1962	5.00	10.00	20.00

7-Inch Extended Plays

Number	Title (A Side/B Side)	Yr	VG	VG+	NM
DECCA					
❑ 9-65 [(4)]	Merry Christmas	1950	12.50	25.00	50.00
—Includes records 23281, 23777, 23778 and 23779 (also priced separately) and box					
❑ 9-66 [(4)]	Christmas Greetings	1950	12.50	25.00	50.00
—Includes records and box					
❑ ED 547 [PS]	Merry Christmas	195?	6.25	12.50	25.00
—Cover for 2-EP set					
❑ ED 581 [PS]	Stardust	195?	5.00	10.00	20.00
—Cover for 2-EP set					
❑ ED 662 [PS]	Down Memory Lane	195?	5.00	10.00	20.00
—Cover for 2-EP set					
❑ ED 2000	Red Sails in the Sunset/Far Away Places//Harbor Lights/On Treasure Island	195?	3.00	6.00	12.00
❑ ED 2000 [PS]	Bing Crosby, Vol. 1	195?	3.00	6.00	12.00
❑ ED 2107	Do You Ever Think of Me/I Never Knew//Somebody Loves Me/After You've Gone	195?	3.00	6.00	12.00
❑ ED 2107 [PS]	Some Fine Old Chestnuts, Vol. 1	195?	3.00	6.00	12.00
❑ ED 2427	Prisoner of Love/Ain't Misbehavin'//Paper Doll/This Love of Mine	1956	3.75	7.50	15.00
❑ ED 2427 [PS]	Song I Wish I Had Sung the First Time Around... Part 2	1956	3.75	7.50	15.00
❑ ED 2547	(contents unknown)	195?	3.00	6.00	12.00
❑ ED 2547 [PS]	Christmas Time	195?	3.00	6.00	12.00
❑ ED 2659	Silver Bells/The Christmas Song//Christmas Carols/God Rest Ye Merry Gentlemen	195?	3.00	6.00	12.00
❑ ED 2659 [PS]	Christmas Songs	195?	3.00	6.00	12.00
❑ 7-38274	The First Nowell/Medley: Deck The Hall-Away In A Manger-I Saw Three Ships//God Rest Ye Merry, Gentlemen/Jingle Bells	196?	3.00	6.00	12.00
❑ 7-38274 [PS]	General Electric Wishes You a Merry Christmas	196?	3.00	6.00	12.00
❑ 91123	Silent Night/Adeste Fideles//White Christmas/God Rest Ye Merry Gentlemen	195?	3.00	6.00	12.00
—Part of 2-EP set ED 547					
❑ 91124	I'll Be Home for Christmas/Faith of Our Fathers//Jingle Bells/Santa Claus Is Comin' to Town	195?	3.00	6.00	12.00
—Part of 2-EP set ED 547					
❑ 91168	I Cried for You/My Melancholy Baby//Star Dust/Deep Purple	195?	3.00	6.00	12.00
—Part of 2-EP set ED 581					
❑ 91169	The One Rose/Moonlight and Shadows//A Blue Serenade/S'posin'	195?	3.00	6.00	12.00
—Part of 2-EP set ED 581					
❑ 91289	Please/I Found a Million Dollar Baby//I Wonder What's Become of Sally/Mary's a Grand Old Name	195?	3.00	6.00	12.00
—Part of 2-EP set ED 662					
❑ 91290	I'm Waiting for Ships That Never Come In/When Day Is Done//I Don't Want to Walk Without You/Moonlight Cocktail	195?	3.00	6.00	12.00
—Part of 2-EP set ED 662					
RCA VICTOR					
❑ EPA 3-1473	Mack the Knife/Tell Me//Down Among the Sheltering Palms/Mama Loved Papa	1957	2.00	4.00	8.00
❑ EPA 3-1473 [PS]	Bing with a Beat	1957	2.50	5.00	10.00

CROSBY, BING, AND LOUIS ARMSTRONG

Number	Title (A Side/B Side)	Yr	VG	VG+	NM
DECCA					
❑ 27623	Gone Fishin'/We All Have a Song in My Heart	1951	3.75	7.50	15.00
MGM					
❑ SB 26 [S]	Muskrat Ramble/Way Down in New Orleans	1960	3.75	7.50	15.00
❑ SB 27 [S]	Dardanella/Brother Bill	1960	3.75	7.50	15.00
❑ SB 28 [S]	Preacher/Little Ol' Tune	1960	3.75	7.50	15.00
❑ SB 29 [S]	Let's Sing Like a Dixieland Band/At the Jazz Band Ball	1960	3.75	7.50	15.00
❑ SB 30 [S]	Rocky Mountain Moon/Bye Bye Blues	1960	3.75	7.50	15.00
—The above five are 33 1/3 rpm jukebox singles					
❑ 12961	Dardanella/Muskrat Ramble	1960	2.50	5.00	10.00

CROSBY, BING, AND PEGGY LEE

Also see each artist's individual listings.

Number	Title (A Side/B Side)	Yr	VG	VG+	NM
DECCA					
❑ 28238	Watermelon Weather/The Moon Came Up with a Great Idea Last Night	1952	3.00	6.00	12.00

CROSBY, DAVID

Also see THE BYRDS; CROSBY, STILLS AND NASH; CROSBY, STILLS, NASH AND YOUNG; GRAHAM NASH AND DAVID CROSBY.

Number	Title (A Side/B Side)	Yr	VG	VG+	NM
ATLANTIC					
❑ 2792	Laughing/Music Is Love	1971	—	2.50	5.00
❑ 2809	Orleans/Traction in the Rain	1971	—	2.50	5.00
❑ 87360	Hero/Coverage	1993	—	—	3.00
—A-side: David Crosby and Phil Collins					

CROSBY, DAVID, AND GRAHAM NASH

See GRAHAM NASH AND DAVID CROSBY.

CROSBY, STILLS AND NASH

Also see DAVID CROSBY; GRAHAM NASH; STEPHEN STILLS.

Number	Title (A Side/B Side)	Yr	VG	VG+	NM
ATLANTIC					
❑ 2652	Marrakesh Express/Helplessly Hoping	1969	—	3.00	6.00
❑ 2676	Suite: Judy Blue Eyes/Long Time Gone	1969	—	3.00	6.00
❑ 3401	Just a Song Before I Go/Dark Star	1977	—	2.00	4.00
❑ 3401 [PS]	Just a Song Before I Go/Dark Star	1977	—	2.50	5.00
❑ 3432	Fair Game/Anything at All	1977	—	2.00	4.00
❑ 3453	I Give You Give Blind/Carried Away	1978	—	2.00	4.00
❑ 3784	Carry On/Shadow Captain	1980	—	2.50	5.00
❑ 4058	Wasted on the Way/Delta	1982	—	—	3.00
❑ 4058 [PS]	Wasted on the Way/Delta	1982	—	2.00	4.00
❑ 87909	Live It Up/Chuck's Lament	1990	—	2.00	4.00
❑ 89775	Raise a Voice/For What It's Worth	1983	—	—	3.00
❑ 89812	War Games/Shadow Captain	1983	—	—	3.00
❑ 89812 [PS]	War Games/Shadow Captain	1983	—	2.00	4.00
❑ 89888	Too Much Love to Hide/Song for Susan	1983	—	—	3.00
❑ 89969	Southern Cross/Into the Darkness	1982	—	—	3.00
❑ 89969 [PS]	Southern Cross/Into the Darkness	1982	—	2.00	4.00

CROSBY, STILLS, NASH & YOUNG

Also see DAVID CROSBY; GRAHAM NASH; STEPHEN STILLS; NEIL YOUNG.

Number	Title (A Side/B Side)	Yr	VG	VG+	NM
ATLANTIC					
❑ 2723	Woodstock/Helpless	1970	—	3.00	6.00
❑ 2735	Teach Your Children/Carry On	1970	—	3.00	6.00
❑ 2740	Ohio/Find the Cost of Freedom	1970	—	3.00	6.00
❑ 2740 [PS]	Ohio/Find the Cost of Freedom	1970	3.00	6.00	12.00
❑ 2760	Our House/Deja Vu	1970	—	3.00	6.00
❑ 88966	Got It Made/This Old House	1989	—	—	3.00
❑ 88966 [PS]	Got It Made/This Old House	1989	—	—	3.00
❑ 89003	American Dream/Compass	1988	—	—	3.00
❑ 89003 [PS]	American Dream/Compass	1988	—	—	3.00

CROSS, JIMMY

Number	Title (A Side/B Side)	Yr	VG	VG+	NM
CHICKEN					
❑ 101	Hey Little Girl/Hey Little Girl (Part 2)	1966	3.00	6.00	12.00
RECORDO					
❑ 502	Pretty Girls Everywhere/Suntan Sally	1961	3.75	7.50	15.00
RED BIRD					
❑ 10-042	Hey Little Girl/Super Duper Man	1965	3.75	7.50	15.00
TOLLIE					
❑ 9039	I Want My Baby Back/Play the Other Side	1965	5.00	10.00	20.00
❑ 9044	The Ballad of James Bong/Play the Other Side Again	1965	3.75	7.50	15.00

CROSS COUNTRY

Includes three members of THE TOKENS.

Number	Title (A Side/B Side)	Yr	VG	VG+	NM
ATCO					
❑ 6932	Rock and Roll Music/Just a Thought	1973	2.00	4.00	8.00
❑ 6934	In the Midnight Hour/The Smile Song	1973	2.00	4.00	8.00
❑ 6947	Tastes So Good to Me/A Ball Song	1973	2.00	4.00	8.00

CROSSFIRES, THE (1)

Group evolved into THE TURTLES.

Number	Title (A Side/B Side)	Yr	VG	VG+	NM
CAPCO					
❑ 104	Fiberglass Jungle/Dr. Jekyll and Mr. Hyde	1963	20.00	40.00	80.00
LUCKY TOKEN					
❑ 112	One Potato, Two Potato/That'll Be the Day	1965	12.50	25.00	50.00

CROSSFIRES, THE (2)

Number	Title (A Side/B Side)	Yr	VG	VG+	NM
CUCA					
❑ 1027	Young Love/When My Blue Moon Turns to Gold Again	1961	3.00	6.00	12.00

CROSSFIRES, THE (4)

Number	Title (A Side/B Side)	Yr	VG	VG+	NM
TOWER					
❑ 278	Who'll Be the Next One/Making Love Is Fun	1966	5.00	10.00	20.00

CROW

Number	Title (A Side/B Side)	Yr	VG	VG+	NM
AMARET					
❑ 106	Busy Day/Time to Make a Turn	1969	—	3.00	6.00
❑ 112	Evil Woman Don't Play Your Games with Me/Gonna Leave a Mark	1969	2.00	4.00	8.00
❑ 119	Cottage Cheese/Slow Down	1970	—	3.00	6.00
❑ 119	Cottage Cheese/Busy Day	1970	—	3.00	6.00
❑ 125	Don't Try to Lay No Boogie-Woogie on the "King of Rock 'n' Roll"/Satisfied	1970	—	3.00	6.00
❑ 129	Watching Can Waste Up the Time/Yellow Dawg	1971	—	2.50	5.00
❑ 133	Something in Your Blood/Yellow Dawg	1971	—	2.50	5.00
❑ 145	Everything Has Got to Be Free/Mobile Blues	1972	—	2.50	5.00
❑ 148	If It Feels Good, Do It/Cado Queen	1972	—	2.50	5.00

CROW, SHERYL

Number	Title (A Side/B Side)	Yr	VG	VG+	NM
A&M					
❑ 31458 0638 7	Can't Cry Anymore/We Do What We Can	1995	—	—	3.00
❑ 31458 0638 7 [PS]	Can't Cry Anymore/We Do What We Can	1995	—	—	3.00
❑ 31458 0836 7	All I Wanna Do/Leaving Las Vegas	1994	—	—	3.00
❑ 31458 0932 7	Strong Enough/Run, Baby, Run	1995	—	—	3.00
❑ 31458 1874 7	If It Makes You Happy/I'm Gonna Be a Wheel Someday	1996	—	—	3.00
❑ 31458 2032 7	Everyday Is a Winding Road/Sad Sad World	1997	—	—	3.00
❑ 31458 2776 7	My Favorite Mistake/There Goes the Neighborhood	1998	—	—	3.00
❑ 069-4970867	Anything But Down/The Difficult Kind	1999	—	—	3.00

CROWN, BOBBY

Number	Title (A Side/B Side)	Yr	VG	VG+	NM
FELCO					
❑ 102	One Way Ticket/Your Conscience	1960	200.00	400.00	800.00
MANCO					
❑ 1005	I've Never Had a Broken Heart/Wait a Minute	1960	10.00	20.00	40.00

CROWNS, THE (1)

Number	Title (A Side/B Side)	Yr	VG	VG+	NM
CHORDETTE					
❑ 1001	Party Time/Amazon Basin Pop	1962	5.00	10.00	20.00

CROWNS, THE (2)

Number	Title (A Side/B Side)	Yr	VG	VG+	NM
OLD TOWN					
❑ 1171	Possibility/Watch Out	1964	10.00	20.00	40.00
—Old light blue Old Town label					
❑ 1171	Possibility/Watch Out	1964	3.75	7.50	15.00
—Black label with moon					

CROWNS, THE (3)

Four members of THE FIVE CROWNS plus Benjamin Nelson (BEN E. KING). Also see THE DRIFTERS.

Number	Title (A Side/B Side)	Yr	VG	VG+	NM
R&B					
❑ 6901	Kiss and Make Up/I'll Forget About You	1958	20.00	40.00	80.00

CROWNS, THE (4)

Number	Title (A Side/B Side)	Yr	VG	VG+	NM
VEE JAY					
❑ 546	Better Luck Next Time/You Make Me Blue	1963	3.75	7.50	15.00

CROWS, THE

Number	Title (A Side/B Side)	Yr	VG	VG+	NM
RAMA					
❑ 3	Seven Lonely Days/No Help Wanted	1953	125.00	250.00	500.00
❑ 5	Gee/I Love You So	1953	17.50	35.00	70.00
—Blue label, black vinyl					
❑ 5	Gee/I Love You So	1953	100.00	200.00	400.00
—Blue label, red vinyl					
❑ 5	Gee/I Love You So	1955	7.50	15.00	30.00
—Red label, black vinyl					
❑ 10	Heartbreaker/Call a Doctor	1953	100.00	200.00	400.00
—Black vinyl					
❑ 10	Heartbreaker/Call a Doctor	1953	200.00	400.00	800.00
—Red vinyl					
❑ 10	Heartbreaker/Call a Doctor	1953	150.00	300.00	600.00
—Black vinyl, label says "The Jewels"					
❑ 10	Heartbreaker/Call a Doctor	1953	150.00	300.00	600.00
—Black vinyl, label says "The Jewels" on one side, "The Crows" on the other					
❑ 10	Heartbreaker/Call a Doctor	1953	400.00	800.00	1200.
—Red vinyl; label says "The Jewels"					
❑ 29	Baby/Untrue	1954	50.00	100.00	200.00
❑ 30	Miss You/I Really, Really Love You So	1954	100.00	200.00	400.00
—Black vinyl					
❑ 30	Miss You/I Really, Really Love You So	1954	250.00	500.00	1000.
—Red vinyl					
❑ 50	Baby Doll/Sweet Sue (It's You)	1954	100.00	200.00	400.00
TICO					
❑ 1082	Mambo Shevitz/Mambo #5	1955	50.00	100.00	200.00
—B-side by Melino and Orchestra; black vinyl					
❑ 1082	Mambo Shevitz/Mambo #5	1955	75.00	150.00	300.00
—B-side by Melino and Orchestra; red vinyl					

CRUDUP, ARTHUR

Number	Title (A Side/B Side)	Yr	VG	VG+	NM
ACE					
❑ 503	I Wonder/My Baby Boogies All the Time	1955	50.00	100.00	200.00
FIRE					
❑ 1501	Rock Me Mama/Mean Ole Frisco	1962	3.75	7.50	15.00
❑ 1502	Katie Mae/Dig Myself a Hole	1962	3.75	7.50	15.00
GROOVE					
❑ 0011	I Love My Baby/Fall on Your Knees and Pray	1954	10.00	20.00	40.00
❑ 0026	She's Got No Hair/If You Ever Been to Georgia	1954	10.00	20.00	40.00
RCA VICTOR					
❑ 47-4367	Love Me Mama/Where Did You Stay Last Night	1951	25.00	50.00	100.00
❑ 47-4572	Goin' Back to Georgia/Mr. So and So	1952	20.00	40.00	80.00
❑ 47-4753	Worried 'Bout You Baby/Late in the Evening	1952	20.00	40.00	80.00
❑ 47-4933	Second Man Blues/Do It If You Want	1952	20.00	40.00	80.00
❑ 47-5070	Lookin' for My Baby/Pearly Lee	1952	20.00	40.00	80.00
❑ 47-5167	Keep On Drinkin'/Nelvina	1953	20.00	40.00	80.00
❑ 47-5563	War Is Over/My Wife and Woman	1953	20.00	40.00	80.00
❑ 50-0000	That's All Right/Crudup's After Hours	1949	100.00	200.00	400.00
—Gray label, orange vinyl; the first R&B 45 rpm record!					
❑ 50-0001	Boy Friend Blues/Katie May	1949	25.00	50.00	100.00
—Gray label, orange vinyl					
❑ 50-0013	Shout Sister Shout/Crudup's Vicksburg Blues	1949	25.00	50.00	100.00
—Gray label, orange vinyl					
❑ 50-0032	Hoodoo Lady Blues/Tired of Worry	1949	25.00	50.00	100.00
—Gray label, orange vinyl					
❑ 50-0046	Come Back Baby/Mercy Blues	1949	25.00	50.00	100.00
—Gray label, orange vinyl					
❑ 50-0074	Dust My Broom/You Know That I Love You	1950	25.00	50.00	100.00
—Gray label, orange vinyl					
❑ 50-0092	Mean Old Santa Fe/Oo Wee Baby	1950	25.00	50.00	100.00
—Gray label, orange vinyl					
❑ 50-0100	Lonesome World to Me/Hand Me Down My Walking Cane	1950	25.00	50.00	100.00
—Gray label, orange vinyl					
❑ 50-0105	She's Just Like Caldonia/(B-side unknown)	1951	25.00	50.00	100.00
—Gray label, orange vinyl					
❑ 50-0109	My Baby Left Me/Anytime Is the Right Time	1951	37.50	75.00	150.00
—Gray label, orange vinyl					
❑ 50-0117	Nobody Wants Me/Star Bootlegger	1951	25.00	50.00	100.00
—Gray label, black vinyl					
❑ 50-0126	Roberta Blues/Behind Closed Doors	1951	25.00	50.00	100.00
—Gray label, black vinyl					
❑ 50-0141	I'm Gonna Dig Myself a Hole/Too Much Competition	1951	25.00	50.00	100.00
—Gray label, black vinyl					

CRUSADERS, THE (1)

Jazz and soul band. Originally recorded as "The Jazz Crusaders"; all releases on Pacfic Jazz and World Pacific use that name.

Number	Title (A Side/B Side)	Yr	VG	VG+	NM
ABC BLUE THUMB					
❑ 261	Stomp and Buck Dance/A Ballad for Joe (Louis)	1975	—	2.50	5.00
❑ 267	Creole/I Feel the Love	1975	—	2.50	5.00
❑ 269	Keep That Same Old Feeling/'Til the Sun Shines	1976	—	2.50	5.00
❑ 270	And Then There Was the Blues/Feeling Funky	1976	—	2.50	5.00
❑ 272	Feel It/The Way We Was	1977	—	2.50	5.00
❑ 273	Free as the Wind/The Way We Was	1977	—	2.50	5.00
❑ 278	Bayou Bottoms/Covert Action	1978	—	2.50	5.00
BLUE THUMB					
❑ 208	Put It Where You Want It/Mosadi	1972	—	2.50	5.00
❑ 217	So Far Away/That's How I Feel	1972	—	2.50	5.00
❑ 225	Don't Let It Get You Down/Journey from Within	1973	—	2.50	5.00
❑ 232	Take It or Leave It/That's How I Feel	1973	—	2.50	5.00
❑ 245	Lay It On the Line/Let's Boogie	1974	—	2.50	5.00
❑ 249	Scratch/Way Back Home	1974	—	2.50	5.00
CHISA					
❑ 8010	Way Back Home/Jackson	1970	—	3.00	6.00
—As "Jazz Crusaders"					
❑ 8013	Pass the Plate/Greasy Spoon	1971	—	3.00	6.00

Number	Title (A Side/B Side)	Yr	VG	VG+	NM
MCA					
❑ 41054	Street Life/Hustler	1979	—	2.00	4.00
❑ 41295	Sweet Gentle Love/Soul Shadows	1980	—	2.00	4.00
❑ 51029	Last Call/Honky Tonk Struttin'	1980	—	2.00	4.00
❑ 51177	I'm So Glad I'm Standing Here Today/Standing Tall	1981	—	2.00	4.00
—A-side with Joe Cocker					
❑ 51222	This Old World's Too Funky for Me/Standing Tall	1981	—	2.00	4.00
—A-side with Joe Cocker					
❑ 52098	Street Life/Overture	1982	—	2.00	4.00
—With B.B. King and the London Symphony Orchestra					
❑ 52365	New Move/Mr. Cool	1984	—	2.00	4.00
❑ 52398	Dream Street/Dead End	1984	—	2.00	4.00
❑ 52454	Gotta Lotta Shakalada/Zalal 'E Mini	1984	—	2.00	4.00
❑ 52966	The Way It Goes/Good Times	1986	—	2.00	4.00
❑ 53330	A.C. (Alternating Currents)/Mulholland Nights	1988	—	—	3.00
MOWEST					
❑ 5028	Spanish Harlem/Papa Hooper's Barrelhouse Groove	1972	—	3.00	6.00
PACIFIC JAZZ					
❑ 340	Sinnin' Sam/Tonight	1962	3.00	6.00	12.00
❑ 342	Young Rabbits/(B-side unknown)	1962	3.00	6.00	12.00
❑ 371	No Name Samba/Tough Talk	1963	2.50	5.00	10.00
❑ 88125	Uptight (Everything's Alright)/Scratch	1966	2.00	4.00	8.00
❑ 88144	Eleanor Rigby/Ooga Boogaloo	1968	—	3.00	6.00
❑ 88146	Hey Jude/Love and Peace	1969	—	3.00	6.00
❑ 88153	Get Back/Willie and Laura Mae Jones	1969	—	3.00	6.00
WORLD PACIFIC					
❑ 388	Boopie/Turkish Black	1963	2.50	5.00	10.00
—As "Jazz Crusaders"					
❑ 401	Heat Wave/On Broadway	1964	2.50	5.00	10.00
❑ 412	I Remember Tomorrow/Long John	1964	2.50	5.00	10.00
❑ 77800	The Thing/Tough Talk	1965	2.00	4.00	8.00
❑ 77806	Aqua Dulce/Soul Bourgeoise	1966	2.00	4.00	8.00

CRUSADERS, THE (U)

None of these are by group (1).

Number	Title (A Side/B Side)	Yr	VG	VG+	NM
CAMEO					
❑ 285	Boogie Woogie/At the Club	1963	3.00	6.00	12.00
DKR					
❑ (no #)	Seminole/Busted Surfboard	1962	10.00	20.00	40.00
DOOTO					
❑ 472	Swinging Week-End/I Found Someone	1963	3.75	7.50	15.00
TOWER					
❑ 286	The Little Drummer Boy/Battle Hymn of the Republic	1966	2.50	5.00	10.00
❑ 328	Make a Joyful Noise/Praise We the Lord	1967	2.50	5.00	10.00

CRYAN' SHAMES, THE

Number	Title (A Side/B Side)	Yr	VG	VG+	NM
COLUMBIA					
❑ 43836	I Wanna Meet You/We Could Be Happy	1966	2.50	5.00	10.00
❑ 44037	Mr. Unreliable/Georgia	1967	2.50	5.00	10.00
❑ 44191	It Could Be We're in Love/I Was Lonely When	1967	2.50	5.00	10.00
❑ 44191 [PS]	It Could Be We're in Love/I Was Lonely When	1967	5.00	10.00	20.00
❑ 44457	Up On the Roof/The Sailing Ship	1968	2.50	5.00	10.00
❑ 44545	Young Birds Fly/Sunshine Psalm	1968	2.00	4.00	8.00
❑ 44638	Greenburg, Blickstein, Charles, David Smith & Jones/The Warm	1968	2.00	4.00	8.00
❑ 44759	First Train to California/A Master's Fool	1969	2.00	4.00	8.00
❑ 45027	Rainmaker/Bits and Pieces	1969	2.00	4.00	8.00
DESTINATION					
❑ 624	Sugar and Spice/Ben Franklin's Almanac	1966	3.75	7.50	15.00

CRYIN' SHAMES, THE

Not the same group as THE CRYAN' SHAMES.

Number	Title (A Side/B Side)	Yr	VG	VG+	NM
LONDON					
❑ 1001	What's New Pussycat/Please Stay (Don't Go)	1966	2.50	5.00	10.00

CRYSTAL, RONETTE AND CHIFFON

Trio that used the names of famous 1960s girl groups as their stage names.

Number	Title (A Side/B Side)	Yr	VG	VG+	NM
GEFFEN					
❑ 7-28393	Little Shop of Horrors/Grow for Me	1987	2.00	4.00	8.00
—B-side by Rick Moranis					

CRYSTALS, THE (1)

Well-known girl group.

Number	Title (A Side/B Side)	Yr	VG	VG+	NM
GUSTO					
❑ 2090	Da Doo Ron Ron/Then He Kissed Me	1979	—	2.00	4.00
—Re-recordings					
MICHELLE					
❑ 4113	Ring-a-Ting-a-Ling/Should I Keep On Waiting	1967	2.50	5.00	10.00
PAVILLION					
❑ 03333	Rudolph the Red-Nosed Reindeer/I Saw Mommy Kissing Santa Claus	1982	—	2.50	5.00
—B-side by The Ronettes					
PHILLES					
❑ 100	There's No Other (Like My Baby)/Oh Yeah, Maybe Baby	1961	10.00	20.00	40.00
❑ 102	Uptown/What a Nice Way to Turn Seventeen	1962	10.00	20.00	40.00
❑ 105	He Hit Me (And It Felt Like a Kiss)/No One Ever Tells You	1962	25.00	50.00	100.00
❑ 106	He's a Rebel/I Love You Eddie	1962	15.00	30.00	60.00
—Orange label					
❑ 106	He's a Rebel/I Love You Eddie	1962	10.00	20.00	40.00
—Light blue label					
❑ 106	He's a Rebel/I Love You Eddie	1964	6.25	12.50	25.00
—Yellow and red label					
❑ 109	He's Sure the Boy I Love/Walkin' Along (La-La-La)	1962	7.50	15.00	30.00
❑ 111 [DJ]	(Let's Dance) The Screw — Part 1/(Let's Dance) The Screw — Part 2	1963	2000.	3000.	4000.
—White label					
❑ 111 [DJ]	(Let's Dance) The Screw — Part 1/(Let's Dance) The Screw — Part 2	1963	3000.	4500.	6000.
—Light blue label. Matrix numbers are stamped in dead wax. Counterfeits have numbers hand-etched.					
❑ 112	Da Do Ron Ron (When He Walked Me Home)/Git' It	1963	7.50	15.00	30.00
❑ 115	Then He Kissed Me/Brother Julius	1963	10.00	20.00	40.00
—Light blue label					
❑ 115	Then He Kissed Me/Brother Julius	1963	6.25	12.50	25.00
—Yellow and red label					
❑ 119X	Little Boy/Harry (From West Virginia) and Milt	1964	5.00	10.00	20.00
❑ 119	Little Boy/Harry (From West Virginia) and Milt	1964	6.25	12.50	25.00
❑ 122	All Grown Up/Irving (Jaggered Sixteenths)	1964	6.25	12.50	25.00
—Possible Rolling Stones involvement on instrumental B-side; "Jaggered" refers to Mick					
PHILLES/COLLECTABLES					
❑ 3200	He's a Rebel/He Hit Me (And It Felt Like a Kiss)	1985	—	3.00	6.00
—Red vinyl; part of box set "Phil Spector Wall of Sound Series Vol. 2"					
❑ 3200	He's a Rebel/He Hit Me (And It Felt Like a Kiss)	1986	—	2.50	5.00
—Black vinyl					
❑ 3201	Then He Kissed Me/Puddin' and Tain	1985	—	3.00	6.00
—Red vinyl; part of box set "Phil Spector Wall of Sound Series Vol. 2"; B-side by the Alley Cats					
❑ 3201	Then He Kissed Me/Puddin' and Tain	1986	—	2.50	5.00
—Black vinyl					
❑ 3202	Uptown/He's Sure the Boy I Love	1985	—	3.00	6.00
—Red vinyl; part of box set "Phil Spector Wall of Sound Series Vol. 2"					
❑ 3202	Uptown/He's Sure the Boy I Love	1986	—	2.50	5.00
—Black vinyl					
❑ 3204	There's No Other (Like My Baby)/Not Too Young to Get Married	1985	—	3.00	6.00
—Gold vinyl; part of box set "Phil Spector Wall of Sound Series Vol. 1"; B-side by Bob B. Soxx and the Blue Jeans					
❑ 3204	There's No Other (Like My Baby)/Not Too Young to Get Married	1986	—	2.50	5.00
—Black vinyl; B-side by Bob B. Soxx and the Blue Jeans					
❑ 3206	Da Doo Ron Ron/All Grown Up	1985	—	3.00	6.00
—Gold vinyl; part of box set "Phil Spector Wall of Sound Series Vol. 1"					
❑ 3206	Da Doo Ron Ron/All Grown Up	1986	—	2.50	5.00
—Black vinyl					
UNITED ARTISTS					
❑ 927	You Can't Tie a Good Girl Down/My Place	1965	3.75	7.50	15.00
❑ 994	I Got a Man/Are You Trying to Get Rid of Me, Baby	1966	3.75	7.50	15.00

CRYSTALS, THE (2)

Number	Title (A Side/B Side)	Yr	VG	VG+	NM
ALADDIN					
❑ 3355	I Love My Baby/I Do Believe	1957	15.00	30.00	60.00

CRYSTALS, THE (3)

Number	Title (A Side/B Side)	Yr	VG	VG+	NM
BRENT					
❑ 7011	Malaguena/Gypsy Ribbon	1960	3.75	7.50	15.00
CUB					
❑ 9064	Oh My You/Watching You	1960	3.75	7.50	15.00
INDIGO					
❑ 114	Dreams and Wishes/Mr. Brush	1961	5.00	10.00	20.00
METRO					
❑ 20026	Better Come Back to Me/That's Where I Belong	1960	3.75	7.50	15.00
REGALIA					
❑ 17	Pony in Dixie/Espresso	1961	3.75	7.50	15.00

CRYSTALS, THE (4)

Number	Title (A Side/B Side)	Yr	VG	VG+	NM
DELUXE					
❑ 6013	Four Women/My Dear	1953	500.00	1000.	2000.
❑ 6037	Have Faith in Me/My Love	1954	500.00	1000.	2000.
❑ 6077	God Only Knows/My Girl	1955	50.00	100.00	200.00
LUNA					
❑ 100	Squeeze Me Baby/Come to Me, Darling	1954	100.00	200.00	400.00
❑ 5001	Squeeze Me Baby/Come to Me, Darling	1954	50.00	100.00	200.00
ROCKIN'					
❑ 518	My Girl/Don't You Go	1953	62.50	125.00	250.00

CRYSTALS, THE (5)

Number	Title (A Side/B Side)	Yr	VG	VG+	NM
FELSTED					
❑ 8566	Mary Ellen/Blind Date	1959	5.00	10.00	20.00
MERCURY					
❑ 71381	Vampire/Tropical Illusion	1958	3.75	7.50	15.00
SPECIALTY					
❑ 657	In the Deep/Love You So	1959	3.75	7.50	15.00

CUES, THE

Number	Title (A Side/B Side)	Yr	VG	VG+	NM
CAPITOL					
❑ F3245	Burn That Candle/Oh My Darling	1955	5.00	10.00	20.00
❑ F3310	Charlie Brown/You're On My Mind	1956	5.00	10.00	20.00
❑ F3400	Destination 2100 and 65/Don't Make Believe	1956	5.00	10.00	20.00
❑ F3483	The Girl I Love/Crackerjack	1956	5.00	10.00	20.00
❑ F3582	Why/Prince or Pauper	1956	5.00	10.00	20.00
JUBILEE					
❑ 5201	Only You/I Feel for Your Loving	1955	5.00	10.00	20.00
LAMP					
❑ 8007	Forty 'Leven Dozen Ways/Scoochie Scoochie	1954	5.00	10.00	20.00
PREP					
❑ 104	I Pretend/Crazy, Crazy Party	1957	5.00	10.00	20.00

CUFF LINKS, THE (1)

Studio band with RON DANTE as lead singer.

Number	Title (A Side/B Side)	Yr	VG	VG+	NM
ATCO					
❑ 6867	Sandi/The Oke-Fen-Okee Electric Harmonica Band	1972	—	2.50	5.00
DECCA					
❑ 32533	Tracy/Where Do You Go	1969	—	3.00	6.00

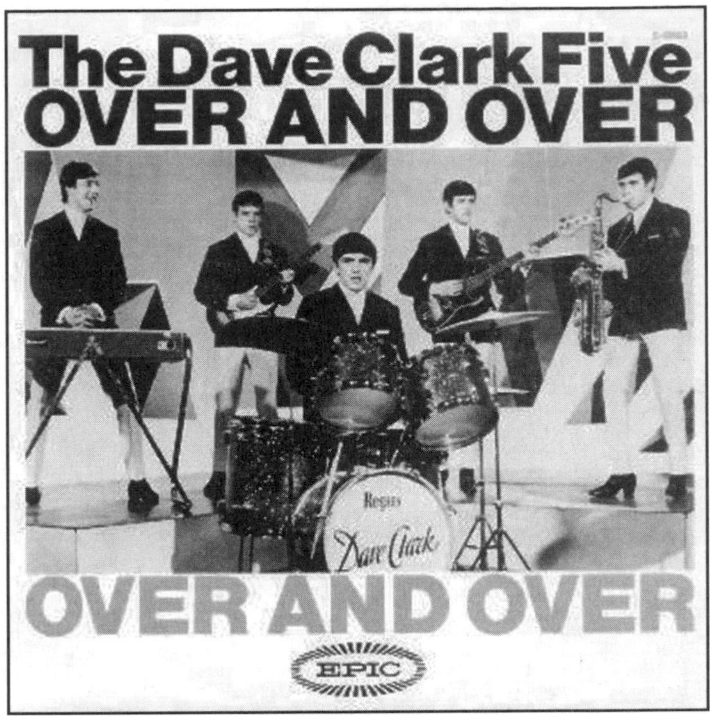

(Top left) Before there was a "group" called the Carpenters, Karen Carpenter made one record for the Magic Lamp label. As her brother Richard was involved, it in essence is a Carpenters record. Near-mint copies of this single can go for four figures. (Top right) In addition to the more common stock sleeve, this promotional-only sleeve for the Dave Clark Five's "Over and Over" exists. It is by far their most sought-after picture cover. (Bottom left) Until recently, Bing Crosby's "White Christmas" was the biggest-selling song in recording industry history. One of the many reissues of this song was in 1978, and it came with this obscure picture sleeve. (Bottom right) One of the 1960s' most difficult picture sleeves to find is the Cyrkle's "Red Rubber Ball." It's rare enough that its existence has sometimes been doubted.

Number	Title (A Side/B Side)	Yr	VG	VG+	NM
❑ 32533 [PS]	Tracy/Where Do You Go	1969	6.25	12.50	25.00
—Three-piece gatefold sleeve					
❑ 32592	When Julie Comes Around/Sally Ann	1969	—	2.50	5.00
❑ 32639	Run, Sally, Run/I Remember	1970	—	2.50	5.00
❑ 32687	Lay a Little Love on Me/Robin's World	1970	—	2.50	5.00
❑ 32732	Thank You Pretty Baby/Kiss	1970	—	2.50	5.00
❑ 32791	All Because of You/Wake Up Judy	1971	—	2.50	5.00

CUFF LINKS, THE (2)

Black vocal group.

Number	Title (A Side/B Side)	Yr	VG	VG+	NM
DOOTO					
❑ 409	Guided Missiles/My Heart	1957	20.00	40.00	80.00
❑ 413	How You Lied/The Winner	1957	10.00	20.00	40.00
❑ 414	Twinkle/One Day Blues	1957	10.00	20.00	40.00
❑ 422	It's Too Late Now/Saxophone Rag	1957	12.50	25.00	50.00
❑ 474	Changing My Love/I Don't Want Nobody	1963	6.25	12.50	25.00
DOOTONE					
❑ 409	Guided Missiles/My Heart	1956	50.00	100.00	200.00

CULMER, LITTLE IRIS, AND THE MAJESTICS

Also see THE MAJESTICS.

Number	Title (A Side/B Side)	Yr	VG	VG+	NM
MARLIN					
❑ 803	Frankie, My Eyes Are On You/(B-side unknown)	1957	1000.	1500.	2500.

CUMMINGS, BURTON

Also see THE GUESS WHO.

Number	Title (A Side/B Side)	Yr	VG	VG+	NM
ALFA					
❑ 7008	You Saved My Soul/Real Good	1981	—	2.00	4.00
❑ 7008 [PS]	You Saved My Soul/Real Good	1981	—	2.00	4.00
❑ 7014	Someone to Lean On/Mother, Keep Your Daughters In	1982	—	2.00	4.00
PORTRAIT					
❑ 8100	Stand Tall/Takes a Fool to Love a Fool	1981	—	2.00	4.00
—Reissue					
❑ 70001	Stand Tall/Burch Magic	1976	—	2.50	5.00
❑ 70002	I'm Scared/Sugartime Flashback Joys	1977	—	2.50	5.00
❑ 70003	Timeless Love/Never Had a Lady Before	1977	—	2.50	5.00
❑ 70007	My Own Way to Rock/A Song for Him	1977	—	2.50	5.00
❑ 70011	Is It Really Right/Your Back Yard	1978	—	2.50	5.00
❑ 70016	Break It To Them Gently/Roll with the Punches	1978	—	2.50	5.00
❑ 70016 [PS]	Break It To Them Gently/Roll with the Punches	1978	2.00	4.00	8.00
❑ 70024	Takes a Fool to Love a Fool/I Will Play a Rhapsody	1978	—	2.50	5.00

CUNNINGHAM, BUDDY

Number	Title (A Side/B Side)	Yr	VG	VG+	NM
SUN					
❑ 208	Right or Wrong/Why Do I Care	1954	500.00	1000.	1500.

CUPIDS, THE (1)

Number	Title (A Side/B Side)	Yr	VG	VG+	NM
AANKO					
❑ 1002	Brenda/For You	1963	25.00	50.00	100.00
KC					
❑ 115	Brenda/For You	1963	12.50	25.00	50.00

CUPIDS, THE (2)

Number	Title (A Side/B Side)	Yr	VG	VG+	NM
ALADDIN					
❑ 3404	Now You Tell Me/Lillie Mae	1957	15.00	30.00	60.00
—Maroon label					
❑ 3404	Now You Tell Me/Lillie Mae	1958	6.25	12.50	25.00
—Black label					

CUPIDS, THE (3)

Number	Title (A Side/B Side)	Yr	VG	VG+	NM
DECCA					
❑ 30279	The Answer to Your Prayer/My Dog Likes Your Dog	1957	10.00	20.00	40.00

CUPIDS, THE (U)

Some of these may be groups (1), (2) or (3), but more likely they aren't. It's also likely they aren't all the same.

Number	Title (A Side/B Side)	Yr	VG	VG+	NM
CHAN					
❑ 107	I Don't Know/Troubles Not At End	1956	20.00	40.00	80.00
MUSICNOTE					
❑ 119	Lorraine/Little Girl of Mine	1963	3.75	7.50	15.00
TIMES SQUARE					
❑ 1	Pretty Baby/Let's Rock	1964	3.75	7.50	15.00
UWR					
❑ 4241/2	True Love, True Love/Let's Twist	1962	10.00	20.00	40.00

CURE, THE

Number	Title (A Side/B Side)	Yr	VG	VG+	NM
ELEKTRA					
❑ 64928	Never Enough/Harold and Joe	1990	—	2.00	4.00
❑ 65936	Love Song/Fascination Street	1990	—	—	3.00
—"Spun Gold" reissue					
❑ 65967	Why Can't I Be You/Hot Hot Hot!!	1990	—	—	3.00
—"Spun Gold" reissue					
❑ 69249	Lullaby/Homesick	1989	—	—	3.00
❑ 69280	Love Song/2 Late	1989	—	—	3.00
—First pressing: Red and black label					
❑ 69280	Love Song/2 Late	1989	—	2.00	4.00
—Second pressing: Gray label					
❑ 69300	Fascination Street/Babble	1989	—	—	3.00
❑ 69300 [PS]	Fascination Street/Babble	1989	—	—	3.00
❑ 69424	Hot Hot Hot!!!/Hey You!!!	1988	—	2.00	4.00
❑ 69424 [PS]	Hot Hot Hot!!!/Hey You!!!	1988	—	2.00	4.00
❑ 69443	Just Like Heaven/Breathe	1987	2.50	5.00	10.00
❑ 69443 [PS]	Just Like Heaven/Breathe	1987	2.50	5.00	10.00
❑ 69474	Why Can't I Be You?/Japanese Dream	1987	—	2.50	5.00
❑ 69474 [PS]	Why Can't I Be You?/Japanese Dream	1987	—	2.50	5.00
❑ 69537	Let's Go to Bed/Boys Don't Cry	1986	—	3.00	6.00
❑ 69537 [PS]	Let's Go to Bed/Boys Don't Cry	1986	—	3.00	6.00
❑ 69551	Close to Me/Sinking	1986	—	2.00	4.00
❑ 69604	In Between Days (Without You)/Stop Dead	1985	—	2.50	5.00
❑ 69604 [PS]	In Between Days (Without You)/Stop Dead	1985	—	2.50	5.00
SIRE					
❑ PRO-A-2022 [DJ]	Let's Go to Bed (same on both sides)	1983	5.00	10.00	20.00
❑ 29376	The Love Cats/Speak My Language	1984	2.50	5.00	10.00
❑ 29490	The Walk/The Dream	1983	2.50	5.00	10.00

CURLEY AND THE JADES

Number	Title (A Side/B Side)	Yr	VG	VG+	NM
MUSIC MAKERS					
❑ 109	Bullfighter/Boom Stix	1962	15.00	30.00	60.00
REPRISE					
❑ 20046	Bullfighter/Boom Stix	1962	7.50	15.00	30.00

CURRENTS, THE

Number	Title (A Side/B Side)	Yr	VG	VG+	NM
LAURIE					
❑ 3205	Night Run/Riff Raff	1963	7.50	15.00	30.00

CURTIS, MAC

Number	Title (A Side/B Side)	Yr	VG	VG+	NM
DOT					
❑ 16315	You're the One/Dance Her By Me (One More Time)	1962	2.50	5.00	10.00
EPIC					
❑ 10257	Too Close to Home/Too Good to Be True	1967	—	3.00	6.00
❑ 10324	The Quiet Kind/Love's Been Good to Me	1968	—	3.00	6.00
❑ 10385	The Sunshine Man/It's My Way	1968	—	3.00	6.00
❑ 10438	Almost Persuaded/The Friendly City	1969	—	3.00	6.00
❑ 10468	Happiness Lives in This House/Little Ole Wine Drinker Me	1969	—	3.00	6.00
❑ 10530	Don't Make Love/Us	1969	—	3.00	6.00
❑ 10574	Honey Don't/Today's Teardrops	1970	—	3.00	6.00
FELSTED					
❑ 8592	Come Back Baby/No, Never Alone	1959	5.00	10.00	20.00
GRT					
❑ 26	Early in the Morning/When the Hurt Moves In	1970	—	2.50	5.00
❑ 41	Gulf Stream Line/I'd Run a Mile	1971	—	2.50	5.00
KING					
❑ 4927	If I Had Me a Woman/Just So You Call Me	1956	37.50	75.00	150.00
❑ 4949	Grandaddy's Rockin'/Half Hearted Love	1956	37.50	75.00	150.00
❑ 4965	You Ain't Treatin' Me Right/The Low Road	1956	37.50	75.00	150.00
❑ 4995	That Ain't Nothin' But Right/Don't You Love Me	1956	37.50	75.00	150.00
❑ 5007	What You Want/To Protect the Innocent	1957	25.00	50.00	100.00
❑ 5059	Say So/I'll Be Gentle	1957	10.00	20.00	40.00
❑ 5107	What You Want/You Are My Special Baby	1958	15.00	30.00	60.00
❑ 5121	Missy Ann/Little Miss Linda	1958	15.00	30.00	60.00
RANWOOD					
❑ 1017	Pistol Packin' Mama/Asphalt Cowboy, Parking Lot Lover	1975	—	2.50	5.00
❑ 1033	Keep Doin' What You're Doin' Now/She Knows All the Good Ways to Be Bad	1975	—	2.50	5.00
❑ 1041	More Like I Do Now/Nine Times Out of Ten	1975	—	2.50	5.00
❑ 1050	We Made It All the Way/West Texas Women	1976	—	2.50	5.00
TOWER					
❑ 319	Ties That Bind/Stepping Out on You	1967	—	3.00	6.00

CURTIS, SONNY

Also see THE CRICKETS (1).

Number	Title (A Side/B Side)	Yr	VG	VG+	NM
'STEEM					
❑ 110185	Now I've Got a Heart of Gold/(B-side unknown)	1985	—	3.00	6.00
A&M					
❑ 1359	Lights of L.A./Sunny Mornin'	1972	7.50	15.00	30.00
❑ 1408	Love Is All Around/Last Days of Childhood	1973	—	—	—
—Unreleased?					
CAPITOL					
❑ 4158	Lovesick Blues/It's Only a Question of Time	1975	3.00	6.00	12.00
❑ 4227	It's Only a Question of Time/When It's Just You and Me	1976	3.00	6.00	12.00
❑ 4240	Where's Patricia Now/When It's Just You and Me	1976	3.00	6.00	12.00
CORAL					
❑ 60954	Someday You're Gonna Be Sorry/Forever Yours	1953	6.25	12.50	25.00
❑ 61023	No More Tears/The Best Way to Hold a Girl	1953	6.25	12.50	25.00
❑ 62207	Red Headed Stranger/Talk About My Baby	1960	10.00	20.00	40.00
DIMENSION					
❑ 1017	So Used to Loving You/The Last Song I'm Ever Gonna Sing	1963	5.00	10.00	20.00
❑ 1024	A Beatle I Want to Be/So Used to Loving You	1964	6.25	12.50	25.00
DOT					
❑ 15754	Wrong Again/Laughing Stock	1958	10.00	20.00	40.00
❑ 15799	A Pretty Girl/Willa May Jones	1958	7.50	15.00	30.00
ELEKTRA					
❑ 46526	The Cowboy Singer/Cheatin' Clouds	1979	—	2.50	5.00
❑ 46568	Do You Remember Roll Over Beethoven/Walk Right Back	1979	—	2.50	5.00
❑ 46616	The Real Buddy Holly Story/Ain't Nobody Honest	1980	—	3.00	6.00
❑ 46643	Love Is All Around/The Clone Song	1980	—	2.50	5.00
❑ 47048	You Made My Life a Song/50 Ways to Leave Your Lover	1980	—	2.50	5.00
❑ 47129	Good Ol' Girls/So Used to Loving You	1981	—	2.50	5.00
❑ 47176	Married Woman/I Live Your Music	1981	—	2.50	5.00
❑ 47231 [DJ]	The Christmas Song/Little Drummer Boy	1981	2.00	4.00	8.00
—B-side by Hank Williams, Jr.					
❑ 69942	Together Alone/Dream Well All of You Children	1982	—	2.50	5.00
LIBERTY					
❑ 55710	Bo Diddley Bach/I Pledge My Love to You	1964	5.00	10.00	20.00
MERCURY					
❑ 73438	Rock and Rol (I Gave You the Best Years of My Life)/My Mama Sure Left Me Some Good Old Days	1973	3.75	7.50	15.00
OVATION					
❑ 1006	Love Is All Around/Here, There and Everywhere	1970	5.00	10.00	20.00
❑ 1023	Unsaintly Judy/You Don't Belong in This Place	1970	3.75	7.50	15.00
VIVA					
❑ 602	My Way of Life/Last Call	1966	3.75	7.50	15.00
❑ 607	The Collection/Destiny's Child	1966	3.75	7.50	15.00

Number	Title (A Side/B Side)	Yr	VG	VG+	NM
❑ 617	I'm a Gypsy Man/I Wanna Go Bummin' Around	1967	3.75	7.50	15.00
❑ 626	Day Drinker/Atlanta, Georgia Stray	1968	3.75	7.50	15.00
❑ 630	The Straight Life/How Little Men Care	1968	3.75	7.50	15.00
❑ 634	Holiday for Clowns/Day Gig	1969	3.75	7.50	15.00
❑ 636	Girl of the North/Hung Up in Your Eyes	1969	3.75	7.50	15.00

CUSTER AND THE SURVIVORS

Number	Title (A Side/B Side)	Yr	VG	VG+	NM
ASCOT					
❑ 2207	I Saw Her Walking/Flapjacks	1965	4.00	8.00	16.00
GOLDEN STATE					
❑ 1657	I Saw Her Walking/Flapjacks	1965	3.00	6.00	12.00
VARDAN					
❑ 202	I Saw Her Walking/Flapjacks	1965	5.00	10.00	20.00

CUTE-TEENS, THE

Number	Title (A Side/B Side)	Yr	VG	VG+	NM
ALADDIN					
❑ 3458	When My Teenage Days Are Over/From This Day Forward	1959	62.50	125.00	250.00

CYCLONE III

Number	Title (A Side/B Side)	Yr	VG	VG+	NM
PHILIPS					
❑ 40258	You've Got a Bomb/Surfnanny	1965	10.00	20.00	40.00

CYKLE, THE

Number	Title (A Side/B Side)	Yr	VG	VG+	NM
LABEL					
❑ 101	If You Can/(B-side unknown)	1969	7.50	15.00	30.00
❑ 101 [PS]	If You Can/(B-side unknown)	1969	15.00	30.00	60.00

CYMBAL, JOHNNY

Includes releases as "Derek" on the Bang label. Also see CYMBAL AND CLINGER.

Number	Title (A Side/B Side)	Yr	VG	VG+	NM
AMARET					
❑ 110	Big River/Girl from Willow County	1969	2.00	4.00	8.00
❑ 111	Ode to Bubblegum/Save All Your Lovin' (Hold It for Me)	1969	2.00	4.00	8.00
BANG					
❑ 558	Cinnamon/This Is My Story	1968	2.00	4.00	8.00
❑ 566	Back Door Man/Tell Your Soul	1969	—	3.00	6.00
❑ 571	Inside Out-Outside In/Sell Your Soul	1969	—	3.00	6.00
COLUMBIA					
❑ 43842	Good Morning Blues/Jessica	1966	2.00	4.00	8.00
DCP					
❑ 1135	Go, VW, Go/Sorrow and Pain	1965	7.50	15.00	30.00
❑ 1146	My Last Day/Summertime's Here at Last	1965	3.75	7.50	15.00
KAPP					
❑ 503	Mr. Bass Man/Sacred Lovers' Vow	1963	5.00	10.00	20.00
❑ 524	Teenage Heaven/Cinderella Baby	1963	3.75	7.50	15.00
❑ 539	Surfin' at Tiajuana/Dum Dum Dee Dum	1963	3.75	7.50	15.00
❑ 556	Marshmallow/Hurdy Gurdy Man	1963	3.75	7.50	15.00
❑ 576	There Goes a Bad Girl/Refreshment Time	1964	3.75	7.50	15.00
❑ 594	Robinson Crusoe on Mars/Mitsu	1964	3.75	7.50	15.00
❑ 614	Connie/Little Miss Lonely	1964	3.75	7.50	15.00
❑ 634	Cheat, Cheat/16 Shades of Blue	1964	3.75	7.50	15.00
KEDLEN					
❑ 2001	Bachelor Man/Growing Up with You	1962	5.00	10.00	20.00
MGM					
❑ 12935	It'll Be Me/Always, Always	1960	5.00	10.00	20.00
❑ 12970	The Water Was Red/The Bunny	1961	5.00	10.00	20.00
MUSICOR					
❑ 1261	It Looks Like Love/May I Get to Know You	1967	3.00	6.00	12.00
❑ 1272	Breaking Your Balloon/The Marriage of Charlotte Brown	1967	3.00	6.00	12.00
VEE JAY					
❑ 495	Bachelor Man/Growing Up with You	1963	3.75	7.50	15.00

CYMBAL & CLINGER

Also see JOHNNY CYMBAL.

Number	Title (A Side/B Side)	Yr	VG	VG+	NM
CHELSEA					
❑ 78-0106	God Bless You Rock & Roll/Forever and Forever	1972	—	2.50	5.00
❑ 78-0112	Dying River/Little Bit No, Little Bit Yes	1973	—	2.50	5.00
MARINA					
❑ 502	Pool Shooter/Mookie Mookie Man	1971	—	3.00	6.00
MGM					
❑ 14256	Pool Shooter/Mookie Mookie Man	1971	—	2.50	5.00

CYRKLE, THE

Number	Title (A Side/B Side)	Yr	VG	VG+	NM
COLUMBIA					
❑ CSM-466	Camaro/SS 396	1967	6.25	12.50	25.00
—B-side by Paul Revere and the Raiders					
❑ CSM-466 [PS]	Camaro/SS 396	1967	12.50	25.00	50.00
—B-side by Paul Revere and the Raiders					
❑ 43589	Red Rubber Ball/How Can I Leave Her	1966	3.00	6.00	12.00
❑ 43589 [DJ]	Red Rubber Ball (same on both sides)	1966	10.00	20.00	40.00
—Promo only on red vinyl					
❑ 43589 [PS]	Red Rubber Ball/How Can I Leave Her	1966	100.00	200.00	400.00
❑ 43729	Turn-Down Day/Big, Little Woman	1966	2.50	5.00	10.00
❑ 43729 [PS]	Turn-Down Day/Big, Little Woman	1966	3.75	7.50	15.00
❑ 43871	Please Don't Ever Leave Me/Money to Burn	1966	2.00	4.00	8.00
❑ 43965	I Wish You Could Be Here/The Visit (She Was Here)	1967	2.00	4.00	8.00
❑ 43965 [PS]	I Wish You Could Be Here/The Visit (She Was Here)	1967	3.00	6.00	12.00
❑ 44108	We Had a Good Thing Goin'/Two Rooms	1967	2.00	4.00	8.00
❑ 44224	Penny Arcade/The Words	1967	2.00	4.00	8.00
❑ 44366	Turn of the Century/Don't Cry, No Fears, No Tears Comin'	1967	2.00	4.00	8.00
❑ 44426	Friends/Reading Her Papers	1968	2.00	4.00	8.00
❑ 44491	Red Chair Fade Away/Where Are You Going	1968	2.00	4.00	8.00

CYRUS ERIE

Early ERIC CARMEN.

Number	Title (A Side/B Side)	Yr	VG	VG+	NM
EPIC					
❑ 10451	Sparrow/Get the Message	1969	3.00	6.00	12.00

D

D'ABO, MIKE

Lead singer of MANFRED MANN in the "Mighty Quinn" era.

Number	Title (A Side/B Side)	Yr	VG	VG+	NM
A&M					
❑ 1374	Little Miss Understood/Belinda	1972	—	2.50	5.00
❑ 1628	Fuel to Burn/Hold On Sweet Darling	1974	—	2.00	4.00
BELL					
❑ 956	Miss Me in the Morning/Arabella Cinderella	1971	—	3.00	6.00

D-MEN, THE

Early incarnation of THE FIFTH ESTATE.

Number	Title (A Side/B Side)	Yr	VG	VG+	NM
KAPP					
❑ 691	So Little Time/Every Moment of Every Day	1965	3.00	6.00	12.00
VEEP					
❑ 1206	Don't You Know/No Hope for Me	1965	3.75	7.50	15.00
❑ 1209	Just Don't Care/Mousin' Around	1965	3.75	7.50	15.00

DA-PREES, THE

Number	Title (A Side/B Side)	Yr	VG	VG+	NM
TWIST					
❑ 70913	Pay Day/Sometimes	1963	37.50	75.00	150.00

DACHE, BERTELL

TONY ORLANDO with CAROLE KING on backing vocals.

Number	Title (A Side/B Side)	Yr	VG	VG+	NM
DIAMOND					
❑ 201	Don't Stop the World for Me/Anchors Awaeigh Girl	1966	3.75	7.50	15.00
UNITED ARTISTS					
❑ 260	All the World Loves a Lover/You Gotta Have Chicks	1960	6.25	12.50	25.00
❑ 290	Not Just Tomorrow, But Today/Love Eyes	1961	6.25	12.50	25.00

DAISIES, THE

Number	Title (A Side/B Side)	Yr	VG	VG+	NM
CAPITOL					
❑ 5667	Cold Wave/Put Your Arms Around Me	1966	6.25	12.50	25.00
ROULETTE					
❑ 4571	I Wanna Swim with Him/You Just Said You Loved Me	1964	3.00	6.00	12.00

DAKIL, FLOYD

Number	Title (A Side/B Side)	Yr	VG	VG+	NM
EARTH					
❑ 402	Bad Boy/Stoppin' Traffic	1965	10.00	20.00	40.00
❑ 403	Kitty Kitty/It Takes a Lot to Hurt	1965	7.50	15.00	30.00
❑ 404	Stronger Than Dirt/You're the Kind of Girl	1965	7.50	15.00	30.00
GUYDEN					
❑ 2111	Dance, Franny, Dance/Look What You've Gone and Done	1964	7.50	15.00	30.00
JETSTAR					
❑ 103	Dance, Franny, Dance/Look What You've Gone and Done	1964	25.00	50.00	100.00
POMPEII					
❑ 66687	Merry Christmas, Baby/One Girl	1968	6.25	12.50	25.00

DAKOTAS, THE

Also see BILLY J. KRAMER AND THE DAKOTAS.

Number	Title (A Side/B Side)	Yr	VG	VG+	NM
LIBERTY					
❑ 55618	The Cruel Surf/The Millionaire	1963	10.00	20.00	40.00

DALE, DICK, AND THE DEL-TONES

Number	Title (A Side/B Side)	Yr	VG	VG+	NM
ACCENT					
❑ 1243	Eyes of a Child/Just a-Waitin'	1968	2.00	4.00	8.00
CAPITOL					
❑ 4963	King of the Surf Guitar/Havah Nagilah	1963	5.00	10.00	20.00
❑ 4963 [PS]	King of the Surf Guitar/Havah Nagilah	1963	20.00	40.00	80.00
❑ 5010	Secret Surfin' Spot/Surfin' and a-Swingin'	1963	5.00	10.00	20.00
❑ 5048	Wild Ideas/Scavenger	1963	5.00	10.00	20.00
❑ 5098	The Wedge/Night Rider	1963	5.00	10.00	20.00
❑ 5140	The Victor/Mr. Eliminator	1964	3.75	7.50	15.00
❑ 5187	Wild, Wild Mustang/Grunge Run	1964	3.75	7.50	15.00
❑ 5225	Never on Sunday/Glory Wave	1964	3.75	7.50	15.00
❑ 5290	Oh Marie/Who Can It Be	1964	3.75	7.50	15.00
❑ 5389	Let's Go Trippin' '65/Watusi Jo	1965	3.75	7.50	15.00
COLUMBIA					
❑ 07340	Pipeline/Love Struck Baby	1987	—	2.00	4.00
—B-side by Stevie Ray Vaughan					
❑ 07340 [PS]	Pipeline/Love Struck Baby	1987	—	3.00	6.00
CONCERT ROOM					
❑ 371	We'll Never Hear the End of It/Fairest of Them All	1963	6.25	12.50	25.00
COUGAR					
❑ 711	Ramblin' Man/You're Hurtin' Now	1967	3.75	7.50	15.00
❑ 712	Taco Wagon/Spanish Kiss	1967	3.75	7.50	15.00
CUPID					
❑ 106	We'll Never Hear the End of It/Fairest of Them All	1960	7.50	15.00	30.00
—Black vinyl					
❑ 106	We'll Never Hear the End of It/Fairest of Them All	1960	20.00	40.00	80.00
—Gold vinyl					
DELTONE					
❑ 4939	Misirlou/Eight Till Midnight	1963	5.00	10.00	20.00
❑ 4940	Surf Beat/Peppermint Man	1963	5.00	10.00	20.00
—Deltone 4939 and 4940 were part of the Capitol numbering system					
❑ 5012	Oh Whee Marie/Breaking Heart	1959	15.00	30.00	60.00
❑ 5013	Stop Teasin'/Without Your Love	1959	15.00	30.00	60.00
❑ 5014	Jessie Pearl/St. Louis Blues	1960	25.00	50.00	100.00
❑ 5017	Let's Go Trippin'/Del-Tone Rock	1961	7.50	15.00	30.00
❑ 5018	Shake and Stomp/Jungle Fever	1962	10.00	20.00	40.00
❑ 5019	Misirlou/Eight Till Midnight	1962	6.25	12.50	25.00
❑ 5020	Peppermint Man/Surf Beat	1962	6.25	12.50	25.00
❑ 5028	Run for Your Life/Lovin' on My Brain	1963	7.50	15.00	30.00
GNP CRESCENDO					
❑ 804	Let's Go Trippin'/Those Memories of You	1975	—	3.00	6.00

Number	Title (A Side/B Side)	Yr	VG	VG+	NM
RENDEZVOUS					
❑ 204	Reincarnation (Part 1)/Reincarnation (Part 2)	1963	5.00	10.00	20.00
SATURN					
❑ 401	We'll Never Hear the End of It/Fairest of Them All	1963	7.50	15.00	30.00
U.S. ARMY					
❑ 1301 [DJ]	The Enlistment Twist/Dream Girl Waltz	1962	7.50	15.00	30.00
—B-side by Craig Adams and His Country Cousins; blue vinyl					
❑ 1301 [PS]	The Enlistment Twist/Dream Girl Waltz	1962	7.50	15.00	30.00
YES					
❑ 7014	We'll Never Hear the End of It/Fairest of Them All	1963	7.50	15.00	30.00
❑ 7014 [PS]	We'll Never Hear the End of It/Fairest of Them All	1963	10.00	20.00	40.00

DALE AND GRACE

Number	Title (A Side/B Side)	Yr	VG	VG+	NM
GUYDEN					
❑ 6002	What's Happening to Me/Darling It's Wonderful	1972	—	2.50	5.00
HANNA-BARBERA					
❑ 472	Let Them Talk/I'd Rather Be Free	1966	2.00	4.00	8.00
MICHELLE					
❑ 921	I'm Leaving It Up to You/That's What I Like	1963	6.25	12.50	25.00
❑ 923	Stop and Think It Over/Bad Luck	1963	3.75	7.50	15.00
❑ 928	The Loneliest Night/I'm Not Free	1964	3.75	7.50	15.00
❑ 930	Darling It's Wonderful/What's Happening to Me	1964	3.75	7.50	15.00
❑ 936	Cool Water/Rules of Love	1964	3.75	7.50	15.00
MONTEL					
❑ 921	I'm Leaving It Up to You/That's What I Like About You	1963	3.00	6.00	12.00
❑ 922	Stop and Think It Over/Bad Luck	1963	3.00	6.00	12.00
❑ 928	The Loneliest Night/I'm Not Free	1964	3.00	6.00	12.00
❑ 930	Darling It's Wonderful/What's Happening to Me	1964	3.00	6.00	12.00
❑ 936	Cool Water/Rules of Love	1964	3.00	6.00	12.00
❑ 958	Make the World Go Away/Stranger	1965	3.00	6.00	12.00
❑ 989	It Keeps Right On a-Hurtin'/So Fine	1967	3.00	6.00	12.00
MONTEL/MICHELLE					
❑ 942	Something Special/What Am I Living For	1964	3.00	6.00	12.00

DALEY, JIMMY, AND THE DING-A-LINGS

Number	Title (A Side/B Side)	Yr	VG	VG+	NM
DECCA					
❑ 30163	Rock, Pretty Baby/Can I Steal a Little Love	1956	10.00	20.00	40.00
❑ 30358	Red Lips and Green Eyes/How's About a Little Kiss?	1957	10.00	20.00	40.00
❑ 30532	Hole in the Wall/Bongo Rock	1957	10.00	20.00	40.00

7-Inch Extended Plays

Number	Title (A Side/B Side)	Yr	VG	VG+	NM
DECCA					
❑ ED 2481	Rockabye Lullaby Blues/Teen Age Bop/The Most//(B-side unknown)	195?	12.50	25.00	50.00
❑ ED 2481 [PS]	(title unknown)	195?	12.50	25.00	50.00
❑ ED 2482	Happy Is a Boy Named Me/Hot Rod/Big Band Rock and Roll//(B-side unknown)	195?	12.50	25.00	50.00
❑ ED 2482 [PS]	(title unknown)	195?	12.50	25.00	50.00

DALTON BOYS, THE

Number	Title (A Side/B Side)	Yr	VG	VG+	NM
SKYLA					
❑ 1124	I'm Thinkin'/It's Much More Stronger	1962	7.50	15.00	30.00
TEEN					
❑ 505	Who's Gonna Hold Your Hand/Walkin'	1959	12.50	25.00	50.00
V.I.P.					
❑ 25025	I've Been Cheated/Something's Bothering You	1965	12.50	25.00	50.00
❑ 25025	I've Been Cheated/Take My Hand	1965	50.00	100.00	200.00

DALTREY, ROGER

Also see THE WHO.

Number	Title (A Side/B Side)	Yr	VG	VG+	NM
ATLANTIC					
❑ 89419	Under a Raging Moon/The Pride You Hide	1986	—	—	3.00
❑ 89457	Quicksilver Lightning/Love Me Like You Do	1986	—	—	3.00
❑ 89457 [PS]	Quicksilver Lightning/Love Me Like You Do	1986	—	2.50	5.00
❑ 89471	Let Me Down Easy/Fallen Angel	1985	—	—	3.00
❑ 89471 [PS]	Let Me Down Easy/Fallen Angel	1985	—	—	3.00
❑ 89491	After the Fire/Don't Satisfy Me	1985	—	—	3.00
❑ 89491 [PS]	After the Fire/Don't Satisfy Me	1985	—	—	3.00
❑ 89667	Parting Would Be Painless/Is There Anyone Out There?	1984	—	—	3.00
❑ 89704	Walking in My Sleep/Somebody Told Me	1984	—	—	3.00
❑ 89704 [PS]	Walking in My Sleep/Somebody Told Me	1984	—	—	3.00
A&M					
❑ 1779	Love's Dream/Orpheus Song	1975	—	2.50	5.00
—With Rick Wakeman					
MCA					
❑ 40453	Come and Get Your Love/Heart's Right	1975	—	2.50	5.00
❑ 40512	Oceans Away/Feeling	1976	—	2.50	5.00
❑ 40761	One of the Boys/Doing It All Again	1977	—	2.50	5.00
❑ 40765	Satin and Lace/Say It Ain't So, Joe	1977	—	2.00	4.00
❑ 40800	Avenging Annie/The Prisoner	1977	—	2.00	4.00
❑ 40862	Leon/The Prisoner	1978	—	2.00	4.00
❑ 52051	Martyrs and Madmen/Avenging Annie	1982	—	2.00	4.00
ODE					
❑ 66040	I'm Free/Underture	1973	—	2.50	5.00
POLYDOR					
❑ 2105	Free Me/McVicar	1980	—	2.00	4.00
❑ 2105 [PS]	Free Me/McVicar	1980	—	2.00	4.00
❑ 2121	Without Your Love/Escape (Part 1)	1980	—	2.00	4.00
❑ 2153	Waiting for a Friend/Bitter and Twisted	1981	—	2.00	4.00
❑ 2153 [DJ]	Waiting for a Friend (same on both sides)	1981	—	3.00	6.00
—One label has name misspelled as "Rodger Daltrey"					
❑ 15098	See Me, Feel Me-Listening to You/Overture from Tommy	1975	—	2.50	5.00
—B-side by Pete Townshend					
❑ 15098 [PS]	See Me, Feel Me-Listening to You/Overture from Tommy	1975	—	2.50	5.00
TRACK					
❑ 40053	Giving It All Away/Way of the World	1973	—	3.00	6.00
—B-side by Bryan Daly & the London Festival Orchestra					
❑ 40084	Thinking/There Is Love	1973	2.00	4.00	8.00

DAMITA JO

Also see BROOK BENTON AND DAMITA JO.

Number	Title (A Side/B Side)	Yr	VG	VG+	NM
ABC-PARAMOUNT					
❑ 9822	How Will I Know/I'll Never Cry	1957	3.75	7.50	15.00
❑ 9849	My Heart Is Home/Disillusioned Lovers	1957	3.75	7.50	15.00
❑ 10176	How Will I Know/Disillusioned Lovers	1961	2.50	5.00	10.00
EPIC					
❑ 9766	Tomorrow Night/Silver Dollar	1965	2.00	4.00	8.00
❑ 9797	Gotta Travel On/Something You Got	1965	2.00	4.00	8.00
❑ 9821	Nobody Knows You When You're Down and Out/Whispering Grass (Don't Tell the Trees)	1965	2.00	4.00	8.00
❑ 9860	Sweet Pussycat/Who Could Ask for More	1965	2.00	4.00	8.00
❑ 9887	That Special Way/Tossin' and Turnin'	1966	2.00	4.00	8.00
❑ 10061	If You Go Away/When the Fog Rolls In to San Francisco	1966	2.00	4.00	8.00
❑ 10176	No Guilty Feelings/Yellow Days	1967	2.00	4.00	8.00
❑ 10235	Dinner For One/Please, James	1967	2.00	4.00	8.00
MERCURY					
❑ 71493	The Dance Was Over/Look at Yourself	1959	3.00	6.00	12.00
❑ 71568	What Would You Do/Widow Talk	1960	3.00	6.00	12.00
❑ 71608	Little Things Mean a Lot/I Burned Your Letter	1960	3.00	6.00	12.00
❑ 71690	I'll Save the Last Dance for You/Forgive	1960	3.75	7.50	15.00
❑ 71760	Keep Your Hands Off of Him/Hush, Somebody's Calling My Name	1961	3.00	6.00	12.00
❑ 71793	Sweet Georgia Brown/Do What You Want	1961	3.00	6.00	12.00
❑ 71840	I'll Be There/Love Laid Its Hands on Me	1962	3.75	7.50	15.00
❑ 71840 [PS]	I'll Be There/Love Laid Its Hands on Me	1962	6.25	12.50	25.00
❑ 71871	Dance with a Dolly (With a Hole in Her Stocking)/You're Nobody 'Til Somebody Loves You	1962	3.00	6.00	12.00
❑ 71929	I Didn't Know I Was Crying/I Built My World Around a Dream	1962	3.00	6.00	12.00
❑ 71946	Joey/You're Nobody 'Til Somebody Loves You	1962	3.00	6.00	12.00
❑ 71984	Another Dancing Partner/Please Send Me Someone to Love	1962	3.00	6.00	12.00
❑ 72019	The Window Up Above/Tennessee Waltz	1962	3.00	6.00	12.00
❑ 72056	Dance Him By Me/Las Vegas	1962	3.00	6.00	12.00
❑ 72086	Little Things/Mr. Blue	1963	2.50	5.00	10.00
❑ 72121	Drama of Love/Hobo Flats	1963	2.50	5.00	10.00
❑ 72162	In the Dark/Melancholy Baby	1963	2.50	5.00	10.00
RANWOOD					
❑ 820	Loving You/Reason to Believe	1968	—	3.00	6.00
❑ 826	Grown-Up Games/Lonely Letters	1968	—	3.00	6.00
❑ 844	Brother Love's Traveling Salvation Show/I'll Save the Last Dance for You	1969	—	3.00	6.00
❑ 857	Lonely Teardrops/Ain't Misbehavin'	1969	—	3.00	6.00
❑ 869	Paint Me Loving You/Tomorrow Is the First Day of the Rest of My Life	1970	—	3.00	6.00
❑ 884	Mrs. Robinson/Two Worlds	1970	—	2.50	5.00
❑ 894	Hallelujah Baby/Two Worlds	1971	—	2.50	5.00
RCA VICTOR					
❑ 47-4685	Lonesome and Blue/I Need You	1952	3.75	7.50	15.00
—By John Greer, vocals by Damita Jo					
❑ 47-5022	I'd Do It Again/I Don't Care	1952	3.75	7.50	15.00
❑ 47-5120	Go 'Way From My Window/Let Me Share Your Name	1953	3.75	7.50	15.00
❑ 47-5253	Missing/The Widow Walk	1953	3.75	7.50	15.00
❑ 47-5328	Do Me a Favor/Don't You Care	1953	3.75	7.50	15.00
❑ 47-5570	Face to Face/Sadie Thompson's Song	1953	3.75	7.50	15.00
❑ 47-5987	Win or Lose/My Tzatskele	1955	3.75	7.50	15.00
❑ 47-6096	Feelin' Kinda Happy/Nuff of That Stuff	1955	3.75	7.50	15.00
—B-side by Steve Gibson and His Red Caps					
❑ 47-6185	In My Heart/Abracadabra	1955	3.75	7.50	15.00
❑ 47-6281	Always/Freehearted	1955	3.75	7.50	15.00
VEE JAY					
❑ 661	I'm Waiting for Ships That Never Come In/Hurt a Fool	1965	2.00	4.00	8.00

DAMN YANKEES

Also see TED NUGENT; TOMMY SHAW.

Number	Title (A Side/B Side)	Yr	VG	VG+	NM
WARNER BROS.					
❑ 18612	Silence Is Broken/Double Coyote	1993	—	—	3.00
❑ 18728	Where You Goin' Now/This Side of Hell	1992	—	—	3.00
❑ 19408	Come Again (Radio Mix)/Come Again (Single Mix)	1991	—	—	3.00
❑ 19595	High Enough/Pile Driver	1990	—	—	3.00

DAMON, LIZ, 'S ORIENT EXPRESS

Number	Title (A Side/B Side)	Yr	VG	VG+	NM
ANTHEM					
❑ 51005	Loneliness Remembers/Quiet Sound	1971	2.50	5.00	10.00
❑ 51006	All in All/Walking Backwards Down the Road	1971	2.50	5.00	10.00
MAKAHA					
❑ 503	1900 Yesterday/You're Falling in Love	1970	3.00	6.00	12.00
WHITE WHALE					
❑ 368	1900 Yesterday/You're Falling in Love	1970	—	3.00	6.00
❑ 370	But For Love/You Make Me Feel Like Someone	1970	—	3.00	6.00

DAN AND DALE

Number	Title (A Side/B Side)	Yr	VG	VG+	NM
TIFTON					
❑ 125	Batman Theme/(B-side unknown)	1966	2.50	5.00	10.00
❑ 125 [PS]	Batman Theme/(B-side unknown)	1966	5.00	10.00	20.00

DANCER, PRANCER, AND NERVOUS

Number	Title (A Side/B Side)	Yr	VG	VG+	NM
CAPITOL					
❑ 4300	The Happy Reindeer/Dancer's Waltz	1959	3.00	6.00	12.00
❑ 4300 [PS]	The Happy Reindeer/Dancer's Waltz	1959	6.25	12.50	25.00
❑ 4353	I Wanta Be an Easter Bunny/The Happy Birthday Song	1960	3.00	6.00	12.00
—As "The Singing Reindeer"					

DANDERLIERS, THE

Number	Title (A Side/B Side)	Yr	VG	VG+	NM
B&F					
❑ 150	Shu-Wop/My Loving Partner	1960	6.25	12.50	25.00
❑ 160	My Love/She's Mine	1960	6.25	12.50	25.00
❑ 1344	Chop Chop Boom/My Autumn Love	1961	5.00	10.00	20.00
MIDAS					
❑ 9004	All the Way/Walk On with Your Nose Up	196?	5.00	10.00	20.00
STATES					
❑ 147	Chop Chop Boom/My Autumn Love	1955	100.00	200.00	400.00
—Black vinyl					
❑ 147	Chop Chop Boom/My Autumn Love	1955	300.00	600.00	1200.
—Red vinyl					
❑ 150	Shu-Wop/My Loving Partner	1955	50.00	100.00	200.00
❑ 152	May God Be With You/Little Man	1956	50.00	100.00	200.00
❑ 160	My Love/She's Mine	1956	62.50	125.00	250.00

DANDLEERS, THE

See THE DANLEERS.

DANETTA AND THE STARLETS

Number	Title (A Side/B Side)	Yr	VG	VG+	NM
OKEH					
❑ 7155	You Belong to Me (We're Going Steady)/ Impression	1962	25.00	50.00	100.00

DANIELS, CHARLIE, BAND

Number	Title (A Side/B Side)	Yr	VG	VG+	NM
EPIC					
❑ 02154	In America/The Legend of Wooley Swamp	1981	—	—	3.00
—Reissue					
❑ 02185	Sweet Home Alabama/Falling in Love for the Night	1981	—	2.00	4.00
❑ 02828	Still in Saigon/Blowing Along with the Wind	1982	—	2.00	4.00
❑ 02995	Ragin' Cajun/Universal Hand	1982	—	2.00	4.00
❑ 03251	We Had It All One Time/Makes You Want to Go Home	1982	—	2.00	4.00
❑ 03918	Stroker's Theme/(B-side unknown)	1983	—	2.00	4.00
❑ 05638	American Farmer/Runnin' with That Crowd	1985	—	—	3.00
❑ 05699	Still Hurtin' Me/American Rock and Roll	1985	—	—	3.00
❑ 05835	Drinkin' My Baby Goodbye/Ever Changing Lady	1986	—	—	3.00
❑ 08002	Boogie Woogie Fiddle Country Blues/Working Man You Got It All	1988	—	—	3.00
❑ 08519	Uneasy Rider '88/Boogie Woogie Fiddle	1988	—	2.00	4.00
❑ 50243	Wichita Jail/It's My Life	1976	—	2.00	4.00
❑ 50278	Sweet Louisiana/Sweetwater, Texas	1976	—	2.00	4.00
❑ 50322	Billy the Kid/Slow Song	1976	—	2.00	4.00
❑ 50456	Heaven Can Be Anywhere (Twin Pines Theme)/ Good Ole Boy	1977	—	2.00	4.00
❑ 50516	Sugar Hill Saturday Night/Maria Teresa	1977	—	2.00	4.00
❑ 50637	Sweet Lousiana/Trudy	1978	—	2.00	4.00
❑ 50700	The Devil Went Down to Georgia/Rainbow Ride	1979	—	2.00	4.00
❑ 50768	Mississippi/Passing Lane	1979	—	2.00	4.00
❑ 50806	Behind Your Eyes/Blue Star	1979	—	2.00	4.00
❑ 50845	Long Haired Country Boy/Sweet Lousiana	1980	—	2.00	4.00
❑ 50888	In America/Blue Star	1980	—	2.00	4.00
❑ 50921	The Legend of Wooley Swamp/Money	1980	—	2.00	4.00
❑ 50955	Carolina (I Remember You)/South Sea Song	1980	—	2.00	4.00
❑ 68542	Cowboy Hat in Dallas/Easy Rider	1988	—	—	3.00
❑ 68738	Midnight Train/Back to Dixie	1989	—	—	3.00
❑ 73030	Simple Man/Ill Wind	1989	—	—	3.00
❑ 73236	Mister DJ/It's My Life	1990	—	—	3.00
❑ 73426	(What This World Needs Is) A Few More Rednecks/It's My Life	1990	—	—	3.00
❑ 73577	Oh Atlanta/What Is 26	1990	—	—	3.00
❑ 73768	Honky Tonk Life/Willie Jones	1991	—	—	3.00
❑ 74061	Little Folks/Let Freedom Ring	1991	—	—	3.00
❑ 74866	The Twang Factor/Old Rock 'n Roll	1991	—	2.00	4.00
HANOVER					
❑ 4541	Robot Bomp/Rover Had a Party	1959	7.50	15.00	30.00
KAMA SUTRA					
❑ 553	Great Big Bunches of Love/(B-side unknown)	1972	—	3.00	6.00
❑ 576	Uneasy Rider/Funky Junky	1973	—	3.00	6.00
❑ 590	Whiskey/(B-side unknown)	1974	—	2.50	5.00
❑ 593	Way Down Yonder/I've Been Down	1974	—	2.50	5.00
❑ 595	Land of Opportunity/(B-side unknown)	1974	—	2.50	5.00
❑ 598	The South's Gonna Do It/King Size Rosewood Bed	1974	—	2.50	5.00
❑ 601	Long Haired Country Boy/I've Been Down	1975	—	2.50	5.00
❑ 606	Birmingham Blues/Damn Good Cowboy	1975	—	2.50	5.00
❑ 607	Texas/Everything Is Kinda Alright	1975	—	2.50	5.00
LIBERTY					
❑ S7-17398	All Night Long/America, I Believe in You	1993	—	2.50	5.00
PAULA					
❑ 246	The Middle of a Heartache/Skip It	1966	3.75	7.50	15.00
❑ 418	The Middle of a Heartache/Skip It	1976	—	2.00	4.00

DANIELS, JEFF

Number	Title (A Side/B Side)	Yr	VG	VG+	NM
ASTRO					
❑ 108	Foxy Dan/Someday You'll Remember	1960	25.00	50.00	100.00
BIG HOWDY					
❑ 777	Switch Blade Sam/You're Still on My Mind	1959	25.00	50.00	100.00
❑ 8120	Uh-Huh/Table for Two	196?	25.00	50.00	100.00
❑ 8121	Foxy Dan/Someday You'll Remember	1961	25.00	50.00	100.00
MELADEE					
❑ 117	Daddy-O Rock/Hey Woman	1958	100.00	200.00	400.00

DANKO, RICK

Also see THE BAND.

Number	Title (A Side/B Side)	Yr	VG	VG+	NM
ARISTA					
❑ 0306	What a Town/Shake It	1978	—	2.00	4.00
❑ 0320	Java Blues/Shake It	1978	—	2.00	4.00

DANLEERS, THE

Number	Title (A Side/B Side)	Yr	VG	VG+	NM
AMP 3					
❑ 2115	One Summer Night/Wheelin' and Dealin'	1958	50.00	100.00	200.00
—By "Dandleers"					
❑ 2115	One Summer Night/Wheelin' and Dealin'	1958	10.00	20.00	40.00
—Corrected group name on label					
EPIC					
❑ 9367	I Live Half a Block from an Angel/If You Don't Care	1960	7.50	15.00	30.00
❑ 9421	I'll Always Be in Love with You/Little Lover	1960	7.50	15.00	30.00
EVEREST					
❑ 19412	Foolish/I'm Looking Around	1961	7.50	15.00	30.00
LEMANS					
❑ 004	The Truth Hurts/Baby You've Got It	1963	2.50	5.00	10.00
❑ 008	I'm Sorry/This Thing Called Love	1963	2.50	5.00	10.00
MERCURY					
❑ 71322	One Summer Night/Wheelin' and Dealin'	1958	5.00	10.00	20.00
❑ 71356	I Really Love You/My Flaming Heart	1958	5.00	10.00	20.00
❑ 71401	A Picture of You/Prelude to Love	1959	5.00	10.00	20.00
❑ 71441	I Can't Sleep/Your Love	1959	5.00	10.00	20.00
SMASH					
❑ 1872	Were You There/If	1964	3.00	6.00	12.00
❑ 1895	Where Is Love/The Angels Sent You	1964	3.00	6.00	12.00

DANNY AND JERRY

"Danny" is Danny Rapp of DANNY AND THE JUNIORS.

Number	Title (A Side/B Side)	Yr	VG	VG+	NM
RONN					
❑ 5	We've Got a Groovy Thing Goin'/You Must Be Fooling	1966	3.00	6.00	12.00
❑ 12	I've Got Pride/Connection	1967	3.00	6.00	12.00
❑ 24	I Can't See Nobody/Mo'Reen	1967	3.00	6.00	12.00

DANNY AND THE JUNIORS

Number	Title (A Side/B Side)	Yr	VG	VG+	NM
ABC-PARAMOUNT					
❑ 9871	At the Hop/Sometimes (When I'm All Alone)	1957	7.50	15.00	30.00
❑ 9888	Rock and Roll Is Here to Stay/School Boy Romance	1958	7.50	15.00	30.00
❑ 9926	Dottie/In the Meantime	1958	6.25	12.50	25.00
❑ 9953	A Thief/Crazy Cave	1958	6.25	12.50	25.00
❑ 9978	Sassy Fran/I Feel So Lonely	1958	12.50	25.00	50.00
❑ 10004	Do You Love Me/Somehow I Can't Forget	1959	6.25	12.50	25.00
❑ 10052	Playing Hard to Get/Of Love	1959	6.25	12.50	25.00
CRUNCH					
❑ 018001	At the Hop/Let the Good Times Roll	1973	—	2.50	5.00
GUYDEN					
❑ 2076	Oo-La-La-Limbo/Now and Then	1962	5.00	10.00	20.00
LUV					
❑ 252	Rock and Roll Is Here to Stay/Sometimes (When I'm All Alone)	1968	2.50	5.00	10.00
MERCURY					
❑ 72240	Sad Girl/Let's Go Ski-ing	1964	5.00	10.00	20.00
SINGULAR					
❑ 711	At the Hop/Sometimes	1957	250.00	500.00	1000.
—Blue label, machine-stamped in dead wax, no mention of Artie Singer on label					
❑ 711	At the Hop/Sometimes	1957	250.00	500.00	1000.
—Blue label, machine-stamped in dead wax, with "Orchestra Directed by Artie Singer" credit. Both versions have a "count-in" before the song starts. Singular records on black labels or without the count-in are probably reproductions.					
SWAN					
❑ 4060	Twistin' U.S.A./A Thousand Miles Away	1960	5.00	10.00	20.00
❑ 4064	Candy Cane. Sugary Plum/Oh Holy Night	1960	6.25	12.50	25.00
❑ 4064 [PS]	Candy Cane. Sugary Plum/Oh Holy Night	1960	62.50	125.00	250.00
❑ 4068	Daydreamer/Pony Express	1961	5.00	10.00	20.00
❑ 4072	Cha Cha Go Go (Chicago Cha-Cha)/Mister Whisper	1961	5.00	10.00	20.00
❑ 4082	Back to the Hop/The Charleston Fish	1961	5.00	10.00	20.00
❑ 4082 [PS]	Back to the Hop/The Charleston Fish	1961	25.00	50.00	100.00
❑ 4084	Just Because/You Hair's Too Long	1961	—	—	—
—Unreleased?					
❑ 4092	Twistin' All Night Long/Some Kind of Nut	1962	5.00	10.00	20.00
❑ 4100	(Do the) Mashed Potatoes/Doin' the Continental Walk	1962	5.00	10.00	20.00
❑ 4113	We Got Soul/Funny	1962	5.00	10.00	20.00

7-Inch Extended Plays

Number	Title (A Side/B Side)	Yr	VG	VG+	NM
ABC-PARAMOUNT					
❑ EP-11	At The Hop/School Boy Romance//Rock And Roll Is Here To Stay/Sometimes (When I'm All Alone)	1958	150.00	300.00	600.00
❑ EP-11 [PS]	At the Hop	1958	225.00	450.00	900.00

DANNY AND THE MEMORIES

"Danny" is Danny Whitten, later of CRAZY HORSE.

Number	Title (A Side/B Side)	Yr	VG	VG+	NM
VALIANT					
❑ 705	Can't Help Lovin' That Girl of Mine/Don't Go	1965	6.25	12.50	25.00
❑ 6049	Can't Help Lovin' That Girl of Mine/Don't Go	1964	6.25	12.50	25.00

DANNY AND THE OTHER GUYS

Number	Title (A Side/B Side)	Yr	VG	VG+	NM
CP					
❑ (# unknown)	Hard Times/(B-side unknown)	196?	200.00	400.00	800.00

DANTE

Number	Title (A Side/B Side)	Yr	VG	VG+	NM
A&M					
❑ 788	Speedoo/Sweet Lover	1966	2.50	5.00	10.00
DARROW					
❑ 515	How Much I Care/Baby Baby	1960	10.00	20.00	40.00
DECCA					
❑ 31178	If You Don't Know/Leave Your Tears Behind You	1960	3.75	7.50	15.00
❑ 31268	Bye Bye Baby/That's Why	1961	3.75	7.50	15.00
❑ 31319	Ring or Write or Call/Say It to Me	1961	3.75	7.50	15.00
IMPERIAL					
❑ 5798	Something Happens/Are You Just My Friend	1961	3.75	7.50	15.00
❑ 5827	Miss America/Now I've Got You	1962	3.75	7.50	15.00

Number	Title (A Side/B Side)	Yr	VG	VG+	NM
❑ 5867	Magic Ring/Am I the One	1962	3.75	7.50	15.00
—Imperial titles as "Dante and His Friends"					
MADISON					
❑ 130	Alley Oop/The Right Time	1960	5.00	10.00	20.00
—As "Dante and the Evergreens"					
❑ 135	Time Machine/Dream Land	1960	3.75	7.50	15.00
❑ 143	What Are You Doing New Year's Eve/Yeah Baby	1960	3.75	7.50	15.00
—As "Dante and the Evergreens"					
❑ 154	Think Sweet Thoughts/Da Doo	1961	3.75	7.50	15.00
MERCURY					
❑ 71621	How Much I Care/Baby Baby	1960	5.00	10.00	20.00
TIDE					
❑ 003	My Lament/Aching Heart	1960	5.00	10.00	20.00

DANTE, RON

Also see THE ARCHIES; THE CUFF LINKS (1); THE DETERGENTS.

Number	Title (A Side/B Side)	Yr	VG	VG+	NM
ALMONT					
❑ 307	Little Lollypop/Funny	1963	3.75	7.50	15.00
BELL					
❑ 45460	Christine/Don't Call It Love	1974	—	2.50	5.00
—As "Bo Cooper"					
❑ 45610	Charmer/Yesterday Dreamin'	1974	—	2.00	4.00
❑ 45619	Midnight Show/The Christian	1974	—	2.00	4.00
COLUMBIA					
❑ 43720	Think/221 East Maple	1966	2.50	5.00	10.00
❑ 43862	I Give You Things/Janie, Janie	1966	2.50	5.00	10.00
DOT					
❑ 17023	Absence of Lisa/Gypsy Be Mine	1967	2.50	5.00	10.00
HANDSHAKE					
❑ 02107	Show and Tell/God Bless Rock and Roll	1981	—	2.00	4.00
❑ 02552	Letter from Zowie/God Bless Rock and Roll	1981	—	2.00	4.00
INFINITY					
❑ 50008	Ain't Misbehavin' (One Never Knows, Do One?)/'Round About Midnight	1979	—	2.50	5.00
❑ 50018	Fire Island/They're Playing Our Song	1979	—	2.50	5.00
❑ 50038	Brand New Key/They're Playing Our Song	1979	—	2.50	5.00
—Infinity sides as "Dante's Inferno"					
KIRSHNER					
❑ 63-1010	How Do You Know/Let Me Bring You Up	1970	—	3.00	6.00
❑ 63-1010 [PS]	How Do You Know/Let Me Bring You Up	1970	2.50	5.00	10.00
❑ 63-5007	Sweet Taste of Love/C'mon Girl	1970	—	3.00	6.00
MERCURY					
❑ 72812	Follow a Dream/He's Raining in My Sunshine	1968	2.50	5.00	10.00
MUSIC VOICE					
❑ 503	If You Love Me, Laurie/Don't Stand Up in a Canoe	1964	3.75	7.50	15.00
MUSICOR					
❑ 1058	Look at Me/There's Love	1965	3.00	6.00	12.00
❑ 1090	In the Rain/Poor Boys	1965	3.00	6.00	12.00
❑ 1105	If You Love Me, Laurie/Don't Stand Up in a Canoe	1965	3.00	6.00	12.00
❑ 1134	Hey Mom, Hey Pop/(Heart) Stop Calling Her Name	1965	3.00	6.00	12.00
RCA					
❑ PB-10898	How Am I to Know/Sky Rider	1977	—	2.00	4.00
RCA VICTOR					
❑ PB-10340	Sugar, Sugar/Sugar, Sugar (Disco)	1975	—	2.50	5.00
SCEPTER					
❑ 12333 [DJ]	That's What Life Is All About (mono/stereo)	1971	—	3.00	6.00
—Stock copy may not exist					

DANZIG, GLENN

Also see THE MISFITS; SAMHAIN.

Number	Title (A Side/B Side)	Yr	VG	VG+	NM
PLAN 9					
❑ PL 1015	Who Killed Marilyn?/Spook City USA	1981	16.25	32.50	65.00
—Black vinyl (5,000 made)					
❑ PL 1015	Who Killed Marilyn?/Spook City USA	1981	33.75	67.50	135.00
—Purple vinyl (500 made)					
❑ PL 1015	Who Killed Marilyn?/Spook City USA	1981	125.00	250.00	500.00
—Black and purple swirl vinyl (25 made); value is conjecture					
❑ PL 1015 [PS]	Who Killed Marilyn?/Spook City USA	1981	16.25	32.50	65.00

DAPPERS, THE

Probably more than one group.

Number	Title (A Side/B Side)	Yr	VG	VG+	NM
EPIC					
❑ 9423	My Love Is Real/Baby You Know You're Wrong	1960	6.25	12.50	25.00
FOXIE					
❑ 7005	Chicken Twist/Lonely Street	1961	10.00	20.00	40.00
GROOVE					
❑ 0156	Unwanted Love/That's All, That's All, That's All	1956	50.00	100.00	200.00
PEACOCK					
❑ 1651	Come Back to Me/Mambo Oongh	1955	37.50	75.00	150.00
RAINBOW					
❑ 373	Bop Bop Bu/How I Need You Baby	1956	10.00	20.00	40.00
STAR-X					
❑ 505	We're in Love/Spellbound	1958	62.50	125.00	250.00

DAPPERS QUINTET, THE

Number	Title (A Side/B Side)	Yr	VG	VG+	NM
FLAYR					
❑ 500	Look What I've Found/(B-side unknown)	1955	500.00	1000.	1500.

DAPS, THE

Number	Title (A Side/B Side)	Yr	VG	VG+	NM
MARTERRY					
❑ 5429	When You're Alone/Down and Out	1956	15.00	30.00	60.00

DARIN, BOBBY

Number	Title (A Side/B Side)	Yr	VG	VG+	NM
ATCO					
❑ 6092	Million Dollar Baby/Talk to Me	1957	7.50	15.00	30.00
❑ 6103	Don't Call My Name/Pretty Betty	1957	7.50	15.00	30.00
❑ 6109	Just in Case You Change Your Mind/So Mean	1958	7.50	15.00	30.00
❑ 6117	Splish Splash/Judy, Don't Be Moody	1958	5.00	10.00	20.00
❑ 6121	Early in the Morning/Now We're One	1958	5.00	10.00	20.00
❑ 6121	Early in the Morning/Now We're One	1958	10.00	20.00	40.00
—As "The Rinky Dinks"					
❑ 6127	Queen of the Hop/Lost Love	1958	5.00	10.00	20.00
❑ 6128	Mighty Mighty Man/You're Gone	1958	5.00	10.00	20.00
❑ 6128	Mighty Mighty Man/You're Gone	1958	10.00	20.00	40.00
—As "The Rinky Dinks"					
❑ 6133 [M]	Plain Jane/While I'm Gone	1959	5.00	10.00	20.00
❑ 6133 [PS]	Plain Jane/While I'm Gone	1959	12.50	25.00	50.00
❑ SD-45-6133 [S]	Plain Jane/While I'm Gone	1959	10.00	20.00	40.00
❑ 6140	Dream Lover/Bullmoose	1959	5.00	10.00	20.00
❑ 6140 [PS]	Dream Lover/Bullmoose	1959	12.50	25.00	50.00
❑ 6147	Mack the Knife/Was There a Call for Me	1959	5.00	10.00	20.00
❑ 6147 [PS]	Mack the Knife/Was There a Call for Me	1959	10.00	20.00	40.00
❑ 6158	Beyond the Sea/That's the Way Love Is	1960	5.00	10.00	20.00
❑ 6158 [PS]	Beyond the Sea/That's the Way Love Is	1960	10.00	20.00	40.00
❑ 6161	Clementine/Tall Story	1960	5.00	10.00	20.00
❑ 6161 [PS]	Clementine/Tall Story	1960	10.00	20.00	40.00
❑ 6167	Won't You Come Home Bill Bailey/I'll Be There	1960	5.00	10.00	20.00
❑ 6167 [PS]	Won't You Come Home Bill Bailey/I'll Be There	1960	7.50	15.00	30.00
❑ 6173	Beachcomber/Autumn Blues	1960	5.00	10.00	20.00
❑ 6173 [PS]	Beachcomber/Autumn Blues	1960	7.50	15.00	30.00
❑ 6179	Artificial Flowers/Somebody to Love	1960	5.00	10.00	20.00
❑ 6179 [PS]	Artificial Flowers/Somebody to Love	1960	7.50	15.00	30.00
❑ 6183	Christmas Auld Lang Syne/Child of God	1960	6.25	12.50	25.00
❑ 6183 [PS]	Christmas Auld Lang Syne/Child of God	1960	10.00	20.00	40.00
❑ 6188	Lazy River/Oo-Ee Train	1961	3.00	6.00	12.00
❑ 6188 [PS]	Lazy River/Oo-Ee Train	1961	5.00	10.00	20.00
❑ 6196	Nature Boy/Look for My True Love	1961	3.00	6.00	12.00
❑ 6196 [PS]	Nature Boy/Look for My True Love	1961	5.00	10.00	20.00
❑ 6200	Come September/Walk Back to Me	1961	3.75	7.50	15.00
❑ 6200 [PS]	Come September/Walk Back to Me	1961	12.50	25.00	50.00
❑ 6206	You Must Have Been a Beautiful Baby/Sorrow Tomorrow	1961	3.00	6.00	12.00
❑ 6206 [PS]	You Must Have Been a Beautiful Baby/Sorrow Tomorrow	1961	5.00	10.00	20.00
❑ 6211	Ave Maria/O Come All Ye Faithful	1961	3.00	6.00	12.00
❑ 6211 [PS]	Ave Maria/O Come All Ye Faithful	1961	40.00	80.00	160.00
❑ 6214	Irresistible You/Multiplication	1961	3.00	6.00	12.00
❑ 6214 [PS]	Irresistible You/Multiplication	1961	5.00	10.00	20.00
❑ 6221	What'd I Say (Part 1)/What'd I Say (Part 2)	1962	3.00	6.00	12.00
❑ 6221 [PS]	What'd I Say (Part 1)/What'd I Say (Part 2)	1962	5.00	10.00	20.00
❑ 6229	Things/Jalier Bring Me Water	1962	3.00	6.00	12.00
❑ 6236	Baby Face/You Know How	1962	3.00	6.00	12.00
❑ 6244	I Found a New Baby/Keep a-Walkin'	1962	3.00	6.00	12.00
❑ 6297	Milord/Golden Earrings	1964	2.50	5.00	10.00
❑ 6316	Swing Low Sweet Chariot/Similau	1964	2.50	5.00	10.00
❑ 6334	Minnie the Moocher/Hard Hearted Hannah	1965	2.50	5.00	10.00
❑ (no #) [DJ]	She's Tanfastic!/Moments of Love	1960	10.00	20.00	40.00
—Ferrion Inc. "Special Premium Record"					
ATLANTIC					
❑ 2305	Funny What Love Can Do/We Didn't Ask to Be Brought Here	1965	2.00	4.00	8.00
❑ 2317	Silver Dollar/The Breaking Point	1966	2.00	4.00	8.00
❑ 2329	Mame/Walking in the Shadow of Love	1966	2.00	4.00	8.00
❑ 2341	Who's Afraid of Virginia Woolf?/Merci, Cheri	1966	2.00	4.00	8.00
❑ 2350	If I Were a Carpenter/Rainin'	1966	2.50	5.00	10.00
❑ 2367	The Girl That Stood Beside Me/Reason to Believe	1966	2.00	4.00	8.00
❑ 2376	Lovin' You/Amy	1967	2.00	4.00	8.00
❑ 2395	The Lady Came from Baltimore/I Am	1967	2.00	4.00	8.00
❑ 2420	Darlin' Be Home Soon/Hello, Sunshine	1967	2.00	4.00	8.00
❑ 2433	Talk to the Animals/After Today	1967	2.00	4.00	8.00
❑ 2433	Talk to the Animals/She Knows	1967	2.00	4.00	8.00
❑ 89166	Beyond the Sea/Mack the Knife	1987	—	—	3.00
❑ 89166 [PS]	Beyond the Sea/Mack the Knife	1987	—	—	3.00
—From the movie "Big Town"					
BRUNSWICK					
❑ 55073	Early in the Morning/Now We're One	1958	20.00	40.00	80.00
—As "The Ding Dongs"; also see Atco 6121					
CAPITOL					
❑ 4837	If a Man Answers/True, True Love	1962	2.50	5.00	10.00
❑ 4837 [PS]	If a Man Answers/True, True Love	1962	3.75	7.50	15.00
❑ 4897	You're the Reason I'm Living/Now You're Gone	1962	2.50	5.00	10.00
❑ 4897 [PS]	You're the Reason I'm Living/Now You're Gone	1962	3.75	7.50	15.00
❑ 4970	18 Yellow Roses/Not for Me	1963	2.50	5.00	10.00
❑ 4970 [PS]	18 Yellow Roses/Not for Me	1963	3.75	7.50	15.00
❑ 5019	Treat My Baby Good/Down So Long	1963	2.50	5.00	10.00
❑ 5079	Be Mad Little Girl/Since You've Been Gone	1963	2.50	5.00	10.00
❑ 5126	I Wonder Who's Kissing Her Now/As Long As I'm Singing	1964	2.50	5.00	10.00
❑ 5257	The Things in This House/Wait by the Water	1964	2.50	5.00	10.00
❑ 5359	Hello, Dolly!/Golden Earrings	1965	2.50	5.00	10.00
❑ 5399	A World Without You/Venice Blue	1965	2.50	5.00	10.00
❑ 5443	When I Get Home/Lonely Road	1965	2.50	5.00	10.00
❑ 5443 [PS]	When I Get Home/Lonely Road	1965	6.25	12.50	25.00
❑ 5481	Gyp the Cat/That Funny Feeling	1965	2.50	5.00	10.00
DECCA					
❑ 29883	Rock Island Line/Timber	1956	10.00	20.00	40.00
❑ 29922	Silly Willy/Blue Eyed Mermaid	1956	12.50	25.00	50.00
❑ 30031	The Greatest Builder (Of Them All)/Hear Them Bells	1956	10.00	20.00	40.00
❑ 30225	Dealer in Dreams/Help Me	1957	10.00	20.00	40.00
❑ 30737	Silly Willy/Dealer in Dreams	1958	7.50	15.00	30.00
DIRECTION					
❑ 350	Long Line Rider/Change	1968	2.00	4.00	8.00
❑ 351	Song for a Dollar/Mr. and Mrs. Hohner	1969	2.00	4.00	8.00
❑ 352	Distractions (Part 1)/Jive	1969	2.00	4.00	8.00
❑ 4000	Sugar Man/(9 to 5) Jive's Alive	1970	2.00	4.00	8.00
❑ 4001	Baby May/Sweet Reason	1970	2.00	4.00	8.00
❑ 4002	Maybe We Can Get It Together/Rx Pyro (Prescription: Fire)	1970	2.00	4.00	8.00

Number	Title (A Side/B Side)	Yr	VG	VG+	NM
MOTOWN					
❑ 1183	Melodie/Someday We'll Be Together	1971	—	3.00	6.00
❑ 1193	Simple Song of Freedom/I'll Be Your Baby Tonight	1971	—	3.00	6.00
❑ 1203	Sail Away/Something in Her Love	1972	—	3.00	6.00
❑ 1212	Average People/Something in Her Love	1972	—	3.00	6.00
❑ 1217	Happy/Something in Her Love	1973	—	3.00	6.00
7-Inch Extended Plays					
ATCO					
❑ 4502	*Splish Splash/Judy, Don't Be Moody/I Found a Million Dollar Baby/(Since You're Gone) I Can't Go On	1959	12.50	25.00	50.00
❑ 4502 [PS]	Bobby Darin	1959	12.50	25.00	50.00
❑ 4504	Mack the Knife/That's the Way Love Is//Beyond the Sea/That's All	1959	12.50	25.00	50.00
❑ 4504 [PS]	That's All	1959	12.50	25.00	50.00
❑ 4505	Queen of the Hop/Lost Love//Plain Jane/While I'm Gone	1960	12.50	25.00	50.00
❑ 4505 [PS]	Bobby Darin	1960	12.50	25.00	50.00
❑ 4508	Clementine/My Gal Sal//Guys and Dolls/Down with Love	1960	12.50	25.00	50.00
❑ 4508 [PS]	This Is Darin	1960	12.50	25.00	50.00
❑ 4512	I Got A Woman/You'd Be So Nice To Come Home To//Medley: By Myself-When Your Lover Has Gone/Love For Sale	1960	12.50	25.00	50.00
❑ 4512 [PS]	Darin at the Copa	1960	12.50	25.00	50.00
❑ EP 4513-D	Hush, Somebody's Calling My Name/Keep a-Walkin'//I Want You With Me/You Know How	1960	17.50	35.00	70.00
❑ EP 4513-D [PS]	For Teenagers Only	1960	17.50	35.00	70.00
—Special promotional sleeve; has photo of LP 1001					
CAPITOL CUSTOM					
❑ TB-2262/3	18 Yellow Roses/Not for Me/The Things in This House//You're the Reason I'm Living/Treat My Baby Good/Wait by the Water, Lillian	1963	7.50	15.00	30.00
—Small hole, plays at 33 1/3 rpm					
❑ TB-2262/3 [PS]	Bobby Darin Presents	1963	10.00	20.00	40.00
—"Manufactured by Capitol Records, Inc., Custom Services Department for Artistic Records"					
❑ MB-2849/50	If a Man Answers/True, True Love//Sermon of Samson/All By Myself	1962	5.00	10.00	20.00
❑ MB-2849/50 [PS]	Scripto Inc. Presents Bobby Darin	1962	7.50	15.00	30.00
—Value is for sleeve alone; the pen that came with the package is very rare					
DECCA					
❑ ED 2676	(contents unknown)	1957	25.00	50.00	100.00
❑ ED 2676 [PS]	Hear Them Bells	1957	25.00	50.00	100.00
MOTOWN					
❑ PR-4 [DJ]	If I Were a Carpenter/Moritat (Mack the Knife)//Blue Monday/Happy	1973	3.75	7.50	15.00
❑ PR-4 [PS]	(title unknown)	1973	5.00	10.00	20.00

DARLING, JOHNNY

Number	Title (A Side/B Side)	Yr	VG	VG+	NM
DELUXE					
❑ 6167	I Don't Want to Wind Up in Love/Baseball Baby	1956	37.50	75.00	150.00

DARNELL, LARRY

Number	Title (A Side/B Side)	Yr	VG	VG+	NM
ANNA					
❑ 1109	With Tears in My Eyes/I'll Get Along Somehow	1960	100.00	200.00	400.00
ARGO					
❑ 5372	With Tears in My Eyes/I'll Get Along Somehow	1960	6.25	12.50	25.00
DELUXE					
❑ 6123	Ramblin' Man/I Care	1957	7.50	15.00	30.00
❑ 6136	If You Go/Fing Fang Foy	1957	7.50	15.00	30.00
❑ 6141	Just Tell Me When/It Must Be Love	1957	7.50	15.00	30.00
OKEH					
❑ 6848	Work Baby Work/Left My Baby	1952	6.25	12.50	25.00
❑ 6869	Darlin'/Boogie-Oogie	1952	6.25	12.50	25.00
❑ 6902	What's On Your Mind/Better Be on My Way	1952	6.25	12.50	25.00
❑ 6916	No Time at All/Singin' My Blues	1952	6.25	12.50	25.00
❑ 6919	I'll Get Along Somehow (Part 1)/I'll Get Along Somehow (Part 2)	1952	6.25	12.50	25.00
❑ 6926	Christmas Blues/I Am the Sparrow	1952	6.25	12.50	25.00
❑ 6954	I'll Be Sittin', I'll Be Rockin'/Crazy She Calls Me	1953	6.25	12.50	25.00
❑ 7024	I'll Carry On/What More Do You Want Me to Do	1954	5.00	10.00	20.00
❑ 7039	I'm Gonna Change/Thank You, Darlin'	1954	5.00	10.00	20.00
❑ 7056	My Love for You/Feelin' Mighty Sad and Low	1955	5.00	10.00	20.00
REGAL					
❑ 3328	Do You Love Me Baby/Sad and Lonesome	1951	6.25	12.50	25.00
—Larry Darnell records on Regal before 3328 are unconfirmed on 45 rpm					
SAVOY					
❑ 1151	That's All I Want from You/Who Showed My Baby How to Love Me	1955	7.50	15.00	30.00
WARWICK					
❑ 506	If I Had You/Thankful	1959	5.00	10.00	20.00
7-Inch Extended Plays					
EPIC					
❑ 7072	(contents unknown)	1961	5.00	10.00	20.00
❑ 7072 [PS]	For You My Love	1961	5.00	10.00	20.00

DARNELLS, THE

See THE MARVELETTES.

DARRELL AND THE OXFORDS

See THE TOKENS.

DARREN, JAMES

Number	Title (A Side/B Side)	Yr	VG	VG+	NM
BUDDAH					
❑ 177	That's My World/Wheeling, West Virginia	1970	—	2.50	5.00
COLPIX					
❑ 102	There's No Such Thing/Mighty Pretty Territory	1959	3.75	7.50	15.00
❑ 102 [PS]	There's No Such Thing/Mighty Pretty Territory	1959	7.50	15.00	30.00
❑ 113	Gidget/You	1959	3.75	7.50	15.00
❑ 119 [M]	Angel Face/I Don't Wanna Lose Ya	1959	3.75	7.50	15.00
❑ 119 [PS]	Angel Face/I Don't Wanna Lose Ya	1959	7.50	15.00	30.00
❑ SCP-119 [S]	Angel Face/I Don't Wanna Lose Ya	1959	10.00	20.00	40.00
❑ 128	I Ain't Sharin' Sharon/Love Among the Young	1959	3.75	7.50	15.00
❑ 130	Teenage Tears/Let There Be Love	1959	3.75	7.50	15.00
❑ 138	You Are My Dream/Your Smile	1960	3.75	7.50	15.00
❑ 142	Because They're Young/Tears in My Eyes	1960	3.75	7.50	15.00
❑ 142 [PS]	Because They're Young/Tears in My Eyes	1960	7.50	15.00	30.00
❑ 145	P.S. I Love You/Traveling Down a Lonesome Road	1960	3.75	7.50	15.00
❑ 155	How Sweet You Are/All the Young Men	1960	3.75	7.50	15.00
❑ 168	Man About Town/Come On My Love	1960	3.75	7.50	15.00
❑ 181	Walking My Baby Back Home/Goodbye My Lady	1960	3.75	7.50	15.00
—Colpix 102-181 by "Jimmy Darren"					
❑ 185	Fool's Paradise/Gotta Have Love	1961	3.75	7.50	15.00
❑ 189	Gidget Goes Hawaiian/Wild About the Girl	1961	3.75	7.50	15.00
❑ 194	Hand in Hand/You Are My Dream	1961	3.75	7.50	15.00
❑ 609	Goodbye Cruel World/Valerie	1961	3.75	7.50	15.00
❑ 609 [PS]	Goodbye Cruel World/Valerie	1961	6.25	12.50	25.00
❑ 622	Her Royal Majesty/If I Could Only Tell You	1962	3.00	6.00	12.00
❑ 630	Conscience/Dream Big	1962	3.00	6.00	12.00
❑ 644	Mary's Little Lamb/The Life of the Party	1962	3.00	6.00	12.00
❑ 655	Hail to the Conquering Hero/Too Young to Go Steady	1962	3.00	6.00	12.00
❑ 664	Hear What I Want to Hear/I'll Be Loving You	1962	3.00	6.00	12.00
❑ 672	Pin a Medal on Joey/Diamond Head	1963	3.00	6.00	12.00
❑ 685	They Should Have Given You the Oscar/Blame It on My Youth	1963	3.00	6.00	12.00
❑ 696	Gegetta/Grande Luna, Italiana	1963	3.00	6.00	12.00
❑ 708	Under the Yum Yum Tree/Backstage	1963	3.00	6.00	12.00
❑ 758	Punch and Judy/Just Think of Tonight	1964	5.00	10.00	20.00
❑ 765	A Married Man/Baby, Talk to Me	1964	2.50	5.00	10.00
KIRSHNER					
❑ 63-1012	I Think Somebody Loves Me/Ain't Been Home in a Long Time	1970	—	2.50	5.00
❑ 63-5013	Bring Me Down Slow/More and More	1971	—	2.50	5.00
❑ 63-5015	Mammy Blue/As Long As You Love Me	1971	—	2.50	5.00
❑ 63-5025	Brian's Song/Thnak Heaven for Little Girls	1973	—	2.50	5.00
MGM					
❑ 14558	Let the Heartaches Begin/Sad Song	1973	—	2.00	4.00
❑ 14667	Sad-Eyed Romany Woman/Stay	1973	—	2.00	4.00
PRIVATE STOCK					
❑ 45050	Love on the Screen/Losing You	1975	—	2.00	4.00
❑ 45064	One Has My Name, The Other Has My Heart/Sleepin' in a Bed of Lies	1975	—	2.00	4.00
❑ 45136	You Take My Heart Away/You Take My Heart Away (Disco)	1977	—	2.00	4.00
❑ 45152 [DJ]	Only a Dream Away (mono/stereo)	1977	—	2.50	5.00
—Stock copies may not exist					
RCA					
❑ PB-11316	Let Me Take You in My Arms Again/California	1978	—	2.00	4.00
❑ PB-11419	Next Time/Something Like Nothing Before	1978	—	2.00	4.00
WARNER BROS.					
❑ 5648	Because You're Mine/Millions of Roses	1965	2.00	4.00	8.00
❑ 5689	I Want to Be Lonely/Tom Hawk	1966	2.00	4.00	8.00
❑ 5812	Where Did We Go Wrong/Counting the Cracks	1966	2.00	4.00	8.00
❑ 5838	Crazy Me/They Don't Know	1966	2.00	4.00	8.00
❑ 5856	Love Is Where You Find It/(Let's Worry About) Tomorrow Tomorrow	1966	2.00	4.00	8.00
❑ 5874	All/Misty Morning Eyes	1966	2.00	4.00	8.00
❑ 7013	I Miss You So/Since I Don't Have You	1967	2.00	4.00	8.00
❑ 7053	Didn't We/Counting the Cracks	1967	2.00	4.00	8.00
❑ 7071	The House Song/They Don't Know	1967	2.00	4.00	8.00
❑ 7152	Cherie/Wait Until Dark	1967	2.00	4.00	8.00
❑ 7206	A Little Bit of Heaven/Each and Every Part of Me	1968	2.00	4.00	8.00

DARTELLS, THE

Number	Title (A Side/B Side)	Yr	VG	VG+	NM
ARLEN					
❑ 509	Hot Pastrami/Dartell Stomp	1963	6.25	12.50	25.00
❑ 513	Dance, Everybody, Dance/The Scoobie Song	1963	6.25	12.50	25.00
DOT					
❑ 16453	Hot Pastrami/Dartell Stomp	1963	5.00	10.00	20.00
❑ 16502	Dance, Everybody, Dance/The Scoobie Song	1963	5.00	10.00	20.00
❑ 16551	Convicted/Sweet Pea	1963	3.75	7.50	15.00
❑ 16646	Swiss Cheese/Dartell Stomp	1964	3.75	7.50	15.00
HANNA-BARBERA					
❑ 457	Clap Your Hands/Where Do We Stand	1965	3.75	7.50	15.00
SANDE					
❑ 103	The Girl Can't Help It/Stranger on the Shore	1964	7.50	15.00	30.00

DARVELL, BARRY

Number	Title (A Side/B Side)	Yr	VG	VG+	NM
ATLANTIC					
❑ 2128	Lost Love/Silver Dollar	1961	5.00	10.00	20.00
❑ 2138	Adam and Eve/A King for Tonight	1962	5.00	10.00	20.00
COLT 45					
❑ 104	Teenage Love/(B-side unknown)	1959	5.00	10.00	20.00
❑ 107	Geronimo Stomp/How Will It End	1959	15.00	30.00	60.00
❑ 110	Butterfly Baby/Send Me Some Loving	1960	6.25	12.50	25.00
❑ 301	Run Little Billy/All I Need Is You	1961	5.00	10.00	20.00
COLUMBIA					
❑ 44197	My World of Make Believe/Beggar's Paradise	1967	2.00	4.00	8.00
CUB					
❑ 9088	Little Angel Lost/Fountain of Love	1961	5.00	10.00	20.00
PROVIDENCE					
❑ 404	When You're Alone/It's Rainin', It's Pourin'	1964	3.00	6.00	12.00
WORLD ARTISTS					
❑ 1042	I'll Remember/Where Is the Love for Me	1965	3.00	6.00	12.00
❑ 1058	I Found a Daisy (in the City)/Kissable Lips	1965	3.00	6.00	12.00

DATE WITH SOUL, A
See HALE AND THE HUSHABYES.

DAVE AND THE CARDIGANS

Number	Title (A Side/B Side)	Yr	VG	VG+	NM
BAY					
❑ 216	My Falling Star/Cha Cha Baby	1963	50.00	100.00	200.00

DAVE AND THE MARKSMEN
With Dave Marks, former member of THE BEACH BOYS.

Number	Title (A Side/B Side)	Yr	VG	VG+	NM
A&M					
❑ 730	Cruisin'/Kustom Kar Show	1964	12.50	25.00	50.00
WARNER BROS.					
❑ 5485	I Wanna Cry/I Could Make You Mine	1964	7.50	15.00	30.00
WESTCO					
❑ 10	Down the Tubes/Ooh Poo Pa Doo	1963	12.50	25.00	50.00
—Black vinyl					
❑ 10	Down the Tubes/Ooh Poo Pa Doo	1963	25.00	50.00	100.00
—Yellow vinyl					

DAVE DEE, DOZY, BEAKY, MICK & TICH

Number	Title (A Side/B Side)	Yr	VG	VG+	NM
ATLANTIC					
❑ 89757 [DJ]	Staying With It (same on both sides)	1983	—	2.50	5.00
—May be promo only					
BELL					
❑ 905	Kelly/Annabella	1970	—	3.00	6.00
—As "Dave Dee"					
❑ 942	Frisco Annie/Hey! Mr. President	1970	—	3.00	6.00
—As "D.B.M. & T."					
COTILLION					
❑ 44061	Bad News/Tonight-Today	1970	—	3.00	6.00
—As "Dozy, Beaky, Mick & Tich"					
❑ 44061 [PS]	Bad News/Tonight-Today	1970	2.50	5.00	10.00
—As "Dozy, Beaky, Mick & Tich"					
FONTANA					
❑ 1537	You Make It Move/No Time	1965	2.50	5.00	10.00
❑ 1545	Hold Tight/You Know What I Want	1966	2.50	5.00	10.00
❑ 1553	Hideaway/Here's a Heart	1966	2.50	5.00	10.00
❑ 1559	Bend It/She's So Good	1966	3.00	6.00	12.00
—With "clean" lyrics that refer to a dance; matrix number of "Bend It" is 38890					
❑ 1559	Bend It/She's So Good	1966	3.00	6.00	12.00
—With "dirty" lyrics that don't mention a dance; matrix number of "Bend It" is 39024					
❑ 1569	Save Me/Shame	1967	2.50	5.00	10.00
❑ 1591	Okay/Master Llewellyn	1967	2.50	5.00	10.00
IMPERIAL					
❑ 66270	Zabadak/The Sun Goes Down	1968	2.50	5.00	10.00
❑ 66287	Legend of Xanadu/Please	1968	2.00	4.00	8.00
❑ 66309	Break Out/Mrs. Thursday	1968	2.00	4.00	8.00
❑ 66325	Break Out/Mrs. Thursday	1968	2.00	4.00	8.00
❑ 66339	Wreck of the Antoinette/Margarita Linman	1968	2.00	4.00	8.00

DAVENPORT SISTERS, THE

Number	Title (A Side/B Side)	Yr	VG	VG+	NM
TRI-PHI					
❑ 1008	You've Got Me Crying Again/Hoy Hoy	1962	15.00	30.00	60.00

DAVI

Number	Title (A Side/B Side)	Yr	VG	VG+	NM
SPARK					
❑ 110	Reason for Love/Go, Charley, Go	1962	75.00	150.00	300.00

DAVID, THE

Number	Title (A Side/B Side)	Yr	VG	VG+	NM
20TH CENTURY FOX					
❑ 6663	40 Miles/Bus Token	1966	7.50	15.00	30.00
V.M.C.					
❑ 716	I'm Not Alone/(B-side unknown)	1968	6.25	12.50	25.00

DAVID AND JONATHAN

Number	Title (A Side/B Side)	Yr	VG	VG+	NM
20TH FOX					
❑ 6641	Modesty/Willie Waltz	1966	2.00	4.00	8.00
AMY					
❑ 11012	Softly Whispering I Love You/Something's Gotten Hold of My Heart	1968	—	3.00	6.00
CAPITOL					
❑ 5563	Michelle/How Bitter the Taste of Love	1965	2.50	5.00	10.00
❑ 5625	I Know/Speak Her Name	1966	2.00	4.00	8.00
❑ 5700	On My Word/Lovers of the World, Unite	1966	2.00	4.00	8.00
❑ 5777	The Magic Book/Time	1966	2.00	4.00	8.00
❑ 5870	Ten Stories High/Looking for My Life	1967	2.00	4.00	8.00
❑ 5934	She's Leaving Home/One Born Every Minute	1967	2.00	4.00	8.00

DAVIES, CYRIL

Number	Title (A Side/B Side)	Yr	VG	VG+	NM
DOT					
❑ 16515	Chicago Calling/Country Line Special	1963	3.00	6.00	12.00

DAVIES, DAVE
Also see THE KINKS.

Number	Title (A Side/B Side)	Yr	VG	VG+	NM
RCA					
❑ PB-12089	Imagination's Real/Wild Man	1980	2.50	5.00	10.00
❑ PB-12089 [PS]	Imagination's Real/Wild Man	1980	3.75	7.50	15.00
❑ PB-12147	Doing the Best for You/Got No More to Lose	1981	2.50	5.00	10.00
REPRISE					
❑ 0614	Death of a Clown/Love Me Till the Sun Shines	1967	10.00	20.00	40.00
❑ 0660	Suzannah's Still Alive/Funny Face	1968	10.00	20.00	40.00
WARNER BROS.					
❑ 29425	Mean Disposition/Cold Winter	1983	—	—	—
—Unreleased?					
❑ 29425 [DJ]	Mean Disposition (same on both sides)	1983	2.50	5.00	10.00
❑ 29509	Love Gets You/One Night with You	1983	12.50	25.00	50.00
❑ 29509 [DJ]	Love Gets You (same on both sides)	1983	2.50	5.00	10.00

DAVIS, AL

Number	Title (A Side/B Side)	Yr	VG	VG+	NM
MANCO					
❑ 1052	Ricky Tic/Time	196?	10.00	20.00	40.00
❑ 1067	Go Baby Go/Camy	196?	75.00	150.00	300.00

DAVIS, ANDREA
See MINNIE RIPERTON.

DAVIS, BO

Number	Title (A Side/B Side)	Yr	VG	VG+	NM
CREST					
❑ 1027	Let's Coast Awhile/Drownin' All My Sorrows	1956	37.50	75.00	150.00
—Eddie Cochran plays guitar on this record.					

DAVIS, EUNICE

Number	Title (A Side/B Side)	Yr	VG	VG+	NM
ATLANTIC					
❑ 992	Go to Work Pretty Daddy/My Beat Is 125th Street	1953	15.00	30.00	60.00
CORAL					
❑ 65075	Work Daddy Work/What Do You Want	1952	5.00	10.00	20.00
DELUXE					
❑ 6068	Get Your Enjoys/24 Hours a Day	1954	7.50	15.00	30.00
DERBY					
❑ 760	Evening Train/I'm a Wild West Woman	1951	7.50	15.00	30.00
❑ 768	Good News for You Baby/Tell Me I'm the Baby	1951	7.50	15.00	30.00
GRAND					
❑ 130	Let's Have a Party/Every Time Your Lips Meet Mine	1955	5.00	10.00	20.00

DAVIS, HAL

Number	Title (A Side/B Side)	Yr	VG	VG+	NM
ALDEN					
❑ 1301	My Young Heart/(B-side unknown)	1959	10.00	20.00	40.00
❑ 1303	King of Lovers/(B-side unknown)	1959	10.00	20.00	40.00
DEL-FI					
❑ 4146	You're Playing with Me/Read the Book of Love	1960	7.50	15.00	30.00
DYNAMITE					
❑ 1010	I Don't Want Nobody/(B-side unknown)	195?	50.00	100.00	200.00
FEDERAL					
❑ 12429	My Only Flower/You're the Girl	1961	3.00	6.00	12.00
GARDENA					
❑ 125	One More Chance/Show Me	1962	7.50	15.00	30.00
GSP					
❑ 2	I Don't Know/(B-side unknown)	1963	7.50	15.00	30.00
KELLEY					
❑ 105	Way to My Heart/(B-side unknown)	196?	25.00	50.00	100.00
—Red vinyl					
MINASA					
❑ 6714	It's You/(B-side unknown)	196?	7.50	15.00	30.00
MJC					
❑ 104	You'll Find Love/(B-side unknown)	196?	7.50	15.00	30.00
VEE JAY					
❑ 387	Merchant of Love/What Do You Mean to Me	1961	5.00	10.00	20.00
WIZARD					
❑ 101	Merchant of Love/What Do You Mean to Me	1961	17.50	35.00	70.00
❑ 102	I Need Someone/(B-side unknown)	1961	7.50	15.00	30.00

DAVIS, LARRY

Number	Title (A Side/B Side)	Yr	VG	VG+	NM
DUKE					
❑ 192	I Tried/Texas Flood	1958	7.50	15.00	30.00
❑ 313	My Little Girl/Angels in Houston	1959	5.00	10.00	20.00
❑ 328	Come Home/Will She Come Home	1960	5.00	10.00	20.00
KENT					
❑ 507	Driving Wheel/Sweet Little Angel	1969	3.75	7.50	15.00

DAVIS, SAMMY, JR.

Number	Title (A Side/B Side)	Yr	VG	VG+	NM
20TH CENTURY					
❑ 2236	Snap Your Fingers/Song and Dance Man	1975	—	2.00	4.00
❑ 2282	Chico and the Man (Main Theme)/(I'd Be) A Legend in My Time	1976	—	2.50	5.00
—May be promo only					
❑ 2292	Baretta's Theme (Keep Your Eye on the Sparrow)/I Heard a Song	1976	—	2.00	4.00
APPLAUSE					
❑ 100	Smoke, Smoke, Smoke (That Cigarette)/We Could Have Been the Closest of Friends	1982	—	2.50	5.00
DDR					
❑ 101/2	Who Needs Spring/(B-side unknown)	197?	2.00	4.00	8.00
—Red vinyl					
DECCA					
❑ 29199	Hey There/And This Is My Beloved	1954	3.00	6.00	12.00
❑ 29200	Because of You (Part 1)/Because of You (Part 2)	1954	3.00	6.00	12.00
❑ 29310	Glad to Be Unhappy/Red Grapes	1954	3.00	6.00	12.00
❑ 29393	The Birth of the Blues/Love	1954	3.00	6.00	12.00
❑ 29402	All of You/Six Bridges to Cross	1955	3.00	6.00	12.00
❑ 29484	Love Me or Leave Me/Something's Gotta Give	1955	3.00	6.00	12.00
❑ 29541	That Old Black Magic/A Man with a Dream	1955	3.00	6.00	12.00
❑ 29620	I Go for You/A Fine Romance	1955	3.00	6.00	12.00
—With Carmen McRae					
❑ 29649	Back Track/It's Bigger Than You and Me	1955	3.00	6.00	12.00
❑ 29672	I'll Know/Adelaide	1955	3.00	6.00	12.00
❑ 29737	Ac-Cent-Tchu-Ate the Positive/Beat Me, Daddy, Eight to the Bar	1955	3.00	6.00	12.00
—With Gary Crosby					
❑ 29759	The Man with the Golden Arm/In a Persian Blanket	1955	3.00	6.00	12.00
❑ 29795	Frankie and Johnny/Circus	1956	3.00	6.00	12.00
❑ 29861	Too Close for Comfort/Jacques d'Iraque	1956	3.00	6.00	12.00
❑ 29929	Without You I'm Nothing/Get Out of the Car	1956	3.00	6.00	12.00
❑ 29976	Five/You're Sensational	1956	3.00	6.00	12.00
❑ 30035	Earthbound/Just One of Those Things	1956	3.00	6.00	12.00
❑ 30111	New York's My Home/Never Like This	1956	3.00	6.00	12.00
❑ 30158	All About Love/Dangerous	1956	3.00	6.00	12.00
❑ 30189	The Golden Key/Long Before I Knew You	1957	2.50	5.00	10.00
❑ 30300	Good Bye, So Long, I'm Gone/French Friend Potatoes and Ketchup	1957	2.50	5.00	10.00
❑ 30371	Doncha Go 'Way Mad/'Specially for Little Girls	1957	2.50	5.00	10.00
❑ 30400	Baby It's Cold Outside/Happy to Make Your Acquaintance	1957	2.50	5.00	10.00

Number	Title (A Side/B Side)	Yr	VG	VG+	NM
❑ 30441	Mad Ball/Cool Credo	1957	2.50	5.00	10.00
❑ 30479	All Dressed Up and No Place to Go/Moment of Madness	1957	2.50	5.00	10.00
❑ 30536	Hallelujah I Love Her So/I'm Comin' Home	1958	2.50	5.00	10.00
❑ 30611	No Fool Like an Old Fool/Unspoken	1958	2.50	5.00	10.00
❑ 30679	Song and Dance Man/I Ain't Gonna Change	1958	2.50	5.00	10.00
❑ 30769	That's Anna/I Never Got Out of Paris	1958	2.50	5.00	10.00
❑ 30898	Fair Warning/You'll Never Get Away from Me	1959	2.50	5.00	10.00
❑ 30915	I Got Plenty of Nothin'/There's a Boat Dat's Leaving Soon for New York	1959	2.50	5.00	10.00
❑ 31136	I Got a Woman/Mess Around	1960	2.50	5.00	10.00
❑ 31177	This Little Girl of Mine/Face to Face	1960	2.50	5.00	10.00
❑ 32470	Rhythm of Life/(B-side unknown)	1969	—	3.00	6.00
MGM					
❑ 14320	The Candy Man/I Want to Be Happy	1971	—	3.00	6.00
❑ 14426	Mr. Bojangles/The People Tree	1972	—	2.50	5.00
❑ 14513	(I'd Be) A Legend in My Time/I'm Not Anyone	1973	—	2.50	5.00
❑ 14685	Singin' in the Rain/Chattanooga Choo Choo	1973	—	2.50	5.00
❑ 14736	That's Entertainment/Singin' in the Rain	1974	—	2.00	4.00
❑ 14759	Sing/This Is the House of the People	1974	—	2.00	4.00
MOTOWN					
❑ 1738	Hello Detroit (Part 1)/Hello Detroit (Part 2)	1984	—	2.00	4.00
REPRISE					
❑ (no #) [DJ]	Here's a Kiss for Christmas (The Christmas Seal Song)/What Kind of Fool Am I	1963	3.75	7.50	15.00
❑ OE-DJ-2 [DJ]	Open End Disc Jockey Interview	196?	10.00	20.00	40.00
—Small hole, plays at 33 1/3 rpm					
❑ 0248	What Kind of Fool Am I/Gonna Buila a Mountain	1963	2.00	4.00	8.00
❑ 0278	Choose/Bee Bom	1964	2.00	4.00	8.00
❑ 0289	Not for Me/Night Song	1964	2.00	4.00	8.00
❑ 0321	Hello, Dolly!/Take the Moment	1964	3.75	7.50	15.00
—Possibly released only outside the U.S.					
❑ 0322	Don't Shut Me Out/Disorderly Orderly	1964	2.00	4.00	8.00
❑ 0345	If I Ruled the World/Flash, Bang, Wallop	1965	2.00	4.00	8.00
❑ 0361	Hello, Dolly!/Take the Moment	1965	2.00	4.00	8.00
❑ 0370	Unforgettable/No One Can Live Forever	1965	2.00	4.00	8.00
❑ 0399	Love, At Last You Have Found Me/Courage	1965	2.00	4.00	8.00
❑ 0416	Yes I Can/Courage	1965	2.00	4.00	8.00
❑ 0425	If You Want This Love of Mine/Second-Best Secret Agent in the Whole Wide World	1965	2.00	4.00	8.00
❑ 0437	Lonely Weekends/More Than One Way	1965	2.00	4.00	8.00
❑ 0502	All That Jazz/Ev'ry Time We Say Goodbye	1966	—	3.00	6.00
❑ 0521	The Good Life/We'll Be Together Again	1966	—	3.00	6.00
❑ 0549	The Birth of the Blues/With a Song in My Heart	1967	—	3.00	6.00
❑ 0566	Don't Blame the Children/She Believes in Me	1967	—	3.00	6.00
❑ 0621	Talk to the Animals/Something in Your Smile	1967	—	3.00	6.00
❑ 0673	Lonely Is the Name/Flash, Bang, Wallop	1968	—	3.00	6.00
❑ 0720	What Kind of Fool Am I/Gonna Build a Mountain	1968	—	2.00	4.00
—"Back to Back Hits" series					
❑ 0733	I've Gotta Be Me/Lonely Is the Name	1970	—	2.00	4.00
—"Back to Back Hits" series					
❑ 0757	Break My Mind/Children, Children	1968	—	3.00	6.00
❑ 0779	I've Gotta Be Me/Bein' Natural Bein' Me	1968	2.00	4.00	8.00
❑ 0827	I Have But One Life to Live/The Goin's Great	1969	—	3.00	6.00
❑ 0989	She Is Today/Runaround	1971	—	2.50	5.00
❑ 20003	I'm a Fool to Want You/Back in Your Own Back Yard	1961	2.50	5.00	10.00
❑ 20018	One More Time (A Tribute to Ray Charles)/There Was a Tavern in the Town	1961	2.50	5.00	10.00
❑ 20048	What Kind of Fool Am I/Gonna Build a Mountain	1962	2.50	5.00	10.00
❑ 20079	The Fool I Used to Be/Everybody Calls Me Joe	1962	2.50	5.00	10.00
❑ 20087	Once in a Lifetime/Someone Nice Like You	1962	2.50	5.00	10.00
❑ 20128	Me and My Shadow/Sam's Song	1962	3.75	7.50	15.00
—A-side: With Frank Sinatra; B-side: With Dean Martin					
❑ 20128 [PS]	Me and My Shadow/Sam's Song	1962	7.50	15.00	30.00
❑ 20138	As Long As She Needs Me/Two for the Seesaw	1963	2.50	5.00	10.00
❑ 20187	Smile/This Way, My Love	1963	5.00	10.00	20.00
—Released only in England					
❑ 20207	If I Ruled the World/Flash, Bang, Wallop	1963	5.00	10.00	20.00
—Released only in England					
❑ 20212	We Kiss in a Shadow/Bye, Bye Blackbird	1963	2.50	5.00	10.00
❑ 20216	The Shelter of Your Arms/This Was My Love	1963	2.50	5.00	10.00
❑ 20227	The Shelter of Your Arms/Falling in Love with Love	1963	5.00	10.00	20.00
—Released only in England					
UNITED ARTISTS					
❑ 50334	Salt and Pepper/I Like the Way You Dance	1968	—	3.00	6.00
VERVE					
❑ 10219	Ain't That a Kick in the Head/Eee-O Eleven	1960	2.00	4.00	8.00
WARNER BROS.					
❑ 49047	Showtime/That Old Black Magic	1979	—	2.00	4.00

7-Inch Extended Plays

Number	Title (A Side/B Side)	Yr	VG	VG+	NM
DECCA					
❑ ED 2214	Hey There/Glad to Be Unhappy//And This Is My Beloved/Easy to Love	195?	3.00	6.00	12.00
❑ ED 2214 [PS]	Starring Sammy Davis, Jr.	195?	3.00	6.00	12.00

DAVIS, SKEETER

Also see THE DAVIS SISTERS.

Number	Title (A Side/B Side)	Yr	VG	VG+	NM
MERCURY					
❑ 73818	I Love Us/It Feels So Good	1976	—	2.00	4.00
❑ 73898	If You Loved Me Now/It's Love That I Feel	1977	—	2.00	4.00
RCA VICTOR					
❑ APBO-0188	Don't Forget to Remember/Baby Get That Leavin' Off Your Mind	1973	—	2.00	4.00
❑ APBO-0277	One More Time/Stay Awhile with Me	1974	—	2.00	4.00
❑ PB-10048	Come Mornin'/Lovin' Touch	1974	—	2.00	4.00
❑ 47-7034	He Left His Heart for Me/Don't Let Your Lips Say Yes	1957	3.75	7.50	15.00
❑ 47-7084	Lost to a Geisha Girl/I'm Going Steady with a Heartache	1957	3.75	7.50	15.00
❑ 47-7189	Walk Softly Darling/I Need You All the Time	1958	3.75	7.50	15.00
❑ 47-7293	Wave Bye Bye/I Forgot More Than You'll Ever Know	1958	3.75	7.50	15.00
❑ 47-7401	I Ain't A-Talkin'/Slave	1958	3.75	7.50	15.00
❑ 47-7471	Set Him Free/The Devil's Doll	1959	3.00	6.00	12.00
❑ 47-7570	Homebreaker/Give Me Death	1959	3.00	6.00	12.00
❑ 47-7671	Am I That Easy to Forget/Wishful Thinking	1960	3.00	6.00	12.00
❑ 47-7767	(I Can't Help You) I'm Falling Too/No, Never	1960	3.00	6.00	12.00
❑ 47-7825	My Last Date (With You)/Someone I'd Like to Forget	1960	3.00	6.00	12.00
❑ 47-7863	The Hand You're Holding Now/Someday Someday	1961	3.00	6.00	12.00
❑ 47-7928	Optimistic/Blueberry Hill	1961	3.00	6.00	12.00
❑ 47-7979	Where I Ought to Be/Something Precious	1962	2.50	5.00	10.00
❑ 47-8055	The Little Music Box/The Final Stop	1962	2.50	5.00	10.00
❑ 47-8098	The End of the World/Somebody Loves You	1962	3.00	6.00	12.00
❑ 47-8176	I'm Saving My Love/Somebody Else on Your Mind	1963	2.50	5.00	10.00
❑ 47-8219	I Can't Stay Mad at You/It Was Only a Heart	1963	2.50	5.00	10.00
❑ 47-8219 [PS]	I Can't Stay Mad at You/It Was Only a Heart	1963	5.00	10.00	20.00
❑ 47-8288	He Says the Same Things to Me/How Much Can a Lonely Heart Stand	1963	2.50	5.00	10.00
❑ 47-8347	Gonna Get Along Without You Now/Now You're Gone	1964	2.50	5.00	10.00
❑ 47-8397	Let Me Get Close to You/Face of a Clown	1964	2.50	5.00	10.00
❑ 47-8450	What Am I Going to Do with You/Don't Let Me Stand in Your Way	1964	2.50	5.00	10.00
❑ 47-8496	A Dear John Letter/Too Used to Being with You	1965	2.50	5.00	10.00
—With Bobby Bare					
❑ 47-8543	You Taught Me Everything I Know/I Can't Help It	1965	2.00	4.00	8.00
❑ 47-8642	Sun Glasses/He Loved Me Too Little	1965	2.00	4.00	8.00
❑ 47-8765	I Can't See Me Without You/Don't Anybody Need My Love	1965	2.00	4.00	8.00
❑ 47-8837	If I Ever Get to Heaven/If I Had Wheels	1966	2.00	4.00	8.00
❑ 47-8932	Goin' Down the Road/I Can't Stand the Sight of You	1966	2.00	4.00	8.00
❑ 47-9058	Fuel to the Flame/You Call This Love	1966	2.00	4.00	8.00
❑ 47-9242	What Does It Take (To Keep a Man Satisfied)/What I Go Through	1967	—	3.00	6.00
❑ 47-9371	Set Him Free/Is It Worth It to You	1967	—	3.00	6.00
❑ 47-9459	How in the World/Instinct for Survival	1968	—	3.00	6.00
❑ 47-9543	There's a Fool Born Every Minute/I Can't See Past the Tears	1968	—	3.00	6.00
❑ 47-9625	I Look Up (And See You on My Mind)/Timothy	1968	—	3.00	6.00
❑ 47-9695	The Closest Thing to Love/Mama Your Big Girl's About to Cry	1968	—	3.00	6.00
❑ 47-9789	Your Husband, My Wife/Before the Sunshine	1969	—	3.00	6.00
—With Bobby Bare					
❑ 47-9818	It's Hard to Be a Woman/What a Little Girl Don't Know	1969	—	3.00	6.00
❑ 47-9871	We Need a Lot More Jesus/When You Gonna Bring Our Soldiers Home	1970	—	2.50	5.00
❑ 47-9893	Let's Get Together/Everything Is Beautiful	1970	—	3.00	6.00
—With George Hamilton IV					
❑ 47-9896	Bridge Over Troubled Water/How in the World Do You Kill a Memory	1970	—	2.50	5.00
❑ 47-9961	Bus Fare to Kentucky/From Her Arms Into Mine	1971	—	2.50	5.00
❑ 47-9997	Love Takes a Lot of Time/Love, Love, Love	1971	—	2.50	5.00
❑ 74-0148	Baby Sweet Baby/Keep Baltimore Beautiful	1969	—	3.00	6.00
❑ 74-0203	Teach Me to Love You/Bobby Blows a Blue Note	1969	—	3.00	6.00
❑ 74-0292	I Didn't Cry Today/I'm a Lover (Not a Fighter)	1969	—	3.00	6.00
❑ 74-0608	One Tin Soldier/Rachel	1971	—	2.50	5.00
❑ 74-0681	Sad Situation/All I Ever Wanted Was Love	1972	—	2.00	4.00
❑ 74-0827	Hillbilly Song/Once	1972	—	2.00	4.00
❑ 74-0968	I Can't Believe That It's All Over/Try Jesus	1973	—	2.00	4.00

DAVIS, SKEETER, AND DON BOWMAN

Number	Title (A Side/B Side)	Yr	VG	VG+	NM
RCA VICTOR					
❑ 47-9415	For Loving You/Baby, It's Cold Outside	1967	2.00	4.00	8.00

DAVIS, SPENCER, GROUP

Includes Spencer Davis solo. Also see STEVE WINWOOD.

Number	Title (A Side/B Side)	Yr	VG	VG+	NM
ATCO					
❑ 6400	Keep On Running/High Time Baby	1966	3.75	7.50	15.00
❑ 6416	Somebody Help Me/Stevie's Blues	1966	3.75	7.50	15.00
FONTANA					
❑ 1960	I Can't Stand It/Midnight Train	1964	3.75	7.50	15.00
UNITED ARTISTS					
❑ SP 78 [DJ]	Voter Registration Spots	1972	3.75	7.50	15.00
—Two ads, 30 and 60 seconds in length					
❑ 0115	Gimme Some Lovin'/Keep On Running	1973	—	2.00	4.00
—"Silver Spotlight Series" reissue					
❑ 0116	I'm a Man/Somebody Help Me	1973	—	2.00	4.00
—"Silver Spotlight Series" reissue					
❑ 50108	Gimme Some Lovin'/Blues in F	1966	3.00	6.00	12.00
❑ 50144	I'm a Man/Can't Get Enough of It	1967	3.00	6.00	12.00
❑ 50162	Somebody Help Me/On the Green Light	1967	2.50	5.00	10.00
❑ 50202	Time Seller/Don't Want You No More	1967	2.50	5.00	10.00
❑ 50202 [PS]	Time Seller/Don't Want You No More	1967	5.00	10.00	20.00
❑ 50286	Looking Back/After Tea	1968	2.50	5.00	10.00
❑ 50922	Listen to the Rhythm/Sunday Walk in the Rain	1972	—	3.00	6.00
—Spencer Davis solo					
❑ 50993	Rainy Season/Tumble-Down Tenement Row	1972	—	3.00	6.00
—Spencer Davis solo					
VERTIGO					
❑ 110	Don't You Let It Bring You Down/Today Gluggo, Tomorrow the World	1973	—	2.50	5.00
❑ 112	Living in a Back Street/Need a Helping Hand	1974	—	2.50	5.00

DAVIS, TYRONE

Number	Title (A Side/B Side)	Yr	VG	VG+	NM
ABC					
❑ 11030	Bet You Win/What If a Man	1967	3.00	6.00	12.00

Number	Title (A Side/B Side)	Yr	VG	VG+	NM
COLUMBIA					
❑ 02269	Just My Luck/Let's Be Closer Together	1981	—	2.00	4.00
❑ 02634	Leave Well Enough Alone/I Won't Let Go	1981	—	2.00	4.00
❑ 10388	Give It Up (Turn It Loose)/You're Too Much	1976	—	2.50	5.00
❑ 10457	Close to You/Wrong Doers	1976	—	2.50	5.00
❑ 10528	This I Swear/Givin' Myself to You	1977	—	2.50	5.00
❑ 10604	All You Got/I Got Carried Away	1977	—	2.50	5.00
❑ 10684	Get It Up (Disco)/It's You, It's You	1978	—	2.50	5.00
❑ 10773	Can't Help But Say/Bunky	1978	—	2.00	4.00
❑ 10904	In the Mood/I Can't Wait	1979	—	2.00	4.00
❑ 11035	Ain't Nothing I Can Do/The Love I Need	1979	—	2.00	4.00
❑ 11128	Be With Me/Love You Forever	1979	—	2.00	4.00
❑ 11199	Can't You Tell It's Me/I Don't Think You Heard Me	1980	—	2.00	4.00
❑ 11246	Keep On Dancin'/Heart Failure	1980	—	2.00	4.00
❑ 11344	How Sweet It Is (To Be Loved By You)/I Can't Wait	1980	—	2.00	4.00
❑ 11415	I Just Can't Keep On Going/We Don't Need No Music	1980	—	2.00	4.00
DAKAR					
❑ 602	Can I Change My Mind/A Woman Needs to Be Loved	1968	2.50	5.00	10.00
❑ 605	Is It Something You've Got/Undying Love	1969	2.00	4.00	8.00
❑ 609	All the Waiting Is Not in Vain/Need Your Lovin' Everybody	1969	2.00	4.00	8.00
❑ 611	If It's Love That You're After/When I'm Not Around	1969	2.00	4.00	8.00
❑ 615	If I Didn't Love You/You Can't Keep a Good Man Down	1969	2.00	4.00	8.00
❑ 616	Turn Back the Hands of Time/I Keep Coming Back	1970	2.00	4.00	8.00
❑ 618	I'll Be Right Here/Just Because of You	1970	—	3.00	6.00
❑ 621	Let Me Back In/Love Bones	1970	—	3.00	6.00
❑ 623	Could I Forget You/Just My Way of Loving You	1971	—	3.00	6.00
❑ 624	One-Way Ticket/We Got a Love	1971	—	3.00	6.00
❑ 626	You Keep Me Holding On/We Got a Love No One Can Deny	1971	—	3.00	6.00
❑ 1452	Can I Change My Mind/A Woman Needs to Be Loved	1968	3.00	6.00	12.00
❑ 4501	I Had It All the Time/You Wouldn't Believe	1972	—	2.50	5.00
❑ 4507	Was I Just a Fool/After All This Time	1972	—	2.50	5.00
❑ 4510	Come and Get This Ring/After All This Time	1972	—	2.50	5.00
❑ 4513	If You Had a Change in Mind/Was It Just a Feelin'	1972	—	2.50	5.00
❑ 4519	Without You in My Life/How Could I Forget You	1973	—	2.50	5.00
❑ 4523	There It Is/You Wouldn't Believe	1973	—	2.50	5.00
❑ 4526	Wrapped Up in Your Warm and Tender Love/True Love Is Hard to Find	1973	—	2.50	5.00
❑ 4529	I Wish It Was Me/You Don't Have to Beg Me to Stay	1974	—	2.50	5.00
❑ 4532	What Goes Up (Must Come Down)/There's Got to Be an Answer	1974	—	2.50	5.00
❑ 4536	Happiness Is Being with You/Where Lovers Meet	1974	—	2.50	5.00
❑ 4538	I Can't Make It Without You/You Wouldn't Believe	1974	—	2.50	5.00
❑ 4541	Homewreckers/This Time	1975	—	2.50	5.00
❑ 4545	A Woman Needs to Be Loved/Just Because of You (I Can See My Way Through)	1975	—	2.50	5.00
❑ 4550	Turning Point/Don't Let It Be Too Late	1975	—	2.50	5.00
❑ 4553	So Good (To Be Home with You)/I Can't Bump	1976	—	2.50	5.00
❑ 4558	I Can't Bump, Part 2/Saving My Love for You	1976	—	2.50	5.00
❑ 4561	Ever Lovin' Girl/Forever	1976	—	2.50	5.00
❑ 4563	Where Lovers Meet (At the Dark End of the Street)/It's All in the Game	1977	—	2.50	5.00
FUTURE					
❑ 101	Sexy Thing/Save Me	1987	—	2.50	5.00
❑ 102	I'm in Love Again/Serious Love	1987	—	2.00	4.00
❑ 103	Do You Feel It/(Instrumental)	1988	—	2.00	4.00
❑ 104	It's a Miracle/Wrong Doers	1988	—	2.00	4.00
❑ 204	Flashin' Back/Flashin' Back (LP Version)	1988	—	2.00	4.00
HIGHRISE					
❑ 2005	Are You Serious/Overdrive	1982	—	2.00	4.00
❑ 2009	A Little Bit of Loving (Goes a Long Way)/Where Did We Lose	1983	—	2.00	4.00
ICHIBAN					
❑ 139	Can I Change My Mind/Hey There Lonely Girl	1989	—	2.00	4.00
—B-side by Eddie Holman					
❑ 226	I'll Always Love You/Can I Change My Mind	1991	—	—	3.00
❑ 237	Mom's Apple Pie/Do U Still Love Me	1991	—	—	3.00
❑ 255	Something's Mighty Wrong/Let Me Love You	1992	—	—	3.00
❑ 261	Running In and Out of My Life/I've Gotta Get Over You	1992	—	—	3.00
❑ 273	Don't Make Me Choose/Ain't Gonna Get It	1992	—	—	3.00
❑ 285	It's a Miracle/Do You Feel It	1993	—	—	3.00
❑ 292	I Found Myself When I Lost You/Something About a Woman	1993	—	—	3.00
OCEAN-FRONT					
❑ 2001	I Found Myself When I Lost You/(Instrumental)	1983	—	2.00	4.00
❑ 2004	Let Me Be Your Pacifier/Turning Point	1984	—	2.00	4.00

DAVIS SISTERS, THE

SKEETER DAVIS and Betty Davis (replaced by Georgia Davis).

Number	Title (A Side/B Side)	Yr	VG	VG+	NM
FORTUNE					
❑ 170	Jealous Love/Going Down the Road	1952	10.00	20.00	40.00
—B-side by Roy Hall					
❑ 174	Kaw-Liga/Sorrow and Pain	1952	6.25	12.50	25.00
❑ 175	Heartbreak Ahead/Steelwood	1952	6.25	12.50	25.00
RCA VICTOR					
❑ 47-5345	I Forgot More Than You'll Ever Know/Rock-a-Bye Boogie	1953	6.25	12.50	25.00
❑ 47-5460	You're Gone/Sorrow and Pain	1953	3.75	7.50	15.00
❑ 47-5607	Takin' Time Out for Tears/Gotta Get a-Goin'	1954	3.75	7.50	15.00
❑ 47-5701	You Weren't Ashamed to Kiss Me Last Night/Foggy Mountain Top	1954	3.75	7.50	15.00
❑ 47-5843	Show Me/Just Like Me	1954	3.75	7.50	15.00
❑ 47-5906	The Christmas Boogie/Tomorrow I'll Cry	1954	3.75	7.50	15.00
❑ 47-5966	Everlovin'/Tomorrow's Just Another Day to Cry	1954	3.75	7.50	15.00
❑ 47-6086	Fiddle Diddle Diddle/Come Back to Me	1955	3.75	7.50	15.00
❑ 47-6187	I'll Get Him Back/I've Closed the Door	1955	3.75	7.50	15.00
❑ 47-6291	Baby Be Mine/It's the Girl Who Gets the Blame	1955	3.75	7.50	15.00
❑ 47-6409	Don't Take HIm for Granted/Blues for Company	1956	3.75	7.50	15.00
❑ 47-6490	Lonely and Blue/Lying Brown Eyes	1956	3.75	7.50	15.00

DAWN (1)

One-man, two-woman vocal group featuring TONY ORLANDO. Includes records issued as "Dawn Featuring Tony Orlando" and "Tony Orlando and Dawn."

Number	Title (A Side/B Side)	Yr	VG	VG+	NM
ARISTA					
❑ 0105	Gimme a Good Old Mammy Song/Little Heads in Bunk Beds	1975	—	2.00	4.00
❑ 0156	Skybird/That's the Way a Wallflower Grows	1975	—	2.00	4.00
❑ 0301	Tie a Yellow Ribbon Round the Ole Oak Tree/Say, Has Anybody Seen My Sweet Gypsy Rose	1978	—	2.00	4.00
BELL					
❑ 903	Candida/Look At...	1970	—	3.00	6.00
❑ 938	Knock Three Times/Home	1970	—	3.00	6.00
❑ 970	I Play and Sing/Get Out from Where We Are	1971	—	2.50	5.00
❑ 45107	Summer Sand/The Sweet Soft Sounds of Love	1971	—	2.50	5.00
❑ 45141	What Are You Doing Sunday/The Sweet Soft Sounds of Love	1971	—	2.50	5.00
❑ 45175	Runaway-Happy Together/Don't Act Like a Baby	1972	—	2.50	5.00
❑ 45225	Vaya Con Dios/I Can't Believe How Much I Love You	1972	—	2.50	5.00
❑ 45285	You're a Lady/In the Park	1972	—	2.00	4.00
❑ 45318	Tie a Yellow Ribbon Round the Ole Oak Tree/I Can't Believe How Much I Love You	1973	—	2.50	5.00
❑ 45375	Say, Has Anybody Seen My Sweet Gypsy Rose/The Spark of Love Is Kindlin'	1973	—	2.00	4.00
❑ 45424	Who's in the Strawberry Patch with Sally/Ukulele Man	1973	—	2.00	4.00
❑ 45450	It Only Hurts When I Try to Smile/Sweet Summer Days of My Life	1974	—	2.00	4.00
❑ 45601	Steppin' Out (Gonna Boogie Tonight)/She Can't Hold a Candle to You	1974	—	2.00	4.00
❑ 45620	Look in My Eyes Pretty Woman/My Love Has No Pride	1974	—	2.00	4.00
ELEKTRA					
❑ 45240	He Don't Love You (Like I Love You)/Pick It Up	1975	—	2.00	4.00
❑ 45260	Mornin' Beautiful/Dance, Rosalie, Dance	1975	—	2.00	4.00
❑ 45275	You're All I Need to Get By/Know You Like a Book	1975	—	2.00	4.00
❑ 45302	Cupid/You're Growin' on Me	1976	—	2.00	4.00
❑ 45319	Midnight Love Affair/The Selfish Ones	1976	—	2.00	4.00
❑ 45387	Sing/Sweet on Candy	1977	—	2.00	4.00
❑ 45432	Growin' on Me/You're All I Need to Get By	1977	—	2.00	4.00
❑ 45501	Bring It On Home to Me/Don't Let Go	1978	—	2.00	4.00
❑ 45542	I Count the Tears/A Lover's Question	1978	—	2.00	4.00
❑ 45542	I Count the Tears/This Is Rock and Roll	1978	—	2.00	4.00

DAWN (2)

Girl group.

Number	Title (A Side/B Side)	Yr	VG	VG+	NM
ABC-PARAMOUNT					
❑ 10791	Baby's Gone Away/Gotta Get Away	1966	2.00	4.00	8.00
APT					
❑ 25088	Can't Get Him Off My Mind/Two of a Kind	1965	3.75	7.50	15.00

DAWN (3)

Said to be THE FIVE DISCS in disguise.

Number	Title (A Side/B Side)	Yr	VG	VG+	NM
LAURIE					
❑ 3388	I'm Afraid They're All Talking About Me/Lovers' Melody	1967	3.00	6.00	12.00
❑ 3417	Sandy/For the Love of Money	1968	3.00	6.00	12.00
RUST					
❑ 5128	Baby I Love You/Bring It On Home	1968	3.00	6.00	12.00

DAWN (U)

Definitely not groups (1) or (3), these may be by group (2), but we're not sure.

Number	Title (A Side/B Side)	Yr	VG	VG+	NM
CADET					
❑ 5644	The Fifth Day of June/Ballad of Gene	1969	—	3.00	6.00
UNITED ARTISTS					
❑ 50096	Love Is a Magic Word/How Can I Get Off This Merry-Go-Round	1966	3.00	6.00	12.00

DAY, BING

Number	Title (A Side/B Side)	Yr	VG	VG+	NM
FEDERAL					
❑ 12320	Pony Tail Partner/Since You Left Me	1958	17.50	35.00	70.00
MERCURY					
❑ 71446	I Can't Help It/Mama's Place	1959	15.00	30.00	60.00
❑ 71494	How Do I Do It/Mary's Place	1959	5.00	10.00	20.00

DAY, BOBBY

Number	Title (A Side/B Side)	Yr	VG	VG+	NM
CASH					
❑ 1031	The Truth Hurts/Let's Live Together As One	1956	25.00	50.00	100.00
—As "Bobby Byrd and the Birds"					
CLASS					
❑ 207	Come Seven/So Long Baby	1957	5.00	10.00	20.00
❑ 211	Little Bitty Pretty One/When the Swallows Come Back to Capistrano	1957	6.25	12.50	25.00
❑ 215	Beep-Beep-Beep/Darling, If I Had You	1957	5.00	10.00	20.00
❑ 225	Little Turtle Dove/Saving My Life for You	1958	5.00	10.00	20.00
❑ 229	Rock-N Robin/Over and Over	1958	7.50	15.00	30.00
❑ 241	The Bluebird, the Buzzard, and the Oriole/Alone Too Long	1959	5.00	10.00	20.00
❑ 245	That's All I Want/Say Yes	1959	3.75	7.50	15.00
❑ 252	Mr. and Mrs. Rock & Roll/Gotta New Girl	1959	3.75	7.50	15.00
❑ 255	Ain't Gonna Cry No More/Love Is a One-Time Affair	1959	3.75	7.50	15.00
❑ 257	Unchained Melody/Three Young Rebs from Georgia	1959	3.75	7.50	15.00
❑ 263	My Blue Heaven/I Don't Want To	1960	3.75	7.50	15.00
❑ 705	Don't Leave Me Hangin' on a String/When I Started Dancin'	1965	3.00	6.00	12.00

Number	Title (A Side/B Side)	Yr	VG	VG+	NM
CORVET					
❑ 1017	Why/Gotta Girl	1958	15.00	30.00	60.00
—As "Bobby Byrd and the Impalas"					
JAMIE					
❑ 1039	Bippin' and Boppin' Over You/Strawberry Stomp	1957	7.50	15.00	30.00
—As "Robert Byrd and His Birdies"					
RCA VICTOR					
❑ 47-8133	Another Country, Another World/Know-It-All	1963	2.50	5.00	10.00
❑ 47-8196	Buzz Buzz Buzz/Pretty Little Girl Next Door	1963	2.50	5.00	10.00
❑ 47-8230	Down on My Knees/Jole Blon, Little Darling	1963	2.50	5.00	10.00
❑ 47-8316	When I See My Baby Smile/On the Street Where You Live	1964	2.50	5.00	10.00
RENDEZVOUS					
❑ 130	Teenage Philosopher/Undecided	1960	3.00	6.00	12.00
❑ 133	Rockin' Robin/Over and Over	1960	3.00	6.00	12.00
❑ 136	Gee Whiz/Over and Over	1960	3.00	6.00	12.00
❑ 146	I Need Help/Life Can Be Beautiful	1961	3.00	6.00	12.00
❑ 158	King's Highway/What Fools We Mortals Be	1961	3.00	6.00	12.00
❑ 167	Don't Worry 'Bout Me/Oop-E-Du-Pers Ball	1962	3.00	6.00	12.00
❑ 175	Undecided/Slow Pokey Joe	1962	3.00	6.00	12.00
SAGE AND SAND					
❑ 203	Please Don't Hurt Me/Delicious Are Your Kisses	1955	10.00	20.00	40.00
—As "Bobby Byrd"					
SPARK					
❑ 501	Bippin' and Boppin' Over You/Strawberry Stomp	1957	12.50	25.00	50.00
—As "Robert Byrd and His Birdies"					
SURE SHOT					
❑ 5036	So Lonely/Spicks and Specks	1967	2.00	4.00	8.00
ZEPHYR					
❑ 70-018	If We Should Meet Again/Looby Loo	1957	7.50	15.00	30.00
—As "Bobby Byrd"					
DAY, DARLENE					
MUSIC MAKERS					
❑ 106	I Love You So/Will	1961	25.00	50.00	100.00
DAY, DORIS					
COLUMBIA					
❑ 1-108 (?)	If You Will Marry Me/You Was	1949	10.00	20.00	40.00
—Microgroove 7-inch, 33 1/3 rpm single					
❑ 1-113	Powder Your Face with Sunshine (Smile! Smile! Smile!)/I'll String Along with You	1949	10.00	20.00	40.00
—Microgroove 7-inch, 33 1/3 rpm single					
❑ 1-125 (?)	Beginning to Miss You/Don't Gamble with Romance	1949	10.00	20.00	40.00
—Microgroove 7-inch, 33 1/3 rpm single					
❑ 1-185 (?)	How It Lies, How It Lies/If I Could Be with You	1949	10.00	20.00	40.00
—Microgroove 7-inch, 33 1/3 rpm single					
❑ 1-211	Again/Everywhere You Go	1949	10.00	20.00	40.00
—Microgroove 7-inch, 33 1/3 rpm single					
❑ 1-251	(Where Are You) Now That I Need You/Blame My Absent-Minded Heart	1949	10.00	20.00	40.00
—Microgroove 7-inch, 33 1/3 rpm single					
❑ 1-266 (?)	At the Café Rendezvous/It's a Great Feeling	1949	10.00	20.00	40.00
—Microgroove 7-inch, 33 1/3 rpm single					
❑ 1-353	Canadian Capers (Cuttin' Capers)/Better To Conceal Than Reveal	1949	10.00	20.00	40.00
—Microgroove 7-inch, 33 1/3 rpm single					
❑ 1-376	(There's a) Bluebird on Your Windowsill/The River Seine	1949	10.00	20.00	40.00
—Microgroove 7-inch, 33 1/3 rpm single					
❑ 1-381 (?)	The Three Rivers/Festival of Roses	1949	10.00	20.00	40.00
—Microgroove 7-inch, 33 1/3 rpm single					
❑ 1-406 (?)	The Game of Broken Hearts/I'll Never Slip Around Again	1949	10.00	20.00	40.00
—Microgroove 7-inch, 33 1/3 rpm single					
❑ 1-407	Quicksilver/Crocodile Tears	1949	10.00	20.00	40.00
—Microgroove 7-inch, 33 1/3 rpm single					
❑ 1-454 (?)	Mama, What'll I Do/Save a Little Sunbeam	1950	10.00	20.00	40.00
—Microgroove 7-inch, 33 1/3 rpm single					
❑ 1-457 (?)	I Don't Wanna Be Kissed/With You Anywhere You Are	1950	10.00	20.00	40.00
—Microgroove 7-inch, 33 1/3 rpm single					
❑ 1-480	Bewitched/Imagination	1950	10.00	20.00	40.00
—Microgroove 7-inch, 33 1/3 rpm single					
❑ 1-497	I Said My Pajamas (And Put On My Prayers)/Enjoy Yourself (It's Later Than You Think)	1950	10.00	20.00	40.00
—Microgroove 7-inch, 33 1/3 rpm single					
❑ 1-591	Hoop-Dee-Doo/Marriage Ties	1950	10.00	20.00	40.00
—Microgroove 7-inch, 33 1/3 rpm single					
❑ 1-637	I Didn't Slip — I Wasn't Pushed — I Fell/Before I Loved You	1950	10.00	20.00	40.00
—Microgroove 7-inch, 33 1/3 rpm single					
❑ 1-708	Darn That Dream/I've Forgotten You	1950	10.00	20.00	40.00
—Microgroove 7-inch, 33 1/3 rpm single					
❑ 6-708	Darn That Dream/I've Forgotten You	1950	7.50	15.00	30.00
❑ 1-838 (?)	A Bushel and a Peck/The Best Thing for You	1950	10.00	20.00	40.00
—Microgroove 7-inch, 33 1/3 rpm single					
❑ 6-838 (?)	A Bushel and a Peck/The Best Thing for You	1950	7.50	15.00	30.00
❑ 1-859 (?)	If I Were a Bell/I've Never Been in Love Before	1950	10.00	20.00	40.00
—Microgroove 7-inch, 33 1/3 rpm single					
❑ 6-859 (?)	If I Were a Bell/I've Never Been in Love Before	1950	7.50	15.00	30.00
❑ 1-908 (?)	Nobody's Chasing Me/It's a Lovely Day Today	1950	10.00	20.00	40.00
—Microgroove 7-inch, 33 1/3 rpm single					
❑ 6-908 (?)	Nobody's Chasing Me/It's a Lovely Day Today	1950	7.50	15.00	30.00
❑ 31084 [S]	(contents unknown)	1961	2.50	5.00	10.00
❑ 31085 [S]	(contents unknown)	1961	2.50	5.00	10.00
❑ 31086 [S]	(contents unknown)	1961	2.50	5.00	10.00
❑ 31087 [S]	(contents unknown)	1961	2.50	5.00	10.00
❑ 31088 [S]	(contents unknown)	1961	2.50	5.00	10.00
—Anyone who can fill in these gaps -- the above 5 all are Columbia "Stereo 7" singles -- please let us know.					
❑ 4-38542	You're My Thrill/That Old Feeling	1950	3.75	7.50	15.00
—Alternate numbers are "B 189-1" and "B 189-2"					
❑ 4-38543	Bewitched/When Your Lover Has Gone	1950	3.75	7.50	15.00
—Alternate numbers are "B 189-3" and "B 189-4"					
❑ 4-38544	I'm Confessin'/I Didn't Know What Time It Was	1950	3.75	7.50	15.00
—Alternate numbers are "B 189-5" and "B 189-6"					
❑ 4-38545	You Go to My Head/Sometimes I'm Happy	1950	3.75	7.50	15.00
—Alternate numbers are "B 189-7" and "B 189-8"; the above four comprise box set B 189					
❑ 38584	Here Comes Santa Claus/Ol' Saint Nicholas	1949	—	—	—
—Unconfirmed on 45 rpm					
❑ 39008	A Bushel and a Peck/The Best Thing for You	1950	5.00	10.00	20.00
❑ 39031	If I Were a Bell/I've Never Been in Love Before	1950	5.00	10.00	20.00
❑ 39032	Christmas Story/Silver Bells	1950	3.00	6.00	12.00
❑ 39055	Nobody's Chasing Me/It's a Lovely Day Today	1950	5.00	10.00	20.00
❑ 39143	You Are My Sunshine/Comb and Paper Polka	1951	3.75	7.50	15.00
❑ 3-39143	You Are My Sunshine/Comb and Paper Polka	1951	7.50	15.00	30.00
—Microgroove 7-inch, 33 1/3 rpm single					
❑ 39159	Would I Love You (Love You, Love You)/Lullaby of Broadway	1951	3.75	7.50	15.00
❑ 3-39159	Would I Love You (Love You, Love You)/Lullaby of Broadway	1951	7.50	15.00	30.00
—Microgroove 7-inch, 33 1/3 rpm single					
❑ 39191	I'll Be Around/I Love the Way You Say Goodnight	1951	3.75	7.50	15.00
❑ 39197	Lullaby of Broadway/Please Don't Talk About Me When I'm Gone	1951	3.00	6.00	12.00
❑ 39198	Fine and Dandy/I Love the Way You Say Goodnight	1951	3.00	6.00	12.00
❑ 39199	In a Shanty in Old Shanty Town/You're Getting to Be a Habit with Me	1951	3.00	6.00	12.00
❑ 39200	Somebody Loves Me/Just One of Those Things	1951	3.00	6.00	12.00
—The above four comprise a box set					
❑ 39255	I Can't Get Over Pumpernickel/You Are My Sunshine	1951	3.75	7.50	15.00
❑ 39293	We Kissed in a Shadow/Something Wonderful	1951	3.75	7.50	15.00
❑ 39295	It's So Laughable/Very Good Advice	1951	3.75	7.50	15.00
❑ 39423	(Why Did I Tell You I Was Going to) Shanghai/My Life's Desire	1951	3.75	7.50	15.00
❑ 39450	Moonlight Bay/Tell Me (Tell Me Why)	1951	3.00	6.00	12.00
❑ 39451	Till We Meet Again/Every Little Movement	1951	3.00	6.00	12.00
❑ 39452	Love You/Cuddle Up a Little Closer	1951	3.00	6.00	12.00
❑ 39453	Christmas Story/I'm Forever Blowing Bubbles	1951	3.00	6.00	12.00
—The above four comprise a box set					
❑ 39490	Ask Me/Lonesome and Sorry	1951	3.75	7.50	15.00
❑ 39534	Kiss Me Goodbye/Got Him Offa My Hands	1951	3.75	7.50	15.00
❑ 39596	Domino/If That Doesn't Do It	1951	3.75	7.50	15.00
❑ 39622	I'll See You in My Dreams/Ain't We Got Fun	1951	3.00	6.00	12.00
❑ 39623	The One I Love/Makin' Whoopee	1951	3.00	6.00	12.00
❑ 39624	My Buddy/I Wish I Had a Girl	1951	3.00	6.00	12.00
❑ 39625	It Had to Be You/Nobody's Sweetheart	1951	3.00	6.00	12.00
—The above four comprise a box set					
❑ 39637	Oops/Baby Doll	1952	3.00	6.00	12.00
❑ 39673	A Guy Is a Guy/Who, Who, Who	1952	3.00	6.00	12.00
❑ 39693	Sugarbush/When I Look Into Your Eyes	1952	3.00	6.00	12.00
—A-side with Frankie Laine					
❑ 39714	Gentle Johnny/Little Kiss Goodnight	1952	3.00	6.00	12.00
❑ 39729	A Guy Is a Guy/What's the Use?	1952	2.50	5.00	10.00
—B-side by Johnnie Ray					
❑ 39738	It's Magic/Too Fat Polka	1952	2.50	5.00	10.00
—B-side by Arthur Godfrey					
❑ 39786	When I Fall in Love/Take Me in Your Arms	1952	3.00	6.00	12.00
❑ 39817	Make It Soon/My Love and Devotion	1952	3.00	6.00	12.00
❑ 39863	No Two People/You Can't Lose Me	1952	3.00	6.00	12.00
—A-side with Donald O'Connor					
❑ 39881	April in Paris/Cherries	1952	3.00	6.00	12.00
❑ 39906	Mister Tap Toe/Your Mother and Mine	1952	3.00	6.00	12.00
❑ 39913	You Have My Symphony/Second Star to the Right	1953	3.00	6.00	12.00
❑ 39970	When the Red, Red Robin Comes Bob, Bob, Bobbin' Along/Beautiful Music to Love By	1953	2.00	4.00	8.00
❑ 39971	Little Silvery Moon/King Chant	1953	2.00	4.00	8.00
❑ 39972	Your Eyes Have Told Me So/I'll Forget You	1953	2.00	4.00	8.00
❑ 39973	Just One Girl/Be Bumble Bee	1953	2.00	4.00	8.00
❑ 39974	Ain't We Got Fun?/If You Were the Only Girl	1953	2.00	4.00	8.00
—The above five comprise a box set					
❑ 40020	Kiss Me Again Stranger/A Purple Cow	1953	2.50	5.00	10.00
❑ 40063	Chho Choo Train (Ch-Ch-Foo)/This Too Shall Pass Away	1953	2.50	5.00	10.00
❑ 40094	The Deadwood Stage (Whip Crack Away!)/I Can Do Without You	1953	2.00	4.00	8.00
❑ 40095	The Black Hills of Dakota/Just Blew In from the Windy City	1953	2.00	4.00	8.00
❑ 40096	A Woman's Touch/Higher Than the Hawk	1953	2.00	4.00	8.00
❑ 40097	Secret Love/'Tis Harry I'm Planning to Marry	1953	2.00	4.00	8.00
—The above four comprise a box set					
❑ 40108	Secret Love/The Deadwood Stage (Whip Crack Away!)	1953	2.50	5.00	10.00
❑ 40168	Lost in Loveliness/What Every Girl Should Know	1954	2.50	5.00	10.00
❑ 40210	I Speak to the Stars/The Blue Belles of Broadway	1954	2.50	5.00	10.00
❑ 40234	Someone Else's Roses/Kay-Muleta	1954	2.50	5.00	10.00
❑ 40300	If I Give My Heart to You/Anyone Can Fall in Love	1954	2.50	5.00	10.00
❑ 40371	Ready, Willing and Able/Hold Me In Your Arms	1954	2.50	5.00	10.00
❑ 40372	Till My Love Comes to Me/Ready and Able	1954	2.00	4.00	8.00
❑ 40373	Ready, Willing and Able/One for My Baby	1954	2.00	4.00	8.00
❑ 40374	Hold Me in Your Arms/There's a Rising Moon	1954	2.00	4.00	8.00
❑ 40375	Someone to Watch Over Me/Just One of Those Things	1954	2.00	4.00	8.00
—The above four comprise a box set					
❑ 40408	There's a Rising Moon/Till Your Love Comes to Me	1954	2.50	5.00	10.00
❑ 40483	Two Hearts, Two Kisses/Foolishly Yours	1955	2.50	5.00	10.00

Number	Title (A Side/B Side)	Yr	VG	VG+	NM
❑ 40505	I'll Never Stop Loving You/Never Look Back	1955	2.50	5.00	10.00
❑ 40581	Ooh Bang Jiggily Bang/Jimmy Unknown	1955	2.50	5.00	10.00
❑ 40618	Let It Ring/Love's Little Island	1955	2.50	5.00	10.00
❑ 40673	We'll Love Again/Somebody Somewhere	1956	2.50	5.00	10.00
❑ 40704	Whatever Will Be, Will Me (Que Sera, Sera)/I've Gotta Sing Away the Blues	1956	2.50	5.00	10.00
❑ 40758	Julie/Love in a Home	1956	2.50	5.00	10.00
❑ 40798	The Party's Over/What'ya Put in That Kiss	1956	2.50	5.00	10.00
❑ 40870	Twelve O'Clock Tonight/Today Will Be Yesterday Tomorrow	1957	2.50	5.00	10.00
❑ 40952	Nothing in the World/Through the Eyes of Love	1957	2.50	5.00	10.00
❑ 41015	Rickety-Rackety Rendezvous/The Man Who Invented Love	1957	2.00	4.00	8.00
❑ 41071	Walk a Chalk Line/Soft As the Starlight	1957	2.00	4.00	8.00
❑ 41123	Teacher's Pet/A Very Precious Love	1958	2.00	4.00	8.00
❑ 41195	Everybody Loves a Lover/Instant Love	1958	2.00	4.00	8.00
❑ 41195 [PS]	Everybody Loves a Lover/Instant Love	1958	3.75	7.50	15.00
❑ 41252	Tunnel of Love/Run Away Skidaddle Skidoo	1958	2.00	4.00	8.00
❑ 41252 [PS]	Tunnel of Love/Run Away Skidaddle Skidoo	1958	3.75	7.50	15.00
❑ 41307	I Enjoy Being a Girl/Kissin' My Honey	1958	2.00	4.00	8.00
❑ 41354	Love Me in the Daytime/He's So Married	1959	2.00	4.00	8.00
❑ 41391	Be Prepared/It Happened to Jane	1959	2.00	4.00	8.00
❑ 41450	Roly Poly/Possess Me	1959	2.00	4.00	8.00
❑ 41463	Pillow Talk/Inspiration	1959	2.00	4.00	8.00
❑ 41463 [PS]	Pillow Talk/Inspiration	1959	3.75	7.50	15.00
❑ 41542	The Sound of Music/Heart Full of Love	1959	2.00	4.00	8.00
❑ 41569	Anyway the Wind Blows/Soft As the Starlight	1960	2.00	4.00	8.00
❑ 41630	Please Don't Eat the Daisies/Here We Go Again	1960	2.00	4.00	8.00
❑ 41703	The Blue Train/A Perfect Understanding	1960	2.00	4.00	8.00
❑ 41791	What Does a Woman Do/Daffa Down Dilly	1960	2.00	4.00	8.00
❑ 41944	Make Someone Happy/Bright and Shiny	1961	2.00	4.00	8.00
❑ 41993	Twinkle and Shine/Gotta Feelin'	1961	2.00	4.00	8.00
❑ 42260	Should I Surrender/Who Knows What Might Have Been	1962	2.00	4.00	8.00
❑ 42295	Lover Come Back/Falling	1962	2.00	4.00	8.00
❑ 42912	Move Over Darling/Twinkle Lullaby	1963	2.00	4.00	8.00
❑ 43153	Send Me No Flowers/Rainbow's End	1964	2.00	4.00	8.00
❑ 43174	Christmas Present/Be a Child at Christmas Time	1964	2.00	4.00	8.00
❑ 43278	How Insensitive/Meditation	1965	2.00	4.00	8.00
❑ 43314	Summer Has Gone/Catch the Bouquet	1965	2.00	4.00	8.00
❑ 43440	Another Go-Round/Not Only Should You Love Him	1965	2.00	4.00	8.00
❑ 43459	Au Revoir Is Goodbye with a Smile/Do Not Disturb	1965	2.00	4.00	8.00
❑ 43606	Every Now and Then/There They Are	1966	—	3.50	7.00
❑ 43688	Glass Bottom Boat/Soft As the Starlight	1966	—	3.50	7.00
❑ 44150	Caprice/Sorry	1967	—	3.50	7.00
❑ JZSP 55070/1	[DJ]Let No Walls Divide/God Rest Ye Merry, Gentlemen	1961	3.00	6.00	12.00

—B-side by Andre Previn

Number	Title (A Side/B Side)	Yr	VG	VG+	NM
❑ JZSP 79171/2	[DJ]Silver Bells/Winter Wonderland	1963	2.50	5.00	10.00

—"Special Album Excerpt" promo

7-Inch Extended Plays

COLUMBIA

Number	Title (A Side/B Side)	Yr	VG	VG+	NM
❑ B-2585	*A Bushel and a Peck/Hoop-Dee-Doo/If I Were a Bell/Lullaby of Broadway	1959	3.75	7.50	15.00
❑ B-2585 [PS]	Doris Day (Hall of Fame Series)	1959	3.75	7.50	15.00

DAY, DORIS/JOHNNIE RAY

Also see each artist's individual listings.

COLUMBIA

Number	Title (A Side/B Side)	Yr	VG	VG+	NM
❑ 39898	A Full Time Job/Ma Says, Pa Says	1952	3.00	6.00	12.00
❑ 40001	Candy Lips/Let's Walk That-A-Way	1953	2.50	5.00	10.00

DAY, LITTLE SUNNY, AND THE CLOUDS

TANDEM

Number	Title (A Side/B Side)	Yr	VG	VG+	NM
❑ 7001	Lou Ann/Baby Doll	1961	100.00	200.00	400.00

DAY, MARGIE

CAT

Number	Title (A Side/B Side)	Yr	VG	VG+	NM
❑ 118	Ho Ho/Pitty Pat Bank	1955	10.00	20.00	40.00

DAY, TERRY

See TERRY MELCHER.

DAYBREAKERS, THE (1)

ALADDIN

Number	Title (A Side/B Side)	Yr	VG	VG+	NM
❑ 3434	I Wonder Why/Up, Up and Away	1958	10.00	20.00	40.00

LAMP

Number	Title (A Side/B Side)	Yr	VG	VG+	NM
❑ 2016	I Wonder Why/Up, Up and Away	1958	15.00	30.00	60.00

DAYBREAKERS, THE (2)

DIAL

Number	Title (A Side/B Side)	Yr	VG	VG+	NM
❑ 4066	Psychedelic Siren/Afterthoughts	1967	7.50	15.00	30.00

DAYTONAS, THE

Also see RONNY AND THE DATYONAS.

AMY

Number	Title (A Side/B Side)	Yr	VG	VG+	NM
❑ 961	Hey Little Girl/Please Go Away	1966	5.00	10.00	20.00

DAYTONES, THE

JUBILEE

Number	Title (A Side/B Side)	Yr	VG	VG+	NM
❑ 5452	Krambuli/Bless My Love	1963	5.00	10.00	20.00

DAYTONS, THE

NORGOLDE

Number	Title (A Side/B Side)	Yr	VG	VG+	NM
❑ 101	King of Broken Hearts/Friday Better Come	1959	50.00	100.00	200.00

DE BONAIRS

PING

Number	Title (A Side/B Side)	Yr	VG	VG+	NM
❑ 1000	Lanky Linda/Mother's Son	1956	75.00	150.00	300.00
❑ 1001	Say a Prayer for Me/Cracker-Jack Daddy	1956	100.00	200.00	400.00

DE-FENDERS, THE

DEL-FI

Number	Title (A Side/B Side)	Yr	VG	VG+	NM
❑ 4226	Little Deuce Coupe/Hayburner	1963	7.50	15.00	30.00

—B-side by the Deuce Coupes

WORLD PACIFIC

Number	Title (A Side/B Side)	Yr	VG	VG+	NM
❑ 382	(Dance to the) Yakety Sax/Wild One	1963	10.00	20.00	40.00

DEACON AND THE ROCK 'N' ROLLERS

NAU-VOO

Number	Title (A Side/B Side)	Yr	VG	VG+	NM
❑ 804	Rockin' on the Moon/I Don't Wanna Leave	1959	500.00	1000.	1500.

DEAD KENNEDYS

ALTERNATIVE TENTACLES

Number	Title (A Side/B Side)	Yr	VG	VG+	NM
❑ VIRUS 2	Too Drunk to Fuck/The Prey	1981	2.00	4.00	8.00
❑ VIRUS 2 [PS]	Too Drunk to Fuck/The Prey	1981	2.00	4.00	8.00

—Picture sleeve and lyric insert

Number	Title (A Side/B Side)	Yr	VG	VG+	NM
❑ VIRUS 6	Nazi Punks Fuck Off/Moral Majority	1981	—	3.75	7.50
❑ VIRUS 6 [PS]	Nazi Punks Fuck Off/Moral Majority	1981	—	3.75	7.50

—Lyric sheet and armband in plastic bag, not actually a picture sleeve

Number	Title (A Side/B Side)	Yr	VG	VG+	NM
❑ VIRUS 23	Bleed for Me/Life Sentence	1982	—	2.50	5.00
❑ VIRUS 23 [PS]	Bleed for Me/Life Sentence	1982	—	2.50	5.00
❑ VIRUS 28	Halloween/Saturday Night Holocaust	1982	—	2.50	5.00
❑ VIRUS 28 [PS]	Halloween/Saturday Night Holocaust	1982	—	2.50	5.00
❑ AT-95-41	California Uber Alles/The Man with the Dogs	1979	5.00	10.00	20.00
❑ AT-95-41 [PS]	California Uber Alles/The Man with the Dogs	1979	5.00	10.00	20.00

—Picture sleeve and lyric insert

I.R.S./FAULTY PRODUCTS

Number	Title (A Side/B Side)	Yr	VG	VG+	NM
❑ 9016	Holiday in Cambodia/Policetruck	1980	2.50	5.00	10.00
❑ 9016 [PS]	Holiday in Cambodia/Policetruck	1980	2.50	5.00	10.00

OPTIONAL MUSIC

Number	Title (A Side/B Side)	Yr	VG	VG+	NM
❑ OPT-2	California Uber Alles/The Man with the Dogs	1979	3.00	6.00	12.00
❑ OPT-2 [PS]	California Uber Alles/The Man with the Dogs	1979	3.00	6.00	12.00
❑ OPT-4	Holiday in Cambodia/Policetruck	1980	2.50	5.00	10.00
❑ OPT-4 [PS]	Holiday in Cambodia/Policetruck	1980	2.50	5.00	10.00

—Picture sleeve and lyric insert

SUBTERRANEAN

Number	Title (A Side/B Side)	Yr	VG	VG+	NM
❑ SUB 24	Nazi Punks Fuck Off/Moral Majority	1981	2.50	5.00	10.00
❑ SUB 24 [PS]	Nazi Punks Fuck Off/Moral Majority	1981	2.50	5.00	10.00

—Lyric sheet and armband in plastic bag, not actually a picture sleeve

DEAL, BILL, AND THE RHONDELS

BUDDAH

Number	Title (A Side/B Side)	Yr	VG	VG+	NM
❑ 318	It's Too Late/So What If It Rains	1972	—	3.00	6.00
❑ 330	Everybody's Got Something to Hide/I Live in the Night	1972	—	3.00	6.00

GIG/WAY

Number	Title (A Side/B Side)	Yr	VG	VG+	NM
❑ 902006	Freak 'N' Freeze/(Instrumental)	1978	—	2.50	5.00

HERITAGE

Number	Title (A Side/B Side)	Yr	VG	VG+	NM
❑ 803	May I/Day By Day My Love Grows	1968	2.00	4.00	8.00
❑ 812	I've Been Hurt/I've Got My Seeds	1969	2.00	4.00	8.00
❑ 812 [PS]	I've Been Hurt/I've Got My Seeds	1969	3.75	7.50	15.00
❑ 817	What Kind of Fool Do You Think I Am/Are You Ready for This	1969	2.00	4.00	8.00
❑ 818	Swingin' Tight/Tuck's Theme	1969	2.00	4.00	8.00
❑ 818 [PS]	Swingin' Tight/Tuck's Theme	1969	3.75	7.50	15.00
❑ 821	Nothing Succeeds Like Success/Swingin' Tight	1969	2.00	4.00	8.00
❑ 824	I'm Gonna Make You Love Me/Hey Bulldog	1970	—	3.00	6.00

MALA

Number	Title (A Side/B Side)	Yr	VG	VG+	NM
❑ 502	Big Toe in the Wind/Don't Put Me Down	1965	7.50	15.00	30.00

—As "Bill Deal and the Big Deals"

POLYDOR

Number	Title (A Side/B Side)	Yr	VG	VG+	NM
❑ 14042	Do I Love You/Won't You Set Me Free	1970	—	3.00	6.00
❑ 14061	19 Years (Everything I Do Is Wrong)/Sea of Life	1971	—	3.00	6.00
❑ 14103	Sea of Life/You Can Make It	1971	—	3.00	6.00

DEAN, BOBBY

CHESS

Number	Title (A Side/B Side)	Yr	VG	VG+	NM
❑ 1673	Just Go Wild Over Rock and Roll/Dime Store Pony Tail	1958	7.50	15.00	30.00
❑ 1710	I'm Ready/Go Mr. Dillon	1959	7.50	15.00	30.00

PROFILE

Number	Title (A Side/B Side)	Yr	VG	VG+	NM
❑ 4006	Just Between Tears/It's a Fad	1959	10.00	20.00	40.00

DEAN, CHARLES

BENTON

Number	Title (A Side/B Side)	Yr	VG	VG+	NM
❑ 103	Itchy/(B-side unknown)	1958	62.50	125.00	250.00

DEAN, DEBBIE

MOTOWN

Number	Title (A Side/B Side)	Yr	VG	VG+	NM
❑ 1007	Don't Let Him Shop Around/A New Girl	1961	10.00	20.00	40.00
❑ 1014	Itty, Bitty, Pity Love/But I'm Afraid	1961	7.50	15.00	30.00
❑ 1025	Everybody's Talking About My Baby/I Cried All Night	1962	10.00	20.00	40.00
❑ 1025 [PS]	Everybody's Talking About My Baby/I Cried All Night	1962	20.00	40.00	80.00

V.I.P.

Number	Title (A Side/B Side)	Yr	VG	VG+	NM
❑ 25044	Why Am I Lovin' You/Stay My Love	1967	75.00	150.00	300.00

DEAN, JIMMY

4 STAR

Number	Title (A Side/B Side)	Yr	VG	VG+	NM
❑ 1613	Bumming Around/Picking Sweethearts	1953	6.25	12.50	25.00
❑ 1640	Queen of Hearts/I'm Feeling For You	1953	5.00	10.00	20.00
❑ 1654	Release Me/Sweet Darling	1954	5.00	10.00	20.00
❑ 1732	Bumming Around/Release Me	1959	3.00	6.00	12.00

CASINO

Number	Title (A Side/B Side)	Yr	VG	VG+	NM
❑ 052	I.O.U./Let's Pick Up the Pieces	1976	—	2.00	4.00
❑ 074	To a Sleeping Beauty/I Didn't Have Time	1976	—	2.00	4.00
❑ 108	Where Is That Man/(B-side unknown)	1976	—	2.00	4.00

CHURCHILL

Number	Title (A Side/B Side)	Yr	VG	VG+	NM
❑ 94024	I.O.U./To a Sleeping Beauty	1983	—	2.00	4.00

COLUMBIA

Number	Title (A Side/B Side)	Yr	VG	VG+	NM
❑ 31550 [S]	Basin Street Blues/Please Pass the Biscuits	1962	5.00	10.00	20.00

Number	Title (A Side/B Side)	Yr	VG	VG+	NM
❑ 31551 [S]	Have You Ever Been Lonely/Nobody	1962	5.00	10.00	20.00
❑ 31552 [S]	I Was Just Walking Out the Door/The Dark Town Poker Club	1962	5.00	10.00	20.00
❑ 31553 [S]	You're Nobody Until Somebody Loves You/ Kentucky Means Paradise	1962	5.00	10.00	20.00
❑ 31554 [S]	Little Black Book/Old Pappy's New Banjo	1962	5.00	10.00	20.00
—The above five are "Stereo Seven" 33 1/3 rpm jukebox singles from set "JS 7-63"					
❑ 40995	Deep Blue Sea/Love Me So I'll Know	1957	3.00	6.00	12.00
❑ 41025	Little Sandy Sleighfoot/When They Ring the Golden Bells	1957	3.75	7.50	15.00
❑ 41025 [PS]	Little Sandy Sleighfoot/When They Ring the Golden Bells	1957	6.25	12.50	25.00
❑ 41118	Starlight, Starbright/Makin' My Mind Up	1958	3.00	6.00	12.00
❑ 41196	School of Love/You Should See Tennessee, Mam'selle	1958	3.00	6.00	12.00
❑ 41265	My Heart Is An Open Book/Shark in the Bathtub	1958	3.00	6.00	12.00
❑ 41395	Sing Along/Weekend Blues	1959	3.00	6.00	12.00
❑ 41453	Stay a Little Longer/Counting Tears	1959	3.00	6.00	12.00
❑ 41543	Thanks for the Dream/There's Still Time, Brother	1959	3.00	6.00	12.00
❑ 41710	Little Boy Lost/There'll Be No Teardrops Tonight	1960	3.00	6.00	12.00
❑ 41956	Give Me Back My Heart/It's Been a Long, Long Time	1961	2.50	5.00	10.00
❑ 42175	Big John/I Won't Go Huntin' with You Jake (But I'll Go Chasin' Wimmin)	1961	5.00	10.00	20.00
—Lyrics say: "At the bottom of this mine lies one hell of a man."					
❑ 42175	Big Bad John/I Won't Go Huntin' with You Jake (But I'll Go Chasin' Wimmin)	1961	2.50	5.00	10.00
—Lyrics say: "At the bottom of this mine lies a big, big man." We think the song title was changed with the lyric, but we're not 100 percent sure. In other words, this title may exist with the "hell of a man" lyrics.					
❑ 42175 [PS]	Big Bad John/I Won't Go Huntin' with You Jake (But I'll Go Chasin' Wimmin)	1961	3.75	7.50	15.00
❑ 42248	Oklahoma Bill/To a Sleeping Beauty	1961	2.50	5.00	10.00
❑ 42259	Dear Ivan/Smoke, Smoke, Smoke That Cigarette	1962	2.50	5.00	10.00
❑ 42259 [PS]	Dear Ivan/Smoke, Smoke, Smoke That Cigarette	1962	3.75	7.50	15.00
❑ 42282	To a Sleeping Beauty/The Cajun Queen	1962	2.50	5.00	10.00
❑ 42282 [PS]	To a Sleeping Beauty/The Cajun Queen	1962	3.75	7.50	15.00
❑ 42338	P.T. 109/Walk On, Boy	1962	2.50	5.00	10.00
❑ 42338 [PS]	P.T. 109/Walk On, Boy	1962	3.75	7.50	15.00
❑ 42483	Steel Men/Little Bitty Big John	1962	2.50	5.00	10.00
❑ 42483 [PS]	Steel Men/Little Bitty Big John	1962	3.75	7.50	15.00
❑ 42529	Little Black Book/Please Pass the Biscuits	1962	2.50	5.00	10.00
❑ 42529 [PS]	Little Black Book/Please Pass the Biscuits	1962	3.75	7.50	15.00
❑ 42600	Gonna Raise a Rukus Tonight/A Day That Changed the World	1962	2.50	5.00	10.00
❑ 42600 [PS]	Gonna Raise a Rukus Tonight/A Day That Changed the World	1962	3.75	7.50	15.00
❑ 42738	Mile Long Train/This Ole House	1963	2.00	4.00	8.00
❑ 42861	The Funniest Thing I Ever Heard/Thumb Pick Pete	1963	2.00	4.00	8.00
❑ 42934	Mind Your Own Business/I Really Don't Want to Know	1963	2.00	4.00	8.00
❑ 43021	Shenandoah/Waitin' for the Wagon	1964	2.00	4.00	8.00
❑ 43159	Sam Hill/When I Grow Too Old to Dream	1964	2.00	4.00	8.00
❑ 43172	Yes, Patricia, There Is a Santa Claus/Little Sandy Sleighfoot	1964	2.50	5.00	10.00
❑ 43263	The First Thing Ev'ry Morning (And the Last Thing Ev'ry Night)/Awkward Situation	1965	—	3.00	6.00
❑ 43382	Harvest of Sunshine/Under the Sun	1965	—	3.00	6.00
❑ 43457	Blue Christmas/Yes, Patricia, There Is a Santa Claus	1965	2.00	4.00	8.00
❑ 43540	Things Have Gone to Pieces/Striker Bill	1966	—	3.00	6.00
❑ 43754	Once a Day/Let's Pretend	1966	—	3.00	6.00
❑ 45922	Your Sweet Love (Keeps Me Homeward Bound)/ I'm Gonna Be Gone	1973	—	2.50	5.00
❑ 45981	Who's Gonna Love Me Tomorrow/The Days When Jim Liked Jimmy	1973	—	2.50	5.00
❑ 46039	I've Been Down Some Road/Your Sweet Love	1974	—	2.50	5.00
❑ JZSP 111915/6 [DJ]	Blue Christmas/Yes, Patricia, There Is a Santa Claus	1965	5.00	10.00	20.00
—Promo only on green vinyl					
KING					
❑ 5862	There Stands the Glass/Bumming Around	1964	2.00	4.00	8.00
MERCURY					
❑ 70691	False Pride/Big Blue Diamonds	1955	3.75	7.50	15.00
❑ 70745	Find 'Em, Fool 'Em, and Leave 'Em Alone/My World Is You	1955	3.75	7.50	15.00
❑ 70786	Freight Train Blues/Glad Rags	1956	3.75	7.50	15.00
❑ 70855	Hello Mr. Blues/I Found Out	1956	3.75	7.50	15.00
❑ 71120	Losing Game/Happy Child	1957	3.75	7.50	15.00
❑ 71172	Look on the Good Side/Do You Love Me	1957	3.75	7.50	15.00
❑ 71240	Bumming Around/Nothing Can Stop My Love	1957	3.75	7.50	15.00
❑ 71313	What This Old World Needs/A Fool in Love	1958	3.75	7.50	15.00
RCA VICTOR					
❑ 47-8971	Stand Beside Me/A Tiny Drop of Sadness	1966	2.00	4.00	8.00
❑ 47-9091	Sweet Misery/When Someone Mentions Your Name	1967	2.00	4.00	8.00
❑ 47-9241	Ninety Days/In the Same Old Way	1967	2.00	4.00	8.00
❑ 47-9350	I'm a Swinger/Your Country Boy	1967	2.00	4.00	8.00
❑ 47-9454	A Thing Called Love/One Last Time	1968	2.00	4.00	8.00
❑ 47-9567	Born to Be By Your Side/Read 'Em and Weep	1968	2.00	4.00	8.00
❑ 47-9652	A Hammer and Nails/I Taught Her Everything She Knows	1968	2.00	4.00	8.00
❑ 47-9800	When Judy Smiled/My Hometown Sweetheart	1969	—	3.00	6.00
❑ 47-9859	Down Comes the Rain/Us	1970	—	3.00	6.00
❑ 47-9915	Weakness in a Man/Aunt Maudie's Fun Garden	1970	—	3.00	6.00
❑ 47-9947	Slowly/Sweet Thang	1971	—	3.00	6.00
—With Dottie West					
❑ 47-9966	Everybody Knows/Ain't Life Sweet	1971	—	3.00	6.00
❑ 74-0122	A Rose Is a Rose Is a Rose/She's Mine	1969	—	3.00	6.00
❑ 74-0600	And I'm Still Missing You/The One You Say Good Mornin' To	1971	—	3.00	6.00

DEAN, LARRY

Number	Title (A Side/B Side)	Yr	VG	VG+	NM
USA					
❑ 620	Outside Chance/(B-side unknown)	1989	—	3.00	6.00
❑ 620 [PS]	Outside Chance/(B-side unknown)	1989	2.00	4.00	8.00

DEAN AND JEAN

Number	Title (A Side/B Side)	Yr	VG	VG+	NM
EMBER					
❑ 1048	We're Gonna Get Married/Too Young to Know	1958	3.00	6.00	12.00
❑ 1054	Turn It Off/Never Let Your Love Fade Away	1959	3.00	6.00	12.00
RUST					
❑ TR 1	Seven Day Wonder/The Man Who Will Never Grow Old	196?	3.00	6.00	12.00
❑ 5044	Come Take a Walk with Me/Dance the Roach	1962	2.50	5.00	10.00
❑ 5046	Mack the Knife/You Can't Be Happy by Yourself	1962	2.50	5.00	10.00
❑ 5067	Tra La La La Suzy/I Love the Summertime	1963	2.50	5.00	10.00
❑ 5075	Hey Jean, Hey Dean/Please Don't Tell Me Now	1964	3.75	7.50	15.00
❑ 5081	I Wanna Be Loved/Thread Your Needle	1964	2.50	5.00	10.00
❑ 5085	Goddess of Love/The Man Who Will Never Grow Old	1964	2.50	5.00	10.00
❑ 5089	Sticks and Stones/In My Way	1964	2.50	5.00	10.00
❑ 5100	Lovingly Yours/Goddess of Love	1965	2.50	5.00	10.00
❑ 5107	She's Too Respectable/I Love the Summertime	1965	2.50	5.00	10.00

DEAN AND MARC

Also see THE NEWBEATS.

Number	Title (A Side/B Side)	Yr	VG	VG+	NM
BULLSEYE					
❑ 1025	Tell Him No/Change of Heart	1959	12.50	25.00	50.00
❑ 1026	Cry/The Beginning of Love	1959	6.25	12.50	25.00
CHECKMATE					
❑ 1008	Boogie Woogie Twist (Parts 1 & 2)	1962	3.75	7.50	15.00
HICKORY					
❑ 1227	With Tears in My Eyes/Kissin' Game	1963	2.50	5.00	10.00
—Hickory titles as "Dean and Mark" unless noted					
❑ 1249	When I Stop Dreaming/There Oughta Be a Law	1964	2.50	5.00	10.00
❑ 1294	Just a Step Away/A Falling Star	1965	2.50	5.00	10.00
❑ 1353	In the Middle of the Night/You'll Never Really Know	1965	2.50	5.00	10.00
❑ 1414	When I Stop Dreaming/With Tears in My Eyes	1966	2.50	5.00	10.00
—As "The Mathis Brothers"					
MAY					
❑ 135	Somebody's Smiling (While I'm Crying)/Pins and Needles (In My Heart)	1963	3.00	6.00	12.00
—As "Dean and Mark"					

DEANS, THE

Number	Title (A Side/B Side)	Yr	VG	VG+	NM
LAURIE					
❑ 3114	I Don't Want to Wait/Little White Gardenia	1961	5.00	10.00	20.00
MOHAWK					
❑ 114	My Heart Is Low/I'll Love You Forever	1960	6.25	12.50	25.00
❑ 119	Humpty Dumpty/La Chiam	1960	6.25	12.50	25.00
❑ 126	It's You/I Don't Wanna Wait	1960	10.00	20.00	40.00
STAR MAKER					
❑ 1928	Oh Little Star/You Got Me Baby	1961	25.00	50.00	100.00
❑ 1931	Chills, Chills, Chills/(Lady of the) Caravan	1962	15.00	30.00	60.00

DEAUVILLE, RONNIE

Number	Title (A Side/B Side)	Yr	VG	VG+	NM
ERA					
❑ 1055	I Concentrate on You/As Children Go	1957	5.00	10.00	20.00
❑ 1056	Laura/It Wasn't Much of a Town	1957	5.00	10.00	20.00
❑ 1056 [PS]	Laura/It Wasn't Much of a Town	1957	15.00	30.00	60.00
❑ 1066	Hong Kong Affair/Crazy, Wonderful	1957	5.00	10.00	20.00
IMPERIAL					
❑ 5559	King of Fools/Blame Your Eyes	1959	3.75	7.50	15.00

DEBBIE AND THE TEEN DREAMS

Number	Title (A Side/B Side)	Yr	VG	VG+	NM
VERNON					
❑ 101	Santa, Teach Me How To Dance/The Time	1962	6.25	12.50	25.00

DEBERRY, JIMMY

Number	Title (A Side/B Side)	Yr	VG	VG+	NM
SUN					
❑ 185	Take a Little Chance/Time Has Made a Change	1953	750.00	1500.	3000.

DEBONAIRES, THE (1)

Number	Title (A Side/B Side)	Yr	VG	VG+	NM
DORE					
❑ 526	Every Once in a While/Mama Don't Care	1959	20.00	40.00	80.00
—As "The Debonairs"					
❑ 592	Every Once in a While/Gert's Skirt	1961	7.50	15.00	30.00
❑ 654	Hold Back the Dawn/Mama Don't Care	1962	6.25	12.50	25.00
❑ 702	Every Once in a While/Gert's Skirt	1964	5.00	10.00	20.00
❑ 712	Everybody's Movin'/Mama Don't Care	1964	5.00	10.00	20.00
GEE					
❑ 1008	Won't You Tell Me/I'm Gone	1956	20.00	40.00	80.00
❑ 1054	We'll Wait/Make Believe Lover	1960	6.25	12.50	25.00
HERALD					
❑ 509	Darlin'/Whispering Blues	1957	15.00	30.00	60.00
❑ 509	Darlin'/Whispering Blues	1957	50.00	100.00	200.00
—As "The Five Debonaires"					

DEBONAIRES, THE (2)

Number	Title (A Side/B Side)	Yr	VG	VG+	NM
ELMONT					
❑ 1004	This Must Be Paradise/I Need You Darling	1958	50.00	100.00	200.00

DEBONAIRES, THE (3)

Number	Title (A Side/B Side)	Yr	VG	VG+	NM
GOLDEN WORLD					
❑ 17	A Little Too Long/Please Don't Say We're Through	1964	5.00	10.00	20.00
❑ 26	Eenie Meenie Gypsaleenie/Please Don't Say We're Through	1965	5.00	10.00	20.00
❑ 38	Big Time Fun/How's Your New Love Treating You	1966	5.00	10.00	20.00
❑ 44	C.O.D./How's Your New Love Treating You	1966	5.00	10.00	20.00

DEBONAIRES, THE (4)

MTM

Number	Title (A Side/B Side)	Yr	VG	VG+	NM
❑ B-72051	I'm on Fire/Loving You's All That's On My Mind	1985	—	3.00	6.00

DEBONAIRES, THE (U)

This may be one of groups (1), (2) or (3), or it may be a completely different group.

MASKE

Number	Title (A Side/B Side)	Yr	VG	VG+	NM
❑ 804	Every Other Day/Jivin' Guy	1959	10.00	20.00	40.00

DEBS, THE

More than one group.

BRUCE

Number	Title (A Side/B Side)	Yr	VG	VG+	NM
❑ 129	Shoo-Doo-De-Doo/Whadaya Want	1955	15.00	30.00	60.00

CROWN

Number	Title (A Side/B Side)	Yr	VG	VG+	NM
❑ 153	If You Were Here Tonight/Look What You're Doin' to Me	1955	10.00	20.00	40.00

DOUBLE L

Number	Title (A Side/B Side)	Yr	VG	VG+	NM
❑ 727	Danger Ahead/Just Another Fool	1964	3.00	6.00	12.00

KEEN

Number	Title (A Side/B Side)	Yr	VG	VG+	NM
❑ 34003	Johnny Darling/Doom-a-Roca	1957	6.25	12.50	25.00

MERCURY

Number	Title (A Side/B Side)	Yr	VG	VG+	NM
❑ 72458	Give Him My Love/Goodbye Boy	1965	5.00	10.00	20.00
❑ 72566	My Best Friend/The Life and Soul of the Party	1966	3.75	7.50	15.00

DEBUTANTES, THE (1)

KAYO

Number	Title (A Side/B Side)	Yr	VG	VG+	NM
❑ 928	Going Steady/Memories	1958	62.50	125.00	250.00

DEBUTANTES, THE (2)

LUCKY ELEVEN

Number	Title (A Side/B Side)	Yr	VG	VG+	NM
❑ 237	Love Is Strange/A New Love Today	196?	3.75	7.50	15.00

DEBUTANTES, THE (3)

SAVOY

Number	Title (A Side/B Side)	Yr	VG	VG+	NM
❑ 1191	Just Leave It to Me/Is It Too Soon	1956	7.50	15.00	30.00

DECEMBER'S CHILDREN

CAPITOL

Number	Title (A Side/B Side)	Yr	VG	VG+	NM
❑ 5883	A Girl Like You/Makin' Music	1967	3.00	6.00	12.00

LIBERTY

Number	Title (A Side/B Side)	Yr	VG	VG+	NM
❑ 56195	You're My Girl/Dirty City	1970	2.50	5.00	10.00

MAINSTREAM

Number	Title (A Side/B Side)	Yr	VG	VG+	NM
❑ 728	Sweet Talking Woman/(B-side unknown)	1970	3.75	7.50	15.00

WORLD PACIFIC

Number	Title (A Side/B Side)	Yr	VG	VG+	NM
❑ 77887	Backwards and Forwards/Kissin' Time	1968	2.50	5.00	10.00
❑ 77895	Lovin' Things/Extraordinary Man	1968	2.50	5.00	10.00
❑ 77910	I've Been Hurt/Good Time Boy	1969	2.50	5.00	10.00

DEE, DONNA

ABC-PARAMOUNT

Number	Title (A Side/B Side)	Yr	VG	VG+	NM
❑ 10296	Television/Nobody's Gonna Hurt You	1962	5.00	10.00	20.00

DEE, FRANKIE

20TH FOX

Number	Title (A Side/B Side)	Yr	VG	VG+	NM
❑ 146	Swingin' in a Hammock/I Had the Craziest Dream	1959	7.50	15.00	30.00

ABCO

Number	Title (A Side/B Side)	Yr	VG	VG+	NM
❑ 1002	Walking in the Rain/Everybody's Doin' It	195?	5.00	10.00	20.00

RCA VICTOR

Number	Title (A Side/B Side)	Yr	VG	VG+	NM
❑ 47-7276	Shake It Up Baby/After Graduation	1958	15.00	30.00	60.00

DEE, JACKIE

See JACKIE DeSHANNON.

DEE, JIMMY

DOT

Number	Title (A Side/B Side)	Yr	VG	VG+	NM
❑ 15664	Henrietta/Don't Cry No More	1957	10.00	20.00	40.00
❑ 15721	Here I Come/You're Late, Miss Kate	1958	10.00	20.00	40.00

TNT

Number	Title (A Side/B Side)	Yr	VG	VG+	NM
❑ 148	Henrietta/Don't Cry No More	1957	20.00	40.00	80.00
❑ 152	Here I Come/You're Late, Miss Kate	1958	20.00	40.00	80.00
❑ 161	Feel Like Rockin'/Rock-Tick-Rock	1958	15.00	30.00	60.00

DEE, JOEY, AND THE STARLITERS

BONUS

Number	Title (A Side/B Side)	Yr	VG	VG+	NM
❑ 7009	Lorraine/The Girl I Walk to School	1963	12.50	25.00	50.00
❑ 7009 [PS]	Lorraine/The Girl I Walk to School	1963	20.00	40.00	80.00

JUBILEE

Number	Title (A Side/B Side)	Yr	VG	VG+	NM
❑ 5532	Feel Good About It Part 1/Feel Good About It Part 2	1966	3.75	7.50	15.00
❑ 5539	Dancing on the Beach/Good Little You	1966	3.75	7.50	15.00
❑ 5554	She's So Exceptional/It's Got You	1966	3.75	7.50	15.00
❑ 5566	Can't Sit Down/Put Your Heart In It	1967	3.75	7.50	15.00

—Stock copy may not exist

LITTLE

Number	Title (A Side/B Side)	Yr	VG	VG+	NM
❑ 813/4	Lorraine/The Girl I Walk to School	1958	100.00	200.00	400.00

MONUMENT

Number	Title (A Side/B Side)	Yr	VG	VG+	NM
❑ (# unknown) [DJ]	Ya Ya Twist/Runaround Sue	1962	6.25	12.50	25.00

—B-side by Dion

ROULETTE

Number	Title (A Side/B Side)	Yr	VG	VG+	NM
❑ 4401	Peppermint Twist — Part 1/Peppermint Twist — Part 2	1961	4.00	8.00	16.00
❑ 4408	Hey, Let's Twist/Roly Poly	1962	3.75	7.50	15.00
❑ 4408 [PS]	Hey, Let's Twist/Roly Poly	1962	6.25	12.50	25.00
❑ 4416	Shout — Part 1/Shout — Part 2	1962	3.75	7.50	15.00
❑ 4416 [PS]	Shout — Part 1/Shout — Part 2	1962	6.25	12.50	25.00
❑ 4431	Every Time (I Think About You) Part 1/Every Time (I Think About You) Part 2	1962	3.00	6.00	12.00
❑ 4438	What Kind of Love Is This/Wing Ding	1962	3.00	6.00	12.00
❑ 4438 [PS]	What Kind of Love Is This/Wing Ding	1962	6.25	12.50	25.00
❑ 4456	I Lost My Baby/Keep Your Mind on What You're Doing	1962	3.00	6.00	12.00
❑ 4456 [PS]	I Lost My Baby/Keep Your Mind on What You're Doing	1962	6.25	12.50	25.00
❑ 4467	Baby You're Driving Me Crazy/Help Me Pick Up the Pieces	1963	3.00	6.00	12.00
❑ 4488	Hot Pastrami with Mashed Potatoes — Part 1/Hot Pastrami with Mashed Potatoes — Part 2	1963	3.00	6.00	12.00
❑ 4503	Dance, Dance, Dance/Let's Have a Party	1963	3.00	6.00	12.00
❑ 4523	Ya Ya/Fanny Mae	1963	3.00	6.00	12.00
❑ 4539	Down by the Riverside/Getting Nearer	1963	5.00	10.00	20.00
❑ 4617	Cry a Little Sometime/Wing Ding	1965	3.00	6.00	12.00

SCEPTER

Number	Title (A Side/B Side)	Yr	VG	VG+	NM
❑ 1210	Face of An Angel/Shimmy Baby	1960	7.50	15.00	30.00

—Originals have "Scepter" at top of label and are credited as "Joey Dee and the Starlights"

Number	Title (A Side/B Side)	Yr	VG	VG+	NM
❑ 1210	Face of An Angel/Shimmy Baby	1961	5.00	10.00	20.00

—Reissues have "Scepter Records" at side of label and are credited as listed

Number	Title (A Side/B Side)	Yr	VG	VG+	NM
❑ 1225	Three Memories/(Bad) Bulldog	1961	7.50	15.00	30.00

VASELINE HAIR TONIC

Number	Title (A Side/B Side)	Yr	VG	VG+	NM
❑ (no #)	Learn to Dance the Authentic Peppermint Twist (Parts 1 & 2)	1962	3.75	7.50	15.00
❑ (no #) [PS]	Learn to Dance the Authentic Peppermint Twist (Parts 1 & 2)	1962	3.75	7.50	15.00

DEE, JOHNNY

See JOHN D. LOUDERMILK.

DEE, KIKI

Also see ELTON JOHN AND KIKI DEE.

FONTANA

Number	Title (A Side/B Side)	Yr	VG	VG+	NM
❑ 1649	On a Magic Carpet Ride/Now the Flowers Die	1969	—	2.50	5.00

LIBERTY

Number	Title (A Side/B Side)	Yr	VG	VG+	NM
❑ 55994	Stop and Think/I	1967	—	3.00	6.00
❑ 56030	I'm Going Out/Patterns	1968	—	3.00	6.00
❑ 56089	On a Magic Carpet Ride/Now the Flowers Die	1969	—	3.00	6.00

POSSE

Number	Title (A Side/B Side)	Yr	VG	VG+	NM
❑ 5008	Nothing Can Stop Us Now/(B-side unknown)	1981	—	2.00	4.00

RARE EARTH

Number	Title (A Side/B Side)	Yr	VG	VG+	NM
❑ 5025	Love Makes the World Go Round/Jimmy	1970	—	2.50	5.00

RCA

Number	Title (A Side/B Side)	Yr	VG	VG+	NM
❑ PB-12347	Star/There's a Need	1981	—	2.00	4.00
❑ PB-13043	Loving You Is Sweeter Than Ever/Twenty-Four Hours	1982	—	—	—

—Unreleased

ROCKET

Number	Title (A Side/B Side)	Yr	VG	VG+	NM
❑ YB-11413	One Step/Dark Side of Your Soul	1978	—	2.00	4.00
❑ YB-11490	Don't Stop Loving Me/One Step Ahead of the Storm	1979	—	2.00	4.00
❑ 40095	The Last Good Man in My Life/Lonnie and Josie	1973	—	2.00	4.00
❑ 40157	Amoureuse/Rest My Head	1973	—	2.00	4.00
❑ 40256	Super Cool/Loving and Free	1974	—	2.00	4.00
❑ 40293	I've Got the Music in Me/Simple Melody	1974	—	2.50	5.00
❑ 40355	Step by Step/Amoureuse	1975	—	2.00	4.00
❑ 40401	How Glad I Am/Peter	1975	—	2.00	4.00
❑ 40506	Once a Fool/Someone to Me	1976	—	2.00	4.00
❑ 40730	Chicago/Bad Day Child	1977	—	2.00	4.00

TAMLA

Number	Title (A Side/B Side)	Yr	VG	VG+	NM
❑ 54193	The Day Will Come Between Sunday and Monday/My Whole World Ended (The Moment You Left Me)	1970	—	2.50	5.00

WORLD PACIFIC

Number	Title (A Side/B Side)	Yr	VG	VG+	NM
❑ 77820	I Dig You Baby/Small Town	1966	2.00	4.00	8.00

DEE, TOMMY

CHALLENGE

Number	Title (A Side/B Side)	Yr	VG	VG+	NM
❑ 59083	The Hobo and the Puppy/There's a Star Spangled Banner Waving Somewhere	1960	5.00	10.00	20.00
❑ 59087	Ballad of a Drag Race/The Story of Susie	1960	5.00	10.00	20.00

CREST

Number	Title (A Side/B Side)	Yr	VG	VG+	NM
❑ 1057 [M]	Three Stars/I'll Never Change	1959	7.50	15.00	30.00

—With backing group and B-side credited to "The Teen Tones and Orchestra"

Number	Title (A Side/B Side)	Yr	VG	VG+	NM
❑ 1057 [M]	Three Stars/I'll Never Change	1959	6.25	12.50	25.00

—With backing group and B-side credited to "Carol Kay and the Teen-Aires"

Number	Title (A Side/B Side)	Yr	VG	VG+	NM
❑ 1057 [S]	Three Stars/I'll Never Change	1959	12.50	25.00	50.00

—With backing group and B-side credited to "Carol Kay and the Teen-Aires"

Number	Title (A Side/B Side)	Yr	VG	VG+	NM
❑ 1061	The Chair/Hello Lonesome	1959	5.00	10.00	20.00
❑ 1067	Merry Christmas, Mary/Angel of Love	1959	6.25	12.50	25.00

—With Carol Kay

PIKE

Number	Title (A Side/B Side)	Yr	VG	VG+	NM
❑ 5906	Loving You (On Someone Else's Time)/Halfway to Hell	1961	5.00	10.00	20.00
❑ 5909	A Little Dog Cried/Look Homeward, Dear Angel	1961	5.00	10.00	20.00
❑ 5917	Missing on a Mountain/Look Homeward, Dear Angel	1962	5.00	10.00	20.00

SIMS

Number	Title (A Side/B Side)	Yr	VG	VG+	NM
❑ 260	Missing While Surfing/Goodbye High School	1966	5.00	10.00	20.00
❑ 308	How's Your Mama Em/Goodbye High School	1966	3.75	7.50	15.00

DEEP PURPLE

MERCURY

Number	Title (A Side/B Side)	Yr	VG	VG+	NM
❑ 880477-7	Knocking at Your Back Door/Wasted Sunset	1984	—	2.00	4.00
❑ 880477-7 [PS]	Knocking at Your Back Door/Wasted Sunset	1984	—	2.50	5.00
❑ 885617-7	Call of the Wild/Dead or Alive	1987	—	—	3.00
❑ 885617-7 [PS]	Call of the Wild/Dead or Alive	1987	—	—	3.00
❑ 885820-7	Bad Attitude/Black and White	1987	—	—	3.00

TETRAGRAMMATON

Number	Title (A Side/B Side)	Yr	VG	VG+	NM
❑ 1503	Hush/One More Rainy Day	1968	3.00	6.00	12.00
❑ 1503 [PS]	Hush/One More Rainy Day	1968	7.50	15.00	30.00
❑ 1508	Kentucky Woman/Hard Road	1968	3.00	6.00	12.00
❑ 1508 [PS]	Kentucky Woman/Hard Road	1968	3.75	7.50	15.00
❑ 1514	River Deep, Mountain High/Listen, Learn, Read On	1969	2.50	5.00	10.00
❑ 1519	The Bird Has Flown/Emmaretta	1969	2.50	5.00	10.00
❑ 1537	Hallelujah (I Am the Preacher)/April Part 1	1969	2.50	5.00	10.00

WARNER BROS.

Number	Title (A Side/B Side)	Yr	VG	VG+	NM
❑ 7405	Black Night/Into the Fire	1970	2.00	4.00	8.00
❑ 7493	Strange Kind of Woman/I'm Alone	1971	2.00	4.00	8.00
❑ 7528	Fire Ball/I'm Alone	1971	2.00	4.00	8.00
❑ 7572	Never Before/When a Blind Man Cries	1972	—	3.00	6.00
❑ 7595	Lazy/When a Blind Man Cries	1972	—	3.00	6.00
❑ 7634	Highway Star (Part 1)/Highway Star (Part 2)	1972	—	3.00	6.00
❑ 7654	Hush/Kentucky Woman	1972	—	3.00	6.00
❑ 7672	Woman from Tokyo/Super Trouper	1972	—	3.00	6.00
❑ 7710	Smoke on the Water (Edited Version) Studio/ Smoke on the Water (Edited Version) Live	1973	—	2.50	5.00
❑ 7737	Woman from Tokyo/Super Trouper	1973	—	2.50	5.00
❑ 7784	Might Just Take Your Life/Coronorias Regid	1974	—	2.50	5.00
❑ 7784 [DJ]	Might Just Take Your Life (Mono 3:35/Stereo 4:36)	1974	2.00	4.00	8.00
❑ 7809	Burn/Coronarias Regid	1974	—	2.50	5.00
❑ 8049	High Ball Shooter/You Can't Do It Right	1974	—	2.50	5.00
❑ 8069	Stormbringer/Love Don't Mean a Thing	1975	—	2.50	5.00
❑ 8182	Gettin' Tighter/Love Child	1976	—	2.50	5.00

DEES, RICK

ATLANTIC

Number	Title (A Side/B Side)	Yr	VG	VG+	NM
❑ 89462	We Are the Weird/Merry Christmas (Wherever You Are)	1985	—	2.00	4.00
❑ 89481	I Wanna Be Elvis/(Instrumental)	1985	2.00	4.00	8.00
❑ 89601	Eat My Shorts/Get Nekked	1984	—	2.00	4.00
❑ 89601 [PS]	Eat My Shorts/Get Nekked	1984	—	2.00	4.00

FRETONE

Number	Title (A Side/B Side)	Yr	VG	VG+	NM
❑ 040	Disco Duck (Part 1)/Disco Duck (Part 2)	1976	2.50	5.00	10.00

NO BUDGET

Number	Title (A Side/B Side)	Yr	VG	VG+	NM
❑ 1680	Merry Christmas (Wherever You Are)/Hurt Me Baby, Make Me Write Bad Checks	1984	2.50	5.00	10.00

RSO

Number	Title (A Side/B Side)	Yr	VG	VG+	NM
❑ 857	Disco Duck (Part 1)/Disco Duck (Part 2)	1976	—	2.00	4.00
❑ 866	Dis-Gorilla (Part 1)/Dis-Gorilla (Part 2)	1976	—	2.00	4.00
❑ 870	He Ate Too Many Jelly Doughnuts/Barely White	1977	2.50	5.00	10.00

—A-side is an Elvis novelty. It only appears on stock copies, as "Barely White" was promoted as the hit

Number	Title (A Side/B Side)	Yr	VG	VG+	NM
❑ 939	Meatballs/Run with the Pack	1979	—	2.00	4.00

STAX

Number	Title (A Side/B Side)	Yr	VG	VG+	NM
❑ 3207	Big Foot/Big Toe	1978	—	2.00	4.00
❑ 3213	You Got Those Lips (Part 1)/You Got Those Lips (Part 2)	1978	—	2.00	4.00

DEF LEPPARD

MERCURY

Number	Title (A Side/B Side)	Yr	VG	VG+	NM
❑ 76064	Rock Brigade/When the Walls Came Tumbling Down	1980	2.50	5.00	10.00
❑ 76120 [DJ]	Let It Go (same on both sides)	1981	2.50	5.00	10.00

—May be promo only

Number	Title (A Side/B Side)	Yr	VG	VG+	NM
❑ 562151-7	Promises/Pour Some Sugar on Me	1999	—	—	3.00
❑ 811215-7	Photograph/Action, Not Words	1983	—	2.50	5.00

—Chicago skyline label

Number	Title (A Side/B Side)	Yr	VG	VG+	NM
❑ 811215-7	Photograph/Action, Not Words	1983	—	2.00	4.00

—Black label

Number	Title (A Side/B Side)	Yr	VG	VG+	NM
❑ 811215-7 [PS]	Photograph/Action, Not Words	1983	2.50	5.00	10.00
❑ 812604-7	Rock of Ages/Billy's Got a Gun	1983	—	2.00	4.00
❑ 814178-7	Foolin'/Comin' Under Fire	1983	—	2.00	4.00
❑ 818779-7	Bringin' On the Heartbreak/Me and My Wine	1984	—	2.00	4.00
❑ 818779-7 [PS]	Bringin' On the Heartbreak/Me and My Wine	1984	—	2.50	5.00
❑ 852424-7	When Love & Hate Collide/Can't Keep Away from the Flame	1995	—	—	3.00
❑ 858080-7	Miss You in a Heartbeat/Let's Get Rocked	1993	—	2.00	4.00
❑ 864038-7	Make Love Like a Man/Miss You in a Heartbeat	1992	—	2.00	4.00
❑ 864136-7	Have You Ever Needed Someone So Bad/ Elected	1992	—	2.00	4.00
❑ 864604-7	Stand Up (Kick Love Into Motion)/From the Inside	1993	—	2.00	4.00
❑ 866568-7	Let's Get Rocked/Only After Dark	1992	—	2.00	4.00
❑ 870004-7	Hysteria/Ride Into the Sun	1988	—	—	3.00
❑ 870004-7 [PS]	Hysteria/Ride Into the Sun	1988	—	—	3.00
❑ 870298-7	Pour Some Sugar on Me/Ring of Fire	1988	—	—	3.00
❑ 870298-7 [PS]	Pour Some Sugar on Me/Ring of Fire	1988	—	—	3.00
❑ 870402-7	Love Bites/Billy's Got a Gun	1988	—	—	3.00
❑ 870402-7 [PS]	Love Bites/Billy's Got a Gun	1988	—	—	3.00
❑ 870692-7	Armageddon It/Release Me	1988	—	—	3.00

—B-side by "Stumpus Maximus and the Good Ol' Boys" (Def Leppard in disguise)

Number	Title (A Side/B Side)	Yr	VG	VG+	NM
❑ 870692-7 [PS]	Armageddon It/Release Me	1988	—	—	3.00
❑ 872614-7	Rocket/Women	1989	—	—	3.00
❑ 872614-7 [PS]	Rocket/Women	1989	—	—	3.00
❑ 888757-7	Women/Tear It Down	1987	—	—	3.00
❑ 888757-7 [PS]	Women/Tear It Down	1987	—	—	3.00
❑ 888832-7	Animal/I Wanna Be Your Hero	1987	—	—	3.00
❑ 888832-7 [PS]	Animal/I Wanna Be Your Hero	1987	—	—	3.00

DEFRANCO FAMILY, THE

20TH CENTURY

Number	Title (A Side/B Side)	Yr	VG	VG+	NM
❑ 2030	Heartbeat — It's a Lovebeat/Sweet, Sweet Loretta	1973	—	2.00	4.00
❑ 2030 [PS]	Heartbeat — It's a Lovebeat/Sweet, Sweet Loretta	1973	—	3.00	6.00
❑ 2070	Abra-Ca-Dabra/Some Kind a' Love	1973	—	2.00	4.00
❑ 2070 [PS]	Abra-Ca-Dabra/Some Kind a' Love	1973	—	3.00	6.00
❑ 2088	Save the Last Dance for Me/Because We Both Are Young	1974	—	2.00	4.00
❑ 2088 [PS]	Save the Last Dance for Me/Because We Both Are Young	1974	—	3.00	6.00
❑ 2128	Baby Blue/Write Me a Letter	1974	—	2.00	4.00
❑ 2214	We Belong Together/Time Enough for Love	1975	2.00	4.00	8.00

DEKKER, DESMOND, AND THE ACES

UNI

Number	Title (A Side/B Side)	Yr	VG	VG+	NM
❑ 55129	Israelites/My Precious World	1969	—	3.00	6.00
❑ 55150	It Mek/Problems	1969	—	3.00	6.00
❑ 55261	You Can Get It If You Really Want It/ Perseverance	1970	—	3.00	6.00

DEL-AIRES, THE

CORAL

Number	Title (A Side/B Side)	Yr	VG	VG+	NM
❑ 62370	Elaine/Just Wigglin' and a-Wobblin'	1963	10.00	20.00	40.00
❑ 62404	The Drag/My Funny Valentine	1964	10.00	20.00	40.00

—As "Ronnie and the Del-Aires"

Number	Title (A Side/B Side)	Yr	VG	VG+	NM
❑ 62419	Arlene/I'm Yours Baby	1964	17.50	35.00	70.00

DEL AND THE ESCORTS

ROME

Number	Title (A Side/B Side)	Yr	VG	VG+	NM
❑ 103	Baby Doll/Someone to Watch Over Me	1961	12.50	25.00	50.00

SYMBOL

Number	Title (A Side/B Side)	Yr	VG	VG+	NM
❑ 913	You Don't Love Me/Skokiian	1960	—	—	—

—Unreleased?

TAURUS

Number	Title (A Side/B Side)	Yr	VG	VG+	NM
❑ 350/1	Happy/You're for Me (And I'm for You)	1961	7.50	15.00	30.00

DEL-PHIS, THE

Early incarnation of MARTHA AND THE VANDELLAS.

CHECKMATE

Number	Title (A Side/B Side)	Yr	VG	VG+	NM
❑ 1005	I'll Let You Know/It Takes Two	1961	50.00	100.00	200.00

DEL RAYS, THE

CORD

Number	Title (A Side/B Side)	Yr	VG	VG+	NM
❑ 1001	Our Love Is True/One Kiss, One Smile and a Dream	1958	1000.	2000.	4000.

MOON

Number	Title (A Side/B Side)	Yr	VG	VG+	NM
❑ 110	Have a Heart/Around the Corner	1959	75.00	150.00	300.00

WARNER BROS.

Number	Title (A Side/B Side)	Yr	VG	VG+	NM
❑ 5022	My Darling/The One I Adore	1958	20.00	40.00	80.00

DEL-RHYTHMETTES

JVB

Number	Title (A Side/B Side)	Yr	VG	VG+	NM
❑ 5000	Chic-a-Boomer/I Need Your Love	1959	15.00	30.00	60.00

DEL RIOS, THE

Probably more than one group.

BET-T

Number	Title (A Side/B Side)	Yr	VG	VG+	NM
❑ 7001	Heavenly Angel/Dangerous Lover	1962	300.00	600.00	1200.

METEOR

Number	Title (A Side/B Side)	Yr	VG	VG+	NM
❑ 5038	Lizzie/Alone on a Rainy Night	1956	200.00	400.00	800.00

NEPTUNE

Number	Title (A Side/B Side)	Yr	VG	VG+	NM
❑ 108	Wait Wait Wait/I'm Crying	1959	15.00	30.00	60.00

RUST

Number	Title (A Side/B Side)	Yr	VG	VG+	NM
❑ 5066	Valerie/Mystery	1963	15.00	30.00	60.00

STAX

Number	Title (A Side/B Side)	Yr	VG	VG+	NM
❑ 125	There's a Love/Just Across the Street	1962	12.50	25.00	50.00

DEL SATINS

B.T. PUPPY

Number	Title (A Side/B Side)	Yr	VG	VG+	NM
❑ 506	Hang Around/Candy Apple 'Vette	1965	3.75	7.50	15.00
❑ 509	Sweets for My Sweet/A Girl Named Arlene	1965	7.50	15.00	30.00
❑ 514	Relief/Throwaway Song	1966	3.75	7.50	15.00
❑ 563	I'll Do My Crying Tomorrow/A Girl Named Arlene	1970	3.00	6.00	12.00

COLUMBIA

Number	Title (A Side/B Side)	Yr	VG	VG+	NM
❑ 42802	Feelin' No Pain/Who Cares	1963	6.25	12.50	25.00
❑ 42802 [PS]	Feelin' No Pain/Who Cares	1963	25.00	50.00	100.00

DIAMOND

Number	Title (A Side/B Side)	Yr	VG	VG+	NM
❑ 216	A Little Rain Must Fall/Love, Hate, Revenge (If I Want You to Cry)	1967	3.75	7.50	15.00

END

Number	Title (A Side/B Side)	Yr	VG	VG+	NM
❑ 1096	I'll Pray for You/I Remember the Night	1961	50.00	100.00	200.00

LAURIE

Number	Title (A Side/B Side)	Yr	VG	VG+	NM
❑ 3132	Teardrops Follow Me/Best Wishes, Good Luck, Goodbye	1962	6.25	12.50	25.00
❑ 3149	Ballad of a Deejay/Does My Love Stand a Chance	1962	6.25	12.50	25.00

MALA

Number	Title (A Side/B Side)	Yr	VG	VG+	NM
❑ 475	Believe in Me/Two Broken Hearts	1964	5.00	10.00	20.00

WIN

Number	Title (A Side/B Side)	Yr	VG	VG+	NM
❑ 702	Counting Teardrops/Remember	1961	40.00	80.00	120.00

—Black label

Number	Title (A Side/B Side)	Yr	VG	VG+	NM
❑ 702	Counting Teardrops/Remember	1961	15.00	30.00	60.00

—Orange label

DEL-VETTS, THE

DUNWICH

Number	Title (A Side/B Side)	Yr	VG	VG+	NM
❑ 125	Last Time Around/Everytime	1966	5.00	10.00	20.00
❑ 142	I Call My Baby STP/That's the Way It Is	1966	5.00	10.00	20.00
❑ 142 [PS]	I Call My Baby STP/That's the Way It Is	1966	7.50	15.00	30.00

—Some sleeves contain an STP decal.

SEEBERG

Number	Title (A Side/B Side)	Yr	VG	VG+	NM
❑ 3018 [M]	Ram Charger/Little Latin Lupe Lu	1965	7.50	15.00	30.00
❑ 3018 [S]	Ram Charger/Little Latin Lupe Lu	1965	10.00	20.00	40.00

—Some copies were pressed in stereo. We don't know if it's marked on the label or trail-off wax or if it must be played to identify.

7-Inch Extended Plays

SUNDAZED

Number	Title (A Side/B Side)	Yr	VG	VG+	NM
❑ SEP 124	Last Time Around/Everytime//I Call My Baby STP/That's the Way It Is	1997	—	—	3.00

—Gold vinyl

Number	Title (A Side/B Side)	Yr	VG	VG+	NM
❑ SEP 124 [PS]	The Del-Vetts	1997	—	—	3.00

DEL VIKINGS, THE

Usually considered to be one group, but actually three: Two of them splintered from the original group, one featuring Kripp Johnson, the other featuring Gus Backus. For convenience's sake, all are listed together.

ABC-PARAMOUNT

Number	Title (A Side/B Side)	Yr	VG	VG+	NM
❑ 10208	I'll Never Stop Crying/Bring Back Your Heart	1961	6.25	12.50	25.00

Number	Title (A Side/B Side)	Yr	VG	VG+	NM
❑ 10248	I Hear Bells (Wedding Bells)/Don't Get Slick on Me	1961	12.50	25.00	50.00
❑ 10278	Kiss Me/Face the Music	1961	6.25	12.50	25.00
❑ 10304	Big Silence/One More River to Cross	1962	6.25	12.50	25.00
❑ 10341	Confession of Love/Kilimanjaro	1962	6.25	12.50	25.00
❑ 10385	An Angel Up in Heaven/Fishing Chant	1962	12.50	25.00	50.00
❑ 10425	Too Many Miles/Sorcerer's Apprentice	1963	6.25	12.50	25.00
ALPINE					
❑ 66	Pistol Packin' Mama/The Sun	1960	20.00	40.00	80.00
❑ 66 [PS]	Pistol Packin' Mama/The Sun	1960	25.00	50.00	100.00
BIM BAM BOOM					
❑ 111	Cold Feet/A Little Man Cried	1972	—	2.50	5.00
❑ 113	Watching the Moon/You Say You Love Me	1972	—	2.50	5.00
❑ 115	I'm Spinning/Girl Girl	1972	—	2.50	5.00
DOT					
❑ 15538	Come Go with Me/How Can I Find True Love	1957	7.50	15.00	30.00
❑ 15571	What Made Maggie Run/Little Billy Boy	1957	7.50	15.00	30.00
❑ 15592	Whispering Bells/Don't Be a Fool	1957	7.50	15.00	30.00
❑ 15636	I'm Spinning/When I Come Home	1957	7.50	15.00	30.00
—As "Kripp Johnson with the Dell-Vikings"					
❑ 16092	Come Go with Me/How Can I Find True Love	1960	5.00	10.00	20.00
❑ 16236	Come Go with Me/Whispering Bells	1961	5.00	10.00	20.00
❑ 16248	I Hear Bells (Wedding Bells)/Don't Get Slick on Me	1961	5.00	10.00	20.00
DRC					
❑ 101	Can't You See/Oh I	196?	10.00	20.00	40.00
FEE BEE					
❑ 173	Welfare Blues/Hollywood and Vine	1977	—	2.50	5.00
❑ 205	Come Go with Me/How Can I Find True Love	1957	125.00	250.00	500.00
—Orange label, bee on top					
❑ 205	Come Go with Me/How Can I Find True Love	1957	62.50	125.00	250.00
—Orange label, one side has bee, the other side doesn't					
❑ 205	Come Go with Me/How Can I Find True Love	1961	7.50	15.00	30.00
—Orange label, no bee					
❑ 205	Come Go with Me/Whispering Bells	1964	5.00	10.00	20.00
❑ 206	Down in Bermuda/Maggie	1964	20.00	40.00	80.00
❑ 210	What Made Maggie Run/Uh Uh Baby	1957	20.00	40.00	80.00
❑ 210	What Made Maggie Run/When I Come Home	1957	40.00	80.00	120.00
❑ 210	What Made Maggie Run/Down by the Stream	1964	7.50	15.00	30.00
❑ 214	Whispering Bells/Don't Be a Fool	1957	100.00	200.00	400.00
❑ 218	I'm Spinning/You Say You Love Me	1957	30.00	60.00	120.00
—Bee on label					
❑ 218	I'm Spinning/You Say You Love Me	1964	7.50	15.00	30.00
—No bee on label					
❑ 221	Willette/Woke Up This Morning	1958	25.00	50.00	100.00
❑ 221	Willette/I Want to Marry You	1958	20.00	40.00	80.00
❑ 227	Tell Me/Finger Poppin' Woman	1959	20.00	40.00	80.00
❑ 902	True Love/Baby, Let Me Know	1964	7.50	15.00	30.00
—As "The Original Dell Vikings"					
GATEWAY					
❑ 743	We Three/I've Got to Know	1964	7.50	15.00	30.00
JOJO					
❑ 108	Keep On Walkin'/My Body, Your Shadow	1976	—	2.50	5.00
LUNIVERSE					
❑ 106	Somewhere Over the Rainbow/Hey, Senorita	1957	25.00	50.00	100.00
❑ 110	Yours/Heaven and Paradise	1958	5.00	10.00	20.00
❑ 113	In the Still of the Night/The White Cliffs of Dover	1958	5.00	10.00	20.00
❑ 114	There I Go/Girl Girl	1958	5.00	10.00	20.00
—The above three Luniverse 45s are bootlegs, but they perversely do have collector's value!					
MERCURY					
❑ 71132	Cool Shake/Jitterbug Mary	1957	7.50	15.00	30.00
❑ 71180	Come Along with Me/Whatcha Gonna Lose	1957	7.50	15.00	30.00
❑ 71198	I'm Spinning/When I Come Home	1957	7.50	15.00	30.00
❑ 71241	Snowbound/Your Book of Life	1957	7.50	15.00	30.00
❑ 71266	The Voodoo Man/Can't Wait	1958	7.50	15.00	30.00
❑ 71345	You Cheated/Pretty Little Things Called Girls	1958	7.50	15.00	30.00
—Black label					
❑ 71345	You Cheated/Pretty Little Things Called Girls	1958	10.00	20.00	40.00
—Blue label					
❑ 71390	How Could You/Flat Tire	1958	7.50	15.00	30.00
SCEPTER					
❑ 12367	Come Go with Me/When You're Asleep	1973	—	2.50	5.00
SHIP					
❑ 214	Sunday Kind of Love/Over the Rainbow	197?	—	2.00	4.00
7-Inch Extended Plays					
DOT					
❑ DEP-1058	(contents unknown)	1957	25.00	50.00	100.00
❑ DEP-1058 [PS]	Come Go with Us	1957	50.00	100.00	200.00
MERCURY					
❑ EP 1-3359	Come Along with Me/A Sunday Kind of Love//(There'll Be Blue Birds Over) The White Cliffs of Dover/Now Is the Hour	1957	25.00	50.00	100.00
❑ EP 1-3359 [PS]	They Sing — They Swing, Vol. 1	1957	37.50	75.00	150.00
❑ EP 1-3362	*Heart and Soul/Down in Bermuda/My Foolish Heart/I'm Sitting on Top of the World	1957	25.00	50.00	100.00
❑ EP 1-3362 [PS]	They Sing — They Swing, Vol. 2	1957	37.50	75.00	150.00
❑ EP 1-3363	(contents unknown)	1957	25.00	50.00	100.00
❑ EP 1-3363 [PS]	They Sing — They Swing, Vol. 3	1957	37.50	75.00	150.00

DEL-VUES, THE

Number	Title (A Side/B Side)	Yr	VG	VG+	NM
U-TOWN					
❑ 8008	After New Year's/My Confession	195?	150.00	300.00	600.00

DELACARDOS, THE (1)

Number	Title (A Side/B Side)	Yr	VG	VG+	NM
ELGEY					
❑ 1001	A Letter to a School Girl/I'll Never Let You Down	1959	12.50	25.00	50.00
SHELL					
❑ 308	Dream Girl/I Just Want to Know	1961	5.00	10.00	20.00
❑ 311	Love Is the Greatest Thing/Girl-Girl	1962	5.00	10.00	20.00
UNITED ARTISTS					
❑ 276	I Got It/Thing-A-Ma-Jig	1960	3.75	7.50	15.00
❑ 310	Hold Back the Tears/Mr. Dillon	1961	5.00	10.00	20.00

DELACARDOS, THE (2)

Number	Title (A Side/B Side)	Yr	VG	VG+	NM
ATLANTIC					
❑ 2368	Got No One/She's the One I Love	1966	2.50	5.00	10.00
❑ 2389	I Know I'm Not Much/You Don't Have to See Me	1967	2.50	5.00	10.00
❑ 2419	They Put a Spell on You/A Fool for You	1967	2.50	5.00	10.00

DELACARDOS, THE (U)

These may be group (1) or (2), or they may be a completely different group or groups.

Number	Title (A Side/B Side)	Yr	VG	VG+	NM
DIMENSION					
❑ 1040	Forget About the Guy/Dance, Gypsy, Dance	1964	5.00	10.00	20.00
IMPERIAL					
❑ 5992	On the Beach/Everybody's Rockin'	1963	3.75	7.50	15.00

DELANCEYS, THE

Number	Title (A Side/B Side)	Yr	VG	VG+	NM
ABC-PARAMOUNT					
❑ 10353	High Voltage/The Scratch	1962	6.25	12.50	25.00

DELANEY AND BONNIE

Also see BONNIE BRAMLETT; DELANEY BRAMLETT.

Number	Title (A Side/B Side)	Yr	VG	VG+	NM
ATCO					
❑ 6725	Groupie (Superstar)/Comin' Home	1969	2.00	4.00	8.00
❑ 6756	Soul Shake/Free the People	1970	2.00	4.00	8.00
❑ 6788	Miss Ann/They Call It Rock and Roll Music	1970	2.00	4.00	8.00
❑ 6804	Never Ending Song of Love/Don't Deceive Me	1971	2.00	4.00	8.00
❑ 6838	Only You Know and I Know/God Knows I Love You	1971	—	3.00	6.00
❑ 6866	Sing My Way Home/Move 'Em Out	1972	—	2.50	5.00
❑ 6883	Where There's a Will There's a Way/Lonesome and a Long Way from Home	1972	—	2.50	5.00
❑ 6904	Sing My Way Home/Will the Circle Be Unbroken	1972	—	2.50	5.00
COLUMBIA					
❑ 45608	Country Life/Walk in the River Jordan	1972	—	2.50	5.00
ELEKTRA					
❑ 45660	Soldiers of the Cross/Get Ourselves Together	1969	2.50	5.00	10.00
❑ 45662	When the Battle Is Over/Get Ourselves Together	1969	2.50	5.00	10.00
GARPAX					
❑ 44184	Cherry Pie/Hey Mr. Weatherman	1964	3.75	7.50	15.00
—As "Lani & Boni"					
INDEPENDENCE					
❑ 78	You've Lost That Lovin' Feelin'/Don't Let It (Be the Last Time)	1967	3.00	6.00	12.00
STAX					
❑ 0003	It's Been a Long Time Coming/We've Just Been Feeling Bad	1968	2.50	5.00	10.00
❑ 0057	Hard to Say Goodbye/Just Plain Beautiful	1969	2.50	5.00	10.00

DELEGATES, THE (1)

Novelty group.

Number	Title (A Side/B Side)	Yr	VG	VG+	NM
MAINSTREAM					
❑ 5525	Convention '72/Funky Butt	1972	2.50	5.00	10.00
❑ 5525	Convention '72 (same on both sides)	1972	2.00	4.00	8.00
—Stock copy; "Funky Butt" deleted because of retailers' protests to the title					
❑ 5530	Richard M. Nixon Faces the Issues (same on both sides)	1972	2.00	4.00	8.00
❑ 5530	Richard M. Nixon Faces the Issues/Touzie's Blues	1972	2.50	5.00	10.00

DELEGATES, THE (3)

DEE CLARK was a member.

Number	Title (A Side/B Side)	Yr	VG	VG+	NM
VEE JAY					
❑ 212	The Convention/Jay's Rock	1956	15.00	30.00	60.00
—B-side by Big Jay McNeely					
❑ 243	Mother's Son/I'm Gonna Be Glad	1957	15.00	30.00	60.00

DELFONICS, THE

Also see MAJOR HARRIS.

Number	Title (A Side/B Side)	Yr	VG	VG+	NM
ARISTA					
❑ 0308	Don't Throw It All Away/I Don't Care What People Say	1978	—	2.00	4.00
CAMEO					
❑ 472	You've Been Untrue/I Was There	1967	3.75	7.50	15.00
MOON SHOT					
❑ 6703	He Don't Really Love You/Without You	1967	3.75	7.50	15.00
PHILLY GROOVE					
❑ 150	La-La Means I Love You/Can't Get Over Losing You	1968	2.50	5.00	10.00
❑ 151	I'm Sorry/You're Gone	1968	2.50	5.00	10.00
❑ 152	Break Your Promise/Alfie	1968	2.50	5.00	10.00
❑ 154	Ready Or Not Here I Come (Can't Hide from Love)/Somebody Loves You	1968	2.50	5.00	10.00
❑ 156	Funny Feeling/My New Love	1969	2.50	5.00	10.00
❑ 157	You Got Yours and I'll Get Mine/Loving Him	1969	2.50	5.00	10.00
❑ 161	Didn't I (Blow Your Mind This Time)/Down Is Up, Up Is Down	1970	2.50	5.00	10.00
❑ 162	Trying to Make a Fool of Me/Baby I Love You	1970	2.50	5.00	10.00
❑ 163	When You Get Right Down To It/I Gave to You	1970	2.50	5.00	10.00
❑ 166	Over and Over/Hey! Love	1971	2.00	4.00	8.00
❑ 169	Walk Right Up to the Sun/Round and Round	1971	2.00	4.00	8.00
❑ 172	Tell Me This Is a Dream/I'm a Man	1972	2.00	4.00	8.00
❑ 174	Think It Over/I'm a Man	1972	2.00	4.00	8.00
❑ 176	I Don't Want to Make You Wait/Baby I Miss You	1973	2.00	4.00	8.00
❑ 177	Alfie/Start All Over Again	1973	2.00	4.00	8.00
❑ 182	I Told You So/Seventeen and In Love	1973	2.00	4.00	8.00
❑ 184	Lying to Myself/Hey Baby	1974	2.00	4.00	8.00

DELICATES, THE
More than one group?

CELESTE

Number	Title (A Side/B Side)	Yr	VG	VG+	NM
❑ 676	My Pillow/I Played 1,2,3,4	1961	7.50	15.00	30.00

CHALLENGE

Number	Title (A Side/B Side)	Yr	VG	VG+	NM
❑ 59232	I've Been Hurt/Come On Everybody	1964	3.75	7.50	15.00
❑ 59267	I Want to Get Married/Home from Camp	1965	3.75	7.50	15.00
❑ 59304	Stop Shovin' Me Around/Comin' Down with Love	1965	3.75	7.50	15.00

DEE DEE

Number	Title (A Side/B Side)	Yr	VG	VG+	NM
❑ 677	My Pillow/I Played 1,2,3,4	1961	7.50	15.00	30.00

ROULETTE

Number	Title (A Side/B Side)	Yr	VG	VG+	NM
❑ 4321	Little Ship/Not Tomorrow	1961	5.00	10.00	20.00
❑ 4360	Little Boy of Mine/Dickie Went and Did It	1961	5.00	10.00	20.00
❑ 4387	I Don't Know Why (I Just Do)/Strange Love	1961	5.00	10.00	20.00

UNART

Number	Title (A Side/B Side)	Yr	VG	VG+	NM
❑ 2017	Black and White Thunderbird/Ronnie Is My Lover	1959	6.25	12.50	25.00
❑ 2024	Ringa Ding/Meusurry	1959	6.25	12.50	25.00

UNITED ARTISTS

Number	Title (A Side/B Side)	Yr	VG	VG+	NM
❑ 210	Flip Flip/Your Happiest Years	1960	5.00	10.00	20.00
❑ 228	The Kiss/Too Young to Date	1960	5.00	10.00	20.00

DELL, DICKEY, AND THE BING BONGS
DRAGON

Number	Title (A Side/B Side)	Yr	VG	VG+	NM
❑ 10205	Ding-a-Ling-a-Ling-Ding-Dong/The Cling	1958	37.50	75.00	150.00

DELL, EVELYN, AND THE VIBRATIONS
ABC-PARAMOUNT

Number	Title (A Side/B Side)	Yr	VG	VG+	NM
❑ 10218	Sincerely/Please Tell Me Why	1961	6.25	12.50	25.00

DELL, LENNY, AND THE DEMENSIONS
See THE DEMENSIONS.

DELL, RICHIE
KING

Number	Title (A Side/B Side)	Yr	VG	VG+	NM
❑ 5888	Come On Let's Sing/King Lover	1964	5.00	10.00	20.00

DELL, TONY
KING

Number	Title (A Side/B Side)	Yr	VG	VG+	NM
❑ 5766	My Girl/Magic Wand	1963	12.50	25.00	50.00

DELL-COEDS, THE
DOT

Number	Title (A Side/B Side)	Yr	VG	VG+	NM
❑ 16314	Hey Mr. Banjo/Love in Return	1962	3.00	6.00	12.00

DELL VIKINGS, THE
See THE DEL-VIKINGS.

DELLS, THE
20TH CENTURY

Number	Title (A Side/B Side)	Yr	VG	VG+	NM
❑ 2463	I Touched a Dream/All About the Paper	1980	—	2.00	4.00
❑ 2475	Passionate Breezes/Your Song	1980	—	2.00	4.00
❑ 2504	Happy Song/Look at Us Now	1981	—	2.00	4.00
❑ 2602	Ain't It a Shame/Stay in My Corner	1982	—	2.00	4.00

ABC

Number	Title (A Side/B Side)	Yr	VG	VG+	NM
❑ 12386	Super Woman/My Life Is So Wonderful	1978	—	2.50	5.00
❑ 12422	(I Wanna) Testify/Don't Save Me	1978	—	2.50	5.00
❑ 12422	(I Wanna) Testify/Drowning for Your Love	1978	—	2.50	5.00
❑ 12440	(You Bring Out) The Best in Me/Wrapped Up Tight	1978	—	2.50	5.00

ARGO

Number	Title (A Side/B Side)	Yr	VG	VG+	NM
❑ 5415	God Bless the Child/I'm Going Home	1962	3.00	6.00	12.00
❑ 5428	The (Bossa Nova) Bird/Eternally	1962	3.00	6.00	12.00
❑ 5442	Hi Diddle Dee Dum Dum (It's a Good Feelin')/If It Ain't One Thing, It's Another	1963	3.00	6.00	12.00
❑ 5456	After You/Goodbye Mary Ann	1963	3.00	6.00	12.00

CADET

Number	Title (A Side/B Side)	Yr	VG	VG+	NM
❑ 5538	Thinkin' About You/The Change We Go Thru (For Love)	1966	—	3.00	6.00
❑ 5551	Over Again/Run for Cover	1967	—	3.00	6.00
❑ 5563	You Belong to Someone Else/Inspiration	1967	—	3.00	6.00
❑ 5574	O-O, I Love You/There Is	1967	—	3.00	6.00
❑ 5590	There Is/Show Me	1968	2.00	4.00	8.00
❑ 5599	Wear it On Our Face/Please Don't Change Me Now	1968	—	3.00	6.00
❑ 5612	Stay in My Corner/Love Is So Simple	1969	—	3.00	6.00
❑ 5621	Always Together/I Want My Mama	1968	—	3.00	6.00
❑ 5631	Does Anybody Know I'm Here/Make Sure (You Have Somebody to Love You)	1968	—	3.00	6.00
❑ 5636	I Can't Do Enough/Hallways of My Mind	1969	—	3.00	6.00
❑ 5641	I Can Sing a Rainbow-Love Is Blue/Hallelujah Baby	1969	—	3.00	6.00
❑ 5649	Oh What a Night/Believe Me	1969	—	3.00	6.00
❑ 5658	On the Dock of the Bay/When I'm in Your Arms	1969	—	3.00	6.00
❑ 5663	Oh What a Day/The Change We Go Thru (For Love)	1970	—	3.00	6.00
❑ 5667	Open Up My Heart/Nadine	1970	—	3.00	6.00
❑ 5672	Long Lonely Nights/A Little Understanding	1970	—	3.00	6.00
❑ 5679	The Glory of Love/A Whiter Shade of Pale	1970	—	3.00	6.00
❑ 5683	The Love We Had (Stays on My Mind)/Freedom Means	1971	—	3.00	6.00
❑ 5689	It's All Up to You/Oh, My Dear	1972	—	3.00	6.00
❑ 5691	Walk On By/This Guy's in Love with You	1972	—	3.00	6.00
❑ 5694	Just As Long As We're in Love/I'd Rather Be with You	1972	—	3.00	6.00
❑ 5696	Give Your Baby a Standing Ovation/Closer	1973	—	3.00	6.00
❑ 5698	My Pretending Days Are Over/Let's Make It Last	1973	—	3.00	6.00
❑ 5700	I Miss You/Don't Make Me a Storyteller	1973	—	3.00	6.00
❑ 5702	I Wish It Was Me You Loved/Two Together Is Better Than One	1974	—	3.00	6.00
❑ 5703	Bring Back the Love of Yesterday/Learning to Love You Was Easy (It's So Hard Trying to Get Over You)	1974	—	3.00	6.00
❑ 5703	Sweeter as the Days Go By/Learning to Love You Was Easy (It's So Hard Trying to Get Over You)	1974	—	3.00	6.00
—A-side is the same song with a new title					
❑ 5707	The Glory of Love/You're the Greatest	1975	—	3.00	6.00
❑ 5711	We Got to Get Our Thing Together/The Power of Love	1975	2.00	4.00	8.00

CHECKER

Number	Title (A Side/B Side)	Yr	VG	VG+	NM
❑ 794	Darling I Know/Christine	1954	400.00	800.00	1200.
—As "The El Rays"					

MCA

Number	Title (A Side/B Side)	Yr	VG	VG+	NM
❑ 41051	Plastic People/What I Could	1979	—	2.50	5.00

MERCURY

Number	Title (A Side/B Side)	Yr	VG	VG+	NM
❑ 73723	We Got to Get Our Thing Together/Reminiscing	1975	—	2.50	5.00
❑ 73759	The Power of Love/Gotta Get Home to My Baby	1976	—	2.50	5.00
❑ 73807	Slow Motion/Ain't No Black and White in Music	1976	—	2.50	5.00
❑ 73842	No Way Back/Too Late for Love	1976	—	2.50	5.00
❑ 73901	Betcha Never Been Loved (Like This Before)/Get On Down	1977	—	2.50	5.00
❑ 73909	Our Love/Could It Be	1977	—	2.50	5.00
❑ 73977	Private Property/Teaser	1977	—	2.50	5.00

PHILCO-FORD

Number	Title (A Side/B Side)	Yr	VG	VG+	NM
❑ HP-32	There Is/Show Me	1968	5.00	10.00	20.00
—4-inch plastic "Hip Pocket Record" with color sleeve					

PRIVATE I

Number	Title (A Side/B Side)	Yr	VG	VG+	NM
❑ 04343	Don't Want Nobody/You Can't Just Walk Away	1984	—	2.00	4.00
❑ 04448	One Step Closer/Come On Back to Me	1984	—	2.00	4.00
❑ 04540	Love On/Don't Want Nobody	1984	—	2.00	4.00

SKYLARK

Number	Title (A Side/B Side)	Yr	VG	VG+	NM
❑ 558	I Can't Help Myself/She's Just an Angel	198?	—	2.00	4.00
❑ 581	Someone to Call Me Darling/Now I Pray	198?	—	2.00	4.00

VEE JAY

Number	Title (A Side/B Side)	Yr	VG	VG+	NM
❑ 134	Tell the World/Blues at Three	1955	2500.	3750.	5000.
—Red vinyl					
❑ 134	Tell the World/Blues at Three	1955	500.00	1000.	2000.
❑ 166	Dreams of Contentment/Zing, Zing, Zing	1955	50.00	100.00	200.00
❑ 204	Oh What a Nite/Jo-Jo	1956	30.00	60.00	120.00
❑ 230	Movin' On/I Wanna Go Home	1956	10.00	20.00	40.00
❑ 236	Why Do You Have to Go/Dance, Dance, Dance	1957	10.00	20.00	40.00
❑ 251	A Distant Love/O-Bop She-Bop	1957	10.00	20.00	40.00
❑ 258	Pain in My Heart/Time Makes You Change	1957	10.00	20.00	40.00
❑ 274	The Springer/What You Say Baby	1958	7.50	15.00	30.00
❑ 292	I'm Calling/Jeepers Creepers	1958	7.50	15.00	30.00
❑ 300	Wedding Day/My Best Girl	1958	25.00	50.00	100.00
❑ 324	Dry Your Eyes/Baby Open Up Your Heart	1959	10.00	20.00	40.00
❑ 338	Oh What a Nite/I Wanna Go Home	1960	5.00	10.00	20.00
❑ 376	Hold On to What You've Got/Swingin' Teens	1961	5.00	10.00	20.00
❑ 595	Shy Girl/What Do We Prove	1964	3.00	6.00	12.00
❑ 615	Wait Till Tomorrow/Oh What a Good Night	1964	3.00	6.00	12.00
❑ 674	Stay in My Corner/It's Not Unusual	1965	3.00	6.00	12.00
❑ 712	Poor Little Boy/Hey Sugar (Don't Get Serious)	1966	3.00	6.00	12.00

VETERAN

Number	Title (A Side/B Side)	Yr	VG	VG+	NM
❑ 7-101	Thought of You Just a Little Too Much/(B-side unknown)	1989	—	2.50	5.00

DELLS, THE, AND THE DRAMATICS
Also see each artist's individual listings.

CADET

Number	Title (A Side/B Side)	Yr	VG	VG+	NM
❑ 5710	Love Is Missing from Our Lives/I'm in Love	1975	—	3.00	6.00

DELLTONES, THE
BATON

Number	Title (A Side/B Side)	Yr	VG	VG+	NM
❑ 212	Don't Be Long/Baby Say You Love Me	1955	7.50	15.00	30.00
❑ 223	My Special Love/Believe It	1956	7.50	15.00	30.00

BRUNSWICK

Number	Title (A Side/B Side)	Yr	VG	VG+	NM
❑ 84015	My Heart's on Fire/Yours Alone	1953	50.00	100.00	200.00

RAINBOW

Number	Title (A Side/B Side)	Yr	VG	VG+	NM
❑ 244	I'm Not in Love with You/Little Short Daddy	1954	25.00	50.00	100.00

DELMIRAS, THE
DADE

Number	Title (A Side/B Side)	Yr	VG	VG+	NM
❑ 1821	Dry Your Eyes/The Big Sound	1961	75.00	150.00	300.00

DELRONS, THE
See REPARATA AND THE DELRONS.

DELTAIRS, THE
FELSTED

Number	Title (A Side/B Side)	Yr	VG	VG+	NM
❑ 8525	Who Would Have Thought It/You Won't Be Satisfied	1959	7.50	15.00	30.00

IVY

Number	Title (A Side/B Side)	Yr	VG	VG+	NM
❑ 101	Lullaby of the Bells/It's Only You Dear	1957	37.50	75.00	150.00
—Yellow label					
❑ 101	Lullaby of the Bells/It's Only You Dear	1958	7.50	15.00	30.00
❑ 105	Standing at the Altar/I Might Like It	1958	7.50	15.00	30.00

DELTAS, THE
More than one group?

CAMBRIDGE

Number	Title (A Side/B Side)	Yr	VG	VG+	NM
❑ 124	Goodnight My Love/Give My Love a Chance	1962	10.00	20.00	40.00

GONE

Number	Title (A Side/B Side)	Yr	VG	VG+	NM
❑ 5010	Let Me Share Your Dream/Lamplight	1957	750.00	1500.	3000.
—Black label					
❑ 5010	Let Me Share Your Dream/Lamplight	1957	20.00	40.00	80.00
—Multi-color label					

PHILIPS

Number	Title (A Side/B Side)	Yr	VG	VG+	NM
❑ 40023	My Own True Love/Work Song	1962	5.00	10.00	20.00
❑ 40023	My Own True Love/Hold Me, Thrill Me, Kiss Me	1962	3.75	7.50	15.00

DELTONES, THE
JUBILEE

Number	Title (A Side/B Side)	Yr	VG	VG+	NM
❑ 5374	La La La/Bow-Legged Annie	1959	6.25	12.50	25.00

Number	Title (A Side/B Side)	Yr	VG	VG+	NM
VEE JAY					
❑ 288	I'm Coming Home/Early Morning Rock	1958	10.00	20.00	40.00
❑ 303	A Lover's Prayer/First Man to the Moon	1958	10.00	20.00	40.00

DELVETTS, THE

Number	Title (A Side/B Side)	Yr	VG	VG+	NM
END					
❑ 1106	I Want a Boy for Christmas/Repeat After Me	1961	7.50	15.00	30.00
❑ 1107	Will You Love Me in Heaven/Repeat After Me	1962	5.00	10.00	20.00

DEMARCO, RALPH

Number	Title (A Side/B Side)	Yr	VG	VG+	NM
GUARANTEED					
❑ 202	More Than Riches/Old Shep	1959	5.00	10.00	20.00
❑ 202 [PS]	More Than Riches/Old Shep	1959	10.00	20.00	40.00
SHELLEY					
❑ 1011	Donna/For All We Know	1960	10.00	20.00	40.00

DEMENS, THE

Number	Title (A Side/B Side)	Yr	VG	VG+	NM
TEENAGE					
❑ 1006	Take Me As I Am/You Broke My Heart	1958	50.00	100.00	200.00
❑ 1007	I'm Not in Love with You/Short Daddy	1958	50.00	100.00	200.00
❑ 1008	The Greatest of Them All/Hey Young Girl	1958	50.00	100.00	200.00

DEMENSIONS, THE

Number	Title (A Side/B Side)	Yr	VG	VG+	NM
CORAL					
❑ 62277	Again/Count Your Blessings Instead of Sheep	1961	6.25	12.50	25.00
❑ 62293	As Time Goes By/Seven Days a Week	1961	6.25	12.50	25.00
❑ 62323	Young at Heart/Your Cheatin' Heart	1962	5.00	10.00	20.00
❑ 62344	My Foolish Heart/Just One More Chance	1963	7.50	15.00	30.00
❑ 62359	Fly Me to the Moon/You'll Never Know	1963	6.25	12.50	25.00
❑ 62382	Just a Shoulder to Cry On/Don't Worry About Bobby	1963	6.25	12.50	25.00
❑ 62392	A Little White Gardenia/Don't Cry Pretty Baby	1964	5.00	10.00	20.00
❑ 62432	This Time Next Year/My Old Girlfriend	1964	5.00	10.00	20.00
—As "Lenny Dell and the Demensions"					
❑ 62444	Once a Day/Ting Along Ting Toy	1965	5.00	10.00	20.00
—As "Lenny Dell and the Demensions"					
❑ 65559	Over the Rainbow/Zing Went the Strings of My Heart	1962	5.00	10.00	20.00
❑ 65611	As Time Goes By/My Foolish Heart	1967	3.75	7.50	15.00
MOHAWK					
❑ 116	Over the Rainbow/Nursery Rhyme Rock	1960	12.50	25.00	50.00
—Maroon label					
❑ 116	Over the Rainbow/Nursery Rhyme Rock	1960	7.50	15.00	30.00
—Brown label					
❑ 116	Over the Rainbow/Nursery Rhyme Rock	1960	6.25	12.50	25.00
—Red label					
❑ 120	Zing Went the Strings of My Heart/Don't Take Your Love from Me	1960	6.25	12.50	25.00
—As "The Dimensions"					
❑ 121	God's Christmas/Ave Maria	1960	15.00	30.00	60.00
❑ 123	A Tear Fell/Theresa	1961	15.00	30.00	60.00

DEMIAN

Number	Title (A Side/B Side)	Yr	VG	VG+	NM
ABC					
❑ 11297	Face the Crowd/Love People	1970	5.00	10.00	20.00

DEMILLES, THE

Number	Title (A Side/B Side)	Yr	VG	VG+	NM
LAURIE					
❑ 3230	Donna Lee/Um Ba Pa	1964	7.50	15.00	30.00
❑ 3247	Lazy Love/Cry and Be On Your Way	1964	12.50	25.00	50.00

DEMOLYRS, THE

Number	Title (A Side/B Side)	Yr	VG	VG+	NM
JASON SCOTT					
❑ 7	Rain/Hey Little Rosie	1978	—	3.00	6.00
U.W.R.					
❑ 900	Rain/Hey Little Rosie	1964	125.00	250.00	500.00

DEMOTRONS, THE

Number	Title (A Side/B Side)	Yr	VG	VG+	NM
ATLANTIC					
❑ 2589	I Want a Home in the Country/I Don't Want to Play No More	1969	2.50	5.00	10.00
CAMEO					
❑ 456	Beg, Borrow and Steal/Midnight in New York	1967	2.50	5.00	10.00
DORSET					
❑ 5010	Frisky/Steel Driving Man	196?	5.00	10.00	20.00
ENRICA					
❑ 1003	Rock-A-Way Special/Bugle Boy	1959	7.50	15.00	30.00
RADAR					
❑ 2615	Hombre/Swinging Soiree	1962	5.00	10.00	20.00
❑ 2616	Pretzel Twist/Meet Mister Callaghan	1962	5.00	10.00	20.00
❑ 2621	Sticks and Stones/Theme from "Adventures in Paradise"	1962	5.00	10.00	20.00
RUST					
❑ 5025	Rockin' with Mother Goose/Home on the Pad	1960	5.00	10.00	20.00
SCEPTER					
❑ 12148	Take This Love I Have/Sleep, Sleep, Sleep	1966	3.00	6.00	12.00
❑ 12174	Brother Where Are You/Take This Love I Have	1966	3.00	6.00	12.00

DEMURES, THE

Number	Title (A Side/B Side)	Yr	VG	VG+	NM
BRUNSWICK					
❑ 55284	Raining Teardrops/He's Got Your Number	1965	25.00	50.00	100.00

DENBY, JUNIOR

Number	Title (A Side/B Side)	Yr	VG	VG+	NM
KING					
❑ 4717	With This Ring/I'm Still Lonesome	1954	15.00	30.00	60.00
❑ 4725	This Fool Has Learned/If You Only Have Faith in Me	1954	15.00	30.00	60.00
❑ 5217	With This Ring/I'm Still Lonesome	1959	7.50	15.00	30.00

DENNIS AND THE EXPLORERS

See THE EXPLORERS.

DENSON, LEE

Number	Title (A Side/B Side)	Yr	VG	VG+	NM
ENTERPRISE					
❑ 9086	A Mom and Dad for Christmas/The Miracle of the Rosary	1973	—	2.50	5.00
KENT					
❑ 306	High School Hop/Devil Doll	1958	15.00	30.00	60.00
VIK					
❑ 0251	Heart of a Fool/The Pied Piper	1957	10.00	20.00	40.00
❑ 0281	New Shoes/Climb Love Mountain	1957	20.00	40.00	80.00
—With Eddie Cochran on guitar					

DENTON, MICKEY

Number	Title (A Side/B Side)	Yr	VG	VG+	NM
AMY					
❑ 902	Top Ten/Now I'm Mr. Blue	1964	3.00	6.00	12.00
BIG TOP					
❑ 3078	Steady Kind/Now You Can't Give Them Away	1961	6.25	12.50	25.00
❑ 3094	Nature Boy/Ain't Nobody	1962	5.00	10.00	20.00
❑ 3114	Tell Her/How Mighty Hath Fallen	1962	5.00	10.00	20.00
❑ 3142	Dance With Me Mary/The Other Side of Betty	1963	5.00	10.00	20.00
IMPACT					
❑ 1002	Ain't Love Grand/Mi Amore	1965	5.00	10.00	20.00
❑ 1011	Heartache Is My Name/King Lonely the Blue	1966	5.00	10.00	20.00
WORLD ARTISTS					
❑ 1043	One More Time/Don't Throw My Toys Away	1965	3.00	6.00	12.00

DENVER, JOHN

Also see DENVER, BOISE & JOHNSON; THE MITCHELL TRIO.

Number	Title (A Side/B Side)	Yr	VG	VG+	NM
CHERRY MOUNTAIN					
❑ 01/02	Let Us Begin (What Are We Making Weapons For)/Flying for Me	1986	—	2.00	4.00
COLUMBIA					
❑ 02679	Perhaps Love/Annie's Song	1982	—	2.00	4.00
—With Placido Domingo					
❑ 03148	Perhaps Love/Annie's Song	1982	—	—	3.00
—With Placido Domingo; reissue					
LEGACY					
❑ 77993	For You/Rocky Mountain High (Live)	1995	—	—	2.00
❑ 77993 [PS]	For You/Rocky Mountain High (Live)	1995	—	—	3.00
RCA					
❑ 5086-7-R	Love Again/Let Us Begin (What Are We Making Weapons For)	1987	—	—	3.00
❑ PB-10774	Like a Sad Song/Pegasus	1976	—	2.00	4.00
❑ PB-10854	Baby, You Look Good to Me Tonight/Wrangle Mountain Song	1976	—	2.00	4.00
❑ PB-10911	My Sweet Lady/Welcome to My Morning	1977	—	2.00	4.00
❑ GB-10940	I'm Sorry/Fly Away	1977	—	—	3.00
—Gold Standard Series					
❑ PB-11036	How Can I Leave You Again/To the Wild Country	1977	—	2.00	4.00
❑ PB-11214	It Amazes Me/Druthers	1978	—	2.00	4.00
❑ PB-11267	I Want to Live/Tradewinds	1978	—	2.00	4.00
❑ GB-11327	My Sweet Lady/Like a Sad Song	1978	—	—	3.00
—Gold Standard Series					
❑ PB-11479	Downhill Stuff/Life Is So Good	1979	—	2.00	4.00
❑ PB-11535	Sweet Melinda/What's On Your Mind	1979	—	2.00	4.00
❑ PB-11637	Garden Song/Berkeley Woman	1979	—	2.00	4.00
❑ PB-11915	Autograph/The Mountain Song	1980	—	2.00	4.00
❑ PB-11915 [PS]	Autograph/The Mountain Song	1980	—	2.00	4.00
❑ PB-12017	Dancing with the Mountains/American Child	1980	—	2.00	4.00
❑ PB-12246	Some Days Are Diamonds (Some Days Are Stone)/Country Love	1981	—	2.00	4.00
❑ PB-12345	The Cowboy and the Lady/Till You Opened My Eyes	1981	—	2.00	4.00
❑ PB-13071	Shanghai Breezes/What One Man Can Do	1982	—	2.00	4.00
❑ PB-13270	Seasons of the Heart/Islands	1982	—	2.00	4.00
❑ PB-13371	Opposite Tables/Relatively Speaking	1982	—	2.00	4.00
❑ PB-13562	Wild Montana Skies/I Remember Romance	1983	—	2.00	4.00
—A-side with Emmylou Harris					
❑ PB-13642	Flight (The Higher We Fly)/Hold On Tightly	1983	—	2.00	4.00
❑ PB-13740	World Games/It's About Time	1984	—	—	3.00
❑ PB-13782	The Way I Am/The Gold and Beyond	1984	—	—	3.00
❑ PB-13931	Love Again/It's About Time	1984	—	—	3.00
—A-side: With Sylvie Vartan					
❑ GB-14075	Calypso/Some Days Are Diamonds (Some Days Are Stone)	1985	—	—	3.00
—Gold Standard Series					
❑ PB-14115	Don't Close Your Eyes Tonight/A Wild Heart Looking for Home	1985	—	—	3.00
❑ PB-14227	Dreamland Express/African Sunrise	1985	—	—	3.00
❑ PB-14227 [PS]	Dreamland Express/African Sunrise	1985	—	2.00	4.00
❑ PB-14366 [DJ]	Flying for Me (same on both sides)	1986	—	2.00	4.00
—No stock copies were issued					
❑ PB-14406	Along for the Ride ('56 T-Bird)/Let Us Begin (What Are We Making Weapons For)	1986	—	—	3.00
RCA VICTOR					
❑ APBO-0067	Farewell Andromeda (Welcome to My Morning)/Whiskey Basin Blues	1973	—	2.00	4.00
❑ APBO-0182	Please, Daddy (Don't Get Drunk This Christmas)/Rocky Mountain High	1973	—	2.50	5.00
❑ APBO-0213	Sunshine on My Shoulders/Around and Around	1974	—	2.00	4.00
❑ APBO-0295	Annie's Song/Cool An' Green An' Shady	1974	—	2.00	4.00
❑ PB-10065	Back Home Again/It's Up to You	1974	—	2.00	4.00
❑ PB-10148	Sweet Surrender/Summer	1974	—	2.00	4.00
❑ PB-10239	Thank God I'm a Country Boy/My Sweet Lady	1975	—	2.00	4.00
❑ PB-10353	I'm Sorry/Calypso	1975	—	2.00	4.00
❑ PB-10464	Christmas for Cowboys/Silent Night, Holy Night	1975	—	2.00	4.00
❑ GB-10472	Annie's Song/Cool An' Green An' Shady	1975	—	—	3.00
—Gold Standard Series					

Number	Title (A Side/B Side)	Yr	VG	VG+	NM
❑ GB-10473	Back Home Again/It's Up to You	1975	—	—	3.00
—Gold Standard Series					
❑ GB-10474	Sunshine on My Shoulders/Around and Around	1975	—	—	3.00
—Gold Standard Series					
❑ GB-10475	Farewell Andromeda (Welcome to My Morning)/ Whiskey Basin Blues	1975	—	—	3.00
—Gold Standard Series					
❑ GB-10476	Thank God I'm a Country Boy/My Sweet Lady	1975	—	—	3.00
—Gold Standard Series					
❑ GB-10477	Rocky Mountain High/Spring	1975	—	—	3.00
—Gold Standard Series					
❑ GB-10478	Sweet Surrender/Summer	1975	—	—	3.00
—Gold Standard Series					
❑ PB-10517	Fly Away/Two Shots	1975	—	2.00	4.00
❑ PB-10586	Looking for Space/Windsong	1976	—	2.00	4.00
❑ PB-10687	It Makes Me Giggle/Spirit	1976	—	2.00	4.00
❑ 74-0275	Daydream/I Wish I Knew How It Would Feel to Be Free	1969	2.50	5.00	10.00
❑ 74-0305	Anthem (Revelation)/Sticky Summer Weather	1970	2.50	5.00	10.00
❑ 74-0332	Follow Me/Isabel	1970	2.50	5.00	10.00
❑ 74-0376	Sail Away Home/I Wish I Could Have Been There	1970	2.50	5.00	10.00
❑ 74-0391	Whose Garden Is This/Mr. Bojangles	1970	2.50	5.00	10.00
❑ 74-0445	Take Me Home, Country Roads/Poems, Prayers and Promises	1971	2.00	4.00	8.00
—With Fat City					
❑ 74-0567	Friends with You/Starwood in Aspen	1971	—	3.00	6.00
❑ 74-0647	Everyday/City of New Orleans	1972	—	3.00	6.00
❑ 74-0737	Goodbye Again/The Eagle and the Hawk	1972	—	3.00	6.00
❑ 74-0801	Late Winter, Early Spring/Hard Life Hard Times	1972	—	3.00	6.00
❑ 74-0829	Rocky Mountain High/Spring	1972	—	2.50	5.00
❑ 74-0955	I'd Rather Be a Cowboy/Sunshine on My Shoulders	1973	—	2.00	4.00
WINDSTAR					
❑ 75720	Country Girl in Paris/Bread and Roses	1988	—	2.50	5.00
❑ 75720 [PS]	Country Girl in Paris/Bread and Roses	1988	—	3.00	6.00

DENVER, JOHN, AND THE MUPPETS

Number	Title (A Side/B Side)	Yr	VG	VG+	NM
RCA					
❑ PB-11767	Have Yourself a Merry Little Christmas//We Wish You a Merry Christmas/A Baby Just Like You	1979	—	2.50	5.00
❑ PB-11767 [PS]	Have Yourself a Merry Little Christmas//We Wish You a Merry Christmas/A Baby Just Like You	1979	—	2.50	5.00

DENVER, JOHN, AND THE NITTY GRITTY DIRT BAND

Also see each artist's individual listings.

Number	Title (A Side/B Side)	Yr	VG	VG+	NM
UNIVERSAL					
❑ UVL-66008	And So It Goes/Amazing Grace	1989	—	2.00	4.00

DENVER, KARL

Number	Title (A Side/B Side)	Yr	VG	VG+	NM
LONDON					
❑ 2020	Marcheta/Joe Sweeney	1961	3.75	7.50	15.00
❑ 9521	Wimoweh/Sleepy Lagoon	1962	3.00	6.00	12.00
❑ 9534	Zimba/Uska Dara	1962	3.00	6.00	12.00
❑ 9576	Blue Weekend/Pastures of Plenty	1963	3.00	6.00	12.00

DENVER, BOISE, & JOHNSON

Also see JOHN DENVER.

Number	Title (A Side/B Side)	Yr	VG	VG+	NM
REPRISE					
❑ 0695	Take Me to Tomorrow/'68 Nixon (This Year's Model)	1968	3.00	6.00	12.00

DEPECHE MODE

Number	Title (A Side/B Side)	Yr	VG	VG+	NM
REPRISE					
❑ 17314	Home/Useless	1997	—	—	3.00
❑ 17390	It's No Good/Slowblow	1997	—	—	3.00
❑ 17409	Barrel of a Gun/Painkiller	1997	—	—	3.00
SIRE					
❑ 18506	Walking in My Shoes/My Joy	1993	—	—	3.00
❑ 18600	I Feel You/One Caress	1993	—	—	3.00
❑ 18889	Personal Jesus/Policy of Truth	1992	—	—	3.00
—First U.S. 45 release of A-side					
❑ 18890	World in My Eyes/Enjoy the Silence	1992	—	—	3.00
—First U.S. 45 release of A-side					
❑ 19842	Policy of Truth/Kaleid	1990	—	—	3.00
❑ 19885	Enjoy the Silence/Memphisto	1990	—	—	3.00
❑ 21886	Strangelove/Behind the Wheel	198?	—	—	3.00
—"Back to Back Hits" reissue					
❑ 21994	People Are People/A Question of Lust	198?	—	—	3.00
—"Back to Back Hits" reissue					
❑ 22993	Nothing/Nothing (instrumental)	1989	—	—	3.00
❑ 27777	Strangelove/Nothing	1988	—	—	3.00
❑ 27777 [PS]	Strangelove/Nothing	1988	—	—	3.00
❑ 27991	Route 66/Behind the Wheel//Behind the Wheel	1988	—	—	3.00
❑ 27991 [PS]	Route 66/Behind the Wheel//Behind the Wheel	1988	—	—	3.00
❑ 28189	Never Let Me Down Again/Pleasure-Little Treasure	1987	—	—	3.00
❑ 28189 [PS]	Never Let Me Down Again/Pleasure-Little Treasure	1987	—	—	3.00
❑ 28366	Strangelove/FPMIP	1987	—	—	3.00
❑ 28366 [PS]	Strangelove/FPMIP	1987	—	—	3.00
❑ 28564	But Not Tonight/Stripped	1986	—	—	3.00
❑ 28697	A Question of Lust/Christmas Island	1986	—	—	3.00
❑ 28697 [PS]	A Question of Lust/Christmas Island	1986	—	—	3.00
❑ 28835	Share the Disease/Flexible	1985	—	2.50	5.00
❑ 28918	Master and Servant/(Set Me Free) Remotivate Me	1985	—	—	3.00
❑ 28918 [PS]	Master and Servant/(Set Me Free) Remotivate Me	1985	—	—	3.00
❑ 29221	People Are People/In Your Memory	1984	—	—	3.00
❑ 29221 [PS]	People Are People/In Your Memory	1984	—	—	3.00
❑ 29482	Everything Counts/Work Hard	1983	—	—	3.00
❑ 29482 [PS]	Everything Counts/Work Hard	1983	—	—	3.00
❑ 50029	Just Can't Get Enough/Tora, Tora, Tora	1982	2.00	4.00	8.00

DERBY-HATVILLE

Number	Title (A Side/B Side)	Yr	VG	VG+	NM
SEA ELL					
❑ 102	You'll Forget Me/(B-side unknown)	1967	10.00	20.00	40.00
❑ 104	Instant Replay/(B-side unknown)	1967	10.00	20.00	40.00

DEREK

See JOHNNY CYMBAL.

DEREK AND THE DOMINOS

Also see ERIC CLAPTON.

Number	Title (A Side/B Side)	Yr	VG	VG+	NM
ATCO					
❑ 6780	Tell the Truth/Roll It Over	1970	6.25	12.50	25.00
—Produced by Phil Spector; withdrawn shortly after release					
❑ 6803	Bell Bottom Blues/Keep On Growing	1971	2.50	5.00	10.00
❑ 6809	Layla (2:43)/I Am Yours	1971	2.50	5.00	10.00
❑ 6809	Layla (7:10)/I Am Yours	1972	—	3.00	6.00
POLYDOR					
❑ 15040	Layla/I Am Yours	1972	—	—	—
—Unreleased?					
RSO					
❑ 400	Presence of the Lord/Why Does Love Got to Be So Sad	1973	—	3.00	6.00

DERRINGER, RICK

Also see THE McCOYS.

Number	Title (A Side/B Side)	Yr	VG	VG+	NM
BLUE SKY					
❑ 2751	Rock and Roll Hoochie Koo/Time Warp	1974	—	2.50	5.00
❑ 2752	Teenage Love Affair/Slide Over Slinky	1974	—	2.00	4.00
❑ 2753	It's Raining/Cheqap Tequila	1974	—	2.00	4.00
❑ 2755	Hang On Sloopy/Skyscraper Blues	1975	—	2.00	4.00
❑ 2757	Don't Ever Say Goodbye/Gimme More	1975	—	2.00	4.00
❑ 2765	Let Me In/You Can Have Me	1976	—	2.00	4.00
—As "Derringer"					
❑ 2767	Don't Stop Loving Me/Let's Make It	1977	—	2.00	4.00
—As "Derringer"					
❑ 2770	Lawyers, Guns and Money/Sleepless	1977	—	2.00	4.00
—As "Derringer"					
❑ 2774	Midnight Road/Rocka-Rolla	1978	—	2.00	4.00
—As "Derringer"					
❑ 2783	Need a Little Girl (Just Like You)/Something Warm	1979	—	2.00	4.00
❑ 2788	Don't Ever Say Godbye/Timeless	1980	—	2.00	4.00
❑ 2793	Runaway/Teenage Love Affair	1980	—	2.00	4.00
❑ 2794	Let the Music Play/You'll Get Yours	1980	—	2.00	4.00
EPIC					
❑ 05830	The Real America/Grab Them Cakes	1986	—	—	3.00
—As "Derringer"					

DESHANNON, JACKIE

Number	Title (A Side/B Side)	Yr	VG	VG+	NM
AMHERST					
❑ 725	I Don't Think I Can Wait/Don't Let the Flame Burn Out	1978	3.00	6.00	12.00
❑ 728	To Love Somebody/Just to Feel This Love from You	1978	3.00	6.00	12.00
❑ 733	You're the Only Dancer/Tonight You're Doin' It Right	1979	3.00	6.00	12.00
❑ 737	Things We Said Today/Way Above the Angels	1979	3.00	6.00	12.00
ATLANTIC					
❑ 2871	Only Love Can Break Your Heart/Vanilla Olay	1972	2.50	5.00	10.00
❑ 2895	I Wanna Roo You/Paradise	1972	2.50	5.00	10.00
❑ 2919	Sweet Sixteen/Speak Out to Me	1972	2.50	5.00	10.00
❑ 2924	Chains on My Soul/Peaceful in My Soul	1972	2.50	5.00	10.00
❑ 2994	Your Baby Is a Lady/(If You Never Have a Big Hit Record) You're Still Gonna Be My Star	1973	2.50	5.00	10.00
❑ 3041	You've Changed/Jimmie, Just Sing Me One More Song	1974	2.50	5.00	10.00
CAPITOL					
❑ 3130	Salinas/Keep Me Warm	1971	2.50	5.00	10.00
❑ 3185	Stone Cold Soul/West Virginia Mine	1971	2.50	5.00	10.00
COLUMBIA					
❑ 10221	Boat to Sail/Let the Sailors Dance	1975	3.75	7.50	15.00
—With Brian Wilson on backing vocal					
❑ 10340	Fire in the City/All Night Desire	1976	2.50	5.00	10.00
DOT					
❑ 15928	Cajun Blues/Just Another Lie	1959	6.25	12.50	25.00
—As "Jackie Shannon"					
❑ 15980	Trouble/Lies	1959	6.25	12.50	25.00
—As "Jackie Shannon"					
EDISON INTERNATIONAL					
❑ 416	I Wanna Go Home/So Warm	1960	25.00	50.00	100.00
❑ 418	Put My Baby Down/The Foolish One	1960	25.00	50.00	100.00
GONE					
❑ 5008	How Wrong I Was/I'll Be True	1957	7.50	15.00	30.00
—As "Jackie Dee"					
IMPERIAL					
❑ 66110	What the World Needs Now Is Love/I Remember the Boy	1965	2.00	4.00	8.00
❑ 66132	A Lifetime of Loneliness/Don't Turn Your Back on Me	1965	—	3.00	6.00
❑ 66171	Come and Get Me/Splendor in the Grass	1966	—	3.00	6.00
❑ 66194	Will You Love Me Tomorrow/Are You Ready for This	1966	—	3.00	6.00
❑ 66196	So Long Johnny/Windows and Doors	1966	—	3.00	6.00
❑ 66202	I Can Make It with You/To Be Myself	1966	—	3.00	6.00
❑ 66224	Come On Down/Find Me Love	1967	—	3.00	6.00
❑ 66236	Where Does the Sun Go/Wishing Doll	1967	—	3.00	6.00
❑ 66251	It's All in the Game/Changin' My Mind	1967	—	3.00	6.00
❑ 66281	Me About You/I Keep Wanting You	1968	—	3.00	6.00
❑ 66301	Nobody's Home to Go Home To/Nicole	1968	—	3.00	6.00
❑ 66312	Didn't Want to Have to Do It/Splendor in the Grass	1968	—	3.00	6.00
❑ 66313	The Weight/Splendor in the Grass	1968	—	3.00	6.00

Number	Title (A Side/B Side)	Yr	VG	VG+	NM
66342	Holly Would/My Heart's Been Marching	1968	—	3.00	6.00
66370	What Is This/Trust Me	1969	—	2.50	5.00
66385	Put a Little Love in Your Heart/Always Be Together	1969	—	3.00	6.00
66419	Love Will Find a Way/I Let Go Completely	1969	—	2.50	5.00
66430	One Christmas/Do You Know How Christmas Trees Are Grown	1969	—	3.00	6.00
66438	Brighton Hill/You Can Come to Me	1970	—	2.50	5.00
66452	You Keep Me Hangin' On-Hurt So Bad/What Was Your Day Like	1970	—	2.50	5.00

LIBERTY

Number	Title (A Side/B Side)	Yr	VG	VG+	NM
55148	Buddy/Strolypso Dance	1958	6.25	12.50	25.00

—As "Jackie Dee"

Number	Title (A Side/B Side)	Yr	VG	VG+	NM
55288	Lonely Girl/Teach Me	1960	3.75	7.50	15.00
55342	Think About You/Heaven Is Being with You	1961	3.75	7.50	15.00
55358	I Won't Turn You Down/Wish I Could Find a Boy	1961	3.75	7.50	15.00
55387	Baby (When You Kiss Me)/Ain't That Love	1961	3.75	7.50	15.00
55425	The Prince/I'll Drown in My Own Tears	1962	3.75	7.50	15.00
55425	The Prince/That's What Boys Are Made Of	1962	3.75	7.50	15.00
55484	Guess Who/Just Like in the Movies	1962	3.75	7.50	15.00
55497	You Won't Forget Me/I Don't Think So Much of Myself	1962	3.75	7.50	15.00
55526	Faded Love/Dancing Silhouettes	1962	3.75	7.50	15.00
55526 [PS]	Faded Love/Dancing Silhouettes	1962	10.00	20.00	40.00
55563	Needles and Pins/Did He Call Today, Mama?	1963	3.75	7.50	15.00
55602	Little Yellow Roses/Oh Sweet Chariot	1963	3.75	7.50	15.00
55602	Little Yellow Roses/500 Miles	1963	3.75	7.50	15.00
55602 [DJ]	Little Yellow Roses	1963	20.00	40.00	80.00

—Yellow vinyl promo

Number	Title (A Side/B Side)	Yr	VG	VG+	NM
55645	When You Walk in the Room/Til You Say You're Mine	1963	3.75	7.50	15.00
55673	I'm Gonna Be Strong/Should I Cry	1964	3.75	7.50	15.00
55678	Oh Boy/I'm Looking for Someone to Love	1964	3.75	7.50	15.00
55705	Hold Your Head High/She Don't Understand Him Like I Do	1964	3.75	7.50	15.00
55730	He's Got the Whole World in His Hands/It's Love Baby	1964	3.75	7.50	15.00
55735	When You Walk in the Room/Over You	1964	3.00	6.00	12.00
55787	What the World Needs Now Is Love/A Lifetime of Loneliness	1965	—	—	—

—Unreleased

Number	Title (A Side/B Side)	Yr	VG	VG+	NM
56187	Mediterranean Sky/It's So Nice	1970	—	3.00	6.00

PJ

Number	Title (A Side/B Side)	Yr	VG	VG+	NM
101	Trouble/Lies	1959	10.00	20.00	40.00

—As "Jackie Shannon"

RCA

Number	Title (A Side/B Side)	Yr	VG	VG+	NM
PB-11902	I Don't Need You Anymore/Find Love	1980	—	2.50	5.00

SAGE AND SAND

Number	Title (A Side/B Side)	Yr	VG	VG+	NM
290	Just Another Lie/Cajun Blues	1960	6.25	12.50	25.00
330	Trouble/Lies	1960	6.25	12.50	25.00

UNITED ARTISTS

Number	Title (A Side/B Side)	Yr	VG	VG+	NM
0033	What the World Needs Now Is Love/Needles and Pins	1973	—	3.00	6.00

—"Silver Spotlight Series" reissue

Number	Title (A Side/B Side)	Yr	VG	VG+	NM
0034	Put a Little Love in Your Heart/When You Walk in the Room	1973	—	3.00	6.00

—"Silver Spotlight Series" reissue

DESIRES, THE

More than one group.

20TH FOX

Number	Title (A Side/B Side)	Yr	VG	VG+	NM
195	I Don't Know Why/Longing	1960	6.25	12.50	25.00

DASA

Number	Title (A Side/B Side)	Yr	VG	VG+	NM
102	Phyllis Beloved/The Girl for Me	1962	7.50	15.00	30.00

HERALD

Number	Title (A Side/B Side)	Yr	VG	VG+	NM
532	Bobby You/Cold Lonely Heart	1958	6.25	12.50	25.00

HULL

Number	Title (A Side/B Side)	Yr	VG	VG+	NM
730	Hey Lena/Let It Please Be You	1959	20.00	40.00	80.00
733	Set Me Free/Rendezvous with You	1960	20.00	40.00	80.00

SEVILLE

Number	Title (A Side/B Side)	Yr	VG	VG+	NM
118	The Story of Love/I Ask You	1962	7.50	15.00	30.00

SMASH

Number	Title (A Side/B Side)	Yr	VG	VG+	NM
1763	There I Go Again/I Never Loved Like This	1962	6.25	12.50	25.00

DETERGENTS, THE

Also see RON DANTE.

KAPP

Number	Title (A Side/B Side)	Yr	VG	VG+	NM
735	I Can Never Eat Home Anymore/Igor's Cellar	1966	3.75	7.50	15.00
753	Pushin' the Panic Button/Some Sunday Morning	1966	3.75	7.50	15.00

ROULETTE

Number	Title (A Side/B Side)	Yr	VG	VG+	NM
4590	Leader of the Laundromat/Ulcers	1964	5.00	10.00	20.00
4590 [PS]	Leader of the Laundromat/Ulcers	1964	10.00	20.00	40.00
4603	Double-O-Seven/The Blue Kangaroo	1965	3.75	7.50	15.00
4616	Tea and Trumpets/Mrs. Jones (How "Bout It)	1965	3.75	7.50	15.00
4626	Little Dum-Dum/Soldier Girl	1965	3.75	7.50	15.00
4642	Bad Girl/Here She Comes	1965	3.75	7.50	15.00

DETOURS, THE

ATCO

Number	Title (A Side/B Side)	Yr	VG	VG+	NM
6448	Who Do You Love/Peace of Mind	1966	6.25	12.50	25.00

MCSHERRY

Number	Title (A Side/B Side)	Yr	VG	VG+	NM
1285	Bring Back My Beatles to Me/Money	1964	6.25	12.50	25.00
1285	Bring Back My Beatles/Money	1964	6.25	12.50	25.00

DETROIT

Mitch Ryder's post-Detroit Wheels band.

PARAMOUNT

Number	Title (A Side/B Side)	Yr	VG	VG+	NM
0094	It Ain't Easy/Long Neck Goose	1971	—	3.00	6.00
0133	Rock 'N Roll/Box of Old Roses	1971	—	3.00	6.00
0158	Gimmie Shelter/Oh Oh La La La Dee Da Doo	1972	—	3.00	6.00

DETROIT EMERALDS

RIC TIC

Number	Title (A Side/B Side)	Yr	VG	VG+	NM
135	Show Time/(Instrumental)	1968	3.00	6.00	12.00
138	Shades Down/Ode to Billie Joe	1968	3.00	6.00	12.00
141	Take Me the Way I Am/I'll Keep On Coming Back	1968	3.00	6.00	12.00

WESTBOUND

Number	Title (A Side/B Side)	Yr	VG	VG+	NM
147	Holding On/Things Are Looking Up	1969	2.00	4.00	8.00
156	If I Lose Your Love/I Bet You Get the One	1969	2.00	4.00	8.00
161	I Can't See Myself Doing Without You/Just Now and Then	1970	2.00	4.00	8.00
172	Do Me Right/Just Now and Then	1970	2.00	4.00	8.00
181	Wear This Ring (With Love)/Bet You Got the One Who Loves You	1971	—	3.00	6.00
192	You Want It, You Got It/Till You Decide to Come Home	1971	—	3.00	6.00
203	Baby Let Me Take You (In My Arms)/I'll Never Sail the Sea Again	1972	—	3.00	6.00
209	Feel the Need in Me/There's a Love for Me Somewhere	1972	—	3.00	6.00
213	You're Gettin' a Little Too Smart/Heaven Couldn't Be Like This	1973	—	3.00	6.00
220	Lee/Whatcha Gonna Wear Tomorrow	1973	—	3.00	6.00
226	I'm Qualified/Set It Out	1974	—	3.00	6.00
5005	Yes I Know I'm in Love/Rosetta Stone	1974	—	3.00	6.00
55401	Feel the Need/Love Has Come to Me	1977	—	2.50	5.00
55404	Set It Out (Part 1)/Set It Out (Part 2)	1977	—	2.50	5.00
55410	Turn On Lady/Just Don't Know About This Girl of Mine	1977	—	2.50	5.00

DETROIT JR.

FOXY

Number	Title (A Side/B Side)	Yr	VG	VG+	NM
002	This Time Last Christmas/Christmas Day	1961	3.00	6.00	12.00

DETROIT WHEELS, THE

Mitch Ryder's band after he went solo.

INFERNO

Number	Title (A Side/B Side)	Yr	VG	VG+	NM
5002	Linda Sue Dixon/Tally Ho	1968	5.00	10.00	20.00
5003	Think (Part 1)/Think (Part 2)	1968	5.00	10.00	20.00

DEUCES OF RHYTHM AND THE TEMPO TOPPERS, THE

Also see LITTLE RICHARD.

PEACOCK

Number	Title (A Side/B Side)	Yr	VG	VG+	NM
1616	Ain't That Good News/A Fool at the Wheel	1953	20.00	40.00	80.00
1628	Always/Rice, Red Beans and Turnip Greens	1954	20.00	40.00	80.00

DEVAURS, THE

D-TONE

Number	Title (A Side/B Side)	Yr	VG	VG+	NM
3	Baby Doll/Teenager	1958	62.50	125.00	250.00

MOON

Number	Title (A Side/B Side)	Yr	VG	VG+	NM
105	Where Are You/Boy in Mexico	1959	50.00	100.00	200.00

RED FOX

Number	Title (A Side/B Side)	Yr	VG	VG+	NM
104	Where Are You/Boy in Mexico	1965	10.00	20.00	40.00

DEVO

BACKSTREET

Number	Title (A Side/B Side)	Yr	VG	VG+	NM
52215	Theme from Doctor Detroit/King of Soul	1983	—	—	3.00

—B-side by James Brown

BOOJI BOY

Number	Title (A Side/B Side)	Yr	VG	VG+	NM
7033-14	Jocko Homo/Mongoloid	1977	2.00	4.00	8.00
7033-14 [PS]	Jocko Homo/Mongoloid	1977	2.00	4.00	8.00
72843/75677	Satisfaction/Sloppy	1978	—	—	3.00
72843/75677 [PS]	Satisfaction/Sloppy	1978	2.00	4.00	8.00

ENIGMA

Number	Title (A Side/B Side)	Yr	VG	VG+	NM
75023	Disco Dancer/Disco Dancer	1989	—	—	3.00
75029	Baby Doll (Ivan Ivan Mix)/Baby Doll (Devo Mix)	1988	—	—	3.00
75029 [PS]	Baby Doll (Ivan Ivan Mix)/Baby Doll (Devo Mix)	1988	—	—	3.00

FULL MOON/ASYLUM

Number	Title (A Side/B Side)	Yr	VG	VG+	NM
47204	Working in the Coal Mine/Planet Earth	1981	—	—	3.00
47204 [PS]	Working in the Coal Mine/Planet Earth	1981	—	—	3.00

REFLEX

Number	Title (A Side/B Side)	Yr	VG	VG+	NM
5	Bush Whacked	1988	—	—	3.00

—One-sided flexi-disc given away with Reflex magazine

WARNER BROS.

Number	Title (A Side/B Side)	Yr	VG	VG+	NM
GWB 0400	Whip It/Girl U Want	198?	—	—	3.00

—Back to Back Hits series

Number	Title (A Side/B Side)	Yr	VG	VG+	NM
EP 3595	Working in the Coal Mine (same on both sides)	1981	—	—	3.00

—Issued with the New Traditionalists LP

Number	Title (A Side/B Side)	Yr	VG	VG+	NM
8675	(I Can't Get No) Satisfaction/Uncontrollable Urge	1978	—	—	3.00
8745	Come Back Jonee/Praying Hands	1979	—	—	3.00
29133	Are You Experienced/Growing Pains	1984	—	—	3.00
29133 [PS]	Are You Experienced/Growing Pains	1984	—	—	3.00
29811	That's Good/What I Must Do	1983	—	—	3.00
29931	Peek-A-Boo/Find Out	1982	—	—	3.00
29931 [PS]	Peek-A-Boo/Find Out	1982	—	—	3.00
49028	Secret Agent Man/Red Eye	1979	—	—	3.00
49524	Girl U Want/Mr. B's Ballroom	1980	—	—	3.00
49550	Whip It/Turn Around	1980	—	—	3.00
49621	Freedom of Choice/Snowball (Remix)	1980	—	—	3.00
49621 [PS]	Freedom of Choice/Snowball (Remix)	1980	—	—	3.00
49715	Gates of Steel (Live)/Be Still (Live)	1981	—	—	3.00
49834	Beautiful World/Enough Said	1981	—	—	3.00
50010	Jerkin' Back 'N' Forth/Mecha Mania Boy	1982	—	—	3.00
50048	Through Being Cool/Going Under	1982	—	—	3.00

DEVONS, THE (1)

DECCA

Number	Title (A Side/B Side)	Yr	VG	VG+	NM
31777	Honda Bike/Free Fall	1965	20.00	40.00	80.00
31822	Are You Really Real/It's All Over Now, Baby Blue	1965	10.00	20.00	40.00
31899	Come On/A Little Extra Effort	1966	10.00	20.00	40.00

DEVONS, THE (2)

KING

Number	Title (A Side/B Side)	Yr	VG	VG+	NM
❑ 6226	Someone to Treat Me (The Way You Used To)/ Soul Party	1969	2.00	4.00	8.00

DEVONS, THE (3)

Also recorded as SIR DOUGLAS QUINTET.

PIC ONE

Number	Title (A Side/B Side)	Yr	VG	VG+	NM
❑ 111	Wine, Wine, Wine/Joey's Guitar	1965	20.00	40.00	80.00

DEVONS, THE (U)

May be group (2), but we're not sure.

MR. G

Number	Title (A Side/B Side)	Yr	VG	VG+	NM
❑ 825	Groovin' with My Thing/Wise Up	1968	3.00	6.00	12.00

DEVORZON, BARRY

Also see BARRY AND THE TAMERLANES; BARRY DeVORZON AND PERRY BOTKIN, JR.

Number	Title (A Side/B Side)	Yr	VG	VG+	NM
A&M					
❑ 2129	Theme from "The Warriors"/Baseball Furies' Chase	1979	—	2.00	4.00
COLUMBIA					
❑ 41464	Betty, Betty/Across the Street from Your House	1959	7.50	15.00	30.00
❑ 41612	Hey Little Darlin'/Rosemary	1960	6.25	12.50	25.00
❑ 41663	Love You Baby/Can-Can Ladies	1960	6.25	12.50	25.00
❑ 42031	Penny Moved Away/Lindy Lou	1961	6.25	12.50	25.00
❑ 3-42031	Penny Moved Away/Lindy Lou	1961	10.00	20.00	40.00
—"Compact 33" single with small hole					
RCA VICTOR					
❑ 47-7124	Barbara Jean/Baby Doll	1957	7.50	15.00	30.00
❑ 47-7226	False Love/Raindrops at My Window	1958	7.50	15.00	30.00
❑ 47-7406	Honey Bunny/Too Soon	1958	7.50	15.00	30.00
❑ 47-7510	Cora Lee/Blue, Green and Gold	1959	7.50	15.00	30.00

DEVORZON, BARRY, AND PERRY BOTKIN, JR.

Also see each artist's individual listings.

A&M

Number	Title (A Side/B Side)	Yr	VG	VG+	NM
❑ 1856	Nadia's Theme (The Young and the Restless)/ Down the Line	1976	—	2.00	4.00
—Reissue; the original is listed under PERRY BOTKIN, JR.					
❑ 1856 [PS]	Nadia's Theme (The Young and the Restless)/ Down the Line	1976	—	2.00	4.00
—Green sleeve					
❑ 1856 [PS]	Nadia's Theme (The Young and the Restless)/ Down the Line	1976	—	3.00	6.00
—Blue sleeve					
❑ 1856 [PS]	Nadia's Theme (The Young and the Restless)/ Down the Line	1976	—	3.00	6.00
—Black sleeve					
❑ 1890	Bless the Beasts and Children/Down the Line	1976	—	2.00	4.00

DEVOTIONS, THE

Number	Title (A Side/B Side)	Yr	VG	VG+	NM
DELTA					
❑ 1001	Rip Van Winkle/I Love You for Sentimental Reasons	1961	37.50	75.00	150.00
KAPE					
❑ 701	(How Do You Speak) To An Angel/Teardrops Follow Me	1966	3.00	6.00	12.00
ROULETTE					
❑ 4406	Rip Van Winkle/I Love You for Sentimental Reasons	1962	10.00	20.00	40.00
❑ 4541	Rip Van Winkle/I Love You for Sentimental Reasons	1964	5.00	10.00	20.00
❑ 4556	A Sunday Kind of Love/Tears from a Broken Heart	1964	7.50	5.00	30.00
❑ 4580	Snow White/Zindy Lou	1964	7.50	5.00	30.00

DEWEY, GEORGE AND JACK

RAVEN

Number	Title (A Side/B Side)	Yr	VG	VG+	NM
❑ 700	The Flying Saucers Have Landed/The Flying Saucers Have Landed (Part 2)	195?	7.50	15.00	30.00

DEY, TRACEY

Number	Title (A Side/B Side)	Yr	VG	VG+	NM
AMY					
❑ 894	Teddy's the Boy I Love/Here Comes the Boy	1963	3.75	7.50	15.00
❑ 901	Gonna Get Along Without You Now/Go Away	1964	3.75	7.50	15.00
❑ 908	Hangin' On to My Baby/Ska-Doo-Dee-Yah	1964	3.75	7.50	15.00
❑ 912	I Won't Tell/Any Kind of Love	1964	3.75	7.50	15.00
❑ 917	Blue Turns to Grey/Didn't Ya	1964	5.00	10.00	20.00
❑ 928	Hanky Panky/Shakin' the Blues Away	1965	3.75	7.50	15.00
LIBERTY					
❑ 55604	Teenage Cleopatra/Who's That	1963	3.75	7.50	15.00
VEE JAY					
❑ 467	Jerry (I'm Your Sherry)/Once in a Blue Moon	1962	6.25	12.50	25.00
❑ 506	Jealous Eyes/Long Time, No See	1963	5.00	10.00	20.00

DEY AND KNIGHT

COLUMBIA

Number	Title (A Side/B Side)	Yr	VG	VG+	NM
❑ 43466	Young Love/I'm Gonna Love You Tomorrow	1965	3.00	6.00	12.00
❑ 43693	Sayin' Somethin'/Ooh Da La Da Lay	1966	3.00	6.00	12.00

DEYOUNG, CLIFF

Also see CLEAR LIGHT.

MCA

Number	Title (A Side/B Side)	Yr	VG	VG+	NM
❑ 40156	My Sweet Lady/Sunshine on My Shoulders	1973	—	2.00	4.00
❑ 40156 [PS]	My Sweet Lady/Sunshine on My Shoulders	1973	—	2.50	5.00
❑ 40239	Escaping Reality/She Bent Me Straight Again	1974	—	2.00	4.00
❑ 40294	It Hurts a Little Even Now/Lives	1974	—	2.00	4.00
❑ 40388	If I Could Put You in My Song/You Will Never Know	1975	—	2.00	4.00

DEYOUNG, DENNIS

Also see STYX.

Number	Title (A Side/B Side)	Yr	VG	VG+	NM
A&M					
❑ 2666	Desert Moon/Gravity	1984	—	—	3.00
❑ 2666 [PS]	Desert Moon/Gravity	1984	—	—	3.00
❑ 2692	Don't Wait for Heroes/Gravity	1984	—	—	3.00
❑ 2709	Dear Darling/Suspicious	1985	—	—	3.00
❑ 2816	Call Me/Please	1986	—	—	3.00
❑ 2816 [PS]	Call Me/Please	1986	—	—	3.00
❑ 2839	This Is the Time/Southbound Ryan	1986	—	—	3.00
MCA					
❑ 53293	Beneath the Moon/Boomchild	1988	—	—	3.00
❑ 53376	Outside Looking In Again/Boomchild	1988	—	—	3.00

DIABLOS, THE (1)

See NOLAN STRONG AND THE DIABLOS.

DIABLOS, THE (2)

JUBILEE

Number	Title (A Side/B Side)	Yr	VG	VG+	NM
❑ 5553	Hombre/El Bandito	1966	5.00	10.00	20.00

DIABLOS, THE (3)

PYRAMID

Number	Title (A Side/B Side)	Yr	VG	VG+	NM
❑ 159	White Christmas/Danny Boy	19??	5.00	10.00	20.00

DIALS, THE

Number	Title (A Side/B Side)	Yr	VG	VG+	NM
HILLTOP					
❑ 219	No Hard Feelings/Win Yourself a Lover	1961	12.50	25.00	50.00
❑ 2009	Wondering About Your Love/Sorrento	1960	37.50	75.00	150.00
❑ 2010	School Bells Are Ringing/Ring Ting-a-Ling	1960	75.00	150.00	300.00
NORGOLDE					
❑ 105	Ring Ting-a Ling/All Kinds of Twistin'	1961	20.00	40.00	80.00
PHILIPS					
❑ 40040	These Foolish Things/At the Start of a New Romance	1962	10.00	20.00	40.00
TIME					
❑ 1068	Monkey Dance/Monkey Walk	1963	5.00	10.00	20.00

DIALTONES, THE (1)

DIAL

Number	Title (A Side/B Side)	Yr	VG	VG+	NM
❑ 4054	Don't Let the Sun Shine on Me/You Don't Know, You Just Don't Know	1967	5.00	10.00	20.00

DIALTONES, THE (2)

GOLDISC

Number	Title (A Side/B Side)	Yr	VG	VG+	NM
❑ 3005	Till I Heard It from You/Johnny	1960	7.50	15.00	30.00
❑ 3020	Till I Heard It from You/Johnny	1961	5.00	10.00	20.00

DIALTONES, THE (U)

Probably neither (1) nor (2), but we're not sure.

LAWN

Number	Title (A Side/B Side)	Yr	VG	VG+	NM
❑ 203	So Young/Chicago Bird	1963	6.25	12.50	25.00

DIAMOND, BRIAN, AND THE CUTTERS

HICKORY

Number	Title (A Side/B Side)	Yr	VG	VG+	NM
❑ 1321	Big Bad Wolf/See If I Care	1965	2.50	5.00	10.00

DIAMOND, NEIL

Also see BARBRA AND NEIL; NEIL AND JACK; TEN BROKEN HEARTS.

Number	Title (A Side/B Side)	Yr	VG	VG+	NM
BANG					
❑ 105	Cherry, Cherry/Girl, You'll Be a Woman Soon	1973	—	2.00	4.00
—Reissue					
❑ 108	Solitary Man/I'm a Believer	1973	—	2.00	4.00
—Reissue					
❑ 519	Solitary Man/Do It	1966	3.75	7.50	15.00
❑ 528	Cherry, Cherry/I'll Come Running	1966	3.00	6.00	12.00
❑ 536	I Got the Feelin' (Oh No No)/The Boat That I Row	1966	3.00	6.00	12.00
❑ 540	You Got to Me/Someday Baby	1967	3.00	6.00	12.00
❑ 542	Girl, You'll Be a Woman Soon/You'll Forget	1967	3.00	6.00	12.00
❑ 547	I Thank the Lord for the Night Time/The Long Way Home	1967	3.75	7.50	15.00
❑ 547	Thank the Lord for the Night Time/The Long Way Home	1967	2.50	5.00	10.00
—Title altered on second pressing					
❑ 551	Kentucky Woman/The Time Is Now	1967	2.50	5.00	10.00
❑ 554	New Orleans/Hanky Panky	1968	2.50	5.00	10.00
❑ 556	Red Red Wine/Red Rubber Ball	1968	2.00	4.00	8.00
❑ 561	Shilo/La Bamba	1968	2.00	4.00	8.00
❑ 575	Shilo/La Bamba	1970	—	3.00	6.00
❑ 578	Solitary Man/The Time Is Now	1970	—	3.00	6.00
❑ 580	Do It/Hanky Panky	1970	—	3.00	6.00
❑ 586	I'm a Believer/Crooked Street	1971	—	3.00	6.00
❑ 586	I'm a Believer/Crooked Street	1971	3.75	7.50	15.00
—Rare pressing with both sides in stereo					
❑ 703	The Long Way Home/Monday, Monday	1973	—	2.50	5.00
CAPITOL					
❑ 4939	Love on the Rocks/Acapulco	1980	—	2.00	4.00
❑ 4939 [PS]	Love on the Rocks/Acapulco	1980	—	2.00	4.00
❑ 4960	Hello Again/Amazed and Confused	1981	—	2.00	4.00
❑ 4960 [PS]	Hello Again/Amazed and Confused	1981	—	2.00	4.00
❑ 4994	America/Songs of Life	1981	—	2.00	4.00
❑ 4994 [PS]	America/Songs of Life	1981	—	2.00	4.00
COLUMBIA					
❑ AE7 1115 [DJ]	Song Sung Blue (mono/stereo)	1977	3.75	7.50	15.00
—Live version from "Love at the Greek"					
❑ 02604	Yesterday's Songs/Guitar Heaven	1981	—	—	3.00
❑ 02604 [PS]	Yesterday's Songs/Guitar Heaven	1981	—	—	3.00
❑ 02712	On the Way to the Sky/Save Me	1982	—	—	3.00
❑ 02712 [PS]	On the Way to the Sky/Save Me	1982	—	—	3.00
❑ 02928	Be Mine Tonight/Right By You	1982	—	—	3.00
❑ 03219	Heartlight/You Don't Know Me	1982	—	—	3.00
❑ 03219 [PS]	Heartlight/You Don't Know Me	1982	—	2.00	4.00
❑ CNR-03345	Heartlight	1982	—	2.50	5.00
—One-sided budget release					
❑ 03503	I'm Alive/Lost Among the Stars	1983	—	—	3.00
❑ CNR-03572	I'm Alive	1983	—	2.50	5.00
—One-sided budget release					

Number	Title (A Side/B Side)	Yr	VG	VG+	NM
❑ 03801	Front Page Story/I'm Guilty	1983	—	—	3.00
❑ 03801 [PS]	Front Page Story/I'm Guilty	1983	—	—	3.00
❑ 04541	Turn Around/Brooklyn on a Saturday Night	1984	—	—	3.00
❑ 04541 [PS]	Turn Around/Brooklyn on a Saturday Night	1984	—	—	3.00
❑ 04646	Sleep with Me Tonight/One by One	1984	—	—	3.00
❑ 04719	You Make It Feel Like Christmas/Crazy	1984	2.00	4.00	8.00
❑ 05889	Headed for the Future/Angel	1986	—	—	3.00
❑ 05889 [PS]	Headed for the Future/Angel	1986	—	—	3.00
❑ 06136	The Story of My Life/Love Doesn't Live Here Anymore	1986	—	—	3.00
❑ 06136 [PS]	The Story of My Life/Love Doesn't Live Here Anymore	1986	—	—	3.00
❑ 07614	I Dreamed a Dream/Sweet Caroline	1987	—	—	3.00
❑ 07614 [PS]	I Dreamed a Dream/Sweet Caroline	1987	—	—	3.00
❑ 07751	Cherry, Cherry/America	1988	—	—	3.00
❑ 08514	This Time/If I Couldn't See You Again	1988	—	—	3.00
❑ 10043	Longfellow Serenade/Rosemary's Wine	1974	—	2.50	5.00
❑ 10084	I've Been This Way Before/Reggae Strut	1975	—	2.50	5.00
❑ 10138	The Last Picasso/The Gift of Song	1975	—	2.50	5.00
❑ 10366	If You Know What I Mean/Street Life	1976	—	2.50	5.00
❑ 10405	Don't Think...Feel/Home Is a Wounded Heart	1976	—	2.50	5.00
❑ 10452	Beautiful Noise/Signs	1976	—	2.50	5.00
❑ 10657	Desiree/Once in a While	1977	—	2.50	5.00
❑ 10897	Forever in Blue Jeans/Remember Me	1979	—	2.00	4.00
❑ 10945	Say Maybe/Diamond Girls	1979	—	2.00	4.00
❑ 11175	September Morn/I'm a Believer	1980	—	2.00	4.00
❑ 11232	The Good Lord Loves You/Jazz Time	1980	—	2.00	4.00
❑ 42809	Clown Town/At Night	1963	125.00	250.00	500.00
❑ 42809 [DJ]	Clown Town/At Night	1963	62.50	125.00	250.00
❑ 45942	Be/Flight of the Gull	1973	—	2.50	5.00
❑ 45998	Skybird/Lonely Looking Sky	1974	—	2.50	5.00
❑ 68741	The Best Years of Our Lives/Carmelita's Eyes	1989	—	—	3.00
❑ 78242	One Good Love/Kentucky Woman	1996	—	—	3.00

—A-side: Duet with Waylon Jennings

MCA

Number	Title (A Side/B Side)	Yr	VG	VG+	NM
❑ 40017	Cherry, Cherry from Hot August Night/Morningside	1973	—	2.50	5.00
❑ 40092	The Last Thing on My Mind/Canta Libra	1973	—	2.50	5.00

PHILCO-FORD

Number	Title (A Side/B Side)	Yr	VG	VG+	NM
❑ HP-5	Girl, You'll Be a Woman Soon/Cherry, Cherry	1967	3.75	7.50	15.00

—4-inch plastic "Hip Pocket Record" with color sleeve

Number	Title (A Side/B Side)	Yr	VG	VG+	NM
❑ HP-17	Solitary Man/You Got to Me	1967	3.75	7.50	15.00

—4-inch plastic "Hip Pocket Record" with color sleeve

UNI

Number	Title (A Side/B Side)	Yr	VG	VG+	NM
❑ 55065	Brooklyn Roads/Holiday Inn Blues	1968	2.00	4.00	8.00
❑ 55075	Two-Bit Manchild/Broad Old Woman	1968	2.00	4.00	8.00
❑ 55075 [DJ]	Two-Bit Manchild (same on both sides)	1968	20.00	40.00	80.00

—Red vinyl

Number	Title (A Side/B Side)	Yr	VG	VG+	NM
❑ 55075 [PS]	Two-Bit Manchild/Broad Old Woman	1968	6.25	12.50	25.00
❑ 55084	Sunday Sun/Honey-Drippin' Times	1968	2.00	4.00	8.00
❑ 55109	Brother Love's Travelling Salvation Show/A Modern-Day Version of Love	1969	—	3.00	6.00
❑ 55136	Sweet Caroline (Good Times Never Seemed So Good)/Dig In	1969	—	3.00	6.00
❑ 55175	Holly Holy/Hurtin' You Don't Come Easy	1969	—	3.00	6.00
❑ 55204	Until It's Time for You to Go/And the Singer Sings His Song	1970	—	3.00	6.00
❑ 55224	Soolaimon (African Trilogy II)/And the Grass Won't Pay No Mind	1970	—	3.00	6.00
❑ 55224 [PS]	Soolaimon (African Trilogy II)/And the Grass Won't Pay No Mind	1970	3.75	7.50	15.00
❑ 55250	Cracklin' Rosie/Lordy	1970	—	3.00	6.00
❑ 55264	He Ain't Heavy...He's My Brother/Free Life	1970	—	3.00	6.00
❑ 55278	I Am...I Said/Done Too Soon	1971	—	2.50	5.00
❑ 55310	Stones/Crunchy Granola Suite	1971	—	2.50	5.00
❑ 55326	Song Sung Blue/Gitchy Goomy	1972	—	2.50	5.00
❑ 55346	Play Me/Porcupine Pie	1972	—	2.50	5.00
❑ 55352	Walk on Water/High Rolling Man	1972	—	2.50	5.00

DIAMOND, RONNIE

IMPERIAL

Number	Title (A Side/B Side)	Yr	VG	VG+	NM
❑ 5554	Zig Zag/Close to My Heart	1958	3.75	7.50	15.00
❑ 5570	Candy Store/Something's Wrong with Me	1959	3.75	7.50	15.00
❑ 5588	Life Begins at 4 O'Clock/Tell Me	1959	12.50	25.00	50.00
❑ 5605	When We Kiss/Pretty Please	1959	3.75	7.50	15.00

DIAMONDS, THE (1)

CORAL

Number	Title (A Side/B Side)	Yr	VG	VG+	NM
❑ 61502	Black Denim Trousers and Motorcycle Boots/Nip Sip	1955	5.00	10.00	20.00
❑ 61577	Be My Lovin' Baby/Smooch Me	1956	5.00	10.00	20.00

GUSTO

Number	Title (A Side/B Side)	Yr	VG	VG+	NM
❑ 2019	Little Darlin'/The Stroll	1979	—	2.00	4.00

—Re-recordings

MERCURY

Number	Title (A Side/B Side)	Yr	VG	VG+	NM
❑ 70790	Why Do Fools Fall in Love/You Baby You	1956	5.00	10.00	20.00
❑ 70835	The Church Bells May Ring/Little Girl of Mine	1956	5.00	10.00	20.00
❑ 70889	Love, Love, Love/Every Night About This Time	1956	5.00	10.00	20.00
❑ 70934	Ka-Ding-Dong/Soft Summer Breeze	1956	5.00	10.00	20.00
❑ 70983	My Judge and My Jury/Put Your House in Order	1956	5.00	10.00	20.00
❑ 71021	A Thousand Miles Away/Ev'ry Minute of the Day	1956	5.00	10.00	20.00
❑ 71060	Little Darlin'/Faithful and True	1957	10.00	20.00	40.00

—The only "cover version" generally considered a significant improvement over the original (by The Gladiolas)

Number	Title (A Side/B Side)	Yr	VG	VG+	NM
❑ 71128	Words of Love/Don't Say Goodbye	1957	5.00	10.00	20.00
❑ 71165	Zip Zip/Oh How I Wish	1957	5.00	10.00	20.00
❑ 71197	Silhouettes/Daddy Cool	1957	5.00	10.00	20.00
❑ 71242	The Stroll/Land of Beauty	1957	7.50	15.00	30.00
❑ 71291	High Sign/Chick-Lets (Don't Let Me Down)	1958	3.75	7.50	15.00
❑ 71291 [PS]	High Sign/Chick-Lets (Don't Let Me Down)	1958	25.00	50.00	100.00
❑ 71330	Kathy-O/Happy Years	1958	3.75	7.50	15.00
❑ 71366	Walking Along/Eternal Lovers	1958	3.75	7.50	15.00
❑ 71404	She Say (Oom Dooby Doom)/From the Bottom of My Heart	1959	5.00	10.00	20.00
❑ 71449	A Mother's Love/Gretchen	1959	3.75	7.50	15.00
❑ 71468	Sneaky Alligator/Holding Your Hand	1959	3.75	7.50	15.00
❑ 71505	Young in Years/The Twenty-Second Day	1959	3.75	7.50	15.00
❑ 71534	Walking the Stroll/Batman, Wolfman, Frankenstein or Dracula	1959	5.00	10.00	20.00
❑ 71586	Real True Love/Tell the Truth	1960	3.75	7.50	15.00
❑ 71633	The Pencil Song/Slave Girl	1960	3.75	7.50	15.00
❑ 71734	The Crumble/You'd Be Mine	1960	3.75	7.50	15.00
❑ 71782	You Sure Changed Me/I Sure Lawd Will	1961	3.75	7.50	15.00
❑ 71818	The Munch/Woomai Ling	1961	3.75	7.50	15.00
❑ 71831	One Summer Night/It's a Doggone Shame	1961	3.75	7.50	15.00
❑ 71956	The Vanishing American/The Horizontal Lieutenant	1962	3.75	7.50	15.00

7-Inch Extended Plays

BRUNSWICK

Number	Title (A Side/B Side)	Yr	VG	VG+	NM
❑ EB 71031	(contents unknown)	1957	37.50	75.00	150.00
❑ EB 71031 [PS]	The Diamonds	1957	37.50	75.00	150.00

MERCURY

Number	Title (A Side/B Side)	Yr	VG	VG+	NM
❑ EP 1-3356	(contents unknown)	1957	10.00	20.00	40.00
❑ EP 1-3356 [PS]	The Diamonds	1957	10.00	20.00	40.00
❑ EP 1-3357	(contents unknown)	1957	10.00	20.00	40.00
❑ EP 1-3357 [PS]	The Diamonds	1957	10.00	20.00	40.00
❑ EP 1-3358	Till My Baby Comes Home/Girl of Mine//One and Only/Honey	1957	10.00	20.00	40.00
❑ EP 1-3358 [PS]	The Diamonds: America's Number One Singing Stylists	1957	10.00	20.00	40.00
❑ EP 1-3367	Silhouettes/Daddy Cool//Passion Flower/Sweet Wild Honey	1957	10.00	20.00	40.00
❑ EP 1-3367 [PS]	The Diamonds	1957	10.00	20.00	40.00
❑ EP 1-3390	(contents unknown)	1958	10.00	20.00	40.00
❑ EP 1-3390 [PS]	The Stroll	1958	10.00	20.00	40.00

DIAMONDS, THE (2)

Black vocal group.

ATLANTIC

Number	Title (A Side/B Side)	Yr	VG	VG+	NM
❑ 981	A Beggar for Your Kisses/Call, Baby, Call	1952	375.00	750.00	1500.
❑ 1003	I'll Live Again/Two Loves Have I	1953	150.00	300.00	600.00
❑ 1017	Romance in the Dark/Cherry	1954	150.00	300.00	600.00

DIAMONDS, THE (3)

Direct descendant of group (1), but with no original members.

CHURCHILL

Number	Title (A Side/B Side)	Yr	VG	VG+	NM
❑ 94101	Just a Little Bit/(B-side unknown)	1987	—	3.00	6.00
❑ 94102	Two Kinds of Woman/(B-side unknown)	1987	—	3.00	6.00

DIANE AND THE DARLETTES

DUNES

Number	Title (A Side/B Side)	Yr	VG	VG+	NM
❑ 2016	Just You/The Wobble	1962	6.25	12.50	25.00
❑ 2026	Here She Comes/Just You	1963	3.75	7.50	15.00

—As "The Darlettes"

DICK AND DEEDEE

Also see DICK ST. JOHN.

DOT

Number	Title (A Side/B Side)	Yr	VG	VG+	NM
❑ 17145	Escape Suite/I'm Not Gonna Get Hung-Up About It	1968	3.75	7.50	15.00
❑ 17261	We'll Sing in the Sunshine/In the Season of Our Love	1969	2.50	5.00	10.00
❑ 17305	Do I Love You/You Came Back to Haunt Me	1970	2.50	5.00	10.00

LAMA

Number	Title (A Side/B Side)	Yr	VG	VG+	NM
❑ 7778	The Mountain's High/I Want Someone	1961	5.00	10.00	20.00
❑ 7780	Goodbye to Love/Swing Low	1961	4.00	8.00	16.00
❑ 7783	Tell Me/Will You Always Love Me	1961	4.00	8.00	16.00

LIBERTY

Number	Title (A Side/B Side)	Yr	VG	VG+	NM
❑ 55350	The Mountain's High/I Want Someone	1961	3.75	7.50	15.00
❑ 55382	Goodbye to Love/Swing Low	1961	3.00	6.00	12.00
❑ 55412	Tell Me/Will You Always Love Me	1962	3.00	6.00	12.00
❑ 55478	All I Want/Life's Just a Play	1962	3.00	6.00	12.00

UNITED ARTISTS

Number	Title (A Side/B Side)	Yr	VG	VG+	NM
❑ 0036	The Mountain's High/Tell Me	1973	—	2.50	5.00

—"Silver Spotlight Series" reissue

WARNER BROS.

Number	Title (A Side/B Side)	Yr	VG	VG+	NM
❑ 5320	The River Took My Baby/My Lonely Self	1962	2.50	5.00	10.00
❑ 5320 [PS]	The River Took My Baby/My Lonely Self	1962	6.25	12.50	25.00
❑ 5342	Young and In Love/Say to Me	1963	3.00	6.00	12.00
❑ 5364	Love Is a Once in a Lifetime Thing/Chug-a Chug-a Choo Choo	1963	2.50	5.00	10.00
❑ 5383	Where Did the Good Times Go/Guess Our Love Must Show	1963	2.50	5.00	10.00
❑ 5396	Turn Around/Don't Leave Me	1963	2.50	5.00	10.00
❑ 5411	All My Trials/Don't Think Twice, It's All Right	1964	2.50	5.00	10.00
❑ 5426	Not Fade Away/The Gift	1964	2.50	5.00	10.00
❑ 5451	You Were Mine/Remember Then	1964	2.50	5.00	10.00
❑ 5470	The Riddle Song/Without Your Love	1964	2.50	5.00	10.00
❑ 5482	Thou Shalt Not Steal/Just 'Round the River Bend	1964	3.75	7.50	15.00

—Red label with arrows

Number	Title (A Side/B Side)	Yr	VG	VG+	NM
❑ 5482	Thou Shalt Not Steal/Just 'Round the River Bend	1964	2.50	5.00	10.00

—Orange label

Number	Title (A Side/B Side)	Yr	VG	VG+	NM
❑ 5482 [PS]	Thou Shalt Not Steal/Just 'Round the River Bend	1964	6.25	12.50	25.00
❑ 5608	Be My Baby/Room 404	1965	2.50	5.00	10.00
❑ 5627	Blue Turns to Grey/Some Things Just Stick in Your Mind	1965	5.00	10.00	20.00

—Both sides are Mick Jagger-Keith Richards songs produced by Andrew Loog Oldham

Number	Title (A Side/B Side)	Yr	VG	VG+	NM
❑ 5652	The World Is Waiting/Vini, Vini	1965	2.50	5.00	10.00
❑ 5671	P.S. 1402 (Your Local Charm School)/Use What You've Got	1965	2.50	5.00	10.00
❑ 5680	New Orleans/Use What You've Got	1965	2.50	5.00	10.00
❑ 5699	Till/Sha-Ta	1966	2.50	5.00	10.00
❑ 5830	She Didn't Even Say Goodbye/So Many Things We Didn't Know	1966	2.50	5.00	10.00

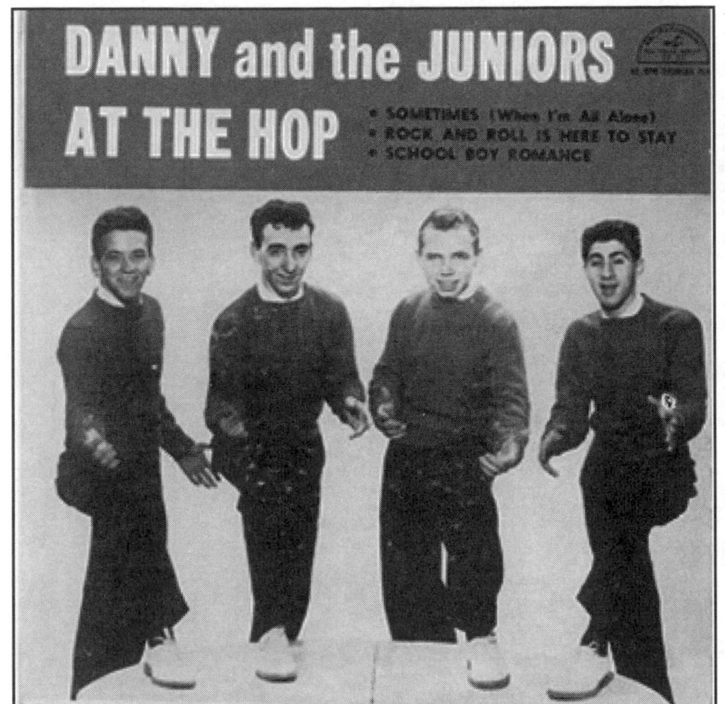

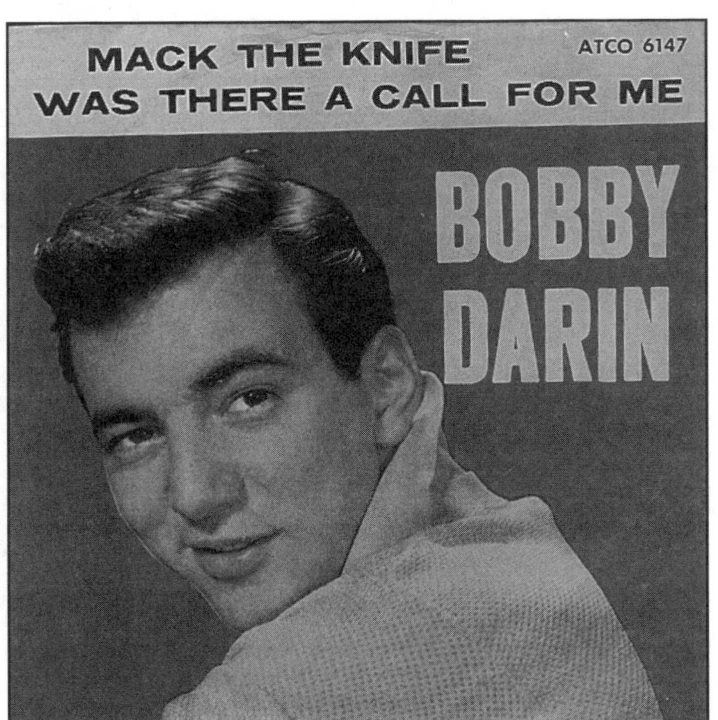

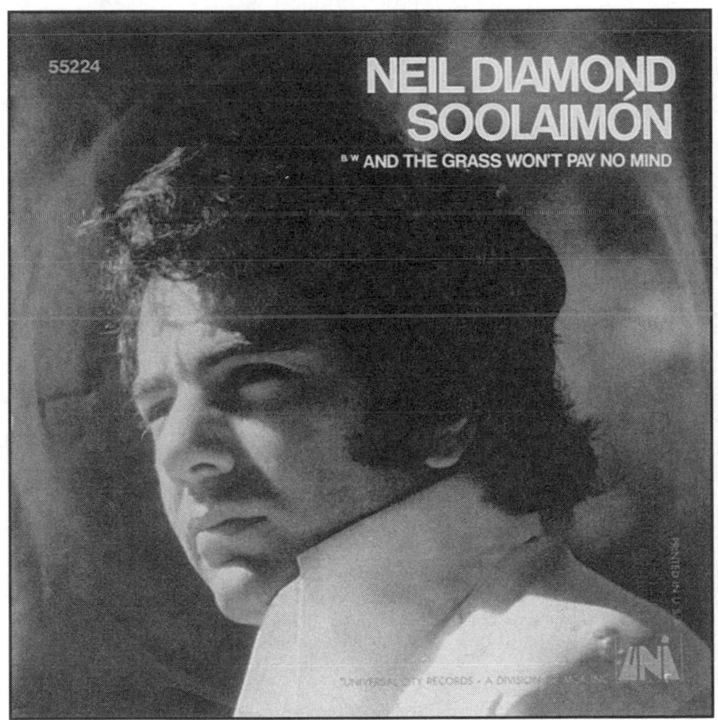

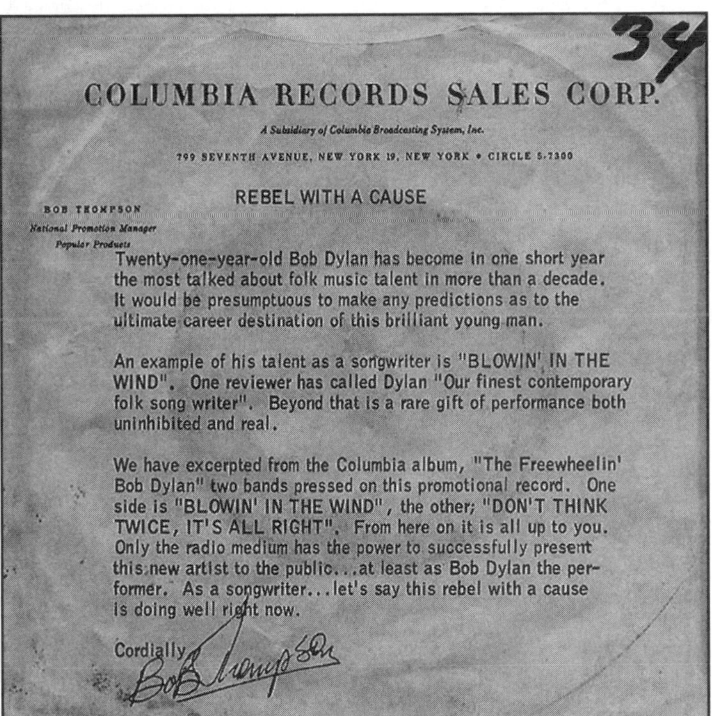
34

COLUMBIA RECORDS SALES CORP.

A Subsidiary of Columbia Broadcasting System, Inc.

799 SEVENTH AVENUE, NEW YORK 19, NEW YORK • CIRCLE 5-7300

BOB THOMPSON
National Promotion Manager
Popular Products

REBEL WITH A CAUSE

Twenty-one-year-old Bob Dylan has become in one short year the most talked about folk music talent in more than a decade. It would be presumptuous to make any predictions as to the ultimate career destination of this brilliant young man.

An example of his talent as a songwriter is "BLOWIN' IN THE WIND". One reviewer has called Dylan "Our finest contemporary folk song writer". Beyond that is a rare gift of performance both uninhibited and real.

We have excerpted from the Columbia album, "The Freewheelin' Bob Dylan" two bands pressed on this promotional record. One side is "BLOWIN' IN THE WIND", the other; "DON'T THINK TWICE, IT'S ALL RIGHT". From here on it is all up to you. Only the radio medium has the power to successfully present this new artist to the public...at least as Bob Dylan the performer. As a songwriter...let's say this rebel with a cause is doing well right now.

Cordially,
Bob Thompson

(Top left) If you think that finding either original blue-label pressing of the Singular label edition of "At the Hop" is tough, try finding Danny and the Juniors' ABC-Paramount EP with the same name. Then try to find its picture cover. Then try to find both in near-mint condition. (Top right) It has been recorded dozens of times before and since, but in 1959, Bobby Darin went beyond his early teen-idol music and did the definitive version of "Mack the Knife." (Bottom left) Relatively few Neil Diamond 45s were issued with picture sleeves until he recorded for Columbia. One of his early, tougher-to-find sleeves was from his mostly forgotten hit "Soolaimon." (Bottom right) In 1963, Columbia sent DJs a Bob Dylan single of "Blowin' in the Wind" backed with "Don't Think Twice, It's All Right." In hopes of getting play, some copies were sent with a sleeve comprising a letter from the Columbia promotion department Because of the headline, it's known as the "Rebel with a Cause" sleeve, and very few copies are known to remain today.

Number	Title (A Side/B Side)	Yr	VG	VG+	NM
❑ 5860	Make Up Before We Break Up/Can't Get Enough of Your Love	1966	2.50	5.00	10.00
❑ 7017	Long Lonely Nights/I'll Always Be Around	1967	2.50	5.00	10.00
❑ 7069	One in a Million/Baby, I Need You	1967	2.50	5.00	10.00
❑ 7109	Young and In Love/Thou Shalt Not Steal	1968	2.00	4.00	8.00

—"Back to Back Hits" series; originals have green labels with "W7" logo

DICKENS, THE
See NRBQ.

DICKENS, CHARLES
WARNER BROS.

Number	Title (A Side/B Side)	Yr	VG	VG+	NM
❑ 5657	That's the Way Love Goes/In the City	1965	3.00	6.00	12.00

DICKIE G. AND THE DON'TS
See DICKIE GOODMAN.

DICKIES, THE
A&M

Number	Title (A Side/B Side)	Yr	VG	VG+	NM
❑ 2092	Silent Night/Sounds of Silence	1978	2.50	5.00	10.00
—All copies on white vinyl					
❑ 2092 [DJ]	Silent Night/Sounds Of Silence	1978	2.00	4.00	8.00
—All copies on white vinyl					
❑ 2092 [PS]	Silent Night/Sounds of Silence	1978	2.50	5.00	10.00
❑ 2225	Nights in White Satin/Manny, Moe and Jack	1980	2.50	5.00	10.00
❑ 2225 [PS]	Nights in White Satin/Manny, Moe and Jack	1980	12.50	25.00	50.00
—Withdrawn; shows Dickies in KKK robes					
❑ 2241	Banana Splits (The Tra La La Song)/Sounds of Silence	1980	2.50	5.00	10.00
❑ 2241 [PS]	Banana Splits (The Tra La La Song)/Sounds of Silence	1980	2.50	5.00	10.00

DICKY DOO AND THE DON'TS

Number	Title (A Side/B Side)	Yr	VG	VG+	NM
ASCOT					
❑ 2178	Click Clack '65/Don't Count Me Out	1965	2.50	5.00	10.00
CASINO					
❑ 106	Click Clack/Lonely Hours Lady	196?	3.00	6.00	12.00
❑ 107	Flip Top Box/That's Life (That's Tough)	196?	3.00	6.00	12.00
DANNA					
❑ 4001	The Judge/Doo Plus Two	1967	2.50	5.00	10.00
SWAN					
❑ 4001	Click Clack/Did You Cry	1958	5.00	10.00	20.00
❑ 4006	Ne Ne Na Na Na Na Nu Nu/Flip Top Box	1959	6.25	12.50	25.00
❑ 4014	Leave Me Alone (Let Me Cry)/Wild Party	1959	5.00	10.00	20.00
❑ 4025	Teardrops Will Fall/Come with Us	1959	5.00	10.00	20.00
❑ 4033	Ballad of a Train/Dear Heart, Don't Cry	1959	5.00	10.00	20.00
❑ 4046	Wabash Cannonball/The Drums of Richard A. Doo	1960	5.00	10.00	20.00
UNITED ARTISTS					
❑ 238	Teen Scene/Pity, Pity	1960	5.00	10.00	20.00
❑ 362	The Judge/The Little Dog Cried	1961	5.00	10.00	20.00

DIDDLEY, BO

Number	Title (A Side/B Side)	Yr	VG	VG+	NM
CHECKER					
❑ 814	Bo Diddley/I'm a Man	1955	12.50	25.00	50.00
❑ 819	Diddley Daddy/She's Fine, She's Mine	1955	15.00	30.00	60.00
—A-side backing vocals: The Moonglows					
❑ 827	Pretty Thing/Bring It to Jerome	1955	12.50	25.00	50.00
❑ 832	Diddy Wah Diddy/I Am Looking for a Woman	1956	12.50	25.00	50.00
❑ 842	Who Do You Love?/In Bad	1956	15.00	30.00	60.00
❑ 842	Who Do You Love?/I'm Bad	1956	10.00	20.00	40.00
—Note altered B-side title					
❑ 850	Cops and Robbers/Down Home Special	1956	10.00	20.00	40.00
❑ 860	Hey! Bo Diddley/Mona	1957	12.50	25.00	50.00
—Originals of Checker 816-860 have "Checker" over a checkerboard on top of label					
❑ 878	Say! Boss Man/Before You Accuse Me	1957	6.25	12.50	25.00
❑ 896	Dearest Darling/Hush Your Mouth	1958	6.25	12.50	25.00
❑ 907	Bo Meets the Monster/Willie and Lillie	1958	7.50	15.00	30.00
❑ 914	I'm Sorry/Oh Yeah	1959	6.25	12.50	25.00
❑ 924	Crackin' Up/The Great Grandfather	1959	6.25	12.50	25.00
❑ 931	Say Man/Clock Strikes Twelve	1959	7.50	15.00	30.00
❑ 931 [PS]	Say Man/Clock Strikes Twelve	1959	100.00	200.00	400.00
❑ 936	Say Man, Back Again/She's Alright	1959	6.25	12.50	25.00
❑ 942	Road Runner/My Story	1960	5.00	10.00	20.00
❑ 951	Walkin' and Talkin'/Crawdad	1960	5.00	10.00	20.00
❑ 965	Gun Slinger/Signifying	1960	5.00	10.00	20.00
❑ 976	No Guilty/Aztec	1961	5.00	10.00	20.00
❑ 985	Pills/Call Me	1961	7.50	15.00	30.00
❑ 997	Bo Diddley/I'm a Man	1961	5.00	10.00	20.00
❑ 1019	You Can't Judge a Book By Its Cover/I Can Tell	1962	6.25	12.50	25.00
❑ 1045	Surfers' Love Call/Greatest Lover in the World	1963	5.00	10.00	20.00
❑ 1058	Memphis/Monkey Diddle	1963	5.00	10.00	20.00
❑ 1083	Jo Ann/Mama, Keep Your Big Mouth Shut	1964	5.00	10.00	20.00
❑ 1089	Bo's Beat/Chuck's Beat	1964	5.00	10.00	20.00
—B-side by Chuck Berry					
❑ 1098	Hey, Good Lookin'/You Ain't Bad	1965	3.75	7.50	15.00
❑ 1123	500% More Man/Let the Kids Dance	1965	3.75	7.50	15.00
❑ 1142	We're Gonna Get Married/Do the Frog	1966	3.75	7.50	15.00
❑ 1158	Ooh Baby/Back to School	1966	3.75	7.50	15.00
❑ 1168	Bo-Ga-Loo Before You Go/Wrecking My Love Life	1967	3.75	7.50	15.00
❑ 1200	Another Sugardaddy/I'm High Again	1968	3.75	7.50	15.00
❑ 1213	Bo Diddley 1969/Soul Train	1969	3.00	6.00	12.00
❑ 1238	The Shape I'm In/Pollution	1970	3.00	6.00	12.00
CHESS					
❑ 2117	I Love You More Than You'll Ever Know/I Said Shut Up Woman	1971	2.50	5.00	10.00
❑ 2129	Bo Diddley-Itis/Infatuation	1972	2.50	5.00	10.00
❑ 2134	Bo-Jam/Husband-in-Law	1972	2.50	5.00	10.00
❑ 2142	I Don't Want No Lyin' Woman/Make a Hit Record	1973	2.50	5.00	10.00
PHILCO-FORD					
❑ HP-33	I'm a Man/Song of Bo Diddley	1968	7.50	15.00	30.00
—4-inch plastic "Hip Pocket Record" with color sleeve					
RCA VICTOR					
❑ PB-10618	Not Fade Away/Drag On	1976	2.50	5.00	10.00
7-Inch Extended Plays					
CHECKER					
❑ 5125	(contents unknown)	1958	30.00	60.00	120.00
❑ 5125 [PS]	Bo Diddley	1958	45.00	90.00	180.00

DILL, DANNY

Number	Title (A Side/B Side)	Yr	VG	VG+	NM
ABC-PARAMOUNT					
❑ 9681	My Girl and His Girl/Geisha Sweetheart	1956	7.50	15.00	30.00
❑ 9734	I'm Hungry for Your Lovin'/The Stranger of Abilene	1956	12.50	25.00	50.00
CUB					
❑ 9045	He's Biding His Time/He Ain't Gonna Study War	1959	5.00	10.00	20.00

DILLARD, VARETTA

Number	Title (A Side/B Side)	Yr	VG	VG+	NM
CUB					
❑ 9073	Teaser/I Know I'm Good for You	1960	3.00	6.00	12.00
❑ 9083	Little Bitty Tear/Mercy Mr. Percy	1961	3.00	6.00	12.00
❑ 9091	You Better Come Home/I Don't Know What It Is, But I Like It	1961	3.00	6.00	12.00
GROOVE					
❑ 0139	Darling, Listen to the Words of This Song/Mama Don't Want (What Poppa Don't Want)	1956	10.00	20.00	40.00
❑ 0152	Gonna Tell My Daddy/Cherry Blossom	1956	6.25	12.50	25.00
❑ 0159	Got You On My Mind/Skinny Jimmy	1956	6.25	12.50	25.00
❑ 0167	I Miss You Jimmy/If You Want to Be My Baby	1956	6.25	12.50	25.00
❑ 0177	One More Time/I Can't Help Myself	1956	6.25	12.50	25.00
RCA VICTOR					
❑ 47-6869	Pray for Me Mother/Leave a Happy Fool Alone	1957	5.00	10.00	20.00
❑ 47-6936	Time Was/I Got a Lot of Love	1957	5.00	10.00	20.00
❑ 47-7057	Undecided/That's Why I Cry	1957	5.00	10.00	20.00
❑ 47-7144	Star of Fortune/The Blues of Love	1958	5.00	10.00	20.00
❑ 47-7285	What'll I Do/Just Multiply	1958	5.00	10.00	20.00
SAVOY					
❑ 822	Love and Wine/Please Come Back to Me	1951	12.50	25.00	50.00
❑ 839	Hurry Up/Please Tell Me Why	1952	10.00	20.00	40.00
❑ 847	Easy, Easy Baby/A Letter in Blue	1952	10.00	20.00	40.00
❑ 851	I'm Yours/Here in My Heart	1952	10.00	20.00	40.00
❑ 871	I Cried and Cried/Double Crossing Daddy	1952	10.00	20.00	40.00
❑ 884	Three Lies/Getting Ready for My Daddy	1953	10.00	20.00	40.00
❑ 897	Mercy, Mr. Percy/No Kinda Good No How	1953	10.00	20.00	40.00
❑ 1118	I Ain't Gonna Tell/(That's the Way) My Mind Is Working	1953	7.50	15.00	30.00
❑ 1137	Send Me Some Money/Love	1954	7.50	15.00	30.00
❑ 1153	Johnny Has Gone/So Many Ways	1955	7.50	15.00	30.00
❑ 1160	You're the Answer to My Prayer/Promise Mr. Thomas	1955	7.50	15.00	30.00
❑ 1166	I'll Never Forget You/I Can't Stop Now	1955	7.50	15.00	30.00
TRIUMPH					
❑ 608	Good Gravy Baby/Scorched	1959	3.75	7.50	15.00

DING DONGS, THE
See BOBBY DARIN.

DINNING, MARK

Number	Title (A Side/B Side)	Yr	VG	VG+	NM
CAMEO					
❑ 299	January/Joey	1964	2.50	5.00	10.00
❑ 313	Should We Do It/Call Her Your Sweetheart	1964	2.50	5.00	10.00
HICKORY					
❑ 1293	Dial AL1-4883/I'm Glad We Fell in Love	1965	2.00	4.00	8.00
❑ 1368	Last Rose/There Stands a Lady	1966	2.00	4.00	8.00
❑ 1404	Run, Opie, Run/He Reminds Me of Me	1966	2.00	4.00	8.00
MGM					
❑ 12447	A Million Years Ago/Shameful Ways	1957	6.25	12.50	25.00
❑ 12553	School Fool/When You're Tired of Breaking Hearts	1957	6.25	12.50	25.00
❑ 12691	You Thrill Me/Do You Know	1958	6.25	12.50	25.00
❑ 12732	Blackeyed Gypsy/Secretly in Love with You	1958	6.25	12.50	25.00
❑ 12775	Cutie, Cutie/A Life of Love	1959	6.25	12.50	25.00
❑ 12845	Teen Angel/Bye Now Baby	1959	6.25	12.50	25.00
❑ 12888	A Star Is Born (A Love Has Died)/You Win Again	1960	5.00	10.00	20.00
❑ 12888 [PS]	A Star Is Born (A Love Has Died)/You Win Again	1960	6.25	12.50	25.00
❑ 12929	The Lovin' Touch/Come Back to Me (My Love)	1960	5.00	10.00	20.00
❑ 12929 [PS]	The Lovin' Touch/Come Back to Me (My Love)	1960	6.25	12.50	25.00
❑ 12958	She Cried On My Shoulder (When She Talked About You)/(Where Can You Hide Away) The World Is Getting Smaller	1960	5.00	10.00	20.00
❑ 12980	Top Forty, News, Weather and Sports/Suddenly (There's Only You)	1961	3.75	7.50	15.00
❑ 13007	Another Lonely Girl/Can't Forget	1961	3.75	7.50	15.00
❑ 13024	Lonely Island/Turn Me On	1961	3.75	7.50	15.00
❑ 13048	What Will My Mary Say/In a Matter of Moments	1961	3.75	7.50	15.00
❑ 13061	The Pickup/All of This for Sally	1962	3.75	7.50	15.00
❑ 13091	She's Changed/I Catch Myself Crying	1962	3.00	6.00	12.00
❑ 13150	The Twelfth of Never/Somebody Catch Me Kissin' Mary	1963	3.00	6.00	12.00
UNITED ARTISTS					
❑ 50169	It's Such a Pretty World Today/Atlanta, Georgia Stray	1967	2.00	4.00	8.00
❑ 50225	Hangin' On/Maggie (I Wish We'd Never Met)	1967	2.00	4.00	8.00
❑ 50305	Throw a Little Love My Way/Dissatisfied Man	1968	2.00	4.00	8.00
❑ 50540	How Little Men Care/Lemon Yellow	1969	2.00	4.00	8.00

DINO, KENNY

Number	Title (A Side/B Side)	Yr	VG	VG+	NM
COLUMBIA					
❑ 43062	Betty Jean/Show Me	1964	5.00	10.00	20.00
DOT					
❑ 16207	Just Wait and See/A Little Bit	1961	3.00	6.00	12.00
MUSICOR					
❑ 1013	You Ma Said You Cried in Your Sleep Last Night/Dream a Girl	1962	5.00	10.00	20.00

Number	Title (A Side/B Side)	Yr	VG	VG+	NM
❑ 1015	Rosie, Why Do You Wear My Ring/What Did I Do	1962	3.75	7.50	15.00
❑ 1021	What Good Are Dreams/What Did I Do	1962	3.75	7.50	15.00
❑ 1027	Remembering Helps Me to Forget/Heartless Moon	1962	3.75	7.50	15.00
SMASH					
❑ 1827	Time Will Tell/I Wanna Know	1963	3.00	6.00	12.00
❑ 1861	You Had Your Chance/Danhoff's Theme	1963	3.00	6.00	12.00

DINO AND THE DIPLOMATS

Number	Title (A Side/B Side)	Yr	VG	VG+	NM
LAURIE					
❑ 3103	I Can't Believe/My Dream	1961	7.50	15.00	30.00
VIDA					
❑ 100/101	Hushabye My Love/Homework	1961	7.50	15.00	30.00
❑ 102/103	Soft Wind/Such a Fool for You	1961	7.50	15.00	30.00

DINO, DESI AND BILLY

Number	Title (A Side/B Side)	Yr	VG	VG+	NM
COLUMBIA					
❑ 4-44975	Hawley/Let's Talk It Over	1969	3.00	6.00	12.00
REPRISE					
❑ 0324	We Know/Since You Broke My Heart	1964	3.75	7.50	15.00
❑ 0367	I'm a Fool/So Many Ways	1965	3.00	6.00	12.00
❑ 0367 [PS]	I'm a Fool/So Many Ways	1965	5.00	10.00	20.00
❑ 0401	Not the Lovin' Kind/Chimes of Freedom	1965	2.50	5.00	10.00
❑ 0401 [PS]	Not the Lovin' Kind/Chimes of Freedom	1965	5.00	10.00	20.00
❑ 0426	Please Don't Fight It/The Rebel Kind	1965	2.50	5.00	10.00
❑ 0426 [PS]	Please Don't Fight It/The Rebel Kind	1965	5.00	10.00	20.00
❑ 0444	Superman/I Can't Get Her Out of My Mind	1966	2.00	4.00	8.00
❑ 0462	It's Just the Way You Are/Tie Me Down	1966	2.00	4.00	8.00
❑ 0496	Look Out Girls/She's So Far Out She's In	1966	2.00	4.00	8.00
❑ 0529	I Hope She's There Tonight/Josephine	1966	2.00	4.00	8.00
❑ 0544	If You're Thinkin' What I'm Thinkin'/Pretty Flamingo	1966	2.00	4.00	8.00
❑ 0579	Two in the Afternoon/Good Luck, Best Wishes to You	1967	2.50	5.00	10.00
❑ 0619	Kitty Doyle/Without Hurtin' Some	1967	2.50	5.00	10.00
❑ 0653	My What a Shame/The Inside Outside Caspar Milquetoast Eskimo Flash	1967	3.00	6.00	12.00
❑ 0653 [PS]	My What a Shame/The Inside Outside Caspar Milquetoast Eskimo Flash	1967	5.00	10.00	20.00
❑ 0698	Tell Someone You Love Them/General Outline	1968	3.00	6.00	12.00
❑ 0716	I'm a Fool/Not the Lovin' Kind	1968	2.00	4.00	8.00
—"Back to Back Hits" series; originals have both "W7" and "r:" logos					
❑ 0965	Lady Love/A Certain Sound	1970	7.50	15.00	30.00
—A-side is a Brian Wilson composition					
UNI					
❑ 55127	Someday/Thru Spray Colored Glasses	1969	3.00	6.00	12.00

DIO, ANDY

Number	Title (A Side/B Side)	Yr	VG	VG+	NM
CRUSADE					
❑ 1023	Bonnie Jean/Rough and Bold	1961	10.00	20.00	40.00
GONE					
❑ 5038	Daisy Belle/Hey Little Bluebird	1958	12.50	25.00	50.00
JOHNSON					
❑ 114	You Are My Sunshine/Satellite	1962	5.00	10.00	20.00
JOY					
❑ 283	Daisy Belle/Some of These Days	1964	10.00	20.00	40.00
MUSICOR					
❑ 1118	Sass-Afrass/Shout	1965	2.50	5.00	10.00
❑ 1162	Dancing Bull/Sorrento	1966	2.50	5.00	10.00

DIO, RONNIE

Opinions differ as to whether this is the same person as the Ronnie James Dio who was popular in hard-rock circles in the 1980s. Ronnie, are you out there?

Number	Title (A Side/B Side)	Yr	VG	VG+	NM
ATLANTIC					
❑ 2145	Love Pains/Ooh-Poo-Pah-Do	1962	5.00	10.00	20.00
KAPP					
❑ 697	Say You're Mine Again/Where You Gonna Run To, Girl	1965	3.75	7.50	15.00
❑ 725	Dear Darlin' (I Won't Be Comin' Home)/Smiling by Day	1965	3.75	7.50	15.00
❑ 770	The Way of Love/Walking Alone	1966	3.75	7.50	15.00
LAWN					
❑ 218	Gonna Make It Alone/Swingin' Street	1963	6.25	12.50	25.00
PARKWAY					
❑ 143	Walking in Different Circles/Ten Days with Brenda	1967	5.00	10.00	20.00
SWAN					
❑ 4165	Mr. Misery/Our Year	1963	5.00	10.00	20.00

DION

Also see DION AND THE BELMONTS; DION AND THE TIMBERLANES.

Number	Title (A Side/B Side)	Yr	VG	VG+	NM
ARISTA					
❑ 9797	And the Night Stood Still/Tower of Love	1989	—	2.00	4.00
❑ 9797 [PS]	And the Night Stood Still/Tower of Love	1989	—	2.00	4.00
BIG TREE/SPECTOR					
❑ 16063	Born to Be with You/Running Close Behind You	1976	3.75	7.50	15.00
—Produced by Phil Spector					
COLUMBIA					
❑ 42662	Ruby Baby/He'll Only Hurt You	1962	5.00	10.00	20.00
❑ 42662 [PS]	Ruby Baby/He'll Only Hurt You	1962	10.00	20.00	40.00
❑ 42776	This Little Girl/The Loneliest Man in the World	1963	3.75	7.50	15.00
❑ 42810	Be Careful of Stones That You Throw/I Can't Believe (That You Don't Love Me Anymore)	1963	3.75	7.50	15.00
❑ 42810 [DJ]	Be Careful of Stones That You Throw (same on both sides)	1963	25.00	50.00	100.00
—Colored vinyl (some sources say blue, others red)					
❑ 42852	Donna the Prima Donna/You're Mine	1963	5.00	10.00	20.00
❑ 42852 [DJ]	Donna the Prima Donna (same on both sides)	1963	20.00	40.00	80.00
—Promo only on red vinyl					
❑ 42917	Drip Drop/No One's Waiting for Me	1963	3.75	7.50	15.00
❑ 42977	I'm the Hoochie Coochie Man/The Road I'm On	1964	3.75	7.50	15.00
❑ 42977 [PS]	I'm the Hoochie Coochie Man/The Road I'm On	1964	10.00	20.00	40.00
❑ 43096	Johnny B. Goode/Chicago Blues	1964	3.75	7.50	15.00
❑ 43213	Sweet Sweet Baby/Unloved, Unwanted Me	1965	3.75	7.50	15.00
❑ 43293	Spoonful/Kickin' Child	1965	3.75	7.50	15.00
❑ 43423	Tomorrow Won't Bring the Rain/You Move Me Babe	1965	3.75	7.50	15.00
❑ 43423 [PS]	Tomorrow Won't Bring the Rain/You Move Me Babe	1965	37.50	75.00	150.00
❑ 43483	Time in My Heart for You/Wake Up Baby	1965	3.75	7.50	15.00
❑ 43692	So Much Younger/Two-Ton Feather	1966	3.75	7.50	15.00
❑ 44719	I Can't Help But Wonder Where I'm Bound/Southern Train	1968	2.50	5.00	10.00
❑ (no #) [PS]	"Dion Is Now on Columbia Records"	1962	12.50	25.00	50.00
—Promo-only sleeve issued with promos of Columbia 42662					
DAYSPRING					
❑ 622 [DJ]	The Best (mono/stereo)	197?	—	2.50	5.00
LAURIE					
❑ 3070	Lonely Teenager/Little Miss Blue	1960	5.00	10.00	20.00
❑ 3070 [PS]	Lonely Teenager/Little Miss Blue	1960	12.50	25.00	50.00
❑ 3081	Havin' Fun/Northeast End of the Corner	1961	5.00	10.00	20.00
❑ 3081 [PS]	Havin' Fun/Northeast End of the Corner	1961	12.50	25.00	50.00
❑ 3090	Kissin Game/Heaven Help Me	1961	5.00	10.00	20.00
❑ 3090 [PS]	Kissin Game/Heaven Help Me	1961	12.50	25.00	50.00
❑ 3101	Somebody Nobody Wants/Could Somebody Take My Place Tonight	1961	5.00	10.00	20.00
❑ 3110 [M]	Runaround Sue/Runaway Girl	1961	6.25	12.50	25.00
❑ 3110 [PS]	Runaround Sue/Runaway Girl	1961	10.00	20.00	40.00
❑ 3110 [S]	Runaround Sue/Runaway Girl	1961	12.50	25.00	50.00
—"Stereo" in white area at right of label					
❑ 3115 [M]	The Wanderer/The Majestic	1961	6.25	12.50	25.00
❑ 3115 [M]	The Wanderer/The Majestic	1979	2.50	5.00	10.00
—Reissue on regular Laurie label with "From the Orion Motion Picture 'The Wanderers'" on label					
❑ 3115 [PS]	The Wanderer/The Majestic	1961	10.00	20.00	40.00
❑ 3115 [S]	The Wanderer/The Majestic	1961	12.50	25.00	50.00
—"Stereo" in white area at right of label					
❑ 3123	Lovers Who Wander/(I Was) Born to Cry	1962	5.00	10.00	20.00
❑ 3123 [PS]	Lovers Who Wander/(I Was) Born to Cry	1962	10.00	20.00	40.00
❑ 3134	Little Diane/Lost for Sure	1962	5.00	10.00	20.00
❑ 3134 [PS]	Little Diane/Lost for Sure	1962	10.00	20.00	40.00
❑ 3145	Love Came to Me/Little Girl	1962	5.00	10.00	20.00
❑ 3153	Sandy/Faith	1963	5.00	10.00	20.00
❑ 3171	Come Go with Me/King Without a Queen	1963	5.00	10.00	20.00
❑ 3187	Lonely World/Tag Along	1963	5.00	10.00	20.00
❑ 3225	After the Dance/Then I'll Be Tired of You	1964	5.00	10.00	20.00
❑ 3240	Shout/Little Girl	1964	5.00	10.00	20.00
❑ 3303	I Got the Blues/(I Was) Born to Cry	1965	5.00	10.00	20.00
❑ 3464	Abraham, Martin, and John/Daddy Rollin' (In Your Arms)	1968	3.00	6.00	12.00
❑ 3478	Purple Haze/The Dolphins	1969	3.00	6.00	12.00
❑ 3495	From Both Sides Now/Sun Fun Song	1969	3.00	6.00	12.00
❑ 3504	Loving You Is Sweeter Than Ever/He Looks a Lot Like Me	1969	3.00	6.00	12.00
LAURIE DOUBLE GOLD					
❑ 100	Runaround Sue/I Wonder Why	197?	—	2.00	4.00
—B-side by Dion and the Belmonts					
❑ 101	The Wanderer/No One Knows	197?	—	2.00	4.00
—B-side by Dion and the Belmonts					
❑ 103	Lonely Teenager/Little Diane	197?	—	2.00	4.00
❑ 104	Lovers Who Wander/Where or When	197?	—	2.00	4.00
—B-side by Dion and the Belmonts					
❑ 105	Love Came to Me/Sandy	197?	—	2.00	4.00
❑ 118	Abraham, Martin and John/From Both Sides Now	197?	—	2.00	4.00
LIFESONG					
❑ 1765	Heart of Saturday Night/You've Awakened Something in Me	1978	—	3.00	6.00
❑ 1770	Midtown American Main Street Gang/Guitar Queen	1978	—	3.00	6.00
❑ 1785	(I Used to Be a) Brooklyn Dodger/Streetheart Theme	1979	—	3.00	6.00
❑ 45082	Fire in the Night/Street Mama	1980	6.25	12.50	25.00
MONUMENT					
❑ (# unknown) [DJ]	Runaround Sue/Ya Ya Twist	1962	6.25	12.50	25.00
—B-side by Joey Dee and the Starliters					
THE RIGHT STUFF					
❑ S7-17651	Christmas (Baby Please Come Home)/Jingle Bell Rock	1993	—	2.50	5.00
—Red vinyl					
❑ S7-19769	Please Come Home for Christmas/Wintertime	1997	—	2.00	4.00
—B-side by the Belmonts on United Artists					
WARNER BROS.					
❑ PRO-537 [DJ]	Seagull/Soft Parade	1972	3.75	7.50	15.00
❑ PRO-814 [DJ]	The Wanderer (same on both sides)	1979	3.75	7.50	15.00
❑ 7356	Natural Man/If We Only Have Love	1969	2.50	5.00	10.00
❑ 7401	Your Own Back Yard/Sit Down Old Friend	1970	2.50	5.00	10.00
❑ 7469	Let It Be/Close to It All	1970	2.50	5.00	10.00
❑ 7491	Josie/Sunniland	1970	2.50	5.00	10.00
❑ 7537	Sanctuary/Brand New Morning	1971	2.50	5.00	10.00
❑ 7537 [PS]	Sanctuary/Brand New Morning	1971	5.00	10.00	20.00
❑ 7663	Seagull/Running Close Behind You	1972	2.50	5.00	10.00
❑ 7704	Doctor Rock and Roll/Sunshine Lady	1973	2.50	5.00	10.00
❑ 7793	New York City Song/Richer Than a Rich Man	1974	2.50	5.00	10.00
❑ 8234	Hey My Love/Lover Boy Supreme	1976	—	3.00	6.00
❑ 8258	The Way You Do the Things You Do/Lover Boy Supreme	1976	—	3.00	6.00
❑ 8293	Oh the Night/Queen of '59	1976	—	3.00	6.00
❑ 8406	Young Virgin Eyes (I'm All Wrapped Up)/Oh the Night	1977	—	3.00	6.00
WARNER/SPECTOR					
❑ 0403	Make the Woman Love Me/Running Close Behind You	1975	3.75	7.50	15.00
—Produced by Phil Spector					

DION AND THE BELMONTS

Also see THE BELMONTS; CARLO; DION.

Number	Title (A Side/B Side)	Yr	VG	VG+	NM
ABC					
❑ 10868	My Girl the Month of May/Berimbau	1966	3.00	6.00	12.00
❑ 10896	For Bobbie/Movin' Man	1967	3.00	6.00	12.00
LAURIE					
❑ ST-607 [S]	In the Still of the Night/All the Things You Are	196?	20.00	40.00	80.00
—Small hole, plays at 33 1/3 rpm					
❑ ST-608 [S]	Swinging on a Star/In Other Words	196?	20.00	40.00	80.00
—Small hole, plays at 33 1/3 rpm					
❑ ST-610 [S]	I've Cried Before/September Song	196?	20.00	40.00	80.00
—Small hole, plays at 33 1/3 rpm					
❑ 3013	I Wonder Why/Teen Angel	1958	15.00	30.00	60.00
—Gray label					
❑ 3013	I Wonder Why/Teen Angel	1958	7.50	15.00	30.00
—Light blue label					
❑ 3013	I Wonder Why/Teen Angel	1958	5.00	10.00	20.00
—Black, red and white label					
❑ 3015	No One Knows/I Can't Go On (Rosalie)	1958	12.50	25.00	50.00
—Gray label					
❑ 3015	No One Knows/I Can't Go On (Rosalie)	1958	7.50	15.00	30.00
—Light blue label					
❑ 3015	No One Knows/I Can't Go On (Rosalie)	1958	5.00	10.00	20.00
—Black, red and white label					
❑ 3021	Don't Pity Me/Just You	1958	6.25	12.50	25.00
❑ 3027 [M]	A Teenager in Love/I've Cried Before	1959	6.25	12.50	25.00
❑ S-3027 [S]	A Teenager in Love/I've Cried Before	1959	12.50	25.00	50.00
❑ 3035	Every Little Thing I Do/A Lover's Prayer	1959	6.25	12.50	25.00
❑ 3035 [PS]	Every Little Thing I Do/A Lover's Prayer	1959	12.50	25.00	50.00
❑ 3044	Where or When/That's My Desire	1959	6.25	12.50	25.00
❑ 3044 [PS]	Where or When/That's My Desire	1959	12.50	25.00	50.00
❑ 3052	When You Wish Upon a Star/Wonderful Girl	1960	6.25	12.50	25.00
❑ 3052 [PS]	When You Wish Upon a Star/Wonderful Girl	1960	12.50	25.00	50.00
❑ 3059	In the Still of the Night/A Funny Feeling	1960	6.25	12.50	25.00
❑ 3059 [PS]	In the Still of the Night/A Funny Feeling	1960	12.50	25.00	50.00
LAURIE DOUBLE GOLD					
❑ 100	I Wonder Why/Runaround Sue	197?	—	2.00	4.00
—B-side by Dion					
❑ 101	No One Knows/The Wanderer	197?	—	2.00	4.00
—B-side by Dion					
❑ 102	A Teenager in Love/A Lover's Prayer	197?	—	2.00	4.00
❑ 104	Where or When/Lovers Who Wander	197?	—	2.00	4.00
—B-side by Dion					
MOHAWK					
❑ 106	Teenage Clementine/Santa Margarita	1957	15.00	30.00	60.00
—May be listed as "The Belmonts"					
❑ 107	Tag Along/We Went Away	1957	15.00	30.00	60.00

7-Inch Extended Plays

Number	Title (A Side/B Side)	Yr	VG	VG+	NM
LAURIE					
❑ 301	(contents unknown)	1958	30.00	60.00	120.00
❑ 301 [PS]	Dion and the Belmonts: Their Hits	1958	45.00	90.00	180.00
❑ 302	(contents unknown)	1959	25.00	50.00	100.00
❑ 302 [PS]	Where or When	1959	37.50	75.00	150.00

DION AND THE TIMBERLANES

Early version of DION AND THE BELMONTS.

Number	Title (A Side/B Side)	Yr	VG	VG+	NM
JUBILEE					
❑ 5294	The Chosen Few/Out in Colorado	1957	7.50	15.00	30.00
MOHAWK					
❑ 105	The Chosen Few/Out in Colorado	1957	15.00	30.00	60.00

DIONNE AND FRIENDS

DIONNE WARWICK with ELTON JOHN, GLADYS KNIGHT and STEVIE WONDER.

Number	Title (A Side/B Side)	Yr	VG	VG+	NM
ARISTA					
❑ 9422	That's What Friends Are For/Two Ships Passing in the Night	1985	—	—	3.00
❑ 9422 [PS]	That's What Friends Are For/Two Ships Passing in the Night	1985	—	—	3.00

DIPPERS QUINTET, THE

Number	Title (A Side/B Side)	Yr	VG	VG+	NM
FLAYR					
❑ 500	It's Almost Christmas/Look What I've Found	1955	2000.	3000.	4000.

DIRE STRAITS

Also see MARK KNOPFLER.

Number	Title (A Side/B Side)	Yr	VG	VG+	NM
WARNER BROS.					
❑ 8736	Sultans of Swing/Southbound Again	1979	—	3.00	6.00
—With "Burbank" palm trees label					
❑ 8736	Sultans of Swing/Southbound Again	1979	—	2.00	4.00
—With white label					
❑ 19094	Heavy Fuel/Kingdom Come	1992	—	—	3.00
❑ 19199	Calling Elvis/Millionaire Blues	1992	—	—	3.00
❑ 28789	So Far Away/If I Had You	1986	—	—	3.00
❑ 28789 [PS]	So Far Away/If I Had You	1986	—	—	3.00
❑ 28878	Walk of Life/One World	1985	—	—	3.00
❑ 28878 [PS]	Walk of Life/One World	1985	—	—	3.00
❑ 28950	Money for Nothing/Love Over Gold (Live)	1985	—	2.00	4.00
❑ 28950 [PS]	Money for Nothing/Love Over Gold (Live)	1985	—	2.00	4.00
❑ 29013	Walk of Life/One World	1985	—	2.50	5.00
❑ 29706	Twisting by the Pool/Badges, Posters, Stickers, T-Shirts	1983	—	2.50	5.00
❑ 29880	Industrial Disease/Badges, Posters, Stickers, T-Shirts	1982	—	2.50	5.00
❑ 49006	Lady Writer/Where Do You Think You're Going	1979	—	2.50	5.00
❑ 49006 [PS]	Lady Writer/Where Do You Think You're Going	1979	—	2.50	5.00
❑ 49082	Once Upon a Time in the West/News	1979	2.50	5.00	10.00
—Price is for stock copy (deduct 50% for double A-sided promo)					
❑ 49632	Skateaway/Solid Rock	1980	—	2.50	5.00
❑ 49632 [PS]	Skateaway/Solid Rock	1980	—	2.50	5.00
❑ 49688	Romeo and Juliet/Solid Rock	1981	—	2.50	5.00

DIRKSEN, SENATOR EVERETT MCKINLEY

Number	Title (A Side/B Side)	Yr	VG	VG+	NM
CAPITOL					
❑ 2034	The First Time the Christmas Story Was Told/I Heard the Bells on Christmas Day	1967	2.00	4.00	8.00
❑ 5805	Gallant Men/The New Colossus	1966	—	3.00	6.00
❑ 5805 [PS]	Gallant Men/The New Colossus	1966	2.00	4.00	8.00
❑ 5912	Man Is Not Alone/The Shepherd and His Flock	1967	—	2.50	5.00

DIRT BAND, THE

See NITTY GRITTY DIRT BAND.

DISENTRI, TURNER

Actually Bob Gaudio of THE ROYAL TEENS and THE FOUR SEASONS.

Number	Title (A Side/B Side)	Yr	VG	VG+	NM
TOPIX					
❑ 6001	10,000,000 Tears/Spanish Lace	1961	25.00	50.00	100.00

DISTANTS, THE

Number	Title (A Side/B Side)	Yr	VG	VG+	NM
NORTHERN					
❑ 3732	Come On/Always	1960	150.00	300.00	600.00
WARWICK					
❑ 546	Come On/Always	1960	25.00	50.00	100.00
❑ 577	Always/Open Up Your Heart	1960	25.00	50.00	100.00

DIXIE BLUES BOYS

Number	Title (A Side/B Side)	Yr	VG	VG+	NM
FLAIR					
❑ 1072	My Baby Left Town/Monte Carlo❑ My Baby Left Town/Monte Carlo	1955	75.00	150.00	300.00

DIXIE CHICKS

Number	Title (A Side/B Side)	Yr	VG	VG+	NM
DIXIE CHICKS					
❑ (# unknown)	Christmas Swing/The Flip Side	1991	12.50	25.00	50.00
❑ (# unknown)	[PS]Home on the Radar Range	1991	12.50	25.00	50.00
—Sleeve for above record					
MONUMENT					
❑ 31-79047	Wide Open Spaces/There's Your Trouble	1998	—	2.00	4.00
❑ 31-79204	Tonight the Heartache's on Me/Give It Up or Let Me Go	1999	—	2.00	4.00
❑ 31-79352	Goodbye Earl/Cowboy Take Me Away	2000	—	2.00	4.00

DIXIE CUPS, THE

Number	Title (A Side/B Side)	Yr	VG	VG+	NM
ABC					
❑ 10855	Love Ain't So Bad (After All)/Daddy Said No	1966	3.00	6.00	12.00
ABC-PARAMOUNT					
❑ 10692	That's Where It's At/Two-Way-Poc-A-Way	1965	3.00	6.00	12.00
❑ 10715	I'm Not the Kind of Girl (To Marry)/What Goes Up Must Go Down	1965	3.00	6.00	12.00
❑ 10755	A-B-C Song/That's What the Kids Said	1965	3.00	6.00	12.00
ANTILLES					
❑ 707	Iko Iko/Hey Hey (Indian's Coming)	1987	—	2.00	4.00
—B-side by The Wild Tchoupitoulas					
❑ 707 [PS]	Iko Iko/Hey Hey (Indian's Coming)	1987	—	2.00	4.00
RED BIRD					
❑ 10-001	Chapel of Love/Ain't That Nice	1964	7.50	15.00	30.00
❑ 10-006	People Say/Girls Can Tell	1964	5.00	10.00	20.00
❑ 10-012	You Should Have Seen the Way He Looked at Me/No True Love	1964	5.00	10.00	20.00
❑ 10-017	Little Bell/Another Boy Like Me	1964	5.00	10.00	20.00
❑ 10-024	Iko Iko/Gee, Baby, Gee	1965	5.00	10.00	20.00
❑ 10-024	Iko Iko/I'm Gonna Get You Yet	1965	5.00	10.00	20.00
❑ 10-032	Gee, the Moon Is Shining Bright/I'm Gonna Get You Yet	1965	5.00	10.00	20.00

DIXIEBELLES, THE

Number	Title (A Side/B Side)	Yr	VG	VG+	NM
SOUND STAGE 7					
❑ 2507	(Down at) Papa Joe's/Rock, Rock, Rock	1963	2.50	5.00	10.00
❑ 2517	Southtown U.S.A./Why Don't You Set Me Free	1964	2.50	5.00	10.00
❑ 2521	New York Town/The Beale Street Dog	1964	2.50	5.00	10.00

DIXIES, THE

Number	Title (A Side/B Side)	Yr	VG	VG+	NM
AUTUMN					
❑ 12	He's Got You/Geisha Girl	1965	3.75	7.50	15.00

DIXON, BILLY, AND THE TOPICS

See THE FOUR SEASONS.

DIXON, FLOYD

Number	Title (A Side/B Side)	Yr	VG	VG+	NM
ALADDIN					
❑ 3101	Do I Love You/Time and Place	1951	50.00	100.00	200.00
—Earlier Floyd Dixon 45s on Aladdin may exist					
❑ 3111	Too Much Jelly Roll/Baby, Let's Go to the Woods	1952	50.00	100.00	200.00
❑ 3121	Blues for Cuba/Bad Neighborhood	1952	50.00	100.00	200.00
❑ 3135	Wine, Wine, Wine/Call Operator 210	1952	50.00	100.00	200.00
❑ 3144	Red Cherries/The River	1952	75.00	150.00	300.00
—Black vinyl					
❑ 3144	Red Cherries/The River	1952	175.00	350.00	700.00
—Red vinyl					
❑ 3151	Tired, Broke and Busted/Come Back Baby	1952	37.50	75.00	150.00
❑ 3166	You Played Me for a Fool/Broken Hearted Traveler	1953	37.50	75.00	150.00
❑ 3196	Lovin'/Married Woman	1953	37.50	75.00	150.00
❑ 3230	You Need Me Now/A Long Time Ago	1954	25.00	50.00	100.00
CASH					
❑ 1057	Oh Baby/Never Can Tell	1957	12.50	25.00	50.00
CAT					
❑ 106	Moonshine/Roll Baby Roll	1954	15.00	30.00	60.00
❑ 114	Hey Bartender/It Is True	1955	15.00	30.00	60.00
CHATTAHOOCHIE					
❑ 652	Tell Me, Tell Me/There Goes My Heart	1964	2.50	5.00	10.00
CHECKER					
❑ 857	Alarm Clock Blues/I'm Ashamed of Myself	1957	7.50	15.00	30.00
DODGE					
❑ 807	Opportunity Blues/Daisy	1961	3.75	7.50	15.00

Number	Title (A Side/B Side)	Yr	VG	VG+	NM
EBB					
❑ 105	What Is Life Without a Home/Oh-Ee Little Girl	1957	7.50	15.00	30.00
IMPERIAL					
❑ 5849	Tired, Broke and Busted/Call Operator 210	1962	3.00	6.00	12.00
KENT					
❑ 311	Change Your Mind/Dance the Thing	1958	5.00	10.00	20.00
SPECIALTY					
❑ 468	Hard Living Alone/Please Don't Go	1953	20.00	40.00	80.00
—Black vinyl					
❑ 468	Hard Living Alone/Please Don't Go	1953	50.00	100.00	200.00
—Red vinyl					
❑ 477	Hole in the Wall/Old Memories	1953	20.00	40.00	80.00
❑ 486	Ooh-Eee Ooh-Eee/Nose Job	1954	20.00	40.00	80.00
SWINGIN'					
❑ 626	Tight Skirts/Wake Up and Live	1960	5.00	10.00	20.00

DOBKINS, CARL, JR.

Number	Title (A Side/B Side)	Yr	VG	VG+	NM
ATCO					
❑ 6283	If Teardrops Were Diamonds/I'm So Sorry Little Girl	1964	3.00	6.00	12.00
CHALET					
❑ 1053	Days of Sand and Shovel/Linda the Motel Maid	1969	2.50	5.00	10.00
❑ 1056	My Heart Is an Open Book/Pictures	1969	2.50	5.00	10.00
COLPIX					
❑ 762	His Loss Is My Gain/A Little Bit Later On Down the Line	1965	3.00	6.00	12.00
DECCA					
❑ 30656	Love Is Everything/If You Don't Want My Lovin'	1958	5.00	10.00	20.00
❑ 30803	My Heart Is an Open Book/My Pledge to You	1959	6.25	12.50	25.00
❑ 31020	Lucky Devil/In My Heart	1959	5.00	10.00	20.00
❑ 31020 [PS]	Lucky Devil/In My Heart	1959	7.50	15.00	30.00
❑ 31088	Exclusively Yours/One Little Girl	1960	3.75	7.50	15.00
❑ 31088 [PS]	Exclusively Yours/One Little Girl	1960	7.50	15.00	30.00
❑ 31143	Different Kind of Love/Genie	1960	3.75	7.50	15.00
❑ 31182	Lovelight/Take Time Out	1960	3.75	7.50	15.00
❑ 31260	Pretty Little Girl in the Yellow Dress/That's What I Call True Love	1961	3.75	7.50	15.00
❑ 31301	Sawdust Dolly/A Chance to Belong	1961	3.75	7.50	15.00
❑ 31353	Ask Me No Questions/Promise Me	1962	3.75	7.50	15.00
FRATERNITY					
❑ 794	That's Why I'm Asking/Take Hold of My Hand	1958	7.50	15.00	30.00
7-Inch Extended Plays					
DECCA					
❑ ED 2664	My Heart Is An Open Book/My Pledge to You//Love Is Everything/If You Don't Want My Lovin'	1959	10.00	20.00	40.00
❑ ED 2664 [PS]	My Heart Is An Open Book	1959	10.00	20.00	40.00

DOBRO, JIMMY

See JAMES BURTON.

DOBRO, LON

Number	Title (A Side/B Side)	Yr	VG	VG+	NM
4 STAR					
❑ 1754	I Just Like You/All the Time	1961	15.00	30.00	60.00
TROY					
❑ 1003	Undercurrent/Mid-Night Surf	1963	12.50	25.00	50.00

DR. FEELGOOD AND THE INTERNS

Also see PIANO RED.

Number	Title (A Side/B Side)	Yr	VG	VG+	NM
COLUMBIA					
❑ 43372	Doctor of Love/Let the House Rock On	1965	2.00	4.00	8.00
❑ 43615	Where Did You Go/Don't Tell Me No Dirty	1966	2.00	4.00	8.00
OKEH					
❑ 7144	Mr. Moonlight/Dr. Feel-Good	1962	3.00	6.00	12.00
❑ 7153	Bald Headed Lena/What's Up Doc	1962	3.00	6.00	12.00
❑ 7156	The Right String But the Wrong Yo-Yo/What's Up Doc	1962	3.00	6.00	12.00
❑ 7161	Let's Have a Good Time Tonight/The Same Old Things Keep Happening	1962	3.00	6.00	12.00
❑ 7167	My Gal Jo/Bald Headed Lena	1963	3.00	6.00	12.00
❑ 7185	The Doctor's Boogie/Blang Dong	1963	3.00	6.00	12.00

DR. HOOK

Includes records as "Dr. Hook and the Medicine Show." Also see RAY SAWYER.

Number	Title (A Side/B Side)	Yr	VG	VG+	NM
CAPITOL					
❑ 4081	Levitate/Cooky and Lila	1975	—	2.00	4.00
❑ 4104	The Millionaire/Cooky and Lila	1975	—	2.00	4.00
❑ 4171	Only Sixteen/Let Me Be Your Lover	1975	—	2.50	5.00
❑ 4280	A Little Bit More/A Couple More Years	1976	—	2.50	5.00
❑ 4364	If Not You/Bad Eye Bill	1976	—	2.00	4.00
❑ 4423	Walk Right In/Sexy Energy	1977	—	2.00	4.00
❑ 4534	Making Love and Music/Who Dat	1978	—	2.00	4.00
❑ 4615	I Don't Want to Be Alone Tonight/You Make My Pants Want to Get Up and Dance	1978	—	2.00	4.00
❑ 4621	Sharing the Night Together/You Make My Pants Want to Get Up and Dance	1978	—	2.00	4.00
❑ 4677	All the Time in the World/Dooley Jones	1979	—	2.00	4.00
❑ 4705	When You're in Love with a Beautiful Woman/Knowing She's There	1979	—	2.00	4.00
❑ 4785	Better Love Next Time/Mountain Mary	1979	—	2.00	4.00
❑ 4831	Sexy Eyes/Help Me Mama	1980	—	2.00	4.00
❑ 4885	Years from Now/I Don't Feel Much Like Smilin'	1980	—	2.00	4.00
❑ 4885 [PS]	Years from Now/I Don't Feel Much Like Smilin'	1980	—	2.50	5.00
CASABLANCA					
❑ 2314	Girls Can Get It/Doin' It	1980	—	2.00	4.00
❑ 2325	S.O.S. For Love/99 and Me	1981	—	2.00	4.00
❑ 2347	Baby Makes Her Blue Jeans Talk/The Turn On	1981	—	2.00	4.00
❑ 2347 [PS]	Baby Makes Her Blue Jeans Talk/The Turn On	1981	—	2.50	5.00
❑ 2351	Loveline/Pity the Fool	1981	—	2.00	4.00
COLUMBIA					
❑ 3-10032	Make It Easy/Ballad of Lucy Jordan	1974	—	3.00	6.00
—All as "Dr. Hook and the Medicine Show"					
❑ 4-45392	Last Morning/One More Ride (Lucille and Bunky)	1971	—	3.00	6.00
❑ 4-45562	Sylvia's Mother/Makin' It Natural	1972	—	3.00	6.00
—Orange label with "Columbia" background print					
❑ 4-45562	Sylvia's Mother/Makin' It Natural	1972	—	2.50	5.00
—Gray label					
❑ 4-45667	Carry Me, Carrie/Call That True Love	1972	—	2.50	5.00
❑ 4-45667 [PS]	Carry Me, Carrie/Call That True Love	1972	—	3.00	6.00
❑ 4-45732	The Cover of "Rolling Stone"/Queen of the Silver Dollar	1972	—	3.00	6.00
—Gray label					
❑ 4-45732	The Cover of "Rolling Stone"/Queen of the Silver Dollar	1972	—	2.50	5.00
—Orange label					
❑ 4-45878	Roland the Roadie and Gertrude the Groupie/Put a Little Bit on Me	1973	—	2.50	5.00
❑ 4-45925	Life Ain't Easy/Wonderful Stone Soup	1973	—	2.50	5.00
❑ 4-46026	Monterey Jack/Cops and Robbers	1974	—	2.50	5.00

DR. HOOK AND THE MEDICINE SHOW

See DR. HOOK.

DR. JOHN

Number	Title (A Side/B Side)	Yr	VG	VG+	NM
ACE					
❑ 611	Good Times/Sahara	1961	6.25	12.50	25.00
—As "Mac Rebennack"					
ATCO					
❑ 6607	I Walk on Gilded Splinters (Part 1)/I Walk on Gilded Splinters (Part 2)	1968	3.00	6.00	12.00
❑ 6635	Jump Sturdy/Mama Roox	1968	3.00	6.00	12.00
❑ 6697	Patriotic Flag Waver (Long)/Patriotic Flag Waver (Short)	1969	2.00	4.00	8.00
❑ 6755	Wash, Mama, Wash/Loup Gardo	1970	3.00	6.00	12.00
❑ 6882	Iko Iko/The Huey Smith Medley	1972	2.50	5.00	10.00
❑ 6898	Wang Dang Doodle/Big Chief	1972	—	3.00	6.00
❑ 6900	Let the Good Times Roll/Stack-A-Lee	1972	—	3.00	6.00
❑ 6914	Right Place Wrong Time/I Been Hoodood	1973	—	3.00	6.00
❑ 6937	Such a Night/Cold, Cold, Cold	1973	—	3.00	6.00
❑ 6957	(Everybody Wanna Get Rich) Rite Away/Mos'Scocious	1974	—	3.00	6.00
❑ 6971	Let's Make a Better World/Me Minus You Equals Loneliness	1974	—	3.00	6.00
A.F.O.					
❑ 309	The Point/One Naughty Flat	1962	6.25	12.50	25.00
—As "Mac Rebenack"					
HORIZON					
❑ 117	Wild Honey/Dance the Night Away with You	1979	—	2.00	4.00
❑ 125	Keep That Music Simple/I Thought I Heard New Orleans	1979	—	2.00	4.00
RCA					
❑ PB-11285	Take Me Higher/Sweet Rider	1978	—	2.00	4.00
REX					
❑ 1008	Storm Warning/Foolish Little Girl	1959	12.50	25.00	50.00
—As "Mac Rebennack"					
SCEPTER					
❑ 12393	One Night Late/She's Just a Square	1974	—	2.50	5.00
WARNER BROS.					
❑ 22976	Makin' Whoopee!/More Than You Know	1989	—	—	3.00
❑ 22976 [PS]	Makin' Whoopee!/More Than You Know	1989	—	—	3.00
❑ 49703	The Sailor and the Mermaid/One Good Turn	1981	—	2.00	4.00
—A-side with Libby Titus; B-side by Al Jarreau					

DOCTOR ROSS

Number	Title (A Side/B Side)	Yr	VG	VG+	NM
HI-Q					
❑ 5027	Cannonball/Numbers Blues	1963	5.00	10.00	20.00
❑ 5033	Call the Doctor/New York Breakdown	1963	5.00	10.00	20.00
SUN					
❑ 193	Chicago Breakdown/Come Back Baby	1954	200.00	400.00	600.00
❑ 212	The Boogie Disease/Juke Box Boogie	1954	500.00	1000.	2000.

DR. WEST'S MEDICINE SHOW AND JUG BAND

Also see NORMAN GREENBAUM.

Number	Title (A Side/B Side)	Yr	VG	VG+	NM
GO GO					
❑ 100	The Eggplant That Ate Chicago/You Can't Fight City Hall Blues	1966	3.00	6.00	12.00
❑ 102	Gondoliers, Shakespeares, Overseers, Playboys and Bums/Daddy, I Know	1967	2.50	5.00	10.00
❑ 102 [PS]	Gondoliers, Shakespeares, Overseers, Playboys and Bums/Daddy, I Know	1967	5.00	10.00	20.00
❑ 104	You Can Fly/The Circus Left Town Today	1967	2.50	5.00	10.00
GREGAR					
❑ 71-0100	Gondoliers, Shakespeares, Overseers, Playboys and Bums/Daddy, I Know	1969	2.50	5.00	10.00
❑ 106	Bullets Laverne/Jigsaw	1968	2.50	5.00	10.00

DODD, DICK

Also see THE STANDELLS.

Number	Title (A Side/B Side)	Yr	VG	VG+	NM
ATTARACK					
❑ 102	Guilty/Requiem 820	1970	2.50	5.00	10.00
TOWER					
❑ 447	Lonely Weekends/Little Star	1968	3.00	6.00	12.00
❑ 447 [PS]	Lonely Weekends/Little Star	1968	7.50	15.00	30.00
❑ 490	Fanny/Don't Be Ashamed to Call My Name	1969	3.00	6.00	12.00

DODD, JIMMIE

Number	Title (A Side/B Side)	Yr	VG	VG+	NM
ABC-PARAMOUNT					
❑ 9665	Mouseketeer Theme/Hi to You	1956	5.00	10.00	20.00
❑ 9680	Mickey Mouse Mambo/Humphrey Hop-Pussy Cat	1956	5.00	10.00	20.00
❑ 9691	Zip-A-Dee-Doo-Dah/Song of the South	1956	5.00	10.00	20.00
—B-side by Jeanne Gayle					

DODDS, MALCOLM

Number	Title (A Side/B Side)	Yr	VG	VG+	NM
AMY					
❑ 861	A Rendezvous with a Broken Heart/All My Wildest Dreams	1962	2.00	4.00	8.00
AURORA					
❑ 3250	Ich Bin Verry Happy (Merry, Merry Christmas)/ Perfect Strangers	1962	2.50	5.00	10.00
DECCA					
❑ 30653	The Swingin' Platoon/Your Voice	1958	3.00	6.00	12.00
❑ 30766	I'll Always Be with You/This Is Real (This Is Love)	1958	3.00	6.00	12.00
❑ 30857	Deep Inside/Tremble	1959	3.00	6.00	12.00
❑ 30922	I've Waited So Long/Somehow	1959	3.00	6.00	12.00
❑ 30970	I Feel Peculiar/Only for You	1959	3.00	6.00	12.00
END					
❑ 1000	It Took a Long Time/Beauty and the Beast	1957	15.00	30.00	60.00
❑ 1004	Fools Rush In/Can't See You	1957	20.00	40.00	80.00
❑ 1010	Tonight/Unspoken Love	1958	15.00	30.00	60.00
MGM					
❑ 12975	All for the Love of a Woman/Come, Oh Come	1961	2.50	5.00	10.00
❑ 13029	Without a Song/Laugh My Heart	1961	2.50	5.00	10.00
PROJECT 3					
❑ 1319	Hey World/I Don't Want to Cry	196?	—	3.00	6.00
❑ 1338	I Love, I Live, I Love/Mr. Broadloom	196?	—	3.00	6.00

DODDS, NELLA

Number	Title (A Side/B Side)	Yr	VG	VG+	NM
WAND					
❑ 167	Come See About Me/You Don't Love Me Anymore	1964	3.75	7.50	15.00
❑ 171	Finders Keepers Losers Weepers/A Girl's Life	1964	3.00	6.00	12.00
❑ 178	Your Love Back/P's and Q's	1965	3.00	6.00	12.00
❑ 187	Come Back Baby/Dream Boy	1965	3.00	6.00	12.00
❑ 1111	Gee Whiz/Maybe Baby	1966	3.75	7.50	15.00
❑ 1136	Honey Boy/I Just Gotta Have You	1966	20.00	40.00	80.00

DODO, JOE, AND THE GROOVERS

Number	Title (A Side/B Side)	Yr	VG	VG+	NM
RCA VICTOR					
❑ 47-7207	Groovy/Goin' Steady	1958	6.25	12.50	25.00

DOHERTY, DENNY

Also see THE MAMAS AND THE PAPAS; THE MUGWUMPS.

Number	Title (A Side/B Side)	Yr	VG	VG+	NM
ABC					
❑ 11318	To Claudia on Thursday/Tuesday Morning	1972	—	3.00	6.00
COLUMBIA					
❑ 45779	Baby Catch the Moon/Indian Girl	1973	—	2.50	5.00
❑ 45866	My Song/Indian Girl	1973	—	2.50	5.00
PARAMOUNT					
❑ 0286	Good Night and Good Morning/You'll Never Know	1974	—	2.50	5.00
PLAYBOY					
❑ 6066	Simone (mono/stereo)	1976	—	2.50	5.00
—May be promo only					

DOLENZ, MICKEY

Also see DOLENZ, JONES & TORK; DOLENZ, JONES, BOYCE & HART; THE MONKEES.

Number	Title (A Side/B Side)	Yr	VG	VG+	NM
BELL					
❑ 986	Do It in the Name of Love/Lady Jane	1971	12.50	25.00	50.00
—With Davy Jones; value is for stock copy (promos worth about 50% of this)					
CHALLENGE					
❑ 59353	Don't Do It/Plastic Symphony III	1967	5.00	10.00	20.00
❑ 59353 [PS]	Don't Do It/Plastic Symphony III	1967	15.00	30.00	60.00
❑ 59372	Huff Puff/(The Obvious) Fate	1967	5.00	10.00	20.00
❑ 59372 [PS]	Huff Puff/(The Obvious) Fate	1967	15.00	30.00	60.00
CHRYSALIS					
❑ 2297	Alicia/Love Light	1979	—	3.00	6.00
MGM					
❑ 14309	Easy on You/Oh Someone	1971	5.00	10.00	20.00
❑ 14395	A Lover's Prayer/Unattended in the Dungeon	1972	5.00	10.00	20.00
ROMAR					
❑ 710	Daybreak/Love War	1973	5.00	10.00	20.00
❑ 715	Buddy Holly Tribute/Ooh, Se's So Young	1974	5.00	10.00	20.00

DOLENZ, MICKEY, AND PETER TORK (OF THE MONKEES)

See THE MONKEES.

DOLENZ, JONES & TORK

Also see MICKEY DOLENZ; DAVY JONES; THE MONKEES.

Number	Title (A Side/B Side)	Yr	VG	VG+	NM
CHRISTMAS					
❑ 700	Christmas Is My Time of Year/White Christmas	1976	5.00	10.00	20.00
❑ 700 [PS]	Christmas Is My Time of Year/White Christmas	1976	10.00	20.00	40.00

DOLENZ, JONES, BOYCE & HART

Also see TOMMY BOYCE; TOMMY BOYCE AND BOBBY HART; MICKEY DOLENZ; BOBBY HART; DAVY JONES; THE MONKEES.

Number	Title (A Side/B Side)	Yr	VG	VG+	NM
CAPITOL					
❑ 4180	You and I/I Remember the Feeling	1975	2.50	5.00	10.00
❑ 4271	Savin' My Love for You/I Love You (And I'm Glad I Said It)	1976	2.50	5.00	10.00

DOLLS, THE

Number	Title (A Side/B Side)	Yr	VG	VG+	NM
LOMA					
❑ 2036	The Reason Why/And That Reminds Me	1966	3.75	7.50	15.00
OKEH					
❑ 7122	In Love/Please Come Home	1959	3.00	6.00	12.00
TEENAGE					
❑ 1010	Just Before You Leave/I Love	1958	250.00	500.00	1000.

DOMINO, FATS

Number	Title (A Side/B Side)	Yr	VG	VG+	NM
ABC					
❑ 10902	I Don't Want to Set the World on Fire/I'm Living Right	1967	2.50	5.00	10.00
ABC-PARAMOUNT					
❑ 10444	There Goes (My Heart Again)/Can't Go On Without You	1963	2.50	5.00	10.00
❑ 10475	When I'm Walking (Let Me Walk)/I've Got a Right to Cry	1963	2.50	5.00	10.00
❑ 10484	Red Sails in the Sunset/Song for Rosemary	1963	3.00	6.00	12.00
❑ 10512	Who Cares/Just a Lonely Man	1963	2.50	5.00	10.00
❑ 10531	Lazy Lady/I Don't Want to Set the World on Fire	1964	2.50	5.00	10.00
❑ 10545	If You Don't Know What Love Is/Something You Got, Baby	1964	2.50	5.00	10.00
❑ 10567	Mary, Oh Mary/Packin' Up	1964	2.50	5.00	10.00
❑ 10584	Sally Was a Good Old Girl/For You	1964	2.50	5.00	10.00
❑ 10596	Heartbreak Hill/Kansas City	1964	2.50	5.00	10.00
❑ 10631	Why Don't You Do Right/Wigs	1965	2.50	5.00	10.00
❑ 10644	Let Me Call You Sweetheart/Goodnight Sweetheart	1965	2.50	5.00	10.00
BROADMOOR					
❑ 104	The Lady in Black/Work My Way Up Steady	1967	3.75	7.50	15.00
❑ 105	Big Mouth/Wait 'Til It Happens to You	1968	5.00	10.00	20.00
IMPERIAL					
❑ 5058	The Fat Man/Detroit City Blues	1950	500.00	1000.	2000.
—Blue-label "script" logo; pressed in 1952 or so; counterfeits exist					
❑ 5099	Korea Blues/Every Night About This Time	1950	200.00	400.00	800.00
—Blue-label "script" logo; pressed in 1952 or so					
❑ 5167	You Know I Miss You/I'll Be Gone	1952	125.00	250.00	500.00
—Fats Domino records on Imperial before 5167 are unconfirmed on 45 rpm, except those listed above.					
❑ 5180	Goin' Home/Reeling and Rocking	1952	75.00	150.00	300.00
❑ 5197	Poor Poor Me/Trust in Me	1952	50.00	100.00	200.00
❑ 5209	How Long/Dreaming	1952	20.00	40.00	80.00
—Black vinyl					
❑ 5209	How Long/Dreaming	1952	75.00	150.00	300.00
—Red vinyl					
❑ 5220	Nobody Loves Me/Cheatin'	1953	20.00	40.00	80.00
—Black vinyl					
❑ 5220	Nobody Loves Me/Cheatin'	1953	75.00	150.00	300.00
—Red vinyl					
❑ 5231	Going to the River/Mardi Gras in New Orleans	1953	25.00	50.00	100.00
—Black vinyl					
❑ 5231	Going to the River/Mardi Gras in New Orleans	1953	125.00	250.00	500.00
—Red vinyl					
❑ 5240	Please Don't Leave Me/The Girl I Love	1953	15.00	30.00	60.00
—Black vinyl					
❑ 5240	Please Don't Leave Me/The Girl I Love	1953	75.00	150.00	300.00
—Red vinyl					
❑ 5251	You Said You Loved Me/Rose Mary	1953	15.00	30.00	60.00
❑ 5262	Something's Wrong/Don't Leave Me This Way	1954	12.50	25.00	50.00
—Black vinyl					
❑ 5262	Something's Wrong/Don't Leave Me This Way	1954	62.50	125.00	250.00
—Red vinyl					
❑ 5272	Little School Girl/You Done Me Wrong	1954	15.00	30.00	60.00
❑ 5283	Baby, Please/Where Did You Stay	1954	15.00	30.00	60.00
❑ 5301	You Can Pack Your Suitcase/I Lived My Life	1954	10.00	20.00	40.00
❑ 5313	Love Me/Don't You Hear Me Calling You	1954	10.00	20.00	40.00
❑ 5323	I Know/Thinking of You	1955	12.50	25.00	50.00
—Black vinyl					
❑ 5323	I Know/Thinking of You	1955	125.00	250.00	500.00
—Red vinyl					
❑ 5340	Don't You Know/Helping Hand	1955	10.00	20.00	40.00
❑ 5348	Ain't It a Shame/La La	1955	10.00	20.00	40.00
❑ 5357	All By Myself/Troubles of My Own	1955	20.00	40.00	80.00
—Red label, script logo					
❑ 5357	All By Myself/Troubles of My Own	1955	6.25	12.50	25.00
—Red or maroon label, block logo					
❑ 5369	Poor Me/I Can't Go On	1955	6.25	12.50	25.00
❑ 5375	Bo Weevil/Don't Blame It on Me	1956	6.25	12.50	25.00
❑ 5386	I'm in Love Again/My Blue Heaven	1956	6.25	12.50	25.00
❑ 5396	When My Dreamboat Comes Home/So-Long	1956	6.25	12.50	25.00
❑ 5407	Blueberry Hill/Honey Chile	1956	6.25	12.50	25.00
—Black vinyl, red label					
❑ 5407	Blueberry Hill/Honey Chile	1956	37.50	75.00	150.00
—Red vinyl					
❑ 5407	Blueberry Hill/Honey Chile	1957	3.75	7.50	15.00
—Black vinyl, black label					
❑ 5417	Blue Monday/What's the Reason I'm Not Pleasing You	1957	6.25	12.50	25.00
❑ 5428	I'm Walkin'/I'm in the Mood for Love	1957	6.25	12.50	25.00
❑ 5428 [PS]	I'm Walkin'/I'm in the Mood for Love	1957	12.50	25.00	50.00
❑ 5442	Valley of Tears/It's You I Love	1957	6.25	12.50	25.00
❑ 5454	When I See You/How Will I Tell My Heart	1957	6.25	12.50	25.00
❑ 5467	Wait and See/I Still Love You	1957	6.25	12.50	25.00
❑ 5477	The Big Beat/I Want You to Know	1957	6.25	12.50	25.00
❑ 5477 [PS]	The Big Beat/I Want You to Know	1957	15.00	30.00	60.00
❑ 5492	Yes, My Darling/Don't You Know I Love You	1958	6.25	12.50	25.00
—Black vinyl					
❑ 5492	Yes, My Darling/Don't You Know I Love You	1958	37.50	75.00	150.00
—Red vinyl					
❑ 5515	Sick and Tired/No, No	1958	6.25	12.50	25.00
❑ 5526	Little Mary/The Prisoner's Song	1958	6.25	12.50	25.00
❑ 5537	Young School Girl/It Must Be Love	1958	6.25	12.50	25.00
❑ 5553	Whole Lotta Loving/Coquette	1958	7.50	15.00	30.00
—Red label					
❑ 5553	Whole Lotta Loving/Coquette	1958	6.25	12.50	25.00
—Black label					
❑ 5553	Whole Lotta Loving/Coquette	1958	37.50	75.00	150.00
—Red vinyl (translucent)					
❑ 5569	Telling Lies/When the Saints Go Marching In	1959	3.75	7.50	15.00
❑ 5585	I'm Ready/Margie	1959	3.75	7.50	15.00
❑ 5606	I Want to Walk You Home/I'm Gonna Be a Wheel Some Day	1959	5.00	10.00	20.00
❑ 5629	Be My Guest/I've Been Around	1959	3.75	7.50	15.00
❑ 5629 [PS]	Be My Guest/I've Been Around	1959	12.50	25.00	50.00
❑ 5645	Country Boy/If You Need Me	1960	3.75	7.50	15.00
❑ 5660	Tell Me That You Love Me/Before I Grow Too Old	1960	3.75	7.50	15.00

Number	Title (A Side/B Side)	Yr	VG	VG+	NM
❑ 5675	Walking to New Orleans/Don't Come Knockin'	1960	5.00	10.00	20.00
❑ 5687	Three Nights a Week/Put Your Arms Around Me Honey	1960	3.75	7.50	15.00
❑ 5704	My Girl Josephine/Natural Born Lover	1960	5.00	10.00	20.00
❑ 5723	What a Price/Ain't That Just Like a Woman	1961	3.75	7.50	15.00
❑ 5734	Shu Rah/Fell in Love on Monday	1961	3.75	7.50	15.00
❑ 5753	It Keeps Rainin'/I Just Cry	1961	3.75	7.50	15.00
❑ 5764	Let the Four Winds Blow/Good Hearted Man	1961	3.75	7.50	15.00
❑ 5779	What a Party/Rockin' Bicycle	1961	3.75	7.50	15.00
❑ 5796	Jambalaya (On the Bayou)/I Hear You Knocking	1961	3.75	7.50	15.00
❑ 5816	You Win Again/Ida Jane	1962	3.75	7.50	15.00
❑ 5833	My Real Name/My Heart Is Bleeding	1962	3.75	7.50	15.00
❑ 5863	Nothing New (Same Old Thing)/Dance with Mr. Domino	1962	3.75	7.50	15.00
❑ 5875	Did You Ever See a Dream Walking/Stop the Clock	1962	3.75	7.50	15.00
❑ 5895	Won't You Come On Back/Hands Across the Table	1962	3.75	7.50	15.00
❑ 5895	Won't You Come On Back/Your Cheatin' Heart	1962	3.75	7.50	15.00
❑ 5909	Hum Diddy Doo/Those Eyes	1963	3.75	7.50	15.00
❑ 5937	You Always Hurt the One You Love/Trouble Blues	1963	3.75	7.50	15.00
❑ 5959	Isle of Capri/True Confession	1963	3.75	7.50	15.00
❑ 5980	One Night/I Can't Go On This Way	1963	3.75	7.50	15.00
❑ 5999	Your Cheatin' Heart/Goin' Home	1963	3.75	7.50	15.00
❑ 66005	I Can't Give You Anything But Love/Goin' Home	1963	3.00	6.00	12.00
❑ 66016	When I Was Young/Your Cheatin' Heart	1964	3.00	6.00	12.00
MERCURY					
❑ 72463	I Left My Heart in San Francisco/I Done Got Over You	1965	2.50	5.00	10.00
❑ 72485	It's Never Too Late/What's That You Got	1965	2.50	5.00	10.00
❑ 72485 [PS]	It's Never Too Late/What's That You Got	1965	5.00	10.00	20.00
REPRISE					
❑ 0696	One for the Highway/Honest Papas Love Their Mamas Better	1968	3.75	7.50	15.00
❑ 0763	Lady Madonna/One for the Highway	1968	3.75	7.50	15.00
❑ 0775	Lovely Rita/Wait Till It Happens to You	1968	3.75	7.50	15.00
❑ 0810	Everybody's Got Someting to Hide (Except Me and My Monkey)/So Swell When You're Well	1969	3.75	7.50	15.00
❑ 0891	Have You Seen My Baby?/Make Me Belong to You	1970	3.75	7.50	15.00
❑ 0944	New Orleans Ain't the Same/Sweet Patootie	1970	3.75	7.50	15.00
THE RIGHT STUFF					
❑ S7-18216	Christmas Is a Special Day/Please Come Home for Christmas (Christmas Once Again)	1994	—	2.00	4.00
—Red vinyl					
❑ S7-19768	Frosty the Snowman/Every Heart Is Home at Christmas	1997	—	2.50	5.00
—B-side by the Five Keys on Aladdin					
TOOT TOOT					
❑ 001	My Toot Toot/My Toot Toot (Rock)	1985	—	2.50	5.00
—With Doug Kershaw					
❑ 002	Don't Mess with My Popeye's/My Toot Toot	1985	—	2.50	5.00
—With Doug Kershaw					
UNITED ARTISTS					
❑ 0001	Ain't That a Shame/Goin' Home	1973		2.00	4.00
❑ 0002	Blue Monday/I'm Gonna Be a Wheel Someday	1973	—	2.00	4.00
❑ 0003	I'm in Love Again/Whole Lotta Lovin'	1973	—	2.00	4.00
❑ 0004	Blueberry Hill/Bo Weevil	1973	—	2.00	4.00
❑ 0005	I'm Walkin'/One Night	1973	—	2.00	4.00
❑ 0006	I Hear You Knockin'/My Blue Heaven	1973	—	2.00	4.00
❑ 0007	Walkin' to New Orleans/Country Boy	1973	—	2.00	4.00
❑ 0008	I Want to Walk You Home/It's You I Love	1973	—	2.00	4.00
❑ 0009	I'm Ready/Wait and See	1973	—	2.00	4.00
❑ 0010	My Girl Josephine/When My Dreamboat Comes Home	1973	—	2.00	4.00
❑ 0011	Three Nights a Week/Let the Four Winds Blow	1973	—	2.00	4.00
—0001 through 0011 are "Silver Spotlight Series" reissues					
❑ XW 514	The Fat Man/Valley of Tears	1974	—	2.50	5.00
—Reissue					
WARNER BROS.					
❑ 49610	Whiskey Heaven/Beers to You	1980	—	2.00	4.00
—B-side by Texas Opera Company					

7-Inch Extended Plays

Number	Title (A Side/B Side)	Yr	VG	VG+	NM
IMPERIAL					
❑ IMP 127	(contents unknown)	1955	37.50	75.00	150.00
—"Script" label					
❑ IMP 127	(contents unknown)	1955	25.00	50.00	100.00
—Maroon label, block-letter logo					
❑ IMP 127	(contents unknown)	1958	6.25	12.50	25.00
—Black label					
❑ IMP 127 [PS]	Fats Domino	1955	12.50	25.00	50.00
❑ IMP 138	(contents unknown)	1956	25.00	50.00	100.00
—Maroon label, block-letter logo					
❑ IMP 138	(contents unknown)	1958	6.25	12.50	25.00
—Black label					
❑ IMP 138 [PS]	Rock and Rollin' with Fats Domino	1956	12.50	25.00	50.00
❑ IMP 139	Rosemary/All By Myself//Tired of Crying/You Said You Loved Me	1956	25.00	50.00	100.00
—Maroon label, block-letter logo					
❑ IMP 139	Rosemary/All By Myself//Tired of Crying/You Said You Loved Me	1958	6.25	12.50	25.00
—Black label					
❑ IMP 139 [PS]	Rock and Rollin' with Fats Domino	1956	12.50	25.00	50.00
❑ IMP 140	Ain't It a Shame/Poor Me//Bo Weevil/Don't Blame It on Me	1956	25.00	50.00	100.00
—Maroon label, block-letter logo					
❑ IMP 140	Ain't It a Shame/Poor Me//Bo Weevil/Don't Blame It on Me	1958	6.25	12.50	25.00
—Black label					
❑ IMP 140 [PS]	Rock and Rollin' with Fats Domino	1956	12.50	25.00	50.00
❑ IMP 141	(contents unknown)	1956	25.00	50.00	100.00
—Maroon label, block-letter logo					
❑ IMP 141	(contents unknown)	1958	6.25	12.50	25.00
—Black label					
❑ IMP 141 [PS]	Rock and Rollin'	1956	12.50	25.00	50.00
❑ IMP 142	Careless Love/I Love Her//I'm in Love Again/When My Dreamboat Comes Home	1956	25.00	50.00	100.00
—Maroon label, block-letter logo					
❑ IMP 142	Careless Love/I Love Her//I'm in Love Again/When My Dreamboat Comes Home	1958	6.25	12.50	25.00
—Black label					
❑ IMP 142 [PS]	Rock and Rollin'	1956	12.50	25.00	50.00
❑ IMP 143	Are Your Going My Way/If You Need Me//My Heart Is In Your Hands/Fats Frenzy	1956	25.00	50.00	100.00
—Maroon label, block-letter logo					
❑ IMP 143	Are Your Going My Way/If You Need Me//My Heart Is In Your Hands/Fats Frenzy	1958	6.25	12.50	25.00
—Black label					
❑ IMP 143 [PS]	Rock and Rollin'	1956	12.50	25.00	50.00
❑ IMP 144	Blueberry Hill/Honey Chile//Troubles of My Own/You Done Me Wrong	1956	25.00	50.00	100.00
—Maroon label, block-letter logo					
❑ IMP 144	Blueberry Hill/Honey Chile//Troubles of My Own/You Done Me Wrong	1958	6.25	12.50	25.00
—Black label					
❑ IMP 144 [PS]	This Is Fats Domino	1956	12.50	25.00	50.00
❑ IMP 145	What's the Reason I'm Not Pleasing You/Blue Monday//Reeling and Rocking/The Fat Man's Hop	1956	25.00	50.00	100.00
—Maroon label, block-letter logo					
❑ IMP 145	What's the Reason I'm Not Pleasing You/Blue Monday//Reeling and Rocking/The Fat Man's Hop	1958	6.25	12.50	25.00
—Black label					
❑ IMP 145 [PS]	This Is Fats Domino	1956	12.50	25.00	50.00
❑ IMP 146	So Long/La La//Poor, Poor Me/Trust in Me	1956	25.00	50.00	100.00
—Maroon label, block-letter logo					
❑ IMP 146	So Long/La La//Poor, Poor Me/Trust in Me	1958	6.25	12.50	25.00
—Black label					
❑ IMP 146 [PS]	This Is Fats Domino	1956	12.50	25.00	50.00
❑ IMP 147	The Rooster Song/My Happiness//As Time Goes By/Hey La Bas	1956	25.00	50.00	100.00
—Maroon label, block-letter logo					
❑ IMP 147	The Rooster Song/My Happiness//As Time Goes By/Hey La Bas	1958	6.25	12.50	25.00
—Black label					
❑ IMP 147 [PS]	Here Comes Fats	1956	12.50	25.00	50.00
❑ IMP 148	Detroit City Blues/Hide Away Blues//She's My Baby/New Baby	1957	25.00	50.00	100.00
—Maroon label, block-letter logo					
❑ IMP 148	Detroit City Blues/Hide Away Blues//She's My Baby/New Baby	1958	6.25	12.50	25.00
—Black label					
❑ IMP 148 [PS]	Here Stands Fats Domino	1957	12.50	25.00	50.00
❑ IMP 149	I'm Walkin'/Cheatin'//Little Bee/Every Night About This Time	1957	25.00	50.00	100.00
—Maroon label, block-letter logo					
❑ IMP 149	I'm Walkin'/Cheatin'//Little Bee/Every Night About This Time	1958	6.25	12.50	25.00
—Black label					
❑ IMP 149 [PS]	Here Stands Fats Domino	1957	12.50	25.00	50.00
❑ IMP 150	I'm in the Mood for Love/You Can Pack Your Suitcase//Hey! Fat Man/I'll Be Gone	1957	25.00	50.00	100.00
—Maroon label, block-letter logo					
❑ IMP 150	I'm in the Mood for Love/You Can Pack Your Suitcase//Hey! Fat Man/I'll Be Gone	1958	6.25	12.50	25.00
—Black label					
❑ IMP 150 [PS]	Here Stands Fats Domino	1957	12.50	25.00	50.00
❑ IMP 151	Love Me/Don't You Hear Me Calling You//It's You I Love/Valley of Tears	1957	25.00	50.00	100.00
—Maroon label, block-letter logo					
❑ IMP 151	Love Me/Don't You Hear Me Calling You//It's You I Love/Valley of Tears	1958	6.25	12.50	25.00
—Black label					
❑ IMP 151 [PS]	Cookin' with Fats	1957	12.50	25.00	50.00
❑ IMP 152	Thinking of You/You Know I Miss You//Where Did You Stay/Baby Please	1957	25.00	50.00	100.00
—Maroon label, block-letter logo					
❑ IMP 152	Thinking of You/You Know I Miss You//Where Did You Stay/Baby Please	1958	6.25	12.50	25.00
—Black label					
❑ IMP 152 [PS]	Rockin' with Fats	1957	12.50	25.00	50.00

DOMINOES, THE

See BILLY WARD AND THE DOMINOES.

DON AND DEWEY

Number	Title (A Side/B Side)	Yr	VG	VG+	NM
FIDELITY					
❑ 3017	Jump Awhile/H.B. Boogie	1960	3.75	7.50	15.00
❑ 3018	Kill Me/Little Sally Walker	1960	3.75	7.50	15.00
SHADE					
❑ 100	Miss Sue/My Heart Is Aching	195?	37.50	75.00	150.00
SPECIALTY					
❑ 599	Jungle Hop/A Little Love	1957	6.25	12.50	25.00
❑ 610	Leavin' It All Up to You/Jelly Bean	1957	7.50	15.00	30.00
❑ 617	Just a Little Lovin'/When the Sun Has Begun to Shine	1957	6.25	12.50	25.00
❑ 631	Justine/Bim Bam	1958	6.25	12.50	25.00
❑ 639	The Letter/Koko Joe	1958	6.25	12.50	25.00
❑ 659	Farmer John/Big Boy Pete	1959	6.25	12.50	25.00
❑ 691	Annie Lee/Get Your Hat	196?	3.00	6.00	12.00

DON AND HIS ROSES

DOT

Number	Title (A Side/B Side)	Yr	VG	VG+	NM
❑ 15755	Since You Went Away to School/Right Now	1958	12.50	25.00	50.00
❑ 15874	Leave Those Cats Alone/Don't Try to Change Me	1958	37.50	75.00	150.00

DON AND JUAN

BIG TOP

Number	Title (A Side/B Side)	Yr	VG	VG+	NM
❑ 3079	What's Your Name/Chicken Necks	1961	6.25	12.50	25.00
❑ 3106	Two Fools Are We/Pot Luck	1962	5.00	10.00	20.00
❑ 3121	Magic Wand/What I Really Meant to Say	1962	10.00	20.00	40.00
❑ 3145	True Love Never Runs Smooth/Is It All Right If I Love You	1963	12.50	25.00	50.00

LANA

Number	Title (A Side/B Side)	Yr	VG	VG+	NM
❑ 150	What's Your Name/Chicken Necks	196?	—	3.00	6.00

—Early reissue

MALA

Number	Title (A Side/B Side)	Yr	VG	VG+	NM
❑ 469	Lonely Man/Could This Be Love	1963	3.00	6.00	12.00
❑ 479	Pledging My Love/Molinda	1964	3.00	6.00	12.00
❑ 484	Sincerely/Maryana Cherie	1964	3.00	6.00	12.00
❑ 494	I Can't Help Myself/All That's Missing Is You	1964	3.00	6.00	12.00
❑ 509	The Heartbreaking Truth/Thank Goodness	1965	7.50	15.00	30.00

TWIRL

Number	Title (A Side/B Side)	Yr	VG	VG+	NM
❑ 2021	Because I Love You/Are You Putting Me on the Shelf	1966	7.50	15.00	30.00

DON AND THE CHEVELLS

"Don" is Don Ciccone, later of THE CRITTERS and THE FOUR SEASONS.

SPEEDWAY

Number	Title (A Side/B Side)	Yr	VG	VG+	NM
❑ 1000	Inner Limits/The Only Girl	1964	20.00	40.00	80.00

DON AND THE GOODTIMES

BURDETTE

Number	Title (A Side/B Side)	Yr	VG	VG+	NM
❑ 3	Colors of Life/You Did It Before	196?	5.00	10.00	20.00

DUNHILL

Number	Title (A Side/B Side)	Yr	VG	VG+	NM
❑ 4008	Little Green Thing/Little Sally Tease	1965	2.50	5.00	10.00
❑ 4015	I'll Be Down Forever/Big Big Knight (On a Big White Horse)	1965	2.50	5.00	10.00
❑ 4022	Sweets for My Sweet/Hey There Mary Mae	1966	2.50	5.00	10.00

EPIC

Number	Title (A Side/B Side)	Yr	VG	VG+	NM
❑ 10145	I Could Be So Good to You/And It's So Good	1967	2.50	5.00	10.00
❑ 10145 [PS]	I Could Be So Good to You/And It's So Good	1967	3.75	7.50	15.00
❑ 10199	If You Love Her, Cherish Her and Such/Happy and Me	1967	2.50	5.00	10.00
❑ 10241	Bambi/Sally (Studio A at 6 O'Clock in the Morning)	1967	2.50	5.00	10.00
❑ 10280	Ball of Fire/May My Heart Be Cast Into Stone	1968	2.50	5.00	10.00

JERDEN

Number	Title (A Side/B Side)	Yr	VG	VG+	NM
❑ 762	You'll Never Walk Away/Little Sally Tease	1965	3.00	6.00	12.00

WAND

Number	Title (A Side/B Side)	Yr	VG	VG+	NM
❑ 165	Turn On/Make It	1964	2.50	5.00	10.00
❑ 184	Straight Scepter/There's Something on Your Mind	1965	2.50	5.00	10.00

DON JUANS, THE

ONEZY

Number	Title (A Side/B Side)	Yr	VG	VG+	NM
❑ 101	The Girl of My Dreams/Dolores	1959	500.00	1000.	2000.

DONAYS, THE

BRENT

Number	Title (A Side/B Side)	Yr	VG	VG+	NM
❑ 7033	Devil in His Heart/Bad Boy	1962	10.00	20.00	40.00

—The Beatles re-made the A-side as "Devil in Her Heart"

DONEGAN, LONNIE

APT

Number	Title (A Side/B Side)	Yr	VG	VG+	NM
❑ 25067	Pick a Bale of Cotton/Ramblin' Round	1962	2.50	5.00	10.00

ATLANTIC

Number	Title (A Side/B Side)	Yr	VG	VG+	NM
❑ 2058	My Old Man's a Dustman/The Golden Vanity	1960	3.00	6.00	12.00
❑ 2063	Take This Hammer/Nobody Understands Me	1960	3.00	6.00	12.00
❑ 2081	Lorelei/Junco Partner	1960	3.00	6.00	12.00
❑ 2108	Have a Drink On Me/Beyond the Sunset	1961	3.00	6.00	12.00
❑ 2123	Wreck of the John B/Sorry, But I'm Gonna Have to Pass	1961	3.00	6.00	12.00

DOT

Number	Title (A Side/B Side)	Yr	VG	VG+	NM
❑ 15792	The Grand Coulee Dam/Nobody Loves Like an Irishman	1958	5.00	10.00	20.00
❑ 15873	Sally Don't You Grieve/Times Are Getting Hard, Boys	1958	5.00	10.00	20.00
❑ 15911	Does Your Chewing Gum Lose Its Flavor (On the Bedpost Overnight)/Aunt Rhody	1959	5.00	10.00	20.00

—Reissued in 1961 with the same number

Number	Title (A Side/B Side)	Yr	VG	VG+	NM
❑ 15953	Fort Worth Jail/Whoa, Back, Back	1959	5.00	10.00	20.00
❑ 16263	Whoa, Back, Back/Light from the Lighthouse	1961	3.75	7.50	15.00

FELSTED

Number	Title (A Side/B Side)	Yr	VG	VG+	NM
❑ 8630	Rock Island Line/John Henry	1961	3.00	6.00	12.00

HICKORY

Number	Title (A Side/B Side)	Yr	VG	VG+	NM
❑ 1247	Lemon Tree/A Very Good Year	1964	2.50	5.00	10.00
❑ 1267	Fisherman's Luck/There's a Big Wheel	1964	2.50	5.00	10.00
❑ 1274	Bad News/Interstate 40	1964	2.50	5.00	10.00
❑ 1299	Louisiana Man/Lovey Told Me Goodbye	1965	2.50	5.00	10.00
❑ 1345	Cajun Jo (Bully of the Bayou)/Nothing to Gain	1965	2.50	5.00	10.00

LONDON

Number	Title (A Side/B Side)	Yr	VG	VG+	NM
❑ 1650	Rock Island Line/John Henry	1956	7.50	15.00	30.00
❑ 20055	Juanita/Who Knows Where the Time Goes	1969	—	3.00	6.00

MERCURY

Number	Title (A Side/B Side)	Yr	VG	VG+	NM
❑ 70872	Lost John/Stewball	1956	6.25	12.50	25.00
❑ 70949	Bring a Little Water, Sylvie/Dead or Alive	1956	6.25	12.50	25.00
❑ 71026	Don't You Rock Me Daddy-O/How Long, How Long Blues	1957	6.25	12.50	25.00
❑ 71094	Cumberland Gap/Wabash Cannonball	1957	6.25	12.50	25.00
❑ 71181	Puttin' On the Style/Gamblin' Man	1957	6.25	12.50	25.00
❑ 71248	My Dixie Darling/I'm Just a Rolling Stone	1957	6.25	12.50	25.00

DONLEY, JIMMY

CHESS

Number	Title (A Side/B Side)	Yr	VG	VG+	NM
❑ 1843	Santa, Don't Pass Me By/Think It Over	1962	3.00	6.00	12.00

CRAZY CAJUN

Number	Title (A Side/B Side)	Yr	VG	VG+	NM
❑ 9001	Santa, Don't Pass Me By/Think It Over	197?	—	2.50	5.00
❑ 9002	Forever Lillie Mae/I Still Care	197?	—	3.00	6.00
❑ 9003	Love Bug/I Still Care	197?	—	3.00	6.00
❑ 9004	I Really Got the Blues/Just a Game	197?	—	3.00	6.00
❑ 9005	You're Why I'm So Lonely/Let Me Hold You	197?	—	3.00	6.00
❑ 9006	Baby, Heaven Sent Me You/Door to My Heart	197?	—	3.00	6.00
❑ 9007	A Woman's Gotta Have Her Way/Hello, Remember Me	197?	—	3.00	6.00
❑ 9008	Please Mr. Sandman/Honey Stop	197?	—	3.00	6.00
❑ 9009	Lovin' Cajun Style/(B-side unknown)	197?	—	3.00	6.00
❑ 9010	Born to Be a Loser/Now I Know	197?	—	3.00	6.00

DECCA

Number	Title (A Side/B Side)	Yr	VG	VG+	NM
❑ 30308	Kickin' My Hound Around/Come Along	1957	20.00	40.00	80.00
❑ 30392	South of the Border/The Trail of the Lonesome Pine	1957	6.25	12.50	25.00
❑ 30519	Baby How Long/I Gotta Go	1957	6.25	12.50	25.00
❑ 30574	Please Baby Come Home/Born to Be a Loser	1958	6.25	12.50	25.00
❑ 30738	Radio, Jukebox and TV/I'm Alone	1958	6.25	12.50	25.00
❑ 30887	What Must I Do/The Shape You Left Me In	1959	6.25	12.50	25.00
❑ 31005	Now I Know/I Can't Love You	1959	6.25	12.50	25.00
❑ 31116	My Baby's Gone/Our Love	1960	10.00	20.00	40.00

TEARDROP

Number	Title (A Side/B Side)	Yr	VG	VG+	NM
❑ 3005	Honey Stop Twistin'/Hello, Remember Me	1962	3.75	7.50	15.00
❑ 3007	Santa, Don't Pass Me By/Forever Lillie Mae	1962	3.00	6.00	12.00
❑ 3007	Think It Over/Forever Lillie Mae	1962	3.00	6.00	12.00
❑ 3009	Baby, Heaven Sent Me You/Loving Cajun Style	1963	3.00	6.00	12.00
❑ 3017	You're Why I'm So Lonely/Let Me Hold You	1963	3.00	6.00	12.00
❑ 3021	Santa, Don't Pass Me By/Santa's Alley	1963	3.00	6.00	12.00
❑ 3026	I Really Got the Blues/Just a Game	1964	2.50	5.00	10.00
❑ 3034	I'm So Lonesome Without the Blues/Forget the Past	1964	2.50	5.00	10.00
❑ 3051	Love Bug/I'm to Blame	196?	2.50	5.00	10.00
❑ 3119	My Forbidden Love/Strange, Strange Feeling	196?	2.00	4.00	8.00

DONNER, RAL

CHICAGO FIRE

Number	Title (A Side/B Side)	Yr	VG	VG+	NM
❑ 7402	The Wedding Song/Godfather Per Me	1974	2.00	4.00	8.00

END

Number	Title (A Side/B Side)	Yr	VG	VG+	NM
❑ GG-19	You Don't Know What You've Got (Until You Lose It)/She's Everything (I Wanted You to Be)	1963	7.50	15.00	30.00

—An early, and sought-after, reissue

FONTANA

Number	Title (A Side/B Side)	Yr	VG	VG+	NM
❑ 1502	Poison Ivy League/You Finally Said Something Good	1965	6.25	12.50	25.00
❑ 1502	Poison Ivy League/A Tear in My Eye	1965	6.25	12.50	25.00
❑ 1515	Good Lovin'/The Other Side of Me	1965	6.25	12.50	25.00

GONE

Number	Title (A Side/B Side)	Yr	VG	VG+	NM
❑ 5102	Girl of My Best Friend/It's Been a Long, Long Time	1961	10.00	20.00	40.00

—Black label

Number	Title (A Side/B Side)	Yr	VG	VG+	NM
❑ 5102	Girl of My Best Friend/It's Been a Long, Long Time	1961	6.25	12.50	25.00

—Multi-color label

Number	Title (A Side/B Side)	Yr	VG	VG+	NM
❑ 5108	You Don't Know What You've Got (Until You Lose It)/So Close to Heaven	1961	7.50	15.00	30.00
❑ 5108	To Love/And Then	1961	10.00	20.00	40.00

—Deleted shortly after release

Number	Title (A Side/B Side)	Yr	VG	VG+	NM
❑ 5114	Please Don't Go/I Didn't Figure on Him	1961	6.25	12.50	25.00
❑ 5119	School of Heartbreakers/Because We're Young	1961	10.00	20.00	40.00
❑ 5121	She's Everything (I Wanted You to Be)/Because We're Young	1961	6.25	12.50	25.00
❑ 5121	She's Everything (I Wanted You to Be)/Will You Love Me in Heaven	1961	7.50	15.00	30.00

—B-side sung by a girl group, not Ral Donner.

Number	Title (A Side/B Side)	Yr	VG	VG+	NM
❑ 5125	To Love Someone/Will You Love Me in Heaven	1962	6.25	12.50	25.00

—B-side sung by Ral Donner as advertised

Number	Title (A Side/B Side)	Yr	VG	VG+	NM
❑ 5129	Loveless Life/Bells of Love	1962	6.25	12.50	25.00
❑ 5133	To Love/Sweetheart	1962	6.25	12.50	25.00

MID-EAGLE

Number	Title (A Side/B Side)	Yr	VG	VG+	NM
❑ 101	(If I Had My) Life to Live Over/Lost	1968	2.50	5.00	10.00
❑ 275	The Wedding Song/So Much Lovin'	1976	—	3.00	6.00

MJ

Number	Title (A Side/B Side)	Yr	VG	VG+	NM
❑ 222	(All of a Sudden) My Heart Sings/Lovin' Place	1970	—	3.00	6.00
❑ 222 [PS]	(All of a Sudden) My Heart Sings/Lovin' Place	1970	—	3.00	6.00

RED BIRD

Number	Title (A Side/B Side)	Yr	VG	VG+	NM
❑ 10-057	Love Isn't Like That/It Will Only Make You Love	1966	37.50	75.00	150.00

REPRISE

Number	Title (A Side/B Side)	Yr	VG	VG+	NM
❑ 20135	(These Are the Things That Make Up) Christmas Day/Second Miracle (Of Christmas)	1962	10.00	20.00	40.00
❑ 20141	I Got Burned/A Tear in My Eye	1963	10.00	20.00	40.00
❑ 20141 [PS]	I Got Burned/A Tear in My Eye	1963	45.00	90.00	180.00
❑ 20176	I Wish This Night Would Never End/Don't Put Your Heart in His Hand	1963	12.50	25.00	50.00
❑ 20192	Beyond the Heartbreak/Run Little Linda	1963	15.00	30.00	60.00

RISING SONS

Number	Title (A Side/B Side)	Yr	VG	VG+	NM
❑ 714	Just a Little Sunshine (In the Rain)/If I Promise	1968	2.50	5.00	10.00

SCOTTIE

Number	Title (A Side/B Side)	Yr	VG	VG+	NM
❑ 1310	Tell Me Why/That's All Right with Me	1959	62.50	125.00	250.00

SMASH

Number	Title (A Side/B Side)	Yr	VG	VG+	NM
❑ 34774/5 [DJ]	Good Lovin'/The Other Side of Me	1964	10.00	20.00	40.00

—A Fontana promo using Smash labels in error and omitting the Fontana number?

STARFIRE

Number	Title (A Side/B Side)	Yr	VG	VG+	NM
❑ 100	Don't Let It Slip Away/Wait a Minute Now	1978	2.50	5.00	10.00

—Black vinyl

Number	Title (A Side/B Side)	Yr	VG	VG+	NM
❑ 100	Don't Let It Slip Away/Wait a Minute Now	1978	2.50	5.00	10.00

—White vinyl

Number	Title (A Side/B Side)	Yr	VG	VG+	NM
❑ 100 [PS]	Don't Let It Slip Away/Wait a Minute Now	1978	2.50	5.00	10.00

Number	Title (A Side/B Side)	Yr	VG	VG+	NM
❑ 103	(Things That Make Up) Christmas Day/Second Miracle (Of Christmas)	1978	2.50	5.00	10.00
—Green vinyl					
❑ 103 [PS]	(Things That Make Up) Christmas Day/Second Miracle (Of Christmas)	1978	2.50	5.00	10.00
❑ 114	Rip It Up/Don't Leave Me Now	1979	2.50	5.00	10.00
❑ 114	Rip It Up/Don't Leave Me Now	1979	6.25	12.50	25.00
—Picture disc					
❑ 114 [PS]	Rip It Up/Don't Leave Me Now	1979	2.50	5.00	10.00
SUNLIGHT					
❑ 1006	Don't Let It Slip Away/Wait a Minute Now	1972	3.00	6.00	12.00
TAU					
❑ 105	Loneliness of a Star/And Then	1963	12.50	25.00	50.00
—Blue label					
❑ 105	Loneliness of a Star/And Then	1963	7.50	15.00	30.00
—Yellow label					
THUNDER					
❑ 7801	The Day the Beat Stopped/Rock on Me	1978	—	3.00	6.00

DONNIE AND THE DARLINGTONS

Number	Title (A Side/B Side)	Yr	VG	VG+	NM
ABC-PARAMOUNT					
❑ 10633	Poppin' My Clutch/Since Grandpa Got a Rail Job	1965	6.25	12.50	25.00

DONNIE AND THE DELCHORDS

Number	Title (A Side/B Side)	Yr	VG	VG+	NM
EPIC					
❑ 9495	So Lonely/When You're Alone	1962	6.25	12.50	25.00
TAURUS					
❑ 352	So Lonely/When You're Alone	1962	10.00	20.00	40.00
❑ 357	I Don't Care/I'll Be With You in Apple Blossom Time	1963	6.25	12.50	25.00
❑ 361	Transylvania Mist/That Old Feeling	1963	6.25	12.50	25.00
❑ 363	Be with You/I Found Heaven	1963	6.25	12.50	25.00
❑ 364	I'm in the Mood for Love/I've Got a Woman	1964	6.25	12.50	25.00

DONNIE AND THE DREAMERS

Number	Title (A Side/B Side)	Yr	VG	VG+	NM
DECCA					
❑ 31312	Carole/Ruby My Love	1961	12.50	25.00	50.00
WHALE					
❑ 500	Dorothy/Count Every Star	1961	6.25	12.50	25.00
❑ 505	Teenage Love/My Memories of You	1961	10.00	20.00	40.00

DONNYBROOKS, THE

Number	Title (A Side/B Side)	Yr	VG	VG+	NM
CALICO					
❑ 108	Every Time We Kiss/Break the Glass	1959	5.00	10.00	20.00
❑ 112	Coming Home from School/Mandolins of Love	1959	5.00	10.00	20.00

DONOVAN

Number	Title (A Side/B Side)	Yr	VG	VG+	NM
ALLEGIANCE					
❑ 3910	Lady of the Stars/(B-side unknown)	1983	—	2.00	4.00
ARISTA					
❑ 0280	Dare to Be Different/International Man	1977	—	2.00	4.00
EPIC					
❑ 10045	Sunshine Superman/The Trip	1966	2.50	5.00	10.00
❑ 10045 [DJ]	Sunshine Superman/The Trip	1966	10.00	20.00	40.00
—Promo only on red vinyl					
❑ 10045 [PS]	Sunshine Superman/The Trip	1966	3.75	7.50	15.00
❑ 10098	Mellow Yellow/Sunny South Kensington	1966	2.50	5.00	10.00
❑ 10098 [PS]	Mellow Yellow/Sunny South Kensington	1966	3.75	7.50	15.00
❑ 10127	Epistle to Dippy/Preachin' Love	1967	2.00	4.00	8.00
❑ 10127 [PS]	Epistle to Dippy/Preachin' Love	1967	3.00	6.00	12.00
❑ 10212	There Is a Mountain/Sand and Foam	1967	2.00	4.00	8.00
❑ 10253	Wear Your Love Like Heaven/Oh Gosh	1967	2.00	4.00	8.00
❑ 10253 [PS]	Wear Your Love Like Heaven/Oh Gosh	1967	3.00	6.00	12.00
❑ 10300	Jennifer Juniper/Poor Cow	1968	2.00	4.00	8.00
❑ 10300 [PS]	Jennifer Juniper/Poor Cow	1968	3.00	6.00	12.00
❑ 10345	Hurdy Gurdy Man/Teen Angel	1968	2.00	4.00	8.00
—Features John Paul Jones, Jimmy Page, and possibly John Bonham, all later of Led Zeppelin					
❑ 10345 [PS]	Hurdy Gurdy Man/Teen Angel	1968	3.00	6.00	12.00
❑ 10393	Lalena/Aye My Love	1968	2.00	4.00	8.00
❑ 10393 [PS]	Lalena/Aye My Love	1968	3.00	6.00	12.00
❑ 10434	Atlantis/To Susan on the West Coast Waiting	1969	2.00	4.00	8.00
❑ 10434 [PS]	Atlantis/To Susan on the West Coast Waiting	1969	3.00	6.00	12.00
❑ 10510	Goo Goo Barabajagal (Love Is Hot)/Trust	1969	2.00	4.00	8.00
❑ 10510 [PS]	Goo Goo Barabajagal (Love Is Hot)/Trust	1969	3.00	6.00	12.00
—With the Jeff Beck Group					
❑ 10649	Riki Tiki Tavi/Roots of Oak	1970	2.00	4.00	8.00
❑ 10649 [PS]	Riki Tiki Tavi/Roots of Oak	1970	3.00	6.00	12.00
❑ 10694	Celia of the Seals/Song of the Wandering Aengus	1971	2.00	4.00	8.00
❑ 10694 [PS]	Celia of the Seals/Song of the Wandering Aengus	1971	3.00	6.00	12.00
❑ 10983	I Like You/Earth Sign Man	1973	—	2.50	5.00
❑ 11023	Maria Magenta/Intergalactic Laxative	1973	—	2.50	5.00
❑ 11108	Yellow Star/Sailing Homeward	1974	—	2.50	5.00
❑ 50016	Rock and Roll with Me/Divine Daze of Deathless Delight	1974	—	2.50	5.00
❑ 50077	Rock and Roll Souljer/How Silly	1975	—	2.50	5.00
❑ 50237	Dark Eyed Blue Jean Angel/Well Known Has-Been	1976	—	2.50	5.00
HICKORY					
❑ 1309	Catch the Wind/Why Do You Treat Me Like You Do	1965	3.75	7.50	15.00
❑ 1324	Colours/Josie	1965	3.00	6.00	12.00
❑ 1338	Universal Soldier/Do You Hear Me Now	1965	3.00	6.00	12.00
❑ 1375	You're Gonna Need Somebody on Your Mind/Little Tin Soldier	1966	3.00	6.00	12.00
❑ 1402	Turquoise/To Try for the Sun	1966	3.00	6.00	12.00
❑ 1417	Hey Gyp/The War Drags On	1966	3.00	6.00	12.00
❑ 1470	Sunny Goodge Street/Summer Day Reflection Song	1967	2.50	5.00	10.00
❑ 1492	Do You Hear Me Now/Why Do You Treat Me Like You Do	1968	2.50	5.00	10.00
JANUS					
❑ 138	Keep On Truckin'/Hey Gyp	1971	2.00	4.00	8.00

DONTELS, THE

Number	Title (A Side/B Side)	Yr	VG	VG+	NM
BELTONE					
❑ 2040	Lover's Reunion/Make a Chance	1963	62.50	125.00	250.00

DOO RON RON AND THE PRESIDENTIAL PLAYERS

Number	Title (A Side/B Side)	Yr	VG	VG+	NM
EUREKA					
❑ 102	Bill Clinton — Face the Music/Bill Clinton — Sweatin' to the Oldies	1998	—	2.00	4.00
—Blue vinyl					

DOOBIE BROTHERS, THE

Also see MICHAEL McDONALD; PATRICK SIMMONS.

Number	Title (A Side/B Side)	Yr	VG	VG+	NM
ASYLUM					
❑ 46630	Power/Cape Fear River	1980	—	2.50	5.00
—A-side: With John Hall and James Taylor; B-side by Sweet Honey in the Rock					
CAPITOL					
❑ B-44376	The Doctor/Too High a Price	1989	—	—	3.00
❑ B-44376 [PS]	The Doctor/Too High a Price	1989	—	—	3.00
❑ 7PRO-79723 [DJ]	Need a Little Taste of Love (same on both sides)	1989	—	3.00	6.00
—Vinyl is promo only					
SESAME STREET					
❑ 49642	Wynken, Blynken and Nod/In Harmony	1980	—	2.50	5.00
—B-side by Kate Taylor and the Simon-Taylor Family					
❑ 49642 [PS]	Wynken, Blynken and Nod/In Harmony	1980	—	2.50	5.00
WARNER BROS.					
❑ 7495	Nobody/Slippery St. Paul	1971	—	3.00	6.00
❑ 7527	Travelin' Man/Feelin' Down Partner	1971	—	3.00	6.00
❑ 7544	Beehive State/Closer Every Day	1971	—	3.00	6.00
❑ 7619	Listen to the Music/Toulouse Street	1972	—	2.50	5.00
❑ 7661	Jesus Is Just Alright/Rockin' Down the Highway	1972	—	2.50	5.00
❑ 7698	Long Train Runnin'/Without You	1973	—	2.00	4.00
❑ 7728	China Grove/Evil Woman	1973	—	2.00	4.00
❑ 7795	Another Park, Another Sunday/Black Water	1974	—	2.50	5.00
❑ 7832	Eyes of Silver/You Just Can't Stop It	1974	—	2.50	5.00
❑ 8011	Eyes of Silver/You Just Can't Stop It	1974	—	2.00	4.00
❑ 8041	Nobody/Flying Cloud	1974	—	2.00	4.00
❑ 8062	Black Water/Song to See You Through	1974	—	2.00	4.00
❑ 8092	Take Me in Your Arms (Rock Me)/Slat Key Soquel Rag	1975	—	2.00	4.00
❑ 8126	Sweet Maxine/Double Dealin' Four Flusher	1975	—	2.00	4.00
❑ 8161	I Cheat the Hangman/Music Man	1975	—	2.00	4.00
❑ 8196	Takin' It to the Streets/For Someone Special	1976	—	2.00	4.00
❑ 8233	Wheels of Fortune/Slat Key Soquel Rag	1976	—	2.00	4.00
❑ 8282	It Keeps You Runnin'/Turn It Loose	1976	—	2.00	4.00
❑ 8408	Little Darling (I Need You)/Losin' End	1977	—	2.00	4.00
❑ 8471	Echoes of Love/There's a Light	1977	—	2.00	4.00
❑ 8500	Livin' on the Fault Line/Nothin' but a Heartache	1977	—	2.00	4.00
❑ 8725	What a Fool Believes/Don't Stop to Watch the Wheels	1978	—	2.00	4.00
❑ 8725 [PS]	What a Fool Believes/Don't Stop to Watch the Wheels	1978	—	2.50	5.00
❑ 8828	Minute by Minute/Sweet Feelin'	1979	—	2.00	4.00
❑ 29552	You Belong to Me/South City Midnight Lady	1983	—	2.00	4.00
❑ 29552 [PS]	You Belong to Me/South City Midnight Lady	1983	—	2.50	5.00
❑ 49029	Dependin' on You/How Do the Fools Survive	1979	—	2.00	4.00
❑ 49503	Real Love/Thank You Love	1980	—	2.00	4.00
❑ 49503 [PS]	Real Love/Thank You Love	1980	—	2.50	5.00
❑ 49622	One Step Closer/South Bay Street	1980	—	2.00	4.00
❑ 49670	Keep This Train A-Rollin'/Just in Time	1981	—	2.00	4.00
❑ 50001	Here to Love You/Wynken, Bliinken and Nod	1982	—	2.00	4.00

7-Inch Extended Plays

Number	Title (A Side/B Side)	Yr	VG	VG+	NM
WARNER BROS.					
❑ S 2750 [DJ]	Eyes of Silver/Pursuit on 53rd St./Spirit//Road Angel/Tell Me What You Want	1974	2.00	4.00	8.00
—Jukebox issue, small hole, plays at 33 1/3 rpm					
❑ S 2750 [PS]	What Were Once Vices Are Now Habits	1974	2.50	5.00	10.00
—Part of Little LP series (LLP #247)					

DOONICAN, VAL

Number	Title (A Side/B Side)	Yr	VG	VG+	NM
DECCA					
❑ 32252	I'd Rather Think of You/If the Whole World Stopped Lovin'	1968	—	2.50	5.00
❑ 32337	The Sun Always Shines When You're Young/Now	1968	—	2.50	5.00
LONDON					
❑ 1014	Two Streets/It Must Be You	1967	—	3.00	6.00
❑ 9717	Walk Tall/Only the Heartaches	1964	2.50	5.00	10.00
❑ 9735	The Special Years/Traveling Home	1965	2.50	5.00	10.00
❑ 9753	I'm Gonna Get There Somehow/How Can I Find Her	1965	2.50	5.00	10.00
PRESS					
❑ 5008	Gentle Mary/What Would I Be	1967	—	3.00	6.00

DOORS, THE

Also see BUTTS BAND; RAY MANZAREK.

Number	Title (A Side/B Side)	Yr	VG	VG+	NM
ELEKTRA					
❑ 45051	Light My Fire/Love Me Two Times	1972	—	3.00	6.00
—"Spun Gold" series; originals have a very dark gold label					
❑ 45051	Light My Fire/Love Me Two Times	1975	—	2.00	4.00
—"Spun Gold" series; reissues have a lighter gold label					
❑ 45052	Touch Me/Hello, I Love You	1972	—	3.00	6.00
—"Spun Gold" series; originals have a very dark gold label					
❑ 45052	Touch Me/Hello, I Love You	1975	—	2.00	4.00
—"Spun Gold" series; reissues have a lighter gold label					
❑ 45059	Riders on the Storm/Love Her Madly	1973	—	3.00	6.00
—"Spun Gold" series; originals have a very dark gold label					
❑ 45059	Riders on the Storm/Love Her Madly	1975	—	2.00	4.00
—"Spun Gold" series; reissues have a lighter gold label					
❑ 45122	L.A. Woman/Roadhouse Blues	1983	—	2.00	4.00
—"Spun Gold" series; lighter gold label					

Number	Title (A Side/B Side)	Yr	VG	VG+	NM
❑ 45123	People Are Strange/Break On Through	1983	—	2.00	4.00
—"Spun Gold" series; lighter gold label					
❑ 45611	Break On Through (To the Other Side)/End of the Night	1966	7.50	15.00	30.00
—Originals have a yellow and black label					
❑ 45611	Break On Through (To the Other Side)/End of the Night	1967	5.00	10.00	20.00
—Second pressings have a red, black and white label					
❑ 45611 [PS]	Break On Through (To the Other Side)/End of the Night	1966	30.00	60.00	120.00
❑ 45615	Light My Fire/The Crystal Ship	1967	7.50	15.00	30.00
—Originals have a yellow and black label					
❑ 45615	Light My Fire/The Crystal Ship	1967	3.00	6.00	12.00
—Second pressings have a red, black and white label					
❑ 45621	People Are Strange/Unhappy Girl	1967	3.00	6.00	12.00
❑ 45621 [PS]	People Are Strange/Unhappy Girl	1967	10.00	20.00	40.00
❑ 45624	Love Me Two Times/Moonlight Drive	1967	3.00	6.00	12.00
❑ 45628	The Unknown Soldier/We Could Be So Good Together	1968	3.00	6.00	12.00
❑ 45628 [PS]	The Unknown Soldier/We Could Be So Good Together	1968	7.50	15.00	30.00
❑ 45635	Hello, I Love You, Won't You Tell Me Your Name?/Love Street	1968	5.00	10.00	20.00
—Original pressings have longer title					
❑ 45635	Hello, I Love You/Love Street	1968	3.00	6.00	12.00
❑ 45646	Touch Me/Wild Child	1968	3.00	6.00	12.00
❑ 45656	Wishful Sinful/Who Scared You?	1969	2.50	5.00	10.00
❑ 45663	Tell All the People/Easy Ride	1969	2.50	5.00	10.00
❑ 45663 [PS]	Tell All the People/Easy Ride	1969	6.25	12.50	25.00
❑ 45675	Runnin' Blue/Do It	1969	2.50	5.00	10.00
❑ 45685	You Make Me Real/Roadhouse Blues	1970	2.50	5.00	10.00
❑ 45726	Love Her Madly/(You Need Meat) Don't Go No Further	1971	2.00	4.00	8.00
❑ 45738	Riders on the Storm/Changeling	1971	2.00	4.00	8.00
❑ 45757	Tightrope Ride/Variety Is the Spice of Life	1971	2.00	4.00	8.00
❑ 45768	Ships w/ Sails/In the Eye of the Sun	1972	2.00	4.00	8.00
❑ 45793	Get Up and Dance/Treetrunk	1972	2.00	4.00	8.00
❑ 45807	The Mosquito/It Slipped My Mind	1972	2.00	4.00	8.00
❑ 45825	The Piano Bird/Good Rockin'	1972	2.00	4.00	8.00
❑ 46005	Roadhouse Blues (Live)/Albinoni/Adagio	1979	—	2.50	5.00
❑ 47097	People Are Strange/Not to Touch the Earth	1980	—	2.00	4.00
❑ 47097 [PS]	People Are Strange/Not to Touch the Earth	1980	2.00	4.00	8.00
—Also has an insert with photos of Doors albums					
❑ 69770	Gloria/Moonlight Drive	1983	—	2.00	4.00
—Contrary to prior reports, this was not issued with a picture sleeve					
PHILCO-FORD					
❑ HP-9	Light My Fire/Break On Through	1968	10.00	20.00	40.00
—4-inch plastic "Hip Pocket Record" with color sleeve					

DOOTONES, THE

Number	Title (A Side/B Side)	Yr	VG	VG+	NM
DOOTONE					
❑ 366	Teller of Fortune/Ay Si Si	1955	50.00	100.00	200.00
❑ 470	Strange Love Affair/The Day You Said Goodbye	1962	7.50	15.00	30.00
❑ 471	Sailor Boy/Down the Road	1962	7.50	15.00	30.00

DORELLS, THE

Number	Title (A Side/B Side)	Yr	VG	VG+	NM
ATLANTIC					
❑ 2244	Beating of My Heart/Maybe Baby	1964	3.75	7.50	15.00
GEI					
❑ 4401	Beating of My Heart/Maybe Baby	1963	7.50	15.00	30.00

DORMAN, HAROLD

Number	Title (A Side/B Side)	Yr	VG	VG+	NM
RITA					
❑ 1003	Mountain of Love/To Be with You	1960	6.25	12.50	25.00
❑ 1008	I'll Come Running/River of Tears	1960	5.00	10.00	20.00
❑ 1012	Moved to Kansas City/Take a Chance on Me	1960	5.00	10.00	20.00
SANTO					
❑ 9005	In an Instant/There on Yonder Hill	1962	3.75	7.50	15.00
❑ 9051	Ain't Gonna Change/What Comes Next	1962	3.75	7.50	15.00
SUN					
❑ 362	I'll Stick By You/There They Go	1961	5.00	10.00	20.00
❑ 370	Just One Step/Uncle Jonah's Place	1961	5.00	10.00	20.00
❑ 377	Wait 'Til Saturday Night/In the Beginning	1962	5.00	10.00	20.00

DORN, JERRY

Number	Title (A Side/B Side)	Yr	VG	VG+	NM
ARWIN					
❑ 122	Brother, Can You Spare a Dime/Disappointed Lover	1959	3.00	6.00	12.00
FLING					
❑ 711	Rocking Chair Rock/Prayer of Love	1959	12.50	25.00	50.00
KING					
❑ 4932	Wishing Well/Sentimental Heaven	1956	20.00	40.00	80.00
❑ 4968	I'm So in Love with You/Nightmare	1956	3.75	7.50	15.00
❑ 5029	Quicksand/The Key	1957	3.75	7.50	15.00

DORRELLES, THE

Number	Title (A Side/B Side)	Yr	VG	VG+	NM
RSVP					
❑ 1108	You Are/Good Luck to the Lucky Girl	1965	3.00	6.00	12.00

DORSAM, TOM

Number	Title (A Side/B Side)	Yr	VG	VG+	NM
LOREN					
❑ 5001	Baby of Mine/(B-side unknown)	1964	125.00	250.00	500.00

DORSEY, GERRY

See ENGELBERT HUMPERDINCK.

DORSEY, JACK

Number	Title (A Side/B Side)	Yr	VG	VG+	NM
PARKWAY					
❑ 938	Ringo's Dog/March of the Gonks	1965	3.00	6.00	12.00

DORSEY, LEE

Number	Title (A Side/B Side)	Yr	VG	VG+	NM
ABC					
❑ 12326	Night People/Can I Be the One	1978	—	2.00	4.00
❑ 12361	God Must Have Blessed America/Say It Again	1978	—	2.00	4.00
ABC-PARAMOUNT					
❑ 10192	Lottie Mo/Lover of Love	1961	3.75	7.50	15.00
ACE					
❑ 640	Lonely Evening/Rock	1961	3.75	7.50	15.00
AMY					
❑ 927	Ride Your Pony/The Kitty Cat Song	1965	2.00	4.00	8.00
❑ 939	Can You Hear Me/Work, Work, Work	1965	2.00	4.00	8.00
❑ 945	Get Out of My Life, Woman/So Long	1965	2.00	4.00	8.00
❑ 952	Confusion/The Neighbors' Daughter	1966	2.00	4.00	8.00
❑ 958	Workin' in the Coal Mine/Mexico	1966	2.50	5.00	10.00
❑ 965	Holy Cow/Operation Heartache	1966	2.00	4.00	8.00
❑ 974	Gotta Find a Job/Rain, Rain, Go Away	1967	—	3.00	6.00
❑ 987	My Old Car/Why Wait Until Tomorrow	1967	—	3.00	6.00
❑ 994	Can't Get Away/Vista Vista	1967	—	3.00	6.00
❑ 998	Go-Go Girl/I Can Hear You Callin'	1967	—	3.00	6.00
❑ 11010	I Can't Get Away/Cynthia	1968	—	3.00	6.00
❑ 11020	Wonder Woman/A Little Dab A Do Ya	1968	—	3.00	6.00
❑ 11031	Four Corners (Part 1)/Four Corners (Part 2)	1968	—	3.00	6.00
❑ 11048	I'm Gonna Sit Right Down/Little Ba-By	1968	—	3.00	6.00
❑ 11052	What Now My Love/A Lover Was Born	1969	—	3.00	6.00
❑ 11055	Everything I Do Gonna be Funky (From Now On)/There Should Be a Book	1969	—	3.00	6.00
❑ 11057	Give It Up/Candy Man	1969	—	3.00	6.00
BELL					
❑ 908	I Can Hear You Callin'/What You Want	1970	—	2.50	5.00
CONSTELLATION					
❑ 115	Organ Grinder's Swing/I Gotta Find a New Love	1964	5.00	10.00	20.00
❑ 135	You're Breaking Me Up/Messed Around and Fell in Love	1964	5.00	10.00	20.00
FURY					
❑ 1053	Ya Ya/Give Me You	1961	3.75	7.50	15.00
❑ 1056	Do-Re-Mi/People Gonna' Talk	1961	3.00	6.00	12.00
❑ 1061	Eenie Meenie Miny Moe/Behind the 8-Ball	1962	3.00	6.00	12.00
❑ 1066	You Are My Sunshine/Give Me Your Love	1962	3.00	6.00	12.00
❑ 1074	Hoodlum Joe/When I Met My Baby	1963	3.00	6.00	12.00
POLYDOR					
❑ 14038	Yes We Can — Part 1/O Me O, My O	1970	—	2.50	5.00
❑ 14055	Sneakin' Sally Through the Alley/Tears, Tears and More Tears	1971	—	2.50	5.00
❑ 14106	Freedom for the Stallion/If She Won't (Find Someone Who Will)	1971	—	2.50	5.00
❑ 14147	When Can I Come Home/Gator Tail	1972	—	2.50	5.00
❑ 14181	On Your Way Down/Freedom for the Stallion	1973	—	2.50	5.00
REX					
❑ 1005	Rock/Lonely Evening	1959	6.25	12.50	25.00
SANSU					
❑ 474	Love Lots of Lovin'/Take Care of Our Love	1967	3.00	6.00	12.00
—With Betty Harris					
SMASH					
❑ 1842	Hello Good Looking/Someday	1963	2.50	5.00	10.00
SPRING					
❑ 114	Occapella/Tears, Tears and More Tears	1971	—	2.50	5.00
VALIANT					
❑ 1001	Lottie Mo/Lover of Love	1958	10.00	20.00	40.00

DOTS, THE

Number	Title (A Side/B Side)	Yr	VG	VG+	NM
CADDY					
❑ 101	I Confess/I Wish I Could Meet You	1956	20.00	40.00	80.00
❑ 107	I Lost You/Johnny	1957	20.00	40.00	80.00
❑ 111	Good Luck to You/Heartsick and Lonely	1957	20.00	40.00	80.00
REV					
❑ 3512	Ring Chimes/Wolf Call	1958	375.00	750.00	1500.

DOUBLE SIX OF PARIS, THE

Number	Title (A Side/B Side)	Yr	VG	VG+	NM
CAPITOL					
❑ 4394	French Rat Race/Meet Benny Bailey	1960	3.75	7.50	15.00
PHILIPS					
❑ 40192	One Mint Julep/Hallelujah I Love Her So	1964	6.25	12.50	25.00
❑ 40220	Lonely Avenue/Sherri	1964	6.25	12.50	25.00

DOUGLAS, KELLIE

Number	Title (A Side/B Side)	Yr	VG	VG+	NM
RCA VICTOR					
❑ 47-8005	My Mama Don't Like Him/Big Hunky Baby	1962	3.00	6.00	12.00

DOUGLAS, KIRK

Number	Title (A Side/B Side)	Yr	VG	VG+	NM
DECCA					
❑ 29355	A Whale of a Tale/The Moon Grew Brighter and Brighter	1954	6.25	12.50	25.00

DOUGLAS, SCOTT, AND THE VENTURE QUINTET

See THE VENTURES.

DOUGLAS, STEVE

Number	Title (A Side/B Side)	Yr	VG	VG+	NM
CAPITOL					
❑ 5527	Yesterday (Part 1)/Yesterday (Part 2)	1965	3.00	6.00	12.00
GRAPEVINE					
❑ 601	Rockin' Green Sleeves/(B-side unknown)	1961	5.00	10.00	20.00
MGM					
❑ 13218	Snowplows Schussing (Part 1)/Snowplows Schussing (Part 2)	1964	3.00	6.00	12.00
PHILLES					
❑ 104	Yes Sir, That's My Baby/Lt. Col. Bogey's Parade	1962	6.25	12.50	25.00
TANDEM					
❑ 7000	Magic Sound/There You Go	1961	5.00	10.00	20.00

DOUGLAS, WAYNE

See DOUG SAHM.

DOVAL, JIM, AND THE GAUCHOS

Number	Title (A Side/B Side)	Yr	VG	VG+	NM
ABC-PARAMOUNT					
❑ 10621	Annie Ya Ya/Out of Sight	1965	2.50	5.00	10.00
❑ 10637	I Know You're Fooling Around/Uptown Caballero	1965	2.50	5.00	10.00

Number	Title (A Side/B Side)	Yr	VG	VG+	NM
DIPLOMACY					
❑ 3	Donna/The Scrub	1964	5.00	10.00	20.00
❑ 5	Stranded in the Pool/Right Now	1964	5.00	10.00	20.00
❑ 6	Beatles Rule/Pink Elephant	1964	6.25	12.50	25.00
❑ 7	She's a Very Nice Girl/Bony Moronie	1964	25.00	50.00	100.00
❑ 8	The Good and the Bad/Fireballed	1965	5.00	10.00	20.00
❑ 17	She's So Fine/Mama, Keep Your Big Mouth Shut	1965	5.00	10.00	20.00
❑ 1000	Love Me One More Time (Part 1)/Love Me One More Time (Part 2)	1963	5.00	10.00	20.00
—As "Jim SanDoval and the Gauchos"					
DOT					
❑ 16468	Fire Ball/Good and Bad	1963	3.75	7.50	15.00
❑ 16548	Love Me One More Time (Part 1)/Love Me One More Time (Part 2)	1963	3.75	7.50	15.00
❑ 16571	Barracuda/The Scrub	1964	3.75	7.50	15.00

DOVE, RONNIE

Number	Title (A Side/B Side)	Yr	VG	VG+	NM
DECCA					
❑ 31288	Yes Darling, I'll Be Around/Party Doll	1961	5.00	10.00	20.00
❑ 32853	Just the Other Side of Nowhere/If I Cried	1971	—	3.00	6.00
❑ 32919	Kiss the Hurt Away/He Cries Like a Baby	1972	—	3.00	6.00
❑ 32997	It's No Sin/My World of Memories	1972	—	3.00	6.00
❑ 33038	Lilacs in Winter/Is It Wrong	1972	—	3.00	6.00
DIAMOND					
❑ 163	Sweeter Than Sugar/I Believe in You	1964	2.50	5.00	10.00
❑ 167	Say You/Let Me Stay Today	1964	2.50	5.00	10.00
❑ 173	Right or Wrong/Baby Put Your Arms Around Me	1964	2.00	4.00	8.00
❑ 176	Hello Pretty Girl/Keep It a Secret	1965	2.00	4.00	8.00
❑ 179	One Kiss for Old Times' Sake/No Greater Love	1965	2.00	4.00	8.00
❑ 179	One Kiss for Old Times' Sake/Bluebird	1965	2.00	4.00	8.00
❑ 184	A Little Bit of Heaven/If I Live to Be a Hundred	1965	2.00	4.00	8.00
❑ 188	I'll Make All Your Dreams Come True/I Had to Lose You	1965	2.00	4.00	8.00
❑ 191	Kiss Away/Where in the World	1965	2.00	4.00	8.00
❑ 195	When Liking Turns to Loving/I'm Learning How to Smile Again	1965	2.00	4.00	8.00
❑ 198	Let's Start All Over Again/That Empty Feeling	1966	2.00	4.00	8.00
❑ 205	Happy Summer Days/Long After	1966	2.00	4.00	8.00
❑ 205 [PS]	Happy Summer Days/Long After	1966	3.75	7.50	15.00
❑ 208	I Really Don't Want to Know/Years of Tears	1966	2.00	4.00	8.00
❑ 214	Cry/Autumn Rhapsody	1966	2.00	4.00	8.00
❑ 217	One More Mountain to Climb/All	1967	2.00	4.00	8.00
❑ 221	My Babe/Put My Mind at Ease	1967	2.50	5.00	10.00
—A-side written and produced by Neil Diamond					
❑ 227	I Want to Love You for What You Are/I Thank You for Your Love	1967	2.00	4.00	8.00
❑ 233	Dancin' Out of My Heart/Back from Baltimore	1967	5.00	10.00	20.00
—B-side written and produced by Neil Diamond, who also supplies backing vocals					
❑ 240	In Some Time/Livin' for Your Lovin'	1968	2.00	4.00	8.00
❑ 244	Mountain of Love/Never Gonna Cry	1968	2.00	4.00	8.00
❑ 249	Tomboy/Tell Me Tomorrow	1968	2.00	4.00	8.00
❑ 256	What's Wrong with My World/That Empty Feeling	1969	—	3.00	6.00
❑ 260	I Need You Now/Bluebird	1969	—	3.00	6.00
❑ 271	Chains of Love/If I Live to Be a Hundred	1970	—	3.00	6.00
❑ 378	Heart/(B-side unknown)	1987	—	2.50	5.00
❑ 378 [PS]	Heart/(B-side unknown)	1987	—	2.50	5.00
❑ 379	Rise and Shine/(B-side unknown)	1987	—	2.50	5.00
DOVE					
❑ 1021	Lover Boy/(B-side unknown)	1955	250.00	500.00	1000.
HITSVILLE					
❑ 6038	Tragedy/Songs We Sang As Children	1976	—	2.50	5.00
❑ 6045	The Morning After the Night Before/Why Daddy	1976	—	2.50	5.00
JALO					
❑ 1406	No Greater Love/Saddest Hour	1962	6.25	12.50	25.00
MCA					
❑ 40106	So Long Dixie/Take My Love	1973	—	2.50	5.00
MELODYLAND					
❑ 6004	Please Come to Nashville/Pictures on Paper	1975	—	2.50	5.00
❑ 6011	Things/Here We Go Again	1975	—	2.50	5.00
❑ 6021	Drina (Take Your Lady Off for Me)/Your Sweet Love	1975	—	2.50	5.00
❑ 6030	Right or Wrong/Guns	1976	—	2.50	5.00
M.C.					
❑ 5013	The Angel in Your Eyes (Brings Out the Devil in Me)/Songs We Sang As Children	1978	—	3.00	6.00

DOVELLS, THE

Also see LEN BARRY.

Number	Title (A Side/B Side)	Yr	VG	VG+	NM
ABKCO					
❑ 4011	Bristol Stomp/You Can't Sit Down	1972	—	2.00	4.00
❑ 4029	Baby Workout/Hully Gully Baby	1973	2.50	5.00	10.00
❑ 4032	Bristol Twistin' Annie/Betty in Bermudas	1973	—	2.00	4.00
EVENT					
❑ 216	Dancing in the Street/Back on the Road Again	1974	—	2.50	5.00
❑ 3310	Roll Over Beethoven/Something About You Boy	1970	—	2.50	5.00
JAMIE					
❑ 1369	Our Winter Love/Blue	1969	2.50	5.00	10.00
MGM					
❑ 13628	There's a Girl/Love Is Everywhere	1966	2.50	5.00	10.00
❑ 14568	Don't Vote for Luke McCabe/Mary's Magic Show	1973	—	2.50	5.00
PARAMOUNT					
❑ 0134	L-O-V-E Love/We're All In This Together	1971	—	2.50	5.00
PARKWAY					
❑ 819	No, No, No/Letters of Love	1961	5.00	10.00	20.00
❑ 827	Bristol Stomp/Out in the Cold Again	1961	7.50	15.00	30.00
❑ 827	Bristol Stomp/Letters of Love	1961	3.75	7.50	15.00
❑ 833	Do the New Continental/Mope-Itty Mope Stomp	1962	3.75	7.50	15.00
❑ 833 [PS]	Do the New Continental/Mope-Itty Mope Stomp	1962	7.50	15.00	30.00
❑ 838	Bristol Twistin' Annie/The Actor	1962	3.75	7.50	15.00
❑ 838 [PS]	Bristol Twistin' Annie/The Actor	1962	7.50	15.00	30.00
❑ 845	Hully Gully Baby/Your Last Chance	1962	3.75	7.50	15.00
❑ 845 [PS]	Hully Gully Baby/Your Last Chance	1962	7.50	15.00	30.00
❑ 855	The Jitterbug/Kissin' in the Kitchen	1962	3.75	7.50	15.00
❑ 855 [PS]	The Jitterbug/Kissin' in the Kitchen	1962	7.50	15.00	30.00
❑ 861	Save Me Baby/You Can't Run Away from Yourself	1963	5.00	10.00	20.00
❑ 861 [PS]	Save Me Baby/You Can't Run Away from Yourself	1963	7.50	15.00	30.00
❑ 867	You Can't Sit Down/Stompin' Everywhere	1963	3.00	6.00	12.00
❑ 867	You Can't Sit Down/Wildwood Days	1963	3.75	7.50	15.00
❑ 867 [PS]	You Can't Sit Down/Stompin' Everywhere	1963	10.00	20.00	40.00
❑ 867 [PS]	You Can't Sit Down/Wildwood Days	1963	10.00	20.00	40.00
❑ 882	Betty in Bermudas/Dance the Froog	1963	3.00	6.00	12.00
❑ 882 [PS]	Betty in Bermudas/Dance the Froog	1963	7.50	15.00	30.00
❑ 889	Stop Monkeyin' Aroun'/No, No, No	1963	3.00	6.00	12.00
❑ 889 [PS]	Stop Monkeyin' Aroun'/No, No, No	1963	7.50	15.00	30.00
❑ 901	Be My Girl/Dragster on the Prowl	1964	5.00	10.00	20.00
❑ 911	One Potato/Happy Birthday Just the Same	1964	3.75	7.50	15.00
❑ 925	Watusi with Lucy/What in the World's Come Over You	1964	3.00	6.00	12.00
❑ 925 [PS]	Watusi with Lucy/What in the World's Come Over You	1964	7.50	15.00	30.00
SWAN					
❑ 4231	Happy/(Hey, Hey, Hey) Alright	1965	5.00	10.00	20.00
VERVE					
❑ 10701	Far Away/Sometimes	1973	—	2.50	5.00

DOWD, LARRY

Number	Title (A Side/B Side)	Yr	VG	VG+	NM
SPINNING					
❑ 6004	Why, Oh Why/Forbidden Love	1958	6.25	12.50	25.00
❑ 6009	Blue Swinging Mama/Pink Cadillac	1959	37.50	75.00	150.00

DOWELL, JOE

Number	Title (A Side/B Side)	Yr	VG	VG+	NM
JOURNEY					
❑ 1238 [DJ]	Homeward on the Wind (mono/stereo)	1973	—	3.00	6.00
—Stock copy not known to exist					
❑ 1238 [PS]	Homeward on the Wind (mono/stereo)	1973	—	3.00	6.00
MONUMENT					
❑ 952	If I Could Find Out What Is Wrong/Indian Summer Days	1966	2.00	4.00	8.00
SMASH					
❑ 1708	Wooden Heart/Little Bo Peep	1961	3.75	7.50	15.00
❑ 1708 [PS]	Wooden Heart/Little Bo Peep	1961	6.25	12.50	25.00
❑ 1717	The Bridge of Love/Just Love Me	1961	3.00	6.00	12.00
❑ 1717 [PS]	The Bridge of Love/Just Love Me	1961	4.00	8.00	16.00
❑ 1728	(I Wonder) Who's Spending Christmas with You/A Kiss for Christmas	1961	3.75	7.50	15.00
❑ 1730	The Sound of Sadness/The Thorn on the Rose	1962	3.00	6.00	12.00
❑ 1759	Little Red Rented Rowboat/The One I Left for You	1962	3.00	6.00	12.00
❑ 1759 [PS]	Little Red Rented Rowboat/The One I Left for You	1962	3.00	6.00	12.00
❑ 1786	Poor Little Cupid/No Secrets	1962	3.00	6.00	12.00
❑ 1786 [PS]	Poor Little Cupid/No Secrets	1962	4.00	8.00	16.00
❑ 1799	Our School Days/Bringa-Branga-Brought	1963	3.00	6.00	12.00
❑ 1799 [PS]	Our School Days/Bringa-Branga-Brought	1963	4.00	8.00	16.00
❑ 1816	Bobby Blue Loves Linda Lou/My Darling Wears White Today	1963	3.00	6.00	12.00
❑ 1816 [PS]	Bobby Blue Loves Linda Lou/My Darling Wears White Today	1963	4.00	8.00	16.00

DOWLANDS, THE

Number	Title (A Side/B Side)	Yr	VG	VG+	NM
TOLLIE					
❑ 9002	All My Loving/Hey Sally	1964	3.75	7.50	15.00

DOWNBEATS, THE (1)

Number	Title (A Side/B Side)	Yr	VG	VG+	NM
GEE					
❑ 1019	My Girl/China Girl	1956	200.00	400.00	800.00
—Red label					
❑ 1019	My Girl/China Girl	1958	7.50	15.00	30.00
—Gray label					
PEACOCK					
❑ 1689	You're So Fine/Someday She'll Come Along	1958	6.25	12.50	25.00

DOWNBEATS, THE (2)

Number	Title (A Side/B Side)	Yr	VG	VG+	NM
SARG					
❑ 168	Darling of Mine/Come On Over	1959	10.00	20.00	40.00
❑ 173	Run to Me Baby/I Need Your Love	1959	10.00	20.00	40.00
❑ 197	Falling Stars/I Just Can't Understand	1960	10.00	20.00	40.00
—As "O.S. Grant and the Downbeats"					
❑ 200	You Did Me Wrong/This Woman I Love	1960	10.00	20.00	40.00
❑ 223	Greyhound (Part 1)/Greyhound (Part 2)	196?	5.00	10.00	20.00
❑ 228	Grant's Soul Blues/Sock It Uptight	196?	5.00	10.00	20.00
❑ 233	Soul Bag/Darling Dear	196?	5.00	10.00	20.00
—As "O.S. Grant and the Downbeats"					

DOWNBEATS, THE (4)

Number	Title (A Side/B Side)	Yr	VG	VG+	NM
WILCO					
❑ 9	Alfalfa/Red X	1960	5.00	10.00	20.00
❑ 16	Playin' Possum/One at a Time	1960	5.00	10.00	20.00

DOWNING, BIG AL

Number	Title (A Side/B Side)	Yr	VG	VG+	NM
CARLTON					
❑ 489	Miss Lucy/Just Around the Corner	1959	12.50	25.00	50.00
❑ 507	It Must Be Love/When My Blue Moon Turns to Gold Again	1959	10.00	20.00	40.00
CHALLENGE					
❑ 59006	Down on the Farm/Oh Babe	1958	12.50	25.00	50.00
CHESS					
❑ 1817	The Story of My Life/I'd Love to Be Loved	1962	3.00	6.00	12.00
❑ 2158	I'll Be Holding On/Baby Let's Talk It Over	1974	—	2.50	5.00
COLUMBIA					
❑ 43028	I'm Just Nobody/All I Want Is You	1964	2.50	5.00	10.00
❑ 43185	I Feel Good/Georgia Slop	1964	2.50	5.00	10.00
DOOR KNOB					
❑ 328	I Guess By Now/(B-side unknown)	1989	—	2.50	5.00

Number	Title (A Side/B Side)	Yr	VG	VG+	NM
❑ 340	Bound for Baltimore/(B-side unknown)	1989	—	2.50	5.00
❑ 345	Father #1/(B-side unknown)	1989	—	2.50	5.00
JANUS					
❑ 211	Thank You Baby/(B-side unknown)	1974	—	3.00	6.00
❑ 234	I'll Be Holding On/Hands	1974	—	3.00	6.00
LENOX					
❑ 5565	You Never Miss Your Water (Till the Well Runs Dry)/If You Want It (I Got It)	1963	3.00	6.00	12.00
—As "Little Esther Phillips and Big Al Downing"					
❑ 5572	Mr. Hurt Walked In/If I Had Our Love to Live Over	1963	3.00	6.00	12.00
POLYDOR					
❑ 14311	I Love to Love/I'm Just Nobody	1976	—	2.50	5.00
SILVER FOX					
❑ 3	Cornbreak Row/The Saints	1969	2.00	4.00	8.00
❑ 11	Medley of Soul/These Arms You Push Away	1969	2.00	4.00	8.00
TEAM					
❑ 1001	I'll Be Loving You/Don't Mess with an Angel	1982	—	2.50	5.00
❑ 1002	Darlene/(B-side unknown)	1982	—	2.50	5.00
❑ 1003	Let's Sing About Love/We Can Only Say Goodbye	1983	—	2.50	5.00
❑ 1004	It Takes Love/If You're Leaving	1983	—	2.50	5.00
❑ 1007	The Best of Families/Fool of the Year	1983	—	2.50	5.00
❑ 1008	There'll Never Be a Better Night for Bein' Wrong/(B-side unknown)	1984	—	2.50	5.00
V-TONE					
❑ 215	Yes, I'm Loving You/Please Come Home	1960	3.00	6.00	12.00
❑ 220	If I Had Our Love to Live Over/Words of Love	1961	3.00	6.00	12.00
❑ 230	So Many Memories/There'll Come a Time	1961	3.00	6.00	12.00
VINE ST.					
❑ 103	How Beautiful You Are (To Me)/The Only Thing Missing Is You	1986	—	3.00	6.00
❑ 105	Just One Night Won't Do/How Beautiful You Are (To Me)	1987	—	3.00	6.00
❑ 106	How Ya Gonna Do It/The Only Thing Missing Is You	1987	—	3.00	6.00
WARNER BROS.					
❑ 8716	Mr. Jones/I Don't Cry (The Onion Song)	1978	—	2.50	5.00
❑ 8787	Touch Me (I'll Be Your Fool Once More)/I Ain't No Fool	1979	—	2.50	5.00
❑ 49034	Midnight Lace/Counting Highway Signs	1979	—	2.00	4.00
❑ 49141	I Ain't No Fool/Mr. Jones	1979	—	2.00	4.00
❑ 49161	The Story Behind the Story/Daddy Played the Banjo	1980	—	2.00	4.00
❑ 49270	Bring It On Home/Beer Drinking People	1980	—	2.00	4.00
WHITE ROCK					
❑ 1111	Down on the Farm/Oh Babe	1958	37.50	75.00	150.00
❑ 1113	Miss Lucy/Just Around the Corner	1958	37.50	75.00	150.00

DOWNLINERS SECT, THE

SMASH

Number	Title (A Side/B Side)	Yr	VG	VG+	NM
❑ 1954	Little Egypt/I Feel Good	1965	3.00	6.00	12.00

DOZIER, LAMONT

Also see HOLLAND-DOZIER.

ABC

Number	Title (A Side/B Side)	Yr	VG	VG+	NM
❑ 11407	Trying to Hold On to My Woman/We Don't Want Nobody to Come Between Us	1973	—	2.00	4.00
—Also see "Holland-Dozier"					
❑ 11438	Fish Ain't Bitin'/Breaking Out All Over	1974	—	2.00	4.00
❑ 12012	Fish Ain't Bitin'/Breaking Out All Over	1974	—	2.00	4.00
❑ 12044	Let Me Start Tonite/I Wanna Be with You	1974	—	2.00	4.00
❑ 12076	All Cried Out/Rose	1975	—	2.00	4.00
❑ 12234	Out Here on My Own/Take Off Your Make-Up	1976	—	2.00	4.00
ANNA					
❑ 1125	Let's Talk It Over/Benny the Skinny Man	1960	6.25	12.50	25.00
—As "Lamont Anthony"					
❑ 1125	Let's Talk It Over/Popeye	1960	62.50	125.00	250.00
—As "Lamont Anthony"					
CHECKMATE					
❑ 1001	Just to Be Loved/I Didn't Know	1961	62.50	125.00	250.00
—As "Lamont Anthony"					
COLUMBIA					
❑ 02035	Cool Me Out/Starting Over (We've Made the Necessary Changes)	1981	—	2.00	4.00
❑ 02238	Too Little Too Long/Chained (To Your Love)	1981	—	2.00	4.00
MEL-O-DY					
❑ 102	Dearest One/Fortune Teller Please Tell Me	1962	25.00	50.00	100.00
M&M					
❑ 502	Shout About It/(Instrumental)	1982	—	2.50	5.00
WARNER BROS.					
❑ 8432	Sight for Sore Eyes/Tear Down the Walls	1977	—	2.00	4.00
❑ 8792	Boogie Business/True Love Is Bittersweet	1979	—	2.00	4.00

DOZY, BEAKY, MICK & TICH

See DAVE DEE, DOZY, BEAKY, MICK & TICH.

DRAG KINGS, THE

UNITED ARTISTS

Number	Title (A Side/B Side)	Yr	VG	VG+	NM
❑ 676	Bearing Burners/Nitro	1963	7.50	15.00	30.00

DRAGONS, THE

With Daryl Dragon, later of THE CAPTAIN AND TENNILLE.

CAPITOL

Number	Title (A Side/B Side)	Yr	VG	VG+	NM
❑ 5278	Elephant Stomp/Troll	1964	5.00	10.00	20.00

DRAKE, CHARLIE

UNITED ARTISTS

Number	Title (A Side/B Side)	Yr	VG	VG+	NM
❑ 398	My Boomerang Won't Come Back/She's My Girl	1961	7.50	15.00	30.00
—With A-side lyric "Practiced 'til I was black in the face."					
❑ 398	My Boomerang Won't Come Back/She's My Girl	1961	3.75	7.50	15.00
—With A-side lyric "Practiced 'til I was blue in the face."					
❑ 437	Tanglefoot/Drake's Progress	1962	3.00	6.00	12.00
❑ 477	Sweet Freddie Green/Zulu Drake	1962	3.00	6.00	12.00

DRAKES, THE

CONQUEST

Number	Title (A Side/B Side)	Yr	VG	VG+	NM
❑ 1001	Oo Wee So Good/Kitty	1958	150.00	300.00	600.00
OLIMPIC					
❑ 252	I Made a Wish/Ole King Cole	1965	30.00	60.00	120.00

DRAMATICS, THE

Probably all the same group. Also see THE DELLS AND THE DRAMATICS.

ABC

Number	Title (A Side/B Side)	Yr	VG	VG+	NM
❑ 12090	Mr. and Mrs. Jones/I Cried All the Way Home	1975	—	2.50	5.00
❑ 12125	(I'm Going By) The Stars in Your Eyes/Trying to Get Over You	1975	—	2.50	5.00
❑ 12150	You're Fooling You/I'll Make It So Good	1975	—	2.50	5.00
❑ 12180	Treat Me Like a Man/I Was the Life of the Party	1976	—	2.50	5.00
❑ 12220	Finger Fever/Say the Word	1976	—	2.50	5.00
❑ 12235	Be My Girl/The Nicest Man Alive	1976	—	2.50	5.00
❑ 12258	I Can't Get Over You/Sundown Is Coming (Hold Back the Night)	1977	—	2.50	5.00
❑ 12299	Shake It Well/That Heaven Kind of Feeling	1977	—	2.50	5.00
❑ 12331	Ocean of Thoughts and Dreams/Come Inside	1978	—	2.50	5.00
❑ 12372	Stop Your Weeping/California Sunrise	1978	—	2.50	5.00
❑ 12400	Do What You Want to Do/Jane	1978	—	2.50	5.00
❑ 12429	Why Do You Wanna Do Me Wrong/Yo' Love (Can Only Bring Me Happiness)	1978	—	2.50	5.00
❑ 12460	I Just Wanna Dance with You/I've Got a Schoolboy Crush on You	1979	—	2.50	5.00
CADET					
❑ 5704	Door to Your Heart/Choosing Up on You	1974	—	3.00	6.00
❑ 5706	Don't Make Me No Promises/Tune Up	1974	—	3.00	6.00
❑ 5710	Love Is Missing from Our Lives/I'm in Love	1975	—	3.00	6.00
—With the Dells					
CAPITOL					
❑ B-5103	Live It Up/She's My Kind of Girl	1982	—	2.00	4.00
❑ B-5140	Treat Me Right/Night Life	1982	—	2.00	4.00
CRACKERJACK					
❑ 4015	Toy Soldier/Hello Summer	1968	15.00	30.00	60.00
FANTASY					
❑ 966	Luv's Calling/Dream Lady	1985	—	—	3.00
❑ 967	One Love Ago/Dream Lady	1986	—	—	3.00
MAINSTREAM					
❑ 5571	No Rebate on Love/Feel It	1976	—	2.50	5.00
MCA					
❑ 12460	I Just Wanna Dance with You/I've Got a Schoolboy Crush on You	1979	—	2.00	4.00
❑ 41017	I Just Wanta Dance With You/I've Got a Schoolboy Crush on You	1979	—	2.00	4.00
❑ 41056	That's My Favorite Song/Bottom Line Woman	1979	—	2.00	4.00
❑ 41178	Welcome Back Home/Marriage on Paper Only	1980	—	2.00	4.00
❑ 41241	Be With the One You Love/If You Feel Like You Wanna Dance, Dance	1980	—	2.00	4.00
❑ 51004	Share Your Love with Me/Get It	1980	—	2.00	4.00
❑ 51041	(We Need More) Lovin' Time/You're the Best Thing in My Life	1980	—	2.00	4.00
SPORT					
❑ 101	All Because of You/If You Haven't Got Love	1967	15.00	30.00	60.00
VOLT					
❑ 302	Bridge Over Troubled Water/(B-side unknown)	1989	—	2.00	4.00
❑ 4029	Since I've Been in Love/Your Love Was Strange	1969	2.00	4.00	8.00
❑ 4058	Whatcha See Is Whatcha Get/Thankful for Your Love	1971	2.00	4.00	8.00
❑ 4071	Get Up and Get Down/Fall in Love, Lady Love	1971	2.00	4.00	8.00
❑ 4075	In the Rain/Good Soul Music	1972	2.00	4.00	8.00
❑ 4082	Toast to the Fool/Your Love Was Strange	1972	2.00	4.00	8.00
❑ 4090	Hey You! Get Off My Mountain/The Devil Is Dope	1973	2.00	4.00	8.00
❑ 4099	Fell for You/Now You Got Me Loving You	1973	2.00	4.00	8.00
❑ 4105	And I Panicked/Beware of the Man	1974	2.00	4.00	8.00
❑ 4108	I Made Myself Lonely/Highway to Heaven	1974	2.00	4.00	8.00
WINGATE					
❑ 18	Somewhere/Bingo!	1966	12.50	25.00	50.00
—As "The Dynamics"					
❑ 22	Baby I Need You/Inky Dinky Wang Dang Doo	1966	12.50	25.00	50.00
—As "The Dynamics"					

DREAM GIRLS, THE

BIG TOP

Number	Title (A Side/B Side)	Yr	VG	VG+	NM
❑ 3059	Don't Break My Heart/I Could Write a Book	1960	5.00	10.00	20.00
❑ 3085	Wanted/Mr. Fine	1961	5.00	10.00	20.00
—The rest of the Big Top singles as "Bobbie Smith and the Dream Girls"					
❑ 3100	Duchess of Earl/Mine All Mine	1962	5.00	10.00	20.00
❑ 3111	Here Comes Baby/I Got a Feeling My Love	1962	5.00	10.00	20.00
❑ 3129	Your Lovey Dovey Ways/Now He's Gone	1962	5.00	10.00	20.00
CAMEO					
❑ 165	Don't Break My Heart/Oh This Is Why	1959	6.25	12.50	25.00
METRO					
❑ 20029	I'm in Love with You/Cryin' in the Night	1960	7.50	15.00	30.00
❑ 20034	Heartaches/Love Hen	1961	6.25	12.50	25.00
TWIRL					
❑ 1002	Don't Break My Heart/Oh This Is Why	1959	12.50	25.00	50.00

DREAM KINGS, THE

CHECKER

Number	Title (A Side/B Side)	Yr	VG	VG+	NM
❑ 858	M.T.Y.L.T.T./Oh What a Baby	1957	37.50	75.00	150.00

DREAM TEAM, THE

EPIC

Number	Title (A Side/B Side)	Yr	VG	VG+	NM
❑ 9701	I'm Not Afraid/Inka Dinka Doo	1964	3.00	6.00	12.00

DREAM WEAVERS, THE

DECCA

Number	Title (A Side/B Side)	Yr	VG	VG+	NM
❑ 29683	It's Almost Tomorrow/You've Got Me Wondering	1955	3.75	7.50	15.00
❑ 29818	You're Mine/Into the Night	1956	3.00	6.00	12.00
❑ 29905	A Little Love Can Go a Long, Long Way/Is There Somebody Else	1956	3.00	6.00	12.00
❑ 29990	Give Us This Day/Why I Chose You	1956	3.00	6.00	12.00
❑ 30156	Till We Meet Again/All This Is Home	1956	3.00	6.00	12.00
❑ 30276	Fool's Gold/I'll Try, I'll Try	1957	3.00	6.00	12.00

DREAMERS, THE

Several different groups.

Number	Title (A Side/B Side)	Yr	VG	VG+	NM
ABC-PARAMOUNT					
❑ 9746	The Girl Down the Street/The Right Time for Love	1956	5.00	10.00	20.00
ALADDIN					
❑ 3303	My Plea/Charles My Darling	1955	37.50	75.00	150.00
APT					
❑ 25053	Mary's Little Lamb/I Sing This Song	1960	6.25	12.50	25.00
BLUE STAR					
❑ 8001	I Really Love You/You Made Me Darling	1960	6.25	12.50	25.00
COUSINS					
❑ 1005	Because of You/Little Girl	1961	25.00	50.00	100.00
EVENT					
❑ 4270	Rock 'N Roll Baby/Ding Dong	1958	7.50	15.00	30.00
FAIRMOUNT					
❑ 612	Daydreamin' of You/The Promise	1963	5.00	10.00	20.00
FLIP					
❑ 319	Since You've Been Gone/Do Not Forget	1956	10.00	20.00	40.00
❑ 354	Since You've Been Gone/Do Not Forget	1961	5.00	10.00	20.00
GOLDISC					
❑ 3015	Teenage Vows of Love/Natalie	1961	7.50	15.00	30.00
GRAND					
❑ 131	Tears in My Eyes/535	1955	75.00	150.00	300.00
GUARANTEED					
❑ 219	Mary, Mary/Canadian Sunset	1961	3.75	7.50	15.00
JUBILEE					
❑ 5053	These Things I Miss/Can't Get You Off My Mind	1951	75.00	150.00	300.00
MANHATTAN					
❑ 503	Lips Were Meant for Kissing/No Obligation	1956	25.00	50.00	100.00
MAY					
❑ 133	Because of You/Little Girl	1963	10.00	20.00	40.00
MERCURY					
❑ 5843	I'm Gonna Hate Myself in the Morning/Ain't Gonna Worry No More	1952	37.50	75.00	150.00
❑ 70019	Please Don't Leave Me/Walkin' My Blues	1953	37.50	75.00	150.00
NUGGET					
❑ 1000	Don't Cry/It's Gonna Be Alright	1959	7.50	15.00	30.00
ROLLIN'					
❑ 1001	No Man Is an Island/Melba	1954	81.25	162.50	325.00
UNITED ARTISTS					
❑ 841	Henry, Henry, Henry/Love, Love, Love	1965	3.00	6.00	12.00

DREAMETTES, THE

Number	Title (A Side/B Side)	Yr	VG	VG+	NM
UNITED ARTISTS					
❑ 921	Gonna Make That Little Boy Mine/Run, Steven, Run	1965	5.00	10.00	20.00

DREAMLOVERS, THE

The Cameo, Casino, Mercury, Swan and Warner Bros. are all by the same group.

Number	Title (A Side/B Side)	Yr	VG	VG+	NM
CAMEO					
❑ 326	These Will Be the Good Old Days/Oh Baby Mine (I Get So Lonely)	1964	3.75	7.50	15.00
CASINO					
❑ 1308	Amazons and Coyotes/Together	1963	3.75	7.50	15.00
COLUMBIA					
❑ 42698	Sad, Sad Boy/If I Were a Magician	1963	5.00	10.00	20.00
❑ 42752	Sad, Sad Boy/Black Bottom	1963	3.00	6.00	12.00
❑ 42842	Pretty Little Girl/I'm Through with You	1963	12.50	25.00	50.00
END					
❑ 1114	If I Should Lose You/I Miss You	1962	5.00	10.00	20.00
HERITAGE					
❑ 102	When We Get Married/Just Because	1961	5.00	10.00	20.00
❑ 104	Welcome Home/Let Them Love (And Be Loved)	1961	3.75	7.50	15.00
❑ 107	Zoom, Zoom, Zoom/While We Were Dancing	1962	3.75	7.50	15.00
LEN					
❑ 1006	Take It from a Fool/For the First Time	1958	50.00	100.00	200.00
MERCURY					
❑ 72595	Bless Your Soul/Bad Time Make the Good Times	1966	2.50	5.00	10.00
❑ 72630	Calling Jo-Ann/You Gave Me Someone to Love	1966	2.50	5.00	10.00
SWAN					
❑ 4167	Amazons and Coyotes/Together	1963	5.00	10.00	20.00
—White label					
❑ 4167	Amazons and Coyotes/Together	1963	3.00	6.00	12.00
—Black label					
V-TONE					
❑ 211	Annabelle Lee/Home Is Where the Heart Is	1960	5.00	10.00	20.00
❑ 229	May I Kiss the Bride/Time	1961	5.00	10.00	20.00
WARNER BROS.					
❑ 5619	You Gave Me Someone to Love/Doin' Things Together with You	1965	6.25	12.50	25.00

DREAMS, THE

Number	Title (A Side/B Side)	Yr	VG	VG+	NM
SAVOY					
❑ 1130	Darlene/A Letter to My Girl	1954	50.00	100.00	200.00
❑ 1140	Under the Willow/I'm Losing My Mind	1954	30.00	60.00	120.00
—A copy on gold vinyl with a blue Savoy label has shown up; its authenticity is unknown					
❑ 1157	I'll Be Faithful/My Little Honeybun	1955	25.00	50.00	100.00

DRIFTERS, THE

Several different groups with a common heritage, thus we list them together. Also see BEN E. KING; RUDY LEWIS; CLYDE McPHATTER; BILL PINKNEY.

Number	Title (A Side/B Side)	Yr	VG	VG+	NM
ATLANTIC					
❑ 1006	Money Honey/The Way I Feel	1953	20.00	40.00	80.00
❑ 1019	Such a Night/Lucille	1954	17.50	35.00	70.00
❑ 1029	Honey Love/Warm Your Heart	1954	12.50	25.00	50.00
❑ 1043	Bip Bam/Someday You'll Want Me to Want You	1954	10.00	20.00	40.00
❑ 1048	White Christmas/The Bells of St. Mary's	1954	15.00	30.00	60.00
—Yellow label, no spinner (original)					
❑ 1048	White Christmas/The Bells of St. Mary's	1956	6.25	12.50	25.00
—Red label, no "fan" logo at lower left					
❑ 1048	White Christmas/The Bells of St. Mary's	1962	2.00	4.00	8.00
—Red label with "fan" logo at lower left					
❑ 1048	White Christmas/The Bells of St. Mary's	197?	—	2.50	5.00
—Glossy yellow label with "fan" logo					
❑ 1048 [DJ]	White Christmas/The Bells of St. Mary's	196?	6.25	12.50	25.00
—White/red label promo, no "fan" logo, with holly leaves encircling "45 R.P.M."					
❑ 1055	What'Cha Gonna Do/Gone	1955	12.50	25.00	50.00
❑ 1078	Adorable/Steamboat	1955	10.00	20.00	40.00
❑ 1089	Ruby Baby/Your Promise to Be Mine	1956	7.50	15.00	30.00
❑ 1101	Soldier of Fortune/I Got to Get Myself a Woman	1956	7.50	15.00	30.00
❑ 1123	Fools Fall in Love/It Was a Tear	1957	7.50	15.00	30.00
❑ 1141	Hypnotized/Drifting Away from You	1957	7.50	15.00	30.00
❑ 1161	I Know/Yodee Yakee	1957	7.50	15.00	30.00
❑ 1187	Drip Drop/Moonlight Bay	1958	7.50	15.00	30.00
—Last record by the "old" Drifters. The below Atlantic 45s are by a completely different group, although personnel changes resulted in at least one "old" Drifter (Johnny Moore) spending time with the "new" Drifters.					
❑ 2025	There Goes My Baby/Oh My Love	1959	6.25	12.50	25.00
❑ 2040	Dance with Me/(If You Cry) True Love, True Love	1959	5.00	10.00	20.00
❑ 2050	This Magic Moment/Baltimore	1960	5.00	10.00	20.00
❑ 2062	Lonely Winds/Hey Senorita	1960	5.00	10.00	20.00
❑ 2071	Save the Last Dance for Me/Nobody But Me	1960	5.00	10.00	20.00
❑ 2087	I Count the Tears/Suddenly There's a Valley	1960	3.75	7.50	15.00
❑ 2096	Some Kind of Wonderful/Honey Bee	1961	3.75	7.50	15.00
❑ 2105	Please Stay/No Sweet Lovin'	1961	3.75	7.50	15.00
❑ 2117	Sweets for My Sweet/Loneliness or Happiness	1961	3.75	7.50	15.00
❑ 2127	Room Full of Tears/Somebody New Dancin' with You	1961	3.75	7.50	15.00
❑ 2134	When My Little Girl Is Smiling/Mexican Divorce	1962	3.75	7.50	15.00
❑ 2143	Stranger on the Shore/What to Do	1962	3.75	7.50	15.00
❑ 2151	Sometimes I Wonder/Jackpot	1962	3.75	7.50	15.00
❑ 2162	Up On the Roof/Another Night with the Boys	1962	5.00	10.00	20.00
❑ 2182	On Broadway/Let the Music Play	1963	3.75	7.50	15.00
❑ 2191	Rat Race/If You Don't Come Back	1963	3.75	7.50	15.00
❑ 2201	I'll Take You Home/I Feel Good All Over	1963	3.75	7.50	15.00
❑ 2216	Vaya Con Dios/In the Land of Make Believe	1964	3.75	7.50	15.00
❑ 2225	One Way Love/Didn't It	1964	3.75	7.50	15.00
❑ 2237	Under the Boardwalk/I Don't Want to Go On Without You	1964	3.75	7.50	15.00
❑ 2253	I've Got Sand in My Shoes/He's Just a Playboy	1964	3.00	6.00	12.00
❑ 2260	Saturday Night at the Movies/Spanish Lace	1964	3.00	6.00	12.00
❑ 2260 [PS]	Saturday Night at the Movies/Spanish Lace	1964	10.00	20.00	40.00
❑ 2261	The Christmas Song/I Remember Christmas	1964	3.00	6.00	12.00
❑ 2261 [PS]	The Christmas Song/I Remember Christmas	1964	7.50	15.00	30.00
❑ 2268	At the Club/Answer the Phone	1965	2.50	5.00	10.00
❑ 2285	Come On Over to My Place/Chains of Love	1965	2.50	5.00	10.00
❑ 2292	Follow Me/The Outside World	1965	2.50	5.00	10.00
❑ 2298	I'll Take You Where the Music's Playing/Far from the Maddening Crowd	1965	2.50	5.00	10.00
❑ 2310	Nylon Stockings/We Gotta Sing	1965	2.50	5.00	10.00
❑ 2325	Memories Are Made of This/My Islands in the Sun	1966	2.00	4.00	8.00
❑ 2336	Up in the Streets of Harlem/You Can't Love Them All	1966	2.00	4.00	8.00
❑ 2366	Aretha/Baby What I Mean	1966	2.00	4.00	8.00
❑ 2426	Up Jumped the Devil/Ain't It the Truth	1967	2.00	4.00	8.00
❑ 2471	I Need You Now/Still Burning in My Heart	1968	2.00	4.00	8.00
❑ 2624	Your Best Friend/Steal Away	1969	2.00	4.00	8.00
❑ 2746	You Got to Pay Your Dues/Black Silk	1970	2.50	5.00	10.00
❑ 2786	A Rose By Any Other Name/Be My Lady	1971	2.50	5.00	10.00
❑ 89189	Ruby Baby/Fever	1987	—	2.00	4.00
—B-side by Little Willie John					
❑ 89189 [PS]	Ruby Baby/Fever	1987	—	2.00	4.00
—From the movie "Big Town"					
BELL					
❑ 45320	You've Got Your Troubles/I'm Feelin' Sad	1973	—	2.50	5.00
❑ 45387	The Songs We Used to Sing/Like Sister and Brother	1973	—	2.50	5.00
❑ 45600	Kissin' in the Back Row of the Movies/I'm Feelin' Sad	1974	—	2.50	5.00
CROWN					
❑ 108	The World Is Changing/Sacroiliac Swing	1954	50.00	100.00	200.00
EMI-CAPITOL MUSIC					
❑ S7-19351	Christmas Time Is Here/I'll Be Home for Christmas	1996	—	—	3.00
—As "The Drifters Featuring Rick Sheppard"					
MUSICOR					
❑ 1498	Midsummer Night in Harlem/Lonely Drifter, Don't Cry	1974	—	2.50	5.00
—As "Charlie Thomas and the Drifters"					
S&J					
❑ 800826	(More Than a Number in My) Little Red Book/I Count the Tears	196?	2.50	5.00	10.00
—As "Bill Pinkney and the Original Drifters"					

7-Inch Extended Plays

Number	Title (A Side/B Side)	Yr	VG	VG+	NM
ATLANTIC					
❑ 534	(contents unknown)	1954	50.00	100.00	200.00
❑ 534 [PS]	Clyde McPhatter and the Drifters	1954	75.00	150.00	300.00

Number	Title (A Side/B Side)	Yr	VG	VG+	NM
❑ 592	Fools Fall in Love/Adorable//Steamboat/Ruby Baby	1957	25.00	50.00	100.00
❑ 592 [PS]	The Drifters	1957	50.00	100.00	200.00

DRIFTERS, THE (2)

Instrumental group from England, and backing band for CLIFF RICHARD. They had one record in the US on Capitol; see THE SHADOWS, the name they adopted after the R&B Drifters became popular.

DRIFTERS, THE (3)

Number	Title (A Side/B Side)	Yr	VG	VG+	NM
CORAL					
❑ 65037	Wine Head Woman/I'm the Caring Kind	1950	75.00	150.00	300.00
❑ 65040	And I Shook/I Had to Find Out for Myself	1951	75.00	150.00	300.00

DRIFTERS, THE (4)

Number	Title (A Side/B Side)	Yr	VG	VG+	NM
RAMA					
❑ 22	Besame Mucho/Summertime	1953	50.00	100.00	200.00

DRIFTERS, THE (U)

Definitely not group (2), (3) or (4), though it could be one of the many variants of group (1).

Number	Title (A Side/B Side)	Yr	VG	VG+	NM
STEELTOWN					
❑ 671	Peace of Mind/The Struggler	1973	—	2.50	5.00

DRIFTING COWBOYS, THE

Backing band for HANK WILLIAMS.

Number	Title (A Side/B Side)	Yr	VG	VG+	NM
EPIC					
❑ 8-50543	Rag Mop/Mud Hut	1978	—	3.00	6.00
MGM					
❑ K11497	Mud Hut/Corn Crib	1953	6.25	12.50	25.00
❑ K11590	Canal Street Parade/Swing Shift Boogie	1953	6.25	12.50	25.00
❑ K11691	Fish Tail/Rock Point	1954	6.25	12.50	25.00

DRIFTWOOD, JIMMIE

Number	Title (A Side/B Side)	Yr	VG	VG+	NM
MONUMENT					
❑ 825	Lonesome Ape/What Is the Color of the Soul of Man	1963	3.00	6.00	12.00
RCA VICTOR					
❑ 47-7534	The Battle of New Orleans/Damyankee Lad	1959	3.75	7.50	15.00
❑ 47-7571	The Answer to The Battle of New Orleans/Sal's Got a Sugar Lip	1959	3.75	7.50	15.00
❑ 47-7603	John Paul Jones/The Bear Flew Over the Ocean	1959	3.75	7.50	15.00

DRIVERS, THE

More than one group.

Number	Title (A Side/B Side)	Yr	VG	VG+	NM
COMET					
❑ 2142	High Gear/Low Gear	1961	6.25	12.50	25.00
DELUXE					
❑ 6094	Women/Smooth, Slow and Easy	1956	25.00	50.00	100.00
❑ 6104	My Lonely Prayer/Midnight Hours	1957	50.00	100.00	200.00
❑ 6117	Dangerous Lips/Oh Miss Nellie	1957	20.00	40.00	80.00
KING					
❑ 5645	Mr. Astronaut/Dry Bones Twist	1962	3.00	6.00	12.00
LIN					
❑ 1002	A Man's Glory/Teeter Totter	1954	100.00	200.00	400.00
RCA VICTOR					
❑ 47-7023	Blue Moon/I Get Weak	1957	15.00	30.00	60.00

DRONGOS, THE

Number	Title (A Side/B Side)	Yr	VG	VG+	NM
WHITE WHALE					
❑ 235	Under My Thumb/If You Wanna Know	1966	5.00	10.00	20.00

DRUIDS OF STONEHENGE, THE

Number	Title (A Side/B Side)	Yr	VG	VG+	NM
UNI					
❑ 55021	A Garden Where Nothing Grows/Painted Woman	1967	5.00	10.00	20.00

DRYSDALE, DON

Number	Title (A Side/B Side)	Yr	VG	VG+	NM
REPRISE					
❑ 20162	Give Her Love/Our Love	1963	2.50	5.00	10.00
❑ 20162 [PS]	Give Her Love/Our Love	1963	5.00	10.00	20.00

DU DROPPERS, THE

Number	Title (A Side/B Side)	Yr	VG	VG+	NM
GROOVE					
❑ 0001	Speed King/Dead Broke	1954	20.00	40.00	80.00
❑ 0013	Just Whisper/How Much Longer	1954	25.00	50.00	100.00
❑ 0036	Boot 'Em Up/Let Nature Take Its Course	1955	12.50	25.00	50.00
❑ 0104	Talk That Talk/Give Me Some Consideration	1955	12.50	25.00	50.00
❑ 0120	I Wanna Love You/You're Mine Already	1955	12.50	25.00	50.00
RCA VICTOR					
❑ 47-5229	I Wanna Know/Laughing Blues	1953	10.00	20.00	40.00
❑ 47-5321	I Found Out/Little Girl, Little Girl	1953	10.00	20.00	40.00
❑ 47-5425	Whatever You're Doin'/Somebody Work on My Baby's Mind	1953	10.00	20.00	40.00
❑ 47-5504	Don't Pass Me By/Get Lost	1953	10.00	20.00	40.00
❑ 47-5543	The Note in the Bottle/Mama's Gone Goodbye	1953	10.00	20.00	40.00
RED ROBIN					
❑ 108	Can't Do Sixty No More/Chain Me Baby (Blues of Desire)	1952	125.00	250.00	500.00
—Red vinyl					
❑ 108	Can't Do Sixty No More/Chain Me Baby (Blues of Desire)	1952	50.00	100.00	200.00
❑ 116	Come On and Love Me Baby/Go Back	1953	37.50	75.00	150.00

7-Inch Extended Plays

Number	Title (A Side/B Side)	Yr	VG	VG+	NM
GROOVE					
❑ 2	(contents unknown)	1955	50.00	100.00	200.00
❑ 2 [PS]	Talk That Talk	1955	50.00	100.00	200.00
❑ 5	(contents unknown)	1955	50.00	100.00	200.00
❑ 5 [PS]	Tops in Rhythm and Blues	1955	50.00	100.00	200.00

DUALS, THE

Number	Title (A Side/B Side)	Yr	VG	VG+	NM
ARC					
❑ 4446	Nearest to My Heart/Bye Bye	1959	5.00	10.00	20.00
FURY					
❑ 1013	Wait Up Baby/Forever and Ever	1958	10.00	20.00	40.00
INFINITY					
❑ 032	Oozy Groove/The Big Race	1964	6.25	12.50	25.00
JUGGY					
❑ 321	Oozy Groove/The Big Race	1964	12.50	25.00	50.00
STAR REVUE					
❑ 1031	Stick Shift/Cruising	1961	200.00	400.00	800.00
SUE					
❑ 745	Stick Shift/Cruising	1961	7.50	15.00	30.00
❑ 758	Travelin' Guitar/Cha Cha Guitar	1962	6.25	12.50	25.00
UNITED ARTISTS					
❑ 0128	Stick Shift/Keem-O-Sabe	1973	—	2.00	4.00
—"Silver Spotlight Series" reissue; B-side by The Electric Indian					

DU'AMBRA, JOEY

Number	Title (A Side/B Side)	Yr	VG	VG+	NM
ABC-PARAMOUNT					
❑ 9917	Baby Sue/Come Back-A Little Mama	1958	7.50	15.00	30.00

DUANE, DICK

Number	Title (A Side/B Side)	Yr	VG	VG+	NM
ABC-PARAMOUNT					
❑ 9656	Sobony/Now	1955	7.50	15.00	30.00
❑ 9677	To Make a Mistake/Blue Prelude	1956	7.50	15.00	30.00
❑ 9709	Fame and Fortune/Mean Don't Cry	1956	7.50	15.00	30.00

DUBS, THE

Number	Title (A Side/B Side)	Yr	VG	VG+	NM
ABC-PARAMOUNT					
❑ 10056	No One/Early in the Evening	1959	6.25	12.50	25.00
❑ 10100	Don't Laugh at Me/You Never Belong to Me	1960	12.50	25.00	50.00
❑ 10150	For the First Time/Ain't That So	1960	6.25	12.50	25.00
❑ 10198	If I Only Had Magic/Joogie Boogie	1961	7.50	15.00	30.00
❑ 10269	Lullaby/Down, Down, Down I Go	1961	7.50	15.00	30.00
CLIFTON					
❑ 2	Where Do We Go from Here/I Only Have Eyes for You	1973	—	3.00	6.00
END					
❑ 1108	Now That We Broke Up/This to Me Is Love	1962	12.50	25.00	50.00
GONE					
❑ 5002	Don't Ask Me (To Be Lonely)/Darling	1957	25.00	50.00	100.00
—Black label, "shadow" logo					
❑ 5002	Don't Ask Me (To Be Lonely)/Darling	1957	15.00	30.00	60.00
—Black label, clown-face logo					
❑ 5002	Don't Ask Me (To Be Lonely)/Darling	1957	6.25	12.50	25.00
—Multi-color label					
❑ 5011	Could This Be Magic/Such Lovin'	1957	12.50	25.00	50.00
—Black label					
❑ 5011	Could This Be Magic/Such Lovin'	1957	6.25	12.50	25.00
—Multi-color label					
❑ 5020	Beside My Love/Gonna Make a Change	1957	15.00	30.00	60.00
❑ 5034	Song in My Heart/Be Sure (My Love)	1958	15.00	30.00	60.00
❑ 5046	Chapel of Dreams/Is There a Love for Me	1958	15.00	30.00	60.00
❑ 5069	Chapel of Dreams/Is There a Love for Me	1959	12.50	25.00	50.00
❑ 5138	You're Free to Go/Is There a Love for Me	1962	12.50	25.00	50.00
JOHNSON					
❑ 097	Connie/Home Under My Hat	1973	—	3.00	6.00
❑ 098	Somebody Goofed/I Won't Have You Breaking My Heart	1973	—	3.00	6.00
❑ 102	Don't Ask Me (To Be Lonely)/Darling	1957	500.00	1000.	1500.
JOSIE					
❑ 911	Wisdom of a Fool/This I Swear	1963	5.00	10.00	20.00
LANA					
❑ 115	Could This Be Magic/Blue Velvet	1964	2.00	4.00	8.00
—A-side is an alternate take of the hit version					
❑ 116	Don't Ask Me (To Be Lonely)/Your Very First Love	1964	2.00	4.00	8.00
—A-side is an alternate take of the hit version					
MARK-X					
❑ 8008	Be Sure My Love/Song in My Heart	1960	5.00	10.00	20.00
VICKIE					
❑ 229	I'm Downtown/Lost in the Wilderness	1971	2.50	5.00	10.00
—As "Richard Blandon and the Dubs"					
WILSHIRE					
❑ 201	Just You/Your Very First Love	1963	10.00	20.00	40.00

DUFF, ARLIE

Number	Title (A Side/B Side)	Yr	VG	VG+	NM
DECCA					
❑ 9-29243	Courtin' in the Rain/She's a Housewife	1954	6.25	12.50	25.00
❑ 9-29428	I Dreamed of a Hill-Billy Heaven/Lie Detector	1955	6.25	12.50	25.00
❑ 9-29589	Pass the Plate of Happiness Around/Take It Easy on Me	1955	6.25	12.50	25.00
❑ 9-29866	Home Boy/Oh, How I Cried	1956	6.25	12.50	25.00
❑ 9-29987	Alligator Came Across/So Close and Yet So Far	1956	6.25	12.50	25.00
STARDAY					
❑ 103	You All Come/Poor Ole Teacher	1953	10.00	20.00	40.00
❑ 105	Stuck-in-a-Mud Hole/A Million Tears	1953	7.50	15.00	30.00
❑ 132	Let Me Be Your Salty Dog/Back to the Country	1954	15.00	30.00	60.00
❑ 176	Courtin's Here to Stay/Fifteen Cents a Pop	1955	7.50	15.00	30.00
❑ 302	What a Way to Die/You've Done It Right	1957	25.00	50.00	100.00

DUKAYS, THE

Also see GENE CHANDLER.

Number	Title (A Side/B Side)	Yr	VG	VG+	NM
NAT					
❑ 4001	The Big Lie/The Girl's a Devil	1961	5.00	10.00	20.00
❑ 4002	Nite Owl/Festival of Love	1961	5.00	10.00	20.00
VEE JAY					
❑ 430	Nite Owl/Festival of Love	1962	3.75	7.50	15.00
❑ 442	I'm Gonna Love You So/Please Help	1962	3.75	7.50	15.00
❑ 460	I Feel Good All Over/I Never Knew	1962	3.75	7.50	15.00
❑ 491	Combination/Every Step	1963	3.75	7.50	15.00

DUKE, PATTY

Number	Title (A Side/B Side)	Yr	VG	VG+	NM
UNITED ARTISTS					
❑ 0127	Don't Just Stand There/Say Something Funny	1973	—	2.00	4.00
—"Silver Spotlight Series" reissue					

Number	Title (A Side/B Side)	Yr	VG	VG+	NM
❑ 875	Don't Just Stand There/Everything But Love	1965	2.50	5.00	10.00
❑ 875 [PS]	Don't Just Stand There/Everything But Love	1965	5.00	10.00	20.00
❑ 915	Funny Little Butterflies/Say Something Funny	1965	2.00	4.00	8.00
❑ 915 [PS]	Funny Little Butterflies/Say Something Funny	1965	5.00	10.00	20.00
❑ 958	Why Don't They Understand/Ribbons and Roses	1965	—	—	—

—Unreleased

Number	Title (A Side/B Side)	Yr	VG	VG+	NM
❑ 978	Whenever She Holds You/Nothing But Me	1966	2.00	4.00	8.00
❑ 50034	Little Things Mean a Lot/The World Is Watching Us	1966	2.00	4.00	8.00
❑ 50034 [PS]	Little Things Mean a Lot/The World Is Watching Us	1966	6.25	12.50	25.00
❑ 50057	The Wall Came Tumbling Down/What Makes You Special	1966	2.00	4.00	8.00
❑ 50073	Why Don't They Understand/Danke Schoen	1966	2.00	4.00	8.00
❑ 50216	Come Live with Me/My Own Little Place	1967	—	3.00	6.00
❑ 50299	Dona, Dona/And We Were Strangers	1968	—	3.00	6.00

DUKE OF EARL, THE

See GENE CHANDLER.

DUKES, THE

Possibly more than one group.

FLIP

Number	Title (A Side/B Side)	Yr	VG	VG+	NM
❑ 343	Looking for You/Groceries Sir	1959	7.50	15.00	30.00
❑ 345	I Love You/Leap Year Cha Cha	1959	10.00	20.00	40.00

IMPERIAL

Number	Title (A Side/B Side)	Yr	VG	VG+	NM
❑ 5401	Teardrop Eyes/Shimmies and Shakes	1956	62.50	125.00	250.00
❑ 5415	Wini Brown/Cotton Pickin' Hands	1956	30.00	60.00	120.00

SPECIALTY

Number	Title (A Side/B Side)	Yr	VG	VG+	NM
❑ 543	Ooh Bop She Bop/Oh-Kay	1954	18.75	37.50	75.00

DUMAURIERS, THE

FURY

Number	Title (A Side/B Side)	Yr	VG	VG+	NM
❑ 1011	Baby I Love You/All Night Long	1957	25.00	50.00	100.00

DUNAVAN, TERRY

FANFARE

Number	Title (A Side/B Side)	Yr	VG	VG+	NM
❑ 727	Rock It on Mars/(B-side unknown)	195?	100.00	200.00	400.00

DUNCAN, HERBIE

GLENN

Number	Title (A Side/B Side)	Yr	VG	VG+	NM
❑ 1400	Hot Lips Baby/Little Angel	1961	100.00	200.00	400.00
❑ 1401	Roll Along/Escape	1961	30.00	60.00	120.00
❑ 1402	That's All/End of the Rainbow	1961	20.00	40.00	80.00

MAR-VEL

Number	Title (A Side/B Side)	Yr	VG	VG+	NM
❑ 1400	Hot Lips Baby/Little Angel	1960	25.00	50.00	100.00

DUNDEE, CARLYLE, AND THE DUNDEES

SPACE

Number	Title (A Side/B Side)	Yr	VG	VG+	NM
❑ 201	Never/Evil One	1954	100.00	200.00	400.00

DUNGAREE DARLINGS, THE

KAREN

Number	Title (A Side/B Side)	Yr	VG	VG+	NM
❑ 1005	Boy of My Dreams/Little Wallflower	1959	25.00	50.00	100.00

REGO

Number	Title (A Side/B Side)	Yr	VG	VG+	NM
❑ 1003	Boy of My Dreams/Little Wallflower	1958	62.50	125.00	250.00

—As "The Dungaree Dolls"

DUNGAREE DOLLS, THE

See THE DUNGAREE DARLINGS.

DUPONTS, THE

Little Anthony's group before joining the Imperials. They are NOT the same group as the Imperials.

ROULETTE

Number	Title (A Side/B Side)	Yr	VG	VG+	NM
❑ 4060	Half Past Nothing/A Screamin' Ball (At Dracula Hall)	1958	6.25	12.50	25.00

ROYAL ROOST

Number	Title (A Side/B Side)	Yr	VG	VG+	NM
❑ 627	Somebody/Prove It Tonight	1957	12.50	25.00	50.00

SAVOY

Number	Title (A Side/B Side)	Yr	VG	VG+	NM
❑ 1552	Must Be Falling in Love/You	1958	6.25	12.50	25.00

—As "Little Anthony Guardine and the Duponts"

WINLEY

Number	Title (A Side/B Side)	Yr	VG	VG+	NM
❑ 212	Must Be Falling in Love/You	1957	20.00	40.00	80.00

DUPREE, CHAMPION JACK

ATLANTIC

Number	Title (A Side/B Side)	Yr	VG	VG+	NM
❑ 2032	Frankie and Johnny/Strollin'	1959	3.00	6.00	12.00

—As "Champion Jack"

Number	Title (A Side/B Side)	Yr	VG	VG+	NM
❑ 2095	My Mother-in-Law/Evil Woman	1961	2.50	5.00	10.00

EVERLAST

Number	Title (A Side/B Side)	Yr	VG	VG+	NM
❑ 5025	Shake Baby Shake/Walking Down the Highway	1963	2.50	5.00	10.00
❑ 5032	Highway Blues/Shake Baby Shake	1964	2.00	4.00	8.00

FEDERAL

Number	Title (A Side/B Side)	Yr	VG	VG+	NM
❑ 12408	Two Below Zero/Sharp Harp	1961	3.00	6.00	12.00

GROOVE

Number	Title (A Side/B Side)	Yr	VG	VG+	NM
❑ 0171	Lonely Road Blues/When I Get Married	1956	10.00	20.00	40.00

—With Mr. Bear

KING

Number	Title (A Side/B Side)	Yr	VG	VG+	NM
❑ 4695	Hard Feeling/Walking Upside Your Head	1954	7.50	15.00	30.00
❑ 4706	Camille/Rub a Little Boogie	1954	7.50	15.00	30.00
❑ 4779	Blues for Everybody/Two Below Zero	1955	7.50	15.00	30.00
❑ 4797	Let the Doorbell Ring/Harelip Blues	1955	7.50	15.00	30.00
❑ 4812	Walking the Blues/Daybreak Rock	1955	7.50	15.00	30.00

—B-side by Mr. Bear and the Bearcats

Number	Title (A Side/B Side)	Yr	VG	VG+	NM
❑ 4827	That's My Pa/Stumbling Block	1955	7.50	15.00	30.00
❑ 4859	Silent Partner/She Cooks Me Cabbage	1955	7.50	15.00	30.00
❑ 4876	Me and My Mule/Failing Health Blues	1956	7.50	15.00	30.00
❑ 4906	So Sorry, So Sorry/Overhead	1956	7.50	15.00	30.00
❑ 4938	Big Leg Woman/Mail Order Woman	1956	7.50	15.00	30.00
❑ 6299	Blues for Everybody/Tongue-Tied Blues	1970	—	3.00	6.00

RED ROBIN

Number	Title (A Side/B Side)	Yr	VG	VG+	NM
❑ 109	Stumblin' Block Blues/Number Nine Blues	1952	100.00	200.00	400.00
❑ 112	Shake Baby Shake/Highway Blues	1952	50.00	100.00	200.00
❑ 130	Drunk Again/Shim Sham Shimmy	1954	50.00	100.00	200.00

VIK

Number	Title (A Side/B Side)	Yr	VG	VG+	NM
❑ 0260	Just Like a Woman/Dirty Woman	1957	10.00	20.00	40.00
❑ 0279	Old Time Rock and Roll/Rocky Mountain	1957	10.00	20.00	40.00
❑ 0304	Shake Baby Shake/Lollipop Baby	1957	10.00	20.00	40.00

DUPREE, DAVE

See DAVE BURGESS.

DUPREES, THE

COED

Number	Title (A Side/B Side)	Yr	VG	VG+	NM
❑ 569	You Belong to Me/Take Me As I Am	1962	5.00	10.00	20.00
❑ 571	My Own True Love/Ginny	1962	5.00	10.00	20.00
❑ 574	I'd Rather Be Here in Your Arms/I Wish You Could Believe Me	1963	3.75	7.50	15.00
❑ 576	Gone with the Wind/Let's Make Love Again	1963	3.75	7.50	15.00
❑ 580	I Gotta Tell Her Now/Take Me As I Am	1963	3.75	7.50	15.00
❑ 584	Why Don't You Believe Me/The Things I Love	1963	7.50	15.00	30.00
❑ 584	Why Don't You Believe Me/My Dearest One	1963	3.75	7.50	15.00
❑ 585	Have You Heard/Love Eyes	1963	3.75	7.50	15.00
❑ 587	(It's No) Sin/The Sand and the Sea	1964	3.75	7.50	15.00
❑ 591	Please Let Her Know/Where Are You	1964	3.75	7.50	15.00
❑ 593	Unbelievable/So Many Have Told Me	1964	3.75	7.50	15.00
❑ 595	So Little Time/It Isn't Fair	1964	3.75	7.50	15.00
❑ 596	I'm Yours/Wishing Ring	1964	3.75	7.50	15.00

COLOSSUS

Number	Title (A Side/B Side)	Yr	VG	VG+	NM
❑ 110	Check Yourself/The Sky's the Limit	1970	—	3.00	6.00

—As "The Italian Asphalt and Pavement Company" or "The I.A.P. Co." for short

Number	Title (A Side/B Side)	Yr	VG	VG+	NM
❑ 110 [PS]	Check Yourself/The Sky's the Limit	1970	—	3.00	6.00

—As "The Italian Asphalt and Pavement Company" or "The I.A.P. Co." for short

COLUMBIA

Number	Title (A Side/B Side)	Yr	VG	VG+	NM
❑ 43336	Around the Corner/They Said It Couldn't Be Done	1965	3.00	6.00	12.00
❑ 43464	Norma Jean/She Waits for Him	1965	3.00	6.00	12.00
❑ 43577	The Exodus Song/Let Them Talk	1966	3.00	6.00	12.00
❑ 43802	It's Not Time Now/Don't Want to Have to Do It	1966	2.50	5.00	10.00
❑ 44078	Be My Love/I Understand	1967	2.50	5.00	10.00

HERITAGE

Number	Title (A Side/B Side)	Yr	VG	VG+	NM
❑ 804	My Special Angel/Ring of Love	1968	2.50	5.00	10.00
❑ 805	Goodnight My Love/Ring of Love	1968	2.50	5.00	10.00
❑ 805 [PS]	Goodnight My Love/Ring of Love	1968	5.00	10.00	20.00
❑ 808	My Love, My Love/The Sky's the Limit	1968	2.50	5.00	10.00
❑ 808 [PS]	My Love, My Love/The Sky's the Limit	1968	5.00	10.00	20.00
❑ 811	Two Different Worlds/Hope	1969	2.50	5.00	10.00
❑ 811 [PS]	Two Different Worlds/Hope	1969	5.00	10.00	20.00
❑ 826	Have You Heard/My Love, My Love	1970	2.50	5.00	10.00

RCA VICTOR

Number	Title (A Side/B Side)	Yr	VG	VG+	NM
❑ PB-10407	The Sky's the Limit/Delicious	1975	2.50	5.00	10.00

DURAN DURAN

Also see ARCADIA; THE POWER STATION; ANDY TAYLOR; JOHN TAYLOR.

CAPITOL

Number	Title (A Side/B Side)	Yr	VG	VG+	NM
❑ 5215	Rio/Hold Back the Rain	1983	—	—	3.00
❑ 5215 [PS]	Rio/Hold Back the Rain	1983	—	3.00	6.00
❑ 5233	Is There Something I Should Know/Careless Memories	1983			3.00
❑ 5233 [PS]	Is There Something I Should Know/Careless Memories	1983	—	2.00	4.00
❑ 5290	Union of the Snake/Secret Oktober	1983	—	—	3.00

—Custom label

Number	Title (A Side/B Side)	Yr	VG	VG+	NM
❑ 5290 [PS]	Union of the Snake/Secret Oktober	1983	—	—	3.00
❑ 5309	New Moon on Monday/Tiger Tiger	1984	—	—	3.00
❑ 5309 [PS]	New Moon on Monday/Tiger Tiger	1984	—	—	3.00
❑ 5345	The Reflex/New Religion	1984	—	2.00	4.00
❑ 5345 [PS]	The Reflex/New Religion	1984	2.00	4.00	8.00

—Foldout poster sleeve

Number	Title (A Side/B Side)	Yr	VG	VG+	NM
❑ 5345 [PS]	The Reflex/New Religion	1984	—	2.00	4.00

—Standard picture sleeve; though less sought-after, this is actually much scarcer than the poster

Number	Title (A Side/B Side)	Yr	VG	VG+	NM
❑ 5417	The Wild Boys/(I'm Looking for) Cracks in the Pavement	1984	—	—	3.00
❑ 5417 [PS]	The Wild Boys/(I'm Looking for) Cracks in the Pavement	1984	—	—	3.00
❑ 5438	Save a Prayer/Save a Prayer (From the Arena)	1985	—	—	3.00
❑ 5438 [PS]	Save a Prayer/Save a Prayer (From the Arena)	1985	—	—	3.00
❑ 5475	A View to a Kill/A View to a Kill (That Fatal Kiss)	1985	—	—	3.00
❑ 5475 [PS]	A View to a Kill/A View to a Kill (That Fatal Kiss)	1985	—	2.00	4.00
❑ 5648	Notorious/Winter Marches On	1986	—	—	3.00
❑ 5648 [DJ]	Notorious (same on both sides)	1986	2.50	5.00	10.00

—Clear vinyl in heavy clear plastic sleeve

Number	Title (A Side/B Side)	Yr	VG	VG+	NM
❑ 5648 [PS]	Notorious/Winter Marches On	1986	—	—	3.00
❑ 5670	Skin Trade/We Need You	1987	—	—	3.00
❑ 5670 [DJ]	Skin Trade (same on both sides)	1987	2.50	5.00	10.00

—Red vinyl in heavy clear plastic sleeve

Number	Title (A Side/B Side)	Yr	VG	VG+	NM
❑ 5670 [PS]	Skin Trade/We Need You	1987	—	—	3.00

—American all-red sleeve

Number	Title (A Side/B Side)	Yr	VG	VG+	NM
❑ 5670 [PS]	Skin Trade/We Need You	1987	6.25	12.50	25.00

—Canada-only nude sleeve

Number	Title (A Side/B Side)	Yr	VG	VG+	NM
❑ S7-17316	Come Undone/Skin Trade	1993	—	—	3.00
❑ S7-17438	Too Much Information/Drowning Man	1993	—	—	3.00
❑ S7-18488	White Lines/Watching the Detectives	1995	—	—	3.00
❑ S7-18577	Perfect Day/Success	1995	—	—	3.00
❑ S7-19721	Electric Barbarella/Out of My Mind	1997	—	—	3.00
❑ 44001	Meet El Presidente/Vertigo (Do the Demolition)	1987	—	—	3.00
❑ 44001 [DJ]	Meet El Presidente (same on both sides)	1987	2.50	5.00	10.00

—White vinyl in heavy clear plastic sleeve

Number	Title (A Side/B Side)	Yr	VG	VG+	NM
❑ 44001 [PS]	Meet El Presidente/Vertigo (Do the Demolition)	1987	—	2.00	4.00

—Foldout poster sleeve

Number	Title (A Side/B Side)	Yr	VG	VG+	NM
❑ 44237	I Don't Want Your Love/(instrumental)	1988	—	—	3.00
❑ 44237 [PS]	I Don't Want Your Love/(instrumental)	1988	—	—	3.00
❑ 44287	All She Wants Is/Medley: I Believe-All I Need to Know	1988	—	—	3.00
❑ 44287 [PS]	All She Wants Is/Medley: I Believe-All I Need to Know	1988	—	—	3.00

Number	Title (A Side/B Side)	Yr	VG	VG+	NM
❑ 44337	Do You Believe in Shame?/Edge of America-Lakeshore Driving	1989	—	—	3.00
❑ 44337 [PS]	Do You Believe in Shame?/Edge of America-Lakeshore Driving	1989	—	—	3.00
❑ S7-56945	Ordinary World/Save a Prayer	1993	—	—	3.00

HARVEST

Number	Title (A Side/B Side)	Yr	VG	VG+	NM
❑ 5017	Planet Earth/To the Shore	1981	6.25	12.50	25.00
❑ 5070	Girls on Film/Faster Than Light	1981	6.25	12.50	25.00
❑ 5134	Hungry Like the Wolf (3:23)/Careless Memories	1982	3.00	6.00	12.00
❑ 5175	Rio/Hold Back the Rain	1982	3.00	6.00	12.00
—Custom label					
❑ 5195	Hungry Like the Wolf (4:11)/Hungry Like the Wolf (5:14)	1982	—	—	3.00
❑ 5195 [PS]	Hungry Like the Wolf (4:11)/Hungry Like the Wolf (5:14)	1982	2.50	5.00	10.00
—A fairly scarce sleeve					

DURANTE, JIMMY

WARNER BROS.

Number	Title (A Side/B Side)	Yr	VG	VG+	NM
❑ 5843	Bill Bailey (Won't You Please Come Home)/Margie	1966	2.00	4.00	8.00

DUSK

With Peggy Santaglia of THE ANGELS.

BELL

Number	Title (A Side/B Side)	Yr	VG	VG+	NM
❑ 961	Angel Baby/If We Just Leave Today	1971	—	3.00	6.00
❑ 961	Angel Baby/Reach Out and Speak My Name	1971	—	3.00	6.00
❑ 990	I Hear Those Church Bells Ringing/I Cannot See to See You	1971	—	3.00	6.00
❑ 45148	Suburbia U.S.A./Treat Me Like a Good Piece of Candy	1971	—	3.00	6.00
❑ 45207	Point of No Return/(B-side unknown)	1972	—	3.00	6.00

DUSTERS, THE (1)

ABC-PARAMOUNT

Number	Title (A Side/B Side)	Yr	VG	VG+	NM
❑ 9887	Pretty Girl/Coolation	1958	7.50	15.00	30.00

CUPID

Number	Title (A Side/B Side)	Yr	VG	VG+	NM
❑ 5003	Rock at the Hop/She's Mine	1958	17.50	35.00	70.00

GLORY

Number	Title (A Side/B Side)	Yr	VG	VG+	NM
❑ 287	Darling Love/Teen-Age Jamboree	1958	12.50	25.00	50.00

DUSTERS, THE (2)

TOMMY TUCKER was a member of this group.

ARC

Number	Title (A Side/B Side)	Yr	VG	VG+	NM
❑ 3000	Give Me Time/Sallie Mae	1956	75.00	150.00	300.00

DUVALL, HUELYN

CHALLENGE

Number	Title (A Side/B Side)	Yr	VG	VG+	NM
❑ 1012	Teen Queen/Comin' or Goin'	1957	25.00	50.00	100.00
—Blue label					
❑ 1012	Teen Queen/Comin' or Goin'	1957	7.50	15.00	30.00
—Maroon label					
❑ 59002	Hum-Dinger/You Knock Me Out	1958	7.50	15.00	30.00
❑ 59014	Little Boy Blue/Three Months to Kill	1958	10.00	20.00	40.00
❑ 59025	Friday Night on a Dollar Bill/Juliette	1958	7.50	15.00	30.00
❑ 59069	Pucker Paint/Boom Boom Baby	1960	7.50	15.00	30.00

DYKE AND THE BLAZERS

ORIGINAL SOUND

Number	Title (A Side/B Side)	Yr	VG	VG+	NM
❑ 64	Funky Broadway — Part 1/Funky Broadway — Part 2	1966	2.50	5.00	10.00
❑ 69	So Sharp/Don't Bug Me	1967	2.00	4.00	8.00
❑ 79	Funky Walk Part 1 — East/Funky Walk Part 2 — West	1967	2.00	4.00	8.00
❑ 83	Funky Bull — Part 1/Funky Bull — Part 2	1968	2.00	4.00	8.00
❑ 86	We Got More Soul/Shotgun Slim	1969	2.00	4.00	8.00
❑ 89	Let a Woman Be a Woman — Let a Man Be a Man/Uhh	1969	2.00	4.00	8.00
❑ 90	You Are My Sunshine/City Dump	1969	2.00	4.00	8.00
❑ 91	Uhh/My Sister's and My Brother's Day Is Coming	1970	2.00	4.00	8.00
❑ 96	Runaway People/I'm So All Alone	1970	2.00	4.00	8.00

DYLAN, BOB

ASYLUM

Number	Title (A Side/B Side)	Yr	VG	VG+	NM
❑ 11033	On a Night Like This/You Angel You	1974	—	3.00	6.00
❑ 11035	Something There Is About You/Going, Going, Gone	1974	—	3.00	6.00
❑ 11043	Most Likely You Go Your Way (And I'll Go Mine)/Stage Fright	1974	—	3.00	6.00
—With The Band					
❑ 45212	All Along the Watchtower/It Ain't Me Babe	1974	3.00	6.00	12.00

COLUMBIA

Number	Title (A Side/B Side)	Yr	VG	VG+	NM
❑ AE 25 [DJ]	All the Tired Horses (mono/stereo)	1970	10.00	20.00	40.00
❑ AE7 1039 [DJ]	If Not for You/Tomorrow Is a Long Time	1971	10.00	20.00	40.00
❑ 02510	Heart of Mine/The Groom's Still Waiting at the Altar	1981	—	2.00	4.00
❑ 02510 [PS]	Heart of Mine/The Groom's Still Waiting at the Altar	1981	—	2.50	5.00
❑ 04301	Sweetheart Like You/Union Sundown	1983	—	2.00	4.00
❑ 04301 [PS]	Sweetheart Like You/Union Sundown	1983	—	2.50	5.00
❑ 04425	Jokerman/Isis	1984	—	2.50	5.00
❑ 04933	Tight Connection to My Heart (Has Anybody Seen My Love)/We Better Talk This Over	1985	—	2.00	4.00
❑ 04933 [PS]	Tight Connection to My Heart (Has Anybody Seen My Love)/We Better Talk This Over	1985	—	2.00	4.00
❑ 05697	Emotionaly Yours/When the Night Comes Falling from the Sky	1985	—	2.00	4.00
❑ 07970	Silvio/Too Far from Home	1988	—	2.50	5.00
❑ 10106	Tangled Up in Blue/If You See Her Say Hello	1975	—	3.00	6.00
❑ 10217	Million Dollar Bash/Tears of Rage	1975	2.50	5.00	10.00
❑ 10245	Hurricane (Part 1)/Hurricane (Part 2)	1975	—	3.00	6.00
❑ 10245 [DJ]	Hurricane (mono/stereo)	1975	5.00	10.00	20.00
—Plays at 33 1/3 rpm; does not have "Special Rush Reservice" on label					
❑ 10245 [DJ]	Hurricane (mono/stereo)	1975	3.75	7.50	15.00
—Plays at 33 1/3 rpm; has "Special Rush Reservice" on label					
❑ 10245 [PS]	Hurricane (mono/stereo)	1975	3.75	7.50	15.00
—Special sleeve for above record					
❑ 10245 [PS]	Hurricane (Part 1)/Hurricane (Part 2)	1975	3.00	6.00	12.00
❑ 10298	Mozambique/Oh, Sister	1976	—	3.00	6.00
❑ 10454	Stuck Inside of Mobile with the Memphis Blues Again/Rita Mae	1976	—	2.50	5.00
❑ 10454 [PS]	Stuck Inside of Mobile with the Memphis Blues Again/Rita Mae	1976	—	3.00	6.00
❑ 10805	Baby Stop Crying/New Pony	1978	—	2.50	5.00
❑ 10851	Changing of the Guards/Senor (Tales of Yankee Power)	1978	—	2.00	4.00
❑ 11072	Gotta Serve Somebody/Trouble in Mind	1979	—	2.00	4.00
❑ 11168	Man Gave Names to All the Animals/When You Gonna Wake Up	1979	—	2.00	4.00
❑ 11235	Slow Train/Do Right to Me Baby (Do Unto Others)	1980	—	2.00	4.00
❑ 11235 [PS]	Slow Train/Do Right to Me Baby (Do Unto Others)	1980	—	2.50	5.00
❑ 11318	Solid Rock/Covenant Woman	1980	—	2.00	4.00
❑ 11370	Saved/Are You Ready	1980	6.25	12.50	25.00
—Scarce on stock copy (promos worth about 20%)					
❑ 42656	Mixed-Up Confusion/Corrina, Corrina	1962	500.00	1000.	1500.
—Orange label					
❑ 42656 [DJ]	Mixed-Up Confusion/Corrina, Corrina	1962	125.00	250.00	500.00
—White label					
❑ 42856	Blowin' in the Wind/Don't Think Twice, It's All Right	1963	125.00	250.00	500.00
❑ 42856 [DJ]	Blowin' in the Wind/Don't Think Twice, It's All Right	1963	75.00	150.00	300.00
—Regular promo					
❑ 42856 [PS]	Blowin' in the Wind/Don't Think Twice, It's All Right	1963	200.00	400.00	800.00
—"Rebel with a Cause" promotional flyer					
❑ 43242	Subterranean Homesick Blues/She Belongs to Me	1965	5.00	10.00	20.00
❑ 43242	Subterranean Homesick Blues/She Belongs to Me	1972	7.50	15.00	30.00
—Briefly issued on gray label, which was used for about six months in 1972					
❑ 43242 [DJ]	Subterranean Homesick Blues (same on both sides)	1965	62.50	125.00	250.00
—Promo only on red vinyl					
❑ 43242 [PS]	Subterranean Homesick Blues/She Belongs to Me	1965	500.00	1000.	1500.
—Only issued with some promos					
❑ 43346	Like a Rolling Stone/Gates of Eden	1965	5.00	10.00	20.00
❑ 43346 [DJ]	Like a Rolling Stone (same on both sides)	1965	50.00	100.00	200.00
—Promo only on red vinyl					
❑ 43389	Positively 4th Street/From a Buick 6	1965	5.00	10.00	20.00
—Standard version					
❑ 43389	Positively 4th Street/From a Buick 6	1965	37.50	75.00	150.00
—A-side contains alternate version of "Can You Please Crawl Out Your Window." Evidently must be heard to identify.					
❑ 43389	Positively 4th Street/From a Buick 6	1965	7.50	15.00	30.00
—Odd version, possibly pressed for export, that plays at 45 but has a small center hole					
❑ 43389	Positively 4th Street/From a Buick 6	1972	6.25	12.50	25.00
—Briefly issued on gray label, which was used for about six months in 1972					
❑ 43389 [DJ]	Positively 4th Street/From a Buick 6	1965	30.00	60.00	120.00
—A-side contains alternate version of "Can You Please Crawl Out Your Window." Evidently must be heard to identify.					
❑ 43389 [DJ]	Positively 4th Street (same on both sides)	1965	37.50	75.00	150.00
—Promo only on red vinyl					
❑ 43389 [PS]	Positively 4th Street/From a Buick 6	1965	17.50	35.00	70.00
❑ 43477	Can You Please Crawl Out Your Window?/Highway 61 Revisited	1965	5.00	10.00	20.00
❑ 43541	Queen Jane Approximately/One of Us Must Know (Sooner or Later)	1966	5.00	10.00	20.00
❑ 43592	Rainy Day Women #12 and 35/Pledging My Time	1966	3.75	7.50	15.00
❑ 43592 [DJ]	Rainy Day Women #12 and 35 (same on both sides)	1966	37.50	75.00	150.00
—Promo only on red vinyl					
❑ 43683	I Want You/Just Like Tom Thumb's Blues (Live)	1966	3.75	7.50	15.00
❑ 43683 [DJ]	I Want You (same on both sides)	1966	37.50	75.00	150.00
—Promo only on red vinyl					
❑ 43683 [PS]	I Want You/Just Like Tom Thumb's Blues (Live)	1966	20.00	40.00	80.00
❑ 43792	Just Like a Woman/Obviously 5 Believers	1966	3.75	7.50	15.00
❑ 44069	Leopard-Skin Pill-Box Hat/Most Likely You'll Go Your Way and I'll Go Mine	1967	5.00	10.00	20.00
❑ 44826	I Threw It All Away/Drifter's Escape	1969	2.00	4.00	8.00
❑ 44926	Lay Lady Lay/Peggy Day	1969	2.00	4.00	8.00
❑ 45004	Tonight I'll Be Staying Here with You/Country Pie	1969	2.50	5.00	10.00
❑ 45199	Wigwam/Copper Kettle (The Pale Moonlight)	1970	—	3.00	6.00
—Red label, black print					
❑ 45199	Wigwam/Copper Kettle (The Pale Moonlight)	1970	—	3.00	6.00
—Red label, "Columbia" repeated around outside of label					
❑ 45199	Wigwam/Copper Kettle (The Pale Moonlight)	1970	—	3.00	6.00
—Orange label with "Columbia" background print					
❑ 45409	Watching the River Flow/Spanish Is the Loving Tongue	1971	—	3.00	6.00
❑ 45516	George Jackson (Acoustic Version)/George Jackson (Big Band Version)	1971	2.50	5.00	10.00
❑ 45913	Knockin' on Heaven's Door/Turkey Chase	1973	—	2.50	5.00
❑ 45982	A Fool Such As I/Lily of the West	1973	—	3.00	6.00
❑ 73042	Everything Is Broken/Dead Man, Dead Man	1989	2.00	4.00	8.00
❑ JZSP 75606/7 [DJ]	Blowin' in the Wind/Don't Think Twice, It's All Right	1963	75.00	150.00	300.00
—"Special Album Excerpt" promo					
❑ JZSP 110939/40 [DJ]	Like a Rolling Stone (Part 1)/Like a Rolling Stone (Part 2)	1965	15.00	30.00	60.00
❑ JZSP 113096/147 [DJ]	One Of Us Must Know (Sooner or Later) (4:49)/(3:07)	1966	25.00	50.00	100.00
—Promo only, long and short versions					

Number	Title (A Side/B Side)	Yr	VG	VG+	NM
MCA					
❑ 52811	Band of the Hand/Theme from Joe's Death	1986	—	—	3.00
—By "Bob Dylan and the Heartbreakers"					
❑ 52811 [PS]	Band of the Hand/Theme from Joe's Death	1986	—	—	3.00

DYNA-SORES, THE

Number	Title (A Side/B Side)	Yr	VG	VG+	NM
RENDEZVOUS					
❑ 120	Alley-Oop/Jungle Walk	1960	6.25	12.50	25.00

DYNAMICS, THE (1)

Detroit R&B group with several charted hits.

Number	Title (A Side/B Side)	Yr	VG	VG+	NM
BIG TOP					
❑ 516	And That's a Natural Fact/I Wanna Know	1964	3.75	7.50	15.00
❑ 3161	Misery/I'm the Man	1963	3.75	7.50	15.00
BLACK GOLD					
❑ 8	What a Shame/Shucks, I Love You	1973	—	3.00	6.00
❑ 9	Funkey Key/Count Your Chips	1973	—	3.00	6.00
❑ 11	She's for Real (Bless You)/(B-side unknown)	1974	—	3.00	6.00
COTILLION					
❑ 44004	Ain't No Sun/Murder in the First Degree	1968	2.50	5.00	10.00
❑ 44021	Ice Cream Song/The Love That I Need	1969	2.50	5.00	10.00
❑ 44038	What Would I Do/Ain't No Love at All	1969	2.50	5.00	10.00
❑ 44045	Dum-De-Dum/I Want to Thank You	1969	2.50	5.00	10.00

DYNAMICS, THE (2)

Mostly an instrumental group.

Number	Title (A Side/B Side)	Yr	VG	VG+	NM
BOLO					
❑ 730	At the Mardi Gras/J.A.J.	1962	2.50	5.00	10.00
❑ 735	Wild Child/Spongy	1962	2.50	5.00	10.00
❑ 740	Tennessee Boy/Tough Talk	1963	2.50	5.00	10.00
❑ 751	Knee Poppin'/Who's Afraid of Virginia Woolf?	1964	2.50	5.00	10.00
GUARANTEED					
❑ 201	Aces Up/Baby	1959	5.00	10.00	20.00
PENGUIN					
❑ 1006	Aces Up/Baby	1959	12.50	25.00	50.00
SEAFAIR					
❑ 100	Onion Salad/Lonesome Llama	1960	5.00	10.00	20.00
❑ 107	At the Mardi Gras/J.A.J.	1961	5.00	10.00	20.00

DYNAMICS, THE (3)

Early version of ANTHONY AND THE SOPHOMORES.

Number	Title (A Side/B Side)	Yr	VG	VG+	NM
HERALD					
❑ 569	Forever/Betty My Own	1962	125.00	250.00	500.00

DYNAMICS, THE (4)

Band from Chicago (probably).

Number	Title (A Side/B Side)	Yr	VG	VG+	NM
U.S.A.					
❑ 769	Summertime in the U.S.A./Coast to Coast	1964	6.25	12.50	25.00

DYNAMICS, THE (U)

Some of these may be groups (1) or (2). We're pretty sure that none of these are groups (3), (4) or (5). It's possible that five more groups, if not more, are represented below. Any help in grouping these correctly will be appreciated.

Number	Title (A Side/B Side)	Yr	VG	VG+	NM
ARC					
❑ 4450	Enchanted Love/Happiness and Love	1959	10.00	20.00	40.00
CAPRI					
❑ 104	No One but You/Always, I Have Loved You	1959	100.00	200.00	400.00
CINDY					
❑ 3005	When the Saints Come Marching In/Gone Is My Love	1957	20.00	40.00	80.00
COLUMBIA					
❑ 3-10666	We Found Love/You Can Make It If You Try	1978	—	2.50	5.00
DECCA					
❑ 31046	How Should I Feel/Seems Like Only Yesterday	1960	7.50	15.00	30.00
❑ 31129	At the End of Each Day/Girl by the Gate	1960	7.50	15.00	30.00
❑ 31450	How Should I Feel/Seems Like Only Yesterday	1962	3.75	7.50	15.00
DELTA					
❑ 1002	Blue Moon/Pigeon-Toed	1959	7.50	15.00	30.00
DO-KAY-LO					
❑ 101	I Guess You Don't Love Me (No More)/Oh Night of Nights	1963	7.50	15.00	30.00
DOUGLAS					
❑ 200	I Love to Be Loved/You Don't Seem to Realize	1961	7.50	15.00	30.00
DYNAMIC					
❑ 109	Don't Be Late/Eenie Meenie	1959	10.00	20.00	40.00
❑ 504	The Girl I Met Last Night/Nobody's Going Out with Me	1959	10.00	20.00	40.00
❑ 578/9	Christmas Plea/Dream Girl	1962	17.50	35.00	70.00
❑ 1001	Don't Leave Me/Wasted	1959	12.50	25.00	50.00
❑ 1002	So Fine/Delsinia	1963	10.00	20.00	40.00
❑ 1008	If She Should Call/Dream Girl	1961	10.00	20.00	40.00
FARRALL					
❑ 964	Later On/Departure	196?	7.50	15.00	30.00
IMPALA					
❑ 501	Moonlight/Someone	1959	30.00	60.00	120.00
JERDEN					
❑ 800	I'll Be Standing There/All She Said	1966	2.50	5.00	10.00
LAVERE					
❑ 186	Wrap Your Troubles in Dreams/I Can't Give You Anything But Love	1961	6.25	12.50	25.00
LIBAN					
❑ 1006	If I Give My Heart to You/Blind Date	1962	20.00	40.00	80.00
LIBERTY					
❑ 55628	Chapel on a Hill/Conquistador	1963	10.00	20.00	40.00
PANORAMA					
❑ 51	Stop and Take a Look Around/(B-side unknown)	1967	2.50	5.00	10.00
RCA VICTOR					
❑ 47-9084	Love Me/I Need Your Love	1967	10.00	20.00	40.00
❑ 47-9278	Lights Out/You Make Me Feel So Good	1967	15.00	30.00	60.00
—As "Zerben R. Hicks and the Dynamics"					
REPRISE					
❑ 20183	So Fine/Delsinia	1963	3.75	7.50	15.00
SEECO					
❑ 6008	Moonlight/Someone	1959	10.00	20.00	40.00
TOP TEN					
❑ 100	Yes I Love You Baby/Soul Sloopy	1965	20.00	40.00	80.00
❑ 927	Love to a Guy/Whenever I'm Without You	196?	15.00	30.00	60.00
WARNER					
❑ 1016	A Hundred Million Les/Ka Joom	1957	20.00	40.00	80.00

DYNAMO, SKINNY

Number	Title (A Side/B Side)	Yr	VG	VG+	NM
EXCELLO					
❑ 2097	So Long, So Long/Jingle Bell	1956	7.50	15.00	30.00

DYNATONES, THE

Number	Title (A Side/B Side)	Yr	VG	VG+	NM
HANNA-BARBERA					
❑ 494	The Fife Piper/And I Always Will	1966	2.50	5.00	10.00
ST. CLAIR					
❑ 117	The Fife Piper/And I Always Will	1966	7.50	5.00	30.00

E

E-TYPES, THE

Number	Title (A Side/B Side)	Yr	VG	VG+	NM
DOT					
❑ 16864	I Can't Do It/Long Before	1966	3.00	6.00	12.00
LINK					
❑ 1	I Can't Do It/Long Before	1966	7.50	15.00	30.00
❑ 1 [PS]	I Can't Do It/Long Before	1966	7.50	15.00	30.00
SUNBURST					
❑ 001	Love of the Loved/She Moves Me	1966	6.25	12.50	25.00
TOWER					
❑ 325	Put the Clock Back On the Wall/14th Street	1967	6.25	12.50	25.00
UPTOWN					
❑ 754	Big City/Back to Me	1967	6.25	12.50	25.00

EADY, ERNESTINE

Number	Title (A Side/B Side)	Yr	VG	VG+	NM
JUNIOR					
❑ 1007	The Change/That's the Way It Goes	1963	7.50	15.00	30.00
SCEPTER					
❑ 12102	The Change/That's the Way It Goes	1965	3.00	6.00	12.00

EAGER, BRENDA LEE

Also see JERRY BUTLER.

Number	Title (A Side/B Side)	Yr	VG	VG+	NM
MERCURY					
❑ 73292	I'm a Lonely Woman/In My World	1972	—	3.00	6.00
❑ 73450	Let Me Be/When I'm With You	1974	—	2.50	5.00
❑ 73607	Ah, Sweet Mystery of Life/There Ain't No Way	1974	—	2.50	5.00
❑ 73627	You Gave Me Everything/When I'm With You	1974	—	2.50	5.00
PLAYBOY					
❑ 6047	Good Old Fashioned Lovin'/I'll Get By	1975	—	2.50	5.00
PRIVATE I					
❑ 04621	Watch My Body Talk/(Instrumental)	1984	—	2.00	4.00

EAGER, JIMMY

Number	Title (A Side/B Side)	Yr	VG	VG+	NM
SABRE					
❑ 100	Please Mr. Doctor/I Should Have Loved Her More	1953	50.00	100.00	200.00

EAGER, VINCE

Number	Title (A Side/B Side)	Yr	VG	VG+	NM
LONDON INT'L.					
❑ 10527	It's Only Make Believe/I Shall Not Be Moved	1964	3.00	6.00	12.00

EAGLES

Also see DON FELDER; GLENN FREY; DON HENLEY; RANDY MEISNER; TIMOTHY B. SCHMIT; JOE WALSH.

Number	Title (A Side/B Side)	Yr	VG	VG+	NM
ASYLUM					
❑ 11005	Take It Easy/Get You in the Mood	1972	—	2.50	5.00
❑ 11008	Witchy Woman/Early Bird	1972	—	2.00	4.00
❑ 11013	Peaceful Easy Feeling/Trying	1973	—	2.00	4.00
❑ 11013	Tequila Sunrise/21	1973	—	2.00	4.00
❑ 11025	Outlaw Man/Certain Kind of Fool	1973	—	2.00	4.00
❑ 11036	Already Gone/Is It True	1974	—	2.00	4.00
❑ 45202	James Dean/Good Day in Hell	1974	—	2.00	4.00
❑ 45218	Best of My Love/Ol' 55	1974	—	2.00	4.00
❑ 45257	One of These Nights/Visions	1975	—	2.00	4.00
❑ 45279	Lyin' Eyes/Too Many People	1975	—	2.00	4.00
❑ 45293	Take It to the Limit/After the Thrill Is Gone	1975	—	2.00	4.00
❑ 45373	New Kid in Town/Victim of Love	1976	—	2.00	4.00
❑ 45386	Hotel California/Pretty Maids All in a Row	1977	—	2.00	4.00
❑ 45403	Life in the Fast Lane/The Last Resort	1977	—	2.00	4.00
❑ 45555	Please Come Home for Christmas/Funky New Year	1978	—	2.00	4.00
—Original with "clouds" label					
❑ 45555	Please Come Home for Christmas/Funky New Year	1984	—	—	3.00
—Reissue with black and yellow label					
❑ 45555 [PS]	Please Come Home for Christmas/Funky New Year	1978	—	2.00	4.00
—Sleeve was available with both original and reissue					
❑ 46545	Heartache Tonight/Teenage Jail	1979	—	2.00	4.00
❑ 46569	The Long Run/The Disco Strangler	1979	—	2.00	4.00
❑ 46608	I Can't Tell You Why/The Greeks Don't Want No Freaks	1980	—	2.00	4.00
❑ 47100	Seven Bridges Road/The Long Run	1980	—	2.00	4.00
FULL MOON					
❑ 49654	I Can't Tell You Why/Outside	1981	—	2.50	5.00
—B-side by Ambrosia					
FULL MOON/ASYLUM					
❑ 47004	Lyin' Eyes/Looking for Love	1980	—	2.00	4.00
—B-side by Johnny Lee; contains the full-length version of "Lyin' Eyes"					

Number	Title (A Side/B Side)	Yr	VG	VG+	NM
❑ 47004 [PS]	Lyin' Eyes/Looking for Love	1980	—	2.50	5.00
❑ 47073	Lyin' Eyes/Hello Texas	1980	—	2.50	5.00

—B-side by Jimmy Buffett

GEFFEN

Number	Title (A Side/B Side)	Yr	VG	VG+	NM
❑ 19376	Get Over It/Get Over It (Live)	1994	—	2.50	5.00

EAGLES, THE (2)

MERCURY

Number	Title (A Side/B Side)	Yr	VG	VG+	NM
❑ 70391	Tryin' to Get to You/Please, Please	1954	7.50	15.00	30.00
❑ 70464	Such a Fool/Don't You Wanna Be Mine	1954	7.50	15.00	30.00
❑ 70524	I Told Myself/What a Crazy Feeling	1955	7.50	15.00	30.00

EAGLES, THE (3)

British group.

SMASH

Number	Title (A Side/B Side)	Yr	VG	VG+	NM
❑ 1837	Christine/Stalactite	1963	3.00	6.00	12.00

EAGLES, THE (U)

The record on Prep may be group (2); the record on Warner Bros. may be group (3). Then again, maybe not.

PREP

Number	Title (A Side/B Side)	Yr	VG	VG+	NM
❑ 18	Kiss Them for Me/Ladies in the Sky	1957	5.00	10.00	20.00

WARNER BROS.

Number	Title (A Side/B Side)	Yr	VG	VG+	NM
❑ 5654	Ballad to a Lady/Eagle	1965	3.00	6.00	12.00

EARL-JEAN

COLPIX

Number	Title (A Side/B Side)	Yr	VG	VG+	NM
❑ 729	I'm Into Somethin' Good/We Love and Learn	1964	3.00	6.00	12.00
❑ 748	Randy/They're Jealous of Me	1964	2.50	5.00	10.00

EARLS, JACK, AND THE JIMBOS

SUN

Number	Title (A Side/B Side)	Yr	VG	VG+	NM
❑ 240	Slow Down/A Fool for Loving You	1956	15.00	30.00	60.00

EARLS, THE (1)

All of the below are by the same group or closely related.

ABC

Number	Title (A Side/B Side)	Yr	VG	VG+	NM
❑ 11109	It's Been a Long Time Coming/My Lonely, Lonely Room	1968	3.75	7.50	15.00

BARRY

Number	Title (A Side/B Side)	Yr	VG	VG+	NM
❑ 1021	I Believe/Don't Forget	1963	10.00	20.00	40.00

CLIFTON

Number	Title (A Side/B Side)	Yr	VG	VG+	NM
❑ 39	Lookin' for My Baby/Cross My Heart	1974	—	2.50	5.00
❑ 43	Lost Love/My Heart's Desire	1974	—	2.50	5.00
❑ 47	Dreams Come True/My Heart's Desire	1974	—	2.50	5.00

COLUMBIA

Number	Title (A Side/B Side)	Yr	VG	VG+	NM
❑ 3-10225	Goin' Uptown/Mrs. Woman	1975	2.00	4.00	8.00

GONE

Number	Title (A Side/B Side)	Yr	VG	VG+	NM
❑ 5117	I'll Never Cry/My Heart's Desire	1961	15.00	30.00	60.00

HARVEY

Number	Title (A Side/B Side)	Yr	VG	VG+	NM
❑ 100	A Sunday Kind of Love/Teenage Dreams	1975	2.00	4.00	8.00

MR. G

Number	Title (A Side/B Side)	Yr	VG	VG+	NM
❑ 801	If I Could Do It Over Again/Papa	1967	3.75	7.50	15.00

OLD TOWN

Number	Title (A Side/B Side)	Yr	VG	VG+	NM
❑ 1130	Remember Then/Let's Waddle	1963	12.50	25.00	50.00
—Blue label					
❑ 1130	Remember Then/Let's Waddle	1963	6.25	12.50	25.00
—Mostly black label with moon					
❑ 1133	Never/I Keep a-Telling You	1963	10.00	20.00	40.00
—Blue label					
❑ 1133	Never/I Keep a-Telling You	1963	5.00	10.00	20.00
—Mostly black label with moon					
❑ 1141	Eyes/Look My Way	1963	5.00	10.00	20.00
❑ 1145	Cry, Cry, Cry/Kissin'	1963	5.00	10.00	20.00
❑ 1149	I Believe/Don't Forget	1963	10.00	20.00	40.00
—Blue label					
❑ 1149	I Believe/Don't Forget	1963	5.00	10.00	20.00
—Mostly black label with moon					
❑ 1169	Oh What a Time/Ask Anybody	1964	7.50	15.00	30.00
❑ 1181 [DJ]	Remember Me Baby/Amor	1965	12.50	25.00	50.00
—Assigned 1181 in error, as another record had been released with the number					
❑ 1182	Remember Me Baby/Amor	1965	5.00	10.00	20.00
—Error was corrected on stock copies					

POWER MARTIN

Number	Title (A Side/B Side)	Yr	VG	VG+	NM
❑ 1005	Stormy Weather/Could This Be Magic	1975	—	2.50	5.00

—B-side by the Pretenders

ROME

Number	Title (A Side/B Side)	Yr	VG	VG+	NM
❑ 101	Life Is But a Dream/It's You	1961	30.00	60.00	120.00
❑ 101	Life Is But a Dream/Without You	1961	10.00	20.00	40.00
❑ 102	Lookin' for My Baby/Cross My Heart	1961	10.00	20.00	40.00
❑ 111	Stormy Weather/Could This Be Magic	1976	—	2.50	5.00
—B-side by the Pretenders					
❑ 112/3	Little Boy and Girl/Lost Love	1976	—	2.00	4.00
❑ 114/5	All Through Our Teens/Whoever You Are	1976	2.00	4.00	8.00
—Black vinyl					
❑ 114/5	All Through Our Teens/Whoever You Are	1976	3.00	6.00	12.00
—Colored vinyl					

WOODBURY

Number	Title (A Side/B Side)	Yr	VG	VG+	NM
❑ 101	Tonight (Could Be the Night)/Meditation	1977	2.00	4.00	8.00

EARLS, THE (2)

GEM

Number	Title (A Side/B Side)	Yr	VG	VG+	NM
❑ 221	Believe Me My Love/Spinnin'	1954	100.00	200.00	400.00
❑ 227	My Marie/Out of This World	197?	2.00	4.00	8.00

—There are differences of opinion on this record. Some claim that it was released in 1954 not long after Gem 221; others claim that it's a 1970s reproduction on a number that Gem never used. As no 78s are known to exist of this title, we lean toward the latter, but would appreciate positive evidence one way or the other.

EARLY, SAM

APT

Number	Title (A Side/B Side)	Yr	VG	VG+	NM
❑ 25041	Do You Love Me/You Are the Greatest of Them All	1960	6.25	12.50	25.00

EARTH AND FIRE

Produced by members of GOLDEN EARRING.

ATCO

Number	Title (A Side/B Side)	Yr	VG	VG+	NM
❑ 6744	Seasons/Hazy Paradise	1970	2.50	5.00	10.00

EARTH QUAKE

A&M

Number	Title (A Side/B Side)	Yr	VG	VG+	NM
❑ 1301	Tickler/Guarding You	1971	2.00	4.00	8.00
❑ 1338	I Get the Sweetest Feeling/Live and Let Live	1972	2.00	4.00	8.00
❑ 1365	Bright Lights/Live and Let Live	1972	2.00	4.00	8.00

BESERKLEY

Number	Title (A Side/B Side)	Yr	VG	VG+	NM
❑ 5701	Friday on My Mind/Roadrunner	1975	2.50	5.00	10.00
—B-side by Jonathan Richman and the Modern Lovers					
❑ 5701 [PS]	Friday on My Mind/Roadrunner	1975	2.50	5.00	10.00
❑ 5734/5	Mr. Security/Madness	1975	—	2.50	5.00
❑ 5736/7	Friday on My Mind/Tall Order for a Short Guy	1975	—	2.50	5.00
❑ 5742	Hit the Floor/Don't Want to Go Back	1976	—	2.50	5.00
❑ 5747	Kicks/Trainride	1977	—	2.50	5.00

EARTH, WIND, AND FIRE

Also see WADE FLEMONS.

ARC

Number	Title (A Side/B Side)	Yr	VG	VG+	NM
❑ 02536	Let's Groove/(Instrumental)	1981	—	2.00	4.00
❑ 02688	Wanna Be with You/Kalimba Tree	1982	—	2.00	4.00
❑ 10854	September/Love's Holiday	1978	—	2.50	5.00
❑ 11033	After the Love Has Gone/Rock That!	1979	—	2.50	5.00
❑ 11093	In the Stone/You and I	1979	—	2.00	4.00
❑ 11165	Star/You and I	1979	—	2.00	4.00
❑ 11366	Let Me Talk/(Instrumental)	1980	—	2.00	4.00
❑ 11366 [PS]	Let Me Talk/(Instrumental)	1980	—	2.50	5.00
❑ 11407	You/Share Your Love	1980	—	2.00	4.00
❑ 11434	And Love Goes On/Win or Lose	1981	—	2.00	4.00

COLUMBIA

Number	Title (A Side/B Side)	Yr	VG	VG+	NM
❑ 13-03136	Let's Groove/Sing a Song	1982	—	—	3.00
—Reissue					
❑ 38-03375	Fall in Love with Me/(Instrumental)	1982	—	2.00	4.00
❑ 38-03375 [PS]	Fall in Love with Me/(Instrumental)	1982	—	2.00	4.00
❑ CNR-03566	Fall in Love with Me	1983	—	3.00	6.00
—One-sided budget release					
❑ 38-03814	Side by Side/Something Special	1983	—	2.00	4.00
❑ 38-04002	Spread Your Love/Freedom of Choice	1983	—	2.00	4.00
❑ 38-04210	Magnetic/Speed of Love	1983	—	2.00	4.00
❑ 38-04210 [PS]	Magnetic/Speed of Love	1983	—	2.00	4.00
❑ 38-04329	Touch/Sweet Sassy Lady	1984	—	2.00	4.00
❑ 38-04329 [PS]	Touch/Sweet Sassy Lady	1984	—	2.00	4.00
❑ 38-04427	Moonwalk/We're Living in Our Own Time	1984	—	2.00	4.00
❑ 38-07608	System of Survival/Writing on the Wall	1987	—	—	3.00
❑ 38-07608 [PS]	System of Survival/Writing on the Wall	1987	—	—	3.00
❑ 38-07678	You and I/Musical Interlude: New Horizons	1988	—	—	3.00
❑ 38-07687	Evil Roy/(Instrumental)	1988	—	—	3.00
❑ 38-07695	Thinking of You/Money Tight	1988	—	—	3.00
❑ 38-07695 [PS]	Thinking of You/Money Tight	1988	—	—	3.00
❑ 38-08107	Turn On (The Beat Box)/(Instrumental)	1988	—	—	3.00
❑ 3-10026	Devotion/Fair But So Uncool	1974	—	3.00	6.00
❑ 3-10056	Hot Dawgit/R.L. Tambura	1974	—	2.50	5.00
—With Ramsey Lewis					
❑ 3-10090	Shining Star/Yearnin', Learnin'	1975	—	2.50	5.00
❑ 3-10090 [PS]	Shining Star/Yearnin', Learnin'	1975	2.50	5.00	10.00
❑ 3-10103	Sun Goddess/Jungle Strut	1975	—	2.50	5.00
—With Ramsey Lewis					
❑ 3-10172	That's the Way of the World/Africano	1975	—	2.50	5.00
❑ 3-10251	Singasong/(Instrumental)	1975	—	3.00	6.00
—Original pressings have title as one word					
❑ 3-10251	Sing a Song/(Instrumental)	1975	—	2.50	5.00
—Later pressings have title as three words					
❑ 3-10309	Can't Hide Love/Gratitude	1976	—	2.50	5.00
❑ 3-10373	Getaway/(Instrumental)	1976	—	2.50	5.00
❑ 3-10373 [PS]	Getaway/(Instrumental)	1976	2.50	5.00	10.00
❑ 3-10439	Saturday Nite/Departure	1976	—	2.50	5.00
❑ 3-10492	On Your Face/Biyo	1977	—	2.50	5.00
❑ 3-10625	Serpentine Fire/(Instrumental)	1977	—	2.50	5.00
❑ 3-10688	Fantasy/Runnin'	1978	—	2.50	5.00
❑ 3-10796	Got to Get You Into My Life/I'll Write a Song for You	1978	—	2.50	5.00
❑ 4-45747	Power/M-O-M	1972	—	3.00	6.00
❑ 4-45800	Tims Is On Your Side/Where Have All the Flowers Gone	1973	—	3.00	6.00
❑ 4-45888	Evil/Clover	1973	—	2.50	5.00
❑ 4-45888 [PS]	Evil/Clover	1973	2.50	5.00	10.00
❑ 4-45953	Keep Your Head to the Sky/Build Your Nest	1973	—	2.50	5.00
❑ 4-46007	Mighty Mighty/Drum Song	1974	—	2.50	5.00
❑ 4-46007 [PS]	Mighty Mighty/Drum Song	1974	2.50	5.00	10.00
❑ 4-46070	Kalimba Story/Tee Nine Chee Bit	1974	—	2.50	5.00
❑ 73205	Heritage/Gotta Find Out	1990	—	2.50	5.00

WARNER BROS.

Number	Title (A Side/B Side)	Yr	VG	VG+	NM
❑ 7480	Fan the Fire/This World Today	1971	—	3.00	6.00
❑ 7492	Love Is Life/This World Today	1971	—	3.00	6.00
❑ 7549	I Think About Lovin' You/C'mon Children	1972	—	3.00	6.00

EARTH, WIND, AND FIRE WITH THE EMOTIONS

ARC

Number	Title (A Side/B Side)	Yr	VG	VG+	NM
❑ 10956	Boogie Wonderland/(Instrumental)	1979	—	2.50	5.00

EASTWOOD, CLINT

CAMEO

Number	Title (A Side/B Side)	Yr	VG	VG+	NM
❑ 240	Rowdy/Cowboy Wedding Song	1963	5.00	10.00	20.00
❑ 240 [PS]	Rowdy/Cowboy Wedding Song	1963	12.50	25.00	50.00

CERTRON

Number	Title (A Side/B Side)	Yr	VG	VG+	NM
❑ 10010	Burning Bridges/When I Loved Her	1970	2.50	5.00	10.00
❑ 10010 [PS]	Burning Bridges/When I Loved Her	1970	6.25	12.50	25.00

GNP CRESCENDO

Number	Title (A Side/B Side)	Yr	VG	VG+	NM
❑ 177	Get Yourself Another Fool/For You, For Me, Forevermore	1962	10.00	20.00	40.00
❑ 177 [PS]	Get Yourself Another Fool/For You, For Me, Forevermore	1962	25.00	50.00	100.00

GOTHIC

Number	Title (A Side/B Side)	Yr	VG	VG+	NM
❑ 005	Unknown Girl of My Dreams/For All We Know	1961	6.25	12.50	25.00
❑ 005 [PS]	Unknown Girl of My Dreams/For All We Know	1961	12.50	25.00	50.00

PARAMOUNT

Number	Title (A Side/B Side)	Yr	VG	VG+	NM
❑ 0010	Best Things/Wand'rin' Star	1969	3.00	6.00	12.00

—B-side by Lee Marvin

WARNER BROS.

Number	Title (A Side/B Side)	Yr	VG	VG+	NM
❑ 49760	Cowboy in a Three-Piece Business Suit/Dark Blue Feeling	1981	—	2.50	5.00

EASYBEATS, THE

ASCOT

Number	Title (A Side/B Side)	Yr	VG	VG+	NM
❑ 2214	In My Book/Make You Feel Alright (Women)	1966	3.75	7.50	15.00
❑ 2214 [PS]	In My Book/Make You Feel Alright (Women)	1966	10.00	20.00	40.00

RARE EARTH

Number	Title (A Side/B Side)	Yr	VG	VG+	NM
❑ 5009	St. Louis/Can't Find Love	1969	3.75	7.50	15.00

UNITED ARTISTS

Number	Title (A Side/B Side)	Yr	VG	VG+	NM
❑ 0114	Friday on My Mind/Gonna Have a Good Time	1973	—	2.00	4.00
—"Silver Spotlight Series" reissue					
❑ 50106	Friday on My Mind/Made My Bed; Gonna Lie in It	1966	3.75	7.50	15.00
❑ 50187	Pretty Girl/Heaven and Hell	1967	2.50	5.00	10.00
❑ 50206	Falling Off the Edge of the World/Remember Sam	1967	2.50	5.00	10.00
❑ 50289	Come In, You'll Get Pneumonia/Hello, How Are You	1968	2.50	5.00	10.00
❑ 50488	Gonna Have a Good Time/Lay Me Down and Die	1969	2.50	5.00	10.00

EBB TIDES, THE

See NINO AND THE EBB TIDES.

EBBTIDES, THE

May be four different groups!

DUANE

Number	Title (A Side/B Side)	Yr	VG	VG+	NM
❑ 1022	Star of Love/First Love	1964	2000.	3000.	4000.

JAN-LAR

Number	Title (A Side/B Side)	Yr	VG	VG+	NM
❑ 101	Love Doctor/Lonesome	1959	75.00	150.00	300.00

MONUMENTAL

Number	Title (A Side/B Side)	Yr	VG	VG+	NM
❑ 520	Come On and Cry/Straightaway	1960	10.00	20.00	40.00

TEEN

Number	Title (A Side/B Side)	Yr	VG	VG+	NM
❑ 121	What Is Your Name Dear/Only Be Mine	1957	2000.	3000.	4000.

EBBTONES, THE

EBB

Number	Title (A Side/B Side)	Yr	VG	VG+	NM
❑ 100	I've Got a Feeling/Danny's Blues	1957	37.50	75.00	150.00

PORT

Number	Title (A Side/B Side)	Yr	VG	VG+	NM
❑ 70026	Rockin' on the Range/Ram Induction	1961	6.25	12.50	25.00

EBON-KNIGHTS, THE

STEPHENY

Number	Title (A Side/B Side)	Yr	VG	VG+	NM
❑ 1817	Poor Butterfly/The Way the Ball Bounces	1958	6.25	12.50	25.00
❑ 1822	First Date/Only Only You	1958	6.25	12.50	25.00

EBONAIRES, THE

ALADDIN

Number	Title (A Side/B Side)	Yr	VG	VG+	NM
❑ 3211	3 O'Clock in the Morning/Baby, You're the One	1953	125.00	250.00	500.00
❑ 3212	You're Nobody 'Til Somebody Loves You/Lawd, Lawd, Lawd	1954	125.00	250.00	500.00

COLONIAL

Number	Title (A Side/B Side)	Yr	VG	VG+	NM
❑ 117	We're in Love/Thinkin' and Thinkin'	1959	30.00	60.00	120.00

HOLLYWOOD

Number	Title (A Side/B Side)	Yr	VG	VG+	NM
❑ 1046	Love For Christmas/Jingle Bell Hop	1955	100.00	200.00	400.00
❑ 1062	Let's Kiss and Say Hello Again/Jivarama Hop	1956	100.00	200.00	400.00

LENA

Number	Title (A Side/B Side)	Yr	VG	VG+	NM
❑ 101	Love Call/Somewhere in My Heart	1959	50.00	100.00	200.00

MONEY

Number	Title (A Side/B Side)	Yr	VG	VG+	NM
❑ 220	The Very Best Luck in the World/Hey Baby Stop	1956	20.00	40.00	80.00

EBONYS, THE

BUDDAH

Number	Title (A Side/B Side)	Yr	VG	VG+	NM
❑ 537	Makin' Love Ain't No Fun (Without the One You Love) Part 1/Part 2	1976	—	3.00	6.00

PHILADELPHIA INT'L.

Number	Title (A Side/B Side)	Yr	VG	VG+	NM
❑ 3503	You're the Reason Why/Sexy Ways	1971	2.00	4.00	8.00
❑ 3510	Determination/Do It	1971	2.00	4.00	8.00
❑ 3513 [DJ]	(Christmas Ain't Christmas, New Year's Ain't New Year's) Without The One You Love (mono/stereo)	1971	2.00	4.00	8.00
❑ 3514	Do You Like the Way I Love/I'm So Glad I'm Me	1972	2.00	4.00	8.00
❑ 3529	It's Forever/Sexy Ways	1973	—	3.50	7.00
❑ 3541	I Believe/Nation Time	1974	—	3.50	7.00
❑ 3548	Life in the Country/Hook Up and Get Down	1974	—	3.50	7.00

SOUL CLOCK

Number	Title (A Side/B Side)	Yr	VG	VG+	NM
❑ 108	Don't Knock Me/Can't Get Enough	1969	3.75	7.50	15.00

ECHO VALLEY BOYS, THE

ISLAND

Number	Title (A Side/B Side)	Yr	VG	VG+	NM
❑ 1/2	Ramblin' Man/Wash Machine Boogie	195?	75.00	150.00	300.00

ECHOES, THE (1)

SEG-WAY

Number	Title (A Side/B Side)	Yr	VG	VG+	NM
❑ 103	Baby Blue/Boomerang	1961	6.25	12.50	25.00
❑ 106	Sad Eyes (Don't You Cry)/It's Raining	1961	6.25	12.50	25.00
❑ 1002	Angel of My Heart/Gee Oh Gee	1962	10.00	20.00	40.00

SMASH

Number	Title (A Side/B Side)	Yr	VG	VG+	NM
❑ 1766	Bluebirds Over the Mountain/A Chicken Ain't Nothin' But a Bird	1962	3.75	7.50	15.00
❑ 1807	Keep an Eye on Her/A Million Miles from Nowhere	1963	3.75	7.50	15.00
❑ 1850	Annabelle Lee/If Love Is	1963	3.75	7.50	15.00

SRG

Number	Title (A Side/B Side)	Yr	VG	VG+	NM
❑ 101	Baby Blue/Boomerang	1960	50.00	100.00	200.00

ECHOES, THE (2)

Early version of THE INNOCENTS.

ANDEX

Number	Title (A Side/B Side)	Yr	VG	VG+	NM
❑ 22102	Time/Dee Dee Di Oh	1958	7.50	15.00	30.00

ECHOES, THE (3)

Eddie Sulik was the singer of this group, which used Nashville professionals as backing musicians.

COLUMBIA

Number	Title (A Side/B Side)	Yr	VG	VG+	NM
❑ 4-41549	Bye-Bye My Baby/Do I Love You?	1960	3.75	7.50	15.00
❑ 4-41709	Loving and Losing/Ecstasy	1960	3.75	7.50	15.00

HARD ROCK HATTIE

Number	Title (A Side/B Side)	Yr	VG	VG+	NM
❑ LS 1000-05	Bye-Bye My Baby/Do I Love You? ('Deed I Do)	2000	—	—	3.00
—Red vinyl; credited to "The Echoes - Eddie Sulik"; came as part of a 7x7 package called "Sweet Memories," which includes a CD, gatefold sleeve and poster					
❑ LS 1000-06	Loving and Losing/Ecstasy	2000	—	—	3.00

—Blue vinyl

ECHOES, THE (4)

COMBO

Number	Title (A Side/B Side)	Yr	VG	VG+	NM
❑ 128	My Little Honey/Aye Senorita	1957	10.00	20.00	40.00

ECHOES, THE (5)

BONNIE GUITAR was in this group.

DOLTON

Number	Title (A Side/B Side)	Yr	VG	VG+	NM
❑ 18	Born to Be With You/My Guiding Light	1960	5.00	10.00	20.00

ECHOES, THE (6)

ROCKIN'

Number	Title (A Side/B Side)	Yr	VG	VG+	NM
❑ 523	All That Wine Is Gone/Please Say You're Mine	1953	100.00	200.00	400.00

ECHOES, THE (U)

Some of these may belong with the above groups. The record on Felsted is a reissue of the Hi Tide release.

ASCOT

Number	Title (A Side/B Side)	Yr	VG	VG+	NM
❑ 2188	I Love Candy/Paper Roses	1965	12.50	25.00	50.00

FELSTED

Number	Title (A Side/B Side)	Yr	VG	VG+	NM
❑ 8614	Angel of Love/Twistin' Town	1961	12.50	25.00	50.00

GEE

Number	Title (A Side/B Side)	Yr	VG	VG+	NM
❑ 1028	Ding Dong/My Heart Beats for You	1957	15.00	30.00	60.00

HI TIDE

Number	Title (A Side/B Side)	Yr	VG	VG+	NM
❑ 106	Angel of Love/Twistin' Town	1961	50.00	100.00	200.00
—Black vinyl					
❑ 106	Angel of Love/Twistin' Town	1961	100.00	200.00	400.00

—Colored vinyl

SPECIALTY

Number	Title (A Side/B Side)	Yr	VG	VG+	NM
❑ 601	Over the Rainbow/Someone	1957	7.50	15.00	30.00

SWAN

Number	Title (A Side/B Side)	Yr	VG	VG+	NM
❑ 4013	Scratch My Back/The Little Green Man	1959	3.00	6.00	12.00

ECSTASIES, THE

AMY

Number	Title (A Side/B Side)	Yr	VG	VG+	NM
❑ 853	That Lucky Old Sun/Time for Love	1962	12.50	25.00	50.00

CLIFTON

Number	Title (A Side/B Side)	Yr	VG	VG+	NM
❑ 40	White Christmas/Silent Night	19??	3.75	7.50	15.00

EDDIE AND THE EVERGREENS

See SHA NA NA.

EDDIE AND THE SHOWMEN

LIBERTY

Number	Title (A Side/B Side)	Yr	VG	VG+	NM
❑ 55566	Toes on the Nose/Border Town	1963	7.50	15.00	30.00
❑ 55608	Squad Car/Scratch	1963	7.50	15.00	30.00
❑ 55659	Movin'/Mr. Rebel	1963	7.50	15.00	30.00
❑ 55695	Faw Away Places/Lanky Bones	1964	7.50	15.00	30.00
❑ 55720	We Are the Young/Young and Lonely	1964	7.50	15.00	30.00

EDDIE AND THE STARLITES

ALJON

Number	Title (A Side/B Side)	Yr	VG	VG+	NM
❑ 1260	Come On Home/(B-side unknown)	1963	7.50	15.00	30.00

SCEPTER

Number	Title (A Side/B Side)	Yr	VG	VG+	NM
❑ 1202	To Make a Long Story Short/Pretty Little Girl	1958	15.00	30.00	60.00
—White label					
❑ 1202	To Make a Long Story Short/Pretty Little Girl	1958	7.50	15.00	30.00

—Red label

EDDY, DUANE

Also see AL CASEY; DUANE AND MIRRIAM EDDY.

BIG TREE

Number	Title (A Side/B Side)	Yr	VG	VG+	NM
❑ 157	Renegade/Nightly News	1972	2.00	4.00	8.00

CAPITOL

Number	Title (A Side/B Side)	Yr	VG	VG+	NM
❑ B-44018	Spies/Rockabilly Holiday	1987	—	2.50	5.00
❑ B-44018 [PS]	Spies/Rockabilly Holiday	1987	—	2.50	5.00

CHINA

Number	Title (A Side/B Side)	Yr	VG	VG+	NM
❑ 42986	Peter Gunn/Something Always Happens	1986	—	—	3.00
—With Art of Noise; B-side does not feature Eddy					
❑ 42986 [PS]	Peter Gunn/Something Always Happens	1986	—	—	3.00

COLPIX

Number	Title (A Side/B Side)	Yr	VG	VG+	NM
❑ 779	Trash/South Phoenix	1965	3.75	7.50	15.00
❑ 788	Don't Think Twice, It's All Right/House of the Rising Sun	1965	3.75	7.50	15.00
❑ 788 [PS]	Don't Think Twice, It's All Right/House of the Rising Sun	1965	12.50	25.00	50.00
❑ 795	El Rancho Grande/Poppa's Movin' On	1966	3.75	7.50	15.00

Number	Title (A Side/B Side)	Yr	VG	VG+	NM
CONGRESS					
❑ 6010	Freight Train/Put a Little Love in Your Heart	1970	3.75	7.50	15.00
ELEKTRA					
❑ 45359	You Are My Sunshine/From 8 to 7	1977	—	2.50	5.00
FORD					
❑ 500	Ramrod/Caravan	1957	500.00	1000.	1500.
—As "Duane Eddy and His Rock-A-Billies"					
GREGMARK					
❑ 5	Caravan (Part 1)/Caravan (Part 2)	1961	3.75	7.50	15.00
—Credited to Duane Eddy, but is actually Al Casey					
GUSTO					
❑ 2047	Rebel Rouser/40 Miles of Bad Road	1979	—	2.00	4.00
—Re-recordings					
JAMIE					
❑ JLP-71 [S]	Lonesome Road/I Almost Lost My Mind	1960	6.25	12.50	25.00
❑ JLP-72 [S]	Loving You/Anything	1960	6.25	12.50	25.00
❑ JLP-73 [S]	Peter Gunn/Along the Navaho Trail	1960	6.25	12.50	25.00
❑ JLP-74 [S]	Hard Times/Along Came Linda	1960	6.25	12.50	25.00
❑ JLP-75 [S]	The Battle/You Are My Sunshine	1960	6.25	12.50	25.00
—The above five are 33 1/3 rpm singles with small holes					
❑ 1101	Moovin N' Groovin'/Up and Down	1958	12.50	25.00	50.00
—Originals have pink labels					
❑ 1101	Moovin N' Groovin'/Up and Down	1958	6.25	12.50	25.00
—All-yellow label, "Jamie" at top					
❑ 1104	Rebel-'Rouser/Stalkin'	1958	6.25	12.50	25.00
❑ 1109	Ramrod/The Walker	1958	6.25	12.50	25.00
❑ 1111	Cannonball/Mason Dixon Line	1958	5.00	10.00	20.00
❑ 1117 [M]	The Lonely One/Detour	1959	5.00	10.00	20.00
❑ 1117 [S]	The Lonely One/Detour	1959	12.50	25.00	50.00
❑ 1122	Yep!/Three-30-Blues	1959	5.00	10.00	20.00
❑ 1122 [PS]	Yep!/Three-30-Blues	1959	12.50	25.00	50.00
❑ 1126 [M]	Forty Miles of Bad Road/The Quiet Three	1959	5.00	10.00	20.00
❑ 1126 [PS]	Forty Miles of Bad Road/The Quiet Three	1959	12.50	25.00	50.00
❑ 1126 [S]	Forty Miles of Bad Road/The Quiet Three	1959	12.50	25.00	50.00
❑ 1130 [M]	Some Kind-a Earthquake/First Love, First Tears	1959	5.00	10.00	20.00
❑ 1130 [PS]	Some Kind-a Earthquake/First Love, First Tears	1959	10.00	20.00	40.00
❑ 1130 [S]	Some Kind-a Earthquake/First Love, First Tears	1959	12.50	25.00	50.00
❑ 1144	Bonnie Came Back/Lost Island	1959	5.00	10.00	20.00
❑ 1144 [PS]	Bonnie Came Back/Lost Island	1959	10.00	20.00	40.00
❑ 1151	Shazam!/The Secret Seven	1960	3.75	7.50	15.00
❑ 1151 [PS]	Shazam!/The Secret Seven	1960	7.50	15.00	30.00
❑ 1156	Because They're Young/Rebel Walk	1960	3.75	7.50	15.00
❑ 1156 [PS]	Because They're Young/Rebel Walk	1960	7.50	15.00	30.00
❑ 1163	Kommotion/Theme for Moon Children	1960	3.75	7.50	15.00
❑ 1163 [PS]	Kommotion/Theme for Moon Children	1960	7.50	15.00	30.00
❑ 1168	Peter Gunn/Along the Navaho Trail	1960	3.75	7.50	15.00
❑ 1168 [PS]	Peter Gunn/Along the Navaho Trail	1960	7.50	15.00	30.00
❑ 1175	"Pepe"/Lost Friend	1960	3.75	7.50	15.00
❑ 1175 [PS]	"Pepe"/Lost Friend	1960	10.00	20.00	40.00
—Red sleeve					
❑ 1175 [PS]	"Pepe"/Lost Friend	1960	7.50	15.00	30.00
—Yellow sleeve					
❑ 1183	Theme from Dixie/Gidget Goes Hawaiian	1961	3.75	7.50	15.00
❑ 1183 [PS]	Theme from Dixie/Gidget Goes Hawaiian	1961	7.50	15.00	30.00
❑ 1187	Ring of Fire/Bobbie	1961	3.75	7.50	15.00
❑ 1187 [PS]	Ring of Fire/Bobbie	1961	7.50	15.00	30.00
❑ 1195	Drivin' Home/Tammy	1961	3.75	7.50	15.00
❑ 1195 [PS]	Drivin' Home/Tammy	1961	7.50	15.00	30.00
❑ 1200	My Blue Heaven/Along Came Linda	1961	3.75	7.50	15.00
❑ 1200 [PS]	My Blue Heaven/Along Came Linda	1961	7.50	15.00	30.00
❑ 1206	The Avenger/Londonderry Air	1961	3.75	7.50	15.00
❑ 1209	The Battle/Trambone	1962	3.75	7.50	15.00
❑ 1224	Runaway Pony/Just Because	1962	3.75	7.50	15.00
❑ 1303	Rebel Rouser/Movin' N' Groovin'	1965	3.00	6.00	12.00
RCA VICTOR					
❑ 47-7999	Deep in the Heart of Texas/Saints and Sinners	1962	3.00	6.00	12.00
❑ 47-7999 [PS]	Deep in the Heart of Texas/Saints and Sinners	1962	6.25	12.50	25.00
❑ 47-8047	The Ballad of Paladin/The WIld Westerner	1962	3.00	6.00	12.00
❑ 47-8047 [PS]	The Ballad of Paladin/The WIld Westerner	1962	6.25	12.50	25.00
❑ 47-8087	(Dance with the) Guitar Man/Stretchin' Out	1962	3.75	7.50	15.00
❑ 47-8087 [PS]	(Dance with the) Guitar Man/Stretchin' Out	1962	7.50	15.00	30.00
❑ 47-8131	Boss Guitar/Desert Rat	1963	3.00	6.00	12.00
❑ 47-8131 [PS]	Boss Guitar/Desert Rat	1963	6.25	12.50	25.00
❑ 47-8180	Lonely Boy, Lonely Guitar/Joshin'	1963	3.00	6.00	12.00
❑ 47-8180 [PS]	Lonely Boy, Lonely Guitar/Joshin'	1963	6.25	12.50	25.00
❑ 47-8214	Your Baby's Gone Surfin'/Shuckin'	1963	3.75	7.50	15.00
❑ 47-8214 [PS]	Your Baby's Gone Surfin'/Shuckin'	1963	7.50	15.00	30.00
❑ 47-8276	The Son of Rebel Rouser/The Story of Three Loves	1963	3.00	6.00	12.00
❑ 47-8276 [PS]	The Son of Rebel Rouser/The Story of Three Loves	1963	6.25	12.50	25.00
❑ 47-8335	Guitar Child/Jerky Jalopy	1964	3.00	6.00	12.00
❑ 47-8376	Water Skiing/Theme from A Summer Place	1964	3.00	6.00	12.00
❑ 47-8442	Guitar Star/The Iguana	1964	3.00	6.00	12.00
❑ 47-8442 [PS]	Guitar Star/The Iguana	1964	7.50	15.00	30.00
❑ 47-8507	Moonshot/Roughneck	1965	3.00	6.00	12.00
❑ 47-8507 [PS]	Moonshot/Roughneck	1965	30.00	60.00	120.00
REPRISE					
❑ 0504	Daydream/This Guitar Was Made for Twangin'	1966	2.50	5.00	10.00
❑ 0557	Roarin'/Monsoon	1967	2.50	5.00	10.00
❑ 0662	There Is a Mountain/This Town	1968	2.50	5.00	10.00
❑ 0690	Niki-Hoeky/Velvet Nights	1968	2.50	5.00	10.00
UNI					
❑ 55237	The Five-Seventeen/Something	1970	3.75	7.50	15.00

7-Inch Extended Plays

Number	Title (A Side/B Side)	Yr	VG	VG+	NM
JAMIE					
❑ JEP-100	Cannonball/Moovin' N' Groovin'//Mason-Dixon Lion/The Lonely One	1958	12.50	25.00	50.00
❑ JEP-100 [PS]	Duane Eddy	1958	12.50	25.00	50.00
❑ JEP-301	Lonesome Road/I Almost Lost My Mind//Detour/Loving You	1959	12.50	25.00	50.00
❑ JEP-301 [PS]	Detour	1959	12.50	25.00	50.00
❑ JEP-302	Yep/Three-30 Blues//Anytime/Stalkin'	1959	12.50	25.00	50.00
❑ JEP-302 [PS]	Yep!	1959	12.50	25.00	50.00
❑ JEP-303	Shazam/Tiger Love//My Blue Heaven/Night Train To Memphis	1960	12.50	25.00	50.00
❑ JEP-303 [PS]	Shazam!	1960	12.50	25.00	50.00
❑ JEP-304	Because They're Young/Easy//Rebel Walk/The Battle	1960	12.50	25.00	50.00
❑ JEP-304 [PS]	Because They're Young	1960	12.50	25.00	50.00

EDDY, DUANE AND MIRRIAM

Also see DUANE EDDY.

Number	Title (A Side/B Side)	Yr	VG	VG+	NM
REPRISE					
❑ 0622	Guitar on My Mind/Wicked Women from Wickenborg	1967	2.50	5.00	10.00

EDEN'S CHILDREN

Number	Title (A Side/B Side)	Yr	VG	VG+	NM
ABC					
❑ 11053	Goodbye Girl/Just Let Go	1968	3.00	6.00	12.00

EDGE, GRAEME

Of THE MOODY BLUES.

Number	Title (A Side/B Side)	Yr	VG	VG+	NM
LONDON					
❑ 1071	Everybody Needs Somebody/Be My Eyes	1977	—	2.50	5.00
—With Adrian Gurvitz					
THRESHOLD					
❑ 67018	We Like to Do It/Shotgun	1974	—	2.50	5.00
❑ 67022	The Tunnel/Bareback Rider	1975	—	2.50	5.00

EDISON LIGHTHOUSE

Number	Title (A Side/B Side)	Yr	VG	VG+	NM
BELL					
❑ 858	Love Grows (Where My Rosemary Goes)/Every Lonely Day	1970	—	3.00	6.00
❑ 907	She Works in a Woman's Way/It's Gonna Be a Lonely Summer	1970	—	2.50	5.00
❑ 960	It's Up to You Petula/Let's Make It Up	1971	—	2.50	5.00
❑ 989	Take a Little Time/What's Happening	1971	—	2.50	5.00

EDMUNDS, DAVE

Also see LOVE SCULPTURE.

Number	Title (A Side/B Side)	Yr	VG	VG+	NM
CAPITOL					
❑ 7PRO-79973 [DJ]	Closer to the Flame (same on both sides)	1990	2.50	5.00	10.00
COLUMBIA					
❑ 02960	From Small Things (Big Things One Day Come)/Warmed Over Kisses (Left Over Love)	1982	—	2.00	4.00
—A-side is a Bruce Springsteen composition.					
❑ 03428	Run Rudolph Run/Deep in the Heart of Texas	1982	—	2.00	4.00
❑ 03428 [PS]	Run Rudolph Run/Deep in the Heart of Texas	1982	2.00	4.00	8.00
❑ 03877	Slipping Away/Don't Call Me Tonight	1983	—	—	3.00
❑ 04080	Information/What Have I Got to Do to Win	1983	—	—	3.00
❑ 04585	Something About You/You Can't Get Enough	1984	—	—	3.00
❑ 04700	Breaking Out/How Could I Be So Wrong	1984	—	—	3.00
❑ 04762	High School Nights/Porky's Revenge	1985	—	—	2.50
❑ 04762 [PS]	High School Nights/Porky's Revenge	1985	—	—	2.50
❑ 04887	Queen of the Hop/I Don't Want to Do It	1985	5.00	10.00	20.00
—B-side by George Harrison, thus accounting for this 45's value					
❑ 04923	Do You Want to Dance/Don't Call Me Tonight	1985	—	—	3.00
❑ 05487	Run Rudolph Run/From Small Things (Big Things One Day Come)	198?	—	—	3.00
—"Golden Oldies" reissue					
❑ 06599	The Wanderer/Information	1987	—	—	3.00
❑ 07040	Paralyzed/Here Comes the Weekend	1987	—	—	3.00
MAM					
❑ 3601	I Hear You Knocking/Black Bill	1970	2.00	4.00	8.00
❑ 3608	I'm Coming Home/Country Roll	1971	—	3.00	6.00
❑ 3611	Blue Monday/I'll Get Along	1971	—	3.00	6.00
MCA					
❑ 53256	Gonna Move/Red River Rock	1988	—	—	2.50
—B-side by Silicon Teens					
❑ 53256 [PS]	Gonna Move/Red River Rock	1988	—	—	2.50
—B-side by Silicon Teens					
RCA VICTOR					
❑ LPBO-5000	Born to Be with You/Pick Axe Rag	1973	—	3.00	6.00
❑ PB-10118	Let It Be Me/Need a Shot of Rhythm and Blues	1974	—	2.50	5.00
❑ 74-0882	Baby I Love You/Maybe	1973	—	3.00	6.00
SWAN SONG					
❑ 70113	I Knew the Bride/Little Darlin'	1978	—	2.00	4.00
❑ 70116	Get Out of Denver/Work Out Suits	1978	—	2.00	4.00
❑ 70118	Trouble Boys/What Looks Best on You	1978	—	2.00	4.00
❑ 71001	Girls Talk/Creature from the Black Lagoon	1979	—	2.50	5.00
❑ 71002	Crawling from the Wreckage/Queen of Hearts	1979	—	2.50	5.00
❑ 72000	Almost Saturday Night/You'll Never Get Me Up	1981	—	—	3.00
❑ 72000 [PS]	Almost Saturday Night/You'll Never Get Me Up	1981	—	—	3.00
❑ 72003	The Race Is On/Singin' the Blues	1981	—	2.50	5.00
—Backing group: Stray Cats					

EDMUNDS, DAVE, AND NICK LOWE

Also see each artist's individual listings.

Number	Title (A Side/B Side)	Yr	VG	VG+	NM
COLUMBIA					
❑ AE7-1219	Take a Message to Mary/Crying in the Rain//Poor Jenny/When Will I Be Loved	1980	—	3.00	6.00
—Bonus EP included in the Rockpile LP "Seconds of Pleasure"					
❑ AE7-1219 [PS]	Nick Lowe and Dave Edmunds Sing The Everly Brothers	1980	—	3.00	6.00

EDSELS, THE

Number	Title (A Side/B Side)	Yr	VG	VG+	NM
CAPITOL					
❑ 4588	Bone Shaker Joe/My Jealous One	1961	5.00	10.00	20.00
❑ 4675	If Your Pillow Could Talk/Shake Shake Sherry	1961	5.00	10.00	20.00
❑ 4836	Shaddy Daddy Dip Dip/Don't You Feel	1962	5.00	10.00	20.00

Number	Title (A Side/B Side)	Yr	VG	VG+	NM
DOT					
❑ 16311	My Whispering Heart/Could It Be	1962	6.25	12.50	25.00
DUB					
❑ 2843	Lama Rama Ding Dong/Bells	1958	17.50	35.00	70.00
—Originals have the wrong title and the same recording as on Twin 700					
❑ 2843	Rama Lama Ding Dong/Bells	1958	12.50	25.00	50.00
—Repress with corrected title and the same recording as on Twin 700					
❑ 2843	Rama Lama Ding Dong/Bells	197?	—	2.50	5.00
—Reproduction with an alternate take of the A-side; this has confused many who believe that the original Dub and Twin records are different.					
EMBER					
❑ 1078	Three Precious Words/Let's Go	1961	6.25	12.50	25.00
MUSICTONE					
❑ 1144	Rama Lama Ding Dong/Bells	1961	3.00	6.00	12.00
ROULETTE					
❑ 4151	Do You Love Me/Rink-a-Dink-a-Doo	1959	6.25	12.50	25.00
TAMMY					
❑ 1010	What Brought Us Together/Don't Know What to Do	1960	12.50	25.00	50.00
❑ 1014	Three Precious Words/Let's Go	1960	12.50	25.00	50.00
❑ 1023	The Girl I Love/Got to FInd Out About Love	1961	10.00	20.00	40.00
❑ 1027	Count the Tears/Twenty-Four Hours	1961	10.00	20.00	40.00
TWIN					
❑ 700	Rama Lama Ding Dong/Bells	1961	6.25	12.50	25.00

EDWARD BEAR

Number	Title (A Side/B Side)	Yr	VG	VG+	NM
CAPITOL					
❑ 2801	You, Me and Mexico/Sinking Ship	1970	—	3.00	6.00
❑ 2955	You Can't Deny It/Toe Jam	1970	—	3.00	6.00
❑ 3351	Masquerade/The Pirate King	1972	—	2.00	4.00
❑ 3452	Last Song/Best Friend	1972	—	2.50	5.00
❑ 3452 [PS]	Last Song/Best Friend	1972	2.00	4.00	8.00
❑ 3581	Close Your Eyes/Cachet County	1973	—	2.00	4.00
❑ 3683	I Love Her (You Love Me)/Walking On Back	1973	—	2.00	4.00
❑ 3780	Coming Home Christmas/Does Your Mother Know	1973	2.00	4.00	8.00
❑ 3804	Same Old Feeling/Fool	1973	—	2.00	4.00
❑ 3869	I Had Dreams/You, Me and Mexico	1974	—	2.00	4.00
❑ 3978	Freedom for the Stallion/Why Don't You Marry Me	1974	—	2.00	4.00

EDWARDS, BOBBY

Number	Title (A Side/B Side)	Yr	VG	VG+	NM
CAPITOL					
❑ 4674	What's the Reason/Walk Away Slowly	1961	2.00	4.00	8.00
❑ 4726	Singing the Blues/What'll I Do Without You	1962	2.00	4.00	8.00
❑ 4789	Someone New/Here's My Heart	1962	2.00	4.00	8.00
❑ 4874	Remember Who Brought You Here/The Way I Am	1962	2.00	4.00	8.00
❑ 5006	Don't Pretend/Help Me	1963	2.00	4.00	8.00
CHART					
❑ 1020	I'm Sorry to See You Go/Once a Fool (Always a Fool)	1968	—	2.50	5.00
❑ 1045	Each Time You Cross My Mind/Just Ain't My Day	1968	—	2.50	5.00
❑ 5016	Bring My Baby Home/Loving You Is Killing Me	1969	—	2.50	5.00
❑ 5061	You're the Reason/Don't Pretend	1970	—	2.50	5.00
CREST					
❑ 1075	You're the Reason/I'm a Fool for Loving You	1961	2.50	5.00	10.00
MANCO					
❑ 1026	Jealous Heart/I've Lost Everything But the Memories	1962	2.00	4.00	8.00
MUSICOR					
❑ 1101	A Little Less Heartache/Within Your Arms	1965	—	3.00	6.00

EDWARDS, J.D.

Number	Title (A Side/B Side)	Yr	VG	VG+	NM
IMPERIAL					
❑ 5245	Crying/Hobo	1953	30.00	60.00	120.00

EDWARDS, JOHNNY, AND THE WHITE CAPS

Number	Title (A Side/B Side)	Yr	VG	VG+	NM
NORTHLAND					
❑ 90-7002	Rock 'n Roll Saddles/Why'd You Leave Me?	1957	50.00	100.00	200.00

EDWARDS, TOMMY

Number	Title (A Side/B Side)	Yr	VG	VG+	NM
MGM					
❑ 10884	Once There Lived a Fool/A Friend of Johnny's	1951	5.00	10.00	20.00
❑ 10921	Gypsy Heart/Operetta	1951	5.00	10.00	20.00
❑ 10973	I'll Never Know Why/A Beggar in Love	1951	5.00	10.00	20.00
❑ 10989	The Morning Side of the Mountain/For Instance	1951	6.25	12.50	25.00
❑ 11035	It's All in the Game/All Over Again	1951	6.25	12.50	25.00
❑ 11077	Solitaire/My Concerto	1951	5.00	10.00	20.00
❑ 11097	Christmas Is for Children/Kris Kringle	1951	5.00	10.00	20.00
❑ 11134	Please Mr. Sun/I May Live with You	1952	6.25	12.50	25.00
❑ 11170	Forgive Me/The Bridge	1952	5.00	10.00	20.00
❑ 11209	My Girl/Piano, Bass and Drums	1952	5.00	10.00	20.00
❑ 11268	Easy to Say/The Greatest Sinner of Them All	1952	5.00	10.00	20.00
❑ 11326	You Win Again/Sinner and Saint	1952	5.00	10.00	20.00
❑ 11395	(Now and Then, There's) A Fool Such As I/I Can't Love Another	1953	5.00	10.00	20.00
❑ 11465	Au Revoir/I Lived When I Met You	1953	5.00	10.00	20.00
❑ 11485	Take These Chains from My Heart/Paging Mr. Jackson	1953	5.00	10.00	20.00
❑ 11541	Lover's Waltz/Baby, Baby, Baby	1953	5.00	10.00	20.00
❑ 11582	So Little Time/Blue Bird	1953	5.00	10.00	20.00
❑ 11604	That's All/Secret Love	1953	5.00	10.00	20.00
❑ 11624	Every Day Is Christmas/It's Christmas Once Again	1953	5.00	10.00	20.00
❑ 11668	There Was a Time/Wall of Ice	1954	5.00	10.00	20.00
❑ 11718	The Joker (In the Card Game of Life)/Within My Heart	1954	5.00	10.00	20.00
❑ 11763	Linger in My Arms/If You Would Love Me Again	1954	5.00	10.00	20.00
❑ 11821	You Walk By/I Have That Kind of Heart	1954	5.00	10.00	20.00
❑ 11932	Serenade to a Fool/It Could Have Been Me	1955	5.00	10.00	20.00
❑ 11993	Welcome to My Heart/Spring Never Came Around This Year	1955	5.00	10.00	20.00
❑ 12054	Teardrop on a Rose/To Those Who Wait	1955	5.00	10.00	20.00
❑ 12095	Baby, Let Me Take You Dreaming/My Sweetheart	1955	5.00	10.00	20.00
❑ 12248	Love Is a Child/There Must Be a Way to Your Heart	1956	5.00	10.00	20.00
❑ 12342	The Day That I Lost You/My Ship	1956	5.00	10.00	20.00
❑ 12514	We're Not Children Anymore/Any Place, Any Time	1957	5.00	10.00	20.00
❑ 12688	It's All in the Game/Please Love Me Forever	1958	3.75	7.50	15.00
❑ 12722	Love Is All We Need/Mr. Music Man	1958	3.75	7.50	15.00
❑ 12757	Please Mr. Sun/The Morning Side of the Mountain	1959	3.75	7.50	15.00
❑ 12794	My Melancholy Baby/It's Only the Good Times	1959	3.75	7.50	15.00
❑ 12814	I've Been There/I Looked at Heaven	1959	3.75	7.50	15.00
❑ 12837	Honestly and Truly/(New In) The Ways of Love	1959	3.75	7.50	15.00
❑ 12871	Don't Fence Me In/I'm Building Castles Again	1960	3.00	6.00	12.00
❑ 12890	I Really Don't Want to Know/Unloved	1960	3.00	6.00	12.00
❑ 12890 [PS]	I Really Don't Want to Know/Unloved	1960	7.50	15.00	30.00
❑ 12916	It's Not the End of Everything/Blue Heartaches	1960	3.00	6.00	12.00
❑ 12959	Suzie Wong/As You Desire Me	1960	3.00	6.00	12.00
❑ 12981	Vaya Con Dios/One and Twenty	1961	3.00	6.00	12.00
❑ 13002	The Golden Chain/That's the Way with Love	1961	3.00	6.00	12.00
❑ 13032	I'm So Lonesome I Could Cry/My Heart Would Know	1961	3.00	6.00	12.00
❑ 13057	I'll Cry You Out of My Heart/Tables Are Turning	1962	3.00	6.00	12.00
❑ 13100	Please Don't Tell Me/Tonight I Won't Be There	1962	3.00	6.00	12.00
❑ 13128	May I/Sometimes You Win, Sometimes You Lose	1963	2.50	5.00	10.00
❑ 13172	Country Boy/Love Is Best of All	1963	2.50	5.00	10.00
❑ 13317	Take These Chains from My Heart/You WIn Again	1965	2.50	5.00	10.00
MUSICOR					
❑ 1046	Left-Over Dreams/9 Chances Out of 10	1964	2.50	5.00	10.00
❑ 1159	I Must Be Doing Something Wrong/I Cried, I Cried	1966	2.50	5.00	10.00
7-Inch Extended Plays					
MGM					
❑ X-1003	(contents unknown)	1952	10.00	20.00	40.00
❑ X-1003 [PS]	It's All in the Game	1952	10.00	20.00	40.00
❑ X-1614	*It's All in the Game/My Sugar, My Sweet/I'll Always Be with You/That's All	1958	5.00	10.00	20.00
❑ X-1614 [PS]	It's All in the Game, Vol. 1	1958	5.00	10.00	20.00
❑ SX-1666 [PS]	For Young Lovers, Vol. 1	1959	6.25	12.50	25.00
❑ SX-1666 [S]	(contents unknown)	1959	6.25	12.50	25.00
❑ X-1666 [M]	(contents unknown)	1959	5.00	10.00	20.00
❑ X-1666 [PS]	For Young Lovers, Vol. 1	1959	5.00	10.00	20.00
❑ SX-1667 [PS]	For Young Lovers, Vol. 2	1959	6.25	12.50	25.00
❑ SX-1667 [S]	(contents unknown)	1959	6.25	12.50	25.00
❑ X-1667 [M]	(contents unknown)	1959	5.00	10.00	20.00
❑ X-1667 [PS]	For Young Lovers, Vol. 2	1959	5.00	10.00	20.00
❑ SX-1668 [PS]	For Young Lovers, Vol. 3	1959	6.25	12.50	25.00
❑ SX-1668 [S]	(contents unknown)	1959	6.25	12.50	25.00
❑ X-1668 [M]	(contents unknown)	1959	5.00	10.00	20.00
❑ X-1668 [PS]	For Young Lovers, Vol. 3	1959	5.00	10.00	20.00

EDWARDS, VERN

Number	Title (A Side/B Side)	Yr	VG	VG+	NM
PROBE					
❑ 100	Cool Baby, Cool/Glenda	1959	50.00	100.00	200.00

EDWARDS, VINCENT

Number	Title (A Side/B Side)	Yr	VG	VG+	NM
CAPITOL					
❑ 4819	Lollipop/As You Desire Me	1962	2.50	5.00	10.00
COLPIX					
❑ 771	No, Not Much/See That Girl	1965	2.00	4.00	8.00
❑ 771 [PS]	No, Not Much/See That Girl	1965	2.50	5.00	10.00
DECCA					
❑ 31413	Don't Worry 'Bout Me/And Now	1962	2.00	4.00	8.00
❑ 31426	I Got It Bad (And That Ain't Good)/Say It Isn't So	1962	2.00	4.00	8.00
❑ 31426 [PS]	I Got It Bad (And That Ain't Good)/Say It Isn't So	1962	3.00	6.00	12.00
❑ 31460	To Kill a Mockingbird/You'll Still Have Me	1963	2.00	4.00	8.00
❑ 31534	This Train/Looking for Someone	1963	2.00	4.00	8.00
❑ 31563	Does Goodnight Mean Goodbye/Per Te Per Me	1963	2.00	4.00	8.00
KAMA SUTRA					
❑ 221	Nylon Stockings/To Be with You	1967	—	3.00	6.00
❑ 221 [PS]	Nylon Stockings/To Be with You	1967	2.50	5.00	10.00
MAGIC LAMP					
❑ 701	I'm Not the Marrying Kind/What Colors Are You	1964	2.00	4.00	8.00
RUSS-FI					
❑ 1	Oh Babe/Squealin' Parrot Twist	196?	3.00	6.00	12.00
❑ 7001	Why Did You Leave Me/Squealin' Parrot Twist	1962	2.50	5.00	10.00

EELY, JACK

Sang lead on THE KINGSMEN's version of "Louie Louie."

Number	Title (A Side/B Side)	Yr	VG	VG+	NM
BANG					
❑ 520	Louie Louie '66/David's Mood	1966	3.75	7.50	15.00
❑ 534	Louie Go Home/Ride Ride Baby	1966	3.75	7.50	15.00

EHRET, BOB

Number	Title (A Side/B Side)	Yr	VG	VG+	NM
ALADDIN					
❑ 3377	Stop the Clock/So Lonely	1957	37.50	75.00	150.00

EIFFEL 65

Number	Title (A Side/B Side)	Yr	VG	VG+	NM
REPUBLIC/UNIVERSAL					
❑ 012-156662-7	Blue (Da Ba Dee)/Move Your Body	2000	—	—	3.00

8TH DAY, THE

Probably all the same group.

Number	Title (A Side/B Side)	Yr	VG	VG+	NM
A&M					
❑ 2539	Call Me Up/I've Got My Heart in the Right Place	1983	—	2.00	4.00
❑ 2595 [DJ]	In the Valley (same on both sides)	1983	—	2.00	4.00
INVICTUS					
❑ 9087	She's Not Just Another Woman/I Can't Fool Myself	1971	—	2.50	5.00
❑ 9098	You've Got to Crawl (Before You Walk)/It's Instrumental to Be Free	1971	—	2.50	5.00
❑ 9107	If I Could See the Light/If I Could See the Light (Part 2)	1971	—	2.50	5.00

Number	Title (A Side/B Side)	Yr	VG	VG+	NM
❑ 9117	Eeny-Meeny-Miny-Mo (Three's a Crowd)/Rocks in My Head	1972	—	2.50	5.00
❑ 9124	Good Book/I Gotta Get Home	1972	—	2.50	5.00
KAPP					
❑ 862	Hey Boy (The Girl's in Love with You)/Million Lights	1967	2.00	4.00	8.00
❑ 894	Raining Sunshine/That Good Old Fashioned Way	1968	2.00	4.00	8.00
❑ 916	Glory/Building with a Steeple	1968	2.00	4.00	8.00

EIRE APPARENT, THE

Number	Title (A Side/B Side)	Yr	VG	VG+	NM
BUDDAH					
❑ 67	Yes I Need Someone/Let Me Stay	1968	3.75	7.50	15.00

EL CAPRIS

Number	Title (A Side/B Side)	Yr	VG	VG+	NM
ARGYLE					
❑ 1010	Ooh But She Did/(Shimmy, Shimmy) Ko Ko Wop	1961	7.50	15.00	30.00
BULLSEYE					
❑ 102	Ooh But She Did/(Shimmy Shimmy) Ko Ko Wop	1956	50.00	100.00	200.00
❑ 102	Oh But She Did/(Shimmy Shimmy) Ko Ko Wop	1956	37.50	75.00	150.00
—Note slight difference in A-side title					
FEE BEE					
❑ 216	Your Star/To Live Again	1957	10.00	20.00	40.00
HI-Q					
❑ 5006	Girl of Mine/These Lonely Nights	1958	25.00	50.00	100.00
—Blue label					
❑ 5006	Girl of Mine/These Lonely Nights	1958	10.00	20.00	40.00
—Yellow label					
PARIS					
❑ 525	They're Always Laughing at Me/Ivy League Clean	1958	10.00	20.00	40.00
RING-O					
❑ 308	Safari/Quit Pulling My Woman	1960	7.50	15.00	30.00

EL CLOD

Number	Title (A Side/B Side)	Yr	VG	VG+	NM
CHALLENGE					
❑ 9159	Tijuana Border (Wolverton Mountain)/Pedro's Piano Roll Twist	1962	5.00	10.00	20.00
MERCURY					
❑ 72082	He's Not a Rebel/Holiday in Havana	1963	3.75	7.50	15.00
VEE JAY					
❑ 647	Tijuana Watusi/Gringo	1965	3.75	7.50	15.00

EL DOMINGOS

Number	Title (A Side/B Side)	Yr	VG	VG+	NM
CANDLELITE					
❑ 418	Made in Heaven/Lucky Me, I'm in Love	1963	6.25	12.50	25.00
CHELSEA					
❑ 1009	Made in Heaven/Lucky Me, I'm in Love	1962	50.00	100.00	200.00
KARMIN					
❑ 1001	Are You Ready to Say "I Do"/I Want to Know	1964	75.00	150.00	300.00

EL DORADOS

Number	Title (A Side/B Side)	Yr	VG	VG+	NM
PAULA					
❑ 347	Looking In from the Outside/Since You Came Into My Life	1971	2.50	5.00	10.00
❑ 369	Loose Booty (Part 1)/Loose Booty (Part 2)	1971	2.50	5.00	10.00
TORRID					
❑ 100	In Over My Head/You Make My Heart Sing	1970	3.75	7.50	15.00
VEE JAY					
❑ 115	Baby I Need You/My Loving Baby	1954	100.00	200.00	400.00
—Red vinyl					
❑ 115	Baby I Need You/My Loving Baby	1954	20.00	40.00	80.00
❑ 118	Annie's Answer/Living with Vivian	1954	75.00	150.00	300.00
—Red vinyl					
❑ 118	Annie's Answer/Living with Vivian	1954	20.00	40.00	80.00
❑ 127	One More Chance/Little Miss Love	1954	50.00	100.00	200.00
❑ 147	At My Front Door/What's Buggin' You Baby	1955	17.50	35.00	70.00
❑ 165	I'll Be Forever Lovin' You/I Began to Realize	1955	15.00	30.00	60.00
❑ 180	Now That You've Gone/Rock 'N' Roll's for Me	1956	12.50	25.00	50.00
❑ 197	Fallen Tear/Chop Ling Soon	1956	12.50	25.00	50.00
❑ 211	Bim Bam Boom/There in the Night	1956	20.00	40.00	80.00
❑ 250	Tears on My Pillow/A Rose for My Darling	1957	7.50	15.00	30.00
❑ 263	Three Reasons Why/Boom Diddle Boom	1958	37.50	75.00	150.00
❑ 302	Oh What a Girl/The Lights Are Low	1958	37.50	75.00	150.00

EL RAYS, THE

See THE DELLS.

EL VENOS, THE

Number	Title (A Side/B Side)	Yr	VG	VG+	NM
GROOVE					
❑ 0170	Now We're Together/Geraldine	1956	20.00	40.00	80.00
RCA VICTOR					
❑ 47-8303	My Heart Beats Faster/You Won't Be There	1963	6.25	12.50	25.00
VIK					
❑ 0305	My Heart Beats Faster/You Must Be True	1957	20.00	40.00	80.00

ELBERT, DONNIE

Number	Title (A Side/B Side)	Yr	VG	VG+	NM
ALL PLATINUM					
❑ 2330	Where Did Our Love Go/That's If You Love Me	1971	—	3.00	6.00
❑ 2333	Sweet Baby/Can't Get Over Losing You	1971	—	3.00	6.00
❑ 2336	If I Can't Have You/Can't Get Over Losing You	1972	—	3.00	6.00
❑ 2337	Little Piece of Leather/Sweet Baby	1972	—	3.00	6.00
❑ 2338	That's If You Love Me/Can't Get Over Losing You	1972	—	3.00	6.00
❑ 2346	This Feeling of Losing You/Can't Stand These Lonely Nights	1973	—	3.00	6.00
❑ 2351	Love Is Strange/(Instrumental)	1973	—	3.00	6.00
❑ 2367	What Do You Do/Will You Love Me Tomorrow	1974	—	2.50	5.00
❑ 2374	You Should Be Dancing/What Do You Do	1974	—	2.50	5.00
ATCO					
❑ 6550	Too Far Gone/In Between the Heartaches	1968	2.00	4.00	8.00
AVCO					
❑ 4587	I Can't Help Myself/Love Is Here and Now You're Gone	1972	—	3.00	6.00
❑ 4598	Ooh, Baby Baby/Tell Her for Me	1972	—	3.00	6.00
CUB					
❑ 9125	Don't Cry My Love/Love Stew	1963	3.00	6.00	12.00
DELUXE					
❑ 6125	What Can I Do/Hear My Plea	1957	5.00	10.00	20.00
❑ 6143	Believe It or Not/Tell Me So	1957	5.00	10.00	20.00
❑ 6148	Leona/Have I Sinned	1957	5.00	10.00	20.00
❑ 6156	Wild Child/Let's Do the Stroll	1958	5.00	10.00	20.00
❑ 6161	My Confession of Love/Peek-a-Boo	1958	5.00	10.00	20.00
❑ 6168	I Want to Be Near You/Come On Sugar	1958	5.00	10.00	20.00
❑ 6175	Just a Little Bit of Lovin'/When You're Near Me	1958	5.00	10.00	20.00
DERAM					
❑ 7526	Without You/Baby Please Come Home	1969	2.00	4.00	8.00
PARKWAY					
❑ 844	Set My Heart at Ease/Baby Cares	1962	3.75	7.50	15.00
RARE BULLET					
❑ 101	Can't Get Over Losing You/Got to Get Myself Together	1970	—	3.00	6.00
VEE JAY					
❑ 336	Hey Baby/Will You Ever Be Mine	1960	3.75	7.50	15.00
❑ 353	Baby Let Me Love You Tonight/Half as Old	1960	3.75	7.50	15.00
❑ 370	I've Loved You Baby/I Beg of You	1960	3.75	7.50	15.00

ELCHORDS, THE

Number	Title (A Side/B Side)	Yr	VG	VG+	NM
GOOD					
❑ 544	Peppermint Stick/Gee, I'm in Love	1958	20.00	40.00	80.00
—Straight lines on label					
❑ 544	Peppermint Stick/Gee, I'm in Love	1962	15.00	30.00	60.00
—Red vinyl					
❑ 544	Peppermint Stick/Gee, I'm in Love	1962	5.00	10.00	20.00
—Sawtooth lines on label					
❑ 544	Peppermint Stick/Gee, I'm in Love	1962	3.75	7.50	15.00
—No lines on label					

ELECTRIC FLAG, THE

Number	Title (A Side/B Side)	Yr	VG	VG+	NM
ATLANTIC					
❑ 3222	Sweet Soul Music/Every Now and Then	1974	—	2.00	4.00
❑ 3237	Doctor Oh Doctor/The Band Kept Playing	1975	—	2.00	4.00
COLUMBIA					
❑ 44307	Groovin' Is Easy/Over-Lovin' You	1967	2.00	4.00	8.00
❑ 44307 [PS]	Groovin' Is Easy/Over-Lovin' You	1967	5.00	10.00	20.00
❑ 44376	Soul Searchin'/Sunny	1967	2.00	4.00	8.00
❑ 44765	Soul Searchin'/Sunny	1969	—	3.00	6.00
SIDEWALK					
❑ 929	Green and Gold/Peter's Trip	1967	3.75	7.50	15.00

ELECTRIC INDIAN, THE

Number	Title (A Side/B Side)	Yr	VG	VG+	NM
MARMADUKE					
❑ 4001	Keem-O-Sabe/Broad Street	1969	5.00	10.00	20.00
UNITED ARTISTS					
❑ 0128	Keem-O-Sabe/Stick Shift	1973	—	2.00	4.00
—"Silver Spotlight Series" reissue; B-side by The Duals					
❑ 50563	Keem-O-Sabe/Broad Street	1969	—	3.00	6.00
❑ 50613	Geronimo/Land of 1,000 Dances	1969	—	2.50	5.00
❑ 50647	Rain Dance/Storm Warning	1970	—	2.50	5.00
❑ 50701	Apotchee/Chicago Hawk	1970	—	2.50	5.00
❑ 50744	Geronimo/My Cherie Amour	1971	—	2.50	5.00

ELECTRIC LIGHT ORCHESTRA

Evolved from THE MOVE. Also see JEFF LYNNE; ROY WOOD.

Number	Title (A Side/B Side)	Yr	VG	VG+	NM
CBS ASSOCIATED					
❑ 05766	Calling America/Caught in a Trap	1986	—	—	3.00
❑ 05766 [PS]	Calling America/Caught in a Trap	1986	—	—	3.00
❑ 05892	So Serious/Endless Lies	1986	—	—	3.00
❑ 05892 [PS]	So Serious/Endless Lies	1986	—	—	3.00
JET					
❑ XW 1099	Turn to Stone/Mister Kingdom	1977	—	2.00	4.00
❑ XW 1099 [PS]	Turn to Stone/Mister Kingdom	1977	2.00	4.00	8.00
❑ XW 1145	Sweet Talkin' Woman/Fire on High	1978	—	2.50	5.00
—Purple vinyl					
❑ XW 1145	Sweet Talkin' Woman/Fire on High	1978	—	2.00	4.00
❑ XW 1145 [PS]	Sweet Talkin' Woman/Fire on High	1978	—	2.50	5.00
❑ 02408	Hold On Tight/When Time Stood Still	1981	—	2.00	4.00
❑ 02559	Twilight/Julie Don't Live Here	1981	—	2.00	4.00
❑ 02693	Rain Is Falling/Another Heart Broke	1982	—	2.00	4.00
❑ 03086	Hold On Tight/Mr. Blue Sky	1982	—	—	3.00
—Reissue					
❑ 03964	Rock and Roll Is King/After All	1983	—	2.00	4.00
❑ 04130	Four Little Diamonds/Letter from Spain	1983	—	2.00	4.00
❑ 04208	Stranger/Train of Gold	1983	—	2.00	4.00
❑ 5050	Mr. Blue Sky/One Summer Dream	1978	—	2.00	4.00
❑ 5052	It's Over/The Whale	1978	—	2.00	4.00
❑ 5057	Shine a Little Love/Jungle	1979	—	2.00	4.00
❑ 5057 [PS]	Shine a Little Love/Jungle	1979	2.00	4.00	8.00
❑ 5060	Don't Bring Me Down/Dreaming of 4000	1979	—	2.00	4.00
❑ 5064	Confusion/Poker	1979	—	2.00	4.00
❑ 5067	Last Train to London/Down Home Town	1979	—	2.00	4.00
MCA					
❑ 41246	I'm Alive/Drum Dreams	1980	—	2.00	4.00
❑ 41246 [PS]	I'm Alive/Drum Dreams	1980	—	2.50	5.00
❑ 41285	Xanadu/Whenever You're Away from Me	1980	—	2.00	4.00
—A-side: Olivia Newton-John/Electric Light Orchestra					
❑ 41289	All Over the World/Drum Dreams	1980	—	2.00	4.00
❑ 41289 [PS]	All Over the World/Drum Dreams	1980	—	2.50	5.00
UNITED ARTISTS					
❑ XW 173	Roll Over Beethoven/Queen of the Hours	1973	—	3.00	6.00
❑ XW 337	Showdown/In Old England Town	1973	—	3.00	6.00
❑ XW 405	Daybreaker/Ma-Ma-Ma-Belle	1974	—	3.00	6.00
❑ XW 513	Roll Over Beethoven/Showdown	1974	—	2.00	4.00
—Reissue					
❑ XW 573	Can't Get It Out of My Head/Illusions in G Major	1974	—	2.00	4.00
❑ XW 573 [PS]	Can't Get It Out of My Head/Illusions in G Major	1974	—	3.00	6.00

Number	Title (A Side/B Side)	Yr	VG	VG+	NM
❑ XW 634	Boy Blue/Eldorado	1975	—	2.50	5.00
❑ XW 729	Evil Woman/10538 Overture (Live)	1975	—	2.00	4.00
❑ XW 770	Strange Magic/New World Rising	1976	—	2.00	4.00
❑ XW 770 [PS]	Strange Magic/New World Rising	1976	—	3.00	6.00
❑ XW 842	Showdown/Daybreaker (Live)	1976	—	2.50	5.00
❑ XW 888	Livin' Thing/Ma-Ma-Ma-Belle	1976	—	2.00	4.00
❑ XW 939	Do Ya/Nightrider	1977	—	2.00	4.00
❑ XW 1000	Telephone Line/Poorboy (The Greenwood)	1977	—	2.50	5.00
—Green vinyl					
❑ XW 1000	Telephone Line/Poorboy (The Greenwood)	1977	—	2.00	4.00
❑ XW 1000 [PS]	Telephone Line/Poorboy (The Greenwood)	1977	—	2.50	5.00
—Picture sleeves were not issued with black vinyl versions					
❑ XW 1176	Can't Get It Out of My Head/Strange Magic	1978	—	2.00	4.00
❑ XW 1177	Evil Woman/Livin' Thing	1978	—	2.00	4.00
❑ XW 1178	Do Ya/Nightrider	1978	—	2.00	4.00
❑ XW 1179	Boy Blue/Telephone Line	1978	—	2.00	4.00
❑ XW 1180	Ma-Ma-Ma-Belle/10538 Overture	1978	—	2.00	4.00
—1176 through 1180 were available for a very short time just before ELO's rights transfered from UA to CBS.					
❑ 50914	10538 Overture/(Battle of) Marston Moor	1972	2.00	4.00	8.00

ELECTRIC PRUNES, THE

Number	Title (A Side/B Side)	Yr	VG	VG+	NM
REPRISE					
❑ PRO 277 [DJ]	Sanctus/Credo	1968	12.50	25.00	50.00
❑ PRO 305 [DJ]	Help Us (Our Father, Our King)/The Adoration	1968	10.00	20.00	40.00
❑ 0473	Ain't It Hard/Little Olive	1966	10.00	20.00	40.00
❑ 0532	I Had Too Much to Dream (Last Night)/Lovin	1966	5.00	10.00	20.00
❑ 0564	Get Me to the World on Time/Are You Lovin' Me	1967	6.25	12.50	25.00
❑ 0594	Hideaway/Dr. Do-Good	1967	6.25	12.50	25.00
❑ 0607	The Great Banana Hoax/Wind-Up Toys	1967	6.25	12.50	25.00
❑ 0652	You Never Had It So Good/Everybody Knows You're Not in Love	1967	10.00	20.00	40.00
❑ 0704	I Had Too Much to Dream (Last Night)/Get Me to the World On Time	1968	—	2.50	5.00
—"Back to Back Hits" series -- originals have "W7" and "r:" logos					
❑ 0805	Hey, Mr. President/Flowing Smoothly	1969	6.25	12.50	25.00
❑ 0833	Violent Rose/Sell	1969	10.00	20.00	40.00
❑ 0858	Love Grows/Finders Keepers, Losers Weepers	1969	6.25	12.50	25.00

ELEGANTS, THE

Also see PAT CORDEL.

Number	Title (A Side/B Side)	Yr	VG	VG+	NM
ABC-PARAMOUNT					
❑ 10219	I've Seen Everything/Tiny Cloud	1961	10.00	20.00	40.00
APT					
❑ 25005	Little Star/Getting Dizzy	1958	12.50	25.00	50.00
—All-black label					
❑ 25005	Little Star/Getting Dizzy	1958	10.00	20.00	40.00
—Black label with rainbow					
❑ 25017	Goodnight/Please Believe Me	1958	7.50	15.00	30.00
❑ 25029	Pay Day/True Love Affair	1959	7.50	15.00	30.00
BANGAR					
❑ 613	Minor Chaos/Lost Souls	1964	7.50	15.00	30.00
BIM BAM BOOM					
❑ 121	It's Just a Matter of Time/Lonesome Weekends	1974	—	3.00	6.00
—Colored vinyl					
❑ 121	It's Just a Matter of Time/Lonesome Weekends	1974	—	2.00	4.00
—Black vinyl					
CRYSTAL BALL					
❑ 139	Maybe/Woo Woo Train	197?	—	2.50	5.00
HULL					
❑ 732	Little Boy Blue/Get Well Soon	1960	25.00	50.00	100.00
LAURIE					
❑ 3283	A Letter from Viet Nam/Barbara Beware	1965	7.50	15.00	30.00
❑ 3298	Wake Up/Bring Back Wendy	1965	12.50	25.00	50.00
❑ 3324	Belinda/Lazy Love	1965	6.25	12.50	25.00
—As "Vito and the Elegants"					
PHOTO					
❑ 2662	Dressin' Up/A Dream Can Come True	1963	12.50	25.00	50.00
❑ 2662 [PS]	Dressin' Up/A Dream Can Come True	1963	37.50	75.00	150.00
UNITED ARTISTS					
❑ 230	Speak Low/Let My Prayers Be With You	1960	10.00	20.00	40.00
❑ 295	Happiness/Spiritual	1961	12.50	25.00	50.00

ELENA

Number	Title (A Side/B Side)	Yr	VG	VG+	NM
ROULETTE					
❑ 4605	Evening Time/Road of Love	1965	3.75	7.50	15.00

ELEPHANTS MEMORY

Number	Title (A Side/B Side)	Yr	VG	VG+	NM
APPLE					
❑ 1854	Liberation Special/Madness	1972	2.00	4.00	8.00
❑ 1854	Liberation Special/Power Boogie	1972	100.00	200.00	400.00
❑ 1854 [PS]	Liberation Special/Madness	1972	2.50	5.00	10.00
ATLANTIC					
❑ 3257	Shakedown/Brother Can You Spare Me a Dime	1975	—	2.50	5.00
BUDDAH					
❑ 98	Cross Roads of the Stepping Stones/Jungle Gym at the Zoo	1969	2.00	4.00	8.00
❑ 209	Don't Put Me on Trial No More/Hot Dog	1971	2.00	4.00	8.00
METROMEDIA					
❑ 182	Mongoose/I Couldn't Dream	1970	—	3.00	6.00
❑ 182 [PS]	Mongoose/I Couldn't Dream	1970	—	3.00	6.00
❑ 210	Skyscraper Commando/Power	1971	—	3.00	6.00
RCA VICTOR					
❑ APBO-0268	Rock and Roll Streaker/Angels Forever	1974	—	2.50	5.00

ELGINS, THE (1)

Detroit R&B group.

Number	Title (A Side/B Side)	Yr	VG	VG+	NM
LUMMTONE					
❑ 113	Your Lovely Ways/Finding a Sweetheart	1963	6.25	12.50	25.00
TAMLA					
❑ 54056	Request of a Fool/Your Baby's Back	1962	75.00	150.00	300.00
—As "The Downbeats"; with "Tamla" circling globe at top of label					
❑ 54056	Request of a Fool/Your Baby's Back	1962	7.50	15.00	30.00
—As "The Downbeats"; with "Tamla" in globe at top of label					
V.I.P.					
❑ 25029	Darling Baby/Put Yourself in My Place	1965	50.00	100.00	200.00
—First pressings credited "The Downbeats"					
❑ 25029	Darling Baby/Put Yourself in My Place	1965	5.00	10.00	20.00
❑ 25037	Heaven Must Have Sent You/Stay in My Lonely Arms	1965	5.00	10.00	20.00
❑ 25043	It's Been a Long, Long Time/I Understand My Man	1966	5.00	10.00	20.00
❑ 25065	Heaven Must Have Sent You/Stay in My Lonely Arms	1970	2.50	5.00	10.00

ELGINS, THE (2)

Number	Title (A Side/B Side)	Yr	VG	VG+	NM
A.B.S.					
❑ 113	Pretending/Lonesome	1961	100.00	200.00	400.00

ELGINS, THE (3)

Number	Title (A Side/B Side)	Yr	VG	VG+	NM
CONGRESS					
❑ 214	The Times We've Wasted/Ritha Mae	1964	6.25	12.50	25.00
❑ 225	Here in Your Arms/We're Gonna Have a Good Time	1964	7.50	15.00	30.00

ELGINS, THE (4)

Number	Title (A Side/B Side)	Yr	VG	VG+	NM
LUMMTONE					
❑ 109	A Winner Never Quits/Johnny I'm Sorry	1962	6.25	12.50	25.00
❑ 110	You Got Your Magnet on Me Baby/Johnny I'm Sorry	1962	6.25	12.50	25.00
❑ 112	Finally/I Lost My Love in the Big City	1963	6.25	12.50	25.00

ELGINS, THE (U)

Some of these may be by group (3) or (4), but not all.

Number	Title (A Side/B Side)	Yr	VG	VG+	NM
DOT					
❑ 16563	Cheryl/Tell Gina	1963	15.00	30.00	60.00
FLIP					
❑ 353	Uncle Sam's Man/Casey Cop	1961	7.50	15.00	30.00
JOED					
❑ 716	Once Upon a Time/The Huddle	1964	175.00	350.00	700.00
MGM					
❑ 12670	A Picture of You/Mademoiselle	1958	15.00	30.00	60.00
TITAN					
❑ 1724	My Illness/Extra, Extra	1962	62.50	125.00	250.00
❑ 1724	My Illness/Heartache Heartbreak	1962	50.00	100.00	200.00
VALIANT					
❑ 712	Street Scene/You Found Yourself Another Fool	1965	5.00	10.00	20.00

ELIGIBLES, THE

Number	Title (A Side/B Side)	Yr	VG	VG+	NM
CAPITOL					
❑ 4203	Car Trouble/I Wrote a Song	1959	3.00	6.00	12.00
❑ 4265	Faker, Faker/24 Hours	1959	3.00	6.00	12.00
❑ 4304	My First Christmas with You/Little Engine	1959	3.75	7.50	15.00
❑ 4409	East of West Berlin/Young Is My Lover	1960	3.00	6.00	12.00
MERCURY					
❑ 72000	That Carmen Twist/Come Back, Music	1962	2.50	5.00	10.00
WARNER BROS.					
❑ 5344	Gabie/See What You Can Do For Me	1963	2.50	5.00	10.00

ELLEN, IVY, & FAMILY

Number	Title (A Side/B Side)	Yr	VG	VG+	NM
FELSTED					
❑ 8609	Go Tell Santa/(Instrumental)	1960	3.75	7.50	15.00
—B-side by the Reindeers					
❑ 8609 [PS]	Go Tell Santa/(Instrumental)	1960	5.00	10.00	20.00

ELLIE POP

Number	Title (A Side/B Side)	Yr	VG	VG+	NM
MAINSTREAM					
❑ 686	Can't Be Love/Seven North Frederick	1968	5.00	10.00	20.00

ELLIOT, CASS

Also see THE BIG THREE; THE MAMAS AND THE PAPAS; DAVE MASON; THE MUGWUMPS.

Number	Title (A Side/B Side)	Yr	VG	VG+	NM
ABC DUNHILL					
❑ 4145	Dream a Little Dream of Me/Midnight Voyage	1968	2.00	4.00	8.00
—Label credit: "Featuring Mama Cass with the Mamas and the Papas"					
❑ 4166	California Earthquake/Talkin' to Your Toothbrush	1968	—	3.00	6.00
❑ 4184	Move In a Little Closer, Baby/All for Me	1969	—	3.00	6.00
❑ 4195	It's Getting Better/Who's to Blame	1969	—	3.00	6.00
—The above three as "Mama Cass"					
❑ 4214	Make Your Own Kind of Music/Ladylove	1969	—	3.00	6.00
❑ 4225	New World Coming/Blow Me a Kiss	1970	—	3.00	6.00
❑ 4244	A Song That Never Comes/I Can Dream, Can't I?	1970	—	3.00	6.00
❑ 4253	Good Times Are Coming/Welcome to the World	1970	—	3.00	6.00
❑ 4264	Don't Let the Good Times Pass You By/A Song That Never Comes	1971	—	3.00	6.00
—The above five as "Mama Cass Elliott"					
DUNHILL					
❑ 4145	Dream a Little Dream of Me/Midnight Voyage	1968	6.25	12.50	25.00
—Label credit: "Featuring Mama Cass with the Mamas and the Papas"; no "ABC" at top of label					
RCA VICTOR					
❑ 74-0644	Baby, I'm Yours/Cherries Jubilee	1972	—	3.00	6.00
❑ 74-0693	That Song/When It Doesn't Work Out	1972	—	3.00	6.00
❑ 74-0764	Disney Girls/Break Another Heart	1972	—	3.00	6.00
❑ 74-0830	The Road Is No Place for a Lady/Does Anybody Love You	1972	—	3.00	6.00
❑ 74-0957	I Think a Lot About You/Listen to the World	1973	—	3.00	6.00

ELLIOTT, BERN, AND THE FENMEN

Number	Title (A Side/B Side)	Yr	VG	VG+	NM
LONDON					
❑ 9670	New Orleans/Everybody Needs a Little Love	1964	3.00	6.00	12.00
❑ 9733	Money/Nobody But Me	1965	3.00	6.00	12.00

ELLIOTT, BILL, AND THE ELASTIC OZ BAND

Also see JOHN LENNON; YOKO ONO.

Number	Title (A Side/B Side)	Yr	VG	VG+	NM
APPLE					
❑ 1835	God Save Us/Do the Oz	1971	2.00	4.00	8.00
❑ 1835 [PS]	God Save Us/Do the Oz	1971	2.50	5.00	10.00
❑ P-1835 [DJ]	God Save Us/Do the Oz	1971	6.25	12.50	25.00
—Has black star on A-side and unsliced apple on both sides					

ELLIS, JIMMY

Also see ORION.

Number	Title (A Side/B Side)	Yr	VG	VG+	NM
BOBLO					
❑ 526	Tupelo Woman/The Closer He Gets	1976	—	2.00	4.00
❑ 531	There You Go/Here Comes That Wonderful Feeling	1977	—	2.00	4.00
❑ 532	Movin' On/My Baby's Out of Sight	1977	—	2.00	4.00
❑ 536	I'm Not Trying to Be Like Elvis/Games You've Been Playing	1978	—	2.00	4.00
❑ 536 [PS]	I'm Not Trying to Be Like Elvis/Games You've Been Playing	1978	2.50	5.00	10.00
DRADCO					
❑ 1892	Don't Count Your Chickens/Love Is But Love	1964	3.75	7.50	15.00
GOLDBAND					
❑ 1191	Woman in the Picture/What Swinging Doors Did to Me	196?	2.50	5.00	10.00
KRIS					
❑ 8115	Outskirts of Town (Part 1)/Outskirts of Town (Part 2)	196?	2.00	4.00	8.00
MCA					
❑ 40060	There Ya Go/Here Comes That Feeling Again	1973	—	2.00	4.00
RIDE					
❑ 146	Baby I Love You/Kiddio	196?	2.00	4.00	8.00
—As "Jimmie Ellis"; may not be the same performer as the others					
SOUTHERN TRACKS					
❑ 1069	I Make the Livin' (You Make the Livin' Worthwhile)/Thank God for America	1986	—	2.00	4.00
❑ 1080	Sunday Fathers/Thank God for America	1987	—	2.00	4.00
SUN					
❑ 1129	That's All Right/Blue Moon of Kentucky	1973	—	2.50	5.00
—Originals have no artist on label in an attempt to make people believe these were lost Elvis Presley outtakes					
❑ 1129	That's All Right/Blue Moon of Kentucky	1973	—	2.00	4.00
—Second pressings credit Jimmy Ellis					
❑ 1131	I Use Her to Remind Me of You/Changing	1974	—	2.00	4.00
❑ 1136	D.O.A./Misty/That's All Right/Blue Moon of Kentucky	1977	—	2.00	4.00

ELLIS, JIMMY (2)

Number	Title (A Side/B Side)	Yr	VG	VG+	NM
ATLANTIC					
❑ 2572	I Don't Mind/Take the Lord With You	1968	2.00	4.00	8.00

ELLIS, LORRAINE

Number	Title (A Side/B Side)	Yr	VG	VG+	NM
BULLSEYE					
❑ 100	Perfidia/Piano Player Play a Tune	1955	15.00	30.00	60.00
GEE					
❑ 1	Perfidia/Piano Player Play a Tune	1953	75.00	150.00	300.00

ELLIS, SHIRLEY

Number	Title (A Side/B Side)	Yr	VG	VG+	NM
COLUMBIA					
❑ 43829	Truly, Truly, Truly/Birds, Bees, Cupids and Bows	1966	2.00	4.00	8.00
❑ 44021	Soul Time/Waitin'	1967	2.00	4.00	8.00
❑ 44137	Sugar Let's Shing-a-Ling/How Lonely Is Lonely	1967	2.00	4.00	8.00
CONGRESS					
❑ 202	The Nitty Gritty/Give Me a List	1963	3.75	7.50	15.00
❑ 208	(That's) What the Nitty Gritty Is/Get Out	1964	2.50	5.00	10.00
❑ 210	Shy One/Takin' Care of Business	1964	2.50	5.00	10.00
❑ 221	Such a Night/Bring It On Home to Me	1964	2.50	5.00	10.00
❑ 230	The Name Game/Whisper to the Wind	1964	3.00	6.00	12.00
❑ 230 [PS]	The Name Game/Whisper to the Wind	1964	5.00	10.00	20.00
❑ 234	The Clapping Song (Clap Pat Clap Slap)/This Is Beautiful	1965	2.50	5.00	10.00
❑ 234 [PS]	The Clapping Song (Clap Pat Clap Slap)/This Is Beautiful	1965	5.00	10.00	20.00
❑ 238	The Puzzle Song (A Puzzle in Song)/I See It, I Like It, I Want It	1965	2.50	5.00	10.00
❑ 246	I Never Will Forget/I Told You So	1965	2.50	5.00	10.00
❑ 251	One Sour Note/You Better Be Good, World	1965	2.50	5.00	10.00
❑ 260	Ever See a Diver Kiss His Wife While the Bubbles Bounce About Above the Water/Stardust	1965	2.50	5.00	10.00

EMANONS, THE

Number	Title (A Side/B Side)	Yr	VG	VG+	NM
ABC-PARAMOUNT					
❑ 9913	Dear One/We Teenagers (Know What We Want)	1958	5.00	10.00	20.00
GEE					
❑ 1005	Change of Time/Hindu Baby	1956	30.00	60.00	120.00
JOSIE					
❑ 801	Blue Moon/Wish I Had My Baby	1956	25.00	50.00	100.00
WINLEY					
❑ 226	Dear One/We Teenagers (Know What We Want)	1958	10.00	20.00	40.00

EMBERS, THE

Several different groups.

Number	Title (A Side/B Side)	Yr	VG	VG+	NM
ATLANTIC					
❑ 2627	Where Did I Go Wrong/You Got What You Want	1969	2.50	5.00	10.00
BELL					
❑ 664	It Ain't No Big Thing/It Ain't Necessary	1967	5.00	10.00	20.00
COLUMBIA					
❑ 40287	Sweet Lips/There'll Be No One Else But You	1954	10.00	20.00	40.00
DOT					
❑ 16101	Wait for Me/Couldn't Wait Any Longer	1960	3.75	7.50	15.00
❑ 16162	Please Mr. Sun/My Dearest Darling	1960	3.75	7.50	15.00
EMBER					
❑ 101	Sound of Love/Paradise Hill	1953	200.00	400.00	800.00
EMPRESS					
❑ 101	Solitaire/I'm Feeling All Right Again	1961	7.50	15.00	30.00
❑ 104	I Won't Cry Anymore/I Was Too Careful	1961	7.50	15.00	30.00
❑ 107	Abigail/I Was Too Careful	1962	7.50	15.00	30.00
❑ 108	What a Surprise/I Was Too Careful	1962	10.00	20.00	40.00
HERALD					
❑ 410	Sound of Love/Paradise Hill	1953	50.00	100.00	200.00
—Black label					
❑ 410	Sound of Love/Paradise Hill	1953	20.00	40.00	80.00
—Yellow label					
❑ 410	Sound of Love/Paradise Hill	1953	37.50	75.00	150.00
—Red vinyl					
JCP					
❑ 1008	In My Lonely Room/Good Good Lovin'	1964	15.00	30.00	60.00
LIBERTY					
❑ 55944	Evelyn/And Now I'm Blue	1967	2.50	5.00	10.00
MGM					
❑ 14167	Watch Out Girl/Far Away Places	1970	7.50	15.00	30.00
WYNNE					
❑ 101	Peter Gunn Cha Cha/Chinny Chin Cha Cha	1958	3.75	7.50	15.00

EMBRY, TED

Number	Title (A Side/B Side)	Yr	VG	VG+	NM
ACCENT					
❑ 1057	New Shoes/Teen Age Confession	1958	15.00	30.00	60.00

EMERALDS, THE

Several different groups.

Number	Title (A Side/B Side)	Yr	VG	VG+	NM
ABC-PARAMOUNT					
❑ 9889	You Belong to My Heart/The One I Adore	1958	6.25	12.50	25.00
❑ 9948	I'm Dreaming/Confess	1958	6.25	12.50	25.00
ALLIED					
❑ 10002	Sally Lou/Why Must I Wonder	1958	10.00	20.00	40.00
BOBBIN					
❑ 107	That's the Way It's Got to Be/Maria's Cha-Cha	1959	12.50	25.00	50.00
❑ 121	Lover's Cry/Rumblin' Tumblin' Baby	1960	10.00	20.00	40.00
JUBILEE					
❑ 5474	Dancing Alone/Wanna Make Him Mine	1964	3.00	6.00	12.00
❑ 5489	Did You Ever Love a Guy/I'm Gonna Ask That Boy to Dance	1964	3.00	6.00	12.00
KICKS					
❑ 3	Sally Lou/Why Must I Wonder	1954	175.00	350.00	700.00
KING					
❑ 6078	Baby You've Got Me/Promises	1967	6.25	12.50	25.00
MOONGLOW					
❑ 230	Ooh Poo Pah Doo/Sally's Snake	1964	7.50	15.00	30.00
❑ 232	Moonlight Surf/Little D Special	1964	7.50	15.00	30.00
—Black vinyl					
❑ 232	Moonlight Surf/Little D Special	1964	20.00	40.00	80.00
—Green vinyl					
REX					
❑ 1004	All the Time/Gotta Be on Time	1959	7.50	15.00	30.00
❑ 1013	I Kneel at Your Throne/Custer's Last Stand	1960	7.50	15.00	30.00
TOY					
❑ 7734	Silver/Roadrunner	1961	5.00	10.00	20.00
VENUS					
❑ 1002	Mademoiselle/The Lover	1959	25.00	50.00	100.00
❑ 1003	Marsha/You're Driving Me Crazy	1959	37.50	75.00	150.00
YALE					
❑ 232	The Web/Trapped	1960	5.00	10.00	20.00

EMERALS, THE

Number	Title (A Side/B Side)	Yr	VG	VG+	NM
TRIPLE X					
❑ 100/101	Please Don't Crush My Dreams/Jukebox Rock	1960	150.00	300.00	600.00

EMERSON, BILLY

Number	Title (A Side/B Side)	Yr	VG	VG+	NM
CHESS					
❑ 1711	Give Me a Little Love/Woodchuck	1959	5.00	10.00	20.00
❑ 1728	Holy Mackerel Baby/Believe Me	1959	5.00	10.00	20.00
❑ 1740	Uh Huh, My Baby/I'll Get to You	1959	5.00	10.00	20.00
CONSTELLATION					
❑ 148	Aunt Molly (Part 1)/Aunt Molly (Part 2)	1965	3.75	7.50	15.00
SUN					
❑ 195	No Teasin' Around/If Lovin' Is Believin'	1954	100.00	200.00	400.00
❑ 203	I'm Not Going Home/The Woodchuck	1954	200.00	400.00	600.00
❑ 214	Move, Baby, Move/When It Rains, It Pours	1955	12.50	25.00	50.00
❑ 219	Red Hot/No Greater Love	1955	25.00	50.00	100.00
❑ 233	Something for Nothing/Little Fine Healthy Thing	1956	12.50	25.00	50.00
VEE JAY					
❑ 219	Every Woman I Know/Tomorrow Never Comes	1956	7.50	15.00	30.00
❑ 247	Somebody Show Me/The Pleasure Is All Mine	1957	7.50	15.00	30.00
❑ 261	You Never Miss the Water/Do Yourself a Favor Billy	1957	7.50	15.00	30.00

EMERSON, LAKE AND PALMER

Also see GREG LAKE.

Number	Title (A Side/B Side)	Yr	VG	VG+	NM
ATLANTIC					
❑ 3398	Fanfare for the Common Man/Brain Salad Surgery	1977	—	2.50	5.00
❑ 3555	All I Want Is You/Tiger in a Spotlight	1979	—	2.50	5.00
❑ 3641	Peter Gunn Theme/Tiger in a Spotlight	1980	—	2.50	5.00
COTILLION					
❑ 44106	Lucky Man/Knife's Edge	1971	—	3.00	6.00
❑ 44131	A Time and a Place/Stone of Years	1971	—	2.50	5.00
❑ 44151	Nutrocker/The Great Gates of Kiev	1972	—	2.50	5.00
❑ 44158	From the Beginning/Living Sin	1972	—	2.50	5.00
MANTICORE					
❑ 2003	Still...You Turn Me On/Brain Salad Surgery	1973	—	2.50	5.00
❑ 2003 [PS]	Still...You Turn Me On/Brain Salad Surgery	1973	2.50	5.00	10.00

EMOTIONS, THE (1)
Female R&B vocal group. Also see EARTH, WIND AND FIRE WITH THE EMOTIONS.

Number	Title (A Side/B Side)	Yr	VG	VG+	NM
ARC					
❑ 18-02239	Turn It Out/When You Gonna Wake Up	1981	—	2.00	4.00
❑ 18-02535	Now That I Know/Here You Come Again	1981	—	2.00	4.00
❑ 11134	What's the Name of Your Love?/Layed Back	1979	—	2.50	5.00
❑ 11205	Where Is Your Love?/Layed Back	1980	—	2.50	5.00
COLUMBIA					
❑ 3-10347	Flowers/I Don't Wanna Lose Your Love	1976	—	2.50	5.00
❑ 3-10544	Best of My Love/A Feeling Is	1977	—	2.50	5.00
❑ 3-10622	Don't Ask My Neighbors/Love's What's Happenin'	1977	—	2.50	5.00
❑ 3-10791	Smile/Changes	1978	—	2.50	5.00
❑ 3-10828	Whole Lotta Shakin'/Time Is Passing By	1978	—	2.50	5.00
❑ 3-10874	Walking the Line/Ain't No Doubt About It	1978	—	2.50	5.00
MOTOWN					
❑ 1784	I Can't Wait to Make You Mine/I'm Gonna Miss Your Love	1985	—	2.00	4.00
❑ 1792	If I Only Knew Then (What I Know Now)/Eternally	1985	—	2.00	4.00
RED LABEL					
❑ 001-1	You're the One/I Can Do Anything	1984	—	2.50	5.00
❑ 001-2	You're the Best/(B-side unknown)	1984	—	2.50	5.00
❑ 001-3	Are You Through with My Heart/(B-side unknown)	1984	—	2.50	5.00
STAX					
❑ 1056	What Do The Lonely Do At Christmas?/Santa Claus Wants Some Lovin'	197?	—	3.00	6.00
—B-side by Albert King; reissue					
❑ 3200	Shouting Out Love/Baby, I'm Through	1977	—	2.50	5.00
❑ 3205	Baby, I'm Through/Any Way You Look at It	1978	—	2.50	5.00
❑ 3215	What Do the Lonely Do at Christmas/(Instrumental)	1978	—	2.50	5.00
TWIN STACKS					
❑ 126	Somebody New/Brushfire	1968	2.50	5.00	10.00
❑ 130	I Love You But I'll Leave You/Brushfire	1968	2.50	5.00	10.00
VOLT					
❑ 4010	So I Can Love You/Got to Be the Man	1969	2.00	4.00	8.00
❑ 4021	The Best Part of a Love Affair/I Like It	1969	2.00	4.00	8.00
❑ 4031	Stealing Love/When Tomorrow Comes	1970	2.00	4.00	8.00
❑ 4045	Heart Association/The Touch of Your Lips	1970	2.00	4.00	8.00
❑ 4053	Black Christmas/(Instrumental)	1970	2.50	5.00	10.00
❑ 4054	You Make Me Want to Love You/What You See Is What You Get	1971	—	3.50	7.00
❑ 4062	If You Think It/Love Ain't Easy One-Sided	1971	—	3.50	7.00
❑ 4066	Show Me How/Boss Love Maker	1971	—	3.50	7.00
❑ 4077	My Honey and Me/Blind Alley	1972	—	3.50	7.00
❑ 4083	I Could Never Be Happy/I've Fallen in Love	1972	—	3.50	7.00
❑ 4088	From Toys to Boys/I Call This Loving You	1972	—	3.50	7.00
❑ 4095	Runnin' Back (And Forth)/I Wanna Come Back	1973	—	3.50	7.00
❑ 4100	Peace Be Still/Runnin' Back (And Forth)	1973	—	3.50	7.00
❑ 4104	What Do the Lonely Do at Christmas/(Instrumental)	1973	2.00	4.00	8.00
❑ 4106	Put a Little Love Away/I Call This Loving You	1974	—	3.50	7.00
❑ 4110	Baby I'm Through/I Wanna Come Back	1974	—	3.50	7.00
❑ 4113	Any Way You Look At It/There Are More Questions Than Answers	1974	—	3.50	7.00

EMOTIONS, THE (2)
Brooklyn-based male vocal group.

Number	Title (A Side/B Side)	Yr	VG	VG+	NM
20TH FOX					
❑ 430	A Story Untold/One Life. One Love, One You	1963	5.00	10.00	20.00
❑ 452	Rainbow/Little Miss Blue	1963	5.00	10.00	20.00
❑ 478	Boomerang/I Love You Madly	1964	5.00	10.00	20.00
❑ 6623	Heart Strings/Every Time	1966	3.75	7.50	15.00
CALLA					
❑ 122	Baby I Need Your Lovin'/She's My Baby (I Just Can't Let Her Go)	1966	3.75	7.50	15.00
KAPP					
❑ 490	Echo/Come Dance Baby	1962	6.25	12.50	25.00
❑ 513	L-O-V-E/A Million Reasons	1963	6.25	12.50	25.00

EMOTIONS, THE (U)
It's unlikely than any of these are group (1). Some of these may be group (2). Others are different.

Number	Title (A Side/B Side)	Yr	VG	VG+	NM
BRAINSTORM					
❑ 125	Can't Stand No More Heartaches/You'd Better Get Used to It	1968	2.00	4.00	8.00
❑ 129	Never Let Me Go/I Can't Control These Emotions	1968	2.00	4.00	8.00
CARD					
❑ 600	(By the Light of the) Silvery Moon/Do You Love Me	1962	37.50	75.00	150.00
FLIP					
❑ 356	I Ran to You/Keep Lookin' Your Way	1961	7.50	15.00	30.00
FURY					
❑ 1010	Candlelight/It's Love	1958	10.00	20.00	40.00
KARATE					
❑ 506	Hey Baby/I Wonder	1964	5.00	10.00	20.00
LAURIE					
❑ 3167	Fool's Paradise/Starlit Night	1963	5.00	10.00	20.00
VARDAN					
❑ 201	Love of a Girl/Do This for Me	1965	5.00	10.00	20.00

EMPERORS, THE (1)
Band from Harrisburg, Pa.

Number	Title (A Side/B Side)	Yr	VG	VG+	NM
BRUNSWICK					
❑ 55333	Karate Boogaloo/Mumble Shing-a-Ling	1967	2.50	5.00	10.00
MALA					
❑ 543	Karate/I've Got to Have Her	1966	3.75	7.50	15.00
❑ 554	My Baby Likes to Boogaloo/You Got Me Where You Want Me	1967	3.00	6.00	12.00
❑ 561	Searchin'/Lookin' for My Baby	1967	3.00	6.00	12.00

EMPERORS, THE (2)
Sometimes called "The Emperors with Rhythm."

Number	Title (A Side/B Side)	Yr	VG	VG+	NM
HAVEN					
❑ 511	I May Be Wrong/Come Back, Come Back	1954	2000.	3000.	4000.

EMPERORS, THE (3)

Number	Title (A Side/B Side)	Yr	VG	VG+	NM
OLIMPIC					
❑ 245	Darlin' in the Moonlight/Steve Allen	1964	10.00	20.00	40.00

EMPERORS, THE (4)

Number	Title (A Side/B Side)	Yr	VG	VG+	NM
SABRA					
❑ 5555	I Want My Woman/(B-side unknown)	196?	10.00	20.00	40.00

EMPIRES, THE (1)
LES COOPER was a member of this group.

Number	Title (A Side/B Side)	Yr	VG	VG+	NM
AMP 3					
❑ 132	If I'm a Fool/Zippety Zip	1957	25.00	50.00	100.00
HARLEM					
❑ 2325	Corn Whiskey/My Baby, My Baby	1954	100.00	200.00	400.00
❑ 2333	Magic Mirror/Make Me or Break Me	1955	100.00	200.00	400.00
WHIRLIN' DISC					
❑ 104	Linda/Whispering Heart	1957	17.50	35.00	70.00
WING					
❑ 90023	I Want to Know/Shirley	1955	12.50	25.00	50.00
❑ 90050	By the Riverside/Tell Me Pretty Baby	1956	10.00	20.00	40.00
❑ 90080	Don't Touch My Gal/My First Discovery	1956	10.00	20.00	40.00

EMPIRES, THE (2)

Number	Title (A Side/B Side)	Yr	VG	VG+	NM
CALICO					
❑ 121	Definition of Love/Only in My Dreams	1960	5.00	10.00	20.00
CANDI					
❑ 1026	Love You So Bad/Come Back Girl	1962	6.25	12.50	25.00
❑ 1033	You're on Top, Girl/Slide On By	1963	10.00	20.00	40.00
CHAVIS					
❑ 1026	Love You So Bad/Come Back Girl	1962	3.75	7.50	15.00
COLPIX					
❑ 680	Everyone Knew But Me/Three Little Fishes	1963	5.00	10.00	20.00
DCP					
❑ 1116	Have Mercy/Love Is Strange	1964	3.00	6.00	12.00
LAKE					
❑ 711	Over the Summer Vacation/You're So Popular	1961	5.00	10.00	20.00

EMPIRES, THE (3)
Featuring David Blatt, later known as JAY BLACK of JAY AND THE AMERICANS.

Number	Title (A Side/B Side)	Yr	VG	VG+	NM
EPIC					
❑ 5-9527	A Time and a Place/Punch Your Nose	1962	10.00	20.00	40.00

ENALOUISE AND THE HEARTS

Number	Title (A Side/B Side)	Yr	VG	VG+	NM
ARGYLE					
❑ 1635	From a Cap and a Gown/A Prisoner to You	1959	12.50	25.00	50.00

ENCHANTERS, THE (1)

Number	Title (A Side/B Side)	Yr	VG	VG+	NM
BALD EAGLE					
❑ 3001	Come On Baby, Let's Do the Stroll/Rock Around	1958	7.50	15.00	30.00
BAMBOO					
❑ 513	Touch of Love/Cafe Bohemian	1961	6.25	12.50	25.00
CANDELITE					
❑ 432	Oh Rose Marie/Bewildered	1964	3.00	6.00	12.00
EP-SOM					
❑ 103	I Need Your Love/Goddess of Love	1962	100.00	200.00	400.00
J.J. & M.					
❑ 1562	Oh Rose Marie/Bewildered	1962	50.00	100.00	200.00
MUSITRON					
❑ 1072	I Lied to My Heart/Talk While You Walk	1961	10.00	20.00	40.00
ORBIT					
❑ 532	Touch of Love/Cafe Bohemian	1959	12.50	25.00	50.00
SHARP					
❑ 105	We Make Mistakes/The Decision	1960	6.25	12.50	25.00
STARDUST					
❑ 102	Spellbound by the Moon/Know It All	1956	375.00	750.00	1500.

ENCHANTERS, THE (2)
Also see GARNET MIMMS AND THE ENCHANTERS.

Number	Title (A Side/B Side)	Yr	VG	VG+	NM
LOMA					
❑ 2012	I Want to Be Loved/I Paid for the Party	1965	2.50	5.00	10.00
❑ 2035	You Were Meant to Be My Baby/God Bless the Girl, and Me	1966	2.50	5.00	10.00
❑ 2054	We Got Love/I've Lost All Communications	1966	2.50	5.00	10.00
WARNER BROS.					
❑ 5460	I Wanna Thank You/I'm a Good Man	1964	3.75	7.50	15.00

ENCHANTERS, THE (3)

Number	Title (A Side/B Side)	Yr	VG	VG+	NM
CORAL					
❑ 61756	True Love Gone/Wait a Minute Baby	1956	15.00	30.00	60.00
❑ 61832	There Goes (A Pretty Girl)/Fan Me Baby	1957	20.00	40.00	80.00
—Full-length version of A-side; matrix number is "100,974"					
❑ 61832	There Goes (A Pretty Girl)/Fan Me Baby	1957	6.25	12.50	25.00
—Edited version of A-side; matrix number is "102,966"					
❑ 61916	Mambo Santa Mambo/Bottle Up and Go	1957	10.00	20.00	40.00
❑ 62373	True Love Gone/The Day	1963	5.00	10.00	20.00
❑ 65610	True Love Gone/Today Is Your Birthday	1963	3.00	6.00	12.00
MERCER					
❑ 992	True Love Gone/Wait a Minute Baby	1956	500.00	1000.	2000.

ENCHANTERS, THE (4)

Number	Title (A Side/B Side)	Yr	VG	VG+	NM
JUBILEE					
❑ 5072	Today Is Your Birthday/How Could You	1952	62.50	125.00	250.00
❑ 5080	I've Lost/Housewife Blues	1952	50.00	100.00	200.00

ENCHANTERS, THE (U)
May be group (1); may be a fifth different group also.

Number	Title (A Side/B Side)	Yr	VG	VG+	NM
TOM TOM					
❑ 301	Surf Blast/Tom Tiki	1963	12.50	25.00	50.00

ENCHANTMENTS, THE

Number	Title (A Side/B Side)	Yr	VG	VG+	NM
FARO					
❑ 620	I'm in Love with Your Daughter/(B-side unknown)	1964	25.00	50.00	100.00
GONE					
❑ 5130	(I Love You) Sherry/Come On Home	1962	7.50	15.00	30.00
RITZ					
❑ 17003	I Love You Baby/Pains in My Heart	1963	25.00	50.00	100.00

ENCHORDS, THE

Number	Title (A Side/B Side)	Yr	VG	VG+	NM
LAURIE					
❑ 3089	Zoom Zoom Zoom/I Need You Baby	1961	12.50	25.00	50.00

ENCORES, THE
More than one group.

Number	Title (A Side/B Side)	Yr	VG	VG+	NM
BOW					
❑ 302	Barbara/Thank You	1958	25.00	50.00	100.00
CHECKER					
❑ 760	When I Look at You/Young Girls, Young Girls	1952	2000.	3000.	4000.
HOLLYWOOD					
❑ 1034	Time Is Moving On/Ha-Chi-Bi-Ri-Bi-Ri	1955	20.00	40.00	80.00
LOOK					
❑ 105	Time Is Moving On/Ha-Chi-Bi-Ri-Bi-Ri	1955	100.00	200.00	400.00
MGM					
❑ 11947	Chloe/Wa Va Ga Dot	1955	3.00	6.00	12.00

ENCOUNTERS, THE

Number	Title (A Side/B Side)	Yr	VG	VG+	NM
SWAN					
❑ 4206	Don't Stop Now/Place in Your Heart	1964	37.50	75.00	150.00

END, THE

Number	Title (A Side/B Side)	Yr	VG	VG+	NM
LONDON					
❑ 1016	Shades of Orange/Loving, Sacred Loving	1968	5.00	10.00	20.00
PHILIPS					
❑ 40323	Hey Little Girl/I Can't Get Any Joy	1965	2.50	5.00	10.00

ENDEAVORS, THE (1)

Number	Title (A Side/B Side)	Yr	VG	VG+	NM
J&S					
❑ 254	Suffering with My Heart/I Got the Feeling	1960	300.00	600.00	1200.

ENDEAVORS, THE (2)
Country group.

Number	Title (A Side/B Side)	Yr	VG	VG+	NM
STOP					
❑ 372	Shattered Dreams/I Know You Don't Want Me	1971	2.50	5.00	10.00

ENDORSERS, THE

Number	Title (A Side/B Side)	Yr	VG	VG+	NM
MOON					
❑ 109	Crying/Hold My Hand	1959	500.00	1000.	2000.

ENEMYS, THE
With Cory Wells, later of THREE DOG NIGHT.

Number	Title (A Side/B Side)	Yr	VG	VG+	NM
MGM					
❑ 13485	Glitter and Gold/Too Much Monkey Business	1966	3.75	7.50	15.00
❑ 13525	Hey Joe/My Dues Have Been Paid	1966	3.75	7.50	15.00
❑ 13573	Mo-Jo Woman/My Dues Have Been Paid	1966	3.75	7.50	15.00
VALIANT					
❑ 714	Say Goodbye to Donna/Sinner Man	1965	6.25	12.50	25.00
—As "Corey Wells and the Enemys"					

ENGEL, SCOTT
Also see THE WALKER BROTHERS.

Number	Title (A Side/B Side)	Yr	VG	VG+	NM
CHALLENGE					
❑ 9206	Devil Surfer/Your Guess	1963	5.00	10.00	20.00
LIBERTY					
❑ 55312	Mr. Jones/Anything Will Do	1961	5.00	10.00	20.00
❑ 55428	Anything Will Do/Forever More	1962	5.00	10.00	20.00
MARTAY					
❑ 2004	Devil Surfer/Your Guess	1963	10.00	20.00	40.00
ORBIT					
❑ 506	The Livin' End/Good for Nothin'	1958	5.00	10.00	20.00
❑ 506 [PS]	The Livin' End/Good for Nothin'	1958	12.50	25.00	50.00
❑ 511	Charley Bop/All I Do Is Dream	1958	7.50	15.00	30.00
❑ 511 [PS]	Charley Bop/All I Do Is Dream	1958	15.00	30.00	60.00
❑ 512	Blue Bell/Paper Doll	1958	5.00	10.00	20.00
❑ 512 [PS]	Blue Bell/Paper Doll	1958	12.50	25.00	50.00
❑ 537	The Golden Rule/Sunday	1959	5.00	10.00	20.00
❑ 537 [PS]	The Golden Rule/Sunday	1959	12.50	25.00	50.00
❑ 545	Comin' Home/I Don't Wanna Know	1959	5.00	10.00	20.00
RKO UNIQUE					
❑ 386	Steady As a Rock/When Is a Boy a Man	1957	6.25	12.50	25.00

ENGLAND, BENNY

Number	Title (A Side/B Side)	Yr	VG	VG+	NM
SNAP					
❑ 400	Eloping/Some How	1958	75.00	150.00	300.00

ENGLER, JERRY, AND THE FOUR EKKOS

Number	Title (A Side/B Side)	Yr	VG	VG+	NM
BRUNSWICK					
❑ 55037	Sputnik (Satellite Girl)/Unfaithful One	1957	20.00	40.00	80.00
—BUDDY HOLLY appears on this record					

ENGLISH, BARBARA
Also includes records as "Barbara Jean English." Also see THE FASHIONS (1).

Number	Title (A Side/B Side)	Yr	VG	VG+	NM
ALITHIA					
❑ 6040	I'm Living a Lie/All This	1972	—	3.00	6.00
❑ 6041	So Many Ways to Die/(B-side unknown)	1972	—	3.00	6.00
❑ 6042	I'm Sorry/Lil' Baby	1972	—	3.00	6.00
❑ 6046	Baby I'm-a Want You/Don't Make Me Over	1973	—	3.00	6.00
❑ 6053	You're Gonna Need Somebody to Love (While You're Looking for Someone to Love)/All This	1973	—	3.00	6.00
❑ 6059	Comin' or Goin'/Love's Arrangement	1973	—	3.00	6.00
❑ 6064	Breakin' Up a Happy Home/Guess Who	1974	—	3.00	6.00
AURORA					
❑ 155	Standin' on Tip-Toe/(You Got Me) Sittin' in the Corner	1965	20.00	40.00	80.00
MALA					
❑ 488	Easy Come, Easy Go/I Don't Deserve a Boy Like You	1964	6.25	12.50	25.00
REPRISE					
❑ 0290	I've Gotta Date/Shoo Fly	1964	6.25	12.50	25.00
❑ 0349	Small Town Girl/Tell It Like It Is	1965	6.25	12.50	25.00
ROULETTE					
❑ 4428	We Need Them/La-Ta-Tee-Ta-Ta	1962	7.50	15.00	30.00
❑ 4450	Fever/Bad News	1962	7.50	15.00	30.00
WARNER BROS.					
❑ 5685	All Because I Love Somebody/All the Good Times Are Gone	1965	5.00	10.00	20.00

ENGLISH, SCOTT

Number	Title (A Side/B Side)	Yr	VG	VG+	NM
DOT					
❑ 16099	White Cliffs of Dover/4000 Miles Away	1960	7.50	15.00	30.00
JANUS					
❑ 171	Brandy/Lead Me Back	1971	3.00	6.00	12.00
—A-side later recorded by Barry Manilow as "Mandy"					
❑ 192	Woman in My Life/Ballad of the Unloved	1972	—	2.50	5.00
JOKER					
❑ 777	Ugly Pills (You're Takin')/When	1962	12.50	25.00	50.00
SPOKANE					
❑ 4003	High on a Hill/When	1964	6.25	12.50	25.00
❑ 4007	Here Comes the Pain/All I Want Is You	1964	10.00	20.00	40.00
SULTAN					
❑ 1003	High on a Hill/When	1963	12.50	25.00	50.00

ENJOYABLES, THE

Number	Title (A Side/B Side)	Yr	VG	VG+	NM
CAPITOL					
❑ 5321	Push a Little Harder/We'll Make Our Way	1964	3.00	6.00	12.00
SHRINE					
❑ 118	Shame/(B-side unknown)	1966	100.00	200.00	400.00

ENO, BRIAN
Also see ROXY MUSIC.

Number	Title (A Side/B Side)	Yr	VG	VG+	NM
ISLAND					
❑ 036	The Lion Sleeps Tonight/I'll Come Running (To Tie Your Shoes)	1975	6.25	12.50	25.00
❑ 036 [DJ]	The Lion Sleeps Tonight (mono/stereo)	1975	3.75	7.50	15.00

ENTWISTLE, JOHN
Also see THE WHO.

Number	Title (A Side/B Side)	Yr	VG	VG+	NM
ATCO					
❑ 7337	Too Late the Hero/Dancin' Master	1981	—	2.00	4.00
❑ 7344	Talk Dirty/Try Me	1982	—	2.00	4.00
DECCA					
❑ 32896	I Believe in Everything/My Size	1971	—	3.00	6.00
❑ 33052	I Wonder/Who Cares	1973	—	3.00	6.00
TRACK					
❑ 40066	Made in Japan/Roller Skate Kate	1973	—	2.50	5.00

EPICS, THE

Number	Title (A Side/B Side)	Yr	VG	VG+	NM
HANNA-BARBERA					
❑ 480	Blue Turns to Grey/Goes to Show	1966	3.75	7.50	15.00

EPISODE SIX

Number	Title (A Side/B Side)	Yr	VG	VG+	NM
CHAPTER ONE					
❑ 2902	Lucky Sunday/Mr. Universe	1968	3.00	6.00	12.00
COMPASS					
❑ 7007	Morning Dew/Sunshine Girl	1967	3.75	7.50	15.00
ELEKTRA					
❑ 45617	Baby, Baby, Baby/Love-Hate-Revenge	1967	3.75	7.50	15.00
WARNER BROS.					
❑ 5851	Here, There and Everywhere/Mighty Morris Ten	1966	3.75	7.50	15.00

EPISODES, THE

Number	Title (A Side/B Side)	Yr	VG	VG+	NM
FOUR SEASONS					
❑ 1014	The Christmas Tree/Where Is My Love	1965	37.50	75.00	150.00

EPPS, PRESTON

Number	Title (A Side/B Side)	Yr	VG	VG+	NM
ADMIRAL					
❑ 901	Bongo Express/Flamenco Bongo	1963	3.75	7.50	15.00
DONNA					
❑ 1367	Mister Bongo/B'Wana Bongo	1962	3.75	7.50	15.00
EMBASSY					
❑ 203	Rockin' in the Congo/Sing Donna Go	1961	3.75	7.50	15.00
JO JO					
❑ 106	Afro Mania/Love Is the Only Good Thing	1969	—	3.00	6.00
MAJESTY					
❑ 1300	Bongo Boogie/Flamenco Bongo	1962	3.75	7.50	15.00
ORIGINAL SOUND					
❑ 4 [M]	Bongo Rock/Bongo Party	1959	5.00	10.00	20.00
❑ 4 [S]	Bongo Rock/Bongo Party	1959	12.50	25.00	50.00
❑ 9	Bongo, Bongo, Bongo/Hully Gully Bongo	1960	5.00	10.00	20.00
❑ 14	Bongo Shuffle/Bongo in the Congo	1960	3.75	7.50	15.00
❑ 17	Bongo Rocket/Jungle Drums	1961	3.75	7.50	15.00
POLO					
❑ 218	Bongo Rock 1965/Bongo Waltz	1965	3.00	6.00	12.00
TOP RANK					
❑ 2067	Blue Bongo/Bongola	1960	3.75	7.50	15.00
❑ 2091	Bongo Hop/Caravan	1960	3.75	7.50	15.00

Number	Title (A Side/B Side)	Yr	VG	VG+	NM

7-Inch Extended Plays

ORIGINAL SOUND

Number	Title (A Side/B Side)	Yr	VG	VG+	NM
❑ EP 1001	Bongo Rock/Doin' the Cha Cha Cha//Bongos in Pastel/Bongo Party	1959	10.00	20.00	40.00
❑ EP 1001 [PS]	Bongo Rock	1959	10.00	20.00	40.00

EQUADORS, THE

ARGO

Number	Title (A Side/B Side)	Yr	VG	VG+	NM
❑ 5353	Say You'll Be Mine/Let Me Sleep, Woman	1959	15.00	30.00	60.00

MIRACLE

Number	Title (A Side/B Side)	Yr	VG	VG+	NM
❑ 7	You're My Desire/Someone to Call My Own	1961	37.50	75.00	150.00

EQUALLOS, THE

M&M

Number	Title (A Side/B Side)	Yr	VG	VG+	NM
❑ 1296	Beneath the Sun/In Between Tears	1962	375.00	750.00	1500.

EQUALS, THE

BANG

Number	Title (A Side/B Side)	Yr	VG	VG+	NM
❑ 582	Ain't Got Nothing to Give You/Black Skin, Blue Eyed Boys	1971	2.50	5.00	10.00

PRESIDENT

Number	Title (A Side/B Side)	Yr	VG	VG+	NM
❑ 103	Fire/I Won't Be There	1967	3.00	6.00	12.00
❑ 105	My Life Ain't Easy/You Got Too Many Boyfriends	1967	3.00	6.00	12.00
❑ 108	Giddy Up a Ding-Dong/I Get So Excited	1968	3.00	6.00	12.00
❑ 109	Lovely Rita/Softly, Softly	1968	3.00	6.00	12.00
❑ 110	Honey Gun/Michael and the Slipper Tree	1968	3.00	6.00	12.00
❑ 111	I Can't Let You Go/Viva Bobby Joe	1969	3.00	6.00	12.00

RCA VICTOR

Number	Title (A Side/B Side)	Yr	VG	VG+	NM
❑ 47-9186	Baby Come Back/Hold Me Closer	1967	3.75	7.50	15.00
❑ 47-9583	Baby Come Back/Hold Me Closer	1968	2.50	5.00	10.00

SHOUT

Number	Title (A Side/B Side)	Yr	VG	VG+	NM
❑ 247	Ain't Got Nothing to Give You/Black Skin, Blue Eyed Boys	1970	3.00	6.00	12.00

EQUIPE 84

IMPERIAL

Number	Title (A Side/B Side)	Yr	VG	VG+	NM
❑ 66266	The Twenty-Ninth of September/Auschwitz	1967	5.00	10.00	20.00

ERASURE

MAVERICK/MUTE

Number	Title (A Side/B Side)	Yr	VG	VG+	NM
❑ 17371	In My Arms/Heart of Glass	1997	—	2.00	4.00

SIRE

Number	Title (A Side/B Side)	Yr	VG	VG+	NM
❑ PRO-S-3409 [DJ]	She Won't Be Home (Lonely Christmas)/God Rest Ye Merry Gentlemen	1988	3.00	6.00	12.00
—Released with promo insert (add 50%), no picture sleeve					
❑ 21863	Chains of Love/A Little Respect	199?	—	—	3.00
—Reissue					
❑ 22879	Stop!/Ship of Fools	1989	—	—	3.00
❑ 27738	A Little Respect/Like Zsa Zsa Gabor	1988	—	—	3.00
❑ 27738 [PS]	A Little Respect/Like Zsa Zsa Gabor	1988	—	—	3.00
❑ 27844	Chains of Love/Don't Suppose	1988	—	—	3.00
❑ 27844 [PS]	Chains of Love/Don't Suppose	1988	—	—	3.00
❑ 28238	Victim of Love/Soldier's Return	1987	—	—	3.00
❑ 28238 [PS]	Victim of Love/Soldier's Return	1987	—	—	3.00
❑ 28362	Sometimes/It Doesn't Have to Be	1987	—	2.50	5.00
❑ 28614	Oh L'Amour/Gimme! Gimme! Gimme!	1986	—	2.50	5.00
❑ 28728	Who Needs Love (Like That)/Push Me Shove Me	1986	—	2.50	5.00

ERLENE AND HER GIRLFRIENDS

OLD TOWN

Number	Title (A Side/B Side)	Yr	VG	VG+	NM
❑ 1150	A Guy Is a Guy/My Dada Say	1963	5.00	10.00	20.00
❑ 1152	Because of You/Casanova	1963	5.00	10.00	20.00

ERMINES, THE

See CORNEL GUNTER.

ERNIE AND THE EMPERORS

REPRISE

Number	Title (A Side/B Side)	Yr	VG	VG+	NM
❑ 0414	Got a Lot I Want to Say/Meet Me at the Corner	1965	7.50	15.00	30.00

ERVIN SISTERS, THE

TRI PHI

Number	Title (A Side/B Side)	Yr	VG	VG+	NM
❑ 1014	Changing Baby/Do It Right	1962	15.00	30.00	60.00
❑ 1022	Every Day's a Holiday/Why I Love Him	1963	20.00	40.00	80.00

ERWIN, DEE

See BIG DEE IRWIN.

ESCORTS, THE (1)

Group from Rahway State Prison in New Jersey.

ALITHIA

Number	Title (A Side/B Side)	Yr	VG	VG+	NM
❑ 6048	All We Need (Is Another Chance) (Short)/All We Need (Is Another Chance) (Long)	1973	—	3.00	6.00
❑ 6052	Look Over Your Shoulder/By the Time I Get to Phoenix	1973	—	2.50	5.00
❑ 6055	I'll Be Sweeter Tomorrow/I'm So Glad I Found You	1973	—	2.50	5.00
❑ 6062	Disrespect Can Wreck/All We Need	1974	—	2.50	5.00
❑ 6066	Let's Make Love (At Home Sometime)/Within Without	1974	—	2.50	5.00

ESCORTS, THE (2)

CORAL

Number	Title (A Side/B Side)	Yr	VG	VG+	NM
❑ 62302	Gloria/Seven Wonders of the World	1961	10.00	20.00	40.00
❑ 62317	As I Love You/Gaudeamus	1962	10.00	20.00	40.00
❑ 62336	Somewhere/Submarine Race Watching	1962	6.25	12.50	25.00
❑ 62349	One Hand. One Heart/I Can't Be Free	1963	6.25	12.50	25.00
❑ 62372	Back Home Again/Something Has Changed Him	1963	6.25	12.50	25.00
—As "Goldie and the Escorts"					
❑ 62385	Give Me Tomorrow/My Heart Cries for You	1963	6.25	12.50	25.00

ESCORTS, THE (3)

British group.

FONTANA

Number	Title (A Side/B Side)	Yr	VG	VG+	NM
❑ 1512	Come On Home Baby/She Gets No Loving	1965	3.75	7.50	15.00
❑ 1912	Dizzy Miss Lizzy/All I Want Is You	1964	3.75	7.50	15.00

ESCORTS, THE (U)

None of these are group (1) or (3). Some could be group (2) or (4). More likely, they are more than one other group.

BOOMERANG

Number	Title (A Side/B Side)	Yr	VG	VG+	NM
❑ 621	Little Big Horn/Wiped Out	1962	10.00	20.00	40.00

JUDD

Number	Title (A Side/B Side)	Yr	VG	VG+	NM
❑ 1014	My First Year/Clap Happy	1959	3.75	7.50	15.00

RCA VICTOR

Number	Title (A Side/B Side)	Yr	VG	VG+	NM
❑ 47-6834	Bad Boy/Tore Up Over You	1957	3.75	7.50	15.00
❑ 47-6963	So Hard to Laugh, So Easy to Cry/Lonely Man	1957	3.75	7.50	15.00
❑ 47-8228	You Can't Even Be My Friend/Itchy Coo	1963	3.00	6.00	12.00
❑ 47-8327	The Hurt/No City Folks Allowed	1964	3.00	6.00	12.00

SCARLET

Number	Title (A Side/B Side)	Yr	VG	VG+	NM
❑ 4005	I Will Be Home Again/Leaky Heart and His Red Go-Kart	1960	15.00	30.00	60.00

SCEPTER

Number	Title (A Side/B Side)	Yr	VG	VG+	NM
❑ 1201	Why Why Why/Ugly Duckling	1958	10.00	20.00	40.00
—With Don Crawford					

SOMA

Number	Title (A Side/B Side)	Yr	VG	VG+	NM
❑ 1144	Main Drag/Judy or Jo Ann	1961	6.25	12.50	25.00

ESQUERITA

CAPITOL

Number	Title (A Side/B Side)	Yr	VG	VG+	NM
❑ F4007	Please Come On Home/Oh Baby	1958	7.50	15.00	30.00
❑ F4058	Rockin' the Joint/Esquerita and the Voola	1958	7.50	15.00	30.00
❑ F4145	Laid Off/Just Another Lie	1959	7.50	15.00	30.00

ESQUIRES, THE (1)

Milwaukee-based R&B group.

BUNKY

Number	Title (A Side/B Side)	Yr	VG	VG+	NM
❑ 7750	Get On Up/Listen to Me	1967	2.50	5.00	10.00
❑ 7752	And Get Away/Everybody's Laughin'	1967	2.50	5.00	10.00
❑ 7753	You Say/State Fair	1968	2.50	5.00	10.00
❑ 7755	Why Can't I Stop/The Feeling's Gone	1968	2.50	5.00	10.00
❑ 7756	How Could It Be/I Know I Can	1968	2.50	5.00	10.00

CAPITOL

Number	Title (A Side/B Side)	Yr	VG	VG+	NM
❑ 2650	Reach Out/Listen to Me	1969	2.00	4.00	8.00

CIGAR MAN

Number	Title (A Side/B Side)	Yr	VG	VG+	NM
❑ 79880	The Show Ain't Over/What Good Is Music?	1980	—	3.00	6.00

JU-PAR

Number	Title (A Side/B Side)	Yr	VG	VG+	NM
❑ 104	Get On Up '76/Feeling's Gone (Also Known As Disco Dancing)	1976	—	3.00	6.00

LAMARR

Number	Title (A Side/B Side)	Yr	VG	VG+	NM
❑ 1001	Girls in the City/Ain't Gonna Give It Up	1971	2.00	4.00	8.00

SCEPTER

Number	Title (A Side/B Side)	Yr	VG	VG+	NM
❑ 12232	You've Got the Power/No Doubt About It	1968	—	—	—
—Unreleased? (Possibly reassigned to Wand?)					

WAND

Number	Title (A Side/B Side)	Yr	VG	VG+	NM
❑ 1193	You've Got the Power/No Doubt About It	1968	2.00	4.00	8.00
❑ 1195	I Don't Know/Part Angel	1969	2.00	4.00	8.00
❑ 11201	Whip It On Me/It Was Yesterday	1969	2.00	4.00	8.00

ESQUIRES, THE (2)

ARGO

Number	Title (A Side/B Side)	Yr	VG	VG+	NM
❑ 5435	Boat of Love/With a Feeling	1963	5.00	10.00	20.00

ESQUIRES, THE (3)

EPIC

Number	Title (A Side/B Side)	Yr	VG	VG+	NM
❑ 5-9024	If You Only Knew What a Three-Cent Stamp Can Do/Now, Now, Now	1954	375.00	750.00	1500.
—This may not exist on 45, though it certainly should.					

HI-PO

Number	Title (A Side/B Side)	Yr	VG	VG+	NM
❑ 1003	Only the Angels Know/One Word for This	1955	500.00	1000.	2000.

ESQUIRES, THE (U)

None of these are groups (1) or (3), but they may not all be the same group, either.

COLUMBIA

Number	Title (A Side/B Side)	Yr	VG	VG+	NM
❑ 4-43815	It's a Dirty Shame/Love Hides a Multitude of Sins	1966	5.00	10.00	20.00

DOT

Number	Title (A Side/B Side)	Yr	VG	VG+	NM
❑ 16954	Misfortune/She's My Woman	1966	3.75	7.50	15.00

DURCO

Number	Title (A Side/B Side)	Yr	VG	VG+	NM
❑ 1001	Flashin' Red/What a Burn	1964	10.00	20.00	40.00

TOWER

Number	Title (A Side/B Side)	Yr	VG	VG+	NM
❑ 174	Love's Made a Fool of You/Summertime	1965	3.75	7.50	15.00

ESQUIVEL

RCA VICTOR

Number	Title (A Side/B Side)	Yr	VG	VG+	NM
❑ 47-5969	Beasme Mucho/Vereda Tropical	1954	5.00	10.00	20.00
—As "Juan Garcia Esquivel"					
❑ 47-6008	Nocturnal/Amor	1955	5.00	10.00	20.00
❑ 47-6496	Nightingale/Jungle Drums	1956	3.75	7.50	15.00
❑ 47-6514	Port Au Prince/To Love Again	1956	3.75	7.50	15.00
❑ 47-7316	That Old Black Magic/Cielito Lindo	1958	3.75	7.50	15.00
❑ 47-7360	It Had to Be You/Begin the Beguine	1958	3.75	7.50	15.00
❑ 47-7361	Night and Day/Ballerina	1958	3.75	7.50	15.00
❑ 47-7462	I Feel Merely Marvelous/Whatchamacallit	1959	3.75	7.50	15.00

ESSEX, DAVID

COLUMBIA

Number	Title (A Side/B Side)	Yr	VG	VG+	NM
❑ 10005	America/Dance Little Girl	1974	—	2.50	5.00
❑ 10005 [PS]	America/Dance Little Girl	1974	2.00	4.00	8.00
❑ 10039	Gonna Make You a Star/Window	1974	—	2.50	5.00
❑ 10183	Rolling Stone/Coconut Ice	1975	—	2.50	5.00
❑ 10183 [PS]	Rolling Stone/Coconut Ice	1975	2.00	4.00	8.00
❑ 10256	Good Ol' Rock 'N' Roll/Hold Me Close	1975	—	2.50	5.00
❑ 45940	Rock On/On and On	1973	—	2.50	5.00
❑ 45940 [PS]	Rock On/On and On	1973	2.50	5.00	10.00
❑ 46041	Lamplight/We're All Insane	1974	—	2.50	5.00
❑ 46041 [PS]	Lamplight/We're All Insane	1974	2.50	5.00	10.00

Number	Title (A Side/B Side)	Yr	VG	VG+	NM
RSO					
❑ 1006	Oh What a Circus (From Evita)/Ships That Pass in the Night	1979	—	2.00	4.00
UNI					
❑ 55020	She's Leaving Home/He's a Better Man Than Me	1967	2.50	5.00	10.00

ESSEX, THE
Also see ANITA HUMES.

Number	Title (A Side/B Side)	Yr	VG	VG+	NM
BANG					
❑ 537	The Eagle/Moonlight, Music, and You	1966	2.00	4.00	8.00
ROULETTE					
❑ 4494	Easier Said Than Done/Are You Going My Way	1963	3.75	7.50	15.00
❑ 4515	A Walkin' Miracle/What I Don't Know Won't Hurt Me	1963	3.75	7.50	15.00
❑ 4530	She's Got Everything/Out of Sight, Out of Mind	1964	2.50	5.00	10.00
❑ 4542	What Did I Do/Curfew Lover	1964	2.50	5.00	10.00

ESTELLE
Estelle Bennett, formerly of THE RONETTES.

Number	Title (A Side/B Side)	Yr	VG	VG+	NM
LAURIE					
❑ 3449	The Year 2000/The Naked Boy	1968	25.00	50.00	100.00

ESTRADA, ROY, AND THE ROCKETEERS

Number	Title (A Side/B Side)	Yr	VG	VG+	NM
KING					
❑ 5368	Jungle Dream (Part 1)/Jungle Dream (Part 2)	1960	12.50	25.00	50.00

ETERNALS, THE (1)

Number	Title (A Side/B Side)	Yr	VG	VG+	NM
HOLLYWOOD					
❑ 68	Rockin' in the Jungle/Rock and Roll Cha Cha	1959	15.00	30.00	60.00
—White label					
❑ 68	Rockin' in the Jungle/Rock and Roll Cha Cha	1959	10.00	20.00	40.00
—Blue label					
❑ 68	Rockin' in the Jungle/Rock and Roll Cha Cha	1959	5.00	10.00	20.00
—Yellow label					
❑ 70	Babalu's Wedding Day/My Girl	1959	12.50	25.00	50.00
—Red label					
❑ 70	Babalu's Wedding Day/My Girl	1959	6.25	12.50	25.00
—Blue label					
WARWICK					
❑ 611	Blind Date/Today	1961	5.00	10.00	20.00

ETERNALS, THE (2)

Number	Title (A Side/B Side)	Yr	VG	VG+	NM
QUALITY					
❑ 1902	Falling Tears/Sticks and Stones	1968	5.00	10.00	20.00

ETERNITY'S CHILDREN

Number	Title (A Side/B Side)	Yr	VG	VG+	NM
A&M					
❑ 866	Rumors/Wait and See	1967	2.50	5.00	10.00
LIBERTY					
❑ 56162	Alone Again/From You Unto Us	1970	2.00	4.00	8.00
TOWER					
❑ 416	Mrs. Bluebird/Little Boy	1968	2.50	5.00	10.00
❑ 416 [PS]	Mrs. Bluebird/Little Boy	1968	6.25	12.50	25.00
❑ 439	Rupert White/Sunshine Among Us	1968	2.50	5.00	10.00
❑ 449	Till I Hear from You/I Wanna Be with You	1968	2.50	5.00	10.00
❑ 476	Sidewalks of the Ghetto/Look Away	1969	2.50	5.00	10.00
❑ 498	Blue Horizon/Lifetime Day	1969	2.50	5.00	10.00

ETTA AND HARVEY
Also see HARVEY; ETTA JAMES.

Number	Title (A Side/B Side)	Yr	VG	VG+	NM
CHESS					
❑ 1760	If I Can't Have You/My Heart Cries	1960	6.25	12.50	25.00
❑ 1771	Spoonful/It's a Crying Shame	1960	6.25	12.50	25.00

EUPHORIA (1)

Number	Title (A Side/B Side)	Yr	VG	VG+	NM
BAND BOX					
❑ 393	Somebody Listen/Dedication of Sally and Cher	196?	7.50	15.00	30.00
MAINSTREAM					
❑ 655	Hungry Women/No Me Tomorrow	1967	5.00	10.00	20.00

EUPHORIA (2)

Number	Title (A Side/B Side)	Yr	VG	VG+	NM
HERITAGE					
❑ 831	You Must Forget/(B-side unknown)	1971	3.00	6.00	12.00

EVANS, BARBARA

Number	Title (A Side/B Side)	Yr	VG	VG+	NM
RCA VICTOR					
❑ 47-7519	Souvenirs/Play for Me, Mother	1959	5.00	10.00	20.00
❑ 47-7576	Oo La La La La/The Little Girl Cried	1959	5.00	10.00	20.00
❑ 47-7634	Beatnik Daddy/A Game of Poker	1959	5.00	10.00	20.00

EVANS, MAUREEN

Number	Title (A Side/B Side)	Yr	VG	VG+	NM
COLUMBIA					
❑ 43189	Get Away/I've Often Wondered	1964	2.50	5.00	10.00
❑ 43354	Never Let Me Go/Poco Sole	1965	2.50	5.00	10.00
DOT					
❑ 16678	Time and Time Again/Tomorrow Is Another Day	1964	2.50	5.00	10.00
LITTLE DARLIN'					
❑ 0019	Touch My Heart/(B-side unknown)	1967	2.50	5.00	10.00
LONDON INT'L.					
❑ 10407	Like I Do/Starlight, Starbright	1963	3.00	6.00	12.00
❑ 10409	Melancholy Me/Pick the Petals	1963	3.00	6.00	12.00

EVANS, PAUL

Number	Title (A Side/B Side)	Yr	VG	VG+	NM
ATCO					
❑ 6138	At My Party/Beat Generation	1959	3.75	7.50	15.00
❑ 6170	Long Gone/Mickey, My Love	1960	3.75	7.50	15.00
BIG TREE					
❑ 16050	Happy Birthday. America/You Made Me Over	1975	—	2.50	5.00
CARLTON					
❑ 539	Show Folk/I Love to Make Love to You	1961	3.75	7.50	15.00
❑ 543	After the Hurricane/Not Me	1961	3.75	7.50	15.00
❑ 554	Just Because I Love You/This Pullover	1961	3.75	7.50	15.00
❑ 558	Over the Mountain, Across the Sea/Sisal Twine	1961	3.75	7.50	15.00
CINNAMON					
❑ 604	One Night Led to Two/Hangin' Out and Hangin' In	1980	—	2.50	5.00
COLUMBIA					
❑ 44472	One Red Rose/Bound to Silence	1968	—	3.00	6.00
DECCA					
❑ 30680	I Think About You All the Time/Oh No	1958	5.00	10.00	20.00
DOT					
❑ 17463	That's What Loving You Is All About/Do You Remember	1973	—	2.50	5.00
EPIC					
❑ 9726	Bewitched/I Think I'm Gonna Kill Myself	1964	2.50	5.00	10.00
—By Paul & Mimi Evans					
❑ 9751	Little Miss Tease/Gina Marina Petunia	1964	2.50	5.00	10.00
❑ 9842	I Wonder What to Do/Always Thinking of the Roses	1965	2.50	5.00	10.00
GUARANTEED					
❑ 200	Seven Little Girls Sitting in the Back Seat/Worshipping an Idol	1959	5.00	10.00	20.00
❑ 205	Midnite Special/Since I Met You Baby	1960	3.75	7.50	15.00
❑ 208	Happy-Go-Lucky Me/Fish in the Ocean	1960	3.75	7.50	15.00
❑ 210	The Brigade of Broken Hearts/Twins	1960	3.75	7.50	15.00
❑ 213	Hushabye Little Guitar/Blind Boy	1960	3.75	7.50	15.00
KAPP					
❑ 473	A Picture of You/Feelin' No Pain	1962	3.00	6.00	12.00
❑ 486	D-Darling/Gonna Build a Mountain	1962	3.00	6.00	12.00
❑ 499	The Bell That Couldn't Jingle/Gilding the Lily	1962	3.00	6.00	12.00
❑ 520	(Mama and Papa) We've Got Something On You/What Are the Lips of Janet	1963	3.00	6.00	12.00
❑ 527	Ten Thousand Years/Evan Tan	1963	3.00	6.00	12.00
LAURIE					
❑ 3571	Think Summer/For Old Times Sake	1971	—	3.00	6.00
❑ 3581	The Man in a Row Boat/Here We Go Around Again	1971	—	3.00	6.00
MERCURY					
❑ 73499	But I Was Born in New York City/Just As Long As You Are There	1974	—	2.50	5.00
❑ 73650	All My Children/Move In with Me	1975	—	2.50	5.00
MUSICOR					
❑ 6305	Roses Are Red Medley/If I Had My Life to Live Over	1977	—	2.00	4.00
RANWOOD					
❑ 928	Try It, You'll Like It/We Liked It	1972	—	3.00	6.00
RCA VICTOR					
❑ 47-6806	What Do You Know/Dorothy	1957	5.00	10.00	20.00
❑ 47-6924	Looking for a Sweetie/Any Little Thing	1957	5.00	10.00	20.00
❑ 47-6992	Caught/Poor Broken Heart	1957	5.00	10.00	20.00
SPRING					
❑ 183	Hello, This Is Joanie (The Telephone Answering Machine Song)/Lullabye Tissue Paper Company	1978	—	2.00	4.00
❑ 187	Down at the Bluebird/I'm Givin' Up My Baby	1978	—	2.00	4.00
❑ 193	Disneyland Daddy/Build An Ark	1979	—	2.00	4.00

EVELS, THE

Number	Title (A Side/B Side)	Yr	VG	VG+	NM
TRA-X					
❑ 14	The Magic of Love/Wonderful Guy	1960	15.00	30.00	60.00

EVERCLEAR

Number	Title (A Side/B Side)	Yr	VG	VG+	NM
CAPITOL					
❑ S7-19018	Santa Monica/Heroin Girl (Acoustic)	1996	—	—	3.00
❑ S7-19166	Heartspark Dollarsign/Queen of the Air	1996	—	—	3.00
❑ S7-19900	I Will Buy You a New Life/Like a California King	1998	—	—	3.00
❑ 58751	Santa Baby/Hating You for Christmas	1998	—	—	3.00
❑ 58856	Wonderful/Unemployed Boyfriend	2000	—	—	3.00
❑ 58893	AM Radio/Here We Go Again	2000	—	2.00	4.00
TIM/KERR					
❑ 937055	Nervous and Weird/Electra Made Me Blind	1993	—	2.00	4.00
—Red and clear vinyl (half and half)					
❑ 937055 [PS]	Nervous and Weird/Electra Made Me Blind	1993	—	2.00	4.00

EVERETT, BETTY

Number	Title (A Side/B Side)	Yr	VG	VG+	NM
ABC					
❑ 10829	In Your Arms/Nothing I Wouldn't Do	1966	2.00	4.00	8.00
❑ 10861	Bye, Bye Baby/Your Love Is Important to Me	1966	2.00	4.00	8.00
❑ 10919	Love Comes Tumbling Down/People Around Me	1967	2.00	4.00	8.00
❑ 10978	I Can't Say/My Baby Loving My Best Friend	1967	2.00	4.00	8.00
CJ					
❑ 611	Why Did You Have to Go/Please Come Back	1961	5.00	10.00	20.00
—As "Bettie Everett & Daylighters"					
❑ 619	Your Lovin' Arms/Happy I Long to Be	1961	5.00	10.00	20.00
❑ 674	Days Gone By/Her New Love	1964	3.75	7.50	15.00
COBRA					
❑ 5019	My Love/My Life Depends on You	1957	7.50	15.00	30.00
❑ 5024	Ain't Gonna Cry/Killer Diller	1958	6.25	12.50	25.00
❑ 5031	Weep No More/Tell Me Darling	1959	6.25	12.50	25.00
FANTASY					
❑ 652	I Got to Tell Somebody/Why Are You Leaving Me	1970	—	2.50	5.00
❑ 658	Ain't Nothing Gonna Change Me/What Is It?	1971	—	2.50	5.00
❑ 667	I'm a Woman/Prove It	1971	—	2.50	5.00
❑ 687	Black Girl/Innocent Bystanders	1972	—	2.50	5.00
❑ 687	Black Girl/What Is It?	1972	—	2.50	5.00
❑ 696	Danger/Just a Matter of Time Till You're Gone	1973	—	2.50	5.00
❑ 714	Sweet Dan/Who Will Your Next Fool Be	1973	—	2.50	5.00
❑ 725	Try It, You'll Like It/Wondering	1974	—	2.50	5.00
❑ 738	Happy Endings/Keep It Up	1974	—	2.50	5.00
ONE-DERFUL					
❑ 4806	I've Got a Claim on You/Your Love Is Important to Me	1962	3.75	7.50	15.00
❑ 4823	I'll Be There/Please Love Me	1964	3.00	6.00	12.00

UNI

Number	Title (A Side/B Side)	Yr	VG	VG+	NM
❑ 55100	Take Me/There'll Come a Time	1968	—	3.00	6.00
❑ 55122	I Can't Say No to You/Better Tomorrow Than Today	1969	—	3.00	6.00
❑ 55141	1900 Yesterday/Maybe	1969	—	3.00	6.00
❑ 55174	Just a Man's Way/Been a Long Time	1969	—	3.00	6.00
❑ 55189	Sugar/Just Another Winter	1969	—	3.00	6.00
❑ 55219	Unlucky Girl/Better Tomorrow Than Today	1970	—	3.00	6.00

UNITED ARTISTS

Number	Title (A Side/B Side)	Yr	VG	VG+	NM
❑ XW1200	True Love (You Took My Heart)/You Can Do It	1978	—	2.00	4.00

VEE JAY

Number	Title (A Side/B Side)	Yr	VG	VG+	NM
❑ 513	By My Side/Prince of Players	1963	3.75	7.50	15.00
❑ 566	You're No Good/Chained to Your Love	1963	5.00	10.00	20.00
❑ 585	The Shoop Shoop Song (It's In His Kiss)/Hands Off	1964	5.00	10.00	20.00
❑ 599	I Can't Hear You/Can I Get to Know You	1964	3.75	7.50	15.00
❑ 610	It Hurts to Be in Love/Until You Were Gone	1964	3.75	7.50	15.00
❑ 628	Getting Mighty Crowded/Chained to a Memory	1964	3.75	7.50	15.00
❑ 683	The Real Thing/Gonna Be Ready	1965	3.75	7.50	15.00
❑ 699	I Don't Hurt Anymore/Too Hot to Hold	1965	3.75	7.50	15.00
❑ 716	Trouble Over the Weekend/My Shoe Won't Fly	1966	3.75	7.50	15.00

EVERETT, BETTY, AND JERRY BUTLER

Also see each artist's individual listings.

VEE JAY

Number	Title (A Side/B Side)	Yr	VG	VG+	NM
❑ 613	Let It Be Me/Ain't That Loving You Baby	1964	3.00	6.00	12.00
❑ 633	Smile/Love Is Strange	1964	3.00	6.00	12.00
❑ 676	Since I Don't Have You/Just Be True	1965	3.00	6.00	12.00
❑ 691	Fever/The Way You Do the Things You Do	1965	3.00	6.00	12.00

EVERETT, VINCE

ABC-PARAMOUNT

Number	Title (A Side/B Side)	Yr	VG	VG+	NM
❑ 10313	Such a Night/Don't Go	1962	15.00	30.00	60.00
❑ 10360	I Ain't Gonna Be Your Low Down Dog No More/Sugaree	1962	12.50	25.00	50.00
❑ 10472	Baby, Let's Play House/Livin' High	1963	20.00	40.00	80.00
❑ 10538	Sweet Flavors/Box Candy	1964	10.00	20.00	40.00
❑ 10624	Big Brother/To Have, to Hold and Let Go	1965	10.00	20.00	40.00

TOWN

Number	Title (A Side/B Side)	Yr	VG	VG+	NM
❑ 1964	Buttercup/Land of No Return	1960	10.00	20.00	40.00

EVERGREENS, THE

BIRTHSTONE

Number	Title (A Side/B Side)	Yr	VG	VG+	NM
❑ 1022	They Came A Long Way To Christmas (Part 1)/They Came A Long Way To Christmas (Part 2)	19??	—	2.00	4.00

CHART

Number	Title (A Side/B Side)	Yr	VG	VG+	NM
❑ 605	Very Truly Yours/Guitar Player	1955	37.50	75.00	150.00

EVERLY, DON

Also see THE EVERLY BROTHERS.

ABC HICKORY

Number	Title (A Side/B Side)	Yr	VG	VG+	NM
❑ 54002	Love at Last Sight/Oh I'd Like to Go Away	1976	—	3.00	6.00
❑ 54005	Since You Broke My Heart/Deep Water	1977	—	3.00	6.00
❑ 54012	Brother Juke-Box/Oh, What a Feeling	1977	—	3.00	6.00

HICKORY/MGM

Number	Title (A Side/B Side)	Yr	VG	VG+	NM
❑ 368	Yesterday Just Passed My Way Again/Never Like This	1976	—	3.00	6.00

ODE

Number	Title (A Side/B Side)	Yr	VG	VG+	NM
❑ 66009	Only Me/Tumbling Tumbleweeds	1970	2.00	4.00	8.00
❑ 66046	Warming Up the Band/Evelyn Swing	1974	2.00	4.00	8.00

EVERLY, PHIL

Also see THE EVERLY BROTHERS.

CAPITOL

Number	Title (A Side/B Side)	Yr	VG	VG+	NM
❑ B-5197	One Way Love/Who's Gonna Keep Me Warm	1983	2.50	5.00	10.00

CURB

Number	Title (A Side/B Side)	Yr	VG	VG+	NM
❑ 02116	Sweet Southern Love/In Your Eyes	1981	2.50	5.00	10.00
❑ 5401	Dare to Dream Again/Lonely Days, Lonely Nights	1980	2.50	5.00	10.00

ELEKTRA

Number	Title (A Side/B Side)	Yr	VG	VG+	NM
❑ 46007	Don't Say You Don't Love Me No More/I Seek the Night	1979	—	2.50	5.00

—A-side: With Sondra Locke; B-side: Sondra Locke solo

Number	Title (A Side/B Side)	Yr	VG	VG+	NM
❑ 46519	Living Alone/I Just Don't Feel Like Dancing	1979	—	2.50	5.00
❑ 46556	Buy Me a Beer/You Broke It	1979	—	2.50	5.00

PYE

Number	Title (A Side/B Side)	Yr	VG	VG+	NM
❑ 71014	Old Kentucky River/Summershine	1975	2.00	4.00	8.00
❑ 71036	New Old Song/Better Than Now	1975	2.00	4.00	8.00
❑ 71050	You and I Are a Song/Better Than Now	1975	2.00	4.00	8.00
❑ 71055	Words in Your Eyes/Back When the Bands Played in Rag Time	1976	2.00	4.00	8.00
❑ 71056	God Bless Older Ladies/Sweet Grass Country	1976	—	3.00	6.00

RCA VICTOR

Number	Title (A Side/B Side)	Yr	VG	VG+	NM
❑ APBO-0064	God Bless Older Ladies/Sweet Grass Country	1973	2.00	4.00	8.00

EVERLY BROTHERS, THE

Also see DON EVERLY; PHIL EVERLY.

BARNABY

Number	Title (A Side/B Side)	Yr	VG	VG+	NM
❑ 500	('Til) I Kissed You/Oh, What a Feeling	197?	—	2.50	5.00
❑ 501	Wake Up Little Susie/Maybe Tomorrow	197?	—	2.50	5.00
❑ 502	Bye, Bye Love/I Wonder If I Care As Much	197?	—	2.50	5.00
❑ 503	This Little Girl of Mine/Should We Tell Him?	197?	—	2.50	5.00
❑ 504	Problems/Love of My Life	197?	—	2.50	5.00
❑ 505	Take a Message to Mary/Poor Jenny	197?	—	2.50	5.00
❑ 506	Let It Be Me/Since You Broke My Heart	197?	—	2.50	5.00
❑ 507	When Will I Be Loved/Be Bop A-Lula	197?	—	2.50	5.00
❑ 508	Like Strangers/Brand New Heartache	197?	—	2.50	5.00
❑ 509	All I Have to Do Is Dream/Claudette	197?	—	2.50	5.00
❑ 510	Bird Dog/Devoted to You	197?	—	2.50	5.00
❑ 511	I'm Here to Get My Baby Out of Jail/Lightning Express	197?	—	2.50	5.00

—All Barnaby records are reissues of original Cadence recordings

CADENCE

Number	Title (A Side/B Side)	Yr	VG	VG+	NM
❑ 1315	Bye, Bye Love/I Wonder If I Care As Much	1957	6.25	12.50	25.00
❑ 1337	Wake Up Little Susie/Maybe Tomorrow	1957	7.50	15.00	30.00
❑ 1337 [PS]	Wake Up Little Susie/Maybe Tomorrow	1957	62.50	125.00	250.00
❑ 1342	This Little Girl of Mine/Should We Tell Him?	1958	6.25	12.50	25.00
❑ 1348	All I Have to Do Is Dream/Claudette	1958	6.25	12.50	25.00
❑ 1348	All I Have to Do Is Dream/Claudette	1961	5.00	10.00	20.00

—Reissue with red and black label; scarcer than original

Number	Title (A Side/B Side)	Yr	VG	VG+	NM
❑ 1350	Bird Dog/Devoted to You	1958	6.25	12.50	25.00
❑ 1355	Problems/Love of My Life	1958	6.25	12.50	25.00
❑ 1355 [PS]	Problems/Love of My Life	1958	12.50	25.00	50.00
❑ 1364	Take a Message to Mary/Poor Jenny	1959	6.25	12.50	25.00
❑ 1369	('Til) I Kissed You/Oh, What a Feeling	1959	6.25	12.50	25.00
❑ 1369 [PS]	('Til) I Kissed You/Oh, What a Feeling	1959	12.50	25.00	50.00
❑ 1376	Let It Be Me/Since You Broke My Heart	1959	6.25	12.50	25.00
❑ 1376 [PS]	Let It Be Me/Since You Broke My Heart	1959	12.50	25.00	50.00
❑ 1380	When Will I Be Loved/Be Bop A-Lula	1960	6.25	12.50	25.00
❑ 1388	Like Strangers/Brand New Heartache	1960	6.25	12.50	25.00
❑ 1429	I'm Here to Get My Baby Out of Jail/Lightning Express	1962	5.00	10.00	20.00
❑ 1429 [PS]	I'm Here to Get My Baby Out of Jail/Lightning Express	1962	10.00	20.00	40.00

CAPITOL

Number	Title (A Side/B Side)	Yr	VG	VG+	NM
❑ B-44297	Don't Worry Baby/Tequila Dreams	1989	—	2.00	4.00

—A-side: With the Beach Boys; B-side by Dave Grusin

Number	Title (A Side/B Side)	Yr	VG	VG+	NM
❑ B-44297 [PS]	Don't Worry Baby/Tequila Dreams	1989	2.50	5.00	10.00

COLUMBIA

Number	Title (A Side/B Side)	Yr	VG	VG+	NM
❑ 4-21496	Keep A Lovin' Me/The Sun Keeps Shining	1956	150.00	300.00	600.00

—Maroon label

Number	Title (A Side/B Side)	Yr	VG	VG+	NM
❑ 4-21496 [DJ]	Keep A Lovin' Me/The Sun Keeps Shining	1956	62.50	125.00	250.00

—White label

MERCURY

Number	Title (A Side/B Side)	Yr	VG	VG+	NM
❑ 872098-7	Ride the Wind/Don't Worry Baby	1988	—	—	3.00
❑ 872420-7	Ballad of a Teenage Queen/Get Rhythm	1988	—	—	3.00

—With Johnny Cash and Roseanne Cash

Number	Title (A Side/B Side)	Yr	VG	VG+	NM
❑ 880213-7	On the Wings of a Nightingale/Asleep	1984	—	2.50	5.00

—A-side written and produced by Paul McCartney

Number	Title (A Side/B Side)	Yr	VG	VG+	NM
❑ 880423-7	The Story of Me/First in Line	1984	—	2.00	4.00
❑ 884428-7	Don't Say Goodnight/Born Yesterday	1986	—	2.00	4.00
❑ 884694-7	I Know Love/These Shoes	1986	—	2.00	4.00
❑ 884694-7 [PS]	I Know Love/These Shoes	1986	—	2.00	4.00

RCA VICTOR

Number	Title (A Side/B Side)	Yr	VG	VG+	NM
❑ SP-45-409 [DJ]	Pass the Chicken and Listen	1971	7.50	15.00	30.00

—Promo-only interview record

Number	Title (A Side/B Side)	Yr	VG	VG+	NM
❑ 74-0717	Stories We Could Tell/Ridin' High	1972	2.50	5.00	10.00
❑ 74-0849	Lay It Down/Paradise	1972	2.50	5.00	10.00
❑ 74-0901	Not Fade Away/Ladies Love Outlaws	1973	2.50	5.00	10.00

WARNER BROS.

Number	Title (A Side/B Side)	Yr	VG	VG+	NM
❑ GWB 0311	That's Old Fashioned/Bowling Green	197?	—	2.00	4.00

—"Back to Back Hits" series; originals have palm-tree labels

Number	Title (A Side/B Side)	Yr	VG	VG+	NM
❑ GWB 0314	Ebony Eyes/Walk Right Back	197?	—	2.00	4.00

—"Back to Back Hits" series; originals have palm-tree labels

Number	Title (A Side/B Side)	Yr	VG	VG+	NM
❑ 5151 [DJ]	Cathy's Clown/Always It's You	1960	25.00	50.00	100.00

—Promo-only gold vinyl pressing

Number	Title (A Side/B Side)	Yr	VG	VG+	NM
❑ 5151 [M]	Cathy's Clown/Always It's You	1960	5.00	10.00	20.00

—Original stock copies have pink labels

Number	Title (A Side/B Side)	Yr	VG	VG+	NM
❑ 5151 [M]	Cathy's Clown/Always It's You	1960	3.75	7.50	15.00

—Second-pressing stock copies have red labels with arrows

Number	Title (A Side/B Side)	Yr	VG	VG+	NM
❑ 5151 [PS]	Cathy's Clown/Always It's You	1960	12.50	25.00	50.00
❑ S-5151 [S]	Cathy's Clown/Always It's You	1960	12.50	25.00	50.00
❑ 5163	So Sad (To Watch Good Love Go Bad)/Lucille	1960	3.75	7.50	15.00
❑ 5163 [DJ]	So Sad (To Watch Good Love Go Bad)/Lucille	1960	25.00	50.00	100.00

—Promo-only gold vinyl pressing

Number	Title (A Side/B Side)	Yr	VG	VG+	NM
❑ 5163 [PS]	So Sad (To Watch Good Love Go Bad)/Lucille	1960	12.50	25.00	50.00
❑ 5199	Ebony Eyes/Walk Right Back	1961	3.75	7.50	15.00
❑ 5199 [DJ]	Ebony Eyes/Walk Right Back	1961	25.00	50.00	100.00

—Promo-only gold vinyl pressing

Number	Title (A Side/B Side)	Yr	VG	VG+	NM
❑ 5199 [PS]	Ebony Eyes/Walk Right Back	1961	6.25	12.50	25.00
❑ 5220	Temptation/Stick With Me, Baby	1961	3.75	7.50	15.00
❑ 5220 [PS]	Temptation/Stick With Me, Baby	1961	7.50	15.00	30.00
❑ 5250	Crying in the Rain/I'm Not Angry	1961	3.75	7.50	15.00
❑ 5250 [PS]	Crying in the Rain/I'm Not Angry	1961	5.00	10.00	20.00
❑ 5273	That's Old Fashioned (That's the Way Love Should Be)/How Can I Meet Her?	1962	3.75	7.50	15.00
❑ 5273 [PS]	That's Old Fashioned (That's the Way Love Should Be)/How Can I Meet Her?	1962	7.50	15.00	30.00
❑ 5297	Don't Ask Me to Be Friends/No One Can Make My Sunshine Smile	1962	5.00	10.00	20.00
❑ 5297 [PS]	Don't Ask Me to Be Friends/No One Can Make My Sunshine Smile	1962	7.50	15.00	30.00
❑ 5346	(So It Was...So It Is...) So It Always Will Be/Nancy's Minuet	1963	3.75	7.50	15.00
❑ 5362	I'm Afraid/It's Been Nice	1963	3.75	7.50	15.00
❑ 5389	Love Her/The Girl Sang the Blues	1963	3.75	7.50	15.00
❑ 5422	Hello, Amy/Ain't That Loving You, Baby	1964	3.75	7.50	15.00
❑ 5441	The Ferris Wheel/Don't Forget to Cry	1964	3.75	7.50	15.00
❑ 5466	You're the One I Love/Ring Around My Rosie	1964	3.75	7.50	15.00
❑ 5478	Gone, Gone, Gone/Torture	1964	3.75	7.50	15.00
❑ 5501	Don't Blame Me/Walk Right Back//Muskrat/Lucille	1961	5.00	10.00	20.00
❑ 5501 [PS]	Don't Blame Me/Walk Right Back//Muskrat/Lucille	1961	10.00	20.00	40.00

—Part of Warner Bros. "+2" series, with two new songs and excerpts of two prior hits

Number	Title (A Side/B Side)	Yr	VG	VG+	NM
❑ 5600	You're My Girl/Don't Let the World Know	1965	3.00	6.00	12.00
❑ 5611	That'll Be the Day/Give Me a Sweetheart	1965	3.00	6.00	12.00
❑ 5628	The Price of Love/It Only Costs a Dime	1965	3.00	6.00	12.00
❑ 5639	I'll Never Get Over You/Follow Me	1965	3.00	6.00	12.00
❑ 5649	Love Is Strange/A Man with Money	1965	3.00	6.00	12.00
❑ 5649 [PS]	Love Is Strange/A Man with Money	1965	7.50	15.00	30.00
❑ 5682	It's All Over/I Used to Love You	1965	3.00	6.00	12.00
❑ 5698	The Doll House Is Empty/Lovey Kravezit	1966	3.00	6.00	12.00

Number	Title (A Side/B Side)	Yr	VG	VG+	NM
❑ 5808	The Power of Love/Leave My Girl Alone	1966	3.00	6.00	12.00
❑ 5833	Somebody Help Me/Hard, Hard Year	1966	3.00	6.00	12.00
❑ 5857	Fifi the Flea/Like Every Time Before	1966	5.00	10.00	20.00
	—A-side listed as "Don Everly Brother," B-side as "Phil Everly Brother"				
❑ 5901	She Never Smiles Anymore/Devil Child	1967	3.00	6.00	12.00
❑ 7020	Bowling Green/I Don't Want to Love You	1967	3.00	6.00	12.00
❑ 7062	Mary Jane/Talking to the Flowers	1967	3.00	6.00	12.00
❑ 7088	Love of the Common People/The Voice Within	1967	3.00	6.00	12.00
❑ 7110	Cathy's Clown/So Sad	1968	2.00	4.00	8.00
	—"Back to Back Hits" series; originals have green "W7" label				
❑ 7111	Crying in the Rain/Lucille	1968	2.00	4.00	8.00
	—"Back to Back Hits" series; originals have green "W7" label				
❑ 7120	Wake Up Little Susie/Bird Dog	1969	2.00	4.00	8.00
	—"Back to Back Hits" series; originals have green "W7" label; re-recordings				
❑ 7121	Bye Bye Love/All I Have to Do Is Dream	1969	2.00	4.00	8.00
	—"Back to Back Hits" series; originals have green "W7" label; re-recordings				
❑ 7192	Empty Boxes/It's My Time	1968	3.00	6.00	12.00
❑ 7226	Lord of the Manor/Milk Train	1968	3.00	6.00	12.00
❑ 7262	T for Texas/I Wonder If I Care As Much	1969	3.00	6.00	12.00
❑ 7290	I'm On My Way Home Again/Cuckoo Bird	1969	3.00	6.00	12.00
❑ 7326	Carolina on My Mind/My Little Yellow Bird	1969	3.75	7.50	15.00
❑ 7425	Yves/The Human Race	1970	3.75	7.50	15.00

7-Inch Extended Plays

CADENCE

Number	Title (A Side/B Side)	Yr	VG	VG+	NM
❑ CLLP-3	Bye Bye Love/('Til) I Kissed You/Bird Dog//Wake Up Little Susie/When Will I Be Loved/Problems	1961	10.00	20.00	40.00
	—33 1/3 rpm, small hole jukebox issue				
❑ CLLP-3 [PS]	Rockin' with the Everly Brothers	1961	10.00	20.00	40.00
❑ CEP-104	Wake Up Little Susie/Maybe Tomorrow//Bye Bye Love/I Wonder If I Care As Much	1957	12.50	25.00	50.00
❑ CEP-104 [PS]	The Everly Brothers	1957	12.50	25.00	50.00
❑ CEP-105	This Little Girl of Mine/Leave My Woman Alone//Should We Tell Him/Be-Bop-a-Lula	1957	12.50	25.00	50.00
❑ CEP-105 [PS]	The Everly Brothers	1957	12.50	25.00	50.00
❑ CEP-107	Brand New Heartache/Keep a Knockin'//Rip It Up/Hey Doll Baby	1957	12.50	25.00	50.00
❑ CEP-107 [PS]	The Everly Brothers	1957	12.50	25.00	50.00
❑ CEP-108	Roving Gambler/Oh So Many Years//Put My Little Shoes Away/That Silver Haired Daddy Of Mine	1958	12.50	25.00	50.00
❑ CEP-108 [PS]	Songs Our Daddy Taught Us, Vol. 1	1958	12.50	25.00	50.00
❑ CEP-109	Barbara Allen/Long Time Gone//Lightning Express/Who's Gonna Shoe Your Pretty Little Feet	1958	12.50	25.00	50.00
❑ CEP-109 [PS]	Songs Our Daddy Taught Us, Vol. 2	1958	12.50	25.00	50.00
❑ CEP-110	*Down in the Willow Garden/Kentucky/I'm Here to Get My Baby Out of Jail/Rockin' Alone in My Old Rockin' Chair	1958	12.50	25.00	50.00
❑ CEP-110 [PS]	Songs Our Daddy Taught Us, Vol. 3	1958	12.50	25.00	50.00
❑ CEP-111	Bird Dog/Devoted to You//All I Have to Do Is Dream/Claudette	1959	12.50	25.00	50.00
❑ CEP-111 [PS]	The Everly Brothers	1959	12.50	25.00	50.00
❑ CEP-118	(contents unknown)	1959	12.50	25.00	50.00
❑ CEP-118 [PS]	The Everly Brothers	1959	12.50	25.00	50.00
❑ CEP-121	Let It Be Me/Since You Broke My Heart//'Til I Kissed You/Oh, What a Feeling	1960	6.25	12.50	25.00
❑ CEP-121 [PS]	The Very Best of the Everly Brothers	1960	6.25	12.50	25.00

WARNER BROS.

Number	Title (A Side/B Side)	Yr	VG	VG+	NM
❑ EA 1381	So Sad (To Watch Good Love Go Bad)/You Thrill Me (Through and Through)//Memories Are Made of This/Oh, True Love	1960	10.00	20.00	40.00
❑ EA 1381 [PS]	Foreverly Yours	1960	10.00	20.00	40.00
❑ EB 1381	Sleepless Nights/Carol Jane//Nashville Blues/That's What You Do to Me	1960	10.00	20.00	40.00
❑ EB 1381 [PS]	Especially for You	1960	10.00	20.00	40.00

EVERPRESENT FULLNESS, THE

WHITE WHALE

Number	Title (A Side/B Side)	Yr	VG	VG+	NM
❑ 233	Wild About My Lovin'/Doin' a Number	1966	3.75	7.50	15.00
❑ 233	Wild About My Lovin'/Fine and Dandy	1966	3.75	7.50	15.00
❑ 248	Darlin' You Can Count On Me/Yeah	1967	3.75	7.50	15.00

EVERY FATHER'S TEENAGE SON

BUDDAH

Number	Title (A Side/B Side)	Yr	VG	VG+	NM
❑ 25	A Letter to Dad/Josephine's Song	1968	2.00	4.00	8.00

EVERY MOTHER'S SON

MGM

Number	Title (A Side/B Side)	Yr	VG	VG+	NM
❑ 13733	Come On Down to My Boat/I Believe in You	1967	2.50	5.00	10.00
❑ 13788	Put Your Mind at Ease/Proper Four Leaf Clover	1967	2.00	4.00	8.00
❑ 13788 [PS]	Put Your Mind at Ease/Proper Four Leaf Clover	1967	3.00	6.00	12.00
❑ 13844	Pony with the Golden Mane/Dolls in the Clock	1967	2.00	4.00	8.00
❑ 13887	No One Knows/What Became of Mary	1968	2.00	4.00	8.00
❑ 13987	Rainflowers/For Brandy	1968	2.00	4.00	8.00

EVIL, THE

CAPITOL

Number	Title (A Side/B Side)	Yr	VG	VG+	NM
❑ 2038	Whatcha Gonna Do About It/Always Runnin' Around	1967	5.00	10.00	20.00

LIVING LEGEND

Number	Title (A Side/B Side)	Yr	VG	VG+	NM
❑ 108	Whatcha Gonna Do About It/Always Runnin' Around	1967	10.00	20.00	40.00

EVIL ENCORPORATED

SCENE

Number	Title (A Side/B Side)	Yr	VG	VG+	NM
❑ 101	Hey You/The Thing Is...	1967	7.50	15.00	30.00
❑ 102	Baby It's You/All I Really Want to Do	1967	7.50	15.00	30.00

EXCALIBURS, THE

TRENT TOWN

Number	Title (A Side/B Side)	Yr	VG	VG+	NM
❑ 1017	Christmas Dreaming/Peace On Earth	19??	25.00	50.00	100.00

EXCELLENTS, THE

BLAST

Number	Title (A Side/B Side)	Yr	VG	VG+	NM
❑ 205	Coney Island Baby/You Baby You	1962	7.50	15.00	30.00
	—All-red label				
❑ 205	Coney Island Baby/You Baby You	1962	5.00	10.00	20.00
	—Red and white label				
❑ 205	Coney Island Baby/You Baby You	1965	6.25	12.50	25.00
	—Purple label				
❑ 207	I Hear a Rhapsody/Why Did You Laugh	1963	15.00	30.00	60.00

MERMAID

Number	Title (A Side/B Side)	Yr	VG	VG+	NM
❑ 106	Love No One But You/Red Red Robin	1961	50.00	100.00	200.00
	—With mermaid on label				
❑ 106	Love No One But You/Red Red Robin	1961	12.50	25.00	50.00
	—No mermaid on label				

EXCELS, THE (1)

GONE

Number	Title (A Side/B Side)	Yr	VG	VG+	NM
❑ 5094	My Foolish Heart/Just You and I Together	1960	6.25	12.50	25.00

RSVP

Number	Title (A Side/B Side)	Yr	VG	VG+	NM
❑ 111	Can't Help Lovin' That Girl of Mine/Till You	1961	12.50	25.00	50.00

EXCELS, THE (2)

CARLA

Number	Title (A Side/B Side)	Yr	VG	VG+	NM
❑ 1901	Little Innocent Girl/Some Kind of Fun	1968	5.00	10.00	20.00
❑ 2529	Gonna Make You Mine Girl/Goodbye Poor Boy	1966	5.00	10.00	20.00
❑ 2534	I Wanna Be Free/Too Much Too Soon	1967	5.00	10.00	20.00
❑ 2536	California on My Mind/Arrival of Mary	1967	5.00	10.00	20.00

EXCELS, THE (3)

CENTRAL

Number	Title (A Side/B Side)	Yr	VG	VG+	NM
❑ 2601	You're Mine Forever/Baby Doll	1957	12.50	25.00	50.00

RELIC

Number	Title (A Side/B Side)	Yr	VG	VG+	NM
❑ 1007	You're Mine Forever/Baby Doll	1965	2.50	5.00	10.00

EXCEPTION, THE

PETER CETERA (later of CHICAGO) was a member of this group.

CAPITOL

Number	Title (A Side/B Side)	Yr	VG	VG+	NM
❑ 2046	Business As Usual/My Mind Goes Traveling	1967	3.00	6.00	12.00
❑ 2120	You Always Hurt Me/You Don't Know Like I Know	1968	3.00	6.00	12.00
❑ 5982	The Girl from New York City/As Far As I Can See	1967	3.00	6.00	12.00

EXCITERS, THE

BANG

Number	Title (A Side/B Side)	Yr	VG	VG+	NM
❑ 515	A Little Bit of Soap/I'm Gonna Get Him Someday	1966	3.00	6.00	12.00
❑ 518	You Better Come Home/Weddings Make Me Cry	1966	7.50	15.00	30.00

FARGO

Number	Title (A Side/B Side)	Yr	VG	VG+	NM
❑ 1400	Alone Again, Naturally/(B-side unknown)	1972	2.00	4.00	8.00

RCA VICTOR

Number	Title (A Side/B Side)	Yr	VG	VG+	NM
❑ 47-9633	Take One Step (I'll Take Two)/If You Want My Love	1968	7.50	15.00	30.00
❑ 47-9723	You Don't Know What You're Missing ('Til It's Gone!)/Blowing Up My Mind	1969	7.50	15.00	30.00
❑ 48-1035	You Don't Know What You're Missing ('Til It's Gone!)/Blowing Up My Mind	1972	3.75	7.50	15.00

ROULETTE

Number	Title (A Side/B Side)	Yr	VG	VG+	NM
❑ 4591	I Want You to Be My Boy/Tonight, Tonight	1965	3.00	6.00	12.00
❑ 4591 [PS]	I Want You to Be My Boy/Tonight, Tonight	1965	12.50	25.00	50.00
❑ 4594	Are You Satisfied/Just Not Ready	1965	3.00	6.00	12.00
❑ 4614	My Father/Run Mascara	1965	3.00	6.00	12.00
❑ 4632	I Knew You Would/There They Go	1965	3.00	6.00	12.00

SHOUT

Number	Title (A Side/B Side)	Yr	VG	VG+	NM
❑ 205	Number One/You Got Love	1966	2.50	5.00	10.00
❑ 214	Soulmotion/You Know It Ain't Right	1967	2.50	5.00	10.00

TODAY

Number	Title (A Side/B Side)	Yr	VG	VG+	NM
❑ 1002	Learning How to Fly/Life, Love and Peace	1970	2.00	4.00	8.00

UNITED ARTISTS

Number	Title (A Side/B Side)	Yr	VG	VG+	NM
❑ 0029	Tell Him/Do Wah Diddy	1973	—	2.00	4.00
	—"Silver Spotlight Series" reissue				
❑ 544	Tell Him/Hard Way to Go	1963	3.75	7.50	15.00
❑ 572	Drama of Love/He's Got the Power	1963	3.00	6.00	12.00
❑ 604	Get Him/It's So Exciting	1963	3.00	6.00	12.00
❑ 662	Do-Wah-Diddy/If Love Came Your Way	1963	3.00	6.00	12.00
❑ 721	Having My Fun/We Were Lovers (When the Party Began)	1964	3.00	6.00	12.00
❑ 830	Having My Fun/We Were Lovers (When the Party Began)	1965	2.50	5.00	10.00

EXODUS

WAND

Number	Title (A Side/B Side)	Yr	VG	VG+	NM
❑ 11248	M&M/Silhouettes-You Cheated	1972	25.00	50.00	100.00
	—Black and white label				
❑ 11248	M&M/Silhouettes-You Cheated	1972	7.50	15.00	30.00
	—Multi-colored label				

EXOTICS, THE

More than one group.

BOLO

Number	Title (A Side/B Side)	Yr	VG	VG+	NM
❑ 722	Oasis/Chattanooga Choo Choo	1962	3.00	6.00	12.00

CORAL

Number	Title (A Side/B Side)	Yr	VG	VG+	NM
❑ 62268	That's My Desire/Darking, I Want to Get Married	1961	5.00	10.00	20.00
❑ 62289	The Gang That Sang (Heart of My Heart)/Hotcha Mighty Knows	1961	5.00	10.00	20.00
❑ 62310	Fortune Hunter/Manpower	1962	5.00	10.00	20.00
❑ 62343	My Life's Desire (Part 1)/My Life's Desire (Part 2)	1963	3.75	7.50	15.00
❑ 62399	Let's Get Together/Sad, Sad Song	1964	3.75	7.50	15.00
❑ 62439	Like You Hurt Me/Big Time Charlie	1964	5.00	10.00	20.00

EXCELLO

Number	Title (A Side/B Side)	Yr	VG	VG+	NM
❑ 2284	Boogaloo Investigator/I Won't Ever Stop Loving You	1967	2.00	4.00	8.00
❑ 2292	Let Me Be a Part of You/Let's Try to Build a Love Affair	1968	2.00	4.00	8.00

Number	Title (A Side/B Side)	Yr	VG	VG+	NM
JERDEN					
❑ 106	Four Banger/Cat Hairs	1960	3.75	7.50	15.00
MONUMENT					
❑ 984	Fire Engine Red/Morning Sun	1966	3.00	6.00	12.00
SEAFAIR					
❑ 108	Ginger Snap/(B-side unknown)	1962	2.50	5.00	10.00
❑ 113	Jerk Time/For the Winds	1965	2.50	5.00	10.00
SPRINGBOARD					
❑ 101	Gee/Lorraine	1963	5.00	10.00	20.00
❑ 101 [PS]	Gee/Lorraine	1963	10.00	20.00	40.00

EXPLORERS, THE

Number	Title (A Side/B Side)	Yr	VG	VG+	NM
CORAL					
❑ 62147	Vision of Love/On a Clear Night	1959	15.00	30.00	60.00
❑ 62175	Don't Be a Fool/In the Wee Small Hours of the Morning	1960	25.00	50.00	100.00
❑ 62295	Remember/Every Road (I Walk Along)	1961	15.00	30.00	60.00
—As "Dennis and the Explorers"					
❑ 65575	Don't Be a Fool/Vision of Love	196?	7.50	15.00	30.00
—Was listed in the last edition under "The Visions"					

EXPORTS, THE

Number	Title (A Side/B Side)	Yr	VG	VG+	NM
KING					
❑ 5917	Car Hop/Seat Belts Please	1964	6.25	12.50	25.00
❑ 5985	Mustang '65/Always It's You	1965	6.25	12.50	25.00

EXPRESSIONS, THE

More than one group.

Number	Title (A Side/B Side)	Yr	VG	VG+	NM
ARLISS					
❑ 1012	My Love, My Love/The Sign of Happiness	1962	12.50	25.00	50.00
FEDERAL					
❑ 12533	You Better Know It/Out of My Life	1964	2.50	5.00	10.00
GUYDEN					
❑ 2122	Be-Bop-a-Lula/Skinnie Minnie	1965	3.75	7.50	15.00
—As "J-D and the Expressions"					
PARKWAY					
❑ 892	On the Corner/To Cry	1963	3.75	7.50	15.00
REPRISE					
❑ 0360	Playboy/One Plus One	1965	5.00	10.00	20.00
SMASH					
❑ 1848	Karen/Thrill	1963	3.75	7.50	15.00
TEEN					
❑ 101	Now That You've Gone/Crazy	1957	50.00	100.00	200.00

EXTERMINATORS, THE

Number	Title (A Side/B Side)	Yr	VG	VG+	NM
CHANCELLOR					
❑ 1143	The Beetle Bomb/Stomp 'Em Out	1963	6.25	12.50	25.00
❑ 1148	Beatle Stomp/Stomp 'Em Out	1964	3.75	7.50	15.00
—A-sides are the same song with different titles					
GOLDEN WEST					
❑ 1002	Beatle Stomp/Stomp 'Em Out	1964	5.00	10.00	20.00

EXTREMES, THE

Number	Title (A Side/B Side)	Yr	VG	VG+	NM
EVERLAST					
❑ 5013	Come Next Spring/Let's Elope	1958	37.50	75.00	150.00
PARO					
❑ 733	The Bells/That's All I Want	1962	75.00	150.00	300.00

F

FABARES, SHELLEY

Number	Title (A Side/B Side)	Yr	VG	VG+	NM
COLPIX					
❑ 621	Johnny Angel/Where's It Gonna Get Me	1962	5.00	10.00	20.00
❑ 621 [PS]	Johnny Angel/Where's It Gonna Get Me	1962	125.00	250.00	500.00
❑ 631	What Did They Do Before Rock and Roll/Very Unlikely	1962	5.00	10.00	20.00
—With Paul Petersen					
❑ 631 [PS]	What Did They Do Before Rock and Roll/Very Unlikely	1962	100.00	200.00	400.00
❑ 636	Johnny Loves Me/I'm Growing Up	1962	5.00	10.00	20.00
❑ 636 [PS]	Johnny Loves Me/I'm Growing Up	1962	30.00	60.00	120.00
❑ 654	The Things We Did Last Summer/Breaking Up Is Hard to Do	1962	5.00	10.00	20.00
❑ 667	Big Star/Telephone (Don't You Ring)	1962	5.00	10.00	20.00
❑ 682	Ronnie, Call Me When You Get a Chance/I Left a Note to Say Goodbye	1963	5.00	10.00	20.00
❑ 705	Welcome Home/Billy Boy	1963	5.00	10.00	20.00
❑ 721	Football Season's Over/He Don't Love Me	1963	25.00	50.00	100.00
—Produced by Jan Berry of Jan and Dean					
DUNHILL					
❑ 4001	My Prayer/Pretty Please	1965	7.50	15.00	30.00
❑ 4041	See Ya 'Round on the Rebound/Pretty Please	1966	7.50	15.00	30.00
VEE JAY					
❑ 632	I Know You'll Be There/Lost Summer Love	1964	10.00	20.00	40.00

FABIAN

Number	Title (A Side/B Side)	Yr	VG	VG+	NM
CHANCELLOR					
❑ 1020	I'm in Love/Shivers	1958	6.25	12.50	25.00
❑ 1024	Be My Steady Date/Lilly Lou	1958	6.25	12.50	25.00
❑ 1029 [M]	I'm a Man/Hypnotized	1959	5.00	10.00	20.00
❑ 1029 [PS]	I'm a Man/Hypnotized	1959	10.00	20.00	40.00
❑ 1029 [PS]	I Am a Man/Hypnotized	1959	12.50	25.00	50.00
—Incorrect title on A-side of sleeve					
❑ S-1029 [S]	I'm a Man/Hypnotized	1959	12.50	25.00	50.00
❑ 1033 [M]	Turn Me Loose/Stop Thief!	1959	5.00	10.00	20.00
❑ 1033 [PS]	Turn Me Loose/Stop Thief!	1959	10.00	20.00	40.00
❑ S-1033 [S]	Turn Me Loose/Stop Thief!	1959	12.50	25.00	50.00
❑ 1037 [M]	Tiger/Mighty Cold (To a Warm, Warm Heart)	1959	5.00	10.00	20.00
❑ 1037 [PS]	Tiger/Mighty Cold (To a Warm, Warm Heart)	1959	10.00	20.00	40.00
❑ S-1037 [S]	Tiger/Mighty Cold (To a Warm, Warm Heart)	1959	12.50	25.00	50.00
❑ 1041 [M]	Come On and Get Me/Got the Feeling	1959	5.00	10.00	20.00
❑ 1041 [PS]	Come On and Get Me/Got the Feeling	1959	10.00	20.00	40.00
❑ S-1041 [S]	Come On and Get Me/Got the Feeling	1959	12.50	25.00	50.00
❑ 1044	Hound Dog Man/Friendly World	1959	6.25	12.50	25.00
❑ 1044 [M]	Hound Dog Man/This Friendly World	1959	5.00	10.00	20.00
—Note difference in B-side title					
❑ 1044 [PS]	Hound Dog Man/This Friendly World	1959	10.00	20.00	40.00
❑ S-1044 [S]	Hound Dog Man/This Friendly World	1959	12.50	25.00	50.00
❑ 1047 [M]	About This Thing Called Love/String Along	1960	3.00	6.00	12.00
❑ 1047 [PS]	About This Thing Called Love/String Along	1960	7.50	15.00	30.00
❑ S-1047 [S]	About This Thing Called Love/String Along	1960	12.50	25.00	50.00
❑ 1051	I'm Gonna Sit Right Down and Write Myself a Letter/Strollin' in the Springtime	1960	3.00	6.00	12.00
❑ 1051 [PS]	I'm Gonna Sit Right Down and Write Myself a Letter/Strollin' in the Springtime	1960	7.50	15.00	30.00
❑ 1055	Tomorrow/King of Love	1960	3.00	6.00	12.00
❑ 1055 [PS]	Tomorrow/King of Love	1960	7.50	15.00	30.00
❑ 1061	Kissin' and Twistin'/Long Before	1960	3.00	6.00	12.00
❑ 1061 [PS]	Kissin' and Twistin'/Long Before	1960	7.50	15.00	30.00
❑ 1067	You Know You Belong to Someone Else/Hold On	1961	3.00	6.00	12.00
❑ 1067 [PS]	You Know You Belong to Someone Else/Hold On	1961	7.50	15.00	30.00
❑ 1072	Grapevine/David and Goliath	1961	3.00	6.00	12.00
❑ 1079	The Love That I'm Giving to You/You're Only Young Once	1961	3.75	7.50	15.00
❑ 1079 [PS]	The Love That I'm Giving to You/You're Only Young Once	1961	10.00	20.00	40.00
❑ 1084	A Girl Like You/Dream Factory	1961	3.00	6.00	12.00
❑ 1084 [PS]	A Girl Like You/Dream Factory	1961	7.50	15.00	30.00
❑ 1086	Tongue-Tied/Kansas City	1961	5.00	10.00	20.00
❑ 1092	Wild Party/Made You	1961	5.00	10.00	20.00
❑ 1092	Wild Party/The Gospel Truth	1961	6.25	12.50	25.00
❑ 1092 [PS]	Wild Party/Made You	1961	10.00	20.00	40.00
CREAM					
❑ 7717	Ease On (Into My Life)/The American East	1977	—	2.50	5.00
❑ 7717 [PS]	Ease On (Into My Life)/The American East	1977	—	2.50	5.00
DOT					
❑ 16413	Break Down and Cry/She's Staying Inside with Me	1963	2.50	5.00	10.00
7-Inch Extended Plays					
CHANCELLOR					
❑ A-301	*Hound Dog Man/This Friendly World/Pretty Little Girl/I'm Growin' Up/Single	1960	12.50	25.00	50.00
❑ A-301 [PS]	5 Songs from Hound Dog Man	1960	12.50	25.00	50.00
❑ A-5003	*Hold Me (In Your Arms)/Just One More Time/Please Don't Stop/Ooh, What You Do!	1959	15.00	30.00	60.00
❑ A-5003 [PS]	Hold That Tiger! Volume 1	1959	15.00	30.00	60.00
❑ B-5003	(contents unknown)	1959	15.00	30.00	60.00
❑ B-5003 [PS]	Hold That Tiger! Volume 2	1959	15.00	30.00	60.00
❑ C-5003	Turn Me Loose/Steady Date//Don't You Think It's Time?/Cuddle Up a Little Closer	1959	15.00	30.00	60.00
❑ C-5003 [PS]	Hold That Tiger! Volume 3	1959	15.00	30.00	60.00
❑ A-5005	Remember Me/I'm Sincere//Everything Is Just Right/You'll Never Tame Me	1959	15.00	30.00	60.00
❑ A-5005 [PS]	The Fabulous Fabian, Volume 1	1959	15.00	30.00	60.00
❑ B-5005	(contents unknown)	1959	15.00	30.00	60.00
❑ B-5005 [PS]	The Fabulous Fabian, Volume 2	1959	15.00	30.00	60.00
❑ C-5005	(contents unknown)	1959	15.00	30.00	60.00
❑ C-5005 [PS]	The Fabulous Fabian, Volume 3	1959	15.00	30.00	60.00
❑ A-9802	Young and Wonderful/Think of Me//Take Me/Exactly Like You	1960	12.50	25.00	50.00
❑ A-9802 [PS]	Young and Wonderful	1960	12.50	25.00	50.00

FABS, THE

Number	Title (A Side/B Side)	Yr	VG	VG+	NM
COTTON BALL					
❑ 1005	That's the Bag I'm In/Dinah Wants Religion	1966	37.50	75.00	150.00

FABULAIRES, THE

Number	Title (A Side/B Side)	Yr	VG	VG+	NM
EASTWEST					
❑ 103	While Walking/No No	1957	75.00	150.00	300.00
MAIN LINE					
❑ 103	While Walking/No No	1958	50.00	100.00	200.00

FABULONS, THE (1)

Number	Title (A Side/B Side)	Yr	VG	VG+	NM
EMBER					
❑ 1069	Smoke From Your Cigarette/Give Me Back My Ring	1960	12.50	25.00	50.00
—White label					
❑ 1069	Smoke From Your Cigarette/Give Me Back My Ring	1960	6.25	12.50	25.00
—Black label					

FABULONS, THE (2)

Also see THE TIKIS AND THE FABULONS.

Number	Title (A Side/B Side)	Yr	VG	VG+	NM
TOWER					
❑ 259	Since You've Been Gone/Don't Ask Me	1966	3.75	7.50	15.00

FABULOUS FIVE, THE

Number	Title (A Side/B Side)	Yr	VG	VG+	NM
KING					
❑ 5220	Janie Made a Monster/Gettin' Old	1959	3.75	7.50	15.00

FABULOUS FLAMES, THE (1)

Number	Title (A Side/B Side)	Yr	VG	VG+	NM
BAY-TONE					
❑ 102	Do You Remember/Get to Stepping	1961	10.00	20.00	40.00
❑ 105	Lover/I'm So All Alone	1961	12.50	25.00	50.00
REX					
❑ 3000	Josephine/My Joan	1958	30.00	60.00	120.00

FABULOUS FOUR, THE

Number	Title (A Side/B Side)	Yr	VG	VG+	NM
BRASS					
❑ 311	Now You Cry/Got to Get Her Back	1964	5.00	10.00	20.00
❑ 314	Who Could It Be/Happy	1964	5.00	10.00	20.00

Number	Title (A Side/B Side)	Yr	VG	VG+	NM
❑ 316	I'm Always Doing Something Wrong/Young Blood	1964	5.00	10.00	20.00
CHANCELLOR					
❑ 1062	In the Chapel in the Moonlight/Mr. Twist	1960	6.25	12.50	25.00
❑ 1068	Let's Try Again/Precious Moments	1961	6.25	12.50	25.00
❑ 1078	Why Do Fools Fall in Love/Sounds of Summer	1961	10.00	20.00	40.00
❑ 1085	Prisoner of Love/Betty Ann	1961	20.00	40.00	80.00
❑ 1090	Everybody Knows/I'm Coming Home	1961	5.00	10.00	20.00
❑ 1098	Mr. Twist/Everybody Knows	1961	5.00	10.00	20.00
❑ 1102	Forever/(It's No) Sin	1962	6.25	12.50	25.00
CORAL					
❑ 62479	Now You Cry/Got to Get Her Back	1966	3.75	7.50	15.00
MELIC					
❑ 4114	Welcome Me Home/Oop Shoobee Doop	1962	12.50	25.00	50.00

FABULOUS PACK, THE
See TERRY KNIGHT AND THE PACK.

FABULOUS PEARL DEVINES, THE

Number	Title (A Side/B Side)	Yr	VG	VG+	NM
ALCO					
❑ 101	You've Been Gone/So Lonely	1963	100.00	200.00	400.00

FABULOUS PEPS, THE

Number	Title (A Side/B Side)	Yr	VG	VG+	NM
D-TOWN					
❑ 1049	You Never Had It So Good/Detroit, Michigan	1965	10.00	20.00	40.00
—As "The Peps"					
❑ 1060	Thinking About You/This I Pray	1965	10.00	20.00	40.00
—As "The Peps"					
❑ 1065	My Love Looks Good on You/Speak Your Peace	1966	12.50	25.00	50.00
GE GE					
❑ 503	This Love I Have for You/She's Going to Leave You	1965	10.00	20.00	40.00
PREMIUM STUFF					
❑ 1	Why Are You Blowing My Mind/I Can't Get Right	1967	10.00	20.00	40.00
❑ 3	So Fine/I'll Never Be the Same Again	1967	10.00	20.00	40.00
❑ 7	Gypsy Woman/Why Are You Blowing My Mind	1967	10.00	20.00	40.00
WEE-3					
❑ 233	With These Eyes/I've Been Trying	1967	7.50	15.00	30.00
WHEELSVILLE					
❑ 109	With These Eyes/Light of My Life	1968	3.00	6.00	12.00

FABULOUS UPTONES, THE

Number	Title (A Side/B Side)	Yr	VG	VG+	NM
TULIP					
❑ 100	New Love I've Found/Turtle	1962	75.00	150.00	300.00

FABULOUS VALIENTS, THE

Number	Title (A Side/B Side)	Yr	VG	VG+	NM
HOLIDAY					
❑ 61005	Your Golden Teardrops/Carmelita	1962	62.50	125.00	250.00

FACENDA, TOMMY

Number	Title (A Side/B Side)	Yr	VG	VG+	NM
ATLANTIC					
❑ 45-51	High School U.S.A.-Virginia/Plea of Love	1959	10.00	20.00	40.00
❑ 45-52	High School U.S.A.-New York City/Plea of Love	1959	10.00	20.00	40.00
❑ 45-53	High School U.S.A.-North & South Carolina/Plea of Love	1959	10.00	20.00	40.00
❑ 45-54	High School U.S.A.-Washington, D.C./Plea of Love	1959	10.00	20.00	40.00
❑ 45-55	High School U.S.A.-Philadelphia/Plea of Love	1959	10.00	20.00	40.00
❑ 45-56	High School U.S.A.-Detroit/Plea of Love	1959	10.00	20.00	40.00
❑ 45-57	High School U.S.A.-Pittsburgh/Plea of Love	1959	10.00	20.00	40.00
❑ 45-58	High School U.S.A.-Minneapolis-St. Paul/Plea of Love	1959	10.00	20.00	40.00
❑ 45-59	High School U.S.A.-Florida/Plea of Love	1959	10.00	20.00	40.00
❑ 45-60	High School U.S.A.-Newark, N.J./Plea of Love	1959	10.00	20.00	40.00
❑ 45-61	High School U.S.A.-Boston/Plea of Love	1959	10.00	20.00	40.00
❑ 45-62	High School U.S.A.-Cleveland/Plea of Love	1959	10.00	20.00	40.00
❑ 45-63	High School U.S.A.-Buffalo/Plea of Love	1959	10.00	20.00	40.00
❑ 45-64	High School U.S.A.-Hartford, Conn./Plea of Love	1959	10.00	20.00	40.00
❑ 45-65	High School U.S.A.-Nashville/Plea of Love	1959	10.00	20.00	40.00
❑ 45-66	High School U.S.A.-Indianapolis/Plea of Love	1959	10.00	20.00	40.00
❑ 45-67	High School U.S.A.-Chicago/Plea of Love	1959	10.00	20.00	40.00
❑ 45-68	High School U.S.A.-New Orleans/Plea of Love	1959	10.00	20.00	40.00
❑ 45-69	High School U.S.A.-St. Louis & Kansas City/Plea of Love	1959	10.00	20.00	40.00
❑ 45-70	High School U.S.A.-Georgia, Alabama/Plea of Love	1959	10.00	20.00	40.00
❑ 45-71	High School U.S.A.-Cincinnati/Plea of Love	1959	10.00	20.00	40.00
❑ 45-72	High School U.S.A.-Memphis/Plea of Love	1959	10.00	20.00	40.00
❑ 45-73	High School U.S.A.-Los Angeles/Plea of Love	1959	10.00	20.00	40.00
❑ 45-74	High School U.S.A.-San Francisco/Plea of Love	1959	10.00	20.00	40.00
❑ 45-75	High School U.S.A.-Texas/Plea of Love	1959	10.00	20.00	40.00
❑ 45-76	High School U.S.A.-Seattle, Portland/Plea of Love	1959	10.00	20.00	40.00
❑ 45-77	High School U.S.A.-Denver/Plea of Love	1959	10.00	20.00	40.00
❑ 45-78	High School U.S.A.-Oklahoma/Plea of Love	1959	10.00	20.00	40.00
❑ 2057	Bubba Ditty/I Don't Know	1960	5.00	10.00	20.00
LEGRAND					
❑ 1001	High School U.S.A./Give Me Another Chance	1959	6.25	12.50	25.00
—Original pressings have purple labels					
NASCO					
❑ 6018	Little Baby/You Are My Everything	1958	6.25	12.50	25.00

FACES
Also see SMALL FACES; ROD STEWART; RONNIE WOOD.

Number	Title (A Side/B Side)	Yr	VG	VG+	NM
WARNER BROS.					
❑ 7393	Around the Phynth/Wicked Messenger	1970	2.50	5.00	10.00
—As "Small Faces"					
❑ 7442	Real Good Time/Real Wheel Skid	1970	2.50	5.00	10.00
❑ 7483	Maybe I'm Amazed/Oh Lord I'm Browned Off	1971	2.00	4.00	8.00
❑ 7545	Stay with Me/You're So Rude	1971	—	3.00	6.00
❑ 7681	Cindy Incidentally/Skewiff (Mend the Fuse)	1973	—	2.50	5.00
❑ 7681 [PS]	Cindy Incidentally/Skewiff (Mend the Fuse)	1973	—	3.00	6.00
❑ 7711	Ooh-La-La/Borstal Boys	1973	—	2.50	5.00

FACES, THE

Number	Title (A Side/B Side)	Yr	VG	VG+	NM
IGUANA					
❑ 601	Christmas/New Year's Resolution	1965	25.00	50.00	100.00
REGINA					
❑ 326	Skier Jones/What Is This Dream (I Have)	1965	6.25	12.50	25.00
❑ 328	I'll Walk Alone/I Didn't Want Her	1965	6.25	12.50	25.00

FACTORY, THE
Lowell George was in this group before LITTLE FEAT.

Number	Title (A Side/B Side)	Yr	VG	VG+	NM
UNI					
❑ 55005	Smile, Let Your Life Begin/When I Was An Apple	1967	3.00	6.00	12.00

FAGEN, DONALD
Also see STEELY DAN.

Number	Title (A Side/B Side)	Yr	VG	VG+	NM
FULL MOON/ASYLUM					
❑ 47244	True Companion/All of You	1981	—	2.50	5.00
REPRISE					
❑ 18502	Tomorrow's Girls/Confide in Me	1993	—	—	3.00
WARNER BROS.					
❑ 27972	Century's End/Shanghai Confidential	1988	—	2.50	5.00
❑ 27972 [PS]	Century's End/Shanghai Confidential	1988	—	2.50	5.00
❑ 29792	New Frontier/Maxine	1983	—	2.00	4.00
❑ 29900	I.G.Y. (What a Beautiful World)/Walk Between Raindrops	1982	—	2.00	4.00
❑ 29900 [PS]	I.G.Y. (What a Beautiful World)/Walk Between Raindrops	1982	—	2.50	5.00

FAIR, YVONNE

Number	Title (A Side/B Side)	Yr	VG	VG+	NM
DADE					
❑ 1851	Straighten Up/Say Yeah Yeah	1963	3.00	6.00	12.00
❑ 5006	Straighten Up/Say Yeah Yeah	1963	5.00	10.00	20.00
KING					
❑ 5594	I Found You/If I Knew	1962	3.75	7.50	15.00
—With the James Brown Band					
❑ 5654	Tell Me Why/Say So Long	1962	3.75	7.50	15.00
—With James Brown					
❑ 5687	It Hurts to Be in Love/You Can Make It If You Try	1962	3.75	7.50	15.00
—With James Brown					
❑ 6017	Tell Me Why/You Can Make It If You Try	1966	2.00	4.00	8.00
MOTOWN					
❑ 1306	Funky Music Sho Nuff Turns Me On/Let Your Hair Down	1974	—	2.50	5.00
❑ 1323	Walk Out the Door If You Wanna/It Should Have Been Me	1974	—	2.50	5.00
❑ 1344	You Can't Judge a Book By Its Cover/It's Bad for Me to See You	1975	—	2.50	5.00
❑ 1354	Love Ain't No Toy/It's Bad for Me to See You	1975	—	2.50	5.00
❑ 1384	It Should Have Been Me/Tell Me Something Good	1976	—	2.50	5.00
SMASH					
❑ 2030	Just As Sure (As You Play, You Must Pay)/Baby, Baby, Baby	1966	2.50	5.00	10.00
SOUL					
❑ 35075	Stay a Little Longer/We Should Never Be Lonely My Love	1970	—	3.00	6.00

FAIRBURN, WERLY

Number	Title (A Side/B Side)	Yr	VG	VG+	NM
CAPITOL					
❑ F2770	Good Deal Lucille/Baby He's a Wolf	1954	7.50	15.00	30.00
❑ F2844	Love Spelled Backwards Is Evol/Nothing But Lovin'	1954	7.50	15.00	30.00
❑ F2963	Prison Cell of Love/I Feel Like Cryin'	1954	7.50	15.00	30.00
❑ F3101	It's a Cold, Weary World/Spiteful Heart	1955	7.50	15.00	30.00
COLUMBIA					
❑ 4-21432	I Guess I'm Crazy/That Sweet Love of Mine	1955	7.50	15.00	30.00
❑ 4-21483	Broken Hearted Me/Stay Close to Me	1956	7.50	15.00	30.00
❑ 4-21528	Everybody's Rockin'/It's Heaven	1956	25.00	50.00	100.00
SAVOY					
❑ 1503	All the Time/I'm a Fool About Your Love	1956	6.25	12.50	25.00
❑ 1509	My Heart's on Fire/Speak to Me Baby	1957	6.25	12.50	25.00
❑ 1521	Telephone Baby/No Blues Tomorrow	1957	6.25	12.50	25.00
TRUMPET					
❑ 195	Camping with Marie/Let's Think It Over	195?	10.00	20.00	40.00
❑ 196	Baby, Call on Me/I Feel Like Crying	195?	—	—	—
—Canceled					

FAIRLANES, THE

Number	Title (A Side/B Side)	Yr	VG	VG+	NM
ARGO					
❑ 5357	Little Girl, Little Girl/Comin' After You	1960	7.50	15.00	30.00
CONTINENTAL					
❑ 1001	Writing This Letter/Playboy	1961	75.00	150.00	300.00
DART					
❑ 109	Just for Me/Bullseye	1959	20.00	40.00	80.00
LUCKY SEVEN					
❑ 102	Seventeen Steps/Johnny Rhythm	1959	15.00	30.00	60.00
MINARET					
❑ 103	The Dagwood/I'm Not the Kind of Guy	1962	5.00	10.00	20.00
RADIANT					
❑ 101	Baby Baby/Tell Me	1964	62.50	125.00	250.00
REPRISE					
❑ 20213	Surf Train/Lonely Weekends	1963	7.50	15.00	30.00

FAIRPORT CONVENTION

Number	Title (A Side/B Side)	Yr	VG	VG+	NM
A&M					
❑ 1108	Fotheringay/I'll Keep It with Mine	1969	3.00	6.00	12.00
❑ 1155	Genesis Hall/Si Tu Dois Partie	1969	3.00	6.00	12.00
❑ 1333	Journeyman's Grace/The World Has Surely Lost Its Head	1972	2.00	4.00	8.00
❑ 1348	John Lee/The Time Is Near	1972	2.00	4.00	8.00

FAITH, ADAM

Number	Title (A Side/B Side)	Yr	VG	VG+	NM
AMY					
895	The First Time/So Long Baby	1964	3.75	7.50	15.00
899	We Are in Love/What Now	1964	3.75	7.50	15.00
913	It's Alright/I Just Don't Know	1964	3.75	7.50	15.00
922	Talk About Love/Stop Feeling Sorry for Yourself	1965	3.75	7.50	15.00
936	Don't You Know/Someone's Taken Marie Away	1965	3.75	7.50	15.00
CAPITOL					
5543	I'm Used to Losing You/I Don't Need That Kind of Lovin'	1965	2.50	5.00	10.00
5699	To Make a Big Man Cry/Here's Another Day	1966	2.50	5.00	10.00
CUB					
9061	What Do You Want/From Now Until September	1960	5.00	10.00	20.00
9068	Poor Me/The Reason	1960	5.00	10.00	20.00
9074	I Did What You Told Me/When Johnny Comes Marching Home	1960	5.00	10.00	20.00
DOT					
16405	Don't That Beat All/Mix Me a Person	1962	3.75	7.50	15.00
EMI					
2691	What Do You Want/Lonely Pup (In A Christmas Shop)//How About That/Someone Else's Baby	1977	2.00	4.00	8.00
—U.K. import					
LAURIE					
3455	Daddy, What'll Happen to Me/Cowman, Milk Your Cow	1968	2.00	4.00	8.00

FAITHFULL, MARIANNE

Number	Title (A Side/B Side)	Yr	VG	VG+	NM
COLLECTABLES					
2605	Broken English/Why D'Ya Do It	199?	—	—	3.00
—Reissue					
4238	As Tears Go By/Gloria	199?	—	—	3.00
—Reissue; B-side by Them					
ISLAND					
49121	Broken English/Brain Drain	1979	—	2.50	5.00
49873	Sweetheart/For Beauty's Sake	1981	—	2.00	4.00
94997	Broken English/Why D'Ya Do It?	198?	2.50	5.00	10.00
—Gold label "Revival of the Fittest" series					
99888	Running for Our Lives/(B-side unknown)	1983	—	2.00	4.00
LONDON					
1022	Sister Morphine/Something Better	1969	25.00	50.00	100.00
—Promo worth about 50% of these values.					
9697	As Tears Go By/Greensleeves	1964	3.00	6.00	12.00
9731	Come and Stay with Me/What Have I Done Wrong				
	Come and Stay with Me/What Have I Done Wrong	1965	2.50	5.00	10.00
9759	This Little Bird/Morning Sun	1965	2.50	5.00	10.00
9780	Summer Nights/The Sha-La-La Song	1965	2.50	5.00	10.00
9802	Go Away from My World/Oh Look Around You	1965	2.50	5.00	10.00
9802 [PS]	Go Away from My World/Oh Look Around You	1965	5.00	10.00	20.00
20012	Counting/Tomorrow's Calling	1966	2.50	5.00	10.00
20012 [PS]	Counting/Tomorrow's Calling	1966	5.00	10.00	20.00
20020	Is This What I Get for Loving You/Tomorrow's Calling	1966	2.50	5.00	10.00

FALCONS, THE (1)

Detroit R&B group. Also see EDDIE FLOYD; WILSON PICKETT.

Number	Title (A Side/B Side)	Yr	VG	VG+	NM
ANNA					
1110	Just for Your Love/This Heart of Mine	1959	25.00	50.00	100.00
ATLANTIC					
2153	Darling/Lah-Tee-Lah-Tah	1962	5.00	10.00	20.00
2179	Let's Kiss and Make Up/Take This Love I've Got	1963	5.00	10.00	20.00
2207	Oh Baby/Fine, Fine, Fine	1963	5.00	10.00	20.00
BIG WHEEL					
321	I Must Love You/Love, Love, Love	1966	5.00	10.00	20.00
323/4	I Can't Help It/Standing on Guard	1966	5.00	10.00	20.00
1967	Standing On Guard/I Can't Help It	1966	5.00	10.00	20.00
1972	Good Good Feeling/You Like You Never Been Loved	1966	5.00	10.00	20.00
CHESS					
1743	Just for Your Love/This Heart of Mine	1959	6.25	12.50	25.00
FALCON					
1006	Now That It's Over/My Only Love	1957	50.00	100.00	200.00
FLICK					
001	You're So Fine/Goddess of Angels	1959	100.00	200.00	400.00
008	You Must Know I Love You/That's What I Aim to Do	1960	30.00	60.00	120.00
KUDO					
661	This Heart of Mine/Romanita	1958	100.00	200.00	400.00
LUPINE					
103	I Found a Love/Swim	1962	12.50	25.00	50.00
124	Lonely Nights/Has It Happened to You	1962	25.00	50.00	100.00
1003	I Found a Love/Swim	1962	12.50	25.00	50.00
1024	Lonely Nights/Has It Happened to You	1962	10.00	20.00	40.00
UNART					
2013-S [S]	You're So Fine/Goddess of Angels	1959	25.00	50.00	100.00
—Though labeled as stereo, this seems to be rechanneled					
2013 [M]	You're So Fine/Goddess of Angels	1959	7.50	15.00	30.00
2022	You're Mine/Country Shack	1959	6.25	12.50	25.00
UNITED ARTISTS					
0108	You're So Fine/Showtime	1973	—	2.00	4.00
—"Silver Spotlight Series" reissue					
229	The Teacher/Waiting for You	1960	5.00	10.00	20.00
255	I Plus Love Plus You/Wonderful Love	1960	5.00	10.00	20.00
289	Pow! You're in Love/Workin' Man's Song	1961	5.00	10.00	20.00
420	You're So Fine/Goddess of Angels	1962	5.00	10.00	20.00
1624	You're So Fine/Goddess of Angels	196?	2.00	4.00	8.00
—"Silver Spotlight Series" issue					
7-Inch Extended Plays					
UNITED ARTISTS					
10010	*The Teacher/Waiting for You/You're So Fine/Goddess of Angels	1960	75.00	150.00	300.00
10010 [PS]	The Falcons	1960	75.00	150.00	300.00

FALCONS, THE (2)

Number	Title (A Side/B Side)	Yr	VG	VG+	NM
CASH					
1002	Tell Me Why/I Miss You Darling	1955	125.00	250.00	500.00
FLIP					
301	Stay Mine/Du-Bi-A-Do	1954	50.00	100.00	200.00
302	You Are the Only One/Mambo Baby Tonight	1954	50.00	100.00	200.00

FALCONS, THE (U)

These may be by group (1) or by group (2) or by neither.

Number	Title (A Side/B Side)	Yr	VG	VG+	NM
MERCURY					
70940	Baby That's It/This Day	1956	15.00	30.00	60.00
SILHOUETTE					
522	Can This Be Christmas/Sent Up	1957	75.00	150.00	300.00

FALLEN ANGELS, THE

Number	Title (A Side/B Side)	Yr	VG	VG+	NM
LAURIE					
3343	Eveytime I Fall in Love/I Have Found	1966	6.25	12.50	25.00
3369	Have You Ever Lost a Love/A Little Love from You Will Do	1966	6.25	12.50	25.00
PHILCO-FORD					
HP-23	Room at the Top/Most Children Do	1968	5.00	10.00	20.00
—4-inch plastic "Hip Pocket Record" with color sleeve					
ROULETTE					
4770	Room at the Top/Your Friends Here in Dunderville	1967	5.00	10.00	20.00
4785	Most Children Do/Hello Girl	1967	5.00	10.00	20.00
TOLLIE					
9049	Up on the Mountain/So Young, So Fine	1965	6.25	12.50	25.00

FALLING PEBBLES, THE

Early version of THE BUCKINGHAMS.

Number	Title (A Side/B Side)	Yr	VG	VG+	NM
ALLEY CAT					
201	Lawdy Miss Clawdy/Virginia Wolf	1964	6.25	12.50	25.00

FALLOWS, SCOTT, AND THE EBBTONES

Number	Title (A Side/B Side)	Yr	VG	VG+	NM
DOT					
16577	Surfing Boop-Boop-A-Do/King of Lovers	1964	5.00	10.00	20.00

FAME, GEORGIE

Number	Title (A Side/B Side)	Yr	VG	VG+	NM
EPIC					
10166	Because I Love You/Bidin' My Time ('Cos I Love You)	1967	2.00	4.00	8.00
10203	The Ballad of Bonnie and Clyde/Beware of the Dog	1968	2.50	5.00	10.00
10347	Hideaway/Runaway Child	1968	—	3.00	6.00
10402	Someone to Watch Over Me/For Your Pleasure	1968	—	3.00	6.00
10477	I'll Be Your Baby Tonight/Down Along the Cove	1969	—	3.00	6.00
10546	Peaceful/Hideaway	1969	—	3.00	6.00
10640	Fire and Rain/The Movie Star Song	1970	—	3.00	6.00
IMPERIAL					
66086	Yeh, Yeh/Preach and Teach	1965	3.00	6.00	12.00
66104	Let the Sunshine In/In the Meantime	1965	2.50	5.00	10.00
66125	Blue Monday/Like We Used to Be	1965	2.50	5.00	10.00
66189	El Bandido/Get Away	1966	2.50	5.00	10.00
66220	Last Night/Sitting in the Park	1966	2.50	5.00	10.00
66299	Funny How Time Slips Away/Last Night	1968	2.00	4.00	8.00
ISLAND					
035	Everlovin' Woman/Ozone	1975	—	2.50	5.00

FAMOUS FLAMES, THE

Backing group for JAMES BROWN.

Number	Title (A Side/B Side)	Yr	VG	VG+	NM
KING					
6341	Nobody Knows But My Baby and Me/Who Am I	1970	2.00	4.00	8.00

FANADOS, THE

Number	Title (A Side/B Side)	Yr	VG	VG+	NM
CARTER					
2050	The One I Love/She Must Be from a Different Planet	195?	200.00	400.00	800.00

FANS, THE

Number	Title (A Side/B Side)	Yr	VG	VG+	NM
DOT					
16688	I Want a Beatle for Christmas/How Far Should I Let My Heart Go Tonight	1964	3.75	7.50	15.00

FANTASTIC BAGGYS, THE

Also see STEVE BARRI; P.F. SLOAN.

Number	Title (A Side/B Side)	Yr	VG	VG+	NM
IMPERIAL					
66047	Tell 'Em I'm Surfin'/Surfer Boy's Dream	1964	17.50	35.00	70.00
66072	Anywhere the Girls Are/Debbie Be True	1964	12.50	25.00	50.00
66092	Alone on the Beach/It Was I	1965	12.50	25.00	50.00

FANTASTIC FOUR, THE

Number	Title (A Side/B Side)	Yr	VG	VG+	NM
EASTBOUND					
609	I Had the Whole World to Choose From/If You Need Me	1973	—	3.00	6.00
620	I'm Falling in Love (I Feel Good All Over)/I Believe in Miracles	1974	—	3.00	6.00
RIC-TIC					
113	Can't Stop Looking for My Baby/Can't Stop Looking for My Baby (Part 2)	1966	50.00	100.00	200.00
119	Girl Have Pity/Live Up to What She Thinks	1967	3.75	7.50	15.00
121	Can't Stop Looking for My Baby/Just the Lonely	1967	25.00	50.00	100.00
122	The Whole World Is a Stage/Ain't Love Wonderful	1967	3.75	7.50	15.00
128	You Gave Me Something (And Everything's Alright)/I Don't Wanna Live Without You	1967	3.75	7.50	15.00
130	To Share Your Love/As Long As I Live (I Live for You)	1967	3.75	7.50	15.00

Number	Title (A Side/B Side)	Yr	VG	VG+	NM
❑ 134	Goddess of Love/As Long As the Feeling Is There	1968	3.75	7.50	15.00
❑ 136	Love Is a Many-Splendored Thing/Goddess of Love	1968	3.75	7.50	15.00
❑ 137	No Love Like Your Love/A Man in Love	1968	3.75	7.50	15.00
❑ 139	I've Got to Have You/Win or Lose	1968	3.75	7.50	15.00
❑ 144	I Love You Madly/(Instrumental)	1968	5.00	10.00	20.00

SOUL

Number	Title (A Side/B Side)	Yr	VG	VG+	NM
❑ 35052	I Love You Madly/(Instrumental)	1968	3.00	6.00	12.00
❑ 35058	I Feel Like I'm Falling in Love/Pin Point It Out	1969	3.75	7.50	15.00
❑ 35065	Just Another Lonely Night/I Don't Care Why You Want Me	1969	3.75	7.50	15.00
❑ 35072	On the Brighter Side of a Blue World/I'm Gonna Hurry On	1970	3.00	6.00	12.00

WESTBOUND

Number	Title (A Side/B Side)	Yr	VG	VG+	NM
❑ 5009	Alvin Stone (The Birth & Death of a Gangster)/I Believe in Miracles, I Believe in You	1975	—	2.50	5.00
❑ 5017	Have a Little Mercy/County Line	1975	—	2.50	5.00
❑ 5030	Don't Risk Your Happiness On Foolish Things/They Took the Show on the Road	1976	—	2.50	5.00
❑ 5032	Hideaway/They Took the Show on the Road	1976	—	2.50	5.00
❑ 55403	I Got to Have Your Love/Ain't I Been Good to You	1977	—	2.50	5.00
❑ 55408	Mixed Up Moods and Attitudes/Disco Fool Blues	1978	—	2.50	5.00
❑ 55417	Sexy Lady/If This Is Love	1979	—	2.50	5.00
❑ 55419	B.Y.O.F. (Bring Your Own Funk)/If This Is Love	1979	—	2.50	5.00

FANTASTIC JOHNNY C, THE

KAMA SUTRA

Number	Title (A Side/B Side)	Yr	VG	VG+	NM
❑ 511	Let's Do It Together/Peace Treaty	1970	—	2.50	5.00
❑ 515	Good Love/You Got Your Hooks in Me	1970	—	2.50	5.00

PHILCO-FORD

Number	Title (A Side/B Side)	Yr	VG	VG+	NM
❑ HP-39	Boogaloo Down Broadway/Got What You Need	1969	5.00	10.00	20.00

—4-inch plastic "Hip Pocket Record" with color sleeve

PHIL.-LA OF SOUL

Number	Title (A Side/B Side)	Yr	VG	VG+	NM
❑ 305	Boogaloo Down Broadway/Look What Love Can Make You Do	1967	2.00	4.00	8.00
❑ 309	Got What You Need/New Love	1968	—	3.00	6.00
❑ 315	Hitch It to the Horse/Cool Broadway	1968	—	3.00	6.00
❑ 320	Baby I Need You/Some Kind of Wonderful	1968	—	3.00	6.00
❑ 327	Is There Anything Better Than Making Love/New Love	1969	—	3.00	6.00
❑ 361	Don't Depend on Me/Waitin' for the Rain	1973	—	2.00	4.00
❑ 363	Just Say the Word/I'm a Man	1973	—	2.00	4.00

FANTASTICS, THE (1)

Male R&B group.

BELL

Number	Title (A Side/B Side)	Yr	VG	VG+	NM
❑ 977	Something Old, Something New/High and Dry	1971	5.00	10.00	20.00
❑ 45157	(Love Me) Love the Life I Lead/Old Rags and Tatters	1971	3.75	7.50	15.00

DERAM

Number	Title (A Side/B Side)	Yr	VG	VG+	NM
❑ 7528	Face to Face with Heartache/This Must Be My Rainy Day	1970	3.75	7.50	15.00

FANTASTICS, THE (2)

RCA VICTOR

Number	Title (A Side/B Side)	Yr	VG	VG+	NM
❑ 47-7572	There Goes My Love/Millionaire Hobo	1959	10.00	20.00	40.00

—Black label, dog on top

Number	Title (A Side/B Side)	Yr	VG	VG+	NM
❑ 47-7572	There Goes My Love/I Wanna Be a Millionaire Hobo	1965	3.75	7.50	15.00

—Evidenly, a reissue with the same number, but the dog on side of label rather than on top, exists

Number	Title (A Side/B Side)	Yr	VG	VG+	NM
❑ 47-7664	This Is My Wedding Day/I Got a Zero	1960	10.00	20.00	40.00

UNITED ARTISTS

Number	Title (A Side/B Side)	Yr	VG	VG+	NM
❑ 309	Dancing Doll/I Told You Once	1961	12.50	25.00	50.00

FANTASTICS, THE (U)

Neither group (1) nor group (2), but are they both the same?

SCORPIO

Number	Title (A Side/B Side)	Yr	VG	VG+	NM
❑ 407	Malaguena/Dance for an Unnamed Gypsy Queen	1966	6.25	12.50	25.00

SOUND STAGE 7

Number	Title (A Side/B Side)	Yr	VG	VG+	NM
❑ 2565	Have a Little You/Me and You	1966	3.00	6.00	12.00

FARDON, DON

CAPITOL

Number	Title (A Side/B Side)	Yr	VG	VG+	NM
❑ 3929	St. Matthew, St. Mark, St. Luke and St. John/Lola	1974	—	2.50	5.00

CHELSEA

Number	Title (A Side/B Side)	Yr	VG	VG+	NM
❑ 78-0115	Delta Queen/Home Town Baby	1973	—	3.00	6.00

DECCA

Number	Title (A Side/B Side)	Yr	VG	VG+	NM
❑ 32696	Belfast Boy/Echoes of the Cheers	1970	—	3.00	6.00

GNP CRESCENDO

Number	Title (A Side/B Side)	Yr	VG	VG+	NM
❑ 405	(The Lament of the Cherokee) Indian Reservation/Dreaming Room	1968	2.00	4.00	8.00
❑ 418	Take a Heart/How Do You Break a Broken Heart	1968	—	3.00	6.00
❑ 421	Sally Goes 'Round the Moon/How Do You Break a Broken Heart	1969	—	3.00	6.00
❑ 424	Running Bear/Ruby's Picture	1969	—	3.00	6.00

ROXBURY

Number	Title (A Side/B Side)	Yr	VG	VG+	NM
❑ BRBO-0159	Louisiana/Lady Zelda	1973	—	2.50	5.00

FARLOWE, CHRIS

GENERAL AMERICAN

Number	Title (A Side/B Side)	Yr	VG	VG+	NM
❑ 718	What You Gonna Do/Just a Dream	1964	3.75	7.50	15.00

IMMEDIATE

Number	Title (A Side/B Side)	Yr	VG	VG+	NM
❑ 5002	Paint It Black/You're So Good to Me	1967	2.50	5.00	10.00
❑ 5005	Handbags and Gladrags/Everyone Makes a Mistake	1968	2.50	5.00	10.00
❑ 5011	What Have I Been Doing/Paint It Black	1968	2.50	5.00	10.00

MGM

Number	Title (A Side/B Side)	Yr	VG	VG+	NM
❑ 13567	Out of Time/Baby Make It Soon	1966	5.00	10.00	20.00

—A-side is a Mick Jagger-Keith Richards composition only later recorded by the Rolling Stones.

POLYDOR

Number	Title (A Side/B Side)	Yr	VG	VG+	NM
❑ 14008	Circles 'Round the Sun/Save Your Tears	1969	2.00	4.00	8.00
❑ 14013	Medicated Goo/Betty Lou	1970	2.00	4.00	8.00

FARNER, MARK

Of GRAND FUNK RAILROAD.

ATLANTIC

Number	Title (A Side/B Side)	Yr	VG	VG+	NM
❑ 3448	You and Me Baby/Second Chance to Dance	1977	—	2.00	4.00
❑ 3510	When a Man Loves a Woman/If It Took All Day	1978	—	2.00	4.00
❑ 3529	Just One Look/Crystal Eyes	1978	—	2.00	4.00

LUCKY ELEVEN

Number	Title (A Side/B Side)	Yr	VG	VG+	NM
❑ 352	Down in the Valley/I Got News for You	1968	2.50	5.00	10.00

FARNER, MARK, AND DON BREWER

Both later of GRAND FUNK RAILROAD.

LUCKY ELEVEN

Number	Title (A Side/B Side)	Yr	VG	VG+	NM
❑ 366	Does It Matter to You Girl/We Gotta Have Love	1968	3.00	6.00	12.00

FARON'S FLAMINGOS

COLUMBIA

Number	Title (A Side/B Side)	Yr	VG	VG+	NM
❑ 43018	Let's Stomp/I Can Tell	1964	6.25	12.50	25.00

—B-side by Rory Storm and the Hurricanes

FARR, GARY, AND THE T-BONES

EPIC

Number	Title (A Side/B Side)	Yr	VG	VG+	NM
❑ 9832	Don't Stop and Stare/Give All She's Got	1965	3.00	6.00	12.00

FARR, LITTLE JOEY

BAND BOX

Number	Title (A Side/B Side)	Yr	VG	VG+	NM
❑ 286	Rock & Roll Santa/Big White Cadillac	196?	12.50	25.00	50.00

FARRELL AND THE FLAMES

FRANSIL

Number	Title (A Side/B Side)	Yr	VG	VG+	NM
❑ 14	Dreams and Memories/You'll Be Sorry	1961	100.00	200.00	400.00

FASCINATIONS, THE (1)

Female vocal group.

ABC-PARAMOUNT

Number	Title (A Side/B Side)	Yr	VG	VG+	NM
❑ 10387	Mama Didn't Lie/Someone Like You	1962	5.00	10.00	20.00

—Some of the ABC-Paramount pressings are misspelled "Fasinations"

Number	Title (A Side/B Side)	Yr	VG	VG+	NM
❑ 10443	Tears In My Eyes/You're Gonna Be Sorry	1963	6.25	12.50	25.00

MAYFIELD

Number	Title (A Side/B Side)	Yr	VG	VG+	NM
❑ 7711	(Say It Isn't So) Say You'd Never Go/(B-side unknown)	1966	2.50	5.00	10.00
❑ 7714	Girls Are Out to Get You/You'll Be Sorry	1966	2.50	5.00	10.00
❑ 7716	I Can't Stay Away from You/(B-side unknown)	1967	2.50	5.00	10.00

FASCINATIONS, THE (2)

DORE

Number	Title (A Side/B Side)	Yr	VG	VG+	NM
❑ 593	If I Had Your Love/Why	1961	12.50	25.00	50.00

PAXLEY

Number	Title (A Side/B Side)	Yr	VG	VG+	NM
❑ 750	If I Had Your Love/Why	1960	37.50	75.00	150.00

FASCINATIONS, THE (U)

It's doubtful that any of these are group (1), but they could be group (2).

A&G

Number	Title (A Side/B Side)	Yr	VG	VG+	NM
❑ 101	I'm Gonna Cry/Since You Went Away	1972	5.00	10.00	20.00

SURE

Number	Title (A Side/B Side)	Yr	VG	VG+	NM
❑ 106	It's Midnight/Boom Bada Boom	1960	20.00	40.00	80.00
❑ 106	Midnight/Boom Bada Boom	1960	30.00	60.00	120.00

FASCINATORS, THE (1)

BIM BAM BOOM

Number	Title (A Side/B Side)	Yr	VG	VG+	NM
❑ 110	Oh, Rose Marie/Forgive Me, My Darling	1974	2.50	5.00	10.00

CAPITOL

Number	Title (A Side/B Side)	Yr	VG	VG+	NM
❑ F-4053	Chapel Bells/I Wonder Who	1958	37.50	75.00	150.00
❑ F-4137	Come to Paradise/Who Do You Think You Are	1959	50.00	100.00	200.00
❑ F-4247	Oh Rose Marie/Fried Chicken and Macaroni	1959	50.00	100.00	200.00
❑ 4544	Chapel Bells/I Wonder Who	1961	20.00	40.00	80.00

FASCINATORS, THE (2)

BLUE LAKE

Number	Title (A Side/B Side)	Yr	VG	VG+	NM
❑ 112	Can't Stop/Don't Give My Love Away	1953	500.00	1000.	2000.

FASCINATORS, THE (3)

BURN

Number	Title (A Side/B Side)	Yr	VG	VG+	NM
❑ 845	I'll Be Gone/Can't You See I'm Lonely	1965	5.00	10.00	20.00

FASCINATORS, THE (4)

DOOTO

Number	Title (A Side/B Side)	Yr	VG	VG+	NM
❑ 441	Teardrop Eyes/Shivers and Shakes	1958	15.00	30.00	60.00

FASCINATORS, THE (5)

YOUR COPY

Number	Title (A Side/B Side)	Yr	VG	VG+	NM
❑ 1135	The Bells of My Heart/Sweet Baby	1954	250.00	500.00	1000.

—Black vinyl

Number	Title (A Side/B Side)	Yr	VG	VG+	NM
❑ 1135	The Bells of My Heart/Sweet Baby	1954	500.00	1000.	2000.

—Red vinyl

Number	Title (A Side/B Side)	Yr	VG	VG+	NM
❑ 1136	My Beauty, My Own/Don't Give It Away	1954	250.00	500.00	1000.

FASCINATORS, THE (U)

If these are not completely different groups, these are most likely by group (3) or (4).

KING

Number	Title (A Side/B Side)	Yr	VG	VG+	NM
❑ 5119	Cuddle Up with Carolyn/Tee Hee	1958	12.50	25.00	50.00

TRANS ATLAS

Number	Title (A Side/B Side)	Yr	VG	VG+	NM
❑ 688	You're to Blame/Revived	196?	7.50	15.00	30.00

FASHIONS, THE (1)

BARBARA ENGLISH was a member of this group.

CAMEO

Number	Title (A Side/B Side)	Yr	VG	VG+	NM
❑ 331	Baby That's Me/Nick and Joe Callin'	1964	2.50	5.00	10.00

ELMOR

Number	Title (A Side/B Side)	Yr	VG	VG+	NM
❑ 301	Please Let It Be Me/Fairy Tales	1961	6.25	12.50	25.00

EMBER

Number	Title (A Side/B Side)	Yr	VG	VG+	NM
❑ 1084	I Just Got a Letter/Try My Love	1962	3.00	6.00	12.00

Number	Title (A Side/B Side)	Yr	VG	VG+	NM
V-TONE					
❑ 202	I'm Dreaming of You/Lonesome Road	1959	12.50	25.00	50.00
❑ 202	I'm Dreaming of You/I Love You So	1959	7.50	15.00	30.00
—Orange label					
❑ 202	I'm Dreaming of You/I Love You So	1959	5.00	10.00	20.00
—Blue label					
WARWICK					
❑ 646	All I Want/Dearest One	1961	5.00	10.00	20.00

FASHIONS, THE (2)

Number	Title (A Side/B Side)	Yr	VG	VG+	NM
FELSTED					
❑ 8689	Surfer's Memories/Surfin' Back to School	1964	7.50	15.00	30.00

FASHIONS, THE (3)

Number	Title (A Side/B Side)	Yr	VG	VG+	NM
PHIL-L.A. OF SOUL					
❑ 354	I Don't Mind Doin' It/What Goes Up (Must Come Down)	1972	—	3.00	6.00

FASHIONS, THE (4)

Number	Title (A Side/B Side)	Yr	VG	VG+	NM
20TH CENTURY FOX					
❑ 6710	Lover's Stand/Only Those in Love	1968	2.00	4.00	8.00

FASTBALL

Number	Title (A Side/B Side)	Yr	VG	VG+	NM
HOT HITS					
❑ A0001	Fire Escape/The Hardest Part	1998	—	—	3.00
—B-side by the Pistoleros					
JBO/HOLLYWOOD					
❑ 5298	The Way (same on both sides)	1998	—	—	3.00

FASTEST GROUP ALIVE, THE

Number	Title (A Side/B Side)	Yr	VG	VG+	NM
TEEN					
❑ 100	The Bears/Beside	1966	7.50	15.00	30.00
VALIANT					
❑ 754	The Bears/Beside	1966	5.00	10.00	20.00
❑ 759	Lullabye/5:15 Sports	1967	5.00	10.00	20.00

FATBOY SLIM

Number	Title (A Side/B Side)	Yr	VG	VG+	NM
ASTRALWERKS					
❑ 38659	The Rockafeller Skank (Radio Edit)/Praise You	1999	—	3.00	6.00

FAUN

Number	Title (A Side/B Side)	Yr	VG	VG+	NM
GREGAR					
❑ 7000	Better Dig What You Find/I Asked My Mother	1969	5.00	10.00	20.00
❑ 7001	Son of a Literate Man/Yes I'm Really Lonely	1969	5.00	10.00	20.00

FAWNS, THE

Number	Title (A Side/B Side)	Yr	VG	VG+	NM
APT					
❑ 25015	Come On/Until I Die	1958	6.25	12.50	25.00

FEATHERBED

Early BARRY MANILOW.

Number	Title (A Side/B Side)	Yr	VG	VG+	NM
BELL					
❑ 971	Amy/Morning	1971	15.00	30.00	60.00
—Stock copies are much scarcer than promo copies					
❑ 45133 [DJ]	Could It Be Magic (mono/stereo)	1971	25.00	50.00	100.00
—Stock copy may not exist					

FEATHERS, CHARLIE

Number	Title (A Side/B Side)	Yr	VG	VG+	NM
FLIP					
❑ 503	I've Been Deceived/Peeping Eyes	1955	125.00	250.00	500.00
HOLIDAY INN					
❑ 114	Deep Elm Blues/Nobody's Darling	1962	50.00	100.00	200.00
KAY					
❑ 1001	Jungle Fever/Why Don't You	1960	50.00	100.00	200.00
KING					
❑ 4971	Can't Hardly Stand It/Everybody's Lovin' My Baby	1956	150.00	300.00	600.00
❑ 4997	One Hand Loose/Bottle to the Baby	1956	125.00	250.00	500.00
❑ 5022	Nobody's Woman/When You Decide	1957	100.00	200.00	400.00
❑ 5043	When You Come Around/Too Much Alike	1957	100.00	200.00	400.00
MEMPHIS					
❑ 103	Wild, Wild Party/Today and Tomorrow	1961	25.00	50.00	100.00
METEOR					
❑ 5032	Tongue-Tied Jill/Get With It	1956	500.00	1000.	1500.
—Maroon label					
❑ 5032	Tongue-Tied Jill/Get With It	1956	100.00	200.00	400.00
—Blue label					
PHILWOOD					
❑ 223	Tear It Up/Stutterin' Cindy	197?	2.00	4.00	8.00
POMPADOUR					
❑ 231	Uh-Huh Honey/A Wedding Gown of White	1974	2.00	4.00	8.00
ROLLIN' ROCK					
❑ 45-025	That Certain Female/She Set Me Free	1978	2.00	4.00	8.00
SUN					
❑ 231	Defrost Your Heart/Wedding Gown of White	1956	200.00	400.00	600.00
❑ 503	I've Been Deceived/Peeping Eyes	1956	200.00	400.00	600.00
WAL-MAY					
❑ 101	Dinky John/South of Chicago	1960	50.00	100.00	200.00

FEATHERS, THE (1)

Number	Title (A Side/B Side)	Yr	VG	VG+	NM
ALADDIN					
❑ 3267	Johnny Darling/Shake 'Em Up	1954	50.00	100.00	200.00
❑ 3277	I Need a Girl/Standing Right There	1955	50.00	100.00	200.00
HOLLYWOOD					
❑ 1051	Dear One/Lonesome Tonight	1956	1000.	2000.	3000.
SHOW TIME					
❑ 1104	Nona/Johnny Darling	1954	75.00	150.00	300.00
❑ 1105	Why Don't You Write Me/Busy as a Bee	1954	50.00	100.00	200.00
❑ 1105	Why Don't You Write Me/Where Did Caledonia Go	1954	37.50	75.00	150.00
❑ 1106	Love Only You/Crashing the Party	1955	50.00	100.00	200.00

FEATHERS, THE (2)

Number	Title (A Side/B Side)	Yr	VG	VG+	NM
KAPP					
❑ 887	Give Him Love/To Be Loved by You	1968	2.00	4.00	8.00

FEATHERS, THE (U)

May or may not be by group (2).

Number	Title (A Side/B Side)	Yr	VG	VG+	NM
VEEP					
❑ 1200	The Dummy/Them Onions	1964	2.00	4.00	8.00

FEDERALS, THE (1)

British group.

Number	Title (A Side/B Side)	Yr	VG	VG+	NM
CAPITOL					
❑ 5526	Bucketful of Love/Leah	1965	2.50	5.00	10.00

FEDERALS, THE (2)

Number	Title (A Side/B Side)	Yr	VG	VG+	NM
DELUXE					
❑ 6112	Come Go with Me/Cold Cash	1957	20.00	40.00	80.00
FURY					
❑ 1005	While Our Hearts Are Young/You're the One I Love	1957	25.00	50.00	100.00
❑ 1009	Dear Lorraine/She's My Girl	1958	25.00	50.00	100.00

FELDER, DON

Also see EAGLES.

Number	Title (A Side/B Side)	Yr	VG	VG+	NM
ASYLUM					
❑ 69673	Winters/(B-side unknown)	1984	—	—	3.00
❑ 69743	Who Tonight/Winters	1984	—	—	3.00
❑ 69784	Bad Girls/Night Owl	1983	—	2.00	4.00
❑ 69976	Never Surrender/Raised on the Radio	1982	—	2.00	4.00
—B-side by Ravyns					
❑ 69976 [PS]	Never Surrender/Raised on the Radio	1982	—	2.00	4.00
FULL MOON/ASYLUM					
❑ 47175	Heavy Metal (Takin' a Ride)/All of You	1981	—	2.00	4.00
❑ 47175 [PS]	Heavy Metal (Takin' a Ride)/All of You	1981	—	2.00	4.00

FELDERS ORIOLES

Number	Title (A Side/B Side)	Yr	VG	VG+	NM
MERCURY					
❑ 72480	Down Home Girl/Misty	1965	2.50	5.00	10.00

FELICITY

Either Don Henley or Glenn Frey was a member of this group (sources conflict).

Number	Title (A Side/B Side)	Yr	VG	VG+	NM
WILSON					
❑ 101	Hurtin'/I'll Try It	1965	7.50	15.00	30.00

FELIX AND THE ESCORTS

An early version of THE (YOUNG) RASCALS. "Felix" is FELIX CAVALIERE.

Number	Title (A Side/B Side)	Yr	VG	VG+	NM
JAG					
❑ 685	The Syracuse/Save	1964	37.50	75.00	150.00

FELTS, NARVEL

Number	Title (A Side/B Side)	Yr	VG	VG+	NM
ABC					
❑ 12338	Runaway/Free	1978	—	2.50	5.00
❑ 12374	Just Keep It Up/Lonely Lady	1978	—	2.50	5.00
❑ 12414	One Run for the Roses/Lie to Me (Darling)	1978	—	2.50	5.00
❑ 12441	Everlasting Love/Small Enough to Crawl	1978	—	2.50	5.00
ABC DOT					
❑ 17549	Reconsider Me/Foggy Misty Morning	1975	—	2.50	5.00
❑ 17569	Funny How Time Slips Away/No One Knows	1975	—	2.50	5.00
❑ 17598	Somebody Hold Me (Until She Passes By)/Away	1975	—	2.50	5.00
❑ 17620	Lonely Teardrops/I Remember You	1976	—	2.50	5.00
❑ 17643	My Prayer/If Ever Two Were One (Then Surely We Are)	1976	—	2.50	5.00
❑ 17664	My Good Thing's Gone/I'm Afraid to Be Alone	1976	—	2.50	5.00
❑ 17680	The Feeling's Right/Another Crazy Dream	1977	—	2.50	5.00
❑ 17700	I Don't Hurt Anymore/When We Were Together	1977	—	2.50	5.00
❑ 17715	To Love Somebody/Remember	1977	—	2.50	5.00
❑ 17731	Please/Blue Darlin'	1977	—	2.50	5.00
ARA					
❑ 203	Four Seasons of Life/All That Heaven Sent	1964	5.00	10.00	20.00
❑ 207	You Were Mine/You Didn't Tell Me, I Didn't Know	1965	5.00	10.00	20.00
❑ 211	Night Creature/One Boy and One Night	1965	5.00	10.00	20.00
❑ 213	Welcome Home Mr. Blues/Your True Love	1965	5.00	10.00	20.00
CELEBRITY CIRCLE					
❑ 6903	Welcome Home Mr. Blues/Back Street	1965	3.00	6.00	12.00
❑ 6905	What's Wrong with Me/It All Depends	1965	3.00	6.00	12.00
CINNAMON					
❑ 756	Rockin' Little Angel/The Twelfth of Never	1973	—	3.00	6.00
❑ 763	Drift Away/Foggy Misty Morning	1973	—	3.00	6.00
❑ 771	All in the Name of Love/Before You Have to Go	1973	—	3.00	6.00
❑ 779	When Your Good Love Was Mine/Fraulein	1973	—	3.00	6.00
❑ 798	I Want to Stay/Wrap My Arms Around the World	1974	—	3.00	6.00
❑ 809	Raindrops/Tilted Cup of Love	1974	—	3.00	6.00
COLLAGE					
❑ 101	Because of Losing You/After You	1979	—	3.00	6.00
COMPLEAT					
❑ 101	Smoke Gets in Your Eyes/You're the Reason	1982	—	2.50	5.00
❑ 104	Cry Baby/Now I Don't Have to Love You	1983	—	2.50	5.00
EVERGREEN					
❑ 1011	Anytime You're Ready/Nobody's Fool	1983	—	2.50	5.00
❑ 1014	Fool/Anytime You're Ready	1983	—	2.50	5.00
❑ 1017	You Lay So Easy on My Mind/Nobody's Fool	1984	—	2.50	5.00
❑ 1022	Let's Live This Dream Together/Nobody's Fool	1984	—	2.50	5.00
❑ 1025	I'm Glad You Couldn't Sleep Last Night/It Amazes Me	1984	—	2.50	5.00
❑ 1027	Hey Lady/Anytime You're Ready	1984	—	2.50	5.00
❑ 1030	If It Was Any Better (I Couldn't Stand It)/Nobody's Fool	1985	—	2.50	5.00
❑ 1034	Out of Sight Out of Mind/It Amazes Me	1985	—	2.50	5.00
❑ 1041	Rockin' My Angel/Anytime You're Ready	1986	—	2.50	5.00
❑ 1054	When a Man Loves a Woman/Hey Lady	1987	—	2.50	5.00
❑ 1083	I Need Somebody Bad/(B-side unknown)	1988	—	3.00	6.00

Number	Title (A Side/B Side)	Yr	VG	VG+	NM
GMC					
❑ 114	Louisiana Lonely/Look What Love Has Done	1981	—	2.50	5.00
❑ 115	Fire in the Night/Look What Love Has Done	1981	—	2.50	5.00
GROOVE					
❑ 58-0029	Mountain of Love/The End of My World Is Near	1963	5.00	10.00	20.00
HI					
❑ 2110	The Greatest Gift/I'll Trade All My Tomorrows	1966	3.75	7.50	15.00
❑ 2118	Bells/86 Miles	1967	3.00	6.00	12.00
❑ 2126	Don't Let Me Cross Over/Like Magic	1967	3.00	6.00	12.00
❑ 2137	Starry Eyes/Dee-Dee	1968	3.00	6.00	12.00
❑ 2141	Since I Met You Baby/I Had to Cry Again	1968	3.00	6.00	12.00
❑ 2305	This Time/I Had to Cry Again	1976	—	2.50	5.00
HI COUNTRY					
❑ 8001	Endless Love/Walkin' to the Pearly Gates	1972	2.00	4.00	8.00
❑ 8002	A Little Bit of Soap/You're Out of My Reach	1972	2.00	4.00	8.00
❑ 8003	Butterfly/Closed by a Dream	1973	2.00	4.00	8.00
KARI					
❑ 110	Love the One You're With/When There's a Will (There's a Way)	1980	—	3.00	6.00
LOBO					
❑ III	I'd Love You to Want Me/The First Time We Made Love	1982	—	3.00	6.00
❑ VIII	Sweet Southern Moonlight/The First Time We Made Love	1982	—	3.00	6.00
❑ XI	Roll Over Beethoven/I'd Love You to Want Me	1982	—	3.00	6.00
MCA					
❑ 41011	Moment by Moment/Never Again	1979	—	2.50	5.00
❑ 41055	Tower of Strength/You're a Heartbreaker	1979	—	2.50	5.00
MERCURY					
❑ 71140	Kiss-a-Me Baby/Foolish Thoughts	1957	7.50	15.00	30.00
❑ 71190	Cry, Cry, Cry/Lonesome Feeling	1957	7.50	15.00	30.00
❑ 71249	Rocket Ride/Dream World	1957	7.50	15.00	30.00
❑ 71275	Rocket Ride Stroll/Dream World	1958	7.50	15.00	30.00
❑ 71347	Little Girl Step This Way/Vadalou	1958	7.50	15.00	30.00
PINK					
❑ 701	Three Thousand Miles/Cutie Baby	1959	10.00	20.00	40.00
❑ 702	Honey Love/Genavee	1959	10.00	20.00	40.00
❑ 706	Darling Sue/Tony	1960	10.00	20.00	40.00

FELTS, NARVEL, AND SHARON VAUGHN

Number	Title (A Side/B Side)	Yr	VG	VG+	NM
CINNAMON					
❑ 793	Until the End of Time/Someone to Give My Love To	1974	—	3.00	6.00

FEMALE BEATLES, THE

Number	Title (A Side/B Side)	Yr	VG	VG+	NM
20TH FOX					
❑ 531	I Don't Want to Cry/I Want You	1964	5.00	10.00	20.00

FEMININE COMPLEX, THE

Number	Title (A Side/B Side)	Yr	VG	VG+	NM
ATHENA					
❑ 5003	Six O'Clock in the Morning/I've Been Workin' on You	1969	3.00	6.00	12.00
❑ 5006	I Won't Run/Forgetting	1969	3.00	6.00	12.00
❑ 5008	Are You Lonesome Like Me/Run That Through Your Mind	1969	3.00	6.00	12.00

FENDER, FREDDY

Number	Title (A Side/B Side)	Yr	VG	VG+	NM
ABC					
❑ 12339	Louisiana Woman/If You're Looking for a Fool	1978	—	2.00	4.00
❑ 12370	Talk to Me/Please Mr. Sun	1978	—	2.00	4.00
❑ 12415	I'm Leaving It All Up to You/Whe It Rains It Really Pours	1978	—	2.00	4.00
❑ 12453	Sweet Summer Day/Walking Piece of Heaven	1979	—	2.00	4.00
ABC/DOT					
❑ 17540	Before the Next Teardrop Falls/Waiting for Your Love	1974	—	2.50	5.00
❑ 17558	Wasted Days and Wasted Nights/I Love My Rancho Grande	1975	—	2.50	5.00
❑ 17585	Secret Love/Loving Cajun Style	1975	—	2.00	4.00
❑ 17607	You'll Lose a Good Thing/I'm to Blame	1976	—	2.00	4.00
❑ 17627	Vaya Con Dios/My Happiness	1976	—	2.00	4.00
❑ 17652	Living It Down/Take Her a Message, I'm Lonely	1976	—	2.00	4.00
❑ 17686	The Rains Came/Sugar Coated Love	1977	—	2.00	4.00
❑ 17713	If You Don't Love Me (Why Don't You Just Leave Me Alone)/Thank You, My Love	1977	—	2.00	4.00
❑ 17730	Think About Me/If That's the Way You Want It	1977	—	2.00	4.00
❑ 17734	Christmas Time in the Valley/Please Come Home for Christmas	1977	—	2.50	5.00
ARGO					
❑ 5375	A Man Can Cry/You're Something Else for Me	1960	3.75	7.50	15.00
ARV INTERNATIONAL					
❑ 5083	Crazy Arms/She Thinks I Still Care	196?	2.50	5.00	10.00
❑ 5102	Un Dia de Sol/La Costumbre	196?	2.50	5.00	10.00
❑ 5146	El Rock de la Carcel/No Seasa Cruel	196?	2.50	5.00	10.00
❑ 5216	Crazy Arms/She Thinks I Still Care	198?	—	2.50	5.00
CRAZY CAJUN					
❑ 2002	Before the Next Teardrop Falls/Waiting for Your Love	198?	—	2.50	5.00
❑ 2002	Before the Next Teardrop Falls/Crazy, Crazy Baby	198?	—	2.50	5.00
❑ 2006	Esta Noche Mia Sera/(B-side unknown)	198?	—	2.50	5.00
❑ 2014	No Toquen Ya/I Love My Rancho Grande	198?	—	2.50	5.00
❑ 2019	Vaya Con Dios/No Say El Mismo	198?	—	2.50	5.00
❑ 2037	Fannie Mae/Going Out with the Tide	198?	—	2.50	5.00
—With Tommy McLain					
❑ 2060	My Confession/Goin' Honky Tonkin'	198?	—	2.00	4.00
DUNCAN					
❑ 1000	Mean Woman/Holy One	1959	10.00	20.00	40.00
❑ 1001	Wasted Days and Wasted Nights/San Antonio Walk	1959	6.25	12.50	25.00
❑ 1002	Wild Side of Life/Crazy Baby	1959	6.25	12.50	25.00
❑ 1004	Since I Met You Baby/Little Mama	1959	6.25	12.50	25.00
GOLDBAND					
❑ 1214	My Tears of Love/Carmelia	197?	2.50	5.00	10.00
❑ 1264	Bye, Bye, Little Angel/Oh My Love	1975	—	2.50	5.00
❑ 1272	Three Wishes/Me and My Bottle of Rum	1975	—	2.50	5.00
GRT					
❑ 031	Since I Met You Baby/Little Mama	1975	—	2.50	5.00
❑ 039	Wild Side of Life/Go On Baby	1975	—	2.50	5.00
IMPERIAL					
❑ 5659	Mean Woman/Holy One	1960	5.00	10.00	20.00
❑ 5670	Wasted Days and Wasted Nights/I Can't Remember When I Didn't Love You	1960	5.00	10.00	20.00
INSTANT					
❑ 3332	Some People Say/Today's Your Wedding Day	1972	2.00	4.00	8.00
MCA					
❑ 12453	Sweet Summer Day/Walking Piece of Heaven	1979	—	2.00	4.00
❑ 52003	Across the Borderline/Before the Next Teardrop Falls	1982	—	2.00	4.00
NORCO					
❑ 100	Love's Light Is an Ember/The New Stroll	1963	2.50	5.00	10.00
❑ 102	You Made Me Cry/Never Trust a Cheating Woman	1963	2.50	5.00	10.00
❑ 103	Coming Home Soon/Going Out with the Tide	1964	2.50	5.00	10.00
❑ 104	Just a Little Bit/You Made Me a Fool	1964	2.50	5.00	10.00
❑ 106	Ooh Poo Pah Doo/Three Wishes	1964	2.50	5.00	10.00
❑ 107	Magic of Love/Bony Moronie	1965	2.50	5.00	10.00
—With Noel Vill					
❑ 108	In the Still of the Night/You Don't Have to Go	1965	2.50	5.00	10.00
❑ 111	Donna/Lover's Quarrel	1965	2.50	5.00	10.00
PA GO GO					
❑ 115	Cool Mary Lou/You Are My Sunshine	1967	2.50	5.00	10.00
PACEMAKER					
❑ 1973	Wasted Days and Wasted Nights/Bidin' My Time	197?	—	2.50	5.00
REPRISE					
❑ 19143	It's All in the Game/Before the Next Teardrop Falls	1992	—	—	3.00
STARFLITE					
❑ 4900	Yours/Rock Down in My Shoe	1979	—	2.00	4.00
❑ 4904	Squeeze Box/Turn Around	1979	—	2.00	4.00
❑ 4906	My Special Prayer/(B-side unknown)	1979	—	2.00	4.00
❑ 4908	Please Talk to My Heart/(B-side unknown)	1980	—	2.00	4.00
WARNER BROS.					
❑ 29794	Chokin' Kind/I Might As Well Forget You	1983	—	2.00	4.00

FENDER IV

Number	Title (A Side/B Side)	Yr	VG	VG+	NM
IMPERIAL					
❑ 66061	Mar-Gaya/You Better Tell Me Now	1964	12.50	25.00	50.00
❑ 66098	Malibu Run/Everybody Up	1965	12.50	25.00	50.00

FENDERMEN, THE

Number	Title (A Side/B Side)	Yr	VG	VG+	NM
CUCA					
❑ 1003	Mule Skinner Blues/Torture	1960	50.00	100.00	200.00
SOMA					
❑ 1137	Mule Skinner Blues/Torture	1960	6.25	12.50	25.00
❑ 1142	Don't You Just Know It/Beach Party	1960	5.00	10.00	20.00
❑ 1155	Heartbreakin' Special/Can't You Wait	1960	5.00	10.00	20.00

FENTON, SHANE, AND THE FENTONES

Number	Title (A Side/B Side)	Yr	VG	VG+	NM
20TH FOX					
❑ 439	Don't Do That/I'll Know	1963	3.75	7.50	15.00
LAURIE					
❑ 3287	Don't Do That/I'll Know	1965	2.50	5.00	10.00

FERGUSON, SHEILA

Number	Title (A Side/B Side)	Yr	VG	VG+	NM
LANDA					
❑ 706	How Did That Happen/Little Red Riding Hood	1965	7.50	15.00	30.00
SWAN					
❑ 4217	I Weep for You/Don't (Leave Me Lover)	1965	10.00	20.00	40.00
❑ 4225	And In Return/Are You Satisfied	1965	7.50	15.00	30.00
❑ 4234	Signs of Love/Heartbroken Memories	1965	10.00	20.00	40.00

FERRIS AND THE WHEELS

Number	Title (A Side/B Side)	Yr	VG	VG+	NM
BAMBI					
❑ 801	I Want to Dance (Every Night)/Chop Chop	1961	6.25	12.50	25.00
UNITED ARTISTS					
❑ 458	Moments Like This/He Was a Fortune Teller	1962	25.00	50.00	100.00

FERRY, BRYAN

Also see ROXY MUSIC.

Number	Title (A Side/B Side)	Yr	VG	VG+	NM
ATLANTIC					
❑ 3017	A Hard Rain's Gonna Fall/2 HB	1974	—	2.50	5.00
❑ 3351	Let's Stick Together (Let's Work Together)/Sea Breezes	1976	—	2.00	4.00
❑ 3364	Heart on My Sleeve/Re-Make, Re-Model	1976	—	2.00	4.00
❑ 3399	Tokyo Joe/As the World Turns	1977	—	2.00	4.00
❑ 3539	Sign of the Times/Can't Let Go	1978	—	2.00	4.00
MCA					
❑ 52788	Is Your Love Strong Enough/Windswept	1986	—	—	3.00
❑ 52788 [PS]	Is Your Love Strong Enough/Windswept	1986	—	—	3.00
REPRISE					
❑ 28116	Limbo (Brooklyn Version)/Limbo (Latin Version)	1988	—	—	3.00
❑ 28116 [PS]	Limbo (Brooklyn Version)/Limbo (Latin Version)	1988	—	—	3.00
❑ 28117	Kiss and Tell/Zamba	1988	—	—	3.00
❑ 28117 [PS]	Kiss and Tell/Zamba	1988	—	—	3.00
❑ 28172	The Right Stuff/The Right Stuff (Brooklyn Mix)	1987	—	—	3.00
VIRGIN					
❑ S7-18133	Mamouna/Don't Stop the Dance (Live)	1994	—	2.00	4.00
❑ 38684	As Time Goes By/Falling in Love Again	1999	—	—	3.00
WARNER BROS.					
❑ 28582	Help Me/Broken Wings	1986	—	—	3.00
❑ 28582 [PS]	Help Me/Broken Wings	1986	—	—	3.00
❑ 28887	Don't Stop the Dance/Nocturne	1985	—	—	3.00
❑ 28887 [PS]	Don't Stop the Dance/Nocturne	1985	—	—	3.00

Number	Title (A Side/B Side)	Yr	VG	VG+	NM
❑ 28990	Slave to Love/Valentine	1985	—	—	3.00
❑ 28990 [PS]	Slave to Love/Valentine	1985	—	—	3.00

FERRY AID

Benefit group assembled by PAUL McCARTNEY.

PROFILE

Number	Title (A Side/B Side)	Yr	VG	VG+	NM
❑ 5147	Let It Be/Let It Be (Gospel Jam Mix)	1987	2.50	5.00	10.00
❑ 5147 [PS]	Let It Be/Let It Be (Gospel Jam Mix)	1987	2.50	5.00	10.00

FEVER TREE

AMPEX

Number	Title (A Side/B Side)	Yr	VG	VG+	NM
❑ 11013	She Comes in Colors/You're Not the Same Baby	1970	3.75	7.50	15.00
❑ 11028	I Put a Spell on You/Hey Joe, Where You Gonna Go	1970	3.75	7.50	15.00

MAINSTREAM

Number	Title (A Side/B Side)	Yr	VG	VG+	NM
❑ 661	Hey Mister/I Can Beat Your Drum	1967	3.00	6.00	12.00
❑ 665	Girl, Oh Girl (Don't Push Me)/Steve Lenore	1967	3.00	6.00	12.00

UNI

Number	Title (A Side/B Side)	Yr	VG	VG+	NM
❑ 55060	San Fransisco Girls (Return of the Native)/Come with Me	1968	3.00	6.00	12.00
❑ 55060 [DJ]	San Fransisco Girls (Return of the Native) (same on both sides)	1968	10.00	20.00	40.00
—Promo only on blue vinyl					
❑ 55095	What Time Did You Say It Is in Salt Lake City/Where Do You Go	1968	3.75	7.50	15.00
❑ 55146	Love Makes the Sun Rise/Filigree and Shadow	1969	3.75	7.50	15.00
❑ 55172	The Sun Also Rises/Clancey	1969	3.75	7.50	15.00
❑ 55202	Catcher in the Rye/What Time Did You Say It Is in Salt Lake City?	1970	5.00	10.00	20.00
❑ 55228	I Am/Grand Candy Young Sweet	1970	5.00	10.00	20.00

FI-DELLS, THE

IMPERIAL

Number	Title (A Side/B Side)	Yr	VG	VG+	NM
❑ 5780	What Is Love/Don't Let Me Love You	1961	6.25	12.50	25.00

WARNER

Number	Title (A Side/B Side)	Yr	VG	VG+	NM
❑ 1014	No Other Love/Come Back to Me	1957	5.00	10.00	20.00

FI-TONES, THE

ANGLE TONE

Number	Title (A Side/B Side)	Yr	VG	VG+	NM
❑ 525	You'll Be the Last/Wake Up	1958	25.00	50.00	100.00
❑ 530	It Wasn't a Lie/What Am I Goin' to Do	1958	20.00	40.00	80.00
❑ 536	Deep In My Heart/Minnie	1959	15.00	30.00	60.00

ATLAS

Number	Title (A Side/B Side)	Yr	VG	VG+	NM
❑ 1050	Foolish Dreams/Let's Fall in Love	1955	100.00	200.00	400.00
—Originals identify label as "Atlas Record Company" and have Atlas logo at far upper left					
❑ 1050	Foolish Dreams/Let's Fall in Love	1955	25.00	50.00	100.00
—Second pressings identify label as "Atlas Records" and have Atlas logo at left side					
❑ 1051	It Wasn't a Lie/Lots and Lots of Love	1955	25.00	50.00	100.00
❑ 1052	I Call to You/Love You Baby	1955	25.00	50.00	100.00
❑ 1055	I Belong to You/Silly and Happy	1956	25.00	50.00	100.00
❑ 1056	Waiting for Your Call/My Tired Feet	1956	25.00	50.00	100.00

OLD TOWN

Number	Title (A Side/B Side)	Yr	VG	VG+	NM
❑ 1042	My Faith/My Heart	1957	100.00	200.00	400.00

FIDELITY'S, THE

BUDDY MILES was in this group.

BATON

Number	Title (A Side/B Side)	Yr	VG	VG+	NM
❑ 252	The Things I Love/Hold On to Whatcha Got	1958	6.25	12.50	25.00
❑ 256	Memories of You/Can't You Come Out	1958	6.25	12.50	25.00
❑ 261	Captain of My Ship/My Greatest Thrill	1958	6.25	12.50	25.00

SIR

Number	Title (A Side/B Side)	Yr	VG	VG+	NM
❑ 271	Marie/The Invitation	1959	5.00	10.00	20.00
❑ 274	Walk with the Wind/Only to You	1959	5.00	10.00	20.00
❑ 276	Where in the World/This Girl of Mine	1960	5.00	10.00	20.00
❑ 277	Wishing Star/Broken Love	1960	7.50	15.00	30.00

FIELD, JERRY, AND THE LAWYERS

PARKWAY

Number	Title (A Side/B Side)	Yr	VG	VG+	NM
❑ 801	The Trial/Easy Steppin'	1958	7.50	15.00	30.00
—Blue label					
❑ 801	The Trial/Easy Steppin'	1958	5.00	10.00	20.00
—White label. This is actually a cover of a break-in record (for the original, see HERB B. LOU AND THE LEGAL EAGLES).					

FIELD, SALLY

COLGEMS

Number	Title (A Side/B Side)	Yr	VG	VG+	NM
❑ 66-1008	Felicidad/Find Yourself a Rainbow	1967	2.50	5.00	10.00
❑ 66-1008 [PS]	Felicidad/Find Yourself a Rainbow	1967	3.75	7.50	15.00
❑ 66-1014	Golden Days/You're a Grand Old Flag	1967	2.00	4.00	8.00

FIELDS, BOBBY

ACE

Number	Title (A Side/B Side)	Yr	VG	VG+	NM
❑ 504	Pity Poor Me/Give Me a Helping Hand	1955	15.00	30.00	60.00

FIELDS, ERNIE

CAPITOL

Number	Title (A Side/B Side)	Yr	VG	VG+	NM
❑ 5161	St. Louis Blues/Lilies of the Field	1964	2.00	4.00	8.00
❑ 5326	Swanne River/Chloe	1964	2.00	4.00	8.00

RENDEZVOUS

Number	Title (A Side/B Side)	Yr	VG	VG+	NM
❑ 110	In the Mood/Christopher Columbus	1959	3.00	6.00	12.00
❑ 117	Chattanooga Choo Choo/Workin' Out	1960	2.50	5.00	10.00
❑ 122	Begin the Beguine/Things Ain't What They Used to Be	1960	2.50	5.00	10.00
❑ 129	Teen Flip/Sweet Slumber	1960	2.50	5.00	10.00
❑ 138	The Honeydripper/(B-side unknown)	1960	2.50	5.00	10.00
❑ 142	The Happy Whistler/Monkey	1961	2.50	5.00	10.00
❑ 148	Be Anything (But Be Mine)/Fallin'	1961	2.50	5.00	10.00
❑ 150	The Charleston/12th Street Rag	1961	2.50	5.00	10.00
❑ 161	A String of Pearls/Castle Rock	1961	2.50	5.00	10.00
❑ 170	Hucklebuck (Twist)/Ernie's Tune	1962	2.00	4.00	8.00
❑ 181	Theme from Perry Mason/Me and My Shadow	1962	2.50	5.00	10.00

FIESTAS, THE

CHIMNEYVILLE

Number	Title (A Side/B Side)	Yr	VG	VG+	NM
❑ 10216	Tina, the Disco Queen/I'm No Better Than You	1977	3.00	6.00	12.00
❑ 10221	Is That Long Enough for You/I'm Gonna Make Myself	1977	3.00	6.00	12.00

COTILLION

Number	Title (A Side/B Side)	Yr	VG	VG+	NM
❑ 44117	So Fine/Broken Heart	1971	6.25	12.50	25.00

OLD TOWN

Number	Title (A Side/B Side)	Yr	VG	VG+	NM
❑ 1062	So Fine/Last Night I Dreamed	1958	12.50	25.00	50.00
—Versions pressed by Columbia have a piano intro not available elsewhere. Look for "ZTSP" on label					
❑ 1062	So Fine/Last Night I Dreamed	1958	7.50	15.00	30.00
—Standard version; no "ZTSP" on label					
❑ 1067	Grandma Gave a Party/I'm Your Slave	1959	6.25	12.50	25.00
❑ 1069	Our Anniversary/I'm Your Slave	1959	6.25	12.50	25.00
❑ 1074	Good News/That Was Me	1959	6.25	12.50	25.00
❑ 1080	Dollar Bill/It Don't Make Sense	1960	6.25	12.50	25.00
❑ 1090	So Nice/You Could Be My Girlfriend	1960	6.25	12.50	25.00
❑ 1104	Look at That Girl/Mr. Dillon, Mr. Dillon	1961	6.25	12.50	25.00
❑ 1111	Hobo's Prayer/She's Mine	1961	10.00	20.00	40.00
❑ 1122	Broken Heart/Railroad Song	1962	5.00	10.00	20.00
❑ 1127	I Feel Good All Over/Look at That Girl	1962	5.00	10.00	20.00
❑ 1134	The Gypsy Said/Mama Put the Law Down	1963	5.00	10.00	20.00
❑ 1140	The Party's Over/Try It One More Time	1963	5.00	10.00	20.00
❑ 1148	Foolish Dreamer/Rock-a-By Baby	1963	5.00	10.00	20.00
❑ 1166	All That's Good/Rock-a-By Baby	1964	5.00	10.00	20.00
❑ 1178	Think Smart/Anna	1965	20.00	40.00	80.00
❑ 1187	Love Is Strange/Love Is Good to Me	1965	3.75	7.50	15.00
❑ 1189	Ain't She Sweet/I Gotta Have Your Lovin'	1965	3.75	7.50	15.00

RESPECT

Number	Title (A Side/B Side)	Yr	VG	VG+	NM
❑ 2509	I Can't Shake Your Love (Can't Shake You Loose)/A Sometimes Storm	1972	2.00	4.00	8.00

STRAND

Number	Title (A Side/B Side)	Yr	VG	VG+	NM
❑ 25046	Come On Everybody/Julia	1961	10.00	20.00	40.00

VIGOR

Number	Title (A Side/B Side)	Yr	VG	VG+	NM
❑ 712	So Fine/Darling You've Changed	1974	2.00	4.00	8.00

FIFTH DIMENSION, THE

ABC

Number	Title (A Side/B Side)	Yr	VG	VG+	NM
❑ 12136	Magic in My Life/Lean On Me Always	1975	—	2.00	4.00
❑ 12168	Walk Your Feet in the Sunshine/Speaking with My Heart	1976	—	2.00	4.00
❑ 12181	Love Hangover/Will You Be There	1976	—	2.00	4.00

ARISTA

Number	Title (A Side/B Side)	Yr	VG	VG+	NM
❑ 0101	No Love in the Room/I Don't Know How to Look for Love	1975	—	2.00	4.00

BELL

Number	Title (A Side/B Side)	Yr	VG	VG+	NM
❑ 860	Medley: A Change Is Gonna Come & People Gotta Be Free/The Declaration	1970	—	2.50	5.00
❑ 880	Puppet Man/A Love Like Ours	1970	—	2.50	5.00
❑ 895	Save the Country/Dimension 5	1970	—	2.50	5.00
❑ 913	On the Beach (In the Summertime)/This Is Your Life	1970	—	2.50	5.00
❑ 940	One Less Bell to Answer/Feelin' Alright?	1970	—	2.50	5.00
❑ 965	Love's Lines, Angles and Rhymes/The Singer	1971	—	2.50	5.00
❑ 999	Light Sings/Viva Tirado	1971	—	2.50	5.00
❑ 45134	Never My Love/A Love Like Ours	1971	—	2.50	5.00
❑ 45170	Together Let's Find Love/I Just Wanta Be Your Friend	1972	—	2.50	5.00
❑ 45195	(Last Night) I Didn't Get to Sleep at All/The River Witch	1972	—	2.50	5.00
❑ 45261	If I Could Reach You/Tomorrow Belongs to the Children	1972	—	2.50	5.00
❑ 45310	Living Together, Growing Together/What Do I Need to Be Me	1973	—	2.00	4.00
❑ 45338	Everything's Been Changed/There Never Was a Day	1973	—	2.00	4.00
❑ 45380	Ashes to Ashes/The Singer	1973	—	2.00	4.00
❑ 45425	Flashback/Diggin' for a Livin'	1973	—	2.00	4.00
❑ 45612	Harlem/My Song	1974	—	2.00	4.00

MOTOWN

Number	Title (A Side/B Side)	Yr	VG	VG+	NM
❑ 1437	You Are the Reason (I Feel Like Dancing)/Slipping Into Something New	1978	—	2.00	4.00
❑ 1453	Everybody's Got to Give It Up/You're My Star	1978	—	2.00	4.00

SOUL CITY

Number	Title (A Side/B Side)	Yr	VG	VG+	NM
❑ 752	I'll Be Loving You Forever/Train, Keep On Moving	1966	15.00	30.00	60.00
❑ 753	Go Where You Wanna Go/Too Poor to Die	1967	2.00	4.00	8.00
❑ 753 [PS]	Go Where You Wanna Go/Too Poor to Die	1967	5.00	10.00	20.00
❑ 755	Another Day, Another Heartache/Rosecrans Blvd.	1967	2.50	5.00	10.00
❑ 755 [PS]	Another Day, Another Heartache/Rosecrans Blvd.	1967	5.00	10.00	20.00
❑ 756	Up-Up and Away/Which Way to Nowhere	1967	2.00	4.00	8.00
❑ 760	Paper Cup/Poor Side of Town	1967	2.00	4.00	8.00
❑ 762	Carpet Man/Magic Garden	1968	2.00	4.00	8.00
❑ 766	Stoned Soul Picnic/The Saliboat Song	1968	2.00	4.00	8.00
❑ 766 [PS]	Stoned Soul Picnic/The Saliboat Song	1968	3.75	7.50	15.00
❑ 768	Sweet Blindness/Bobby's Blues	1968	2.00	4.00	8.00
❑ 768 [PS]	Sweet Blindness/Bobby's Blues	1968	3.75	7.50	15.00
❑ 770	California Soul/It'll Never Be the Same	1968	2.00	4.00	8.00
❑ 772	Aquarius/Let the Sunshine In (The Flesh Failures)//Don'tcha Hear Me Callin' To Ya	1969	2.00	4.00	8.00
❑ 772 [PS]	Aquarius/Let the Sunshine In (The Flesh Failures)//Don'tcha Hear Me Callin' To Ya	1969	3.75	7.50	15.00
❑ 776	Workin' on a Groovy Thing/Broken Wing Bird	1969	2.00	4.00	8.00
❑ 779	Wedding Bell Blues/Lovin' Stew	1969	2.00	4.00	8.00
❑ 780	Blowing Away/Skinny Man	1970	—	3.00	6.00
❑ 781	The Girls' Song/It'll Never Be the Same Again	1970	—	3.00	6.00

SUTRA

Number	Title (A Side/B Side)	Yr	VG	VG+	NM
❑ 122	Surrender/Fantasy	1983	—	2.00	4.00

FIFTH ESTATE, THE

Also see THE D-MEN.

Number	Title (A Side/B Side)	Yr	VG	VG+	NM
JUBILEE					
❑ 5573	Ding! Dong! The Witch Is Dead/The Rub-a-Dub	1967	3.00	6.00	12.00
❑ 5588	Lost Generation/The Goofin' Song	1967	2.00	4.00	8.00
❑ 5595	Heigh-Ho/It's Waiting There for You	1967	2.00	4.00	8.00
❑ 5607	Morning, Morning/Tomorrow Is My Turn	1967	2.00	4.00	8.00
❑ 5617	Do Drop Inn/That's Love	1968	2.00	4.00	8.00
❑ 5627	Coney Island Sally/Tomorrow Is My Turn	1968	2.00	4.00	8.00
❑ 5655	Mickey Mouse Club March/I Knew You Before I Met You	1969	2.00	4.00	8.00
❑ 5683 [DJ]	Parade of the Wooden Soldiers (mono/stereo)	1969	2.50	5.00	10.00
—Stock copies may not exist ("I Knew You Before I Met You" was listed as B-side)					
RED BIRD					
❑ 10-064	Love Is All a Game/Like I Love You	1966	3.75	7.50	15.00

FILETS OF SOUL

Number	Title (A Side/B Side)	Yr	VG	VG+	NM
SAVOY					
❑ 1630	Since I Fell for You/C'mon Let's Dance	1968	6.25	12.50	25.00

FINNEGAN, MIKE, AND THE SERFS

Number	Title (A Side/B Side)	Yr	VG	VG+	NM
PARKWAY					
❑ 113	Help Me Somebody/Bread and Water	1966	5.00	10.00	20.00

FIREBALLS, THE

Includes records credited to "Jimmy Gilmer and the Fireballs." Also see JIMMY GILMER.

Number	Title (A Side/B Side)	Yr	VG	VG+	NM
7 ARTS					
❑ 714	Callin' the Sheriff/Don't Stop	1961	—	—	—
—Evidently, record was never released, though its picture sleeve exists					
❑ 714 [PS]	Callin' the Sheriff/Don't Stop	1961	12.50	25.00	50.00
ASTRA					
❑ 1021	Torquay/Sweet Walk	1966	2.50	5.00	10.00
ATCO					
❑ 6491	Bottle of Wine/Can't You See I'm Tryin'	1967	2.50	5.00	10.00
❑ 6569	Goin' Away/Groovy Motions	1968	2.00	4.00	8.00
❑ 6595	Chicken Little/Three Minutes' Time	1968	2.00	4.00	8.00
❑ 6614	Come On, React!/Woman Help Me	1968	2.00	4.00	8.00
❑ 6651	Long Green/Light in the Window	1969	2.00	4.00	8.00
❑ 6678	Watch Her Walk/Good Morning Shame	1969	2.00	4.00	8.00
DOT					
❑ 16487	Sugar Shack/My Heart Is Free	1963	3.75	7.50	15.00
—Jimmy Gilmer and the Fireballs					
❑ 16493	Torquay Two/Peg Leg	1963	3.75	7.50	15.00
❑ 16539	Daisy Petal Pickin'/When My Tears Have Dried	1963	3.00	6.00	12.00
—Jimmy Gilmer and the Fireballs					
❑ 16583	Ain't Gonna Tell Anybody/Young Am I	1964	3.00	6.00	12.00
—Jimmy Gilmer and the Fireballs					
❑ 16591	Daytona Drag/Gently, Gently	1964	3.75	7.50	15.00
❑ 16609	I'll Send for You/Look at Me	1964	2.50	5.00	10.00
—Jimmy Gilmer and the Fireballs					
❑ 16642	Wishing/What Kinda Love	1964	2.50	5.00	10.00
—Jimmy Gilmer and the Fireballs					
❑ 16661	Dumbo/Mr. Reed	1964	3.75	7.50	15.00
❑ 16666	Cry Baby/Thunder 'N' Lightnin'	1964	2.50	5.00	10.00
—Jimmy Gilmer and the Fireballs					
❑ 16687	Break His Heart for Me/Cinnamon Cindy	1965	2.50	5.00	10.00
—Jimmy Gilmer and the Fireballs					
❑ 16692	Yummie Yama Papa/Baby, What's Wrong	1965	3.75	7.50	15.00
❑ 16714	Born to Be with You/Lonesome Tears	1965	2.50	5.00	10.00
—Jimmy Gilmer and the Fireballs					
❑ 16715	More Than I Can Say/Beating of My Heart	1965	3.75	7.50	15.00
❑ 16743	The Fool/Somebody Stole My Watermelon	1965	2.50	5.00	10.00
—Jimmy Gilmer and the Fireballs					
❑ 16745	Ahhh, Soul/Campusology	1965	3.75	7.50	15.00
❑ 16768	Codine/Come to Me	1965	2.50	5.00	10.00
—Jimmy Gilmer and the Fireballs					
❑ 16786	She Belongs to Me/Rambler's Blues	1965	2.50	5.00	10.00
—Jimmy Gilmer and the Fireballs					
❑ 16833	Hungry, Hungry, Hungry/Wild Roses	1966	2.50	5.00	10.00
—Jimmy Gilmer and the Fireballs					
❑ 16834	Jada/What I Am	1966	3.75	7.50	15.00
❑ 16881	All I Do Is Dream of You/Ain't That Rain	1966	2.50	5.00	10.00
—Jimmy Gilmer and the Fireballs					
❑ 16918	Torquay Two/Say I Am	1966	3.75	7.50	15.00
❑ 16979	Sugar Shack/Daisy Petal Pickin'	1966	2.50	5.00	10.00
—Jimmy Gilmer and the Fireballs					
❑ 16992	Shy Girl/I Think I'll Catch a Bus	1967	2.50	5.00	10.00
—Jimmy Gilmer and the Fireballs					
HAMILTON					
❑ 50036	Blacksmith Blues/Tuff-a-Nuff	1960	5.00	10.00	20.00
JARO					
❑ 77029	Long, Long Ponytail/Let There Be Love	1960	20.00	40.00	80.00
—Chuck Tharp and the Fireballs					
KAPP					
❑ 248	Fireball/I Don't Know	1958	25.00	50.00	100.00
—Chuck Tharp and the Fireballs					
TOP RANK					
❑ 2008	Torquay/Cry Baby	1959	5.00	10.00	20.00
❑ 2026ST [S]	Bulldog/Nearly Sunrise	1959	12.50	25.00	50.00
❑ 2026 [M]	Bulldog/Nearly Sunrise	1959	5.00	10.00	20.00
❑ 2038ST [S]	Foot Patter/Kissin'	1959	12.50	25.00	50.00
❑ 2038 [M]	Foot Patter/Kissin'	1959	5.00	10.00	20.00
❑ 2054	Vaquero/Chief Whoopin'-Koff	1960	5.00	10.00	20.00
❑ 2081	Almost Paradise/Sweet Talk	1960	5.00	10.00	20.00
❑ 3003	Rick-a-Tic/Tacky Doo	1961	5.00	10.00	20.00
WARWICK					
❑ 630	Rik-A-Tik/Yackey-Doo	1961	4.00	8.00	16.00
❑ 644	Quite a Party/Gunshot	1961	4.00	8.00	16.00

7-Inch Extended Plays

Number	Title (A Side/B Side)	Yr	VG	VG+	NM
TOP RANK					
❑ REX 1000	Bulldog/Torquay//Kissin'/Foot Patter	196?	37.50	75.00	150.00
❑ REX 1000 [PS]	The Fireballs	196?	37.50	75.00	150.00

FIREFLIES, THE

Number	Title (A Side/B Side)	Yr	VG	VG+	NM
CANADIAN AMERICAN					
❑ 117	Marianne/Give All Your Love to Me	1960	5.00	10.00	20.00
RIBBON					
❑ 6901	You Were Mine/Stella Got a Fella	1959	6.25	12.50	25.00
—With "Ribbon" encased in a ribbon on label					
❑ 6901	You Were Mine/Stella Got a Fella	1959	7.50	15.00	30.00
—With "Ribbon" standing alone on label					
❑ 6904	I Can't Say Goodbye/What Did I Do Wrong	1959	5.00	10.00	20.00
❑ 6906	My Girl/Because of My Pride	1960	5.00	10.00	20.00
TAURUS					
❑ 355	One O'Clock Twist/You Were Mine for Awhile	1962	5.00	10.00	20.00
❑ 366	Good Friends/My Prayer for You	1964	5.00	10.00	20.00
❑ 376	Runaround/Could You Mean More	1965	5.00	10.00	20.00
❑ 380	Tonight/A Time for Us	1965	5.00	10.00	20.00

FIRST CHOICE

Number	Title (A Side/B Side)	Yr	VG	VG+	NM
GOLD MIND					
❑ 4004	Doctor Love/I Love You More Than Before	1977	—	2.50	5.00
❑ 4009	Love Having You Around/Indian Giver	1977	—	2.50	5.00
❑ 4017	Hold Your Horses/Now I've Thrown It All Away	1979	—	2.50	5.00
❑ 4019	Double Cross/Game of Love	1979	—	2.50	5.00
❑ 4022	Love Thang/Great Expectations	1980	—	2.50	5.00
❑ 4023	Breakaway/House for Sale	1980	—	2.50	5.00
PHILLY GROOVE					
❑ 175	Armed and Extremely Dangerous/Gonna Keep On Lovin' Him	1973	—	2.50	5.00
❑ 179	Smarty Pants/One Step Away	1973	—	2.50	5.00
❑ 183	Newsy Neighbors/This Little Woman	1974	—	2.50	5.00
❑ 200	The Player — Part 1/The Player — Part 2	1974	—	2.50	5.00
❑ 202	Guilty/Wake Up to Me	1974	—	2.50	5.00
❑ 204	Love Freeze/A Boy Named Junior	1975	—	2.50	5.00
SCEPTER					
❑ 12347	One Step Away/This Is the House	1972	—	3.00	6.00
WARNER BROS.					
❑ 8214	Gotta Get Away (From You Baby)/Yes, Maybe Not	1976	—	2.50	5.00
❑ 8251	Let Him Go/First Choice Theme	1976	—	2.50	5.00

FIRST CLASS (1)

British studio group featuring Tony Burrows on vocals.

Number	Title (A Side/B Side)	Yr	VG	VG+	NM
UK					
❑ 49022	Beach Baby/Both Sides of the Story	1974	—	2.50	5.00
—Most stock copies have the full-length (4:59) version of the A-side					
❑ 49022	Beach Baby/Both Sides of the Story	1974	—	3.00	6.00
—Some stock copies have a short version of the A-side					
❑ 49028	Dreams Are Ten a Penny/Lavender Man	1974	—	2.00	4.00
❑ 49033	Funny How Love Can Be/Surfer Queen	1975	—	2.00	4.00

FIRST CLASS (2)

U.S. R&B group.

Number	Title (A Side/B Side)	Yr	VG	VG+	NM
ALL PLATINUM					
❑ 2365	Me and My Gemini/Me and My Gemini (Part 2)	1976	—	2.50	5.00
❑ 2368	This Is It/Filled with Desire	1977	—	2.50	5.00
❑ 2372	Coming Back to You/This Is It	1977	—	2.50	5.00
EBONY SOUNDS					
❑ 187	The Beginning of My End/(B-side unknown)	1975	—	2.50	5.00
TODAY					
❑ 1528	What About Me/Outside Your World	1974	—	2.50	5.00

FIRST CLASS (U)

This is either group (1) or group (2).

Number	Title (A Side/B Side)	Yr	VG	VG+	NM
PRIVATE STOCK					
❑ 45093	Ain't No Love/Long Time Gone	1976	—	2.00	4.00

FIRST CROW TO THE MOON

Number	Title (A Side/B Side)	Yr	VG	VG+	NM
ROULETTE					
❑ 4774	The Sun Lights Up the Shadows of Your Mind/Spend Your Life	1967	7.50	15.00	30.00

FIRST EDITION, THE

Includes "Kenny Rogers and the First Edition." Also see KENNY ROGERS.

Number	Title (A Side/B Side)	Yr	VG	VG+	NM
JOLLY ROGERS					
❑ 1001	Lady, Play Your Symphony/There's An Old Man in Our Town	1973	—	2.50	5.00
❑ 1003	(Do You Remember) The First Time/Indian Joe	1973	—	2.50	5.00
❑ 1004	Today I Started Loving You Again/She Thinks I Still Care	1973	—	2.50	5.00
❑ 1006	Whatcha Gonna Do/Something About Your Song	1973	—	2.50	5.00
❑ 1007	A Stranger in My Place/Makin' Music for Money	1974	—	2.50	5.00
—All of the above as "Kenny Rogers and the First Edition"					
REPRISE					
❑ 0628	Ticket to Nowhere/I Found a Reason	1967	2.00	4.00	8.00
❑ 0655	Just Dropped In (To See What Condition My Condition Was In)/Shadow in the Corner of Your Mind	1967	3.00	6.00	12.00
—Original pressing has orange and brown label					
❑ 0655	Just Dropped In (To See What Condition My Condition Was In)/Shadow in the Corner of Your Mind	1967	2.50	5.00	10.00
—Second pressing has lighter orange "steamboat" Reprise/W7 label					
❑ 0683	Dream On/Only Me	1968	—	3.00	6.00
❑ 0693	Look Around, I'll Be There/Charlie the Fer-De-Lance	1968	—	3.00	6.00
❑ 0737	Just Dropped In (To See What Condition My Condition Was In)/But You Know I Love You	1971	—	2.00	4.00
—As "Kenny Rogers and the First Edition"; "Back to Back Hits" series					

Number	Title (A Side/B Side)	Yr	VG	VG+	NM
❑ 0738	Ruby, Don't Take Your Love to Town/Reuben James	1971	—	2.00	4.00
—As "Kenny Rogers and the First Edition"; "Back to Back Hits" series					
❑ 0747	Something's Burning/Someone Who Cares	1972	—	2.00	4.00
—As "Kenny Rogers and the First Edition"; "Back to Back Hits" series					
❑ 0748	Tell It All Brother/Heed the Call	1972	—	2.00	4.00
—As "Kenny Rogers and the First Edition"; "Back to Back Hits" series					
❑ 0773	If I Could Only Change Your Mind/Are My Thoughts With You	1968	—	3.00	6.00
❑ 0799	But You Know I Love You/Homemade Lies	1968	—	3.00	6.00
❑ 0822	Good Time Liberator/Once Again She's All Alone	1969	—	2.50	5.00
—Starting above, by "Kenny Rogers and the First Edition"					
❑ 0829	Ruby, Don't Take Your Love to Town/Girl Get a Hold of Yourself	1969	—	2.50	5.00
❑ 0854	Ruben James/Sunshine	1969	—	2.50	5.00
❑ 0854	Reuben James/Sunshine	1969	—	2.50	5.00
❑ 0888	Something's Burning/Mama's Waiting	1970	—	2.50	5.00
❑ 0923	Tell It All Brother/Just Remember You're My Sunshine	1970	—	2.50	5.00
❑ 0953	Heed the Call/A Stranger in My Place	1970	—	2.50	5.00
❑ 0999	Someone Who Cares/Mission of San Mohera	1971	—	2.50	5.00
❑ 1018	Take My Hand/All God's Lonely Children	1971	—	2.50	5.00
❑ 1053	Where Does Rosie Go/What Am I Gonna Do	1971	—	2.50	5.00
❑ 1069	School Teacher/Trigger Happy Kid	1972	—	2.50	5.00

FISCHER, WILD MAN

Number	Title (A Side/B Side)	Yr	VG	VG+	NM
REPRISE					
❑ 0781	Merry-Go-Round/The Circle	1968	5.00	10.00	20.00

FISHER, CHIP

Number	Title (A Side/B Side)	Yr	VG	VG+	NM
20TH FOX					
❑ 202	Junior High/Snow Job	1960	3.00	6.00	12.00
ADDISON					
❑ 15002	No One/Poor Me	1959	3.75	7.50	15.00
RCA VICTOR					
❑ 47-7213	I Love Your Poni-Tail/I Want You to Be My Own	1958	6.25	12.50	25.00
❑ 47-7308	Sugar Bowl Rock/Did You Ever See a Dream Walking	1958	7.50	15.00	30.00

FISHER, SONNY

Number	Title (A Side/B Side)	Yr	VG	VG+	NM
PEACOCK					
❑ 1947	Hurtin'/I'm Goin' All the Way	1966	6.25	12.50	25.00
STARDAY					
❑ 179	Rockin' Daddy/Hold Me Baby	1955	100.00	200.00	400.00
❑ 190	Sneaky Pete/Hey Mama	1955	125.00	250.00	500.00
❑ 207	Rockin' and Rollin'/I Can't Lose	1955	100.00	200.00	400.00
❑ 244	Pink and Black/Little Red Wagon	1956	100.00	200.00	400.00

FISHER, TONI

Number	Title (A Side/B Side)	Yr	VG	VG+	NM
BIG TOP					
❑ 3097	West of the Wall/What Did I Do	1962	3.00	6.00	12.00
❑ 3124	The Music from the House Next Door/Quickly My Love	1962	3.00	6.00	12.00
CAPITOL					
❑ 5901	Train of Love/A Million Heartbeats from Now	1967	2.00	4.00	8.00
COLUMBIA					
❑ 42066	If I Loved You/Love Big	1961	3.00	6.00	12.00
SIGNET					
❑ 275	The Big Hurt/Memphis Belle	1959	3.75	7.50	15.00
❑ 276	How Deep Is the Ocean/Blue, Blue, Blue	1960	3.00	6.00	12.00
❑ 279	Everlasting Love/The Red Sea of Mars	1960	3.00	6.00	12.00
❑ 364	You Never Told Me/Toot Toot Amore	1964	2.00	4.00	8.00
❑ 400	A Man That's Steady/You Never Told Me	196?	2.00	4.00	8.00
❑ 664	Springtime of Love/Train of Love	1964	2.00	4.00	8.00
SMASH					
❑ 1797	Hold Me/Laugh or Cry	1963	2.50	5.00	10.00
❑ 1820	Cry a Little for Me/365 Disappointments	1963	2.50	5.00	10.00
❑ 1832	Lovers, Dreamers, Fools/You Won't Forget Me	1963	2.50	5.00	10.00
❑ 1847	Your Royal Majesty/Billy, Marry Me	1963	2.50	5.00	10.00

FIVE AMERICANS, THE

Number	Title (A Side/B Side)	Yr	VG	VG+	NM
ABC-PARAMOUNT					
❑ 10686	Show Me/Love, Love, Love	1965	—	—	—
ABNAK					
❑ 106	Say That You Love Me/Without You	1965	2.50	5.00	10.00
❑ 106 [DJ]	Say That You Love Me/Without You	1965	6.25	12.50	25.00
—Promo only on yellow vinyl					
❑ 109	I See the Light/The Outcast	1965	5.00	10.00	20.00
❑ 109 [DJ]	I See the Light/The Outcast	1965	6.25	12.50	25.00
—Promo only on yellow vinyl					
❑ 114	Reality/Sympathy	1966	2.50	5.00	10.00
❑ 114 [DJ]	Reality/Sympathy	1966	6.25	12.50	25.00
—Promo only on yellow vinyl					
❑ 116	If I Could/Now That It's Over	1966	2.50	5.00	10.00
❑ 116 [DJ]	If I Could/Now That It's Over	1966	6.25	12.50	25.00
—Promo only on yellow vinyl					
❑ 118	Western Union/Now That It's Over	1967	3.00	6.00	12.00
❑ 118 [DJ]	Western Union/Now That It's Over	1967	6.25	12.50	25.00
—Promo only on yellow vinyl					
❑ 120	Sound of Love/Sympathy	1967	2.00	4.00	8.00
❑ 120 [DJ]	Sound of Love/Sympathy	1967	6.25	12.50	25.00
—Promo only on yellow vinyl					
❑ 123	Zip Code/Sweet Bird of Youth	1967	2.00	4.00	8.00
❑ 123 [DJ]	Zip Code/Sweet Bird of Youth	1967	6.25	12.50	25.00
—Promo only on yellow vinyl					
❑ 125	Stop Light/Tell Ann I Love Her	1967	2.00	4.00	8.00
❑ 125 [DJ]	Stop Light/Tell Ann I Love Her	1967	6.25	12.50	25.00
—Promo only on yellow vinyl					
❑ 125 [PS]	Stop Light/Tell Ann I Love Her	1967	3.75	7.50	15.00
❑ 126	7:30 Guided Tour/See Saw Baby	1967	2.00	4.00	8.00
❑ 126 [DJ]	7:30 Guided Tour/See Saw Baby	1967	6.25	12.50	25.00
—Promo only on yellow vinyl					
❑ 126 [PS]	7:30 Guided Tour/See Saw Baby	1967	3.75	7.50	15.00
❑ 128	The Rain Maker/No Communication	1968	2.00	4.00	8.00
❑ 128 [DJ]	The Rain Maker/No Communication	1968	6.25	12.50	25.00
—Promo only on yellow vinyl					
❑ 131	Con Man/Lovin' Is Lovin'	1968	2.00	4.00	8.00
❑ 131 [DJ]	Con Man/Lovin' Is Lovin'	1968	6.25	12.50	25.00
—Promo only on yellow vinyl					
❑ 132	Generation Gap/The Source	1968	2.00	4.00	8.00
❑ 132 [DJ]	Generation Gap/The Source	1968	6.25	12.50	25.00
—Promo only on yellow vinyl					
❑ 134	Virginia Girl/Call on Me	1969	2.00	4.00	8.00
❑ 134 [DJ]	Virginia Girl/Call on Me	1969	6.25	12.50	25.00
—Promo only on yellow vinyl					
❑ 137	Scrooge/Ignert Woman	1969	2.00	4.00	8.00
❑ 137 [DJ]	Scrooge/Ignert Woman	1969	6.25	12.50	25.00
—Promo only on yellow vinyl					
❑ 139	I See the Light '69/Red Cape	1969	2.00	4.00	8.00
—As "Michael Rabon and the Five Americans"					
❑ 139 [DJ]	I See the Light '69/Red Cape	1969	6.25	12.50	25.00
—As "Michael Rabon and the Five Americans"; promo only on yellow vinyl					
❑ 142	She's Too Good to Me/Molly Black	1969	2.00	4.00	8.00
❑ 142 [DJ]	She's Too Good to Me/Molly Black	1969	6.25	12.50	25.00
—Promo only on yellow vinyl					
HANNA-BARBERA					
❑ 454	I See the Light/The Outcast	1965	3.00	6.00	12.00
❑ 468	Evol-Not Love/Don't Blame Me	1966	3.00	6.00	12.00
❑ 468 [PS]	Evol-Not Love/Don't Blame Me	1966	3.75	7.50	15.00
❑ 483	Good Times/The Losing Game	1966	3.00	6.00	12.00
JETSTAR					
❑ 104	It's You Girl/I'm Gonna Leave You	1966	6.25	12.50	25.00
❑ 105	I'm Feeling OK/Slippin' and Slidin'	1966	7.50	15.00	30.00
PHILCO-FORD					
❑ HP-10	Western Union/Sounds of Love	1968	5.00	10.00	20.00
—4-inch plastic "Hip Pocket Record" with color sleeve					

FIVE BARS, THE

Number	Title (A Side/B Side)	Yr	VG	VG+	NM
MONEY					
❑ 224	Stormy Weather/Somebody Else's Fool	1957	15.00	30.00	60.00

FIVE BELLS, THE

Number	Title (A Side/B Side)	Yr	VG	VG+	NM
BRUNSWICK					
❑ 84002	Till I Waltz Again with You/Can't Wait for Tomorrow	1952	125.00	250.00	500.00
❑ 84004	Till Dawn and Tomorrow/Waiting, Waiting	1952	125.00	250.00	500.00

FIVE BLOBS, THE

Number	Title (A Side/B Side)	Yr	VG	VG+	NM
COLUMBIA					
❑ 41250	The Blob/Saturday Night in Tijuana	1958	6.25	12.50	25.00
JOY					
❑ 226	Rockin' Pow Wow/From the Top of Your Guggle	1959	5.00	10.00	20.00
❑ 230	Juliet/Young and Wild	1959	5.00	10.00	20.00

FIVE BLUE FLAMES, THE

See CHRIS POWELL AND THE FIVE BLUE FLAMES.

FIVE BLUE NOTES, THE

Number	Title (A Side/B Side)	Yr	VG	VG+	NM
SABRE					
❑ 103	My Gal Is Gone/Ooh Baby	1953	250.00	500.00	1000.
❑ 108	The Beat of Our Hearts/You Gotta Go Baby	1954	625.00	1250.	2500.

FIVE BUDDS, THE

Number	Title (A Side/B Side)	Yr	VG	VG+	NM
RAMA					
❑ 1	I Was Such a Fool (To Fall in Love with You)/Midnight	1953	125.00	250.00	500.00
❑ 2	I Guess It's All Over Now/I Want Her Back	1953	125.00	250.00	500.00

FIVE CAMPBELLS, THE

Number	Title (A Side/B Side)	Yr	VG	VG+	NM
MUSIC CITY					
❑ 794	Hey Baby/Morrine	1956	125.00	250.00	500.00

FIVE CARD STUD

Number	Title (A Side/B Side)	Yr	VG	VG+	NM
RED BIRD					
❑ 10-082	Be-Bop-A-Lula/Everybody Needs Somebody	1967	3.75	7.50	15.00
SMASH					
❑ 2080	Bag Me/Once	1967	3.75	7.50	15.00

FIVE CATS, THE

Number	Title (A Side/B Side)	Yr	VG	VG+	NM
RCA VICTOR					
❑ 47-5885	He Follows She/Santa Lucia	1954	6.25	12.50	25.00
❑ 47-6012	Rockin' Chair/Mine, Mine, Mine	1955	7.50	15.00	30.00
❑ 47-6181	I Was So Wrong/Someone's Gonna Cry	1955	10.00	20.00	40.00

FIVE CHANCES, THE

Number	Title (A Side/B Side)	Yr	VG	VG+	NM
ATOMIC					
❑ 2494	Make Love to Me/California	1977	3.00	6.00	12.00
BLUE LAKE					
❑ 115	All I Want/Shake-a-Link	1955	200.00	400.00	800.00
CHANCE					
❑ 1157	I May Be Small/Nagasaki	1954	250.00	500.00	1000.
FEDERAL					
❑ 12303	My Days Are Blue/Tell Me Why	1957	125.00	250.00	500.00
P.S.					
❑ 1510	Is This Love/Need Your Love	1960	75.00	150.00	300.00
STATES					
❑ 156	Gloria/Sugar Lips	1956	200.00	400.00	800.00
—Black vinyl					
❑ 156	Gloria/Sugar Lips	1956	300.00	600.00	1200.
—Red vinyl					

FIVE CROWNS, THE

Probably more than one group.

Number	Title (A Side/B Side)	Yr	VG	VG+	NM
CARAVAN					
❑ 15609	I Can't Pretend/Popcorn Willie	1955	12.50	25.00	50.00

Number	Title (A Side/B Side)	Yr	VG	VG+	NM
DE'BESTH					
❑ 1121/2	A Surprise from Outer Space/Memories of Yesterday	1959	100.00	200.00	400.00
❑ 1123	I Want You/Hillum Boy	1959	100.00	200.00	400.00
GEE					
❑ 1001	Do You Remember/God Bless You	1956	50.00	100.00	200.00
OLD TOWN					
❑ 790	Good Luck Darling/You Could Be My Love	1952	125.00	250.00	500.00
—Black vinyl					
❑ 790	Good Luck Darling/You Could Be My Love	1952	750.00	1500.	3000.
—Red vinyl					
❑ 792	Lullaby of the Bells/Later, Later Baby	1952	—	—	—
—Unconfirmed on 45 rpm					
RAINBOW					
❑ 179	A Star/You're My Inspiration	1952	75.00	150.00	300.00
—Black vinyl					
❑ 179	A Star/You're My Inspiration	1952	200.00	400.00	800.00
—Red vinyl					
❑ 184	Who Can Be True/$19.50 Due	1952	—	—	—
—Unconfirmed on 45 rpm					
❑ 202	Keep It a Secret/Why Don't You Believe Me	1953	1000.	2000.	4000.
—Red vinyl					
❑ 202	Keep It a Secret/Why Don't You Believe Me	1953	250.00	500.00	1000.
—Black vinyl					
❑ 206	Alone Again/Don't Have to Hunt No More	1953	—	—	—
—Unconfirmed on 45 rpm					
❑ 281	I Was Wrong/Hug Me Baby	1954	125.00	250.00	500.00
❑ 335	You Came to Me/Ooh Wee Baby	1956	50.00	100.00	200.00
—Reissued by "The Duvals"					
RIVIERA					
❑ 990	You Came to Me/Ooh Wee Baby	1955	1000.	2000.	4000.
TRANS WORLD					
❑ 717	I Can't Pretend/Popcorn Willie	1956	20.00	40.00	80.00

FIVE DEBONAIRES, THE

See THE DEBONAIRES.

FIVE DELIGHTS, THE

Number	Title (A Side/B Side)	Yr	VG	VG+	NM
ABEL					
❑ 228	The Thought of Losing You/That Love Affair	1959	75.00	150.00	300.00
NEWPORT					
❑ 7002	There'll Be No Goodbye/Okey Dokey Mama	1958	37.50	75.00	150.00
UNART					
❑ 2003	There'll Be No Goodbye/Okey Dokey Mama	1958	7.50	15.00	30.00

FIVE DISCS, THE

Evidently these are all the same group or closely related. Also see DAWN (3).

Number	Title (A Side/B Side)	Yr	VG	VG+	NM
CALO					
❑ 202	Adios/My Baby Loves Me	1961	37.50	75.00	150.00
—Green label					
❑ 202	Adios/My Baby Loves Me	1962	25.00	50.00	100.00
—White label					
CHEER					
❑ 1000	Never Let You Go/That Was the Time	1962	25.00	50.00	100.00
—Black label					
❑ 1000	Never Let You Go/That Was the Time	1962	12.50	25.00	50.00
—Red label					
❑ 1000 [DJ]	Never Let You Go/That Was the Time	1962	75.00	150.00	300.00
—White label, promo only					
CRYSTAL BALL					
❑ 114	Mirror Mirror/Most of All I Wonder Why	1978	2.50	5.00	10.00
❑ 120	Unchained Melody/The Shrine of St. Cecelia	1978	2.50	5.00	10.00
❑ 136	Playing a Game of Love/Bells	1979	2.00	4.00	8.00
❑ 141	This Love of Ours/To the Fair	1979	2.00	4.00	8.00
DWAIN					
❑ 803	My Chinese Girl/Roses	1959	50.00	100.00	200.00
—As "Mario and the Five Discs"					
❑ 803	My Chinese Girl/Roses	1959	37.50	75.00	150.00
❑ 6072	My Chinese Girl/Roses	1959	500.00	1000.	2000.
EMGE					
❑ 1004	I Remember/The World Is a Beautiful Place	1958	100.00	200.00	400.00
LAURIE					
❑ 3601	Rock and Roll Revival/Gypsy Women	1973	3.75	7.50	15.00
MELLO MOOD					
❑ 1002	My Chinese Girl/Roses	1964	3.75	7.50	15.00
PYRAMID					
❑ 166	Let's Fall in Love/That Was the Time	197?	—	3.00	6.00
RUST					
❑ 5027	I Remember/The World Is a Beautiful Place	1961	6.25	12.50	25.00
VIK					
❑ 0327	I Remember/The World Is a Beautiful Place	1958	20.00	40.00	80.00
YALE					
❑ 240	When Love Comes Knocking/Go-Go	1961	100.00	200.00	400.00
❑ 243/4	Come On Baby/I Don't Know What to Do	1961	100.00	200.00	400.00

FIVE DOLLARS, THE

Number	Title (A Side/B Side)	Yr	VG	VG+	NM
FORTUNE					
❑ 821	Harmony of Love/Doctor Baby	1955	25.00	50.00	100.00
❑ 826	So Strange/You Know I Can't Refuse	1956	25.00	50.00	100.00
❑ 830	I Will Wait/Hard Working Mama	1956	25.00	50.00	100.00
❑ 833	You Fool/How Do You Do the Bacon Fat	1957	20.00	40.00	80.00
❑ 854	That's the Way It Goes/My Baby-O	1960	12.50	25.00	50.00
FRATERNITY					
❑ 821	Harmony of Love/Doctor Baby	1958	10.00	20.00	40.00

FIVE ECHOES, THE

Number	Title (A Side/B Side)	Yr	VG	VG+	NM
SABRE					
❑ 102	Baby Come Back to Me/Lonely Mood	1953	150.00	300.00	600.00
—Black vinyl					
❑ 102	Baby Come Back to Me/Lonely Mood	1953	750.00	1125.	1500.
—Red vinyl					
❑ 105	So Lonesome/Broke	1954	150.00	300.00	600.00
—Black vinyl					
❑ 105	So Lonesome/Broke	1954	750.00	1125.	1500.
—Red vinyl					
VEE JAY					
❑ 129	I Really Do/Tell Me Baby	1954	75.00	150.00	300.00
❑ 156	Fool's Prayer/Tastee Freeze	1955	250.00	500.00	1000.
❑ 190	Soldier Boy/Pledging to You	1956	50.00	100.00	200.00

FIVE EMBERS, THE

Number	Title (A Side/B Side)	Yr	VG	VG+	NM
GEM					
❑ 224	Please Come Home/(B-side unknown)	1954	200.00	400.00	800.00

FIVE EMERALDS, THE

Number	Title (A Side/B Side)	Yr	VG	VG+	NM
S.R.C.					
❑ 106	I'll Beg/Let Me Take You Out Tonight	1953	250.00	500.00	1000.
—Label uses numeral "5" in group name, and "S.R.C." has periods in it					
❑ 106	I'll Beg/Let Me Take You Out Tonight	1953	250.00	500.00	1000.
—Label spells out "Five" in group name, and "S-R-C" has hyphens in it					
❑ 107	Darling/Pleasure Me	1954	300.00	600.00	1200.

FIVE EMPREES, THE

Number	Title (A Side/B Side)	Yr	VG	VG+	NM
FREEPORT					
❑ 1001	Little Miss Sad/Hey Lover	1965	3.00	6.00	12.00
❑ 1001	Little Miss Sad/Hey Lover	1965	6.25	12.50	25.00
—Originally released as "The Five Empressions"					
❑ 1002	Hey Baby/Why	1965	3.00	6.00	12.00
❑ 1007	Little Miss Happiness/Over the Mountain	1966	3.00	6.00	12.00
❑ 1009	Pretty Face (Part 1)/Pretty Face (Part 2)	1966	3.00	6.00	12.00
❑ 1010	Johnny B. Goode/Hey Lover	1966	3.00	6.00	12.00
SMASH					
❑ 2065	Gone from My Mind/Hey Diddle Diddle	1966	2.50	5.00	10.00

FIVE FORTUNES, THE

Number	Title (A Side/B Side)	Yr	VG	VG+	NM
RANSOM					
❑ 103	You Are My Only Love/Time Out for Love	1958	250.00	500.00	1000.

FIVE JETS, THE

Number	Title (A Side/B Side)	Yr	VG	VG+	NM
DELUXE					
❑ 6018	I Am in Love/Not a Hand to Shake	1953	37.50	75.00	150.00
❑ 6053	I'm Stuck/I Want a Woman	1954	37.50	75.00	150.00
❑ 6058	Tell Me You're Mine/Give In	1954	50.00	100.00	200.00
❑ 6064	Crazy Chicken/Everybody Do the Chicken	1954	15.00	30.00	60.00
❑ 6071	Down Slow/Please Love Me Baby	1955	20.00	60.00	120.00
KING					
❑ 6058	Tell Me You're Mine/Give In	1966	5.00	10.00	20.00

FIVE KEYS, THE

Number	Title (A Side/B Side)	Yr	VG	VG+	NM
ALADDIN					
❑ 3085	With a Broken Heart/Too Late	1951	—	—	—
—Unconfirmed on 45 rpm					
❑ 3099	The Glory of Love/Hucklebuck with Jimmy	1951	250.00	500.00	1000.
❑ 3113	It's Christmas Time/Old Mac Donald	1951	250.00	500.00	1000.
❑ 3118	Yes Sir That's My Baby/Old Mac Donald	1952	250.00	500.00	1000.
❑ 3119	Darling/Goin' Downtown	1952	250.00	500.00	1000.
❑ 3127	Red Sails in the Sunset/Be Anything, But Be Mine	1952	3000.	4500.	6000.
❑ 3131	How Long/Mistakes	1952	300.00	600.00	1200.
❑ 3136	Hold Me/I Hadn't Anyone Till You	1952	200.00	400.00	800.00
❑ 3158	I Cried for You/Serve Another Round	1953	225.00	450.00	900.00
❑ 3167	Can't Keep From Crying/Come Go My Bail, Louise	1953	200.00	400.00	800.00
❑ 3175	There Ought to Be a Law/Mama (Your Daughter Told a Lie on Me)	1953	200.00	400.00	800.00
❑ 3182	I'll Always Be in Love with You/Rocking and Crying Blues	1953	200.00	400.00	800.00
❑ 3190	These Foolish Things/Lonesome Old Story	1953	1000.	2000.	4000.
❑ 3204	Teardrops in Your Eyes/I'm So High	1953	200.00	400.00	800.00
❑ 3214	My Saddest Hour/Oh! Babe!	1953	200.00	400.00	800.00
❑ 3228	Someday Sweetheart/Love My Loving	1954	200.00	400.00	800.00
❑ 3245	Deep in My Heart/How Do You Expect Me to Get It	1954	200.00	400.00	800.00
❑ 3263	My Love/Why, Oh Why	1954	75.00	150.00	300.00
❑ 3312	Story of Love/Serve Another Round	1956	75.00	150.00	300.00
❑ S7-19768	Every Heart Is Home at Christmas/Frosty the Snowman	1997	—	2.50	5.00
—B-side by Fats Domino on The Right Stuff					
BANGAR					
❑ 661	Run-Around/I Tell My Heart	1965	3.75	7.50	15.00
CAPITOL					
❑ F-2945	Ling, Ting, Tong/I'm Alone	1954	10.00	20.00	40.00
❑ F-3032	Close Your Eyes/Doggone It, You Did It	1955	10.00	20.00	40.00
❑ F-3127	The Verdict/Me Make Um Pow Wow	1955	10.00	20.00	40.00
❑ F-3185	Don't You Know I Love You/I Wish I'd Never Learned to Read	1955	10.00	20.00	40.00
❑ F-3267	'Cause You're My Lover/Gee Whittakers	1955	10.00	20.00	40.00
❑ F-3318	You Broke the Rules of Love/What Goes On	1956	10.00	20.00	40.00
❑ F-3392	She's the Most/I Dreamt I Dwelt in Heaven	1956	10.00	20.00	40.00
—Regular large hole					
❑ F-3392	She's the Most/I Dreamt I Dwelt in Heaven	1956	17.50	35.00	70.00
—Small hole					
❑ F-3455	My Pigeon's Gone/Peace and Love	1956	10.00	20.00	40.00
❑ F-3502	Out of Sight, Out of Mind/That's Right	1956	7.50	15.00	30.00
❑ F-3597	Wisdom of a Fool/Now Don't That Prove I Love You	1956	7.50	15.00	30.00
❑ F-3660	Tiger Lily/Let There Be You	1957	6.25	12.50	25.00
❑ F-3710	Four Walls/It's a Groove	1957	6.25	12.50	25.00
❑ F-3738	This I Promise You/The Blues Don't Care	1957	6.25	12.50	25.00
❑ F-3786	Boom Boom/Face of An Angel	1957	6.25	12.50	25.00
❑ F-3830	Do Anything/It's a Cryin' Shame	1957	6.25	12.50	25.00
❑ F-3861	From Me to You/Whippety Whirl	1957	6.25	12.50	25.00
❑ F-3948	You're for Me/With All My Love	1958	6.25	12.50	25.00
❑ F-4009	Emily Please/Handy Andy	1958	6.25	12.50	25.00

Number	Title (A Side/B Side)	Yr	VG	VG+	NM
❑ F-4092	One Great Love/Really-O, Truly-O	1958	6.25	12.50	25.00
❑ 4828	Out of Sight, Out of Mind/From the Bottom of My Heart	1962	5.00	10.00	20.00
CLASSIC ARTISTS					
❑ 115	I Want You For Christmas/Express Yourself Back Home	1989	—	2.50	5.00
—As "Rudy West and the Five Keys"					
GROOVE					
❑ 0031	I'll Follow You/Lawdy Miss Mary	1954	2000.	3000.	4000.
—There is some debate about whether this record actually exists.					
INFERNO					
❑ 4500	Hey Girl/No Matter	1967	5.00	10.00	20.00
KING					
❑ 5251	I Took Your Love for a Toy/Ziggus	1959	7.50	15.00	30.00
❑ 5273	Dancing Senorita/Dream On	1959	5.00	10.00	20.00
❑ 5302	How Can I Forget You/I Burned Your Letter	1960	5.00	10.00	20.00
❑ 5330	Gonna Be Too Late/Rosetta	1960	5.00	10.00	20.00
❑ 5358	I Didn't Know/No, Says My Heart	1960	5.00	10.00	20.00
❑ 5398	Bimbo/Valley of Love	1960	5.00	10.00	20.00
❑ 5446	You Broke the Only Heart/That's What You're Doing to Me	1961	5.00	10.00	20.00
❑ 5496	Do Something for Me/Stop Your Crying	1961	5.00	10.00	20.00
❑ 5877	I'll Never Stop Loving You/I Can't Escape from You	1964	3.00	6.00	12.00
LIBERTY					
❑ 1394	It's Christmas Time/It's Christmas	1980	2.00	4.00	8.00
—B-side by Marvin and Johnny					
OWL					
❑ 321	A Dreamer/Your Teeth and Your Tongue	1973	2.00	4.00	8.00
SEG-WAY					
❑ 1008	Out of Sight, Out of Mind/You're the One	1962	3.75	7.50	15.00
UNITED ARTISTS					
❑ 0150	The Glory of Love/My Saddest Hour	1973	—	2.00	4.00
—"Silver Spotlight Series" reissue					
7-Inch Extended Plays					
CAPITOL					
❑ EAP 572	(contents unknown)	1955	25.00	50.00	100.00
❑ EAP 572 [PS]	The Five Keys	1955	25.00	50.00	100.00
❑ EAP 1-828	(contents unknown)	1957	25.00	50.00	100.00
❑ EAP 1-828 [PS]	The Five Keys On Stage! Volume 1	1957	37.50	75.00	150.00
—On cover, the far left singer has his thumb sticking out (inadvertently?) in a phallic way					
❑ EAP 1-828 [PS]	The Five Keys On Stage! Volume 1	1957	25.00	50.00	100.00
—On cover, the far left singer's "offending" thumb is airbrushed out					
❑ EAP 2-828	(contents unknown)	1957	25.00	50.00	100.00
❑ EAP 2-828 [PS]	The Five Keys On Stage! Volume 2	1957	37.50	75.00	150.00
—On cover, the far left singer has his thumb sticking out (inadvertently?) in a phallic way					
❑ EAP 2-828 [PS]	The Five Keys On Stage! Volume 2	1957	25.00	50.00	100.00
—On cover, the far left singer's "offending" thumb is airbrushed out					

FIVE KIDS, THE

Number	Title (A Side/B Side)	Yr	VG	VG+	NM
MAXWELL					
❑ 101	Carolyn/Oh Baby	1955	1000.	2000.	3000.

FIVE LYRICS, THE

Number	Title (A Side/B Side)	Yr	VG	VG+	NM
MUSIC CITY					
❑ 799	I'm Traveling Light/My Honeysweet Pea	1956	375.00	750.00	1500.

FIVE MAN ELECTRICAL BAND

Number	Title (A Side/B Side)	Yr	VG	VG+	NM
CAPITOL					
❑ 2368	It Never Rains on Maple Lane/Private Train	1968	—	3.00	6.00
❑ 2517	Baby/Lovin' Look	1969	—	3.00	6.00
❑ 2562	Sunrise to Sunset/Little Bit of Love	1969	—	3.00	6.00
❑ 2628	Riverboat/Good	1969	—	3.00	6.00
LION					
❑ 112	Coming of Age/The Devil and Miss Lucy	1972	—	2.50	5.00
❑ 127	Money Back Guarantee/Find the One	1972	—	2.50	5.00
❑ 149	I'm a Stranger Here/Doin' The Best We Can Rag	1973	—	2.50	5.00
❑ 160	Sweet Paradise/Baby Wanna Boogie	1973	—	2.50	5.00
LIONEL					
❑ 3213	Signs/Hello Melinda Goodbye	1971	2.00	4.00	8.00
—Lists "Hello Melinda Goodbye" as the A-side and contains the full-length version of "Signs"					
❑ 3213	Signs/Hello Melinda Goodbye	1971	—	3.00	6.00
—Lists no A and B sides and contains an edited version (3:20) of "Signs"					
❑ 3220	Absolutely Right/Butterfly	1971	—	2.50	5.00
❑ 3224	Friends and Family/Julianna	1971	—	2.50	5.00
MGM					
❑ 14149	Moonshine/Forever Together	1970	—	3.00	6.00
❑ 14182 [DJ]	Hello Melinda Goodbye/Signs	1970	2.50	5.00	10.00
—Evidently only exists as a promo					
POLYDOR					
❑ 14221	Werewolf/Country Angel	1974	—	2.00	4.00
❑ 14263	Johnnie Get a Gun/And the World Goes Round	1974	—	3.00	6.00

FIVE NOTES, THE

Number	Title (A Side/B Side)	Yr	VG	VG+	NM
CHESS					
❑ 1614	Show Me the Way/Park Your Lover	1955	37.50	75.00	150.00
JEN D					
❑ 4185	You Are So Beautiful/Broken Hearted Baby	1955	125.00	250.00	500.00
JOSIE					
❑ 784	You Are So Beautiful/Broken Hearted Baby	1955	20.00	40.00	80.00

FIVE PLAYBOYS, THE

Number	Title (A Side/B Side)	Yr	VG	VG+	NM
DOT					
❑ 15605	When We Were Young/Pages of My Scrapbook	1957	6.25	12.50	25.00
FEE BEE					
❑ 213	When We Were Young/Pages of My Scrapbook	1958	12.50	25.00	50.00
❑ 232	Angel Mine/She's My Baby	1959	25.00	50.00	100.00
MERCURY					
❑ 71269	Time Will Allow/Why Be a Fool	1958	6.25	12.50	25.00
PETITE					
❑ 504	She's My Baby/Mr. Echo	1959	10.00	20.00	40.00

FIVE ROVERS, THE

Number	Title (A Side/B Side)	Yr	VG	VG+	NM
MUSIC CITY					
❑ 798	Down to the Sea/Change Your Mind	1956	30.00	60.00	120.00

FIVE ROYALES, THE

Also includes "The Five Royals" and "The '5' Royales."

Number	Title (A Side/B Side)	Yr	VG	VG+	NM
ABC-PARAMOUNT					
❑ 10348	Catch That Teardrop/Goof Ball	1962	2.50	5.00	10.00
❑ 10368	What's In Your Heart/I Want It Like That	1962	2.50	5.00	10.00
APOLLO					
❑ 441	Courage to Love/You Know I Know	1952	25.00	50.00	100.00
—Black vinyl					
❑ 441	Courage to Love/You Know I Know	1952	100.00	200.00	400.00
—Red vinyl					
❑ 443	Baby Don't Do It/Take All of Me	1952	25.00	50.00	100.00
—Black vinyl					
❑ 443	Baby Don't Do It/Take All of Me	1952	100.00	200.00	400.00
—Red vinyl					
❑ 446	Help Me, Somebody/Crazy, Crazy, Crazy	1953	25.00	50.00	100.00
❑ 448	Too Much Lovin' (Much Too Much)/Laundromat Blues	1953	30.00	60.00	120.00
❑ 449	I Want to Thank You/All Righty	1953	20.00	40.00	80.00
❑ 452	I Do/Good Things	1954	20.00	40.00	80.00
❑ 454	Cry Some More/I Like It Like That	1954	20.00	40.00	80.00
❑ 458	What's That/Let Me Come Back Home	1954	17.50	35.00	70.00
❑ 467	With All Your Heart/6 O'Clock in the Morning	1955	17.50	35.00	70.00
HOME OF THE BLUES					
❑ 112	Please, Please, Please/I Got to Know	1960	3.75	7.50	15.00
❑ 218	If You Don't Need Me/I'm Gonna Tell Them	1961	3.75	7.50	15.00
❑ 232	Take Me With You Baby/Not Going to Cry	1961	3.75	7.50	15.00
❑ 234	Nuch in Need/They Don't Know	1962	3.75	7.50	15.00
❑ 243	Catch That Teardrop/Goof Ball	1962	3.75	7.50	15.00
KING					
❑ 4740	I'm Gonna Run It Down/Behave Yourself	1954	20.00	40.00	80.00
❑ 4744	Monkey Hips and Rice/Devil with the Rest	1954	20.00	40.00	80.00
❑ 4762	School Girl/One Mistake	1955	20.00	40.00	80.00
❑ 4770	Every Dog Has His Day/You Didn't Learn It at Home	1955	20.00	40.00	80.00
❑ 4785	How I Wonder/Mohawk Squaw	1955	20.00	40.00	80.00
❑ 4806	I Need Your Lovin'/When I Get Like This	1955	12.50	25.00	50.00
❑ 4819	Women About to Make Me Go Crazy/Do Unto You	1955	12.50	25.00	50.00
❑ 4830	I Ain't Gettin' Caught/Someone Made You for Me	1955	12.50	25.00	50.00
❑ 4869	When You Walked Through the Door/Right Around the Corner	1956	12.50	25.00	50.00
❑ 4901	I Could Love You/My Wants for Love	1956	12.50	25.00	50.00
❑ 4952	Get Something Out of It/Come On and Save Me	1956	12.50	25.00	50.00
❑ 4973	Just As I Am/Mine Forevermore	1956	12.50	25.00	50.00
❑ 5032	Tears of Joy/Thirty Second Lover	1957	10.00	20.00	40.00
❑ 5053	Think/I'd Better Make a Move	1957	10.00	20.00	40.00
❑ 5082	Messin' Up/Say It	1957	10.00	20.00	40.00
❑ 5098	Dedicated to the One I Love/Don't Be Ashamed	1958	10.00	20.00	40.00
❑ 5131	Do the Cha Cha Cherry/The Feeling Is Real	1958	6.25	12.50	25.00
❑ 5141	Tell the Truth/Double or Nothing	1958	6.25	12.50	25.00
❑ 5153	The Slummer the Slum/Don't Let It Be in Vain	1958	6.25	12.50	25.00
❑ 5162	Your Only Love/The Real Thing	1958	6.25	12.50	25.00
❑ 5191	Miracle of Love/I Know It's Hard, But It's Fair	1959	6.25	12.50	25.00
❑ 5237	Tell Me You Care/Wonder Where Your Love Has Gone	1959	6.25	12.50	25.00
❑ 5266	My Sugar Sugar/It Hurts Inside	1959	6.25	12.50	25.00
❑ 5329	Don't Give No More Than You Can Take/I'm with You	1960	6.25	12.50	25.00
❑ 5357	Why/Within My Heart	1960	6.25	12.50	25.00
❑ 5453	Dedicated to the One I Love/Miracle of Love	1961	3.75	7.50	15.00
❑ 5756	Dedicated to the One I Love/Tears of Joy	1963	3.75	7.50	15.00
❑ 5892	I Wonder Where Your Love Has Gone/I Need Your Lovin' Baby	1964	3.75	7.50	15.00
—The Five Royals					
SMASH					
❑ 1936	Baby Don't Do It/I Like It Like That	1964	2.50	5.00	10.00
❑ 1963	Never Turn Your Back/Faith	1965	2.50	5.00	10.00
TODD					
❑ 1086	I'm Standing in the Shadows/Doin' Everything	1963	2.50	5.00	10.00
❑ 1088	Baby Don't Do It/There's Somebody Over There	1963	2.50	5.00	10.00
VEE JAY					
❑ 412	Much in Need/They Don't Know	1961	3.75	7.50	15.00
❑ 431	Help Me Somebody/Talk About My Woman	1962	3.75	7.50	15.00

FIVE SATINS, THE

Also see FRED PARRIS; THE WILDWOODS.

Number	Title (A Side/B Side)	Yr	VG	VG+	NM
BUDDAH					
❑ 477	Everybody Stand and Clap Your Hands/Hey There Pretty Lady	1975	—	2.50	5.00
—As "Black Satin"					
CANDELITE					
❑ 411	She's Gone (With the Wind)/Somewhere a Voice Is Calling	1974	—	3.00	6.00
CHANCELLOR					
❑ 1110	The Masquerade Is Over/Raining in My Heart	1962	5.00	10.00	20.00
❑ 1121	Do You Remember/Downtown	1962	5.00	10.00	20.00
CUB					
❑ 9071	Your Memory/I Didn't Know	1960	6.25	12.50	25.00
❑ 9077	These Foolish Things/A Beggar with a Dream	1960	6.25	12.50	25.00
❑ 9090	Golden Earrings/Can I Come Over Tonight	1961	6.25	12.50	25.00
ELEKTRA					
❑ 47411	Memories of Days Gone By Medley/Loving You (Would Be the Sweetest Thing)	1982	5.00	10.00	20.00
—As "Fred Parris and the Five Satins"					

Number	Title (A Side/B Side)	Yr	VG	VG+	NM
❑ 69888	Didn't I (Blow Your Mind)/Loving You (Would Be the Sweetest Thing)	1982	—	2.50	5.00
❑ 69938	Breaking Up/Loving You (Would Be the Sweetest Thing)	1982	—	2.50	5.00
❑ 69984	I'll Be Seeing You/Loving You (Would Be the Sweetest Thing)	1982	—	2.50	5.00
EMBER					
❑ 1005	In the Still of the Nite/The Jones Girl	1956	50.00	100.00	200.00
—Red label; has "6106A" in the trail-off vinyl					
❑ 1005	In the Still of the Nite/The Jones Girl	1956	12.50	25.00	50.00
—Red label; has "E-2105-45" in the trail-off vinyl					
❑ 1005	In the Still of the Nite/The Jones Girl	1956	7.50	15.00	30.00
—Red label; has "E-1005" in the trail-off vinyl					
❑ 1005	I'll Remember (In the Still of the Nite)/The Jones Girl	1956	7.50	15.00	30.00
—Red label					
❑ 1005	I'll Remember (In the Still of the Nite)/The Jones Girl	1959	12.50	25.00	50.00
—Multi-color "logs" label; reads "Special Demand Release"					
❑ 1005	I'll Remember (In the Still of the Nite)/The Jones Girl	1959	7.50	15.00	30.00
—Multi-color "logs" label; no "Special Demand Release"					
❑ 1005	In the Still of the Nite/The Jones Girl	1959	10.00	20.00	40.00
—Multi-color "logs" label with original A-side title					
❑ 1005	I'll Remember (In the Still of the Nite)/The Jones Girl	1961	7.50	15.00	30.00
—Black label					
❑ 1008	Weeping Willow/Wonderful Girl	1956	10.00	20.00	40.00
❑ 1014	Our Love Is Forever/Oh Happy Day	1957	10.00	20.00	40.00
❑ 1019	To the Aisle/Wish I Had My Baby	1957	10.00	20.00	40.00
—Red label					
❑ 1019	To the Aisle/Wish I Had My Baby	1960	7.50	15.00	30.00
—Multi-color "logs" label					
❑ 1019	To the Aisle/Wish I Had My Baby	1961	5.00	10.00	20.00
—Black label					
❑ 1025	Our Anniversary/Pretty Baby	1957	10.00	20.00	40.00
—Red label					
❑ 1025	Our Anniversary/Pretty Baby	1957	5.00	10.00	20.00
—Black label					
❑ 1028	A Million to One/Love with No Love in Return	1957	10.00	20.00	40.00
❑ 1038	A Night to Remember/Senorita Lolita	1958	7.50	15.00	30.00
—As "Fred Parris and the Satins"					
❑ 1056	Shadows/Toni My Love	1959	7.50	15.00	30.00
❑ 1061	I'll Be Seeing You/A Night Like This	1960	7.50	15.00	30.00
❑ 1066	Candlelight/The Time	1960	6.25	12.50	25.00
❑ 1070	Wishing Ring/Tell Me Dear	1961	6.25	12.50	25.00
FIRST					
❑ 104	When Your Love Comes Along/Skippity Doo	1959	10.00	20.00	40.00
—Orange label					
❑ 104	When Your Love Comes Along/Skippity Doo	1959	6.25	12.50	25.00
—Green label					
KIRSHNER					
❑ 4251	Very Precious Oldies/You Are Love	1974	2.50	5.00	10.00
❑ 4252	Two Different Worlds/Love Is Such a Beautiful Thing	1974	2.50	5.00	10.00
KLIK					
❑ 1020	I Love You So/Story to You	1973	2.50	5.00	10.00
MAMA SADIE					
❑ 1001	In the Still of the Night "67"/Heck No (Instrumental)	1967	3.00	6.00	12.00
MUSICTONE					
❑ 1108	To the Aisle/Just to Be Near You	1961	6.25	12.50	25.00
NIGHTRAIN					
❑ 901	All Mine/The Voice	1970	2.50	5.00	10.00
RCA					
❑ 6989-7-R	In the Still of the Night/Yes	1988	—	—	3.00
—B-side by Merry Clayton					
RCA VICTOR					
❑ 74-0478	Summer in New York/Dark at the Top of My Heart	1971	2.50	5.00	10.00
ROULETTE					
❑ 4563	Ain't Gonna Cry/You Can Count on Me	1964	2.50	5.00	10.00
SAMMY					
❑ 103	No One Knows/Musical Chairs	196?	7.50	15.00	30.00
SIGNATURE					
❑ 001	Everybody's Got a Home But Me/Heartache	1990	—	2.50	5.00
STANDORD					
❑ 100	All Mine/Rose Mary	1956	175.00	2350.	700.00
—Red label					
❑ 100	All Mine/Rose Mary	1962	50.00	100.00	200.00
—Maroon label					
❑ 200	In the Still of the Nite/The Jones Girl	1956	300.00	600.00	900.00
❑ 200	In the Still of the Nite/The Jones Girl	1956	1000.	1500.	2000.
—With "Produced by Martin Kuegell" credit					
TIME MACHINE					
❑ 570	Wonder Why/No One Knows	1962	2.00	4.00	8.00
❑ 571	The Masquerade Is Over/Lonely Hearts	1962	2.00	4.00	8.00
TIMES SQUARE					
❑ 4	All Mine/Rose Mary	1962	5.00	10.00	20.00
—Blue vinyl					
❑ 21	Paradise on Earth/Monkey Business	1963	5.00	10.00	20.00
❑ 94	Paradise on Earth/Monkey Business	1964	3.75	7.50	15.00
UNITED ARTISTS					
❑ 368	On a Lover's Island/Till the End	1961	6.25	12.50	25.00
WARNER BROS.					
❑ 5367	Remember Me/Kangaroo	1963	3.00	6.00	12.00
X-BAT					
❑ 1000	When the Swallows Come Back to Capistrano/Dance Girl Dance	1995	—	2.50	5.00
—Red vinyl					
❑ 1000 [PS]	When the Swallows Come Back to Capistrano/Dance Girl Dance	1995	—	2.50	5.00

7-Inch Extended Plays

Number	Title (A Side/B Side)	Yr	VG	VG+	NM
EMBER					
❑ EEP-100	I'll Remember/The Jones Girl//Wonderful Girl/Pretty Baby	1957	50.00	100.00	200.00
❑ EEP-100 [PS]	The Five Satins Sing (Vol. 1)	1957	50.00	100.00	200.00
❑ EEP-101	To the Aisle/Sugar//Our Love Is Forever/Weeping Willow	1957	50.00	100.00	200.00
❑ EEP-101 [PS]	The Five Satins Sing (Vol. 2)	1957	50.00	100.00	200.00
❑ EEP-102	(contents unknown)	1957	50.00	100.00	200.00
❑ EEP-102 [PS]	The Five Satins Sing (Vol. 3)	1957	50.00	100.00	200.00

FIVE SCALDERS, THE

Number	Title (A Side/B Side)	Yr	VG	VG+	NM
DRUMMOND					
❑ 3000	If Only You Were Mine/There Will Come a Time	1956	250.00	500.00	1000.
❑ 3001	Girl Friend/Willow Blues	1956	500.00	1000.	1500.
—Blue label					
❑ 3001	Girl Friend/Willow Blues	1956	250.00	500.00	1000.
—Maroon label					
SUGAR HILL					
❑ 3000	If Only You Were Mine/There Will Come a Time	1956	500.00	1000.	2000.

FIVE SECRETS, THE

Number	Title (A Side/B Side)	Yr	VG	VG+	NM
DECCA					
❑ 30350	See You Next Year/Queen Bee	1957	20.00	40.00	80.00
❑ 30350	See You Next Year/Queen Bee	1957	10.00	20.00	40.00
—As "The Secrets"					

FIVE SHARKS, THE

Number	Title (A Side/B Side)	Yr	VG	VG+	NM
AMBER					
❑ 852	The Lion Sleeps Tonight/Land of 1000 Dances	1966	2.50	5.00	10.00
OLD TIMER					
❑ 604	Gloria/Flames	1964	5.00	10.00	20.00
❑ 605	Stand By Me/I'll Never Let You Go	1964	5.00	10.00	20.00
—Gold vinyl					
❑ 605	Stand By Me/I'll Never Let You Go	1964	4.00	8.00	16.00
—Blue vinyl					
❑ 611	Gloria/Flames	1965	5.00	10.00	20.00
—Red vinyl					
❑ 611	Gloria/Flames	1965	3.75	7.50	15.00
—Black vinyl					
RELIC					
❑ 525	Stormy Weather (2:45)/If You Love Me	1965	2.50	5.00	10.00
SIAMESE					
❑ 404	Gloria/Flames	1965	3.00	6.00	12.00
TIMES SQUARE					
❑ 35	Stormy Weather (3:45)/If You Love Me	1964	15.00	30.00	60.00
—Blue vinyl					
❑ 35	Stormy Weather (3:45)/If You Love Me	1964	10.00	20.00	40.00
—Black vinyl					
❑ 35	Stormy Weather (2:45)/If You Love Me	1964	7.50	15.00	30.00

FIVE SHARPS, THE (1)

Number	Title (A Side/B Side)	Yr	VG	VG+	NM
BIM BAM BOOM					
❑ 103	Stormy Weather/Sleepy Cowboy	1972	2.00	4.00	8.00
—Reissue mastered off the cracked Jubilee 78 (see below); the original master has long since disappeared					
JUBILEE					
❑ 5104	Stormy Weather/Sleepy Cowboy	1952	—	—	—
—Unknown on 45 RPM (3 known copies, one of which is cracked, exist on 78); all known 45s are counterfeits. Known counterfeits do not match the proper typeface of the era for the label, and the blue labels are too bright compared to authentic Jubilee 45s of the early 1950s. Even the cracked 78 would likely sell for $10,000; if a legitimate 45 would be confirmed, it could sell for more than any record ever made!					

FIVE SHARPS, THE (2)

A completely different group than (1), they were assembled by Jubilee to record a new version of "Stormy Weather" in the midst of the hubbub about the first Five Sharps version. (For the full story, see The Complete Book of Doo-Wop by Gribin and Schiff, Krause Publications, 2000.)

Number	Title (A Side/B Side)	Yr	VG	VG+	NM
JUBILEE					
❑ 5478	Stormy Weather/Mammy Jammy	1964	3.00	6.00	12.00

FIVE STAIRSTEPS, THE

Includes records by "Five Stairsteps and Cubie" and "Stairsteps."

Number	Title (A Side/B Side)	Yr	VG	VG+	NM
BUDDAH					
❑ 20	Something's Missing/Tell Me Who	1967	2.00	4.00	8.00
—As "Five Stairsteps and Cubie"					
❑ 20 [PS]	Something's Missing/Tell Me Who	1967	3.75	7.50	15.00
❑ 26	A Million to One/You Make Me So Mad	1968	2.00	4.00	8.00
—As "Five Stairsteps and Cubie"					
❑ 26 [PS]	A Million to One/You Make Me So Mad	1968	3.75	7.50	15.00
❑ 35	The Shadow of Your Love/Bad News	1968	2.00	4.00	8.00
❑ 165	Dear Prudence/O-o-h Child	1970	2.00	4.00	8.00
❑ 165	O-o-h Child/Who Do You Belong To	1970	—	3.00	6.00
❑ 188	Because I Love You/America Standing	1970	—	2.50	5.00
❑ 213	Didn't It Look So Easy/Peace Is Gonna Come	1971	—	2.50	5.00
—Starting with the above, as "Stairsteps"					
❑ 222	Snow/Look Out	1971	—	2.50	5.00
❑ 277	I Love You-Stop/I Feel a Song (In My Heart Again)	1972	—	2.50	5.00
❑ 291	Hush Child/The Easy Way	1972	—	2.50	5.00
❑ 320	Every Single Way/Two Weeks' Notice	1972	—	2.50	5.00
CURTOM					
❑ 1931	Don't Change Your Love/New Dance Craze	1968	—	3.00	6.00
—Curtom releases as "Five Stairsteps and Cubie"					
❑ 1933	I Made a Mistake/Stay Close to Me	1968	—	3.00	6.00
❑ 1936	Baby Make Me Feel So Good/Little Young Lover	1969	—	3.00	6.00
❑ 1944	Madame Mary/Little Boy Blue	1969	—	3.00	6.00
❑ 1945	We Must Be in Love/Little Young Lover	1969	—	3.00	6.00
DARK HORSE					
❑ 10005	From Us to You/Time	1975	—	2.50	5.00

Number	Title (A Side/B Side)	Yr	VG	VG+	NM
❑ 10005 [PS]	From Us to You/Time	1975	—	3.00	6.00
❑ 10009	Tell Me Why/Salaam	1976	—	2.50	5.00
WINDY "C"					
❑ 601	You Waited Too Long/Don't Waste Your Time	1966	2.50	5.00	10.00
❑ 602	World of Fantasy/Playgirl's Love	1966	2.50	5.00	10.00
❑ 603	Come Back/You Don't Love Me	1966	2.50	5.00	10.00
❑ 604	Danger, She's a Stranger/Behind Curtains	1967	2.50	5.00	10.00
❑ 605	Ain't Gonna Rest (Till I Get You)/You Can't See	1967	2.50	5.00	10.00
❑ 607	Oooh, Baby Baby/The Girl I Love	1967	2.50	5.00	10.00
❑ 608	The Touch of You/Change of Face	1967	2.50	5.00	10.00

FIVE STARS, THE (1)

Number	Title (A Side/B Side)	Yr	VG	VG+	NM
ABC-PARAMOUNT					
❑ 9911	Pickin' on the Wrong Chicken/Dreaming	1958	6.25	12.50	25.00
HUNT					
❑ 318	Pickin' on the Wrong Chicken/Dreaming	1959	5.00	10.00	20.00
NOTE					
❑ 10011	Pickin' on the Wrong Chicken/Dreaming	1958	7.50	15.00	30.00
❑ 10016	My Paradise/Friction	1958	10.00	20.00	40.00
❑ 10031	Am I Wasting My Time/Gamblin' Man	1959	7.50	15.00	30.00

FIVE STARS, THE (2)

Number	Title (A Side/B Side)	Yr	VG	VG+	NM
SHOW TIME					
❑ 1102	Where Did Caledonia Go?/Walkin' An' Talkin'	1954	62.50	125.00	250.00

FIVE STARS, THE (U)

Many of these are probably group (1); the Treat release may be group (2).

Number	Title (A Side/B Side)	Yr	VG	VG+	NM
ATCO					
❑ 6065	Take Five/Humpty Dump	1956	7.50	15.00	30.00
BLUES BOYS KINGDOM					
❑ 106	So Lonely, Baby/Hey Juanita	1957	50.00	100.00	200.00
COLUMBIA					
❑ 4-42056	Baby Baby/Blabber Mouth	1961	15.00	30.00	60.00
DOT					
❑ 15579	Atom Bomb Baby/You Sweet Little Thing	1957	6.25	12.50	25.00
END					
❑ 1028	Baby Baby/Blabber Mouth	1958	20.00	40.00	80.00
KERNEL					
❑ 3195	Atom Bomb Baby/You Sweet Little Thing	1957	25.00	50.00	100.00
MARK-X					
❑ 7006	Dead Wrong/Ooh Shucks	1957	25.00	50.00	100.00
TREAT					
❑ 505	Let's Fall in Love/We Danced in the Moonlight	1955	500.00	1000.	2000.

FIVE SUPERIORS, THE

Number	Title (A Side/B Side)	Yr	VG	VG+	NM
GARPAX					
❑ 44170	There's a Fool Born Every Day/Big Shot	1962	37.50	75.00	150.00

FIVE SWANS, THE

Number	Title (A Side/B Side)	Yr	VG	VG+	NM
MUSIC CITY					
❑ 795	Little Girl of My Dreams/Little Tipa Tins	1956	75.00	150.00	300.00

FIVE THRILLS, THE

Number	Title (A Side/B Side)	Yr	VG	VG+	NM
PARROT					
❑ 796	My Baby's Gone/Feel So Good	1954	200.00	400.00	800.00
❑ 800	Gloria/Wee Wee Baby	1954	1000.	1500.	2000.
—Black vinyl					
❑ 800	Gloria/Wee Wee Baby	1954	2000.	3000.	4000.
—Red vinyl					

FIVE TINOS, THE

Number	Title (A Side/B Side)	Yr	VG	VG+	NM
SUN					
❑ 222	Sitting By My Window/Don't Do That	1955	300.00	600.00	1200.

FIVE TRUMPETS, THE

Number	Title (A Side/B Side)	Yr	VG	VG+	NM
GOTHAM					
❑ 681	Stand By Me/Jesus Is Here Today	1951	15.00	30.00	60.00
❑ 693	My Chains Fell Off/The Lord Knows What I Need	1952	15.00	30.00	60.00
❑ 696	No Not One/A Hand I Can See	1952	15.00	30.00	60.00
RCA VICTOR					
❑ 50-0014	Oh Lord/Don't Let Nobody Turn You Around	1949	17.50	35.00	70.00
—Orange vinyl					
❑ 50-0034	Swing Low Sweet Chariot/Sign of the Judgment	1949	17.50	35.00	70.00
—Orange vinyl					
❑ 50-0080	When the Saints Go Marching In/Preach My Word	1950	17.50	35.00	70.00
—Orange vinyl					
SAVOY					
❑ 4060	Amazing Grace/Lord I Want to Be a Christian	1955	6.25	12.50	25.00
❑ 4072	I've Got Jesus/I Shall Not Be Moved	1956	6.25	12.50	25.00

FIVE WILLOWS, THE

Number	Title (A Side/B Side)	Yr	VG	VG+	NM
ALLEN					
❑ 1000	My Dear, Dearest Darling/Rock, Little Francis	1953	75.00	150.00	300.00
❑ 1002	Delores/All Night Long	1953	150.00	300.00	600.00
❑ 1003	The White Cliffs of Dover/With These Hands	1953	175.00	350.00	700.00
HERALD					
❑ 433	Baby Come a Little Closer/Lay Your Head on My Shoulder	1954	75.00	150.00	300.00
❑ 442	Look Me in the Eyes/So Help Me	1954	100.00	200.00	400.00
LOST-NITE					
❑ 174	My Dear, Dearest Darling/Rock, Little Francis	196?	—	3.00	6.00
❑ 183	Delores/All Night Long	196?	—	3.00	6.00
❑ 187	The White Cliffs of Dover/With These Hands	196?	—	3.00	6.00
—Lost-Nite records are reissues					
❑ 192	Love Bells/Please Baby	196?	—	3.00	6.00
PEE DEE					
❑ 290	Love Bells/Please, Baby	1953	375.00	750.00	1500.

FIVE WINGS, THE

Number	Title (A Side/B Side)	Yr	VG	VG+	NM
KING					
❑ 4778	Johnny Has Gone/Johnny's Still Singing	1955	50.00	100.00	200.00
❑ 4781	Teardrops Are Falling/Rock-A-Locka	1955	100.00	200.00	400.00
—Later released on King 5199 as The Checkers.					

FLACK, ROBERTA

Number	Title (A Side/B Side)	Yr	VG	VG+	NM
ANGEL					
❑ S7-19773	The Christmas Song (Chestnuts Roasting on an Open Fire)/25th of Last December	1997	—	2.00	4.00
ATLANTIC					
❑ 2665	Compared to What/That's No Way to Say Goodbye	1969	2.00	4.00	8.00
❑ 2730	How Many Broken Wings/Baby Baby	1970	—	3.00	6.00
—With Les McCann					
❑ 2758	Reverend Lee/Business Goes On As Usual	1970	—	3.00	6.00
❑ 2785	Let It Be Me/Do What Cha Gotta Do	1971	—	3.00	6.00
❑ 2851	Will You Still Love Me Tomorrow/Go Up Moses	1972	—	2.50	5.00
❑ 2864	The First Time Ever I Saw Your Face/Trade Winds	1972	—	2.50	5.00
❑ 2940	Killing Me Softly with His Song/Just Like a Woman	1973	—	2.50	5.00
❑ 2982	Jesse/No Tears	1973	—	2.50	5.00
❑ 3025	Feel Like Makin' Love/When You Smile	1974	—	2.50	5.00
❑ 3203	Feel Like Makin' Love/When You Smile	1974	—	2.00	4.00
❑ 3271	Feelin' That Glow/Some Gospel According to Matthew	1975	—	2.00	4.00
❑ 3441	The 25th of Last December/Move In with Me	1977	—	2.00	4.00
❑ 3483	If Ever I See You Again/I'd Like to Be a Baby to You	1978	—	2.00	4.00
❑ 3521	When It's Over/Come Share My Love	1978	—	2.00	4.00
❑ 3560	You Are Everything/Knowing That We're Made for Each Other	1979	—	2.00	4.00
❑ 3627	You Are My Heaven/I'll Love You Forever and Ever	1979	—	2.00	4.00
❑ 3753	Don't Make Me Wait Too Long/Only Heaven Can Wait (For Love)	1980	—	2.00	4.00
❑ 4005	Making Love/Jesse	1982	—	2.00	4.00
❑ 4005 [PS]	Making Love/Jesse	1982	—	3.00	6.00
❑ 4068	I'm the One/'Til the Morning Comes	1982	—	2.00	4.00
❑ 87607	Set the Night to Music/Natural Thing	1991	—	2.00	4.00
—A-side: With Maxi Priest					
❑ 88898	Shock to My System/You Know What It's Like	1989	—	—	3.00
❑ 88941	Uh-Uh Ooh-Ooh Look Out (Here It Comes)/You Know What It's Like	1989	—	—	3.00
❑ 88941 [PS]	Uh-Uh Ooh-Ooh Look Out (Here It Comes)/You Know What It's Like	1989	—	—	3.00
❑ 88996	Oasis/You Know What It's Like	1988	—	—	3.00
❑ 88996 [PS]	Oasis/You Know What It's Like	1988	—	—	3.00
❑ 89295	We Shall Overcome/We Shall Overcome	1987	—	—	3.00
❑ 89440	Let Me Be a Light to Shine/We Shall Overcome	1986	—	—	3.00
—With Howard Hewett					
❑ 89931	Our Love Will Stop the World/Only Heaven Can Wait (For Love)	1982	—	2.00	4.00
—A-side: With Eric Mercury					
❑ 89932	In the Name of Love/Happiness	1982	—	2.00	4.00
COLUMBIA					
❑ 44050	Si, Si, Senor/This Year	1967	2.50	5.00	10.00
❑ 44448	Cold, Cold Winter/If You Ever Leave Me Now	1968	2.50	5.00	10.00
MCA					
❑ 51126	You Stopped Loving Me/Qual E Maundrinio	1981	—	2.00	4.00
❑ 51173	Lovin' You/Hittin' Me Where It Hurts	1981	—	2.00	4.00
VIVA					
❑ 29401	This Side of Forever/Robbery Suspects	1983	—	2.00	4.00
—B-side by The Enforcers					

FLACK, ROBERTA, AND DONNY HATHAWAY

Also see each artist's individual listings.

Number	Title (A Side/B Side)	Yr	VG	VG+	NM
ATLANTIC					
❑ 2808	You've Got a Friend/Gone Away	1971	—	2.50	5.00
❑ 2837	You've Lost That Lovin' Feeling/Be Real Black for Me	1971	—	2.50	5.00
❑ 2879	Where Is the Love/Mood	1972	—	2.50	5.00
❑ 3463	The Closer I Get to You/Love Is the Healing	1978	—	2.00	4.00
❑ 3661	Back Together Again/God Don't Like Ugly	1980	—	2.00	4.00

FLAGG, BILL

Number	Title (A Side/B Side)	Yr	VG	VG+	NM
MGM					
❑ 12637	Doin' My Time/I Will Always Love You	1958	25.00	50.00	100.00
TETRA					
❑ 4445	Go Cat, Go/A Good Woman's Leaving	1956	37.50	75.00	150.00
❑ 4448	Guitar Rock/(B-side unknown)	1957	37.50	75.00	150.00

FLAIRS, THE (1)

Also see CORNEL GUNTER; SHIRLEY GUNTER.

Number	Title (A Side/B Side)	Yr	VG	VG+	NM
ABC-PARAMOUNT					
❑ 9740	Aladdin's Lamp/Steppin' Out	1956	10.00	20.00	40.00
FLAIR					
❑ 1012	I Had a Love/She Wants to Rock	1953	100.00	200.00	400.00
❑ 1019	Tell Me You Love Me/You Should Care for Me	1953	100.00	200.00	400.00
❑ 1028	Love Me Girl/Gettin' High	1954	100.00	200.00	400.00
❑ 1041	Baby Wants/You Were Untrue	1954	100.00	200.00	400.00
❑ 1044	This Is the Night for Love/Let's Make with Some Love	1954	100.00	200.00	400.00
❑ 1051	Love Me, Love Me, Love Me/My Heart's Crying for You	1954	100.00	200.00	400.00
—As "The Chimes"					
❑ 1056	I'll Never Let You Go/Hold Me, Thrill Me, Chill Me	1955	100.00	200.00	400.00
❑ 1067	She Loves to Dance/My Darling, My Sweet	1955	100.00	200.00	400.00

FLAIRS, THE (3)

Number	Title (A Side/B Side)	Yr	VG	VG+	NM
PALMS					
❑ 726	Roll Over Beethoven/Brazil	1961	12.50	25.00	50.00
—Reissued on Jamie under the name "The Velaires"					

FLAME, THE

With Rikki Fataar and Blondie Chaplin, who later spent time in THE BEACH BOYS. (Fataar also was with THE RUTLES in the studio.)

Number	Title (A Side/B Side)	Yr	VG	VG+	NM
BROTHER					
❑ 3501	See the Light/Got Your Mind Made Up	1970	3.75	7.50	15.00
❑ 3502	Another Day Like Heaven/I'm So Happy	1970	3.75	7.50	15.00

FLAMES, THE

More than one group. Also see THE HOLLYWOOD FLAMES.

Number	Title (A Side/B Side)	Yr	VG	VG+	NM
7-11					
❑ 2106	Keep On Smiling/Baby, Baby, Baby	1953	150.00	300.00	600.00
❑ 2107	Together/Baby, Pretty Baby	1953	125.00	250.00	500.00
BERTRAM					
❑ 203	I'll Never Let You Go/Crazy	1958	6.25	12.50	25.00
DOT					
❑ 15813	The Scramble (Part 1)/The Scramble (Part 2)	1958	3.75	7.50	15.00
FARGO					
❑ 1018	Making Time/Letti Lu	1961	5.00	10.00	20.00
HARLEM					
❑ 114	So Long My Darling/I'm Going to Try to Live My Life All Over	1960	1500.	2250.	3000.
—As "The Fabulous Flames"					
❑ 114	So Long My Darling/I'm Going to Try to Live My Life All Over	1960	200.00	400.00	800.00
—As "The Flames"					
SPIN					
❑ 101	Cryin' for My Baby/Starnge Land Blues	1952	125.00	250.00	500.00

FLAMIN' GROOVIES, THE

Number	Title (A Side/B Side)	Yr	VG	VG+	NM
BOMP!					
❑ 101	You Tore Me Down/Him or Me (What's It Gonna Be?)	1975	2.00	4.00	8.00
EPIC					
❑ 10507	Rockin' Pneumonia & The Boogie Woogie Flu/ The First One's Free	1969	2.50	5.00	10.00
❑ 10564	Somethin' Else/Laurie Did It	1969	2.50	5.00	10.00
KAMA SUTRA					
❑ 527	Have You Seen My Baby/Yesterday's Numbers	1971	2.50	5.00	10.00
RCA					
❑ PB-11266	Too Many Cooks/Watch Me Run	1978	—	3.00	6.00
SIRE					
❑ 731	I Can't Hide/Teenage Confidential	1976	—	3.00	6.00

FLAMING EMBER, THE

Number	Title (A Side/B Side)	Yr	VG	VG+	NM
FORTUNE					
❑ 869	Gone, Gone, Gone/You Can Count on Me	1965	15.00	30.00	60.00
HOT WAX					
❑ 6902	Mind, Body and Soul/Filet de Soul	1969	—	3.00	6.00
❑ 6907	Shades of Green/Don't You Wanna Wanna	1969	—	3.00	6.00
❑ 7003	Westbound #9/Why Don't You Stay	1970	—	3.00	6.00
❑ 7006	I'm Not My Brothers Keeper/Deserted Village	1970	—	3.00	6.00
❑ 7010	Stop the World and Let Me Off/Robot in a Robot's World	1970	—	3.00	6.00
❑ 7103	Sunshine/1200 Miles	1971	—	3.00	6.00
❑ 7109	If It's Good to You (Part 1)/If It's Good to You (Part 2)	1971	—	3.00	6.00
RIC-TIC					
❑ 129	Let's Have a Love-In (Vocal)/Let's Have a Love-In (Instrumental)	1967	5.00	10.00	20.00
—B-side credited to Wingate's Love-In Strings					
❑ 131	She's a Real Live Wire/Let's Have a Love-In (Instrumental)	1967	5.00	10.00	20.00
—B-side credited to Wingate's Love-In Strings					
❑ 132	Hey Mama/Let's Have a Love-In	1967	5.00	10.00	20.00
❑ 140	Bless You (My Love) (Instrumental)/Bless You (My Love) (Vocal)	1968	3.75	7.50	15.00
—B-side by Al Kent					
❑ 143	Children (Vocal)/Children (Instrumental)	1968	3.75	7.50	15.00
❑ 145	Tell It Like It Is/Just Like Children	1968	3.75	7.50	15.00

FLAMINGOS, THE

Number	Title (A Side/B Side)	Yr	VG	VG+	NM
CHANCE					
❑ 1133	If I Can't Have You/Someday, Somehow	1953	200.00	400.00	800.00
—Black vinyl					
❑ 1133	If I Can't Have You/Someday, Somehow	1953	1000.	1500.	2000.
—Red vinyl					
❑ 1140	That's My Desire/Hurry Home Baby	1953	150.00	300.00	600.00
—Black vinyl					
❑ 1140	That's My Desire/Hurry Home Baby	1953	375.00	750.00	1500.
—Red vinyl					
❑ 1145	Golden Teardrops/Carried Away	1953	250.00	500.00	1000.
—Black vinyl					
❑ 1145	Golden Teardrops/Carried Away	1953	750.00	1500.	3000.
—Red vinyl					
❑ 1149	Plan for Love/You Ain't Ready	1953	500.00	1000.	2000.
—Yellow and black label					
❑ 1149	Plan for Love/You Ain't Ready	1953	200.00	400.00	800.00
—Blue and silver label					
❑ 1154	Cross Over the Bridge/Listen to My Plea	1954	250.00	500.00	1000.
❑ 1162	Jump Children/Blues in the Letter	1954	150.00	300.00	600.00
CHECKER					
❑ 815	That's My Baby (Chick-a-Boom)/When	1955	20.00	40.00	80.00
❑ 821	I Want to Love You/Please Come Back Home	1955	20.00	40.00	80.00
❑ 830	I'll Be Home/Need Your Love	1956	20.00	40.00	80.00
❑ 837	A Kiss from Your Lips/Get With It	1956	20.00	40.00	80.00
❑ 846	The Vow/Shilly Dilly	1956	20.00	40.00	80.00
❑ 853	Just for a Kick/Would I Be Crying	1957	20.00	40.00	80.00
—Originals of above Checker singles are maroon with a checkerboard at top of label					
❑ 915	Whispering Stars/Dream of a Lifetime	1959	12.50	25.00	50.00
❑ 1084	Lover Come Back to Me/Your Little Guy	1964	3.75	7.50	15.00
❑ 1091	Goodnight Sweetheart/Does It Really Matter	1964	3.75	7.50	15.00
DECCA					
❑ 30335	The Ladder of Love/Let's Make Up	1957	7.50	15.00	30.00
❑ 30454	Helpless/My Faith in You	1957	7.50	15.00	30.00
❑ 30687	Rock and Roll March/Where Mary Go	1958	7.50	15.00	30.00
❑ 30880	Kiss-A Me/Ever Since I Met Lucy	1959	7.50	15.00	30.00
❑ 30948	Jerri-Lee/Hey Now	1959	7.50	15.00	30.00
END					
❑ 1035	Please Wait for Me/That Love Is You	1958	15.00	30.00	60.00
❑ 1035	Lovers Never Say Goodbye/That Love Is You	1958	10.00	20.00	40.00
—A-sides of End 1035 are the same song, the titles were changed					
❑ 1040	I Shed a Tear at Your Wedding/But Not for Me	1959	7.50	15.00	30.00
❑ 1044	At the Prom/Love Walked In	1959	10.00	20.00	40.00
❑ 1046 [M]	I Only Have Eyes for You/Goodnight Sweetheart	1959	7.50	15.00	30.00
❑ 1046 [M]	I Only Have Eyes for You/At the Prom	1959	6.25	12.50	25.00
❑ 1046 [M]	I Only Have Eyes for You/Love Walked In	1959	6.25	12.50	25.00
❑ 1046 [S]	I Only Have Eyes for You/At the Prom	1959	12.50	25.00	50.00
—This B-side has been confirmed for the stereo version; others are not yet known					
❑ 1055 [M]	Yours/Love Walked In	1959	6.25	12.50	25.00
❑ 1055 [S]	Yours/Love Walked In	1959	12.50	25.00	50.00
❑ 1062	I Was Such a Fool/Heavenly Angel	1959	6.25	12.50	25.00
❑ 1065	Mio Amore/You, Me and the Sea	1960	6.25	12.50	25.00
❑ 1068	Nobody Loves Me Like You/Besame Mucho	1960	7.50	15.00	30.00
❑ 1068	Nobody Loves Me Like You/You, Me and the Sea	1960	6.25	12.50	25.00
❑ 1070	Besame Mucho/You, Me and the Sea	1960	6.25	12.50	25.00
❑ 1073	Mio Amore/At Night	1960	5.00	10.00	20.00
❑ 1079	Beside You/When I Fall in Love	1960	5.00	10.00	20.00
❑ 1081	Your Other Love/Lovers Gotta Cry	1960	5.00	10.00	20.00
❑ 1085	Thatr's Why I Love You/Ko Ko Mo	1961	5.00	10.00	20.00
❑ 1092	Time Was/Dream Girl	1961	5.00	10.00	20.00
❑ 1099	My Memories of You/I Want to Love You	1961	5.00	10.00	20.00
❑ 1111	It Must Be Love/I'm No Fool Anymore	1962	5.00	10.00	20.00
❑ 1116	For All We Know/Near You	1962	5.00	10.00	20.00
❑ 1121	I Know Better/Flame of Love	1963	5.00	10.00	20.00
❑ 1124	(Talk About) True Love/Come to My Party	1963	5.00	10.00	20.00
JULMAR					
❑ 506	Dealin' (Groovin' with Feelin')/Dealin' All the Way	1969	2.50	5.00	10.00
MERCURY					
❑ 72455	Temptation/Call Her on the Phone	1965	—	—	—
—Cancelled					
PARROT					
❑ 808	Dream of a Lifetime/On My Merry Way	1954	200.00	400.00	800.00
—Black vinyl					
❑ 808	Dream of a Lifetime/On My Merry Way	1954	400.00	800.00	1600.
—Red vinyl					
❑ 811	I Really Don't Want to Know/Get With It	1955	4000.	6000.	8000.
—Red vinyl					
❑ 811	I Really Don't Want to Know/Get With It	1955	2500.	2750.	5000.
—Black vinyl					
❑ 812	I'm Yours/Ko Ko Mo	1955	200.00	400.00	800.00
—Black vinyl					
❑ 812	I'm Yours/Ko Ko Mo	1955	400.00	800.00	1600.
—Red vinyl					
PHILIPS					
❑ 40308	Temptation/Call Her on the Phone	1965	3.75	7.50	15.00
❑ 40347	The Boogaloo Party/The Nearness of You	1965	3.75	7.50	15.00
❑ 40378	Brooklyn Boogaloo/Since My Baby Put Me Down	1966	3.75	7.50	15.00
❑ 40413	Itty Bitty Baby/She Shook My World	1966	3.75	7.50	15.00
❑ 40452	Koo Koo/It Keeps the Doctor Away	1967	3.75	7.50	15.00
❑ 40496	Oh Mary Don't You Worry/Do It, Do It	1967	3.75	7.50	15.00
POLYDOR					
❑ 14019	Buffalo Soldier (Long)/Buffalo Soldier (Short)	1970	2.50	5.00	10.00
❑ 14044	Straighten It Up (Get It Together)/Lover Come Back to Me	1970	2.50	5.00	10.00
RONZE					
❑ 111	Welcome Home/Gotta Have All Your Lovin'	1971	—	2.50	5.00
❑ 115	Someone to Watch Over Me/Heavy Hips	1972	—	2.50	5.00
❑ 116	Love Keeps the Doctor Away (Long)/Love Keeps the Doctor Away (Short)	1972	—	2.50	5.00
ROULETTE					
❑ 4524	Ol' Man River (Part 1)/Ol' Man River (Part 2)	1963	5.00	10.00	20.00
SKYLARK					
❑ 541	If I Could Love You/I Found a New Baby	197?	—	2.50	5.00
TIMES SQUARE					
❑ 102	A Lovely Way to Spend an Evening/Walking My Baby Back Home	1964	3.75	7.50	15.00
VEE JAY					
❑ 384	Golden Teardrops/Carried Away	1961	6.25	12.50	25.00
WORLDS					
❑ 103	Think About Me/(Instrumental)	1974	—	2.50	5.00

7-Inch Extended Plays

Number	Title (A Side/B Side)	Yr	VG	VG+	NM
END					
❑ 205	(contents unknown)	1959	50.00	100.00	200.00
❑ 205 [PS]	The Flamingos	1959	50.00	100.00	200.00

FLARES, THE

Number	Title (A Side/B Side)	Yr	VG	VG+	NM
FELSTED					
❑ 8604	Loving You/Hotcha Cha-Cha Brown	1960	5.00	10.00	20.00
❑ 8607	What Do You Want If You Don't Want Love/Jump and Hump	1960	5.00	10.00	20.00
❑ 8624	Foot Stomping — Part 1/Foot Stomping — Part 2	1961	5.00	10.00	20.00
PRESS					
❑ 2800	Rock and Roll Heaven — Part 1/Rock and Roll Heaven — Part 2	1962	3.75	7.50	15.00
❑ 2802	Doing the Hully Gully/Truck and Trailer	1962	3.75	7.50	15.00
❑ 2803	Madhouse/Make It Be Me	1962	3.75	7.50	15.00
❑ 2807	Do It with Me/Yon He Go	1963	3.75	7.50	15.00
❑ 2808	Hand Clappin'/Shimmy and Stomp	1963	3.75	7.50	15.00
❑ 2810	Monkey Walk/Do It If You Wanna	1963	3.75	7.50	15.00
❑ 2814	I Didn't Lose a Doggone Thing/Write a Song About Me	1964	3.75	7.50	15.00

FLEAS, THE

All-star studio group supposedly with DAVE BURGESS, GLEN CAMPBELL, JERRY FULLER and RICK NELSON!

CHALLENGE

Number	Title (A Side/B Side)	Yr	VG	VG+	NM
9115	Scratchin'/Tears	1961	10.00	20.00	40.00

FLEETWOOD, MICK

Also see FLEETWOOD MAC.

RCA

Number	Title (A Side/B Side)	Yr	VG	VG+	NM
PB-12308	You Weren't in Love/O'Niamali	1981	—	2.00	4.00
PB-13621	I Want You Back/Put Me Right	1983	—	2.00	4.00
PB-13621 [PS]	I Want You Back/Put Me Right	1983	—	2.00	4.00
PB-13739	Angel Come Home/I Give	1984	—	2.00	4.00

FLEETWOOD MAC

Also see LINDSEY BUCKINGHAM; BUCKINGHAM NICKS; BILLY BURNETTE; MICK FLEETWOOD; DANNY KIRWAN; DAVE MASON; CHRISTINE McVIE; STEVIE NICKS; JEREMY SPENCER; BOB WELCH.

BLUE HORIZON

Number	Title (A Side/B Side)	Yr	VG	VG+	NM
304	Hungry Country Woman/Walkin'	1970	3.00	6.00	12.00

—A-side by Otis Spann with Fleetwood Mac; B-side by Otis Spann

DJM

Number	Title (A Side/B Side)	Yr	VG	VG+	NM
1007	Man of the World/Best Girl in the World	1976	—	3.00	6.00

—B-side by Danny Kirwan

EPIC

Number	Title (A Side/B Side)	Yr	VG	VG+	NM
10351	Black Magic Woman/Long Grey Mare	1968	3.75	7.50	15.00
10368	Stop Messin' Around/Need Your Love So Bad	1968	3.00	6.00	12.00
10436	Albatross/Jigsaw Puzzle Blues	1969	3.00	6.00	12.00
11029	Albatross/Black Magic Woman	1973	2.00	4.00	8.00

REPRISE

Number	Title (A Side/B Side)	Yr	VG	VG+	NM
GRE 0119	Rhiannon (Will You Ever Win)/Over My Head	1978	—	—	3.00

—"Back to Back Hits" series

Number	Title (A Side/B Side)	Yr	VG	VG+	NM
0860	Rattlesnake Shake/Coming Your Way	1969	5.00	10.00	20.00
0860 [DJ]	Rattlesnake Shake/Coming Your Way	1969	2.50	5.00	10.00
0883	Oh Well, Part 1/Oh Well, Part 2	1970	4.00	8.00	16.00
0883 [DJ]	Oh Well, Part 1/Oh Well, Part 2	1970	2.50	5.00	10.00
0925	The Green Manalishi (With the Two-Prong Crown)/World In Harmony	1970	4.00	8.00	16.00
0925 [DJ]	The Green Manalishi (With the Two-Prong Crown)/World In Harmony	1970	2.50	5.00	10.00
0984	Jewel-Eyed Judy/Station Man	1971	4.00	8.00	16.00
0984 [DJ]	Jewel-Eyed Judy/Station Man	1971	2.50	5.00	10.00
1057	Sands of Time/Lay It All Down	1971	2.00	4.00	8.00
1077	Oh Well, Part 1/The Green Manalishi (With the Two-Prong Crown)	1971	—	2.50	5.00

—"Back to Back Hits" reissue

Number	Title (A Side/B Side)	Yr	VG	VG+	NM
1093	Sentimental Lady/Sunny Side of Heaven	1972	2.00	4.00	8.00
1159	Remember Me/Dissatisfied	1973	—	3.00	6.00
1172	Did You Ever Love Me/Revelation	1973	—	3.00	6.00
1188	For Your Love/Hypnotized	1973	—	3.00	6.00
1188 [DJ]	For Your Love (Long)/For Your Love (Short)	1973	2.50	5.00	10.00
1317	Heroes Are Hard to Find/Born Enchanter	1974	—	3.00	6.00
1339	Over My Head/I'm So Afraid	1975	—	2.00	4.00
1345	Rhiannon (Will You Ever Win)/Sugar Daddy	1976	—	2.00	4.00
1356	Say You Love Me (Edited)/Monday Morning	1976	—	2.00	4.00

—The A-sides of Reprise 1339, 1345 and 1356 feature significantly different mixes than those on their parent album, "Fleetwood Mac."

Number	Title (A Side/B Side)	Yr	VG	VG+	NM
17300	Silver Springs/Go Your Own Way	1997	—	—	2.50
17300 [PS]	Silver Springs/Go Your Own Way	1997	—	—	2.50

WARNER BROS.

Number	Title (A Side/B Side)	Yr	VG	VG+	NM
GWB 0348	Go Your Own Way/Dreams	1979	—	—	3.00

—"Back to Back Hits" series

Number	Title (A Side/B Side)	Yr	VG	VG+	NM
GWB 0388	Tusk/Sara	1981	—	—	3.00

—"Back to Back Hits" series

Number	Title (A Side/B Side)	Yr	VG	VG+	NM
GWB 0439	Hold Me/Gypsy	1984	—	—	3.00

—"Back to Back Hits" series

Number	Title (A Side/B Side)	Yr	VG	VG+	NM
8304	Go Your Own Way/Silver Springs	1976	2.00	4.00	8.00

—Sought-after because of its non-LP B-side

Number	Title (A Side/B Side)	Yr	VG	VG+	NM
8371	Dreams/Songbird	1977	—	2.00	4.00
8413	Don't Stop/Never Going Back Again	1977	—	2.00	4.00
8413 [PS]	Don't Stop/Never Going Back Again	1977	—	2.50	5.00
8483	You Make Loving Fun/Gold Dust Woman	1977	—	2.00	4.00
18661	Paper Doll/The Chain	1993	—	2.00	4.00
19537	Hard Feelings/Freedom	1990	—	3.00	6.00
19866	Save Me/Another Woman	1990	—	2.00	4.00
19867	Skies the Limit/The Second Time	1990	—	2.00	4.00
21888	Little Lies/Everywhere	1989	—	—	3.00

—"Back to Back Hits" series

Number	Title (A Side/B Side)	Yr	VG	VG+	NM
21943	Big Love/Seven Wonders	1988	—	—	3.00

—"Back to Back Hits" series

Number	Title (A Side/B Side)	Yr	VG	VG+	NM
21990	Don't Stop/Silver Springs	1988	—	—	3.00

—"Back to Back Hits" series

Number	Title (A Side/B Side)	Yr	VG	VG+	NM
21991	You Make Loving Fun/Say You Love Me	1988	—	—	3.00

—"Back to Back Hits" series

Number	Title (A Side/B Side)	Yr	VG	VG+	NM
27644	As Long As You Follow/Oh Well (Live)	1988	—	—	3.00
27644 [PS]	As Long As You Follow/Oh Well (Live)	1988	—	—	3.00
28114	Family Man/Down Endless Street	1988	—	—	3.00
28114 [PS]	Family Man/Down Endless Street	1988	—	—	3.00
28143	Everywhere/When I See You Again	1987	—	—	3.00
28143 [PS]	Everywhere/When I See You Again	1987	—	—	3.00
28291	Little Lies/Ricky	1987	—	—	3.00
28291 [PS]	Little Lies/Ricky	1987	—	—	3.00
28317	Seven Wonders/Book of Miracles	1987	—	—	3.00
28317 [PS]	Seven Wonders/Book of Miracles	1987	—	—	3.00
28398	Big Love/You and I, Part 1	1987	—	—	3.00
28398 [PS]	Big Love/You and I, Part 1	1987	—	—	3.00
29698	Oh Diane/That's Alright	1983	—	—	3.00
29848	Love in Store/Can't Go Back	1983	—	—	3.00
29918	Gypsy/Cool Water	1982	—	—	3.00
29918 [PS]	Gypsy/Cool Water	1982	—	—	3.00
29966	Hold Me/Eyes of the World	1982	—	—	3.00
29966 [PS]	Hold Me/Eyes of the World	1982	—	—	3.00
49077	Tusk/Never Make Me Cry	1979	—	2.00	4.00
49077 [PS]	Tusk/Never Make Me Cry	1979	—	2.50	5.00

—Version 1: Brown print, small dog photo

Number	Title (A Side/B Side)	Yr	VG	VG+	NM
49077 [PS]	Tusk/Never Make Me Cry	1979	—	2.00	4.00

—Version 2: Black print, large dog photo

Number	Title (A Side/B Side)	Yr	VG	VG+	NM
49150	Sara/That's Enough for Me	1979	—	2.00	4.00
49150 [PS]	Sara/That's Enough for Me	1979	—	3.00	6.00
49196	Think About Me/Save Me a Place	1980	—	2.00	4.00
49196 [PS]	Think About Me/Save Me a Place	1980	—	3.00	6.00
49500	Sisters of the Moon/Walk a Thin Line	1980	2.50	5.00	10.00

—Scarce on stock copy; A-side is a different mix than the LP version

Number	Title (A Side/B Side)	Yr	VG	VG+	NM
49660	Fireflies/Over My Head (Live)	1981	—	2.00	4.00
49660 [PS]	Fireflies/Over My Head (Live)	1981	—	2.00	4.00
49700	The Farmer's Daughter/Monday Morning (Live)	1982	—	3.00	6.00
49700 [PS]	The Farmer's Daughter/Monday Morning (Live)	1982	—	3.00	6.00

FLEETWOODS, THE

DOLPHIN

Number	Title (A Side/B Side)	Yr	VG	VG+	NM
1	Come Softly to Me/I Care So Much	1959	6.25	12.50	25.00

DOLTON

Number	Title (A Side/B Side)	Yr	VG	VG+	NM
3	Graduation's Here/Oh Lord, Let It Be	1959	5.00	10.00	20.00
S-3 [S]	Graduation's Here/Oh Lord, Let It Be	1959	12.50	25.00	50.00
5	Mr. Blue/You Mean Everything to Me	1959	5.00	10.00	20.00
15	Outside My Window/Magic Star	1960	5.00	10.00	20.00
22	Runaround/Truly Do	1960	5.00	10.00	20.00
22 [PS]	Runaround/Truly Do	1960	12.50	25.00	50.00
27	The Last One to Know/Dormilona	1960	3.75	7.50	15.00
30	Confidential/I Love You So	1960	3.75	7.50	15.00
40	Tragedy/Little Miss Sad One	1961	3.75	7.50	15.00
45	(He's) The Great Impostor/Poor Little Girl	1961	3.75	7.50	15.00
49	Billy Old Buddy/Trouble	1962	3.75	7.50	15.00
62	They Tell Me It's Summer/Lovers by Night, Strangers by Day	1962	3.75	7.50	15.00
74	You Should Have Been There/Sure Is Lonesome Downtown	1963	3.75	7.50	15.00
75	Goodnight My Love/Jimmy Beware	1963	3.75	7.50	15.00
86	Baby Bye-O/What'll I Do	1963	2.50	5.00	10.00
93	Lonesome Town/Ruby Red Baby Blue	1964	2.50	5.00	10.00
97	Ten Times Blue/Ska Light Ska Bright	1964	2.50	5.00	10.00
98	Mr. Sandman/This Is My Prayer	1964	2.50	5.00	10.00
302	Before and After (Losing You)/Lonely Is As Lonely Does	1964	2.50	5.00	10.00
307	Come Softly to Me/I'm Not Jimmy	1965	2.50	5.00	10.00
310	Rainbow/Just As I Need You	1965	2.50	5.00	10.00
315	For Lovin' Me/This Is Where I See Her	1965	2.50	5.00	10.00

LIBERTY

Number	Title (A Side/B Side)	Yr	VG	VG+	NM
62	They Tell Me It's Summer/Lovers by Night, Strangers by Day	1970	3.75	7.50	15.00

—Odd reissue keeping the Dolton number

Number	Title (A Side/B Side)	Yr	VG	VG+	NM
55188 [M]	Come Softly to Me/I Care So Much	1959	6.25	12.50	25.00
77188 [S]	Come Softly to Me/I Care So Much	1959	12.50	25.00	50.00

UNITED ARTISTS

Number	Title (A Side/B Side)	Yr	VG	VG+	NM
0038	Come Softly to Me/Runaround	1973	—	2.00	4.00
0039	Mr. Blue/Tragedy	1973	—	2.00	4.00
0040	He's the Great Impostor/Goodnight My Love	1973	—	2.00	4.00

—0038, 0039 and 0040 are "Silver Spotlight Series" reissues

Number	Title (A Side/B Side)	Yr	VG	VG+	NM
XW515	(He's) The Great Impostor/Goodnight My Love	1974	—	2.00	4.00

—Reissue

7-Inch Extended Plays

DOLTON

Number	Title (A Side/B Side)	Yr	VG	VG+	NM
BEP-502	Runaround/Mr. Blue//Outside My Window/Come Softly to Me	1960	15.00	30.00	60.00
BEP-502 [PS]	The Fleetwoods	1960	22.50	45.00	90.00

FLEMONS, WADE

Also see EARTH, WIND AND FIRE.

VEE JAY

Number	Title (A Side/B Side)	Yr	VG	VG+	NM
295	Here I Stand/My Baby Likes to Rock	1958	7.50	15.00	30.00
309	Hold Me Close/You'll Remain Forever	1959	7.50	15.00	30.00
321	Slow Motion/Wailing by the River	1959	7.50	15.00	30.00
335	Goodnite, It's Time To Go/What's Happening	1959	7.50	15.00	30.00
344	Easy Lovin'/Woops Now	1960	7.50	15.00	30.00
368	Ain't That Lovin' You Baby/I'll Come Runnin'	1960	5.00	10.00	20.00
377	At the Party/Devil in Your Soul	1961	5.00	10.00	20.00
389	Please Send Me Someone to Love/Keep On Loving Me	1961	5.00	10.00	20.00
427	Half a Love/Welcome Stranger	1962	5.00	10.00	20.00
471	Ain't These Tears/I Hope, I Think, I Wish	1962	5.00	10.00	20.00
533	That Time of the Year/I Came Running	1963	3.75	7.50	15.00
578	When It Rains, It Pours/Watch Over Her	1964	3.75	7.50	15.00

—The Four Seasons sing backup on this record

Number	Title (A Side/B Side)	Yr	VG	VG+	NM
614	I Knew You When/That Other Place	1964	3.75	7.50	15.00
668	Where Did You Go Last Night/Empty Balcony	1965	3.00	6.00	12.00

FLESH GORDON AND THE NUDE HOLLYWOOD ARGYLES

Also see THE HOLLYWOOD ARGYLES.

PARAMOUNT

Number	Title (A Side/B Side)	Yr	VG	VG+	NM
0289	Superstreaker/Naked	1974	3.00	6.00	12.00

FLINT, SHELBY

CADENCE

Number	Title (A Side/B Side)	Yr	VG	VG+	NM
1352	Oh, I Miss Him So/I Will Love You	1958	3.75	7.50	15.00

VALIANT

Number	Title (A Side/B Side)	Yr	VG	VG+	NM
701	Angel on My Shoulder/I Will Love You	1965	2.00	4.00	8.00
716	Joy in the Morning/Lonely Cinderella	1965	2.00	4.00	8.00
743	Cast Your Fate to the Wind/The Lily	1966	2.00	4.00	8.00
6001	Angel on My Shoulder/Someday	1960	3.00	6.00	12.00
6010	I Will Love You/Every Night	1961	2.50	5.00	10.00
6014	A Broken Vow/Magic Wand	1961	2.50	5.00	10.00
6017	The Riddle Song/I Love a Wanderer	1962	2.50	5.00	10.00
6022	The Boy I Love/Ugly Duckling	1962	2.50	5.00	10.00

Number	Title (A Side/B Side)	Yr	VG	VG+	NM
❑ 6031	Little Dancing Doll/It Really Doesn't Matter	1963	2.50	5.00	10.00
❑ 6052	Wonderland/Pipes of Keith	1964	2.50	5.00	10.00
❑ 6060	I've Grown Accustomed to Her (Your) Face/Our Town	1964	2.50	5.00	10.00

FLINTSTONE, FRED

EPIC

Number	Title (A Side/B Side)	Yr	VG	VG+	NM
❑ 9475	Bedrock Beat/Stone Age Roll	1961	5.00	10.00	20.00

FLIRTATIONS, THE (1)

Female vocal group.

DERAM

Number	Title (A Side/B Side)	Yr	VG	VG+	NM
❑ 7531	Give Me Love, Love, Love/This Must Be the End	1970	2.00	4.00	8.00
❑ 85036	Christmas Time Is Here Again/Nothing But a Heartache	1968	2.00	4.00	8.00
❑ 85038	Nothing But a Heartache/How Can You Tell Me	1969	—	3.00	6.00
❑ 85048	Need Your Loving/South Caroline	1969	—	3.00	6.00
❑ 85057	I Wanna Be There/Keep On Searching	1970	—	3.00	6.00
❑ 85062	Can't Stop Lovin' You/Everybody Needs Somebody	1970	—	3.00	6.00

PARROT

Number	Title (A Side/B Side)	Yr	VG	VG+	NM
❑ 40028	Somewhere Out There/How Can You Tell Me	1968	3.00	6.00	12.00

FLIRTATIONS, THE (2)

Male vocal group.

FESTIVAL

Number	Title (A Side/B Side)	Yr	VG	VG+	NM
❑ 705	Stronger Than Her Love/Settle Down	1967	15.00	30.00	60.00

FLIRTATIONS, THE (U)

May be group (2), or perhaps a completely different group.

JOSIE

Number	Title (A Side/B Side)	Yr	VG	VG+	NM
❑ 956	Natural Born Lover/Change My Darkness Into Light	1965	3.75	7.50	15.00

FLO AND EDDIE

Also see THE TURTLES.

COLUMBIA

Number	Title (A Side/B Side)	Yr	VG	VG+	NM
❑ 10028	Come to My Rescue, Webelos/Let Me Make Love to You	1974	—	3.00	6.00
❑ 10204	Come to My Rescue, Webelos/Let Me Make Love to You	1975	—	2.50	5.00
❑ 10264	Illegal, Immoral and Fattening/Rebecca	1975	—	2.50	5.00
❑ 10425	Elenore/The Love You Gave Away	1976	—	2.50	5.00
❑ 10458	Keep It Warm/Hot	1976	—	2.50	5.00

REPRISE

Number	Title (A Side/B Side)	Yr	VG	VG+	NM
❑ 1113	Nikki Hoi/Godbye Surprise	1972	—	2.50	5.00
❑ 1142	Afterglow/Original Soundtract from "Carlos & De Bull"	1972	—	2.50	5.00
❑ 1160	If We Only Had the Time/You're a Lady	1973	—	2.50	5.00

FLORIDIANS, THE

ABC-PARAMOUNT

Number	Title (A Side/B Side)	Yr	VG	VG+	NM
❑ 10185	That Lucky Old Sun/I Love Marie	1961	12.50	25.00	50.00

FLOWERPOT MEN, THE

DERAM

Number	Title (A Side/B Side)	Yr	VG	VG+	NM
❑ 7513	Let's Go to San Francisco/Let's Go to San Francisco, Part 2	1967	3.75	7.50	15.00
—As "The Flower Pots"					
❑ 7516	Am I Losing You/A Walk in the Sky	1968	3.75	7.50	15.00
❑ 85051	A Moment of Madness/Young Birds Fly	1969	3.00	6.00	12.00

FLOYD, EDDIE

Also see THE FALCONS.

ATLANTIC

Number	Title (A Side/B Side)	Yr	VG	VG+	NM
❑ 2275	Hush Hush/Drive On	1965	3.00	6.00	12.00

LUPINE

Number	Title (A Side/B Side)	Yr	VG	VG+	NM
❑ 115	Set My Soul on Fire/Will I Be the One	1963	3.75	7.50	15.00

MALACO

Number	Title (A Side/B Side)	Yr	VG	VG+	NM
❑ 1032	Somebody Touch Me/Never Too Old	1976	—	2.50	5.00
❑ 1035	Chi-Town Hustler/In Paradise	1976	—	2.50	5.00
❑ 1039	Special Christmas Day/Mother, My Dear Mother	1976	—	2.50	5.00
❑ 1040	We Should Really Be in Love/I'll Never Be Loved	1977	—	2.50	5.00
—With Dorothy Moore					
❑ 1043	You're Gonna Walk Out on Me/Prove It to Me	1977	—	2.50	5.00

MERCURY

Number	Title (A Side/B Side)	Yr	VG	VG+	NM
❑ 73964	If You Really Love Me/It's Me	1977	—	2.00	4.00
❑ 74003	Disco Summer/Do It in the Water	1978	—	2.00	4.00

SAFICE

Number	Title (A Side/B Side)	Yr	VG	VG+	NM
❑ 336	Can This Be Christmas/I'll Be Home For Christmas	1964	3.00	6.00	12.00

STAX

Number	Title (A Side/B Side)	Yr	VG	VG+	NM
❑ 0002	I've Never Found a Girl (To Love Me Like You Do)/I'm Just the Kind of Fool	1968	—	3.00	6.00
❑ 0012	Bring It On Home to Me/The Sweet Things You Do	1968	—	3.00	6.00
❑ 0025	I've Got to Have Your Love/Girl I Love You	1969	—	3.00	6.00
❑ 0036	Don't Tell Your Mama (Where You've Been)/Consider Me	1969	—	3.00	6.00
❑ 0041	Never Never Let You Go/Ain't That Good	1969	—	3.00	6.00
—With Mavis Staples					
❑ 0051	Why Is the Wine Sweeter (On the Other Side)/People Get It Together	1969	—	3.00	6.00
❑ 0060	California Girl/The Woodman	1970	—	3.00	6.00
❑ 0072	My Girl/Laurie	1970	—	3.00	6.00
❑ 0077	The Best Years of My Life/My Little Girl	1970	—	3.00	6.00
❑ 0087	Oh How It Rained/When My Baby Said Goodbye	1971	—	3.00	6.00
❑ 0095	Blood Is Thicker Than Water/Have You Heard the Word	1971	—	3.00	6.00
❑ 0109	Yum Yum Yum (I Want Some)/Tears of Joy	1971	—	3.00	6.00
❑ 0134	You're Good Enough (To Be My Baby)/Spend All You Have on Love	1972	—	3.00	6.00
❑ 0158	Knock on Wood/Lay Your Loving on Me	1973	—	3.00	6.00
❑ 0171	Baby Lay Your Head Down (Gently on My Bed)/Check Me Out	1973	—	3.00	6.00
❑ 187	Things Get Better/Good Love, Bad Love	1966	3.00	6.00	12.00
❑ 0188	I Wanna Do Things for You/We've Been Through Too Much Together	1973	—	3.00	6.00
❑ 194	Knock on Wood/Got to Make a Comeback	1966	3.75	7.50	15.00
❑ 208	Raise Your Hand/I've Just Been Feeling Bad	1967	2.50	5.00	10.00
❑ 0209	Guess Who/Something to Write Home About	1974	—	3.00	6.00
❑ 0216	Soul Street/Highway Man	1974	—	3.00	6.00
❑ 219	Don't Rock the Boat/This House	1967	2.50	5.00	10.00
❑ 223	Love Is a Doggone Good Thing/Hey Now	1967	2.50	5.00	10.00
❑ 0232	Stealing Love/I Got a Reason to Smile	1974	—	3.00	6.00
❑ 233	On a Saturday Night/Under My Nose	1967	2.50	5.00	10.00
❑ 0239	Talk to the Man/I Got a Reason to Smile	1975	—	3.00	6.00
❑ 246	Holding On with Both Hands/Big Bird	1968	2.50	5.00	10.00
❑ 0251	I'm So Glad I Met You/I'm So Grateful	1975	—	3.00	6.00

FLYERS, THE

ATCO

Number	Title (A Side/B Side)	Yr	VG	VG+	NM
❑ 6088	On Bended Knee/My Only Desire	1957	10.00	20.00	40.00

FLYING BURRITO BROTHERS, THE

Includes records as "The Burrito Brothers." Also see GRAM PARSONS.

A&M

Number	Title (A Side/B Side)	Yr	VG	VG+	NM
❑ 1067	Train Song/Hot Burrito #1	1969	2.00	4.00	8.00
❑ 1166	If You Gotta Go, Go Now/Cody, Cody	1970	2.00	4.00	8.00
❑ 1189	Down in the Churchyard/Older Guys	1970	2.00	4.00	8.00
❑ 1277	White Line Fever/Colorado	1971	2.00	4.00	8.00

COLUMBIA

Number	Title (A Side/B Side)	Yr	VG	VG+	NM
❑ 10229	Building Fires/Hot Burrito No. 3	1975	—	2.50	5.00
❑ 10287	Bon Soir Blues/Hot Burrito No. 3	1976	—	2.50	5.00
❑ 10389	Big Bayou/Waiting for Love to Begin	1976	—	2.50	5.00

CURB

Number	Title (A Side/B Side)	Yr	VG	VG+	NM
❑ 01011	Does She Wish She Was Single Again/Oh Lonesome Me	1981	—	2.00	4.00
—As "Burrito Brothers"					
❑ 02243	She Belongs to Everyone But Me/Why Must the Ending Always Be So Sad	1981	—	2.00	4.00
—As "Burrito Brothers"					
❑ 02641	If Something Should Come Between Us/Damned If I'll Be Lonely Tonight	1981	—	2.00	4.00
—As "Burrito Brothers"					
❑ 02667	If Something Should Come Between Us	1982	—	2.00	4.00
—As "Burrito Brothers"					
❑ 02835	Closer to You/Coast to Coast	1982	—	2.00	4.00
—As "Burrito Brothers"					
❑ 03023	I'm Drinkin' Canada Dry/How'd We Ever Get This Way	1982	—	2.00	4.00
—As "Burrito Brothers"					
❑ 03314	Blue and Broken Hearted Me/Our Roots Are Country Music	1982	—	2.00	4.00
—As "Burrito Brothers"					
❑ 5402	She's a Friend of a Friend/(B-side unknown)	1981	—	2.00	4.00
—As "Burrito Brothers"					

MCA CURB

Number	Title (A Side/B Side)	Yr	VG	VG+	NM
❑ 52329	Almost Saturday Night/Juke Box Kind of Night	1983	—	—	3.00
—As "Burrito Brothers"					
❑ 52379	My Kind of Lady/Dream Chaser	1984	—	—	3.00
—As "Burrito Brothers"					

REGENCY

Number	Title (A Side/B Side)	Yr	VG	VG+	NM
❑ 45001	White Line Fever/(B-side unknown)	1980	—	3.00	6.00

FLYING MACHINE, THE

This is a British group, no relation to the American group that featured JAMES TAYLOR.

CONGRESS

Number	Title (A Side/B Side)	Yr	VG	VG+	NM
❑ 6000	Smile a Little Smile for Me/Maybe We've Been Loving Too Long	1969	2.00	4.00	8.00
❑ 6012	There She Goes/Baby Make It Soon	1970	—	3.00	6.00

JANUS

Number	Title (A Side/B Side)	Yr	VG	VG+	NM
❑ 121	Hanging on the Edge of Sadness/My Baby's Coming Home	1970	—	3.00	6.00
❑ 137	Hey Little Girl/The Devil Has Possession of My Mind	1971	—	3.00	6.00

FOGERTY, JOHN

Includes records as "The Blue Ridge Rangers." Also see CREEDENCE CLEARWATER REVIVAL; TOMMY FOGERTY AND THE BLUE VELVETS; THE GOLLIWOGS.

ASYLUM

Number	Title (A Side/B Side)	Yr	VG	VG+	NM
❑ 45274	Rockin' All Over the World/The Wall	1975	—	2.50	5.00
❑ 45293	Almost Saturday Night/Sea Cruise	1975	—	2.50	5.00
❑ 45309	You Got the Magic/Evil Thing	1976	—	2.50	5.00

ELEKTRA

Number	Title (A Side/B Side)	Yr	VG	VG+	NM
❑ 45309 [DJ]	You Got the Magic (stereo/mono)	1976	2.50	5.00	10.00
—Promo-only version with wrong label					

FANTASY

Number	Title (A Side/B Side)	Yr	VG	VG+	NM
❑ 683	Blue Ridge Mountain Blues/Have Thine Own Way, Lord	1972	—	2.50	5.00
—As "The Blue Ridge Rangers"					
❑ 683 [PS]	Blue Ridge Mountain Blues/Have Thine Own Way, Lord	1972	3.75	7.50	15.00
—As "The Blue Ridge Rangers"					
❑ 689	Jambalaya (On the Bayou)/Workin' on a Building	1972	—	3.00	6.00
—As "The Blue Ridge Rangers"; green, red and orange label					
❑ 689	Jambalaya (On the Bayou)/Workin' on a Building	1972	—	2.50	5.00
—As "The Blue Ridge Rangers"; brown label					
❑ 700	Hearts of Stone/Somewhere Listening	1973	—	2.50	5.00
—As "The Blue Ridge Rangers"					
❑ 710	Back in the Hills/You Don't Own Me	1973	—	2.50	5.00
—As "The Blue Ridge Rangers"					
❑ 717	Coming Down the Road/Ricochet	1973	—	2.50	5.00

Number	Title (A Side/B Side)	Yr	VG	VG+	NM
REPRISE					
❑ 17191	Premonition/Born on the Bayou	1998	—	—	3.00
❑ 17192	Almost Saturday Night/Who'll Stop the Rain	1998	—	—	3.00
WARNER BROS.					
❑ 17283	Blueboy/Bad Bad Boy	1997	—	—	3.00
❑ 28535	Change in the Weather/My Toot Toot	1986	—	2.00	4.00
❑ 28535 [PS]	Change in the Weather/My Toot Toot	1986	—	2.00	4.00
❑ 28657	Eye of the Zombie/I Confess	1986	—	2.00	4.00
❑ 28657 [PS]	Eye of the Zombie/I Confess	1986	—	2.00	4.00
❑ 29053	Rock and Roll Girls/Centerfield	1985	—	2.00	4.00
❑ 29053 [PS]	Rock and Roll Girls/Centerfield	1985	—	2.00	4.00
❑ 29100	The Old Man Down the Road/Big Train (From Memphis)	1985	—	2.00	4.00
❑ 29100 [PS]	The Old Man Down the Road/Big Train (From Memphis)	1985	—	2.00	4.00

FOGERTY, TOM

Also see CREEDENCE CLEARWATER REVIVAL; TOMMY FOGERTY AND THE BLUE VELVETS; THE GOLLIWOGS.

Number	Title (A Side/B Side)	Yr	VG	VG+	NM
FANTASY					
❑ 661	Goodbye, Media Man/Goodbye, Media Man (Part 2)	1971	—	2.50	5.00
❑ 661 [PS]	Goodbye, Media Man/Goodbye, Media Man (Part 2)	1971	2.50	5.00	10.00
❑ 680	Cast the First Stone/Lady of Fatima	1972	—	2.50	5.00
❑ 691	Forty Years/Faces, Places, People	1972	—	2.50	5.00
❑ 702	Heartbeat/Joyful Resurrection	1973	—	2.50	5.00
❑ 715	Mystic Island Avalon/Reggie	1973	—	2.50	5.00
❑ 726	It's Been a Good Day/Money	1974	—	2.50	5.00
❑ 737	Sweet Things to Come/There Was a Time	1974	—	2.50	5.00

FOGERTY, TOMMY, AND THE BLUE VELVETS

Early version of THE GOLLIWOGS, which was an early version of CREEDENCE CLEARWATER REVIVAL.

Number	Title (A Side/B Side)	Yr	VG	VG+	NM
ORCHESTRA					
❑ 1010	Have You Ever Been Lonely/Bonita	1961	20.00	40.00	80.00
❑ 6177	Come On Baby/Oh! My Love	1961	20.00	40.00	80.00
❑ (# unknown)	Yes, You Did/Now You're Not Mine	1962	20.00	40.00	80.00

FOGHAT

Number	Title (A Side/B Side)	Yr	VG	VG+	NM
BEARSVILLE					
❑ 0008	I Just Want to Make Love to You/Hole to Hide In	1973	—	2.50	5.00
❑ 0014	What a Shame/Helping Hand	1973	—	2.50	5.00
❑ 0019	That'll Be the Day/Wild Cherry	1974	—	2.50	5.00
❑ 0021	Maybelline/Step Outside	1974	—	2.50	5.00
❑ 0306	Slow Ride/Save Your Loving	1975	—	2.50	5.00
❑ 0307	Fool for the City/Take It or Leave It	1976	—	2.50	5.00
❑ 0313	Drivin' Wheel/Night Shift	1976	—	2.00	4.00
❑ 0315	I'll Be Standing By/Take Me to the River	1977	—	2.00	4.00
❑ 0319	I Just Want to Make Love to You (Live)/Fool for the City (Live)	1977	—	2.00	4.00
❑ 0325	Stone Blue/Chevrolet	1978	—	2.00	4.00
❑ 0329	High on Love/Sweet Home Chicago	1978	—	2.00	4.00
❑ PRO-S-780 [DJ]	Run, Run, Rudolph (same on both sides)	1978	2.50	5.00	10.00
❑ PRO-S-1002 [DJ]	All I Want For Christmas Is You (same on both sides)	1981	2.50	5.00	10.00
❑ 29612	Seven Day Weekend/That's What Love Can Do	1983	—	2.00	4.00
❑ 29860	Slipped, Tripped, Fell in Love/And I Do Just What I Want	1982	—	2.00	4.00
❑ 49125	Third Time Lucky (First Time I Was a Fool)/Love in Motion	1979	—	2.00	4.00
❑ 49125 [PS]	Third Time Lucky (First Time I Was a Fool)/Love in Motion	1979	—	2.50	5.00
❑ 49510	Stranger in My Home Town/Be My Woman	1980	—	2.00	4.00
❑ 49779	Wide Boy/Love Zone	1981	—	2.00	4.00
❑ 49779 [PS]	Wide Boy/Love Zone	1981	—	3.00	6.00
FOGHAT					
❑ 1069	Goin' Home For Christmas/Santa Claus Is Back In Town	1986	—	3.00	6.00
❑ 1069 [PS]	Goin' Home For Christmas/Santa Claus Is Back In Town	1986	—	3.00	6.00

FOLDS, BEN, FIVE

Number	Title (A Side/B Side)	Yr	VG	VG+	NM
550 MUSIC					
❑ 79018	Brick (Radio Mix)/Fair	1998	—	—	3.00
❑ 79186	Army//Leather Jackets/Birds	1999	—	—	2.00
❑ 79186 [PS]	Army//Leather Jackets/Birds	1999	—	—	2.00
D-TOX					
❑ (no #)	Jackson Cannery/Eddie Walker, This Is Your Life	1994	10.00	20.00	40.00
❑ (no #) [PS]	Jackson Cannery/Eddie Walker, This Is Your Life	1994	10.00	20.00	40.00

FONTAINE, EDDIE

Number	Title (A Side/B Side)	Yr	VG	VG+	NM
ARGO					
❑ 5309	Nothin' Shakin'/Don't Ya Know	1958	6.25	12.50	25.00
CHANCELLOR					
❑ 1018	Goodness, It's Gladys/Middle of the Road	1958	5.00	10.00	20.00
DECCA					
❑ 30042	Cool It Baby/Into Each Life Some Rain Must Fall	1956	6.25	12.50	25.00
❑ 30108	A Rose and a Baby Ruth/The Years Before	1956	6.25	12.50	25.00
❑ 30121	As Far As I'm Concerned/'Til Tonight	1956	6.25	12.50	25.00
—With Karen Chandler					
❑ 30202	I'll Be There/East of Mississippi	1957	6.25	12.50	25.00
❑ 30256	Money/Homesick Blues	1957	6.25	12.50	25.00
❑ 30338	Hey Marie, Rock with Me/The One and Only	1957	6.25	12.50	25.00
❑ 30446	Fun Lovin'/Honky Tonk Man	1957	6.25	12.50	25.00
JALO					
❑ 102	Where Is Da Woman/It Ain't Gonna Happen No More	1956	20.00	40.00	80.00
LIBERTY					
❑ 55776	Blue Roses/Way Down Home	1965	2.50	5.00	10.00
❑ 55823	I Need You/It Can Happen to You	1965	2.50	5.00	10.00
SUNBEAM					
❑ 105	Nothin' Shakin'/Oh, Wonderful Night	1958	10.00	20.00	40.00
❑ 112	Nobody Can Handle This Job/I'm Ready As I'll Ever Be	1958	6.25	12.50	25.00
—B-side by Gerry Granahan					
❑ 118	Love Eyes/Something Cha Cha	1958	6.25	12.50	25.00
VIK					
❑ 0184	Turn the Light On/Boom-De-De-Boom	1955	6.25	12.50	25.00
❑ 0193	Here 'Tis/I Look at You	1956	6.25	12.50	25.00
❑ 0203	Stand On That Rock/Baby You Did This to Me	1956	6.25	12.50	25.00
WARNER BROS.					
❑ 5313	My Heart Belongs to You/I'm Gonna Settle Down	1962	3.75	7.50	15.00
❑ 5345	(It's No) Sin/All I Want Is You	1963	3.75	7.50	15.00
"X"					
❑ 0096	Rock Love/All My Love Belongs to You	1955	7.50	15.00	30.00
❑ 0108	On Bended Knees/I Miss You So	1955	7.50	15.00	30.00
❑ 0128	Rollin' Stone/I'm Through Chasin' After You	1955	7.50	15.00	30.00
❑ 0151	Poor Little Monday/The Rain Song	1955	7.50	15.00	30.00
❑ 0184	Turn the Light On/Boom-De-De-Boom	1955	7.50	15.00	30.00
❑ 0193	Here 'Tis/I Look at You	1956	7.50	15.00	30.00
❑ 0203	Stand On That Rock/Baby You Did This to Me	1956	7.50	15.00	30.00

FONTAINE, FRANK

Number	Title (A Side/B Side)	Yr	VG	VG+	NM
ABC-PARAMOUNT					
❑ 10384	When Your Hair Has Turned to Silver/Here in My Heart	1962	2.00	4.00	8.00
❑ 10384 [PS]	When Your Hair Has Turned to Silver/Here in My Heart	1962	3.00	6.00	12.00
❑ 10430	Easter Parade/Always	1963	2.00	4.00	8.00
❑ 10491	Daddy's Little Girl/Oh How I Miss You Tonight	1963	2.00	4.00	8.00
❑ 10517	RSVP/Alouette, Sweet Alouette	1964	2.00	4.00	8.00
❑ 10574	Any Man Who Loves His Mother/When Your Old Wedding Ring Was New	1964	2.00	4.00	8.00
❑ 10618	Mexicali Rose/I'm Counting on You	1965	2.00	4.00	8.00
❑ 10662	I Ain't Got Nobody/Someday	1965	2.00	4.00	8.00
CAPITOL					
❑ 4929	John L.C. Savoney The Sweepstakes Winner/The Maharajah	1963	2.00	4.00	8.00
—B-side by Lou Holtz					
❑ 4929 [PS]	John L.C. Savoney The Sweepstakes Winner/The Maharajah	1963	3.00	6.00	12.00
MGM					
❑ 12129	Everybody Rocks/Livin' It Up	1955	15.00	30.00	60.00

FONTANA, WAYNE

Also see WAYNE FONTANA AND THE MINDBENDERS.

Number	Title (A Side/B Side)	Yr	VG	VG+	NM
BRUT					
❑ 812	Sweet America/Interested	1973	—	2.50	5.00
METROMEDIA					
❑ 133	Say Goodbye to Yesterday/Dayton, Ohio	1969	—	3.00	6.00
MGM					
❑ 13456	It Was Easier to Hurt Her/You Made Me What I Am Today	1966	2.00	4.00	8.00
❑ 13516	Come On Home/My Eyes	1966	2.00	4.00	8.00
❑ 13661	Pamela, Pamela/Something Keeps Calling Me Back	1967	—	3.00	6.00
❑ 13762	From a Boy to a Girl/24 Sycamore	1967	—	3.00	6.00

FONTANA, WAYNE, AND THE MINDBENDERS

Also see WAYNE FONTANA; THE MINDBENDERS.

Number	Title (A Side/B Side)	Yr	VG	VG+	NM
A&M					
❑ 3010	Game of Love/What a Wonderful World	1988	—	2.00	4.00
—B-side by Louis Armstrong					
❑ 3010 [PS]	Game of Love/What a Wonderful World	1988	—	2.00	4.00
—"Good Morning Vietnam" sleeve					
FONTANA					
❑ 1503	Game of Love/Since You've Been Gone	1965	3.75	7.50	15.00
❑ 1509	Game of Love/One More Time	1965	3.00	6.00	12.00
❑ 1514	It's Just a Little Bit Too Late/Long Time Comin'	1965	2.50	5.00	10.00
❑ 1524	She Needs Love/Like I Do	1965	2.50	5.00	10.00
❑ 1917	Stop, Look, Listen/Road Runner	1964	3.00	6.00	12.00
❑ 1945	Um, Um, Um, Um, Um, Um/First Taste of Love	1964	3.00	6.00	12.00

FONTANE SISTERS, THE

Also see PERRY COMO.

Number	Title (A Side/B Side)	Yr	VG	VG+	NM
DOT					
❑ 15171	Happy Days and Lonely Nights/If I Didn't Have You	1954	3.00	6.00	12.00
❑ 15248	Willow Weep for Me/A Love Like You	1954	3.00	6.00	12.00
❑ 15265	Hearts of Stone/Bless Your Heart	1954	3.75	7.50	15.00
❑ 15333	Rock Love/You're Mine	1955	3.00	6.00	12.00
❑ 15352	Most of All/Put Me in the Mood	1955	3.00	6.00	12.00
❑ 15370	Rollin' Stone/Playmates	1955	3.00	6.00	12.00
❑ 15386	Seventeen/If I Could Be with You	1955	3.00	6.00	12.00
❑ 15428	Daddy-O/Adorable	1955	3.00	6.00	12.00
❑ 15434	Nuttin' for Christmas/Silver Bells	1955	3.00	6.00	12.00
❑ 15450	Eddie My Love/Yum, Yum	1956	3.00	6.00	12.00
❑ 15462	I'm in Love Again/You Always Hurt the One You Love	1956	3.00	6.00	12.00
❑ 15480	Voices/Lonesome Lover Blues	1956	3.00	6.00	12.00
❑ 15501	Please Don't Leave Me/Still	1956	3.00	6.00	12.00
❑ 15527	The Banana Boat Song/Honolulu Moon	1957	2.50	5.00	10.00
❑ 15547	Dancing to the Rock and Roll/I'm the One Who Loves You	1957	2.50	5.00	10.00
❑ 15555	I'm Stickin' with You/Let the Rest of the World Go By	1957	2.50	5.00	10.00
❑ 15581	Fool Around/Which Way to Your Heart	1957	2.50	5.00	10.00
❑ 15682	Ain't It the Truth/Love Like a Fool	1957	2.50	5.00	10.00
❑ 15736	Chanson D'Amour/Coconut Grove	1958	2.50	5.00	10.00
❑ 15782	Buttermilk/Take a Step	1958	2.50	5.00	10.00
❑ 15853	Encore D'Amour/Jealous Heart	1958	2.50	5.00	10.00
❑ 15908	Billy Boy/Third Man Theme	1959	2.50	5.00	10.00

Number	Title (A Side/B Side)	Yr	VG	VG+	NM
❑ 15943	You Are My Sunshine/A Lover's Hymn	1959	2.50	5.00	10.00
❑ 16014	Listen to Your Heart/Please Be Kind	1959	2.50	5.00	10.00
❑ 16027	Hearts of Stone/Seventeen	1960	2.00	4.00	8.00
❑ 16059	Theme from "A Summer Place"/Darling, It's Wonderful	1960	2.00	4.00	8.00
❑ 16086	Come Home Eddie/Lover's Leap	1960	2.00	4.00	8.00
❑ 16499	The Tip of My Fingers/Summertime Love	1963	—	3.00	6.00

RCA VICTOR

Number	Title (A Side/B Side)	Yr	VG	VG+	NM
❑ 47-2926	I'm a Little Cuckoo/Turtle Song	1949	3.00	6.00	12.00
—With the Cavanaugh Trio					
❑ 47-2976	The Bumpity Bus/24 Hours of Sunshine	1949	3.00	6.00	12.00
❑ 47-3127	Fairy Tales/The Cinderella Work Song	1949	3.00	6.00	12.00
❑ 47-3713	(If I Knew You Were Comin') I'd've Baked a Cake/Mississippi Mud	1950	3.00	6.00	12.00
❑ 47-3772	I Wanna Be Loved/I Didn't Know What Time It Was	1950	3.00	6.00	12.00
❑ 47-3814	Three Little Rings/Down Home Rag	1950	3.00	6.00	12.00
❑ 47-3940	Sleigh Bells/Jing-a-Ling, Jing-a-Ling	1950	3.00	6.00	12.00
—With Dick Contino					
❑ 47-3979	Tennessee Waltz/I Guess I'll Have to Dream the Rest	1950	3.00	6.00	12.00
❑ 47-4009	Bouncy Bouncy Bally/What Did I Do	1950	3.00	6.00	12.00
❑ 47-4077	Let Me In/Hurry Home to Me	1951	3.75	7.50	15.00
—With Texas Jim Robertson					
❑ 47-4106	The Fortune Teller Song/The Fifth Wheel on the Wagon	1951	3.00	6.00	12.00
❑ 47-4168	Rhumba Boogie/Moon-June-Spoon	1951	3.00	6.00	12.00
❑ 47-4233	Castle Rock/Makin' Like a Train	1951	3.00	6.00	12.00
❑ 47-4274	Cold, Cold Heart/I Get the Blues When It Rains	1951	3.00	6.00	12.00
❑ 47-4322	A Howdy Doody Christmas/The Popcorn Song	1951	5.00	10.00	20.00
—With Howdy Doody					
❑ 47-4387	Alabama Jubilee/Grand Central Station	1951	3.00	6.00	12.00
❑ 47-4449	Snowflakes/River in Moonlight	1952	3.00	6.00	12.00
—With Merv Griffin and Freddie Martin					
❑ 47-4667	When I Dream/I Grabbed for the Ending	1952	3.00	6.00	12.00
❑ 47-4776	If You Would Only Be Mine/There's Doubt in My Mind	1952	3.00	6.00	12.00
❑ 47-5049	Winter's Here Again/Lonesome Road	1952	3.00	6.00	12.00
❑ 47-5162	Walkin' the Floor Over You/The Price I Paid for Loving You	1953	3.00	6.00	12.00
❑ 47-5266	Mexican Joe/He Who Has Love	1953	3.00	6.00	12.00
❑ 47-5383	Please Play Our Song/Falling	1953	3.00	6.00	12.00
❑ 47-5612	Till Then/Baion	1954	3.00	6.00	12.00

FOOTPRINTS

CAPITOL

Number	Title (A Side/B Side)	Yr	VG	VG+	NM
❑ 2052	Never Say Die/Mama Rand's	1967	3.75	7.50	15.00

FORCE FIVE, THE

ASCOT

Number	Title (A Side/B Side)	Yr	VG	VG+	NM
❑ 2206	Gee Too Tiger/I Want You Babe	1966	12.50	25.00	50.00

FORD, BILLY

Of BILLY AND LILLIE.

JOSIE

Number	Title (A Side/B Side)	Yr	VG	VG+	NM
❑ 775	String of Pearls/Stop Lyin' on Me	1955	10.00	20.00	40.00

REPRISE

Number	Title (A Side/B Side)	Yr	VG	VG+	NM
❑ 0265	This Is Worth Fighting For/My Girl	1964	3.00	6.00	12.00

UNITED

Number	Title (A Side/B Side)	Yr	VG	VG+	NM
❑ 142	Smooth Rocking/You Foxie Thing	1954	7.50	15.00	30.00
❑ 167	Confessing/Old Age	1955	7.50	15.00	30.00

VIK

Number	Title (A Side/B Side)	Yr	VG	VG+	NM
❑ 0263	How Can I Be Sure/Billy Boy Blow	1957	6.25	12.50	25.00

FORD, CAROL

KING

Number	Title (A Side/B Side)	Yr	VG	VG+	NM
❑ 6188	Christmas Letters/Please Come Home For Christmas	1968	3.00	6.00	12.00

FORD, DEE DEE

Also see DON GARDNER AND DEE DEE FORD.

ABC-PARAMOUNT

Number	Title (A Side/B Side)	Yr	VG	VG+	NM
❑ 10503	Just Like a Fool (I Keep Hopin')/Shoo-Fly Pie	1963	3.00	6.00	12.00

BRIAR

Number	Title (A Side/B Side)	Yr	VG	VG+	NM
❑ 142	Good Morning Blues/I Just Can't Believe	1962	3.00	6.00	12.00

TODD

Number	Title (A Side/B Side)	Yr	VG	VG+	NM
❑ 1049	Good Morning Blues/I Just Can't Believe	1959	3.75	7.50	15.00

FORD, EMILE, AND THE CHECKMATES

ANDIE

Number	Title (A Side/B Side)	Yr	VG	VG+	NM
❑ 5018	Don't Tell Me Your Troubles/What Do You Want to Make Those Eyes at Me For	1960	3.75	7.50	15.00

FORD, FRANKIE

ABC

Number	Title (A Side/B Side)	Yr	VG	VG+	NM
❑ 11431	All Alone Am I/Blue Monday	1974	—	2.50	5.00

ACE

Number	Title (A Side/B Side)	Yr	VG	VG+	NM
❑ 549	The Last One to Cry/Cheatin' Woman	1958	6.25	12.50	25.00
❑ 554	Sea Cruise/Roberta	1959	7.50	15.00	30.00
❑ 566	Alimony/Can't Tell My Heart (What to Do)	1959	6.25	12.50	25.00
❑ 580	Time After Time/Want to Be Your Man	1960	6.25	12.50	25.00
❑ 592	Chinatown/What's Goin' On	1960	6.25	12.50	25.00
❑ 592 [PS]	Chinatown/What's Goin' On	1960	12.50	25.00	50.00
❑ 8009	Ocean Full of Tears/Hour of Need	1963	3.75	7.50	15.00

BRIARMEADE

Number	Title (A Side/B Side)	Yr	VG	VG+	NM
❑ 7600	I've Found Someone of My Own/Battle Hymn of the Republic	1976	—	2.50	5.00
❑ 7701	Desperado/Mardi Gras in New Orleans	1977	—	2.50	5.00
❑ 7901	Halfway to Paradise/I'm Proud of What I Am	1979	—	2.50	5.00

CINNAMON

Number	Title (A Side/B Side)	Yr	VG	VG+	NM
❑ 752	When I Stop Dreamin'/I'm Proud of What I Am	1972	—	2.50	5.00
❑ 767	Talk to a Carpenter/When I Stop Dreamin'	1973	—	2.50	5.00

CONSTELLATION

Number	Title (A Side/B Side)	Yr	VG	VG+	NM
❑ 101	Chinatown/Ocean Full of Tears	1963	3.75	7.50	15.00

DOUBLOON

Number	Title (A Side/B Side)	Yr	VG	VG+	NM
❑ 101	Half a Crown/I Can't Face Tomorrow	1967	2.50	5.00	10.00

IMPERIAL

Number	Title (A Side/B Side)	Yr	VG	VG+	NM
❑ 5686	You Talk Too Much/If You've Got Troubles	1960	3.75	7.50	15.00
❑ 5706	My Southern Belle/The Groom	1960	3.75	7.50	15.00
❑ 5735	Seventenn/Doghouse	1961	3.75	7.50	15.00
❑ 5749	Saturday Night Fish Fry/Love Don't Love Nobody	1961	3.75	7.50	15.00
❑ 5776	Let 'Em Talk/What Happened to You	1961	3.75	7.50	15.00
❑ 5819	They Said It Couldn't Be Done/A Man Only Does	1962	3.75	7.50	15.00

PAULA

Number	Title (A Side/B Side)	Yr	VG	VG+	NM
❑ 351	Peace of Mind/I'm Proud of What I Am	1971	2.00	4.00	8.00

SYC

Number	Title (A Side/B Side)	Yr	VG	VG+	NM
❑ 1227	Growing Pains/Ups and Downs	1982	—	2.00	4.00
❑ 1228	My Prayer/Gospel Ship	1983	—	2.00	4.00

7-Inch Extended Plays

ACE

Number	Title (A Side/B Side)	Yr	VG	VG+	NM
❑ 105	(contents unknown)	1959	37.50	75.00	150.00
❑ 105 [PS]	The Best of Frankie Ford	1959	37.50	75.00	150.00

FORD, TENNESSEE ERNIE

Includes records issued as "Tennessee Ernie."

CANADA DRY

Number	Title (A Side/B Side)	Yr	VG	VG+	NM
❑ 72-6596 [DJ]	The Real Story Of Christmas from St. Luke, Chapter 2	1972	—	2.50	5.00
—Special promo for his 1972 Christmas TV special					
❑ 72-6596 [PS]	The Real Story Of Christmas from St. Luke, Chapter 2	1972	—	2.50	5.00
—Special promo for his 1972 Christmas TV special					

CAPITOL

Number	Title (A Side/B Side)	Yr	VG	VG+	NM
❑ F-985	I've Got to Feed 'Em in the Morning/My Hobby	1950	3.75	7.50	15.00
❑ F-1124	I'll Never Be Free/Ain't Nobody's Business But My Own	1950	3.75	7.50	15.00
—With Kay Starr					
❑ F-1174	Bright Lights/The Cincinnati Dancing Pig	1950	3.75	7.50	15.00
❑ F-1205	Mama Goes Everywhere Papa Goes/Please Love Me	1950	3.75	7.50	15.00
—With Kay Starr					
❑ F-1275	Bryant's Boogie/Little Juan Pedro	1950	5.00	10.00	20.00
❑ F-1295	The Shot Gun Boogie/I Ain't Gonna Let It Happen No More	1950	5.00	10.00	20.00
❑ F-1349	Tailor Made Woman/Stack-O-Lee	1951	3.75	7.50	15.00
❑ F-1470	Kentucky Waltz/Strange Little Girl	1951	3.75	7.50	15.00
❑ F-1521	Mr. and Mississippi/She's My Baby	1951	3.75	7.50	15.00
❑ F-1567	Oceans of Tears/You're My Sugar	1951	3.75	7.50	15.00
—With Kay Starr					
❑ F-1623	I'll Never Be Free/Ain't Nobody's Business But My Own	1951	3.00	6.00	12.00
—With Kay Starr; reissue					
❑ F1626	The Shot Gun Boogie/Anticipation Blues	1951	3.00	6.00	12.00
❑ F1695	Mule Train/The Cry of the Wild Goose	1951	3.00	6.00	12.00
❑ F1775	Kissin' Bug Boogie/Woman Is a Five-Letter Word	1951	5.00	10.00	20.00
❑ F1809	Hey, Good Lookin'/Cool, Cool Kisses	1951	3.75	7.50	15.00
❑ F1830	A Rootin' Tootin' Santa Claus/Christmas Dinner	1951	3.75	7.50	15.00
❑ F1911	Rock City Boogie/Streamline Cannonball	1951	5.00	10.00	20.00
—With the Dinning Sisters					
❑ F2017	Hambone/Candy Dancers' Ball	1952	3.75	7.50	15.00
❑ F2042	Put Your Arms Around Me/Everybody's Got a Girl But Me	1952	3.75	7.50	15.00
❑ F2066	Snowshoe Thompson/Fatback Louisiana USA	1952	3.75	7.50	15.00
❑ 2145	Talk to the Animals/What a Wonderful World	1968	—	3.00	6.00
❑ F2170	Blackberry Boogie/Tennessee Local	1952	5.00	10.00	20.00
❑ F2179	Smokey Mountain Boogie/Country Junction	1952	5.00	10.00	20.00
❑ F2215	I'm Hog Tied Over You/False Hearted Girl	1952	3.75	7.50	15.00
—With Ella Mae Morse					
❑ 2334	The Little Boy King/Bring a Torch, Jeanette, Isabella	1968	—	3.00	6.00
❑ F2338	Sweet Temptation/I Don't Know	1953	3.75	7.50	15.00
❑ F2443	Hey, Mr. Cotton Picker/Three Things (A Man Must Do)	1953	3.75	7.50	15.00
❑ 2522	Honey-Eyed Girl (That's You That's You)/Good Morning, Dear	1969	—	3.00	6.00
❑ F2602	Catfish Boogie/Kiss Me Big	1953	5.00	10.00	20.00
❑ F2809	The Honeymoon's Over/This Must Be the Place	1954	3.00	6.00	12.00
—With Betty Hutton					
❑ F2810	River of No Return/Give Me Your Word	1954	3.00	6.00	12.00
❑ F2876	Losing You/Eins, Zwei, Drei	1954	3.00	6.00	12.00
❑ 2918	Rainy Night in Georgia/Let the Lovelight in Your Eyes Lead Me On	1970	—	2.50	5.00
❑ F2939	Somebody Bigger Than You and I/There Is Beauty in Everything	1954	3.00	6.00	12.00
❑ F3058	Ballad of Davy Crockett/Farewell	1955	3.75	7.50	15.00
❑ 3079	Happy Songs of Love/Don't Let the Good Life Pass You By	1971	—	2.50	5.00
❑ F3135	I Am a Pilgrim/His Hands	1955	3.00	6.00	12.00
❑ F3262	Sixteen Tons/You Don't Have to Be a Baby to Cry	1955	3.75	7.50	15.00
❑ F-3343	Bright Lights and Blonde Haired Women/That's All	1956	5.00	10.00	20.00
❑ F3421	John Henry/Rovin' Gambler	1956	3.00	6.00	12.00
❑ 3422	Pea-Pickin' Cook/The Song	1972	—	2.50	5.00
❑ F3474	Rock Roll Boogie/Call Me Darling, Call Me Sweetheart	1956	5.00	10.00	20.00
❑ F3553	First Born/Have You Seen Her	1956	3.00	6.00	12.00
❑ 3556	Printers' Alley Stars/Baby	1973	—	2.00	4.00
❑ 3631	Farther Down the River (Where the Fishin's Good)/You've Still Got Love All Over You	1973	—	2.00	4.00
❑ F3649	The Watermelon Song/One Suit	1957	3.00	6.00	12.00
❑ F3700	Lonely Man/False Hearted Girl	1957	3.00	6.00	12.00
❑ 3704	Colorado Country Morning/Daddy Usta Say	1973	—	2.00	4.00
❑ F3762	In the Middle of An Island/Ivy League	1957	3.00	6.00	12.00

Number	Title (A Side/B Side)	Yr	VG	VG+	NM
❑ 3783	She Picked Up the Pieces/Sweet Child of Sunshine	1973	—	2.00	4.00
❑ 3848	I've Got Confidence/I'd Like to Be	1974	—	2.00	4.00
❑ F3868	Bless Your Pea Pickin' Heart/Down Deep	1957	3.00	6.00	12.00
❑ 3916	Come On Down/Bits and Pieces of Life	1974	—	2.00	4.00
❑ F3997	Love Makes the World Go Round/Sunday Barbecue	1958	2.50	5.00	10.00
❑ 4044	Baby/I'd Like to Be	1975	—	2.00	4.00

—With Andra Willis

Number	Title (A Side/B Side)	Yr	VG	VG+	NM
❑ F4107	Sleepin' at the Foot of the Bed/Glad Rags	1958	2.50	5.00	10.00
❑ 4160	The Devil Ain't a Lonely Woman's Friend/Smokey Taverns, Bar Room Girls	1975	—	2.00	4.00
❑ F4173	Code of the Mountains/Black-Eyed Susie	1959	2.50	5.00	10.00
❑ 4285	I Been to Georgia on a Fast Train/Baby's Home	1976	—	2.00	4.00
❑ 4302	Love Is the Only Thing/Sunny Side of Heaven	1959	2.00	4.00	8.00
❑ 4333	Sweet Feelin's/Dogs and Sheriff John	1976	—	2.00	4.00
❑ 4416	Joshua Fit De Battle/Oh Mary, Don't You Weep	1960	2.00	4.00	8.00
❑ 4446	Little Klinker/Jingle-O-The-Brownie	1960	3.00	6.00	12.00
❑ 4446 [PS]	Little Klinker/Jingle-O-The-Brownie	1960	5.00	10.00	20.00
❑ 4468	Bless This Land/Lord of All Creation	1960	2.00	4.00	8.00
❑ 4531	Dark As a Dungeon/His Love (Makes the World Go Round)	1961	2.00	4.00	8.00
❑ 4577	Litttle Red Rockin' Hood/I Gotta Have My Baby Back	1961	2.00	4.00	8.00
❑ 4734	Take Your Girlie to the Movies/There'll Be No New Tunes	1962	2.00	4.00	8.00
❑ 4793	The Work Song/Rags and Old Iron	1962	2.00	4.00	8.00
❑ 4838	How Great Thou Art/Eternal Life	1962	2.00	4.00	8.00
❑ 5425	Sixteen Tons/Hicktown	1965	—	3.00	6.00
❑ 5520	Girl Don't You Know/Now It's All Over	1965	—	3.00	6.00
❑ 5534	Sing We Now of Christmas/The Little Drummer Boy	1965	2.00	4.00	8.00
❑ 5757	God Lives/How Great Thou Art	1966	—	3.00	6.00
❑ 5900	Pearly Shells/Lahaina Luna	1967	—	3.00	6.00
❑ 5996	The Road/Hand Me Down Things	1967	—	3.00	6.00
❑ F40280	The Cry of the Wild Goose/The Donkey Serenade	1950	5.00	10.00	20.00

7-Inch Extended Plays

CAPITOL

Number	Title (A Side/B Side)	Yr	VG	VG+	NM
❑ EAP-413	(contents unknown)	1953	5.00	10.00	20.00
❑ EAP-413 [PS]	Backwoods Boogie and Blues	1953	5.00	10.00	20.00
❑ EAP 1-639	His Hands/Somebody Bigger Than You and I//I Am a Pilgrim/There Is Beauty in Everything	195?	3.75	7.50	15.00
❑ EAP 1-639 [PS]	Tennessee Ernie Ford	195?	3.75	7.50	15.00
❑ EAP-693	(contents unknown)	1956	3.75	7.50	15.00
❑ EAP-693 [PS]	Sixteen Tons	1956	3.75	7.50	15.00
❑ EAP 1-700	John Henry/Trouble in Mind//Gaily the Troubadour/The Lost Letter	1956	3.75	7.50	15.00
❑ EAP 1-700 [PS]	This Lusty Land! Part 1	1956	3.75	7.50	15.00
❑ EAP 2-700	Dark as a Dungeon/False Hearted Girl//I Gave My Love a Cherry/Nine Pound Hammer	1956	3.75	7.50	15.00
❑ EAP 2-700 [PS]	This Lusty Land! Part 2	1956	3.75	7.50	15.00
❑ EAP 3-700	Chicken Road/Who Will Shoe Your Pretty Little Foot//The Rovin' Gambler/In the Pines	1956	3.75	7.50	15.00
❑ EAP 3-700 [PS]	This Lusty Land! Part 3	1956	3.75	7.50	15.00
❑ EAP 1-756	The Ninety and Nine/Softly and Tenderly//Who at My Door Is Standing/Rock of Ages	1956	3.75	7.50	15.00
❑ EAP 1-756 [PS]	Hymns, Part 1	1956	3.75	7.50	15.00
❑ EAP 2-756	When They Ring the Golden Bells/In the Garden//Sweet Hour of Prayer/The Old Rugged Cross	1956	3.75	7.50	15.00
❑ EAP 2-756 [PS]	Hymns, Part 2	1956	3.75	7.50	15.00
❑ EAP 3-756	Let the Lower Lights Be Burning/Others//My Task/Ivory Palaces	1956	3.75	7.50	15.00
❑ EAP 3-756 [PS]	Hymns, Part 3	1956	3.75	7.50	15.00
❑ EAP 1-818	Just a Closer Walk with Thee/Peace in the Valley//Wayfaring Pilgrim/Were You There	195?	3.75	7.50	15.00
❑ EAP 1-818 [PS]	Spirituals, Part 1	195?	3.75	7.50	15.00
❑ EAP 2-818	He'll Understand and Say "Well Done"/I Know the Lord Laid His Hands on Me//Noah Found Grace in the Eyes of the Lord/I Want to Be Ready	195?	3.75	7.50	15.00
❑ EAP 2-818 [PS]	Spirituals, Part 2	195?	3.75	7.50	15.00
❑ EAP 3-818	Take My Hand, Precious Lord/Stand By Me//When God Dips His Love in My Heart/Get On Board, Little Children	195?	3.75	7.50	15.00
❑ EAP 3-818 [PS]	Spirituals, Part 3	195?	3.75	7.50	15.00
❑ EAP 1-888	(contents unknown)	1956	3.75	7.50	15.00
❑ EAP 1-888 [PS]	Ol' Rockin' Ern, Part 1	1956	3.75	7.50	15.00
❑ EAP 2-888	(contents unknown)	1956	3.75	7.50	15.00
❑ EAP 2-888 [PS]	Ol' Rockin' Ern, Part 2	1956	3.75	7.50	15.00
❑ EAP 3-888	Smokey Mountain Boogie/Ain't Nobody's Business But My Own//I Ain't a-Gonna Let It Happen No More/The Lord's Lariat	1956	3.75	7.50	15.00
❑ EAP 3-888 [PS]	Ol' Rockin' Ern, Part 3	1956	3.75	7.50	15.00
❑ EAP 1-1005	*What a Friend We Have in Jesus/Jesus, Savior, Pilot Me/His Eye Is on the Sparrow/Beautiful Isle of Somewhere	1958	2.50	5.00	10.00
❑ EAP 1-1005 [PS]	Nearer the Cross, Part 1	1958	2.50	5.00	10.00
❑ EAP 2-1005	Now the Day Is Over/Nearer My God to Thee//Sweet Peace the Gift of God's Love/Whispering Hope	1958	2.50	5.00	10.00
❑ EAP 2-1005 [PS]	Nearer the Cross, Part 2	1958	2.50	5.00	10.00
❑ EAP 3-1005	(contents unknown)	1958	2.50	5.00	10.00
❑ EAP 3-1005 [PS]	Nearer the Cross, Part 3	1958	2.50	5.00	10.00
❑ EAP 1-1071	*Joy to the World/O Little Town of Bethlehem/The Star Carol/Hark! The Herald Angels Sing	1958	3.00	6.00	12.00
❑ EAP 1-1071 [PS]	The Star Carol, Part 1	1958	3.00	6.00	12.00
❑ EAP 2-1071	(contents unknown)	1958	3.00	6.00	12.00
❑ EAP 2-1071 [PS]	The Star Carol, Part 2	1958	3.00	6.00	12.00
❑ EAP 3-1071	(contents unknown)	1958	3.00	6.00	12.00
❑ EAP 3-1071 [PS]	The Star Carol, Part 3	1958	3.00	6.00	12.00

GREEN GIANT

Number	Title (A Side/B Side)	Yr	VG	VG+	NM
❑ PB-2565 [DJ]	Down in the Valley/Medley: The More We Get Together-Dear Evalina-Keep on the Sunny Side of Life-How Many Biscuits Can We Eat-For He's a Jolly Green Giant/How the Green Giant Found His Song (And Almost Lost His Ho-Ho-Ho)/Good Things from the Garden	1963	2.50	5.00	10.00

—Promotional item for the Green Giant Company/Le Sueur Peas

Number	Title (A Side/B Side)	Yr	VG	VG+	NM
❑ PB-2565 [PS]	When Pea-Pickers Get Together	1963	2.50	5.00	10.00

—Promotional item for the Green Giant Company/Le Sueur Peas

FORD, TENNESSEE ERNIE, AND MOLLY BEE

CAPITOL

Number	Title (A Side/B Side)	Yr	VG	VG+	NM
❑ F2473	Don't Start Courtin' in a Hot Rod/We're a-Growin' Up	1953	5.00	10.00	20.00

FOREIGNER

ATLANTIC

Number	Title (A Side/B Side)	Yr	VG	VG+	NM
❑ 3394	Feels Like the First Time/Woman, Oh Woman	1977	—	2.00	4.00
❑ 3410	Cold As Ice/I Need You	1977	—	2.00	4.00

—Has a different mix (with strings) than the LP version

Number	Title (A Side/B Side)	Yr	VG	VG+	NM
❑ 3439	Long, Long Way from Home/The Damage Is Done	1977	—	2.00	4.00

—Has a different vocal with slightly altered lyrics from the LP version

Number	Title (A Side/B Side)	Yr	VG	VG+	NM
❑ 3488	Hot Blooded/Tramontaine	1978	—	2.00	4.00
❑ 3514	Double Vision/Lonely Children	1978	—	2.00	4.00
❑ 3514 [PS]	Double Vision/Lonely Children	1978	—	2.50	5.00
❑ 3543	Blue Morning, Blue Day/I Have Waited So Long	1978	—	2.00	4.00
❑ 3543 [DJ]	Blue Morning, Blue Day (same on both sides)	1978	2.50	5.00	10.00

—Promo only on blue vinyl

Number	Title (A Side/B Side)	Yr	VG	VG+	NM
❑ 3618	Dirty White Boy/Rev on the Red Line	1979	—	2.00	4.00
❑ 3618 [PS]	Dirty White Boy/Rev on the Red Line	1979	—	2.50	5.00
❑ 3633	Head Games/Do What You Like	1979	—	2.00	4.00
❑ 3633 [PS]	Head Games/Do What You Like	1979	—	2.50	5.00
❑ 3651	Women/The Modern Day	1980	—	2.00	4.00
❑ 3831	Urgent/Girl on the Moon	1981	—	2.00	4.00
❑ 3831 [PS]	Urgent/Girl on the Moon	1981	—	2.00	4.00
❑ 3868	Waiting for a Girl Like You/I'm Gonna Win	1981	—	2.00	4.00
❑ 3868 [PS]	Waiting for a Girl Like You/I'm Gonna Win	1981	—	2.50	5.00
❑ 4017	Juke Box Hero/Night Life	1982	—	2.00	4.00
❑ 4017 [PS]	Juke Box Hero/Night Life	1982	—	2.00	4.00
❑ 4044	Break it Up/Head Games (Live)	1982	—	2.00	4.00
❑ 4044 [PS]	Break it Up/Head Games (Live)	1982	—	2.00	4.00
❑ 4072	Luanne/Fool For You Anyway	1982	—	2.00	4.00
❑ 89046	Heart Turns to Stone/Counting Every Minute	1988	—	—	3.00
❑ 89046 [PS]	Heart Turns to Stone/Counting Every Minute	1988	—	—	3.00
❑ 89101	I Don't Want to Live Without You/Face to Face	1988	—	—	3.00
❑ 89101 [PS]	I Don't Want to Live Without You/Face to Face	1988	—	—	3.00
❑ 89169	Say You Will/A Night to Remember	1987	—	—	3.00
❑ 89169 [PS]	Say You Will/A Night to Remember	1987	—	—	3.00
❑ 89493	Down on Love/Growing Up the Hard Way	1985	—	—	3.00
❑ 89542	Reaction to Action/She's Too Tough	1985	—	—	3.00
❑ 89542 [PS]	Reaction to Action/She's Too Tough	1985	—	—	3.00
❑ 89571	That Was Yesterday/Two Different Worlds	1985	—	—	3.00
❑ 89571 [PS]	That Was Yesterday/Two Different Worlds	1985	—	—	3.00
❑ 89596	I Want to Know What Love Is/Street Thunder	1984	—	2.00	4.00

—Generic red and black Atlantic label

Number	Title (A Side/B Side)	Yr	VG	VG+	NM
❑ 89596	I Want to Know What Love Is/Street Thunder	1984	—	—	3.00

—Custon black and colorblocked label

Number	Title (A Side/B Side)	Yr	VG	VG+	NM
❑ 89596 [PS]	I Want to Know What Love Is/Street Thunder	1984	—	2.00	4.00

FORMATIONS, THE

BANK

Number	Title (A Side/B Side)	Yr	VG	VG+	NM
❑ 1007	At the Top of the Stairs/Magic Melody	1968	7.50	15.00	30.00

MGM

Number	Title (A Side/B Side)	Yr	VG	VG+	NM
❑ 13899	At the Top of the Stairs/Magic Melody	1968	2.50	5.00	10.00
❑ 13963	Love's Not Only for the Heart/Lonely Voice of Love	1968	5.00	10.00	20.00
❑ 14009	Don't Get Close/There's No Room	1968	3.00	6.00	12.00

FORTUNE, JOHNNY

ARENA

Number	Title (A Side/B Side)	Yr	VG	VG+	NM
❑ 102	I'm a Fool for You/Gee But I Miss You	1963	5.00	10.00	20.00

ARHAVEN

Number	Title (A Side/B Side)	Yr	VG	VG+	NM
❑ 1001	I'm a Fool for You/Gee But I Miss You	1962	6.25	12.50	25.00

BEAVER

Number	Title (A Side/B Side)	Yr	VG	VG+	NM
❑ 111	I'm Requesting a Love Song/Stay Just One More Day	1966	3.75	7.50	15.00

CRUSADER

Number	Title (A Side/B Side)	Yr	VG	VG+	NM
❑ 104	If You Love Me/Gee But I Miss You	1964	3.75	7.50	15.00

CURRENT

Number	Title (A Side/B Side)	Yr	VG	VG+	NM
❑ 101	Say You Will/Come On and Love Me	1965	3.75	7.50	15.00
❑ 104	Dan Stole My Girl/You Want Me to Be Your Baby	1965	3.75	7.50	15.00
❑ 105	I Am Lonely for You/I'll Never Let You Go	1965	3.75	7.50	15.00

EMMY

Number	Title (A Side/B Side)	Yr	VG	VG+	NM
❑ 1001	If You Love Me/Alone and Crying	1960	7.50	15.00	30.00
❑ 1002	I'm in Heaven (When You Kiss Me)/Gee But I Miss You	1960	7.50	15.00	30.00

PARK AVENUE

Number	Title (A Side/B Side)	Yr	VG	VG+	NM
❑ 104	Need You/One Less Angel	1963	3.75	7.50	15.00
❑ 110	Midnight Surf/Soul Surfer	1963	3.75	7.50	15.00
❑ 126	Surfer's Trip/Soul Traveler	1963	3.75	7.50	15.00
❑ 130	Dragster/Siboney	1963	3.75	7.50	15.00
❑ 4905	I'm Talkin' About You/My Wandering Love	1963	3.75	7.50	15.00

UNITED ARTISTS

Number	Title (A Side/B Side)	Yr	VG	VG+	NM
❑ 720	Juarez/It Ain't Necessarily So	1964	3.75	7.50	15.00
❑ 780	Don't You Lie to Me/Don't Stay Out After Midnight	1964	3.75	7.50	15.00

VAULT

Number	Title (A Side/B Side)	Yr	VG	VG+	NM
❑ 954	Your True Love/Tell me You Love Me	1969	2.50	5.00	10.00

FORTUNES, THE (1)

British band.

CAPITOL

Number	Title (A Side/B Side)	Yr	VG	VG+	NM
❑ 3086	Here Comes That Rainy Day Feeling Again/I Gotta Dream	1971	—	3.00	6.00

Number	Title (A Side/B Side)	Yr	VG	VG+	NM
❑ 3086	Here Comes That Rainy Day Feeling Again/Bad Side of Town	1971	2.50	5.00	10.00
❑ 3179	Freedom Comes, Freedom Goes/There's a Man	1971	—	2.50	5.00
❑ 3248	Storm in a Teacup/I'm Not Following You	1971	—	2.50	5.00
❑ 3445	Wait Until September/Don't Sing to Me	1972	—	2.50	5.00
❑ 3514	I Can't Remember When the Sun Went In/Secret Love	1973	—	2.50	5.00
❑ 3626	Give Me Some Room/Whenever It's a Sunday	1973	—	2.50	5.00
PRESS					
❑ 9773	You've Got Your Troubles/I've Gotta Go	1965	4.00	8.00	16.00
—White label stock copy					
❑ 9773	You've Got Your Troubles/I've Gotta Go	1965	3.00	6.00	12.00
—Purple label					
❑ 9798	Here It Comes Again/Things I Should Have Known	1965	3.75	7.50	15.00
—White label stock copy					
❑ 9798	Here It Comes Again/Things I Should Have Known	1965	2.50	5.00	10.00
—Purple label					
❑ 9811	This Golden Ring/Someone to Care	1966	2.50	5.00	10.00
❑ 60001	Gone from My Mind/Silent Street	1966	2.50	5.00	10.00
UNITED ARTISTS					
❑ 50211	The Idol/His Smile Was a Lie	1967	2.50	5.00	10.00
❑ 50280	Painting a Shadow/Fire Brigade	1968	2.50	5.00	10.00
WORLD PACIFIC					
❑ 77937	That Same Old Feeling/Lifetime of Love	1970	2.00	4.00	8.00

FORTUNES, THE (U)

None of these are by group (1), but exactly which ones are by the same group as others, we have not yet determined.

Number	Title (A Side/B Side)	Yr	VG	VG+	NM
ARGO					
❑ 5364	Congratulations/Look at Me, Look at You	1960	15.00	30.00	60.00
CHECKER					
❑ 818	Believe in Me/My Baby Is Fine	1955	15.00	30.00	60.00
CUB					
❑ 9123	The Ghoul in School/You Don't Know (What I've Been Through)	1963	3.75	7.50	15.00
DECCA					
❑ 30541	Tarnished Angel/Who Cares?	1958	15.00	30.00	60.00
❑ 30688	How Clever of You/Trees	1958	12.50	25.00	50.00
DRA					
❑ 320	Tell Me/Running Away from Love	1962	75.00	150.00	300.00
LAKE					
❑ 704	St. John's Cha Cha/Runnin'	196?	3.75	7.50	15.00
QUEEN					
❑ 24010	Nothing Matters Anymore/Ugly Duckling	1962	6.25	12.50	25.00
TOP RANK					
❑ 2019	Steady Vows/In the Night	1959	10.00	20.00	40.00
YUCCA					
❑ 168	Laugh of the Train/Chi Wawa	1964	7.50	15.00	30.00
❑ 170	Lonely Teardrops/This Is Love	1964	10.00	20.00	40.00

49TH PARALLEL, THE

Number	Title (A Side/B Side)	Yr	VG	VG+	NM
MAVERICK					
❑ 1004	Close the Barn Door/Twilight Woman	1968	5.00	10.00	20.00
❑ 1011	(Come On Little Child and) Talk to Me/Now That I'm a Man	1968	5.00	10.00	20.00

FORUM, THE

Number	Title (A Side/B Side)	Yr	VG	VG+	NM
MIRA					
❑ 232	The River Is Wide/I Fall in Love	1967	3.00	6.00	12.00
❑ 243	Trip on Me/It's Sunday	1967	3.00	6.00	12.00
❑ 248	A Girl Without a Boy/Go Try to Put Out the Sun	1968	3.00	6.00	12.00
PENTHOUSE					
❑ 504	The River Is Wide/(B-side unknown)	1966	5.00	10.00	20.00

FOSTER, CELL, AND THE AUDIOS

Number	Title (A Side/B Side)	Yr	VG	VG+	NM
ULTRA					
❑ 105	Honest I Do/I Prayed for You	1956	100.00	200.00	400.00
—Yellow label					
❑ 105	Honest I Do/I Prayed for You	1956	62.50	125.00	250.00
—Maroon label					

FOSTER, JOHN, AND SONS BLACK DYKE MILLS BAND

Number	Title (A Side/B Side)	Yr	VG	VG+	NM
APPLE					
❑ 1800	Thingumybob/Yellow Submarine	1968	25.00	50.00	100.00
—With "Thingumybob" on uncut apple side					
❑ 1800	Thingumybob/Yellow Submarine	1968	25.00	50.00	100.00
—With "Yellow Submarine" on uncut apple side					
❑ 1800	Thingumybob/Yellow Submarine	1968	30.00	60.00	120.00
—With black star on uncut apple side					

FOTO-FI FOUR, THE

Some sources say Harry NILSSON is on this recording.

Number	Title (A Side/B Side)	Yr	VG	VG+	NM
FOTO-FI					
❑ 107	Stand Up and Holler!/Ismael	1964	6.25	12.50	25.00
❑ 107 [PS]	Stand Up and Holler!/Ismael	1964	12.50	25.00	50.00
—Sleeve states: "The Beatles arrive in America! Have fun running the film with this specially scored recording." Price does not include film.					

FOTOMAKER

With former members of THE RASCALS and RASPBERRIES.

Number	Title (A Side/B Side)	Yr	VG	VG+	NM
ATLANTIC					
❑ 3471	Where Have You Been All My Life/The Same for One	1978	—	2.00	4.00
❑ 3485	The Other Side/Pain	1978	—	2.00	4.00
❑ 3531	Snowblind/Miles Away	1978	—	2.00	4.00
❑ 3561	Does She Sance/If I Can't Believe in You	1979	—	2.00	4.00
❑ 3621	Love Me Forever/Fooled Again	1979	—	2.00	4.00

FOUNDATIONS, THE

Number	Title (A Side/B Side)	Yr	VG	VG+	NM
UNI -					
❑ 55038	Baby, Now That I've Found You/Come On Back to Me	1967	2.00	4.00	8.00
❑ 55058	Back on My Feet Again/I Can Take or Leave Your Loving	1968	—	3.00	6.00
❑ 55073	We Are Happy People/Any Old Time	1968	—	3.00	6.00
❑ 55101	Build Me Up Buttercup/New Direction	1968	2.00	4.00	8.00
❑ 55117	In the Bad, Bad Old Days (Before You Loved Me)/Give Me Love	1969	—	3.00	6.00
❑ 55137	My Little Chickadee/Solomon Grundy	1969	—	3.00	6.00
❑ 55162	Why Did You Cry/Born to Live, Born to Die	1969	—	3.00	6.00
❑ 55210	Take a Girl Like You/I'm Gonna Be a Rich Man	1970	—	3.00	6.00
❑ 55315	I'll Give You Love/Stoney Ground	1972	—	3.00	6.00

FOUNTAIN OF YOUTH

Number	Title (A Side/B Side)	Yr	VG	VG+	NM
COLGEMS					
❑ 66-1020	Livin' Too Fast/(Angie, Love Me) Make the Hurt Go Away	1968	5.00	10.00	20.00
❑ 66-1024	Take a Giant Step/Don't Blame Me (For Trying)	1968	5.00	10.00	20.00
❑ 66-1032	The Day Don't Come/Sunshine on a Cold Morning	1969	3.75	7.50	15.00
❑ 66-5003	Liza Jane/Mistress People	1969	3.75	7.50	15.00

FOUNTAINS OF WAYNE

Number	Title (A Side/B Side)	Yr	VG	VG+	NM
ATLANTIC					
❑ 84057	I Want an Alien for Christmas/The Man in the Santa Suit	1997	—	2.00	4.00
—Green vinyl					

FOUR ACES

Number	Title (A Side/B Side)	Yr	VG	VG+	NM
ABC-PARAMOUNT					
❑ 10166	Searching/Dolce Par Niente	1960	2.50	5.00	10.00
❑ 10183	Me Without You/The Ballad of Patrick Henry	1961	2.50	5.00	10.00
DECCA					
❑ 27860	Tell Me Why/A Garden in the Rain	1951	5.00	10.00	20.00
❑ 27937	Perfidia/You Brought Me Love	1952	5.00	10.00	20.00
❑ 28073	My Hero/Spring Is a Wonderful Thing	1952	5.00	10.00	20.00
❑ 28162	I'm Yours/I Understand	1952	5.00	10.00	20.00
❑ 28323	Should I/There's Only Tonight	1952	5.00	10.00	20.00
❑ 28390	Heart and Soul/Just Squeeze Me	1952	5.00	10.00	20.00
❑ 28391	I'll Never Smile Again/My Devotion	1952	5.00	10.00	20.00
❑ 28392	Tip-Pi-Tin/Heaven Can Wait	1952	5.00	10.00	20.00
❑ 28393	La Rosita/Take Me in Your Arms	1952	5.00	10.00	20.00
❑ 28650	You Fooled Me/If You Take My Heart Away	1953	3.75	7.50	15.00
❑ 28691	Organ Grinder's Swing/Honey in the Horn	1953	3.75	7.50	15.00
❑ 28744	Don't Forget Me/False Love	1953	3.75	7.50	15.00
❑ 28843	Laughing on the Outisde (Crying on the Inside)/I've Been Waiting a Lifetime	1953	3.75	7.50	15.00
❑ 28927	The Gang That Sang "Heart of My Heart"/Stranger in Paradise	1953	3.75	7.50	15.00
❑ 28979	Bandera (Texas Polka)/What More Is There	1954	3.75	7.50	15.00
❑ 29036	Amor/So Long	1954	3.75	7.50	15.00
❑ 29123	Three Coins in the Fountain/Wedding Bells (Are Breaking Up That Old Gang of Mine)	1954	3.75	7.50	15.00
❑ 29217	Dream/It Shall Come to Pass	1954	3.75	7.50	15.00
❑ 29269	It's a Woman's World/The Cuckoo Bird in the Pickle Tree	1954	3.75	7.50	15.00
❑ 29344	Mister Sandman/(I'll Be With You) In Apple Blossom Time	1954	3.75	7.50	15.00
❑ 29395	Melody of Love/There Is a Tavern in the Town	1954	3.75	7.50	15.00
❑ 29435	There Goes My Heart/You'll Always Be the One	1955	3.00	6.00	12.00
❑ 29476	Heart/Sluefoot	1955	3.00	6.00	12.00
❑ 29625	Love is a Many-Splendored Thing/Shine On Harvest Moon	1955	3.00	6.00	12.00
❑ 29702	The Christmas Song (Merry Christmas to You)/Jingle Bells	1955	3.00	6.00	12.00
❑ 29712	O Holy Night/Silent Night	1955	3.00	6.00	12.00
❑ 29725	A Woman in Love/Of This I'm Sure	1955	3.00	6.00	12.00
❑ 29809	If You Can Dream/The Gal with the Yaller Shoes	1956	3.00	6.00	12.00
❑ 29889	To Love Again/Charlie Was a Boxer	1956	3.00	6.00	12.00
❑ 29989	I Only Know I Love You/Dreamer	1956	3.00	6.00	12.00
❑ 30041	Friendly Persuasion (Thee I Love)/You Can't Run Away from It	1956	3.00	6.00	12.00
❑ 30123	Someone to Love/Written on the Wind	1956	3.00	6.00	12.00
❑ 30242	Bahama Mama/You're Mine	1957	3.00	6.00	12.00
❑ 30348	Three Sheets to the Wind/Yes Sir, That's My Baby	1957	3.00	6.00	12.00
❑ 30384	Half of My Heart/When My Sugar Walks Down the Street	1957	3.00	6.00	12.00
❑ 30466	How Do You Say Goodbye?/I Would Love You Still	1957	3.00	6.00	12.00
❑ 30575	Rock and Roll Rhapsody/I Wish I May, I Wish I Might	1958	3.00	6.00	12.00
❑ 30649	Saturday Swing-Out/Take My Heart	1958	3.00	6.00	12.00
❑ 30695	Two Arms, Two Lips, One Heart/Heartache in Costume	1958	3.00	6.00	12.00
❑ 30721	Roses of Rio/Hangin' Up a Horseshoe	1958	3.00	6.00	12.00
❑ 30764	The World Outside/How Can You Forget	1958	3.00	6.00	12.00
❑ 30775	Ol' Fatso/Christmas Tree	1958	3.00	6.00	12.00
❑ 30822	No Other Arms, No Other Lips/The Inn of the Sixth Happiness	1959	2.50	5.00	10.00
❑ 30874	Ciao, Ciao Bambino/Paradise Island	1959	2.50	5.00	10.00
❑ 30897	The Five Pennies/Anyone Would Love You	1959	2.50	5.00	10.00
❑ 30989	Waltzing Matilda/The Wonder of It All	1959	2.50	5.00	10.00
❑ 31027	I Love Paris/Till Tomorrow	1959	2.50	5.00	10.00
❑ 31081	Poor Butterfly/You Are Music	1960	2.50	5.00	10.00
FLASH					
❑ 103	Who's to Blame/Two Little Kisses	1950	7.50	15.00	30.00
JUBILEE					
❑ 5416	It's All Over But the Crying/Lonely Hill	1962	2.00	4.00	8.00
RADNOR					
❑ 301	Always Keep Me in Your Heart/Didn't We	1968	—	2.50	5.00
❑ 302	I Started a Joke/Summer Won't Be Summer	1969	—	2.50	5.00

VICTORIA

Number	Title (A Side/B Side)	Yr	VG	VG+	NM
❑ 101	Sin/Arizona Moon	1951	15.00	30.00	60.00
—Red vinyl					
❑ 101	Sin/Arizona Moon	1951	6.25	12.50	25.00
—Black vinyl					
❑ 102	There's a Christmas Tree in Heaven/There's a Small Hotel	1951	7.50	15.00	30.00

7-Inch Extended Plays

DECCA

Number	Title (A Side/B Side)	Yr	VG	VG+	NM
❑ ED 2004	Tell Me Why/Perfidia//I Understand/My Hero	195?	3.75	7.50	15.00
❑ ED 2004 [PS]	The Four Aces, Vol. 1	195?	3.75	7.50	15.00
❑ ED 2170	*I Don't Know Why/(I'll Be With You) In Apple Blossom Time/Dream/Among My Souvenirs	195?	3.75	7.50	15.00
❑ ED 2170 [PS]	Dream	195?	3.75	7.50	15.00
❑ ED 2211	I'm in the Mood for Love/What a Difference a Day Makes//Stars Fell on Alabama/Pennies from Heaven	195?	3.00	6.00	12.00
❑ ED 2211 [PS]	Mood for Love, Volume 1	195?	3.00	6.00	12.00
❑ ED 2212	(contents unknown)	195?	3.00	6.00	12.00
❑ ED 2212 [PS]	Mood for Love, Volume 2	195?	3.00	6.00	12.00
❑ ED 2213	(contents unknown)	195?	3.00	6.00	12.00
❑ ED 2213 [PS]	Mood for Love, Volume 3	195?	3.00	6.00	12.00
❑ ED 2309	White Christmas/The Christmas Song//Silent Night/O Little Town of Bethlehem/Joy to the World	1956	3.00	6.00	12.00
❑ ED 2309 [PS]	A Merry Christmas with the Four Aces, Part 1	1956	3.00	6.00	12.00
❑ ED 2310	(contents unknown)	1956	3.00	6.00	12.00
❑ ED 2310 [PS]	A Merry Christmas with the Four Aces, Part 2	1956	3.00	6.00	12.00
❑ ED 2311	(contents unknown)	1956	3.00	6.00	12.00
❑ ED 2311 [PS]	A Merry Christmas with the Four Aces, Part 3	1956	3.00	6.00	12.00
❑ ED 2324	Amor/I'm Yours//Organ Grinder's Swing/So Long	195?	3.00	6.00	12.00
❑ ED 2324 [PS]	Amor	195?	3.00	6.00	12.00
❑ ED 2529	(contents unknown)	195?	3.00	6.00	12.00
❑ ED 2529 [PS]	Shufflin' Along, Volume 1	195?	3.00	6.00	12.00
❑ ED 2565	(contents unknown)	195?	3.00	6.00	12.00
❑ ED 2565 [PS]	Hits from Hollywood	195?	3.00	6.00	12.00
❑ ED 2675	(contents unknown)	1959	3.00	6.00	12.00
❑ ED 2675 [PS]	Beyond the Blue Horizon	1959	3.00	6.00	12.00

FOUR AIMS, THE

See FOUR TOPS.

FOUR BARS, THE

JOSIE

Number	Title (A Side/B Side)	Yr	VG	VG+	NM
❑ 762	Grief by Day, Grief by Night/Hey Baby	1954	75.00	150.00	300.00
❑ 768	If I Give My Heart to You/Stop It! Quit It!	1954	75.00	150.00	300.00
❑ 783	Let Me Live/Why Do You Treat Me This Way	1955	150.00	300.00	600.00

REPUBLIC

Number	Title (A Side/B Side)	Yr	VG	VG+	NM
❑ 7101	Memories of You/When Did You Leave Heaven	1954	150.00	300.00	600.00

FOUR BELLS, THE

GEM

Number	Title (A Side/B Side)	Yr	VG	VG+	NM
❑ 207	Please Tell It to Me/Long Way to Go	1953	200.00	400.00	800.00
❑ 220	Only a Miracle/My Tree	1954	200.00	400.00	000.00

FOUR BROTHERS AND A COUSIN

JAGUAR

Number	Title (A Side/B Side)	Yr	VG	VG+	NM
❑ 3003	Trust in Me/Whistle Stop Blues	1954	100.00	200.00	400.00
❑ 3005	Whispeing Wind/Can It Be	1954	125.00	250.00	500.00

FOUR BUDDIES, THE (1)

Vocal group from Baltimore.

SAVOY

Number	Title (A Side/B Side)	Yr	VG	VG+	NM
❑ 769	I Will Wait/Just to See You Smile Again	1951	100.00	200.00	400.00
❑ 769	I Will Wait/Just to See You Smile Again	1951	125.00	250.00	500.00
—As "The Four Buds"					
❑ 779	Don't Leave Me Now/Sweet Slumber	1951	100.00	200.00	400.00
❑ 789	My Summer's Gone/Why at a Time Like This	1951	75.00	150.00	300.00
❑ 817	Heart and Soul/Sin	1951	75.00	150.00	300.00
❑ 823	Window Eyes/Simply Say Goodbye	1951	75.00	150.00	300.00
❑ 845	You're Part of Me/Story Blues	1952	75.00	150.00	300.00
❑ 866	What's the Matter with Me/Sweet Tooth for My Baby	1952	75.00	150.00	300.00
❑ 888	My Mother's Eyes/Ooh Ow	1953	75.00	150.00	300.00
❑ 891	I'd Climb the Highest Mountain/I Wanna Know	1953	75.00	150.00	300.00
—B-side by Dolly Cooper					

FOUR BUDDIES, THE (2)

Vocal group from Chicago.

CLUB 51

Number	Title (A Side/B Side)	Yr	VG	VG+	NM
❑ 105	Delores/Look Out	1956	50.00	100.00	200.00
—Black vinyl					
❑ 105	Delores/Look Out	1956	1000.	2000.	4000.
—Red vinyl					

FOUR BUDDIES, THE (3)

CORAL

Number	Title (A Side/B Side)	Yr	VG	VG+	NM
❑ 62217	Hurt/Moonglow & Theme from Picnic	1960	5.00	10.00	20.00
❑ 62325	The Light/Cin Cin (Che Bell)	1962	5.00	10.00	20.00

IMPERIAL

Number	Title (A Side/B Side)	Yr	VG	VG+	NM
❑ 66018	I Want to Be the Boy You Love/Just Enough of Your Love	1964	15.00	30.00	60.00

PHILIPS

Number	Title (A Side/B Side)	Yr	VG	VG+	NM
❑ 40122	Lonely Summer/Slow Locomotion	1963	5.00	10.00	20.00

FOUR CAL-QUETTES, THE

CAPITOL

Number	Title (A Side/B Side)	Yr	VG	VG+	NM
❑ 4534	Sparkle and Shine/In This World	1961	7.50	15.00	30.00
—As "The Four Coquettes"					
❑ 4574	Billy, My Billy/Star Bright	1961	7.50	15.00	30.00
❑ 4657	Most of All/I'm Gonna Love Him Anyway	1961	7.50	15.00	30.00
❑ 4725	I'll Never Come Back (Silly Boy)/Again	1962	7.50	15.00	30.00

LIBERTY

Number	Title (A Side/B Side)	Yr	VG	VG+	NM
❑ 55549	I Cried/Movie Magazines	1963	3.75	7.50	15.00

FOUR CHEERS, THE

END

Number	Title (A Side/B Side)	Yr	VG	VG+	NM
❑ 1034	Fatal Charms of Love/Periwinkle Blue	1958	50.00	100.00	200.00

FOUR CHEVELLES, THE

BAND BOX

Number	Title (A Side/B Side)	Yr	VG	VG+	NM
❑ 357	This Is Our Wedding Day/Darling Forever	1957	5.00	10.00	20.00
❑ 358	I Can't Believe/I Know	1957	5.00	10.00	20.00

DELFT

Number	Title (A Side/B Side)	Yr	VG	VG+	NM
❑ 357	This Is Our Wedding Day/Darling Forever	1957	150.00	300.00	600.00

FOUR CHICADEES, THE

CHECKER

Number	Title (A Side/B Side)	Yr	VG	VG+	NM
❑ 849	Ding Dong/Teenage Blues	1956	15.00	30.00	60.00

FOUR CLEFS, THE

RCA VICTOR

Number	Title (A Side/B Side)	Yr	VG	VG+	NM
❑ 47-4507	Dig These Blues/Four Clefs Woogie	1952	12.50	25.00	50.00

FOUR COINS, THE

COLUMBIA

Number	Title (A Side/B Side)	Yr	VG	VG+	NM
❑ 44006	If You Love Me (Really Love Me)/Learning to Live Without Your Love	1967	—	3.00	6.00

EPIC

Number	Title (A Side/B Side)	Yr	VG	VG+	NM
❑ 9074	Once More/We'll Be Married...	1954	3.75	7.50	15.00
❑ 9082	I Love You Madly/Maybe	1954	3.75	7.50	15.00
❑ 9091	My Anxious Heart/Oh Mother Dear	1955	3.75	7.50	15.00
❑ 9104	Promises, Promises/That's the Way	1955	3.75	7.50	15.00
❑ 9107	A Story Untold/Magnolia	1955	3.75	7.50	15.00
❑ 9116	The Song That Brought Us Together/Need You	1955	3.75	7.50	15.00
❑ 9129	Memories of You/Tear Down the Fence	1955	3.75	7.50	15.00
❑ 9148	The Song That God Sings/The Old Professor	1956	3.00	6.00	12.00
❑ 9164	This I Offer You/One Kiss (Is Worth a Thousand Words)	1956	3.00	6.00	12.00
❑ 9183	Manhattan Serenade/Too Late	1956	3.00	6.00	12.00
❑ 9192	Destination Love/The Time of the Year	1956	3.00	6.00	12.00
❑ 9200	Falling Star/My Love Is a Little Kitten	1957	3.00	6.00	12.00
❑ 9213	Shangri-La/First in Line	1957	3.00	6.00	12.00
❑ 9229	My One Sin/This Life	1957	3.00	6.00	12.00
❑ 9253	Follow Your Heart/A Broken Promise	1957	3.00	6.00	12.00
❑ 9258	My Love Loves Me/New World	1957	3.00	6.00	12.00
❑ 9276	Dream World/One Life, One Love	1958	2.50	5.00	10.00
❑ 9286	Wendy, Wendy/Be Still My Heart	1958	2.50	5.00	10.00
❑ 9295	The World Outside/Roselle	1958	2.50	5.00	10.00
❑ 9306	Angel of Love/Who Are You	1959	2.50	5.00	10.00
❑ 9314	My First Love/One Love, One Heart	1959	2.50	5.00	10.00
❑ 9337	Angel in the Rain/First Signs of Love	1959	2.50	5.00	10.00
❑ 9348	Buon Natale/Serenade of the Bells	1959	2.50	5.00	10.00
❑ 9383	My Only Love/You're Breaking My Heart	1960	2.50	5.00	10.00

JOY

Number	Title (A Side/B Side)	Yr	VG	VG+	NM
❑ 287	Answer Me, My Love/Joanna	1964	2.00	4.00	8.00

JUBILEE

Number	Title (A Side/B Side)	Yr	VG	VG+	NM
❑ 5411	Gee, Officer Krupki/The Miracle of St. Marie	1961	2.00	4.00	8.00
❑ 5419	Come a Little Closer/Windows of Heaven	1962	2.00	4.00	8.00
❑ 5429	One Red Rose/I Wish You Were Here	1962	2.00	4.00	8.00

LAURIE

Number	Title (A Side/B Side)	Yr	VG	VG+	NM
❑ 3331	I'll Never Love Again/Try Your Luck	1966	—	3.00	6.00
❑ 3360	Shout Shout (Knock Yourself Out)/People Get Jealous	1966	—	3.00	6.00

MGM

Number	Title (A Side/B Side)	Yr	VG	VG+	NM
❑ 12951	Pledging My Love/I Want a Little Girl	1960	2.00	4.00	8.00
❑ 12977	Love Is Where You Find It/Beat on Your Drum Little Susan	1961	2.00	4.00	8.00
❑ 13003	To Love/From Your Very Own Lips	1961	2.00	4.00	8.00
❑ 13031	Pretty Nina/Moon of Manakoora	1961	2.00	4.00	8.00

VEE JAY

Number	Title (A Side/B Side)	Yr	VG	VG+	NM
❑ 474	They Say/Jimmy San	1962	2.00	4.00	8.00
❑ 551	Take a Bow (Little Darlin')/Nina	1963	2.00	4.00	8.00

7-Inch Extended Plays

EPIC

Number	Title (A Side/B Side)	Yr	VG	VG+	NM
❑ EG-7121	(contents unknown)	195?	3.00	6.00	12.00
❑ EG-7121 [PS]	The Four Coins	195?	3.00	6.00	12.00
❑ EG-7186	(contents unknown)	195?	3.00	6.00	12.00
❑ EG-7186 [PS]	The Four Coins in Shangri-La	195?	3.00	6.00	12.00
❑ EG-7196	(contents unknown)	195?	2.50	5.00	10.00
❑ EG-7196 [PS]	The Four Coins Sing	195?	2.50	5.00	10.00
❑ EG-7197	(contents unknown)	195?	2.50	5.00	10.00
❑ EG-7197 [PS]	The Four Coins Sing	195?	2.50	5.00	10.00

FOUR COQUETTES, THE

See THE FOUR CAL-QUETTES.

FOUR DATES, THE

CHANCELLOR

Number	Title (A Side/B Side)	Yr	VG	VG+	NM
❑ 1014	I'm Happy/Eloise	1958	5.00	10.00	20.00
❑ 1019	I say babe/Hey Roly Poly	1958	5.00	10.00	20.00
❑ 1027	Feel Good/Teenage Neighbor	1958	6.25	12.50	25.00

FOUR DEALS, THE

CAPITOL

Number	Title (A Side/B Side)	Yr	VG	VG+	NM
❑ F-1313	It's Too Late Now/There Ain't No Bears	1950	25.00	50.00	100.00

FOUR DEEP TONES, THE

CORAL

Number	Title (A Side/B Side)	Yr	VG	VG+	NM
❑ 65061	Just in Case You Change Your Mind/Castle Rock	1951	50.00	100.00	200.00
❑ 65062	The Night You Said Goodbye/When the Saints Go Marching In	1951	50.00	100.00	200.00

FOUR DEUCES, THE

Number	Title (A Side/B Side)	Yr	VG	VG+	NM
EVEREST					
❑ 19311	Polly/Yella Shoes	1959	7.50	15.00	30.00
MUSIC CITY					
❑ 790	W-P-L-J/Here Lies My Love	1955	37.50	75.00	150.00
—Maroon label					
❑ 790	W-P-L-J/Here Lies My Love	1955	10.00	20.00	40.00
—Black label					
❑ 796	Down It Went/Goose Is Gone	1955	15.00	30.00	60.00

FOUR DIRECTIONS, THE

Number	Title (A Side/B Side)	Yr	VG	VG+	NM
CORAL					
❑ 62456	(Doin' the) Arthur/Tonight We Love	1965	7.50	15.00	30.00

FOUR DOTS, THE

Number	Title (A Side/B Side)	Yr	VG	VG+	NM
FREEDOM					
❑ 44005	Pleading for Your Love/(B-side unknown)	1958	25.00	50.00	100.00

FOUR DUKES, THE (1)

Number	Title (A Side/B Side)	Yr	VG	VG+	NM
DUKE					
❑ 116	Crying in the Chapel/I Done Done It	1953	200.00	400.00	800.00

FOUR DUKES, THE (2)

Number	Title (A Side/B Side)	Yr	VG	VG+	NM
IMPERIAL					
❑ 5653	Baby Won't You Please Come Home/John Henry	1960	7.50	15.00	30.00

FOUR EPICS, THE

Number	Title (A Side/B Side)	Yr	VG	VG+	NM
HERITAGE					
❑ 109	I'm On My Way to Love/When the Music Ends	1962	25.00	50.00	100.00
LAURIE					
❑ 3155	Again/I Love You Diane	1963	6.25	12.50	25.00
❑ 3183	How I Wish I Was Single Again/Dance Joanne	1963	6.25	12.50	25.00

FOUR ESQUIRES, THE

Number	Title (A Side/B Side)	Yr	VG	VG+	NM
CADENCE					
❑ 1260	Three Things/The Sphinx Won't Tell	1955	5.00	10.00	20.00
❑ 1277	Adorable/Thunderbolt	1955	5.00	10.00	20.00
LONDON					
❑ 1652	Look Homeward Angel/Santo Domingo	1956	6.25	12.50	25.00
PARIS					
❑ 501	Song of April/Everyone's Sweet on My Sugar	1957	5.00	10.00	20.00
❑ 505	The Chopstick Rock/Never Look for Love	1957	5.00	10.00	20.00
❑ 509	Love Me Forever/I Ain't Been Right Since You Left	1957	5.00	10.00	20.00
❑ 512	Always and Forever/I Walk Down the Street	1958	5.00	10.00	20.00
❑ 515	All Around the Clock/The Big Dance	1958	5.00	10.00	20.00
❑ 520	Hideaway/Repeat After Me	1958	5.00	10.00	20.00
—With Rosemary June					
❑ 526	Follow Me/The Land of You and Me	1958	5.00	10.00	20.00
❑ 531	Lucky Old Sun/Non E Cosi	1959	5.00	10.00	20.00
❑ 535	Act Your Age/So Ends the Night	1959	5.00	10.00	20.00
❑ 539	Wonderful One/Wouldn't It Be Wonderful	1959	5.00	10.00	20.00
❑ 544	Make Them Mine/Peg O' My Heart	1960	5.00	10.00	20.00
❑ 549	Sweet Sixteen She'll Never Be/The Chopstick Rock	1960	5.00	10.00	20.00
PILGRIM					
❑ 717	Follow Me/Summer Vacation	1956	6.25	12.50	25.00
TERRACE					
❑ 7502	Can't Help Falling in Love/Merry-Go-Round of Love	1961	3.75	7.50	15.00
❑ 7516	The James Bond Theme (Double-O-Seven)/Summer Vacation	1963	6.25	12.50	25.00
—Betcha didn't know this had lyrics...					

FOUR-EVERS, THE

Number	Title (A Side/B Side)	Yr	VG	VG+	NM
CHATTAHOOCHIE					
❑ 630	Colors/Come Up in the World	1963	3.75	7.50	15.00
COLUMBIA					
❑ 42303	You Belong to Me/Such a Good Night for Dreaming	1962	15.00	30.00	60.00
❑ 43886	A Lovely Way to Spend An Evening/The Girl I Want	1966	5.00	10.00	20.00
CONSTELLATION					
❑ 151	Stormy/Out of the Crowd	1965	7.50	15.00	30.00
JAMIE					
❑ 1247	Everybody South Street/One More Time	1963	3.75	7.50	15.00
RED BIRD					
❑ 10-078	You Never Had It So Good/What a Scene	1966	6.25	12.50	25.00
SMASH					
❑ 1853	Lover Come Back to Me/It's Love	1963	3.75	7.50	15.00
❑ 1887	Please Be Mine/If I Were a Magician	1964	7.50	15.00	30.00
❑ 1887	Be My Girl/If I Were a Magician	1964	3.75	7.50	15.00
—Same A-side, different title					
❑ 1921	(Say I Love You) Do Be Dum/Everlasting	1964	3.75	7.50	15.00

FOUR EXCEPTIONS, THE

Number	Title (A Side/B Side)	Yr	VG	VG+	NM
PARKWAY					
❑ 986	You Got the Power/A Sad Goodbye	1966	12.50	25.00	50.00

FOUR FELLOWS, THE

Number	Title (A Side/B Side)	Yr	VG	VG+	NM
DERBY					
❑ 862	I Tried/Bend of the River	1954	100.00	200.00	400.00
GLORY					
❑ 231	I Wish I Didn't Know You/I Know Love	1955	20.00	40.00	80.00
❑ 234	Soldier Boy/Take Me Back Baby	1955	15.00	30.00	60.00
❑ 236	Angels Say/In the Rain	1955	15.00	30.00	60.00
❑ 238	Fallen Angel/Hold 'Em Joe	1956	15.00	30.00	60.00
❑ 242	Darling You/Please Don't Deprive Me of My Love	1956	20.00	40.00	80.00
❑ 244	I Sit in My Window/Please Play My Song	1956	15.00	30.00	60.00
❑ 248	You Don't Know Me/Sweet Girl	1956	15.00	30.00	60.00
❑ 250	Loving You, Darling/Give Me Back My Broken Heart	1957	15.00	30.00	60.00
NESTOR					
❑ 27	Remember/That Kiss You Gave Me	1958	75.00	150.00	300.00

FOUR FIFTHS, THE

Number	Title (A Side/B Side)	Yr	VG	VG+	NM
COLUMBIA					
❑ 43913	If You Still Want Me/Have You Ever Loved a Girl	1966	3.00	6.00	12.00
HUDSON					
❑ 8101	After Graduation/Come On Girl	1963	100.00	200.00	400.00
—Blue vinyl					
❑ 8101	After Graduation/Come On Girl	1963	37.50	75.00	150.00
—Black vinyl					

FOUR FRESHMEN, THE

Number	Title (A Side/B Side)	Yr	VG	VG+	NM
CAPITOL					
❑ F1293	Mr. B's Blues/Then I'll Be Happy	1950	3.75	7.50	15.00
❑ F1377	Now You Know/Pick Up Tears	1951	3.75	7.50	15.00
❑ F2152	It's a Blue World/Tuxedo Junction	1952	3.00	6.00	12.00
❑ F2286	Stormy Weather/The Day Isn't Long Enough	1952	3.00	6.00	12.00
❑ F2398	Baltimore Oriole/Poinciana	1953	3.00	6.00	12.00
❑ F2564	Holiday/It Happened Once Before	1953	3.00	6.00	12.00
❑ F2745	Seems Like Old Times/Crazy Bones	1954	3.00	6.00	12.00
❑ F2832	I'll Be Seeing You/Please Remember	1954	3.00	6.00	12.00
❑ F2898	We'll Be Together Again/My Heart Stood Still	1954	3.00	6.00	12.00
❑ F2961	Mood Indigo/Love Turns Winter to Spring	1954	3.00	6.00	12.00
❑ F3070	It Never Occurred to Me/Malaya	1955	2.50	5.00	10.00
❑ F3154	Day by Day/How Can I Tell Her	1955	2.50	5.00	10.00
❑ F3292	Charmaine/In This Whole Wide World	1955	2.50	5.00	10.00
❑ F3359	Angel Eyes/Love Is Just Around the Corner	1956	2.50	5.00	10.00
❑ F3410	Graduation Day/Lonely Night in Paris	1956	3.75	7.50	15.00
❑ F3532	You're So Far Above Me/He Who Loves and Runs Away	1956	2.50	5.00	10.00
❑ F3652	That's the Way I Feel/What's It Gonna Be	1957	2.50	5.00	10.00
❑ F3779	Julie Is Her Name/Sometimes I'm Happy	1957	2.50	5.00	10.00
❑ F3832	Grenada/How Can I Begin to Tell	1957	2.50	5.00	10.00
❑ F3930	Whistle Me Some Blues/Nights Are Longer	1958	2.50	5.00	10.00
❑ 4341	Candy/Route 66	1960	2.00	4.00	8.00
❑ 4749	Shangri-La/Teach Me Tonight	1962	2.00	4.00	8.00
❑ 4824	I'm Gonna Go Fishin'/Taps Miller	1962	2.00	4.00	8.00
❑ 5007	Summertime/Baby Won't You Please Come Home	1963	2.00	4.00	8.00
❑ 5083	Charade/Funny How Time Slips Away	1963	2.00	4.00	8.00
❑ 5151	Don't Make Me Sorry/My Baby's Gone	1964	2.00	4.00	8.00
❑ 5471	Those Magnificent Men in Their Flying Machines/Old Cape Cod	1965	2.50	5.00	10.00
DECCA					
❑ 32070	Cry/Nowhere to Go	1966	—	3.00	6.00
LIBERTY					
❑ 56047	Cherish-Windy/Come Fly with Me-Up Up and Away	1968	—	3.00	6.00
❑ 56099	By the Time I Get to Phoenix-My Special Angel/It's a Blue World	1969	—	3.00	6.00

7-Inch Extended Plays

Number	Title (A Side/B Side)	Yr	VG	VG+	NM
CAPITOL					
❑ EAP 1-763	*After You've Gone/Ev'ry Time We Say Goodbye/Easy Street/Good Night Sweetheart	1957	2.50	5.00	10.00
❑ EAP 1-763 [PS]	4 Freshmen and 5 Trumpets, Part 1	1957	2.50	5.00	10.00
❑ EAP 2-763	(contents unknown)	1957	2.50	5.00	10.00
❑ EAP 2-763 [PS]	4 Freshmen and 5 Trumpets, Part 2	1957	2.50	5.00	10.00
❑ EAP 3-763	(contents unknown)	1957	2.50	5.00	10.00
❑ EAP 3-763 [PS]	4 Freshmen and 5 Trumpets, Part 3	1957	2.50	5.00	10.00
❑ EAP 1-844	*Liza/You've Got Me Cryin' Again/This Love of Mine/I Get Along Without You Very Well	1957	2.50	5.00	10.00
❑ EAP 1-844 [PS]	Four Freshmen and Five Saxes, Part 1	1957	2.50	5.00	10.00
❑ EAP 2-844	(contents unknown)	1957	2.50	5.00	10.00
❑ EAP 2-844 [PS]	Four Freshmen and Five Saxes, Part 2	1957	2.50	5.00	10.00
❑ EAP 3-844	(contents unknown)	1957	2.50	5.00	10.00
❑ EAP 3-844 [PS]	Four Freshmen and Five Saxes, Part 3	1957	2.50	5.00	10.00
❑ EAP 1-1255	(contents unknown)	1959	2.50	5.00	10.00
❑ EAP 1-1255 [PS]	The Four Freshmen and Five Guitars, Part 1	1959	2.50	5.00	10.00
❑ EAP 2-1255	(contents unknown)	1959	2.50	5.00	10.00
❑ EAP 2-1255 [PS]	The Four Freshmen and Five Guitars, Part 2	1959	2.50	5.00	10.00
❑ EAP 3-1255	(contents unknown)	1959	2.50	5.00	10.00
❑ EAP 3-1255 [PS]	The Four Freshmen and Five Guitars, Part 3	1959	2.50	5.00	10.00

FOUR GRADUATES, THE

Number	Title (A Side/B Side)	Yr	VG	VG+	NM
CRYSTAL BALL					
❑ 116	May I Have This Dance/Caught in a Lie	1978	—	2.00	4.00
❑ 119	Your Initials/Every Year About This Time	1978	—	2.00	4.00
RUST					
❑ 5062	Picture of An Angel/A Lovely Way to Spend An Evening	1963	25.00	50.00	100.00
❑ 5084	Candy Queen/A Girl in Love	1964	45.00	90.00	180.00

FOUR HAVEN KNIGHTS, THE

Number	Title (A Side/B Side)	Yr	VG	VG+	NM
ANGLETONE					
❑ 1066	In My Lonely Room/I'm Just a Dreamer	1958	12.50	25.00	50.00
❑ 1092	Just to Be in Love/Why Go On Pretending	1958	12.50	25.00	50.00
ATLAS					
❑ 1066	In My Lonely Room/I'm Just a Dreamer	1957	37.50	75.00	150.00
❑ 1092	Just to Be in Love/Why Go On Pretending	1957	37.50	75.00	150.00
JOSIE					
❑ 824	In My Lonely Room/I'm Just a Dreamer	1957	7.50	15.00	30.00

FOUR HORSEMEN, THE

The MGM and United Artists records are probably by two different groups.

Number	Title (A Side/B Side)	Yr	VG	VG+	NM
MGM					
❑ 11300	Indian Love Call/San Antonio Rose	1952	3.75	7.50	15.00
❑ 11345	Memories/By the Waters of the Minnetonka	1952	3.75	7.50	15.00
❑ 11566	A Dear John Letter/No Stone Unturned	1953	3.75	7.50	15.00
❑ 12159	The Iron Horse/Go On with the Wedding	1955	3.75	7.50	15.00
UNITED ARTISTS					
❑ 134	A Long Long Time/My Heartbeat	1958	50.00	100.00	200.00

FOUR HUES, THE

Number	Title (A Side/B Side)	Yr	VG	VG+	NM
CORAL					
❑ 61617	Ivory Tower/Sister Jenny	1956	7.50	15.00	30.00
CROWN					
❑ 159	Rock-a-Bye/Take Me Out of Your Heart	1955	10.00	20.00	40.00

FOUR IMPERIALS, THE

Number	Title (A Side/B Side)	Yr	VG	VG+	NM
CHANT					
❑ 10067	My Girl/Teen Age Fool	1958	12.50	25.00	50.00
DIAL					
❑ 101	Valley of Tears/Time Out	1959	37.50	75.00	150.00
DOT					
❑ 15737	Lazy Bonnie/Let's Make a Scene	1958	6.25	12.50	25.00
FOX					
❑ 102	Give Me One More Chance/Look Up and Live	1958	20.00	40.00	80.00
LORELEI					
❑ 4444	Lazy Bonnie/Let's Make a Scene	1958	25.00	50.00	100.00
TWIRL					
❑ 2005	Santa's Got a Coupe de Ville/Seven Lonely Days	1960	6.25	12.50	25.00

FOUR J'S, THE

Number	Title (A Side/B Side)	Yr	VG	VG+	NM
4-J					
❑ 506	Will You Be My Love/Nursery	1963	3.75	7.50	15.00
CONGRESS					
❑ 6003	Dreamin'/Love My Life	1969	2.50	5.00	10.00
HERALD					
❑ 528	Kissin' at the Drive-In/Dreams Are a Dime a Dozen	1958	7.50	15.00	30.00
JAMIE					
❑ 1267	Here I Am Broken-Hearted/She Said That She Loved Me	1964	6.25	12.50	25.00
❑ 1274	By Love Possessed/My Love, My Love	1964	6.25	12.50	25.00
UNITED ARTISTS					
❑ 125	Rock and Roll Age/Be Nice, Don't Fight	1958	10.00	20.00	40.00

FOUR J'S, THE, AND THE FABULOUS IMPERIALS

Number	Title (A Side/B Side)	Yr	VG	VG+	NM
MGM					
❑ 12687	Class Ring/Weird	1958	20.00	40.00	80.00

FOUR JACKS, THE

Number	Title (A Side/B Side)	Yr	VG	VG+	NM
FEDERAL					
❑ 12075	You Met a Fool/Goodbye Baby	1952	200.00	400.00	800.00
❑ 12087	The Last of the Good Rockin' Men/I'll Be Home Again	1952	125.00	250.00	500.00
MGM					
❑ 11179	You're in Love with Someone Else/Darling, Lonesome for You	1952	5.00	10.00	20.00

FOUR JACKS AND A JILL (1)

Number	Title (A Side/B Side)	Yr	VG	VG+	NM
RCA VICTOR					
❑ 47-9473	Master Jack/I Looked Back	1968	2.00	4.00	8.00
❑ 47-9572	Mister Nico/Hamba Liliwam	1968	—	3.00	6.00
❑ 47-9655	Hey Mister/Sad Little Pigeon	1968	—	3.00	6.00
❑ 47-9728	Stone in My Shoe/Grandfather Dugan	1969	—	3.00	6.00

FOUR JACKS AND A JILL (2)

Number	Title (A Side/B Side)	Yr	VG	VG+	NM
FORTUNE					
❑ 507	Love's Not Love Without You/I'm in Love with Someone	1955	7.50	15.00	30.00

FOUR JACKS AND A JILL (U)

Number	Title (A Side/B Side)	Yr	VG	VG+	NM
HEART SONG					
❑ 103	It's Christmas Time Again/(B-side unknown)	19??	2.50	5.00	10.00

FOUR JETS, THE

See THE SHADOWS.

FOUR JEWELS, THE

Number	Title (A Side/B Side)	Yr	VG	VG+	NM
CHECKER					
❑ 1039	Dapper Dan/Loaded with Goodies	1963	5.00	10.00	20.00
❑ 1069	Time for Love/That's What They Put Erasers on Pencils For	1964	5.00	10.00	20.00
START					
❑ 638	Loaded with Goodies/Fire	1963	10.00	20.00	40.00
❑ 638	Johnny Jealousy/Someone Special	1963	7.50	15.00	30.00
❑ 641	All That's Good/I Love Me Some You	1963	7.50	15.00	30.00
TEC					
❑ 3007	Baby It's You/She's Wrong for You Baby	1964	6.25	12.50	25.00

FOUR JOKERS, THE (1)

Number	Title (A Side/B Side)	Yr	VG	VG+	NM
AMY					
❑ 832	She's a Flirt/Uggaboo	1961	5.00	10.00	20.00

FOUR JOKERS, THE (2)

Number	Title (A Side/B Side)	Yr	VG	VG+	NM
CRYSTALLETTE					
❑ 730	Your Decision/We Met in Catalina	1959	3.75	7.50	15.00
❑ 733	Beyond the Reef/That's the Way	1959	3.75	7.50	15.00

FOUR JOKERS, THE (3)

Jimmy Drake, a.k.a. NERVOUS NORVUS, was in this group.

Number	Title (A Side/B Side)	Yr	VG	VG+	NM
DIAMOND					
❑ 3004	Transfusion/You Dig	1956	7.50	15.00	30.00

FOUR JOKERS, THE (4)

Number	Title (A Side/B Side)	Yr	VG	VG+	NM
MGM					
❑ 11815	Tell Me Now/Caring	1954	7.50	15.00	30.00

FOUR JOKERS, THE (5)

Number	Title (A Side/B Side)	Yr	VG	VG+	NM
SUE					
❑ 703	Written in the Stars/The Run-Around	1958	15.00	30.00	60.00

FOUR JUST MEN

Also see FREDDIE AND THE DREAMERS.

Number	Title (A Side/B Side)	Yr	VG	VG+	NM
TOWER					
❑ 118	That's My Baby/Things Will Never Be the Same	1965	3.00	6.00	12.00

FOUR KINGS, THE

Number	Title (A Side/B Side)	Yr	VG	VG+	NM
CANADIAN AMERICAN					
❑ 173	One Night/Lonely Lovers	1964	6.25	12.50	25.00
—The Four Seasons sing backup					
❑ 173 [DJ]	One Night (no B-side)	1964	10.00	20.00	40.00
—White label promo with blank B-side					

FOUR KNIGHTS, THE

Number	Title (A Side/B Side)	Yr	VG	VG+	NM
CAPITOL					
❑ F1587	I Love the Sunshine of Your Smile/Sentimental Fool	1951	12.50	25.00	50.00
❑ F1707	Walkin' Whistlin' Blues/Who Am I	1951	10.00	20.00	40.00
❑ F1787	I Go Crazy/Get Her Off My Hands	1951	10.00	20.00	40.00
❑ F1806	It's No Sin/The Glory of Love	1951	10.00	20.00	40.00
❑ F1875	Cry/Charmaine	1951	10.00	20.00	40.00
❑ F1914	Marshmallow Moon/Five Foot Two, Eyes of Blue	1951	7.50	15.00	30.00
❑ F1930	The Way I Feel/I Wish I Had a Girl	1952	7.50	15.00	30.00
❑ F1971	There Are Two Sides to Every Heartache/Walkin' in Sunshine	1952	7.50	15.00	30.00
❑ F1998	The More I Go Out with Somebody Else/The Doll with the Sawdust Heart	1952	7.50	15.00	30.00
❑ F2087	I'm the World's Biggest Fool/It's a Sin to Tell a Lie	1952	7.50	15.00	30.00
❑ F2127	Win or Lose/Do-Wacka-Do	1952	7.50	15.00	30.00
❑ F2195	Say No More/That's the Way It's Gonna Be	1952	7.50	15.00	30.00
❑ F2234	Lies/One Way Kisses	1952	7.50	15.00	30.00
❑ F2315	Oh Happy Day/A Million Tears	1953	6.25	12.50	25.00
❑ F2403	Anniversary Song/A Few Kind Words	1953	6.25	12.50	25.00
❑ F2517	Baby Doll/Tennessee Train	1953	6.25	12.50	25.00
❑ F2654	Oh Baby Mine/I Couldn't Stay Away from You	1953	10.00	20.00	40.00
❑ F2654	I Get So Lonely (When I Dream About You)/I Couldn't Stay Away from You	1953	5.00	10.00	20.00
❑ F2782	I Was Meant for You/They Tell Me	1954	5.00	10.00	20.00
❑ F2847	How Wrong Can You Be/Period	1954	5.00	10.00	20.00
❑ F2894	In the Chapel in the Moonlight/Easy Street	1954	5.00	10.00	20.00
❑ F2938	I Don't Wanna See You Cryin'/Saw Your Eyes	1954	5.00	10.00	20.00
❑ F3024	Write Me Baby/Honey Bunch	1955	5.00	10.00	20.00
❑ F3093	Foolishly Yours/Inside You	1955	5.00	10.00	20.00
❑ F3155	Gratefully Yours/Me	1955	5.00	10.00	20.00
❑ F3192	Don't Sit Under the Apple Tree/Believing You	1955	5.00	10.00	20.00
❑ F3250	Perdido/After	1955	5.00	10.00	20.00
❑ F3279	Guilty/You	1955	5.00	10.00	20.00
❑ F3339	I Love You Still/Happy Birthday Baby	1956	3.75	7.50	15.00
❑ F3386	Bottle Up the Moonlight/Mistaken	1956	3.75	7.50	15.00
❑ F3494	Don't Depend on Me/You're a Honey	1956	3.75	7.50	15.00
❑ F3689	It Doesn't Cost Money/How Can You Not Believe	1957	3.75	7.50	15.00
❑ F3730	Walkin' and Whistlin' Blues/I Love That Song	1957	3.75	7.50	15.00
❑ F15895	I Ain't Got Nobody/When My Baby Smiles at Me	1952	7.50	15.00	30.00
❑ F15896	Easy Street/Ida, Sweet As Apple Cider	1952	7.50	15.00	30.00
❑ F15897	Georgia on My Mind/Sentimental Journey	1952	7.50	15.00	30.00
CORAL					
❑ 61936	The Four Minute Mile/When Your Lover Has Gone	1958	3.00	6.00	12.00
❑ 61981	Yes I Do/If You Ever Change Your Mind	1958	3.00	6.00	12.00
❑ 62045	O Falling Star/Foolish Tears	1959	3.00	6.00	12.00
❑ 62110	Where Is the Love/Things to Do Today	1959	3.00	6.00	12.00
DECCA					
❑ 48018	He'll Understand and Say Well Done/Lead Me to That Rock	1952	25.00	50.00	100.00
—Reissue of original 78 from 1947. (Decca 48014 and 48026 are known to exist only on 78s.)					

7-Inch Extended Plays

Number	Title (A Side/B Side)	Yr	VG	VG+	NM
CAPITOL					
❑ EAP 414	(contents unknown)	1953	10.00	20.00	40.00
❑ EAP 414 [PS]	The Four Knights Sing	1953	10.00	20.00	40.00
❑ EAP 506	(contents unknown)	1954	10.00	20.00	40.00
❑ EAP 506 [PS]	I Get So Lonely	1954	10.00	20.00	40.00
MONOGRAM					
❑ 2	Speaking of Angels/What Are You Doing New Year's Eve// + 2	19??	2.50	5.00	10.00

FOUR LADS, THE

Number	Title (A Side/B Side)	Yr	VG	VG+	NM
COLUMBIA					
❑ 39865	Somebody Loves Me/Thanks to You	1952	3.75	7.50	15.00
❑ 39902	Blackberry Boogie/Girl on the Shore	1952	3.75	7.50	15.00
❑ 39958	He Who Has Love/I Wonder, I Wonder, I Wonder	1953	3.75	7.50	15.00
❑ 40005	Down By the Riverside/Take Me Back	1953	3.75	7.50	15.00
❑ 40082	Istanbul (Not Constantinople)/I Should Have Told You Long Ago	1953	3.75	7.50	15.00
❑ 40140	Harmony Brown/Gotta Go to the Fais Do Do	1953	3.75	7.50	15.00
❑ 40204	Long John/The Place Where I Worship	1954	3.75	7.50	15.00
❑ 40220	What Can I Lose by Letting You Know/Oh That'll Be Joyful	1954	3.75	7.50	15.00
❑ 40236	Gilly Gilly Ossenfeffer Katzenelle Bogen by the Sea/I Hear It Everywhere	1954	3.75	7.50	15.00
❑ 40306	Skokiaan (South African Song)/Why Should I Love You So	1954	3.75	7.50	15.00
❑ 40402	Two Ladies in De Shade of De Banana Tree/Dance Calinda	1954	3.75	7.50	15.00
❑ 40436	Pledging My Love/I've Been Thinking	1955	3.00	6.00	12.00
❑ 40490	Too Much! Baby, Baby/The Average Giraffe	1955	3.00	6.00	12.00
❑ 40539	Moments to Remember/Dream On, My Love, Dream On	1955	3.00	6.00	12.00
❑ 40629	No, Not Much!/I'll Never Know	1955	3.00	6.00	12.00
❑ 40674	Standing on the Corner/My Little Angel	1956	3.00	6.00	12.00
❑ 40736	The Bus Stop Song (A Paper of Pins)/A House with Love In It	1956	3.00	6.00	12.00
❑ 40788	Mary's Little Boy Child/The Stingiest Man in Town	1956	3.00	6.00	12.00
❑ 40811	Who Needs You/It's So Easy to Forget	1956	3.00	6.00	12.00

Number	Title (A Side/B Side)	Yr	VG	VG+	NM
❑ 40811 [PS]	Who Needs You/It's So Easy to Forget	1956	5.00	10.00	20.00
❑ 40914	I Just Don't Know/Golly	1957	3.00	6.00	12.00
❑ 40974	The Eyes of God/His Invisible Hand	1957	3.00	6.00	12.00
❑ 41058	Put a Light in the Window/The Things We Did Last Summer	1957	2.50	5.00	10.00
❑ 41136	There's Only One of You/Blue Tattoo	1958	2.50	5.00	10.00
❑ 41194	Enchanted Island/Guess What the Neighbors'll Say	1958	2.50	5.00	10.00
❑ 41194 [PS]	Enchanted Island/Guess What the Neighbors'll Say	1958	3.75	7.50	15.00
❑ 41266	The Mocking Bird/I May Hate Myself in the Morning	1958	2.50	5.00	10.00
❑ 41310	The Girl on Page 44/Sunday	1958	2.50	5.00	10.00
❑ 41365	The Fountain of Youth/Meet Me Tonight in Dreamland	1959	2.50	5.00	10.00
❑ 41409	The Chosen Few/Together Wherever We Go	1959	2.50	5.00	10.00
❑ 41443	Got a Locket in My Pocket/Real Thing	1959	2.50	5.00	10.00
❑ 41497	Happy Anniversary/Who Do You Think You Are	1959	2.50	5.00	10.00
❑ 41497 [PS]	Happy Anniversary/Who Do You Think You Are	1959	3.75	7.50	15.00
❑ 41629	You're Nobody 'Til Somebody Loves You/Goona Goona	1960	2.50	5.00	10.00
❑ 41682	Our Lady of Fatima (Vocal)/Our Lady of Fatima (Recitation)	1960	2.50	5.00	10.00
❑ 41733	Two Other People/The Sheik of Chicago (Mustafa)	1960	2.50	5.00	10.00

DOT

Number	Title (A Side/B Side)	Yr	VG	VG+	NM
❑ 16328	Don't Fly Away, Flamingo/Winter Snow	1962	2.00	4.00	8.00
❑ 16373	The Exodus Song/Never on Sunday	1962	2.00	4.00	8.00
❑ 16390	That's What I Like/Sweet Mama Tree-Top Tall	1962	2.00	4.00	8.00
❑ 16412	Beyond My Heart/Not That I Care	1962	2.00	4.00	8.00

EPIC

Number	Title (A Side/B Side)	Yr	VG	VG+	NM
❑ 9150	The Mocking Bird/I May Hate Myself in the Morning	1956	3.00	6.00	12.00

FONA

Number	Title (A Side/B Side)	Yr	VG	VG+	NM
❑ 1000	You'll Never Know/(B-side unknown)	1977	—	2.00	4.00
❑ 1001	Moments to Remember/Skokiaan	1977	—	2.00	4.00

KAPP

Number	Title (A Side/B Side)	Yr	VG	VG+	NM
❑ 359	Just Young/Goodbye Mr. Love	1960	2.00	4.00	8.00
❑ 359 [PS]	Just Young/Goodbye Mr. Love	1960	2.50	5.00	10.00
❑ 404	555 Times/I Should Know Better	1961	2.00	4.00	8.00
❑ 412	Giuggigla/Oceans of Love	1961	2.00	4.00	8.00

OKEH

Number	Title (A Side/B Side)	Yr	VG	VG+	NM
❑ 6885	The Mocking Bird/I May Hate Myself in the Morning	1952	5.00	10.00	20.00

REPRISE

Number	Title (A Side/B Side)	Yr	VG	VG+	NM
❑ 20163	My Home Town/Cornflower Blue	1963	2.00	4.00	8.00

UNITED ARTISTS

Number	Title (A Side/B Side)	Yr	VG	VG+	NM
❑ 653	It's a Mad, Mad, Mad, Mad World/Stolen Hours	1963	—	3.00	6.00
❑ 702	Love Theme from "Tom Jones"/Theme from "Lilies of the Field"	1964	—	3.00	6.00
❑ 760	Memories of You/Always Thinking of the Roses	1964	—	3.00	6.00
❑ 852	Thanks, Mr. Florist/Barabanchik	1965	—	3.00	6.00
❑ 893	With My Eyes Wide Open/I'm Not a Run-Around	1965	—	3.00	6.00
❑ 962	Give Her My Love/All the Winds	1965	—	3.00	6.00
❑ 50006	No, Not Much/Standing on the Corner	1966	—	2.50	5.00
❑ 50339	Where Do I Go/A Woman	1968	—	2.50	5.00
❑ 50517	My Heart's Symphony/Pardon Me Kiss	1969	—	2.50	5.00
❑ 50585	Moments to Remember/Free Again	1969	—	2.50	5.00

7-Inch Extended Plays

COLUMBIA

Number	Title (A Side/B Side)	Yr	VG	VG+	NM
❑ B-2557	*Standing on the Corner/Take Me Back/Skokiaan/Who Needs You	1958	3.75	7.50	15.00
❑ B-2557 [PS]	The Four Lads (Hall of Fame Series)	1958	3.75	7.50	15.00

FOUR LARKS, THE

TOWER

Number	Title (A Side/B Side)	Yr	VG	VG+	NM
❑ 364	Rain/Another Chance	1967	7.50	15.00	30.00
❑ 402	I Still Love You (From the Bottom of My Heart)/Groovin' at the Go-Go	1968	10.00	20.00	40.00
❑ 450	Can I Have Another Helping, Please/I've Got Plenty	1968	2.50	5.00	10.00

UPTOWN

Number	Title (A Side/B Side)	Yr	VG	VG+	NM
❑ 748	You and Me/That's All That Counts	1967	10.00	20.00	40.00

FOUR LOVERS, THE

Also see THE FOUR SEASONS; FRANKIE VALLI.

EPIC

Number	Title (A Side/B Side)	Yr	VG	VG+	NM
❑ 9255	My Life for Your Love/Pucker Up	1957	500.00	1000.	2000.

RCA VICTOR

Number	Title (A Side/B Side)	Yr	VG	VG+	NM
❑ 47-6518	You're the Apple of My Eye/The Girl of My Dreams	1956	10.00	20.00	40.00
❑ 47-6519	Honey Love/Please Don't Leave Me	1956	10.00	20.00	40.00
❑ 47-6646	Be Lovey Dovey/Jambalaya	1956	7.50	15.00	30.00
❑ 47-6768	Happy Am I/Never Never	1956	7.50	15.00	30.00
❑ 47-6812	Shake a Hand/The Stranger	1957	10.00	20.00	40.00
❑ 47-6819	Night Train/The Stranger	1957	10.00	20.00	40.00

7-Inch Extended Plays

RCA VICTOR

Number	Title (A Side/B Side)	Yr	VG	VG+	NM
❑ EPA-869	Diddley Diddley Babe/Shake a Hand//The Stranger/Night Train	1956	37.50	75.00	150.00
❑ EPA-869 [PS]	The Four Lovers	1956	37.50	75.00	150.00
❑ EPA-871	I Want a Girl Just Like the Girl That Married Dear Old Dad/(I Love You) For Sentimental Reasons//This Is My Story/Memories of You	1956	37.50	75.00	150.00
❑ EPA-871 [PS]	Joyride	1956	37.50	75.00	150.00

FOUR NATURALS, THE

RED TOP

Number	Title (A Side/B Side)	Yr	VG	VG+	NM
❑ 113	How Strange/Blue Moon	1958	12.50	25.00	50.00

—As "The Naturals"

Number	Title (A Side/B Side)	Yr	VG	VG+	NM
❑ 119	I Hear a Rhapsody/When I'm In Your Arms	1959	12.50	25.00	50.00
❑ 125	The Thought of You Darling/Long Long Ago	1959	20.00	40.00	80.00

FOUR PEARLS, THE

DOLTON

Number	Title (A Side/B Side)	Yr	VG	VG+	NM
❑ 26	Look at Me/It's Almost Tomorrow	1960	50.00	100.00	200.00

FOUR PENNIES, THE (1)

See THE CHIFFONS.

FOUR PENNIES, THE (2)

British group.

PHILIPS

Number	Title (A Side/B Side)	Yr	VG	VG+	NM
❑ 40202	Juliet/Tell Me Girl. What Are You Gonna Do	1964	3.75	7.50	15.00
❑ 40333	Until It's Time for You to Go/Till Another Day	1965	3.75	7.50	15.00

FOUR PENNIES, THE (U)

May also be by group (2), but we're not sure.

BRUNSWICK

Number	Title (A Side/B Side)	Yr	VG	VG+	NM
❑ 55304	You Have No Time to Lose/You're a Gas with Your Trash	1966	2.50	5.00	10.00
❑ 55324	Shake a Hand/'Tis the Season	1967	5.00	10.00	20.00

FOUR PREPS, THE

CAPITOL

Number	Title (A Side/B Side)	Yr	VG	VG+	NM
❑ F3576	Dreamy Eyes/Fools Will Be Fools	1956	5.00	10.00	20.00
❑ F3621	Moonstruck in Madrid/I Cried a Million Tears	1957	5.00	10.00	20.00
❑ F3699	Falling Star/Where Wuzz You	1957	5.00	10.00	20.00
❑ F3761	Promise Me Baby/Again 'N Again 'N Again	1957	5.00	10.00	20.00
❑ F3775	Band of Angels/How About That	1957	5.00	10.00	20.00
❑ F3845	26 Miles (Santa Catalina)/It's You	1957	5.00	10.00	20.00
❑ F3960	Big Man/Stop Baby	1958	5.00	10.00	20.00
❑ F4023	Lazy Summer Night/Summertime Lies	1958	5.00	10.00	20.00
❑ F4078	Cinderella/Gidget	1958	5.00	10.00	20.00
❑ F4126	She Was Five and He Was Ten/Riddle of Love	1959	5.00	10.00	20.00
❑ F4218	Big Surprise/Try My Arms	1959	5.00	10.00	20.00
❑ F4256	I Ain't Never/Memories, Memories	1959	5.00	10.00	20.00
❑ 4312	Down by the Station/Listen Honey	1959	3.00	6.00	12.00
❑ 4362	Got a Girl/Wait Till You Hear It from Me	1960	3.00	6.00	12.00
❑ 4400	Sentimental Kid/Madelina	1960	3.00	6.00	12.00
❑ 4435	The Sand and the Sea/Kaw-Liga	1960	3.00	6.00	12.00
❑ 4478	Balboa/I've Already Started In	1960	3.00	6.00	12.00
❑ 4508	Calcutta/Gone Are the Days	1961	3.00	6.00	12.00
❑ 4568	Dream, Boy, Dream/Grounded	1961	7.50	15.00	30.00
❑ 4599	More Money for You and Me/Swing Down Chariot	1961	3.75	7.50	15.00

—With full-length version of A-side

Number	Title (A Side/B Side)	Yr	VG	VG+	NM
❑ 4599	More Money for You and Me/Swing Down Chariot	1961	3.00	6.00	12.00

—With edited version of A-side

Number	Title (A Side/B Side)	Yr	VG	VG+	NM
❑ 4599 [PS]	More Money for You and Me/Swing Down Chariot	1961	5.00	10.00	20.00
❑ 4641	Smoke Gets In Your Eyes/Swing Down Chariot	1961	3.00	6.00	12.00
❑ 4659	Once Around the Block/The Seine	1961	3.00	6.00	12.00
❑ 4716	The Big Draft/Suzy Cockroach	1962	2.50	5.00	10.00
❑ 4716 [PS]	The Big Draft/Suzy Cockroach	1962	2.50	5.00	10.00
❑ 4792	Alice/Goodnight Sweetheart	1962	2.50	5.00	10.00
❑ 4974	Charmaine/Hi-Ho Anybody Home	1963	2.50	5.00	10.00
❑ 5020	Oh Where, Oh Where/Demons and Witches	1963	2.50	5.00	10.00
❑ 5074	The Greatest Surfer Couple/I'm Falling in Love with a Girl	1963	2.50	5.00	10.00
❑ 5143	A Letter to the Beatles/College Cannonball	1964	6.25	12.50	25.00
❑ 5178	I've Known You All My Life/What Kind of Bird Is That	1964	2.00	4.00	8.00
❑ 5236	A Girl Without a Top/Two Wrongs Don't Make a Right	1964	2.00	4.00	8.00
❑ 5274	How to Succeed in Love/My Love, My Love	1964	2.00	4.00	8.00
❑ 5351	Everlasting/I'll Set My Love to Music	1965	2.00	4.00	8.00
❑ 5450	Now I'll Never Be the Same/Our First American Dance	1965	2.00	4.00	8.00
❑ 5609	Annie in Her Granny/Something to Remember You By	1966	2.00	4.00	8.00
❑ 5687	Let's Call It a Day, Girl/The Girl in the Shade of a Striped Umbrella	1966	2.00	4.00	8.00
❑ 5819	Love of the Common People/What I Don't Know Won't Hurt Me	1967	2.00	4.00	8.00
❑ 5921	Draft Dodger Rag/The Hitchhiker	1967	2.00	4.00	8.00

7-Inch Extended Plays

CAPITOL

Number	Title (A Side/B Side)	Yr	VG	VG+	NM
❑ EAP 1-1015	(contents unknown)	1958	6.25	12.50	25.00
❑ EAP 1-1015 [PS]	Twenty-Six Miles	1958	6.25	12.50	25.00
❑ EAP 1-1064	Big Man/Too Young for Love//Stop, Baby/Humble Pie	1958	6.25	12.50	25.00
❑ EAP 1-1064 [PS]	Big Man	1958	6.25	12.50	25.00
❑ EAP 1-1090	(contents unknown)	1959	6.25	12.50	25.00
❑ EAP 1-1090 [PS]	Things We Did Last Summer	1959	6.25	12.50	25.00
❑ EAP 1-1139	(contents unknown)	1959	6.25	12.50	25.00
❑ EAP 1-1139 [PS]	Lazy Summer Night	1959	6.25	12.50	25.00

FOUR SEASONS, THE

Also see THE FOUR LOVERS; FRANKIE VALLI.

COLUMBIA

Number	Title (A Side/B Side)	Yr	VG	VG+	NM
❑ (# unknown)	Big Man's World	1964	7.50	15.00	30.00

—One-sided cardboard soundsheet, a promo for the Columbia Record Club. Number has been reported as both 6675 and 6724.

CREWE

Number	Title (A Side/B Side)	Yr	VG	VG+	NM
❑ 333	And That Reminds Me (My Heart Reminds Me)/The Singles Game	1969	2.00	4.00	8.00
❑ 333 [PS]	And That Reminds Me (My Heart Reminds Me)/The Singles Game	1969	2.50	5.00	10.00

—No shadow behind Frankie Valli's and Joe Long's heads

Number	Title (A Side/B Side)	Yr	VG	VG+	NM
❑ 333 [PS]	And That Reminds Me (My Heart Reminds Me)/The Singles Game	1969	3.00	6.00	12.00

—With shadow behind Frankie Valli's and Joe Long's heads

FBI

Number	Title (A Side/B Side)	Yr	VG	VG+	NM
❑ 7701	East Meets West/Rhapsody	1986	5.00	10.00	20.00

—With the Beach Boys

(Top left) "Move Enterprises Ltd. Presents the Services of The Electric Light Orch." That's the full credit on this, ELO's first American 45, "10538 Overture." The off-shoot soon eclipsed the Move, and once Roy Wood left to form Wizzard, the Move was history. (Top right) Among the rarest picture sleeves by a female singer are those featuring Shelley Fabares. The sleeve for "Johnny Angel" is one of the most sought-after, with a value well into three figures. (Bottom left) Tennessee Ernie Ford was known for "Sixteen Tons" and his many albums of hymns, but he also had a TV show for a few years. As one of his favorite sayings was "Bless your little pea-pickin' hearts," this EP, "When Pea Pickers Get Together," was a natural result. Even more natural is that it was a promotional item for Le Sueur peas! (Bottom right) "Something's on Her Mind" was a wonderful late-1960s single by the Four Seasons. It's all but forgotten today, as is this obscure picture sleeve, because it wasn't a hit.

Number	Title (A Side/B Side)	Yr	VG	VG+	NM
FOUR SEASONS					
❑ 0019	I Saw Mommy Kissing Santa Claus/Santa Claus Is Coming To Town	198?	—	2.00	4.00
GONE					
❑ 5122	Bermuda/Spanish Lace	1961	20.00	40.00	80.00
❑ 5122 [DJ]	Bermuda/Spanish Lace	1961	15.00	30.00	60.00
MCA/CURB					
❑ 52618	Streetfighter/Deep Inside Your Love	1985	—	2.00	4.00
❑ 52724	Moonlight Memories/What About Tomorrow	1985	—	2.00	4.00
❑ 52871	Book of Love/What About Tomorrow	1986	—	2.00	4.00
❑ 53440	Big Girls Don't Cry (Enhanced Original Mix)/Big Girls Don't Cry (Dirty Dancing Rap)	1988	—	2.00	4.00
MOTOWN					
❑ 1255	How Come/Life and Breath	1973	2.50	5.00	10.00
❑ 1288	Hickory/Charisma	1973	2.50	5.00	10.00
MOWEST					
❑ 5026	Walk On, Don't Look Back/Sun Country	1972	2.50	5.00	10.00
OLDIES 45					
❑ #18	Sherry/I've Cried Before	1964	2.00	4.00	8.00
❑ #47	Big Girls Don't Cry/Connie-O	1964	2.00	4.00	8.00
❑ #60	Walk Like a Man/Lucky Ladybug	1964	2.00	4.00	8.00
❑ #116	Candy Girl/Marlena	1964	2.00	4.00	8.00
❑ #319	Stay/Goodnight My Love	1965	2.00	4.00	8.00
PHILIPS					
❑ 40166	Dawn (Go Away)/No Surfin' Today	1964	3.75	7.50	15.00
—Black label					
❑ 40166	Dawn (Go Away)/No Surfin' Today	1967	2.00	4.00	8.00
—Light blue label with "S" stamp					
❑ 40185	Ronnie/Born to Wander	1964	3.00	6.00	12.00
❑ 40185 [PS]	Ronnie/Born to Wander	1964	7.50	15.00	30.00
❑ 40211	Rag Doll/Silence Is Golden	1964	3.75	7.50	15.00
—Black label					
❑ 40211	Rag Doll/Silence Is Golden	1967	2.00	4.00	8.00
—Light blue label with "S" stamp					
❑ 40211 [PS]	Rag Doll/Silence Is Golden	1964	7.50	15.00	30.00
—Yellow sleeve					
❑ 40211 [PS]	Rag Doll/Silence Is Golden	1964	7.50	15.00	30.00
—Green sleeve					
❑ 40225	Save It for Me/Funny Face	1964	2.50	5.00	10.00
❑ 40238	Big Man in Town/Little Angel	1964	2.50	5.00	10.00
❑ 40238 [PS]	Big Man in Town/Little Angel	1964	6.25	12.50	25.00
❑ 40260	Bye, Bye Baby (Baby Goodbye)/Searching Wind	1965	2.50	5.00	10.00
❑ 40260 [PS]	Bye, Bye Baby (Baby Goodbye)/Searching Wind	1965	6.25	12.50	25.00
❑ 40278	Toy Soldier/Betrayed	1965	2.50	5.00	10.00
❑ 40278 [PS]	Toy Soldier/Betrayed	1965	6.25	12.50	25.00
❑ 40305	Girl Come Running/Cry Myself to Sleep	1965	2.50	5.00	10.00
❑ 40305 [PS]	Girl Come Running/Cry Myself to Sleep	1965	6.25	12.50	25.00
❑ 40317	Let's Hang On!/On Broadway Tonight	1965	2.50	5.00	10.00
—Black label					
❑ 40317	Let's Hang On!/On Broadway Tonight	1967	2.00	4.00	8.00
—Light blue label with "S" stamp					
❑ 40324	Don't Think Twice/Sassy	1965	2.50	5.00	10.00
❑ 40324 [PS]	Don't Think Twice/Sassy	1965	6.25	12.50	25.00
—Philips 40324 by "The Wonder Who?"					
❑ 40350	Working My Way Back to You/Too Many Memories	1966	2.50	5.00	10.00
❑ 40370	Opus 17 (Don't You Worry 'Bout Me)/Beggar's Paradise	1966	2.50	5.00	10.00
❑ 40370 [PS]	Opus 17 (Don't You Worry 'Bout Me)/Beggar's Paradise	1966	6.25	12.50	25.00
❑ 40380	On the Good Ship Lollipop/You're Nobody Until Somebody Loves You	1966	2.50	5.00	10.00
❑ 40380 [PS]	On the Good Ship Lollipop/You're Nobody Until Somebody Loves You	1966	6.25	12.50	25.00
—Philips 40380 by "The Wonder Who?"					
❑ 40393	I've Got You Under My Skin/Huggin' My Pillow	1966	2.50	5.00	10.00
❑ 40393 [PS]	I've Got You Under My Skin/Huggin' My Pillow	1966	6.25	12.50	25.00
❑ 40412	Tell It to the Rain/Show Girl	1966	2.50	5.00	10.00
❑ 40412 [PS]	Tell It to the Rain/Show Girl	1966	6.25	12.50	25.00
❑ 40433	Beggin'/Dody	1967	2.50	5.00	10.00
—Black label					
❑ 40433	Beggin'/Dody	1967	2.00	4.00	8.00
—Light blue label					
❑ 40433 [PS]	Beggin'/Dody	1967	6.25	12.50	25.00
❑ 40460	C'mon Marianne/Let's Ride Again	1967	2.50	5.00	10.00
—Black label					
❑ 40460	C'mon Marianne/Let's Ride Again	1967	3.00	6.00	12.00
—Blue label; contains a noticeably different, slowed-down mix of A-side					
❑ 40460 [PS]	C'mon Marianne/Let's Ride Again	1967	6.25	12.50	25.00
❑ 40471	Lonesome Road/Around and Around	1967	2.50	5.00	10.00
❑ 40471 [PS]	Lonesome Road/Around and Around	1967	6.25	12.50	25.00
—Philips 40471 by "The Wonder Who?"; B-side listed as The Four Seasons					
❑ 40490	Watch the Flowers Grow/Raven	1967	2.50	5.00	10.00
❑ 40490 [PS]	Watch the Flowers Grow/Raven	1967	6.25	12.50	25.00
❑ 40500	Donneybrook/Around and Around	1968	5.00	10.00	20.00
—Only released in Canada					
❑ 40523	Will You Love Me Tomorrow/Around and Around	1968	3.00	6.00	12.00
—Black label					
❑ 40523	Will You Love Me Tomorrow/Around and Around	1968	2.50	5.00	10.00
—Blue label					
❑ 40542	Saturday's Father/Good-Bye Girl	1968	—	3.00	6.00
❑ 40542 [PS]	Saturday's Father/Good-Bye Girl	1968	2.50	5.00	10.00
—Standard sleeve					
❑ 40542 [PS]	Saturday's Father/Good-Bye Girl	1968	3.75	7.50	15.00
—Fold-open sleeve					
❑ 40577	Electric Stories/Pity	1968	—	3.00	6.00
❑ 40597	Something's On Her Mind/Idaho	1969	—	3.00	6.00
❑ 40597 [PS]	Something's On Her Mind/Idaho	1969	2.50	5.00	10.00
❑ 40662	Patch of Blue/She Gives Me Light	1970	2.00	4.00	8.00
—As "Frankie Valli & THE 4 SEASONS"					
❑ 40662 [PS]	Patch of Blue/She Gives Me Light	1970	2.50	5.00	10.00

Number	Title (A Side/B Side)	Yr	VG	VG+	NM
❑ 40688	Lay Me Down (Wake Me Up)/Heartaches and Rainbows	1970	6.25	12.50	25.00
❑ 40688 [DJ]	Lay Me Down (Wake Me Up) (mono/stereo)	1970	3.75	7.50	15.00
❑ 40694	Where Are My Dreams?/Any Day Now-Oh Happy Day	1971	6.25	12.50	25.00
❑ 40694 [DJ]	Where Are My Dreams? (mono/stereo)	1971	3.75	7.50	15.00
SEASONS 4-EVER					
❑ 777	Trance/I Am All Alone	1971	3.75	7.50	15.00
—As "Billy Dixon and the Topics"; blue vinyl					
❑ 777	Trance/I Am All Alone	1971	2.00	4.00	8.00
—As "Billy Dixon and the Topics"; green vinyl					
TOPIX					
❑ 6000	Too Young to Start/Red Lips	1960	37.50	75.00	150.00
—As "The Village Voices"; yellow and black label					
❑ 6000	Too Young to Start/Red Lips	1960	25.00	50.00	100.00
—As "The Village Voices"; yellow, black and white label					
❑ 6002	I Am All Alone/Trance	1961	37.50	75.00	150.00
—As "Billy Dixon and the Topics"					
❑ 6008	Lost Lullaby/Trance	1961	50.00	100.00	200.00
—As "Billy Dixon and the Topics"					
VEE JAY					
❑ 456	Sherry/I've Cried Before	1962	6.25	12.50	25.00
—First pressings have black rainbow labels with oval logo					
❑ 456	Sherry/I've Cried Before	1962	6.25	12.50	25.00
—A later pressing has an all-black label					
❑ 465	Big Girls Don't Cry/Connie-O	1962	5.00	10.00	20.00
—First pressings have black rainbow labels with oval logo					
❑ 465	Big Girls Don't Cry/Connie-O	1962	6.25	12.50	25.00
—A later pressing has an all-black label					
❑ 478	Santa Claus Is Coming to Town/Christmas Tears	1962	6.25	12.50	25.00
❑ 485	Walk Like a Man/Lucky Ladybug	1963	3.75	7.50	15.00
❑ 512	Ain't That a Shame!/Soon (I'll Be Home Again)	1963	5.00	10.00	20.00
❑ 539	Candy Girl/Marlena	1963	3.75	7.50	15.00
❑ 562	New Mexican Rose/That's the Only Way	1963	3.75	7.50	15.00
❑ 562 [DJ]	New Mexican Rose/That's the Way It Goes	1963	7.50	15.00	30.00
—Wrong title on B-side; evidently only exists on promos					
❑ 576	Peanuts/Stay	1963	25.00	50.00	100.00
❑ 576 [DJ]	Peanuts/Stay	1963	15.00	30.00	60.00
❑ 582	Stay/Goodnight My Love	1964	3.75	7.50	15.00
❑ 597	Alone/Long, Lonely Nights	1964	3.75	7.50	15.00
—Black rainbow label					
❑ 597	Alone/Long, Lonely Nights	1964	6.25	12.50	25.00
—Plain black label					
❑ 597	Alone/Long, Lonely Nights	1964	7.50	15.00	30.00
—Yellow label					
❑ 597 [PS]	Alone/Long, Lonely Nights	1964	12.50	25.00	50.00
❑ 608	Sincerely/One Song	1964	5.00	10.00	20.00
❑ 618	Happy, Happy Birthday Baby/You're the Apple of My Eye	1964	5.00	10.00	20.00
❑ 626	I Saw Mommy Kissing Santa Claus/Christmas Tears	1964	5.00	10.00	20.00
❑ 626 [PS]	I Saw Mommy Kissing Santa Claus/Christmas Tears	1964	12.50	25.00	50.00
❑ 639	Never on Sunday/Connie-O	1965	5.00	10.00	20.00
❑ 664	Since I Don't Have You/Tonite, Tonite	1965	7.50	15.00	30.00
❑ 713	Little Boy (In Grown Up Clothes)/Silver Wings	1965	5.00	10.00	20.00
—Maroon label					
❑ 713	Little Boy (In Grown Up Clothes)/Silver Wings	1965	7.50	15.00	30.00
—Black label					
❑ 717	Peanuts/My Sugar	1966	7.50	15.00	30.00
—As "The Wonder Who"					
❑ 719	My Mother's Eyes/Stay	1966	3.75	7.50	15.00
❑ 901 [DJ]	Peanuts	1963	25.00	50.00	100.00
—One-sided promo from EP 901					
WABC RADIO					
❑ 77	Cousin Brucie Go Go	1964	37.50	75.00	150.00
—One-sided yellow vinyl; theme song for Cousin Brucie's radio show					
WARNER BROS.					
❑ 8122	Who Loves You/Who Loves You (Disco Version)	1975	—	2.50	5.00
❑ 8168	December, 1963 (Oh, What a Night)/Slip Away	1975	—	2.50	5.00
❑ 8203	Silver Star/Mystic Mr. Sam	1976	—	2.50	5.00
❑ 8407	Down the Hall/I Believe in You	1977	2.00	4.00	8.00
❑ 49585	Heaven Must Have Sent You (Here in the Night)/Silver Star	1981	2.00	4.00	8.00
❑ 49597	Spend the Night in Love/Slip Away	1980	2.00	4.00	8.00
WIBBAGE					
❑ WIBG-	Joey Reynolds Theme/Rats in My Room	1965	25.00	50.00	100.00
—Custom pressing for Philadelphia radio station; B-side by Joey and Danny					
WXYZ DETROIT					
❑ 121003	Joey Reynolds Theme/Rats in My Room	1965	25.00	50.00	100.00
—Custom pressing for Detroit radio station; B-side by Joey and Danny					
7-Inch Extended Plays					
VEE JAY					
❑ EP 1-901	Never on Sunday/Peanuts//I Can't Give You Anything But Love/La Dee Dah	1962	6.25	12.50	25.00
❑ EP 1-901 [PS]	The Four Seasons Sing	1962	6.25	12.50	25.00
❑ EP 1-902	Why Do Fools Fall in Love/Silhouettes//Since I Don't Have You/Alone	1963	6.25	12.50	25.00
❑ EP 1-902 [PS]	The Four Seasons Sing	1963	6.25	12.50	25.00

FOUR SEASONS, THE (2)

Not the same as the better-known group.

Number	Title (A Side/B Side)	Yr	VG	VG+	NM
ALANNA					
❑ 555	Don't Sweat It Baby/That's the Way the Ball Bounces	1959	10.00	20.00	40.00
❑ 555	I'm Still in Love with You, Baby/That's the Way the Ball Bounces	1959	15.00	30.00	60.00
❑ 558	Love Knows No Season/Hot Water Bottle	1959	7.50	15.00	30.00
ROBBEE					
❑ 106	Mirage/Nancy's Trampoline	1960	37.50	75.00	150.00

FOUR SPEEDS, THE

Number	Title (A Side/B Side)	Yr	VG	VG+	NM
CHALLENGE					
❑ 9187	R.P.M./My Sting Ray	1963	10.00	20.00	40.00
❑ 9202	Four on the Floor/Cheater Slicks	1963	10.00	20.00	40.00
FEDERAL					
❑ 6070	I Need You Baby/The Girls Back Home	1954	20.00	40.00	80.00

FOUR STUDENTS, THE

Number	Title (A Side/B Side)	Yr	VG	VG+	NM
GROOVE					
❑ 0110	So Near and Yet So Far/Hot Rotten Soda Pop	1955	12.50	25.00	50.00

FOUR TEENS, THE

Number	Title (A Side/B Side)	Yr	VG	VG+	NM
CHALLENGE					
❑ 59021	Go Little Go Cat/Spark Plug	1958	15.00	30.00	60.00

FOUR TEMPTATIONS, THE

Number	Title (A Side/B Side)	Yr	VG	VG+	NM
ABC-PARAMOUNT					
❑ 9920	Cathy/Rock and Roll Baby	1958	7.50	15.00	30.00

FOUR TOPS, THE

Also see DELORES CARROLL AND THE FOUR TOPS.

Number	Title (A Side/B Side)	Yr	VG	VG+	NM
ABC					
❑ 12096	Seven Lonely Nights/I Can't Hold Out Much Longer	1975	—	2.00	4.00
❑ 12123	We All Gotta Stick Together/(It Would Almost) Drive Me Out of My Mind	1975	—	2.00	4.00
❑ 12155	I'm Glad You Walked Into My Life/Mama, You're All Right with Me	1975	—	2.00	4.00
❑ 12214	Catfish/Look at My Baby	1976	—	2.00	4.00
❑ 12223	Look at My Baby/Catfish	1976	—	2.00	4.00
❑ 12236	Feel Free/I Know You Like It	1976	—	2.00	4.00
❑ 12267	Strung Out for Your Love/You Can't Hold Back on Love	1977	—	2.00	4.00
❑ 12315	Runnin' From Your Love/The Show Must Go On	1977	—	2.00	4.00
❑ 12427	Inside a Brokenhearted Man/H.E.L.P.	1978	—	2.00	4.00
❑ 12457	Just in Time/This House	1978	—	2.00	4.00
ABC DUNHILL					
❑ 4330	Keeper of the Castle/Jubilee with Soul	1972	—	2.50	5.00
❑ 4334	Guardian De Tu Castle/Jubilee with Soul	1972	—	2.50	5.00
❑ 4339	Ain't No Woman (Like the One I've Got)/The Good Lord Knows	1973	—	2.50	5.00
❑ 4354	Are You Man Enough/Peace of Mind	1973	—	2.50	5.00
❑ 4366	Sweet Understanding Love/Main Street People	1973	—	2.50	5.00
❑ 4377	I Just Can't Get You Out of My Mind/Am I My Brother's Keeper?	1973	—	2.50	5.00
❑ 4386	One Chain Don't Make No Prison/Light of Your Love	1974	—	2.50	5.00
❑ 15005	Midnight Flower/All My Love	1974	—	2.50	5.00
ARISTA					
❑ 9706	Indestructible/Are You With Me	1988	—	—	3.00
❑ 9706 [PS]	Indestructible/Are You With Me	1988	—	—	3.00
❑ 9766	If Ever a Love There Was/Let's Jam	1988	—	—	3.00
—A-side: With Aretha Franklin					
❑ 9766 [PS]	If Ever a Love There Was/Let's Jam	1988	—	—	3.00
❑ 9801	Change of Heart/Loco in Acapulco	1989	—	—	3.00
❑ 9850	If Ever a Love There Was/It Wasn't, It Isn't, It Ain't Never Gonna Be	1989	—	—	3.00
—A-side: With Aretha Franklin; B-side: Aretha Franklin and Whitney Houston					
❑ 9850 [PS]	If Ever a Love There Was/It Wasn't, It Isn't, It Ain't Never Gonna Be	1989	—	—	3.00
CASABLANCA					
❑ 2338	When She Was My Girl/Something to Remember	1981	—	2.00	4.00
❑ 2344	Let Me Set You Free/From a Distance	1981	—	2.00	4.00
❑ 2345	Tonight I'm Gonna Love You All Over/I'll Never Leave Again	1981	—	2.00	4.00
❑ 2353	Sad Hearts/I Believe in You and Me	1982	—	2.00	4.00
CHESS					
❑ 1623	Could It Be You?/Kiss Me, Baby	1956	50.00	100.00	200.00
COLUMBIA					
❑ 41755	Ain't That Love/Lonely Summer	1960	15.00	30.00	60.00
❑ 43356	Ain't That Love/Lonely Summer	1965	6.25	12.50	25.00
GRADY					
❑ 012	If Only I Had Known/(B-side unknown)	1956	150.00	300.00	600.00
—As "The Four Aims"					
MOTOWN					
❑ 1062	Baby I Need Your Loving/Call On Me	1964	3.75	7.50	15.00
❑ 1069	Without the One You Love (Life's Not Worth While)/Love Has Gone	1964	3.00	6.00	12.00
❑ 1073	Ask the Lonely/Where Did You Go	1965	3.75	7.50	15.00
❑ 1073 [PS]	Ask the Lonely/Where Did You Go	1965	20.00	40.00	80.00
❑ 1076	I Can't Help Myself/Sad Souvenirs	1965	3.75	7.50	15.00
❑ 1081	It's the Same Old Song/Your Love Is Amazing	1965	3.75	7.50	15.00
❑ 1084	Something About You/Darling, I Hum Our Song	1965	3.75	7.50	15.00
❑ 1090	Shake Me, Wake Me (When It's Over)/Just As Long As You Need Me	1966	3.75	7.50	15.00
❑ 1096	Loving You Is Sweeter Than Ever/I Like Everything About You	1966	3.75	7.50	15.00
❑ 1098	Reach Out I'll Be There/Until You Love Someone	1966	3.75	7.50	15.00
❑ 1098 [PS]	Reach Out I'll Be There/Until You Love Someone	1966	20.00	40.00	80.00
❑ 1102	Standing in the Shadows of Love/Since You've Been Gone	1966	3.75	7.50	15.00
❑ 1104	Bernadette/I Got a Feeling	1967	3.00	6.00	12.00
❑ 1110	7-Rooms of Gloom/I'll Turn to Stone	1967	3.00	6.00	12.00
❑ 1113	You Keep Running Away/If You Don't Want My Love	1967	3.00	6.00	12.00
❑ 1119	Walk Away Renee/Your Love Is Wonderful	1968	3.00	6.00	12.00
❑ 1124	If I Were a Carpenter/Wonderful Baby	1968	3.00	6.00	12.00
❑ 1127	Yesterday's Dreams/For Once In My Life	1968	2.00	4.00	8.00
❑ 1132	I'm in a Different World/Remember When	1968	2.00	4.00	8.00
❑ 1147	What Is a Man/Don't Bring Back Memories	1969	2.00	4.00	8.00
❑ 1159	Don't Let Him Take Your Love from Me/The Key	1969	2.00	4.00	8.00
❑ 1164	It's All in the Game/Love (Is the Answer)	1970	2.00	4.00	8.00
❑ 1164 [PS]	It's All in the Game/Love (Is the Answer)	1970	5.00	10.00	20.00
❑ 1170	Still Water (Love)/Still Water (Peace)	1970	—	3.00	6.00
❑ 1175	Just Seven Numbers (Can Straighten Out My Life)/I Wish I Were Your Mirror	1971	—	3.00	6.00
❑ 1175 [PS]	Just Seven Numbers (Can Straighten Out My Life)/I Wish I Were Your Mirror	1971	5.00	10.00	20.00
❑ 1185	In These Changing Times/Right Before My Eyes	1971	—	3.00	6.00
❑ 1189	MacArthur Park (Part 2)/MacArthur Park (Part 1)	1971	—	3.00	6.00
❑ 1196	A Simple Game/L.A. My Town	1972	—	3.00	6.00
❑ 1198	I Can't Quit Your Love/Happy (Is a Bumpy Road)	1972	—	3.00	6.00
❑ 1210	(It's the Way) Nature Planned It/I'll Never Change	1972	—	3.00	6.00
❑ 1254	Hey Man-We Gotta Get You a Woman/How Can I Forget You	1973	—	—	—
—Unreleased					
❑ 1706	I Just Can't Walk Away/Hang	1983	—	—	3.00
❑ 1718	Make Yourself Right at Home/Sing a Song of Yesterday	1984	—	—	3.00
❑ 1790	Sexy Ways/Body and Soul	1985	—	—	3.00
❑ 1811	Don't Tell Me That It's Over/I'm Ready for Love	1985	—	—	3.00
❑ 1854	Hot Nights/Again	1986	—	—	3.00
RELIANT					
❑ 1691	I'm Here Again/(Instrumental)	198?	—	2.00	4.00
RIVERSIDE					
❑ 4534	Pennies from Heaven/Where Are You?	1962	18.75	37.50	75.00
RSO					
❑ 1069	Back to School Again/Rock-a-Hula Luau	1982	—	—	3.00
❑ 1069 [PS]	Back to School Again/Rock-a-Hula Luau	1982	—	—	3.00
—B-side: by The Cast (from the movie Grease 2)					
TOPPS/MOTOWN					
❑ 5	I Can't Help Myself	1967	18.75	37.50	75.00
❑ 9	Baby I Need Your Loving	1967	18.75	37.50	75.00
—These are cardboard discs					

FOUR TUNES, THE

Number	Title (A Side/B Side)	Yr	VG	VG+	NM
JUBILEE					
❑ 5128	Marie/I Gambled with Love	1953	10.00	20.00	40.00
❑ 5132	I Understand Just How You Feel/Sugar Lump	1953	7.50	15.00	30.00
❑ 5135	My Wild Irish Rose/Do-Do-Do It Again	1954	7.50	15.00	30.00
❑ 5152	Lonesome/The Greatest Feeling in the World	1954	7.50	15.00	30.00
❑ 5165	Don't Cry Darling/L'Amour Toujours, L'Amour	1954	7.50	15.00	30.00
❑ 5174	I Sold My Heart to the Junkman/Let Me Go Lover	1954	7.50	15.00	30.00
❑ 5174	I Sold My Heart to the Junkman/Good News	1954	7.50	15.00	30.00
❑ 5183	I Hope/I Close My Eyes	1955	6.25	12.50	25.00
❑ 5200	Tired of Waitin'/Time Out for Texas	1955	6.25	12.50	25.00
❑ 5212	Brooklyn Bridge/Three Little Chickens	1955	6.25	12.50	25.00
❑ 5218	You Are My Love/At the Steamboat River Ball	1955	6.25	12.50	25.00
❑ 5232	Rock and Roll Call/Our Love	1956	5.00	10.00	20.00
❑ 5239	I Gotta Go/Hold Me Closer	1956	5.00	10.00	20.00
❑ 5245	Far Away Places/Dancing with Tears in My Eyes	1956	5.00	10.00	20.00
❑ 5255	The Ballad of James Dean/Japanses Farewell	1956	5.00	10.00	20.00
❑ 5276	Cool Water/A Little on the Lonely Side	1957	5.00	10.00	20.00
❑ 6000	I Understand/Marie	196?	2.50	5.00	10.00
KAY-RON					
❑ 1000	I Want to Be Loved/Savannah Sings the Blues	1953	10.00	20.00	40.00
❑ 1005	I Understand/Just in Case You Change Your Mind	1953	10.00	20.00	40.00
RCA VICTOR					
❑ 47-3881	Say When/Do I Worry?	1950	12.50	25.00	50.00
❑ 47-3967	How Can You Say That I Don't Care/Cool Water	1950	10.00	20.00	40.00
❑ 47-4102	Wishing You Were Here Tonight/The Last Roundup	1951	10.00	20.00	40.00
❑ 47-4198	Cool Water/Carry Me Back to the Lone Prairie	1951	10.00	20.00	40.00
❑ 47-4241	The Prisoner's Song/I Married An Angel	1951	7.50	15.00	30.00
❑ 47-4305	My Buddy/Early in the Morning	1951	7.50	15.00	30.00
❑ 47-4427	Tell Me Why/I'll See You in My Dreams	1951	10.00	20.00	40.00
❑ 47-4489	Greatest Song I Ever Heard/Come What May	1952	6.25	12.50	25.00
❑ 47-4663	I Wonder/Can I Say Any More?	1952	6.25	12.50	25.00
❑ 47-4828	They Don't Understand/Why Did You Do This	1952	6.25	12.50	25.00
❑ 47-4968	I Don't Want to Set the World On Fire/Let's Give Love Another Chance	1952	10.00	20.00	40.00
❑ 47-5532	Don't Get Around Much Anymore/Water Boy	1953	7.50	15.00	30.00
❑ 50-0008	You're Heartless/Careless Love	1949	50.00	100.00	200.00
—Gray label, orange vinyl					
❑ 50-0016	My Last Affair/I'm the Guy	1949	50.00	100.00	200.00
—Gray label, orange vinyl					
❑ 50-0042	I'm Just a Fool in Love/The Lonesome Road	1949	50.00	100.00	200.00
—Gray label, orange vinyl					
❑ 50-0072	There Goes My Heart/Am I Blue	1950	37.50	75.00	150.00
—Gray label, orange vinyl					
❑ 50-0085	Old Fashioned Love/Kentucky Babe	1950	37.50	75.00	150.00
—Gray label, orange vinyl					
❑ 50-0131	May That Day Never Come/Carry Me Back to the Lone Prairie	1951	37.50	75.00	150.00
—Gray label, orange vinyl					
7-Inch Extended Plays					
RCA VICTOR					
❑ EPA-586	(contents unknown)	1954	10.00	20.00	40.00
❑ EPA-586 [PS]	The Four Tunes	1954	10.00	20.00	40.00

FOUR UPSETTERS, THE

Number	Title (A Side/B Side)	Yr	VG	VG+	NM
SUN					
❑ 381	Crazy Arms/Midnight Soiree	1962	5.00	10.00	20.00
❑ 386	Surfin' Calliope/Wabash Cannonball	1963	7.50	15.00	30.00

FOUR WINDS, THE (1)

Also see THE TOKENS, to which they are related.

Number	Title (A Side/B Side)	Yr	VG	VG+	NM
B.T. PUPPY					
❑ 555	Let It Ride/One Face In the Crowd	1970	2.50	5.00	10.00
CRYSTAL BALL					
❑ 102	Come Softly to Me/Judy	1978	—	2.50	5.00
❑ 105	Arlene/Goodbye, Maureen	1978	2.50	5.00	10.00
—Red vinyl					

Number	Title (A Side/B Side)	Yr	VG	VG+	NM
❑ 105	Arlene/Goodbye, Maureen	1978	—	2.50	5.00
—Black vinyl					
SWING					
❑ 100	Remember Last Summer/Strange, Strange Feeling	1964	5.00	10.00	20.00

FOUR WINDS, THE (U)

None of these are group (1), but they aren't all the same group, either.

Number	Title (A Side/B Side)	Yr	VG	VG+	NM
CHATTAHOOCHIE					
❑ 655	Down and Out/To Love or Not to Love	1964	3.75	7.50	15.00
DECOR					
❑ 175	Short Shorts/Five Minutes More	1961	5.00	10.00	20.00
DERBY					
❑ 10022	Playgirl/Jennifer	1964	7.50	15.00	30.00
DIAL					
❑ 3006	Woe Is Me/Promised Land	1962	3.75	7.50	15.00
FELSTED					
❑ 8703	Playgirl/Jennifer	1964	5.00	10.00	20.00
HIDE-A-WAY					
❑ 101	Mission by the Sea/These Hearts Were Mine	1958	5.00	10.00	20.00
VIK					
❑ 0221	Colorado Moon/Find Someone New	1956	5.00	10.00	20.00
WARWICK					
❑ 633	Daddy's Home/Bull-Moose Stomp	1961	10.00	20.00	40.00

FOURMOST, THE

Number	Title (A Side/B Side)	Yr	VG	VG+	NM
ATCO					
❑ 6280	Hello Little Girl/Just in Case	1963	5.00	10.00	20.00
❑ 6285	I'm in Love/Respectable	1964	3.75	7.50	15.00
❑ 6307	If You Cry/Little Bit of Loving	1964	3.75	7.50	15.00
❑ 6317	How Can I Tell Her/You Got That Way	1964	3.75	7.50	15.00
CAPITOL					
❑ 5591	Girls, Girls, Girls/Why Do Fools Fall in Love	1966	3.00	6.00	12.00
❑ 5738	Here, There and Everywhere/You've Changed	1966	5.00	10.00	20.00

FOWLEY, KIM

Number	Title (A Side/B Side)	Yr	VG	VG+	NM
CAPITOL					
❑ 3403	Forbidden Love/I'm Bad	1972	—	3.00	6.00
❑ 3534	International Heroes/E.S.P. Reader	1973	—	3.00	6.00
❑ 3662	A Born Dancer/Something New	1973	—	3.00	6.00
IMPERIAL					
❑ 66326	Born to Be Wild/Space Odyssey	1968	2.50	5.00	10.00
❑ 66349	Bubble Gum/Wildfire	1969	2.50	5.00	10.00
LIVING LEGEND					
❑ 721	Mr. Responsibility/My Foolish Heart	1965	3.75	7.50	15.00
❑ 725	Underground Lady/Pop Art '66	1966	3.75	7.50	15.00
LOMA					
❑ 2064	Lights/Something New and Different	1966	2.50	5.00	10.00
MIRA					
❑ 209	American Dream/The Statue	1965	2.50	5.00	10.00
ORIGINAL SOUND					
❑ 98	Thunder Road/Born to Make You Cry	1970	2.50	5.00	10.00
RCA VICTOR					
❑ 74-0511	Citizen Kane/The Sky Is On Fire	1971	—	—	—
—Canceled					
REPRISE					
❑ 0569	Don't Be Cruel/Strangers from the Sky	1967	2.50	5.00	10.00
TOWER					
❑ 342	Love Is Alive and Well/Reincarnation	1967	2.50	5.00	10.00

FOX, NORMAN, AND THE ROB ROYS

Number	Title (A Side/B Side)	Yr	VG	VG+	NM
BACK BEAT					
❑ 499	Lover Doll/Little Star	197?	—	2.00	4.00
—Bootleg					
❑ 501	Tell Me Why/Audrey	1957	20.00	40.00	80.00
—White label					
❑ 501	Tell Me Why/Audrey	1957	10.00	20.00	40.00
—Red label					
❑ 508	Dance Girl Dance/My Dearest One	1958	20.00	40.00	80.00
CAPITOL					
❑ 4128	Dream Girl/Pizza Pie	1959	175.00	350.00	700.00
HAMMER					
❑ 544	Dream Girl/Pizza Pie	1958	7.50	15.00	30.00

FOXX, INEZ (AND CHARLIE)

Number	Title (A Side/B Side)	Yr	VG	VG+	NM
DYNAMO					
❑ 102	Baby Take It All/Tightrope	1967	2.00	4.00	8.00
❑ 104	I Stand Accused/Guilty	1967	2.00	4.00	8.00
❑ 109	You Are the Man/Hard to Get	1967	2.00	4.00	8.00
❑ 112	(1-2-3-4-5-6-7) Count the Days/A Stranger I Don't Know	1967	2.00	4.00	8.00
❑ 117	Undecided/I Ain't Goin' for That	1968	2.00	4.00	8.00
❑ 119	Vaya Con Dios/Fellows in Vietnam	1968	2.00	4.00	8.00
❑ 126	Come On In/Baby Drop a Dime	1968	2.00	4.00	8.00
❑ 127	Baby Give It to Me/You Fixed My Heartache	1968	2.00	4.00	8.00
❑ 134	We Got a Chance to Be Free/Speed Ticket	1969	2.00	4.00	8.00
❑ 138	North Carolina (South Carolina)/I Got It	1970	2.00	4.00	8.00
❑ 144	You Shouldn't Have Set My Soul on Fire/Live for Today	1970	2.00	4.00	8.00
MUSICOR					
❑ 1201	No Stranger to Love/Come By Here	1966	2.50	5.00	10.00
SYMBOL					
❑ 20-001	Hurt by Love/Confusion	1964	3.00	6.00	12.00
❑ 201	La De Da, I Love You/Yankee Doodle Dandy	1964	3.00	6.00	12.00
❑ 204	Don't Do It No More/I Fancy You	1964	3.00	6.00	12.00
❑ 206	I Feel Alright/My Mama Told Me	1965	3.00	6.00	12.00
❑ 208	I've Come to One Conclusion/Down by the Seashore	1965	3.00	6.00	12.00
❑ 213	Hummingbird/If I Need Anyone	1966	3.00	6.00	12.00
❑ 919	Mockingbird/Jaybirds	1963	6.25	12.50	25.00
❑ 922	Broken Hearted Fool/He's the One You Love	1963	3.75	7.50	15.00
❑ 924	Hi Diddle Diddle/Talk with Me	1963	3.75	7.50	15.00
❑ 926	Ask Me/I See You My Love	1963	3.75	7.50	15.00
UNITED ARTISTS					
❑ XW510	Mockingbird/I Know (You Don't Love Me No More)	1974	—	2.00	4.00
—Reissue; B-side by Barbara George					
VOLT					
❑ 4087	Watch the Dog/You Hurt Me for the Last Time	1972	—	3.00	6.00
❑ 4093	One Woman's Man/The Time	1973	—	3.00	6.00
❑ 4096	Crossing Over That Bridge/You're Saving Me for a Rainy Day	1973	—	3.00	6.00
❑ 4101	I Had a Talk with My Man/The Lady, The Doctor and the Prescription	1973	—	3.00	6.00
❑ 4107	Circuit's Overloaded/There's a Hand That's Reading Out	1974	—	3.00	6.00

FRACTION

Number	Title (A Side/B Side)	Yr	VG	VG+	NM
ANGELUS					
❑ 5005	Sanc Divided/(B-side unknown)	1971	25.00	50.00	100.00

FRAMPTON, PETER

Also see THE HERD; HUMBLE PIE; THE TAGES.

Number	Title (A Side/B Side)	Yr	VG	VG+	NM
ATLANTIC					
❑ 88820	Holding On to You/Give Me a Little Love That's Real	1990	—	—	3.00
❑ 89395	Hiding from a Heartache/Into View	1986	—	—	3.00
❑ 89426	All Eyes on You/So Far Away	1986	—	—	3.00
❑ 89426 [PS]	All Eyes on You/So Far Away	1986	—	—	3.00
❑ 89463	Lying/Into View	1985	—	—	3.00
❑ 89463 [PS]	Lying/Into View	1985	—	—	3.00
A&M					
❑ 1379	Jumping Jack Flash/On for Another Day	1972	—	3.00	6.00
❑ 1456	Don't Fade Away/All Night Long	1973	—	2.50	5.00
—As "Frampton's Camel"					
❑ 1470	I Believe (When I Fall in Love It Will Be Forever)/Which Way the Wind Blows	1973	—	2.50	5.00
—As "Frampton's Camel"					
❑ 1506	Somethin's Happening/I Wanna Go to the Sun	1974	—	2.50	5.00
❑ 1693	Show Me the Way/Crying Clown	1975	—	2.50	5.00
❑ 1738	Baby I Love Your Way/(I'll Give You) Money	1975	—	2.50	5.00
❑ 1763	Nowhere's Too Far (For My Baby)/(I'll Give You) Money	1975	—	2.50	5.00
❑ 1795	Show Me the Way/Shine On	1976	—	2.00	4.00
❑ 1795 [PS]	Show Me the Way/Shine On	1976	—	3.00	6.00
❑ 1832	Baby, I Love Your Way/It's a Plain Shame	1976	—	2.00	4.00
❑ 1832 [PS]	Baby, I Love Your Way/It's a Plain Shame	1976	—	3.00	6.00
❑ 1867	Do You Feel Like We Do/Penny for Your Thoughts	1976	—	2.00	4.00
❑ 1941	I'm in You/St. Thomas (Know How I Feel)	1977	—	2.50	5.00
❑ 1941	I'm in You/St. Thomas (Don't You Know How I Feel)	1977	—	2.00	4.00
❑ 1941 [PS]	I'm in You/St. Thomas (Know How I Feel)	1977	—	3.50	7.00
❑ 1941 [PS]	I'm in You/St. Thomas (Don't You Know How I Feel)	1977	—	3.00	6.00
❑ 1972	Signed, Sealed, Delivered (I'm Yours)/Rocky's Hot Club	1977	—	2.00	4.00
❑ 1972 [PS]	Signed, Sealed, Delivered (I'm Yours)/Rocky's Hot Club	1977	—	3.00	6.00
❑ 1988	Tried to Love/You Don't Have to Worry	1977	—	2.00	4.00
❑ 1988 [PS]	Tried to Love/You Don't Have to Worry	1977	—	3.00	6.00
❑ 2070	The Long and Winding Road/Tried to Love	1978	—	2.50	5.00
❑ 2148	I Can't Stand It No More/Where Should I Be	1979	—	2.00	4.00
❑ 2148 [PS]	I Can't Stand It No More/Where Should I Be	1979	—	2.50	5.00
❑ 2174	She Don't Reply/St. Thomas (Don't Cha Know How I Feel)	1979	—	2.00	4.00
❑ 2350	Breaking All the Rules/Night Town	1981	—	2.00	4.00
❑ 2362	Wasting the Night Away/You Kill Me	1981	—	2.00	4.00
❑ 2442	Sleepwalk/Theme from Nivram	1982	—	2.00	4.00

FRANCIS, CONNIE

Number	Title (A Side/B Side)	Yr	VG	VG+	NM
GSF					
❑ 6901	The Answer (Should I Tie a Yellow Ribbon Round the Ole Oak Tree?)/Paint the Rain	1973	—	2.50	5.00
IVANHOE					
❑ 508	I Don't Wanna Walk Without You/Don't Turn Around	197?	—	2.50	5.00
MGM					
❑ CS6-5	Celebrity Scene: Connie Francis	1967	15.00	30.00	60.00
—Box set of five singles (13708-13712). Price includes box, all 5 singles, jukebox title strips, bio. Records are sometimes found by themselves, so they are also listed separately.					
❑ SB-9 [S]	Rock-A-Bye Your Baby with a Dixie Melody/Ciao Ciao Bambino	1960	12.50	25.00	50.00
❑ SB-10 [S]	I Almost Lost My Mind/Come Back to Sorrento	1960	12.50	25.00	50.00
❑ 126	Stupid Cupid/I'm Sorry I Made You Cry	196?	2.00	4.00	8.00
—Reissue					
❑ 129	Who's Sorry Now/You Were Only Fooling	196?	2.00	4.00	8.00
—Reissue					
❑ 135	Mama/You're Gonna Miss Me	196?	2.00	4.00	8.00
—Reissue					
❑ 136	Among My Souvenirs/God Bless America	196?	2.00	4.00	8.00
—Reissue					
❑ 139	Lipstick on Your Collar/Frankie	196?	2.00	4.00	8.00
—Reissue					
❑ 141	My Happiness/If I Didn't Care	196?	2.00	4.00	8.00
—Reissue					
❑ 148	My Heart Has a Mind of Its Own/Malaguena	196?	2.00	4.00	8.00
—Reissue					
❑ 150	Where the Boys Are/No One	196?	2.00	4.00	8.00
—Reissue					

Number	Title (A Side/B Side)	Yr	VG	VG+	NM
❑ 153	Breakin' In a Brand New Broken Heart/Somebody Else's Boy	196?	2.00	4.00	8.00
—Reissue					
❑ 155	Together/Too Many Rules	196?	2.00	4.00	8.00
—Reissue					
❑ 156	Many Tears Ago/Senza Mama E Numerata	196?	2.00	4.00	8.00
—Reissue					
❑ 157	Don't Break the Heart That Loves You/Second Hand Love	196?	2.00	4.00	8.00
—Reissue					
❑ 165	Everybody's Somebody's Fool/Al Di La	196?	2.00	4.00	8.00
—Reissue					
❑ 169	Jealous Heart/Forget Domani	196?	2.00	4.00	8.00
—Reissue					
❑ 511	Who's Sorry Now/Stupid Cupid	197?	—	2.50	5.00
—Reissue					
❑ 512	Lipstick on Your Collar/Mama	197?	—	2.50	5.00
—Reissue					
❑ 513	Everybody's Somebody's Fool/Al Di La	197?	—	2.50	5.00
—Reissue					
❑ 524	My Happiness/If I Didn't Care	197?	—	2.50	5.00
—Reissue					
❑ 12015	Freddy/Didn't I Love You Enough	1955	12.50	25.00	50.00
❑ 12056	Oh Please Make Him Jealous/Goody Goodbye	1955	12.50	25.00	50.00
❑ 12122	Are You Satisfied/My Treasure	1956	6.25	12.50	25.00
❑ 12191	My First Real Love/Believe in Me	1956	15.00	30.00	60.00
❑ 12251	Send for My Baby/Forgetting	1956	6.25	12.50	25.00
❑ 12335	My Sailor Boy/Everyone Needs Someone	1956	6.25	12.50	25.00
❑ 12375	I Never Had a Sweetheart/Little Blue Wren	1957	6.25	12.50	25.00
❑ 12440	No Other One/I Leaned on a Man	1957	6.25	12.50	25.00
❑ 12490	Eighteen/Faded Orchid	1957	6.25	12.50	25.00
❑ 12588	Who's Sorry Now?/You Were Only Fooling	1958	5.00	10.00	20.00
❑ 12647	I'm Sorry I Made You Cry/Lock Up Your Heart	1958	5.00	10.00	20.00
❑ 12669	Heartaches/I Miss You So	1958	12.50	25.00	50.00
❑ 12683	Stupid Cupid/Carolina Moon	1958	5.00	10.00	20.00
❑ 12713	Fallin'/Happy Days and Lonely Nights	1958	5.00	10.00	20.00
❑ 12738 [M]	My Happiness/Never Before	1958	5.00	10.00	20.00
❑ 12738 [PS]	My Happiness/Never Before	1958	7.50	15.00	30.00
—Pink sleeve					
❑ 12738 [PS]	My Happiness/Never Before	1958	10.00	20.00	40.00
—White sleeve					
❑ 12769	If I Didn't Care/Toward the End of the Day	1959	5.00	10.00	20.00
❑ 12769 [PS]	If I Didn't Care/Toward the End of the Day	1959	7.50	15.00	30.00
❑ 12793 [M]	Lipstick on Your Collar/Frankie	1959	5.00	10.00	20.00
❑ 12824 [M]	You're Gonna Miss Me/Plenty Good Lovin'	1959	5.00	10.00	20.00
❑ 12841 [M]	Among My Souvenirs/God Bless America	1959	7.50	15.00	30.00
—First pressing has a yellow label					
❑ 12841 [M]	Among My Souvenirs/God Bless America	1959	5.00	10.00	20.00
—Second pressing has a black label					
❑ 12878	Mama/Teddy	1960	3.75	7.50	15.00
❑ 12899	Everybody's Somebody's Fool/Jealous of You	1960	3.75	7.50	15.00
❑ 12899 [PS]	Everybody's Somebody's Fool/Jealous of You	1960	5.00	10.00	20.00
❑ 12923	My Heart Has a Mind of Its Own/Malaguena	1960	3.75	7.50	15.00
❑ 12923 [PS]	My Heart Has a Mind of Its Own/Malaguena	1960	5.00	10.00	20.00
❑ 12964	Many Tears Ago/Senza Mama (With No One)	1960	3.75	7.50	15.00
❑ 12964 [PS]	Many Tears Ago/Senza Mama (With No One)	1960	5.00	10.00	20.00
❑ 12971	Where the Boys Are/No One	1961	3.75	7.50	15.00
❑ 12971 [PS]	Where the Boys Are/No One	1961	5.00	10.00	20.00
❑ 12995	Breakin' In a Brand New Broken Heart/Someone Else's Boy	1961	3.75	7.50	15.00
❑ 12995 [PS]	Breakin' In a Brand New Broken Heart/Someone Else's Boy	1961	5.00	10.00	20.00
❑ 13005	Atashi-No/Swanee	1961	7.50	15.00	30.00
❑ 13019	Together/Too Many Rules	1961	3.75	7.50	15.00
❑ 13019 [PS]	Together/Too Many Rules	1961	5.00	10.00	20.00
❑ 13039	(He's My) Dreamboat/Hollywood	1961	3.75	7.50	15.00
❑ 13039 [PS]	(He's My) Dreamboat/Hollywood	1961	5.00	10.00	20.00
❑ 13051	When the Boy in Your Arms (Is the Boy in Your Heart)/Baby's First Christmas	1961	3.75	7.50	15.00
❑ 13051 [PS]	When the Boy in Your Arms (Is the Boy in Your Heart)/Baby's First Christmas	1961	5.00	10.00	20.00
❑ 13059	Don't Break the Heart That Loves You/Drop It, Joe	1962	3.75	7.50	15.00
❑ 13059 [PS]	Don't Break the Heart That Loves You/Drop It, Joe	1962	5.00	10.00	20.00
❑ 13074	Second Hand Love/Gonna Git That Man	1962	5.00	10.00	20.00
—A-side: Produced by Phil Spector					
❑ 13074 [PS]	Second Hand Love/Gonna Git That Man	1962	6.25	12.50	25.00
❑ 13087	Vacation/The Biggest Sin of All	1962	3.75	7.50	15.00
❑ 13087 [PS]	Vacation/The Biggest Sin of All	1962	5.00	10.00	20.00
❑ 13096	I Was Such a Fool (To Fall in Love with You)/He Thinks I Still Care	1962	3.00	6.00	12.00
❑ 13096 [PS]	I Was Such a Fool (To Fall in Love with You)/He Thinks I Still Care	1962	4.00	8.00	16.00
❑ 13116	I'm Gonna' Be Warm This Winter/Al Di La	1962	3.00	6.00	12.00
❑ 13116 [PS]	I'm Gonna' Be Warm This Winter/Al Di La	1962	4.00	8.00	16.00
❑ 13127	Follow the Boys/Waiting for Billy	1962	3.00	6.00	12.00
❑ 13127 [PS]	Follow the Boys/Waiting for Billy	1962	4.00	8.00	16.00
❑ 13143	If My Pillow Could Talk/You're the Only One Can Hurt Me	1963	3.00	6.00	12.00
❑ 13143 [PS]	If My Pillow Could Talk/You're the Only One Can Hurt Me	1963	4.00	8.00	16.00
❑ 13160	Drownin' My Sorrows/Mala Femmena	1963	3.00	6.00	12.00
❑ 13160 [PS]	Drownin' My Sorrows/Mala Femmena	1963	4.00	8.00	16.00
❑ 13176	Your Other Love/Whatever Happened to Rosemarie?	1963	3.00	6.00	12.00
❑ 13176 [PS]	Your Other Love/Whatever Happened to Rosemarie?	1963	4.00	8.00	16.00
❑ 13203	In the Summer of His Years/My Buddy	1963	3.00	6.00	12.00
❑ 13203 [PS]	In the Summer of His Years/My Buddy	1963	4.00	8.00	16.00
❑ 13214	Blue Winter/You Know You Don't Want Me (So Why Don't You Leave Me Alone)	1964	3.00	6.00	12.00
❑ 13214 [PS]	Blue Winter/You Know You Don't Want Me (So Why Don't You Leave Me Alone)	1964	4.00	8.00	16.00
❑ 13237	Be Anything (But Be Mine)/Tommy	1964	3.00	6.00	12.00
❑ 13237 [PS]	Be Anything (But Be Mine)/Tommy	1964	4.00	8.00	16.00
❑ 13256	Looking for Love/This Is My Happiest Moment	1964	3.00	6.00	12.00
❑ 13256 [PS]	Looking for Love/This Is My Happiest Moment	1964	4.00	8.00	16.00
❑ 13287	Don't Ever Leave Me/We Have Something More (Than a Summer Love)	1964	3.00	6.00	12.00
❑ 13287 [PS]	Don't Ever Leave Me/We Have Something More (Than a Summer Love)	1964	4.00	8.00	16.00
❑ 13303	Whose Heart Are You Breaking Tonight/Come On Jerry	1965	2.50	5.00	10.00
❑ 13303 [PS]	Whose Heart Are You Breaking Tonight/Come On Jerry	1965	3.00	6.00	12.00
❑ 13325	For Mama (La Mamma)/She'll Be Coming 'Round the Mountain	1965	3.00	6.00	12.00
❑ 13331	Wishing It Was You/You're Mine (Just When You're Lonely)	1965	2.50	5.00	10.00
❑ 13331 [PS]	Wishing It Was You/You're Mine (Just When You're Lonely)	1965	3.00	6.00	12.00
❑ 13363	Forget Domani/No One Sends Me Roses	1965	2.50	5.00	10.00
❑ 13389	Roundabout/Bossa Nova Hand Dance	1965	2.50	5.00	10.00
❑ 13420	Jealous Heart/Can I Rely on You	1965	2.50	5.00	10.00
❑ 13470	Love Is Me, Love Is You/I'd Let You Break My Heart All Over Again	1966	2.50	5.00	10.00
❑ 13470 [PS]	Love Is Me, Love Is You/I'd Let You Break My Heart All Over Again	1966	3.00	6.00	12.00
❑ 13505	It's a Different World/Empty Chapel	1966	2.50	5.00	10.00
❑ 13505 [PS]	It's a Different World/Empty Chapel	1966	5.00	10.00	20.00
❑ 13545	A Letter from a Soldier (Dear Mama)/ Somewhere, My Love	1966	2.50	5.00	10.00
❑ 13550 [DJ]	A Nurse in the U.S. Army (same on both sides)	1966	7.50	15.00	30.00
—Promotional item for the U.S, Army					
❑ 13578	All the Love in the World/So Nice	1966	2.50	5.00	10.00
❑ 13610	Spanish Nights and You/Games That Lovers Play	1966	2.50	5.00	10.00
❑ 13610 [PS]	Spanish Nights and You/Games That Lovers Play	1966	5.00	10.00	20.00
❑ 13665	Another Page/Souvenir d'Italie	1967	2.50	5.00	10.00
❑ 13708	Mama/Never on Sunday	1967	2.50	5.00	10.00
—Part of Celebrity Series CS-5					
❑ 13709	My Happiness/Al Di La	1967	2.50	5.00	10.00
—Part of Celebrity Series CS-5					
❑ 13710	Malaguena/I Love You Much Too Much	1967	2.50	5.00	10.00
—Part of Celebrity Series CS-5					
❑ 13711	Once in a Lifetime/Oh Lonesome Me	1967	2.50	5.00	10.00
—Part of Celebrity Series CS-5					
❑ 13712	Jealous Heart/Will You Still Be Mine	1967	2.50	5.00	10.00
—Part of Celebrity Series CS-5					
❑ 13718	Time Alone Will Tell/Born Free	1967	2.50	5.00	10.00
❑ 13773	My Heart Cries for You/Someone Took the Sweetness Out of Sweetheart	1967	2.50	5.00	10.00
❑ 13773 [PS]	My Heart Cries for You/Someone Took the Sweetness Out of Sweetheart	1967	5.00	10.00	20.00
❑ 13814	Lonely Again/When You Care a Lot for Someone	1967	2.50	5.00	10.00
❑ 13876	My World Is Slipping Away/Till We're Together	1967	2.50	5.00	10.00
❑ 13923	Why Say Goodbye/Adios, Me Amore	1968	2.00	4.00	8.00
❑ 13948	Somebody Else Is Taking My Place/Brother, Can You Spare a Dime?	1968	2.00	4.00	8.00
❑ 14004	I Don't Wanna Play House/The Welfare Check	1968	2.00	4.00	8.00
❑ 14034	The Wedding Cake/Over Hill, Under Ground	1969	2.00	4.00	8.00
❑ 14058	Gone Like the Wind/Am I Blue?	1969	2.00	4.00	8.00
❑ 14058 [PS]	Gone Like the Wind/Am I Blue?	1969	5.00	10.00	20.00
❑ 14089	Invierno Trieste/Noches Espanolas Y Tu	1969	—	—	—
—Not known to exist					
❑ 14091	Mr. Love/Zingara	1969	2.00	4.00	8.00
❑ 14091 [PS]	Mr. Love/Zingara	1969	5.00	10.00	20.00
❑ 14853	I'm Me Again/Comme Si, Comme Sa	1976	—	3.00	6.00
❑ SK-50117 [S]	My Happiness/Never Before	1958	12.50	25.00	50.00
❑ SK-50121 [S]	Lipstick on Your Collar/Frankie	1959	15.00	30.00	60.00
❑ SK-50129 [S]	You're Gonna Miss Me/Plenty Good Lovin'	1959	12.50	25.00	50.00
❑ SK-50133 [S]	Among My Souvenirs/God Bless America	1959	12.50	25.00	50.00

POLYDOR

Number	Title (A Side/B Side)	Yr	VG	VG+	NM
❑ 2143	I'm Me Again/Comme Si, Comme Sa	1981	—	2.50	5.00
❑ 810087-7	There's Still a Few Good Love Songs Left in Me/ Let's Make It Love Tonight	1983	—	2.50	5.00

7-Inch Extended Plays

MGM

Number	Title (A Side/B Side)	Yr	VG	VG+	NM
❑ HC5-6 [DJ]	Heart Circuit Interview	1959	25.00	50.00	100.00
❑ X-1599	(contents unknown)	1958	10.00	20.00	40.00
❑ X-1599 [PS]	Connie Francis	1958	10.00	20.00	40.00
❑ X-1603	(contents unknown)	1958	10.00	20.00	40.00
❑ X-1603 [PS]	Who's Sorry Now Vol. I	1958	10.00	20.00	40.00
❑ X-1604	(contents unknown)	1958	10.00	20.00	40.00
❑ X-1604 [PS]	Who's Sorry Now Vol. II	1958	10.00	20.00	40.00
❑ X-1605	*You Always Hurt the One You Love/If I Had You/ How Deep Is the Ocean?/I'll Get By	1958	10.00	20.00	40.00
❑ X-1605 [PS]	Who's Sorry Now Vol. III	1958	10.00	20.00	40.00
❑ X-1655	My Happiness/No Other One//You're My Everything/Never Before	1958	10.00	20.00	40.00
❑ X-1655 [PS]	My Happiness	1958	10.00	20.00	40.00
❑ X-1662	(contents unknown)	1959	10.00	20.00	40.00
❑ X-1662 [PS]	If I Didn't Care	1959	10.00	20.00	40.00
❑ X-1663	(contents unknown)	1959	10.00	20.00	40.00
❑ X-1663 [PS]	The Exciting Connie Francis (Part 1)	1959	10.00	20.00	40.00
❑ X-1664	(contents unknown)	1959	10.00	20.00	40.00
❑ X-1664 [PS]	The Exciting Connie Francis (Part 2)	1959	10.00	20.00	40.00
❑ X-1665	(contents unknown)	1959	10.00	20.00	40.00
❑ X-1665 [PS]	The Exciting Connie Francis (Part 3)	1959	10.00	20.00	40.00
❑ X-1687	You're Gonna Miss Me/Plenty Good Lovin'// Frankie/Lipstick on Your Collar	1959	7.50	15.00	30.00
❑ X-1687 [PS]	Connie Francis	1959	7.50	15.00	30.00
❑ X-1688	(contents unknown)	1960	7.50	15.00	30.00
❑ X-1688 [PS]	Connie's Greatest Hits (Part 1)	1960	7.50	15.00	30.00
❑ X-1689	(contents unknown)	1960	7.50	15.00	30.00
❑ X-1689 [PS]	Connie's Greatest Hits (Part 2)	1960	7.50	15.00	30.00

Number	Title (A Side/B Side)	Yr	VG	VG+	NM
X-1690	(contents unknown)	1960	7.50	15.00	30.00
X-1690 [PS]	Connie's Greatest Hits (Part 3)	1960	7.50	15.00	30.00
X-1691	(contents unknown)	1960	7.50	15.00	30.00
X-1691 [PS]	Rock 'N Roll Million Sellers (Part 1)	1960	7.50	15.00	30.00
X-1692	(contents unknown)	1960	7.50	15.00	30.00
X-1692 [PS]	Rock 'N Roll Million Sellers (Part 2)	1960	7.50	15.00	30.00
X-1693	(contents unknown)	1960	7.50	15.00	30.00
X-1693 [PS]	Rock 'N Roll Million Sellers (Part 3)	1960	7.50	15.00	30.00
X-1694	(contents unknown)	1960	7.50	15.00	30.00
X-1694 [PS]	Country & Western Golden Hits (Part 1)	1960	7.50	15.00	30.00
X-1695	(contents unknown)	1960	7.50	15.00	30.00
X-1695 [PS]	Country & Western Golden Hits (Part 2)	1960	7.50	15.00	30.00
X-1696	(contents unknown)	1960	7.50	15.00	30.00
X-1696 [PS]	Country & Western Golden Hits (Part 3)	1960	7.50	15.00	30.00
X-1703	Valentino/You Made Me Love You//Because of You/Young at Heart	1961	7.50	15.00	30.00
X-1703 [PS]	Connie Francis	1961	7.50	15.00	30.00

—Has paper sleeve rather than a cardboard sleeve

FRANCIS, CONNIE, AND MARVIN RAINWATER

MGM

Number	Title (A Side/B Side)	Yr	VG	VG+	NM
12555	You, My Darlin', You/The Majesty of Love	1957	6.25	12.50	25.00

FRANK, JOE, AND THE KNIGHTS

ABC-PARAMOUNT

Number	Title (A Side/B Side)	Yr	VG	VG+	NM
10782	Can't Find a Way/Won't You Come Home	1966	5.00	10.00	20.00

FRANKIE AND THE C-NOTES

RICHIE

Number	Title (A Side/B Side)	Yr	VG	VG+	NM
2	Forever and Ever/Fade Out	1959	100.00	200.00	400.00

FRANKLIN, ARETHA

ARISTA

Number	Title (A Side/B Side)	Yr	VG	VG+	NM
0569	United Together/Take Me With You	1980	—	2.00	4.00
0591	What a Fool Believes/Love Me Forever	1980	—	2.00	4.00
0600	Come to Me/School Days	1981	—	2.00	4.00
0624	Love All the Hurt Away/Whole Lotta Me	1981	—	2.00	4.00
—Aretha Franklin and George Benson					
0646	It's My Turn/Kind of Man	1981	—	2.00	4.00
0665	Livin' in the Streets/There's a Star for Everyone	1982	—	2.00	4.00
0699	Jump To It/Just My Daydream	1982	—	2.00	4.00
1023	Love Me Right/(It's Just) Your Love	1982	—	2.00	4.00
1043	This Is for Real/I Just Want to Make It Up to You	1983	—	2.00	4.00
2239	Everyday People/You Can't Take Me for Granted	1991	—	2.50	5.00
9034	Get It Right/Giving In	1983	—	2.00	4.00
9095	Every Girl (Wants My Guy)/I Got Your Love	1983	—	2.00	4.00
9354	Freeway of Love/Until You Say You Love Me	1985	—	—	3.00
9354 [PS]	Freeway of Love/Until You Say You Love Me	1985	—	—	3.00
9410	Who's Zoomin' Who/Bittersweet Love	1985	—	—	3.00
9410 [PS]	Who's Zoomin' Who/Bittersweet Love	1985	—	—	3.00
9453	Another Night/Kind of Man	1986	—	—	3.00
9474	Ain't Nobody Ever Loved You/Push	1986	—	—	3.00
—B-side with Peter Wolf					
9528	Jumpin' Jack Flash/Integrity	1986	—	2.50	5.00
—Original pressings on clear vinyl					
9528	Jumpin' Jack Flash/Integrity	1986	—	—	3.00
—Second pressing on black vinyl					
9528 [PS]	Jumpin' Jack Flash/Integrity	1986	—	2.50	5.00
—Picture sleeve with clear vinyl pressing lists catalog number as ALC-9528					
9528 [PS]	Jumpin' Jack Flash/Integrity	1986	—	—	3.00
—Picture sleeve with black vinyl pressing lists catalog number as AL-9528					
9541	Jumpin' Jack Flash/Jumpin' Jack Flash	1986	—	2.00	4.00
—Reissue with two different versions of the song					
9546	Jimmy Lee/If You Need My Love Tonight	1986	—	2.00	4.00
9546 [PS]	Jimmy Lee/If You Need My Love Tonight	1986	—	2.00	4.00
—B-side with Larry Graham					
9557	Jimmy Lee/An Angel Cries	1986	—	—	3.00
9557 [PS]	Jimmy Lee/An Angel Cries	1986	—	—	3.00
9559	I Knew You Were Waiting (For Me)/(Instrumental)	1987	—	—	3.00
—With George Michael					
9559 [PS]	I Knew You Were Waiting (For Me)/(Instrumental)	1987	—	—	3.00
—With George Michael					
9574	Rock-A-Lott/Look to the Rainbow	1987	—	—	3.00
9574 [PS]	Rock-A-Lott/Look to the Rainbow	1987	—	—	3.00
9623	If You Need My Love Tonight/He'll Come Along	1987	—	—	3.00
—A-side with Larry Graham					
9672	Oh Happy Day/The Lord's Prayer	1988	—	2.00	4.00
9766	If Ever a Love There Was/Let's Jam	1988	—	—	3.00
—A-side with the Four Tops; B-side: Four Tops solo					
9809	Through the Storm/Come to Me	1989	—	—	3.00
—A-side: Aretha Franklin and Elton John					
9809 [PS]	Through the Storm/Come to Me	1989	—	—	3.00
9850	It Isn't, It Wasn't, It Ain't Never Gonna Be/If Ever a Love There Was	1989	—	—	3.00
—A-side with Whitney Houston; B-side with the Four Tops					
9850 [PS]	It Isn't, It Wasn't, It Ain't Never Gonna Be/If Ever a Love There Was	1989	—	—	3.00
—A-side with Whitney Houston; B-side with the Four Tops					
9884	Gimme Your Love/Think	1989	—	—	3.00
—With James Brown					
9884 [PS]	Gimme Your Love/Think	1989	—	—	3.00
—With James Brown					

ATLANTIC

Number	Title (A Side/B Side)	Yr	VG	VG+	NM
2386	I Never Loved a Man (The Way I Love You)/Do Right Woman, Do Right Man	1967	2.50	5.00	10.00
2403	Respect/Dr. Feelgood	1967	2.50	5.00	10.00
2427	Baby I Love You/Going Down Now	1967	2.50	5.00	10.00
2441	(You Make Me Feel Like) A Natural Woman/Baby, Baby, Baby	1967	2.50	5.00	10.00
2464	Chain of Fools/Prove It	1967	2.50	5.00	10.00
2486	(Sweet Sweet Baby) Since You've Been Gone/Ain't No Way	1968	2.50	5.00	10.00
2518	Think/You Send Me	1968	2.50	5.00	10.00
2546	I Say a Little Prayer/The House That Jack Built	1968	2.50	5.00	10.00
2574	See Saw/My Song	1968	2.00	4.00	8.00
2603	The Weight/Tracks of My Tears	1969	2.00	4.00	8.00
2619	I Can't See Myself Leaving You/Gentle On My Mind	1969	2.00	4.00	8.00
2650	Share Your Love with Me/Pledging My Love-The Clock	1969	2.00	4.00	8.00
2683	Eleanor Rigby/It Ain't Fair	1969	2.00	4.00	8.00
2706	Call Me/Son of a Preacher Man	1970	2.00	4.00	8.00
2731	Spirit in the Dark/The Thrill Is Gone	1970	2.00	4.00	8.00
2751	Don't Play That Song/Let It Be	1970	2.00	4.00	8.00
2772	Border Song (Holy Moses)/You and Me	1970	2.00	4.00	8.00
2787	You're All I Need to Get By/Pullin'	1971	—	3.00	6.00
2796	Bridge Over Troubled Water/Brand New Me	1971	—	3.00	6.00
2817	Spanish Harlem/Lean On Me	1971	—	3.00	6.00
2838	Rock Steady/Oh Me Oh My (I'm a Fool for You Baby)	1971	—	3.00	6.00
2866	Day Dreaming/I've Been Loving You Too Long	1972	—	3.00	6.00
2883	All the King's Horses/April Fools	1972	—	3.00	6.00
2901	Wholy Holy/Give Yourself to Jesus	1972	—	3.00	6.00
2941	Master of Eyes (The Deepness of Your Eyes)/Moody's Mood for You	1973	—	3.00	6.00
2969	Angel/Hey Hey Now (Sister from Texas)	1973	—	3.00	6.00
2995	Until You Come Back to Me (That's What I'm Gonna Do)/If You Don't Think	1973	—	3.00	6.00
2999	I'm in Love/Oh Baby	1974	—	3.00	6.00
3200	Ain't Nothing Like the Real Thing/Eight Days a Week	1974	—	3.00	6.00
3224	Without Love/Don't Go Breaking My Heart	1974	—	3.00	6.00
3249	With Everything I Feel in Me/Sing It Again, Say It Again	1975	—	3.00	6.00
3289	Mr. D.J. (5 for the D.J.)/As Long As You Are There	1975	—	3.00	6.00
3311	You/Without You	1975	—	3.00	6.00
3326	Something He Can Feel/Loving You, Baby	1976	—	3.00	6.00
3358	Jump/Hooked on Your Love	1976	—	3.00	6.00
3373	Look Into Your Heart/Rock with Me	1977	—	3.00	6.00
3393	Break It To Me Gently/Meadows of Springtime	1977	—	3.00	6.00
3418	When I Think About You/Touch Me Up	1978	—	3.00	6.00
3468	Almighty Fire/I'm Your Speed	1978	—	3.00	6.00
3495	More Than Just a Joy/This You Can Believe	1979	—	3.00	6.00

CHECKER

Number	Title (A Side/B Side)	Yr	VG	VG+	NM
861	Never Grow Old/You Grow Closer	1957	5.00	10.00	20.00
941	Precious Lord, Part 1/Precious Lord, Part 2	1960	3.75	7.50	15.00

COLUMBIA

Number	Title (A Side/B Side)	Yr	VG	VG+	NM
31202 [S]	titles unknown	1961	3.00	6.00	12.00
31203 [S]	titles unknown	1961	3.00	6.00	12.00
31204 [S]	titles unknown	1961	3.00	6.00	12.00
31205 [S]	titles unknown	1961	3.00	6.00	12.00
31206 [S]	titles unknown	1961	3.00	6.00	12.00
—Anyone who can fill in these gaps -- the above five all are Columbia "Stereo 7" singles -- please let us know.					
41793	Today I Sing the Blues/Love Is the Only Thing	1960	3.00	6.00	12.00
41923	Won't Be Long/Right Now	1961	3.00	6.00	12.00
41965	Are You Sure/Maybe I'm a Fool	1961	3.00	6.00	12.00
42157	Rock-A-Bye Your Baby with a Dixie Melody/Operation Heartbreak	1961	3.00	6.00	12.00
42266	I Surrender, Dear/Rough Lover	1962	2.50	5.00	10.00
42266 [PS]	I Surrender, Dear/Rough Lover	1962	7.50	15.00	30.00
42456	Don't Cry, Baby/Without the One You Love	1962	2.50	5.00	10.00
42456 [PS]	Don't Cry, Baby/Without the One You Love	1962	7.50	15.00	30.00
42520	Try a Little Tenderness/Just for a Thrill	1962	2.50	5.00	10.00
42625	Trouble in Mind/God Bless the Child	1962	2.50	5.00	10.00
42796	Here's Where I Came In/Say It Isn't So	1963	2.50	5.00	10.00
42796 [PS]	Here's Where I Came In/Say It Isn't So	1963	7.50	15.00	30.00
42874	Skylark/You've Got Her	1963	2.50	5.00	10.00
42933	Johnny/Kissin' by the Mistletoe	1963	2.50	5.00	10.00
43009	Soulville/Evil Gal Blues	1964	2.50	5.00	10.00
43113	Runnin' Out of Fools/It's Just a Matter of Time	1964	2.50	5.00	10.00
43177	Winter Wonderland/The Christmas Song (Chestnuts Roasting on an Open Fire)	1964	2.50	5.00	10.00
43203	Can't You Just See Me/Little Miss Raggedy Ann	1965	2.50	5.00	10.00
43241	One Step Ahead/I Can't Wait Until I See My Baby's Face	1965	2.50	5.00	10.00
43333	(No, No) I'm Losing You/Sweet Bitter Love	1965	2.50	5.00	10.00
43442	You Made Me Love You/There Is No Greater Love	1966	2.50	5.00	10.00
43515	Hands Off/Tighten Up Your Tie, Button Up Your Jacket	1966	2.50	5.00	10.00
43637	Until You Were Gone/Swanee	1966	2.50	5.00	10.00
43827	Cry Like a Baby/Swanee	1966	2.50	5.00	10.00
44181	Until You Were Gone/Lee Cross	1967	2.50	5.00	10.00
44270	Take a Look/Follow Your Heart	1967	2.50	5.00	10.00
44381	Mockingbird/A Mother's Love	1967	2.00	4.00	8.00
44441	Soulville/If Ever I Would Leave You	1968	2.00	4.00	8.00
44851	Friendly Persuasion/Jim	1969	2.00	4.00	8.00
44951	Today I Sing the Blues/People	1969	2.00	4.00	8.00

JVB

Number	Title (A Side/B Side)	Yr	VG	VG+	NM
47	Never Grow Old/You Grow Closer	1957	7.50	15.00	30.00
75	Precious Lord, Part 1/Precious Lord, Part 2	1959	7.50	15.00	30.00

PHILCO-FORD

Number	Title (A Side/B Side)	Yr	VG	VG+	NM
HP-24	Respect/Soul Serenade	1968	6.25	12.50	25.00

—4-inch plastic "Hip Pocket Record" with color sleeve

FRANKLIN, CAROLYN

RCA VICTOR

Number	Title (A Side/B Side)	Yr	VG	VG+	NM
APBO-0022	You Are Everything/If You Want Me	1973	—	2.50	5.00
PB-10688	I Can't Help My Feeling So Blue/If You Want Me	1976	—	2.00	4.00
47-9734	The Boxer/I Don't Want to Lose You	1969	—	3.00	6.00
74-0188	Reality/It's True I'm Gonna Miss You	1969	—	3.00	6.00
74-0289	Ain't That Groovy/All I Want Is to Be Your Woman	1969	—	3.00	6.00
74-0314	Everybody's Talkin'/Chain Reaction	1970	—	2.50	5.00

Number	Title (A Side/B Side)	Yr	VG	VG+	NM
❑ 74-0373	You Really Didn't Mean It/All I Want Is to Be Your Woman	1970	—	2.50	5.00
❑ 74-0783	As Long As You're There/I Want to Be With You	1972	—	2.50	5.00

FRANKLIN, ERMA

BRUNSWICK

Number	Title (A Side/B Side)	Yr	VG	VG+	NM
❑ 55403	Change My Thoughts from You/Gotta Find Me a Lover	1969	2.00	4.00	8.00
❑ 55415	Saving My Love/You've Been Cancelled	1969	2.00	4.00	8.00
❑ 55424	I Just Don't Need You (At All)/It Could've Been Me	1969	2.00	4.00	8.00
❑ 55430	Whispers (Gettin' Louder)/(I Get the) Swetest Feeling	1970	2.00	4.00	8.00

EPIC

Number	Title (A Side/B Side)	Yr	VG	VG+	NM
❑ 9488	Hello Again/It's Over	1962	5.00	10.00	20.00
❑ 9511	Each Night I Cry/Time After Time	1962	5.00	10.00	20.00
❑ 9516	Dear Mama/Never Again	1962	5.00	10.00	20.00
❑ 9559	Don't Wait Too Long/Time After Time	1962	5.00	10.00	20.00
❑ 9594	Have You Ever Had the Blues/I Don't Want No Mama's Boy	1963	3.75	7.50	15.00
❑ 9610	Abracadabra/Love Is Blind	1963	3.75	7.50	15.00

SHOUT

Number	Title (A Side/B Side)	Yr	VG	VG+	NM
❑ 218	Big Boss Man/Didn't Catch the Dog's Bone	1967	2.50	5.00	10.00
❑ 221	Piece of My Heart/Baby What You Want Me to Do	1967	3.00	6.00	12.00
❑ 230	Open Up Your Soul/I'm Just Not Ready for Love	1967	2.50	5.00	10.00
❑ 234	Right to Cry/I'm Just Not Ready for Love	1968	2.50	5.00	10.00

FRANTIC

LIZARD

Number	Title (A Side/B Side)	Yr	VG	VG+	NM
❑ 20002	Shady Sam/(B-side unknown)	1970	3.75	7.50	15.00

FRANTICS, THE

BOLO

Number	Title (A Side/B Side)	Yr	VG	VG+	NM
❑ 728	Pony Moronie/Meet Me in Seattle Twist	1962	2.50	5.00	10.00
❑ 736	Oh Yeah/Let Our Love Roll On	1962	2.50	5.00	10.00

DOLTON

Number	Title (A Side/B Side)	Yr	VG	VG+	NM
❑ 2	Straight Flush/Young Blues	1959	5.00	10.00	20.00
❑ 6	Fog Cutter/Black Sapphire	1959	5.00	10.00	20.00
❑ 13	Checkerboard/Werewolf	1959	5.00	10.00	20.00
❑ 16	Werewolf/No Werewolf	1960	3.75	7.50	15.00
❑ 24	The Whip/Delilah	1960	3.75	7.50	15.00
❑ 31	Yankee Doodlin'/One Minute of Flamenco	1961	3.75	7.50	15.00
❑ 33	San Antonio Rose/Trees	1961	3.75	7.50	15.00

SEAFAIR

Number	Title (A Side/B Side)	Yr	VG	VG+	NM
❑ 111	San Francisco Swim/Blue Day	1964	2.50	5.00	10.00

FREAK SCENE, THE

COLUMBIA

Number	Title (A Side/B Side)	Yr	VG	VG+	NM
❑ 4-44056	A Million Grains of Sand/Behind the Mind	1967	6.25	12.50	25.00

FREBERG, STAN

CAPITOL

Number	Title (A Side/B Side)	Yr	VG	VG+	NM
❑ F1356	John & Marsha/Ragtime Dan	1951	7.50	15.00	30.00
❑ F1697	St. George and the Dragonet/Little Blue Riding Hood	1954	5.00	10.00	20.00
—Reissue (despite the lower number)					
❑ F1711	That's My Boy/I've Got You Under My Skin	1951	7.50	15.00	30.00
❑ F1962	Maggie/Tele-Vee-Shun	1951	7.50	15.00	30.00
❑ F2029	Try/Pass the Udder Udder	1952	7.50	15.00	30.00
❑ F2125	Abe Snake for President/Ba Ba Ball and Chain	1952	12.50	25.00	50.00
❑ F2279	The World Is Waiting for the Sunrise/Boogie Woogie Banjo Man from Birmingham	1952	6.25	12.50	25.00
❑ F2596	St. George and the Dragonet/Little Blue Riding Hood	1953	7.50	15.00	30.00
❑ F2671	Christmas Dragnet Part 1/Christmas Dragnet Part 2	1953	7.50	15.00	30.00
❑ F2677	C'est Si Bon (It's So Good)/A Dear John & Marsha Letter	1953	6.25	12.50	25.00
❑ F2838	Point of Order/Person to Pearson	1954	6.25	12.50	25.00
❑ F2929	Sh-Boom/Widescreen Mama Blues	1954	6.25	12.50	25.00
❑ F2986	Yulenet (Part 1)/Yulenet (Part 2)	1954	6.25	12.50	25.00
—Same recording as "Christmas Dragnet" (Capitol 2671)					
❑ F3138	The Honey Earthers/The Lone Psychiatrist	1955	7.50	15.00	30.00
—With Daws Butler					
❑ F3249	The Yellow Rose of Texas/Rock Around Stephen Foster	1955	6.25	12.50	25.00
❑ F3280	Nuttin' for Christmas/The Night Before Christmas	1955	6.25	12.50	25.00
❑ 3355	Try/John and Marsha	1972	2.50	5.00	10.00
❑ F3396	The Great Pretender/The Quest for Bridey Hammerschlaugen	1956	6.25	12.50	25.00
❑ F3480	Heartbreak Hotel/Rock Island Line	1956	6.25	12.50	25.00
❑ 3503	Green Chritma (Part 1)/Green Chritma (Part 2)	1972	2.50	5.00	10.00
❑ F3687	Banana Boat (Day-O)/Tele-Vee-Shun	1957	6.25	12.50	25.00
❑ F3815	Wun'erful, Wun'erful! (Part uh-one)/Wun'erful, Wun'erful! (Part uh-two)	1957	6.25	12.50	25.00
❑ F3892	Ya Got Trouble/Gary Indiana	1958	5.00	10.00	20.00
❑ F4097	Green Chritma/The Meaning of Christmas	1958	5.00	10.00	20.00
❑ F4097 [PS]	Green Chritma/The Meaning of Christmas	1958	7.50	15.00	30.00
❑ 4329	The Old Payola Roll Blues Part 1/The Old Payola Roll Blues Part 2	1960	5.00	10.00	20.00
❑ 4329 [PS]	The Old Payola Roll Blues Part 1/The Old Payola Roll Blues Part 2	1960	7.50	15.00	30.00
❑ 4433	Comments for Our Time Part 1/Comments for Our Time Part 2	1960	5.00	10.00	20.00
❑ 5726	Flackman and Reagan Part 1/Flackman and Reagan Part 2	1966	5.00	10.00	20.00
❑ 5726 [PS]	Flackman and Reagan Part 1/Flackman and Reagan Part 2	1966	7.50	15.00	30.00
❑ S7-19761	Green Chritma/The Meaning of Christmas	1997	—	—	3.00
❑ S7-57891	Nuttin' for Christmas/I Yust Go Nuts at Christmas	1992	—	2.00	4.00
—B-side by Yogi Yorgesson					

7-Inch Extended Plays

CAPITOL

Number	Title (A Side/B Side)	Yr	VG	VG+	NM
❑ EAP 496	(contents unknown)	1954	7.50	15.00	30.00
❑ EAP 496 [PS]	Any Requests?	1954	7.50	15.00	30.00
❑ EAP 628	(contents unknown)	1955	7.50	15.00	30.00
❑ EAP 628 [PS]	The Real St. George	1955	7.50	15.00	30.00

FRED, JOHN, AND HIS PLAYBOY BAND

BELL

Number	Title (A Side/B Side)	Yr	VG	VG+	NM
❑ 45382	I'm in Love Again/In the Mood	1973	—	2.50	5.00
—As "John Fred and the Creepers"					

JEWEL

Number	Title (A Side/B Side)	Yr	VG	VG+	NM
❑ 730	The Fool/There'll Be No Teardrops Tonight	1964	2.50	5.00	10.00
❑ 736	Lenne/You're Mad at Me	1964	2.50	5.00	10.00
❑ 737	Boogie Children/My First Love	1964	2.50	5.00	10.00
—As "The Playboys"					
❑ 743	Wrong to Me/How Can I Prove	1965	2.50	5.00	10.00

MONTEL

Number	Title (A Side/B Side)	Yr	VG	VG+	NM
❑ 904	Down in New Orleans/I Love You	1959	3.75	7.50	15.00
❑ 1002	Shirley/My Love for You	1959	3.75	7.50	15.00
❑ 1007	Good Lovin'/You Know You Made Me Cry	1961	2.50	5.00	10.00
❑ 2000	Mirror Mirror (On the Wall)/To Have and to Hold	1962	2.50	5.00	10.00

N-JOY

Number	Title (A Side/B Side)	Yr	VG	VG+	NM
❑ 1005	Boogie Children/My First Love	1965	2.50	5.00	10.00

PAULA

Number	Title (A Side/B Side)	Yr	VG	VG+	NM
❑ 225	Fortune Teller/Making Love to You	1965	2.00	4.00	8.00
❑ 234	Can't I Get a Word In/Sun City	1966	2.00	4.00	8.00
❑ 244	Doin' the Best I Can/Leave Her Never	1966	2.00	4.00	8.00
❑ 247	Outta My Head/Love Comes in Time	1966	2.00	4.00	8.00
❑ 259	Up and Down/Wind-Up Doll	1967	2.00	4.00	8.00
❑ 273	Agnes English/Sad Story	1967	2.00	4.00	8.00
❑ 282	Judy in Disguise (With Glasses)/When the Lights Go Out	1967	3.00	6.00	12.00
—White label					
❑ 282	Judy in Disguise (With Glasses)/When the Lights Go Out	1967	2.50	5.00	10.00
—Yellow label					
❑ 282	Judy in Disguise (With Glasses)/When the Lights Go Out	1967	2.00	4.00	8.00
—Pink label					
❑ 294	Hey Hey Bunny/No Letter Today	1968	2.00	4.00	8.00
❑ 303	Lonely Are the Lonely/We Played Games	1968	2.00	4.00	8.00
❑ 310	Tissue Paper/Little Dum Dum	1968	2.00	4.00	8.00
❑ 315	What Is Happiness/Sometimes You Just Can't Win	1968	2.00	4.00	8.00

PHILCO-FORD

Number	Title (A Side/B Side)	Yr	VG	VG+	NM
❑ HP-25	Judy in Disguise/No Letter Today	1968	5.00	10.00	20.00
—4-inch plastic "Hip Pocket Record" with color sleeve					

SUGARCANE

Number	Title (A Side/B Side)	Yr	VG	VG+	NM
❑ 1001	Keep It Hid/You Had to Be a Woman	1975	—	2.00	4.00
❑ 1002	Jukebox Shirley/Hey, Good Lookin'	1975	—	2.00	4.00

UNI

Number	Title (A Side/B Side)	Yr	VG	VG+	NM
❑ 55135	Back in the U.S.S.R./Silly Sarah Carter	1969	—	3.00	6.00
❑ 55160	Open Doors/Three Deep Is a Feeling	1969	—	3.00	6.00
❑ 55187	Love My Soul/Julia Julia	1969	—	3.00	6.00
❑ 55220	Come with Me/Where's Everybody Going	1970	—	3.00	6.00

FREDDIE AND THE DREAMERS

CAPITOL

Number	Title (A Side/B Side)	Yr	VG	VG+	NM
❑ 5053	I'm Telling You Now/What Have I Done to You	1963	5.00	10.00	20.00
❑ 5137	You Were Made for Me/Send a Letter to Me	1964	5.00	10.00	20.00

MERCURY

Number	Title (A Side/B Side)	Yr	VG	VG+	NM
❑ 72285	I Love You Baby/Don't Make Me Cry	1965	2.50	5.00	10.00
❑ 72285 [PS]	I Love You Baby/Don't Make Me Cry	1965	5.00	10.00	20.00
❑ 72327	Don't Do That to Me/Just for You	1965	2.50	5.00	10.00
❑ 72377	I Understand (Just How You Feel)/I Will	1965	2.50	5.00	10.00
❑ 72428	Do the Freddie/Tell Me When	1965	2.50	5.00	10.00
❑ 72428	Do the Freddie/A Love Like You	1965	3.00	6.00	12.00
❑ 72462	A Little You/Things I'd Like to Say	1965	2.50	5.00	10.00
❑ 72487	I Don't Know/Windmill in Old Amsterdam	1965	2.50	5.00	10.00
❑ 72487 [PS]	I Don't Know/Windmill in Old Amsterdam	1965	5.00	10.00	20.00
❑ 72548	When I'm Home with You/If You Got a Minute Baby	1966	2.50	5.00	10.00
❑ 72604	Some Day/Short Shorts	1966	2.50	5.00	10.00

SUPER K

Number	Title (A Side/B Side)	Yr	VG	VG+	NM
❑ 146	She Needs Me/Susan's Tuba	1970	2.00	4.00	8.00

TOWER

Number	Title (A Side/B Side)	Yr	VG	VG+	NM
❑ 125	I'm Telling You Now/What Have I Done to You	1964	3.75	7.50	15.00
❑ 127	You Were Made for Me/Send a Letter to Me	1965	5.00	10.00	20.00
❑ 127	You Were Made for Me/So Fine	1965	3.75	7.50	15.00
—B-side: "Introducing the Beat Merchants"					
❑ 163	Send a Letter to Me/There's Not One Thing	1965	3.75	7.50	15.00
—B-side by 4 Just Men					

UNITED ARTISTS

Number	Title (A Side/B Side)	Yr	VG	VG+	NM
❑ 50239	Come Back When You Grow Up/Oh What a Lovely Day	1967	—	—	—
—Unreleased					

7-Inch Extended Plays

MERCURY

Number	Title (A Side/B Side)	Yr	VG	VG+	NM
❑ SRC 661-C	Thou Shalt Not Steal/Funny Over You/He Got What He Wanted//I Fell in Love with Your Picture/I Think of You/Some Other Guy	1965	5.00	10.00	20.00
—Jukebox mini-LP					
❑ SRC 661-C [PS]	Fun Lovin' Freddie	1965	5.00	10.00	20.00

FREDDIE AND THE PARLIAMENTS

TWIRL

Number	Title (A Side/B Side)	Yr	VG	VG+	NM
❑ 1003	Darlene/That Girl	1959	25.00	50.00	100.00

Number	Title (A Side/B Side)	Yr	VG	VG+	NM
FREDRIC					
EVOLUTION					
❑ 1001	Five O'Clock Traffic/Red Pier	1968	6.25	12.50	25.00
FORTE					
❑ 3001	Five O'Clock Traffic/Red Pier	1968	10.00	20.00	40.00
FREE					
A&M					
❑ 1099	I'm a Mover/Worry	1969	—	2.00	4.00
❑ 1172	I'll Be Creepin'/Mouthful of Grass	1970	—	2.00	4.00
❑ 1206	All Right Now/Mouthful of Grass	1970	—	2.50	5.00
❑ 1230	Stealer/Broad Daylight	1970	—	2.00	4.00
❑ 1248	Highway Song/Love You So	1971	—	2.00	4.00
❑ 1266	Mr. Big/I'll Be Creepin'	1971	—	2.00	4.00
❑ 1276	My Brother Jake/Only My Soul	1971	—	2.00	4.00
❑ 1352	Little Bit of Love/Sail On	1972	—	2.00	4.00
❑ 1720	All Right Now/Stealer	1975	—	2.00	4.00
ISLAND					
❑ 1212	Wishing Well/Let Me Show You	1972	—	2.00	4.00
FREE DESIGN, THE					
PROJECT 3					
❑ 1324	Kites Are Fun/Proper Ornaments	1967	2.00	4.00	8.00
❑ 1331	You Be You and I'll Be Me/Never Tell the World	1967	2.00	4.00	8.00
❑ 1336	I Found Love/Umbrellas	1968	2.00	4.00	8.00
❑ 1345	Eleanor Rigby/Make the Madness Stop	1968	2.00	4.00	8.00
❑ 1347 [DJ]	Close Your Mouth (It's Christmas)/Christmas Is The Day	1968	2.50	5.00	10.00
—Stock copy may not exist					
❑ 1350	You Could Be Born Again/A Leaf Has Veins	1968	2.00	4.00	8.00
❑ 1356	Where Do I Go/Girls Alone	1969	2.00	4.00	8.00
❑ 1358	Summertime/Dorian Benediction	1969	2.00	4.00	8.00
❑ 1360	If I Were a Carpenter/Now Is the Time	1969	2.00	4.00	8.00
❑ 1366	2002: A Hit Song/Hurry Sundown	1969	2.00	4.00	8.00
❑ 1370	Butterflies Are Free/(B-side unknown)	1970	2.00	4.00	8.00
❑ 1375	I'm a Yogi/Bubbles	1970	2.00	4.00	8.00
❑ 1383	Tomorrow Is the First Day of the Rest of My Life/Kije's Ouija	1970	2.00	4.00	8.00
❑ 1393	Felt So Good/You Are My Sunshine	1971	2.00	4.00	8.00
❑ 1404	Stay Off of Your Frown/Friendly Man	1971	2.00	4.00	8.00
FREE MOVEMENT, THE					
COLUMBIA					
❑ 45512	The Harder I Try (The Bluer I Get)/Comin' Home	1972	—	2.50	5.00
❑ 45567	Could You Believe in a Dream/Love the One You're With	1972	—	2.50	5.00
❑ 45778	Every Step of the Way/I Can't Move No Mountains	1973	—	2.50	5.00
DECCA					
❑ 32818	I've Found Someone of My Own/I Can't Convince My Heart	1971	—	3.00	6.00
FREED, ALAN					
CORAL					
❑ 61626	Right Now, Right Now/Tina's Cantine	1956	7.50	15.00	30.00
❑ 61660	THe Camel Rock/I Don't Need Lotsa Money	1956	7.50	15.00	30.00
❑ 61693	The Space Man/Jazzbo's Theory	1956	7.50	15.00	30.00
—With Al "Jazzbo" Collins and the Modernaires					
❑ 61749	Rock 'N' Roll Boogie/The Grey Bear	1956	10.00	20.00	40.00
❑ 61818	Sentimental Journey/Stop! Look! and Run!	1957	10.00	20.00	40.00
FREEMAN, ART					
FAME					
❑ 1008	I Can't Get You Out of My Mind/Slippin' Around with You	1966	12.50	25.00	50.00
❑ 1012	A Piece of My Heart/Everybody's Got to Cry Sometime	1966	7.50	15.00	30.00
FREEMAN, BOBBY					
AUTUMN					
❑ 1	Come to Me/Let's Surf Again	1964	5.00	10.00	20.00
❑ 2	C'mon and Swim/C'mon and Swim — Part 2	1964	3.00	6.00	12.00
—White label, red print					
❑ 2	C'mon and Swim/C'mon and Swim — Part 2	1964	2.50	5.00	10.00
—Tan label					
❑ 5	S-W-I-M/That Little Old Heartbreaker	1964	2.50	5.00	10.00
❑ 9	I'll Never Fall in Love Again/Friends	1965	2.50	5.00	10.00
❑ 25	Cross My Heart/The Duck	1965	2.50	5.00	10.00
DOUBLE SHOT					
❑ 139	There Oughta Be a Law/Everybody's Got a Hang-Up	1969	—	3.00	6.00
❑ 144	Susie Sunshine/Four Piece Funky Nitty Gritty Junky Band	1969	—	3.00	6.00
❑ 148	Can You Stand the Pressure/Put Another Dime in the Parking Meter	1970	—	3.00	6.00
❑ 152	Do You Wanna Dance 1970/Society for the Prevention of Cruelty to People	1970	—	3.00	6.00
JOSIE					
❑ 835	Do You Want to Dance/Big Fat Woman	1958	5.00	10.00	20.00
❑ 841	Betty Lou Got a New Pair of Shoes/Starlight	1958	5.00	10.00	20.00
❑ 844	Need Your Love/Shame On You, Miss Johnson	1958	3.75	7.50	15.00
❑ 855	A Love to Last a Lifetime/When You're Smiling	1959	3.75	7.50	15.00
❑ 863	Love Me/Mary Ann Thomas	1959	3.75	7.50	15.00
❑ 867	My Guardian Angel/Where Did My Baby Go	1959	3.75	7.50	15.00
❑ 872	Ebb Tide/Sinbad	1959	3.75	7.50	15.00
❑ 879	I Need Someone/First Day of Spring	1960	3.00	6.00	12.00
❑ 886	Miss You So/Baby What Would You Do	1961	3.00	6.00	12.00
❑ 887	The Mess Around/So Much to Do	1961	3.00	6.00	12.00
❑ 889	Put You Down/She Said She Wants to Dance	1961	3.00	6.00	12.00
❑ 896	Love Me/Little Girl Don't You Understand	1962	3.00	6.00	12.00
❑ 928	The Mess Around/Little Girl Don't You Understand	1965	2.50	5.00	10.00
KING					
❑ 5373	Shimmy Shimmy/You Don't Understand	1960	3.00	6.00	12.00

Number	Title (A Side/B Side)	Yr	VG	VG+	NM
❑ 5953	Fever/What Can I Do	1964	2.50	5.00	10.00
❑ 5962	Somebody, Somewhere/Be My Little Chick-A-Dee	1964	2.50	5.00	10.00
❑ 5975	Come to Me/There's Gonna Be a Change	1965	2.50	5.00	10.00
LOMA					
❑ 2056	Shadow of Your Love/Soulful Sound of Music	1966	2.00	4.00	8.00
❑ 2080	I Got a Good Thing/Lies	1967	2.00	4.00	8.00
PARKWAY					
❑ 875	She's a Hippy/Whip It Up Baby	1963	3.00	6.00	12.00
FREEMAN, ERNIE					
AVA					
❑ 176	Raunchy '65/Jivin' Around	1965	2.00	4.00	8.00
CASH					
❑ 1017	Jivin' Around (Part 1)/Jivin' Around (Part 2)	1955	3.75	7.50	15.00
IMPERIAL					
❑ 5381	Rockin' Around/Lost Dreams	1956	3.75	7.50	15.00
❑ 5391	Rainy Day/Funny Face	1956	3.75	7.50	15.00
❑ 5403	Spring Fever/Walking the Beat	1956	3.75	7.50	15.00
❑ 5419	Return to Me/A Touch of the Blues	1957	3.75	7.50	15.00
❑ 5430	Without Love/Night Life	1957	3.75	7.50	15.00
❑ 5444	Swing It/River Boat	1957	3.75	7.50	15.00
❑ 5461	Dumplin's/Beautiful Weekend	1957	3.75	7.50	15.00
❑ 5474	Raunchy/Puddin'	1957	6.25	12.50	25.00
❑ 5486	The Tuttle/Leaps and Bounds	1958	3.00	6.00	12.00
❑ 5518	Indian Love Call/Summer Serenade	1958	3.00	6.00	12.00
❑ 5527	Rose Marie/After Sunset	1958	3.00	6.00	12.00
❑ 5541	Jamboree/Junior Jive	1958	3.00	6.00	12.00
❑ 5551	School Room Rock/Blues After Hours	1958	3.00	6.00	12.00
❑ 5566	Live It Up/Whispering Hope (Freedom and Land)	1959	2.50	5.00	10.00
❑ 5574	Marshmallows, Popcorn & Soda Pop/Honey Dripper	1959	2.50	5.00	10.00
❑ 5612	A Summer Love/Always with You	1959	2.50	5.00	10.00
❑ 5621	Lost Dreams/One More Time Around	1959	2.50	5.00	10.00
❑ 5633	Big River/Night Sounds	1959	2.50	5.00	10.00
❑ 5656	Rockin' Red Wing/Dark Eyes	1960	2.00	4.00	8.00
❑ 5677	Autumn and Eve/Prayer	1960	2.00	4.00	8.00
❑ 5693	Theme from "The Dark at the Top of the Stairs"/Come On Home	1960	2.00	4.00	8.00
❑ 5716	Hawaiian Eye/Heartbreak Hotel	1960	2.00	4.00	8.00
❑ 5732	Swamp Meeting/That's All	1961	2.00	4.00	8.00
❑ 5752	Theme from "Return to Peyton Place"/Warsaw Concerto	1961	2.00	4.00	8.00
❑ 5769	Conquest/Swingin' Preacher	1961	2.00	4.00	8.00
❑ 5793	The Twist/Shine On Harvest Moon	1961	2.00	4.00	8.00
❑ 5815	What Am I Living For/I Didn't Want to Do It	1962	2.00	4.00	8.00
❑ 5841	The Stripper/I Hear You Knocking	1962	2.00	4.00	8.00
❑ 5883	The Freeloader/Say It Isn't So	1962	2.00	4.00	8.00
LIBERTY					
❑ 55515	Half as Much/I'm Sorry for You My Friend	1962	2.00	4.00	8.00
FREEMAN BROTHERS, THE					
MALA					
❑ 553	I'm Counting on You/Everyday It's You	1966	6.25	12.50	25.00
SOUL					
❑ 35011	My Baby/Beautiful Brown Eyes	1965	10.00	20.00	40.00
FREEPORT					
MAINSTREAM					
❑ 730	I Need Your Lovin'/(B-side unknown)	1970	2.50	5.00	10.00
❑ 732	Now That She's Gone/Misunderstood	1970	2.50	5.00	10.00
FREEWHEELERS, THE					
EPIC					
❑ 9664	Walk, Walk/The Best of It	1964	5.00	10.00	20.00
❑ 9700	San Francisco Bay Blues/Susu	1964	5.00	10.00	20.00
❑ 9725	Beach Boy/Annie	1964	3.75	7.50	15.00
FREHLEY, ACE					
Also see KISS.					
ATLANTIC					
❑ 89072	Insane/The Acorn Is Spinning	1988	—	—	3.00
—As "Frehley's Comet"					
❑ 89255	Into the Night/Fractured Too	1987	—	—	3.00
CASABLANCA					
❑ 941	New York Groove/Snowblind	1978	—	2.50	5.00
FREY, GLENN					
Also see EAGLES; LONGBRANCH PENNYWHISTLE.					
ASYLUM					
❑ 47466	I Found Somebody/She Can't Let Go	1982	—	2.00	4.00
❑ 47466 [PS]	I Found Somebody/She Can't Let Go	1982	—	2.50	5.00
❑ 69857	All Those Lies/That Girl	1982	—	2.00	4.00
❑ 69974	The One You Love/All Those Lies	1982	—	2.00	4.00
MCA					
❑ 52413	Sexy Girl/Better in the U.S.A.	1984	—	—	3.00
❑ 52413 [PS]	Sexy Girl/Better in the U.S.A.	1984	—	—	3.00
❑ 52461	The Allnighter/Smuggler's Blues	1984	—	—	3.00
❑ 52461 [PS]	The Allnighter/Smuggler's Blues	1984	—	—	3.00
❑ 52512	The Heat Is On/Shoot Out	1984	—	—	3.00
❑ 52512 [PS]	The Heat Is On/Shoot Out	1984	—	—	3.00
—B-side by Harold Faltermeyer					
❑ 52546	Smuggler's Blues/New Love	1985	—	—	3.00
❑ 52546 [PS]	Smuggler's Blues/New Love	1985	—	—	3.00
❑ 52651	You Belong to the City/Smuggler's Blues	1985	—	—	3.00
❑ 52651 [PS]	You Belong to the City/Smuggler's Blues	1985	—	—	3.00
❑ 53363	True Love/Working Man	1988	—	—	3.00
❑ 53363 [PS]	True Love/Working Man	1988	—	—	3.00
❑ 53452	Soul Searchin'/It's Cold in Here	1988	—	—	3.00
❑ 53497	Livin' Right/Soul Searchin'	1989	—	—	3.00
❑ 53684	Two Hearts/Some Kind of Blue	1989	—	—	3.00
❑ 54429	I've Got Mine/A Walk in the Park	1992	—	—	3.00

Number	Title (A Side/B Side)	Yr	VG	VG+	NM
54461	River of Dreams/He Took Advantage (Blues for Ronald Reagan)	1992	—	—	3.00

FRIAR TUCK

Curt Boetcher was in the group.

BANSHEE

Number	Title (A Side/B Side)	Yr	VG	VG+	NM
100	The Return of Robin Hood/(B-side unknown)	196?	3.75	7.50	15.00

MERCURY

Number	Title (A Side/B Side)	Yr	VG	VG+	NM
72684	Alley Oop/Sweet Pea	1967	2.50	5.00	10.00

FRIEND AND LOVER

ABC

Number	Title (A Side/B Side)	Yr	VG	VG+	NM
10910	Town Called Love/If Tomorrow	1967	3.00	6.00	12.00

CADET CONCEPT

Number	Title (A Side/B Side)	Yr	VG	VG+	NM
7019	Hard Lovin'/Colorado Exile	1970	—	3.00	6.00
7019 [PS]	Hard Lovin'/Colorado Exile	1970	3.75	7.50	15.00

VERVE FORECAST

Number	Title (A Side/B Side)	Yr	VG	VG+	NM
5069	Reach Out of the Darkness/Time on Your Side (You're Only 15 Years Old)	1967	2.50	5.00	10.00
5091	If Love Is In Your Heart/Zig Zag	1968	2.00	4.00	8.00
5100	I Want to Be Free/Circus	1968	2.00	4.00	8.00
5106	Ode to a Dandelion/A Wise Man Changes His Mind	1969	—	3.00	6.00

FRIENDLY TORPEDOES, THE

ORIGINAL SOUND

Number	Title (A Side/B Side)	Yr	VG	VG+	NM
95	Nothing's Too Good for My Car/So Long Ago	1970	6.25	12.50	25.00

FRIENDS OF DISTINCTION, THE

RCA VICTOR

Number	Title (A Side/B Side)	Yr	VG	VG+	NM
PB-10197	Honey Baby Theme Part 1/Honey Baby Theme Part 2	1975	—	2.00	4.00
PB-10220	Love Shack Part 1/Love Shack Part 2	1975	—	2.00	4.00
74-0107	Grazing in the Grass/I Really Hope You Do	1969	—	3.00	6.00
74-0204	Going in Circles/Let Yourself Go	1969	—	3.00	6.00
74-0319	Love Or Let Me Be Lonely/This Generation	1970	—	3.00	6.00
74-0385	Time Waits for No One/Mother Nature	1970	—	2.50	5.00
74-0416	Check It Out/I Need You	1971	—	2.50	5.00
74-0516	It Don't Matter to Me/Down I Go	1971	—	2.50	5.00
74-0562	Let Me Be/Long Time Comin' My Way	1971	—	2.50	5.00
74-0679	Love Is the Way of Life/Jenny Wants to Know	1972	—	2.50	5.00
74-0787	Now Is the Time/Thumb Tripping	1972	—	2.50	5.00
74-0888	Ain't No Woman (Like the One I've Got)/Easy Evil	1973	—	2.50	5.00
74-0956	Check It Out/Love Can Make It Easier	1973	—	2.50	5.00

FRIJID PINK

LION

Number	Title (A Side/B Side)	Yr	VG	VG+	NM
115	Earth Omen/Lazy Day	1972	2.00	4.00	8.00
136	Go Now/Lazy Day	1972	2.00	4.00	8.00
158	Big Betty/Shady Lady	1973	—	3.00	6.00

PARROT

Number	Title (A Side/B Side)	Yr	VG	VG+	NM
334	Tell Me Why/Cryin' Shame	1969	—	3.00	6.00
340	God Gave Me You/Drivin' Blues	1970	—	3.00	6.00
341	House of the Rising Sun/Drivin' Blues	1970	2.00	4.00	8.00
349	Sing a Song for Freedom/End of the Line	1970	—	3.00	6.00
352	Heartbreak Hotel/Bye Bye Blues	1970	—	3.00	6.00
355	Music for the People/Sloony	1971	—	3.00	6.00
358	We're Gonna Be There/Shorty Kline	1971	—	3.00	6.00
360	Lost Son/I Love Her	1971	—	3.00	6.00

FRIZZELL, LEFTY

ABC

Number	Title (A Side/B Side)	Yr	VG	VG+	NM
11350	I Buy the Wine/Let Me Give Her the Flowers	1973	2.00	4.00	8.00
11387	I Can't Get Over You to Save My Life/Somebody's Words	1973	—	3.50	7.00
11416	I Never Go Around Mirrors/That's the Way It Goes	1974	—	3.50	7.00
11442	Railroad Lady/If I Had Half the Sense (A Fool Was Born With)	1974	—	3.50	7.00
12023	Lucky Arms/If She Just Helps Me Get Over You	1974	—	3.50	7.00
12061	Life's Like Poetry/Sittin' and Thinkin'	1975	—	3.50	7.00
12103	Falling/I Love You a Thousand Ways	1975	—	3.50	7.00

COLUMBIA

Number	Title (A Side/B Side)	Yr	VG	VG+	NM
38-04264	Get This Stranger Out of Me/This Just Ain't No Good Day for Leaving	1983	—	2.50	5.00
38-04480	Watermelon Time in Georgia/Everything Keeps Coming Back to You	1984	—	2.50	5.00
4-20739	If You've Got the Money, I've Got the Time/I Love You a Thousand Ways	1950	10.00	20.00	40.00
4-20772	Look What Thoughts Will Do/Shine, Shave, Shower (It's Saturday)	1951	6.25	12.50	25.00
4-20799	I Want to Be With You Always/My Baby's Just Like Money	1951	6.25	12.50	25.00
4-20837	Always Late (With Your Kisses)/Mom and Dad's Waltz	1951	6.25	12.50	25.00
4-20840	Blue Yodel #2/Treasures Untold	1951	5.00	10.00	20.00
4-20841	Brakeman's Blues/My Old Pal	1951	5.00	10.00	20.00
4-20842	Travellin' Blues/Blue Yodel #6	1951	6.25	12.50	25.00
4-20843	My Rough and Rowdy Ways/Lullaby Yodel	1951	5.00	10.00	20.00
—The above four comprise a box set (20842 was also available separately)					
4-20885	Give Me More, More, More (Of Your Kisses)/How Long Will It Take (To Stop Loving You)	1951	6.25	12.50	25.00
4-20911	Don't Stay Away (Till Love Grows Cold)/You're Here, So Everything's All Right	1952	6.25	12.50	25.00
4-20941	Don't Stay Away (Till Love Grows Cold)/Sad Singin', Slow Ridin'	1952	5.00	10.00	20.00
—B-side by Polly Possum; part of a 4-record various-artists box set					
4-20950	If You Can Spare the Time/It's Just You	1952	6.25	12.50	25.00
4-20958	If You've Got the Money, I've Got the Time/Look What Thoughts Will Do	1952	5.00	10.00	20.00
4-20959	I Love You a Thousand Ways/I Want to Be with You Always	1952	5.00	10.00	20.00
4-20960	Always Late (With Your Kisses)/Mom and Dad's Waltz	1952	5.00	10.00	20.00
4-20961	Don't Stay Away (Till Love Grows Cold)/If You Can Spare the Time	1952	5.00	10.00	20.00
—The above four comprise a box set					
4-20997	Forever (And Always)/I Know You're Lonesome While Waiting for Me	1952	6.25	12.50	25.00
4-21034	I'm an Old, Old Man (Tryin' to Live While I Can)/You're Just Mine (Only in My Dreams)	1952	6.25	12.50	25.00
4-21084	(Honey, Baby, Hurry) Bring Your Sweet Self Back to Me/Time Changes Things	1953	6.25	12.50	25.00
4-21100	Never No More Blues/Sleep Baby Sleep	1953	6.25	12.50	25.00
4-21101	California Blues/I'm Lonely and Blue	1953	6.25	12.50	25.00
4-21118	We Crucified Our Jesus/When It Comes to Measuring Love	1953	6.25	12.50	25.00
4-21142	Two Friends of Mine/Before You Go	1953	6.25	12.50	25.00
4-21169	Hopeless Love/Then I'll Come Back to You	1953	6.25	12.50	25.00
4-21194	Run 'Em Off/Darkest Moment	1953	6.25	12.50	25.00
4-21208	My Little Her and Him/I've Been Away Way Too Long	1954	6.25	12.50	25.00
4-21241	King Without a Queen/You Can Always Count on Me	1954	6.25	12.50	25.00
4-21284	You're Too Late/Two Hearts Broken Now	1954	6.25	12.50	25.00
4-21328	I Love You Mostly/Mama	1954	6.25	12.50	25.00
4-21366	Making Believe/A Forest Fire	1955	6.25	12.50	25.00
4-21393	I'll Sit Alone and Cry/Moonlight Darling and You	1955	6.25	12.50	25.00
4-21433	Sweet Lies/I'm Lost Between Right and Wrong	1955	6.25	12.50	25.00
4-21458	It Gets Late So Early/Your Tomorrows Will Never Come	1955	6.25	12.50	25.00
4-21488	First to Have a Second Chance/These Hands	1956	6.25	12.50	25.00
4-21506	Promises Promises/Today Is That Tomorrow	1956	6.25	12.50	25.00
4-21530	Just Can't Live That Fast/Waltz of the Angels	1956	6.25	12.50	25.00
4-21554	Heart's Highway/I'm a Boy Left Alone	1956	6.25	12.50	25.00
4-40818	Glad I Found You/Lullaby Waltz	1957	5.00	10.00	20.00
4-40867	From an Angel to a Devil/Now That You Are Gone	1957	5.00	10.00	20.00
4-40938	Is It Only That You're Lonely/No One to Talk To	1957	5.00	10.00	20.00
4-41080	Time Out for the Blues/Tell Me Dear	1957	5.00	10.00	20.00
4-41161	Silence/The Torch Within My Heart	1958	5.00	10.00	20.00
4-41268	Cigarettes and Coffee Blues/You're Humbuggin' Me	1958	5.00	10.00	20.00
4-41384	The Long Black Veil/Knock Again, True Love	1959	5.00	10.00	20.00
4-41455	Farther Than My Eyes Can See/Ballad of the Blue and Gray	1959	5.00	10.00	20.00
4-41635	She's Gone/My Blues Will Pass	1960	3.75	7.50	15.00
4-41751	What You Gonna Do Leroy/That's All I Can Remember	1960	3.75	7.50	15.00
4-41984	Looking for You/Heaven's Plan	1961	3.75	7.50	15.00
4-42253	I Feel Sorry for Me/So What, Let It Rain	1961	3.75	7.50	15.00
4-42521	Stranger/Just Passing Through	1962	3.75	7.50	15.00
4-42676	Forbidden Lovers/A Few Steps Away	1963	3.00	6.00	12.00
4-42830	Don't Let Her See Me Cry/James River	1963	3.00	6.00	12.00
4-42924	Saginaw, Michigan/When It Rains the Blues	1963	3.00	6.00	12.00
4-43051	The Nester/The Rider	1964	3.00	6.00	12.00
4-43169	'Gator Hollow/Make That One for the Road a Cup of Coffee	1964	3.00	6.00	12.00
4-43256	She's Gone Gone Gone/Confused	1965	2.50	5.00	10.00
4-43364	A Little Unfair/Love Looks Good on You	1965	2.50	5.00	10.00
4-43590	Writing on the Wall/Mama	1966	2.50	5.00	10.00
4-43747	I Just Couldn't See the Forest (For the Trees)/Everything Keeps Coming Back (But You)	1966	2.50	5.00	10.00
4-44023	You Gotta Be Puttin' Me On/A Song from a Lonely Heart	1967	2.50	5.00	10.00
4-44205	Get This Stranger Out of Me/Hobo's Pride	1967	2.50	5.00	10.00
4-44390	Anything You Can Spare/A Prayer on Your Lips	1967	2.50	5.00	10.00
4-44563	The Marriage Bit/When the Grass Grows Green Again	1968	2.50	5.00	10.00
4-44692	Wasted Way of Life/Keep the Flowers Watered When I'm Gone	1968	2.50	5.00	10.00
4-44738	An Article from Life/Only Way to Fly	1969	2.50	5.00	10.00
4-44984	Honky Tonk Hill/Wasted Way of Life	1969	2.50	5.00	10.00
4-45145	My Baby Is a Tramp/She Brought Love, Sweet Love	1970	2.50	5.00	10.00
4-45197	Watermelon Time in Georgia/Out of You	1970	2.50	5.00	10.00
4-45310	Three Cheers for the Good Guys/I Must Be Getting Over You	1971	2.50	5.00	10.00
4-45347	Honyk Tonk Stardust Cowboy/What Am I Gonna Do	1971	2.50	5.00	10.00
4-45652	You, Babe/When It Rains the Blues	1972	2.50	5.00	10.00
4-52019	If You've Got the Money, I've Got the Time/I Love You a Thousand Ways	195?	3.75	7.50	15.00
—Early "Hall of Fame Series" issue with maroon label					

FROGMEN, THE

ASTRA

Number	Title (A Side/B Side)	Yr	VG	VG+	NM
1009	Underwater/The Mad Rush	196?	12.50	25.00	50.00
1010	Beware Below/Tioga	196?	12.50	25.00	50.00
—The above two are East Coast reissues					

CANDIX

Number	Title (A Side/B Side)	Yr	VG	VG+	NM
314	Underwater/The Mad Rush	1961	6.25	12.50	25.00
326	Beware Below/Tioga	1961	6.25	12.50	25.00

SCOTT

Number	Title (A Side/B Side)	Yr	VG	VG+	NM
101	Seahorse Flats/Tioga	1961	12.50	25.00	50.00
102	Underwater/Beware Below	1961	12.50	25.00	50.00

TEE JAY

Number	Title (A Side/B Side)	Yr	VG	VG+	NM
131	Sea Haunt/Diamond Back	1964	20.00	40.00	80.00
—Blue vinyl					

FRONT PAGE NEWS

DIAL

Number	Title (A Side/B Side)	Yr	VG	VG+	NM
4052	Thoughts/You Better Behave	1967	6.25	12.50	25.00

FROST, FRANK

JEWEL

Number	Title (A Side/B Side)	Yr	VG	VG+	NM
765	My Back Scratcher/Harp and Soul	1966	3.75	7.50	15.00
771	Things You Do/Harpin' On It	1966	3.75	7.50	15.00

Number	Title (A Side/B Side)	Yr	VG	VG+	NM
❑ 778	Pocketful of Money/Ride with Your Daddy Tonight	1967	5.00	10.00	20.00
PHILLIPS INTERNATIONAL					
❑ 3578	Jelly Roll King/Crawlback	1962	5.00	10.00	20.00

FROST, MAX, AND THE TROOPERS

Number	Title (A Side/B Side)	Yr	VG	VG+	NM
SIDEWALK					
❑ 938	There Is a Party Going On/Stomper's Ride	1968	3.75	7.50	15.00
TOWER					
❑ 419	Shape of Things to Come/Free Lovin'	1968	3.75	7.50	15.00
❑ 452	52%/Max Frost Theme	1968	3.75	7.50	15.00
❑ 452 [PS]	52%/Max Frost Theme	1968	5.00	10.00	20.00
❑ 478	Paxton Quigley's Had the Course/Sittin' in Circles	1969	3.75	7.50	15.00
❑ 478 [PS]	Paxton Quigley's Had the Course/Sittin' in Circles	1969	5.00	10.00	20.00

FROST, THE

Number	Title (A Side/B Side)	Yr	VG	VG+	NM
DATE					
❑ 1577	Bad Girl/Rainy Day	1967	3.00	6.00	12.00
—As "Dick Wagner and the Frosts"					
❑ 1596	Little Girl/Sunshine	1968	3.00	6.00	12.00
—As "Dick Wagner and the Frosts"					
VANGUARD					
❑ 35099	Linda/Sweet Lady Love	1969	2.00	4.00	8.00
❑ 35111	Rock and Roll Music/Donny's Blues	1969	2.00	4.00	8.00
❑ 35115	A Long Way from Home/Black As Night	1970	2.00	4.00	8.00

FRUMIOUS BANDERSNATCH

7-Inch Extended Plays

Number	Title (A Side/B Side)	Yr	VG	VG+	NM
MUGGLES GRAMOPHONE WORKS					
❑ (no #)	(contents unknown)	1967	62.50	125.00	250.00
—Legitimate copies show purple vinyl when held to a light. All others are bootlegs.					
❑ (no #) [PS]	Frumious Bandersnatch	1967	62.50	125.00	250.00

FUGAZI

Number	Title (A Side/B Side)	Yr	VG	VG+	NM
DISCHORD					
❑ 43	Joe #1/Break In/Song #1	1990	—	—	2.00
❑ 43 [PS]	Joe #1/Break In/Song #1	1990	—	—	2.00
SUB POP					
❑ 52	Joe #1/Break In/Song #1	1989	18.75	37.50	75.00
—Green vinyl pressing of 1,200					
❑ 52	Joe #1/Break In/Song #1	1989	6.25	12.50	25.00
—Black vinyl pressing of 800					
❑ 52 [PS]	Joe #1/Break In/Song #1	1989	6.25	12.50	25.00
—#14 in Sub Pop Singles Club series					

FUGS, THE

Number	Title (A Side/B Side)	Yr	VG	VG+	NM
ESP-DISK'					
❑ 4507	Frenzy/I Want to Know	1966	3.75	7.50	15.00

FULLER, BOBBY, FOUR

Number	Title (A Side/B Side)	Yr	VG	VG+	NM
CAPITOL					
❑ 3038	The Only God I Know/A Name Like Watermelon	1971	5.00	10.00	20.00
DONNA					
❑ 1403	Those Memories of You/Our Favorite Martian	1965	50.00	100.00	200.00
—As "Bobby Fuller and the Fantastics"					
EASTWOOD					
❑ 345	Not Fade Away/Nervous Breakdown	1962	25.00	50.00	100.00
EXETER					
❑ 122	King of the Beach/Wine, Wine, Wine	1964	50.00	100.00	200.00
❑ 124	I Fought the Law/She's My Girl	1964	87.50	175.00	350.00
❑ 126	Fool of Love/Shakedown	1964	30.00	60.00	120.00
LIBERTY					
❑ 55812	Let Her Dance/Another Sad and Lonely Night	1965	7.50	15.00	30.00
MUSTANG					
❑ 3004	She's My Girl/Take My Hand	1965	6.25	12.50	25.00
❑ 3006	Let Her Dance/Another Sad and Lonely Night	1965	3.75	7.50	15.00
❑ 3011	Never to Be Forgotten/You Kissed Me	1965	6.25	12.50	25.00
❑ 3012	Let Her Dance/Another Sad and Lonely Night	1965	3.75	7.50	15.00
❑ 3014	I Fought the Law/Little Annie Lou	1966	3.75	7.50	15.00
❑ 3016	Love's Made a Fool of You/Don't Ever Let Me Know	1966	3.75	7.50	15.00
❑ 3018	Magic Touch/My True Love	1966	3.00	6.00	12.00
TODD					
❑ 1090	Saturday Night/The Stinger	1963	25.00	50.00	100.00
YUCCA					
❑ 140	You're in Love/Guess We'll Fall in Love	1961	20.00	40.00	80.00
—Slow version					
❑ 140	You're in Love/Guess We'll Fall in Love	1961	10.00	20.00	40.00
—Fast version					
❑ 144	My Heart Jumped/Gently My Love	1961	20.00	40.00	80.00

FULLER, JERRY

Also see THE FLEAS; THE FULLER BROTHERS.

Number	Title (A Side/B Side)	Yr	VG	VG+	NM
ABC					
❑ 12436	Salt on the Wound/No Time	1978	—	2.00	4.00
BELL					
❑ 45233	Rhyme/Thumb Tripping	1972	—	2.50	5.00
❑ 45295	Bookends/(B-side unknown)	1972	—	2.50	5.00
❑ 45349	Lazy Susan/How Do We Stand	1973	—	2.50	5.00
❑ 45433	Arianne/(B-side unknown)	1974	—	2.50	5.00
CHALLENGE					
❑ 9114	Guilty of Loving You/First Love Never Dies	1961	5.00	10.00	20.00
❑ 9128	The Place Where I Cry/Poor Little Heart	1961	5.00	10.00	20.00
❑ 9132	Wake Up Sleeping Beauty/Trust Me	1962	5.00	10.00	20.00
❑ 9148	Too Many People/Willingly, I'll Let You Go	1962	5.00	10.00	20.00
❑ 9161	Why Do They Say Goodbye/Let Me Be with You	1962	5.00	10.00	20.00
❑ 9184	Give My Love to Christy/Dear Teresa	1963	5.00	10.00	20.00
❑ 59052	Betty My Angel/Memories of You	1959	7.50	15.00	30.00
❑ 59057	Tennessee Waltz/Charlene	1959	5.00	10.00	20.00
❑ 59068	Two Loves Have I/I Dreamed About My Lover	1960	5.00	10.00	20.00
❑ 59074	Above and Beyond/One Heart	1960	5.00	10.00	20.00
—With Diane Maxwell					
❑ 59085	Gone for the Summer/Anna from Louisiana	1960	5.00	10.00	20.00
❑ 59104	Shy Away/Heavenly	1961	5.00	10.00	20.00
❑ 59217	I Only Came to Dance with You/Young Land	1963	5.00	10.00	20.00
❑ 59235	Footprints in the Snow/Hollywood Star	1964	3.75	7.50	15.00
❑ 59252	Don't Let Go/Roses Love Sunshine	1964	3.75	7.50	15.00
❑ 59269	The Killer/Mi Amora Mi Vidor	1965	3.75	7.50	15.00
❑ 59279	I Get Carried Away/Am I That Easy to Forget	1965	7.50	15.00	30.00
❑ 59307	Don't Look at Me Like That/What Happened to the Music	1965	3.75	7.50	15.00
❑ 59315	Man in Black/Master Plan	1965	3.75	7.50	15.00
❑ 59329	Double Life/Turn to Me	1966	6.25	12.50	25.00
COLUMBIA					
❑ 4-45131	Could It Be/I Know We Can Make It	1970	2.00	4.00	8.00
❑ 4-45209	Go/If I Had a Mind To	1970	2.00	4.00	8.00
LIN					
❑ 5011	Blue Memories/I Found a New Love	1958	7.50	15.00	30.00
❑ 5012	Do You Love Me/Teenage Love	1958	7.50	15.00	30.00
❑ 5015	A Certain Smile/Angel from Above	1958	7.50	15.00	30.00
❑ 5016	The Door Is Open/Through Eternity	1958	7.50	15.00	30.00
❑ 5019	Lipstick and Rouge/Mother Goose at the Bandstand	1959	7.50	15.00	30.00
MCA					
❑ 41022	Lines/Over You	1979	—	2.00	4.00
❑ 41114	Don't Do Anything/Don't Tell Me	1979	—	2.00	4.00

FULLER, JOHNNY

Number	Title (A Side/B Side)	Yr	VG	VG+	NM
ALADDIN					
❑ 3278	Johnny Ace's Last Letter/Fools Paradise	1955	20.00	40.00	80.00
❑ 3286	Cruel, Cruel World/My Heart Beats for You	1955	15.00	30.00	60.00
ART TONE					
❑ 828	No More/The Power	1962	5.00	10.00	20.00
CHECKER					
❑ 899	You Got Me Whistling/All Night Long	1958	6.25	12.50	25.00
FLAIR					
❑ 1054	Buddy/Hard Times	1955	37.50	75.00	150.00
HOLLYWOOD					
❑ 1043	Train Train Blues/Bad Luck Overtook Me	1955	20.00	40.00	80.00
❑ 1057	Mean Old World/How Long	1956	20.00	40.00	80.00
❑ 1063	Comin' Round the Corner/Roughest Place in Town	1956	20.00	40.00	80.00
❑ 1077	My Mama Told Me/Too Late to Change My Mind	1956	20.00	40.00	80.00
❑ 1084	Sunny Road/I Can't Succeed	1957	20.00	40.00	80.00
IMPERIAL					
❑ 5580	Heavenly Love/Whispering Wind	1959	5.00	10.00	20.00
❑ 5697	Miss You/Stop, Look and Listen	1960	5.00	10.00	20.00
IRMA					
❑ 106	Weeping and Mourning/Strange Land	1958	20.00	40.00	80.00
❑ 110	First Stage of the Blues/No More, No More	1958	20.00	40.00	80.00
❑ 112	You Got Me Whistling/All Night Long	1958	15.00	30.00	60.00
MONEY					
❑ 206	I Walk All Night/These Young Girls	1955	15.00	30.00	60.00
SPECIALTY					
❑ 655	Haunted House/The Mighty Hand	1959	5.00	10.00	20.00
❑ 671	Swingin' at the Creek/Many Rivers, Mighty Seas	1959	5.00	10.00	20.00

FULLER BROTHERS, THE

Also see JERRY FULLER.

Number	Title (A Side/B Side)	Yr	VG	VG+	NM
CHALLENGE					
❑ 9119	Moon River/Framed, Convicted and Condemned	1961	5.00	10.00	20.00
❑ 9145	Ballad of the Midnight Special/The Gallows Tree	1962	5.00	10.00	20.00

FULSON, LOWELL

Also recorded as "Lowell Folsom" and "Lowell Fulsom," both included below.

Number	Title (A Side/B Side)	Yr	VG	VG+	NM
ALADDIN					
❑ 3088	Double Trouble/Good Woman Blues	1951	37.50	75.00	150.00
❑ 3104	Night and Day/Stormin' and Rainin'	1951	25.00	50.00	100.00
—Black vinyl					
❑ 3104	Night and Day/Stormin' and Rainin'	1951	50.00	100.00	200.00
—Green vinyl					
❑ 3217	Don't Leave Me Baby/Check with the Boys	1954	20.00	40.00	80.00
❑ 3233	Blues Never Fail/You've Gotta Reap	1954	20.00	40.00	80.00
CASH					
❑ 1051	Love Society Blues/Blue Shadows	1957	10.00	20.00	40.00
CHECKER					
❑ 804	Reconsider Baby/I Believe I'll Give It Up	1954	10.00	20.00	40.00
❑ 812	Loving You (Is All I Crave)/Check Yourself	1955	10.00	20.00	40.00
❑ 820	Lonely Hours/Do Me Right	1955	7.50	15.00	30.00
❑ 829	Trouble, Trouble/I Still Love You Baby	1955	7.50	15.00	30.00
❑ 841	It's Your Fault, Baby/Tollin' Bells	1956	7.50	15.00	30.00
❑ 854	Blues Rhumba/Please Don't Go	1957	6.25	12.50	25.00
❑ 865	Don't Drive Me, Baby/You're Gonna Miss Me	1957	6.25	12.50	25.00
❑ 882	I Want to Make Love to You/Rock This Morning	1958	6.25	12.50	25.00
❑ 937	It Took a Long Time/That's Alright	1960	5.00	10.00	20.00
❑ 952	Comin' Home/Have You Changed Your Mind	1960	5.00	10.00	20.00
❑ 959	I'm Glad You Reconsidered/Blue Shadows	1960	5.00	10.00	20.00
❑ 972	I Want to Know (Part 1)/I Want to Know (Part 2)	1961	3.75	7.50	15.00
❑ 992	So Many Tears/Hung Down Head	1961	3.75	7.50	15.00
❑ 1027	Shed No Tears/Can She	1962	3.75	7.50	15.00
❑ 1046	Trouble with the Blues/Love Grows Cold	1963	3.75	7.50	15.00
GRANITE					
❑ 533	Do You Love Me/A Step at a Time	1975	—	2.50	5.00
❑ 538	The Old Blues Singer/Monday Morning Blues	1976	—	2.50	5.00
HOLLYWOOD					
❑ 567-242	The Original Lonesome Christmas Part 1/The Original Lonesome Christmas Part 2	196?	2.50	5.00	10.00

Number	Title (A Side/B Side)	Yr	VG	VG+	NM
❑ 1022	The Original Lonesome Christmas Part 1/The Original Lonesome Christmas Part 2	1955	5.00	10.00	20.00
❑ 1029	Everyday I Have the Blues/Guitar Shuffle	1955	12.50	25.00	50.00
❑ 1103	Everyday I Have the Blues/Guitar Shuffle	1962	3.75	7.50	15.00

JEWEL

Number	Title (A Side/B Side)	Yr	VG	VG+	NM
❑ 801	Letter Home/Lady in the Rain	1969	2.00	4.00	8.00
❑ 802	Why Don't We Do It in the Road/Too Soon	1969	2.50	5.00	10.00
❑ 805	How Do You Want Your Man/Sleeper	1969	2.00	4.00	8.00
❑ 808	Don't Leave Me/Thug	1970	2.00	4.00	8.00
❑ 811	Do You Feel It/Don't Destroy Me	1970	2.00	4.00	8.00
❑ 813	Lonesome Christmas (Part 1)/Lonesome Christmas (Part 2)	1970	—	3.00	6.00
❑ 818	My Baby/Bluesway	1971	—	3.00	6.00
❑ 820	Teach Me/Man of Motion	1971	—	3.00	6.00
❑ 827	Change of Heart/Every Second a Fool Is Born	1972	—	3.00	6.00
❑ 832	Look at You Baby/Fed Up	1972	—	3.00	6.00

KENT

Number	Title (A Side/B Side)	Yr	VG	VG+	NM
❑ 395	Every Time It Rains/My Heart Belongs to You	1964	3.00	6.00	12.00
❑ 395	Every Time It Rains/Just One More Time	1964	3.00	6.00	12.00
❑ 401	Key to My Heart/Too Many Drivers	1964	3.00	6.00	12.00
❑ 410	Strange Feeling/What's Gonna Be	1965	3.00	6.00	12.00
❑ 422	No More (Part 1)/No More (Part 2)	1965	3.00	6.00	12.00
❑ 431	Black Nights/Little Angel	1965	2.50	5.00	10.00
❑ 440	Sittin' Here Thinkin'/Shattered Dreams	1966	2.50	5.00	10.00
❑ 443	Blues Around Midnight/Talkin' Woman	1966	2.50	5.00	10.00
❑ 448	Change Your Ways/My Aching Back	1966	2.50	5.00	10.00
❑ 452	The Trouble I'm In/Ask at Any Door in Town	1966	2.50	5.00	10.00
❑ 456	Tramp/Pico	1966	2.50	5.00	10.00
❑ 463	Make a Little Love/I'm Sinking	1967	2.50	5.00	10.00
❑ 463 [PS]	Make a Little Love/I'm Sinking	1967	5.00	10.00	20.00
❑ 466	Everyday I Have the Blues/No Hard Feelings	1967	2.50	5.00	10.00
❑ 471	I Cried/The Thing	1967	2.50	5.00	10.00
❑ 474	I'm a Drifter/Hobo Meetin'	1967	2.50	5.00	10.00
❑ 477	I Wanna Spend Christmas with You Part 1/I Wanna Spend Christmas with You Part 2	1967	3.00	6.00	12.00
❑ 479	Tomorrow/Push Me	1968	2.50	5.00	10.00
❑ 486	The Letter/Let's Go Get Stoned	1968	2.50	5.00	10.00
❑ 489	Blues Pain/Mellow Together	1968	2.50	5.00	10.00
❑ 497	Sweetest Thing/What the Heck	1968	2.50	5.00	10.00
❑ 505	Lovin' Touch/Price for Love	1969	2.50	5.00	10.00
❑ 4535	Let's Go Get Stoned/Funky Broadway	1970	2.00	4.00	8.00

MOVIN'

Number	Title (A Side/B Side)	Yr	VG	VG+	NM
❑ 128	Stop and Think/Baby	1964	3.00	6.00	12.00

PARROT

Number	Title (A Side/B Side)	Yr	VG	VG+	NM
❑ 787	I've Been Mistreated/Juke Box Shuffle	1953	25.00	50.00	100.00
—Black vinyl					
❑ 787	I've Been Mistreated/Juke Box Shuffle	1953	50.00	100.00	200.00
—Red vinyl					

SWING TIME

Number	Title (A Side/B Side)	Yr	VG	VG+	NM
❑ 242	Lonesome Christmas (Part 1)/Lonesome Christmas (Part 2)	1951	15.00	30.00	60.00
—78 released in 1950; 45 released in 1951					
❑ 243	I'm a Night Owl (Part 1)/I'm a Night Owl (Part 2)	1951	25.00	50.00	100.00
❑ 272	Why Can't You Cry for Me/Blues with a Feeling	1951			
—Unreleased on 45 rpm?					
❑ 289	Let's Live Right/Best Wishes	1952	12.50	25.00	50.00
❑ 290	Three O'Clock in the Morning Blues/I'm Wild About You Baby	1952	—	—	—
—Unreleased on 45 rpm?					
❑ 295	Guitar Shuffle/Mean Old Lonesome Song	1952	12.50	25.00	50.00
❑ 308	Black Widow Spider/Midnight Showers of Rain	1953	12.50	25.00	50.00
❑ 315	Raggedy Daddy Blues/Goodbye	1953	12.50	25.00	50.00
❑ 320	Ride Until the Sun Goes Down/Good Party Shuffle	1953	12.50	25.00	50.00
❑ 325	Upstairs/Let Me Ride Your Automobile	1953	12.50	25.00	50.00
❑ 330	The Blues Come Rollin' In/I Love My Baby	1954	12.50	25.00	50.00
❑ 335	Cash Box Boogie/My Daily Prayer	1954	12.50	25.00	50.00
❑ 338	I've Been Mistreated/Juke Box Shuffle	1954	12.50	25.00	50.00

FUN AND GAMES

UNI

Number	Title (A Side/B Side)	Yr	VG	VG+	NM
❑ 55086	Elephant Candy/The Way She Smiles	1968	3.00	6.00	12.00
❑ 55098	The Grooviest Girl in the World/It Must Have Been the Wind	1968	3.00	6.00	12.00
❑ 55128	Gotta Say Goodbye/We	1969	3.00	6.00	12.00

FUNKADELIC

Also see GEORGE CLINTON; FUNKADELIC (2); PARLIAMENT; THE PARLIAMENTS.

MCA

Number	Title (A Side/B Side)	Yr	VG	VG+	NM
❑ 53654	By Way of the Drum/(Instrumental)	1989	—	—	3.00

WARNER BROS.

Number	Title (A Side/B Side)	Yr	VG	VG+	NM
❑ 8618	One Nation Under a Groove (Part 1)/One Nation Under a Groove (Part 2)	1978	—	2.50	5.00
❑ 8618 [PS]	One Nation Under a Groove (Part 1)/One Nation Under a Groove (Part 2)	1978	—	2.50	5.00
❑ 8735	Cholly (Funk Getting Ready to Roll)/Into You	1979	—	2.50	5.00
❑ 49040	(Not Just) Knee Deep — Part 1/(Not Just) Knee Deep — Part 2	1979	—	2.50	5.00
❑ 49117	Uncle Jam (Part 1)/Uncle Jam (Part 2)	1979	—	2.50	5.00
❑ 49667	The Electric Spanking of War Babies/The Electric Spanking of War Babies (Part 2)	1981	—	2.00	4.00
❑ 49667 [PS]	The Electric Spanking of War Babies/The Electric Spanking of War Babies (Part 2)	1981	—	2.50	5.00
❑ 49807	Shockwaves/Bullino's Bounce	1981	—	2.00	4.00

WESTBOUND

Number	Title (A Side/B Side)	Yr	VG	VG+	NM
❑ 148	Music for My Mother/(Instrumental)	1969	2.50	5.00	10.00
❑ 150	I'll Bet You/Open Your Eyes	1969	2.50	5.00	10.00
❑ 158	I Got a Thing, You Got a Thing, Everybody's Got a Thing/Fish, Chips and Sweat	1970	2.50	5.00	10.00
❑ 167	I Wanna Know If It's Good to You?/I Wanna Know If It's Good to You? (Part 2)	1970	2.50	5.00	10.00
❑ 175	You and Your Folks, Me and My Folks/Funky Dollar Bill	1971	2.50	5.00	10.00
❑ 185	Can You Get to That/Back in Our Minds	1971	2.50	5.00	10.00
❑ 197	I Miss My Baby/Baby I Owe You Something Good	1972	2.50	5.00	10.00
—As "U.S. Music with Funkadelic"					
❑ 198	Hit It and Quit It/A Whole Lot of B.S.	1972	2.50	5.00	10.00
❑ 205	A Joyful Process/Loose Booty	1972	2.50	5.00	10.00
❑ 218	Cosmic Slop/If You Don't Like the Effects, Don't Produce the Cause	1973	2.50	5.00	10.00
❑ 224	Standing on the Verge of Getting It On/Jimmy's Got a Little Bit of Bitch in Him	1974	2.50	5.00	10.00
❑ 5000	Red Hot Momma/Vital Juices	1975	2.00	4.00	8.00
❑ 5014	Better by the Pound/Stuffs and Things	1975	2.00	4.00	8.00
❑ 5026	Let's Take It to the Stage/Bilogical Speculation	1976	2.00	4.00	8.00
❑ 5029	Undisco Kidd/How Do Yeau View You	1976	2.00	4.00	8.00

FUNKADELIC (2)

Splinter group from the original band, listed separately because GEORGE CLINTON is not involved.

LAX

Number	Title (A Side/B Side)	Yr	VG	VG+	NM
❑ 70055	Connections and Disconnections/The Witch	1981	—	2.00	4.00

FURY, BILLY

LONDON

Number	Title (A Side/B Side)	Yr	VG	VG+	NM
❑ 1857	Maybe Tomorrow/Gonna Type a Letter	1959	5.00	10.00	20.00
❑ 1925	Colette/Baby How I Cried	1960	5.00	10.00	20.00
❑ 1991	Halfway to Paradise/Cross My Heart	1961	5.00	10.00	20.00
❑ 2004	Stick Around/Coming Up in the World	1961	5.00	10.00	20.00
❑ 9515	I'll Never Find Another You/Don't Jump	1962	3.75	7.50	15.00
❑ 9548	Once Upon a Dream/Running Around	1962	3.75	7.50	15.00
❑ 9594	Because of Love/Like I've Never Loved Before	1963	3.75	7.50	15.00
❑ 9615	Don't Walk Away/When Will I Say I Love You	1963	3.75	7.50	15.00
❑ 9662	Hippy Hippy Shake/Glad All Over	1964	3.75	7.50	15.00
❑ 9675	I Will/What Am I Living For	1964	3.75	7.50	15.00
❑ 9740	I'm Lost Without You/Go Ahead and Ask Her	1965	3.75	7.50	15.00

MALA

Number	Title (A Side/B Side)	Yr	VG	VG+	NM
❑ 569	Loving You/I'll Go Along With It	1967	2.50	5.00	10.00
❑ 583	Suzanne in the Mirror/It Just Don't Matter Now	1968	2.50	5.00	10.00
❑ 595	Beyond the Shadow of a Doubt/Baby Do You Love Me	1968	2.50	5.00	10.00
❑ 12018	Silly Boy Blue/One Minute Woman	1968	2.50	5.00	10.00

PARROT

Number	Title (A Side/B Side)	Yr	VG	VG+	NM
❑ 9692	Baby What You Want Me to Do/It's Only Make Believe	1964	3.75	7.50	15.00

UNITED ARTISTS

Number	Title (A Side/B Side)	Yr	VG	VG+	NM
❑ 968	In Thoughts of You/Away from You	1966	3.00	6.00	12.00
❑ 50061	She's So Far Out She's In/Give Me Your Word	1966	3.00	6.00	12.00

FUSE

Early version of CHEAP TRICK.

EPIC

Number	Title (A Side/B Side)	Yr	VG	VG+	NM
❑ 10514	Cruisin' for Burgers/Hound Dog	1969	6.25	12.50	25.00

FUT, THE

Maurice Gibb was in this group, whose single often was bootlegged as a "lost" Beatles track. It has no Beatles involvement whatsoever.

BEACON

Number	Title (A Side/B Side)	Yr	VG	VG+	NM
❑ 160	Have You Heard the Word/Futting	1970	2.50	5.00	10.00

FUT

Number	Title (A Side/B Side)	Yr	VG	VG+	NM
❑ 160	Have You Heard the Word/Futting	1976	—	2.50	5.00

G

G-CLEFS, THE

LOMA

Number	Title (A Side/B Side)	Yr	VG	VG+	NM
❑ 2034	Party '66/Little Lonely Boy	1966	2.50	5.00	10.00
❑ 2048	I Can't Stand It/Whirlwind	1966	2.50	5.00	10.00

PARIS

Number	Title (A Side/B Side)	Yr	VG	VG+	NM
❑ 502	Symbol of Love/Love Her in the Mornin'	1957	7.50	15.00	30.00
❑ 506	Zing Zang Zoo/Is This the Way	1957	6.25	12.50	25.00

PILGRIM

Number	Title (A Side/B Side)	Yr	VG	VG+	NM
❑ 715	Ka-Ding-Dong/Darla My Darlin'	1956	7.50	15.00	30.00
—Purple label					
❑ 715	Ka-Ding-Dong/Darla My Darlin'	1956	5.00	10.00	20.00
—Red label					
❑ 720	'Cause You're Mine/Please Write While I'm Away	1956	7.50	15.00	30.00

REGINA

Number	Title (A Side/B Side)	Yr	VG	VG+	NM
❑ 1314	To the Winner Goes the Prize/I Believe in All I Feel	1964	3.75	7.50	15.00
❑ 1319	Angel Listen to Me/Nobody But Betty	1964	5.00	10.00	20.00

TERRACE

Number	Title (A Side/B Side)	Yr	VG	VG+	NM
❑ 7500	I Understand (Just How You Feel)/Little Girl I Love You	1961	5.00	10.00	20.00
❑ 7503	Girl Has to Know/Lad (There Never Was a Dog Like You)	1962	5.00	10.00	20.00
❑ 7507	Make Up Your Mind/They'll Call Me Away	1962	5.00	10.00	20.00
❑ 7510	A Lover's Prayer/Sitting in the Moonlight	1962	6.25	12.50	25.00
❑ 7514	All My Trials/Big Train	1963	6.25	12.50	25.00

VEEP

Number	Title (A Side/B Side)	Yr	VG	VG+	NM
❑ 1218	I Have/On the Other Side of Town	1965	3.75	7.50	15.00
❑ 1226	This Time/On the Other Side of Town	1965	3.75	7.50	15.00

G.T.O.'S, THE (1)

CLARIDGE

Number	Title (A Side/B Side)	Yr	VG	VG+	NM
❑ 312	She Rides with Me/Rudy Vahoo	1966	5.00	10.00	20.00
—Reissue of Claridge 304 by "Joey and the Continentals"					

PARKWAY

Number	Title (A Side/B Side)	Yr	VG	VG+	NM
❑ 108	Girl from New York City/Missing Out on the Fun	1966	3.75	7.50	15.00

GABRIEL, PETER

Also see GENESIS.

Number	Title (A Side/B Side)	Yr	VG	VG+	NM
ATCO					
❑ 7079	Solsbury Hill/Moribund the Burgermeister	1977	2.50	5.00	10.00
ATLANTIC					
❑ 3479	D.I.Y. (Do It Yourself)/Mother of Violence	1978	2.50	5.00	10.00
❑ 89668	Walk Through the Fire/Making a Big Mistake	1984	—	2.00	4.00
❑ 89668 [PS]	Walk Through the Fire/Making a Big Mistake	1984	—	2.00	4.00
GEFFEN					
❑ GGEF 0481	Shock the Monkey/Solsbury Hill (Live)	198?	—	—	3.00
—Reissue					
❑ 19136	Digging in the Dirt/Quiet Steam	1992	—	2.00	4.00
❑ 19145	Steam/Games Without Frontiers (DB Mix)	1992	—	2.00	4.00
❑ 28247	Red Rain/I Go Swimming	1987	—	—	3.00
❑ 28247 [PS]	Red Rain/I Go Swimming	1987	—	—	3.00
❑ 28463	Don't Give Up/Curtains	1987	—	—	3.00
—A-side: Peter Gabriel/Kate Bush					
❑ 28463 [PS]	Don't Give Up/Curtains	1987	—	—	3.00
❑ 28503	Big Time/We Do What We're Told (milgram's 37)	1986	—	—	3.00
❑ 28503 [PS]	Big Time/We Do What We're Told (milgram's 37)	1986	—	—	3.00
❑ 28622	In Your Eyes/In Your Eyes (Special Mix)	1986	—	—	3.00
❑ 28622 [PS]	In Your Eyes/In Your Eyes (Special Mix)	1986	—	—	3.00
❑ 28718	Sledgehammer/Don't Break This Rhythm	1986	—	—	3.00
❑ 28718 [PS]	Sledgehammer/Don't Break This Rhythm	1986	—	—	3.00
❑ 29542	Solsbury Hill (Live)/I Go Swimming	1983	—	2.50	5.00
❑ 29883	Shock the Monkey/Soft Dog	1982	—	2.50	5.00
MERCURY					
❑ 76063	Games Without Frontiers/Lead a Normal Life	1980	—	—	4.00
❑ 76063 [PS]	Games Without Frontiers/Lead a Normal Life	1980	3.00	6.00	12.00
❑ 76086 [DJ]	I Don't Remember (same on both sides)	1980	2.00	4.00	8.00
—Stock copy may not exist					
WTG					
❑ 68936	In Your Eyes/Skankin' to the Beat	1989	—	2.00	4.00
—B-side by Fishbone					
❑ 68977	In Your Eyes/In Your Eyes (Live Version)	1989	—	—	3.00

GABRIEL AND THE ANGELS

Number	Title (A Side/B Side)	Yr	VG	VG+	NM
AMY					
❑ 802	Chumba/Hey	1960	5.00	10.00	20.00
❑ 823	Zing Went the Strings of My Heart/The Rooster	1961	10.00	20.00	40.00
APRIL					
❑ 1102	Chumba/Hey	1960	12.50	25.00	50.00
NORMAN					
❑ 506	I'm Gabriel/Ginza	1961	3.75	7.50	15.00
❑ 510	Gabriel, Blow Your Horn (Part 1)/Gabriel, Blow Your Horn (Part 2)	1961	3.75	7.50	15.00
❑ 514	Miss You So/See See Rider	1962	3.75	7.50	15.00
—As "Gabriel and His Trumpet"					
SWAN					
❑ 4118	That's Life (That's Tough)/Don't Wanna Twist No More	1962	3.00	6.00	12.00
❑ 4118	That's Life/Don't Wanna Twist No More	1962	3.75	7.50	15.00
—No subtitle on A-side					
❑ 4133	The Peanut Butter Song/All Work and No Play	1963	3.00	6.00	12.00

GADABOUTS, THE

Number	Title (A Side/B Side)	Yr	VG	VG+	NM
JARO					
❑ 77022	Caress Me/Deep Are the Roots of a Happy Home	1960	3.75	7.50	15.00
MERCURY					
❑ 70495	By the Waters of the Minnetonka/Giuseppe Mandolino	1954	6.25	12.50	25.00
❑ 70581	Go Boom Boom/Oochi Pachi	1955	6.25	12.50	25.00
❑ 70823	Busy Body Rock/All My Love Belongs to You	1956	6.25	12.50	25.00
❑ 70898	Stranded in the Jungle/Blues Train	1956	6.25	12.50	25.00
❑ 70978	Too Much Monkey Business/To Be with You	1956	6.25	12.50	25.00
WING					
❑ 90008	Two Things I Love/Glass Heart	1955	6.25	12.50	25.00
❑ 90043	Teenage Rock/If You Only Had a Heart	1955	6.25	12.50	25.00
❑ 90062	Busy Body Rock/All My Love Belongs to You	1956	5.00	10.00	20.00

GADDY, BOB

Number	Title (A Side/B Side)	Yr	VG	VG+	NM
DOT					
❑ 1185	Honey Stealin' Blues/Hold That Train, Conductor	1954	25.00	50.00	100.00
—As "Doctor Gaddy and His Orchestra"					
HARLEM					
❑ 2330	The Blues Has Walked in My Room/Slow Down Baby	1954	37.50	75.00	150.00
JAX					
❑ 308	No Help Wanted/Little Girls Boogie	1952	75.00	150.00	300.00
OLD TOWN					
❑ 1031	I Love My Baby/Operator	1956	6.25	12.50	25.00
❑ 1039	Paper Lady/Out of My Name	1957	6.25	12.50	25.00
❑ 1050	Woe, Woe Is Me/Rip and Run	1958	6.25	12.50	25.00
❑ 1057	You Are the One/Take My Advice	1958	6.25	12.50	25.00
❑ 1064	What Would I Do/Paper Lady	1959	5.00	10.00	20.00
❑ 1070	Till the Day I Die/I'll Go My Way	1959	5.00	10.00	20.00
❑ 1077	Early One Morning/What Wrong Did I Do	1960	5.00	10.00	20.00
❑ 1085	Don't Tell Her/Could I	1960	5.00	10.00	20.00
❑ 1162	I Love My Baby/Operator	1964	3.00	6.00	12.00

GADDY, DOCTOR

See BOB GADDY.

GADSON, MEL

Number	Title (A Side/B Side)	Yr	VG	VG+	NM
BIG TOP					
❑ 3034	Comin' Down with Love/I'm Getting Sentimental Over You	1959	6.25	12.50	25.00

GAILTONES, THE

Number	Title (A Side/B Side)	Yr	VG	VG+	NM
DECCA					
❑ 30726	Lover Boy/Please Don't Go	1958	10.00	20.00	40.00

GAINES, ROY

Number	Title (A Side/B Side)	Yr	VG	VG+	NM
CHART					
❑ 606	Loud Mouth Lucy/I'm Setting You Free	1955	15.00	30.00	60.00
DEL-FI					
❑ 4169	What Is This Thing Called Love/Lizzie	1961	3.75	7.50	15.00
DELUXE					
❑ 6119	Isabella/Gainesville	1957	6.25	12.50	25.00
❑ 6132	You're Right, I'm Left/Stolen Moments	1957	6.25	12.50	25.00
❑ 6147	Annabelle/Night Beat	1957	6.25	12.50	25.00
GROOVE					
❑ 0146	Right Now Baby/De Dat De Dum Dum	1956	7.50	15.00	30.00
❑ 0161	Worried 'Bout You Baby/All My Life	1956	7.50	15.00	30.00
RCA VICTOR					
❑ 47-7243	Skippy Is a Sissy/Weeping Willow	1958	15.00	30.00	60.00

GALAXIES, THE

Several different groups.

Number	Title (A Side/B Side)	Yr	VG	VG+	NM
CAPITOL					
❑ 4427	Big Triangle/Until the Next Time	1960	3.75	7.50	15.00
CHESS					
❑ 1757	This Rock and Roll/6:15	1960	5.00	10.00	20.00
DOT					
❑ 16212	My Blue Heaven/Tremble	1961	6.25	12.50	25.00
ETIQUETTE					
❑ 17	I'm a Worker/Make Love to Me Baby	1965	5.00	10.00	20.00
❑ 20	On the Beach/She Said I Do	1965	5.00	10.00	20.00
❑ 25	I (Who Have Nothing)/I Am Yours	1966	5.00	10.00	20.00
GUARANTEED					
❑ 216	My Tattle Tale/Love Has Its Way	1960	12.50	25.00	50.00
—Eddie Cochran plays guitar on this record					
PANORAMA					
❑ 54	Along Comes the Man/She Said I Do	1966	2.50	5.00	10.00
RICHIE					
❑ 458	Dear Someone/The Leopard	1961	18.75	37.50	75.00
RONNIE					
❑ 201	Just Another Date/Little Man	1976	—	3.00	6.00
SEAFAIR					
❑ 110	Shaken/Tacoma	1964	3.75	7.50	15.00

GALAXYS, THE

Number	Title (A Side/B Side)	Yr	VG	VG+	NM
CARTHAY					
❑ 103	A Lover's Prayer/Jelly Bean	1959	375.00	750.00	1500.

GALE, BARBARA

Number	Title (A Side/B Side)	Yr	VG	VG+	NM
LLOYDS					
❑ 107	Lonely Weather/So Long, Good-Bye Joe	1953	30.00	60.00	120.00
❑ 109	Once Again/Fool Fool Me	1953	30.00	60.00	120.00
❑ 111	When You're Near/Who Walks In	1954	75.00	150.00	300.00
—With the Larks					
❑ 115	Johnny Darlin'/You're Gonna Lose That Gal	1954	75.00	150.00	300.00
—With the Larks					

GALES, THE

Number	Title (A Side/B Side)	Yr	VG	VG+	NM
DEBRA					
❑ 1002	Tommy/Around the Clock with You	1963	10.00	20.00	40.00
JVB					
❑ 34	His Eyes Keep Me in Trouble/Don't Let the Sun Catch You Cryin'	1955	1000.	2000.	3000.
❑ 35	Darling Patricia/All Is Well, All Is Well	1955	125.00	250.00	500.00
J.O.B.					
❑ 3001	Darling Patricia/All Is Well, All Is Well	1956	50.00	100.00	200.00
MEL-O					
❑ 111	Guiding Angel/Boy Come Home	1958	62.50	125.00	250.00
❑ 113	Josephine/If I Could Forget	1958	62.50	125.00	250.00
WINN					
❑ 916	I Love You/Squeeze Me	1960	125.00	250.00	500.00

GALLAGHER, JAMES

Number	Title (A Side/B Side)	Yr	VG	VG+	NM
DECCA					
❑ 29984	Crazy Chicken/Just for You	1956	30.00	60.00	120.00

GALLAHADS, THE (1)

Number	Title (A Side/B Side)	Yr	VG	VG+	NM
CAPITOL					
❑ F-3060	Ooh Ah/Careless	1955	6.25	12.50	25.00
❑ F-3175	Do You Believe Me/If It Wasn't for You	1955	6.25	12.50	25.00
JUBILEE					
❑ 5252	The Fool/The Morning Mail	1956	7.50	15.00	30.00
❑ 5259	Take My Love/I Give You My Word	1956	6.25	12.50	25.00
VIK					
❑ 0291	Take Back My Ring/One Love Alone	1957	6.25	12.50	25.00
❑ 0316	Best Wishes/Steady Man	1958	6.25	12.50	25.00
❑ 0332	Silently/Barracuda	1958	6.25	12.50	25.00

GALLAHADS, THE (2)

Number	Title (A Side/B Side)	Yr	VG	VG+	NM
DEL-FI					
❑ 4137	Lonely Guy/Jo Jo the Big Wheel	1960	10.00	20.00	40.00
—Green label					
❑ 4137	Lonely Guy/Jo Jo the Big Wheel	1960	5.00	10.00	20.00
—Black label					
❑ 4148	Be Fair/I'm Without a Girl Friend	1960	10.00	20.00	40.00
—Green label					
❑ 4148	Be Fair/I'm Without a Girl Friend	1960	5.00	10.00	20.00
—Black label					
DONNA					
❑ 1322	Lonely Guy/Jo Jo the Big Wheel	1960	10.00	20.00	40.00
❑ 1361	This Letter to You/The Answer to Love	1962	12.50	25.00	50.00

GALLAHADS, THE (U)
It's unlikely any of these are group (1). Some of these are probably group (2). Others could be by different groups.

Number	Title (A Side/B Side)	Yr	VG	VG+	NM
BEECHWOOD					
❑ 3001	Keeper of Dreams/Sad Girl	1960	30.00	60.00	120.00
—More than one group.					
NITE OWL					
❑ 20	Gone/So Long	1961	15.00	30.00	60.00
RENDEZVOUS					
❑ 153	Gone/Why Do Fools Fall in Love	1961	10.00	20.00	40.00
SEA CREST					
❑ 6005	Have Love, Will Travel/My Offering	1964	10.00	20.00	40.00
STARLA					
❑ 15	Keeper of Dreams/Sad Girl	1960	5.00	10.00	20.00

GALT, JAMES

Number	Title (A Side/B Side)	Yr	VG	VG+	NM
AURORA					
❑ 158	With My Baby/Most Unusual Feeling	1966	7.50	15.00	30.00

GAMBLE, DEE DEE SHARP
See DEE DEE SHARP.

GAMBLE, KENNY

Number	Title (A Side/B Side)	Yr	VG	VG+	NM
ARCTIC					
❑ 107	Down by the Seashore (Part 1)/Down by the Seashore (Part 2)	1965	50.00	100.00	200.00
❑ 114	Ain't It Baby (Part 1)/Ain't It Baby (Part 2)	1965	50.00	100.00	200.00
❑ 123	The Joke's on You/Don't Stop Loving Me	1966	50.00	100.00	200.00
COLUMBIA					
❑ 43132	Our Love/You Don't Know What You Got Until You Lose It	1964	7.50	15.00	30.00
EPIC					
❑ 9636	Standing in the Shadows/No Mail on Monday	1963	7.50	15.00	30.00

GAMBLERS, THE (1)
BRUCE JOHNSTON and SANDY NELSON were in this group.

Number	Title (A Side/B Side)	Yr	VG	VG+	NM
LAST CHANCE					
❑ 2	Teen Machine/Tonky	1961	10.00	20.00	40.00
❑ 108	Teen Machine/Tonky	1962	6.25	12.50	25.00
WORLD PACIFIC					
❑ 815	Moon Dawg/LSD-25	1960	15.00	30.00	60.00

GAMBLERS, THE (2)
British group.

Number	Title (A Side/B Side)	Yr	VG	VG+	NM
CORAL					
❑ 62525	Cry Me a River/Who Will Buy	1967	2.00	4.00	8.00
PRESS					
❑ 9739	Now I'm All Alone/Find Out What's Happening	1965	3.00	6.00	12.00

GAMMA GOOCHEE

Number	Title (A Side/B Side)	Yr	VG	VG+	NM
COLPIX					
❑ 786	I'm Gonna Buy Me a Dog/(You Got the) Gamma Goochee	1965	5.00	10.00	20.00
❑ 804	I'm So Glad/Sweet Violets	1966	3.75	7.50	15.00
MGM					
❑ 13874	Booga-Loo/Everybody's Somebody's Fool	1967	3.75	7.50	15.00

GANDALF

Number	Title (A Side/B Side)	Yr	VG	VG+	NM
CAPITOL					
❑ 2400	Golden Earrings/Never Too Far	1969	6.25	12.50	25.00

GANEY, JERRY

Number	Title (A Side/B Side)	Yr	VG	VG+	NM
MGM					
❑ 13697	Hi-Heel Sneakers/You Don't Love Me	1967	5.00	10.00	20.00
VERVE					
❑ 10454	Who Am I/Just a Fool	1966	25.00	50.00	100.00

GANT, CECIL

Number	Title (A Side/B Side)	Yr	VG	VG+	NM
DECCA					
❑ 30320	I Wonder/Cecil's Boogie	1957	7.50	15.00	30.00
❑ 48171	Someday You'll Be Sorry (Part 1)/Someday You'll Be Sorry (Part 2)	1950	10.00	20.00	40.00
❑ 48185	It's Christmas Time Again/Hello Santa Claus	1950	10.00	20.00	40.00
❑ 48191	Train Time Blues No. 2/It Ain't Gonna Be Like That	1951	10.00	20.00	40.00
❑ 48200	Shot Gun Boogie/Rock Little Baby	1951	12.50	25.00	50.00
❑ 48212	Don't You Worry/My Little Baby	1951	10.00	20.00	40.00
❑ 48231	Owl Stew/Playin' Myself the Blues	1951	10.00	20.00	40.00
❑ 48249	God Bless My Daddy/The Grass Is Gettin' Greener	1951	10.00	20.00	40.00
DOT					
❑ 1112	All By Myself/It Hurts Me Too	1952	10.00	20.00	40.00
—Earlier singles on Dot may not exist on 45s					
❑ 1121	Sloppy Joes/Train Time Blues	1952	10.00	20.00	40.00
GILT EDGE					
❑ 5090	I Wonder/Cecil's Boogie	1955	10.00	20.00	40.00
—Reissue of 78 first released in 1944					

GANTS, THE
The group on Aladdin is not the same as the others.

Number	Title (A Side/B Side)	Yr	VG	VG+	NM
ALADDIN					
❑ 3387	My Unfaithful Love/Happening After School	1957	15.00	30.00	60.00
LIBERTY					
❑ 55829	Road Runner/My Baby Don't Care	1965	3.75	7.50	15.00
❑ 55853	Smoke Rings/Little Boy Sad	1966	2.50	5.00	10.00
❑ 55884	Dr. Feelgood/Crackin' Up	1966	2.50	5.00	10.00
❑ 55903	I Want Your Lovin'/A Spoonful of Sugar	1966	2.50	5.00	10.00
❑ 55940	Greener Days/I Wonder	1967	2.50	5.00	10.00
❑ 55965	Drifter's Sunrise/Just a Good Show	1967	2.50	5.00	10.00
STATUE					
❑ 605	Road Runner/My Baby Don't Care	1965	12.50	25.00	50.00
❑ 608	What's Happening/Careless Hands	1965	6.25	12.50	25.00
—B-side by the Niteliters					

GARCIA, JERRY
Also see THE GRATEFUL DEAD; NEW RIDERS OF THE PURPLE SAGE.

Number	Title (A Side/B Side)	Yr	VG	VG+	NM
ROUND					
❑ 4504	Let It Rock/Midnight Town	1974	—	3.00	6.00
WARNER BROS.					
❑ 7551	Deal/The Wheel	1972	—	3.00	6.00
❑ 7569	Deep Hour/Sugaree	1972	—	3.00	6.00

GARDENIAS, THE (1)

Number	Title (A Side/B Side)	Yr	VG	VG+	NM
FEDERAL					
❑ 12284	Flaming Love/My Baby's Tops	1956	30.00	60.00	120.00

GARDENIAS, THE (2)

Number	Title (A Side/B Side)	Yr	VG	VG+	NM
FAIRLANE					
❑ 21019	Darling It's You, You, You/What's the Matter with Me	1962	6.25	12.50	25.00

GARDNER, BROTHER DAVE

Number	Title (A Side/B Side)	Yr	VG	VG+	NM
DECCA					
❑ 30548	Hop Along Rock/All By Myself	1958	5.00	10.00	20.00
❑ 30627	Slick Slacks/Wild Streak	1958	10.00	20.00	40.00
OJ					
❑ 1002	White Silver Sands/Fat Charlie	1957	3.75	7.50	15.00
❑ 1006	Love Is My Business/Mad Witch	1958	3.75	7.50	15.00
RCA VICTOR					
❑ 47-7876	Coward at the Alamo/You Are My Love	1961	2.50	5.00	10.00

GARDNER, DON
Also see DON GARDNER AND DEE DEE FORD.

Number	Title (A Side/B Side)	Yr	VG	VG+	NM
BRUCE					
❑ 105	How Do You Speak to an Angel/Sonotone Bounce	1954	15.00	30.00	60.00
❑ 108	I'll Walk Alone/Going Down Mary	1954	12.50	25.00	50.00
❑ 127	It's a Sin to Tell a Lie/I Hear a Rhapsody	1955	12.50	25.00	50.00
DELUXE					
❑ 6133	This Nearly Was Mine/A Dagger in My Chest	1957	6.25	12.50	25.00
❑ 6155	There! I've Said It Again/I Don't Want to Go Home	1958	6.25	12.50	25.00
JUBILEE					
❑ 5482	I Really Love You Baby/Talking About You	1964	2.50	5.00	10.00
❑ 5484	The Bitter with the Sweet/I Don't Know What I'm Gonna Do	1964	2.50	5.00	10.00
❑ 5493	Little Girl Blue/I'm In Such Misery	1964	2.50	5.00	10.00
MR. G					
❑ 824	Your Love Is Driving Me Crazy/There Ain't Gonna Be No Loving	1969	2.00	4.00	8.00

GARDNER, DON, AND DEE DEE FORD

Number	Title (A Side/B Side)	Yr	VG	VG+	NM
FIRE					
❑ 508	I Need Your Loving/Tell Me	1962	5.00	10.00	20.00
—Red label					
❑ 508	I Need Your Loving/Tell Me	1962	3.75	7.50	15.00
—Multicolor label					
❑ 513	Don't You Worry/I'm Coming Home to Stay	1962	3.75	7.50	15.00
❑ 517	Lead Me On/TOD (Taking Care of Business)	1962	3.75	7.50	15.00
KC					
❑ 196	Glory of Love/'Deed I Do	1963	3.00	6.00	12.00
LUDIX					
❑ 104	You Upset My Soul/Son My Son	1963	3.00	6.00	12.00

GARFUNKEL, ART
Also see SIMON AND GARFUNKEL; TOM AND JERRY (1).

Number	Title (A Side/B Side)	Yr	VG	VG+	NM
COLUMBIA					
❑ 02307	A Heart in New York/Is This Love	1981	—	2.00	4.00
❑ 02307 [PS]	A Heart in New York/Is This Love	1981	—	2.00	4.00
❑ 02627	Bright Eyes/The Romance	1981	—	2.00	4.00
❑ 06590	Carol of the Birds/The Decree	1986	—	—	3.00
—With Amy Grant					
❑ 06590 [PS]	Carol of the Birds/The Decree	1986	—	—	3.00
❑ 07711	So Much in Love/King of Tonga	1988	—	—	3.00
❑ 07949	This Is the Moment/Slow Breakup	1988	—	—	3.00
❑ 08511	When a Man Loves a Woman/I Have a Love	1988	—	—	3.00
❑ 10020	Second Avenue/Woyaya	1974	—	2.50	5.00
—As "Garfunkel"					
❑ 10190	I Only Have Eyes for You/Looking for the Right One	1975	—	2.50	5.00
❑ 10274	Breakaway/Disney Girls	1975	—	2.50	5.00
❑ 10608	Crying in My Sleep/Mr. Shuck 'N' Jive	1977	—	2.50	5.00
❑ 10676	(What a) Wonderful World/Wooden Planes	1978	—	3.00	6.00
—A-side: Art Garfunkel with Paul Simon and James Taylor					
❑ 10933	In a Little While (I'll Be On My Way)/And I Know	1979	—	2.00	4.00
❑ 10999	Since I Don't Have You/When Someone Doesn't Want You	1979	—	2.00	4.00
❑ 11050	Bright Eyes/Sail on a Rainbow	1979	—	2.00	4.00
❑ 45926	All I Know/Mary Was An Only Child	1973	—	2.50	5.00
—As "Garfunkel"					
❑ 45926	All I Know/Mary Was An Only Child	1973	—	2.50	5.00
—As "Art Garfunkel"					
❑ 45926 [Q]	All I Know/Mary Was An Only Child	1973	2.50	5.00	10.00
—As "Garfunkel"; promo-only quadraphonic pressing					
❑ 45983	I Shall Sing/Feuilles-Oh: Do Space Men Pass Dead Souls on Their Way to the Moon	1973	—	2.50	5.00
—As "Garfunkel"					
❑ 46030	Traveling Boy/Old Men	1974	—	2.50	5.00
—As "Garfunkel"					
OCTAVIA					
❑ 8002	Forgive Me/Private World	1960	10.00	20.00	40.00
—As "Artie Garr"					
WARWICK					
❑ 515	Beat Love/Dream Alone	1959	10.00	20.00	40.00
—As "Artie Garr"					

Number	Title (A Side/B Side)	Yr	VG	VG+	NM
GARNER, JOHNNY					
IMPERIAL					
❑ 5536	Kiss Me Sweet/Little Starry Eyes	1958	6.25	12.50	25.00
❑ 5548	Didi Didi/The Fool	1958	12.50	25.00	50.00
GARNETT, GALE					
COLUMBIA					
❑ 44479	Breaking Through/Fall in Love Again	1968	—	2.50	5.00
RCA VICTOR					
❑ 47-8388	We'll Sing in the Sunshine/Prism Song	1964	2.50	5.00	10.00
❑ 47-8472	Lovin' Place/I Used to Live Here	1964	2.00	4.00	8.00
❑ 47-8472 [PS]	Lovin' Place/I Used to Live Here	1964	2.00	4.00	8.00
❑ 47-8549	I'll Cry Alone/Where Do You Go to Go Away	1965	2.00	4.00	8.00
❑ 47-8668	I'm Gonna Sit Right Down and Write Myself a Letter/Why Am I Standing in the Window	1965	2.00	4.00	8.00
❑ 47-8824	This Kind of Love/Oh There'll Be Laughter	1966	—	3.00	6.00
❑ 47-8961	It's Been a Lonely Summer/You've Got to Fall in Love Again	1966	—	3.00	6.00
❑ 47-9020	The Sun Is Gray/I Make Him Fly	1966	—	3.00	6.00
❑ 47-9196	Over the Rainbow/The Cats I Know	1967	—	3.00	6.00
GARR, ARTIE					
See ART GARFUNKEL.					
GARRETT, SCOTT					
LAURIE					
❑ 3023	House of Love/So Far So Good	1959	5.00	10.00	20.00
❑ 3029	Love Story/Graduation Souvenir	1959	12.50	25.00	50.00
—With vocal backing by the Mystics					
❑ 3034	Where Are You/Jumpin' Blue Blazes	1959	5.00	10.00	20.00
OKEH					
❑ 7104	In My Heart/The Day I Died	1960	5.00	10.00	20.00
GARRIGAN, EDDIE					
FONTANA					
❑ 1575	I Wish I Was/Mail Call	1966	10.00	20.00	40.00
GARRISON, GLEN					
CREST					
❑ 1047	Lovin' Lorene/You're My Darling	1958	15.00	30.00	60.00
IMPERIAL					
❑ 66191	Green to Blue/You Can't Win 'Em All	1966	2.50	5.00	10.00
❑ 66215	Where Do I Go from Here/Strong and Handsome, Sweet and Simple Side	1966	2.50	5.00	10.00
❑ 66230	Listen, They're Playing My Song/My New Creation	1967	2.50	5.00	10.00
❑ 66257	Goodbye Swingers/Hello Mama	1967	2.50	5.00	10.00
❑ 66279	Your Side of Me/If I Lived Here (I'd Be Home Now)	1968	2.00	4.00	8.00
❑ 66300	I'll Be Your Baby Tonight/You Know I Love You	1968	2.00	4.00	8.00
❑ 66333	That Lucky Old Sun/She Thinks I Still Care	1968	2.00	4.00	8.00
❑ 66401	Goodnight Irene/Change Me	1969	2.00	4.00	8.00
LODE					
❑ 106	Pony Tail Girl/Ballad of Hank Gordon	1959	15.00	30.00	60.00
GARY AND CLYDE					
See SKIP AND FLIP.					
GARY AND THE CASUALS					
VANDAN					
❑ 609	My Own Desire/Someone Like You	1959	15.00	30.00	60.00
GARY AND THE KNIGHT-LITES					
Evolved into THE AMERICAN BREED.					
BELL					
❑ 643	Lonely Soldier's Pledge/So Far Away from Home	1966	3.75	7.50	15.00
NIKE					
❑ 1020	I'm Glad She's Mine/How Can I Forget Her	1963	10.00	20.00	40.00
PRIMA					
❑ 1016	I Can't Love You Anymore/Will You Go Steady	1963	25.00	50.00	100.00
SEEBURG					
❑ 3016	Sweet Little Sixteen/Take Me Back	1965	6.25	12.50	25.00
❑ 3017	Bony Moronie/Glad You're Mine	1965	6.25	12.50	25.00
U.S.A.					
❑ 833	Bid Bad Wolf/I Don't Need Your Help	1966	5.00	10.00	20.00
GAS AND FUNK FACTORY, THE					
BRUNSWICK					
❑ 55434	Goodnight Song/Everybody Get Some Love	1970	7.50	15.00	30.00
GATEMEN, THE					
COLPIX					
❑ 671	Silent Night/White Christmas	1962	5.00	10.00	20.00
MAY					
❑ 141	Goodnight Irene/The Klan	1963	5.00	10.00	20.00
GATES, DAVID					
Also see BREAD; THE MANCHESTERS.					
ARISTA					
❑ 0615	Take Me Now/It's What You Say	1981	—	2.00	4.00
❑ 0653	Come Home for Christmas/Lady Valentine	1981	2.00	4.00	8.00
DEL-FI					
❑ 4206	No One Really Loves a Clown/You Had It Comin' To Ya	1963	6.25	12.50	25.00
EASTWEST					
❑ 123	Walkin' and Talkin'/Swingin' Baby Doll	1959	37.50	75.00	150.00
ELEKTRA					
❑ 45223	Never Let Her Go/Watch Out	1974	—	2.00	4.00
❑ 45245	Part-Time Love/Chain Me	1975	—	2.00	4.00
❑ 45450	Goodbye Girl/Sunday Rider	1977	—	2.00	4.00
❑ 45450 [PS]	Goodbye Girl/Sunday Rider	1977	—	2.50	5.00
—Version 1: Titles on both sides, no photo					
❑ 45450 [PS]	Goodbye Girl/Sunday Rider	1977	—	2.50	5.00
—Version 2: Titles on one side, photo on other side					
❑ 45500	Took the Last Train/Ann	1978	—	2.00	4.00
❑ 45857	Clouds/I Use the Soap	1973	—	2.00	4.00
❑ 45868	Sail Around the World/Help Is On the Way	1973	—	2.00	4.00
❑ 46588	Where Does the Lovin' Go/Starship Ride	1980	—	2.00	4.00
❑ 46646	Can I Call You/Chingo	1980	—	2.00	4.00
❑ 47011	Falling in Love Again/Sweet Desire	1980	—	2.00	4.00
MALA					
❑ 413	You'll Be My Baby/What's This I Hear	1960	12.50	25.00	50.00
❑ 418	The Happiest Man Alive/A Road That Leads to Love	1960	12.50	25.00	50.00
❑ 427	Jo-Baby/Teardrops in My Heart	1961	12.50	25.00	50.00
MANCHESTER					
❑ 101	There's a Heaven/She Don't Cry	196?	10.00	20.00	40.00
—As "Del Ashley"					
PERSPECTIVE					
❑ (no #)	Jo-Baby/Lovin' at Night	1961	37.50	75.00	150.00
PLANETARY					
❑ 103	Little Miss Stuck-Up/The Brighter Side	1965	6.25	12.50	25.00
—As "Del Ashley"					
❑ 108	Let You Go/Once Upon a Time	1965	5.00	10.00	20.00
ROBBINS					
❑ 1008	Jo-Baby/Lovin' at Night	1961	25.00	50.00	100.00
GAUCHOS, THE					
See JIM DOVAL AND THE GAUCHOS.					
GAUDET, JOHN, AND THE LAURELS					
MARY GLEN					
❑ 1001/2	Christmas Will Soon Be Here/Your Name Shall Be Remembered	1961	6.25	12.50	25.00
GAVIN, TONY					
20TH FOX					
❑ 228	Ever Lovin' Baby/I Just Don't Know	1960	10.00	20.00	40.00
GAY KNIGHTS, THE					
PET					
❑ 801	The Loudness of My Heart/Angel	1958	10.00	20.00	40.00
GAY NOTES, THE					
DREXEL					
❑ 905	For Only a Moment/Pu-Pu-Pa-Doo	1955	150.00	300.00	600.00
POST					
❑ 2006	Crossroads/Hear My Plea	1955	15.00	30.00	60.00
VIM					
❑ 501	Something Special/Cherie	1959	15.00	30.00	60.00
GAYE, ELLIE					
May be ELLIE GREENWICH.					
RCA VICTOR					
❑ 47-7231	Silly Isn't It/Cha Cha Charming	1958	10.00	20.00	40.00
GAYE, MARVIN					
Also see THE MARQUEES (5); DIANA ROSS AND MARVIN GAYE.					
COLUMBIA					
❑ 03302	Sexual Healing/(Instrumental)	1982	—	2.00	4.00
❑ CNR-03344	Sexual Healing	1982	—	3.00	6.00
—One-sided budget release					
❑ 03585	Sexual Healing/(Instrumental)	1983	—	—	3.00
—Reissue					
❑ 03589	'Til Tomorrow/Rockin' After Midnight	1983	—	2.00	4.00
❑ 03860	Joy/(Instrumental)	1983	—	2.00	4.00
❑ 03870	Star Spangled Banner/Turn On Some Music	1983	—	—	—
—Unreleased?					
❑ 03935	Joy/Turn On Some Music	1983	—	2.00	4.00
❑ 04861	Sanctified Lady/(Instrumental)	1985	—	2.00	4.00
❑ 05442	It's Madness/Ain't It Funny (How Things Turn Around)	1985	—	2.00	4.00
❑ 05791	Just Like/More	1986	—	2.00	4.00
DETROIT FREE PRESS					
❑ (no #) [DJ]	The Teen Beat Song/Loraine Alterman Interviews Marvin Gaye	1966	37.50	75.00	150.00
TAMLA					
❑ (no #) [DJ]	Masquerade (Is Over)/Witchcraft	1962	150.00	300.00	600.00
—As "Marvin Gay"; label states "Single Not Available extracted from Album (TM-221)"					
❑ S4KM 0741/2 [DJ]	This Is the Life/My Way	1965	12.50	25.00	50.00
❑ 1836	This World Is Rated X/No Greater Love	1986	—	2.50	5.00
❑ 1836 [PS]	This World Is Rated X/No Greater Love	1986	—	2.50	5.00
❑ 54041	Let Your Conscience Be Your Guide/Never Let You Go	1961	100.00	200.00	400.00
❑ 54055	Sandman/I'm Yours, You're Mine	1962	15.00	30.00	60.00
❑ 54062	Masquerade (Is Over)/Witchcraft	1962	—	—	—
—Unreleased					
❑ 54063	Soldier's Plea/Taking My Time	1962	10.00	20.00	40.00
—With label credit "Marvin Gaye Love Tones"					
❑ 54063	Soldier's Plea/Taking My Time	1962	12.50	25.00	50.00
—With label credit "Marvin Gaye"					
❑ 54068	Stubborn Kind of Fellow/It Hurts Me Too	1962	7.50	15.00	30.00
❑ 54075	Hitch Hike/Hello There Angel	1963	5.00	10.00	20.00
❑ 54079	Pride and Joy/One of These Days	1963	5.00	10.00	20.00
❑ 54087	Can I Get a Witness/I'm Crazy 'Bout My Baby	1963	5.00	10.00	20.00
❑ 54093	You're a Wonderful One/When I'm Alone I Cry	1964	3.75	7.50	15.00
❑ 54095	Try It Baby/If My Heart Could Sing	1964	3.75	7.50	15.00
❑ 54095 [PS]	Try It Baby/If My Heart Could Sing	1964	15.00	30.00	60.00
❑ 54101	Baby Don't You Do It/Walk on the Wild Side	1964	3.75	7.50	15.00
❑ 54101 [PS]	Baby Don't You Do It/Walk on the Wild Side	1964	15.00	30.00	60.00
❑ 54107	How Sweet It Is To Be Loved By You/Forever	1964	3.75	7.50	15.00
❑ 54112	I'll Be Doggone/You've Been a Long Time Coming	1965	3.75	7.50	15.00
❑ 54117	Pretty Little Baby/Now That You've Won Me	1965	3.75	7.50	15.00
❑ 54122	Ain't That Peculiar/She's Got to Be Real	1965	3.75	7.50	15.00
❑ 54129	One More Heartache/When I Had Your Love	1966	3.00	6.00	12.00

Number	Title (A Side/B Side)	Yr	VG	VG+	NM
❑ 54132	Take This Heart of Mine/Need Your Lovin' (Want You Back)	1966	3.00	6.00	12.00
❑ 54138	Little Darling, I Need You/Hey Diddle Diddle	1966	3.00	6.00	12.00
❑ 54153	Your Unchanging Love/I'll Take Care of You	1967	2.50	5.00	10.00
❑ 54160	You/Change What You Can	1967	2.50	5.00	10.00
❑ 54170	Chained/At Last I Found a Love	1968	2.50	5.00	10.00
❑ 54176	I Heard It Through the Grapevine/You're What's Happening (In the World Today)	1968	2.50	5.00	10.00
❑ 54181	Too Busy Thinking About My Baby/Wherever I Lay My Hat (That's My Home)	1969	2.00	4.00	8.00
❑ 54185	That's the Way Love Is/Gonna Keep On Tryin' Till I Win Your Love	1969	2.00	4.00	8.00
❑ 54190	Gonna Give Her All the Love I've Got/How Can I Forget You	1970	2.00	4.00	8.00
❑ 54195	The End of Our Road/Me and My Lonely Room	1970	2.00	4.00	8.00
❑ 54201	What's Going On/God Is Love	1971	—	3.00	6.00
❑ 54207	Mercy Mercy Me (The Ecology)/Sad Tomorrows	1971	—	3.00	6.00
❑ 54209	Inner City Blues (Make Me Wanna Holler)/Wholly Holy	1971	—	3.00	6.00
❑ 54221	You're the Man (Part 1)/You're the Man (Part 2)	1972	—	3.00	6.00
❑ 54228	Trouble Man/Don't Mess With Mister "T"	1972	—	3.00	6.00
❑ 54229	Christmas in the City/I Want to Come Home for Christmas	1972	—	—	—
—Canceled					
❑ 54234	Let's Get It On/I Wish It Would Rain	1973	—	2.00	4.00
❑ 54241	Come Get to This/Distant Lover	1973	—	2.00	4.00
❑ 54244	You Sure Love to Ball/Just to Keep You Satisfied	1974	—	2.00	4.00
❑ 54253	Distant Lover/Trouble Man	1974	—	2.00	4.00
❑ 54264	I Want You/I Want You (Instrumental)	1975	—	2.00	4.00
❑ 54273	After the Dance/Feel All My Love Inside	1976	—	2.00	4.00
❑ 54280	Got to Give It Up — Pt. 1/Got to Give It Up — Pt. 2	1977	—	2.00	4.00
❑ 54280 [PS]	Got to Give It Up — Pt. 1/Got to Give It Up — Pt. 2	1977	2.50	5.00	10.00
❑ 54298	Funky Space Reincarnation — Pt. 1/Funky Space Reincarnation — Pt. 2	1979	—	2.00	4.00
❑ 54300	Time to Get It Together/Anger	1979	2.50	5.00	10.00
—Only released in Canada					
❑ 54305	Ego Tripping Out/(Instrumental)	1979	—	2.00	4.00
❑ 54322	Funk Me/Praise	1981	—	2.00	4.00
❑ 54326	Heavy Love Affair/Far Cry	1981	—	2.00	4.00

TOPPS/MOTOWN

Number	Title (A Side/B Side)	Yr	VG	VG+	NM
❑ 6	How Sweet It Is	1967	18.75	37.50	75.00
—Cardboard record					

GAYE, MARVIN, AND TAMMI TERRELL

Also see each artist's individual listings.

TAMLA

Number	Title (A Side/B Side)	Yr	VG	VG+	NM
❑ 54149	Ain't No Mountain High Enough/Give a Little Love	1967	2.00	4.00	8.00
❑ 54156	Your Precious Love/Hold Me Oh My Darling	1967	2.00	4.00	8.00
❑ 54161	If I Could Build My Whole World Around You/If This World Were Mine	1967	2.00	4.00	8.00
❑ 54163	Ain't Nothing Like the Real Thing/Little Ole Boy, Little Ole Girl	1968	2.00	4.00	8.00
❑ 54169	You're All I Need to Get By/Two Can Have a Party	1968	2.00	4.00	8.00
❑ 54173	You Ain't Livin' Till You're Lovin'/Keep On Lovin' Me Honey	1968	—	3.00	6.00
❑ 54179	Good Lovin' Ain't Easy to Come By/Satisfied Feelin'	1969	—	3.00	6.00
❑ 54179 [PS]	Good Lovin' Ain't Easy to Come By/Satisfied Feelin'	1969	5.00	10.00	20.00
❑ 54187	What You Gave Me/How You Gonna Keep It	1969	—	3.00	6.00
❑ 54192	The Onion Song/California Soul	1970	—	3.00	6.00

GAYE, MARVIN, AND MARY WELLS

Also see each artist's individual listings.

MOTOWN

Number	Title (A Side/B Side)	Yr	VG	VG+	NM
❑ 1057	Once Upon a Time/What's the Matter with You Baby	1964	3.75	7.50	15.00
❑ 1057 [PS]	Once Upon a Time/What's the Matter with You Baby	1964	15.00	30.00	60.00

GAYE, MARVIN, AND KIM WESTON

Also see each artist's individual listings.

TAMLA

Number	Title (A Side/B Side)	Yr	VG	VG+	NM
❑ 54104	What Good Am I Without You/I Want You 'Round	1964	3.75	7.50	15.00
❑ 54141	It Takes Two/It's Got to Be a Miracle	1966	3.00	6.00	12.00

GAYLARKS, THE

MUSIC CITY

Number	Title (A Side/B Side)	Yr	VG	VG+	NM
❑ 792	Tell Me Darling/Whole Lot of Love	1956	30.00	60.00	120.00
—B-side by the Rovers					
❑ 793	Romantic Memories/Li'l Dream Girl	1956	30.00	60.00	120.00
❑ 805	My Greatest Sin/Teenage Mambo	1957	25.00	50.00	100.00
❑ 809	Church on the Hill/Mr. Rock-n-Roll	1957	30.00	60.00	120.00
❑ 812	Just One More Chance/Somewhere in This World	1957	15.00	30.00	60.00
❑ 819	Ivy League Clothes/Rockin' Satellite	1958	12.50	25.00	50.00

GAYLES, BILLY, WITH IKE TURNER'S RHYTHM ROCKERS

FEDERAL

Number	Title (A Side/B Side)	Yr	VG	VG+	NM
❑ 12265	I'm Tore Up/If I Had Never Known You	1956	10.00	20.00	40.00
❑ 12272	Let's Call It a Day/Take Your Fine Frame Home	1956	10.00	20.00	40.00
❑ 12282	No Coming Back/Do Right Baby	1956	10.00	20.00	40.00
❑ 12287	Just One More Time/Sad as a Man Can Be	1957	10.00	20.00	40.00

GAYLES, THE

ABC-PARAMOUNT

Number	Title (A Side/B Side)	Yr	VG	VG+	NM
❑ 9707	Shortnin' Bread Rock/You Fool	1956	6.25	12.50	25.00

KING

Number	Title (A Side/B Side)	Yr	VG	VG+	NM
❑ 4846	My Boy, Flat Top/I Get So Happy	1955	5.00	10.00	20.00
❑ 4860	I Had to Love You/Too Late I Learned	1955	5.00	10.00	20.00

GAYTEN, PAUL

Also see THE TUNE WEAVERS.

ANNA

Number	Title (A Side/B Side)	Yr	VG	VG+	NM
❑ 1106	The Hunch/Hot Cross Buns	1959	5.00	10.00	20.00
❑ 1112	Beatnick Beat/Scratch Back	1960	5.00	10.00	20.00

ARGO

Number	Title (A Side/B Side)	Yr	VG	VG+	NM
❑ 5257	The Music Goes Round and Round/Be My Baby	1956	6.25	12.50	25.00
❑ 5263	Driving Home Part 1/Driving Home Part 2	1957	6.25	12.50	25.00
❑ 5267	Old Buttermilk Sky/The Sweeper	1957	6.25	12.50	25.00
❑ 5277	Nervous Boogie/Flatfoot Sam	1957	6.25	12.50	25.00
—B-side by Oscar Wiles					
❑ 5300	Windy/Tickle Toe	1958	6.25	12.50	25.00

CHECKER

Number	Title (A Side/B Side)	Yr	VG	VG+	NM
❑ 801	I'm Tired/Get It	1954	6.25	12.50	25.00
❑ 836	You Better Believe It/Mother Roux	1956	6.25	12.50	25.00

OKEH

Number	Title (A Side/B Side)	Yr	VG	VG+	NM
❑ 6847	Lonesome for My Baby/All Alone and Lovely	1952	7.50	15.00	30.00
❑ 6870	Give Me Liberty or Give Me Death/Happy Days	1952	7.50	15.00	30.00
❑ 6908	True (You Don't Love Me)/They All Ask for You	1952	7.50	15.00	30.00
❑ 6934	Yes You Do, Yes You Do/Don't Worry Me	1953	7.50	15.00	30.00
❑ 6972	Time Is a-Passin'/Ain't Nothin' Happenin'	1953	7.50	15.00	30.00
❑ 6982	Cow Cow Blues/Ooh-Boo	1953	7.50	15.00	30.00
❑ 7003	Hurry Home/Sugar Baby	1953	7.50	15.00	30.00
❑ 7019	Mule Face/It's Over	1954	7.50	15.00	30.00
❑ 7068	True (You Don't Love Me)/Cow Cow Blues	1956	6.25	12.50	25.00

GAYTUNES, THE

JOYCE

Number	Title (A Side/B Side)	Yr	VG	VG+	NM
❑ 101	I Love You/You Left Me	1957	50.00	100.00	200.00
❑ 106	Pen Pal/Plea in the Moonlight	199?	2.00	4.00	8.00
—Black vinyl					
❑ 106	Pen Pal/Plea in the Moonlight	199?	2.50	5.00	10.00
—Red vinyl					

GAZELLES, THE

GOTHAM

Number	Title (A Side/B Side)	Yr	VG	VG+	NM
❑ 315	Honest/Pretty Baby, Baby	1956	75.00	150.00	300.00

GEE, ELLIE

See ELLIE GREENWICH.

GEE, JOEY

ABC-PARAMOUNT

Number	Title (A Side/B Side)	Yr	VG	VG+	NM
❑ 10781	Don't Blow Your Cool/It's More Than I Deserve	1966	6.25	12.50	25.00

SARA

Number	Title (A Side/B Side)	Yr	VG	VG+	NM
❑ 2599	She's Mean/(B-side unknown)	1966	3.75	7.50	15.00

GEE CEES, THE

Also see THE KELLY FOUR.

CREST

Number	Title (A Side/B Side)	Yr	VG	VG+	NM
❑ 1088	Buzz Saw/Annie Had a Party	1961	10.00	20.00	40.00
—Glen Campbell is on A-side; Eddie Cochran is on B-side					
❑ 1088	Buzz Saw Twist/Annie Had a Party	1962	7.50	5.00	30.00

GEILS, J., BAND

ATLANTIC

Number	Title (A Side/B Side)	Yr	VG	VG+	NM
❑ 2784	First I Look at the Purse/Homework	1971	2.00	4.00	8.00
❑ 2802	Cruisin' for a Love/Wait	1971	—	3.00	6.00
❑ 2843	Dead Presidents/I Don't Need You No More	1971	—	3.00	6.00
❑ 2844	Looking for a Love/What's Your Whammer Jammer	1971	—	3.00	6.00
❑ 2929	Hard Drivin' Man/Whammer Jammer	1972	—	3.00	6.00
❑ 2953	Give It To Me/Hold Your Loving	1973	—	2.50	5.00
❑ 2974	Make Up Your Mind/Southside Shuffle	1973	—	2.50	5.00
❑ 2974 [PS]	Make Up Your Mind/Southside Shuffle	1973	2.50	5.00	10.00
❑ 3007	Did You No Wrong/That's Why I'm Thinking of You	1974	—	2.50	5.00
❑ 3214	Must of Got Lost/Funky Judge	1974	—	2.50	5.00
❑ 3251	Givin' It All Up/Gettin' Out	1975	—	2.50	5.00
❑ 3301	Think It Over/Love-Itis	1975	—	2.50	5.00
❑ 3320	Where Did Our Love Go/What's Your Hurry	1976	—	2.50	5.00
❑ 3350	(Ain't Nothing But a) House Party/Give It To Me	1976	—	2.50	5.00
❑ 3378	Peanut Buuter/Magic's Mood	1976	—	2.50	5.00
❑ 3411	You're the Only One/Wreckage	1977	—	2.50	5.00
—As "Geils"					
❑ 3438	Monkey Island (Part 1)/Surrender	1977	—	2.50	5.00
—As "Geils"					
❑ 3454	I Do/Trying to Live My Life Without You	1978	—	2.50	5.00
—As "Geils"					
❑ 3454 [PS]	I Do/Trying to Live My Life Without You	1978	2.00	4.00	8.00
—As "Geils"					

EMI AMERICA

Number	Title (A Side/B Side)	Yr	VG	VG+	NM
❑ 8007	One Last Kiss/Revenge	1978	—	2.00	4.00
❑ 8007 [PS]	One Last Kiss/Revenge	1978	—	3.00	6.00
❑ 8012	Take It Back/I Can't Believe You	1979	—	2.00	4.00
❑ 8016	Wild Man/Just Can't Stop Me	1979	—	2.00	4.00
❑ 8032	Come Back/Takin' You Down	1980	—	2.00	4.00
❑ 8032 [DJ]	Come Back (Long)/Come Back (Edit)	1980	—	2.50	5.00
❑ 8039	Love Stinks/Till the Walls Come Tumblin' Down	1980	—	2.00	4.00
❑ 8039 [PS]	Love Stinks/Till the Walls Come Tumblin' Down	1980	—	2.50	5.00
❑ 8047	Just Can't Wait/No Anchovies, Please	1980	—	2.00	4.00
❑ 8100	Angel in Blue/Rage in the Cage	1982	—	—	3.00
❑ 8100 [PS]	Angel in Blue/Rage in the Cage	1982	—	2.00	4.00
❑ 8102	Centerfold/Rage in the Cage	1981	—	2.50	5.00
—Regular gray EMI America label					
❑ 8102	Centerfold/Rage in the Cage	1981	—	—	3.00
—Custom pink label					
❑ 8102 [PS]	Centerfold/Rage in the Cage	1981	2.50	5.00	10.00
❑ 8108	Freeze-Frame/Flamethrower	1982	—	—	3.00
❑ 8108 [PS]	Freeze-Frame/Flamethrower	1982	—	3.00	6.00
❑ 8148	I Do/Sanctuary	1982	—	—	3.00
❑ 8148 [PS]	I Do/Sanctuary	1982	—	2.00	4.00
❑ 8156	Land of 1000 Dances/Jus' Can't Stop Me	1983	—	—	3.00
❑ 8242	Concealed Weapons/Tell 'Em Jonsey	1984	—	—	3.00
❑ 8242 [PS]	Concealed Weapons/Tell 'Em Jonsey	1984	—	2.00	4.00
❑ 8260	Eenie Meenie Miney Mo/I Will Carry You Home	1985	—	—	3.00

Number	Title (A Side/B Side)	Yr	VG	VG+	NM
PRIVATE I					
❑ 05462	Fright Night/Boppin' Tonight	1985	—	—	3.00
—B-side by The Fabulous Fontaines					
❑ 05462 [PS]	Fright Night/Boppin' Tonight	1985	—	2.00	4.00

GEMS, THE (1)

Number	Title (A Side/B Side)	Yr	VG	VG+	NM
CHESS					
❑ 1863	One More Year/Let Your Hair Down	1963	3.00	6.00	12.00
❑ 1875	If It's the Last Thing I Do/A Girl's Impression	1963	3.00	6.00	12.00
❑ 1882	A Love of Mine/That's Why They Put Erasers On	1964	3.00	6.00	12.00
❑ 1908	I Can't Help Myself/Can't You Take a Hint	1964	3.00	6.00	12.00
❑ 1917	Love For Christmas/All Of It	1964	3.00	6.00	12.00
❑ 1930	He Makes Me Feel So Good/Happy New Love	1965	2.50	5.00	10.00
❑ 2104	Girls Can Do It/Ain't That Loving You	1971	—	3.00	6.00

GEMS, THE (2)

Number	Title (A Side/B Side)	Yr	VG	VG+	NM
DREXEL					
❑ 901	Deed I Do/Talk About the Weather	1954	100.00	200.00	400.00
—Black vinyl					
❑ 901	Deed I Do/Talk About the Weather	1954	625.00	1250.	2500.
—Red vinyl					
❑ 903	I Thought You'd Care/Kitty from New York City	1954	75.00	150.00	300.00
—Black vinyl					
❑ 903	I Thought You'd Care/Kitty from New York City	1954	150.00	300.00	600.00
—Red vinyl					
❑ 904	You're Tired of Love/Ol' Man River	1954	75.00	150.00	300.00
—Black vinyl					
❑ 904	You're Tired of Love/Ol' Man River	1954	150.00	300.00	600.00
—Red vinyl					
❑ 909	One Woman Man/The Darkest Night	1955	100.00	200.00	400.00
❑ 915	Till the Day I Die/Monkey Face Baby	1956	100.00	200.00	400.00

GEMS, THE (U)

These probably are neither group (1) nor (2).

Number	Title (A Side/B Side)	Yr	VG	VG+	NM
MERCURY					
❑ 71819	Crazy Chicken/Hippy Dippy	1961	2.50	5.00	10.00
PAT					
❑ 101	There's No One Like My Love/School Rock	1961	7.50	15.00	30.00
RECORTE					
❑ 407	Waiting/Please Change Your Mind	1959	12.50	25.00	50.00
RIVERSIDE					
❑ 4590	I'll Be There/I Miss Him	1967	7.50	15.00	30.00
WIN					
❑ 701	Nursery Rhymes/The Night Is Over	1958	75.00	150.00	300.00

GENE AND EUNICE

Number	Title (A Side/B Side)	Yr	VG	VG+	NM
ALADDIN					
❑ 3276	Ko Ko Mo (I Need You So)/You and Me	1954	6.25	12.50	25.00
❑ 3282	This Is My Story/Move It Over Baby	1954	6.25	12.50	25.00
❑ 3292	Flim Flam/Can We Forget It	1954	6.25	12.50	25.00
❑ 3305	I Gotta Go Home/Have You Changed Your Mind	1954	6.25	12.50	25.00
❑ 3315	Hootchy Kootchy/I'll Never Believe in You	1955	5.00	10.00	20.00
❑ 3321	Let's Get Together/I'm So in Love with You	1955	5.00	10.00	20.00
❑ 3351	Bom Bom Lulu/Hi Diddle Diddle	1956	5.00	10.00	20.00
❑ 3374	The Vow/Strange World	1957	5.00	10.00	20.00
❑ 3376	Doodle Doodle Doo/Don't Treat Me This Way	1957	5.00	10.00	20.00
❑ 3414	I Mean Love/The Angels Gave You to Me	1958	5.00	10.00	20.00
CASE					
❑ 1001	Poco-Loco/Go-On Kokomo	1959	7.50	15.00	30.00
❑ 1002	Ah! Ah!/You Think I'm Not Thinking	1959	7.50	15.00	30.00
COMBO					
❑ 64	Ko Ko Mo (I Need You So)/You and Me	1954	7.50	15.00	30.00
LILLY					
❑ 512	Everlovin' Baby/Got a Right to Know	1962	3.75	7.50	15.00
UNITED ARTISTS					
❑ 0151	Ko Ko Mo (I Love You So)/This Is My Story	1973	—	2.00	4.00
—"Silver Spotlight Series" reissue					

GENESIS

Also see PHIL COLLINS; PETER GABRIEL.

Number	Title (A Side/B Side)	Yr	VG	VG+	NM
ATCO					
❑ 7013	The Lamb Lies Down on Broadway/Counting Out Time	1975	5.00	10.00	20.00
❑ 7050	Entangled/Ripples	1976	2.50	5.00	10.00
❑ 7076	Your Own Special Way/In That Quiet Earth	1977	2.50	5.00	10.00
ATLANTIC					
❑ 3474	Follow You Follow Me/Inside and Out	1978	—	2.00	4.00
—A radically different mix than the LP version of A-side					
❑ 3511	Go West Young Man (In the Motherlode)/Scene from a Night's Dream	1978	—	2.00	4.00
❑ 3662	Misunderstanding/Behind the Lines	1980	—	2.00	4.00
❑ 3662 [PS]	Misunderstanding/Behind the Lines	1980	—	2.50	5.00
❑ 3751	Turn It On Again/Evidence of Autumn	1980	—	2.00	4.00
❑ 3858	No Reply At All/Heaven Love My Life	1981	—	2.00	4.00
❑ 3891	Abacab/Who Dunnit?	1982	—	2.00	4.00
❑ 3891 [PS]	Abacab/Who Dunnit?	1982	—	2.00	4.00
❑ 4025	Man on the Corner/Submarine	1982	—	2.00	4.00
❑ 4025 [PS]	Man on the Corner/Submarine	1982	—	2.00	4.00
❑ 4053	Paperlate/You Might Recall	1982	—	2.00	4.00
❑ 4053 [PS]	Paperlate/You Might Recall	1982	—	2.50	5.00
❑ 84043	Not About Us/Turn It On Again (Live)	1997	—	—	3.00
❑ 87481	Hold On My Heart/Way of the World	1992	—	2.00	4.00
❑ 87532	I Can't Dance/On the Shoreline	1992	—	2.00	4.00
❑ 87571	No Son of Mine/Living Forever	1991	—	2.00	4.00
❑ 89290	Tonight, Tonight, Tonight/In the Glow of the Night	1987	—	—	3.00
❑ 89290 [PS]	Tonight, Tonight, Tonight/In the Glow of the Night	1987	—	2.00	4.00
—Color sleeve					
❑ 89290 [PS]	Tonight, Tonight, Tonight/In the Glow of the Night	1987	—	2.50	5.00
—Black and white sleeve					
❑ 89316	In Too Deep/I'd Rather Be You	1987	—	—	3.00
❑ 89316 [PS]	In Too Deep/I'd Rather Be You	1987	—	2.00	4.00
❑ 89336	Land of Confusion/Feeding the Fire	1986	—	—	3.00
—Regular Atlantic red and black label					
❑ 89336	Land of Confusion/Feeding the Fire	1986	2.50	5.00	10.00
—Black label with different Atlantic logo					
❑ 89336 [PS]	Land of Confusion/Feeding the Fire	1986	2.50	5.00	10.00
—Sleeve came only with black-label versions					
❑ 89372	Throwing It All Away/Do the Neurotic	1986	—	—	3.00
❑ 89372 [PS]	Throwing It All Away/Do the Neurotic	1986	—	—	3.00
❑ 89407	Invisible Touch/The Last Domino	1986	—	—	3.00
❑ 89407 [PS]	Invisible Touch/The Last Domino	1986	—	—	3.00
❑ 89656	Taking It All Too Hard/Silver Rainbow	1984	—	—	3.00
❑ 89656 [PS]	Taking It All Too Hard/Silver Rainbow	1984	—	—	3.00
❑ 89698	Illegal Alien/Turn It On Again (Live in Philadelphia)	1984	—	—	3.00
❑ 89698 [PS]	Illegal Alien/Turn It On Again (Live in Philadelphia)	1984	—	—	3.00
❑ 89724	That's All/Second Home by the Sea	1983	—	—	3.00
❑ 89724 [PS]	That's All/Second Home by the Sea	1983	—	2.50	5.00
—Brown title sleeve with no center cut-out					
❑ 89724 [PS]	That's All/Second Home by the Sea	1983	—	2.00	4.00
—Brown title sleeve with center cut-out					
❑ 89770	Mama/It's Gonna Get Better	1983	—	—	3.00
❑ 89770 [PS]	Mama/It's Gonna Get Better	1983	—	2.00	4.00
CHARISMA					
❑ 103	Watcher of the Skies/Willow Farm	1973	12.50	25.00	50.00
❑ 26002	I Know What I Like/Twilight Ale House	1973	10.00	20.00	40.00
PARROT					
❑ 3018	Silent Sun/That's Me	1968	100.00	200.00	400.00
—Stock copy with black label and green and yellow bird. This has been proven to exist.					
❑ 3018 [DJ]	Silent Sun/That's Me	1968	25.00	50.00	100.00
—Promotional copy; orangeish label with black bird					

GENESIS (2)

Number	Title (A Side/B Side)	Yr	VG	VG+	NM
BUDDAH					
❑ 132	Journey to the Moon (Part 1)/Journey to the Moon (Part 2)	1969	2.50	5.00	10.00

GENESIS (3)

Number	Title (A Side/B Side)	Yr	VG	VG+	NM
MERCURY					
❑ 72806	Angeline/Suzanne	1968	2.50	5.00	10.00
❑ 72869	Gloomy Sunday/What's It All About	1968	2.50	5.00	10.00

GENESIS (4)

Number	Title (A Side/B Side)	Yr	VG	VG+	NM
RIPCHORD					
❑ 004	Window of Sand/Would You Like To	1967	6.25	12.50	25.00

GENESIS (5)

Number	Title (A Side/B Side)	Yr	VG	VG+	NM
SCEPTER					
❑ 12341	Second Coming/Double Bubble	1972	—	2.50	5.00

GENTEELS, THE

Number	Title (A Side/B Side)	Yr	VG	VG+	NM
CAPITOL					
❑ 4798	Take It Off/Hitchhiker	1962	6.25	12.50	25.00
STAG					
❑ 2930/1	Take It Off/Hitch Hiker	1962	12.50	25.00	50.00
❑ 4949/50	The Force of Gravity/Springboard	1962	12.50	25.00	50.00

GENTLEMEN, THE

Number	Title (A Side/B Side)	Yr	VG	VG+	NM
APOLLO					
❑ 470	Don't Leave Me Baby/(B-side unknown)	1955	25.00	50.00	100.00

GENTLEMEN FOUR, THE

Number	Title (A Side/B Side)	Yr	VG	VG+	NM
WAND					
❑ 1184	It Won't Hurt Baby/You Can't Keep a Good Man Down	1968	20.00	40.00	80.00

GENTRY, BOBBIE

Number	Title (A Side/B Side)	Yr	VG	VG+	NM
BRUNSWICK					
❑ 55517	Another Place — Another Time/I Think I'll Cry Out Loud	1975	—	3.00	6.00
CAPITOL					
❑ 2044	Okolona River Bottom Band/Penduli Pendulum	1967	2.00	4.00	8.00
❑ 2044 [PS]	Okolona River Bottom Band/Penduli Pendulum	1967	3.75	7.50	15.00
❑ 2147	Louisiana Man/Courtyard	1968	2.00	4.00	8.00
❑ 2295	Hushabye Mountain/Sweet Peony	1968	2.00	4.00	8.00
❑ 2501	Touch 'Em With Love/Casket Vignette	1969	—	3.00	6.00
❑ 2675	Fancy/Courtyard	1969	—	3.00	6.00
❑ 2788	He Made a Woman Out of Me/Billy the Kid	1970	—	3.00	6.00
❑ 2849	Apartment 21/Seasons Come, Seasons Go	1970	—	3.00	6.00
❑ 3071	But I Can't Get Back/Marigolds and Tangerines	1971	—	3.00	6.00
❑ 3413	Girl from Cincinnati/You and Me Together	1972	—	3.00	6.00
❑ 4294	Ode to Billie Joe/Mississippi Delta	1976	—	2.50	5.00
❑ 5950	Ode to Billie Joe/Mississippi Delta	1967	2.50	5.00	10.00
❑ 5992	I Saw An Angel Die/Poppa, Won'tcha Let Me Go to Town with You	1967	2.00	4.00	8.00
TITAN					
❑ 1736	Requiem for Love/Stranger in the Mirror	1963	3.75	7.50	15.00
—With Jody Reynolds					
WARNER BROS.					
❑ 8210	Ode to Billie Joe/There'll Be a Time	1976	—	2.50	5.00
—B-side by Michel Legrand					
❑ 8210 [PS]	Ode to Billie Joe/There'll Be a Time	1976	2.50	5.00	10.00
❑ 8532	Steal Away/He Did Me Wrong But He Did It Right	1978	—	2.00	4.00

GENTRY, RAY

Number	Title (A Side/B Side)	Yr	VG	VG+	NM
MAVERICK					
❑ 614	Willie Was a Bad Boy/Do the Fly	1958	100.00	200.00	400.00

GENTRYS, THE

Number	Title (A Side/B Side)	Yr	VG	VG+	NM
BELL					
❑ 720	You Better Come Home/I Can't Go Back to Denver	1968	—	3.00	6.00
❑ 740	Thinking Like a Child/Silky	1968	—	3.00	6.00
❑ 753	Midnight Train/You Tell Me You Care	1968	—	3.00	6.00

Number	Title (A Side/B Side)	Yr	VG	VG+	NM
CAPITOL					
❑ 3459	Changin'/Let Me Put This Ring Upon Your Finger	1972	—	2.50	5.00
HIT					
❑ 229	Keep On Dancing/A Lover's Concerto	1965	5.00	10.00	20.00
—B-side by Alpha Zoe					
MGM					
❑ 13379	Keep On Dancing/Make Up Your Mind	1965	3.75	7.50	15.00
❑ 13432	Spread It On Thick/Brown Paper Bag	1965	3.00	6.00	12.00
❑ 13432 [PS]	Spread It On Thick/Brown Paper Bag	1965	4.00	8.00	16.00
❑ 13495	Everyday I Have to Cry/Don't Let It Be (This Time)	1966	3.00	6.00	12.00
❑ 13561	There Are Two Sides to Every Story/Woman of the World	1966	3.00	6.00	12.00
❑ 13690	There's a Love/You Make Me Feel So Good	1967	6.25	12.50	25.00
❑ 13749	I Can See/90 Pound Weakling	1967	2.50	5.00	10.00
STAX					
❑ 0223	All Hung Up on You/Little Gold Band	1974	—	2.00	4.00
❑ 0242	High Flyer/Little Gold Band	1975	—	2.00	4.00
SUN					
❑ 1108	I Need Love/Why Should I Cry	1969	—	2.50	5.00
❑ 1114	Cinnamon Girl/I Just Got the News	1970	—	2.50	5.00
❑ 1114 [DJ]	Cinnamon Girl/I Just Got the News	1970	2.50	5.00	10.00
—Promo only on blue vinyl					
❑ 1118	I Hate to See You Go/He'll Never Love Me	1970	—	2.50	5.00
❑ 1120	Friends/Goddess of Love	1970	—	2.50	5.00
❑ 1122	Wild World/Sunshine	1971	—	2.50	5.00
❑ 1126	God Save Our Country/Love You All My Life	1971	—	2.50	5.00
YOUNGSTOWN					
❑ 600	Sometimes/Little Drops of Water	1965	6.25	12.50	25.00
❑ 601	Keep On Dancing/Make Up Your Mind	1965	7.50	15.00	30.00

GEORGE, BARBARA

Number	Title (A Side/B Side)	Yr	VG	VG+	NM
A.F.O.					
❑ 302	I Know (You Don't Love Me No More)/Love	1961	3.00	6.00	12.00
—Orange and black label					
❑ 302	I Know (You Don't Love Me No More)/Love	1961	3.75	7.50	15.00
—All-orange label					
❑ 304	You Talk About Love/Whip-O-Will	1962	2.50	5.00	10.00
SUE					
❑ 763	If You Think/If When You've Done the Best You Can	1962	2.00	4.00	8.00
❑ 766	Send for Me (If You Need Some Lovin')/Bless You	1962	2.00	4.00	8.00
❑ 773	Recipe (For Perfect Fools)/Try Again	1962	2.00	4.00	8.00
❑ 796	Something's Definitely Wrong/I Need Something Different	1963	2.50	5.00	10.00
UNITED ARTISTS					
❑ XW516	I Know (You Don't Love Me No More)/ Mockingbird	1974	—	2.00	4.00
—Reissue; B-side by Charles and Inez Foxx					

GEORGE, LLOYD

Number	Title (A Side/B Side)	Yr	VG	VG+	NM
IMPERIAL					
❑ 5837	Twistville/Young Date	1962	3.75	7.50	15.00
❑ 5896	Come On Train/Frog Hunt	1962	3.75	7.50	15.00

GEORGE, LOWELL

Number	Title (A Side/B Side)	Yr	VG	VG+	NM
WARNER BROS.					
❑ 8847	What Do You Want the Girl to Do/A Million Things	1979	—	2.50	5.00

GEORGE AND EARL

Number	Title (A Side/B Side)	Yr	VG	VG+	NM
MERCURY					
❑ 70605	Got Anything Good/Can I?	1955	6.25	12.50	25.00
❑ 70632	Goin' Steady with the Blues/Sweet Little Miss Blue Eyes	1955	6.25	12.50	25.00
❑ 70683	Heartaches/Don't, Don't, Don't	1955	6.25	12.50	25.00
❑ 70773	Cry, Baby, Cry/Take a Look at My Darlin'	1956	6.25	12.50	25.00
❑ 70852	Done Gone/Better Stop, Look and Listen	1956	15.00	30.00	60.00
❑ 70935	Eleven Roses/Remember and Regret	1956	6.25	12.50	25.00

GEORGE AND GREER

Number	Title (A Side/B Side)	Yr	VG	VG+	NM
GOLDWAX					
❑ 313	You Don't Know It, But You Had Me/Good Times	1966	10.00	20.00	40.00
❑ 313	You Don't Know It, But You Had Me/Good Times	1966	7.50	15.00	30.00
—Reissue as "George Jackson and Dan Greer"					

GEORGE AND LOUIS

Number	Title (A Side/B Side)	Yr	VG	VG+	NM
SUN					
❑ 301	The Return of Jerry Lee/Lewis Boogie	1958	7.50	15.00	30.00
—B-side by Jerry Lee Lewis					
❑ 301	The Return of Jerry Lee/The Return of Jerry Lee, Part 2	1958	6.25	12.50	25.00

GERMZ, THE

Number	Title (A Side/B Side)	Yr	VG	VG+	NM
VERTIGO					
❑ 8001	Boy-Girl Love/No Easy Way Down	1967	3.75	7.50	15.00

GERRY AND THE PACEMAKERS

Also see GERRY MARSDEN.

Number	Title (A Side/B Side)	Yr	VG	VG+	NM
LAURIE					
❑ 3162	How Do You Do It/Away From You	1963	5.00	10.00	20.00
❑ 3196	I Like It/It Happened to Me	1963	5.00	10.00	20.00
❑ 3218	You'll Never Walk Alone/It's All Right	1964	5.00	10.00	20.00
❑ 3233	I'm the One/You've Got What I Like	1964	5.00	10.00	20.00
❑ 3233	I'm the One/It's All Right	1964	3.75	7.50	15.00
❑ 3233	I'm the One/How Do You Do It	1964	3.75	7.50	15.00
❑ 3251	Don't Let the Sun Catch You Crying/Away from You	1964	3.75	7.50	15.00
❑ 3261	How Do You Do It/You'll Never Walk Alone	1964	3.00	6.00	12.00
❑ 3271	I Like It/Jambalaya	1964	3.00	6.00	12.00
❑ 3279	I'll Be There/You, You, You	1964	3.00	6.00	12.00
❑ 3284	Ferry Across the Mersey/Pretend	1965	3.00	6.00	12.00
❑ 3293	It's Gonna Be Alright/Skinny Minnie	1965	2.50	5.00	10.00
❑ 3302	You'll Never Walk Alone/Away from You	1965	2.50	5.00	10.00
❑ 3313	Give All Your Love to Me/You're the Reason	1965	2.50	5.00	10.00
❑ 3323	Dreams/Walk Hand in Hand	1965	2.50	5.00	10.00
❑ 3337	La La La/Without You	1966	2.50	5.00	10.00
❑ 3354	Girl on a Swing/The Way You Look Tonight	1966	2.50	5.00	10.00
❑ 3370	The Big Bright Green Pleasure Machine/Looking for My Life	1966	3.00	6.00	12.00

GIBB, ANDY

Number	Title (A Side/B Side)	Yr	VG	VG+	NM
RSO					
❑ 872	I Just Want to Be Your Everything/In the End	1977	—	2.00	4.00
❑ 872 [PS]	I Just Want to Be Your Everything/In the End	1977	—	2.50	5.00
❑ 883	(Love Is) Thicker Than Water/Words and Music	1977	—	2.00	4.00
❑ 893	Shadow Dancing/Let It Be Me	1978	—	2.00	4.00
❑ 904	An Everlasting Love/Flowing Rivers	1978	—	2.00	4.00
❑ 911	(Our Love) Don't Throw It All Away/One More Look at the Night	1978	—	2.00	4.00
❑ 911 [PS]	(Our Love) Don't Throw It All Away/One More Look at the Night	1978	—	2.50	5.00
❑ 1019	Desire/Waiting for You	1980	—	2.00	4.00
—A picture sleeve is rumored to exist, but we haven't seen it					
❑ 1026	I Can't Help It/Someone I Ain't	1980	—	2.00	4.00
—A-side: With Olivia Newton-John					
❑ 1056	Me (Without You)/Melody	1980	—	2.00	4.00
❑ 1059	Time Is Time/I Go for You	1980	—	2.00	4.00
❑ 1065	All I Have to Do Is Dream/Good Feeling	1981	—	2.00	4.00
—With Victoria Principal					
❑ 1065 [PS]	All I Have to Do Is Dream/Good Feeling	1981	—	2.50	5.00

GIBB, BARRY

Also see BEE GEES; BARBRA STREISAND.

Number	Title (A Side/B Side)	Yr	VG	VG+	NM
ATCO					
❑ 6786	One Bad Thing/The Day Your Eyes Met Mine	1970	2.00	4.00	8.00
MCA					
❑ 52443	Shine Shine/She Says	1984	—	—	3.00
❑ 52443 [PS]	Shine Shine/She Says	1984	—	—	3.00
❑ 52501	Stay Alone/Fine Line	1984	—	—	3.00

GIBB, MAURICE

Also see BEE GEES; THE FUT.

Number	Title (A Side/B Side)	Yr	VG	VG+	NM
ATCO					
❑ 6757	Railroad/I've Come Back	1970	2.00	4.00	8.00

GIBB, ROBIN

Also see BEE GEES.

Number	Title (A Side/B Side)	Yr	VG	VG+	NM
ATCO					
❑ 6698	Saved by the Bell/Mother and Jack	1969	2.00	4.00	8.00
❑ 6727	Weekend/One Million Years	1969	2.00	4.00	8.00
❑ 6737	Give Me a Smile/August October	1970	2.00	4.00	8.00
EMI AMERICA					
❑ 8291	Like a Fool/Possession	1985	—	—	3.00
❑ 8291 [PS]	Like a Fool/Possession	1985	—	2.00	4.00
❑ 8304	Toys/Do You Love Her	1986	—	—	3.00
❑ 8304 [PS]	Toys/Do You Love Her	1986	—	2.00	4.00
MIRAGE					
❑ 99688 [DJ]	In Your Diary (same on both sides)	1984	—	2.00	4.00
—Stock copy unknown					
❑ 99712	Secret Agent/Robot	1984	—	—	3.00
❑ 99743	Boys Do Fall in Love/Diamonds	1984	—	—	3.00
❑ 99743 [PS]	Boys Do Fall in Love/Diamonds	1984	—	—	3.00
POLYDOR					
❑ 810895-7	Juliet/Hearts on Fire	1983	—	—	3.00
❑ 810895-7 [PS]	Juliet/Hearts on Fire	1983	—	2.00	4.00
RSO					
❑ 907	Oh Darling/She's Leaving Home	1978	—	2.00	4.00
—B-side by The Bee Gees					
❑ 1047	Help Me/(Instrumental)	1980	—	2.00	4.00
—With Marcy Levy					
❑ 1047 [PS]	Help Me/(Instrumental)	1980	—	2.00	4.00
SESAME STREET					
❑ 99070	Sesame Street Fever/Trash	1978	—	2.50	5.00
❑ 99070 [PS]	Sesame Street Fever/Trash	1978	—	3.00	6.00

GIBBS, GEORGIA

Number	Title (A Side/B Side)	Yr	VG	VG+	NM
BELL					
❑ 608	I Wouldn't Have It Any Other Way/You Can Never Get Away from Me	1965	—	3.00	6.00
❑ 615	Lert Me Cry on Your Shoulder/You Can Never Get Away from Me	1965	—	3.00	6.00
❑ 626	Call Me/Don't Cry Joe	1965	—	3.00	6.00
❑ 635	In Time/Let Me Dream	1965	—	3.00	6.00
❑ 641	Kiss of Fire/Blue Grass	1966	—	3.00	6.00
CORAL					
❑ 60210	I Don't Care If the Sun Don't Shine/I'll Get Myself a Choo-Choo Train (And Go Far, Far Away)	1950	3.75	7.50	15.00
❑ 60227	Simple Melody/A Little Bit Independent	1950	3.75	7.50	15.00
—With Bob Crosby					
❑ 60234	Red Hot Mama/Razz-A-Ma-Tazz	1950	3.75	7.50	15.00
❑ 60255	I Was Dancing with Someone/Then I'll Be Happy	1950	3.75	7.50	15.00
❑ 60310	If I Were a Bell/I'll Know	1950	3.75	7.50	15.00
❑ 60315	Ballin' the Jack/Looks Like a Cold Winter	1950	3.75	7.50	15.00
❑ 60353	I Still Feel the Same About You/Get Out Those Old Records	1951	3.75	7.50	15.00
❑ 60406	Shoo Shoo Baby/Once Upon a Nickel	1951	3.75	7.50	15.00
❑ 60462	Ballin' the Jack/Then I'll Be Happy	1951	3.75	7.50	15.00
❑ 60463	Get Out Those Old Records/I'll Get Myself a Choo-Choo Train (And Go Far, Far Away)	1951	3.75	7.50	15.00
❑ 61525	If I Were a Bell/I'll Know	1955	2.50	5.00	10.00
EPIC					
❑ 9573	Candy Kisses/Nobody's Asking Questions	1963	—	—	—
—Unreleased?					
❑ 9585	I Will Follow Him (You)/Candy Kisses	1963	2.00	4.00	8.00
❑ 9606	Tater Poon/Nine Girls Out of Ten Girls	1963	5.00	10.00	20.00

IMPERIAL

Number	Title (A Side/B Side)	Yr	VG	VG+	NM
❑ 5652	Seven Lonely Days/The Stroll That Stole My Heart	1960	2.50	5.00	10.00
❑ 5688	So in Love/Loch Lomond	1960	2.50	5.00	10.00

KAPP

Number	Title (A Side/B Side)	Yr	VG	VG+	NM
❑ 286	Pretend/Hamburgers, Frankfurters and Potato Chips	1959	2.50	5.00	10.00

MERCURY

Number	Title (A Side/B Side)	Yr	VG	VG+	NM
❑ 5644	Tom's Tune/I Wish, I Wish	1951	3.75	7.50	15.00
❑ 5662	Good Morning Mister Echo/Be Doggone Sure You Call	1951	3.75	7.50	15.00
❑ 5681	While You Danced, Danced, Danced/While We're Young	1951	3.75	7.50	15.00
❑ 5687	Got Him Offa My Hands/Cherry Pink	1951	3.75	7.50	15.00
❑ 5718	What You Do to Me/While We Danced	1951	3.75	7.50	15.00
❑ 5749	Cry/My Old Flame	1951	3.75	7.50	15.00
❑ 5758	Be My Life's Companion/The Oklahoma Polka	1951	3.75	7.50	15.00
❑ 5823	Kiss of Fire/A Lasting Thing	1952	3.00	6.00	12.00
❑ 5874	So Madly in Love/Make Me Love You	1952	3.00	6.00	12.00
❑ 5912	My Favorite Song/Sinner or Saint	1952	3.00	6.00	12.00
❑ 70034	A Moth and a Flame/Photograph on the Piano	1953	3.00	6.00	12.00
❑ 70057	What Does It Mean/Winter's Here Again	1953	3.00	6.00	12.00
❑ 70095	Seven Lonely Days/If I Take My Heart Away	1953	3.00	6.00	12.00
❑ 70172	For Me, For Me/Thunder and Lightning	1953	3.00	6.00	12.00
❑ 70218	Say It Isn't So/He's Funny That Way	1953	3.00	6.00	12.00
❑ 70238	Bridge of Sighs/Hard Lovin' Man	1953	3.00	6.00	12.00
❑ 70274	I Love Paris/Under Paris Skies	1953	3.00	6.00	12.00
❑ 70298	Somebody Bad Stole De Wedding Bell (Who's Got de Ding Dong)/Baubles, Bangles and Beads	1954	3.00	6.00	12.00
❑ 70339	My Sin/I'll Always Be Happy with You	1954	3.00	6.00	12.00
❑ 70386	Wait for Me Darling/Whistle and I'll Wait	1954	3.00	6.00	12.00
❑ 70430	The Man That Got Away/More Than Ever	1954	3.00	6.00	12.00
❑ 70473	Mambo Baby/Love Me	1954	3.00	6.00	12.00
❑ 70517	Tweedle Dee/You're Wrong, All Wrong	1954	3.75	7.50	15.00
❑ 70572	Dance with Me Henry (Wallflower)/Ballin' the Jack	1955	3.75	7.50	15.00
❑ 70647	Sweet and Gentle/Blueberries	1955	3.00	6.00	12.00
❑ 70685	I Want You to Be My Baby/Come Rain or Come Shine	1955	3.00	6.00	12.00
❑ 70743	Goodbye to Rome (Arrividerci Roma)/24 Hours a Day (365 a Year)	1955	3.00	6.00	12.00
❑ 70811	Rock Right/The Greatest Thing	1956	3.00	6.00	12.00
❑ 70850	Kiss Me Another/Fool of the Year	1956	3.00	6.00	12.00
❑ 70920	Happiness Street/Happiness Is a Thing Called Joe	1956	3.00	6.00	12.00
❑ 70998	Tra La La/Morning, Noon and Night	1956	3.00	6.00	12.00
❑ 71058	Silent Lips/Pretty Pretty	1957	3.00	6.00	12.00
❑ 71103	The Sheik of Araby/I Am a Heart, a Heart, a Heart	1957	3.00	6.00	12.00

RCA VICTOR

Number	Title (A Side/B Side)	Yr	VG	VG+	NM
❑ 47-6922	I'm Walking the Floor Over You/Sugar Candy	1957	3.00	6.00	12.00
❑ 47-7047	Fun Lovin' Baby/I Never Had the Blues	1957	3.00	6.00	12.00
❑ 47-7098	Great Balls of Fire/I Miss You	1957	3.00	6.00	12.00
❑ 47-7166	You're Doin' It/Way Way Down	1958	3.00	6.00	12.00
❑ 47-7239	Hello Happiness, Goodbye Blues/It's My Pleasure	1958	3.00	6.00	12.00
❑ 47-9173	Time Will Tell/Where's the Music Coming From	1967	—	3.00	6.00

ROULETTE

Number	Title (A Side/B Side)	Yr	VG	VG+	NM
❑ 4106	The Hula Hoop Song/Keep in Touch	1958	2.50	5.00	10.00
❑ 4126	Ther Hucklebuck/Better Loved You'll Never Be	1959	2.50	5.00	10.00

7-Inch Extended Plays

MERCURY

Number	Title (A Side/B Side)	Yr	VG	VG+	NM
❑ EP1-3061	Say It Isn't So/It Had to Be You//I'll Always Be in Love with You/How Long Has This Been Going On	195?	3.00	6.00	12.00
❑ EP1-3061 [PS]	Georgia Sings Oldies	195?	3.00	6.00	12.00
❑ EP1-3062	(contents unknown)	195?	3.00	6.00	12.00
❑ EP1-3062 [PS]	Her Nibs, Miss Georgia Gibbs	195?	3.00	6.00	12.00
❑ EP1-3082	(contents unknown)	195?	3.00	6.00	12.00
❑ EP1-3082 [PS]	Encores	195?	3.00	6.00	12.00
❑ EP1-3130	My Favorite Song/A Moth and a Flame//Seven Lonely Days/Sinner or Saint	195?	3.00	6.00	12.00
❑ EP1-3130 [PS]	For Gentlemen Only	195?	3.00	6.00	12.00
❑ EP1-3214	(contents unknown)	195?	3.00	6.00	12.00
❑ EP1-3214 [PS]	Bridge of Sighs	195?	3.00	6.00	12.00
❑ EP1-3226	(contents unknown)	195?	3.00	6.00	12.00
❑ EP1-3226 [PS]	Somebody Bad Stole De Wedding Bell	195?	3.00	6.00	12.00
❑ EP1-3241	(contents unknown)	195?	3.00	6.00	12.00
❑ EP1-3241 [PS]	Thunder and Lightning	195?	3.00	6.00	12.00
❑ EP1-3242	(contents unknown)	195?	3.00	6.00	12.00
❑ EP1-3242 [PS]	Kiss of Fire	195?	3.00	6.00	12.00
❑ EP1-3243	(contents unknown)	195?	3.00	6.00	12.00
❑ EP1-3243 [PS]	So Madly in Love	195?	3.00	6.00	12.00
❑ EP1-3266	(contents unknown)	195?	3.00	6.00	12.00
❑ EP1-3266 [PS]	After You've Gone	195?	3.00	6.00	12.00
❑ EP-1-4002	Tweedle Dee/You're Wrong, All Wrong//Melancholy Baby/Ballin' the Jack	195?	3.00	6.00	12.00
❑ EP-1-4002 [PS]	Tops in Pops	195?	3.00	6.00	12.00

ROYALE

Number	Title (A Side/B Side)	Yr	VG	VG+	NM
❑ EP 259	Ballin' the Jack/Old Man Mose//Wrap Your Troubles in Dreams/The One I Love	195?	5.00	10.00	20.00

—Red vinyl

Number	Title (A Side/B Side)	Yr	VG	VG+	NM
❑ EP 259 [PS]	Georgia Gibbs Sings	195?	5.00	10.00	20.00

GIBSON, BOBBY, AND THE VOYAGERS

GIBSON

Number	Title (A Side/B Side)	Yr	VG	VG+	NM
❑ 6003	B-52/Samoa	1959	12.50	25.00	50.00

GIBSON, DEBBIE

ATLANTIC

Number	Title (A Side/B Side)	Yr	VG	VG+	NM
❑ 87793	Anything Is Possible/So Close to Forever	1990	—	2.00	4.00
❑ 88885	No More Rhyme/Over the Wall	1989	—	—	3.00
❑ 88885 [PS]	No More Rhyme/Over the Wall	1989	—	—	3.00
❑ 88896	We Could Be Together/No More Rhyme	1989	—	—	3.00
❑ 88896 [PS]	We Could Be Together/No More Rhyme	1989	—	—	3.00
❑ 88919	Electric Youth/We Could Be Together	1989	—	—	3.00
❑ 88919 [PS]	Electric Youth/We Could Be Together	1989	—	—	3.00
❑ 88970	Lost in Your Eyes/Silence Speaks (A Thousand Words)	1989	—	—	3.00
❑ 88970 [PS]	Lost in Your Eyes/Silence Speaks (A Thousand Words)	1989	—	—	3.00
❑ 89034	Staying Together/Staying Together (Dub Edit)	1988	—	—	3.00
❑ 89034 [PS]	Staying Together/Staying Together (Dub Edit)	1988	3.00	6.00	12.00
❑ 89109	Foolish Beat/(Instrumental)	1988	—	—	3.00
❑ 89109 [PS]	Foolish Beat/(Instrumental)	1988	—	—	3.00
❑ 89129	Out of the Blue/Out of the Blue (Edited Dub)	1988	—	—	3.00
❑ 89129 [PS]	Out of the Blue/Out of the Blue (Edited Dub)	1988	—	—	3.00
❑ 89152	Red Hot/Make It My Night	1988	—	2.50	5.00

—B-side by Donna Allen

Number	Title (A Side/B Side)	Yr	VG	VG+	NM
❑ 89187	Shake Your Love/Shake Your Love (Bad Dub Version)	1987	—	—	3.00
❑ 89187 [PS]	Shake Your Love/Shake Your Love (Bad Dub Version)	1987	—	—	3.00
❑ 89322	Only in My Dreams/Only in My Dreams (Dub)	1986	—	2.00	4.00

—Original pressings do not have bar code on label

Number	Title (A Side/B Side)	Yr	VG	VG+	NM
❑ 89322	Only in My Dreams/Only in My Dreams (Dub)	1987	—	—	3.00

—With bar-coded label

Number	Title (A Side/B Side)	Yr	VG	VG+	NM
❑ 89322 [PS]	Only in My Dreams/Only in My Dreams (Dub)	1987	—	2.00	4.00

GIBSON, DON

Also see DOTTIE WEST.

ABC HICKORY

Number	Title (A Side/B Side)	Yr	VG	VG+	NM
❑ 54001	I'm All Wrapped Up in You/We Live in Two Different Worlds	1976	—	2.50	5.00
❑ 54010	Fan the Flame, Feed the Fire/Bringin' In the Georgia Mail	1977	—	2.50	5.00
❑ 54014	If You Ever Get to Houston (Look Me Down)/It's All Over	1977	—	2.50	5.00
❑ 54019	When Do We Stop Starting Over/Love Is Not the Way (You Told Me)	1977	—	2.50	5.00
❑ 54024	Starting All Over Again/I'd Rather Die Young (Than Grow Old Without You)	1978	—	2.50	5.00
❑ 54029	The Fool/Every Song I Sang Would Be Blue	1978	—	2.50	5.00
❑ 54036	Oh, Such a Stranger/I Love You Because	1978	—	2.50	5.00
❑ 54039	Any Day Now/Baby's Not Home	1978	—	2.50	5.00

COLUMBIA

Number	Title (A Side/B Side)	Yr	VG	VG+	NM
❑ 20999	No Shoulder to Cry On/We're Stepping Out	1952	5.00	10.00	20.00
❑ 21060	Sample Kisses/Let Me Stay in Your Arms	1952	5.00	10.00	20.00
❑ 21109	Just Walkin' in the Moonlight/I Just Love the Way You Tell a Lie	1953	5.00	10.00	20.00
❑ 21156	You Cast Me Out/Waitin' Down the Road	1953	5.00	10.00	20.00
❑ 21231	Symptoms of Love/Many Times I've Waited	1954	5.00	10.00	20.00
❑ 21281	Selfish with Your Kisses/Ice Cold Heart	1954	5.00	10.00	20.00

HICKORY

Number	Title (A Side/B Side)	Yr	VG	VG+	NM
❑ 1559	Don't Take All Your Loving/Pretending Every Day	1970	—	2.50	5.00
❑ 1571	A Perfect Mountain/Would You Believe	1970	—	2.50	5.00
❑ 1579	Someway/Comfort for Your Mind	1970	—	2.50	5.00
❑ 1588	Guess Away the Blues/I Wanna Live	1970	—	2.50	5.00
❑ 1598	(I Heard That) Lonesome Whistle/Window Shopping	1971	2.00	4.00	8.00
❑ 1614	Country Green/Move It On Over	1971	2.00	4.00	8.00
❑ 1623	Far, Far Away/What's Happened to Me	1972	2.00	4.00	8.00
❑ 1638	Woman (Sensuous Woman)/If You Want Me To I'll Go	1972	2.00	4.00	8.00
❑ 1651	Is This the Best I'm Gonna Feel/Watching It Go	1972	2.00	4.00	8.00
❑ 1661	If You're Goin' Girl/Lonesome Number One	1973	2.00	4.00	8.00
❑ 1671	Touch the Morning/Too Much to Know	1973	2.00	4.00	8.00

HICKORY/MGM

Number	Title (A Side/B Side)	Yr	VG	VG+	NM
❑ 301	Touch the Morning/Too Much to Know	1973	—	3.00	6.00
❑ 306	That's What I'll Do/Sweet Dreams	1973	—	3.00	6.00
❑ 312	Snap Your Fingers/Love Is a Lonesome Thing	1973	—	3.00	6.00
❑ 318	One Day at a Time/Rainbow Love	1974	—	3.00	6.00
❑ 327	Bring Back Your Love to Me/Drinking Champagne	1974	—	3.00	6.00
❑ 338	I'll Sing for You/Pocatello	1974	—	3.00	6.00
❑ 345	(There She Goes) I Wish Her Well/Funny Familiar Forgotten Feelings	1975	—	3.00	6.00
❑ 353	Don't Stop Loving Me/Somebody's Words	1975	—	3.00	6.00
❑ 361	I Don't Think I'll Ever (Get Over You)/It Can't Last Always	1975	—	3.00	6.00
❑ 365	You've Got to Stop Hurting Me, Darling/Blues in My Mind	1976	—	3.00	6.00
❑ 372	Doing My Time/The World Is Waiting for the Sunrise	1976	—	3.00	6.00

MCA

Number	Title (A Side/B Side)	Yr	VG	VG+	NM
❑ 41031	Forever One Day at a Time/Look Who's Blue	1979	—	2.00	4.00

MGM

Number	Title (A Side/B Side)	Yr	VG	VG+	NM
❑ 12109	Run Boy/I Must Forget You	1955	7.50	15.00	30.00
❑ 12194	Sweet Dreams/The Road of Life Alone	1956	7.50	15.00	30.00
❑ 12290	I Ain't Gonna Waste My Time/Ah-Ha	1956	10.00	20.00	40.00
❑ 12331	I Believed in You/What a Fool I Was to Fall	1956	7.50	15.00	30.00
❑ 12494	I Ain't a-Studying You Baby/It's Hoppin'	1957	10.00	20.00	40.00

RCA VICTOR

Number	Title (A Side/B Side)	Yr	VG	VG+	NM
❑ 37-7841	What About Me/The World Is Waiting for the Sunrise	1961	5.00	10.00	20.00

—"Compact Single 33" (small hole, plays at LP speed)

Number	Title (A Side/B Side)	Yr	VG	VG+	NM
❑ 47-4364	Red Lips, White Lies and Blue Hours/Just Let Me Love You	1951	6.25	12.50	25.00
❑ 47-4473	Dark Future/Blue Million Tears	1952	6.25	12.50	25.00
❑ 47-6860	I Can't Leave/I Love You Still	1957	5.00	10.00	20.00
❑ 47-6942	Everything Turns Out for the Best/Sittin' Here Cryin'	1957	5.00	10.00	20.00
❑ 47-7010	Blue Blue Day/Too Soon to Know	1957	3.75	7.50	15.00
❑ 47-7133	Oh Lonesome Me/I Can't Stop Lovin' You	1958	3.75	7.50	15.00
❑ 47-7330	Give Myself a Party/Look Who's Blue	1958	3.75	7.50	15.00
❑ 47-7437	Who Cares/A Stranger to Me	1959	3.75	7.50	15.00

Number	Title (A Side/B Side)	Yr	VG	VG+	NM
❑ 47-7505	Lonesome Old House/I Couldn't Care Less	1959	3.75	7.50	15.00
❑ 47-7566	Don't Tell Me Your Troubles/Heartbreak Avenue	1959	3.75	7.50	15.00
❑ 47-7629	I'm Movin' On/Big Hearted Man	1959	3.75	7.50	15.00
❑ 47-7690	Just One Time/I May Never Get to Heaven	1960	3.00	6.00	12.00
❑ 47-7762	Far, Far Away/A Legend in My Time	1960	3.00	6.00	12.00
❑ 47-7805	Sweet Dreams/The Same Street	1960	3.00	6.00	12.00
❑ 47-7841	What About Me/The World Is Waiting for the Sunrise	1961	3.00	6.00	12.00
❑ 47-7890	Sea of Heartbreak/I Think It's Best (To Forget Me)	1961	3.00	6.00	12.00
❑ 47-7959	Lonesome Number One/Same Old Trouble	1961	3.00	6.00	12.00
❑ 47-8017	I Can Mend Your Broken Heart/I Let Her Get Lonely	1962	2.50	5.00	10.00
❑ 47-8085	So How Come (No One Loves Me)/Baby We're Really in Love	1962	2.50	5.00	10.00
❑ 47-8085 [PS]	So How Come (No One Loves Me)/Baby We're Really in Love	1962	3.75	7.50	15.00
❑ 47-8144	Head Over Heels in Love with You/It Was Worth It All	1963	2.50	5.00	10.00
❑ 47-8144 [PS]	Head Over Heels in Love with You/It Was Worth It All	1963	3.75	7.50	15.00
❑ 47-8192	Anything New Gets Old (Except My Love for You)/After the Heartache	1963	2.50	5.00	10.00
❑ 47-8192 [PS]	Anything New Gets Old (Except My Love for You)/After the Heartache	1963	3.75	7.50	15.00
❑ 47-8367	Fireball Mail/Oh, Such a Stranger	1964	2.50	5.00	10.00
❑ 47-8456	Cause I Believe in You/A Love That Can't Be	1964	2.50	5.00	10.00
❑ 47-8589	Again/You're Going Away	1965	2.00	4.00	8.00
❑ 47-8678	Watch Where You're Going/There's a Big Wheel	1965	2.00	4.00	8.00
❑ 47-8732	A Born Loser/All the World Is Lonely Now	1965	2.00	4.00	8.00
❑ 47-8812	(Yes) I'm Hurting/My Whole World Is Hurt	1966	2.00	4.00	8.00
❑ 47-8975	Funny, Familiar, Forgotten, Feelings/Forget Me	1966	2.00	4.00	8.00
❑ 47-9177	Lost Highway/Around the Town	1967	2.00	4.00	8.00
❑ 47-9266	All My Love/No Doubt About It	1967	2.00	4.00	8.00
❑ 47-9395	Satisfied/Where No Man Stands Alone	1967	2.00	4.00	8.00
❑ 47-9460	Ashes of Love/Good Morning, Dear	1968	—	3.00	6.00
❑ 47-9563	It's a Long, Long Way to Georgia/Low and Lonely	1968	—	3.00	6.00
❑ 47-9663	Ever Changing Mind/Thoughts	1968	—	3.00	6.00
❑ 47-9906	Montego Bay/If My Heart Had Windows	1970	—	3.00	6.00
❑ 48-0424	I Love No One But You/Carolina Breakdown	1951	6.25	12.50	25.00
❑ 48-0460	Roses Are Red/Wiggle Wag	1951	6.25	12.50	25.00
❑ 61-7762 [S]	Far, Far Away/A Legend in My Time	1960	6.25	12.50	25.00
—"Living Stereo" (large hole, plays at 45 rpm)					
❑ 74-0143	Solitary/I Just Said Goodbye to My Dreams	1969	—	3.00	6.00
❑ 74-0219	I Will Always/Half As Much	1969	—	3.00	6.00
WARNER BROS.					
❑ 49193	Sweet Sensuous Sensations/Stranger to Me	1980	—	2.00	4.00
❑ 49504	I'd Be Crazy Over You/Somewhere Between Yesterday	1980	—	2.00	4.00
❑ 49602	Love Fires/Come Back and Love Me	1980	—	2.00	4.00
7-Inch Extended Plays					
COLUMBIA					
❑ B-2146	(contents unknown)	1957	5.00	10.00	20.00
❑ B-2146 [PS]	Don Gibson	1957	5.00	10.00	20.00
RCA VICTOR					
❑ EPA-4323	(contents unknown)	1958	3.75	7.50	15.00
❑ EPA-4323 [PS]	Blue, Blue Day	1958	3.75	7.50	15.00
❑ EPA-4335	(contents unknown)	1958	3.75	7.50	15.00
❑ EPA-4335 [PS]	That Lonesome Valley	1958	3.75	7.50	15.00
❑ EPA-5114	Oh Lonesome Me/Look Who's Blue//Who Cares/Blue, Blue Day	1959	3.75	7.50	15.00
❑ EPA-5114 [PS]	Blue and Lonesome	1959	3.75	7.50	15.00

GIBSON, DON, AND SUE THOMPSON

Also see each artist's individual listings.

Number	Title (A Side/B Side)	Yr	VG	VG+	NM
HICKORY					
❑ 1607	The Two of Us Together/Oh Yes, I Love You	1971	2.00	4.00	8.00
❑ 1629	Did You Ever Think/Love Garden	1972	2.00	4.00	8.00
❑ 1646	I Think They Call It Love/Over There's the Door	1972	2.00	4.00	8.00
❑ 1654	Cause I Love You/My Tears Don't Show	1972	2.00	4.00	8.00
❑ 1665	Go with Me/Two of Us Together	1973	2.00	4.00	8.00
HICKORY/MGM					
❑ 303	Warm Love/Fly the Friendly Skies with Jesus	1973	—	3.00	6.00
❑ 324	Good Old Fashioned Country Love/Ages and Ages Ago	1974	—	3.00	6.00
❑ 342	No One Will Ever Know/Put It Off Till Tomorrow	1975	—	3.00	6.00
❑ 350	Oh, How Love Changes/Sweet and Tender Times	1975	—	3.00	6.00
❑ 360	Maybe Tomorrow/I Can't Tell My Heart That	1975	—	3.00	6.00
❑ 367	Get Ready, Here I Come/Once More	1976	—	3.00	6.00
❑ 373	You've Still Got a Place in My Heart/Let's Get Together	1976	—	3.00	6.00

GIBSON, JILL

For a very brief time in late 1966, she was a member of THE MAMAS AND THE PAPAS.

Number	Title (A Side/B Side)	Yr	VG	VG+	NM
IMPERIAL					
❑ 66068	It's as Easy as 1,2,3/Jilly's Flip Side	1964	15.00	30.00	60.00
—Produced by Jan Berry					

GIBSON, STEVE, AND THE RED CAPS

Number	Title (A Side/B Side)	Yr	VG	VG+	NM
ABC-PARAMOUNT					
❑ 9702	Love Me Tenderly/Rock and Roll Stomp	1956	5.00	10.00	20.00
❑ 9750	Write to Me/Cuacho Serenade	1956	5.00	10.00	20.00
❑ 9796	You've Got Me Dizzy/You May Not Love Me	1957	5.00	10.00	20.00
❑ 9856	Silhouettes/Flamingo	1957	5.00	10.00	20.00
❑ 10105	I Went to Your Wedding/Together	1960	3.75	7.50	15.00
BAND BOX					
❑ 325	No More/Peppermint Baby	1962	3.00	6.00	12.00
HUNT					
❑ 326	Bless You/Cheryl Lee	1959	3.75	7.50	15.00
❑ 330	Where Are You/San Antonio Rose	1959	3.75	7.50	15.00
JAY DEE					
❑ 796	It Hurts Me But I Like It/Ouch!	1954	10.00	20.00	40.00
MERCURY					
❑ 5380	I'll Never Love Anyone Else/(B-side unknown)	1950	37.50	75.00	150.00
❑ 8146	Blueberry Hill/I Love You	1951	20.00	40.00	80.00
—78 released in 1949					
❑ 70389	Wedding Bells (Are Breaking Up That Old Gang of Mine)/Second Hand Romance	1954	12.50	25.00	50.00
RCA VICTOR					
❑ 47-3986	The Thing/Am I To Blame?	1950	15.00	30.00	60.00
❑ 47-4076	Did Ya Eat Yet, Joe/$3.98	1951	12.50	25.00	50.00
❑ 47-4294	Shame/Boogie Woogie on Saturday Night	1951	12.50	25.00	50.00
❑ 47-4670	Two Little Kisses/I May Hate Myself in the Morning	1952	10.00	20.00	40.00
❑ 47-4835	I Went to Your Wedding/Wait	1952	10.00	20.00	40.00
❑ 47-5013	Why Don't You Love Me/Truthfully	1952	10.00	20.00	40.00
❑ 47-5130	Big Game Hunter/Do I, Do I, Do I	1953	10.00	20.00	40.00
❑ 47-6096	Nuff of That Stuff/Feelin' Kinda Happy	1955	5.00	10.00	20.00
—B-side by Damita Jo					
❑ 47-6345	How I Cry/Bobbin'	1955	5.00	10.00	20.00
❑ 50-0127	I'm to Blame/Sidewalk Shuffle	1951	15.00	30.00	60.00
❑ 50-0138	Would I Mind/When You Come Back to Me	1951	15.00	30.00	60.00
7-Inch Extended Plays					
MERCURY					
❑ EP1-3215	(contents unknown)	1952	50.00	100.00	200.00
❑ EP1-3215 [PS]	Blueberry Hill	1952	50.00	100.00	200.00

GIGOLOS, THE

More than one group.

Number	Title (A Side/B Side)	Yr	VG	VG+	NM
BROADWAY					
❑ 1000	Movin' Out/Black and Blue	1961	7.50	15.00	30.00
CHESS					
❑ 1715	Luna Rock/La Companola	1959	7.50	15.00	30.00
DAYNITE					
❑ 1	Sqingin' Saints/Night Crawlers	1960	12.50	25.00	50.00
ENTERPRISE					
❑ 5000	Don't You Just Know It/Movin' Out	1965	3.75	7.50	15.00

GILLESPIE, DANA

Number	Title (A Side/B Side)	Yr	VG	VG+	NM
JERDEN					
❑ 764	Donna Donna/It's No Use Saying If	1965	3.00	6.00	12.00

GILLESPIE, DARLENE

Number	Title (A Side/B Side)	Yr	VG	VG+	NM
CORAL					
❑ 62178	I Loved, I Laughed, I Cried/Ring the Bell, Beat the Drum	1960	3.75	7.50	15.00
DISNEYLAND					
❑ F-050	Sittin' in the Balcony/Too Much	1957	7.50	15.00	30.00
❑ F-051	Butterfly/Seven Days	1957	7.50	15.00	30.00
❑ F-052	I've Never Been in Love/Rock-a-Billy	1957	7.50	15.00	30.00
❑ F-060	Together Time/Now to Sleep	1957	6.25	12.50	25.00
—A-side with Jimmie Dodd					
❑ F-061	Break of Day/Perri	1957	6.25	12.50	25.00
—With Jimmie Dodd					

GILLEY, MICKEY

Also see RAY CHARLES.

Number	Title (A Side/B Side)	Yr	VG	VG+	NM
ACT 1					
❑ 101	Say No More/Make Me Believe	1966	2.50	5.00	10.00
AIRBORNE					
❑ 10002	I'm Your Puppet/Don't Show Me Your Memories (And I Won't Show You Mine)	1988	—	2.00	4.00
❑ 10008	She Reminded Me of You/Easy Climb	1988	—	2.00	4.00
❑ 10016	You Still Got a Way with My Heart/It's Killing Me to Watch Love Die	1989	—	2.00	4.00
❑ 75740	There I've Said It Again/It's Killing Me to Watch Love Die	1989	—	2.00	4.00
ASTRO					
❑ 102	Down the Line/Lonely Wine	196?	25.00	50.00	100.00
❑ 103	Is It Wrong/Turn Around	196?	6.25	12.50	25.00
❑ 104	Night After Night/Susie Q	196?	6.25	12.50	25.00
❑ 106	Lotta Lovin'/I Miss You So	196?	6.25	12.50	25.00
❑ 110	A Certain Smile/If I Didn't Have a Dime	196?	6.25	12.50	25.00
❑ 112	Little Egypt/If I Didn't Have a Dime	196?	6.25	12.50	25.00
❑ 5002	Everything Is Yours That Once Was Mine/Don't Throw a Good Love Away	1971	2.00	4.00	8.00
❑ 5003	You Touch My Life/Toast to Mary Ann	1971	2.00	4.00	8.00
❑ 10003	Room Full of Roses/She Called Me Baby	1973	2.50	5.00	10.00
DARYL					
❑ 101	What Have I Done/Three's a Crowd	1963	2.50	5.00	10.00
DOT					
❑ 15706	Call Me Shorty/Come On Baby	1958	50.00	100.00	200.00
EPIC					
❑ AE7 1356 [DJ]	Mickey Gilley's Christmas Medley (2:51)/Mickey Gilley's Christmas Medley (3:34)	1981	2.50	5.00	10.00
❑ AE7 1774	Home to Texas for Christmas/I'm Spending Christmas with You	1982	—	2.50	5.00
❑ 02172	You Don't Know Me/Juke Box Argument	1981	—	—	3.00
❑ 02578	Lonely Nights/We've Watched Another Evening Waste Away	1981	—	—	3.00
❑ 02774	Tears of the Lonely/Ladies Night	1982	—	—	3.00
❑ 03055	Put Your Dreams Away/If I Can't Hold Her on the Outside	1982	—	—	3.00
❑ 03326	Talk to Me/Honky Tonkin' (I Guess I Done Some)	1982	—	—	3.00
❑ 03332	Blue Christmas/Jingle Bell Rock	1982	—	2.00	4.00
❑ 03783	Fool for Your Love/Shakin' a Heartache	1983	—	—	3.00
❑ 04018	Your Love Shines Through/Wish You Were Mine Again	1983	—	—	3.00
❑ 04269	You've Really Got a Hold on Me/Giving Up Getting Over You	1983	—	—	3.00
❑ 04563	Too Good to Stop Now/A Shoulder to Cry On	1984	—	—	3.00
❑ 04746	I'm the One Mama Warned You About/You Can Lie to Me Tonight	1985	—	—	3.00

Number	Title (A Side/B Side)	Yr	VG	VG+	NM
❑ 05460	You've Got Something on Your Mind/I Feel Good About Lovin' You	1985	—	—	3.00
❑ 05744	Your Memory Ain't What It Used to Be/Lonely Nights, Lonely Heartaches	1985	—	—	3.00
❑ 05895	Play, Ruby, Play/After She's Gone	1986	—	—	3.00
❑ 06184	Doo-Wah Days/After She's Gone	1986	—	—	3.00
❑ 07009	Full Grown Fool/To My One and Only	1987	—	—	3.00
❑ 50580	Here Comes the Hurt Again/I Hate It, But I Drink It Anyway	1978	—	2.00	4.00
❑ 50631	The Song We Made Love To/Memphis Memories	1978	—	2.00	4.00
❑ 50672	Just Long Enough to Say Goodbye/Tying One On	1979	—	2.00	4.00
❑ 50740	My Silver Lining/Picture of Our Love	1979	—	2.00	4.00
❑ 50801	A Little Getting Used To/Can't Nobody Love You	1979	—	2.00	4.00
❑ 50876	True Love Ways/The More I Turn the Bottle	1980	—	2.00	4.00
❑ 50940	That's All That Matters/The Blues Don't Care Who's Got 'Em	1980	—	2.00	4.00
❑ 50973	A Headache Tomorrow (Or a Heartache Tonight)/Million Dollar Memories	1981	—	2.00	4.00
❑ 51003	Mamas Don't Let Your Babies Grow Up to Be Cowboys/Cotton-Eyed Joe	1981	—	2.00	4.00
—A-side with Johnny Lee; B-side by Bayou City Beats					
FULL MOON/ASYLUM					
❑ 46640	Stand By Me/Cotton Eyed Joe	1980	—	2.00	4.00
—B-side by the Unstrung Heroes					
❑ 46640 [PS]	Stand By Me/Cotton Eyed Joe	1980	—	2.50	5.00
—"Urban Cowboy" sleeve (John Travolta pictured)					
GOLDBAND					
❑ 1223	I Ain't Goin' Home/No Greater Love	1964	2.50	5.00	10.00
GRT					
❑ 27	I'm Nobody Today (But I Was Somebody Last Night)/She's Not Yours Anymore	1970	2.00	4.00	8.00
❑ 45	Time to Tell Another Lie/Because I Love You	1970	2.00	4.00	8.00
KHOURY'S					
❑ 712	Drive In Movie/Give Me a Chance	1959	75.00	150.00	300.00
LYNN					
❑ 503	Your Selfish Pride/Everything Turned to Love	1960	6.25	12.50	25.00
❑ 508	My Baby's Been Cheating Again/Turn Around	1960	6.25	12.50	25.00
❑ 512	Slippin' and Slidin'/End of the Line	1961	6.25	12.50	25.00
❑ 515	Long Lonely Nights/My Babe	1961	6.25	12.50	25.00
MINOR					
❑ 106	Oo-Ee Baby/Tell Me Why	1957	150.00	300.00	600.00
PAULA					
❑ 256	Make Me Believe/Say No to You	1966	2.50	5.00	10.00
❑ 269	A World of My Own/Love in the Want Ads	1967	2.00	4.00	8.00
❑ 280	Blame It on the Moon/Sounds Like Trouble	1967	2.00	4.00	8.00
❑ 281	One Way Street/Tears in My Eyes	1967	2.00	4.00	8.00
❑ 301	A New Way to Live/That Heart Belongs to Me	1968	2.00	4.00	8.00
❑ 402	Night After Night/I'm to Blame	1974	—	2.50	5.00
❑ 441	She Cheats on Me/You Can Count Me Missing	1983	—	2.00	4.00
❑ 1200	Now I Can Live Again/Without You	1968	2.00	4.00	8.00
❑ 1208	She's Still Got a Hold on You/There's No One Like You	1969	2.00	4.00	8.00
❑ 1215	Watching the Way/It's Just a Matter of Making Up My Mind	1969	2.00	4.00	8.00
PLAYBOY					
❑ 5807	Honky Tonk Memories/Five Foot Two, Eyes of Blue	1977	—	2.00	4.00
❑ 5818	Chains of Love/No. 1 Rock 'n Roll C & W Boogie Blues Man	1977	—	2.00	4.00
❑ 5826	The Power of Positive Drinkin'/Playing My Old Piano	1978	—	2.00	4.00
❑ 6004	I Overlooked an Orchid/Swinging Doors	1974	—	2.50	5.00
❑ 6015	City Lights/Fraulein	1974	—	2.50	5.00
❑ 6031	Window Up Above/I'm Movin' On	1975	—	2.50	5.00
❑ 6041	Bouquet of Roses/If You Were Mine to Lose	1975	—	2.50	5.00
❑ 6045	Roll You Like a Wheel/Let's Sing a Song Together	1975	—	2.50	5.00
—With Barbi Benton					
❑ 6045 [PS]	Roll You Like a Wheel/Let's Sing a Song Together	1975	—	3.00	6.00
—With Barbi Benton					
❑ 6055	Overnight Sensation/I'll Sail My Ship Alone	1975	—	2.50	5.00
❑ 6063	Don't All the Girls Get Prettier at Closing Time/Where Do You Go to Lose a Heartache	1976	—	2.50	5.00
❑ 6075	Bring It On Home to Me/How's My Ex Treating You	1976	—	2.50	5.00
❑ 6089	Lawdy Miss Clawdy/What Is It	1976	—	2.50	5.00
❑ 6095	Pretty Paper/Lonely Christmas Call	1976	—	2.50	5.00
❑ 6100	She's Pulling Me Back Again/Sweet Mama Goodtime	1977	—	2.50	5.00
❑ 50056	Room Full of Roses/She Called Me Baby	1974	—	2.50	5.00
POTOMAC					
❑ 901	Is It Wrong/No Greater Love	1960	3.75	7.50	15.00
PRINCESS					
❑ 4004	Drive-In Movie/Your First Time	1962	10.00	20.00	40.00
❑ 4006	Wild Side of Life/Caught in the Middle	1962	10.00	20.00	40.00
❑ 4011	I'll Keep On Dancing/I'll Keep On Searching	196?	3.75	7.50	15.00
❑ 4015	A World of My Own/I Still Care	196?	3.75	7.50	15.00
RESCO					
❑ 617	You Touch My Life/Toast to Mary Ann	1974	—	3.00	6.00
❑ 622	She Gives Me Love/Quittin' Time	1974	—	3.00	6.00
REX					
❑ 1007	Grapevine/That's How It's Got to Be	1959	7.50	15.00	30.00
SABRA					
❑ 518	Valley of Tears/I Need Your Love	1961	5.00	10.00	20.00
SAN					
❑ 1513	I Ain't No Bo Diddley/I'm to Blame	1966	2.50	5.00	10.00
SUPREME					
❑ 101	Now That I Have You/Happy Birthday	1962	3.75	7.50	15.00
❑ 102	Everything Turned to Love/No One Will Ever Know	1962	3.75	7.50	15.00

Number	Title (A Side/B Side)	Yr	VG	VG+	NM
TCF HALL					
❑ 126	When Two Worlds Collide/Let's Hurt Together	1965	2.00	4.00	8.00

GILMAN, BILLY

Number	Title (A Side/B Side)	Yr	VG	VG+	NM
EPIC					
❑ 34 79527	One Voice/Oklahoma	2000	—	2.00	4.00

GILMER, JIMMY

Also see THE FIREBALLS.

Number	Title (A Side/B Side)	Yr	VG	VG+	NM
ATCO					
❑ 6583	Three Squares (And a Place to Lay Your Head)/Baby	1968	2.00	4.00	8.00
❑ 6716	Sugar in the Woods/Model Child	1969	2.00	4.00	8.00
DECCA					
❑ 30942	Look Alive/Because I Need You	1959	6.25	12.50	25.00
HAMILTON					
❑ 50037	Won't Be Long/I'm Gonna Go Walkin'	1960	3.75	7.50	15.00
WARWICK					
❑ 592	Good Good Lovin'/Do You Think	1960	5.00	10.00	20.00

GILMER, JIMMY, AND THE FIREBALLS

See THE FIREBALLS.

GILMORE, JIMMIE DALE

Number	Title (A Side/B Side)	Yr	VG	VG+	NM
HIGHTONE					
❑ 504	White Freight Liner Blues/Trying to Get to You	1988	—	2.50	5.00
❑ 510	Honky Tonk Song/(B-side unknown)	1989	—	2.50	5.00

GILMOUR, DAVID

Also see PINK FLOYD.

Number	Title (A Side/B Side)	Yr	VG	VG+	NM
COLUMBIA					
❑ 04378	Blue Light/Cruise	1984	—	—	3.00
—Of Pink Floyd					
❑ 04490	Love on the Air/Near the End	1984	—	—	3.00
❑ 10803	There's No Way Out of Here/Deafinitely	1978	—	2.50	5.00

GIN BLOSSOMS

Number	Title (A Side/B Side)	Yr	VG	VG+	NM
A&M					
❑ 31458 0418 7	Found Out About You/Hey Jealousy	1993	—	2.50	5.00
❑ 31458 0862 7	Allison Road/Until I Fall Away	1994	—	—	3.00
❑ 31458 1380 7	Follow You Down/Til I Hear It from You	1996	—	—	3.00
❑ 31458 1672 7	As Long As It Matters/Allison Road (Live)	1996	—	—	3.00
❑ 74021 8735 7	Hey Jealousy/Found Out About You	1996	—	—	3.00
—Oldies reissue					

GINGER

Also see GINGER AND THE SNAPS; THE HONEYS.

Number	Title (A Side/B Side)	Yr	VG	VG+	NM
TITAN					
❑ 1717	Dry Tears/Spare Time	1961	25.00	50.00	100.00

GINGER AND THE CHIFFONS

Number	Title (A Side/B Side)	Yr	VG	VG+	NM
GROOVE					
❑ 58-0003	She/Where Were You Last Night	1963	7.50	15.00	30.00

GINGER AND THE SNAPS

Also see GINGER.

Number	Title (A Side/B Side)	Yr	VG	VG+	NM
MGM					
❑ 13413	Growing Up Is Hard to Do/Seven Days in September	1965	37.50	75.00	150.00
TORE					
❑ 1008	Love Me the Way That I Love You/Truly	1961	18.75	37.50	75.00

GINGER-SNAPS, THE

Number	Title (A Side/B Side)	Yr	VG	VG+	NM
DUNHILL					
❑ 4003	The Sh-Down-Down Song/I've Got Faith in Him	1965	5.00	10.00	20.00

GINO AND THE DELLS

Number	Title (A Side/B Side)	Yr	VG	VG+	NM
GOLDEN CREST					
❑ 567	Altar of Dreams/Baby Don't Go Now	1962	75.00	150.00	300.00
❑ 576	We'll Make It Someday/I'm a Boy in Love	1963	10.00	20.00	40.00
❑ 581	It's Only a Paper Moon/Home Sweet Home	1963	10.00	20.00	40.00

GIORDANO, LOU

Number	Title (A Side/B Side)	Yr	VG	VG+	NM
BRUNSWICK					
❑ 55115	Stay Close to Me/Don'Cha Know	1959	400.00	800.00	1200.
—With Buddy Holly on guitar					

GIRLFRIENDS, THE

Number	Title (A Side/B Side)	Yr	VG	VG+	NM
COLPIX					
❑ 712	My One and Only Jimmy Boy/For My Sake	1963	5.00	10.00	20.00
❑ 744	Baby Don't Cry/I Don't Believe in You	1964	5.00	10.00	20.00
MELIC					
❑ 4125	No More Tears/I Want to Be Happy	1963	3.75	7.50	15.00
PIONEER					
❑ 71833	Four Shy Girls (In Their Itsy Bitsy Teeny Weeny Yellow Polka Dot Bikinis)/Jackie	1961	5.00	10.00	20.00

GIRLS, THE

Two different groups?

Number	Title (A Side/B Side)	Yr	VG	VG+	NM
20TH CENTURY FOX					
❑ 6651	Way, Way Out/Modesty Blaise	1966	5.00	10.00	20.00
CAPITOL					
❑ 5528	My Baby/My Love	1965	5.00	10.00	20.00
❑ 5675	Chico's Girl/The Dumb Song	1966	5.00	10.00	20.00
SCEPTER					
❑ 12242	Perfect Love/Mr. Poster	1969	2.00	4.00	8.00

GLAD, THE

Number	Title (A Side/B Side)	Yr	VG	VG+	NM
ABC					
❑ 11163	Johnny Silver's Ride/Love Needs the World	1969	3.00	6.00	12.00
EQUINOX					
❑ 70004	See What You Mean/(B-side unknown)	1968	5.00	10.00	20.00
❑ 70006	A New Tomorrow/Pickin' Up the Pieces	1968	5.00	10.00	20.00

GLADIATORS, THE

Number	Title (A Side/B Side)	Yr	VG	VG+	NM
DIG					
❑ 135	Girl of My Heart/My Baby Doll	1957	75.00	150.00	300.00

GLADIOLAS, THE

Evolved into MAURICE WILLIAMS AND THE ZODIACS.

Number	Title (A Side/B Side)	Yr	VG	VG+	NM
EXCELLO					
❑ 2101	Little Darlin'/Sweetheart, Please Don't Go	1957	18.75	37.50	75.00
❑ 2110	Run, Run, Little Joe/Comin' Home to You	1957	12.50	25.00	50.00
❑ 2120	Hey Little Girl/I Wanta Know	1957	12.50	25.00	50.00
❑ 2136	Shoop Shoop/Say You'll Be Mine	1958	12.50	25.00	50.00

GLASS HARP

Christian rock pioneer Phil Keaggy was in this group.

Number	Title (A Side/B Side)	Yr	VG	VG+	NM
DECCA					
❑ 32830	Children's Fantasy/Village Queen	1971	2.50	5.00	10.00
❑ 32915	The Answer/Just Always	1972	2.50	5.00	10.00
❑ 32995	La De Da/(B-side unknown)	1972	2.50	5.00	10.00

GLEEMS, THE

Number	Title (A Side/B Side)	Yr	VG	VG+	NM
PARKWAY					
❑ 893	Sandra Baby/You Are the One	1964	5.00	10.00	20.00

GLENN, GLEN

Number	Title (A Side/B Side)	Yr	VG	VG+	NM
DORE					
❑ 523	Goofin' Around/Susie Green from Abilene	1959	3.75	7.50	15.00
ERA					
❑ 1061	Everybody's Movin'/I'm Glad My Baby's Gone	1957	15.00	30.00	60.00
❑ 1074	One Cup of Coffee/Laurie Ann	1958	12.50	25.00	50.00

GLENN, LLOYD

Number	Title (A Side/B Side)	Yr	VG	VG+	NM
ALADDIN					
❑ 3268	Nite Flite/Still Waters	1954	6.25	12.50	25.00
❑ 3288	Footloose/Glen's Glide	1955	6.25	12.50	25.00
❑ 3307	Sunrise/Tiddly Winks	1955	6.25	12.50	25.00
❑ 3327	Southbound Special/Blue Ivories	1956	5.00	10.00	20.00
❑ 3346	After Hours (Part 1)/After Hours (Part 2)	1956	5.00	10.00	20.00
❑ 3353	Chica-Boo/Old Time Shuffle	1957	5.00	10.00	20.00
❑ 3378	The Vamp/Ballroom Shuffle	1957	5.00	10.00	20.00
❑ 3400	Hyde Park/Love for Sale	1957	5.00	10.00	20.00
❑ 3407	Cute-Tee/Black Fantasy	1958	5.00	10.00	20.00
❑ 3446	Petite Fleur/Honky Tonk Train	1959	3.75	7.50	15.00
❑ 3459	Long Gone (Part 1)/Long Gone (Part 2)	1959	3.75	7.50	15.00
HOLLYWOOD					
❑ 1021	Merry Christmas Baby/Sleigh Ride	1954	5.00	10.00	20.00
—B-side by Charles Brown; red label					
❑ 1021	Merry Christmas Baby/Sleigh Ride	196?	2.00	4.00	8.00
—B-side by Charles Brown; color label					
❑ 1021	Merry Christmas Baby/Sleigh Ride	197?	—	2.50	5.00
—B-side by Charles Brown; black label					
❑ 1028	Chica-Boo/Old Time Shuffle	1954	6.25	12.50	25.00
❑ 1033	Sleigh Ride/China Doll	1954	6.25	12.50	25.00
IMPERIAL					
❑ 5839	Twistville/Young Date	1962	3.00	6.00	12.00
SWING TIME					
❑ 254	Chica-Boo/Jungle Town Jubilee	1951	7.50	15.00	30.00
❑ 271	Sleigh Ride/Savage Boy	1951	7.50	15.00	30.00
❑ 277	Day Break Stomp/Jungle Twilight	1952	7.50	15.00	30.00
❑ 278	Cute-Tee/Rhumba	1952	7.50	15.00	30.00
❑ 292	After Hours/Yancey Special	1952	7.50	15.00	30.00
❑ 293	Honky Tonk Train/Pine Top Boogie Woogie	1952	7.50	15.00	30.00
❑ 296	Angora/Cuba Doll	1952	7.50	15.00	30.00
❑ 311	Boogie Woogie on St. Louis Blues/Ugh	1953	7.50	15.00	30.00
❑ 324	Night Time/It Moves Me	1953	7.50	15.00	30.00
❑ 336	Not the Girl for Me/Black Fantasy	1954	7.50	15.00	30.00

GLITTER, GARY

Number	Title (A Side/B Side)	Yr	VG	VG+	NM
ARISTA					
❑ 0173	I Love You Love Me Love/Hands Up! It's a Stick-Up	1976	—	2.50	5.00
BELL					
❑ 45237	Rock and Roll, Part 2/Rock and Roll, Part 1	1972	—	3.00	6.00
❑ 45276	I Didn't Know I Loved You (Till I Saw You Rock and Roll)/Shakey Sue	1972	—	2.50	5.00
❑ 45326	Do You Wanna Touch Me (Oh Yeah)/I Would If I Could But I Can't	1973	—	2.50	5.00
❑ 45345	Baby Please Don't Go/I.O.U.	1973	—	2.50	5.00
❑ 45375	Come On, Come In/Happy Birthday	1973	—	2.50	5.00
❑ 45398	(I'm the) Leader of the Gang (I Am)/(B-side unknown)	1973	—	2.50	5.00
❑ 45438	I Love You Love Me Love/(B-side unknown)	1974	—	2.50	5.00
DECCA					
❑ 32714	Goodbye Seattle/Wait for Me	1970	3.75	7.50	15.00
—As "Paul Raven"					
TOMMY BOY					
❑ 639	Rock 'N' Roll Part 2...The Hey Song (same on both sides)	1995	—	—	3.00
—Original recording with overdubbed crowd sounds					

GLOBETROTTERS, THE

Number	Title (A Side/B Side)	Yr	VG	VG+	NM
BUDDAH					
❑ 309	Don't Rock the Boat/Hatfield Small	1972	2.50	5.00	10.00
KIRSHNER					
❑ 63-5006	Cheer Me Up/Gravy	1970	3.00	6.00	12.00
❑ 63-5006 [PS]	Cheer Me Up/Gravy	1970	3.75	7.50	15.00
❑ 63-5008	Rainy Day Bells/Meadowlark	1970	3.75	7.50	15.00
❑ 63-5012	Duke of Earl/Everybody's Got Hot Pants	1971	3.00	6.00	12.00
❑ 63-5016	Everybody Needs Love/ESP	1971	3.00	6.00	12.00

GLORIES, THE

Number	Title (A Side/B Side)	Yr	VG	VG+	NM
DATE					
❑ 1553	I Stand Accused (Of Loving You)/Wish They Could Write a Song	1967	2.50	5.00	10.00
❑ 1571	Give Me My Freedom/Security	1967	6.25	12.50	25.00
❑ 1579	Sing Me a Love Song/Ooh, That's Love, Baby	1967	6.25	12.50	25.00
❑ 1593	Stand By (I'm Coming Home)/My Sweet, Sweet Baby	1968	6.25	12.50	25.00
❑ 1593 [PS]	Stand By (I'm Coming Home)/My Sweet, Sweet Baby	1968	12.50	25.00	50.00
❑ 1615	I Worship You Baby/Don't Dial My Number	1968	12.50	25.00	50.00
❑ 1622	No News/Oh Baby That's Love	1968	6.25	12.50	25.00
❑ 1636	Try a Little Tenderness/There He Is	1969	6.25	12.50	25.00
❑ 1647	Don't Make the Good Girls Go Bad/The Dark End of the Street	1969	5.00	10.00	20.00

GLORYTONES, THE

Number	Title (A Side/B Side)	Yr	VG	VG+	NM
EPIC					
❑ 9243	You Only Came Back to Hurt Me/Was That the Right Thing to Do	1957	10.00	20.00	40.00

GLOWTONES, THE

Number	Title (A Side/B Side)	Yr	VG	VG+	NM
ATLANTIC					
❑ 1156	The Girl I Love/Ping Pong	1957	—	—	—
—Only known on 78 rpm; 45 rpm release was on EastWest 101					
EASTWEST					
❑ 101	The Girl I Love/Ping Pong	1957	7.50	15.00	30.00

GO-GO'S

Also see BELINDA CARLISLE; JANE WIEDLIN.

Number	Title (A Side/B Side)	Yr	VG	VG+	NM
I.R.S.					
❑ 8001 [PD]	We Got the Beat/Our Lips Are Sealed	1982	2.50	5.00	10.00
—7-inch picture disc					
❑ 8690	Our Lips Are Sealed/We Got the Beat	198?	—	—	3.00
—Amnesia Series reissue					
❑ 8691	Vacation/Cool Jerk	198?	—	—	3.00
—Reissue					
❑ 9901	Our Lips Are Sealed/Surfing and Spying	1981	—	—	3.00
❑ 9901 [PS]	Our Lips Are Sealed/Surfing and Spying	1981	—	3.00	6.00
❑ 9903	We Got the Beat/Can't Stop the World	1982	—	—	3.00
❑ 9903 [PS]	We Got the Beat/Can't Stop the World	1982	—	—	3.00
❑ 9907	Vacation/Beatnik Beach	1982	—	—	3.00
❑ 9907 [PS]	Vacation/Beatnik Beach	1982	—	—	3.00
❑ 9910	Get Up and Go/Speeding	1982	—	—	3.00
❑ 9910 [PS]	Get Up and Go/Speeding	1982	—	—	3.00
❑ 9911	This Old Feeling/It's Everything But Partytime	1982	—	—	3.00
❑ 9911 [PS]	This Old Feeling/It's Everything But Partytime	1982	—	—	3.00
—Die-cut "Go-Go's" sleeve (yellow)					
❑ 9926	Head Over Heels/Good for Gone	1984	—	—	3.00
❑ 9926 [PS]	Head Over Heels/Good for Gone	1984	—	—	3.00
❑ 9928	Turn to You/I'm With You	1984	—	—	3.00
❑ 9928 [PS]	Turn to You/I'm With You	1984	—	—	3.00
❑ 9933	Yes or No/Mercenary	1984	—	—	3.00
❑ S7-18490	Good Girl/The Whole World Lost Its Head	1995	—	—	3.00

GO-GO'S, THE

Number	Title (A Side/B Side)	Yr	VG	VG+	NM
RCA VICTOR					
❑ 47-8370	Lonely Girl/Chicken of the Sea	1964	3.75	7.50	15.00
❑ 47-8435	The Wild One/Saturday's Hero	1964	7.50	15.00	30.00

GODDARD, GEOFF

Number	Title (A Side/B Side)	Yr	VG	VG+	NM
LAWN					
❑ 235	Walk With My Angel/Sky Men	1964	3.00	6.00	12.00

GODLEY AND CREME

Also see 10CC.

Number	Title (A Side/B Side)	Yr	VG	VG+	NM
MERCURY					
❑ 73965	Five O'Clock in the Morning/The Flood	1977	—	2.50	5.00
—As "Lol Creme and Kevin Godley"					
MIRAGE					
❑ 4036 [DJ]	Wedding Bells (same on both sides)	1982	—	2.00	4.00
—May be promo only					
❑ 99587	Wedding Bells/Lonnie	1985	—	—	3.00
POLYDOR					
❑ 880786-7	Cry/Love Bombs	1985	—	—	3.00
❑ 880786-7 [PS]	Cry/Love Bombs	1985	—	2.00	4.00

GODZ, THE

Number	Title (A Side/B Side)	Yr	VG	VG+	NM
ESP-DISK'					
❑ 4503	Lay in the Sun/I Want a Word with You	1966	2.50	5.00	10.00

GOINS, HERBIE, AND THE NIGHT-RIDERS

Number	Title (A Side/B Side)	Yr	VG	VG+	NM
CAPITOL					
❑ 5978	Coming Home to You/The Incredible Miss Brown	1967	2.50	5.00	10.00

GOLD BUGS, THE

Number	Title (A Side/B Side)	Yr	VG	VG+	NM
CORAL					
❑ 62453	Stop That Wedding/It's So Nice	1965	10.00	20.00	40.00

GOLDBERG, BARRY

Also see GOLDBERG-MILLER BLUES BAND.

Number	Title (A Side/B Side)	Yr	VG	VG+	NM
BUDDAH					
❑ 59	Sittin' in Circles/Hole in My Pocket	1968	2.50	5.00	10.00
❑ 103	Jimi the Fox/On the Road Again	1969	2.50	5.00	10.00
EPIC					
❑ 10007	Blowing My Mind/Think	1966	3.75	7.50	15.00
❑ 10033	Ginger Man/Whole Lotta Shakin' Goin' On	1966	3.75	7.50	15.00

GOLDBERG-MILLER BLUES BAND

Also see BARRY GOLDBERG; STEVE MILLER.

Number	Title (A Side/B Side)	Yr	VG	VG+	NM
EPIC					
❑ 9865	More Soul Than Soulful/Mother Song	1965	3.75	7.50	15.00

Number	Title (A Side/B Side)	Yr	VG	VG+	NM
❑ 9865 [DJ]	More Soul Than Soulful/Mother Song	1965	6.25	12.50	25.00
—Promo only on blue vinyl					
❑ 9865 [PS]	More Soul Than Soulful/Mother Song	1965	12.50	25.00	50.00
—Promo only					

GOLDEN EARRING

Number	Title (A Side/B Side)	Yr	VG	VG+	NM
21 RECORDS					
❑ 103	Twilight Zone/King Dark	1982	—	2.00	4.00
❑ 108	The Devil Made Me Do It/Chargin' Batteries	1983	—	2.00	4.00
❑ 112	When the Lady Smiles/Orwell's Ear	1984	—	—	3.00
❑ 112 [PS]	When the Lady Smiles/Orwell's Ear	1984	—	2.50	5.00
❑ 113	Fist in Glove/One Night Moonlight	1984	—	—	3.00
❑ 99515	Love in Motion/Why Do I	1986	—	—	3.00
❑ 99533	Quiet Eyes/Love in Motion	1986	—	—	3.00
❑ 881415-7	Something Heavy Going Down/Enough Is Enough	1984	—	—	3.00
ATLANTIC					
❑ 2710	Eight Miles High/One High Road	1970	—	3.00	6.00
DWARF					
❑ 2001	Back Home/As Long As the Wind Blows	1969	2.50	5.00	10.00
❑ 2001 [PS]	Back Home/As Long As the Wind Blows	1969	5.00	10.00	20.00
MCA					
❑ 40513	Babylon/Sleep Walkin'	1976	—	2.00	4.00
❑ 40802	Radar Love (Live)/Radar Love (Studio)	1977	—	2.00	4.00
POLYDOR					
❑ 2004	Weekend Love/Tiger Bay	1979	—	2.00	4.00
❑ 14001	It's Alright, But I Admit It Could Be Better/Song of a Devil's Servant	1969	2.50	5.00	10.00
❑ 14581	Weekend Love/Tiger Bay	1979	—	—	—
—Unreleased					
TRACK					
❑ 40202	Radar Love/Just Like Vince Taylor	1974	—	3.00	6.00
❑ 40309	Candy's Going Bad/She Flies on Strange Wings	1974	—	2.50	5.00
❑ 40369	Ce Soir/Lucky Numbers	1975	—	2.50	5.00
❑ 40412	The Switch/Lonesome D.J.	1975	—	2.50	5.00

GOLDEN NUGGETS, THE

Two different groups?

Number	Title (A Side/B Side)	Yr	VG	VG+	NM
FUTURA					
❑ 1691	I Was a Fool/Teenage Josephine	1959	150.00	300.00	600.00
HAWK					
❑ 107/8	Surf Everybody/Everybody Bird	1963	10.00	20.00	40.00

GOLDENRODS, THE

Number	Title (A Side/B Side)	Yr	VG	VG+	NM
VEE JAY					
❑ 307	Wish I Was Back in School/Color Cartoons	1959	62.50	125.00	250.00

GOLDENTONES, THE

Number	Title (A Side/B Side)	Yr	VG	VG+	NM
BEACON					
❑ 560	Meaning of Love/(B-side unknown)	1961	6.25	12.50	25.00
JAY-DEE					
❑ 806	Meaning of Love/(B-side unknown)	1955	20.00	40.00	80.00

GOLDIE, DAN

Number	Title (A Side/B Side)	Yr	VG	VG+	NM
TEARDROP					
❑ 3070	Take Our Last Walk Tonight/Walking the Streets	1966	6.25	12.50	25.00
—The Sir Douglas Quintet is the backing band					

GOLDSBORO, BOBBY

Number	Title (A Side/B Side)	Yr	VG	VG+	NM
BUENA VISTA					
❑ 561	These Are the Best Times/(B-side unknown)	1979	—	2.50	5.00
CURB					
❑ 02117	Love Ain't Never Hurt Nobody/Wings of an Angel	1981	—	2.00	4.00
❑ 02583	The Round-Up Saloon/Green-Eyed Woman, Nashville Blues	1981	—	2.00	4.00
❑ 02726	Lucy and the Stranger/Outrun the Sun	1982	—	2.00	4.00
❑ 5400	Goodbye Marie/Love Has Made a Woman Out of You	1980	—	2.00	4.00
❑ 70052	Alice Doesn't Love Here Anymore/Green-Eyed Woman, Nashville Blues	1981	—	2.00	4.00
EPIC					
❑ 50342	Me and the Elephants/I Love Music	1977	—	2.00	4.00
❑ 50413	The Cowboy and the Lady/Me and Millie	1977	—	2.00	4.00
❑ 50480	He'll Have to Go/Too Hot to Handle	1977	—	2.00	4.00
❑ 50535	Life Gets Hard on Easy Street/Black Fool's Gold	1978	—	2.00	4.00
LAURIE					
❑ 3130	Lonely Traveler/You Better Go Home	1962	3.75	7.50	15.00
❑ 3148	Molly/Honey Baby	1962	3.75	7.50	15.00
❑ 3159	The Letter/The Runaround	1963	3.75	7.50	15.00
❑ 3168	Light the Candles/That's What Love Will Do	1963	3.75	7.50	15.00
UNITED ARTISTS					
❑ 0044	See the Funny Little Clown/Little Things	1973	—	2.00	4.00
❑ 0045	It's Too Late/Voodoo Woman	1973	—	2.00	4.00
❑ 0046	Honey/Autumn of My Life	1973	—	2.00	4.00
❑ 0047	Watching Scotty Grow/I'm a Drifter	1973	—	2.00	4.00
—0044 through 0047 are "Silver Spotlight Series" reissues					
❑ XW251	Summer (The First Time)/Childhood 1949	1973	—	2.50	5.00
❑ XW251 [PS]	Summer (The First Time)/Childhood 1949	1973	—	3.00	6.00
❑ XW371	Marlena/Sing Me a Smile	1973	—	2.50	5.00
❑ XW422	I Believe the South Is Gonna Rise Again/She	1974	—	2.00	4.00
❑ XW451	And Then There Was Gina/Quicksand	1974	—	2.00	4.00
❑ XW517	Summer (The First Time)/Marlena	1974	—	2.00	4.00
—Reissue					
❑ XW529	Hello Summertime/And Then There Was Gina	1974	—	2.00	4.00
❑ XW633	And Then There Was Gina/You Pull Me Down (Into Sweet, Sweet Love)	1975	—	2.00	4.00
❑ 672	See the Funny Little Clown/Hello Loser	1963	2.50	5.00	10.00
❑ XW681	I Wrote a Song (Sing Along)/You Pull Me Down (Into Sweet, Sweet Love)	1975	—	2.00	4.00
❑ 710	Whenever He Holds You/If She Was Mine	1964	2.00	4.00	8.00
❑ 710 [PS]	Whenever He Holds You/If She Was Mine	1964	3.75	7.50	15.00
❑ 742	Me Japanese Boy, I Love You/Everyone But Me	1964	2.00	4.00	8.00
❑ 781	I Don't Know You Anymore/Little Drops of Water	1964	2.00	4.00	8.00
❑ XW793	A Butterfly for Bucky/Another Night Alone	1976	—	2.00	4.00
❑ 810	Little Things/I Can't Go On Pretending	1965	2.50	5.00	10.00
❑ 862	Voodoo Woman/It Breaks My Heart	1965	2.00	4.00	8.00
❑ XW866	She Taught Me How to Live Again/Reunion	1976	—	2.00	4.00
❑ 908	If You Wait for Love/If You've Got a Heart	1965	2.00	4.00	8.00
❑ 952	Broomstick Cowboy/Ain't Got Time for Happy	1965	2.00	4.00	8.00
❑ 980	It's Too Late/I'm Goin' Home	1966	2.00	4.00	8.00
❑ 50018	I Know You Better Than That/When Your Love Has Gone	1966	2.00	4.00	8.00
❑ 50018 [PS]	I Know You Better Than That/When Your Love Has Gone	1966	3.75	7.50	15.00
❑ 50044	Longer Than Forever/Take Your Love	1966	2.00	2.00	8.00
❑ 50056	It Hurts Me/Pity the Fool	1966	2.00	2.00	8.00
❑ 50087	Blue Autumn/I Just Don't Love You Anymore	1966	2.00	2.00	8.00
❑ 50138	Love Is/Goodbye to All You Women	1967	2.00	2.00	8.00
❑ 50186	Three in the Morning/Trusty Little Herbert	1967	2.00	2.00	8.00
❑ 50224	Pledge of Love/Jo-Jo's Place	1967	2.00	2.00	8.00
❑ 50283	Honey/Danny	1968	2.50	5.00	10.00
—Black label					
❑ 50283	Honey/Danny	1968	2.00	4.00	8.00
—Orange and pink label					
❑ 50318	Autumn of My Life/She Chased Me	1968	—	3.00	6.00
❑ 50318 [PS]	Autumn of My Life/She Chased Me	1968	3.75	7.50	15.00
❑ 50321	Autumn of My Life/She Chased Me	1968	—	—	—
—Unreleased; these were edits of the versions on UA 50318					
❑ 50461	The Straight Life/Tomorrow Is Forgotten	1968	—	3.00	6.00
❑ 50470	A Christmas Wish/Look Around You (It's Christmas Time)	1968	2.50	5.00	10.00
❑ 50497	Glad She's a Woman/Letter to Emily	1969	—	3.00	6.00
❑ 50525	I'm a Drifter/Hobos and Kings	1969	—	3.00	6.00
❑ 50565	Muddy Mississippi Line/A Richer Man Than I	1969	—	3.00	6.00
❑ 50614	Mornin' Mornin'/Requiem	1969	—	3.00	6.00
❑ 50650	Can You Feel It/Time Good, Time Bad	1970	—	2.50	5.00
❑ 50696	Down on the Bayou/It's Gonna Change	1970	—	2.50	5.00
❑ 50715	My God and I/The World Beyond	1970	—	2.50	5.00
❑ 50727	Watching Scotty Grow/Water Color Days	1970	—	2.50	5.00
❑ 50776	And I Love You So/Gentle of a Man	1971	—	2.50	5.00
❑ 50807	I'll Remember You/Come Back Home	1971	—	2.50	5.00
❑ 50846	Poem for the Little Lady/Danny Is a Mirror to Me	1971	—	2.50	5.00
❑ 50891	California Wine/To Be with You	1972	—	2.50	5.00
❑ 50938	With Pen in Hand/Southern Fried Singin' Sunday Mornin'	1972	—	2.50	5.00
❑ 51107	Country Feelin's/Brand New Kind of Love	1973	—	2.50	5.00

GOLDTONES, THE

Number	Title (A Side/B Side)	Yr	VG	VG+	NM
A&R					
❑ 714	Strike/Gutterball	1963	7.50	15.00	30.00
❑ 714 [PS]	Strike/Gutterball	1963	12.50	25.00	50.00

GOLLIWOGS, THE

Early CREEDENCE CLEARWATER REVIVAL. Also see TOMMY FOGERTY AND THE BLUE VELVETS.

Number	Title (A Side/B Side)	Yr	VG	VG+	NM
FANTASY					
❑ 590	Don't Tell Me No Lies/Little Girl, Does Your Mama Know	1964	15.00	30.00	60.00
❑ 597	Where You Been/You Came Walking	1965	15.00	30.00	60.00
❑ 599	You Got Nothin' on Me/You Can't Be True	1965	12.50	25.00	50.00
SCORPIO					
❑ 404	Brown Eyed Girl/You Better Be Careful	1967	12.50	25.00	50.00
❑ 405	Fragile Child/Fight Fire	1967	12.50	25.00	50.00
❑ 408	Walking on the Water/You Better Get It Before It Gets You	1967	12.50	25.00	50.00
❑ 412 [DJ]	Porterville/Call It Pretending	1968	15.00	30.00	60.00
—Only promos credit the Golliwogs; all known stock copies credit Creedence Clearwater Revival.					

GONE ALL STARS

Number	Title (A Side/B Side)	Yr	VG	VG+	NM
GONE					
❑ 5016	7-11/Down Yonder Rock	1957	6.25	12.50	25.00

GONN

Number	Title (A Side/B Side)	Yr	VG	VG+	NM
EMIR					
❑ 9217	Blackout of Gretley/Pain in My Heart	1966	100.00	200.00	400.00
EMIR/MCCM					
❑ 88-9217	Blackout of Gretley/Pain in My Heart	1988	—	2.50	5.00
—Black vinyl					
❑ 88-9217	Blackout of Gretley/Pain in My Heart	1988	3.75	7.50	15.00
—Colored vinyl					
MERRY JAINE					
❑ 2318	You're Looking Fine/Come with Me	1967	25.00	50.00	100.00

GONZALES, FRANK

Number	Title (A Side/B Side)	Yr	VG	VG+	NM
FESTIVAL					
❑ 1001	Let's Make Up/(B-side unknown)	1961	62.50	125.00	250.00

GOOBERS, THE

Number	Title (A Side/B Side)	Yr	VG	VG+	NM
SURF					
❑ 1001	Hawaiian Holiday/Buyer Beware	1963	12.50	25.00	50.00

GOOD, TOMMY

Number	Title (A Side/B Side)	Yr	VG	VG+	NM
GORDY					
❑ 7034	Baby I Miss You/Leaving Here	1964	10.00	20.00	40.00

GOOD GUYS, THE

Number	Title (A Side/B Side)	Yr	VG	VG+	NM
GNP CRESCENDO					
❑ 326	Asphalt Wipe Out/Scratch	1964	5.00	10.00	20.00

GOOD RATS, THE

Number	Title (A Side/B Side)	Yr	VG	VG+	NM
KAPP					
❑ 946	The Hobo/Truth Is Gone	1968	3.00	6.00	12.00
PASSPORT					
❑ 7912	Just Found a Lady/Coo Coo Coo Blues	1978	—	2.50	5.00

GOOD ROCKIN' SAM

Number	Title (A Side/B Side)	Yr	VG	VG+	NM
EXCELLO					
❑ 2059	Baby I'm Fool Proof/Thing-a-Ma-Jig	1955	12.50	25.00	50.00

GOODMAN, DICKIE

Also see BUCHANAN AND GOODMAN; JOHN AND ERNEST; SPENCER AND SPENCER.

Number	Title (A Side/B Side)	Yr	VG	VG+	NM
20TH FOX					
❑ 443	Senate Hearing/Lock-Up	1963	3.75	7.50	15.00
ASI					
❑ 1013	Rocky and the Angel/Pug Rock	1977	—	3.00	6.00
—As "Dickie G. and the Don'ts"					
AUDIO SPECTRUM					
❑ 75	Presidential Interview (Flying Saucer '64)/Paul Revere	1964	10.00	20.00	40.00
CASH					
❑ 451	Mr. Jaws/Irv's Theme	1975	—	2.50	5.00
COTIQUE					
❑ 158	On Campus/Mombo Suzie	1969	—	3.00	6.00
—B-side by Johnny Colo					
❑ 173	Luna Trip/My Victrola	1969	—	3.00	6.00
—B-side by Joey Pastrana					
DAVY JONES					
❑ 663	White House Happening/President Johnson	1967	6.25	12.50	25.00
❑ 663 [PS]	White House Happening/President Johnson	1967	10.00	20.00	40.00
DIAMOND					
❑ 119	Ben Crazy/Flip Side	1962	3.75	7.50	15.00
EXTRAN					
❑ 601	Hey, E.T./Get a Job	1982	—	2.50	5.00
GOODNAME					
❑ 7100	Safe Sex Report/Safety First	1987	3.75	7.50	15.00
—His last record					
HOT LINE					
❑ 1017	Energy Crisis '79/Pain	1979	—	3.00	6.00
JANUS					
❑ 271	Star Warts/The Boys Tune	1977	—	2.50	5.00
J.M.D.					
❑ 001	Ben Crazy/Flip Side	1962	6.25	12.50	25.00
MARK-X					
❑ 8009	The Touchables/Martian Melody	1961	7.50	15.00	30.00
—Yellow label					
❑ 8009	The Touchables/Martian Melody	1961	5.00	10.00	20.00
—Black label					
❑ 8010	The Touchables in Brooklyn/Mystery	1961	5.00	10.00	20.00
MONTAGE					
❑ 1220	Hey, E.T./The Ride of Paul Revere	1982	3.75	7.50	15.00
❑ 1220 [DJ]	Hey, E.T. (same on both sides)	1982	—	2.50	5.00
M.D.					
❑ 101	Schmonanza/Backwards Theme	1961	5.00	10.00	20.00
ORON					
❑ 101	Washington Uptight/The Cat	1967	6.25	12.50	25.00
—As "The Pennsylvania Players"					
PRELUDE					
❑ 8018	Election '80 (same on both sides)	1980	—	2.50	5.00
RAINY WEDNESDAY					
❑ 202	Watergrate/Friends	1973	—	3.00	6.00
❑ 204	Purple People Eater/Ruthie's Theme	1973	—	3.00	6.00
❑ 205	The Constitution/The End	1973	—	3.00	6.00
❑ 206	Energy Crisis '74/The Mistake	1974	—	3.00	6.00
❑ 206	Energy Crisis '74/Ruthie's Theme	1974	2.00	4.00	8.00
❑ 207	Mr. President/Popularity	1974	—	3.00	6.00
❑ 208	Gerry Ford, A Special Report/Robert	1974	—	3.00	6.00
❑ 209	Inflation in the Nation/Jon and Jed's Theme	1975	—	3.00	6.00
RAMGO					
❑ 501	Speaking of Ecology/Dayton's Theme	1970	6.25	12.50	25.00
RED BIRD					
❑ 10-058	Batman & His Grandmother/Suspense	1966	5.00	10.00	20.00
RHINO					
❑ 019	Radio Russia/Washington Inside Out	1984	—	2.00	4.00
RORI					
❑ 601	Horror Movies/Whoa, Mule	1961	6.25	12.50	25.00
❑ 602	The Berlin Top Ten/Little Tiger	1961	6.25	12.50	25.00
❑ 701	Santa and the Touchables/North Pole Rock	1961	6.25	12.50	25.00
SCEPTER					
❑ 12339	Speaking of Ecology/Dayton's Theme	1971	3.00	6.00	12.00
SHARK					
❑ 1001	Mrs. Jaws/(B-side unknown)	1979	5.00	10.00	20.00
❑ 1002	Super Superman/Chomp Chomp	1979	3.75	7.50	15.00
SHELL					
❑ 711	Election '84/Herb's Theme	1984	—	2.00	4.00
SHOCK					
❑ 6	Kong/Ed's Tune	1977	—	2.50	5.00
TWIRL					
❑ 2015	James Bomb/Seventh Theme	1966	3.75	7.50	15.00
WACKO					
❑ 1001	Mr. President/Dancin' U.S.A.	1981	—	2.50	5.00
❑ 1002	Super-Duper Man/Robert's Tune	1981	—	2.50	5.00
❑ 1381	America '81/(B-side unknown)	1981	2.00	4.00	8.00
Z-100					
❑ 100 [DJ]	Attack of the Z Monster/Mystery	1984	2.50	5.00	10.00
—Promo item for New York radio station					

GOODMAN, SHIRLEY

Of SHIRLEY AND LEE; also of SHIRLEY (AND COMPANY).

Number	Title (A Side/B Side)	Yr	VG	VG+	NM
IMPERIAL					
❑ 5944	When a Boy Meets a Girl/Don't Marry Too Soon	1963	3.00	6.00	12.00

GOODMAN, STEVE

Number	Title (A Side/B Side)	Yr	VG	VG+	NM
ASYLUM					
❑ 45284	Jessie's Jig (Rob's Romp, Beth's Bounce)/It's a Sin to Tell a Lie	1975	—	3.00	6.00
❑ 45331	Between the Lines/Can't Go Back	1976	—	3.00	6.00
❑ 45481	Video Tape/My Old Man	1978	—	3.00	6.00
❑ 46012	Men Who Love Women Who Love Men/The One That Got Away	1979	—	3.00	6.00
❑ 46522	Men Who Love Women Who Love Men/The One That Got Away	1979	—	2.50	5.00
❑ 47107	Bobby Don't Stop/Trust Me	1981	—	2.50	5.00
BUDDAH					
❑ 270	City of New Orleans/(B-side unknown)	1971	3.00	6.00	12.00
❑ 326	Election Year Rag/Someone Else's Troubles	1972	2.50	5.00	10.00
❑ 348	The Dutchman/Song for David	1973	2.50	5.00	10.00
RED PAJAMA					
❑ 1001	A Dying Cub Fan's Last Request/Take Me Out to the Ball Game	1981	2.50	5.00	10.00
WGN					
❑ 784	Go Cubs Go (WGN Radio Cubs Theme) (same on both sides)	1984	2.00	4.00	8.00

GOODMAN, STEVE, AND PHOEBE SNOW

Also see each artist's individual listings.

Number	Title (A Side/B Side)	Yr	VG	VG+	NM
ASYLUM					
❑ 47069	Sometimes Love Forgets/Can't Find My Heart	1980	—	2.50	5.00

GOODTIMERS, THE

See DON COVAY.

GOONS, THE

Number	Title (A Side/B Side)	Yr	VG	VG+	NM
LONDON					
❑ 1684	I'm Walking Backwards for Christmas/Bluebottle Blues	1956	6.25	12.50	25.00

GORDON, BARRY

Number	Title (A Side/B Side)	Yr	VG	VG+	NM
MGM					
❑ 12092	Nuttin' for Christmas/Santa Claus Looks Like Daddy	1955	5.00	10.00	20.00
—With Art Mooney and His Orchestra					
❑ 12367	Zoomah, the Santa Claus from Mars/I Like Christmas (I Like It, I Like It)	1956	5.00	10.00	20.00
❑ 12367 [PS]	Zoomah, the Santa Claus from Mars/I Like Christmas (I Like It, I Like It)	1956	6.25	12.50	25.00

GORDON, MIKE, AND THE AGATES

Number	Title (A Side/B Side)	Yr	VG	VG+	NM
DORE					
❑ 681	Rumble at Newport Beach/Last Call for Dinner	1963	7.50	15.00	30.00
❑ 780	Curfew on the Strip/Last Call for Dinner	1966	3.75	7.50	15.00

GORDON, MIKE, AND THE EL TEMPOS

Number	Title (A Side/B Side)	Yr	VG	VG+	NM
CAT					
❑ 101	Why Don't You Do Right/You Got to Give	1954	12.50	25.00	50.00

GORDON, ROSCOE

Number	Title (A Side/B Side)	Yr	VG	VG+	NM
ABC-PARAMOUNT					
❑ 10351	A Girl to Love/As You Walk Away	1962	3.00	6.00	12.00
❑ 10407	A Little Bit of Magic/I Want Revenge	1963	3.00	6.00	12.00
❑ 10501	I Don't Stand a Chance/That's What You Did	1963	3.00	6.00	12.00
—As "Barbara & Roscoe Gordon"					
CALLA					
❑ 145	Just a Little Bit/I Really Love You	1968	2.00	4.00	8.00
CHESS					
❑ 1487	Booted/I Love You Till the Day I Die	1951	375.00	750.00	1500.
DUKE					
❑ 101	Tell Daddy/Hey Fat Girl	1952	25.00	50.00	100.00
❑ 106	T-Model Boogie/New Orleans Woman	1953	12.50	25.00	50.00
❑ 109	Too Many Women/Wise to You, Baby	1953	12.50	25.00	50.00
❑ 114	Ain't No Use/Roscoe's Mambo	1953	12.50	25.00	50.00
❑ 129	Three Can't Love/You Figure It Out	1954	12.50	25.00	50.00
❑ 165	Keep On Doggin'/Bad Dream	1957	7.50	15.00	30.00
❑ 173	I've Loved and Lost/Tummer Tee	1957	7.50	15.00	30.00
❑ 320	Dilly Bop/You'll Never Know	1960	3.75	7.50	15.00
FLIP					
❑ 227	Weeping Blues/Just Love Me, Baby	1956	75.00	150.00	300.00
❑ 237	The Chicken (Dance with You)/Love for You Baby	1956	12.50	25.00	50.00
OLD TOWN					
❑ 1167	Gotta Keep Rollin'/Just a Little at a Time	1964	2.50	5.00	10.00
❑ 1175	It Ain't Right/Could This Be Love	1965	2.50	5.00	10.00
—As "Roscoe and Barbara"					
RPM					
❑ 324	Saddled the Cow/Ouch, Pretty Baby	1951	100.00	200.00	400.00
❑ 336	Dime a Dozen/A New Remedy for Love	1951	62.50	125.00	250.00
❑ 344	Booted/Cold, Cold Winter	1952	50.00	100.00	200.00
❑ 350	No More Doggin'/Maria	1952	50.00	100.00	200.00
❑ 358	New Orleans Woman/I Remember Your Kisses	1952	25.00	50.00	100.00
❑ 365	What You Got on Your Mind/Two Kinds of Women	1952	25.00	50.00	100.00
❑ 369	Trying/Dream Baby	1952	15.00	30.00	60.00
❑ 373	Lucille/Blues for My Baby	1953	15.00	30.00	60.00
❑ 379	I'm in Love/Just In from Texas	1953	15.00	30.00	60.00
❑ 384	We're All Loaded/Tomorrow May Be Too Late	1953	15.00	30.00	60.00
SUN					
❑ 227	Weeping Blues/Just Love Me, Baby	1956	125.00	250.00	500.00
❑ 237	The Chicken (Dance with You)/Love for You Baby	1956	50.00	100.00	200.00
❑ 257	Shoobie Oobie/Cheese and Crackers	1956	12.50	25.00	50.00
❑ 305	Sally Jo/Torro	1958	6.25	12.50	25.00
VEE JAY					
❑ 316	A Fool in Love/No More Doggin'	1959	3.75	7.50	15.00
❑ 332	Just a Little Bit/Goin' Home	1959	3.75	7.50	15.00
❑ 348	Surely I Love You/What You Do to Me	1960	3.75	7.50	15.00
❑ 385	What I Wouldn't Do/Let 'Em Try	1961	3.00	6.00	12.00

GORE, LESLEY

Number	Title (A Side/B Side)	Yr	VG	VG+	NM
A&M					
❑ 1710	Give It to Me, Sweet Thing/Immortality	1975	—	2.50	5.00
❑ 1710 [PS]	Give It to Me, Sweet Thing/Immortality	1975	—	3.00	6.00
❑ 1830	Sometimes/Give It To Me, Sweet Thing	1976	—	2.50	5.00
CREWE					
❑ 338	Why Doesn't Love Make Me Happy/Tomorrow's Children	1970	2.50	5.00	10.00
❑ 344	When Yesterday Was Tomorrow/Why Me, Why You	1970	2.50	5.00	10.00
❑ 601	Back Together/Quiet Love	1971	2.50	5.00	10.00
MANHATTAN					
❑ 50039	Since I Don't Have You-It's Only Make Believe/Our Love Was Meant to Be	1986	2.00	4.00	8.00
—With Lou Christie					
MERCURY					
❑ 72119	It's My Party/Danny	1963	3.75	7.50	15.00
❑ 72119 [PS]	It's My Party/Danny	1963	7.50	15.00	30.00
❑ 72143	Judy's Turn to Cry/Just Let Me Cry	1963	3.75	7.50	15.00
❑ 72143 [PS]	Judy's Turn to Cry/Just Let Me Cry	1963	6.25	12.50	25.00
❑ 72180	She's a Fool/The Old Crowd	1963	3.75	7.50	15.00
❑ 72180 [PS]	She's a Fool/The Old Crowd	1963	6.25	12.50	25.00
❑ 72206	You Don't Own Me/Run, Bobby, Run	1963	3.75	7.50	15.00
❑ 72206 [PS]	You Don't Own Me/Run, Bobby, Run	1963	10.00	20.00	40.00
—With insert (deduct 25% if missing)					
❑ 72245	Je Ne Sais Plus/Je N'ose Pas	1964	5.00	10.00	20.00
❑ 72259	That's the Way Boys Are/That's the Way the Ball Bounces	1964	2.50	5.00	10.00
❑ 72259 [PS]	That's the Way Boys Are/That's the Way the Ball Bounces	1964	5.00	10.00	20.00
❑ 72270	I Don't Wanna Be a Loser/It's Gotta Be You	1964	2.50	5.00	10.00
❑ 72270 [PS]	I Don't Wanna Be a Loser/It's Gotta Be You	1964	5.00	10.00	20.00
❑ 72309	Maybe I Know/Wonder Boy	1964	2.50	5.00	10.00
❑ 72309 [PS]	Maybe I Know/Wonder Boy	1964	5.00	10.00	20.00
❑ 72352	Hey Now/Sometimes I Wish I Were a Boy	1964	2.50	5.00	10.00
❑ 72352 [PS]	Hey Now/Sometimes I Wish I Were a Boy	1964	5.00	10.00	20.00
❑ 72372	Look of Love/Little Girl Gone Home	1964	2.50	5.00	10.00
❑ 72372 [PS]	Look of Love/Little Girl Gone Home	1964	5.00	10.00	20.00
❑ 72412	All of My Life/I Cannot Hope for Anything	1965	2.50	5.00	10.00
❑ 72412 [PS]	All of My Life/I Cannot Hope for Anything	1965	5.00	10.00	20.00
❑ 72433	Sunshine, Lollipops and Rainbows/You've Come Back	1965	2.50	5.00	10.00
❑ 72433 [PS]	Sunshine, Lollipops and Rainbows/You've Come Back	1965	5.00	10.00	20.00
❑ 72475	My Town, My Guy and Me/Girl in Love	1965	2.50	5.00	10.00
❑ 72475 [PS]	My Town, My Guy and Me/Girl in Love	1965	5.00	10.00	20.00
❑ 72513	I Won't Love You Anymore (Sorry)/No Matter What You Do	1966	2.50	5.00	10.00
❑ 72513 [PS]	I Won't Love You Anymore (Sorry)/No Matter What You Do	1966	5.00	10.00	20.00
❑ 72530	We Know We're in Love/That's What We'll Do	1966	2.50	5.00	10.00
❑ 72553	Young Love/I Just Don't Know If I Can	1966	2.50	5.00	10.00
❑ 72580	Off and Running/I Don't Care	1966	2.50	5.00	10.00
❑ 72611	Maybe Now/Treat Me Like a Lady	1966	2.50	5.00	10.00
❑ 72649	California Nights/I'm Goin' Out	1967	2.50	5.00	10.00
❑ 72683	Summer and Sandy/I'm Fallin' Down	1967	2.50	5.00	10.00
❑ 72683 [PS]	Summer and Sandy/I'm Fallin' Down	1967	5.00	10.00	20.00
❑ 72726	Brink of Disaster/On a Day Like This	1967	2.50	5.00	10.00
❑ 72759	It's a Happening/Magic Colors	1967	2.50	5.00	10.00
❑ 72787	Small Talk/Say What You See	1968	3.00	6.00	12.00
❑ 72819	He Gives Me Love (La, La, La)/Brand New Me	1968	3.00	6.00	12.00
❑ 72842	Where Can I Go/I Can't Make It Without You	1968	3.00	6.00	12.00
❑ 72867	Look the Other Way/I'll Be Standing By	1968	3.00	6.00	12.00
❑ 72892	Take Good Care (Of My Heart)/I Can't Make It Without You	1969	3.00	6.00	12.00
❑ 72892	Take Good Care (Of My Heart)/You Sent Me Silver Bells	1969	3.00	6.00	12.00
❑ 72931	Summer Symphony/98.6-Lazy Day	1969	3.75	7.50	15.00
❑ 72969	Wedding Bell Blues/One by One	1969	3.75	7.50	15.00
MOWEST					
❑ 5029	The Road I Walk/She Said That	1972	2.50	5.00	10.00
❑ 5042	Give It to Me, Sweet Thing/Don't Want to Be One	1973	—	—	—
—Unreleased					
PHILCO-FORD					
❑ HP-21	You Don't Own Me/That's the Way Boys Are	1968	3.75	7.50	15.00
—4-inch plastic "Hip Pocket Record" with color sleeve					

GORMAN, FREDDIE

Number	Title (A Side/B Side)	Yr	VG	VG+	NM
MIRACLE					
❑ 11	The Day Will Come/(B-side unknown)	1962	17.50	35.00	70.00
RIC-TIC					
❑ 101	In a Bad Way/There Can Be Too Much	1964	7.50	15.00	30.00
❑ 102	Take Me Back/Can't Get It Out of My Mind	1965	7.50	15.00	30.00

GOSPEL STARS, THE

Number	Title (A Side/B Side)	Yr	VG	VG+	NM
TAMLA					
❑ 54037	He Lifted Me/Behold the Saints of God	1961	37.50	75.00	150.00
—Horizontal lines logo					
❑ 54037	He Lifted Me/Behold the Saints of God	1961	15.00	30.00	60.00
—Globe logo					

GOTHAM CITY CRIME FIGHTERS, THE

Number	Title (A Side/B Side)	Yr	VG	VG+	NM
BATWING					
❑ 1001	Who Stole the Batmobile/That's Life	1966	7.50	15.00	30.00

GOULDMAN, GRAHAM

Also see THE MOCKINGBIRDS; 10CC.

Number	Title (A Side/B Side)	Yr	VG	VG+	NM
A&M					
❑ 2251	Away from It All/Bionic Boar	1980	—	2.00	4.00
RCA VICTOR					
❑ 47-9453	Impossible Years/No Milk Today	1968	3.00	6.00	12.00
❑ 47-9584	For Your Love/Pamela, Pamela	1968	3.00	6.00	12.00

GOWENS, SAMMY

Number	Title (A Side/B Side)	Yr	VG	VG+	NM
UNITED ARTISTS					
❑ 114	Kissin' at the Drive-In/Rockin' By Myself	1958	25.00	50.00	100.00

GRACIE, CHARLIE

Number	Title (A Side/B Side)	Yr	VG	VG+	NM
20TH CENTURY					
❑ 5033	Head Home, Honey/My Baby Loves Me	1955	12.50	25.00	50.00
❑ 5035	Honey Honey/Wildwood Boogie	1955	15.00	30.00	60.00
CADILLAC					
❑ 141	Boogie Boogie Blues/I'm Gonna Sit Right Down and Write Myself a Letter	1953	37.50	75.00	150.00
❑ 144	Rockin' and Rollin'/(B-side unknown)	1954	37.50	75.00	150.00
CAMEO					
❑ 105	Butterfly/Ninety-Nine Ways	1957	6.25	12.50	25.00
❑ 107	Fabulous/Just Lookin'	1957	5.00	10.00	20.00
❑ 111	I Love You So Much It Hurts/Wandering Eyes	1957	5.00	10.00	20.00
❑ 118	Cool Baby/You've Got a Heart Like a Rock	1957	5.00	10.00	20.00
❑ 127	Crazy Girl/Dressin' Up	1958	5.00	10.00	20.00
❑ 141	Love Bird/Trying	1958	5.00	10.00	20.00
CORAL					
❑ 62073	Hurry Up Buttercup/Doodlebug	1959	3.75	7.50	15.00
❑ 62115	Angel of Love/I'm a Fool, That's Why	1959	3.75	7.50	15.00
❑ 62141	Oh-Well-a/Because I Love You So	1959	3.75	7.50	15.00
DIAMOND					
❑ 178	He'll Never Love You Like I Do/Keep My Love Next to Your Heart	1965	6.25	12.50	25.00
FELSTED					
❑ 8629	W-Wow/Makin' Whoopee	1961	3.75	7.50	15.00
PRESIDENT					
❑ 825	Pretty Baby/Night and Day U.S.A.	1962	3.75	7.50	15.00
❑ 828	Count to Three/Just Like Us	1963	3.75	7.50	15.00
ROULETTE					
❑ 4255	I Look for You/The Race	1960	3.75	7.50	15.00
❑ 4312	Sorry for You/Scenery	1960	3.75	7.50	15.00

GRADS, THE

Number	Title (A Side/B Side)	Yr	VG	VG+	NM
A&M					
❑ 797	Everything in the Garden/Stage Door	1966	2.50	5.00	10.00
MERCURY					
❑ 72346	Cool One/Wild One	1964	5.00	10.00	20.00
MGM					
❑ 13216	Their Hearts Were Full of Spring/It Happened Once Before	1964	2.50	5.00	10.00
VALIANT					
❑ 6023	Once Again/White Steeple	1962	3.75	7.50	15.00

GRADUATES, THE (1)

Number	Title (A Side/B Side)	Yr	VG	VG+	NM
CORSICAN					
❑ 0058	What Good Is Graduation/Lonely	1959	10.00	20.00	40.00
LAWN					
❑ 208	Ballad of a Girl and Boy/Goodbye My Love	1963	5.00	10.00	20.00
SHAN-TODD					
❑ 0055	Ballad of a Girl and Boy/Care	1959	7.50	15.00	30.00

GRADUATES, THE (2)

Number	Title (A Side/B Side)	Yr	VG	VG+	NM
GNP CRESCENDO					
❑ 404	(The Shape of) Things to Come/Listen to the Music	1968	2.50	5.00	10.00

GRADUATES, THE (U)

Definitely not group (1); might not be group (2), either.

Number	Title (A Side/B Side)	Yr	VG	VG+	NM
RISING SONS					
❑ 712	If Ever I Get Out of This Mess I'm In/Seventh Generation Breakthrough	1968	7.50	15.00	30.00

GRAFFITI

Number	Title (A Side/B Side)	Yr	VG	VG+	NM
ABC					
❑ 11123	He's Got the Knack/Love In Spite	1968	7.50	15.00	30.00

GRAHAM, LOU

Number	Title (A Side/B Side)	Yr	VG	VG+	NM
CLYMAX					
❑ 318	Wee Willie Brown/You Were Mean Baby	1957	75.00	150.00	300.00
CORAL					
❑ 61931	Wee Willie Brown/You Were Mean Baby	1958	25.00	50.00	100.00

GRAMMER, BILLY

Number	Title (A Side/B Side)	Yr	VG	VG+	NM
DECCA					
❑ 31226	Columbus Stockade Blues/There's a Rainbow 'Round My Shoulder	1961	2.50	5.00	10.00
❑ 31274	Have a Drink on Me/Finger	1961	2.50	5.00	10.00
❑ 31321	Save Your Tears/I'd Like to Know You	1961	2.50	5.00	10.00
❑ 31396	He Ain't My Buddy No More/Blue Roller Rink	1962	2.50	5.00	10.00
❑ 31449	I Wanna Go Home (Detroit City)/Bottom of the Glass	1962	2.50	5.00	10.00
❑ 31514	Love Gets Better with Time/Lonesome Life	1963	2.50	5.00	10.00
❑ 31562	Old Foolish Me/I'll Leave the Porch Lights a-Burning	1963	2.50	5.00	10.00
❑ 31618	Don't Drop It/I Saw Your Face in the Moon	1964	2.00	4.00	8.00
❑ 31669	Wabash Cannonball/Gonna Lay Down My Old Guitar	1964	2.00	4.00	8.00
❑ 31757	Little Bit of Happiness/I'm Letting You Go (Goodbye)	1965	2.00	4.00	8.00
❑ 31892	Brown's Ferry Blues/Souvenirs of Sorrow	1966	2.00	4.00	8.00
EPIC					
❑ 10052	Bottles/Temporarily	1966	2.00	4.00	8.00
❑ 10103	Heaven Help This Heart of Mine/The Real Thing	1966	2.00	4.00	8.00
❑ 10169	I've Seen That Look on Me (A Thousand Times)/Written on a Jailhouse	1967	2.00	4.00	8.00
EVEREST					
❑ 19353	Unknown Soldier/Princess of Persia	1960	2.50	5.00	10.00
❑ 19384	Big Big Dream/River of Regret	1960	2.50	5.00	10.00

Number	Title (A Side/B Side)	Yr	VG	VG+	NM
JMI					
❑ 9	Nobody's Listening to the Preacher Anymore/(B-side unknown)	1972	2.00	4.00	8.00
MERCURY					
❑ 72785	Money, Love and War/Last of My Future	1968	2.00	4.00	8.00
❑ 72836	The Ballad of John Dillinger/Do You Still Believe	1968	2.00	4.00	8.00
❑ 72893	The Hour of Separation/The Changing Scene	1969	—	3.00	6.00
MONUMENT					
❑ 400	Gotta Travel On/Chasing a Dream	1958	3.75	7.50	15.00
❑ 403	Bonaparte's Retreat/The Kissing Tree	1959	3.00	6.00	12.00
❑ 407	It Takes You/Willie, Quit Your Playing	1959	3.00	6.00	12.00
❑ 413	Loveland/On the Job Too Long	1960	3.00	6.00	12.00
❑ 8653	Family Man/What We Have in Common Is Love	1975	—	2.00	4.00
❑ 8665	Steppin' Out/Mom and Dad's Waltz	1975	—	2.00	4.00
❑ 8685	That's Life/Who's Gonna Buy You the Ribbons	1976	—	2.00	4.00
RICE					
❑ 5025	Mabel (You Have Been a Friend to Me)/Papa and Mama	1967	2.00	4.00	8.00
STONEWAY					
❑ 1129	Tie Me to Your Apron Strings Again/Blue Jay Rag	197?	—	3.00	6.00
STOP					
❑ 321	Jesus Is a Soul Man/Peace on Earth Begins Today	1969	—	3.00	6.00

7-Inch Extended Plays

Number	Title (A Side/B Side)	Yr	VG	VG+	NM
DECCA					
❑ ED 2767	Detroit City/Old Foolish Me//Love Gets Better with Time/Have a Drink on Me	196?	3.00	6.00	12.00
❑ ED 2767 [PS]	Billy Grammer	196?	3.00	6.00	12.00

GRANAHAN, GERRY

Also see JERRY GRANT.

Number	Title (A Side/B Side)	Yr	VG	VG+	NM
20TH CENTURY FOX					
❑ 425	Hang Up the Phone/Too Weak to Win	1963	3.75	7.50	15.00
❑ 541	Racing Fever: Title/Racing Fever: Mainstream	1964	3.75	7.50	15.00
—B-side by Arnold Goland and His Orchestra					
ATCO					
❑ 6122	Sweet Affection/Confess It to Your Heart	1958	7.50	15.00	30.00
CANADIAN AMERICAN					
❑ 116	When Irish Eyes Are Smiling/In My Heart	1960	5.00	10.00	20.00
❑ 119	You'll Never Walk Alone/Where's the Girl	1960	5.00	10.00	20.00
❑ 121	Short Skirts/I'm Afraid You'll Never Know	1960	5.00	10.00	20.00
CAPRICE					
❑ 106	Unchained Melody/Dancing Man	1961	5.00	10.00	20.00
❑ 108	Too Big for Her Bikini/Dance, Girl, Dance	1961	25.00	50.00	100.00
—With backing by the Belmonts or the Five Satins (sources disagree)					
GONE					
❑ 5065	Let the Rumors Fly/Put Me Anywhere	1959	5.00	10.00	20.00
❑ 5081	It Hurts/Look for Me	1959	5.00	10.00	20.00
❑ 5081 [PS]	It Hurts/Look for Me	1959	7.50	15.00	30.00
MARK					
❑ 121	Love's Young Dream/Oh Well-A Watch-A Gonna Do	1957	8.75	17.50	35.00
SUNBEAM					
❑ 102	No Chemise, Please/Girl of My Dreams	1958	7.50	15.00	30.00
❑ 108	Baby Wait/Completely	1958	6.25	12.50	25.00
❑ 112	I'm Ready As I'll Ever Be/Nobody Can Handle This Job	1958	6.25	12.50	25.00
—B-side by Eddie Fontaine					
❑ 122	King Size/I'm Afraid You'll Never Know	1958	6.25	12.50	25.00
❑ 127	A Ring, a Bracelet, a Heart/You're Adorable	1959	6.25	12.50	25.00
VEEP					
❑ 1205	All the Live-Long Day/Sophia	1965	3.00	6.00	12.00

GRAND FUNK RAILROAD

Includes records as "Grand Funk." Also see MARK FARNER; MARK FARNER AND DON BREWER; TERRY KNIGHT AND THE PACK.

Number	Title (A Side/B Side)	Yr	VG	VG+	NM
CAPITOL					
❑ 2567	Time Machine/High on a Horse	1969	—	3.00	6.00
❑ 2691	Mr. Limousine Driver/High Falootin' Woman	1969	—	3.00	6.00
❑ 2732	Heartbreaker/Please Don't Worry	1970	—	3.00	6.00
❑ 2816	Nothing Is the Same/Sin's a Good Man's Brother	1970	—	3.00	6.00
❑ 2877	Closer to Home/Aimless Lady	1970	—	3.00	6.00
❑ 2996	Mean Mistreater/Mark Says Alright	1970	—	3.00	6.00
❑ 3095	Feelin' Alright/I Want Freedom	1971	—	3.00	6.00
❑ 3160	Gimme Shelter/I Can Feel Him in the Morning	1971	—	3.00	6.00
❑ 3160 [PS]	Gimme Shelter/I Can Feel Him in the Morning	1971	2.50	5.00	10.00
❑ 3217	People, Let's Stop the War/Save the Land	1971	—	3.00	6.00
❑ 3255	Footstompin' Music/I Come Tumblin'	1972	—	3.00	6.00
❑ 3316	Upsetter/No Lies	1972	—	3.00	6.00
❑ 3363	Rock 'N Roll Soul/Flight of the Phoenix	1972	—	3.00	6.00
❑ 3660	We're An American Band/Creepin'	1973	—	3.00	6.00
—Originals on gold vinyl					
❑ 3660	We're An American Band/Creepin'	1973	—	2.00	4.00
❑ 3660 [PS]	We're An American Band/Creepin'	1973	—	2.50	5.00
❑ 3760	Walk Like a Man/The Railroad	1973	—	2.00	4.00
❑ 3760 [PS]	Walk Like a Man/The Railroad	1973	—	2.50	5.00
❑ 3840	The Loco-Motion/Destitute and Losin'	1974	—	2.00	4.00
❑ 3840 [PS]	The Loco-Motion/Destitute and Losin'	1974	—	2.50	5.00
❑ 3917	Shinin' On/Mr. Pretty Boy	1974	—	2.00	4.00
❑ 3917 [PS]	Shinin' On/Mr. Pretty Boy	1974	—	2.50	5.00
❑ 4002	Some Kind of Wonderful/Wild	1974	—	2.00	4.00
❑ 4002 [PS]	Some Kind of Wonderful/Wild	1974	—	2.50	5.00
❑ 4046	Bad Time/Good and Evil	1975	—	2.00	4.00
❑ 4199	Take Me/Genevieve	1975	—	2.00	4.00
❑ 4199 [PS]	Take Me/Genevieve	1975	—	2.50	5.00
❑ 4235	Sally/Love Is Dyin'	1976	—	2.00	4.00
❑ 4235 [PS]	Sally/Love Is Dyin'	1976	—	2.50	5.00
FULL MOON					
❑ 49823	Testify/Y.O.U.	1981	—	2.00	4.00
❑ 49866	No Reason Why/Stuck in the Middle	1981	—	2.00	4.00
MCA					
❑ 40590	Can You Do It/1976	1976	—	2.50	5.00
❑ 40590 [PS]	Can You Do It/1976	1976	—	3.00	6.00
❑ 40641	Out to Get You/Just Couldn't Wait	1976	—	2.50	5.00
—The MCA sides were produced by Frank Zappa					

GRANT, AMY

Number	Title (A Side/B Side)	Yr	VG	VG+	NM
A&M					
❑ 31458 0104 7	Grown-Up Christmas List/Have Yourself a Merry Little Christmas	1992	—	2.00	4.00
❑ 31458 0726 7	Lucky One/I Will Remember You	1994	—	2.00	4.00
❑ 31458 0864 7	House of Love/Good for Me	1994	—	2.00	4.00
❑ 1218	Lead Me On/Sure Enough	1988	—	—	3.00
❑ 1218 [PS]	Lead Me On/Sure Enough	1988	—	—	3.00
❑ 1243	If You Have to Go Away/1974	1988	—	—	3.00
❑ 1260	Saved by Love/Say Once More	1989	—	—	3.00
❑ 75021 1549 7	Baby Baby (2 mixes)	1991	—	2.00	4.00
❑ 75021 1557 7	Every Heartbeat (2 mixes)	1991	—	2.00	4.00
❑ 75021 1566 7	That's What Love Is For (2 mixes)	1991	—	2.00	4.00
❑ 2734	Find a Way/Strangers	1985	—	—	3.00
❑ 2734 [PS]	Find a Way/Strangers	1985	—	2.00	4.00
❑ 2762	Wise Up/Straight Ahead	1985	—	—	3.00
❑ 2762 [PS]	Wise Up/Straight Ahead	1985	—	2.00	4.00
❑ 2777	Tennessee Christmas/Little Town	1985	—	2.00	4.00
❑ 2777 [PS]	Tennessee Christmas/Little Town	1985	—	2.50	5.00
❑ 2785	Everywhere I Go/Where Do You Hide Your Heart	1985	—	—	3.00
❑ 2864	Stay for Awhile/Love of Another Kind	1986	—	—	3.00
❑ 2864 [PS]	Stay for Awhile/Love of Another Kind	1986	—	2.00	4.00
❑ 2920	Angels/Love Can Do	1987	—	—	3.00
MYRRH					
❑ 901 6173595	Love Has Come/(B-side unknown)	198?	2.00	4.00	8.00

GRANT, CARY

Number	Title (A Side/B Side)	Yr	VG	VG+	NM
COLUMBIA					
❑ 44377	Christmas Lullaby/Here's to You	1967	7.50	15.00	30.00

GRANT, EARL

Number	Title (A Side/B Side)	Yr	VG	VG+	NM
DECCA					
❑ 25526	Ebb Tide/Deep Purple	1962	2.00	4.00	8.00
❑ 25560	Swingin' Gently/Beyond the Roof	1962	2.00	4.00	8.00
❑ 25574	Sweet Sixteen Bars/Learnin' the Blues	1962	2.00	4.00	8.00
❑ 25601	Caravan/I'll Build a Stariway to Paradise	1963	2.00	4.00	8.00
❑ 25607	More (Theme from "Mondo Cane")/Sukiyaki	1963	2.00	4.00	8.00
❑ 25626	Black Coffee/I'm Just a Lucky So-and-So	1964	2.00	4.00	8.00
❑ 25638	Satin Doll/Just One More Time	1964	2.00	4.00	8.00
❑ 25659	Without a Song/Meditation	1965	2.00	4.00	8.00
❑ 25674	Stand By Me/After Hours	1965	2.00	4.00	8.00
❑ 25683	Rudolph the Red-Nosed Reindeer/Santa Claus Is Comin' to Town	1965	2.00	4.00	8.00
❑ 25697	Blue Velvet/The Sweetest Sounds	1966	—	3.00	6.00
❑ 25703	Jingle Bells/Silver Bells	1966	—	3.00	6.00
❑ 25704	The Lonesome Road/When I Grow Too Old to Dream	1966	—	3.00	6.00
❑ 25713	Summertime/September in the Rain	1967	—	3.00	6.00
❑ 25721	Without a Song/I'm in the Mood for Love	1967	—	3.00	6.00
❑ 25730	I Miss You So/Stormy Weather	1967	—	3.00	6.00
❑ 25737	My Foolish Heart/One Note Samba	1968	—	3.00	6.00
❑ 25743	Bewitched/In Motion	1968	—	3.00	6.00
❑ 30150	Goodnight My Love, Pleasant Dreams/My Consolation	1956	3.75	7.50	15.00
❑ 30244	Thanks for You/Through the Eyes of a Boy and Girl	1956	3.75	7.50	15.00
❑ 30475	Fever/Malaguena	1957	3.75	7.50	15.00
❑ 30561	Honky Tonk/The Next Time You See Me	1958	3.00	6.00	12.00
❑ 30640	Ol' Man River/Kathy-O	1958	3.00	6.00	12.00
❑ 30719	The End/Hunky Dunky Doo	1958	3.75	7.50	15.00
❑ 30719	(At) The End (Of a Rainbow)/Hunky Dunky Doo	1958	3.00	6.00	12.00
—Same song, altered title on A-side					
❑ 30819	Evening Rain/Evening Rain (Instrumental)	1959	2.50	5.00	10.00
❑ 30856	Last Night/Imitation of Life	1959	2.50	5.00	10.00
❑ 30908	The Wish/Don't Point Your Finger at Anyone Else	1959	2.50	5.00	10.00
❑ 30983	All for the Best/Not One Minute More	1959	2.50	5.00	10.00
❑ 31022	Christmas Card/Swingin' Christmas	1959	2.50	5.00	10.00
❑ 31044	House of Bamboo/Two Loves Have I	1960	2.50	5.00	10.00
❑ 31110	Dreamy/Building Castles	1960	2.50	5.00	10.00
❑ 31203	You Thrill Me/Quando La Luna	1961	2.00	4.00	8.00
❑ 31222	Ebb Tide/Next Time	1961	2.00	4.00	8.00
❑ 31263	My Foolish Heart/Sermonette	1961	2.00	4.00	8.00
❑ 31328	Honey/Tender Is the Night	1961	2.00	4.00	8.00
❑ 31468	Steve's Theme (From "Forty Pounds of Trouble")/Yes Sirree	1963	2.00	4.00	8.00
❑ 31716	This Little Girl of Mine/Come to Me (Pretty Baby)	1964	2.00	4.00	8.00
❑ 31902	I'll Drown in My Own Tears/I Can't Stop Loving You	1966	—	3.00	6.00
❑ 32093	I Love You, Yes I Do/Hide Nor Hair	1967	—	3.00	6.00
❑ 32443	It Was a Very Good Year/If I Only Had Time	1969	—	2.50	5.00
❑ 32499	I Wonder/The Importance of the Rose	1969	—	2.50	5.00
❑ 32667	Grant's Pass/Elizabethan Reggae	1970	—	2.50	5.00
MCA					
❑ 65023	Silver Bells/Jingle Bells	1973	—	2.00	4.00
—Black label with rainbow					
❑ 65023	Silver Bells/Jingle Bells	1980	—	—	3.00
—Blue label with rainbow					
PRINCE					
❑ 1201	One Way Street/(B-side unknown)	1956	3.75	7.50	15.00
—Black vinyl					
❑ 1201	One Way Street/(B-side unknown)	1956	6.25	12.50	25.00
—Colored vinyl					

7-Inch Extended Plays

Number	Title (A Side/B Side)	Yr	VG	VG+	NM
DECCA					
❑ ED 2591	(contents unknown)	195?	2.50	5.00	10.00
❑ ED 2591 [PS]	The Versatile Earl Grant	195?	2.50	5.00	10.00

Number	Title (A Side/B Side)	Yr	VG	VG+	NM
❑ ED 2634	(contents unknown)	195?	2.50	5.00	10.00
❑ ED 2634 [PS]	The Versatile Earl Grant	195?	2.50	5.00	10.00
❑ ED 2635	(contents unknown)	195?	2.50	5.00	10.00
❑ ED 2635 [PS]	The Versatile Earl Grant	195?	2.50	5.00	10.00
❑ ED 2639 [M]	(contents unknown)	1959	2.50	5.00	10.00
❑ ED 2639 [PS]	The End	1959	2.50	5.00	10.00
❑ ED 7-2639 [PS]	The End	1959	3.75	7.50	15.00
❑ ED 7-2639 [S]	(contents unknown)	1959	3.75	7.50	15.00
❑ ED 2705	Ebb Tide/My Foolish Heart//Exodus Theme/I'm in the Mood for Love	196?	2.50	5.00	10.00
❑ ED 2705 [PS]	Earl Grant	196?	2.50	5.00	10.00
❑ ED 2722	Swingin' Gently/Beyond the Reef//Yellow Bird/Make Someone Happy	196?	2.50	5.00	10.00
❑ ED 2722 [PS]	Swingin' Gently	196?	2.50	5.00	10.00
❑ ED 2736	Sweet Sixteen Bars/Learnin' the Blues//Because of Rain/Too Close for Comfort	196?	2.50	5.00	10.00
❑ ED 2736 [PS]	Earl Grant	196?	2.50	5.00	10.00

GRANT, GEORGE, AND THE CASTELLES

See THE CASTELLES.

GRANT, GOGI

Number	Title (A Side/B Side)	Yr	VG	VG+	NM
20TH FOX					
❑ 284	Johnny, I Hardly Knew Ye/The Second Time Around	1961	2.50	5.00	10.00
❑ 297	Magic Music/Tender Is the Night	1962	2.50	5.00	10.00
❑ 403	Magic Music/Tender Is the Night	1963	2.00	4.00	8.00
ERA					
❑ 1003	Suddenly There's a Valley/Love Is	1955	3.75	7.50	15.00
❑ 1008	Who Are We/We Believe in Love	1955	3.75	7.50	15.00
❑ 1013	The Wayward Wind/No More Than Forever	1956	4.00	8.00	16.00
❑ 1019	You're in Love/When the Tide Is High	1956	3.75	7.50	15.00
❑ 1053	The Golden Ladder/All of Me	1957	3.00	6.00	12.00
❑ 1062	I Gave You My Heart/I Don't Want to Walk Without You	1957	3.00	6.00	12.00
❑ 3046	The Wayward Wind/The Tide Is High	1961	2.00	4.00	8.00
❑ 3205	The Wayward Wind/Suddenly There's a Valley	1969	—	2.50	5.00
LIBERTY					
❑ 55214	If and When/I'll Never Smile Again	1959	2.50	5.00	10.00
❑ 55229	Goin' Home/All God's Children Got Shoes	1959	2.50	5.00	10.00
❑ 55252	I Never Meant to Fall in Love/Stay Here with Me	1960	2.50	5.00	10.00
❑ 55286	Two Lovers by the Sea/In a Sentimental Mood	1960	2.50	5.00	10.00
❑ 55316	That One Kiss/Adrift on a Star	1961	2.50	5.00	10.00
MONUMENT					
❑ 986	Don't Touch Me/Pathfinder	1966	—	3.00	6.00
❑ 1005	The Sea/How Much Will I Love You	1967	—	3.00	6.00
PETE					
❑ 701	Down Here on the Ground/The Magic of People	1968	—	2.50	5.00
❑ 708	Buy Me Penny Candy/Paradise	1968	—	2.50	5.00
❑ 717	Yesterday, When I Was Young/(B-side unknown)	1969	—	2.50	5.00
❑ 718	On the Mountain/Faure	1969	—	2.50	5.00
RCA VICTOR					
❑ 47-4994	Forget Me Not/Where There's Smoke, There's Fire	1952	5.00	10.00	20.00
❑ 47-5053	Mommy's Little Angel/My Tormented Heart	1952	5.00	10.00	20.00
—B-side by the Three Suns					
❑ 47-5436	Everyone Knows I Love You/Ricochet	1953	5.00	10.00	20.00
❑ 47-5512	Secret Love/Ricochet	1953	5.00	10.00	20.00
❑ 47-6996	That's the Life for Me/It's a Wonderful Thing to Be Loved	1957	2.50	5.00	10.00
❑ 47-7082	Johnny's Dream/What a Beautiful Combination	1957	2.50	5.00	10.00
❑ 47-7146	Chinese Nightingale/Bonjour Tristesse	1958	2.50	5.00	10.00
❑ 47-7215	My Secret Prayer/How Do We Know We're in Love	1958	2.50	5.00	10.00
❑ 47-7294	Strange Are the Ways of Love/Marjolaino	1958	2.50	5.00	10.00
❑ 47-7438	Two Dreams/(Kiss Me) Honey Honey (Kiss Me)	1959	2.50	5.00	10.00
❑ 47-7492	The Ride Back from Boot Hill/A Restless Pair	1959	2.50	5.00	10.00

GRANT, JANIE

Number	Title (A Side/B Side)	Yr	VG	VG+	NM
CAPRICE					
❑ 104	Triangle/She's Going Steady with You	1961	3.75	7.50	15.00
❑ 109	Romeo/Roller Coaster	1961	3.75	7.50	15.00
❑ 111	I Wonder Who's Kissing You Now/Unhappy	1961	3.75	7.50	15.00
❑ 113	Oh Johnny/Oh My Love	1962	3.75	7.50	15.00
❑ 115	That Greasy Kid Stuff/Trying to Forget You	1962	3.75	7.50	15.00
❑ 119	Peggy Got Engaged/Two Is Company and Three's a Crowd	1962	3.75	7.50	15.00
PARKWAY					
❑ 982	My Heart, Your Heart/And That Reminds Me of You	1966	7.50	15.00	30.00
UNITED ARTISTS					
❑ 616	Tell Me Mama/Whose Heart Are You Breaking Now	1963	3.00	6.00	12.00
❑ 649	That Kind of Boy/Priceless Persuasion	1963	3.00	6.00	12.00
❑ 731	Ribbons and Roses/Too Young for Me	1964	3.00	6.00	12.00
❑ 775	After Last Night/All I Did Was Fall in Love	1964	3.00	6.00	12.00
❑ 843	I Shouldn't Care (If You're Using Me)/There Ain't No Party Tonight	1965	3.00	6.00	12.00

GRANT, JERRY

Probably the artist who later recorded as GERRY GRANAHAN.

Number	Title (A Side/B Side)	Yr	VG	VG+	NM
ATCO					
❑ 6100	Talkin' About Love/Some Day, Maybe Tonight	1957	10.00	20.00	40.00

GRANT, JULIE

Number	Title (A Side/B Side)	Yr	VG	VG+	NM
HICKORY					
❑ 1260	Every Day I Have to Cry/Watch What You Do with Your Baby	1964	3.00	6.00	12.00
❑ 1288	You're Nobody 'Til Somebody Loves You/Come to Me	1964	3.00	6.00	12.00

GRAPEFRUIT

Number	Title (A Side/B Side)	Yr	VG	VG+	NM
ABC DUNHILL					
❑ 4178	This Little Man/Round Going Round	1968	2.50	5.00	10.00
EQUINOX					
❑ 70000	Dead Boot/Dear Delilah	1967	3.00	6.00	12.00
❑ 70005	Elevator/Yes	1968	3.00	6.00	12.00
❑ 70008	C'mon Marianne/Ain't It Good	1968	3.00	6.00	12.00
RCA VICTOR					
❑ 74-0241	Thunder and Lightning/Blues in Your Head	1969	2.00	4.00	8.00

GRASS ROOTS, THE

Also see STEVE BARRI; ROB GRILL; P.F. SLOAN.

Number	Title (A Side/B Side)	Yr	VG	VG+	NM
ABC DUNHILL					
❑ 4144	Midnight Confessions/Who Will You Be Tomorrow	1968	2.00	4.00	8.00
❑ 4162	Della Linda/Hot Bright Blues	1968	3.00	6.00	12.00
—Some labels have A-side typographical error as shown					
❑ 4162	Bella Linda/Hot Bright Blues	1968	2.00	4.00	8.00
❑ 4180	Lovin' Things/You and Love Are the Same	1969	2.00	4.00	8.00
❑ 4187	The River Is Wide/(You Gotta) Live for Love	1969	2.00	4.00	8.00
❑ 4198	I'd Wait a Million Years/Fly Me to Havana	1969	—	3.00	6.00
❑ 4217	Heaven Knows/Don't Remind Me	1969	—	3.00	6.00
❑ 4227	Walking Through the Country/Truck Drivin' Man	1970	—	3.00	6.00
❑ 4237	Baby Hold On/Get It Together	1970	—	3.00	6.00
❑ 4237 [PS]	Baby Hold On/Get It Together	1970	2.50	5.00	10.00
❑ 4249	Come On and Say It/Something's Comin' Over Me	1970	—	3.00	6.00
❑ 4249 [PS]	Come On and Say It/Something's Comin' Over Me	1970	2.50	5.00	10.00
❑ 4263	Temptation Eyes/Keepin' Me Down	1971	—	2.50	5.00
❑ 4279	Sooner or Later/I Can Turn Off the Rain	1971	—	2.50	5.00
❑ 4289	Two Divided by Love/Let It Go	1971	—	2.50	5.00
❑ 4302	Glory Bound/The Only One	1972	—	2.50	5.00
❑ 4316	The Runway/Move Along	1972	—	2.50	5.00
❑ 4325	Any Way the Wind Blows/Monday Love	1972	—	2.50	5.00
❑ 4335	Love Is What You Make It/Someone to Love	1973	—	3.00	6.00
❑ 4345	Where There's Smoke There's Fire/Look but Don't Touch	1973	2.50	5.00	10.00
❑ 4371	We Can't Dance to Your Music/Look but Don't Touch	1973	2.50	5.00	10.00
❑ 15006	Stealin' Love (In the Night)/We Almost Made It Together	1974	3.75	7.50	15.00
DUNHILL					
❑ 4013	Mr. Jones (A Ballad of a Thin Man)/You're a Lonely Girl	1965	5.00	10.00	20.00
❑ 4029	Where Were You When I Needed You/(These Are) Bad Times	1966	5.00	10.00	20.00
❑ 4043	Only When You're Lonely/This Is What I Was Made For	1966	5.00	10.00	20.00
❑ 4053	Tip of My Tongue/Look Out, Girl	1966	6.25	12.50	25.00
❑ 4084	Let's Live for Today/Depressed Feeling	1967	3.00	6.00	12.00
❑ 4094	Things I Should Have Said/Tip of My Tongue	1967	2.50	5.00	10.00
❑ 4094 [PS]	Things I Should Have Said/Tip of My Tongue	1967	3.75	7.50	15.00
❑ 4105	Wake Up, Wake Up/No Exit	1967	2.50	5.00	10.00
❑ 4122	A Melody for You/Hey Friend	1968	2.50	5.00	10.00
❑ 4129	Feelings/Here's Where You Belong	1968	2.50	5.00	10.00
❑ 4144	Midnight Confessions/Who Will You Be Tomorrow	1968	7.50	15.00	30.00
—Original label has no "ABC" logo next to "Dunhill"					
HAVEN					
❑ 802	Out in the Open/Optical Illusion	1976	2.00	4.00	8.00
❑ 7015	Mamacita/Last Time Around	1975	—	2.50	5.00
❑ 7021	Naked Man/Nothing Good Comes Easy	1975	—	2.50	5.00
MCA					
❑ 52058	Here Comes That Feeling Again/Temptation Eyes	1982	2.50	5.00	10.00
❑ 52104	She Don't Know Me/Keep On Burning	1982	2.50	5.00	10.00

GRATEFUL DEAD, THE

Also see JERRY GARCIA; MICKEY HART; BOB WEIR.

Number	Title (A Side/B Side)	Yr	VG	VG+	NM
ARISTA					
❑ 0276	Dancin' in the Streets/Terrapin Station	1977	—	3.00	6.00
❑ 0291	Passenger/Terrapin Station	1977	—	3.00	6.00
❑ 0383	Good Lovin'/Stagger Lee	1978	—	3.00	6.00
❑ 0410	France/Shakedown Street	1979	—	3.00	6.00
❑ 0519	Alabama Getaway/Far from Me	1980	—	2.50	5.00
❑ 0519 [PS]	Alabama Getaway/Far from Me	1980	—	2.50	5.00
❑ 0546	Don't Ease Me In/Far from Me	1980	—	2.50	5.00
❑ 9606	Touch of Grey/My Brother Esau	1987	—	2.50	5.00
—Grey vinyl					
❑ 9606	Touch of Grey/My Brother Esau	1987	—	—	3.00
—Black vinyl (not issued with picture sleeve)					
❑ 9606 [PS]	Touch of Grey/My Brother Esau	1987	—	2.50	5.00
—Fold-open poster sleeve (add $2 for sticker attached to original shrink wrap)					
❑ 9643	Throwing Stones (Ashes Ashes) Edit/Throwing Stones (Ashes Ashes) LP Version	1987	—	—	3.00
❑ 9643 [PS]	Throwing Stones (Ashes Ashes) Edit/Throwing Stones (Ashes Ashes) LP Version	1987	—	—	3.00
❑ 9899	Foolish Heart/We Can Run	1989	—	2.00	4.00
❑ 9899 [PS]	Foolish Heart/We Can Run	1989	—	2.00	4.00
GRATEFUL DEAD					
❑ 01	Here Comes Sunshine/Let Me Sing Your Blues Away	1973	3.00	6.00	12.00
❑ 02	Eyes of the World/Weather Report (Part 1)	1974	3.00	6.00	12.00
❑ 03	U.S. Blues/Loose Lucy	1974	2.50	5.00	10.00
❑ 03 [PS]	U.S. Blues/Loose Lucy	1974	6.25	12.50	25.00
❑ XW-718	The Music Never Stopped/Help on the Way	1975	3.75	7.50	15.00
❑ XW-762	Franklin's Tower/Help on the Way	1976	6.25	12.50	25.00
SCORPIO					
❑ 201	Stealin'/Don't Ease Me In	1966	250.00	500.00	1000.

Number	Title (A Side/B Side)	Yr	VG	VG+	NM
WARNER BROS.					
❑ 7016	The Golden Road (To Unlimited Devotion)/ Cream Puff War	1967	6.25	12.50	25.00
❑ 7186	Dark Star/Born Cross-Eyed	1968	6.25	12.50	25.00
❑ 7186 [PS]	Dark Star/Born Cross-Eyed	1968	125.00	250.00	500.00
❑ 7324	Dupree's Diamond Blues/Cosmic Charlie	1969	6.25	12.50	25.00
❑ 7410	Uncle John's Band/New Speedway Boogie	1970	3.75	7.50	15.00
—A picture sleeve for this is rumored to exist					
❑ 7464	Truckin'/Ripple	1971	3.75	7.50	15.00
❑ 7627	Johnny B. Goode/So Fine	1972	5.00	10.00	20.00
—B-side by Elvin Bishop Group					
❑ 7653	Truckin'/Johnny B. Goode	1973	2.00	4.00	8.00
—"Back to Back Hits" series					
❑ 7667	Sugar Magnolia/Mr. Charlie	1972	3.75	7.50	15.00

7-Inch Extended Plays

Number	Title (A Side/B Side)	Yr	VG	VG+	NM
WARNER BROS.					
❑ S 1893 [DJ]	Sugar Magnolia/Operator/Till the Morning Comes//Truckin'/Friend of the Devil	1973	5.00	10.00	20.00
—Jukebox issue, small hole, plays at 33 1/3 rpm					
❑ S 1893 [PS]	American Beauty	1973	7.50	15.00	30.00
—Part of Little LP series (LLP #226)					

GRAVES, BILLY

Number	Title (A Side/B Side)	Yr	VG	VG+	NM
MONUMENT					
❑ 401	The Shag (Is Totally Cool)/Uncertain	1958	5.00	10.00	20.00
❑ 404	Long Journey Home/Midnight Bus	1959	3.75	7.50	15.00
❑ 418	Right or Wrong (I'll Be With You)/Mount Fujiyama	1960	3.00	6.00	12.00
❑ 992	The Lonesome Ape/I've Got a Feeling	1966	2.00	4.00	8.00

GRAVES, JOE

Number	Title (A Side/B Side)	Yr	VG	VG+	NM
PARKWAY					
❑ 103	Debbie/A Boy and a Girl Fall in Love	1966	3.75	7.50	15.00
❑ 964	See Saw/Beautiful Girl	1965	3.75	7.50	15.00

GRAY, BARRY, AND THE SPACEMAKERS

Number	Title (A Side/B Side)	Yr	VG	VG+	NM
ABC-PARAMOUNT					
❑ 10424	Fireball/XL 5	1963	3.00	6.00	12.00

GRAY, BILLY

Also see WANDA JACKSON.

Number	Title (A Side/B Side)	Yr	VG	VG+	NM
DECCA					
❑ 29489	Okie Blondie/I've Had At My Heart	1955	7.50	15.00	30.00
❑ 29678	Harbor of Love/Girls, Girls, Girls	1955	7.50	15.00	30.00
❑ 29800	Tennessee Toddy/It Could Have Been Me	1956	10.00	20.00	40.00
LIBERTY					
❑ 55599	I'll Never Live Long Enough/I Left My Heart in San Francisco	1963	3.00	6.00	12.00
❑ 55712	Last Call for Alcohol/Late Last Night	1964	2.50	5.00	10.00

GRAY, DOBIE

Number	Title (A Side/B Side)	Yr	VG	VG+	NM
ANTHEM					
❑ 200	Guess Who?/Bits and Pieces	1972	—	2.50	5.00
ARISTA					
❑ 1047	One Can Fake It/(B-side unknown)	1983	—	2.00	4.00
CAPITOL					
❑ 2241	We the People/Funny and Groovy	1968	2.50	5.00	10.00
❑ B-5562	Gonna Be a Long Night/That's One to Grown On	1986	—	—	3.00
❑ B-5596	The Dark Side of Life/A Night in the Life of a Country Boy	1986	—	—	3.00
❑ B-5647	From Where I Stand/So Far So Good	1986	—	—	3.00
❑ 5853	River Deep, Mountain High/Tennessee Waltz	1967	3.75	7.50	15.00
❑ B-44087	Take It Real Easy/You Must Have Been Reading My Heart	1987	—	—	3.00
❑ B-44126	Love Letters/Steady As She Goes	1988	—	—	3.00
CAPRICORN					
❑ 0249	If Love Must Go/Lover's Sweat	1975	—	2.00	4.00
❑ 0259	Find 'Em, Fool 'Em and Forget 'Em/Mellow Man	1976	—	2.00	4.00
❑ 0267	Let Go/Mellow Man	1976	—	2.00	4.00
CHARGER					
❑ 105	The "In" Crowd/To Be a Man	1964	3.00	6.00	12.00
❑ 107	See You at the "Go-Go"/Walk with Love	1965	2.50	5.00	10.00
❑ 109	In Hollywood/Mr. Engineer	1965	2.50	5.00	10.00
❑ 113	Monkey Jerk/My Baby	1965	2.50	5.00	10.00
❑ 115	No Room to Cry/Out on the Floor	1966	2.50	5.00	10.00
CORDAK					
❑ 1602	Look at Me/Walkin' and Whistlin'	1962	3.75	7.50	15.00
DECCA					
❑ 33057	Drift Away/City Stars	1973	—	2.50	5.00
INFINITY					
❑ 50003	You Can Do It/Sharing the Night Together	1978	—	2.00	4.00
❑ 50010	Who's Lovin' You/Thank You for Tonight	1979	—	2.00	4.00
❑ 50020	Spending Time, Making Love, and Going Crazy/ Let This Man Take Hold of Your Life	1979	—	2.00	4.00
❑ 50043	The In Crowd/Let This Man Take Hold of Your Life	1979	—	2.00	4.00
MCA					
❑ 40100	Loving Arms/Now That I'm Without You	1973	—	2.00	4.00
❑ 40153	Good Old Song/Reachin' for the Feelin'	1973	—	2.00	4.00
❑ 40188	Rose/Lovin' the Easy Way	1974	—	2.00	4.00
❑ 40201	There's a Honky Tonk Angel (Who'll Take Me Back In)/Lovin' the Easy Way	1974	—	2.00	4.00
❑ 40268	Watch Out for Lucy/Turning On You	1974	—	2.00	4.00
❑ 40315	The Music's Real/Roll On Sweet Mississippi	1974	—	2.00	4.00
ROBOX					
❑ RRS-117	Decorate the Night (same on both sides)	1979	—	2.50	5.00
WHITE WHALE					
❑ 300	Rose Garden/Where's the Girl Gone	1969	2.50	5.00	10.00
❑ 330	What a Way to Go/Do You Really Have a Heart	1969	50.00	100.00	200.00
❑ 342	Honey, You Can't Take It Back	1970	15.00	30.00	60.00

GRAY, GENE, AND THE STINGRAYS

Number	Title (A Side/B Side)	Yr	VG	VG+	NM
DOT					
❑ 16478	Surf Bunny/Surfer's Mood	1963	5.00	10.00	20.00
LINDA					
❑ 110	Surf Bunny/Surfer's Mood	1963	10.00	20.00	40.00

GRAY, MACY

Number	Title (A Side/B Side)	Yr	VG	VG+	NM
EPIC					
❑ 79241	I Try (same on both sides)	2000	—	—	2.00
—Custom gray label					
❑ 79241 [PS]	I Try (same on both sides)	2000	—	—	2.00

GRAY, MAUREEN

Number	Title (A Side/B Side)	Yr	VG	VG+	NM
CHANCELLOR					
❑ 1082	Crazy Over You/Today's the Day	1961	6.25	12.50	25.00
❑ 1091	Come On and Dance/I Don't Want to Cry	1961	6.25	12.50	25.00
❑ 1100	I'm So Young/There's a Boy	1962	6.25	12.50	25.00
LANDA					
❑ 689	Dancin' the Strand/Oh My	1962	3.75	7.50	15.00
❑ 692	People Are Talking/Oh My	1962	3.75	7.50	15.00
MERCURY					
❑ 72131	Story of My Love/Summertime Is Near	1963	3.00	6.00	12.00
❑ 72227	I'm a Happy Girl (Tra La La)/Goodbye Baby	1964	3.00	6.00	12.00

GRAY, RUDY

See RUDY GRAYZELL.

GRAYZELL, RUDY

Number	Title (A Side/B Side)	Yr	VG	VG+	NM
ABBOTT					
❑ 147	Bonita Chiquita/I'm Gone Again	1953	20.00	40.00	80.00
❑ 157	Ocean Paradise/It Ain't My Baby	1954	20.00	40.00	80.00
CAPITOL					
❑ F2946	Hearts Made of Stone/There's Gonna Be a Ball	1954	10.00	20.00	40.00
❑ F3044	You Better Believe It/Ca-Razy	1955	10.00	20.00	40.00
❑ F3149	Please Big Mama/My Heart Is Willing	1955	10.00	20.00	40.00
—Capitol titles as "Rudy Gray"					
MERCURY					
❑ 71138	Let's Get Wild/I Love You So	1957	20.00	40.00	80.00
STARDAY					
❑ 229	The Moon Is Up/Day by Day	1956	20.00	40.00	80.00
❑ 241	Duck Dail/You're Gone	1956	20.00	40.00	80.00
❑ 270	You Hurt Me So/Jig-Ga-Lee-Ga	1956	20.00	40.00	80.00
❑ 321	Let's Get Wild/I Love You So	1957	25.00	50.00	100.00
SUN					
❑ 290	Judy/I Think of You	1958	12.50	25.00	50.00

GREAT BUILDINGS

Two members later formed THE REMBRANDTS.

Number	Title (A Side/B Side)	Yr	VG	VG+	NM
COLUMBIA					
❑ 02008	Combat Zone/Hold On Something	1981	—	3.00	6.00

GREAT SCOTTS, THE

Number	Title (A Side/B Side)	Yr	VG	VG+	NM
EPIC					
❑ 9805	Don't Want Your Love/Give Me Lovin'	1965	5.00	10.00	20.00
❑ 9866	That's My Girl (Rotton to the Core)/Lost in Conversation	1965	10.00	20.00	40.00
TRIUMPH					
❑ 66	Ball and Chain/Run, Run for Your Life	1966	7.50	15.00	30.00
❑ 67	Light Hurts My Eyes/You Know What You Can Do	1966	7.50	15.00	30.00

GREAT SOCIETY, THE

Also see GRACE SLICK.

Number	Title (A Side/B Side)	Yr	VG	VG+	NM
COLUMBIA					
❑ 44583	Sally Go 'Round the Roses/Didn't Think So	1968	5.00	10.00	20.00
NORTH BEACH					
❑ 1001	Someone to Love/Free Advice	1966	62.50	125.00	250.00
—As "The Great!! Society!!"					

GREATS, THE

Number	Title (A Side/B Side)	Yr	VG	VG+	NM
EBB					
❑ 145	Marching Elvis/Fiddler's Rock	1958	12.50	25.00	50.00

GREAVES, R.B.

Number	Title (A Side/B Side)	Yr	VG	VG+	NM
20TH CENTURY					
❑ 2147	Rock and Roll/I'm Married, You're Married	1974	—	2.00	4.00
❑ 2203	Let's Try It Again/My Place or Yours	1975	—	2.00	4.00
ATCO					
❑ 6714	Take a Letter Maria/Big Bad City	1969	2.00	4.00	8.00
❑ 6726	Always Something There to Remind Me/Oh, When I Was a Boy	1969	—	3.00	6.00
❑ 6745	Fire and Rain/The Ballad of Leroy	1970	—	3.00	6.00
❑ 6778	Oh When I Was a Boy/Georgia Took Her Back	1970	—	3.00	6.00
❑ 6789	Whiter Shade of Pale/Show Me the Way to Go	1970	—	3.00	6.00
❑ 6839	Paperback Writer/Over You Now	1971	—	2.50	5.00
BAREBACK					
❑ 523	Margie, Who's Watching the Baby/(B-side unknown)	1977	—	3.00	6.00
MGM					
❑ 14483	Margie, Who's Watching the Baby/Area Code 213	1973	—	2.50	5.00
❑ 14567	All I Want to Do/Long Live the King	1973	—	2.50	5.00
MIDSONG INT'L.					
❑ 72006	Let Me Be the One Tonight/Please Mister Mailman	1980	—	2.00	4.00
SUNFLOWER					
❑ 128	Margie, Who's Watching the Baby/Area Code 213	1972	—	3.00	6.00

GREEN, AL

Number	Title (A Side/B Side)	Yr	VG	VG+	NM
A&M					
❑ 1427	As Long As We're Together/Blessed	1989	—	—	3.00
❑ 2786	Going Away/Building Up	1985	—	2.00	4.00
❑ 2807	True Love/He Is the Light	1986	—	2.00	4.00
❑ 2919	Everything's Gonna Be Alright/So Real to Me	1987	—	—	3.00

Number	Title (A Side/B Side)	Yr	VG	VG+	NM
❑ 2952	You Know and I Know/True Love	1987	—	—	3.00
❑ 2962	Soul Survivor/Jesus Will Fix It	1987	—	—	3.00
BELL					
❑ 45258	Guilty/Let Me Help You	1972	—	2.50	5.00
❑ 45305	Hot Wire/Don't Leave Me	1973	—	2.50	5.00
CAPITOL					
❑ S7-18869	Tired of Being Alone/Walk On By	1995	—	—	3.00
—B-side by Isaac Hayes					
HI					
❑ 2159	I Want to Hold Your Hand/What Am I Gonna Do with Myself	1969	2.00	4.00	8.00
❑ 2164	One Woman/Tomorrow's Dream	1969	2.00	4.00	8.00
❑ 2172	You Say It/Gotta Find a New World	1969	—	3.00	6.00
❑ 2177	Right Now, Right Now/All Because I'm a Foolish One	1970	—	3.00	6.00
❑ 2182	I Can't Get Next to You/Ride Sally Ride	1970	—	3.00	6.00
❑ 2188	Driving Wheel/True Love	1971	—	3.00	6.00
❑ 2194	Tired of Being Alone/Get Back Baby	1971	—	2.50	5.00
❑ 2202	Let's Stay Together/Tomorrow's Dream	1971	—	2.50	5.00
❑ 2211	Look What You Done for Me/La La for You	1972	—	2.50	5.00
❑ 2216	I'm Still in Love with You/Old Time Lovin'	1972	—	2.50	5.00
❑ 2227	You Ought to Be with Me/What Is This Feeling	1972	—	2.50	5.00
❑ 2235	Call Me (Come Back Home)/What a Wonderful Thing Love Is	1973	—	2.50	5.00
❑ 2247	Here I Am (Come and Take Me)/I'm Glad You're Mine	1973	—	2.50	5.00
❑ 2257	Livin' for You/It Ain't No Fun to Me	1973	—	2.50	5.00
❑ 2262	Let's Get Married/So Good to Be Here	1974	—	2.50	5.00
❑ 2274	Sha-La-La (Make Me Happy)/School Days	1974	—	2.50	5.00
❑ 2282	L-O-V-E (Love)/I Wish You Were Here	1975	—	2.50	5.00
❑ 2288	Oh Me, Oh My (Dreams in My Arms)/Strong As Death (Sweet As Love)	1975	—	2.50	5.00
❑ 2300	Full of Fire/Could I Be the One	1975	—	2.50	5.00
❑ 2306	Let It Shine/There's No Way	1976	—	2.50	5.00
❑ 2319	Keep Me Cryin'/There Is Love	1976	—	2.50	5.00
❑ 2322	I Tried to Tell Myself/Something	1977	—	2.50	5.00
❑ 2324	Love and Happiness/Glory Glory	1977	—	2.50	5.00
❑ 77505	Belle/Chariots of Fire	1977	—	2.00	4.00
❑ 77505 [PS]	Belle/Chariots of Fire	1977	—	3.00	6.00
❑ 78511	I Feel Good/Feels Like Summer	1978	—	2.00	4.00
❑ 78522	Wait Here/To Sir with Love	1978	—	2.00	4.00
❑ 78522 [PS]	Wait Here/To Sir with Love	1978	—	3.00	6.00
HOT LINE JOURNAL					
❑ 15000	Back Up Train/Don't Leave Me	1967	6.25	12.50	25.00
❑ 15001	Don't Hurt Me No More/Get Yourself Together	1967	7.50	15.00	30.00
❑ 15002	I'll Be Good to You/Lover's Hideaway	1967	7.50	15.00	30.00
THE RIGHT STUFF					
❑ S7-17524	Let's Stay Together/I'm Still in Love with You	1993	—	—	3.00
❑ S7-18217	I'll Be Home for Christmas/It Feels Like Christmas	1994	—	2.50	5.00

GREEN, FRED

Number	Title (A Side/B Side)	Yr	VG	VG+	NM
BOBBIN					
❑ 111	Wham Slam Baby/It's Funny	1959	25.00	50.00	100.00
❑ 123	Don't Make a Fool Out of Me/If You Ever Try to Leave Me	1960	25.00	50.00	100.00

GREEN, FRED, AND THE MELLARDS

Number	Title (A Side/B Side)	Yr	VG	VG+	NM
BALLAD					
❑ 1012	My Sweetheart/You Can't Keep Love in a Broken Heart	1955	75.00	150.00	300.00
❑ 1016	Love Me Crazy/That's Life	1955	50.00	100.00	200.00

GREEN, JANICE (THE "OH JULIE" GIRL)

Number	Title (A Side/B Side)	Yr	VG	VG+	NM
NASCO					
❑ 6013	With All My Heart/Jackie	1958	5.00	10.00	20.00

GREEN, KEITH

Number	Title (A Side/B Side)	Yr	VG	VG+	NM
DECCA					
❑ 31799	A Go-Go Letter/The Way I Used to Be	1965	5.00	10.00	20.00
❑ 31859	Girl Don't Tell Me/How to Be Your Guy	1965	6.25	12.50	25.00
❑ 31973	Home Town Girls/Hear What's Happening, Baby	1966	5.00	10.00	20.00
ERA					
❑ 108	Sgt. Pepper's Epitaph/Country Store	1970	2.50	5.00	10.00
❑ 3210	Fantastic/L.A. City Smog Blues	1969	2.50	5.00	10.00

GREEN, LIL

Number	Title (A Side/B Side)	Yr	VG	VG+	NM
ATLANTIC					
❑ 951	Every Time/I've Got That Feeling	1952	25.00	50.00	100.00

GREEN, LLOYD

Number	Title (A Side/B Side)	Yr	VG	VG+	NM
CHART					
❑ 1029	Woman, Woman/Mr. Nashville Sound	1968	2.00	4.00	8.00
❑ 1071	Bar Hoppin'/Greenblue	1969	2.00	4.00	8.00
❑ 5014	Orbit/Robin	1969	2.00	4.00	8.00
❑ 5043	Tell Ya What/Steel Blue	1969	2.00	4.00	8.00
❑ 5072	Ride, Ride, Ride/Not Another Time	1970	2.00	4.00	8.00
LITTLE DARLIN'					
❑ 007	Skillet Lickin'/Green Strings	1966	6.25	12.50	25.00
❑ 0023	Pedal Pattle/Little Darlin'	1967	6.25	12.50	25.00
❑ 0050	Sweet Cheeks/Green Strings	1968	2.50	5.00	10.00
MONUMENT					
❑ 8549	Morning Has Broken/Phase Phive	1972	—	3.00	6.00
❑ 8562	I Can See Clearly Now/Steelin' Away	1973	—	3.00	6.00
❑ 8574	Here Comes the Sun/Peace	1973	—	3.00	6.00
❑ 8592	Sleep Walk/Dixie Drive-In	1973	—	3.00	6.00
❑ 8608	Atlantis/San Antonio Rose	1974	—	3.00	6.00
❑ 8615	Seaside/Summer Clouds	1974	—	3.00	6.00
❑ 8624	Canadian Sunset/Spirit of '49	1974	—	3.00	6.00
❑ 8635	Sally G/Lucretia	1974	—	3.00	6.00
❑ 8648	I Can Help/Theme from A Summer Place	1975	—	2.50	5.00
—With Charlie McCoy					
OCTOBER					
❑ 1002	You and Me/Edgewater Beach	1976	—	3.00	6.00
❑ 1009	Feelings/Stainless Steel	1977	—	3.00	6.00
PRIZE					
❑ 01	Midnight Silence/Wide Awake	1971	—	3.50	7.00
❑ 09	Soundwaves/Tom's Tavern Blues	1971	—	3.50	7.00
SOUNDWAVES					
❑ 4560	The Whistler/Afterglow	1977	—	2.50	5.00

GREEN, RUDY

See RUDY GREENE.

GREEN, VERNON, AND THE MEDALLIONS

See THE MEDALLIONS.

GREENBAUM, NORMAN

Also see DR. WEST'S MEDICINE SHOW AND JUG BAND.

Number	Title (A Side/B Side)	Yr	VG	VG+	NM
GREGAR					
❑ 71-0107	Nancy Whiskey/Twentieth Century Fox	1969	2.50	5.00	10.00
REPRISE					
❑ 0739	Spirit in the Sky/Canned Ham	1971	—	2.00	4.00
—"Back to Back Hits" series					
❑ 0752	Children of Paradise/School for Sweet Talk	1968	2.50	5.00	10.00
❑ 0818	Marcy/Children of Paradise	1969	2.50	5.00	10.00
❑ 0846	Jubilee/Skyline	1969	2.50	5.00	10.00
❑ 0885	Spirit in the Sky/Milk Cow	1969	2.00	4.00	8.00
❑ 0919	Canned Ham/Junior Cadillac	1970	—	3.00	6.00
❑ 0956	Rhode Island Red/I.J. Foxx	1970	—	3.00	6.00
❑ 0956 [PS]	Rhode Island Red/I.J. Foxx	1970	7.50	15.00	30.00
❑ 1008	California Earthquake/Rhode Island Red	1971	—	3.00	6.00
❑ 1134	Dairy Queen/Petaluma	1972	—	3.00	6.00

GREENBEATS, THE

Number	Title (A Side/B Side)	Yr	VG	VG+	NM
JERDEN					
❑ 757	You Must Be the One/If This Wine Was Mine	1965	3.00	6.00	12.00
❑ 763	So Sad/I'm on Fire	1965	3.00	6.00	12.00

GREENE, BARBARA

Number	Title (A Side/B Side)	Yr	VG	VG+	NM
ATCO					
❑ 6250	Long Tall Sally/Slippin' and Slidin'	1963	10.00	20.00	40.00
RENEE					
❑ 5001	Young Boy/I Should Have Treated You Right	1968	2.50	5.00	10.00
VIVID					
❑ 105	Young Boy/I Should Have Treated You Right	1968	3.00	6.00	12.00

GREENE, RUDY

Number	Title (A Side/B Side)	Yr	VG	VG+	NM
CHANCE					
❑ 1139	Love Is a Pain/No Need of Your Crying	1953	37.50	75.00	150.00
❑ 1146	The Letter/It's You I Love	1953	37.50	75.00	150.00
❑ 1151	I Had a Feeling/Meet Me Baby	1954	37.50	75.00	150.00
—Black vinyl					
❑ 1151	I Had a Feeling/Meet Me Baby	1954	100.00	200.00	400.00
—Red vinyl					
CLUB 51					
❑ 103	Highway No. 1/You Mean Everything to Me	1956	50.00	100.00	200.00
—With the Four Buddies					
EMBER					
❑ 1012	Juicy Fruit/You're the One for Me	1957	10.00	20.00	40.00
❑ 1020	Lonesome/Wild Life	1957	10.00	20.00	40.00
EXCELLO					
❑ 2074	Cool Lovin' Mama/My Mumblin' Baby	1955	12.50	25.00	50.00
❑ 2090	Teeny Weeny Baby/Queer Feeling	1956	12.50	25.00	50.00

GREENWICH, ELLIE

Also see THE RAINDROPS.

Number	Title (A Side/B Side)	Yr	VG	VG+	NM
BELL					
❑ 855	Ain't That Peculiar/I Don't Want to Be Left Outside	1970	2.50	5.00	10.00
❑ 933	That Certain Someone/It's Like a Sad Old Kind of Movie	1970	2.50	5.00	10.00
MADISON					
❑ 160	Red Corvette/I Go, You Go	1961	7.50	15.00	30.00
—As "Ellie Gee"					
RED BIRD					
❑ 10-034	You Don't Know/Baby	1965	10.00	20.00	40.00
UNITED ARTISTS					
❑ 50151	I Want You to Be My Baby/Goodnight, Goodnight	1967	3.75	7.50	15.00
❑ 50278	A Long Time Comin'/Niki-Hoeky	1968	3.75	7.50	15.00
VERVE					
❑ 10719	Today I Met the Boy I'm Gonna Marry/Maybe I Know	1973	2.50	5.00	10.00
❑ 10724	Chapel of Love/River Deep, Mountain High	1973	2.50	5.00	10.00

GREER, BIG JOHN

Number	Title (A Side/B Side)	Yr	VG	VG+	NM
GROOVE					
❑ 0002	Bottle It Up and Go/You'll Never Be Mine	1954	10.00	20.00	40.00
❑ 0016	When the Roses Bloom in Lover's Lane/Too Long	1954	10.00	20.00	40.00
❑ 0038	We Wanna See Santa Do the Mambo/Wait Till After Christmas	1954	10.00	20.00	40.00
❑ 0108	Soon, Soon, Soon/I'm Glad for Your Sake	1955	10.00	20.00	40.00
❑ 0119	Come Back Maybellene/Night Crawlin'	1955	12.50	25.00	50.00
❑ 0131	A Man and a Woman/Blam	1955	15.00	30.00	60.00
—With the Four Students					
KING					
❑ 4878	Record Hop/Keep On Loving Me	1956	5.00	10.00	20.00
❑ 4941	Let Me Come Home/Come Back, Uncle John	1956	5.00	10.00	20.00
❑ 5006	Midnight Ramble/Sweet Slumber	1957	5.00	10.00	20.00
❑ 5057	Duck Walk/I Still Love You So	1957	5.00	10.00	20.00
RCA VICTOR					
❑ 47-4293	Have Another Drink/I'm Savin' All My Lovin'	1951	10.00	20.00	40.00
❑ 47-4348	Got You on My Mind/Woman Is a Five-Letter Word	1951	10.00	20.00	40.00
❑ 47-4484	Strong Red Whiskey/If You Let Me	1952	10.00	20.00	40.00

Number	Title (A Side/B Side)	Yr	VG	VG+	NM
❑ 47-5037	I'm the Fat Man/Since You Went Away from Me	1952	10.00	20.00	40.00
❑ 47-5170	I'll Never Let You Go/You Played on My Piano	1953	10.00	20.00	40.00
❑ 47-5259	Ride Pretty Baby/Don't Worry 'Bout Me	1953	10.00	20.00	40.00
❑ 47-5531	Drinkin' Fool/Gettin' Mighty Lonesome for You	1953	10.00	20.00	40.00
❑ 50-0007	Drinkin' Wine Spo-Dee-O-Dee/Long Tall Gal	1949	17.50	35.00	70.00
—Orange vinyl					
❑ 50-0029	If I Told You Once/I Found a Dream	1949	17.50	35.00	70.00
—Orange vinyl					
❑ 50-0051	Rockin' Jenny Jones/I've Just Found Love	1950	17.50	35.00	70.00
—Orange vinyl					
❑ 50-0076	I'll Never Do That Again/A Fool Hasn't Got a Chance	1950	15.00	30.00	60.00
—Orange vinyl					
❑ 50-0096	Cheatin'/It's Better to Have Been Taken for Granted	1950	15.00	30.00	60.00
—Orange vinyl					
❑ 50-0104	Red Juice/Big John's a-Blowin'	1950	15.00	30.00	60.00
—Orange vinyl					
❑ 50-0108	Once There Lived a Fool/I Want Ya, I Need Ya	1951	12.50	25.00	50.00
❑ 50-0113	Why Did You Go/Our Wedding Time	1951	12.50	25.00	50.00
❑ 50-0125	Clambake Boogie/When You Love	1951	12.50	25.00	50.00
❑ 50-0137	Big Rock/How Can You Forget?	1951	12.50	25.00	50.00

GREGORY, DICK

B-SHARP

Number	Title (A Side/B Side)	Yr	VG	VG+	NM
❑ 272	Did You Need to Know/(B-side unknown)	1966	75.00	150.00	300.00
—Probably a different performer than the comedian/activist					

VEE JAY

Number	Title (A Side/B Side)	Yr	VG	VG+	NM
❑ 469	They Won't Hire Me/Benefit	1962	3.00	6.00	12.00

GREGORY, IVAN, AND THE BLUE NOTES

G&G

Number	Title (A Side/B Side)	Yr	VG	VG+	NM
❑ 110	Elvis Presley Blues/Kathy	1956	62.50	125.00	250.00

GRIER, FRANKIE, QUARTET

SWAN

Number	Title (A Side/B Side)	Yr	VG	VG+	NM
❑ 4019	Oh, Gloria/Lonesome for You	1958	100.00	200.00	400.00

GRIER, ROOSEVELT

Most of his 1970s records, and scattered earlier ones, were as "Rosey Grier."

Number	Title (A Side/B Side)	Yr	VG	VG+	NM
20TH CENTURY					
❑ 2212	Take the Time to Love Somebody/Your Love Is Right Up My Alley	1975	2.00	4.00	8.00
A					
❑ 105	Sincerely/Why Don't You Do Me Right	1959	6.25	12.50	25.00
❑ 110	Moonlight in Vermont/Smoky Morning	1960	6.25	12.50	25.00
ABC					
❑ 11275	Rat Race/I Don't Want Nobody (To Lead Me On)	1970	—	3.00	6.00
AGP					
❑ 109	Bad News/Ring Around the World	1969	2.00	4.00	8.00
AMY					
❑ 11004	Who's Got the Ball (Y'All)/Halftime	1967	3.00	6.00	12.00
❑ 11015	High Society Woman/C'mon Cupid	1968	3.00	6.00	12.00
❑ 11029	Hard to Forget/People Make the World	1968	3.00	6.00	12.00
A&M					
❑ 1457	Beautiful People/I'll Be Back Tomorrow	1973	—	2.50	5.00
❑ 1500	If You Hit a Good Lick, Lay On It/You're the Violin	1974	—	2.50	5.00
BATTLE					
❑ 45911	Why/Lover Set Me Free	1963	6.25	12.50	25.00
BELL					
❑ 45459	It's All Right to Cry/(B-side unknown)	1974	2.00	4.00	8.00
D-TOWN					
❑ 1058	Pizza Pie Man/Welcome to the Club	1965	10.00	20.00	40.00
LIBERTY					
❑ 55413	Struttin' 'n Twistin'/Let the Cool Wind Blow	1962	3.75	7.50	15.00
❑ 55453	The Mail Must Go Thru/Your Has Been	1962	3.75	7.50	15.00
MGM					
❑ 13698	Slow Drag/Yesterday	1967	3.00	6.00	12.00
❑ 13840	Spanish Harlem/I'm Living Good	1967	3.00	6.00	12.00
RIC					
❑ 102	Fool, Fool, Fool/Since You've Been Gone	1964	5.00	10.00	20.00
❑ 112	Down So Long/In My Tenement	1964	5.00	10.00	20.00
SPINDLE TOP					
❑ 102	I'm Going Home/Jinny	1961	5.00	10.00	20.00
UNITED ARTISTS					
❑ 50893	Bring Back the Time/Oh How I Miss You Baby	1972	—	3.00	6.00
YOUNGSTOWN					
❑ 609	Deputy Dog/(B-side unknown)	1966	7.50	15.00	30.00

GRIFFIN, BUCK

Number	Title (A Side/B Side)	Yr	VG	VG+	NM
HOLIDAY INN					
❑ 109	Pretty Lou/The Girl in Room 1209	1963	10.00	20.00	40.00
LIN					
❑ 1005	Meadowlark Boogie/It Don't Make No Never Mind	1954	15.00	30.00	60.00
❑ 1007	Rollin' Tears/One Day After Pay Day	1955	15.00	30.00	60.00
❑ 1008	Going Home, All Alone/Lookin' for the Green	1955	15.00	30.00	60.00
❑ 1014	Next to Mine/Lord, Give Me Strength	1955	15.00	30.00	60.00
❑ 1015	Bawlin' and Squallin'/Let's Elope, Baby	1955	18.75	37.50	75.00
❑ 1016	Go-Stop-O/Cochise	1955	25.00	50.00	100.00
❑ 1018	Little Dan/Neither Do I	1956	15.00	30.00	60.00
METRO					
❑ 20007	The Party/Every Night	1958	7.50	15.00	30.00
MGM					
❑ 12284	Stutterin' Papa/Watchin' the 7:10 Roll By	1956	25.00	50.00	100.00
❑ 12439	Bow My Back/Old Bee Tree	1957	20.00	40.00	80.00
❑ 12597	Jessie Lee/You'll Never Come Back	1957	20.00	40.00	80.00

GRIFFIN, JIMMY

Some of these were credited to "James Griffin." Also see BREAD.

Number	Title (A Side/B Side)	Yr	VG	VG+	NM
IMPERIAL					
❑ 66108	These Are the Times/Walking to New Orleans	1965	3.00	6.00	12.00
❑ 66152	He Will Break Your Heart/Hard Row to Hoe	1965	3.00	6.00	12.00
POLYDOR					
❑ 14213	Breakin' Up Is Easy/Melody Maker	1973	—	2.50	5.00
❑ 14236	She Knows/Beachwood Band	1974	—	2.50	5.00
❑ 14282	Treat Her Right/How Do You Say Goodbye	1975	—	2.50	5.00
REPRISE					
❑ 0268	All My Loving/My Baby Made Me Cry	1964	3.75	7.50	15.00
❑ 0280	Gotta Lotta Love/Running to You	1964	3.75	7.50	15.00
❑ 0304	You're Nobody Till Somebody Loves You/Try	1964	3.75	7.50	15.00
❑ 20114	Girls Grow Up Faster Than Boys/It's a Free Country	1962	5.00	10.00	20.00
❑ 20161	What Kind of Girl Are You/A Little Like Lovin' You	1963	5.00	10.00	20.00
❑ 20178	Love Letters in the Sand/Summer Holiday	1963	5.00	10.00	20.00
❑ 20221	Little Miss Cool/Marie Is Moving	1963	5.00	10.00	20.00
VIVA					
❑ 611	Miracle Worker/Looking So Much Better	1967	2.50	5.00	10.00
❑ 627	Thank You Love/Light of Your Mind	1968	2.50	5.00	10.00
❑ 642	Miracle Worker/Thank You Love	1970	2.50	5.00	10.00

GRIFFINS, THE

Number	Title (A Side/B Side)	Yr	VG	VG+	NM
MERCURY					
❑ 70558	I Swear By All the Stars Above/Sing to Me	1955	30.00	60.00	120.00
❑ 70650	Bad Little Girl/Scheming	1955	30.00	60.00	120.00
❑ 70913	My Baby's Gone/Why Must You Go	1956	10.00	20.00	40.00
WING					
❑ 90067	Forever More/Leave It to Me	1956	50.00	100.00	200.00

GRIFFITH, PEGGI

DOLTON

Number	Title (A Side/B Side)	Yr	VG	VG+	NM
❑ 35	Lovely Girl/You're In My Dreams to Stay	1961	5.00	10.00	20.00

GRILL, ROB

Also see THE GRASS ROOTS.

MERCURY

Number	Title (A Side/B Side)	Yr	VG	VG+	NM
❑ 76009	Rock Sugar/Have Mercy	1979	—	2.50	5.00
❑ 76068	Where Were You When I Needed You/Rockin' on the Road Again	1979	—	2.50	5.00

GRINER, LINDA

MOTOWN

Number	Title (A Side/B Side)	Yr	VG	VG+	NM
❑ 1037	Good-By Cruel World/Envious	1963	87.50	175.00	350.00
—With incorrect A-side title					
❑ 1037	Good-By Cruel Love/Envious	1963	50.00	100.00	200.00
—With corrected A-side title					

GROGAN, TOBY

VEE JAY

Number	Title (A Side/B Side)	Yr	VG	VG+	NM
❑ 560	Angel/Just a Friend	1963	7.50	15.00	30.00
—The Four Seasons sing on this record.					

GROOMS, SHERRY

Number	Title (A Side/B Side)	Yr	VG	VG+	NM
ABC					
❑ 10812	The Girls' Song/Call of the Wild One	1966	5.00	10.00	20.00
❑ 10875	Night Fall/Take Away the Memories (Of a Love So Fine)	1966	7.50	15.00	30.00
❑ 10907	Forever Is a Long Time/That Same Old Song	1967	5.00	10.00	20.00
PARACHUTE					
❑ 514	Me/Mama's Boys	1978	—	2.50	5.00

GROUNDSPEED

DECCA

Number	Title (A Side/B Side)	Yr	VG	VG+	NM
❑ 32344	In a Dream/L-12 East	1968	6.25	12.50	25.00

GROUP "B"

SCORPIO

Number	Title (A Side/B Side)	Yr	VG	VG+	NM
❑ 402	Stop Calling Me/She's Gone	1967	6.25	12.50	25.00
❑ 406	I Know Your Name Girl/I Never Really Knew	1967	6.25	12.50	25.00

GROUPIES, THE

ATCO

Number	Title (A Side/B Side)	Yr	VG	VG+	NM
❑ 6393	I'm a Hog for You/Primitive	1966	7.50	15.00	30.00

GROWING CONCERN, THE

MAINSTREAM

Number	Title (A Side/B Side)	Yr	VG	VG+	NM
❑ 685	Tomorrow Has Been Canceled/A Boy I Once Knew Well	1968	7.50	15.00	30.00

GRUNION HUNTERS, THE

HIGHLAND

Number	Title (A Side/B Side)	Yr	VG	VG+	NM
❑ 1035	The Four-Eyed, Tongue-Tied, Swimmin' Surfer Biter/Sing Along to the Swimmin' Surfer Biter	1963	10.00	20.00	40.00

GRUNIONS, THE

JOCKO

Number	Title (A Side/B Side)	Yr	VG	VG+	NM
❑ 505	Surfin' Psycho/Big Noise from Winnetka	1963	12.50	25.00	50.00

GTR

ARISTA

Number	Title (A Side/B Side)	Yr	VG	VG+	NM
❑ 9470	When the Heart Rules the Mind/Reach Out (Never Say No)	1986	—	—	3.00
❑ 9470 [PS]	When the Heart Rules the Mind/Reach Out (Never Say No)	1986	—	—	3.00
❑ 9512	The Hunter/Sketches in the Sun	1986	—	—	3.00
❑ 9512 [PS]	The Hunter/Sketches in the Sun	1986	—	—	3.00

GUARALDI, VINCE

FANTASY

Number	Title (A Side/B Side)	Yr	VG	VG+	NM
❑ 563	Cast Your Fate to the Wind/Samba de Orpheus	1962	2.50	5.00	10.00
❑ 567	Zalas/Jitterbug Waltz	1963	2.50	5.00	10.00
❑ 571	Mr. Lucky/Treat Street	1963	2.50	5.00	10.00
❑ 580	Days of Wine and Roses/(B-side unknown)	1963	2.50	5.00	10.00
❑ 593	Linus & Lucy/Oh, Good Grief	1964	5.00	10.00	20.00
❑ 606	Humbly I Adore Thee/Theme to Grace	1965	2.50	5.00	10.00
❑ 608	Christmas Time Is Here/What Child Is This	1966	5.00	10.00	20.00
❑ 613	I'm a Loser/Favela	1966	2.50	5.00	10.00

Number	Title (A Side/B Side)	Yr	VG	VG+	NM

GUARD, DAVE, AND THE WHISKEYHILL SINGERS

Dave Guard had split from THE KINGSTON TRIO.

Number	Title (A Side/B Side)	Yr	VG	VG+	NM
CAPITOL					
❑ 4787	Plane Wreck at Los Gatos/Ride On, Railroad Bill	1962	2.50	5.00	10.00

GUESS WHO, THE

Also see CHAD ALLAN; RANDY BACHMAN; BURTON CUMMINGS.

Number	Title (A Side/B Side)	Yr	VG	VG+	NM
AMY					
❑ 967	And She's Mine/All Right	1966	5.00	10.00	20.00
—The existence of stock copies of this record has been questioned					
❑ 976	His Girl/It's My Pride	1967	7.50	15.00	30.00
—Price is for stock copy; promos go for less					
FONTANA					
❑ 1597	This Time Long Ago/There's No Getting Away from It	1967	7.50	15.00	30.00
HILLTAK					
❑ 7803	C'mon Little Mama/Moon Wave Maker	1979	—	3.00	6.00
❑ 7807	Sweet Young Thing/It's Getting Pretty Bad	1979	—	3.00	6.00
RCA VICTOR					
❑ APBO-0217	Star Baby/Musicione	1974	—	2.50	5.00
❑ SPS-45-223 [DJ]	Friends of Mine (Part 1)/Friends of Mine (Part 2)	1969	3.00	6.00	12.00
❑ APBO-0324	Clap for the Wolfman/Road Food	1974	—	2.50	5.00
❑ PB-10075	Dancin' Fool/Seems Like I Can't Live With You, But I Can't Live Without You	1974	—	2.50	5.00
❑ GB-10161	Clap for the Wolfman/Star Baby	1975	—	2.00	4.00
—Gold Standard Series					
❑ PB-10216	Loves Me Like a Brother/Hoe Down Time	1975	—	2.50	5.00
❑ PB-10360	Dreams/Rosanne	1975	—	2.50	5.00
❑ PB-10410	When the Band Was Singin' (Shakin' All Over)/Women	1975	—	3.00	6.00
❑ PB-10716	Silver Bird/Runnin' Down the Street	1976	3.00	6.00	12.00
❑ 74-0102	These Eyes/Lightfoot	1969	—	3.00	6.00
❑ 74-0195	Laughing/Undun	1969	—	3.00	6.00
❑ 74-0300	No Time/Proper Stranger	1969	—	3.00	6.00
❑ 74-0325	American Woman/No Sugar Tonight	1970	—	2.50	5.00
❑ 74-0367	Hand Me Down World/Runnin' Down the Street	1970	—	2.50	5.00
❑ 74-0388	Share the Land/Bus Rider	1970	—	2.50	5.00
❑ 74-0388 [PS]	Share the Land/Bus Rider	1970	2.50	5.00	10.00
❑ 74-0414	Hang On to Your Life/Do You Miss Me, Darlin'?	1970	—	2.50	5.00
❑ 74-0414 [PS]	Hang On to Your Life/Do You Miss Me, Darlin'?	1970	6.25	12.50	25.00
❑ 74-0458	Albert Flasher/Broker	1971	—	2.50	5.00
❑ 74-0522	Rain Dance/One Divided	1971	—	2.50	5.00
❑ 74-0578	Sour Suite/Life in the Bloodstream	1971	—	2.50	5.00
❑ 74-0659	Heartbroken Bopper/Arrividerci Girl	1972	—	2.50	5.00
❑ 74-0708	Guns, Guns, Guns/Heaven Only Moved Just Once Yesterday	1972	—	2.50	5.00
❑ 74-0803	Runnin' Back to Saskatoon/New Mother Nature	1972	—	2.50	5.00
❑ 74-0880	Follow Your Daughter Home/Bye Bye Babe	1973	—	2.50	5.00
❑ 74-0926	The Watcher/Orly	1973	—	2.50	5.00
❑ 74-0977	Lie Down/Glamour Boy	1973	—	2.50	5.00
SCEPTER					
❑ 1295	Shakin' All Over/Till We Kissed	1965	3.75	7.50	15.00
❑ 1295	Shakin' All Over/Monkey in a Cage	1965	7.50	15.00	30.00
—B-side by the Discotays					
❑ 12108	Hey Ho What You Do to Me/Goodnight Goodnight	1965	3.75	7.50	15.00
❑ 12118	Hurting Each Other/Baby's Birthday	1965	5.00	10.00	20.00
❑ 12131	Believe Me/Baby Feelin'	1966	5.00	10.00	20.00
❑ 12144	One Day/Clock on the Wall	1966	5.00	10.00	20.00

GUIDES, THE

Number	Title (A Side/B Side)	Yr	VG	VG+	NM
GUYDEN					
❑ 2023	How Long Must a Fool Go On/You Must Try	1959	7.50	15.00	30.00
—Originally released under the name "The Swallows"					

GUILLOTEENS, THE

Number	Title (A Side/B Side)	Yr	VG	VG+	NM
COLUMBIA					
❑ 43852	Wild Child/You Think You're Happy	1966	3.75	7.50	15.00
❑ 43852 [PS]	Wild Child/You Think You're Happy	1966	10.00	20.00	40.00
—Sleeve is promo only					
❑ 44089	I Love That Girl/Dear Mrs. Applebee	1967	3.00	6.00	12.00
HANNA-BARBERA					
❑ 446	I Don't Believe/Hey You	1965	3.75	7.50	15.00
❑ 451	Don't Let the Rain Get You Down/For My Own	1965	3.75	7.50	15.00
❑ 451 [PS]	Don't Let the Rain Get You Down/For My Own	1965	7.50	15.00	30.00
❑ 486	I Sit and Cry/Crying All Over My Time	1966	5.00	10.00	20.00

GUITAR, BILLY

Number	Title (A Side/B Side)	Yr	VG	VG+	NM
DECCA					
❑ 30634	Here Comes the Night/You Should Have Loved Her More	1958	17.50	35.00	70.00

GUITAR, BONNIE

Number	Title (A Side/B Side)	Yr	VG	VG+	NM
4 STAR					
❑ 1006	I Wanna Spend My Life with You/Maggie	1975	—	2.50	5.00
❑ 1041	Honey on the Moon/Lonely Eyes	1980	—	2.50	5.00
—Number also listed as 1003. Which is correct? Or are both?					
COLUMBIA					
❑ 4-45643	Just As Soon As I Get Over Loving You/Happy Everything	1972	—	2.50	5.00
DOLTON					
❑ 10	Candy Apple Red/Come to Me, I Love You	1959	3.00	6.00	12.00
❑ 19	Candy Apple Red/Come to Me, I Love You	1960	2.50	5.00	10.00
DOT					
❑ 15550	Dark Moon/Big Mile	1957	3.75	7.50	15.00
❑ 15587	Half Your Heart/If You See My Love Dancing	1957	3.00	6.00	12.00
❑ 15612	There's a New Moon Over My Shoulder/Mister Fire Eyes	1957	3.00	6.00	12.00
❑ 15678	Making Believe/I Saw Your Face in the Moon	1957	3.00	6.00	12.00
❑ 15708	A Very Precious Love/Johnny Vagabond	1958	3.00	6.00	12.00
❑ 15776	I Found You Out/If You'll Be the Teacher	1958	3.00	6.00	12.00
❑ 15862	Rocky Mountain Moon/Whispering Hope	1958	3.00	6.00	12.00
❑ 15894	Baby Moon/Solitude	1959	3.00	6.00	12.00
❑ 16811	I'm Living in Two Worlds/Goodtime Charlie	1965	—	3.00	6.00
❑ 16872	Would You Believe/Get Your Life the Way You Want It	1966	—	3.00	6.00
❑ 16919	Are You SIncere/The Tallest Tree	1966	—	3.00	6.00
❑ 16968	I'll Be Missing You (Under the Mistletoe)/Blue Christmas	1966	5.00	10.00	20.00
❑ 16987	The Kickin' Tree/Only I	1967	—	3.00	6.00
❑ 17007	You Can Steal Me/Ramblin' Man	1967	—	3.00	6.00
❑ 17029	I Want My Baby/Woman in Love	1967	—	3.00	6.00
❑ 17057	Wings of a Dove/Stop the Sun	1967	—	3.00	6.00
❑ 17097	Faded Love/I Believe in Love	1968	—	2.50	5.00
❑ 17150	Almost Like Being with You/Leaves Are the Tears of Autumn	1968	—	2.50	5.00
❑ 17249	Perfect Strangers/I'll Meet You in Denver	1969	—	2.50	5.00
❑ 17276	I'll Pick Up My Heart/That See Me Later Look	1969	—	2.50	5.00
FABOR					
❑ 138	Ra Ta Ta Ta/Leave Weeping to the Willow Tree	1964	2.00	4.00	8.00
❑ 4013	If You See My Love Dancing/Hello, Hello, Please Answer	1956	6.25	12.50	25.00
❑ 4017	Clinging VIne/Dream Dreamers	1956	6.25	12.50	25.00
❑ 4018	Dark Moon/Big Mile	1957	10.00	20.00	40.00
JERDEN					
❑ 707	There'll Be No Teardrops Tonight/The Fool	1963	2.50	5.00	10.00
MCA					
❑ 40192	The Bed I Love In/Wishing Star	1974	—	2.00	4.00
❑ 40306	From This Moment On/Shine	1974	—	2.00	4.00
PARAMOUNT					
❑ 0004	A Truer Love You'll Never Find (Than Mine)/That's When	1969	—	3.50	7.00
—As "Bonnie and Buddy"					
❑ 0045	Allegheny/Red Checkered Blazer	1970	—	3.50	7.00
PLAYBACK					
❑ 1304	Things Songs Are Made Of/Here We Lie	1988	—	3.00	6.00
❑ 1309	Paradise/Wine from My Table	1988	—	3.00	6.00
❑ 1326	What Can I Say/What's In It for Me	1989	—	3.00	6.00
❑ 1341	Lonely Eyes/Honey on the Moon	1989	—	3.00	6.00
❑ 75714	Still the Same/If You Were Here	1989	—	2.50	5.00
RADIO					
❑ 101	Please, My Love/Love Is Over, Love Is Done	1958	3.00	6.00	12.00
❑ 110	Shanty Boat/Only the Moon Man Knows	1958	3.00	6.00	12.00
RCA VICTOR					
❑ 47-7951	I'll Step Down/Tell Her Bye	1961	2.50	5.00	10.00
❑ 47-8063	Broken Hearted Girl/Who Is She	1962	2.50	5.00	10.00

GUITAR SLIM

Number	Title (A Side/B Side)	Yr	VG	VG+	NM
ATCO					
❑ 6072	Oh Yeah/Down Through the Years	1956	10.00	20.00	40.00
❑ 6097	It Hurts to Love Someone/If I Should Lose You	1957	7.50	15.00	30.00
❑ 6108	I Won't Mind at All/Hello, How Ya' Been, Goodbye	1958	7.50	15.00	30.00
❑ 6120	If I Had My Life to Live Over/When There's No Way Out	1958	7.50	15.00	30.00
IMPERIAL					
❑ 5278	Woman Troubles/Cryin' in the Mornin'	1954	15.00	30.00	60.00
❑ 5310	New Arrival/Standing at the Station	1954	15.00	30.00	60.00
SPECIALTY					
❑ 482	The Things That I Used to Do/Well, I Done Got Over It	1954	12.50	25.00	50.00
❑ 490	Story of My Life/A Letter to My Girl Friend	1954	10.00	20.00	40.00
❑ 527	Later for You Baby/Troubles Don't Last	1954	6.25	12.50	25.00
❑ 536	Sufferin' Mind/Twenty-Five Lies	1955	6.25	12.50	25.00
❑ 542	Stand By Me/Our Only Child	1955	6.25	12.50	25.00
❑ 551	You're Gonna Miss Me/I Got Sumpin' for You	1955	6.25	12.50	25.00
❑ 557	Think It Over/Quicksand	1955	6.25	12.50	25.00
❑ 569	Sumthin' to Remember Me By/You Give Me Nothin' But the Blues	1956	6.25	12.50	25.00

GUITARS, INC.

Pseudonym for THE FIREBALLS.

Number	Title (A Side/B Side)	Yr	VG	VG+	NM
HAMILTON					
❑ 50035	Little Toy/Holiday Love	1960	6.25	12.50	25.00

GULLIVER

With DARYL HALL. John Oates joined later, but is not on these records.

Number	Title (A Side/B Side)	Yr	VG	VG+	NM
ELEKTRA					
❑ 45689	Angelina/Every Day's a Lovely Day	1970	2.00	4.00	8.00
❑ 45698	A Truly Good Song/Every Day's a Lovely Day	1970	2.00	4.00	8.00

GUM DROPS, THE

Number	Title (A Side/B Side)	Yr	VG	VG+	NM
CORAL					
❑ 62003	My Own True Love/On the Wings of the Wind	1958	3.75	7.50	15.00
❑ 62102	I Spoke Too Soon/Sie Tu (It's You, It's You)	1959	3.75	7.50	15.00
❑ 62138	It Happens Every Day/They Wake Me	1959	3.75	7.50	15.00
DECCA					
❑ 30584	You're the One/Gum Drop Shoes and Bells in Her Hair	1958	5.00	10.00	20.00
KING					
❑ 1496	Gum Drop/Don't Take It So Hard	1955	5.00	10.00	20.00
❑ 1499	I'll Wait for One More Train/Don't Take It So Hard	1955	5.00	10.00	20.00
❑ 4913	I Wonder and Wonder/I'll Follow You	1956	6.25	12.50	25.00
❑ 4963	Natural Born Lover/Chapel of Hearts	1956	6.25	12.50	25.00
❑ 5051	Ba-Bee Da Boat Is Leaving/Pigeon	1957	5.00	10.00	20.00

GUN

Number	Title (A Side/B Side)	Yr	VG	VG+	NM
EPIC					
❑ 10413	Race with the Devil/Sunshine	1968	2.50	5.00	10.00
❑ 10537	Don't Look Back/Hobo	1969	2.50	5.00	10.00
❑ 10593	Drown Yourself in the River/Long Hair Wildman	1970	2.50	5.00	10.00

GUNHILL ROAD

Number	Title (A Side/B Side)	Yr	VG	VG+	NM
KAMA SUTRA					
❑ 562	Ford, De Soto, Cadillac/(B-side unknown)	1972	—	2.50	5.00

MERCURY

Number	Title (A Side/B Side)	Yr	VG	VG+	NM
❑ 569	Back When My Hair Was Short/We Can't Ride the Roller Coaster Anymore	1973	—	3.00	6.00
❑ 582	Ford, De Soto, Cadillac/Sailing	1973	—	2.50	5.00
❑ 591	She Made a Man Out of Me/(B-side unknown)	1974	—	2.50	5.00

MERCURY

Number	Title (A Side/B Side)	Yr	VG	VG+	NM
❑ 73232	42nd Street/(B-side unknown)	1971	—	3.00	6.00

GUNTER, ARTHUR

EXCELLO

Number	Title (A Side/B Side)	Yr	VG	VG+	NM
❑ 2047	Baby Let's Play House/Blues After Hours	1954	30.00	60.00	120.00
❑ 2053	She's Mine, All Mine/You Are Doin' Me Wrong	1955	15.00	30.00	60.00
❑ 2058	Honey Babe/No Happy Home	1955	15.00	30.00	60.00
❑ 2073	Baby You Better Listen/Trouble with My Baby	1955	7.50	15.00	30.00
❑ 2084	Hear My Plea Baby/Love Has Got Me	1956	7.50	15.00	30.00
❑ 2125	Baby Can't You See/You're Always on My Mind	1958	6.25	12.50	25.00
❑ 2137	Ludella/We're Gonna Shake	1959	6.25	12.50	25.00
❑ 2147	Crazy Me/Don't Leave Me Now	1959	6.25	12.50	25.00
❑ 2164	No Naggin' No Draggin'/I Want Her Back	1959	6.25	12.50	25.00
❑ 2191	Little Blue Jeans/Mind Your Own Business Babe	1960	5.00	10.00	20.00
❑ 2201	My Heart's Always Lonesome/I'm Fallin', Love's Got Me	1961	5.00	10.00	20.00

GUNTER, CORNEL

Also see THE FLAIRS.

ABC-PARAMOUNT

Number	Title (A Side/B Side)	Yr	VG	VG+	NM
❑ 9698	She Loves to Rock/In Self Defense	1956	10.00	20.00	40.00

—As "Cornel Gunter and the Flairs"

CHALLENGE

Number	Title (A Side/B Side)	Yr	VG	VG+	NM
❑ 59281	If I Had the Key to Your Heart/Wishful	1965	2.50	5.00	10.00

DOT

Number	Title (A Side/B Side)	Yr	VG	VG+	NM
❑ 15654	You Send Me/Call Me a Fool	1957	5.00	10.00	20.00

EAGLE

Number	Title (A Side/B Side)	Yr	VG	VG+	NM
❑ 301	Baby Come Home/I Want You Madly	1957	7.50	15.00	30.00

LIBERTY

Number	Title (A Side/B Side)	Yr	VG	VG+	NM
❑ 55096	If We Should Meet Again/Neighborhood Dance	1957	5.00	10.00	20.00

LOMA

Number	Title (A Side/B Side)	Yr	VG	VG+	NM
❑ 701	True Love/Peek, Peek-a-Boo	1955	25.00	50.00	100.00
❑ 703	You Broke My Heart/(Pretty Baby) I'm Used to You Now	1956	37.50	75.00	150.00
❑ 704	Keep Me Alive/Muchacha, Muchacha	1956	20.00	40.00	80.00
❑ 705	I'm Sad/One Thing	1956	25.00	50.00	100.00

—The Loma singles credit "The Ermines," and may or may not mention Gunter.

WARNER BROS.

Number	Title (A Side/B Side)	Yr	VG	VG+	NM
❑ 5266	Lieft Me Up Angel/Hope of Sand	1962	3.00	6.00	12.00
❑ 5292	It Ain't No Use/In a Dream of Love	1962	3.00	6.00	12.00

GUNTER, HARDROCK

DECCA

Number	Title (A Side/B Side)	Yr	VG	VG+	NM
❑ 9-46300	Boogie Woogie on a Saturday Night/Honky Tonk	1951	10.00	20.00	40.00
❑ 9-46350	I've Done Gone Hog Wild/I Believe That Mountain Music	1951	6.25	12.50	25.00
❑ 9-46363	Sixty Minute Man/Tennessee Blues	1951	6.25	12.50	25.00
❑ 9-46367	Dixieland Boogie/If I Could Only Live My Dreams	1951	6.25	12.50	25.00
❑ 9-46383	Hesitation Boogie/Don't You Agree	1951	6.25	12.50	25.00
❑ 9-46401	Silver and Gold/Senator from Tennessee	1952	6.25	12.50	25.00

KING

Number	Title (A Side/B Side)	Yr	VG	VG+	NM
❑ 4858	Turn the Other Cheek/Before My Time	1955	5.00	10.00	20.00

MGM

Number	Title (A Side/B Side)	Yr	VG	VG+	NM
❑ K-11520	Like the Lovers Do/Naptown, Indiana	1953	6.25	12.50	25.00
❑ K-11596	Sunday Angel/Where Have You Been	1953	6.25	12.50	25.00

SUN

Number	Title (A Side/B Side)	Yr	VG	VG+	NM
❑ 201	Fallen Angel/Gonna Dance All Night	1954	500.00	1000.	2000.

GUNTER, SHIRLEY

FLAIR

Number	Title (A Side/B Side)	Yr	VG	VG+	NM
❑ 1020	Send Him Back/Since I Fell for You	1953	10.00	20.00	40.00
❑ 1027	Found Some Good Lovin'/Strange Romance	1954	7.50	15.00	30.00
❑ 1050	Oop Shoop/It's You	1955	7.50	15.00	30.00
❑ 1060	You're Mine/Why	1955	7.50	15.00	30.00
❑ 1065	What Difference Does It Make/Baby I Love You So	1955	7.50	15.00	30.00
❑ 1070	That's the Way I Like It/Gimme, Gimme, Gimme	1955	7.50	15.00	30.00
❑ 1076	How Can I Tell You/Ipsy Gypsy Ooh	1955	15.00	30.00	60.00

—With the Flairs

MODERN

Number	Title (A Side/B Side)	Yr	VG	VG+	NM
❑ 979	Please Tell Me/Come On	1956	6.25	12.50	25.00
❑ 1001	Fortune in Love/Just Got Rid of a Heartache	1956	6.25	12.50	25.00

—With the Flairs

Number	Title (A Side/B Side)	Yr	VG	VG+	NM
❑ 1011	I'm So Sorry/I've Been Searching	1956	6.25	12.50	25.00

TANGERINE

Number	Title (A Side/B Side)	Yr	VG	VG+	NM
❑ 949	Stuck Up/You Let My Love Grow Cold	1965	2.50	5.00	10.00

TENDER

Number	Title (A Side/B Side)	Yr	VG	VG+	NM
❑ 503	Believe Me/Crazy Little Baby	1958	10.00	20.00	40.00

GURUS, THE

UNITED ARTISTS

Number	Title (A Side/B Side)	Yr	VG	VG+	NM
❑ 50089	Come Girl/Blue Snow Night	1966	3.00	6.00	12.00
❑ 50089 [PS]	Come Girl/Blue Snow Night	1966	6.25	12.50	25.00
❑ 50140	It Just Won't Be That Way/Everybody's Got to Be Alone Sometime	1967	3.00	6.00	12.00

GUTHRIE, ARLO

REPRISE

Number	Title (A Side/B Side)	Yr	VG	VG+	NM
❑ PRO 304 [DJ]	Motorcycle Song/The Pause of Mr. Claus	1970	5.00	10.00	20.00
❑ 0644	Motorcycle Song/Now and Then	1967	3.00	6.00	12.00
❑ 0793	Motorcycle Song (Part 1)/Motorcycle Song (Part 2)	1968	3.00	6.00	12.00
❑ 0877	Alice's Rock & Roll Restaurant/Coming Into Los Angeles	1969	3.00	6.00	12.00
❑ 0951	Gabriel's Mother's Hiway/Ballad #16 Blues	1970	2.00	4.00	8.00
❑ 0994	The Ballad of Tricky Fred/Shackles and Chains	1971	—	3.00	6.00
❑ 1103	The City of New Orleans/Days Are Short	1972	—	3.00	6.00
❑ 1137	Ukulele Lady/Cooper's Lament	1972	—	2.50	5.00
❑ 1158	A Week on the Rag/Gypsy Dave	1973	—	2.50	5.00
❑ 1211	Nostalgia Rag/Presidential Rag	1974	—	2.00	4.00
❑ 1363	Patriot's Dream/Ocean Crossing	1976	—	2.00	4.00
❑ 1376	Grocery Blues/Guabi, Guabi	1976	—	2.00	4.00
❑ 1388	Massachusetts/My Love	1977	—	2.00	4.00

WARNER BROS.

Number	Title (A Side/B Side)	Yr	VG	VG+	NM
❑ 49037	Wedding Song/Prologue	1979	—	2.00	4.00
❑ 49796	Slow Boat/If I Could Only Touch Your Life	1981	—	2.00	4.00
❑ 49889	Oklahoma Nights/Power of Love	1981	—	2.00	4.00

GUY, ART

VALIANT

Number	Title (A Side/B Side)	Yr	VG	VG+	NM
❑ 762	Where You Gonna Go/Teenage Millionaire	1967	7.50	15.00	30.00

GUY, BOB

Pseudonym for FRANK ZAPPA.

DONNA

Number	Title (A Side/B Side)	Yr	VG	VG+	NM
❑ 1380	Letter from Jeepers/Dear Jeepers	1963	25.00	50.00	100.00

GUY, BOBBY

APT

Number	Title (A Side/B Side)	Yr	VG	VG+	NM
❑ 25052	A Vow/Good Enough	1960	7.50	15.00	30.00

GUY, BROWLEY, AND THE SKYSCRAPERS

CHECKER

Number	Title (A Side/B Side)	Yr	VG	VG+	NM
❑ 779	Watermelon Man/You Look Good to Me	1954	75.00	150.00	300.00

—Black vinyl

Number	Title (A Side/B Side)	Yr	VG	VG+	NM
❑ 779	Watermelon Man/You Look Good to Me	1954	187.50	375.00	750.00

—Red vinyl

GUYTON, HOWARD

VERVE

Number	Title (A Side/B Side)	Yr	VG	VG+	NM
❑ 10386	I Watched You Slowly Slip Away/I Got My Own Thing Going	1966	25.00	50.00	100.00

GUYTONES, THE

DELUXE

Number	Title (A Side/B Side)	Yr	VG	VG+	NM
❑ 6144	You Won't Let Me Go/Ooh Bop Sha Boo (Give All Your Love to Me)	1957	20.00	40.00	80.00
❑ 6152	She's Mine/Not Wanted	1957	20.00	40.00	80.00
❑ 6159	Hunky Dory/This Is Love	1958	20.00	40.00	80.00
❑ 6163	Baby, I Don't Care/Young Dreamer	1958	15.00	30.00	60.00
❑ 6169	Tell Me (How Was I to Know)/Your Heart's Bigger Than Mine	1958	15.00	30.00	60.00

GYPSIES, THE

Probably two different groups.

ATLAS

Number	Title (A Side/B Side)	Yr	VG	VG+	NM
❑ 1073	Why/Young Girl to Calypso	1957	20.00	40.00	80.00

GROOVE

Number	Title (A Side/B Side)	Yr	VG	VG+	NM
❑ 0117	One, Two, Three, Go/I'm Good to You Baby	1955	5.00	10.00	20.00
❑ 0129	Rock Around the Christmas Tree/You've Been Away Too Long	1955	5.00	10.00	20.00

OLD TOWN

Number	Title (A Side/B Side)	Yr	VG	VG+	NM
❑ 1168	Blue Bird/Hey There Hey There	1964	5.00	10.00	20.00
❑ 1180	Jerk It/Diamonds, Rubies, Gold and Fame	1965	5.00	10.00	20.00
❑ 1184	It's a Woman's World/They're Having a Party	1965	20.00	40.00	80.00
❑ 1193	Oh I Wonder Why/Diamonds, Rubies, Gold and Fame	1966	6.25	12.50	25.00

GYPSY TRIPS, THE

WORLD PACIFIC

Number	Title (A Side/B Side)	Yr	VG	VG+	NM
❑ 77809	Rock 'n Roll Gypsies/Ain't It Hard	1966	7.50	15.00	30.00

H

H.P. LOVECRAFT

MERCURY

Number	Title (A Side/B Side)	Yr	VG	VG+	NM
❑ 73698	Flight/I Feel Better	1975	—	3.00	6.00

—As "Lovecraft"

Number	Title (A Side/B Side)	Yr	VG	VG+	NM
❑ 73707	We Love You (Whoever You Are)/Ain't Gettin' Home	1975	—	3.00	6.00

—As "Lovecraft"

PHILIPS

Number	Title (A Side/B Side)	Yr	VG	VG+	NM
❑ 40464	Anyway That You Want Me/It's All Over for You	1967	3.00	6.00	12.00
❑ 40491	Wayfaring Stranger/The Time Machine	1967	3.00	6.00	12.00
❑ 40491 [PS]	Wayfaring Stranger/The Time Machine	1967	6.25	12.50	25.00
❑ 40506	The White Ship (Part 1)/The White Ship (Part 2)	1967	3.00	6.00	12.00
❑ 40578	Blue Jack of Diamonds/Keeper of the Keys	1968	3.00	6.00	12.00

REPRISE

Number	Title (A Side/B Side)	Yr	VG	VG+	NM
❑ 0996	We Can All Have It Together/Will I Know When My Time Comes	1971	2.00	4.00	8.00

—As "Lovecraft"

HACKERT, VALINE

BRUNSWICK

Number	Title (A Side/B Side)	Yr	VG	VG+	NM
❑ 55151	Billy Boy/Show Me How	1959	50.00	100.00	200.00

HADLEY, RED

METEOR

Number	Title (A Side/B Side)	Yr	VG	VG+	NM
❑ 5017	Ring Out Those Bells/Brother, That's All	1955	27.50	75.00	150.00

HAGAN, SAMMY, AND THE VISCOUNTS

CAPITOL

Number	Title (A Side/B Side)	Yr	VG	VG+	NM
❑ F-3772	Out of Your Heart/Shoochie Poochie	1957	10.00	20.00	40.00
❑ F-3818	Wild Bird/Don't Cry	1957	10.00	20.00	40.00
❑ F-3885	Tail Light/Snuggle Bunny	1958	7.50	15.00	30.00

HAGAR, SAMMY

Also see VAN HALEN.

CAPITOL

Number	Title (A Side/B Side)	Yr	VG	VG+	NM
❑ 4261	Urban Guerilla/Flamingos Fly	1976	—	2.50	5.00
❑ 4388	Catch the Wind/Red	1977	—	2.50	5.00
❑ 4411	Cruisin' and Boozin'/Love Has Found Me	1977	—	2.50	5.00
❑ 4502	Reckless/You Made Me Crazy	1977	—	2.50	5.00
❑ 4550	Turn Up the Music/Hey Boys	1978	—	2.50	5.00
❑ 4596	I've Done Everything for You/Someone Out There	1978	—	2.50	5.00
❑ 4699	(Sittin' On) The Dock of the Bay/I've Done Everything for You	1979	—	2.50	5.00
❑ 4757	Plain Jane/Wounded in Love	1979	—	2.50	5.00
❑ 4825	Growing Pains/Straight to the Top	1980	—	2.50	5.00
❑ 4893	Heartbeat/Miles from Boredom	1980	—	2.50	5.00

COLUMBIA

Number	Title (A Side/B Side)	Yr	VG	VG+	NM
❑ 06647	Winner Takes It All/The Fight	1987	—	—	3.00
—B-side by Giorgio Moroder					
❑ 06647 [PS]	Winner Takes It All/The Fight	1987	—	—	3.00

GEFFEN

Number	Title (A Side/B Side)	Yr	VG	VG+	NM
❑ 28185	Eagles Fly/Hands and Knees	1987	—	—	3.00
❑ 28185 [PS]	Eagles Fly/Hands and Knees	1987	—	—	3.00
❑ 28314	Give to Live/When the Hammer Falls	1987	—	—	3.00
❑ 28314 [PS]	Give to Live/When the Hammer Falls	1987	—	—	3.00
❑ 29090	I'll Only Fall in Love Again/Only the Young	1985	—	2.00	4.00
—B-side by Journey					
❑ 29173	I Can't Drive 55/Dick in the Dirt	1984	—	—	3.00
❑ 29173 [PS]	I Can't Drive 55	1984	—	3.00	6.00
—Promo-only version contains facsimile speeding ticket					
❑ 29173 [PS]	I Can't Drive 55/Dick in the Dirt	1984	—	—	3.00
❑ 29246	Two Sides of Love/Burnin' Down the City	1984	—	2.50	5.00
—Red vinyl					
❑ 29246 [PS]	Two Sides of Love/Burnin' Down the City	1984	—	2.50	5.00
❑ 29718	Fast Times At Ridgemont High/Never Give Up	1983	—	2.00	4.00
❑ 29816	Your Love Is Driving Me Crazy/I Don't Need Love	1982	—	2.00	4.00
❑ 49881	I'll Fall in Love Again/Satisfied	1981	—	2.00	4.00
❑ 50059	Piece of My Heart/Sweet Hitchhiker	1982	—	2.00	4.00

MCA

Number	Title (A Side/B Side)	Yr	VG	VG+	NM
❑ 55574	Mas Tequila/Little White Lie	1999	—	—	3.00

HAGGARD, MERLE

Also see PAYCHECK AND HAGGARD.

CAPITOL

Number	Title (A Side/B Side)	Yr	VG	VG+	NM
❑ 2017	Sing Me Back Home/Good Times	1967	2.00	4.00	8.00
❑ 2017 [PS]	Sing Me Back Home/Good Times	1967	2.00	4.00	8.00
❑ 2123	The Legend of Bonnie and Clyde/Today I Started Loving You Again	1968	2.00	4.00	8.00
❑ 2219	Mama Tried/You'll Never Love Me Now	1968	2.00	4.00	8.00
❑ 2219 [PS]	Mama Tried/You'll Never Love Me Now	1968	2.00	4.00	8.00
❑ 2289	I Take a Lot of Pride in What I Am/Keep Me from Cryin' Today	1968	2.00	4.00	8.00
❑ 2289 [PS]	I Take a Lot of Pride in What I Am/Keep Me from Cryin' Today	1968	2.00	4.00	8.00
❑ 2383	Hungry Eyes/California Blues	1969	2.00	4.00	8.00
❑ 2383 [PS]	Hungry Eyes/California Blues	1969	2.00	4.00	8.00
❑ 2503	Workin' Man Blues/Silver Wings	1969	2.00	4.00	8.00
❑ 2503 [PS]	Workin' Man Blues/Silver Wings	1969	2.00	4.00	8.00
❑ 2626	Okie from Muskogee/If I Had Left It Up to You	1969	2.00	4.00	8.00
❑ 2626 [PS]	Okie from Muskogee/If I Had Left It Up to You	1969	2.00	4.00	8.00
❑ 2719	The Fightin' Side of Me/Every Fool Has a Rainbow	1970	2.00	4.00	8.00
❑ 2719 [PS]	The Fightin' Side of Me/Every Fool Has a Rainbow	1970	2.00	4.00	8.00
❑ 2778	Street Singer/Mexicali Rose	1970	2.00	4.00	8.00
❑ 2838	Jesus, Take a Hold/No Reason to Quit	1970	2.00	4.00	8.00
❑ 2891	I Can't Be Myself/Sidewalks of Chicago	1970	2.00	4.00	8.00
❑ 2891 [PS]	I Can't Be Myself/Sidewalks of Chicago	1970	2.00	4.00	8.00
❑ 3024	Soldier's Last Letter/The Farmer's Daughter	1971	—	3.00	6.00
❑ 3024 [PS]	Soldier's Last Letter/The Farmer's Daughter	1971	2.00	4.00	8.00
❑ 3112	Someday We'll Look Back/It's Great to Be Alive	1971	—	3.00	6.00
❑ 3144	Song from Sleepwalk/Slow 'n Easy	1971	2.00	4.00	8.00
—By "Merle Haggard's Strangers"					
❑ 3198	Daddy Frank (The Guitar Man)/My Heart Would Know	1971	—	3.00	6.00
❑ 3222	Carolyn/When the Feelin' Goes Away	1971	—	3.00	6.00
❑ 3294	Grandma Harp/Turnin' Off a Memory	1972	—	3.00	6.00
❑ 3376	I'm a Light Boy/Shoulder to Cry On	1972	2.50	5.00	10.00
❑ 3419	It's Not Love (But It's Not Bad)/My Woman Keeps Lovin' Her Man	1972	—	3.00	6.00
❑ 3488	I Wonder If They Ever Think of Me/I Forget You Every Day	1972	—	3.00	6.00
❑ 3552	The Emptiest Arms in the World/Radiator Man from Waco	1973	—	2.50	5.00
❑ 3641	Everybody's Had the Blues/Nobody Knows I'm Hurtin'	1973	—	2.50	5.00
❑ 3746	If We Make It Through December/Bobby Wants a Puppy Dog for Christmas	1973	—	2.50	5.00
❑ 3830	Things Aren't Funny Anymore/Honky Tonk Night Time Man	1974	—	2.50	5.00
❑ 3900	Old Man from the Mountain/Holding Things Together	1974	—	2.50	5.00
❑ 3974	Kentucky Gambler/I've Got a Darlin' (For a Wife)	1974	—	2.50	5.00
❑ 3989	Santa Claus and Popcorn/If We Make It Through December	1974	—	2.50	5.00
❑ 4027	Always Wanting You/I've Got a Yearning	1975	—	2.50	5.00
❑ 4085	Movin' On/Here in Frisco	1975	—	2.50	5.00
❑ 4141	It's All in the Movies/Living with the Shades Pulled Down	1975	—	2.50	5.00
❑ 4204	The Roots of My Raising/The Way It Was in '51	1975	—	2.50	5.00
❑ 4267	Here Comes the Freedom Train/I Won't Give Up My Train	1976	—	2.50	5.00
❑ 4326	Cherokee Maiden/What Have You Got Planned Tonight Diana	1976	—	2.50	5.00
❑ 4477	A Workin' Man Can't Get Nowhere Today/Blues Stay Away from Me	1977	—	2.50	5.00
❑ 4525	Running Kind/Making Believe	1978	—	2.50	5.00
❑ 4636	The Way It Was in '51/Moanin' the Blues	1978	—	2.50	5.00
❑ 5460	I'm Gonna Break Every Heart I Can/Falling for You	1965	2.50	5.00	10.00
❑ 5523	This Town's Not Big Enough/Shade Tree	1965	2.50	5.00	10.00
❑ 5600	Swinging Doors/The Girl Turned Ripe	1966	2.50	5.00	10.00
❑ 5704	The Bottle Let Me Down/The Longer You Wait	1966	2.50	5.00	10.00
❑ 5803	The Fugitive/Someone Told My Story	1966	3.00	6.00	12.00
❑ 5803	I'm a Lonesome Fugitive/Someone Told My Story	1967	2.00	4.00	8.00
—Retitled A-side					
❑ 5844	I Threw Away the Rose/Loneliness Is Eating Me Alive	1967	2.00	4.00	8.00
❑ 5844 [PS]	I Threw Away the Rose/Loneliness Is Eating Me Alive	1967	2.00	4.00	8.00
❑ 5931	Branded Man/You Don't Have Very Far to Go	1967	2.00	4.00	8.00
❑ 5931 [PS]	Branded Man/You Don't Have Very Far to Go	1967	2.00	4.00	8.00

CAPITOL NASHVILLE

Number	Title (A Side/B Side)	Yr	VG	VG+	NM
❑ S7-19346	White Christmas/Silver Bells	1996	—	2.00	4.00

CURB

Number	Title (A Side/B Side)	Yr	VG	VG+	NM
❑ 76832	When It Rains It Pours/Me and Crippled Soldiers	1990	—	2.00	4.00
❑ 76846	Blue Jungle/Me and Crippled Soldiers	1990	—	2.00	4.00
❑ 76854	A Bar in Bakersfield/Lucky Old Colorado	1991	—	2.00	4.00

ELEKTRA

Number	Title (A Side/B Side)	Yr	VG	VG+	NM
❑ 46634	Bar Room Buddies/The Not So Great Train Robbery	1980	—	2.00	4.00
—With Clint Eastwood					
❑ 46634 [PS]	Bar Room Buddies/The Not So Great Train Robbery	1980	—	2.50	5.00

EPIC

Number	Title (A Side/B Side)	Yr	VG	VG+	NM
❑ AE7 1777 [DJ]	Santa Claus and Popcorn/Grandma's Homemade Christmas Card	1982	—	2.50	5.00
❑ 02504	My Favorite Memory/Texas Fiddle Song	1981	—	—	3.00
❑ 02686	Big City/I Think I'm Gonna Live Forever	1981	—	—	3.00
❑ 02894	Are the Good Times Really Over (I Wish a Buck Was Still Silver)/I Always Get Lucky with You	1982	—	—	3.00
❑ 03315	Going Where the Lonely Go/Someday You're Gonna Need Your Friends Again	1982	—	—	3.00
❑ 03365	Going Where the Lonely Go	1982	2.00	4.00	8.00
—One-sided budget release					
❑ 03406	Goin' Home for Christmas/If We Make It Through December	1982	—	2.00	4.00
❑ 03723	You Take Me for Granted/I Won't Give Up My Train	1983	—	—	3.00
❑ 04006	What Am I Gonna Do (With the Rest of My Life)/I Think I'll Stay	1983	—	—	3.00
❑ 04226	That's the Way Love Goes/Don't Seem Like We've Been Together All Our Lives	1983	—	—	3.00
❑ 04402	Someday When Things Are Good/If You Hated Me	1984	—	—	3.00
❑ 04512	Let's Chase Each Other Around the Room/All I Want to Do Is Sing My Song	1984	—	—	3.00
❑ 04830	Natural High/I Never Go Home Anymore	1985	—	—	3.00
❑ 05426	Kern River/The Old Water Mill	1985	—	—	3.00
❑ 05659	Amber Waves of Grain/I Wish Things Were Simple Again	1985	—	—	3.00
❑ 05734	American Waltz/The Farmer's Daughter	1985	—	—	3.00
❑ 05782	I Had a Beautiful Time/This Time I Really Do	1986	—	—	3.00
❑ 06097	A Friend in California/Mama's Prayers	1986	—	—	3.00
❑ 06344	Out Among the Stars/Suzie	1986	—	—	3.00
❑ 07036	Almost Persuaded/Love Don't Hurt Everytime	1987	—	—	3.00
❑ 07631	Twinkle, Twinkle, Lucky Star/I Don't Have Any Love Around	1987	—	—	3.00
❑ 07754	Chill Factor/Thanking the Good Lord	1988	—	—	3.00
❑ 07944	We Never Touch at All/Man from Another Time	1988	—	—	3.00
❑ 08111	You Babe/Thirty Again	1988	—	—	3.00
❑ 68598	5:01 Blues/Man from Another Time	1989	—	—	3.00
❑ 68979	A Better Love Next Time/Me and Crippled Soldiers	1989	—	—	3.00
❑ 73076	If You Want to Be My Woman/Someday We'll Know	1989	—	—	3.00
❑ 73303	Broken Friend/Wouldn't That Be Something	1990	—	2.00	4.00

MCA

Number	Title (A Side/B Side)	Yr	VG	VG+	NM
❑ 40700	If We're Not Back in Love By Monday/I Think It's Gone Forever	1977	—	2.00	4.00
❑ 40743	Ramblin' Fever/When My Blue Moon Turns to Gold Again	1977	—	2.00	4.00
❑ 40804	From Graceland to the Promised Land/Are You Lonesome Tonight	1977	—	3.00	6.00
❑ 40869	I'm Always on a Mountain When I Fall/The Life of a Rodeo Cowboy	1978	—	2.00	4.00
❑ 40936	It's Been a Great Afternoon/Love Me When You Can	1978	—	2.00	4.00
❑ 41007	Red Bandana/I Must Have Done Something Bad	1979	—	2.00	4.00
❑ 41112	My Own Kind of Hat/Heaven Was a Drink of Wine	1979	—	2.00	4.00
❑ 41168	If We Make It Through December/The Fightin' Side of Me	1979	—	2.50	5.00
❑ 41200	The Way I Am/Wake Up	1980	—	2.00	4.00
❑ 41255	Misery and Gin/No One to Sing For	1980	—	2.00	4.00
❑ 41255 [PS]	Misery and Gin/No One to Sing For	1980	—	2.50	5.00
❑ 51014	I Think I'll Just Stay Here and Drink/Back to the Barrooms	1980	—	2.00	4.00
❑ 51048	Leonard/Our Paths May Never Cross	1981	—	2.00	4.00
❑ 51120	Rainbow Stew/Blue Yodel No. 9	1981	—	2.00	4.00
❑ 52020	Dealing with the Devil/Fiddle Breakdown	1982	—	2.00	4.00
❑ 52276	It's All in the Game/New Cocaine Blues	1983	—	—	3.00
❑ 52595	Make-Up and Faded Blue Jeans/Love Me When You Can	1985	—	—	3.00

TALLY

Number	Title (A Side/B Side)	Yr	VG	VG+	NM
❑ 152	Singin' My Heart Out/Skid Row	1963	5.00	10.00	20.00
❑ 155	Sing a Sad Song/You Don't Even Try	1963	3.75	7.50	15.00

Number	Title (A Side/B Side)	Yr	VG	VG+	NM
❑ 178	Sam Hill/You Don't Have Far to Go	1964	3.75	7.50	15.00
❑ 179	(My Friends Are Gonna Be) Strangers/Please Mr. D.J.	1964	3.75	7.50	15.00

HAGGARD, MERLE, AND JANIE FRICKE

Number	Title (A Side/B Side)	Yr	VG	VG+	NM
EPIC					
❑ 04663	A Place to Fall Apart/All I Want to Do Is Sing My Song	1984	—	—	3.00

HAGGARD, MERLE, AND JEWEL

Number	Title (A Side/B Side)	Yr	VG	VG+	NM
BNA					
❑ 65895	That's the Way Love Goes/Silver Wings	1999	—	—	3.00

HAGGARD, MERLE, AND GEORGE JONES

Also see each artist's individual listings.

Number	Title (A Side/B Side)	Yr	VG	VG+	NM
EPIC					
❑ 03072	Yesterday's Wine/I Haven't Found Her Yet	1982	—	—	3.00
❑ 03405	C.C. Waterback/After I Sing All My Songs	1982	—	—	3.00

HAGGARD, MERLE, AND WILLIE NELSON

Also see each artist's individual listings.

Number	Title (A Side/B Side)	Yr	VG	VG+	NM
EPIC					
❑ 03494	Reasons to Quit/Half a Man	1983	—	2.00	4.00
❑ ENR-03495	Reasons to Quit	1983	2.00	4.00	8.00
—One-sided budget release					
❑ 03842	Pancho and Lefty/Opportunity to Cry	1983	—	2.00	4.00
❑ 34-07400	If I Could Only Fly/Without You on My Side	1987	—	—	3.00

HAGGARD, MERLE, AND BONNIE OWENS

Number	Title (A Side/B Side)	Yr	VG	VG+	NM
TALLY					
❑ 181	Just Between the Two of Us/Slowly But Sure	1964	5.00	10.00	20.00

HAGGARD, MERLE, AND LEONA WILLIAMS

Number	Title (A Side/B Side)	Yr	VG	VG+	NM
MCA					
❑ 40962	The Bull and the Beaver/I'm Gettin' High	1978	—	2.00	4.00
MERCURY					
❑ 812214-7	We're Strangers Again/Sally Let Your Bangs Hang Down	1983	—	—	3.00
❑ 880139-7	Don't Ever Let Your Lover Sleep Alone/It's Cold in California	1984	—	2.00	4.00

HAGGETT, JIMMY

Number	Title (A Side/B Side)	Yr	VG	VG+	NM
CAPROCK					
❑ 107	All I Have Is You/Without You	1958	10.00	20.00	40.00
METEOR					
❑ 5043	Gonna Shut You Off Baby/Tell Her True	1957	50.00	100.00	200.00
SUN					
❑ 236	No More/They Call Our Love a Sin	1956	150.00	300.00	600.00

HAIG, RONNIE

Number	Title (A Side/B Side)	Yr	VG	VG+	NM
ABC-PARAMOUNT					
❑ 9912	Don't You Hear Me Calling, Baby/Traveler of Love	1958	7.50	15.00	30.00
❑ 10209	Don't You Hear Me Calling, Baby/Traveler of Love	1961	20.00	40.00	80.00
NOTE					
❑ 10010	Don't You Hear Me Calling, Baby/Traveler of Love	1958	7.50	15.00	30.00
❑ 10014	Rockin' with Rhythm and Blues/Money Is a Thing of the Past	1958	25.00	50.00	100.00

HAINES, CONNIE

Number	Title (A Side/B Side)	Yr	VG	VG+	NM
MOTOWN					
❑ 1092	What's Easy for Two Is Hard for One/Walk in Silence	1966	7.50	15.00	30.00

HAIRCUTS, THE

Number	Title (A Side/B Side)	Yr	VG	VG+	NM
PARKWAY					
❑ 899	She Loves You/Love Me Do	1964	5.00	10.00	20.00
❑ 899 [PS]	She Loves You/Love Me Do	1964	10.00	20.00	40.00

HAIRSTON, BROTHER WILL

Number	Title (A Side/B Side)	Yr	VG	VG+	NM
JVB					
❑ 44	The Alabama Bus (Part 1)/The Alabama Bus (Part 2)	1956	75.00	150.00	300.00

HAIRSTON, JACKIE

Number	Title (A Side/B Side)	Yr	VG	VG+	NM
ATCO					
❑ 6464	Monkey on My Back/Hijack	1967	5.00	10.00	20.00

HALE AND THE HUSHABYES

All-star group including BRIAN WILSON, JACKIE DeSHANNON, and SONNY AND CHER.

Number	Title (A Side/B Side)	Yr	VG	VG+	NM
APOGEE					
❑ 104	Yes Sir, That's My Baby/900 Quetzals	1964	75.00	150.00	300.00
REPRISE					
❑ 0299	Yes Sir, That's My Baby/Jack's Theme	1964	50.00	100.00	200.00
—Reissued in 1967 by "A Date With Soul"					
YORK					
❑ 408	Yes Sir, That's My Baby/Bee Side Soul	1967	12.50	25.00	50.00
—As "A Date with Soul"					

HALEE'S COMET

Roy Halee, later producer for SIMON AND GARFUNKEL.

Number	Title (A Side/B Side)	Yr	VG	VG+	NM
EPIC					
❑ 10207	All I Want Is What's Real/From a Parachute	1967	3.00	6.00	12.00

HALEY, BILL, AND HIS COMETS

Includes "Bill Haley and His Saddlemen." Also see THE JODIMARS; THE KINGSMEN (2); SALLY STARR.

Number	Title (A Side/B Side)	Yr	VG	VG+	NM
APT					
❑ 25081	Stop, Look, and Listen/Burn That Candle	1965	5.00	10.00	20.00
❑ 25087	Haley A-Go-Go/Tongue Tied Tony	1965	6.25	12.50	25.00
ARZEE					
❑ 4677	Yodel Your Blues Away/Within This Broken Heart of Mine	1978	6.25	12.50	25.00
❑ 4677 [PS]	Yodel Your Blues Away/Within This Broken Heart of Mine	1978	6.25	12.50	25.00
BUDDAH					
❑ 169	Rock Around the Clock/Framed	1970	3.75	7.50	15.00
DECCA					
❑ 29124	(We're Gonna) Rock Around the Clock/Thirteen Women (And Only One Man in Town)	1954	15.00	30.00	60.00
—With lines on either side of "Decca"					
❑ 29124	(We're Gonna) Rock Around the Clock/Thirteen Women (And Only One Man in Town)	1955	5.00	10.00	20.00
—With star under "Decca"					
❑ 29204	Shake, Rattle and Roll/A.B.C. Boogie	1954	10.00	20.00	40.00
—With lines on either side of "Decca"					
❑ 29204	Shake, Rattle and Roll/A.B.C. Boogie	1954	5.00	10.00	20.00
—With star under "Decca"					
❑ 29317	Dim, Dim the Lights (I Want Some Atmosphere)/Happy Baby	1954	10.00	20.00	40.00
—With lines on either side of "Decca"					
❑ 29317	Dim, Dim the Lights (I Want Some Atmosphere)/Happy Baby	1954	5.00	10.00	20.00
—With star under "Decca"					
❑ 29418	Mambo Rock/Birth of the Boogie	1955	6.25	12.50	25.00
❑ 29552	Razzle-Dazzle/Two Hound Dogs	1955	6.25	12.50	25.00
❑ 29713	Burn That Candle/Rock-a-Beatin' Boogie	1955	6.25	12.50	25.00
❑ 29791	See You Later, Alligator/The Paper Boy (On Main Street, U.S.A.)	1956	6.25	12.50	25.00
❑ 29870	R-O-C-K/The Saints Rock 'N' Roll	1956	6.25	12.50	25.00
❑ 29948	Hot Dog Buddy Buddy/Rockin' Through the Rye	1956	6.25	12.50	25.00
❑ 30028	Rip It Up/Teenager's Mother (Are You Right?)	1956	6.25	12.50	25.00
❑ 30085	Rudy's Rock/Blue Comet Blues	1956	6.25	12.50	25.00
❑ 30148	Don't Knock the Rock/Choo Choo Ch'Boogie	1956	6.25	12.50	25.00
❑ 30214	Forty Cups of Coffeee/Hook, Line and Sinker	1957	6.25	12.50	25.00
❑ 30314	(You Hit the Wrong Note) Billy Goat/Rockin' Rollin' Rover	1957	6.25	12.50	25.00
❑ 30314 [PS]	(You Hit the Wrong Note) Billy Goat/Rockin' Rollin' Rover	1957	30.00	60.00	120.00
❑ 30394	The Dipsy Doodle/Miss You	1957	6.25	12.50	25.00
❑ 30461	Rock the Joint/How Many	1957	6.25	12.50	25.00
❑ 30530	It's a Sin/Mary, Mary Lou	1957	6.25	12.50	25.00
❑ 30530 [PS]	It's a Sin/Mary, Mary Lou	1957	20.00	40.00	80.00
❑ 30592	Skinny Minnie/Sway with Me	1958	7.50	15.00	30.00
❑ 30681	Lean Jean/Don't Nobody Move	1958	6.25	12.50	25.00
❑ 30741	Chiquita Linda/Whoa Mabel	1958	6.25	12.50	25.00
❑ 30781	Corrine, Corrina/B.B. Betty	1958	6.25	12.50	25.00
❑ 30844	Charmaine/I Got a Woman	1959	6.25	12.50	25.00
❑ 30873	(Now and Then, There's) A Fool Such As I/Where Did You Go Last Night	1959	6.25	12.50	25.00
❑ 30926	Caldonia/Shakey	1959	6.25	12.50	25.00
❑ 30956	Joey's Song/Ooh, Look-a-There, Ain't She Pretty	1959	6.25	12.50	25.00
❑ 31030	Skokiaan (South African Song)/Puerto Rican Peddler	1959	6.25	12.50	25.00
❑ 31080	Music, Music, Music/Strictly Instrumental	1960	6.25	12.50	25.00
❑ 31649	The Green Door/Yeah, She's Evil	1964	3.00	6.00	12.00
ESSEX					
❑ 102	Rock Around the Clock/Crazy Man, Crazy	1955	12.50	25.00	50.00
—Actually a bootleg, but highly sought-after nonetheless					
❑ 303	Rock the Joint/Icy Heart	1952	25.00	50.00	100.00
—Black vinyl, block logo ("ESSEX" in all caps)					
❑ 303	Rock the Joint/Icy Heart	1952	15.00	30.00	60.00
—Black vinyl, script logo ("Essex" not in all caps)					
❑ 303	Rock the Joint/Icy Heart	1952	900.00	1350.	1800.
—Red vinyl					
❑ 305	Rocking Chair on the Moon/Dance with a Dolly (With a Hole in Her Stocking)	1952	25.00	50.00	100.00
—Essex 303 and 305 credit "Bill Haley and the Saddlemen"					
❑ 310	Real Rock Drive/Stop Beatin' Round the Mulberry Bush	1952	37.50	75.00	150.00
—Blue label					
❑ 310	Real Rock Drive/Stop Beatin' Round the Mulberry Bush	1952	20.00	40.00	80.00
—Orange label					
❑ 321	Crazy Man, Crazy/Whatcha Gonna Do	1953	15.00	30.00	60.00
❑ 327	Pat-a-Cake/Fractured	1953	10.00	20.00	40.00
❑ 332	Live It Up/Farewell, So Long, Goodbye	1953	10.00	20.00	40.00
❑ 340	Ten Little Indians/I'll Be True	1953	10.00	20.00	40.00
❑ 348	Chattanooga Choo Choo/Straight Jacket	1954	10.00	20.00	40.00
❑ 374	Sundown Boogie/Jukebox Cannonball	1954	18.75	37.50	75.00
❑ 381	Rocket 88/Green Tree Boogie	1955	31.25	62.50	125.00
❑ 399	Rock the Joint/Farewell, So Long, Goodbye	1955	18.75	37.50	75.00
GNP CRESCENDO					
❑ 475	I'm Walkin'/Crazy Man, Crazy	1974	3.00	6.00	12.00
GONE					
❑ 5111	Spanish Twist/My Kind of Woman	1961	6.25	12.50	25.00
❑ 5116	Riviera/War Paint	1961	6.25	12.50	25.00
HOLIDAY					
❑ 113	Sundown Boogie/Jukebox Cannonball	1951	125.00	250.00	500.00
—As "Bill Haley and the Saddlemen"; the only Holiday single known to exist on a 45. Earlier Holiday singles only exist on 78s.					
JANUS					
❑ 162	Travelin' Band/A Little Piece at a Time	1971	3.00	6.00	12.00
KAMA SUTRA					
❑ 508	Rock Around the Clock/Framed	1970	5.00	10.00	20.00
KASEY					
❑ 7006	A.B.C. Boogie/Rock Around the Clock	1961	5.00	10.00	20.00
—B-side by Phil Flowers					
MCA					
❑ 60025	(We're Gonna) Rock Around the Clock/Thirteen Women (And Only One Man in Town)	1973	—	2.50	5.00
—Reissue on black label with rainbow; made the Top 40 in 1974					
NEWTOWN					
❑ 5013	Tenor Man/Up Goes My Love	1962	5.00	10.00	20.00

Number	Title (A Side/B Side)	Yr	VG	VG+	NM
❑ 5024	Dance Around the Clock/What Can I Say After I Say I'm Sorry	1963	5.00	10.00	20.00
NICETOWN					
❑ 5025	You Call Everybody Darling/Tandy	1963	5.00	10.00	20.00
TRANS WORLD					
❑ 718	Real Rock Drive/Yes, Indeed	1954	50.00	100.00	200.00
UNITED ARTISTS					
❑ 50483	Ain't Love Funny, Ha Ha Ha/That's How I Got to Memphis	1969	3.00	6.00	12.00
WARNER BROS.					
❑ 5145	Candy Kisses/Tamiami	1960	6.25	12.50	25.00
❑ 5145 [DJ]	Candy Kisses/Tamiami	1960	12.50	25.00	50.00
—Promo only on yellow vinyl					
❑ 5154	Hawk/Chick Safari	1960	6.25	12.50	25.00
❑ 5171	Let the Good Times Roll, Creole/So Right Tonight	1960	6.25	12.50	25.00
❑ 5228	Flip, Flop and Fly/Honky Tonk	1961	6.25	12.50	25.00
❑ 7124	Rock Around the Clock/Shake, Rattle and Roll	1969	3.75	7.50	15.00

7-Inch Extended Plays

Number	Title (A Side/B Side)	Yr	VG	VG+	NM
CLAIRE					
❑ 4779	*All I Need Is Some More Lovin'/Trouble in Mind/ Life of the Party/I Should Write a Song About You	1978	3.75	7.50	15.00
❑ 4779 [PS]	Bill Haley and the Comets	1978	3.75	7.50	15.00
DECCA					
❑ ED 2168	Shake, Rattle and Roll/A.B.C. Boogie//(We're Gonna) Rock Around the Clock/Thirteen Women (And Only One Man in Town)	1954	15.00	30.00	60.00
❑ ED 2168 [PS]	Shake, Rattle and Roll	1954	15.00	30.00	60.00
❑ ED 2209	Dim, Dim the Lights/Happy Baby//Birth of the Boogie/Mambo Rock	1955	15.00	30.00	60.00
❑ ED 2209 [PS]	Dim, Dim the Lights	1955	15.00	30.00	60.00
❑ ED 2322	Razzle-Dazzle/Two Hound Dogs//Burn That Candle/Rock-a-Beatin' Boogie	1956	15.00	30.00	60.00
❑ ED 2322 [PS]	Rock and Roll	1956	15.00	30.00	60.00
❑ ED 2398	See You Later Alligator/R-O-C-K//The Saints Rock 'n Roll/Burn That Candle	1956	12.50	25.00	50.00
❑ ED 2398 [PS]	He Digs RnR (Music for the Boyfriend)	1956	12.50	25.00	50.00
—Note: In prior editions we listed ED 2399 and ED 2400 in this section. We now know that they have no Bill Haley tracks whatsoever.					
❑ ED 2416	Calling All Comets/Rockin' Through the Rye// Hook, Line and Sinker/Rudy's Rock	1956	12.50	25.00	50.00
❑ ED 2416 [PS]	Rock 'n' Roll Stage Show, Part 1	1956	12.50	25.00	50.00
❑ ED 2417	A Rockin' Little Tune/Hide and Seek//Choo Choo Ch' Boogie/Blue Comet Blues	1956	12.50	25.00	50.00
❑ ED 2417 [PS]	Rock 'n' Roll Stage Show, Part 2	1956	12.50	25.00	50.00
❑ ED 2418	Hey Then, There Now/Goofin' Around//Hot Dog Buddy Buddy/Tonight's the Night	1956	12.50	25.00	50.00
❑ ED 2418 [PS]	Rock 'n' Roll Stage Show, Part 3	1956	12.50	25.00	50.00
❑ ED 2532	*The Dipsy Doodle/Miss You/Is It True What They Say About Dixie?/Carolina in the Morning	1957	12.50	25.00	50.00
❑ ED 2532 [PS]	Rockin' the Oldies	1957	12.50	25.00	50.00
❑ ED 2533	*One Sweet Letter from You/Please Don't Talk About Me When I'm Gone/Apple Blossom Time/ Somebody Else Is Taking My Place	1957	12.50	25.00	50.00
❑ ED 2533 [PS]	Rock 'n' Roll Party	1957	12.50	25.00	50.00
❑ ED 2534	*Moon Over Miami/Ain't Misbehavin'/You Can't Stop Me from Dreaming/I'm Gonna Sit Right Down and Write Myself a Letter	1957	12.50	25.00	50.00
❑ ED 2534 [PS]	Rockin' & Rollin'	1957	12.50	25.00	50.00
❑ ED 2564	*Me Rock-a-Hula/Wooden Shoe Rock/Oriental Rock/Rockin' Matilda	1957	12.50	25.00	50.00
❑ ED 2564 [PS]	Rockin' Around the World	1957	12.50	25.00	50.00
❑ ED 2576	*Piccadilly Rock/Vive La Rock & Roll/Rockin' Rollin' Schnitzlebank/Come Rock with Me	1957	12.50	25.00	50.00
❑ ED 2576 [PS]	Rockin' Around Europe	1957	12.50	25.00	50.00
❑ ED 2577	*Pretty Alouette/El Rocko/Rockin' Rita/Jamaican DJ	1957	12.50	25.00	50.00
❑ ED 2577 [PS]	Rockin' Around the Americas	1957	12.50	25.00	50.00
❑ ED 2615	Rock Lomond/It's a Sin//Move It On Over/New Rock the Joint	1958	10.00	20.00	40.00
❑ ED 2615 [PS]	Rockin' the Joint, Part 1	1958	10.00	20.00	40.00
❑ ED 2616	Rip It Up/The Beak (Speaks)//Sway with Me/Forty Cups of Coffee	1958	10.00	20.00	40.00
❑ ED 2616 [PS]	Rockin' the Joint, Part 2	1958	10.00	20.00	40.00
❑ ED 2638 [M]	*Whoa Mabel!/Ida Sweet as Apple Cider/Eloise/ Dinah	1958	10.00	20.00	40.00
❑ ED 2638 [PS]	Bill Haley's Chicks	1958	10.00	20.00	40.00
❑ ED 7-2638 [PS]	Bill Haley's Chicks	1959	20.00	40.00	80.00
❑ ED 7-2638 [S]	*Whoa Mabel!/Ida Sweet as Apple Cider/Eloise/ Dinah	1959	20.00	40.00	80.00
❑ ED 2670 [M]	Joe's Song/Ooh Look-a There Ain't She Pretty// Shakey/Caledonia	1959	10.00	20.00	40.00
❑ ED 2670 [PS]	Bill Haley and His Comets	1959	10.00	20.00	40.00
❑ ED 7-2670 [PS]	Bill Haley and His Comets	1959	20.00	40.00	80.00
❑ ED 7-2670 [S]	Joe's Song/Ooh Look-a There Ain't She Pretty// Shakey/Caledonia	1959	20.00	40.00	80.00
❑ ED 2671 [M]	Strictly Instrumental/South Africa Song//Mack the Knife/In a Little Spanish Town	1959	10.00	20.00	40.00
❑ ED 2671 [PS]	Strictly Instrumental	1959	10.00	20.00	40.00
❑ ED 7-2671 [PS]	Strictly Instrumental	1959	20.00	40.00	80.00
❑ ED 7-2671 [S]	Strictly Instrumental/South Africa Song//Mack the Knife/In a Little Spanish Town	1959	20.00	40.00	80.00
ESSEX					
❑ TWEP-102	Rock the Joint/Rockin' Chair on the Moon//Crazy Man, Crazy/Pat-a-Cake	1954	25.00	50.00	100.00
❑ TWEP-102 [PS]	For Your Dance Party	1954	30.00	60.00	120.00
❑ EP-117	*Live It Up/Farewell, So Long, Goodbye/Real Rock Drive/Fractured	1954	25.00	50.00	100.00
❑ EP-117 [PS]	Rock with Bill Haley and His Comets, Volume 1	1954	30.00	60.00	120.00
❑ EP-118	*Stop Beatin' Round the Mulberry Bush/Watcha Gonna Do/I'll Be True/Juke Box Cannon Ball	1954	25.00	50.00	100.00
❑ EP-118 [PS]	Rock with Bill Haley and His Comets, Volume 2	1954	30.00	60.00	120.00
❑ EP-119	(contents unknown)	1954	25.00	50.00	100.00
❑ EP-119 [PS]	Rock with Bill Haley and His Comets, Volume 3	1954	30.00	60.00	120.00
SOMERSET					
❑ 460	(contents unknown)	1955	20.00	40.00	80.00
❑ 460 [PS]	Rock with Bill Haley and His Comets	1955	20.00	40.00	80.00
TRANS WORLD					
❑ TWEP-117	(contents unknown)	1955	20.00	40.00	80.00
❑ TWEP-117 [PS]	Rock with Bill Haley and His Comets, Volume 1	1955	20.00	40.00	80.00
❑ TWEP-118	(contents unknown)	1955	20.00	40.00	80.00
❑ TWEP-118 [PS]	Rock with Bill Haley and His Comets, Volume 2	1955	20.00	40.00	80.00
❑ TWEP-119	(contents unknown)	1955	20.00	40.00	80.00
❑ TWEP-119 [PS]	Rock with Bill Haley and His Comets, Volume 3	1955	20.00	40.00	80.00

HALL, DARYL

Also see GULLIVER; DARYL HALL AND JOHN OATES; THE TEMPTONES.

Number	Title (A Side/B Side)	Yr	VG	VG+	NM
AMY					
❑ 11049	The Princess and the Soldier (Part 1)/The Princess and the Soldier (Part 2)	1969	—	3.00	6.00
EPIC					
❑ 77139	I'm in a Philly Mood/Money Changes Everything	1993	—	—	3.00
❑ 77258	Stop Lovin' Me, Stop Lovin' You/Stop Lovin' Me, Stop Lovin' You (Churban Remix)	1993	—	—	3.00
PARALLAX					
❑ 404	A Lonely Girl/(B-side unknown)	196?	7.50	15.00	30.00
RCA					
❑ 5038-7-R	Foolish Pride/What's Gonna Happen to Us	1986	—	—	3.00
❑ 5038-7-R [PS]	Foolish Pride/What's Gonna Happen to Us	1986	—	—	3.00
❑ 5105-7-R	Someone Like You (The Guitar Solo)/Someone Like You (The Sax Solo)	1987	—	—	3.00
❑ 5105-7-R [PS]	Someone Like You (The Guitar Solo)/Someone Like You (The Sax Solo)	1987	—	—	3.00
❑ PB-12001	Something in 4/4 Time/Sacred Songs	1980	—	2.00	4.00
❑ PB-12001 [PS]	Something in 4/4 Time/Sacred Songs	1980	—	2.50	5.00
❑ PB-14387	Dreamtime/Let It Out	1986	—	—	3.00
❑ PB-14387 [PS]	Dreamtime/Let It Out	1986	—	—	3.00

HALL, DARYL, AND JOHN OATES

Also see GULLIVER; DARYL HALL.

Number	Title (A Side/B Side)	Yr	VG	VG+	NM
ARISTA					
❑ 2085	So Close/So Close (Unplugged)	1990	—	—	3.00
❑ 2157	Don't Hold Back Your Love/Change of Season	1990	—	—	3.00
❑ 9684	Everything Your Heart Desires/Real Love	1988	—	—	3.00
❑ 9684 [PS]	Everything Your Heart Desires/Real Love	1988	—	—	3.00
❑ 9727	Missed Opportunity/Soul Love	1988	—	—	3.00
❑ 9727 [PS]	Missed Opportunity/Soul Love	1988	—	—	3.00
❑ 9753	Downtown Life (LP Version)/Downtown Life (Urban Mix)	1988	—	—	3.00
❑ 9753 [PS]	Downtown Life (LP Version)/Downtown Life (Urban Mix)	1988	—	—	3.00
ATLANTIC					
❑ 2922	Goodnight & Good Morning/All Our Love	1972	2.50	5.00	10.00
—As "Whole Oats"					
❑ 2939	Lilly (Are You Happy)/I'm Sorry	1973	2.00	4.00	8.00
❑ 2993	She's Gone/I'm Just a Kid (Don't Make Me Feel Like a Man)	1973	2.00	4.00	8.00
❑ 3026	Lady Rain/When the Morning Comes	1974	—	2.50	5.00
❑ 3239	Can't Stop the Music/70's Scenario	1975	—	2.50	5.00
❑ 3332	She's Gone/I'm Just a Kid (Don't Make Me Feel Like a Man)	1976	—	2.00	4.00
❑ 3332 [DJ]	She's Gone (Long Version)/She's Gone	1976	—	3.00	6.00
❑ 3397	It's Uncanny/Lilly (Are You Happy)	1977	—	2.00	4.00
CHELSEA					
❑ 3063	If That's What Makes You Happy/The Reason Why	1977	—	2.50	5.00
—B-side by "Daryl Hall and Gulliver"					
❑ 3065	Red River Blues/(B-side unknown)	1977	—	2.50	5.00
❑ 3069	Perkiomen/The Provider	1977	—	2.50	5.00
RCA					
❑ PB-10808	Do What You Want, Be What You Are/You'll Never Learn	1976	—	2.00	4.00
❑ PB-10860	Rich Girl/London Luck, & Love	1976	—	2.00	4.00
❑ PB-10860 [PS]	Rich Girl/London Luck, & Love	1976	2.00	4.00	8.00
❑ GB-10942	Sara Smile/Do What You Want, Be What You Are	1977	—	—	3.00
—Gold Standard Series					
❑ PB-10970	Back Together Again/Room to Breathe	1977	—	2.00	4.00
❑ PB-11132	Why Do Lovers (Break Each Other's Heart?)/A Girl Who Used to Be	1977	—	2.00	4.00
❑ PB-11181	Don't Change/The Emptiness	1977	—	2.00	4.00
❑ GB-11324	Rich Girl/Back Together Again	1978	—	—	3.00
—Gold Standard Series					
❑ PB-11371	It's a Laugh/Serious Music	1978	—	2.00	4.00
❑ PB-11424	I Don't Wanna Lose You/August Day	1978	—	2.00	4.00
❑ PB-11747	Wait for Me/No Brain No Pain	1979	—	2.00	4.00
❑ PB-11920	All You Want Is Heaven/Who Said the World Was Fair	1980	—	2.00	4.00
❑ GB-11970	It's a Laugh/I Don't Wanna Lose You	1980	—	—	3.00
—Gold Standard Series					
❑ PB-12048	How Does It Feel to Be Back/United State	1980	—	2.00	4.00
❑ PB-12103	You've Lost That Lovin' Feeling/Diddy Doo Wap (I Hear the Voices)	1980	—	2.00	4.00
❑ PB-12142	Kiss on My List/Africa	1981	—	2.00	4.00
❑ PB-12217	You Make My Dreams/Gotta Lotta Love	1981	—	2.00	4.00
❑ PB-12296	Private Eyes/Tell Me What You Want	1981	—	2.00	4.00
❑ GB-12318	Kiss on My List/You've Lost That Lovin' Feeling	1981	—	—	3.00
—Gold Standard Series					
❑ PB-12357	I Can't Go for That (No Can Do)/Unguarded Minute	1981	—	2.00	4.00
❑ JB-12361 [DJ]	I Can't Go for That (No Can Do)/I Can't Go for That (No Can Do) (Club Mix)	1981	2.50	5.00	10.00
—Promo only					
❑ PB-13065	Did It in a Minute/Head Above Water	1982	—	2.00	4.00
❑ PB-13252	Your Imagination/Sara Smile	1982	—	2.00	4.00

Number	Title (A Side/B Side)	Yr	VG	VG+	NM
❑ PB-13354	Maneater/Delayed Reaction	1982	—	—	3.00
❑ PB-13354 [PS]	Maneater/Delayed Reaction	1982	—	2.00	4.00
❑ PB-13421	One on One/Art of Heartbreak	1983	—	—	3.00
❑ PB-13421 [PS]	One on One/Art of Heartbreak	1983	—	2.00	4.00
❑ GB-13480	Private Eyes/I Can't Go for That (No Can Do)	1983	—	—	3.00

—Gold Standard Series

Number	Title (A Side/B Side)	Yr	VG	VG+	NM
❑ GB-13481	You Make My Dreams/Did It in a Minute	1983	—	—	3.00

—Gold Standard Series

Number	Title (A Side/B Side)	Yr	VG	VG+	NM
❑ PB-13507	Family Man/Open All Night	1983	—	—	3.00
❑ PB-13654	Say It Isn't So/Kiss on My List	1983	—	—	3.00
❑ PB-13654 [PS]	Say It Isn't So/Kiss on My List	1983	—	2.00	4.00
❑ PB-13714	Adult Education/Maneater	1984	—	—	3.00
❑ PB-13714 [PS]	Adult Education/Maneater	1984	—	2.00	4.00
❑ GB-13796	Maneater/One on One	1984	—	—	3.00

—Gold Standard Series

Number	Title (A Side/B Side)	Yr	VG	VG+	NM
❑ GB-13797	Family Man/Say It Isn't So	1984	—	—	3.00

—Gold Standard Series

Number	Title (A Side/B Side)	Yr	VG	VG+	NM
❑ PB-13916	Out of Touch/Cold, Dark, and Yesterday	1984	—	—	3.00
❑ PB-13916 [PS]	Out of Touch/Cold, Dark, and Yesterday	1984	—	—	3.00
❑ PB-13970	Method of Modern Love (Remix Edit)/Method of Modern Love	1984	—	—	3.00
❑ PB-13970 [PS]	Method of Modern Love (Remix Edit)/Method of Modern Love	1984	—	—	3.00
❑ PB-14035	Some Things Are Better Left Unsaid/All American Girl	1985	—	—	3.00
❑ PB-14035 [PS]	Some Things Are Better Left Unsaid/All American Girl	1985	—	—	3.00
❑ GB-14064	Out of Touch/Adult Education	1985	—	—	3.00

—Gold Standard Series

Number	Title (A Side/B Side)	Yr	VG	VG+	NM
❑ PB-14098	Possession Obsession/Dance on Your Knees	1985	—	—	3.00
❑ PB-14098 [PS]	Possession Obsession/Dance on Your Knees	1985	—	—	3.00
❑ PB-14178	A Nite at the Apollo Live! The Way You Do the Things You Do-My Girl/Everytime You Go Away	1985	—	—	3.00

—A-side: With David Ruffin and Eddie Kendrick (sic)

Number	Title (A Side/B Side)	Yr	VG	VG+	NM
❑ PB-14178 [PS]	A Nite at the Apollo Live! The Way You Do the Things You Do-My Girl/Everytime You Go Away	1985	—	—	3.00

—A-side: With David Ruffin and Eddie Kendrick (sic)

Number	Title (A Side/B Side)	Yr	VG	VG+	NM
❑ JR-14259 [DJ]	Jingle Bell Rock from Daryl/Jingle Bell Rock from John	1985	2.50	5.00	10.00

—Promo only on red vinyl

Number	Title (A Side/B Side)	Yr	VG	VG+	NM
❑ JR-14259 [DJ]	Jingle Bell Rock from Daryl/Jingle Bell Rock from John	1985	2.50	5.00	10.00

—Promo only on green vinyl

Number	Title (A Side/B Side)	Yr	VG	VG+	NM
❑ JR-14259 [PS]	Jingle Bell Rock from Daryl/Jingle Bell Rock from John	1985	2.50	5.00	10.00
❑ GB-14340	Method of Modern Love/Possession Obsession	1986	—	—	3.00

—Gold Standard Series

Number	Title (A Side/B Side)	Yr	VG	VG+	NM
❑ GB-14341	Some Things Are Better Left Unsaid/A Nite at the Apollo Live! The Way You Do the Things You Do-My Girl	1986	—	—	3.00

—Gold Standard Series

RCA VICTOR

Number	Title (A Side/B Side)	Yr	VG	VG+	NM
❑ PB-10373	Camellia/Ennui on the Mountain	1975	—	2.50	5.00
❑ PB-10436	Nothing at All/Alone Too Long	1975	—	2.50	5.00
❑ PB-10530	Sara Smile/Soldering	1975	—	2.50	5.00

SIRE

Number	Title (A Side/B Side)	Yr	VG	VG+	NM
❑ 22967	Love Train/"Earth Girls Are Easy" Theme	1989	—	—	3.00
❑ 22967 [PS]	Love Train/"Earth Girls Are Easy" Theme	1989	—	—	3.00

HALL, DICKSON

EPIC

Number	Title (A Side/B Side)	Yr	VG	VG+	NM
❑ 9262	Cowboy/It's a Long Walk Home	1958	3.75	7.50	15.00
❑ 9262 [PS]	Cowboy/It's a Long Walk Home	1958	6.25	12.50	25.00

HALL, FRANCES

SURF

Number	Title (A Side/B Side)	Yr	VG	VG+	NM
❑ 5031	Christmas Lullaby/Jack in the Box	1958	5.00	10.00	20.00

HALL, LARRY

HOT

Number	Title (A Side/B Side)	Yr	VG	VG+	NM
❑ 1	Sandy/Lovin' Tree	1959	12.50	25.00	50.00

STRAND

Number	Title (A Side/B Side)	Yr	VG	VG+	NM
❑ 25007	Sandy/Lovin' Tree	1959	6.25	12.50	25.00
❑ 25013	A Girl Like You/Rosemary	1960	5.00	10.00	20.00
❑ 25016	For Every Boy/I'll Stay Single	1960	5.00	10.00	20.00
❑ 25025	The Girl I Left Behind/Kool Love	1961	5.00	10.00	20.00
❑ 25029	Lips of Wine/Rebel Heart	1961	5.00	10.00	20.00
❑ 25048	Ladder of Love/The One You Left Behind	1961	5.00	10.00	20.00

HALL, ROY

DECCA

Number	Title (A Side/B Side)	Yr	VG	VG+	NM
❑ 29697	Whole Lotta Shakin' Goin' On/All By Myself	1955	20.00	40.00	80.00
❑ 29786	See You Later, Alligator/Don't Stop Now	1956	12.50	25.00	50.00
❑ 29880	Blue Suede Shoes/Luscious	1956	12.50	25.00	50.00
❑ 30060	Three Alley Cats/Diggin' the Boogie	1956	12.50	25.00	50.00

FORTUNE

Number	Title (A Side/B Side)	Yr	VG	VG+	NM
❑ 170	Going Down the Road/Jealous Love	1952	10.00	20.00	40.00

—B-side by the Davis Sisters

Number	Title (A Side/B Side)	Yr	VG	VG+	NM
❑ 521	Corrine, Corrina/Don't Ask Me No Questions	1956	12.50	25.00	50.00

HI-Q

Number	Title (A Side/B Side)	Yr	VG	VG+	NM
❑ 5045	Three Alley Cats/Bedspring Motel	196?	15.00	30.00	60.00
❑ 5050	Go Go Little Queenie/Everybody Dig That Boogie	196?	15.00	30.00	60.00

HALL, TOM T.

MERCURY

Number	Title (A Side/B Side)	Yr	VG	VG+	NM
❑ 55001	It's All in the Game/The Little Green Flowers	1977	—	2.00	4.00
❑ 72700	I Wish My Face in the Morning Dew/Picture of Your Mother	1967	2.00	4.00	8.00
❑ 72749	Beauty Is a Fading Flower/Your Love Is Mine Again	1967	2.00	4.00	8.00
❑ 72786	The World the Way I Want It/Shame on the Rain	1968	2.00	4.00	8.00
❑ 72835	Ain't Got the Time/Hope	1968	2.00	4.00	8.00
❑ 72863	Ballad of Forty Dollars/Highways	1968	—	3.00	6.00
❑ 72913	Strawberry Farms/3	1969	—	3.00	6.00
❑ 72951	Homecoming/Myra	1969	—	3.00	6.00
❑ 72998	A Week in a Country Jail/Flat-Footin' It	1969	—	3.00	6.00
❑ 73039	Shoeshine Man/Kentucky in the Morning	1970	—	3.00	6.00
❑ 73078	Salute to a Switchblade/That'll Be Alright with Me	1970	—	3.00	6.00
❑ 73140	One Hundred Children/I Took a Memory to Lunch	1970	—	3.00	6.00
❑ 73189	Ode to a Half Pound of Ground Round/Pinto the Wonder Horse Is Dead	1971	—	3.00	6.00
❑ 73221	The Year That Clayton Delaney Died/Second Handed Flowers	1971	—	2.50	5.00
❑ 73278	Me and Jesus/Coot Marseilles Blues	1972	—	2.50	5.00
❑ 73297	The Monkey That Became President/She Gave Her Heart to Jethro	1972	—	2.50	5.00
❑ 73327	More About John Henry/Windy City Anne	1972	—	2.50	5.00
❑ 73346	(Old Dogs-Children and) Watermelon Wine/Grandma Whistled	1972	—	2.50	5.00
❑ 73377	Ravishing Ruby/I Flew Over Our House Last Night	1973	—	2.50	5.00
❑ 73394	Watergate Blues/Spokane Motel Blues	1973	—	2.50	5.00
❑ 73436	I Love/Back When We Were Young	1973	—	2.00	4.00
❑ 73488	That Song Is Driving Me Crazy/Forget It	1974	—	2.00	4.00
❑ 73617	Country Is/God Came Through Bellville, Ga.	1974	—	2.00	4.00
❑ 73641	I Care/Sneaky Snake	1974	—	2.00	4.00
❑ 73686	Deal/It Rained in Every Town Except Paducah	1975	—	2.00	4.00
❑ 73704	I Like Beer/From a Mansion to a Honky Tonk	1975	—	2.00	4.00
❑ 73755	Faster Horses (The Cowboy and the Poet)/No New Friends Please	1975	—	2.00	4.00
❑ 73795	Negatory Romance/It's Got to Be Kentucky for Me	1976	—	2.00	4.00
❑ 73850	Fox on the Run/Bluegrass Festival in the Sky	1976	—	2.00	4.00
❑ 73899	Your Man Loves You Honey/One of the Mysteries of Life	1977	—	2.00	4.00
❑ 812835-7	Everything from Jesus to Jack Daniels/(Old Dogs-Children and) Watermelon Wine	1983	—	—	3.00
❑ 814560-7	How'd You Get Home So Soon/The Year That Clayton Delaney Died	1983	—	—	3.00
❑ 870669-7	Let's Play Remember/Fox Hollow's Animal Train	1988	—	—	3.00
❑ 872180-7	Let's Spend Christmas at My House/Let's Go Shopping Today	1988	—	—	3.00
❑ 880030-7	Famous in Missouri/I Only Think About You When I'm Drunk	1984	—	—	3.00
❑ 880216-7	P.S. I Love You/My Heroes Have Always Been Cowboys	1984	—	—	3.00
❑ 880690-7	A Bar with No Beer/Red Sails in the Sunset	1985	—	—	3.00
❑ 884017-7	Down in the Florida Keys/Song in a Seashell	1985	—	—	3.00
❑ 884850-7	Susie's Beauty Shop/Love Letters in the Sand	1986	—	—	3.00
❑ 888155-7	Dowm at the Mall/We're All Through Dancing	1986	—	—	3.00

RCA

Number	Title (A Side/B Side)	Yr	VG	VG+	NM
❑ PB-11158	May the Force Be With You Always/No One Feels My Heart	1977	—	2.50	5.00
❑ PB-11253	I Wish I Loved Somebody Else/Whiskey	1978	—	2.00	4.00
❑ PB-11376	What Have You Got to Lose/The Three Sofa Story	1978	—	2.00	4.00
❑ PB-11453	Son of Clayton Delaney/The Great East Breadway Onion Championship of 1978	1978	—	2.00	4.00
❑ PB-11568	There Is a Miracle in You/Saturday Morning Show	1979	—	2.00	4.00
❑ PB-11713	You Show Me Your Heart (And I'll Show You Mine)/Old Habits Die Hard	1979	—	2.00	4.00
❑ PB-11765	Christmas Is/Thanksgiving Is	1979	—	2.00	4.00
❑ PB-11888	The Old Side of Town/Jesus on the Radio (Daddy on the Phone)	1979	—	2.00	4.00
❑ PB-12005	Soldier of Fortune/The World According to Raymond	1980	—	—	3.00
❑ PB-12066	Back When Gas Was Thirty Cents a Gallon/Texas Never Fell in Love with Me	1980	—	—	3.00
❑ PB-12219	The All New Me/Pour Me (Pour Me Another Drink)	1981	—	—	3.00

HALL, TOM T., AND EARL SCRUGGS

COLUMBIA

Number	Title (A Side/B Side)	Yr	VG	VG+	NM
❑ 18-02858	There Ain't No Country Music on This Jukebox/Don't This Road Look Rough and Rocky	1982	—	2.00	4.00
❑ 18-03033	Song of the South/Shackles and Chains	1982	—	2.00	4.00

HALLIWELL, GERI

Also see SPICE GIRLS.

CAPITOL

Number	Title (A Side/B Side)	Yr	VG	VG+	NM
❑ 58811	Mi Chico Latino/Summertime	1999	—	2.00	4.00

HALLMARKS, THE

The Smash group may not be the same as the others.

DOT

Number	Title (A Side/B Side)	Yr	VG	VG+	NM
❑ 16418	My Little Sailor Boy/Congratulations	1963	5.00	10.00	20.00

EPIC

Number	Title (A Side/B Side)	Yr	VG	VG+	NM
❑ 9681	Let There Be You/Royal King	1964	3.00	6.00	12.00

SMASH

Number	Title (A Side/B Side)	Yr	VG	VG+	NM
❑ 2115	Soul Shakin' Psychedelic Sally/Girl of My Dreams	1967	7.50	15.00	30.00

HALLOWAY, LARRY

PARKWAY

Number	Title (A Side/B Side)	Yr	VG	VG+	NM
❑ 903	Beatle Teen Beat/Going Up	1964	5.00	10.00	20.00

HALLYDAY, JOHNNY

PHILIPS

Number	Title (A Side/B Side)	Yr	VG	VG+	NM
❑ 40024	I Got a Woman/Be-Bop-a-Lula	1962	6.25	12.50	25.00
❑ 40043	Hey Little Girl/Caravan of Lonely Men	1962	6.25	12.50	25.00

HALO OF FLIES

AMPHETAMINE REPTILE

Number	Title (A Side/B Side)	Yr	VG	VG+	NM
❑ (1)	Rubber Room/Thoughts in a Booth/3 More Quarters	1985	37.50	75.00	150.00

—Numbered edition of 300

Number	Title (A Side/B Side)	Yr	VG	VG+	NM
❑ (1) [PS]	Rubber Room/Thoughts in a Booth/3 More Quarters	1985	37.50	75.00	150.00

—With insert

Number	Title (A Side/B Side)	Yr	VG	VG+	NM
❑ Scale 2	Snapping Back Roscoe Bottles: DDT Fin 13-PCP/Can't Touch Her	1985	25.00	50.00	100.00

—Numbered edition of 400

Number	Title (A Side/B Side)	Yr	VG	VG+	NM
❑ Scale 2 [PS]	Snapping Back Roscoe Bottles: DDT Fin 13-PCP/Can't Touch Her	1985	25.00	50.00	100.00

—With lyrics

Number	Title (A Side/B Side)	Yr	VG	VG+	NM
❑ Scale 3	M.D. 20-20/Pipebomb/Sinner Sings	1986	18.75	37.50	75.00

—Yellow vinyl (300 made)

Number	Title (A Side/B Side)	Yr	VG	VG+	NM
❑ Scale 3	M.D. 20-20/Pipebomb/Sinner Sings	1986	6.25	12.50	25.00

—Black vinyl (1,700 made)

Number	Title (A Side/B Side)	Yr	VG	VG+	NM
❑ Scale 3 [PS]	M.D. 20-20/Pipebomb/Sinner Sings	1986	6.25	12.50	25.00
❑ Scale 5	Richie's Dog/How Does It Feel to Feel	1986	6.25	12.50	25.00
❑ Scale 5 [PS]	Richie's Dog/How Does It Feel to Feel	1986	6.25	12.50	25.00
❑ Scale 13	No Time/You Get Nothing	1987	5.00	10.00	20.00
❑ Scale 13 [PS]	No Time/You Get Nothing	1987	5.00	10.00	20.00
❑ Scale 19	Death of a Fly/Sit It Out/There Ain't No Hell	1988	3.75	7.50	15.00
❑ Scale 19 [PS]	Death of a Fly/Sit It Out/There Ain't No Hell	1988	3.75	7.50	15.00
❑ Scale 35	Tired and Cold/Wasted Time	1990	6.25	12.50	25.00

—Burgundy vinyl

Number	Title (A Side/B Side)	Yr	VG	VG+	NM
❑ Scale 35	Tired and Cold/Wasted Time	1990	2.50	5.00	10.00
❑ Scale 35 [PS]	Tired and Cold/Wasted Time	1990	2.50	5.00	10.00
❑ Scale 36	Jagged Time Lapse/She's Just Fifteen	1991	6.75	13.75	27.50

—B-side by Mudhoney; burgundy vinyl

Number	Title (A Side/B Side)	Yr	VG	VG+	NM
❑ Scale 36	Jagged Time Lapse/She's Just Fifteen	1991	—	3.75	7.50

—B-side by Mudhoney; black vinyl

Number	Title (A Side/B Side)	Yr	VG	VG+	NM
❑ Scale 36 [PS]	Jagged Time Lapse/She's Just Fifteen	1991	—	3.75	7.50

FORCED EXPOSURE

Number	Title (A Side/B Side)	Yr	VG	VG+	NM
❑ FE-019	Human Fly/I'ma Big	1989	5.00	10.00	20.00
❑ FE-019 [PS]	Human Fly/I'ma Big	1989	5.00	10.00	20.00

SILTBREEZE

Number	Title (A Side/B Side)	Yr	VG	VG+	NM
❑ 1	Richie's Dog/Garbage Rock/Ballad of Extreme Hate	1989	3.00	6.25	12.50
❑ 1 [PS]	Richie's Dog/Garbage Rock/Ballad of Extreme Hate	1989	3.00	6.25	12.50

—First pressings have a numbered insert; add 80% if insert is enclosed

HALOS, THE

7 ARTS

Number	Title (A Side/B Side)	Yr	VG	VG+	NM
❑ 709	Nag/Copy Cat	1961	5.00	10.00	20.00
❑ 720	Come On/What'd I Say	1962	5.00	10.00	20.00

CONGRESS

Number	Title (A Side/B Side)	Yr	VG	VG+	NM
❑ 244	Do I/Just Keep On Loving Me	1965	3.00	6.00	12.00
❑ 249	Since I Fell for You/You're Never Gonna Find	1965	3.00	6.00	12.00
❑ 253	Baby What You Want Me to Do/Hey, Hey, Love Me	1965	3.00	6.00	12.00
❑ 262 [DJ]	Come Softly to Me/(B-side unknown)	1966	3.00	6.00	12.00

—May be promo-only

HAMILTON, GEORGE

ABC-PARAMOUNT

Number	Title (A Side/B Side)	Yr	VG	VG+	NM
❑ 10734	Loneliness/So Small	1965	2.50	5.00	10.00
❑ 10734 [PS]	Loneliness/So Small	1965	5.00	10.00	20.00

MGM

Number	Title (A Side/B Side)	Yr	VG	VG+	NM
❑ 13178	Don't Envy Me/Little Bitty Falling Star	1963	3.00	6.00	12.00
❑ 13215	Does Goodnight Mean Goodbye/Errand of Mercy	1964	3.00	6.00	12.00

UNI

Number	Title (A Side/B Side)	Yr	VG	VG+	NM
❑ 55303	Evel Knievel/Boy from the Country	1971	2.50	5.00	10.00

HAMILTON, GEORGE, IV

ABC

Number	Title (A Side/B Side)	Yr	VG	VG+	NM
❑ 12342 [DJ]	Only the Best (mono/stereo)	1978	—	2.50	5.00

—May be promo only

Number	Title (A Side/B Side)	Yr	VG	VG+	NM
❑ 12376	One Day at a Time/Take This Heart	1978	—	2.00	4.00

ABC-PARAMOUNT

Number	Title (A Side/B Side)	Yr	VG	VG+	NM
❑ 9765	A Rose and a Baby Ruth/If You Don't Know	1956	7.50	15.00	30.00
❑ 9782	Only One Love/If I Possessed a Printing Press	1957	7.50	15.00	30.00
❑ 9838	High School Romance/Everybody's Baby	1957	7.50	15.00	30.00
❑ 9862	Why Don't They Understand/Even Tho'	1957	7.50	15.00	30.00
❑ 9898	Now and For Always/One Heart	1958	6.25	12.50	25.00
❑ 9924	I Know Where I'm Goin'/Who's Taking You to the Prom	1958	6.25	12.50	25.00
❑ 9946	When Will I Know/Your Cheatin' Heart	1958	6.25	12.50	25.00
❑ 9966	Lucy, Lucy/The Two of Us	1958	6.25	12.50	25.00
❑ 10009	The Steady Game/Can You Blame Us	1959	5.00	10.00	20.00
❑ 10028	Gee/I Know Your Sweetheart	1959	5.00	10.00	20.00
❑ 10059	One Little Acre/Little Tom	1959	5.00	10.00	20.00
❑ 10090	Why I'm Walkin'/Tremble	1960	5.00	10.00	20.00
❑ 10125	Before This Day Ends/Loneliness All Around Me	1960	5.00	10.00	20.00
❑ 10167	A Walk on the Wild Side of Life/It's Just the Idea	1960	5.00	10.00	20.00

ABC/DOT

Number	Title (A Side/B Side)	Yr	VG	VG+	NM
❑ 17687	I Wonder Who's Kissing Her Now/In the Palm of Her Hand	1977	—	2.00	4.00
❑ 17708	Cornbread, Beans and Sweet Potato Pie/May the Wind Be Always at Your Back	1977	—	2.00	4.00
❑ 17723	Everlasting (Everlasting Love)/In the Palm of Your Hand	1977	—	2.00	4.00

COLONIAL

Number	Title (A Side/B Side)	Yr	VG	VG+	NM
❑ 420	A Rose and a Baby Ruth/If You Don't Know	1956	20.00	40.00	80.00
❑ 451	I've Got a Secret/Sam	1956	10.00	20.00	40.00

GRT

Number	Title (A Side/B Side)	Yr	VG	VG+	NM
❑ 063	Blue Jeans, Ice Cream and Saturday Shoes/Bad Romancer	1976	—	2.50	5.00

MCA

Number	Title (A Side/B Side)	Yr	VG	VG+	NM
❑ 41149	Forever Young/'Rangement Blues	1979	—	2.00	4.00
❑ 41215	I'll Be Here in the Morning/Spin Spin	1980	—	2.00	4.00
❑ 41282	Catfish Bates/Mose Rankin	1980	—	2.00	4.00

RCA

Number	Title (A Side/B Side)	Yr	VG	VG+	NM
❑ 2722-7-R	Abilene/Oh So Many Tears	1990	—	2.00	4.00

RCA VICTOR

Number	Title (A Side/B Side)	Yr	VG	VG+	NM
❑ APBO-0084	Second Cup of Coffee/Farmer's Song	1973	—	2.00	4.00
❑ APBO-0203	Claim on Me/Early Mornin' Rain	1973	—	2.00	4.00
❑ APBO-0314	The Ways of a Country Girl/Pictou County Jail	1974	—	2.00	4.00
❑ 47-7881	Three Steps to the Picnic/The Ballad of Widder Jones	1961	3.75	7.50	15.00
❑ 47-7934	To You and Yours (From Me and Mine)/I Want a Girl	1961	3.75	7.50	15.00
❑ 47-8001	China Doll/Commerce Street and Sixth Avenue North	1962	3.75	7.50	15.00
❑ 47-8062	If You Don't Know, I Ain't Gonna Tell You/Where Nobody Knows Me	1962	3.75	7.50	15.00
❑ 47-8118	In This Very Same Room/If You Want Me To	1962	3.75	7.50	15.00
❑ 47-8181	Abilene/Oh So Many Years	1963	3.00	6.00	12.00
❑ 47-8250	There's More Pretty Girls Than One/If You Don't, Somebody Else Will	1963	3.00	6.00	12.00
❑ 47-8304	Linda with the Lonely Eyes/Fair and Tender Ladies	1963	3.00	6.00	12.00
❑ 47-8392	Fort Worth, Dallas or Houston/Life's Railway to Heaven	1964	3.00	6.00	12.00
❑ 47-8462	Truck Driving Man/The Little Grave	1964	3.00	6.00	12.00
❑ 47-8537	The Last Mister Jones/Anymore	1965	2.50	5.00	10.00
❑ 47-8608	Walking the Floor Over You/Driftwood on the River	1965	2.50	5.00	10.00
❑ 47-8690	Write Me a Picture/Twist of the Wrist	1965	2.50	5.00	10.00
❑ 47-8797	Steel Rail Blues/Tobacco	1966	2.50	5.00	10.00
❑ 47-8924	Early Morning Rain/Slightly Used	1966	2.50	5.00	10.00
❑ 47-9059	Urge for Going/Changes	1966	2.50	5.00	10.00
❑ 47-9239	Break My Mind/Something Special to Me	1967	2.00	4.00	8.00
❑ 47-9385	Little World Girl/Song for a Winter's Night	1967	2.00	4.00	8.00
❑ 47-9519	It's My Time/Canadian Railroad Trilogy	1968	2.00	4.00	8.00
❑ 47-9637	Take My Hand for Awhile/Wonderful World of My Dreams	1968	2.00	4.00	8.00
❑ 47-9775	Natividad (The Nativity)/The Little Grave	1969	2.00	4.00	8.00
❑ 47-9829	She's a Little Bit Country/My Nova Scotia Home	1970	—	3.00	6.00
❑ 47-9886	Back Where It's At/Then I Miss You	1970	—	3.00	6.00
❑ 47-9893	Let's Get Together/Everything Is Beautiful	1970	—	3.00	6.00

—With Skeeter Davis

Number	Title (A Side/B Side)	Yr	VG	VG+	NM
❑ 47-9937	Natividad (The Nativity)/The Little Grave	1970	—	3.00	6.00
❑ 47-9945	Anyway/The Best That I Can Do	1971	—	3.00	6.00
❑ 74-0100	Back to Denver/Suzanne	1969	2.00	4.00	8.00
❑ 74-0171	Canadian Pacific/Sisters of Mercy	1969	2.00	4.00	8.00
❑ 74-0256	Carolina in My Mind/I'm Gonna Be a Country Boy Again	1969	2.00	4.00	8.00
❑ 74-0469	Countryfied/My North Country Home	1971	—	3.00	6.00
❑ 74-0531	West Texas Highway/There's No Room in This Rat Race	1971	—	3.00	6.00
❑ 74-0622	10 Degrees and Getting Colder/Tumbleweed	1971	—	3.00	6.00
❑ 74-0697	Country Music in My Soul/Child's Song	1972	—	2.50	5.00
❑ 74-0776	Travelin' Light/Alberta Bound	1972	—	2.50	5.00
❑ 74-0854	Blue Train (Of the Heartbreak Line)/Maritime Farewell	1972	—	2.50	5.00
❑ 74-0948	Dirty Old Man/Abilene	1973	—	2.50	5.00

7-Inch Extended Plays

ABC-PARAMOUNT

Number	Title (A Side/B Side)	Yr	VG	VG+	NM
❑ A-220	Clementine/When I Grow Too Old to Dream//Tell Me Why/Let Me Call You Sweetheart	1958	5.00	10.00	20.00
❑ A-220 [PS]	On Campus	1958	5.00	10.00	20.00

HAMILTON, GEORGE, V

MTM

Number	Title (A Side/B Side)	Yr	VG	VG+	NM
❑ B-72101	She Says/Grass Grows Greener	1988	—	2.00	4.00

HAMILTON, JUDD

AMERICAN INT'L.

Number	Title (A Side/B Side)	Yr	VG	VG+	NM
❑ 151	Rules/Someday Morning	1970	2.00	4.00	8.00
❑ 163	Baltimore/Sunshine Man	1970	2.00	4.00	8.00

DOLTON

Number	Title (A Side/B Side)	Yr	VG	VG+	NM
❑ 80	Dream/Your Only Boy	1963	7.50	15.00	30.00

HAMILTON, ROY

AGP

Number	Title (A Side/B Side)	Yr	VG	VG+	NM
❑ 113	The Dark End of the Street/100 Years	1969	2.00	4.00	8.00
❑ 116	Angelica/Hang Ups	1969	2.00	4.00	8.00
❑ 125	It's Only Make Believe/100 Years	1969	2.00	4.00	8.00

CAPITOL

Number	Title (A Side/B Side)	Yr	VG	VG+	NM
❑ 2057	Let This World Be Free/Wait Until Dark	1967	2.00	4.00	8.00

EPIC

Number	Title (A Side/B Side)	Yr	VG	VG+	NM
❑ 9015	You'll Never Walk Alone/I'm Gonna Sit Right Down and Cry	1954	6.25	12.50	25.00
❑ 9047	So Let There Be Love/If You Loved Me	1954	6.25	12.50	25.00
❑ 9068	Ebb Tide/Beware	1954	6.25	12.50	25.00
❑ 9086	Hurt/Star of Love	1954	6.25	12.50	25.00
❑ 9092	I Believe/If You Are But a Dream	1955	5.00	10.00	20.00
❑ 9102	Unchained Melody/From Here to Eternity	1955	6.25	12.50	25.00
❑ 9111	Forgive This Fool/You Wanted to Change Me	1955	5.00	10.00	20.00
❑ 9118	A Little Voice/All This Is Mine	1955	5.00	10.00	20.00
❑ 9125	Without a Song/Cuban Love Song	1955	5.00	10.00	20.00
❑ 9132	Everybody's Got a Home/Take Me with You	1955	5.00	10.00	20.00
❑ 9147	There Goes My Heart/Walk Along with Kings	1956	5.00	10.00	20.00
❑ 9160	Somebody, Somewhere/Since I Fell for You	1956	5.00	10.00	20.00
❑ 9180	I Took My Grief to Him/Chained	1956	5.00	10.00	20.00
❑ 9203	The Simple Prayer/A Mother's Love	1957	5.00	10.00	20.00
❑ 9212	My Faith, My Hope, My Love/So Long	1957	5.00	10.00	20.00
❑ 9224	The Aisle/That Old Feeling	1957	5.00	10.00	20.00
❑ 9232	(All of a Sudden) My Heart Sings/I'm Gonna Lock You in My Heart	1957	5.00	10.00	20.00
❑ 9257	Don't Let Go/The Night to Love	1957	5.00	10.00	20.00
❑ 9268	Crazy Feelin'/In a Dream	1958	3.75	7.50	15.00
❑ 9274	Lips/Jungle Fever	1958	3.75	7.50	15.00
❑ 9282	Wait for Me/Everything	1958	3.75	7.50	15.00
❑ 9294	Pledging My Love/My One and Only Love	1958	3.75	7.50	15.00
❑ 9301	It's Never Too Late/Somewhere Along the Way	1959	3.75	7.50	15.00
❑ 9307	I Need Your Lovin'/Blue Prelude	1959	3.75	7.50	15.00
❑ 9323	Time Marches On/Take It Easy, Joe	1959	3.75	7.50	15.00
❑ 9342	Great Romance/On My Way Back Home	1959	3.75	7.50	15.00

Number	Title (A Side/B Side)	Yr	VG	VG+	NM
❑ 9354	The Ten Commandments/Nobody Knows the Trouble I've Seen	1959	5.00	10.00	20.00
❑ 9354	The Ten Commandments/Dowm by the Riverside	1959	3.75	7.50	15.00
❑ 9372	Down by the Riverside/Nobody Knows the Trouble I've Seen	1960	3.75	7.50	15.00
❑ 9373	I Let a Song Go Out of My Heart/I Get the Blues When It Rains	1960	3.75	7.50	15.00
❑ 9374	My Story/Please Send Me Someone to Love	1960	3.75	7.50	15.00
❑ 9375	Something's Gotta Give/Cheek to Cheek	1960	—	—	—
—Unreleased?					
❑ 9376	Sing You Sinners/Blow, Gabriel, Blow	1960	3.75	7.50	15.00
❑ 9386	Having Myself a Ball/Slowly	1960	3.75	7.50	15.00
—B-side by Bobby Sykes					
❑ 9388	Never Let Me Go/I Get the Blues When It Rains	1960	—	—	—
—Unreleased?					
❑ 9390	The Clock/I Get the Blues When It Rains	1960	3.75	7.50	15.00
❑ 9398	A Lover's Prayer/Never Let Me Go	1960	3.75	7.50	15.00
❑ 9407	Lonely Hands/Your Love	1960	3.75	7.50	15.00
❑ 9434	You Can Have Her/Abide With Me	1961	3.75	7.50	15.00
❑ 9434 [PS]	You Can Have Her/Abide With Me	1961	7.50	15.00	30.00
❑ 9443	You're Gonna Need Magic/To the One I Love	1961	3.75	7.50	15.00
❑ 9443 [PS]	You're Gonna Need Magic/To the One I Love	1961	7.50	15.00	30.00
❑ 9449	No Substitute for Love/Please Louise	1961	3.75	7.50	15.00
❑ 9449 [PS]	No Substitute for Love/Please Louise	1961	7.50	15.00	30.00
❑ 9460	Excerpts from "You Can Have Her"	1961	3.75	7.50	15.00
❑ 9461	Excerpts from "You Can Have Her"	1961	3.75	7.50	15.00
❑ 9462	Excerpts from "You Can Have Her"	1961	3.75	7.50	15.00
❑ 9463	Excerpts from "You Can Have Her"	1961	3.75	7.50	15.00
❑ 9464	Excerpts from "You Can Have Her"	1961	3.75	7.50	15.00
❑ 9466	There We Were/If	1961	3.00	6.00	12.00
❑ 9492	Don't Come Cryin' to Me/If Only I Had Known	1962	3.00	6.00	12.00
❑ 9520	Climb Ev'ry Mountain/I'll Come Running Back to You	1962	3.00	6.00	12.00
❑ 9538	I Am/Earthquake	1962	3.00	6.00	12.00
❑ 10559	You'll Never Walk Alone/The Golden Boy	1969	2.00	4.00	8.00

MGM

Number	Title (A Side/B Side)	Yr	VG	VG+	NM
❑ 13138	Let Go/You Still Love Him	1963	2.50	5.00	10.00
❑ 13157	Midnight Town-Daybreak City/Intermezzo	1963	2.50	5.00	10.00
❑ 13175	Theme from "The V.I.P.'s" (The Willow)/The Sinner	1963	2.50	5.00	10.00
❑ 13217	The Panic Is On/There She Is	1964	6.25	12.50	25.00
❑ 13247	Answer Me, My Love/Unchained Melody	1964	2.50	5.00	10.00
❑ 13291	You Can Count on Me/She Makes Me Wanna Dance	1964	6.25	12.50	25.00
❑ 13315	Sweet Violets/A Thousand Years Ago	1965	2.50	5.00	10.00

RCA VICTOR

Number	Title (A Side/B Side)	Yr	VG	VG+	NM
❑ 47-8641	Heartache/Ain't It the Truth	1965	2.50	5.00	10.00
❑ 47-8705	And I Love Her/Tore Up Over You	1965	2.50	5.00	10.00
❑ 47-8813	The Impossible Dream/She's Got a Heart	1966	2.50	5.00	10.00
❑ 47-8960	Walk Hand in Hand/Crackin' Up Over You	1966	6.25	12.50	25.00
❑ 47-9061	I Taught Her Everything She Knows/Lament	1967	2.50	5.00	10.00
❑ 47-9171	So High My Love/You Shook Me Up	1967	12.50	25.00	50.00
❑ 48-1034	Walk Hand in Hand/Crackin' Up Over You	1972	2.50	5.00	10.00

7-Inch Extended Plays

EPIC

Number	Title (A Side/B Side)	Yr	VG	VG+	NM
❑ EG-7065	(contents unknown)	195?	5.00	10.00	20.00
❑ EG-7065	(contents unknown)	195?	5.00	10.00	20.00
❑ EG-7065 [PS]	Here's Roy Hamilton	195?	5.00	10.00	20.00
❑ EG-7065 [PS]	You'll Never Walk Alone	195?	5.00	10.00	20.00
❑ EG-7079	Ebb Tide/Beware//If You Are But a Dream/From Here to Eternity	195?	5.00	10.00	20.00
❑ EG-7079 [PS]	Ebb Tide	195?	5.00	10.00	20.00
❑ EG-7080	(contents unknown)	195?	5.00	10.00	20.00
❑ EG-7080 [PS]	Faith, Hope and Hamilton	195?	5.00	10.00	20.00
❑ EG-7133	(contents unknown)	195?	5.00	10.00	20.00
❑ EG-7133 [PS]	Roy Hamilton	195?	5.00	10.00	20.00
❑ EG-7158	(contents unknown)	195?	3.75	7.50	15.00
❑ EG-7158 [PS]	Roy Hamilton	195?	3.75	7.50	15.00
❑ EG-7159	(contents unknown)	195?	3.75	7.50	15.00
❑ EG-7159 [PS]	Roy Hamilton	195?	3.75	7.50	15.00
❑ EG-7200	(contents unknown)	1958	3.75	7.50	15.00
❑ EG-7200 [PS]	Don't Let Go	1958	3.75	7.50	15.00
❑ EG-7205	(contents unknown)	1958	3.75	7.50	15.00
❑ EG-7205 [PS]	Lips	1958	3.75	7.50	15.00
❑ EG-7210	(contents unknown)	195?	3.75	7.50	15.00
❑ EG-7210 [PS]	With All My Love	195?	3.75	7.50	15.00
❑ EG-7214	(contents unknown)	195?	3.75	7.50	15.00
❑ EG-7214 [PS]	You Belong to My Heart	195?	3.75	7.50	15.00

HAMILTON, RUSS

KAPP

Number	Title (A Side/B Side)	Yr	VG	VG+	NM
❑ 184	Rainbow/We Will Make Love	1957	3.75	7.50	15.00
❑ 194	Wedding Ring/I Still Belong to You	1957	3.00	6.00	12.00
❑ 204	My Mother's Eyes/I Had a Dream	1957	3.00	6.00	12.00
❑ 219	Drifting and Dreaming/Tip Toe Through the Tulips	1958	3.00	6.00	12.00
❑ 250	All Alone/The Things I Didn't Say	1958	3.00	6.00	12.00
❑ 281	I Found Out/My Unbreakable Heart	1959	3.00	6.00	12.00
❑ 612	Valley of Love/The Loneliest Boy in Town	1964	2.50	5.00	10.00

MGM

Number	Title (A Side/B Side)	Yr	VG	VG+	NM
❑ 12947	Gonna Find Me a Bluebird/Choir Girl	1960	3.00	6.00	12.00

HAMILTON, JOE FRANK & DENNISON

See HAMILTON, JOE FRANK & REYNOLDS.

HAMILTON, JOE FRANK & REYNOLDS

Includes records as "Hamilton, Joe Frank & Dennison." Also see THE T-BONES.

ABC DUNHILL

Number	Title (A Side/B Side)	Yr	VG	VG+	NM
❑ 4276	Don't Pull Your Love/Funk-In-Wagnall	1971	—	3.00	6.00
❑ 4287	Annabelle/Goin' Down	1971	—	2.50	5.00
❑ 4296	Daisy Mae/It Takes the Best	1971	—	2.50	5.00
❑ 4305	Don't Refuse My Love/One Good Woman	1972	—	2.50	5.00

PLAYBOY

Number	Title (A Side/B Side)	Yr	VG	VG+	NM
❑ 5801	Now That I've Got You/Get On the Bus	1977	—	2.00	4.00
—As "Hamilton, Joe Frank & Dennison"					
❑ 6024	Fallin' in Love/So Good at Lovin' You	1975	—	2.50	5.00
❑ 6054	Winners and Losers/Barroom Blues	1975	—	2.00	4.00
❑ 6068	Everyday Without You/Badman	1976	—	2.00	4.00
❑ 6077	Light Up the World with Sunshine/Houdini	1976	—	2.00	4.00
—As "Hamilton, Joe Frank & Dennison"					
❑ 6077 [PS]	Light Up the World with Sunshine/Houdini	1976	—	2.50	5.00
—As "Hamilton, Joe Frank & Dennison"					
❑ 6088	Don't Fight the Hands (That Need You)/Get On the Bus	1976	—	2.00	4.00
—As "Hamilton, Joe Frank & Dennison"					
❑ 6088 [PS]	Don't Fight the Hands (That Need You)/Get On the Bus	1976	—	2.50	5.00
—As "Hamilton, Joe Frank & Dennison"					

HAMILTON STREETCAR

DOT

Number	Title (A Side/B Side)	Yr	VG	VG+	NM
❑ 17253	Silver Wings/I See I Am	1969	3.00	6.00	12.00
❑ 17279	Brother Speed/Wasn't It You	1969	3.00	6.00	12.00
❑ 17306	Honey and Wine/Now I Taste the Tears	1969	3.00	6.00	12.00

LHI

Number	Title (A Side/B Side)	Yr	VG	VG+	NM
❑ 1206	Confusion/Your Own Come Down	1968	3.75	7.50	15.00
❑ 17016	Invisible People/Flash	1967	3.75	7.50	15.00

HAMMER, MC

BUSTIN'

Number	Title (A Side/B Side)	Yr	VG	VG+	NM
❑ 1987-7	Let's Get It Started/(Instrumental)	1987	5.00	10.00	20.00

CAPITOL

Number	Title (A Side/B Side)	Yr	VG	VG+	NM
❑ B-44229	Let's Get It Started/(Instrumental)	1988	—	—	3.00
❑ B-44266	Pump It Up/(Instrumental)	1988	—	—	3.00
❑ B-44290	Turn This Mutha Out/Ring 'Em	1989	—	—	3.00
❑ B-44353	(Hammer Hammer) They Put Me in the Mix/Cold Go M.C. Hammer	1989	—	—	—
—Unreleased?					
❑ B-44497	Help the Children/(Instrumental)	1989	—	—	3.00
❑ NR-44794	Addams Groove/(Instrumental)	1991	—	2.00	4.00
❑ S7-57700	2 Legit to Quit (Long)/2 Legit to Quit (Short)	1992	—	2.00	4.00
❑ S7-57730	Do Not Pass Me By/Gaining Momentum	1992	—	2.00	4.00
❑ S7-57740	Good to Go/Count It Off	1992	—	2.00	4.00
❑ 7PRO-79072	[DJ]U Can't Touch This (same on both sides)	1990	3.75	7.50	15.00
❑ 7PRO-79150	[DJ]Have You Seen Her (same on both sides)	1990	2.50	5.00	10.00
❑ 7PRO-79284/95	[DJ]Pray (Radio Edit)/Pray (LP Version)	1990	2.50	5.00	10.00
❑ 7PRO-79667	[DJ](Hammer Hammer) They Put Me in the Mix (same on both sides)	1989	—	3.00	6.00
❑ 7PRO-79893	[DJ]Dancin' Machine (same on both sides)	1990	—	3.00	6.00

GIANT

Number	Title (A Side/B Side)	Yr	VG	VG+	NM
❑ 18218	Pumps & a Bump (Radio Edit)/Pumps & a Bump (Album Version)	1994	—	—	3.00
❑ 18271	It's All Good/(Instrumental)	1994	—	—	3.00

HAMMOND, ALBERT

Also see HAMMOND-HAZLEWOOD.

COLUMBIA

Number	Title (A Side/B Side)	Yr	VG	VG+	NM
❑ 02470	Memories/I Want You Back with Me	1981	—	2.00	4.00
❑ 03412	Before You Change the World/Somewhere in America	1982	—	2.00	4.00
❑ 60510	When I'm Gone/World of Love	1981	—	2.00	4.00

EPIC

Number	Title (A Side/B Side)	Yr	VG	VG+	NM
❑ 50277	Moonlight Lady/Cry Baby	1976	—	2.00	4.00

MUMS

Number	Title (A Side/B Side)	Yr	VG	VG+	NM
❑ 6009	Down by the River/The Last One to Know	1972	—	2.00	4.00
❑ 6011	It Never Rains in Southern California/Anyone Here in the Audience	1972	—	2.50	5.00
—Bizarrely, the stock copy is in rechanneled stereo					
❑ 6015	If You Gotta Break Another Heart/That Old American Dream	1973	—	2.00	4.00
❑ 6018	The Free Electric Band/You Taught Me to Sing the Blues	1973	—	2.00	4.00
❑ 6021	The Peacemaker/Who's for Lunch Today	1973	—	2.00	4.00
❑ 6024	Half a Million Miles from Home/I Think I'll Go That Way	1973	—	2.00	4.00
❑ 6026	I'm a Train/Brand New Day	1974	—	2.00	4.00
❑ 6030	Air Disaster/Candlelight, Sweet Candlelight	1974	—	2.00	4.00
❑ 6032	Fountain Avenue/Names, Tags, Numbers, Labels	1974	—	2.00	4.00
❑ 6037	99 Miles from L.A./Rivers Are for Boats	1975	—	2.00	4.00

HAMMOND, JOHN

ATLANTIC

Number	Title (A Side/B Side)	Yr	VG	VG+	NM
❑ 2696	I'm Tore Down/Shake for Me	1969	2.00	4.00	8.00

COLUMBIA

Number	Title (A Side/B Side)	Yr	VG	VG+	NM
❑ 45372	As the Years Go Passing By/Mellow Down Easy	1971	—	3.00	6.00

RED BIRD

Number	Title (A Side/B Side)	Yr	VG	VG+	NM
❑ 10-047	I Wish You Would/I Can Tell	1966	5.00	10.00	20.00

HAMMOND-HAZLEWOOD

Also see ALBERT HAMMOND.

CAPITOL

Number	Title (A Side/B Side)	Yr	VG	VG+	NM
❑ 2616	Wendy, Wendy/Broken Hearts Brigade	1969	2.50	5.00	10.00

HAMPTON, JOHN

UNITED

Number	Title (A Side/B Side)	Yr	VG	VG+	NM
❑ 210	Honey Hush/Shadow Blues	1958	30.00	60.00	120.00

HANDS OF TIME, THE

SIDEWALK

Number	Title (A Side/B Side)	Yr	VG	VG+	NM
❑ 903	Got to Get You Into My Life/Midnight Rider	1966	7.50	15.00	30.00

HANEY, JACK, AND NIKITER ARMSTRONG

MEL-O-DY

Number	Title (A Side/B Side)	Yr	VG	VG+	NM
❑ 107	The Interview/Peaceful	1963	5.00	10.00	20.00

HANGMEN, THE
MONUMENT

Number	Title (A Side/B Side)	Yr	VG	VG+	NM
❑ 910	What a Girl Can't Do/The Girl Who Faded Away	1965	5.00	10.00	20.00
❑ 951	Faces/Bad Goodbye	1966	5.00	10.00	20.00

HANK AND CAROLEE
MALA

Number	Title (A Side/B Side)	Yr	VG	VG+	NM
❑ 424	Go On and Go/I've Never Known	1960	10.00	20.00	40.00

HANNAN, JIMMY
ATLANTIC

Number	Title (A Side/B Side)	Yr	VG	VG+	NM
❑ 2247	Beach Ball/You Gotta Have Love	1964	37.50	75.00	150.00

—Backing Hannan on this record are THE BEE GEES, three years before their first American release!

HANS CHRISTIAN
With Jon Anderson, pre-YES.

TOWER

Number	Title (A Side/B Side)	Yr	VG	VG+	NM
❑ 409	Never My Love/All of the Time	1968	25.00	50.00	100.00

HANSON
ISLAND

Number	Title (A Side/B Side)	Yr	VG	VG+	NM
❑ 562800-7	This Time Around/If Only	2000	—	2.00	4.00

MERCURY

Number	Title (A Side/B Side)	Yr	VG	VG+	NM
❑ 568066-7	I Will Come to You/With You in My Dreams	1997	—	—	2.00
❑ 568066-7 [PS]	I Will Come to You/With You in My Dreams	1997	—	—	2.00
❑ 574260-7	Mmmbop/Where's the Love	1997	—	—	3.00

HAPPENINGS, THE
Also see BOB MIRANDA.

BIG TREE

Number	Title (A Side/B Side)	Yr	VG	VG+	NM
❑ 146	Strawberry Morning/Workin' My Way Back to You	1972	—	2.00	4.00
❑ 153	Me Without You/God Bless Joanna	1972	—	2.00	4.00

B.T. PUPPY

Number	Title (A Side/B Side)	Yr	VG	VG+	NM
❑ 181 [DJ]	Have Yourself a Merry Little Christmas (same on both sides)	1966	7.50	15.00	30.00
—Stock copies do not exist					
❑ 517	Girls on the Go/Go-Go	1966	2.50	5.00	10.00
❑ 520	See You in September/He Thinks He's a Hero	1966	2.50	5.00	10.00
❑ 522	Go Away Little Girl/Tea Time	1966	2.00	4.00	8.00
❑ 523	Goodnight My Love/Lillies By Money	1966	2.00	4.00	8.00
❑ 527	I Got Rhythm/You're in a Bad Way	1967	2.00	4.00	8.00
❑ 530	My Mammy/I Believe in Nothing	1967	2.00	4.00	8.00
❑ 530 [PS]	My Mammy/I Believe in Nothing	1967	3.75	7.50	15.00
❑ 532	Why Do Fools Fall in Love/When the Summer Is Through	1967	2.00	4.00	8.00
❑ 532 [PS]	Why Do Fools Fall in Love/When the Summer Is Through	1967	3.75	7.50	15.00
❑ 538	Music, Music, Music/When I Lock My Door	1968	2.00	4.00	8.00
❑ 538 [PS]	Music, Music, Music/When I Lock My Door	1968	3.75	7.50	15.00
❑ 540	Randy/Love Song of Mommy and Daddy	1968	2.00	4.00	8.00
❑ 542	Sealed with a Kiss/Anyway	1968	2.00	4.00	8.00
❑ 543	Breaking Up Is Hard to Do/Anyway	1968	2.00	4.00	8.00
❑ 545	Crazy Rhythm/Love Song of Mommy and Daddy	1968	2.00	4.00	8.00
❑ 549	That's All I Want from You/He Thinks He's a Hero	1968	2.00	4.00	8.00

JUBILEE

Number	Title (A Side/B Side)	Yr	VG	VG+	NM
❑ 5666	Where Do I Go and Be In/New Day Comin'	1969	—	3.00	6.00
❑ 5677	El Paso County Jail/Won't Anybody Listen	1969	—	3.00	6.00
❑ 5686	Answer Me, My Love/I Need a Woman	1970	—	3.00	6.00
❑ 5698	Tomorrow, Today Will Be Yesterday/Chain of Hands	1970	—	3.00	6.00
❑ 5702	Crazy Love/Chain of Hands	1970	—	3.00	6.00
❑ 5703	Condition Red/Sweet September	1970	2.50	5.00	10.00
—As "The Honor Society"					
❑ 5712	Lullaby in the Rain/I Wish You Could Know Me (Naomi)	1971	—	3.00	6.00
❑ 5721 [DJ]	Make Your Own Kind of Music (mono/stereo)	1971	—	3.00	6.00
—Stock copies may not exist					

MIDLAND INT'L.

Number	Title (A Side/B Side)	Yr	VG	VG+	NM
❑ MB-10897	That's Why I Love You/Beyond the Hurt	1977	—	2.00	4.00
❑ MB-11127	Let Me Stay/Someone Special	1977	—	2.00	4.00

PHILCO-FORD

Number	Title (A Side/B Side)	Yr	VG	VG+	NM
❑ HP-7	Go Away Little Girl/See You in September	1967	5.00	10.00	20.00

—4-inch plastic "Hip Pocket Record" with color sleeve

HAPPY HARTS, THE
KAPP

Number	Title (A Side/B Side)	Yr	VG	VG+	NM
❑ 314	Let's All Sing a Song for Christmas/I Want the South to Win the War for Christmas	1959	5.00	10.00	20.00

—B-side by Spike Jones and the City Slickers

HARBOR LIGHTS, THE
Early JAY AND THE AMERICANS.

JARO

Number	Title (A Side/B Side)	Yr	VG	VG+	NM
❑ 77020	Is That Too Much to Ask/What Would I Do Without You	1960	10.00	20.00	40.00

MALA

Number	Title (A Side/B Side)	Yr	VG	VG+	NM
❑ 422	Angel of Love/Tick-a-Tick-a-Tock	1960	12.50	25.00	50.00

HARBOUR LITES, THE
FONTANA

Number	Title (A Side/B Side)	Yr	VG	VG+	NM
❑ 1544	Run for Your Life/Lonely Journey	1966	2.50	5.00	10.00

HARD, RANDY
NRC

Number	Title (A Side/B Side)	Yr	VG	VG+	NM
❑ 013	Honey Doll/May It Be My Fortune	1959	15.00	30.00	60.00
❑ 044	Let Her Go/Make Me a Dreamer	1959	12.50	25.00	50.00

HARDLY WORTHIT PLAYERS, THE
See SENATOR BOBBY.

HARDWATER
CAPITOL

Number	Title (A Side/B Side)	Yr	VG	VG+	NM
❑ 2230	Not So Hard/City Sidewalks	1968	3.00	6.00	12.00

HARDY BOYS, THE
RCA VICTOR

Number	Title (A Side/B Side)	Yr	VG	VG+	NM
❑ 47-9795	Wheels/Sha-La-La	1969	2.00	4.00	8.00
❑ 47-9831	Good, Good Lovin'/Love Train	1970	2.00	4.00	8.00
❑ 74-0228	Love and Let Love/Sink or Swim	1969	2.00	4.00	8.00

HARGRAVE, RON
CUB

Number	Title (A Side/B Side)	Yr	VG	VG+	NM
❑ 9025	Drive-In Movie/Buttercup	1959	3.00	6.00	12.00

MGM

Number	Title (A Side/B Side)	Yr	VG	VG+	NM
❑ 12344	A Fool Am I/Too Late	1956	5.00	10.00	20.00
❑ 12422	Latch On/Only a Daydream	1957	10.00	20.00	40.00
❑ 12475	Hold Me/Song of the Moonlight	1957	5.00	10.00	20.00
❑ 12571	If You Should Go/Heartbreaker	1957	5.00	10.00	20.00
❑ 12644	Young Romance/Should Have Been Home in Bed	1958	5.00	10.00	20.00

HARLAN, BILLY
BRUNSWICK

Number	Title (A Side/B Side)	Yr	VG	VG+	NM
❑ 55066	I Wanna Bop/School House Rock	1958	50.00	100.00	200.00

HARMONAIRES, THE
ATHENA

Number	Title (A Side/B Side)	Yr	VG	VG+	NM
❑ 6512/13	If I Had One Wish For Christmas/Impact	19??	2.00	4.00	8.00

HOLIDAY

Number	Title (A Side/B Side)	Yr	VG	VG+	NM
❑ 2602	Come Back/Lorraine	1957	75.00	150.00	300.00
—Black label					
❑ 2602	Come Back/Lorraine	1960	15.00	30.00	60.00
—Red label, double horizontal lines					
❑ 2602	Come Back/Lorraine	196?	6.25	12.50	25.00
—Red label, single horizontal line					

HARMONICA FRANK
SUN

Number	Title (A Side/B Side)	Yr	VG	VG+	NM
❑ 205	Rockin' Chair Daddy/The Great Musical Menagerist	1954	1500.	3000.	4500.

HARMONY GRITS, THE
Members of the original DRIFTERS formed this group after their firing.

END

Number	Title (A Side/B Side)	Yr	VG	VG+	NM
❑ 1051	Am I to Be the One/I Could Have Told You	1959	6.25	12.50	25.00
❑ 1063	Gee/I Could Have Told You	1959	6.25	12.50	25.00
❑ 1063	Gee/Santa Claus Is Coming to Town	1959	10.00	20.00	40.00

HAROLD AND THE CASUALS
SCOTTY

Number	Title (A Side/B Side)	Yr	VG	VG+	NM
❑ 628	Darling Do You Love Me/You Can Shake a Tail Feather	1959	75.00	150.00	300.00

HARPER, CHUCK
As "Chuck Fassert," he recorded with THE REGENTS.

FELSTED

Number	Title (A Side/B Side)	Yr	VG	VG+	NM
❑ 8658	Summer Is Thru/Call on Me	1962	7.50	15.00	30.00

HARPER, ROY
EPIC

Number	Title (A Side/B Side)	Yr	VG	VG+	NM
❑ 10268	Midspring Dithering/Zengfm	1967	3.75	7.50	15.00

HARPERS BIZARRE
WARNER BROS.

Number	Title (A Side/B Side)	Yr	VG	VG+	NM
❑ 5890	The 59th Street Bridge Song (Feelin' Groovy)/Lost My Love Today	1967	2.50	5.00	10.00
❑ 7028	Come to the Sunshine/Debutante's Ball	1967	2.00	4.00	8.00
❑ 7063	Anything Goes/Malibu U.	1967	2.00	4.00	8.00
❑ 7090	Chattanooga Choo Choo/Hey, You in the Crowd	1967	2.00	4.00	8.00
❑ 7106	The 59th Street Bridge Song (Feelin' Groovy)/Come to the Sunshine	1968	—	3.00	6.00
—"Back to Back Hits" series -- originals have green labels with "W7" logo					
❑ 7123	Anything Goes/Chattanooga Choo Choo	1969	—	3.00	6.00
—"Back to Back Hits" series -- originals have green labels with "W7" logo					
❑ 7172	Virginia City/Cotton Candy Sandman	1968	—	3.00	6.00
❑ 7200	Both Sides Now/Small Talk	1968	—	3.00	6.00
❑ 7223	Battle of New Orleans/Green Apple Tree	1968	—	3.00	6.00
❑ 7238	I Love You, Alice B. Toklas/Look to the Rainbow	1968	—	3.00	6.00
❑ 7296	Knock on Wood/Witchi-Tai-Yo	1969	—	2.50	5.00
❑ 7377	Poly High/Soft Soundin' Music	1970	—	2.50	5.00
❑ 7388	Anything Goes/Virginia City	1970	—	2.50	5.00
❑ 7399	If We Ever Needed the Lord Before/Mad	1970	—	2.50	5.00
❑ 7647	Knock on Wood/Poly High	1972	—	2.00	4.00

HARPO, SLIM
EXCELLO

Number	Title (A Side/B Side)	Yr	VG	VG+	NM
❑ 2113	I'm a King Bee/I Got Love If You Want It	1957	15.00	30.00	60.00
❑ 2138	Wonderin' and Worryin'/Strange Love	1958	7.50	15.00	30.00
❑ 2162	One More Day/You'll Be Sorry One Day	1959	7.50	15.00	30.00
❑ 2171	Buzz Me Babe/Late Last Night	1960	7.50	15.00	30.00
❑ 2184	Blues Hangover/What a Dream	1960	7.50	15.00	30.00
❑ 2194	Rainin' in My Heart/Don't Start Cryin' Now	1961	5.00	10.00	20.00
❑ 2239	Buzzin'/I Love the Life I'm Livin'	1963	3.75	7.50	15.00
❑ 2246	Little Queen Bee (Got a Brand New King)/I Need Money (Keep Your Alibis)	1964	3.00	6.00	12.00
❑ 2253	Still Rainin' in My Heart/We're Two of a Kind	1964	3.00	6.00	12.00
❑ 2261	Sittin' Here Wondering/What's Goin' On Baby	1964	3.00	6.00	12.00
❑ 2265	Please Don't Turn Me Down/Harpo's Blues	1965	3.00	6.00	12.00
❑ 2273	Baby Scratch My Back/I'm Gonna Miss You (LIke the Devil)	1965	3.00	6.00	12.00
❑ 2276	Goin' Away Blues/Just a Lonely Stranger	1966	2.50	5.00	10.00
❑ 2278	Midnight Blues/Shake Your Hips	1966	2.50	5.00	10.00

Number	Title (A Side/B Side)	Yr	VG	VG+	NM
❑ 2282	I'm Your Bread-Maker, Baby/Loving You (The Way I Do)	1966	2.50	5.00	10.00
❑ 2285	Tip On In (Part 1)/Tip On In (Part 2)	1967	2.50	5.00	10.00
❑ 2289	I'm Gonna Keep What I've Got/I've Got to Be with You Tonight	1967	2.50	5.00	10.00
❑ 2294	Te-Ni-Lee-Ni-Nu/Mailbox Bues	1968	2.50	5.00	10.00
❑ 2301	Mohair Sam/I Just Can't Leave You	1969	2.00	4.00	8.00
❑ 2305	Just for You/That's Why I Love You	1969	2.00	4.00	8.00
❑ 2306	Folsom Prison Blues/Mututal Friend	1969	2.00	4.00	8.00
❑ 2309	I've Got My Finger on Your Trigger/The Price Is Too High	1969	2.00	4.00	8.00
❑ 2316	Rainin' in My Heart/Jody Man	1970	2.00	4.00	8.00

HARPS, THE

See THE CAMELOTS.

HARPTONES, THE

Number	Title (A Side/B Side)	Yr	VG	VG+	NM
AMBIENT SOUND					
❑ 02807	Love Needs a Heart/It's You	1982	—	3.00	6.00
ANDREA					
❑ 100	What Is Your Decision/Gimme Some	1956	10.00	20.00	40.00
BRUCE					
❑ 101	A Sunday Kind of Love/I'll Never Tell	1953	1000.	2000.	3000.
—"Bruce" in script lettering					
❑ 101	A Sunday Kind of Love/I'll Never Tell	1953	20.00	40.00	80.00
—"Bruce" in block lettering					
❑ 102	My Memories of You/It Was Just for Laughs	1954	50.00	100.00	200.00
❑ 102	My Memories of You/The Laughs on You	1954	30.00	60.00	120.00
—Same B-side with different title (and missing the apostrophe)					
❑ 104	I Depended on You/Mambo Boogie	1954	20.00	40.00	80.00
❑ 109	Forever Mine/Why Should I Love You	1954	20.00	40.00	80.00
❑ 113	Since I Fell for You/Oobidee-Oobidee-Oo	1954	20.00	40.00	80.00
❑ 123	High Flying Baby/Loving a Girl Like You	1955	15.00	30.00	60.00
❑ 128	I Almost Lost My Mind/Oh Wee Baby	1955	15.00	30.00	60.00
COED					
❑ 540	Answer Me My Love/Rain Down Kisses	1960	5.00	10.00	20.00
COMPANION					
❑ 102	All in Your Mind/The Last Dance	1961	7.50	15.00	30.00
❑ 103	What Will I Tell My Heart/Foolish Me	1961	20.00	40.00	80.00
CUB					
❑ 9097	Devil in Velvet/Your Love Is a Good Love	1961	5.00	10.00	20.00
GEE					
❑ 1045	Cry Like I Cried/So Good, So Fine, You're Mine	1957	15.00	30.00	60.00
—Red label					
KT					
❑ 201	Sunset/I Gotta Have Your Love	1963	12.50	25.00	50.00
PARADISE					
❑ 101	Life Is But a Dream/You Know You're Doing Me Wrong	1954	37.50	75.00	150.00
—Maroon label					
❑ 101	Life Is But a Dream/You Know You're Doing Me Wrong	1954	15.00	30.00	60.00
—Purple label					
❑ 103	My Success/I've Got a Notion	1955	75.00	150.00	300.00
❑ 105	It All Depends on You/Guitar Shuffle	1955	37.50	75.00	150.00
—Maroon label					
❑ 105	It All Depends on You/Guitar Shuffle	1955	15.00	30.00	60.00
—Purple label					
RAMA					
❑ 203	Three Wishes/That's the Way It Goes	1956	20.00	40.00	80.00
❑ 214	The Masquerade Is Over/On Sunday Afternoon	1956	20.00	40.00	80.00
❑ 221	The Shrine of St. Cecelia/Oo Wee Baby	1957	20.00	40.00	80.00
RAVEN					
❑ 8001	A Sunday Kind of Love/Mambo Boogie	1962	3.75	7.50	15.00
TIP TOP					
❑ 401	My Memories of You/High Flyin' Baby	1956	10.00	20.00	40.00
WARWICK					
❑ 500	I Remember/Laughing on the Outside	1959	6.25	12.50	25.00
❑ 512	Love Me Completely/Hep Teenager	1959	6.25	12.50	25.00
❑ 551	No Greater Miracle/What Kind of a Fool	1960	6.25	12.50	25.00
7-Inch Extended Plays					
BRUCE					
❑ BEP 201	A Sunday Kind of Love/Ou Wee Baby//Forever Mine/I Almost Lost My Mind	1954	2500.	3750.	5000.
❑ BEP 201 [PS]	The Sensational Harptones	1954	2500.	3750.	5000.

HARRIS, ANITA

Number	Title (A Side/B Side)	Yr	VG	VG+	NM
BRUT					
❑ 1345	I Just Need a Lover/Music	197?	—	3.00	6.00
COLUMBIA					
❑ 44236	Just Loving You/Butterfly with Coloured Wings	1967	2.00	4.00	8.00
❑ 44438	Anniversary Waltz/Comes the Night	1968	2.00	4.00	8.00
LONDON					
❑ 9720	Lies/Don't Think About Love	1964	3.00	6.00	12.00
WARNER BROS.					
❑ 5638	Trains and Boats and Planes/Upside Down	1965	2.50	5.00	10.00

HARRIS, EMMYLOU

Number	Title (A Side/B Side)	Yr	VG	VG+	NM
ASYLUM					
❑ 64570	Thanks to You/Lovin' You Again	1993	—	—	3.00
❑ 64610	High Powered Love/Ballad of a Runaway Horse	1992	—	—	3.00
A&M					
❑ 2290	Wish We Were Back in Missouri/Riding with Jesse James	1980	—	2.00	4.00
—B-side by Charlie Daniels					
HUGHES					
❑ 53236	I Still Dream of You/Back in Baby's Arms	1988	—	—	3.00
JUBILEE					
❑ 5679	I'll Be Your Baby Tonight/I'll Never Fall in Love Again	1969	5.00	10.00	20.00
❑ 5697	Paddy/Fugue for the Ox	1970	5.00	10.00	20.00
REPRISE					
❑ 1326	Too Far Gone/Boulder to Birmingham	1975	—	2.50	5.00
❑ 1332	If I Could Only Win Your Love/Boulder to Birmingham	1975	—	2.50	5.00
❑ 1341	Light of the Stable/Bluebird Wine	1975	2.50	5.00	10.00
—A-side is a longer version than later releases					
❑ 1341 [PS]	Light of the Stable/Bluebird Wine	1975	3.00	6.00	12.00
❑ 1346	Together Again/Here, There and Everywhere	1976	—	2.50	5.00
❑ 1353	Till I Gain Control Again/One of These Days	1976	—	2.50	5.00
❑ 1371	Sweet Dreams/Amarillo	1976	—	2.50	5.00
❑ 1379	Light of the Stable/Boulder to Birmingham	1976	—	2.50	5.00
❑ 19281	Rollin' and Ramblin'/Sweet Dreams Of You	1991	—	—	3.00
❑ 19510	Wheels of Love/Better Off Without You	1991	—	—	3.00
❑ 19707	Never Be Anyone Else But You/Red, Red Rose	1990	—	—	3.00
❑ 19870	Gulf Coast Highway/Evangeline	1990	—	—	3.00
—A-side: With Willie Nelson					
❑ 22850	I Still Miss Someone/No Regrets	1989	—	—	3.00
❑ 22999	Heaven Only Knows/A River for Him	1989	—	—	3.00
❑ 27635	Heartbreak Hill/Icy Blue Heart	1989	—	—	3.00
WARNER BROS.					
❑ PRO-S-2872 [DJ]	Light of the Stable/It Came Upon a Midnight Clear	1987	2.50	5.00	10.00
—B-side by Highway 101					
❑ 8329	C'est La Vie (You Never Can Tell)/You're Supposed to Be Feeling Good	1977	—	2.50	5.00
❑ 8388	Making Believe/I'll Be Your San Antone Rose	1977	—	2.50	5.00
❑ 8498	To Daddy/Tulsa Queen	1977	—	2.50	5.00
❑ 8553	Two More Bottles of Wine/I Ain't Living Long Like This	1978	—	2.50	5.00
❑ 8623	Easy from Now On/You're Supposed to Be Feeling Good	1978	—	2.50	5.00
❑ 8732	Too Far Gone/Tulsa Queen	1979	—	2.00	4.00
❑ 8815	Save the Last Dance for Me/Even Cowgirls Get the Blues	1979	—	2.50	5.00
❑ 28302	Someday My Ship Will Sail/When He Calls	1987	—	—	3.00
❑ 28714	Today I Started Loving You Again/When I Was Young	1986	—	—	3.00
❑ 28770	I Had My Heart Set on You/Your Long Journey	1986	—	—	3.00
❑ 28852	Timberline/Sweet Chariot	1985	—	2.00	4.00
❑ 28952	Rhythm Guitar/Diamond in My Crown	1985	—	—	3.00
❑ 29041	White Line/Long Tall Sally Rose	1985	—	2.00	4.00
❑ 29138	Someone Like You/Light of the Stable	1984	—	2.00	4.00
❑ 29218	Pledging My Love/Baby, Better Start Turnin' 'Em Down	1984	—	2.00	4.00
❑ 29329	In My Dreams/Like an Old Fashioned World	1984	—	2.00	4.00
❑ 29443	Drivin' Wheel/Good News	1983	—	2.00	4.00
❑ 29583	So Sad (To Watch Good Love Go Bad)/Amarillo	1983	—	2.00	4.00
❑ 29729	I'm Movin' On/Maybe Tonight	1983	—	2.00	4.00
❑ 29898	(Lost His Love) On Our Last Date/Another Pot O' Tea	1982	—	2.00	4.00
❑ 29993	Born to Run/Colors of My Heart	1982	—	2.00	4.00
❑ 49056	Blue Kentucky Girl/Leaving Louisiana in the Broad Daylight	1979	—	2.00	4.00
❑ 49164	Beneath Still Waters/'Til I Gain Control Again	1980	—	2.00	4.00
❑ 49239	Wayfaring Stranger/Green Pastures	1980	—	2.00	4.00
❑ 49262	That Lovin' You Feeling Again/Lola	1980	—	2.50	5.00
—A-side: With Roy Orbison; B-side by Craig Hundley					
❑ 49551	The Boxer/Precious Love	1980	—	2.00	4.00
❑ 49633	Beautiful Star of Bethlehem/The Little Drummer Boy	1980	—	2.00	4.00
❑ 49645	Light of the Stable/The Little Drummer Boy	1980	—	2.00	4.00
❑ 49684	Mister Sandman/Fools' Thin Air	1981	—	2.00	4.00
❑ 49739	I Don't Have to Crawl/Colors of Your Heart	1981	—	2.00	4.00
❑ 49809	If I Needed You/Ashes By Now	1981	—	2.00	4.00
—A-side with Don Williams					
❑ 49892	Tennessee Rose/Mama Help	1982	—	2.00	4.00

HARRIS, GENEE

Number	Title (A Side/B Side)	Yr	VG	VG+	NM
ABC-PARAMOUNT					
❑ 9900	Bye Bye Elvis/You're Like a Jumping Jack	1958	12.50	25.00	50.00

HARRIS, GEORGIA, AND THE LYRICS

Number	Title (A Side/B Side)	Yr	VG	VG+	NM
HY-TONE					
❑ 111	Let's Exchange Hearts for Christmas/It's Time to Rock	1958	125.00	250.00	500.00
❑ 117	Let's Exchange Hearts for Christmas/Kiss, Kiss, Kiss	1958	125.00	250.00	500.00

HARRIS, JET, AND TONY MEECHAN

Also see THE SHADOWS.

Number	Title (A Side/B Side)	Yr	VG	VG+	NM
LONDON					
❑ 9589	Diamonds/Footstep	1963	3.75	7.50	15.00
❑ 9608	Scarlet O'Hara/(Doin' the) Hully Gully	1963	3.75	7.50	15.00
❑ 9622	Applejack/Tall Texan	1963	3.75	7.50	15.00

HARRIS, KURT

Number	Title (A Side/B Side)	Yr	VG	VG+	NM
DIAMOND					
❑ 158	Go On/Emperor of My Baby's Heart	1964	20.00	40.00	80.00
JOSIE					
❑ 898	Let Her Dance/I Can't Love Nobody Else	1962	5.00	10.00	20.00
❑ 902	Uh-Uh/You Better Shut Your Mouth	1962	5.00	10.00	20.00

HARRIS, MAJOR

Also see THE DELFONICS.

Number	Title (A Side/B Side)	Yr	VG	VG+	NM
ATLANTIC					
❑ 3217	Each Morning I Wake Up/Just a Thing I Do	1974	—	2.50	5.00
❑ 3248	Love Won't Let Me Wait/After Loving You	1975	—	2.00	4.00
❑ 3299 [DJ]	Loving You Is Mellow (mono/stereo)	1975	—	2.50	5.00
—May be promo-only					
❑ 3303	I Got Over Love/Loving You Is Mellow	1975	—	2.00	4.00
❑ 3321	Jealousy/Tynisa (What's Your Hurry)	1976	—	2.00	4.00
❑ 3336	It's Got to Be Magic/Just a Thing That I Do	1976	—	2.00	4.00

Number	Title (A Side/B Side)	Yr	VG	VG+	NM
OKEH					
❑ 7314	Just Love Me/Loving You More	1968	7.50	15.00	30.00
❑ 7327	Like a Rolling Stone/Call Me Tomorrow	1969	15.00	30.00	60.00
WMOT					
❑ 02091	Here We Are/Living's Easy Now	1981	—	2.00	4.00
❑ 4002	Laid Back Love/This Is What You Mean to Me	1976	—	2.00	4.00

HARRIS, PEPPERMINT

Number	Title (A Side/B Side)	Yr	VG	VG+	NM
ALADDIN					
❑ 3097	I Got Loaded/It's You, Yes It's You	1951	25.00	50.00	100.00
—Black vinyl					
❑ 3097	I Got Loaded/It's You, Yes It's You	1951	62.50	125.00	250.00
—Green vinyl					
❑ 3107	Have Another Drink and Talk to Me/Middle of Winter	1951	20.00	40.00	80.00
❑ 3108	Let the Back Door Hit You/P.H. Blues	1951	20.00	40.00	80.00
❑ 3130	Right Back On It/Maggie's Boogie	1952	20.00	40.00	80.00
❑ 3141	I Cry for My Baby/There's a Dead Cat on the Line	1952	20.00	40.00	80.00
❑ 3154	I Sure Do Miss My Baby/Hey Little Schoolgirl	1952	20.00	40.00	80.00
❑ 3177	Wasted Love/Goodbye Blues	1953	20.00	40.00	80.00
❑ 3183	Don't Leave Me Alone/Wet Rat	1953	20.00	40.00	80.00
❑ 3206	I Never Get Enough of You/Three Sheets in the Wind	1953	20.00	40.00	80.00
CASH					
❑ 1003	Cadillac Funeral/Treat Me Like I Treat You	1954	37.50	75.00	150.00
COMBO					
❑ 114	Love at First Sight/I Don't Care	1956	15.00	30.00	60.00
DART					
❑ 103	You Get Me Wondering/Messing Around with the Blues	1959	6.25	12.50	25.00
DUKE					
❑ 319	Ain't No Business/Angel Child	1960	6.25	12.50	25.00
JEWEL					
❑ 742	Marking Time/Bad, Mad Woman	1965	2.50	5.00	10.00
❑ 747	Ma Ma/Anything You Can Do	1965	2.50	5.00	10.00
❑ 762	Raining in My Heart/My Time After Awhile	1966	2.50	5.00	10.00
❑ 772	Anytime Is the Right Time/Wait Until It Happens to You	1966	2.50	5.00	10.00
❑ 789	Bad Bad Whiskey/Lonesome As Can Be	1967	2.50	5.00	10.00
❑ 795	24 Hours/Little Girl	1968	2.50	5.00	10.00
MODERN					
❑ 936	Bye Bye, Fare Thee Well/Black Cat Bone	1951	25.00	50.00	100.00
SITTIN' IN WITH					
❑ 543	Raining in My Heart/My Blues Have Rolled Away	1950	37.50	75.00	150.00
—Other Peppermint Harris 45s on this label may exist.					
"X"					
❑ 0142	Need Your Lovin'/Just Me and You	1955	25.00	50.00	100.00

HARRIS, RAY

Number	Title (A Side/B Side)	Yr	VG	VG+	NM
SUN					
❑ 254	Come On Little Mama/Where'd You Stay Last Night	1956	37.50	75.00	150.00
❑ 272	Greenback Dollar Watch and Chain/Foolish Hearts	1957	25.00	50.00	100.00

HARRIS, ROLF

Number	Title (A Side/B Side)	Yr	VG	VG+	NM
20TH FOX					
❑ 207	Tie Me Kangaroo Down, Sport/Nick Teen & Al K. Hall	1960	5.00	10.00	20.00
—Different versions than the Epic recordings					
❑ 230	Lost Little Boy/The Big Black Hat	1960	3.75	7.50	15.00
❑ 295	Six White Boomers/Tame Eagle	1962	3.75	7.50	15.00
❑ 414	Lost Little Boy/The Big Black Hat	1963	3.00	6.00	12.00
EPIC					
❑ 9567	Sun Arise/Someone's Pinched My Winkles	1963	3.00	6.00	12.00
❑ 9596	Tie Me Kangaroo Down, Sport/The Big Black Hat	1963	3.75	7.50	15.00
❑ 9596 [PS]	Tie Me Kangaroo Down, Sport/The Big Black Hat	1963	5.00	10.00	20.00
❑ 9615	Nick Teen & Al K. Hall/I Know a Man	1963	3.00	6.00	12.00
❑ 9615 [PS]	Nick Teen & Al K. Hall/I Know a Man	1963	5.00	10.00	20.00
❑ 9641	Lost Little Boy/Six White Boomers	1963	2.50	5.00	10.00
❑ 9641 [PS]	Lost Little Boy/Six White Boomers	1963	5.00	10.00	20.00
❑ 9682	The Court of King Caractacus/Two Buffalos	1964	2.50	5.00	10.00
❑ 9721	Ringo for President/Click Go the Shears	1964	3.75	7.50	15.00
❑ 9756	The Thing/Wild Colonial Boy	1965	2.50	5.00	10.00
❑ 9780	Tie My Hunting Dog Down, Jed/Five Young Apprentices	1965	2.50	5.00	10.00
❑ 10037	Jake the Peg/Big Dog	1966	2.50	5.00	10.00
MGM					
❑ 14103	Two Little Boys/I Love My Love	1970	2.50	5.00	10.00

HARRIS, THURSTON

Number	Title (A Side/B Side)	Yr	VG	VG+	NM
ALADDIN					
❑ 3398	Little Bitty Pretty One/I Hope You Won't Hold It Against Me	1957	10.00	20.00	40.00
❑ 3399	Do What You Did/I'm Asking Forgiveness	1957	7.50	15.00	30.00
❑ 3415	Be Baby Leba/I'm Out to Getcha	1958	7.50	15.00	30.00
❑ 3428	Only One Love Is Blessed/Smokey Joe's	1958	7.50	15.00	30.00
❑ 3430	Over and Over/You're Gonna Miss Me	1958	5.00	10.00	20.00
❑ 3435	Over Someone Else's Shoulder/Tears from My Heart	1958	5.00	10.00	20.00
❑ 3440	Purple Stew/I Heard a Rhapsody	1958	5.00	10.00	20.00
❑ 3447	From the Bottom of My Heart/You Don't Know How Much I Love You	1959	5.00	10.00	20.00
❑ 3448	Don't You Know/From the Bottom of My Heart	1959	5.00	10.00	20.00
❑ 3450	Hey Little Girl/My Love Will Last	1959	5.00	10.00	20.00
❑ 3452	Runk Bunk/Bless Your Heart	1959	5.00	10.00	20.00
❑ 3456	Slip SLop/Paradise Hill	1959	5.00	10.00	20.00
❑ 3462	Moonlight Cocktail/Recess in Heaven	1960	5.00	10.00	20.00
❑ 3468	One Scotch, One Bourbon, One Beer/Send Me Some Loving	1960	5.00	10.00	20.00
CUB					
❑ 9108	I'd Like to Start Over Again/Mr. Satan	1962	3.00	6.00	12.00
DOT					
❑ 16415	Quiet As It's Kept/Goddess of Angels	1963	2.50	5.00	10.00
❑ 16427	Poop-A-Loop/She's the One	1963	2.50	5.00	10.00
IMPERIAL					
❑ 5928	Got You on My Mind/Tears from My Heart	1963	2.50	5.00	10.00
❑ 5971	You're Gonna Need Me/I'm Asking Forgiveness	1963	2.50	5.00	10.00
REPRISE					
❑ 0255	Dance On Little Girl/Dancing Silhouettes	1964	2.50	5.00	10.00
UNITED ARTISTS					
❑ 0152	Little Bitty Pretty One/Over and Over	1973	—	2.00	4.00
—"Silver Spotlight Series" reissue					

HARRIS, TONY

Number	Title (A Side/B Side)	Yr	VG	VG+	NM
DEE GEE					
❑ 3014	Super Man/How Much Do I Love You	1966	4.00	8.00	16.00
EBB					
❑ 104	Chicken Baby Chicken/I'll Forever Love You	1957	12.50	25.00	50.00
❑ 120	Try This Little Ol' Heart/When I Get You Back	1957	7.50	15.00	30.00
❑ 128	You Fascinate Me/Swing, Swing, Swing	1957	7.50	15.00	30.00
TRIUMPH					
❑ 60	Go, Go, Little Scrambler/Poor Boy	1964	7.50	15.00	30.00

HARRIS, WEE WILLIE

Number	Title (A Side/B Side)	Yr	VG	VG+	NM
CHARLIE PARKER					
❑ 217	I Go Ape/Trouble in Mind	1963	2.50	5.00	10.00

HARRIS, WYNONIE

Number	Title (A Side/B Side)	Yr	VG	VG+	NM
ATCO					
❑ 6081	Destination Love/Tell a Whale of a Tale	1956	7.50	15.00	30.00
KING					
❑ 4210	Good Rockin' Tonight/Good Morning Mister Blues	1952	37.50	75.00	150.00
—78 originally released in 1948; the only known Wynonie Harris 45 on King before 4461					
❑ 4461	Bloodshot Eyes/Confessin' the Blues	1951	30.00	60.00	120.00
❑ 4468	I'll Never Give Up/Man Have I Got Troubles	1951	30.00	60.00	120.00
❑ 4485	Lovin' Machine/Luscious Woman	1951	30.00	60.00	120.00
—Black vinyl					
❑ 4485	Lovin' Machine/Luscious Woman	1951	100.00	200.00	400.00
—Blue vinyl					
❑ 4507	My Playful Baby's Gone/Here Comes the Night	1952	25.00	50.00	100.00
❑ 4526	Keep On Churnin'/Married Women Stay Married	1952	25.00	50.00	100.00
❑ 4555	Do it Again Please/Night Train	1952	25.00	50.00	100.00
❑ 4565	Drinking Blues/Adam Come and Get Your Rib	1952	25.00	50.00	100.00
❑ 4592	Greyhound/Rot Gut	1953	25.00	50.00	100.00
❑ 4593	Bad News Baby (There'll Be Rockin' Tonight)/Bring It Back	1953	25.00	50.00	100.00
❑ 4620	Mama Your Daughter Done Lied on Me/Wasn't That Good	1953	25.00	50.00	100.00
❑ 4635	Song of the Bayou/The Deacon Doesn't Like It	1953	25.00	50.00	100.00
❑ 4662	Tremblin'/Rot Gut	1953	20.00	40.00	80.00
❑ 4668	Please Louise/Nearer My Love to Thee	1953	20.00	40.00	80.00
❑ 4685	Down Boy Down/Quiet Whiskey	1953	20.00	40.00	80.00
❑ 4716	Shake That Thing/Keep A-Talking	1954	20.00	40.00	80.00
❑ 4724	I Get a Thrill/Don't Take My Whiskey Away from Me	1954	20.00	40.00	80.00
❑ 4763	All She Wants to Do Is Mambo/Christina	1955	15.00	30.00	60.00
❑ 4774	Good Mambo Tonight/Git to Gittin' Baby	1955	15.00	30.00	60.00
❑ 4789	Fishtail Blues/Mr. Dollar	1955	15.00	30.00	60.00
❑ 4814	Drinkin' Sherry Wine/Get With the Guts	1955	12.50	25.00	50.00
❑ 4826	Wine, Wine, Sweet Wine/Man's Best Friend	1955	12.50	25.00	50.00
❑ 4839	Shot Gun Wedding/I Don't Know Where to Go	1955	12.50	25.00	50.00
❑ 4852	Good Morning Judge/Bloodshot Eyes	1955	12.50	25.00	50.00
❑ 5050	Big Ole Country Fool/That's Me Right Now	1957	7.50	15.00	30.00
❑ 5073	There's No Substitute for Love/A Tale of Woe	1957	7.50	15.00	30.00
❑ 5416	Good Rockin' Tonight/Bloodshot Eyes	1960	3.75	7.50	15.00
❑ 6011	Big Old Country Fool/Bloodshot Eyes	1965	2.50	5.00	10.00
❑ 6304	Good Rockin' Tonight/Good Morning Judge	1970	—	3.00	6.00
ROULETTE					
❑ 4291	Bloodshot Eyes/Sweet Lucy Brown	1960	3.00	6.00	12.00
7-Inch Extended Plays					
KING					
❑ 260	(contents unknown)	1954	125.00	250.00	500.00
❑ 260 [PS]	Wynonie Harris	1954	125.00	250.00	500.00

HARRISON, GEORGE

Also see THE BEATLES; TRAVELING WILBURYS.

Number	Title (A Side/B Side)	Yr	VG	VG+	NM
APPLE					
❑ 1828	What Is Life/Apple Scruffs	1971	3.75	7.50	15.00
—With star on A-side label					
❑ 1828	What Is Life/Apple Scruffs	1971	2.00	4.00	8.00
—Without star on A-side label					
❑ 1828 [PS]	What Is Life/Apple Scruffs	1971	10.00	20.00	40.00
❑ 1836	Bangla-Desh/Deep Blue	1971	6.25	12.50	25.00
—Without star on A-side label					
❑ 1836	Bangla-Desh/Deep Blue	1971	2.00	4.00	8.00
—With star on A-side label					
❑ 1836 [PS]	Bangla-Desh/Deep Blue	1971	5.00	10.00	20.00
❑ 1862	Give Me Love (Give Me Peace on Earth)/Miss O'Dell (2:30)	1973	2.00	4.00	8.00
—With incorrect time for B-side listed					
❑ 1862	Give Me Love (Give Me Peace on Earth)/Miss O'Dell (2:20)	1973	2.00	4.00	8.00
—B-side playing time corrected					
❑ P-1862 [DJ]	Give Me Love (Give Me Peace on Earth) (mono/stereo)	1973	12.50	25.00	50.00
❑ 1877	Dark Horse/I Don't Care Anymore	1974	2.00	4.00	8.00
—Light blue and white custom photo label					
❑ 1877	Dark Horse/I Don't Care Anymore	1974	2.50	5.00	10.00
—White label; NOT a promo					

Number	Title (A Side/B Side)	Yr	VG	VG+	NM
❑ 1877 [PS]	Dark Horse/I Don't Care Anymore	1974	20.00	40.00	80.00
❑ P-1877 [DJ]	Dark Horse (full length mono/stereo)	1974	10.00	20.00	40.00
❑ P-1877 [DJ]	Dark Horse (edited mono/stereo)	1974	15.00	30.00	60.00
❑ 1879	Ding Dong, Ding Dong/Hari's on Tour (Express)	1974	5.00	10.00	20.00
—Black and white custom photo label					
❑ 1879	Ding Dong, Ding Dong/Hari's on Tour (Express)	1974	62.50	125.00	250.00
—Blue and white custon photo label					
❑ 1879 [PS]	Ding Dong, Ding Dong/Hari's on Tour (Express)	1974	5.00	10.00	20.00
❑ P-1879 [DJ]	Ding Dong, Ding Dong (remixed mono/edited stereo)	1974	10.00	20.00	40.00
❑ 1884	You/World of Stone	1975	—	3.00	6.00
❑ 1884 [PS]	You/World of Stone	1975	3.75	7.50	15.00
❑ P-1884 [DJ]	You (mono/stereo)	1975	10.00	20.00	40.00
❑ 1885	This Guitar (Can't Keep from Crying)/Maya Love	1975	6.25	12.50	25.00
—The last Apple 45 until 1995					
❑ P-1885 [DJ]	This Guitar (Can't Keep from Crying) (mono/stereo)	1975	12.50	25.00	50.00
❑ 2995	My Sweet Lord/Isn't It a Pity	1970	10.00	20.00	40.00
—With black star on label					
❑ 2995	My Sweet Lord/Isn't It a Pity	1970	2.00	4.00	8.00
—With "Mfd. by Apple" on label					
❑ 2995	My Sweet Lord/Isn't It a Pity	1975	6.25	12.50	25.00
—With "All Rights Reserved" disclaimer					
❑ 2995 [PS]	My Sweet Lord/Isn't It a Pity	1970	10.00	20.00	40.00
CAPITOL					
❑ 1828	What Is Life/Apple Scruffs	1976	7.50	15.00	30.00
—Orange label					
❑ 1828	What Is Life/Apple Scruffs	1978	—	3.00	6.00
—Purple late-1970s label					
❑ 1836	Bangla-Desh/Deep Blue	1976	7.50	15.00	30.00
—Orange label					
❑ 1836	Bangla-Desh/Deep Blue	1978	—	3.00	6.00
—Purple late-1970s label					
❑ 1836	Bangla-Desh/Deep Blue	1983	3.75	7.50	15.00
—Black colorband label					
❑ 1862	Give Me Love (Give Me Peace on Earth)/Miss O'Dell	1978	2.00	4.00	8.00
—Purple late-1970s label					
❑ 1862	Give Me Love (Give Me Peace on Earth)/Miss O'Dell	1978	3.75	7.50	15.00
—Black colorband label					
❑ 1879	Ding Dong, Ding Dong/Hari's on Tour (Express)	1978	2.00	4.00	8.00
—Purple late-1970s label					
❑ 2995	My Sweet Lord/Isn't It a Pity	1976	5.00	10.00	20.00
—Orange label with "Capitol" at bottom					
❑ 2995	My Sweet Lord/Isn't It a Pity	1978	—	3.00	6.00
—Purple label; label has reeded edge					
❑ 2995	My Sweet Lord/Isn't It a Pity	1983	—	3.00	6.00
—Black label with colorband					
❑ 2995	My Sweet Lord/Isn't It a Pity	1988	—	2.50	5.00
—Purple label; label has smooth edge					
❑ 15930 [DJ]	My Sweet Lord/My Sweet Lord 2000	2001	2.50	5.00	10.00
—White label, small hole					
❑ 15930 [PS]	My Sweet Lord/My Sweet Lord 2000	2001	3.75	7.50	15.00
—Promo item for the re-release of the All Things Must Pass CD					
COLUMBIA					
❑ 04887	I Don't Want to Do It/Queen of the Hop	1985	6.25	12.50	25.00
—B-side by Dave Edmunds					
DARK HORSE					
❑ 8294	This Song/Learning How to Love You	1976	2.50	5.00	10.00
—Tan label					
❑ 8294	This Song/Learning How to Love You	1976	2.00	4.00	8.00
—White label, NOT a promo					
❑ 8294 [DJ]	This Song (mono/stereo)	1976	6.25	12.50	25.00
❑ 8294 [PS]	This Song/Learning How to Love You	1976	7.50	15.00	30.00
❑ 8294 [PS]	This Song (mono/stereo)	1976	10.00	20.00	40.00
—Promotional only sleeve, different from stock sleeve					
❑ 8294 [PS]	This Song (mono/stereo)	1976	10.00	20.00	40.00
—Flyer with "The Story Behind This Song"					
❑ 8313	Crackerbox Palace/Learning How to Love You	1977	—	2.50	5.00
❑ 8763	Blow Away/Soft-Hearted Hana	1979	—	2.50	5.00
—With "RE-1" on label					
❑ 8763	Blow Away/Soft-Hearted Hana	1979	5.00	10.00	20.00
—Without "RE-1" on label (no "Loka Productions S.A." on label)					
❑ 8763 [PS]	Blow Away/Soft-Hearted Hana	1979	—	2.50	5.00
❑ 8844	Love Comes to Everyone/Soft Touch	1979	2.50	5.00	10.00
❑ 8844 [PS]	Love Comes to Everyone/Soft Touch	1979	250.00	500.00	750.00
❑ 27913	This Is Love/Breath Away from Heaven	1988	—	2.50	5.00
❑ 27913 [PS]	This Is Love/Breath Away from Heaven	1988	—	2.50	5.00
❑ 28131	When We Was Fab/Zig Zag	1988	—	2.50	5.00
❑ 28131 [PS]	When We Was Fab/Zig Zag	1988	—	2.50	5.00
❑ 28178	Got My Mind Set on You/Lay His Head	1987	—	2.00	4.00
❑ 28178 [PS]	Got My Mind Set on You/Lay His Head	1987	—	2.00	4.00
❑ 29744	I Really Love You/Circles	1983	6.25	12.50	25.00
❑ 29864	Wake Up My Love/Greece	1982	2.50	5.00	10.00
❑ 49725	All Those Years Ago/Writing's on the Wall	1981	—	2.50	5.00
❑ 49725 [PS]	All Those Years Ago/Writing's on the Wall	1981	—	2.50	5.00
❑ 49785	Teardrops/Save the World	1981	2.50	5.00	10.00
WARNER BROS.					
❑ 22807	Cheer Down/That's What It Takes	1989	3.75	7.50	15.00
❑ 22807 [DJ]	Cheer Down (same on both sides)	1989	50.00	100.00	200.00
❑ 22807 [PS]	Cheer Down/That's What It Takes	1989	3.75	7.50	15.00

HARRISON, JERRY

Also see TALKING HEADS.

Number	Title (A Side/B Side)	Yr	VG	VG+	NM
SIRE					
❑ 27977	Rev It Up/Bobby (Aboriginal Mix)	1988	—	—	3.00
❑ 27977 [PS]	Rev It Up/Bobby (Aboriginal Mix)	1988	—	—	3.00

HARRISON, NOEL

Number	Title (A Side/B Side)	Yr	VG	VG+	NM
LONDON					
❑ 9755	One Too Many Mornings/Barbara Allen	1965	2.00	4.00	8.00
❑ 9795	A Young Girl/The Future Mrs. 'Awkins	1965	2.50	5.00	10.00
❑ 9815	It's All Over Now, Baby Blue/Much As I Love You	1966	2.00	4.00	8.00
❑ 20011	The Man Behind the Red Balloon/Marlene	1966	2.00	4.00	8.00
❑ 20017	Cheryl's Going Home/In a Dusty Old Room	1966	2.00	4.00	8.00
❑ 20017 [PS]	Cheryl's Going Home/In a Dusty Old Room	1966	3.00	6.00	12.00
❑ 20021	Out for the Day/Fly Sing Song	1967	2.00	4.00	8.00
REPRISE					
❑ 0599	Sign of the Queen/Mrs. Williams' Rose	1967	—	3.00	6.00
❑ 0615	Life Is a Dream/Suzanne	1967	—	3.00	6.00
❑ 0682	Santa Monica Pier/In Your Chidren	1968	—	3.00	6.00
❑ 0758	The Windmills of Your Mind/Leitch on the Beach	1968	2.00	4.00	8.00
❑ 0795	I'll Be Your Baby Tonight/The Greatest Experiment Is Over	1968	—	3.00	6.00
❑ 0914	Another Virgin Spring/Tin Wedding	1970	—	3.00	6.00

HARRISON, WES

Number	Title (A Side/B Side)	Yr	VG	VG+	NM
LIN					
❑ 5002	There Y'Are/Uncle Winnie's Sound Stories	1956	7.50	15.00	30.00

HARRISON, WILBERT

Number	Title (A Side/B Side)	Yr	VG	VG+	NM
BELL					
❑ 869	C.C. Rider/Since I Fell for You	1970	—	3.00	6.00
BRUNSWICK					
❑ 55511	Lovin' Operator/Love You	1974	—	3.00	6.00
❑ 55519	I'm Going to the River/I Need Some (Honey Honey)	1975	—	3.00	6.00
CHART					
❑ 626	Cool Water/Calypso Man	1956	6.25	12.50	25.00
CONSTELLATION					
❑ 122	New York World's Fair/Mama, Mama, Mama	1964	2.50	5.00	10.00
DELUXE					
❑ 6002	This Woman of Mine/The Letter	1953	15.00	30.00	60.00
❑ 6031	Nobody Knows My Trouble/Gin and Coconut Milk	1954	15.00	30.00	60.00
FURY					
❑ 1023	Kansas City/Listen, My Darling	1959	7.50	15.00	30.00
❑ 1027	Cheating Baby/Don't Wreck My Life	1959	3.75	7.50	15.00
❑ 1028	Goodbye Kansas City/1960	1960	3.75	7.50	15.00
❑ 1031	C.C. Rider/Why Did You Leave	1960	3.75	7.50	15.00
❑ 1037	Since I Fell for You/Little School Girl	1960	3.75	7.50	15.00
❑ 1041	The Horse/Da-De-Ya-Da (I'd Do Anything for You)	1961	3.75	7.50	15.00
❑ 1047	Happy in Love/Calypso Dance	1961	3.75	7.50	15.00
❑ 1055	Drafted/My Heart Is Yours	1961	3.75	7.50	15.00
❑ 1059	Let's Stick Together/Kansas City Twist	1962	3.75	7.50	15.00
❑ 1063	Let's Stick Together/My Heart Is Yours	1962	3.00	6.00	12.00
GLADES					
❑ 603	Gonna Tell You a Story/Letter Edged in Black	1959	3.00	6.00	12.00
PORT					
❑ 3003	Baby Move On/You're Still My Baby	1965	2.00	4.00	8.00
❑ 3009	Don't Take It So Hard/Sugar Lump	1965	2.00	4.00	8.00
ROCKIN'					
❑ 526	This Woman of Mine/The Letter	1952	25.00	50.00	100.00
ROULETTE					
❑ 4752	No One's Love But Yours/Mini-Parade	1967	2.00	4.00	8.00
SAVOY					
❑ 1138	Don't Drop It/The Ways of a Woman	1954	10.00	20.00	40.00
❑ 1149	Women and Whiskey/Da-De-Ya-Da (I'd Do Anything for You)	1955	7.50	15.00	30.00
❑ 1164	Florida Special/Darling, Listen to This Song	1955	7.50	15.00	30.00
❑ 1198	Confessin' My Dream/The Way I Feel	1956	7.50	15.00	30.00
❑ 1517	My Love Is True/I Know My Baby Loves Me	1957	6.25	12.50	25.00
❑ 1531	Baby Don't You Know/My Love for You Lingers On	1958	5.00	10.00	20.00
❑ 1571	Don't Drop It/Baby Don't You Know	1959	3.75	7.50	15.00
SEA HORN					
❑ 502	Say It Again/Near to You	1963	2.00	4.00	8.00
SSS INTERNATIONAL					
❑ 830	My Heart Is Yours/Pretty Little Woman	1971	—	3.00	6.00
❑ 830 [DJ]	My Heart Is Yours (mono/stereo)	1971	2.50	5.00	10.00
—Promo only on blue vinyl					
SUE					
❑ 11	Let's Work Together (Part 1)/Let's Work Together (Part 2)	1969	—	3.00	6.00
WET SOUL					
❑ 4	My Heart Is Yours/Pretty Little Woman	1970	2.00	4.00	8.00

HARRY, DEBBIE

Also see BLONDIE.

Number	Title (A Side/B Side)	Yr	VG	VG+	NM
CHRYSALIS					
❑ 2526	Backfired/Military Rap	1981	—	—	3.00
❑ 2526 [PS]	Backfired/Military Rap	1981	—	—	3.00
❑ 2554	The Jam Was Moving/Inner City Spillover	1981	—	—	3.00
❑ 42745	Rush, Rush, Rush/Dance, Dance, Dance	1983	—	—	3.00
❑ 42745 [PS]	Rush, Rush, Rush/Dance, Dance, Dance	1983	—	—	3.00
❑ 43328	Denis (The '88 Remix)/Rapture (Teddy Riley Remix)	1988	—	—	3.00
❑ 43328 [PS]	Denis (The '88 Remix)/Rapture (Teddy Riley Remix)	1988	—	—	3.00
GEFFEN					
❑ 28476	In Love with Love/Secret Life	1987	—	—	3.00
❑ 28476 [PS]	In Love with Love/Secret Life	1987	—	—	3.00
❑ 28546	French Kissin'/Rockbird	1986	—	—	3.00
❑ 28546 [PS]	French Kissin'/Rockbird	1986	—	—	3.00
REPRISE					
❑ 27792	Liar, Liar/Queen of Voodoo	1988	—	—	3.00
—B-side by Voodooist Corporation					
❑ 27792 [PS]	Liar, Liar/Queen of Voodoo	1988	—	—	3.00

SIRE

Number	Title (A Side/B Side)	Yr	VG	VG+	NM
❑ 22816	I Want That Man/Bike Boy	1989	—	—	3.00

HARSHMAN, ROBERT LUKE
See BOBBY HART.

HART, BILLY AND DON
ROULETTE

Number	Title (A Side/B Side)	Yr	VG	VG+	NM
❑ 4133	Rock-a-Bop-a-Lena/More and More	1959	15.00	30.00	60.00
❑ 4172	Check-Mated and Bingoed/Blabbermouth	1959	7.50	15.00	30.00

HART, BOBBY
Also see TOMMY BOYCE AND BOBBY HART; DOLENZ, JONES, BOYCE & HART.

Number	Title (A Side/B Side)	Yr	VG	VG+	NM
ARIOLA AMERICA					
❑ 809	Lovers for the Night/You Get Smoke in Your Eyes	1980	—	2.50	5.00
BAMBOO					
❑ 507	The Girl I Used to Know/The Spider and the Fly	1961	7.50	15.00	30.00
CHELSEA					
❑ BCBO-0026	Easy Evil/California	1973	—	2.50	5.00
DCP					
❑ 1113	That'll Be the Day/Turn On Your Lovelight	1964	5.00	10.00	20.00
❑ 1142	Baby Let Your Hair Down/Jealous Feeling	1965	6.25	12.50	25.00
❑ 1152	Around the Corner/Cry My Eyes Out	1966	5.00	10.00	20.00
ERA					
❑ 3039	Girl in the Window/Journey of Love	1961	5.00	10.00	20.00
GUYDEN					
❑ 2022	Is You Is Or Is You Ain't My Baby/Girl of My Dreams	1959	7.50	15.00	30.00
—As "Robert Luke Harshman"					
INFINITY					
❑ 017	Too Many Teardrops/The People Next Door	1963	5.00	10.00	20.00
❑ 022	Lovesick Blues/I Think It's Called a Heartache	1963	5.00	10.00	20.00
RADIO					
❑ 122	Stop Talkin', Start Lovin'/Love Whatcha Doin' to Me	1959	10.00	20.00	40.00
—As "Robert Luke Harshman"					
REEL					
❑ 100	Girl in the Window/Journey of Love	1961	10.00	20.00	40.00
WARNER BROS.					
❑ 8058	Hard Core Man/To Keep from Crying	1974	—	2.50	5.00
❑ 8058 [PS]	Hard Core Man/To Keep from Crying	1974	2.00	4.00	8.00
❑ 49079	The Loneliest Night/Sometimes Love	1979	—	2.50	5.00

HART, FREDDIE

Number	Title (A Side/B Side)	Yr	VG	VG+	NM
CAPITOL					
❑ F2524	Butterfly Love/My Heart Is a Playground	1953	6.25	12.50	25.00
❑ F2588	Secret Kisses/Whole Hog or None	1953	5.00	10.00	20.00
❑ 2692	The Whole World Holding Hands/Without You	1969	2.00	4.00	8.00
❑ F2726	Loose Talk/The Curtain Never Falls	1954	5.00	10.00	20.00
❑ 2768	One More Mountain to Climb/Just Another Girl	1970	2.00	4.00	8.00
❑ 2839	Fingerprints/I Can't Keep My Hands Off of You	1970	2.00	4.00	8.00
❑ F2873	Caught at Last/It Just Don't Seem Like Home	1954	5.00	10.00	20.00
❑ 2933	California Grapevine/What's Wrong with Your Head, Fred	1970	2.00	4.00	8.00
❑ F2991	I'm Going Out on the Front Porch and Cry/Please Don't Tell Her	1954	5.00	10.00	20.00
❑ F3090	Miss Lonely Heart/Oh Heart Let Her Go	1955	5.00	10.00	20.00
❑ 3115	Easy Loving/Brother Bluebird	1971	—	3.00	6.00
❑ F3203	Canada to Tennessee/No Thanks to You	1955	5.00	10.00	20.00
❑ 3261	My Hang-Up Is You/Big Bad Wolf	1972	—	3.00	6.00
❑ F3299	Hiding in Darkness/That's What You Gave to Me	1955	5.00	10.00	20.00
❑ 3353	Bless Your Heart/Conscience Makes Cowards (Of Us All)	1972	—	3.00	6.00
❑ 3453	Got the All Overs for You (All Over Me)/Just Another Girl	1972	—	3.00	6.00
❑ 3524	Super Kind of Woman/Mother Nature Made a Believer Out of Me	1973	—	3.00	6.00
❑ 3612	Trip to Heaven/Look-a Here	1973	—	3.00	6.00
❑ 3730	If You Can't Feel It (It Ain't There)/Skid Row Street	1973	—	3.00	6.00
❑ 3789	Blue Christmas/I Believe in Santa Claus	1973	—	3.50	7.00
❑ 3827	Hang In There Girl/You Belong to Me	1974	—	3.00	6.00
❑ 3898	The Want-To's/Phenix City, Alabama	1974	—	3.00	6.00
❑ 3970	My Woman's Man/Let's Clean Up the Country	1974	—	3.00	6.00
❑ 4031	I'd Like to Sleep Til I Get Over You/Nothing's Better Than That	1975	—	3.00	6.00
❑ 4099	The First Time/Sexy	1975	—	3.00	6.00
❑ 4152	Warm Side of You/I Love You, I Just Don't Like You	1975	—	3.00	6.00
❑ 4210	You Are the Song (Inside of Me)/I Can Almost See Houston from Here	1976	—	3.00	6.00
❑ 4251	She'll Throw Stones at You/Love Makes It Alright	1976	—	3.00	6.00
❑ 4313	That Look in Her Eyes/Try My Love for Size	1976	—	3.00	6.00
❑ 4363	Why Lovers Turn to Strangers/Paper Sack Full of Memories	1976	—	3.00	6.00
❑ 4409	Thank God She's Mine/Falling All Over Me	1977	—	2.00	4.00
❑ 4448	The Pleasure's Been All Mine/It's Heaven Loving You	1977	—	2.00	4.00
❑ 4498	The Search/Honky Tonk Toys	1977	—	2.50	5.00
❑ 4530	So Good, So Rare, So Fine/There's an Angel Living There	1978	—	2.50	5.00
❑ 4561	Only You/I Love You, I Just Don't Like You	1978	—	2.50	5.00
❑ 4609	Toe to Toe/And Then Some	1978	—	2.50	5.00
❑ 4684	My Lady/Guilty	1979	—	2.50	5.00
❑ 4720	Wasn't It Easy Baby/My Lady Loves	1979	—	2.50	5.00
COLUMBIA					
❑ 21512	Dig Boy Dig/Two of a Kind	1956	12.50	25.00	50.00
❑ 21550	Snatch It and Grab It/Human Thing to Do	1956	3.75	7.50	15.00
❑ 21558	Drink Up and Go Home/Blue	1956	3.75	7.50	15.00
❑ 40821	On the Prowl/Extra	1957	3.75	7.50	15.00
❑ 40896	Fraulein/Baby Don't Leave	1957	3.75	7.50	15.00
❑ 41005	Say No More/The Outside World	1957	3.75	7.50	15.00
❑ 41081	You Are My World/Heaven Only Knows	1957	3.75	7.50	15.00
❑ 41144	I Won't Be Home Tonight/Love, Come to Me	1958	3.75	7.50	15.00
❑ 41269	I'm No Angel/Midnight Date	1958	3.75	7.50	15.00
❑ 41345	The Wall/Davy Jones	1959	3.00	6.00	12.00
❑ 41439	Farther Than My Eyes Can See/My Kind of Love	1959	—	—	—
—Unreleased					
❑ 41456	Chain Gang/Rock Bottom	1959	3.00	6.00	12.00
❑ 41597	The Key's in the Mailbox/Starvation Days	1960	3.00	6.00	12.00
❑ 41805	Lying Again/Do My Heart a Favor	1960	3.00	6.00	12.00
❑ 42146	What a Laugh!/Heart Attack	1961	3.00	6.00	12.00
❑ 42285	Some Do, Some Don't, Some Will, Some Won't/Like You Are	1962	3.00	6.00	12.00
❑ 42491	Stand Up/Ugly Duckling	1962	3.00	6.00	12.00
❑ 42679	I'll Hit It with a Stick/Stranger Drive Away	1963	3.00	6.00	12.00
❑ 42769	Angels Like You/Mary Ann	1963	3.00	6.00	12.00
EL DORADO					
❑ 101	I Don't Want to Lose You/My Favorite Entertainer	1985	—	3.50	7.00
FIFTH ST.					
❑ 1091	Best Love I Never Had/I'm Not Going Hungry	1987	—	3.00	6.00
KAPP					
❑ 632	Love Can Make or Break a Heart/Hurts Feel So Good	1964	2.50	5.00	10.00
❑ 661	Moon Gal/You've Got It Coming To Ya	1965	2.50	5.00	10.00
❑ 694	Hank Williams' Guitar/I Created a Monster	1965	2.50	5.00	10.00
❑ 743	Why Should I Cry Over You/Keys in the Mailbox	1966	2.50	5.00	10.00
❑ 765	Together Again/Waiting for a Train	1966	2.50	5.00	10.00
❑ 794	Misty Blue/Elm Street Pawn Shop	1966	2.50	5.00	10.00
❑ 820	I'll Hold You in My Heart/Too Much of You (Left of Me)	1967	2.50	5.00	10.00
❑ 841	Anna Maria/Leon and the Rain	1967	2.50	5.00	10.00
❑ 879	Togetherness/Portrait of a Lonely Man	1967	2.50	5.00	10.00
❑ 879 [PS]	Togetherness/Portrait of a Lonely Man	1967	3.75	7.50	15.00
❑ 910	Born a Fool/Hands of a Man	1968	2.50	5.00	10.00
❑ 944	Don't Cry Baby/Here Lies a Heart	1968	2.50	5.00	10.00
❑ 976	Why Leave Something I Can't Use/Hang On to Her	1969	2.50	5.00	10.00
❑ 993	I Lost All My Tomorrows/That's How High a Man Can Go	1969	2.50	5.00	10.00
❑ 2183	Don't Cry Baby/Loving You Again	1972	—	3.50	7.00
MCA					
❑ 40011	Born a Fool/My Anna Maria	1973	—	3.00	6.00
MONUMENT					
❑ 826	For a Second There/The Almighty Dollar	1963	3.00	6.00	12.00
❑ 838	First You Go Through Me/Valentino	1964	3.00	6.00	12.00
SUNBIRD					
❑ 110	Sure Thing/Makin' Love to a Memory	1980	—	3.00	6.00
❑ 7550	Sure Thing/Makin' Love to a Memory	1980	—	2.50	5.00
❑ 7553	Roses Are Red/Battle of the Sexes	1980	—	2.50	5.00
❑ 7560	You're Crazy Man/Playboy's Centerfolk	1981	—	2.50	5.00
❑ 7565	You Were There/The Weaker Sex	1981	—	2.50	5.00

HART, MICKEY
Also see THE GRATEFUL DEAD.

WARNER BROS.

Number	Title (A Side/B Side)	Yr	VG	VG+	NM
❑ 7644	Blind John/Pump Man	1972	2.50	5.00	10.00

HART, RITCHIE

Number	Title (A Side/B Side)	Yr	VG	VG+	NM
FELSTED					
❑ 8593	The Great Duane/I'm Hypnotized	1959	25.00	50.00	100.00
MCI					
❑ 1025	Choo Choo Train/I Want You	1960	6.25	12.50	25.00

HART, ROCKY

Number	Title (A Side/B Side)	Yr	VG	VG+	NM
BIG TOP					
❑ 3069	Crying/Baby You've Got It Made	1961	7.50	15.00	30.00
CUB					
❑ 9052	Every Day/Come with Me	1959	7.50	15.00	30.00
GLO					
❑ 216	I Play the Part of a Fool/Someone Stole My Baby While Doing the Twist	1961	50.00	100.00	200.00

HARTFORD, KEN
SOUTHERN SOUND

Number	Title (A Side/B Side)	Yr	VG	VG+	NM
❑ 119	Jay Walker/Little Joe, Go Lightly	1963	6.25	12.50	25.00
—With Frankie Valli					

HARVESTERS, THE
COLUMBIA

Number	Title (A Side/B Side)	Yr	VG	VG+	NM
❑ 4-21457	Let God Abide/I Just Telephone Upstairs	1955	6.25	12.50	25.00
❑ 4-21495	I Want You to Be More Like Jesus/When I'm Alone	1956	6.25	12.50	25.00
❑ 4-21511	Jacob's Ladder/He's Everywhere	1956	6.25	12.50	25.00
❑ 4-40897	These Are the Things That Matter/That Will Be a Great Day	1957	5.00	10.00	20.00
❑ 4-41074	I Shall Not Be Moved/Closer Than a Brother	1957	5.00	10.00	20.00

HARVEY
Also see ETTA AND HARVEY; THE MOONGLOWS.

Number	Title (A Side/B Side)	Yr	VG	VG+	NM
CHESS					
❑ 1713	I Want Somebody/Da Da Goo Goo	1959	10.00	20.00	40.00
❑ 1725	Twelve Months of the Year/Don't Be Afraid of Love	1959	10.00	20.00	40.00
❑ 1749	Blue Skies/Ooh, Ouch, Stop!	1960	6.25	12.50	25.00
❑ 1760	If I Can't Have You/My Heart Cries	1960	6.25	12.50	25.00
—As "Etta and Harvey" (Etta is Etta James)					
❑ 1771	Spoonful/It's a Crying Shame	1960	6.25	12.50	25.00
—As "Etta and Harvey" (Etta is Etta James)					
❑ 1781	The First Time/Mama	1961	6.25	12.50	25.00
—As "Harvey Fuqua"					
HARVEY					
❑ 121	What Can You Do Now/Will I Do	1962	10.00	20.00	40.00
—As "Harvey and Ann"					
TRI-PHI					
❑ 1017	She Loves Me So/Any Way You Wanta	1962	10.00	20.00	40.00

Number	Title (A Side/B Side)	Yr	VG	VG+	NM
❑ 1024	Memories of You/Come On and Answer Me	1963	15.00	30.00	60.00

HARVEY, ALEX (1)

Number	Title (A Side/B Side)	Yr	VG	VG+	NM
ATLANTIC					
❑ 3293	Delilah/Soul in Chains	1975	—	2.50	5.00
DECCA					
❑ 31649	New Orleans/I Just Wanna Make Love to You	1964	5.00	10.00	20.00
VERTIGO					
❑ 113	Swamp Snake/Gang Bang	1974	—	2.50	5.00
❑ 200	Tomahawk Kid/Sergeant Fury	1974	—	2.50	5.00

HARVEY, PHIL

Actually PHIL SPECTOR.

Number	Title (A Side/B Side)	Yr	VG	VG+	NM
IMPERIAL					
❑ 5583	Willy Boy/Bumbershoot	1959	37.50	75.00	150.00

HARVEY AND THE MOONGLOWS

See THE MOONGLOWS.

HASLAM, ANNIE

Also see RENAISSANCE.

Number	Title (A Side/B Side)	Yr	VG	VG+	NM
SIRE					
❑ 1016	I Never Believed in Love/Inside My Life	1978	—	3.00	6.00

HASSAN, ALI

Also see B. BUMBLE AND THE STINGERS.

Number	Title (A Side/B Side)	Yr	VG	VG+	NM
PHILLES					
❑ 103	Malaguena/Chop Sticks	1962	7.50	15.00	30.00

HASSLES, THE

BILLY JOEL was in this group.

Number	Title (A Side/B Side)	Yr	VG	VG+	NM
UNITED ARTISTS					
❑ 50215	You've Got Me Hummin'/I'm Thinkin'	1967	3.00	6.00	12.00
❑ 50215 [PS]	You've Got Me Hummin'/I'm Thinkin'	1967	5.00	10.00	20.00
❑ 50258	I Hear Voices/Every Step I Take	1968	3.00	6.00	12.00
❑ 50450	4 O'Clock in the Morning/Let Me Bring You to the Sunshine	1968	3.00	6.00	12.00
❑ 50513	Night After Day/Country Boy	1969	3.00	6.00	12.00
❑ 50586	Traveling Band/Great Balls of Fire	1969	3.00	6.00	12.00

HATCHER, WILLIE

Number	Title (A Side/B Side)	Yr	VG	VG+	NM
COLUMBIA					
❑ 44259	Good Things Come to Those Who Wait/Searching	1968	12.50	25.00	50.00
KING					
❑ 6360	Head Over Heels/Who's Gotta Woman Like Mine	1971	7.50	15.00	30.00

HATFIELD, BOBBY

Also see THE RIGHTEOUS BROTHERS.

Number	Title (A Side/B Side)	Yr	VG	VG+	NM
MOONGLOW					
❑ 220	I Need a Girl/Hot Tamale	1963	6.25	12.50	25.00
VERVE					
❑ 10598	Hang-Ups/Soul Cafe	1968	2.00	4.00	8.00
❑ 10621	Brothers/What's the Matter Baby	1968	2.00	4.00	8.00
❑ 10634	Only You/The Wonder of You	1969	2.00	4.00	8.00
❑ 10639	My Prayer/I Wish I Didn't Love You So	1969	2.00	4.00	8.00
❑ 10641	Answer Me My Love/I Only Have Eyes for You	1969	2.00	4.00	8.00
WARNER BROS.					
❑ 7566	Rock 'N Roll Woman/Oo Wee Baby, I Love You	1972	—	2.50	5.00
❑ 7649	Stay with Me/Rock 'N Roll Woman	1972	—	2.50	5.00

HATFIELD, JULIANA, THREE

Number	Title (A Side/B Side)	Yr	VG	VG+	NM
MAMMOTH					
❑ MR 0053	My Sister//A Dame with a Rod/Put It Away	1993	—	2.50	5.00
—Gray vinyl; limited edition of 1,500					
❑ MR 0053 [PS]	My Sister//A Dame with a Rod/Put It Away	1993	—	2.50	5.00

HATHAWAY, DONNY

Also see ROBERTA FLACK.

Number	Title (A Side/B Side)	Yr	VG	VG+	NM
ATCO					
❑ 6719	The Ghetto (Part 1)/The Ghetto (Part 2)	1969	—	3.00	6.00
❑ 6759	Thank You Master/Je Vous Aime	1970	—	2.50	5.00
❑ 6768	Tryin' Times/Voices Inside	1970	—	2.50	5.00
❑ 6799	This Christmas/Be There	1970	2.00	4.00	8.00
❑ 6817	Take a Love Song/Magnificent Sanctuary Band	1971	—	2.50	5.00
❑ 6828	A Song for You/Put Your Hand in the Hand	1971	—	2.50	5.00
❑ 6880	Little Ghetto Boy/We're Still Friends	1972	—	2.50	5.00
❑ 6884	Giving Up/Jealous Love	1972	—	2.50	5.00
❑ 6899	Bossa Nova/Come Back Charleston Blue	1972	—	2.50	5.00
—With Margie Joseph					
❑ 6903	I Love You More Than You'll Ever Know/Lord Help Me	1972	—	2.50	5.00
❑ 6928	Love, Love, Love/Someday We'll All Be Free	1973	—	2.50	5.00
❑ 6951	Come Little Children/The Slums	1973	—	2.50	5.00
❑ 7066	This Christmas/Be There	1975	—	2.50	5.00
❑ 7092	You Were Meant for Me/Valdez in the Country	1978	—	2.00	4.00
❑ 7320	This Christmas/Be There	1980	—	2.00	4.00
❑ 99956	This Christmas/Be There	1982	—	2.00	4.00
CURTOM					
❑ 1935	I Thank You Baby/What's This I See	1969	2.00	4.00	8.00
—By "June and Donnie"					
❑ 1971	I Thank You/Just Another Reason	1972	—	2.50	5.00
—By "June Conquest and Donnie Hathaway"; same A-side as 1935 but with revised title					

HAVEN, SHIRLEY

Number	Title (A Side/B Side)	Yr	VG	VG+	NM
FEDERAL					
❑ 12092	Troubles of My Own/Stop Foolin' Around	1952	75.00	150.00	300.00
—With the Four Jacks					

HAWK, THE

See JERRY LEE LEWIS.

HAWKETTS, THE

Number	Title (A Side/B Side)	Yr	VG	VG+	NM
CHESS					
❑ 1591	Mardi Gras Mambo/Your Time Is Up	1955	25.00	50.00	100.00

HAWKINS, DALE

Number	Title (A Side/B Side)	Yr	VG	VG+	NM
ABC-PARAMOUNT					
❑ 10668	I'll Fly High/La La Song	1965	2.50	5.00	10.00
ABNAK					
❑ 110	The Flag/And I Believed You	1965	3.00	6.00	12.00
ATLANTIC					
❑ 2126	Stay at Home, Lulu/I Can't Erase You	1961	5.00	10.00	20.00
❑ 2150	What a Feeling/Women, That's What's Happening	1962	5.00	10.00	20.00
BELL					
❑ 807	Back Street/Little Rain Cloud	1969	2.00	4.00	8.00
❑ 827	Heavy on My Mind/Joe	1969	2.00	4.00	8.00
CHECKER					
❑ 843	See You Soon, Baboon/Four Letter Word	1956	7.50	15.00	30.00
❑ 863	Susie-Q/Don't Treat Me This Way	1957	12.50	25.00	50.00
❑ 876	Baby, Baby/Mrs. Merguitory's Daughter	1957	7.50	15.00	30.00
❑ 892	Little Pig/Tornado	1958	6.25	12.50	25.00
❑ 900	La-Do-Dada/Cross Ties	1958	6.25	12.50	25.00
❑ 906	My Babe/A House, a Car, and a Wedding Ring	1958	6.25	12.50	25.00
❑ 913	Someday, One Day/Take My Heart	1959	6.25	12.50	25.00
❑ 916	Class Cutter (Yeah Yeah)/Lonely Nights	1959	6.25	12.50	25.00
❑ 923	Ain't That Lovin' You Baby/My Dream	1959	6.25	12.50	25.00
❑ 929	Our Turn/Lifeguard Man	1959	6.25	12.50	25.00
❑ 934	Liza Jane/Back to School Blues	1959	6.25	12.50	25.00
❑ 940	Hot Dog/Don't Break Your Promise to Me	1960	5.00	10.00	20.00
❑ 944	Poor Little Rhode Island/Every Little Girl	1960	5.00	10.00	20.00
❑ 944 [PS]	Poor Little Rhode Island/Every Little Girl	1960	75.00	150.00	300.00
❑ 962	Linda/Who	1960	5.00	10.00	20.00
❑ 970	Grandma's House/I Want to Love You	1961	5.00	10.00	20.00
LINCOLN					
❑ 002	Johnny B. Goode/Baby We Had It	196?	2.00	4.00	8.00
PAULA					
❑ 424	First Cut Is the Deepest/Nothing Left to Do But Say Goodbye	1977	—	2.50	5.00
TILT					
❑ 781	Money Honey/The Same Old Way	1962	5.00	10.00	20.00
❑ 783	Forbidden Love/Wish I Hadn't Called Home	1962	5.00	10.00	20.00
❑ 785	Hawk Blows, Band Plays (Part 1)/Hawk Blows, Band Plays (Part 2)	1962	5.00	10.00	20.00
ZONK					
❑ 1002	Gotta Dance/Peaches	1973	—	2.50	5.00

HAWKINS, HAWKSHAW

Number	Title (A Side/B Side)	Yr	VG	VG+	NM
COLUMBIA					
❑ 4-41419	Soldier's Joy/Big Red Benson	1959	5.00	10.00	20.00
❑ 4-41574	Alaska Lil and Texas Bill/Patanio	1960	5.00	10.00	20.00
❑ 4-41714	Put a Nickel in the Jukebox/Your Conscience	1960	5.00	10.00	20.00
❑ 4-41011	You Know Me Too Well/My Story	1960	5.00	10.00	20.00
❑ 4-42002	No Love for Me/The Love I Have for You	1961	3.75	7.50	15.00
❑ 4-42223	Twenty Miles from Shore/Big Ole Heartache	1961	3.75	7.50	15.00
❑ 4-42441	I Can't Seem to Say Goodbye/Darkness on the Face of the Earth	1962	3.75	7.50	15.00
KING					
❑ 969	I'm Waiting Just for You/A Heartache to Recall	1951	10.00	20.00	40.00
❑ 997	Sunny Side of the Mountain/Blue Skies in Your Eyes	1951	10.00	20.00	40.00
❑ 998	Slow Poke/Two Roads	1951	10.00	20.00	40.00
❑ 1039	Be My Life's Companion/Everybody's Got a Girl But Me	1952	7.50	15.00	30.00
❑ 1047	Over the Hill/I Am Slowly Dying of a Broken Heart	1952	7.50	15.00	30.00
❑ 1062	Unwanted/Got You on My Mind	1952	7.50	15.00	30.00
❑ 1081	Loaded with Love/I Love the Way You Say Goodnight	1952	7.50	15.00	30.00
❑ 1133	Heavenly Road/An Empty Mansion	1952	7.50	15.00	30.00
❑ 1134	I'm a Lone Wolf/I Hope You're Cryin' Too	1952	7.50	15.00	30.00
❑ 1154	Tangled Heart/Betty Lorraine	1953	7.50	15.00	30.00
❑ 1174	The Life Story of Hank Williams/Picking Sweethearts	1953	10.00	20.00	40.00
❑ 1175	Kaw-Liga/If I Ever Get Rich Mom	1953	7.50	15.00	30.00
❑ 1190	Barbara Allen/The Life Story of Hank Williams	1953	7.50	15.00	30.00
❑ 5404	Nothing More to Say/Between the Lines	1960	3.75	7.50	15.00
❑ 5692	Silver Threads and Golden Needles/Girl Without a Name	1962	3.75	7.50	15.00
❑ 5695	Bad News Travels Fast/Let Them Talk	1962	3.75	7.50	15.00
❑ 5712	Lonesome 7-7203/Everything Has Changed	1963	3.75	7.50	15.00
❑ 5765	Love Died Tonight/Sunny Side of the Mountain	1963	3.75	7.50	15.00
❑ 5810	Caught in the Middle of Two Hearts/If I Ever Get Rich Mom	1963	3.75	7.50	15.00
❑ 5871	I'm Beginning to Forget/Teardrops on Your Letter	1964	3.75	7.50	15.00
❑ 5909	This Particular Baby/The Shadows	1964	3.75	7.50	15.00
❑ 6047	The Last Letter/Never Mind the Tears	1967	3.00	6.00	12.00
❑ 6074	Jealous Fate/It's Easy to Remember	1967	3.00	6.00	12.00
RCA VICTOR					
❑ 47-5333	I'll Trade Yours for Mine/Long Way	1953	6.25	12.50	25.00
❑ 47-5444	A Heap of Lovin'/Mark Round My Finger	1953	6.25	12.50	25.00
❑ 47-5549	I'll Never Close My Heart to You/When You Say Yes	1953	6.25	12.50	25.00
❑ 47-5623	Flashing Lights/Waitin' for My Baby	1954	6.25	12.50	25.00
❑ 47-5702	Rebound/Why Didn't I Hear It from You	1954	6.25	12.50	25.00
❑ 47-5808	One White Rose/I Wanna Be Hugged to Death	1954	6.25	12.50	25.00
❑ 47-5890	I'll Take a Chance with You/Why Don't You Leave This Town	1954	6.25	12.50	25.00
❑ 47-6022	Ling Ting Tong/Ko Ko Mo, I Love You So	1955	6.25	12.50	25.00
—With Rita Robbins					

Number	Title (A Side/B Side)	Yr	VG	VG+	NM
❑ 47-6103	How Can Anything So Pretty Be So Doggone Mean/Pedro Gonzalez Tennessee Lopez	1955	6.25	12.50	25.00
❑ 47-6211	Car Hoppin' Mama/The Love You Steal	1955	6.25	12.50	25.00
❑ 47-6298	I Gotta Have You/Standing at the End of My World	1955	6.25	12.50	25.00
❑ 47-6396	If It Ain't on the Menu/Borrowing	1956	6.25	12.50	25.00
❑ 47-6509	It Would Be a Doggone Lie/Sunny Side of the Mountain	1956	6.25	12.50	25.00
❑ 47-6716	I'll Be Gone/My Fate Is In Your Hands	1956	6.25	12.50	25.00
❑ 47-6794	Action/Oh How I Cried	1957	5.00	10.00	20.00
❑ 47-6910	Dark Moon/With This Pen	1957	5.00	10.00	20.00
❑ 47-7054	Is My Ring on Your Finger/Sensation	1957	5.00	10.00	20.00
❑ 47-7145	Guilty of Dreaming/It's Easier Said Than Done	1958	5.00	10.00	20.00
❑ 47-7222	I Don't Apologize/I'll Get Even with You	1958	5.00	10.00	20.00
❑ 47-7389	I've Got It Again/Freedom	1958	5.00	10.00	20.00
❑ 47-7486	Are You Happy/She Was Here	1959	5.00	10.00	20.00

HAWKINS, JALACY

See SCREAMIN' JAY HAWKINS.

HAWKINS, RONNIE

His backing band, The Hawks, evolved into THE BAND.

Number	Title (A Side/B Side)	Yr	VG	VG+	NM
COTILLION					
❑ 44060	Matchbox/Down in the Alley	1970	—	3.00	6.00
❑ 44067	Forty Days/Bitter Green	1970	—	3.00	6.00
❑ 44076	Little Bird/One More Night	1970	—	3.00	6.00
MONUMENT					
❑ 8548	Lawdy Miss Clawdy/Cora Mae	1972	—	2.50	5.00
❑ 8561	Lonesome Town/Kinky	1973	—	2.50	5.00
❑ 8573	Diddley Daddy/Cora Mae	1973	—	2.50	5.00
❑ 8583	Bo Diddley/Lonely Hours	1973	—	2.50	5.00
ROULETTE					
❑ 4154 [M]	Forty Days/One of These Days	1959	6.25	12.50	25.00
❑ SSR-4154 [S]	Forty Days/One of These Days	1959	12.50	25.00	50.00
❑ 4177 [M]	Mary Lou/Need Your Lovin'	1959	7.50	15.00	30.00
❑ SSR-4177 [S]	Mary Lou/Need Your Lovin'	1959	12.50	25.00	50.00
❑ 4209	Southern Love/Love Me Like You Can	1959	5.00	10.00	20.00
❑ 4228	Lonely Hours/Clara	1960	5.00	10.00	20.00
❑ 4231	The Ballad of Caryl Chessman/The Tale of Floyd Collins	1960	5.00	10.00	20.00
❑ 4249	Ruby Baby/Hayride	1960	5.00	10.00	20.00
❑ 4267	Sumemrtime/Mister and Mississippi	1960	5.00	10.00	20.00
❑ 4311	Cold, Cold Heart/Nobody's Lonesome for Me	1960	5.00	10.00	20.00
❑ 4400	Come Love/I Feel Good	1961	5.00	10.00	20.00
❑ 4483	Bo Diddley/Who Do You Love	1963	5.00	10.00	20.00
❑ 4502	High Blood Pressure/There's a Screw Loose	1963	5.00	10.00	20.00

HAWKINS, SCREAMIN' JAY

Number	Title (A Side/B Side)	Yr	VG	VG+	NM
APOLLO					
❑ 506	Please Try to Understand/Not Anymore	1957	6.25	12.50	25.00
❑ 528	Baptize Me in Wine/Not Anymore	1958	6.25	12.50	25.00
CHANCELLOR					
❑ 1117	Ashes/Nitty Gritty	1962	3.75	7.50	15.00
DECCA					
❑ 32019	All Night/I'm Not Made of Clay	1966	3.75	7.50	15.00
❑ 32100	I Put a Spell on You/You're an Exception to the Rule	1967	10.00	20.00	40.00
ENRICA					
❑ 1010	I Hear Voices/I Just Don't Care	1962	6.25	12.50	25.00
GRAND					
❑ 135	Take Me Back/I Is	1957	6.25	12.50	25.00
MERCURY					
❑ 70549	This Is All/She Put the Whammee on Me	1955	20.00	40.00	80.00
OKEH					
❑ 7072	I Put a Spell on You/Little Demon	1956	12.50	25.00	50.00
❑ 7084	You Made Me Love You/Darling, Please Forgive Me	1957	7.50	15.00	30.00
❑ 7087	Person to Person/Frenzy	1957	7.50	15.00	30.00
❑ 7101	Alligator Wine/There's Something Wrong with You	1958	7.50	15.00	30.00
PHILIPS					
❑ 40606	Stone Crazy/I'm Lonely	1969	—	3.00	6.00
❑ 40636	Too Many Teardrops/Makaka Ways	1969	—	3.00	6.00
❑ 40645	Constipation Blues/Do You Really Love Me	1969	—	3.00	6.00
❑ 40668	Moanin'/Do You Really Love Me	1970	—	3.00	6.00
❑ 40674	Our Love Is Not for Three/Take Me Back	1970	—	3.00	6.00
PROVIDENCE					
❑ 411	My Kind of Love/Po' Folks	1965	3.00	6.00	12.00
QUEEN BEE					
❑ 1314	Monkberry Moon Delight/Sweet Ginny	1973	—	3.00	6.00
RCA VICTOR					
❑ PB-10127	You Put the Spell on Me/Voodoo	1974	—	2.50	5.00
ROULETTE					
❑ 4579	The Whammy/Strange	1964	3.00	6.00	12.00
TIMELY					
❑ 1004	Baptize Me in Wine/Not Anymore	1954	20.00	40.00	80.00
❑ 1005	I Found My Way to Wine/Please Try to Understand	1954	20.00	40.00	80.00
WING					
❑ 90005	Well, I Tried/You're All of Life to Me	1955	10.00	20.00	40.00
❑ 90055	Even Though/Talk About Me	1956	7.50	15.00	30.00

HAWKINS, SOPHIE B.

Number	Title (A Side/B Side)	Yr	VG	VG+	NM
COLUMBIA					
❑ 74164	Damn I Wish I Was Your Lover/Don't Stop Swaying	1992	—	2.00	4.00
❑ 74349	California Here I Come/Saviour Child	1992	—	2.00	4.00
❑ 74747	I Want You/Live and Let Love	1992	—	2.00	4.00

HAWKS, THE (1)

Number	Title (A Side/B Side)	Yr	VG	VG+	NM
IMPERIAL					
❑ 5266	Joe the Grinder/Candy Girl	1954	62.50	125.00	250.00
❑ 5281	She's All Right/Good News	1954	50.00	100.00	200.00
❑ 5292	It Ain't That Way/I-Yi	1954	25.00	50.00	100.00
❑ 5306	Nobody But You/Give It Up	1954	25.00	50.00	100.00
❑ 5317	All Women Are the Same/That's What You Are	1954	25.00	50.00	100.00
❑ 5332	It's Too Late Now/I Can't See for Lookin'	1955	25.00	50.00	100.00
MODERN					
❑ 990	It's All Over/Ever Since You Been Gone	1956	62.50	125.00	250.00
POST					
❑ 2004	These Blues/Why Oh Why	1955	75.00	150.00	300.00

HAWKS, THE (U)

None of these are group (1), but we don't know how many groups are represented below.

Number	Title (A Side/B Side)	Yr	VG	VG+	NM
ABC-PARAMOUNT					
❑ 10116	Grasshopper/The Grissle	1960	6.25	12.50	25.00
DEL-FI					
❑ 4108	A Little More Wine, My Dear?/Fussy	1958	10.00	20.00	40.00
MALA					
❑ 401	Cupcake/Lupp!!	1959	5.00	10.00	20.00

HAWLEY, DEANE

Number	Title (A Side/B Side)	Yr	VG	VG+	NM
DORE					
❑ 524	New Fad/Pretty Little Mary	1959	3.75	7.50	15.00
❑ 536	Good Morning, Mr. Sun/Bossman	1959	3.75	7.50	15.00
❑ 543	Where Is My Angel/I'll Never Be a Fool Again	1960	3.75	7.50	15.00
❑ 554	Look for a Star/Bossman	1960	3.75	7.50	15.00
❑ 569	Like a Fool/Stay at Home Blues	1960	3.75	7.50	15.00
❑ 577	Hey There/Rainbow	1960	3.75	7.50	15.00
LIBERTY					
❑ 55359	Pocketful of Rainbows/That Dream Could Never Be	1961	5.00	10.00	20.00
❑ 55446	Queen of the Angels/You Conquered Me	1962	6.25	12.50	25.00
SUNDOWN					
❑ 111	I Hate to See Me Go/Love of the Common People	196?	2.50	5.00	10.00
❑ 113	That's the Name of the Game/Canterbury Station	196?	2.50	5.00	10.00
VALOR					
❑ 2003	Mummy's Bracelet/Don't Keep Me Guessin'	1961	7.50	15.00	30.00
WARNER BROS.					
❑ 5484	I Know She'll Be There/You'll Never Have to Cry Again	1964	3.00	6.00	12.00

HAYES, BILL

Number	Title (A Side/B Side)	Yr	VG	VG+	NM
ABC-PARAMOUNT					
❑ 9785	Wringle, Wrangle/Westward Ho the Wagons	1957	3.00	6.00	12.00
❑ 9785 [PS]	Wringle, Wrangle/Westward Ho the Wagons	1957	5.00	10.00	20.00
❑ 9809	Ramshackle Daddy/On the Outside	1957	3.00	6.00	12.00
❑ 9895	Bop Boy/Uh Huh Oh Yeah	1958	15.00	30.00	60.00
CADENCE					
❑ 1245	I Knew an Old Lady/(B-side unknown)	1954	3.00	6.00	12.00
❑ 1256	The Ballad of Davy Crockett/Farewell	1955	3.75	7.50	15.00
❑ 1261	The Berry Tree/Blue Back Hair	1955	3.00	6.00	12.00
❑ 1274	That Do Make It Nice/Kwela Kwela	1955	3.00	6.00	12.00
❑ 1275	The Legend of Wyatt Earp/White Buffalo	1955	3.75	7.50	15.00
❑ 1294	I Knew an Old Lady/Das Ist Music	1956	3.00	6.00	12.00
❑ 1301	A Message from James Dean/The Trail's End	1956	3.75	7.50	15.00
KAPP					
❑ 258	Wimoweh/Goin' Down the Road Feelin' Bad	1959	2.50	5.00	10.00
❑ 298	Choppin' Mountains/Tall Teller of Tall Tales	1959	2.50	5.00	10.00
MERCURY					
❑ 5599	Too Young/Shenandoah Waltz	1951	5.00	10.00	20.00
MGM					
❑ 11006	Waltz of the Wind/Mine	1951	3.75	7.50	15.00
❑ 11042	The Love of a Gypsy/I've Got an Idea for a Song	1951	3.75	7.50	15.00
❑ 11064	I Love You/Never	1951	3.75	7.50	15.00
❑ 11112	Charmaine/For All We Know	1951	3.75	7.50	15.00
❑ 11142	We Won't Live in A.../Tulips and Heather	1952	3.75	7.50	15.00
❑ 11205	April Sings/Golden Haired Boy	1952	3.75	7.50	15.00
❑ 11210	When I Dream/Don't Send Me Home	1952	3.75	7.50	15.00
—With Judy Johnson					
❑ 11266	High Noon/Padam Padam	1952	3.75	7.50	15.00
❑ 11296	Say You'll Wait for Me/My Search for You	1952	3.75	7.50	15.00
❑ 11384	My Ever Lovin'/As Long As You Care	1952	3.75	7.50	15.00
❑ 11394	How Do You Speak to An Angel/The Donkey Song	1953	3.75	7.50	15.00
❑ 11492	I'm So Lonesome/There's Music in You	1953	3.75	7.50	15.00
❑ 11556	A Little Kiss Each Morning/Love You	1953	3.75	7.50	15.00
—With Judy Johnson					
❑ 12004	Wanderin'/You're Nearer	1955	3.00	6.00	12.00

HAYES, ISAAC

Number	Title (A Side/B Side)	Yr	VG	VG+	NM
ABC/HBS					
❑ 12118	Chocolate Chip/(Instrumental)	1975	—	2.00	4.00
❑ 12138	Come Live with Me/Body Language	1975	—	2.00	4.00
❑ 12171	Disco Connection/St. Thomas Square	1976	—	2.00	4.00
—By the "Isaac Hayes Movement"					
❑ 12176	Rock Me Easy Baby (Pt. 1)/Rock Me Easy Baby (Pt. 2)	1976	—	2.00	4.00
❑ 12206	Juicy Fruit (Disco Freak) (Pt. 1)/Juicy Fruit (Disco Freak) (Pt. 2)	1976	—	2.00	4.00
BRUNSWICK					
❑ 55258	Sweet Temptation/Laura	1964	2.50	5.00	10.00
CAPITOL					
❑ S7-18869	Walk On By/Tired of Being Alone	1995	—	—	3.00
—B-side by Al Green					
COLUMBIA					
❑ 06363	Ike's Rap/Hey Girl (Edited)	1986	—	—	3.00
❑ 06363 [PS]	Ike's Rap/Hey Girl (Edited)	1986	—	2.00	4.00
❑ 06655	Thing for You/Thank God for Love	1987	—	—	3.00
❑ 07104	If You Want My Lovin' (Do Me Right)/(Instrumental)	1987	—	—	3.00
❑ 07978	Showdown/(Instrumental)	1988	—	—	3.00
❑ 08116	Let Me Be Your Everything/Curious	1988	—	—	3.00

Number	Title (A Side/B Side)	Yr	VG	VG+	NM
ENTERPRISE					
❑ 002	Precious Precious/Going to Chicago Blues	1969	2.00	4.00	8.00
❑ 9003	By the Time I Get to Phoenix/Walk On By	1969	—	3.00	6.00
❑ 9006	The Mistletoe and Me/Winter Snow	1969	—	3.00	6.00
❑ 9017	I Stand Accused/I Just Don't Know What to Do with Myself	1970	—	2.50	5.00
❑ 9028	The Look of Love/Ike's Mood	1970	—	2.50	5.00
❑ 9031	Never Can Say Goodbye/I Can't Help It If I'm Still in Love with You	1971	—	2.50	5.00
❑ 9038	Theme from Shaft/Cafe Regio's	1971	—	2.50	5.00
❑ 9042	Do Your Thing/Ellie's Love Theme	1972	—	2.50	5.00
❑ 9045	Let's Stay Together/Soulville	1972	—	2.50	5.00
❑ 9049	Ain't That Loving You (For More Reasons Than One)/Baby I'm-a Want You	1972	—	2.50	5.00
—With David Porter					
❑ 9058	Theme from The Men/Type Thang	1972	—	2.50	5.00
❑ 9065	(If Loving You Is Wrong) I Don't Want to Be Right/Rolling Down a Mountainside	1973	—	2.50	5.00
❑ 9085	Joy (Part 1)/Joy (Part 2)	1973	—	2.50	5.00
❑ 9095	Wonderful/Someone Made You for Me	1974	—	2.50	5.00
❑ 9104	Title Theme/Hung Up on My Baby	1974	—	2.50	5.00
POLYDOR					
❑ 2011	Don't Let Go/You Can't Hold Your Woman	1979	—	2.00	4.00
❑ 2068	A Few More Kisses to Go/What Does It Take	1980	—	2.00	4.00
❑ 2090	I Ain't Never/Love Has Been Good to Us	1980	—	2.00	4.00
❑ 2102	It's All in the Game/Wherever You Are	1980	—	2.00	4.00
❑ 2182	I'm So Proud/I'm Gonna Make Me Love You	1981	—	2.00	4.00
❑ 2192	Fugitive/Lifetime Thing	1981	—	2.00	4.00
❑ 14446	Out of the Ghetto/It's Heaven to Me	1977	—	2.00	4.00
❑ 14464	Moonlight Lovin' (Menage a Trois)/It's Heaven to Me	1978	—	2.00	4.00
❑ 14521	Zeke the Freak/If We Ever Needed Peace	1978	—	2.00	4.00
❑ 14534	Just the Way You Are (Part 1)/Just the Way You Are (Part 2)	1979	—	2.00	4.00
STAX					
❑ 3209	Feel Like Makin' Love (Part 1)/Feel Like Makin' Love (Part 2)	1978	—	2.50	5.00
VIRGIN					
❑ 38759	Only If You Were Here/Oh Come All Ye Faithful	2000	—	2.00	4.00
—B-side by Ideal					

HAYES, ISAAC, AND DIONNE WARWICK

Also see each artist's individual listings.

Number	Title (A Side/B Side)	Yr	VG	VG+	NM
ABC/HBS					
❑ 12253	By the Time I Get to Phoenix—I Say a Little Prayer/That's the Way I Like It—Cry Down	1977	—	2.00	4.00

HAYES, JIMMY, AND THE SOUL SURFERS

Number	Title (A Side/B Side)	Yr	VG	VG+	NM
IMPERIAL					
❑ 5986	Summer Surfin'/Down on the Beach	1963	6.25	12.50	25.00

HAYES, LINDA

Number	Title (A Side/B Side)	Yr	VG	VG+	NM
ANTLER					
❑ 4000	I Had a Dream/You Ain't Movin' Me	1956	7.50	15.00	30.00
DECCA					
❑ 29644	Our Love's Forever Blessed/You're the Only One for Me	1955	7.50	15.00	30.00
HOLLYWOOD					
❑ 1003	Take Me Back/Yours for the Asking	1953	12.50	25.00	50.00
❑ 1009	No Next Time/Don't Do Nothin' Baby	1954	10.00	20.00	40.00
❑ 1016	Play It Right/Your Back's Out	1954	10.00	20.00	40.00
❑ 1019	Non-Cooperation/Grrr! Mambo	1954	10.00	20.00	40.00
❑ 1027	Change of Heart/Darling Angel	1954	10.00	20.00	40.00
❑ 1031	Johnny Ace's Last Letter/Why Johnny Why	1955	12.50	25.00	50.00
—With Johnny Moore					
❑ 1032	Our Love's Forever Blessed/You're the Only One for Me	1955	15.00	30.00	60.00
KING					
❑ 4752	My Name Ain't Annie/Let's Babalu	1954	18.75	37.50	75.00
❑ 4773	Please Have Mercy/Oochi Poochi	1955	12.50	25.00	50.00
RECORDED IN HOLLYWOOD					
❑ 244	Yes! I Know (What You're Putting Down)/Sister Ann	1953	12.50	25.00	50.00
❑ 246	Big City (Part 1)/Big City (Part 2)	1953	12.50	25.00	50.00

HAYES, TOMMY

Number	Title (A Side/B Side)	Yr	VG	VG+	NM
PHILIPS					
❑ 40259	Trance/Glistening Lights	1965	7.50	15.00	30.00
—The Four Seasons sing backup					

HAYWARD, JUSTIN

Also see THE MOODY BLUES.

Number	Title (A Side/B Side)	Yr	VG	VG+	NM
COLUMBIA					
❑ 10799	Forever Autumn/The Fighting Machine	1978	2.00	4.00	8.00
DERAM					
❑ 401	Night Flight/Suitcase	1980	—	2.00	4.00
❑ 402	A Face in the Crowd/It's Not On	1980	—	2.00	4.00
❑ 7541	Lay It On Me/Songwriter Part 2	1977	—	2.00	4.00
❑ 7542	Country Girl/Songwriter Part 2	1977	—	2.00	4.00
RED BIRD					
❑ 10-049	London Is Behind Me/Day Must Come	1966	5.00	10.00	20.00

HAYWARD, JUSTIN, AND JOHN LODGE

Also see each artist's individual listings; THE MOODY BLUES.

Number	Title (A Side/B Side)	Yr	VG	VG+	NM
THRESHOLD					
❑ 67019	I Dreamed Last Night/Remember Me, My Friend	1975	—	2.00	4.00
❑ 67021	Blue Guitar/When You Wake Up	1975	—	2.00	4.00
❑ 67021 [PS]	Blue Guitar/When You Wake Up	1975	—	2.50	5.00

HAYWOOD, LEON

Number	Title (A Side/B Side)	Yr	VG	VG+	NM
20TH CENTURY					
❑ 2003	One Way Ticket to Loveland/There Ain't Enough Love Around	1972	—	3.00	6.00
❑ 2022	La La Song/Sweet Loving Fair	1973	—	3.00	6.00
❑ 2065	Keep It in the Family/Long As There's You (I Got Love)	1974	—	2.50	5.00
❑ 2103	Sugar Lump/That Sweet Woman of Mine	1974	—	2.50	5.00
❑ 2146	Believe Half of What You See (And None of What You Hear)/The Day I Laid Eyes on You	1974	—	2.50	5.00
❑ 2191	Come an' Get Yourself Some/B.M.F. Beautiful	1975	—	3.00	6.00
❑ 2191	Come an' Get Yourself Some/Who You Been Givin' It Up To	1975	—	2.50	5.00
❑ 2228	I Want'a Do Something Freaky to You/I Know What Love Is	1975	—	2.50	5.00
❑ 2264	Just Your Fool/Consider the Source	1975	—	2.50	5.00
❑ 2285	Strokin' (Part 1)/Strokin' (Part 2)	1976	—	2.50	5.00
❑ 2443	Don't Push It Don't Force It/Who You Been Givin' It Up To	1980	—	2.00	4.00
❑ 2454	If You're Lookin' for a Night of Fun (Look Past Me, I'm Not the One)/That's What Time It Is	1980	—	2.00	4.00
❑ 2469	Daydream/Love Is What We Came Here For	1980	—	2.00	4.00
ATLANTIC					
❑ 2799	You and Your Moody Ways/You Know What	1971	—	3.00	6.00
❑ 2858	Clean Up Your Own Back Yard/String Bean	1972	—	3.00	6.00
CAPITOL					
❑ 2584	Just Your Fool/Consider the Source	1969	3.75	7.50	15.00
❑ 2752	I Wanna Thank You/I Was Sent to Love You	1970	3.75	7.50	15.00
CASABLANCA					
❑ 812164-7	I'm Out to Catch/Keep It in the Family	1983	—	—	3.00
—With Karen Roberts					
❑ 814217-7	T.V. Mama/Steppin' Out	1983	—	—	3.00
COLUMBIA					
❑ 10413	The Streets Will Love You to Death - Part 1/The Streets Will Love You to Death - Part 2	1976	—	2.00	4.00
❑ 10477	Dream Dream/Let Me Make It Good	1977	—	2.00	4.00
DECCA					
❑ 32164	It's Got to Be Mellow/Cornbread & Buttermilk	1967	2.00	4.00	8.00
❑ 32230	Mellow Moonlight/Tennessee Waltz	1967	2.00	4.00	8.00
❑ 32310	Mercy, Mercy, Mercy/It's the Last Time	1968	2.00	4.00	8.00
❑ 32348	I Want to Talk About My Baby/You Don't Have to See Me Cry	1968	2.00	4.00	8.00
❑ 32414	Blues Get Off My Shoulder/Everyday Will Be Like a Holiday	1968	2.00	4.00	8.00
FANTASY					
❑ 581	The Truth About Money/Would I	1964	6.25	12.50	25.00
FAT FISH					
❑ 8005	Soul Cargo/(B-side unknown)	1966	7.50	15.00	30.00
IMPERIAL					
❑ 66123	She's With Her Other Love/Pain in My Heart	1965	3.75	7.50	15.00
—As "Leon Hayward"					
❑ 66149	Soul-On/1-2-3	1965	3.00	6.00	12.00
MCA					
❑ 40793	Super Sexy/Life Goes On	1977	—	2.00	4.00
❑ 40849	Double My Pleasure/It's Gonna Be Alright	1978	—	2.00	4.00
❑ 40889	Fine and Healthy Thing/She's Built, She's Stacked	1978	—	2.00	4.00
❑ 40941	Party/Life Goes On	1978	—	2.00	4.00
❑ 40989	Disco Fever/Self Respect	1979	—	2.00	4.00
❑ 41035	Energy/You Bring Out the Freak in Me	1979	—	2.00	4.00
MODERN					
❑ 99708	Tenderoni/(Instrumental)	1984	—	—	3.00

HEAD, MURRAY

Number	Title (A Side/B Side)	Yr	VG	VG+	NM
A&M					
❑ 1796	Say It Ain't So, Joe/She's Such a Drag	1976	—	2.00	4.00
❑ 1836	Somebody's Rockin' My Dreamboat/She's Such a Drag	1976	—	2.00	4.00
DECCA					
❑ 32603	Superstar/John Nineteen Forty-One	1969	—	3.00	6.00
—First pressings use this reference on the A-side: "Superstar (From JESUS CHRIST)"					
❑ 32603	Superstar/John Nineteen Forty-One	1970	—	2.50	5.00
—Reissues have the word "Superstar" without a subtitle, and small print mentions the LP "Jesus Christ Superstar"					
❑ 32603 [PS]	Superstar/John Nineteen Forty-One	1970	2.00	4.00	8.00
—Picture sleeve accompanies second pressings					
❑ 32709	Heaven on Their Minds/Strange Thing (Mystifying)	1970	—	2.50	5.00
❑ 32709 [PS]	Heaven on Their Minds/Strange Thing (Mystifying)	1970	2.00	4.00	8.00
RCA					
❑ PB-13988	One Night in Bangkok/Merano	1985	—	2.00	4.00
❑ PB-13988 [PS]	One Night in Bangkok/Merano	1985	—	2.00	4.00
❑ PB-14152	Pity the Child/The Deal (No Deal)	1985	—	2.00	4.00
❑ GB-14339	One Night in Bangkok/Pity the Child	1986	—	—	3.00
—Gold Standard Series					

HEAD, ROY

Number	Title (A Side/B Side)	Yr	VG	VG+	NM
ABC					
❑ 12346	How You See 'Em, Now You Don't/Smooth Whiskey	1978	—	2.00	4.00
❑ 12383	Tonight's the Night/A Lady in My Room	1978	—	2.00	4.00
❑ 12418	Dixie/Love Survived	1978	—	2.00	4.00
❑ 12462 [DJ]	Kiss You and Make It Better (mono/stereo)	1979	—	2.00	4.00
—May be promo only					
ABC DOT					
❑ 17608	Lady Luck and Mother Nature/The Door I Used to Close	1976	—	2.00	4.00
❑ 17629	Ain't It Funny (How Times Haven't Changed)/A Bridge for Crawling Back	1976	—	2.00	4.00
❑ 17650	One Night/Deep Elem Blues	1976	—	2.00	4.00

Number	Title (A Side/B Side)	Yr	VG	VG+	NM
❑ 17669	Just Because/Angel with a Broken Wing	1976	—	2.00	4.00
❑ 17706	Julianne/Velvet Strings	1977	—	2.00	4.00
❑ 17722	Come to Me/Georgia on My Mind	1977	—	2.00	4.00

ABC DUNHILL

Number	Title (A Side/B Side)	Yr	VG	VG+	NM
❑ 4240	I'm Not a Fool Anymore/Mama Mama	1970	—	3.00	6.00

ATLANTIC AMERICA

Number	Title (A Side/B Side)	Yr	VG	VG+	NM
❑ 99529	There's Something on Your Mind/Everything A Man Can Do (And I Love You)	1986	—	—	3.00

AVION

Number	Title (A Side/B Side)	Yr	VG	VG+	NM
❑ 105	Where Did He Go Right/(B-side unknown)	1983	—	3.50	7.00

BACK BEAT

Number	Title (A Side/B Side)	Yr	VG	VG+	NM
❑ 543	Teenage Letter/Pain	1965	3.00	6.00	12.00
❑ 546	Treat Her Right/So Long, My Love	1965	4.00	8.00	16.00
❑ 555	Apple of My Eye/I Pass the Day	1965	3.00	6.00	12.00
❑ 560	My Babe/Pain	1966	3.00	6.00	12.00
❑ 563	Driving Wheel/Wigglin' and Gigglin'	1966	3.00	6.00	12.00
❑ 571	Don't Cry No More/To Make a Big Man Cry	1966	3.00	6.00	12.00
❑ 576	You're (Almost) Tough/Tush Hog	1966	3.00	6.00	12.00
❑ 582	Nobody But Me/A Good Man Is Hard to Find	1967	2.50	5.00	10.00

CHURCHILL

Number	Title (A Side/B Side)	Yr	VG	VG+	NM
❑ 7778	After Texas/California Day	1981	—	2.50	5.00

ELEKTRA

Number	Title (A Side/B Side)	Yr	VG	VG+	NM
❑ 46549	In Our Room/Things I Never Could Have Left Behind	1979	—	2.00	4.00
❑ 46582	The Fire of Two Old Flames/Under Suspicion	1980	—	2.00	4.00
❑ 46653	Long Drop/Gonna Save It for My Baby	1980	—	2.00	4.00
❑ 47029	Drinking Them Long Necks/Baby's Found Another Way to Love Me	1980	—	2.00	4.00
❑ 47081	I've Never Gone to Bed With an Ugly Woman/All Night Long Is Gone	1981	—	2.00	4.00

MEGA

Number	Title (A Side/B Side)	Yr	VG	VG+	NM
❑ 1219	Baby's Not Home/Do What You Can Do	1974	—	2.50	5.00

MERCURY

Number	Title (A Side/B Side)	Yr	VG	VG+	NM
❑ 72750	Got Down on Saturday (Sunday in the Rain)/The Grass Was Green	1967	2.00	4.00	8.00
❑ 72799	Broadway Walk/Turn Out the Lights	1968	2.00	4.00	8.00
❑ 72848	Ain't Goin' Down Right/Lovin' Man on Your Hands	1968	2.00	4.00	8.00
❑ 72922	I Miss You Baby/I Want Some Action	1969	2.00	4.00	8.00

NSD

Number	Title (A Side/B Side)	Yr	VG	VG+	NM
❑ 129	Play Another Gettin' Drunk and Take Somebody Home Song/Your Next One and Only	1982	—	2.50	5.00
❑ 146	The Trouble with Hearts/Naughty Smile	1982	—	2.50	5.00
❑ 156	Your Mama Don't Dance/Party Time	1982	—	2.50	5.00

SCEPTER

Number	Title (A Side/B Side)	Yr	VG	VG+	NM
❑ 12116	Just a Little Bit/Treat Me Right	1965	2.50	5.00	10.00
❑ 12117	Won't Be Blue/One More Time	1965	2.50	5.00	10.00
❑ 12124	Get Back — Part 1/Get Back — Part 2	1965	2.50	5.00	10.00
❑ 12138	Convicted/One More Time	1966	2.50	5.00	10.00

SHANNON

Number	Title (A Side/B Side)	Yr	VG	VG+	NM
❑ 829	The Most Wanted Woman in Town/Gingerbread Man	1975	—	2.50	5.00
❑ 833	Help Yourself to Me/To Make a Big Man Cry	1975	—	2.50	5.00
❑ 838	I'll Take It/The One That Got Away	1975	—	2.50	5.00

TEXAS CRUDE

Number	Title (A Side/B Side)	Yr	VG	VG+	NM
❑ 614	Break Out the Good Stuff/She Needs Time	1985	2.00	4.00	8.00

TMI

Number	Title (A Side/B Side)	Yr	VG	VG+	NM
❑ 75-0103	Rock and Roll Mood/You Got the Power	1972	—	2.50	5.00
❑ 75-0106	Why Don't We Go Somewhere and Love/Smell-A-Woman	1972	—	2.50	5.00
❑ BTBO-0111	Small Town Girl/Chug All Night	1973	—	2.50	5.00
❑ 75-0113	Carol/Clyde O'Riley	1973	—	2.50	5.00
❑ 9000	Puff of Smoke/Lord Take a Bow	1971	—	3.00	6.00
❑ 9010	Bit By Bit/Wait Till I Arrive	1972	—	3.00	6.00

TNT

Number	Title (A Side/B Side)	Yr	VG	VG+	NM
❑ 194	Don't Be Blue/One More Time	1965	3.75	7.50	15.00

HEART

Well-known Pacific Northwest-based group featuring the Wilson sisters, Ann and Nancy. Also see BORDERSONG; ANN WILSON; ANN AND NANCY WILSON.

CAPITOL

Number	Title (A Side/B Side)	Yr	VG	VG+	NM
❑ B-5481	What About Love/Heart of Darkness	1985	—	—	3.00
❑ B-5481 [PS]	What About Love/Heart of Darkness	1985	—	—	3.00
❑ B-5512	Never (Remix)/Shell Shock	1985	—	—	3.00
—A-side eventually replaced original mix on "Heart" LP					
❑ B-5512 [PS]	Never (Remix)/Shell Shock	1985	—	—	3.00
❑ B-5541	These Dreams/Shell Shock	1985	—	—	3.00
❑ B-5541 [PS]	These Dreams/Shell Shock	1985	—	—	3.00
❑ B-5572	Nothin' at All/The Wolf	1986	—	—	3.00
❑ B-5572 [PS]	Nothin' at All/The Wolf	1986	—	—	3.00
❑ B-5605	If Looks Could Kill/What He Don't Know	1986	—	—	3.00
❑ B-5605 [PS]	If Looks Could Kill/What He Don't Know	1986	—	—	3.00
❑ S7-17799	Will You Be There (In the Morning)/Back to Avalon	1994	—	—	3.00
❑ S7-17904	The Woman in Me/Risin' Suspicion	1994	—	—	3.00
❑ B-44002	Alone/Barracuda (Live)	1987	—	—	3.00
❑ B-44002 [PS]	Alone/Barracuda (Live)	1987	—	—	3.00
❑ B-44040	Who Will You Run To/Magic Man (Live)	1987	—	—	3.00
❑ B-44040 [PS]	Who Will You Run To/Magic Man (Live)	1987	—	—	3.00
❑ B-44089	There's the Girl/Bad Animals	1987	—	—	3.00
❑ B-44089 [PS]	There's the Girl/Bad Animals	1987	—	—	3.00
❑ B-44116	I Want You So Bad/Easy Target	1988	—	—	3.00
❑ NR-44507	All I Wanna Do Is Make Love to You/Call of the Wild	1990	—	—	3.00
❑ NR-44507 [PS]	All I Wanna Do Is Make Love to You/Call of the Wild	1990	—	2.00	4.00
❑ NR-44553	I Didn't Want to Need You/The Night	1990	—	—	3.00

EPIC

Number	Title (A Side/B Side)	Yr	VG	VG+	NM
❑ 02925	This Man Is Mine/America	1982	—	—	3.00
❑ 02925 [PS]	This Man Is Mine/America	1982	—	—	3.00
❑ 03071	Private Audition/Bright Light Girl	1982	—	—	3.00
❑ 04047	How Can I Refuse/Johnny Moon	1983	—	—	3.00
❑ 04047 [PS]	How Can I Refuse/Johnny Moon	1983	—	—	3.00
❑ 04184	Allies/Together Now	1983	—	—	3.00
❑ 04184 [PS]	Allies/Together Now	1983	—	—	3.00
❑ 08101	Barracuda/Straight On	1988	—	—	3.00
—Reissue					
❑ 50847	Even It Up/Pilot	1980	—	2.00	4.00
❑ 50874	Raised on You/Down on Me	1980	—	2.00	4.00
❑ 50892	Bebe Le Strange/Silver Wheels	1980	—	2.00	4.00
❑ 50950	Tell It Like It Is/Strange Euphoria	1980	—	2.00	4.00
❑ 51010	Unchained Melody/Mistral Wind	1981	—	2.00	4.00

MUSHROOM

Number	Title (A Side/B Side)	Yr	VG	VG+	NM
❑ 7011	Magic Man/How Deep It Goes	1976	—	2.50	5.00
❑ 7021	Crazy on You/Dreamboat Annie	1976	—	2.50	5.00
❑ 7023	Dreamboat Annie/Sing Child	1976	—	2.50	5.00
—Bizarre version of A-side with part of the intro to "Crazy on You" grafted on.					
❑ 7031	Heartless/Just the Wine	1978	—	2.00	4.00
❑ 7035	Without You/Here Song	1978	—	2.00	4.00
❑ 7043	Magazine/Devil Delight	1978	—	2.00	4.00

PORTRAIT

Number	Title (A Side/B Side)	Yr	VG	VG+	NM
❑ 8101	Barracuda/Straight On	1981	—	—	3.00
—Reissue					
❑ 70004	Barracuda/Cry to Me	1977	—	2.00	4.00
❑ 70008	Little Queen/Treat Me Well	1977	—	2.00	4.00
❑ 70010	Kick It Out/Go On, Cry	1977	—	2.00	4.00
❑ 70020	Straight On/Lighter Touch	1978	—	2.00	4.00
❑ 70025	Dog and Butterfly/Mistral Wind	1979	—	2.00	4.00

HEART (2)

EMI

Number	Title (A Side/B Side)	Yr	VG	VG+	NM
❑ 4008	Beautiful Woman/Lovemaker	1974	—	2.00	4.00

HEART (3)

LOOK

Number	Title (A Side/B Side)	Yr	VG	VG+	NM
❑ 5023	Give Me a Happy Heart/Now	1969	—	3.00	6.00
❑ 5029	I Love You/Love	1970	—	3.00	6.00

HEART (U)

This could be group (3), or it might not be. It is definitely not by the most famous Heart.

REPRISE

Number	Title (A Side/B Side)	Yr	VG	VG+	NM
❑ 0772	Heartbeat/The Train	1968	—	3.00	6.00

HEART-THROBS, THE

ALADDIN

Number	Title (A Side/B Side)	Yr	VG	VG+	NM
❑ 3394	So Glad/All the Way Home	1957	10.00	20.00	40.00

LAMP

Number	Title (A Side/B Side)	Yr	VG	VG+	NM
❑ 2010	So Glad/All the Way Home	1957	10.00	20.00	40.00

HEARTBEATS, THE

Also see SHEP AND THE LIMELITES.

GEE

Number	Title (A Side/B Side)	Yr	VG	VG+	NM
❑ 1043	When I Found You/Hands Off My Baby	1957	12.50	25.00	50.00
❑ 1047	500 Miles to Go/After New Year's Eve	1958	10.00	20.00	40.00
—Red label					
❑ 1047	500 Miles to Go/After New Year's Eve	1958	5.00	10.00	20.00
—Gray label					
❑ 1061	People Are Talking/Your Way	1960	5.00	10.00	20.00
❑ 1062	Darling How Long/Hurry Home Baby	1960	5.00	10.00	20.00

GUYDEN

Number	Title (A Side/B Side)	Yr	VG	VG+	NM
❑ 2011	One Million Years/Let's Get Married	1959	10.00	20.00	40.00
—Yellow label					
❑ 2011	One Million Years/Let's Get Married	1959	7.50	15.00	30.00
—Purple label					

HULL

Number	Title (A Side/B Side)	Yr	VG	VG+	NM
❑ 711	Crazy for You/Rockin-N-Rollin-N-Rhythm-N-Blues-N	1955	75.00	150.00	300.00
—Pink label, "Sheppard-Miller" as A-side composers					
❑ 711	Crazy for You/Rockin-N-Rollin-N-Rhythm-N-Blues-N	1955	50.00	100.00	200.00
—Pink label, "Miller" as A-side composer					
❑ 711	Crazy for You/Rockin-N-Rollin-N-Rhythm-N-Blues-N	1955	25.00	50.00	100.00
—Black label					
❑ 711 [DJ]	Crazy for You/Rockin-N-Rollin-N-Rhythm-N-Blues-N	1955	150.00	300.00	600.00
—White label					
❑ 713	Darling How Long/Hurry Home Baby	1956	50.00	100.00	200.00
❑ 716	People Are Talking/Your Way	1956	50.00	100.00	200.00
❑ 720	A Thousand Miles Away/Oh Baby Don't	1957	62.50	125.00	250.00
—Black label					
❑ 720	A Thousand Miles Away/Oh Baby Don't	1957	20.00	450.00	80.00
—Red label					

JUBILEE

Number	Title (A Side/B Side)	Yr	VG	VG+	NM
❑ 5202	Finally/Boil and Bubble	1955	7.50	15.00	30.00

NETWORK

Number	Title (A Side/B Side)	Yr	VG	VG+	NM
❑ 71200	Tormented/After Everybody's Gone	1955	75.00	150.00	300.00
—Cream label, black vinyl					
❑ 71200	Tormented/After Everybody's Gone	195?	30.00	60.00	120.00
—Yellow label, black vinyl					
❑ 71200	Tormented/After Everybody's Gone	195?	6.25	12.50	25.00
—Red vinyl The Network release as "The Heart Beats Quintet"					

RAMA

Number	Title (A Side/B Side)	Yr	VG	VG+	NM
❑ 216	A Thousand Miles Away/Oh Baby Don't	1956	20.00	40.00	80.00
❑ 222	Wedding Bells/I Won't Be the Fool Anymore	1957	25.00	50.00	100.00
❑ 231	I Want to Know/Everybody's Somebody's Fool	1957	25.00	50.00	100.00

ROULETTE

Number	Title (A Side/B Side)	Yr	VG	VG+	NM
❑ 4054	I Found a Job/Down on My Knees	1958	7.50	15.00	30.00
❑ 4091	One Day Next Year/Sometimes I Wonder	1958	7.50	15.00	30.00
❑ 4194	Crazy for You/Down on My Knees	1959	7.50	15.00	30.00

HEARTBREAKERS, THE

Several different groups.

Number	Title (A Side/B Side)	Yr	VG	VG+	NM
ATCO					
❑ 6258	The Willow Wept/You Had Time	1963	5.00	10.00	20.00
BRENT					
❑ 7037	I'm Leaving It All Up to You/Corrido Mash	1962	7.50	15.00	30.00
DONNA					
❑ 1381	Everytime I See You/Cradle Rock	1963	30.00	60.00	120.00
—Frank Zappa plays guitar on this record					
LINDA					
❑ 114	Please Answer/She Is My Baby	1964	3.75	7.50	15.00
MARKAY					
❑ 106	Since You've Been Gone/John Law	1962	20.00	40.00	80.00
MAX'S KANSAS CITY					
❑ 213	All By Myself/Milk Me	1979	6.25	12.50	25.00
MGM					
❑ 13129	It's Hard Being a Girl/Special Occasions	1963	3.75	7.50	15.00
RCA VICTOR					
❑ 47-4327	Heartbreaker/Wanda	1951	150.00	300.00	600.00
❑ 47-4508	You're So Necessary to Me/I'm Only Following My Heart	1952	150.00	300.00	600.00
❑ 47-4662	Why Don't I/Rockin' Daddy-O	1952	125.00	250.00	500.00
❑ 47-4849	There Is Time/It's OK With Me	1952	125.00	250.00	500.00
SWAN					
❑ 4242	Baby Baby/I Told You So	1966	3.75	7.50	15.00
VIK					
❑ 0261	Without a Cause/One, Two, I Love You	1957	37.50	75.00	150.00
❑ 0299	My Love/Love You Till the Day I Die	1957	62.50	125.00	250.00

HEARTS, THE

Number	Title (A Side/B Side)	Yr	VG	VG+	NM
BATON					
❑ 208	Lonely Nights/Oo-Wee	1955	12.50	25.00	50.00
❑ 211	All My Love Belongs to You/Talk About Him Girlie	1955	12.50	25.00	50.00
❑ 215	Gone, Gone, Gone/Until the Real Thing Comes Along	1955	12.50	25.00	50.00
❑ 222	Disappointed Bride/Going Home to Stay	1956	7.50	15.00	30.00
❑ 228	He Drives Me Crazy/I Had a Guy	1956	6.25	12.50	25.00
J&S					
❑ 425/6	My Love Has Gone/You or Me Have Got to Go	1959	12.50	25.00	50.00
❑ 995	A Thousand Years from Today/I Feel So Good	1960	10.00	20.00	40.00
❑ 1180/1	You Weren't Home/I Couldn't Let You See Me Crying	1961	12.50	25.00	50.00
❑ 1626/7	I Want Your Love Tonight/Like Later Baby	1958	12.50	25.00	50.00
❑ 1657	Dancing in a Dream World/You Needn't Tell, I Know	1957	15.00	30.00	60.00
❑ 1660	So Long, Baby/You Say You Love Me	1957	15.00	30.00	60.00
❑ 4571/2	Goodbye Baby/There Is No Love at All	1959	10.00	20.00	40.00
❑ 10002/3	If I Had Known/There Are So Many Ways	1958	12.50	25.00	50.00
TUFF					
❑ 370	Dear Abby/(Instrumental)	1963	3.75	7.50	15.00

HEATHERTON, JOEY

Number	Title (A Side/B Side)	Yr	VG	VG+	NM
CORAL					
❑ 62422	That's How It Goes/I'll Be Seeing You	1964	7.50	15.00	30.00
❑ 62422 [PS]	That's How It Goes/I'll Be Seeing You	1964	10.00	20.00	40.00
❑ 62451	Hullaballoo/My Blood Runs Cold	1965	6.25	12.50	25.00
❑ 62459	Tomorrow Is Another Day/But He's Not Mine	1965	6.25	12.50	25.00
DECCA					
❑ 31962	Live and Learn/When You Call Me Baby	1966	15.00	30.00	60.00
❑ 31962 [PS]	Live and Learn/When You Call Me Baby	1966	20.00	40.00	80.00
MGM					
❑ 14387	Gone/The Road I Took to You	1972	—	2.50	5.00
❑ 14387 [PS]	Gone/The Road I Took to You	1972	2.50	5.00	10.00
❑ 14434	I'm Sorry/Crazy	1972	—	3.00	6.00
❑ 14434	I'm Sorry/Someone to Watch Over Me	1972	—	2.50	5.00
❑ 14499	Crazy/God Only Knows	1973	—	2.50	5.00

HEBB, BOBBY

Number	Title (A Side/B Side)	Yr	VG	VG+	NM
BOOM					
❑ 60017	Betty Jo from Ohio/Sam Hall Jr.	1966	2.00	4.00	8.00
CADET					
❑ 5690	I Was a Boy When You Needed a Man/Woman in the Window	1972	—	2.50	5.00
LAURIE					
❑ 3632	True, I Love You/Proud Soul Heritage	1975	—	2.50	5.00
❑ 3638	Sunny '76/Sunny Disco	1976	—	2.50	5.00
PHILIPS					
❑ 40365	Sunny/Bread	1966	2.50	5.00	10.00
❑ 40400	A Satisfied Mind/Love, Love, Love	1966	2.00	4.00	8.00
❑ 40400 [PS]	A Satisfied Mind/Love, Love, Love	1966	3.00	6.00	12.00
❑ 40421	Love Me/Crazy Baby	1966	2.00	4.00	8.00
❑ 40431	My Pretty Sunshine/Ooh La La	1967	2.00	4.00	8.00
❑ 40448	I Love Everything About You/Some Kind of Magic	1967	2.00	4.00	8.00
❑ 40482	Everything Is Coming Up Roses/Bound by Love	1967	2.00	4.00	8.00
❑ 40551	Dreamy/You Want to Change Me	1968	2.00	4.00	8.00
RICH					
❑ 1006	Cherry/Feel So Good	1960	3.75	7.50	15.00
❑ 1740	Just a Little Bit More/Walk Me On Alone	1962	3.75	7.50	15.00
SCEPTER					
❑ 12166	I Love Mary (Part 1)/I Love Mary (Part 2)	1966	2.00	4.00	8.00

HEDGEHOPPERS ANONYMOUS

Number	Title (A Side/B Side)	Yr	VG	VG+	NM
PARROT					
❑ 3002	Remember/Baby (You're My Everything)	1966	2.50	5.00	10.00
❑ 9800	It's Good News Week/Afraid of Love	1965	3.00	6.00	12.00
❑ 9817	Don't Push Me/Please Don't Hurt Your Heart for Me	1966	2.50	5.00	10.00

HEINZ

Number	Title (A Side/B Side)	Yr	VG	VG+	NM
LONDON					
❑ 9619	Just Like Eddie/Don't You Knock on My Door	1963	3.75	7.50	15.00
TOWER					
❑ 110	Questions I Can't Answer/The Beating of My Heart	1964	5.00	10.00	20.00
❑ 172	Digging My Potatoes/Don't Think Twice, It's All Right	1965	5.00	10.00	20.00
❑ 195	Don't Worry Baby/Heart Full of Sorrow	1966	7.50	15.00	30.00
❑ 253	I'm Not a Bad Boy/Movin' In	1966	5.00	10.00	20.00

HELM, LEVON

Also see THE BAND; LEVON AND THE HAWKS.

Number	Title (A Side/B Side)	Yr	VG	VG+	NM
ABC					
❑ 12336	Milk Cow Boogie/Blues So Bad	1978	—	2.00	4.00
❑ 12416	Ain't No Way to Forget You/Standing on a Mountaintop	1978	—	2.00	4.00
A&M					
❑ 2291	The Death of Me/One More Shot	1980	—	2.00	4.00
—With Johnny Cash					
MCA					
❑ 41202	Working in the Coal Mine/Blue Moon of Kentucky	1980	—	2.00	4.00
❑ 41242	America's Farm/Blue Moon of Kentucky	1980	—	2.00	4.00

HELMS, BOBBY

Number	Title (A Side/B Side)	Yr	VG	VG+	NM
CAPITOL					
❑ 3003	The Only Thing That Matters/Just Hold My Hand and Sing	1970	2.00	4.00	8.00
CERTRON					
❑ 10002	Mary Goes 'Round/Cold Winds Blow on Me	1970	2.00	4.00	8.00
❑ 10021	Jingle Bell Rock/The Old Year Is Gone	1970	2.00	4.00	8.00
❑ 10023	I Wouldn't Take the World for You/Look What You've Done	1970	2.00	4.00	8.00
COLUMBIA					
❑ 4-42801	Fraulein/My Special Angel	1963	2.50	5.00	10.00
❑ 4-43031	It's a Girl/Put Your Arms Around Him	1964	2.50	5.00	10.00
DECCA					
❑ 9-29947	Tennessee Rock 'N' Roll/I Don't Owe You Nothing	1956	12.50	25.00	50.00
❑ 9-30194	Fraulein/(Got a) Heartsick Feeling	1957	5.00	10.00	20.00
❑ 9-30194 [PS]	Fraulein/(Got a) Heartsick Feeling	1957	12.50	25.00	50.00
❑ 9-30423	My Special Angel/Standing at the End of My World	1957	6.25	12.50	25.00
❑ 9-30513	Jingle Bell Rock/Captain Santa Claus	1957	6.25	12.50	25.00
—Black label with star					
❑ 9-30513	Jingle Bell Rock/Captain Santa Claus	1960	3.00	6.00	12.00
—Black label with color bars					
❑ 9-30513 [PS]	Jingle Bell Rock/Captain Santa Claus	1957	12.50	25.00	50.00
❑ 9-30557	Just a Little Lonesome/Love My Baby	1958	5.00	10.00	20.00
❑ 9-30619	Jacqueline/Living in the Shadow of the Past	1958	5.00	10.00	20.00
❑ 9-30682	Schoolboy Crush/Borrowed Dreams	1958	5.00	10.00	20.00
❑ 9-30749	A Hundred Hearts/The Fool and the Angel	1958	5.00	10.00	20.00
❑ 9-30831	New River Train/Miss Memory	1959	3.75	7.50	15.00
❑ 9-30886	Soon It Can Be Told/I Guess I'll Miss the Prom	1959	3.75	7.50	15.00
❑ 9-30928	No Other Baby/You're No Longer Mine	1959	3.75	7.50	15.00
❑ 9-30976	My Lucky Day/Hurry Baby	1959	3.75	7.50	15.00
❑ 9-31041	To My Sorrow/Someone Was Already There	1960	3.75	7.50	15.00
❑ 31103	Let Me Be the One/I Wanna Be with You	1960	3.75	7.50	15.00
❑ 31148	Lonely River Rhine/Guess We Thought the World Would End	1960	3.75	7.50	15.00
❑ 31230	Sad-Eyed Baby/You're the One	1961	3.00	6.00	12.00
❑ 31287	How Can You Divide a Little Child/My Greatest Weakness	1961	3.00	6.00	12.00
❑ 31356	One Deep Love/Once in a Lifetime	1962	3.00	6.00	12.00
❑ 31403	Then Came You/Yesterday's Champagne	1962	3.00	6.00	12.00
GUSTO					
❑ 116	That Heart Belongs to Me/With Jenny on My Mind	1974	—	3.00	6.00
❑ 119	Work Things Out with Annie/With Jenny on My Mind	1974	—	3.00	6.00
KAPP					
❑ 708	I'm the Man/Have This Love on Me	1965	2.50	5.00	10.00
❑ 719	Jingle Bell Rock/The Bell That Couldn't Jingle	1965	3.00	6.00	12.00
❑ 732	Those Snowy Glowy Blowy Days of Winter/Sailor	1965	2.50	5.00	10.00
❑ 777	The Things I Remember Most/Sorry, My Name Isn't Fred	1966	2.50	5.00	10.00
❑ 876	I Miss My Fraulein/Where Does a Shadow Go	1967	2.00	4.00	8.00
LITTLE DARLIN'					
❑ 0030	He Thought He'd Die Laughing/You'd Better Make Up Your Mind	1967	2.50	5.00	10.00
❑ 0034	The Day You Stop Loving Me/You Can Tell the World	1967	2.50	5.00	10.00
❑ 0038	Jingle Bell Rock/I Wanta Go to Santa Claus Land	1967	3.00	6.00	12.00
❑ 0041	I Feel You, I Love You/The Day You Stop Loving Me	1968	2.50	5.00	10.00
❑ 0049	Or Is It Love/Touch My Heart	1968	2.50	5.00	10.00
❑ 0054	My Special Angel/Expressing My Love	1968	2.50	5.00	10.00
❑ 0062	So Long/Just Do the Best You Can	1969	2.50	5.00	10.00
❑ 0073	Echoes and Shadows/Step Into My Soul	1969	2.50	5.00	10.00
❑ 7801	I'm Gonna Love the Devil Out of You/I Can't Promise You	1978	—	3.00	6.00
❑ 7807	The Things I Remember Most/I'm Not Sorry	1978	—	3.00	6.00
❑ 7809	Jingle Bell Rock/I Wanta Go to Santa Claus Land	1978	—	3.00	6.00
❑ 7916	One More Dollar for the Band/Touch My Heart	1979	—	3.00	6.00
MCA					
❑ 65026	Jingle Bell Rock/Captain Santa Claus	1973	—	2.50	5.00
—Black label with rainbow					
❑ 65026	Jingle Bell Rock/Captain Santa Claus	1980	—	—	3.00
—Blue label with rainbow					
❑ 65029	Jingle Bell Rock/The Bell That Couldn't Jingle	1973	—	2.50	5.00
—Black label with rainbow; this contains the 1965 Kapp re-recording of the A-side					
❑ 65029	Jingle Bell Rock/The Bell That Couldn't Jingle	1980	—	—	3.00
—Blue label with rainbow					

Number	Title (A Side/B Side)	Yr	VG	VG+	NM
MILLION					
❑ 5	It's the Little Things/Love's Sweet Mystery	1972	—	3.50	7.00
❑ 22	It's Starting to Rain Again/Wouldn't Give Up on You	1972	—	3.50	7.00
MISTLETOE					
❑ 802	Jingle Bell Rock/Jingle Bells	197?	—	2.50	5.00
❑ 802 [PS]	Jingle Bell Rock/Jingle Bells	197?	2.00	4.00	8.00
PLAYBACK					
❑ 1305	Lay Me Down Look/Dance with Me	1988	—	3.00	6.00
❑ 1322	Somebody Wrong Is Looking Right/This Song for You	1988	—	3.00	6.00
❑ 1328	Southern Belle/Troubles Wall to Wall	1989	—	3.00	6.00
❑ 75709	Southern Belle/Troubles Wall to Wall	1989	—	2.50	5.00
SPEED					
❑ 45-114	Yesterday's Lovin'/Hanging Around	1957	7.50	15.00	30.00

7-Inch Extended Plays

Number	Title (A Side/B Side)	Yr	VG	VG+	NM
DECCA					
❑ ED 2555	If Only I Knew/Far Away Heart//My Shoes Keep Walking Back to You/Sugar Moon	1957	5.00	10.00	20.00
❑ ED 2555 [PS]	(title unknown)	1957	5.00	10.00	20.00
❑ ED 2586	Plaything/Magic Song//Tonight's the Night/Just a Little Lonesome	1957	5.00	10.00	20.00
❑ ED 2586 [PS]	Tonight's the Night	1957	5.00	10.00	20.00
❑ ED 2629	Jacqueline/My Special Angel//Borrowed Dreams/Schoolboy Crush	1957	5.00	10.00	20.00
❑ ED 2629 [PS]	Bobby Helms	1957	5.00	10.00	20.00

HEMLOCKS, THE

Number	Title (A Side/B Side)	Yr	VG	VG+	NM
FURY					
❑ 1004	Cora Lee/Joys of Love	1957	25.00	50.00	100.00

HENCHMEN, THE

Number	Title (A Side/B Side)	Yr	VG	VG+	NM
PUNCH					
❑ 1009	Please Tell Me/Livin'	1966	12.50	25.00	50.00
SWAN					
❑ 4249	Rockin' Robin/Baby What's Wrong	1966	10.00	20.00	40.00
❑ 4264	The James Brown (Part 1)/The James Brown (Part 2)	1966	10.00	20.00	40.00

HENDERSON, JOE

Number	Title (A Side/B Side)	Yr	VG	VG+	NM
FONTANA					
❑ 1638	Help Yourself/A Man Without Love	1969	—	3.00	6.00
❑ 1658	Don't Forget to Catch Me/Please Don't Go	1969	—	3.00	6.00
KAPP					
❑ 590	If We Could Start All Over/You Take One Step, I'll Take Two	1964	2.50	5.00	10.00
RIC					
❑ 141	I Ain't Never/The River or the Railroad Track	1964	2.00	4.00	8.00
❑ 149	Honey on My Lips/Like a Child	1965	2.00	4.00	8.00
❑ 181	Sweet Lovin' Baby/Too Much to Lose	1966	2.00	4.00	8.00
TODD					
❑ 1066	Baby Don't Leave Me/Right Now	1961	3.75	7.50	15.00
❑ 1072	Snap Your Fingers/If You See Me Cry	1962	3.75	7.50	15.00
❑ 1077	Big Love/After Loving You	1962	3.00	6.00	12.00
❑ 1079	Three Steps/The Searching Is Over	1962	3.00	6.00	12.00
❑ 1082	Cause We're in Love/Sad Teardrops at Dawn	1963	3.00	6.00	12.00
❑ 1083	You Can't Lose/All Day Every Day	1963	3.00	6.00	12.00
❑ 1085	Love Me Sweet/My Hands Are Tied	1963	3.00	6.00	12.00
❑ 1091	Lovin' Part Time/Blues for a Four-String Guitar	1963	3.00	6.00	12.00
❑ 1096	If We Could Start All Over/You Take One Step, I'll Take Two	1964	3.00	6.00	12.00

HENDRICKS, BOBBY

Number	Title (A Side/B Side)	Yr	VG	VG+	NM
MERCURY					
❑ 71788	Happy Hearts/Pleasing You	1961	3.00	6.00	12.00
❑ 71810	Good Lovin'/Honey Crisp	1961	3.00	6.00	12.00
❑ 71881	I'm Comin' Home/Every Other Night	1961	3.00	6.00	12.00
MGM					
❑ 13179	Let's Get It Over/Love in My Heart	1963	5.00	10.00	20.00
SUE					
❑ 706	Itchy Twitchy Feeling/A Thousand Dreams	1958	7.50	15.00	30.00
❑ 708	Dreamy Eyes/Molly Be Good	1958	5.00	10.00	20.00
❑ 710	Cast Your Vote/It's Misery	1959	5.00	10.00	20.00
❑ 712	I'm a Big Boy Now/Good Things Will Come	1959	5.00	10.00	20.00
❑ 717	Little John Green/Sincerely, Your Lover	1959	5.00	10.00	20.00
❑ 727	City of Angels/If I Just Had Your Love	1960	5.00	10.00	20.00
❑ 732	Psycho/Too Good to Be True	1960	5.00	10.00	20.00
UNITED ARTISTS					
❑ 0142	Itchy Twitchy Feeling/Psycho	1973	—	2.00	4.00
—"Silver Spotlight Series" reissue					

HENDRIX, AL

Number	Title (A Side/B Side)	Yr	VG	VG+	NM
ABC-PARAMOUNT					
❑ 9901	Rhonda Lee/Go, Daddy. Rock	1958	6.25	12.50	25.00
LEGREE					
❑ 701	Young and Wild/I Need You	1960	30.00	60.00	120.00
TALLY					
❑ 119	Rhonda Lee/Go, Daddy Rock	1957	20.00	40.00	80.00

HENDRIX, JIMI

Number	Title (A Side/B Side)	Yr	VG	VG+	NM
AUDIO FIDELITY					
❑ 167	No Such Animal (Part 1)/No Such Animal (Part 2)	1970	3.75	7.50	15.00
❑ 167 [PS]	No Such Animal (Part 1)/No Such Animal (Part 2)	1970	10.00	20.00	40.00
EXPERIENCE HENDRIX					
❑ RTH-1007	The Jimi Hendrix Classic Singles Collection	1998	15.00	30.00	60.00
—Boxed set of 10 45s, each with picture sleeves and white sleeve, with booklet					
❑ 5651-7	Little Drummer Boy-Auld Lang Syne/Three Little Bears	1999	3.00	6.00	12.00
—Red vinyl, small hole					
❑ 5651-7 [PS]	Little Drummer Boy-Auld Lang Syne/Three Little Bears	1999	3.00	6.00	12.00
❑ 13487 [DJ]	Star Spangled Banner/Purple Haze	1999	3.75	7.50	15.00
—Promo-only picture disc					
MCA					
❑ 55336 [DJ]	Dolly Dagger/Night Bird Flying	1997	2.50	5.00	10.00
—Promo only on purple vinyl					
❑ 55336 [PS]	Dolly Dagger/Night Bird Flying	1997	2.50	5.00	10.00
❑ 55454 [DJ]	Can You Please Crawl Out Your Window?/Burning of the Midnight Lamp	1998	—	2.00	5.00
—Promo only on orange vinyl					
❑ 55454 [PS]	Can You Please Crawl Out Your Window?/Burning of the Midnight Lamp	1998	—	2.00	5.00
—Cardboard sleeve					
REPRISE					
❑ 0572	Hey Joe/51st Anniversary	1967	25.00	50.00	100.00
❑ 0572 [PS]	Hey Joe/51st Anniversary	1967	250.00	500.00	1000.
❑ PRO 595 [DJ]	Medley: The Little Drummer Boy-Silent Night/Auld Lang Syne	1974	37.50	75.00	150.00
❑ PRO 595 [PS]	...And a Happy New Year	1974	20.00	40.00	80.00
❑ 0597	Purple Haze/The Wind Cries Mary	1967	6.25	12.50	25.00
❑ 0641	Foxey Lady/Hey Joe	1967	6.25	12.50	25.00
❑ 0665	Up from the Skies/One Rainy Wish	1968	7.50	15.00	30.00
❑ 0728	Purple Haze/Foxey Lady	1968	3.75	7.50	15.00
—"Back to Back Hits" series -- originals have both "r:" and "W7" logos					
❑ 0742	All Along the Watchtower/Crosstown Traffic	1971	—	3.00	6.00
—"Back to Back Hits" series					
❑ 0767	All Along the Watchtower/Burning of the Midnight Lamp	1968	7.50	15.00	30.00
❑ 0792	Crosstown Traffic/Gypsy Eyes	1968	7.50	15.00	30.00
❑ 0853	If 6 Was 9/Stone Free	1969	10.00	20.00	40.00
❑ 0905	Stepping Stone/Izabella	1970	25.00	50.00	100.00
❑ 1000	Freedom/Angel	1971	3.75	7.50	15.00
❑ 1044	Star Spangled Banner/Dolly Dagger	1971	3.75	7.50	15.00
❑ 1082	Johnny B. Goode/Lover Man	1972	3.75	7.50	15.00
❑ 1118	The Wind Cries Mary/Little Wing	1972	3.75	7.50	15.00
❑ EP 2239	Gloria (B-side blank)	1979	—	2.50	5.00
❑ EP 2239 [PS]	Gloria (B-side blank)	1979	—	2.50	5.00
—Above was a bonus record in "The Essential Jimi Hendrix, Volume 2"					
❑ 29845	Fire/Little Wing	1982	—	3.00	6.00
TRIP					
❑ 3002	Hot Trigger/Suspicious	1972	—	2.50	5.00

HENDRIX, JIMI, AND LITTLE RICHARD

Also see each artist's individual listings.

Number	Title (A Side/B Side)	Yr	VG	VG+	NM
ALA					
❑ 1175	Goodnight Irene/Why Don't You Love Me	1972	2.00	4.00	8.00

HENHOUSE FIVE PLUS TOO

See RAY STEVENS.

HENLEY, DON

Also see EAGLES; STEVIE NICKS; SHILOH.

Number	Title (A Side/B Side)	Yr	VG	VG+	NM
ASYLUM					
❑ 69831	Nobody's Business/Long Way Home	1983	—	2.00	4.00
❑ 69894	Dirty Laundry/Lilah	1982	—	2.00	4.00
❑ 69894 [PS]	Dirty Laundry/Lilah	1982	—	3.00	6.00
❑ 69931	I Can't Stand Still/Them and Us	1982	—	2.00	4.00
❑ 69971	Johnny Can't Read/Long Way Home	1982	—	2.00	4.00
❑ 69971 [PS]	Johnny Can't Read/Long Way Home	1982	—	2.50	5.00
GEFFEN					
❑ 19660	New York Minute/The Heart of the Matter	1990	—	—	3.00
❑ 22771	The Last Worthless Evening/Gimme What You Got	1989	—	—	3.00
❑ 22771 [PS]	The Last Worthless Evening/Gimme What You Got	1989	—	—	3.00
❑ 22925	The End of the Innocence/If Dirt Were Dollars	1989	—	—	3.00
❑ 22925 [PS]	The End of the Innocence/If Dirt Were Dollars	1989	—	—	3.00
❑ 28906	Sunset Grill/Man with a Mission	1985	—	2.00	4.00
❑ 29012	Not Enough Love in the World/Man with a Mission	1985	—	—	3.00
❑ 29012 [PS]	Not Enough Love in the World/Man with a Mission	1985	—	—	3.00
❑ 29065	All She Wants to Do Is Dance/Building the Perfect Beast	1985	—	—	3.00
❑ 29065 [PS]	All She Wants to Do Is Dance/Building the Perfect Beast	1985	—	—	3.00
❑ 29141	The Boys of Summer/A Month of Sundays	1984	—	—	3.00
❑ 29141 [PS]	The Boys of Summer/A Month of Sundays	1984	—	—	3.00

HENRY, CLARENCE

Number	Title (A Side/B Side)	Yr	VG	VG+	NM
ARGO					
❑ 5259	Ain't Got No Home/Troubles, Troubles	1956	5.00	10.00	20.00
❑ 5266	I'm a Country Boy/Lonely Tramp	1957	4.00	8.00	16.00
❑ 5273	Found a Home/It Won't Be Long	1957	4.00	8.00	16.00
❑ 5305	I'm in Love/Baby Baby Please	1958	4.00	8.00	16.00
❑ 5378	I Don't Know Why/Just Baby and Me	1960	5.00	10.00	20.00
❑ 5378	But I Do/Just Baby and Me	1960	4.00	8.00	16.00
—A-side: Same song, new title					
❑ 5388	You Always Hurt the One You Love/Hello, Hello	1961	4.00	8.00	16.00
❑ 5395	Lonely Street/Why Can't You	1961	3.75	7.50	15.00
❑ 5401	On Bended Knees/Standing in the Need of Love	1961	3.75	7.50	15.00
❑ 5408	A Little Too Much/I Wish I Could Stay the Same	1962	3.00	6.00	12.00
❑ 5414	Dream Myself a Sweetheart/Lost Without You	1962	3.00	6.00	12.00
❑ 5426	Jealous Kind/Come On and Dance	1962	3.00	6.00	12.00
❑ 5448	If I Didn't Care/It Takes Two to Tango	1963	3.00	6.00	12.00
❑ 5480	Looking Back/Long Lost and Worried	1964	2.50	5.00	10.00
CADET					
❑ 5259	Ain't Got No Home/Troubles, Troubles	1966	2.00	4.00	8.00
DIAL					
❑ 4057	This Time/Hummin' a Heartache	1967	—	3.00	6.00
❑ 4072	Shake Your Money Maker/That's When I Guessed	1968	—	3.00	6.00
PARROT					
❑ 45004	Have You Ever Been Lonely/Little Green Frog	1964	2.50	5.00	10.00
❑ 45009	I Told My Pillow/Can't Hide My Tear	1964	2.50	5.00	10.00

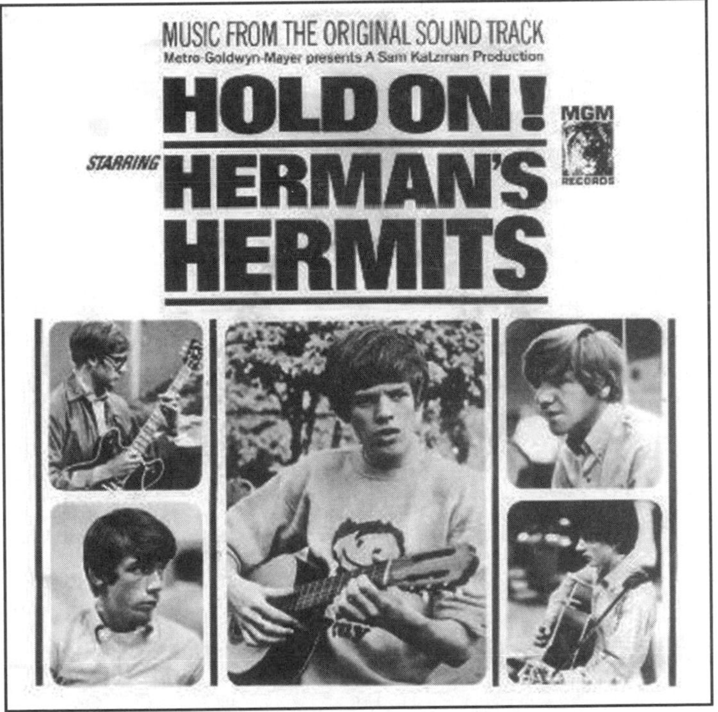

(Top left) Vee Jay Records, which misspelled the famous British band's name "The Beattles" on first editions of their first single, was not the only label that had problems like this. On this rare promo-only single of "Witchcraft," notice the spelling of Marvin Gaye's name! (Top right) Picture discs, on which the entire record, including the playing surface, were far more commonly done on albums than on singles. One 7-inch record that bucked the trend was this 1982 release of the Go-Go's first two hits, "We Got the Beat" and "Our Lips Are Sealed," on the same picture disc. (Bottom left) Even with the reissue of the Jimi Hendrix recording of his Christmas medley in 1999 - the 45 version of which is already a collectible in its own right - this promo sleeve from the first promo-only issue of the material is still a highly sought-after Hendrix item. (Bottom right) Exactly what 45 was contained inside this promo-only picture sleeve, which has the same design as the LP cover for the "Hold On!" soundtrack, is not known. Our best guess is "Leaning on the Lamp Post," but we're not certain. We do know that this is the rarest Herman's Hermits picture sleeve.

Number	Title (A Side/B Side)	Yr	VG	VG+	NM
❑ 45015	I Might As Well/Tore Up Over You	1965	2.50	5.00	10.00

HENRY, EARL

DOT

Number	Title (A Side/B Side)	Yr	VG	VG+	NM
❑ 15756	Whatcha Gonna Do?/I Am the Man	1958	12.50	25.00	50.00
❑ 15875	My Suzanne/Believe a Traveler	1958	7.50	15.00	30.00

HENRY TREE

MAINSTREAM

Number	Title (A Side/B Side)	Yr	VG	VG+	NM
❑ 729	Penfield Town/(B-side unknown)	1970	3.00	6.00	12.00

HENSLEE, GENE

IMPERIAL

Number	Title (A Side/B Side)	Yr	VG	VG+	NM
❑ 8227	Diggin' and Datin'/A Girl Named Haertbreak	1954	17.50	35.00	70.00
❑ 8260	Naughty and Nice/Try As I May	1954	15.00	30.00	60.00
❑ 8277	Rockin' Baby/What Will I Do	1954	15.00	30.00	60.00

MEL-O-DY

Number	Title (A Side/B Side)	Yr	VG	VG+	NM
❑ 110	Beautiful Women/Shambles	1963	5.00	10.00	20.00

UNITED ARTISTS

Number	Title (A Side/B Side)	Yr	VG	VG+	NM
❑ 946	I Don't Wanna Go Home/Shambles	1964	3.75	7.50	15.00

HEP STARS, THE

With Benny Andersson, later of BJORN & BENNY and ABBA.

CHARTMAKER

Number	Title (A Side/B Side)	Yr	VG	VG+	NM
❑ 414	It's Now Winter's Day/Musty Dusty	1969	5.00	10.00	20.00

DUNHILL

Number	Title (A Side/B Side)	Yr	VG	VG+	NM
❑ 4040	Sunny Girl/No Response	1966	6.25	12.50	25.00

HEPSTERS, THE

RONEL

Number	Title (A Side/B Side)	Yr	VG	VG+	NM
❑ 107	Rockin' N' Rollin' with Santa Claus/I Had To Let You Go	1955	100.00	200.00	400.00
❑ 110	I Gotta Sing the Blues/This-a-Way	1956	75.00	150.00	300.00

XMAS

Number	Title (A Side/B Side)	Yr	VG	VG+	NM
❑ 3711	Rockin' & Rollin' With Santa Claus/Sleigh Bell Rock	19??	2.00	4.00	8.00

—B-side by Three Aces and a Joker; reissue of rare R&B sides

HERALDS, THE

HERALD

Number	Title (A Side/B Side)	Yr	VG	VG+	NM
❑ 435	Eternal Love/Gonna Love You	1954	62.50	125.00	250.00

HERD, THE

PETER FRAMPTON was in this group.

FONTANA

Number	Title (A Side/B Side)	Yr	VG	VG+	NM
❑ 1588	I Can Fly/Understand Me	1967	2.50	5.00	10.00
❑ 1602	Sweet William/From the Underworld	1967	2.50	5.00	10.00
❑ 1610	Paradise Lost/Come On, Believe Me	1968	2.50	5.00	10.00
❑ 1618	Our Fairy Tale/I Don't Want Our Loving to Die	1968	2.50	5.00	10.00
❑ 1646	The Game/Beauty Queen	1969	2.50	5.00	10.00

HERMAN'S HERMITS

Also see PETER NOONE.

ABKCO

Number	Title (A Side/B Side)	Yr	VG	VG+	NM
❑ 4021	Mrs. Brown You've Got a Lovely Daughter/I'm Henry VIII, I Am	1972	—	2.50	5.00
❑ 4022	I'm Into Something Good/Can't You Hear My Heartbeat	1972	—	2.50	5.00
❑ 4023	There's a Kind of Hush (All Over the World)/Wonderful World	1972	—	2.50	5.00
❑ 4024	Listen People/Dandy	1972	—	2.50	5.00
❑ 4042	Silhouettes/Just a Little Bit Better	1973	—	2.50	5.00
❑ 4043	A Must to Avoid/Leaning on the Lamp Post	1973	—	2.50	5.00

BUDDAH

Number	Title (A Side/B Side)	Yr	VG	VG+	NM
❑ 516	Lonely Situation (Love Is All I Need)/Blond Haired Blue Eyed Boy	1976	2.00	4.00	8.00

MGM

Number	Title (A Side/B Side)	Yr	VG	VG+	NM
❑ (no #) [PS]	Hold On	1966	62.50	125.00	250.00

—Promo-only sleeve similar to the LP cover of the same name; it's not known which single this came with

Number	Title (A Side/B Side)	Yr	VG	VG+	NM
❑ 13280	I'm Into Something Good/Your Hand in Mine	1964	2.50	5.00	10.00
❑ 13310	Can't You Hear My Heartbeat/I Know Why	1964	2.50	5.00	10.00
❑ 13310 [PS]	Can't You Hear My Heartbeat/I Know Why	1964	3.75	7.50	15.00
❑ 13332	Silhouettes/Walkin' With My Angel	1965	2.50	5.00	10.00
❑ 13341	Mrs. Brown You've Got a Lovely Daughter/I Gotta Dream On	1965	2.50	5.00	10.00
❑ 13341 [PS]	Mrs. Brown You've Got a Lovely Daughter/I Gotta Dream On	1965	3.75	7.50	15.00
❑ 13354	Wonderful World/Traveling Light	1965	2.50	5.00	10.00
❑ 13354 [PS]	Wonderful World/Traveling Light	1965	3.75	7.50	15.00
❑ 13367	I'm Henry VIII, I Am/The End of the World	1965	2.50	5.00	10.00
❑ 13367 [PS]	I'm Henry VIII, I Am/The End of the World	1965	5.00	10.00	20.00
❑ 13398	Just a Little Bit Better/Sea Cruise	1965	2.50	5.00	10.00
❑ 13398 [PS]	Just a Little Bit Better/Sea Cruise	1965	3.75	7.50	15.00
❑ 13437	A Must to Avoid/The Man with the Cigar	1966	2.00	4.00	8.00
❑ 13462	Listen People/Got a Feeling	1966	2.00	4.00	8.00
❑ 13500	Leaning on the Lamp Post/Hold On	1966	2.00	4.00	8.00
❑ 13548	This Door Swings Both Ways/For Love	1966	2.00	4.00	8.00
❑ 13603	Dandy/My Reservation's Been Confirmed	1966	2.00	4.00	8.00
❑ 13603 [PS]	Dandy/My Reservation's Been Confirmed	1966	3.75	7.50	15.00
❑ 13639	East West/What Is Wrong What Is Right	1966	2.00	4.00	8.00
❑ 13681	There's a Kind of Hush/No Milk Today	1967	2.00	4.00	8.00
❑ 13681	There's a Kind of Hush (All Over the World)/No Milk Today	1967	2.50	5.00	10.00
❑ 13681 [PS]	There's a Kind of Hush/No Milk Today	1967	3.75	7.50	15.00
❑ 13761	Don't Go Out Into the Rain (You're Going to Melt)/Moonshine Man	1967	2.00	4.00	8.00
❑ 13761 [PS]	Don't Go Out Into the Rain (You're Going to Melt)/Moonshine Man	1967	3.75	7.50	15.00
❑ 13787	Museum/Last Bus Home	1967	2.00	4.00	8.00
❑ 13787 [PS]	Museum/Last Bus Home	1967	3.75	7.50	15.00
❑ 13885	I Can Take or Leave Your Loving/Marcel's	1967	2.00	4.00	8.00
❑ 13934	Sleepy Joe/Just One Girl	1968	2.50	5.00	10.00

—Black label

Number	Title (A Side/B Side)	Yr	VG	VG+	NM
❑ 13934	Sleepy Joe/Just One Girl	1968	2.00	4.00	8.00

—Blue and gold label

Number	Title (A Side/B Side)	Yr	VG	VG+	NM
❑ 13973	Sunshine Girl/Nobody Needs to Know	1968	2.50	5.00	10.00
❑ 13994	Ooh, She's Done It Again/The Most Beautiful Thing in My Life	1968	2.50	5.00	10.00
❑ 14035	Something's Happening/Little Miss Sorrow, Child of Tomorrow	1969	2.50	5.00	10.00
❑ 14060	My Lady/My Sentimental Friend	1969	2.50	5.00	10.00
❑ 14100	It's Alright Now/(Here Comes) The Star	1969	2.50	5.00	10.00

PRIVATE STOCK

Number	Title (A Side/B Side)	Yr	VG	VG+	NM
❑ 45019	Ginny Go Softly/Blond Haired, Blue Eyed Boy	1975	2.00	4.00	8.00

ROULETTE

Number	Title (A Side/B Side)	Yr	VG	VG+	NM
❑ 7213	Truck Stop Mama/Heart Get Ready for Love	1977	3.75	7.50	15.00

HERROLD, DENNIS

IMPERIAL

Number	Title (A Side/B Side)	Yr	VG	VG+	NM
❑ 5482	Hip Hip Baby/Make with the Lovin'	1957	20.00	40.00	80.00

HESITATIONS, THE

GWP

Number	Title (A Side/B Side)	Yr	VG	VG+	NM
❑ 504	Is This the Way to Treat a Girl/Yes I'm Ready	1969	2.00	4.00	8.00

KAPP

Number	Title (A Side/B Side)	Yr	VG	VG+	NM
❑ 790	Soul Superman/I'm Not Built That Way	1966	2.50	5.00	10.00
❑ 810	Soul Kind of Love/Wait a Minute	1967	2.50	5.00	10.00
❑ 822	I'll Be Right There/She Won't Come Back	1967	2.50	5.00	10.00
❑ 848	You Can't Bypass Love/You'll Never Know	1967	2.50	5.00	10.00
❑ 878	Born Free/Love Is Everywhere	1967	2.50	5.00	10.00
❑ 899	The Impossible Dream/Nobody Knows You When You're Down and Out	1968	2.50	5.00	10.00
❑ 911	Climb Every Mountain/My World	1968	2.50	5.00	10.00
❑ 926	Who Will Answer/If You Ever Need a Hand	1968	2.50	5.00	10.00
❑ 948	A Whiter Shade of Pale/With Pen in Hand	1968	2.50	5.00	10.00

HEWITT, BEN

MERCURY

Number	Title (A Side/B Side)	Yr	VG	VG+	NM
❑ 71413	You Break Me Up/I Ain't Givin' Up Nothin'	1959	25.00	50.00	100.00
❑ 71472	Patricia June/For Quite a While	1959	12.50	25.00	50.00
❑ 71577	My Search/I Want a New Girl Now	1960	10.00	20.00	40.00
❑ 71612	The Queen in the Kingdom/Whirlwind Blues	1960	10.00	20.00	40.00

HEWITT, JENNIFER LOVE

WARNER BROS.

Number	Title (A Side/B Side)	Yr	VG	VG+	NM
❑ 17105	How Do I Deal/Try to Say Goodbye	1999	—	—	3.00

—B-side by Jory Eve

HI-FI-DELS, THE

ATLANTIC

Number	Title (A Side/B Side)	Yr	VG	VG+	NM
❑ 2121	Did I Cry/Tricky Tricky	1961	3.75	7.50	15.00

HI-FIVES, THE (1)

BELL

Number	Title (A Side/B Side)	Yr	VG	VG+	NM
❑ 634	Julie/Son of Raunchy	1965	10.00	20.00	40.00

JERDEN

Number	Title (A Side/B Side)	Yr	VG	VG+	NM
❑ 730	Goin' Away/Tort	1964	3.75	7.50	15.00

HI-FIVES, THE (2)

BINGO

Number	Title (A Side/B Side)	Yr	VG	VG+	NM
❑ 1006	Felicia/Windy City Special	1960	7.50	15.00	30.00

DECCA

Number	Title (A Side/B Side)	Yr	VG	VG+	NM
❑ 30576	My Friend/How Can I Win?	1958	10.00	20.00	40.00
❑ 30657	Dorothy/Just a Shoulder to Cry On	1958	12.50	25.00	50.00
❑ 30744	Lonely/What's New	1958	10.00	20.00	40.00

HI-LITERS, THE (1)

With King Bassie and His Three Aces...Ben Vereen was a member.

HICO

Number	Title (A Side/B Side)	Yr	VG	VG+	NM
❑ 2432	Let Me Be True to You/In the Night	1958	25.00	50.00	100.00
❑ 2433	Over the Rainbow/(B-side unknown)	1958	37.50	75.00	150.00

HI-LITERS, THE (U)

Probably not group (1), but we don't know if these are the same group or two different groups.

VEE JAY

Number	Title (A Side/B Side)	Yr	VG	VG+	NM
❑ 184	Bobby Sox Baby/Hello Dear	1956	250.00	500.00	1000.

WEN-DEE

Number	Title (A Side/B Side)	Yr	VG	VG+	NM
❑ 1927	Baby Don't Treat Me This Way/Route 66	1955	15.00	30.00	60.00

HI-LITES, THE (1)

For records on Daran, see THE CHI-LITES.

HI-LITES, THE (2)

JULIA

Number	Title (A Side/B Side)	Yr	VG	VG+	NM
❑ 1105	Gloria/For Your Precious Love	1962	30.00	60.00	120.00

MONOGRAM

Number	Title (A Side/B Side)	Yr	VG	VG+	NM
❑ 119	Everybody's Somebody's Fool/Moonlight	1976	2.00	4.00	8.00
❑ 120	Zoom Zoom Zoom/To the Aisle	1976	2.00	4.00	8.00
❑ 121	Pretty Face/Maybe You'll Be There	1976	2.00	4.00	8.00

RECORD FAIR

Number	Title (A Side/B Side)	Yr	VG	VG+	NM
❑ 500	I'm Falling in Love/Walking My Baby Back Home	1961	12.50	25.00	50.00
❑ 501	For Sentimental Reasons/For Your Precious Love	1962	12.50	25.00	50.00

HI-LITES, THE (U)

None of these are group (1). Some could be group (2). The rest could be several more groups.

BRUNSWICK

Number	Title (A Side/B Side)	Yr	VG	VG+	NM
❑ 55102	Friday Night Go Go/Chicka-Rocka-Chee-Chi-Cho (Cha Cha)	1958	5.00	10.00	20.00

JET

Number	Title (A Side/B Side)	Yr	VG	VG+	NM
❑ 501	The Pony (Part 1)/The Pony (Part 2)	1961	5.00	10.00	20.00
❑ 502	4000 Miles Away/Woke Up This Morning	1961	7.50	15.00	30.00

KING

Number	Title (A Side/B Side)	Yr	VG	VG+	NM
❑ 5730	Death of an Angel/Our Winter Love	1963	5.00	10.00	20.00

Number	Title (A Side/B Side)	Yr	VG	VG+	NM
MERCURY					
❑ 70987	The Next Four Years/The Girls with the Bells	1956	6.25	12.50	25.00
OKEH					
❑ 7046	I Found a Love/Zanzee	1954	125.00	250.00	500.00
RENO					
❑ 1030	Please Believe Me I Love You/Sweet and Lovely	1958	62.50	125.00	250.00
TWIST TIME					
❑ 12	Twistin' Time/Twistin' Pony	1962	3.75	7.50	15.00
WASSEL					
❑ 701	Groovy/Hey Baby	1965	2.50	5.00	10.00

HI-LO'S, THE

Number	Title (A Side/B Side)	Yr	VG	VG+	NM
COLUMBIA					
❑ 40915	A Face in the Crowd/Autumn Rain	1957	2.50	5.00	10.00
❑ 41050	A Very Special Love/My Sugar Is So Refined	1957	2.50	5.00	10.00
❑ 41197	Whistlin' Down the Lane/When I Remember	1958	2.50	5.00	10.00
❑ 41465	Goody Goody/Indiana	1959	2.50	5.00	10.00
❑ 41647	Cindy's Prayer/A Lot of Livin' to Do	1960	2.50	5.00	10.00
❑ 41867	The Trolley Song/Five Foot Two, Eyes of Blue	1960	2.50	5.00	10.00
7-Inch Extended Plays					
COLUMBIA					
❑ B-10231	Sunnyside Up/Laura//A Shine on Your Shoes/The Heather on the Hill	195?	3.00	6.00	12.00
❑ B-10231 [PS]	Sunnyside Up	195?	3.00	6.00	12.00

HIBBLER, AL

Number	Title (A Side/B Side)	Yr	VG	VG+	NM
ALADDIN					
❑ 3328	Don't Take Your Love from Me/I Got It So Bad and That Ain't Good	1956	3.75	7.50	15.00
ATLANTIC					
❑ 911	Danny Boy/Song of the Wanderer	1950	—	—	—
—Unconfirmed on 45 rpm					
❑ 925	The Blues Come Falling Down/Old Folks	1951	12.50	25.00	50.00
❑ 932	Travelin' Light/If I Knew You Were There	1951	12.50	25.00	50.00
❑ 945	Now I Lay Me Down to Dream/This Is Always	1951	12.50	25.00	50.00
❑ 1071	Danny Boy/Now I Lay Me Down	1955	7.50	15.00	30.00
BRUNSWICK					
❑ 55027	Star Dust/Stormy Weather	1957	3.75	7.50	15.00
CLEF					
❑ 89095	I'm Getting Sentimental Over You/As Time Goes By	1954	3.75	7.50	15.00
DECCA					
❑ 29441	Unchained Melody/Daybreak	1955	5.00	10.00	20.00
❑ 29543	I Can't Put My Arms Around a Memory/They Say You're Laughing at Me	1955	3.75	7.50	15.00
❑ 29660	He/Breeze (Blow My Baby Back to Me)	1955	5.00	10.00	20.00
❑ 29789	11th Hour Melody/Let's Try Again	1956	3.75	7.50	15.00
❑ 29950	Away All Boats/Never Turn Back	1956	3.75	7.50	15.00
❑ 29982	After the Lights Go Down Low/I Was Telling Her About You	1956	3.75	7.50	15.00
❑ 30100	Nightfall/I'm Free	1956	3.75	7.50	15.00
❑ 30127	White Christmas/Silent Night	1956	3.75	7.50	15.00
❑ 30176	Trees/The Town Crier	1957	3.00	6.00	12.00
❑ 30268	Sweet Slumber/Because of You	1957	3.00	6.00	12.00
❑ 30337	Around the Corner from the Blues/I Complain	1957	3.00	6.00	12.00
❑ 30397	When Will I Forget You/Be Fair	1957	3.00	6.00	12.00
❑ 30483	The Crying Wind/A Wish	1957	3.00	6.00	12.00
❑ 30547	My Heart Tells Me/I'm Glad I'm Not Young Anymore	1958	3.00	6.00	12.00
❑ 30622	Honeysuckle Rose/Ain't Nothin' Wrong with That Baby	1958	3.00	6.00	12.00
❑ 30684	Softly, My Love/Your Hands	1958	3.00	6.00	12.00
❑ 30752	Love Land/Love Me Long, Hold Me Close	1958	3.00	6.00	12.00
❑ 30817	Warm Heart-Cold Feet/Mine All Mine	1959	3.00	6.00	12.00
❑ 30870	He Is Always There/What 'Tis, What 'Tis, 'Tis Spring	1959	3.00	6.00	12.00
❑ 30946	It Won't Be Easy/Lonesome and Cold	1959	3.00	6.00	12.00
MERCURY					
❑ 89011	Please/Believe It Love	1952	3.75	7.50	15.00
REPRISE					
❑ 20035	Look Away/Tall the Sky	1961	2.50	5.00	10.00
❑ 20077	Walk Away/I've Convinced Everyone But You	1962	2.50	5.00	10.00
TOP RANK					
❑ 2089	Strawberry Hill/Stranger	1960	2.50	5.00	10.00
7-Inch Extended Plays					
DECCA					
❑ ED 2410	*After the Lights Go Down Low/September in the Rain/You'll Never Know/Where Are You?	195?	5.00	10.00	20.00
❑ ED 2410 [PS]	Starring Al Hibbler, Part 1	195?	5.00	10.00	20.00

HICKEY, ERSEL

Number	Title (A Side/B Side)	Yr	VG	VG+	NM
APOLLO					
❑ 761	Upside Down Love/The Millionaire	1949	12.50	25.00	50.00
EPIC					
❑ 9263	Bluebirds Over the Mountain/Hangin' Around	1958	7.50	15.00	30.00
❑ 9278	Goin' Down That Road/Lovers' Land	1958	6.25	12.50	25.00
❑ 9298	You Never Can Tell/Wedding Day	1958	6.25	12.50	25.00
❑ 9309	Don't Be Afraid of Love/You Threw a Dart	1959	6.25	12.50	25.00
❑ 9320	I Can't Love Another/People Gotta Talk	1959	6.25	12.50	25.00
❑ 9357	Love in Bloom/What Do You Want	1960	6.25	12.50	25.00
❑ 9395	Another Wasted Day/Money Brought Me You	1960	6.25	12.50	25.00
JANUS					
❑ 151	Bluebirds Over the Mountain/Self Made Man	1971	—	2.50	5.00
KAPP					
❑ 372	Teardrops at Dawn/I Guess You Can Call It Love	1961	5.00	10.00	20.00
LAURIE					
❑ 3165	Some Enchanted Evening/Put Your Mind at Ease	1963	5.00	10.00	20.00
RAMESES II					
❑ 2003	Waitin' for Baby/In Spite of the Fool That I Am	1976	—	3.00	6.00
TOOT					
❑ 602	Tryin' to Get to You/Blue Skies	196?	2.50	5.00	10.00
7-Inch Extended Plays					
EPIC					
❑ EG-7206	(contents unknown)	1958	25.00	50.00	100.00
❑ EG-7206 [PS]	Ersel Hickey in Lover's Land	1958	25.00	50.00	100.00

HICKMAN, DWAYNE

Starred as Dobie Gillis on TV.

Number	Title (A Side/B Side)	Yr	VG	VG+	NM
ABC-PARAMOUNT					
❑ 9908	School Dance/Pretty Baby	1958	6.25	12.50	25.00
❑ 9908 [PS]	School Dance/Pretty Baby	1958	10.00	20.00	40.00
CAPITOL					
❑ 4445	I'm a Lover, Not a Fighter/I Pass Your House	1960	5.00	10.00	20.00

HIDE-A-WAYS, THE

Number	Title (A Side/B Side)	Yr	VG	VG+	NM
LOST-NITE					
❑ 119	Can't Help Loving That Girl of Mine/I'm Coming Home	196?	—	2.50	5.00
—Reissue label					
MGM					
❑ 55004	Cherie/Me Make Em Powwow	1955	125.00	250.00	500.00
RONNI					
❑ 1000	Can't Help Lovin' That Girl of Mine/I'm Coming Home	1954	2000.	4000.	6000.

HIGH NUMBERS, THE

See THE WHO.

HIGHLIGHTS, THE

Number	Title (A Side/B Side)	Yr	VG	VG+	NM
BALLY					
❑ 1016	City of Angels/Listen, My Love	1956	7.50	15.00	30.00
❑ 1027	To Be with You/Will I Ever Know	1957	7.50	15.00	30.00
❑ 1044	Indian Style/Turn Around Shoes	1957	6.25	12.50	25.00

HIGHWAYMEN, THE

Number	Title (A Side/B Side)	Yr	VG	VG+	NM
ABC					
❑ 10801	She's Not There/Little Bird, Little Bird	1966	2.00	4.00	8.00
❑ 10824	Fling/My Foolish Pride	1966	2.00	4.00	8.00
ABC-PARAMOUNT					
❑ 10688	Should I Go, Should I Stay/Permit to Be a Hermit	1965	2.00	4.00	8.00
❑ 10716	I'll Show You the Way/Never a Thought for Tomorrow	1965	2.00	4.00	8.00
UNITED ARTISTS					
❑ 258	Michael/Santiano	1960	3.75	7.50	15.00
❑ 370	Cotton Fields/Gypsy Rover	1961	3.00	6.00	12.00
❑ 439	Whiskey in the Jar/I'm On My Way	1962	3.00	6.00	12.00
❑ 475	Cindy, Oh Cindy/The Birdman	1962	3.00	6.00	12.00
❑ 540	I Know Where I'm Going/Well, Well, Well	1963	3.00	6.00	12.00
❑ 568	I Never Will Marry/Pretoria	1963	3.00	6.00	12.00
❑ 602	All My Trials/Midnight Train	1963	3.00	6.00	12.00
❑ 647	Universal Soldier/I'll Fly Away	1963	3.00	6.00	12.00
❑ 679	Roll On Columbia, Roll On/The Tale of Michael Flynn	1963	3.00	6.00	12.00
❑ 696	The Sinking of the Reuben James/Bon Soir	1964	2.50	5.00	10.00
❑ 752	Nellie/Sweet Mama Tree Top Tall	1964	2.50	5.00	10.00
❑ 788	Puttin' On the Style/Michael	1964	2.50	5.00	10.00
❑ 801	Michael '65/Puttin' On the Style	1964	2.50	5.00	10.00

HIGHWAYMEN, THE (2)

See JOHNNY CASH; WAYLON JENNINGS; KRIS KRISTOFFERSON; WILLIE NELSON.

HILDEBRAND, RAY

See PAUL AND PAULA.

Number	Title (A Side/B Side)	Yr	VG	VG+	NM
PHILIPS					
❑ 40174	It's All Over, Paula/Snow Girl	1964	2.50	5.00	10.00
—As "Paul"					
❑ 40318	Hey Little Julie/The Way of the DJ	1965	2.00	4.00	8.00
❑ 40339	Hello Viet Nam (Goodbye My Love)/You, Wonderful You	1965	2.00	4.00	8.00
TOWER					
❑ 304	Paper Clown/Patsy	1966	2.00	4.00	8.00
—As "Paul (Paul and Paula)"					

HILDEGARDE

Number	Title (A Side/B Side)	Yr	VG	VG+	NM
YULETIDE					
❑ 752	Christmas Is Christmas All Over the World/(Instrumental)	19??	—	2.00	4.00

HILL, BUNKER

Number	Title (A Side/B Side)	Yr	VG	VG+	NM
MALA					
❑ 451	Hide and Go Seek (Part 1)/Hide and Go Seek (Part 2)	1962	5.00	10.00	20.00
❑ 457	Red Ridin' Hood and the Wolf/Nobody Knows	1962	5.00	10.00	20.00
❑ 464	The Girl Can't Dance/You Can't Make Me Doubt My Baby	1963	6.25	12.50	25.00

HILL, FAITH

Number	Title (A Side/B Side)	Yr	VG	VG+	NM
WARNER BROS.					
❑ 7-16773	If My Heart Had Wings/It Will Be Me	2001	—	2.00	4.00
❑ 7-16792	Let's Make Love/There Will Come a Day	2000	—	—	3.00
—A-side with Tim McGraw					
❑ 7-16818	The Way You Love Me/Never Gonna Be Your Lady	2000	—	—	3.00
❑ 7-16884	Breathe/It All Comes Down to Love	2000	—	2.00	4.00
❑ 7-17247	This Kiss/Better Days	1998	—	2.00	4.00
❑ 7-17531	I Can't Do That Anymore/Take Me As I Am	1996	—	2.00	4.00
❑ 7-17718	It Matters to Me/Keep Walkin' On	1995	—	2.00	4.00
❑ 7-17817	Let's Go to Vegas/You Will Be Mine	1995	—	2.00	4.00
❑ 7-18179	But I Will/Love's Too Short to Love Like That	1994	—	—	3.00
❑ 7-18261	Piece of My Heart/I Would Be Stronger Than That	1994	—	2.00	4.00
❑ 7-18411	Wild One/Go the Distance	1993	—	2.00	4.00

HILL, JESSIE

BLUE THUMB

Number	Title (A Side/B Side)	Yr	VG	VG+	NM
❑ 204	Naturally/Livin' a Lie	1971	—	3.00	6.00

DOWNEY

Number	Title (A Side/B Side)	Yr	VG	VG+	NM
❑ 115	Chip Chop/Woodshed	1964	2.50	5.00	10.00
❑ 117	Understanding/Down the Street	1964	2.50	5.00	10.00
❑ 124	Never Thought/TV Guide	1964	2.50	5.00	10.00

MINIT

Number	Title (A Side/B Side)	Yr	VG	VG+	NM
❑ 607	Ooh Poo Pah Doo — Part 1/Ooh Poo Pah Doo — Part 2	1960	3.75	7.50	15.00
❑ 611	Whip It On Me/I Need Your Love	1960	3.00	6.00	12.00
❑ 616	Scoop Scoobie Doobie/Highland Blues	1960	3.00	6.00	12.00
❑ 622	Oh My Oh My/I Got Mine	1961	3.00	6.00	12.00
❑ 628	Oogsey Moo/My Love	1961	3.00	6.00	12.00
❑ 638	Sweet Jelly Roll/It's My Fault	1961	3.00	6.00	12.00
❑ 646	Can't Get Enough of That Ooh Pah Doo/Pot's on a Strike	1962	3.00	6.00	12.00

UNITED ARTISTS

Number	Title (A Side/B Side)	Yr	VG	VG+	NM
❑ 0081	Ooh Poo Pah Doo — Part 1/Ooh Poo Pah Doo — Part 2	1973	—	2.00	4.00

—"Silver Spotlight Series" reissue

HILL, LAURYN

RUFFHOUSE

Number	Title (A Side/B Side)	Yr	VG	VG+	NM
❑ 78868	Doo Wop (That Thing)/Lost Ones (Remix)	1998	—	—	2.00
❑ 78868 [PS]	Doo Wop (That Thing)/Lost Ones (Remix)	1998	—	—	2.00
❑ 79077	Ex-Factor/When It Hurts So Bad	1999	—	—	3.00
❑ 79206	Everything Is Everything/Ex-Factor	1999	—	—	3.00

HILL, RAYMOND

SUN

Number	Title (A Side/B Side)	Yr	VG	VG+	NM
❑ 204	Bourbon Street Jump/The Snuggle	1954	250.00	500.00	750.00

HILLMAN, CHRIS

Also see THE BYRDS; McGUINN AND HILLMAN; McGUINN, CLARK AND HILLMAN.

ASYLUM

Number	Title (A Side/B Side)	Yr	VG	VG+	NM
❑ 45330	Step On Out/Take It on the Run	1976	—	2.00	4.00
❑ 45350	Falling Again/Love Is the Sweetest Amnesty	1976	—	2.00	4.00
❑ 45428	Heartbreaker/Lucky in Love	1977	—	2.00	4.00

SUGAR HILL

Number	Title (A Side/B Side)	Yr	VG	VG+	NM
❑ 4105	Somebody's Back in Town/Desert Rose	1984	—	2.50	5.00
❑ 4106	Running the Roadblocks/Turn Your Radio On	1985	—	2.50	5.00

HILLMAN, CHRIS, AND ROGER MCGUINN

See McGUINN AND HILLMAN.

HILLSIDERS, THE

MEL-O-DY

Number	Title (A Side/B Side)	Yr	VG	VG+	NM
❑ 120	You Only Pass This Way One Time/Rain Is a Lonesome Thing	1964	7.50	15.00	30.00

HILLTOPPERS, THE

DOT

Number	Title (A Side/B Side)	Yr	VG	VG+	NM
❑ 15018	Trying/You Made Up My Mind	1952	5.00	10.00	20.00
—As "The Hill Toppers"					
❑ 15034	Must I Cry Again/I Keep Telling Myself	1952	4.00	8.00	16.00
❑ 15055	If I Were King/I Can't Lie to Myself	1953	4.00	8.00	16.00
❑ 15085	P.S. I Love You/I'd Rather Die Young	1953	4.00	8.00	16.00
❑ 15105	Love Walked In/To Be Alone	1953	4.00	8.00	16.00
❑ 15127	From the Vine Came the Grape/Time Will Tell	1954	4.00	8.00	16.00
❑ 15156	Wrapped in a Dream/Poor Butterfly	1954	4.00	8.00	16.00
❑ 15201	Sweetheart/Old Cabaret	1954	4.00	8.00	16.00
❑ 15220	If I Didn't Care/Bertha	1954	4.00	8.00	16.00
❑ 15249	You Try Somebody Else/Time Waits for No One	1954	4.00	8.00	16.00
❑ 15318	D-A-R-L-I-N/Frivolette	1955	3.75	7.50	15.00
❑ 15351	The Door Is Still Open/Tears from My Eyes	1955	3.75	7.50	15.00
❑ 15375	The Kentuckian Song/I Must Be Dreaming	1955	3.75	7.50	15.00
❑ 15415	Searching/All I Need Is You	1955	3.75	7.50	15.00
❑ 15423	Only You (And You Alone)/Until the Real Thing Comes Along	1955	3.75	7.50	15.00
❑ 15437	My Treasure/The Last Word in Love	1955	3.75	7.50	15.00
❑ 15451	Do the Bop/When You're Alone	1956	3.75	7.50	15.00
❑ 15459	So Tired/Faded Rose	1956	3.75	7.50	15.00
❑ 15468	I'm Walking Thru Heaven/Eyes of Fire, Lips of Wine	1956	3.75	7.50	15.00
❑ 15489	Ka-Ding-Dong/Into Each Life Some Rain Must Fall	1956	3.75	7.50	15.00
—Originals have maroon labels					
❑ 15489	Ka-Ding-Dong/Into Each Life Some Rain Must Fall	1956	3.00	6.00	12.00
—Second pressings have black labels					
❑ 15511	Until You're Mine/No Regrets	1956	3.00	6.00	12.00
❑ 15537	Marianne/You're Wasting Your Time	1957	3.00	6.00	12.00
❑ 15560	I Love My Girl/I'm Serious	1957	3.00	6.00	12.00
❑ 15594	A Fallen Star/Footsteps	1957	3.00	6.00	12.00
❑ 15626	My Cabin of Dreams/Dedicated to You	1957	3.00	6.00	12.00
❑ 15662	The Joker (That's What They Call Me)/Chicken Chicken	1957	3.00	6.00	12.00
❑ 15712	Starry Eyes/You Sure Look Good to Me	1958	3.00	6.00	12.00
❑ 15814	Signorina/Peggy's Sister	1958	3.00	6.00	12.00
❑ 15857	You're Nobody Till Somebody Loves You/Trying	1958	3.00	6.00	12.00
❑ 15889	I'd Rather Die Young/Welcome to My Heart	1959	2.50	5.00	10.00
❑ 15958	Lots of Luck/Lizzie Darlin'	1959	2.50	5.00	10.00
❑ 16010	The Prisoner's Song/Phone	1959	2.50	5.00	10.00
❑ 16022	Trying/P.S. I Love You	1960	2.50	5.00	10.00
❑ 16024	From the Vine Came the Grape/Love Walked In	1960	2.50	5.00	10.00
❑ 16025	Only You (And You Alone)/Till Then	1960	2.50	5.00	10.00
❑ 16039	Marianne/To Be Alone	1960	2.50	5.00	10.00
❑ 16054	To Be Alone/P.S. I Love You	1960	2.50	5.00	10.00
❑ 16556	Only You/No Longer Lonely	1963	2.00	4.00	8.00

MGM

Number	Title (A Side/B Side)	Yr	VG	VG+	NM
❑ 14515	Jamaica Farewell/Sunshine and Love	1973	—	2.50	5.00
—As "Jimmy Sacca and the Hilltoppers"					
❑ 14603	Little Things You Do/Sunshine and Love	1973	—	2.50	5.00
—As "Jimmy Sacca and the Hilltoppers"					

7-Inch Extended Plays

DOT

Number	Title (A Side/B Side)	Yr	VG	VG+	NM
❑ DEP-1006	(contents unknown)	195?	3.75	7.50	15.00
❑ DEP-1006 [PS]	The Hilltoppers Sing	195?	3.75	7.50	15.00
❑ DEP-1007	(contents unknown)	195?	3.75	7.50	15.00
❑ DEP-1007 [PS]	The Hilltoppers Sing	195?	3.75	7.50	15.00
❑ DEP-1008	(contents unknown)	195?	3.75	7.50	15.00
❑ DEP-1008 [PS]	The Hilltoppers Sing	195?	3.75	7.50	15.00
❑ DEP-1009	(contents unknown)	195?	3.75	7.50	15.00
❑ DEP-1009 [PS]	The Hilltoppers Sing	195?	3.75	7.50	15.00
❑ DEP-1011	(contents unknown)	195?	3.75	7.50	15.00
❑ DEP-1011 [PS]	The Hilltoppers Sing	195?	3.75	7.50	15.00
❑ DEP-1012	(contents unknown)	195?	3.75	7.50	15.00
❑ DEP-1012 [PS]	The Hilltoppers Sing	195?	3.75	7.50	15.00

HIM

See DOUG SAHM.

HINDU LOVE GODS

Also see R.E.M.

I.R.S.

Number	Title (A Side/B Side)	Yr	VG	VG+	NM
❑ 52867	Gonna Have a Good Time Tonight/Narrator	1986	2.00	4.00	8.00
❑ 52867 [PS]	Gonna Have a Good Time Tonight/Narrator	1986	2.00	4.00	8.00

HINTON, JOE

ARVEE

Number	Title (A Side/B Side)	Yr	VG	VG+	NM
❑ 5028	My Love Is Real/I Won't Be Your Fool	1961	3.00	6.00	12.00
—Arvee titles as "Little Joe Hinton"					
❑ 5029	Your Kind of Love/Let's Start a Romance	1961	3.00	6.00	12.00

BACK BEAT

Number	Title (A Side/B Side)	Yr	VG	VG+	NM
❑ 519	I Know/Ladder of Prayer	1958	3.75	7.50	15.00
❑ 526	Pretty Little Mama/Will You	1959	3.75	7.50	15.00
❑ 526 [PS]	Pretty Little Mama/Will You	1959	7.50	15.00	30.00
❑ 532	If You Love Me/A Thousand Cups of Happiness	1960	3.75	7.50	15.00
❑ 535	The Girls in My Life/Come On Baby	1961	3.75	7.50	15.00
❑ 537	You Know It Ain't Right/Lovre Sick Blues	1963	3.00	6.00	12.00
❑ 539	Better to Give Than Receive/There Is No In Between	1963	3.00	6.00	12.00
❑ 540	There Oughta Be a Law/You're My Girl	1964	3.00	6.00	12.00
❑ 541	Funny/You Gotta Have Love	1964	3.75	7.50	15.00
❑ 545	I Want a Little Girl/True Love	1965	3.00	6.00	12.00
❑ 547	Darling Come and Talk to Me/Everything	1965	3.00	6.00	12.00
❑ 550	Pledging My Love/Just a Kid Named Joe	1965	3.00	6.00	12.00
❑ 565	I'm Waiting/How Long Can I Last	1966	2.50	5.00	10.00
❑ 574	If I Had Only Known/Lots of Love	1966	2.50	5.00	10.00
❑ 581	Close to MyHeart/You've Been Good to Me	1967	2.50	5.00	10.00
❑ 589	I'm Satisfied/Be Ever Wonderful	1968	2.50	5.00	10.00
❑ 594	Got You on My Mind/Please	1968	2.50	5.00	10.00

SOUL

Number	Title (A Side/B Side)	Yr	VG	VG+	NM
❑ 35080	Let's Save the Children/You Are Blue	1971	6.25	12.50	25.00

HIPPIES, THE

PARKWAY

Number	Title (A Side/B Side)	Yr	VG	VG+	NM
❑ 863	Memory Lane/A Lonely Piano	1963	5.00	10.00	20.00

—Originally released as "The Tams"; B-side by Reggie Harrison

HIPPY DIPPYS, THE

UNI

Number	Title (A Side/B Side)	Yr	VG	VG+	NM
❑ 55004	Thoroughly Modern Millie/Jimmy	1967	3.00	6.00	12.00

HIT PACK, THE

SOUL

Number	Title (A Side/B Side)	Yr	VG	VG+	NM
❑ 35010	Never Say No to Your Baby/Let's Dance	1965	12.50	25.00	50.00

HITCHCOCK, ROBYN, AND THE EGYPTIANS

A&M

Number	Title (A Side/B Side)	Yr	VG	VG+	NM
❑ 1409	Madonna of the Wasps/Ruling Class	1989	2.50	5.00	10.00
❑ 3023	Balloon Man/A Globe of Frogs (Electric)	1988	—	2.00	4.00

RELATIVITY

Number	Title (A Side/B Side)	Yr	VG	VG+	NM
❑ 8076 [DJ]	Heaven/Listening to the Higsons	1985	2.50	5.00	10.00

HO-DADS, THE

IMPERIAL

Number	Title (A Side/B Side)	Yr	VG	VG+	NM
❑ 66001	Legends/Honey	1963	7.50	15.00	30.00
❑ 66023	After Dark/Space Race	1964	7.50	15.00	30.00

HOBBITS, THE

DECCA

Number	Title (A Side/B Side)	Yr	VG	VG+	NM
❑ 32226	Sunny Day Girl/Daffodil Days	1967	3.00	6.00	12.00
❑ 32270	Pretty Young Thing/Strawberry Children	1968	3.00	6.00	12.00

ZAR

Number	Title (A Side/B Side)	Yr	VG	VG+	NM
❑ 25	Frodo Lives/Jolly Good Fellow	1967	5.00	10.00	20.00

HOBBS, BUD

MGM

Number	Title (A Side/B Side)	Yr	VG	VG+	NM
❑ 11579	Goose Rock/Rightfully Yours	1953	20.00	40.00	80.00

HODGE, CHRIS

APPLE

Number	Title (A Side/B Side)	Yr	VG	VG+	NM
❑ 1850	We're On Our Way/Supersoul	1972	2.00	4.00	8.00
❑ 1850 [PS]	We're On Our Way/Supersoul	1972	2.50	5.00	10.00
❑ 1858	Goodnight Sweet Lorraine/Contact Love	1973	2.00	4.00	8.00

RCA VICTOR

Number	Title (A Side/B Side)	Yr	VG	VG+	NM
❑ APBO-0289	Beautiful Love/Sweet Lady from the Sky	1974	—	2.50	5.00

HODGES, EDDIE

AURORA

Number	Title (A Side/B Side)	Yr	VG	VG+	NM
❑ 150	Across the Street (Is a Million Miles Away)/She Doesn't Love Me	1965	2.50	5.00	10.00
❑ 153	New Orleans/Hard Times for Young Lovers	1965	2.50	5.00	10.00
❑ 156	Love Minus Zero (No Limit)/The Water Is Over My Head	1965	2.50	5.00	10.00

Number	Title (A Side/B Side)	Yr	VG	VG+	NM
❑ 161	Hitch Hike/Old Man Rag	1966	2.50	5.00	10.00
CADENCE					
❑ 1397	I'm Gonna Knock on Your Door/Ain't Gonna Wash for a Week	1961	3.75	7.50	15.00
❑ 1397 [PS]	I'm Gonna Knock on Your Door/Ain't Gonna Wash for a Week	1961	6.25	12.50	25.00
❑ 1410	Bandit of My Dreams/Mugmates	1962	5.00	10.00	20.00
❑ 1421	(Girls, Girls, Girls) Made to Love/I Make Believe It's You	1962	3.75	7.50	15.00
COLUMBIA					
❑ 42649	Seein' Is Believin'/Secret	1962	3.00	6.00	12.00
❑ 42649 [PS]	Seein' Is Believin'/Secret	1962	4.00	8.00	16.00
❑ 42697	Would You Come Back?/Too Soon to Know	1962	3.00	6.00	12.00
❑ 42811	Rainin' in My Heart/Halfway	1963	3.00	6.00	12.00
DECCA					
❑ 30675	That Funny Little Dog/What Would It Be Like in Heaven	1958	3.75	7.50	15.00
❑ 30903	High Hopes/Don't Dance on Momma's Rug	1959	3.75	7.50	15.00
MGM					
❑ 13219	Avalanche/Just a Kid in Love	1964	2.50	5.00	10.00

HODGES, JESSE

Number	Title (A Side/B Side)	Yr	VG	VG+	NM
FABLE					
❑ 603	I Think It's Almost Christmas Time/My Christmas Prayer	19??	—	3.00	6.00
—B-side by Donna Zuker					

HOG HEAVEN

The Shondells after Tommy James went solo.

Number	Title (A Side/B Side)	Yr	VG	VG+	NM
ROULETTE					
❑ 7091	Theme from a Thought/(B-side unknown)	1970	2.00	4.00	8.00
❑ 7101	Happy/Prayer	1971	2.00	4.00	8.00
❑ 7106	If It Feels Good/(B-side unknown)	1971	2.00	4.00	8.00

HOGG, SMOKEY

Number	Title (A Side/B Side)	Yr	VG	VG+	NM
COMBO					
❑ 11	Where Have You Been/Believe I'll Change My Towns	1952	50.00	100.00	200.00
—Also had releases on Combo 4 and 9, but these are unknown on 45					
EBB					
❑ 127	Good Morning Baby/Sure 'Nuff	1958	6.25	12.50	25.00
FEDERAL					
❑ 12109	Keep a-Walkin'/Do It No More	1953	25.00	50.00	100.00
❑ 12117	Your Little Wagon/Penny Pinching Mama	1953	25.00	50.00	100.00
❑ 12127	Gone, Gone, Gone/I Ain't Got Over It Yet	1953	25.00	50.00	100.00
IMPERIAL					
❑ 5269	When I've Been Drinkin'/Tear Me Down	1954	25.00	50.00	100.00
❑ 5290	My Baby's Gone/Train Whistle	1954	25.00	50.00	100.00
METEOR					
❑ 5021	I Declare/Dark Clouds	1955	25.00	50.00	100.00
SPECIALTY					
❑ 753	I Want My Baby for Christmas/I Want My Baby for Christmas	197?	2.50	5.00	10.00
—B-side by Jimmy Liggins					

HOGS, THE

Early version of THE CHOCOLATE WATCH BAND.

Number	Title (A Side/B Side)	Yr	VG	VG+	NM
HANNA-BARBERA					
❑ 511	Loose Lip Sync Ships/Blues Theme	1967	37.50	75.00	150.00
—A-side produced by Frank Zappa					

HOLDEN, RON

Number	Title (A Side/B Side)	Yr	VG	VG+	NM
CHALLENGE					
❑ 59360	I Tried/I'll Forgive and Forget	1967	10.00	20.00	40.00
DONNA					
❑ 1315	Love You So/My Babe	1959	7.50	15.00	30.00
❑ 1324	Gee, But I'm Lonesome/Susie Jane	1960	6.25	12.50	25.00
❑ 1328	True Love Can Be/Everything's Gonna Be Alright	1960	6.25	12.50	25.00
❑ 1331	Who Says There Ain't No Santa Claus/Your Line Is Busy	1960	6.25	12.50	25.00
❑ 1335	The Big Shoe/Rock and Roll Call	1961	5.00	10.00	20.00
ELDO					
❑ 117	I'll Be Happy/I'll Always Have You	1961	5.00	10.00	20.00
NITE OWL					
❑ 10	Love You So/My Babe	1959	200.00	400.00	800.00
NOW					
❑ 6	Can You Talk?/I Need Ya	1974	—	3.00	6.00
RAMPART					
❑ 645	Girl I Love You/Nothing I Wouldn't Do	1965	3.00	6.00	12.00

HOLE

Number	Title (A Side/B Side)	Yr	VG	VG+	NM
DGC					
❑ 19379	Doll Parts/Plump (Live)	1994	—	2.00	4.00
❑ 97087	Malibu/Celebrity Skin	1999	—	—	3.00
SUB POP					
❑ 93	Dicknail/Burn Black	1991	11.25	22.50	45.00
—First 3,500 on gray marble vinyl					
❑ 93	Dicknail/Burn Black	1991	—	2.50	5.00
—Later pressings on green or black vinyl					
❑ 93 [PS]	Dicknail/Burn Black	1991	—	2.50	5.00
SYMPATHY FOR THE RECORD INDUSTRY					
❑ 53	Retard Girl//Phonebillsong/Johnnie's in the Bathroom	1990	—	—	2.50
❑ 53	Retard Girl//Phonebillsong/Johnnie's in the Bathroom	1990	9.25	18.75	37.50
—First pressing on pink vinyl					
❑ 53 [PS]	Retard Girl//Phonebillsong/Johnnie's in the Bathroom	1990	—	—	2.50
TIM/KERR					
❑ 947081	Miss World/Over the Edge	1994	—	2.00	4.00
—Pink vinyl					
❑ 947081 [PS]	Miss World/Over the Edge	1994	—	2.00	4.00

HOLIDAY, JOHN E.

Number	Title (A Side/B Side)	Yr	VG	VG+	NM
ATLANTIC					
❑ 2091	Yes I Will Love You Tomorrow/Till the End of Time	1961	5.00	10.00	20.00

HOLIDAYS, THE (1)

Detroit-based R&B group.

Number	Title (A Side/B Side)	Yr	VG	VG+	NM
GOLDEN WORLD					
❑ 36	Makin' Up Time/I'll Love You Forever	1966	6.25	12.50	25.00
❑ 47	No Greater Love/Watch Out Girl	1966	6.25	12.50	25.00
GROOVE CITY					
❑ 206	Easy Living/I've Lost You	196?	25.00	50.00	100.00
—As "The New Holidays"					
REVILOT					
❑ 205	Love's Creeping Up on Me/Never Alone	1967	7.50	15.00	30.00
❑ 210	I Know She Cares/I Keep Holding On	1967	7.50	15.00	30.00
❑ 226	I'll Keep Coming Back/All That Is Required of You	1968	6.25	12.50	25.00

HOLIDAYS, THE (U)

None of these are group (1), but exactly how many groups are represented here is not known.

Number	Title (A Side/B Side)	Yr	VG	VG+	NM
ANDIE					
❑ 5019	The Stars Will Remember/Who Knows, Who Cares	1960	15.00	30.00	60.00
BRENT					
❑ 7018	Come Back to Me/No Other Love	1961	5.00	10.00	20.00
BRUNSWICK					
❑ 55084	Sands of Gold/French Riviera	1958	3.75	7.50	15.00
CORAL					
❑ 62430	Love and Learn/I Want You to Love Me	1964	5.00	10.00	20.00
DIXIE					
❑ 1156	Little Miss Hurt/I Got News for You	196?	7.50	15.00	30.00
GALAXY					
❑ 714	Send Back My Love/Deacon Brown	1962	5.00	10.00	20.00
❑ 714 [DJ]	Send Back My Love/Deacon Brown	1962	7.50	15.00	30.00
—Promo on colored vinyl					
KING					
❑ 1217	I'm a-Like a-You (Pizza Pie)/Rolling River	1953	7.50	15.00	30.00
❑ 1246	Just Out of Reach/Let the Dice Decide	1953	7.50	15.00	30.00
MELBA					
❑ 112	The Robin/Desperately	1957	75.00	150.00	300.00
MONUMENT					
❑ 431	Merry Christmas Song/A Very Merry Christmas	1960	3.75	7.50	15.00
NIX					
❑ 537	One Little Kiss/My Girl	1961	7.50	15.00	30.00
PAM					
❑ 111	Refreshing/Crazy Discharge	1959	50.00	100.00	200.00
ROBBEE					
❑ 103	Them There Eyes/The Kiss Cha Cha	1960	15.00	30.00	60.00
❑ 107	Lonely Summer/Then I'll Be Tired of You	1960	12.50	25.00	50.00
SPECIALTY					
❑ 533	Irene/Aw-Aw Baby	1954	10.00	20.00	40.00
TRACK					
❑ 101	Patty Ann/Big Brown Eyes	1962	3.75	7.50	15.00

HOLLAND, BRIAN

Number	Title (A Side/B Side)	Yr	VG	VG+	NM
INVICTUS					
❑ 1265	I'm So Glad (Part 1)/I'm So Glad (Part 2)	1974	—	2.50	5.00
❑ 1272	Super Woman/Let's Get Together	1974	—	2.50	5.00
KUDO					
❑ 667	(Where's the Joy?) In Nature Boy/Shock	1958	150.00	300.00	600.00
—First name as "Briant"					

HOLLAND, EDDIE

Also see HOLLAND-DOZIER.

Number	Title (A Side/B Side)	Yr	VG	VG+	NM
MERCURY					
❑ 71290	You/Little Miss Ruby	1958	25.00	50.00	100.00
MOTOWN					
❑ 1021	Jamie/Take a Chance on Me	1961	6.25	12.50	25.00
❑ 1026	You Deserve What You Got/Last Night I Had a Vision	1962	6.25	12.50	25.00
❑ 1030	If Cleopatra Took a Chance/What About Me	1962	6.25	12.50	25.00
❑ 1030 [PS]	If Cleopatra Took a Chance/What About Me	1962	25.00	50.00	100.00
❑ 1031	If It's Love (It's All Right)/It's Not Too Late	1962	6.25	12.50	25.00
❑ 1036	Darling I Hum Our Song/Just a Few Memories	1963	6.25	12.50	25.00
❑ 1043	Brenda/Baby Shake	1963	6.25	12.50	25.00
❑ 1049	I'm On the Outside Looking In/I Couldn't Cry If I Wanted To	1963	37.50	75.00	150.00
❑ 1052	Leaving Here/Brenda	1964	3.75	7.50	15.00
❑ 1058	Just Ain't Enough Love/Last Night I Had a Vision	1964	3.75	7.50	15.00
❑ 1063	Candy to Me/If You Don't Want My Love	1964	3.75	7.50	15.00
TAMLA					
❑ 102	Merry-Go-Round/It Moves Me	1959	62.50	125.00	250.00
UNITED ARTISTS					
❑ 172	Merry-Go-Round/It Moves Me	1959	7.50	15.00	30.00
❑ 191	Because I Love Her/Everybody's Going	1959	7.50	15.00	30.00
❑ 207	Magic Mirror/Will You Love Me	1960	7.50	15.00	30.00
❑ 280	The Last Laugh/Why Do You Want to Let Me Go	1960	7.50	15.00	30.00

HOLLAND-DOZIER

Also see LAMONT DOZIER; EDDIE HOLLAND.

Number	Title (A Side/B Side)	Yr	VG	VG+	NM
INVICTUS					
❑ 1253	Slipping Away/Can't Get Enough	1973	—	2.50	5.00
❑ 1254	If You Don't Wanta Be in My Life/New Breed Kinda Woman	1973	—	2.50	5.00
❑ 1258	You Took Me from a World Outside/I'm Gonna Hijack Ya, Kidnap Ya, Take What I Want	1973	—	2.50	5.00
❑ 9110	Don't Leave Me (Part 1)/Don't Leave Me (Part 2)	1972	—	2.50	5.00
❑ 9125	Why Can't We Be Lovers/Don't Leave Me	1972	—	2.50	5.00

Number	Title (A Side/B Side)	Yr	VG	VG+	NM
❑ 9133	Don't Leave Me Starvin' for Your Love (Part 1)/ Don't Leave Me Starvin' for Your Love (Part 2)	1972	—	2.50	5.00

MOTOWN

Number	Title (A Side/B Side)	Yr	VG	VG+	NM
❑ 1045	What Goes Up Must Come Down/Come On Home	1963	6.25	12.50	25.00

HOLLIDAY, MICHAEL

CAPITOL

Number	Title (A Side/B Side)	Yr	VG	VG+	NM
❑ F3720	Good Luck, Good Health, God Bless You/John and Julie	1957	3.00	6.00	12.00
❑ F4018	Rooney/Keep Your Heart	1958	3.00	6.00	12.00

HOLLIES, THE

Also see ALLAN CLARKE; GRAHAM NASH; TERRY SYLVESTER; THE TREMELOES/THE HOLLIES.

ATLANTIC

Number	Title (A Side/B Side)	Yr	VG	VG+	NM
❑ 89768 [DJ]	Casualty (same on both sides)	1983	—	2.50	5.00
—May be promo only					
❑ 89784	Someone Else's Eyes/If the Lights Go Out	1983	—	—	3.00
❑ 89819	Stop in the Name of Love/Musical Pictures	1983	—	—	3.00
❑ 89819 [PS]	Stop in the Name of Love/Musical Pictures	1983	—	2.50	5.00

EPIC

Number	Title (A Side/B Side)	Yr	VG	VG+	NM
❑ 10180	Carrie-Anne/Signs That Will Never Change	1967	2.00	4.00	8.00
❑ 10180 [PS]	Carrie-Anne/Signs That Will Never Change	1967	3.75	7.50	15.00
❑ 10234	King Midas in Reverse/Water on the Brain	1967	2.00	4.00	8.00
❑ 10234 [PS]	King Midas in Reverse/Water on the Brain	1967	3.75	7.50	15.00
❑ 10251	Dear Eloise/When Your Light's Turned On	1967	2.00	4.00	8.00
❑ 10251 [PS]	Dear Eloise/When Your Light's Turned On	1967	3.75	7.50	15.00
❑ 10298	Jennifer Eccles/Try It	1968	2.00	4.00	8.00
❑ 10361	Do the Best You Can/Elevated Observations	1968	2.00	4.00	8.00
❑ 10400	Listen to Me/Everything Is Sunshine	1968	2.00	4.00	8.00
❑ 10454	Sorry Suzanne/Not That Way at All	1969	2.00	4.00	8.00
❑ 10532	He Ain't Heavy, He's My Brother/Cos You Like to Love Me	1969	—	3.00	6.00
—A-side: Elton John on piano					
❑ 10613	I Can't Tell the Bottom from the Top/Mad Professor Blythe	1970	—	3.00	6.00
❑ 10677	Gasoline Alley Bred/Dandelion Wine	1970	2.50	5.00	10.00
❑ 10716	Survival of the Fittest/Man Without a Heart	1971	3.00	6.00	12.00
❑ 10754	Hey Willy/Row the Boat Together	1971	2.50	5.00	10.00
❑ 10842	The Baby/Oh Granny	1972	2.50	5.00	10.00
❑ 10842 [PS]	The Baby/Oh Granny	1972	12.50	25.00	50.00
❑ 10871	Long Cool Woman (In a Black Dress)/Look What We've Got	1972	—	2.50	5.00
❑ 10920	Long Dark Road/Indian Girl	1972	—	2.50	5.00
❑ 10951	Magic Woman Touch/Blue in the Morning	1973	—	2.50	5.00
❑ 10989	Jesus Was a Crossmaker/I Had a Dream	1973	—	2.50	5.00
❑ 11025	Won't We Feel Good/Slow Down	1973	—	2.50	5.00
❑ 11051	The Day That Curley Billy Shot Down Crazy Sam McGee/Born a Man	1973	—	2.50	5.00
❑ 11100	The Air That I Breathe/No More Riders	1974	—	2.50	5.00
❑ 50029	Don't Let Me Down/Layin' to the Music	1974	—	2.50	5.00
❑ 50086	Sandy/Second Hand Hangups	1975	—	2.50	5.00
❑ 50110	Another Night/Time Machine Jive	1975	—	2.00	4.00
❑ 50144	Look Out Johnny/I'm Down	1975	—	2.00	4.00
❑ 50204	Crocodile Woman (She Bites)/Write On	1976	—	2.00	4.00
❑ 50359	Sandy/Second Hand Hangups	1977	—	2.00	4.00
❑ 50422	Draggin' My Heels/I Won't Move Over	1977	—	2.00	4.00
❑ 50522	Burn Out/Writing on the Wall	1978	—	2.00	4.00

IMPERIAL

Number	Title (A Side/B Side)	Yr	VG	VG+	NM
❑ 54050	Look Through My Window/I'm Alive	196?	3.75	7.50	15.00
—"The Golden Series" gold label reissue with incorrect A-side title					
❑ 66026	Just One Look/Keep Off That Friend of Mine	1964	5.00	10.00	20.00
❑ 66044	Here I Go Again/Lucille	1964	3.75	7.50	15.00
❑ 66070	Come On Back/We're Through	1964	3.75	7.50	15.00
❑ 66099	Yes I Will/Nobody	1965	10.00	20.00	40.00
❑ 66119	I'm Alive/You Know He Did	1965	3.75	7.50	15.00
❑ 66134	Look Through Any Window/So Lonely	1965	3.00	6.00	12.00
❑ 66158	I Can't Let Go/I've Got a Way of My Own	1966	3.75	7.50	15.00
❑ 66186	Bus Stop/Don't Run and Hide	1966	3.00	6.00	12.00
❑ 66214	Stop Stop Stop/It's You	1966	3.00	6.00	12.00
❑ 66231	On a Carousel/All the World Is Love	1967	3.00	6.00	12.00
❑ 66231 [PS]	On a Carousel/All the World Is Love	1967	7.50	15.00	30.00
❑ 66240	Pay You Back With Interest/Whatcha Gonna Do 'Bout It	1967	3.00	6.00	12.00
❑ 66258	Just One Look/Running Through the Night	1967	3.00	6.00	12.00
❑ 66271	If I Needed Someone/I'll Be True to You (Yes I Will)	1968	10.00	20.00	40.00

LIBERTY

Number	Title (A Side/B Side)	Yr	VG	VG+	NM
❑ 55674	Stay/Now's the Time	1964	15.00	30.00	60.00

UNITED ARTISTS

Number	Title (A Side/B Side)	Yr	VG	VG+	NM
❑ 50079	After the Fox/The Fox Trot	1966	5.00	10.00	20.00
—With Peter Sellers					

HOLLOWAY, BRENDA

DONNA

Number	Title (A Side/B Side)	Yr	VG	VG+	NM
❑ 1358	Echo/Hey Fool	1962	10.00	20.00	40.00
❑ 1366	Game of Love/Echo-Echo-Echo	1962	12.50	25.00	50.00
❑ 1370	I'll Give My Life/More Echo	1962	12.50	25.00	50.00

TAMLA

Number	Title (A Side/B Side)	Yr	VG	VG+	NM
❑ 54094	Every Little Bit Hurts/Land of 1,000 Boys	1964	3.00	6.00	12.00
❑ 54099	I'll Always Love You/Sad Song	1964	3.75	7.50	15.00
❑ 54111	When I'm Gone/I've Been Good to You	1965	3.75	7.50	15.00
❑ 54111 [PS]	When I'm Gone/I've Been Good to You	1965	25.00	50.00	100.00
❑ 54115	Operator/I'll Be Available	1965	3.75	7.50	15.00
❑ 54121	You Can Cry on My Shoulder/How Many Times Did You Mean It	1965	5.00	10.00	20.00
❑ 54125	Sad Song/Together 'Til the End of Time	1965	5.00	10.00	20.00
❑ 54137	Hurt a Little Every Day/Where Were You	1966	7.50	15.00	30.00
❑ 54144	'Til Johnny Comes/Where Were You	1967	50.00	100.00	200.00
❑ 54148	Just Look What You've Done/Starting the Hurt All Over Again	1967	6.25	12.50	25.00
❑ 54155	You've Made Me So Very Happy/I've Got to Find It	1967	5.00	10.00	20.00
❑ 206312 [DJ]	Play It Cool, Stay in School	1966	150.00	300.00	600.00
—Promo for Women's Ad Club of Detroit					

HOLLOWAY, PATRICE

Also see JOSIE AND THE PUSSYCATS.

CAPITOL

Number	Title (A Side/B Side)	Yr	VG	VG+	NM
❑ 5680	Stolen Hours/Lucky My Boy	1966	20.00	40.00	80.00
❑ 5778	Love and Desire/Ecstasy	1967	15.00	30.00	60.00
❑ 5985	Stay with Your Own Kind/That's All You Got to Do	1967	12.50	25.00	50.00

TASTE

Number	Title (A Side/B Side)	Yr	VG	VG+	NM
❑ 125	Do the Del Viking (Pt. 1)/Do the Del Viking (Pt. 2)	1963	7.50	15.00	30.00

HOLLY, BUDDY

Also see THE CRICKETS (1).

CORAL

Number	Title (A Side/B Side)	Yr	VG	VG+	NM
❑ 61852	Words of Love/Mailman, Bring Me No More Blues	1957	150.00	250.00	400.00
—Promos for any Coral title valued at $50 or under Near Mint are worth 2-4 times the stock copy value.					
❑ 61885	Peggy Sue/Everyday	1957	12.50	25.00	50.00
—Orange label					
❑ 61885	Peggy Sue/Everyday	196?	6.25	12.50	25.00
—Black color bars label					
❑ 61947	I'm Gonna Love You Too/Listen to Me	1958	12.50	25.00	50.00
❑ 61985	Rave On/Take Your Time	1958	12.50	25.00	50.00
❑ 62006	Early in the Morning/Now We're One	1958	12.50	25.00	50.00
❑ 62051	Heartbeat/Well...All Right	1958	12.50	25.00	50.00
❑ 62074	It Doesn't Matter Anymore/Raining in My Heart	1959	10.00	20.00	40.00
❑ 62134	Peggy Sue Got Married/Crying, Waiting, Hoping	1959	15.00	30.00	60.00
❑ 62210	True Love Ways/That Makes It Tough	1960	12.50	25.00	50.00
❑ 62283	You're So Square (Baby I Don't Care)/Valley of Tears	1961	40.00	80.00	160.00
—Evidently only released in Canada					
❑ 62329	Reminiscing/Wait Till the Sun Shines, Nellie	1962	7.50	15.00	30.00
❑ 62352	True Love Ways/Bo Diddley	1963	15.00	30.00	60.00
❑ 62369	Brown Eyed Handsome Man/Wishing	1963	10.00	20.00	40.00
❑ 62390	Rock Around with Ollie Vee/I'm Gonna Love You Too	1963	10.00	20.00	40.00
❑ 62448	Slippin' and Slidin'/What to Do	1965	25.00	50.00	100.00
❑ 62554	Rave On/Early in the Morning	1968	7.50	15.00	30.00
❑ 62558	Love Is Strange/You're the One	1969	5.00	10.00	20.00
❑ 62558 [PS]	Love Is Strange/You're the One	1969	7.50	15.00	30.00

DECCA

Number	Title (A Side/B Side)	Yr	VG	VG+	NM
❑ 29854	Blue Days, Black Nights/Love Me	1956	150.00	300.00	600.00
—With lines on either side of "Decca"					
❑ 29854	Blue Days, Black Nights/Love Me	1956	75.00	150.00	300.00
—With star under "Decca"					
❑ 29854 [DJ]	Blue Days, Black Nights/Love Me	1956	100.00	200.00	400.00
—Promos have pink labels					
❑ 30166	Modern Don Juan/You Are My One Desire	1956	125.00	250.00	500.00
—With lines on either side of "Decca"					
❑ 30166	Modern Don Juan/You Are My One Desire	1956	62.50	125.00	250.00
—With star under "Decca"					
❑ 30166 [DJ]	Modern Don Juan/You Are My One Desire	1956	75.00	150.00	300.00
—Promos have pink labels					
❑ 30434	That'll Be the Day/Rock Around with Ollie Vee	1957	62.50	125.00	250.00
—With star under "Decca"					
❑ 30434	That'll Be the Day/Rock Around with Ollie Vee	1957	100.00	200.00	400.00
—With lines on either side of "Decca"					
❑ 30434 [DJ]	That'll Be the Day/Rock Around with Ollie Vee	1957	62.50	125.00	250.00
—Promos have pink labels					
❑ 30543	Love Me/You Are My One Desire	1958	75.00	150.00	300.00
❑ 30543 [DJ]	Love Me/You Are My One Desire	1958	75.00	150.00	300.00
—Green label promos					
❑ 30543 [DJ]	Love Me/You Are My One Desire	1958	50.00	100.00	200.00
—Pink label promos					
❑ 30650	Ting-a-Ling/Girl on My Mind	1958	75.00	150.00	300.00
❑ 30650 [DJ]	Ting-a-Ling/Girl on My Mind	1958	50.00	100.00	200.00
—Promos have pink labels					

MCA

Number	Title (A Side/B Side)	Yr	VG	VG+	NM
❑ 40905	It Doesn't Matter Anymore/Peggy Sue	1978	—	2.50	5.00
❑ 40905 [PS]	It Doesn't Matter Anymore/Peggy Sue	1978	—	2.50	5.00

7-Inch Extended Plays

CORAL

Number	Title (A Side/B Side)	Yr	VG	VG+	NM
❑ EC 81169	Listen to Me/Peggy Sue//I'm Gonna Love You Too/Everyday	1958	75.00	150.00	300.00
❑ EC 81169 [PS]	Listen to Me	1958	75.00	150.00	300.00
❑ EC 81182	It Doesn't Matter Anymore/Heartbeat//Raining in My Heart/Early in the Morning	1959	75.00	150.00	300.00
❑ EC 81182 [PS]	The Buddy Holly Story	1959	75.00	150.00	300.00
❑ EC 81191	Peggy Sue Got Married/Crying, Waiting, Hoping//Learning the Game/That Makes It Tough	1961	62.50	125.00	250.00
❑ EC 81191 [PS]	Buddy Holly	1961	62.50	125.00	250.00
❑ EC 81193	Brown Eyed Handsome Man/Wishing//Bo Diddley/True Love Ways	1961	62.50	125.00	250.00
❑ EC 81193 [PS]	Brown Eyed Handsome Man	1961	62.50	125.00	250.00

DECCA

Number	Title (A Side/B Side)	Yr	VG	VG+	NM
❑ ED 2575	*That'll Be the Day/Blue Days — Black Nights/Ting-a-Ling/You Are My One Desire	1958	150.00	300.00	600.00
❑ ED 2575 [PS]	That'll Be the Day	1958	500.00	1000.	2000.
—Sleeve has liner notes on back					
❑ ED 2575 [PS]	That'll Be the Day	1958	150.00	300.00	600.00
—Sleeve has other EP ads on back					

HOLLY TWINS, THE

LIBERTY

Number	Title (A Side/B Side)	Yr	VG	VG+	NM
❑ 55015	Take Me Back/It's Easy	1956	6.25	12.50	25.00
❑ 55048	I Want Elvis for Christmas/The Tender Age	1956	12.50	25.00	50.00

RENDEZVOUS

Number	Title (A Side/B Side)	Yr	VG	VG+	NM
❑ 180	Okee-Feenokee/Potato Chips	1962	3.00	6.00	12.00

HOLLYHAWKS, THE
With Niki Sullivan, ex-CRICKETS (1).

Number	Title (A Side/B Side)	Yr	VG	VG+	NM
JUBILEE					
❑ 5441	I Cry All the Time/When Came the Fall	1962	20.00	40.00	80.00

HOLLYWOOD ARGYLES, THE
Also see FLESH GORDON AND THE NUDE HOLLYWOOD ARGYLES; GARY PAXTON.

Number	Title (A Side/B Side)	Yr	VG	VG+	NM
BRENT					
❑ 7004	Vacation Days Are Over/It Takes Time	1959	7.50	15.00	30.00
—As "The Argyles"					
CHATTAHOOCHIE					
❑ 691	Long Hair, Unsquare Dude Called Jack/Ole	1965	3.75	7.50	15.00
FELSTED					
❑ 8674	Bossy Nover/Find Another Way	1963	5.00	10.00	20.00
FINER ARTS					
❑ 1002	The Morning After/See You in the Morning	1961	5.00	10.00	20.00
KAMMY					
❑ 105	Alley-Oop '65/Do the Funky Foot	1965	5.00	10.00	20.00
—As "The New Hollywood Argyles"					
LUTE					
❑ 5905	Alley Oop/Sho' Know a Lot About Love	1960	6.25	12.50	25.00
❑ 5908	Gun Totin' Critter Called Jack/Bug Eyed Man	1960	5.00	10.00	20.00
❑ 6002	Hully Gully/So Fine	1960	5.00	10.00	20.00
PAXLEY					
❑ 200	Unemployment (same on both sides)	196?	2.50	5.00	10.00
❑ 752	You've Been Torturing Me/The Grubble	1960	5.00	10.00	20.00
TRILL					
❑ 6311	The Watermelon Song/Short Fat Outlaw	196?	6.25	12.50	25.00

HOLLYWOOD FLAMES, THE
Also see BOBBY DAY.

Number	Title (A Side/B Side)	Yr	VG	VG+	NM
ATCO					
❑ 6155	Every Day, Every Way/If I Thought I Needed You	1959	3.75	7.50	15.00
❑ 6164	Ball and Chain/I Found a Boy	1960	3.75	7.50	15.00
❑ 6171	Devil or Angel/Do You Ever Think of Me	1960	3.75	7.50	15.00
❑ 6180	Money Honey/My Heart's On Fire	1960	3.75	7.50	15.00
CHESS					
❑ 1787	Gee/Yes They Do	1961	3.00	6.00	12.00
DECCA					
❑ 29285	Peggy/Ooh La La	1954	18.75	37.50	75.00
❑ 48331	Let's Talk It Over/I Know	1955	18.75	37.50	75.00
EBB					
❑ 119	Buzz-Buzz-Buzz/Crazy	1957	7.50	15.00	30.00
❑ 131	Give Me Back My Heart/A Little Bird	1958	6.25	12.50	25.00
❑ 144	Frankenstein's Den/Strollin' on the Beach	1958	6.25	12.50	25.00
❑ 146	Chains of Love/Let's Talk It Over	1958	6.25	12.50	25.00
❑ 149	A Star Fell/I'll Get By	1958	6.25	12.50	25.00
❑ 153	I'll Be Seeing You/Just for You	1959	7.50	15.00	30.00
❑ 158	So Good/There Is Something on Your Mind	1959	6.25	12.50	25.00
❑ 162	Now That You're Gone/Hawaiian Dream	1959	6.25	12.50	25.00
❑ 163	Much Too Much/In the Dark	1959	6.25	12.50	25.00
LUCKY					
❑ 001	One Night with a Fool/Ride, Helen, Ride	1954	150.00	300.00	600.00
❑ 006	Peggy/Ooh-La-La	1954	150.00	300.00	600.00
❑ 009	Let's Talk It Over/I Know	1954	100.00	200.00	400.00
MONA-LEE					
❑ 135	Buzz-Buzz-Buzz/Crazy	1958	6.25	12.50	25.00
MONEY					
❑ 202	Fare Thee Well/I'm Leaving	1954	100.00	200.00	400.00
SWING TIME					
❑ 345	Let's Talk It Over/I Know	1953	125.00	250.00	500.00
❑ 346	Go and Get Some More/Another Soldier Gone	1953	125.00	250.00	500.00
—B-side by the Question Marks					
SYMBOL					
❑ 211	Dance Senorita/Annie Don't Love Me Anymore	1965	3.00	6.00	12.00
❑ 215	I'm Coming Home/I'm Gonna Stand By You	1966	3.00	6.00	12.00
VEE JAY					
❑ 515	Drop Me a Line/Letter to My Love	1963	3.75	7.50	15.00

HOLLYWOOD PERSUADERS, THE

Number	Title (A Side/B Side)	Yr	VG	VG+	NM
ORIGINAL SOUND					
❑ 39	Tijuana/Grunion Run	1964	12.50	25.00	50.00
❑ 39	Tijuana Surf/Grunion Run	1964	12.50	25.00	50.00
❑ 44	Persuasion/Juarez	1964	6.25	12.50	25.00
❑ 50	Drums-A-Go-Go/Agua Caliente	1965	6.25	12.50	25.00
❑ 58	Hollywood A-Go-Go/Eve of Destruction	1965	6.25	12.50	25.00

HOLLYWOOD PLAYBOYS, THE
With Nick Massi, later of THE FOUR SEASONS.

Number	Title (A Side/B Side)	Yr	VG	VG+	NM
SURE					
❑ 105	Ding Dong School Is Out/Talk to Audrey	1960	7.50	15.00	30.00

HOLLYWOOD PRODUCERS, THE

Number	Title (A Side/B Side)	Yr	VG	VG+	NM
PARKWAY					
❑ 993	Whits Silk Glove/You're Not Welcome	1966	7.50	15.00	30.00

HOLMAN, EDDIE

Number	Title (A Side/B Side)	Yr	VG	VG+	NM
ABC					
❑ 11149	I Love You/I Surrender	1968	2.50	5.00	10.00
❑ 11240	Hey There Lonely Girl/It's All in the Game	1969	—	3.00	6.00
❑ 11261	Don't Stop Now/Since I Don't Have You	1970	—	3.00	6.00
❑ 11265	I'll Be There/Cause You're Mine Little Girl	1970	—	3.00	6.00
❑ 11276	Cathy Called/I Need Somebody	1970	—	3.00	6.00
❑ 11292	Love Story/Four Walls	1971	—	3.00	6.00
ASCOT					
❑ 2142	Go Get Your Own/Laughing at Me	1963	3.75	7.50	15.00
BELL					
❑ 712	I'm Not Gonna Give Up/I'll Cry 1,000 Tears	1968	5.00	10.00	20.00
GSF					
❑ 6873	My Mind Keeps Telling Me (That I Really Love You, Girl)/Stranded in a Dream	1972	—	3.00	6.00
❑ 6885	Young Girl/I'll Call You Joy	1972	—	3.00	6.00
PARKWAY					
❑ 106	Am I a Loser/You Know That I Will	1966	5.00	10.00	20.00
❑ 133	Somewhere Waits a Lonely Girl/Stay Mine for Heaven's Sake	1967	5.00	10.00	20.00
❑ 157	Why Do Fools Fall in Love/Never Let Me Go	1967	5.00	10.00	20.00
❑ 960	This Can't Be True/A Free Country	1965	5.00	10.00	20.00
❑ 981	Don't Stop Now/Eddie's My Name	1966	5.00	10.00	20.00
❑ 994	Return to Me/Stay Mine for Heaven's Sake	1966	5.00	10.00	20.00
SALSOUL					
❑ 2026	This Will Be a Night to Remember/Time Will Tell	1977	—	2.50	5.00
❑ 2043	You Make My Life Complete/Somehow You Make Me Feel	1977	—	2.50	5.00
SILVER BLUE					
❑ 807	You're My Lady (Right Or Wrong)/(Instrumental)	1974	—	2.50	5.00
❑ 815	Just Say I Love Her/Darling Take Me Back	1974	—	2.50	5.00
UNITED ARTISTS					
❑ 609	Go Get Your Own/Laughing at Me	1963	—	—	—
—Unreleased					

HOLMES, MARVIN

Number	Title (A Side/B Side)	Yr	VG	VG+	NM
UNI					
❑ 55111	Ooh, Ooh, The Dragon (Part 1)/Ooh, Ooh, The Dragon (Part 2)	1969	6.25	12.50	25.00
❑ 55233	Sweet Talk/Thang	1970	6.25	12.50	25.00

HOLMES, RUPERT

Number	Title (A Side/B Side)	Yr	VG	VG+	NM
EPIC					
❑ 11014	Philly/Talk	1973	—	3.00	6.00
❑ 11117	Our National Pastime/Phantom of the Opera	1974	—	3.00	6.00
❑ 50013	Terminal/Bagdad	1974	—	3.00	6.00
❑ 50096	I Don't Wanna Hold Your Hand/The Man Behind the Woman	1975	—	3.00	6.00
❑ 50161	Deco Lady/Terminal	1975	—	3.00	6.00
❑ 50223	Weekend Lover/Weekend Lover	1976	—	2.50	5.00
❑ 50295	You Make Me Real/Who, What, When, Where, How	1976	—	2.50	5.00
INFINITY					
❑ 50035	Escape (The Pina Colada Song)/Drop It	1979	—	2.50	5.00
❑ 50051	Him/Get Outta Yourself	1980	—	—	—
—Canceled					
MCA					
❑ 41173	Him/Get Outta Yourself	1980	—	2.00	4.00
❑ 41235	Answering Machine/Lunch Hour	1980	—	2.00	4.00
❑ 50035	Escape (The Pina Colada Song)/Drop It	1980	—	2.00	4.00
❑ 51019	Morning Man/The Mask	1980	—	2.00	4.00
❑ 51045	Blackjack/Crowd Pleaser	1981	—	2.00	4.00
❑ 51092	I Don't Need You/Cold	1981	—	2.00	4.00
PRIVATE STOCK					
❑ 45183	Bedside Companions/So Beautiful It Hurts	1978	—	2.50	5.00
❑ 45199	Let's Get Crazy Tonight/Long Way Home	1978	—	2.50	5.00

HOLY MODAL ROUNDERS, THE

Number	Title (A Side/B Side)	Yr	VG	VG+	NM
ELEKTRA					
❑ 45644	Bird Song/Dame Fortune	1968	3.75	7.50	15.00
METROMEDIA					
❑ 223	Boobs a Lot/Love Is the Closest Thing	1971	2.50	5.00	10.00

HOMBRES, THE

Number	Title (A Side/B Side)	Yr	VG	VG+	NM
SUN					
❑ 1104	If This Ain't Loving You Baby/You Made Me What I Am	1969	2.50	5.00	10.00
VERVE FORECAST					
❑ 5058	Let It All Hang Out/Go Girl, Go	1967	3.75	7.50	15.00
❑ 5058	Let It Out (Let It All Hang Out)/Go Girl, Go	1967	3.00	6.00	12.00
❑ 5076	It's a Gas/Am I High	1967	2.50	5.00	10.00
❑ 5083	The Prodigal/Mau, Mau, Mau	1968	2.50	5.00	10.00
❑ 5093	Pumpkin Man/Take My Overwhelming Love	1968	2.50	5.00	10.00

HOMEMADE THEATER

Number	Title (A Side/B Side)	Yr	VG	VG+	NM
A&M					
❑ 1776	Santa Jaws (Part 1)/Santa Jaws (Part 2)	1975	3.75	7.50	15.00
❑ 1887	C.B. Santa/Soup of the Day	1976	3.75	7.50	15.00

HOMER

Number	Title (A Side/B Side)	Yr	VG	VG+	NM
UNITED					
❑ 123-6	I Never Cared for You/(B-side unknown)	1969	6.25	12.50	25.00
❑ 123-8	Texas Lights/(B-side unknown)	1970	5.00	10.00	20.00
❑ 123-10	Dandelion Wine/(B-side unknown)	1970	5.00	10.00	20.00

HONDELLS, THE

Number	Title (A Side/B Side)	Yr	VG	VG+	NM
AMOS					
❑ 131	Follow the Bouncing Ball/The Legend of Frankie and Johnny	1969	3.00	6.00	12.00
❑ 150	Shine On Ruby Mountain/The Legend of Frankie and Johnny	1970	3.00	6.00	12.00
COLUMBIA					
❑ 44361	Just One More Chance/Yes to You	1967	5.00	10.00	20.00
❑ 44557	Another Woman/Atlanta Georgia Stray	1968	5.00	10.00	20.00
MERCURY					
❑ 72324	Little Honda/Hot Rod High	1964	5.00	10.00	20.00
❑ 72366	My Buddy Seat/You're Gonna Ride with Me	1964	5.00	10.00	20.00
❑ 72366 [PS]	My Buddy Seat/You're Gonna Ride with Me	1964	6.25	12.50	25.00
❑ 72405	Little Sidewalk Surfer Girl/Come On Baby (Pack It In)	1965	5.00	10.00	20.00
❑ 72443	Sea of Love/Do As I Say	1965	5.00	10.00	20.00
❑ 72479	You Meet the Nicest People on a Honda/Sea Cruise	1965	5.00	10.00	20.00

Number	Title (A Side/B Side)	Yr	VG	VG+	NM
❑ 72479 [PS]	You Meet the Nicest People on a Honda/Sea Cruise	1965	7.50	15.00	30.00
❑ 72523	Endless Sleep/Follow Your Heart	1966	3.75	7.50	15.00
❑ 72563	Younger Girl/All American Girl	1966	3.75	7.50	15.00
❑ 72605	Country Love/Kissin' My Life Away	1966	3.75	7.50	15.00
❑ 72626	Cheryl's Goin' Home/Show Me	1966	3.75	7.50	15.00

HONEY BEES, THE (1)

Number	Title (A Side/B Side)	Yr	VG	VG+	NM
FONTANA					
❑ 1505	You Turn Me On Boy/Some of Your Lovin'	1965	5.00	10.00	20.00
❑ 1939	One Wonderful Night/She Don't Deserve You	1964	5.00	10.00	20.00
GARRISON					
❑ 3005	Never in a Million Years/Let's Get Back Together	1966	62.50	125.00	250.00
VEE JAY					
❑ 611	One Girl, One Boy/No Guy	1964	6.25	12.50	25.00
WAND					
❑ 1141	Never in a Million Years/Let's Get Back Together	1966	3.00	6.00	12.00

HONEY BEES, THE (2)

Number	Title (A Side/B Side)	Yr	VG	VG+	NM
IMPERIAL					
❑ 5400	Endless/Let's See What's Happening	1956	10.00	20.00	40.00
❑ 5436	Just to Live Again/What's to Become of Me	1957	10.00	20.00	40.00

HONEY CONE, THE

Number	Title (A Side/B Side)	Yr	VG	VG+	NM
HOT WAX					
❑ 6901	While You're Out Looking for Sugar?/The Feeling's Gone	1969	—	3.00	6.00
❑ 6903	Girls It Ain't Easy/The Feeling's Gone	1969	—	3.00	6.00
❑ 7001	Take Me With You/Take My Love	1970	—	3.00	6.00
❑ 7005	When Will It End/Take Me With You	1970	—	3.00	6.00
❑ 7011	Want Ads/We Belong Together	1970	—	3.00	6.00
—Mostly white label					
❑ 7011	Want Ads/We Belong Together	1970	—	2.50	5.00
—Mostly orange label					
❑ 7106	Stick-Up/V.I.P.	1971	—	3.00	6.00
❑ 7110	One Monkey Don't Stop No Show Part I/One Monkey Don't Stop No Show Part II	1971	—	3.00	6.00
❑ 7113	The Day I Found Myself/When Will It End	1971	—	3.00	6.00
❑ 7205	Sittin' on a Time Bomb (Waitin' for the Hurt to Come)/It's Better to Have Loved and Lost	1972	—	3.00	6.00
❑ 7208	Innocent Till Proven Guilty/Don't Send Me an Invitation	1972	—	3.00	6.00
❑ 7212	Ace in the Hole/Ooo Baby Baby	1972	—	3.00	6.00
❑ 7301	If I Can't Fly/Woman Can't Live by Bread Alone	1973	—	3.00	6.00
❑ 9255	The Truth Will Come Out/Somebody Is Always Messing Up a Good Thing	1974	—	3.00	6.00

HONEYCOMBS, THE

Number	Title (A Side/B Side)	Yr	VG	VG+	NM
INTERPHON					
❑ 7707	Have I the Right?/Please Don't Pretend Again	1964	3.00	6.00	12.00
❑ 7713	I Can't Stop/I'll Cry Tomorrow	1964	2.50	5.00	10.00
❑ 7713 [PS]	I Can't Stop/I'll Cry Tomorrow	1964	6.25	12.50	25.00
❑ 7716	Color Slide/That's the Way	1965	2.50	5.00	10.00
❑ 7716 [PS]	Colour Slide/That's the Way	1965	6.25	12.50	25.00
—Yes, the American sleeve spells the A-side the British way					
WARNER BROS.					
❑ 5634	I'll See You Tomorrow/Something Better Beginning	1965	2.50	5.00	10.00
❑ 5655	I Can't Get Through to You/That's the Way	1965	2.50	5.00	10.00
❑ 5803	How Will I Know/Who Is Sylvia	1966	2.50	5.00	10.00

HONEYCONES, THE

Number	Title (A Side/B Side)	Yr	VG	VG+	NM
EMBER					
❑ 1033	Betty Moretti/Cool It Baby	1958	5.00	10.00	20.00
❑ 1036	Op/Vision of You	1958	6.25	12.50	25.00
❑ 1042	Gee Whiz/Rockin' in the Knees	1958	5.00	10.00	20.00
❑ 1049	Tell Me Baby/Your Face	1959	5.00	10.00	20.00

HONEYCUTT, GLENN

Number	Title (A Side/B Side)	Yr	VG	VG+	NM
FERNWOOD					
❑ 142	Campus Love/Tombigbee Queen	1964	25.00	50.00	100.00
SUN					
❑ 264	I'll Be Around/I'll Wait Forever	1957	7.50	15.00	30.00

HONEYDRIPPERS, THE

Also see JEFF BECK; JIMMY PAGE; ROBERT PLANT.

Number	Title (A Side/B Side)	Yr	VG	VG+	NM
ES PARANZA					
❑ 99686	Rockin' at Midnight/Young Boy Blues	1984	—	—	3.00
❑ 99686 [PS]	Rockin' at Midnight/Young Boy Blues	1984	—	—	3.00
❑ 99701	Sea of Love/Rockin' at Midnight	1984	—	2.50	5.00
❑ 99701	Sea of Love/I Get a Thrill	1984	—	—	3.00
❑ 99701 [PS]	Sea of Love/Rockin' at Midnight	1984	—	2.50	5.00
❑ 99701 [PS]	Sea of Love/I Get a Thrill	1984	—	—	3.00

HONEYS, THE

Number	Title (A Side/B Side)	Yr	VG	VG+	NM
CAPITOL					
❑ 2454	Goodnight My Love/Tonight You Belong to Me	1969	20.00	40.00	80.00
❑ 4952	Surfin' Down the Swanee River/Shoot the Curl	1963	37.50	75.00	150.00
❑ 4952 [PS]	Surfin' Down the Swanee River/Shoot the Curl	1963	200.00	400.00	800.00
❑ 5034	Hide Go Seek/Pray for Surf	1963	50.00	100.00	200.00
❑ 5093	The One You Can't Have/From Jimmy With Tears	1963	50.00	100.00	200.00
WARNER BROS.					
❑ 5430	He's a Doll/The Love of a Boy and Girl	1964	150.00	300.00	600.00
—Stock copy; red label					
❑ 5430 [DJ]	He's a Doll/The Love of a Boy and Girl	1964	50.00	100.00	200.00
—Promotional copy; white label					

HONEYTONES, THE

Number	Title (A Side/B Side)	Yr	VG	VG+	NM
BIG TOP					
❑ 3002	Don't Look Now, But/I Know, I Know	1958	5.00	10.00	20.00
MERCURY					
❑ 70557	Too Bad/Somewhere, Sometime, Someday	1955	6.25	12.50	25.00
WING					
❑ 90013	False Alarm/Honeybun Cha Cha	1955	7.50	15.00	30.00

HONOR SOCIETY, THE

See THE HAPPENINGS.

HOOK, THE

Number	Title (A Side/B Side)	Yr	VG	VG+	NM
UNI					
❑ 55057	Son of Fantasy/Plug Your Head In	1968	2.50	5.00	10.00
❑ 55077	Love Theme in E Major/Homes	1968	2.50	5.00	10.00
❑ 55149	In the Beginning/Show You the Way	1969	2.50	5.00	10.00

HOOKER, JOHN LEE

Number	Title (A Side/B Side)	Yr	VG	VG+	NM
ABC					
❑ 11298	Doin' the Shout/Kick Hit 4 Hit Kix U	1971	—	3.00	6.00
❑ 11320	Never Get Out of These Blues Alive/Boogie with the Hook	1972	—	3.00	6.00
BATTLE					
❑ 45901	No More Doggin'/I Need Some Money	1962	2.50	5.00	10.00
BLUESWAY					
❑ 61010	Motor City Is Burning/Want Ad Blues	1967	2.00	4.00	8.00
❑ 61014	Mr. Lucky/Cry Before I Go	1968	—	3.00	6.00
❑ 61017	Back Biters and Syndicators/Think Twice Before You Go	1968	—	3.00	6.00
❑ 61023	I Don't Wanna Go to Vietnam/Simply the Truth	1969	—	3.00	6.00
CHANCE					
❑ 1108	Miss Lorraine/Talkin' Boogie	1951	750.00	1500.	3000.
—As "John Lee Booker"					
❑ 1110	Graveyard Blues/I Love to Boogie	1952	750.00	1500.	3000.
—As "John Lee Booker"					
❑ 1122	609 Boogie/Road Trouble	1952	500.00	1000.	2000.
—As "John L. Booker"					
CHART					
❑ 609	Going South/Wobbling Baby	1955	12.50	25.00	50.00
CHESS					
❑ 1505	High Priced Woman/Union Station Blues	1952	300.00	600.00	1200.
❑ 1513	Sugar Mama/Walkin' the Boogie	1952	250.00	500.00	1000.
❑ 1562	It's My Own Fault/Women and Money	1954	62.50	125.00	250.00
❑ 1965	Let's Go Out Tonight/In the Mood	1966	2.50	5.00	10.00
DELUXE					
❑ 6004	Blue Monday/Lovin' Guitar Man	1953	125.00	250.00	500.00
—As "John Lee Booker"					
❑ 6009	I Came to See You Baby/I'm a Boogie Man	1953	200.00	400.00	800.00
—As "Johnny Lee"					
❑ 6032	Stuttering Blues/Pouring Down Rain	1954	100.00	200.00	400.00
—As "John Lee Booker"					
❑ 6046	My Baby Don't Love Me/Real, Real Gone	1954	100.00	200.00	400.00
—As "John Lee Booker"					
ELMOR					
❑ 303	Blues for Christmas/Big Fine Woman	1959	5.00	10.00	20.00
FEDERAL					
❑ 12377	Late Last Night/Don't You Remember Me	1960	3.75	7.50	15.00
FORTUNE					
❑ 853	Cry Baby/Love You Baby	1960	5.00	10.00	20.00
❑ 855	Crazy About That Walk/We're All God's Chillun	1960	5.00	10.00	20.00
GALAXY					
❑ 716	I Lost My Job/You Gotta Shake It Up and Go	1963	2.50	5.00	10.00
HI-Q					
❑ 5018	Blues for Christmas/Big Fine Woman	1960	5.00	10.00	20.00
IMPULSE					
❑ 242	Honey/Bottle Up and Go	1966	2.50	5.00	10.00
JEWEL					
❑ 824	I Feel Good (Part 1)/I Feel Good (Part 2)	1971	—	2.50	5.00
❑ 852	Stand By (Part 1)/Stand By (Part 2)	1977	—	2.00	4.00
JVB					
❑ 30	Boogie Rambler/No More Doggin'	1953	375.00	750.00	1500.
KING					
❑ 4504	Moaning Blues/Stomp Boogie	1952	250.00	500.00	1000.
—As "John Lee Cooker"					
❑ 6298	Don't Go Baby/Moanin' and Stompin' Blues	1970	—	3.00	6.00
LAUREN					
❑ 361	Ballad to Abraham Lincoln (He Got Assassinated)/Mojo Hand (Louisiana Voodoo)	1961	5.00	10.00	20.00
❑ 362	I Lost My Job/You Gotta Shake It Up and Go	1961	5.00	10.00	20.00
MODERN					
❑ 835	How Can You Do It/I'm in the Mood	1951	100.00	200.00	400.00
❑ 847	Anybody Seen My Baby? (Johnny Says Come Back)/Turn Over a New Leaf	1951	75.00	150.00	300.00
❑ 852	Ground Hog Blues/Louise	1951	30.00	60.00	120.00
❑ 862	Cold Chills All Over Me/Rock Me, Mama	1952	20.00	40.00	80.00
❑ 876	It Hurts Me So/I Got Eyes for You	1952	20.00	40.00	80.00
—With Little Eddie Kirkland					
❑ 886	Key to the Highway/Bluebird Blues	1952	20.00	40.00	80.00
❑ 893	New Boogie Chillen/I Tried	1952	20.00	40.00	80.00
❑ 897	It's Been a Long Time Baby/Rock House Boogie	1952	20.00	40.00	80.00
❑ 901	Ride Till I Die/It's Stormin' and Rainin'	1953	15.00	30.00	60.00
❑ 908	Please Take Me Back/Love Money Can't Buy	1953	15.00	30.00	60.00
❑ 916	Too Much Boogie/Need Somebody	1953	15.00	30.00	60.00
❑ 923	Gotta Boogie/Down Child	1953	15.00	30.00	60.00
❑ 931	Jump Me/I Wonder Little Darling	1954	15.00	30.00	60.00
❑ 935	I Tried Hard/Let's Talk It Over	1954	12.50	25.00	50.00
❑ 942	Cool Little Car/Bad Boy	1954	12.50	25.00	50.00
❑ 948	Half a Stranger/Shake, Holler and Run	1954	12.50	25.00	50.00
❑ 958	Taxi Driver/You Receive Me	1955	12.50	25.00	50.00
❑ 966	Hug and Squeeze/The Syndicator	1955	12.50	25.00	50.00
❑ 978	Looking for a Woman/I'm Ready	1955	15.00	30.00	60.00
POINTBLANK					
❑ S7-19518	Dimples/Don't Look Back	1997	—	2.00	4.00
❑ 38664	Burnin' Hell/Boogie at Russian Hill	1999	—	—	3.00

Number	Title (A Side/B Side)	Yr	VG	VG+	NM
RIVERSIDE					
❑ 438	I Need Some Money/No More Diggin'	1960	6.25	12.50	25.00
ROCKIN'					
❑ 524	Blue Monday/Lovin' Guitar Man	1953	250.00	500.00	1000.
—As "John Lee Booker"					
❑ 525	Stuttering Blues/Pouring Down Rain	1953	250.00	500.00	1000.
—As "John Lee Booker"					
SPECIALTY					
❑ 528	Everybody's Blues/I'm Mad	1954	10.00	20.00	40.00
STAX					
❑ 0053	Slow and Easy/Grinder Man	1969	—	3.00	6.00
VEE JAY					
❑ 164	Mambo Chillen/Time Is Marching	1955	7.50	15.00	30.00
❑ 188	Every Night/Trouble Blues	1956	7.50	15.00	30.00
❑ 205	Dimples/Baby Lee	1956	7.50	15.00	30.00
❑ 233	The Road Is So Rough/I'm So Worried Baby	1957	6.25	12.50	25.00
❑ 245	I'm So Excited/I See You When You're Weak	1957	6.25	12.50	25.00
❑ 255	Little Wheel/Rosie Mae	1957	6.25	12.50	25.00
❑ 265	You Can Lead Me, Baby/Unfriendly Baby	1958	6.25	12.50	25.00
❑ 293	I Love You Honey/You've Taken My Woman	1958	6.25	12.50	25.00
❑ 308	Maudie/I'm In the Mood	1959	6.25	12.50	25.00
❑ 319	Tennessee Blues/Boogie Chillun	1959	6.25	12.50	25.00
❑ 331	Hobo Blues/Crawlin' King Snake	1959	6.25	12.50	25.00
❑ 349	No Shoes/Solid Sender	1960	6.25	12.50	25.00
❑ 366	Dusty Road/Tupelo	1960	6.25	12.50	25.00
❑ 379	I'm Mad Again/I'm Going Upstairs	1961	6.25	12.50	25.00
❑ 397	Want Ad Blues/Take Me As I Am	1961	6.25	12.50	25.00
❑ 438	Boom Boom/Drug Store Woman	1962	6.25	12.50	25.00
❑ 453	She's Mine/A New Leaf	1962	6.25	12.50	25.00
❑ 493	Take a Look at Yourself/I Love Her	1963	12.50	25.00	50.00
❑ 493	Take a Look at Yourself/Frisco Blues	1963	5.00	10.00	20.00
❑ 538	I'm Leaving/Birmingham Blues	1963	3.75	7.50	15.00
❑ 575	Send Me Your Pillow/Don't Look Back	1964	3.75	7.50	15.00
❑ 670	Big Legs, Tight Skirt/Your Baby Ain't Sweet Like Mine	1965	3.00	6.00	12.00
❑ 708	It Serves Me Right/Flowers on the Hour	1966	2.50	5.00	10.00

HOOKER, JOHN LEE, AND CANNED HEAT

Also see each artist's individual listings.

Number	Title (A Side/B Side)	Yr	VG	VG+	NM
UNITED ARTISTS					
❑ 50779	Whiskey and Wimmen/Let's Make It	1971	—	2.50	5.00

HOOTERS

Also see BABY GRAND.

Number	Title (A Side/B Side)	Yr	VG	VG+	NM
ANTENNA					
❑ HOO 84	Hangin' on a Heartbeat/Concubine	1984	2.50	5.00	10.00
❑ HOO 84 [PS]	Hangin' on a Heartbeat/Concubine	1984	2.50	5.00	10.00
COLUMBIA					
❑ 04854	All You Zombies/Nervous Night	1985	—	2.00	4.00
—Not issued with picture sleeve in U.S.					
❑ 05568	And We Danced/Blood from a Stone	1985	—	—	3.00
❑ 05568 [PS]	And We Danced/Blood from a Stone	1985	—	—	3.00
❑ 05730	Day By Day/South Ferry Road	1985	—	—	3.00
❑ 05730 [PS]	Day By Day/South Ferry Road	1985	—	—	3.00
❑ 05854	Where Do the Children Go/Nervous Night	1986	—	—	3.00
❑ 05854 [PS]	Where Do the Children Go/Nervous Night	1986	—	—	3.00
❑ 07241	Johnny B/Lucy in the Sky with Diamonds	1987	—	—	3.00
❑ 07241 [PS]	Johnny B/Lucy in the Sky with Diamonds	1987	—	—	3.00
❑ 07607	Satellite/One Way Home	1987	—	—	3.00
❑ 07607 [PS]	Satellite/One Way Home	1987	—	—	3.00
❑ 07666	Karla with a K/Washington's Day	1988	—	—	3.00
❑ 08384	And We Danced/All You Zombies	1988	—	—	3.00
—Reissue					
❑ 73013	500 Miles/The House of Wolfgang	1989	—	—	3.00
—Backing vocals on A-side: Peter, Paul and Mary					
EIGHTY PERCENT					
❑ HOO 80	Fightin' on the Same Side/Wireless	1980	2.50	5.00	10.00
❑ HOO 80 [PS]	Fightin' on the Same Side/Wireless	1980	2.50	5.00	10.00
❑ HOO 82	All You Zombies (Live)/Rescue Me	1982	2.50	5.00	10.00
❑ HOO 82 [PS]	All You Zombies (Live)/Rescue Me	1982	2.50	5.00	10.00

HOOTIE & THE BLOWFISH

Number	Title (A Side/B Side)	Yr	VG	VG+	NM
ATLANTIC					
❑ 84411	I Will Wait/Wishing	1998	—	—	3.00
❑ 85050	Use Me/I Go Blind	2000	—	—	3.00
❑ 87051	Tucker's Town/Araby	1996	—	—	3.00
❑ 87057	Old Man & Me (When I Get to Heaven)/Before the Heartache Rolls In	1996	—	—	3.00
—Large center hole, regular label					
❑ 87074	Old Man & Me (When I Get to Heaven)/Before the Heartache Rolls In	1996	—	—	3.00
—Small center hole, photo label					
❑ 87074 [PS]	Old Man & Me (When I Get to Heaven)/Before the Heartache Rolls In	1996	—	—	3.00
—Cardboard sleeve					
❑ 87095	Time/Only Wanna Be with You	1995	—	—	3.00
❑ 87231	Let Her Cry/Hold My Hand	1995	—	—	3.00

HOPE, LYNN

Number	Title (A Side/B Side)	Yr	VG	VG+	NM
ALADDIN					
❑ 3095	Blue Moon/Blow, Lynn, Blow	1951	10.00	20.00	40.00
❑ 3103	Too Young/Free and Easy	1951	10.00	20.00	40.00
❑ 3109	She's Funny That Way/Eleven Till Two	1951	10.00	20.00	40.00
❑ 3134	Driftin'/Sentimental Journey	1952	7.50	15.00	30.00
❑ 3155	Move It/Don't Worry 'Bout Me	1952	7.50	15.00	30.00
❑ 3165	September Song/Blues for Anna Bocoa	1953	6.25	12.50	25.00
❑ 3178	Broken Heart/Morocco	1953	6.25	12.50	25.00
❑ 3185	Jet/Tenderly	1953	6.25	12.50	25.00
❑ 3208	Swing Train/Rose Room	1953	6.25	12.50	25.00
❑ 3229	Brazil/C. Jam Blues	1954	6.25	12.50	25.00
❑ 3297	All of Me/Summertime	1955	6.25	12.50	25.00
❑ 3322	Cherry/Blues in F	1956	6.25	12.50	25.00
KING					
❑ 5336	Tenderly/Full Moon	1960	3.00	6.00	12.00
❑ 5352	Body and Soul/Sands of Sahara	1960	3.00	6.00	12.00
❑ 5378	A Ghost of a Chance/Little Landslide	1960	3.00	6.00	12.00
❑ 5431	Shockin'/Blue and Sentimental	1960	3.00	6.00	12.00

HOPKIN, MARY

Number	Title (A Side/B Side)	Yr	VG	VG+	NM
APPLE					
❑ 1801	Those Were the Days/Turn, Turn, Turn	1968	2.50	5.00	10.00
❑ 1806	Goodbye/Sparrow	1969	2.00	4.00	8.00
❑ 1806 [PS]	Goodbye/Sparrow	1969	3.00	6.00	12.00
❑ 1816	Temma Harbour/Lantano Dagli Occhi	1970	2.00	4.00	8.00
❑ 1816 [PS]	Temma Harbour/Lantano Dagli Occhi	1970	3.00	6.00	12.00
❑ 1823	Que Sera, Sera (Whatever Will Be, Will Be)/Fields of St. Etienne	1970	2.00	4.00	8.00
❑ 1825	Think About Your Children/Heritage	1970	2.00	4.00	8.00
❑ 1825	Think About Your Children/Heritage	1970	3.00	6.00	12.00
—With star on A-side label					
❑ 1825 [PS]	Think About Your Children/Heritage	1970	3.00	6.00	12.00
❑ 1843	Water, Paper and Clay/Streets of London	1972	2.00	4.00	8.00
❑ 1843	Water, Paper and Clay/Streets of London	1972	3.00	6.00	12.00
—With star on A-side label					
❑ 1855	Knock Knock Who's There/International	1972	2.00	4.00	8.00
APPLE/AMERICOM					
❑ 1801P/M-238	Those Were the Days/Turn, Turn, Turn	1969	150.00	300.00	600.00
—Four-inch flexi-disc sold from vending machines					
RCA VICTOR					
❑ PB-10694	Tell Me Now/If You Love Me	1976	—	2.00	4.00

HOPKINS, LIGHTNIN'

Number	Title (A Side/B Side)	Yr	VG	VG+	NM
ACE					
❑ 516	Bad Boogie/Wonder What Is Wrong with Me	1956	10.00	20.00	40.00
ALADDIN					
❑ 3063	Shotgun Blues/Rolling Blues	1950	175.00	350.00	700.00
❑ 3077	Moonrise Blues/Honey, Honey Blues	1951	50.00	100.00	200.00
❑ 3096	Miss Me Blues/Abilene	1951	50.00	100.00	200.00
❑ 3117	You Are Not Going to Worry About My Life Anymore/Daddy Will Be Home Someday	1951	50.00	100.00	200.00
❑ 3262	So Long/My California	1954	25.00	50.00	100.00
ARHOOLIE					
❑ 508	My Woman/Lousiana Blues	1965	3.00	6.00	12.00
❑ 513	Come On Baby/Money Taker	1965	3.00	6.00	12.00
BLUESVILLE					
❑ 813	So Sorry to Leave You/Got to Move Your Baby	1960	5.00	10.00	20.00
❑ 814	Death Bells/Sail On	1961	5.00	10.00	20.00
❑ 817	Back to New Orleans/Hard to Love a Woman	1961	5.00	10.00	20.00
❑ 820	Happy Blues for John Glenn (Part 1)/Happy Blues for John Glenn (Part 2)	1962	5.00	10.00	20.00
❑ 821	Last Night Blues/Walkin' Blues	1962	5.00	10.00	20.00
❑ 822	Sinner's Prayer/Angel Child	1962	5.00	10.00	20.00
❑ 823	The Business You're Doing/Wake Up Old Lady	1963	5.00	10.00	20.00
❑ 824	Going Away/Better Stop Her	1963	5.00	10.00	20.00
❑ 825	Katie Mae/My Babe	1963	5.00	10.00	20.00
CHART					
❑ 636	Walkin' the Streets/Mussy Haired Woman	1957	7.50	15.00	30.00
DART					
❑ 123	Grievance Blues/Unsuccessful Blues	1959	5.00	10.00	20.00
❑ 152	Mary Lou/Wait to Go Home	1960	5.00	10.00	20.00
DECCA					
❑ 28841	The War Is Over/Policy Game	1953	20.00	40.00	80.00
❑ 48306	Merry Christmas/Happy New Year	1953	20.00	40.00	80.00
❑ 48312	Highway Blues/Cemetery Blues	1954	20.00	40.00	80.00
❑ 48321	I'm Wild About You Baby/Bad Things on My Mind	1954	25.00	50.00	100.00
FIRE					
❑ 1034	Mojo Hand/Glory Be	1961	5.00	10.00	20.00
HARLEM					
❑ 2321	Contrary Mary/I'm Begging You	1954	50.00	100.00	200.00
❑ 2324	Mad Man's Boogie/Nobody Cares for Me	1954	50.00	100.00	200.00
❑ 2331	Fast Life/The Jackstropper	1955	50.00	100.00	200.00
❑ 2336	Good Old Woman/Untrue	1955	50.00	100.00	200.00
HERALD					
❑ 425	Lightnin's Boogie/Don't Think 'Cause You're Pretty	1954	7.50	15.00	30.00
❑ 428	Lightnin's Special/Life Is Used to Live	1954	7.50	15.00	30.00
❑ 436	Movin' On Out Boogie/Sick Feelin' Blues	1954	7.50	15.00	30.00
❑ 443	Nothin' But the Blues/Early Morning Boogie	1954	7.50	15.00	30.00
❑ 449	Evil Hearted Woman/They Wonder Who I Am	1955	7.50	15.00	30.00
❑ 456	My Baby's Gone/Don't Need No Job	1955	6.25	12.50	25.00
❑ 465	I Had a Gal Named Sal/Blues for My Cookie	1955	6.25	12.50	25.00
❑ 471	Hopkins Sky Hop/Lonesome in Your Home	1956	6.25	12.50	25.00
❑ 476	Grandma's Boogie/I Love You Baby	1956	6.25	12.50	25.00
❑ 483	Finally Met My Baby/That's Alright Baby	1956	6.25	12.50	25.00
❑ 490	Shine On Moon/Sitting and Thinking	1956	6.25	12.50	25.00
❑ 497	Remember Me/Please Don't Go Baby	1957	6.25	12.50	25.00
❑ 504	Boogie Woogie Dance/The Blues Is a Mighty Bad Feeling	1957	5.00	10.00	20.00
❑ 520	Little Kewpie Doll/Lightnin' Don't Feel Well	1958	5.00	10.00	20.00
❑ 531	Hear Me Talkin'/Lightnin's Stomp	1958	5.00	10.00	20.00
❑ 542	Let's Move/I'm Achin'	1959	5.00	10.00	20.00
❑ 547	Flash Lightnin'/Gonna Change My Ways	1960	5.00	10.00	20.00
IMPERIAL					
❑ 5834	Feel So Bad/Shotgun	1962	3.75	7.50	15.00
❑ 5852	Picture on the Wall/Lightnin's Boogie	1962	3.75	7.50	15.00
IVORY					
❑ 91272	Got Me a Lousiana Woman/War Is Starting Again	196?	3.75	7.50	15.00
JAX					
❑ 315	No Good Woman/Been a Bad Man	1953	75.00	150.00	300.00
❑ 318	Automobile/Organ Blues	1953	75.00	150.00	300.00
❑ 321	Contrary Mary/I'm Begging You	1953	75.00	150.00	300.00
❑ 635	Coffee Blues/New Short Haired Woman	1954	62.50	125.00	250.00

Number	Title (A Side/B Side)	Yr	VG	VG+	NM
❑ 642	You Caused My Heart to Weep/Tap Dance Boogie	1954	62.50	125.00	250.00
JEWEL					
❑ 788	Back Door Friends/Fishing Clothes	1968	—	3.00	6.00
❑ 796	Wig Wearin' Woman/Move On Out, Part 2	1968	—	3.00	6.00
❑ 803	Lovin' Arms/Ride in Your New Auto	1969	—	3.00	6.00
❑ 807	Play with Your Poodle/Breakfast Time	1970	—	3.00	6.00
❑ 809	I'm Comin' Home/You're Too Fast	1970	—	3.00	6.00
❑ 816	My Charlie (Part 1)/My Charlie (Part 2)	1970	—	3.00	6.00
❑ 819	Rock Me Mama/Love Me This Morning	1971	—	3.00	6.00
❑ 825	Uncle Sam the Hip Hit Record Man/Found My Baby Crying	1971	—	3.00	6.00
LIGHTNING					
❑ 104	Unsuccessful Blues/(B-side unknown)	1955	125.00	250.00	500.00
MERCURY					
❑ 8274	Sad News from Korea/Let Me Fly Your Kite	1952	25.00	50.00	100.00
❑ 8293	Gone with the Wind/She's Almost Dead	1952	25.00	50.00	100.00
❑ 70081	Ain't It a Shame/Crazy About My Baby	1953	25.00	50.00	100.00
❑ 70191	My Mama Told Me/What's the Matter Now	1953	25.00	50.00	100.00
PRESTIGE					
❑ 326	I Like to Boogie/Let's Go Sit on the Lawn	1964	2.50	5.00	10.00
❑ 343	Mojo Hand/Automobile Blues	1964	2.50	5.00	10.00
❑ 374	T Model Blues/You Cook Alright	1965	2.50	5.00	10.00
❑ 391	Sinner's Prayer/Got to Move Your Baby	1965	2.50	5.00	10.00
❑ 405	I'm Gonna Build Me a Heaven (Part 1)/I'm Gonna Build Me a Heaven (Part 2)	1966	2.50	5.00	10.00
❑ 452	Mama Blues/Pneumonia Blues	1968	2.00	4.00	8.00
RPM					
❑ 337	Beggin' You to Stay/Bad Luck and Trouble	1951	150.00	300.00	600.00
❑ 346	Lonesome Dog Blues/Jake Head	1952	200.00	400.00	800.00
❑ 351	Don't Keep My Baby Long/Last Affair	1952	100.00	200.00	400.00
❑ 359	Needed Time/One Kind Favor	1952	100.00	200.00	400.00
❑ 378	Another Fool in Town/Candy Kitchen	1953	75.00	150.00	300.00
❑ 388	Black Cat/Mistreated Blues	1953	75.00	150.00	300.00
❑ 398	Santa Fe Blues/Some Day Baby	1954	50.00	100.00	200.00
SHAD					
❑ 5011	Hello Central/Mad As I Can Be	1959	3.75	7.50	15.00
SITTIN' IN WITH					
❑ 621	Give Me Central 209/New York Boogie	1951	125.00	250.00	500.00
❑ 621	Hello Central/New York Boogie	1952	100.00	200.00	400.00
❑ 635	Coffee Blues/New Short Haired Woman	1952	125.00	250.00	500.00
❑ 642	You Caused My Heart to Weep/Tap Dance Boogie	1952	125.00	250.00	500.00
❑ 644	Jail House Blues/"T" Model Blues	1952	125.00	250.00	500.00
❑ 647	Bald Headed Woman/Dirty House	1952	125.00	250.00	500.00
❑ 649	New Worried Life Blues/One Kind of Favor	1952	—	—	—
—Unreleased on 45 rpm?					
❑ 652	Papa Bones Boogie/Everything Happens to Me	1953	125.00	250.00	500.00
❑ 658	Freight Train Blues (When I Started Hoboing)/Broken Hearted Blues	1953	125.00	250.00	500.00
❑ 660	Mad Blues/Why	1953	125.00	250.00	500.00
❑ 661	Gone Again/Down to the River	1953	125.00	250.00	500.00
SPHERE SOUND					
❑ 710	Santa/Black Mare Trot	196?	2.50	5.00	10.00
TNT					
❑ 8002	Lightnin' Jump/Late in the Evening	1954	175.00	350.00	700.00
❑ 8003	Moanin' Blues/Leavin' Blues	1954	175.00	350.00	700.00
VAULT					
❑ 965	Easy on Your Heels/No Education	1970	—	3.00	6.00

HOPKINS, NICKY

Prominent session keyboardist who played on BEATLES and ROLLING STONES sessions, among dozens of others.

Number	Title (A Side/B Side)	Yr	VG	VG+	NM
COLUMBIA					
❑ 45869	Speed On/Sundown in Mexico	1973	—	2.50	5.00
DECCA					
❑ 32139	Mister Pleasant/Nothing As Yet	1967	3.00	6.00	12.00

HORNETS, THE

More than one group.

Number	Title (A Side/B Side)	Yr	VG	VG+	NM
COLUMBIA					
❑ 42999	Fruit Cake/Seven Days to Tahiti	1964	15.00	30.00	60.00
EMERALD					
❑ 501	Runt/Breakfast in Bed	196?	7.50	15.00	30.00
FLASH					
❑ 125	Crying Over You/Tango Moon	1957	62.50	125.00	250.00
LIBERTY					
❑ 55688	Motorcycle U.S.A./On the Track	1964	7.50	15.00	30.00
REV					
❑ 3515	Slow Dance/Strollin'	1958	6.25	12.50	25.00
STATES					
❑ 127	I Can't Believe/Lonesome Baby	1953	4000.	6000.	8000.
—Black vinyl					
❑ 127	I Can't Believe/Lonesome Baby	1953	7500.	10000.	15000.
—Red vinyl					
V.I.P.					
❑ 25004	She's My Baby/Give Me a Kiss	1964	15.00	30.00	60.00

HORSLIPS

Number	Title (A Side/B Side)	Yr	VG	VG+	NM
ATCO					
❑ 6935	High Reel/Furniture	1973	2.00	4.00	8.00
DJM					
❑ 1026	Warm Sweet Breath of Love/(B-side unknown)	1977	—	2.50	5.00
❑ 1032	Trouble (With a Capital T)/(B-side unknown)	1978	—	2.50	5.00
❑ 1036	Sure the Boy Was Green/Exiles	1978	2.50	5.00	10.00
—Green vinyl					
❑ 1105	Loneliness/Homesick	1979	—	2.50	5.00
MERCURY					
❑ 76030	Rescue Me/Soap Opera	1979	—	2.50	5.00
❑ 76072 [DJ]	Shakin' All Over (mono/stereo)	1979	—	3.00	6.00
—May be promo only					
RCA VICTOR					
❑ PB-10123	Nighttown Boys/We Bring the Summer With Me	1974	—	3.00	6.00

HORTON, JAY

Number	Title (A Side/B Side)	Yr	VG	VG+	NM
MUSTANG					
❑ 3010	I Trip on You Girl/(B-side unknown)	1965	7.50	15.00	30.00
❑ 3021	It's Love/Come What May	1966	7.50	15.00	30.00

HORTON, JOHNNY

Number	Title (A Side/B Side)	Yr	VG	VG+	NM
ABBOTT					
❑ 100	Candy Jones/Devilish Lovelight	1951	10.00	20.00	40.00
❑ 101	Happy Millionaire/Mean Mean Son of a Gun	1951	10.00	20.00	40.00
❑ 102	Plaid and Calico/Done Roving	1951	10.00	20.00	40.00
—B-side by Bill Thompson's Westerners					
❑ 103	Birds and Butteflies/Coal Smoke, Valve Oil and Steam	1951	10.00	20.00	40.00
❑ 104	Go and Wash (Those Dirty Feet)/In My Home in Shelby County	1951	10.00	20.00	40.00
❑ 105	Shadows on the Old Bayou/Talk Gobbler Talk	1951	10.00	20.00	40.00
❑ 106	Smokey Joe's Barbeque/Words	1951	10.00	20.00	40.00
❑ 107	Long Rocky Road/On the Banks of the Beautiful Nile	1952	10.00	20.00	40.00
❑ 108	Somebody Rocking in My Broken Chair/Betty Lorraine	1952	10.00	20.00	40.00
—With Hillbilly Barton					
❑ 109	Rhythm in My Baby's Walk/Bowlin' Baby	1952	10.00	20.00	40.00
❑ 135	Plaid and Calico/Shadows on the Old Bayou	1953	7.50	15.00	30.00
COLUMBIA					
❑ 21504	Honky Tonk Man/I'm Ready If You're Willing	1956	7.50	15.00	30.00
❑ 21538	I'm a One Woman Man/I Don't Like I Did	1956	6.25	12.50	25.00
❑ 30568 [S]	Sink the Bismarck/The Same Old Tale the Crow Told Me	1960	6.25	12.50	25.00
—"Stereo Single 33"; small hole, plays at 33 1/3 rpm					
❑ 31104 [S]	North to Alaska/Whispering Pines	1961	5.00	10.00	20.00
❑ 31105 [S]	Johnny Reb/The Mansion You Stole	1961	5.00	10.00	20.00
❑ 31106 [S]	When It's Springtime in Alaska/The Battle of New Orleans	1961	5.00	10.00	20.00
❑ 31107 [S]	All for the Love of a Girl/Sink the Bismarck	1961	5.00	10.00	20.00
❑ 31108 [S]	The Brave Comanche/Jim Bridger	1961	5.00	10.00	20.00
—The above five all are Columbia "Stereo 7" singles with small center holes					
❑ 40813	I'm Coming Home/I Got a Hole in My Picture	1957	7.50	15.00	30.00
❑ 40919	She Knows Why/The Woman I Need	1957	5.00	10.00	20.00
❑ 40986	I'll Do It Every Time/Let's Take the Long Way Home	1957	5.00	10.00	20.00
❑ 41043	You're My Baby/Lover's Rock	1957	7.50	15.00	30.00
❑ 41110	Honky Tonk Hardwood Floor/The Wild One	1958	15.00	30.00	60.00
❑ 41210	All Grown Up/Counterfeit Love	1958	5.00	10.00	20.00
❑ 41308	When It's Springtime in Alaska (It's Forty Below)/Whispering Pines	1958	3.75	7.50	15.00
❑ 41308 [PS]	When It's Springtime in Alaska (It's Forty Below)/Whispering Pines	1958	7.50	15.00	30.00
—Promo-only black and white sleeve					
❑ 41339	The Battle of New Orleans/All for the Love of a Girl	1959	3.75	7.50	15.00
❑ 41339 [PS]	The Battle of New Orleans/All for the Love of a Girl	1959	5.00	10.00	20.00
❑ 41437	Johnny Reb/Sal's Got a Sugar Lip	1959	3.75	7.50	15.00
❑ 41502	I'm Ready If You're Willing/Take Me Like I Am	1959	3.75	7.50	15.00
❑ 41522	They Shined Up Rudolph's Nose/The Electrified Donkey	1959	3.75	7.50	15.00
❑ 41568	Sink the Bismarck/The Same Old Tale the Crow Told Me	1960	3.00	6.00	12.00
❑ 41568 [PS]	Sink the Bismarck/The Same Old Tale the Crow Told Me	1960	5.00	10.00	20.00
❑ 41685	Johnny Freedom/Comanche	1960	3.00	6.00	12.00
❑ 41685 [PS]	Johnny Freedom/Comanche	1960	5.00	10.00	20.00
❑ 41782	North to Alaska/The Mansion You Stole	1960	3.00	6.00	12.00
❑ 41782 [PS]	North to Alaska/The Mansion You Stole	1960	5.00	10.00	20.00
❑ 41963	Sleepy Eyed John/They'll Never Take Her Love from Me	1961	3.00	6.00	12.00
❑ 41963 [PS]	Sleepy Eyed John/They'll Never Take Her Love from Me	1961	5.00	10.00	20.00
❑ 42063	Ole Slewfoot/Miss Marcy	1961	3.00	6.00	12.00
❑ 42063 [PS]	Ole Slewfoot/Miss Marcy	1961	5.00	10.00	20.00
❑ 42302	Honky Tonk Man/Words	1962	3.75	7.50	15.00
❑ 42302 [PS]	Honky Tonk Man/Words	1962	5.00	10.00	20.00
❑ 42653	All Grown Up/I'm a One Woman Man	1962	3.00	6.00	12.00
❑ 42653 [PS]	All Grown Up/I'm a One Woman Man	1962	5.00	10.00	20.00
❑ 42774	Sugar Coated Baby/When It's Springtime in Alaska (It's Forty Below)	1963	2.50	5.00	10.00
❑ 42993	Hooray for That Little Difference/Tell My Baby I Love Her	1964	2.50	5.00	10.00
❑ 42993 [PS]	Hooray for That Little Difference/Tell My Baby I Love Her	1964	5.00	10.00	20.00
❑ 43143	Lost Highway/The Same Old Tale the Crow Told Me	1964	2.50	5.00	10.00
❑ 43228	Rock Island Line/I Just Don't Like This Kind of Lovin'	1965	2.50	5.00	10.00
❑ 43719	Sam Magee/All for the Love of a Girl	1966	2.00	4.00	8.00
❑ 44156	The Battle of New Orleans/All for the Love of a Girl	1967	—	3.00	6.00
CORMAC					
❑ 1193	Plaid and Calico/Done Roving	1951	30.00	60.00	120.00
❑ 1197	Birds and Butteflies/Coal Smoke, Valve Oil and Steam	1951	30.00	60.00	120.00
DOT					
❑ 15966	Plaid and Calico/Shadows on the Old Bayou	1959	3.00	6.00	12.00
MERCURY					
❑ 6412	The Devil Sent Me You/First Train Headin' South	1952	7.50	15.00	30.00
❑ 6418	The Rest of Your Life/This Won't Be the First Time	1952	7.50	15.00	30.00
❑ 70014	I Won't Forget/The Child's Side of Life	1952	7.50	15.00	30.00
❑ 70100	Tennessee Jive/The Mansion You Stole	1953	7.50	15.00	30.00
❑ 70156	S.S. Loveline/I Won't Get Dreamy-Eyed	1953	7.50	15.00	30.00

Number	Title (A Side/B Side)	Yr	VG	VG+	NM
❑ 70198	You, You, You/Red Lips and Warm Red Wine	1953	7.50	15.00	30.00
❑ 70227	All for the Love of a Girl/Broken Hearted	1953	7.50	15.00	30.00
❑ 70325	Move On Down the Line/Train with the Rhumba Beat	1954	7.50	15.00	30.00
❑ 70399	The Door of Your Mansion/Ha Ha and Moonface	1954	7.50	15.00	30.00
❑ 70462	No True Love/There'll Never Be Another Mary	1954	7.50	15.00	30.00
❑ 70636	Journey with No End/Ridin' the Sunshine Special	1955	7.50	15.00	30.00
❑ 70707	Big Wheels Rollin'/Hey Sweet, Sweet Thing	1955	7.50	15.00	30.00

7-Inch Extended Plays

COLUMBIA

Number	Title (A Side/B Side)	Yr	VG	VG+	NM
❑ B-13621	The Battle of New Orleans/Whispering Pines//The First Train Heading South/Lost Highway	1960	3.00	6.00	12.00
❑ B-13621 [PS]	The Spectacular Johnny Horton, Vol. 1	1960	4.00	8.00	16.00
❑ B-13622	Joe's Been a-Gettin' There/Sam Magee//When It's Springtime in Alaska/Cherokee Boogie	1960	3.00	6.00	12.00
❑ B-13622 [PS]	The Spectacular Johnny Horton, Vol. 2	1960	4.00	8.00	16.00
❑ B-13623	All for the Love of a Girl/The Golden Rocket//Mr. Moonlight/Got the Bull by the Horns	1960	3.00	6.00	12.00
❑ B-13623 [PS]	The Spectacular Johnny Horton, Vol. 3	1960	4.00	8.00	16.00

HOSEA, DON

SUN

Number	Title (A Side/B Side)	Yr	VG	VG+	NM
❑ 368	Since I Met You/Uh Huh Huh	1961	5.00	10.00	20.00

HOT CHOCOLATE

APPLE

Number	Title (A Side/B Side)	Yr	VG	VG+	NM
❑ 1812	Give Peace a Chance/Living Without Tomorrow	1969	2.50	5.00	10.00

—As "Hot Chocolate Band"

BELL

Number	Title (A Side/B Side)	Yr	VG	VG+	NM
❑ 45390	Rumors/(B-side unknown)	1973	—	2.50	5.00
❑ 45466	Emma/(B-side unknown)	1974	—	3.50	7.00

BIG TREE

Number	Title (A Side/B Side)	Yr	VG	VG+	NM
❑ 16031	Emma/A Love Like Yours	1975	—	2.50	5.00
❑ 16038	Disco Queen/Makin' Music	1975	—	2.50	5.00
❑ 16047	You Sexy Thing/Amazing Skin Song	1975	—	2.50	5.00
❑ 16060	Don't Stop It Now/Beautiful Lady	1976	—	2.50	5.00
❑ 16078	Heaven Is in the Back Seat of My Cadillac/(B-side unknown)	1976	—	2.50	5.00
❑ 16096	So You Win Again/Part of Being with You	1977	—	2.50	5.00
❑ 16101	Man to Man/(B-side unknown)	1977	—	2.50	5.00

EMI-CAPITOL

Number	Title (A Side/B Side)	Yr	VG	VG+	NM
❑ S7-19894	You Sexy Thing/So You Win Again	1998	—	—	3.00

EMI AMERICA

Number	Title (A Side/B Side)	Yr	VG	VG+	NM
❑ 8143	Are You Getting Enough Happiness/One Night's Not Enough	1982	—	2.00	4.00
❑ 8157	Bed Games/It Started with a Kiss	1983	—	2.00	4.00

INFINITY

Number	Title (A Side/B Side)	Yr	VG	VG+	NM
❑ 50002	Every 1's a Winner/Power of Love	1978	—	2.00	4.00
❑ 50016	Going Through the Motions/Don't Turn It Off	1979	—	2.00	4.00
❑ 50033	I Just Love What You're Doing/Congas Man	1979	—	2.00	4.00
❑ 50048	Mindless Boogie/Dance (Get Down To It)	1979	—	2.00	4.00

RAK

Number	Title (A Side/B Side)	Yr	VG	VG+	NM
❑ 4503	You Could Have Been a Lady/Everybody's Laughing	1972	—	3.00	6.00
❑ 4506	I Believe in Love/Caveman Billy	1972	—	3.00	6.00
❑ 4508	Mary Anne/Ruth	1972	—	3.00	6.00
❑ 4513	Brother Louie/I Want to Be Free	1973	—	3.00	6.00

HOT-TODDYS, THE

See ROCKIN' REBELS.

HOT TUNA

Offshoot of JEFFERSON AIRPLANE.

GRUNT

Number	Title (A Side/B Side)	Yr	VG	VG+	NM
❑ 65-0502	Water Song/Keep On Truckin'	1972	—	3.00	6.00
❑ 65-0502 [PS]	Water Song/Keep On Truckin'	1972	3.00	6.00	12.00
❑ PB-10443	Hot Jellyroll Blues/Surphase Tension	1975	—	2.50	5.00
❑ PB-10776	It's So Easy/I Can't Be Satisfied	1976	—	2.50	5.00

RCA VICTOR

Number	Title (A Side/B Side)	Yr	VG	VG+	NM
❑ 74-0528	Candy Man/Been So Long	1971	—	3.00	6.00

HOTLEGS

Early incarnation of 10CC. Also see GRAHAM GOULDMAN.

CAPITOL

Number	Title (A Side/B Side)	Yr	VG	VG+	NM
❑ 2886	Neanderthal Man/You Didn't Like It, Because You Didn't Think of It	1970	2.50	5.00	10.00
❑ 3043	Run Baby Run/How Many Times	1971	3.75	7.50	15.00

HOUND DOG CLOWNS

UNI

Number	Title (A Side/B Side)	Yr	VG	VG+	NM
❑ 55047	Superfox/Wicked Witch	1968	5.00	10.00	20.00

HOUR GLASS, THE

Also see DUANE AND GREGG ALLMAN; GREGG ALLMAN.

LIBERTY

Number	Title (A Side/B Side)	Yr	VG	VG+	NM
❑ 56002	Heartbeat/Nothing But Tears	1967	3.00	6.00	12.00
❑ 56029	Power of Love/I Still Want Your Love	1968	3.00	6.00	12.00
❑ 56053	D-I-V-O-R-C-E/Changing of the Guard	1968	3.00	6.00	12.00
❑ 56065	She Is My Woman/Going Nowhere	1968	3.00	6.00	12.00
❑ 56072	Now Is the Time/She Is My Woman	1968	3.00	6.00	12.00
❑ 56091	I've Been Trying/Silently	1969	3.00	6.00	12.00

HOUSE OF SCHOCK

Featuring Gina Schock of the GO-GO'S.

CAPITOL

Number	Title (A Side/B Side)	Yr	VG	VG+	NM
❑ B-44135	Middle of Nowhere/World Goes 'Round	1988	—	—	3.00
❑ B-44135 [PS]	Middle of Nowhere/World Goes 'Round	1988	—	—	3.00
❑ B-44202	Love in Return/Middle of Nowhere	1988	—	—	3.00

HOUSTON, CISSY

COLUMBIA

Number	Title (A Side/B Side)	Yr	VG	VG+	NM
❑ 11058	Warning-Danger (This Love Affair May Be Hazardous to You)/An Umbrella Song	1979	—	2.00	4.00
❑ 11208	Break It To Me Gently/Gonna Take the Easy Way Out	1980	—	2.00	4.00

COMMONWEALTH UNITED

Number	Title (A Side/B Side)	Yr	VG	VG+	NM
❑ 3010	I'll Be There/So I Believe	1970	—	3.00	6.00

CONGRESS

Number	Title (A Side/B Side)	Yr	VG	VG+	NM
❑ 268	Bring Him Back/World of Broken Hearts	1966	15.00	30.00	60.00

—As "Susie Houston"

JANUS

Number	Title (A Side/B Side)	Yr	VG	VG+	NM
❑ 131	I Just Don't Know What to Do with Myself/Empty Place	1970	—	3.00	6.00
❑ 145	Be My Baby/I'll Be There	1971	—	3.00	6.00
❑ 159	Hang On to a Dream/Darling Take Me Back	1971	—	3.00	6.00
❑ 177	I Love You/Making Love	1971	—	3.00	6.00
❑ 190	Didn't We/It's Not Easy	1972	—	3.00	6.00
❑ 206	Midnight Train to Georgia/Will You Still Love Me Tomorrow	1972	—	3.00	6.00
❑ 230	I'm So Glad I Can Love Again/One Time You Say You Love Me	1973	—	3.00	6.00
❑ 255	I Believe/Nothing Can Stop Me	1975	—	3.00	6.00

KAPP

Number	Title (A Side/B Side)	Yr	VG	VG+	NM
❑ 814	Don't Come Running to Me/One Broken Heart for Sale	1967	7.50	15.00	30.00

—As "Sissie Houston"

PRIVATE STOCK

Number	Title (A Side/B Side)	Yr	VG	VG+	NM
❑ 45137	Love Is Something That Leads You/If I Ever Lose This Heaven	1977	—	2.50	5.00
❑ 45137	Love Is Something That Leads You/It Never Really Ended	1977	—	2.50	5.00
❑ 45153	Tomorrow/Love Is Holding On	1977	—	2.50	5.00
❑ 45171	Things to Do/It Never Really Ended	1977	—	2.50	5.00
❑ 45204	Think It Over/The Umbrella Song	1978	—	2.50	5.00

HOUSTON, DAVID

COLONIAL

Number	Title (A Side/B Side)	Yr	VG	VG+	NM
❑ 101	Waltz of the Angels/(B-side unknown)	1978	2.00	4.00	8.00

COUNTRY INT'L.

Number	Title (A Side/B Side)	Yr	VG	VG+	NM
❑ 145	You're the Perfect Reason/We Couldn't Make It Love	1980	—	3.00	6.00
❑ 148	Sad Love Song Lady/Thanks for Being You and Loving Me	1980	—	3.00	6.00
❑ 149	The Bottom Line/We Couldn't Make It Love	1980	—	3.00	6.00
❑ 155	Bandera Waltz/(B-side unknown)	1981	—	3.00	6.00
❑ 220	A Penny for Your Thoughts Tonight Virginia/(B-side unknown)	1989	—	3.00	6.00

DERRICK

Number	Title (A Side/B Side)	Yr	VG	VG+	NM
❑ 126	Let Your Love Fall Back on Me/Take Me to Your Heart	1979	—	3.00	6.00
❑ 127	Here's to All the Hard Working Husbands (In the World)/Next Sunday I'm Gonna Be Saved	1979	—	3.00	6.00

ELEKTRA

Number	Title (A Side/B Side)	Yr	VG	VG+	NM
❑ 45513	Sunday I'm Gonna Be Saved/Waltz of the Angels	1978	—	2.00	4.00
❑ 45552	Best Friends Make the Worst Enemies/There Won't Be a Wedding	1978	—	2.00	4.00
❑ 46028	Faded Love and Winter Roses/Beyond the Blue Horizon	1979	—	2.00	4.00

EPIC

Number	Title (A Side/B Side)	Yr	VG	VG+	NM
❑ 9625	Mountain of Love/Angeline	1963	2.00	4.00	8.00
❑ 9658	Chickashay/Passing Through	1964	2.00	4.00	8.00
❑ 9690	One If For Him, Two If For Me/Your Memories	1964	2.00	4.00	8.00
❑ 9720	Love Looks Good on You/My Little Lady	1964	2.00	4.00	8.00
❑ 9746	Sweet, Sweet Judy/Too Many Times (Away from You)	1964	2.00	4.00	8.00
❑ 9782	Rose Colored Glasses/Ballad of the Fool Killer	1965	2.50	5.00	10.00
❑ 9831	Livin' in a House Full of Love/Cowpoke	1965	2.00	4.00	8.00
❑ 9884	Sammy/I'll Take You Home Again, Kathleen	1966	2.00	4.00	8.00
❑ 9884 [PS]	Sammy/I'll Take You Home Again, Kathleen	1966	2.50	5.00	10.00
❑ 10025	Almost Persuaded/We Got Love	1966	2.00	4.00	8.00
❑ 10102	A Loser's Cathedral/Where Could I Go? (But to Her)	1966	—	3.00	6.00
❑ 10102 [PS]	A Loser's Cathedral/Where Could I Go? (But to Her)	1966	2.50	5.00	10.00
❑ 10154	With One Exception/Sweet, Sweet Judy	1967	—	3.00	6.00
❑ 10154 [PS]	With One Exception/Sweet, Sweet Judy	1967	2.50	5.00	10.00
❑ 10224	You Mean the World to Me/Don't Mention Tomorrow	1967	—	3.00	6.00
❑ 10224 [PS]	You Mean the World to Me/Don't Mention Tomorrow	1967	2.50	5.00	10.00
❑ 10291	Have a Little Faith/Too Far Gone	1968	—	3.00	6.00
❑ 10291 [PS]	Have a Little Faith/Too Far Gone	1968	2.50	5.00	10.00
❑ 10338	Already It's Heaven/Lighter Shade of Pale	1968	—	3.00	6.00
❑ 10338 [PS]	Already It's Heaven/Lighter Shade of Pale	1968	2.50	5.00	10.00
❑ 10394	Where Love Used to Live/I Love a Rainbow	1968	—	3.00	6.00
❑ 10430	My Woman's Good to Me/Lullaby to a Little Girl	1968	—	3.00	6.00
❑ 10488	I'm Down to My Last "I Love You"/Watching My World Walk Away	1969	—	3.00	6.00
❑ 10539	Baby, Baby (I Know You're a Lady)/True Love's a Lasting Thing	1969	—	3.00	6.00
❑ 10596	I Do My Swinging at Home/Then I'll Know You Care	1970	—	3.00	6.00
❑ 10643	Wonders of the Wine/If God Can Forgive Me	1970	—	3.00	6.00
❑ 10696	A Woman Always Knows/The Rest of My Life	1970	—	3.00	6.00
❑ 10748	Nashville/That's Why I Cry	1971	—	3.00	6.00
❑ 10778	Maiden's Prayer/Home Sweet Home	1971	—	3.00	6.00
❑ 10830	The Day That Love Walked In/Sweet Lovin'	1972	—	3.00	6.00
❑ 10870	Soft, Sweet and Warm/The Rest of My Life	1972	—	3.00	6.00
❑ 10911	I Wonder How John Felt (When He Baptized Jesus)/Will the Circle Be Unbroken	1972	2.00	4.00	8.00
❑ 10939	Good Things/The Love She Gives	1973	—	3.00	6.00
❑ 10995	She's All Woman/Sweet Lovin'	1973	—	2.50	5.00
❑ 11048	The Lady of the Night/Thank You Teardrop	1973	—	2.50	5.00
❑ 11096	That Same Ol' Look of Love/Clinging Vine	1974	—	2.50	5.00
❑ 50009	Can't You Feel It/I Walk and I Walk and I Walk	1974	—	2.50	5.00

Number	Title (A Side/B Side)	Yr	VG	VG+	NM
❑ 50066	A Man Needs Love/Flower of Love	1975	—	2.50	5.00
❑ 50113	I'll Be Your Steppin' Stone/Then I'll Know You Care	1975	—	2.50	5.00
❑ 50134	Sweet Molly/Old Blind Fiddler	1975	—	2.50	5.00
—With Calvin Crawford					
❑ 50156	The Woman on My Mind/I Can't Sit Still	1975	—	2.50	5.00
❑ 50186	What a Night/From the Bottom of My Heart	1976	—	2.50	5.00
❑ 50241	Lullaby Song/White Circle	1976	—	2.50	5.00
❑ 50275	Come On Down (To Our Favorite Forget-About-Her Place)/Me and Susan Wright	1976	—	2.50	5.00
EXCELSIOR					
❑ 1007	My Lady/Something You've Never Heard	1981	—	2.50	5.00
❑ 1012	Texas Ida Red/(B-side unknown)	1981	—	3.00	6.00
❑ 1015	After All/(B-side unknown)	1981	—	2.00	4.00
GUSTO					
❑ 156	So Many Ways/Touch My World	1977	—	3.00	6.00
❑ 161	Amazing Grace/Return to Me	1977	—	—	—
—Canceled					
❑ 162	Ain't That Lovin' You Baby/Love Is a Mystery	1977	—	3.00	6.00
❑ 168	The Twelfth of Never/Barroom Champagne	1977	—	3.00	6.00
❑ 172	It Started All Over Again/Touch My World	1977	—	3.00	6.00
❑ 184	No Tell Motel/Hate to Tell Baby a Lie	1978	—	3.00	6.00
IMPERIAL					
❑ 8291	I'm Sorry I Made You Cry/Blue Prelude	1955	10.00	20.00	40.00
NRC					
❑ 005	Waited So Long/All I Do Is Dream of You	1958	5.00	10.00	20.00
❑ 012	The Key/So Young, So Unknowing	1958	5.00	10.00	20.00
❑ 047	It's Been So Long/Kalua	1959	5.00	10.00	20.00
PHILLIPS INTERNATIONAL					
❑ 3583	Sherry's Lips/Miss Brown	1961	7.50	15.00	30.00
RCA VICTOR					
❑ 47-6611	Sugar Sweet/Hasta Luego	1956	7.50	15.00	30.00
❑ 47-6696	Blue Prelude/I'll Always Have It on My Mind	1956	7.50	15.00	30.00
❑ 47-6837	Someone Else's Arms/Ain't Going There No More	1957	7.50	15.00	30.00
❑ 47-6927	One and Only/Hackin' Around	1957	12.50	25.00	50.00
❑ 47-7001	The Teenage Frankie and Johnny/I'll Follow	1957	7.50	15.00	30.00
SOUNDWAVES					
❑ 4712	E.T. Still Means Ernest Tubb to Me/One Good Cry Away from Happiness	1982	—	2.00	4.00
SUN					
❑ 403	Sherry's Lips/Miss Brown	1966	5.00	10.00	20.00
❑ 1127	Sherry's Lips/Miss Brown	1972	2.00	4.00	8.00

HOUSTON, DAVID, AND JOY FORD

Number	Title (A Side/B Side)	Yr	VG	VG+	NM
COUNTRY INT'L.					
❑ 146	(Making the Best of) A Bad Situation/(B-side unknown)	1980	—	2.50	5.00

HOUSTON, DAVID, AND BARBARA MANDRELL

Number	Title (A Side/B Side)	Yr	VG	VG+	NM
EPIC					
❑ 10656	After Closing Time/My Song of Love	1970	2.00	4.00	8.00
❑ 10779	We've Got Everything But Love/Try a Little Harder	1971	2.00	4.00	8.00
❑ 10908	A Perfect Match/Almost Persuaded	1972	2.00	4.00	8.00
❑ 11068	I Love You, I Love You/Let's Go Down Together	1973	—	3.00	6.00
❑ 11120	Lovin' You Is Worth It/How Can It Be Wrong	1974	—	3.00	6.00
❑ 20005	Ten Commandments of Love/Try a Little Harder	1974	—	3.00	6.00

HOUSTON, DAVID, AND TAMMY WYNETTE

Also see each artist's individual listings.

Number	Title (A Side/B Side)	Yr	VG	VG+	NM
EPIC					
❑ 10194	My Elusive Dreams/Marriage on the Rocks	1967	2.50	5.00	10.00
❑ 10274	It's All Over/Together We Stand	1967	2.50	5.00	10.00

HOUSTON, JOHNNY

Number	Title (A Side/B Side)	Yr	VG	VG+	NM
EVENT					
❑ 4277	Slick Chick/Playboy	1959	7.50	15.00	30.00
❑ 4280	Torrid Tessie Lee/Our Very First Kiss	1959	7.50	15.00	30.00

HOUSTON, SOLDIER BOY

Number	Title (A Side/B Side)	Yr	VG	VG+	NM
ATLANTIC					
❑ 971	Western Rider Blues/Hug Me Baby	1952	62.50	125.00	250.00

HOUSTON, THELMA

Number	Title (A Side/B Side)	Yr	VG	VG+	NM
ABC DUNHILL					
❑ 11 [DJ]	Everybody Gets to Go to the Moon (same on both sides)	1969	3.75	7.50	15.00
—Special Apollo 11 promotional item					
❑ 11 [PS]	Everybody Gets to Go to the Moon (same on both sides)	1969	5.00	10.00	20.00
—Special Apollo 11 promotional item					
❑ 4197	Sunshower/If This Was the Last Song	1969	2.50	5.00	10.00
❑ 4212	Jumpin' Jack Flash/This Is Your Life	1969	2.50	5.00	10.00
❑ 4222	Save the Country/I Just Can't Stay Away	1970	2.00	4.00	8.00
❑ 4260	The Good Earth/Ride, Louie, Ride	1970	2.00	4.00	8.00
CAPITOL					
❑ 5767	Baby Mine/Woman Behind Her Man	1966	12.50	25.00	50.00
❑ 5882	Don't Cry, My Soldier Boy/Let's Try to Make It	1967	12.50	25.00	50.00
MCA					
❑ 52196	Working Girl/Running in Circles	1983	—	—	3.00
❑ 52239	Make It Last/Just Like All the Rest	1983	—	—	3.00
❑ 52489	(I Guess) It Must Be Love/Running in Circles	1984	—	—	3.00
❑ 52491	Love Is a Dangerous Game/You Used to Hold Me So Tight	1984	—	—	3.00
❑ 52574	Keep It Light/My Lucille	1985	—	—	3.00
—B-side by B.B. King					
❑ 52582	What a Woman Feels Inside/Fantasy and Heartbreak	1985	—	—	3.00
MOTOWN					
❑ 1245	I'm Just a Part of Yesterday/Piano Man	1973	—	2.50	5.00
❑ 1260	Do You Know Where You're Going/Together	1973	—	2.50	5.00
❑ 1316	You've Been Doing Wrong for So Long/Pick Up the Week	1974	—	2.50	5.00
❑ 1385	The Bingo Long Song/Razzle Dazzle	1976	—	2.50	5.00
—B-side by William Goldstein					
❑ 1385 [PS]	The Bingo Long Song/Razzle Dazzle	1976	—	3.00	6.00
—B-side by William Goldstein					
MOWEST					
❑ 5008	I Want to Go Back There Again/Pick Up the Week	1972	—	3.00	6.00
❑ 5013	Me and Bobby McGee/No One's Gonna Be a Fool Forever	1972	—	3.00	6.00
❑ 5023	Piano Man/Me and Bobby McGee	1972	—	3.00	6.00
❑ 5027	What If/There Is a Fool	1972	—	3.00	6.00
❑ 5046	If It's the Last Thing I Do/And I Never Did	1973	—	—	—
—Unreleased					
❑ 5050	I'm Just a Part of Yesterday/Piano Man	1973	—	3.00	6.00
RCA					
❑ PB-11913	Suspicious Minds/Gone	1980	—	2.50	5.00
❑ PB-12215	If You Feel It/Hollywood	1981	—	2.00	4.00
❑ PB-12285	96 Tears/There's No Runnin' Away from Love	1981	—	2.00	4.00
TAMLA					
❑ 54275	One Out of Every Six (Censored)/Pick of the Week	1976	2.50	5.00	10.00
❑ 54278	Don't Leave Me This Way (Short Version)/Today Will Soon Be Yesterday	1977	—	2.00	4.00
❑ 54278 [DJ]	Don't Leave Me This Way (Long Version)/Don't Leave Me This Way (Short Version)	1977	—	3.00	6.00
❑ 54283	If It's the Last Thing I Do/If You Won't Let Me Walk on the Water	1977	—	2.00	4.00
❑ 54287	I'm Here Again/Sharin' Something Perfect	1977	—	2.00	4.00
❑ 54292	I Can't Go On Living Without Your Love/Any Way You Like It	1978	—	2.00	4.00
❑ 54295	I'm Not Strong Enough to Love You/Triplin'	1978	—	2.00	4.00
❑ 54297	Saturday Night, Sunday Morning/Come to Me	1979	—	2.00	4.00

HOUSTON, THELMA, AND JERRY BUTLER

Also see each artist's individual listings.

Number	Title (A Side/B Side)	Yr	VG	VG+	NM
MOTOWN					
❑ 1422	It's a Lifetime Thing/Kiss Me Now	1977	—	2.50	5.00

HOWELL, BILL

Number	Title (A Side/B Side)	Yr	VG	VG+	NM
PALLADIUM					
❑ 513	Rocket Rollin' Blues/Bayou City Blues	195?	12.50	25.00	50.00

HOWLIN' WOLF

Number	Title (A Side/B Side)	Yr	VG	VG+	NM
CADET CONCEPT					
❑ 7013	Evil/Tail Dragger	1969	2.00	4.00	8.00
CHESS					
❑ 1528	Oh! Red/My Last Affair	1952	175.00	350.00	700.00
—Note: Howlin' Wolf releases on Chess before 1528 are unknown on 45 rpm					
❑ 1557	All Night Boogie/I Love My Baby	1953	75.00	150.00	300.00
❑ 1566	No Place to Go/Rockin' Daddy	1954	25.00	50.00	100.00
❑ 1575	How Long/Evil Is Going On	1954	25.00	50.00	100.00
❑ 1584	I'll Be Around/Forty Four	1955	12.50	25.00	50.00
❑ 1593	Who Will Be Next/I Have a Little Girl	1955	10.00	20.00	40.00
❑ 1607	Come to Me Baby/Don't Mess with My Baby	1955	10.00	20.00	40.00
❑ 1618	Smoke Stack Lightning/You Can't Be Beat	1956	10.00	20.00	40.00
❑ 1632	I Asked for Water/So Glad	1956	10.00	20.00	40.00
❑ 1648	Goin' Back Home/My Life	1957	10.00	20.00	40.00
❑ 1668	Somebody in My Home/Nature	1957	10.00	20.00	40.00
❑ 1679	Sittin' On Top of the World/Poor Boy	1958	10.00	20.00	40.00
❑ 1695	Moaning for My Baby/I Didn't Know	1958	10.00	20.00	40.00
❑ 1712	I'm Leaving You/Change My Way	1959	10.00	20.00	40.00
❑ 1726	Howlin' Blues/I Better Go Now	1959	10.00	20.00	40.00
❑ 1735	Mr. Airplane Man/I've Been Abused	1959	10.00	20.00	40.00
❑ 1744	The Natchez Burning/You Gonna Wreck My Life	1959	10.00	20.00	40.00
❑ 1762	Spoonful/Howlin' for My Baby	1960	7.50	15.00	30.00
❑ 1777	Wang Dang Doodle/Back Door Man	1961	7.50	15.00	30.00
❑ 1793	Little Baby/Down in the Bottom	1961	7.50	15.00	30.00
❑ 1804	The Red Rooster/Shake for Me	1961	6.25	12.50	25.00
❑ 1813	You'll Be Mine/Goin' Down Slow	1962	6.25	12.50	25.00
❑ 1823	Just Like I Treat You/I Ain't Superstitious	1962	6.25	12.50	25.00
❑ 1844	Do the Do/Mama's Baby	1962	6.25	12.50	25.00
❑ 1870	300 Pounds of Joy/Built for Comfort	1963	5.00	10.00	20.00
❑ 1890	Tail Dragger/Hidden Charms	1964	5.00	10.00	20.00
❑ 1911	Love Me Darlin'/My Country Sugar Mama	1964	5.00	10.00	20.00
❑ 1923	Killin' Floor/Louise	1965	5.00	10.00	20.00
❑ 1928	Tell Me What I've Done/Ooh Baby	1965	3.75	7.50	15.00
❑ 1945	I Walked from Dallas/Don't Laugh at Me	1965	3.75	7.50	15.00
❑ 1968	New Crawlin' King Snake/Wild Ramblin'	1966	3.75	7.50	15.00
❑ 2009	I Had a Dream/Pop It to Me	1967	3.75	7.50	15.00
❑ 2081	Mary Sue/Hard Luck	1970	2.00	4.00	8.00
❑ 2108	I Smell a Rat/Just As Long	1971	2.00	4.00	8.00
❑ 2118	Do the Do/Red Rooster	1971	2.00	4.00	8.00
❑ 2145	Back Door Wolf/Coon on the Moon	1973	2.00	4.00	8.00
RPM					
❑ 340	Passing By Blues/Crying at Daybreak	1952	1000.	2000.	3000.
—Note: Howlin' Wolf releases on RPM before 340 are unknown on 45 rpm					
❑ 347	My Baby Stole Off/I Want Your Picture	1952	800.00	1600.	2400.

HOYA, OSCAR DE LA

Number	Title (A Side/B Side)	Yr	VG	VG+	NM
EMI LATIN					
❑ 58882	Run to Me/Ven A Mi	2000	—	2.00	4.00

HUBCAPS, THE

ERNIE MARESCA is in this group.

Number	Title (A Side/B Side)	Yr	VG	VG+	NM
LAURIE					
❑ 3219	Hot Rod City (Vocal)/Hot Rod City (Instrumental)	1964	3.75	7.50	15.00

HUDDLE, JACK

Number	Title (A Side/B Side)	Yr	VG	VG+	NM
KAPP					
❑ 207	Starlight/Believe Me	1959	50.00	100.00	200.00
—Buddy Holly plays guitar on these tracks					
PETSY					
❑ 1002	Starlight/Believe Me	1958	125.00	250.00	500.00

HUDSON, POOKIE

Lead singer with THE SPANIELS.

DOUBLE L

Number	Title (A Side/B Side)	Yr	VG	VG+	NM
❑ 711	Jealous Heart/I Know, I Know	1963	5.00	10.00	20.00
❑ 720	I Love You For Sentimental Reasons/Miracles	1963	5.00	10.00	20.00

JAMIE

Number	Title (A Side/B Side)	Yr	VG	VG+	NM
❑ 1319	This Gets To Me/All the Places I've Been	1966	15.00	30.00	60.00

PARKWAY

Number	Title (A Side/B Side)	Yr	VG	VG+	NM
❑ 839	John Brown/Turn Out the Lights	1962	5.00	10.00	20.00

HUDSON, ROCK

DECCA

Number	Title (A Side/B Side)	Yr	VG	VG+	NM
❑ 30966	Pillow Talk/Roly Poly	1959	3.75	7.50	15.00
❑ 30966 [PS]	Pillow Talk/Roly Poly	1959	6.25	12.50	25.00

HUDSON BROTHERS, THE

ARISTA

Number	Title (A Side/B Side)	Yr	VG	VG+	NM
❑ 0208	Help Wanted/Last Time I Looked	1976	—	2.50	5.00
❑ 0286	I Don't Wanna Be Lonely/Pauline	1977	—	2.50	5.00
❑ 0371	The Runaway/You Can't Make Me Cry	1978	—	2.50	5.00

CASABLANCA

Number	Title (A Side/B Side)	Yr	VG	VG+	NM
❑ 0108	So You Are a Star/Ma Ma Ma Baby	1974	—	3.00	6.00
—With long version of A-side					
❑ 801	So You Are a Star/Ma Ma Ma Baby	1974	—	2.50	5.00
—With short version of A-side					
❑ 816	Me and My Guitar/Coochie Coochie Coo	1975	—	2.50	5.00

COLUMBIA

Number	Title (A Side/B Side)	Yr	VG	VG+	NM
❑ 03976	Don't Try to Fight It/You Keep Me Up	1983	—	2.00	4.00
—As "The Hudsons"					

DECCA

Number	Title (A Side/B Side)	Yr	VG	VG+	NM
❑ 32634	Love Is a Word/Laugh, Funny, Funny	1970	—	3.00	6.00
—As "Everyday Hudson"					

ELEKTRA

Number	Title (A Side/B Side)	Yr	VG	VG+	NM
❑ 46648	Annie/Joni	1980	—	2.00	4.00
—As "Hudson"					
❑ 47049	Afraid to Love/Sidewalk	1980	—	2.00	4.00
—As "Hudson"					

LIONEL

Number	Title (A Side/B Side)	Yr	VG	VG+	NM
❑ 3211	Love Nobody/The World Would Be a Little Bit Better	1971	—	3.00	6.00
—As "Hudson"					

PLAYBOY

Number	Title (A Side/B Side)	Yr	VG	VG+	NM
❑ 50001	Someday/Leavin' It's Over	1972	—	3.00	6.00

ROCKET

Number	Title (A Side/B Side)	Yr	VG	VG+	NM
❑ 40141	America — Fight Back/If You Really Need Me	1973	—	3.00	6.00
—As "Hudson"					
❑ 40317	Sunday Driver/Be a Man	1974	—	3.00	6.00
❑ 40417	Rendezvous/Medley	1975	—	2.50	5.00
❑ 40464	Lonely School Year/If You Really Need Me	1975	—	2.50	5.00
❑ 40464 [PS]	Lonely School Year/If You Really Need Me	1975	2.00	4.00	8.00
❑ 40508	Spinning the Wheel (With the Girl You Love)/ Bernie Was a Friend of Ours	1976	—	2.50	5.00

HUGHES, JIMMY

ATLANTIC

Number	Title (A Side/B Side)	Yr	VG	VG+	NM
❑ 2454	Uncle Sam/It Ain't What You've Got	1967	2.00	4.00	8.00

FAME

Number	Title (A Side/B Side)	Yr	VG	VG+	NM
❑ 1000	Midnight Affair/When It Comes to Dancing	1965	2.50	5.00	10.00
❑ 1003	Neighbor, Neighbor/It's a Good Thing	1966	2.00	4.00	8.00
❑ 1006	I Worship the Ground You Walk On/A Shot of Rhythm and Blues	1966	2.00	4.00	8.00
❑ 1011	Why Not Tonight/I'm a Man of Action	1967	2.00	4.00	8.00
❑ 1014	Don't Lose Your Good Thing/You Can't Believe Everything That You Hear	1967	2.00	4.00	8.00
❑ 1015	Hi-Heel Sneakers/Time Will Bring You Back	1967	2.00	4.00	8.00
❑ 6401	Steal Away/Lollipops, Lace and Lipstick	1964	5.00	10.00	20.00
—Black label					
❑ 6401	Steal Away/Lollipops, Lace and Lipstick	1964	3.00	6.00	12.00
—Red label					
❑ 6403	Try Me/Lovely Ladies	1964	2.50	5.00	10.00
❑ 6404	I Want Justice/I'm Getting Better	1964	2.50	5.00	10.00
❑ 6407	Goodbye My Lover, Goodbye/It Was Nice	1965	2.50	5.00	10.00
❑ 6410	You Really Know How to Hurt a Guy/The Loving Physician	1965	2.50	5.00	10.00

GUYDEN

Number	Title (A Side/B Side)	Yr	VG	VG+	NM
❑ 2075	I'm Qualified/My Loving Time	1962	5.00	10.00	20.00

JAMIE

Number	Title (A Side/B Side)	Yr	VG	VG+	NM
❑ 1280	I'm Qualified/My Loving Time	1964	3.75	7.50	15.00

VOLT

Number	Title (A Side/B Side)	Yr	VG	VG+	NM
❑ 4002	I Like Everything About You/What Side of the Door	1968	2.00	4.00	8.00
❑ 4008	Let 'Em Down Baby/The Sweet Things You Do	1969	2.00	4.00	8.00
❑ 4017	Chains of Love/I'm Not Ashamed to Beg or Plead	1969	2.00	4.00	8.00
❑ 4024	I'm So Glad/Lay It on the Line	1969	2.00	4.00	8.00

HULLABALLOOS, THE

ROULETTE

Number	Title (A Side/B Side)	Yr	VG	VG+	NM
❑ 4587	I'm Gonna Love You Too/Party Doll	1964	5.00	10.00	20.00
❑ 4587 [PS]	I'm Gonna Love You Too/Party Doll	1964	10.00	20.00	40.00
❑ 4593	Beware/Did You Ever	1965	5.00	10.00	20.00
❑ 4593 [PS]	Beware/Did You Ever	1965	10.00	20.00	40.00
❑ 4612	Learning the Game/Don't Stop	1965	5.00	10.00	20.00
❑ 4612 [PS]	Learning the Game/Don't Stop	1965	10.00	20.00	40.00
❑ 4622	I Won't Turn Around Now/My Heart Keeps Telling Me	1965	5.00	10.00	20.00
❑ 4622 [PS]	I Won't Turn Around Now/My Heart Keeps Telling Me	1965	10.00	20.00	40.00

HUMAN BEINZ, THE

CAPITOL

Number	Title (A Side/B Side)	Yr	VG	VG+	NM
❑ 2119	Turn On Your Love Light/It's Fun to Be Clean	1968	2.50	5.00	10.00
❑ 2119 [PS]	Turn On Your Love Light/It's Fun to Be Clean	1968	5.00	10.00	20.00
❑ 2198	Every Time Woman/The Face	1968	2.50	5.00	10.00
❑ 2431	I've Got to Keep On Pushin'/This Little Girl of Mine	1969	2.50	5.00	10.00
❑ 5990	Nobody But Me/Sueno	1967	3.75	7.50	15.00

GATEWAY

Number	Title (A Side/B Side)	Yr	VG	VG+	NM
❑ 828	Gloria/The Times They Are a-Changin'	1967	3.75	7.50	15.00
❑ 838	You Can't Make Me Cry/The Pied Piper	1967	3.75	7.50	15.00

HUMAN EXPRESSION, THE

ACCENT

Number	Title (A Side/B Side)	Yr	VG	VG+	NM
❑ 1214	Every Night/Love at Psychedelic Velocity	1967	50.00	100.00	200.00
❑ 1226	Calm Me Down/Optical Sound	1967	25.00	50.00	100.00
❑ 1252	I Don't Need Nobody/Sweet Child of Nothingness	1967	25.00	50.00	100.00

HUMBLE PIE

Also see PETER FRAMPTON.

ATCO

Number	Title (A Side/B Side)	Yr	VG	VG+	NM
❑ 7216	Fool for a Pretty Face/You Soppy Pratt	1980	—	2.50	5.00

A&M

Number	Title (A Side/B Side)	Yr	VG	VG+	NM
❑ 1282	I Don't Need No Doctor/Song for Jenny	1971	—	2.00	4.00
❑ 1282 [PS]	I Don't Need No Doctor/Song for Jenny	1971	—	3.00	6.00
❑ 1349	Hot and Nasty/You're So Good for Me	1972	—	2.00	4.00
❑ 1349 [PS]	Hot and Nasty/You're So Good for Me	1972	—	3.00	6.00
❑ 1366	Sweet Peace and Time/30 Days in the Hole	1972	—	2.00	4.00
❑ 1406	Say No More/Black Coffee	1973	—	2.00	4.00
❑ 1440	Honky Tonk Woman/Get Down to It	1973	—	2.00	4.00
❑ 1484	Oh La De Da/The Out Crowd	1974	—	2.00	4.00
❑ 1530	Rally with Ali/Ninety-Nine Pounds	1974	—	2.00	4.00
❑ 1711	Road Hog/Rock and Roll Music	1975	—	2.00	4.00

IMMEDIATE

Number	Title (A Side/B Side)	Yr	VG	VG+	NM
❑ 001	Natural Born Woman/I'll Go Alone	1969	2.00	4.00	8.00

HUMBLEBUMS, THE

GERRY RAFFERTY was in this group.

UNITED ARTISTS

Number	Title (A Side/B Side)	Yr	VG	VG+	NM
❑ 50771	All the Best People Do It/Cruisin'	1971	2.50	5.00	10.00

HUMES, ANITA

Also see THE ESSEX.

ROULETTE

Number	Title (A Side/B Side)	Yr	VG	VG+	NM
❑ 4564	Don't Fight It Baby/When Somethin's Hard to Get	1964	3.75	7.50	15.00
❑ 4575	I'm Making It Over/Just for the Boy	1964	3.75	7.50	15.00
❑ 4750	Are You Going My Way/Everybody's Got You	1967	2.50	5.00	10.00

HUMPERDINCK, ENGELBERT

EPIC

Number	Title (A Side/B Side)	Yr	VG	VG+	NM
❑ AE7 1170 [DJ]	Christmas Song/Silent Night	1978	—	2.00	4.00
❑ AE7 1170 [PS]	Christmas Song/Silent Night	1978	—	2.00	4.00
❑ 02060	Don't You Love Me Anymore/Till I Get It Right	1981	—	—	3.00
❑ 02245	Maybe This Time/When the Night Ends	1981	—	—	3.00
❑ 03817	Till You and Your Lover Are Lovers Again/What Will I Write	1983	—	—	3.00
❑ 50270	After the Lovin'/Let's Remember the Good Times	1976	—	2.50	5.00
❑ 50365	I Believe in Miracles/Goodbye My Friend	1977	—	2.00	4.00
❑ 50447	A Lover's Holiday/Look at Me	1977	—	2.00	4.00
❑ 50488	A Night to Remember/Silent Night	1977	—	2.00	4.00
❑ 50526	The Last of the Romantics/I Have Paid the Toll	1978	—	2.00	4.00
❑ 50566	Love Me Tender/This Time One Year Ago	1978	—	2.00	4.00
❑ 50579	Love's In Need of Love Today/Sweet Marjorene	1978	—	2.00	4.00
❑ 50632	This Moment in Time/And the Day Begins	1978	—	2.00	4.00
❑ 50692	Can't Help Falling in Love/You Know Me	1979	—	2.00	4.00
❑ 50732	Lovin' Too Well/Much, Much Greater Love	1979	—	2.00	4.00
❑ 50844	Love's Only Love/Burning Ember	1980	—	—	3.00
❑ 50899	A Chance to Be a Hero/Any Kind of Love at All	1980	—	—	3.00
❑ 50933	Don't Cry Out Loud/Don't Touch That Dial	1980	—	—	3.00
❑ 50958	It's Not Easy to Live Together/Royal Affair	1980	—	—	3.00

HICKORY

Number	Title (A Side/B Side)	Yr	VG	VG+	NM
❑ 1337	Baby Turn Around/If I Could Do the Things I Want to Do	1965	4.00	8.00	16.00
—As "Gerry Dorsey"					

PARROT

Number	Title (A Side/B Side)	Yr	VG	VG+	NM
❑ 40011 [M]	Release Me (And Let Me Love Again)/Ten Guitars	1967	2.00	4.00	8.00
❑ 40011 [S]	Release Me (And Let Me Love Again)/Ten Guitars	1967	5.00	10.00	20.00
—Both sides in true stereo. Letters "XDR" are stamped in run-off area before the matrix number					
❑ 40015	There Goes My Everything/You Love	1967	2.00	4.00	8.00
❑ 40019	The Last Waltz/That Promise	1967	2.00	4.00	8.00
❑ 40019 [PS]	The Last Waltz/That Promise	1967	3.00	6.00	12.00
❑ 40023	Am I That Easy to Forget/Pretty Ribbons	1967	2.00	4.00	8.00
❑ 40023 [PS]	Am I That Easy to Forget/Pretty Ribbons	1967	3.00	6.00	12.00
❑ 40027	A Man Without Love/Call on Me	1968	2.00	4.00	8.00
❑ 40032	Les Bicyclettes De Belsize/Three Little Words	1968	2.00	4.00	8.00
❑ 40032 [PS]	Les Bicyclettes De Belsize/Three Little Words	1968	3.00	6.00	12.00
❑ 40036	The Way It Used to Be/A Good Thing Going	1969	—	3.00	6.00
❑ 40036 [PS]	The Way It Used to Be/A Good Thing Going	1969	2.50	5.00	10.00
❑ 40040	I'm a Better Man/Cafe	1969	—	3.00	6.00
❑ 40044	Winter World of Love/Take My Heart	1969	—	3.00	6.00
❑ 40044 [PS]	Winter World of Love/Take My Heart	1969	2.50	5.00	10.00
❑ 40049	My Marie/Our Song (La Paloma)	1970	—	3.00	6.00
❑ 40049 [PS]	My Marie/Our Song (La Paloma)	1970	2.00	4.00	8.00
❑ 40054	Sweetheart/Born to Be Wanted	1970	—	3.00	6.00
❑ 40054 [PS]	Sweetheart/Born to Be Wanted	1970	2.00	4.00	8.00
❑ 40059	When There's No You/Stranger, Step In My World	1971	—	3.00	6.00
❑ 40059 [PS]	When There's No You/Stranger, Step In My World	1971	2.00	4.00	8.00
❑ 40065	Another Time, Another Place/You're the Window of My World	1971	—	3.00	6.00
❑ 40069	Too Beautiful to Last/A Hundred Times a Day	1972	—	2.50	5.00
❑ 40071	In Time/How Does It Feel	1972	—	2.50	5.00
❑ 40072	I Never Said Goodbye/Time After Time	1972	—	2.50	5.00
❑ 40073	I'm Leavin' You/My Summer Song	1973	—	2.00	4.00
❑ 40076	Love Is All/Lady of the Night	1973	—	2.00	4.00
❑ 40077	Free as the Wind/My Friend the Wind	1974	—	2.00	4.00
❑ 40079	Catch Me I'm Falling/Love, Oh Precious Love	1974	—	2.00	4.00

Number	Title (A Side/B Side)	Yr	VG	VG+	NM
❑ 40082	Forever and Ever/Precious Love	1974	—	2.00	4.00
❑ 40085	This Is What You Mean to Me/A World Without Music	1975	—	2.00	4.00

HUNS, THE

Number	Title (A Side/B Side)	Yr	VG	VG+	NM
GOD					
❑ 001	Busy Kids/Glad He's Dead	1979	25.00	50.00	100.00
❑ 001 [PS]	Busy Kids/Glad He's Dead	1979	25.00	50.00	100.00
—Oversized sleeve with insert					

HUNT, D.A.

Number	Title (A Side/B Side)	Yr	VG	VG+	NM
SUN					
❑ 183	Lonesome Ol' Jail/Greyhound Blues	1953	—	—	—
—Unknown on 45 rpm, although both Sun 182 and 184 exist on 45s.					

HUNT, DANNY

Number	Title (A Side/B Side)	Yr	VG	VG+	NM
DYNAMITE					
❑ 8663	What's Happening to Our Love Affair/(B-side unknown)	1974	5.00	10.00	20.00

HUNT, GERALDINE

Number	Title (A Side/B Side)	Yr	VG	VG+	NM
ABC					
❑ 10859	Winner Take All/For Lovers Only	1966	7.50	15.00	30.00
BOMBAY					
❑ 4501	He's for Real/(B-side unknown)	1964	25.00	50.00	100.00
CHECKER					
❑ 1028	I Let Myself Go/I Wished I Had Listened	1962	7.50	15.00	30.00
PRISM					
❑ 315	Can't Fake the Feeling/(B-side unknown)	1980	—	2.00	4.00
❑ 323	Heart Heart/(B-side unknown)	1981	—	2.00	4.00
ROULETTE					
❑ 7068	Never, Never Leave Me/Push, Sweet	1970	—	3.00	6.00
❑ 7109	Now That There's You/Shades of Blue	1971	—	3.00	6.00
❑ 7129	Baby, I Need Your Loving/(B-side unknown)	1972	—	3.00	6.00
❑ 7132	Cold Blood/Just Believe in Me	1972	—	3.00	6.00
❑ 7149	You Brought Joy/Shades of Blue	1973	—	3.00	6.00
U.S.A.					
❑ 732	Sneak Around/It Never Happened Before	1962	7.50	15.00	30.00
❑ 737	Sneak Around/It Never Happened Before	1963	6.25	12.50	25.00

HUNTER, CHRISTINE

Number	Title (A Side/B Side)	Yr	VG	VG+	NM
ROULETTE					
❑ 4589	Santa Bring Me Ringo/Where Were You Daddy	1964	3.75	7.50	15.00

HUNTER, IAN

Also see MOTT THE HOOPLE.

Number	Title (A Side/B Side)	Yr	VG	VG+	NM
CHRYSALIS					
❑ 2324	When the Daylight Comes/Life After Death	1979	—	2.50	5.00
❑ 2352	Cleveland Rocks/Just Another Night	1979	—	2.50	5.00
❑ 2405	We Gotta Get Out of Here/Sons and Daughters	1980	—	2.00	4.00
❑ 2542	I Need Your Love/(B-side unknown)	1981	—	2.00	4.00
❑ 2569	Central Park 'N' West/(B-side unknown)	1981	—	2.00	4.00
COLUMBIA					
❑ 03929	All of the Good Ones Are Taken/Death 'N' Glory Boys	1983	—	2.00	4.00
❑ 04166	Seeing Double/That Girl Is Rock 'N' Roll	1983	—	2.00	4.00
❑ 10161	Once Bitten Twice Shy/3000 Miles from Here	1975	—	3.00	6.00

HUNTER, IVORY JOE

Number	Title (A Side/B Side)	Yr	VG	VG+	NM
ATLANTIC					
❑ 1049	It May Sound Silly/I Got to Learn to Do the Mambo	1954	6.25	12.50	25.00
❑ 1066	I Want Somebody/Heven Came Down to Earth	1955	6.25	12.50	25.00
❑ 1086	A Tear Fell/I Need You By My Side	1956	6.25	12.50	25.00
❑ 1095	You Mean Everything to Me/That's Why I Dream	1956	6.25	12.50	25.00
❑ 1111	Since I Met You Baby/You Can't Stop This Rocking and Rolling	1956	7.50	15.00	30.00
❑ 1128	Empty Arms/Love's a Hurting Game	1957	5.00	10.00	20.00
❑ 1151	She's Gone/Everytime I Hear That Song	1957	5.00	10.00	20.00
❑ 1164	All About the Blues/If Only You Were Here with Me	1957	5.00	10.00	20.00
❑ 1173	You're On My Mind/Baby, Baby, Count on Me	1958	5.00	10.00	20.00
❑ 1183	I'm So Glad I Found You/Shooty Booty	1958	5.00	10.00	20.00
❑ 1191	You Flip Me Baby/Yes, I Want You	1958	5.00	10.00	20.00
❑ 2020	I Just Want to Love You/Now I Don't Worry No More	1959	3.75	7.50	15.00
CAPITOL					
❑ 4587	I'm Hooked/Because I Love You	1961	3.00	6.00	12.00
❑ 4648	May the Best Man Win/You Better Believe It Baby	1961	3.00	6.00	12.00
❑ 4688	The Life I Live/A Great Big Heart Full of Love	1962	3.00	6.00	12.00
DOT					
❑ 15880	City Lights/Stolen Moments	1958	3.75	7.50	15.00
❑ 15930	Old Fashioned Love/Cottage for Sale	1959	3.75	7.50	15.00
❑ 15957	I Love You So Much It Hurts/Welcome Home Baby	1959	3.75	7.50	15.00
❑ 15986	My Search Was Ended/Did You Mean It	1959	3.75	7.50	15.00
EPIC					
❑ 10725	Heartbreak and Misery/We All Like That Groovy Feeling	1971	—	3.00	6.00
❑ 10725	Heartbreak and Misery/I'm Coming Down with the Blues	1971	—	3.00	6.00
GOLDISC					
❑ 3010	It's Love, It's Love, It's Love/You Satisfy Me Baby	1960	3.75	7.50	15.00
GOLDWAX					
❑ 307	Every Little Bit Helped Me/I Can Make You Happy	1966	5.00	10.00	20.00
KING					
❑ 4424	False Friend Blues/Send Me Pretty Mama	1951	10.00	20.00	40.00
—Ivory Joe Hunter records on King before 4422 are unconfirmed on 45 rpm					
❑ 4443	She's Gone Blues/Stop Rockin' That Train	1951	10.00	20.00	40.00
❑ 4455	Old Gal and New Gal Blues/Woo Wee Blues	1951	10.00	20.00	40.00
❑ 5166	Jealous Heart/I Like It	1958	3.75	7.50	15.00
❑ 5271	Guess Who/Don't Fall in Love with Me	1959	—	—	—
—Unreleased					
❑ 5280	Guess Who/Don't Fall in Love with Me	1959	3.75	7.50	15.00
MGM					
❑ 8011	I Almost Lost My Mind/If I Give You My Love	1949	12.50	25.00	50.00
—Original 45 issue of this record					
❑ 10578	I Almost Lost My Mind/If I Give You My Love	1949	10.00	20.00	40.00
❑ 10618	S.P. Blues/Why Fool Yourself	1950	7.50	15.00	30.00
❑ 10663	I Need You So/Leave Her Alone	1950	7.50	15.00	30.00
❑ 10733	Let Me Dream/Gimme a Pound of Round Ground	1950	7.50	15.00	30.00
❑ 10761	Old Man's Boogie/Living a Lie	1950	7.50	15.00	30.00
❑ 10818	It's A Sin/Don't You Believe Me	1950	7.50	15.00	30.00
❑ 10899	I Found My Baby/I Ain't Got No Gal	1951	7.50	15.00	30.00
❑ 10951	I Can't Get You Off My Mind/I Can't Resist You	1951	7.50	15.00	30.00
❑ 10995	You Lied/When I Lost You	1951	7.50	15.00	30.00
❑ 11052	I'm Yours/Wrong Woman Blues	1951	7.50	15.00	30.00
❑ 11132	Blue Moon/U Name It	1952	7.50	15.00	30.00
❑ 11165	Laugh/Where Shall I Go	1952	7.50	15.00	30.00
❑ 11195	I'm Sorry for You My Friend/I Will Be	1952	7.50	15.00	30.00
❑ 11263	I Get That Lonesome Feeling/I Thought I Had Loved	1952	7.50	15.00	30.00
❑ 11325	Big Bounce/Tell Her for Me	1952	7.50	15.00	30.00
❑ 11378	Rockin' Chair Boogie/Music Before Dawn	1952	7.50	15.00	30.00
❑ 11459	I Had a Girl/If You See My Baby	1953	7.50	15.00	30.00
❑ 11549	I'm Afraid/Don't Make Me Cry	1953	7.50	15.00	30.00
❑ 11599	I Must Be Talking to Myself/My Best Wishes	1953	7.50	15.00	30.00
❑ 11702	I Have a Secret/I Feel So Good	1954	6.25	12.50	25.00
❑ 11818	Do You Miss Me/Whose Arms Are You Missing	1954	6.25	12.50	25.00
PARAMOUNT					
❑ 0253	He'll Never Love You/San Antonio Rose	1973	—	3.00	6.00
SMASH					
❑ 1825	My Arms Are Waiting/Congratulations	1963	3.00	6.00	12.00
❑ 1860	There's No Forgetting You/My Lover's Prayer	1963	3.00	6.00	12.00
SOUND STAGE 7					
❑ 2623	Ivory Tower/I'll Give You All Night to Stop	1968	2.00	4.00	8.00
❑ 2635	Until the Day I Die/I Built a Wall Around Me	1969	2.00	4.00	8.00
❑ 2643	Straighten Up Baby/Baby Me Baby	1969	2.00	4.00	8.00
STAX					
❑ 155	This Kind of Woman/Can't Explain Why It Happened	1964	3.00	6.00	12.00
TEARDROP					
❑ 3058	I've Asked You for the Last Time/Heart	196?	2.50	5.00	10.00
VEE JAY					
❑ 452	Somebody's Stealing My Love/You Only Want Me When You Need Me	1962	3.00	6.00	12.00
VEEP					
❑ 1258	What's the Matter Baby/Don't You Believe Me	1967	2.00	4.00	8.00
❑ 1270	Did She Ask About Me/From the First Time We Met	1967	2.00	4.00	8.00

7-Inch Extended Plays

Number	Title (A Side/B Side)	Yr	VG	VG+	NM
ATLANTIC					
❑ 589	*Since I Met You Baby/I Got to Learn to Do the Mambo/It May Sound Silly/A Tear Fell	1958	12.50	25.00	50.00
❑ 589 [PS]	Ivory Joe Hunter (Since I Met You Baby)	1958	12.50	25.00	50.00
❑ 608	(contents unknown)	1958	15.00	30.00	60.00
❑ 608 [PS]	Rock with Ivory Joe Hunter	1958	15.00	30.00	60.00
KING					
❑ 265	(contents unknown)	1954	20.00	40.00	80.00
❑ 265 [PS]	Ivory Joe Hunter	1954	20.00	40.00	80.00
MGM					
❑ X-1376	(contents unknown)	1957	12.50	25.00	50.00
❑ X-1376 [PS]	I Get That Lonesome Feeling, Volume 1	1957	12.50	25.00	50.00
❑ X-1377	(contents unknown)	1957	12.50	25.00	50.00
❑ X-1377 [PS]	I Get That Lonesome Feeling, Volume 2	1957	12.50	25.00	50.00
❑ X-1378	(contents unknown)	1957	12.50	25.00	50.00
❑ X-1378 [PS]	I Get That Lonesome Feeling, Volume 3	1957	12.50	25.00	50.00

HURRICANES, THE

Number	Title (A Side/B Side)	Yr	VG	VG+	NM
KING					
❑ 4817	Poor Little Dancin' Girl/Pistol Packin' Mama	1955	50.00	100.00	200.00
❑ 4867	Maybe It's All for the Best/Yours	1956	50.00	100.00	200.00
❑ 4898	Raining in My Heart/Tell Me Baby	1956	50.00	100.00	200.00
❑ 4926	Little Girl of Mine/Your Promise to Me	1956	37.50	75.00	150.00
❑ 4947	Dear Mother/You May Not Know	1956	30.00	60.00	120.00
❑ 5018	Fallen Angel/I'll Always Be in Love with You	1957	25.00	50.00	100.00
❑ 5042	Priceless/Now That I Need You	1957	25.00	50.00	100.00

HUSKER DU

Also see BOB MOULD.

Number	Title (A Side/B Side)	Yr	VG	VG+	NM
NEW ALLIANCE					
❑ 010	In a Free Land/What Do I Want/M.I.C.	1982	17.50	35.00	70.00
❑ 010 [PS]	In a Free Land/What Do I Want/M.I.C.	1982	12.50	25.00	50.00
REFLEX					
❑ A	Statues/Amusement (Live)	1980	10.00	20.00	40.00
❑ A [PS]	Statues/Amusement (Live)	1980	15.00	30.00	60.00
SST					
❑ 025	Eight Miles High/Masochism World (Live)	1984	—	—	2.00
❑ 025	Eight Miles High/Masochism World (Live)	199?	—	—	3.00
—Reissue on purple vinyl					
❑ 025	Eight Miles High/Masochism World (Live)	199?	—	—	4.00
—Reissue on blue vinyl					
❑ 025 [PS]	Eight Miles High/Masochism World (Live)	1984	—	—	2.00
❑ PSST 031 [DJ]	Celebrated Summer/New Day Rising	1984	3.75	7.50	15.00
❑ PSST 031 [PS]	Celebrated Summer/New Day Rising	1984	3.75	7.50	15.00
—Rubber-stamped sleeve with sticker and enclosed press release					
❑ 051	Makes No Sense at All/Love Is All Around	1985	—	—	2.00
❑ 051	Makes No Sense at All/Love Is All Around	199?	—	—	3.00
—Reissue on white vinyl					
❑ 051 [PS]	Makes No Sense at All/Love Is All Around	1985	—	—	2.00

HUSKY, FERLIN

4 STAR

Number	Title (A Side/B Side)	Yr	VG	VG+	NM
❑ 1516	Guilty Feeling/Road to Heaven	1950	12.50	25.00	50.00
—All 4 Star records as "Terry Preston"; it's possible that not all these exist on 45s					
❑ 1518	Let's Keep the Communists Out/The Sabbath	1950	12.50	25.00	50.00
❑ 1542	Irma/Put Me in Your Pocket	1950	12.50	25.00	50.00
❑ 1566	Wise Guy/Cross Eyed Gal from the Ozarks	1951	10.00	20.00	40.00
❑ 1571	Jezebel/Tennessee Hillbilly Ghost	1951	10.00	20.00	40.00
❑ 1572	Crying Heart Blues/If You Don't Believe I'm Leaving (Just Count the Days I'm Gone)	1951	10.00	20.00	40.00
❑ 1573	Rotation Blues/Deadly Weapon	1951	10.00	20.00	40.00

ABC

Number	Title (A Side/B Side)	Yr	VG	VG+	NM
❑ 11345	True True Lovin'/A Legend in My Time	1973	—	3.00	6.00
❑ 11360	Between Me and Blue/(B-side unknown)	1973	—	3.00	6.00
❑ 11381	Baby's Blue/One	1973	—	3.00	6.00
❑ 11395	Rosie Cries a Lot/Shoes	1973	—	3.00	6.00
❑ 11432	Freckles and Polliwog Days/Everything Is Nothing Without You	1974	—	3.00	6.00
❑ 12020	Drinkin' Man/Cuzz Yore So Sweet	1974	—	3.00	6.00
—As "Simon Crum"					
❑ 12021	A Room for a Boy...Never Used/A Ring of String	1974	—	2.50	5.00
❑ 12048	Champagne Ladies and Blue Ribbon Babies/I Feel Better All Over	1974	—	2.50	5.00
❑ 12085	Burning/A Touch of Yesterday	1975	—	2.50	5.00

ABC DOT

Number	Title (A Side/B Side)	Yr	VG	VG+	NM
❑ 17574	An Old Memory (Got in My Eye)/She's Not Yours Anymore	1975	—	2.50	5.00

CAPITOL

Number	Title (A Side/B Side)	Yr	VG	VG+	NM
❑ F1861	China Doll/Tennessee Central #9	1951	6.25	12.50	25.00
❑ F1947	I Want You So/Time	1952	5.00	10.00	20.00
—As "Terry Preston"					
❑ 2023	Christmas Dream/Christmas Is Holy	1967	2.00	4.00	8.00
❑ F2024	Words/I'm Missin' Lots of Lovin'	1952	5.00	10.00	20.00
—As "Terry Preston"					
❑ 2048	Just for You/Don't Hurt Me Anymore	1967	2.00	4.00	8.00
❑ F2105	Counting My Heartaches/I Love You	1952	5.00	10.00	20.00
—As "Terry Preston"					
❑ 2154	I Promised You the World/You Should Live My Life	1968	2.00	4.00	8.00
❑ F2211	I'm Only Wishing/Are You Afraid	1952	5.00	10.00	20.00
—As "Terry Preston"					
❑ 2288	White Fences and Evergreen Trees/Love's Been Good to Me	1968	2.00	4.00	8.00
❑ F2298	Gone/Out of Reach	1952	7.50	15.00	30.00
—As "Terry Preston"					
❑ F2391	My Foolish Heart/Undesired	1953	5.00	10.00	20.00
—As "Terry Preston"					
❑ F2397	Hank's Song/I'll Never Have You	1953	5.00	10.00	20.00
❑ 2411	Flat River, Mo./One Life to Live	1969	2.00	4.00	8.00
❑ F2467	I've Got a Woman's Love/Watch the Company You Keep	1953	5.00	10.00	20.00
—As "Terry Preston"					
❑ F2495	Mini Ha Cha/I Lost My Love Today	1953	5.00	10.00	20.00
❑ 2512	That's Why I Love You So Much/Forever Yours	1969	2.00	4.00	8.00
❑ F2558	How Much Are You Mine/You'll Die a Thousand Deaths	1953	5.00	10.00	20.00
❑ F2627	Walkin' and Hummin'/I Wouldn't Treat a Dog Like You're Treating Me	1953	5.00	10.00	20.00
❑ 2666	Every Step of the Way/That's What I'd Do	1969	2.00	4.00	8.00
❑ F2746	Eli the Camel/Somebody Lied	1954	5.00	10.00	20.00
❑ 2793	Heavenly Sunshine/All My Little Loving Ways	1970	—	3.00	6.00
❑ F2814	Each Time You Leave/Deceived	1954	5.00	10.00	20.00
—As "Terry Preston"					
❑ F2835	The Drunken Driver/Homesick	1954	5.00	10.00	20.00
❑ 2882	Your Sweet Love Lifted Me/You're the Happy Song I Sing	1970	—	3.00	6.00
❑ F2914	King of a Lonely Castle/Very Seldom Frequently Ever	1954	5.00	10.00	20.00
❑ 2999	Sweet Misery/Because You're Mine	1970	—	3.00	6.00
❑ F3001	I Feel Better All Over (More Than Anywhere's Else)/Little Tom	1954	3.75	7.50	15.00
❑ F3063	Cuzz Yore So Sweet/My Gallina	1955	5.00	10.00	20.00
—As "Simon Crum"					
❑ 3069	One More Time/Don't Let the Good Life Pass You By	1971	—	3.00	6.00
❑ F3097	I'll Baby Sit with You/She's Always There	1955	3.75	7.50	15.00
❑ 3165	Open Up the Book (And Take a Look)/Even If It's True	1971	—	3.00	6.00
❑ F3183	Don't Blame the Children/Saith the Lord	1955	3.75	7.50	15.00
❑ F3233	Dear Mr. Brown/I'll Be Here for a Lifetime	1955	3.75	7.50	15.00
❑ F3270	A Hillbilly Deck of Cards/Ooh I Want You	1955	5.00	10.00	20.00
—As "Simon Crum"					
❑ 3308	Just Plain Lonely/Always in All Ways	1972	—	3.00	6.00
❑ F3316	A Sinful Secret/Slow Down Brother	1956	3.75	7.50	15.00
❑ 3415	How Could You Be Anything But Love/I'd Walk a Mile for a Smile	1972	—	3.00	6.00
❑ F3428	Aladdin's Lamp/That Big Old Moon	1956	3.75	7.50	15.00
❑ F3460	Bop Cat Bop/Muki Ruki	1956	5.00	10.00	20.00
—As "Simon Crum"					
❑ F3522	Nothing Looks As Good As You/Waiting	1956	3.75	7.50	15.00
❑ F3628	Gone/Missing Persons	1957	3.75	7.50	15.00
❑ F3742	A Fallen Star/Prize Possession	1957	3.00	6.00	12.00
❑ F3790	Make Me Live Again/This Moment of Love	1957	3.00	6.00	12.00
❑ F3862	What'cha Doin' After School/Wang Dang Doo	1957	3.00	6.00	12.00
❑ F3943	Kingdom of Love/Terrific Together	1958	3.00	6.00	12.00
❑ F4000	I Saw God/I Feel That Old Heartache Again	1958	3.00	6.00	12.00
❑ F4046	I Will/All of the Time	1958	3.00	6.00	12.00
❑ F4073	Country Music Is Here to Stay/Stand Up, Sit Down, Shut Your Mouth	1958	5.00	10.00	20.00
—As "Simon Crum"					
❑ F4123	My Reason for Living/Wrong	1959	3.00	6.00	12.00
❑ F4186	Draggin' the River/Sea Sand	1959	3.00	6.00	12.00
❑ F4252	Morgan Poisoned the Water Hole/I Fell Out of Love with You	1959	3.75	7.50	15.00
—As "Simon Crum"					
❑ F4278	Black Sheep/I'll Always Return	1959	3.00	6.00	12.00
❑ 4343	My Love for You/Asi Es La Vida	1960	3.00	6.00	12.00
❑ 4406	Wings of a Dove/Next to Jimmy	1960	3.00	6.00	12.00
❑ 4464	Country Music Fiddler/I Feel Better All Over	1960	3.75	7.50	15.00
—As "Simon Crum"					
❑ 4499	Enormity in Motion/Cuzz Yore So Sweet	1961	3.75	7.50	15.00
—As "Simon Crum"					
❑ 4548	Before I Lose My Mind/What Good Will I Ever Be	1961	3.00	6.00	12.00
❑ 4594	Willow Tree/Take a Look	1961	3.00	6.00	12.00
❑ 4650	The Waltz You Saved for Me/Out of a Clear Blue Sky	1961	3.00	6.00	12.00
❑ 4721	Somebody Save Me/Just Another Lonely Night	1962	2.50	5.00	10.00
❑ 4779	Stand Up/It Scares Me	1962	2.50	5.00	10.00
❑ 4853	It Was You/Near You	1962	2.50	5.00	10.00
❑ 4908	You Hurt Me/My Reason for Living	1963	2.50	5.00	10.00
❑ 4966	Don't Be Mad/Little Red Webb	1963	3.00	6.00	12.00
—As "Simon Crum"					
❑ 4977	Who's Next/As Close As We'll Ever Be	1963	2.50	5.00	10.00
❑ 5067	Face of a Clown/Love Looks Good on You	1963	2.50	5.00	10.00
❑ 5111	Timber I'm Falling/Don't Count the Diamonds	1964	2.50	5.00	10.00
❑ 5206	Up on the Mountain Top/Weaker Moments	1964	2.50	5.00	10.00
❑ 5355	True, True Lovin'/Love Built the House	1965	2.50	5.00	10.00
❑ 5438	Willie Was a Gamblin' Man/Picking Up the Pieces	1965	2.50	5.00	10.00
❑ 5522	Money Greases the Wheels/Lasting Love	1965	2.50	5.00	10.00
❑ 5615	I Could Sing All Night/What Does Your Conscience Say to You	1966	2.50	5.00	10.00
❑ 5679	I Hear Little Rock Calling/Stand Beside Me	1966	2.50	5.00	10.00
❑ 5775	Once/Why Do I Put Up with You	1966	2.50	5.00	10.00
❑ 5852	What Am I Gonna Do Now/General G	1967	2.00	4.00	8.00
❑ 5938	You Pushed Me Too Far/A Bridge I Have Never Crossed	1967	2.00	4.00	8.00

KING

Number	Title (A Side/B Side)	Yr	VG	VG+	NM
❑ 5434	Irma/Cotton Pickin' Heart	1960	3.00	6.00	12.00
❑ 5476	Electrified Donkey/Guilty Feeling	1961	3.00	6.00	12.00

7-Inch Extended Plays

CAPITOL

Number	Title (A Side/B Side)	Yr	VG	VG+	NM
❑ EAP 1-609	(contents unknown)	1955	5.00	10.00	20.00
❑ EAP 1-609 [PS]	Ferlin Husky	1955	5.00	10.00	20.00
❑ EAP 1-718	Hang Your Head in Shame/That Silver Haired Daddy of Mine//Honky-Tonkin' Party Girl/Useless	1956	3.75	7.50	15.00
❑ EAP 1-718 [PS]	Songs of the Home and Heart, Part 1	1956	3.75	7.50	15.00
❑ EAP 2-718	I Can't Go On This Way/That Little Girl of Mine//You Make Me Feel Funny, Honey/Rockin' Alone in an Old Rockin' Chair	1956	3.75	7.50	15.00
❑ EAP 2-718 [PS]	Songs of the Home and Heart, Part 2	1956	3.75	7.50	15.00
❑ EAP 3-718	Farther and Farther Apart/Never Have, Never Will//I Dreamed of an Old Love Affair/Daddy's Little Girl	1956	3.75	7.50	15.00
❑ EAP 3-718 [PS]	Songs of the Home and Heart, Part 3	1956	3.75	7.50	15.00
❑ EAP 1-880	(contents unknown)	1957	3.75	7.50	15.00
❑ EAP 1-880 [PS]	Boulevard of Broken Dreams, Part 1	1957	3.75	7.50	15.00
❑ EAP 2-880	(contents unknown)	1957	3.75	7.50	15.00
❑ EAP 2-880 [PS]	Boulevard of Broken Dreams, Part 2	1957	3.75	7.50	15.00
❑ EAP 3-880	(contents unknown)	1957	3.75	7.50	15.00
❑ EAP 3-880 [PS]	Boulevard of Broken Dreams, Part 3	1957	3.75	7.50	15.00
❑ EAP 1-921	Don't Walk Away/Somewhere There's Sunshine//My Home Town/This Whole Wide World	1958	3.00	6.00	12.00
❑ EAP 1-921 [PS]	Country Music Holiday	1958	3.00	6.00	12.00
❑ EAP 1-1280	(contents unknown)	1960	3.00	6.00	12.00
❑ EAP 1-1280 [PS]	Ferlin Favorites, Part 1	1960	3.00	6.00	12.00
❑ EAP 2-1280	(contents unknown)	1960	3.00	6.00	12.00
❑ EAP 2-1280 [PS]	Ferlin Favorites, Part 2	1960	3.00	6.00	12.00
❑ EAP 3-1280	(contents unknown)	1960	3.00	6.00	12.00
❑ EAP 3-1280 [PS]	Ferlin Favorites, Part 3	1960	3.00	6.00	12.00
❑ EAP 1-1516	(contents unknown)	1961	3.00	6.00	12.00
❑ EAP 1-1516 [PS]	Wings of a Dove	1961	3.00	6.00	12.00

HUTCH, WILLIE

DUNHILL

Number	Title (A Side/B Side)	Yr	VG	VG+	NM
❑ 4012	The Duck/Love Runs Out	1965	15.00	30.00	60.00

MAVERICK

Number	Title (A Side/B Side)	Yr	VG	VG+	NM
❑ 1003	Use What You Got (Part 1)/Use What You Got (Part 2)	1968	3.75	7.50	15.00

MODERN

Number	Title (A Side/B Side)	Yr	VG	VG+	NM
❑ 1021	I Can't Get Enough/Your Love Has Made Me a Man	1966	10.00	20.00	40.00

MOTOWN

Number	Title (A Side/B Side)	Yr	VG	VG+	NM
❑ 1222	Brother's Gonna Work It Out/I Choose You	1973	—	2.50	5.00
❑ 1252	Slick/Mother's Theme	1973	—	2.50	5.00
❑ 1252 [PS]	Slick/Mother's Theme	1973	—	3.00	6.00
❑ 1282	Sunshine Lady/I Just Wanted to Make Her Happy	1973	—	2.50	5.00
❑ 1287	If You Ain't Got No Money (You Can't Get No Honey) Pt. 1/Pt. 2	1974	—	2.50	5.00
❑ 1292	Theme of Foxy Brown/Give Me Some of That Good Old Love	1974	—	2.50	5.00
❑ 1331	I'm Gonna Stay/Woman You Touched Me	1975	—	2.50	5.00
❑ 1339	Get Ready for the Get Down/Don't Let Nobody Tell You How to Do Your Thing	1975	—	2.50	5.00
❑ 1360	Love Power/Talk to Me	1975	—	2.00	4.00
❑ 1371	Party Down/Just Another Day	1976	—	2.00	4.00
❑ 1406	Let Me Be the One, Baby/She's Just Doing Her Thing	1976	—	2.00	4.00
❑ 1411	Shake It, Shake It/I Feel Like We Can Make It	1976	—	2.00	4.00
❑ 1416	We Gonna Have a House Party/Never Had It So Good	1977	—	2.00	4.00
❑ 1424	We Gonna Party Tonight/Precious Pearl	1977	—	2.00	4.00

Number	Title (A Side/B Side)	Yr	VG	VG+	NM
❑ 1433	What You Gonna Do After the Party/I Feel Like We Can Make It	1977	—	2.00	4.00
❑ 1637	In and Out/Girl	1982	—	2.00	4.00
RCA VICTOR					
❑ 74-0189	Ain't Gonna Stop/Do What You Wanna Do	1969	2.50	5.00	10.00
❑ 74-0294	When a Boy Falls in Love (Part 1)/When a Boy Falls in Love (Part 2)	1969	2.50	5.00	10.00
❑ 74-0327	Magic of Love/Walking on My Love	1970	2.50	5.00	10.00
WHITFIELD					
❑ 8615	All American Funkathon/And All Hell Broke Loose	1978	—	2.00	4.00
❑ 8689	Paradise/Hip Shakin' Sexy Lady	1978	—	2.00	4.00
❑ 49015	Deep in Your Love/Everybody Needs Money	1979	—	2.00	4.00
❑ 49102	Down Here on Disco Street/Kelly Green	1979	—	2.00	4.00

HUTTO, J.B.

Number	Title (A Side/B Side)	Yr	VG	VG+	NM
CHANCE					
❑ 1155	Now She's Gone/Combination Boogie	1954	250.00	500.00	1000.
❑ 1160	Lovin' You/Pet Cream Man	1954	1000.	2000.	4000.
—The above two may be listed on the label as "J.B. and the Hawks"					
❑ 1165	Dim Lights/Things Are So Slow	1955	750.00	1500.	3000.

HUTTON, DANNY

Also see THREE DOG NIGHT.

Number	Title (A Side/B Side)	Yr	VG	VG+	NM
ALMO					
❑ 213	Why Don't You Love Me Anymore/Home in Pasadena	1964	5.00	10.00	20.00
—As "Daring Dan Hutton"					
HANNA-BARBERA					
❑ 447	Roses and Rainbows/Monster Shindig	1965	3.75	7.50	15.00
❑ 447 [PS]	Roses and Rainbows/Monster Shindig	1965	7.50	15.00	30.00
❑ 453	Big Bright Eyes/Monester Shindig (Part 2)	1965	3.75	7.50	15.00
MGM					
❑ 13502	Funny How Love Can Be/Dreamin' Isn't Good for You	1966	2.50	5.00	10.00
❑ 13502 [PS]	Funny How Love Can Be/Dreamin' Isn't Good for You	1966	5.00	10.00	20.00
❑ 13613	Hang On to a Dream/Hit the Wall	1966	2.50	5.00	10.00

HYLAND, BRIAN

Number	Title (A Side/B Side)	Yr	VG	VG+	NM
ABC-PARAMOUNT					
❑ 10236	Let Me Belong to You/Let It Die	1961	2.50	5.00	10.00
❑ 10262	I'll Never Stop Wanting You/The Night I Cried	1961	2.50	5.00	10.00
❑ 10262 [PS]	I'll Never Stop Wanting You/The Night I Cried	1961	5.00	10.00	20.00
❑ 10294	Ginny Come Lately/I Should Be Gettin' Better	1962	2.50	5.00	10.00
❑ 10294 [PS]	Ginny Come Lately/I Should Be Gettin' Better	1962	5.00	10.00	20.00
❑ 10336	Sealed with a Kiss/Summer Job	1962	3.00	6.00	12.00
❑ 10336 [PS]	Sealed with a Kiss/Summer Job	1962	5.00	10.00	20.00
❑ 10359	Warmed Over Kisses (Left Over Love)/Walk a Lonely Mile	1962	2.50	5.00	10.00
❑ 10359 [PS]	Warmed Over Kisses (Left Over Love)/Walk a Lonely Mile	1962	5.00	10.00	20.00
❑ 10374	I May Not Live to See Tomorrow/It Ain't That Way at All	1962	2.50	5.00	10.00
❑ 10374 [PS]	I May Not Live to See Tomorrow/It Ain't That Way at All	1962	5.00	10.00	20.00
❑ 10400	If Mary's There/Remember Me	1963	2.50	5.00	10.00
❑ 10400 [PS]	If Mary's There/Remember Me	1963	5.00	10.00	20.00
❑ 10427	Somewhere in the Night/I Wish Today Was Yesterday	1963	2.50	5.00	10.00
❑ 10452	I'm Afraid to Go Home/Save Your Heart for Me	1963	2.50	5.00	10.00
❑ 10494	Nothing Matters But You/Let Us Make Our Own Mistakes	1963	2.50	5.00	10.00
❑ 10549	Act Naturally/Out of Sight, Out of Mind	1964	2.50	5.00	10.00
DOT					
❑ 17050	Apologize/Words on Paper	1967	—	3.00	6.00
❑ 17061	It's Christmas Time Once Again/Words on Paper	1967	3.00	6.00	12.00
❑ 17078	Come with Me/Delilah	1968	—	3.00	6.00
❑ 17109	The Lover/Springfield, Illinois	1968	—	3.00	6.00
❑ 17176	Tragedy/You'd Better Stop and Think It Over	1968	—	3.00	6.00
❑ 17222	A Million to One/It Could All Begin Again	1969	—	3.00	6.00
❑ 17258	Early April Morning/Stay and Love Me All Summer	1969	—	3.00	6.00
❑ 17291	Dreamy Eyes/Gonna Make a Woman Out of You	1970	—	3.00	6.00
KAPP					
❑ 342	Itsy Bitsy Teeny Weeny Yellow Polka Dot Bikini/Don't Dilly Dally, Sally	1960	3.75	7.50	15.00
❑ 342 [PS]	Itsy Bitsy Teeny Weeny Yellow Polka Dot Bikini/Don't Dilly Dally, Sally	1960	7.50	15.00	30.00
❑ 352	Four Little Heels (The Clickety Clack Song)/That's How Much	1960	3.00	6.00	12.00
❑ 352 [PS]	Four Little Heels (The Clickety Clack Song)/That's How Much	1960	6.25	12.50	25.00
❑ 363	I Gotta Go/Lopsided, Over Loaded	1960	3.00	6.00	12.00
❑ 363 [PS]	I Gotta Go/Lopsided, Over Loaded	1960	6.25	12.50	25.00
❑ 401	Lipstick on Your Lips/When Will I Know	1961	3.00	6.00	12.00
LEADER					
❑ 801	Library Love Affair/Rosemary	1960	5.00	10.00	20.00
❑ 805	Itsy Bitsy Teeny Weeny Yellow Polka Dot Bikini/Don't Dilly Dally, Sally	1960	7.50	15.00	30.00
PHILIPS					
❑ 40179	Here's to Our Love/Two Kinds of Girls	1964	2.00	4.00	8.00
❑ 40179 [PS]	Here's to Our Love/Two Kinds of Girls	1964	3.00	6.00	12.00
❑ 40203	Devoted to You/Pledging My Love	1964	2.00	4.00	8.00
❑ 40203 [PS]	Devoted to You/Pledging My Love	1964	3.00	6.00	12.00
❑ 40221	Now I Belong to You/One Step Forward, Two Steps Back	1964	2.00	4.00	8.00
❑ 40263	He Don't Understand You/Love Will Find a Way	1965	2.00	4.00	8.00
❑ 40263 [PS]	He Don't Understand You/Love Will Find a Way	1965	3.00	6.00	12.00
❑ 40306	Stay Away from Her/I Can't Keep a Secret	1965	2.00	4.00	8.00
❑ 40354	3000 Miles/Sometimes They Do, Sometimes They Don't	1966	2.00	4.00	8.00
❑ 40377	The Joker Went Wild/I Can Hear the Rain	1966	2.50	5.00	10.00
❑ 40405	Why Did You Do It/Run, Run, Look and See	1966	2.00	4.00	8.00
❑ 40424	Hung Up in Your Eyes/Why Mine	1967	2.00	4.00	8.00
❑ 40424 [PS]	Hung Up in Your Eyes/Why Mine	1967	3.00	6.00	12.00
❑ 40444	Holiday for Clowns/Yesterday I Had a Girl	1967	2.00	4.00	8.00
❑ 40472	Get the Message/Kinda Groovy	1967	—	3.00	6.00
UNI					
❑ 55193	You and Me/Could You Dig It	1970	—	3.00	6.00
❑ 55240	Gypsy Woman/You and Me (#2)	1970	—	3.00	6.00
❑ 55272	Lonely Teardrops/Lorraine	1971	—	2.50	5.00
❑ 55287	So Long, Marianne/No Place to Run	1971	—	2.50	5.00
❑ 55306	Out of the Blue/If You Came Back	1971	—	2.50	5.00
❑ 55323	I Love Every Little Thing About You/With My Eyes Wide Open	1972	—	2.50	5.00
❑ 55334	Only Wanna Make You Happy/When You're Lovin' Me	1972	—	2.50	5.00

I

I.V. LEAGUERS, THE

Number	Title (A Side/B Side)	Yr	VG	VG+	NM
DOT					
❑ 15677	Ring Chimes/The Story	1957	5.00	10.00	20.00
NAU-VOO					
❑ 803	Told by the Stars/Jim Jam	1959	100.00	200.00	400.00
PORTER					
❑ 1004	Ring Chimes/The Story	1957	12.50	25.00	50.00

IAN, JANIS

Number	Title (A Side/B Side)	Yr	VG	VG+	NM
CAPITOL					
❑ 3107	He's a Rainbow/Here in Spain	1971	2.00	4.00	8.00
CASABLANCA					
❑ 2245	Night Rains/Fly Too High	1980	—	2.50	5.00
COLUMBIA					
❑ 02176	Sugar Mountain/Under the Covers	1981	—	2.00	4.00
❑ 02546	Restless Eyes/I Remember Yesterday	1981	—	2.00	4.00
❑ 10119	When the Party's Over/Bright Lights and Promises	1975	—	2.50	5.00
❑ 10154	At Seventeen/Stars	1975	—	2.50	5.00
❑ 10154 [PS]	At Seventeen/Stars	1975	2.00	4.00	8.00
❑ 10228	In the Winter/Thankyouse	1975	—	2.50	5.00
❑ 10297	Aftertones/Boy, I Really Tied One On	1976	—	2.50	5.00
❑ 10331	I Would Like to Dance/Goodbye to Morning	1976	—	2.50	5.00
❑ 10391	Roses/Love Is Blind	1976	—	2.50	5.00
❑ 10484	Miracle Row/Take It to the Sky	1977	—	2.50	5.00
❑ 10526	Candlelight/I Want to Make You Love Me	1977	—	2.50	5.00
❑ 10813	That Grand Illusion/Hopper Paining	1978	—	2.50	5.00
❑ 10864	The Bridge/Do You Wanna Dance	1978	—	2.50	5.00
❑ 10979	Here Comes the Night/Tonight Will Last Forever	1979	—	2.00	4.00
❑ 11111	Night Rains/Fly Too High	1979	—	2.00	4.00
❑ 11327	The Other Side of the Sun/Memories	1980	—	2.00	4.00
❑ 46034	Jesse/The Man You Are in Me	1974	—	2.50	5.00
POLYDOR					
❑ 14299	Society's Child (Baby I've Been Thinking)/I'll Give You a Stone If You Throw It	1975	—	3.00	6.00
VERVE					
❑ 5027	Society's Child (Baby I've Been Thinking)/Letter to Jon	1967	2.50	5.00	10.00
VERVE FOLKWAYS					
❑ 5027	Society's Child (Baby I've Been Thinking)/Letter to Jon	1966	3.00	6.00	12.00
VERVE FORECAST					
❑ 5027	Society's Child (Baby I've Been Thinking)/Letter to Jon	1967	2.00	4.00	8.00
❑ 5041	I'll Give You a Stone If You'll Throw It/Younger Generation Blues	1967	2.00	4.00	8.00
❑ 5072	Insanity Comes Quietly to the Structured Mind/Snowflakes Fall, Snowrays Call	1967	2.00	4.00	8.00
❑ 5079	Somg for All the Seasons of Your Mind/Lonely One	1968	2.00	4.00	8.00
❑ 5090	Lady of the Night/Friends Again	1968	2.00	4.00	8.00
❑ 5099	Everybody Knows/Janey's Blues	1968	2.00	4.00	8.00
❑ 5113	Month of May/Calling Your Name	1969	2.00	4.00	8.00

IAN AND THE ZODIACS

Number	Title (A Side/B Side)	Yr	VG	VG+	NM
PHILIPS					
❑ 40244	The Cryin' Game/Livin' Lovin' Wreck	1964	2.50	5.00	10.00
❑ 40277	Good Morning Little Schoolgirl/Message to Martha	1965	2.50	5.00	10.00
❑ 40291	So Much in Love with You/This Empty Place	1965	2.50	5.00	10.00
❑ 40291 [PS]	So Much in Love with You/This Empty Place	1965	6.25	12.50	25.00
❑ 40343	Why Can't It Be Me/Leave It to Me	1965	2.50	5.00	10.00
❑ 40369	No Money, No Honey/Where Were You	1966	2.50	5.00	10.00

ID, THE

Number	Title (A Side/B Side)	Yr	VG	VG+	NM
RCA VICTOR					
❑ 47-9136	Short Circuit/Boil the Kettle, Mother	1967	3.00	6.00	12.00
❑ 47-9195	Wild Times/The Take	1967	3.00	6.00	12.00

IDEALS, THE (1)

Chicago-based group that, at one time, featured MAJOR LANCE. He is not on the Satellite singles, however.

Number	Title (A Side/B Side)	Yr	VG	VG+	NM
PASO					
❑ 6401	Together/What's the Matter with You Sam	1961	12.50	25.00	50.00
❑ 6402	Magic/Teens	1961	12.50	25.00	50.00
SATELLITE					
❑ 2007	You Lost and I Won/You Hurt Me	1965	6.25	12.50	25.00
❑ 2009	Kissing/I Had a Dream	1966	6.25	12.50	25.00
❑ 2011	Go Go Gorilla/Kissing Won't Go Out of Style	1966	6.25	12.50	25.00

IDEALS, THE (2)

Number	Title (A Side/B Side)	Yr	VG	VG+	NM
CHECKER					
❑ 920	Knee Socks/Mary's Lamb	1959	6.25	12.50	25.00
❑ 979	Knee Socks/Mary's Lamb	1961	3.75	7.50	15.00
—As "Johnny Brantley and the Ideals"					

IDEALS, THE (U)

Some of these could be groups (1) or (2), but others are likely other groups.

Number	Title (A Side/B Side)	Yr	VG	VG+	NM
COOL					
❑ 108	Do I Have the Right/You Won't Like It	1958	75.00	150.00	300.00
CORTLAND					
❑ 110	Don Juan/Gorilla	1963	5.00	10.00	20.00
❑ 113	Mo Joe Hanna/Simple Simon	1964	3.75	7.50	15.00
❑ 115	Feeling of a Kiss/You Came a Long Way from St. Louis	1964	3.75	7.50	15.00
❑ 117	Local Boy/L.A.	1964	3.75	7.50	15.00
DECCA					
❑ 30720	Annie Has a Stroller/My Girl	1959	10.00	20.00	40.00
❑ 30800	Ivy League Lover/Don't Be a Baby, Baby	1959	6.25	12.50	25.00
FARGO					
❑ 1024	The Duchess/Trans Zizstor	1962	5.00	10.00	20.00
STARS OF HOLLYWOOD					
❑ 1001	Please, Jan/Always Yours	1959	10.00	20.00	40.00
ST. LAWRENCE					
❑ 1001	Cathy's Clown/Go Get a Wig	1965	3.00	6.00	12.00
❑ 1020	I Got Lucky (When I Found You)/Tell Her I Apologize	1966	3.75	7.50	15.00

IDES OF MARCH, THE

Also see JIM PETERIK.

Number	Title (A Side/B Side)	Yr	VG	VG+	NM
KAPP					
❑ 992	Nobody Loves Me/Strawberry Sunday	1969	2.50	5.00	10.00
PARROT					
❑ 304	I'll Keep Searching/You Wouldn't Listen	1966	2.50	5.00	10.00
❑ 310	Roller Coaster/Things Aren't Always What They Seem	1966	2.50	5.00	10.00
❑ 312	You Need Love/Sha-La-La-La-Lee	1966	2.50	5.00	10.00
❑ 321	My Foolish Pride/Give Your Mind Wings	1967	2.50	5.00	10.00
❑ 326	Hole in My Soul/Girls Don't Grow on Trees	1967	2.50	5.00	10.00
RCA VICTOR					
❑ APBO-0052	Hot Water/Heavy on the Country	1973	—	2.50	5.00
❑ 74-0850	Mother America/Ladyland	1972	—	2.50	5.00
SUNDAZED					
❑ 142	I'm Gonna Say My Prayers/The Sun Ain't Gonna Shine Anymore	1999	—	—	2.00
❑ 142 [PS]	I'm Gonna Say My Prayers/The Sun Ain't Gonna Shine Anymore	1999	—	—	2.00
WARNER BROS.					
❑ 7140	Vehicle/L.A. Goodbye	1972	—	2.00	4.00
—"Back to Back Hits" series -- originals have green labels					
❑ 7334	High on a Hillside/One Woman Man	1969	—	3.00	6.00
❑ 7378	Vehicle/Lead Me Down, Gently	1970	2.00	4.00	8.00
❑ 7403	Superman/Home	1970	—	3.00	6.00
❑ 7426	Melody/The Sky Is Falling	1970	—	3.00	6.00
❑ 7466	L.A. Goodbye/Mrs. Grayson's Farm	1071	—	3.00	6.00
❑ 7507	Tie-Dye Princess/Friends of Feeling	1971	—	3.00	6.00
❑ 7526	Giddy-Up, Ride Me/Freedom Sweet	1971	—	3.00	6.00

IDLE RACE, THE

JEFF LYNNE, later of THE MOVE and ELECTRIC LIGHT ORCHESTRA, was in this group.

Number	Title (A Side/B Side)	Yr	VG	VG+	NM
LIBERTY					
❑ 55997	Here We Go 'Round the Lemon Tree/My Father's Son	1967	5.00	10.00	20.00
❑ 56064	The End of the Road/The Morning Sunshine	1968	6.25	12.50	25.00

IDOLS, THE

Probably more than one group.

Number	Title (A Side/B Side)	Yr	VG	VG+	NM
DOT					
❑ 16210	Just a Little Bit More/Why Must I Cry	1961	3.75	7.50	15.00
—B-side by the Swans					
E-Z					
❑ 1	Jeannine/Can't Tag Along	1961	10.00	20.00	40.00
RCA VICTOR					
❑ 47-7339	30 Days/The Prowler	1958	5.00	10.00	20.00
❑ 47-7417	Here in My Heart/The Counterfeiter	1958	5.00	10.00	20.00
REVEILLE					
❑ 1002	Just a Little Bit More/Why Must I Cry	1961	7.50	15.00	30.00
—B-side by the Swans					

IFIELD, FRANK

Number	Title (A Side/B Side)	Yr	VG	VG+	NM
CAPITOL					
❑ 5032	I'm Confessin' (That I Love You)/Waltzing Matilda	1963	2.50	5.00	10.00
❑ 5089	Please/Mule Train	1963	2.50	5.00	10.00
❑ 5134	Don't Blame Me/Say It Isn't So	1964	2.50	5.00	10.00
❑ 5170	Sweet Lorraine/You Came a Long Way from St. Louis	1964	2.50	5.00	10.00
❑ 5275	True Love Ways/I Should Care	1964	2.50	5.00	10.00
❑ 5349	Without You/Don't Make Me Laugh	1965	2.50	5.00	10.00
HICKORY					
❑ 1397	No One Will Ever Know/I'm Saving All My Love (For You)	1966	2.00	4.00	8.00
❑ 1411	Call Her Your Sweetheart/Give Myself a Party	1966	2.00	4.00	8.00
❑ 1435	I Remember You/Stranger to You	1967	2.00	4.00	8.00
❑ 1454	Kaw-Liga/Out of Nowhere	1967	2.00	4.00	8.00
❑ 1473	Just Let Me Make Believe/Fireball Mail	1967	2.00	4.00	8.00
❑ 1486	Oh, Such a Stranger/Then You Can Tell Me Goodbye	1967	2.00	4.00	8.00
❑ 1499	Adios Matador/Movin' Lover	1968	2.00	4.00	8.00
❑ 1507	Don't Forget to Cry/Morning in Your Eyes	1968	2.00	4.00	8.00
❑ 1514	Good Morning Dear/Innocent Years	1968	2.00	4.00	8.00
❑ 1525	Maurie/I'm Learning Child	1968	2.00	4.00	8.00
❑ 1540	Let Me Into Your Life/Mary in the Morning	1969	—	3.00	6.00
❑ 1550	I Love You Because/It's My Time	1969	—	3.00	6.00
❑ 1556	Lights of Home/Love Hurts	1969	—	3.00	6.00
❑ 1574	Sweet Memories/You've Still Got a Place in My Heart	1970	—	3.00	6.00
❑ 1595	Someone/One More Mile, One More Town (One More Time)	1971	—	3.00	6.00
MAM					
❑ 3612	Lonesome Jubilee/Teach Me Little Children	1971	—	2.50	5.00
VEE JAY					
❑ 457	I Remember You/I Listen to My Heart	1962	3.75	7.50	15.00
—With Frank Ifield's name spelled correctly on label					
❑ 457	I Remember You/I Listen to My Heart	1962	5.00	10.00	20.00
—With both labels misspelled "Farnk Ifield"					
❑ 477	Lovesick Blues/Anytime	1962	3.00	6.00	12.00
❑ 499	The Wayward Wind/I'm Smiling Now	1963	3.00	6.00	12.00
❑ 525	Unchained Melody/Nobody's Darlin' But Mine	1963	3.00	6.00	12.00
❑ 553	I'm Confessin' (That I Love You)/Heart and Soul	1963	3.00	6.00	12.00
WARNER BROS.					
❑ 8730	Why Don't We Leave Together/Crawling Back	1979	—	2.00	4.00
❑ 8853	Crystal/Touch the Morning	1979	—	2.00	4.00
❑ 49095	Play Born to Lose Again/Yesterday Just Passed My Way Again	1979	—	2.00	4.00

IGGY AND THE STOOGES

Includes records as "The Stooges." Also see IGGY POP.

Number	Title (A Side/B Side)	Yr	VG	VG+	NM
BOMP!					
❑ 139	I Got a Right/Gimme Some Skin	1991	—	—	2.00
❑ 139 [PS]	I Got a Right/Gimme Some Skin	1991	—	—	2.00
COLUMBIA					
❑ 45877	Search and Destroy/Penetration	1973	2.50	5.00	10.00
ELEKTRA					
❑ 45664	I Wanna Be Your Dog (Part 1)/I Wanna Be Your Dog (Part 2)	1970	7.50	15.00	30.00
—As "The Stooges"					
❑ 45695	Down on the Street/I Feel Alright	1970	7.50	15.00	30.00
—As "The Stooges"					
SIAMESE					
❑ 001	I Got a Right/Gimme Some Skin	1977	6.25	12.50	25.00
❑ 001	I Got a Right/Gimme Some Skin	1977	2.50	5.00	10.00
—Second pressing: "Siamese" in fake Asian lettering with iguana logo					
❑ 001 [PS]	I Got a Right/Gimme Some Skin	1977	—	3.00	6.00
—Only issued with Bomp!-distributed copies; has "Iggy & & The Stooges" on cover					
7-Inch Extended Plays					
BOMP!					
❑ 114	Jesus Loves the Stooges	1977	—	3.75	7.50
❑ 114 [PS]	Jesus Loves the Stooges	1977	—	3.75	7.50

IGGY POP

Also see IGGY AND THE STOOGES.

Number	Title (A Side/B Side)	Yr	VG	VG+	NM
ARISTA					
❑ 0438	I'm Bored/African Man	1979	—	2.00	4.00
A&M					
❑ 2874	Cry for Love/Winners and Losers	1900	—	2.00	4.00
❑ 2909	Real Wild Child (Wild One)/Little Miss Emperor	1987	—	2.00	4.00
RCA					
❑ PB-10989	Baby/Sister Midnight	1977	—	3.00	6.00

IGLESIAS, ENRIQUE

Number	Title (A Side/B Side)	Yr	VG	VG+	NM
INTERSCOPE					
❑ 069 490366-7	Be with You/Sad Eyes	2000	—	2.00	4.00

IKETTES, THE

Also see THE MIRETTES.

Number	Title (A Side/B Side)	Yr	VG	VG+	NM
ATCO					
❑ 6212	I'm Blue (The Gong-Gong Song)/Find My Baby	1961	5.00	10.00	20.00
❑ 6223	Troubles on My Mind/Come On and Truck	1962	3.75	7.50	15.00
❑ 6232	Zizzy Zee Zum Zum/Heavenly Love	1962	3.75	7.50	15.00
❑ 6243	I Do Love You/I Had a Dream the Other Night	1962	3.75	7.50	15.00
MODERN					
❑ 1005	Peaches 'N' Cream/The Biggest Players	1965	2.50	5.00	10.00
❑ 1008	(He's Gonna Be) Fine, Fine, Fine/How Come	1965	2.50	5.00	10.00
❑ 1011	I'm So Thankful/Don't Feel Sorry for Me	1965	2.00	4.00	8.00
❑ 1015	Sally Go Round the Roses/Lonely for You	1965	2.00	4.00	8.00
❑ 1024	Da Doo Ron Ron/Not That I Recall	1966	2.00	4.00	8.00
PHI-DAN					
❑ 5009	Down Down/What'cha Gonna Do	1966	2.50	5.00	10.00
POMPEII					
❑ 66683	Beauty Is Just Skin Deep/Make Them Wait	1968	—	3.00	6.00
UNITED ARTISTS					
❑ 50866	If You Take a Close Look/Got What It Takes	1971	—	2.50	5.00
❑ 51103	I'm Just Not Ready for Love/Two Timin' Double Dealin'	1973	—	2.50	5.00

ILL WIND, THE

Number	Title (A Side/B Side)	Yr	VG	VG+	NM
ABC					
❑ 11107	In My Dark World/Walkin' and Singin'	1968	6.25	12.50	25.00

ILL WINDS, THE

Later incarnation of CHANTAY'S.

Number	Title (A Side/B Side)	Yr	VG	VG+	NM
REPRISE					
❑ 0423	So Be On Your Way (I Won't Cry)/Fear of the Rain	1965	3.75	7.50	15.00
❑ 0492	I Idolize You/A Letter	1966	3.75	7.50	15.00

ILLUSION, THE

Number	Title (A Side/B Side)	Yr	VG	VG+	NM
DYNO VOICE					
❑ 914	It's Groovy Time/My Party	1968	2.50	5.00	10.00
STEED					
❑ 712	Did You See Her Eyes/Falling in Love	1969	2.50	5.00	10.00
❑ 717	Run Run Run/I Love You Yes I Do	1969	2.00	4.00	8.00
❑ 718	Did You See Her Eyes/Falling in Love	1969	—	3.00	6.00

Number	Title (A Side/B Side)	Yr	VG	VG+	NM
❑ 721	How Does It Feel/Once in a Lifetime	1969	—	3.00	6.00
❑ 722	Together/Don't Push It	1969	—	3.00	6.00
❑ 726	Let's Make Each Other Happy/Beside You	1970	—	3.00	6.00
❑ 732	Collection/Wait a Minute	1970	—	3.00	6.00

ILLUSIONS, THE
More than one group.

Number	Title (A Side/B Side)	Yr	VG	VG+	NM
COLUMBIA					
❑ 43700	I Know/Take My Heart	1966	2.50	5.00	10.00
CORAL					
❑ 62173	The Letter/Henry and Henrietta	1960	10.00	20.00	40.00
DIAL					
❑ 4004	I Don't Believe It/The World Outside	1965	2.50	5.00	10.00
DOT					
❑ 16752	Secrets of Love/Don't Put Me Down	1965	5.00	10.00	20.00
EMBER					
❑ 1071	How High Is the Mountain/Can't We Fall in Love	1961	7.50	15.00	30.00
KAPE					
❑ 1001	The Closer You Are/For Sentimental Reasons	196?	2.50	5.00	10.00
LAURIE					
❑ 3245	Maybe/In the Beginning	1964	5.00	10.00	20.00
LITTLE DEBBIE					
❑ 105	Story of My Life/Walking Boy	1964	37.50	75.00	150.00
MALI					
❑ 104	Hey Boy/Lonely Soldier	1962	12.50	25.00	50.00
NORTHEAST					
❑ 801	Hey Boy/Lonely Soldier	1962	3.75	7.50	15.00
RELIC					
❑ 512	Hey Boy/Lonely Soldier	1964	2.50	5.00	10.00
ROUND					
❑ 1018	Jezebel/Nightmare	1963	20.00	40.00	80.00
SHERATON					
❑ 104	Hey Boy/Lonely Soldier	1962	6.25	12.50	25.00

IMAGINATIONS, THE (1)

Number	Title (A Side/B Side)	Yr	VG	VG+	NM
BALLAD					
❑ 500	Wait a Little Longer Son/Mama's Little Baby	1962	5.00	10.00	20.00
BO MARC					
❑ 301	Guardian Angel/Hey You	1961	10.00	20.00	40.00
DUEL					
❑ 507	Guardian Angel/Hey You	1961	5.00	10.00	20.00
MUSIC MAKERS					
❑ 103	Goodnight Baby/The Search Is Over	1961	12.50	25.00	50.00
❑ 108	Guardian Angel/Hey You	1961	12.50	25.00	50.00

IMAGINATIONS, THE (2)
Another concoction of STEVE BARRI and P.F. SLOAN.

Number	Title (A Side/B Side)	Yr	VG	VG+	NM
DUNHILL					
❑ 4092	I Love You When You're Mad/Summer in New York	1967	5.00	10.00	20.00

IMAGINATIONS, THE (3)

Number	Title (A Side/B Side)	Yr	VG	VG+	NM
FRATERNITY					
❑ 1001	I Just Can't Get Over Losing You/Strange Neighborhood	1967	7.50	15.00	30.00
❑ 1006	No One Ever Lost More/Strange Voice	1968	6.25	12.50	25.00

IMPACTS, THE
Several different groups.

Number	Title (A Side/B Side)	Yr	VG	VG+	NM
ANDERSON					
❑ 104	Summer/Linda	1964	12.50	25.00	50.00
CARLTON					
❑ 548	Darling, No You're Mine/Help Me Somebody	1961	12.50	25.00	50.00
—With incorrect A-side title					
❑ 548	Darling, Now You're Mine/Help Me Somebody	1961	7.50	15.00	30.00
DCP					
❑ 1147	Wishing Well/Heartaches	1965	12.50	25.00	50.00
—As "Kenny and the Impacts"					
❑ 1150	Just Because/Pigtails	1965	10.00	20.00	40.00
KIP					
❑ 1890	Burnt Valves/Chrome Reverse	1963	12.50	25.00	50.00
RCA VICTOR					
❑ 47-7583	Bobby Sox Squaw/Croc-O-Doll	1959	5.00	10.00	20.00
❑ 47-7609	Canadian Sunset/They Say	1959	12.50	25.00	50.00
WATTS					
❑ 5599	Now Is the Time/Soup	1959	20.00	40.00	80.00

IMPALAS, THE

Number	Title (A Side/B Side)	Yr	VG	VG+	NM
20TH FOX					
❑ 428	Last Night I Saw a Girl/There Is Nothin' Like a Dame	1963	3.00	6.00	12.00
BUNKY					
❑ 7760	Whay Should He Do/I Still Love You	1969	2.00	4.00	8.00
❑ 7762	Whip it On Me/I Still Love You	1969	2.00	4.00	8.00
CAPITOL					
❑ 2709	Speed Up/Soul	1969	2.00	4.00	8.00
CHECKER					
❑ 999	For the Love of Mike/I Need You So Much	1961	3.00	6.00	12.00
CUB					
❑ 9022	Sorry (I Ran All the Way Home)/Fool, Fool, Fool	1959	5.00	10.00	20.00
❑ 9022	I Ran All the Way Home/Fool, Fool, Fool	1959	15.00	30.00	60.00
—Original A-side title					
❑ 9033	Oh What a Fool/Sandy Went Away	1959	5.00	10.00	20.00
❑ 9053	Peggy Darling/Bye Everybody	1959	5.00	10.00	20.00
❑ 9066	All Alone/When My Heart Does All the Talking	1960	5.00	10.00	20.00
—As "Speedo and the Impalas"					
HAMILTON					
❑ 50026	I Was a Fool/First Date	1960	5.00	10.00	20.00
RED BOY					
❑ 113	When You Dance/I Can't See Me Without You	1966	6.25	12.50	25.00
RITE-ON					
❑ 101	I Can't See Me Without You/Old Man Mose	196?	5.00	10.00	20.00
STEADY					
❑ 044	When You Dance/I Can't See Me Without You	1967	5.00	10.00	20.00
SUNDOWN					
❑ 115	The Lonely One/Lost Boogie	1959	3.75	7.50	15.00
7-Inch Extended Plays					
CUB					
❑ 5000	(contents unknown)	1959	100.00	200.00	400.00
❑ 5000 [PS]	Sorry (I Ran All the Way Home)	1959	100.00	200.00	400.00

IMPERIALITES, THE

Number	Title (A Side/B Side)	Yr	VG	VG+	NM
IMPERIAL					
❑ 66015	Have Love, Will Travel/Let's Get One	1964	5.00	10.00	20.00

IMPERIALS, THE (2)

Number	Title (A Side/B Side)	Yr	VG	VG+	NM
BUZZY					
❑ 1	My Darling/You Should Have Told Me	1962	5.00	10.00	20.00
—Red vinyl					
SAVOY					
❑ 1104	My Darling/You Should Have Told Me	1954	50.00	100.00	200.00

IMPERIALS, THE (3)

Number	Title (A Side/B Side)	Yr	VG	VG+	NM
NEWTIME					
❑ 503	A Short Prayer/Where Will You Be	1962	3.75	7.50	15.00
❑ 505	The Letter/Go and Get Your Heart Broken	1962	3.75	7.50	15.00

IMPERIALS, THE (4)

Number	Title (A Side/B Side)	Yr	VG	VG+	NM
OMNI					
❑ 5501	Who's Gonna Love Me/Better Take Time to Love	1978	—	2.50	5.00

IMPERIALS, THE (U)
We're not sure which group these are.

Number	Title (A Side/B Side)	Yr	VG	VG+	NM
CAPITOL					
❑ 4921	I'm Still Dancing/Bermuda Wonderful	1963	3.75	7.50	15.00
CARLTON					
❑ 566	Faithfully Yours/Vut Vut	1961	5.00	10.00	20.00

IMPERIALS MINUS TWO, THE

Number	Title (A Side/B Side)	Yr	VG	VG+	NM
IMPERIAL					
❑ 5787	A Swingin' Dream/In Any Language	1961	5.00	10.00	20.00

IMPOSSIBLES, THE
More than one group.

Number	Title (A Side/B Side)	Yr	VG	VG+	NM
BLANCHE					
❑ 029	Chapel Bells/Little by Little	1960	100.00	200.00	400.00
REPRISE					
❑ 0305	Lonely Bluebird/Paint Me a Pretty Picture	1964	6.25	12.50	25.00
RMP					
❑ 501	Everywhere I Go/Well, It's Alright	1966	6.25	12.50	25.00
❑ 1030	Mr. Maestro/Well, It's Alright	1964	6.25	12.50	25.00
ROULETTE					
❑ 4745	I Wanna Know/It's All Right	1967	5.00	10.00	20.00

IMPRESSIONS, THE
Also see JERRY BUTLER; CURTIS MAYFIELD.

Number	Title (A Side/B Side)	Yr	VG	VG+	NM
20TH FOX					
❑ 172	All Through the Night/Meanwhile, Back in My Heart	1959	10.00	20.00	40.00
ABC					
❑ 10831	Can't Satisfy/This Must End	1966	2.00	4.00	8.00
❑ 10869	Love's a-Comin'/Wade in the Water	1966	2.00	4.00	8.00
❑ 10900	You Always Hurt Me/Little Girl	1967	2.00	4.00	8.00
❑ 10932	It's Hard to Believe/You've Got Me Runnin'	1967	2.00	4.00	8.00
❑ 10964	I Can't Stay Away from You/You Ought to Be in Heaven	1967	2.00	4.00	8.00
❑ 11022	We're a Winner/It's All Over	1967	2.00	4.00	8.00
❑ 11071	We're Rolling On (Part 1)/We're Rolling On (Part 2)	1968	2.00	4.00	8.00
❑ 11103	I Loved and I Lost/Up, Up and Away	1968	2.00	4.00	8.00
❑ 11135	Don't Cry My Love/Sometimes I Wonder	1968	2.00	4.00	8.00
❑ 11188	East of Java/Just Before Sunrise	1969	2.00	4.00	8.00
ABC-PARAMOUNT					
❑ 10241	Gypsy Woman/As Long As You Love Me	1961	3.75	7.50	15.00
❑ 10289	Grow Closer Together/Can't You See	1962	3.75	7.50	15.00
❑ 10328	Little Young Lover/Never Let Me Go	1962	3.75	7.50	15.00
❑ 10357	You've Come Home/Minstrel and Queen	1962	3.75	7.50	15.00
❑ 10386	I'm the One Who Loves You/I Need Your Love	1962	3.75	7.50	15.00
❑ 10431	Sad, Sad Girl and Boy/Twist and Limbo	1963	3.75	7.50	15.00
❑ 10487	It's All Right/You'll Want Me Back	1963	3.75	7.50	15.00
❑ 10511	Talking About My Baby/Never Too Much Love	1963	3.75	7.50	15.00
❑ 10537	Girl You Don't Know Me/A Woman Who Loves Me	1964	3.75	7.50	15.00
❑ 10544	I'm So Proud/I Made a Mistake	1964	3.75	7.50	15.00
❑ 10554	Keep On Pushing/I Love You (Yeah)	1964	3.75	7.50	15.00
❑ 10581	You Must Believe Me/See the Real Me	1964	3.75	7.50	15.00
❑ 10602	Amen/Long, Long Winter	1964	3.75	7.50	15.00
❑ 10622	People Get Ready/I've Been Trying	1965	3.75	7.50	15.00
❑ 10647	Woman's Got Soul/Get Up and Move	1965	3.00	6.00	12.00
❑ 10670	Meeting Over Yonder/I've Found That I've Lost	1965	3.00	6.00	12.00
❑ 10710	I Need You/Never Could You Be	1965	3.00	6.00	12.00
❑ 10725	Just One Kiss from You/Twilight Time	1965	3.00	6.00	12.00
❑ 10750	You've Been Cheatin'/Man, Oh Man	1965	3.00	6.00	12.00
❑ 10761	Since I Lost the One I Love/Falling in Love with You	1966	2.50	5.00	10.00
❑ 10789	Too Slow/No One Else	1966	2.50	5.00	10.00
ABNER					
❑ 1013	For Your Precious Love/Sweet Was the Wine	1958	10.00	20.00	40.00
—As "Jerry Butler and the Impressions"					
❑ 1017	Come Back My Love/Love Me	1958	7.50	15.00	30.00
❑ 1023	The Gift of Love/At the County Fair	1959	7.50	15.00	30.00

Number	Title (A Side/B Side)	Yr	VG	VG+	NM
❑ 1025	Lonely One/Senorita I Love You	1959	7.50	15.00	30.00
❑ 1034	Say That You Love Me/A New Love	1960	7.50	15.00	30.00

BANDERA

Number	Title (A Side/B Side)	Yr	VG	VG+	NM
❑ 2504	Listen/Shorty's Got to Go	1959	12.50	25.00	50.00

CHI-SOUND

Number	Title (A Side/B Side)	Yr	VG	VG+	NM
❑ 2418	Sorry/All I Wanna Do Is Make Love to You	1979	—	2.50	5.00
❑ 2438	Maybe I'm Mistaken/All I Wanna Do Is Make Love to You	1980	—	2.50	5.00
❑ 2491	For Your Precious Love/You're Mine	1981	—	2.50	5.00
❑ 2499	Love, Love, Love/Fan the Fire	1981	—	2.50	5.00

COTILLION

Number	Title (A Side/B Side)	Yr	VG	VG+	NM
❑ 44210	This Time/I'm a Fool for Love	1976	—	2.50	5.00
❑ 44211	Silent Night/I Saw Mommy Kissing Santa Claus	1976	—	3.00	6.00
❑ 44214	You'll Never Find/Stardust	1977	—	2.50	5.00
❑ 44222	Can't Get Along/You're So Right for Me	1977	—	2.50	5.00

CURTOM

Number	Title (A Side/B Side)	Yr	VG	VG+	NM
❑ SP-3 [DJ]	Merry Christmas Happy New Year	197?	3.00	6.00	12.00
❑ 0103	Sooner or Later/Miracle Woman	1975	—	2.50	5.00
❑ 0106	Same Thing It Took/I'm So Glad	1975	—	2.50	5.00
❑ 0110	Loving Power/First Impressions	1975	—	2.50	5.00
❑ 0116	Sunshine/I Wish I'd Stayed in Bed	1976	—	2.50	5.00
❑ 1932	Fool for You/I'm Loving Nothing	1968	—	3.00	6.00
❑ 1932 [PS]	Fool for You/I'm Loving Nothing	1968	3.75	7.50	15.00
❑ 1934	This Is My Country/My Woman's Love	1968	—	3.00	6.00
❑ 1937	My Deceiving Heart/You Want Somebody Else	1969	—	3.00	6.00
❑ 1940	Seven Years/The Girl I Find	1969	—	3.00	6.00
❑ 1943	Choice of Colors/Mighty Mighty Spade and Whitey	1969	—	3.00	6.00
❑ 1946	Say You Love Me/You'll Be Always Mine	1969	—	3.00	6.00
❑ 1948	Wherever She Leadeth Me/Amen (1970)	1970	—	3.00	6.00
❑ 1951	Check Out Your Mind/Can't You See	1970	—	3.00	6.00
❑ 1954	(Baby) Turn On to Me/Soulful Love	1970	—	3.00	6.00
❑ 1957	Ain't Got Time/I'm So Proud	1971	—	3.00	6.00
❑ 1959	Love Me/Do You Wanna Win	1971	—	3.00	6.00
❑ 1966	Inner City Blues/We Must Be in Love	1971	—	3.00	6.00
❑ 1970	This Loves for Real/Times Have Changed	1972	—	3.00	6.00
❑ 1973	I Need to Belong to Someone/Love Me	1972	—	3.00	6.00
❑ 1982	Preacher Man/Times Have Changed	1973	—	3.00	6.00
❑ 1985	Thin Line/I'm Loving You	1973	—	3.00	6.00
❑ 1994	If It's In You to Do Wrong/Times Have Changed	1973	—	3.00	6.00
❑ 1997	Finally Got Myself Together (I'm a Changed Man)/I'll Always Be Here	1974	—	3.00	6.00
❑ 2003	Something's Mighty, Mighty Wrong/Three the Hard Way	1974	—	3.00	6.00

FALCON

Number	Title (A Side/B Side)	Yr	VG	VG+	NM
❑ 1013	For Your Precious Love/Sweet Was the Wine	1958	15.00	30.00	60.00

—As "Jerry Butler and the Impressions"

MCA

Number	Title (A Side/B Side)	Yr	VG	VG+	NM
❑ 52995	Can't Wait 'Til Tomorrow/Love Workin' On Me	1987	—	—	3.00

PORT

Number	Title (A Side/B Side)	Yr	VG	VG+	NM
❑ 70031	Listen/Shorty's Got to Go	1962	3.75	7.50	15.00

SWIRL

Number	Title (A Side/B Side)	Yr	VG	VG+	NM
❑ 107	I Need Your Love/Don't Leave Me	1962	5.00	10.00	20.00

VEE JAY

Number	Title (A Side/B Side)	Yr	VG	VG+	NM
❑ 280	For Your Precious Love/Sweet Was the Wine	1958	4000.	6000.	8000.

—As "Jerry Butler and the Impressions"

Number	Title (A Side/B Side)	Yr	VG	VG+	NM
❑ 424	Say That You Love Me/Senorita I Love You	1962	5.00	10.00	20.00
❑ 574	The Gift of Love/At the County Fair	1963	3.75	7.50	15.00
❑ 621	Say That You Love Me/Senorita I Love You	1964	3.75	7.50	15.00

IN-BETWEENS, THE

Early incarnation of SLADE.

HIGHLAND

Number	Title (A Side/B Side)	Yr	VG	VG+	NM
❑ 1173	Girl Child, I Am An Evil Witchman/Security	1966	75.00	150.00	300.00

IN CROWD, THE (1)

Also see JON AND ROBIN & THE IN CROWD.

ABNAK

Number	Title (A Side/B Side)	Yr	VG	VG+	NM
❑ 121	Inside Out/Big Cities	1967	2.00	4.00	8.00
❑ 121 [DJ]	Inside Out/Big Cities	1967	3.00	6.00	12.00

—Promo only on yellow vinyl

Number	Title (A Side/B Side)	Yr	VG	VG+	NM
❑ 129	Let's Take a Walk/Hangin' From Your Lovin' Tree	1968	2.00	4.00	8.00
❑ 129 [DJ]	Let's Take a Walk/Hangin' From Your Lovin' Tree	1968	3.00	6.00	12.00

—Promo only on yellow vinyl

IN CROWD, THE (2)

Includes two members of THE ELIGIBLES.

VIVA

Number	Title (A Side/B Side)	Yr	VG	VG+	NM
❑ 604	Questions and Answers/Happiness in My Heart	1966	2.00	4.00	8.00
❑ 610	If I Knew a Magic Word/Never Ending Symphony	1967	2.00	4.00	8.00

IN CROWD, THE (3)

British group.

TOWER

Number	Title (A Side/B Side)	Yr	VG	VG+	NM
❑ 147	That's How Strong My Love Is/Things She Says	1965	6.25	12.50	25.00
❑ 196	Why Must They Criticize/I Don't Mind	1966	6.25	12.50	25.00

IN CROWD, THE (U)

It's doubtful that any of these are group (1) or (3). Some may be group (2), though.

BRENT

Number	Title (A Side/B Side)	Yr	VG	VG+	NM
❑ 7046	Grapevine/Cat Dance	1965	3.75	7.50	15.00

HICKORY

Number	Title (A Side/B Side)	Yr	VG	VG+	NM
❑ 1378	Speed Queen/Cry, Boy, Cry	1966	3.75	7.50	15.00
❑ 1413	In the Midnight Hour/Just Give Me Time	1966	3.00	6.00	12.00

MUSICOR

Number	Title (A Side/B Side)	Yr	VG	VG+	NM
❑ 1111	Do the Surfer Jerk/Girl in the Black Bikini	1965	5.00	10.00	20.00

RONN

Number	Title (A Side/B Side)	Yr	VG	VG+	NM
❑ 1	In the Midnight Hour/Nothing You Do	1967	2.50	5.00	10.00

SWAN

Number	Title (A Side/B Side)	Yr	VG	VG+	NM
❑ 4204	Let's Shindig/Klink	1965	3.75	7.50	15.00

INDIGO GIRLS

EPIC

Number	Title (A Side/B Side)	Yr	VG	VG+	NM
❑ 68912	Closer to Fine/Cold As Ice	1989	2.50	5.00	10.00

INGMANN, JORGEN

ATCO

Number	Title (A Side/B Side)	Yr	VG	VG+	NM
❑ 6184	Apache/Echo Boogie	1960	3.75	7.50	15.00
❑ 6195	Anna/Cherokee	1961	3.00	6.00	12.00
❑ 6205	Milord/Oceans of Love	1961	2.50	5.00	10.00
❑ 6216	Violetta/Pinetop's Boogie Woogie	1962	2.50	5.00	10.00
❑ 6235	Africa/Johnny's Tune	1962	2.50	5.00	10.00
❑ 6265	I Loved You/My Little Boy	1963	2.00	4.00	8.00

—As "Grethe and Jorgen Ingmann"

Number	Title (A Side/B Side)	Yr	VG	VG+	NM
❑ 6277	Fourth Man Theme/Drina	1963	2.00	4.00	8.00
❑ 6305	Tovarisch/Desert March	1964	2.00	4.00	8.00
❑ 6370	Theme from "Zorba the Greek"/Gorilla	1965	2.00	4.00	8.00
❑ 6403	Corfu/Seven Roses	1966	2.00	4.00	8.00

PARROT

Number	Title (A Side/B Side)	Yr	VG	VG+	NM
❑ 45006	Sunrise Serenade/Tokyo Melody	1964	2.50	5.00	10.00

INGRAM, LUTHER

DECCA

Number	Title (A Side/B Side)	Yr	VG	VG+	NM
❑ 31794	Ain't That Nice/You Never Miss Your Water	1965	3.00	6.00	12.00

HIB

Number	Title (A Side/B Side)	Yr	VG	VG+	NM
❑ 698	If It's All the Same To You Babe/Exus Trek	1967	20.00	40.00	80.00

KOKO

Number	Title (A Side/B Side)	Yr	VG	VG+	NM
❑ 101	I Can't Stop/You Got to Give Love to Get Love	1968	2.50	5.00	10.00
❑ 103	Missing You/Since You Don't Want Me	1968	2.50	5.00	10.00
❑ 721	Ain't Good for Nothing/These Are the Things	1976	—	3.00	6.00
❑ 724	Let's Steal Away to the Hideaway/I've Got Your Love in My Life	1977	—	3.00	6.00
❑ 725	I Like the Feeling/Gonna Be the Next Time	1977	—	3.00	6.00
❑ 728	Do You Love Somebody/How I Miss My Baby	1977	—	3.00	6.00
❑ 731	Get to Me/Trying to Find My Love	1978	—	3.00	6.00
❑ 2101	You Can Depend on Me/Looking for a New Love	1969	2.00	4.00	8.00
❑ 2102	Pity for the Lonely/Looking for a New Love	1969	2.00	4.00	8.00
❑ 2103	Puttin' Game Down/Since You Don't Want Me	1969	2.00	4.00	8.00
❑ 2104	My Honey and Me/I Can't Stop	1969	2.00	4.00	8.00
❑ 2105	Ain't That Loving You (For More Reasons Than One)/Home Don't Seem Like Home	1970	2.00	4.00	8.00
❑ 2106	To the Other Man/I'll Just Call You Honey	1970	2.00	4.00	8.00
❑ 2107	Be Good to Me Baby/Since You Don't Want Me	1971	2.00	4.00	8.00
❑ 2108	I'll Love You Until the End/Ghetto Train	1971	2.00	4.00	8.00
❑ 2110	You Were Made for Me/Missing You	1972	2.00	4.00	8.00
❑ 2111	(If Loving You Is Wrong) I Don't Want to Be Right/Puttin' Game Down	1972	2.00	4.00	8.00
❑ 2113	I'll Be Your Shelter (In Time of Storm)/I Can't Stop	1972	2.00	4.00	8.00
❑ 2115	Always/Help Me Love	1973	2.00	4.00	8.00
❑ 2116	Love Ain't Gonna Run Me Away/To the Other Man	1973	2.00	4.00	8.00

PROFILE

Number	Title (A Side/B Side)	Yr	VG	VG+	NM
❑ 5125	Baby Don't Go Too Far/How Sweet It Would Be	1986	—	—	3.00
❑ 5132	Don't Turn Around/(B-side unknown)	1987	—	—	3.00
❑ 5143	Gotta Serve Somebody/All in the Name of Love	1987	—	—	3.00

SMASH

Number	Title (A Side/B Side)	Yr	VG	VG+	NM
❑ 2019	(I Spy) For the F.B.I./Foxey Devil	1966	5.00	10.00	20.00

INITIALS, THE (1)

CONGRESS

Number	Title (A Side/B Side)	Yr	VG	VG+	NM
❑ 207	School Day/The Song Is Number One	1964	3.00	6.00	12.00
❑ 219	Dancing on the Sand/Seventeen Guys on a Blanket at the Beach	1964	3.00	6.00	12.00
❑ 229	Someday She'll Love Me/I Should Have Listened	1964	3.00	6.00	12.00

—As "Angelo and the Initials"

INITIALS, THE (2)

DEE

Number	Title (A Side/B Side)	Yr	VG	VG+	NM
❑ 1001	You/Bells of Joy	1959	50.00	100.00	200.00

SHERRY

Number	Title (A Side/B Side)	Yr	VG	VG+	NM
❑ 667	You/Bells of Joy	1959	12.50	25.00	50.00

INK SPOTS

DECCA

Number	Title (A Side/B Side)	Yr	VG	VG+	NM
❑ 9-5 [PS]	Ink Spots, Volume 2	1950	3.75	7.50	15.00

—Box for 25238, 25239 and 25240

Number	Title (A Side/B Side)	Yr	VG	VG+	NM
❑ 23632	If I Didn't Care/Whispering Grass (Don't Tell the Trees)	1950	6.25	12.50	25.00

—Black label, lines on either side of "Decca"

Number	Title (A Side/B Side)	Yr	VG	VG+	NM
❑ 23632	If I Didn't Care/Whispering Grass (Don't Tell the Trees)	1955	3.00	6.00	12.00

—Black label, star under "Decca"

Number	Title (A Side/B Side)	Yr	VG	VG+	NM
❑ 23632	If I Didn't Care/Whispering Grass (Don't Tell the Trees)	1961	2.50	5.00	10.00

—Black label, color bars at right

Number	Title (A Side/B Side)	Yr	VG	VG+	NM
❑ 25238	I'll Get By (As Long As I Have You)/Just for a Thrill	1950	5.00	10.00	20.00

—Side 1 and 6 of "Album No. 9-5"

Number	Title (A Side/B Side)	Yr	VG	VG+	NM
❑ 25239	I'd Climb the Highest Mountain/I'm Gettin' Sentimental Over You	1950	5.00	10.00	20.00

—From "Album No. 9-5"

Number	Title (A Side/B Side)	Yr	VG	VG+	NM
❑ 25240	Coquette/When the Swallows Come Back to Capistrano	1950	5.00	10.00	20.00

—From "Album No. 9-5"

Number	Title (A Side/B Side)	Yr	VG	VG+	NM
❑ 25505	It's a Sin to Tell a Lie/That's When Your Heartaches Begin	1961	2.50	5.00	10.00
❑ 25533	All My Life/You Were Only Fooling	1961	3.00	6.00	12.00
❑ 27102	Sometime/I Was Dancing with Someone	1950	6.25	12.50	25.00
❑ 27214	The Way It Used to Be/Right About Now	1950	6.25	12.50	25.00
❑ 27256	Our Lady of Fatima/Stranger in the City	1950	6.25	12.50	25.00
❑ 27259	Dream Awhile/Time Out for Tears	1950	6.25	12.50	25.00
❑ 27391	If/A Friend of Johnny's	1951	5.00	10.00	20.00
❑ 27464	Tell Me You Love Me/Castles in the Sand	1951	5.00	10.00	20.00
❑ 27493	Do Something for Me/A Fool Grows Wise	1951	5.00	10.00	20.00
❑ 27632	More of the Same Sweet You/What Can You Do	1951	5.00	10.00	20.00

Number	Title (A Side/B Side)	Yr	VG	VG+	NM
❑ 27742	I Don't Stand a Ghost of a Chance/I'm Lucky I Have You	1951	5.00	10.00	20.00
❑ 27996	Honest and Truly/All My Life	1952	5.00	10.00	20.00
❑ 29750	Memories of You/It's Funny to Everyone But Me	1955	5.00	10.00	20.00
❑ 29991	My Prayer/Bewildered	1956	5.00	10.00	20.00
❑ 30058	The Best Things in Life Are Free/I Don't Stand a Ghost of a Chance	1956	3.75	7.50	15.00
GRAND AWARD					
❑ 1001	Rock and Roll Rag/Do I Worry	1956	5.00	10.00	20.00
KING					
❑ 1297	Ebb Tide/If You Should Say Goodbye	1953	15.00	30.00	60.00
❑ 1304	Changing Partners/Stranger in Paradise	1954	17.50	35.00	70.00
❑ 1336	Melody of Love/Am I Too Late	1954	17.50	35.00	70.00
❑ 1378	Yesterdays/Planting Rice	1954	15.00	30.00	60.00
❑ 1425	When You Come to the End of the Day/ Someone's Rocking My Dreamboat	1955	12.50	25.00	50.00
❑ 1429	Melody of Love/There Is Something Missing	1955	10.00	20.00	40.00
❑ 1512	Don't Laugh at Me/Keep It Movin'	1955	10.00	20.00	40.00
❑ 4670	Here in My Lonely Room/A Fool in Love	1953	37.50	75.00	150.00
❑ 4857	Command Me/I'll Walk a Country Mile	1955	10.00	20.00	40.00
SWIFT					
❑ 1001	If I Didn't Care//Into Each Life Some Rain Must Fall/We Three	195?	3.75	7.50	15.00
VERVE					
❑ 10198	Secret Love/A Little Bird Told Me	1960	3.00	6.00	12.00

7-Inch Extended Plays

Number	Title (A Side/B Side)	Yr	VG	VG+	NM
DECCA					
❑ ED 2047	*It's Funny to Everyone But Me/It's a Sin to Tell a Lie/Don't Get Around Much Anymore/My Prayer	195?	6.25	12.50	25.00
❑ ED 2047 [PS]	The Ink Spots, Volume 2	195?	6.25	12.50	25.00

INNER CIRCLE, THE

Another STEVE BARRI and P.F. SLOAN creation.

Number	Title (A Side/B Side)	Yr	VG	VG+	NM
DUNHILL					
❑ 4128	So Long Mary Ann/Goes to Show	1968	5.00	10.00	20.00
IMPACT					
❑ 1019	Sally Go Round the Roses/Sugar	1967	5.00	10.00	20.00

INNOCENCE, THE

Also see ANDERS AND PONCIA.

Number	Title (A Side/B Side)	Yr	VG	VG+	NM
KAMA SUTRA					
❑ 214	There's Got to Be a Word!/It's Not Gonna Take Too Long	1966	2.00	4.00	8.00
❑ 222	Mairzy Doats/Lifetime Lovin' You	1967	2.50	5.00	10.00
❑ 228	All I Do Is Think About You/Whence, I Make Thee Mine	1967	2.00	4.00	8.00
❑ 232	Someone Got Caught in My Eye/Your Show Is Over	1967	2.00	4.00	8.00
❑ 237	Day Turns Me On (The Bufferin Song)/It's Not Gonna Take Too Long	1967	2.00	4.00	8.00

INNOCENTS, THE

Also see KATHY YOUNG AND THE INNOCENTS.

Number	Title (A Side/B Side)	Yr	VG	VG+	NM
DECCA					
❑ 31519	Don't Cry/Come On Lover	1963	5.00	10.00	20.00
INDIGO					
❑ 105	Honest I Do/My Baby Hully Gullys	1960	5.00	10.00	20.00
❑ 111	Gee Whiz/Please Mr. Sun	1960	5.00	10.00	20.00
❑ 116	Kathy/In the Beginning	1961	5.00	10.00	20.00
❑ 124	Beware/Because I Love You	1961	5.00	10.00	20.00
❑ 128	Donna/You Got Me Goin'	1961	5.00	10.00	20.00
❑ 132	Pains in My Heart/When I Become a Man	1961	5.00	10.00	20.00
PORT					
❑ 3026	Gee Whiz/Please Mr. Sun	196?	2.00	4.00	8.00
REPRISE					
❑ 20112	Be Mine/Oh How I Miss My Baby	1962	6.25	12.50	25.00
❑ 20122	Be Mine/Oh How I Miss My Baby	1962	—	—	—
—Unreleased					
❑ 20125	You're Never Satisfied/Oh How I Miss My Baby	1962	5.00	10.00	20.00
TRANS WORLD					
❑ 7001	Tick Tock/The Rut	196?	5.00	10.00	20.00
WARNER BROS.					
❑ 5450	My Heart Stood Still/Don't Call Me Lonely Anymore	1964	7.50	15.00	30.00

INSECTS, THE

Number	Title (A Side/B Side)	Yr	VG	VG+	NM
APPLAUSE					
❑ 1002	Let's Bug the Beatles/Dear Beatles	1964	6.25	12.50	25.00
—B-side by the Little Lady Beatles					

INSIDERS, THE

Number	Title (A Side/B Side)	Yr	VG	VG+	NM
RCA VICTOR					
❑ 47-9225	I'm Just a Man/I'm Better Off Without You	1967	6.25	12.50	25.00
❑ 47-9325	If You Had a Heart/Movin' On	1967	3.75	7.50	15.00
RED BIRD					
❑ 10-055	Chapel Bells Are Calling/I'm Stuck on You	1966	3.75	7.50	15.00

INSIGHT, THE

Number	Title (A Side/B Side)	Yr	VG	VG+	NM
CASCADE					
❑ 364	Please Come Home For Christmas/Out Of Sight	1964	7.50	15.00	30.00

INSPIRATIONS, THE

More than one group.

Number	Title (A Side/B Side)	Yr	VG	VG+	NM
AL-BRITE					
❑ 1651	Angel in Disguise/Stool Pigeon	1960	20.00	40.00	80.00
BELTONE					
❑ 2037	The Girl By My Side/Neckin'	1963	15.00	30.00	60.00
GONE					
❑ 5097	Angel in Disguise/Stool Pigeon	1961	6.25	12.50	25.00
JAMIE					
❑ 1034	Dry Your Eyes/Good-Bye	1956	18.75	37.50	75.00
❑ 1212	Dry Your Eyes/Good-Bye	1962	5.00	10.00	20.00
RONDAK					
❑ 9787	Ring Those Bells/The Cumberland and the Merrimac	1961	200.00	400.00	800.00
SPARKLE					
❑ 102	Angel in Disguise/Stool Pigeon	1960	37.50	75.00	150.00
SULTAN					
❑ 1	The Genie/The Feeling of Her Kiss	1959	7.50	15.00	30.00
❑ 1 [PS]	The Genie/The Feeling of Her Kiss	1959	12.50	25.00	50.00

INTENTIONS, THE

Probably more than one group.

Number	Title (A Side/B Side)	Yr	VG	VG+	NM
JAMIE					
❑ 1253	Summertime Angel/Mr. Misery	1963	375.00	750.00	1500.
MELRON					
❑ 5014	I'm in Love with a Go-Go Girl/Wonderful Girl	1965	50.00	100.00	200.00
PHILIPS					
❑ 40428	Don't Forget That I Love You/Night Rider	1967	6.25	12.50	25.00

INTERLUDES, THE

Probably more than one group.

Number	Title (A Side/B Side)	Yr	VG	VG+	NM
ABC-PARAMOUNT					
❑ 10213	Number 1 in the Nation/Beautiful, Wonderful, Heavenly You	1961	3.75	7.50	15.00
KING					
❑ 5633	Darling I'll Be True/Wilted Rose Bud	1962	7.50	15.00	30.00
RCA VICTOR					
❑ 47-7281	I Shed a Million Tears/Oo-Wee	1958	6.25	12.50	25.00
STAR-HI					
❑ 103	I Want You to Know/Split a Kiss	1959	3.75	7.50	15.00
VALLEY					
❑ 105	Heartbreaker/Scandalous	1959	3.75	7.50	15.00
❑ 106	No One for Me/Fort Lauderdale	1960	3.75	7.50	15.00
❑ 107	White Sailor Hat/Evil	1960	3.75	7.50	15.00

INTERNATIONAL SUBMARINE BAND, THE

Also see GRAM PARSONS.

Number	Title (A Side/B Side)	Yr	VG	VG+	NM
ASCOT					
❑ 2218	The Russians Are Coming/Truck Driving Man	1966	3.75	7.50	15.00
❑ 2218 [PS]	The Russians Are Coming/Truck Driving Man	1966	12.50	25.00	50.00
—Counterfeit identification: Fake copies are missing the Ascot logo and catalog number.					
COLUMBIA					
❑ 43935	Sum Up Broke/One Day Week	1966	7.50	15.00	30.00
LHI					
❑ 1205	Luxury Liner/Blue Eyes	1968	3.75	7.50	15.00
❑ 1217	Miller's Cave/I Must Be Somebody Else	1968	3.75	7.50	15.00

INTERNS, THE

Number	Title (A Side/B Side)	Yr	VG	VG+	NM
CAPITOL					
❑ 5747	Is It Really What You Want/Just Like Me	1966	3.00	6.00	12.00
UPTOWN					
❑ 730	Hard to Get/And I'm Glad	1966	3.00	6.00	12.00

INTRUDERS, THE (1)

Early Philly Soul group.

Number	Title (A Side/B Side)	Yr	VG	VG+	NM
GAMBLE					
❑ 201	(We'll Be) United/Up and Down the Ladder	1966	2.50	5.00	10.00
❑ 203	Devil with an Angel's Smile/A Book for the Broken Hearted	1966	2.50	5.00	10.00
❑ 203 [PS]	Devil with an Angel's Smile/A Book for the Broken Hearted	1966	3.75	7.50	15.00
❑ 204	It Must Be Love/Check Yourself	1966	2.50	5.00	10.00
❑ 205	Together/Up and Down the Ladder	1967	2.50	5.00	10.00
❑ 209	Baby I'm Lonely/A Love That's Real	1967	2.50	5.00	10.00
❑ 214	Cowboys to Girls/Turn the Hands of Time	1968	2.50	5.00	10.00
❑ 217	(Love Is Like a) Baseball Game/Friends No More	1968	2.50	5.00	10.00
❑ 221	Slow Drag/So Glad I'm Yours	1968	2.50	5.00	10.00
❑ 223	Give Her a Transplant/Girls, Girls, Girls	1969	2.50	5.00	10.00
❑ 225	Me Tarzan You Jane/Favorite Candidate	1969	2.50	5.00	10.00
❑ 231	Lollipop (I Like You)/Don't Give It Away	1969	2.50	5.00	10.00
❑ 235	Sad Girl/Let's Go Downtown	1969	2.50	5.00	10.00
❑ 240	Old Love/Every Day Is a Holiday	1969	2.50	5.00	10.00
❑ 2501	(Win, Place or Show) She's a Winner/Memories Are Here to Stay	1972	2.00	4.00	8.00
❑ 2506	I'll Always Love My Mama (Part 1)/I'll Always Love My Mama (Part 2)	1973	2.00	4.00	8.00
❑ 2508	I Wanna Know Your Name/Hang On In There	1973	2.00	4.00	8.00
❑ 4001	Tender (Was the Love We Knew)/By the Time I Get to Phoenix	1970	2.00	4.00	8.00
❑ 4004	When We Get Married/Doctor Doctor	1970	2.00	4.00	8.00
❑ 4007	This Is My Love Song/Let Me in Your Mind	1970	2.00	4.00	8.00
❑ 4009	I'm Girl Scoutin'/Wonder What Kind of Bag She's In	1971	2.00	4.00	8.00
❑ 4014	Pray for Me/Best Days of My Life	1971	2.00	4.00	8.00
❑ 4016	I Bet He Don't Love You (Like I Love You)/Do You Remember Yesterday	1971	2.00	4.00	8.00
❑ 4019	(Win, Place or Show) She's a Winner/Memories Are Here to Stay	1972	2.50	5.00	10.00
GOWEN					
❑ 1401	I'm Sold on You/Come Home Soon	1961	10.00	20.00	40.00
PHILADELPHIA INT'L.					
❑ 3624	I'll Always Love My Mama (Part 1)/I'll Always Love My Mama (Part 2)	1977	—	2.50	5.00
❑ 3689	I'll Always Love My Mama/Save the Children	1979	—	2.50	5.00
TSOP					
❑ 4758	A Nice Girl Like You/To Be Happy Is the Real Thing	1974	—	3.00	6.00
❑ 4766	Rainy Days and Mondays/Be on Time	1975	—	3.00	6.00
❑ 4771	Plain Old Fashioned Girl/Energy of Love	1975	—	3.00	6.00

INTRUDERS, THE (2)

Instrumental group from New Jersey.

Number	Title (A Side/B Side)	Yr	VG	VG+	NM
BELTONE					
❑ 1009	Camptown Rock/Morse Code	1961	3.75	7.50	15.00
FAME					
❑ 101	Fried Eggs/Jeffrie's Rock	1959	6.25	12.50	25.00
❑ 313	Creepin'/Frankfurters and Sauerkraut	1959	6.25	12.50	25.00
❑ 616	Rock-A-Ma-Roll/Era-Rock-A	1959	6.25	12.50	25.00

INVITATIONS, THE

Number	Title (A Side/B Side)	Yr	VG	VG+	NM
DIAMOND					
❑ 253	Got to Have It Now/Swingin' on the Love Vine	1968	3.00	6.00	12.00
DYNO VOICE					
❑ 206	Written on the Wall/Hallelujah	1965	7.50	15.00	30.00
❑ 210	What's Wrong with Me Baby/Why Did My Baby Turn Bad	1965	7.50	15.00	30.00
❑ 215	Skiing in the Snow/Why Did My Baby Turn Bad	1966	15.00	30.00	60.00
MGM					
❑ 13574	The Skate/Girl I'm Leavin' You	1966	3.75	7.50	15.00
❑ 13666	Watch Out Little Girl/You're Like a Mystery	1967	3.75	7.50	15.00
SILVER BLUE					
❑ 801	They Say the Girl's Crazy/For Your Precious Love	1973	2.00	4.00	8.00
❑ 804	Let's Love/Love Has to Grow	1973	2.00	4.00	8.00
❑ 809	Living Together Is Keeping Us Apart/I Didn't Know	1974	2.00	4.00	8.00
❑ 818	Look on the Good Side/Look on the Good Side (Part 2)	1974	2.00	4.00	8.00

IRIDESCENTS, THE

Number	Title (A Side/B Side)	Yr	VG	VG+	NM
HUDSON					
❑ 8102	Three Coins in the Fountain/Strong Love	1963	25.00	50.00	100.00
—Blue vinyl					
❑ 8102	Three Coins in the Fountain/Strong Love	1963	6.25	12.50	25.00
ULTRASONIC					
❑ 109	I Know/The Angels Sang	1960	100.00	200.00	400.00

IRIS, DONNIE

Also see THE JAGGERZ; WILD CHERRY.

Number	Title (A Side/B Side)	Yr	VG	VG+	NM
HME					
❑ 04734	Injured in the Game of Love/I Want You Back	1985	—	—	3.00
❑ 04734 [PS]	Injured in the Game of Love/I Want You Back	1985	—	2.00	4.00
❑ 04885	State of the Heart/You're My Serenity	1985	—	—	3.00
MCA					
❑ 51025	Ah! Leah!/Joking	1980	—	3.00	6.00
❑ 51093	She's So Wild/You're Only Dreaming	1981	—	2.50	5.00
❑ 51153	The Rapper/Ah! Leah!	1981	—	2.50	5.00
❑ 51198	Sweet Merilee/Back on the Streets	1981	—	2.50	5.00
❑ 51223	Love Is Like a Rock/Agnes	1981	—	2.50	5.00
❑ 52031	My Girl/The Last to Know	1982	—	2.00	4.00
❑ 52127	Tough World/You're Gonna Miss Me	1982	—	2.00	4.00
❑ 52127 [PS]	Tough World/You're Gonna Miss Me	1982	—	2.50	5.00
❑ 52169	This Time It Must Be Love/You're Gonna Miss Me	1983	—	2.00	4.00
❑ 52230	Do You Compute?/I Belong	1983	—	2.00	4.00
❑ 52230 [PS]	Do You Compute?/I Belong	1983	—	2.00	4.00

IRISH ROVERS, THE

Also see THE ROVERS.

Number	Title (A Side/B Side)	Yr	VG	VG+	NM
DECCA					
❑ 32254	The Unicorn/Black Velvet Band	1968	2.50	5.00	10.00
❑ 32333	(The Puppet Song) Whiskey on a Sunday/The Orange and the Green	1968	2.00	4.00	8.00
❑ 32371	Liverpool Lou/The Bi-Plane, Ever More	1968	2.00	4.00	8.00
❑ 32444	Lily the Pink/Mrs. Crandall's Boardinghouse	1969	2.00	4.00	8.00
❑ 32529	Peter Knight/Did She Mention My Name	1969	2.00	4.00	8.00
❑ 32575	Fifi O'Toole/Winkin', Blinkin', and Nod	1969	2.00	4.00	8.00
❑ 32616	Rhymes and Reasons/Penny Whistler Peddler	1970	—	3.00	6.00
❑ 32616 [PS]	Rhymes and Reasons/Penny Whistler Peddler	1970	2.50	5.00	10.00
❑ 32723	Two Little Boys/Years May Come, Years May Go	1970	—	3.00	6.00
❑ 32775	The Marvelous Toy/Marika's Lullaby	1970	—	3.00	6.00

IRON BUTTERFLY

Number	Title (A Side/B Side)	Yr	VG	VG+	NM
ATCO					
❑ 6573	Possession/Unconscious Power	1968	2.00	4.00	8.00
❑ 6606	In-A-Gadda-Da-Vida/Iron Butterfly Theme	1968	2.50	5.00	10.00
❑ 6647	Soul Experience/In the Crowds	1969	2.00	4.00	8.00
❑ 6676	In the Times of Our Lives/It Must Be Love	1969	2.00	4.00	8.00
❑ 6712	Little Girl/I Can't Help But Deceive You	1969	2.00	4.00	8.00
❑ 6782	Easy Rider (Let the Wind Pay the Way)/Soldier in Town	1970	2.00	4.00	8.00
❑ 6818	Silly Sally/Stone Believer	1971	—	3.00	6.00
MCA					
❑ 40379	Pearly Gates/Searchin' Circles	1975	—	2.00	4.00
❑ 40493	Beyond the Milky Way/Get It Out	1975	—	2.00	4.00

IRON CITY HOUSEROCKERS

Number	Title (A Side/B Side)	Yr	VG	VG+	NM
MCA					
❑ 41076	Hideaway/Blondie	1979	—	3.00	6.00
❑ 41290	Hypnotized/Old Man Bar	1980	—	3.00	6.00
❑ 51002	Rock-Ola/Junior's Bar	1980	—	3.00	6.00
❑ 51219	Friday Night/No Easy Way Out	1981	—	3.00	6.00

IRON MAIDEN

Number	Title (A Side/B Side)	Yr	VG	VG+	NM
CAPITOL					
❑ B-5248	Flight of Icarus/I've the Fire	1983	2.50	5.00	10.00
❑ B-44154	Can I Play with Madness/Black Bart Blues	1988	2.00	4.00	8.00

IRRIDESCENTS, THE

Number	Title (A Side/B Side)	Yr	VG	VG+	NM
HAWK					
❑ 4001	Bali Ha'i/Swamp Surfer	1963	12.50	25.00	50.00
INFINITY					
❑ 037	Bali Ha'i/Swamp Surfer	1963	6.25	12.50	25.00
OLDIES 45					
❑ 183	Bali Ha'i/Swamp Surfer	1964	3.00	6.00	12.00

IRWIN, BIG DEE

Number	Title (A Side/B Side)	Yr	VG	VG+	NM
CUB					
❑ 9155	I Only Get This Feeling/Wrong Direction	1968	2.00	4.00	8.00
—As "Dee Erwin"					
DIMENSION					
❑ 1021	The Christmas Song/I Wish You a Merry Christmas	1963	3.75	7.50	15.00
—With Little Eva					
IMPERIAL					
❑ 66295	Wrong Direction/I Only Get This Feeling	1968	2.50	5.00	10.00
—As "Dee Irwin"					
❑ 66320	I Can't Stand the Pain/My Hope to Die Girl	1968	2.50	5.00	10.00
❑ 66334	All I Want for Christmas Is Your Love//By the Time I Get to Phoenix/I Say a Little Prayer	1968	3.00	6.00	12.00
—With Mamie Galore					
❑ 66359	Day Tripper/I Didn't Wanna Do It, But I Did	1969	2.00	4.00	8.00
—With Mamie Galore					
❑ 66420	Ain't No Way/Cherish	1969	2.00	4.00	8.00
PHIL-LA OF SOUL					
❑ 303	Better to Have Loved and Lost/Linda	1967	3.75	7.50	15.00
—As "Dee Erwin"					
ROULETTE					
❑ 4596	Discotheque/The Sun's Gonna Shine Tomorrow	1965	2.50	5.00	10.00
—As "Big Dee Erwin"					

ISLE, JIMMY

Number	Title (A Side/B Side)	Yr	VG	VG+	NM
BALLY					
❑ 1034	Baby-O/Hssle	1957	6.25	12.50	25.00
EVEREST					
❑ 19320	Oh Judy/Billy Boy	1959	6.25	12.50	25.00
MALA					
❑ 459	Our Town/Everybody Gotta Little Girl But Me	1963	5.00	10.00	20.00
ROULETTE					
❑ 4065	Goin' Wild/You and Johnny Smith	1958	7.50	15.00	30.00
SUN					
❑ 306	Diamond Ring/I've Been Waiting	1958	6.25	12.50	25.00
❑ 318	Time Will Tell/Without a Love	1959	6.25	12.50	25.00
❑ 332	What a Life/Together	1959	6.25	12.50	25.00

ISLEY BROTHERS, THE

Number	Title (A Side/B Side)	Yr	VG	VG+	NM
ATLANTIC					
❑ 2092	Jeepers Creepers/Teach Me How to Shimmy	1961	3.75	7.50	15.00
❑ 2100	Shine On Harvest Moon/Standing on the Dance Floor	1961	3.75	7.50	15.00
❑ 2110	Your Old Lady/Write to Me	1961	3.75	7.50	15.00
❑ 2122	A Fool for You/Just One More Time	1961	3.75	7.50	15.00
❑ 2263	Looking for a Love/The Last Girl	1964	2.50	5.00	10.00
❑ 2277	Simon Says/Wild As a Tiger	1965	2.50	5.00	10.00
❑ 2303	Move Over and Let Me Dance/Have You Ever Been Disappointed	1965	3.75	7.50	15.00
CINDY					
❑ 3009	Don't Be Jealous/This Is the End	1958	37.50	75.00	150.00
—"Cindy" in shadow print					
❑ 3009	Don't Be Jealous/This Is the End	1958	18.75	37.50	75.00
—"Cindy" in regular print					
GONE					
❑ 5022	I Wanna Know/Everybody's Gonna Rock and Roll	1958	20.00	40.00	80.00
❑ 5048	My Love/The Drag	1958	20.00	40.00	80.00
MARK-X					
❑ 7003	The Drag/Rockin' MacDonald	1957	25.00	50.00	100.00
❑ 8000	The Drag/Rockin' MacDonald	1959	7.50	15.00	30.00
PHILCO-FORD					
❑ HP-41	Twist and Shout/Rubberleg Twist	1969	6.25	12.50	25.00
—4-inch plastic "Hip Pocket Record" with color sleeve					
RCA					
❑ 447-0589	Shout (Part 1)/Shout (Part 2)	1976	—	2.00	4.00
—Gold Standard Series; black label, dog near top					
RCA VICTOR					
❑ 47-7537	I'm Gonna Knock on Your Door/Turn to Me	1959	6.25	12.50	25.00
❑ 47-7588	Shout (Part 1)/Shout (Part 2)	1959	7.50	15.00	30.00
❑ 47-7657	Respectable/Without a Song	1959	6.25	12.50	25.00
❑ 47-7718	He's Got the Whole World in His Hands/How Deep Is the Ocean	1960	6.25	12.50	25.00
❑ 47-7746	Gypsy Love Song/Open Up Your Heart	1960	6.25	12.50	25.00
❑ 47-7787	Say You Love Me Too/Tell Me Who	1960	6.25	12.50	25.00
❑ 61-7588 [S]	Shout (Part 1)/Shout (Part 2)	1959	15.00	30.00	60.00
—"Living Stereo" (large hole, plays at 45 rpm)					
❑ 447-0589	Shout (Part 1)/Shout (Part 2)	1962	3.00	6.00	12.00
—Gold Standard Series; black label, dog on top (this charted with this number in 1962)					
❑ 447-0589	Shout (Part 1)/Shout (Part 2)	1965	2.00	4.00	8.00
—Gold Standard Series; black label, dog on side					
❑ 447-0589	Shout (Part 1)/Shout (Part 2)	1969	—	2.50	5.00
—Gold Standard Series; red label					
T-NECK					
❑ 501	Testify (Part 1)/Testify (Part 2)	1964	3.75	7.50	15.00
❑ 901	It's Your Thing/Don't Give It Away	1969	—	3.00	6.00
❑ 902	I Turned You On/I Know Who You Been Socking It To	1969	—	3.00	6.00
❑ 906	Black Berries — Pt. 1/Black Berries — Pt. 2	1969	—	3.00	6.00
❑ 908	Was It Good to You/I Got to Get Myself Together	1969	—	3.00	6.00
❑ 912	Bless Your Heart/Give the Women What They Want	1969	—	3.00	6.00
❑ 914	Keep On Doin'/Save Me	1970	—	3.00	6.00
❑ 919	If He Can, You Can/Holdin' On	1970	—	3.00	6.00
❑ 921	Girls Will Be Girls, Boys Will Be Boys/Get Down Off of the Train	1970	—	3.00	6.00
❑ 924	Get Into Something/Get Into Something (Part 2)	1970	—	3.00	6.00

Number	Title (A Side/B Side)	Yr	VG	VG+	NM
❑ 927	Freedom/I Need You So	1970	—	3.00	6.00
❑ 929	Warpath/I Got to Find Me One	1971	—	3.00	6.00
❑ 930	Love the One You're With/He's Got Your Love	1971	—	3.00	6.00
❑ 932	Spill the Wine/Take Inventory	1971	—	3.00	6.00
❑ 933	Lay Lady Lay/Vacuum Cleaner	1971	—	3.00	6.00
❑ 934	Lay-Away/Feel Like the World	1972	—	3.00	6.00
❑ 935	Pop That Thang/I Got to Find Me One	1972	—	3.00	6.00
❑ 936	Work to Do/Beautiful	1972	—	3.00	6.00
❑ 937	It's Too Late/Nothing to Do But Today	1973	—	3.00	6.00
❑ 02033	Hurry Up and Wait/(Instrumental)	1981	—	2.50	5.00
❑ 02151	Don't Say Goodnight (It's Time for Love) (Parts 1 & 2)	1981	—	2.00	4.00
—Reissue					
❑ 02179	I Once Had Your Love (And I Can't Let Go)/(Instrumental)	1981	—	2.50	5.00
❑ 2251	That Lady (Part 1)/That Lady (Part 2)	1973	—	2.50	5.00
❑ 2252	What It Comes Down To/Highways of My Life	1973	—	2.50	5.00
❑ 2253	Summer Breeze (Part 1)/Summer Breeze (Part 2)	1974	—	2.50	5.00
❑ 2254	Live It Up (Part 1)/Live It Up (Part 2)	1974	—	2.50	5.00
❑ 2255	Midnight Sky (Part 1)/Midnight Sky (Part 2)	1974	—	2.50	5.00
❑ 2256	Fight the Power Part 1/Fight the Power Part 2	1975	—	2.50	5.00
❑ 2259	For the Love of You (Part 1&2)/You Walk Your Way	1975	—	2.50	5.00
❑ 2260	Who Loves You Better-Part 1/Who Loves You Better-Part 2	1976	—	2.50	5.00
❑ 2261	Harvest for the World/Harvest for the World (Part 2)	1976	—	2.50	5.00
❑ 2262	The Pride (Part 1)/The Pride (Part 2)	1977	—	2.50	5.00
❑ 2264	Livin' in the Life/Go for Your Guns	1977	—	2.50	5.00
❑ 2270	Voyage to Atlantis/Do You Wanna Stay Down	1977	—	2.50	5.00
❑ 02270	Voyage to Atlantis/Do You Wanna Stay Down	1981	—	2.00	4.00
—Reissue					
❑ 2272	Take Me to the Next Phase (Part 1)/Take Me to the Next Phase (Part 2)	1978	—	2.50	5.00
❑ 2277	Groove with You/Footsteps in the Dark	1978	—	2.50	5.00
❑ 2278	Showdown (Part 1)/Showdown (Part 2)	1978	—	2.50	5.00
❑ 2279	I Wanna Be with You (Part 1)/I Wanna Be with You (Part 2)	1979	—	2.50	5.00
❑ 2284	Winner Takes All/Fun and Games	1979	—	2.50	5.00
❑ 2287	It's a Disco Night (Rock Don't Stop)/Ain't Givin' Up on Love	1979	—	2.50	5.00
❑ 2290	Don't Say Goodnight (It's Time for Love) (Part 1)/Don't Say Goodnight (It's Time for Love) (Part 2)	1980	—	2.50	5.00
❑ 2291	Here We Go Again (Part 1)/Here We Go Again (Part 2)	1980	—	2.50	5.00
❑ 2292	Say You Will (Part 1)/Say You Will (Part 2)	1980	—	2.50	5.00
❑ 2293	Who Said?/(Can't You See) What You've Done to Me	1980	—	2.50	5.00
❑ 02293	Who Said?/(Can't You See) What You Do to Me	1981	—	2.00	4.00
—Reissue					
❑ 02531	Inside You (Part 1)/Inside You (Part 2)	1981	—	2.50	5.00
❑ 02705	Party Night/Welcome Into My Night	1982	—	2.50	5.00
❑ 02985	The Real Deal/(Instrumental)	1982	—	2.50	5.00
❑ 03281	It's Alright with Me/(Instrumental)	1982	—	2.50	5.00
❑ 03797	Between the Sheets/(Instrumental)	1983	—	2.50	5.00
❑ 03994	Choosey Lover/(Instrumental)	1983	—	2.50	5.00
❑ 04320	Let's Make Love Tonight/(Instrumental)	1984	—	2.50	5.00
TAMLA					
❑ 54128	This Old Heart of Mine (Is Weak for You)/There's No Love Left	1966	3.75	7.50	15.00
❑ 54133	Take Some Time Out for Love/Who Could Ever Doubt My Love	1966	3.00	6.00	12.00
❑ 54135	I Guess I'll Always Love You/I Hear a Symphony	1966	3.00	6.00	12.00
❑ 54146	Got to Have You Back/Just Ain't Enough Love	1967	3.00	6.00	12.00
❑ 54154	One Too Many Heartaches/That's the Way Love Is	1967	3.00	6.00	12.00
❑ 54164	Take Me in Your Arms (Rock Me a Little While)/Why When Love Is Gone	1968	3.00	6.00	12.00
❑ 54175	Behind a Painted Smile/All Because I Love You	1968	3.00	6.00	12.00
❑ 54182	Take Some Time Out for Love/Just Ain't Enough Love	1969	3.00	6.00	12.00
TEENAGE					
❑ 1004	Angels Cried/The Cow Jumped Over the Moon	1957	200.00	400.00	800.00
UNITED ARTISTS					
❑ 605	She's Gone/Tango	1963	5.00	10.00	20.00
❑ 638	Surf and Shout/Whatcha Gonna Do	1963	5.00	10.00	20.00
❑ 659	Please, Please, Please/You'll Never Leave Him	1963	5.00	10.00	20.00
❑ 714	Who's That Lady/My Little Girl	1964	5.00	10.00	20.00
❑ 798	Love Is a Wonderful Thing/Open Up Her Eyes	1964	—	—	—
—Unreleased					
❑ 923	Love Is a Wonderful Thing/Open Up Her Eyes	1965	—	—	—
—Unreleased					
VEEP					
❑ 1230	Love Is a Wonderful Thing/Open Up Her Eyes	1966	2.50	5.00	10.00
V.I.P.					
❑ 25020	I Hear a Symphony/Who Could Ever Doubt My Love	1965	200.00	400.00	800.00
WAND					
❑ 118	Right Now/The Snake	1962	3.75	7.50	15.00
❑ 124	Twist and Shout/Spanish Twist	1962	5.00	10.00	20.00
❑ 127	Twistin' with Linda/You Better Come Home	1962	3.00	6.00	12.00
❑ 131	Nobody But Me/I'm Laughing to Keep from Crying	1963	3.00	6.00	12.00
❑ 137	I Say Love/Hold On Baby	1963	3.00	6.00	12.00
WARNER BROS.					
❑ 22748	One of a Kind/You'll Never Walk Alone	1989	—	—	3.00
❑ 22900	Spend the Night (Ce Soir)/(Instrumental)	1989	—	—	3.00
❑ 22900 [PS]	Spend the Night (Ce Soir)/(Instrumental)	1989	—	—	3.00
❑ 27954	It Takes a Good Woman/(Instrumental)	1988	—	2.00	4.00
❑ 28129	I Wish/(Instrumental)	1988	—	2.00	4.00
❑ 28129 [PS]	I Wish/(Instrumental)	1988	—	2.00	4.00
❑ 28241	Come My Way/(Instrumental)	1987	—	2.00	4.00
❑ 28385	Smooth Sailin' Tonight/(Instrumental)	1987	—	2.00	4.00
❑ 28385 [PS]	Smooth Sailin' Tonight/(Instrumental)	1987	—	2.00	4.00
❑ 28764	May I?/(Instrumental)	1986	—	2.00	4.00
❑ 28860	Colder Are My Nights/(Instrumental)	1985	—	2.00	4.00

IT'S A BEAUTIFUL DAY

Number	Title (A Side/B Side)	Yr	VG	VG+	NM
COLUMBIA					
❑ 44928	White Bird/Wasted Union Blues	1969	2.00	4.00	8.00
❑ 45152	Good Lovin'/Soapstone Mountain	1970	—	3.00	6.00
❑ 45309	Do You Remember the Sun/Dolphin	1971	—	2.50	5.00
❑ 45536	Anytime/Apples and Oranges	1972	—	2.50	5.00
❑ 45788	White Bird/Wasted Union Blues	1973	—	2.50	5.00
❑ 45853	Ain't That Lovin' You Baby/Time	1973	—	3.00	6.00
SAN FRANCISCO SOUND					
❑ 11680	Aquarian Dream/Bulgaria	198?	2.50	5.00	10.00

ITALIAN ASPHALT AND PAVEMENT COMPANY, THE

See THE DUPREES.

IVAN

Number	Title (A Side/B Side)	Yr	VG	VG+	NM
CORAL					
❑ 62017	Real Wild Child/Oh You Beautiful Doll	1958	50.00	100.00	200.00
—With Buddy Holly on guitar					
❑ 62081	That'll Be Alright/Frankie Frankenstein	1959	100.00	200.00	400.00
❑ 65607	Real Wild Child/That'll Be Alright	1967	12.50	25.00	50.00

IVEYS, THE

See BADFINGER.

IVOLEERS, THE

Number	Title (A Side/B Side)	Yr	VG	VG+	NM
BUZZ					
❑ 101	Lover's Quarrel/Come with Me	1959	100.00	200.00	400.00

IVORYS, THE

Number	Title (A Side/B Side)	Yr	VG	VG+	NM
DARLA					
❑ 1000	Wishing Well/Deep Freeze	1962	100.00	200.00	400.00
SPARTA					
❑ 001	Why Don't You Write Me/Deep Freeze	1962	20.00	40.00	80.00

IVY LEAGUE, THE

Number	Title (A Side/B Side)	Yr	VG	VG+	NM
CAMEO					
❑ 343	Wait a Minute/What More Do You Want	1965	3.75	7.50	15.00
❑ 356	Lonely Room/Funny How Love Can Be	1965	3.75	7.50	15.00
❑ 365	A Girl Like You/That's Why I'm Crying	1965	3.75	7.50	15.00
❑ 377	Tossing & Turning/Graduation Day	1965	3.75	7.50	15.00
❑ 388	Our Love Is Slipping Away/I Could Make You Fall in Love	1966	3.75	7.50	15.00
❑ 388 [PS]	Our Love Is Slipping Away/I Could Make You Fall in Love	1966	6.25	12.50	25.00
❑ 402	Rain Rain Go Away/Running Around in Circles	1966	3.75	7.50	15.00
❑ 449	When You're Young/My World Fell Down	1966	3.75	7.50	15.00

IVY THREE, THE

Number	Title (A Side/B Side)	Yr	VG	VG+	NM
SHELL					
❑ 302	Nine Out of Ten/I've Cried Enough for Two	1961	7.50	15.00	30.00
—Gold label					
❑ 302	Nine Out of Ten/I've Cried Enough for Two	1961	5.00	10.00	20.00
—Multicolored label					
❑ 306	Bagoo/Suicide	1961	3.75	7.50	15.00
❑ 720	Yogi/Was Judy There	1960	5.00	10.00	20.00
—Originals have blue labels					
❑ 720	Yogi/Was Judy There	1961	3.75	7.50	15.00
—Reissues have multicolored labels					
❑ 723	Alone in the Chapel/Hush Little Baby	1960	6.25	12.50	25.00

J

J.B. AND THE HAWKS
See J.B. HUTTO.

J.B.'S, THE
See FRED WESLEY.

JACKIE AND JILL

Number	Title (A Side/B Side)	Yr	VG	VG+	NM
U.S.A.					
❑ 791	I Want a Beatle for Christmas/Jingle Bells	1964	5.00	10.00	20.00

JACKIE AND THE RAINDROPS

Number	Title (A Side/B Side)	Yr	VG	VG+	NM
COLPIX					
❑ 738	Down Our Street/My Heart Is Your Heart	1964	2.50	5.00	10.00

JACKS, THE
Also see THE CADETS.

Number	Title (A Side/B Side)	Yr	VG	VG+	NM
KENT					
❑ 344	Why Don't You Write Me/This Empty Heart	1960	3.75	7.50	15.00
RPM					
❑ 428	Why Don't You Write Me/Smack Dab in the Middle	1955	50.00	100.00	200.00
❑ 428	Why Don't You Write Me/My Darling	1955	15.00	30.00	60.00
❑ 433	I'm Confessin'/Since My Baby's Been Gone	1955	15.00	30.00	60.00
❑ 444	This Empty Heart/My Clumsy Heart	1955	12.50	25.00	50.00
❑ 454	So Wrong/How Soon	1956	12.50	25.00	50.00
❑ 458	Sugar Baby/Why Did I Fall in Love	1956	15.00	30.00	60.00
❑ 467	Let's Make Up/Dream a Little Longer	1956	15.00	30.00	60.00

JACKSON, ALAN

Number	Title (A Side/B Side)	Yr	VG	VG+	NM
ARISTA					
❑ 2032	Wanted/Dog River Blues	1990	—	2.00	4.00
❑ 2095	Chasin' That Neon Rainbow/Short Sweet Ride	1990	—	2.00	4.00
❑ 2166	I'd Love You All Over Again/Home	1990	—	2.00	4.00
❑ 2220	Don't Rock the Jukebox/Home	1991	—	2.00	4.00
❑ 9892	Blue Blooded Woman/Home	1989	2.50	5.00	10.00
—Issued on blue vinyl					
❑ 9922	Here in the Real World/Blue Blooded Woman	1989	—	2.00	4.00
❑ 12335	Someday/From a Distance	1991	—	2.00	4.00
❑ 12372	I Only Want You for Christmas/Merry Christmas to Me	1991	—	2.00	4.00
❑ 12385	Dallas/Just Playin' Possum	1991	—	2.00	4.00
❑ 12418	Midnight in Montgomery/Working Class Hero	1992	—	2.00	4.00
❑ 12447	Love's Got a Hold on You/That's All I Need to Know	1992	—	2.00	4.00
❑ 12463	She's Got the Rhythm (And I Got the Blues)/She Likes It Too	1992	—	2.00	4.00
❑ 12514	Tonight I Climbed the Wall/Up to My Ears in Tears	1993	—	—	3.00
❑ 12535	Here in the Real World/Wanted	1993	—	—	3.00
—Reissue with "Collectables" logo on label					
❑ 12536	Don't Rock the Jukebox/I'd Love You All Over Again	1993	—	—	3.00
—Reissue with "Collectables" logo on label					
❑ 12537	Chasin' That Neon Rainbow/Midnight in Montgomery	1993	—	—	3.00
—Reissue with "Collectables" logo on label					
❑ 12538	Love's Got a Hold on You/Someday	1993	—	—	3.00
—Reissue with "Collectables" logo on label					
❑ 12560	Chattahoochee/I Don't Need the Booze (To Get a Buzz On)	1993	—	2.00	4.00
❑ 12607	Mercury Blues/Chattahoochee (Club Mix)	1993	—	2.00	4.00
❑ 12611	Honky Tonk Christmas/The Angels Cried	1993	—	—	3.00
—B-side with Alison Krauss					
❑ 12649	(Who Says) You Can't Have It All/If It Ain't One Thing (It's You)	1993	—	—	3.00
❑ 12697	Summertime Blues/Hole in the Wall	1994	—	2.00	4.00
❑ 12745	Livin' on Love/Let's Get Back to Me and You	1994	—	2.00	4.00
❑ 12775	Gone Country/All American Country Boy	1994	—	2.00	4.00
❑ 12792	Song for the Life/You Can't Give Up on Love	1995	—	—	3.00
❑ 12830	I Don't Even Know Your Name/If I Had You	1995	—	—	3.00
❑ 12879	Tall, Tall Trees/Home	1995	—	—	3.00
❑ 12942	Home/I'll Try	1996	—	—	3.00
ARISTA NASHVILLE					
❑ 13048	Little Bitty/Must've Had a Ball	1996	—	—	3.00
❑ 13060	Rudolph the Red-Nosed Reindeer/We Three Kings (Star of Wonder)	1996	—	2.00	4.00
—B-side by Blackhawk					
❑ 13068	Everything I Love/It's Time You Learned About Good-Bye	1996	—	—	3.00
❑ 13069	Who's Cheatin' Who/Buicks to the Moon	1997	—	—	3.00
❑ 13070	There Goes/A House with No Curtains	1997	—	—	3.00
❑ 13106	Between the Devil and Me/Walk on the Rocks	1997	—	—	3.00
❑ 13135	I'll Go On Loving You/Chattahoochee	1998	—	—	3.00
❑ 13136	Right On the Money/A Woman's Love	1998	—	—	3.00
❑ 13145	Little Man/Hurtin' Comes Easy	1999	—	—	3.00
❑ 13155	Gone Crazy/Amarillo	1999	—	—	3.00
❑ 13183	Pop a Top/Revenooer Man	1999	—	—	3.00
❑ 13193	The Blues Man/My Own Kind of Hat	2000	—	—	3.00
❑ 69020	www.memory/It's Alright to Be a Redneck	2000	—	—	3.00
ARISTA/FOX					
❑ 10001	A Holly Jolly Christmas/I Only Want You for Christmas	1992	—	2.00	4.00

JACKSON, BULL MOOSE

Number	Title (A Side/B Side)	Yr	VG	VG+	NM
KING					
❑ 4181	I Love You Yes I Do/Sneaky Pete	1951	15.00	30.00	60.00
—78 originally released in 1947					
❑ 4189	I Want a Bowlegged Woman/All My Love Belongs to You	1951	20.00	40.00	80.00
—78 originally released in 1948 -- 5191 and 5198 are the only legitimate 45s known before 4451					
❑ 4451	Trust in Me/Wonder When My Baby's Coming Home	1951	15.00	30.00	60.00
❑ 4462	Unless/End This Misery	1951	15.00	30.00	60.00
❑ 4472	Cherokee Boogie/I'm Lucky I Have You	1951	15.00	30.00	60.00
❑ 4493	I'll Be Home for Christmas/I Never Loved Anyone But You	1951	15.00	30.00	60.00
❑ 4524	Nosey Joe/Sad	1952	20.00	40.00	80.00
❑ 4535	(Let Me Love You) All Night Long/Bootsie	1952	15.00	30.00	60.00
❑ 4551	Bearcat Blues/There Is No Greater Love	1952	15.00	30.00	60.00
❑ 4580	Big Ten Inch Record/I Needed You	1952	50.00	100.00	200.00
❑ 4634	Meet Me with Your Black Dress On/Try to Forget Him	1953	10.00	20.00	40.00
❑ 4655	If You'll Let Me/Hodge Podge	1953	10.00	20.00	40.00
❑ 4775	If You Ain't Lovin'/I Wanna Hug Ya, Kiss Ya	1955	6.25	12.50	25.00
❑ 4802	I'm Glad for Your Sake/Must You Keep On Pretending	1955	6.25	12.50	25.00
SEVEN ARTS					
❑ 705	I Love YouYes I Do/Aw Shucks Baby	1961	5.00	10.00	20.00
WARWICK					
❑ 575	I Found My Love/More of the Same	1960	5.00	10.00	20.00

JACKSON, CHUCK

Number	Title (A Side/B Side)	Yr	VG	VG+	NM
ABC					
❑ 11368	I Only Get This Feeling/Slowly But Surely	1973	—	3.00	6.00
❑ 11398	I Can't Break Away/Just a Little Tear	1973	—	3.00	6.00
❑ 11423	If Only You Believe/Maybe This Will Be the Morning	1974	—	3.00	6.00
❑ 12024	Take Off Your Make-Up/Talk a Little Less	1974	—	3.00	6.00
ALL PLATINUM					
❑ 2357	Love Lights/(Instrumental)	1975	—	2.50	5.00
❑ 2360	I'm Needing You, Wanting You/We Can't Hide It Anymore	1975	—	2.50	5.00
❑ 2363	If You Were My Woman (Part 1)/If You Were My Woman (Part 2)	1976	—	2.50	5.00
❑ 2370	One of Those Yesterdays/Love Lights	1976	—	2.50	5.00
❑ 2373	I Fell Asleep/One of Those Yesterdays	1976	—	2.50	5.00
AMY					
❑ 849	Come On and Love Me/Ooh Baby	1962	3.75	7.50	15.00
❑ 868	I'm Yours/Hula Lula	1962	3.75	7.50	15.00
ATCO					
❑ 6197	Never Let Me Go/Baby I Want to Marry You	1961	3.00	6.00	12.00
BELTONE					
❑ 1005	Mr. Price/Hula Lula	1961	5.00	10.00	20.00
CLOCK					
❑ 1015	Come On and Love Me/Ooh Baby	1959	6.25	12.50	25.00
—Clock sides as "Charles Jackson"					
❑ 1022	Hula Hula/I'm Yours	1960	6.25	12.50	25.00
❑ 1027	This Is It/Mr. Pride	1960	6.25	12.50	25.00
DAKAR					
❑ 4512	I Forgot to Tell You/The Man and the Woman	1972	—	3.00	6.00
DOT					
❑ 15673	Woke Up This Morning/Wilette	1957	7.50	15.00	30.00
—With Kripp Johnson					
EMI AMERICA					
❑ 8042	I Wanna Give You Some Love/Waiting in Vain	1980	—	2.00	4.00
❑ 8056	After You/Let's Get Together	1980	—	2.00	4.00
MOTOWN					
❑ 1118	(Don't Let the Boy Overpower) The Man in You/Girls, Girls, Girls	1968	2.50	5.00	10.00
❑ 1144	Are You Lonely for Me Baby/Your Wonderful Love	1969	2.50	5.00	10.00
❑ 1152	Honey Come Back/What Am I Gonna Do Without You	1969	2.50	5.00	10.00
❑ 1160	The Day My World Stood Still/Baby, I'll Get It	1970	125.00	250.00	500.00
SUGARHILL					
❑ 764	Sometimes When We Touch/(B-side unknown)	1981	—	2.00	4.00
VIBRATION					
❑ 569	We Can't Hide It Anymore/I'm Needing You, Wanting You	1977	—	2.50	5.00
—With Sylvia					
V.I.P.					
❑ 25052	The Day My World Stood Still/Baby, I'll Get It	1970	2.50	5.00	10.00
❑ 25056	Let Somebody Love Me/Two Feet from Happiness	1970	2.50	5.00	10.00
❑ 25059	Is There Anything Love Can't Do/Pet Names	1971	2.50	5.00	10.00
❑ 25067	Who You Gonna Run To/Forgive My Jealousy	1971	100.00	200.00	400.00
WAND					
❑ 106	I Don't Want to Cry/Just Once	1961	3.00	6.00	12.00
❑ 108	(It Never Happens) In Real Life/The Same Old Story	1961	3.00	6.00	12.00
❑ 110	I Wake Up Crying/Everybody Needs Love	1961	3.00	6.00	12.00
❑ 115	The Breaking Point/My Willow Tree	1961	3.00	6.00	12.00
❑ 119	What'cha Gonna Say Tomorrow/Angel of Angels	1962	3.00	6.00	12.00
❑ 122	Any Day Now (My Wild Beautiful Bird)/The Prophet	1962	3.75	7.50	15.00
❑ 126	I Keep Forgetting/Who's Gonna Pick Up the Pieces	1962	2.50	5.00	10.00
❑ 128	Gettin' Ready for the Heartbreak/In Between Tears	1962	2.50	5.00	10.00
❑ 132	Tell Him I'm Not Home/Lonely Am I	1963	2.50	5.00	10.00
❑ 132 [PS]	Tell Him I'm Not Home/Lonely Am I	1963	6.25	12.50	25.00
❑ 138	I Will Never Turn My Back on You/Tears of Joy	1963	2.50	5.00	10.00
❑ 141	Any Other Way/Big New York	1963	2.50	5.00	10.00
❑ 149	Hand It Over/Look Over Your Shoulder	1964	2.00	4.00	8.00
❑ 154	Beg Me/This Broken Heart	1964	2.00	4.00	8.00
❑ 161	Somebody New/Stand By Me	1964	2.00	4.00	8.00
❑ 169	Since I Don't Have Yopu/Hand It Over	1964	2.00	4.00	8.00
❑ 179	I Need You/Soul Brother Twist	1965	2.00	4.00	8.00
❑ 188	If I Didn't Love You/Just a Little Bit of Your Soul	1965	2.00	4.00	8.00
❑ 1105	Good Things Come to Those Who Wait/Yah	1965	2.00	4.00	8.00
❑ 1119	All in My Mind/And That's Saying a Lot	1966	2.00	4.00	8.00
❑ 1129	These Chains of Love/Theme to the Blues	1966	2.00	4.00	8.00
❑ 1142	I've Got to Be Strong/Where Did She Stay	1967	2.00	4.00	8.00

Number	Title (A Side/B Side)	Yr	VG	VG+	NM
❑ 1151	Every Man Needs a Down Home Girl/Need You There	1967	2.00	4.00	8.00
❑ 1159	Hound Dog/Love Me Tender	1967	2.00	4.00	8.00
❑ 1166	Shame on Me/Candy	1967	2.00	4.00	8.00
❑ 1178	My Child's Child/Theme to the Blues	1968	2.00	4.00	8.00

JACKSON, CHUCK, AND MAXINE BROWN

Also see each artist's individual listings.

Number	Title (A Side/B Side)	Yr	VG	VG+	NM
WAND					
❑ 181	Something You Got/Baby Take Me	1965	2.00	4.00	8.00
❑ 191	Don't Go/Can't Let You Out of My Sight	1965	2.00	4.00	8.00
❑ 198	I Need You So/Cause We're in Love	1965	2.00	4.00	8.00
❑ 1109	Plerase Don't Hurt Me/I'm Satisfied	1966	2.00	4.00	8.00
❑ 1148	Hold On I'm Comin'/Never Had It So Good	1967	2.00	4.00	8.00
❑ 1155	Daddy's Home/Don't Go	1967	2.00	4.00	8.00
❑ 1162	See See Rider/Tennessee Waltz	1967	2.00	4.00	8.00

JACKSON, DEON

Number	Title (A Side/B Side)	Yr	VG	VG+	NM
ATLANTIC					
❑ 2213	Hush Little Baby/You Said You Loved Me	1963	2.50	5.00	10.00
❑ 2252	Come Back Home/Nursery Rhymes	1964	2.50	5.00	10.00
CARLA					
❑ 1900	I Can't Go On/I Need a Love Like Yours	1968	2.00	4.00	8.00
❑ 1903	You'll Wake Up Wiser Baby/You Gotta Love	1968	2.00	4.00	8.00
❑ 2526	Love Makes the World Go Round/You Said You Loved Me	1966	2.50	5.00	10.00
❑ 2527	Love Takes a Long Time Growing/Hush Little Baby	1966	2.00	4.00	8.00
❑ 2530	I Can't Do Without You/That's What You Do to Me	1966	2.00	4.00	8.00
❑ 2533	When Your Love Has Gone/Hard to Get Thing Called Love	1967	2.00	4.00	8.00
❑ 2537	Ooh Baby/All on a Sunny Day	1967	2.00	4.00	8.00
SHOUT					
❑ 254	I'll Always Love You/Life Can Be That Way	1969	6.25	12.50	25.00

JACKSON, GEORGE

Number	Title (A Side/B Side)	Yr	VG	VG+	NM
ATLANTIC					
❑ 1024	Uh Huh/I'm Sorry	1954	12.50	25.00	50.00
CAMEO					
❑ 460	When I Stop Lovin' You/That Lonely Night	1967	3.00	6.00	12.00
CHESS					
❑ 2167	Things Are Gettin' Better/Mackin' on You	1975	—	3.00	6.00
DOT					
❑ 16724	Blinkety Blink/There Goes My Pride	1965	3.00	6.00	12.00
FAME					
❑ 1457	Find 'Em, Fool 'Em, and Forget 'Em/My Desires Are Getting the Best of Me	1969	2.00	4.00	8.00
❑ 1468	That's How Much You Mean to Me/I'm Gonna Hold On	1970	2.00	4.00	8.00
HI					
❑ 2130	I'm Gonna Wait/So Good to Me	1967	3.00	6.00	12.00
❑ 2212	Aretha, Sing One for Me/I'm Gonna Wait	1972	2.00	4.00	8.00
❑ 2236	Let Them Know You Care/Patricia	1973	2.00	4.00	8.00
MERCURY					
❑ 72736	Kiss Me/Tossin' and Turnin'	1967	2.50	5.00	10.00
❑ 72782	I Don't Have the Time to Love You/Don't Use Me	1968	2.50	5.00	10.00
MGM					
❑ 14680	We've Only Just Begun/You Can't Run Away from Love	1973	—	3.00	6.00
❑ 14732	Willie Lump Lump/How Can I Get Next to You	1974	—	3.00	6.00
❑ 14767	Soul Train/Smoking and Drinking	1974	—	3.00	6.00
RPM					
❑ 441	Hold Me Up/Heaven on Earth	1955	6.25	12.50	25.00
VERVE					
❑ 10658	Love Highjacker/I Found What I Wanted	1970	6.25	12.50	25.00

JACKSON, GEORGE, AND DAN GREER

See GEORGE AND GREER.

JACKSON, J.J.

Number	Title (A Side/B Side)	Yr	VG	VG+	NM
CALLA					
❑ 119	But It's Alright/Boogaloo Baby	1966	3.00	6.00	12.00
❑ 125	I Dig Girls/That Ain't Right	1966	2.50	5.00	10.00
❑ 130	Til Love Goes Out of Style/Seems Like I've Been Here Before	1967	2.50	5.00	10.00
❑ 133	Four Walls (Three Windows and Two Doors)/ Here We Go Again	1967	2.50	5.00	10.00
CONGRESS					
❑ 6008	Fat, Black and Together/That Woman Loving	1969	2.00	4.00	8.00
EVEREST					
❑ 2012	False Face/Ring Telephone	1963	3.00	6.00	12.00
LOMA					
❑ 2082	Try Me/Sho Nuff (Gotta Good Thing Goin')	1967	2.00	4.00	8.00
❑ 2090	Down But Not Out/Why Does It Take So Long	1968	2.00	4.00	8.00
❑ 2096	Come See Me (I'm Your Man)/I Don't Want to Live My Life Alone	1968	2.00	4.00	8.00
❑ 2102	Too Late/You Do It Cause You Wanna	1968	2.00	4.00	8.00
❑ 2104	That Ain't Right/Courage Ain't Strength	1968	2.00	4.00	8.00
PERCEPTION					
❑ 7	Nobody's Gonna Help You/Help Me Get to My Grits	1970	2.00	4.00	8.00
WARNER BROS.					
❑ 7130	But It's Alright/Four Walls (Three Windows and Two Doors)	1970	—	3.00	6.00
—"Back to Back Hits" series					
❑ 7278	But It's Alright/Ain't Too Proud to Beg	1969	2.00	4.00	8.00
❑ 7321	Four Walls (Three Windows and Two Doors)/That Ain't Right	1969	2.00	4.00	8.00

JACKSON, JACKIE

Also see THE JACKSONS.

Number	Title (A Side/B Side)	Yr	VG	VG+	NM
POLYDOR					
❑ 871548-7	Stay/Who's Loving You Now	1989	—	—	3.00
❑ 871548-7 [PS]	Stay/Who's Loving You Now	1989	—	—	3.00
❑ 889034-7	Cruzin/(B-side unknown)	1989	—	—	3.00
❑ 889034-7 [PS]	Cruzin/(B-side unknown)	1989	—	—	3.00

JACKSON, JANET

Number	Title (A Side/B Side)	Yr	VG	VG+	NM
A&M					
❑ 31458 1194 7	Runaway/When I Think of You (Morales House Mix 95)	1995	—	—	2.00
❑ 31458 1194 7 [PS]	Runaway/When I Think of You (Morales House Mix 95)	1995	—	—	2.00
❑ 1445	Miss You Much/You Need Me	1989	—	2.00	4.00
❑ 1455	Rhythm Nation/(Instrumental)	1989	—	—	3.00
❑ 1475	Come Back to Me/Vuelva A Mi	1990	—	2.00	4.00
—First pressing: No bar code					
❑ 75021 1475 7	Come Back to Me/Vuelva A Mi	1990	—	—	3.00
—Second pressing: Longer number with bar code					
❑ 75021 1477 7	Black Cat (2 mixes)	1990	—	—	3.00
❑ 1479	Alright (2 mixes)	1990	—	2.00	4.00
—First pressing: No bar code					
❑ 75021 1479 7	Alright (2 mixes)	1990	—	—	3.00
—Second pressing: Longer number with bar code					
❑ 1490	Escapade/(Instrumental)	1990	—	—	3.00
❑ 75021 1538 7	Love Will Never Do (Without You)/Work It Out	1990	—	—	3.00
❑ 2440	Young Love/The Magic Is Working	1982	—	2.00	4.00
❑ 2440 [PS]	Young Love/The Magic Is Working	1982	—	2.00	4.00
❑ 2522	Come Give Your Love to Me/Forever Yours	1983	—	2.00	4.00
❑ 2522 [PS]	Come Give Your Love to Me/Forever Yours	1983	—	2.00	4.00
❑ 2537	Say You Do/Don't Mess Up a Good Thing	1983	—	2.00	4.00
❑ 2545	Say You Do/You'll Never Find (A Love Like Mine)	1983	—	2.00	4.00
❑ 2660	Don't Stand Another Chance/Rock 'N' Roll	1984	—	2.00	4.00
❑ 2682	Dream Street/Love and My Best Friend	1984	—	2.00	4.00
❑ 2693	Fast Girls/Love and My Best Friend	1984	—	2.00	4.00
❑ 2812	What Have You Done for Me Lately/He Doesn't Know I'm Alive	1986	—	—	3.00
❑ 2812 [PS]	What Have You Done for Me Lately/He Doesn't Know I'm Alive	1986	—	—	3.00
❑ 2830	Nasty/You'll Never Find (A Love Like Mine)	1986	—	—	3.00
❑ 2830 [PS]	Nasty/You'll Never Find (A Love Like Mine)	1986	—	2.50	5.00
❑ 2855	When I Think of You/Pretty Boy	1986	—	—	3.00
❑ 2855 [PS]	When I Think of You/Pretty Boy	1986	—	—	3.00
❑ 2877	Control/Fast Girls	1986	—	—	3.00
❑ 2877 [PS]	Control/Fast Girls	1986	—	—	3.00
❑ 2906	Let's Wait Awhile/Pretty Boy	1987	—	—	3.00
❑ 2906 [PS]	Let's Wait Awhile/Pretty Boy	1987	—	—	3.00
❑ 2927	The Pleasure Principle/Fast Girls	1987	—	—	3.00
❑ 2927 [PS]	The Pleasure Principle/Fast Girls	1987	—	—	3.00
DEF JAM/DEF SOUL					
❑ 314-562913-7	Doesn't Really Matter/Doesn't Really Matter	2000	—	2.00	4.00
—As "Janet"					
PERSPECTIVE					
❑ 28968 0010 7	The Best Things in Life Are Free (2 mixes)	1992	—	2.00	4.00
—And Luther Vandross with BBD and Ralph Tresvant					
VIRGIN					
❑ S7-17332	That's the Way Love Goes/(Instrumental)	1993	—	2.50	5.00
—Original pressing on red vinyl					
❑ S7-17332	That's the Way Love Goes/(Instrumental)	1993	—	—	3.00
—Reissue on black vinyl					
❑ S7-17446	If/One More Chance	1993	—	—	3.00
❑ S7-17582	Again/Again (Piano Vocal)	1993	—	2.00	4.00
—Yellow vinyl					
❑ S7-17807	Because of Love/Funky Big Band	1994	—	—	3.00
❑ S7-18095	Any Time, Any Place (R. Kelly Mix)/Throb	1994	—	—	3.00
❑ S7-18307	You Want This/New Agenda	1995	—	—	3.00
❑ NR-38623	Together Again/Got 'Til It's Gone	1997	—	—	2.00
❑ NR-38623 [PS]	Together Again/Got 'Til It's Gone	1997	—	—	2.00
❑ NR-38631	I Get Lonely (TNT Remix Edit)/I Get Lonely (Jam & Lewis Feel My Bass Mix - Radio Edit)	1998	—	—	2.00
❑ NR-38631 [PS]	I Get Lonely (TNT Remix Edit)/I Get Lonely (Jam & Lewis Feel My Bass Mix - Radio Edit)	1998	—	—	2.00

JACKSON, JERMAINE

Also see THE JACKSONS.

Number	Title (A Side/B Side)	Yr	VG	VG+	NM
ARISTA					
❑ 2029	I'd Like to Get to Know You/Spare the Rod, Love the Child	1990	—	—	3.00
❑ 9190	Dynamite/Tell Me I'm Not Dreaming (Too Good to Be True) (Instrumental)	1984	—	—	3.00
❑ 9190 [PS]	Dynamite/Tell Me I'm Not Dreaming (Too Good to Be True) (Instrumental)	1984	—	—	3.00
❑ 9275	Take Good Care of My Heart/Tell Me I'm Not Dreaming (Too Good to Be True) (Instrumental)	1984	—	—	3.00
—A-side with Whitney Houston					
❑ 9279	Do What You Do/Tell Me I'm Not Dreaming (Too Good to Be True)	1984	—	—	3.00
❑ 9356	(Closest Thing to) Perfect/(Instrumental)	1985	—	—	3.00
❑ 9356 [PS]	(Closest Thing to) Perfect/(Instrumental)	1985	—	—	3.00
❑ 9444	I Think It's Love/Voices in the Dark	1985	—	—	3.00
❑ 9444 [PS]	I Think It's Love/Voices in the Dark	1985	—	—	3.00
❑ 9495	Words Into Action/Our Love Story	1986	—	—	3.00
❑ 9495 [PS]	Words Into Action/Our Love Story	1986	—	—	3.00
❑ 9502	Do You Remember Me/Whatcha' Doin'	1986	—	—	3.00
❑ 9502 [PS]	Do You Remember Me/Whatcha' Doin'	1986	—	—	3.00
❑ 9690	If You Say My Eyes Are Beautiful/Just the Lonely Talking Again	1988	—	—	3.00
—A-side with Whitney Houston; B-side: Whitney Houston solo					
❑ 9788	Clean Up Your Act/I'm Gonna Git Ya Sucka	1988	—	—	3.00
—B-side by the Gap Band					
❑ 9788 [PS]	Clean Up Your Act/I'm Gonna Git Ya Sucka	1988	—	—	3.00

Number	Title (A Side/B Side)	Yr	VG	VG+	NM
❑ 9875	Don't Take It Personal/Clean Up Your Act	1989	—	—	3.00
❑ 9875 [PS]	Don't Take It Personal/Clean Up Your Act	1989	—	—	3.00
❑ 9933	Two Ships (In the Night)/Next to You	1990	—	—	3.00
❑ 9933 [PS]	Two Ships (In the Night)/Next to You	1990	—	—	3.00

LAFACE

Number	Title (A Side/B Side)	Yr	VG	VG+	NM
❑ 24003	You Said, You Said/(Instrumental)	1991	—	—	3.00

MCA CURB

Number	Title (A Side/B Side)	Yr	VG	VG+	NM
❑ 52521	When the Rain Begins to Fall/Substitute	1984	—	—	3.00
—With Pia Zadora					
❑ 52521 [PS]	When the Rain Begins to Fall/Substitute	1984	—	—	3.00

MOTOWN

Number	Title (A Side/B Side)	Yr	VG	VG+	NM
❑ 1201	That's How Love Goes/I Lost My Love in the Big City	1972	—	2.50	5.00
❑ 1216	Daddy's Home/Take Me in Your Arms (Rock Me a Little While)	1972	—	2.50	5.00
❑ 1244	You're in Good Hands/Does Your Mama Know About Me	1973	—	2.50	5.00
❑ 1386	She's the Ideal Girl/I'm So Glad You Chose Me	1976	—	—	—
—Unreleased					
❑ 1401	Let's Be Young Tonight/Boss Odyssey	1976	—	2.50	5.00
❑ 1409	You Need to Be Loved/My Touch of Madness	1977	—	2.50	5.00
❑ 1441	Castles of Sand/I Love Every Little Thing About You	1978	—	2.50	5.00
❑ 1469	Let's Get Serious/Je Vous Aime Beaucoups	1980	—	2.00	4.00
❑ 1490	You're Supposed to Keep Your Love for Me/Let It Ride	1980	—	2.00	4.00
❑ 1499	Little Girl Don't You Worry/We Can Put It Back Together	1980	—	2.00	4.00
❑ 1503	You Like Me Don't You/(Instrumental)	1981	—	2.00	4.00
❑ 1525	I'm Just Too Shy/All Because of You	1981	—	2.00	4.00
❑ 1600	Paradise in Your Eyes/I'm My Brother's Keeper	1982	—	2.00	4.00
❑ 1628	Let Me Tickle Your Fancy/Maybe Next Time	1982	—	2.00	4.00
—Devo is the backing group					
❑ 1649	Very Special Part/You're Givin' Me the Runaround	1982	—	2.00	4.00

JACKSON, JERRY

CAPITOL

Number	Title (A Side/B Side)	Yr	VG	VG+	NM
❑ 2112	Miss You/Take Over Now	1968	2.50	5.00	10.00

COLUMBIA

Number	Title (A Side/B Side)	Yr	VG	VG+	NM
❑ 43056	Shrimp Boats/Always	1964	3.00	6.00	12.00
❑ 43158	Tell Her Johnny Said Goodbye/Are You Glad When We're Apart	1964	3.00	6.00	12.00
❑ 43231	You're Mine (And I Love You)/Hey, Sugarfoot	1965	3.00	6.00	12.00

KAPP

Number	Title (A Side/B Side)	Yr	VG	VG+	NM
❑ 387	Time/Se Habla Espanol	1961	5.00	10.00	20.00
❑ 420	I Don't Play Games/You Might Be There With Him	1961	5.00	10.00	20.00
❑ 438	If I Had Only Know How to Keep Her (She Would Never Have Gone to You)/Till the End of Time	1961	5.00	10.00	20.00
❑ 448	La-Dee-Dah (Ha-Ha-Ha)/You Don't Wanna Hurt Me	1962	3.75	7.50	15.00
❑ 464	They Really Don't Know You/Blues in the Night	1962	3.75	7.50	15.00
❑ 496	She Lied/Wide Awake in a Dream	1962	3.75	7.50	15.00
❑ 511	Gypsy Eyes/Turn Back	1963	3.75	7.50	15.00
❑ 543	Blowin' in the Wind (Part 1)/Blowin' in the Wind (Part 2)	1963	3.75	7.50	15.00

PARKWAY

Number	Title (A Side/B Side)	Yr	VG	VG+	NM
❑ 100	It's Rough Out There/I'm Gonna Paint a Picture	1966	5.00	10.00	20.00

TOP RANK

Number	Title (A Side/B Side)	Yr	VG	VG+	NM
❑ 2042	A Chance to Prove My Love/For Every One There's Someone	1960	5.00	10.00	20.00
❑ 2072	Every Time You Kiss Me/Meaning of My Love	1960	5.00	10.00	20.00

JACKSON, JILL

Also see PAUL AND PAULA.

REPRISE

Number	Title (A Side/B Side)	Yr	VG	VG+	NM
❑ 0297	Hey Handsome Boy/All Over Again	1964	3.75	7.50	15.00
❑ 0323	Pixie Girl/I Just Don't Know What to Do With Myself	1964	3.75	7.50	15.00
❑ 0362	Born Too Late/Here Comes the Night	1965	3.75	7.50	15.00
❑ 0411	Treasure of Love/I'll Love You for a While	1965	3.75	7.50	15.00

JACKSON, JUNE

BELL

Number	Title (A Side/B Side)	Yr	VG	VG+	NM
❑ 45173	Little Dog Heaven/Tenderly with Feeling	1972	5.00	10.00	20.00

IMPERIAL

Number	Title (A Side/B Side)	Yr	VG	VG+	NM
❑ 66185	It's What's Up Front That Counts/Fifty Per Cent Won't Do	1966	7.50	15.00	30.00

JACKSON, LIL' SON

IMPERIAL

Number	Title (A Side/B Side)	Yr	VG	VG+	NM
❑ 5204	Journey Back Home/Rockin' and Rollin' #2	1952	25.00	50.00	100.00
—Note: Lil' Son Jackson records on Imperial before 5204 are unconfirmed on 45 rpm					
❑ 5218	Black and Brown/Sad Letter Blues	1953	25.00	50.00	100.00
❑ 5229	Lonely Blues/Freight Train Blues	1953	25.00	50.00	100.00
❑ 5237	Spending Money Blues/All Alone	1953	25.00	50.00	100.00
❑ 5248	Movin' to the Country/Confession	1953	25.00	50.00	100.00
❑ 5259	Dirty Work/Little Girl	1953	25.00	50.00	100.00
❑ 5267	Thrill Me, Baby/Doctor, Doctor	1954	20.00	40.00	80.00
❑ 5276	Big Rat/Piggly Wiggly	1954	20.00	40.00	80.00
❑ 5286	Trouble Don't Last Always/Blues by the Hour	1954	20.00	40.00	80.00
❑ 5300	Get High Everybody/Let Me Down Easy	1954	20.00	40.00	80.00
❑ 5312	How Long/Good Ole Wagon	1954	20.00	40.00	80.00
❑ 5319	My Younger Days/I Wish to Go Home	1954	20.00	40.00	80.00
❑ 5339	Sugar Mama/Messin' Up	1955	20.00	40.00	80.00
❑ 5703	Rockin' and Rollin'/Peace Breaking People	1960	3.75	7.50	15.00
❑ 5851	Everybody's Blues/Travelin' Woman	1962	3.75	7.50	15.00
❑ 5963	Prison Bound/Rolling Mill	1963	3.00	6.00	12.00

POST

Number	Title (A Side/B Side)	Yr	VG	VG+	NM
❑ 2014	No Money/Lonely Blues	1955	10.00	20.00	40.00

JACKSON, MARLON

Also see THE JACKSONS.

CAPITOL

Number	Title (A Side/B Side)	Yr	VG	VG+	NM
❑ B-5675	(Let Your Love Find) The Chosen One/Sardo and the Child	1987	—	—	3.00
❑ B-44047	Don't Go/(Instrumental)	1987	—	—	3.00
❑ B-44047 [PS]	Don't Go/(Instrumental)	1987	—	—	3.00
❑ B-44092	Baby Tonight (Radio Edit)/Baby Tonight (Video Version)	1987	—	—	3.00
❑ B-44092 [PS]	Baby Tonight (Radio Edit)/Baby Tonight (Video Version)	1987	—	—	3.00
❑ B-44122	Lovely Eyes/(Instrumental)	1988	—	—	3.00

JACKSON, MICHAEL

Also see THE JACKSONS.

EPIC

Number	Title (A Side/B Side)	Yr	VG	VG+	NM
❑ 02156	Rock with You/Off the Wall	1981	—	—	3.00
—Reissue					
❑ 02157	She's Out of My Life/Lovely One	1981	—	—	3.00
—Reissue; B-side by The Jacksons					
❑ 03509	Billie Jean/Can't Get Outta the Rain	1983	—	2.00	4.00
❑ 03575	Billie Jean	1983	3.00	6.00	12.00
—One-sided budget release					
❑ 03759	Beat It/Get On the Floor	1983	—	2.00	4.00
❑ 03914	Wanna Be Startin' Somethin'/(Instrumental)	1983	—	2.00	4.00
❑ 03914 [PS]	Wanna Be Startin' Somethin'/(Instrumental)	1983	—	2.50	5.00
❑ 04026	Human Nature/Baby Be Mine	1983	—	2.00	4.00
❑ 04026 [PS]	Human Nature/Baby Be Mine	1983	—	2.50	5.00
❑ 04165	P.Y.T. (Pretty Young Thing)/Working Day and Night	1983	—	2.00	4.00
❑ 04165 [PS]	P.Y.T. (Pretty Young Thing)/Working Day and Night	1983	—	2.50	5.00
❑ 04364	Thriller/Can't Get Outta the Rain	1984	—	2.00	4.00
❑ 07253	I Just Can't Stop Loving You/Baby Be Mine	1987	—	—	3.00
❑ 07253 [PS]	I Just Can't Stop Loving You/Baby Be Mine	1987	—	—	3.00
❑ 07418	Bad/I Can't Help It	1987	—	—	3.00
❑ 07418 [PS]	Bad/I Can't Help It	1987	—	—	3.00
❑ 07645	The Way You Make Me Feel/(Instrumental)	1987	—	—	3.00
❑ 07645 [PS]	The Way You Make Me Feel/(Instrumental)	1987	—	—	3.00
❑ 07668	Man in the Mirror/(Instrumental)	1988	—	—	3.00
❑ 07668 [PS]	Man in the Mirror/(Instrumental)	1988	—	—	3.00
❑ 07739	Dirty Diana/(Instrumental)	1988	—	—	3.00
❑ 07739 [PS]	Dirty Diana/(Instrumental)	1988	—	—	3.00
❑ 07962	Another Part of Me/(Instrumental)	1988	—	—	3.00
❑ 07962 [PS]	Another Part of Me/(Instrumental)	1988	—	—	3.00
❑ 08044	Smooth Criminal/(Instrumental)	1988	—	—	3.00
❑ 08044 [PS]	Smooth Criminal/(Instrumental)	1988	—	—	3.00
❑ 50654	You Can't Win (Part 1)/You Can't Win (Part 2)	1979	—	3.00	6.00
❑ 50742	Don't Stop 'Til You Get Enough/I Can't Help It	1979	—	2.00	4.00
❑ 50797	Rock with You/Working Day and Night	1979	—	2.00	4.00
❑ 50838	Off the Wall/Get On the Floor	1980	—	2.00	4.00
❑ 50871	She's Out of My Life/Get On the Floor	1980	—	2.00	4.00
❑ 74100	Black or White/(Instrumental)	1991	—	—	3.00
❑ 74200	Remember the Time/Black or White (The Underground Club Mix)	1992	—	—	3.00
❑ 74266	In the Closet (7" Edit)/In the Closet (The Mission Radio Edit)	1992	—	—	3.00
❑ 74333	Jam/Rock with You (Masters At Work Remix)	1992	—	—	3.00
❑ 74406	Who Is It/Wanna Be Startin' Somethin'	1992	—	—	3.00
❑ 74708	Heal the World/She Drives Me Wild	1992	—	—	3.00
❑ 77060	Will You Be There/(Instrumental)	1993	—	—	3.00
❑ 77312	Gone Too Soon/(Instrumental)	1993	—	—	3.00
❑ 78000	Scream/Childhood	1995	—	—	3.00
—A-side: With Janet Jackson					
❑ 78002	You Are Not Alone/Scream Louder	1995	—	—	3.00
❑ 78007	Blood on the Dance Floor/Dangerous (Roger's Dangerous Edit)	1997	—	—	3.00
❑ 78012	Stranger in Moscow (Radio Edit)/(Tee's Radio Mix)	1997	—	—	3.00
❑ 78264	They Don't Care About Us/Rock with You (Frankie Knuckles Mix)	1996	—	—	3.00

MCA

Number	Title (A Side/B Side)	Yr	VG	VG+	NM
❑ S45-1786 [DJ]	Someone in the Dark (same on both sides)	1982	12.50	25.00	50.00
❑ S45-1786 [PS]	Someone in the Dark (same on both sides)	1982	12.50	25.00	50.00
❑ 40947	Ease On Down the Road/Poppy Girls	1978	—	2.50	5.00
❑ 40947 [PS]	Ease On Down the Road/Poppy Girls	1978	—	2.50	5.00
—With Diana Ross					

MOTOWN

Number	Title (A Side/B Side)	Yr	VG	VG+	NM
❑ 1191	Got to Be There/Maria (You Were the Only One)	1971	—	2.50	5.00
❑ 1197	Rockin' Robin/Love Is Here and Now You're Gone	1972	—	2.50	5.00
❑ 1202	I Wanna Be Where You Are/We Got a Good Thing Going	1972	—	2.50	5.00
❑ 1202 [PS]	I Wanna Be Where You Are/We Got a Good Thing Going	1972	2.50	5.00	10.00
❑ 1207	Ben/You Can Cry on My Shoulder	1972	—	2.50	5.00
❑ 1218	With a Child's Heart/Morning Glow	1973	—	2.50	5.00
❑ 1270	Doggin' Around/Up Again	1974	—	—	—
—Unreleased					
❑ 1341	We're Almost There/Take Me Back	1975	—	2.50	5.00
❑ 1349	Just a Little Bit of You/Dear Michael	1975	—	2.50	5.00
❑ 1512	One Day in Your Life/Take Me Back	1981	—	2.00	4.00
❑ 1739	Farewell My Summer Love/Call On Me	1984	—	2.00	4.00
❑ 1739 [PS]	Farewell My Summer Love/Call On Me	1984	—	2.50	5.00
❑ 1757	Girl You're So Together/Touch the One You Love	1984	—	2.00	4.00
❑ 1914	Twenty-Five Miles/Up on the House Top	1987	2.00	4.00	8.00
❑ 1914 [PS]	Twenty-Five Miles/Up on the House Top	1987	2.00	4.00	8.00

JACKSON, MICHAEL, AND PAUL MCCARTNEY

Also see each artist's individual listings.

COLUMBIA

Number	Title (A Side/B Side)	Yr	VG	VG+	NM
❑ 04168	Say, Say, Say/Ode to a Koala Bear	1983	—	2.00	4.00
—B-side by Paul McCartney					

Number	Title (A Side/B Side)	Yr	VG	VG+	NM
❑ 04168 [PS]	Say, Say, Say/Ode to a Koala Bear	1983	—	2.00	4.00
EPIC					
❑ 03288	The Girl Is Mine/Can't Get Outta the Rain	1982	—	2.50	5.00
—B-side by Michael Jackson					
❑ 03288 [PS]	The Girl Is Mine/Can't Get Outta the Rain	1982	—	2.50	5.00
❑ 03372	The Girl Is Mine	1982	2.50	5.00	10.00
—One-sided budget release					

JACKSON, RUDY

Number	Title (A Side/B Side)	Yr	VG	VG+	NM
IMPERIAL					
❑ 5425	Teasing Me/Give Me Your Hand	1957	10.00	20.00	40.00
❑ 5945	Go On Lover, Go On/Who Do You Think You Are	1963	3.00	6.00	12.00
R & B					
❑ 1310	I'm Crying/Enfold Me	1955	20.00	40.00	80.00

JACKSON, TONY, AND THE VIBRATIONS

Number	Title (A Side/B Side)	Yr	VG	VG+	NM
KAPP					
❑ 639	This Little Girl of Mine/You Beat Me to the Punch	1965	3.75	7.50	15.00
RED BIRD					
❑ 10-038	That's What I Want/Stage Door	1965	3.75	7.50	15.00

JACKSON, WALTER

Number	Title (A Side/B Side)	Yr	VG	VG+	NM
BRUNSWICK					
❑ 55502	It Doesn't Take Much/Let Me Come Back	1973	—	3.00	6.00
CHI-SOUND					
❑ XW908	Feelings/Words (Are Impossible)	1976	—	2.50	5.00
❑ XW964	Baby, I Love Your Way/What Would You Do	1977	—	2.50	5.00
❑ XW1044	It's All Over/Gonna Find Me an Angel	1977	—	2.50	5.00
❑ XW1140	If I Had My Way/We Could Fly	1978	—	2.50	5.00
❑ XW1216	Manhattan Skyline/I Won't Remember Ever Loving You	1978	—	2.50	5.00
❑ 2426	Magic Man/Golden Rays	1979	—	2.00	4.00
COLUMBIA					
❑ 02037	Tell Me Where It Hurts/When I See You	1981	—	2.00	4.00
❑ 02294	What If I Walked Out on You/Come to Me	1981	—	2.00	4.00
❑ 42528	This World of Mine/I Don't Want to Suffer	1962	6.25	12.50	25.00
❑ 42659	Starting Tomorrow/Then, Only Then	1963	5.00	10.00	20.00
❑ 42823	Opportunity/It Will Be the Last Time	1963	5.00	10.00	20.00
COTILLION					
❑ 44053	Anyway That You Want Me/Life Has Its Ups and Downs	1969	2.00	4.00	8.00
EPIC					
❑ 10408	Ad Lib/No Butterflies	1968	2.00	4.00	8.00
KELLI-ARTS					
❑ 1006	If I Had a Chance/(B-side unknown)	1982	—	2.50	5.00
OKEH					
❑ 7189	That's What Mama Say/What Would You Do	1964	3.00	6.00	12.00
❑ 7204	It's All Over/Lee Cross	1964	2.50	5.00	10.00
❑ 7215	Suddenly I'm All Alone/Special Love	1965	2.50	5.00	10.00
❑ 7219	Welcome Home/Blowin' in the Wind	1965	2.50	5.00	10.00
❑ 7229	I'll Keep On Trying/Where Have All the Flowers Gone	1965	2.50	5.00	10.00
❑ 7236	Funny (Not Much)/One Heart Lonely	1965	2.50	5.00	10.00
❑ 7247	It's an Uphill Climb to the Bottom/Tear for Tear	1966	2.00	4.00	8.00
❑ 7247 [PS]	It's an Uphill Climb to the Bottom/Tear for Tear	1966	5.00	10.00	20.00
❑ 7256	After You There Can Be Nothing/My Funny Valentine	1966	2.00	4.00	8.00
❑ 7260	A Corner in the Sun/Not You	1966	2.00	4.00	8.00
❑ 7272	Speak Her Name/They Don't Give Medals (To Yesterday's Heroes)	1967	2.00	4.00	8.00
❑ 7272 [PS]	Speak Her Name/They Don't Give Medals (To Yesterday's Heroes)	1967	5.00	10.00	20.00
❑ 7285	Deep in the Heart of Harlem/My One Chance to Make It	1967	2.00	4.00	8.00
❑ 7285 [PS]	Deep in the Heart of Harlem/My One Chance to Make It	1967	5.00	10.00	20.00
❑ 7295	Cold, Cold Winter/My Ship Is Comin' In	1967	2.00	4.00	8.00
❑ 7305	Everything/Road to Ruin	1968	2.00	4.00	8.00
U.S.A.					
❑ 104	Fool for You/Walls That Separate	196?	3.00	6.00	12.00

JACKSON, WANDA

Number	Title (A Side/B Side)	Yr	VG	VG+	NM
ABC					
❑ 12116	Take a Look/I Can't Stand to Hear You Say Goodbye	1975	—	2.50	5.00
CAPITOL					
❑ 2021	A Girl Don't Have to Drink to Have Fun/My Days Are Darker Than Your Nights	1967	2.50	5.00	10.00
❑ 2085	By the Time You Get to Phoenix/Wishing Well	1968	2.00	4.00	8.00
❑ 2151	My Baby Walked Right Out on Me/No Place to Go But Home	1968	2.00	4.00	8.00
❑ 2245	Little Boy Soldier/I Talk a Pretty Story	1968	2.00	4.00	8.00
❑ 2315	I Wish I Was Your Friend/Poor Old Me	1968	2.00	4.00	8.00
❑ 2379	If I Had a Hammer/The Pain of It All	1969	2.00	4.00	8.00
❑ 2472	Your Tender Love/As the Day Wears On	1969	2.00	4.00	8.00
❑ 2524	Everything's Leaving/You Cheated Me	1969	2.00	4.00	8.00
❑ 2614	My Big Iron Skillet/The Hunter	1969	2.00	4.00	8.00
❑ 2693	Two Separate Bar Stools/Two Wrongs Don't Make a Right	1969	2.00	4.00	8.00
❑ 2761	A Woman Lives for Love/What Have We Done	1970	—	3.00	6.00
❑ 2872	Who Shot John/Stop the World	1970	—	3.00	6.00
❑ 2986	Fancy Satin Pillows/Why Don't We Love Like That Anymore	1970	—	3.00	6.00
❑ 3070	People Gotta Be Loving/Glory Hallelujah	1971	—	3.00	6.00
❑ 3143	Back Then/I'm Gonna Walk Out of Your Life	1971	—	3.00	6.00
❑ 3218	I Already Know (What I'm Gettin' for My Birthday)/The Man You Could Have Been	1971	—	3.00	6.00
❑ 3293	I'll Be Whatever You Say/The More You See Me Less	1972	—	3.00	6.00
❑ 3385	I Wouldn't Want You Any Other Way/Song of the Wind	1972	—	3.00	6.00
❑ F3485	I Gotta Know/Half As Good a Girl	1956	10.00	20.00	40.00
❑ 3498	Roll with the Tide/Tennessee Women's Prison	1972	—	3.00	6.00
❑ F3575	The Hot Dog That Made Him Mad/Silver Threads and Golden Needles	1956	10.00	20.00	40.00
❑ 3599	I Don't Know How to Tell Him/Your Memory Comes and Gets Me	1973	—	3.00	6.00
❑ F3637	Cryin' Through the Night/Baby Loves Him	1957	12.50	25.00	50.00
❑ F3683	Don'a Wana/Let Me Explain	1957	7.50	15.00	30.00
❑ F3764	Cool Love/Did You Miss Me	1957	7.50	15.00	30.00
❑ F3843	Fujiyama Mama/No Wedding Bells for Joe	1957	7.50	15.00	30.00
❑ F3941	Just a Queen for a Day/Honey Bop	1958	7.50	15.00	30.00
❑ F4026	(Every Time They Play) Our Song/Mean, Mean Man	1958	7.50	15.00	30.00
❑ F4081	Sinful Heart/Rock Your Baby	1958	7.50	15.00	30.00
❑ F4142	Savin' My Love/I Wanna Waltz	1959	6.25	12.50	25.00
❑ F4207	A Date with Jerry/You're the One for Me	1959	6.25	12.50	25.00
❑ F4286	Reaching/I'd Rather Have You	1959	6.25	12.50	25.00
❑ 4354	My Destiny/Please Call Today	1960	6.25	12.50	25.00
❑ 4397	Let's Have a Party/Cool Love	1960	10.00	20.00	40.00
❑ 4469	Mean, Mean Man/Happy, Happy Birthday	1960	6.25	12.50	25.00
❑ 4520	Riot in Cell Black #9/Little Charm Bracelet	1961	6.25	12.50	25.00
❑ 4553	Right or Wrong/Funnel of Love	1961	6.25	12.50	25.00
❑ 4635	In the Middle of a Heartache/I'd Be Ashamed	1961	6.25	12.50	25.00
❑ 4681	A Little Bitty Tear/I Don't Wanta Go	1962	5.00	10.00	20.00
❑ 4723	If I Cried Every Time You Hurt Me/Let My Love Walk In	1962	5.00	10.00	20.00
❑ 4723 [PS]	If I Cried Every Time You Hurt Me/Let My Love Walk In	1962	7.50	15.00	30.00
❑ 4785	I Misunderstood/Between the Window and the Phone	1962	3.75	7.50	15.00
❑ 4833	The Greatest Actor/You Bug Me Bad	1962	3.75	7.50	15.00
❑ 4884	Whirlpool/One Teardrop at a Time	1962	3.75	7.50	15.00
❑ 4917	But I Was Lying/Sympathy	1963	3.75	7.50	15.00
❑ 4973	This Should Go On Forever/We Haven't a Moment to Lose	1963	3.75	7.50	15.00
❑ 5015	Memory Mountain/Let Me Talk to You	1963	3.75	7.50	15.00
❑ 5072	Slippin'/Just for You	1963	3.75	7.50	15.00
❑ 5142	The Violet and a Rose/To Tell You the Truth	1964	3.00	6.00	12.00
❑ 5228	Leave My Baby Alone/I'm Mad at Me	1964	3.00	6.00	12.00
❑ 5287	Candy Man/Weary Blues From Waitin'	1964	3.00	6.00	12.00
❑ 5364	My Baby's Gone/If I Were You	1965	3.00	6.00	12.00
❑ 5433	Have I Grown Used to Missing You/Take Me Home	1965	3.00	6.00	12.00
❑ 5491	My First Day Without You/Send Me No Roses	1965	3.00	6.00	12.00
❑ 5559	The Box It Came In/Look Out Heart	1965	3.00	6.00	12.00
❑ 5645	Because It's You/Long As I Have You	1966	2.50	5.00	10.00
❑ 5712	This Gun Don't Care/I Wonder If She Knows	1966	2.50	5.00	10.00
❑ 5789	Tears Will Be the Chaser for Your Wine/Reckless Love Affair	1967	2.50	5.00	10.00
❑ 5863	Both Sides of the Line/Famous Last Words	1967	2.50	5.00	10.00
❑ 5960	My Heart Gets All the Breaks/You'll Always Have My Love	1967	2.50	5.00	10.00
DECCA					
❑ 29140	You Can't Have My Love/Lovin' Country Style	1954	15.00	30.00	60.00
—With Billy Gray					
❑ 29253	The Right to Love/If You Knew What I Know	1954	15.00	30.00	60.00
❑ 29267	If You Don't, Somebody Else Will/You'd Be the First One to Know	1954	12.50	25.00	50.00
—With Billy Gray					
❑ 29514	Tears at the Grand Ole Opry/Nobody's Darlin' But Mine	1955	12.50	25.00	50.00
❑ 29677	Don't Do the Things He'd Do/It's the Same World	1955	7.50	15.00	30.00
❑ 29803	Wasted/I Cried Again	1956	12.50	25.00	50.00
❑ 30153	You Won't Forget (About Me)/A Heart You Could Have Had	1956	7.50	15.00	30.00
JIN					
❑ 300	Lonely Days, Lonely Nights/My Memories	197?	—	2.50	5.00
MYRRH					
❑ 122	When It's Time to Fall in Love Again/Say "I Do"	1973	—	2.50	5.00
❑ 126	Come On Home (To This Lonely Heart)/It's a Long, Long Time to Cry	1973	—	2.50	5.00
❑ 143	Jesus Put a Yodel in My Soul/(B-side unknown)	1974	—	2.50	5.00
❑ 152	Where Do I Put His Memory/Take a Look	1975	—	2.50	5.00

JACKSON FIVE, THE

See THE JACKSONS.

JACKSONS, THE

Includes records as "The Jackson Five." Also see JACKIE JACKSON; JERMAINE JACKSON; MARLON JACKSON; MICHAEL JACKSON.

Number	Title (A Side/B Side)	Yr	VG	VG+	NM
DYNAMO					
❑ 146	You Don't Have to Be Over Twenty-One to Fall in Love/Some Girls Want Me for Their Love	1971	10.00	20.00	40.00
EPIC					
❑ 01032	Can You Feel It/Everybody	1981	—	2.00	4.00
❑ 02132	Walk Right Now/Your Ways	1981	—	2.00	4.00
❑ 02157	Lovely One/She's Out of My Life	1981	—	—	3.00
—Reissue; B-side by Michael Jackson					
❑ 02720	The Things I Do for You/Working Day and Night	1982	—	2.00	4.00
❑ 04503	State of Shock/Your Ways	1984	—	2.00	4.00
—A-side: With Mick Jagger					
❑ 04503 [PS]	State of Shock/Your Ways	1984	—	2.00	4.00
❑ 04575	Torture/(Instrumental)	1984	—	2.00	4.00
❑ 04575 [PS]	Torture/(Instrumental)	1984	—	2.00	4.00
❑ 04673	Body/(Instrumental)	1984	—	2.00	4.00
❑ 04673 [PS]	Body/(Instrumental)	1984	—	2.00	4.00
❑ 50595	Blame It on the Boogie/Ease On Down the Road	1978	—	2.00	4.00
❑ 50656	Shake Your Body (Down to the Ground)/That's What You Get (For Being Polite)	1979	—	2.50	5.00
—Original issue has orange label					
❑ 50656	Shake Your Body (Down to the Ground)/That's What You Get (For Being Polite)	1979	—	2.00	4.00
—Second issue has dark blue label					

Number	Title (A Side/B Side)	Yr	VG	VG+	NM
❑ 50938	Lovely One/Bless His Soul	1980	—	2.00	4.00
❑ 50959	Heartbreak Hotel/The Things I Do for You	1980	—	2.00	4.00
❑ 68688	Nothing (That Compares 2 U)/Alright with Me	1989	—	—	3.00
❑ 69022	2300 Jackson Street/When I Look at You	1989	—	—	3.00
EPIC/PHILA. INT'L.					
❑ 50289	Enjoy Yourself/Style of Life	1976	—	2.50	5.00
❑ 50350	Show You the Way to Go/Blues Away	1977	—	2.50	5.00
❑ 50454	Goin' Places/Do What You Wanna	1977	—	2.50	5.00
❑ 50496	Find Me a Girl/Different Kind of Lady	1977	—	2.50	5.00
MCA					
❑ 53032	Time Out for the Burglar/News at Eleven	1987	—	—	3.00
—B-side by the Distants					
❑ 53032 [PS]	Time Out for the Burglar/News at Eleven	1987	—	—	3.00
MOTOWN					
❑ 1157	I Want You Back/Who's Lovin' You	1969	2.00	4.00	8.00
❑ 1163	ABC/The Young Folks	1970	2.00	4.00	8.00
❑ 1166	The Love You Save/I Found That Girl	1970	2.00	4.00	8.00
❑ 1166 [DJ]	I Found That Girl (same on both sides)	1970	5.00	10.00	20.00
—Red vinyl					
❑ 1166 [DJ]	The Love You Save	1970	7.50	15.00	30.00
—Blank back promo					
❑ 1171	I'll Be There/One More Chance	1970	2.00	4.00	8.00
❑ 1174	Santa Claus Is Coming to Town/Christmas Won't Be the Same This Year	1970	3.00	6.00	12.00
❑ 1177	Mama's Pearl/Darling Dear	1971	—	3.00	6.00
❑ 1177 [PS]	Mama's Pearl/Darling Dear	1971	3.75	7.50	15.00
❑ 1179	Never Can Say Goodbye/She's Good	1971	—	3.00	6.00
❑ 1186	Maybe Tomorrow/I Will Find a Way	1971	—	3.00	6.00
❑ 1194	Sugar Daddy/I'm So Happy	1971	—	3.00	6.00
❑ 1199	Little Bitty Pretty One/If I Had to Move a Mountain	1972	—	3.00	6.00
❑ 1205	Looking Through the Windows/Love Song	1972	—	3.00	6.00
❑ 1214	Corner of the Sky/To Know	1972	—	3.00	6.00
❑ 1224	Hallelujah Day/You Made Me What I Am	1973	—	3.00	6.00
❑ 1230	Boogie Man/Don't Let Your Baby Catch You	1973	—	—	—
—Unreleased					
❑ 1277	Get It Together/Touch	1973	—	3.00	6.00
❑ 1286	Dancing Machine/It's Too Late to Change the Time	1974	—	3.00	6.00
❑ 1308	Whatever You Got, I Want/I Can't Quit Your Love	1974	—	3.00	6.00
❑ 1310	I Am Love (Parts 1 & 2)/I Am Love (Part 2)	1975	—	3.00	6.00
❑ 1310	I Am Love (Part 1)/I Am Love (Part 2)	1975	2.00	4.00	8.00
❑ 1356	Forever Came Today/All I Do Is Think of You	1975	—	3.00	6.00
❑ 1365	Body Language/Call of the Wild	1975	—	—	—
—Unreleased					
❑ 2193	Who's Lovin' You/In the Still of the Night (I'll Remember)	1992	—	2.00	4.00
—B-side by Boyz II Men					
STEELTOWN					
❑ 681	Big Boy/You've Changed	1968	25.00	50.00	100.00
❑ 684	You Don't Have to Be Over Twenty-One to Fall in Love/Some Girls Want Me for Their Love	1968	25.00	50.00	100.00
❑ 689	Let Me Carry Your School Books/I Never Had a Girl	1969	20.00	40.00	80.00
—By "The Ripples and Waves plus Michael"					

JADE, FAINE

Number	Title (A Side/B Side)	Yr	VG	VG+	NM
RSVP					
❑ 1130	Introspection/(B-side unknown)	1968	6.25	12.50	25.00

JADES, THE

Many different groups.

Number	Title (A Side/B Side)	Yr	VG	VG+	NM
ADONA					
❑ 1445	Hey Senorita/(B-side unknown)	1962	7.50	15.00	30.00
CAPITOL					
❑ 2281	Ain't It Funny What Love Can Do/Baby I Need Your Love	1968	—	3.00	6.00
CHRISTY					
❑ 110	Oh Why/Big Beach Party	1959	125.00	250.00	500.00
❑ 111	Tell Me Pretty Baby/Applesauce	1959	62.50	125.00	250.00
❑ 113	Don't Be a Fool/Friday Night with My Baby	1959	125.00	250.00	500.00
❑ 114	Look for a Lie/Blue Memories	1959	375.00	750.00	1500.
DORE					
❑ 687	Hold Back the Dawn/When They Ask About You	1963	5.00	10.00	20.00
DOT					
❑ 15822	I'm Pretending/Beverly	1958	20.00	40.00	80.00
GAITY					
❑ 2-23-64	Surfin' Crow/Blue Black Hair	1964	45.00	90.00	180.00
IMPERIAL					
❑ 66383	Wheel of Fortune/Gotta Find Somebody to Love	1969	—	3.00	6.00
❑ 66425	L-O-V-E I Love You/Don't Give What's Mine Away	1969	—	3.00	6.00
LIBERTY					
❑ 56192	All's Quiet on West 23rd/Love of a Woman	1970	—	2.50	5.00
MGM					
❑ 13399	There's a Kinder Way to Say Goodbye/You're So Right for Me	1965	3.00	6.00	12.00
NAU VOO					
❑ 807	Walking All Alone/Hey Little Girl	1959	37.50	75.00	150.00
OXBORO					
❑ 2002	Surfin' Crow/Blue Black Hair	1964	30.00	60.00	120.00
❑ 2005	Little Marlene/Shake Baby Shake	1965	30.00	60.00	120.00
PORT					
❑ 70042	He's My Guy/There Will Come a Day	1964	6.25	12.50	25.00
TIME					
❑ 1002	Leave Her For Me/So Blue	1957	50.00	100.00	200.00
—Lou Reed is alleged to have been in this group, but he would have been 15 at the time.					
UNI					
❑ 55019	The Glide/Flower Power	1967	2.00	4.00	8.00
❑ 55032 [DJ]	Privilege (same on both sides)	1967	2.00	4.00	8.00
VERVE					
❑ 10385	For Just Another Day/I'm By Your Side (Baby)	1966	3.00	6.00	12.00

JAGGED EDGE, THE

Number	Title (A Side/B Side)	Yr	VG	VG+	NM
RCA VICTOR					
❑ 47-8880	Baby You Don't Know/Deep Inside	1966	2.50	5.00	10.00
TWIRL					
❑ 2024	How Many Times/Midnight to Six Man	1966	7.50	15.00	30.00

JAGGER, MICK

Also see THE ROLLING STONES.

Number	Title (A Side/B Side)	Yr	VG	VG+	NM
ATLANTIC					
❑ 87410	Sweet Thing/Whispering Spirit	1992	—	2.00	4.00
COLUMBIA					
❑ 04743	Just Another Night/Turn the Girl Loose	1985	—	—	3.00
❑ 04743 [PS]	Just Another Night/Turn the Girl Loose	1985	—	2.00	4.00
❑ 04893	Lucky in Love/Running Out of Luck	1985	—	—	3.00
❑ 04893 [PS]	Lucky in Love/Running Out of Luck	1985	—	2.00	4.00
❑ 07306	Let's Work/Catch as Catch Can	1987	—	—	3.00
❑ 07306 [PS]	Let's Work/Catch as Catch Can	1987	—	—	3.00
❑ 07653	Throwaway/Peace for the Wicked	1987	—	—	3.00
❑ 07653 [PS]	Throwaway/Peace for the Wicked	1987	—	—	3.00
❑ 07703	Say You Will/Shoot Off Your Mouth	1988	—	—	3.00
EPIC					
❑ 06211	Ruthless People/I'm Ringing	1986	—	—	3.00
❑ 06211 [PS]	Ruthless People/I'm Ringing	1986	—	2.00	4.00

JAGGERZ, THE

Also see DONNIE IRIS.

Number	Title (A Side/B Side)	Yr	VG	VG+	NM
GAMBLE					
❑ 218	(That's Why) Baby I Love You/Bring It Back	1968	2.00	4.00	8.00
❑ 226	Gotta Find My Way Back Home/Forever Together, Together Forever	1968	2.00	4.00	8.00
❑ 238	Together/Let Me Be the One	1969	2.00	4.00	8.00
❑ 4008	Higher and Higher/Ain't No Sun	1970	2.00	4.00	8.00
❑ 4012	Need Your Love/Here's a Heart	1970	2.00	4.00	8.00
KAMA SUTRA					
❑ 502	The Rapper/Born Poor	1970	2.00	4.00	8.00
❑ 509	I Call My Baby Candy/Will She Believe Me	1970	—	3.00	6.00
❑ 513	What a Bummer/Memories of the Traveller	1970	—	3.00	6.00
❑ 517	Let's Talk About Love/I'll Never Forget You	1971	—	2.50	5.00
❑ 583	Let's Talk About Love/Ain't That Sad	1973	—	2.00	4.00
WOODEN NICKEL					
❑ PB-10194	Don't It Make You Want to Dance/2 Plus 2	1975	—	2.00	4.00

JAGUARS, THE (1)

Number	Title (A Side/B Side)	Yr	VG	VG+	NM
AARDELL					
❑ 0003	Rock It Davy, Rock It/I Wanted You	1955	12.50	25.00	50.00
❑ 0006	Be My Sweetie/Why Don't You Believe Me	1956	12.50	25.00	50.00
❑ 0011	The Way You Look Tonight/Moonlight and You	1956	62.50	125.00	250.00
—Black vinyl					
❑ 0011	The Way You Look Tonight/Moonlight and You	1956	150.00	300.00	600.00
—Red vinyl					
BARONET					
❑ 1	The Way You Look Tonight/Baby, Baby, Baby	1962	6.25	12.50	25.00
CLASSIC ARTISTS					
❑ 117	Happy Holiday/More Than Enough for Me	1989	—	3.00	6.00
—B-side by Johnny Staton and the Feathers					
❑ 136	Merry Christmas, Darling/Lost and Found	1990	—	3.00	6.00
ORIGINAL SOUND					
❑ 6	Thinking of You/Look Into My Eyes	1959	20.00	40.00	80.00
❑ 20	Thinking of You/Look Into My Eyes	1962	10.00	20.00	40.00
❑ 59	The Way You Look Tonight/Baby, Baby, Baby	1966	5.00	10.00	20.00
R-DELL					
❑ 11	The Way You Look Tonight/Baby, Baby, Baby	1956	12.50	25.00	50.00
❑ 16	I Love You Baby/Baby, Baby, Baby	1957	30.00	60.00	120.00
❑ 45	Rock It Davy, Rock It/I Wanted You	1958	10.00	20.00	40.00
❑ 107	Rock It Davy, Rock It/The Big Bear	1958	10.00	20.00	40.00
❑ 117	Girl of My Dreams/Don't Go Home	1960	15.00	30.00	60.00

JAGUARS, THE (2)

Number	Title (A Side/B Side)	Yr	VG	VG+	NM
DOT					
❑ 16723	Dead Sea/Supersonic	1965	2.50	5.00	10.00
❑ 16931	The Gorilla/He'll Turn Away	1966	2.50	5.00	10.00

JAGUARS, THE (3)

Number	Title (A Side/B Side)	Yr	VG	VG+	NM
EPIC					
❑ 9325	Drive-In/Exit 6	1959	5.00	10.00	20.00

JAGUARS, THE (4)

Number	Title (A Side/B Side)	Yr	VG	VG+	NM
FARO					
❑ 618	Where Lovers Go/Discover a Lover	1965	3.00	6.00	12.00

JAGUARS, THE (U)

Some of these could be the above groups.

Number	Title (A Side/B Side)	Yr	VG	VG+	NM
EBB					
❑ 129	Hold Me Tight/Piccadilly	1958	25.00	50.00	100.00
RENDEZVOUS					
❑ 159	Fine, Fine, Fine/It Finally Happened	1961	5.00	10.00	20.00
❑ 216	Fine, Fine, Fine/It Finally Happened	1963	3.00	6.00	12.00
SKOOP					
❑ 1067	It's Gonna Be Alright/(B-side unknown)	1966	6.25	12.50	25.00
SPAY					
❑ 121	Rendezvous/(B-side unknown)	196?	15.00	30.00	60.00

JAMES, ELMORE

Some of the below were as "Elmo James."

Number	Title (A Side/B Side)	Yr	VG	VG+	NM
ACE					
❑ 508	I Believe My Time Ain't Long/I Wish I Was a Catfish	1955	62.50	125.00	250.00
CHECKER					
❑ 777	Country Boogie/She Just Won't Do Right	1953	250.00	500.00	1000.
CHESS					
❑ 1756	I Can't Hold Out/The Sun Is Shining	1960	3.75	7.50	15.00

Number	Title (A Side/B Side)	Yr	VG	VG+	NM
CHIEF					
❑ 7001	The Twelve Year Old Boy/Coming Home	1957	20.00	40.00	80.00
❑ 7004	It Hurts Me Too/Elmore's Contribution to Jazz	1957	20.00	40.00	80.00
❑ 7006	Cry for Me Baby/Take Me Where You Go	1957	15.00	30.00	60.00
❑ 7020	Knocking at Your Door/Calling All Blues	1960	10.00	20.00	40.00
ENJOY					
❑ 2015	It Hurts Me Too/Bleeding Heart	1965	5.00	10.00	20.00
❑ 2015	It Hurts Me Too/Pickin' the Blues	1965	3.75	7.50	15.00
❑ 2020	Mean Mistreatin' Mama/Bleeding	1965	3.75	7.50	15.00
❑ 2027	Dust My Broom/Everyday I Have the Blues	1965	3.75	7.50	15.00
FIRE					
❑ 504	Shake Your Moneymaker/Look on Yonder Wall	1962	10.00	20.00	40.00
❑ 1011	Make My Dreams Come True/Bobby's Rock	1960	7.50	15.00	30.00
❑ 1016	The Sky Is Crying/Held My Baby Last Night	1960	10.00	20.00	40.00
❑ 1024	I'm Worried/Rollin' and Tumblin'	1960	5.00	10.00	20.00
❑ 1031	Fine Little Mama/Done Somebody Wrong	1961	5.00	10.00	20.00
❑ 1503	Stranger Blues/Anna Lee	1963	3.75	7.50	15.00
❑ 2020	It Hurts Me Too/Pickin' the Blues	196?	3.75	7.50	15.00
—Red vinyl					
FLAIR					
❑ 1011	Early in the Morning/Hawaiian Boogie	1953	125.00	250.00	500.00
❑ 1014	Can't Stop Lovin'/Make a Little Love	1953	50.00	100.00	200.00
❑ 1022	Strange Kinda Feeling/Please Find My Baby	1953	50.00	100.00	200.00
❑ 1031	Make My Dreams Come True/Hand in Hand	1954	75.00	150.00	300.00
❑ 1039	Sho'nuff, I Do/1839 Blues	1954	75.00	150.00	300.00
❑ 1048	Dark and Dreary/Rock My Baby Right	1954	75.00	150.00	300.00
❑ 1057	Standing at the Cross Roads/Sunny Land	1955	62.50	125.00	250.00
❑ 1062	Late Hours at Midnight/The Way You Treat Me	1955	37.50	75.00	150.00
❑ 1069	Happy Home/No Love in My Heart	1955	37.50	75.00	150.00
❑ 1074	Dust My Blues/I Was a Fool	1955	62.50	125.00	250.00
❑ 1079	Blues Before Sunrise/Goodbye Baby	1955	50.00	100.00	200.00
JEWEL					
❑ 764	Dust My Broom/Gotta Find My Baby	1966	2.50	5.00	10.00
❑ 783	Catfish Blues/Make a Little Love	1967	2.50	5.00	10.00
KENT					
❑ 331	Dust My Blues/Happy Home	1960	3.00	6.00	12.00
❑ 394	Dust My Blues/Happy Home	1964	2.50	5.00	10.00
❑ 465	Sunnyland/Goodbye Baby	1967	2.00	4.00	8.00
❑ 508	I Believe/1839 Blues	1969	—	3.00	6.00
M-PAC					
❑ 7231	Cry for Me/Take Me Where You Go	1966	2.50	5.00	10.00
MEL					
❑ 7011	Cry for Me Baby/(B-side unknown)	197?	—	3.00	6.00
METEOR					
❑ 5000	I Believe/I Held My Baby Last Night	1953	200.00	400.00	800.00
❑ 5003	Baby What's Wrong/Sinful Woman	1953	125.00	250.00	500.00
❑ 5016	Saxony Boogie/Dumb Woman Blues	1954	75.00	150.00	300.00
❑ 5024	San Symphonic Boogie/Flaming Blues	1955	62.50	125.00	250.00
MODERN					
❑ 983	Wild About You/Long Tall Woman	1956	75.00	150.00	300.00
VEE JAY					
❑ 249	Coming Home/The 12-Year-Old Boy	1957	6.25	12.50	25.00
❑ 259	It Hurts Me Too/Elmore's Contribution to Jazz	1957	6.25	12.50	25.00
❑ 269	Cry for Me Baby/Take Me Where You Go	1958	6.25	12.50	25.00

JAMES, ETTA

Also see ETTA AND HARVEY.

Number	Title (A Side/B Side)	Yr	VG	VG+	NM
ARGO					
❑ 5359	All I Could Do Was Cry/Girl of My Dreams	1960	3.00	6.00	12.00
❑ 5368	My Dearest Darling/Tough Mary	1960	3.00	6.00	12.00
❑ 5380	At Last/I Just Want to Make Love to You	1961	3.75	7.50	15.00
❑ 5385	Trust in Me/Anything to Say You're Mine	1961	2.50	5.00	10.00
❑ 5390	Dream/Fool That I Am	1961	2.50	5.00	10.00
❑ 5393	Sunday Kind of Love/Don't Cry, Baby	1961	2.50	5.00	10.00
❑ 5402	It's Too Soon to Know/Seven Day Fool	1961	2.50	5.00	10.00
❑ 5409	Something's Got a Hold on Me/Waiting for Charlie to Come Home	1962	2.50	5.00	10.00
❑ 5418	Stop the Wedding/Street of Tears	1962	2.50	5.00	10.00
❑ 5424	Next Door to the Blues/Fools Rush In	1962	2.50	5.00	10.00
❑ 5430	How Do You Speak to An Angel/Would It Make Any Difference to You	1962	2.50	5.00	10.00
❑ 5437	Pushover/I Can't Hold It In Anymore	1963	2.50	5.00	10.00
❑ 5445	Be Honest with Me/Pay Back	1963	2.50	5.00	10.00
❑ 5452	Two Sides (To Every Story)/Worry 'Bout You	1963	2.50	5.00	10.00
❑ 5459	Baby What You Want Me to Do/What I Say	1964	2.50	5.00	10.00
❑ 5465	Look Who's Blue/Loving You More Every Day	1964	2.50	5.00	10.00
❑ 5477	Breaking Point/That Man Belongs Back Here with Me	1964	2.50	5.00	10.00
❑ 5485	Mellow Fellow/Bobby Is His Name	1964	2.50	5.00	10.00
CADET					
❑ 5519	Somewhere Down the Line/Do I Make Myself Clear	1966	2.00	4.00	8.00
—With Sugar Pie DeSanto					
❑ 5526	Only Time Will Tell/I'm Sorry for You	1966	2.00	4.00	8.00
❑ 5539	In the Basement — Part 1/In the Basement — Part 2	1966	2.00	4.00	8.00
—With Sugar Pie DeSanto					
❑ 5552	I Prefer You/I'm So Glad	1966	2.00	4.00	8.00
❑ 5564	Don't Take Me for Your Fool/It Must Be Your Love	1967	2.00	4.00	8.00
❑ 5568	Happiness/842-3089 (Call My Name)	1967	2.00	4.00	8.00
❑ 5578	Tell Mama/I'd Rather Go Blind	1967	2.00	4.00	8.00
❑ 5594	Security/I'm Gonna Take What He's Got	1968	2.00	4.00	8.00
❑ 5606	I Got You Babe/I Worship the Ground You Walk On	1968	2.00	4.00	8.00
❑ 5620	Fire/You Got It	1968	2.00	4.00	8.00
❑ 5630	Almost Persuaded/Steal Away	1968	2.00	4.00	8.00
❑ 5655	Miss Pitiful/Bobby Is His Name	1969	2.00	4.00	8.00
❑ 5664	Tighten Up Your Own Thing/What Fools We Mortals Be	1970	2.00	4.00	8.00
❑ 5671	The Sound of Love/When I Stop Dreaming	1970	2.00	4.00	8.00
❑ 5676	Losers Weepers — Part 1/Losers Weepers — Part 2	1970	2.00	4.00	8.00
CAPITOL					
❑ B-44333	Avenue D/My Head Is a City	1989	—	2.00	4.00
—With David A. Stewart					
CHESS					
❑ 2100	The Love of My Man/Nothing from Nothing Leaves Nothing	1971	—	3.00	6.00
❑ 2112	I Think It's You/Take Out Some Insurance	1971	—	3.00	6.00
❑ 2125	I Found a Love/Nothing from Nothing Leaves Nothing	1972	—	3.00	6.00
❑ 2144	All the Way Down/Lay Back Daddy	1973	—	3.00	6.00
❑ 2148	Leave Your Hat On/Only a Fool	1974	—	3.00	6.00
❑ 2153	Out on the Street Again/Feeling Uneasy	1974	—	3.00	6.00
❑ 2171	Lovin' Arms/Take Out Some Insurance	1975	—	3.00	6.00
❑ 31001	Jump Into Love/(B-side unknown)	1976	—	2.50	5.00
EPIC					
❑ 68593	Baby What You Want Me to Do/Max's Theme (Instrumental)	1989	—	2.00	4.00
KENT					
❑ 304	Baby, Baby, Every Night/Sunshine of Love	1958	7.50	15.00	30.00
❑ 345	Roll with Me Henry/Good Rockin' Daddy	1960	6.25	12.50	25.00
❑ 352	How Big a Fool/Good Rockin' Daddy	1961	6.25	12.50	25.00
❑ 370	Do Something Crazy/Good Rockin' Daddy	1962	6.25	12.50	25.00
MODERN					
❑ 947	The Wallflower (Roll With Me Henry)/Hold Me, Squeeze Me	1955	10.00	20.00	40.00
❑ 947	The Wallflower (Dance With Me Henry)/Hold Me, Squeeze Me	1955	6.25	12.50	25.00
❑ 957	Hey Henry (Doin' Fine, Henry)/Be Mine	1955	6.25	12.50	25.00
❑ 962	Good Rockin' Daddy/Crazy Feeling	1955	7.50	15.00	30.00
❑ 972	That's All/W-O-M-A-N	1955	6.25	12.50	25.00
❑ 984	I'm a Fool/Number One (My One and Only)	1956	6.25	12.50	25.00
❑ 988	Shortnin' Bread Rock/Tears of Joy	1956	6.25	12.50	25.00
❑ 998	Fools We Mortals Be/Tough Lover	1956	7.50	15.00	30.00
❑ 1007	Good Lookin'/Then I'll Care	1957	6.25	12.50	25.00
❑ 1016	The Pick-Up/Market Place	1957	6.25	12.50	25.00
❑ 1022	By the Light of the Silvery Moon/Come What May	1957	6.25	12.50	25.00
PHILCO-FORD					
❑ HP-31	Tell Mama/Security	1968	5.00	10.00	20.00
—4-inch plastic "Hip Pocket Record" with color sleeve					
T-ELECTRIC					
❑ 41264	It Takes Love to Keep a Woman/Mean Mother	1980	—	2.50	5.00
WARNER BROS.					
❑ 8545	Piece of My Heart/Lovesick Blues	1978	—	2.50	5.00
❑ 8611	Sugar on the Floor/Lovesick Blues	1978	—	2.50	5.00

JAMES, JONI

Number	Title (A Side/B Side)	Yr	VG	VG+	NM
MGM					
❑ 11223	Let There Be Love/My Baby Just Cares for Me	1952	6.25	12.50	25.00
❑ 11295	You Belong to Me/Yes, Yes, Yes	1952	6.25	12.50	25.00
❑ 11333	Why Don't You Believe Me/Purple Shades	1952	7.50	15.00	30.00
❑ 11390	Have You Heard/Wishing Ring	1953	5.00	10.00	20.00
❑ 11426	Your Cheatin' Heart/I'll Be Waiting for You	1953	5.00	10.00	20.00
❑ 11470	Is It Any Wonder/Almost Always	1953	5.00	10.00	20.00
❑ 11543	My Love, My Love/You're Fooling Someone	1953	5.00	10.00	20.00
❑ 11606	I'll Never Stand in Your Way/Why Can't I	1953	5.00	10.00	20.00
❑ 11637	Christmas and You/Nina-Non	1953	5.00	10.00	20.00
❑ 11696	Am I in Love/Maybe Next Time	1954	5.00	10.00	20.00
❑ 11753	In a Garden of Roses/Every Day	1954	5.00	10.00	20.00
❑ 11802	Mama, Don't Cry at My Wedding/Pa Pa Pa	1954	5.00	10.00	20.00
❑ 11865	Everytime You Tell Me You Love Me/When We Come of Age	1954	5.00	10.00	20.00
❑ 11919	How Important Can It Be?/This Is My Confession	1955	5.00	10.00	20.00
❑ 11960	When You Wish Upon a Star/Is This the End of the Line	1955	5.00	10.00	20.00
❑ 12020	The Moment I Saw You/Where Is That Someone for Me	1955	5.00	10.00	20.00
❑ 12066	You Are My Love/I Lay Me Down to Sleep	1955	5.00	10.00	20.00
❑ 12091	The Christmas Song/Have Yourself a Merry Little Christmas	1955	6.25	12.50	25.00
❑ 12126	My Believing Heart/You Never Fall in Love Again	1955	5.00	10.00	20.00
❑ 12175	Don't Tell Me Not to Love You/Somewhere Someone Is Lonely	1956	3.75	7.50	15.00
❑ 12213	I Woke Up Crying/The Maverick Queen	1956	3.75	7.50	15.00
❑ 12288	Give Us This Day/How Lucky You Are	1956	3.75	7.50	15.00
❑ 12353	Love Letters/Don't Take Your Love from Me	1956	3.75	7.50	15.00
❑ 12368	White Christmas/I'll Be Home for Christmas	1956	5.00	10.00	20.00
❑ 12369	Danny Boy/To You I Give My Heart	1956	3.75	7.50	15.00
❑ 12450	I Need You So/Only Trust Your Heart	1957	3.75	7.50	15.00
❑ 12480	Summer Love/I'm Sorry for You, My Friend	1957	3.75	7.50	15.00
❑ 12531	Crying in the Shadows/Day Dreaming	1957	3.75	7.50	15.00
❑ 12565	Never 'Til Now/I Give You My Heart	1957	3.75	7.50	15.00
❑ 12565 [PS]	Never 'Til Now/I Give You My Heart	1957	6.25	12.50	25.00
❑ 12607	Dansero/Love Works Miracles	1958	3.75	7.50	15.00
❑ 12627	Nothing Will Ever Change/Does It Show	1958	3.75	7.50	15.00
❑ 12639	Arrividerci Roma/Non Dimenticar	1958	3.75	7.50	15.00
❑ 12660	Coming from You/Junior Prom	1958	3.75	7.50	15.00
❑ 12706	There Goes My Heart/Funny	1958	3.75	7.50	15.00
❑ 12706 [PS]	There Goes My Heart/Funny	1958	12.50	25.00	50.00
❑ SK-12706 [S]	There Goes My Heart/Funny	1958	10.00	20.00	40.00
—Note different prefix. Also, label will say "Stereo."					
❑ 12746	There Must Be a Way/Sorry for Myself	1959	3.75	7.50	15.00
❑ 12779	I Still Get a Thrill (Thinking of You)/Perhaps	1959	3.75	7.50	15.00
❑ 12779 [PS]	I Still Get a Thrill (Thinking of You)/Perhaps	1959	6.25	12.50	25.00
❑ 12807	I Still Get Jealous/My Prayer of Love	1959	3.75	7.50	15.00
❑ 12828	Are You Sorry/What I Don't Know Won't Hurt Me	1959	3.75	7.50	15.00
❑ 12849	Little Things Mean a Lot/I Laughed at Love	1959	3.75	7.50	15.00
❑ 12885	I Need You Now/You Belong to Me	1960	3.00	6.00	12.00
❑ 12895	They Really Don't Know You/We Know	1960	3.00	6.00	12.00

Number	Title (A Side/B Side)	Yr	VG	VG+	NM
❑ 12933	My Last Date (With You)/I Can't Give You Anything But Love	1960	3.00	6.00	12.00
❑ 12933 [PS]	My Last Date (With You)/I Can't Give You Anything But Love	1960	5.00	10.00	20.00
❑ 12948	Be My Love/Tall As a Tree	1960	3.00	6.00	12.00
❑ 12948 [PS]	Be My Love/Tall As a Tree	1960	5.00	10.00	20.00
❑ 12990	Theme from "Carnival"/Can You Imagine That	1961	3.00	6.00	12.00
❑ 13016	Go Away (Bother Me No More)/I Gave My Love	1961	3.00	6.00	12.00
❑ 13037	Somebody Else Is Taking My Place/You Were Wrong	1961	3.00	6.00	12.00
❑ 13037 [PS]	Somebody Else Is Taking My Place/You Were Wrong	1961	5.00	10.00	20.00
❑ 13080	It's Magic/Tender and True	1962	3.00	6.00	12.00
❑ 13092	You Are My Sunshine/Lend Me Your Handkerchief	1962	3.75	7.50	15.00
❑ 13117	Anyone But Her/Forgive a Fool	1962	3.75	7.50	15.00
❑ 13159	Hey, Good Lookin'/He Says the Same Things to Me	1963	3.75	7.50	15.00
❑ 13180	Red Sails in the Sunset/Every Time I Meet You	1963	3.75	7.50	15.00
❑ 13206	Teach Me to Forget You/Un Cafe	1964	5.00	10.00	20.00
❑ 13243	Break, My Heart, Break/Don't Let the Neighbors Know	1964	5.00	10.00	20.00
❑ 13267	Pearly Shells/Hawaiian War Chant	1964	5.00	10.00	20.00
❑ 13288	Sentimental Me/You're Nearer	1964	20.00	40.00	80.00
❑ 13304	Dondi/Once I Loved	1964	5.00	10.00	20.00
❑ 13365	There Goes My Heart/I Still Get Jealous	1965	5.00	10.00	20.00
❑ SK-50111 [S]	There Must Be a Way/Sorry for Myself	1959	7.50	15.00	30.00

SHARP

Number	Title (A Side/B Side)	Yr	VG	VG+	NM
❑ 46	Let There Be Love/My Baby Just Cares for Me	1952	75.00	150.00	300.00
❑ 50	You Belong to Me/Yes, Yes, Yes	1952	62.50	125.00	250.00

7-Inch Extended Plays

MGM

Number	Title (A Side/B Side)	Yr	VG	VG+	NM
❑ X-222 [PS]	Let There Be Love	1953	12.50	25.00	50.00
—Cover for X-4047 and X-4048					
❑ X-234 [PS]	Joni James	1954	12.50	25.00	50.00
—Cover with X-4090 and X-4091					
❑ X-1160	I'm in the Mood for Love/Where Can I Go Without You//People Will Say We're in Love/Love Letters	1955	15.00	30.00	60.00
❑ X-1160 [PS]	Joni James	1955	15.00	30.00	60.00
❑ X-1172	(contents unknown)	1955	15.00	30.00	60.00
❑ X-1172 [PS]	Have Yourself a Merry Little Christmas	1955	15.00	30.00	60.00
❑ X-1211	(contents unknown)	1956	10.00	20.00	40.00
❑ X-1211 [PS]	In the Still of the Night, Part 1	1956	10.00	20.00	40.00
❑ X-1212	(contents unknown)	1956	10.00	20.00	40.00
❑ X-1212 [PS]	In the Still of the Night, Part 2	1956	10.00	20.00	40.00
❑ X-1213	In the Still of the Night/What's New//Deep Purple/You'd Be So Nice to Come Home To	1956	10.00	20.00	40.00
❑ X-1213 [PS]	In the Still of the Night, Vol. 3	1956	10.00	20.00	40.00
❑ X-1219	(contents unknown)	1956	10.00	20.00	40.00
❑ X-1219 [PS]	Award Winning Album, Part 1	1956	10.00	20.00	40.00
❑ X-1220	(contents unknown)	1956	10.00	20.00	40.00
❑ X-1220 [PS]	Award Winning Album, Part 2	1956	10.00	20.00	40.00
❑ X-1221	(contents unknown)	1956	10.00	20.00	40.00
❑ X-1221 [PS]	Award Winning Album, Part 3	1956	10.00	20.00	40.00
❑ X-1223	In Love in Vain/Too Late Now//Autumn Leaves/That Old Feeling	1956	10.00	20.00	40.00
❑ X-1223 [PS]	Little Girl Blue	1956	10.00	20.00	40.00
❑ X-1227	I Need You Now/This Is My Confession//The Moment I Saw You/Am I in Love	1956	10.00	20.00	40.00
❑ X-1227 [PS]	Let There Be Love	1956	10.00	20.00	40.00
❑ X-1343	My Foolish Heart/I Don't Stand a Ghost of a Chance with You//Stella by Starlight/A Hundred Years from Today	1956	10.00	20.00	40.00
❑ X-1343 [PS]	Joni Sings Songs by Victor Young (Vol. 1)	1956	10.00	20.00	40.00
❑ X-1344	Song of Surrender/Everything I Do//If I Were a Bell.My Darling, My Darling	1956	10.00	20.00	40.00
❑ X-1344 [PS]	Joni Sings Songs by Victor Young/Songs by Frank Loesser (Vol. 2)	1956	10.00	20.00	40.00
❑ X-1345	On a Slow Boat to China/I'll Know//Spring Will Be a Little Late This Year/Anywhere I Wander	1956	10.00	20.00	40.00
❑ X-1345 [PS]	Joni Sings Songs by Frank Loesser (Vol. 3)	1956	10.00	20.00	40.00
❑ X-1389	(contents unknown)	1957	10.00	20.00	40.00
❑ X-1389 [PS]	Give Us This Day, Vol. 1	1957	10.00	20.00	40.00
❑ X-1390	Look for the Silver Lining/Panis Angelicus//I Believe/The Rosary	1957	10.00	20.00	40.00
❑ X-1390 [PS]	Give Us This Day, Vol. 2	1957	10.00	20.00	40.00
❑ X-1391	Count Your Blessings/Ave Maria (Gounod)//Abide with Me/May the Good Lord Bles and Keep You	1957	10.00	20.00	40.00
❑ X-1391 [PS]	Give Us This Day, Vol. 3	1957	10.00	20.00	40.00
❑ X-1399	(contents unknown)	1957	15.00	30.00	60.00
❑ X-1399 [PS]	Merry Christmas from Joni, Part 1	1957	15.00	30.00	60.00
❑ X-1400	(contents unknown)	1957	15.00	30.00	60.00
❑ X-1400 [PS]	Merry Christmas from Joni, Part 2	1957	15.00	30.00	60.00
❑ X-1401	(contents unknown)	1957	15.00	30.00	60.00
❑ X-1401 [PS]	Merry Christmas from Joni, Part 3	1957	15.00	30.00	60.00
❑ X-1545	Always/When You Were Sweet Sixteen//Let Me Call You Sweetheart/Alice Blue Gown	1957	10.00	20.00	40.00
❑ X-1545 [PS]	Among My Souvenirs, Vol. I	1957	10.00	20.00	40.00
❑ X-1546	(contents unknown)	1957	10.00	20.00	40.00
❑ X-1546 [PS]	Among My Souvenirs, Vol. II	1957	10.00	20.00	40.00
❑ X-1547	(contents unknown)	1957	10.00	20.00	40.00
❑ X-1547 [PS]	Among My Souvenirs, Vol. III	1957	10.00	20.00	40.00
❑ X-1652	(contents unknown)	1959	10.00	20.00	40.00
❑ X-1652 [PS]	Songs of Hank Williams, Part 1	1959	10.00	20.00	40.00
❑ X-1653	(contents unknown)	1959	10.00	20.00	40.00
❑ X-1653 [PS]	Songs of Hank Williams, Part 2	1959	10.00	20.00	40.00
❑ X-1654	(contents unknown)	1959	10.00	20.00	40.00
❑ X-1654 [PS]	Songs of Hank Williams, Part 3	1959	10.00	20.00	40.00
❑ X-1656	(contents unknown)	1959	10.00	20.00	40.00
❑ X-1656 [PS]	100 Strings and Joni, Part 1	1959	10.00	20.00	40.00
❑ X-1657	(contents unknown)	1959	10.00	20.00	40.00
❑ X-1657 [PS]	100 Strings and Joni, Part 2	1959	10.00	20.00	40.00
❑ X-1658	(contents unknown)	1959	10.00	20.00	40.00
❑ X-1658 [PS]	100 Strings and Joni, Part 3	1959	10.00	20.00	40.00
❑ X-4047	Let There Be Love/My Romance//The Nearness of You/You're Mine You	1953	12.50	25.00	50.00
—One record of "X222"					
❑ X-4048	You're My Everything/You're Nearer//Love Is Here to Stay/I'll Be Seeing You	1953	12.50	25.00	50.00
—One record of "X222"					
❑ X-4090	Have You Heard/Almost Always//Purple Shades/Your Cheatin' Heart	1954	12.50	25.00	50.00
—One record of "X234"					
❑ X-4091	Why Don't You Believe Me/Is It Any Wonder//Wishing Ring/My Love, My Love	1954	12.50	25.00	50.00
—One record of "X234"					

JAMES, RICK

A&M

Number	Title (A Side/B Side)	Yr	VG	VG+	NM
❑ 1615	Funkin' Around/My Mama	1974	6.25	12.50	25.00

GORDY

Number	Title (A Side/B Side)	Yr	VG	VG+	NM
❑ 1619	Dance Wit' Me — Part 1/Dance Wit' Me — Part 2	1982	—	2.00	4.00
❑ 1619 [PS]	Dance Wit' Me — Part 1/Dance Wit' Me — Part 2	1982	—	2.50	5.00
❑ 1634	Hard to Get/My Love	1982	—	2.00	4.00
❑ 1646	She Blew My Mind (69 Times)/(B-side unknown)	1982	—	2.00	4.00
❑ 1658	Teardrops/Throwdown	1983	—	2.00	4.00
❑ 1687	Cold Blooded/(Instrumental)	1983	—	2.00	4.00
❑ 1703	U Bring the Freak Out/He Talks	1983	—	2.00	4.00
❑ 1714	Ebony Eyes/1,2,3	1983	—	2.50	5.00
—As "Rick James and Friend"					
❑ 1714	Ebony Eyes/1,2,3	1983	—	2.00	4.00
—As "Rick James and Smokey Robinson"					
❑ 1730	17/(Instrumental)	1984	—	2.00	4.00
❑ 1763	You Turn Me On/Fire and Desire	1984	—	2.00	4.00
❑ 1776	Can't Stop/Oh What a Night	1985	—	2.00	4.00
❑ 1776 [PS]	Can't Stop/Oh What a Night	1985	—	2.50	5.00
❑ 1796	Glow/(Instrumental)	1985	—	2.00	4.00
❑ 1806	Spend the Night with Me/(Instrumental)	1985	—	2.00	4.00
❑ 7156	You & I/Hollywood	1978	—	2.50	5.00
❑ 7162	Mary Jane/Dream Maker	1978	—	2.50	5.00
❑ 7164	High on Your Love Suite/Stone City Band High	1979	—	2.50	5.00
❑ 7164 [PS]	High on Your Love Suite/Stone City Band High	1979	—	3.00	6.00
❑ 7167	Bustin' Out/Sexy Lady	1979	—	2.50	5.00
❑ 7171	Fool on the Street/Jefferson Hall	1979	—	2.50	5.00
❑ 7176	Love Gun/Stormy Love	1979	—	2.50	5.00
❑ 7177	Come Into My Life (Part 1)/Come Into My Life (Part 2)	1980	—	2.50	5.00
❑ 7185	Big Time/Island Lady	1980	—	2.50	5.00
❑ 7191	Gettin' it On (In the Summertime)/Summer Love	1980	—	2.50	5.00
❑ 7197	Give It to Me Baby/Don't Give Up on Love	1981	—	2.00	4.00
❑ 7205	Super Freak (Part 1)/Super Freak (Part 2)	1981	—	2.00	4.00
❑ 7215	Ghetto Life/Below the Funk (Pass the J)	1981	—	2.00	4.00

MOTOWN

Number	Title (A Side/B Side)	Yr	VG	VG+	NM
❑ 1844	Sweet and Sexy Thing/(Instrumental)	1986	—	—	3.00
❑ 1862	Forever and a Day/(Instrumental)	1986	—	—	3.00

REPRISE

Number	Title (A Side/B Side)	Yr	VG	VG+	NM
❑ 27764	Sexual Love Affair/In the Girls' Room	1988	—	—	3.00
❑ 27828	Wonderful/(Instrumental)	1988	—	—	3.00
❑ 27828 [PS]	Wonderful/(Instrumental)	1988	—	—	3.00
❑ 27885	Loosey's Rap/(Instrumental)	1988	—	—	3.00
—With Roxanne Shante					
❑ 27885 [PS]	Loosey's Rap/(Instrumental)	1988	—	—	3.00

WARNER BROS.

Number	Title (A Side/B Side)	Yr	VG	VG+	NM
❑ 27763	This Magic Moment-Dance with Me/(Instrumental)	1989	—	—	3.00
❑ 27763 [PS]	This Magic Moment-Dance with Me/(Instrumental)	1989	—	—	3.00

JAMES, SONNY

CAPITOL

Number	Title (A Side/B Side)	Yr	VG	VG+	NM
❑ 2067	A World of Our Own/An Old Sweetheart of Mine	1967	2.50	5.00	10.00
❑ 2067 [PS]	A World of Our Own/An Old Sweetheart of Mine	1967	3.75	7.50	15.00
❑ 2155	Heaven Says Hello/Fairy Tales	1968	2.50	5.00	10.00
❑ 2155 [PS]	Heaven Says Hello/Fairy Tales	1968	3.75	7.50	15.00
❑ F2164	Short Cut/It's So Nice to Make Up	1952	6.25	12.50	25.00
❑ F2259	That's Me Without You/Cool, Cold and Colder	1952	6.25	12.50	25.00
❑ 2271	Born to Be With You/In Waikiki	1968	2.50	5.00	10.00
❑ 2271 [PS]	Born to Be With You/In Waikiki	1968	3.00	6.00	12.00
❑ 2370	Only the Lonely/The Journey	1968	2.50	5.00	10.00
❑ 2370 [PS]	Only the Lonely/The Journey	1968	3.00	6.00	12.00
❑ F2399	The One I Can't Forget/Somebody's Heartache	1953	6.25	12.50	25.00
❑ 2486	Running Bear/Midnight Mood	1969	2.50	5.00	10.00
❑ 2486 [PS]	Running Bear/Midnight Mood	1969	3.00	6.00	12.00
❑ F2508	I Forgot More Than You'll Ever Know/Poor Boy, Rich Lovin'	1953	6.25	12.50	25.00
❑ 2595	Since I Met You, Baby/Clinging to a Hope	1969	2.50	5.00	10.00
❑ 2595 [PS]	Since I Met You, Baby/Clinging to a Hope	1969	3.00	6.00	12.00
❑ F2641	Won't Somebody Tell Me/My Greatest Thrill	1953	6.25	12.50	25.00
❑ 2700	It's Just a Matter of Time/This World of Ours	1969	2.50	5.00	10.00
❑ 2700 [PS]	It's Just a Matter of Time/This World of Ours	1969	3.00	6.00	12.00
❑ F2734	I've Always Wanted You/That's How I Need You	1954	6.25	12.50	25.00
❑ 2782	My Love/Blue for You	1970	2.00	4.00	8.00
❑ 2782 [PS]	My Love/Blue for You	1970	2.50	5.00	10.00
❑ F2829	Table Next to Mine/Believe Another's Lips	1954	6.25	12.50	25.00
❑ 2834	Don't Keep Me Hangin' On/Woodbine Valley	1970	2.00	4.00	8.00
❑ 2834 [PS]	Don't Keep Me Hangin' On/Woodbine Valley	1970	2.50	5.00	10.00
❑ F2906	She Done Give Her Heart to Me/Oceans of Tears	1954	6.25	12.50	25.00
❑ 2914	Endlessly/Happy Memories	1970	2.00	4.00	8.00
❑ 2914 [PS]	Endlessly/Happy Memories	1970	2.50	5.00	10.00
❑ F2958	Christmas in My Home Town/I Forgot to Remember Santa Claus	1954	7.50	15.00	30.00
❑ 3015	Empty Arms/Everything Begins and Ends with You	1971	2.00	4.00	8.00

Number	Title (A Side/B Side)	Yr	VG	VG+	NM
❑ 3015 [PS]	Empty Arms/Everything Begins and Ends with You	1971	2.50	5.00	10.00
❑ F3025	Lovin' Season/This Kiss Must Last Forever	1955	6.25	12.50	25.00
❑ F3112	Deceive Me Once Again/Ain't Gonna Take No Chance	1955	6.25	12.50	25.00
❑ 3114	Bright Lights, Big City/True Love Lasts Forever	1971	2.00	4.00	8.00
❑ 3114 [PS]	Bright Lights, Big City/True Love Lasts Forever	1971	2.50	5.00	10.00
❑ F3163	Til the Last Leaf Shall Fall/You Don't Have to Walk Alone	1955	6.25	12.50	25.00
❑ 3174	Here Comes Honey Again/The Only Ones We Truly Hurt	1971	2.00	4.00	8.00
❑ 3174 [PS]	Here Comes Honey Again/The Only Ones We Truly Hurt	1971	2.50	5.00	10.00
❑ F3198	Too Much/Let's Go Bunny Huggin'	1955	6.25	12.50	25.00
❑ 3232	Only Love Can Break a Heart/He Has Walked This Way Before	1971	2.00	4.00	8.00
❑ 3232 [PS]	Only Love Can Break a Heart/He Has Walked This Way Before	1971	2.50	5.00	10.00
❑ F3281	Careless with My Heart/Pigtails and Ribbons	1955	6.25	12.50	25.00
❑ 3322	That's Why I Love You Like I Do/Still Water Runs Deep	1972	2.00	4.00	8.00
❑ F3357	For Rent (One Empty Heart)/My Stolen Love	1956	5.00	10.00	20.00
❑ 3398	Traces/I'm in Love with You	1972	—	3.50	7.00
❑ F3441	Twenty Feet of Muddy Water/All Mixed Up	1956	5.00	10.00	20.00
❑ 3475	Downfall of Me/I'll Follow You	1972	—	3.50	7.00
❑ F3542	The Cat Came Back/Hello, Old Broken Heart	1956	5.00	10.00	20.00
❑ 3564	Reach Out Your Hand and Touch Me/Just Keep Thinking of Me	1973	—	3.50	7.00
❑ F3602	Young Love/You're the Reason I'm in Love	1956	5.50	11.00	22.00
❑ 3653	Heaven on Earth/She Believes in Me	1973	—	3.50	7.00
❑ F3674	First Date, First Kiss, First Love/Speak to Me	1957	5.00	10.00	20.00
❑ F3734	Lovesick Blues/Dear Love	1957	5.00	10.00	20.00
❑ 3779	Surprise, Surprise/What Am I Living For	1973	—	3.50	7.00
❑ F3792	Love Conquered/Mighty Loveable Man	1957	5.00	10.00	20.00
❑ F3840	Uh Huh-mm/Why Can't They Remember	1957	5.00	10.00	20.00
❑ F3888	Kathleen/Walk to the Dance	1958	5.00	10.00	20.00
❑ 3931	All the Way Together/Clinging Vine	1974	—	3.00	6.00
❑ F3962	Are You Mine/Let's Play Love	1958	5.00	10.00	20.00
❑ F4020	You Got That Touch/I Can See It in Your Eyes	1958	5.00	10.00	20.00
❑ F4066	Let Me Be the One to Love You/I Can't Stay Away from You	1958	5.00	10.00	20.00
❑ F4127	Yo-Yo/Dream Big	1959	5.00	10.00	20.00
❑ F4178	Talk of the School/The Table	1959	5.00	10.00	20.00
❑ F4229	Pure Love/This Love of Mine	1959	5.00	10.00	20.00
❑ F4268	Who's Next in Line/Red Mud	1959	5.00	10.00	20.00
❑ F4268 [PS]	Who's Next in Line/Red Mud	1959	10.00	20.00	40.00
❑ 4307	Till Tomorrow/I Forgot More Than You'll Ever Know	1959	5.00	10.00	20.00
❑ 4969	The Minute You're Gone/Gold and Silver	1963	3.00	6.00	12.00
❑ 5057	Going Through the Motions (Of Living)/Bad Times a-Comin'	1963	3.00	6.00	12.00
❑ 5129	Baltimore/Least of All You	1964	3.00	6.00	12.00
❑ 5197	Ask Marie/Sugar Lump	1964	3.00	6.00	12.00
❑ 5280	You're the Only World I Know/Tying Pieces Together	1964	3.00	6.00	12.00
❑ 5280	You're the Only World I Know/Tying Pieces Together	1964	5.00	10.00	20.00
❑ 5375	I'll Keep Holding On (Just to Your Love)/I'm Getting Gray from Being Blue	1965	3.00	6.00	12.00
❑ 5375 [PS]	I'll Keep Holding On (Just to Your Love)/I'm Getting Gray from Being Blue	1965	5.00	10.00	20.00
❑ 5454	Behind the Tear/Runnin'	1965	3.00	6.00	12.00
❑ 5454 [PS]	Behind the Tear/Runnin'	1965	5.00	10.00	20.00
❑ 5536	True Love's a Blessing/Just Ask Your Heart	1965	3.00	6.00	12.00
❑ 5536 [PS]	True Love's a Blessing/Just Ask Your Heart	1965	5.00	10.00	20.00
❑ 5612	Take Good Care of Her/On the Fingers of One Hand	1966	3.00	6.00	12.00
❑ 5612 [PS]	Take Good Care of Her/On the Fingers of One Hand	1966	5.00	10.00	20.00
❑ 5690	Room in Your Heart/How Many Times Can a Man Be a Fool	1966	3.00	6.00	12.00
❑ 5690 [PS]	Room in Your Heart/How Many Times Can a Man Be a Fool	1966	5.00	10.00	20.00
❑ 5733	My Christmas Dream/Barefoot Santa Claus	1966	3.00	6.00	12.00
❑ 5733 [PS]	My Christmas Dream/Barefoot Santa Claus	1966	5.00	10.00	20.00
❑ 5833	Need You/On and On	1967	3.00	6.00	12.00
❑ 5833 [PS]	Need You/On and On	1967	5.00	10.00	20.00
❑ 5914	I'll Never Find Another You/Goodbye, Maggie, Goodbye	1967	3.00	6.00	12.00
❑ 5914 [PS]	I'll Never Find Another You/Goodbye, Maggie, Goodbye	1967	3.75	7.50	15.00
❑ 5987	It's the Little Things/Don't Cut Timber on a Windy Day	1967	3.00	6.00	12.00
❑ 5987 [PS]	It's the Little Things/Don't Cut Timber on a Windy Day	1967	3.75	7.50	15.00
COLUMBIA					
❑ 3-10001	A Mi Esposa Con Amor (To My Wife with Love)/Just Don't Stop Lovin' Me	1974	—	2.50	5.00
❑ 3-10001 [PS]	A Mi Esposa Con Amor (To My Wife with Love)/Just Don't Stop Lovin' Me	1974	2.00	4.00	8.00
❑ 3-10072	A Little Bit South of Saskatoon/Home Style Lovin'	1974	—	2.50	5.00
❑ 3-10072 [PS]	A Little Bit South of Saskatoon/Home Style Lovin'	1974	2.00	4.00	8.00
❑ 3-10121	Little Band of Gold/Pop and Me	1975	—	2.50	5.00
❑ 3-10121 [PS]	Little Band of Gold/Pop and Me	1975	2.00	4.00	8.00
❑ 3-10139	Indian Love Call/Maria Elena	1975	—	2.50	5.00
—As "The Guitars of Sonny James"					
❑ 3-10184	What in the World's Come Over You/Walking the Railroad Trestle	1975	—	2.50	5.00
❑ 3-10184 [PS]	What in the World's Come Over You/Walking the Railroad Trestle	1975	—	3.00	6.00
❑ 3-10249	Eres Tu (Touch the Wind)/Apache	1975	—	2.50	5.00
❑ 3-10276	The Prisoner's Song/Back in the Saddle Again	1975	—	2.50	5.00
❑ 3-10276 [PS]	The Prisoner's Song/Back in the Saddle Again	1975	—	3.00	6.00

Number	Title (A Side/B Side)	Yr	VG	VG+	NM
❑ 3-10335	When Something Is Wrong with My Baby/Big Silver Bird	1976	—	2.50	5.00
❑ 3-10392	Come On In/Baby's Eyes	1976	—	2.50	5.00
❑ 3-10466	You're Free to Go/Puttin' On the Dog Tonight	1976	—	2.50	5.00
❑ 3-10551	In the Jailhouse Now/Amazing Grace	1977	—	2.50	5.00
❑ 3-10551 [PS]	In the Jailhouse Now/Amazing Grace	1977	—	2.50	5.00
❑ 3-10628	Abilene/Pistol Packin' Mama	1977	—	2.50	5.00
❑ 3-10703	This Is the Love/It'll Still Be Worth It All	1978	—	2.50	5.00
❑ 3-10703 [PS]	This Is the Love/It'll Still Be Worth It All	1978	—	3.00	6.00
❑ 3-10764	Caribbean/Each Time I Look at You	1978	—	2.50	5.00
❑ 3-10852	Building Memories/Little Band of Gold	1978	—	2.50	5.00
❑ 4-45644	When the Snow Is On the Roses/Love is a Rainbow	1972	—	3.50	7.00
❑ 4-45644 [PS]	When the Snow Is On the Roses/Love is a Rainbow	1972	2.50	5.00	10.00
❑ 4-45706	White Silver Sands/Why Is It I'm the Last to Know	1972	—	3.50	7.00
❑ 4-45770	I Love You More and More Everyday/I'll Think About That Tomorrow	1973	—	3.50	7.00
❑ 4-45770 [PS]	I Love You More and More Everyday/I'll Think About That Tomorrow	1973	2.50	5.00	10.00
❑ 4-45871	If She Just Helps Me Get Over You/I Won't Think About It Now	1973	—	3.00	6.00
❑ 4-46003	Is It Wrong (For Loving You)/Suddenly There's a Valley	1974	—	3.00	6.00
DIMENSION					
❑ 1026	Innocent Lies/Don't Let the Stars Get in Your Eyes	1981	—	2.50	5.00
❑ 1026 [PS]	Innocent Lies/Don't Let the Stars Get in Your Eyes	1981	2.00	4.00	8.00
❑ 1033	A Place in the Sun/Lean On Me Girl	1982	—	2.50	5.00
❑ 1033 [PS]	A Place in the Sun/Lean On Me Girl	1982	2.00	4.00	8.00
❑ 1036	I'm Looking Over the Rainbow/Something's Got a Hold on Me	1982	—	2.50	5.00
❑ 1036 [PS]	I'm Looking Over the Rainbow/Something's Got a Hold on Me	1982	2.00	4.00	8.00
❑ 1040	The Fool in Me/Little Rainbow	1982	—	2.50	5.00
❑ 1045	A Free Roamin' Mind/Don't Let the Stars Get In Your Eyes	1983	—	2.50	5.00
DOT					
❑ 16381	A Mile and a Quarter/Just One More Lie	1962	3.75	7.50	15.00
❑ 16419	On the Longest Day/The Only Cure	1963	3.75	7.50	15.00
GROOVE					
❑ 1	Young Love/Broken Wings	1961	5.00	10.00	20.00
MONUMENT					
❑ 45280	Hold What You've Got/Hanging On to Yesterday	1979	—	2.50	5.00
❑ 45280 [PS]	Hold What You've Got/Hanging On to Yesterday	1979	—	3.00	6.00
❑ 45288	Lorelei/If I Ever Wanted You	1979	—	2.50	5.00
NRC					
❑ 050	Jenny Lou/Passin' Through	1960	6.25	12.50	25.00
❑ 050 [PS]	Jenny Lou/Passin' Through	1960	12.50	25.00	50.00
❑ 056	Cold in the Morning/Wondering	1960	6.25	12.50	25.00
❑ 061	Bimbo/I Wish This Night Would Never End	1960	5.00	10.00	20.00
RCA VICTOR					
❑ 47-7858	Apache/Magnetism	1961	3.75	7.50	15.00
❑ 47-7919	Innocent Angel/Hey Little Ducky	1961	3.75	7.50	15.00
❑ 47-7998	The Day's Not Over Yet/The Legend of Brown Mountain Light	1962	3.75	7.50	15.00

7-Inch Extended Plays

Number	Title (A Side/B Side)	Yr	VG	VG+	NM
CAPITOL					
❑ SU-111 [PS]	Born to Be with You	1969	3.75	7.50	15.00
—Above "For Coin Operated Phonographs Only"					
❑ SU-111 [S]	(contents unknown)	1969	3.75	7.50	15.00
❑ EAP 1-779	Can't Get Over Missin' You/Cold, Cold Heart//Only One Heart to Give/I Got the Feeling	1957	5.00	10.00	20.00
❑ EAP 1-779 [PS]	Southern Gentleman, Part 1	1957	5.00	10.00	20.00
❑ EAP 2-779	I Wish I Knew/Forgive Me//I'll Always Wonder (But I'll Never Know)/Lonesome	1957	5.00	10.00	20.00
❑ EAP 2-779 [PS]	Southern Gentleman, Part 2	1957	5.00	10.00	20.00
❑ EAP 3-779	'Til the Last Leaf Shall Fall/Only a Shadow Between//May God Be With You/My God and I	1957	5.00	10.00	20.00
❑ EAP 3-779 [PS]	Southern Gentleman, Part 3	1957	5.00	10.00	20.00
❑ EAP 1-827	Young Love/Twenty Feet of Muddy Water//For Rent/Hello Old Broken Heart	1957	6.25	12.50	25.00
❑ EAP 1-827 [PS]	Young Love	1957	6.25	12.50	25.00

JAMES, TOMMY

Also see TOMMY JAMES AND THE SHONDELLS.

Number	Title (A Side/B Side)	Yr	VG	VG+	NM
21 RECORDS					
❑ 105	Two-Time Lover/Say Please	1983	—	—	3.00
❑ 105 [PS]	Two-Time Lover/Say Please	1983	—	2.00	4.00
FANTASY					
❑ 761	I Love You Love Me Love/Devil Gate Drive	1976	—	2.00	4.00
❑ 761 [PS]	I Love You Love Me Love/Devil Gate Drive	1976	—	2.50	5.00
❑ 776	Tighter, Tighter/Comin' Down	1976	—	2.50	5.00
❑ 811	Love Is Gonna Find a Way/I Don't Love You Anymore	1977	—	2.50	5.00
❑ 886	Tighter, Tighter/Comin' Down	1980	—	2.00	4.00
MCA					
❑ 40289	Glory, Glory/Comin' Down	1974	—	2.50	5.00
MILLENNIUM					
❑ YB-11785	Three Times in Love/I Just Wanna Play the Music	1980	—	2.00	4.00
❑ YB-11787	No Hay Dos Sin Tres (Three Times in Love)/I Just Wanna Play the Music	1980	—	2.50	5.00
❑ YB-11787 [PS]	No Hay Dos Sin Tres (Three Times in Love)/I Just Wanna Play the Music	1980	2.50	5.00	10.00
❑ YB-11788	It's Alright (For Now)/You Got Me	1980	—	2.00	4.00
❑ YB-11802	You're So Easy to Love/Halfway to Heaven	1981	—	2.00	4.00
❑ YB-11814	The Lady in White/Payin' for My Lover's Mistake	1981	—	2.00	4.00
ROULETTE					
❑ 7084	Ball and Chain/Candy Maker	1970	—	3.00	6.00
❑ 7093	Church Street Soul Revival/Draggin' the Line	1970	2.00	4.00	8.00
❑ 7100	Adrienne/Light of Day	1971	—	3.00	6.00
❑ 7103	Draggin' the Line/Bits & Pieces	1971	—	3.00	6.00

Number	Title (A Side/B Side)	Yr	VG	VG+	NM
❑ 7110	I'm Coming Home/Sing, Sing, Sing	1971	—	2.50	5.00
❑ 7114	Nothing to Hide/Walk a Country Mile	1971	—	2.50	5.00
❑ 7119	Tell 'Em Willie Boy's A-Comin'/Forty Days and Dorty Nights	1972	—	2.50	5.00
❑ 7126	Cat's Eye in the Window/Dark Is the Night	1972	—	2.50	5.00
❑ 7130	Love Song/Kingston Highway	1972	—	2.50	5.00
❑ 7135	Celebration/The Last One to Know	1972	—	2.50	5.00
❑ 7140	Boo, Boo, Don't Cha Be Blue/Rings and Things	1973	—	2.50	5.00
❑ 7147	Calico/Hey, My Lady	1973	—	2.50	5.00

JAMES, TOMMY, AND THE SHONDELLS

Also see HOG HEAVEN; TOMMY JAMES.

Number	Title (A Side/B Side)	Yr	VG	VG+	NM
PHILCO-FORD					
❑ HP-1	Mirage/I Think We're Alone Now	1967	3.75	7.50	15.00
—4-inch plastic "Hip Pocket Record" with color sleeve					
❑ HP-2	Hanky Panky/Gettin' Together	1967	3.75	7.50	15.00
—4-inch plastic "Hip Pocket Record" with color sleeve					
RED FOX					
❑ 110	Hanky Panky/Thunderbolt	1966	10.00	20.00	40.00
—As "The Shondells"					
ROULETTE					
❑ 4686	Hanky Panky/Thunderbolt	1966	2.50	5.00	10.00
❑ 4695	Say I Am (What I Am)/Lots of Pretty Girls	1966	2.00	4.00	8.00
❑ 4695 [PS]	Say I Am (What I Am)/Lots of Pretty Girls	1966	3.75	7.50	15.00
❑ 4710	It's Only Love/Don't Let My Love Pass You By	1966	2.00	4.00	8.00
❑ 4710	It's Only Love/Ya Ya	1966	3.00	6.00	12.00
❑ 4720	I Think We're Alone Now/Gone, Gone, Gone	1967	2.50	5.00	10.00
❑ 4720 [PS]	I Think We're Alone Now/Gone, Gone, Gone	1967	3.75	7.50	15.00
❑ 4736	Mirage/Run, Run, Baby, Run	1967	2.00	4.00	8.00
❑ 4736 [PS]	Mirage/Run, Run, Baby, Run	1967	3.75	7.50	15.00
❑ 4756	I Like the Way/(Baby) Baby I Can't Take It No More	1967	2.00	4.00	8.00
❑ 4762	Gettin' Together/Real Girl	1967	2.00	4.00	8.00
❑ 4762 [PS]	Gettin' Together/Real Girl	1967	3.75	7.50	15.00
❑ 4775	Out of the Blue/Love's Closin' In on Me	1967	2.00	4.00	8.00
❑ 7000	Get Out Now/Wish It Were True	1968	2.00	4.00	8.00
❑ 7008	Mony Mony/One Two Three and I Fell	1968	2.50	5.00	10.00
❑ 7016	Somebody Cares/Do Unto Me	1968	2.00	4.00	8.00
❑ 7024	Do Something to Me/Ginger Bread Man	1968	2.00	4.00	8.00
❑ 7028	Crimson and Clover/(I'm) Taken	1968	3.75	7.50	15.00
❑ 7028	Crimson and Clover/Some Kind of Love	1968	2.50	5.00	10.00
❑ 7039	Sweet Cherry Wine/Breakaway	1969	2.00	4.00	8.00
❑ 7050	Crystal Blue Persuasion/I'm Alive	1969	2.50	5.00	10.00
❑ 7060	Ball of Fire/Makin' Good Time	1969	2.00	4.00	8.00
❑ 7066	She/Loved One	1969	2.00	4.00	8.00
❑ 7071	Gotta Get Back to You/Red Rover	1970	2.00	4.00	8.00
❑ 7076	Come to Me/Talkin' and Signifyin'	1970	2.00	4.00	8.00
SNAP					
❑ 102	Hanky Panky/Thunderbolt	1963	20.00	40.00	80.00
—As "The Shondells"; no mention of Red Fox Records on label					
❑ 102	Hanky Panky/Thunderbolt	1966	7.50	15.00	30.00
—As "The Shondells"; with "Dist. by Red Fox Records, Pgh, Pa." on label					

JAMES GANG, THE (1)

Also see TOMMY BOLIN; JOE WALSH.

Number	Title (A Side/B Side)	Yr	VG	VG+	NM
ABC					
❑ 11272	Funk #49/Thanks	1970	—	3.00	6.00
❑ 11301	Walk Away/Yadig?	1971	—	3.00	6.00
❑ 11312	White Man—Black Man/Midnight	1971	—	3.00	6.00
❑ 11325	Looking for My Lady/Hairy Hypochondriac	1972	—	3.00	6.00
❑ 11336	Had Enough/Kick Back Man	1972	—	3.00	6.00
ATCO					
❑ 6953	Must Be Love/Got No Time for Trouble	1974	—	2.50	5.00
❑ 6966	Standing in the Rain/From Another Time	1974	—	2.50	5.00
❑ 7006	Cruisin' Down the Highway/Miami Two-Step	1974	—	2.50	5.00
❑ 7021	Merry Go Round/Red Satin Lover	1975	—	2.50	5.00
❑ 7067	I Need Love/Feelin' Alright	1975	—	2.50	5.00
BLUESWAY					
❑ 61027	I Don't Have the Time/Fred	1969	2.00	4.00	8.00
❑ 61030	Funk #48/Collage	1969	2.50	5.00	10.00
❑ 61033	Take a Look Around/Stop	1970	2.00	4.00	8.00

JAMES GANG, THE (2)

Number	Title (A Side/B Side)	Yr	VG	VG+	NM
ASCOT					
❑ 2168	Everybody Knows/Ladies' Man	1965	3.00	6.00	12.00
❑ 2196	Georgia Pines/Baby Take Me Back	1965	3.00	6.00	12.00
❑ 2205	Right String But the Wrong Yo-Yo/Satin and Lace	1966	3.00	6.00	12.00

JAMESON, BOBBY

Number	Title (A Side/B Side)	Yr	VG	VG+	NM
CURRENT					
❑ 103	All Alone/Your Sweet Lovin'	1964	3.00	6.00	12.00
LONDON					
❑ 9730	All I Want Is My Baby/Each and Everyday	1965	10.00	20.00	40.00

JAMIE AND JANE

"Jamie" is GENE PITNEY.

Number	Title (A Side/B Side)	Yr	VG	VG+	NM
DECCA					
❑ 30862	Snuggle Up Baby/Strollin' Thru the Park	1959	7.50	15.00	30.00
❑ 30934	Faithful Our Love/Classical Rock and Roll	1959	7.50	15.00	30.00

JAMIES, THE

Number	Title (A Side/B Side)	Yr	VG	VG+	NM
EPIC					
❑ 9281	Summertime, Summertime/Searching for You	1958	3.00	6.00	12.00
—Reissued in 1962 with the same catalog number and label design					
❑ 9281 [PS]	Summertime, Summertime/Searching for You	1958	5.00	10.00	20.00
❑ 9299	When the Sun Goes Down/Snow Train	1958	5.00	10.00	20.00
❑ 9565	When the Sun Goes Down/Snow Train	1963	3.00	6.00	12.00
❑ 11129	Summertime, Summertime/Searching for You	1974	—	2.50	5.00
UNITED ARTISTS					
❑ 193	The Evening Star/Don't Darken My Door	1959	5.00	10.00	20.00

JAN AND ARNIE

Also see JAN AND DEAN.

Number	Title (A Side/B Side)	Yr	VG	VG+	NM
ARWIN					
❑ 108	Jennie Lee/Gotta Getta Date	1958	10.00	20.00	40.00
❑ 111	Gas Money/Bonnie Lou	1958	10.00	20.00	40.00
❑ 113	I Love Linda/The Beat That Can't Be Beat	1958	15.00	30.00	60.00
DORE					
❑ 522	Baby Talk/Jeannette Get Your Hair Done	1959	150.00	300.00	600.00
—Actually by Jan and Dean, but incorrectly credited					
DOT					
❑ 16116	Gas Money/Gotta Getta Date	1960	12.50	25.00	50.00
7-Inch Extended Plays					
DOT					
❑ DEP-1097	Jennie Lee/Gas Money//Gotta Getta Date/The Beat That Can't Be Beat	1960	125.00	250.00	500.00
❑ DEP-1097 [PS]	Jan and Arnie	1960	125.00	250.00	500.00

JAN AND DEAN

Also see JAN BERRY; JAN AND ARNIE; THE LEGENDARY MASKED SURFERS; THE RALLY PACKS.

Number	Title (A Side/B Side)	Yr	VG	VG+	NM
CHALLENGE					
❑ 9111	Heart and Soul/Those Words	1961	10.00	20.00	40.00
❑ 9111	Heart and Soul/A Midsummer Night's Dream	1961	5.00	10.00	20.00
❑ 9120	Wanted: One Girl/Something a Little Bit Different	1961	7.50	15.00	30.00
COLUMBIA					
❑ 44036	Yellow Balloon/Taste of Rain	1967	7.50	15.00	30.00
DORE					
❑ 522	Baby Talk/Jeannette Get Your Hair Done	1959	7.50	15.00	30.00
❑ 531	There's a Girl/My Heart Sings	1959	6.25	12.50	25.00
❑ 539	Clementine/You're On My Mind	1960	6.25	12.50	25.00
❑ 548	Cindy/Whiter Tennis Sneakers	1960	6.25	12.50	25.00
❑ 555	We Go Together/Rosilane	1960	6.25	12.50	25.00
❑ 555	We Go Together/Rosie Lane	1960	6.25	12.50	25.00
—B-side title was altered after the record no longer was issued with picture sleeve					
❑ 555 [PS]	We Go Together/Rosilane	1960	30.00	60.00	120.00
❑ 576	Gee/Such a Good Night to Be Together	1960	6.25	12.50	25.00
❑ 576 [PS]	Gee/Such a Good Night to Be Together	1960	75.00	150.00	300.00
❑ 583	Baggy Pants/Judy's an Angel	1961	7.50	15.00	30.00
❑ 610	Julie/Don't Fly Away	1961	7.50	15.00	30.00
EVATONE					
❑ 7801X	Surf Bunkey	1980	2.00	4.00	8.00
—6-inch red flexi-disc; Dutch version of "Surf City"					
JAN & DEAN					
❑ 10	Hawaii/Tijuana	1966	18.75	37.50	75.00
❑ 11	Fan Tan/Love and Hate	1966	30.00	60.00	120.00
J&D					
❑ 001	California Lullabye/Summertime	1966	7.50	15.00	30.00
❑ 402	Like a Summer Rain/Louiciana Man	1966	7.50	15.00	30.00
❑ 1271 [DJ]	Ocean Park Angel/Wipe Out	1981	2.50	5.00	10.00
—B-side by the Surfaris					
LIBERTY					
❑ S7-19770	Frosty (The Snow Man)/Rudolph the Red-Nosed Reindeer	1997	—	—	3.00
—B-side by the Ventures on Dolton					
❑ 55397	A Sunday Kind of Love/Poor Little Puppet	1961	6.25	12.50	25.00
❑ 55454	Tennessee/Your Heart Has Changed Its Mind	1962	6.25	12.50	25.00
❑ 55496	Who Put the Bomp/My Favorite Dream	1962	12.50	25.00	50.00
❑ 55522	Frosty (The Snow Man)/(She's Still Talking) Baby Talk	1962	37.50	75.00	150.00
—Promos worth about half this value					
❑ 55531	Linda/When I Learn How to Cry	1963	6.25	12.50	25.00
❑ 55580	Surf City/She's My Summer Girl	1963	3.75	7.50	15.00
❑ 55580 [PS]	Surf City/She's My Summer Girl	1963	10.00	20.00	40.00
❑ 55613	Honolulu Lulu/Someday	1963	3.75	7.50	15.00
❑ 55613 [PS]	Honolulu Lulu/Someday	1963	10.00	20.00	40.00
❑ 55641	Drag City/Schlock Rod (Part 1)	1963	3.75	7.50	15.00
❑ 55641 [PS]	Drag City/Schlock Rod (Part 1)	1963	10.00	20.00	40.00
❑ 55672	Dead Man's Curve/The New Girl in School	1964	3.75	7.50	15.00
❑ 55672 [PS]	Dead Man's Curve/The New Girl in School	1964	10.00	20.00	40.00
❑ 55704	The Little Old Lady (From Pasadena)/My Mighty G.T.O.	1964	3.75	7.50	15.00
❑ 55704 [PS]	The Little Old Lady (From Pasadena)/My Mighty G.T.O.	1964	10.00	20.00	40.00
❑ 55724	Ride the Wild Surf/The Anaheim, Azusa and Cucamonga Sewing Circle, Book Review and Timing Association	1964	3.75	7.50	15.00
❑ 55724 [PS]	Ride the Wild Surf/The Anaheim, Azusa and Cucamonga Sewing Circle, Book Review and Timing Association	1964	10.00	20.00	40.00
❑ 55727	Sidewalk Surfin'/When It's Over	1964	3.75	7.50	15.00
❑ 55727 [PS]	Sidewalk Surfin'/When It's Over	1964	10.00	20.00	40.00
❑ 55766	(Here They Come) From All Over the World/Freeway Flyer	1965	3.00	6.00	12.00
❑ 55766 [PS]	(Here They Come) From All Over the World/Freeway Flyer	1965	50.00	100.00	200.00
❑ 55792	You Really Know How to Hurt a Guy/It's As Easy As 1-2-3	1965	3.00	6.00	12.00
❑ 55792 [PS]	You Really Know How to Hurt a Guy/It's As Easy As 1-2-3	1965	7.50	15.00	30.00
❑ 55816	It's a Shame to Say Goodbye/The Submarine Races	1965	—	—	—
—Unreleased					
❑ 55833	I Found a Girl/It's a Shame to Say Goodbye	1965	3.00	6.00	12.00
❑ 55849	Folk City/A Beginning from an End	1965	3.00	6.00	12.00
❑ 55849 [PS]	Folk City/A Beginning from an End	1965	7.50	15.00	30.00
❑ 55856	Norwegian Wood/I Can't Wait to Love You	1966	—	—	—
—Unreleased					
❑ 55860	Batman/Bucket "T"	1966	6.25	12.50	25.00
❑ 55886	Popsicle/Norwegian Wood	1966	3.00	6.00	12.00
❑ 55905	Fiddle Around/Surfer's Dream	1966	3.00	6.00	12.00
❑ 55923	The New Girl in School/School Days	1966	3.00	6.00	12.00

MAGIC LAMP

Number	Title (A Side/B Side)	Yr	VG	VG+	NM
❑ 401	California Lullabye/Summertime	1966	7.50	15.00	30.00

ODE

Number	Title (A Side/B Side)	Yr	VG	VG+	NM
❑ 66111	Fun City/Totally Wild	1975	6.25	12.50	25.00

UNITED ARTISTS

Number	Title (A Side/B Side)	Yr	VG	VG+	NM
❑ 0089	Jennie Lee/Baby Talk	1973	3.75	7.50	15.00
❑ 0090	Linda/The New Girl in School	1973	3.75	7.50	15.00
❑ 0091	Surf City/Ride the Wild Surf	1973	3.75	7.50	15.00
❑ 0092	Dead Man's Curve/Drag City	1973	3.75	7.50	15.00
❑ 0093	Honolulu Lulu/Sidewalk Surfin'	1973	3.75	7.50	15.00
❑ 0094	The Little Old Lady (From Pasadena)/Popsicle	1973	3.75	7.50	15.00

—0089 through 0094 are "Silver Spotlight Series" reissues

Number	Title (A Side/B Side)	Yr	VG	VG+	NM
❑ XW670	Sidewalk Surfin'/Gonna Hustle You	1975	3.75	7.50	15.00
❑ 50859	Jennie Lee/Vegetables	1971	3.75	7.50	15.00
❑ 50859 [PS]	Jennie Lee/Vegetables	1971	6.25	12.50	25.00

WARNER BROS.

Number	Title (A Side/B Side)	Yr	VG	VG+	NM
❑ 7151	Only a Boy/Love and Hate	1967	10.00	20.00	40.00
❑ 7219	Laurel and Hardy/I Know My Mind	1968	12.50	25.00	50.00
❑ 7240 [DJ]	In the Still of the Night/Girl, You're Blowing My Mind	1968	20.00	40.00	80.00

—Stock copy may not exist

7-Inch Extended Plays

SUNDAZED

Number	Title (A Side/B Side)	Yr	VG	VG+	NM
❑ SEP 125	Yellow Balloon/Raindrops//California Lullaby/Here Comes the Rain	1996	—	—	2.50

—Light blue marbled vinyl; instrumental versions of songs on the reissue of the "Save for a Rainy Day" LP

Number	Title (A Side/B Side)	Yr	VG	VG+	NM
❑ SEP 125 [PS]	Sounds for a Rainy Day	1996	—	—	2.50

JANE'S ADDICTION

WARNER BROS.

Number	Title (A Side/B Side)	Yr	VG	VG+	NM
❑ 27520	Mountain Song/Standing in the Shower...Thinking	1989	2.50	5.00	10.00
❑ 27520 [PS]	Mountain Song/Standing in the Shower...Thinking	1989	2.50	5.00	10.00

JAPANESE BEATLES, THE

GOLDEN CREST

Number	Title (A Side/B Side)	Yr	VG	VG+	NM
❑ 584	The Beatle Song (Japanese Style) (Part 1)/The Beatle Song (Japanese Style) (Part 2)	1964	5.00	10.00	20.00

JARMELS, THE

LAURIE

Number	Title (A Side/B Side)	Yr	VG	VG+	NM
❑ 3085	Little Lonely One/She Loves to Dance	1961	3.75	7.50	15.00
❑ 3098	A Little Bit of Soap/The Way You Look Tonight	1961	5.00	10.00	20.00
❑ 3116	I'll Follow You/Gee Oh Gosh	1962	3.75	7.50	15.00
❑ 3124	Red Sails in the Sunset/Loneliness	1962	3.75	7.50	15.00
❑ 3142	Little Bug/One By One	1962	3.75	7.50	15.00
❑ 3174	Come On Girl/Keep Your Mind on Me	1963	3.75	7.50	15.00

JARVIS, FELTON

ABC-PARAMOUNT

Number	Title (A Side/B Side)	Yr	VG	VG+	NM
❑ 10570	Be-I-Bye/Ski King	1964	3.75	7.50	15.00
❑ 10610	Honky Tonk Song/Everybody's Going to the Party	1964	3.75	7.50	15.00
❑ 10641	Too Many Tigers/Knuckie, Knuckie	1965	3.75	7.50	15.00

MGM

Number	Title (A Side/B Side)	Yr	VG	VG+	NM
❑ 12982	Indian Love Call/Goin' Downtown	1961	5.00	10.00	20.00

THUNDER INT'L.

Number	Title (A Side/B Side)	Yr	VG	VG+	NM
❑ 1023	Swingin' Cat/Honest John the Workin' Man's Friend	1960	25.00	50.00	100.00

VIVA

Number	Title (A Side/B Side)	Yr	VG	VG+	NM
❑ 1001	Don't Knock Elvis/Honest John	1959	10.00	20.00	40.00

JAXON, BOB

20TH CENTURY FOX

Number	Title (A Side/B Side)	Yr	VG	VG+	NM
❑ 441	Weep, Mary, Weep/Do the People	1963	2.50	5.00	10.00

ABC-PARAMOUNT

Number	Title (A Side/B Side)	Yr	VG	VG+	NM
❑ 10364	It's a Cruel, Cruel Thing/One Way to Love Me	1962	3.00	6.00	12.00

CADENCE

Number	Title (A Side/B Side)	Yr	VG	VG+	NM
❑ 1264	Ali Baba/Why Does a Woman Cry	1955	3.75	7.50	15.00

RCA VICTOR

Number	Title (A Side/B Side)	Yr	VG	VG+	NM
❑ 47-6945	Beach Party/I'm Hangin' Around	1957	3.75	7.50	15.00
❑ 47-7006	(Gotta Have Something in the) Bank Frank/Come On Down	1957	5.00	10.00	20.00
❑ 47-7106	Declaration of Love/I'm Hurtin' Inside	1957	3.75	7.50	15.00
❑ 47-7168	Me! Please! Me!/All About Me	1958	3.75	7.50	15.00
❑ 47-7232	For the Love of You/(Well It's) No Lie	1958	3.75	7.50	15.00

JAY, IRA

SUN

Number	Title (A Side/B Side)	Yr	VG	VG+	NM
❑ 351	You Don't Love Me/More Than Anything	1960	5.00	10.00	20.00

JAY, JERRY

California DJ, better known as Jerry Osborne.

QUALITY

Number	Title (A Side/B Side)	Yr	VG	VG+	NM
❑ 201	The King's Country/Merry Christmas To You	1966	50.00	100.00	200.00

JAY, PETER, AND THE JAYWALKERS

WAND

Number	Title (A Side/B Side)	Yr	VG	VG+	NM
❑ 180	What's Easy/Parchment Farm	1965	2.50	5.00	10.00

JAY AND THE AMERICANS

Also see JAY BLACK; JAY TRAYNOR.

EEOC

Number	Title (A Side/B Side)	Yr	VG	VG+	NM
❑ 1140	Things Are Changing/Things Are Changing	1965	37.50	75.00	150.00
❑ 1140 [PS]	Things Are Changing/Things Are Changing	1965	37.50	75.00	150.00

—Promotional item for the Equal Employment Opportunity Commission

UNITED ARTISTS

Number	Title (A Side/B Side)	Yr	VG	VG+	NM
❑ 0026	She Cried/Come a Little Bit Closer	1973	—	2.50	5.00
❑ 0027	Cara Mia/Let's Lock the Door (And Throw Away the Key)	1973	—	2.50	5.00
❑ 0028	This Magic Moment/Walking in the Rain	1973	—	2.50	5.00

—0026, 0027, 0028 are "Silver Spotlight Series" reissues

Number	Title (A Side/B Side)	Yr	VG	VG+	NM
❑ 353	Tonight/The Other Girls	1961	3.00	6.00	12.00
❑ 415	She Cried/Dawning	1962	3.75	7.50	15.00
❑ 479	It's My Turn to Cry/This Is It	1962	3.00	6.00	12.00
❑ 504	Tomorrow/Yes	1962	3.00	6.00	12.00
❑ 566	What's the Use/Strangers Tomorrow	1963	2.50	5.00	10.00
❑ 626	Only in America/My Clair De Lune	1963	2.50	5.00	10.00
❑ 669	Come Dance with Me/Look in My Eyes Maria	1963	2.50	5.00	10.00
❑ 693	To Wait for Love/Friday	1964	2.50	5.00	10.00
❑ 759	Come a Little Bit Closer/Goodbye Boys, Goodbye	1964	2.50	5.00	10.00
❑ 805	Let's Lock the Door (And Throw Away the Key)/I'll Remember You	1965	2.50	5.00	10.00
❑ 845	Think of the Good Times/If You Were Mine, Girl	1965	2.50	5.00	10.00
❑ 881	Cara Mia/When It's All Over	1965	2.50	5.00	10.00
❑ 919	Some Enchanted Evening/Girl	1965	2.50	5.00	10.00
❑ 919 [PS]	Some Enchanted Evening/Girl	1965	3.75	7.50	15.00
❑ 948	Sunday and Me/Through This Doorway	1965	2.50	5.00	10.00
❑ 948 [PS]	Sunday and Me/Through This Doorway	1965	12.50	25.00	50.00
❑ 992	Why Can't You Bring Me Home/Baby Stop Your Cryin'	1966	2.00	4.00	8.00
❑ 50016	Crying/I Don't Need a Friend	1966	2.00	4.00	8.00
❑ 50016 [PS]	Crying/I Don't Need a Friend	1966	3.00	6.00	12.00
❑ 50046	Livin' Above Your Head/Look at Me, What Do You See	1966	2.00	4.00	8.00
❑ 50046 [PS]	Livin' Above Your Head/Look at Me, What Do You See	1966	3.00	6.00	12.00
❑ 50086	Baby Come Home/Stop the Clock	1966	2.00	4.00	8.00
❑ 50094	(He's) Raining in My Sunshine/The Reason for Living (For You My Darling)	1966	2.00	4.00	8.00
❑ 50139	Nature Boy/You Ain't As Hip As All That, Baby	1967	2.00	4.00	8.00
❑ 50196	(We'll Meet in the) Yellow Forest/Got Hung Up Along the Way	1967	2.00	4.00	8.00
❑ 50222	Shanghai Noodle Factory/French Provincial	1967	2.00	4.00	8.00
❑ 50282	No Other Love/No, I Don't Know Her	1968	2.00	4.00	8.00
❑ 50448	You Ain't Gonna Wake Up Cryin'/Gemini	1968	2.00	4.00	8.00
❑ 50475	This Magic Moment/Since I Don't Have You	1969	3.00	6.00	12.00
❑ 50510	When You Dance/No, I Don't Know Her	1969	—	3.00	6.00
❑ 50535	Hushabye/Gypsy Woman	1969	—	3.00	6.00
❑ 50567	(I'd Kill) For the Love of a Lady/Learnin' How to Fly	1969	—	3.00	6.00
❑ 50605	Walkin' in the Rain/(I'd Kill) For the Love of a Lady	1969	2.00	4.00	8.00
❑ 50654	Do You Ever Think of Me/Capture the Moment	1970	—	3.00	6.00
❑ 50683	Do I Love You?/Tricia (Tell Your Daddy)	1970	—	3.00	6.00
❑ 50858	There Goes My Baby/Solitary Man	1971	—	3.00	6.00

JAY AND THE DELTAS

WARNER BROS.

Number	Title (A Side/B Side)	Yr	VG	VG+	NM
❑ 5404	Bells Are Ringing/Super Hawk	1964	12.50	25.00	50.00

JAY AND THE TECHNIQUES

EVENT

Number	Title (A Side/B Side)	Yr	VG	VG+	NM
❑ 222	I Feel Love Coming On/World of Mine	1975	—	2.50	5.00
❑ 228	Number Onederful/Don't Forget to Ask	1975	—	2.50	5.00

GORDY

Number	Title (A Side/B Side)	Yr	VG	VG+	NM
❑ 7123	I'll Be Here/Robot Man	1973	—	3.00	6.00

PHILCO-FORD

Number	Title (A Side/B Side)	Yr	VG	VG+	NM
❑ HP-22	Apples Peaches Pumpkin Pie/Loving for Money	1968	3.75	7.50	15.00

—4-inch plastic "Hip Pocket Record" with color sleeve

SMASH

Number	Title (A Side/B Side)	Yr	VG	VG+	NM
❑ 2086	Apples, Peaches, Pumpkin Pie/Stronger Than Dirt	1967	2.00	4.00	8.00
❑ 2124	Keep the Ball Rollin'/Here We Go Again	1967	2.00	4.00	8.00
❑ 2124 [PS]	Keep the Ball Rollin'/Here We Go Again	1967	3.00	6.00	12.00
❑ 2142	Strawberry Shortcake/Still (In Love with You)	1967	2.00	4.00	8.00
❑ 2142 [PS]	Strawberry Shortcake/Still (In Love with You)	1967	3.00	6.00	12.00
❑ 2154	Baby Make Your Own Sweet Music/Help Yourself to All My Lovin'	1968	2.00	4.00	8.00
❑ 2154 [PS]	Baby Make Your Own Sweet Music/Help Yourself to All My Lovin'	1968	3.00	6.00	12.00
❑ 2171	The Singles Game/Baby How Easy Your Heart Forgets Me	1968	2.00	4.00	8.00
❑ 2171 [PS]	The Singles Game/Baby How Easy Your Heart Forgets Me	1968	3.00	6.00	12.00
❑ 2185	Hey Diddle Diddle/If I Should Lose You	1968	2.00	4.00	8.00
❑ 2217	Change Your Mind/Are You Ready for This	1969	2.00	4.00	8.00
❑ 2237	Dancin' Mood/If I Should Lose You	1969	2.00	4.00	8.00

JAYBEES, THE

RCA VICTOR

Number	Title (A Side/B Side)	Yr	VG	VG+	NM
❑ 47-8904	Do You Think I'm in Love/I'm a Lover	1966	5.00	10.00	20.00

JAYHAWKS, THE

Also see THE MARATHONS; THE VIBRATIONS.

ALADDIN

Number	Title (A Side/B Side)	Yr	VG	VG+	NM
❑ 3393	Everyone Should Know/The Creature	1957	20.00	40.00	80.00

ARGYLE

Number	Title (A Side/B Side)	Yr	VG	VG+	NM
❑ 1005	Lonely Highway/La Macerena	1961	6.25	12.50	25.00

EASTMAN

Number	Title (A Side/B Side)	Yr	VG	VG+	NM
❑ 792	Start the Fire/I Wish the World Owed Me a Living	1958	37.50	75.00	150.00
❑ 798	New Love/Betty Brown	1958	37.50	75.00	150.00

FLASH

Number	Title (A Side/B Side)	Yr	VG	VG+	NM
❑ 105	Counting Teardrops/The Devil's Cousin	1955	50.00	100.00	200.00
❑ 109	Starnded in the Jungle/My Only Darling	1956	12.50	25.00	50.00
❑ 111	Love Train/Don't Mind Dyin'	1956	7.50	15.00	30.00

JAYNELLS, THE

CAMEO

Number	Title (A Side/B Side)	Yr	VG	VG+	NM
❑ 286	I'll Stay Home New Year's Eve/Down Home	1963	5.00	10.00	20.00

DIAMOND

Number	Title (A Side/B Side)	Yr	VG	VG+	NM
❑ 153	I'll Stay Home (New Year's Eve)/Down Home	1963	10.00	20.00	40.00

JAYNETTS, THE

J&S

Number	Title (A Side/B Side)	Yr	VG	VG+	NM
❑ 1177	Out Behind the Daisies/Is It My Imagination	196?	2.00	4.00	8.00
❑ 1468/9	Chicken, Chicken, Crance or Crow/Winky Dinky	196?	2.00	4.00	8.00
❑ 1473	Peepin' In and Out the Window/Extra, Extra, Read All About It	196?	2.00	4.00	8.00
❑ 1477	Who Stole the Cookie/That's My Boy	196?	2.50	5.00	10.00
❑ 1686	Looking for Wonderland, My Lover/Make It an Extra	1965	2.00	4.00	8.00
❑ 1765/6	I Wanted to Be Free/Where Are You Tonight	196?	2.50	5.00	10.00
❑ 4418/9	Vangie Don't You Cry/My Guy Is As Sweet As Can Be	196?	2.00	4.00	8.00

TUFF

Number	Title (A Side/B Side)	Yr	VG	VG+	NM
❑ 369	Sally, Go 'Round the Roses/(Instrumental)	1963	3.75	7.50	15.00
❑ 371	Keep an Eye on Her/(Instrumental)	1963	2.50	5.00	10.00
❑ 374	Snowman, Snowman, Sweet Potato Nose/(Instrumental)	1963	3.75	7.50	15.00
❑ 377	No Love at All/Tonight You Belong to Me	1964	3.00	6.00	12.00

JAYTONES, THE

BRUNSWICK

Number	Title (A Side/B Side)	Yr	VG	VG+	NM
❑ 55087	The Clock/Gasoline	1958	30.00	60.00	120.00

CUB

Number	Title (A Side/B Side)	Yr	VG	VG+	NM
❑ 9057	My Only Love/Absolutely Right	1960	15.00	30.00	60.00

TIMELY

Number	Title (A Side/B Side)	Yr	VG	VG+	NM
❑ 1003/4	My Darling/The Bells	1958	375.00	750.00	1500.

JAZZ CRUSADERS, THE

See THE CRUSADERS.

JEFFERSON

Also see ROCKIN' BERRIES.

DECCA

Number	Title (A Side/B Side)	Yr	VG	VG+	NM
❑ 32501	The Colour of My Love/Look No Further	1969	2.00	4.00	8.00

JANUS

Number	Title (A Side/B Side)	Yr	VG	VG+	NM
❑ 106	Baby Take Me in Your Arms/I Fell Flat on My Face	1969	2.00	4.00	8.00
❑ 117	You Know How It Is with a Woman/Are You Growing Tired of My Love	1970	2.00	4.00	8.00

JEFFERSON AIRPLANE

Also see MARTY BALIN; PAPA JOHN CREACH; HOT TUNA; JEFFERSON STARSHIP; PAUL KANTNER; GRACE SLICK; STARSHIP.

EPIC

Number	Title (A Side/B Side)	Yr	VG	VG+	NM
❑ 73044	Summer of Love/Panda	1989	—	2.50	5.00

GRUNT

Number	Title (A Side/B Side)	Yr	VG	VG+	NM
❑ 65-0500	Pretty As You Feel/Wild Turkey	1971	—	2.50	5.00
❑ 65-0500 [PS]	Pretty As You Feel/Wild Turkey	1971	2.50	5.00	10.00
❑ 65-0506	Long John Silver/Milk Train	1972	—	2.50	5.00
❑ 65-0506 [PS]	Long John Silver/Milk Train	1972	3.75	7.50	15.00
❑ 65-0511	Trial by Fire/Twilight Double Leader	1972	—	2.50	5.00
❑ JB-10988 [DJ]	White Rabbit (mono/stereo)	1978	7.50	15.00	30.00

—White vinyl

RCA

Number	Title (A Side/B Side)	Yr	VG	VG+	NM
❑ 5156-7-R	White Rabbit/Plastic Fantastic Lover	1987	—	2.50	5.00

—White vinyl

Number	Title (A Side/B Side)	Yr	VG	VG+	NM
❑ 5156-7-R [PS]	White Rabbit/Plastic Fantastic Lover	1987	—	2.50	5.00

RCA VICTOR

Number	Title (A Side/B Side)	Yr	VG	VG+	NM
❑ 47-8769	It's No Secret/Runnin' 'Round This World	1966	3.75	7.50	15.00
❑ 47-8848	Come Up the Years/Blues from an Airplane	1966	3.75	7.50	15.00
❑ 47-8967	Bringing Me Down/Let Me In	1966	3.75	7.50	15.00
❑ 47-9063	My Best Friend/How Do You Feel	1967	3.75	7.50	15.00
❑ 47-9140	Somebody to Love/She Has Funny Cars	1967	3.75	7.50	15.00
❑ 47-9248	White Rabbit/Plastic Fantastic Lover	1967	3.75	7.50	15.00
❑ 47-9297	Ballad of You & Me & Pooneil/Two Heads	1967	2.50	5.00	10.00
❑ 47-9389	Watch Her Ride/Martha	1967	2.50	5.00	10.00
❑ 47-9496	Greasy Heart/Share a Little Joke (With the World)	1968	2.00	4.00	8.00
❑ 47-9644	Crown of Creation/Lather	1968	2.00	4.00	8.00
❑ 47-9644 [PS]	Crown of Creation/Lather	1968	5.00	10.00	20.00
❑ 74-0150	Plastic Fantastic Lover/Other Side of This Life	1969	—	3.00	6.00
❑ 74-0150 [PS]	Plastic Fantastic Lover/Other Side of This Life	1969	5.00	10.00	20.00
❑ 74-0245	Volunteers/We Can Be Together	1969	—	3.00	6.00
❑ 74-0245 [PS]	Volunteers/We Can Be Together	1969	3.75	7.50	15.00
❑ 74-0343	Have You Seen the Saucers/Mexico	1970	—	3.00	6.00
❑ 74-0343 [PS]	Have You Seen the Saucers/Mexico	1970	3.75	7.50	15.00

JEFFERSON STARSHIP

See cross-references under JEFFERSON AIRPLANE.

GRUNT

Number	Title (A Side/B Side)	Yr	VG	VG+	NM
❑ FB-10080	Ride the Tiger/Devil's Den	1974	—	2.00	4.00
❑ FB-10206	Caroline/Be Young You	1975	—	2.00	4.00
❑ FB-10367	Miracles/Al Garimaso (There Is Love)	1975	—	2.50	5.00
❑ FB-10456	Play on Love/I Want to See Another World	1975	—	2.00	4.00
❑ FB-10746	With Your Love/Switchblade	1976	—	2.50	5.00
❑ FB-10791	St. Charles/Love Lovely Day	1976	—	2.00	4.00
❑ GB-10941	Miracles/With Your Love	1977	—	—	3.00

—Gold Standard Series

Number	Title (A Side/B Side)	Yr	VG	VG+	NM
❑ FB-11196	Count on Me/Show Yourself	1978	—	2.00	4.00
❑ FB-11196 [PS]	Count on Me/Show Yourself	1978	—	2.50	5.00
❑ FB-11274	Runaway/Hot Water	1978	—	2.00	4.00
❑ FB-11274 [PS]	Runaway/Hot Water	1978	—	2.50	5.00
❑ JB-11274 [DJ]	Runaway (Long)/Runaway (Short)	1978	—	2.50	5.00
❑ JB-11274 [PS]	Runaway (Long)/Runaway (Short)	1978	—	3.00	6.00

—Promo-only sleeve (one song listed on jacket)

Number	Title (A Side/B Side)	Yr	VG	VG+	NM
❑ FB-11374	Crazy Feelin'/Love Too Good	1978	—	2.00	4.00
❑ FB-11374 [PS]	Crazy Feelin'/Love Too Good	1978	—	2.50	5.00
❑ FB-11426	Light the Sky On Fire/Hyperdrive	1978	—	2.00	4.00
❑ FB-11426 [PS]	Light the Sky On Fire/Hyperdrive	1978	—	2.50	5.00
❑ GB-11506	Count on Me/Runaway	1979	—	—	3.00

—Gold Standard Series

Number	Title (A Side/B Side)	Yr	VG	VG+	NM
❑ FB-11750	Jane/Freedom at Point Zero	1979	—	2.00	4.00
❑ FB-11750 [PS]	Jane/Freedom at Point Zero	1979	—	2.50	5.00
❑ FB-11921	Girl with the Hungry Eyes/Just the Same	1980	—	2.00	4.00
❑ FB-11921 [PS]	Girl with the Hungry Eyes/Just the Same	1980	—	2.50	5.00
❑ FB-11961	Rock Music/Lightning Rose	1980	—	2.00	4.00
❑ FB-12211	Find Your Way Back/Modern Times	1981	—	2.00	4.00
❑ FB-12212	Mary/Modern Times	1981	—	—	—

—Unreleased

Number	Title (A Side/B Side)	Yr	VG	VG+	NM
❑ FB-12275	Stranger/Free	1981	—	2.00	4.00
❑ FB-12332	Save Your Love/Wild Eyes	1981	—	2.00	4.00
❑ FB-13350	Be My Lady/Out of Control	1982	—	2.00	4.00
❑ FB-13439	Winds of Change/Black Widow	1983	—	2.00	4.00
❑ FB-13531	Can't Find Love/I Will Stay	1983	—	2.00	4.00
❑ FB-13811	No Way Out/Rose Goes to Yale	1984	—	2.00	4.00
❑ FB-13872	Layin' It on the Line/Showdown	1984	—	2.00	4.00
❑ FB-13872 [PS]	Layin' It on the Line/Showdown	1984	—	2.00	4.00

JELLY BEAN BANDITS, THE

MAINSTREAM

Number	Title (A Side/B Side)	Yr	VG	VG+	NM
❑ 674	Country Woman/Generation	1967	7.50	15.00	30.00

JELLY BEANS, THE

ESKEE

Number	Title (A Side/B Side)	Yr	VG	VG+	NM
❑ 001	I'm Hip to You/You Don't Mean No Good to Me	1965	3.75	7.50	15.00

RED BIRD

Number	Title (A Side/B Side)	Yr	VG	VG+	NM
❑ 10-003	I Wanna Love Him So Bad/So Long	1964	5.00	10.00	20.00
❑ 10-011	The Kind of Boy You Can't Forget/Baby Be Mine	1964	5.00	10.00	20.00

JENNIFER

See JENNIFER WARNES.

JENNINGS, WAYLON

Also see JOHNNY CASH; WAYLON AND JESSI; WAYLON AND WILLIE.

ARK 21

Number	Title (A Side/B Side)	Yr	VG	VG+	NM
❑ S7-58711	I Know About Me, Don't Know About You/Closing In on the Fire	1998	—	—	3.00

A&M

Number	Title (A Side/B Side)	Yr	VG	VG+	NM
❑ 722	Rave On/Love, Denise	1963	5.00	10.00	20.00
❑ 739	Four Strong Winds/Just to Satisfy You	1964	3.75	7.50	15.00
❑ 753	The Race Is On/Sing the Girls a Song	1964	3.75	7.50	15.00

BAT

Number	Title (A Side/B Side)	Yr	VG	VG+	NM
❑ 121636	White Lightning/(B-side unknown)	1962	12.50	25.00	50.00
❑ 121639	Dream Baby/Crying	1962	10.00	20.00	40.00

BRUNSWICK

Number	Title (A Side/B Side)	Yr	VG	VG+	NM
❑ 55130	Jole Blon/When Sin Stops	1959	75.00	150.00	300.00

COLUMBIA

Number	Title (A Side/B Side)	Yr	VG	VG+	NM
❑ 04881	Highwayman/The Human Condition	1985	—	—	3.00

—A-side: Willie Nelson/Waylon Jennings/Johnny Cash/Kris Kristofferson; B-side: Nelson, Cash

Number	Title (A Side/B Side)	Yr	VG	VG+	NM
❑ 04881 [PS]	Highwayman/The Human Condition	1985	—	2.00	4.00

—A-side: Willie Nelson/Waylon Jennings/Johnny Cash/Kris Kristofferson; B-side: Nelson, Cash

Number	Title (A Side/B Side)	Yr	VG	VG+	NM
❑ 05594	Desperadoes Waiting for a Train/The Twentieth Century Is Almost Over	1985	—	—	3.00

—A-side: Willie Nelson/Waylon Jennings/Johnny Cash/Kris Kristofferson; B-side: Nelson, Cash

Number	Title (A Side/B Side)	Yr	VG	VG+	NM
❑ 08406	Highwayman/Desperadoes Waiting for a Train	1988	—	—	3.00

—Waylon Jennings/Willie Nelson/Johnny Cash/Kris Kristofferson; reissue

Number	Title (A Side/B Side)	Yr	VG	VG+	NM
❑ 73233	Silver Stallion/America Remains	1990	—	—	3.00

—Waylon Jennings/Willie Nelson/Johnny Cash/Kris Kristofferson

Number	Title (A Side/B Side)	Yr	VG	VG+	NM
❑ 73381	Born and Raised in Black and White/Texas	1990	—	—	3.00

—The Highwaymen (Waylon Jennings/Willie Nelson/Johnny Cash/Kris Kristofferson)

Number	Title (A Side/B Side)	Yr	VG	VG+	NM
❑ 73572	American Remains/Texas	1990	—	—	3.00

—The Highwaymen (Waylon Jennings/Willie Nelson/Johnny Cash/Kris Kristofferson)

EPIC

Number	Title (A Side/B Side)	Yr	VG	VG+	NM
❑ 73352	Wrong/Waking Up with You	1990	—	—	3.00
❑ 73519	Where Corn Don't Grow/Waking Up with You	1990	—	—	3.00
❑ 73647	What Bothers Me Most/Wrong	1990	—	—	3.00
❑ 73718	The Eagle/What Bothers Me Most	1991	—	—	3.00
❑ 74403	Just Talkin'/I've Got My Faults	1992	—	—	3.00
❑ 74705	Too Dumb for New York City, Too Smart for L.A./I've Got My Faults	1992	—	—	3.00

LIBERTY

Number	Title (A Side/B Side)	Yr	VG	VG+	NM
❑ S7-18486	It Is What It Is/The Devil's Right Hand	1995	—	—	3.00

—By The Highwaymen

MCA

Number	Title (A Side/B Side)	Yr	VG	VG+	NM
❑ 52776	Working Without a Net/They Ain't Got 'Em All	1986	—	—	3.00
❑ 52830	Will the Wolf Survive/I've Got Me a Woman	1986	—	—	3.00
❑ 52915	What You'll Do When I'm Gone/That Dog Won't Hurt	1986	—	—	3.00
❑ 53009	Rose in Paradise/Crying Don't Even Come Close	1987	—	—	3.00
❑ 53088	Fallin' Out/Deep in the West	1987	—	—	3.00
❑ 53158	My Rough and Rowdy Days/Love Song (I Can't Sing Anymore)	1987	—	—	3.00
❑ 53243	If Ole Hank Could Only See Us Now (Chapter Five...Nashville)/You Went Out with Rock 'n' Roll	1988	—	—	3.00
❑ 53314	How Much Is It Worth to Live in L.A./G.I. Joe	1988	—	—	3.00
❑ 53476	Which Way Do I Go (Now That I'm Gone)/Hey Willie	1988	—	—	3.00
❑ 53634	Trouble Man/Yoyos, Bozos, Bimbos and Heroes	1989	—	—	3.00
❑ 53710	You Put the Soul in the Song/Woman I Hate It	1989	—	—	3.00

RAMCO

Number	Title (A Side/B Side)	Yr	VG	VG+	NM
❑ 1997	My World/Another Blue Day	1968	3.00	6.00	12.00

RCA

Number	Title (A Side/B Side)	Yr	VG	VG+	NM
❑ 5034-7-R	The Broken Promise Land/I Don't Have Any More Love Songs	1986	—	2.00	4.00
❑ PB-10842	Are You Ready for the Country/So Good Woman	1976	—	2.50	5.00
❑ PB-10924	Luckenbach, Texas (Back to the Basics of Love)/Belle of the Ball	1977	—	2.50	5.00
❑ GB-10927	Dreaming My Dreams with You/Can't You See	1977	—	—	3.00

—Gold Standard Series

Number	Title (A Side/B Side)	Yr	VG	VG+	NM
❑ PB-11118	The Wurlitzer Prize (I Don't Want to Get Over You)/Lookin' for a Feeling	1977	—	2.50	5.00
❑ PB-11344	I've Always Been Crazy/I Never Said It Would Be Easy	1978	—	2.00	4.00

Number	Title (A Side/B Side)	Yr	VG	VG+	NM
❑ PB-11390	Don't You Think This Outlaw Bit's Done Got Out of Hand/Girl I Can Tell (You're Trying to Work It Out)	1978	—	2.00	4.00
❑ GB-11500	Are You Ready for the Country/The Wurlitzer Prize (I Don't Want to Get Over You)	1978	—	—	3.00
—Gold Standard Series					
❑ PB-11596	Amanda/Lonesome, On'ry and Mean	1979	—	2.00	4.00
❑ PB-11596 [PS]	Amanda/Lonesome, On'ry and Mean	1979	—	2.50	5.00
❑ PB-11723	Come with Me/Mes'kin	1979	—	2.00	4.00
❑ GB-11757	Luckenbach, Texas (Back to the Basics of Love)/ Belle of the Ball	1979	—	—	3.00
—Gold Standard Series					
❑ PB-11898	I Ain't Living Long Like This/The World's Crazy	1979	—	2.00	4.00
❑ GB-11991	I've Always Been Crazy/Don't You Think This Outlaw Bit's Done Got Out of Hand	1980	—	—	3.00
—Gold Standard Series					
❑ PB-12007	Clyde/I Came Here to Party	1980	—	2.00	4.00
❑ PB-12067	Theme from "The Dukes of Hazzard" (Good Ol' Boys)/It's Alright	1980	—	2.00	4.00
❑ PB-12067 [PS]	Theme from "The Dukes of Hazzard" (Good Ol' Boys)/It's Alright	1980	—	2.50	5.00
❑ GB-12187	Theme from "The Dukes of Hazzard" (Good Ol' Boys)/Come with Me	1981	—	—	3.00
—Gold Standard Series					
❑ GB-12313	Amanda/I Ain't Living Long Like This	1981	—	—	3.00
—"Gold Standard Series" reissue					
❑ PB-12367	Shine/White Water	1981	—	2.00	4.00
❑ PB-13257	Women Do Know How to Carry On/Honky Tonk Blues	1982	—	2.00	4.00
❑ PB-13465	Lucille (You Won't Do Your Daddy's Will)/Medley of Hits	1983	—	2.00	4.00
❑ PB-13543	Breakin' Down/Livin' Legends (A Dyin' Breed)	1983	—	2.00	4.00
❑ PB-13631	The Conversation/Fancy Free	1983	—	2.00	4.00
—A-side with Hank Williams, Jr.					
❑ PB-13729	I May Be Used (But Baby I Ain't Used Up)/So You Want to Be a Cowboy Singer	1984	—	2.00	4.00
❑ PB-13827	Never Could Toe the Mark/Talk Good Boogie	1984	—	2.00	4.00
❑ PB-13903	Silent Night, Holy Night/Precious Memories	1984	—	2.00	4.00
—A-side with Jessi Colter					
❑ PB-13908	America/People Up in Texas	1984	—	2.00	4.00
❑ PB-13984	Waltz Me to Heaven/Dream On	1984	—	2.00	4.00
❑ PB-14094	Drinkin' and Dreamin'/Prophets Show Up in Strange Places	1985	—	2.00	4.00
❑ PB-14215	The Devil's on the Loose/Good Morning John	1985	—	2.00	4.00
❑ PB-14291	Sweet Mother Texas/Hanging On	1985	—	2.00	4.00
RCA VICTOR					
❑ APBO-0086	You Asked Me To/Willy, the Wandering Gypsy and Me	1973	2.00	4.00	8.00
❑ AMAO-0122	MacArthur Park/The Taker	1973	—	2.50	5.00
❑ APBO-0251	This Time/Mona	1974	—	3.00	6.00
❑ PB-10020	I'm a Ramblin' Man/Got a Lot Going for Me	1974	—	3.00	6.00
❑ PB-10142	Rainy Day Woman/Let's All Help the Cowboys (Sing the Blues)	1974	—	3.00	6.00
❑ GB-10169	This Time/You Asked Me To	1975	—	2.00	4.00
—Gold Standard Series					
❑ PB-10270	Dreaming My Dreams with You/Waymore's Blues	1975	—	3.00	6.00
❑ PB-10379	Are You Sure Hank Done It This Way/Bob Wills Is Still the King	1975	—	3.00	6.00
❑ GB-10498	I'm a Ramblin' Man/Got a Lot Going for Me	1975	—	2.00	4.00
—Gold Standard Series					
❑ GB-10499	Rainy Day Woman/Let's All Help the Cowboys (Sing the Blues)	1975	—	2.00	4.00
—Gold Standard Series					
❑ GB-10673	Are You Sure Hank Done It This Way/Bob Wills Is Still the King	1976	—	2.00	4.00
—Gold Standard Series					
❑ PB-10721	Can't You See/I'll Go Back to Her	1976	—	2.50	5.00
❑ 47-8572	That's the Chance I'll Have to Take/I Wonder Just Where I Went Wrong	1965	2.50	5.00	10.00
❑ 47-8652	Stop the World (And Let Me Off)/The Dark Side of Fame	1965	2.50	5.00	10.00
❑ 47-8729	Anita, You're Dreaming/Look Into My Teardrops	1965	2.50	5.00	10.00
❑ 47-8822	Time to Bum Again/Norwegian Wood	1966	2.50	5.00	10.00
❑ 47-8917	(That's What You Get) For Lovin' Me/Time Will Tell the Story	1966	2.50	5.00	10.00
❑ 47-9025	Green River/Silver Ribbons	1966	2.50	5.00	10.00
❑ 47-9146	Mental Revenge/Born to Love You	1967	2.50	5.00	10.00
❑ 47-9259	The Chokin' Kind/Love of the Common People	1967	2.50	5.00	10.00
❑ 47-9414	Walk On Out of My Mind/Julie	1967	2.50	5.00	10.00
❑ 47-9480	I Got You/No One's Gonna Miss Me	1968	2.50	5.00	10.00
—A-side with Anita Carter					
❑ 47-9561	Only Daddy That'll Walk the Line/Right Before My Eyes	1968	2.50	5.00	10.00
❑ 47-9642	Yours Love/Six Strings Away	1968	2.50	5.00	10.00
❑ 47-9819	Singer of Sad Songs/Lila	1970	2.00	4.00	8.00
❑ 47-9885	The Taker/Shadows of the Gallows	1970	2.00	4.00	8.00
❑ 47-9925	(Don't Let the Sun Set on You) Tulsa/You'll Look for Me	1970	2.00	4.00	8.00
❑ 47-9967	Mississippi Woman/Life Goes On	1971	2.00	4.00	8.00
❑ 48-1003	Cedartown, Georgia/I Think It's Time She Learned	1971	2.00	4.00	8.00
❑ 74-0105	Something's Wrong in California/Farewell Party	1969	2.00	4.00	8.00
❑ 74-0157	The Days of Sand and Shovels/Delia's Gone	1969	2.00	4.00	8.00
❑ 74-0210	MacArthur Park/But You Know I Love You	1969	2.00	4.00	8.00
❑ 74-0281	Brown Eyed Handsome Man/Sorrow (Breaks a Good Man Down)	1969	2.00	4.00	8.00
❑ 74-0615	Good Hearted Woman/It's All Over Now	1971	2.00	4.00	8.00
❑ 74-0716	Sweet Dream Woman/Sure Didn't Take Him Long	1972	2.00	4.00	8.00
❑ 74-0808	Pretend I Never Happened/Nothin' Worth Takin' or Leavin'	1972	2.00	4.00	8.00
❑ 74-0886	You Can Have Her/Gone to Denver	1973	2.00	4.00	8.00
❑ 74-0961	We Had It All/Do No Good Woman	1973	2.00	4.00	8.00

Number	Title (A Side/B Side)	Yr	VG	VG+	NM
TREND					
❑ 102	Another Blue Day/Never Again	1962	7.50	15.00	30.00
❑ 106	The Stage/My Baby Walks All Over Me	1963	25.00	50.00	100.00

JENNINGS, WAYLON, AND JERRY REED

Also see each artist's individual listings.

Number	Title (A Side/B Side)	Yr	VG	VG+	NM
RCA					
❑ PB-13580	Hold On, I'm Comin'/Waiting On Down the Line	1983	—	2.00	4.00
❑ GB-13789	Hold On, I'm Comin'/The Conversation	1984	—	—	3.00
—Gold Standard Series; B-side by Waylon and Hank Williams, Jr.					

JENSON, JIMMY

Number	Title (A Side/B Side)	Yr	VG	VG+	NM
BANGAR					
❑ 0650	Walkin' in My Vinter Underwear/Copenhagen	1964	3.75	7.50	15.00
❑ 0651	I Yust Go Nuts At Christmas/Yingle Bells	1964	3.75	7.50	15.00

JERRY AND WAYNE

Number	Title (A Side/B Side)	Yr	VG	VG+	NM
ABC-PARAMOUNT					
❑ 9806	Baby Baby Baby/I'm Sad, Blue and Lonesome	1957	5.00	10.00	20.00
❑ 9808	Baby Baby Baby, Be Mine/I'm Sad, Blue and Lonesome	1957	6.25	12.50	25.00

JESSE AND MARVIN

"Jesse" is JESSE BELVIN. "Marvin" later was with MARVIN AND JOHNNY.

Number	Title (A Side/B Side)	Yr	VG	VG+	NM
SPECIALTY					
❑ 447	Dream Girl/Daddy Loves Baby	1952	50.00	100.00	200.00
—Red vinyl					
❑ 447	Dream Girl/Daddy Loves Baby	1952	18.75	37.50	75.00
—Black vinyl					

JESTERS, THE

Number	Title (A Side/B Side)	Yr	VG	VG+	NM
AMY					
❑ 859	Alexander Graham Bell/Buffalo	1962	2.00	4.00	8.00
CYCLONE					
❑ 5011	I Laughed/Now That You're Gone	1958	12.50	25.00	50.00
FEATURE					
❑ 101	Panther Pounce/Tiger Tail	1964	12.50	25.00	50.00
SIDEWALK					
❑ 910	Leave Me Alone/Don't Try to Crawl Back	1967	2.50	5.00	10.00
❑ 916	Hands of Time/If You Love Her, Tell Her So	1967	2.50	5.00	10.00
SUN					
❑ 400	Cadillac Man/My Babe	1966	7.50	15.00	30.00
ULTIMA					
❑ 705	Drag Like Boogie/A-Rab	1964	7.50	15.00	30.00
WINLEY					
❑ 218	So Strange/Love No One But You	1957	12.50	25.00	50.00
❑ 221	I'm Falling in Love/Please Let Me Love You	1957	12.50	25.00	50.00
❑ 225	The Plea/Oh Baby	1958	10.00	20.00	40.00
❑ 242	The Wind/Sally Green	1959	10.00	20.00	40.00
❑ 248	That's How It Goes/Tutti Frutti	1961	12.50	25.00	50.00
—Red vinyl					
❑ 248	That's How It Goes/Tutti Frutti	1961	7.50	15.00	30.00
—Black vinyl					
❑ 252	Come Let Me Show You/Uncle Henry's Basement	1961	7.50	15.00	30.00

JET SET, THE

Number	Title (A Side/B Side)	Yr	VG	VG+	NM
CAPITOL					
❑ 5358	True to You/You Got Me Hooked	1965	6.25	12.50	25.00
❑ 5421	How Can I Know/Dancing Yet	1965	6.25	12.50	25.00
—As "Liza and the Jet Set"					

JETHRO TULL

Number	Title (A Side/B Side)	Yr	VG	VG+	NM
CHRYSALIS					
❑ 2006	Living in the Past/Christmas Song	1972	—	3.00	6.00
❑ 2012	A Passion Play (Edit #9)/A Passion Play (Edit #8)	1973	—	3.00	6.00
❑ 2017	A Passion Play (Edit #6)/A Passion Play (Edit #10)	1973	—	2.50	5.00
❑ 2101	Bungle in the Jungle/Back Door Angels	1974	—	2.50	5.00
❑ 2101 [PS]	Bungle in the Jungle/Back Door Angels	1974	2.50	5.00	10.00
❑ 2103	Skating Away (On the Thin Ice of a New Day)/ Sealion	1975	—	2.50	5.00
❑ 2106	Minstrel in the Gallery/Sumer Day Sand	1975	—	2.50	5.00
❑ 2110	Locomotive Breath/Fat Man	1975	—	2.50	5.00
❑ 2114	Too Old to Rock and Roll, Too Young to Die/Bad Eyed and Loveless	1976	—	2.50	5.00
❑ 2135	The Whistler/Strip Cartoon	1977	—	2.50	5.00
❑ 2387	Home/Warm Sporran	1979	—	2.50	5.00
❑ 2613	Fallen on Hard Times/Pussy Willow	1982	—	2.00	4.00
❑ S7-18211	Christmas Song/Skating Away on the Thin Ice of a New Day	1994	—	2.50	5.00
—Green vinyl					
❑ 43172	Steel Monkey/Down at the End of Your Road	1987	—	2.00	4.00
REPRISE					
❑ 0815 [DJ]	Love Story/Song for Jeffrey	1969	3.75	7.50	15.00
—May be promo-only					
❑ 0845 [DJ]	Living in the Past/Driving Song	1969	5.00	10.00	20.00
—May be promo-only					
❑ 0886	Reasons for Waiting/Sweet Dream	1970	3.75	7.50	15.00
❑ 0899	Teacher/Witch's Promise	1970	3.75	7.50	15.00
❑ 0927	Inside/Time for Everything	1970	—	2.50	5.00
❑ 1024	Hymn 43/Mother Goose	1971	—	2.50	5.00
❑ 1054	Locomotive Breath/Wind-Up	1971	—	2.50	5.00
❑ 1153	Thick as a Brick (Edit)/Hymn 43	1972	—	2.50	5.00
—"Back to Back Hits" series					

JETS, THE

Number	Title (A Side/B Side)	Yr	VG	VG+	NM
GEE					
❑ 1020	Heaven Above Me/(B-side unknown)	1956	500.00	1000.	2000.

JEWEL AND EDDIE
JEWEL AKENS and Eddie Daniels; EDDIE COCHRAN plays guitar.

SILVER

Number	Title (A Side/B Side)	Yr	VG	VG+	NM
❑ 1004	Opportunity/Doin' the Hully Gully	1960	10.00	20.00	40.00
❑ 1004	Opportunity/Strollin' Guitar	1960	7.50	15.00	30.00
❑ 1008	My Eyes Are Cryin' for You/Sixteen Tons	1960	7.50	15.00	30.00

JEWELL AND THE RUBIES
ABC-PARAMOUNT

Number	Title (A Side/B Side)	Yr	VG	VG+	NM
❑ 10485	The Kidnapper/A Thrill	1963	3.00	6.00	12.00

LA LOUISIANNE

Number	Title (A Side/B Side)	Yr	VG	VG+	NM
❑ 8041	The Kidnapper/A Thrill	1963	7.50	15.00	30.00

JEWELS, THE (1)
Female vocal group.

DIMENSION

Number	Title (A Side/B Side)	Yr	VG	VG+	NM
❑ 1034	Opportunity/Gotta Find a Way	1964	5.00	10.00	20.00
❑ 1048	Smokey Joe/But I Do	1965	3.75	7.50	15.00

JEWELS, THE (2)
Male vocal group, did the original version of the hit "Hearts of Stone."

ANTLER

Number	Title (A Side/B Side)	Yr	VG	VG+	NM
❑ 1102	The Wind/Pearlie Mae	1959	10.00	20.00	40.00

IMPERIAL

Number	Title (A Side/B Side)	Yr	VG	VG+	NM
❑ 5351	Angel in My Life/Hearts Can Be Broken	1955	25.00	50.00	100.00
❑ 5362	Natural, Natural Ditty/Please Return	1955	25.00	50.00	100.00
❑ 5377	How/Rickety Rock	1956	25.00	50.00	100.00
❑ 5387	My Baby/Goin', Goin', Goin'	1956	25.00	50.00	100.00

ORIGINAL SOUND

Number	Title (A Side/B Side)	Yr	VG	VG+	NM
❑ 38	Hearts of Stone/Oh Yes I Know	1964	5.00	10.00	20.00

RPM

Number	Title (A Side/B Side)	Yr	VG	VG+	NM
❑ 474	She's a Flirt/Be-Bomp Baby	1956	17.50	35.00	70.00

R&B

Number	Title (A Side/B Side)	Yr	VG	VG+	NM
❑ 1301	Hearts of Stone/Runnin'	1954	50.00	100.00	200.00
❑ 1303	Oh Yes I Know/A Fool in Paradise	1954	75.00	150.00	300.00

JEWELS, THE (3)
DYNAMITE

Number	Title (A Side/B Side)	Yr	VG	VG+	NM
❑ 2000	Papa Left Mama Holdin' the Bag/This Is My Story	1966	3.75	7.50	15.00

FEDERAL

Number	Title (A Side/B Side)	Yr	VG	VG+	NM
❑ 12541	My Song/This Is My Story	1966	5.00	10.00	20.00

KING

Number	Title (A Side/B Side)	Yr	VG	VG+	NM
❑ 6068	Smokie Joe's/Lookie Lookie	1967	3.00	6.00	12.00

JEWELS, THE (4)
Probably an instrumental group.

FERN

Number	Title (A Side/B Side)	Yr	VG	VG+	NM
❑ 806	Jewel Rock/Space Guitar	1961	5.00	10.00	20.00

JEWELS, THE (U)
We can't definitely put these with any of the above groups. This could be as many as three more groups!

MGM

Number	Title (A Side/B Side)	Yr	VG	VG+	NM
❑ 13577	We Got Togetherness/I'm Forever Blowing Bubbles	1966	5.00	10.00	20.00

OLIMPIC

Number	Title (A Side/B Side)	Yr	VG	VG+	NM
❑ 244	Jimmy Lee/The Hash	1964	7.50	15.00	30.00

SHASTA

Number	Title (A Side/B Side)	Yr	VG	VG+	NM
❑ 115	I Worry 'Bout You/Are You Coming to the Party	1959	5.00	10.00	20.00

JIANTS, THE
CLAUDRA

Number	Title (A Side/B Side)	Yr	VG	VG+	NM
❑ 112	Tornado/She's My Woman	1959	50.00	100.00	200.00

JILL AND RAY
See PAUL AND PAULA.

JIMMY AND DUANE
"Duane" is DUANE EDDY.

EB X. PRESTON

Number	Title (A Side/B Side)	Yr	VG	VG+	NM
❑ 213	Soda Fountain Girl/(B-side unknown)	1955	62.50	125.00	250.00

JIMMY AND WALTER
SUN

Number	Title (A Side/B Side)	Yr	VG	VG+	NM
❑ 180	Before Long/Easy	1953	500.00	1000.	2000.
—The earliest known 45 on Sun					

JIV-A-TONES, THE
FELSTED

Number	Title (A Side/B Side)	Yr	VG	VG+	NM
❑ 8506	Flirty Gertie/Fire Engine Baby	1958	15.00	30.00	60.00

JIVE BOMBERS, THE
SAVOY

Number	Title (A Side/B Side)	Yr	VG	VG+	NM
❑ 1508	Bad Boy/When Your Hair Has Turned to Silver	1957	6.25	12.50	25.00
❑ 1513	If I Had a Talking Picture of You/The Blues Don't Mean a Thing	1957	5.00	10.00	20.00
❑ 1515	You Took My Love/Cherry	1957	5.00	10.00	20.00
❑ 1535	Just Around the Corner/Is This the End	1958	5.00	10.00	20.00
❑ 1560	Star Dust/You Give Your Love to Me	1959	5.00	10.00	20.00

JIVE FIVE, THE
AMBIENT SOUND

Number	Title (A Side/B Side)	Yr	VG	VG+	NM
❑ 02742	Magic Maker, Music Maker/Oh Baby	1982	—	2.50	5.00
❑ 03053	Hey Sam/Don't Believe Him Donna	1982	—	2.50	5.00

AVCO

Number	Title (A Side/B Side)	Yr	VG	VG+	NM
❑ 4568	Come Down in Time/Love Is Pain	1971	—	3.00	6.00
❑ 4589	Follow the Lamb/Let the Feeling Belong	1972	—	3.00	6.00
❑ 4589	Follow the Lamb/Lay Lady Lay	1972	—	3.00	6.00

BELTONE

Number	Title (A Side/B Side)	Yr	VG	VG+	NM
❑ 1006	My True Story/When I Was Single	1961	7.50	15.00	30.00
❑ 1014	Never, Never/People from Another World	1961	5.00	10.00	20.00
❑ 2019	Hully Gully Calling Time/No, Not Again	1962	5.00	10.00	20.00
❑ 2024	What Time Is It?/Beggin' You Please	1962	5.00	10.00	20.00
❑ 2029	These Golden Rings/Do You Hear Wedding Bells	1962	5.00	10.00	20.00
❑ 2030	Lily Marlene/Johnny Never Knew	1963	5.00	10.00	20.00
❑ 2034	She's My Girl/Rain	1963	5.00	10.00	20.00

BRUT

Number	Title (A Side/B Side)	Yr	VG	VG+	NM
❑ 814	All I Ever Do Is Dream About You/Super Woman (Part 2)	1973	—	3.00	6.00

DECCA

Number	Title (A Side/B Side)	Yr	VG	VG+	NM
❑ 32671	(If You Let Me Make Love to You) Why Can't I Touch You/You Showed Me the Light of Love	1970	2.00	4.00	8.00
❑ 32736	I Want You to Be My Baby/Give Me Just a Chance	1970	2.00	4.00	8.00

LANA

Number	Title (A Side/B Side)	Yr	VG	VG+	NM
❑ 105	My True Story/When I Was Single	196?	2.00	4.00	8.00
—Early reissue					

MUSICOR

Number	Title (A Side/B Side)	Yr	VG	VG+	NM
❑ 1250	Crying Like a Baby/You'll Fall in Love	1967	3.00	6.00	12.00
❑ 1270	No More Tears/You'll Fall in Love	1967	3.00	6.00	12.00
❑ 1305	Sugar (Don't Take Away My Candy)/Blues in the Ghetto	1968	3.00	6.00	12.00

SKETCH

Number	Title (A Side/B Side)	Yr	VG	VG+	NM
❑ 219	United/Prove Every Word You Say	1964	3.75	7.50	15.00

UNITED ARTISTS

Number	Title (A Side/B Side)	Yr	VG	VG+	NM
❑ 0100	I'm a Happy Man/It Will Stand	1973	—	2.50	5.00
—"Silver Spotlight Series" reissue; B-side by The Showmen					
❑ 807	United/Prove Every Word You Say	1965	5.00	10.00	20.00
❑ 853	I'm a Happy Man/Kiss Kiss Kiss	1965	5.00	10.00	20.00
❑ 936	Please Baby Please/A Bench in the Park	1965	5.00	10.00	20.00
❑ 50004	Goin' Wild/Main Street	1966	3.75	7.50	15.00
❑ 50033	In My Neighborhood/Then Came Heartbreak	1966	3.75	7.50	15.00
❑ 50069	You're a Puzzle/Ha Ha	1966	3.75	7.50	15.00
❑ 50107	You/You Promised Me Great Things	1966	3.75	7.50	15.00

JIVERS, THE
ALADDIN

Number	Title (A Side/B Side)	Yr	VG	VG+	NM
❑ 3329	Cherie/Little Mama	1956	40.00	80.00	160.00
❑ 3347	Ray Pearl/Dear Little One	1956	30.00	60.00	120.00

JO ANN AND TROY
Also see JO ANN CAMPBELL.

ATLANTIC

Number	Title (A Side/B Side)	Yr	VG	VG+	NM
❑ 2256	Who Do You Love/I Found a Love, Oh What a Love	1964	3.75	7.50	15.00
❑ 2293	Same Old Feeling/Just Because	1965	3.75	7.50	15.00

JODIMARS, THE
Contains ex-members of BILL HALEY AND HIS COMETS.

CAPITOL

Number	Title (A Side/B Side)	Yr	VG	VG+	NM
❑ F3285	Well Now — Dig This/Let's All Rock Together	1955	6.25	12.50	25.00
❑ F3360	Dancin' the Bop/Boom Boom My Bayou Baby	1956	6.25	12.50	25.00
❑ F3436	Lotsa Love/Rattle My Bones	1956	6.25	12.50	25.00
❑ F3512	Rattle Shakin' Daddy/Eat Your Heart Out, Annie	1956	6.25	12.50	25.00
❑ F3588	Clarabella/Midnight	1956	6.25	12.50	25.00
❑ F3633	Cloud 99/Later	1957	6.25	12.50	25.00

PRESIDENT

Number	Title (A Side/B Side)	Yr	VG	VG+	NM
❑ 1017	Shoo-Sue/Story-Telling Baby	1957	5.00	10.00	20.00

JOEL, BILLY
Also see THE HASSLES.

COLUMBIA

Number	Title (A Side/B Side)	Yr	VG	VG+	NM
❑ 02518	Say Goodbye to Hollywood/Summer, Highland Falls	1981	—	2.00	4.00
❑ 02518 [PS]	Say Goodbye to Hollywood/Summer, Highland Falls	1981	—	2.00	4.00
❑ 02628	She's Got a Way/The Ballad of Billy the Kid	1981	—	2.00	4.00
❑ 02628 [PS]	She's Got a Way/The Ballad of Billy the Kid	1981	—	2.00	4.00
❑ 03238	It's Still Rock and Roll to Me/Don't Ask Me Why	1982	—	—	3.00
—Reissue					
❑ 03239	You May Be Right/She's Got a Way	1982	—	—	3.00
—Reissue					
❑ 03241	Honesty/Sometimes a Fantasy	1982	—	—	3.00
—Reissue					
❑ 03244	Pressure/Laura	1982	—	2.00	4.00
❑ 03244 [PS]	Pressure/Laura	1982	—	2.00	4.00
❑ CNR-03321	Pressure	1982	—	3.00	6.00
—One-sided budget release (Large hole)					
❑ 03413	Allentown/Elvis Presley Blvd.	1982	—	2.00	4.00
❑ 03413 [PS]	Allentown/Elvis Presley Blvd.	1982	—	2.00	4.00
❑ CNR-03426	Allentown	1982	—	3.00	6.00
—One-sided budget release					
❑ 03780	Goodnight Saigon/A Room of Our Own	1983	—	2.00	4.00
❑ 03780 [PS]	Goodnight Saigon/A Room of Our Own	1983	—	2.00	4.00
❑ 04012	Tell Her About It/Easy Money	1983	—	—	3.00
❑ 04012 [PS]	Tell Her About It/Easy Money	1983	—	2.00	4.00
❑ 04149	Uptown Girl/Careless Talk	1983	—	—	3.00
❑ 04149 [PS]	Uptown Girl/Careless Talk	1983	—	2.00	4.00
❑ 04259	An Innocent Man/I'll Cry Instead	1983	—	—	3.00
❑ 04259 [PS]	An Innocent Man/I'll Cry Instead	1983	—	2.00	4.00
❑ 04400	The Longest Time/Christie Lee	1984	—	—	3.00
❑ 04400 [PS]	The Longest Time/Christie Lee	1984	—	2.00	4.00
❑ 04514	Leave a Tender Moment Alone/This Night	1984	—	—	3.00
❑ 04514 [PS]	Leave a Tender Moment Alone/This Night	1984	—	2.00	4.00
❑ 04681	Keeping the Faith (Special Mix)/She's Right On Time	1984	—	—	3.00
❑ 04681 [PS]	Keeping the Faith (Special Mix)/She's Right On Time	1984	—	2.00	4.00
❑ 05417	You're Only Human (Second Wind)/Surprises	1985	—	—	3.00
❑ 05417 [PS]	You're Only Human (Second Wind)/Surprises	1985	—	—	3.00
❑ 05657	The Night Is Still Young/Summer, Highland Falls	1985	—	—	3.00
❑ 05657 [PS]	The Night Is Still Young/Summer, Highland Falls	1985	—	2.00	4.00
❑ 05657 [PS]	The Night Is Still Young/Summer, Highland Falls	1985	2.50	5.00	10.00
—Promotional sleeve, different that stock sleeve					
❑ 06108	A Matter of Trust/Getting Closer	1986	—	—	3.00
❑ 06526	This Is the Time/Code of Silence	1986	—	—	3.00

Number	Title (A Side/B Side)	Yr	VG	VG+	NM
❑ 06526 [PS]	This Is the Time/Code of Silence	1986	—	—	3.00
❑ 06994	Baby Grand/Big Man on Mulberry Street	1987	—	—	3.00
—A-side: With Ray Charles					
❑ 06994 [PS]	Baby Grand/Big Man on Mulberry Street	1987	—	—	3.00
❑ 07626	Back in the U.S.S.R./Big Shot	1987	—	—	3.00
❑ 07626 [PS]	Back in the U.S.S.R./Big Shot	1987	—	2.00	4.00
❑ 07664	The Times They Are a-Changin'/Back in the U.S.S.R.	1987	—	2.00	4.00
❑ 08415	Tell Her About It/Easy Money	1988	—	—	3.00
—Reissue					
❑ 08416	An Innocent Man/I'll Cry Instead	1988	—	—	3.00
—Reissue					
❑ 08417	The Longest Time/Christie Lee	1988	—	—	3.00
—Reissue					
❑ 08418	Leave a Tender Moment Alone/This Night	1988	—	—	3.00
—Reissue					
❑ 08419	Keeping the Faith/She's Right on Time	1988	—	—	3.00
—Reissue					
❑ 08420	You're Only Human (Second Wind)/Surprises	1988	—	—	3.00
—Reissue					
❑ 10015	Travelin' Prayer/Ain't No Crime	1974	—	3.00	6.00
❑ 10064	The Entertainer/The Mexican Connection	1974	—	3.00	6.00
❑ 10412	James/Summer, Highland Falls	1976	—	3.00	6.00
❑ 10562	Say Goodbye to Hollywood/I've Loved These Days	1977	—	3.00	6.00
❑ 10624	Movin' Out (Anthony's Song)/She's Always a Woman	1977	2.50	5.00	10.00
❑ 10646	Just the Way You Are/Get It Right the First Time	1977	—	2.50	5.00
❑ 10708	Movin' Out (Anthony's Song)/Everybody Has a Dream	1978	—	2.50	5.00
❑ 10750	Only the Good Die Young/Get It Right the First Time	1978	—	2.50	5.00
❑ 10788	She's Always a Woman/Vienna	1978	—	2.50	5.00
❑ 10853	My Life/52nd Street	1978	—	2.50	5.00
❑ 10913	Big Shot/Root Beer Rag	1979	—	2.50	5.00
❑ 10959	Honesty/The Mexican Connection	1979	—	2.50	5.00
❑ 11229	All for Leyna/Souvenir	1980	—	—	—
—Canceled					
❑ 11231	You May Be Right/Close to the Borderline	1980	—	2.00	4.00
❑ 11231 [PS]	You May Be Right/Close to the Borderline	1980	—	3.00	6.00
❑ 11276	It's Still Rock and Roll to Me/Through the Long Night	1980	—	2.00	4.00
❑ 11276 [PS]	It's Still Rock and Roll to Me/Through the Long Night	1980	—	3.00	6.00
❑ 11331	Don't Ask Me Why/C'etait Toi (You Were the One)	1980	—	2.00	4.00
❑ 11331 [PS]	Don't Ask Me Why/C'etait Toi (You Were the One)	1980	—	3.00	6.00
❑ 11379	Sometimes a Fantasy/All for Leyna	1980	—	2.50	5.00
❑ 11379 [PS]	Sometimes a Fantasy/All for Leyna	1980	2.00	4.00	8.00
❑ 45963	Piano Man/You're My Home	1973	—	3.00	6.00
❑ 46055	Worse Comes to Worst/Somewhere Along the Line	1974	—	3.00	6.00
❑ 73021	We Didn't Start the Fire/House of Blue Light	1989	—	—	3.00
❑ 73091	I Go to Extremes/When in Rome	1989	—	—	3.00
❑ 73333	The Downeaster "Alexa"/And So It Goes	1990	—	—	—
—This is said to exist as a U.S. 45, but we have not confirmed this					
❑ 73442	That's Not Her Style/And So It Goes	1990	—	—	3.00
❑ 77086	The River of Dreams/No Man's Land	1993	—	—	3.00
❑ 77254	All About Soul/Picked a Real Bad Time	1993	—	—	3.00
❑ 77363	Lullabye (Goodnight, My Angel)/Two Thousand Years	1994	—	—	3.00
❑ 78641	To Make You Feel My Love//Intro/Summer, Highland Falls/Summer, Highland Falls	1997	—	—	3.00

EPIC

Number	Title (A Side/B Side)	Yr	VG	VG+	NM
❑ 06118	Modern Woman/Sleeping with the Television On	1986	—	—	3.00
❑ 06118 [PS]	Modern Woman/Sleeping with the Television On	1986	—	2.00	4.00
❑ 74422	All Shook Up/Wear My Ring Around Your Neck	1992	—	—	3.00
—B-side is instrumental track of Ricky Van Shelton's recording					

FAMILY PRODUCTIONS

Number	Title (A Side/B Side)	Yr	VG	VG+	NM
❑ 0900	She's Got a Way/Everybody Loves You Now	1971	6.25	12.50	25.00
❑ 0906	Tomorrow Is Today/Everybody Loves You Now	1971	6.25	12.50	25.00

JOEY AND DANNY

SWAN

Number	Title (A Side/B Side)	Yr	VG	VG+	NM
❑ 4276	Santa's Got a Brand New Bag/Rats in My Room	1967	5.00	10.00	20.00

JOEY AND THE CONTINENTALS

CLARIDGE

Number	Title (A Side/B Side)	Yr	VG	VG+	NM
❑ 304	She Rides with Me/Rudy Vahoo	1966	6.25	12.50	25.00
—Reissued on Claridge 312 as "The G.T.O.'s"					

KOMET

Number	Title (A Side/B Side)	Yr	VG	VG+	NM
❑ 1001	Linda/Will Love Ever Come My Way	196?	3.75	7.50	15.00

LAURIE

Number	Title (A Side/B Side)	Yr	VG	VG+	NM
❑ 3294	Sad Girl/Baby	1965	6.25	12.50	25.00

JOEY AND THE LEXINGTONS

COMET

Number	Title (A Side/B Side)	Yr	VG	VG+	NM
❑ 2154	Heaven/The Girl I Love	1962	37.50	75.00	150.00

DUNES

Number	Title (A Side/B Side)	Yr	VG	VG+	NM
❑ 2029	Bobbie/Tears from My Eyes	1963	25.00	50.00	100.00

JOEY AND THE TEENAGERS

COLUMBIA

Number	Title (A Side/B Side)	Yr	VG	VG+	NM
❑ 42054	What's On Your Mind/The Draw	1961	20.00	40.00	80.00

JOHN, ELTON

CONGRESS

Number	Title (A Side/B Side)	Yr	VG	VG+	NM
❑ 6017	Lady Samantha/It's Me That You Need	1970	12.50	25.00	50.00
❑ 6017 [DJ]	Lady Samantha/It's Me That You Need	1970	7.50	15.00	30.00
❑ 6022	Border Song/Bad Side of the Moon	1970	12.50	25.00	50.00
❑ 6022 [DJ]	Border Song/Bad Side of the Moon	1970	7.50	15.00	30.00

DJM

Number	Title (A Side/B Side)	Yr	VG	VG+	NM
❑ 70008	Lady Samantha/All Across the Havens	1969	75.00	150.00	300.00
❑ 70008 [DJ]	Lady Samantha/All Across the Havens	1969	25.00	50.00	100.00

GEFFEN

Number	Title (A Side/B Side)	Yr	VG	VG+	NM
❑ 28578	Heartache All Over the World/Highlander	1986	—	—	3.00
❑ 28578 [PS]	Heartache All Over the World/Highlander	1986	—	—	3.00
❑ 28800	Nikita/Restless	1985	—	—	3.00
❑ 28800 [PS]	Nikita/Restless	1985	—	—	3.00
❑ 28873	Wrap Her Up/The Man Who Never Died	1985	—	—	3.00
❑ 28873 [PS]	Wrap Her Up/The Man Who Never Died	1985	—	—	3.00
❑ 29111	In Neon/Tactics	1984	—	—	3.00
❑ 29189	Who Wears These Shoes?/Lonely Boy	1984	—	—	3.00
❑ 29189 [PS]	Who Wears These Shoes?/Lonely Boy	1984	—	—	3.00
❑ 29292	Sad Songs (Say So Much)/A Simple Man	1984	—	—	3.00
❑ 29292 [DJ]	Sad Songs (Say So Much) (2 mixes)	1984	2.50	5.00	10.00
—One side features a 4:05 mix unavailable elsewhere					
❑ 29402	Cold As Christmas (In the Middle of the Year)/(B-side unassigned)	1983	—	—	—
—Unreleased					
❑ 29460	I Guess That's Why They Call It the Blues/The Retreat	1983	—	—	3.00
❑ 29460 [PS]	I Guess That's Why They Call It the Blues/The Retreat	1983	—	—	3.00
❑ 29568	Kiss the Bride/Choc Ice Goes Mental	1983	—	—	3.00
❑ 29568 [PS]	Kiss the Bride/Choc Ice Goes Mental	1983	—	—	3.00
❑ 29639	I'm Still Standing/Love So Cold	1983	—	—	3.00
❑ 29639 [PS]	I'm Still Standing/Love So Cold	1983	—	—	3.00
❑ 29846	Ball & Chain/Where Have All the Good Times Gone?	1982	—	2.00	4.00
❑ 29954	Blue Eyes/Hey Papa Legba	1982	—	2.00	4.00
❑ 29954 [PS]	Blue Eyes/Hey Papa Legba	1982	—	2.50	5.00
❑ 49722	Nobody Wins/Fools in Fashion	1981	—	2.00	4.00
❑ 49722 [PS]	Nobody Wins/Fools in Fashion	1981	—	2.50	5.00
❑ 49788	Chloe/Tortured	1981	—	2.00	4.00
❑ 49788 [DJ]	Chloe//Fanfare/Chloe	1981	2.00	4.00	8.00
—B-side of this promo-only single is full-length version					
❑ 50049	Empty Garden (Hey Hey Johnny)/Take Me Down to the Ocean	1982	—	2.00	4.00
❑ 50049 [DJ]	Empty Garden (LP version)/Empty Garden (Edit)	1982	2.00	4.00	8.00
❑ 50049 [PS]	Empty Garden (Hey Hey Johnny)/Take Me Down to the Ocean	1982	—	2.50	5.00

MCA

Number	Title (A Side/B Side)	Yr	VG	VG+	NM
❑ S45-1938	Love Song (Long)/Love Song (Short)	1976	5.00	10.00	20.00
—Promo-only release from the Here And There live album					
❑ 40000	Crocodile Rock/Elderberry Wine	1972	—	3.00	6.00
—Original pressings have a solid black label					
❑ 40046	Daniel/Skyline Pigeon	1973	—	2.50	5.00
❑ 40105	Saturday Night's Alright for Fighting//Jack Rabbit/Whenever You're Ready	1973	—	2.50	5.00
❑ 40148	Goodbye Yellow Brick Road/Young Man's Blues	1973	—	2.50	5.00
❑ 40198	Bennie and the Jets/Harmony	1974	—	2.50	5.00
❑ 40259	Don't Let the Sun Go Down on Me/Sick City	1974	—	2.50	5.00
❑ 40297	The Bitch Is Back/Cold Highway	1974	—	2.50	5.00
❑ 40344	Lucy in the Sky with Diamonds/One Day at a Time	1974	—	2.50	5.00
—Both sides feature "Dr. Winston O'Boogie" (John Lennon)					
❑ 40344 [PS]	Lucy in the Sky with Diamonds/One Day at a Time	1974	2.50	5.00	10.00
❑ 40364	Philadelphia Freedom/I Saw Her Standing There	1975	—	2.50	5.00
—B-side features John Lennon					
❑ 40364 [PS]	Philadelphia Freedom/I Saw Her Standing There	1975	—	3.00	6.00
❑ 40364 [PS]	Philadelphia Freedom/I Saw Her Standing There	1975	10.00	20.00	40.00
—Promo-only sleeve from WFIL radio in Philadelphia					
❑ 40421	Someone Saved My Life Tonight/House of Cards	1975	—	2.50	5.00
—Original copies have "Captain Fantastic" label					
❑ 40421	Someone Saved My Life Tonight/House of Cards	1975	—	2.00	4.00
—With MCA black/rainbow label					
❑ 40461	Island Girl/Sugar on the Floor	1975	—	2.00	4.00
❑ 40505	Grow Some Funk of Your Own/I Feel Like a Bullet (in the Gun of Robert Ford)	1976	—	2.00	4.00
❑ 40892	Ego/Flinstone Boy	1978	—	2.00	4.00
❑ 40892 [PS]	Ego/Flinstone Boy	1978	2.50	5.00	10.00
❑ 40973	Part-Time Love/I Cry at Night	1978	—	2.00	4.00
❑ 40973 [PS]	Part-Time Love/I Cry at Night	1978	—	2.00	4.00
❑ 40993	Song for Guy/Lovesick	1979	2.50	5.00	10.00
—The stock copy is much scarcer than the promo, the only Elton John MCA single where this is the case.					
❑ 40993 [DJ]	Song for Guy/Lovesick	1979	—	2.50	5.00
❑ 40993 [PS]	Song for Guy/Lovesick	1979	—	2.50	5.00
❑ 41042	Mama Can't Buy You Love/Three Way Love Affair	1979	—	2.00	4.00
❑ 41042 [PS]	Mama Can't Buy You Love/Three Way Love Affair	1979	—	2.00	4.00
❑ 41126	Victim of Love/Strangers	1979	2.00	4.00	8.00
—Label incorrectly says "From the MCA LP...'Thunder in the Night'"					
❑ 41126	Victim of Love/Strangers	1979	—	2.00	4.00
—Label correctly says "From the MCA LP...'Victim of Love'"					
❑ 41159	Johnny B. Goode/Georgia	1980	—	2.50	5.00
❑ 41236	Little Jeannie/Conquer the Sun	1980	—	2.00	4.00
—Originals have a colorful custom label					
❑ 41236 [PS]	Little Jeannie/Conquer the Sun	1980	—	2.50	5.00
❑ 41293	(Sartorial Eloquence) Don't Ya Wanna Play This Game No More?//Cartier/White Man Danger	1980	—	2.00	4.00
❑ 53196	Candle in the Wind/Sorry Seems to Be the Hardest Word	1987	—	—	3.00
❑ 53196 [PS]	Candle in the Wind/Sorry Seems to Be the Hardest Word	1987	—	2.00	4.00
—White sleeve					
❑ 53196 [PS]	Candle in the Wind/Sorry Seems to Be the Hardest Word	1987	—	—	3.00
—Yellow sleeve with album jackets pictured on back					
❑ 53260	Take Me to the Pilot/Tonight	1988	—	2.00	4.00
❑ 53260 [PS]	Take Me to the Pilot/Tonight	1988	—	2.00	4.00
❑ 53345	I Don't Wanna Go On with You Like That/Rope Around a Fool	1988	—	—	3.00
❑ 53345 [PS]	I Don't Wanna Go On with You Like That/Rope Around a Fool	1988	—	—	3.00
❑ 53408	A Word in Spanish/Heavy Traffic	1988	—	—	3.00

Number	Title (A Side/B Side)	Yr	VG	VG+	NM
53408 [PS]	A Word in Spanish/Heavy Traffic	1988	—	—	3.00
53692	Healing Hands/Dancing in the End Zone	1989	—	—	3.00
53750	Sacrifice/Love Is a Cannibal	1989	—	—	3.00
54423	The One/Suit of Wolves	1992	—	—	3.00
54452	Runaway Train/Understanding Women	1992	—	—	3.00
—A-side: Elton John and Eric Clapton					
54581	Simple Life/The North	1993	—	—	3.00
65018	Step Into Christmas/Ho! Ho! Ho! (Who'd Be a Turkey at Christmas)	1973	—	2.50	5.00
—Originals have black labels with rainbow					
65018	Step Into Christmas/Ho! Ho! Ho! (Who'd Be a Turkey at Christmas)	1978	—	2.00	4.00
—Second edition: Tan label					
65018	Step Into Christmas/Ho! Ho! Ho! (Who'd Be a Turkey at Christmas)	1980	—	—	3.00
—Third edition: Blue label with rainbow					
79026	Club at the End of the Street/Sacrifice	1990	—	—	3.00
POLYDOR					
PRO-002	Pinball Wizard/Acid Queen	1975	10.00	20.00	40.00
—Promo-only release; B-side by Tina Turner					
ROCKET					
31456 8108 7	Something About the Way You Look Tonight/Candle in the Wind 1997	1997	—	2.50	5.00
40645	Sorry Seems to Be the Hardest Word/Shoulder Holster	1976	—	2.00	4.00
40677	Bite Your Lip (Get up and dance!)/Chameleon	1977	—	2.00	4.00
852172-7	Made in England/Lucy in the Sky with Diamonds	1995	—	2.00	4.00
—B-side recorded live at Madison Square Garden in 1974 with John Lennon					
852394-7	Blessed/Latitude	1995	—	2.00	4.00
856014-7	Believe/The One (Live)	1995	—	—	3.00
856014-7 [PS]	Believe/The One (Live)	1995	—	—	3.00
UNI					
55246	Border Song/Bad Side of the Moon	1970	—	3.00	6.00
55265	Your Song/Take Me to the Pilot	1970	—	3.00	6.00
55277	Friends/Honey Roll	1971	—	3.00	6.00
55314	Levon/Goodbye	1971	—	3.00	6.00
55318	Tiny Dancer/Razor Face	1971	—	3.00	6.00
—Stock copies have full-length version of A-side					
55318 [DJ]	Tiny Dancer/Razor Face	1971	2.50	5.00	10.00
—With a severely truncated version of the A-side					
55328	Rocket Man/Suzie (Dramas)	1972	—	3.00	6.00
55343	Honky Cat/Slave	1972	—	3.00	6.00
VIKING					
1010	From Denver to L.A./Warm Summer Rain	1970	15.00	30.00	60.00
—B-side by The Barbara Moore Singers					
1010 [DJ]	From Denver to L.A. (same on both sides)	1970	6.25	12.50	25.00
—The promo version of this has been counterfeited; some say all are counterfeits.					

7-Inch Extended Plays

Number	Title (A Side/B Side)	Yr	VG	VG+	NM
UNI					
1903 [DJ]	Come Down in Time/Country Comfort//Amoreena/Love Song	1971	3.75	7.50	15.00
—Jukebox issue, small hole, plays at 33 1/3 rpm					
1903 [PS]	Tumbleweed Connection	1971	3.75	7.50	15.00
—Part of Little LP series (LLP 143)					

JOHN, ELTON, AND KIKI DEE

Also see each artist's individual listings.

Number	Title (A Side/B Side)	Yr	VG	VG+	NM
MCA					
54762	True Love/Runaway Train	1993	—	—	3.00
—B-side by Elton John and Eric Clapton					
ROCKET					
40585	Don't Go Breakin' My Heart/Snow Queen	1976	—	2.00	4.00
40585 [PS]	Don't Go Breakin' My Heart/Snow Queen	1976	—	2.50	5.00

JOHN, ELTON, AND MILLIE JACKSON

Number	Title (A Side/B Side)	Yr	VG	VG+	NM
GEFFEN					
28956	Act of War, Part 1/Act of War, Part 2	1985	—	2.00	4.00
28956 [PS]	Act of War, Part 1/Act of War, Part 2	1985	—	2.00	4.00

JOHN, LITTLE WILLIE

Number	Title (A Side/B Side)	Yr	VG	VG+	NM
ATLANTIC					
89189	Fever/Ruby Baby	1987	—	—	3.00
—B-side by the Drifters					
89189 [PS]	Fever/Ruby Baby	1987	—	—	3.00
—From the movie "Big Town"					
KING					
4818	All Around the World/Don't Leave Me Dear	1955	6.25	12.50	25.00
4841	Need Your Love So Bad/Home at Last	1955	6.25	12.50	25.00
4893	Are You Ever Coming Back/I'm Stickin' with You Baby	1956	6.25	12.50	25.00
4935	Fever/Letter from My Darling	1956	7.50	15.00	30.00
4960	Do Something for Me/My Nerves	1956	6.25	12.50	25.00
4989	I've Been Around/Suffering with the Blues	1956	6.25	12.50	25.00
5003	Will the Sun Shine Tomorrow/A Little Bit of Loving	1956	6.25	12.50	25.00
5023	Love, Life and Money/You Got to Get Up Early in the Morning	1957	6.25	12.50	25.00
5045	I've Got to Go Cry/Look What You've Done to Me	1957	6.25	12.50	25.00
5066	Young Girl/If I Thought You Needed Me	1957	6.25	12.50	25.00
5083	Uh Uh Baby/Summer Date	1957	6.25	12.50	25.00
5091	Person to Person/Until You Do	1957	6.25	12.50	25.00
5108	Talk to Me, Talk to Me/Spasms	1958	6.25	12.50	25.00
5142	Let's Rock While the Rockin's Good/You're a Sweetheart	1958	6.25	12.50	25.00
5147	Tell It Like It Is/Don't Be Ashamed to Call My Name	1958	6.25	12.50	25.00
5154	All My Love Belongs to You/Why Don't You Haul Off and Love Me	1958	6.25	12.50	25.00
5170	No Regrets/I'll Carry Your Love Wherever I Go	1959	5.00	10.00	20.00
5179	Made for Me/Do More in Life	1959	5.00	10.00	20.00
5219	Leave My Kitten Alone/Let Nobody Love You	1959	5.00	10.00	20.00
5274	Let Them Talk/Right There	1959	5.00	10.00	20.00
5318	Loving Care/My Love Is	1960	5.00	10.00	20.00
5342	I'm Shakin'/Cottage for Sale	1960	5.00	10.00	20.00
5356	Heartbreak (It's Hurtin' Me)/Do You Love Me	1960	5.00	10.00	20.00
5394	Sleep/There's a Difference	1960	5.00	10.00	20.00
5428	Walk Slow/You Hurt Me	1960	3.75	7.50	15.00
5452	Leave My Kitten Alone/I'll Never Go Back on My Word	1961	3.75	7.50	15.00
5458	I'm Sorry/The Very Thought of You	1961	3.75	7.50	15.00
5503	(I've Got) Spring Fever/Flamingo	1961	3.75	7.50	15.00
5516	Take My Love (I Want to Give It All to You)/Now You Know	1961	3.75	7.50	15.00
5539	Need Your Love So Bad/Drive Me Home	1961	3.75	7.50	15.00
5577	There Is Someone in This World for Me/Autumn Leaves	1961	3.75	7.50	15.00
5591	Fever/Bo-Da-Ley Dino-Ley	1962	3.75	7.50	15.00
5602	The Masquerade Is Over/Katanga	1962	3.75	7.50	15.00
5628	Until Again My Love/Mister Glenn	1962	3.75	7.50	15.00
5641	Every Beat of My Heart/I Wish I Could Cry	1962	3.75	7.50	15.00
5667	She Thinks I Still Care/Come Back to Me	1962	3.75	7.50	15.00
5681	Doll Face/Big Blue Diamonds	1962	3.75	7.50	15.00
5694	Without a Friend/Half a Love	1962	3.75	7.50	15.00
5717	Don't Play with Love/Heaven All Around Me	1963	3.00	6.00	12.00
5744	My Baby's in Love with Another Guy/Come On Sugar	1963	3.00	6.00	12.00
5799	Let Them Talk/Talk to Me	1963	3.00	6.00	12.00
5818	So Lovely/Inside Information	1963	3.00	6.00	12.00
5823	Person to Person/I'm Shakin'	1963	3.00	6.00	12.00
5850	Bill Bailey/My Love Will Never Change	1964	3.00	6.00	12.00
5870	Rock Love/It Only Hurts for a Little While	1964	3.00	6.00	12.00
5886	All Around the World/All My Love Belongs to You	1964	3.00	6.00	12.00
5949	Do Something for Me/Don't You Know I'm in Love	1964	3.00	6.00	12.00
6003	Talk to Me/Take My Love	1965	2.50	5.00	10.00
6170	Fever/Let Them Talk	1968	2.50	5.00	10.00
6302	All Around the World/Need Your Love So Bad	1970	2.00	4.00	8.00

7-Inch Extended Plays

Number	Title (A Side/B Side)	Yr	VG	VG+	NM
KING					
423	(contents unknown)	1958	62.50	125.00	250.00
423 [PS]	Talk to Me	1958	62.50	125.00	250.00

JOHN, MABLE

Number	Title (A Side/B Side)	Yr	VG	VG+	NM
MOTOWN					
54031	Who Wouldn't Love a Man Like That/You Made a Fool Out of Me	1960	125.00	250.00	500.00
—Mispress with wrong label; may have been promo only					
STAX					
0016	Running Out/Shouldn't I Love Him	1968	5.00	10.00	20.00
192	Your Good Thing (Is About to End)/It's Catching	1966	5.00	10.00	20.00
205	If You Give Up What You Got/You're Taking Up Another Man's Place	1967	5.00	10.00	20.00
215	Same Time, Same Place/Bigger and Better	1967	5.00	10.00	20.00
225	I'm a Big Girl Now/Wait You Dog	1967	5.00	10.00	20.00
234	Don't Hit Me No More/Left Over Love	1967	5.00	10.00	20.00
249	Don't Get Caught/Able Mable	1968	5.00	10.00	20.00
TAMLA					
54031	Who Wouldn't Love a Man Like That/You Made a Fool Out of Me	1960	37.50	75.00	150.00
54040	No Love/Looking for a Love	1961	30.00	60.00	120.00
—Version with long intro					
54040	No Love/Looking for a Love	1961	25.00	50.00	100.00
—Version with no intro					
54050	Take Me/Action Speaks Louder Than Words	1962	20.00	40.00	80.00
54081	Who Wouldn't Love a Man Like That/Say You'll Never Let Me Go	1963	30.00	60.00	120.00

JOHN, ROBERT

Number	Title (A Side/B Side)	Yr	VG	VG+	NM
ARIOLA AMERICA					
7693	Poor Side of Town/Give a Little More	1978	—	2.00	4.00
ATLANTIC					
2846	The Lion Sleeps Tonight (Wimoweh) (Mbube)/Janet	1971	—	3.00	6.00
2884	Hushabye/To Touch, To Feel	1972	—	2.50	5.00
2906	The Way You Do the Things You Do/To Touch, To Feel	1972	—	2.50	5.00
2930	You and Me/You Don't Need a Gypsy	1973	—	2.50	5.00
A&M					
1210	When the Party Is Over/Raindrops, Love and Sunshine	1970	—	2.50	5.00
1250	You Can't Hold On/You're What's Been Missing from My Life	1971	—	2.50	5.00
1341	I'm Gonna Be Strong/I Don't Want to Make You Love Me	1972	—	2.50	5.00
BIG TOP					
3004	White Bucks and Saddle Shoes/Stranded	1958	12.50	25.00	50.00
—As "Bobby Pedrick, Jr."					
3008	Betty Blue Eyes/Pajama Party	1958	10.00	20.00	40.00
—As "Bobby Pedrick, Jr."					
3024	My Private Joy/Summer Nights	1959	10.00	20.00	40.00
—As "Bobby Pedrick, Jr."					
COLUMBIA					
44435	If You Don't Want My Love/Don't Go	1968	2.00	4.00	8.00
44639	Don't Leave Me/Children	1968	2.00	4.00	8.00
44697	Can't Stop Loving You/Thirteen Times	1968	3.00	6.00	12.00
44706	Ooh Baby Baby/Children	1968	2.00	4.00	8.00
44950	Who Could Ever Believe It/Children in the Making	1969	2.00	4.00	8.00
DUEL					
504	That Girl Is You/I'm Scared	1962	5.00	10.00	20.00
—As "Bobby Pedrick, Jr."					
516	Dining and Dancing/Two Ton Tessie	1962	5.00	10.00	20.00
—As "Bobby Pedrick, Jr."					
525	If I Had My Life to Live Over/If Mary Only Knew	1963	5.00	10.00	20.00
—As "Bobby Pedrick, Jr."					

Number	Title (A Side/B Side)	Yr	VG	VG+	NM
EMI AMERICA					
❑ 8013	Only Time/That's What Keeps Us Together	1979	—	2.00	4.00
❑ 8015	Sad Eyes/Am I Ever Gonna Hold You	1979	—	2.00	4.00
❑ 8023	Stay a Little Longer/Only Time	1979	—	2.00	4.00
❑ 8030	Lonely Eyes/Dance the Night Away	1979	—	2.00	4.00
❑ 8049	Hey There Lonely Girl/You Could Have Told Me	1980	—	2.00	4.00
❑ 8061	Sherry/On My Own	1980	—	2.00	4.00
MGM					
❑ 13384	Don't Try to Change My Ways/(I Have to) Teach Myself How to Cry	1965	3.75	7.50	15.00
—As "Bobby Pedrick"					
MOSAIC					
❑ 04445	Greased Lightning/(Instrumental)	1984	—	—	3.00
MOTOWN					
❑ 1664	Bread and Butter/If You Don't Want My Love	1983	—	—	3.00
SHELL					
❑ 722	School Crush/Come Out, Come Out	1960	5.00	10.00	20.00
—As "Bobby Pedrick"					
VERVE					
❑ 10402	Maybe/Karine	1966	12.50	25.00	50.00
—As "Bobby Pedrick"					

JOHN AND ERNEST

Also see DICKIE GOODMAN.

Number	Title (A Side/B Side)	Yr	VG	VG+	NM
RAINY WEDNESDAY					
❑ 201	Super Fly Meets Shaft/Problems	1973	—	2.50	5.00
❑ 201	Super Fly Meets Shaft/Part Two	1973	—	2.50	5.00
❑ 203	Soul President Number One/Crossover	1973	—	2.50	5.00

JOHN'S CHILDREN

Number	Title (A Side/B Side)	Yr	VG	VG+	NM
WHITE WHALE					
❑ 239	Strange Affair/Smashed, Blocked	1966	5.00	10.00	20.00

JOHNNIE AND JOE

Number	Title (A Side/B Side)	Yr	VG	VG+	NM
ABC-PARAMOUNT					
❑ 10079	I Adore You/I Want You Here Beside Me	1960	3.75	7.50	15.00
❑ 10117	Your Love/Why Do You Hurt Me So	1960	3.75	7.50	15.00
AMBIENT SOUND					
❑ 03410	Kingdom of Love/Tossin' Turnin' (Yearnin' Burnin' For Your Love)	1982	—	2.50	5.00
CHESS					
❑ 1641	I'll Be Spinning/Feel Alright	1956	5.00	10.00	20.00
❑ 1654	Over the Mountain; Across the Sea/My Baby's Gone, On, On	1957	6.25	12.50	25.00
—Originals with blue and silver "chess pieces" label					
❑ 1654	Over the Mountain; Across the Sea/My Baby's Gone, On, On	1958	3.00	6.00	12.00
—Reissues on blue labels					
❑ 1654	Over the Mountain; Across the Sea/My Baby's Gone, On, On	1963	2.50	5.00	10.00
—Reissues on other labels (multicolor, black)					
❑ 1677	I Was So Lonely/If You Tell Me You're Mine	1957	5.00	10.00	20.00
❑ 1693	Why Oh Why/Why Did She Go	1958	5.00	10.00	20.00
❑ 1706	My Baby's Gone/Darling	1958	5.00	10.00	20.00
❑ 1769	Across the Sea/You Said It, And Don't Forget It	1960	3.75	7.50	15.00
GONE					
❑ 5024	Who Do You Love/Trust in Me	1958	7.50	15.00	30.00
J&S					
❑ 1008	Over the Mountain (Part 2)/Won't You Come Back to Me	1959	6.25	12.50	25.00
❑ 1603	I Was So Lonely/If You Tell Me You're Mine	1957	6.25	12.50	25.00
❑ 1605/6	Who Do You Love/Trust in Me	1958	6.25	12.50	25.00
❑ 1630/1	Warm, Soft and Lovely/False Love Has Got to Go	1958	6.25	12.50	25.00
❑ 1654	Over the Mountain; Across the Sea/My Baby's Gone, On, On	1957	37.50	75.00	150.00
—With horizontal lines on label					
❑ 1654	Over the Mountain; Across the Sea/My Baby's Gone, On, On	1962	5.00	10.00	20.00
—Without horizontal lines on label					
❑ 1659	It Was There/There Goes My Heart	1957	6.25	12.50	25.00
❑ 1701	Where Did She Go/Red Sails in the Sunset	1959	6.25	12.50	25.00
❑ 4420	The Devil Said No, Gone With You Bad Self/You Can Always Count on Me	196?	3.75	7.50	15.00
❑ 8719	Tell Me/Sincere Love	196?	3.75	7.50	15.00
❑ 42832	You're the Loveliest Song/Let Your Mind Do the Walking	196?	3.75	7.50	15.00
❑ 87187	False Love Has Got to Go/Jamaica — Our Thing	196?	3.75	7.50	15.00
TUFF					
❑ 379	Here We Go Baby/That's the Way You Go	1964	3.00	6.00	12.00

JOHNNY AND JON

Number	Title (A Side/B Side)	Yr	VG	VG+	NM
JEWEL					
❑ 776	Christmas in Viet Nam/Why Did You Leave Me Crawl	1966	7.50	15.00	30.00

JOHNNY AND THE DREAMS

Number	Title (A Side/B Side)	Yr	VG	VG+	NM
RICHIE					
❑ 457	You're Too Young/Are You for Me	1961	125.00	250.00	500.00
—Red vinyl					
❑ 457	You're Too Young/Are You for Me	1961	62.50	125.00	250.00
—Black vinyl					

JOHNNY AND THE HURRICANES

Number	Title (A Side/B Side)	Yr	VG	VG+	NM
ATILA					
❑ 211	Saga of the Beatles/Rene	1967	2.50	5.00	10.00
❑ 214	Judy's Moody/I Love You	1967	2.50	5.00	10.00
❑ 215	Because I Love You/Wisdom's 5th Take	1967	2.50	5.00	10.00
❑ 216	Red River Rock '67/The Psychedlic Woman	1967	2.50	5.00	10.00
BIG TOP					
❑ 3036	Down Yonder/Sheba	1960	5.00	10.00	20.00
❑ 3036 [PS]	Down Yonder/Sheba	1960	10.00	20.00	40.00
❑ 3051	Revival/Rocking Goose	1960	5.00	10.00	20.00
❑ 3051 [PS]	Revival/Rocking Goose	1960	10.00	20.00	40.00
❑ 3056	You Are My Sunshine/Molly-O	1960	5.00	10.00	20.00
❑ 3056 [PS]	You Are My Sunshine/Molly-O	1960	10.00	20.00	40.00
❑ 3063	Ja-Da/Mr. Lonely	1961	5.00	10.00	20.00
❑ 3063 [PS]	Ja-Da/Mr. Lonely	1961	10.00	20.00	40.00
❑ 3076	Old Smokey/High Voltage	1961	5.00	10.00	20.00
❑ 3076 [PS]	Old Smokey/High Voltage	1961	10.00	20.00	40.00
❑ 3090	Traffic Jam/Farewell, Farewell	1961	5.00	10.00	20.00
❑ 3103	Misirlou/Salvation	1962	5.00	10.00	20.00
❑ 3113	San Antonio Rose/Come On Train	1962	5.00	10.00	20.00
❑ 3125	Shiek of Araby/Minnesota Fats	1962	5.00	10.00	20.00
❑ 3132	Whatever Happened to Baby Jane/Greens and Beans	1963	5.00	10.00	20.00
❑ 3146	James Bond Theme/Hungry Eye	1963	5.00	10.00	20.00
❑ 3159	Rough road/Kaw-Liga	1963	5.00	10.00	20.00
JEFF					
❑ 211	Saga of the Beatles/Rene	1964	3.75	7.50	15.00
MALA					
❑ 470	It's a Mad, Mad, Mad, Mad World/Shadows	1963	2.50	5.00	10.00
❑ 483	That's All/Honey, Honey	1964	2.50	5.00	10.00
TWIRL					
❑ 1001	Crossfire/Lazy	1958	12.50	25.00	50.00
WARWICK					
❑ 502	Crossfire/Lazy	1959	6.25	12.50	25.00
❑ 509 ST [S]	Red River Rock/Buckeye	1959	12.50	25.00	50.00
❑ 509 [M]	Red River Rock/Buckeye	1959	6.25	12.50	25.00
❑ 513 ST [S]	Reveille Rock/Time Bomb	1959	12.50	25.00	50.00
❑ 513 [M]	Reveille Rock/Time Bomb	1959	6.25	12.50	25.00
❑ 520	Beatnik Fly/Sand Storm	1960	5.00	10.00	20.00
❑ 520 [PS]	Beatnik Fly/Sand Storm	1960	15.00	30.00	60.00
7-Inch Extended Plays					
WARWICK					
❑ EX-700	Red River Rock/Storm Warning//Joy Ride/Bam Boo	1959	20.00	40.00	80.00
❑ EX-700 [PS]	Johnny and the Hurricanes	1959	30.00	60.00	120.00
—Came with paper sleeve rather than cardboard sleeve					

JOHNNY AND THE JAMMERS

"Johnny" is JOHNNY WINTER. His debut single.

Number	Title (A Side/B Side)	Yr	VG	VG+	NM
DART					
❑ 131	School Day Blues/You Know I Love You	1959	75.00	150.00	300.00

JOHNNY AND THE TOKENS

Also see THE TOKENS.

Number	Title (A Side/B Side)	Yr	VG	VG+	NM
WARWICK					
❑ 658	The Taste of a Tear/Never Till Now	1961	5.00	10.00	20.00

JOHNSON, BETTY

Number	Title (A Side/B Side)	Yr	VG	VG+	NM
ATLANTIC					
❑ 1169	The Little Blue Man/Winter in Miami	1958	3.75	7.50	15.00
❑ 1186	Dream/How Much	1958	3.00	6.00	12.00
❑ 2002	Hoopa Hoola/One More Time	1958	3.00	6.00	12.00
❑ 2009	You Can't Get to Heaven on Roller Skates/I Want a Good Home for My Cat	1958	3.00	6.00	12.00
❑ 2019	Does Your Heart Beat for Me?/You and Only You	1959	3.00	6.00	12.00
❑ 2039	The Lonely Willow Tree/Waltz Me Around	1959	3.00	6.00	12.00
❑ 2056	Fantastic/Don't You Care a Rowboat	1960	3.00	6.00	12.00
BALLY					
❑ 1000	I'll Wait/Please Tell Me Why	1956	3.00	6.00	12.00
❑ 1005	Honky Tonk Rock/Say It Ain't So, Joe	1956	3.75	7.50	15.00
❑ 1013	Clay Idol/Why Do You Cry?	1956	3.00	6.00	12.00
❑ 1020	I Dreamed/If It's Wrong to Love You	1956	3.00	6.00	12.00
❑ 1033	Little White Lies/1492	1957	3.00	6.00	12.00
❑ 1041	The Song You Heard When You Fell in Love/I'm Beginning to Wonder	1957	3.00	6.00	12.00
COED					
❑ 532	There's a Star Spangled Banner Waving Somewhere/Take a Little Look (In the Good Book)	1960	2.50	5.00	10.00
DOT					
❑ 16127	Slipping Around/One Has My Name, The Other Has My Heart	1960	2.50	5.00	10.00
NEW-DISC					
❑ 10013	I Want Eddie Fisher For Christmas/Show Me	1954	6.25	12.50	25.00
RCA VICTOR					
❑ 47-6034	Seven Pretty Dreams/Be a Lover	1955	3.00	6.00	12.00
❑ 47-6158	That's Happiness/Give Me Something I Can Dream About	1955	3.00	6.00	12.00
❑ 47-6268	I'm a Sinner/Beginner's Luck	1955	3.00	6.00	12.00
❑ 47-8143	Betty's Bossa Nova/Ginny's Got a Phone	1963	2.00	4.00	8.00
REPUBLIC					
❑ 2011	Depend on Me/I Don't Want to Go to Sleep Tonight	1961	2.50	5.00	10.00
❑ 2017	Let Me Be the One/Only When I Dream	1961	2.50	5.00	10.00
❑ 2021	My Kind of Guy/A Gal's Best Friend Is Her Makeup	1961	2.50	5.00	10.00
❑ 2025	How Do You Tell Your Heart/Why, Why	1961	2.50	5.00	10.00
❑ 2026	I Dreamed/Luna Caprese	1962	2.50	5.00	10.00
WORLD ARTISTS					
❑ 1014	Wednesday's Child/What's the Matter	1963	2.00	4.00	8.00

JOHNSON, BILL

Number	Title (A Side/B Side)	Yr	VG	VG+	NM
SUN					
❑ 340	Bobaloo/Bad Times Ahead	1960	5.00	10.00	20.00

JOHNSON, CLIFF

Number	Title (A Side/B Side)	Yr	VG	VG+	NM
COLUMBIA					
❑ 40865	Go 'Way Hound Dog/Twenty Four Hours a Day	1957	20.00	40.00	80.00

JOHNSON, JIMMY

Number	Title (A Side/B Side)	Yr	VG	VG+	NM
ALLIGATOR					
❑ 792	Serves Me Right to Suffer/Your Turn to Cry	1979	—	2.00	4.00

Number	Title (A Side/B Side)	Yr	VG	VG+	NM
CLASS					
❑ 237	Cool, Cool School/Lone Ranger Gonna Get Married	1958	15.00	30.00	60.00
MID WEST					
❑ 1002	Mean Woman Blues/(B-side unknown)	195?	62.50	125.00	250.00
RENDEZVOUS					
❑ 145	Cool, Cool School/Lone Ranger Gonna Get Married	1961	6.25	12.50	25.00
VIV					
❑ 3001	How About Me? Pretty Baby/Cat Daddy	1956	50.00	100.00	200.00

JOHNSON, LONNIE

Number	Title (A Side/B Side)	Yr	VG	VG+	NM
BLUESVILLE					
❑ 806	Don't Ever Love/You Don't Move Me	196?	3.00	6.00	12.00
❑ 812	I'll Get Along Somehow/Memories of You	196?	3.00	6.00	12.00
FEDERAL					
❑ 12376	Friendless Blues/What a Real Woman	1960	3.75	7.50	15.00
KING					
❑ 4201	Tomorrow Night/What a Woman	1951	15.00	30.00	60.00
—78 released in 1948					
❑ 4459	Take Me I'm Yours/Why Should I Cry	1951	10.00	20.00	40.00
❑ 4473	It Was All in Vain/You Only Want Me When You're Lonely	1951	10.00	20.00	40.00
❑ 4492	Happy New Year, Darling/Christmas Blues	1951	12.50	25.00	50.00
—B-side by Gatemouth Moore					
❑ 4503	Seven Long Days/Darlin'	1951	10.00	20.00	40.00
❑ 4510	My Mother's Eyes/My Crazy Self	1951	10.00	20.00	40.00
❑ 4553	I'm Guilty/Can't Sleep Anymore	1952	10.00	20.00	40.00
❑ 4572	You Can't Buy Love/Just Another Day	1952	10.00	20.00	40.00
❑ 4758	Tomorrow Night/Pleasing You	1954	10.00	20.00	40.00
❑ 5293	Tomorrow Night/Pleasing You	1959	3.75	7.50	15.00
❑ 5907	Love Me Tonight/Brenda	1964	2.50	5.00	10.00
❑ 6303	Tomorrow Night/Blues Stay Away from Me	1970	—	3.00	6.00
PRESTIGE					
❑ 310	Mr. Jelly Roll Baker/I'll Get Along Somehow	1964	2.50	5.00	10.00
RAMA					
❑ 9	My Woman Is Gone/Don't Make Me Cry Baby	1953	15.00	30.00	60.00
—Black vinyl					
❑ 9	My Woman Is Gone/Don't Make Me Cry Baby	1953	37.50	75.00	150.00
—Red vinyl					
❑ 14	Stick With It Baby/Will You Remember	1953	15.00	30.00	60.00
❑ 19	It's Been So Long/Vaya Con Dios	1953	15.00	30.00	60.00
❑ 20	This Love of Mine/I Love a Dream	1953	15.00	30.00	60.00

JOHNSON, MARV

Number	Title (A Side/B Side)	Yr	VG	VG+	NM
GORDY					
❑ 7042	Why Do You Want to Let Me Go/I'm Not a Plaything	1965	3.75	7.50	15.00
❑ 7051	Just the Way You Are/Miss You Baby	1966	3.75	7.50	15.00
❑ 7077	I'll Pick a Rose for My Rose/You Got the Love I Love	1968	3.75	7.50	15.00
KUDO					
❑ 663	My Baby-O/Once Upon a Time	1958	150.00	300.00	600.00
TAMLA					
❑ 101	Come to Me/Whisper	1959	75.00	150.00	300.00
—No address on label					
❑ 101	Come to Me/Whisper	1959	62.50	125.00	250.00
—With Gladstone St., Detroit, address on label					
UNITED ARTISTS					
❑ 0030	You've Got What It Takes/I Love the Way You Love	1973	—	2.50	5.00
—"Silver Spotlight Series" reissue					
❑ 0031	Move Two Mountains/Come to Me	1973	—	2.50	5.00
—"Silver Spotlight Series" reissue					
❑ 160	Come to Me/Whisper	1959	6.25	12.50	25.00
❑ 175	River of Tears/I'm Coming Home	1959	5.00	10.00	20.00
❑ 185	You Got What It Takes/Don't Leave Me	1959	5.00	10.00	20.00
❑ 208	I Love the Way You Love/Let Me Love You	1960	5.00	10.00	20.00
❑ 226	Ain't Gonna Be That Way/All the Love I've Got	1960	5.00	10.00	20.00
❑ 241	(You've Got to) Move Two Mountains/I Need You	1960	3.75	7.50	15.00
❑ 273	Happy Days/Baby, Baby	1960	3.75	7.50	15.00
❑ 294	Merry-Go-Round/Tell Me That You Love Me	1961	3.75	7.50	15.00
❑ 322	How Can We Tell Him/I've Got a Notion	1961	5.00	10.00	20.00
❑ 359	Show Me/Oh Mary	1961	5.00	10.00	20.00
❑ 386	Easier Said Than Done/Johnny One Stop	1961	5.00	10.00	20.00
❑ 423	Magic Mirror/With All That's In Me	1962	5.00	10.00	20.00
❑ 454	He Gave Me You/That's How Bad	1962	5.00	10.00	20.00
❑ 483	Let Yourself Go/That's Where I Lost My Baby	1962	5.00	10.00	20.00
❑ 556	Keep Tellin' Yourself/Everyone Who's Been in Love with You	1963	5.00	10.00	20.00
❑ 590	He's Got the Whole World In His Hands/Another Tear Falls	1963	5.00	10.00	20.00
❑ 617	Come On and Stop/Not Available	1963	5.00	10.00	20.00
❑ 643	Congratulations, You've Hurt Me Again/Crying on My Pillow	1963	5.00	10.00	20.00
❑ 691	Unbreakable Love/A Man Who Don't Believe in Love	1964	6.25	12.50	25.00
7-Inch Extended Plays					
UNITED ARTISTS					
❑ 10,007	I Love the Way You Love/Let Me Love You//You Got What It Takes/Don't Leave Me	1960	25.00	50.00	100.00
❑ 10,007 [PS]	Marv Johnson	1960	25.00	50.00	100.00
❑ 10,009	(contents unknown)	1960	25.00	50.00	100.00
❑ 10,009 [PS]	Marv Johnson	1960	25.00	50.00	100.00

JOHNSON, MIRRIAM

See JESSI COLTER.

JOHNSON, TERRY

Number	Title (A Side/B Side)	Yr	VG	VG+	NM
GORDY					
❑ 7091	My Springtime/Suzie	1969	30.00	60.00	120.00
❑ 7095	Whatcha Gonna Do/Suzie	1970	6.25	12.50	25.00

JOHNSON BROTHERS, THE

Number	Title (A Side/B Side)	Yr	VG	VG+	NM
IMPERIAL					
❑ 5550	Love Ain't Got a Thing/Find Another Heart	1958	5.00	10.00	20.00
VALOR					
❑ 2006	Zombie Lou/Castin' My Spell	1958	25.00	50.00	100.00

JOHNSTON, BRUCE

Also see THE BEACH BOYS; BRUCE AND TERRY; THE GAMBLERS; THE KUSTOM KINGS; PAPA DOO RUN RUN; THE REVERES (3); THE VETTES.

Number	Title (A Side/B Side)	Yr	VG	VG+	NM
COLUMBIA					
❑ 10568	Pipeline/Disney Girls	1977	2.50	5.00	10.00
—Promos (with "Pipeline" on both sides) worth 50% less					
DEL-FI					
❑ 4202	The Original Surfer Stomp/Pajama Party	1963	15.00	30.00	60.00
—Originals credit "The Surf Stompers"					
❑ 4202	The Original Surfer Stomp/Pajama Party	1963	7.50	15.00	30.00
DONNA					
❑ 1354	Do the Surfer Stomp (Part 1)/Do the Surfer Stomp (Part 2)	1962	12.50	25.00	50.00
—Originals credit "The Surf Stompers"					
❑ 1354	Do the Surfer Stomp (Part 1)/Do the Surfer Stomp (Part 2)	1962	7.50	15.00	30.00
❑ 1354 [PS]	Do the Surfer Stomp (Part 1)/Do the Surfer Stomp (Part 2)	1962	25.00	50.00	100.00
❑ 1364	Soupy Shuffle Stomp (SSS)/Moon Shot	1962	7.50	15.00	30.00
❑ 1374	The Original Surfer Stomp (Part 1)/The Original Surfer Stomp (Part 2)	1962	7.50	15.00	30.00
RONDA					
❑ 1003	Do the Surfer Stomp (Part 1)/Do the Surfer Stomp (Part 2)	1962	10.00	20.00	40.00

JOHNSTON, BRUCE, AND TERRY MELCHER

See BRUCE AND TERRY.

JOLSON, AL

Number	Title (A Side/B Side)	Yr	VG	VG+	NM
DECCA					
❑ 9-27024	The Old Piano Roll Blues/Way Down Yonder in New Orleans	1950	5.00	10.00	20.00
❑ 9-27043	Are You Lonesome Tonight/No Sad Songs for Me	1950	5.00	10.00	20.00
❑ 9-27181	De Camptown Races/Oh Susannah	1950	5.00	10.00	20.00
❑ 9-27362	Beautiful Dreamer/Old Folks at Home	1951	3.75	7.50	15.00
❑ 9-27364	I Dream of Jeannie with the Light Brown Hair/Old Black Joe	1951	3.75	7.50	15.00
❑ 9-27365	Massa's in De Cold, Cold Ground/My Old Kentucky Home	1951	3.75	7.50	15.00
—The above four comprise a box set					
❑ 9-27410	In Our House/I'm Crying Just for You	1951	3.75	7.50	15.00
MCA					
❑ 60037	Swanee/April Showers	1973	—	2.50	5.00
—Black label with rainbow					
❑ 60038	Avalon/Anniversary Song	1973	—	2.50	5.00
—Black label with rainbow					
❑ 60048	You Made Me Love You/Ma Blushin' Rosie	1973	—	2.50	5.00
—Black label with rainbow					
❑ 60096	My Mammy/Sonny Boy	197?	—	2.50	5.00
—Black label with rainbow					
❑ 60136	California Here I Come/Rock-a-Bye Your Baby with a Dixie Melody	197?	—	2.50	5.00
—Black label with rainbow					

JON AND ROBIN AND THE IN CROWD

Also see THE IN CROWD (1).

Number	Title (A Side/B Side)	Yr	VG	VG+	NM
ABNAK					
❑ 111	Lonely One/How Come	1965	2.50	5.00	10.00
❑ 111 [DJ]	Lonely One/How Come	1965	3.75	7.50	15.00
—Promo only on yellow vinyl					
❑ 113	Can't Make It With You/If I Need Someone	1966	2.50	5.00	10.00
❑ 113 [DJ]	Can't Make It With You/If I Need Someone	1966	3.75	7.50	15.00
—Promo only on yellow vinyl					
❑ 115	Hey Girl/If I Need Someone	1966	2.50	5.00	10.00
❑ 115 [DJ]	Hey Girl/If I Need Someone	1966	3.75	7.50	15.00
—Promo only on yellow vinyl					
❑ 119	Do It Again A Little Bit Slower/If I Need Someone	1967	3.00	6.00	12.00
❑ 119 [DJ]	Do It Again A Little Bit Slower/If I Need Someone	1967	4.00	8.00	16.00
—Promo only on yellow vinyl					
❑ 122	Drums/You Don't Care	1967	2.50	5.00	10.00
❑ 122 [DJ]	Drums/You Don't Care	1967	3.75	7.50	15.00
—Promo only on yellow vinyl					
❑ 124	I Want Some More/Love Me Baby	1967	2.50	5.00	10.00
❑ 124 [DJ]	I Want Some More/Love Me Baby	1967	3.75	7.50	15.00
—Promo only on yellow vinyl					
❑ 127	Dr. Jon (The Medicine Man)/Love Me Baby	1968	2.00	4.00	8.00
❑ 127 [DJ]	Dr. Jon (The Medicine Man)/Love Me Baby	1968	3.00	6.00	12.00
—Promo only on yellow vinyl					
❑ 130	You Got Style/Thursday Morning	1968	2.00	4.00	8.00
❑ 130 [DJ]	You Got Style/Thursday Morning	1968	3.00	6.00	12.00
—Promo only on yellow vinyl					
❑ 133	Save Me, Save Me/Thursday Morning	1968	2.00	4.00	8.00
—As "Jon and the In Crowd"					
❑ 133 [DJ]	Save Me, Save Me/Thursday Morning	1968	3.00	6.00	12.00
—Promo only on yellow vinyl					
❑ 135	Gift of Love/Gift of Love (Country Style)	1969	2.00	4.00	8.00
❑ 135 [DJ]	Gift of Love/Gift of Love (Country Style)	1969	3.00	6.00	12.00
—Promo only on yellow vinyl					
❑ 138	Give Me Your Love/Lonely One	1969	2.00	4.00	8.00
❑ 138 [DJ]	Give Me Your Love/Lonely One	1969	3.00	6.00	12.00
—Promo only on yellow vinyl					
❑ 140	There's An American Flag on the Moon (Part 1)/There's An American Flag on the Moon (Part 2)	1969	2.00	4.00	8.00

Number	Title (A Side/B Side)	Yr	VG	VG+	NM
❑ 140 [DJ]	There's An American Flag on the Moon (Part 1)/There's An American Flag on the Moon (Part 2)	1969	3.00	6.00	12.00
—Promo only on yellow vinyl					
❑ 141	If You Got It, Flaunt It/I'll Come Running to You	1969	2.00	4.00	8.00
❑ 141 [DJ]	If You Got It, Flaunt It/I'll Come Running to You	1969	3.00	6.00	12.00
—Promo only on yellow vinyl					

JONES, CORKY

See BUCK OWENS.

JONES, DAVY

Also see DOLENZ, JONES & TORK; DOLENZ, JONES, BOYCE & HART; THE MONKEES.

Number	Title (A Side/B Side)	Yr	VG	VG+	NM
BELL					
❑ 45111	Rainy Jane/Welcome to My Love	1971	2.50	5.00	10.00
❑ 45136	I Really Love You/Sitting in the Apple Tree	1971	2.50	5.00	10.00
❑ 45159	Girl/Take My Love	1971	12.50	25.00	50.00
❑ 45178	I'll Believe in You/The Road to Love	1972	5.00	10.00	20.00
COLPIX					
❑ 764	Dream Girl/Take Me to Paradise	1965	5.00	10.00	20.00
—Colpix sides as "David Jones"					
❑ 764 [PS]	Dream Girl/Take Me to Paradise	1965	7.50	15.00	30.00
❑ 784	What Are We Going to Do/This Bouquet	1965	5.00	10.00	20.00
❑ 784 [PS]	What Are We Going to Do/This Bouquet	1965	7.50	15.00	30.00
❑ 789	The Girl from Chelsea/Theme for a New Love	1965	5.00	10.00	20.00
❑ 789 [PS]	The Girl from Chelsea/Theme for a New Love	1965	10.00	20.00	40.00
MGM					
❑ 14458	You're a Lady/Who Was It	1972	7.50	15.00	30.00
❑ 14524	Rubberene/Who Was It	1973	7.50	15.00	30.00

JONES, GEORGE

Also see GENE PITNEY.

Number	Title (A Side/B Side)	Yr	VG	VG+	NM
D					
❑ 1226	New Baby for Christmas/Maybe Next Christmas	1961	3.00	6.00	12.00
EPIC					
❑ 02526	Still Doin' Time/Good Ones and Bad Ones	1981	—	—	3.00
❑ 02696	Same Ol' Me/Together Alone	1982	—	—	3.00
❑ 03489	Shine On (Shine All Your Sweet Love on Me)/Memories of Mama	1982	—	—	3.00
❑ 03883	I Always Get Lucky with You/I'd Rather Have What We Had	1983	—	—	3.00
❑ 04082	Tennessee Whiskey/Almost Persuaded	1983	—	—	3.00
❑ 04413	You've Still Got a Place in My Heart/I'm Ragged But Right	1984	—	—	3.00
❑ 04609	She's My Rock/(What Love Can Do) The Second Time Around	1984	—	—	3.00
❑ 04876	Size Seven Round (Made of Gold)/All I Want to Do in Life	1985	—	—	3.00
—A-side with Lacy J. Dalton; B-side with Janie Frickie					
❑ 05439	Who's Gonna Fill Their Shoes/A Whole Lot of Trouble for You	1985	—	—	3.00
❑ 05698	The One I Loved Back Then (The Corvette Song)/If Only You'd Love Me Again	1985	—	—	3.00
❑ 05862	Somebody Wants Me Out of the Way/Call the Wrecker for My Heart	1986	—	—	3.00
❑ 06296	Wine Colored Roses/These Old Eyes Have Seen It All	1986	—	—	3.00
❑ 06593	The Right Left Hand/The Very Best on Me	1986	—	—	3.00
❑ 07107	I Turn to You/Don't Leave Without Taking Your Silver	1987	—	—	3.00
❑ 07655	The Bird/I'm Goin' Home Like I Never Did Before	1987	—	—	3.00
❑ 07748	I'm a Survivor/The Real McCoy	1988	—	—	3.00
❑ 07913	The Old Man No One Loves/One Hell of a Song	1988	—	—	3.00
❑ 08011	If I Could Bottle This Up/I Always Get It Right with You	1988	—	—	3.00
—With Shelby Lynne					
❑ 08509	I'm a One Woman Man/Pretty Little Lady from Beaumont, Texas	1988	—	—	3.00
❑ 10831	We Can Make It/One of These Days	1972	—	2.50	5.00
❑ 10858	Loving You Could Never Be Better/Try It, You'll Like It	1972	—	2.50	5.00
❑ 10917	A Picture of Me (Without You)/The Man Worth Loving You	1972	—	2.50	5.00
❑ 10959	What My Woman Can't Do/My Loving Wife	1973	—	2.50	5.00
❑ 11006	Nothing Ever Hurt Me (Half As Bad As Losing You)/Wine	1973	—	2.50	5.00
❑ 11053	Once You've Had the Best/Mary Don't Go Round	1973	—	2.50	5.00
❑ 11122	The Grand Tour/Our Private Life	1974	—	2.50	5.00
❑ 50038	The Door/Wean Me	1974	—	2.50	5.00
❑ 50088	These Days (I Barely Get By)/Baby, There's Nothing Like You	1975	—	2.50	5.00
❑ 50127	Memories of Us/I Just Don't Give a Damn	1975	—	2.50	5.00
❑ 50187	The Battle/I'll Come Back	1976	—	2.50	5.00
❑ 50227	You Always Look Your Best (Here in My Arms)/Have You Seen My Chicken	1976	—	2.50	5.00
❑ 50271	Her Name Is.../Diary of My Mind	1976	—	2.50	5.00
❑ 50385	Old King Kong/It's a 10-33 (Let's Get Jesus on the Line)	1977	—	2.00	4.00
❑ 50423	If I Could Put Them All Together (I'd Have You)/You've Got the Best of Me Again	1977	—	2.00	4.00
❑ 50495	Bartender's Blues/Rest in Peace	1977	—	2.00	4.00
❑ 50564	I'll Just Take It Out in Love/Leaving Love All Over the Place	1978	—	2.00	4.00
❑ 50684	Someday My Day Will Come/We Oughta Be Ashamed	1979	—	2.00	4.00
❑ 50867	He Stopped Loving Her Today/A Hard Act to Follow	1980	—	3.00	6.00
❑ 50922	I'm Not Ready Yet/Garage Sale Today	1980	—	2.00	4.00
❑ 50968	If Drinkin' Don't Kill Me (Her Memory Will)/Brother to the Blues	1980	—	2.00	4.00
❑ 68743	Ya Ba Da Ba Do (So Are You)/Don't You Ever Get Tired (Of Hurting Me)	1989	—	2.50	5.00
❑ 68743	The King Is Gone (So Are You)/Don't You Ever Get Tired (Of Hurting Me)	1989	—	—	3.00
—Same song, different title (changed for legal reasons)					
❑ 68743 [PS]	Ya Ba Da Ba Do (So Are You)/Don't You Ever Get Tired (Of Hurting Me)	1989	—	2.50	5.00
❑ 68991	Writing on the Wall/Burning Bridges	1989	—	—	3.00
❑ 73070	Radio Lover/Burning Bridges	1989	—	—	3.00
❑ 73424	Six Foot Deep, Six Foot Down/He Never Got the Picture at All	1990	—	2.00	4.00
MCA					
❑ 54187	You Couldn't Get the Picture/Heckle and Jeckle	1991	—	2.00	4.00
❑ 54272	She Loved a Lot in Her Time/Come Home to Me	1991	—	2.00	4.00
❑ 54370	Honky Tonk Myself to Death/Where the Tall Grass Grows	1992	—	2.00	4.00
❑ 54470	I Don't Need Your Rockin' Chair/Finally Friday	1992	—	2.50	5.00
❑ 54604	Wrong's What I Do Best/The Bottle Let Me Down	1993	—	2.00	4.00
❑ 54687	Walls Can Fall/You Must Have Walked Across My Mind Again	1993	—	—	3.00
❑ 54749	High-Tech Redneck/Forever's Here to Stay	1993	—	2.00	4.00
❑ 54969	A Good Year for the Roses/I've Still Got Some Hurtin' Left to Do	1994	—	2.00	4.00
—A-side with Alan Jackson					
❑ 55228	Honky Tonk Song/The Lone Ranger	1996	—	2.00	4.00
❑ 55287	Billy B. Bad/Back Down to Hung Up on You	1996	—	2.00	4.00
❑ 72038	Wild Irish Rose/No Future for Me in Our Past	1998	—	—	3.00
MERCURY					
❑ 7045 [S]	White Lightning/Treasure of Love	196?	10.00	20.00	40.00
❑ 7046 [S]	Why Baby Why/Hearts in My Dream	196?	10.00	20.00	40.00
❑ 7047 [S]	The Window Up Above/Color of the Blues	196?	10.00	20.00	40.00
❑ 7048 [S]	Tall, Tall Trees/Don't Stop the Music	196?	10.00	20.00	40.00
❑ 7049 [S]	Who Shot Sam/Accidentally on Purpose	196?	10.00	20.00	40.00
❑ 71029	Don't Stop the Music/Uh, Uh, No	1957	6.25	12.50	25.00
❑ 71049	Just One More/Gonna Come Get You	1957	6.25	12.50	25.00
❑ 71096	Too Much Water/All I Want to Do	1957	6.25	12.50	25.00
❑ 71139	Nothing Can Stop Me/I'm With the Wrong One	1957	6.25	12.50	25.00
❑ 71176	Tall, Tall Trees/Hearts in My Dream	1957	5.00	10.00	20.00
❑ 71224	Take the Devil Out of Me/A Cup of Loneliness	1957	5.00	10.00	20.00
❑ 71225	New Baby for Christmas/Maybe Next Christmas	1957	5.00	10.00	20.00
❑ 71257	Color of the Blues/Eskimo Pie	1958	5.00	10.00	20.00
❑ 71340	Wandering Soul/Jesus Wants Me	1958	5.00	10.00	20.00
❑ 71373	Treasure of Love/If I Don't Love You (Grits Ain't Groceries)	1958	5.00	10.00	20.00
❑ 71406	White Lightning/Long Time to Forget	1959	3.75	7.50	15.00
❑ 71464	Who Shot Sam/Into My Arms Again	1959	3.75	7.50	15.00
❑ 71506	My Lord Has Called Me/If You Want to Wear a Crown	1959	5.00	10.00	20.00
❑ 71514	Money to Burn/Big Harlan Taylor	1959	3.75	7.50	15.00
❑ 71583	Accidently on Purpose/Sparkling Blue Eyes	1960	3.75	7.50	15.00
❑ 71615	Have Mercy on Me/If You Believe	1960	5.00	10.00	20.00
❑ 71636	Family Bible/Your Old Standby	1960	5.00	10.00	20.00
❑ 71641	Out of Control/Just Little Boy Blue	1960	3.75	7.50	15.00
❑ 71700	The Window Up Above/Candy Hearts	1960	3.75	7.50	15.00
❑ 71721	Family Bible/Taggin' Along	1961	3.75	7.50	15.00
❑ 71804	Tender Years/Battle of Love	1961	3.00	6.00	12.00
❑ 71804 [PS]	Tender Years/Battle of Love	1961	3.75	7.50	15.00
❑ 71910	Aching, Breaking Heart/When My Heart Hurts No More	1962	3.00	6.00	12.00
❑ 71910 [PS]	Aching, Breaking Heart/When My Heart Hurts No More	1962	3.75	7.50	15.00
❑ 72010	You're Still on My Mind/Cold, Cold Heart	1962	3.00	6.00	12.00
❑ 72010 [PS]	You're Still on My Mind/Cold, Cold Heart	1962	3.75	7.50	15.00
❑ 72087	I Love You Because/Revenoor Man	1963	3.00	6.00	12.00
❑ 72087 [PS]	I Love You Because/Revenoor Man	1963	3.75	7.50	15.00
❑ 72159	Are You Mine/I Didn't Hear You	1963	3.00	6.00	12.00
❑ 72200	Mr. Fool/One Is a Lonely Number	1963	3.00	6.00	12.00
❑ 72233	The Last Town I Painted/Tarnished Angel	1964	3.00	6.00	12.00
❑ 72233 [PS]	The Last Town I Painted/Tarnished Angel	1964	3.75	7.50	15.00
❑ 72293	Oh Lonesome Me/Life to Go	1964	3.00	6.00	12.00
❑ 72293 [PS]	Oh Lonesome Me/Life to Go	1964	3.75	7.50	15.00
❑ 72362	I Wouldn't Know About That/You Better Treat Your Man Right	1964	3.00	6.00	12.00
MUSICOR					
❑ 1067	Things Have Gone to Pieces/Wearing My Heart Away	1965	2.00	4.00	8.00
❑ 1067 [PS]	Things Have Gone to Pieces/Wearing My Heart Away	1965	3.75	7.50	15.00
❑ 1098	Love Bug/I Can't Get Used to Being Lonely	1965	2.00	4.00	8.00
❑ 1117	Take Me/Ship of Love	1965	2.00	4.00	8.00
❑ 1143	I'm a People/I Woke Up from Dreaming	1966	2.00	4.00	8.00
❑ 1174	Old Brush Arbors/Flowers for Mama	1966	2.00	4.00	8.00
❑ 1181	Four-O-Thirty Three/Don't Think I Don't	1966	2.00	4.00	8.00
❑ 1226	Walk Through This World with Me/Developing My Pictures	1967	2.00	4.00	8.00
❑ 1243	I Can't Get There from Here/A Poor Man's Riches	1967	2.00	4.00	8.00
❑ 1244	A Cup of Loneliness/That the World But Give Me Jesus	1967	3.00	6.00	12.00
❑ 1267	If My Heart Had Windows/Honky Tonk Downstairs	1967	2.00	4.00	8.00
❑ 1289	Say It's Not You/Poor Chinee	1968	2.00	4.00	8.00
❑ 1297	Small Time Laboring Man/Well It's Alright	1968	2.00	4.00	8.00
❑ 1298	As Long As I Live/Your Angel Steps Out of Heaven	1968	2.00	4.00	8.00
❑ 1333	When the Grass Grows Over Me/Heartaches and Hangovers	1968	2.00	4.00	8.00
❑ 1339	Lonely Christmas Call/My Mom and Santa Claus	1968	2.00	4.00	8.00
❑ 1351	I'll Share My World with You/I'll See You a While Ago	1969	2.00	4.00	8.00
❑ 1366	If Not for You/When the Wife Runs Off	1969	2.00	4.00	8.00
❑ 1381	She's Mine/No Blues Is Good News	1969	2.00	4.00	8.00
❑ 1392	Where Grass Won't Grow/Shoulder to Shoulder	1970	—	3.00	6.00
❑ 1404	Going Life's Way/Uncloudy Day	1970	—	3.00	6.00

Number	Title (A Side/B Side)	Yr	VG	VG+	NM
❑ 1408	Tell Me My Lying Eyes Are Wrong/You've Become My Everything	1970	—	3.00	6.00
❑ 1425	A Good Year for the Roses/Let a Little Loving Come In	1970	2.00	4.00	8.00
❑ 1432	Sometimes You Just Can't Win/Brothers of a Bottle	1971	—	3.00	6.00
❑ 1440	Right Won't Touch a Hand/Someone Sweet to Love	1971	—	3.00	6.00
❑ 1446	I'll Follow You (Up to Our Cloud)/Getting Over the Storm	1971	—	3.00	6.00
RCA VICTOR					
❑ AMBO-0123	Tender Years/White Lightnin'	1973	—	2.50	5.00
❑ APBO-0218	My Favorite Lies/You Gotta Be My Baby	1974	—	2.50	5.00
❑ PB-10052	I Can Love You Enough/Talk to Me Lonesome Heart	1974	—	2.50	5.00
❑ 74-0625	A Day in the Life of a Fool/Old, Old House	1971	—	3.00	6.00
❑ 74-0700	I Made Leaving (Easy for You)/How Proud I Would Have Been	1972	—	3.00	6.00
❑ 74-0792	Wrapped Around Her Finger/With Half a Heart	1972	—	3.00	6.00
❑ 74-0878	I Can Still See Him in Your Eyes/She's Mine	1973	—	3.00	6.00
STARDAY					
❑ 130	No Money in This Deal/You're in My Heart	1954	25.00	50.00	100.00
❑ 146	Play It Cool, Man/Wrong About You	1954	15.00	30.00	60.00
—B-side with Sonny Burns					
❑ 160	Let Him Know/Let Me Catch My Breath	1954	15.00	30.00	60.00
❑ 162	You All Goodnight/Let Him Know	1954	15.00	30.00	60.00
❑ 165	Tell Her/Heartbroken Me	1954	15.00	30.00	60.00
—B-side with Sonny Burns					
❑ 188	Hold Everything/What's Wrong with You	1955	12.50	25.00	50.00
❑ 202	Why Baby Why/Season of My Heart	1955	12.50	25.00	50.00
❑ 216	What Am I Worth/Still Hurtin'	1955	10.00	20.00	40.00
❑ 234	I'm Ragged But I'm Right/Your Heart	1956	10.00	20.00	40.00
❑ 240	Rock It/How Come It	1956	50.00	100.00	200.00
—As "Thumper Jones"					
❑ 247	You Gotta Be My Baby/It's OK	1956	10.00	20.00	40.00
❑ 256	Boat of Life/Taggin' Along	1956	10.00	20.00	40.00
❑ 264	Just One More/Gonna Come Get You	1956	10.00	20.00	40.00
❑ 7003	Seasons of My Heart/I'm Ragged But I'm Right	197?	—	2.50	5.00
❑ 7020	Wasted Words/Any Old Time	197?	—	2.50	5.00
❑ 7036	Why Baby Why/You Gotta Be My Baby	197?	—	2.50	5.00
❑ 8012	Why Baby Why/Seasons of My Heart	197?	—	2.50	5.00
UNITED ARTISTS					
❑ 424	She Thinks I Still Care/Sometimes You Just Can't Win	1962	2.50	5.00	10.00
❑ 424 [PS]	She Thinks I Still Care/Sometimes You Just Can't Win	1962	3.75	7.50	15.00
❑ 442	Beacon in the Night/He Made Me Free	1962	3.00	6.00	12.00
❑ 462	Open Pit Mine/Geronimo	1962	2.50	5.00	10.00
❑ 463	He Is So Good to Me/Magic Valley	1962	3.00	6.00	12.00
❑ 500	A Girl I Used to Know/Big Fool of the Year	1962	2.50	5.00	10.00
❑ 528	Not What I Had in Mind/I Saw Me	1962	2.50	5.00	10.00
❑ 530	Lonely Christmas Call/My Mom and Santa Claus	1962	3.75	7.50	15.00
❑ 578	You Comb Her Hair/Ain't It Funny What a Fool Will Do	1963	2.50	5.00	10.00
❑ 578 [PS]	You Comb Her Hair/Ain't It Funny What a Fool Will Do	1963	3.75	7.50	15.00
❑ 683	Your Heart Turned Left (And I Was On the Right)/My Tears Are Overdue	1964	2.50	5.00	10.00
❑ 724	Where Does a Little Tear Come From/Something I Dreamed	1964	2.50	5.00	10.00
❑ 751	The Race Is On/She's Lonesome Again	1964	2.50	5.00	10.00
❑ 804	Least of All/Brown to Blue	1965	2.50	5.00	10.00
❑ 858	Wrong Number/Old Old House	1965	2.50	5.00	10.00
❑ 901	What's Money/I Get Lonely in a Hurry	1965	2.50	5.00	10.00
❑ 965	World's Worse Loser/I Can't Change Overnight	1965	2.50	5.00	10.00
❑ 50014	Best Guitar Picker/A Good Old Fashioned Cry	1966	2.50	5.00	10.00

JONES, GEORGE, AND BRENDA CARTER

Number	Title (A Side/B Side)	Yr	VG	VG+	NM
MUSICOR					
❑ 1325	Milwaukee, Here I Come/Great Big Spirit of Love	1968	2.00	4.00	8.00
❑ 1375	Lonesome End of the Line/Just Your Average Couple	1969	2.00	4.00	8.00

JONES, GEORGE, AND JEANETTE HICKS

Number	Title (A Side/B Side)	Yr	VG	VG+	NM
MERCURY					
❑ 71061	Yearning/Cry, Cry	1957	6.25	12.50	25.00
STARDAY					
❑ 279	Yearning/So Near Yet So Far Away	1956	7.50	15.00	30.00

JONES, GEORGE, AND BRENDA LEE

Number	Title (A Side/B Side)	Yr	VG	VG+	NM
EPIC					
❑ 04723	Hallelujah I Love Her So/(What Love Can Do) The Second Time Around	1984	—	2.00	4.00

JONES, GEORGE, AND MELBA MONTGOMERY

Number	Title (A Side/B Side)	Yr	VG	VG+	NM
MUSICOR					
❑ 1204	Close Together (As You and Me)/Long As We're Dreaming	1966	2.00	4.00	8.00
❑ 1238	Party Pickin'/Simply Divine	1967	2.00	4.00	8.00
UNITED ARTISTS					
❑ 575	We Must Have Been Out of Our Minds/Until Then	1963	2.50	5.00	10.00
❑ 635	Let's Invite Them Over/What's In Our Hearts	1963	2.50	5.00	10.00
❑ 704	There's a Friend in the Way/Suppose Tonight Would Be Our Last	1964	2.50	5.00	10.00
❑ 732	Please Be My Love/Will There Ever Be Another	1964	2.50	5.00	10.00
❑ 784	Multiply the Heartaches/Once More	1964	2.50	5.00	10.00
❑ 828	House of Gold/I Dreamed My Baby Came Home	1965	2.50	5.00	10.00
❑ 899	Don't Go/I Let You Go	1965	2.50	5.00	10.00
❑ 941	Blue Moon of Kentucky/I Can't Get Over You	1965	2.50	5.00	10.00
❑ 50015	Afraid/Now Tell Me	1966	2.50	5.00	10.00

JONES, GEORGE, AND JOHNNY PAYCHECK

Also see each artist's individual listings.

Number	Title (A Side/B Side)	Yr	VG	VG+	NM
EPIC					
❑ 50647	Mabellene/Don't Want No Stranger Sleepin' in My Bed	1978	—	2.00	4.00
❑ 50708	You Can Have Her/Along Came Jones	1979	—	2.00	4.00
❑ 50891	When You're Ugly Like Us (You Just Naturally Got to Be Cool)/Kansas City	1980	—	2.00	4.00
❑ 50949	You Better Move On/Smack Dab in the Middle	1980	—	2.00	4.00

JONES, GEORGE, AND MARGIE SINGLETON

Number	Title (A Side/B Side)	Yr	VG	VG+	NM
MERCURY					
❑ 71856	Did I Ever Tell You/Not Even Friends	1961	3.00	6.00	12.00
❑ 71955	Waltz of the Angels/Talk About Lovin'	1962	3.00	6.00	12.00

JONES, GEORGE, AND TAMMY WYNETTE

Also see each artist's individual listings; TINA WITH DADDY AND MOMMY.

Number	Title (A Side/B Side)	Yr	VG	VG+	NM
EPIC					
❑ 10815	Take Me/We Go Together	1971	—	2.50	5.00
❑ 10881	The Ceremony/The Great Divide	1972	—	2.50	5.00
❑ 10923	Old Fashioned Singing/We Love to Sing About Jesus	1972	—	2.50	5.00
❑ 10963	Let's Build a World Together/Touching Shoulders	1973	—	2.50	5.00
❑ 11031	We're Gonna Hold On/My Elusive Dreams	1973	—	2.50	5.00
❑ 11077	Mr. and Mrs. Santa Claus/The Greatest Christmas Gift	1973	—	2.50	5.00
❑ 11083	(We're Not) The Jet Set/The Crawdad Song	1974	—	2.50	5.00
❑ 11151	We Loved It Away/Ain't It Been Good	1974	—	2.50	5.00
❑ 50099	God's Gonna Getcha (For That)/Those Were the Good Times	1975	—	2.50	5.00
❑ 50235	Golden Ring/We're Putting It Back Together	1976	—	2.50	5.00
❑ 50314	Near You/Tattletale Eyes	1976	—	2.50	5.00
❑ 50418	Southern California/Keep the Change	1977	—	2.00	4.00
❑ 50849	Two Story House/It Sure Was Good	1980	—	2.00	4.00
❑ 50930	A Pair of Old Sneakers/We'll Talk About It Later	1980	—	2.00	4.00
MCA					
❑ 55048	One/Golden Ring	1995	—	2.00	4.00

JONES, JIMMY

Number	Title (A Side/B Side)	Yr	VG	VG+	NM
ABC-PARAMOUNT					
❑ 10094	Blue and Lonely/Daddy Needs Baby	1960	37.50	75.00	150.00
—As "Jimmy Jones and the Pretenders"					
ARROW					
❑ 717	Heaven in Your Eyes/The Whistlin' Man	1957	45.00	90.00	180.00
—As "Jimmy Jones and the Jones Boys"					
BELL					
❑ 682	Personal Property/39-21-40	1967	2.00	4.00	8.00
❑ 689	True Love Ways/Snap My Fingers	1967	2.00	4.00	8.00
CAPITOL					
❑ 3849	If I Knew Then (What I Know Now)/Everything's Gonna Be All Right	1974	—	2.50	5.00
CONCHILLO					
❑ 1	Ain't Nothing Wrong Makin' Love the First Night/Time and Changes	1976	—	3.00	6.00
CUB					
❑ 9049	Handy Man/The Search Is Over	1959	6.25	12.50	25.00
❑ 9067	Good Timin'/My Precious Angel	1960	6.25	12.50	25.00
❑ 9072	That's When I Cried/I Just Go for You	1960	5.00	10.00	20.00
❑ 9072 [PS]	That's When I Cried/I Just Go for You	1960	12.50	25.00	50.00
❑ 9076	Itchin'/Ee-I-Ee-I-Oh	1960	5.00	10.00	20.00
❑ 9082	Ready for Love/For You	1960	5.00	10.00	20.00
❑ 9085	I Told You So/You Got It	1961	3.75	7.50	15.00
❑ 9093	Dear One/I Say Love	1961	3.75	7.50	15.00
❑ 9102	Mr. Music Man/Holler Hey	1961	3.75	7.50	15.00
❑ 9110	You're Much Too Young/Nights of Mexico	1962	3.75	7.50	15.00
EPIC					
❑ 9339	Whenever You Need Me/You for Me to Love	1959	30.00	60.00	120.00
PARKWAY					
❑ 988	Don't You Just Know It/Dynamite	1966	2.50	5.00	10.00
RAMA					
❑ 210	Lover/Plain Old Love	1956	30.00	60.00	120.00
—As "Jimmy Jones and the Pretenders"					
ROULETTE					
❑ 4232	Lover/Plain Old Love	1960	7.50	15.00	30.00
—As "Jimmy 'Handyman' Jones"					
VEE JAY					
❑ 505	No Insurance (For a Broken Heart)/Mr. Fix-It	1963	3.75	7.50	15.00

JONES, JOE

Number	Title (A Side/B Side)	Yr	VG	VG+	NM
CAPITOL					
❑ F2951	Adam Bit the Apple/Will Call	1954	10.00	20.00	40.00
HERALD					
❑ 488	You Done Me Wrong/When Your Hair Has Turned to Silver	1956	10.00	20.00	40.00
RIC					
❑ 972	You Talk Too Much/I Love You Still	1960	6.25	12.50	25.00
ROULETTE					
❑ 4304	You Talk Too Much/I Love You Still	1960	3.75	7.50	15.00
❑ 4316	One Big Mouth/Here's What You Gotta Do	1960	3.00	6.00	12.00
❑ 4344	California Sun/Please Don't Talk About Me When I'm Gone	1961	3.00	6.00	12.00
❑ 4377	The Big Mule/I've Got a Uh Uh Wife	1961	3.00	6.00	12.00

JONES, JOHN PAUL

Also see LED ZEPPELIN.

Number	Title (A Side/B Side)	Yr	VG	VG+	NM
COTILLION					
❑ 44102	Got to Get Together Now/Man from Nazareth	1971	6.25	12.50	25.00
JERDEN					
❑ 761	Sound City/Broken Promises	1965	7.50	15.00	30.00
—B-side by Rosemary and Howard					

PARKWAY

Number	Title (A Side/B Side)	Yr	VG	VG+	NM
❑ 915	Baja/A Foggy Day in Vietnam	1964	10.00	20.00	40.00

JONES, LITTLE JOHNNY

ATLANTIC

Number	Title (A Side/B Side)	Yr	VG	VG+	NM
❑ 1045	Hoy, Hoy/Doin' the Best I Can	1954	20.00	40.00	80.00

FLAIR

Number	Title (A Side/B Side)	Yr	VG	VG+	NM
❑ 1010	Sweet Little Woman/I May Be Wrong	1953	200.00	400.00	800.00

JONES, LITTLE SONNY

IMPERIAL

Number	Title (A Side/B Side)	Yr	VG	VG+	NM
❑ 5275	I Got Booted/Tend to Your Business Blues	1954	25.00	50.00	100.00
❑ 5287	Winehead Baby/Going to the Country	1954	25.00	50.00	100.00

SPECIALTY

Number	Title (A Side/B Side)	Yr	VG	VG+	NM
❑ 443	Is Everything All Right/Do You Really Love Me	1952	20.00	40.00	80.00

JONES, PAUL

Original lead singer for MANFRED MANN.

BELL

Number	Title (A Side/B Side)	Yr	VG	VG+	NM
❑ 805	It's Getting Better/Not Before Time	1969	2.00	4.00	8.00

CAPITOL

Number	Title (A Side/B Side)	Yr	VG	VG+	NM
❑ 5745	I Can't Hold On Much Longer/Baby Tomorrow	1966	2.00	4.00	8.00
❑ 5800	High Time/It Is Coming Closer	1966	2.00	4.00	8.00
❑ 5857	Sonny Boy Williamson/I've Been a Bad, Bad Boy	1967	2.00	4.00	8.00
❑ 5970	Privilege/Free Me	1967	2.00	4.00	8.00

LONDON

Number	Title (A Side/B Side)	Yr	VG	VG+	NM
❑ 168	Mighty Ship/Who Are the Masters	1972	—	2.50	5.00
❑ 178	The Pod That Came Back/Construction Worker's Song	1972	—	2.50	5.00

PRIVATE STOCK

Number	Title (A Side/B Side)	Yr	VG	VG+	NM
❑ 45004	Love Enough	1974	—	2.50	5.00

JONES, RONNIE, AND THE CLASSMATES

END

Number	Title (A Side/B Side)	Yr	VG	VG+	NM
❑ 1002	Teenage Rock/Little Girl Next Door	1957	30.00	60.00	120.00
❑ 1014	Lonely Boy/Baby Cries	1958	30.00	60.00	120.00
❑ 1125	Teenage Rock/Little Girl Next Door	1963	6.25	12.50	25.00

JONES, THUMPER

See GEORGE JONES.

JONES, TOM

CHINA

Number	Title (A Side/B Side)	Yr	VG	VG+	NM
❑ 871038-7	Kiss/E.F.L.	1989	—	—	3.00
—A-side: The Art of Noise with Tom Jones; B-side by Art of Noise					
❑ 871038-7 [PS]	Kiss/E.F.L.	1989	—	—	3.00

EPIC

Number	Title (A Side/B Side)	Yr	VG	VG+	NM
❑ 50308	Say You'll Stay Until Tomorrow/Lady Lay	1976	—	2.00	4.00
❑ 50382	Take Me Tonight/I Hope You'll Understand	1977	—	2.00	4.00
❑ 50468	What a Night/That's Where I Belong	1977	—	2.00	4.00
❑ 50506	There's Nothing Stronger Than Our Love/No One Gave Me Love	1978	—	2.00	4.00
❑ 50636	Hey Love/Baby, As You Turn Away	1978	—	2.00	4.00

MCA

Number	Title (A Side/B Side)	Yr	VG	VG+	NM
❑ 41127	Dancing Endlessly/Never Had a Lady Before	1979	—	2.00	4.00

MERCURY

Number	Title (A Side/B Side)	Yr	VG	VG+	NM
❑ 76100	Darlin'/I Don't Want to Know You That Way	1981	—	2.00	4.00
❑ 76115	What in the World's Come Over You/The Things That Matter Most to Me	1981	—	2.00	4.00
❑ 76125	Lady Lay Down/A Daughter's Question	1981	—	2.00	4.00
❑ 76172	A Woman's Touch/I'll Never Get Over You	1982	—	2.00	4.00
❑ 810445-7	Touch Me (I'll Be Your Fool Once More)/We're Wasting Our Time	1983	—	—	3.00
❑ 812631-7	It'll Be Me/If I Ever Had to Say Goodbye to You	1983	—	—	3.00
❑ 814820-7	I've Been Rained On Too/That Old Piano	1983	—	—	3.00
❑ 818801-7	This Time/Memphis, Tennessee	1984	—	—	3.00
❑ 870233-7	Things That Matter Most to Me/Green, Green Grass of Home	1988	—	—	3.00
❑ 880173-7	All the Love Is On the Radio/(B-side unknown)	1984	—	—	3.00
❑ 880402-7	I'm an Old Rock and Roller (Dancin' to a Different Beat)/My Kind of Girl	1984	—	—	3.00
❑ 880569-7	Give Her All the Roses (Don't Wait Until Tomorrow)/A Picture of You	1985	—	—	3.00
❑ 884039-7	Not Another Heart Song/Only My Heart Knows	1985	—	—	3.00
❑ 884252-7	It's Four in the Morning/I'll Never Get Over You	1985	—	—	3.00
❑ 888911-7	Lover to Lover/A Daughter's Question	1987	—	—	3.00

PARROT

Number	Title (A Side/B Side)	Yr	VG	VG+	NM
❑ 9737	It's Not Unusual/To Wait for Love (Is to Waste Your Life Away)	1965	2.50	5.00	10.00
❑ 9765	What's New Pussycat/Once Upon a Time	1965	2.50	5.00	10.00
❑ 9765 [PS]	What's New Pussycat/Once Upon a Time	1965	3.75	7.50	15.00
❑ 9787	With These Hands/Some Other Guy	1965	2.00	4.00	8.00
❑ 9787 [PS]	With These Hands/Some Other Guy	1965	3.00	6.00	12.00
❑ 9801	Thunderball/Key to My Heart	1965	2.00	4.00	8.00
❑ 9801 [PS]	Thunderball/Key to My Heart	1965	5.00	10.00	20.00
—Version 1: with a dead female and a spear gun					
❑ 9801 [PS]	Thunderball/Key to My Heart	1965	3.00	6.00	12.00
—Version 2: without the above elements on sleeve					
❑ 9809	Promise Her Anything/Little You	1966	2.00	4.00	8.00
❑ 40006	Not Responsible/Once There Was a Time	1966	2.00	4.00	8.00
❑ 40008	City Girl/What a Party	1966	2.00	4.00	8.00
❑ 40009	Green, Green Grass of Home/If I Had You	1966	2.00	4.00	8.00
❑ 40012	Detroit City/Ten Guitars	1967	2.00	4.00	8.00
❑ 40014	Funny Familiar Forgotten Feelings/I'll Never Let You Go	1967	2.00	4.00	8.00
❑ 40016	Sixteen Tons/Things I Wanna Do	1967	2.00	4.00	8.00
❑ 40018	I'll Never Fall in Love Again/Once Upon a Time	1967	3.00	6.00	12.00
—First pressings contain the full-length version of the A-side; time is listed at over four minutes					
❑ 40018	I'll Never Fall in Love Again/Once Upon a Time	1967	2.00	4.00	8.00
—Later pressings delete a verse from the A-side; time is listed at 2:55					
❑ 40020	Land of a Thousand Dances/I Can't Stop Loving You	1967	5.00	10.00	20.00
—May be promo only					
❑ 40024	I'm Coming Home/Lonely One	1967	2.00	4.00	8.00
❑ 40025	Delilah/Smile Away Your Blues	1968	2.00	4.00	8.00
❑ 40029	Help Yourself/Day by Day	1968	2.00	4.00	8.00
❑ 40035	A Minute of Your Time/Looking Out My Window	1968	2.00	4.00	8.00
❑ 40038	Love Me Tonight/Hide and Seek	1969	—	3.00	6.00
❑ 40038 [PS]	Love Me Tonight/Hide and Seek	1969	2.00	4.00	8.00
❑ 40045	Without Love (There Is Nothing)/The Man Who Knows Too Much	1969	—	3.00	6.00
❑ 40045 [PS]	Without Love (There Is Nothing)/The Man Who Knows Too Much	1969	2.00	4.00	8.00
❑ 40048	Daughter of Darkness/Tupelo Mississippi Flash	1970	—	3.00	6.00
❑ 40048 [PS]	Daughter of Darkness/Tupelo Mississippi Flash	1970	2.00	4.00	8.00
❑ 40051	I (Who Have Nothing)/Stop Breaking My Heart	1970	—	3.00	6.00
❑ 40051 [PS]	I (Who Have Nothing)/Stop Breaking My Heart	1970	2.00	4.00	8.00
❑ 40056	Can't Stop Loving You/Never Give Away Love	1970	—	3.00	6.00
❑ 40056 [PS]	Can't Stop Loving You/Never Give Away Love	1970	2.00	4.00	8.00
❑ 40058	She's a Lady/My Way	1971	—	3.00	6.00
❑ 40058 [PS]	She's a Lady/My Way	1971	2.00	4.00	8.00
❑ 40062	Puppet Man/Every Mile	1971	—	3.00	6.00
❑ 40062 [PS]	Puppet Man/Every Mile	1971	3.75	7.50	15.00
❑ 40064	Puppet Man/Resurrection Shuffle	1971	—	2.50	5.00
❑ 40067	Till/One Day Soon	1971	—	2.50	5.00
❑ 40070	The Young New Mexican Puppeteer/All That I Need Is Time	1972	—	2.50	5.00
❑ 40074	Letter to Lucille/Thank the Lord	1973	—	2.50	5.00
❑ 40078	La, La, La (Just Having You Here)/Love, Love, Love	1973	—	2.50	5.00
❑ 40080	Somethin' 'Bout You Baby I Like/Keep a-Talkin' 'Bout Love	1973	—	2.50	5.00
❑ 40081	Pledging My Love/I'm Too Far Gone	1974	—	2.50	5.00
❑ 40083	Ain't No Love/When the Band Goes Home	1974	—	2.50	5.00
❑ 40084	I Got Your Number/The Pain of Love	1974	—	2.50	5.00
❑ 40086	Memories Don't Leave Like People Do/Helping Hand	1975	—	2.50	5.00

TOWER

Number	Title (A Side/B Side)	Yr	VG	VG+	NM
❑ 126	Little Lonely One/That's What We'll All Do	1965	3.00	6.00	12.00
❑ 126 [PS]	Little Lonely One/That's What We'll All Do	1965	5.00	10.00	20.00
❑ 176	Lonely One/I Was a Fool	1965	3.00	6.00	12.00
❑ 176 [PS]	Lonely One/I Was a Fool	1965	5.00	10.00	20.00
❑ 190	Baby I'm in Love/Chills and Fever	1966	2.50	5.00	10.00

JONES, TOM (2)

SYMBOL

Number	Title (A Side/B Side)	Yr	VG	VG+	NM
❑ 205	Nothing But Fine/Trying to Get to My Grits	1965	3.00	6.00	12.00

JONES BROTHERS, THE

SUN

Number	Title (A Side/B Side)	Yr	VG	VG+	NM
❑ 213	Every Night/Look to Jesus	1954	200.00	400.00	800.00

JOPLIN, JANIS

Also see BIG BROTHER AND THE HOLDING COMPANY.

COLUMBIA

Number	Title (A Side/B Side)	Yr	VG	VG+	NM
❑ 45023	Kozmik Blues/Little Girl Blue	1969	—	3.00	6.00
❑ 45080	One Good Man/Try (Just a Little Bit Harder)	1970	—	3.00	6.00
❑ 45128	Wake Me, Lord/Maybe	1970	—	3.00	6.00
❑ 45314	Me and Bobby McGee/Half Moon	1971	—	2.50	5.00
❑ 45379	Mercedez Benz/Cry Baby	1971	—	2.50	5.00
❑ 45433	Get It While You Can/Move Over	1971	—	2.50	5.00
❑ 45630	Bye Bye Baby/Down on Me	1972	—	2.50	5.00

JORDANAIRES, THE

CAPITOL

Number	Title (A Side/B Side)	Yr	VG	VG+	NM
❑ F1254	Working on the Building/I Want to Rest	1950	7.50	15.00	30.00
❑ F1363	David and Goliath/Journey to the Sky	1951	6.25	12.50	25.00
❑ F1407	One Day/Something Within	1951	6.25	12.50	25.00
❑ F1499	He Bought My Soul/Read That Book	1951	6.25	12.50	25.00
❑ F2725	Tattler's Wagon/In My Saviour's Loving Arms	1954	5.00	10.00	20.00
❑ F2815	Bugle Call from Heaven/Oh Lord Stand By Me	1954	5.00	10.00	20.00
❑ F2915	This Ole House/Be Prepared	1954	5.00	10.00	20.00
❑ F3022	When the Saints Go Marching In/All the Way	1955	5.00	10.00	20.00
❑ F3158	Let's Make a Joyful Noise/Will You Be Ready	1955	5.00	10.00	20.00
❑ F3265	Shaking Bridges/What Will the Verdict Be	1955	5.00	10.00	20.00
❑ F3356	A House of Gold/Blow, Whistle, Blow	1956	5.00	10.00	20.00
❑ F3420	Rock 'n Roll Religion/Do Unto Others	1956	5.00	10.00	20.00
❑ F3492	Hands of God/Fighting for the Lord	1956	5.00	10.00	20.00
❑ F3610	Sugaree/Baby Won't You Please Come Home	1957	5.00	10.00	20.00
❑ F3684	Walk Away/Ridin' for a Fall	1957	5.00	10.00	20.00
❑ F3750	Summer Vacation/Each Day	1957	5.00	10.00	20.00
❑ F3807	Any Which-a-Way/Mood for the Blues	1957	5.00	10.00	20.00
❑ F3940	Little Miss Ruby/All I Need Is You	1958	3.75	7.50	15.00
❑ F4025	Wella Wella Honey/Where Many Go	1958	3.75	7.50	15.00
❑ 4431	Sit Down/Girl in the Valley	1960	3.00	6.00	12.00

COLUMBIA

Number	Title (A Side/B Side)	Yr	VG	VG+	NM
❑ 4-43283	Malibu Run/Who Does He Think He Is	1965	2.50	5.00	10.00
—Said to be a different group than the rest.					

DECCA

Number	Title (A Side/B Side)	Yr	VG	VG+	NM
❑ 9-46242	Dig a Little Deeper/I'm Free Again	1950	10.00	20.00	40.00
❑ 9-46366	Loafin' on a Lazy River/Sweet Roses of Morn	1951	6.25	12.50	25.00

DECCA FAITH SERIES

Number	Title (A Side/B Side)	Yr	VG	VG+	NM
❑ 9-14530	Peace in the Valley/(B-side unknown)	1950	7.50	15.00	30.00

RCA VICTOR

Number	Title (A Side/B Side)	Yr	VG	VG+	NM
❑ 47-4378	The Four Horsemen (Of the Apocalypse)/Mansion Over the Hilltop	1951	6.25	12.50	25.00
❑ 47-4607	Who Can He Be/Gonna Walk Those Golden Stairs	1952	6.25	12.50	25.00
❑ 47-4645	Goodbye Pharaoh/Roll, Jordan, Roll	1952	6.25	12.50	25.00
❑ 47-4943	Rag Mama/I Never Will Marry	1952	6.25	12.50	25.00
❑ 47-4948	My Rock/I'll Tell It Wherever I Go	1952	6.25	12.50	25.00
❑ 47-5021	He'll Understand and Say Well Done/I'm Moving On to Glory	1952	6.25	12.50	25.00

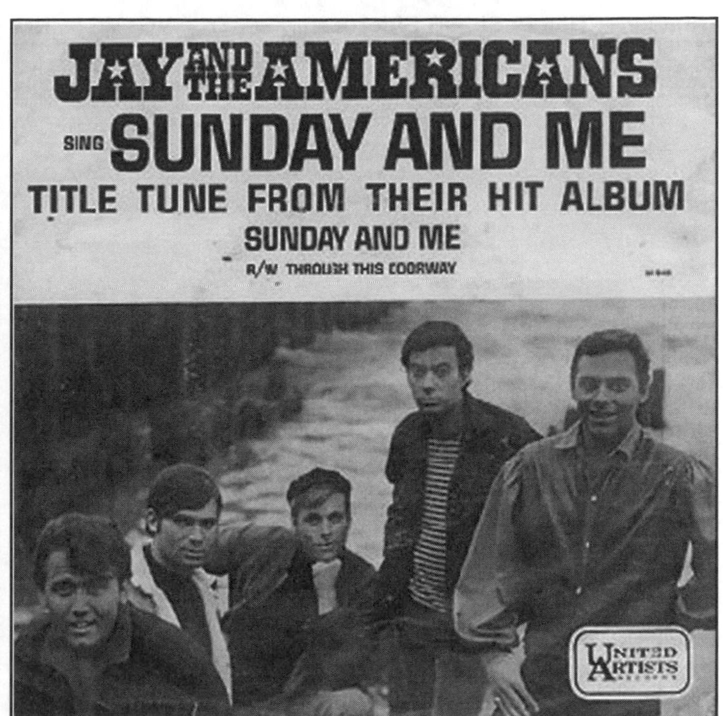

(Top left) Many Jan and Dean picture sleeves from their hit-making era are not that hard to find. But "From All Over the World" is a tough onc. (Top right) Speaking of tough picture sleeves, this one, from Jay and the Americans' top 20 hit single "Sunday and Me," is pretty obscure as well. The song itself was the first major songwriting success for Neil Diamond. (Bottom left) Elton John's first British single, "I've Been Loving You," was not issued in the U.S. until the CD era. His second one, "Lady Samantha," actually came out twice in the States. The first time was on a short-lived American branch of the British DJM Records in 1969. It had its original U.K. B-side, "All Across the Havens," and is by far the rarest of Elton's regular U.S. 45 issues. The single was later reissued on Congress with a different flip side. (Bottom right) Of all the "cartoon groups" that sprang up in the late 1960s and early 1970s, the most collectible is Josie and the Pussycats. Part of the reason is that one of the singers on the music (though not one of the voices on the TV show) was a pre-Charlie's Angels Cheryl Ladd.

Number	Title (A Side/B Side)	Yr	VG	VG+	NM
❑ 47-5076	Beautiful City/Stand by Me	1952	5.00	10.00	20.00
❑ 47-5077	By the River of Life/Noah	1952	5.00	10.00	20.00
❑ 47-5078	You Better Run/Dry Bones	1952	5.00	10.00	20.00
❑ 47-5079	When Dey Ring Dem Golden Bells/Didn't They Crucify My Lord	1952	5.00	10.00	20.00
❑ 47-5373	On the Jericho Road/The Lord Will Make a Way Somehow	1953	6.25	12.50	25.00
❑ 47-5458	Is He Satisfied/I Am So Glad Jesus Lifted Me	1953	6.25	12.50	25.00

STOP

Number	Title (A Side/B Side)	Yr	VG	VG+	NM
❑ 259	You're Wasting Your Time Girl/A Hundred Years of Real Estate	1969	2.00	4.00	8.00

"X"

Number	Title (A Side/B Side)	Yr	VG	VG+	NM
❑ 0034	Say It Again/I Can't Smoke You Out of My Heart	1954	5.00	10.00	20.00

7-Inch Extended Plays

SESAC

Number	Title (A Side/B Side)	Yr	VG	VG+	NM
❑ AD 46	Wanderin'/John Henry//Honey Baby Mine/ Twenty-One Froggies	195?	5.00	10.00	20.00
❑ AD 46 [PS]	Songs of the Plains	195?	5.00	10.00	20.00

JOSHUA FOX

TETRAGRAMMATON

Number	Title (A Side/B Side)	Yr	VG	VG+	NM
❑ 1527	Goin' Down for Big Numbers/Moontime Bore	1969	3.00	6.00	12.00
❑ 1532	Don't Tell Me a Story/It's Just Meant to Be	1969	3.00	6.00	12.00

JOSIE AND THE PUSSYCATS

Also see PATRICE HOLLOWAY; CHERYL LADD.

CAPITOL

Number	Title (A Side/B Side)	Yr	VG	VG+	NM
❑ CP 58-1	Letter to Mama/Inside, Outside, Upside Down	1970	5.00	10.00	20.00
❑ CP 58-1 [PS]	Letter to Mama/Inside, Outside, Upside Down	1970	7.50	15.00	30.00
❑ CP 59-2	With Every Beat of My Heart/Josie	1970	5.00	10.00	20.00
❑ CP 59-2 [PS]	With Every Beat of My Heart/Josie	1970	7.50	15.00	30.00
❑ CP 60-3	Voodoo/If That Isn't Love	1970	5.00	10.00	20.00
❑ CP 60-3 [PS]	Voodoo/If That Isn't Love	1970	7.50	15.00	30.00
❑ CP 61-4	I Wanna Make You Happy/It's Gotta Be Him	1970	5.00	10.00	20.00
❑ CP 61-4 [PS]	I Wanna Make You Happy/It's Gotta Be Him	1970	7.50	15.00	30.00
❑ 2967	Every Beat of My Heart/It's All Right with Me	1970	5.00	10.00	20.00

—Same song as CP 59, but a slightly different title and a mono mix

Number	Title (A Side/B Side)	Yr	VG	VG+	NM
❑ 3045	Stop, Look and Listen/You've Come a Long Way, Baby	1971	5.00	10.00	20.00

JOURNEYMEN, THE (1)

Also see SCOTT McKENZIE; JOHN PHILLIPS.

AMY

Number	Title (A Side/B Side)	Yr	VG	VG+	NM
❑ 821	Cup-E-Co/Hush Storm	1961	3.00	6.00	12.00

CAPITOL

Number	Title (A Side/B Side)	Yr	VG	VG+	NM
❑ 4625	500 Miles/The River She Comes Down	1961	2.50	5.00	10.00
❑ 4678	Soft Blow the Summer Winds/Kumbaya	1962	2.50	5.00	10.00
❑ 4737	Don't Turn Around/Hush Now Sally	1962	2.50	5.00	10.00
❑ 4829	What'll I Do/Loadin' Coal	1962	2.50	5.00	10.00
❑ 4943	Rag Mama/I Never Will Marry	1963	2.50	5.00	10.00
❑ 4943 [PS]	Rag Mama/I Never Will Marry	1963	10.00	20.00	40.00
❑ 5031	Kumbaya/Ja Da	1963	2.50	5.00	10.00

JOURNEYMEN, THE (2)

IONA

Number	Title (A Side/B Side)	Yr	VG	VG+	NM
❑ 1111	Work Out/Bag's Groove	1961	12.50	25.00	50.00
❑ 1115	Surfer's Blues/Surfer's Rule	1963	12.50	25.00	50.00
❑ 1115	Surfer's Blues/Surfer's Rule	1963	10.00	20.00	40.00

—Rerelease as "The Baylanders"

JOY, BENNY

ANTLER

Number	Title (A Side/B Side)	Yr	VG	VG+	NM
❑ 4011	Crash the Party/Little Red Book	1959	125.00	250.00	500.00

DECCA

Number	Title (A Side/B Side)	Yr	VG	VG+	NM
❑ 31199	New York, Hey Hey/Sincerely, Your Friend	1961	3.75	7.50	15.00
❑ 31280	Birds of a Feather Fly Together/You Go Your Way (And I'll Go Mine)	1961	3.75	7.50	15.00

DIXIE

Number	Title (A Side/B Side)	Yr	VG	VG+	NM
❑ 2001	Steady with Betty/Spin the Bottle	1958	125.00	250.00	500.00

DOT

Number	Title (A Side/B Side)	Yr	VG	VG+	NM
❑ 16445	I'm of No More Use to You Old Earth/Harry's Harem	1963	3.75	7.50	15.00

RAM

Number	Title (A Side/B Side)	Yr	VG	VG+	NM
❑ 1107	Ittie Bittie Everything/(B-side unknown)	1959	125.00	250.00	500.00

TRI-DEC

Number	Title (A Side/B Side)	Yr	VG	VG+	NM
❑ 8667	Steady with Betty/Spin the Bottle	1958	150.00	300.00	600.00

JOY, RODDIE

PARKWAY

Number	Title (A Side/B Side)	Yr	VG	VG+	NM
❑ 101	Something Strange Is Going On/Stop	1966	3.00	6.00	12.00
❑ 134	Every Breath I Take/Walkin' Back	1967	3.00	6.00	12.00
❑ 151	I Want You Back/Let's Start All Over	1967	3.00	6.00	12.00
❑ 991	A Boy Is Just a Toy/Stop	1966	3.75	7.50	15.00

RED BIRD

Number	Title (A Side/B Side)	Yr	VG	VG+	NM
❑ 10-021	Love Hit Me with a Wallop/Come Back Baby	1965	5.00	10.00	20.00
❑ 10-031	The La La Song/He's So Easy to Love	1965	6.25	12.50	25.00
❑ 10-037	If There's Anything Else You Want (Let Me Know)/ Stop	1965	10.00	20.00	40.00

JOY DIVISION

Also see NEW ORDER.

FACTORY

Number	Title (A Side/B Side)	Yr	VG	VG+	NM
❑ FACTUS 23	Love Will Tear Us Apart/These Days	1980	3.00	6.25	12.50
❑ FACTUS 23 [PS]	Love Will Tear Us Apart/These Days	1980	3.00	6.25	12.50
❑ FACUS 23 [DJ]	Love Will Tear Us Apart/These Days	1980	25.00	50.00	100.00

—White label promo

Number	Title (A Side/B Side)	Yr	VG	VG+	NM
❑ FAC 28	Komakino/Incubation/Dub	1980	3.75	7.50	15.00

—Flexi-disc with no picture sleeve, "Evatone" on label

Number	Title (A Side/B Side)	Yr	VG	VG+	NM
❑ FAC 28	Komakino/Incubation/Dub	1980	2.50	5.00	10.00

—Flexi-disc, with below picture sleeve

Number	Title (A Side/B Side)	Yr	VG	VG+	NM
❑ FAC 28 [PS]	Komakino/Incubation/Dub	1980	6.25	12.50	25.00

—Numbered sleeve from fanzine "The Other Sound"

JOY TONES, THE

COED

Number	Title (A Side/B Side)	Yr	VG	VG+	NM
❑ 600	This Love (That I'm Giving You)/I Wanna Party Some More	1965	3.00	6.00	12.00

JOYE, COL, AND THE JOY BOYS

DECCA

Number	Title (A Side/B Side)	Yr	VG	VG+	NM
❑ 30933	(Rockin' Rollin') Clementine/Bye Bye Baby Goodbye	1959	7.50	15.00	30.00

JOYETTES, THE

ONYX

Number	Title (A Side/B Side)	Yr	VG	VG+	NM
❑ 502	Story of Love/The Boy Next Door	1956	25.00	50.00	100.00

JOYTONES, THE

RAMA

Number	Title (A Side/B Side)	Yr	VG	VG+	NM
❑ 191	All My Love Belongs to You/You Just Won't Treat Me Right	1956	37.50	75.00	150.00
❑ 202	Gee What a Boy/Is This Really the End	1956	75.00	150.00	300.00
❑ 215	My Foolish Heart/Jimbo Jango	1956	125.00	250.00	500.00

JULIAN, DON, AND THE MEADOWLARKS

Also see THE LARKS.

CLASSIC ARTISTS

Number	Title (A Side/B Side)	Yr	VG	VG+	NM
❑ 101	Quickie Wedding/Our Love	1988	—	2.00	4.00
❑ 105	White Christmas/Marry Christmas, Baby	1988	—	3.00	6.00

DOOTO

Number	Title (A Side/B Side)	Yr	VG	VG+	NM
❑ 424	Blue Moon/Big Mama Wants to Rock	1957	12.50	25.00	50.00

DOOTONE

Number	Title (A Side/B Side)	Yr	VG	VG+	NM
❑ 359	Heaven and Paradise/Embarrassing Moments	1955	75.00	150.00	300.00
❑ 367	Always and Always/I Got Tore Up	1955	18.75	37.50	75.00

—Red label

Number	Title (A Side/B Side)	Yr	VG	VG+	NM
❑ 367	Always and Always/I Got Tore Up	1955	12.50	25.00	50.00

—Maroon label

Number	Title (A Side/B Side)	Yr	VG	VG+	NM
❑ 372	This Must Be Paradise/Mine All Mine	1955	15.00	30.00	60.00
❑ 394	Please Love a Fool/Oop Boopy Oop	1956	12.50	25.00	50.00
❑ 405	I Am a Believer/Boogie Woogie Teenager	1956	20.00	40.00	80.00

DYNAMITE

Number	Title (A Side/B Side)	Yr	VG	VG+	NM
❑ 1112	Heaven Only Knows/Popeye	1962	7.50	15.00	30.00

ORIGINAL SOUND

Number	Title (A Side/B Side)	Yr	VG	VG+	NM
❑ 3	Please Say You Want Me/Doin' the Cha Cha Cha	1959	10.00	20.00	40.00
❑ 12	There's a Girl/Blue Moon	1960	7.50	15.00	30.00

RPM

Number	Title (A Side/B Side)	Yr	VG	VG+	NM
❑ 399	Love Only You/Real Pretty Mama	1954	75.00	150.00	300.00

—As "The Meadow Larks"

Number	Title (A Side/B Side)	Yr	VG	VG+	NM
❑ 406	LSMFT Blues (Lord Find My Sweet Theresa)/ Pass the Gin	1954	750.00	1500.	3000.

—As "The Meadow Larks"

7-Inch Extended Plays

DOOTO

Number	Title (A Side/B Side)	Yr	VG	VG+	NM
❑ 203	(contents unknown)	1958	50.00	100.00	200.00
❑ 203 [PS]	Don Julian and the Meadowlarks	1958	50.00	100.00	200.00

—Reissue of Dootone 203

DOOTONE

Number	Title (A Side/B Side)	Yr	VG	VG+	NM
❑ 203	(contents unknown)	1956	100.00	200.00	400.00
❑ 203 [PS]	Don Julian and the Meadowlarks	1956	100.00	200.00	400.00

JULIANA

RCA VICTOR

Number	Title (A Side/B Side)	Yr	VG	VG+	NM
❑ 47-7906	You Can Have Any Boy/You're Saying Goodnight	1961	15.00	30.00	60.00

JUMPIN' JACKS, THE

DECCA

Number	Title (A Side/B Side)	Yr	VG	VG+	NM
❑ 29973	You'll Wonder Where the Yellow Went/A Frantic Antic	1956	7.50	15.00	30.00
❑ 29973 [PS]	You'll Wonder Where the Yellow Went/A Frantic Antic	1956	10.00	20.00	40.00

JUNIOR AND HIS FRIENDS

ABC-PARAMOUNT

Number	Title (A Side/B Side)	Yr	VG	VG+	NM
❑ 10089	Who's Our Pet, Annette!/A.B.C. Love	1960	7.50	15.00	30.00

JUSTIS, BILL

BELL

Number	Title (A Side/B Side)	Yr	VG	VG+	NM
❑ 921	Electric Dreams/Dark Continent Contribution	1970	—	2.50	5.00

MCA

Number	Title (A Side/B Side)	Yr	VG	VG+	NM
❑ 40810	Foxy Lady/Orange Blossom Special	1977	—	2.00	4.00

MONUMENT

Number	Title (A Side/B Side)	Yr	VG	VG+	NM
❑ 956	Yellow Summer/So Until I See You	1966	2.50	5.00	10.00
❑ 8699	Sea Dream/Touching, Feeling, Dreaming	1976	—	2.50	5.00

NRC

Number	Title (A Side/B Side)	Yr	VG	VG+	NM
❑ 1119	Blowing Rock/Boogie Woogie Rock	1959	5.00	10.00	20.00

PHILLIPS INTERNATIONAL

Number	Title (A Side/B Side)	Yr	VG	VG+	NM
❑ 3519	Raunchy/Midnight Man	1957	5.00	10.00	20.00
❑ 3522	College Man/The Stranger	1958	5.00	10.00	20.00
❑ 3525	Wild Ride/Scroungie	1958	5.00	10.00	20.00
❑ 3529	Cattywampus/Summer Holiday	1958	5.00	10.00	20.00
❑ 3535	Bop Train/String of Pearls	1958	5.00	10.00	20.00
❑ 3544	Flea Circus/Cloud Nine	1959	5.00	10.00	20.00

SMASH

Number	Title (A Side/B Side)	Yr	VG	VG+	NM
❑ 1812	I'm Gonna Learn to Dance/Tamoure	1963	2.50	5.00	10.00
❑ 1812 [PS]	I'm Gonna Learn to Dance/Tamoure	1963	4.00	8.00	16.00
❑ 1851	Sunday in Madrid/Satin and Velvet	1963	2.50	5.00	10.00
❑ 1902	Lavender Sax/Fia, Fia	1964	2.50	5.00	10.00
❑ 1955	How Soon/Ska-Ha	1964	2.50	5.00	10.00
❑ 1977	Late Game/Last Farewell	1965	2.50	5.00	10.00

K

K-CI AND JOJO

MCA

Number	Title (A Side/B Side)	Yr	VG	VG+	NM
❑ 55604	Tell Me It's Real/All My Life	1999	—	—	3.00

K-DOE, ERNIE

Number	Title (A Side/B Side)	Yr	VG	VG+	NM
DUKE					
❑ 378	My Mother-in-Law (Is In My Hair Again)/Looking Into the Future	1964	2.00	4.00	8.00
❑ 387	Little Bit of Everything/Someone	1965	2.00	4.00	8.00
❑ 400	Please Don't Stop/Boomerang	1966	2.00	4.00	8.00
❑ 404	Little Marie/Somebody Told Me	1966	2.00	4.00	8.00
❑ 411	Later for Tomorrow/Dancin' Man	1966	2.00	4.00	8.00
❑ 420	Love Me Like I Wanna/Don't Kill My Groove	1967	2.00	4.00	8.00
❑ 423	(It Will Have to Do) Until the Real Thing Comes Along/Little Marie	1967	2.00	4.00	8.00
❑ 437	Gotta Pack My Bag/How Sweet You Are	1968	2.00	4.00	8.00
❑ 450	I'm Sorry/Trying to Make You Love Me	1969	2.00	4.00	8.00
❑ 456	I'll Make Everything Be Alright/Wishing in Vain	1969	2.00	4.00	8.00
EMBER					
❑ 1050	My Love for You/Tuff-Enuff	1959	6.25	12.50	25.00
❑ 1075	My Love for You/Shirley's Tuff	1961	3.75	7.50	15.00
INSTANT					
❑ 3260	Baby, Since I Met You/Sufferin' So	1963	2.50	5.00	10.00
❑ 3264	Reaping What I Sow/Talking Out of My Head	1964	2.50	5.00	10.00
ISLAND					
❑ 031	Let Me Love You/So Good	1975	—	3.00	6.00
JANUS					
❑ 167	Here Come the Girls/Long Way Home	1971	—	3.00	6.00
MINIT					
❑ 604	Make You Love Me/There's a Will, There's a Way	1959	7.50	15.00	30.00
❑ 614	'Tain't It the Truth/Hello My Lover	1960	5.00	10.00	20.00
❑ 623	Mother-in-Law/Wanted, $10,000 Reward	1961	6.25	12.50	25.00
—Side 1 is at the correct speed. Trail-off number is "SO-738-2"					
❑ 623	Mother-in-Law/Wanted, $10,000 Reward	1961	50.00	100.00	200.00
—Side 1 was accidentally mis-mastered at 33 1/3 rpm. Trail-off number is "45-SO-738"					
❑ 627	Te-Ta-Te-Ta-Ta/Real Man	1961	3.75	7.50	15.00
❑ 634	A Certain Girl/I Cried My Last Tear	1961	3.75	7.50	15.00
❑ 641	Popeye Joe/Come On Home	1962	3.75	7.50	15.00
❑ 645	Hey Hey Hey/Love You the Best	1962	3.75	7.50	15.00
❑ 651	Beating Like a Tom-Tom/I Got to Find Somebody	1962	3.75	7.50	15.00
❑ 656	Loving You/Get Out of My House	1962	3.75	7.50	15.00
❑ 661	Easier Said Than Done/Be Sweet	1963	3.75	7.50	15.00
❑ 665	I'm the Boss/Pennies Worth o' Happiness	1963	3.75	7.50	15.00
SANSU					
❑ 1006	Stoop Down/(B-side unknown)	197?	5.00	10.00	20.00
❑ 1016	Hotcha Mama/She Gave It All to Me	197?	5.00	10.00	20.00
SPECIALTY					
❑ 563	Eternity/Do Baby Do	1955	10.00	20.00	40.00
—As "Ernest Kador"					
UNITED ARTISTS					
❑ 0110	Mother-in-Law/A Wonderful Dream	1973	—	2.50	5.00
—"Silver Spotlight Series" reissue; B-side by the Majors					

KACT-TIES, THE

Number	Title (A Side/B Side)	Yr	VG	VG+	NM
ATCO					
❑ 6299	Oh What a Night/Let Me In Your Life	1964	3.75	7.50	15.00
—As "The Kac-Ties"					
KAPE					
❑ 501	Happy Birthday/Girl in My Heart	1965	3.75	7.50	15.00
—As "The Kac-Ties"					
❑ 502	Walkin' in the Rain/Smile	1965	3.75	7.50	15.00
—As "The Kac-Ties"					
❑ 503	Let Your Love Light Shine/Were-Wolf	1965	3.75	7.50	15.00
—As "The Kac-Ties"					
SHELLEY					
❑ 163	Let Your Love Light Shine/Were-Wolf	1963	6.25	12.50	25.00
❑ 165	Oh What a Night/Let Me In Your Life	1963	6.25	12.50	25.00
TRANS ATLAS					
❑ 695	Walkin' in the Rain/Smile	1962	75.00	150.00	300.00
—With thunderstorm sound effects					
❑ 695	Walkin' in the Rain/Smile	1962	37.50	75.00	150.00
—Without thunderstorm sound effects					

KAK

Gary Yoder of BLUE CHEER was in this group.

Number	Title (A Side/B Side)	Yr	VG	VG+	NM
EPIC					
❑ 10383 [DJ]	Everything's Changing (Long Version)/ Everything's Changing (Edited Version)	1968	5.00	10.00	20.00
—May be promo only					
❑ 10446	I've Got Time/Disbelievin'	1969	5.00	10.00	20.00

KALEIDOSCOPE, THE

Number	Title (A Side/B Side)	Yr	VG	VG+	NM
EPIC					
❑ 10117	Elevator Man/Please	1967	7.50	15.00	30.00
❑ 10219	Little Orphan Annie/Why Try	1967	7.50	15.00	30.00
❑ 10239	I Found Out/Rampe Rampe	1967	7.50	15.00	30.00
❑ 10332	Just a Taste/Hello Trouble	1968	7.50	15.00	30.00
❑ 10481	Lie to Me/Let the Good Love Flow	1969	7.50	15.00	30.00
❑ 10500	Killing Floor/Lie to Me	1969	7.50	15.00	30.00
FONTANA					
❑ 1633	Jimmy Artichoke/Just How Much You Are	1968	—	—	—
—Unreleased					

KALIN TWINS, THE

Number	Title (A Side/B Side)	Yr	VG	VG+	NM
AMY					
❑ 969	Thinkin' About You Baby/Sometimes It Comes	1966	2.00	4.00	8.00
DECCA					
❑ 30552	Jumpin' Jack/Walkin' to School	1958	5.00	10.00	20.00
❑ 30642	When/Three O'Clock Thrill	1958	6.25	12.50	25.00
❑ 30745	Forget Me Not/Dream of Me	1958	6.25	12.50	25.00
❑ 30807	It's Only the Beginning/Oh My Goodness	1959	5.00	10.00	20.00
❑ 30868	Cool/When I Look in the Mirror	1959	5.00	10.00	20.00
❑ 30911	Sweet Sugar Lips/Moody	1959	5.00	10.00	20.00
❑ 30977	Why Don't You Believe Me/The Meaning of the Blues	1959	5.00	10.00	20.00
❑ 30977 [PS]	Why Don't You Believe Me/The Meaning of the Blues	1959	7.50	15.00	30.00
❑ 31064	Loneliness/Chicken Thief	1960	3.75	7.50	15.00
❑ 31111	True to You/Blue, Blue Town	1960	3.75	7.50	15.00
❑ 31169	Zing! Went the Strings of My Heart/No Money Can Buy	1960	3.75	7.50	15.00
❑ 31220	Momma-Poppa/You Mean the World to Me	1961	3.75	7.50	15.00
❑ 31286	Bubbles (I'm Forever Blowing Bubbles)/One More Time	1961	3.75	7.50	15.00
❑ 31410	Trouble/A Picture of You	1962	3.75	7.50	15.00
7-Inch Extended Plays					
DECCA					
❑ ED 2623	(contents unknown)	1958	15.00	30.00	60.00
❑ ED 2623 [PS]	When	1958	20.00	40.00	80.00
❑ ED 2641	(contents unknown)	1958	12.50	25.00	50.00
❑ ED 2641 [PS]	Forget Me Not	1958	15.00	30.00	60.00

KALLEN, KITTY

Number	Title (A Side/B Side)	Yr	VG	VG+	NM
20TH CENTURY FOX					
❑ 471	Make Somebody Love You/Lies and More Lies	1964	2.00	4.00	8.00
BELL					
❑ 673	Summer, Summer Wind/Oba, Oba	1967	2.00	4.00	8.00
COLUMBIA					
❑ 40298	The High and the Mighty/Still You'd Break My Heart	1954	3.75	7.50	15.00
—With Harry James					
❑ 41236	When Will I Know/Love Is a Sacred Thing	1958	3.00	6.00	12.00
❑ 41473	If I Give My Heart to You/The Door That Won't Open	1959	3.00	6.00	12.00
❑ 41546	That Old Feeling/Need Me	1959	3.00	6.00	12.00
❑ 41622	Always in My Heart/Got a Date with an Angel	1960	3.00	6.00	12.00
❑ 41671	Make Love to Me/Heaven Help Me	1960	3.00	6.00	12.00
❑ 41769	Come Live with Me/Be True to Me	1960	3.00	6.00	12.00
❑ 41857	I Believe in You/The Things You Left in My Heart	1960	3.00	6.00	12.00
❑ 41934	Hey Good Lookin'/Raining in My Heart	1961	3.00	6.00	12.00
❑ 42038	Summertime Lies/Yassu	1961	3.00	6.00	12.00
❑ 42247	It Wasn't God Who Made Honky Tonk Angels/ You Are My Sunshine	1961	3.00	6.00	12.00
DECCA					
❑ 28813	Lonely/Heartless Heart	1953	3.75	7.50	15.00
❑ 28904	A Little Lie/Are You Looking for a Sweetheart	1953	3.75	7.50	15.00
❑ 29037	Little Things Mean a Lot/I Don't Think You Love Me Anymore	1954	3.75	7.50	15.00
❑ 29130	In the Chapel in the Moonlight/Take Everything But You	1954	3.75	7.50	15.00
❑ 29268	I Want You All to Myself (Just You)/Don't Let the Kitty Geddin	1954	3.75	7.50	15.00
❑ 29315	The Spirit of Christmas/Baby Brother (Santa Claus, Dear Santa Claus)	1954	3.00	6.00	12.00
❑ 29417	I'd Never Forgive Myself/Honestly	1955	3.00	6.00	12.00
❑ 29473	By Bayou Bay/Kitty Who?	1955	3.00	6.00	12.00
❑ 29548	If It's a Dream/Forgive Me	1955	3.00	6.00	12.00
❑ 29593	Let's Make the Most of Tonight/Just Between Friends	1955	3.00	6.00	12.00
❑ 29663	Only Forever/Come Spring	1955	3.00	6.00	12.00
❑ 29708	Sweet Kentucky Rose/How Lonely Can I Get?	1955	3.00	6.00	12.00
❑ 29959	True Love/Will I Always Be Your Sweetheart	1956	3.00	6.00	12.00
❑ 30049	How About Me/The Lonely One	1956	3.00	6.00	12.00
❑ 30144	Saturday Blues/Ah, Ah, Ah (The Song That Haunts)	1956	3.00	6.00	12.00
❑ 30267	Star Bright/Gently, Johnny	1957	3.00	6.00	12.00
❑ 30346	Teen-Age Heart/Hideaway Heart	1957	3.00	6.00	12.00
❑ 30516	Crying Roses/I Never Was the One	1957	3.00	6.00	12.00
❑ 88181	The Spirit of Christmas/Baby Brother (Santa Claus, Dear Santa Claus)	1954	3.00	6.00	12.00
—Children's Series issue					
❑ 88181 [PS]	The Spirit of Christmas/Baby Brother (Santa Claus, Dear Santa Claus)	1954	5.00	10.00	20.00
—Children's Series issue					
MERCURY					
❑ 5417	Juke Box Annie/Choo'n Gum	1950	5.00	10.00	20.00
❑ 5587	If You Want Some Lovin'/Last Night	1951	3.75	7.50	15.00
❑ 5700	I Wish I Had a Daddy in the White House/The Old Soft Shoe	1951	3.75	7.50	15.00
❑ 5727	Another Human Being of the Opposite Sex/More, More, More	1951	3.75	7.50	15.00
PHILIPS					
❑ 40375	One Grain of Sand/From Your Lips to the Arms of an Angel	1966	2.00	4.00	8.00
RCA VICTOR					
❑ 47-8124	My Coloring Book/Here's to Us	1962	2.50	5.00	10.00
❑ 47-8202	I'll Teach You How to Cry/We'll Cross That Bridge	1963	2.50	5.00	10.00
7-Inch Extended Plays					
DECCA					
❑ ED 2164	*Little Things Mean a Lot/I Don't Think You Love Me Anymore/In the Chapel in the Moonlight/ Take Everything But You	1954	10.00	20.00	40.00
❑ ED 2164 [PS]	Kitty Kallen Sings	1954	10.00	20.00	40.00
❑ ED 2467	(contents unknown)	1956	6.25	12.50	25.00
❑ ED 2467 [PS]	It's a Lonesome Old Town, Part 1	1956	6.25	12.50	25.00
❑ ED 2468	(contents unknown)	1956	6.25	12.50	25.00
❑ ED 2468 [PS]	It's a Lonesome Old Town, Part 2	1956	6.25	12.50	25.00

Number	Title (A Side/B Side)	Yr	VG	VG+	NM
❑ ED 2469	(contents unknown)	1956	6.25	12.50	25.00
❑ ED 2469 [PS]	It's a Lonesome Old Town, Part 3	1956	6.25	12.50	25.00

MERCURY

Number	Title (A Side/B Side)	Yr	VG	VG+	NM
❑ EP 1-3293	(contents unknown)	1955	10.00	20.00	40.00
❑ EP 1-3293 [PS]	Pretty Kitty Kallen Sings, Vol. 1	1955	10.00	20.00	40.00
❑ EP 1-3294	(contents unknown)	1955	10.00	20.00	40.00
❑ EP 1-3294 [PS]	Pretty Kitty Kallen Sings, Vol. 2	1955	10.00	20.00	40.00

KALLEN, KITTY (WITH RICHARD HAYES)

MERCURY

Number	Title (A Side/B Side)	Yr	VG	VG+	NM
❑ 5466	Our Lady of Fatima/Honestly I Love You	1950	3.75	7.50	15.00
❑ 5499	Halls of Ivy/Dream	1950	3.75	7.50	15.00
❑ 5501	Silver Bells/A Bushel and a Peck	1950	3.75	7.50	15.00
❑ 5532	Silver Bells/Jing-a-Ling	1950	3.75	7.50	15.00
❑ 5564	It Is No Secret (What God Can Do)/Get Out the Old Records	1950	3.75	7.50	15.00
❑ 5586	The Aba Daba Honeymoon/I Don't Want to Love	1951	3.75	7.50	15.00
❑ 5661	Everyone Is Welcome (In the House of the Lord)/Good Luck	1951	3.75	7.50	15.00

KALLEN, KITTY, AND GEORGIE SHAW

DECCA

Number	Title (A Side/B Side)	Yr	VG	VG+	NM
❑ 29776	Go On with the Wedding/The Second Greatest Sex	1955	3.00	6.00	12.00

KANE, EDEN

FONTANA

Number	Title (A Side/B Side)	Yr	VG	VG+	NM
❑ 1891	Boys Cry/Don't Come Crying to Me	1964	3.00	6.00	12.00
❑ 1961	Hangin' Around/Do Something About You	1964	3.00	6.00	12.00

LONDON

Number	Title (A Side/B Side)	Yr	VG	VG+	NM
❑ 1993	Well, I Ask You/Before I Lose My Mind	1961	3.75	7.50	15.00
❑ 9508	Get Lost/I'm Telling You	1961	3.75	7.50	15.00
❑ 9516	Forget Me Not/New Kind of Lovin'	1962	3.75	7.50	15.00
❑ 9532	I Don't Know Why/Music for Strings	1962	3.75	7.50	15.00

T-A

Number	Title (A Side/B Side)	Yr	VG	VG+	NM
❑ 193	Reason to Believe/(B-side unknown)	1970	—	3.00	6.00

KANE, PAUL

See PAUL SIMON.

KANTNER, PAUL

RCA

Number	Title (A Side/B Side)	Yr	VG	VG+	NM
❑ PB-13661	The Planet Earth Rock 'N' Roll Orchestra/The Sky Is No Limit	1983	—	2.00	4.00

KANTNER, PAUL/JEFFERSON STARSHIP

Also see JEFFERSON STARSHIP.

RCA VICTOR

Number	Title (A Side/B Side)	Yr	VG	VG+	NM
❑ 74-0426	Let's Go Together/A Child Is Coming	1971	—	2.50	5.00
❑ 74-0426 [PS]	Let's Go Together/A Child Is Coming	1971	2.00	4.00	8.00

KANTNER, PAUL, AND GRACE SLICK

Also see JEFFERSON AIRPLANE; JEFFERSON STARSHIP; GRACE SLICK.

GRUNT

Number	Title (A Side/B Side)	Yr	VG	VG+	NM
❑ BFBO-0094	Sketches of China/Ballad of Chrome Men	1973	—	2.50	5.00
—With David Freiberg					
❑ 65-0503	Sunfighter/China	1971	—	2.50	5.00
❑ 65-0503 [PS]	Sunfighter/China	1971	—	3.00	6.00

KARTUNES, THE

MGM

Number	Title (A Side/B Side)	Yr	VG	VG+	NM
❑ 12598	Raindrops/Will You Marry Me	1957	7.50	15.00	30.00
❑ 12680	Dedicated to Love/Willie the Weeper	1958	6.25	12.50	25.00

KASENETZ-KATZ SINGING ORCHESTRAL CIRCUS

BELL

Number	Title (A Side/B Side)	Yr	VG	VG+	NM
❑ 966	When He Come/Ah-La	1970	2.50	5.00	10.00
—As "Kasenetz-Katz Fighter Squadron"					

BUDDAH

Number	Title (A Side/B Side)	Yr	VG	VG+	NM
❑ 52	Down in Tennessee/Mrs. Green	1968	2.00	4.00	8.00
❑ 64	Quick Joey Small (Run Joey Run)/Mr. Jensen	1968	2.00	4.00	8.00
❑ 82	I'm in Love with You/To You, With Love	1969	2.00	4.00	8.00
❑ 90	Embrasez-Moi/Mrs. Green	1969	2.00	4.00	8.00

EPIC

Number	Title (A Side/B Side)	Yr	VG	VG+	NM
❑ 50443	Heart Get Ready for Love/Jungle Junk	1977	—	2.50	5.00
—As "K&K Super Cirkus"					

SUPER K

Number	Title (A Side/B Side)	Yr	VG	VG+	NM
❑ 109	Bubblegum March/Dong-Dong-Diki-Di-Ki-Dong	1970	2.00	4.00	8.00

KAY, JOHN

Also see SPARROW; STEPPENWOLF.

ABC DUNHILL

Number	Title (A Side/B Side)	Yr	VG	VG+	NM
❑ 4309	I'm Movin' On/Walk Beside Me	1972	—	2.00	4.00
❑ 4319	You Win Again/Somebody	1972	—	2.00	4.00
❑ 4351	Moonshine/Nobody Lives Here Anymore	1973	—	2.00	4.00
❑ 4360	Dance to My Song/Easy Evil	1973	—	2.00	4.00

COLUMBIA

Number	Title (A Side/B Side)	Yr	VG	VG+	NM
❑ 44769	Twistin'/Square-Headed People	1969	2.00	4.00	8.00

MERCURY

Number	Title (A Side/B Side)	Yr	VG	VG+	NM
❑ 74004	Say You Will/Give Me Some News I Can Use	1978	—	2.00	4.00

KAYLI, BOB

ANNA

Number	Title (A Side/B Side)	Yr	VG	VG+	NM
❑ 1104	Never More/Peppermint (You Know What to Do)	1959	10.00	20.00	40.00

CARLTON

Number	Title (A Side/B Side)	Yr	VG	VG+	NM
❑ 482	Everyone Was There/I Took a Dare	1958	7.50	15.00	30.00

GORDY

Number	Title (A Side/B Side)	Yr	VG	VG+	NM
❑ 7004	Toodle Loo/Everyone Was There	1962	20.00	40.00	80.00
❑ 7008	Toodle Loo/Hold On Pearl	1962	7.50	15.00	30.00

TAMLA

Number	Title (A Side/B Side)	Yr	VG	VG+	NM
❑ 54051	Small Sad Sam/Tie Me Tight	1962	7.50	15.00	30.00

KEEN, BILL, AND THE TRADEWINDS

LESLEY

Number	Title (A Side/B Side)	Yr	VG	VG+	NM
❑ 1922	Don't Call Me/Summer in the Lowlands	1961	7.50	15.00	30.00

KEGGS, THE

ORBIT

Number	Title (A Side/B Side)	Yr	VG	VG+	NM
❑ 20959	To Find Out/(B-side unknown)	1967	1000.	2000.	4000.
—Counterfeit identification: The producer's first name, "Yolanda," is misspelled "Yalanda" on fakes.					

KEITH

COLUMBIA

Number	Title (A Side/B Side)	Yr	VG	VG+	NM
❑ 43268	Dream/Caravan of Lonely Men	1965	3.75	7.50	15.00
—As "Keith and the Admirations"					

DISCREET

Number	Title (A Side/B Side)	Yr	VG	VG+	NM
❑ 1193	What Did You Do in the Revolution, Dad/In and Out of Love	1974	—	2.50	5.00

MERCURY

Number	Title (A Side/B Side)	Yr	VG	VG+	NM
❑ 72596	Ain't Gonna Lie/Our Love Started All Over Again	1966	2.00	4.00	8.00
❑ 72639	98.6/The Teenie Bopper Song	1966	2.50	5.00	10.00
❑ 72639 [PS]	98.6/The Teenie Bopper Song	1966	3.75	7.50	15.00
❑ 72652	Tell Me To My Face/Pretty Little Shy One	1967	2.00	4.00	8.00
❑ 72652 [PS]	Tell Me To My Face/Pretty Little Shy One	1967	3.75	7.50	15.00
❑ 72695	Daylight Savin' Time/Happy Walking Around	1967	2.00	4.00	8.00
❑ 72695 [PS]	Daylight Savin' Time/Happy Walking Around	1967	3.00	6.00	12.00
❑ 72715	Easy-As-Pie/Sugar Man	1967	2.00	4.00	8.00
❑ 72715 [PS]	Easy-As-Pie/Sugar Man	1967	3.00	6.00	12.00
❑ 72746	I'm So Proud/Candy Candy	1967	2.00	4.00	8.00
❑ 72794	Hurry/Pleasure of Your Company	1968	2.00	4.00	8.00
❑ 72824	Always Tomorrow/I Can't Go Wrong	1968	2.00	4.00	8.00

PHILCO-FORD

Number	Title (A Side/B Side)	Yr	VG	VG+	NM
❑ HP-20	98.6/Ain't Gonna Lie	1968	3.75	7.50	15.00
—4-inch plastic "Hip Pocket Record" with color sleeve					

RCA VICTOR

Number	Title (A Side/B Side)	Yr	VG	VG+	NM
❑ 74-0140	Marstrand/The Problem	1969	—	3.00	6.00
❑ 74-0222	Trixin's Election/A Fairy Tale or Two	1969	—	3.00	6.00

KELLER, JERRY

CAPITOL

Number	Title (A Side/B Side)	Yr	VG	VG+	NM
❑ 4630	Never Wake Up/Be Careful How You Drive, Young Joey	1961	3.00	6.00	12.00
❑ 4668	I'll Get By/My Year of Love	1961	3.00	6.00	12.00

CORAL

Number	Title (A Side/B Side)	Yr	VG	VG+	NM
❑ 62348	It's Too Late/What Will I Tell My Darling	1963	2.50	5.00	10.00
❑ 62361	Sume Summer/Goodnight Pretty Girl	1963	2.50	5.00	10.00
❑ 62378	Sea Shell Sherry/What Happens When He Comes Home	1963	2.50	5.00	10.00
❑ 62409	Small Wonder/The Tears Keep Falling Down	1964	2.50	5.00	10.00

KAPP

Number	Title (A Side/B Side)	Yr	VG	VG+	NM
❑ 277 [M]	Here Comes Summer/Time Has a Way	1959	3.75	7.50	15.00
❑ 277 [PS]	Here Comes Summer/Time Has a Way	1959	6.25	12.50	25.00
❑ KS-277 [S]	Here Comes Summer/Time Has a Way	1959	7.50	15.00	30.00
❑ 295	If I Had a Girl/Lovable	1959	3.00	6.00	12.00
❑ 295 [PS]	If I Had a Girl/Lovable	1959	6.25	12.50	25.00
❑ 310	Now, Now, Now/There Are Such Things	1959	3.00	6.00	12.00
❑ 322	American Beauty Rose/Lonesome Lullaby	1960	3.00	6.00	12.00
❑ 337	My Name Ain't Joe/White for You and Bless for Me	1960	3.00	6.00	12.00
❑ 353	What More Can I Say/Whole-Heartedly	1960	3.00	6.00	12.00

RCA VICTOR

Number	Title (A Side/B Side)	Yr	VG	VG+	NM
❑ 47-9221	You're Leanin' On My Mind/My Heart Loves the Samba (Best of All)	1967	2.00	4.00	8.00

REPRISE

Number	Title (A Side/B Side)	Yr	VG	VG+	NM
❑ 0351	Fickle Finger of Fate/Glory of Love	1965	2.00	4.00	8.00
❑ 0397	Ma (She's Such a Quiet Girl)/The Mack	1965	2.00	4.00	8.00

KELLUM, MURRY

CINNAMON

Number	Title (A Side/B Side)	Yr	VG	VG+	NM
❑ 765	Walking Tall/Huckleberry's Ferry Boat Building Blues	1973	—	2.50	5.00
❑ 777	Lovely Lady/Alive and Doing Well	1973	—	2.50	5.00
❑ 794	Girl of My Life/Since You've Been Gone	1974	—	2.50	5.00

EPIC

Number	Title (A Side/B Side)	Yr	VG	VG+	NM
❑ 10741	Joy to the World/In a Phone Booth on My Knees	1971	—	2.50	5.00
❑ 10784	Train Train (Carry Me Away)/What's Made Milwaukee Famous	1971	—	2.50	5.00
❑ 10832	Love You to Sleep Tonight/You Do the Callin' (I'll Do the Crawlin')	1972	—	2.50	5.00

M.O.C.

Number	Title (A Side/B Side)	Yr	VG	VG+	NM
❑ 653	Long, Tall Texan/I Gotta Leave This Town	1963	3.00	6.00	12.00
—B-side by Glenn Sutton					
❑ 657	Red Ryder/Texas Lil	1964	3.00	6.00	12.00
❑ 658	I Dreamed I Was a Beatle/Oh How Sweet It Could Be	1964	5.00	10.00	20.00

PLANTATION

Number	Title (A Side/B Side)	Yr	VG	VG+	NM
❑ 176 [DJ]	Memphis Sun (mono/stereo)	1978	—	2.50	5.00
—Released only as a promo					

RANWOOD

Number	Title (A Side/B Side)	Yr	VG	VG+	NM
❑ 1047	Shoot Low Sheriff/How Long Has It Been (Since They Played Something You Could Dance To)	1976	—	2.50	5.00

KELLY, PAUL

DIAL

Number	Title (A Side/B Side)	Yr	VG	VG+	NM
❑ 4021	Chills and Fever/Only Your Love	1965	2.50	5.00	10.00
❑ 4025	Since I Found You/Can't Help It	1966	2.50	5.00	10.00
❑ 4088	Call Another Doctor/We're Gonna Make It	1968	2.50	5.00	10.00

HAPPY TIGER

Number	Title (A Side/B Side)	Yr	VG	VG+	NM
❑ 541	Stealing in the Name of the Lord/Day After Forever	1970	—	3.00	6.00
❑ 555	Sailing/509	1970	—	3.00	6.00
❑ 568	Poor But Proud/Hot Runnin' Soul	1971	—	3.00	6.00
❑ 573	Hangin' On In There/Soul Flow	1971	—	3.00	6.00

Number	Title (A Side/B Side)	Yr	VG	VG+	NM
PHILIPS					
❑ 40409	I Need Your Love So Bad/Nine Times Out of Ten	1966	3.75	7.50	15.00
❑ 40457	Cryin' for My Baby/Sweet Sweet Lovin'	1967	3.75	7.50	15.00
❑ 40480	If This Old House Could Talk/You Don't Know, You Just Don't Know	1967	3.75	7.50	15.00
❑ 40513	Glad to Be Sad/My Love Is Growing Stronger	1968	3.75	7.50	15.00
WARNER BROS.					
❑ 7614	Travelin' Man/Here Comes Old Jezebel	1972	—	2.50	5.00
❑ 7657	Don't Burn Me/Love Me Now	1972	—	2.50	5.00
❑ 7707	Come Lay Some Lovin' on Me/Come By Here	1973	—	2.50	5.00
❑ 7765	I'm Into Something I Can't Shake Loose/Joy	1974	—	2.50	5.00
❑ 7823	Hooked, Hogtied & Collared/I Wanna Be Close to You	1974	—	2.50	5.00
❑ 8040	Let Your Love Come Down (Let It Fall on Me)/I Wanna Be Close to You	1974	—	2.50	5.00
❑ 8067	Take It Away from Him (Put It On Me)/Try My Love	1975	—	2.50	5.00
❑ 8120	Get Sexy/I Believe I Can	1975	—	2.50	5.00
❑ 8187	Play Me a Love Song/Stealin' Love on the Side	1976	—	2.50	5.00

KELLY FOUR, THE

Also see THE GEE CEES; JEWEL AND EDDIE.

Number	Title (A Side/B Side)	Yr	VG	VG+	NM
CANDIX					
❑ 325	Annie Had a Party/Sweet Angelina	1961	6.25	12.50	25.00
—A-side is an alternate take of Silver 1006					
❑ 325	Annie Had a Party/Sweet Angelina	1961	6.25	12.50	25.00
—As "Big Daddy Greenfield"; same recordings as above					
SILVER					
❑ 1001	Strollin' Guitar/Guybo	1959	10.00	20.00	40.00
—A-side was reissued on Silver 1004 by "Jewel and Eddie"					
❑ 1006	Annie Had a Party/So Fine, Be Mine	1960	10.00	20.00	40.00
—A-side was reissued on Crest 1088 by "The Gee Cees"					

KEMPER, JIMMY, AND THE TIERS

Number	Title (A Side/B Side)	Yr	VG	VG+	NM
LE MANS					
❑ 002	Lonely for Kathy/I'm Free to Choose	1964	37.50	75.00	150.00

KENDRICK, NAT, AND THE SWANS

James Brown's backing band, later known as the J.B.'s. Also see FRED WESLEY.

Number	Title (A Side/B Side)	Yr	VG	VG+	NM
DADE					
❑ 1804	(Do the) Mashed Potatoes (Part 1)/(Do the) Mashed Potatoes (Part 2)	1959	3.75	7.50	15.00
❑ 1808	Dish Rag (Part 1)/Dish Rag (Part 2)	1960	3.75	7.50	15.00
❑ 1812	Hot Chili/Slow Down	1960	3.75	7.50	15.00
❑ 5003	Wobble Wobble (Part 1)/Wobble Wobble (Part 2)	1961	3.75	7.50	15.00
❑ 5004	(Do the) Mashed Potatoes (Part 1)/(Do the) Mashed Potatoes (Part 2)	1961	3.00	6.00	12.00

KENDRICKS, EDDIE

Also see DARYL HALL AND JOHN OATES; DAVID RUFFIN AND EDDIE KENDRICK; THE TEMPTATIONS.

Number	Title (A Side/B Side)	Yr	VG	VG+	NM
ARISTA					
❑ 0325	Ain't No Smoke Without Fire/Love, Love, Love	1978	—	2.00	4.00
❑ 0346	The Best of Strangers Now/Don't Underestimate the Power of Love	1978	—	2.00	4.00
❑ 0466	I Just Want to Be the One in Your Life/I Can't Let You Walk Away	1979	—	2.00	4.00
❑ 0500	Your Love Has Been So Good/I Never Used to Dance	1980	—	2.00	4.00
ATLANTIC					
❑ 3796	Looking for Love/Need Your Lovin'	1981	—	2.00	4.00
❑ 3874 [DJ]	I Don't Need Nobody Else (same on both sides)	1981	—	2.50	5.00
—May be promo only					
CORNER STONE					
❑ 1001	Surprise Attack/(B-side unknown)	1984	—	2.00	4.00
TAMLA					
❑ 54203	It's So Hard for Me to Say Good-Bye/This Used to Be the Home of Johnnie Mae	1971	—	2.50	5.00
❑ 54210	Can I/I Did It All for You	1971	—	2.50	5.00
❑ 54218	Eddie's Love/Let Me Run Into Your Lonely Heart	1972	—	2.50	5.00
❑ 54222	If You Let Me/Just Memories	1972	—	2.50	5.00
❑ 54230	Girl You Need a Change of Mind (Part 1)/Girl You Need a Change of Mind (Part 2)	1973	—	2.50	5.00
❑ 54236	Darling Come Back Home/Loving You the Second Time Around	1973	—	2.50	5.00
❑ 54238	Keep On Truckin' (Part 1)/Keep On Truckin' (Part 2)	1973	—	2.50	5.00
❑ 54243	Boogie Down/Can't Help What I Am	1974	—	2.50	5.00
❑ 54247	Son of Sagittarius/Trust Your Heart	1974	—	2.50	5.00
❑ 54249	Tell Her Love Has Felt the Need/Loving You the Second Time Around	1974	—	2.50	5.00
❑ 54255	One Tear/The Thin Man	1974	—	2.50	5.00
❑ 54257	Shoeshine Boy/Hooked on Your Love	1975	—	2.50	5.00
❑ 54260	Get the Cream Off the Top/Honey Brown	1975	—	2.50	5.00
❑ 54263	Happy/Deep and Quiet Love	1975	—	2.50	5.00
❑ 54266	He's a Friend/All of My Life	1976	—	2.50	5.00
❑ 54270	Get It While It's Hot/Never Gonna Leave You	1976	—	2.50	5.00
❑ 54277	Goin' Up in Smoke/Thanks for the Memories	1976	—	2.50	5.00
❑ 54285	Date with the Rain/Born Again	1977	—	2.50	5.00
❑ 54289	Baby/I Want to Live (My Life with You)	1977	—	—	—
—Unreleased					
❑ 54290	Baby/Intimate Friends	1977	—	2.50	5.00

KENNER, CHRIS

Number	Title (A Side/B Side)	Yr	VG	VG+	NM
BATON					
❑ 220	Grandma's House/Don't Let Her Pin That Charge	1956	10.00	20.00	40.00
IMPERIAL					
❑ 5448	Sick and Tired/Nothing Will Keep Me from You	1957	6.25	12.50	25.00
❑ 5488	Will You Be Mine/I Have News for You	1958	6.25	12.50	25.00
❑ 5767	Sick and Tired/Nothing Will Keep Me from You	1961	3.00	6.00	12.00
INSTANT					
❑ 3229	I Like It Like That, Part 1/I Like It Like That, Part 2	1961	3.75	7.50	15.00
❑ 3234	A Very True Story/Packin' Up	1961	3.00	6.00	12.00
❑ 3237	Something You Got/Come See About Me	1961	3.00	6.00	12.00
❑ 3244	How Far/Time	1962	3.00	6.00	12.00
❑ 3247	Let Me Show You How (To Twist)/Johnny Little	1962	3.00	6.00	12.00
❑ 3252	Land of 1000 Dances/That's My Girl	1962	3.00	6.00	12.00
❑ 3257	Come Back and See/Go Thru Life	1963	3.00	6.00	12.00
❑ 3263	What's Wrong with Life/Never Reach Perfection	1963	3.00	6.00	12.00
❑ 3265	She Can Dance/Anybody Here See My Baby	1964	3.00	6.00	12.00
❑ 3277	I'm Lonely, Take Me/Cinderella	1966	2.50	5.00	10.00
❑ 3280	All Night Rambler, Part 1/All Night Rambler, Part 2	1966	2.50	5.00	10.00
❑ 3283	Shoo Rah/Stretch My Hands to You	1967	2.50	5.00	10.00
❑ 3286	Fumigate Funky Broadway/Wind the Clock	1967	2.50	5.00	10.00
❑ 3290	Memories of a King (Let Freedom Ring), Part 1/Memories of a King (Let Freedom Ring), Part 2	1968	3.00	6.00	12.00
❑ 3293	Mini-Skirts and Soul/Sad Mistake	1968	2.50	5.00	10.00
RON					
❑ 335	Rocket to the Moon/Life's Just a Struggle	1961	3.00	6.00	12.00
UPTOWN					
❑ 708	Life of My Baby/They Took My Money	1965	2.50	5.00	10.00
❑ 716	I'm the Greatest/Get On This Train	1965	2.50	5.00	10.00
VALIANT					
❑ 3229	I Like It Like That, Part 1/I Like It Like That, Part 2	1960	10.00	20.00	40.00

KENNY AND CORKY

Number	Title (A Side/B Side)	Yr	VG	VG+	NM
BIG TOP					
❑ 3031	Nuttin' for Christmas/Suzy Snowflake	1959	5.00	10.00	20.00
❑ 3031 [PS]	Nuttin' for Christmas/Suzy Snowflake	1959	10.00	20.00	40.00

KENNY AND THE CADETS

Also see THE BEACH BOYS.

Number	Title (A Side/B Side)	Yr	VG	VG+	NM
RANDY					
❑ 422	Barbie/What Is a Young Man Made Of	1962	100.00	200.00	400.00
—Pink label original (white labels are counterfeits)					
❑ 422	Barbie/What Is a Young Man Made Of	1962	250.00	500.00	1000.
—Red and gold vinyl					

KENNY AND THE FIENDS

Number	Title (A Side/B Side)	Yr	VG	VG+	NM
DOT					
❑ 16568	House on Haunted Hill (Part 1)/House on Haunted Hill (Part 2)	1963	5.00	10.00	20.00
❑ 16596	Moon Shot/One-Two-Three-Four	1964	5.00	10.00	20.00
POSEA					
❑ 80	The Raven (Part 1)/The Raven (Part 2)	1963	7.50	15.00	30.00
❑ 87	House on Haunted Hill/Green Door	1963	10.00	20.00	40.00
—As "Kenny and the Beach Fiends"					
PRINCESS					
❑ 51	House on Haunted Hill (Part 1)/House on Haunted Hill (Part 2)	1963	7.50	15.00	30.00

KENNY AND THE KASUALS

Number	Title (A Side/B Side)	Yr	VG	VG+	NM
MARK IV					
❑ 911	Nothin' Better to Do/Floatin'	1965	7.50	15.00	30.00
❑ 1002	Don't Let Your Baby Go/(B-side unknown)	1966	7.50	15.00	30.00
❑ 1003	It's All Right/You Make Me Feel So Good	1966	7.50	15.00	30.00
❑ 1004	Strings of Time/(B-side unknown)	1966	7.50	15.00	30.00
❑ 1006	I'm Gonna Make It/Journey to Tyme	1966	10.00	20.00	40.00
❑ 1008	See-Saw Ride/As I Knew	1967	7.50	15.00	30.00
UNITED ARTISTS					
❑ 50085	I'm Gonna Make It/Journey to Tyme	1966	5.00	10.00	20.00

KENNY AND THE SOCIALITES

Number	Title (A Side/B Side)	Yr	VG	VG+	NM
CROSSTOWN					
❑ 001	I'll Have to Decide/King Tut Rock	1958	37.50	75.00	150.00

KENT, AL

Number	Title (A Side/B Side)	Yr	VG	VG+	NM
BARITONE					
❑ 942	Hold Me/Tell Me Why	1960	37.50	75.00	150.00
CHECKER					
❑ 881	Dat's Why (I Love You So)/Am I the Man	1958	15.00	30.00	60.00
RIC-TIC					
❑ 123	The Way You Been Acting Lately/(Instrumental)	1967	5.00	10.00	20.00
❑ 127	You've Got to Pay the Price/Where Do I Go from Here	1967	5.00	10.00	20.00
❑ 133	Finders Keepers/Ooh! Pretty Lady	1967	5.00	10.00	20.00
❑ 140	Bless You (My Love)/(Instrumental)	1968	3.75	7.50	15.00
WINGATE					
❑ 004	You Know I Love You/Country Boy	1965	6.25	12.50	25.00
WIZARD					
❑ 100	Hold Me/You Know Me	1959	25.00	50.00	100.00

KENT, BILLY, AND THE ANDANTES

Number	Title (A Side/B Side)	Yr	VG	VG+	NM
MAH'S					
❑ 000.2	Your Love/Take All of Me	1960	30.00	60.00	120.00
—First pressing, with Detroit address on label					
❑ 000.2	Your Love/Take All of Me	1960	15.00	30.00	60.00
—Second pressing, without address and with Roulette distribution mentioned on label					

KENTS, THE

Number	Title (A Side/B Side)	Yr	VG	VG+	NM
ARGO					
❑ 5299	I Found My Girl/With All My Heart and Soul	1958	7.50	15.00	30.00
DOME					
❑ 501	I Love You So/Happy Beat	1958	125.00	250.00	500.00

KESTRELS, THE

Number	Title (A Side/B Side)	Yr	VG	VG+	NM
LAURIE					
❑ 3053	There Comes a Time/In the Chapel in the Moonlight	1960	6.25	12.50	25.00

KEYES, TROY

Number	Title (A Side/B Side)	Yr	VG	VG+	NM
ABC					
❑ 11027	Love Explosion/I'm Crying (Inside)	1967	2.50	5.00	10.00
❑ 11060	No Sad Songs/You Told Your Story (Now Let Me Tell Mine)	1968	3.75	7.50	15.00

Number	Title (A Side/B Side)	Yr	VG	VG+	NM
❑ 11116	A Good Love Gone Bad/I Can Wait My Turn	1968	5.00	10.00	20.00

—With Norma Jenkins

KEYMEN, THE

ABC-PARAMOUNT

Number	Title (A Side/B Side)	Yr	VG	VG+	NM
❑ 9976	Sentimental Journey/Like Help, Man	1958	3.75	7.50	15.00
❑ 9977 [M]	Miss You/Isle of Capri	1958	3.75	7.50	15.00
❑ S-9977 [S]	Miss You/Isle of Capri	1958	6.25	12.50	25.00
❑ 9991 [M]	Gazachstahagen/Miss You	1959	3.75	7.50	15.00
❑ S-9991 [S]	Gazachstahagen/Miss You	1959	6.25	12.50	25.00
❑ 10016	Dream/Nancy Lee	1959	3.00	6.00	12.00
❑ 10039	Camilia/Cha Cha Marcha Congo	1959	3.00	6.00	12.00

KEYNOTES, THE

Possibly all the same group.

APOLLO

Number	Title (A Side/B Side)	Yr	VG	VG+	NM
❑ 478	Suddenly/Zenda	1955	37.50	75.00	150.00
❑ 484	I Don't Know/A Star	1955	20.00	40.00	80.00
❑ 493	Really Wish You Were Here/Bye Bye Baby	1956	30.00	60.00	120.00
❑ 498	Now I Know/Zup Zup	1956	25.00	50.00	100.00
❑ 503	In the Evening/O Yeah Hm-m-m	1956	20.00	40.00	80.00
❑ 513	One Little Kiss/Now I Know	1957	20.00	40.00	80.00

DOT

Number	Title (A Side/B Side)	Yr	VG	VG+	NM
❑ 15225	Who/They Say	1954	7.50	15.00	30.00

POP

Number	Title (A Side/B Side)	Yr	VG	VG+	NM
❑ 111	Carelessly/Congratulations Baby	1957	20.00	40.00	80.00

TOP RANK

Number	Title (A Side/B Side)	Yr	VG	VG+	NM
❑ 2005	With These Rings/We're Not Getting Along	1959	3.75	7.50	15.00

KEYSTONERS, THE

EPIC

Number	Title (A Side/B Side)	Yr	VG	VG+	NM
❑ 9187	The Magic Kiss/After I Propose	1956	15.00	30.00	60.00

G&M

Number	Title (A Side/B Side)	Yr	VG	VG+	NM
❑ 102	The Magic Kiss/I'd Write About the Blues	1956	75.00	150.00	300.00

OKEH

Number	Title (A Side/B Side)	Yr	VG	VG+	NM
❑ 7210	The Magic Kiss/After I Propose	1964	5.00	10.00	20.00

RIFF

Number	Title (A Side/B Side)	Yr	VG	VG+	NM
❑ 202	Sleep and Dream/T.V. Gal	1961	50.00	100.00	200.00

KEYTONES, THE

OLD TOWN

Number	Title (A Side/B Side)	Yr	VG	VG+	NM
❑ 1041	Wonders of the World/A Fool in Love	1957	75.00	150.00	300.00
❑ 1041	Seven Wonders of the World/A Fool in Love	1957	25.00	50.00	100.00

KID, THE

RUMBLE

Number	Title (A Side/B Side)	Yr	VG	VG+	NM
❑ 1347	Sleep Tight/True Love	1959	45.00	90.00	180.00

KIDD, JOHNNY, AND THE PIRATES

APT

Number	Title (A Side/B Side)	Yr	VG	VG+	NM
❑ 25040	Shakin' All Over/Yes Sir, That's My Baby	1960	6.25	12.50	25.00

CAPITOL

Number	Title (A Side/B Side)	Yr	VG	VG+	NM
❑ 5065	I'll Never Get Over You/Then I Got Everything	1963	3.75	7.50	15.00

KIDDS, THE

IMPERIAL

Number	Title (A Side/B Side)	Yr	VG	VG+	NM
❑ 5335	Are You Forgetting Me/Drunk, Drunk, Drunk	1955	125.00	250.00	500.00

POST

Number	Title (A Side/B Side)	Yr	VG	VG+	NM
❑ 2003	You Broke My Heart/I Won't Be Back	1955	75.00	150.00	300.00

KIM, ANDY

20TH CENTURY FOX

Number	Title (A Side/B Side)	Yr	VG	VG+	NM
❑ 6709	Give Me Your Love/That Girl	1968	2.00	4.00	8.00

CAPITOL

Number	Title (A Side/B Side)	Yr	VG	VG+	NM
❑ 3895	Rock Me Gently/Rock Me Gently (Part 2)	1974	—	2.50	5.00
❑ 3962	Fire, Baby, I'm on Fire/Here Comes the Mornin'	1974	—	2.00	4.00
❑ 3962 [PS]	Fire, Baby, I'm on Fire/Here Comes the Mornin'	1974	—	3.00	6.00
❑ 4032	Hang Up Those Rock 'N' Roll Shoes/Essence of Joan	1975	—	2.00	4.00
❑ 4086	Mary Ann/You Are My Everything	1975	—	2.00	4.00
❑ 4130	(She Got Me) Dancin'/Baby, You're All I Got	1975	—	2.00	4.00
❑ 4234	Oh, Pretty Woman/Baby You're All I Got	1976	—	2.00	4.00

RED BIRD

Number	Title (A Side/B Side)	Yr	VG	VG+	NM
❑ 10-040	I Hear You Say (I Love You Baby)/Falling in Love	1965	3.75	7.50	15.00

STEED

Number	Title (A Side/B Side)	Yr	VG	VG+	NM
❑ 707	How'd We Ever Get This Way/Are You Ever Coming Home	1968	2.00	4.00	8.00
❑ 710	Shoot 'Em Up Baby/Ordinary Kind of Girl	1968	2.00	4.00	8.00
❑ 711	Rainbow Ride/Resurrection	1968	2.00	4.00	8.00
❑ 715	Foundation of My Soul/Tricia Tell Your Daddy	1969	2.00	4.00	8.00
❑ 716	Baby I Love You/Gee Girl	1969	2.00	4.00	8.00
❑ 720	So Good Together/I Got to Know	1969	—	3.00	6.00
❑ 720 [PS]	So Good Together/I Got to Know	1969	3.00	6.00	12.00
❑ 723	A Friend in the City/You	1970	—	3.00	6.00
❑ 723 [PS]	A Friend in the City/You	1970	3.00	6.00	12.00
❑ 727	It's Your Life/To Be Continued	1970	—	3.00	6.00
❑ 729	Be My Baby/Love That Little Woman	1970	—	3.00	6.00
❑ 731	I Wish I Were/Walking My La De La	1971	—	3.00	6.00
❑ 734	I Been Moved/If I Had You Here	1971	—	3.00	6.00
❑ 734 [PS]	I Been Moved/If I Had You Here	1971	3.00	6.00	12.00

TCF

Number	Title (A Side/B Side)	Yr	VG	VG+	NM
❑ 5	Give Me Your Love/Li'l Liz (I Love You)	1964	3.75	7.50	15.00

UNI

Number	Title (A Side/B Side)	Yr	VG	VG+	NM
❑ 55332	Who Has the Answers?/Shady Hollow Dreamers	1972	—	2.50	5.00
❑ 55353	Love Song/Love the Poor Boy	1972	—	2.50	5.00
❑ 55356	Oh What a Day/Sunshine	1972	—	2.50	5.00

UNITED ARTISTS

Number	Title (A Side/B Side)	Yr	VG	VG+	NM
❑ 591	Love Me, Love Me/I Loved You Once	1963	3.75	7.50	15.00

KIMBERLY, ADRIAN

Actually DON EVERLY.

CALLIOPE

Number	Title (A Side/B Side)	Yr	VG	VG+	NM
❑ 6501	The Graduation Song...Pomp and Circumstance/Black Mountain Stomp	1961	10.00	20.00	40.00
❑ 6503	Greensleeves/God Bless America	1961	10.00	20.00	40.00
❑ 6504	When You Wish Upon a Star/Draggin' Dragon	1961	10.00	20.00	40.00

KING, ALBERT

ATLANTIC

Number	Title (A Side/B Side)	Yr	VG	VG+	NM
❑ 2604	The Hunter/As the Years Go Passing By	1969	2.00	4.00	8.00

BOBBIN

Number	Title (A Side/B Side)	Yr	VG	VG+	NM
❑ 114	Why Are You So Mean to Me/Ooh-Ee Baby	1959	6.25	12.50	25.00
❑ 119	Need You By My Side/The Time Has Come	1960	6.25	12.50	25.00
❑ 126	Blues at Sunrise/Let's Have a Natural Ball	1960	6.25	12.50	25.00
❑ 129	I Walked All Night Long/I've Made Nights By Myself	1961	6.25	12.50	25.00
❑ 130	Travelin' to California/Dyna-Flow	1961	6.25	12.50	25.00
❑ 131	Don't Thow Your Love on Me So Strong/This Morning	1961	6.25	12.50	25.00
❑ 135	I Get Evil/What Can I Do to Change Your Mind	1962	6.25	12.50	25.00
❑ 141	I'll Do Anything for You/Got to Be Some Changes Made	1963	6.25	12.50	25.00
❑ 143	Old Blue Ribbon/I've Made Nights By Myself	1963	6.25	12.50	25.00

KING

Number	Title (A Side/B Side)	Yr	VG	VG+	NM
❑ 5575	Don't Throw Your Love on Me So Strong/This Morning	1961	3.00	6.00	12.00
❑ 5588	Travelin' to California/Dyna-Flow	1961	3.00	6.00	12.00
❑ 5751	This Funny Feeling/Had You Told It Like It Was	1963	3.00	6.00	12.00
❑ 6265	Travelin' to California/Don't Throw Your Love on Me So Strong	1969	2.00	4.00	8.00

PARROT

Number	Title (A Side/B Side)	Yr	VG	VG+	NM
❑ 798	Bad Luck Blues/Be On Your Merry Way	1954	400.00	800.00	1200.

STAX

Number	Title (A Side/B Side)	Yr	VG	VG+	NM
❑ 0020	Night Stomp/Blues Power	1968	2.00	4.00	8.00
❑ 0034	Drowning on Dry Land (Vocal)/(Instrumental)	1969	2.00	4.00	8.00
❑ 0058	Wrapped Up in Love Again/Cockroach	1969	2.00	4.00	8.00
❑ 0069	Can't You See What You're Doing to Me/Cold Sweat	1970	2.00	4.00	8.00
❑ 0101	Everybody Wants to Go to Heaven/Lovejoy, Ill.	1971	—	3.50	7.00
❑ 0121	Angel of Mercy/Funky London	1972	—	3.50	7.00
❑ 0135	I'll Play the Blues for You (Part 1)/I'll Play the Blues for You (Part 2)	1972	—	3.50	7.00
❑ 0147	Breaking Up Somebody's Home/Little Brother	1972	—	3.50	7.00
❑ 0166	The High Cost of Loving/Playing on Me	1973	—	3.50	7.00
❑ 0189	That's What the Blues Is All About/I Wanna Get Funky	1973	—	3.50	7.00
❑ 190	Laundromat Blues/Overall Junction	1966	2.50	5.00	10.00
❑ 197	Funk-Shun/Pretty Woman (Can't Make You Love Me)	1966	2.50	5.00	10.00
❑ 201	Crosscut Saw/Down Don't Bother Me	1966	2.50	5.00	10.00
❑ 217	Born Under a Bad Sign/Personal Manager	1967	2.50	5.00	10.00
❑ 0217	I Can Hear Nothing But the Blues/Flat Tire	1974	—	3.50	7.00
❑ 0228	Crosscut Saw/Don't Burn Down the Bridge	1974	—	3.50	7.00
❑ 0234	Santa Claus Wants Some Lovin'/Don't Burn Down the Bridges	1974	—	3.50	7.00
❑ 241	Cold Feet/Drive a Hard Bargain	1967	2.50	5.00	10.00
❑ 252	(I Love) Lucy/You're Gonna Need Me	1968	2.50	5.00	10.00
❑ 1056	What Do The Lonely Do At Christmas?/Santa Claus Wants Some Lovin'	197?	—	3.00	6.00

—B-side by Emotions; reissue

Number	Title (A Side/B Side)	Yr	VG	VG+	NM
❑ 1073	Christmas Comes Once A Year/I'll Be Your Santa Claus	197?	—	2.50	5.00

—B-side by Rufus Thomas; reissue

Number	Title (A Side/B Side)	Yr	VG	VG+	NM
❑ 3203	The Pinch Paid Off (Part 1)/The Pinch Paid Off (Part 2)	1978	—	2.50	5.00
❑ 3225	Santa Claus Wants Some Lovin'/Don't Burn Down the Bridges	1979	—	3.00	6.00

TOMATO

Number	Title (A Side/B Side)	Yr	VG	VG+	NM
❑ 10001	Call My Job/Love Shack	1978	—	2.50	5.00
❑ 10002	Chump Change/Good Time Charlie	1978	—	2.50	5.00
❑ 10009	The Very Thought of You/I Get Evil	1979	—	2.50	5.00
❑ 10012	Born Under a Bad Sign/I've Got the Blues	1979	—	2.50	5.00

UTOPIA

Number	Title (A Side/B Side)	Yr	VG	VG+	NM
❑ PB-10544	Cadillac Assembly Line/Nobody Wants a Loser	1976	—	2.50	5.00
❑ PB-10682	Sensation, Communication Together/Gonna Make It Somehow	1976	—	2.50	5.00
❑ PB-10770	Guitar Man/Rub My Back	1976	—	2.50	5.00
❑ PB-10879	Ain't Nothing You Can Do/I Don't Care What My Baby Do	1977	—	2.50	5.00

KING, ALBERT/STEVE CROPPER/POP STAPLES

STAX

Number	Title (A Side/B Side)	Yr	VG	VG+	NM
❑ 0047	Tupelo (Part 1)/Tupelo (Part 2)	1969	2.00	4.00	8.00
❑ 0048	Water/Opus de Soul	1969	2.00	4.00	8.00

KING, B.B.

Also see BOBBY BLAND AND B.B. KING.

ABC

Number	Title (A Side/B Side)	Yr	VG	VG+	NM
❑ 10856	Don't Answer the Door (Part 1)/Don't Answer the Door (Part 2)	1966	3.75	7.50	15.00
❑ 10889	Waitin' on You/Night Life	1966	3.75	7.50	15.00
❑ 11268	Hummingbird/Ask Me No Questions	1970	2.00	4.00	8.00
❑ 11280	Chains and Things/King's Special	1970	2.00	4.00	8.00
❑ 11290	Ask Me No Questions/Nobody Loves Me But My Mother	1971	2.00	4.00	8.00
❑ 11302	Help the Poor/Lucille's Granny	1971	2.00	4.00	8.00
❑ 11310	Ghetto Woman/Seven Minutes	1971	2.00	4.00	8.00
❑ 11316	Ain't Nobody Home/Alexi's Boogie	1971	2.00	4.00	8.00
❑ 11319	Sweet Sixteen/I've Been Blue Too Long	1972	—	3.00	6.00
❑ 11321	I Got Some Help I Don't Need/Lucille's Granny	1972	—	3.00	6.00
❑ 11330	Guess Who/Better Lovin' Man	1972	—	3.00	6.00

Number	Title (A Side/B Side)	Yr	VG	VG+	NM
❑ 11339	Summer in the City/Five Long Years	1972	—	3.00	6.00
❑ 11373	To Know You Is to Love You/I Can't Leave	1973	—	3.00	6.00
❑ 11406	I Like to Live the Love/Love	1973	—	3.00	6.00
❑ 11433	Who Are You/On to Me	1974	—	3.00	6.00
❑ 12029	Philadelphia/Up at 5 A.M.	1974	—	3.00	6.00
❑ 12053	Friends/My Song	1974	—	3.00	6.00
❑ 12158	When I'm Wrong/Have Faith	1976	—	3.00	6.00
❑ 12247	Slow and Easy/I Wonder Why	1977	—	3.00	6.00
❑ 12380	Never Make a Move Too Soon/Let Me Make You Cry a Little Longer	1978	—	3.00	6.00
❑ 12412	I Just Can't Leave Your Love Alone/Midnight Believer	1978	—	3.00	6.00
ABC-PARAMOUNT					
❑ 10316	I'm Gonna Sit In Till You Give In/You Ask Me	1962	3.75	7.50	15.00
❑ 10334	Blues at Midnight/My Baby's Coming Home	1962	3.75	7.50	15.00
❑ 10361	Chains of Love/Sneakin' Around	1962	3.75	7.50	15.00
❑ 10367	Tomorrow Night/Mother's Love	1962	3.75	7.50	15.00
❑ 10390	Guess Who/By Myself	1962	3.75	7.50	15.00
❑ 10455	On My Word of Honor/Young Dreamers	1963	3.75	7.50	15.00
❑ 10486	How Do I Love You/Slowly Losing My Mind	1963	3.75	7.50	15.00
❑ 10527	How Blue Can You Get/Please Accept My Love	1964	3.75	7.50	15.00
❑ 10552	Help the Poor/I Wouldn't Have It Any Other Way	1964	3.75	7.50	15.00
❑ 10576	Whole Lotta Lovin'/The Hurt	1964	3.75	7.50	15.00
❑ 10597	Never Trust a Woman/Worryin' Blues	1964	3.75	7.50	15.00
❑ 10616	Please Send Me Someone to Love/The Worst Thing in My Life	1965	3.75	7.50	15.00
❑ 10634	Everyday I Have the Blues/It's My Own Fault	1965	3.75	7.50	15.00
❑ 10675	Tired of Your Jive/Night Owl	1965	3.75	7.50	15.00
❑ 10724	All Over Again/The Things You Put Me Through	1965	3.75	7.50	15.00
❑ 10754	Goin' to Chicago Blues/I'd Rather Drink Muddy Water	1965	3.75	7.50	15.00
❑ 10766	Tormented/You're Still a Square	1966	3.75	7.50	15.00
BLUESWAY					
❑ 61004	Think It Over/I Don't Want You Cutting Off Your Hair	1967	2.50	5.00	10.00
❑ 61007	Worried Dream/That's Wrong, Little Mama	1967	2.50	5.00	10.00
❑ 61011	Raining in My Heart/Heartbreaker	1967	2.50	5.00	10.00
❑ 61012	Sweet Sixteen (Part 1)/Sweet Sixteen (Part 2)	1968	2.50	5.00	10.00
❑ 61015	Paying the Cost to Be the Boss/Having My Say	1968	2.50	5.00	10.00
❑ 61018	I'm Gonna Do What They Do to Me/Losing Faith in You	1968	2.50	5.00	10.00
❑ 61019	You Put It On Me/B.B. Jones	1968	2.50	5.00	10.00
❑ 61021	Dance with Me/Please Send Me Someone to Love	1968	2.50	5.00	10.00
❑ 61022	Don't Waste My Time/Get Myself Somebody	1969	2.50	5.00	10.00
❑ 61024	Why I Sing the Blues/Friends	1969	2.50	5.00	10.00
❑ 61026	Get Off My Back Woman/I Want You So Bad	1969	2.50	5.00	10.00
❑ 61029	Just a Little Love/My Mood	1969	2.50	5.00	10.00
❑ 61032	The Thrill Is Gone/You're Mean	1969	3.00	6.00	12.00
❑ 61032 [PS]	The Thrill Is Gone/You're Mean	1969	5.00	10.00	20.00
❑ 61035	So Excited/Confessin' the Blues	1970	2.00	4.00	8.00
KENT					
❑ 301	You Know I Go for You/Why Do Everything Happen to Me	1958	5.00	10.00	20.00
❑ 307	Days of Old/Don't Look Now, But You Got the Blues	1958	5.00	10.00	20.00
❑ 315	Please Accept My Love/You've Been an Angel	1958	6.25	12.50	25.00
—With the Vocal Chords					
❑ 317	Worry Worry/I Am	1959	5.00	10.00	20.00
❑ 319	The Fool/Come By Here	1959	5.00	10.00	20.00
❑ 325	A Lonely Lover's Plea/Woman in Love	1959	5.00	10.00	20.00
❑ 327	Everyday I Have the Blues/Time to Say Goodbye	1959	5.00	10.00	20.00
❑ 329	Sugar Mama/Mean Old Friend	1959	5.00	10.00	20.00
❑ 330	Sweet Sixteen, Pt. 1/Sweet Sixteen, Pt. 2	1960	5.00	10.00	20.00
❑ 333	Got a Right to Love My Baby/My Own Fault	1960	3.75	7.50	15.00
❑ 336	Please Love Me/Crying Won't Help You	1960	3.75	7.50	15.00
❑ 337	Blind Love/You Upset Me Baby	1960	3.75	7.50	15.00
❑ 338	Ten Long Years/Everyday I Have the Blues	1960	3.75	7.50	15.00
❑ 339	Did You Ever Love a Woman/Three O'Clock Blues	1960	3.75	7.50	15.00
❑ 340	Sweet Little Angel/You Done Lost Your Good Thing Now	1960	3.75	7.50	15.00
❑ 346	Partin' Time/Good Man Gone Bad	1960	3.75	7.50	15.00
❑ 350	Waking Dr. Bill/You Done Lost Your Good Thing Now	1960	3.75	7.50	15.00
❑ 351	Things Are Not the Same/Fishin' After Me	1961	3.75	7.50	15.00
❑ 353	Bad Luck Soul/Get Out of Here	1961	3.75	7.50	15.00
❑ 358	Hold That Train/Understand	1961	3.75	7.50	15.00
❑ 360	Peace of Mind/Someday	1961	3.75	7.50	15.00
❑ 362	You're Breaking My Heart/Bad Case of Love	1961	3.75	7.50	15.00
❑ 365	My Sometime Baby/Lonely	1962	3.00	6.00	12.00
❑ 372	Gonna Miss You Around Here/Hully Gully Twist	1962	3.00	6.00	12.00
❑ 373	3 O'Clock Stomp/Mashed Potato Twist	1962	3.00	6.00	12.00
❑ 381	Tell Me Baby/Mashing the Popeye	1962	3.00	6.00	12.00
❑ 383	Going Down Slow/When My Heart Beats Like a Hammer	1962	3.00	6.00	12.00
❑ 386	Your Letter/Blues for Me	1962	3.00	6.00	12.00
❑ 387	Christmas Celebration/Easy Listening	1962	3.00	6.00	12.00
❑ 388	Whole Lot of Loving/Down Now	1963	3.00	5.00	10.00
❑ 389	Trouble in Mind/Long Nights	1963	3.00	5.00	10.00
❑ 390	My Reward/The Road I Travel	1963	3.00	5.00	10.00
❑ 391	The Letter/You Never Know	1963	3.00	5.00	10.00
❑ 392	Army of the Lord/Precious Lord	1964	3.00	7.50	15.00
❑ 393	Rock Me Baby/I Can't Lose	1964	3.00	5.00	10.00
❑ 396	Let Me Love You/You're Gonna Miss Me	1964	3.00	5.00	10.00
❑ 403	Beautician Blues/I Can Hear My Name	1964	3.00	5.00	10.00
❑ 412	Christmas Celebration/Easy Listening	1964	3.00	6.00	12.00
❑ 415	Got 'Em Bad/The Worst Thing in My Life	1965	3.00	6.00	12.00
❑ 421	Please Love Me/Baby Look at You	1965	3.00	6.00	12.00
❑ 426	Blue Shadows/And Like That	1965	3.00	6.00	12.00
❑ 429	Just a Dream/Why Do Everything Happen to Me	1965	3.00	6.00	12.00
❑ 435	Mercy, Mercy, Mercy/Broken Promise	1965	3.00	6.00	12.00
❑ 441	Eyesight to the Blind/Just Like a Woman	1966	3.00	6.00	12.00
❑ 445	Five Long Years/Love, Honor and Obey	1966	3.00	6.00	12.00
❑ 447	Ain't Nobody's Business/I Wonder Why	1966	3.00	6.00	12.00
❑ 450	I Stay in the Mood/Early Every Morning	1966	3.00	6.00	12.00
❑ 458	It's a Mean World/Blues Stay Away	1966	2.00	4.00	8.00
❑ 462	The Jungle/Long Gone Baby	1967	2.00	4.00	8.00
❑ 467	Treat Me Right/Who Can Your Good Man Be	1967	2.00	4.00	8.00
❑ 470	Bad Breaks/Growing Old	1967	2.00	4.00	8.00
❑ 475	Sweet Thing/Soul Beat	1967	2.00	4.00	8.00
❑ 484	Worry, Worry, Worry/Why Do Everything Happen to Me	1968	—	3.00	6.00
❑ 492	The Woman I Love/Blues for Me	1968	—	3.00	6.00
❑ 499	Slow Burn/3 O'Clock Blues	1968	—	3.00	6.00
❑ 510	Your Fool/Shoutin' the Blues	1969	—	3.00	6.00
❑ 4513	I'm Cracking Up Over You/Powerhouse	1969	2.50	5.00	10.00
❑ 4515	Dreams/House Rocker	1970	2.50	5.00	10.00
❑ 4526	Worried Life/Walkin' Dr. Bill	1970	2.50	5.00	10.00
❑ 4542	That Evil Child/Tell Me Baby	1971	2.00	4.00	8.00
❑ 4549	I'll Survive/Long Nights	1971	2.00	4.00	8.00
❑ 4562	Precious Lord/Swing Low, Sweet Chariot	1972	2.00	4.00	8.00
❑ 4566	Don't Get Around Much Anymore/Poontanging	1972	2.00	4.00	8.00
❑ 4572	Recession Blues/Walkin' Dr. Bill	1972	2.00	4.00	8.00
MCA					
❑ 41062	Happy Birtday Blues/Better Not Look Down	1979	—	2.00	4.00
❑ 51101	There Must Be a Better World Somewhere/You're Going with Me	1981	—	2.00	4.00
❑ 52057	Since I Met You Baby/One of Those Nights	1982	—	—	3.00
❑ 52098	Street Life/Overture	1982	—	—	3.00
—With the Crusaders and the London Symphony Orchestra					
❑ 52125	Love Me Tender/The World I Never Made	1982	—	—	3.00
❑ 52218	Sell My Monkey/Inflation Blues	1983	—	—	3.00
❑ 52530	Into the Night/Century City Chase of J.B. in Teheran	1985	—	—	3.00
❑ 52530 [PS]	Into the Night/Century City Chase of J.B. in Teheran	1985	—	—	3.00
❑ 52574	My Lucille/Keep It Light	1985	—	—	3.00
—B-side by Thelma Houston					
❑ 52675	Big Boss Man/My Guitar Sings the Blues	1985	—	—	3.00
❑ 52751	Memory Lane/Six Silver Strings	1985	—	—	3.00
❑ 53269	(You've Become a) Habit to Me/(You've Become a) Habit to Me (Long)	1988	—	—	3.00
❑ 53644	Lay Another Log on the Fire/Go On	1989	—	—	3.00
❑ 54339	The Blues Come Over Me (Wild & Bluesy Club Mix Edit)/The Blues Come Over Me (Integrity Mix)	1992	—	2.00	4.00
POINTBLANK					
❑ 58820	Christmas Celebration/White Christmas	1999	—	—	3.00
—B-side by Hadda Brooks					
RPM					
❑ 339	3 O'Clock Blues/That Ain't the Way to Do It	1951	225.00	450.00	900.00
—B.B. King singles on RPM before 339 are unconfirmed on 45 rpm					
❑ 348	Fine Lookin' Woman/She Don't Move Me No More	1952	75.00	150.00	300.00
❑ 355	Shake It Up and Go/My Own Fault, Darling	1952	37.50	75.00	150.00
❑ 360	Gotta Find My Baby/Someday Somewhere	1952	25.00	50.00	100.00
❑ 363	You Know I Love You/You Didn't Want Me	1952	20.00	40.00	80.00
❑ 374	Story from My Heart and Soul/Boogie Woogie Woman	1952	37.50	75.00	150.00
❑ 380	Woke Up This Morning (My Baby She Was Gone)/Don't Have to Cry	1953	25.00	50.00	100.00
❑ 386	Please Love Me/Highway Bound	1953	37.50	75.00	150.00
❑ 391	Please Hurry Home/Neighborhood Affair	1953	20.00	40.00	80.00
❑ 395	Why Did You Leave Me/Blind Love	1953	20.00	40.00	80.00
❑ 403	Praying to the Lord/Please Help Me	1954	7.50	15.00	30.00
❑ 408	Love Me Baby/The Woman I Love	1954	7.50	15.00	30.00
❑ 411	Everything I Do Is Wrong/Don't You Want a Man Like Me	1954	7.50	15.00	30.00
❑ 412	When My Heart Beats Like a Hammer/Bye Bye Baby	1954	7.50	15.00	30.00
❑ 416	You Upset Me Baby/Whole Lotta' Love	1954	7.50	15.00	30.00
❑ 421	Every Day I Have the Blues/Sneakin' Around	1955	7.50	15.00	30.00
❑ 425	Lonely and Blue/Jump with You Baby	1955	7.50	15.00	30.00
❑ 430	I'm in Love/Shut Your Mouth	1955	7.50	15.00	30.00
❑ 435	Talkin' the Blues/Boogie Rock	1955	7.50	15.00	30.00
❑ 437	Ten Long Years/What Can I Do	1955	7.50	15.00	30.00
❑ 450	I'm Cracking Up Over You/Ruby Lee	1956	6.25	12.50	25.00
❑ 451	Crying Won't Help You/Sixteen Tons	1956	6.25	12.50	25.00
❑ 451	Crying Won't Help You/Can't We Talk It Over	1956	6.25	12.50	25.00
❑ 457	Did You Ever Love a Woman/Let's Do the Boogie	1956	6.25	12.50	25.00
❑ 459	Dark Is the Night (Part 1)/Dark Is the Night (Part 2)	1956	6.25	12.50	25.00
❑ 468	Bad Luck/Sweet Little Angel	1956	6.25	12.50	25.00
❑ 479	On My Word of Honor/Bim Bam	1956	6.25	12.50	25.00
❑ 486	You Don't Know/Early in the Morning	1957	6.25	12.50	25.00
❑ 490	How Do I Love You/You Can't Fool My Heart	1957	6.25	12.50	25.00
❑ 492	Troubles, Troubles, Troubles/I Want to Get Married	1957	6.25	12.50	25.00
❑ 494	Quit My Baby/Be Careful with a Fool	1957	6.25	12.50	25.00
❑ 498	I Wonder/I Need You So Bad	1957	6.25	12.50	25.00
❑ 501	The Key to My Kingdom/My Heart Belongs to Only You	1957	6.25	12.50	25.00

KING, B.B./ERIC CLAPTON

Also see each artist's individual listings.

Number	Title (A Side/B Side)	Yr	VG	VG+	NM
REPRISE					
❑ 7-16831	Riding with the King/Key to the Highway	2000	—	—	3.00
❑ 7-16832	Worried Life Blues/Days of Old	2000	—	—	3.00
❑ 7-16833	Marry You/Three O'Clock Blues (Edit)	2000	—	—	3.00
❑ 7-16834	When My Heart Beats Like a Hammer (Edit)/I Wanna Be	2000	—	—	3.00
❑ 7-16835	Help the Poor/Hold On I'm Coming	2000	—	—	3.00
❑ 7-16836	Come Rain or Come Shine/Ten Long Years	2000	—	—	3.00

KING, BEN E.

Also see AVERAGE WHITE BAND; THE DRIFTERS.

ATCO

Number	Title (A Side/B Side)	Yr	VG	VG+	NM
❑ 6166	Show Me the Way/Brace Yourself	1960	4.00	8.00	16.00
❑ 6185	Spanish Harlem/First Taste of Love	1960	5.00	10.00	20.00
❑ 6194	Stand By Me/On the Horizon	1961	5.00	10.00	20.00
❑ 6203	Amor/Souvenir of Mexico	1961	4.00	8.00	16.00
❑ 6207	Young Boy Blues/Here Comes the Night	1961	4.00	8.00	16.00
❑ 6215	Ecstasy/Yes	1962	4.00	8.00	16.00
❑ 6222	Don't Play That Song (You Lied)/Hermit of Misty Mountain	1962	4.00	8.00	16.00
❑ 6231	Too Bad/My Heart Cries for You	1962	3.00	6.00	12.00
❑ 6237	I'm Standing By/Walking in the Footsteps of a Fool	1962	3.00	6.00	12.00
❑ 6246	Tell Daddy/Auf Weidersehn, My Dear	1962	3.00	6.00	12.00
❑ 6256	How Can I Forget/Gloria Gloria	1963	3.00	6.00	12.00
❑ 6267	I (Who Have Nothing)/The Beginning of Time	1963	3.00	6.00	12.00
❑ 6275	I Could Have Danced All Night/Gypsy	1963	3.00	6.00	12.00
❑ 6284	What Now My Love/Groovin'	1964	2.50	5.00	10.00
❑ 6288	That's When It Hurts/Around the Corner	1964	2.50	5.00	10.00
❑ 6303	What Can a Man Do/Si, Senor	1964	2.50	5.00	10.00
❑ 6315	It's All Over/Let the Water Run Down	1964	2.50	5.00	10.00
❑ 6328	Seven Letters/River of Tears	1964	2.50	5.00	10.00
❑ 6343	The Record (Baby I Love You)/The Way You Shake It	1965	2.50	5.00	10.00
❑ 6357	She's Gone Again/Not Now (I'll Tell You When)	1965	2.50	5.00	10.00
❑ 6371	Cry No More/There's No Place to Hide	1965	2.50	5.00	10.00
❑ 6390	Goodnight My Love/I Can't Break the News to Myself	1965	2.50	5.00	10.00
❑ 6413	So Much Love/Don't Drive Me Away	1966	2.00	4.00	8.00
❑ 6431	Get in a Hurry/I Swear by Stars Above	1966	2.00	4.00	8.00
❑ 6454	They Don't Give Medals to Yesterday's Heroes/What Is Soul	1966	2.00	4.00	8.00
❑ 6472	A Man Without a Dream/Tears, Tears, Tears	1967	2.00	4.00	8.00
❑ 6493	Katherine/Teeny Weeny Little Bit	1967	2.00	4.00	8.00
❑ 6527	Don't Take Your Sweet Love Away/She Knows What to Do for Me	1967	2.50	5.00	10.00
❑ 6557	We Got a Thing Goin' On/What 'Cha Gonna Do About It	1968	2.00	4.00	8.00
—With Dee Dee Sharp					
❑ 6571	Don't Take Your Love from Me/Forgive This Soul	1968	2.00	4.00	8.00
❑ 6596	Where's the Girl/It's Amazing	1968	2.00	4.00	8.00
❑ 6637	It Ain't Fair/Till I Can't Take It Anymore	1968	2.00	4.00	8.00
❑ 6666	Hey Little One/When You Love Someone	1969	2.50	5.00	10.00

ATLANTIC

Number	Title (A Side/B Side)	Yr	VG	VG+	NM
❑ 3241	Supernatural Thing — Part 1/Supernatural Thing — Part 2	1975	—	2.50	5.00
❑ 3274	Do It in the Name of Love/Imagination	1975	—	2.50	5.00
❑ 3308	We Got Love/I Had a Love	1975	—	2.50	5.00
❑ 3337	I Betch'a You Didn't Know/Smooth Sailing	1976	—	2.50	5.00
❑ 3359	One More Time/Somebody's Knocking	1976	—	2.50	5.00
❑ 3402	Get It Up/Keepin' It To Myself	1977	—	2.50	5.00
—With the Average White Band					
❑ 3427	A Star in the Ghetto/What Is Soul?	1977	—	2.50	5.00
—With the Average White Band					
❑ 3444	Fool for You Anyway/The Message	1977	—	2.50	5.00
—With the Average White Band					
❑ 3494	I See the Light/Tippin'	1978	—	2.50	5.00
❑ 3535	Fly Away to My Wonderland/Spoiled	1978	—	2.50	5.00
❑ 3635	Music Trance/And This Is Love	1979	—	2.00	4.00
❑ 3808	Street Tough/Why Is the Question	1981	—	2.00	4.00
❑ 3839	You Made the Difference in My Life/Souvenirs of Love	1981	—	2.00	4.00
❑ 89234	Spanish Harlem/First Taste of Love	1987	—	—	3.00
❑ 89361	Stand By Me/Yakety Yak	1986	—	—	3.00
—B-side by the Coasters					
❑ 89361 [DJ]	Stand By Me Medley (same on both sides)	1986	2.00	4.00	8.00
—Contains excerpts from all 10 songs on the "Stand By Me" soundtrack album. It is listed here because it uses the same number as the stock release of "Stand By Me."					
❑ 89361 [PS]	Stand By Me/Yakety Yak	1986	—	—	3.00
❑ 89361 [PS]	Stand By Me Medley	1986	2.00	4.00	8.00
—Promo-only sleeve accompanying above medley. Stock and promo sleeves are identical in front but different on back.					

ICHIBAN

Number	Title (A Side/B Side)	Yr	VG	VG+	NM
❑ 254	You've Got All of Me/It's All Right	1992	—	—	3.00
❑ 257	You Still Move Me/I'm Gonna Be Somebody	1992	—	—	3.00

MANDALA

Number	Title (A Side/B Side)	Yr	VG	VG+	NM
❑ 2512	Take Me to the Pilot/I Guess It's Goodbye	1972	—	2.50	5.00
❑ 2513	Into the Mystic/White Moon	1972	—	2.50	5.00
❑ 2518	Spread Myself Around/Travellin' Woman	1973	—	2.50	5.00

MANHATTAN

Number	Title (A Side/B Side)	Yr	VG	VG+	NM
❑ 50078	Save the Last Dance for Me/Wheel of Love	1987	—	—	3.00
❑ 50078 [PS]	Save the Last Dance for Me/Wheel of Love	1987	—	—	3.00

MAXWELL

Number	Title (A Side/B Side)	Yr	VG	VG+	NM
❑ 800	I Can't Take It Like a Man/(B-side unknown)	1969	2.00	4.00	8.00

THE RIGHT STUFF

Number	Title (A Side/B Side)	Yr	VG	VG+	NM
❑ S7-19728	4th of July, Asbury Park (Sandy)/Janey, Don't You Lose Heart	1997	—	—	3.00
—B-side by Mrs. Fun/Tina & The B-Side Movement					

KING, CAROLE

Also see THE CITY; BERTELL DACHE.

ABC-PARAMOUNT

Number	Title (A Side/B Side)	Yr	VG	VG+	NM
❑ 9921	Goin' Wild/The Right Girl	1958	37.50	75.00	150.00
❑ 9986	Baby Sittin'/Under the Stars	1958	37.50	75.00	150.00

ALPINE

Number	Title (A Side/B Side)	Yr	VG	VG+	NM
❑ 57	Oh, Neil/A Very Special Boy	1959	175.00	350.00	700.00

ATLANTIC

Number	Title (A Side/B Side)	Yr	VG	VG+	NM
❑ 4026	One to One/Goat Annie	1982	—	2.00	4.00
❑ 4026 [PS]	One to One/Goat Annie	1982	—	2.50	5.00
❑ 4062	Read Between the Lines/Life Without Love	1982	—	2.00	4.00
❑ 89694 [DJ]	Speeding Time (same on both sides)	1984	—	2.00	4.00
—May be promo only					
❑ 89756	Crying in the Rain/Sacred Heart of Stone	1983	—	2.00	4.00

CAPITOL

Number	Title (A Side/B Side)	Yr	VG	VG+	NM
❑ 4455	Hard Rock Cafe/To Know That I Love You	1977	—	2.00	4.00
❑ 4455 [PS]	Hard Rock Cafe/To Know That I Love You	1977	—	2.50	5.00
❑ 4497	Simple Things/Hold On	1977	—	2.00	4.00
❑ 4593	Main Street Saturday Night/Changes	1978	—	2.00	4.00
❑ 4649	Sunbird/Morning Sun	1978	—	2.00	4.00
❑ 4718	Move Lightly/Whiskey	1979	—	2.00	4.00
❑ 4718 [PS]	Move Lightly/Whiskey	1979	—	2.50	5.00
❑ 4766	Time Gone By/Dreamlike I Wander	1979	—	2.00	4.00
❑ 4864	One Fine Day/Rulers of This World	1980	—	2.00	4.00
❑ 4864 [PS]	One Fine Day/Recipients of History	1980	2.00	4.00	8.00
—First pressing sleeves list the wrong title for the B-side (no records are known to exist with this title)					
❑ 4864 [PS]	One Fine Day/Rulers of This World	1980	—	2.00	4.00
—Second pressing sleeves don't list a B-side at all					
❑ 4911	The Locomotion/Oh No Not My Baby	1980	—	2.00	4.00
❑ 4941	Chains/Bad Girl	1980	—	2.00	4.00
❑ B-44336	City Streets/Time Heals All Wounds	1989	—	—	3.00
❑ B-44336 [PS]	City Streets/Time Heals All Wounds	1989	—	—	3.00
❑ 7PRO-79520 [DJ]	City Streets (same on both sides)	1989	—	2.00	4.00
❑ 7PRO-79520 [PS]	City Streets (same on both sides)	1989	—	2.00	4.00
❑ 7PRO-79873 [DJ]	Lovelight (same on both sides)	1989	—	2.50	5.00
—Vinyl is promo only					

COMPANION

Number	Title (A Side/B Side)	Yr	VG	VG+	NM
❑ 2000	It Might As Well Rain Until September/Nobody's Perfect	1962	75.00	150.00	300.00

DIMENSION

Number	Title (A Side/B Side)	Yr	VG	VG+	NM
❑ 1004	School Bells Are Ringing/I Didn't Have Any Summer Romance	1962	5.00	10.00	20.00
❑ 1009	He's a Bad Boy/We Grew Up Together	1963	5.00	10.00	20.00
❑ 2000	It Might As Well Rain Until September/Nobody's Perfect	1962	3.00	6.00	12.00

ODE

Number	Title (A Side/B Side)	Yr	VG	VG+	NM
❑ 66006	Eventually/Up On the Roof	1970	2.00	4.00	8.00
❑ 66015	It's Too Late/I Feel the Earth Move	1971	—	2.00	4.00
❑ 66015 [PS]	It's Too Late/I Feel the Earth Move	1971	—	2.50	5.00
❑ 66019	So Far Away/Smackwater Jack	1971	—	2.00	4.00
❑ 66019 [PS]	So Far Away/Smackwater Jack	1971	—	2.50	5.00
❑ 66022	Sweet Seasons/Pocket Money	1971	—	2.00	4.00
❑ 66022 [PS]	Sweet Seasons/Pocket Money	1971	—	2.50	5.00
❑ 66026	It's Going to Take Some Time/Brother Brother	1972	—	3.00	6.00
❑ 66031	Been to Canaan/Bitter with the Sweet	1972	—	2.00	4.00
❑ 66031 [PS]	Been to Canaan/Bitter with the Sweet	1972	—	2.50	5.00
❑ 66035	Believe in Humanity/You Light Up My Life	1973	—	2.00	4.00
❑ 66035 [PS]	Believe in Humanity/You Light Up My Life	1973	—	2.50	5.00
❑ 66039	Corazon/That's How Things Go Down	1973	—	2.00	4.00
❑ 66047	Jazzman/You Go Your Way, I'll Go Mine	1974	—	2.50	5.00
❑ 66047 [PS]	Jazzman/You Go Your Way, I'll Go Mine	1974	—	3.00	6.00
❑ 66101	Jazzman/You Go Your Way, I'll Go Mine	1974	—	2.00	4.00
❑ 66101 [PS]	Jazzman/You Go Your Way, I'll Go Mine	1974	—	2.50	5.00
❑ 66106	Nightingale/You're Something New	1975	—	2.00	4.00
❑ 66112 SP	Chicken Soup with Rice/Pierre	1975	2.00	4.00	8.00
—33 1/3 rpm 7-inch record					
❑ 66112 SP [PS]	Chicken Soup with Rice/Pierre	1975	2.50	5.00	10.00
❑ 66119	Only Love Is Real/Still Here Thinking of You	1976	—	2.00	4.00
❑ 66123	High Out of Time/I'd Like to Know You Better	1976	—	2.00	4.00

RCA VICTOR

Number	Title (A Side/B Side)	Yr	VG	VG+	NM
❑ 47-7560	Short Mort/Queen of the Beach	1959	25.00	50.00	100.00

TOMORROW

Number	Title (A Side/B Side)	Yr	VG	VG+	NM
❑ 7502	A Road to Nowhere/Some of Your Lovin'	1966	10.00	20.00	40.00

KING, CLYDIE

IMPERIAL

Number	Title (A Side/B Side)	Yr	VG	VG+	NM
❑ 66109	The Thrill Is Gone/If You Were a Man	1965	5.00	10.00	20.00
❑ 66139	My Love Grows Deeper/Missin' My Baby	1965	5.00	10.00	20.00
❑ 66172	He Always Comes Back to Me/Soft and Gentle Ways	1966	5.00	10.00	20.00

LIZARD

Number	Title (A Side/B Side)	Yr	VG	VG+	NM
❑ 21007	'Bout Love/(B-side unknown)	1971	—	3.00	6.00

MINIT

Number	Title (A Side/B Side)	Yr	VG	VG+	NM
❑ 32025	Good for Cryin' Over You Days/Mistakes of Yesterday	1967	3.00	6.00	12.00
❑ 32054	Love Now, Pay Later/One Part, Two Part	1969	2.00	4.00	8.00

PHILIPS

Number	Title (A Side/B Side)	Yr	VG	VG+	NM
❑ 40001	Boys in My Life/Promises	1962	5.00	10.00	20.00
❑ 40051	Turn Around/Don't Hang Up the Phone	1962	5.00	10.00	20.00
❑ 40107	Only the Guilty Cry/By Noro	1963	5.00	10.00	20.00

SPECIALTY

Number	Title (A Side/B Side)	Yr	VG	VG+	NM
❑ 605	Our Romance/Written on the Wall	1957	7.50	15.00	30.00

KING, CURTIS

No, not King Curtis.

COLUMBIA

Number	Title (A Side/B Side)	Yr	VG	VG+	NM
❑ 44096	Bad Habits/So Nice While It Lasted	1967	5.00	10.00	20.00

KING, EARL

ACE

Number	Title (A Side/B Side)	Yr	VG	VG+	NM
❑ 509	Those Lonely, Lonely Nights/Baby You Can Get Your Gun	1955	15.00	30.00	60.00
❑ 514	My Love Is Strong/Little Girl	1956	12.50	25.00	50.00
❑ 517	It Must Have Been Love/I'll Take You Back Home	1956	12.50	25.00	50.00
❑ 520	Is Everything Alright/Mother Told Me Not to Go	1956	12.50	25.00	50.00
❑ 529	Those Lonely, Lonely Feelings/You Can Fly High	1957	12.50	25.00	50.00
❑ 543	I'll Never Get Tired/Well'o, Well'o, Well'o Baby	1958	12.50	25.00	50.00
❑ 564	Weary Silent Night/Everybody's Carried Away	1959	10.00	20.00	40.00
❑ 598	Don't You Know You're Wrong/Buddy It's Time to Go	1960	10.00	20.00	40.00

IMPERIAL

Number	Title (A Side/B Side)	Yr	VG	VG+	NM
❑ 5713	Come On — Part 1/Come On — Part 2	1960	6.25	12.50	25.00

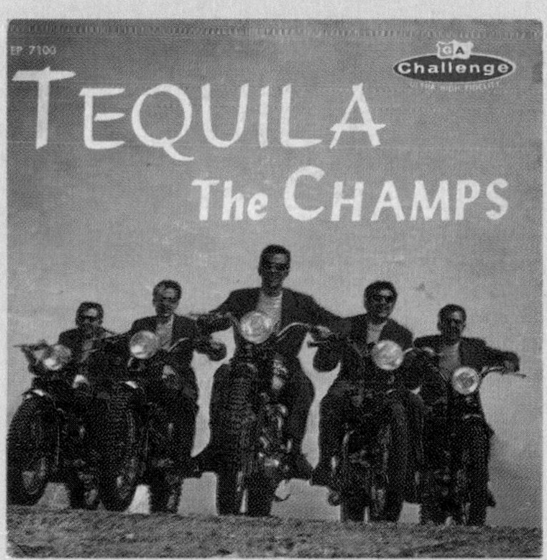

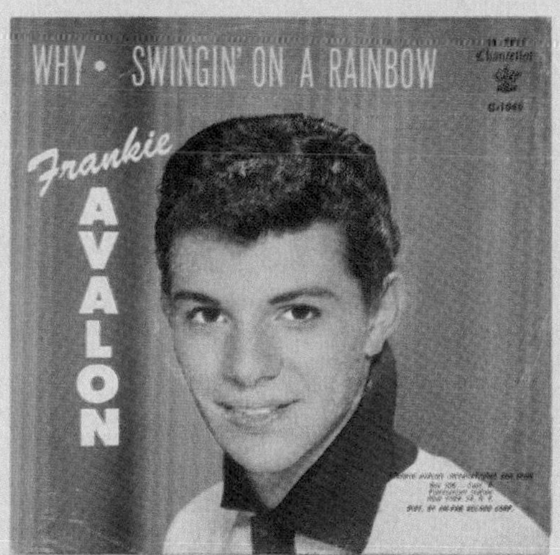

Picture sleeves, or special sleeves that promote the artist on the record within, go back to the days of Enrico Caruso. But not until the introduction of the 45 rpm in 1949 did their use become more common. The introduction of extended-play singles, which came with cardboard covers, made for some attractive sleeves as well. (**Top left**) The first Decca EP for Bill Haley and His Comets, "Shake, Rattle, and Roll," featured the A and B sides of his first two Decca 45s, one of which was "Rock Around the Clock" ($60). (**Top right**) One of the rarest of all Elvis Presley picture sleeves came with a special edition of the EP "Elvis Presley." The records inside contained three songs on each side rather than the two on the normal edition. In near-mint condition this sleeve alone can bring $1,500. (**Middle left**) Buddy Holly's first commercial recordings appeared on the Decca label and flopped. When he became successful, his original label re-released some of that material in this sought-after EP. With liner notes on the back, the cover alone can go for $2,000. (**Middle right**) Ricky Nelson is probably the most collectible "teen idol," because his music transcends the teen-idol stereotype and stands on its own. One of his earliest sleeves was from the 1958 hit "Stood Up" ($70). (**Bottom left**) The Champs were a revolving-door group that at various times included Dave Burgess, Chuck Rio, Glen Campbell, Jim Seals and Dash Crofts. Their only EP release was named after their biggest hit, "Tequila" ($150 record, $150 sleeve). (**Bottom right**) The last chart-topper of the 1950s was "Why" by Frankie Avalon, which came with this sleeve ($30).

When RCA Victor introduced 45s in 1949, it initially color-coded the records by type of music. That experiment was pretty much over by 1951, but ever since, colored vinyl 45s have remained a staple of record collecting. (**Top left**) The most sought-after of the early RCA colored vinyl singles are the orange (officially "cerise") releases from the "blues and rhythm" series. Here's "Rockin' with Red" by Piano Red. (**Top right**) Mercury issued some red-vinyl singles in the early 1950s, including this pressing of Patti Page's "Mister and Mississippi." (**Bottom left**) From 1961, here's an unusual orange-vinyl pressing of Chubby Checker's "Let's Twist Again," one we were not aware of until research started for the third edition of this book. (**Bottom right**) Early copies of Electric Light Orchestra's 1977 hit "Telephone Line" were on green vinyl.

More examples of colored vinyl 45s: (**Top left**) Most copies of Prince's "Purple Rain," from 1984, came out on purple vinyl. An earlier single, "When Doves Cry," is quite hard to find on purple wax, though it exists. (**Top right**) The first run of Madonna's 1986 hit "True Blue" was issued on blue vinyl. (**Bottom left**) When Capitol issued Crazy Diamond, a box set of Syd Barrett's solo material, it also released this EP on, appropriately, pink vinyl. (**Bottom right**) Colored vinyl is still made to this day. From 2000, here's a reissue single of John Lennon's "Woman" on see-through clear vinyl.

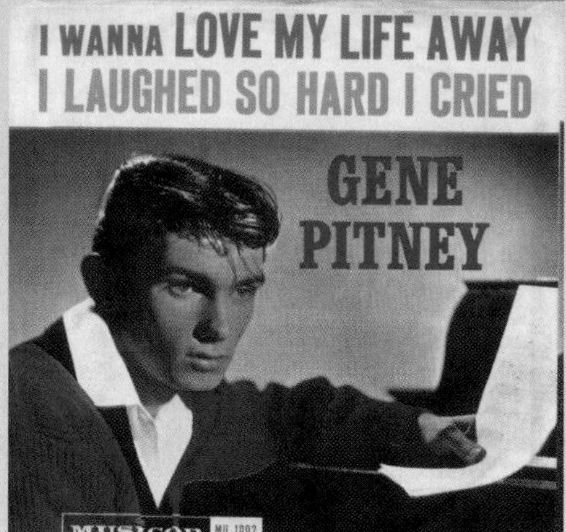

Some of the neatest, and most sought-after, picture sleeves were released in the 1960s. Here's a sample. (**Top left**) "I'm Hurtin'," from late 1960, was Roy Orbison's first hit single to have a picture sleeve ($120). (**Top right**) Gene Pitney's "I Wanna Love My Life Away," his debut single in 1961, had this attractive sleeve of Gene at a piano ($40). (**Middle left**) Shelley Fabares had a couple hit singles in 1962. "Johnny Loves Me," the follow-up to the chart-topping "Johnny Angel," came with this color sleeve ($120). (**Middle right**) One of the rarest Beach Boys picture sleeves came with their second Capitol single, 1962's "Ten Little Indians" ($400). (**Bottom left**) The most valuable Beatles-related stock picture sleeve isn't from a Beatles 45. It's from George Martin's instrumental version of "A Hard Day's Night" on United Artists ($2,000). (**Bottom right**) This is an American picture sleeve for the Honeycombs' third single on Interphon. Curiously, though the record label has the American spelling of "color," the British spelling, "colour," is on the sleeve ($25).

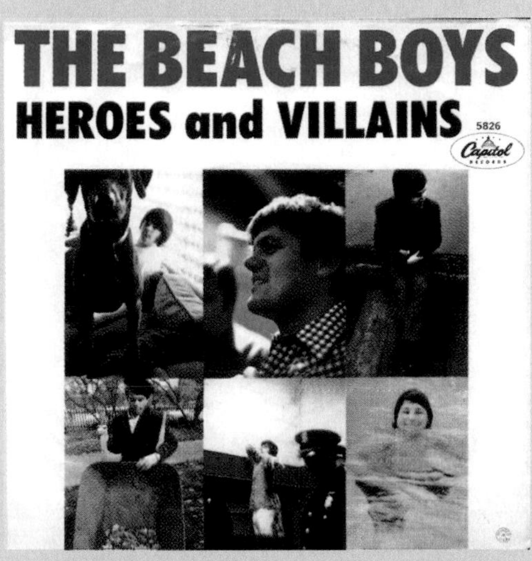

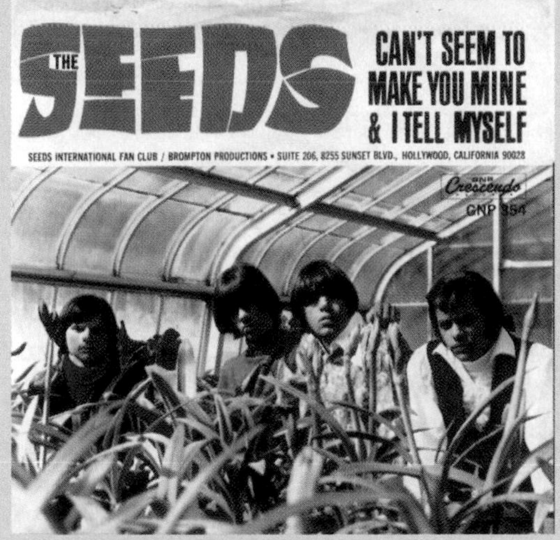

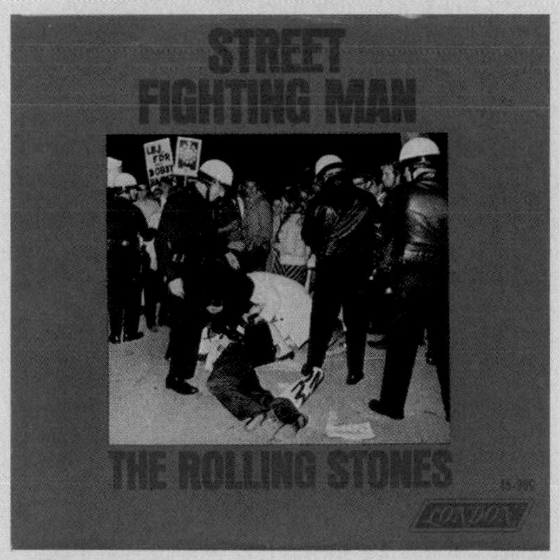

Some more 1960s picture sleeves: (**Top left**) The Doors' first single, 1967's "Break On Through," was a flop that didn't even make the Hot 100. The single's relatively hard to find today, but this picture sleeve is even more difficult ($120). (**Top right**) The Turtles' biggest hit, "Happy Together," came with this somewhat tough sleeve ($40). (**Middle left and middle right**) Here are both sides of the Beach Boys' rarest picture sleeve, the officially unreleased Capitol 5826 version of "Heroes and Villains." ($400) It was prepared in advance as the first single from the never-issued Smile LP. Only later did the song come out, but on Brother 1001 with a completely different sleeve. (**Bottom left**) The Seeds are best known for their two-chord gem "Pushin' Too Hard." An earlier song that charted, "Can't Seem to Make You Mine," came with this attractive picture sleeve of Sky Saxon and the gang ($50). (**Bottom right**) The Holy Grail of all picture sleeves, the Rolling Stones' "Street Fighting Man" ($10,000). By the way, if you have a copy of this with the same picture on both sides, it's a counterfeit. The B-side, "No Expectations," has a completely different photo.

Capitol Records 45s: A Pictorial Chronology

1949-55: Capitol logo at top. Some early singles also exist with maroon, red or yellow labels. Singles from 1949 used a "54" prefix; from 1950 on, an "F."

1956-59: The size of "Capitol" has shrunk considerably.

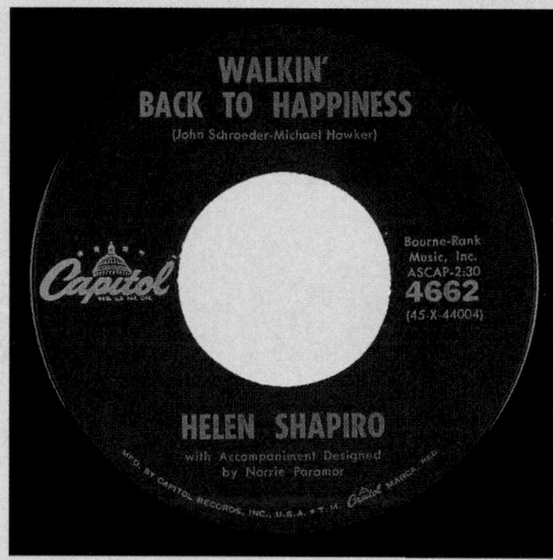

1960-61: The "Capitol" is even smaller and at the left.

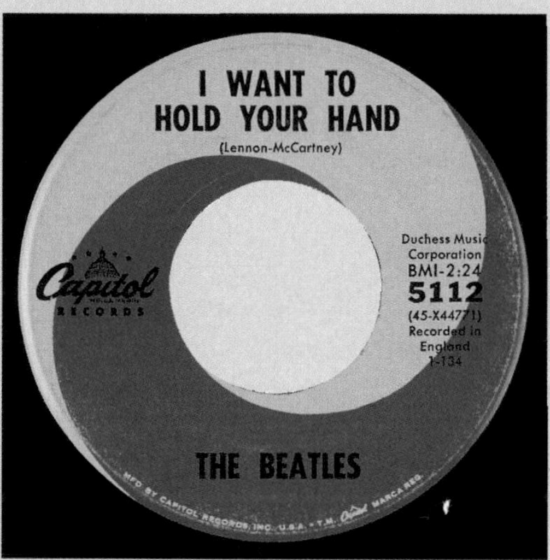

1962-68: A classic; "swirl" label, Capitol logo at left.

1968-69: Short-lived variation with much smaller print and "A Subsidiary of Capitol Industries" in the fine print.

1969: An even shorter-lived variation with the new "target" label and Capitol logo in an oval at left.

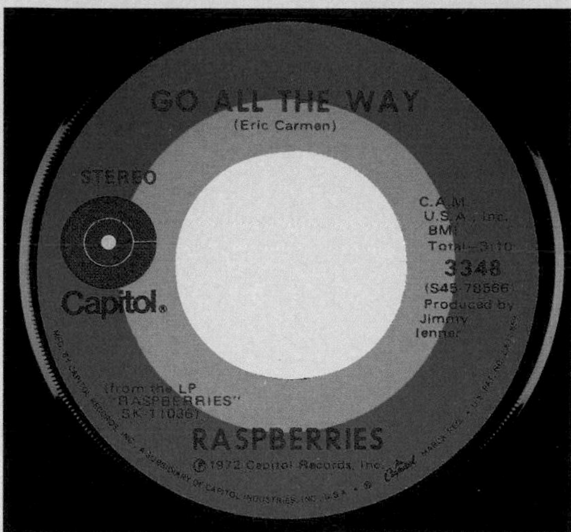

1969-72: "Target" label with new Capitol logo at left. It can be found with or without a white circle in the middle of the logo.

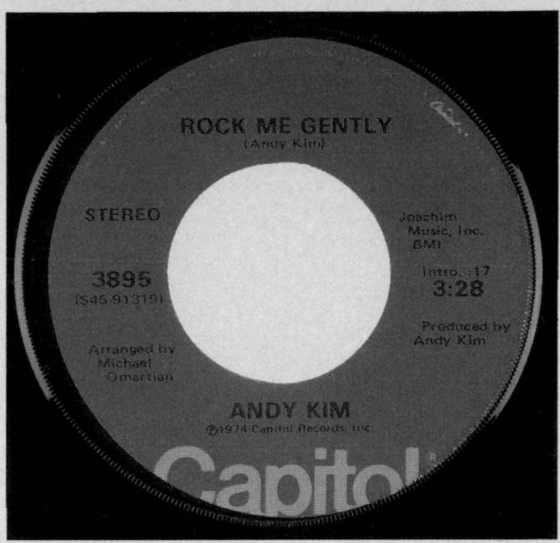

1972-78: Capitol logo moves to bottom. Some records are red with a black logo.

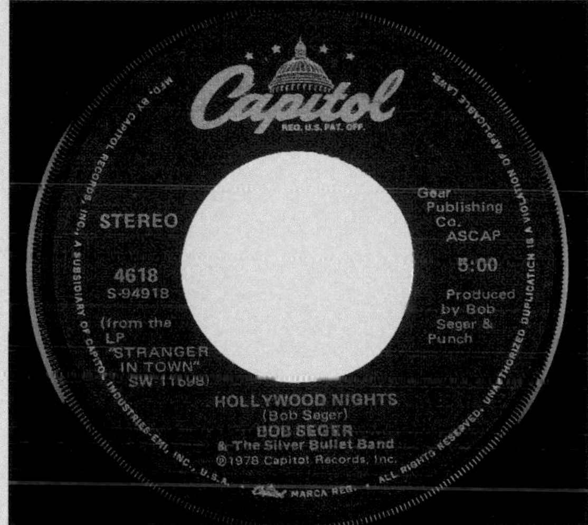

1978-83: A return to the old purple, but with some subtle changes.

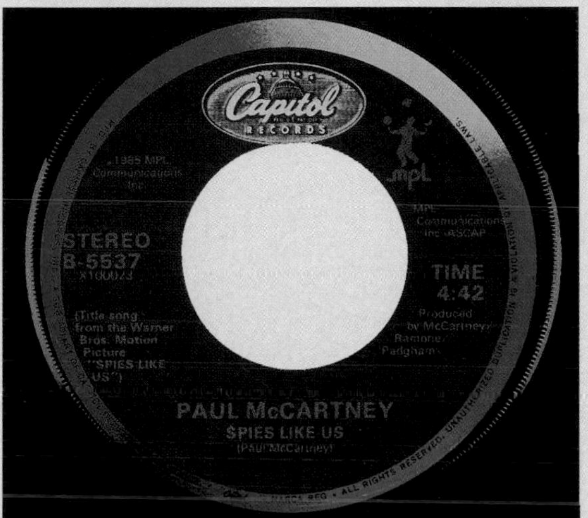

1983-88: For the first time, the 1960s album label design gets used on 45s.

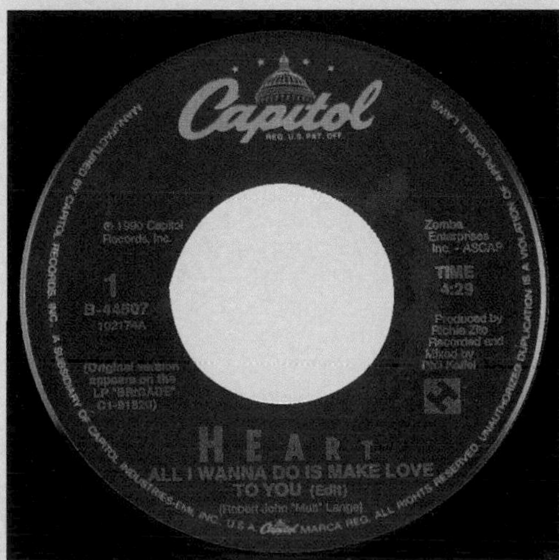

1989-91: Purple returns, this time with a much wider label than in 1978-83.

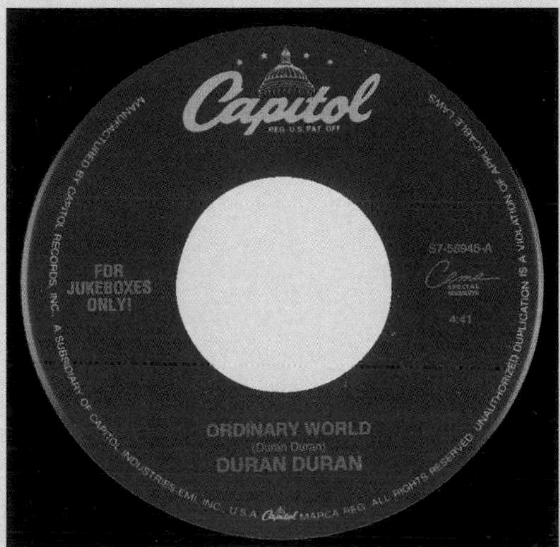

1992-present: "For Jukeboxes Only!" is added to the left of most 45s of this era. Also, some stock singles are issued with white labels.

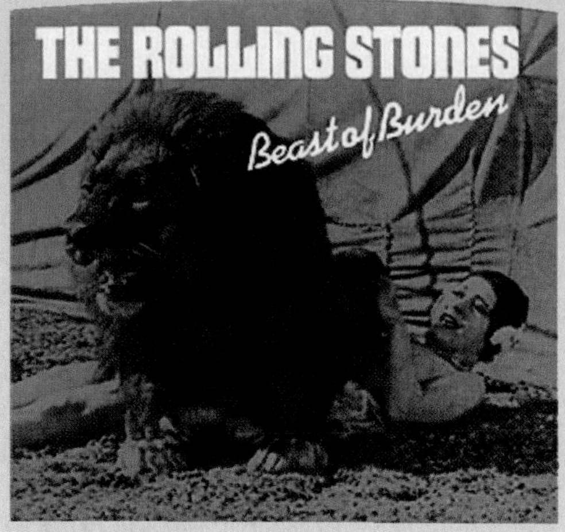

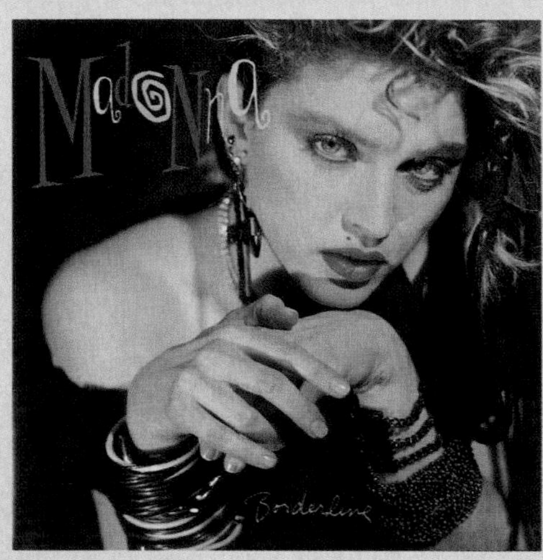

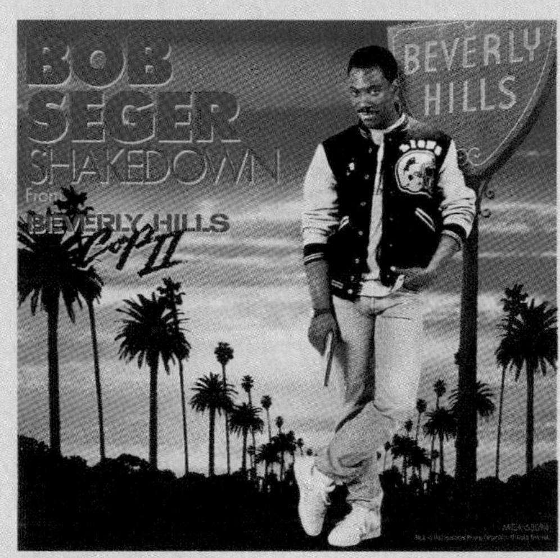

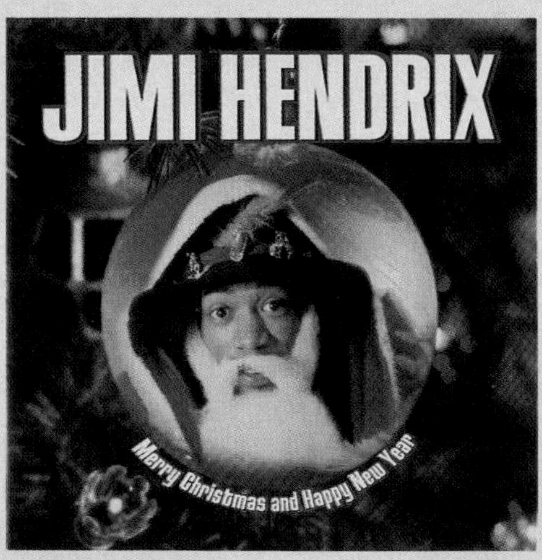

Here are some more recent picture sleeves, from the late 1970s to the present. Most sleeves from this period bring modest amounts, but there are exceptions. (**Top left**) The most sought-after 1970s picture sleeve is from the 1978 Rolling Stones single "Beast of Burden" ($2,000). The record itself is common, but few sleeves exist. Like its 1960s counterpart, "Street Fighting Man," this has been counterfeited, but the phonies are a much lighter pink color than the originals, which are lavender. (**Top right**) Pink Floyd's 1982 single "When the Tigers Broke Free" came in a cardboard, fold-open sleeve with scenes from the movie The Wall ($10). (**Middle left**) The first U.S. picture sleeve from Madonna is a beauty. "Borderline" folds open into a beautiful poster of the popular singer ($80). (**Middle right**) Much scarcer than previously suspected is this alternate picture sleeve of Bob Seger's only No. 1 hit single, "Shakedown." Copies with Seger's photo on the title side are common, but the version with Eddie Murphy on the title side isn't ($15). (**Bottom left**) "Real Love" was one of the two John Lennon demos that the surviving Beatles made into their own. This 1996 single release, obscure on 45, has this beautiful sleeve, which is not that hard to find ($3). (**Bottom right**) From the holiday season of 1999 came this cardboard picture sleeve of a Jimi Hendrix Christmas medley ($12).

Number	Title (A Side/B Side)	Yr	VG	VG+	NM
❑ 5730	Love Me Now/The Things That I Used to Do	1961	6.25	12.50	25.00
❑ 5750	Come Along with Me/You're More to Me Than Gold	1961	6.25	12.50	25.00
❑ 5774	You Better Know/Mama and Papa	1961	6.25	12.50	25.00
❑ 5811	Trick Bag/Always a First Time	1962	6.25	12.50	25.00
❑ 5858	We Are Just Friends/You're More to Me That Gold	1962	6.25	12.50	25.00
❑ 5891	Come Along with Me/Case of Love	1962	6.25	12.50	25.00
REX					
❑ 1015	I Can't Help Myself/Darling Honey, Angel Child	1961	5.00	10.00	20.00
SPECIALTY					
❑ 495	A Mother's Love/I'm Your Best Bet Baby	1954	15.00	30.00	60.00
❑ 531	No One But Me/Eating and Sleeping	1954	15.00	30.00	60.00
❑ 558	Funny Face/Sittin' and Wonderin'	1955	15.00	30.00	60.00

KING, FREDDIE

Number	Title (A Side/B Side)	Yr	VG	VG+	NM
COTILLION					
❑ 44015	Funky/Play It Cool	1968	2.00	4.00	8.00
❑ 44058	I Wonder Why/Yonder Wall	1970	2.00	4.00	8.00
EL-BEE					
❑ 157	Country Boy/That's What You Think	1956	100.00	200.00	400.00
FEDERAL					
❑ 12384	Have You Ever Loved a Woman/You've Got to Love Her with a Feeling	1960	10.00	20.00	40.00
❑ 12401	Hideaway/I Love the Woman	1961	7.50	15.00	30.00
❑ 12415	Lonesome Whistle Blues/It's Too Bad Things Are Going So Tough	1961	7.50	15.00	30.00
❑ 12428	San-Ho-Zay/See See Baby	1961	7.50	15.00	30.00
❑ 12432	I'm Tore Down/Sen-Say-Shun	1961	7.50	15.00	30.00
❑ 12439	Christmas Tears/I Hear Jingle Bells	1961	7.50	15.00	30.00
❑ 12443	If You Believe in What You Do/Heads Up	1961	5.00	10.00	20.00
❑ 12450	Takin' Care of Business/The Stumble	1962	5.00	10.00	20.00
❑ 12456	Side Tracked/Sittin' on the Boat Dock	1962	5.00	10.00	20.00
❑ 12462	What About Love/Texas Oil	1962	5.00	10.00	20.00
❑ 12470	Come On/Just Pickin'	1962	5.00	10.00	20.00
❑ 12475	In the Open/I'm On My Way to Atlanta	1962	5.00	10.00	20.00
❑ 12482	The Bossa Nova Watusi Twist/Look Ma, I'm Crying	1963	3.75	7.50	15.00
❑ 12491	(I'd Love To) Make Love to You/One Hundred Years	1963	3.75	7.50	15.00
❑ 12499	(The Welfare) Turns Its Back on You/You're Barkin' Up the Wrong Tree	1963	3.75	7.50	15.00
❑ 12509	Surf Monkey/Monkey Donkey	1963	5.00	10.00	20.00
❑ 12515	Meet Me at the Station/Ting-a-Ling	1964	3.75	7.50	15.00
❑ 12518	Driving Sideways/Someday After Awhile (You'll Be Gone)	1964	3.00	6.00	12.00
❑ 12521	She Put the Whammy on Me/High Rise	1964	3.00	6.00	12.00
❑ 12529	Now I've Got a Woman/Onion Rings	1964	3.00	6.00	12.00
❑ 12532	Some Other Day, Some Other Time/Manhole	1965	3.00	6.00	12.00
❑ 12535	If You Have It/I Love You More Every Day	1965	3.00	6.00	12.00
❑ 12537	Full Time Love/She's the One	1965	3.00	6.00	12.00
KING					
❑ 6057	Use What You've Got/Double Eyed Whammy	1966	3.00	6.00	12.00
❑ 6080	You've Got Me Licked/The Girl from Kookamunga	1967	3.00	6.00	12.00
❑ 6264	Have You Ever Loved a Woman/Hideaway	1969	2.00	4.00	8.00
RSO					
❑ 505	My Credit Didn't Go Through/Texas Flyer	1975	—	2.50	5.00
❑ 516	Boogie Bump/It's Your Love	1975	—	2.50	5.00
SHELTER					
❑ 7303	Going Down/Toke Down	1971	—	3.00	6.00
❑ 7320	Me and My Guitar/Downtown in Lodi	1972	—	3.00	6.00
❑ 7333	Woman Across the River/Help Me Through the Day	1973	—	3.00	6.00
❑ 40410	Going Down/Me and My Guitar	1975	—	2.50	5.00

KING, JONATHAN

Number	Title (A Side/B Side)	Yr	VG	VG+	NM
PARROT					
❑ 3005	Just Like a Woman/Land of the Golden Tree	1966	2.00	4.00	8.00
❑ 3008	Icicles (Fell from the Heart of a Bluebird)/In a Hundred Years from Now	1966	2.00	4.00	8.00
❑ 3011	Round, Round/Time and Motion	1967	2.00	4.00	8.00
❑ 3021	1968 (Message to the Presidential Candidates)/ Colloquial Sex	1968	2.00	4.00	8.00
❑ 3027	Lazy Bones/Just Want to Say Thank You	1968	2.00	4.00	8.00
❑ 3029	Hooked on a Feeling/I Don't Want to Be Gay	1969	—	3.00	6.00
❑ 3030	Flirt/Hey Jim	1969	—	3.00	6.00
❑ 9774	Everyone's Gone to the Moon/Summer's Coming	1965	2.50	5.00	10.00
❑ 9804	Green Is the Grass/Where the Sun Has Never Shown	1965	2.00	4.00	8.00
❑ 40047	Let It All Hang Out/Colloquial Sex	1970	—	3.00	6.00
❑ 40055	Cherry Cherry/Gay Girl	1970	—	3.00	6.00
UK					
❑ 49002	It's a Tall Order for a Short Guy/Learned Tax Counsel	1972	—	2.50	5.00
❑ 49014	Mary, My Love/A Little Bit Left of Right	1973	—	2.50	5.00
❑ 49018	The Kung Fu Anthem/A Little Bit Left of Right	1973	—	2.50	5.00
❑ 49034	The Way You Look Tonight/The True Story of Molly Malone	1974	—	2.50	5.00

KING, REV. MARTIN LUTHER

Number	Title (A Side/B Side)	Yr	VG	VG+	NM
GORDY					
❑ 7023	I Have a Dream/We Shall Overcome	1963	7.50	15.00	30.00
❑ 7023	I Have a Dream/We Shall Overcome	1968	2.00	4.00	8.00
—B-side by Liz Lands; "Gordy" on side of label					
MERCURY					
❑ 72814	I Have a Dream/I've Been to the Mountain Top-Eulogy	1968	2.00	4.00	8.00

KING, SID

Number	Title (A Side/B Side)	Yr	VG	VG+	NM
COLUMBIA					
❑ 4-21361	I Like It/Put Something in the Pot Now	1955	12.50	25.00	50.00
—As "The Five Strings"					
❑ 4-21403	Drinkin' Wine Spoli-Oli/Crazy Little Heart	1955	15.00	30.00	60.00
—As "The Five Strings"					
❑ 4-21449	Sag, Drag and Fall/But I Don't Care	1955	12.50	25.00	50.00
❑ 4-21489	Mama I Want You/Purr, Kitty, Purr	1956	12.50	25.00	50.00
❑ 4-21505	Blue Suede Shoes/Let 'Er Roll	1956	15.00	30.00	60.00
❑ 4-21564	Good Rockin' Baby/Gonna Shake This	1956	15.00	30.00	60.00
❑ 4-40680	Oobie Doobie/Boozer Red	1956	12.50	25.00	50.00
❑ 4-40833	It's True, I'm Blue/When My Baby Left Me	1957	12.50	25.00	50.00
❑ 4-41019	I've Got the Blues/What Have Ya Got to Lose	1957	12.50	25.00	50.00
DOT					
❑ 16293	Hello There Rockin' Chair/Once Upon a Time	1961	7.50	15.00	30.00
SOUNDWAVES					
❑ 4612	Back Door Man/I'd Rather Hear Willie	1980	2.00	4.00	8.00

KING BEES, THE

More than one group.

Number	Title (A Side/B Side)	Yr	VG	VG+	NM
CHECKER					
❑ 909	Buzzin'/Good Rockin' Tonight	1958	20.00	40.00	80.00
FLIP					
❑ 323	Puppy Love/Give Me Your Number	1957	10.00	20.00	40.00
KRC					
❑ 302	Lovely Love/Can't You Understand?	1957	10.00	20.00	40.00
NOBLE					
❑ 715	Tender Love/What Could Have Been Can't Be	1959	62.50	125.00	250.00
RCA VICTOR					
❑ 47-8688	What She Does to Me/That Ain't Love	1965	3.00	6.00	12.00
❑ 47-8787	On Your Way Down the Drain/Rhythm and Blues	1966	3.00	6.00	12.00
❑ 47-8979	Lost in the Shuffle/Hardly (Part 3)	1966	3.00	6.00	12.00

KING CRIMSON

Number	Title (A Side/B Side)	Yr	VG	VG+	NM
ATLANTIC					
❑ 2702	In the Court of the Crimson King (Part 1)/In the Court of the Crimson King (Part 2)	1970	3.00	6.00	12.00
❑ 3016	Night Watch/The Great Deceiver	1974	—	3.00	6.00
WARNER BROS.					
❑ 29309	Sleepless/Nuages (That Which Passes, Passes Like Clouds)	1984	—	2.50	5.00
❑ 29964	Heartbeat/Requiem	1982	—	2.50	5.00

KING CURTIS

Number	Title (A Side/B Side)	Yr	VG	VG+	NM
ABC-PARAMOUNT					
❑ 10133	Beatnick Hoedown/King Neptune's Guitar	1960	3.75	7.50	15.00
ALCOR					
❑ 1016	Jay Walk/The Lone Prairie	1961	5.00	10.00	20.00
APOLLO					
❑ 507	King's Rock/Dynamite at Midnight	1957	7.50	15.00	30.00
ATCO					
❑ 6114	The Birth of the Blues/Just Smoochin'	1958	5.00	10.00	20.00
❑ 6124	You Made Me Love You/Ific	1958	5.00	10.00	20.00
❑ 6135	Castle Rock/Chili	1959	5.00	10.00	20.00
❑ 6143	Honey Dripper (Part 1)/Honey Dripper (Part 2)	1959	5.00	10.00	20.00
❑ 6152	Heavenly Blues/Restless Guitar	1959	5.00	10.00	20.00
❑ 6387	Spanish Harlem/The Boss	1965	2.50	5.00	10.00
❑ 6406	On Broadway/Quicksand	1966	2.00	4.00	8.00
❑ 6419	Make the World Go Away/You've Lost That Lovin' Feeling	1966	2.00	4.00	8.00
❑ 6429	Dancing in the Streets/He'll Have to Go	1966	2.00	4.00	8.00
❑ 6447	Pots and Pans (Part 1)/Pots and Pans (Part 2)	1966	2.00	4.00	8.00
❑ 6457	Something on Your Mind/Soul Theme	1966	2.00	4.00	8.00
❑ 6476	Jump Back/When Something Is Wrong with My Baby	1967	2.00	4.00	8.00
❑ 6496	You Don't Miss Your Water/Green Onions	1967	2.00	4.00	8.00
❑ 6511	Memphis Soul Stew/Blue Nocturne	1967	2.00	4.00	8.00
❑ 6516	Ode to Billie Joe/In the Pocket	1967	2.00	4.00	8.00
—As "The Kingpins"					
❑ 6534	For What It's Worth/Cook Out	1968	2.00	4.00	8.00
❑ 6547	I Never Loved a Man (The Way I Love You)/I Was Made to Love Her	1968	2.00	4.00	8.00
❑ 6562	(Sittin' On) The Dock of the Bay/This Is Soul	1968	2.00	4.00	8.00
❑ 6582	(Theme from) Valley of the Dolls/Eighth Wonder	1968	2.00	4.00	8.00
❑ 6598	I Heard It Through the Grapevine/Whiter Shade of Pale	1968	2.00	4.00	8.00
❑ 6613	Harper Valley P.T.A./Makin' Hey	1968	2.00	4.00	8.00
❑ 6630	The Christmas Song/What Are You Doing New Year's Eve?	1968	3.00	6.00	12.00
❑ 6664	Games People Play/Foot Pattin' (Part 2)	1969	2.00	4.00	8.00
❑ 6680	Instant Groove/Sweet Inspiration	1969	2.00	4.00	8.00
❑ 6695	Little Green Apples/La Jeanne	1969	2.00	4.00	8.00
❑ 6711	C.C. Rider/Rocky Roll	1969	2.00	4.00	8.00
❑ 6720	Pop Corn Willie/Patty Cake	1969	2.00	4.00	8.00
❑ 6738	Soulin'/Teasin'	1970	—	3.00	6.00
❑ 6762	Get Ready/Bridge Over Troubled Water	1970	—	3.00	6.00
❑ 6779	Whole Lotta Love/Floatin'	1970	—	3.00	6.00
❑ 6785	Changes (Part 1)/Changes (Part 2)	1970	—	3.00	6.00
❑ 6834	Changes (Part 1)/Changes (Part 2)	1971	—	3.00	6.00
❑ 6908	Ridin' Thumb (Part 1)/Ridin' Thumb (Part 2)	1972	—	3.00	6.00
CAPITOL					
❑ 4788	Beach Party/Turn 'Em On	1962	2.50	5.00	10.00
❑ 4841	Beautiful Brown Eyes/Your Cheatin' Heart	1962	2.50	5.00	10.00
❑ 4891	Strollin' Home/Mess Around	1962	2.50	5.00	10.00
❑ 4998	Do the Monkey/Feel All Right	1963	2.50	5.00	10.00
❑ 5061	Theme from "Lilies of the Field" (Part 1)/Theme from "Lilies of the Field" (Part 2)	1963	2.50	5.00	10.00
❑ 5109	Soul Serenade/More Soul	1964	2.50	5.00	10.00
❑ 5212	Summer Dream/Melancholy Serenade	1964	2.50	5.00	10.00
❑ 5270	Stranger on the Shore/Hide Away	1964	2.50	5.00	10.00
❑ 5324	Sister Sadie/Tanya	1964	2.50	5.00	10.00
❑ 5377	Bill Bailey/Soul Twine	1965	2.50	5.00	10.00
❑ 5490	The Prance/Slow Drag	1965	2.50	5.00	10.00
DELUXE					
❑ 6142	The Stranger/Steel Guitar Rag	1957	6.25	12.50	25.00

Number	Title (A Side/B Side)	Yr	VG	VG+	NM
❑ 6157	Wicky Wacky (Part 1)/Wicky Wacky (Part 2)	1958	6.25	12.50	25.00
ENJOY					
❑ 1000	Soul Twist/Twisting Time	1962	3.75	7.50	15.00
❑ 1001	Twisting with the King/Wobble Twist	1962	3.75	7.50	15.00
EVEREST					
❑ 19406	Jay Walk/The Lone Prairie	1961	3.75	7.50	15.00
EVERLAST					
❑ 5030	Soul Twist/Twisting Time	1965	2.50	5.00	10.00
GEM					
❑ 208	Tenor in the Sky/No More Crying on My Pillow	1954	10.00	20.00	40.00
GROOVE					
❑ 1060	Movin' On/Rockabye Baby	1956	6.25	12.50	25.00
KING					
❑ 5647	King Curtis Stomp/Steel Guitar Rag	1962	3.00	6.00	12.00
MONARCH					
❑ 702	Wine Head/I've Got News for You Baby	1953	15.00	30.00	60.00
NEW JAZZ					
❑ 45-510	Soul Meeting/All the Way	1961	3.75	7.50	15.00
SEG-WAY					
❑ 1006	Hot Rod/Bonaparte's Retreat	1962	3.75	7.50	15.00
SKY ROCKET					
❑ 106	Madisonville (Part 1)/Madisonville (Part 2)	1960	5.00	10.00	20.00
TRU SOUND					
❑ 401	Trouble in Mind/But That's Alright	1961	3.75	7.50	15.00
❑ 406	Twistin' and Jivin'/I Have to Worry	1961	3.75	7.50	15.00
❑ 412	So Rare/Hucklebuck Twist	1961	3.75	7.50	15.00
❑ 415	Free for All/When the Saints Go Marching In	1962	3.75	7.50	15.00
❑ 422	Low Down/I'll Wait for You	1962	3.75	7.50	15.00

KING HARVEST

Number	Title (A Side/B Side)	Yr	VG	VG+	NM
A&M					
❑ 1726	Little Bit Like Magic/Vaea	1975	—	2.00	4.00
❑ 1761	Lovestruck/Hickory	1975	—	2.00	4.00
PERCEPTION					
❑ 515	Dancing in the Moonlight/Marty and the Captain	1972	—	2.50	5.00
❑ 527	A Little Bit Like Magic/Elmore Bacon	1973	—	2.00	4.00
❑ 534	Take It Slow/Idaho	1973	—	2.00	4.00
❑ 556	Celestial Navigator/Angels of Mercy	1974	—	2.00	4.00

KING PINS, THE (1)

Number	Title (A Side/B Side)	Yr	VG	VG+	NM
FEDERAL					
❑ 12480	Believe in Me/Don't Wait Pretty Baby	1963	5.00	10.00	20.00
❑ 12484	It Won't Be This Way (Always)/How Long Will It Last	1963	5.00	10.00	20.00
❑ 12505	The Monkey One More Time/With the Other Guy	1963	3.75	7.50	15.00
❑ 12512	Hop Scotch/Wonderful One	1964	3.75	7.50	15.00
❑ 12517	Two Hearts/I Won't Have It	1964	3.75	7.50	15.00
❑ 12519	I Got the Monkey Off My Back/You're Using Me	1964	3.75	7.50	15.00

KING PINS, THE (2)

Number	Title (A Side/B Side)	Yr	VG	VG+	NM
LARSE					
❑ 101	94 Second Turf/Rod Hot Rod	1966	10.00	20.00	40.00
MGM					
❑ 13535	Rod Hot Rod/Door Banger	1966	7.50	15.00	30.00

KINGS, THE

Several different groups.

Number	Title (A Side/B Side)	Yr	VG	VG+	NM
BATON					
❑ 245	Long Lonely Nights/Let Me Know	1957	10.00	20.00	40.00
ELEKTRA					
❑ 47006	Switchin' to Glide/My Habit	1980	—	2.50	5.00
❑ 47052	Switchin' to Glide/This Beat Goes On	1980	—	—	3.00
❑ 47110	Don't Let Me Know/Partyitis	1981	—	—	3.00
❑ 47213	All the Way/Loading Zone	1981	—	—	3.00
EPIC					
❑ 9370	I Want to Know/Bomp-I-Ty Bump	1960	7.50	15.00	30.00
GONE					
❑ 5013	Don't Go/Love Is Something from Within	1957	25.00	50.00	100.00
GOTHAM					
❑ 316	God Made You Mine/The Good Book	1956	25.00	50.00	100.00
HARLEM					
❑ 2322	Fire in My Heart/You Never Know	1954	37.50	75.00	150.00
JALO					
❑ 203	Angel/Come On Little Baby	1958	10.00	20.00	40.00
JAY-WING					
❑ 5805	Surrender/Hold Me	1959	37.50	75.00	150.00
JOX					
❑ 052	I've Got a License/Just a Little Bit of You	1965	10.00	20.00	40.00
LOOKIE					
❑ 18	I Want to Know/Bomp-I-Ty Bump	1960	10.00	20.00	40.00
RCA VICTOR					
❑ 47-7419	Till You/Elephant Walk	1958	6.25	12.50	25.00
❑ 47-7544	Troubles Don't Last/Your Sweet Love	1959	6.25	12.50	25.00
SPECIALTY					
❑ 497	What Can I Do/Till I Say Well Done	1954	30.00	60.00	120.00

KINGSMEN, THE (1)

Northwest garage band. Also see JACK EELY.

Number	Title (A Side/B Side)	Yr	VG	VG+	NM
JERDEN					
❑ 712	Louie Louie/Haunted Castle	1963	15.00	30.00	60.00
WAND					
❑ 143	Louie, Louie/Haunted Castle	1963	5.00	10.00	20.00
❑ 143	Louie Louie 64-65-66.../Haunted Castle	1966	3.75	7.50	15.00
❑ 143	Louie Louie/Little Green Thing	196?	3.75	7.50	15.00
❑ 150	Money/Bent Scepter	1964	3.00	6.00	12.00
❑ 157	Little Latin Lupe Lu/David's Mood	1964	2.50	5.00	10.00
❑ 164	Death of an Angel/Searchin' for Love	1964	2.50	5.00	10.00
❑ 172	The Jolly Green Giant/Long Green	1965	3.00	6.00	12.00
❑ 183	The Climb/I'm Waiting	1965	2.50	5.00	10.00
❑ 189	Annie Fanny/Give Her Lovin'	1965	2.50	5.00	10.00
❑ 1107	(You Got) Gamma Goochie/It's Only the Dog	1965	3.75	7.50	15.00
❑ 1115	Killer Joe/Little Green Thing	1966	3.75	7.50	15.00
❑ 1118	The Krunch/The Climb	1966	3.75	7.50	15.00
❑ 1118 [PS]	The Krunch/The Climb	1966	6.25	12.50	25.00
❑ 1127	My Wife Can't Dance/Little Sally Tease	1966	2.50	5.00	10.00
❑ 1137	If I Need Someone/The Grass Is Green	1966	2.50	5.00	10.00
❑ 1147	Trouble/Daytime Shadows	1967	2.00	4.00	8.00
❑ 1154	The Wolf of Manhattan/Children's Caretaker	1967	2.00	4.00	8.00
❑ 1157	(I Have Found) Another Girl/Don't Say No	1967	2.00	4.00	8.00
❑ 1164	Bo Diddley Bach/Just Before the Break of Day	1968	2.00	4.00	8.00
❑ 1174	Get Out of My Life Woman/Since You've Been Gone	1968	2.00	4.00	8.00
❑ 1180	I Guess I Was Dreamin'/Oh Love	1968	2.00	4.00	8.00

KINGSMEN, THE (2)

Instrumental group composed of former members of BILL HALEY AND HIS COMETS.

Number	Title (A Side/B Side)	Yr	VG	VG+	NM
EASTWEST					
❑ 115	Week End/Better Believe It	1958	10.00	20.00	40.00
❑ 120	Conga Rock/The Cat Walk	1958	10.00	20.00	40.00

KINGSMEN, THE (3)

Number	Title (A Side/B Side)	Yr	VG	VG+	NM
ALL STAR					
❑ 500	Guardian Angel/I'm Your Lover Man	1957	20.00	40.00	80.00

KINGSMEN, THE (U)

Some of these could have been by groups (1), (2) or (3).

Number	Title (A Side/B Side)	Yr	VG	VG+	NM
ARNOLD					
❑ 2106	Goodnight Sweetheart/Humpty Dumpty	196?	30.00	60.00	120.00
CAPITOL					
❑ 3576	You Better Do Right/Today	1973	—	2.50	5.00
JALYNNE					
❑ 108	Ladies Choice/Dig This	1960	5.00	10.00	20.00
NEIL					
❑ 102	One Foolish Mistake/Stranded Love	1956	15.00	30.00	60.00

KINGSTON TRIO, THE

Also see DAVE GUARD AND THE WHISKEYHILL SINGERS; BOB SHANE; JOHN STEWART.

Number	Title (A Side/B Side)	Yr	VG	VG+	NM
CAPITOL					
❑ PRO 856 [DJ]	The Merry Minuet/Tick, Tick, Tick	1959	10.00	20.00	40.00
❑ X1-1407 [S]	When I Was Young/Leave My Woman Alone	1960	5.00	10.00	20.00
—33 1/3 rpm, small hole jukebox pressing					
❑ X2-1407 [S]	This Mornin', This Evenin', So Soon/Everglades	1960	5.00	10.00	20.00
—33 1/3 rpm, small hole jukebox pressing					
❑ X3-1407 [S]	Buddy Better Get On Down the Line/South Wind	1960	5.00	10.00	20.00
—33 1/3 rpm, small hole jukebox pressing					
❑ X4-1407 [S]	Who's Gonna Hold Her Hand/To Morrow	1960	5.00	10.00	20.00
—33 1/3 rpm, small hole jukebox pressing					
❑ X5-1407 [S]	Colorado Trail/The Tattooed Lady	1960	5.00	10.00	20.00
—33 1/3 rpm, small hole jukebox pressing					
❑ XE1-1446 [S]	We Wish You a Merry Christmas/The Last Month of the Year	1960	3.75	7.50	15.00
—33 1/3 rpm, small hole jukebox pressing					
❑ XE2-1446 [S]	Sing We Noel/Go Where I Send Thee	1960	3.75	7.50	15.00
—33 1/3 rpm, small hole jukebox pressing					
❑ XE3-1446 [S]	The White Snows of Winter/All Through the Night	1960	3.75	7.50	15.00
—33 1/3 rpm, small hole jukebox pressing					
❑ XE4-1446 [S]	Follow Now, Oh Shepherd/Somerset Gloucestershire Wassail	1960	3.75	7.50	15.00
—33 1/3 rpm, small hole jukebox pressing					
❑ XE5-1446 [S]	Bye Bye Thou Little Tiny Child/Mary Mild	1960	3.75	7.50	15.00
—33 1/3 rpm, small hole jukebox pressing					
❑ SM-1705 [S]	Billy Goat Hill/Take Her Out of Pity	1962	3.75	7.50	15.00
—Small hole, plays at 33 1/3 rpm					
❑ SXE1-1809 [S]	Some Fool Made a Soldier Out of Me/To Be Redeemed	1963	3.75	7.50	15.00
—33 1/3 rpm, small hole jukebox pressing					
❑ SXE2-1809 [S]	Honey, Are You Mad at Your Man/Adios Farewell	1963	3.75	7.50	15.00
—33 1/3 rpm, small hole jukebox pressing					
❑ SXE3-1809 [S]	Poor Ellie Smith/My Lord What a Mornin'	1963	3.75	7.50	15.00
—33 1/3 rpm, small hole jukebox pressing					
❑ SXE4-1809 [S]	Long Black Veil/Genny Glen	1963	3.75	7.50	15.00
—33 1/3 rpm, small hole jukebox pressing					
❑ SXE5-1809 [S]	The First Time/Dogie's Lament	1963	3.75	7.50	15.00
—33 1/3 rpm, small hole jukebox pressing					
❑ 2006/7 [DJ]	Farewell Adelita/Corey, Corey	1960	3.75	7.50	15.00
❑ 2006/7 [PS]	Farewell Adelita/Corey, Corey	1960	6.25	12.50	25.00
—Promo item for Welgrume Sportswear					
❑ 2782/3 [DJ]	Molly Dee/Haul Away	1959	3.75	7.50	15.00
❑ 2782/3 [PS]	Molly Dee/Haul Away	1959	6.25	12.50	25.00
—Promo item for "The New March of Dimes"					
❑ 3149	Tell the Riverboat Captain/Windy Wakefield	1971	2.50	5.00	10.00
—As "The New Kingston Trio"					
❑ F3970	Scarlet Ribbons (For Her Hair)/Three Jolly Coachmen	1958	5.00	10.00	20.00
❑ F4049	Tom Dooley/Ruby Red	1958	6.25	12.50	25.00
❑ F4114	Raspberries, Strawberries/Sally	1959	5.00	10.00	20.00
❑ F4167 [M]	The Tijuana Jail/Oh Cindy	1959	5.00	10.00	20.00
❑ SF4167 [S]	The Tijuana Jail/Oh Cindy	1959	12.50	25.00	50.00
❑ F4221	M.T.A./All My Sorrows	1959	5.00	10.00	20.00
❑ F4271	A Worried Man/San Miguel	1959	5.00	10.00	20.00
❑ 4303	Coo Coo-U/Green Grasses	1959	3.75	7.50	15.00
❑ 4338	El Matador/Home from the Hill	1960	3.75	7.50	15.00
❑ 4338 [PS]	El Matador/Home from the Hill	1960	10.00	20.00	40.00
—This sleeve's existence has been confirmed					
❑ 4379	Bad Man Blunder/Escape of Old John Webb	1960	3.75	7.50	15.00
❑ 4441	Everglades/This Mornin', This Evenin', So Soon	1960	3.75	7.50	15.00
❑ 4475	Somerset Gloucestershire Wassail/Goodnight My Baby	1960	3.75	7.50	15.00
❑ 4475 [PS]	Somerset Gloucestershire Wassail/Goodnight My Baby	1960	15.00	30.00	60.00
❑ 4536	You're Gonna Miss Me/En El Aqua	1961	3.75	7.50	15.00

Number	Title (A Side/B Side)	Yr	VG	VG+	NM
❑ 4642	Coming from the Mountains/Nothing More to Look Forward To	1961	3.75	7.50	15.00
❑ 4671	Where Have All the Flowers Gone/O Ken Karanga	1961	3.75	7.50	15.00
❑ 4740	Scotch and Soda/Jane, Jane, Jane	1962	2.50	5.00	10.00
❑ 4740 [PS]	Scotch and Soda/Jane, Jane, Jane	1962	7.50	15.00	30.00
❑ 4808	Old Joe Clark/C'mon Betty Home	1962	2.50	5.00	10.00
❑ 4842	One More Town/She Was Too Good to Me	1962	2.50	5.00	10.00
❑ 4842 [PS]	One More Town/She Was Too Good to Me	1962	7.50	15.00	30.00
❑ 4898	Greenback Dollar/New Frontier	1963	2.50	5.00	10.00
❑ 4898 [PS]	Greenback Dollar/New Frontier	1963	10.00	20.00	40.00
❑ 4951	Reverend Mr. Black/One More Round	1963	2.50	5.00	10.00
❑ 5005	Desert Pete/Ballad of the Thresher	1963	2.50	5.00	10.00
❑ 5078	Ally Ally Oxen Free/Marcelle Vanine	1963	2.50	5.00	10.00
❑ 5132	Last Night I Had the Strangest Dream/Patriot Game	1964	2.50	5.00	10.00
❑ 5166	Seasons in the Sun/If You Don't Look Around	1964	2.50	5.00	10.00
❑ 6002	Tom Dooley/M.T.A.	1962	2.00	4.00	8.00

—Originals have two-tone green swirl labels

Number	Title (A Side/B Side)	Yr	VG	VG+	NM
❑ 6046	A Worried Man/Scotch and Soda	1964	2.00	4.00	8.00

—Originals have two-tone green swirl labels

Number	Title (A Side/B Side)	Yr	VG	VG+	NM
❑ 6071	Greenback Dollar/Reverend Mr. Black	1965	2.00	4.00	8.00

—Originals have two-tone green swirl labels; "Greenback Dollar" does NOT have the word "damn" obliterated by a guitar chord, as the original 45 does

Number	Title (A Side/B Side)	Yr	VG	VG+	NM
❑ S7-19762	Somerset Gloucestershire Wassail/Goodnight My Baby	1997	—	2.00	4.00

CAPITOL CUSTOM

Number	Title (A Side/B Side)	Yr	VG	VG+	NM
❑ KB-2670/1	Tom Dooley/A Worried Man//The Hunter/With You My Johnny	1960	7.50	15.00	30.00
❑ KB-2670/1 [PS]	Cool Cargo	1960	7.50	15.00	30.00

—Promotional item for 7-Up

DECCA

Number	Title (A Side/B Side)	Yr	VG	VG+	NM
❑ 31702	My Ramblin' Boy/Hope You Understand	1964	3.75	7.50	15.00
❑ 31702 [PS]	My Ramblin' Boy/Hope You Understand	1964	6.25	12.50	25.00
❑ 31730	Little Play Soldiers/I'm Going Home	1965	2.50	5.00	10.00
❑ 31790	Stay Awhile/Yes I Can Feel It	1965	2.50	5.00	10.00
❑ 31790 [PS]	Stay Awhile/Yes I Can Feel It	1965	6.25	12.50	25.00
❑ 31860	The Runaway Song/Parchment Farm (Blues)	1965	2.50	5.00	10.00
❑ 31860 [PS]	The Runaway Song/Parchment Farm (Blues)	1965	6.25	12.50	25.00
❑ 31922	Norwegian Wood/Put Your Money Away	1966	2.50	5.00	10.00
❑ 31961	The Spinnin' of the World/A Little Soul Is Born	1966	2.50	5.00	10.00
❑ 32010	Lock All the Windows/Hit and Run	1966	2.50	5.00	10.00
❑ 32040	Babe, You've Been On My Mind/Texas Across the River	1966	2.50	5.00	10.00

MOUNTAIN CREEK

Number	Title (A Side/B Side)	Yr	VG	VG+	NM
❑ 301/2	Big Ship Glory/Johnson Party of Four	1977	6.25	12.50	25.00

NAUTILUS

Number	Title (A Side/B Side)	Yr	VG	VG+	NM
❑ NR2-45	Aspen Gold/Longest Beer of the Night	1979	—	2.50	5.00

TETRAGRAMMATON

Number	Title (A Side/B Side)	Yr	VG	VG+	NM
❑ 1526	One Too Many Mornings/Scotch and Soda	1969	2.50	5.00	10.00

XERES

Number	Title (A Side/B Side)	Yr	VG	VG+	NM
❑ 10004	Looking for the Sunshine/Reverend Mr. Black	1982	—	2.00	4.00
❑ 10004 [PS]	Looking for the Sunshine/Reverend Mr. Black	1982	—	2.00	4.00

7-Inch Extended Plays

CAPITOL

Number	Title (A Side/B Side)	Yr	VG	VG+	NM
❑ EAP 1-996	Three Jolly Coachmen/Wreck of the "John B"//Bay of Mexico/Saro Jane	1958	7.50	15.00	30.00
❑ EAP 1-996 [PS]	The Kingston Trio	1958	7.50	15.00	30.00
❑ EAP 1-1119	M.T.A./Como Se Viene//All My Sorrows/Sail Away Ladies	1959	7.50	15.00	30.00
❑ EAP 1-1119 [PS]	M.T.A.	1959	7.50	15.00	30.00
❑ EAP 1-1129	The Tijuana Jail/Oh Cindy//Coplas/Tom Dooley	1959	7.50	15.00	30.00
❑ EAP 1-1129 [PS]	Tijuana Jail	1959	7.50	15.00	30.00
❑ EAP 1-1136	Tom Dooley/Coplas//Banua/Santy Ano	1959	7.50	15.00	30.00
❑ EAP 1-1136 [PS]	Tom Dooley	1959	7.50	15.00	30.00
❑ EAP 1-1182	Raspberries, Strawberries/Ruby Red//Sally/Scarlet Ribbons	1959	7.50	15.00	30.00
❑ EAP 1-1182 [PS]	Raspberries, Strawberries	1959	7.50	15.00	30.00
❑ EAP 1-1199	M.T.A./All My Sorrows//Scarlet Ribbons/Remember the Alamo	1959	6.25	12.50	25.00
❑ EAP 1-1199 [PS]	The Kingston Trio at Large, Part 1	1959	6.25	12.50	25.00
❑ EAP 2-1199	Blow Ye Winds/Corey Corey//The Long Black Rifle/Early in the Mornin'	1959	6.25	12.50	25.00
❑ EAP 2-1199 [PS]	The Kingston Trio at Large, Part 2	1959	6.25	12.50	25.00
❑ EAP 3-1199	The Seine/I Bawled//Good News/Getaway John	1959	6.25	12.50	25.00
❑ EAP 3-1199 [PS]	The Kingston Trio at Large, Part 3	1959	6.25	12.50	25.00
❑ EAP 1-1258	Molly Dee/Across the Wide Missouri//Goober Peas/A Worried Man	1959	6.25	12.50	25.00
❑ EAP 1-1258 [PS]	Here We Go Again! Part 1	1959	6.25	12.50	25.00
❑ EAP 2-1258	Haul Away/The Wanderer//E Inu Tatou E/A Rollin' Stone	1959	6.25	12.50	25.00
❑ EAP 2-1258 [PS]	Here We Go Again! Part 2	1959	6.25	12.50	25.00
❑ EAP 3-1258	Round About a Mountain/Oleanna//The Unfortunate Miss Bailey/San Miguel	1959	6.25	12.50	25.00
❑ EAP 3-1258 [PS]	Here We Go Again! Part 3	1959	6.25	12.50	25.00
❑ EAP 1-1322	A Worried Man/Molly Dee//San Miguel/Oleanna	1959	6.25	12.50	25.00
❑ EAP 1-1322 [PS]	A Worried Man	1959	6.25	12.50	25.00
❑ EAP 1-1352	El Matador/The Mountains o' Mourne//The Hunter/Farewell Adelita	1960	6.25	12.50	25.00
❑ EAP 1-1352 [PS]	Sold Out, Part 1	1960	6.25	12.50	25.00
❑ EAP 2-1352	Don't Cry Katie/Medley: Tanga Tiki-Toerau//Mangwani Mpulele/With You My Johnny	1960	6.25	12.50	25.00
❑ EAP 2-1352 [PS]	Sold Out, Part 2	1960	6.25	12.50	25.00
❑ EAP 3-1352	With Her Head Tucked Underneath Her Arm/Carrier Pigeon//Bimini/Raspberries, Strawberries	1960	6.25	12.50	25.00
❑ EAP 3-1352 [PS]	Sold Out, Part 3	1960	6.25	12.50	25.00
❑ EAP 1-1407	Bad Man Blunder/The Escape of Old John Webb//Colorado Trail/The Tattooed Lady	1960	6.25	12.50	25.00
❑ EAP 1-1407 [PS]	String Along, Part 1	1960	6.25	12.50	25.00
❑ EAP 2-1407	When I Was Young/Leave My Woman Alone//Who's Gonna Hold Her Hand/To Morrow	1960	6.25	12.50	25.00
❑ EAP 2-1407 [PS]	String Along, Part 2	1960	6.25	12.50	25.00
❑ EAP 3-1407	This Mornin', This Evenin', So Soon/Everglades//Buddy Better Get On Down the Line/South Wind	1960	6.25	12.50	25.00
❑ EAP 3-1407 [PS]	String Along, Part 3	1960	6.25	12.50	25.00
❑ EAP 1-1446	Bye Bye Thou Little Tiny Child/The Snows of Winter//Sing We Noel/The Last Month of the Year	1960	6.25	12.50	25.00
❑ EAP 1-1446 [PS]	The Last Month of the Year, Part 1	1960	6.25	12.50	25.00
❑ EAP 2-1446	We Wish You a Merry Christmas/All Through the Night//Mary Mild/A Round About Christmas	1960	6.25	12.50	25.00
❑ EAP 2-1446 [PS]	The Last Month of the Year, Part 2	1960	6.25	12.50	25.00
❑ EAP 3-1446	Goodnight My Baby Goodnight/Go Where I Send Thee//Follow Now, Oh Shepherds/Somerset Gloucestershire Wassail	1960	6.25	12.50	25.00
❑ EAP 3-1446 [PS]	The Last Month of the Year, Part 3	1960	6.25	12.50	25.00
❑ EAP 1-1474	En El Agua/Come All You Fair and Tender Ladies//Blow the Candle Out/Blue Eyed Gal	1961	6.25	12.50	25.00
❑ EAP 1-1474 [PS]	Make Way, Part 1	1961	6.25	12.50	25.00
❑ EAP 2-1474	The Jug of Punch/Bonny Heilan' Laddie//The River Is Wide/Oh Yes, Oh	1961	6.25	12.50	25.00
❑ EAP 2-1474 [PS]	Make Way, Part 2	1961	6.25	12.50	25.00
❑ EAP 3-1474	Utawena/Hear Travelin'//Hangman/Speckled Roan	1961	6.25	12.50	25.00
❑ EAP 3-1474 [PS]	Make Way, Part 3	1961	6.25	12.50	25.00
❑ EAP 1-1642	Coming from the Mountains/Oh Sail Away//Weeping Willow/Reuben James	1961	6.25	12.50	25.00
❑ EAP 1-1642 [PS]	Close Up, Part 1	1961	6.25	12.50	25.00
❑ EAP 2-1642	Take Her Out of Pity/Don't You Weep, Mary//When My Love Was Here/Karu	1961	6.25	12.50	25.00
❑ EAP 2-1642 [PS]	Close Up, Part 2	1961	6.25	12.50	25.00
❑ EAP 3-1642	The Whistling Gypsy/O Ken Karanga//Jessie James/Glorious Kingdom	1961	6.25	12.50	25.00
❑ EAP 3-1642 [PS]	Close Up, Part 3	1961	6.25	12.50	25.00

KINKS, THE

Also see DAVE DAVIES.

ARISTA

Number	Title (A Side/B Side)	Yr	VG	VG+	NM
❑ SP-5 [DJ]	Sleepwalker/All the Kids on the Street	1977	2.50	5.00	10.00

—Gold vinyl; B-side by the Hollywood Stars

Number	Title (A Side/B Side)	Yr	VG	VG+	NM
❑ SP-5 [PS]	Sleepwalker/All the Kids on the Street	1977	2.50	5.00	10.00
❑ 0240	Sleepwalker/Full Moon	1977	—	2.00	4.00
❑ 0247	Life Goes On/Juke Box Music	1977	—	2.00	4.00
❑ 0296	Father Christmas/Prince of the Punks	1977	—	2.50	5.00
❑ 0296 [PS]	Father Christmas/Prince of the Punks	1977	—	2.50	5.00
❑ 0342	A Rock and Roll Fantasy/Live Life	1978	—	2.00	4.00
❑ 0372	Black Messiah/Live Life	1978	—	2.00	4.00
❑ 0409	Superman/Low Budget	1979	—	2.50	5.00
❑ 0409	(Wish I Could Fly Like) Superman/Party Line	1979	—	2.00	4.00
❑ 0448	Low Budget/A Gallon of Gas	1979	—	2.00	4.00
❑ 0458	Catch Me Now I'm Falling/Low Budget	1979	—	2.00	4.00
❑ 0541	Lola/Celluloid Heroes	1980	—	2.00	4.00
❑ 0541 [PS]	Lola/Celluloid Heroes	1980	—	2.50	5.00
❑ 0577	You Really Got Me/Attitude	1980	—	2.00	4.00
❑ 0619	Destroyer/Back to Back	1981	—	2.00	4.00
❑ 0649	Better Things/Yo-Yo	1981	—	2.00	4.00
❑ 1054	Come Dancing/Noise	1983	—	2.00	4.00
❑ 1054 [PS]	Come Dancing/Noise	1983	—	2.00	4.00
❑ 9016	Come Dancing/Noise	1983	—	—	3.00
❑ 9016 [PS]	Come Dancing/Noise	1983	—	—	3.00
❑ 9075	Don't Forget to Dance/Young Conservatives	1983	—	—	3.00
❑ 9309	Do It Again/Guilty	1984	—	—	3.00
❑ 9309 [PS]	Do It Again/Guilty	1984	—	—	3.00
❑ 9334	Summer's Gone/Going Solo	1985	—	—	3.00

CAMEO

Number	Title (A Side/B Side)	Yr	VG	VG+	NM
❑ 308	Long Tall Sally/I Took My Baby Home	1964	150.00	300.00	600.00
❑ 345	Long Tall Sally/I Took My Baby Home	1965	75.00	150.00	300.00
❑ 348	You Still Want Me/You Do Something to Me	1965	—	—	—

—Canceled. NOTE: An EP on Cameo, which contains the four songs assigned to Cameo in the U.S., is a bootleg with little collector value.

MCA

Number	Title (A Side/B Side)	Yr	VG	VG+	NM
❑ 52960	Rock 'N' Roll Cities/Sleazy Town	1986	—	—	3.00
❑ 52960 [PS]	Rock 'N' Roll Cities/Sleazy Town	1986	—	—	3.00
❑ 53015	Lost and Found/Killing Time	1987	—	—	3.00
❑ 53015 [PS]	Lost and Found/Killing Time	1987	—	—	3.00
❑ 53093	Working at the Factory/How Are You	1987	2.50	5.00	10.00
❑ 53699	How Do I Get Close/War Is Over	1989	2.50	5.00	10.00

RCA VICTOR

Number	Title (A Side/B Side)	Yr	VG	VG+	NM
❑ APBO-0275	Money Talks/Here Comes Flash	1974	2.50	5.00	10.00
❑ DJBO-0275 [DJ]	Money Talks (short/long versions)	1974	2.00	4.00	8.00
❑ LPBO-5001	Sitting in the Midday Sun/Sweet Lady Genevieve	1973	2.50	5.00	10.00
❑ PB-10019	Mirror of Love/It's Evil	1974	—	3.00	6.00
❑ PB-10121	Preservation/Salvation Road	1974	—	3.00	6.00
❑ PB-10251	Everybody's a Star (Starmaker)/Ordinary People	1975	—	3.00	6.00
❑ PB-10551	I'm in Disgrace/The Hard Way	1976	—	3.00	6.00
❑ 74-0620	20th Century Man/Skin and Bones	1971	2.00	4.00	8.00
❑ 74-0807	Supersonic Rocket Ship/You Don't Know My Name	1972	2.00	4.00	8.00
❑ 74-0852	Celluloid Heroes/Hot Potatoes	1972	2.00	4.00	8.00
❑ 74-0940	One of the Survivors/Scrap Heap City	1973	50.00	100.00	200.00

—Released with acoustic versions of the two songs rather than the LP versions and quickly deleted

REPRISE

Number	Title (A Side/B Side)	Yr	VG	VG+	NM
❑ 0306	You Really Got Me/It's All Right	1964	6.25	12.50	25.00

—Originals have peach labels

Number	Title (A Side/B Side)	Yr	VG	VG+	NM
❑ 0306	You Really Got Me/It's All Right	1964	3.75	7.50	15.00

—Second pressings have orange and brown labels

Number	Title (A Side/B Side)	Yr	VG	VG+	NM
❑ 0334	All Day and All of the Night/I Gotta Move	1964	5.00	10.00	20.00
❑ 0347	Tired of Waiting for You/Come On Now	1965	5.00	10.00	20.00
❑ 0366	Who'll Be the Next in Line/Everybody's Gonna Be Happy	1965	5.00	10.00	20.00
❑ 0379	Set Me Free/I Need You	1965	5.00	10.00	20.00

Number	Title (A Side/B Side)	Yr	VG	VG+	NM
❑ 0409	See My Friends/Never Met a Girl Like You Before	1965	3.75	7.50	15.00
❑ 0420	A Well Repected Man/Such a Shame	1965	3.75	7.50	15.00
❑ 0454	Till the End of the Day/Where Have All the Good Times Gone	1966	3.75	7.50	15.00
❑ 0471	Dedicated Follower of Fashion/Sittin' on My Sofa	1966	3.75	7.50	15.00
❑ 0497	Sunny Afternoon/I'm Not Like Everybody Else	1966	3.75	7.50	15.00
❑ 0540	Dead End Street/Big Black Smoke	1966	10.00	20.00	40.00
❑ 0587	Mr. Pleasant/Harry Rag	1967	10.00	20.00	40.00
❑ 0612	Waterloo Sunset/Two Sisters	1967	10.00	20.00	40.00
❑ 0647	Autumn Almanac/David Watts	1967	10.00	20.00	40.00
❑ 0691	Wonderboy/Polly	1968	10.00	20.00	40.00
❑ 0708	Sunny Afternoon/Dead End Street	1968	2.50	5.00	10.00
❑ 0712	Dedicated Follower of Fashion/Who'll Be the Next in Line	1968	2.50	5.00	10.00
❑ 0715	A Well Respected Man/Set Me Free	1968	2.50	5.00	10.00
❑ 0719	Tired of Waiting for You/All Day and All of the Night	1968	2.50	5.00	10.00
❑ 0722	You Really Got Me/It's All Right	1968	2.50	5.00	10.00

—0708 through 0722 are "Back to Back Hits" series -- originals have both "r:" and "W7" on label

Number	Title (A Side/B Side)	Yr	VG	VG+	NM
❑ 0743	Lola/Apeman	1972	—	2.50	5.00

—"Back to Back Hits" series

Number	Title (A Side/B Side)	Yr	VG	VG+	NM
❑ 0762	Days/She's Got Everything	1968	10.00	20.00	40.00
❑ 0806	Starstruck/Picture Book	1969	10.00	20.00	40.00
❑ 0847	The Village Green Preservation Society/Do You Remember Walter	1969	10.00	20.00	40.00
❑ 0863	Victoria/Brainwashed	1969	3.75	7.50	15.00
❑ 0930	Lola/Mindless Child of Motherhood	1970	2.50	5.00	10.00
❑ 0979	Apeman/Rats	1970	2.50	5.00	10.00
❑ 1017	God's Children/The Way Love Used to Be	1971	5.00	10.00	20.00
❑ 1094	King Kong/Waterloo Sunset	1972	3.75	7.50	15.00

7-Inch Extended Plays

CAMEO

Number	Title (A Side/B Side)	Yr	VG	VG+	NM
❑ 315	Long Tall Sally/I Took My Baby Home//You Still Want Me/You Do Something To Me	196?	—	—	—

—Bootleg; also comes with bootleg title sleeve

KIPPINGTON LODGE

Also see NICK LOWE.

CAPITOL

Number	Title (A Side/B Side)	Yr	VG	VG+	NM
❑ 2236	And She Cried/Rumors	1968	7.50	15.00	30.00

KIRBY, KATHY

ASCOT

Number	Title (A Side/B Side)	Yr	VG	VG+	NM
❑ 2232	In All the World/Time	1967	2.00	4.00	8.00

LONDON

Number	Title (A Side/B Side)	Yr	VG	VG+	NM
❑ 9572	(He's a) Big Man/Slowly	1963	3.75	7.50	15.00
❑ 9621	Dance On/Playboy	1963	3.75	7.50	15.00
❑ 9628	Secret Love/Too Bad for Johnny	1964	3.75	7.50	15.00
❑ 9645	Let Me Go Lover/Sweetest Sounds	1964	3.75	7.50	15.00
❑ 9677	Love Me Baby/You're the One	1964	3.75	7.50	15.00
❑ 9750	I Belong/I'll Try Not to Cry	1965	3.75	7.50	15.00

PARROT

Number	Title (A Side/B Side)	Yr	VG	VG+	NM
❑ 9767	Secret Love/Soon I'll Wed My Love	1965	3.00	6.00	12.00
❑ 9775	The Way of Love/Oh Darling How I Miss You	1965	3.00	6.00	12.00
❑ 9805	Where in the World/Wonderful Feeling of Love	1965	3.00	6.00	12.00
❑ 9827	Till the End of Time/Spanish Flea	1966	2.50	5.00	10.00

KIRK, DAVE

HI-Q

Number	Title (A Side/B Side)	Yr	VG	VG+	NM
❑ 5024	Oh! Baby/Those Lonely Blue Nights	1962	12.50	25.00	50.00

KISS

Also see PETER CRISS; ACE FREHLEY; GENE SIMMONS; PAUL STANLEY.

CASABLANCA

Number	Title (A Side/B Side)	Yr	VG	VG+	NM
❑ 0004	Love Theme from Kiss/Nothin' to Lose	1974	3.00	6.00	12.00
❑ 0011	Kissin' Time/Nothin' to Lose	1974	3.00	6.00	12.00
❑ 0015	Strutter/100,000 Years	1974	3.00	6.00	12.00
❑ 823	Let Me Go, Rock and Roll/Hotter Than Hell	1975	3.00	6.00	12.00
❑ 829	Rock and Roll All Nite/Getaway	1975	3.00	6.00	12.00
❑ 841	C'mon and Love Me/Getaway	1975	3.00	6.00	12.00
❑ 850	Rock and Roll All Nite (Live)/Rock and Roll All Night (Studio)	1975	2.50	5.00	10.00
❑ 854	Shout It Out Loud/Sweet Pain	1976	2.50	5.00	10.00
❑ 858	Flaming Youth/God of Thunder	1976	2.50	5.00	10.00
❑ 858 [PS]	Flaming Youth/God of Thunder	1976	15.00	30.00	60.00
❑ 863	Detroit Rock City/Beth	1976	2.50	5.00	10.00

—With "Detroit Rock City" listed as "Side A"

Number	Title (A Side/B Side)	Yr	VG	VG+	NM
❑ 863	Beth/Detroit Rock City	1976	—	2.50	5.00

—With "Beth" listed as "Side A"

Number	Title (A Side/B Side)	Yr	VG	VG+	NM
❑ 873	Hard Luck Woman/Mr. Speed	1976	—	3.00	6.00
❑ 880	Calling Dr. Love/Take Me	1977	—	3.00	6.00
❑ 889	Christine Sixteen/Shock Me	1977	—	3.00	6.00
❑ 895	Love Gun/Hooligan	1977	—	3.00	6.00
❑ 906	Shout It Out Loud (Live)/Nothin' to Lose	1977	—	3.00	6.00
❑ 915	Rocket Ride/Tomorrow and Tonight	1978	—	3.00	6.00
❑ 928	Strutter '78/Shock Me	1978	—	3.00	6.00
❑ 983	I Was Made for Lovin' You/Hard Times	1979	—	2.50	5.00
❑ 2205	Sure Know Something/Dirty Livin'	1979	—	2.50	5.00
❑ 2282	Shandi/She's So European	1980	—	2.50	5.00
❑ 2299	Tomorrow/Naked City	1980	—	2.50	5.00
❑ 2343	A World Without Heroes/Dark Light	1981	—	2.50	5.00
❑ 2365	I Love It Loud/Danger	1982	—	2.50	5.00
❑ 2365 [PS]	I Love It Loud/Danger	1982	5.00	10.00	20.00

MERCURY

Number	Title (A Side/B Side)	Yr	VG	VG+	NM
❑ 814671-7	Lick It Up/Dance All Over Your Face	1983	—	2.00	4.00
❑ 818216-7	Young and Wasted/All Hell Is Breaking Loose	1984	—	2.00	4.00
❑ 858894-7	Detroit Rock City/Detroit Rock City	1994	—	2.00	4.00

—B-side by Mighty Mighty Bosstones; small center hole; green vinyl

Number	Title (A Side/B Side)	Yr	VG	VG+	NM
❑ 858894-7 [PS]	Detroit Rock City/Detroit Rock City	1994	—	2.00	4.00
❑ 870022-7	Reason to Live/Thief in the Night	1987	—	2.00	4.00
❑ 870022-7 [PS]	Reason to Live/Thief in the Night	1987	—	2.50	5.00
❑ 870215-7	Turn On the Night/Hell or High Water	1988	—	2.00	4.00
❑ 870215-7 [PS]	Turn On the Night/Hell or High Water	1988	—	2.50	5.00
❑ 872244-7	Let's Put the X in Sex/Calling Dr. Love	1989	—	2.50	5.00
❑ 872244-7 [PS]	Let's Put the X in Sex/Calling Dr. Love	1989	—	3.00	6.00
❑ 876146-7	Hide Your Heart/Betrayed	1989	—	2.50	5.00
❑ 876716-7	Forever/The Street Giveth and the Street Taketh Away	1990	—	2.50	5.00
❑ 880205-7	Heaven's on Fire/Lonely Is the Hunter	1984	—	2.00	4.00
❑ 880535-7	Thrills in the Night/Burn Bitch Burn	1985	—	2.00	4.00
❑ 884141-7	Tears Are Falling/Any Way You Slice It	1985	—	2.00	4.00
❑ 884141-7 [PS]	Tears Are Falling/Any Way You Slice It	1985	—	2.50	5.00
❑ 888796-7	Crazy Crazy Nights/No, No, No	1987	—	2.00	4.00
❑ 888796-7 [PS]	Crazy Crazy Nights/No, No, No	1987	—	2.50	5.00

KISSOON, MAC AND KATIE

ABC

Number	Title (A Side/B Side)	Yr	VG	VG+	NM
❑ 11306	Chirpy Chirpy Cheep Cheep/Walking Around	1971	—	3.00	6.00

BELL

Number	Title (A Side/B Side)	Yr	VG	VG+	NM
❑ 45198	I Found My Freedom/Love Game Today	1972	—	2.50	5.00
❑ 45436	Love Will Keep Us Together/I'm Up in Heaven	1974	—	2.50	5.00

MCA

Number	Title (A Side/B Side)	Yr	VG	VG+	NM
❑ 40409	Black Rose/Sugar Candy Kisses	1975	—	2.00	4.00
❑ 40482	Like a Butterfly/Beautiful Day	1975	—	2.00	4.00
❑ 40550	Two of Us/Dream of Me	1976	—	2.00	4.00
❑ 40609	Fly Away/Where Would Our Love Be	1976	—	2.00	4.00

KIT AND THE OUTLAWS

PHILIPS

Number	Title (A Side/B Side)	Yr	VG	VG+	NM
❑ 40420	Midnight Hour/Don't Tread on Me	1966	3.00	6.00	12.00

KIT KATS, THE

JAMIE

Number	Title (A Side/B Side)	Yr	VG	VG+	NM
❑ 1321	That's the Way/Won't Find Better Than Me	1966	3.00	6.00	12.00
❑ 1326	Let's Get Lost on a Country Road/Find Someone (Who'll Make You Happy)	1966	3.00	6.00	12.00
❑ 1331	You've Got to Know/Cold Walls	1967	3.00	6.00	12.00
❑ 1337	Breezy/Won't Find Better Than Me	1967	3.00	6.00	12.00
❑ 1343	Sea of Love/Cold Walls	1967	3.00	6.00	12.00
❑ 1345	Distance/Find Someone	1968	2.50	5.00	10.00
❑ 1346	I Got the Feeling/That's the Way	1968	2.50	5.00	10.00
❑ 1353	I Want to Be/Need You	1968	2.50	5.00	10.00
❑ 1354	You're So Good to Me/Need You	1968	2.50	5.00	10.00
❑ 1362	Hey Saturday Noon/That's the Way	1968	2.50	5.00	10.00
❑ 1381	Won't Find Better (Than Me)/(They Call It) Love	1969	2.00	4.00	8.00

—As "New Hope"

Number	Title (A Side/B Side)	Yr	VG	VG+	NM
❑ 1385	Rain/Let's Get Lost on a Country Road	1970	2.00	4.00	8.00

—As "New Hope"

Number	Title (A Side/B Side)	Yr	VG	VG+	NM
❑ 1388	Look Away/The Money Game	1970	2.00	4.00	8.00

—As "New Hope"

Number	Title (A Side/B Side)	Yr	VG	VG+	NM
❑ 1422	Find Someone/Breezy	1974	—	3.00	6.00

—As "New Hope"

LAURIE

Number	Title (A Side/B Side)	Yr	VG	VG+	NM
❑ 3186	Good Luck Charlie/Aba Daba Honeymoon	1963	5.00	10.00	20.00

LAWN

Number	Title (A Side/B Side)	Yr	VG	VG+	NM
❑ 249	You're No Angel/Cold Walls	1964	3.75	7.50	15.00

PARAMOUNT

Number	Title (A Side/B Side)	Yr	VG	VG+	NM
❑ 0110	That You Love/Taking My Time	1971	2.00	4.00	8.00

KITCHEN CINQ, THE

DECCA

Number	Title (A Side/B Side)	Yr	VG	VG+	NM
❑ 32262	Good Lovin'/For Never We Met	1968	2.50	5.00	10.00
❑ 32374	She's So Fine/The Minstrel	1968	2.50	5.00	10.00

LHI

Number	Title (A Side/B Side)	Yr	VG	VG+	NM
❑ 17000	You'll Be Sorry Someday/Determination	1966	3.00	6.00	12.00
❑ 17005	If You Think/Ride the Wind	1967	3.00	6.00	12.00
❑ 17010	Still in Love with You Baby/Ride the Wind	1967	3.00	6.00	12.00
❑ 17015	Street Song/When the Rain Disappears	1967	3.00	6.00	12.00

KITTENS, THE

Probably more than one group.

ABC

Number	Title (A Side/B Side)	Yr	VG	VG+	NM
❑ 10835	The Masquerade Is Over/It's Gotta Be Love	1966	2.50	5.00	10.00

ABC-PARAMOUNT

Number	Title (A Side/B Side)	Yr	VG	VG+	NM
❑ 10619	Shindig/I Got to Know Him	1965	3.00	6.00	12.00
❑ 10730	Lookie Lookie/We Find Him Guilty	1965	3.00	6.00	12.00
❑ 10783	Is It Our Baby/Undecided You	1966	3.00	6.00	12.00

ALPINE

Number	Title (A Side/B Side)	Yr	VG	VG+	NM
❑ 64	Dark, Dark Sunglasses/Itsy Bitsy Teeny Weeny Yellow Polka Dot Bikini	1960	7.50	15.00	30.00
❑ 67	A Letter on His Sweater/Broken Dreams	1960	7.50	15.00	30.00

CHESS

Number	Title (A Side/B Side)	Yr	VG	VG+	NM
❑ 2027	Hey Operator/Ain't No More Room	1967	2.00	4.00	8.00
❑ 2055	How Long Can I Go On/I've Got to Get Over You	1968	2.00	4.00	8.00

CHESTNUT

Number	Title (A Side/B Side)	Yr	VG	VG+	NM
❑ 203	Count Every Star/I'm Worried	1963	12.50	25.00	50.00

DON-EL

Number	Title (A Side/B Side)	Yr	VG	VG+	NM
❑ 122	Walter/Lite Bulb	1963	3.75	7.50	15.00
❑ 205	I Need Your Love Tonight/Johnny's Place	1963	3.75	7.50	15.00

MURBO

Number	Title (A Side/B Side)	Yr	VG	VG+	NM
❑ 1015	Joey Has a New Love/Lonely Summer	1967	2.50	5.00	10.00

UNART

Number	Title (A Side/B Side)	Yr	VG	VG+	NM
❑ 2010	It's All Over Now/Letter to Donna	1959	12.50	25.00	50.00

KLAATU

CAPITOL

Number	Title (A Side/B Side)	Yr	VG	VG+	NM
❑ 4377	Calling Occupants/Doctor Marvello	1976	2.00	4.00	8.00
❑ 4412	Calling Occupants/Sub-Rosa Subway	1977	—	2.50	5.00
❑ 4516	Around the Universe in 80 Days/We're Off You Know	1977	—	2.50	5.00
❑ 4627	Dear Christine/Older	1978	—	2.50	5.00
❑ 4866	Knee Deep in Love/Dog Star	1980	—	2.50	5.00

Number	Title (A Side/B Side)	Yr	VG	VG+	NM
ISLAND					
❑ 011	California Jam/Doctor Marvello	1975	2.50	5.00	10.00

KLARK KENT
Stewart Copeland of THE POLICE in disguise.

Number	Title (A Side/B Side)	Yr	VG	VG+	NM
KRYPTONE/I.R.S.					
❑ 9012	Away from Home/Office Talk	1980	—	2.50	5.00
—Green vinyl, custom label, small hole					
❑ 9012 [PS]	Away from Home/Office Talk	1980	—	2.50	5.00

KLEIN, GEORGE

Number	Title (A Side/B Side)	Yr	VG	VG+	NM
SUN					
❑ 358	U.T. Party (Part 1)/U.T. Party (Part 2)	1961	5.00	10.00	20.00

KNICKERBOCKERS, THE

Number	Title (A Side/B Side)	Yr	VG	VG+	NM
CHALLENGE					
❑ 59268	All I Need Is You/Bite, Bite Barracuda	1965	10.00	20.00	40.00
❑ 59293	Jerktown/Room for One More	1965	3.75	7.50	15.00
❑ 59321	Lies/The Coming Generation	1965	4.00	8.00	16.00
❑ 59326	One Track Mind/I Must Be Doing Something Right	1966	3.75	7.50	15.00
❑ 59332	High on Love/Stick with Me	1966	3.75	7.50	15.00
❑ 59335	Just One Girl/Chapel in the Fields	1966	3.75	7.50	15.00
❑ 59341	Love Is a Bird/Rumors, Gossip, Words Untrue	1966	3.75	7.50	15.00
❑ 59348	Can You Help Me/Please Don't Love Him	1966	3.75	7.50	15.00
❑ 59359	What Does That Make You/Sweet Green Fields	1967	3.75	7.50	15.00
❑ 59366	Come and Get It/Wishful Thinking	1967	3.75	7.50	15.00
❑ 59380	You'll Never Walk Alone/I Can Do It Better	1967	3.75	7.50	15.00
❑ 59384	As a Matter of Fact/They Ran for Their Lives	1968	3.75	7.50	15.00

KNIGHT, CHRIS
"Peter Brady" of THE BRADY BUNCH.

Number	Title (A Side/B Side)	Yr	VG	VG+	NM
PARAMOUNT					
❑ 0177	Good for Each Other/Over and Over	1972	3.75	7.50	15.00
❑ 0177 [PS]	Good for Each Other/Over and Over	1972	3.75	7.50	15.00

KNIGHT, CHRIS, AND MAUREEN MCCORMICK
Also see each artist's individual listings; THE BRADY BUNCH.

Number	Title (A Side/B Side)	Yr	VG	VG+	NM
PARAMOUNT					
❑ 0246	Little Bird/Just a-Singin' Along	1973	3.75	7.50	15.00

KNIGHT, GLADYS, AND THE PIPS
Includes Gladys Knight solo and the Pips without Gladys.

Number	Title (A Side/B Side)	Yr	VG	VG+	NM
BRUNSWICK					
❑ 55048	Whistle My Love/Ching Ching	1958	30.00	60.00	120.00
BUDDAH					
❑ 363	Where Peaceful Waters Flow/Perfect Love	1973	—	2.50	5.00
❑ 363 [PS]	Where Peaceful Waters Flow/Perfect Love	1973	2.00	4.00	8.00
❑ 383	Midnight Train to Georgia/(Instrumental)	1973	—	3.00	6.00
❑ 383	Midnight Train to Georgia/Window Raising Granny	1973	—	2.50	5.00
❑ 393	I've Got to Use My Imagination/I Can See Clearly Now	1973	—	2.50	5.00
❑ 403	Best Thing That Ever Happened to Me/Once in a Lifetime	1974	—	2.50	5.00
❑ 423	On and On/The Makings of You	1974	—	2.50	5.00
❑ 423 [PS]	On and On/The Makings of You	1974	2.00	4.00	8.00
❑ 433	I Feel a Song (In My Heart)/Don't Burn Down the Bridge	1974	—	2.50	5.00
❑ 453	Love FInds It's Own Way/Better You Go Your Way	1975	—	2.50	5.00
❑ 463	The Way We Were-Try to Remember/The Need to Be	1975	—	2.50	5.00
❑ 487	Money/Street Brothers	1975	—	2.50	5.00
❑ 513	Part Time Love/Where Did I Put His Memory	1975	—	2.50	5.00
❑ 523	Make Yours a Happy Home/The Going Up and the Coming Down	1976	—	2.50	5.00
❑ 544	So Sad the Song/(Instrumental)	1976	—	2.50	5.00
❑ 569	Baby Don't Change Your Mind/I Love to Feel That Feelin'	1977	—	2.50	5.00
❑ 584	Sorry Doesn't Always Make It Right/You Put a New Life in My Body	1977	—	2.50	5.00
❑ 592	The One and Only/Pipe Dreams	1978	—	2.50	5.00
❑ 598	It's a Better Than Good Time/Everybody's Got to Find a Way	1978	—	2.50	5.00
❑ 601	I'm Coming Home Again/Love Gives You the Power	1978	—	2.50	5.00
❑ 605	Sail Away/I'm Still Caught Up with You	1979	—	2.50	5.00
❑ 1974 [DJ]	Do You Hear What I Hear/Silent Night	1974	—	3.00	6.00
❑ 1974 [PS]	Do You Hear What I Hear/Silent Night	1974	—	3.00	6.00
CASABLANCA					
❑ 912	If I Could Bring Back Yesterday/Since I Found Love	1978	—	2.00	4.00
—As "The Pips"					
❑ 949	Baby I'm Your Fool/Lights of the City	1978	—	2.00	4.00
—As "The Pips"					
COLUMBIA					
❑ 02113	Forever Yesterday (For the Children)/(Instrumental)	1981	—	2.00	4.00
❑ 02113 [PS]	Forever Yesterday (For the Children)/(Instrumental)	1981	—	2.50	5.00
❑ 02413	If That'll Make You Happy/Love Was Made for Two	1981	—	2.00	4.00
❑ 02549	I Will Fight/God Is	1981	—	2.00	4.00
❑ 02706	Friend of Mine/Reach High	1982	—	2.00	4.00
❑ 03418	That Special Time of Year/Santa Claus Is Comin' to Town	1982	—	2.00	4.00
❑ 03761	Save the Overtime (For Me)/Ain't No Greater Love	1983	—	2.00	4.00
❑ 04033	You're Number 1 in My Book/Oh La De Dah	1983	—	2.00	4.00
❑ 04219	Hero (The Wind Beneath My Wings)/Seconds	1983	—	2.50	5.00
❑ 04333	Here's That Sunny Day/Oh La De Da	1984	—	2.00	4.00
❑ 04369	When You're Far Away/Seconds	1984	—	2.00	4.00
❑ 04761	My Time/(Instrumental)	1985	—	2.00	4.00
❑ 04761 [PS]	My Time/(Instrumental)	1985	—	2.50	5.00
❑ 04873	Keep Givin' Me Love/Do You Wanna Have Some Fun	1985	—	2.00	4.00
❑ 05679	Till I See You Again/Strivin'	1985	—	2.00	4.00
❑ 10922	Am I Too Late/It's the Same Old Song	1979	—	2.00	4.00
❑ 10997	You Bring Out the Best in Me/You Loved Away the Pain	1979	—	2.00	4.00
❑ 11088	The Best Thing We Can Do Is Say Goodbye/You Don't Have to Say I Love You	1979	—	2.00	4.00
❑ 11239	Landlord/We Need Hearts	1980	—	2.00	4.00
❑ 11330	Taste of Bitter Love/Add It Up	1980	—	2.00	4.00
❑ 11375	Bourgie', Bourgie'/Get the Love	1980	—	2.00	4.00
❑ 11409	When a Child Is Born/The Lord's Prayer	1980	—	2.00	4.00
—With Johnny Mathis					
ENJOY					
❑ 2012	What Shall I Do/Love Call	1964	3.75	7.50	15.00
EVERLAST					
❑ 5025	Happiness/I Had a Dream Last Night	1963	6.25	12.50	25.00
—As "The Pips"					
FURY					
❑ 1050	Every Beat of My Heart/Room in Your Heart	1961	6.25	12.50	25.00
—Re-recordings of the same songs on Huntom and Vee Jay					
❑ 1052	Guess Who/Stop Running Around	1961	3.75	7.50	15.00
❑ 1054	Letter Full of Tears/You Broke Your Promise	1961	3.75	7.50	15.00
❑ 1064	Operator/I'll Trust in You	1962	3.75	7.50	15.00
❑ 1067	Darling/Linda	1962	5.00	10.00	20.00
—As "The Pips"					
❑ 1073	Come See About Me/I Want That Kind of Love	1963	7.50	15.00	30.00
HUNTOM					
❑ 2510	Every Beat of My Heart/Room in Your Heart	1961	125.00	250.00	500.00
—As "The Pips"					
MAXX					
❑ 326	Giving Up/Maybe, Maybe Baby	1964	3.75	7.50	15.00
❑ 329	Lovers Always Forget/Another Love	1964	3.75	7.50	15.00
❑ 331	Either Way I Lose/Go Away, Stay Away	1964	3.75	7.50	15.00
❑ 334	Who Knows/Stop and Get a Hold of Myself	1965	3.75	7.50	15.00
❑ 335	Tell Her You're Mine/If I Should Ever Be in Love	1965	3.75	7.50	15.00
MCA					
❑ 53002	Send It to Me/When You Love Somebody (It's Christmas Every Day)	1987	—	—	3.00
❑ 53002 [PS]	Send It to Me/When You Love Somebody (It's Christmas Every Day)	1987	—	—	3.00
❑ 53210	Love Overboard/(Instrumental)	1987	—	—	3.00
❑ 53210 [PS]	Love Overboard/(Instrumental)	1987	—	—	3.00
❑ 53211	Lovin' on Next to Nothin'/(Instrumental)	1988	—	—	3.00
❑ 53211 [PS]	Lovin' on Next to Nothin'/(Instrumental)	1988	—	—	3.00
❑ 53351	It's Gonna Take All Our Love/(Instrumental)	1988	—	—	3.00
❑ 53657	Licence to Kill/You	1989	—	—	3.00
❑ 53676	Licence to Kill/Pam	1989	—	—	3.00
—B-side by National Philharmonic Orchestra					
❑ 54117	Men/(Instrumental)	1991	—	—	3.00
SCOTTI BROS.					
❑ 06267	Loving on Borrowed Time (Love Theme from Cobra)/Angel of the City	1986	—	—	3.00
—A-side: Gladys Knight and Bill Medley; B-side: Robert Tepper					
SOUL					
❑ 35023	Just Walk in My Shoes/Stepping Closer to Your Heart	1966	2.00	4.00	8.00
❑ 35033	Take Me in Your Arms and Love Me/Do You Love Me Just a Little More?	1967	2.00	4.00	8.00
❑ 35034	Everybody Needs Love/Since I've Lost You	1967	2.00	4.00	8.00
❑ 35039	I Heard It Through the Grapevine/It's Time to Go Now	1967	2.50	5.00	10.00
❑ 35042	The End of Our Road/Don't Let Her Take Your Love from Me	1968	2.00	4.00	8.00
❑ 35045	It Should Have Been Me/You Don't Love MeNo More	1968	2.00	4.00	8.00
❑ 35047	I Wish It Would Rain/It's Summer	1968	2.00	4.00	8.00
❑ 35057	Didn't You Know (You'd Have to Cry Sometime)/Keep an Eye	1969	2.00	4.00	8.00
❑ 35063	The Nitty Gritty/Got Myself a Good Man	1969	2.00	4.00	8.00
❑ 35068	Friendship Train/Cloud Nine	1969	2.00	4.00	8.00
❑ 35071	You Need Love Like I Do (Don't You)/You're My Everything	1970	2.00	4.00	8.00
❑ 35078	If I Were Your Woman/The Tracks of My Tears	1970	—	3.50	7.00
❑ 35083	I Don't Want to Do Wrong/Is There a Place In His Heart for Me	1971	—	3.00	6.00
❑ 35091	Make Me the Woman You Come Home To/If You're Gonna Leave (Just Leave)	1972	—	3.00	6.00
❑ 35094	Help Me Make It Through the Night/If You're Gonna Leave (Just Leave)	1972	—	3.00	6.00
❑ 35098	Neither One of Us (Wants to Be the First to Say Goodbye)/Can't Give It Up No More	1972	—	3.00	6.00
❑ 35105	Daddy Could Swear I Declare/For Once In My LIfe	1973	—	3.00	6.00
❑ 35107	All I Need Is Time/The Only Time You Love Me (Is When You're Losing Me)	1973	—	3.00	6.00
❑ 35111	Betwen Her Goodbye and My Hello/This Child Needs Its Father	1974	—	3.00	6.00
TRIP					
❑ 3004	It Hurt Me So Bad/What Will Become of Me	1973	—	3.00	6.00
❑ 3004 [PS]	It Hurt Me So Bad/What Will Become of Me	1973	3.00	6.00	12.00
VEE JAY					
❑ 386	Every Beat of My Heart/Room in Your Heart	1961	5.00	10.00	20.00
—By "The Pips"					
❑ 386	Every Beat of My Heart/Ain'tcha Got Some Room (In Your Heart for Me)	1961	5.00	10.00	20.00
—By "The Pips"; same B-side, different title					
❑ 545	A Love Like Mine/Queen of Tears	1963	5.00	10.00	20.00

KNIGHT, JEAN

Number	Title (A Side/B Side)	Yr	VG	VG+	NM
CHELSEA					
❑ 3020	Don't Ask for 24 Hours/Hold Back the Night	1975	—	2.50	5.00
❑ 3035	Jesse James Is an Outlaw/Hold Back the Night	1975	—	2.50	5.00
COTILLION					
❑ 46020	You Got the Papers (But I Got the Man)/Anything You Can Do (I Can Do As Well)	1981	—	2.00	4.00
❑ 46027	Keep It Comin'/One on One	1981	—	2.00	4.00
❑ 47002	You Show Me Yours, I'll Show You Mine/(B-side unknown)	1982	—	2.00	4.00
—All of the above with Premium					
DIAL					
❑ 1026	Dirt/Jesse Joe	1974	—	2.50	5.00
ICHIBAN					
❑ 97-422	Bill/Bus Stop	1997	—	—	3.00
JETSTREAM					
❑ 706	Doggin' Around/The Man That Left Me	1965	2.50	5.00	10.00
MIRAGE					
❑ 99606	Let the Good Times Roll/Magic	1985	—	—	3.00
❑ 99643	My Toot Toot/My Heart Is Willing (And My Body Is Too)	1985	—	—	3.00
❑ 99643 [PS]	My Toot Toot/My Heart Is Willing (And My Body Is Too)	1985	—	—	3.00
STAX					
❑ 0088	Mr. Big Stuff/Why I Keep Living These Memories	1971	—	3.00	6.00
❑ 0105	You Think You're Hot Stuff/Don't Talk About Jody	1971	—	2.50	5.00
❑ 0116	Carry On/Call Me Your Fool	1972	—	2.50	5.00
❑ 0136	Helping Man/Pick Up the Pieces	1972	—	2.50	5.00
❑ 0150	Do Me/Save the Last Kiss for Me	1972	—	2.50	5.00
TRIBE					
❑ 8304	Lonesome Tonight/Love	1964	3.00	6.00	12.00
❑ 8306	T'Ain't It the Truth/I'm So Glad for Your Sake	1965	3.00	6.00	12.00
❑ 8313	Anyone Can Love Him/A Tear	1966	3.00	6.00	12.00

KNIGHT, ROBERT

Number	Title (A Side/B Side)	Yr	VG	VG+	NM
DOT					
❑ 16256	Because/Dance Only with Me	1961	3.00	6.00	12.00
❑ 16303	Free Me/The Other Half of Man	1962	3.00	6.00	12.00
ELF					
❑ 90019	Isn't It Lonely Together/We'd Better Stop	1968	—	3.00	6.00
❑ 90030	Smokey/If I Had My Way	1969	—	3.00	6.00
❑ 90037	I Only Have Eyes for You/I'm Sticking with You	1969	—	3.00	6.00
MONUMENT					
❑ 8612	Better Get Ready for Love/Somebody's Baby	1974	—	2.50	5.00
❑ 8629	Dynamite/The Outsider	1974	—	2.50	5.00
PRIVATE STOCK					
❑ 45038	I'm Coming Home to You/(B-side unknown)	1975	—	2.50	5.00
❑ 45069	Second Chance/Glitter Lady	1976	—	2.50	5.00
❑ 45118	I've Got News for You/(B-side unknown)	1976	—	2.50	5.00
RISING SONS					
❑ 705	Everlasting Love/Somebody's Baby	1967	2.00	4.00	8.00
❑ 707	Blessed Are the Lonely/It's Been Worth It All	1967	—	3.00	6.00
❑ 708	Power of Love/Love on a Mountain Top	1968	—	3.00	6.00

KNIGHT, SONNY

Number	Title (A Side/B Side)	Yr	VG	VG+	NM
ALADDIN					
❑ 3357	But Officer/Dear Wonderful God	1957	7.50	15.00	30.00
AURA					
❑ 403	If You Want This Love/I Just Called to Say Hello	1964	2.00	4.00	8.00
❑ 4505	Love Me As Though There Were No Tomorrow/Fool Like Me	1964	2.00	4.00	8.00
❑ 4505 [PS]	Love Me As Though There Were No Tomorrow/Fool Like Me	1964	5.00	10.00	20.00
❑ 4508	Rose Mary/(B-side unknown)	1965	2.00	4.00	8.00
A&M					
❑ 718	Evil Minded Woman/Georgia Town	1963	2.50	5.00	10.00
❑ 728	Be True to Your Dog/State Street	1964	2.50	5.00	10.00
DOT					
❑ 15507	Confidential/Jailbird	1956	5.00	10.00	20.00
—Originals have maroon labels					
❑ 15507	Confidential/Jailbird	1956	3.75	7.50	15.00
—Second pressings have black labels					
❑ 15542	End of a Dream/Worthless and Lowdown	1957	3.75	7.50	15.00
❑ 15597	Lovesick Blues/Insha Allot	1957	3.75	7.50	15.00
❑ 15635	Dedicated to You/Short Walk	1957	3.75	7.50	15.00
FIFO					
❑ 102	Cold, Cold Night/Saving My Love	1961	3.75	7.50	15.00
❑ 105	A Swingin' Door/(B-side unknown)	1961	3.75	7.50	15.00
MERCURY					
❑ 72033	Just One More Chance/Lost Child	1962	2.50	5.00	10.00
ORIGINAL SOUND					
❑ 2	Once in Awhile/School's Out	1959	5.00	10.00	20.00
❑ 18	Those Oldies But Goodies Are Dedicated to You/She Had Me Reelin'	1961	3.75	7.50	15.00
SPECIALTY					
❑ 594	Keep a-Walkin'/My Baby Don't Want Me	1957	3.75	7.50	15.00
STARLA					
❑ 1	Dedicated to You/Short Walk	1957	7.50	15.00	30.00
❑ 10	Once in a While/School's Out	1958	3.75	7.50	15.00
VITA					
❑ 137	Confidential/Jailbird	1956	10.00	20.00	40.00
WORLD PACIFIC					
❑ 403	If You Want This Love/I Just Called to Say Hello	1964	3.00	6.00	12.00
❑ 77811	If I May/Need Your Love So Bad	1966	2.00	4.00	8.00
❑ 77832	Angel Love/If I Ruled the World	1966	2.00	4.00	8.00
❑ 77858	A Quiet Man/I Can't Let You Go	1966	6.25	12.50	25.00
—This record exists as a promo at least (we have listed it as "Unreleased" in the past)					

KNIGHT, TERRY, AND THE PACK

Group evloved into GRAND FUNK RAILROAD.

Number	Title (A Side/B Side)	Yr	VG	VG+	NM
A&M					
❑ 769	Kids Will Be the Same/You Lie	1965	3.75	7.50	15.00
CAMEO					
❑ 482	Forever and a Day/Lizbeth Peach	1967	2.50	5.00	10.00
❑ 495	Come Home Baby/Dirty Lady	1967	2.50	5.00	10.00
CAPITOL					
❑ 2174	Without a Woman/Let Me Stand Next to Your Fire	1968	3.00	6.00	12.00
—As "The Pack"					
❑ 2409	Such a Lonely Life/Lullaby	1969	2.50	5.00	10.00
❑ 2506	St. Paul/(Legend of) William and Mary	1969	2.50	5.00	10.00
❑ 2737	I'll Keep Waiting Patiently/Lullaby	1970	2.50	5.00	10.00
LUCKY ELEVEN					
❑ 003	Harlem Shuffle/I've Got News for You	1965	4.00	8.00	16.00
—As "The Pack"					
❑ 007	Does It Matter to You Girl/Wide Trackin'	1965	4.00	8.00	16.00
—As "The Fabulous Pack"					
❑ 007 [PS]	Does It Matter to You Girl/Wide Trackin'	1965	6.25	12.50	25.00
—As "The Fabulous Pack"					
❑ 225	How Much More/I've Been Told	1966	3.75	7.50	15.00
❑ 226	I Got Love/Better Man Than I	1966	3.75	7.50	15.00
❑ 228	Lady Jane/Lovin' Kind	1966	3.75	7.50	15.00
❑ 229	What's On Your Mind/A Change on the Way	1966	3.75	7.50	15.00
❑ 230	I (Who Have Nothing)/Numbers	1966	3.75	7.50	15.00
❑ 235	This Precious Time/Love, Love, Love, Love, Love	1967	3.75	7.50	15.00
❑ 236	One Monkey Don't Stop No Show/The Train	1967	3.75	7.50	15.00
WINGATE					
❑ 007	The Tears Come Rollin'/The Colour of My Love	1965	6.25	12.50	25.00
—As "The Pack"					

KNIGHT RIDERS, THE

Featuring BILLY VERA.

Number	Title (A Side/B Side)	Yr	VG	VG+	NM
UNITED ARTISTS					
❑ 366	Annie's Place/Unchained Melody	1961	6.25	12.50	25.00

KNIGHTS, THE

Both are probably by different groups.

Number	Title (A Side/B Side)	Yr	VG	VG+	NM
CAPITOL					
❑ 5302	Hot Rod High/Theme for Teen Love	1964	12.50	25.00	50.00
FELSTED					
❑ 8640	White Fang/Night Train	1962	3.00	6.00	12.00

KNOCKOUTS, THE (1)

Number	Title (A Side/B Side)	Yr	VG	VG+	NM
SHAD					
❑ 5013	Darling Lorraine/Riot in Room 3C	1959	12.50	25.00	50.00
—With long ending on A-side					
❑ 5013	Darling Lorraine/Riot in Room 3C	1959	6.25	12.50	25.00
—With short ending on A-side					
❑ 5018	Please Be Mine/Rich Boy, Poor Boy	1960	6.25	12.50	25.00

KNOCKOUTS, THE (U)

The records on Scepter and Tribute are by the same group, but we're not sure if they are by group (1) or a different group. The MGM group may be different or the same, too; again, we're not sure.

Number	Title (A Side/B Side)	Yr	VG	VG+	NM
MGM					
❑ 13010	Fever/You Can Take My Girl	1961	5.00	10.00	20.00
SCEPTER					
❑ 1269	Got My Mojo Workin'/Every Day of the Week	1964	3.00	6.00	12.00
TRIBUTE					
❑ 199	Got My Mojo Working (Part 1)/Got My Mojo Working (Part 2)	1964	3.75	7.50	15.00
❑ 201	Tweet-Tweet/What's On Your Mind	1964	4.00	8.00	16.00

KNOPFLER, MARK

Also see DIRE STRAITS.

Number	Title (A Side/B Side)	Yr	VG	VG+	NM
WARNER BROS.					
❑ 7-16779	The Last Laugh/Who's Your Baby Now	2000	—	2.50	5.00
—Withdrawn on day of release; Van Morrison appears on A-side but is not credited					
❑ 7-16780	What It Is/Silvertown Blues	2000	—	—	3.00

KNOTT SISTERS, THE

Number	Title (A Side/B Side)	Yr	VG	VG+	NM
BIG TOP					
❑ 3003	Undivided Attention/Sun Glasses	1958	25.00	50.00	100.00

KNOX, BUDDY

Number	Title (A Side/B Side)	Yr	VG	VG+	NM
LIBERTY					
❑ 55290	Lovey Dovey/I Got You	1960	3.00	6.00	12.00
❑ 55305	Ling, Ting, Tong/The Kisses	1961	3.00	6.00	12.00
❑ 55305 [PS]	Ling, Ting, Tong/The Kisses	1961	7.50	15.00	30.00
❑ 55366	All By Myself/Three Eyed Man	1961	3.00	6.00	12.00
❑ 55411	Cha-Hua-Hua/Open	1962	3.00	6.00	12.00
❑ 55473	She's Gone/There's Only Me	1962	3.00	6.00	12.00
❑ 55503	Dear Abby/Three Way Love Affair	1962	3.00	6.00	12.00
❑ 55592	Shadaroom/Tomorrow Is a-Comin'	1963	2.50	5.00	10.00
❑ 55650	Thanks a Lot/Hitchhike Back to Georgia	1963	2.50	5.00	10.00
❑ 55694	Good Lovin'/All Time Loser	1964	2.50	5.00	10.00
REPRISE					
❑ 0395	Livin' in a House Full of Love/Good Time Girl	1965	2.50	5.00	10.00
❑ 0431	A Lover's Question/You Said Goodbye	1965	2.50	5.00	10.00
❑ 0463	A White Sport Coat/That Don't Do Me No Good	1966	2.50	5.00	10.00
❑ 0501	Love Has Many Ways/Sixteen Feet of Patio	1966	2.50	5.00	10.00
ROULETTE					
❑ 4002	Party Doll/My Baby's Gone	1957	12.50	25.00	50.00
—Maroon label, silver print, with roulette wheel around outside					
❑ 4002	Party Doll/My Baby's Gone	1957	7.50	15.00	30.00
—Red label, roulette wheel on top half of label					
❑ 4002	Party Doll/My Baby's Gone	1957	6.25	12.50	25.00
—Red label, no roulette wheel					
❑ 4002	Party Doll/My Baby's Gone	1957	10.00	20.00	40.00
—Red label, black print, with roulette wheel around outside					

Number	Title (A Side/B Side)	Yr	VG	VG+	NM
❑ 4002	Party Doll/My Baby's Gone	1958	3.75	7.50	15.00
—White label with color spokes					
❑ 4009	Rock Your Little Baby to Sleep/Don't Make Me Cry	1957	10.00	20.00	40.00
—Red label with roulette wheel around outside					
❑ 4009	Rock Your Little Baby to Sleep/Don't Make Me Cry	1957	6.25	12.50	25.00
—Red label, roulette wheel on top half of label					
❑ 4009	Rock Your Little Baby to Sleep/Don't Make Me Cry	1957	5.00	10.00	20.00
—Red label, no roulette wheel					
❑ 4018	Hula Love/Devil Woman	1957	6.25	12.50	25.00
❑ 4042	Swingin' Daddy/Whenever I'm Lonely	1958	6.25	12.50	25.00
❑ 4082	Somebody Touched Me/C'mon Baby	1958	6.25	12.50	25.00
❑ 4120	That's Why I Cry/Teaseable, Pleaseable You	1958	6.25	12.50	25.00
❑ 4140	I Think I'm Gonna Kill Myself/To Be with You	1959	6.25	12.50	25.00
❑ 4179	Taste of the Blues/I Ain't Sharin' Sharon	1959	6.25	12.50	25.00
❑ 4262	Long Lonely Nights/Storm Clouds	1960	6.25	12.50	25.00
RUFF					
❑ 1001	Jo-Ann/Don't Make a Ripple	1965	2.50	5.00	10.00
TRIPLE D					
❑ 798	Party Doll/I'm Stickin' With You	1956	250.00	500.00	1000.
—B-side by Jimmy Bowen					
UNITED ARTISTS					
❑ 50301	This Time Tomorrow/Gypsy Man	1968	2.00	4.00	8.00
❑ 50463	Today My Sleepless Nights Came Back to Town/A Million Years or So	1968	2.00	4.00	8.00
❑ 50526	God Knows I Love You/Night Runners	1969	2.00	4.00	8.00
❑ 50596	Salt Lake City/I'm Only Rockin'	1969	2.00	4.00	8.00
❑ 50644	Yesterday Is Gone/Back to New Orleans	1970	—	3.00	6.00
❑ 50722	White Dove/Glory Train	1970	—	3.00	6.00
❑ 50789	Come Softly to Me/Travelin' Light	1971	—	3.00	6.00

KODAKS, THE

FURY

Number	Title (A Side/B Side)	Yr	VG	VG+	NM
❑ 1007	Teenager's Dream/Little Boy and Girl	1957	20.00	40.00	80.00
❑ 1015	Oh Gee Oh Gosh/(B-side unknown)	1957	15.00	30.00	60.00
❑ 1020	Runaround Baby/Guardian Angel	1958	15.00	30.00	60.00

KOKOMO (1)

Pseudonym for producer Jimmy "Wiz" Wisner.

FELSTED

Number	Title (A Side/B Side)	Yr	VG	VG+	NM
❑ 8612	Asia Minor/Roy's Tune	1961	2.50	5.00	10.00
❑ 8612 [PS]	Asia Minor/Roy's Tune	1961	3.75	7.50	15.00
❑ 8622	Humorous/Theme from a Silent Movie	1961	2.00	4.00	8.00
❑ 8628	Piano Rhapsody/Sweet Memories	1961	2.00	4.00	8.00
❑ 8635	Journey Home/Like Teen	1961	2.00	4.00	8.00
❑ 8641	Poinciana/The Good Earth	1962	2.00	4.00	8.00

KOKOMO (2)

COLUMBIA

Number	Title (A Side/B Side)	Yr	VG	VG+	NM
❑ 3-10207	Kitty Sittin' Pretty/It Ain't Cool (To Be Cool No More)	1975	—	2.50	5.00
❑ 3-10213	Kitty Sittin' Pretty/Anytime	1975	—	2.50	5.00
❑ 3-10283	Rise and Shine/Do It Right	1976	—	2.50	5.00
❑ 3-10380	Use Your Imagination/That's Enough	1976	—	2.50	5.00

KOKOMOS, THE

Number	Title (A Side/B Side)	Yr	VG	VG+	NM
GONE					
❑ 5134	Mama's Boy/Yours Truly	1962	3.75	7.50	15.00
JOSIE					
❑ 906	Open House Party/No Lies	1963	3.00	6.00	12.00

KOOBAS, THE

Number	Title (A Side/B Side)	Yr	VG	VG+	NM
CAPITOL					
❑ 2416	First Cut Is the Deepest/Walking Out	1969	2.00	4.00	8.00
KAPP					
❑ 737	Take Me for a Little While/Give a Little Bit	1965	3.75	7.50	15.00
❑ 737 [PS]	Take Me for a Little While/Give a Little Bit	1965	5.00	10.00	20.00

KOOL AND THE GANG

DE-LITE

Number	Title (A Side/B Side)	Yr	VG	VG+	NM
❑ 519	Kool and the Gang/Raw Hamburger	1969	—	3.00	6.00
❑ 523	The Gangs Back Again/Kools Back Again	1969	—	3.00	6.00
❑ 525	Kool It (Here Comes the Fuzz)/Can't Stop	1970	—	3.00	6.00
❑ 529	Let the Music Take Your Mind/Chocolate Buttermilk	1970	—	3.00	6.00
❑ 534	Funky Man/1,2,3,4,5,6,7,8	1970	—	3.00	6.00
❑ 538	Who's Gonna Take the Weight (Part One)/Who's Gonna Take the Weight (Part Two)	1970	—	3.00	6.00
❑ 540	I Want to Take You Higher/Pneumonia	1971	—	3.00	6.00
❑ 543	The Penguin/Lucky for Me	1971	—	3.00	6.00
❑ 544	N.T. (Part One)/N.T. (Part Two)	1971	—	3.00	6.00
❑ 546	Love the Life You Live, Part I/Love the Life You Live, Part II	1972	—	3.00	6.00
❑ 547	You've Lost That Lovin' Feeling/Ike's Mood	1972	—	3.00	6.00
❑ 550	Music Is the Messenger, Part I/Music Is the Messenger, Part II	1972	—	3.00	6.00
❑ 552	Good Times/The Frog	1972	—	3.00	6.00
❑ 553	Funky Granny/Blowing with the Wind	1973	—	3.00	6.00
❑ 555	Country Junkie/I Remember John W. Coltrane	1973	—	3.00	6.00
❑ 557	Funky Stuff/More Funky Stuff	1973	—	3.00	6.00
❑ 559	Jungle Boogie/North, East, South, West	1973	—	2.50	5.00
❑ 561	Hollywood Swinging/Dujii	1974	—	2.50	5.00
❑ 801	Ladies Night/If You Feel Like Dancin'	1979	—	2.00	4.00
❑ 802	Too Hot/Tonight's the Night	1979	—	2.00	4.00
❑ 804	Hangin' Out/Got You Into My Life	1980	—	2.00	4.00
❑ 807	Celebration/Morning Star	1980	—	2.00	4.00
❑ 810	Take It to the Top/Love Affair	1981	—	2.00	4.00
❑ 813	Jones Vs. Jones/Night People	1981	—	2.00	4.00
❑ 815	Take My Heart/Just Friends	1981	—	2.50	5.00
—First pressings have no subtitle					
❑ 815	Take My Heart (You Can Have It If You Want It)/Just Friends	1981	—	2.00	4.00
❑ 816	Steppin' Out/Love Festival	1982	—	2.00	4.00
❑ 818	Get Down On It/Steppin' Out	1982	—	2.00	4.00
❑ 822	Big Fun/No Show	1982	—	2.00	4.00
❑ 824	Let's Go Dancin' (Ooh, La, La, La)/Be My Lady	1982	—	2.00	4.00
❑ 825	Street Kids/As One	1983	—	2.00	4.00
❑ 829	Joanna/A Place for Us	1983	—	—	3.00
❑ 830	Tonight/September Love	1984	—	—	3.00
❑ 831	Straight Ahead/September Love	1984	—	—	3.00
❑ 901	Slick Superchick/Life's a Song	1978	—	2.50	5.00
❑ 905	A Place in Space/The Force	1978	—	2.50	5.00
❑ 909	I Like Music/It's All You Need	1978	—	2.50	5.00
❑ 910	Everybody's Dancin'/Stay Awhile	1978	—	2.50	5.00
❑ 1562	Higher Plane/Wild Is Love	1974	—	2.50	5.00
❑ 1563	Rhyme Tyme People/Father, Father	1974	—	2.50	5.00
❑ 1567	Spirit of the Boogie/Summer Madness	1975	—	2.50	5.00
❑ 1573	Caribbean Festival/Caribbean Festival (Disco Version)	1975	—	2.50	5.00
❑ 1577	Winter Sadness/Father, Father	1975	—	2.50	5.00
❑ 1579	Love and Understanding (Come Together)/Sunshine and Love	1976	—	2.50	5.00
❑ 1583	Universal Sound/Ancestral Ceremony	1976	—	2.50	5.00
❑ 1586	Open Sesame — Part 1/Open Sesame — Part 2	1976	—	2.50	5.00
❑ 1590	Super Band/Sunshine	1977	—	2.50	5.00
❑ 880431-7	Misled/Rollin'	1984	—	—	3.00
❑ 880623-7	Fresh/In the Heart	1985	—	—	3.00
❑ 880623-7 [PS]	Fresh/In the Heart	1985	—	2.00	4.00
❑ 880869-7	Cherish/(Instrumental)	1985	—	—	3.00
❑ 880869-7 [PS]	Cherish/(Instrumental)	1985	—	2.00	4.00
❑ 884199-7	Emergency/You Are the One	1985	—	—	3.00
MERCURY					
❑ 870513-7	Rags to Riches/Rags to Riches (Remix)	1988	—	—	3.00
❑ 870513-7 [PS]	Rags to Riches/Rags to Riches (Remix)	1988	—	—	3.00
❑ 872038-7	Strong/Funky Stuff	1988	—	—	3.00
❑ 874402-7	Raindrops/(B-side unknown)	1989	—	—	3.00
❑ 876072-7	Never Give Up/(B-side unknown)	1989	—	—	3.00
❑ 888074-7	Victory/Bad Woman	1986	—	—	3.00
❑ 888074-7 [PS]	Victory/Bad Woman	1986	—	—	3.00
❑ 888292-7	Stone Love/Dance Champion	1987	—	—	3.00
❑ 888292-7 [PS]	Stone Love/Dance Champion	1987	—	—	3.00
❑ 888712-7	Holiday/Holiday (Jam Mix)	1987	—	—	3.00
❑ 888712-7 [PS]	Holiday/Holiday (Jam Mix)	1987	—	—	3.00
❑ 888867-7	In a Special Way/God's Country	1987	—	—	3.00
❑ 888867-7 [PS]	In a Special Way/God's Country	1987	—	—	3.00

KOOL GENTS

DEE CLARK was a member of this group.

VEE JAY

Number	Title (A Side/B Side)	Yr	VG	VG+	NM
❑ 173	This Is the Night/Do Ya Do	1956	50.00	100.00	200.00
❑ 207	You Know/I Can't Help Myself	1956	50.00	100.00	200.00

KOOPER, AL

Also see BLOOD, SWEAT AND TEARS; THE BLUES PROJECT.

Number	Title (A Side/B Side)	Yr	VG	VG+	NM
AURORA					
❑ 164	New York's My Town/My Voice, My Piano	1967	3.00	6.00	12.00
COLUMBIA					
❑ 03312	Two Sides (To Every Situation)/Snowblind	1982	—	2.00	4.00
❑ 44748	You Never Know Who Your Friends Are/Soft Landing on the Moon	1969	—	2.50	5.00
❑ 44811	I Stand Alone/Hey, Western Union Man	1969	—	2.50	5.00
❑ 45093	One Room Country Shack/Bury My Body	1970	—	2.50	5.00
❑ 45148	She Gets Me Where I Live/God Sheds His Grace on Thee	1970	—	2.50	5.00
❑ 45179	Love Theme from "The Landlord"/Brand New Day	1970	—	2.50	5.00
❑ 45243	I Got a Woman/Easy Does It	1970	—	2.50	5.00
❑ 45412	John the Baptist/Back on My Feet	1971	—	2.50	5.00
❑ 45566	The Monkey Time/Bended Knees (Please Don't Let Me Down)	1972	—	2.50	5.00
❑ 45691	Sam Stone/Be Real	1972	—	2.50	5.00
❑ 45735	Jolie/Be Real	1972	—	2.50	5.00
UNITED ARTISTS					
❑ XW879	This Diamond Ring/Hollywood Vampire	1976	—	2.00	4.00
VERVE FOLKWAYS					
❑ 5026	Changes/Pack Up Your Sorrows	1966	3.00	6.00	12.00

KORNER, ALEXIS

COLUMBIA

Number	Title (A Side/B Side)	Yr	VG	VG+	NM
❑ 10166	Get Off My Cloud/Strange N' Deranged	1975	2.00	4.00	8.00

KRAFTWERK

Number	Title (A Side/B Side)	Yr	VG	VG+	NM
CAPITOL					
❑ 4211	Radioactivity/Antenna	1976	—	2.50	5.00
❑ 4211 [PS]	Radioactivity/Antenna	1976	2.00	4.00	8.00
❑ 4460	Trans-Europe Express/Franz Schubert	1977	—	2.50	5.00
❑ 4620	Neon Lights/The Robots	1978	—	2.50	5.00
VERTIGO					
❑ 203	Autobahn/Morgan Spaziergance	1975	2.00	4.00	8.00
❑ 204	Mitternacht (Midnight)/Kometen Melodie (Comet Melody 2)	1975	2.00	4.00	8.00
WARNER BROS.					
❑ 28441	The Telephone Call/Der Telefon Anruf	1987	—	—	3.00
❑ 28441 [PS]	The Telephone Call/Der Telefon Anruf	1987	—	—	3.00
❑ 28532	Musique Non-Stop (Long)/Musique Non-Stop (Short)	1986	—	—	2.00
❑ 28532 [PS]	Musique Non-Stop (Long)/Musique Non-Stop (Short)	1986	—	—	2.00
❑ 29342	Tour de France (Remix)/Tour de France (French)	1984	—	—	3.00
❑ 49723	Pocket Calculator/Dentaku	1981	—	—	3.00
❑ 49723	Pocket Calculator/Dentaku	1981	—	2.50	5.00
—Yellow vinyl					

Number	Title (A Side/B Side)	Yr	VG	VG+	NM
❑ 49723 [PS]	Pocket Calculator/Dentaku	1981	—	2.50	5.00
—Plastic sleeve that goes with yellow vinyl pressing					
❑ 49795	Numbers/Computer Love	1981	—	—	3.00

KRAMER, BILLY J., AND THE DAKOTAS

Also see THE DAKOTAS.

Number	Title (A Side/B Side)	Yr	VG	VG+	NM
EPIC					
❑ 10331	1941/His Love Is Just a Lie	1968	2.50	5.00	10.00
IMPERIAL					
❑ 66027	Little Children/Bad to Me	1964	3.00	6.00	12.00
❑ 66048	I'll Keep You Satisfied/I Know	1964	3.00	6.00	12.00
❑ 66051	From a Window/I'll Be On My Way	1964	3.00	6.00	12.00
❑ 66051 [PS]	From a Window/I'll Be On My Way	1964	6.25	12.50	25.00
❑ 66085	It's Gotta Last Forever/They Remind Me of You	1965	3.00	6.00	12.00
❑ 66115	Trains and Boats and Planes/I'll Be On My Way	1965	3.00	6.00	12.00
❑ 66115	Trains and Boats and Planes/That's the Way I Feel	1965	2.50	5.00	10.00
❑ 66135	Irresistible You/Twilight Time	1965	2.50	5.00	10.00
❑ 66143	I'll Be Doggone/Neon City	1965	2.50	5.00	10.00
❑ 66210	You Make Me Feel Like Someone/Take My Hand	1966	2.50	5.00	10.00
LIBERTY					
❑ 55586	Do You Want to Know a Secret/I'll Be On My Way	1963	7.50	15.00	30.00
❑ 55618	The Cruel Surf/The Millionaire	1963	10.00	20.00	40.00
❑ 55626	Bad to Me/I Call Your Name	1963	7.50	15.00	30.00
❑ 55643	I'll Keep You Satisfied/I Know	1963	7.50	15.00	30.00
❑ 55667	Bad to Me/Do You Want to Know a Secret	1964	6.25	12.50	25.00
❑ 55687	Little Children/They Remind Me of You	1964	—	—	—
—Unreleased					

KRISTOFFERSON, KRIS

Also see WILLIE NELSON.

Number	Title (A Side/B Side)	Yr	VG	VG+	NM
COLUMBIA					
❑ 04881	Highwayman/The Human Condition	1985	—	—	3.00
—A-side: Willie Nelson/Waylon Jennings/Johnny Cash/Kris Kristofferson; B-side: Nelson, Cash					
❑ 04881 [PS]	Highwayman/The Human Condition	1985	—	2.00	4.00
—A-side: Willie Nelson/Waylon Jennings/Johnny Cash/Kris Kristofferson; B-side: Nelson, Cash					
❑ 05594	Desperadoes Waiting for a Train/The Twentieth Century Is Almost Over	1985	—	—	3.00
—A-side: Willie Nelson/Waylon Jennings/Johnny Cash/Kris Kristofferson; B-side: Nelson, Cash					
❑ 08406	Highwayman/Desperadoes Waiting for a Train	1988	—	—	3.00
—Waylon Jennings/Willie Nelson/Johnny Cash/Kris Kristofferson; reissue					
❑ 08406	Highwayman/Desperadoes Waiting for a Train	1988	—	—	3.00
—Waylon Jennings/Willie Nelson/Johnny Cash/Kris Kristofferson; reissue					
❑ 10525	Watch Closely Now/Crippled Crow	1977	—	2.00	4.00
❑ 10731	The Fighter/Forever in Your Love	1978	—	2.00	4.00
❑ 11160	Prove It to You One More Time Again/Fallen Angel	1979	—	2.00	4.00
❑ 11383	I'll Take Any Chance I Can with You/Maybe You Heard	1980	—	2.00	4.00
❑ 60507	Nobody Loves Anybody Anymore/Maybe You Heard	1981	—	2.00	4.00
❑ 73381	Born and Raised in Black and White/Texas	1990	—	—	3.00
—The Highwaymen (Waylon Jennings/Willie Nelson/Johnny Cash/Kris Kristofferson)					
❑ 73572	American Remains/Texas	1990	—	—	3.00
—The Highwaymen (Waylon Jennings/Willie Nelson/Johnny Cash/Kris Kristofferson)					
EPIC					
❑ 10225	Golden Idol/Killing Time	1967	3.75	7.50	15.00
LIBERTY					
❑ S7-18486	It Is What It Is/The Devil's Right Hand	1995	—	—	3.00
—By The Highwaymen					
MERCURY					
❑ 888345-7	They Killed Him/Anthem '84	1987	—	—	3.00
❑ 888554-7	Love Is the Way/This Old Road	1987	—	—	3.00
❑ 888723-7	El Coyote/They Killed Him	1987	—	—	3.00
MONUMENT					
❑ 1210	Sunday Morning Comin' Down/To Beat the Devil	1970	2.00	4.00	8.00
❑ 8525	Loving Her Was Easier (Than Anything I'll Ever Do Again)/Epitaph	1971	—	3.00	6.00
❑ 8531	The Taker/Pilgrim: Chapter 33	1971	—	3.00	6.00
❑ 8536	Josie/Border Lord	1972	—	3.00	6.00
❑ 8558	Jesus Was a Capricorn/Enough for You	1972	—	3.00	6.00
❑ 8564	Jesse Younger/Give It Time to Be Tender	1973	—	3.00	6.00
❑ 8571	Why Me/Help Me	1973	—	2.50	5.00
❑ 8618	I May Smoke Too Much/Lights of Magdala	1974	—	2.50	5.00
❑ 8658	Easy, Come On/Rocket to Star	1975	—	2.00	4.00
❑ 8679	If It's All the Same to You/The Year 2000 Minus 25	1975	—	2.00	4.00
❑ 8707	The Prisoner/It's Never Gonna Be the Same Again	1976	—	2.00	4.00
❑ 21000	Here Comes That Rainbow Again/(B-side unknown)	1981	—	2.00	4.00

KRISTOFFERSON, KRIS, AND RITA COOLIDGE

Number	Title (A Side/B Side)	Yr	VG	VG+	NM
A&M					
❑ 1475	A Song I'd Like to Sing/From the Bottle to the Bottom	1973	—	2.00	4.00
❑ 1475 [PS]	A Song I'd Like to Sing/From the Bottle to the Bottom	1973	—	3.00	6.00
❑ 1498	Loving Arms/I'm Down	1974	—	2.00	4.00
❑ 2121	Not Everyone Knows/Blue As I Do	1979	—	2.00	4.00
MONUMENT					
❑ 8630	Rain/What'cha Gonna Do	1974	—	2.00	4.00
❑ 8636	Lover Please/Slow Down	1975	—	2.00	4.00
❑ 8646	We Must Have Been Out of Our Minds/Sweet Susannah	1975	—	2.00	4.00

KUBAN, BOB, AND THE IN-MEN

Also see WALTER SCOTT.

Number	Title (A Side/B Side)	Yr	VG	VG+	NM
MUSICLAND U.S.A.					
❑ 20001	The Cheater/Try Me Baby	1966	5.00	10.00	20.00
—With "Vocal by Walter Scott" on both sides' labels					
❑ 20001	The Cheater/Try Me Baby	1966	3.00	6.00	12.00
—With "Vocal by Walter Scott" on only B-side label					
❑ 20001	The Cheater/Try Me Baby	1966	2.50	5.00	10.00
—With no mention of "Vocal by Walter Scott"					
❑ 20006	The Teaser/All I Want	1966	2.50	5.00	10.00
❑ 20007	Drive My Car/The Pretzel	1966	2.50	5.00	10.00
❑ 20013	Harlem Shuffle/Theme from "Virginia Wolff"	1967	2.00	4.00	8.00
❑ 20017	Batman Theme/You Better Run, You Better Hide	1967	2.00	4.00	8.00
NORMAN					
❑ 558	Jerkin' Time/Turn On Your Lovelight	1965	3.00	6.00	12.00
❑ 567	Little Girl/I Don't Want to Know	1965	3.00	6.00	12.00
REPRISE					
❑ 0937	Soul Man/Hard to Handle	1970	2.00	4.00	8.00

KUF-LINX, THE

Number	Title (A Side/B Side)	Yr	VG	VG+	NM
CHALLENGE					
❑ 1013	So Tough/What'cha Gonna Do	1957	10.00	20.00	40.00
❑ 1013	So Tough/What'cha Gonna Do	1958	6.25	12.50	25.00
❑ 59004	Eyeballin'/Service with a Smile	1958	3.75	7.50	15.00
❑ 59015	Climb Love Mountain/All That's Good	1958	3.75	7.50	15.00
❑ 59102	So Tough/What'cha Gonna Do	1961	3.00	6.00	12.00

KUSTOM KINGS, THE

BRUCE JOHNSTON appears on the below.

Number	Title (A Side/B Side)	Yr	VG	VG+	NM
SMASH					
❑ 1883	In My '40 Ford/Clutch Rider	1964	12.50	25.00	50.00

L

LABEEF, SLEEPY

Number	Title (A Side/B Side)	Yr	VG	VG+	NM
COLUMBIA					
❑ 43452	Everybody's Got to Have Somebody (To Love)/You Can't Catch Me	1965	3.00	6.00	12.00
❑ 43875	I Feel a Lot More Like I Do Now/I'm Too Broke	1966	3.00	6.00	12.00
❑ 44068	Sure Beats the Heck Out of Settlin' Down/Schneider	1967	2.50	5.00	10.00
❑ 44261	Completely Destroyed/Go Ahead On Baby	1967	2.50	5.00	10.00
❑ 44455	Every Day/If I'm Right I'm Wrong	1968	2.50	5.00	10.00
CRESCENT					
❑ 102	Turn Me Loose/(B-side unknown)	195?	50.00	100.00	200.00
MERCURY					
❑ 71112	I'm Through/All Alone	1957	25.00	50.00	100.00
❑ 71179	All the Time/Lonely	1957	25.00	50.00	100.00
PICTURE					
❑ 1937	Ride On Josephine/(B-side unknown)	1959	37.50	75.00	150.00
PLANTATION					
❑ 55	Too Much Monkey Business/Got You on My Mind	1970	6.25	12.50	25.00
❑ 66	Asphalt Cowboy/Got You on My Mind	1971	2.50	5.00	10.00
❑ 74	Blackland Farmer/Got You on My Mind	1971	2.50	5.00	10.00
❑ 74 [DJ]	Blackland Farmer (mono/stereo)	1971	3.00	6.00	12.00
—Promo only on green vinyl					
STARDAY					
❑ 292	I'm Through/All Alone	1957	37.50	75.00	150.00
SUN					
❑ 1132	Thunder Road/A Hundred Pounds of Lovin'	1974	—	2.00	4.00
❑ 1133 [DJ]	Ghost Riders in the Sky (same on both sides)	1975	—	2.00	4.00
—Promo only					
❑ 1134	There Ain't Much After Taxes/A Hundred Pounds of Lovin'	1976	—	2.00	4.00
❑ 1137	Good Rockin' Boogie (Part 1)/Good rockin' Boogie (Part 2)	1978	—	2.00	4.00
❑ 1145	Flying Saucers Rock and Roll/Boogie Woogie Country Girl	1979	—	2.00	4.00
WAYSIDE					
❑ 1651	Ride On Josephine/(B-side unknown)	1959	50.00	100.00	200.00
—Wayside titles as "Tommy LaBeef"					
❑ 1652	Walkin' Slowly/(B-side unknown)	1959	62.50	125.00	250.00
❑ 1654	Tore Up/Lonely	1959	75.00	150.00	300.00

LABELLE

Also see PATTI LaBELLE; PATTI LaBELLE AND THE BLUE BELLES.

Number	Title (A Side/B Side)	Yr	VG	VG+	NM
EPIC					
❑ 50048	Lady Marmalade/Space Children	1974	—	3.00	6.00
❑ 50097	Night Bird/What Can I Do for You	1975	—	3.00	6.00
❑ 50140	Messin' My Mind/Take the Night Off	1975	—	3.00	6.00
❑ 50168	Slow Burn/Far As We Felt Like Going	1975	—	3.00	6.00
❑ 50262	Get You Somebody New/Who's Watching the Watcher	1976	—	3.00	6.00
❑ 50315	Isn't It a Shame/Gypsy Moths	1976	—	3.00	6.00
RCA VICTOR					
❑ APBO-0157	Mr. Sunshine Man/Sunshine	1973	2.00	4.00	8.00
❑ 74-0965	Open Up Your Heart/Going Up a Holiday	1973	2.00	4.00	8.00
WARNER BROS.					
❑ 7512	Morning Much Better/Shades of Difference	1971	2.00	4.00	8.00
❑ 7579	Moonshadow/If I Can't Have You	1972	2.00	4.00	8.00
❑ 7624	Touch Me All Over/Ain't It Sad It's All Over	1972	2.00	4.00	8.00

LABELLE, PATTI

Also see LaBELLE; PATTI LaBELLE AND THE BLUE BELLES.

Number	Title (A Side/B Side)	Yr	VG	VG+	NM
ARISTA					
❑ 12929	My Love, Sweet Love/Sittin' Up in My Room	1996	—	—	3.00
—B-side by Brandy					
BEVERLY GLEN					
❑ 2012	Love Has Finally Come at Last/American Dream	1984	—	2.00	4.00
—With Bobby Womack					
❑ 2018	It Takes a Lot of Strength to Say Goodbye/Who's Foolin' Who	1984	—	2.00	4.00
—With Bobby Womack					

Number	Title (A Side/B Side)	Yr	VG	VG+	NM
ELEKTRA					
❑ 69887	The Best Is Yet to Come/Bye Bye Love	1982	—	2.00	4.00
—With Grover Washington Jr.					
EPIC					
❑ 50445	Joy to Have Your Love/Do I Stand a Chance	1977	—	3.00	6.00
❑ 50487	You Are My Friend/I Think About You	1977	—	3.00	6.00
❑ 50510	Since I Don't Have You/Dan Swit Me	1978	—	3.00	6.00
❑ 50550	Teach Me Tonight/Quiet Time	1978	—	3.00	6.00
❑ 50583	Little Girls/You Make It So Hard	1978	—	3.00	6.00
❑ 50659	It's Alright with Me/Music Is My Way of Life	1979	—	2.50	5.00
❑ 50718	Music Is My Way of Life/My Best Was Good Enough	1979	—	2.50	5.00
❑ 50763	Love Is Just a Touch Away/Love and Learn	1979	—	2.50	5.00
❑ 50852	Come and Dance with Me/Release	1980	—	2.50	5.00
❑ 50872	I Don't Go Shopping/Come and Dance with Me	1980	—	2.50	5.00
❑ 50910	Ain't That Enough/Don't Make Your Angel Cry	1980	—	2.50	5.00
MCA					
❑ 52517	New Attitude/Shoot Out	1984	—	2.00	4.00
—B-side by Harold Faltermeyer					
❑ 52517 [PS]	New Attitude/Shoot Out	1984	—	2.00	4.00
❑ 52610	Stir It Up/The Discovery	1985	—	2.00	4.00
—B-side by Harold Faltermeyer					
❑ 52610 [PS]	Stir It Up/The Discovery	1985	—	2.00	4.00
❑ 52770	On My Own/Stir It Up	1986	—	—	3.00
—A-side: With Michael McDonald					
❑ 52770 [PS]	On My Own/Stir It Up	1986	—	2.00	4.00
❑ 52876	Something Special (Is Gonna Happen Tonight)/(Instrumental)	1986	—	—	3.00
❑ 52877	Oh, People/Love Attack	1986	—	—	3.00
❑ 52877 [PS]	Oh, People/Love Attack	1986	—	2.00	4.00
❑ 52945	Kiss Away the Pain/(Instrumental)	1986	—	—	3.00
❑ 53064	The Last Unbroken Heart/Miami Vice: New York Theme	1987	—	—	3.00
—A-side: With Bill Champlin; B-side by Harold Faltermeyer					
❑ 53064 [PS]	The Last Unbroken Heart/Miami Vice: New York Theme	1987	—	—	3.00
❑ 53100	Just the Facts/(Instrumental)	1987	—	—	3.00
❑ 53358	If You Asked Me To/(Instrumental)	1988	—	—	3.00
❑ 53728	Yo Mister/I Can Fly	1989	—	—	3.00
❑ 53774	I Can't Complain/I Can Fly	1989	—	—	3.00
❑ 54481	When You Love Somebody (I'm Saving My Love for You)/Temptation	1992	—	—	3.00
❑ 54513	All Right Now/All Right Now (Remix Dub)	1992	—	—	3.00
❑ 54673	The Right Kinda Lover/(Instrumental)	1993	—	—	3.00
PHILADELPHIA INT'L.					
❑ 02309	Rocking Pneumonia and the Boogie Woogie Flu/Over the Rainbow	1981	—	2.00	4.00
❑ 02655	The Spirit's In It/The Family	1981	—	2.00	4.00
❑ 04248	If Only You Knew/I'll Never, Never Give Up	1983	—	2.00	4.00
❑ 04399	I'm in Love Again/Love, Need and Want It	1984	—	2.00	4.00
❑ 05436	I Can't Forget You/Living Doubt	1985	—	2.00	4.00
❑ 05755	If You Don't Know Me By Now/(Instrumental)	1986	—	2.00	4.00
❑ 05877	Look to the Rainbow/What Can I Do for You	1986	—	2.00	4.00

LABELLE, PATTI, AND THE BLUE BELLES

Also see THE BLUE BELLES; LaBELLE; PATTI LaBELLE AND THE BLUE BELLES.

Number	Title (A Side/B Side)	Yr	VG	VG+	NM
ATLANTIC					
❑ 2311	All or Nothing/You Forgot How to Love	1965	3.00	6.00	12.00
❑ 2318	A Groovy Kind of Love/Over the Rainbow	1966	2.50	5.00	10.00
❑ 2333	Ebb Tide/Patti's Prayer	1966	2.50	5.00	10.00
❑ 2347	I'm Still Waiting/Family Man	1966	2.50	5.00	10.00
❑ 2373	Take Me for a Little While/I Don't Want to Go On Without You	1967	2.50	5.00	10.00
❑ 2390	(There's) Always Something There to Remind Me/Tender Words	1967	2.50	5.00	10.00
❑ 2408	Unchained Melody/Dreamer	1967	2.50	5.00	10.00
❑ 2446	Oh My Love/I Need Your Love	1967	2.50	5.00	10.00
❑ 2548	He's My Man/Wonderful	1968	2.50	5.00	10.00
❑ 2610	Dance to the Rhythm of Love/He's Gone	1969	2.50	5.00	10.00
❑ 2629	Loving Blues/Pride's No Match for Love	1969	2.50	5.00	10.00
❑ 2712	Suffer/Trustin' in You	1970	2.50	5.00	10.00
KING					
❑ 5777	Down the Aisle (Wedding Song)/C'est La Vie	1963	3.75	7.50	15.00
NEWTIME					
❑ 510	Love Me Just a Little/The Joke's On You	1962	5.00	10.00	20.00
NEWTOWN					
❑ 5000	I Sold My Heart to the Junkman/Itty Bitty Twist	1962	5.00	10.00	20.00
—Credited to "The Blue-Belles" but actually recorded by The Starlets					
❑ 5006	I Found a New Love/Pitter Patter	1962	5.00	10.00	20.00
—Most of the Newtown sides credit "The Blue-Belles"					
❑ 5007	Tear After Tear/Go On, This Is Goodbye	1962	5.00	10.00	20.00
❑ 5009	Cool Water/When Johnny Comes Marching Home	1962	5.00	10.00	20.00
❑ 5019	Academy Award/Decatur Street	1963	5.00	10.00	20.00
❑ 5777	Down the Aisle (Wedding Song)/C'est La Vie	1963	3.75	7.50	15.00
NICETOWN					
❑ 5020	You'll Never Walk Alone/Where Are You	1963	3.75	7.50	15.00
PARKWAY					
❑ 896	You'll Never Walk Alone/Decatur Street	1964	3.00	6.00	12.00
❑ 896 [PS]	You'll Never Walk Alone/Decatur Street	1964	20.00	40.00	80.00
❑ 913	One Phone Call/You Will Fill My Eyes No More	1964	3.00	6.00	12.00
❑ 935	Danny Boy/I Believe	1964	3.00	6.00	12.00
PEAK					
❑ 7042	I've Got to Let Him Know/I Sold My Heart to the Junkman	1962	6.25	12.50	25.00
—Credited to "The Blue-Belles" but actually recorded by The Starlets					

LACEWING

Number	Title (A Side/B Side)	Yr	VG	VG+	NM
MAINSTREAM					
❑ 731	Paradox/(B-side unknown)	1971	3.00	6.00	12.00

LADD, CHERYL

Also see JOSIE AND THE PUSSYCATS.

Number	Title (A Side/B Side)	Yr	VG	VG+	NM
CAPITOL					
❑ 4215	Country Love/He's Lookin' More Everyday Like the Man Who Broke My Heart	1976	—	2.50	5.00
❑ 4599	Think It Over/Here Is a Song	1978	—	2.00	4.00
❑ 4599 [PS]	Think It Over/Here Is a Song	1978	—	3.00	6.00
❑ 4650	Good Good Lovin'/Skinnydippin'	1978	—	2.00	4.00
❑ 4650 [PS]	Good Good Lovin'/Skinnydippin'	1978	—	3.00	6.00
❑ 4698	Missing You/Thunder in the Distance	1979	—	2.00	4.00
❑ B-5115	Can't Say No to You/You Make It Beautiful	1982	—	2.00	4.00
—With Frankie Valli					
❑ B-5115 [PS]	Can't Say No to You/You Make It Beautiful	1982	—	2.00	4.00
WARNER BROS.					
❑ 7821	Mama Don't Be Blue/The Family	1974	—	3.00	6.00
❑ 7821 [PS]	Mama Don't Be Blue/The Family	1974	2.50	5.00	10.00

LADDERS, THE

Number	Title (A Side/B Side)	Yr	VG	VG+	NM
HOLIDAY					
❑ 2611	Counting the Stars/I Want to Know	1957	75.00	150.00	300.00
—Red label, double lines					
❑ 2611	Counting the Stars/I Want to Know	196?	20.00	40.00	80.00
—Red label, single line					
VEST					
❑ 826	My Love Is Gone/Hey, Pretty Baby	1959	37.50	75.00	150.00
—No stars around "Vest" logo					
❑ 826	My Love Is Gone/Hey, Pretty Baby	1960	12.50	25.00	50.00
—With stars around "Vest" logo					

LADDINS, THE

Number	Title (A Side/B Side)	Yr	VG	VG+	NM
CENTRAL					
❑ 2602	Now You're Gone/(B-side unknown)	1957	175.00	350.00	700.00
—Black label					
❑ 2602	Now You're Gone/(B-side unknown)	1957	100.00	200.00	400.00
—Yellow label					
❑ 2602	Now You're Gone/(B-side unknown)	1957	25.00	50.00	100.00
—Pink label					
GREY CLIFF					
❑ 721	Yes, Oh Baby Yes/Light a Candle	1959	7.50	15.00	30.00

LADY BUGS, THE

May be three different groups, two different groups, or all the same group.

Number	Title (A Side/B Side)	Yr	VG	VG+	NM
CHATTAHOOCHIE					
❑ 637	How Do You Do It/Liverpool	1964	3.75	7.50	15.00
DEL-FI					
❑ 4233	Sooner or Later/It's the Last Time	1964	5.00	10.00	20.00
LEGRAND					
❑ 1033	Who Sends the Love Note/Fraternity U.S.A.	1964	5.00	10.00	20.00

LADYBIRDS, THE

Number	Title (A Side/B Side)	Yr	VG	VG+	NM
ATCO					
❑ 6329	Memories/Lady Bird	1964	3.00	6.00	12.00
LAWN					
❑ 231	Handsome Boy/Yes I Know	1964	2.50	5.00	10.00

LAINE, DENNY

Also see THE MOODY BLUES; WINGS.

Number	Title (A Side/B Side)	Yr	VG	VG+	NM
ARISTA					
❑ 0511	Japanese Tears/Guess I'm Only Fooling	1980	—	2.00	4.00
CAPITOL					
❑ 4340	It's So Easy-Listen to Me/I'm Lookin' for Someone to Love	1976	—	3.00	6.00
❑ 4425	Heartbeat/Moondreams	1977	—	3.00	6.00
DERAM					
❑ 7509	Ask the People/Say You Don't Mind	1967	3.75	7.50	15.00

LAINE, FRANKIE

Number	Title (A Side/B Side)	Yr	VG	VG+	NM
ABC					
❑ 10891	I'll Take Care of Your Cares/Every Street's a Boulevard	1966	—	3.00	6.00
❑ 10924	Making Memories/Moment of Truth	1967	—	3.00	6.00
❑ 10946	You Wanted Someone to Play With (I Wanted Someone to Love)/The Real Meaning of Love	1967	—	3.00	6.00
❑ 10967	Laura, What's He Got That I Ain't Got/Sometimes (I Just Can't Stand You)	1967	—	3.00	6.00
❑ 10983	You, No One But You/Somewhere There's Someone	1967	—	3.00	6.00
❑ 11032	To Each His Own/I'm Happy to Hear You're Sorry	1967	—	3.00	6.00
❑ 11057	I Don't Want to Set the World On Fire/I Found You	1968	—	3.00	6.00
❑ 11097	Forsaking All Others/Take Me Back	1968	—	3.00	6.00
❑ 11129	Please Forgive Me/Pretty Little Princess	1968	—	3.00	6.00
❑ 11174	You Gave Me a Mountain/The Secret of Happiness	1969	—	3.00	6.00
❑ 11224	Dammit Isn't God's Last Name/Fresh Out of Tears	1969	—	3.00	6.00
❑ 11231	If I Didn't Believe in You/Allegra	1969	—	3.00	6.00
AMOS					
❑ 138	I Believe/On the Sunny Side of the Street	1970	—	2.50	5.00
❑ 153	Put Your Hand in the Hand/Going to Newport	1971	—	2.50	5.00
❑ 161	Don't Blame the Child/My God and I	1971	—	2.50	5.00
CAPITOL					
❑ 5299	Go On With Your Dancing/Halfway	1964	2.00	4.00	8.00
❑ 5472	House of Laughter/A Girl	1965	2.00	4.00	8.00
❑ 5525	Seven Days of Love/Heartaches Can Be Fun	1965	2.00	4.00	8.00
❑ 5569	The Meaning of It All/Pray and He Will Answer You	1966	2.00	4.00	8.00
❑ 5658	Johnny Willow/What Do You Know	1966	2.00	4.00	8.00
COLUMBIA					
❑ 39367	Jezebel/Rose, Rose, I Love You	1951	3.75	7.50	15.00
❑ 39489	Wonderful, Wasn't It?/The Girl in the Wood	1951	3.75	7.50	15.00
❑ 39585	Jealousy (Jalousie)/Flamenco	1951	3.75	7.50	15.00
❑ 39597	One for My Baby/Tomorrow Mountain	1951	3.00	6.00	12.00

Number	Title (A Side/B Side)	Yr	VG	VG+	NM
❑ 39598	Song of the Islands/Necessary Evil	1951	3.00	6.00	12.00
❑ 39599	She Reminds Me of You/Love Is Such a Cheat	1951	3.00	6.00	12.00
❑ 39600	Sleepy Time Down South/To Be Worthy	1951	3.00	6.00	12.00
—The above four comprise a box set					
❑ 39662	Jealousy (Jalousie)/Charmaine	1952	3.00	6.00	12.00
—B-side by Paul Weston; part of a box set					
❑ 39665	The Gandy Dancers' Ball/When You're in Love	1952	3.75	7.50	15.00
❑ 39716	That's How It Goes/Snow in Lover's Lane	1952	3.75	7.50	15.00
❑ 39770	High Noon (Do Not Forsake Me)/Rock of Gibraltar	1952	3.75	7.50	15.00
❑ 39798	There's a Rainbow 'Round My Shoulder/She's Funny That Way	1952	3.00	6.00	12.00
❑ 39799	Wonderful, Wasn't It?/The Girl in the Wood	1952	3.00	6.00	12.00
❑ 39862	The Mermaid/The Ruby and the Pearl	1952	3.75	7.50	15.00
❑ 39903	I'm Just a Poor Bachelor/Tonight You Belong to Me	1952	3.75	7.50	15.00
❑ 39938	I Believe/Your Cheatin' Heart	1953	3.75	7.50	15.00
❑ 39979	Ramblin' Man/I Let Her Go	1953	3.75	7.50	15.00
❑ 40022	When the Wind Blows/Te Amo	1953	3.75	7.50	15.00
❑ 40036	Hey Joe!/Sittin' in the Sun	1953	3.75	7.50	15.00
❑ 40079	Another Me/Blowing Wild	1953	3.75	7.50	15.00
❑ 40136	Granada/I'd Give My Life	1953	3.75	7.50	15.00
❑ 40178	The Kid's Last Fight/Long Distance Love	1954	3.75	7.50	15.00
❑ 40235	Some Day/There Must Be a Reason	1954	3.75	7.50	15.00
❑ 40295	Rain, Rain, Rain/Your Heart, My Heart	1954	3.75	7.50	15.00
—With the Four Lads					
❑ 40378	In the Beginning/Old Shoes	1954	3.75	7.50	15.00
❑ 40433	The Tarrier Song/Bubbles	1955	3.00	6.00	12.00
❑ 40457	Cool Water/Strange Lady in Town	1955	3.00	6.00	12.00
❑ 40526	Humming Bird/My Little One	1955	3.00	6.00	12.00
❑ 40558	Hawk-Eye/Your Love	1955	3.00	6.00	12.00
❑ 40583	A Woman in Love/Walking the Night Away	1955	3.00	6.00	12.00
❑ 40600	I Heard the Angels Singing/Ain't It a Pity and a Shame	1955	3.00	6.00	12.00
—With the Four Lads					
❑ 40663	Hell Hath No Fury/The Most Happy Fella	1956	3.00	6.00	12.00
❑ 40669	Moby Dick/A Capitol Ship	1956	3.00	6.00	12.00
❑ 40693	Don't Cry/Ticky Ticky Tick (I'm Gonna Tell on You)	1956	3.00	6.00	12.00
—With Paul Weston					
❑ 40720	Make Me a Child Again/The Thief	1956	3.00	6.00	12.00
❑ 40741	On the Road to Mandalay/Only If We Love	1956	3.00	6.00	12.00
❑ 40780	Moonlight Gambler/Lotus Land	1956	3.00	6.00	12.00
❑ 40780 [PS]	Moonlight Gambler/Lotus Land	1956	6.25	12.50	25.00
❑ 40856	Love Is a Golden Ring/There's Not a Moment to Spare	1957	3.00	6.00	12.00
❑ 40916	Gunfight at the O.K. Corral/Without Him	1957	3.00	6.00	12.00
❑ 40962	The 3:10 to Yuma/You Know How It Is	1957	3.00	6.00	12.00
❑ 41036	East Is East/The Greater Sin	1957	3.00	6.00	12.00
❑ 41106	Annabelle Lee/All of These…And More	1958	3.00	6.00	12.00
❑ 41139	My Gal and a Prayer/Lonesome Road	1958	3.00	6.00	12.00
❑ 41163	Lovin' Up a Storm/A Kiss Can Change the World	1958	3.00	6.00	12.00
❑ 41187	I Have to Cry/Choombala Bay	1958	3.00	6.00	12.00
❑ 41230	Rawhide/Magnificent Obsession	1958	6.25	12.50	25.00
❑ 41283	A Cottage for Sale/When I Speak Your Name	1958	3.00	6.00	12.00
❑ 41299	When I Speak Your Name/Midnight on a Rainy Monday	1958	3.00	6.00	12.00
❑ 41331	That's My Desire/In My Wildest Dreams	1959	2.50	5.00	10.00
❑ 41376	My Little Love/Journey's End	1959	2.50	5.00	10.00
❑ 41430	El Diablo/The Valley of a Hundred Hills	1959	2.50	5.00	10.00
❑ 41486	Rockin' Mother/Rocks and Gravel	1959	2.50	5.00	10.00
❑ 41613	St. James Infirmary/Et Voila	1960	2.50	5.00	10.00
❑ 41700	Seven Women/And Doesn't She Roll	1960	2.50	5.00	10.00
❑ 41787	Kisses That Shake the World/Here She Comes Now	1960	2.50	5.00	10.00
❑ 41974	Gunslinger/Wanted Man	1961	2.50	5.00	10.00
❑ 42233	Miss Satan/Ride Through the Night	1961	2.50	5.00	10.00
❑ 42383	A Wedded Man/We'll Be Together Again	1962	2.50	5.00	10.00
❑ 42767	The Moment of Truth/Don't Make Me Baby Blue	1963	2.50	5.00	10.00
❑ 42843	I'm Gonna Be Strong/And Doesn't She Roll	1963	2.50	5.00	10.00
❑ 42884	Take Her/I'm Gonna Be Strong	1963	2.50	5.00	10.00
❑ 42966	Lonely Days of Winter/Up Among the Stars	1964	2.50	5.00	10.00
❑ 50006	Jezebel/(B-side unknown)	1954	2.50	5.00	10.00
—Early "Hall of Fame Series" issue					
MAINSTREAM					
❑ 5579	Tell Me 'Bout the Hard Times/(B-side unknown)	1975	—	2.00	4.00
MERCURY					
❑ 526	Exactly Like You/You're Wonderful	195?	5.00	10.00	20.00
❑ 1026	Black and Blue/Wrap Your Troubles in Dreams	195?	6.25	12.50	25.00
❑ 1275	The Cry of the Wild Goose/Don't Cry Little Children	195?	5.00	10.00	20.00
—Part of box set A-113					
❑ 1277	Mule Train/God Bless the Child	195?	5.00	10.00	20.00
—Part of box set A-113					
❑ 5028	Stay As Sweet As You Are/I May Be Wrong	1950	6.25	12.50	25.00
—Reissue of 78 rpm					
❑ 5177	You're All I Want for Christmas/Tara Talara Tara	1950	7.50	15.00	30.00
—Reissue of 78 rpm					
❑ 5316	That Lucky Old Sun/I Get Sentimental Over Nothing	1950	6.25	12.50	25.00
—Reissue of 78 rpm					
❑ 5358	Satan Wears a Satin Gown/Baby Just for Me	1950	6.25	12.50	25.00
❑ 5363	The Cry of the Wild Goose/Black Lace	1950	6.25	12.50	25.00
—Maroon label					
❑ 5363	The Cry of the Wild Goose/Black Lace	1950	7.50	15.00	30.00
—Turquoise label					
❑ 5390	Swamp Girl/A Kiss for Tomorrow	1950	6.25	12.50	25.00
❑ 5421	Stars and Stripes Forever/Thanks for the Kisses	1950	6.25	12.50	25.00
❑ 5458	Music, Maestro, Please/Dream a Little Dream of Me	1950	5.00	10.00	20.00
❑ 5495	Nevertheless/I Was Dancing with Someone	1950	5.00	10.00	20.00
❑ 5500	If I Were a Bell/Sleepy Ol' River	1950	5.00	10.00	20.00
❑ 5544	I'm Gonna Live 'Til I Die/A Man Gets Awfully Lonesome	1950	5.00	10.00	20.00
❑ 5553	Merry Christmas Everywhere/What Am I Gonna Do This Christmas	1950	5.00	10.00	20.00
❑ 5580	Dear, Dear, Dear/May the Good Lord Bless and Keep You	1951	5.00	10.00	20.00
❑ 5581	Metro Polka/The Jalopy Song	1951	5.00	10.00	20.00
❑ 5656	The Gang That Sang Heart of My Heart/Out in the Rain	1951	5.00	10.00	20.00
❑ 5685	Isle of Capri/The Day Isn't Long Enough	1951	5.00	10.00	20.00
❑ 5733	Get Happy/I Would Do Most Anything for You	1951	5.00	10.00	20.00
❑ 5768	Baby I Need You/Yes My Darling Daughter	1951	5.00	10.00	20.00
❑ 5892	All of Me/South of the Border	1952	5.00	10.00	20.00
❑ 70099	Ain't Misbehavin'/How Rhythm Was Born	1953	3.75	7.50	15.00
❑ 70262	(The Gang That Sang) Heart of My Heart/South of the Border	1953	3.75	7.50	15.00
❑ 70275	West End Blues/I Can't Believe That You're in Love with Me	1953	3.75	7.50	15.00
SUNFLOWER					
❑ 125	My Own True Love/Time to Ride	1972	—	2.50	5.00
WARNER BROS.					
❑ 7774	Blazing Saddles/I'm Tired	1974	—	3.00	6.00
—B-side by Madeline Kahn					

7-Inch Extended Plays

Number	Title (A Side/B Side)	Yr	VG	VG+	NM
COLUMBIA					
❑ 5-1169	There's a Rainbow 'Round My Shoulder/She's Funny That Way//Wonderful Wasn't It?/The Girl in the Wood	195?	5.00	10.00	20.00
—Alternate number is B-1512					
❑ 5-1325	Jezebel/Jealousy (Jalousie)//The Gandy Dancers' Ball/When You're in Love	195?	5.00	10.00	20.00
—Alternate number is B-1582					
❑ B-1512 [PS]	Rainbow 'Round My Shoulder	195?	5.00	10.00	20.00
❑ 5-1569	Your Cheatin' Heart/I Believe//Love Is Such a Cheat/High Noon (Do Not Forsake Me)	195?	5.00	10.00	20.00
—Alternate number is B-1685					
❑ B-1582 [PS]	Frankie Laine Spotlite	195?	5.00	10.00	20.00
❑ B-1685 [PS]	Frankie Laine Favorites	195?	5.00	10.00	20.00
❑ B-1897	(contents unknown)	195?	5.00	10.00	20.00
❑ B-1897 [PS]	Popular Favorites	195?	5.00	10.00	20.00
❑ B-2086	(contents unknown)	1956	5.00	10.00	20.00
❑ B-2086 [PS]	Bring Your Smile Along	1956	5.00	10.00	20.00
❑ B-2121	(contents unknown)	1957	5.00	10.00	20.00
❑ B-2121 [PS]	Moonlight Gambler	1957	5.00	10.00	20.00
❑ B-2132	(contents unknown)	1957	5.00	10.00	20.00
❑ B-2132 [PS]	Love Is a Golden Ring and Other Hits	1957	5.00	10.00	20.00
❑ B-2590	*Shine/That's My Desire/That Lucky Old Sun/Moonlight Gambler	1960	3.75	7.50	15.00
❑ B-2590 [PS]	Frankie Laine (Hall of Fame Series)	1960	3.75	7.50	15.00
❑ B-11161	(contents unknown)	195?	5.00	10.00	20.00
❑ B-11161 [PS]	Foreign Affair	195?	5.00	10.00	20.00
❑ B-11162	(contents unknown)	195?	5.00	10.00	20.00
❑ B-11162 [PS]	Foreign Affair	195?	5.00	10.00	20.00
MERCURY					
❑ EP 1-3001	(contents unknown)	195?	6.25	12.50	25.00
❑ EP 1-3001 [PS]	Music, Maestro, Please	195?	6.25	12.50	25.00
❑ EP 1-3010	Two Loves Have I/I May Be Wrong//All of Me/Old Fashioned Love	195?	6.25	12.50	25.00
❑ EP 1-3010 [PS]	Frankie Laine	195?	6.25	12.50	25.00
❑ EP 1-3021	But Beautiful/That's My Desire//We Will Be Together Again/Shine	195?	6.25	12.50	25.00
❑ EP 1-3021 [PS]	Frankie Laine Favorites	195?	6.25	12.50	25.00
❑ EP 1-3028	(contents unknown)	195?	6.25	12.50	25.00
❑ EP 1-3028 [PS]	Christmas Favorites	195?	6.25	12.50	25.00
❑ EP-1-3057	I May Be Wrong/On the Sunny Side of the Street//Too Marvelous for Words/I Get a Kick Out of You	195?	5.00	10.00	20.00
—B-side by Billy Daniels					
❑ EP-1-3057	(title unknown)	195?	5.00	10.00	20.00
❑ EP 1-3071	(contents unknown)	195?	6.25	12.50	25.00
❑ EP 1-3071 [PS]	Georgia on My Mind	195?	6.25	12.50	25.00
❑ EP 1-3165	(contents unknown)	195?	6.25	12.50	25.00
❑ EP 1-3165 [PS]	Get Happy	195?	6.25	12.50	25.00
❑ EP 1-3175	(contents unknown)	195?	6.25	12.50	25.00
❑ EP 1-3175 [PS]	With All My Heart	195?	6.25	12.50	25.00

LAINE, FRANKIE, AND JIMMY BOYD

Number	Title (A Side/B Side)	Yr	VG	VG+	NM
COLUMBIA					
❑ 39945	Tell Me a Story/The Little Boy and the Old Man	1953	3.75	7.50	15.00
❑ 40069	Let's Go Fishin'/Poor Little Piggy Bank	1953	3.75	7.50	15.00
❑ 40650	Little Child/Let's Go Fishin'	1956	3.00	6.00	12.00

LAINE, FRANKIE, AND PATTI PAGE

Also see each artist's individual listings.

Number	Title (A Side/B Side)	Yr	VG	VG+	NM
MERCURY					
❑ 5442	I Love You for That/If I Were You Baby, I'd Love Me	1950	5.00	10.00	20.00

LAINE, FRANKIE, AND JO STAFFORD

Number	Title (A Side/B Side)	Yr	VG	VG+	NM
COLUMBIA					
❑ 39388	Pretty Eyed Baby/That's One for Me	1951	3.75	7.50	15.00
❑ 39466	In the Cool of the Evening/That's Good, That's Bad	1951	3.75	7.50	15.00
❑ 39570	Hey, Good Lookin'/Gambella (The Gamblin' Lady)	1951	3.75	7.50	15.00
❑ 39672	Hambone/Let's Have a Party	1952	3.75	7.50	15.00
❑ 39867	Settin' the Woods on Fire/Piece a-Puddin'	1952	3.75	7.50	15.00
❑ 39893	Christmas Roses/Chow Willy	1952	3.75	7.50	15.00
❑ 40116	Way Down Yonder in New Orleans/Floatin' Down to Cotton Town	1953	3.75	7.50	15.00
❑ 40198	Rollin' Down the Line/Goin' Like Wildfire	1954	3.75	7.50	15.00
❑ 40401	High Society/Back Where I Belong	1954	3.75	7.50	15.00

LAINE, LINDA, AND THE SINNERS

Number	Title (A Side/B Side)	Yr	VG	VG+	NM
TOWER					
❑ 108	Low Grades and High Fever/After Today	1964	3.00	6.00	12.00

LAKE, GREG

Also see EMERSON, LAKE AND PALMER.

Number	Title (A Side/B Side)	Yr	VG	VG+	NM
ATLANTIC					
❑ 3305	I Believe in Father Christmas/Humbug	1975	—	3.00	6.00
❑ 3305 [PS]	I Believe in Father Christmas/Humbug	1975	2.50	5.00	10.00
❑ 3405	C'est La Vie/Jeremy Bender	1977	—	2.50	5.00
CHRYSALIS					
❑ 2517	Let Me Love You Once/(B-side unknown)	1981	—	2.00	4.00
❑ 2571	Retribution Drive/Let Me Love You Once	1981	—	2.00	4.00

LAKE, KAREN

Number	Title (A Side/B Side)	Yr	VG	VG+	NM
ABC-PARAMOUNT					
❑ 10050	Nine O'Clock/Will I Know	1959	5.00	10.00	20.00
❑ 10087	Kiss Me Quick and Go/When I'm Not Teen Age Anymore	1960	5.00	10.00	20.00
BIG TOP					
❑ 3077	Air Mail Special Delivery/I'd Like to Miss My Graduation	1961	7.50	15.00	30.00

—Produced by Phil Spector

LALA AND THE LALARETTES

Number	Title (A Side/B Side)	Yr	VG	VG+	NM
ELPECO					
❑ 2922	This Day of Ours/Getting Ready for Freddy	1963	15.00	30.00	60.00

LAMARR, GENE

Number	Title (A Side/B Side)	Yr	VG	VG+	NM
SPRY					
❑ 113	Crazy Little House on the Hill/You Don't Love Me Anymore	1959	37.50	75.00	150.00
❑ 114	You Can Count on Me/Just a Little Bit Longer	1959	37.50	75.00	150.00
❑ 115	Close to Me/Moon Eyes	1959	25.00	50.00	100.00

LAMB, BECKY

Number	Title (A Side/B Side)	Yr	VG	VG+	NM
WARNER BROS.					
❑ 7154	Little Becky's Christmas Wish/Go to Sleep, Little Lambs	1967	3.00	6.00	12.00

—B-side by Bill Lamb

LAMBERT, RUDY

See THE MONDELLOS.

LAMM, ROBERT

Of CHICAGO.

Number	Title (A Side/B Side)	Yr	VG	VG+	NM
COLUMBIA					
❑ 10068	Skinny Boy/Temporary Jones	1974	—	2.50	5.00

LAMONT, BILLY

Number	Title (A Side/B Side)	Yr	VG	VG+	NM
KING					
❑ 5403	Come On Right Now/Hear Me Now	1960	3.00	6.00	12.00
OKEH					
❑ 7125	Country Boy/Can't Make It By Myself	1959	6.25	12.50	25.00
❑ 7131	I'm Gonna Try/Now Darling	1960	6.25	12.50	25.00
SAVOY					
❑ 1522	I'm So Lonely/I Got a Rock 'n' Roll Gal	1957	3.75	7.50	15.00
THREE-D					
❑ 850	Country Boy/Can't Make It By Myself	1959	37.50	75.00	150.00

LAMP, BUDDY

Number	Title (A Side/B Side)	Yr	VG	VG+	NM
ABC-PARAMOUNT					
❑ 10398	I'm Comin' Home/Promised Land	1963	3.75	7.50	15.00
D-TOWN					
❑ 1064	Next Best Thing/Just a Little Bit of Lovin'	1966	7.50	15.00	30.00
DOUBLE L					
❑ 716	Thank You Love/My Tears	1963	7.50	15.00	30.00
DUKE					
❑ 438	I'm Coming Home/Where Have You Been	1968	2.50	5.00	10.00
❑ 461	Devil's Gonna Get You/Wall Around Your Heart	1970	2.00	4.00	8.00
❑ 468	Hen Pecked/If You See Kate	1971	2.00	4.00	8.00
GONE					
❑ 5104	Good News/What Here Can I Do	1961	3.75	7.50	15.00
WHEELSVILLE					
❑ 113	You've Got the Lovin' Touch/I Wanna Go Home	196?	10.00	20.00	40.00
❑ 120	Confusion/I Wanna Go Home	196?	10.00	20.00	40.00
❑ 122	Save Your Love/I Wanna Go Home	196?	17.50	35.00	70.00

LAMPLIGHTERS, THE

Number	Title (A Side/B Side)	Yr	VG	VG+	NM
FEDERAL					
❑ 12149	Part of Me/Turn Me Loose	1953	75.00	150.00	300.00
❑ 12152	Give Me/Be-Bop Wino	1953	37.50	75.00	150.00
❑ 12166	Smootchie/I Can't Stand It	1954	37.50	75.00	150.00
❑ 12176	Tell Me You Came/I Used to Cry Mercy, Mercy	1954	37.50	75.00	150.00
❑ 12182	Salty Dog/Ride, Jockey, Ride	1954	37.50	75.00	150.00
❑ 12192	Five Minutes Longer/You Hear	1954	37.50	75.00	150.00
❑ 12197	Yum! Yum!/Goody Good Times	1954	37.50	75.00	150.00
❑ 12206	I Wanna Know/Believe in Me	1955	37.50	75.00	150.00
❑ 12212	Roll On/Love, Rock and Thrill	1955	37.50	75.00	150.00
❑ 12242	Don't Make It So Good/Hug a Little, Kiss a Little	1955	37.50	75.00	150.00
❑ 12255	You Were Sent Down from Heaven/Bo-Peep	1956	25.00	50.00	100.00
❑ 12261	It Ain't Right/Everything's All Right	1956	25.00	50.00	100.00
KING					
❑ 5890	Be-Bop Wino/Thunderbird	1964	3.75	7.50	15.00

—B-side by Dossie Terry

LANCASTRIANS, THE

Number	Title (A Side/B Side)	Yr	VG	VG+	NM
CAPITOL					
❑ 5501	Never Gonna Come On Home/There'll Be No More Goodbyes	1965	2.50	5.00	10.00
JERDEN					
❑ 798	The World Keeps Going Round/Not the Same Anymore	1966	2.50	5.00	10.00

LANCE, MAJOR

Number	Title (A Side/B Side)	Yr	VG	VG+	NM
COLUMBIA					
❑ 10488	Come On, Have Yourself a Good Time/Come What May	1977	—	2.50	5.00
CURTOM					
❑ 1953	Stay Away from Me (I Love You Too Much)/Gypsy Woman	1970	—	3.00	6.00
❑ 1956	Must Be Love Coming Down/Little Young Lover	1970	—	3.00	6.00
DAKAR					
❑ 608	Follow the Leader/Since You've Been Gone	1969	2.00	4.00	8.00
❑ 612	Shadows of a Memory/Sweeter As the Days Go By	1969	2.00	4.00	8.00
KAT FAMILY					
❑ 03024	I Wanna Go Home/(Instrumental)	1982	—	2.00	4.00
❑ 04185	Are You Leaving Me/I Wanna Go Home	1983	—	2.00	4.00
MERCURY					
❑ 71582	I've Got a Girl/Phyllis	1960	7.50	15.00	30.00
OKEH					
❑ 7175	The Monkey Time/Mama Didn't Know	1963	3.75	7.50	15.00
❑ 7181	Hey Little Girl/Crying in the Rain	1963	3.00	6.00	12.00
❑ 7187	Um, Um, Um, Um, Um, Um/Sweet Music	1964	3.75	7.50	15.00
❑ 7187 [PS]	Um, Um, Um, Um, Um, Um/Sweet Music	1964	7.50	15.00	30.00
❑ 7191	The Matador/Gonna Get Married	1964	2.50	5.00	10.00
❑ 7197	It Ain't No Use/Girls	1964	2.50	5.00	10.00
❑ 7200	Think Nothing About It/It's Alright	1964	12.50	25.00	50.00
❑ 7203	Rhythm/Please Don't Say No More	1964	2.50	5.00	10.00
❑ 7203 [PS]	Rhythm/Please Don't Say No More	1964	3.75	7.50	15.00
❑ 7209	Sometimes I Wonder/I'm So Lost	1965	2.50	5.00	10.00
❑ 7216	Come See/You Belong to Me My Love	1965	2.50	5.00	10.00
❑ 7216 [PS]	Come See/You Belong to Me My Love	1965	3.75	7.50	15.00
❑ 7223	Ain't It a Shame/Gotta Get Away	1965	2.50	5.00	10.00
❑ 7226	Too Hot to Hold/Dark and Lovely	1965	2.50	5.00	10.00
❑ 7233	Everybody Loves a Good Time/I Just Can't Help It	1965	3.75	7.50	15.00
❑ 7250	Little Young Lover/Investigate	1966	3.75	7.50	15.00
❑ 7250 [PS]	Little Young Lover/Investigate	1966	5.00	10.00	20.00
❑ 7255	It's the Beat/You'll Want Me Back	1966	2.50	5.00	10.00
❑ 7266	Ain't No Soul (In These Shoes)/I	1966	3.75	7.50	15.00
❑ 7284	You Don't Want Me No More/Wait Till I Get You in Your Arms	1967	12.50	25.00	50.00
❑ 7298	Without a Doubt/Forever	1967	2.50	5.00	10.00
OSIRIS					
❑ 001	You're Everything I Need/(Instrumental)	1975	—	2.50	5.00
PLAYBOY					
❑ 6017	Um, Um, Um, Um, Um/Last of the Red Hot Lovers	1974	—	2.50	5.00
❑ 6020	Sweeter/Wild and Free	1975	—	2.50	5.00
SOUL					
❑ 35123	I Never Thought I'd Be Losing You/Chicago Disco	1977	—	2.50	5.00
VOLT					
❑ 4079	I Wanna Make Up/That's the Story of My Life	1972	—	3.00	6.00
❑ 4085	Ain't No Sweat/Since I Lost My Baby's Love	1972	—	3.00	6.00

LANCELOT LINK AND THE EVOLUTION REVOLUTION

Number	Title (A Side/B Side)	Yr	VG	VG+	NM
ABC					
❑ 11278	Sha La Love You/Blind Date	1970	2.50	5.00	10.00
❑ 11285	Daydreams/Magic Feelings	1970	2.50	5.00	10.00

LANCERS, THE

Number	Title (A Side/B Side)	Yr	VG	VG+	NM
CLOUD					
❑ 500	Baja/When Johnny Comes Draggin' Home	1965	6.25	12.50	25.00
CORAL					
❑ 61288	Mr. Sandman/Little White Light	1954	3.00	6.00	12.00
❑ 61314	'Twas the Night Before Christmas/I Wanna Do More Than Whistle (Under the Mistletoe)	1954	3.00	6.00	12.00
❑ 61332	Tweedlee Dee/Open Up Your Heart (And Let the Sun Shine In)	1955	3.00	6.00	12.00
❑ 61343	Timberjack/Crazy Music	1955	3.00	6.00	12.00
—With Lawrence Welk and His Orchestra					
❑ 61374	Somebody Else Is Taking My Place/Cherry	1955	3.00	6.00	12.00
❑ 61382	Two Hearts, Two Kisses/Afraid	1955	3.00	6.00	12.00
❑ 61416	Leave the Door Partly Open/The Lucky Black Cat	1955	3.00	6.00	12.00
❑ 61468	It Shouldn't Hurt to Love You/It Takes a Heap of Livin'	1955	3.00	6.00	12.00
❑ 61527	Alphabet Rock/How Lonely Can I Get	1955	3.00	6.00	12.00
❑ 61550	Rock Around the Island/The Walking Doll	1956	3.00	6.00	12.00
❑ 61611	Sorry/A Man Is As Good As His Word	1956	3.00	6.00	12.00
❑ 61614	Joey, Joey, Joey/When You're in Love	1956	3.00	6.00	12.00
❑ 61616	Little Fool/A Man Is As Good As His Word	1956	3.00	6.00	12.00
❑ 61665	The First Traveling Saleslady/Free	1956	3.00	6.00	12.00
❑ 61686	The Bonnie Banks of Loch Lomon'/Maybe Now	1956	3.00	6.00	12.00
❑ 61712	I Came Back to Say I'm Sorry/Never Leave Me	1956	3.00	6.00	12.00
❑ 61769	Freckle Face Sara Jane/It Happened in Monterey	1957	3.00	6.00	12.00
❑ 61831	Charm Bracelets/And I Don't Feel Bad	1957	3.00	6.00	12.00
❑ 61866	Lover's Rendezvous/Follow the River	1957	3.00	6.00	12.00
❑ 61887	I'm Awfully Strong for You/I'd Move Heaven and Earth	1957	3.00	6.00	12.00
❑ 61899	Don't Go Near the Water/A Hundred Heartbeats	1957	3.00	6.00	12.00
❑ 61930	The Stroll/Jo-Ann	1958	3.00	6.00	12.00
❑ 61966	Sorry/The Sound	1958	3.00	6.00	12.00
❑ 61998	It Was Great While It Lasted/The Lord Is a Generous Man	1958	3.00	6.00	12.00
OLD TIMER					
❑ 604	Baja/When Johnny Comes Draggin' Home	1965	10.00	20.00	40.00
—Black vinyl					
❑ 604	Baja/When Johnny Comes Draggin' Home	1965	2.50	5.00	10.00
—Red vinyl (reissue)					
VEE JAY					
❑ 654	The Warmth of the Sun/Hush-A-Bye	1965	2.50	5.00	10.00

LANDIS, JERRY
See PAUL SIMON.

LANDS, HOAGY

Number	Title (A Side/B Side)	Yr	VG	VG+	NM
ABC-PARAMOUNT					
❑ 10171	(I'm Gonna) Cry Some Tears/Lighted Windows	1960	6.25	12.50	25.00
❑ 10392	Tender Years/I'm Yours	1963	3.75	7.50	15.00
ATLANTIC					
❑ 2217	Baby Come On Home/Baby Let Me Hold Your Hand	1964	3.75	7.50	15.00
JUDI					
❑ 054	(I'm Gonna) Cry Some Tears/Lighted Windows	1960	20.00	40.00	80.00
LAURIE					
❑ 3349	Theme from The Other Side/Friends and Lovers Don't Go Together	1966	5.00	10.00	20.00
❑ 3372	Yesterday/Forever	1967	5.00	10.00	20.00
❑ 3381	The Next in Line/Please Don't Talk About Me When I'm Gone	1967	6.25	12.50	25.00
—Backing group: THE CHIFFONS.					
MGM					
❑ K-13041	My Tears Are Dry/It's Gonna Be Morning	1961	5.00	10.00	20.00
❑ K-13062	Goodnight Irene/It Ain't As Easy As That	1962	5.00	10.00	20.00

LANDS, LIZ

Number	Title (A Side/B Side)	Yr	VG	VG+	NM
GORDY					
❑ 7023	We Shall Overcome/I Have a Dream	1963	6.25	12.50	25.00
—B-side by Rev. Martin Luther King					
❑ 7026	May What He Lived For Live/He's Got the Whole World in His Hands	1963	7.50	15.00	30.00
❑ 7030	Midnight Journey/Keep Me	1964	12.50	25.00	50.00
—The Temptations sing backup					
ONE-DERFUL					
❑ 4847	One Man's Poison/Don't Shut Me Out	1967	3.75	7.50	15.00
T&L					
❑ 201	Silent Night (Part 1)/Silent Night (Part 2)	19??	2.00	4.00	8.00

LANE, BILLY

Number	Title (A Side/B Side)	Yr	VG	VG+	NM
TABA					
❑ 201	Beginner in Love/Space Ship Blues	196?	40.00	80.00	160.00

LANE, MICKEY

Number	Title (A Side/B Side)	Yr	VG	VG+	NM
BRUNSWICK					
❑ 55098	Daddy's Little Baby/Toasted Love	1958	5.00	10.00	20.00
LAURIE					
❑ 3071	Dum Dee Dee Dum/Night Cap	1960	6.25	12.50	25.00

LANE, ROCKI, AND THE GROSS GROUP

Number	Title (A Side/B Side)	Yr	VG	VG+	NM
EPIC					
❑ 10556	Happy Hairy Hippy Harry Claus/Santa Soul	1969	6.25	12.50	25.00

LANE, RONNIE
Also see SMALL FACES.

Number	Title (A Side/B Side)	Yr	VG	VG+	NM
RCA					
❑ PB-11914	You're So Right/Kuschty Rye	1980	—	2.50	5.00

LANG, K.D.

Number	Title (A Side/B Side)	Yr	VG	VG+	NM
SIRE					
❑ 18289	Just Keep Me Moving/In Perfect Dreams	1994	—	2.00	4.00
❑ 18608	Miss Chatelaine/Outside Myself	1993	—	—	3.00
❑ 18942	Constant Craving/Season of Hollow Soul	1992	—	2.00	4.00
❑ 19793	Seven Lonely Days/Ridin' the Rails	1990	—	2.00	4.00
❑ 22734	Three Days/Trail of Broken Hearts	1989	—	—	3.00
❑ 22734 [PS]	Three Days/Trail of Broken Hearts	1989	—	3.00	6.00
❑ 22932	Full Moon of Love/Wallpaper Waltz	1989	—	—	3.00
❑ 22932 [PS]	Full Moon of Love/Wallpaper Waltz	1989	—	2.50	5.00
❑ 27813	Lock, Stock and Teardrop/Don't Let the Stars Get In Your Eyes	1988	—	—	3.00
❑ 27813 [PS]	Lock, Stock and Teardrop/Don't Let the Stars Get In Your Eyes	1988	—	2.00	4.00
❑ 27919	I'm Down to My Last Cigarette/Western Stars	1988	—	—	3.00
❑ 27919 [PS]	I'm Down to My Last Cigarette/Western Stars	1988	—	—	3.00
❑ 28338	Turn Me Around/Diet of Strange Places	1987	—	—	3.00
❑ 28465	Rose Garden/High Time for a Detour	1987	—	—	3.00
WARNER BROS.					
❑ 17747	If I Were You/Get Some	1995	—	—	3.00

LANI & BONI
See DELANEY AND BONNIE.

LAPELS, THE

Number	Title (A Side/B Side)	Yr	VG	VG+	NM
DOT					
❑ 16129	Sneakin' Around/Sneakin' Blues	1960	3.00	6.00	12.00
MELKER					
❑ 103	Sneakin' Around/Sneakin' Blues	1960	10.00	20.00	40.00

LARADOS, THE
Members of this group were later in THE REFLECTIONS.

Number	Title (A Side/B Side)	Yr	VG	VG+	NM
FOX					
❑ 962/3	Now the Parting Begins/Bad Guitar Man	1958	50.00	100.00	200.00
MADOG					
❑ 801	Will You Love Me Tomorrow/You Didn't Care	1980	3.75	7.50	15.00

LARKIN, BILLY

Number	Title (A Side/B Side)	Yr	VG	VG+	NM
AURA					
❑ 4504	Pigmy (Part 1)/Pigmy (Part 2)	1965	3.75	7.50	15.00
—As "The Delegates"					
❑ 4508	The Peeper/Hainty	1965	3.75	7.50	15.00
—As "The Delegates"					
WORLD PACIFIC					
❑ 4504	Pigmy (Part 1)/Pigmy (Part 2)	1965	3.00	6.00	12.00
—As "The Delegates"					
❑ 88120	Pigmy (Part 1)/The Peeper	1966	2.50	5.00	10.00
—As "The Delegates"					

LARKS, THE (1)
Also see DON JULIAN AND THE MEADOWLARKS.

Number	Title (A Side/B Side)	Yr	VG	VG+	NM
MONEY					
❑ 106	The Jerk/Forget Me	1964	5.00	10.00	20.00
❑ 109	Mickey's East Coast Jerk/Soul Jerk	1965	3.00	6.00	12.00
❑ 110	The Slauson Shuffle/Soul Jerk	1965	3.00	6.00	12.00
❑ 112	The Roman/Heavenly Father	1965	3.00	6.00	12.00
❑ 115	Can You Do the Duck/Sad Sad Boy	1965	3.00	6.00	12.00
❑ 119	Lost My Love Yesterday/The Answer Came Too Late	1966	3.00	6.00	12.00
❑ 122	Philly Dog/Heaven Only Knows	1966	3.00	6.00	12.00
❑ 127	The Skate/Come Back Baby	1967	3.00	6.00	12.00
❑ 601	I Love You/I Want You Back	1973	—	3.00	6.00
❑ 604	My Favorite Beer Joint/(Instrumental)	1973	—	3.00	6.00
❑ 607	Shorty the Pimp (Part 1)/Shorty the Pimp (Part 2)	1974	—	3.00	6.00
—Money 604 and 607 as "Don Julian and the Larks"					

LARKS, THE (2)

Number	Title (A Side/B Side)	Yr	VG	VG+	NM
SHERYL					
❑ 334	It's Unbelievable/I Can't Believe It	1961	7.50	15.00	30.00
❑ 338	There Is a Girl/Let's Drink a Toast	1961	6.25	12.50	25.00

LARKS, THE (3)

Number	Title (A Side/B Side)	Yr	VG	VG+	NM
APOLLO					
❑ 429	Little Side Car/Hey Little Girl	1951	1000.	2000.	4000.
❑ 430	Ooh, It Feels So Good/I Don't Believe in Tomorrow	1951	1000.	2000.	4000.
❑ 435	My Lost Love/How Long Must I Wait for You	1952	250.00	500.00	1000.
❑ 437	Darlin'/Lucy Brown	1952	250.00	500.00	1000.
❑ 475	No Mama No/Honey from the Bee	1955	100.00	200.00	400.00
❑ 1180	Hopefully Yours/When I Leave These Prison Walls	1951	1000.	2000.	4000.
❑ 1184	My Reverie/Let's Say a Prayer	1951	500.00	1000.	2000.
—Black vinyl					
❑ 1184	My Reverie/Let's Say a Prayer	1951	4000.	6000.	8000.
—Red vinyl					
❑ 1189	Shadrack/Honey in the Rock	1952	500.00	1000.	2000.
❑ 1190	Stolen Love/In My Lonely Room	1952	625.00	1250.	2500.
—Black vinyl					
❑ 1190	Stolen Love/In My Lonely Room	1952	2500.	3750.	5000.
—Red vinyl					
❑ 1194	I Live True to You/Hold Me	1952	250.00	500.00	1000.
LLOYDS					
❑ 108	Margie/Rockin' in the Rockin' Room	1954	200.00	400.00	800.00
❑ 110	Tippin' In/If It's a Crime	1954	200.00	400.00	800.00
❑ 112	No Other Girl/The World Is Waiting for the Sunrise	1954	200.00	400.00	800.00
❑ 114	Forget It/I Live True to You	1954	150.00	300.00	600.00

LARKS, THE (U)
It's doubtful that any of these are groups (1) or (3). Some could be by group (2).

Number	Title (A Side/B Side)	Yr	VG	VG+	NM
CROSS FIRE					
❑ 74-49/50	Fabulous Cars and Diamond Rings/Life Is Sweeter Now	1961	5.00	10.00	20.00
GUYDEN					
❑ 2098	I Want Her to Love Me/(Instrumental)	1963	3.00	6.00	12.00
❑ 2103	Fabulous Cars and Diamond Rings/Life Is Sweeter Now	1964	3.00	6.00	12.00
JETT					
❑ 3001	Love You So/Love Me True	1965	15.00	30.00	60.00
NASCO					
❑ 028	I Love You/I Want You Back	1972	2.00	4.00	8.00
STACY					
❑ 969	Food Sticks/Scavenger	1963	3.00	6.00	12.00
VIOLET					
❑ 1051	I Want Her to Love Me/(Instrumental)	1962	5.00	10.00	20.00

LARKTONES, THE

Number	Title (A Side/B Side)	Yr	VG	VG+	NM
ABC-PARAMOUNT					
❑ 9909	The Letter/Rockin' Swingin' Man	1958	7.50	15.00	30.00
RIKI					
❑ 140	Why Are You Tearing Us Apart/Nosy Neighbor	1960	15.00	30.00	60.00

LAROSA, JULIUS

Number	Title (A Side/B Side)	Yr	VG	VG+	NM
ABC					
❑ 10959	For Once in My Life/Summer Love	1967	—	3.00	6.00
CADENCE					
❑ 1230	Anywhere I Wander/This Is Heaven	1953	3.75	7.50	15.00
❑ 1231	My Lady Loves to Dance/Let's Make Up Before We Say Goodnight	1953	3.75	7.50	15.00
❑ 1232	Eh, Cumpari/Till They're All Gone Home	1953	3.75	7.50	15.00
❑ 1235	The Big Bell and the Little Bell/I Couldn't Believe My Eyes	1954	3.00	6.00	12.00
❑ 1236	My Funny Valentine/Roseanne	1954	3.00	6.00	12.00
❑ 1237	When You're in Love/Have a Heart	1954	3.00	6.00	12.00
❑ 1240	Three Coins in the Fountain/Me Gotta Have You	1954	3.00	6.00	12.00
❑ 1244	My Heart's on a Fast Express/In My Own Quiet Way	1954	3.00	6.00	12.00
❑ 1251	Mobile/I Hate to Say Hello	1954	3.00	6.00	12.00
❑ 1252	Campanelle (Jingle Bells)/I Hope You'll Be Very Happy	1954	3.00	6.00	12.00
❑ 1253	Jingle Dingle/Campanelle (Jingle Bells)	1954	3.00	6.00	12.00
❑ 1258	Let's Stay Home Tonight/Pass It On	1955	3.00	6.00	12.00
❑ 1265	Domani (Tomorrow)/Mama Rosa	1955	3.00	6.00	12.00
❑ 1270	Suddenly There's a Valley/Everytime That I Kiss Carrie	1955	3.00	6.00	12.00
❑ 1440	David and Lisa's Love Song/Suddenly There's a Valley	1963	2.00	4.00	8.00
❑ 1444	Gonna Build a Mountain/JE	1964	2.00	4.00	8.00
GP					
❑ 592	A Christmas Gift/To Find Our Children	1981	—	3.00	6.00
KAPP					
❑ 323	Green Fields/Your Hand in Mine	1960	2.00	4.00	8.00

Number	Title (A Side/B Side)	Yr	VG	VG+	NM
❑ 348	Bewitched/It's Alright with Me	1960	2.00	4.00	8.00
❑ 371	Let Your Lips Tell Me/Seventeen	1961	2.00	4.00	8.00
❑ 417	There's No Other Love/Caress Me	1961	2.00	4.00	8.00
❑ 444	You Can't Keep Me from Loving You/If I Had My Way	1962	2.00	4.00	8.00

METROMEDIA

Number	Title (A Side/B Side)	Yr	VG	VG+	NM
❑ 186	Brooklyn Roads/Being Alive	1970	—	2.50	5.00

MGM

Number	Title (A Side/B Side)	Yr	VG	VG+	NM
❑ CS5-5	Celebrity Scene: Julius LaRosa	1967	12.50	25.00	50.00

—Box set of five singles (13671-13675). Price includes box, all 5 singles, jukebox title strips, bio. Records are sometimes found by themselves, so they are also listed separately.

Number	Title (A Side/B Side)	Yr	VG	VG+	NM
❑ 13454	Small, Small World/Unless	1966	—	3.00	6.00
❑ 13497	Lonely As I Leave You/You're Gonna Hear from Me	1966	—	3.00	6.00
❑ 13575	I Think It's Going to Rain Today/You Only See Her	1966	—	3.00	6.00
❑ 13651	We Need A Little Christmas/Our Venetian Affair	1966	2.00	4.00	8.00
❑ 13671	(titles unknown)	1967	2.00	4.00	8.00
❑ 13672	Somethin' Special/You're Gonna Hear from Me	1967	2.00	4.00	8.00
❑ 13673	(titles unknown)	1967	2.00	4.00	8.00
❑ 13674	What Did I Have That I Don't Have/Spring	1967	2.00	4.00	8.00
❑ 13675	Who Am I/What'll I Do	1967	2.00	4.00	8.00

RCA VICTOR

Number	Title (A Side/B Side)	Yr	VG	VG+	NM
❑ 47-6416	Lipstick and Candy and Rubber Sole Shoes/Winter in New England	1956	2.50	5.00	10.00
❑ 47-6499	I've Got Love/Augustine	1956	2.50	5.00	10.00
❑ 47-6567	Get Me to the Church On Time/I've Grown Accustomed to Her Face	1956	2.50	5.00	10.00
❑ 47-6648	The Opposite Sex/Namely You	1956	2.50	5.00	10.00
❑ 47-6700	All I Want/Priscilla	1956	2.50	5.00	10.00
❑ 47-6802	Jeanette/Stashu Pandowski	1957	2.50	5.00	10.00
❑ 47-6878	Mama Guitar/Man to Man	1957	2.50	5.00	10.00
❑ 47-6923	Crying My Heart Out for You/When You're With the One You Love	1957	2.50	5.00	10.00
❑ 47-6998	Worlds Apart/Famous Last Words	1957	2.50	5.00	10.00
❑ 47-7059	Just Forever/Since When (Is It a Sin)	1957	2.50	5.00	10.00
❑ 47-7186	Lover, Lover/A Heart for a Heart	1958	2.50	5.00	10.00
❑ 47-7227	Torero/Milano	1958	2.50	5.00	10.00
❑ 74-0938	The Good Life/Sing Me a Song	1973	—	2.50	5.00

ROULETTE

Number	Title (A Side/B Side)	Yr	VG	VG+	NM
❑ 4135	Where's the Girl/Protect Me	1959	2.50	5.00	10.00
❑ 4162	Honey Bunch/Port of Love	1959	2.50	5.00	10.00

7-Inch Extended Plays

CADENCE

Number	Title (A Side/B Side)	Yr	VG	VG+	NM
❑ EP 1233	No Other Love/I Believe//My Funny Valentine/Roseanne	1953	3.75	7.50	15.00
❑ EP 1233 [PS]	(title unknown)	1953	3.75	7.50	15.00
❑ EP 1234	Ave Maria/Adeste Fideles//Silent Night/Oh Holy Night	1953	3.75	7.50	15.00
❑ EP 1234 [PS]	Julius LaRosa Sings...	1953	3.75	7.50	15.00

RCA VICTOR

Number	Title (A Side/B Side)	Yr	VG	VG+	NM
❑ EPA 841	(contents unknown)	1956	3.75	7.50	15.00
❑ EPA 841 [PS]	Julius LaRosa	1956	3.75	7.50	15.00

LARRY AND THE CROSSFIRES

SEARCY

Number	Title (A Side/B Side)	Yr	VG	VG+	NM
❑ 711	Torquay '65/Wee Wee Hours	1965	12.50	25.00	50.00

LARRY AND THE LEGENDS

ATLANTIC

Number	Title (A Side/B Side)	Yr	VG	VG+	NM
❑ 2220	Don't Pick On My Baby/The Creep	1964	6.25	12.50	25.00

—With the Four Seasons

LASALLE, DENISE

ABC

Number	Title (A Side/B Side)	Yr	VG	VG+	NM
❑ 12225	Hellfire Loving/I Get What I Want	1976	—	2.50	5.00
❑ 12238	Freedom to Express Yourself/Second Breath	1977	—	2.00	4.00
❑ 12312	Love Me Right/Fool Me Good	1977	—	2.00	4.00
❑ 12353	One Life to Live/Before You Take It to the Streets	1978	—	2.00	4.00
❑ 12419	Workin' Overtime/No Matter What They Say	1978	—	2.00	4.00
❑ 12443	P.A.R.T.Y. (Where It Is)/Under the Influence	1979	—	2.00	4.00

CHESS

Number	Title (A Side/B Side)	Yr	VG	VG+	NM
❑ 2005	A Love Reputation/One Little Thing	1967	2.50	5.00	10.00
❑ 2044	Private Property/I've Been Waiting	1968	2.50	5.00	10.00
❑ 2058	Count Down (And Fly Me to the Moon)/A Promise Is a Promise	1968	2.50	5.00	10.00

MALACO

Number	Title (A Side/B Side)	Yr	VG	VG+	NM
❑ 2089	Lady in the Street/I Was Not the Best Woman	198?	—	2.00	4.00
❑ 2092	Lay Me Down/I Was Telling Him About You	198?	—	2.00	4.00
❑ 2095	Down Home Blues/Down Home Blues (X-Rated)	198?	—	2.00	4.00
❑ 2098	Right Place, Right Time/He's Not Available	1984	—	2.00	4.00

—With Latimore

Number	Title (A Side/B Side)	Yr	VG	VG+	NM
❑ 2105	Treat Your Man Like a Baby/Come to Bed	1985	—	2.00	4.00
❑ 2112	My Tu-Tu/Give Me Yo' Strongest Whiskey	1985	—	2.00	4.00
❑ 2124	Santa Claus Got the Blues/Love Is a Five Letter Word	1985	—	2.50	5.00
❑ 2131	What's Going On in My House/He's That Way Sometime	1986	—	2.00	4.00
❑ 2138	Hold What You Got/Footsteps of a Fool	1986	—	2.00	4.00
❑ 2152	Bring It On Home to Me/Write This One Off (As Actors)	1987	—	2.00	4.00
❑ 2156	Caught in Your Mess/I Forgot to Remember	1987	—	2.00	4.00
❑ 2167	Drop That Zero/Chain Letter	1988	—	2.00	4.00

MCA

Number	Title (A Side/B Side)	Yr	VG	VG+	NM
❑ 41222	I'm So Hot/Miracle, You and Me	1980	—	2.00	4.00
❑ 51046	I'm Trippin' on You/I'll Get You Some Help	1981	—	2.00	4.00
❑ 51098	Sharing Your Love/I'll Get You Some Help	1981	—	2.00	4.00

TARPEN

Number	Title (A Side/B Side)	Yr	VG	VG+	NM
❑ 6603	A Love Reputation/One Little Thing	1967	6.25	12.50	25.00

WESTBOUND

Number	Title (A Side/B Side)	Yr	VG	VG+	NM
❑ 162	Heartbreaker of the Year/Hung Up, Strung Out	1971	2.00	4.00	8.00
❑ 182	Trapped by a Thing Called Love/Keep It Coming	1971	—	3.00	6.00
❑ 201	Now Run and Tell That/The Deeper I Go	1972	—	3.00	6.00
❑ 206	Man Sized Job/I'm Over You	1972	—	3.00	6.00
❑ 215	What It Takes to Get a Good Woman (That's What It's Gonna Take to Keep Her)/Making a Good Thing Better	1973	—	3.00	6.00
❑ 219	Your Man and Your Best Friend/What Am I Doing Wrong	1973	—	3.00	6.00
❑ 221	Don't Nobody Live Here (By the Name of Fool)/Goody Goody Getter	1973	—	3.00	6.00
❑ 223	Get Up Off My Mind/The Best Thing I Ever Had	1974	—	3.00	6.00
❑ 229	Trying to Forget/We've Got Love	1974	—	3.00	6.00
❑ 5004	My Brand on You/Anytime Is the Right Time	1975	—	2.50	5.00
❑ 5008	Here I Am Again/Hung Up, Strung Out	1975	—	2.50	5.00
❑ 5019	Married, But Not to Each Other/Who's the Fool	1976	—	2.50	5.00

LAST POETS, THE

BLUE THUMB

Number	Title (A Side/B Side)	Yr	VG	VG+	NM
❑ 216	Tribute to Orabi/Bird's Word	1972	3.00	6.00	12.00

DOUGLAS

Number	Title (A Side/B Side)	Yr	VG	VG+	NM
❑ ADS 8	O.D./Black Thighs	1971	3.75	7.50	15.00
❑ ADS 8 [PS]	O.D./Black Thighs	1971	7.50	15.00	30.00

LAUGHING GRAVY

WHITE WHALE

Number	Title (A Side/B Side)	Yr	VG	VG+	NM
❑ 261	Vegetables/Snow Flakes on Laughing Gravy's Whiskers	1968	50.00	100.00	200.00

LAUPER, CYNDI

Also see BLUE ANGEL.

EPIC

Number	Title (A Side/B Side)	Yr	VG	VG+	NM
❑ 07940	Hole in My Heart (All the Way to China)/Boy Blue	1988	—	—	3.00
❑ 07940 [PS]	Hole in My Heart (All the Way to China)/Boy Blue	1988	—	—	3.00
❑ 08443	True Colors/What's Going On	1988	—	—	3.00

—Reissue

Number	Title (A Side/B Side)	Yr	VG	VG+	NM
❑ 68759	I Drove All Night/Maybe He'll Know	1989	—	—	3.00
❑ 68945	My First Night Without You/Unabbreviated Love	1989	—	—	3.00
❑ 73031	A Night to Remember/Insecurious	1989	—	—	3.00
❑ 74942	Who Let In the Rain/Cold	1993	—	—	3.00
❑ 77233	That's What I Think/That's What I Think (Live)	1993	—	—	3.00

PORTRAIT

Number	Title (A Side/B Side)	Yr	VG	VG+	NM
❑ 04120	Girls Just Want to Have Fun/Right Track Wrong Train	1983	—	—	3.00
❑ 04120 [PS]	Girls Just Want to Have Fun/Right Track Wrong Train	1983	2.00	4.00	8.00
❑ 04120 [PS]	Girls Just Want to Have Fun	1983	2.00	4.00	8.00

—"Demonstration -- Not for Sale" on back

Number	Title (A Side/B Side)	Yr	VG	VG+	NM
❑ 04432	Time After Time/I'll Kiss You	1984	—	—	3.00
❑ 04516	She Bop/Witness	1984	—	—	3.00
❑ 04516 [PS]	She Bop/Witness	1984	—	—	3.00
❑ 04639	All Through the Night/Witness	1984	—	—	3.00
❑ 04639 [PS]	All Through the Night/Witness	1984	—	—	3.00
❑ 04737	Money Changes Everything (Studio)/Money Changes Everything (Live)	1984	—	—	3.00
❑ 04737 [PS]	Money Changes Everything (Studio)/Money Changes Everything (Live)	1984	—	—	3.00
❑ 04918	The Goonies 'R' Good Enough/What a Thrill	1985	—	—	3.00
❑ 04918 [PS]	The Goonies 'R' Good Enough/What a Thrill	1985	—	—	3.00
❑ 05480	Girls Just Want to Have Fun/Time After Time	198?	—	—	3.00

—Reissue

Number	Title (A Side/B Side)	Yr	VG	VG+	NM
❑ 05537	She Bop/All Through the Night	198?	—	—	3.00

—Reissue

Number	Title (A Side/B Side)	Yr	VG	VG+	NM
❑ 06247	True Colors/Heading for the Moon	1986	—	—	3.00
❑ 06247 [PS]	True Colors/Heading for the Moon	1986	—	—	3.00
❑ 06431	Change of Heart/Witness	1986	—	—	3.00
❑ 06431 [PS]	Change of Heart/Witness	1986	—	—	3.00
❑ 06970	What's Going On/One Track Mind	1987	—	—	3.00
❑ 06970 [PS]	What's Going On/One Track Mind	1987	—	—	3.00
❑ 07181	Boy Blue/The Faraway Nearby	1987	—	—	3.00
❑ 07181 [PS]	Boy Blue/The Faraway Nearby	1987	2.00	4.00	8.00

LAURELS, THE (1)

ABC-PARAMOUNT

Number	Title (A Side/B Side)	Yr	VG	VG+	NM
❑ 10048	Hand in Hand/Picture of Love	1959	12.50	25.00	50.00

LAURELS, THE (2)

"X"

Number	Title (A Side/B Side)	Yr	VG	VG+	NM
❑ 0143	Truly, Truly/'Tis Night	1955	62.50	125.00	250.00

LAURELS, THE (U)

May also be by group (2), but we're not sure.

SPRING

Number	Title (A Side/B Side)	Yr	VG	VG+	NM
❑ 1112	Baby Talk/You Left Me	1959	15.00	30.00	60.00

LAUREN, ROD

CHANCELLOR

Number	Title (A Side/B Side)	Yr	VG	VG+	NM
❑ 1126	I Ain't Got You/Mexicali Rose	1962	3.00	6.00	12.00
❑ 1132	Oh How I Miss You Tonight/Blame Your Friends	1963	3.00	6.00	12.00
❑ 1136	Yesterday's Lovers/I Know	1963	3.00	6.00	12.00
❑ 1141	I Wanna Know/Searcher for Love	1963	3.00	6.00	12.00
❑ 1146	Let Me Tell You 'Bout My Baby/I can't Get You Out of My Heart	1963	3.00	6.00	12.00

RCA VICTOR

Number	Title (A Side/B Side)	Yr	VG	VG+	NM
❑ 47-7645	If I Had a Girl/No Wonder	1959	3.75	7.50	15.00
❑ 47-7645 [PS]	If I Had a Girl/No Wonder	1959	5.00	10.00	20.00
❑ 47-7720	Listen My Love/This I Know	1960	3.75	7.50	15.00
❑ 47-7786	A Wild Imagination/The One Finger Symphony	1960	3.75	7.50	15.00
❑ 47-8020	I Dreamed/A Wondrous Place	1962	3.00	6.00	12.00

LAURIE, ANNIE

DELUXE

Number	Title (A Side/B Side)	Yr	VG	VG+	NM
❑ 6107	It Hurts to Be in Love/Hand in Hand	1957	5.00	10.00	20.00
❑ 6135	It Must Be Honey/Please Honey Don't Go	1957	3.75	7.50	15.00
❑ 6140	You're the Only One for Me/Out of My Mind	1957	3.75	7.50	15.00

Number	Title (A Side/B Side)	Yr	VG	VG+	NM
❑ 6151	Love Is a Funny Thing/Nobody's Gonna Hurt You Baby	1957	3.75	7.50	15.00
❑ 6173	Someday Someway/Hold On to What You Got	1958	3.75	7.50	15.00
❑ 6182	Since I Fell for You/Lost Love	1959	3.75	7.50	15.00
❑ 6189	If You're Lonely/It's Gonna Come Out in the Wash Someday	1960	3.75	7.50	15.00

OKEH

Number	Title (A Side/B Side)	Yr	VG	VG+	NM
❑ 6915	You Belong to Me/I Feel So Right Tonight	1952	6.25	12.50	25.00
❑ 6933	Stop Talkin' and Start Walkin'/Give Me Half a Chance	1953	6.25	12.50	25.00
❑ 6973	It's Been a Long, Long Time/I Ain't Got It Bad No More	1953	6.25	12.50	25.00
❑ 7025	I'm in the Mood for You/Feeling the Need	1954	5.00	10.00	20.00

SAVOY

Number	Title (A Side/B Side)	Yr	VG	VG+	NM
❑ 1197	You Promised Love/Rockin' and Rollin' Again	1956	5.00	10.00	20.00

LAURIE, LINDA

ANDIE

Number	Title (A Side/B Side)	Yr	VG	VG+	NM
❑ 5015	All Winter Long/Stay with Me	1960	3.00	6.00	12.00

GLORY

Number	Title (A Side/B Side)	Yr	VG	VG+	NM
❑ 290	Ambrose (Part Five)/Ooh! What a Lover	1958	3.75	7.50	15.00
❑ 294	Forever Ambrose/Wherever He Goes, I Go	1959	3.00	6.00	12.00

KEETCH

Number	Title (A Side/B Side)	Yr	VG	VG+	NM
❑ 6001	Jose He Say/Chico	197?	—	2.50	5.00

MCA

Number	Title (A Side/B Side)	Yr	VG	VG+	NM
❑ 40119	Leave Me Alone (Ruby Red Dress)/Sweet Deceiver	1973	—	3.00	6.00

RUST

Number	Title (A Side/B Side)	Yr	VG	VG+	NM
❑ 5022	Prince Charming/Soupin' Up Your Motor	1960	2.50	5.00	10.00
❑ 5042	Stay at Home Sue/Lazy Love	1961	2.50	5.00	10.00
❑ 5061	The Return of Ambrose/Chicken Little	1963	2.50	5.00	10.00

LAVETTE, BETTY

ATCO

Number	Title (A Side/B Side)	Yr	VG	VG+	NM
❑ 6891	Heart of Gold/You'll Wake Up Wisely	1972	—	3.00	6.00
❑ 6913	Your Turn to Cry/Soul Tambourine	1973	—	3.00	6.00

ATLANTIC

Number	Title (A Side/B Side)	Yr	VG	VG+	NM
❑ 2160	My Man — He's a Lovin' Man/Shut Your Mouth	1962	3.00	6.00	12.00
—As "Betty LaVett"					
❑ 2198	You'll Never Change/Here I Am	1963	3.00	6.00	12.00
—As "Betty LaVett"					

CALLA

Number	Title (A Side/B Side)	Yr	VG	VG+	NM
❑ 102	Let Me Down Easy/What I Don't Know (Won't Hurt Me)	1965	2.50	5.00	10.00
❑ 104	I Feel Good (All Over)/Only Your Love Can Save Me	1965	2.50	5.00	10.00
❑ 106	Stand Up Like a Man/I'm Just a Fool for You	1965	2.50	5.00	10.00

KAREN

Number	Title (A Side/B Side)	Yr	VG	VG+	NM
❑ 1540	Love Makes the World Go Round/Almost	1968	2.00	4.00	8.00
❑ 1544	Get Away/What Condition My Condition Was In	1968	2.00	4.00	8.00
❑ 1545	With a Little Help from My Friends/Hey Love	1969	2.00	4.00	8.00
❑ 1548	Ticket to the Moon/Let Me Down Easy	1969	2.00	4.00	8.00

LUPINE

Number	Title (A Side/B Side)	Yr	VG	VG+	NM
❑ 123	Witch Craft in the Air/You Killed the Love	1964	10.00	20.00	40.00
—As "Betty LaVett"					
❑ 1021	Witch Craft in the Air/You Killed the Love	1964	6.25	12.50	25.00
—As "Betty LaVett"					

MOTOWN

Number	Title (A Side/B Side)	Yr	VG	VG+	NM
❑ 1532	Right in the Middle (Of Falling in Love)/You Seen One, You Seen 'Em All	1981	—	2.50	5.00
—As "Bettye LaVette"					
❑ 1614	Either Way, We Lose/I Can't Stop	1982	—	2.50	5.00
—As "Bettye LaVette"					

SILVER FOX

Number	Title (A Side/B Side)	Yr	VG	VG+	NM
❑ 17	He Made a Woman Out of Me/Nearer to You	1969	—	3.00	6.00
❑ 21	Do Your Duty/Love's Made a Fool Out of Me	1970	—	3.00	6.00
❑ 24	Games People Play/My Train's Comin' In	1970	—	3.00	6.00

SSS INTERNATIONAL

Number	Title (A Side/B Side)	Yr	VG	VG+	NM
❑ 839	Take Another Piece of My Heart/At the Mercy of a Man	1971	—	3.00	6.00

WEST END

Number	Title (A Side/B Side)	Yr	VG	VG+	NM
❑ 1213	Doin' the Best That I Can/(Instrumental)	1983	—	2.50	5.00
—As "Bettye LaVette"					

LAVOIE, KENT

See LOBO.

LAWRENCE, SYD

COSMIC

Number	Title (A Side/B Side)	Yr	VG	VG+	NM
❑ 1001	The Answer to the Flying Saucer/Haunted Guitar	1956	10.00	20.00	40.00
—B-side by Billy Mure					

LAWRENCE, WALT

HOLLYWOOD INT'L.

Number	Title (A Side/B Side)	Yr	VG	VG+	NM
❑ 2	Cascade/Twilight Adrift	195?	10.00	20.00	40.00

LEADERS, THE

GLORY

Number	Title (A Side/B Side)	Yr	VG	VG+	NM
❑ 235	Stormy Weather/(B-side unknown)	1955	15.00	30.00	60.00

LEAPING FERNS, THE

Also recorded as CHANTAY'S.

X-PANDED SOUND

Number	Title (A Side/B Side)	Yr	VG	VG+	NM
❑ 103	It Never Works Out for Me/Maybe Baby	1964	7.50	15.00	30.00

LEAPY LEE

CADET

Number	Title (A Side/B Side)	Yr	VG	VG+	NM
❑ 5635	It's All Happening/It's Great	1969	—	3.50	7.00

DECCA

Number	Title (A Side/B Side)	Yr	VG	VG+	NM
❑ 32380	Little Arrows/Time Will Tell	1968	2.00	4.00	8.00
❑ 32436	Here Comes the Rain/I'm Gonna Spend My Love	1969	—	3.50	7.00
❑ 32492	Little Yellow Aeroplane/Boom Boom (That's How My Heart Beats)	1969	—	3.50	7.00
❑ 32584	Someone's in Love/Best to Forget	1969	—	3.50	7.00
❑ 32625	Good Morning/Teresa	1970	—	3.50	7.00
❑ 32692	Tupelo Mississippi Flash/Green Green Trees	1970	—	3.00	6.00
❑ 32808	Best to Forget/I'll Be Your Baby Tonight	1971	—	3.00	6.00

MAM

Number	Title (A Side/B Side)	Yr	VG	VG+	NM
❑ 3618	Just Another Night/My Advice to You	1972	—	3.00	6.00
❑ 3622	Summer Rain/No Full Moon	1972	—	3.00	6.00

MCA

Number	Title (A Side/B Side)	Yr	VG	VG+	NM
❑ 40470	Every Road Leads Back to You/Honey Go Drift Away	1975	—	2.50	5.00

LEARY, DR. TIMOTHY

MERCURY

Number	Title (A Side/B Side)	Yr	VG	VG+	NM
❑ 72713	Turn On, Tune In, Drop Out (Part 1)/Turn On, Tune In, Drop Out (Part 2)	1967	7.50	15.00	30.00

LEATHER BOY

FLOWER

Number	Title (A Side/B Side)	Yr	VG	VG+	NM
❑ 100	My Prayer/You Gotta Have Soul	1968	7.50	15.00	30.00

MGM

Number	Title (A Side/B Side)	Yr	VG	VG+	NM
❑ 13724	I'm a Leather Boy/Shadows	1967	7.50	15.00	30.00
❑ 13724 [PS]	I'm a Leather Boy/Shadows	1967	15.00	30.00	60.00
❑ 13790	On the Go/Soulin'	1967	7.50	15.00	30.00

PARKWAY

Number	Title (A Side/B Side)	Yr	VG	VG+	NM
❑ 125	Jersey Thursday/Black Friday	1966	7.50	15.00	30.00

LEAVES, THE

CAPITOL

Number	Title (A Side/B Side)	Yr	VG	VG+	NM
❑ 5799	Lemon Princess/Twilight Sanctuary	1966	3.00	6.00	12.00

MIRA

Number	Title (A Side/B Side)	Yr	VG	VG+	NM
❑ 202	Love Minus Zero-No Limit/Too Many People	1965	12.50	25.00	50.00
❑ 207	Hey Joe, Where You Gonna Go/Be with You	1965	25.00	50.00	100.00
❑ 213	You Better Move On/A Different Story	1966	12.50	25.00	50.00
❑ 220	Be with You/Funny Little World	1966	12.50	25.00	50.00
❑ 222	Hey Joe/Funny Little World	1966	12.50	25.00	50.00
❑ 222	Hey Joe/Girl from the East	1966	10.00	20.00	40.00
❑ 227	Too Many People/Girl from the East	1966	10.00	20.00	40.00
❑ 231	Get Out of My Life Woman/Girl from the East	1966	10.00	20.00	40.00
❑ 234	Be with You/You Better Move On	1966	10.00	20.00	40.00

LED ZEPPELIN

Also see JOHN PAUL JONES; JIMMY PAGE; ROBERT PLANT.

ATLANTIC

Number	Title (A Side/B Side)	Yr	VG	VG+	NM
❑ PR 157 [DJ]	Gallows Pole (mono/stereo)	1971	50.00	100.00	200.00
❑ PR 175 [DJ]	Stairway to Heaven (mono/stereo)	1972	25.00	50.00	100.00
❑ PR 175 [PS]	Stairway to Heaven (mono/stereo)	1972	62.50	125.00	250.00
❑ PR 269 [DJ]	Stairway to Heaven (stereo/stereo)	1973	12.50	25.00	50.00
❑ 2613	Communication Breakdown/Good Times Bad Times	1969	6.25	12.50	25.00
❑ 2690	Whole Lotta Love/Living Loving Maid (She's Just a Woman)	1969	3.75	7.50	15.00
—With A-side time of 3:12					
❑ 2690	Whole Lotta Love/Living Loving Maid (She's Just a Woman)	1969	5.00	10.00	20.00
—With A-side time of 5:33					
❑ 2777	Immigrant Song/Hey, Hey, What Can I Do	1970	6.25	12.50	25.00
—First pressings with "Do What Thou Wilt Shalt Be the Whole of the Law" in trail-off					
❑ 2777	Immigrant Song/Hey, Hey, What Can I Do	1970	3.75	7.50	15.00
—Second pressings without "Do What Thou Wilt Shalt Be the Whole of the Law" in trail-off					
❑ 2777	Immigrant Song/Hey, Hey, What Can I Do	1970	—	2.50	5.00
—Third pressings with smaller, bolder type; in print well into the late 1980s					
❑ 2777 [DJ]	Immigrant Song	1970	30.00	60.00	120.00
—One-sided promo					
❑ 2849	Black Dog/Misty Mountain Hop	1971	2.50	5.00	10.00
❑ 2865	Rock and Roll/Four Sticks	1972	2.50	5.00	10.00
❑ 2970	Over the Hills & Far Away/Dancing Days	1973	2.50	5.00	10.00
❑ 2986	D'yer Mak'er/The Crunge	1973	—	3.00	6.00
—Defective pressing -- the left channel starts to fade out midway through the A-side, making it sound like rechanneled stereo. The number "3" follows the matrix number in the trail-off wax of those copies we've encountered.					
❑ 2986	D'yer Mak'er/The Crunge	1973	2.50	5.00	10.00
—Normal pressing in true stereo throughout.					

SWAN SONG

Number	Title (A Side/B Side)	Yr	VG	VG+	NM
❑ 70102	Trampled Under Foot/Black Country Woman	1975	—	3.00	6.00
❑ 70110	Candy Store Rock/Royal Orleans	1976	—	3.00	6.00
❑ 71003	Fool in the Rain/Hot Dog	1979	—	3.00	6.00

LEE

See LEE MARENO.

LEE, ARTHUR

Also see LOVE.

A&M

Number	Title (A Side/B Side)	Yr	VG	VG+	NM
❑ 1361	Everybody's Gotta Live/Love Jumped Through My Window	1972	—	2.00	4.00
❑ 1381	Sad Song/You Want Change for Your Re-Run	1972	—	2.00	4.00

CAPITOL

Number	Title (A Side/B Side)	Yr	VG	VG+	NM
❑ 4980	Ninth Wave/Rumble Still Skins	1963	7.50	15.00	30.00

LEE, BILLY, AND THE RIVIERAS

Early version of MITCH RYDER AND THE DETROIT WHEELS.

HYLAND

Number	Title (A Side/B Side)	Yr	VG	VG+	NM
❑ 3016	Won't You Dance with Me/You Know	1964	6.25	12.50	25.00

LEE, BRENDA

DECCA

Number	Title (A Side/B Side)	Yr	VG	VG+	NM
❑ 30050	Jambalaya (On the Bayou)/Bigelow 6-2000	1956	7.50	15.00	30.00
❑ 30107	Christy Christmas/I'm Gonna Lasso Santa Claus	1956	6.25	12.50	25.00
❑ 30198	One Step at a Time/Fairyland	1957	6.25	12.50	25.00
❑ 30333	Dynamite/Love You 'Til I Die	1957	6.25	12.50	25.00
❑ 30411	Ain't That Love/One Teenager to Another	1957	6.25	12.50	25.00

Number	Title (A Side/B Side)	Yr	VG	VG+	NM
❑ 30535	Rock-a-Bye Baby Blues/Rock the Bop	1958	6.25	12.50	25.00
❑ 30673	Ring-a My Phone/Little Jonah	1958	7.50	15.00	30.00
❑ 30776	Rockin' Around the Christmas Tree/Papa Noel	1958	6.25	12.50	25.00
—Originals have black labels with star under "Decca"					
❑ 30776	Rockin' Around the Christmas Tree/Papa Noel	1960	3.75	7.50	15.00
—Reissues have black labels with color bars					
❑ 30776 [PS]	Rockin' Around the Christmas Tree/Papa Noel	1960	12.50	25.00	50.00
❑ 30806	Bill Bailey Won't You Please Come Home/ Hummin' the Blues	1959	6.25	12.50	25.00
❑ 30885	Let's Jump the Broomstick/One of These Days	1959	7.50	15.00	30.00
❑ 30967	Sweet Nothin's/Weep No More My Baby	1959	5.00	10.00	20.00
❑ 30967 [PS]	Sweet Nothin's/Weep No More My Baby	1959	30.00	60.00	120.00
❑ 31093	I'm Sorry/That's All You Gotta Do	1960	5.00	10.00	20.00
❑ 31093 [PS]	I'm Sorry/That's All You Gotta Do	1960	12.50	25.00	50.00
❑ 31149	I Want to Be Wanted/Just a Little	1960	3.75	7.50	15.00
❑ 31149 [PS]	I Want to Be Wanted/Just a Little	1960	10.00	20.00	40.00
❑ 31195	Emotions/I'm Learning About Love	1961	3.75	7.50	15.00
❑ 31195 [PS]	Emotions/I'm Learning About Love	1961	7.50	15.00	30.00
❑ 31231	You Can Depend on Me/It's Never Too Late	1961	3.75	7.50	15.00
❑ 31231 [PS]	You Can Depend on Me/It's Never Too Late	1961	7.50	15.00	30.00
❑ 31272	Dum Dum/Eventually	1961	3.75	7.50	15.00
❑ 31309	Fool #1/Anybody But Me	1961	3.75	7.50	15.00
❑ 31309 [PS]	Fool #1/Anybody But Me	1961	7.50	15.00	30.00
❑ 31348	Break It To Me Gently/So Deep	1962	3.75	7.50	15.00
❑ 31348 [PS]	Break It To Me Gently/So Deep	1962	6.25	12.50	25.00
❑ 31379	Everybody Loves Me But You/Here Comes That Feelin'	1962	3.75	7.50	15.00
❑ 31407	Heart in Hand/It Started All Over Again	1962	3.75	7.50	15.00
❑ 31424	All Alone Am I/Save All Your Lovin' for Me	1962	3.75	7.50	15.00
❑ 31424 [PS]	All Alone Am I/Save All Your Lovin' for Me	1962	6.25	12.50	25.00
❑ 31454	Your Used to Be/She'll Never Know	1963	3.75	7.50	15.00
❑ 31454 [PS]	Your Used to Be/She'll Never Know	1963	6.25	12.50	25.00
❑ 31478	Losing You/He's So Heavenly	1963	3.75	7.50	15.00
❑ 31478 [PS]	Losing You/He's So Heavenly	1963	6.25	12.50	25.00
❑ 31510	My Whole World Is Falling Down/I Wonder	1963	3.75	7.50	15.00
❑ 31510 [PS]	My Whole World Is Falling Down/I Wonder	1963	6.25	12.50	25.00
❑ 31539	The Grass Is Greener/Sweet Impossible You	1963	3.75	7.50	15.00
❑ 31539 [PS]	The Grass Is Greener/Sweet Impossible You	1963	6.25	12.50	25.00
❑ 31570	As Usual/Lonely Lonely Lonely Me	1963	3.75	7.50	15.00
❑ 31599	Think/The Waiting Game	1964	2.50	5.00	10.00
❑ 31599 [PS]	Think/The Waiting Game	1964	3.75	7.50	15.00
❑ 31628	Alone with You/My Dreams	1964	2.50	5.00	10.00
❑ 31628 [PS]	Alone with You/My Dreams	1964	3.75	7.50	15.00
❑ 31654	When You Loved Me/He's Sure to Remember Me	1964	2.50	5.00	10.00
❑ 31654 [PS]	When You Loved Me/He's Sure to Remember Me	1964	3.75	7.50	15.00
❑ 31687	Jingle Bell Rock/Winter Wonderland	1964	3.00	6.00	12.00
❑ 31687 [PS]	Jingle Bell Rock/Winter Wonderland	1964	4.00	8.00	16.00
❑ 31688	This Time of the Year/Christmas Will Be Just Another Lonely Day	1964	3.00	6.00	12.00
❑ 31688 [PS]	This Time of the Year/Christmas Will Be Just Another Lonely Day	1964	4.00	8.00	16.00
❑ 31690	Is It True/Just Behind the Rainbow	1964	2.50	5.00	10.00
❑ 31690 [PS]	Is It True/Just Behind the Rainbow	1964	3.75	7.50	15.00
❑ 31728	Thanks a Lot/The Crying Game	1965	2.50	5.00	10.00
❑ 31762	Truly, Truly, True/I Still Miss Someone	1965	2.50	5.00	10.00
❑ 31762 [PS]	Truly, Truly, True/I Still Miss Someone	1965	3.75	7.50	15.00
❑ 31792	Too Many Rivers/No One	1965	2.50	5.00	10.00
❑ 31849	Rusty Bells/If You Don't (Not Like You)	1965	2.50	5.00	10.00
❑ 31917	Too Little Time/Time and Time Again	1966	2.00	4.00	8.00
❑ 31970	Ain't Gonna Cry No More/It Takes One to Know One	1966	2.00	4.00	8.00
❑ 32018	Coming On Strong/You Keep Coming Back to Me	1966	2.00	4.00	8.00
❑ 32079	Ride, Ride, Ride/Lonely People Do Foolish Things	1967	2.00	4.00	8.00
❑ 32119	Born to Be By Your Side/Take Me	1967	2.00	4.00	8.00
❑ 32161	My Heart Keeps Hangin' On/Where Love Is	1967	2.00	4.00	8.00
❑ 32213	Where's the Melody/Save Me for a Rainy Day	1967	2.00	4.00	8.00
❑ 32248	That's All Right/Fantasy	1967	2.00	4.00	8.00
❑ 32299	Cabaret/Mood Indigo	1968	2.00	4.00	8.00
—With Pete Fountain					
❑ 32330	Kansas City/Each Day Is a Rainbow	1968	2.00	4.00	8.00
❑ 32428	Johnny One Time/I Must Have Been Out of My Mind	1968	2.00	4.00	8.00
❑ 32428 [PS]	Johnny One Time/I Must Have Been Out of My Mind	1968	3.75	7.50	15.00
❑ 32491	You Don't Need Me for Anything Anymore/Bring Me Sunshine	1969	—	3.00	6.00
❑ 32560	Let It Be Me/You Better Move On	1969	—	3.00	6.00
❑ 32675	I Think I Love You Again/Hello Love	1970	—	3.00	6.00
❑ 32734	Do Right Woman, Do Right Man/Sisters in Sorrow	1970	—	3.00	6.00
❑ 32848	If This Is Our Last Time/Everybody's Reaching Out for Someone	1971	—	3.00	6.00
❑ 32918	I'm a Memory/Misty Memories	1972	—	3.00	6.00
❑ 32975	Always on My Mind/That Ain't Right	1972	—	3.00	6.00
❑ 34060 [S]	Lazy River/You Always Hurt the One You Love	1962	5.00	10.00	20.00
❑ 34061 [S]	It's the Talk of the Town/You've Got Me Crying Again	1962	5.00	10.00	20.00
❑ 34062 [S]	How Deep Is the Ocean (How High Is the Sky)/ Send Me Some Lovin'	1962	5.00	10.00	20.00
❑ 34063 [S]	Fools Rush In (Where Angels Fear to Tread)/I'll Always Be in Love with You	1962	5.00	10.00	20.00
❑ 34064 [S]	I'll Be Seeing You/Hold Me	1962	5.00	10.00	20.00
—The above five are 7-inch 33 1/3 rpm singles with small holes					
❑ 34494 [DJ]	Where's the Melody? (same on both sides)	1967	3.75	7.50	15.00
—Promo-only number, pink label					
❑ 38236 [DJ]	Voice Tracks by Brenda Lee: For Brenda Lee Day, March 29, 1961/Introduction and Station Breaks for General Use	1961	10.00	20.00	40.00
—Pink label promo					
❑ 38275 [S]	If You Love Me (Really Love Me)/Just Another Lie	1961	5.00	10.00	20.00
❑ 38276 [S]	When I Fall in Love/Crazy Talk	1961	5.00	10.00	20.00
❑ 38277 [S]	Swanee River Rock/Around the World	1961	5.00	10.00	20.00
❑ 38278 [S]	Will You Love Me Tomorrow/Georgia on My Mind	1961	5.00	10.00	20.00
❑ 38279 [S]	I'm in the Mood for Love/Cry	1961	5.00	10.00	20.00
—The above five are 7-inch 33 1/3 rpm singles with small holes					
❑ 88215	Christy Christmas/I'm Gonna Lasso Santa Claus	1956	12.50	25.00	50.00
—As "Little Brenda Lee" on Decca's Children's Series					
❑ 88215 [PS]	Christy Christmas/I'm Gonna Lasso Santa Claus	1956	20.00	40.00	80.00
ELEKTRA					
❑ 45492	Left-Over Love/Could It Be I Found Love Tonight	1978	—	2.50	5.00
MCA					
❑ 40003	Nobody Wins/We Had a Good Thing Goin'	1973	—	2.50	5.00
❑ 40107	Sunday Sunrise/Must I Believe	1973	—	2.50	5.00
❑ 40171	Wrong Ideas/Something For A Rainy Day	1973	—	2.50	5.00
❑ 40262	Big Four Poster Bed/Castles In The Sand	1974	—	2.50	5.00
❑ 40318	Rock On Baby/More Than A Memory	1974	—	2.50	5.00
❑ 40385	He's My Rock/Feel Free	1975	—	2.50	5.00
❑ 40442	Bringing It Back/Papa's Knee	1975	—	2.50	5.00
❑ 40511	Find Yourself Another Puppet/What I Had With You	1976	—	2.50	5.00
❑ 40584	Brother Shelton/Now He's Coming Home	1976	—	2.50	5.00
❑ 40640	Takin' What I Can Get/Your Favorite Wornout Nightmare's Coming Home	1976	—	2.50	5.00
❑ 40683	Ruby's Lounge/Oklahoma Superstar	1977	—	2.50	5.00
❑ 41130	Tell Me What It's Like/Let Your Love Fall Back On Me	1979	—	2.50	5.00
❑ 41187	The Cowgirl And The Dandy/Do You Wanna Spend The Night	1980	—	2.50	5.00
❑ 41262	Keeping Me Warm For You/At The Moonlight	1980	—	2.50	5.00
❑ 41270	Don't Promise Me Anything (Do It)/You Only Broke My Heart	1980	—	2.50	5.00
❑ 41322	Broken Trust/Right Behind The Rain	1980	—	2.50	5.00
—With the Oak Ridge Boys					
❑ 51047	Every Now And Then/He'll Play The Music	1981	—	2.00	4.00
❑ 51113	Fool, Fool/Right Behind The Rain	1981	—	2.00	4.00
❑ 51154	Enough For You/What Am I Gonna Do	1981	—	2.00	4.00
❑ 51195	Only When I Laugh/Too Many Nights Alone	1981	—	2.00	4.00
❑ 51230	From Levis To Calvin Klein Jeans/I Know A Lot About Love	1982	—	2.00	4.00
❑ 52060	Keeping Me Warm For You/There's More To Me Than You Can See	1982	—	2.00	4.00
❑ 52124	Just For The Moment/Love Letters	1982	—	2.00	4.00
—With the Oak Ridge Boys					
❑ 52268	Didn't We Do It Good/We're So Close	1983	—	2.00	4.00
❑ 52394	A Sweeter Love (I'll Never Know)/A Woman's Mind	1984	—	2.00	4.00
❑ 52654	I'm Takin' My Time/That's The Way It Was Then	1985	—	2.00	4.00
❑ 52720	Why You Been Gone So Long/He Can't Make Your Kind of Love	1985	—	2.00	4.00
❑ 52720 [PS]	Why You Been Gone So Long/He Can't Make Your Kind of Love	1985	—	2.00	4.00
❑ 52804	Two Hearts/Loving Arms	1986	—	2.00	4.00
❑ 52804 [DJ]	Two Hearts (same on both sides)	1986	2.50	5.00	10.00
—Promo only on red vinyl					
❑ 60069	Sweet Nothin's/I Want to Be Wanted	197?	—	2.00	4.00
—Reissue; originals have black rainbow label					
❑ 60070	I'm Sorry/All Alone Am I	197?	—	2.00	4.00
—Reissue; originals have black rainbow label					
❑ 65027	Rockin' Around the Christmas Tree/Papa Noel	1973	—	2.00	4.00
—Black label with rainbow					
❑ 65027	Rockin' Around the Christmas Tree/Papa Noel	1980	—	—	3.00
—Blue label with rainbow					
❑ 65028	Jingle Bell Rock/Winter Wonderland	1973	—	2.00	4.00
—Black label with rainbow					
❑ 65028	Jingle Bell Rock/Winter Wonderland	1980	—	—	3.00
—Blue label with rainbow					
MONUMENT					
❑ 03781	You're Gonna Love Yourself (In the Morning)/ What Do You Think About Lovin'	1983	—	2.00	4.00
—A-side: With Willie Nelson; B-side: With Dolly Parton					
WARNER BROS.					
❑ 19303	A Little Unfair/Some of These Days	1991	—	—	3.00
❑ 19397	Your One and Only/You Better Do Better	1991	—	—	3.00

7-Inch Extended Plays

Number	Title (A Side/B Side)	Yr	VG	VG+	NM
DECCA					
❑ ED 2678	(contents unknown)	1960	5.00	10.00	20.00
❑ ED 2678 [PS]	Sweet Nothin's	1960	5.00	10.00	20.00
❑ ED 2682	Be My Love Again/Just Let Me Dream// Jambalaya/Wee Wee Willie	1960	5.00	10.00	20.00
❑ ED 2682 [PS]	(title unknown)	1960	5.00	10.00	20.00
❑ ED 2683	Dynamite/Heading Home//I'm Sorry/That's All You Gotta Do	1960	5.00	10.00	20.00
❑ ED 2683 [PS]	I'm Sorry	1960	5.00	10.00	20.00
❑ ED 2695	I Want to Be Wanted/Just a Little//Teach Me Tonite/Walkin' to New Orleans	1961	5.00	10.00	20.00
❑ ED 2695 [PS]	(title unknown)	1961	5.00	10.00	20.00
❑ ED 2702	Dum Dum/Eventually//When I Fall in Love/Build a Big Fence	1961	5.00	10.00	20.00
❑ ED 2702 [PS]	(title unknown)	1961	5.00	10.00	20.00
❑ ED 2704	Lover Come Back to Me/All the Way//Kansas City/On the Sunny Side of the Street	1961	5.00	10.00	20.00
❑ ED 2704 [PS]	Lover Come Back to Me	1961	5.00	10.00	20.00
❑ ED 2712	Fool #1/Anybody But Me//You Can Depend on Me/It's Never Too Late	1961	5.00	10.00	20.00
❑ ED 2712 [PS]	(title unknown)	1961	5.00	10.00	20.00
❑ ED 2716	Break It to Me Gently/Will You Love Me Tomorrow//Tragedy/So Deep	1962	5.00	10.00	20.00
❑ ED 2716 [PS]	Break It to Me Gently	1962	5.00	10.00	20.00
❑ ED 2725	Here Comes That Feeling/Everybody Loves Me But You//You've Got Me Crying Again/Lazy River	1962	5.00	10.00	20.00
❑ ED 2725 [PS]	Everybody Loves Me But You	1962	5.00	10.00	20.00

Number	Title (A Side/B Side)	Yr	VG	VG+	NM
❑ ED 2730	It Started All Over Again/Heart in Hand//You Always Hurt the One You Love/Cry	1962	5.00	10.00	20.00
❑ ED 2730 [PS]	(title unknown)	1962	5.00	10.00	20.00
❑ ED 2738	All Alone Am I/Why Me//It's a Lonely Old Town/ Save All Your Loving for Me	1962	5.00	10.00	20.00
❑ ED 2738 [PS]	All Alone Am I	1962	5.00	10.00	20.00
❑ ED 2745	My Coloring Book/I Left My Heart in San Francisco//What Kind of Fool Am I/Fly Me to the Moon	1962	5.00	10.00	20.00
❑ ED 2745 [PS]	Fly Me to the Moon	1962	5.00	10.00	20.00
❑ ED 2764	The Grass Is Greener/I Wonder//My Whole World Is Falling Down/Losing You	1963	5.00	10.00	20.00
❑ ED 2764 [PS]	The Grass Is Greener	1963	5.00	10.00	20.00
❑ ED 2775	As Usual/The End of the World//There Goes My Heart/Out in the Cold Again	1963	5.00	10.00	20.00
❑ ED 2775 [PS]	As Usual	1963	5.00	10.00	20.00
❑ ED 2801	Thanks a Lot/Think//Is It True/When You Love Me	1965	5.00	10.00	20.00
❑ ED 2801 [PS]	(title unknown)	1965	5.00	10.00	20.00
❑ 7-4216 [DJ]	You Always Hurt the One You Love/Lazy River/ You've Got Me Crying//I Miss You So/Fools Rush In/I'll Be Seeing You	1962	5.00	10.00	20.00
—Jukebox EP, stereo, small hole, plays at 33 1/3 rpm					
❑ 7-4216 [PS]	Sincerely	1962	5.00	10.00	20.00
❑ 7-4439 [DJ]	I Wanna Be Around/Our Day Will Come/You're the Reason I'm in Love//End of the World/Losing You/Break It to Me Gently	1963	5.00	10.00	20.00
—Jukebox EP, stereo, small hole, plays at 33 1/3 rpm					
❑ 7-4439 [PS]	Let Me Sing	1963	5.00	10.00	20.00
❑ 7-4825 [DJ]	What Now My Love/You Don't Have to Say You Love Me/You've Got Your Troubles//Up Tight/ Strangers in the Night/Call Me	1966	5.00	10.00	20.00
—Jukebox EP, stereo, small hole, plays at 33 1/3 rpm					
❑ 7-4825 [PS]	Coming On Strong	1966	5.00	10.00	20.00
❑ 7-34254	This Time of the Year/Blue Christmas/Jingle Bell Rock//Rockin' Around the Christmas Tree/ Marshmallow World/Winter Wonderland	1964	6.25	12.50	25.00
—Jukebox EP, stereo, small hole, plays at 33 1/3 rpm					
❑ 7-34254 [PS]	Merry Christmas	1964	6.25	12.50	25.00
—Sleeve says this is "DL 74583"; price includes title strips					
❑ 7-34363	Bye Bye Blues/September in the Rain/What a Difference a Day Makes//The Good Life/Shadow of Your Smile/Softly As I Leave You	1966	5.00	10.00	20.00
—Jukebox EP, stereo, small hole, plays at 33 1/3 rpm					
❑ 7-34363 [PS]	Bye Bye Blues	1966	5.00	10.00	20.00

LEE, BRENDA (2)

Not the same Brenda Lee as the others; this one's real name is Brenda Lee Jones.

Number	Title (A Side/B Side)	Yr	VG	VG+	NM
APOLLO					
❑ 490	I Ain't Gonna Give Nobody None/I'll Never Get Rich Again	1956	7.50	15.00	30.00

LEE, CURTIS

Also see C.L. AND THE PICTURES.

Number	Title (A Side/B Side)	Yr	VG	VG+	NM
DUNES					
❑ 801	California GH-903/Then I'll Know	1960	5.00	10.00	20.00
❑ 2001	Special Love/"D" in Love	1960	5.00	10.00	20.00
❑ 2003	Pledge of Love/Then I'll Know	1961	5.00	10.00	20.00
❑ 2003 [PS]	Pledge of Love/Then I'll Know	1961	6.25	12.50	25.00
❑ 2007	Pretty Little Angel Eyes/Gee, How I Wish	1961	6.25	12.50	25.00
❑ 2008	Under the Moon of Love/Beverly Jean	1961	6.25	12.50	25.00
—2007 and 2208 were Phil Spector productions					
❑ 2012	Just Another Fool/A Night at Daddy G's	1962	5.00	10.00	20.00
❑ 2015	Does He Mean That Much to You/The Wobble	1962	5.00	10.00	20.00
❑ 2020	Lonely Weekends/Better Him Than Me	1963	5.00	10.00	20.00
❑ 2021	Pickin' Up the Pieces of My Heart/Mr. Mistaker	1963	5.00	10.00	20.00
HOT					
❑ 7	I Never Knew What Love Could Do/Gotta Have You	1960	18.75	37.50	75.00
MIRA					
❑ 240	Sweet Baby/Is She In Your Town	1967	5.00	10.00	20.00
ROJAC					
❑ 114	Get In My Bag/Everybody's Going Wild	1967	3.00	6.00	12.00
SABRA					
❑ 517	Let's Take a Ride/I'm Asking Forgiveness	1960	6.25	12.50	25.00
WARRIOR					
❑ 1555	With All My Heart/Pure Love	1959	7.50	15.00	30.00

LEE, DICKEY

Number	Title (A Side/B Side)	Yr	VG	VG+	NM
ATCO					
❑ 6546	Run Right Back/Red, Green, Yellow, Blue	1968	2.00	4.00	8.00
❑ 6580	All My Life/Hang-Ups	1968	2.00	4.00	8.00
❑ 6609	You're Young and You'll Forget/Waitin' for Love to Come My Way	1968	2.00	4.00	8.00
DIAMOND					
❑ 266	Ruby Baby/I Remember Barbara	1969	2.00	4.00	8.00
DOT					
❑ 16087	Life in a Teenage World/Why Don't You Write On	1960	3.75	7.50	15.00
HALLWAY					
❑ 1924	Big Brother/She's Walking Away	1964	2.50	5.00	10.00
MERCURY					
❑ 55068	I'm Just a Heartache Away/Midnight Flyer	1979	—	2.00	4.00
❑ 57005	He's an Old Rock 'N' Roller/It Hurts to Be in Love	1979	—	2.00	4.00
❑ 57017	Don't Look Back/I'm Trustin' a Feelin'	1980	—	2.00	4.00
❑ 57027	Workin' My Way to Your Heart/If You Want Me	1980	—	2.00	4.00
❑ 57036	Lost in Love/Again	1980	—	2.00	4.00
—A-side with Kathy Burdick					
❑ 57052	Honky Tonk Hearts/Best I Hit the Road	1981	—	2.00	4.00
❑ 57056	I Wonder If I Care As Much/Further Than a Country Mile	1981	—	2.00	4.00
❑ 76129	Everybody Loves a Winner/You Won't Be Here Tonight	1982	—	2.00	4.00
RCA					
❑ PB-10764	9,999,999 Tears/I Never Will Get Over You	1976	—	2.00	4.00
❑ PB-10914	If You Gotta Make a Fool of Somebody/My Love Shows Thru	1977	—	2.00	4.00
❑ GB-10929	Rocky/9,999,999 Tears	1977	—	—	3.00
—Gold Standard Series					
❑ PB-11009	Virginia, How Far Will You Go/My Love Shows Thru	1977	—	2.00	4.00
❑ PB-11125	Peanut Butter/Breezy Was Her Name	1977	—	2.00	4.00
❑ PB-11191	Love Is a Word/I'll Be Leaving Alone	1978	—	2.00	4.00
❑ PB-11294	My Heart Won't Cry Anymore/Danna	1978	—	2.00	4.00
❑ PB-11389	It's Not Easy/I've Been Honky-Tonkin' Too Long	1978	—	2.00	4.00
RCA VICTOR					
❑ APBO-0082	Sparklin' Brown Eyes/Country Song	1973	—	2.50	5.00
❑ APBO-0227	I Use the Soap/Strawberry Women	1974	—	2.50	5.00
❑ PB-10014	Give Me One Good Reason/Sweet Fever	1974	—	2.50	5.00
❑ PB-10091	The Busiest Memory in Town/Way to Go On	1974	—	2.50	5.00
❑ PB-10289	You Make It Look So Easy/The Door's Always Open	1975	—	2.00	4.00
❑ PB-10361	Rocky/The Closest Thing to You	1975	—	2.00	4.00
❑ PB-10543	Angels, Roses and Rain/Danna	1976	—	2.00	4.00
❑ PB-10684	Makin' Love Don't Always Make Love Grow/I Never Will Get Over You	1976	—	2.00	4.00
❑ 47-9862	All Too Soon/Charlie	1970	—	3.00	6.00
❑ 47-9941	Home To/Special	1971	—	3.00	6.00
❑ 47-9988	The Mahogany Pulpit/Everybody's Reaching Out for Someone	1971	—	3.00	6.00
❑ 48-1013	Never Ending Song of Love/On the Southbound	1971	—	3.00	6.00
❑ 74-0623	I Saw My Lady/What We Used to Hang On To	1971	—	3.00	6.00
❑ 74-0710	Ashes of Love/The Kingdom I Call Home	1972	—	2.50	5.00
❑ 74-0798	Baby, Bye Bye/She Thinks I Still Care	1972	—	2.50	5.00
❑ 74-0892	Crying Over You/My World Around You	1973	—	2.50	5.00
❑ 74-0980	Put Me Down Softly/If She Turns Up in Atlanta	1973	—	2.50	5.00
RENDEZVOUS					
❑ 188	Dream Boy/Stay True Baby	1962	6.25	12.50	25.00
SMASH					
❑ 1758	Patches/More or Less	1962	3.75	7.50	15.00
❑ 1791	I Saw Linda Yesterday/The Girl I Can't Forget	1962	3.00	6.00	12.00
❑ 1808	Don't Wanna Talk About Paula/Just a Friend	1963	3.00	6.00	12.00
❑ 1822	I Go Lonely/Ten Million Faces	1963	3.00	6.00	12.00
❑ 1844	She Wants to Be Bobby's Girl/The Day the Sawmill Closed Down	1963	3.00	6.00	12.00
❑ 1871	To the Aisle/Mother Nature	1964	3.00	6.00	12.00
❑ 1913	Me and My Teardrops/Only Trust in Me	1964	3.00	6.00	12.00
SUN					
❑ 280	Good Lovin'/Memories Never Grow Old	1957	7.50	15.00	30.00
❑ 297	Dreamy Nights/Fool, Fool, Fool	1958	20.00	40.00	80.00
TAMPA					
❑ 131	Dream Boy/Stay True Baby	1957	7.50	15.00	30.00
TCF HALL					
❑ 102	Laurie (Strange Things Happen)/Party Doll	1965	2.50	5.00	10.00
❑ 111	The Girl from Peyton Place/The Girl I Used to Know	1965	2.50	5.00	10.00
❑ 118	Good Girl Goin' Bad/Pretty White Dress	1965	2.50	5.00	10.00
❑ 128	Good Guy/Annie	1966	2.50	5.00	10.00

LEE, JACKIE (1)

Male R&B singer whose biggest hit was "The Duck."

Number	Title (A Side/B Side)	Yr	VG	VG+	NM
ABC					
❑ 11146	One for the Road/Darkest Days	1968	5.00	10.00	20.00
CAPITOL					
❑ 3145	25 Miles to Louisiana/Pershing Square	1971	—	3.00	6.00
KEYMEN					
❑ 109	Glory of Love/Bring It Home	1968	2.50	5.00	10.00
❑ 114	African Boo-Ga-Loo/(B-side unknown)	1968	2.50	5.00	10.00
MIRWOOD					
❑ 5502	The Duck/Let Your Conscience Be Your Guide	1965	3.00	6.00	12.00
❑ 5509	Your P-E-R-S-O-N-A-L-I-T-Y/Try My Method	1966	2.50	5.00	10.00
❑ 5510	The Shotgun and the Duck/Do the Temptation Walk	1966	2.50	5.00	10.00
❑ 5519	You're Everything/Would You Believe	1966	2.50	5.00	10.00
❑ 5527	Don't Be Ashamed/Oh, My Darlin'	1966	2.50	5.00	10.00
❑ 5528	Baby I'm Satisfied/Whether It's Right or Wrong	1966	2.50	5.00	10.00
—With Dolores Hall					
UNI					
❑ 55206	The Chicken/I Love You	1970	2.00	4.00	8.00
❑ 55259	Your Sweetness Is My Weakness/You Were Searching for a Love	1970	2.00	4.00	8.00

LEE, JACKIE (2)

Philadelphia-based keyboard player.

Number	Title (A Side/B Side)	Yr	VG	VG+	NM
ABC-PARAMOUNT					
❑ 9892	The Storm/Bye Bye Blues	1958	2.50	5.00	10.00
CORAL					
❑ 61214	The Donkey Serenade/Mr. Hot Piano	1954	3.00	6.00	12.00
❑ 61259	Bei Mir Bist Du Schoen/Missouri Waltz	1954	3.00	6.00	12.00
❑ 61304	I Can't Give You Anything But Love/Blue Boogie	1954	3.00	6.00	12.00
❑ 61400	Chop Sticks/Luigi's Wedding	1955	3.00	6.00	12.00
❑ 61461	Cannibal King/The Spoon Song	1955	3.00	6.00	12.00
❑ 61534	Aloha Oe/More, More, More	1955	3.00	6.00	12.00
❑ 61579	A String of Pearls/Always Love Me	1956	2.50	5.00	10.00
❑ 61638	Crazy Polka/Elmer's Tune	1956	2.50	5.00	10.00
❑ 61734	Chatterbox/Dardanella	1956	2.50	5.00	10.00
❑ 61827	Baby Buggy Boogie/Sippin' Soda	1957	2.50	5.00	10.00
SURE					
❑ 1738	Do the New Hully Gully/Patricia	1962	2.50	5.00	10.00
❑ 1767	Hungarian Rhapsody Boogie/Bumpy	1962	2.50	5.00	10.00
SWAN					
❑ 4034	Happy Vacation/The Hucklebuck	1959	3.00	6.00	12.00
❑ 4039	Like Sunset/Rancho	1959	3.00	6.00	12.00

LEE, JACKIE (3)

Female singer.

EPIC

Number	Title (A Side/B Side)	Yr	VG	VG+	NM
❑ 9807	I Cry Alone/'Cause I Love Him	1965	2.50	5.00	10.00
❑ 10183	Love Is Gone/The Lonely Clown	1967	2.00	4.00	8.00

LEE, JACKIE, AND THE RAINDROPS

LONDON INT'L.

Number	Title (A Side/B Side)	Yr	VG	VG+	NM
❑ 10602	The Last One to Know/There's No One in the Whole Wide World	1962	3.00	6.00	12.00

LEE, JENNY, AND THE STARLETS

CONGRESS

Number	Title (A Side/B Side)	Yr	VG	VG+	NM
❑ 107	What I Gotta Do/Show Me a Man	1962	3.75	7.50	15.00

LEE, JOHNNY

For records on DeLuxe, see JOHN LEE HOOKER.

LEE, NANCY

ACME

Number	Title (A Side/B Side)	Yr	VG	VG+	NM
❑ 711	So They Say/(B-side unknown)	1957	20.00	40.00	80.00

LEE, PEGGY

Number	Title (A Side/B Side)	Yr	VG	VG+	NM
ATLANTIC					
❑ 3215	Let's Love/Always	1974	—	2.00	4.00
A&M					
❑ 1771	I Remember/Some Cats Know	1975	—	2.00	4.00
CAPITOL					
❑ F791	The Old Master Painter/Bless You	1949	6.25	12.50	25.00
—With Mel Torme					
❑ F801	My Small Senor/When You Speak with Your Eyes	1950	5.00	10.00	20.00
❑ F810	Save Your Sorrow for Tomorrow/Sugar	1950	5.00	10.00	20.00
❑ F849	Sunshine Cake/Goodbye John	1950	5.00	10.00	20.00
❑ F898	Crazy He Calls Me/Them There Eyes	1950	5.00	10.00	20.00
❑ F961	Cry, Cry, Cry/Once Around the Moon	1950	5.00	10.00	20.00
❑ F1105	Show Me the Way to Get Out of This World ('Cause That's Where Everything Is)/Happy Music	1950	5.00	10.00	20.00
❑ F1161	Lover Come Back to Me/Helpless	1950	5.00	10.00	20.00
❑ F1244	Once in a Lifetime/Love Is So Peculiar	1950	5.00	10.00	20.00
❑ F1298	Where Are You/Ay-Ay-Chug-a-Lug	1950	5.00	10.00	20.00
❑ F1366	Climb Up the Mountain/The Mill on the Floss	1951	3.75	7.50	15.00
❑ F1428	Yeah, Yeah, Yeah/Rock Me to Sleep	1951	3.75	7.50	15.00
❑ F1450	That Ol' Devil/Cannonball Express	1951	3.75	7.50	15.00
❑ F1513	He's Only Wonderful/It Never Happens to Me	1951	3.75	7.50	15.00
❑ F1544	Boulevard Café/If You Turn Me Down	1951	3.75	7.50	15.00
❑ F1573	(When I Dance with You) I Get Ideas/Tonight You Belong to Me	1951	3.75	7.50	15.00
❑ F1586	My Magic Heart/So Far So Good	1951	3.75	7.50	15.00
❑ F1601	It's a Good Day/Them There Eyes	1951	3.75	7.50	15.00
—Reissue of 78 rpm recordings from the 1940s					
❑ F1602	Manana (Is Soon Enough for Me)/Why Don't You Do It Right	1951	3.75	7.50	15.00
—Reissue of 78 rpm recordings from the 1940s					
❑ F1609	That Old Feeling/Solitude	1951	3.75	7.50	15.00
—B-side by the Capitol Jazzmen; reissue of 1940s material					
❑ F1667	I Can't Give You Anything But Love/I Don't Know Enough About You	1951	3.75	7.50	15.00
—Reissue of 78 rpm recordings from the 1940s					
❑ F1683	While We're Young/Golden Earrings	195?	3.00	6.00	12.00
—Reissue					
❑ F1749	I Love You But I Don't Like You/Wandering Swallow	1951	3.75	7.50	15.00
❑ F1776	While We're Young/Birmingham Jail	1951	3.75	7.50	15.00
❑ SM-1857 [S]	Mack the Knife/(B-side unknown)	1963	3.75	7.50	15.00
—Small hole, plays at 33 1/3 rpm					
❑ F1926	Shame on You/Would You Dance	1952	3.75	7.50	15.00
❑ F2025	Everytime/Goin' On a Hayride	1952	3.75	7.50	15.00
❑ 2171	Reason to Believe/Didn't Want to Have to Do It	1968	—	3.00	6.00
❑ 2308	Misty Roses/It'll Never Happen Again	1968	—	3.00	6.00
❑ 2477	Spinning Wheel/Lean On Me	1969	—	3.00	6.00
❑ 2602	Is That All There Is/Me and My Shadow	1969	—	3.00	6.00
❑ 2696	Something/Whistle for Happiness	1969	—	3.00	6.00
❑ 2721	My Old Flame/Love Story	1970	—	2.50	5.00
❑ 2817	Have You Seen My Baby/You'll Remember Me	1970	—	2.50	5.00
❑ 2910	One More Ride on the Merry-Go-Round/Pieces of Dreams	1970	—	2.50	5.00
❑ 3113	Where Did They Go/All I Want	1971	—	2.50	5.00
❑ 3439	Someone Who Cares/Love Song	1972	—	2.50	5.00
❑ F3722	Every Night/Baby, Baby, Wait for Me	1957	3.00	6.00	12.00
❑ F3811	Listen to the Rockin' Bird/Uninvited Dream	1957	3.00	6.00	12.00
❑ F3998	Fever/You Don't Know	1958	3.00	6.00	12.00
❑ F4071	Light of Love/Sweetheart	1958	3.00	6.00	12.00
❑ F4115	Alright, OK, You Win/My Man	1959	3.00	6.00	12.00
❑ F4189	Hallelujah I Love Him So/I'm Looking Out the Window	1959	3.00	6.00	12.00
❑ F4243	You Came a Long Way from St. Louis/I Lost My Sugar in Salt Lake City	1959	3.00	6.00	12.00
❑ 4298	You Deserve/Where Do I Go from Here	1959	3.00	6.00	12.00
❑ 4311	The Tree/The Christmas List	1959	3.75	7.50	15.00
❑ 4311 [PS]	The Tree/The Christmas List	1959	5.00	10.00	20.00
❑ 4349	Heart/C'est Magnifique	1960	2.50	5.00	10.00
❑ 4449	I'm Gonna Go Fishin'/My Gentle Young Johnny	1960	2.50	5.00	10.00
❑ 4474	I Like a Sleighride (Jingle Bells)/Christmas Carousel	1960	3.00	6.00	12.00
❑ 4474 [PS]	I Like A Sleighride (Jingle Bells)/Christmas Carousel	1960	10.00	20.00	40.00
❑ 4498	Bucket of Tears/I Love Being Here with You	1961	2.50	5.00	10.00
❑ 4576	Boston Beans/Yes Indeed	1961	2.50	5.00	10.00
❑ 4610	Hey, Look Me Over/When He Makes Music	1961	2.50	5.00	10.00
❑ 4750	The Sweetest Sounds/Loads of Love	1962	2.50	5.00	10.00
❑ 4812	Tell All the World About You/Amazing	1962	2.50	5.00	10.00
❑ 4888	I'm a Woman/Big Bad Bill	1962	2.50	5.00	10.00
❑ 4942	Alley Cat Song/O Barquinho (Little Boat)	1963	2.50	5.00	10.00
❑ 5001	The Doodlin' Song/Got That Magic	1963	2.50	5.00	10.00
❑ 5121	I Can't Stop Loving You/A Lot of Livin' to Do	1964	2.50	5.00	10.00
❑ 5241	In the Name of Love/My Sin	1964	2.50	5.00	10.00
❑ 5289	Talk to Me Baby/After You've Gone	1964	2.50	5.00	10.00
❑ 5346	That's What It Takes/Pass Me By	1965	2.00	4.00	8.00
❑ 5404	Bewitched/Sneakin' Up on You	1965	2.00	4.00	8.00
❑ 5469	The Sandpiper Love Theme (The Shadow of Your Smile)/Maybe This Summer	1965	2.00	4.00	8.00
❑ 5488	I Go to Sleep/Stop Living in the Past	1965	2.00	4.00	8.00
❑ 5521	Everybody Has the Right to Be Wrong/Free Spirits	1965	2.00	4.00	8.00
❑ 5557	Big Spender/Trapped	1965	2.00	4.00	8.00
❑ 5605	That Man/You Don't Know	1966	2.00	4.00	8.00
❑ 5653	Come Back to Me/You've Got Possibilities	1966	2.00	4.00	8.00
❑ 5678	Stay with Me/Happy Feet	1966	2.00	4.00	8.00
❑ 5758	So What's New/Walking Happy	1966	2.00	4.00	8.00
❑ 5988	I Feel It/Lonesome Road	1967	—	3.00	6.00
❑ S7-19343	Happy Holiday/Auld Lang Syne	1996	—	—	3.00
—B-side by Guy Lombardo					
❑ 54-90035	The Christmas Spell/Song at Midnight	1949	10.00	20.00	40.00
DECCA					
❑ 27238	Watermelon Weather/The Moon Came Up	1950	3.75	7.50	15.00
—With Bing Crosby					
❑ 27813	Just One of Those Things/I'm Glad There Is You	1951	3.75	7.50	15.00
❑ 28142	Be Anything/Forgive Me	1952	3.75	7.50	15.00
❑ 28215	Lover/You Go to My Head	1952	3.75	7.50	15.00
❑ 28313	Just One of Those Things/I'm Glad There Is You	1952	3.75	7.50	15.00
❑ 28395	San Souci/River, River	1952	3.75	7.50	15.00
❑ 28565	This Is a Very Special Day/I Hear the Music Now	1953	3.75	7.50	15.00
❑ 28631	Who's Gonna Pay the Check/Sorry, Baby, You Let My Love Get Cold	1953	3.75	7.50	15.00
❑ 28737	I've Got You Under My Skin/My Heart Belongs to Daddy	1953	3.75	7.50	15.00
❑ 28889	Apples, Peaches and Cherries/Night Holds No Fear	1953	3.75	7.50	15.00
❑ 28890	Baubles, Bangles and Beads/Love You So	1953	3.75	7.50	15.00
❑ 28939	Ring Those Christmas Bells/It's Christmas Time Again	1953	3.75	7.50	15.00
❑ 29003	Go You Where You Go/Where Can I Go Without You	1954	3.75	7.50	15.00
❑ 29076	Juhnny Guitar/Autumn in Rome	1954	3.75	7.50	15.00
❑ 29164	Summer Vacation/That's What a Woman Is For	1954	3.75	7.50	15.00
❑ 29250	Love, You Didn't Do Right by Me/Sisters	1954	3.75	7.50	15.00
❑ 29342	God Rest Ye Merry Gentlemen/White Christmas	1954	3.75	7.50	15.00
—A-side with Trudi Stevens; B-side by Bing Crosby and Danny Kaye					
❑ 29359	It Must Be So/Straight Ahead	1954	3.00	6.00	12.00
—With the Mills Brothers					
❑ 29373	Let Me Go Lover/Bouquet of Roses	1954	3.00	6.00	12.00
❑ 29427	He's a Tramp/The Siamese Cat Song	1955	3.00	6.00	12.00
❑ 29429	I Belong to You/How Bitter, My Sweet	1955	3.00	6.00	12.00
❑ 29460	Bella Notte/La La Lu	1955	3.00	6.00	12.00
❑ 29534	Ooh, That Kiss/Oh! No!	1955	3.00	6.00	12.00
❑ 29605	Sing a Rainbow/He Needs Me	1955	3.00	6.00	12.00
❑ 29608	What Can I Say After I Say I'm Sorry/Sugar	1955	3.00	6.00	12.00
❑ 29681	Me/Pablo Pasablo	1955	3.00	6.00	12.00
❑ 29834	Mr. Wonderful/Crazy in the Heart	1956	3.00	6.00	12.00
❑ 29837	The Comeback/You've Got to See Mamma Every Night	1956	3.00	6.00	12.00
❑ 29877	Joey, Joey, Joey/They Can't Take That Away from Me	1956	3.00	6.00	12.00
❑ 29994	That's Alright Honey/We Laughed at Love	1956	3.00	6.00	12.00
❑ 30059	You Oughta Be Mine/I Don't Know Enough About You	1956	3.00	6.00	12.00
❑ 30117	Where Flamingos Fly/Gypsy with Fire in Her Shoes	1956	3.00	6.00	12.00
❑ 30494	Never Mind/Wrong, Wrong, Wrong	1957	2.50	5.00	10.00
❑ 30879	It Ain't Necessarily So/Swing Low Sweet Chariot	1959	2.50	5.00	10.00

LEE AND THE LEOPARDS

Number	Title (A Side/B Side)	Yr	VG	VG+	NM
FORTUNE					
❑ 867	What About Me/Don't Press Your Luck	1964	12.50	25.00	50.00
GORDY					
❑ 7002	Come Into My Palace/Trying to Make It	1962	15.00	30.00	60.00
LAURIE					
❑ 3197	Come Into My Palace/Trying to Make It	1963	6.25	12.50	25.00

LEFT BANKE, THE

Number	Title (A Side/B Side)	Yr	VG	VG+	NM
CAMERICA					
❑ 005	Queen of Paradise/And One Day	1978	—	2.50	5.00
SMASH					
❑ 2041	Walk Away Renee/I Haven't Got the Nerve	1966	3.75	7.50	15.00
❑ 2074	Pretty Ballerina/Lazy Day	1966	3.75	7.50	15.00
❑ 2089	Ivy, Ivy/And Suddenly	1967	3.00	6.00	12.00
❑ 2097	She May Call You Up Tonight/Barterers and Their Wives	1967	3.00	6.00	12.00
❑ 2119	Desiree/I've Got Something on My Mind	1967	3.00	6.00	12.00
❑ 2119 [PS]	Desiree/I've Got Something on My Mind	1967	6.25	12.50	25.00
❑ 2165	Dark Is the Bark/My Friend Today	1968	3.00	6.00	12.00
❑ 2198	Goodbye Holly/Sing, Little Bird, Sing	1968	3.00	6.00	12.00
❑ 2209	Bryant Hotel/Give the Man a Hand	1969	3.00	6.00	12.00
❑ 2243	Myrah/Pedestal	1969	10.00	20.00	40.00
—Picture sleeves are bootlegs					

LEGENDARY MASKED SURFERS, THE

Also see JAN AND DEAN.

UNITED ARTISTS

Number	Title (A Side/B Side)	Yr	VG	VG+	NM
❑ XW270	Summer Means Fun/Gonna Hustle You	1973	5.00	10.00	20.00
—Original pressings have a Jan & Dean recording on them by mistake					
❑ XW270	Summer Means Fun/Gonna Hustle You	1973	30.00	60.00	120.00
—With the intended recording, a newly-recorded vocal track					
❑ XW270 [PS]	Summer Means Fun/Gonna Hustle You	1973	7.50	15.00	30.00

Number	Title (A Side/B Side)	Yr	VG	VG+	NM
❑ 50958	Summertime, Summertime/Gonna Hustle You	1972	7.50	15.00	30.00

LEGENDARY STARDUST COWBOY, THE

MERCURY

Number	Title (A Side/B Side)	Yr	VG	VG+	NM
❑ 72862	Paralyzed/Who's Knocking on My Door	1968	5.00	10.00	20.00
❑ 72891	Down in the Wrecking Yard/I Took a Trip on a Gemini Spaceship	1969	5.00	10.00	20.00
❑ 72912	Everything's Getting Bigger But Our Love/Kiss and Run	1969	5.00	10.00	20.00

NORTON

Number	Title (A Side/B Side)	Yr	VG	VG+	NM
❑ 012	I Hate CD's/Linda	199?	—	—	2.00
❑ 012 [PS]	I Hate CD's/Linda	199?	—	—	2.00

PSYCHO-SUAVE

Number	Title (A Side/B Side)	Yr	VG	VG+	NM
❑ 1033	Paralyzed/Who's Knocking on My Door	1968	7.50	15.00	30.00

LEGENDS, THE

Several different groups.

BRIDGE SOCIETY

Number	Title (A Side/B Side)	Yr	VG	VG+	NM
❑ 2204	Keep On Running/Cheating	1968	10.00	20.00	40.00

CALDWELL

Number	Title (A Side/B Side)	Yr	VG	VG+	NM
❑ 410	Go Away with Me/Jungle Lullaby	1962	6.25	12.50	25.00

CAPITOL

Number	Title (A Side/B Side)	Yr	VG	VG+	NM
❑ 5014	Summertime Blues/Run to the Movies	1963	5.00	10.00	20.00

COLUMBIA

Number	Title (A Side/B Side)	Yr	VG	VG+	NM
❑ 41949	Theme from "Exodus"/Later	1961	3.00	6.00	12.00

DOC HOLLIDAY

Number	Title (A Side/B Side)	Yr	VG	VG+	NM
❑ 107	Surf's Up/Dance with the Drummer Man	1963	10.00	20.00	40.00
❑ 107 [PS]	Surf's Up/Dance with the Drummer Man	1963	12.50	25.00	50.00

EPIC

Number	Title (A Side/B Side)	Yr	VG	VG+	NM
❑ 10937	Rock and Roll Woman/Problems	1973	2.00	4.00	8.00

ERMINE

Number	Title (A Side/B Side)	Yr	VG	VG+	NM
❑ 39	My Love for You/Say Mama	1962	12.50	25.00	50.00
❑ 41	Lariat/Late Train	1962	10.00	20.00	40.00
❑ 43	Bop-A-Lena/I Wish I Knew	1962	12.50	25.00	50.00
❑ 45	Temptation/Marionette	1962	10.00	20.00	40.00

HART-VAN

Number	Title (A Side/B Side)	Yr	VG	VG+	NM
❑ 18003	Traction/As Long As I Live	1962	7.50	15.00	30.00

HEART

Number	Title (A Side/B Side)	Yr	VG	VG+	NM
❑ 7672	Rock and Roll Woman/Problems	1972	5.00	10.00	20.00

HULL

Number	Title (A Side/B Side)	Yr	VG	VG+	NM
❑ 727	The Legend of Love/Now I'm Telling You	1958	25.00	50.00	100.00
—Red label					
❑ 727	The Legend of Love/Now I'm Telling You	1962	7.50	15.00	30.00
—Multicolor label					

JAMIE

Number	Title (A Side/B Side)	Yr	VG	VG+	NM
❑ 1228	Tell the Truth/You'll Never See the Forest	1962	5.00	10.00	20.00

KEY

Number	Title (A Side/B Side)	Yr	VG	VG+	NM
❑ 1002	Lariat/Gail	1961	10.00	20.00	40.00
❑ 1002	Lariat/Late Train	1961	10.00	20.00	40.00

MELBA

Number	Title (A Side/B Side)	Yr	VG	VG+	NM
❑ 109	I'll Never Fall in Love Again/Eyes of an Angel	1957	37.50	75.00	150.00
—Label with double horizontal lines					
❑ 109	I'll Never Fall in Love Again/Eyes of an Angel	1961	10.00	20.00	40.00
—Label with no horizontal lines					

PARROT

Number	Title (A Side/B Side)	Yr	VG	VG+	NM
❑ 45010	Just in Case/If I Only Had Her Back	1965	3.00	6.00	12.00
❑ 45011	Alright/How Can I Find Her	1965	3.00	6.00	12.00

RAILROAD HOUSE

Number	Title (A Side/B Side)	Yr	VG	VG+	NM
❑ 12003	High Towers/Fever Games	1969	5.00	10.00	20.00
❑ 12003 [PS]	High Towers/Fever Games	1969	7.50	15.00	30.00

THAMES

Number	Title (A Side/B Side)	Yr	VG	VG+	NM
❑ 104	Raining in My Heart/(B-side unknown)	1964	7.50	15.00	30.00

UP

Number	Title (A Side/B Side)	Yr	VG	VG+	NM
❑ 2202	Baby, Get Your Head Screwed On/Why	1968	12.50	25.00	50.00

WARNER BROS.

Number	Title (A Side/B Side)	Yr	VG	VG+	NM
❑ 5457	Here Comes the Rain/Don't Be Ashamed	1964	3.75	7.50	15.00

LEHRER, TOM

REPRISE

Number	Title (A Side/B Side)	Yr	VG	VG+	NM
❑ 0862	Pollution/Who's Next	1969	2.00	4.00	8.00

LEIGH, LINDA

AMERICAN INT'L.

Number	Title (A Side/B Side)	Yr	VG	VG+	NM
❑ 540	I Promise You/My Guy	1959	6.25	12.50	25.00
❑ 543	Beri-Beri/The Plan	1959	12.50	25.00	50.00
❑ 546	Foolish Dreams/The Scent	1960	5.00	10.00	20.00

KASH

Number	Title (A Side/B Side)	Yr	VG	VG+	NM
❑ 1028	Heart/Here I Go Out of Your Life	1965	3.00	6.00	12.00

RENDEZVOUS

Number	Title (A Side/B Side)	Yr	VG	VG+	NM
❑ 103	Move Out/It's Real	1958	5.00	10.00	20.00
❑ 106	Please Please (Let Me Go Steady)/Teardrops	1959	5.00	10.00	20.00

REPRISE

Number	Title (A Side/B Side)	Yr	VG	VG+	NM
❑ 20060	Someone Special/Please	1962	3.00	6.00	12.00
❑ 20078	Lover's Beach/A Thousand Violins	1962	3.00	6.00	12.00

LEMON PIPERS, THE

BUDDAH

Number	Title (A Side/B Side)	Yr	VG	VG+	NM
❑ 11	Turn Around and Take a Look/Danger	1967	2.50	5.00	10.00
❑ 23	Green Tambourine/No Help from Me	1967	3.00	6.00	12.00
❑ 31	Rice Is Nice/Blueberry Blue	1968	2.50	5.00	10.00
❑ 31 [PS]	Rice Is Nice/Blueberry Blue	1968	3.75	7.50	15.00
❑ 41	Jelly Jungle (Of Orange Marmalade)/Shoe Shine Boy	1968	2.50	5.00	10.00
❑ 63	Wine and Violet/Lonely Atmosphere	1968	2.50	5.00	10.00
❑ 136	I Was Not Born to Follow/Rainbow Tree	1969	2.00	4.00	8.00

CAROL

Number	Title (A Side/B Side)	Yr	VG	VG+	NM
❑ 107	Quiet Please/Monaural 78	1966	3.75	7.50	15.00

LENNON, FREDDIE

JERDEN

Number	Title (A Side/B Side)	Yr	VG	VG+	NM
❑ 792	That's My Life (My Love and My Home)/Next Time You Feel Important	1966	20.00	40.00	80.00

LENNON, JOHN

Includes records as "Plastic Ono Band," "John Ono Lennon," "John Lennon/Plastic Ono Band" and other records he made with Yoko Ono. Also see THE BEATLES.

APPLE

Number	Title (A Side/B Side)	Yr	VG	VG+	NM
❑ 1809	Give Peace a Chance/Remember Love	1969	—	2.50	5.00
—As "Plastic Ono Band"					
❑ 1809 [PS]	Give Peace a Chance/Remember Love	1969	3.75	7.50	15.00
—As "Plastic Ono Band"					
❑ 1813	Cold Turkey/Don't Worry Kyoko (Mummy's Only Looking for a Hand in the Snow)	1969	—	2.50	5.00
—As "Plastic Ono Band"; most copies skip on A-side on the third chorus because of a pressing defect					
❑ 1813	Cold Turkey/Don't Worry Kyoko (Mummy's Only Looking for a Hand in the Snow)	1969	2.50	5.00	10.00
—As "Plastic Ono Band"; some copies don't skip on A-side. They tend to have wider, bolder print than those that do.					
❑ 1813 [PS]	Cold Turkey/Don't Worry Kyoko (Mummy's Only Looking for a Hand in the Snow)	1969	10.00	20.00	40.00
—As "Plastic Ono Band"					
❑ 1818	Instant Karma! (We All Shine On)/Who Has Seen the Wind?	1970	—	2.00	4.00
—As "John Ono Lennon"; B-side by "Yoko Ono Lennon"					
❑ 1818 [DJ]	Instant Karma! (We All Shine On)	1970	50.00	100.00	200.00
—As "John Ono Lennon"; one-sided promo					
❑ 1818 [PS]	Instant Karma! (We All Shine On)/Who Has Seen the Wind?	1970	3.75	7.50	15.00
—As "John Ono Lennon"; B-side by "Yoko Ono Lennon"					
❑ 1827	Mother/Why	1970	2.00	4.00	8.00
—As "John Lennon/Plastic Ono Band"; B-side by "Yoko Ono/Plastic Ono Band"					
❑ 1827	Mother/Why	1970	3.00	6.00	12.00
—As "John Lennon/Plastic Ono Band"; star on A-side label					
❑ 1827	Mother/Why	1970	10.00	20.00	40.00
—As "John Lennon/Plastic Ono Band"; "MONO" on A-side label					
❑ 1827 [PS]	Mother/Why	1970	30.00	60.00	120.00
—As "John Lennon/Plastic Ono Band"; B-side by "Yoko Ono/Plastic Ono Band"					
❑ 1830	Power to the People/Touch Me	1971	2.00	4.00	8.00
—As "John Lennon/Plastic Ono Band"; B-side by "Yoko Ono/Plastic Ono Band"					
❑ 1830	Power to the People/Touch Me	1971	2.00	4.00	8.00
—As "John Lennon/Plastic Ono Band"; with star on A-side label					
❑ 1830 [PS]	Power to the People/Touch Me	1971	7.50	15.00	30.00
—As "John Lennon/Plastic Ono Band"; B-side by "Yoko Ono/Plastic Ono Band"					
❑ 1840	Imagine/It's So Hard	1971	2.00	4.00	8.00
—As "John Lennon Plastic Ono Band"; tan label					
❑ 1840	Imagine/It's So Hard	1975	3.00	6.00	12.00
—As "John Lennon Plastic Ono Band"; green label with "All Rights Reserved"					
❑ 1842	Happy Xmas (War Is Over)/Listen, the Snow Is Falling	1971	3.75	7.50	15.00
—As "John & Yoko/Plastic Ono Band with the Harlem Community Choir"; green vinyl, faces label					
❑ 1842	Happy Xmas (War Is Over)/Listen, the Snow Is Falling	1971	2.50	5.00	10.00
—As "John & Yoko/Plastic Ono Band with the Harlem Community Choir"; green vinyl, Apple label					
❑ 1842 [PS]	Happy Xmas (War Is Over)/Listen, the Snow Is Falling	1971	5.00	10.00	20.00
—As "John & Yoko/Plastic Ono Band with the Harlem Community Choir"					
❑ 1848	Woman Is the Nigger of the World/Sisters O Sisters	1972	2.00	4.00	8.00
—As "John Lennon/Plastic Ono Band..."; B-side by "Yoko Ono/Plastic Ono Band..."					
❑ 1848 [PS]	Woman Is the Nigger of the World/Sisters O Sisters	1972	6.25	12.50	25.00
—As "John Lennon/Plastic Ono Band..."; B-side by "Yoko Ono/Plastic Ono Band..."					
❑ 1868	Mind Games/Meat City	1973	—	3.00	6.00
❑ 1868 [PS]	Mind Games/Meat City	1973	3.75	7.50	15.00
❑ P-1868 [DJ]	Mind Games (mono/stereo)	1973	12.50	25.00	50.00
❑ 1874	Whatever Gets You Thru the Night/Beef Jerky	1974	—	3.00	6.00
—As "John Lennon and the Plastic Ono Nuclear Band"					
❑ P-1874 [DJ]	Whatever Gets You Thru the Night (mono/stereo)	1974	12.50	25.00	50.00
—As "John Lennon and the Plastic Ono Nuclear Band"					
❑ 1878	#9 Dream/What You Got	1974	2.00	4.00	8.00
❑ P-1878 [DJ]	#9 Dream (edited mono/stereo)	1974	12.50	25.00	50.00
❑ P-1878 [DJ]	What You Got (mono/stereo)	1974	25.00	50.00	100.00
❑ 1881	Stand By Me/Move Over Ms. L.	1975	2.00	4.00	8.00
❑ P-1881 [DJ]	Stand By Me (mono/stereo)	1975	12.50	25.00	50.00
❑ P-1883 [DJ]	Ain't That a Shame (mono/stereo)	1975	50.00	100.00	200.00
—No stock copies issued					
❑ P-1883 [DJ]	Slippin' and Slidin' (mono/stereo)	1975	50.00	100.00	200.00
—No stock copies issued					
❑ S45X-47663/4 [DJ]	Happy Xmas (War Is Over)/Listen, the Snow Is Falling	1971	187.50	375.00	750.00
—As "John & Yoko/Plastic Ono Band with the Harlem Community Choir"; white label on styrene					

APPLE/AMERICOM

Number	Title (A Side/B Side)	Yr	VG	VG+	NM
❑ 1809P/M-435	Give Peace a Chance/Remember Love	1969	187.50	375.00	750.00
—As "Plastic Ono Band"; four-inch flexi-disc sold in vending machines					

ATLANTIC

Number	Title (A Side/B Side)	Yr	VG	VG+	NM
❑ PR-104/5 [DJ]	John Lennon on Ronnie Hawkins: The Short Rap/The Long Rap	1970	25.00	50.00	100.00

CAPITOL

Number	Title (A Side/B Side)	Yr	VG	VG+	NM
❑ 1840	Imagine/It's So Hard	1978	—	3.00	6.00
—As "John Lennon Plastic Ono Band"; purple late 1970s label					
❑ 1840	Imagine/It's So Hard	1983	—	3.00	6.00
—As "John Lennon Plastic Ono Band"; black colorband label					
❑ 1840	Imagine/It's So Hard	1988	—	2.50	5.00
—As "John Lennon Plastic Ono Band"; purple late-1980s label (wider)					
❑ 1842	Happy Xmas (War Is Over)/Listen, the Snow Is Falling	1976	12.50	25.00	50.00
—As "John & Yoko/Plastic Ono Band with the Harlem Community Choir"; orange label					

Number	Title (A Side/B Side)	Yr	VG	VG+	NM
❑ 1842	Happy Xmas (War Is Over)/Listen, the Snow Is Falling	1978	—	3.00	6.00
—As "John & Yoko/Plastic Ono Band with the Harlem Community Choir"; purple late-1970s label					
❑ 1842	Happy Xmas (War Is Over)/Listen, the Snow Is Falling	1983	—	3.00	6.00
—As "John & Yoko/Plastic Ono Band with the Harlem Community Choir"; black colorband label					
❑ 1842	Happy Xmas (War Is Over)/Listen, the Snow Is Falling	1988	5.00	10.00	20.00
—As "John & Yoko/Plastic Ono Band with the Harlem Community Choir"; purple late-1980s label (wider)					
❑ 1868	Mind Games/Meat City	1978	—	3.00	6.00
—Purple late-1970s label					
❑ 1868	Mind Games/Meat City	1983	3.00	6.00	12.00
—Black colorband label					
❑ 1874	Whatever Gets You Thru the Night/Beef Jerky	1978	—	3.00	6.00
—Purple late-1970s label					
❑ 1874	Whatever Gets You Thru the Night/Beef Jerky	1983	—	3.00	6.00
—Black colorband label					
❑ 1874	Whatever Gets You Thru the Night/Beef Jerky	1988	—	3.00	6.00
—Purple late-1980s label					
❑ 1878	#9 Dream/What You Got	1976	10.00	20.00	40.00
—Orange label					
❑ 1878	#9 Dream/What You Got	1978	—	3.00	6.00
—Purple late-1970s label					
❑ 1878	#9 Dream/What You Got	1983	2.50	5.00	10.00
—Black colorband label					
❑ S7-17644	Happy Xmas (War Is Over)/Listen, the Snow Is Falling	1993	—	2.00	4.00
—John & Yoko/The Plastic Ono Band; green vinyl					
❑ S7-17783	Give Peace a Chance/Remember Love	1994	25.00	50.00	100.00
—CEMA Special Markets issue; meant for gold-plating in a special plaque. About 100 were not.					
❑ B-44230	Jealous Guy/Give Peace a Chance	1988	—	2.50	5.00
❑ B-44230 [PS]	Jealous Guy/Give Peace a Chance	1988	—	2.50	5.00
❑ S7-57849	Imagine/It's So Hard	1992	12.50	25.00	50.00
—CEMA Special Markets issue; meant for gold-plating in a special plaque. About 1,000 were not.					
❑ 58894	(Just Like) Starting Over/Watching the Wheels	2000	—	2.50	5.00
—Blue vinyl					
❑ 58895	Woman/Walking on Thin Ice	2000	—	2.50	5.00
—Clear vinyl; B-side as "John Lennon and Yoko Ono" though originally issued as a Yoko Ono solo single					
COTILLION					
❑ PR-104/5 [DJ]	John Lennon on Ronnie Hawkins: The Short Rap/The Long Rap	1970	20.00	40.00	80.00
—White label with promo markings					
❑ PR-104/5 [DJ]	John Lennon on Ronnie Hawkins: The Short Rap/The Long Rap	1970	22.50	45.00	90.00
—No promo markings on white label					
GEFFEN					
❑ 29855	Happy Xmas (War Is Over)/Beautiful Boy (Darling Boy)	1982	—	2.50	5.00
❑ 29855 [PS]	Happy Xmas (War Is Over)/Beautiful Boy (Darling Boy)	1982	—	2.50	5.00
❑ 49604	(Just Like) Starting Over/Kiss Kiss Kiss	1980	—	2.00	4.00
—B-side by Yoko Ono					
❑ 49604 [PS]	(Just Like) Starting Over/Kiss Kiss Kiss	1980	—	2.00	4.00
—B-side by Yoko Ono					
❑ 49644	Woman/Beautiful Boys	1980	—	2.00	4.00
—B-side by Yoko Ono					
❑ 49644 [PS]	Woman/Beautiful Boys	1980	—	2.00	4.00
—B-side by Yoko Ono					
❑ 49695	Watching the Wheels/Yes, I'm Your Angel	1981	—	2.00	4.00
—B-side by Yoko Ono					
❑ 49695 [PS]	Watching the Wheels/Yes, I'm Your Angel	1981	—	2.00	4.00
—B-side by Yoko Ono					
KYA					
❑ 1260 [DJ]	The KYA 1969 Peace Talk	1969	50.00	100.00	200.00
NOISEVILLE					
❑ 43	John Lennon Talks About David Peel	199?	10.00	20.00	40.00
—Red vinyl, signed by David Peel					
❑ 43	John Lennon Talks About David Peel	199?	2.50	5.00	10.00
—Black vinyl					
❑ 43 [PS]	John Lennon Talks About David Peel	199?	2.50	5.00	10.00
POLYDOR					
❑ 817254-7	Nobody Told Me/O' Sanity	1983	2.50	5.00	10.00
—With "Manufactured by Polydor Incorporated..." on label; B-side by Yoko Ono					
❑ 817254-7	Nobody Told Me/O' Sanity	1983	—	2.50	5.00
—With "Manufactured and Marketed by Polygram..." on label; B-side by Yoko Ono					
❑ 817254-7 [PS]	Nobody Told Me/O' Sanity	1983	—	2.50	5.00
❑ 821107-7	I'm Stepping Out/Sleepless Night	1984	—	2.00	4.00
—B-side by Yoko Ono					
❑ 821107-7 [PS]	I'm Stepping Out/Sleepless Night	1984	—	2.00	4.00
❑ 821204-7	Borrowed Time/Your Hands	1984	—	2.50	5.00
—B-side by Yoko Ono					
❑ 821204-7 [PS]	Borrowed Time/Your Hands	1984	—	2.50	5.00
❑ 881378-7	Every Man Has a Woman Who Loves Him/It's Alright	1984	2.00	4.00	8.00
—B-side by Sean Ono Lennon					
❑ 881378-7 [PS]	Every Man Has a Woman Who Loves Him/It's Alright	1984	2.00	4.00	8.00
QUAKER GRANOLA DIPPS					
❑ (no #)	A Tribute to John Lennon	1986	3.75	7.50	15.00
—Cardboard record included in specially marked boxes of Quaker Granola Dipps					
QUAYE/TRIDENT					
❑ SK 3419 [DJ]	Rock 'N' Roll	1975	125.00	250.00	500.00
—Radio spot to promote the album Rock 'N' Roll					

LENNON, JULIAN

Number	Title (A Side/B Side)	Yr	VG	VG+	NM
ATLANTIC					
❑ 88890	You're the One/(B-side unknown)	1989	—	2.00	4.00
❑ 88925	Now You're in Heaven/Second Time	1989	—	2.00	4.00
❑ 88925 [PS]	Now You're in Heaven/Second Time	1989	—	2.00	4.00
❑ 89385	This Is My Day/Everyday	1986	—	2.00	4.00
❑ 89405	Want Your Body/Everyday	1986	—	2.00	4.00
❑ 89437	Stick Around/Always Think Twice	1986	—	2.00	4.00
❑ 89437 [PS]	Stick Around/Always Think Twice	1986	—	2.00	4.00
❑ 89529	Jesse/Bebop	1985	—	2.00	4.00
❑ 89529 [PS]	Jesse/Bebop	1985	—	2.00	4.00
❑ 89567	Say You're Wrong/Big Mama	1985	—	2.00	4.00
❑ 89567 [PS]	Say You're Wrong/Big Mama	1985	—	2.00	4.00
❑ 89589	Too Late for Goodbyes/Let Me Go	1985	—	2.00	4.00
❑ 89589 [PS]	Too Late for Goodbyes/Let Me Go	1985	—	2.00	4.00
❑ 89609	Valotte/Well I Don't Know	1984	—	2.00	4.00
❑ 89609 [PS]	Valotte/Well I Don't Know	1984	—	2.00	4.00
CAPITOL					
❑ B-5618	Time Will Teach Us All/(Instrumental)	1986	—	2.00	4.00

LENNON, SEAN

Also see JOHN LENNON.

Number	Title (A Side/B Side)	Yr	VG	VG+	NM
GRAND ROYAL					
❑ GR 058	Home/ 5/8	1998	—	—	2.00
—Also includes insert					
❑ GR 058	Home/ 5/8	1998	—	—	2.00

LENOIR, J.B.

Number	Title (A Side/B Side)	Yr	VG	VG+	NM
CHECKER					
❑ 844	Let Me Die with the One I Love/If I Give My Love to You	1956	10.00	20.00	40.00
❑ 856	Don't Touch My Head/I've Been Down So Long	1957	10.00	20.00	40.00
❑ 874	What About Your Daughter/Five Years	1957	7.50	15.00	30.00
❑ 901	Daddy Talk to Your Son/She Don't Know	1958	7.50	15.00	30.00
J.O.B.					
❑ 1012	The Mojo/How Can I Leave	1952	50.00	100.00	200.00
❑ 1102	Play a Little While/Louise	1952	30.00	60.00	120.00
PARROT					
❑ 802	Eisenhower Blues/I'm in Korea	1954	100.00	200.00	400.00
❑ 802	Tax Paying Blues/I'm in Korea	1954	250.00	500.00	1000.
—A-side is similar, though not identical, to "Eisenhower Blues"					
❑ 802	Tax Paying Blues/I'm in Korea	1954	500.00	1000.	2000.
—Red vinyl					
❑ 809	Mama Talk to Your Daughter/Man, Watch Your Woman	1955	20.00	40.00	80.00
❑ 814	Mama Your Daughter Is Going to Miss Me/What Have I Done	1955	25.00	50.00	100.00
❑ 821	Fine Girls/I Lost My Baby	1955	37.50	75.00	150.00
SHAD					
❑ 5012	Back Door/Louella	1959	5.00	10.00	20.00
U.S.A.					
❑ 744	I Feel So Good/Sing Um the Way I Feel	1963	5.00	10.00	20.00
VEE JAY					
❑ 352	Do What I Say/Oh Baby	1960	3.00	6.00	12.00
—As "J.B. Lenore"					

LESTER, BOBBY, AND THE MOONLIGHTERS

The Moonlighters are THE MOONGLOWS.

Number	Title (A Side/B Side)	Yr	VG	VG+	NM
CHECKER					
❑ 806	So All Alone/Shoo Doo-Be Do (My Loving Baby)	1954	25.00	50.00	100.00
—Maroon label with checkerboard top					
❑ 806	So All Alone/Shoo Doo-Be Do (My Loving Baby)	1958	10.00	20.00	40.00
—Maroon label, vertical logo					
❑ 813	New Gal/The Hug and a Kiss	1955	20.00	40.00	80.00

LESTER, KETTY

Number	Title (A Side/B Side)	Yr	VG	VG+	NM
ERA					
❑ 3068	Love Letters/I'm a Fool to Want You	1962	3.00	6.00	12.00
❑ 3080	But Not for Me/Once Upon a Time	1962	2.50	5.00	10.00
❑ 3088	You Can't Lie to a Liar/River of Salt	1962	2.50	5.00	10.00
❑ 3094	This Land Is Your Land/Love Is for Everyone	1962	2.50	5.00	10.00
❑ 3103	Fallen Angel/Lullaby for Lovers	1963	2.50	5.00	10.00
EVEREST					
❑ 20007	Queen for a Day/I Said Goodbye to My Love	1962	2.50	5.00	10.00
PETE					
❑ 706	I Wil Lead You/Now That I Need Him	1968	—	3.00	6.00
❑ 710	Measure of a Man/Cracker Box Living	1968	—	3.00	6.00
❑ 714	Show Me/Since I Fell for You	1969	—	3.00	6.00
RCA VICTOR					
❑ 47-8331	The House Is Haunted/Some Things Are Better Left Unsaid	1964	2.00	4.00	8.00
❑ 47-8371	Please Don't Cry Anymore/Roses Grow With Thorns	1964	2.00	4.00	8.00
❑ 47-8424	I Trust You Baby/Theme from The Luck of Ginger Coffey	1964	2.00	4.00	8.00
❑ 47-8471	You Go Your Way/Variations on a Theme by Byrd	1964	2.00	4.00	8.00
❑ 47-8573	(Looking for a) Better World/Pretty Lies, Pretty Make Believes	1965	2.00	4.00	8.00
TOWER					
❑ 166	I'll Be Looking Back/West Coast	1965	2.00	4.00	8.00
❑ 208	Secret Love/Love Me Just a Little Bit	1966	2.00	4.00	8.00
❑ 236	When a Woman Loves a Man/We'll Be Together Again	1966	2.00	4.00	8.00

LETTERMEN, THE

Number	Title (A Side/B Side)	Yr	VG	VG+	NM
ALPHA OMEGA					
❑ 078501	It Feels Like Christmas/I Believe	1985	—	2.00	4.00
❑ 078501 [PS]	It Feels Like Christmas/I Believe	1985	—	2.00	4.00
APPLAUSE					
❑ 104	What I Did for Love/Cherish-Precious and Few	1983	—	2.00	4.00
CAPITOL					
❑ 2054	Goin' Out of My Head-Can't Take My Eyes Off You/I Believe	1967	2.00	4.00	8.00
❑ 2132	Sherry Don't Go/Never My Love	1968	—	3.00	6.00

Number	Title (A Side/B Side)	Yr	VG	VG+	NM
❑ 2196	Anyone Who Had a Heart/All the Gray-Haired Men	1968	—	3.00	6.00
❑ 2218	Love Is Blue-Greensleeves/Where Were You When the Lights Went Out	1968	—	3.00	6.00
❑ 2254	Playing the Piano/Sally Le Roy	1968	—	3.00	6.00
❑ 2324	Put Your Head on My Shoulder/Mary's Rainbow	1968	—	3.00	6.00
❑ 2414	I Have Dreamed/The Pendulum Swings Both Ways	1969	—	3.00	6.00
❑ 2482	Hurt So Bad/Catch the Wind	1969	—	3.00	6.00
❑ 2643	Shangri-La/When Summer Ends	1969	—	3.00	6.00
❑ 2697	Traces-Memories Medley/For Once in a Lifetime	1969	—	3.00	6.00
❑ 2774	Hang On Sloopy/For Love	1970	—	2.50	5.00
❑ 2820	She Cried/For Love	1970	—	2.50	5.00
❑ 2938	Hey Girl/Worlds	1970	—	2.50	5.00
❑ 3020	Everything Is Good About You/It's Over	1971	—	2.50	5.00
❑ 3098	Love Is a Hurtin' Thing/Feelings	1971	—	2.50	5.00
❑ 3192	Love/Maybe Tomorrow	1971	—	2.50	5.00
❑ 3285	Oh My Love/An Old Fashioned Love Song	1972	—	2.00	4.00
❑ 3449	Maybe We Should/Spin Away	1972	—	2.00	4.00
❑ 3512	Sandman/Love Song	1973	—	2.00	4.00
❑ 3619	A Summer Song/Mac Arthur Park	1973	—	2.00	4.00
❑ 3810	Goodbye/The You Part of Me	1973	—	2.00	4.00
❑ 3912	The Way We Were-Isn't It a Shame/Touch Me in the Morning	1974	—	2.00	4.00
❑ 4005	Song from Some Came Running (To Love and Be Loved)/Eastward	1974	—	2.00	4.00
❑ 4096	You Are My Sunshine Girl/Make a Time for Lovin'	1975	—	2.00	4.00
❑ 4161	If You Feel the Way I Do/Love Me Like a Stranger	1975	—	2.00	4.00
❑ 4226	Storms of Troubled Times/The Way You Look Tonight	1976	—	2.00	4.00
❑ 4586	The Way You Look Tonight/That's My Desire	1961	3.00	6.00	12.00
❑ 4586 [PS]	The Way You Look Tonight/That's My Desire	1961	5.00	10.00	20.00
❑ 4658	When I Fall in Love/Smile	1961	3.00	6.00	12.00
❑ 4658 [PS]	When I Fall in Love/Smile	1961	5.00	10.00	20.00
❑ 4699	Come Back Silly Girl/A Song for Young Love	1962	3.00	6.00	12.00
❑ 4699 [PS]	Come Back Silly Girl/A Song for Young Love	1962	5.00	10.00	20.00
❑ 4746	How Is Julie?/Turn Around, Look at Me	1962	3.00	6.00	12.00
❑ 4746 [PS]	How Is Julie?/Turn Around, Look at Me	1962	5.00	10.00	20.00
❑ 4810	Silly Boy (She Doesn't Love You)/I Told the Stars	1962	3.00	6.00	12.00
❑ 4810 [PS]	Silly Boy (She Doesn't Love You)/I Told the Stars	1962	5.00	10.00	20.00
❑ 4851	Again/Tree in the Meadow	1962	3.00	6.00	12.00
❑ 4914	No Other Love/Heartache on Heartache	1963	2.50	5.00	10.00
❑ 4976	Two Brothers/The Allentown Jail	1963	2.50	5.00	10.00
❑ 5091	Where or When/Be My Girl	1963	2.50	5.00	10.00
❑ 5218	Put Away Your Teardrops/Seventh Dawn Theme	1964	2.50	5.00	10.00
❑ 5273	When Summer Ends/You Don't Know Just How Lucky You Are	1964	2.50	5.00	10.00
❑ 5370	The Girl with a Little Tin Heart/It's Over	1965	2.00	4.00	8.00
❑ 5437	Theme from "A Summer Place"/Sealed with a Kiss	1965	2.00	4.00	8.00
❑ 5499	Secretly/The Things We Did Last Summer	1965	2.00	4.00	8.00
❑ 5499 [PS]	Secretly/The Things We Did Last Summer	1965	3.00	6.00	12.00
❑ 5544	I Believe/Sweet September	1965	2.00	4.00	8.00
❑ 5583	You'll Be Needin' Me/Run to My Loving Arms	1966	2.00	4.00	8.00
❑ 5649	I Only Have Eyes for You/Love Letters	1966	2.00	4.00	8.00
❑ 5649 [PS]	I Only Have Eyes for You/Love Letters	1966	3.00	6.00	12.00
❑ 5749	Chanson D'Amour/She Don't Want Me Now	1966	2.00	4.00	8.00
❑ 5813	Our Winter Love/Warm	1966	2.00	4.00	8.00
❑ 5913	Volare/Mr. Sun	1967	2.00	4.00	8.00

WARNER BROS.

Number	Title (A Side/B Side)	Yr	VG	VG+	NM
❑ 5152	Their Hearts Were Full of Spring/When	1960	3.75	7.50	15.00
❑ 5178	Two Hearts/Magic Sound	1960	3.75	7.50	15.00

LETTERMEN, THE (2)

Different group from above.

LIBERTY

Number	Title (A Side/B Side)	Yr	VG	VG+	NM
❑ 55141	Hey, Big Brain/Guiro	1958	2.50	5.00	10.00

LEVON AND THE HAWKS

Also see THE BAND; LEVON HELM.

ATCO

Number	Title (A Side/B Side)	Yr	VG	VG+	NM
❑ 6383	He Don't Love You (And He'll Break Your Heart)/Stones I Throw	1965	7.50	15.00	30.00
❑ 6625	He Don't Love You (And He'll Break Your Heart)/Go Go Lisa Jane	1968	7.50	15.00	30.00

LEWIS, BARBARA

ATLANTIC

Number	Title (A Side/B Side)	Yr	VG	VG+	NM
❑ 2141	My Heart Went Do Dat Da/The Longest Night of the Year	1962	3.00	6.00	12.00
❑ 2159	My Mama Told Me/Gonna Love You Till the Day I Die	1962	3.00	6.00	12.00
❑ 2184	Hello Stranger/Think a Little Sugar	1963	5.00	10.00	20.00
❑ 2200	Straighten Up Your Heart/If You Love Her	1963	3.00	6.00	12.00
❑ 2214	Puppy Love/Snap Your Fingers	1963	3.00	6.00	12.00
❑ 2227	Someday We're Gonna Love Again/Spend a Little Time	1964	2.50	5.00	10.00
❑ 2255	Come Home/Pushin' a Good Thing Too Far	1964	2.50	5.00	10.00
❑ 2283	Baby, I'm Yours/I Say Love	1965	3.75	7.50	15.00
❑ 2300	Make Me Your Baby/Love to Be Loved	1965	3.75	7.50	15.00
❑ 2316	Don't Forget About Me/It's Magic	1965	2.50	5.00	10.00
❑ 2346	Make Me Belong to You/Girls Need Loving Care	1966	2.00	4.00	8.00
❑ 2361	I Remember the Feeling/Baby What You Want Me to Do	1966	2.00	4.00	8.00
❑ 2400	Love Makes the World Go Round/I'll Make Him Love Me	1967	2.00	4.00	8.00
❑ 2413	Fool, Fool, Fool/Only All the Time	1967	2.00	4.00	8.00
❑ 2482	Thankful for What I Got/Sho Nuff	1968	2.00	4.00	8.00
❑ 2514	On Bended Knees/I'll Keep Believing	1968	2.00	4.00	8.00
❑ 2550	I'm All You've Got/You're a Dream Maker	1968	2.00	4.00	8.00

ENTERPRISE

Number	Title (A Side/B Side)	Yr	VG	VG+	NM
❑ 9012	You Made Me a Woman/Just the Way You Are Today	1970	—	3.00	6.00
❑ 9027	Ask the Lonely/Why Did It Take You So Long	1970	—	3.00	6.00
❑ 9029	Anyway/That's the Way I Like It	1970	—	3.00	6.00

KAREN

Number	Title (A Side/B Side)	Yr	VG	VG+	NM
❑ 313	My Heart Went Do Dat Da/The Longest Night of the Year	1961	7.50	15.00	30.00

REPRISE

Number	Title (A Side/B Side)	Yr	VG	VG+	NM
❑ 1146	Rock and Roll Lullaby/I'm So Thankful	1972	—	2.50	5.00

7-Inch Extended Plays

ATLANTIC

Number	Title (A Side/B Side)	Yr	VG	VG+	NM
❑ LSD 8110 [DJ]	Baby I'm Yours/Hy Heart Went Do Da Dat/Puppy Love//Hello Stranger/Someday We're Gonna Love Again/Snap Your Fingers	196?	3.75	7.50	15.00

—Jukebox mini-LP, small hole, plays at 33 1/3 rpm

Number	Title (A Side/B Side)	Yr	VG	VG+	NM
❑ LSD 8110 [PS]	Baby I'm Yours	196?	3.75	7.50	15.00

LEWIS, BOBBY (1)

R&B singer.

ABC-PARAMOUNT

Number	Title (A Side/B Side)	Yr	VG	VG+	NM
❑ 10565	That's Right/Fannie Lewis	1964	3.00	6.00	12.00
❑ 10592	Jealous Love/Stark Raving Wild	1964	3.00	6.00	12.00

BELTONE

Number	Title (A Side/B Side)	Yr	VG	VG+	NM
❑ 1002	Tossin' and Turnin'/Oh Yes I Love You	1961	6.25	12.50	25.00
❑ 1012	One Track Mind/Are You Ready	1961	6.25	12.50	25.00
❑ 1015	What a Walk/Cry No More	1961	3.75	7.50	15.00
❑ 1016	Yes, Oh Yes, It Did/Mamie in the Afternoon	1962	3.75	7.50	15.00
❑ 2018	A Man's Gotta Be a Man/Day by Day I Need Your Love	1962	3.75	7.50	15.00
❑ 2023	I'm Tossin' and Turnin' Again/Nothin' But the Blues	1962	3.75	7.50	15.00
❑ 2026	Lonely Teardrops/Boom-a-Chick-Chick	1962	3.75	7.50	15.00
❑ 2035	Nothin' But the Blues/Intermission	1963	3.75	7.50	15.00

MERCURY

Number	Title (A Side/B Side)	Yr	VG	VG+	NM
❑ 71245	Mumbles Blues/Oh Baby	1957	6.25	12.50	25.00

PHILIPS

Number	Title (A Side/B Side)	Yr	VG	VG+	NM
❑ 40519	Soul Seekin'/Give Me Your Yesterdays	1968	5.00	10.00	20.00

ROULETTE

Number	Title (A Side/B Side)	Yr	VG	VG+	NM
❑ 4182	You Better Stop/Fire of Love	1959	3.75	7.50	15.00
❑ 4382	Solid as a Rock/Oh Mr. Somebody	1961	3.75	7.50	15.00

SPOTLIGHT

Number	Title (A Side/B Side)	Yr	VG	VG+	NM
❑ 394	Mumbles Blues/Oh Baby	1957	7.50	15.00	30.00
❑ 397	Solid as a Rock/You Even Forgot My Name	1957	7.50	15.00	30.00

LEWIS, BOBBY (2)

Country singer.

ACE OF HEARTS

Number	Title (A Side/B Side)	Yr	VG	VG+	NM
❑ 0463	Already Gone to My Heart/Mr. President	1973	—	3.00	6.00
❑ 0466	Here with You/Where Happiness Is	1973	—	3.00	6.00
❑ 0472	Too Many Memories/With Meaning	1973	—	3.00	6.00
❑ 0480	I Never Get Through Missing You/Lady Lover	1974	—	3.00	6.00
❑ 0502	Let Me Take Care of You/Where Happiness Is	1975	—	3.00	6.00
❑ 7503	It's So Nice to Be with You/(B-side unknown)	1975	—	3.00	6.00

CAPRICORN

Number	Title (A Side/B Side)	Yr	VG	VG+	NM
❑ 0318	She's Been Keeping Me Up Nights/I Keep Falling in Love with You	1979	—	2.50	5.00
❑ 0331	Love Won't Be Love Without You/This Is a Man and Woman Kind of Night	1979	—	2.50	5.00

GRT

Number	Title (A Side/B Side)	Yr	VG	VG+	NM
❑ 007	Lady Lover/I Never Get Through Missing You	1974	—	3.00	6.00
❑ 008	I See Love/Your Love	1974	—	3.00	6.00

HME

Number	Title (A Side/B Side)	Yr	VG	VG+	NM
❑ 04853	Love Is An Overload/Treat Her Like a Stranger	1985	—	2.00	4.00

RPA

Number	Title (A Side/B Side)	Yr	VG	VG+	NM
❑ 7603	For Your Love/(B-side unknown)	1976	—	3.00	6.00
❑ 7613	I'm Getting High Remembering/With Meaning	1976	—	3.00	6.00
❑ 7622	What a Diff'rence a Day Made/I Can Feel It	1977	—	3.00	6.00

UNITED ARTISTS

Number	Title (A Side/B Side)	Yr	VG	VG+	NM
❑ 842	Everybody's Baby/Perfect Example of a Fool	1965	2.50	5.00	10.00
❑ 920	Why Me/Six Days a Week, Twice on Sunday	1965	2.50	5.00	10.00
❑ 50009	You Remind Me Of Myself/I Hope You Find in Him What You Were Looking For in Me	1966	2.00	4.00	8.00
❑ 50067	How Long Has It Been/Easy to Say, Hard to Do	1966	2.00	4.00	8.00
❑ 50133	Two of the Usual/Your B.A.B.Y. Baby Don't Love You	1967	2.00	4.00	8.00
❑ 50161	Love Me and Make It All Better/My Tears Don't Care (They Fall Anywhere)	1967	2.00	4.00	8.00
❑ 50208	I Doubt It/Laughing Girl, She's Not Happy	1967	2.00	4.00	8.00
❑ 50263	Ordinary Miracle/These Are Things I Miss	1968	2.00	4.00	8.00
❑ 50327	From Heaven to Heartache/Only for Me	1968	2.00	4.00	8.00
❑ 50476	Each and Every Part of Me/My (Is Such a Lonely Word)	1969	2.00	4.00	8.00
❑ 50528	Til Something Better Comes Along/I'm Only a Man	1969	2.00	4.00	8.00
❑ 50573	Things for You and I/Somebody Lied to Me	1969	2.00	4.00	8.00
❑ 50620	I'm Going Home/I May Never Be Free	1969	2.00	4.00	8.00
❑ 50668	Hello Mary Lou/Love, Wonderful Love	1970	—	3.50	7.00
❑ 50719	Simple Days and Simple Ways/Love's Garden	1970	—	3.50	7.00
❑ 50754	Come Sundown/He Gives Us All His Love	1971	—	3.50	7.00
❑ 50791	If I Had You/Doggone This Heartache	1971	—	3.50	7.00
❑ 50850	Today's Teardrops/Love's Satisfaction	1971	—	3.50	7.00
❑ 50885	Only Love Can Break a Heart/We Ran Out of Time	1972	—	3.50	7.00

LEWIS, CLARENCE

FURY

Number	Title (A Side/B Side)	Yr	VG	VG+	NM
❑ 1032	Cupid's Little Helper/Half a Heart	1960	3.75	7.50	15.00

RED ROBIN

Number	Title (A Side/B Side)	Yr	VG	VG+	NM
❑ 136	Lost Everything/Your Heart Must Be Made of Stone	1955	20.00	40.00	80.00

LEWIS, EARL, AND THE CHANNELS
See THE CHANNELS.

LEWIS, GARY, AND THE PLAYBOYS

EPIC

Number	Title (A Side/B Side)	Yr	VG	VG+	NM
❑ 50068	One Good Woman/Ooh Baby	1975	2.00	4.00	8.00

—Gary Lewis solo

LIBERTY

Number	Title (A Side/B Side)	Yr	VG	VG+	NM
❑ (no #) [DJ]	Way Way Out (same on both sides)	1967	125.00	250.00	500.00
❑ 65-227 [DJ]	Doin' the Flake//This Diamond Ring/Little Miss Go-Go	1965	6.25	12.50	25.00
❑ 65-227 [PS]	Doin' the Flake//This Diamond Ring/Little Miss Go-Go	1965	12.50	25.00	50.00

—Kellogg's Corn Flakes giveaway

Number	Title (A Side/B Side)	Yr	VG	VG+	NM
❑ 55756	This Diamond Ring/Hard to Find	1964	3.00	6.00	12.00
❑ 55756	This Diamond Ring/Tijuana Wedding	1964	2.50	5.00	10.00
❑ 55778	Count Me In/Little Miss Go-Go	1965	2.50	5.00	10.00
❑ 55809	Save Your Heart for Me/Without a Word of Warning	1965	2.50	5.00	10.00
❑ 55818	Everybody Loves a Clown/Time Stands Still	1965	2.50	5.00	10.00
❑ 55818 [PS]	Everybody Loves a Clown/Time Stands Still	1965	3.75	7.50	15.00
❑ 55846	She's Just My Style/I Won't Make That Mistake Again	1965	2.50	5.00	10.00
❑ 55846 [PS]	She's Just My Style/I Won't Make That Mistake Again	1965	3.75	7.50	15.00
❑ 55865	Sure Gonna Miss Her/I Don't Wanna Say Goodnight	1966	2.50	5.00	10.00
❑ 55865 [PS]	Sure Gonna Miss Her/I Don't Wanna Say Goodnight	1966	3.75	7.50	15.00
❑ 55880	Green Grass/I Can Read Between the Lines	1966	2.50	5.00	10.00
❑ 55880 [PS]	Green Grass/I Can Read Between the Lines	1966	3.75	7.50	15.00
❑ 55898	My Heart's Symphony/Tina	1966	2.50	5.00	10.00
❑ 55898 [PS]	My Heart's Symphony/Tina	1966	3.75	7.50	15.00
❑ 55914	(You Don't Have to) Paint Me a Picture/Looking for the Stars	1966	2.50	5.00	10.00
❑ 55914 [PS]	(You Don't Have to) Paint Me a Picture/Looking for the Stars	1966	3.75	7.50	15.00
❑ 55932	Down on the Sloop John B/Ice Melts in the Sun	1966	—	—	—

—Unreleased

Number	Title (A Side/B Side)	Yr	VG	VG+	NM
❑ 55933	Where Will the Words Come From/May the Best Man Win	1966	2.50	5.00	10.00
❑ 55949	The Loser (With a Broken Heart)/Ice Melts in the Sun	1967	2.50	5.00	10.00
❑ 55949 [PS]	The Loser (With a Broken Heart)/Ice Melts in the Sun	1967	3.75	7.50	15.00
❑ 55971	Girls in Love/Let's Be More Than Friends	1967	2.00	4.00	8.00
❑ 55985	Jill/New in Town	1967	2.00	4.00	8.00
❑ 56011	Has She Got the Nicest Eyes/Happiness	1967	2.00	4.00	8.00
❑ 56037	Sealed with a Kiss/Sara Jane	1968	2.00	4.00	8.00
❑ 56075	C.C. Rider/Main Street	1968	—	3.00	6.00
❑ 56093	Rhythm of the Rain/Mister Memory	1969	—	3.00	6.00
❑ 56093	Every Day I Have to Cry Some/Mister Memory	1969	—	3.00	6.00
❑ 56121	Hayride/Gary's Groove	1969	—	3.00	6.00
❑ 56144	I Saw Elvis Presley Last Night/Something Is Wrong	1969	3.00	6.00	12.00
❑ 56158	Great Balls of Fire/I'm On the Road Right Now	1970	—	3.00	6.00

SCEPTER

Number	Title (A Side/B Side)	Yr	VG	VG+	NM
❑ 12359	Peace of Mind/Then Again Maybe	1972	2.00	4.00	8.00

—Gary Lewis solo

UNITED ARTISTS

Number	Title (A Side/B Side)	Yr	VG	VG+	NM
❑ 0064	This Diamond Ring/My Heart's Symphony	1973	—	2.00	4.00
❑ 0065	Count Me In/Save Your Heart for Me	1973	—	2.00	4.00
❑ 0066	Everybody Loves a Clown/Sure Gonna Miss Her	1973	—	2.00	4.00
❑ 0067	She's Just My Style/Green Grass	1973	—	2.00	4.00

—0064 through 0067 are "Silver Spotlight Series" reissues

LEWIS, JERRY

CAPITOL

Number	Title (A Side/B Side)	Yr	VG	VG+	NM
❑ F1045	I'm a Little Busybody/Sunday Driving	1950	5.00	10.00	20.00
❑ F1385	The Navy Gets the Gravy/Pa-Pa-Pa Polka	1951	3.75	7.50	15.00
❑ F1482	A-Hunting We Will Go/Never Been Kissed	1951	3.75	7.50	15.00
❑ F1740	I Like It, I Like It/I'll Tell a Policeman on You	1951	3.75	7.50	15.00
❑ F1868	I Love Girls/Lay Something on the Bar	1951	3.75	7.50	15.00
❑ F1969	The Book Was So Much Better Than the Picture/North Dakota, South Dakota	1952	3.75	7.50	15.00
❑ F2141	Crazy Words/I Can't Carry a Tune	1952	3.75	7.50	15.00
❑ F2202	They Go Wild, Simply Wild Over Me/I Keep Her Picture Hanging	1952	3.75	7.50	15.00
❑ F2317	I've Had a Very Merry Christmas/Strictly for the Birds	1952	5.00	10.00	20.00
❑ F2481	If You Love Me Truly/Little Man You've Had a Busy Day	1953	3.75	7.50	15.00

—With Patti Lewis

Number	Title (A Side/B Side)	Yr	VG	VG+	NM
❑ F2576	Give Me a Little Kiss, Will Ya Huh/Yyyup	1953	3.75	7.50	15.00

DECCA

Number	Title (A Side/B Side)	Yr	VG	VG+	NM
❑ 30124	Rock-a-Bye Your Baby with a Dixie Melody/Come Rain or Come Shine	1956	3.00	6.00	12.00
❑ 30263	Let Me Sing and I'm Happy/It All Depends on You	1957	2.50	5.00	10.00
❑ 30345	My Mammy/With These Arms	1957	2.50	5.00	10.00
❑ 30370	By Myself/No One	1957	2.50	5.00	10.00
❑ 30503	Sad Sack/The Lord Loves a Laughing Man	1957	2.50	5.00	10.00
❑ 30607	Long Black Nylons/Back to Kenya	1958	2.50	5.00	10.00
❑ 30664	Dormi-Dormi-Dormi/Love Is a Lonely Thing	1958	2.50	5.00	10.00
❑ 30808	Song from "The Geisha Boy"/The More I See	1959	2.50	5.00	10.00
❑ 31019	Makin' Whoopee/Have a Girl, Have a Boy	1959	2.50	5.00	10.00
❑ 31115	Smile/Everything's Coming Up Roses	1960	2.00	4.00	8.00
❑ 31400	My Mammy/Let Me Sing and I'm Happy	1962	2.00	4.00	8.00

DOT

Number	Title (A Side/B Side)	Yr	VG	VG+	NM
❑ 16164	Somebody/Turn It On	1960	2.00	4.00	8.00
❑ 16772	Green, Green/I'll See Your Light	1965	—	3.00	6.00

—As "The Jerry Lewis Singers"

LIBERTY

Number	Title (A Side/B Side)	Yr	VG	VG+	NM
❑ 55633	Kids/Witchcraft	1963	2.00	4.00	8.00

7-Inch Extended Plays

DECCA

Number	Title (A Side/B Side)	Yr	VG	VG+	NM
❑ ED 2455	(contents unknown)	1957	3.75	7.50	15.00
❑ ED 2455 [PS]	Jerry Lewis Just Sings, Vol. 1	1957	3.75	7.50	15.00
❑ ED 2456	(contents unknown)	1957	3.75	7.50	15.00
❑ ED 2456 [PS]	Jerry Lewis Just Sings, Vol. 2	1957	3.75	7.50	15.00
❑ ED 2457	Birth of the Blues/Bye Bye Baby//Back in Your Own Backyard/Sometimes I'm Happy	1957	3.75	7.50	15.00
❑ ED 2457 [PS]	Jerry Lewis Just Sings, Vol. 3	1957	3.75	7.50	15.00

LEWIS, JERRY LEE

ELEKTRA

Number	Title (A Side/B Side)	Yr	VG	VG+	NM
❑ 46030	Rockin' My Life Away/I Wish I Was Eighteen Again	1979	—	2.00	4.00
❑ 46067	Who Will the Next Fool Be/Rita May	1979	—	2.00	4.00
❑ 46591	When Two Worlds Collide/Good News Travels Fast	1980	—	2.00	4.00
❑ 46642	Honky Tonk Stuff/Rockin' Jerry Lee	1980	—	2.00	4.00
❑ 47026	Over the Rainbow/Folsom Prison Blues	1980	—	2.00	4.00
❑ 47095	Thirty-Nine and Holding/Change Places with Me	1980	—	2.00	4.00
❑ 69962	I'd Do It All Again/Who Will Buy the Wine	1982	—	2.00	4.00

MCA

Number	Title (A Side/B Side)	Yr	VG	VG+	NM
❑ 52151	My Fingers Do the Talkin'/Forever Forgiving	1983	—	—	3.00
❑ 52188	Come As You Were/Circumstantial Evidence	1983	—	—	3.00
❑ 52233	She Sings Amazing Grace/Why You Been Gone So Long	1983	—	—	3.00
❑ 52369	I Am What I Am/That Was the Way It Was Then	1984	—	—	3.00

MERCURY

Number	Title (A Side/B Side)	Yr	VG	VG+	NM
❑ 55011	Middle Age Crazy/Georgia on My Mind	1977	—	3.00	6.00
❑ 55021	Come On In/Who's Sorry Now	1977	—	3.00	6.00
❑ 55028	I'll Find It Where I Can/Don't Let the Stars Get In Your Eyes	1977	—	3.00	6.00
❑ 73099	There Must Be More to Love Than This/Home Away from Home	1970	2.00	4.00	8.00
❑ 73155	I Can't Have a Merry Christmas, Mary (Without You)/In Loving Memories	1970	2.50	5.00	10.00
❑ 73192	Touching Home/Woman, Woman	1971	2.00	4.00	8.00
❑ 73227	When He Walks on You (Like You Have Walked on Me)/Foolish Kind of Man	1971	2.00	4.00	8.00
❑ 73248	Would You Take Another Chance on Me/Me and Bobby McGee	1971	2.00	4.00	8.00
❑ 73273	Chantilly Lace/Think About It Darlin'	1972	2.00	4.00	8.00
❑ 73296	Lonely Weekends/Turn On Your Love Light	1972	2.00	4.00	8.00
❑ 73328	Who's Gonna PlayThis Old Piano/No Honky Tonks in Heaven	1972	2.00	4.00	8.00
❑ 73361	No More Hanging On/Mercy of a Letter	1973	2.00	4.00	8.00
❑ 73374	Drinking Wine Spo-Dee O'Dee/Rock and Roll Medley	1973	2.00	4.00	8.00
❑ 73402	No Headstone on My Grave/Jack Daniels	1973	2.00	4.00	8.00
❑ 73423	Sometimes a Memory Ain't Enough/I Think I Need to Pray	1973	2.00	4.00	8.00
❑ 73452	I'm Left, You're Right, She's Gone/I've Fallen to the Bottom	1974	2.00	4.00	8.00
❑ 73462	Meat Man/Just a Little Bit	1974	2.00	4.00	8.00
❑ 73491	Tell Tale Signs/Cold, Cold Morning Light	1974	2.00	4.00	8.00
❑ 73618	He Can't Fill My Shoes/Tomorrow's Taking Baby Away	1974	—	3.00	6.00
❑ 73661	I Can Still Hear the Music in the Restroom/Remember Me	1975	—	3.00	6.00
❑ 73685	Boogie Woogie Country Man/I'm Still Jealous of You	1975	—	3.00	6.00
❑ 73729	A Damn Good Country Song/When I Take My Vacation in Heaven	1975	—	3.00	6.00
❑ 73763	Don't Boogie Woogie/That Kind of Fool	1976	—	3.00	6.00
❑ 73822	Let's Put It Back Together Again/Jerry Lee's Rock and Roll Revival Show	1976	—	3.00	6.00
❑ 73872	The Closest Thing to You/You Belong to Me	1976	—	3.00	6.00
❑ 76148	I'm So Lonesome I Could Cry/Pick Me Up on Your Way Down	1982	—	2.50	5.00

PHILLIPS INT'L.

Number	Title (A Side/B Side)	Yr	VG	VG+	NM
❑ 3559	In the Mood/I Get the Blues When It Rains	1960	12.50	25.00	50.00

—As "The Hawk"

POLYDOR

Number	Title (A Side/B Side)	Yr	VG	VG+	NM
❑ 889312-7	Breathless/Great Balls of Fire	1989	—	2.00	4.00
❑ 889312-7 [PS]	Breathless/Great Balls of Fire	1989	—	2.00	4.00
❑ 889798-7	Crazy Arms/Great Balls of Fire	1989	—	2.00	4.00

SCR

Number	Title (A Side/B Side)	Yr	VG	VG+	NM
❑ 386	Get Out Your Big Roll, Daddy/Honky Tonkin' Rock 'N' Roll Piano Man	1985	—	2.50	5.00

SIRE

Number	Title (A Side/B Side)	Yr	VG	VG+	NM
❑ 19809	It Was the Whiskey Talkin' (Not Me)/same (Rock and Roll Version)	1990	—	—	3.00
❑ 64423	Goose Bumps/Crown Victoria 51	1995	—	2.50	5.00

SMASH

Number	Title (A Side/B Side)	Yr	VG	VG+	NM
❑ 1857	Pen and Paper/Hit the Road Jack	1963	3.75	7.50	15.00
❑ 1886	I'm on Fire/Bread and Butter Man	1964	10.00	20.00	40.00
❑ 1906	She Was My Baby (He Was My Friend)/The Hole He Said He'd Dig for Me	1964	3.75	7.50	15.00
❑ 1930	High Heel Sneakers/You Went Back on Your Word	1964	3.75	7.50	15.00
❑ 1969	Baby Hold Me Close/I Believe in You	1965	3.75	7.50	15.00
❑ 1992	This Must Be the Place/Rocking Pneumonia and the Boogie Woogie Flu	1965	3.75	7.50	15.00
❑ 2006	Green, Green Grass of Home/You've Got What It Takes	1965	3.75	7.50	15.00
❑ 2027	Sticks and Stones/What a Heck of a Mess	1966	3.00	6.00	12.00
❑ 2053	If I Had It All to Do Over/Memphis Beat	1966	3.00	6.00	12.00
❑ 2103	Holding On/It's a Hang-Up, Baby	1967	3.00	6.00	12.00
❑ 2122	Turn On Your Love Light/Shotgun Man	1967	3.00	6.00	12.00

Number	Title (A Side/B Side)	Yr	VG	VG+	NM
❑ 2146	Another Place, Another Time/Walking the Floor Over You	1968	2.50	5.00	10.00
❑ 2164	What's Made Milwaukee Famous (Has Made a Loser Out of Me)/All the Good Is Gone	1968	2.50	5.00	10.00
❑ 2186	She Still Comes Around (To Love What's Left of Me)/Slipping Around	1968	2.50	5.00	10.00
❑ 2202	To Make Love Sweeter for You/Let's Talk About Us	1968	2.50	5.00	10.00
❑ 2224	One Has My Name (The Other Has My Heart)/I Can't Stop Loving You	1969	2.50	5.00	10.00
❑ 2244	She Even Woke Me Up to Say Goodbye/Echoes	1969	2.50	5.00	10.00
❑ 2257	Once More with Feeling/You Went Out of Your Way (To Walk on Me)	1970	2.50	5.00	10.00
❑ 884934-7	Sixteen Candles/Rock and Roll (Fais-Do-Do)	1986	—	2.00	4.00
—B-side with Roy Orbison, Carl Perkins and Johnny Cash					
❑ 888142-7	We Remember the King/Class of '55	1987	—	2.00	4.00
—With Johnny Cash, Roy Orbison and Carl Perkins; B-side by Carl Perkins solo					

SUN

Number	Title (A Side/B Side)	Yr	VG	VG+	NM
❑ 259	Crazy Arms/End of the Road	1957	25.00	50.00	100.00
—As "Jerry Lee Lewis"					
❑ 259	Crazy Arms/End of the Road	1957	12.50	25.00	50.00
—As "Jerry Lee Lewis and His Pumping Piano"					
❑ 267	Whole Lot of Shakin' Going On/It'll Be Me	1957	10.00	20.00	40.00
❑ 281	Great Balls of Fire/You Win Again	1957	10.00	20.00	40.00
❑ 281 [PS]	Great Balls of Fire/You Win Again	1957	20.00	40.00	80.00
❑ 288	Breathless/Down the Line	1958	10.00	20.00	40.00
❑ 296	High School Confidential/Fools Like Me	1958	7.50	15.00	30.00
❑ 296 [PS]	High School Confidential/Fools Like Me	1958	20.00	40.00	80.00
❑ 301	Lewis Boogie/The Return of Jerry Lee	1958	7.50	15.00	30.00
—B-side by George and Louis					
❑ 303	I'll Make It All Up to You/Break-Up	1958	6.25	12.50	30.00
❑ 312	I'll Sail My Ship Alone/It Hurt Me So	1958	6.25	12.50	25.00
❑ 317	Lovin' Up a Storm/Big Blon' Baby	1959	6.25	12.50	25.00
❑ 324	Let's Talk About Us/Ballad of Billy Joe	1959	6.25	12.50	25.00
❑ 330	Little Queenie/I Could Never Be Ashamed of You	1959	6.25	12.50	25.00
❑ 337	Old Black Joe/Baby Baby, Bye Bye	1960	5.00	10.00	20.00
❑ 344	Hang Up My Rock and Roll Shoes/John Henry	1960	5.00	10.00	20.00
❑ 352	Love Made a Fool of Me/When I Get Paid	1960	5.00	10.00	20.00
❑ 356	What'd I Say/Livin' Lovin' Wreck	1961	5.00	10.00	20.00
❑ 364	Cold, Cold Heart/It Won't Happen with Me	1961	5.00	10.00	20.00
❑ 367	Save the Last Dance for Me/As Long As I Live	1961	5.00	10.00	20.00
❑ 371	Money/Bonnie B	1961	5.00	10.00	20.00
❑ 374	I've Been Twistin'/Ramblin' Rose	1962	5.00	10.00	20.00
❑ 379	Sweet Little Sixteen/How's My Ex Treating You	1962	5.00	10.00	20.00
❑ 382	Good Golly Miss Molly/I Can't Trust Me	1962	5.00	10.00	20.00
❑ 384	Teenage Letter/Seasons of My Heart	1963	5.00	10.00	20.00
❑ 396	Carry Me Back to Old Virginny/I Know What It Means	1965	5.00	10.00	20.00
❑ 1101	Invitation to Your Party/I Could Never Be Ashamed of You	1969	—	3.00	6.00
❑ 1107	One Minute Past Eternity/Frankie and Johnny	1969	—	3.00	6.00
❑ 1115	I Can't Seem to Say Goodbye/Goodnight Irene	1970	—	2.50	5.00
❑ 1119	Waiting for the Train (All Around the Watertank)/Big Legged Woman	1970	—	2.50	5.00
❑ 1125	Love on Broadway/Matchbox	1971	—	2.50	5.00
❑ 1128	Your Loving Ways/I Can't Trust Me in Your Arms Anymore	1972	—	2.50	5.00
❑ 1130	Good Rockin' Tonight/I Can't Trust Me in Your Arms Anymore	1973	—	2.50	5.00
❑ 1138	Matchbox/Am I to Be the One	1978	—	2.00	4.00
❑ 1139	Save the Last Dance for Me/Am I to Be the One	1978	—	2.00	4.00
—With uncredited "duet" partner, actually Orion (Jimmy Ellis); a shameless attempt to concoct a "lost Elvis Presley duet"					
❑ 1141	Cold, Cold Heart/Hello Josephine	1979	—	2.00	4.00
❑ 1151	Be-Bop-a-Lula/The Breakup	1980	—	2.00	4.00
—B-side by Charlie Rich; both sides are duets with Orion					

7-Inch Extended Plays

SUN

Number	Title (A Side/B Side)	Yr	VG	VG+	NM
❑ EPA-107	Mean Woman Blues/I'm Feelin' Sorry//Whole Lot of Shakin' Goin' On/Turn Around	1958	20.00	30.00	80.00
❑ EPA-107 [PS]	The Great Ball of Fire	1958	20.00	30.00	80.00
❑ EPA-108	Don't Be Cruel/Goodnight Irene//Put Me Down/It All Depends	1958	12.50	25.00	50.00
❑ EPA-108 [PS]	Jerry Lee Lewis	1958	12.50	25.00	50.00
❑ EPA-109	(contents unknown)	1958	12.50	25.00	50.00
❑ EPA-109 [PS]	Jerry Lee Lewis	1958	12.50	25.00	50.00
❑ EPA-110	(contents unknown)	1958	12.50	25.00	50.00
❑ EPA-110 [PS]	Jerry Lee Lewis	1958	12.50	25.00	50.00

LEWIS, JERRY LEE, AND LINDA GAIL LEWIS

Also see each artist's individual listings.

MERCURY

Number	Title (A Side/B Side)	Yr	VG	VG+	NM
❑ 73303	Writing on the Wall/Me and Jesus	1972	—	3.50	7.00

SMASH

Number	Title (A Side/B Side)	Yr	VG	VG+	NM
❑ 2220	Don't Let Me Cross Over/We Live in Two Different Worlds	1969	2.50	5.00	10.00
❑ 2254	Roll Over Beethoven/Secret Places	1969	2.50	5.00	10.00

LEWIS, LINDA GAIL

Also see JERRY LEE LEWIS.

MERCURY

Number	Title (A Side/B Side)	Yr	VG	VG+	NM
❑ 73113	Before the Snow Flies/What Is Love	1970	—	3.50	7.00
❑ 73245	Paper Roses/Working Girl	1971	—	3.50	7.00
❑ 73316	Smile, Somebody Loves You/Louisiana	1972	—	3.50	7.00
❑ 73343	Ivory Tower/He's Loved Me Much Too Much	1972	—	3.50	7.00
❑ 73463	I Wanna Be a Sensuous Woman/I Should Not Have Fallen in Love with You	1974	—	3.00	6.00
❑ 73473	The Joy and Love You Bring/A Lover and a Friend	1974	—	3.00	6.00

SMASH

Number	Title (A Side/B Side)	Yr	VG	VG+	NM
❑ 2193	Turn Back the Hands of Time/Good	1968	2.50	5.00	10.00
❑ 2211	T-H-E E-N-D/Then We Said Goodbye	1969	2.00	4.00	8.00
❑ 2240	He's Loved Me Much Too Much (Much Too Long)/Southside Soul Society Chapter No. 1	1969	2.00	4.00	8.00
❑ 2261	My Heart Was the Last One to Know/Gather Round Children	1970	2.00	4.00	8.00

LEWIS, RUDY

Also see THE DRIFTERS.

ATLANTIC

Number	Title (A Side/B Side)	Yr	VG	VG+	NM
❑ 2193	I've Loved You So Long/Baby I Dig Love	1963	3.00	6.00	12.00

RCA VICTOR

Number	Title (A Side/B Side)	Yr	VG	VG+	NM
❑ 47-7792	Moonbeam/Beer, Beer and More Beer	1960	5.00	10.00	20.00
—With the Sputnicks					

LEWIS, SABBY

ABC-PARAMOUNT

Number	Title (A Side/B Side)	Yr	VG	VG+	NM
❑ 9685	Ding-a-Ling/Kenny's Blues	1956	10.00	20.00	40.00
❑ 9687	Forgive Me, My Love/Regretting	1956	10.00	20.00	40.00

GONE

Number	Title (A Side/B Side)	Yr	VG	VG+	NM
❑ 5074	Swana/Sabby	1959	6.25	12.50	25.00
—With the Uniques					

LEWIS, SAMMIE

SUN

Number	Title (A Side/B Side)	Yr	VG	VG+	NM
❑ 218	So Long Baby Goodbye/I Feel So Worried	1955	20.00	40.00	80.00

LEWIS, SMILEY

DOT

Number	Title (A Side/B Side)	Yr	VG	VG+	NM
❑ 16674	I Wonder/Lookin' for My Woman	1964	2.50	5.00	10.00

IMPERIAL

Number	Title (A Side/B Side)	Yr	VG	VG+	NM
❑ 5194	The Bells Are Ringing/Lillie Mae	1952	30.00	60.00	120.00
—Note: Smiley Lewis records on Imperial before 5194 are unconfirmed on 45 rpm					
❑ 5208	Gumbo Blues/It's So Peaceful	1952	25.00	50.00	100.00
❑ 5224	Gypsy Blues/You're Not the One	1953	25.00	50.00	100.00
❑ 5234	Play Girl/Big Mamou	1953	20.00	40.00	80.00
❑ 5234	Play Girl/Big Mamou	1953	62.50	125.00	250.00
—Red vinyl					
❑ 5241	Caldonia's Party/Oh Baby	1953	20.00	40.00	80.00
❑ 5252	Little Fernandez/It's Music	1953	20.00	40.00	80.00
❑ 5268	Down the Road/Blue Monday	1954	20.00	40.00	80.00
❑ 5279	I Love You for Sentimental Reasons/The Rocks	1954	20.00	40.00	80.00
❑ 5296	Can't Stop Loving You/That Certain Door	1954	20.00	40.00	80.00
❑ 5316	Too Many Drivers/Ooh La La	1954	20.00	40.00	80.00
❑ 5325	Jailbird/Farewell	1955	20.00	40.00	80.00
❑ 5349	Real Gone Lover/Nobody Knows	1955	20.00	40.00	80.00
❑ 5356	I Hear You Knocking/Bumpity Bump	1955	20.00	40.00	80.00
❑ 5372	Queen of Hearts/Come On	1956	20.00	40.00	80.00
❑ 5380	One Night/Ain't Gonna Do It	1956	20.00	40.00	80.00
❑ 5389	She's Got Me (Hook, Line and Sinker)/Please Listen to Me	1956	20.00	40.00	80.00
❑ 5404	Down Yonder We Go Ballin'/Someday You'll Want Me	1956	20.00	40.00	80.00
❑ 5418	Shame, Shame, Shame/No No	1957	15.00	30.00	60.00
❑ 5431	You Are My Sunshine/Sweeter Words Have Never Been Spoken	1957	10.00	20.00	40.00
❑ 5450	Go On Fool/Goin' to Jump and Shout	1957	7.50	15.00	30.00
❑ 5470	Rootin' and Tootin'/I Can't Believe	1957	7.50	15.00	30.00
❑ 5478	Bad Luck Blues/School Days Are Back Again	1957	7.50	15.00	30.00
❑ 5531	Lil' Liza Jane/My Love Is Gone	1958	6.25	12.50	25.00
❑ 5662	Oh Red!/I Want to Be with Her	1960	3.75	7.50	15.00
❑ 5676	Last Night/Ain't Goin' There No More	1960	3.75	7.50	15.00
❑ 5719	Stormy Monday Blues/Tell Me Who	1961	3.75	7.50	15.00
❑ 5820	Gumbo Blues/Tee Nah Nah	1962	3.75	7.50	15.00

KNIGHT

Number	Title (A Side/B Side)	Yr	VG	VG+	NM
❑ 2007	Baby Please/I Shall Not Be Moved	1959	3.75	7.50	15.00
❑ 2011	Lost Weekend/By the Water	1959	3.75	7.50	15.00

LOMA

Number	Title (A Side/B Side)	Yr	VG	VG+	NM
❑ 2024	Bells Are Ringing/Walkin' the Girl	1965	2.50	5.00	10.00

OKEH

Number	Title (A Side/B Side)	Yr	VG	VG+	NM
❑ 7146	I'm Coming Down with the Blues/Tune-Up	1962	3.00	6.00	12.00

LEWIS AND CLARKE EXPEDITION, THE

CHARTMAKER

Number	Title (A Side/B Side)	Yr	VG	VG+	NM
❑ 402	Expedition West/For Your Freedom Tonight	1966	2.00	4.00	8.00

COLGEMS

Number	Title (A Side/B Side)	Yr	VG	VG+	NM
❑ 66-1006	I Feel Good (I Feel Bad)/Blue Revelations	1967	2.00	4.00	8.00
❑ 66-1006 [PS]	I Feel Good (I Feel Bad)/Blue Revelations	1967	3.75	7.50	15.00
❑ 66-1011	Destination Unknown/Freedom Bird	1967	2.00	4.00	8.00
❑ 66-1011 [PS]	Destination Unknown/Freedom Bird	1967	3.75	7.50	15.00
❑ 66-1022	Chain Around the Flowers/Why Need They Pretend	1968	2.00	4.00	8.00
❑ 66-1028	Daddy's Plastic Child/Gypsy Song Man	1968	2.00	4.00	8.00

LIFEGUARDS, THE (1)

ABC-PARAMOUNT

Number	Title (A Side/B Side)	Yr	VG	VG+	NM
❑ 10021	Everybody Out'a the Pool/Teenage Tango	1959	10.00	20.00	40.00

CASA BLANCA

Number	Title (A Side/B Side)	Yr	VG	VG+	NM
❑ 5535	Everybody Out'a the Pool/Teenage Tango	1959	12.50	25.00	50.00

DR

Number	Title (A Side/B Side)	Yr	VG	VG+	NM
❑ 69	Everybody Out'a the Pool/Teenage Tango	1965	3.75	7.50	15.00

LIFEGUARDS, THE (2)

Yet another production of STEVE BARRI and P.F. SLOAN.

CATCH

Number	Title (A Side/B Side)	Yr	VG	VG+	NM
❑ 104	State Beach/Big Swim	1964	7.50	15.00	30.00

REPRISE

Number	Title (A Side/B Side)	Yr	VG	VG+	NM
❑ 0277	Swim Party/Swimtime U.S.A.	1964	6.25	12.50	25.00

LIGHTFOOT, GORDON

ABC-PARAMOUNT

Number	Title (A Side/B Side)	Yr	VG	VG+	NM
❑ 10352	Daisy-Doo/I'm the One (Remember Me)	1962	6.25	12.50	25.00
—As "Gord Lightfoot"					
❑ 10373	It's Too Late, He Wins/Negotiations	1962	6.25	12.50	25.00

CHATEAU

Number	Title (A Side/B Side)	Yr	VG	VG+	NM
❑ 142	Daisy-Doo/I'm the One (Remember Me)	1962	12.50	25.00	50.00
❑ 148	It's Too Late, He Wins/Negotiations	1962	12.50	25.00	50.00
❑ 152	I'll Meet You in Michigan/Is My Baby Blue Tonight	1962	10.00	20.00	40.00

REPRISE

Number	Title (A Side/B Side)	Yr	VG	VG+	NM
❑ 0744	If You Could Read My Mind/Me and Bobby McGee	1972	—	2.00	4.00
—"Back to Back Hits" series					
❑ 0745	Talking in Your Sleep/Summer Side of Life	1972	—	2.00	4.00
—"Back to Back Hits" series					
❑ 0926	Me and Bobby McGee/Pony Man	1970	—	2.50	5.00
❑ 0974	If You Could Read My Mind/Poor Little Allison	1970	—	3.00	6.00
❑ 1020	Talking in Your Sleep/Nous Vivons Ensemble	1971	—	2.50	5.00
❑ 1035	Summer Side of Life/Love and Maple Syrup	1971	—	2.50	5.00
❑ 1088	Beautiful/Don Quixote	1972	—	2.50	5.00
❑ 1128	You Are What I Am/The Same Old Obsession	1972	—	2.50	5.00
❑ 1145	Can't Depend on You/It's Worth Believin'	1972	—	2.50	5.00
❑ 1194	Sundown/Too Late for Prayin'	1974	—	2.00	4.00
❑ 1309	Carefree Highway/Seven Island Suite	1974	—	2.00	4.00
❑ 1328	Rainy Day People/Cherokee Bend	1975	—	2.00	4.00
❑ 1369	The Wreck of the Edmund Fitzgerald/The House You Live In	1976	—	2.00	4.00
❑ 1380	Race Among the Ruins/Protocol	1976	—	2.00	4.00

UNITED ARTISTS

Number	Title (A Side/B Side)	Yr	VG	VG+	NM
❑ 929	Just Like Tom Thumb's Blues/Ribbon of Darkness	1965	2.50	5.00	10.00
❑ 50055	For Lovin' Me/Spin, Spin	1966	2.00	4.00	8.00
❑ 50114	I'll Be Alright/Go Go Round	1967	2.00	4.00	8.00
❑ 50152	The Way I Feel/Peaceful Waters	1967	2.00	4.00	8.00
❑ 50281	Pussywillows, Cat-Tails/Black Day in July	1968	2.00	4.00	8.00
❑ 50447	Does Your Mother Know/Bitter Green	1968	2.00	4.00	8.00
❑ 50765	If I Could/Softly	1971	—	2.50	5.00

WARNER BROS.

Number	Title (A Side/B Side)	Yr	VG	VG+	NM
❑ 5621	For Lovin' Me/I'm Not Sayin'	1965	3.75	7.50	15.00
❑ 8518	The Circle Is Small/Sweet Guinevere	1978	—	2.50	5.00
—Without A-side subtitle					
❑ 8518	The Circle Is Small (I Can See It In Your Eyes)/Sweet Guinevere	1978	—	2.00	4.00
—Subtitle added to later pressings					
❑ 8579	Daylight Katy/Hangdog Hotel Room	1978	—	2.00	4.00
❑ 8644	Dreamland/Songs the Minstrel Sang	1978	—	2.00	4.00
❑ 28222	Ecstasy Made Easy/Morning Glory	1987	—	—	3.00
❑ 28422	East of Midnight/I'll Tag Along	1987	—	—	3.00
❑ 28553	Stay Loose/Morning Glory	1986	—	—	3.00
❑ 28655	Anything for Love/Let It Ride	1986	—	—	3.00
❑ 28655 [PS]	Anything for Love/Let It Ride	1986	—	2.00	4.00
❑ 29466	Someone to Believe In/Without You	1983	—	2.00	4.00
❑ 29511	Knotty Pine/Salute	1983	—	2.00	4.00
❑ 29859	Shadows/In My Fashion	1982	—	2.00	4.00
❑ 29963	Blackberry Wine/(B-side unknown)	1982	—	2.00	4.00
❑ 49230	Dream Street Rose/Make Way for the Lady	1980	—	2.00	4.00
❑ 49516	If You Need Me/Mister Rock of Ages	1980	—	2.00	4.00
❑ 50012	Baby Step Back/Thank You for the Promises	1982	—	2.00	4.00

LIGHTFOOT, PAPA

ALADDIN

Number	Title (A Side/B Side)	Yr	VG	VG+	NM
❑ 3171	After a While (Blue Lights)/P.L.'s Blues	1953	50.00	100.00	200.00
❑ 3304	Blue Lights/Jumpin' with Jarvis	1955	37.50	75.00	150.00

IMPERIAL

Number	Title (A Side/B Side)	Yr	VG	VG+	NM
❑ 5289	Wine, Women, Whiskey/Mean Old Train	1954	37.50	75.00	150.00

SAVOY

Number	Title (A Side/B Side)	Yr	VG	VG+	NM
❑ 1161	Mean Old Train/Wild Fire	1955	7.50	15.00	30.00

LIGHTNIN' SLIM

ACE

Number	Title (A Side/B Side)	Yr	VG	VG+	NM
❑ 505	Bad Feeling Blues/Lightning Slim Boogie	1955	37.50	75.00	150.00

EXCELLO

Number	Title (A Side/B Side)	Yr	VG	VG+	NM
❑ 2066	I Can't Be Successful/Lightnin' Blues	1955	10.00	20.00	40.00
❑ 2075	Sugar Plum/Just Made Twenty One	1956	7.50	15.00	30.00
❑ 2080	Goin' Home/Wonderin' and Goin'	1956	7.50	15.00	30.00
❑ 2096	Have Your Way/Bad Luck and Trouble	1956	7.50	15.00	30.00
❑ 2106	Mean Old Lonesome Train/I'm Grown	1957	7.50	15.00	30.00
❑ 2116	I'm a Rollin' Stone/Love Me Mama	1957	7.50	15.00	30.00
❑ 2131	Hoo-Doo Blues/It's Mighty Crazy	1958	7.50	15.00	30.00
❑ 2142	My Starter Won't Work/Long Leanie Mama	1958	7.50	15.00	30.00
❑ 2150	Feelin' Awful Blues/I'm Leavin' You Baby	1959	7.50	15.00	30.00
❑ 2160	Sweet Little Woman/Lightnin's Troubles	1959	7.50	15.00	30.00
❑ 2169	Rooster Blues/G.I. Slim	1959	7.50	15.00	30.00
❑ 2179	My Little Angel Child/Too Close Blues	1960	6.25	12.50	25.00
❑ 2186	Cool Down Baby/Nothin' But the Devil	1960	6.25	12.50	25.00
❑ 2195	Somebody Knockin'/I Just Don't Know	1961	6.25	12.50	25.00
❑ 2203	Hello Mary Lee/I'm Tired Waitin' Baby	1961	6.25	12.50	25.00
❑ 2215	Mind Your Own Business/You're Old Enough to Understand	1962	6.25	12.50	25.00
❑ 2224	Winter Time Blues/I'm Warnin' You Baby	1962	6.25	12.50	25.00
❑ 2228	If You Ever Need Me/I'm Evil	1963	6.25	12.50	25.00
❑ 2234	Loving Around the Clock/You Know You're So Fine	1963	6.25	12.50	25.00
❑ 2240	Blues at Night/Don't Mistreat Me Baby	1963	6.25	12.50	25.00
❑ 2245	You Give Me the Blues/Strangest Feelin'	1964	6.25	12.50	25.00
❑ 2252	Greyhound Blues/She's My Crazy Little Baby	1964	6.25	12.50	25.00
❑ 2258	Baby Please Come Back/You Move Me Baby	1964	6.25	12.50	25.00
❑ 2262	Have Mercy on Me Baby/I've Been a Fool for You Darlin'	1965	6.25	12.50	25.00
❑ 2267	Bad Luck Blues/Can't Live This Life No More	1965	6.25	12.50	25.00
❑ 2269	Don't Start Me Talkin'/Darlin' You're the One	1965	5.00	10.00	20.00
❑ 2272	I Hate to See You Leave/Love Is Just a Gamble	1965	5.00	10.00	20.00
❑ 2320	My Babe/Good Morning Heartaches	1971	2.50	5.00	10.00

FEATURE

Number	Title (A Side/B Side)	Yr	VG	VG+	NM
❑ 3006	Rock Me, Mama/Bad Luck	1954	75.00	150.00	300.00
❑ 3008	I Can't Live Happy/New Orleans Bound	1954	15.00	30.00	60.00
❑ 3012	Bugger Bugger Boy/Ethel Mae	1954	15.00	30.00	60.00

LIMELIGHTERS, THE

JOSIE

Number	Title (A Side/B Side)	Yr	VG	VG+	NM
❑ 795	Cabin Hideaway/My Sweet Norma Lee	1956	37.50	75.00	150.00

LIMEYS, THE

DOT

Number	Title (A Side/B Side)	Yr	VG	VG+	NM
❑ 16725	Don't Cry/I Can't Find My Way Through	1965	3.75	7.50	15.00

SCEPTER

Number	Title (A Side/B Side)	Yr	VG	VG+	NM
❑ 12156	Come Back/Scraped: Green and Blue	1966	3.75	7.50	15.00

LINDEN, KATHY

CAPITOL

Number	Title (A Side/B Side)	Yr	VG	VG+	NM
❑ 4700	Remember Me (To Jimmy)/Beautiful Brown Eyes	1962	2.00	4.00	8.00
❑ 4770	Words/There'll Always Be Sadness	1962	2.00	4.00	8.00
❑ 4811	If You Really Love Me/Jimmy	1962	2.00	4.00	8.00
❑ 5018	People Say/There'll Always Be Sadness	1963	2.00	4.00	8.00

FELSTED

Number	Title (A Side/B Side)	Yr	VG	VG+	NM
❑ 8510	Billy/If I Could Hold You in My Arms	1958	3.75	7.50	15.00
❑ 8521	You'd Be Surprised/Why Oh Why	1958	3.75	7.50	15.00
❑ 8533	Oh Johnny Oh/Georgie	1958	3.75	7.50	15.00
❑ 8544	Kissin' Conversation/Just a Sandy Haired Boy Called Sandy	1958	3.75	7.50	15.00
❑ 8554	Somebody Loves You/You Walked Into My Life	1959	3.75	7.50	15.00
❑ 8571	Goodbye, Jimmy, Goodbye/Heartaches at Sweet Sixteen	1959	3.75	7.50	15.00
❑ 8587	You Don't Know Girls/So Close to My Heart	1959	3.00	6.00	12.00
❑ 8596	Think Love/Mary Lou Wilson and Johnny Brown	1959	3.00	6.00	12.00

MONUMENT

Number	Title (A Side/B Side)	Yr	VG	VG+	NM
❑ 420	Allentown Jail/That's What Love Is	1960	2.50	5.00	10.00
❑ 423	Midnight/The Willow Weeps	1960	2.50	5.00	10.00
❑ 428	Take Me Home (To My Lover)/We Had Words	1960	2.50	5.00	10.00
❑ 436	So in Love (With You)/Take Me Home, Jimmy	1961	2.50	5.00	10.00

LINDSAY, MARK

Also see PAUL REVERE AND THE RAIDERS; THE UNKNOWNS.

COLUMBIA

Number	Title (A Side/B Side)	Yr	VG	VG+	NM
❑ 10081	Mamacita/Song for a Friend	1974	—	2.50	5.00
❑ 10114	Photograph/Song for a Friend	1975	—	2.50	5.00
❑ 44875	The Old Man at the Fair/First Hymn from Grand Terrace	1969	—	3.00	6.00
❑ 45037	Arizona/Man from Houston	1969	—	3.00	6.00
❑ 45125	Miss America/Small Town Woman	1970	—	3.00	6.00
❑ 45180	Silver Bird/So Hard to Leave You	1970	—	3.00	6.00
❑ 45229	And the Grass Won't Pay No Mind/Funny How Little Men Care	1970	—	3.00	6.00
❑ 45286	Problem Child/Bookends	1970	—	3.00	6.00
❑ 45385	Been Too Long on the Road/All I Really See Is You	1971	—	2.50	5.00
❑ 45462	Are You Old Enough/Don't You Know	1971	—	2.50	5.00
❑ 45506	Pretty Pretty/Something Big	1971	—	2.50	5.00
❑ 45895	California/Someone's Been Hiding	1973	—	2.50	5.00

ELKA

Number	Title (A Side/B Side)	Yr	VG	VG+	NM
❑ 310	Sing Your Own Song/Sing Your Own Song (Theme)	1976	2.50	5.00	10.00

GREEDY

Number	Title (A Side/B Side)	Yr	VG	VG+	NM
❑ 106	Sing Your Own Song/Sing Your Own Song (Theme)	1976	—	3.00	6.00

WARNER BROS.

Number	Title (A Side/B Side)	Yr	VG	VG+	NM
❑ 8359	Sing Me High, Sing Me Low/Flips-Eyed	1977	—	2.00	4.00
❑ 8479	Little Ladies of the Night/Flips-Eyed	1977	—	2.00	4.00

LINK-EDDY COMBO

REPRISE

Number	Title (A Side/B Side)	Yr	VG	VG+	NM
❑ 20002	Big Mr. C./The Man with the Golden Arm	1961	3.75	7.50	15.00
❑ 20008	Katrina/The Cat's Pajamas	1961	3.75	7.50	15.00

LINKLETTER, BOB

CHATTAHOOCHIE

Number	Title (A Side/B Side)	Yr	VG	VG+	NM
❑ 702	The Out Crowd/Final Season	1965	5.00	10.00	20.00

LINKS, THE

TEENAGE

Number	Title (A Side/B Side)	Yr	VG	VG+	NM
❑ 1009	Ba-Bee/She's the One	1958	250.00	500.00	1000.

LIPTON, PEGGY

ODE

Number	Title (A Side/B Side)	Yr	VG	VG+	NM
❑ 111	Let Me Pass By/Stoney End	1968	2.00	4.00	8.00
❑ 114	San Francisco Glide/Stoney End	1968	2.00	4.00	8.00
❑ 114 [PS]	San Francisco Glide/Stoney End	1968	3.00	6.00	12.00
❑ 118	Just a Little Lovin' (Early in the Morning)/Red Clay County Line	1969	2.00	4.00	8.00
❑ 124	Lu/Let Me Pass By	1969	2.00	4.00	8.00
❑ 124 [PS]	Lu/Let Me Pass By	1969	3.00	6.00	12.00
❑ 66001	Wear Your Love Like Heaven/Honey Won't Let Me	1970	—	3.00	6.00
❑ 66001 [PS]	Wear Your Love Like Heaven/Honey Won't Let Me	1970	3.00	6.00	12.00

LISTEN

With ROBERT PLANT, later of LED ZEPPELIN.

COLUMBIA

Number	Title (A Side/B Side)	Yr	VG	VG+	NM
❑ 43967	You Better Run/Everybody's Gonna Say	1967	75.00	150.00	300.00
—Promotional copies go for about half these values					

LITTER

PROBE

Number	Title (A Side/B Side)	Yr	VG	VG+	NM
❑ 461	Silly People/Feeling	1968	6.25	12.50	25.00
❑ 467	Blue Ice/On Our Minds	1969	6.25	12.50	25.00

SCOTTY

Number	Title (A Side/B Side)	Yr	VG	VG+	NM
❑ 6710	Action Woman/A Legal Matter	1967	25.00	50.00	100.00

WARICK

Number	Title (A Side/B Side)	Yr	VG	VG+	NM
❑ 6711	Somebody Help Me/I'm a Man	1967	50.00	100.00	200.00
❑ 6712	Action Woman/Whatcha Gonna Do About It	1967	37.50	75.00	150.00

LITTLE ANTHONY AND THE IMPERIALS

APOLLO

Number	Title (A Side/B Side)	Yr	VG	VG+	NM
❑ 521	The Fires Burn No More/Lift Up Your Hands	1957	15.00	30.00	60.00

—As "The Chesters"

AVCO

Number	Title (A Side/B Side)	Yr	VG	VG+	NM
❑ 4635	I'm Falling in Love with You/What Good Am I Without You	1974	—	2.50	5.00
❑ 4645	I Don't Have to Worry/Loneliest House on the Block	1974	—	2.50	5.00
❑ 4651	Hold On (Just a Little Bit Longer)/I've Got to Let You Go (Part 1)	1975	—	2.50	5.00
❑ 4655	I'll Be Loving You Sooner or Later/Young Girl	1975	—	2.50	5.00

DCP

Number	Title (A Side/B Side)	Yr	VG	VG+	NM
❑ 1104	I'm On the Outside (Looking In)/Please Go	1964	2.50	5.00	10.00
❑ 1119	Goin' Out of My Head/Make It Easy on Yourself	1964	2.50	5.00	10.00
❑ 1128	Hurt So Bad/Reputation	1965	2.50	5.00	10.00
❑ 1128 [PS]	Hurt So Bad/Reputation	1965	10.00	20.00	40.00
❑ 1136	Take Me Back/Our Song	1965	2.00	4.00	8.00
❑ 1149	I Miss You So/Get Out of My Life	1965	2.00	4.00	8.00
❑ 1154	Hurt/Never Again	1966	2.00	4.00	8.00

END

Number	Title (A Side/B Side)	Yr	VG	VG+	NM
❑ 1027	Tears on My Pillow/Two People in the World	1958	10.00	20.00	40.00
—As "The Imperials"					
❑ 1027	Tears on My Pillow/Two People in the World	1958	6.25	12.50	25.00
—As "Little Anthony and the Imperials"					
❑ 1036	So Much/Oh Yeah	1958	6.25	12.50	25.00
❑ 1038	The Diary/Cha Cha Henry	1959	6.25	12.50	25.00
❑ 1039	When You Wish Upon a Star/Wishful Thinking	1959	6.25	12.50	25.00
❑ 1047	A Prayer and a Juke Box/River Path	1959	6.25	12.50	25.00
❑ 1053	So Near and Yet So Far/I'm Alright	1959	6.25	12.50	25.00
❑ 1060	Shimmy, Shimmy, Ko-Ko Bop/I'm Still in Love with You	1959	7.50	15.00	30.00
❑ 1067	My Empty Room/Bayou, Bayou, Baby	1960	3.75	7.50	15.00
❑ 1074	I'm Taking a Vacation from Love/Only Sympathy	1960	3.75	7.50	15.00
❑ 1080	Limbo (Part 1)/Limbo (Part 2)	1960	3.75	7.50	15.00
❑ 1083	Formula of Love/Dream	1961	3.75	7.50	15.00
❑ 1086	Please Say You Want Me/So Near and Yet So Far	1961	3.75	7.50	15.00
❑ 1091	Traveling Stranger/Say Yea	1961	3.75	7.50	15.00
❑ 1104	Dream/A Lovely Way to Spend an Evening	1961	3.75	7.50	15.00

JANUS

Number	Title (A Side/B Side)	Yr	VG	VG+	NM
❑ 160	Father, Father/Each One, Teach One	1971	—	3.00	6.00
❑ 166	Madeline/Universe	1971	—	3.00	6.00
❑ 178	(Where Do I Begin) Love Story/There's an Island	1972	—	3.00	6.00

LIBERTY

Number	Title (A Side/B Side)	Yr	VG	VG+	NM
❑ 55119	The Glory of Love/C'mon Tiger (Gimme a Growl)	1958	7.50	15.00	30.00

—As "The Imperials"

MCA

Number	Title (A Side/B Side)	Yr	VG	VG+	NM
❑ 41258	Daylight/Your Love	1980	—	2.00	4.00

—Little Anthony solo

PCM

Number	Title (A Side/B Side)	Yr	VG	VG+	NM
❑ 202	This Time We're Winning/Your Love	1983	—	2.00	4.00

PURE GOLD

Number	Title (A Side/B Side)	Yr	VG	VG+	NM
❑ 101	Nothing from Nothing/Running with the Wrong Crowd	1976	—	2.50	5.00

ROULETTE

Number	Title (A Side/B Side)	Yr	VG	VG+	NM
❑ 4379	That Lil' Ole Lovemaker Me/It Just Ain't Fair	1961	3.00	6.00	12.00
—Little Anthony solo					
❑ 4477	Lonesome Romeo/I've Got a Lot to Offer Darling	1963	3.00	6.00	12.00
—Little Anthony solo					

UNITED ARTISTS

Number	Title (A Side/B Side)	Yr	VG	VG+	NM
❑ 0117	Goin' Out of My Head/I'm On the Outside (Looking In)	1973	—	2.00	4.00
—"Silver Spotlight Series" reissue					
❑ 0118	Hurt So Bad/Take Me Back	1973	—	2.00	4.00
—"Silver Spotlight Series" reissue					
❑ 50552	Out of Sight, Out of Mind/Summer's Comin'	1969	—	3.00	6.00
❑ 50598	The Ten Commandments of Love/Let the Sunshine In	1969	—	3.00	6.00
❑ 50625	It'll Never Be the Same Again/Don't Get Close	1970	—	3.00	6.00
❑ 50677	World of Darkness/The Change	1970	—	3.00	6.00
❑ 50720	Help Me Find a Way (To Say I Love You)/If I Love You	1970	—	3.00	6.00

VEEP

Number	Title (A Side/B Side)	Yr	VG	VG+	NM
❑ 1228	Better Use Your Head/The Wonder of It All	1966	2.00	4.00	8.00
❑ 1228 [PS]	Better Use Your Head/The Wonder of It All	1966	10.00	20.00	40.00
❑ 1233	You Better Take It Easy Baby/Gonna Fix You Good (Every Time You're Bad)	1966	2.00	4.00	8.00
❑ 1239	Tears on My Pillow/Who's Sorry Now	1966	—	3.00	6.00
❑ 1240	I'm On the Outside (Looking In)/Please Go	1966	—	3.00	6.00
❑ 1241	Goin' Out of My Head/Shing-a-Ling	1966	—	3.00	6.00
❑ 1242	Hurt So Bad/Reputation	1966	—	3.00	6.00
❑ 1243	Take Me Back/Our Song	1966	—	3.00	6.00
❑ 1244	I Miss You So/Get Out of My Life	1966	—	3.00	6.00
❑ 1245	Hurt/Never Again	1966	—	3.00	6.00
❑ 1248	It's Not the Same/Down on Love	1966	2.00	4.00	8.00
❑ 1255	Don't Tie Me Down/Where There's a Will There's a Way	1967	2.00	4.00	8.00
❑ 1262	Hold On to Someone/Lost in Love	1967	2.00	4.00	8.00
❑ 1269	You Only Live Twice/Hungry Heart	1967	2.00	4.00	8.00
❑ 1275	Beautiful People/If I Remember to Forget	1967	2.00	4.00	8.00
❑ 1278	I'm Hypnotized/Hungry Heart	1968	2.00	4.00	8.00
❑ 1283	What Greater Love/In the Back of My Heart	1968	2.00	4.00	8.00
❑ 1285	Yesterday Has Gone/My Love Is a Rainbow	1968	2.00	4.00	8.00
❑ 1293	The Flesh Failures (Let the Sunshine In)/Gentle Rain	1969	2.00	4.00	8.00
❑ 1303	Anthem (Revelation)/Goodbye Good Times	1969	2.00	4.00	8.00

7-Inch Extended Plays

END

Number	Title (A Side/B Side)	Yr	VG	VG+	NM
❑ 203	(contents unknown)	1959	50.00	100.00	200.00
❑ 203 [PS]	Little Anthony and the Imperials	1959	75.00	150.00	300.00
❑ 204	(contents unknown)	1959	50.00	100.00	200.00
❑ 204 [PS]	We Are Little Anthony and the Imperials	1959	75.00	150.00	300.00

LITTLE BILL AND THE BLUENOTES

DOLTON

Number	Title (A Side/B Side)	Yr	VG	VG+	NM
❑ 4	I Love an Angel/Bye Bye Baby	1959	7.50	15.00	30.00

LITTLE BILLY

ABC-PARAMOUNT

Number	Title (A Side/B Side)	Yr	VG	VG+	NM
❑ 9896	I Found Me a Girl/Say It Like You Mean It	1958	3.75	7.50	15.00

LITTLE BOOKER

ACE

Number	Title (A Side/B Side)	Yr	VG	VG+	NM
❑ 547	Open the Door/Teen-Age Rock	1958	6.25	12.50	25.00

IMPERIAL

Number	Title (A Side/B Side)	Yr	VG	VG+	NM
❑ 5293	Thinkin' 'Bout My Baby/Doing the Ham Bone	1954	25.00	50.00	100.00

LITTLE BOY BLUES

FONTANA

Number	Title (A Side/B Side)	Yr	VG	VG+	NM
❑ 1623	It's Only You/Is Love?	1968	3.75	7.50	15.00

IRC

Number	Title (A Side/B Side)	Yr	VG	VG+	NM
❑ 6928	Look at the Sun/Love for a Day	1966	5.00	10.00	20.00
❑ 6936	I'm Ready/Little Boy Blues' Blues	1966	7.50	15.00	30.00
❑ 6939	I Can Only Give You Everything/You Don't Love Me	1966	7.50	15.00	30.00

LITTLE BUBBER

IMPERIAL

Number	Title (A Side/B Side)	Yr	VG	VG+	NM
❑ 5225	High Class Woman/Come Back Baby	1953	20.00	40.00	80.00
❑ 5238	Runnin' Around/Never Trust a Woman	1953	20.00	40.00	80.00

LITTLE CAESAR

BIG TOWN

Number	Title (A Side/B Side)	Yr	VG	VG+	NM
❑ 106	Can't Stand It All Alone/Big Eyes	195?	15.00	30.00	60.00
❑ 110	What Kind of Fool Is He/Wonder Why I'm Leaving (Rat Song)	195?	15.00	30.00	60.00

RCA VICTOR

Number	Title (A Side/B Side)	Yr	VG	VG+	NM
❑ 47-7270	Who Slammed the Door/I'm Reachin'	1958	6.25	12.50	25.00

RECORDED IN HOLLYWOOD

Number	Title (A Side/B Side)	Yr	VG	VG+	NM
❑ 234	Long Time Baby/(Going Down to) The River	1952	15.00	30.00	60.00
❑ 235	Goodbye Baby/If I Could See My Baby	1952	15.00	30.00	60.00
❑ 236	Move Me/Lying Woman	1953	15.00	30.00	60.00
❑ 237	You're Part of Me/Here Is a Letter	1953	15.00	30.00	60.00
❑ 238	Do Right/Money Ain't Long Enough	1953	15.00	30.00	60.00
❑ 239	Atomic Love/You Can't Bring Me Down	1953	15.00	30.00	60.00

RPM

Number	Title (A Side/B Side)	Yr	VG	VG+	NM
❑ 393	Chains of Love Have Disappeared/Tried to Reason with You Baby	1953	15.00	30.00	60.00

LITTLE CAESAR AND THE CONSULS

MALA

Number	Title (A Side/B Side)	Yr	VG	VG+	NM
❑ 512	(My Girl) Sloopy/Poison Ivy	1965	3.75	7.50	15.00
❑ 518	You've Really Got a Hold on Me/It's So Easy	1965	3.00	6.00	12.00
❑ 523	Hey Girl/You Laugh Too Much	1966	3.00	6.00	12.00

LITTLE CAESAR AND THE EMPIRE

PARKWAY

Number	Title (A Side/B Side)	Yr	VG	VG+	NM
❑ 152	Everybody Dance Now/(Instrumental)	1967	6.25	12.50	25.00

LITTLE CAESAR AND THE ROMANS

DEL-FI

Number	Title (A Side/B Side)	Yr	VG	VG+	NM
❑ 4158	Those Oldies But Goodies (Remind Me of You)/She Don't Wanna Dance	1961	7.50	15.00	30.00
❑ 4164	Hully Gully Again/Frankie and Johnny	1961	6.25	12.50	25.00
❑ 4166	Memories of Those Oldies But Goodies/Fever	1961	15.00	30.00	60.00
❑ 4170	Ten Commandments of Love/C.C. Rider	1961	12.50	25.00	50.00
❑ 4176	Popeye One More Time/Yoyo Yo Yoyo	1962	6.25	12.50	25.00

SCEPTER

Number	Title (A Side/B Side)	Yr	VG	VG+	NM
❑ 12237	Baby Love/When Will I Get Over You	1969	2.00	4.00	8.00
—As "Caesar and the Romans"					
❑ 12264	Jailhouse Rock/Leavin' My Past Behind	1969	2.00	4.00	8.00
—As "Caesar and the Romans"					

LITTLE CHARLES AND THE SIDEWINDERS

DECCA

Number	Title (A Side/B Side)	Yr	VG	VG+	NM
❑ 31980	I'm Available/It's a Heartache	1966	10.00	20.00	40.00
❑ 32095	Talkin' About You, Babe/A Taste of the Good Life	1967	7.50	15.00	30.00
❑ 32233	The Loner (Part 1)/The Loner (Part 2)	1967	5.00	10.00	20.00
❑ 32321	Sweet Lorene/Twice as Much for My Baby	1968	5.00	10.00	20.00

JEWEL

Number	Title (A Side/B Side)	Yr	VG	VG+	NM
❑ 752	Give Me a Chance/Guess I'll Have to Take What's Left	1965	5.00	10.00	20.00

LITTLE CHERYL

CAMEO

Number	Title (A Side/B Side)	Yr	VG	VG+	NM
❑ 270	Heaven Only Knows/Can't We Just Be Friends	1963	10.00	20.00	40.00
❑ 276	Mama Let the Phone Bell Ring/Can't We Just Be Friends	1963	3.00	6.00	12.00
❑ 292	Come On Home/I Love You Conrad	1964	3.00	6.00	12.00
❑ 307	Yeh Yeh We Love 'Em All/Nick and Joe Callin'	1964	4.00	8.00	16.00

REPRISE

Number	Title (A Side/B Side)	Yr	VG	VG+	NM
❑ 20109	Jim/Pocketful of Money	1962	3.75	7.50	15.00

LITTLE COOLBREEZERS, THE

See THE COOLBREEZERS.

LITTLE DOUG

See DOUG SAHM.

LITTLE ESTHER

See LITTLE ESTHER PHILLIPS.

LITTLE EVA

AMY

Number	Title (A Side/B Side)	Yr	VG	VG+	NM
❑ 943	Stand By Me/That's My Man	1965	2.00	4.00	8.00

Number	Title (A Side/B Side)	Yr	VG	VG+	NM
BELL					
❑ 45264	The Loco-Motion/Will You Love Me Tomorrow	1972	—	2.50	5.00
DIMENSION					
❑ 1000	The Loco-Motion/He Is the Boy	1962	5.00	10.00	20.00
❑ 1003	Keep Your Hands Off/Where Do I Go	1962	3.75	7.50	15.00
—Some copies have this shortened title					
❑ 1003	Keep Your Hands Off My Baby/Where Do I Go	'1962	3.00	6.00	12.00
—Most copies have longer, and correct, title					
❑ 1006	Let's Turkey Trot/Down Home	1963	3.00	6.00	12.00
❑ 1011	Old Smokey Locomotion/Just a Little Girl	1963	3.00	6.00	12.00
❑ 1013	The Trouble with Boys/What I Gotta Do	1963	3.00	6.00	12.00
❑ 1019	Let's Start the Party Again/Please Hurt Me	1963	3.00	6.00	12.00
❑ 1021	The Christmas Song/I Wish You a Merry Christmas	1963	3.75	7.50	15.00
—With Big Dee Irwin					
❑ 1021 [PS]	The Christmas Song/I Wish You a Merry Christmas	1963	10.00	20.00	40.00
—With Big Dee Irwin					
❑ 1035	Makin' with the Magilla/Run to Her	1964	2.50	5.00	10.00
❑ 1035	Makin' with the Magilla/Conga	1964	2.50	5.00	10.00
❑ 1035 [PS]	Makin' with the Magilla/Run to Her	1964	10.00	20.00	40.00
❑ 1042	Wake Up John/Takin' Back What I Said	1964	2.50	5.00	10.00
SPRING					
❑ 101	Mama Said/Something About You Boy	1970	—	3.00	6.00
❑ 107	Night After Night/Something About You Boy	1970	—	3.00	6.00
VERVE					
❑ 10459	Bend It/Just One Word Isn't Enough	1966	2.00	4.00	8.00
❑ 10529	Everything Is Beautiful About You Boy/Take a Step in My Direction	1967	2.00	4.00	8.00

LITTLE FEAT

Number	Title (A Side/B Side)	Yr	VG	VG+	NM
WARNER BROS.					
❑ 7431	Strawberry Flats/Hamburger Midnight	1970	2.00	4.00	8.00
❑ 7553	Easy to Slip/Cat Fever	1972	2.00	4.00	8.00
❑ 7689	Dixie Chicken/Lafayette Railroad	1973	—	3.00	6.00
❑ 8054	Oh Atlanta/Down the Road	1974	—	2.50	5.00
❑ 8174	Long Distance Love/Romance Dance	1975	—	2.50	5.00
❑ 8219	All That You Dream/One Love Stand	1976	—	2.50	5.00
❑ 8420	Time Loves a Hero/Sailin' Shoes	1977	—	2.50	5.00
❑ 8566	Oh Atlanta/Willin'	1978	—	2.50	5.00
❑ 27684	One Clear Moment/Changin' Luck	1988	—	—	3.00
❑ 27684 [PS]	One Clear Moment/Changin' Luck	1988	—	—	3.00
❑ 27728	Hate to Lose Your Lovin'/Cajun Girl	1988	—	—	3.00
❑ 27728 [PS]	Hate to Lose Your Lovin'/Cajun Girl	1988	—	—	3.00
❑ 49169	Wake Up Dreaming/Front Page News	1980	—	2.50	5.00
❑ 49801	Front Page News/Easy to Sleep	1981	—	2.50	5.00
❑ 49841	Strawberry Flats/Gringo	1981	—	2.50	5.00

LITTLE GUY AND THE GIANTS

Number	Title (A Side/B Side)	Yr	VG	VG+	NM
LAWN					
❑ 103	It's You/So Young	1960	50.00	100.00	200.00

LITTLE IVA AND HER BAND

Number	Title (A Side/B Side)	Yr	VG	VG+	NM
MIRACLE					
❑ 2	When I Needed You/Continental Strut	1960	500.00	1000.	1500.

LITTLE JOE AND THE THRILLERS

Number	Title (A Side/B Side)	Yr	VG	VG+	NM
ENJOY					
❑ 2011	Peanuts and Popcorn/Chicken Little Boo Boo	1964	2.50	5.00	10.00
EPIC					
❑ 9293	Mine/It's Too Bad We Had to Say Goodbye	1958	3.75	7.50	15.00
❑ 9431	Run Little Girl/Public Opinion	1961	3.00	6.00	12.00
MGM					
❑ 14129	Somehow, Someway/Days 'Til Morning	1970	—	2.50	5.00
❑ 14230	People Show/Baby I Could Be So Good at Lovin' You	1971	—	2.50	5.00
❑ 14290	Don't Take the Rain Away/The Children	1971	—	2.50	5.00
❑ 14361	Shelly Made Me Smile/Words and Music	1972	—	2.50	5.00
❑ 14466	Baby I Could Be So Good at Lovin' You/Cherry Pink and Apple Blossom White	1972	—	2.50	5.00
❑ 14662	Folks Who Live on the Hill/Baby I Could Be So Good at Lovin' You	1973	—	2.50	5.00
OKEH					
❑ 7075	Let's Do the Slop/This I Know	1956	3.75	7.50	15.00
❑ 7088	Peanuts/Lilly Lou	1957	5.00	10.00	20.00
❑ 7094	Lonesome/The Echoes Keep Calling Me	1957	3.75	7.50	15.00
❑ 7099	Don't Leave Me Alone/What's Happened to Your Halo	1958	3.75	7.50	15.00
❑ 7107	Mine/It's Too Bad We Had to Say Goodbye	1958	3.75	7.50	15.00
❑ 7116	Cherry (Part 1)/Cherry (Part 2)	1959	3.00	6.00	12.00
❑ 7121	I'm Tryin'/Strange Dreams	1959	3.00	6.00	12.00
❑ 7127	Give Me All Your Love/I'll Never Let You Go	1959	3.00	6.00	12.00
❑ 7134	Ev'ry Now and Then/Goodnight, Little Girl	1960	3.00	6.00	12.00
❑ 7136	Stay/Please Don't Go	1960	3.00	6.00	12.00
❑ 7140	Run Little Girl/Public Opinion	1961	3.00	6.00	12.00
REPRISE					
❑ 20142	Peanuts/No, No, I Can't Stop	1963	2.50	5.00	10.00

7-Inch Extended Plays

Number	Title (A Side/B Side)	Yr	VG	VG+	NM
EPIC					
❑ EG-7198	(contents unknown)	1958	25.00	50.00	100.00
❑ EG-7198 [PS]	Little Joe and the Thrillers	1958	25.00	50.00	100.00

LITTLE JUNIOR'S BLUE FLAMES

See JUNIOR PARKER.

LITTLE LADY BEATLES, THE

See THE INSECTS.

LITTLE MILTON

Number	Title (A Side/B Side)	Yr	VG	VG+	NM
BOBBIN					
❑ 101	I'm a Lonely Man/That Will Never Do	1958	6.25	12.50	25.00
❑ 103	Long Distance Operator/I Found Me a New Love	1959	6.25	12.50	25.00
❑ 112	Strange Dreams/I'm Tryin'	1959	6.25	12.50	25.00
❑ 117	Hold Me Tight/Same Old Blues	1959	6.25	12.50	25.00
❑ 120	Dead Love/My Baby Pleases Me	1960	6.25	12.50	25.00
❑ 125	Let It Be Known/Hey Girl	1960	6.25	12.50	25.00
❑ 128	I'm in Love/Cross My Heart	1961	6.25	12.50	25.00
CHECKER					
❑ 977	Saving My Love for You/Lonely No More	1961	3.75	7.50	15.00
❑ 994	So Mean to Me/I Need Somebody	1961	3.75	7.50	15.00
❑ 1012	Satisfied/Someone to Love	1962	3.75	7.50	15.00
❑ 1020	I Wonder Why/Losing Hand	1962	3.75	7.50	15.00
❑ 1048	She Put a Spell on Me/Never Too Old	1963	3.75	7.50	15.00
❑ 1063	Meddlin'/One of These Old Days	1963	3.75	7.50	15.00
❑ 1078	Sacrifice/What Kind of Love Is This	1964	3.75	7.50	15.00
❑ 1096	Blind Man/Blues in the Night	1964	3.75	7.50	15.00
❑ 1105	We're Gonna Make It/Can't Hold Back the Tears	1965	3.75	7.50	15.00
❑ 1113	Who's Cheating Who?/Ain't No Big Deal on You	1965	3.75	7.50	15.00
❑ 1118	Help Me Help You/Without My Sweet Baby	1965	3.75	7.50	15.00
❑ 1128	My Baby's Something Else/Your People	1965	3.75	7.50	15.00
❑ 1132	Sometimes/We Got the Winning Hand	1965	3.75	7.50	15.00
❑ 1138	I'm Mighty Grateful/When Does Heartache End	1966	3.75	7.50	15.00
❑ 1149	Man Loves Two/Believe in Me	1966	3.75	7.50	15.00
❑ 1162	Feel So Bad/You Colored My Blues Right	1966	5.00	10.00	20.00
❑ 1172	I'll Never Turn My Back on You/Don't Leave Her	1967	3.00	6.00	12.00
❑ 1178	I'm Shorty/Sitting Home Alone	1967	3.00	6.00	12.00
❑ 1186	A Whole Lot of Fun Before the Weekend Is Done/Real True Love	1967	3.00	6.00	12.00
❑ 1189	More and More/Cost of Living	1967	3.00	6.00	12.00
❑ 1194	I Know What I Want/You Mean Everything to Me	1968	3.00	6.00	12.00
❑ 1203	At the Dark End of the Street/I (Who Have Nothing)	1968	3.00	6.00	12.00
❑ 1208	Let Me Down Easy/Lonely Drifter	1968	3.00	6.00	12.00
❑ 1212	Grits Ain't Groceries (All Around the World)/I Can't Quit You Baby	1969	3.00	6.00	12.00
❑ 1217	Just a Little Bit/Spring	1969	3.00	6.00	12.00
❑ 1221	Poor Man/So Blue	1969	3.00	6.00	12.00
❑ 1225	Let's Get Together/I'll Always Love You	1969	3.00	6.00	12.00
❑ 1226	If Walls Could Talk/Loving You	1969	3.00	6.00	12.00
❑ 1227	Baby I Love You/Don't Talk Back	1970	3.00	6.00	12.00
❑ 1231	Somebody's Changin' My Sweet Baby's Mind/I'm Tired	1970	3.00	6.00	12.00
—As "Little Milton Campbell"					
❑ 1236	Many Rivers to Cross/Mother's Love	1970	3.00	6.00	12.00
❑ 1239	I Play Dirty/Nothing Beats a Failure	1971	2.00	4.00	8.00
GLADES					
❑ 1734	Friend of Mine/(Instrumental)	1976	—	2.50	5.00
❑ 1738	Baby It Ain't No Way/Bring It On Back	1976	—	2.50	5.00
❑ 1741	Just One Step/(Instrumental)	1977	—	2.50	5.00
❑ 1743	Loving You (Is the Best Thing to Happen to Me)/9:59 A.M.	1977	—	2.50	5.00
❑ 1747	Me for You, You for Me/My Thing Is You	1977	—	2.50	5.00
MALACO					
❑ 2104	The Blues Is All Right/Come Back Kind of Loving	1985	—	2.00	4.00
❑ 2108	Misty Blue/Catch You on the Way Down	1985	—	2.00	4.00
❑ 2123	Lonesome Christmas/Come To Me	1985	—	2.00	4.00
❑ 2127	I Will Survive/4:59 A.M.	1986	—	2.00	4.00
❑ 2134	Real Good Woman/Annie Mae's Café	198?	—	2.00	4.00
❑ 2147	His Old Lady and My Old Lady/(B-side unknown)	198?	—	2.00	4.00
❑ 2162	Bad Dream/The Woman I Love	198?	—	2.00	4.00
MCA					
❑ 52184	Age Ain't Nothin' But a Number/(Instrumental)	1983	—	2.00	4.00
❑ 52254	Living on the Dark Side of Love/Why Are You So Hard to Please	1983	—	2.00	4.00
METEOR					
❑ 5040	Love at First Sight/Let's Boogie Baby	1957	50.00	100.00	200.00
❑ 5045	Let My Baby Be/Oh My Little Baby	1957	200.00	400.00	800.00
STAX					
❑ 0100	If That Ain't a Reason (For Your Woman to Leave You)/Mr. Mailman	1971	—	3.00	6.00
❑ 0111	That's What Love Will Make You Do/I'm Livin' Off the Love You Give	1972	—	3.00	6.00
❑ 0124	Walking the Back Streets and Crying/Before the Honeymoon	1972	—	3.00	6.00
❑ 0141	I'm Gonna Cry a River/What It Is	1972	—	3.00	6.00
❑ 0148	Lovin' Stick/Rainy Day	1972	—	3.00	6.00
❑ 0174	What It Is/Who Can Handle Me Is You	1973	—	3.00	6.00
❑ 0191	Tin Pan Alley/Sweet Woman of Mine	1974	—	3.00	6.00
❑ 0210	Behind Closed Doors/Bet You I Win	1974	—	3.00	6.00
❑ 0229	Let Me Back In/Let Your Loss Be Your Lesson	1974	—	3.00	6.00
❑ 0238	If You Talk in Your Sleep/Sweet Woman of Mine	1975	—	3.00	6.00
❑ 0252	How Could You Do It to Me/Packed Up and Took My Mind	1975	—	3.00	6.00
SUN					
❑ 194	Beggin' My Baby/Somebody Told Me	1954	75.00	150.00	300.00
❑ 200	If You Love Me/Alone and Blue	1954	150.00	300.00	600.00
❑ 220	Looking for My Baby/Lonesome for My Baby	1955	200.00	400.00	800.00

LITTLE MISS CORNSHUCKS

Number	Title (A Side/B Side)	Yr	VG	VG+	NM
CHESS					
❑ 1785	No Teasing Around/It Do Me No Good	1961	3.75	7.50	15.00

LITTLE OTIS

Number	Title (A Side/B Side)	Yr	VG	VG+	NM
TAMLA					
❑ 54058	I Out-Duked the Duke/Baby I Need You	1962	7.50	15.00	30.00

LITTLE RICHARD

Also see THE DEUCES OF RHYTHM AND THE TEMPO TOPPERS; JIMI HENDRIX.

Number	Title (A Side/B Side)	Yr	VG	VG+	NM
ATLANTIC					
❑ 2181	Crying in the Chapel/Hole in the Wall	1963	3.00	6.00	12.00
❑ 2192	It Is No Secret (What God Can Do)/Travelin' Shoes	1963	3.00	6.00	12.00
BELL					
❑ 45385	Good Golly Miss Molly/Good Golly Miss Molly (Part 2)	1973	—	2.50	5.00

Number	Title (A Side/B Side)	Yr	VG	VG+	NM
BRUNSWICK					
❑ 55362	She's Together/Try Some of Mine	1968	2.00	4.00	8.00
❑ 55377	Stingy Jenny/Baby Don't You Tear My Clothes	1968	2.00	4.00	8.00
❑ 55386	Soul Train/Can I Count on You	1968	2.00	4.00	8.00
CORAL					
❑ 62366	Milky White Way/Need Him	1963	2.50	5.00	10.00
CRITIQUE					
❑ 99392	Happy Endings/California Girls	1987	—	—	3.00
—A-side: With the Beach Boys; B-side: The Beach Boys without Little Richard					
ELEKTRA					
❑ 69370	Tutti Frutti/Rave On	1988	—	—	3.00
—B-side by John Cougar Mellencamp					
❑ 69384	Tutti Frutti/Powerful Stuff	1988	—	—	3.00
—B-side by the Fabulous Thunderbirds					
❑ 69385	Tutti Frutti/Kokomo	1988	—	—	3.00
—B-side by the Beach Boys					
END					
❑ 1057	Troubles of the World/Save Me Lord	1959	3.75	7.50	15.00
❑ 1058	Milky White Way/I've Just Come From the Fountain	1959	3.75	7.50	15.00
GREEN MOUNTAIN					
❑ 413	In the Middle of the Night/Where Will I Find a Place to Sleep This Evening	1973	—	2.50	5.00
KENT					
❑ 4567	Mississippi/In the Name	1972	—	—	—
—Unreleased					
❑ 4568	Don't You Know I/In the Name	1972	—	2.50	5.00
MAINSTREAM					
❑ 5572	Try to Help Your Brother/Funk Proof	1975	—	2.50	5.00
MANTICORE					
❑ 7007	Call My Name/Steal Miss Liza (Miss Liza Jane)	1975	—	2.00	4.00
MCA					
❑ 52780	Great Gosh A-Mighty! (It's a Matter of Time)/The Ride	1986	—	—	3.00
—B-side by Charlie Midnight					
❑ 52780 [PS]	Great Gosh A-Mighty! (It's a Matter of Time)/The Ride	1986	—	—	3.00
MERCURY					
❑ 71884	He's Not Just a Soldier/Joy, Joy, Joy	1962	3.75	7.50	15.00
❑ 71911	Do You Care/Ride On King Jesus	1962	3.75	7.50	15.00
❑ 71965	Why Don't You Change Your Ways/He Got What He Wanted	1962	3.75	7.50	15.00
MODERN					
❑ 1018	Holy Mackeral/Baby, Don't You Want a Man Like Me	1966	3.00	6.00	12.00
❑ 1018 [PS]	Holy Mackeral/Baby, Don't You Want a Man Like Me	1966	5.00	10.00	20.00
❑ 1019	Do You Feel It (Part 1)/Do You Feel It (Part 2)	1966	3.00	6.00	12.00
❑ 1022	Directly from My Heart to You/I'm Back	1966	3.00	6.00	12.00
❑ 1030	Slippin' and Slidin'/Bring It Back Home to Me	1967	3.00	6.00	12.00
❑ 1043	Baby What You Want Me to Do (Part 1)/Baby What You Want Me to Do (Part 2)	1967	3.00	6.00	12.00
OKEH					
❑ 7251	Poor Dog (Who Can't Wag His Own Tail)/Well	1966	3.75	7.50	15.00
❑ 7251 [PS]	Poor Dog (Who Can't Wag His Own Tail)/Well	1966	6.25	12.50	25.00
❑ 7262	I Need Love/Commandments of Love	1966	3.00	6.00	12.00
❑ 7271	Hurry Sundown/I Don't Want to Discuss It	1967	3.00	6.00	12.00
❑ 7278	Don't Deceive Me (Please Don't Go)/Never Gonna Let You Go	1967	3.00	6.00	12.00
❑ 7286	Money/Little Bit of Something	1967	3.00	6.00	12.00
❑ 7325	Lucille/Whole Lotta Shakin' Goin' On	1969	2.50	5.00	10.00
PEACOCK					
❑ 1658	Little Richard's Boogie/Directly from My Heart to You	1956	37.50	75.00	150.00
❑ 1673	Maybe I'm Right/I Love My Baby	1957	20.00	40.00	80.00
RCA VICTOR					
❑ 47-4392	Taxi Blues/Every Hour	1951	225.00	450.00	900.00
❑ 47-4582	Get Rich Quick/Thinkin' 'Bout My Mother	1952	200.00	400.00	800.00
❑ 47-4772	Why Did You Leave Me?/Ain't Nothin' Happenin'	1952	200.00	400.00	800.00
❑ 47-5025	Please Have Mercy on Me/I Brought It All on Myself	1952	150.00	300.00	600.00
REPRISE					
❑ 0907	Freedom Blues/Dew Drop Inn	1970	2.50	5.00	10.00
❑ 0942	Greenwood Mississippi/I Saw Her Standing There	1970	2.50	5.00	10.00
❑ 1005	Shake a Hand (If You Can)/Somebody Saw You	1971	2.00	4.00	8.00
❑ 1043	Green Power/Dancing in the Street	1971	2.00	4.00	8.00
❑ 1062	Money Is/Money Runner	1972	2.00	4.00	8.00
—B-side by Quincy Jones					
❑ 1130	Mockingbird Sally/Nuki Suki	1972	2.00	4.00	8.00
SPECIALTY					
❑ 561	Tutti-Frutti/I'm Just a Lonely Guy	1955	12.50	25.00	50.00
❑ 572	Long Tall Sally/Slippin' and Slidin' (Peepin' and Hidin')	1956	10.00	20.00	40.00
❑ 579	Rip It Up/Ready Teddy	1956	10.00	20.00	40.00
❑ 584	Heebie-Jeebies/She's Got it	1956	10.00	20.00	40.00
❑ 591	The Girl Can't Help It/All Around the World	1956	10.00	20.00	40.00
❑ 598	Lucille/Send Me Some Lovin'	1957	10.00	20.00	40.00
❑ 606	Jenny, Jenny/Miss Ann	1957	10.00	20.00	40.00
❑ 606 [PS]	Jenny, Jenny/Miss Ann	1957	15.00	30.00	60.00
❑ 611	Keep a Knockin'/Can't Believe You Wanna Leave	1957	7.50	15.00	30.00
❑ 611 [PS]	Keep a Knockin'/Can't Believe You Wanna Leave	1957	15.00	30.00	60.00
❑ 624	Good Golly, Miss Molly/Hey-Hey-Hey-Hey!	1958	7.50	15.00	30.00
❑ 624 [PS]	Good Golly, Miss Molly/Hey-Hey-Hey-Hey!	1958	12.50	25.00	50.00
❑ 633	Ooh! My Soul/True, Fine Mama	1958	6.25	12.50	25.00
❑ 633 [PS]	Ooh! My Soul/True, Fine Mama	1958	12.50	25.00	50.00
❑ 645	Baby Face/I'll Never Let You Go	1958	6.25	12.50	25.00
❑ 652	She Knows How to Rock/Early One Morning	1958	6.25	12.50	25.00
❑ 660	By the Light of the Silvery Moon/Wonderin'	1959	6.25	12.50	25.00
❑ 664	Kansas City/Lonesome and Blue	1959	6.25	12.50	25.00
❑ 670	Shake a Hand/All Night Long	1959	6.25	12.50	25.00
❑ 680	Whole Lotta Shakin' Goin' On/Maybe I'm Right	1959	6.25	12.50	25.00
❑ 681	I Got It/Baby	1960	6.25	12.50	25.00
❑ 686	The Most I Can Offer/Directly from My Heart	1964	3.75	7.50	15.00
❑ 692	Bama Lama Bama Loo/Annie's Back	1964	3.75	7.50	15.00
❑ 697	Keep a Knockin'/Bama Lama Bama Loo	1964	3.75	7.50	15.00
❑ 699	Poor Boy Paul/Wonderin'	1964	3.75	7.50	15.00
❑ 734	Chicken Little Baby/Oh Why	1974	—	3.00	6.00
VEE JAY					
❑ 612	Whole Lotta Shakin' Goin' On/Goodnight Irene	1964	2.50	5.00	10.00
❑ 625	Blueberry Hill/Cherry Red	1964	2.50	5.00	10.00
❑ 652	It Ain't Whatcha Do/Cross Over	1965	2.50	5.00	10.00
❑ 665	Without Love/Dance What You Wanna	1965	2.50	5.00	10.00
❑ 698	I Don't Know What You've Got But It's Got Me — Part I/I Don't Know What You've Got But It's Got Me — Part II	1965	2.50	5.00	10.00
WARNER BROS.					
❑ 28491	Big House Reunion/Somebody's Comin'	1987	—	2.00	4.00
WTG					
❑ 08492	Twins (Long)/Twins (Short)	1988	—	2.00	4.00
—With Philip Bailey					

7-Inch Extended Plays

Number	Title (A Side/B Side)	Yr	VG	VG+	NM
RCA CAMDEN					
❑ CAE-416	Ain't Nothin' Happenin'/Why Did You Leave Me//Every Hour/I Brought It All on Myself	1955	37.50	75.00	150.00
❑ CAE-416 [PS]	Little Richard	1955	37.50	75.00	150.00
❑ CAE-446	Taxi Blues/Please Have Mercy on Me//Get Rich Quick/Thinkin' 'Bout My Mother	1956	25.00	50.00	100.00
❑ CAE-446 [PS]	Little Richard Rocks	1956	25.00	50.00	100.00
SPECIALTY					
❑ SEP-400	Long Tall Sally/Miss Ann//She's Got It/Can't Believe You Wanna Leave	1957	25.00	50.00	100.00
❑ SEP-400 [PS]	Here's Little Richard	1957	25.00	50.00	100.00
❑ SEP-401	Slippin' and Slidin'/Oh Why//Ready Teddy/Baby	1957	25.00	50.00	100.00
❑ SEP-401 [PS]	Here's Little Richard	1957	25.00	50.00	100.00
❑ SEP-402	Tutti-Frutti/True, Fine Mama//Rip It Up/Jenny, Jenny	1957	25.00	50.00	100.00
❑ SEP-402 [PS]	Here's Little Richard	1957	25.00	50.00	100.00
❑ SEP-403	(contents unknown)	1958	20.00	40.00	80.00
❑ SEP-403 [PS]	Little Richard	1958	20.00	40.00	80.00
❑ SEP-404	Ooh! My Soul/All Around the World//Good Golly, Miss Molly/Babyface	1958	20.00	40.00	80.00
❑ SEP-404 [PS]	Little Richard	1958	20.00	40.00	80.00
❑ SEP-405	(contents unknown)	1958	20.00	40.00	80.00
❑ SEP-405 [PS]	Little Richard	1958	20.00	40.00	80.00

LITTLE SAMMY AND THE TONES

Number	Title (A Side/B Side)	Yr	VG	VG+	NM
JACLYN					
❑ 1761	Christine/Over the Rainbow	1962	12.50	25.00	50.00

LITTLE TOMMY AND THE ELGINS

Number	Title (A Side/B Side)	Yr	VG	VG+	NM
ABC-PARAMOUNT					
❑ 10358	Never Love Again/I Walk On	1962	6.25	12.50	25.00
ELMAR					
❑ 1084	Never Love Again/I Walk On	1962	15.00	30.00	60.00

LITTLE WALTER

Number	Title (A Side/B Side)	Yr	VG	VG+	NM
CHANCE					
❑ 1116	That's All Right/Just Keep Loving Her	1952	1000.	2000.	3000.
—As "Little Walter J."					
CHECKER					
❑ 758	Juke/Can't Hold On Much Longer	1952	50.00	100.00	200.00
❑ 764	Mean Old World/Sad Hours	1952	30.00	60.00	120.00
❑ 767	Don't Have to Hunt No More/Tonight with a Fool	1953	20.00	40.00	80.00
❑ 770	Off the Wall/Tell Me Mama	1953	20.00	40.00	80.00
—Black vinyl					
❑ 770	Off the Wall/Tell Me Mama	1953	750.00	1500.	3000.
—Red vinyl					
❑ 780	Blues with a Feeling/Quarter to Twelve	1953	25.00	50.00	100.00
❑ 786	Lights Out/You're So Fine	1953	12.50	25.00	50.00
❑ 793	Oh Baby/Rocker	1954	10.00	20.00	40.00
❑ 799	You'd Better Watch Yourself/Blue Light	1954	10.00	20.00	40.00
—Black vinyl					
❑ 799	You'd Better Watch Yourself/Blue Light	1954	25.00	50.00	100.00
—Red vinyl					
❑ 805	Last Night/Mellow Down Easy	1954	15.00	30.00	60.00
❑ 811	My Babe/Thunder Bird	1955	10.00	20.00	40.00
❑ 817	Roller Coaster/I Got to Go	1955	10.00	20.00	40.00
❑ 825	Too Late/I Hate to See You Go	1955	10.00	20.00	40.00
❑ 833	Who/It Ain't Right	1956	10.00	20.00	40.00
❑ 838	Flying Saucer/One More Chance with You	1956	10.00	20.00	40.00
❑ 845	Teenage Beat/What a Feeling	1956	10.00	20.00	40.00
❑ 852	It's Too Late Brother/Take Me Back	1957	10.00	20.00	40.00
❑ 859	Everybody Needs Somebody/Nobody But You	1957	10.00	20.00	40.00
❑ 867	Boom, Boom — Out Goes the Light/Temperature	1957	10.00	20.00	40.00
❑ 890	The Toddle/Confessin' the Blues	1958	7.50	15.00	30.00
❑ 904	Key to the Highway/Rock Bottom	1958	7.50	15.00	30.00
❑ 919	My Baby's Sweeter/Crazy Mixed-Up World	1959	6.25	12.50	25.00
❑ 930	Everything's Gonna Be All Right/Back Track	1959	6.25	12.50	25.00
❑ 938	Break It Up/Me and Piney Brown	1960	5.00	10.00	20.00
❑ 945	Ah'w Baby/I Had My Fun	1960	5.00	10.00	20.00
❑ 955	My Babe/Blue Midnight	1960	5.00	10.00	20.00
❑ 968	I Don't Play/As Long As I Have You	1961	5.00	10.00	20.00
❑ 986	Crazy Legs/Crazy for My Baby	1961	5.00	10.00	20.00
❑ 1013	Just You Fool/I Got to Find My Baby	1962	3.75	7.50	15.00
❑ 1043	Up the Line/Southern Feeling	1963	3.75	7.50	15.00
❑ 1071	Diggin' My Potatoes/Snake Dancer	1963	3.75	7.50	15.00
❑ 1081	Dead Presidents/I'm a Business Man	1964	3.75	7.50	15.00
❑ 1117	Mean Ole Frisco/Blue and Lonesome	1965	3.75	7.50	15.00

LITTLE WHEELS, THE
With RAY HILDEBRAND and JILL JACKSON, better known as PAUL AND PAULA.

DOT

Number	Title (A Side/B Side)	Yr	VG	VG+	NM
❑ 16676	Four Wheeles, Ball Bearing Surfing Board/The Bumper	1964	7.50	15.00	30.00

LITTLEFIELD, LITTLE WILLIE
BULLSEYE

Number	Title (A Side/B Side)	Yr	VG	VG+	NM
❑ 1005	Ruby-Ruby/Easy Go	1958	7.50	15.00	30.00

FEDERAL

Number	Title (A Side/B Side)	Yr	VG	VG+	NM
❑ 12101	Sticking on You Baby/Blood Is Redder Than Wine	1952	25.00	50.00	100.00
❑ 12110	K.C. Loving/Pleading at Midnight	1953	25.00	50.00	100.00
❑ 12137	The Midnight Hour Was Shining/My Best Wishes and Regards	1953	25.00	50.00	100.00
❑ 12148	Miss K.C.'s Fine/Rock-a-Bye Baby	1953	25.00	50.00	100.00
❑ 12163	Please Don't Go-o-o-o-oh/Don't Take My Heart Little Girl	1954	20.00	40.00	80.00
❑ 12174	Goofy Dust Blues/Falling Tears	1954	20.00	40.00	80.00
❑ 12221	Jim Wilson's Boogie/Sitting on the Curbstone	1955	15.00	30.00	60.00
❑ 12351	Kansas City/Midnight Hour Was Shining	1959	7.50	15.00	30.00

RHYTHM

Number	Title (A Side/B Side)	Yr	VG	VG+	NM
❑ 107	Baby Shame/Mistreated	1956	37.50	75.00	150.00
❑ 108	Ruby-Ruby/Easy Go	1956	37.50	75.00	150.00
❑ 115	I Need a Pay Day/I Want a Little Girl	195?	25.00	50.00	100.00
❑ 124	Theresa/The Day the Rains Came	195?	20.00	40.00	80.00
❑ 130	I Wanna Love You/Goodbye Baby	195?	20.00	40.00	80.00

LITTLES, HATTIE
GORDY

Number	Title (A Side/B Side)	Yr	VG	VG+	NM
❑ 7004	Back in My Arms Again/(B-side unknown)	1962	200.00	400.00	800.00
❑ 7007	Here You Come/Your Love Is Wonderful	1962	20.00	40.00	80.00

LIVELY ONES, THE
DEL-FI

Number	Title (A Side/B Side)	Yr	VG	VG+	NM
❑ 4184	Guitarget/Crying Guitar	1962	7.50	15.00	30.00
❑ 4189	Misirlou/Blue Tears	1962	7.50	15.00	30.00
❑ 4189	Misirlou/Livin'	1962	7.50	15.00	30.00
❑ 4196	Surf Rider/Surfer's Lament	1963	7.50	15.00	30.00
❑ 4205	Surfer Boogie/Ric-a-Tic	1963	6.25	12.50	25.00
❑ 4210	High Tide/Goofy Foot	1963	6.25	12.50	25.00
❑ 4217	Surf City/Telstar Surf	1963	6.25	12.50	25.00

MGM

Number	Title (A Side/B Side)	Yr	VG	VG+	NM
❑ 13691	Bugalu Movement/Take It While You Can	1967	3.75	7.50	15.00

SMASH

Number	Title (A Side/B Side)	Yr	VG	VG+	NM
❑ 1880	Night and Day/Hey Scrounge	1964	6.25	12.50	25.00

LIVERPOOL SPINNERS, THE
FONTANA

Number	Title (A Side/B Side)	Yr	VG	VG+	NM
❑ 1574	Seth Davey/All For Me Grog	1967	2.50	5.00	10.00

LIVERS, THE
CONSTELLATION

Number	Title (A Side/B Side)	Yr	VG	VG+	NM
❑ 118	Beatle Time/This Is the Night	1964	3.75	7.50	15.00

LLOYD, JIMMY
ROULETTE

Number	Title (A Side/B Side)	Yr	VG	VG+	NM
❑ 4062	I Got a Rocket in My Pocket/You're Gone Baby	1958	25.00	50.00	100.00
❑ 7001	Where the Rio De Rosa Flows/The Beginning of the End	1957	15.00	30.00	60.00

LOAD OF MISCHIEF
HOLIDAY INN

Number	Title (A Side/B Side)	Yr	VG	VG+	NM
❑ 2205	I'm a Lover/Back in My Arms Again	1967	5.00	10.00	20.00

SUN

Number	Title (A Side/B Side)	Yr	VG	VG+	NM
❑ 407	I'm a Lover/Back in My Arms Again	1967	20.00	40.00	80.00

—The last of the Sam Phillips Sun 45s

LOBO
ATLANTIC

Number	Title (A Side/B Side)	Yr	VG	VG+	NM
❑ 3851 [DJ]	Caribbean Carnival (same on both sides)	1981	—	2.50	5.00

—May be promo only

BIG TREE

Number	Title (A Side/B Side)	Yr	VG	VG+	NM
❑ 112	Me and You and a Dog Named Boo/Walk Away from It All	1971	—	3.00	6.00
❑ 116	She Didn't Do Magic/I'm the Only One	1971	—	2.50	5.00
❑ 119	California Kid and Reemo/A Little Different	1971	—	2.50	5.00
❑ 134	The Albatross/We'll Make It, I Know We Will	1972	—	2.50	5.00
❑ 141	A Simple Man/Don't Expect Me to Be Your Friend	1972	—	2.50	5.00
❑ 147	I'd Love You to Want Me/Am I True to Myself	1972	—	2.50	5.00
❑ 158	Don't Expect Me to Be Your Friend/A Simple Man	1973	—	2.00	4.00
❑ 15001	Standing at the End of the Line/Stoney	1974	—	2.00	4.00
❑ 15008	Rings/I'm Just Dreaming	1974	—	2.00	4.00
❑ 16001	It Sure Took a Long, Long Time/Running Deer	1973	—	2.00	4.00
❑ 16004	How Can I Tell Her/Hope You're Proud of Me Girl	1973	—	2.00	4.00
❑ 16012	There Ain't No Way/Love Me for What I Am	1973	—	2.00	4.00
❑ 16033	Don't Tell Me Goodnight/My Mama Had Soul	1975	—	2.00	4.00
❑ 16040	Would I Still Have You/Morning Sun	1975	—	2.00	4.00

ELEKTRA

Number	Title (A Side/B Side)	Yr	VG	VG+	NM
❑ 47099	I Can't Believe You Anymore/Fight Fire with Fire	1980	—	2.00	4.00

EVERGREEN

Number	Title (A Side/B Side)	Yr	VG	VG+	NM
❑ 1028	Am I Going Crazy (Or Just Out of My Mind)/I Don't Want to Want You	1985	—	2.50	5.00

—Stock copies have corrected title

Number	Title (A Side/B Side)	Yr	VG	VG+	NM
❑ 1028 [DJ]	Am I Going Crazy (Or Just Out of Her Mind) (same on both sides)	1985	—	3.00	6.00

—Promo copies have incorrect title

LAURIE

Number	Title (A Side/B Side)	Yr	VG	VG+	NM
❑ 3526	Happy Days in New York City/My Friend Is Here	1969	3.75	7.50	15.00

—As "Kent LaVoie"

LOBO

Number	Title (A Side/B Side)	Yr	VG	VG+	NM
❑ I	I Don't Want to Want You/No One Will Ever Know	1981	—	2.50	5.00
❑ IV	Come Looking for Me/I Don't Want to Want You	1982	—	2.50	5.00
❑ X	Living My Life Without You/A Simple Man	1982	—	2.50	5.00

MCA

Number	Title (A Side/B Side)	Yr	VG	VG+	NM
❑ 41065	Where Were You When I Was Falling in Love/I Don't Wanna Make Love Anymore	1979	—	2.00	4.00
❑ 41152	Holdin' On for Dear Love/Gus, the Dancing Dog	1979	—	2.00	4.00

WARNER BROS.

Number	Title (A Side/B Side)	Yr	VG	VG+	NM
❑ 8493	Afterglow/Our Best Time	1977	—	2.00	4.00
❑ 8537	You Are All I'll Ever Need/Our Best Time	1978	—	2.00	4.00

LODGE, JOHN
Also see JUSTIN HAYWARD AND JOHN LODGE; THE MOODY BLUES.

LONDON

Number	Title (A Side/B Side)	Yr	VG	VG+	NM
❑ 1069	Natural Avenue/Say You Love Me	1977	—	2.50	5.00
❑ 1072	Summer Breeze/(B-side unknown)	1977	—	2.50	5.00

LOE AND JOE
HARVEY

Number	Title (A Side/B Side)	Yr	VG	VG+	NM
❑ 112	Little Ole Boy, Little Ole Girl/That's How I Am Without You	1962	7.50	15.00	30.00

LOGGINS, KENNY
Also see LOGGINS AND MESSINA.

COLUMBIA

Number	Title (A Side/B Side)	Yr	VG	VG+	NM
❑ 02167	I'm Alright (Theme from Caddyshack)/This Is It	1981	—	—	3.00
—Reissue					
❑ 03192	Don't Fight It/The More We Try	1982	—	—	3.00
—A-side: Kenny Loggins with Steve Perry					
❑ 03192 [PS]	Don't Fight It/The More We Try	1982	—	2.00	4.00
—A-side: Kenny Loggins with Steve Perry					
❑ CNR-03270	Don't Fight It	1982	—	3.00	6.00
—Kenny Loggins with Steve Perry; one-sided budget release					
❑ 03377	Heart to Heart/The More We Try	1982	—	—	3.00
❑ CNR-03427	Heart to Heart	1982	—	3.00	6.00
—One-sided budget release					
❑ 03555	Welcome to Heartlight/Only a Miracle	1983	—	—	3.00
❑ 03555 [PS]	Welcome to Heartlight/Only a Miracle	1983	—	2.00	4.00
❑ 04310	Footloose/Swear Your Love	1984	—	—	3.00
❑ 04310 [PS]	Footloose/Swear Your Love	1984	—	2.50	5.00
❑ 04452	I'm Free (Heaven Helps the Man)/Welcome to Heartlight (Live)	1984	—	—	3.00
❑ 04452 [PS]	I'm Free (Heaven Helps the Man)/Welcome to Heartlight (Live)	1984	—	—	3.00
❑ 04849	Vox Humana/Love Will Follow	1985	—	—	3.00
❑ 04849 [PS]	Vox Humana/Love Will Follow	1985	—	—	3.00
❑ 04931	Forever/At Last	1985	—	—	3.00
❑ 04931 [PS]	Forever/At Last	1985	—	—	3.00
❑ 05625	I'll Be There/No Lookin' Back	1985	—	—	3.00
❑ 05893	Danger Zone/I'm Gonna Do It Right	1986	—	—	3.00
❑ 05893 [PS]	Danger Zone/I'm Gonna Do It Right	1986	—	—	3.00
❑ 05902	Playing with the Boys/Love Will Follow	1986	—	—	3.00
❑ 05902 [PS]	Playing with the Boys/Love Will Follow	1986	—	—	3.00
❑ 06690	Meet Me Half Way/Semifinal	1987	—	—	3.00
❑ 06690 [PS]	Meet Me Half Way/Semifinal	1987	—	—	3.00
❑ 07971	Nobody's Fool (Theme from Caddyshack II)/I'm Gonna Do It Right	1988	—	—	3.00
❑ 07971 [PS]	Nobody's Fool (Theme from Caddyshack II)/I'm Gonna Do It Right	1988	—	—	3.00
❑ 08091	I'm Gonna Miss You/Isabella's Eyes	1988	—	—	3.00
❑ 08091 [PS]	I'm Gonna Miss You/Isabella's Eyes	1988	—	—	3.00
❑ 10569	I Believe in Love/Enter My Dream	1977	—	2.50	5.00
❑ 10652	Celebrate Me Home/Why Do People Lie	1977	—	2.50	5.00
❑ 10794	Whenever I Call You "Friend"/Angelique	1978	—	2.50	5.00
—With Stevie Nicks on A-side (uncredited)					
❑ 10866	Easy Driver/Somebody Knows	1978	—	2.50	5.00
❑ 11109	This Is It/Will It Last	1979	—	2.50	5.00
❑ 11215	Keep the Fire/Now and Then	1980	—	2.00	4.00
❑ 11290	Love Has Come of Age/Junkaroo Holiday (Fallin', Flyin')	1980	—	2.00	4.00
❑ 11317	I'm Alright (Theme from "Caddyshack")/Lead the Way	1980	—	2.00	4.00
❑ 11417	Celebrate Me Home (Live)/Celebrate Me Home (Studio)	1980	—	2.00	4.00
❑ 68531	Tell Her/Hope for the Runaway	1989	—	—	3.00
❑ 74029	Conviction of the Heart/My Father's House	1991	—	—	3.00

LOGGINS AND MESSINA
Also see KENNY LOGGINS; JIM MESSINA.

COLUMBIA

Number	Title (A Side/B Side)	Yr	VG	VG+	NM
❑ JBQ 507	Your Mama Don't Dance/Thinking of You	1973	2.50	5.00	10.00
—Quadraphonic single, "Special Coin Operator Release"					
❑ 10077	Changes/Get a Hold	1974	—	2.50	5.00
❑ 10118	Growin'/Keep Me in Mind	1975	—	2.50	5.00
❑ 10188	I Like It Like That/Angry Eyes	1975	—	2.50	5.00
❑ 10222	A Lover's Question/Oh, Lonesome Me	1975	—	2.50	5.00
❑ 10311	When I Was a Child/Peacemaker	1976	—	2.50	5.00
❑ 10376	Native Son/Pretty Princess	1976	—	2.50	5.00
❑ 10444	Angry Eyes/Watching the River Run	1976	—	2.50	5.00
❑ 45550	Same Old Wine/Vahevela	1972	—	3.00	6.00
—As "Kenny Loggins and Jim Messina"					
❑ 45617	Nobody But You/Danny's Song	1972	—	3.00	6.00
—As "Kenny Loggins and Jim Messina"					
❑ 45664	Peace of Mind/House at Pooh Corner	1972	—	3.00	6.00
—As "Kenny Loggins and Jim Messina"					
❑ 45719	Your Mama Don't Dance/Golden Ribbons	1972	—	3.00	6.00
—As "Kenny Loggins and Jim Messina"; gray label					
❑ 45719	Your Mama Don't Dance/Golden Ribbons	1972	—	2.50	5.00
—As "Kenny Loggins and Jim Messina"; orange label					
❑ 45815	Thinking of You/Till the Ends Meet	1973	—	2.50	5.00
—A-side is a different version than on most LPs					
❑ 45952	My Music/A Love Song	1973	—	2.50	5.00
❑ 46010	Watching the River Run/Travelin' Blues	1974	—	2.50	5.00

LOLITA

Number	Title (A Side/B Side)	Yr	VG	VG+	NM
4 CORNERS OF THE WORLD					
❑ 131	Come Back/When Our Father Is Happy	1965	—	3.50	7.00
KAPP					
❑ 349	Sailor (Your Home Is the Sea)/La Luna (Quando La Luna)	1960	3.00	6.00	12.00
—Maroon and silver label					
❑ 349	Sailor (Your Home Is the Sea)/La Luna (Quando La Luna)	1960	2.00	4.00	8.00
—Black label					
❑ 349 [PS]	Sailor (Your Home Is the Sea)/La Luna (Quando La Luna)	1960	5.00	10.00	20.00
❑ 370	Cowboy Jimmy Joe (Die Sterne Der Prarie)/ Theme from "A Summer Place"	1961	2.00	4.00	8.00
❑ 370 [PS]	Cowboy Jimmy Joe (Die Sterne Der Prarie)/ Theme from "A Summer Place"	1961	5.00	10.00	20.00
❑ 402	For the First Time (I've Fallen in Love)/Souvenir d'Amour	1961	2.00	4.00	8.00

LOLLIPOP SHOPPE, THE

Number	Title (A Side/B Side)	Yr	VG	VG+	NM
SHAMLEY					
❑ 44005	Someone I Know/Through My Window	1969	3.00	6.00	12.00
UNI					
❑ 55050	You Must Be a Witch/Don't Close the Door	1968	3.75	7.50	15.00
❑ 55050 [PS]	You Must Be a Witch/Don't Close the Door	1968	6.25	12.50	25.00

LOLLIPOPS, THE (1)

Number	Title (A Side/B Side)	Yr	VG	VG+	NM
ATCO					
❑ 6787	Nothing's Gonna Stop Our Love/I Believe in Love	1970	—	3.00	6.00
GORDY					
❑ 7089	Cheating Is Telling On You/Need Your Love	1969	200.00	400.00	800.00
IMPACT					
❑ 1021	Lovin' Good Feelin'/Step Aside Baby	1967	7.50	15.00	30.00
V.I.P.					
❑ 25051	Cheating Is Telling On You/Need Your Love	1968	6.25	12.50	25.00

LOLLIPOPS, THE (2)

Number	Title (A Side/B Side)	Yr	VG	VG+	NM
SSS INTERNATIONAL					
❑ 777	You Don't Know/Feel So Comfortable	1969	3.75	7.50	15.00

LOLLIPOPS, THE (3)

Number	Title (A Side/B Side)	Yr	VG	VG+	NM
WARNER BROS.					
❑ 5122	Mister Santa/Little Donkey (Carry Mary Safely on Her Way)	1959	3.00	6.00	12.00

LOLLIPOPS, THE (U)

Some of these could be group (1).

Number	Title (A Side/B Side)	Yr	VG	VG+	NM
RCA VICTOR					
❑ 47-8344	Peggy Got Engaged/I'll Set My Love to Music	1964	5.00	10.00	20.00
❑ 47-8390	Don't Monkey With Me/Love Is the Only Answer	1964	5.00	10.00	20.00
❑ 47-8430	Billy, Billy Baby/Big Brother	1964	5.00	10.00	20.00
❑ 47-8494	Busy Signal/I Want You Back Again	1965	3.75	7.50	15.00
SMASH					
❑ 2057	He's the Boy/Gee Whiz Baby	1966	3.00	6.00	12.00

LOLLYPOPS, THE

Number	Title (A Side/B Side)	Yr	VG	VG+	NM
HOLLAND					
❑ 7420	My Love Is Real/Believe in Me	1958	750.00	1500.	3000.
UNIVERSAL INT'L.					
❑ 7420	My Love Is Real/Believe in Me	1958	1000.	2000.	4000.

LOMAX, JACKIE

Number	Title (A Side/B Side)	Yr	VG	VG+	NM
APPLE					
❑ 1802	Sour Milk Sea/The Eagle Laughs at You	1968	5.00	10.00	20.00
—With B-side author listed as "(George Harrison)"					
❑ 1802	Sour Milk Sea/The Eagle Laughs at You	1968	5.00	10.00	20.00
—With B-side author listed as "(Jackie Lomax)"					
❑ 1807	New Day/Thumbin' a Ride	1969	18.75	37.50	75.00
—With star on A-side label					
❑ 1807	New Day/Thumbin' a Ride	1969	15.00	30.00	60.00
—Without star on A-side label					
❑ 1819	How the Web Was Woven/I Fall Inside Your Eyes	1970	2.00	4.00	8.00
❑ 1819 [PS]	How the Web Was Woven/I Fall Inside Your Eyes	1970	2.50	5.00	10.00
❑ 1834	Sour Milk Sea/(I) Fall Inside Your Eyes	1971	2.00	4.00	8.00
❑ PRO-6240/1 [DJ]	Sour Milk Sea/(I) Fall Inside Your Eyes	1971	7.50	15.00	30.00
CAPITOL					
❑ 4384	More (Livin' for Lovin')/I Remember (Memorabilia)	1976	—	2.50	5.00
EPIC					
❑ 10270	One Minute Woman/Genuine Imitation of Life	1967	3.00	6.00	12.00
WARNER BROS.					
❑ 7503	Helluva Woman/Higher Ground	1971	—	3.00	6.00
❑ 7564	Lavender Dream/Lost	1972	—	3.00	6.00
❑ 7589	Roll On/Hellfire, Night Crier	1972	—	3.00	6.00

LONDON, JULIE

Number	Title (A Side/B Side)	Yr	VG	VG+	NM
BETHLEHEM					
❑ 11003	Sometimes I Feel Like a Motherless Child/A Foggy Day	1958	5.00	10.00	20.00
❑ 11015	Don't Worry 'Bout Me/You're Blase	1959	3.00	6.00	12.00
LIBERTY					
❑ 33007 [S]	When I Fall in Love/The More I See You	1960	5.00	10.00	20.00
❑ 33008 [S]	Blue Moon/I Guess I'll Have to Change My Plan	1960	5.00	10.00	20.00
❑ 33009 [S]	Bye Bye Blues/Basin Street Blues	1960	5.00	10.00	20.00
❑ 33010 [S]	Daddy/Bye Bye Blackbird	1960	5.00	10.00	20.00
—The above four are 33 1/3 rpm jukebox singles					
❑ 55006	Cry Me a River/S'Wonderful	1955	3.00	6.00	12.00
❑ 55009	Baby, Baby, All the Time/Shadow Woman	1955	2.50	5.00	10.00
❑ 55025	September in the Rain/Lonely Girl	1956	2.50	5.00	10.00
❑ 55032	Tall Boy/Now, Baby, Now	1956	2.50	5.00	10.00
❑ 55052	The Meaning of the Blues/Boy on a Dolphin	1957	2.50	5.00	10.00
❑ 55074	It Had to Be You/Dark	1957	2.50	5.00	10.00
❑ 55108	I'd Like You for Christmas/Saddle the Wind	1957	3.00	6.00	12.00
❑ 55131	Tell Me You're Home/The Freshman	1958	2.50	5.00	10.00
❑ 55139	It's Easy/Voice in the Mirror	1958	2.50	5.00	10.00
❑ 55157	Blue Moon/Man of the West	1958	2.50	5.00	10.00
❑ 55175	Come On-a My House/My Strange Affair	1959	2.50	5.00	10.00
❑ 55182	Must Be Catchin'/Something I Dreamed Last Night	1959	2.50	5.00	10.00
❑ 55216	Comin' Through the Rye/Makin' Whoopee	1959	2.50	5.00	10.00
❑ 55227	Cry Me a River/It's a Blue World	1959	2.50	5.00	10.00
❑ 55269	In the Wee Small Hours of the Morning/Time for Lovers	1960	2.50	5.00	10.00
❑ 55300	Send for Me/Evenin'	1961	2.00	4.00	8.00
❑ 55309	Sanctuary/Every Chance I Get	1961	2.00	4.00	8.00
❑ 55337	My Darling, My Darling/My Love, My Love	1961	2.00	4.00	8.00
❑ 55512	Desafinado/Where Did the Gentleman Go	1962	2.00	4.00	8.00
❑ 55605	I'm Coming Back to You/When Snowflakes Fall in the Summer	1963	2.00	4.00	8.00
❑ 55666	Guilty Heart/I Want to Find Out for Myself	1964	—	3.00	6.00
❑ 55702	Girl (Boy) from Ipanema/My Lover Is a Stranger	1964	—	3.00	6.00
❑ 55759	We Proved Them Wrong/You're Free to Go	1964	—	3.00	6.00
❑ 55830	Girl Talk/Won't Somebody Please Belong to Me	1965	—	3.00	6.00
❑ 55911	Nice Girls Don't Stay for Breakfast/Bill Bailey (Won't You Please Come Home)	1966	—	3.00	6.00
❑ 55966	Mickey Mouse March/Baby Won't You Please	1967	—	3.00	6.00
❑ 56074	Yummy, Yummy, Yummy/Come to Me Slowly	1968	—	2.50	5.00
❑ 56085	Louie Louie/Hushabye Mountain	1969	—	2.50	5.00
❑ 56112	Too Much of a Man/Sittin' Pretty	1969	—	—	—
—Unreleased					
UNITED ARTISTS					
❑ 0013	Cry Me a River/Come On-a My House	1973	—	2.00	4.00
—"Silver Spotlight Series" reissue					
7-Inch Extended Plays					
LIBERTY					
❑ LEP-1-3006	Laura/S' Wonderful//I'm in the Mood for Love/ Can't Help Lovin' That Man	1956	3.00	6.00	12.00
❑ LEP-1-3006 [PS]	Julie Is Her Name, Part One	1956	3.00	6.00	12.00
❑ LEP-2-3006	(contents unknown)	1956	3.00	6.00	12.00
❑ LEP-2-3006 [PS]	Julie Is Her Name, Part Two	1956	3.00	6.00	12.00
❑ LEP-3-3006	(contents unknown)	1956	3.00	6.00	12.00
❑ LEP-3-3006 [PS]	Julie Is Her Name, Part Three	1956	3.00	6.00	12.00
❑ LEP-1-3012	*Lonely Girl/Fools Rush In/How Deep Is the Ocean/Mean to Me	195?	3.00	6.00	12.00
❑ LEP-1-3012 [PS]	Lonely Girl, Part One	195?	3.00	6.00	12.00
❑ LEP-2-3012	(contents unknown)	195?	3.00	6.00	12.00
❑ LEP-2-3012 [PS]	Lonely Girl, Part Two	195?	3.00	6.00	12.00
❑ LEP-3-3012	(contents unknown)	195?	3.00	6.00	12.00
❑ LEP-3-3012 [PS]	Lonely Girl, Part Three	195?	3.00	6.00	12.00

LONDON, LAURIE

Number	Title (A Side/B Side)	Yr	VG	VG+	NM
CAPITOL					
❑ F3891	He's Got the Whole World (In His Hands)/Handed Down	1958	3.75	7.50	15.00
❑ F3973	Joshua/I Gotta Robe	1958	3.00	6.00	12.00
❑ F4133	My Mother/Three O'Clock	1959	3.00	6.00	12.00
ROULETTE					
❑ 4176	Pretty Eyed Baby/Boom Ladda Boom Boom	1959	2.50	5.00	10.00

LONESOME DRIFTER, THE

Number	Title (A Side/B Side)	Yr	VG	VG+	NM
K					
❑ 5812	Eager Boy/Teardrop Valley	1958	500.00	1000.	2000.

LONG, HUEY

Number	Title (A Side/B Side)	Yr	VG	VG+	NM
FIDELITY					
❑ 4054	How to Tell My Heart/Waiting for a Letter	1962	5.00	10.00	20.00
❑ 4055	Elvis Stole My Gal/Ballad of John Glenn	1962	12.50	25.00	50.00

LONG, SHORTY (1)

R&B singer.

Number	Title (A Side/B Side)	Yr	VG	VG+	NM
SOUL					
❑ 35001	Devil with the Blue Dress/Wind It Up	1964	6.25	12.50	25.00
❑ 35005	It's a Crying Shame/Out to Get You	1964	6.25	12.50	25.00
❑ 35021	Function at the Junction/Call On Me	1966	3.75	7.50	15.00
❑ 35031	Chantilly Lace/Your Love Is Amazing	1966	3.75	7.50	15.00
❑ 35040	Night Fo' Last/(Instrumental)	1968	2.50	5.00	10.00
❑ 35044	Here Comes the Judge/Sing What You Wanna	1968	2.50	5.00	10.00
❑ 35054	I Had a Dream/Ain't No Justice	1969	2.50	5.00	10.00
❑ 35064	A Whiter Shade of Pale/When You Are Available	1969	2.50	5.00	10.00
TRI-PHI					
❑ 1006	I'll Be There/Bad Willie	1962	12.50	25.00	50.00
❑ 1015	Too Smart/I'll Be There	1962	17.50	35.00	70.00
❑ 1021	What's the Matter/Going Away	1963	15.00	30.00	60.00

LONG, SHORTY (2)

C&W singer.

Number	Title (A Side/B Side)	Yr	VG	VG+	NM
DOT					
❑ 1154	Pretend/Crying Street Guitar Waltz	1953	6.25	12.50	25.00
KING					
❑ 953	Goodnight Cincinnati/Just Like Two Drops of Water	1951	10.00	20.00	40.00
❑ 5605	Take Me to the Happy Land/Mary, Oh Mary	1962	6.25	12.50	25.00
RCA VICTOR					
❑ 47-6472	Hey, Doll Baby/Luscious	1956	25.00	50.00	100.00
❑ 47-6572	Vacation Rock/Burnt Toast and Black Coffee	1956	25.00	50.00	100.00
❑ 47-6804	Another Love Has Ended/Little White Horse	1957	25.00	50.00	100.00
❑ 47-6873	You Don't Have to Be a Baby to Cry/I'd Crawl Back	1957	25.00	50.00	100.00
❑ 48-0057	The Morning After/Please Daddy Forgive	1949	10.00	20.00	40.00
—Originals on green vinyl; second pressing on black vinyl is unconfirmed					
❑ 48-0098	The Warm Red Wine/I Got Mine	1949	10.00	20.00	40.00
—Originals on green vinyl; second pressing on black vinyl is unconfirmed					
❑ 48-0134	I Wasted a Nickel/This Cold War with You	1950	10.00	20.00	40.00
—Originals on green vinyl; second pressing on black vinyl is unconfirmed					

Number	Title (A Side/B Side)	Yr	VG	VG+	NM
❑ 48-0347	A Bottle and a Blonde/Waltz of Colorado	1950	10.00	20.00	40.00
—Originals on green vinyl; second pressing on black vinyl is unconfirmed					
"X"					
❑ 0024	Standing in the Station/Make with Me De Love	1954	5.00	10.00	20.00

LONGBRANCH PENNYWHISTLE

GLENN FREY, J.D. SOUTHER and RY COODER all were members of this group.

Number	Title (A Side/B Side)	Yr	VG	VG+	NM
AMOS					
❑ 121	Don't Talk Now/Jubilee Anne	1969	3.75	7.50	15.00
❑ 129	Lucky Love/Rebecca	1969	3.75	7.50	15.00
❑ 148	Star Spangled Bus/Bring Back Founky Women	1970	3.75	7.50	15.00

LONNIE AND THE CAROLLONS

Number	Title (A Side/B Side)	Yr	VG	VG+	NM
MOHAWK					
❑ 108	Chapel of Tears/My Heart	1958	37.50	75.00	150.00
—Green label					
❑ 108	Chapel of Tears/My Heart	1961	7.50	15.00	30.00
—Red label					
❑ 108	Chapel of Tears/My Heart	1965	5.00	10.00	20.00
—White label					
❑ 111	Hold Me Close/Trudy	1958	12.50	25.00	50.00
❑ 112	Back Yard Rock/You Say	1958	12.50	25.00	50.00
❑ 113	The Gang All Knows/Ike Hammer	1959	15.00	30.00	60.00
❑ 122	Need Your Lovin'/Beeline	1960	6.25	12.50	25.00
—As "Lonnie"					

LONNIE AND THE CRISIS

Number	Title (A Side/B Side)	Yr	VG	VG+	NM
RELIC					
❑ 532	Bells in the Chapel/Santa Town USA	196?	—	3.00	6.00
—Reissue of Universal 103					
TIMES SQUARE					
❑ 25	Bells in the Chapel/Santa Town USA	196?	2.00	4.00	8.00
—Reissue of Universal 103					
UNIVERSAL					
❑ 103	Bells in the Chapel/Santa Town USA	1961	50.00	100.00	200.00

LOOKINLAND, MIKE

"Bobby Brady" of THE BRADY BUNCH.

Number	Title (A Side/B Side)	Yr	VG	VG+	NM
CAPITOL					
❑ 3914	Gum Drop/Love Doesn't Care Who's In It	1974	2.50	5.00	10.00
❑ 3914 [PS]	Gum Drop/Love Doesn't Care Who's In It	1974	3.75	7.50	15.00

LOPEZ, JENNIFER

Number	Title (A Side/B Side)	Yr	VG	VG+	NM
WORK					
❑ 79163	If You Had My Love/No Me Ames (Duet with Marc Anthony)	1999	—	—	2.00
❑ 79163 [PS]	If You Had My Love/No Me Ames (Duet with Marc Anthony)	1999	—	—	2.00
❑ 32-79387	Feelin' So Good (Bad Boy Alternate Mix)/(Album Version)	2000	—	—	2.00
—Issued with small hole					
❑ 32-79387 [PS]	Feelin' So Good (Bad Boy Alternate Mix)/(Album Version)	2000	—	—	2.00

LOPEZ, TRINI

Number	Title (A Side/B Side)	Yr	VG	VG+	NM
CAPITOL					
❑ 3195	Some Kind of a Summer/Poor Old Billy	1971	—	2.50	5.00
❑ 3312	Ruby Mountain/Y Voluere	1972	—	2.50	5.00
❑ 3402	Mammy Blue/Viva	1972	—	2.50	5.00
D.R.A.					
❑ 7008	Rosita/Only in My Dreams	1962	3.75	7.50	15.00
GRIFFIN					
❑ 504	Butterfly/Don't Burn Your Bridges Behind You	1973	—	2.50	5.00
❑ 508	Bring Back the Sunshine/We Gotta Make It Together	1974	—	2.50	5.00
KING					
❑ 5173	Rosalia/Nola	1959	5.00	10.00	20.00
❑ 5187	Since I Don't Have You/Rock On	1959	6.25	12.50	25.00
❑ 5198	Love Me Tonight/Here Comes Sally	1959	5.00	10.00	20.00
❑ 5234	Don't Let Your Sweet Love Die/I'm Grateful	1959	5.00	10.00	20.00
❑ 5284	Nobody Loves Me/Nobody Listens to Our Teenage Problems	1959	5.00	10.00	20.00
❑ 5304	Chain of Love/Sweet Thing	1960	5.00	10.00	20.00
❑ 5324	Schemes/Jeannie Marie	1960	5.00	10.00	20.00
❑ 5344	It Hurts to Be in Love/The Search Goes On	1960	5.00	10.00	20.00
❑ 5418	Don't Treat Me That Way/Then You Know	1960	5.00	10.00	20.00
❑ 5487	One Heart, One Life, One Love/You Broke the Only Heart	1961	5.00	10.00	20.00
❑ 5801	Jeannie Marie/Love Me Tonight	1963	3.00	6.00	12.00
❑ 5820	Don't Go/It Seems	1963	3.00	6.00	12.00
❑ 5824	Nobody Loves Me/The Club for Broken Hearts	1963	3.00	6.00	12.00
❑ 5849	Yes You Do/Won't You Be	1964	3.00	6.00	12.00
❑ 6000	Jeannie Marie/Nobody Listens, Nobody Cares	1965	2.00	4.00	8.00
❑ 6021	The Search Goes On/Chain of Love	1966	2.00	4.00	8.00
PRIVATE STOCK					
❑ 45024	Somethin' 'Bout You Baby I Like/Sweet Life	1975	—	2.50	5.00
❑ 45035	Seco Sulto Y Tonton	1975	—	2.50	5.00
❑ 45044	Heavy Makes You Happy (Sha-La-Boom-Boom-Yeah)/Satisfaction	1975	—	2.50	5.00
REPRISE					
❑ 0239	La Bamba/Granada	1963	3.75	7.50	15.00
—Released only in Latin America					
❑ 0260	Jailer, Bring Me Water/You Can't Say Goodbye	1964	2.00	4.00	8.00
❑ 0276	Ya Ya/What Have I Got of My Own	1964	2.00	4.00	8.00
❑ 0300	Michael/San Francisco De Assisi	1964	2.00	4.00	8.00
❑ 0328	Sad Tomorrows/I've Lost My Love for You	1964	2.00	4.00	8.00
❑ 0328 [PS]	Sad Tomorrows/I've Lost My Love for You	1964	3.75	7.50	15.00
❑ 0336	Lemon Tree/Pretty Eyes	1965	2.50	5.00	10.00
❑ 0336 [PS]	Lemon Tree/Pretty Eyes	1965	3.75	7.50	15.00
❑ 0376	Are You Sincere/You'll Be Sorry	1965	2.00	4.00	8.00
❑ 0405	Sinner Man/Double Trouble	1965	2.00	4.00	8.00
❑ 0405 [PS]	Sinner Man/Double Trouble	1965	3.75	7.50	15.00
❑ 0421	Regressa A Mi/Mi Felicidad	1965	2.00	4.00	8.00
❑ 0435	Made in Paris/Pretty Little Girl	1965	2.00	4.00	8.00
❑ 0435 [PS]	Made in Paris/Pretty Little Girl	1965	3.75	7.50	15.00
❑ 0455	The 32nd of May/I'm Coming Home, Cindy	1966	2.00	4.00	8.00
❑ 0480	La Bamba — Part 1/Trini's Tune	1966	2.00	4.00	8.00
❑ 0508	Hall of Fame/Pancho Lopez	1966	2.00	4.00	8.00
❑ 0536	Your Ever Changin' Mind/Takin' the Back Roads	1966	2.00	4.00	8.00
❑ 0547	Gonna Get Along Without Ya' Now/Love Letters	1967	—	3.00	6.00
❑ 0574	In the Land of Plenty/Up To Now	1967	—	3.00	6.00
❑ 0596	Ballad of the Dirty Dozen/The Bramble Bush	1967	—	3.00	6.00
❑ 0618	I Wanna Be Free/Together	1967	—	3.00	6.00
❑ 0648	It's a Great Life/Let's Take a Walk	1967	—	3.00	6.00
❑ 0659	Sally Was a Good Old Girl/It's a Great Life	1968	—	3.00	6.00
❑ 0687	Good Old Mountain Dew/Mental Journey	1968	—	3.00	6.00
❑ 0700	If I Had a Hammer/Lemon Tree	1968	—	2.50	5.00
—"Back to Back Hits" series					
❑ 0725	La Bamba/Kansas City	1968	—	2.50	5.00
—"Back to Back Hits" series					
❑ 0770	Something Tells Me/Malaguena Salerosa	1968	—	3.00	6.00
❑ 0801 [DJ]	El Nino Del Tambor/Nocho De Paz (Let There Be Peace)	1968	2.00	4.00	8.00
—Stock copy may not exist					
❑ 0814	Come a Little Bit Closer/My Baby Loves Sad Songs	1969	—	3.00	6.00
❑ 0825	Don't Let the Sun Catch You Crryin'/My Baby Loves Sad Songs	1969	—	3.00	6.00
❑ 0879	Games People Play/Love Story	1969	—	3.00	6.00
❑ 0912	5 O'Clock World/You Make My Day	1970	—	2.50	5.00
❑ 0933	Mexican Medicine Man/Time to Get It Together	1970	—	2.50	5.00
❑ 0947	Su-Kal-De-Don/Mexican Medicine Man	1970	—	2.50	5.00
❑ 0975	Let's Think About Living/There Was a Crooked Man	1970	—	2.50	5.00
❑ 20168	A-M-E-R-I-C-A/Let It Be Known	1963	2.50	5.00	10.00
❑ 20190	La Bamba (Part 1)/La Bamba (Part 2)	1963	2.50	5.00	10.00
❑ 20198	If I Had a Hammer/Unchain My Heart	1963	3.00	6.00	12.00
❑ 20218	If I Had a Hammer/La Bamba	1963	3.75	7.50	15.00
—Released only in Italy					
❑ 20223	This Land Is Your Land/Cielito Lindo	1963	3.75	7.50	15.00
—Released only in Holland					
❑ 20224	Bye Bye Blackbird/Medley	1963	3.75	7.50	15.00
—Released only in Holland					
❑ 20234	This Land Is Your Land/La Bamba	1963	3.75	7.50	15.00
—Released only in West Germany					
❑ 20236	Kansas City/Lonesome Traveler	1963	2.00	4.00	8.00
ROULETTE					
❑ 7214	Beautiful People/Helplessly	1977	—	2.50	5.00
VOLK					
❑ 101	The Right to Rock/Just Once More	1958	7.50	15.00	30.00
7-Inch Extended Plays					
FRESCA					
❑ ZTEP-124178	If I Had a Hammer/A-Me-Ri-Ca//Kansas City/The Blizzard Song	1967	2.50	5.00	10.00
❑ ZTEP-124178 [PS]	Trini Lopez Sings His Greatest Hits	1967	3.75	7.50	15.00
—Available on specially marked packages of Fresca soda					
KING					
❑ EP-483	Jeanie Marie/It Seems//Don't Go/Love Me Tonight	1963	10.00	20.00	40.00
—Possibly promo only; not known if issued with sleeve					

LORD, BRIAN, AND THE MIDNIGHTERS

FRANK ZAPPA was a member of this group.

Number	Title (A Side/B Side)	Yr	VG	VG+	NM
CAPITOL					
❑ 4981	Big Surfer/Not Another One	1963	37.50	75.00	150.00
VIGAH					
❑ 001	Big Surfer/Not Another One	1963	75.00	150.00	300.00

LORD ROCKINGHAM'S XI

Number	Title (A Side/B Side)	Yr	VG	VG+	NM
LONDON					
❑ 1810	Fried Onions/The Squelch	1958	3.00	6.00	12.00
❑ 1839	Hoots Mon/Blue Train	1958	3.00	6.00	12.00

LORD SITAR

Sometimes rumored to be GEORGE HARRISON, but it's not.

Number	Title (A Side/B Side)	Yr	VG	VG+	NM
CAPITOL					
❑ 5972	Black Is Black/Have You Seen Your Mother, Baby, Standing in the Shadow	1967	5.00	10.00	20.00

LORDAN, JERRY

Number	Title (A Side/B Side)	Yr	VG	VG+	NM
CAPITOL					
❑ 4389	Who Could Be Bluer/Do I Worry	1960	3.75	7.50	15.00

LORDS OF LONDON, THE

Number	Title (A Side/B Side)	Yr	VG	VG+	NM
DECCA					
❑ 32196	Time Waits for No One/Cornflakes and Ice Cream	1967	5.00	10.00	20.00
MGM					
❑ 13919	Candy Rainbow/Within Your Mind	1968	5.00	10.00	20.00

LOS BRAVOS

Number	Title (A Side/B Side)	Yr	VG	VG+	NM
PARROT					
❑ 3020	Bring a Little Lovin'/Make It Last	1968	3.00	6.00	12.00
❑ 3023	Dirty Street/Two People in Me	1968	2.50	5.00	10.00
PRESS					
❑ 60002	Black Is Black/I Want a Name	1966	3.75	7.50	15.00
❑ 60003	Going Nowhere/Brand New Baby	1966	2.50	5.00	10.00
❑ 60004	You'll Never Get the Chance Again/I'm All Ears	1967	2.50	5.00	10.00

LOST, THE

Number	Title (A Side/B Side)	Yr	VG	VG+	NM
CAPITOL					
❑ 5519	Back Door Blues/Maybe More Than You Do	1965	3.75	7.50	15.00
❑ 5708	Mean Motorcycle/Violet Gown	1966	3.75	7.50	15.00
❑ 5725	No Reason Why/Violet Gown	1966	3.75	7.50	15.00

JANUS

Number	Title (A Side/B Side)	Yr	VG	VG+	NM
❑ 109	I Shall Be Released/Shame	1969	2.50	5.00	10.00

LOST & FOUND

INTERNATIONAL ARTISTS

Number	Title (A Side/B Side)	Yr	VG	VG+	NM
❑ 120	Everybody's Here/Forever Lasting Plastic Words	1968	6.25	12.50	25.00
❑ 125	When Will You Come Through/Professor Black	1968	6.25	12.50	25.00

LOTHAR AND THE HAND PEOPLE

CAPITOL

Number	Title (A Side/B Side)	Yr	VG	VG+	NM
❑ 2008	Have Mercy (Mercy, Mercy, Mercy)/Let the Boy Pretend	1967	2.50	5.00	10.00
❑ 2376	Machines/Milkweed Love	1969	2.00	4.00	8.00
❑ 2556	Midnight Ranger/Yes, I Love You	1969	2.00	4.00	8.00
❑ 5874	L-O-V-E/Rose Colored Glasses	1967	2.50	5.00	10.00
❑ 5945	Comic Strip/Every Single Word	1967	2.50	5.00	10.00

LOU, HERB B., AND THE LEGAL EAGLES

Break-in record with HERB ALPERT involvement.

ARCH

Number	Title (A Side/B Side)	Yr	VG	VG+	NM
❑ 1607	The Trial/Kiss Me	1958	10.00	20.00	40.00

LOUDERMILK, JOHN D.

Includes records as "Johnny Dee."

COLONIAL

Number	Title (A Side/B Side)	Yr	VG	VG+	NM
❑ 430	Sittin' in the Balcony/A-Plus in Love *—As "Johnny Dee"*	1957	7.50	15.00	30.00
❑ 430 [PS]	Sittin' in the Balcony/A-Plus in Love *—As "Johnny Dee"*	1957	100.00	200.00	400.00
❑ 433	Teenage Queen/It's Gotta Be You *—As "Johnny Dee"*	1957	7.50	15.00	30.00
❑ 435	1000 Concrete Blocks/In My Simple Way *—As "Johnny Dee"*	1958	7.50	15.00	30.00

COLUMBIA

Number	Title (A Side/B Side)	Yr	VG	VG+	NM
❑ 4-41165	Yearbook/Susie's House	1958	3.75	7.50	15.00
❑ 4-41165 [PS]	Yearbook/Susie's House	1958	6.25	12.50	25.00
❑ 4-41209	Lover's Lane/Yo Yo	1958	3.75	7.50	15.00
❑ 4-41247	Goin' Away to School/This Cold War with You	1958	3.75	7.50	15.00
❑ 4-41507	The Happy Wanderer/Red Headed Stranger	1959	3.75	7.50	15.00
❑ 4-41562	Tobacco Road/Midnight Bus	1960	5.00	10.00	20.00

DOT

Number	Title (A Side/B Side)	Yr	VG	VG+	NM
❑ 15699	Somebody Sweet/They Were Right *—As "Johnny Dee"*	1958	7.50	15.00	30.00

RCA VICTOR

Number	Title (A Side/B Side)	Yr	VG	VG+	NM
❑ 47-7938	Language of Love/Darling Jane	1961	3.00	6.00	12.00
❑ 47-7993	Thou Shalt Not Steal/Mister Jones	1962	3.00	6.00	12.00
❑ 47-8054	Callin' Doctor Casey/Oh How Sad	1962	3.00	6.00	12.00
❑ 47-8101	Road Hog/Angela Jones	1962	3.00	6.00	12.00
❑ 47-8101 [PS]	Road Hog/Angela Jones	1962	5.00	10.00	20.00
❑ 47-8154	Bad News/The Guitar Player	1963	3.00	6.00	12.00
❑ 47-8308	Blue Train (Of the Heartbreak Line)/Rhythm and Blues	1962	3.00	6.00	12.00
❑ 47-8389	Th' Wife/Nothing to Gain	1964	3.00	6.00	12.00
❑ 47-8579	That Ain't All/Then You Can Tell Me Goodbye *—B-side is the original version of the future hit*	1965	3.00	6.00	12.00
❑ 47-8826	Run On Home Baby Brother/Silver Cloud Talking Blues	1966	2.50	5.00	10.00
❑ 47-8973	I Hear It Now/You're the Guilty One	1966	2.50	5.00	10.00
❑ 47-9189	It's My Time/Bahama Mama	1967	2.50	5.00	10.00
❑ 47-9592	Sidewalks/The Odd Folks of Okracoke	1968	2.00	4.00	8.00
❑ 74-0121	Brown Girl/The Jones'	1969	2.00	4.00	8.00

WARNER BROS.

Number	Title (A Side/B Side)	Yr	VG	VG+	NM
❑ 7489	When I Was Nine/Lord Have Mercy	1971	—	3.50	7.00

LOUIS, BOBBY

CAPITOL

Number	Title (A Side/B Side)	Yr	VG	VG+	NM
❑ F4224	Adult Western/Love at First Sight	1959	7.50	15.00	30.00
❑ F4272	I'm a Coward/Cell of Love	1959	7.50	15.00	30.00

LOVE

Also see ARTHUR LEE.

BLUE THUMB

Number	Title (A Side/B Side)	Yr	VG	VG+	NM
❑ 106	Stand Out/I'll Pray for You	1970	—	3.00	6.00
❑ 7116	Keep On Shining/Everlasting First	1970	—	3.00	6.00

ELEKTRA

Number	Title (A Side/B Side)	Yr	VG	VG+	NM
❑ 45603	My Little Red Book/Message to Pretty	1966	2.50	5.00	10.00
❑ 45605	7 and 7 Is/No. Fourteen	1966	2.50	5.00	10.00
❑ 45608	Stephanie Knows Who/Orange Sky	1966	7.50	15.00	30.00
❑ 45608	She Comes in Colors/Orange Sky	1966	2.50	5.00	10.00
❑ 45613	Que Vida/Hey Joe	1967	12.50	25.00	50.00
❑ 45629	Alone Again Or/A House Is Not a Motel	1968	2.50	5.00	10.00
❑ 45633	Laughing Stock/You're Mine and We Belong Together	1968	3.75	7.50	15.00
❑ 45700	Alone Again Or/Good Times	1970	2.00	4.00	8.00

RSO

Number	Title (A Side/B Side)	Yr	VG	VG+	NM
❑ 502	Time Is Like a River/With a Little Energy	1974	—	2.50	5.00
❑ 506	Good Old Fashioned Dream/You Said You Would	1975	—	2.50	5.00

LOVE, DARLENE

Also see THE BLOSSOMS; THE CRYSTALS.

COLUMBIA

Number	Title (A Side/B Side)	Yr	VG	VG+	NM
❑ 07984	He's Sure the Man I Love/Everybody Needs	1988	—	2.50	5.00

ELEKTRA

Number	Title (A Side/B Side)	Yr	VG	VG+	NM
❑ 69647	River Deep, Mountain High/Leader of the Pack *—B-side by Leader of the Pack*	1985	—	2.00	4.00
❑ 69647 [PS]	River Deep, Mountain High/Leader of the Pack	1985	—	2.00	4.00

PASSPORT

Number	Title (A Side/B Side)	Yr	VG	VG+	NM
❑ 7926	Christmas (Baby Please Come Home)/Playing for Keeps	1983	3.00	6.00	12.00

PHILLES

Number	Title (A Side/B Side)	Yr	VG	VG+	NM
❑ 111	(Today I Met) The Boy I'm Gonna Marry/My Heart Beat a Little Faster	1963	7.50	15.00	30.00
❑ 111	(Today I Met) The Boy I'm Gonna Marry/Playing for Keeps	1963	5.00	10.00	20.00
❑ 114	Wait 'Til My Bobby Gets Home/Take It From Me	1963	5.00	10.00	20.00
❑ 117	A Fine Fine Boy/Nino & Sonny (Big Trouble)	1963	5.00	10.00	20.00
❑ 119	Christmas (Baby Please Come Home)/Harry and Milt Meet Hal B.	1963	10.00	20.00	40.00
❑ 123	Stumble and Fall/(He's a) Quiet Guy *—Yellow and red label stock copy; has been verified to exist*	1964	200.00	400.00	800.00
❑ 123	Stumble and Fall/(He's a) Quiet Guy *—Yellow and red label, "D.J. Copy Not for Sale" on label*	1964	75.00	150.00	300.00
❑ 123 [DJ]	Stumble and Fall/(He's a) Quiet Guy *—White label promo*	1964	37.50	75.00	150.00
❑ 125X	Christmas (Baby Please Come Home)/Winter Wonderland	1965	6.25	12.50	25.00
❑ 125	Christmas (Baby Please Come Home)/X-Mas Blues	1964	100.00	200.00	400.00

REPRISE

Number	Title (A Side/B Side)	Yr	VG	VG+	NM
❑ 0534	Too Late to Say You're Sorry/If	1966	2.50	5.00	10.00

WARNER/SPECTOR

Number	Title (A Side/B Side)	Yr	VG	VG+	NM
❑ 0401	Christmas (Baby Please Come Home)/Winter Wonderland	1974	2.50	5.00	10.00
❑ 0410	Lord, If You're a Woman/Stumble and Fall	1975	2.50	5.00	10.00

LOVE, HOT SHOT

SUN

Number	Title (A Side/B Side)	Yr	VG	VG+	NM
❑ 196	Wolf Call Boogie/Harmonica Jam	1954	1000.	2000.	4000.

LOVE, MIKE

Also see THE BEACH BOYS; CELEBRATION FEATURING MIKE LOVE; BRIAN WILSON AND MIKE LOVE.

BOARDWALK

Number	Title (A Side/B Side)	Yr	VG	VG+	NM
❑ NB7-11-128	Looking Back with Love/One Good Reason	1981	—	2.00	4.00

LOVE, MIKE, AND DEAN TORRENCE

Also see JAN AND DEAN; MIKE LOVE.

HITBOUND

Number	Title (A Side/B Side)	Yr	VG	VG+	NM
❑ X-2	Jingle Bell Rock/Jingle Bells *—B-side by Paul Revere and the Raiders*	1983	3.00	6.00	12.00
❑ X-2 [PS]	Jingle Bell Rock/Jingle Bells *—B-side by Paul Revere and the Raiders*	1983	5.00	10.00	20.00

LOVE NOTES, THE (1)

HOLIDAY

Number	Title (A Side/B Side)	Yr	VG	VG+	NM
❑ 2605	United/Tonight *—Glossy label*	1957	15.00	30.00	60.00
❑ 2605	United/Tonight *—Flat (matte) label*	1957	5.00	10.00	20.00
❑ 2607	If I Could Make You Mine/Don't Go	1957	10.00	20.00	40.00

LOVE NOTES, THE (2)

IMPERIAL

Number	Title (A Side/B Side)	Yr	VG	VG+	NM
❑ 5254	Surrender Your Heart/Get On My Train	1953	300.00	600.00	1200.

RAINBOW

Number	Title (A Side/B Side)	Yr	VG	VG+	NM
❑ 266	I'm Sorry/Sweet Lulu	1954	75.00	150.00	300.00

RIVIERA

Number	Title (A Side/B Side)	Yr	VG	VG+	NM
❑ 970	I'm Sorry/Sweet Lulu	1954	200.00	400.00	800.00
❑ 975	Since I Fell for You/Don't Be No Fool *—Authentic copies have a lavender (light purple) label, counterfeits have a pink label*	1954	250.00	500.00	1000.

LOVE NOTES, THE (3)

WILSHIRE

Number	Title (A Side/B Side)	Yr	VG	VG+	NM
❑ 200	Nancy/Our Songs of Love	1963	10.00	20.00	40.00
❑ 203	Gloria/The Mathematics of Love	1963	25.00	50.00	100.00

LOVE SCULPTURE

DAVE EDMUNDS was in this group.

PARROT

Number	Title (A Side/B Side)	Yr	VG	VG+	NM
❑ 335	Sabre Dance/Think of Love	1969	3.75	7.50	15.00
❑ 362	In the Land of the Few/Farandole	1970	3.75	7.50	15.00

LOVE SOCIETY, THE

MERCURY

Number	Title (A Side/B Side)	Yr	VG	VG+	NM
❑ 73130	America/Wanda	1970	3.75	7.50	15.00

RCA VICTOR

Number	Title (A Side/B Side)	Yr	VG	VG+	NM
❑ 74-0257	Don't Worry Baby/You Know How I Feel (And Why)	1969	2.50	5.00	10.00

SCEPTER

Number	Title (A Side/B Side)	Yr	VG	VG+	NM
❑ 12223	Without You/Do You Wanna Dance	1968	3.00	6.00	12.00
❑ 12236	Tobacco Road/Drops of Rain	1969	3.00	6.00	12.00

LOVEJOYS, THE

RED BIRD

Number	Title (A Side/B Side)	Yr	VG	VG+	NM
❑ 10-004	Payin'/It's Mighty Nice	1964	7.50	15.00	30.00

LOVERS, THE (1)

Husband-and-wife R&B duo.

ALADDIN

Number	Title (A Side/B Side)	Yr	VG	VG+	NM
❑ 3419	Tell Me/Love Bug Bit Me	1958	10.00	20.00	40.00

IMPERIAL

Number	Title (A Side/B Side)	Yr	VG	VG+	NM
❑ 5845	Darling It's Wonderful/I Want to Be Loved	1962	5.00	10.00	20.00
❑ 5960	Tell Me/Let's Elope	1963	5.00	10.00	20.00
❑ 66055	Darling It's Wonderful/I Want to Be Loved	1964	3.75	7.50	15.00

LAMP

Number	Title (A Side/B Side)	Yr	VG	VG+	NM
❑ 2005	Darling It's Wonderful/Gotta Whole Lot of Livin' to Do	1957	12.50	25.00	50.00
❑ 2013	I Wanna Be Loved/Let's Elope	1957	12.50	25.00	50.00
❑ 2018	Tell Me/Love Bug Bit Me	1958	12.50	25.00	50.00

POST

Number	Title (A Side/B Side)	Yr	VG	VG+	NM
❑ 10007	Darling It's Wonderful/Gotta Whole Lot of Livin' to Do	1963	3.75	7.50	15.00

LOVERS, THE (2)

Number	Title (A Side/B Side)	Yr	VG	VG+	NM
AGON					
❑ 1011	Caravan of Lonely Men/In My Tenement	1965	6.25	12.50	25.00
GATE					
❑ 501	Someone/Do This For Me	1965	25.00	50.00	100.00
PHILIPS					
❑ 40353	Someone/Do This for Me	1966	5.00	10.00	20.00

LOVERS, THE (3)

Number	Title (A Side/B Side)	Yr	VG	VG+	NM
CASINO					
❑ 103	Let's/Big Axe	1958	5.00	10.00	20.00

LOVERS, THE (4)

Number	Title (A Side/B Side)	Yr	VG	VG+	NM
MARLIN					
❑ 3313	Discomania (Part 1)/Discomania (Part 2)	1977	—	2.50	5.00

LOVERS, THE (U)

These could be groups (1) or (2).

Number	Title (A Side/B Side)	Yr	VG	VG+	NM
CHECKER					
❑ 1100	It's Too Late/Security	1965	2.50	5.00	10.00
DECCA					
❑ 29862	Don't Touch Me/Let Me Be the First to Know	1956	10.00	20.00	40.00
KELLER					
❑ 101	Party Line/Strange As It Seems	1961	10.00	20.00	40.00

LOVETONES, THE

Number	Title (A Side/B Side)	Yr	VG	VG+	NM
LOVE-TONE					
❑ 101	You Can Tell Me That This Is Christmas/When I Asked My Love	1961	5.00	10.00	20.00
PLUS					
❑ 108	Talk to an Angel/Take It Easy, Baby	1956	125.00	250.00	500.00

LOVIN' SPOONFUL, THE

Also see JOHN SEBASTIAN; ZALMAN YANOVSKY.

Number	Title (A Side/B Side)	Yr	VG	VG+	NM
KAMA SUTRA					
❑ 201	Do You Believe in Magic/On the Road Again	1965	3.75	7.50	15.00
—Originals have a mostly red-orange label					
❑ 201	Do You Believe in Magic/On the Road Again	1965	2.50	5.00	10.00
—Second pressings have a mostly yellow label with "Kama Sutra" in red					
❑ 201	Do You Believe in Magic/On the Road Again	1965	2.00	4.00	8.00
—Third pressings have a mostly yellow label with "Kama Sutra" in black					
❑ 205	You Didn't Have to Be So Nice/My Gal	1965	3.00	6.00	12.00
—Originals have a mostly red-orange label					
❑ 205	You Didn't Have to Be So Nice/My Gal	1965	2.50	5.00	10.00
—Second pressings have a mostly yellow label with "Kama Sutra" in red					
❑ 205	You Didn't Have to Be So Nice/My Gal	1965	2.00	4.00	8.00
—Third pressings have a mostly yellow label with "Kama Sutra" in black					
❑ 205 [PS]	You Didn't Have to Be So Nice/My Gal	1965	3.75	7.50	15.00
❑ 208	Daydream/Night Owl Blues	1966	3.00	6.00	12.00
—Originals have a mostly yellow label with "Kama Sutra" in red					
❑ 208	Daydream/Night Owl Blues	1966	2.50	5.00	10.00
—Second pressings have a mostly yellow label with "Kama Sutra" in black					
❑ 208 [PS]	Daydream/Night Owl Blues	1966	3.75	7.50	15.00
❑ 209	Did You Ever Have to Make Up Your Mind/Didn't Want to Have to Do It	1966	2.50	5.00	10.00
❑ 209 [PS]	Did You Ever Have to Make Up Your Mind/Didn't Want to Have to Do It	1966	3.75	7.50	15.00
❑ 211	Summer in the City/Butchie's Tune	1966	2.50	5.00	10.00
❑ 211 [PS]	Summer in the City/Butchie's Tune	1966	3.75	7.50	15.00
❑ 216	Rain on the Roof/Pow	1966	2.50	5.00	10.00
❑ 216 [PS]	Rain on the Roof/Pow	1966	3.75	7.50	15.00
❑ 219	Nashville Cats/Full Measure	1966	2.50	5.00	10.00
❑ 219 [PS]	Nashville Cats/Full Measure	1966	3.75	7.50	15.00
❑ 220	Darling Be Home Soon/Darlin' Companion	1967	2.50	5.00	10.00
❑ 220 [PS]	Darling Be Home Soon/Darlin' Companion	1967	3.75	7.50	15.00
❑ 225	Six O'Clock/The Finale	1967	2.50	5.00	10.00
❑ 225 [PS]	Six O'Clock/The Finale	1967	3.75	7.50	15.00
❑ 231	Lonely (Amy's Theme)/You're a Big Boy Now	1967	3.75	7.50	15.00
❑ 239	She Is Still a Mystery/Only Pretty, What a Pity	1967	2.50	5.00	10.00
❑ 239 [PS]	She Is Still a Mystery/Only Pretty, What a Pity	1967	3.75	7.50	15.00
❑ 241	Money/Close Your Eyes	1967	2.00	4.00	8.00
❑ 250	Never Going Back/Forever	1968	2.00	4.00	8.00
❑ 251	Revelation Revolution '69/Run with You	1968	2.00	4.00	8.00
❑ 255	Me About You/Amazing Air	1968	2.00	4.00	8.00
❑ 551	Summer in the City/You and Me and Rain on the Roof	1972	—	3.00	6.00
❑ 608 [DJ]	Daydream (mono/stereo)	1976	—	3.00	6.00
—Stock copy not known to exist					

LOWE, JIM

Number	Title (A Side/B Side)	Yr	VG	VG+	NM
20TH CENTURY FOX					
❑ 426	Hootenanny Granny/These Bones Gonna Rise Again	1963	2.00	4.00	8.00
BUDDAH					
❑ 44	Michael J. Polalrd for President/The Ol' Racetrack	1968	—	3.00	6.00
DECCA					
❑ 31153	Someone Else's Arms/Man of the Cloth	1960	2.50	5.00	10.00
❑ 31198	That Do Make It Nice/Two Sides to Every Story	1961	2.50	5.00	10.00
DOT					
❑ 15381	Close the Door/Nuevo Laredo	1955	3.00	6.00	12.00
❑ 15407	Maybellene/Rene La Rue	1955	3.00	6.00	12.00
❑ 15429	John Jacob Jingleheimer Smith/St. James Avenue	1955	3.00	6.00	12.00
❑ 15456	The Sixty-Four Thousand Dollar Question/Blue Suede Shoes	1956	3.00	6.00	12.00
❑ 15486	The Green Door/(The Story of) The Little Man in Chinatown	1956	3.75	7.50	15.00
—Originals have maroon labels					
❑ 15486	The Green Door/(The Story of) The Little Man in Chinatown	1956	3.00	6.00	12.00
—Second pressings have black labels					
❑ 15525	By You, By You, By You/I Feel the Beat	1957	2.50	5.00	10.00
❑ 15569	Four Walls/Talkin' to the Blues	1957	3.00	6.00	12.00
❑ 15611	From a Jack to a King/Slow Train	1957	2.50	5.00	10.00
❑ 15665	Rick-a-Chickie/The Bright Light	1957	2.50	5.00	10.00
❑ 15693	Kewpie Doll/The Lady from Johannesburg	1958	2.50	5.00	10.00
❑ 15753	Take Us To Your President/Later On Tonight	1958	2.50	5.00	10.00
❑ 15832	Chapel Bells on Chapel Hill/Ja, Ja, Ja	1958	2.50	5.00	10.00
❑ 15869	Play Number Eleven/Come Away from Her Arms	1958	2.50	5.00	10.00
❑ 15954	I'm Movin' On/Without You	1959	2.50	5.00	10.00
❑ 16046	He'll Have to Go/Dress Rehearsal	1960	2.50	5.00	10.00
❑ 16074	The Midnight Ride of Paul Revere/A Tomorrow That Never Comes	1960	2.50	5.00	10.00
❑ 16636	Addis Ababa/Have You Ever Been Lonely	1964	—	3.00	6.00
MERCURY					
❑ 70163	Gambler's Guitar/The Martins and the Coys	1953	5.00	10.00	20.00
❑ 70265	Santa Claus Rides a Strawberry Roan/Love in Both Directions	1953	5.00	10.00	20.00
❑ 70319	Goodbye Little Sweetheart/River Boat	1954	5.00	10.00	20.00
❑ 71016	Prince of Peace/Santa Claus Rides a Strawberry Roan	1956	3.75	7.50	15.00
UNITED ARTISTS					
❑ 874	Mr. Moses/Make Your Back Strong	1965	—	3.00	6.00
❑ 50124	Gambler's Guitar/Blotson Bottom	1967	—	3.00	6.00

LOWE, NICK

Also see BRINSLEY SCHWARZ; DAVE EDMUNDS; KIPPINGTON LODGE; ROCKPILE.

Number	Title (A Side/B Side)	Yr	VG	VG+	NM
COLUMBIA					
❑ 02813	Stick It Where the Sun Don't Shine/My Heart Hurts	1982	—	—	3.00
❑ 03837	Wish You Were Here/How Do You Talk to An Angel	1983	—	—	3.00
❑ 03837 [DJ]	Cool Reaction (same on both sides)	1983	—	—	3.00
❑ 04486	Half a Boy and Half a Man/Awesome	1984	—	—	3.00
❑ 05570	I Knew the Bride (When She Used to Rock and Roll)/Long Walk Back	1985	—	—	3.00
—Label credit: Nick Lowe And His Cowboy Outfit					
❑ 07734	Lovers Jamboree/Crying in My Sleep	1988	—	—	3.00
❑ 10734	So It Goes/Heart of the City (Live)	1978	—	2.50	5.00
❑ 10844	(I Love the Sound of) Breaking Glass/Endless Sleep	1978	—	2.50	5.00
❑ 11018	Cruel to Be Kind/Endless Grey Ribbon	1979	—	2.50	5.00
❑ 11131	Switch Board Susan/Basin Street	1979	—	2.50	5.00
❑ 33398	Cruel to Be Kind/So It Goes	198?	—	—	3.00
—"Hall of Fame" reissue					

LOWE, VIRGINIA

Number	Title (A Side/B Side)	Yr	VG	VG+	NM
MELBA					
❑ 107	I'm in Love with Elvis Presley/Empty Feeling	1956	12.50	25.00	50.00

LUKE, ROBIN

Number	Title (A Side/B Side)	Yr	VG	VG+	NM
BERTRAM INTERNATIONAL					
❑ 206	Susie Darlin'/Living's Loving You	1958	15.00	30.00	60.00
❑ 206 [PS]	Susie Darlin'/Living's Loving You	1958	25.00	50.00	100.00
❑ 208	My Girl/Chicka Chicka Honey	1958	7.50	15.00	30.00
❑ 210	Strollin' Blues/You Can't Stop Me from Dreaming	1959	7.50	15.00	30.00
❑ 212	Five Minutes More/Who's Gonna Hold Your Hand	1959	7.50	15.00	30.00
DOT					
❑ 15781	Susie Darlin'/Living's Loving You	1958	6.25	12.50	25.00
❑ 15839	My Girl/Chicka Chicka Honey	1958	5.00	10.00	20.00
❑ 15899	Strollin' Blues/You Can't Stop Me from Dreaming	1959	5.00	10.00	20.00
❑ 15959	Five Minutes More/Who's Gonna Hold Your Hand	1959	5.00	10.00	20.00
❑ 16001	Make Me a Dreamer/Walkin' in the Moonlight	1959	5.00	10.00	20.00
❑ 16040	Bad Boy/School Bus Love Affair	1960	5.00	10.00	20.00
❑ 16096	Everlovin'/Well Oh Well Oh	1960	5.00	10.00	20.00
❑ 16096 [PS]	Everlovin'/Well Oh Well Oh	1960	15.00	30.00	60.00
❑ 16170	So Alone/All Because of You	1960	5.00	10.00	20.00
❑ 16229	Part of a Fool/Poor Little Rich Boy	1961	3.75	7.50	15.00
❑ 16366	Foggin' Up the Windows/Time	1962	3.75	7.50	15.00
—With Roberta Shore					
INTERNATIONAL					
❑ 206	Susie Darlin'/Living's Loving You	1958	250.00	500.00	1000.
—Light blue label					

7-Inch Extended Plays

Number	Title (A Side/B Side)	Yr	VG	VG+	NM
DOT					
❑ DEP-1092	(contents unknown)	1958	100.00	200.00	400.00
❑ DEP-1092 [PS]	Susie Darlin'	1958	100.00	200.00	400.00

LUKE THE DRIFTER

See HANK WILLIAMS.

LUKE THE DRIFTER, JR.

See HANK WILLIAMS, JR.

LULU

Number	Title (A Side/B Side)	Yr	VG	VG+	NM
ALFA					
❑ 7006	I Could Never Miss You (More Than I Do)/Dance to the Feeling	1981	—	2.00	4.00
❑ 7006 [PS]	I Could Never Miss You (More Than I Do)/Dance to the Feeling	1981	—	2.50	5.00
—With Lulu wearing a spotted headband					
❑ 7006 [PS]	I Could Never Miss You (More Than I Do)/Dance to the Feeling	1981	—	3.00	6.00
—With Lulu not wearing a headband (original)					
❑ 7011	If I Were You/You Win, I Lose	1981	—	2.00	4.00
❑ 7011 [PS]	If I Were You/You Win, I Lose	1981	—	2.50	5.00
❑ 7021	Who's Foolin' Who/You Win, I Lose	1982	—	2.00	4.00
ATCO					
❑ 6722	Oh Me Oh My (I'm a Fool for You Baby)/Sweep Around Your Own Back Door	1969	2.00	4.00	8.00
❑ 6749	Hum a Song (From Your Heart)/Where's Eddie	1970	—	3.00	6.00
❑ 6761	Good Day Sunshine/After the Feeling Is Gone	1970	—	3.00	6.00
❑ 6774	Melody Fair/To the Other Woman	1970	—	3.00	6.00

Number	Title (A Side/B Side)	Yr	VG	VG+	NM
❑ 6819	Goodbye My Love, Goodbye/Everybody's Got to Clap	1971	—	3.00	6.00
❑ 6885	It Takes a Real Man/You Ain't Wrong, You Just Ain't Right	1972	—	3.00	6.00

CHELSEA

Number	Title (A Side/B Side)	Yr	VG	VG+	NM
❑ 78-0121	Make Believe World/Help Me Help You	1973	2.00	4.00	8.00
❑ 3001	The Man Who Sold the World/Watch That Man	1974	7.50	15.00	30.00
—A David Bowie song on the A-side...and produced by Bowie, too					
❑ 3009	The Man with a Golden Gun/Baby I Don't Care	1974	5.00	10.00	20.00
❑ 3011	Take Your Mama for a Ride (Long)/Take Your Mama for a Ride (Short)	1975	2.50	5.00	10.00
❑ 3019	Boy Meets Girl/(B-side unknown)	1975	2.50	5.00	10.00
❑ 3038	Heaven and Earth and the Stars/(B-side unknown)	1976	5.00	10.00	20.00

EPIC

Number	Title (A Side/B Side)	Yr	VG	VG+	NM
❑ 10187	To Sir with Love/The Boat That I Row	1967	2.50	5.00	10.00
❑ 10210	Dreamy Nights and Days/Let's Pretend	1967	2.00	4.00	8.00
❑ 10260/65 [DJ]	Best of Both Worlds/Everybody Knows	1968	6.25	12.50	25.00
—B-side by the Dave Clark Five; odd promo					
❑ 10260	Best of Both Worlds/Love Loves to Love Love	1967	2.00	4.00	8.00
❑ 10260 [PS]	Best of Both Worlds/Love Loves to Love Love	1967	5.00	10.00	20.00
❑ 10302	Me, the Peaceful Heart/Look Out	1968	2.00	4.00	8.00
❑ 10302 [PS]	Me, the Peaceful Heart/Look Out	1968	5.00	10.00	20.00
❑ 10346	Sad Memories/Boy	1968	2.00	4.00	8.00
❑ 10367	Morning Dew/You and I	1968	2.00	4.00	8.00
❑ 10403	Without Him/This Time	1968	2.00	4.00	8.00
❑ 10420	Rattler/I'm a Tiger	1968	2.00	4.00	8.00

PARROT

Number	Title (A Side/B Side)	Yr	VG	VG+	NM
❑ 9678	Shout/Forget Me Baby	1964	5.00	10.00	20.00
❑ 9714	Here Comes the Night/I'll Come Running	1964	5.00	10.00	20.00
❑ 9778	Leave a Little Love/He Don't Want Your Love Anymore	1965	5.00	10.00	20.00
❑ 9791	Try to Understand/Not in This Whole World	1965	5.00	10.00	20.00
❑ 40021	Shout/When He Touches Me	1967	2.50	5.00	10.00

ROCKET

Number	Title (A Side/B Side)	Yr	VG	VG+	NM
❑ YB-11355	Don't Take Love for Granted/Love Is the Sweetest Mistake	1978	—	2.50	5.00

7-Inch Extended Plays

EPIC

Number	Title (A Side/B Side)	Yr	VG	VG+	NM
❑ 5-26339 [DJ]	To Sir With Love/Morning Dew/Love Loves to Love Love//Best of Both Worlds/Day Tripper/Take Me in Your Arms (And Love Me)	1967	3.75	7.50	15.00
—Jukebox mini-LP, small hole, plays at 33 1/3 rpm					
❑ 5-26339 [PS]	To Sir With Love	1967	3.75	7.50	15.00

LUMAN, BOB

CAPITOL

Number	Title (A Side/B Side)	Yr	VG	VG+	NM
❑ F3972	Try Me/I Know My Baby Cares	1958	7.50	15.00	30.00
❑ F4059	Precious/Svengali	1958	7.50	15.00	30.00

EPIC

Number	Title (A Side/B Side)	Yr	VG	VG+	NM
❑ 10312	Ain't Got Time to Be Unhappy/I Can't Remember to Forget	1968	—	3.00	6.00
❑ 10381	I Like Trains/A World of Unhappiness	1968	—	3.00	6.00
❑ 10416	I'm In This Town for Good/A Woman Without Love	1968	—	3.00	6.00
❑ 10439	Come On Home and Sing the Blues to Daddy/Big, Big World	1969	—	3.00	6.00
❑ 10480	Every Day I Have to Cry Some/Livin' in a House Full of Love	1969	—	3.00	6.00
❑ 10535	The Gun/Cleanin' Up the Streets of Memphis	1969	—	3.00	6.00
❑ 10581	Gettin' Back to Norma/Maybelline	1970	—	3.00	6.00
❑ 10631	Honky Tonk Man/I Ain't Built That Way	1970	—	3.00	6.00
❑ 10667	What About the Hurt/The Time to Remember	1970	—	3.00	6.00
❑ 10699	Is It Any Wonder That I Love You?/Give Us One More Chance	1971	—	2.50	5.00
❑ 10755	I Got a Woman/One Hundred Songs on the Jukebox	1971	—	2.50	5.00
❑ 10786	A Chain Don't Take to Me/Don't Let Love Pass You By	1971	—	2.50	5.00
❑ 10823	When You Say Love/Have a Little Faith	1972	—	2.50	5.00
❑ 10869	It Takes You/Let's Think About Livin'	1972	—	2.50	5.00
❑ 10905	Lonely Women Make Good Lovers/Love Ought to Be a Happy Thing	1972	—	2.50	5.00
❑ 10943	Neither One of Us/Anything But Lonesome	1973	—	2.00	4.00
❑ 10994	A Good Love Is Like a Good Song/Have I Ever Said "I Love You" to a Lady	1973	—	2.00	4.00
❑ 11039	Still Loving You/I'm Gonna Write a Song	1973	—	2.00	4.00
❑ 11087	Just Enough to Make Me Stay/Baby Make It Good	1974	—	2.00	4.00
❑ 11138	Let Me Make the Bright Lights Shine for You/The Closest Thing to Heaven That I Love	1974	—	2.00	4.00
❑ 50065	Proud of You Baby/Tonight Your Baby's Coming Home	1975	—	2.00	4.00
❑ 50136	Shame on Me/How Do You Start Over	1975	—	2.00	4.00
❑ 50183	A Satisfied Mind/Cleanin' Up the Streets of Memphis	1975	—	2.00	4.00
❑ 50216	The Man from Bowling Green/It's Only Make Believe	1976	—	2.00	4.00
❑ 50247	How Do You Start Over/Red Cadillac and Black Mustache	1976	—	2.00	4.00
❑ 50297	Labor of Love/Blond Haired Woman	1976	—	2.00	4.00
❑ 50323	He's Got a Way with Women/Here We Are Making Love Again	1976	—	2.00	4.00

HICKORY

Number	Title (A Side/B Side)	Yr	VG	VG+	NM
❑ 1201	You're Welcome/Interstate 40	1963	3.00	6.00	12.00
❑ 1219	Can't Take the Country from the Boy/I'm Gonna Write a Song of Love	1963	3.00	6.00	12.00
❑ 1221	Too Hot to Dance/I Like Your Kind of Love	1963	3.00	6.00	12.00
—With Sue Thompson					
❑ 1238	The File/Bigger Men Than I (Have Cried)	1964	3.00	6.00	12.00
❑ 1266	Lonely Room (Empty Walls)/Run On Home Baby Brother	1964	3.00	6.00	12.00
❑ 1277	Fire Engine Red/Old George Dickel	1964	3.00	6.00	12.00
❑ 1289	Bad, Bad Day/Tears from Out of Nowhere	1965	2.50	5.00	10.00
❑ 1307	Jealous Heart/Go On Home Boy	1965	2.50	5.00	10.00
❑ 1333	I Love You Because/Love Worked a Miracle	1965	2.50	5.00	10.00
❑ 1355	Five Miles from Home (Soon I'll See Mary)/(I Get So) Sentimental	1965	2.50	5.00	10.00
❑ 1382	Poor Boy Blues/(Can't Get You) Off My Mind	1966	2.50	5.00	10.00
❑ 1410	Come On and Sing/It's a Sin	1966	2.50	5.00	10.00
❑ 1430	Hardly Anymore/Freedom of Living	1967	2.00	4.00	8.00
❑ 1460	If You Don't Love Me (Then Why Don't You Leave Me Alone)/Throwin' Kisses	1967	2.00	4.00	8.00
❑ 1481	Running Scared/The Best Years of My Wife	1967	2.00	4.00	8.00
❑ 1536	It's All Over (But the Shouting)/Still Loving You	1969	—	3.00	6.00
❑ 1564	Still Loving You/Meet Mr. Mud	1970	—	3.00	6.00

IMPERIAL

Number	Title (A Side/B Side)	Yr	VG	VG+	NM
❑ 5705	A Red Cadillac and a Black Moustache/All Night Long	1960	6.25	12.50	25.00
❑ 8311	A Red Cadillac and a Black Moustache/All Night Long	1957	20.00	40.00	80.00
❑ 8313	Red Hot/Whenever You're Ready	1957	20.00	40.00	80.00
❑ 8315	Make Up Your Mind, Baby/Your Love	1958	15.00	30.00	60.00
—The same coupling was slated for Imperial 8314 but not released.					

POLYDOR

Number	Title (A Side/B Side)	Yr	VG	VG+	NM
❑ 14408	I'm a Honky-Tonk Woman's Man/Lonely Women Make Good Lovers	1977	—	2.00	4.00
❑ 14431	The Pay Phone/He'll Be the One	1977	—	2.00	4.00
❑ 14444	A Christmas Tribute/Give Someone You Love (A Little Bit of Love This Year)	1977	—	2.00	4.00
❑ 14454	Proud Lady/Let Me Love Him Out of You	1978	—	2.00	4.00

ROLLIN' ROCK

Number	Title (A Side/B Side)	Yr	VG	VG+	NM
❑ 028	Stranger Than Fiction/You're the Cause of It All	1978	—	2.00	4.00

WARNER BROS.

Number	Title (A Side/B Side)	Yr	VG	VG+	NM
❑ 5081	My Baby Walks All Over Me/Class of '59	1959	6.25	12.50	25.00
❑ 5105	Dreamy Doll/Buttercup	1959	6.25	12.50	25.00
❑ 5172	Let's Think About Living/You've Got Everything	1960	5.00	10.00	20.00
❑ 5172 [PS]	Let's Think About Living/You've Got Everything	1960	10.00	20.00	40.00
❑ 5184	Why, Why, Bye, Bye/Oh Lonesome Me	1960	5.00	10.00	20.00
❑ 5184 [PS]	Why, Why, Bye, Bye/Oh Lonesome Me	1960	10.00	20.00	40.00
❑ 5204	The Great Snow Man/The Pig Latin Song	1961	5.00	10.00	20.00
❑ 5204 [PS]	The Great Snow Man/The Pig Latin Song	1961	10.00	20.00	40.00
❑ 5233	Private Eyes/You've Turned Down the Lights	1961	5.00	10.00	20.00
❑ 5233 [PS]	Private Eyes/You've Turned Down the Lights	1961	10.00	20.00	40.00
❑ 5255	Louisiana Man/Rocks of Reno	1962	5.00	10.00	20.00
❑ 5272	Big River Rose/Belonging to You	1962	5.00	10.00	20.00
❑ 5299	Hey Joe/The Fool	1962	5.00	10.00	20.00
❑ 5321	You're Everything/Envy	1962	5.00	10.00	20.00
❑ 5506	Boston Rocker/Old Friends//Bad Bad Day/Let's Think About Living	1960	25.00	50.00	100.00
—Part of Warner Bros. "+2" series, with two new songs and excerpts of two prior hits					
❑ 5506 [PS]	Boston Rocker/Old Friends//Bad Bad Day/Let's Think About Living	1960	25.00	50.00	100.00

LUMPKIN, HENRY

MOTOWN

Number	Title (A Side/B Side)	Yr	VG	VG+	NM
❑ 1005	I've Got a Notion/We Really Love Each Other	1961	20.00	40.00	80.00
❑ 1013	What Is a Man/Don't Leave Me	1961	10.00	20.00	40.00
❑ 1029	Mo Jo Hanna/Break Down and Sing	1962	10.00	20.00	40.00

LUREX, LARRY

See FREDDIE MERCURY.

LY-DELLS, THE

MASTER

Number	Title (A Side/B Side)	Yr	VG	VG+	NM
❑ 111	Genie of the Lamp/Teenage Tears	1961	62.50	125.00	250.00
❑ 251	Wizard of Love/Let This Night Last	1961	15.00	30.00	60.00

PAM

Number	Title (A Side/B Side)	Yr	VG	VG+	NM
❑ 103	There Goes the Boy/Talking to Myself	1959	50.00	100.00	200.00

PARKWAY

Number	Title (A Side/B Side)	Yr	VG	VG+	NM
❑ 897	There Goes the Boy/Talking to Myself	1964	5.00	10.00	20.00

ROULETTE

Number	Title (A Side/B Side)	Yr	VG	VG+	NM
❑ 4493	Karen/Doing the Wiggle Wobble	1963	6.25	12.50	25.00

SCA

Number	Title (A Side/B Side)	Yr	VG	VG+	NM
❑ 18001	Book of Songs/Hear That Train	1962	10.00	20.00	40.00

SOUTHERN SOUND

Number	Title (A Side/B Side)	Yr	VG	VG+	NM
❑ 122	Three Little Monkeys/Playing Hide and Seek	1965	15.00	30.00	60.00

LYMAN, JONI

REPRISE

Number	Title (A Side/B Side)	Yr	VG	VG+	NM
❑ 0378	Happy Birthday Blue/I Just Don't Know What to Do with Myself	1965	10.00	20.00	40.00

LYMON, FRANKIE

Also see FRANKIE LYMON AND THE TEENAGERS.

BIG KAT

Number	Title (A Side/B Side)	Yr	VG	VG+	NM
❑ 7008	I Want You to Be My Girl/Portable on My Shoulder	1968	2.50	5.00	10.00
❑ 7008 [PS]	I Want You to Be My Girl/Portable on My Shoulder	1968	3.00	6.00	12.00

COLUMBIA

Number	Title (A Side/B Side)	Yr	VG	VG+	NM
❑ 43094	Somewhere/Sweet and Lovely	1964	12.50	25.00	50.00

GEE

Number	Title (A Side/B Side)	Yr	VG	VG+	NM
❑ 1039	Goody Goody/Creation of Love	1957	6.25	12.50	25.00
❑ 1052	I'm Not Too Young to Dream/Goody Good Girl	1959	6.25	12.50	25.00

ROULETTE

Number	Title (A Side/B Side)	Yr	VG	VG+	NM
❑ 4026	So Goes My Love/My Girl	1957	6.25	12.50	25.00
❑ 4035	It's Christmas Once Again/Little Girl	1957	6.25	12.50	25.00
❑ 4044	Footsteps/Thumb Thumb	1958	5.00	10.00	20.00
❑ 4068	Mama Don't Allow It/Portable on My Shoulder	1958	5.00	10.00	20.00
❑ 4093	Melinda/The Only Way to Love	1958	5.00	10.00	20.00
❑ 4128	No Matter What You've Done/Up Jumped a Rabbit	1959	5.00	10.00	20.00
❑ 4150	Before I Fall Asleep/What a Little Moonlight Can Do	1959	5.00	10.00	20.00
❑ 4257	Little Bitty Pretty One/Creation of Love	1960	5.00	10.00	20.00
❑ 4283	Buzz, Buzz, Buzz/Waitin' in School	1960	5.00	10.00	20.00
❑ 4310	Jailhouse Rock/Silhouettes	1961	5.00	10.00	20.00

(Top left) In 1959, Neil Sedaka had a major hit with his "Oh! Carol," which was written about Carole King. Well, the subject answered with "Oh, Neil." Carole's record was not a hit, and today is highly sought after. (Top right) "Rockin' Around the Christmas Tree," which today is a holiday staple, was pretty much ignored when Brenda Lee's version first came out in 1958. Two years later, after Lee had had two No. 1 singles, the two-year-old stiff was rediscovered and became a big hit. (Bottom left) "Great Balls of Fire," Jerry Lee Lewis' biggest pop hit, was issued with this tough picture sleeve. (Bottom right) Among the most sought-after country singles are Loretta Lynn's early issues on the Zero label. "I'm a Honky Tonk Girl" even charted nationally, but that hasn't stopped this record from soaring well into the hundreds for top-condition examples.

Number	Title (A Side/B Side)	Yr	VG	VG+	NM
❑ 4348	Change Partners/So Young	1961	5.00	10.00	20.00
❑ 4391	I Put the Bomp/So Young	1962	5.00	10.00	20.00

TCF

Number	Title (A Side/B Side)	Yr	VG	VG+	NM
❑ 11	Teacher Teacher/To Each His Own	1964	3.75	7.50	15.00

7-Inch Extended Plays

ROULETTE

Number	Title (A Side/B Side)	Yr	VG	VG+	NM
❑ EPR-1-304	Let's Fall in Love/My Baby Just Cares for Me//Goody Goody/Somebody Loves Me	1958	50.00	100.00	200.00
❑ EPR-1-304 [PS]	Frankie Lymon at the London Palladium	1958	50.00	100.00	200.00

LYMON, FRANKIE, AND THE TEENAGERS

Also see FRANKIE LYMON.

GEE

Number	Title (A Side/B Side)	Yr	VG	VG+	NM
❑ 1002	Why Do Fools Fall in Love/Please Be Mine	1956	20.00	40.00	80.00
—Red and gold label					
❑ 1002	Why Do Fools Fall in Love/Please Be Mine	1956	12.50	25.00	50.00
—Red and black label; vocal duet on B-side					
❑ 1002	Why Do Fools Fall in Love/Please Be Mine	1956	7.50	15.00	30.00
—Red and black label; vocal solo on B-side. All of the above credit "The Teenagers featuring Frankie Lymon"					
❑ 1002	Why Do Fools Fall in Love/My Girl	1958	6.25	12.50	25.00
—White label, "Gee Records" at top; note different B-side					
❑ 1012	I Want You to Be My Girl/I'm Not a Know-It-All	1956	12.50	25.00	50.00
—As "The Teenagers featuring Frankie Lymon"					
❑ 1012	I Want You to Be My Girl/I'm Not a Know-It-All	1956	7.50	15.00	30.00
—As "Frankie Lymon and the Teenagers"					
❑ 1018	I Promise to Remember/Who Can Explain	1956	7.50	15.00	30.00
❑ 1022	The ABC's of Love/Share	1956	7.50	15.00	30.00
❑ 1026	I'm Not a Juvenile Delinquent/Baby Baby	1957	7.50	15.00	30.00
❑ 1032	Teenage Love/Paper Castles	1957	7.50	15.00	30.00
❑ 1035	Am I Fooling Myself Again/Love Is a Clown	197?	—	—	—
—Evidently a 1970s bootleg to fill in a gap in the Gee Records discography					
❑ 1036	Miracle of Love/Out in the Cold Again	1957	7.50	15.00	30.00
❑ 1039	Goody Goody/Creation of Love	1957	10.00	20.00	40.00
—Actually a Frankie Lymon solo recording; the first pressing credited the entire group					

7-Inch Extended Plays

GEE

Number	Title (A Side/B Side)	Yr	VG	VG+	NM
❑ GEP-601	Teenage Love/Why Do Fools Fall in Love//I Want You to Be My Girl/Love Is a Clown	1956	37.50	75.00	150.00
❑ GEP-601 [PS]	The Teenagers Go Rock'n	1956	50.00	100.00	200.00
❑ GEP-602	Paper Castles/Share//Am I Fooling Myself Again/I'm Not a Know-It-All	1957	50.00	100.00	200.00
❑ GEP-602 [PS]	The Teenagers Go Romantic	1957	50.00	100.00	200.00

LYMON, LEWIS, AND THE TEENCHORDS

END

Number	Title (A Side/B Side)	Yr	VG	VG+	NM
❑ 1003	Too Young/Your Last Chance	1957	25.00	50.00	100.00
❑ 1007	I Found Out Why/Tell Me Love	1958	20.00	40.00	80.00
❑ 1113	Too Young/Your Last Chance	1962	5.00	10.00	20.00

FURY

Number	Title (A Side/B Side)	Yr	VG	VG+	NM
❑ 1000	I'm So Happy (Tra-La-La-La-La-La)/Lydia	1957	50.00	100.00	200.00
—Maroon label					
❑ 1000	I'm So Happy (Tra-La-La-La-La-La)/Lydia	1958	10.00	20.00	40.00
—Yellow label					
❑ 1003	Honey, Honey (You Don't Know)/Please Tell the Angels	1957	20.00	40.00	80.00
❑ 1006	I'm Not Too Young to Fall in Love/Falling in Love	1957	20.00	40.00	80.00

JUANITA

Number	Title (A Side/B Side)	Yr	VG	VG+	NM
❑ 101	Dance Girl/Them There Eyes	1958	12.50	25.00	50.00

LYNCH, KENNY

ARLEN

Number	Title (A Side/B Side)	Yr	VG	VG+	NM
❑ 750	Make It Easy on Yourself/Monument	1964	3.00	6.00	12.00

BIG TOP

Number	Title (A Side/B Side)	Yr	VG	VG+	NM
❑ 3140	Poof (Up in Smoke)/Happy That's Me	1963	3.00	6.00	12.00

IMPERIAL

Number	Title (A Side/B Side)	Yr	VG	VG+	NM
❑ 66088	So Much to Love You For/My Own Two Feet	1964	3.00	6.00	12.00

LIBERTY

Number	Title (A Side/B Side)	Yr	VG	VG+	NM
❑ 55740	That's What Girls Are Made For/What Am I to You	1964	3.00	6.00	12.00
❑ 55811	For Lovin' You Baby/I'll Stay By You	1965	2.50	5.00	10.00

WHITE WHALE

Number	Title (A Side/B Side)	Yr	VG	VG+	NM
❑ 307	Along Comes Love/Sweet Situation	1969	—	3.00	6.00

LYNN, BARBARA

ATLANTIC

Number	Title (A Side/B Side)	Yr	VG	VG+	NM
❑ 2450	This Is the Thanks I Get/Ring, Telephone, Ring	1967	2.00	4.00	8.00
❑ 2513	Why Can't You Love Me/You're Losing Me	1968	2.00	4.00	8.00
❑ 2553	Love Ain't Never Hurt Nobody/You're Gonna See a Lot More	1968	2.00	4.00	8.00
❑ 2585	People Like Me/He Ain't Gonna Do Right	1968	2.00	4.00	8.00
❑ 2812	(Until Then) I'll Suffer/Take Your Love and Run	1971	—	3.00	6.00
❑ 2853	Nice and Easy/I'm a One Woman Man	1972	—	3.00	6.00
❑ 2880	(Daddy Hotstuff) You're Too Hot to Hold/You Better Quit It	1972	—	3.00	6.00
❑ 2931	You Make Me So Hot/It Ain't No Good to Be Too Good	1973	—	3.00	6.00

JAMIE

Number	Title (A Side/B Side)	Yr	VG	VG+	NM
❑ 1220	You'll Lose a Good Thing/Lonely Heartache	1962	5.00	10.00	20.00
❑ 1233	Second Fiddle Girl/Letter to Mommy and Daddy	1962	3.00	6.00	12.00
❑ 1240	You're Gonna Need Me/I'm Sorry I Met You	1962	3.00	6.00	12.00
❑ 1244	Don't Be Cruel/You Can't Be Satisfied	1963	3.00	6.00	12.00
❑ 1251	To Love or Not to Love/Promises	1963	3.00	6.00	12.00
❑ 1260	(I Cried at) Laura's Wedding/You Better Stop	1963	3.00	6.00	12.00
❑ 1265	Everybody Loves Somebody/Dedicate the Blues to Me	1963	3.00	6.00	12.00
❑ 1269	Money/Jealous Love	1964	3.00	6.00	12.00
❑ 1277	Oh! Baby (We Got a Good Thing Goin')/Unfair	1964	3.00	6.00	12.00
❑ 1286	Don't Spread It Around/Let Her Knock Herself Out	1964	3.00	6.00	12.00
❑ 1292	It's Better to Have It/People Gonna Talk	1964	3.00	6.00	12.00
❑ 1295	(Don't Pretend) Just Lay It on the Line/Careless Hands	1965	2.00	4.00	8.00
—With Lee Maye					
❑ 1297	Keep On Pushing Your Luck/I've Taken All I'm Gonna Take	1965	2.00	4.00	8.00
❑ 1301	Can't Buy Me Love/That's What Friends Are For	1965	2.00	4.00	8.00
❑ 1304	All I Need Is Your Love/You're Gonna Be Sorry	1965	2.00	4.00	8.00

TRIBE

Number	Title (A Side/B Side)	Yr	VG	VG+	NM
❑ 8316	Running Back/I'm a Good Woman	1966	2.00	4.00	8.00
❑ 8319	You Left the Water Running/Until I'm Free	1966	2.00	4.00	8.00
❑ 8322	Watch the One That Brings Bad News/AUB A-Go-Go	1967	2.00	4.00	8.00
❑ 8324	I Don't Want a Playboy/New Kind of Love	1967	2.00	4.00	8.00

LYNN, DONNA

CAPITOL

Number	Title (A Side/B Side)	Yr	VG	VG+	NM
❑ 5087	Ronnie/That's Me, I'm the Brother	1963	3.75	7.50	15.00
❑ 5127	My Boyfriend Got a Beatle Haircut/That Winter Weekend	1964	5.00	10.00	20.00
❑ 5156	Java Jones/Things That I Feel	1964	3.75	7.50	15.00
❑ 5213	Silly Girl/There Goes the Boy I Love with Mary	1964	3.75	7.50	15.00
❑ 5378	I'd Much Rather Be with the Girls/I'm Sorry More Than You Know	1965	3.00	6.00	12.00
❑ 5456	True Blue/When Your Heart Rings, Answer	1965	3.00	6.00	12.00

PALMER

Number	Title (A Side/B Side)	Yr	VG	VG+	NM
❑ 5016	Don't You Dare/I Was Raining	1967	6.25	12.50	25.00

LYNN, LORETTA

DECCA

Number	Title (A Side/B Side)	Yr	VG	VG+	NM
❑ 31323	The Girl That I Am Now/I Walked Away from the Wreck	1961	3.75	7.50	15.00
❑ 31384	Success/Hundred Proof Heartache	1962	3.00	6.00	12.00
❑ 31435	World of Forgotten People/Get Set for a Heartache	1962	3.75	7.50	15.00
❑ 31471	The Other Woman/Who'll Help Me Get Over You	1963	2.50	5.00	10.00
❑ 31541	Before I'm Over You/Where Were You	1963	2.50	5.00	10.00
❑ 31608	Wine, Women and Song/This Haunted House	1964	2.50	5.00	10.00
❑ 31707	Happy Birthday/When Lonely Hits Your Heart	1964	2.50	5.00	10.00
❑ 31769	Blue Kentucky Girl/Two Steps Forward	1965	2.50	5.00	10.00
❑ 31836	The Home You're Tearin' Down/The Farther You Go	1965	2.50	5.00	10.00
❑ 31879	When I Hear My Children Play/Everybody Wants to Go to Heaven	1965	3.00	6.00	12.00
❑ 31893	Dear Uncle Sam/Hurtin' for Certain	1966	2.50	5.00	10.00
❑ 31966	You Ain't Woman Enough/God Gave Me a Heart to Forgive	1966	2.50	5.00	10.00
❑ 32043	It Won't Seem Like Christmas/To Heck with Santa Claus	1966	2.50	5.00	10.00
❑ 32043 [PS]	It Won't Seem Like Christmas/To Heck with Santa Claus	1966	3.75	7.50	15.00
❑ 32045	Don't Come Home a-Drinkin' (With Lovin' on Your Mind)/A Saint to a Sinner	1966	2.50	5.00	10.00
❑ 32127	If You're Not Gone Too Long/A Man I Hardly Know	1967	2.50	5.00	10.00
❑ 32184	What Kind of a Girl (Do You Think I Am?)/Bargain Basement Dress	1967	2.50	5.00	10.00
❑ 32264	Fist City/Slowly Killing Me	1968	2.00	4.00	8.00
❑ 32332	You've Just Stepped In (From Stepping Out on Me)/Taking the Place of My Man	1968	2.00	4.00	8.00
❑ 32392	Your Squaw Is On the Warpath/Let Me Go, You're Hurtin' Me	1968	2.00	4.00	8.00
❑ 32439	Woman of the World (Leave My World Alone)/Sneakin' In	1969	2.00	4.00	8.00
❑ 32513	To Make a Man (Feel Like a Man)/One Little Reason	1969	2.00	4.00	8.00
❑ 32586	Wings Upon Your Horns/Let's Get Back Down to Earth	1969	2.00	4.00	8.00
❑ 32637	I Know How/The End of My World	1970	2.00	4.00	8.00
❑ 32693	You Wanna Give Me a Lift/What's the Bottle Done Today Baby	1970	2.00	4.00	8.00
❑ 32749	Coal Miner's Daughter/Man of the House	1970	2.50	5.00	10.00
❑ 32749 [PS]	Coal Miner's Daughter/Man of the House	1970	3.00	6.00	12.00
❑ 32763	I Love You/That Ain't a Woman's Way	1970	2.00	4.00	8.00
❑ 32796	I Wanna Be Free/If I Never Love Again	1971	—	3.50	7.00
❑ 32851	You're Lookin' at Country/When You're Poor	1971	—	3.50	7.00
❑ 32900	Here in Topeka/Kinfolks Holler	1971	5.00	10.00	20.00
❑ 32900	One's On the Way/Kinfolks Holler	1971	—	3.50	7.00
—Retitled version of A-side					
❑ 32974	Here I Am Again/My Kind of Man	1972	—	3.50	7.00
❑ 33039	Rated "X"/'Til the Pain Outwears the Shame	1972	—	3.50	7.00

MCA

Number	Title (A Side/B Side)	Yr	VG	VG+	NM
❑ 40058	Love Is the Foundation/What Sundown Does to You	1973	—	2.50	5.00
❑ 40150	Hey Loretta/Turn Me Any Way But Loose	1973	—	2.50	5.00
❑ 40223	They Don't Make 'Em Like My Daddy/Nothin'	1974	—	2.50	5.00
❑ 40283	Trouble in Paradise/We've Already Tasted Love	1974	—	2.50	5.00
❑ 40358	The Pill/Will You Be There	1975	—	2.50	5.00
❑ 40438	Home/You Take Me to Heaven Every Night	1975	—	2.50	5.00
❑ 40484	When the Tingle Becomes a Chill/All I Want from You (Is Away)	1975	—	2.50	5.00
❑ 40541	Red, White and Blue/Sounds of a New Love (Being Born)	1976	—	2.50	5.00
❑ 40607	Somebody Somewhere (Don't Know What He's Missin' Tonight)/Sundown Tavern	1976	—	2.50	5.00
❑ 40679	She's Got You/The Lady That Lived Here Before	1977	—	2.50	5.00
❑ 40747	Why Can't He Be You/I Keep On Putting On	1977	—	2.50	5.00
❑ 40832	Out of My Head and Back in My Bed/Old Rooster	1977	—	2.50	5.00
❑ 40910	Spring Fever/God Bless the Children	1978	—	2.00	4.00
❑ 40954	We've Come a Long Way, Baby/I Can't Feel You Anymore	1978	—	2.00	4.00
❑ 40954 [PS]	We've Come a Long Way, Baby/I Can't Feel You Anymore	1978	—	3.00	6.00
❑ 41021	I Can't Feel You Anymore/True Love Needs to Keep in Touch	1979	—	2.00	4.00

Number	Title (A Side/B Side)	Yr	VG	VG+	NM
❑ 41129	I've Got a Picture of Us on My Mind/I Don't Feel Like a Movie Tonight	1979	—	2.00	4.00
❑ 41185	Pregnant Again/You're a Cross I Can't Bear	1980	—	2.00	4.00
❑ 41250	Naked in the Rain/I Should Be Over You by Now	1980	—	2.00	4.00
❑ 51015	Cheatin' On a Cheater/Until I Met You	1980	—	2.00	4.00
❑ 51058	Somebody Led Me Away/Everybody's Lookin' for Somebody New	1981	—	2.00	4.00
❑ 51226	I Lie/If I Ain't Got It	1982	—	2.50	5.00
❑ 52005	I Lie/If I Ain't Got It	1982	—	2.00	4.00
❑ 52092	Making Love from Memory/Don't It Feel Good	1982	—	2.00	4.00
❑ 52158	Breakin' It/There's All Kinds of Smoke (In the Barroom)	1983	—	2.00	4.00
❑ 52219	Lyin', Cheatin', Woman Chasin', Honky Tonkin', Whiskey Drinkin' You/Star Light, Star Bright	1983	—	2.00	4.00
❑ 52289	Walking with My Memories/It's Gone	1983	—	2.00	4.00
❑ 52621	Heart Don't Do This to Me/Adam's Rib	1985	—	—	3.00
❑ 52706	Wouldn't It Be Great/One Man Band	1985	—	—	3.00
❑ 52766	Just a Woman/Take Me in Your Arms (And Hold Me)	1986	—	—	3.00
❑ 53320	Who Was That Stranger/Elsie Banks	1988	—	—	3.00
❑ 53397	Fly Away/Your Used to Be	1988	—	—	3.00
❑ 65034	Shadrack, the Black Reindeer/Let's Put Christ Back in Christmas	1974	—	2.00	4.00

—Black label with rainbow

Number	Title (A Side/B Side)	Yr	VG	VG+	NM
❑ 65034	Shadrack, the Black Reindeer/Let's Put Christ Back in Christmas	1980	—	—	3.00

—Blue label with rainbow

ZERO

Number	Title (A Side/B Side)	Yr	VG	VG+	NM
❑ 107	I'm a Honky Tonk Girl/Whispering Sea	1960	125.00	250.00	500.00
❑ 110	New Rainbow/Heartaches Meet Mr. Blues	1960	100.00	200.00	400.00
❑ 112	The Darkest Day/Gonna Pack My Troubles	1961	100.00	200.00	400.00

7-Inch Extended Plays

DECCA

Number	Title (A Side/B Side)	Yr	VG	VG+	NM
❑ ED 2762	The Other Woman/Where Were You//Success/Before I'm Over You	1964	5.00	10.00	20.00
❑ ED 2762 [PS]	The Other Woman	1964	5.00	10.00	20.00
❑ ED 2784	(contents unknown)	1965	5.00	10.00	20.00
❑ ED 2784 [PS]	Wine, Women and Song	1965	5.00	10.00	20.00
❑ ED 2793	(contents unknown)	1965	5.00	10.00	20.00
❑ ED 2793 [PS]	The End of the World	1965	5.00	10.00	20.00
❑ ED 2800	(contents unknown)	1965	5.00	10.00	20.00
❑ ED 2800 [PS]	Songs from the Heart	1965	5.00	10.00	20.00

LYNNE, JEFF

Also see ELECTRIC LIGHT ORCHESTRA; THE IDLE RACE; THE MOVE.

A&M

Number	Title (A Side/B Side)	Yr	VG	VG+	NM
❑ 2658	Video!/Sooner or Later	1984	—	—	—

—Unreleased?

JET

Number	Title (A Side/B Side)	Yr	VG	VG+	NM
❑ XW1060	Doin' That Crazy Thing/Going Down to Rio	1977	—	2.50	5.00

VIRGIN/EPIC

Number	Title (A Side/B Side)	Yr	VG	VG+	NM
❑ 04570	Video!/Sooner or Later	1984	—	2.00	4.00

LYNOTT, PHILIP

Also see THIN LIZZY.

WARNER BROS.

Number	Title (A Side/B Side)	Yr	VG	VG+	NM
❑ 49272	Ode to a Black Man/King's Call	1980	—	2.00	4.00

LYNYRD SKYNYRD

Also see ROSSINGTON COLLINS BAND.

ATINA

Number	Title (A Side/B Side)	Yr	VG	VG+	NM
❑ 129	Need All My Friends/Michelle	1978	3.75	7.50	15.00

COLUMBIA

Number	Title (A Side/B Side)	Yr	VG	VG+	NM
❑ 78284	White Knuckle Ride/Tearin' It Up	1996	—	2.00	4.00

—B-side by Joe Diffie

MCA

Number	Title (A Side/B Side)	Yr	VG	VG+	NM
❑ L45-1966 [DJ]	Gimme Back My Bullets (same on both sides)	1976	6.25	12.50	25.00
❑ 40258	Sweet Home Alabama/Take Your Time	1974	—	2.50	5.00
❑ 40328	Free Bird/Down South Jukin'	1974	—	2.50	5.00
❑ 40416	Saturday Night Special/Made in the Shade	1975	—	2.50	5.00
❑ 40532	Double Trouble/Roll Gypsy Roll	1975	—	2.50	5.00
❑ 40565	Gimme Back My Bullets/All I Can Do Is Write About It	1976	—	2.50	5.00
❑ 40647	Gimme Three Steps/Travelin' Man	1976	—	2.50	5.00
❑ 40665	Free Bird/Searching	1976	—	2.50	5.00
❑ 40819	What's Your Name/I Know a Little	1977	—	2.50	5.00

—"What's Your Name" is a different mix than that on the Street Survivors LP.

Number	Title (A Side/B Side)	Yr	VG	VG+	NM
❑ 40888	You Got That Right/Ain't No Good Life	1978	—	2.50	5.00
❑ 40957	Down South Jukin'/Wino	1978	—	2.50	5.00
❑ 53206	When You Got Good Friends/Truck Drivin' Man	1987	—	2.00	4.00
❑ 60191	Sweet Home Alabama/Saturday Night Special	1976	—	2.00	4.00

—Reissue

SHADE TREE

Number	Title (A Side/B Side)	Yr	VG	VG+	NM
❑ 101	Need All My Friends/Michelle	1971	375.00	750.00	1500.

—As "Lynard Skynard"; approximately 300 copies pressed

SOUNDS OF THE SOUTH

Number	Title (A Side/B Side)	Yr	VG	VG+	NM
❑ 40158	Gimme Three Steps/Mr. Banker	1973	2.00	4.00	8.00
❑ 40231	Don't Ask Me No Questions/Take Your Time	1974	2.00	4.00	8.00
❑ 40258	Sweet Home Alabama/Take Your Time	1974	2.00	4.00	8.00

LYRICS, THE

Several different groups.

ABC-PARAMOUNT

Number	Title (A Side/B Side)	Yr	VG	VG+	NM
❑ 10560	So Hard to Get Along/Side Wind	1964	3.00	6.00	12.00

CORAL

Number	Title (A Side/B Side)	Yr	VG	VG+	NM
❑ 62322	The Girl I Love/Oh, Please Love Me	1962	6.25	12.50	25.00

FERNWOOD

Number	Title (A Side/B Side)	Yr	VG	VG+	NM
❑ 129	Let's Bee Sweethearts Again/You and Your Fellow	1960	200.00	400.00	800.00

—This edition misspelled the A-side

FLEETWOOD

Number	Title (A Side/B Side)	Yr	VG	VG+	NM
❑ 233	Let's Be Sweethearts Again/You and Your Fellow	1961	100.00	200.00	400.00

—This edition spelled the A-side correctly

VEE JAY

Number	Title (A Side/B Side)	Yr	VG	VG+	NM
❑ 285	Come On Home/Why Don't You Stop	1958	20.00	40.00	80.00

M

M.C. HAMMER

See HAMMER, MC.

M.H. ROYALS, THE

ABC

Number	Title (A Side/B Side)	Yr	VG	VG+	NM
❑ 10907	Tomorrow's Dead/She's Gone Forever	1967	6.25	12.50	25.00
❑ 10957	Old Town/Now She's Crying	1967	6.25	12.50	25.00

M-3'S, THE

ABC-PARAMOUNT

Number	Title (A Side/B Side)	Yr	VG	VG+	NM
❑ 10772	Funny Cafe/So Give Me Love	1966	6.25	12.50	25.00

UNITED ARTISTS

Number	Title (A Side/B Side)	Yr	VG	VG+	NM
❑ 737	When the Party's Over/Magic Kiss	1964	3.00	6.00	12.00
❑ 889	Three Lonely Nights/I See a Rainbow	1965	3.00	6.00	12.00

MACH, LEON

LAVENDER

Number	Title (A Side/B Side)	Yr	VG	VG+	NM
❑ 1554	You Hurt Me So/It's You I Love	1960	25.00	50.00	100.00

MACK, LONNIE

BUCCANEER

Number	Title (A Side/B Side)	Yr	VG	VG+	NM
❑ 3001	Memphis/Lonnie on the Move	196?	2.00	4.00	8.00

—Reissue of Fraternity material

CAPITOL

Number	Title (A Side/B Side)	Yr	VG	VG+	NM
❑ 4441	Running Wild/Funky Country Living	1977	—	2.50	5.00

ELEKTRA

Number	Title (A Side/B Side)	Yr	VG	VG+	NM
❑ 45638	Memphis/Why	1968	2.50	5.00	10.00
❑ 45652	Save Your Money/In the Band	1969	2.50	5.00	10.00
❑ 45715	She Even Woke Me Up to Say Goodbye/Lay It Down	1971	2.00	4.00	8.00
❑ 45761	Rings/Florida	1972	2.00	4.00	8.00

EPIC

Number	Title (A Side/B Side)	Yr	VG	VG+	NM
❑ 07973	Too Rock for Country, Too Country for Rock and Roll/Lucille	1988	—	2.00	4.00
❑ 08117	Hard Life/50's-60's Man	1988	—	2.00	4.00

FRATERNITY

Number	Title (A Side/B Side)	Yr	VG	VG+	NM
❑ 906	Memphis/Down In the Dumps	1963	3.75	7.50	15.00
❑ 912	Wham!/Susie-Q	1963	3.75	7.50	15.00
❑ 918	Baby, What's Wrong/Where There's a Will	1963	3.00	6.00	12.00
❑ 920	Say Something Nice to Me/Lonnie on the Move	1964	3.00	6.00	12.00
❑ 925	I've Had It/Nashville	1964	3.00	6.00	12.00
❑ 932	Chicken Pickin'/Sa-Ba-Hoola	1964	3.00	6.00	12.00
❑ 938	Don't Make My Baby Blue/Georgia Boy	1964	3.00	6.00	12.00
❑ 942	Crying Over You/Coastin'	1965	3.00	6.00	12.00
❑ 946	Tonky Go Go/When I'm Alone	1965	3.00	6.00	12.00
❑ 951	Honky Tonk '65/Chicken Pickin'	1965	3.00	6.00	12.00
❑ 957	Crying Over You/Are You Guilty	1966	3.00	6.00	12.00
❑ 959	The Circus/Bucaroo	1966	3.00	6.00	12.00
❑ 967	Tension (Part 1)/Tension (Part 2)	1966	3.00	6.00	12.00
❑ 969	Wildwood Flower/Snow on the Mountain	1966	3.00	6.00	12.00
❑ 981	I Left My Heart in San Francisco/Omaha	1967	2.50	5.00	10.00
❑ 986	Save Your Money/Snow on the Mountain	1967	2.50	5.00	10.00
❑ 1004	Soul Express/Down and Out	1968	2.50	5.00	10.00
❑ 1278	Soul Express/I Found a Love	197?	—	3.00	6.00

ROULETTE

Number	Title (A Side/B Side)	Yr	VG	VG+	NM
❑ 7175	All We Need Is Love, You and Me/Highway 56	1975	—	3.00	6.00

MACKENZIE, GISELE

CAPITOL

Number	Title (A Side/B Side)	Yr	VG	VG+	NM
❑ F1722	Jolie Jacqueline/Fairyland	1951	3.75	7.50	15.00
❑ F1768	J'Attendrai/My Greatest Love	1951	3.75	7.50	15.00
❑ F1807	On Rosary Hill/Lovers' Waltz	1951	3.75	7.50	15.00

—With Gordon MacRae

Number	Title (A Side/B Side)	Yr	VG	VG+	NM
❑ F1826	Sans Souci/I Never Was Loved by Anyone Else	1951	3.75	7.50	15.00
❑ F1865	Sweetheart/It's All Over But the Memories	1951	3.75	7.50	15.00
❑ F1907	La Fiacre/Thu Pocket Thu Pocket	1951	3.75	7.50	15.00
❑ F1959	My Buick, My Lover and I/Lovers' Waltz	1952	3.00	6.00	12.00

—With Gordon MacRae

Number	Title (A Side/B Side)	Yr	VG	VG+	NM
❑ F1983	Wishin'/Goodbye Sweetheart	1952	3.00	6.00	12.00
❑ F1997	Eggbert the Easter Egg/Benny the Bob-Tailed Bunny	1952	3.75	7.50	15.00
❑ F2059	What'll I Do/I'm So Easy to Satisfy	1952	3.00	6.00	12.00
❑ F2110	Johnny/Whistle My Love	1952	3.00	6.00	12.00
❑ F2156	Adios/Darling You Can't Love Two	1952	3.00	6.00	12.00
❑ F2256	Don't Let the Stars Get In Your Eyes/My Favorite Song	1952	3.00	6.00	12.00
❑ F2307	Gone/The New Wears Off Too Fast	1952	3.00	6.00	12.00
❑ F2354	Let Me Know/Friend of the Family	1953	3.00	6.00	12.00
❑ F2404	Lipstick and Powder and Paint/Get It While You're Young	1953	3.00	6.00	12.00

—With Helen O'Connell

Number	Title (A Side/B Side)	Yr	VG	VG+	NM
❑ F2501	I'd Rather Die Young/I Didn't Want to Love You	1953	3.00	6.00	12.00
❑ F2521	Give Me a Name/When the Hands of the Clock Pray at Midnight	1953	3.00	6.00	12.00

—With Helen O'Connell

Number	Title (A Side/B Side)	Yr	VG	VG+	NM
❑ F2556	Half Hearted/Till They've All Come Home	1953	3.00	6.00	12.00
❑ F2600	Walkin' Tune/Embrasse	1953	3.00	6.00	12.00
❑ F2695	A Letter and a Ring/Le Gros Bill	1954	3.00	6.00	12.00
❑ F2743	Doggone It Baby, I'm in Love/Ridin' to Tennessee	1954	3.00	6.00	12.00
❑ F2827	El Recicario/The One Who Broke My Heart Is Back in Town	1954	3.00	6.00	12.00

EVEREST

Number	Title (A Side/B Side)	Yr	VG	VG+	NM
❑ 19352	In Milano/You Dream of Me (And I'll Dream of You)	1960	2.00	4.00	8.00

MERCURY

Number	Title (A Side/B Side)	Yr	VG	VG+	NM
❑ 72113	Loser's Lullaby/By Myself	1963	—	3.50	7.00

RCA VICTOR

Number	Title (A Side/B Side)	Yr	VG	VG+	NM
❑ 47-7086	Never Go Away/This I Know	1957	2.50	5.00	10.00
❑ 47-7183	They're Playing Our Song/Come to Me My True Love	1958	2.00	4.00	8.00

VIK

Number	Title (A Side/B Side)	Yr	VG	VG+	NM
❑ 0233	The Star You Wished Upon Last Night/It's Delightful to Be Married	1956	2.50	5.00	10.00
❑ 0249	He Knows/Hello There	1957	2.50	5.00	10.00
❑ 0274	The Waltz That Broke My Heart/Oh Pain, Oh Agony	1957	2.50	5.00	10.00
❑ 0300	Too Fat for the Chimney/Jingle Bells	1957	3.00	6.00	12.00
❑ 0300 [PS]	Too Fat for the Chimney/Jingle Bells	1957	5.00	10.00	20.00

"X"

Number	Title (A Side/B Side)	Yr	VG	VG+	NM
❑ 0137	Hard to Get/Boston Fancy	1955	3.00	6.00	12.00
❑ 0137 [PS]	Hard to Get/Boston Fancy	1955	5.00	10.00	20.00
❑ 0172	Pepper Hot Baby/That's the Chance I've Got to Take	1955	2.50	5.00	10.00
❑ 0189	Reserved/The Little Child	1956	2.50	5.00	10.00
—With Billy Quinn					
❑ 0202	Mr. Telephone/Dance If You Want to Dance	1956	2.50	5.00	10.00

MAD HATTERS, THE

ASCOT

Number	Title (A Side/B Side)	Yr	VG	VG+	NM
❑ 2197	I Need Love/Blowin' in the Wind	1965	6.25	12.50	25.00

FONTANA

Number	Title (A Side/B Side)	Yr	VG	VG+	NM
❑ 1582	I'll Come Running/Hello Girl	1967	5.00	10.00	20.00

IGL

Number	Title (A Side/B Side)	Yr	VG	VG+	NM
❑ 117	Her Love/Route 66	196?	3.75	7.50	15.00

MAD LADS, THE

CAPITOL

Number	Title (A Side/B Side)	Yr	VG	VG+	NM
❑ 5284	Don't Cry at the Party/I'll Survive	1964	3.75	7.50	15.00

STAX

Number	Title (A Side/B Side)	Yr	VG	VG+	NM
❑ 160	Surf Jerk/Sidewalk Surf	1964	3.75	7.50	15.00

VOLT

Number	Title (A Side/B Side)	Yr	VG	VG+	NM
❑ 127	Don't Have to Shop Around/Tear-Maker	1965	2.50	5.00	10.00
❑ 131	I Want Someone/Nothing Can Break Through	1965	2.50	5.00	10.00
❑ 135	Come Closer to Me/Sugar Sugar	1966	2.50	5.00	10.00
❑ 137	I Want a Girl/What Will Love Tend to Make You Do	1966	2.50	5.00	10.00
❑ 139	Patch My Heart/You Mean So Much to Me	1966	2.50	5.00	10.00
❑ 143	These Simple Reasons/I Don't Want to Lose Your Love	1967	2.50	5.00	10.00
❑ 150	My Inspiration/Mr. Fix-It	1967	2.50	5.00	10.00
❑ 162	Whatever Hurts You/No Time Is Better Than Right Now	1968	2.50	5.00	10.00
❑ 4003	So Nice/Make Room	1968	2.00	4.00	8.00
❑ 4009	Love Is Here Today and Gone Tomorrow/Make This Young Lady Mine	1969	2.00	4.00	8.00
❑ 4016	By the Time I Get to Phoenix/No Strings Attached	1969	2.00	4.00	8.00
❑ 4041	Seeing Is Believing/These Old Memories	1970	2.00	4.00	8.00
❑ 4068	Gone! The Promises of Yesterday/I'm So Glad I Fell in Love with You	1971	2.00	4.00	8.00
❑ 4080	Let Me Repair Your Heart/Did My Baby Call	1972	2.00	4.00	8.00
❑ 4098	I Forgot to Be Your Lover/I'm So Glad I Fell in Love with You	1973	2.00	4.00	8.00

WAND

Number	Title (A Side/B Side)	Yr	VG	VG+	NM
❑ 11221	Let's Have Some Fun (Part 1)/Let's Have Some Fun (Part 2)	1970	2.50	5.00	10.00

MAD MILO

COMBO

Number	Title (A Side/B Side)	Yr	VG	VG+	NM
❑ 131	Elvis on Trial/A Date with Elvis	1957	12.50	25.00	50.00

MILLION

Number	Title (A Side/B Side)	Yr	VG	VG+	NM
❑ 20018	Elvis for Christmas/New Year	1957	12.50	25.00	50.00
—B-side by Ron Tan and Combo					

MAD RIVER

CAPITOL

Number	Title (A Side/B Side)	Yr	VG	VG+	NM
❑ 2310	A Gazelle/High All the Time	1968	3.00	6.00	12.00
❑ 2559	Copper Plates/Harfy Magnum	1969	3.00	6.00	12.00

MADHATTANS, THE

ATLANTIC

Number	Title (A Side/B Side)	Yr	VG	VG+	NM
❑ 1142	Wowie/A Basketful of Blueberries	1957	5.00	10.00	20.00

MADISONS, THE

LAWN

Number	Title (A Side/B Side)	Yr	VG	VG+	NM
❑ 240	Can You Imagine It/The Wind and the Rain	1964	10.00	20.00	40.00

LIMELIGHT

Number	Title (A Side/B Side)	Yr	VG	VG+	NM
❑ 3018	Bad Baboon/Because I Got You	1964	5.00	10.00	20.00

MGM

Number	Title (A Side/B Side)	Yr	VG	VG+	NM
❑ 13312	Cheryl Anne/Looking for True Love	1965	10.00	20.00	40.00

MADONNA

GEFFEN

Number	Title (A Side/B Side)	Yr	VG	VG+	NM
❑ GGEF 0540	Gambler/Crazy for You	198?	—	—	3.00
—"Back to Back Hits" series; first issue of A-side on U.S. 45					
❑ 29051	Crazy for You/No More Words	1985	—	—	3.00
—B-side by Berlin					
❑ 29051 [PS]	Crazy for You/No More Words	1985	—	—	3.00

MAVERICK

Number	Title (A Side/B Side)	Yr	VG	VG+	NM
❑ 16825	Don't Tell Me (Album Version)/Don't Tell Me (Thunderpuss' 2001 Hands in the Air Radio)	2001	—	2.00	4.00
❑ 16826	Music/Cyberraga	2000	—	2.00	4.00
❑ 17102	Nothing Really Matters/To Have and Not to Hold	1999	—	2.00	4.00
❑ 17160	The Power of Good-Bye/Mer Girl	1998	—	—	3.00
❑ 17206	Ray of Light/Has to Be	1998	—	—	3.00
❑ 17244	Frozen/Shanti-Ashtangi	1998	—	—	3.00
❑ 17714	Love Don't Live Here Anymore (Soulpower Radio Remix)/Love Don't Live Here Anymore (Album Remix)	1996	—	—	3.00
❑ 17719	You'll See/Live to Tell (Live Edit)	1995	—	—	3.00
❑ 17882	Human Nature/Sanctuary	1995	—	—	3.00
❑ 17924	Bedtime Story/Survival	1995	—	—	3.00
❑ 18000	Take a Bow/Take a Bow (In Da Soul Mix)	1994	—	—	3.00
❑ 18035	Secret/Secret (instrumental)	1994	—	—	3.00
❑ 18247	I'll Remember/Secret Garden	1994	—	—	3.00
❑ 18505	Rain/Waiting	1993	—	—	3.00
❑ 18639	Deeper and Deeper/Deeper and Deeper (instrumental)	1992	—	—	3.00
❑ 18650	Bad Girl/Fever	1993	—	—	3.00
❑ 18782	Erotica/Erotica (instrumental)	1992	—	—	3.00

SIRE

Number	Title (A Side/B Side)	Yr	VG	VG+	NM
❑ GSRE 0494	Borderline/Holiday	198?	—	—	3.00
—"Back to Back Hits" reissue					
❑ GSRE 0506	Live a Virgin/Lucky Star	198?	—	—	3.00
—"Back to Back Hits" reissue					
❑ GSRE 0507	Material Girl/Angel	198?	—	—	3.00
—"Back to Back Hits" reissue					
❑ GSRE 0539	Into the Groove/Dress You Up	198?	—	—	3.00
—"Back to Back Hits" series; first issue of A-side on U.S. 45					
❑ PRO-S-2023 [DJ]	Physical Attraction/Physical Attraction	1983	12.50	25.00	50.00
❑ 18822	This Used to Be My Playground/This Used to Be My Playground (Long Version)	1992	—	—	3.00
❑ 19485	Justify My Love/Express Yourself 1990	1990	—	—	3.00
❑ 19490	Rescue Me/Rescue Me (Alternate Single Mix)	1990	—	—	3.00
❑ 19789	Hanky Panky/More	1990	—	—	3.00
❑ 19863	Vogue (Single Version)/Vogue (Bette Davis Dub)	1990	—	—	3.00
❑ 19986	Keep It Together/Keep It Together (instrumental)	1990	—	—	3.00
❑ 19986 [PS]	Keep It Together/Keep It Together (instrumental)	1990	20.00	40.00	80.00
❑ 21860	Express Yourself/Cherish	199?	—	—	3.00
—"Back to Back Hits" reissue					
❑ 21861	Like a Prayer/Oh Father	199?	—	—	3.00
—"Back to Back Hits" reissue					
❑ 21940	Who's That Girl/Causing a Commotion	198?	—	—	3.00
—"Back to Back Hits" reissue					
❑ 21941	La Isla Bonita/Open Your Heart	198?	—	—	3.00
—"Back to Back Hits" reissue					
❑ 21985	Live to Tell/True Blue	198?	—	—	3.00
—"Back to Back Hits" reissue					
❑ 21986	Papa Don't Preach/Everybody	198?	—	—	3.00
—"Back to Back Hits" reissue					
❑ 22723	Oh Father/Pray for Spanish Eyes	1989	—	—	3.00
❑ 22723 [PS]	Oh Father/Pray for Spanish Eyes	1989	—	—	—
—The purported sleeve, the front cover of which was printed in the prior edition of this guide, appears to be fake. Current opinion is that there is NO genuine U.S. picture sleeve.					
❑ 22883	Cherish/Supernatural	1989	—	—	3.00
❑ 22883 [PS]	Cherish/Supernatural	1989	—	—	3.00
❑ 22948	Express Yourself/The Look of Love	1989	—	—	3.00
❑ 22948 [PS]	Express Yourself/The Look of Love	1989	—	—	3.00
❑ 27539	Like a Prayer/Act of Contrition	1989	—	—	3.00
❑ 27539 [DJ]	Like a Prayer (7" Remix Edit)/Like a Prayer (7" Version with Fade)	1989	2.50	5.00	10.00
❑ 27539 [PS]	Like a Prayer/Act of Contrition	1989	—	—	3.00
❑ 28224	Causing a Commotion/Jimmy, Jimmy	1987	—	—	3.00
❑ 28224 [PS]	Causing a Commotion/Jimmy, Jimmy	1987	—	—	3.00
❑ 28341	Who's That Girl?/White Heat	1987	—	—	3.00
❑ 28341 [PS]	Who's That Girl?/White Heat	1987	—	—	3.00
❑ 28425	La Isla Bonita/La Isla Bonita (instrumental)	1987	—	—	3.00
❑ 28425 [PS]	La Isla Bonita/La Isla Bonita (instrumental)	1987	—	—	3.00
❑ 28508	Open Your Heart/White Heat	1986	—	—	3.00
❑ 28508 [PS]	Open Your Heart/White Heat	1986	—	—	3.00
❑ 28591	True Blue/Ain't No Big Deal	1986	—	2.50	5.00
—Blue vinyl					
❑ 28591	True Blue/Ain't No Big Deal	1986	—	—	3.00
❑ 28591 [PS]	True Blue/Ain't No Big Deal	1986	—	2.50	5.00
—"Limited edition blue vinyl pressing" on sleeve					
❑ 28591 [PS]	True Blue/Ain't No Big Deal	1986	—	—	3.00
—No mention of limited edition on sleeve					
❑ 28660	Papa Don't Preach/Pretender	1986	—	—	3.00
❑ 28660 [PS]	Papa Don't Preach/Pretender	1986	—	—	3.00
❑ 28717	Live to Tell/Live to Tell (instrumental)	1986	—	—	3.00
❑ 28717 [PS]	Live to Tell/Live to Tell (instrumental)	1986	—	—	3.00
❑ 28919	Dress You Up/Shoo-Be-Doo	1985	—	—	3.00
❑ 28919 [PS]	Dress You Up/Shoo-Be-Doo	1985	12.50	25.00	50.00
❑ 29008	Angel/Angel (12" Remix Edit)	1985	—	—	3.00
❑ 29008 [PS]	Angel/Angel (12" Remix Edit)	1985	—	—	3.00
❑ 29083	Material Girl/Pretender	1985	—	—	3.00
❑ 29083 [PS]	Material Girl/Pretender	1985	—	—	3.00
❑ 29177	Lucky Star/I Know It	1984	—	2.00	4.00
❑ 29210	Like a Virgin/Stay	1984	—	—	3.00
❑ 29210 [PS]	Like a Virgin/Stay	1984	—	—	3.00
❑ 29354	Borderline/Think of Me	1984	—	2.00	4.00
❑ 29354 [PS]	Borderline/Think of Me	1984	20.00	40.00	80.00
—Fold-out poster sleeve					
❑ 29478	Holiday/(Instrumental)	1983	—	2.00	4.00
❑ 29478	Holiday/I Know It	1983	—	2.00	4.00
❑ 29841	Everybody/(Instrumental)	1982	5.00	10.00	20.00
—Deduct 50% for promo copy					

WARNER BROS.

Number	Title (A Side/B Side)	Yr	VG	VG+	NM
❑ 17495	You Must Love Me/Rainbow High	1996	—	—	3.00

MAESTRO, JOHNNY

Also see THE BROOKLYN BRIDGE; THE CRESTS.

APT

Number	Title (A Side/B Side)	Yr	VG	VG+	NM
❑ 25075	Phone Booth on the Highway/She's All Mine Alone	1965	12.50	25.00	50.00

Number	Title (A Side/B Side)	Yr	VG	VG+	NM
BUDDAH					
❑ 201	The Rains Came/Never Knew THis Kind of Hurt Before	1971	2.50	5.00	10.00
❑ 236	Yours Until Tomorrow/Man in a Band	1971	2.50	5.00	10.00
❑ 289 [DJ]	Snow (mono/stereo)	1971	2.50	5.00	10.00
—May be promo only					
CAMEO					
❑ 256	Over the Weekend/I'll Be There	1963	7.50	15.00	30.00
❑ 305	Lean on Me/(It's Harder to) Make Up My Mind	1964	5.00	10.00	20.00
COED					
❑ 527	Say It Isn't So/The Great Physician	1960	6.25	12.50	25.00
—As "Johnny Masters"					
❑ 545	Model Girl/We've Got to Tell Them	1961	6.25	12.50	25.00
—As "Johnny Mastro"					
❑ 549	What a Surprise/Warning Voice	1961	6.25	12.50	25.00
❑ 552	Mr. Happiness/Test of Love	1961	6.25	12.50	25.00
❑ 557	I.O.U./The Way You Look Tonight	1961	7.50	15.00	30.00
❑ 562	Besame Baby/It Must Be Love	1962	25.00	50.00	100.00
PARKWAY					
❑ 118	My Times/Is It You	1966	5.00	10.00	20.00
❑ 987	Heartburn/Try Me	1966	3.75	7.50	15.00
❑ 987 [DJ]	Heartburn	1966	15.00	30.00	60.00
—One-sided white label promo					
❑ 999	I Care About You/Come See Me (I'm Your Man)	1966	3.75	7.50	15.00
UNITED ARTISTS					
❑ 474	Before I Loved Her/Fifty Million Heartbeats	1962	10.00	20.00	40.00

MAGIC CHRISTIANS, THE

Number	Title (A Side/B Side)	Yr	VG	VG+	NM
COMMONWEALTH UNITED					
❑ 3006	Come and Get It/Nats	1970	3.00	6.00	12.00

MAGIC FERN, THE

Number	Title (A Side/B Side)	Yr	VG	VG+	NM
JERDEN					
❑ 813	Maggie/I Wonder Why	1966	5.00	10.00	20.00
PICCADILLY					
❑ 240	Nellie/Candy Day	1967	3.75	7.50	15.00

MAGIC LANTERNS

Contrary to some opinions, Ozzy Osbourne was never in this group. (The bass player was Michael "Oz" Osborne; notice the difference in last name spelling.) But ALBERT HAMMOND was.

Number	Title (A Side/B Side)	Yr	VG	VG+	NM
ATLANTIC					
❑ 2560	Shame, Shame/Baby, I Gotta Go Now	1968	2.50	5.00	10.00
❑ 2600	Give Me Love/Biding My Time	1969	2.00	4.00	8.00
❑ 2626	Melt All Your Troubles Away/Bossa Nova 1940-Hello You Lovers	1969	2.00	4.00	8.00
❑ 2715	One Night Stand/Frisco Annie	1970	2.00	4.00	8.00
BIG TREE					
❑ 109	One Night Stand/Frisco Annie	1970	—	3.00	6.00
❑ 113	Let the Sunshine In/Old Pa Bradley	1971	—	3.00	6.00
CHARISMA					
❑ 100	Country Woman/Pa Bradley	1972	—	2.50	5.00
EPIC					
❑ 10062	Excuse Me Baby/Greedy Girl	1966	2.00	4.00	8.00
❑ 10062 [PS]	Excuse Me Baby/Greedy Girl	1966	5.00	10.00	20.00
❑ 10111	Knight in Rusty Armour/Simple Things	1966	2.00	4.00	8.00

MAGIC MUSHROOM, THE

Number	Title (A Side/B Side)	Yr	VG	VG+	NM
WARNER BROS.					
❑ 5846	I'm Gone/Cry Baby	1966	6.25	12.50	25.00

MAGIC MUSHROOMS, THE

Number	Title (A Side/B Side)	Yr	VG	VG+	NM
A&M					
❑ 815	It's a-Happening/Never More	1966	3.75	7.50	15.00
PHILIPS					
❑ 40483	Look in My Face/Never Let Go	1968	3.75	7.50	15.00

MAGISTRATES, THE

Number	Title (A Side/B Side)	Yr	VG	VG+	NM
MGM					
❑ 13946	Here Comes the Judge/Girl	1968	3.00	6.00	12.00
❑ 13980	After the Fox/Tear Down the Walls	1968	3.00	6.00	12.00

MAGNETS, THE (1)

Number	Title (A Side/B Side)	Yr	VG	VG+	NM
GROOVE					
❑ 58-0058	Surprise/You Just Say the Word	1965	10.00	20.00	40.00

MAGNETS, THE (2)

Number	Title (A Side/B Side)	Yr	VG	VG+	NM
LONDON INT'L.					
❑ 10036	Drag Race/Joker	1963	6.25	12.50	25.00

MAGNETS, THE (3)

Number	Title (A Side/B Side)	Yr	VG	VG+	NM
RCA VICTOR					
❑ 47-7391	When the School Bells Ring/Don't Tarry, Little Mary	1958	6.25	12.50	25.00

MAGNIFICENT FOUR, THE

Number	Title (A Side/B Side)	Yr	VG	VG+	NM
BLAST					
❑ 210	The Closer You Are/Uncle Sam	1963	10.00	20.00	40.00
WHALE					
❑ 506	The Closer You Are/Uncle Sam	1961	20.00	40.00	80.00

MAGNIFICENT 7, THE

Number	Title (A Side/B Side)	Yr	VG	VG+	NM
DIAL					
❑ 4074	Ooh, Baby Baby/Never Will I (Make My Baby Cry)	1968	6.25	12.50	25.00
DIMENSION					
❑ 1050	Show Me/Boogidy	1965	5.00	10.00	20.00
—As "Magnificent VII"					
EASTERN					
❑ 611	She's Called a Woman/Since You've Been Gone So Long	1966	10.00	20.00	40.00

MAGNIFICENTS, THE

Number	Title (A Side/B Side)	Yr	VG	VG+	NM
CHECKER					
❑ 1016	The Dribble Twist/Do You Mind	1962	3.75	7.50	15.00
KANSOMA					
❑ 03	The Dribble Twist/Do You Mind	1962	7.50	15.00	30.00
VEE JAY					
❑ 183	Up On the Mountain/Why Did She Go	1956	18.75	37.50	75.00
❑ 208	Hiccup/Caddy Bo	1956	25.00	50.00	100.00
❑ 235	Off the Mountain/Lost Lovers	1957	18.75	37.50	75.00
❑ 281	Don't Leave Me/Ozeta	1958	25.00	50.00	100.00
❑ 367	Up On the Mountain/Let's Do the Cha Cha	1960	5.00	10.00	20.00

MAJESTICS, THE (1)

Number	Title (A Side/B Side)	Yr	VG	VG+	NM
CHESS					
❑ 1802	Oasis (Part 1)/Oasis (Part 2)	1961	5.00	10.00	20.00
V.I.P.					
❑ 25028 [DJ]	Say You/All for Someone	1965	250.00	500.00	1000.
—Promo only; stock copies credited "The Monitors"					

MAJESTICS, THE (2)

Number	Title (A Side/B Side)	Yr	VG	VG+	NM
CHEX					
❑ 1000	Give Me a Cigarette/Shoppin' and Hoppin'	1962	25.00	50.00	100.00
❑ 1000	Give Me a Cigarette/So I Can Forget	1962	10.00	20.00	40.00
❑ 1004	Unhappy and Blue/Treat Me Like You Want	1962	12.50	25.00	50.00
❑ 1006	Lonely Heart/Gwendolyn	1962	7.50	15.00	30.00
❑ 1009	Baby/Teach Me How to Limbo	1963	6.25	12.50	25.00

MAJESTICS, THE (3)

Number	Title (A Side/B Side)	Yr	VG	VG+	NM
20TH FOX					
❑ 171	The Lone Stranger/Sweet One	1959	6.25	12.50	25.00
CONTOUR					
❑ 501	Teen Age Gossip/Hard Times	1960	20.00	40.00	80.00
FARO					
❑ 592	TV Cowboys/So You Want to Rock	1959	6.25	12.50	25.00
FOXIE					
❑ 7004	The Lone Stranger/Sweet One	1960	5.00	10.00	20.00
NRC					
❑ 502	Please Don't Say No/Divided Heart	1958	62.50	125.00	250.00
SIOUX					
❑ 91459	The Lone Stranger/Sweet One	1959	12.50	25.00	50.00

MAJESTICS, THE (4)

Number	Title (A Side/B Side)	Yr	VG	VG+	NM
DUNES					
❑ 2014	The Boss Walk (Part 1)/The Boss Walk (Part 2)	1962	10.00	20.00	40.00
SAM					
❑ 112	Jaguar/Blue Feeling	1962	12.50	25.00	50.00
❑ 117	Riptide/Big Noise from Makaba	1962	12.50	25.00	50.00
❑ 123	XL-3/My Little Baby	1963	12.50	25.00	50.00

MAJESTICS, THE (5)

Number	Title (A Side/B Side)	Yr	VG	VG+	NM
JORDAN					
❑ 1057	Angel of Love/Searching for a New Love	1961	75.00	150.00	300.00
—Yellow vinyl					
❑ 1057	Angel of Love/Searching for a New Love	1961	12.50	25.00	50.00
—Black vinyl					
LINDA					
❑ 111	Strange World/Everything Is Gonna Be All Right	1963	15.00	30.00	60.00
❑ 121	Girl of My Dreams/It Hurts Me	1963	25.00	50.00	100.00
NU-TONE					
❑ 123	Angel of Love/Searching for a New Love	1961	17.50	35.00	70.00
PIXIE					
❑ 6901	Angel of Love/Searching for a New Love	1961	7.50	15.00	30.00

MAJESTICS, THE (6)

Sam Moore of SAM AND DAVE was in this group.

Number	Title (A Side/B Side)	Yr	VG	VG+	NM
MARLIN					
❑ 802	Nitey Nite/Cave Man Rock	1956	250.00	500.00	1000.

MAJESTICS, THE (7)

Number	Title (A Side/B Side)	Yr	VG	VG+	NM
MGM					
❑ 13488	Love Has Forgotten Me/Smile Through My Tears	1966	3.00	6.00	12.00

MAJORETTES, THE

Number	Title (A Side/B Side)	Yr	VG	VG+	NM
TROY					
❑ 1000	White Levi's/Please Come Back	1963	5.00	10.00	20.00
❑ 1000 [PS]	White Levi's/Please Come Back	1963	10.00	20.00	40.00

MAJORS, THE (1)

Number	Title (A Side/B Side)	Yr	VG	VG+	NM
IMPERIAL					
❑ 5855	A Wonderful Dream/Time Will Tell	1962	5.00	10.00	20.00
❑ 5879	She's a Troublemaker/A Little Bit Now, A Little Bit Later	1962	3.75	7.50	15.00
❑ 5914	What in the World/Anything You Can Do	1963	3.00	6.00	12.00
❑ 5936	Tra La La/What Have You Been Doin'	1963	3.00	6.00	12.00
❑ 5968	One Happy Ending/Get Up Now	1963	3.00	6.00	12.00
❑ 5991	Which Way Did She Go/Your Life Begins (Sweet 16)	1963	3.00	6.00	12.00
❑ 66009	I'll Be There/Ooh Wee Baby	1963	3.00	6.00	12.00
UNITED ARTISTS					
❑ 0110	A Wonderful Dream/Mother-in-Law	1973	—	2.50	5.00
—"Silver Spotlight Series" reissue; B-side by Ernie K-Doe					

MAJORS, THE (2)

Number	Title (A Side/B Side)	Yr	VG	VG+	NM
DERBY					
❑ 763	At Last/You Ran Away from My Heart	1951	200.00	400.00	800.00
❑ 779	Laughing on the Outside/Come On Up to My Room	1951	150.00	300.00	600.00

MAJORS, THE (3)

Number	Title (A Side/B Side)	Yr	VG	VG+	NM
FELSTED					
❑ 8501	Blue Sunset/Rockin' the Boogie	1958	7.50	15.00	30.00
❑ 8576	Come Go with Me/Les Qua	1959	6.25	12.50	25.00
❑ 8707	Come Go with Me/Les Qua	1964	3.75	7.50	15.00

MAJORS, THE (4)

ORIGINAL

Number	Title (A Side/B Side)	Yr	VG	VG+	NM
❑ 1003	Big Eyes/Go 'Way	1954	100.00	200.00	400.00

MALLETT, SAUNDRA, AND THE VANDELLAS

Also see MARTHA AND THE VANDELLAS.

TAMLA

Number	Title (A Side/B Side)	Yr	VG	VG+	NM
❑ 54067	Camel Walk/It's Gonna Be Hard Times	1962	250.00	500.00	1000.

MAMA CASS

See CASS ELLIOT.

MAMAS AND THE PAPAS, THE

Also see DENNY DOHERTY; CASS ELLIOT; JILL GIBSON; JOHN PHILLIPS; MICHELLE PHILLIPS.

ABC DUNHILL

Number	Title (A Side/B Side)	Yr	VG	VG+	NM
❑ 4125	Safe in My Garden/Too Late	1968	2.00	4.00	8.00
❑ 4150	For the Love of Ivy/Strange Young Girls	1968	2.00	4.00	8.00
❑ 4171	Do You Wanna Dance/My Girl	1968	2.00	4.00	8.00
❑ 4301	Step Out/Shooting Star	1972	—	3.00	6.00

DUNHILL

Number	Title (A Side/B Side)	Yr	VG	VG+	NM
❑ 4018 [DJ]	Go Where You Wanna Go/Somebody Groovy	1966	5.00	10.00	20.00
—Withdrawn before stock copies were released					
❑ 4018 [PS]	Go Where You Wanna Go/Somebody Groovy	1966	100.00	200.00	400.00
—Yes, a picture sleeve has been confirmed!					
❑ 4020	California Dreamin'/Somebody Groovy	1966	2.50	5.00	10.00
—Most of the 1966 Dunhill singles credited "The Mama's and the Papa's"					
❑ 4020 [PS]	California Dreamin'/Somebody Groovy	1966	75.00	150.00	300.00
—Sleeve is promo only					
❑ 4026	Monday, Monday/Got a Feeling	1966	2.50	5.00	10.00
❑ 4031	I Saw Her Again/Even If I Could	1966	2.50	5.00	10.00
❑ 4050	Look Through My Window/Once Was a Time I Thought	1966	2.50	5.00	10.00
❑ 4057	Words of Love/Dancing in the Street	1966	2.50	5.00	10.00
❑ 4077	Dedicated to the One I Love/Free Advice	1967	2.50	5.00	10.00
❑ 4083	Creeque Alley/Did You Ever Want to Cry	1967	2.50	5.00	10.00
❑ 4083 [PS]	Creeque Alley/Did You Ever Want to Cry	1967	10.00	20.00	40.00
—Sleeve is promo only					
❑ 4099	Twelve Thirty (Young Girls Are Coming to the Canyon)/Straight Shooter	1967	2.50	5.00	10.00
❑ 4107	Glad to Be Unhappy/Hey Girl	1967	2.50	5.00	10.00
❑ 4113	Dancing Bear/John's Music Box	1967	2.50	5.00	10.00
❑ 4113 [PS]	Dancing Bear/John's Music Box	1967	3.00	6.00	12.00
❑ 4125	Safe in My Garden/Too Late	1968	6.25	12.50	25.00
—Without the "ABC" logo at top of label					

MANCHA, STEVE

GROOVESVILLE

Number	Title (A Side/B Side)	Yr	VG	VG+	NM
❑ 1001	You're Still in My Heart/She's So Good	1965	6.25	12.50	25.00
❑ 1002	I Don't Want to Lose You/Need to Be Needed	1966	5.00	10.00	20.00
❑ 1004	Friday Night/Monday Through Thursday	1966	25.00	50.00	100.00
❑ 1005	Don't Make Me a Storyteller/I Won't Love and Leave You	1967	5.00	10.00	20.00
❑ 1007	Just Keep On Loving Me/Sweet Baby Don't Ever Be Untrue	1967	6.25	12.50	25.00

WHEELSVILLE

Number	Title (A Side/B Side)	Yr	VG	VG+	NM
❑ 102	Did My Baby Call/Whirlpool	1965	37.50	75.00	150.00

MANCHESTERS, THE (2)

Featuring DAVID GATES.

VEE JAY

Number	Title (A Side/B Side)	Yr	VG	VG+	NM
❑ 700	I Don't Come from England/Dragonfly	1965	6.25	12.50	25.00

MANHATTANS, THE (1)

Well-known male R&B vocal group.

CARNIVAL

Number	Title (A Side/B Side)	Yr	VG	VG+	NM
❑ 504	I've Got Everything But You/For the Very First Time	1964	5.00	10.00	20.00
❑ 506	There Goes a Fool/Call Somebody Please	1964	10.00	20.00	40.00
❑ 507	I Wanna Be (Your Everything)/What's It Gonna Be	1965	3.75	7.50	15.00
❑ 509	Searchin' for My Baby/I'm the One That Love Forgot	1965	3.75	7.50	15.00
❑ 512	Follow Your Heart/The Boston Money	1965	3.75	7.50	15.00
❑ 514	Baby I Need You/Teach Me the Philly Dog	1966	3.75	7.50	15.00
❑ 517	Can I/That New Girl	1966	3.75	7.50	15.00
❑ 522	I Betcha (Couldn't Love Me)/Sweet Little Girl	1966	3.75	7.50	15.00
❑ 524	It's That Time of the Year/Alone on New Year's Eve	1966	5.00	10.00	20.00
❑ 526	All I Need Is Your Love/Our Love Will Never Die	1967	3.75	7.50	15.00
❑ 529	When We're Made As One/Baby I'm Sorry	1967	3.75	7.50	15.00
❑ 533	I Call It Love/Manhattan Stomp	1967	3.75	7.50	15.00
❑ 542	I Don't Wanna Go/Love Is Breaking Out	1968	3.75	7.50	15.00
❑ 545	Til You Come Back to Me/Call Somebody Please	1968	3.75	7.50	15.00

COLUMBIA

Number	Title (A Side/B Side)	Yr	VG	VG+	NM
❑ 02164	Shining Star/Summertime in the City	1981	—	—	3.00
—Reissue					
❑ 02191	Just One Moment Away/When I Leave Tomorrow	1981	—	2.00	4.00
❑ 02548	Let Your Love Come Down/I Gotta Thank You	1981	—	2.00	4.00
❑ 02666	Money, Money/I Wanta Thank You	1982	—	2.00	4.00
❑ 03939	Crazy/Gonna Find You	1983	—	2.00	4.00
❑ 04110	Forever By Your Side/Locked Up in Your Love	1983	—	2.00	4.00
❑ 04754	You Send Me/You're Gonna Love Being Loved By Me	1985	—	2.00	4.00
❑ 04754 [PS]	You Send Me/You're Gonna Love Being Loved By Me	1985	—	2.00	4.00
❑ 04930	Don't Say No/Dreamin'	1985	—	2.00	4.00
❑ 06376	Where Did We Go Wrong/Maybe Tomorrow	1986	—	2.00	4.00
—With Regina Belle					
❑ 07010	Mr. D.J./All I Need	1987	—	2.00	4.00
❑ 10045	Don't Take Your Love/The Day the Robins Sang to Me	1974	—	2.50	5.00
❑ 10140	Hurt/Nursery Rhymes	1975	—	2.50	5.00
❑ 10310	Kiss and Say Goodbye/Wonderful World of Love	1976	—	2.50	5.00
❑ 10430	I Kinda Miss You/Gypsy Man	1976	—	2.50	5.00
❑ 10495	It Feels So Good to Be Loved By You/On the Street (Where I Live)	1977	—	2.50	5.00
❑ 10586	We Never Danced to a Love Song/Let's Start It All Over Again	1977	—	2.50	5.00
❑ 10674	Am I Losing You/Movin'	1978	—	2.50	5.00
❑ 10766	Everybody Has a Dream/Happiness	1978	—	2.50	5.00
❑ 10921	Here Comes the Hurt Again/Don't Say Goodbye	1979	—	2.50	5.00
❑ 11024	The Way We Were-Memories/New York City	1979	—	2.50	5.00
❑ 11222	Shining Star/I'll Never Run Away from Love Again	1980	—	2.00	4.00
❑ 11321	Girl of My Dreams/The Closer You Are	1980	—	2.00	4.00
❑ 11398	I'll Never Find Another (Another Just Like You)/Rendezvous	1980	—	2.00	4.00
❑ 45838	There's No Me Without You/I'm Not a Run-Around	1973	—	3.00	6.00
❑ 45927	You'd Better Believe It/Soul Train	1973	—	3.00	6.00
❑ 45971	Wish That You Were Mine/It's So Hard Loving You	1973	—	3.00	6.00
❑ 46081	Summertime in the City/The Other Side of Me	1974	—	3.00	6.00
❑ 60511	Do You Really Mean Goodbye/Rendezvous	1981	—	2.00	4.00

DELUXE

Number	Title (A Side/B Side)	Yr	VG	VG+	NM
❑ 109	The Picture Became Quite Clear/Oh Lord, How I Wish I Could Sleep	1969	2.50	5.00	10.00
❑ 115	It's Gonna Take a Lot to Bring Me Back/Give Him Up	1970	2.50	5.00	10.00
❑ 122	If My Heart Could Speak/Loneliness	1970	2.50	5.00	10.00
❑ 129	From Atlanta to Goodbye/Fantastic Journey	1970	2.50	5.00	10.00
❑ 132	Let Them Talk/Straight to My Heart	1970	2.50	5.00	10.00
❑ 136	Do You Ever/I Can't Stand for You to Leave Me	1971	2.50	5.00	10.00
❑ 137	A Million to One/Cry If You Wanna Cry	1971	2.50	5.00	10.00
❑ 139	One Life to Live/It's the Only One	1972	2.50	5.00	10.00
❑ 144	Back Up/Fever	1972	2.50	5.00	10.00
❑ 146	Rainbow Week/Loneliness	1973	2.50	5.00	10.00
❑ 152	Do You Ever/If My Heart Could Speak	1973	2.50	5.00	10.00

STARFIRE

Number	Title (A Side/B Side)	Yr	VG	VG+	NM
❑ 121	Alone on New Year's Eve/It's That Time of the Year	1979	—	2.50	5.00

VALLEY VUE

Number	Title (A Side/B Side)	Yr	VG	VG+	NM
❑ 75723	Sweet Talk/(B-side unknown)	1989	—	3.00	6.00
❑ 75749	Why You Wanna Love Me Like That/(B-side unknown)	1989	—	3.00	6.00

MANHATTANS, THE (2)

COLPIX

Number	Title (A Side/B Side)	Yr	VG	VG+	NM
❑ 115	Big Wheel Express/Powder Blue	1959	7.50	15.00	30.00

MANHATTANS, THE (U)

Some of these are likely group (1); others could be group (2); others are probably neither.

AVANTI

Number	Title (A Side/B Side)	Yr	VG	VG+	NM
❑ 1401	What Should I Do/Later for You	1963	6.25	12.50	25.00

BIG MACK

Number	Title (A Side/B Side)	Yr	VG	VG+	NM
❑ 3911	Why Should I Cry/The Feeling Is Mutual	196?	50.00	100.00	200.00

CAPITOL

Number	Title (A Side/B Side)	Yr	VG	VG+	NM
❑ 4591	Molly Brown Medley/I Ain't Down Yet	1961	5.00	10.00	20.00
❑ 4730	La La La/Sing All the Day	1962	5.00	10.00	20.00

ENJOY

Number	Title (A Side/B Side)	Yr	VG	VG+	NM
❑ 2008	Come On Back/Long Time No See	1964	5.00	10.00	20.00
—As "Ronnie and the Manhattans"					

GOLDEN WORLD

Number	Title (A Side/B Side)	Yr	VG	VG+	NM
❑ 14	Just a Little Loving/Beautiful Brown Eyes	1964	7.50	15.00	30.00

KING

Number	Title (A Side/B Side)	Yr	VG	VG+	NM
❑ 5228	Ebb Tide (Part 1)/Ebb Tide (Part 2)	1959	3.75	7.50	15.00
❑ 5259	Sugar Tooth/Like Saying Something	1959	3.75	7.50	15.00

PINEY

Number	Title (A Side/B Side)	Yr	VG	VG+	NM
❑ 107	Live It Up/Go Baby Go	1962	15.00	30.00	60.00
❑ 108	Crazy Love/The Hawk and the Crow	1962	12.50	25.00	50.00

WARNER

Number	Title (A Side/B Side)	Yr	VG	VG+	NM
❑ 1015	How Do I Say I'm Sorry/Love Is Where You Find It	1958	30.00	60.00	120.00

MANILOW, BARRY

Also see FEATHERBED.

ARISTA

Number	Title (A Side/B Side)	Yr	VG	VG+	NM
❑ SP-11 [DJ]	It's Just Another New Year's Eve (same on both sides)	1977	2.00	4.00	8.00
❑ SP-11 [PS]	It's Just Another New Year's Eve (same on both sides)	1977	3.00	6.00	12.00
❑ SP-25 [DJ]	Ready to Take a Chance Again (same on both sides)	1978	2.00	4.00	8.00
❑ SP-25 [PS]	Ready to Take a Chance Again (same on both sides)	1978	3.00	6.00	12.00
❑ 0108	It's a Miracle/One of These Days	1975	—	2.00	4.00
❑ 0126	Could It Be Magic/I Am Your Child	1975	—	2.00	4.00
❑ 0157	I Write the Songs/A Nice Boy Like Me	1975	—	2.00	4.00
❑ 0172	Tryin' to Get the Feeling Again/Beautiful Music	1976	—	2.00	4.00
❑ 0206	This One's for You/Riders to the Stars	1976	—	2.00	4.00
❑ 0212	Weekend in New England/Say the Words	1976	—	2.00	4.00
❑ 0244	Looks Like We Made It/New York City Rhythm	1977	—	2.00	4.00
❑ 0273	Daybreak/Jump Shout Boogie	1977	—	2.00	4.00
❑ 0305	Can't Smile Without You/Sunrise	1978	—	2.00	4.00
❑ 0330	Even Now/I Was a Fool (To Let You Go)	1978	—	2.00	4.00
❑ 0330 [PS]	Even Now/I Was a Fool (To Let You Go)	1978	—	2.00	4.00
❑ 0339	Copacabana (Short Version)/Copacabana (Long Version)	1978	—	2.00	4.00
❑ 0357	Ready to Take a Chance Again/Sweet Life	1978	—	2.00	4.00
❑ 0382	Somewhere in the Night/Leavin' in the Morning	1978	—	2.00	4.00
❑ 0464	Ships/They Gave In to the Blues	1979	—	2.00	4.00
❑ 0481	When I Wanted You/Bobbie Lee (What's the Difference I Gotta Live)	1979	—	2.00	4.00
❑ 0501	I Don't Want to Walk Without You/One Voice	1980	—	2.00	4.00
❑ 0566	I Made It Through the Rain/Only in Chicago	1980	—	2.00	4.00
❑ 0596	Lonely Together/The Last Duet	1981	—	2.00	4.00
—B-side with Lily Tomlin					

Number	Title (A Side/B Side)	Yr	VG	VG+	NM
❑ 0633	The Old Songs/Don't Fall in Love with Me	1981	—	2.00	4.00
❑ 0658	Somewhere Down the Road/Let's Take All Night to Say Goodbye	1982	—	2.00	4.00
❑ 0675	Let's Hang On/No Other Love	1982	—	2.00	4.00
❑ 0698	Oh Julie/Break Down the Door	1982	—	2.00	4.00
❑ 1025	Memory/Heart of Steel	1982	—	2.00	4.00
❑ 1046	Some Kind of Friend/Heaven	1983	—	2.00	4.00
❑ 2094	Jingle Bells/Because It's Christmas (For All the Children)	1990	—	—	3.00
—A-side with Expose					
❑ 9003	Some Kind of Friend/Heaven	1983	—	—	3.00
❑ 9101	Read 'Em and Weep/One Voice	1983	—	—	3.00
❑ 9185	You're Lookin' Hot Tonight/Put a Quarter in the Jukebox	1984	—	—	3.00
—B-side with Ronnie Milsap					
❑ 9666	Hey Mambo/When October Goes	1988	—	—	3.00
—With Kid Creole and the Coconuts					
❑ 9666 [PS]	Hey Mambo/When October Goes	1988	—	—	3.00
❑ 9811	Please Don't Be Scared/A Little Traveling Music, Please	1989	—	—	3.00
❑ 9838	Keep Each Other Warm/A Little Traveling Music, Please	1989	—	2.50	5.00
❑ 9838 [PS]	Keep Each Other Warm/A Little Traveling Music, Please	1989	—	2.50	5.00
BELL					
❑ 45357	Sweetwater Jones/One of These Days	1973	—	3.00	6.00
❑ 45422	Cloudburst/Could It Be Magic	1973	—	3.00	6.00
❑ 45443	Let's Take Some Time to Say Goodbye/Seven More Years	1974	—	3.00	6.00
❑ 45613	Mandy/Something's Comin' Up	1974	—	2.50	5.00
RCA					
❑ PB-14223	In Search of Love/At the Dance	1985	—	—	3.00
❑ PB-14223 [PS]	In Search of Love/At the Dance	1985	—	2.00	4.00
❑ PB-14302	He Doesn't Care (But I Do)/It's All Behind Us Now	1986	—	—	3.00
❑ PB-14302 [PS]	He Doesn't Care (But I Do)/It's All Behind Us Now	1986	—	2.00	4.00
❑ PB-14397	I'm Your Man/I'm Your Man (Dub)	1986	—	—	3.00
❑ PB-14397 [PS]	I'm Your Man/I'm Your Man (Dub)	1986	—	—	3.00
SBK					
❑ S7-17906	Let Me Be Your Wings/Follow Your Heart	1994	—	2.00	4.00
—A-side with Debra Byrd; B-side by Gino Conforti					

MANN, BARRY

Number	Title (A Side/B Side)	Yr	VG	VG+	NM
ABC-PARAMOUNT					
❑ 10143	War Paint/Counting Teardrops	1960	5.00	10.00	20.00
❑ 10180	Happy Birthday, Broken Heart/Millionaire	1961	5.00	10.00	20.00
❑ 10237	Who Put the Bomp (In the Bomp, Bomp, Bomp)/Love, True Love	1961	6.25	12.50	25.00
❑ 10263	Little Miss U.S.A./Find Another Fool	1961	5.00	10.00	20.00
❑ 10356	Hey Baby I'm Dancin'/Like I Don't Love You	1962	5.00	10.00	20.00
❑ 10380	Teenage Has-Been/Bless You	1962	5.00	10.00	20.00
ARISTA					
❑ 0194	The Princess and the Punk/Jennifer	1976	—	2.00	4.00
CAPITOL					
❑ 2082	Young Electric Psychedelic Hippy Flippy Folk & Funky Philosophic Turned On Groovy Twelve-String Band/Take Your Love	1968	3.75	7.50	15.00
❑ 2217	I Just Can't Help Believin'/Where Do I Go from Here	1968	2.50	5.00	10.00
❑ 5695	Looking at Tomorrow/Angelica	1966	2.50	5.00	10.00
❑ 5894	Where Do I Go from Here/She Is Today	1967	2.50	5.00	10.00
CASABLANCA					
❑ 2287	Brown-Eyed Woman/In My Own Way	1980	—	2.00	4.00
COLPIX					
❑ 691	Graduation Time/Johnny Surfboard	1963	5.00	10.00	20.00
JDS					
❑ 5002	I Love to Last a Lifetime/All the Things You Are	1959	7.50	15.00	30.00
NEW DESIGN					
❑ 1000	Carry Me Home/Sundown	1971	—	2.50	5.00
❑ 1005	When You Get Right Down to It/Don't Give Up on Me	1972	—	2.50	5.00
❑ 1006	Too Many Mornings/On Broadway	1972	—	2.50	5.00
❑ 1006	Too Many Mornings/Lay It All Out	1972	—	2.50	5.00
RCA VICTOR					
❑ PB-10104	Nobody But You/Woman, Woman, Woman	1974	—	2.50	5.00
❑ PB-10230	Nothing Good Comes Easy/Woman, Woman, Woman	1975	—	2.50	5.00
❑ PB-10319	Don't Seem Right/I'm a Survivor	1975	—	2.50	5.00
RED BIRD					
❑ 10-015	Talk to Me Baby/Amy	1964	3.75	7.50	15.00
SCEPTER					
❑ 12281	Feelings/Let Me Stay with You	1970	—	3.00	6.00
UNITED ARTISTS					
❑ XW1021	Best That I Know How/Lettin' Good Times Get Away	1977	—	2.00	4.00
WARNER BROS.					
❑ 8752	For No Reason at All/Almost Gone	1979	—	2.00	4.00
❑ 8752 [PS]	For No Reason at All/Almost Gone	1979	—	2.50	5.00

MANN, BOBBY

See BOBBY BLOOM.

MANN, CARL

Number	Title (A Side/B Side)	Yr	VG	VG+	NM
ABC					
❑ 12035	Burnin' Holes in the Eyes of Abraham Lincoln/Ballad of Johnny Clyde	1974	—	2.50	5.00
❑ 12071	Neon Lights/Just About Out	1975	—	2.50	5.00
❑ 12092	It's Not the Coffee/Cheatin' Time	1975	—	2.50	5.00
ABC/DOT					
❑ 17596	Back Loving/Annie Over Time	1975	—	2.50	5.00
❑ 17621	Twilight Time/Belly-Rubbin' Country Soul	1976	—	2.50	5.00
JAXON					
❑ 502	Gonna Rock and Roll Tonight/Rockin' Love	1957	750.00	1500.	3000.
MONUMENT					
❑ 974	Down to My Last I Forgive You/Serenade of the Bells	1966	3.75	7.50	15.00
PHILLIPS INT'L.					
❑ 3539	Mona Lisa/Foolish One	1959	6.25	12.50	25.00
❑ 3546	Pretend/Rockin' Love	1959	6.25	12.50	25.00
❑ 3550	Some Enchanted Evening/I Can't Forget	1960	6.25	12.50	25.00
❑ 3555	South of the Border/I'm Comin' Home	1960	6.25	12.50	25.00
❑ 3564	The Wayward Wind/Born to Be Bad	1961	6.25	12.50	25.00
❑ 3569	I Ain't Got No Home/If I Could Change You	1961	6.25	12.50	25.00
❑ 3579	When I Grow Too Old to Dream/Mountain Dew	1962	6.25	12.50	25.00

MANN, MANFRED

Also see MIKE D'ABO; PAUL JONES; MANFRED MANN'S EARTH BAND.

Number	Title (A Side/B Side)	Yr	VG	VG+	NM
ASCOT					
❑ 2151	Hubble Bubble (Toil and Trouble)/I'm Your Kingpin	1964	50.00	100.00	200.00
❑ 2157	Do Wah Diddy Diddy/What You Gonna Do?	1964	3.75	7.50	15.00
❑ 2165	Sha La La/John Hardy	1964	2.50	5.00	10.00
❑ 2165 [PS]	Sha La La/John Hardy	1964	6.25	12.50	25.00
❑ 2170	Come Tomorrow/What Did I Do Wrong	1965	2.50	5.00	10.00
❑ 2170 [PS]	Come Tomorrow/What Did I Do Wrong	1965	6.25	12.50	25.00
❑ 2181	Poison Ivy/I Can't Believe What You Say	1965	—	—	—
—Unreleased?					
❑ 2184	My Little Red Book/What Am I Doing Wrong	1965	2.50	5.00	10.00
❑ 2194	If You Gotta Go, Go Now/The One in the Middle	1965	2.50	5.00	10.00
❑ 2210	She Needs Company/Hi Lili, Hi Lo	1966	2.50	5.00	10.00
❑ 2241	My Little Red Book/I Can't Believe What You Say	1967	2.50	5.00	10.00
MERCURY					
❑ 72607	Just Like a Woman/I Wanna Be Rich	1966	2.50	5.00	10.00
❑ 72607 [PS]	Just Like a Woman/I Wanna Be Rich	1966	6.25	12.50	25.00
❑ 72629	Semi-Detached Suburban Mr. Jones/Each and Every Day	1966	2.50	5.00	10.00
❑ 72675	Ha, Ha, Said the Clown/Feeling So Good	1967	2.50	5.00	10.00
❑ 72770	The Mighty Quinn (Quinn the Eskimo)/By Request — Edwin Garvey	1968	2.50	5.00	10.00
—Orange and red swirl label					
❑ 72770	The Mighty Quinn (Quinn the Eskimo)/By Request — Edwin Garvey	1968	3.00	6.00	12.00
—Red label with "Mercury" in all capital letters					
❑ 72770	The Mighty Quinn (Quinn the Eskimo)/By Request — Edwin Garvey	1968	2.00	4.00	8.00
—Red label with white "Mercury" in a circle					
❑ 72770	Quinn the Eskimo/By Request — Edwin Garvey	1968	3.00	6.00	12.00
—Orange and red swirl label					
❑ 72770	Quinn the Eskimo/By Request — Edwin Garvey	1968	2.50	5.00	10.00
—Red label with white "Mercury" in a circle					
❑ 72822	My Name Is Jack/There Is a Man	1968	2.00	4.00	8.00
❑ 72822 [PS]	My Name Is Jack/There Is a Man	1968	3.75	7.50	15.00
❑ 72879	Fox on the Run/Too Many People	1968	2.00	4.00	8.00
❑ 72921	Ragamuffin Man/A B Side	1969	2.00	4.00	8.00
POLYDOR					
❑ 14026	Sometimes/Snakeskin Garter	1970	—	3.00	6.00
❑ 14074	California Coastline/Part Time	1971	—	—	—
—Unreleased					
❑ 14097	Please Mrs. Henry/Prayers	1971	—	2.50	5.00
PRESTIGE					
❑ 312	5-4-3-2-1/Without You	1964	10.00	20.00	40.00
❑ 314	Blue Brave/Brother Jack	1964	25.00	50.00	100.00
UNITED ARTISTS					
❑ 0048	Do Wah Diddy Diddy/Sha La La	1973	—	2.50	5.00
—"Silver Spotlight Series" reissue					
❑ 0049	Pretty Flamingo/Come Tomorrow	1973	—	2.50	5.00
—"Silver Spotlight Series" reissue					
❑ 50040	Pretty Flamingo/You're Standing By	1966	2.50	5.00	10.00
❑ 50066	When Will I Be Loved/Do You Have to Do That	1966	2.50	5.00	10.00

MANN, MANFRED'S, EARTH BAND

Also see MANFRED MANN; CHRIS THOMPSON.

Number	Title (A Side/B Side)	Yr	VG	VG+	NM
ARISTA					
❑ 9143	Runner/Where Do They Send Them	1984	—	2.00	4.00
—First pressing has whitish label					
❑ 9143	Runner/Where Do They Send Them	1984	—	—	3.00
—Second pressing has black label					
❑ 9203	Rebel/Figures on a Rock	1984	—	—	3.00
POLYDOR					
❑ 14113	Living Without You/Tribute	1972	—	2.50	5.00
❑ 14130	I'm Up and Leaving/Part Time Man	1972	—	2.50	5.00
❑ 14130 [PS]	I'm Up and Leaving/Part Time Man	1972	2.50	5.00	10.00
❑ 14160	It's All Over Now, Baby Blue/Ashes	1973	—	2.50	5.00
❑ 14173	Mardi Gras Day/Sad Joy	1973	—	2.50	5.00
❑ 14191	Get Your Rocks Off/Wind	1973	—	2.50	5.00
❑ 14205	Joybringer/Cloudy Eyes	1973	—	2.50	5.00
❑ 14225	Father of Night/Solar Fire Two	1974	—	2.50	5.00
WARNER BROS.					
❑ 8152	Spirit in the Night/As Above So Below	1975	—	—	—
—Unreleased?					
❑ 8176	Spirit in the Night/As Above So Below	1976	—	3.00	6.00
❑ 8176 [DJ]	Spirit in the Night (Long)/Spirit in the Night (Short)	1976	—	3.00	6.00
❑ 8252	Blinded by the Light/Starbird No. 2	1976	—	2.50	5.00
❑ 8252 [PS]	Blinded by the Light/Starbird No. 2	1976	2.00	4.00	8.00
❑ 8355	Spirit in the Night/Questions	1977	—	2.50	5.00
—This has newly-recorded vocal tracks by Chris Thompson					
❑ 8574	California/Bouillabaise	1978	—	2.50	5.00
❑ 8620	Davy's on the Road Again/Bouillabaise	1978	—	2.50	5.00
❑ 8850	You Angel You/"Belle" of the Earth	1979	—	2.00	4.00
❑ 49678	For You/Fool I Am	1981	—	2.50	5.00
❑ 49762	Adolescent Dream/Lies (Through the 80's)	1981	—	2.00	4.00

MANN, REV. COLUMBUS

Number	Title (A Side/B Side)	Yr	VG	VG+	NM
CYE					
❑ 1001	Soon Very Soon (He's Coming Back)/(B-side unknown)	196?	10.00	20.00	40.00
TAMLA					
❑ 54047	Jesus Loves/They Shall Be Mine	1961	12.50	25.00	50.00

MANZAREK, RAY

Also see THE DOORS; RICK AND THE RAVENS.

Number	Title (A Side/B Side)	Yr	VG	VG+	NM
MERCURY					
❑ 73477	Solar Boat/Moorish Idol	1974	—	2.50	5.00
❑ 73601	Downbound Train/Choose Up and Choose Off	1974	—	2.50	5.00
❑ 73644	The Whole Thing Started with Rock and Roll (And Now It's Out of Control)/Art Deco Fandango	1974	—	2.50	5.00

MAR-KEYS

Number	Title (A Side/B Side)	Yr	VG	VG+	NM
SATELLITE					
❑ 107	Last Night/Night Before	1960	7.50	15.00	30.00
STAX					
❑ 112	Morning After/Diana	1961	3.00	6.00	12.00
❑ 114	About Noon/Sack-O-Woe	1961	3.00	6.00	12.00
❑ 115	Foxy/One Degree North	1961	3.00	6.00	12.00
❑ 121	Pop-Eye Stroll/Po-Dunk	1962	3.00	6.00	12.00
❑ 124	What's Happening/You Got It	1962	3.00	6.00	12.00
❑ 129	Sailor Man Waltz/Sack-O-Woe	1963	3.00	6.00	12.00
❑ 133	The Dribble/Bo Time	1963	3.00	6.00	12.00
❑ 156	Beach Bash/Bush Bash	1964	2.50	5.00	10.00
❑ 166	The Shovel/Banana Juice	1965	2.50	5.00	10.00
❑ 181	Grab This Thing (Part 1)/Grab This Thing (Part 2)	1965	2.50	5.00	10.00
❑ 185	Philly Dog/Honey Pot	1966	2.50	5.00	10.00

MAR-VELS, THE

Number	Title (A Side/B Side)	Yr	VG	VG+	NM
ANGIE					
❑ 1005	Go On and Have Yourself a Ball/How Do I Keep the Girls Away	1963	5.00	10.00	20.00
BUTANE					
❑ 778	Go On and Have Yourself a Ball/How Do I Keep the Girls Away	1963	3.75	7.50	15.00
IN					
❑ 102	Surfing at Makeha/Endless Nights	1964	12.50	25.00	50.00
LOVE					
❑ 5011/2	Cherry Lips/Could Be You	1958	7.50	15.00	30.00
TAMMY					
❑ 1016	Somewhere in Life/Voo Doo Hurt	1961	75.00	150.00	300.00
❑ 1019	My Guardian Angel/Marble Stomp	1961	75.00	150.00	300.00

MARAINEY, BIG MEMPHIS

Number	Title (A Side/B Side)	Yr	VG	VG+	NM
SUN					
❑ 184	Call Me Anything, But Call Me/Baby No, No	1953	2000.	3000.	4000.

MARATHONS, THE (1)

Two different groups posing as one. After the success of "Peanut Butter" on Arvee, the label hired another group to be The Marathons after losing a legal battle to keep the "real" group, which was really THE VIBRATIONS in disguise. And the Vibrations had formerly been THE JAYHAWKS. Confused yet?

Number	Title (A Side/B Side)	Yr	VG	VG+	NM
ARGO					
❑ 5389	Peanut Butter/Down in New Orleans	1961	3.75	7.50	15.00
—As "Vibrations Named By Others As MARATHONS"					
ARVEE					
❑ 5027	Peanut Butter/Talkin' Trash	1961	5.00	10.00	20.00
❑ 5038	Tight Sweater/C. Percy Mercy of Scotland	1961	3.00	6.00	12.00
❑ 5048	Chicken Spaceman/You Bug Me Baby	1962	3.00	6.00	12.00
CHESS					
❑ 1790	Peanut Butter/Down in New Orleans	1961	4.00	8.00	16.00
PLAZA					
❑ 507	Mashed Potatoes One More Time/Little Pancho	1962	3.00	6.00	12.00

MARATHONS, THE (2)

Completely unrelated to groups (1).

Number	Title (A Side/B Side)	Yr	VG	VG+	NM
SABRINA					
❑ 334	Don't Know Why/The Stranger	1959	30.00	60.00	120.00

MARAUDERS, THE

More than one group.

Number	Title (A Side/B Side)	Yr	VG	VG+	NM
ALMO					
❑ 221	Like You/Slippin' and Slidin'	1965	3.75	7.50	15.00
HAWK					
❑ 4002	Sand Flea/Stomp Watch	1962	12.50	25.00	50.00
LAURIE					
❑ 3356	Out of Sight, Out of Mind/Jug Band Music	1966	5.00	10.00	20.00
LEE					
❑ 9449	Nightmare/Lovin'	1965	7.50	15.00	30.00
SKYVIEW					
❑ 001	Since I Met You/I Don't Know How	1966	5.00	10.00	20.00
❑ 001 [PS]	Since I Met You/I Don't Know How	1966	12.50	25.00	50.00

MARBLE PHROGG, THE

Number	Title (A Side/B Side)	Yr	VG	VG+	NM
DERRICK					
❑ 8568	Fire/(B-side unknown)	1968	20.00	40.00	80.00

MARCELS, THE

Number	Title (A Side/B Side)	Yr	VG	VG+	NM
888					
❑ 101	How Deep Is the Ocean/Lonely Boy	1964	3.75	7.50	15.00
ALL EARS					
❑ 810085	Blue Moon/Clap Your Hands (When I Clap My Hands)	1981	—	3.00	6.00
BARON					
❑ 109	Betty Lou/Take Me Back	197?	2.00	4.00	8.00
CHARTBOUND					
❑ 009	Letter Full of Tears/Tell Me	197?	2.00	4.00	8.00
COLPIX					
❑ 186	Blue Moon/Goodybe to Love	1961	7.50	15.00	30.00
❑ 186 [PS]	Blue Moon/Goodybe to Love	1961	15.00	30.00	60.00
❑ 196	Summertime/Teeter-Totter Love	1961	6.25	12.50	25.00
❑ 606	You Are My Sunshine/Find Another Fool	1961	6.25	12.50	25.00
❑ 612	Heartaches/My Love for You	1961	6.25	12.50	25.00
❑ 612 [PS]	Heartaches/My Love for You	1961	25.00	50.00	100.00
❑ 617	Merry Twist-Mas/Don't Cry for Me This Christmas	1961	6.25	12.50	25.00
❑ 617 [PS]	Merry Twist-Mas/Don't Cry for Me This Christmas	1961	30.00	60.00	120.00
❑ 624	My Melancholy Baby/Really Need Your Love	1962	5.00	10.00	20.00
❑ 629	Footprints in the Sand/Twistin' Fever	1962	12.50	25.00	50.00
❑ 640	Flowerpot/Hold On	1962	7.50	15.00	30.00
❑ 651	Loved Her the Whole Week Through/Friendly Loans	1962	6.25	12.50	25.00
❑ 665	Alright, Okay, You Win/Lollipop Baby	1962	6.25	12.50	25.00
❑ 683	That Old Black Magic/Don't Turn Your Back on Me	1963	6.25	12.50	25.00
❑ 687	Give Me Back Your Love/I Wanna Be the Leader	1963	7.50	15.00	30.00
❑ 694	One Last Kiss/Teeter-Totter Love	1963	25.00	50.00	100.00
❑ 694	One Last Kiss/You Got to Be Sincere	1963	50.00	100.00	200.00
KYRA					
❑ 100	Comes Love/Your Red Wagon	1964	25.00	50.00	100.00
—Red vinyl					
❑ 100	Comes Love/Your Red Wagon	1964	12.50	25.00	50.00
MONOGRAM					
❑ 112	I'll Be Forever Loving You/A Fallen Tear	1974	3.00	6.00	12.00
❑ 113	Sweet Was the Wine/Over the Rainbow	1974	3.00	6.00	12.00
❑ 115	Two People in the World/Most of All	1974	3.00	6.00	12.00
OWL					
❑ 324	(You Gave Me) Peace of Mind/Crazy Bells	197?	2.00	4.00	8.00
QUEEN BEE					
❑ 47001	In the Still of the Night/High on a Hill	1973	3.75	7.50	15.00
ROCKY					
❑ 13711	(You Gave Me) Peace of Mind/That Lucky Old Sun	1975	2.00	4.00	8.00
—As "The Fabulous Marcels"					
ST. CLAIR					
❑ 13711	(You Gave Me) Peace of Mind/That Lucky Old Sun	1975	2.50	5.00	10.00
—As "The Fabulous Marcels"					

MARCH, LITTLE PEGGY

Number	Title (A Side/B Side)	Yr	VG	VG+	NM
OLDE WORLD					
❑ 1105	Average People/Isn't This the Way We Are	1975	2.00	4.00	8.00
RCA VICTOR					
❑ 47-8107	Little Me/Pagan Love Song	1962	3.75	7.50	15.00
❑ 47-8139	I Will Follow Him/Wind-Up Doll	1963	5.00	10.00	20.00
❑ 47-8189	I Wish I Were a Princess/My Teenage Castle	1963	3.75	7.50	15.00
❑ 47-8189 [PS]	I Wish I Were a Princess/My Teenage Castle	1963	7.50	15.00	30.00
❑ 47-8221	Hello Heartache, Goodbye Love/Boy Crazy	1963	3.75	7.50	15.00
❑ 47-8221 [PS]	Hello Heartache, Goodbye Love/Boy Crazy	1963	7.50	15.00	30.00
❑ 47-8267	The Impossible Happened/Waterfall	1963	3.00	6.00	12.00
❑ 47-8291	My Heart Keeps Telling Me/His	1963	—	—	—
—Unreleased					
❑ 47-8302	(I'm Watching) Every Little Move You Make/After You	1963	3.00	6.00	12.00
❑ 47-8357	Takin' the Long Way Home/Leave Me Alone	1964	2.50	5.00	10.00
—All records from 1964 on are as "Peggy March"					
❑ 47-8418	Oh My, What a Guy/Only You Could Do That to My Heart	1964	2.50	5.00	10.00
❑ 47-8460	Watch What You Do With My Baby/Can't Stop Thinking About Him	1964	2.50	5.00	10.00
❑ 47-8534	Why Can't He Be You/Losin' My Touch	1965	2.50	5.00	10.00
❑ 47-8605	Let Her Go/Your Girl	1965	2.50	5.00	10.00
❑ 47-8710	He Couldn't Care Less/Heaven for Lovers	1965	2.50	5.00	10.00
❑ 47-8840	Ein Boy Wie Du (A Boy Like You)/Sechs Tage Lang (Six Long Days)	1966	5.00	10.00	20.00
❑ 47-8877	Play a Simple Melody/Old Fashioned Wedding	1966	2.50	5.00	10.00
—With Gary Marshall					
❑ 47-8903	He's Back Again/Running Scared	1966	2.50	5.00	10.00
❑ 47-9033	Fool, Fool, Fool (Look in the Mirror)/Try to See It My Way	1966	2.50	5.00	10.00
❑ 47-9143	January First/How Can I Tell Him	1967	2.50	5.00	10.00
❑ 47-9223	Mama Dear, Papa Dear/Your Good Girl's Gonna Go Bad	1967	2.50	5.00	10.00
❑ 47-9283	This Heart Wasn't Made to Kick Around/Foolin' Around	1967	2.50	5.00	10.00
❑ 47-9359	Have a Good Time/Let Me Down Hard	1967	2.50	5.00	10.00
❑ 47-9494	If You Would Love Me/Thinking Through My Tears	1968	2.50	5.00	10.00
❑ 47-9566	Roses on the Sea/Time and Time Again	1968	2.50	5.00	10.00
❑ 47-9627	I've Been Here Before/Aren't You Glad	1968	2.50	5.00	10.00
❑ 47-9718	Purple Hat/Try to See It My Way	1969	2.50	5.00	10.00
❑ 74-0136	Boom Bang-a Bang/Lilac Skies	1969	2.50	5.00	10.00

MARCHAN, BOBBY

Number	Title (A Side/B Side)	Yr	VG	VG+	NM
ACE					
❑ 523	Chickee Wah-Wah/Don't Take Your Love from Me	1956	10.00	20.00	40.00
❑ 532	I'll Never Let You Go/I Can't Stop Loving You	1957	7.50	15.00	30.00
❑ 557	Rockin' Behind the Iron Curtain/You Can't Stop Her	1959	7.50	15.00	30.00
❑ 3004	Push the Button/My Day Is Coming	1974	—	2.50	5.00
❑ 3008	God Bless Our Love/My Day Is Coming	1975	—	2.50	5.00
❑ 3016	Baby Get Your Yo-Yo/What Can I Do	1975	—	2.50	5.00
ALADDIN					
❑ 3189	Just a Little Walk/Have Mercy	1953	15.00	30.00	60.00
BOBBY ROBINSON					
❑ (# unknown)	There's Something on Your Mind/(B-side unknown)	1973	—	3.00	6.00

Number	Title (A Side/B Side)	Yr	VG	VG+	NM
CAMEO					
❑ 405	There's Something About My Baby/Everything a Poor Fool Needs	1966	2.50	5.00	10.00
❑ 429	Shake Your Tambourine/Just Be Yourself	1966	2.50	5.00	10.00
❑ 453	Meet Me in Church/Hooked	1967	2.00	4.00	8.00
❑ 469	You Better Hold On/Help Yourself	1967	2.00	4.00	8.00
❑ 489	Rockin' Pneumonia/Someone to Take Your Place	1967	2.00	4.00	8.00
DIAL					
❑ 1152	Bump Your Bootie/Ain't Nothing Wrong with Whitey	1975	—	2.50	5.00
❑ 3022	I Gotta Sit Down and Cry/I Got a Thing Going	1964	2.50	5.00	10.00
❑ 4002	Get Down to It/Half a Mind	1964	2.50	5.00	10.00
❑ 4007	Hello Happiness/Funny Style	1965	2.50	5.00	10.00
❑ 4020	I Feel It Coming/Gimme Your Love	1965	2.50	5.00	10.00
❑ 4065	I Just Want What Belongs to Me/Sad Sack	1967	2.00	4.00	8.00
FIRE					
❑ 510	Yes It's Written All Over Your Face/Look at My Heart	1962	3.75	7.50	15.00
❑ 1014	Snoopin' and Accusin'/This Is the Life	1959	3.75	7.50	15.00
❑ 1022	There's Something On Your Mind (Part 1)/There's Something On Your Mind (Part 2)	1960	6.25	12.50	25.00
❑ 1027	Booty Green/It Hurts Me to My Heart	1960	3.75	7.50	15.00
❑ 1028	You're Still My Baby (Part 1)/You're Still My Baby (Part 2)	1960	3.75	7.50	15.00
❑ 1035	All in My Mind/I Miss You So	1961	3.75	7.50	15.00
❑ 1037	What You Don't Know Don't Hurt You/I Need Someone (I Need You)	1961	3.75	7.50	15.00
GALE					
❑ 4M-101	Chickee Wah Wah/Give a Helping Hand	1957	6.25	12.50	25.00
GAMBLE					
❑ 216	(Ain't No Reason) For Girls to Be Lonely Part 1/Part 2	1968	2.00	4.00	8.00
MERCURY					
❑ 73908	I Wanna Bump with the Big Fat Woman/Disco Rabbit	1977	—	2.50	5.00
VOLT					
❑ 108	What Can I Do (Part 1)/What Can I Do (Part 2)	1963	3.00	6.00	12.00

MARCY PLAYGROUND

Number	Title (A Side/B Side)	Yr	VG	VG+	NM
CAPITOL					
❑ S7-19864	Sex and Candy/Ancient Walls of Flowers	1998	—	2.00	4.00
❑ S7-19972	Sherry Fraser/Saint Joe on the School Bus	1998	—	2.00	4.00
❑ 58797	It's Saturday/Pigeon Farm	1999	—	—	3.00
❑ 58821	Keegan's Christmas/Last Christmas	1999	—	—	3.00
—B-side by Dexter Freebish					

MARENO, LEE

Number	Title (A Side/B Side)	Yr	VG	VG+	NM
NEW ART					
❑ 103	Goddess of Love/He's Gone	1961	30.00	60.00	120.00
SCEPTER					
❑ 1222	Goddess of Love/He's Gone	1961	7.50	15.00	30.00
❑ 12222	Goddess of Love/Lonely Summer	1968	3.00	6.00	12.00
—As "Lee"					

MARESCA, ERNIE

Number	Title (A Side/B Side)	Yr	VG	VG+	NM
LAURIE					
❑ 3345	The Good Life/A Bum Can't Cry	1966	2.50	5.00	10.00
❑ 3371	My Son/My Shadow and Me	1967	2.50	5.00	10.00
❑ 3447	What Is a Marine/The Night My Papa Died	1968	2.00	4.00	8.00
❑ 3496	Blind Date/People Get Jealous	1969	2.00	4.00	8.00
❑ 3519	The Spirit of Woodstock/Web of Love	1969	2.00	4.00	8.00
❑ 3671	The Night My Poppa Died/Please Don't Play Me a Seven	1978	—	3.00	6.00
❑ 3698	You're the Only Girl for Me/Medley	1980	—	3.00	6.00
—B-side by the Belmonts					
PROVIDENCE					
❑ 417	Rockin' Blvd. St./Am I Better Off Than Them	1965	12.50	25.00	50.00
RUST					
❑ 5076	The Beetle Dance/Theme from Lilly, Lilly	1964	3.75	7.50	15.00
SEVILLE					
❑ 107	Lonesome Blues/I Don't Know Why	1960	3.75	7.50	15.00
❑ 117	Shout! Shout! (Knock Yourself Out)/Crying Like a Baby	1962	6.25	12.50	25.00
❑ 119	Down on the Beach/Mary Jane	1962	3.75	7.50	15.00
❑ 119 [PS]	Down on the Beach/Mary Jane	1962	5.00	10.00	20.00
❑ 122	Something to Shout About/How Many Times	1962	3.75	7.50	15.00
❑ 125	Love Express/Lorelei	1963	12.50	25.00	50.00
❑ 129	The Rovin' Kind/Please Be Fair	1963	3.75	7.50	15.00
❑ 138	I Can't Dance/It's Their World	1965	3.75	7.50	15.00

MARGO AND THE MARVETTES

Number	Title (A Side/B Side)	Yr	VG	VG+	NM
AMERICAN ARTS					
❑ 8	Cherry Pie/Say You Will	1965	3.75	7.50	15.00

MARGO, MARGO, MEDRESS AND SIEGEL

See THE TOKENS.

MARIE AND THE DECCORS

Number	Title (A Side/B Side)	Yr	VG	VG+	NM
CUB					
❑ 9115	I'm the One/Queen of Fools	1962	6.25	12.50	25.00

MARILLION

Number	Title (A Side/B Side)	Yr	VG	VG+	NM
CAPITOL					
❑ B-5493	Kayleigh/Heart of Lothian	1985	—	2.00	4.00
❑ B-5493 [PS]	Kayleigh/Heart of Lothian	1985	—	2.50	5.00
❑ B-5539	Lavender/Freak	1985	—	2.00	4.00
❑ B-5561	Lady Nina/Heart of Lothian	1986	—	2.00	4.00
❑ B-5561 [PS]	Lady Nina/Heart of Lothian	1986	—	3.00	6.00
❑ B-44043	Incommunicado/Going Under	1987	—	2.00	4.00
❑ B-44060	Sugar Mice/Tux On	1987	—	2.00	4.00
❑ 7PRO-79890/911 [DJ]	Hooks in You (7" Mix)/Hooks in You (Meaty Mix)	1989	5.00	10.00	20.00
—Vinyl is promo only					

MARIONETTES, THE

Number	Title (A Side/B Side)	Yr	VG	VG+	NM
LONDON					
❑ 9738	Whirlpool of Love/Nobody But You	1965	3.00	6.00	12.00

MARKETTS, THE

Number	Title (A Side/B Side)	Yr	VG	VG+	NM
ARVEE					
❑ 5063	Beach Bum/Sweet Potatoes	1962	5.00	10.00	20.00
CALLIOPE					
❑ 8003	Mary Hartman, Mary Hartman/(B-side unknown)	1977	—	2.50	5.00
—As "The New Marketts"					
❑ 8009	City Nights/Soul Coaxing	1977	—	2.50	5.00
—As "The New Marketts"					
FARR					
❑ 007	Song from M.A.S.H./Song from M.A.S.H. (Disco Version)	1976	—	2.50	5.00
—As "The New Marketts"					
❑ 019	The Hustle/Song from M.A.S.H.	1977	—	2.50	5.00
—As "The New Marketts"					
❑ 021	Looking for Mr. Goodbar (Terry's Theme)/Black	1977	—	2.50	5.00
—As "Danny Welton and the New Marketts"					
LIBERTY					
❑ 55401	Surfer's Stomp/Start	1962	5.00	10.00	20.00
—As "The Mar-Kets"					
❑ 55443	Balboa Blue/Stompede	1962	5.00	10.00	20.00
—As "The Mar-Kets"					
❑ 55506	Stomping Room Only/Canadian Sunset	1962	5.00	10.00	20.00
—As "The Mar-Kets"					
MERCURY					
❑ 73433	Mystery Movie Theme/Sister Candy	1973	2.00	4.00	8.00
SEMINOLE					
❑ 501	Song from M.A.S.H./Song from M.A.S.H. (Disco Version)	1976	2.00	4.00	8.00
—As "The New Marketts"					
UNI					
❑ 55173	The Undefeated/They Call the Wind Maria	1969	2.00	4.00	8.00
UNION					
❑ 501	Surfer's Stomp/Start	1961	7.50	15.00	30.00
❑ 504	Balboa Blue/Stompede	1962	7.50	15.00	30.00
❑ 507	Stomping Room Only/Canadian Sunset	1962	7.50	15.00	30.00
UNITED ARTISTS					
❑ 0043	Surfer's Stomp/Balboa Blue	1973	—	2.50	5.00
—"Silver Spotlight Series" reissue					
WARNER BROS.					
❑ 5365	Woody Wagon/Cobra	1963	3.75	7.50	15.00
❑ 5391	Outer Limits/Bella Dalena	1963	7.50	15.00	30.00
—Original title of A-side					
❑ 5391	Out of Limits/Bella Dalena	1963	5.00	10.00	20.00
❑ 5423	Vanishing Point/Borealis	1964	3.00	6.00	12.00
❑ 5468	Come See, Come Ska/Look for a Star	1964	3.00	6.00	12.00
❑ 5641	Miami's Blue/Napoleon's Solo	1965	2.50	5.00	10.00
❑ 5670	Ready Steady Go/Lady in the Cage	1965	2.50	5.00	10.00
❑ 5696	Batman Theme/Richie's Theme	1966	3.00	6.00	12.00
❑ 5814	Theme from "The Avengers"/A Touch of Velvet, a Sting of Brass	1966	5.00	10.00	20.00
❑ 5847	Tarzan/Stirrin' Up Some Soul	1966	2.50	5.00	10.00
❑ 7116	Out of Limits/Batman Theme	1968	—	3.00	6.00
—"Back to Back Hits" series -- originals have green labels with "W7" logo					
WORLD PACIFIC					
❑ 77874	Sunshine Girl/Sun Power	1967	2.50	5.00	10.00
❑ 77899	California Summer (People Moving West)/Groovin' Time	1968	2.50	5.00	10.00

MARKEYS, THE

No relation to THE MAR-KEYS.

Number	Title (A Side/B Side)	Yr	VG	VG+	NM
20TH CENTURY					
❑ 1210	Eternal Love/You've Got Me on a String	1956	12.50	25.00	50.00
GONE					
❑ 5028	Special Delivery/Along Came Love	1958	7.50	15.00	30.00
RCA VICTOR					
❑ 47-7256	Hot Rod/Yakkaty Yal	1958	6.25	12.50	25.00
❑ 47-7412	Time to Love/Make a Record Man	1958	6.25	12.50	25.00

MARKSMEN, THE (1)

With Don Wilson of THE VENTURES.

Number	Title (A Side/B Side)	Yr	VG	VG+	NM
BLUE HORIZON					
❑ 6052	Night Run/Scratch	1960	37.50	75.00	150.00

MARKSMEN, THE (2)

Number	Title (A Side/B Side)	Yr	VG	VG+	NM
JUBILEE					
❑ 5531	Coming In on a Wing and a Prayer/Just One More Mile	1966	3.00	6.00	12.00

MARLEY, BOB, AND THE WAILERS

Number	Title (A Side/B Side)	Yr	VG	VG+	NM
COTILLION					
❑ 46023	Reggae on Broadway/Gonna Get You	1981	—	2.50	5.00
❑ 46029	Chances Are/(B-side unknown)	1981	—	2.50	5.00
ISLAND					
❑ 004	I Shot the Sheriff/Put It On	1974	—	3.00	6.00
❑ 027	Lively Up Yourself/So Jah Seh	1975	—	3.00	6.00
❑ 037	No Woman, No Cry/Kinky Reggae	1975	—	3.00	6.00
❑ 060	Roots, Rock, Reggae/Cry to Me	1976	—	3.00	6.00
❑ 072	Who the Cap Fit/(B-side unknown)	1976	—	3.00	6.00
❑ 089	Exodus/(Instrumental)	1977	—	3.00	6.00
❑ 092	Waiting in Vain/Roots	1977	—	3.00	6.00
❑ 099	Is This Love/Crisis	1978	—	3.00	6.00
❑ 1211	Rock It Baby/Stop That Train	1972	2.00	4.00	8.00
❑ 1215	Concrete Jungle/No More Trouble	1973	2.00	4.00	8.00

Number	Title (A Side/B Side)	Yr	VG	VG+	NM
❑ 1218	Get Up, Stand Up/Slave Driver	1973	2.00	4.00	8.00
❑ 49080	Wake Up and Live/Wake Up and Live (Dub)	1979	—	3.00	6.00
❑ 49156	Kaya/One Drop	1980	—	3.00	6.00
❑ 49547	Ride Natty Ride/Could You Be Loved	1980	—	3.00	6.00
❑ 49636	Redemption Song/Coming In from the Cold	1980	—	3.00	6.00
❑ 49755	Jamming/No Woman, No Cry	1981	—	3.00	6.00
❑ 99740	Blackman Redemption/Is This Love	1984	—	2.00	4.00
❑ 99837	Mix Up, Mix Up/(B-side unknown)	1983	—	2.00	4.00
❑ 99882	Buffalo Soldier/Buffalo Dub	1983	—	2.00	4.00
❑ 99882 [PS]	Buffalo Soldier/Buffalo Dub	1983	—	3.00	6.00
❑ 562356-7	Kinky Reggae (Raga Mix)/Kinky Reggae (Kinky Mix)	1999	—	2.00	4.00

SHELTER

Number	Title (A Side/B Side)	Yr	VG	VG+	NM
❑ 7309	Doppy Conquer/Justice	1971	3.00	6.00	12.00

—B-side by the Upsetters

MARLO, MICKI

ABC-PARAMOUNT

Number	Title (A Side/B Side)	Yr	VG	VG+	NM
❑ 9762	Little By Little/It All Started With Your Kiss	1956	6.25	12.50	25.00
❑ 9807	Ain't That Love/The Beginning of Love	1957	3.75	7.50	15.00
❑ 9841	What You've Done to Me/That's Right	1957	7.50	15.00	30.00
—With "Vocal assist by Paul Anka"					
❑ 9841	What You've Done to Me/That's Right	1957	3.75	7.50	15.00
—New mix, without "Vocal assist by Paul Anka"					

CAPITOL

Number	Title (A Side/B Side)	Yr	VG	VG+	NM
❑ F2736	I'm Gonna Rock, Rock, Rock/Love's Like That	1954	5.00	10.00	20.00
❑ F2801	I'm Going to Sit Right Down and Cry Over You/Forever Is Now	1954	5.00	10.00	20.00
❑ F2874	I'm Flying/Why Should I Cry	1954	3.75	7.50	15.00
❑ F2932	Show Me/Every Road Must Have a Turning	1954	3.75	7.50	15.00
❑ F3016	Don't Go, Don't Go, Don't Go/Can You	1955	3.75	7.50	15.00
❑ F3062	Prize of Gold/Foolish Notion	1955	3.75	7.50	15.00
❑ F3148	I've Got Rhythm in My Nursery Rhymes/Dream Boy	1955	3.75	7.50	15.00
❑ F3266	Pet Me, Poppa/Like I Love Nobody Before	1955	3.75	7.50	15.00
❑ F3346	How Come You Love Me Like You Do/Way Down by the Cherry Tree	1956	3.75	7.50	15.00

MARMALADE, THE

ARIOLA AMERICA

Number	Title (A Side/B Side)	Yr	VG	VG+	NM
❑ 7619	Falling Apart at the Seams/Fly, Fly, Fly	1976	—	2.00	4.00
❑ 7631	My Everything/Walking a Tightrope	1976	—	2.00	4.00

EMI

Number	Title (A Side/B Side)	Yr	VG	VG+	NM
❑ 3676	Engine Driver/Wishing Well	1973	—	2.00	4.00

EPIC

Number	Title (A Side/B Side)	Yr	VG	VG+	NM
❑ 10162	Can't Stop Now/There Ain't No Use in Hanging On	1967	2.50	5.00	10.00
❑ 10236	Otherwise It's Been a Perfect Day/I See the Rain	1967	2.50	5.00	10.00
❑ 10284	Cry/Man in a Shop	1968	2.00	4.00	8.00
❑ 10340	Hey Joe/Lovin' Things	1968	2.00	4.00	8.00
❑ 10404	Wait for Me Mary-Ann/Mess Around	1968	2.00	4.00	8.00
❑ 10428	Ob-La-Di, Ob-La-Da/Chains	1969	2.50	5.00	10.00
❑ 10493	Time Is On My Side/Baby Make It Soon	1969	2.00	4.00	8.00

LONDON

Number	Title (A Side/B Side)	Yr	VG	VG+	NM
❑ 20058	Reflections of My Life/Rollin' Thing	1970	—	3.00	6.00
❑ 20059	Rainbow/The Ballad of Cherry Flavar	1970	—	2.50	5.00
❑ 20066	My Little One/Is Your Life Your Own	1971	—	2.50	5.00
❑ 20068	Lonely Man/Cousin Norman	1971	—	2.50	5.00
❑ 20072	Just One Woman/Radancer	1971	—	2.50	5.00

MARQUEES, THE (1)

DAY-SEL

Number	Title (A Side/B Side)	Yr	VG	VG+	NM
❑ 1001	Ecstasy/Close to Me	1959	150.00	300.00	600.00

MARQUEES, THE (2)

GRAND

Number	Title (A Side/B Side)	Yr	VG	VG+	NM
❑ 141	The Bells/The Rain	1956	75.00	150.00	300.00
—With no address on label					
❑ 141	The Bells/The Rain	195?	12.50	25.00	50.00
—With address on label					

MARQUEES, THE (3)

JO-ANN

Number	Title (A Side/B Side)	Yr	VG	VG+	NM
❑ 128	Stay with Me/That's the Way I Feel	1960	37.50	75.00	150.00
❑ 130	I Need a Helping Hand/Don't You Do Me Like That	1961	25.00	50.00	100.00

MARQUEES, THE (4)

LEN

Number	Title (A Side/B Side)	Yr	VG	VG+	NM
❑ 100	Say Hey/I'm in Misery	1958	25.00	50.00	100.00

MARQUEES, THE (5)

MARVIN GAYE was in this group.

OKEH

Number	Title (A Side/B Side)	Yr	VG	VG+	NM
❑ 7096	Hey Little School Girl/Wyatt Earp	1957	30.00	60.00	120.00

MARQUEES, THE (6)

WARNER BROS.

Number	Title (A Side/B Side)	Yr	VG	VG+	NM
❑ 5072	Who Will Be the First One/Love Machine	1959	10.00	20.00	40.00
❑ 5127	Christmas in the Crowd/Sunset to Sunrise	1959	10.00	20.00	40.00
❑ 5139	Until the Day I Die/Don't Be Mean, Geraldine	1960	20.00	40.00	80.00

MARQUIS, THE

ONYX

Number	Title (A Side/B Side)	Yr	VG	VG+	NM
❑ 505	Bohemian Daddy/(B-side unknown)	1956	500.00	1000.	2000.

MARSDEN, BERYL

CAPITOL

Number	Title (A Side/B Side)	Yr	VG	VG+	NM
❑ 5552	Who You Gonna Hurt/Gonna Make Him My Baby	1965	2.50	5.00	10.00

MARSDEN, GERRY

Also see GERRY AND THE PACEMAKERS.

COLUMBIA

Number	Title (A Side/B Side)	Yr	VG	VG+	NM
❑ 44309	Gilbert Green/Please Let Them Be	1967	2.50	5.00	10.00

MARSH, RICHIE

Also known as Dick Marsh, he later recorded as "Sky Saxon" in THE SEEDS.

ACAMA

Number	Title (A Side/B Side)	Yr	VG	VG+	NM
❑ 125	Baby, Baby, Baby/Half Angel	1960	7.50	15.00	30.00

AVA

Number	Title (A Side/B Side)	Yr	VG	VG+	NM
❑ 122	Goodbye/Crying Inside My Heart	1963	5.00	10.00	20.00

ROSCO

Number	Title (A Side/B Side)	Yr	VG	VG+	NM
❑ 412	There's Only One Girl/What Chance Have I	1960	5.00	10.00	20.00

SHEPHERD

Number	Title (A Side/B Side)	Yr	VG	VG+	NM
❑ 2203	They Say Darling/I Swear That It's True	1962	6.25	12.50	25.00

MARSHALL TUCKER BAND, THE

CAPRICORN

Number	Title (A Side/B Side)	Yr	VG	VG+	NM
❑ 0021	Can't You See/See You Later, I'm Gone	1973	—	3.00	6.00
❑ 0030	Take the Highway/Jesus Told Me So	1973	—	3.00	6.00
❑ 0049	Another Cruel Love/Blue Ridge Mountain Sky	1974	—	2.50	5.00
❑ 0228	This Ol' Cowboy/Try One More Time	1975	—	2.50	5.00
❑ 0244	Fire on the Mountain/Bop Away My Blues	1975	—	2.50	5.00
❑ 0251	Searchin' for a Rainbow/Walkin' and Talkin'	1976	—	2.50	5.00
❑ 0258	Long Hard Ride/Windy City Blues	1976	—	2.50	5.00
❑ 0270	Heard It in a Love Song/Life in a Song	1977	—	2.50	5.00
❑ 0278	Can't You See/Fly Like an Eagle	1977	—	2.50	5.00
❑ 0300	Dream Lover/A Change Is Gonna Come	1978	—	2.50	5.00
❑ 0307	I'll Be Seeing You/Everybody Needs Somebody	1978	—	2.50	5.00

MERCURY

Number	Title (A Side/B Side)	Yr	VG	VG+	NM
❑ 870050-7	Once You Get the Feel of It/Slow Down	1987	—	—	3.00
❑ 870505-7	Dancin' Shoes/I'm Glad It's Gone	1988	—	—	3.00
❑ 872096-7	Still Holdin' On/Same Old Moon	1989	—	—	3.00
❑ 888774-7	Hangin' Out in Smokey Places/He Don't Know	1987	—	—	3.00

WARNER BROS.

Number	Title (A Side/B Side)	Yr	VG	VG+	NM
❑ 8841	Last of the Singing Cowboys/Pass It On	1979	—	2.50	5.00
❑ 8841 [PS]	Last of the Singing Cowboys/Pass It On	1979	—	3.00	6.00
❑ 29355	I May Be Easy But You Make It Hard/Shot Down Where You Stand	1984	—	2.00	4.00
❑ 29619	A Place I've Never Been/8:05	1983	—	2.00	4.00
❑ 29939	Reachin' for a Little Bit More/Sweet Elaine	1982	—	2.00	4.00
❑ 29995	Mr. President/The Sea, Dreams and Fairy Tales	1982	—	2.00	4.00
❑ 49068	Running Like the Wind/(B-side unknown)	1979	—	2.50	5.00
❑ 49215	It Takes Time/Jimi	1980	—	2.50	5.00
❑ 49259	Disillusioned/Without You	1980	—	2.00	4.00
❑ 49724	This Time I Believe/Tell the Blues to Take Off the Night	1981	—	2.00	4.00
❑ 49764	Time Has Come/Love Some	1981	—	2.00	4.00

MARSHANS, THE

ETIQUETTE

Number	Title (A Side/B Side)	Yr	VG	VG+	NM
❑ 8	I Remember/It's Almost Tomorrow	1964	5.00	10.00	20.00

JOHNSON

Number	Title (A Side/B Side)	Yr	VG	VG+	NM
❑ 736	My Letter To Santa/Main Man	1966	5.00	10.00	20.00

MARTELLS, THE

BELLA

Number	Title (A Side/B Side)	Yr	VG	VG+	NM
❑ 20	Rockin' Santa Claus/Carol Lee	1959	10.00	20.00	40.00
—B-side by Eulis Mason					
❑ 45	Forgotten Spring/Va Va Voom	1961	12.50	25.00	50.00

CESSNA

Number	Title (A Side/B Side)	Yr	VG	VG+	NM
❑ 477	Forgotten Spring/Va Va Voom	1961	20.00	40.00	80.00

RELIC

Number	Title (A Side/B Side)	Yr	VG	VG+	NM
❑ 517	Forgotten Spring/Va Va Voom	1964	2.50	5.00	10.00

MARTHA AND THE VANDELLAS

Also see SAUNDRA MALLETT AND THE VANDELLAS; MARTHA REEVES; THE VELLS.

A&M

Number	Title (A Side/B Side)	Yr	VG	VG+	NM
❑ 3022	Nowhere to Run/I Got You (I Feel Good)	1988	—	2.00	4.00
—B-side by James Brown					
❑ 3022 [PS]	Nowhere to Run/I Got You (I Feel Good)	1988	—	2.00	4.00
—"Good Morning Vietnam" sleeve					

GORDY

Number	Title (A Side/B Side)	Yr	VG	VG+	NM
❑ 7011	I'll Have to Let Him Go/My Baby Won't Come Back	1962	6.25	12.50	25.00
❑ 7014	Come and Get These Memories/Jealous Love	1963	7.50	15.00	30.00
❑ 7022	Heat Wave/A Love Like Yours	1963	5.00	10.00	20.00
❑ 7025	Quicksand/Darling, I Hum Our Song	1963	3.75	7.50	15.00
❑ 7027	Live Wire/Old Love	1964	3.75	7.50	15.00
❑ 7031	In My Lonely Room/A Tear for the Girl	1964	3.75	7.50	15.00
❑ 7033	Dancing in the Street/There He Is (At My Door)	1964	3.75	7.50	15.00
❑ 7033 [PS]	Dancing in the Street/There He Is (At My Door)	1964	30.00	60.00	120.00
❑ 7036	Wild One/Dancing Slow	1964	3.00	6.00	12.00
❑ 7039	Nowhere to Run/Motoring	1965	3.00	6.00	12.00
❑ 7045	You've Been in Love Too Long/Love (Makes You Do Foolish Things)	1965	3.00	6.00	12.00
❑ 7048	My Baby Loves Me/Never Leave Your Baby's Side	1965	3.00	6.00	12.00
❑ 7053	What Am I Gonna Do Without Your Love/Go Ahead and Laugh	1966	3.00	6.00	12.00
❑ 7056	I'm Ready for Love/He Doesn't Love Her Anymore	1966	3.00	6.00	12.00
❑ 7058	Jimmy Mack/Third Finger, Left Hand	1967	2.50	5.00	10.00
❑ 7062	Love Bug Leave My Heart Alone/One Way Out	1967	2.50	5.00	10.00
❑ 7067	Honey Chile/Show Me the Way	1967	2.50	5.00	10.00
—Starting here, as "Martha Reeves and the Vandellas"					
❑ 7070	I Promise to Wait My Love/Forget Me Not	1968	2.50	5.00	10.00
❑ 7075	I Can't Dance to That Music You're Playin'/I Tried	1968	2.50	5.00	10.00
❑ 7080	Sweet Darlin'/Without You	1968	2.50	5.00	10.00
❑ 7085	(We've Got) Honey Love/I'm In Love (And I Know It)	1969	2.00	4.00	8.00
❑ 7094	Taking My Love (And Leaving Me)/Heartless	1969	2.00	4.00	8.00
❑ 7098	I Should Be Pround/Love, Guess Who	1970	2.00	4.00	8.00
❑ 7103	I Gotta Let You Go/You're the Loser Now	1970	2.00	4.00	8.00
❑ 7110	Bless You/Hope I Don't Get My Heart Broke	1971	2.00	4.00	8.00
❑ 7113	In and Out of My Life/Your Love Makes It All Worthwhile	1972	2.00	4.00	8.00
❑ 7118	Tear It On Down/I Want You Back	1972	2.00	4.00	8.00

Number	Title (A Side/B Side)	Yr	VG	VG+	NM
❑ 7127	Baby Don't Leave Me/I Won't Be the Fool I've Been Again	1973	2.00	4.00	8.00

TOPPS/MOTOWN

Number	Title (A Side/B Side)	Yr	VG	VG+	NM
❑ 7	Dancing in the Street	1967	18.75	37.50	75.00
—Cardboard record					
❑ 14	Love Is Like a Heat Wave	1967	18.75	37.50	75.00
—Cardboard record					

MARTIN, BARRY

FREEDOM

Number	Title (A Side/B Side)	Yr	VG	VG+	NM
❑ 44019	Minnie the Moocher/The Willies	1959	3.00	6.00	12.00

RCA VICTOR

Number	Title (A Side/B Side)	Yr	VG	VG+	NM
❑ 47-7834	Got a Whole Lot of Lovin' to Do/Why'd I Have to Fa;;	1961	5.00	10.00	20.00

MARTIN, BENNY

DECCA

Number	Title (A Side/B Side)	Yr	VG	VG+	NM
❑ 9-30712	Border Baby/My Fortune	1958	5.00	10.00	20.00
❑ 9-30935	Untrue You/If I Can Stay Away Long Enough	1959	5.00	10.00	20.00
❑ 9-31050	Top Gun/Going Down This Road	1960	5.00	10.00	20.00

GULF REEF

Number	Title (A Side/B Side)	Yr	VG	VG+	NM
❑ 1005	Thinking About Love/The Man Next Door	196?	5.00	10.00	20.00

JAB

Number	Title (A Side/B Side)	Yr	VG	VG+	NM
❑ 9002	I'm a Father Alone/Salvation Army	1967	2.00	4.00	8.00

MERCURY

Number	Title (A Side/B Side)	Yr	VG	VG+	NM
❑ 70476	Read Between the Lines/Secret of Your Heart	1954	7.50	15.00	30.00
❑ 70508	Me and My Fiddle/The Law of My Heart	1954	7.50	15.00	30.00
❑ 70560	Ice Cold Love/You Know That I Know	1955	7.50	15.00	30.00
❑ 70664	Take My Word/Who Put Those Tears in Your Eyes	1955	7.50	15.00	30.00
❑ 70731	Yes, It's True/I'm Right and You're Wrong	1955	7.50	15.00	30.00
❑ 70794	If I Didn't Have a Conscience/You're Guilty Darlin'	1956	7.50	15.00	30.00
❑ 70883	Lover of the Town/Whippoor-Will	1956	7.50	15.00	30.00

RCA VICTOR

Number	Title (A Side/B Side)	Yr	VG	VG+	NM
❑ 47-6855	That's the Story of My Life/Look What You've Done	1957	6.25	12.50	25.00
❑ 47-7003	I Saw Your Face in the Moon/Torch of Love	1957	6.25	12.50	25.00
❑ 47-7100	Do Me a Favor/(B-side unknown)	1957	6.25	12.50	25.00

STARDAY

Number	Title (A Side/B Side)	Yr	VG	VG+	NM
❑ 519	A Dime's Worth of Dreams/Pretty Girl	1960	5.00	10.00	20.00
❑ 536	You Are the One/No One But You	1961	3.75	7.50	15.00
❑ 623	Rosebuds and You/Sinful Cinderella	1963	3.75	7.50	15.00
❑ 646	Down in the Shinnery/Two Take Away One Equals Lonesome	1963	3.75	7.50	15.00
❑ 705	Stick Your Finger in a Glass of Water/The Other Me	1964	3.75	7.50	15.00
❑ 725	One Way or the Other/Weekend Ellie	1965	3.00	6.00	12.00
❑ 743	Hello City Limits/I'll Never Get Over Loving You	1965	3.00	6.00	12.00

MARTIN, DEAN

CAPITOL

Number	Title (A Side/B Side)	Yr	VG	VG+	NM
❑ 54-691	Just for Fun/My One, My Only, My All	1949	5.00	10.00	20.00
—Note: Dean Martin singles on Capitol before 691 are unconfirmed on 45 rpm					
❑ 54-726	That Lucky Old Sun/Vieni Su	1949	5.00	10.00	20.00
❑ F937	Rain/Zing-a, Zing-a, Boom	1950	3.75	7.50	15.00
❑ F948	Muskrat Ramble/I'm Gonna Paper All My Walls with Love Letters	1950	3.75	7.50	15.00
❑ F981	Choo'n Gum/I Don't Care If the Sun Don't Shine	1950	3.75	7.50	15.00
❑ F1002	I Still Get a Thrill/Be Honest with Me	1950	3.75	7.50	15.00
❑ F1028	I'll Always Love You/Baby Obey Me	1950	3.75	7.50	15.00
❑ F1052	Bye Bye Blackbird/Happy Feet	1950	3.75	7.50	15.00
❑ F1139	Peddler's Serenade/Wham, Bam, Thank You, Ma'am	1950	3.75	7.50	15.00
❑ F1160	Don't Rock the Boat/I'm in Love with You	1950	3.75	7.50	15.00
—With Margaret Whiting					
❑ F1342	If/I Love the Way	1950	3.75	7.50	15.00
❑ F1358	You and Your Beautiful Eyes/Tonda Wanda Hoy	1951	3.75	7.50	15.00
❑ F1458	Beside You/Who's Sorry Now	1951	3.75	7.50	15.00
❑ F1682	Oh Marie/I'll Always Love You	1951	3.00	6.00	12.00
❑ F1703	In the Cool, Cool, Cool of the Evening/Bonne Nuit	1951	3.75	7.50	15.00
❑ F1797	Hanging Around with You/Aw C'mon	1951	3.75	7.50	15.00
❑ F1811	Meanderin'/Bella Bimba	1951	3.75	7.50	15.00
❑ F1817	Solitaire/I Ran All the Way Home	1951	3.75	7.50	15.00
❑ F1885	Night Train to Memphis/Blue Smoke	1951	3.75	7.50	15.00
❑ F1901	Never Before/Sailors Polka	1951	3.75	7.50	15.00
❑ F1921	As You Are/Oh Boy	1952	3.75	7.50	15.00
❑ F1938	Until/My Heart Found Home	1952	3.75	7.50	15.00
❑ F1975	All I Have to Give/When You're Smiling	1952	3.75	7.50	15.00
❑ F2001	Pretty as a Picture/Won't You Surrender	1952	3.75	7.50	15.00
❑ F2071	Bet-i-Cha/I Passed Your House Tonight	1952	3.75	7.50	15.00
❑ F2140	Oh Marie/Come Back to Sorrento	1952	3.75	7.50	15.00
❑ F2165	You Belong to Me/Hominy Grits	1952	3.75	7.50	15.00
❑ F2240	I Know a Dream When I See One/Second Chance	1952	3.75	7.50	15.00
❑ F2319	What Could Be More Beautiful/The Kiss	1953	3.00	6.00	12.00
❑ F2378	Little Did We Know/There's My Lover	1953	3.00	6.00	12.00
❑ F2485	Love Me, Love Me/Till I Find You❑ Love Me, Love Me/Till I Find You	1953	3.00	6.00	12.00
❑ F2555	If I Could Sing Like Bing/Don't You Remember	1953	3.00	6.00	12.00
❑ F2589	That's Amore/You're the Right One	1953	3.75	7.50	15.00
❑ F2640	The Christmas Blues/If I Should Love Again	1953	3.00	6.00	12.00
❑ F2749	Hey Brother Pass the Wine/I'd Cry Like a Baby	1954	3.00	6.00	12.00
❑ F2818	Money Burns a Hole in My Pocket/Sway	1954	3.00	6.00	12.00
❑ F2870	That's What I Like/Peddler Man	1954	3.00	6.00	12.00
❑ F2911	Try Again/One More Time	1954	3.00	6.00	12.00
❑ F2985	Open Up the Doghouse/Long, Long Ago	1954	3.75	7.50	15.00
—With Nat King Cole					
❑ F3011	Confused/Belle from Barcelona	1955	2.50	5.00	10.00
❑ F3036	Young and Foolish/Under the Bridges of Paris	1955	2.50	5.00	10.00
❑ F3133	Chee Chee Oo-Chee/Ridin' Into Love	1955	2.50	5.00	10.00
❑ F3153	Simpatico/Love Is All That Matters	1955	2.50	5.00	10.00
❑ F3196	Two Sleepy People/Relax Ay Voo	1955	2.50	5.00	10.00
—With Line Renaud					
❑ F3238	I Like Them All/In Napoli	1955	2.50	5.00	10.00
❑ F3295	Memories Are Made of This/Change of Heart	1955	3.00	6.00	12.00
❑ F3352	Innamorata/Lady with a Big Umbrella	1956	2.50	5.00	10.00
❑ F3414	Standing on the Corner/Watching the World Go By	1956	2.50	5.00	10.00
❑ F3468	Street of Love/I'm Gonna Steal You Away	1956	2.50	5.00	10.00
❑ F3521	Mississippi Dreamboat/Test of Time	1956	2.50	5.00	10.00
❑ F3577	The Look/Give Me a Sign	1956	2.50	5.00	10.00
❑ F3604	Just Kiss Me/I Know I Can't Forget	1956	2.50	5.00	10.00
❑ F3648	Captured/The Man Who Plays the Mandolino	1957	2.50	5.00	10.00
❑ F3680	Bamboozled/Only Trust Your Heart	1957	2.50	5.00	10.00
❑ F3718	I Can't Give You Anything But Love/I Never Had a Chance	1957	2.50	5.00	10.00
❑ F3752	Write to Me from Naples/Beau James	1957	2.50	5.00	10.00
❑ F3787	Promise Her Anything/Triche Trache	1957	2.50	5.00	10.00
❑ F3842	Makin' Love Ukulele Style/Good Morning Life	1957	2.50	5.00	10.00
❑ F3894	Return to Me/Forgetting You	1958	2.00	4.00	8.00
❑ F3988	Angel Baby/I'll Gladly Make the Same Mistake Again	1958	2.00	4.00	8.00
❑ F4028	Volare (Nel Blu Dipinto Di Blu)/Outa My Mind	1958	2.00	4.00	8.00
❑ F4028 [PS]	Volare (Nel Blu Dipinto Di Blu)/Outa My Mind	1958	6.25	12.50	25.00
❑ F4065	Once Upon a Time/The Magician	1958	2.00	4.00	8.00
❑ F4124	It Takes So Long/You Were Made for Love	1959	2.00	4.00	8.00
❑ F4174	Rio Bravo/My Rifle, My Pony and Me	1959	2.00	4.00	8.00
❑ F4222	On an Evening in Roma/You Can't Love 'Em All	1959	2.00	4.00	8.00
❑ F4222 [PS]	On an Evening in Roma/You Can't Love 'Em All	1959	6.25	12.50	25.00
❑ F4287	I Ain't Gonna Lead This Life No More/Career	1959	2.00	4.00	8.00
❑ 4328	Love Me, My Love/Who Was That Lady	1960	2.00	4.00	8.00
❑ 4361	Napoli/Professor, Professor	1960	2.00	4.00	8.00
❑ 4391	Just in Time/Buttercup a Golden Hair	1960	2.00	4.00	8.00
❑ 4420	Ain't That a Kick in the Head/Humdinger	1960	2.00	4.00	8.00
❑ 4472	How Sweet It Is/Sogni D'Oro	1960	2.00	4.00	8.00
❑ 4518	Sparklin' Eyes/Tu Sei Bella Signorina	1961	2.00	4.00	8.00
❑ 4551	Bella, Bella Bambina/All in a Night's Work	1961	2.00	4.00	8.00
❑ 4570	The Story of Life/Giuggiola	1961	2.00	4.00	8.00
❑ B-44153	That's Amore/It Must Be Him	1988	—	2.00	4.00
—B-side by Vikki Carr					
❑ S7-57889	Rudolph, the Red-Nosed Reindeer/White Christmas	1992	—	2.50	5.00
❑ 58742	The Christmas Blues/Let It Snow! Let It Snow! Let It Snow!	1998	—	—	3.00

MCA

Number	Title (A Side/B Side)	Yr	VG	VG+	NM
❑ 52662	L.A. Is My Home/Drinking Champagne	1985	—	2.00	4.00

REPRISE

Number	Title (A Side/B Side)	Yr	VG	VG+	NM
❑ PRO 248 [DJ]	White Christmas (same on both sides)	1966	2.50	5.00	10.00
❑ 0252	La Giostra (Merry-Go-Round)/Grazie, Prego, Scusi	1964	2.00	4.00	8.00
❑ 0281	Everybody Loves Somebody/A Little Voice	1964	2.50	5.00	10.00
❑ 0307	The Door Is Still Open to My Heart/Every Minute, Every Hour	1964	2.00	4.00	8.00
❑ 0333	You're Nobody Till Somebody Loves You/You'll Always Be the One I Love	1964	2.00	4.00	8.00
❑ 0344	Send Me the Pillow You Dream On/I'll Be Seeing You	1965	2.00	4.00	8.00
❑ 0369	(Remember Me) I'm the One Who Loves You/Born to Lose	1965	2.00	4.00	8.00
❑ 0393	Houston/Bumming Around	1965	2.00	4.00	8.00
❑ 0415	I Will/You're the Reason I'm in Love	1965	2.00	4.00	8.00
❑ 0443	Somewhere There's a Someone/That Old Clock on the Wall	1965	2.00	4.00	8.00
❑ 0466	Come Running Back/Bouquet of Roses	1966	—	3.00	6.00
❑ 0500	A Million and One/Shades	1966	—	3.00	6.00
❑ 0516	Nobody's Baby Again/It Just Happened That Way	1966	—	3.00	6.00
❑ 0538	(Open Up the Door) Let the Good Times In/I'm Not the Marrying Kind	1966	—	3.00	6.00
❑ 0542	Blue Christmas/A Marshmallow World	1966	—	3.00	6.00
❑ 0571	Lay Some Happiness on Me/Think About Me	1967	—	3.00	6.00
❑ 0601	In the Chapel in the Moonlight/Welcome to My World	1967	—	3.00	6.00
❑ 0608	Little Ole Wine Drinker, Me/I Can't Help Remembering You	1967	—	3.00	6.00
❑ 0640	In the Misty Moonlight/Wallpaper Roses	1967	—	3.00	6.00
❑ 0640	In the Misty Moonlight/The Glory of Love	1967	—	3.00	6.00
❑ 0672	You've Still Got a Place in My Heart/Old Yellow Line	1968	—	2.50	5.00
❑ 0703	Lay Some Happiness on Me/(Open Up the Door) Let the Good Times In	1968	—	2.50	5.00
❑ 0709	Everybody Loves Somebody/A Million and One	1968	—	2.50	5.00
❑ 0711	Somewhere There's a Someone/Come Running Back	1968	—	2.50	5.00
❑ 0714	Houston/I Will	1968	—	2.50	5.00
❑ 0717	You're Nobody Till Somebody Loves You/(Remember Me) I'm the One Who Loves You	1968	—	2.50	5.00
❑ 0718	Send Me the Pillow You Dream On/The Door Is Still Open to My Heart	1968	—	2.50	5.00
❑ 0730	In the Chapel in the Moonlight/Little Ole Wine Drinker, Me	1968	—	2.50	5.00
❑ 0735	In the Misty Moonlight/Not Enough Indians	1970	—	2.00	4.00
—0703 through 0735 are "Back to Back Hits" reissues					
❑ 0761	April Again/That Old Time Feelin'	1968	—	2.50	5.00
❑ 0765	Five Card Stud/One Lonely Boy	1968	—	2.50	5.00
❑ 0780	Not Enough Indians/Rainbows Are Back in Style	1968	—	2.50	5.00
❑ 0812	Gentle on My Mind/That's When I See the Blues	1969	—	2.50	5.00
❑ 0841	I Take a Lot of Pride in What I Am/Drowning in My Tears	1969	—	2.50	5.00
❑ 0857	Crying TIme/One Cup of Happiness	1969	—	2.50	5.00
❑ 0893	Down Home/Come On Down	1970	—	2.50	5.00
❑ 0915	For the Love of a Woman/The Tracks of My Tears	1970	—	2.50	5.00
❑ 0934	My Woman, My Woman, My Wife/Here We Go Again	1970	—	2.50	5.00
❑ 0955	Detroit City/Turn the World Around	1970	—	2.50	5.00
❑ 0973	For the Good Times/Georgia Sunshine	1970	—	2.50	5.00
❑ 1004	She's a Little Bit Country/Raining in My Heart	1971	—	2.50	5.00

Number	Title (A Side/B Side)	Yr	VG	VG+	NM
❑ 1060	What's Yesterday/The Right Kind of Woman	1971	—	2.50	5.00
❑ 1085	I Can Give You What You Want Now/Guess Who	1972	—	2.50	5.00
❑ 1141	Amor Mio/You Made Me Love You	1972	—	2.50	5.00
❑ 1166	Smile/Get On With Your Livin'	1973	—	2.50	5.00
❑ 1178	You're the Best Thing That Ever Happened to Me/ Free to Carry On	1973	—	2.50	5.00
❑ 20058	Just Close Your Eyes/Tik-A-Tee Tik-A-Tay	1962	3.00	6.00	12.00
❑ 20076	C'est Si Bon/The Poor People of Paris	1962	6.25	12.50	25.00

—Released only in Italy

Number	Title (A Side/B Side)	Yr	VG	VG+	NM
❑ 20082	Baby-O/Dame Su Amor	1962	2.50	5.00	10.00
❑ 20116	From the Bottom of My Heart (Dammi, Dammi, Dammi)/Who's Got the Action	1962	2.50	5.00	10.00
❑ 20116 [PS]	From the Bottom of My Heart (Dammi, Dammi, Dammi)/Who's Got the Action	1962	5.00	10.00	20.00
❑ 20128	Sam's Song/Me and My Shadow	1962	3.75	7.50	15.00

—A-side: With Sammy Davis, Jr.; B-side: Sammy Davis Jr. and Frank Sinatra

Number	Title (A Side/B Side)	Yr	VG	VG+	NM
❑ 20140	Who's Got the Action/Send a Fine	1963	2.50	5.00	10.00
❑ 20150	Ain't Gonna Try Anymore/A Face in the Crowd	1963	2.50	5.00	10.00
❑ 20194	Corrine, Corrina/My Sugar's Gone	1963	2.50	5.00	10.00
❑ 20215	Via Veneto/Mama Roma	1963	2.50	5.00	10.00
❑ 20217	Fugue for Tinhorns/The Oldest Established (Permanent Floating Crap Game in New York)	1963	3.75	7.50	15.00

—By Frank Sinatra/Bing Crosby/Dean Martin

Number	Title (A Side/B Side)	Yr	VG	VG+	NM
❑ 20217 [PS]	Fugue for Tinhorns/The Oldest Established (Permanent Floating Crap Game in New York)	1963	20.00	40.00	80.00

—By Frank Sinatra/Bing Crosby/Dean Martin

WARNER BROS.

Number	Title (A Side/B Side)	Yr	VG	VG+	NM
❑ 29480	Drinking Champagne/Since I Met You Baby	1983	—	2.00	4.00
❑ 29584	My First Country Song/Hangin' Around	1983	—	2.00	4.00

7-Inch Extended Plays

CAPITOL

Number	Title (A Side/B Side)	Yr	VG	VG+	NM
❑ EAP 1-401	(contents unknown)	195?	5.00	10.00	20.00
❑ EAP 1-401 [PS]	Dean Martin Sings	195?	5.00	10.00	20.00
❑ EAP 1-481	That's Amore/Oh Marie//Come Back to Sorrento/ Luna Mezzo Mare	1954	5.00	10.00	20.00
❑ EAP 1-481 [PS]	Sunny Italy	1954	5.00	10.00	20.00
❑ EAP 1-576	(contents unknown)	195?	3.75	7.50	15.00
❑ EAP 1-576 [PS]	Swingin' Down Yonder, Part 1	195?	3.75	7.50	15.00
❑ EAP 2-576	(contents unknown)	195?	3.75	7.50	15.00
❑ EAP 2-576 [PS]	Swingin' Down Yonder, Part 2	195?	3.75	7.50	15.00
❑ EAP 3-576	Alabamy Bound/Dinah//Carolina in the Morning/ Way Down Yonder in New Orleans	195?	3.75	7.50	15.00
❑ EAP 3-576 [PS]	Swingin' Down Yonder, Part 3	195?	3.75	7.50	15.00
❑ EAP 1-701	(contents unknown)	1956	3.75	7.50	15.00
❑ EAP 1-701 [PS]	Memories Are Made of This	1956	3.75	7.50	15.00
❑ EAP 1-702	(contents unknown)	1956	3.75	7.50	15.00
❑ EAP 1-702 [PS]	Artists and Models	1956	3.75	7.50	15.00
❑ EAP 1-806	(contents unknown)	1957	3.75	7.50	15.00
❑ EAP 1-806 [PS]	Hollywood or Bust	1957	3.75	7.50	15.00
❑ EAP 1-840	(contents unknown)	1957	3.75	7.50	15.00
❑ EAP 1-840 [PS]	Ten Thousand Bedrooms	1957	3.75	7.50	15.00
❑ EAP 1-849	(contents unknown)	1957	3.00	6.00	12.00
❑ EAP 1-849 [PS]	Pretty Baby, Part 1	1957	3.00	6.00	12.00
❑ EAP 2-849	(contents unknown)	1957	3.00	6.00	12.00
❑ EAP 2-849 [PS]	Pretty Baby, Part 2	1957	3.00	6.00	12.00
❑ EAP 3-849	(contents unknown)	1957	3.00	6.00	12.00
❑ EAP 3-849 [PS]	Pretty Baby, Part 3	1957	3.00	6.00	12.00
❑ EAP 1-939	*Return to Me/Don't You Remember/Forgetting You/Buona Sera	1958	3.75	7.50	15.00
❑ EAP 1-939 [PS]	Return to Me	1958	3.75	7.50	15.00
❑ EAP 1-1285	(contents unknown)	1959	3.00	6.00	12.00
❑ EAP 1-1285 [PS]	A Winter Romance, Part 1	1959	3.00	6.00	12.00
❑ EAP 2-1285	(contents unknown)	1959	3.00	6.00	12.00
❑ EAP 2-1285 [PS]	A Winter Romance, Part 2	1959	3.00	6.00	12.00
❑ EAP 3-1285	(contents unknown)	1959	3.00	6.00	12.00
❑ EAP 3-1285 [PS]	A Winter Romance, Part 3	1959	3.00	6.00	12.00

MARTIN, DEAN, AND JERRY LEWIS

7-Inch Extended Plays

CAPITOL

Number	Title (A Side/B Side)	Yr	VG	VG+	NM
❑ EAP 1-533	(contents unknown)	1954	20.00	40.00	80.00
❑ EAP 1-533 [PS]	Livin' It Up	1954	20.00	40.00	80.00
❑ EAP 1-733	(contents unknown)	1956	15.00	30.00	60.00
❑ EAP 1-733 [PS]	Pardners	1956	15.00	30.00	60.00

MARTIN, DEWEY, AND MEDICINE BALL

Dewey is a former member of BUFFALO SPRINGFIELD.

RCA VICTOR

Number	Title (A Side/B Side)	Yr	VG	VG+	NM
❑ 74-0489	There Must Be a Reason/Caress Me Pretty Music	1971	2.00	4.00	8.00

UNI

Number	Title (A Side/B Side)	Yr	VG	VG+	NM
❑ 55178	Jambalaya (On the Bayou)/Ala-Bam	1969	2.00	4.00	8.00
❑ 55245	Indian Child/I Do Believe	1970	2.00	4.00	8.00

MARTIN, GEORGE

UNITED ARTISTS

Number	Title (A Side/B Side)	Yr	VG	VG+	NM
❑ 745	Ringo's Theme (This Boy)/And I Love Her	1964	6.25	12.50	25.00
❑ 745 [PS]	Ringo's Theme (This Boy)/And I Love Her	1964	75.00	150.00	300.00
❑ 750	A Hard Day's Night/I Should Have Known Better	1964	25.00	50.00	100.00
❑ 750 [PS]	A Hard Day's Night/I Should Have Known Better	1964	500.00	1000.	2000.
❑ 831	All Quiet on the Mersey Front/Cast Your Fate to the Wind	1965	3.75	7.50	15.00
❑ 873	I Feel Fine/Downtown	1965	3.75	7.50	15.00
❑ 50148	Love in the Open Air/Bahama Sound	1967	7.50	15.00	30.00

MARTIN, JANIS

PALETTE

Number	Title (A Side/B Side)	Yr	VG	VG+	NM
❑ 5058	Hard Times Ahead/Here Today and Gone Tomorrow	1960	6.25	12.50	25.00
❑ 5071	Teen Street/Cry Guitar	1961	6.25	12.50	25.00

RCA VICTOR

Number	Title (A Side/B Side)	Yr	VG	VG+	NM
❑ 47-6491	Drugstore Rock and Roll/Will You, Willyum	1956	10.00	20.00	40.00
❑ 47-6560	Ooby-Dooby/One More Year to Go	1956	10.00	20.00	40.00
❑ 47-6652	My Boy Elvis/Little Bit	1956	17.50	35.00	70.00
❑ 47-6744	Let's Elope, Baby/Barefoot Baby	1956	7.50	15.00	30.00
❑ 47-6832	Love Me to Pieces/Two Long Years	1957	7.50	15.00	30.00
❑ 47-6983	Love and Kisses/I'll Never Be Free	1957	7.50	15.00	30.00
❑ 47-7104	All Right Baby/Billy Boy, Billy Boy	1957	7.50	15.00	30.00
❑ 47-7184	Cracker Jack/Good Love	1958	7.50	15.00	30.00

7-Inch Extended Plays

RCA VICTOR

Number	Title (A Side/B Side)	Yr	VG	VG+	NM
❑ EPA-4093	Just Squeeze Me (But Don't Tease Me)/My Confession//I Don't Hurt Anymore/Half Loved	1957	37.50	75.00	150.00
❑ EPA-4093 [PS]	Just Squeeze Me	1957	50.00	100.00	200.00

MARTINI, LUIGI, AND THE BAY CITY 5

JAGUAR

Number	Title (A Side/B Side)	Yr	VG	VG+	NM
❑ 3001	Basin Street Blues/Please Don't Talk About Me	1954	75.00	150.00	300.00
❑ 3002	Oh Marie/I'm Sorry I Made You Cry	1954	75.00	150.00	300.00

MARTY

NOVELTY

Number	Title (A Side/B Side)	Yr	VG	VG+	NM
❑ 101	Marty on Planet Mars (Part 1)/Marty on Planet Mars (Part 2)	1956	10.00	20.00	40.00

MARTY AND THE SYMBOLS

GRAPHIC ARTS

Number	Title (A Side/B Side)	Yr	VG	VG+	NM
❑ 1000	You're the One/Rip Van Winkle	1963	20.00	40.00	80.00

MARVELETTES, THE

A&M

Number	Title (A Side/B Side)	Yr	VG	VG+	NM
❑ 1201	Danger Heartbreak Dead Ahead/Baby Please Don't Go	1988	—	2.00	4.00

—B-side by Them

Number	Title (A Side/B Side)	Yr	VG	VG+	NM
❑ 1201 [PS]	Danger Heartbreak Dead Ahead/Baby Please Don't Go	1988	—	2.00	4.00

—"Good Morning Vietnam" sleeve

GORDY

Number	Title (A Side/B Side)	Yr	VG	VG+	NM
❑ 7024	Too Hurt to Cry, Too Much in Love to Say Goodbye/Come On Home	1963	20.00	40.00	80.00

—As "The Darnells"

TAMLA

Number	Title (A Side/B Side)	Yr	VG	VG+	NM
❑ 54046	Please Mr. Postman/So Long Baby	1961	6.25	12.50	25.00
❑ 54046 [PS]	Please Mr. Postman/So Long Baby	1961	30.00	60.00	120.00
❑ 54054	Twistin' Postman/I Want a Guy	1962	5.00	10.00	20.00
❑ 54054 [PS]	Twistin' Postman/I Want a Guy	1962	25.00	50.00	100.00
❑ 54060	Playboy/All the Love I've Got	1962	5.00	10.00	20.00
❑ 54065	Beechwood 4-5789/Someday, Someway	1962	5.00	10.00	20.00
❑ 54072	Strange I Know/Too Strong to Be Strung Along	1962	3.75	7.50	15.00
❑ 54077	Forever/Locking Up My Heart	1963	3.75	7.50	15.00
❑ 54082	Tie a String Around My Finger/My Daddy Knows Best	1963	5.00	10.00	20.00
❑ 54088	As Long As I Know He's Mine/Little Girl Blue	1963	3.00	6.00	12.00
❑ 54091	He's a Good Guy (Yes He Is)/Goddess of Love	1964	3.00	6.00	12.00
❑ 54091 [DJ]	Yes He Is	1964	18.75	37.50	75.00

—One-sided promo with different title than stock copy

Number	Title (A Side/B Side)	Yr	VG	VG+	NM
❑ 54097	You're My Remedy/A Little Bit of Sympathy, A Little Bit of Love	1964	2.50	5.00	10.00
❑ 54097 [PS]	You're My Remedy/A Little Bit of Sympathy, A Little Bit of Love	1964	15.00	30.00	60.00
❑ 54105	Too Many Fish in the Sea/A Need for Love	1964	2.50	5.00	10.00
❑ 54116	I'll Keep Holding On/No Time for Tears	1965	2.50	5.00	10.00
❑ 54120	Danger, Heartbreak Dead Ahead/Your Cheating Ways	1965	2.50	5.00	10.00
❑ 54126	Don't Mess with Bill/Anything You Wanna Do	1965	2.50	5.00	10.00
❑ 54131	You're the One/Paper Boy	1966	2.50	5.00	10.00
❑ 54143	The Hunter Gets Captured by the Game/I Think I Can Change You	1967	2.50	5.00	10.00
❑ 54150	When You're Young and In Love/The Day You Take One, You Have to Take the Other	1967	2.50	5.00	10.00
❑ 54158	My Baby Must Be a Magician/I Need Someone	1967	2.50	5.00	10.00
❑ 54166	Here I Am Baby/Keep Off, No Trespassing	1968	2.50	5.00	10.00
❑ 54171	Destination: Anywhere/What's So Easy for Two Is So Hard for One	1968	2.50	5.00	10.00
❑ 54177	I'm Gonna Hold On Long As I Can/Don't Make Hurting Me a Habit	1968	2.50	5.00	10.00
❑ 54186	That's How Heartaches Are Made/Rainy Mourning	1969	2.50	5.00	10.00
❑ 54198	Marionette/After All	1970	2.00	4.00	8.00
❑ 54213	A Breath Taking Guy/You're the One for Me Baby	1972	2.00	4.00	8.00

TOPPS/MOTOWN

Number	Title (A Side/B Side)	Yr	VG	VG+	NM
❑ 12	Please Mr. Postman	1967	18.75	37.50	75.00

—Cardboard record

MARVELLOS, THE (1)

CHA CHA

Number	Title (A Side/B Side)	Yr	VG	VG+	NM
❑ 756	Come Back My Love/Boyee Yoing	1963	7.50	15.00	30.00

STEPHENY

Number	Title (A Side/B Side)	Yr	VG	VG+	NM
❑ 1818	Come Back My Love/Boyee Yoing	1958	50.00	100.00	200.00

MARVELLOS, THE (2)

EXODUS

Number	Title (A Side/B Side)	Yr	VG	VG+	NM
❑ 6214	Salty Sam/She Told Me Lies	1962	50.00	100.00	200.00
❑ 6216	I Ask of You/Hip Enough	1962	30.00	60.00	120.00

REPRISE

Number	Title (A Side/B Side)	Yr	VG	VG+	NM
❑ 20088	Salty Sam/She Told Me Lies	1962	7.50	15.00	30.00

MARVELLOS, THE (3)

LOMA

Number	Title (A Side/B Side)	Yr	VG	VG+	NM
❑ 2045	Something's Burning/We Go Together	1966	3.00	6.00	12.00
❑ 2061	You're Such a Sweet Thing/Why Do You Want to Hurt the One You Love	1966	3.00	6.00	12.00

MODERN

Number	Title (A Side/B Side)	Yr	VG	VG+	NM
❑ 1054	Down in the City/In the Sunshine	1967	2.50	5.00	10.00

Number	Title (A Side/B Side)	Yr	VG	VG+	NM
WARNER BROS.					
❑ 7011	Don't Play with My Heart/Let Me Keep You Satisfied	1967	2.50	5.00	10.00
❑ 7054	Piece of Silk/Yes I Do	1967	2.50	5.00	10.00

MARVELLOS, THE (U)

Could be group (1); it's doubtful that these could be either of the other two.

Number	Title (A Side/B Side)	Yr	VG	VG+	NM
MARVELLO					
❑ 5005	Red Hot Momma/I Need a Girl	1955	75.00	150.00	300.00
THERON					
❑ 117	You're the Dream/Calypso Mama	1957	100.00	200.00	400.00

MARVELOWS, THE

Number	Title (A Side/B Side)	Yr	VG	VG+	NM
ABC					
❑ 10820	Fade Away/You've Been Going to Sally	1966	2.50	5.00	10.00
❑ 11011	In the Morning/Talkin' 'Bout Ya, Baby	1967	2.00	4.00	8.00
—As "The Mighty Marvelows"					
❑ 11073	I'm So Confused/I'm Without a Girl	1968	2.00	4.00	8.00
—As "The Mighty Marvelows"					
❑ 11139	Hey, Hey Girl/Wait, Be Cool	1968	2.00	4.00	8.00
—As "The Mighty Marvelows"					
❑ 11189	You're Breaking My Heart/This Town's Too Much	1969	2.00	4.00	8.00
—As "The Mighty Marvelows"					
ABC-PARAMOUNT					
❑ 10613	A Friend/Hey, Hey Baby	1965	2.50	5.00	10.00
❑ 10629	I Do/My Heart	1965	3.75	7.50	15.00
❑ 10708	Shim Sham/Your Little Sister	1965	2.50	5.00	10.00
❑ 10756	Do It/I've Got My Eyes on You	1965	2.50	5.00	10.00

MARVELS, THE (1)

Early version of THE DUBS.

Number	Title (A Side/B Side)	Yr	VG	VG+	NM
ABC-PARAMOUNT					
❑ 9771	I Won't Have You Breaking My Heart/Jump Rock and Roll	1956	150.00	300.00	600.00

MARVELS, THE (2)

Number	Title (A Side/B Side)	Yr	VG	VG+	NM
LAURIE					
❑ 3106	I Shed So Many Tears/So Young, So Sweet	1958	17.50	35.00	70.00
—Also released as "The Marvells"					

MARVELS, THE (3)

Number	Title (A Side/B Side)	Yr	VG	VG+	NM
MUN-RAB					
❑ 1008	Just Another Fool/You Crack Me Up	1959	375.00	750.00	1500.

MARVELS, THE (U)

May be group (2).

Number	Title (A Side/B Side)	Yr	VG	VG+	NM
WINN					
❑ 1916	For Sentimental Reasons/Come Back	1961	50.00	100.00	200.00

MARVIN AND JOHNNY

Also see JESSE AND MARVIN.

Number	Title (A Side/B Side)	Yr	VG	VG+	NM
ALADDIN					
❑ 3371	Yak Yak/Pretty Eyes	1957	7.50	15.00	30.00
❑ 3408	You're In My Heart/Smack Smack	1958	7.50	15.00	30.00
❑ 3439	It's Christmas/The Valley of Love	1958	7.50	15.00	30.00
FELSTED					
❑ 8681	Hot Biscuits and Gravy/Tired of Being Alone	1963	3.00	6.00	12.00
JAMIE					
❑ 1188	Once Upon a Time/Tick Tock	1961	3.00	6.00	12.00
LIBERTY					
❑ 1394	It's Christmas/It's Christmas Time	1980	—	2.50	5.00
—B-side by the Five Keys					
MODERN					
❑ 933	Tick Tock/Cherry Pie	1954	18.75	37.50	75.00
❑ 941	Sugar/Kiss Me	1954	12.50	25.00	50.00
❑ 946	Little Honey/Honey Girl	1955	12.50	25.00	50.00
❑ 949	Ko Ko Mo/Sometimes I Wonder	1955	10.00	20.00	40.00
❑ 952	I Love You, Yes I Do/Baby Won't You Marry Me	1955	10.00	20.00	40.00
❑ 959	Butler Ball/Sugar Mama	1955	10.00	20.00	40.00
❑ 968	Will You Love Me/Sweet Dreams	1956	7.50	15.00	30.00
❑ 974	Ain't That Right/Let Me Know	1956	7.50	15.00	30.00
SPECIALTY					
❑ 479	Baby Doll/I'm Not a Fool	1953	15.00	30.00	60.00
❑ 479	Baby Doll/I'm Not a Fool	1953	25.00	50.00	100.00
—Red vinyl					
❑ 488	Jo Jo/How Long Has She Been Gone	1954	15.00	30.00	60.00
❑ 498	School of Love/Boy Loves Girl	1954	15.00	30.00	60.00
❑ 530	Day In — Day Out/Flip	1954	15.00	30.00	60.00
❑ 554	Ding Dong Baby/Mamo Mamo	1955	12.50	25.00	50.00
SWINGIN'					
❑ 641	I'm Tired of Being Alone/Baby You Don't Know	1962	3.00	6.00	12.00
❑ 645	Pretty One/Second Helping of Cherry Pie	1963	3.00	6.00	12.00

MARVIN AND THE CHIRPS

Number	Title (A Side/B Side)	Yr	VG	VG+	NM
TIP TOP					
❑ 202	I'll Miss You This Christmas/Sixteen Tons	1958	50.00	100.00	200.00

MARX, THE

Number	Title (A Side/B Side)	Yr	VG	VG+	NM
CHANTE					
❑ 1002	One Minute More/You Are My Love	19??	50.00	100.00	200.00
DAHLIA					
❑ 1002	One Minute More/You Are My Love	19??	25.00	50.00	100.00

MARYLANDERS, THE

Number	Title (A Side/B Side)	Yr	VG	VG+	NM
JUBILEE					
❑ 5079	I'm a Sentimental Fool/Sittin' By the River	1952	100.00	200.00	400.00
❑ 5091	Make Me Thrill Again/Please Love Me	1952	100.00	200.00	400.00
❑ 5114	Fried Chicken/Good Old 99	1953	100.00	200.00	400.00
—Red vinyl					
❑ 5114	Fried Chicken/Good Old 99	1953	75.00	150.00	300.00

MASCOTS, THE (1)

Number	Title (A Side/B Side)	Yr	VG	VG+	NM
ABC					
❑ 11152	Baby, You're So Wrong/Moreen	1968	2.00	4.00	8.00

MASCOTS, THE (2)

Number	Title (A Side/B Side)	Yr	VG	VG+	NM
BLAST					
❑ 206	Once Upon a Love/Hey Little Angel	1963	10.00	20.00	40.00
—Red label					
❑ 206	Once Upon a Love/Hey Little Angel	1963	5.00	10.00	20.00
—White label					
MERMAID					
❑ 107	Bluebirds Over the Mountain/Timberlands	1962	20.00	40.00	80.00

MASCOTS, THE (3)

Later recorded as THE O'JAYS.

Number	Title (A Side/B Side)	Yr	VG	VG+	NM
KING					
❑ 5377	The Story of My Heart/Do the Wiggle	1960	25.00	50.00	100.00
❑ 5435	Lonely Rain/That's the Way I Feel	1960	15.00	30.00	60.00

MASCOTS, THE (4)

Number	Title (A Side/B Side)	Yr	VG	VG+	NM
MGM					
❑ 12027	Relax-Ay-Voo/The Others I Like	1955	5.00	10.00	20.00
❑ 12107	Nobody's Arms/Little Mustard Seed	1955	5.00	10.00	20.00
❑ 12236	Who Put the Devil in Evelyn's Eyes/Java Jive	1956	5.00	10.00	20.00

MASCOTS, THE (U)

If this is any of the above groups, it's most likely group (1).

Number	Title (A Side/B Side)	Yr	VG	VG+	NM
RUMBLE					
❑ 4197	I Want Love/Waited So Long	196?	5.00	10.00	20.00

MASH, THE

Number	Title (A Side/B Side)	Yr	VG	VG+	NM
COLUMBIA					
❑ 45130	Suicide Is Painless/M*A*S*H March	1970	3.00	6.00	12.00
❑ 45130	Song from M*A*S*H/M*A*S*H March	1970	2.00	4.00	8.00
—Alternate A-side title					

MASKED MARAUDERS, THE

Number	Title (A Side/B Side)	Yr	VG	VG+	NM
DEITY					
❑ 0870	I Can't Get No Nookie/Cow Pie	1969	3.75	7.50	15.00

MASON, BARBARA

Number	Title (A Side/B Side)	Yr	VG	VG+	NM
ARCTIC					
❑ 102	Girls Have Feelings Too/Come to Me	1964	3.00	6.00	12.00
❑ 105	Yes I'm Ready/Keep Him	1965	5.00	10.00	20.00
❑ 108	Sad, Sad Girl/Come to Me	1965	3.00	6.00	12.00
❑ 112	You Got What It Takes/If You Don't (Love Me, Tell Me So)	1965	3.00	6.00	12.00
❑ 116	Don't Ever Want to Lose Your Love/Is It Me	1965	3.00	6.00	12.00
❑ 120	I Need Love/Bobby Is My Baby	1966	2.50	5.00	10.00
❑ 126	Hello Baby/Poor Girl I'm in Trouble	1966	2.50	5.00	10.00
❑ 134	You Can Depend on Me/Game of Love	1967	2.00	4.00	8.00
❑ 137	Oh, How It Hurts/Ain't Got Nobody	1967	2.00	4.00	8.00
❑ 140	Dedicated to the One I Love/Half a Love	1968	2.00	4.00	8.00
❑ 142	Half a Love/(I Can Feel Your Love) Slipping Away	1968	2.00	4.00	8.00
❑ 146	Don't Ever Go Away/I'm No Good for You	1968	2.00	4.00	8.00
❑ 148	Take It Easy/You Never Loved Me	1969	2.00	4.00	8.00
❑ 154	You Better Stop It/Happy Girl	1969	2.00	4.00	8.00
BUDDAH					
❑ 249	The Pow Pow Song (Sorry Sorry Baby)/Your Old Flame	1971	—	3.00	6.00
❑ 296	Bed and Board/Yes It's You	1972	—	2.50	5.00
❑ 319	Woman and Man/Who Will You Hurt Next	1972	—	2.50	5.00
❑ 331	Give Me Your Love/You Can Be with the One You Don't Love	1972	—	2.50	5.00
❑ 355	Yes I'm Ready/Who Will You Hurt Next	1973	—	2.50	5.00
❑ 375	Child of Tomorrow/Out of This World	1973	—	2.50	5.00
❑ 395	Caught in the Middle/Give Him Up	1973	—	2.50	5.00
❑ 405	World War III/I Miss You Gordon	1974	—	2.50	5.00
❑ 424	Our Day Will Come/Half Sister, Half Brother	1974	—	2.50	5.00
❑ 441	From His Woman to You/When You Wake Up in Georgia	1974	—	2.50	5.00
❑ 459	Shackin' Up/One Man Between Us	1975	—	2.50	5.00
❑ 481	Make It Last/We Got Each Other	1975	—	2.50	5.00
—With the Futures					
❑ 481 [PS]	Make It Last/We Got Each Other	1975	2.00	4.00	8.00
CRUSADER					
❑ 111	Dedicated to You/Trouble Child	1965	2.50	5.00	10.00
NATIONAL GENERAL					
❑ 005	Raindrops Keep Fallin' on My Head/If You Knew Him Like I Do	1970	—	3.00	6.00
PRELUDE					
❑ 71103	I Am Your Woman, She Is Your Wife/Take Me Tonight	1978	—	2.50	5.00
❑ 71111	Darling Come Back Home Soon/It Was You Boy	1978	—	2.50	5.00
WEST END					
❑ 1264	Another Man (Vocal) (Short)/Another Man (Instrumental)	1984	—	2.00	4.00
WMOT					
❑ 02506	She's Got the Papers (But I've Got the Man)/(Instrumental)	1981	—	2.00	4.00
❑ 5352	I'll Never Love the Same Way Twice/(B-side unknown)	1980	—	2.00	4.00
❑ 70077	On and Off/You're All Inside of Me	1981	—	2.00	4.00

MASON, BONNIE JO

See CHER.

MASON, DAVE

Also see FLEETWOOD MAC; DAVE MASON AND CASS ELLIOT; TRAFFIC.

Number	Title (A Side/B Side)	Yr	VG	VG+	NM
BLUE THUMB					
❑ 112	World and Changes/Can't Stop Worrying	1970	—	3.00	6.00
❑ 114	Only You Know and I Know/Sad and Deep As You	1970	—	3.00	6.00

Number	Title (A Side/B Side)	Yr	VG	VG+	NM
❑ 205	A Heartache, a Shadow, a Lifetime/Can't Stop Worrying	1972	—	3.00	6.00
❑ 209	To Be Free/Pearly Queen	1972	—	3.00	6.00
❑ 276	Only You Know and I Know/Sad and Deep As You	1975	—	2.50	5.00
❑ 7117	Satin and Red Velvet Woman/Shouldn't Have Took More Than You Gave	1971	—	3.00	6.00
❑ 7122	Just a Song/Waitin' on You	1971	—	3.00	6.00

COLUMBIA

Number	Title (A Side/B Side)	Yr	VG	VG+	NM
❑ 10074	Bring it On Home to Me/Harmony and Melody	1974	—	2.50	5.00
❑ 10104	Every Woman/Relationships	1975	—	2.50	5.00
❑ 10162	Show Me Some Affection/Get a Hold on Love	1975	—	2.50	5.00
❑ 10246	Long Lost Friend/Split Coconut	1975	—	2.50	5.00
❑ 10469	All Along the Watchtower/Sad and Deep As You	1976	—	2.50	5.00
❑ 10509	So High (Rock Me Baby and Roll Me Away)/You Just Have to Wait Now	1977	—	2.50	5.00
❑ 10575	We Just Disagree/Mystic Traveler	1977	—	2.50	5.00
❑ 10662	Let it Go, Let It Flow/Takin' the Time to Find	1978	—	2.50	5.00
❑ 10749	Will You Still Love Me Tomorrow/Mystic Traveler	1978	—	2.50	5.00
❑ 10819	Warm Desire/Don't It Make You Wonder	1978	—	2.50	5.00
❑ 11289	Save Me/Tryin' to Get Back to You	1980	—	2.00	4.00
❑ 45947	Baby... Please/Side-Tracked	1973	—	2.50	5.00

MCA

Number	Title (A Side/B Side)	Yr	VG	VG+	NM
❑ 53205	Dreams I Dream/Fighting for Love	1987	—	2.00	4.00
—A-side with Phoebe Snow					

MASON, DAVE, AND CASS ELLIOT

Also see each artist's individual listings.

ABC DUNHILL

Number	Title (A Side/B Side)	Yr	VG	VG+	NM
❑ 4266	Something to Make You Happy/Next to You	1971	—	3.00	6.00
❑ 4271	Walking to the Point/Too Much Truth, Too Much Love	1971	—	3.00	6.00

MASTER-TONES, THE

BRUCE

Number	Title (A Side/B Side)	Yr	VG	VG+	NM
❑ 111	What'll You Do/Tell Me	1954	125.00	250.00	500.00
—Black vinyl, "New York 19, N.Y." address					
❑ 111	What'll You Do/Tell Me	1954	75.00	150.00	300.00
—Blue vinyl					
❑ 111	What'll You Do/Tell Me	1962	12.50	25.00	50.00
—Black vinyl, "New York, N.Y." address					

MASTERETTES, THE

LE SAGE

Number	Title (A Side/B Side)	Yr	VG	VG+	NM
❑ 716	Never Ever/Follow the Leader	1961	37.50	75.00	150.00

MASTERS, JOHNNY; MASTRO, JOHNNY

See JOHNNY MAESTRO.

MASTERS, KEN

DECCA

Number	Title (A Side/B Side)	Yr	VG	VG+	NM
❑ 31084	Too Late/Parting Hour	1960	5.00	10.00	20.00

MATADORS, THE (1)

CHART MAKER

Number	Title (A Side/B Side)	Yr	VG	VG+	NM
❑ 404	Let Me Dream/Wiggle Wobble	1966	37.50	75.00	150.00

FORBES

Number	Title (A Side/B Side)	Yr	VG	VG+	NM
❑ 230	Let Me Dream/Wiggle Wobble	1966	6.25	12.50	25.00

MATADORS, THE (2)

COLPIX

Number	Title (A Side/B Side)	Yr	VG	VG+	NM
❑ 698	Ace of Hearts/Perfidia	1963	6.25	12.50	25.00
❑ 718	I've Gotta Drive/La Corrida	1963	12.50	25.00	50.00
—A-side is a Jan and Dean track with a new spoken introduction					
❑ 741	C'mon, Let Yourself Go (Part 1)/C'mon, Let Yourself Go (Part 2)	1964	6.25	12.50	25.00

MATADORS, THE (3)

KEITH

Number	Title (A Side/B Side)	Yr	VG	VG+	NM
❑ 6502	If You Left Me Today/It Ain't Nothin' But Rock 'N' Roll	1962	10.00	20.00	40.00
❑ 6504	You'd Be Crying, Too/My Foolish Heart	1963	20.00	40.00	80.00

MATADORS, THE (4)

SUE

Number	Title (A Side/B Side)	Yr	VG	VG+	NM
❑ 700	Pennies from Heaven/Vengeance	1957	30.00	60.00	120.00
❑ 701	Be Good to Me/Have Mercy Baby	1957	20.00	40.00	80.00

MATADORS, THE (U)

Could be group (2) or (3).

JAMIE

Number	Title (A Side/B Side)	Yr	VG	VG+	NM
❑ 1226	Listen/So Near	1962	5.00	10.00	20.00

MATCHBOX 20

ATLANTIC

Number	Title (A Side/B Side)	Yr	VG	VG+	NM
❑ 84704	Bent/Push (Acoustic)	2000	—	—	3.00

LAVA/ATLANTIC

Number	Title (A Side/B Side)	Yr	VG	VG+	NM
❑ 84410	Back 2 Good/Push	1998	—	—	3.00

MATHERS, JERRY

Better known as "The Beaver."

ATLANTIC

Number	Title (A Side/B Side)	Yr	VG	VG+	NM
❑ 2156	Don'tcha Cry/Wind-Up Toy	1962	5.00	10.00	20.00
❑ 2156 [PS]	Don'tcha Cry/Wind-Up Toy	1962	10.00	20.00	40.00

MATHIS, BOBBY, AND THE SEVILLES

SIOUX

Number	Title (A Side/B Side)	Yr	VG	VG+	NM
❑ 51860	Girl in the Drugstore/Going to the City	1960	37.50	75.00	150.00

MATHIS, JOHNNY

COLUMBIA

Number	Title (A Side/B Side)	Yr	VG	VG+	NM
❑ (no #) [DJ]	Columbia Records Presents Johnny Mathis — Take 2	1957	7.50	15.00	30.00
—Promo-only gatefold sleeve containing white-label promos of 40784 and 40851					
❑ SS-7 [S]	The Best of Everything/The Theme from "A Summer Place"	1960	3.75	7.50	15.00
—B-side by Percy Faith; "Stereo Seven" single, small hole, plays at 33 1/3 rpm					
❑ AS 93 [DJ]	The Heart of a Woman (same on both sides)	1974	2.50	5.00	10.00
—Promo release for the Helena Rubenstein cosmetics firm					
❑ AS 93 [PS]	Helena Rubenstein Presents Johnny Mathis for Courant	1974	3.75	7.50	15.00
—Promo sleeve with above single					
❑ AE7 1148 [DJ]	Christmas Is/Sleigh Ride	1977	2.00	4.00	8.00
❑ AE7 1148 [PS]	Christmas Is/Sleigh Ride	1977	3.00	6.00	12.00
—Above single and sleeve were the 1977 Christmas Seals record					
❑ 02194	Nothing Between Us But Love/Deep Purple	1981	—	—	3.00
❑ 03222	When the Lovin' Goes Out of the Lovin'/Warm	1982	—	—	3.00
❑ 04468	Simple/Lead Me to Your Love	1984	—	—	3.00
❑ 04856	Right From the Heart/Hold On	1985	—	—	3.00
❑ 05588	Just One Touch/I Need You (The Journey)	1985	—	—	3.00
❑ 06561	Where Can I Find Christmas?/It's Beginning to Look a Lot Like Christmas	1986	—	2.00	4.00
❑ 07797	I'm on the Outside Looking In/Just Like You	1988	—	—	3.00
❑ 08524	Daydreamin'/Love Brought Us Here Tonight	1988	—	—	3.00
❑ 10080	Sail On White Moon/The Heart of a Woman	1974	—	2.50	5.00
❑ 10112	I'm Stone in Love with You/Foolish	1975	—	2.50	5.00
❑ 10175	The Greatest Gift/You're As Right As Rain	1975	—	2.50	5.00
❑ 10250	Stardust/What I Did for Love	1975	—	2.50	5.00
❑ 10291	One Day in Your Life/Midnight Blue	1976	—	2.50	5.00
❑ 10350	Yellow Roses on Her Gown/Every Time You Touch Me (I Get High)	1976	—	2.50	5.00
❑ 10404	Do Me Wrong, But Do Me/Send In the Clowns	1976	—	2.50	5.00
❑ 10447	When a Child Is Born/Turn the Lights Down	1976	—	2.50	5.00
❑ 10496	Loving You, Losing You/World of Laughter	1977	—	2.50	5.00
❑ 10574	Arianne/99 Miles from L.A.	1977	—	2.50	5.00
❑ 10611	Hold Me, Thrill Me, Kiss Me/The Most Beautiful Girl	1977	—	2.50	5.00
❑ 10640	When a Child Is Born/Every Time You Touch Me (I Get High)	1977	—	2.50	5.00
❑ 10902	The Last Time I Felt Like This/As Time Goes By	1979	—	2.00	4.00
—A-side with Jane Olivor					
❑ 11001	Begin the Beguine/Gone, Gone, Gone	1979	—	2.00	4.00
❑ 11091	No One Else But the One You Love/To the Ends of the Earth	1979	—	2.00	4.00
—A-side with Stephanie Lawrence					
❑ 11158	Christmas in the City of the Angels/The Very First Christmas Day	1979	—	2.50	5.00
❑ 11313	Different Kinda Different/The Lights of Rio	1980	—	2.00	4.00
—A-side with Paulette					
❑ 11409	When a Child Is Born/The Lord's Prayer	1980	—	2.00	4.00
—With Gladys Knight and the Pips					
❑ 30355 [S]	Someone/Very Much in Love	1959	5.00	10.00	20.00
—"Stereo Seven" single, small hole, plays at 33 1/3 rpm					
❑ 30410 [S]	Small World/You Are Everything to Me	1959	5.00	10.00	20.00
—"Stereo Seven" single, small hole, plays at 33 1/3 rpm					
❑ 30483 [S]	Misty/The Story of Our Love	1959	5.00	10.00	20.00
—"Stereo Seven" single, small hole, plays at 33 1/3 rpm					
❑ 30583 [S]	The Best of Everything/Cherie	1959	5.00	10.00	20.00
—"Stereo Seven" single, small hole, plays at 33 1/3 rpm					
❑ 30598 [S]	Heavenly/Hello, Young Lovers	1959	3.75	7.50	15.00
—"Stereo Seven" single, small hole, plays at 33 1/3 rpm					
❑ 30599 [S]	Misty/Stranger in Paradise	1959	3.75	7.50	15.00
—"Stereo Seven" single, small hole, plays at 33 1/3 rpm					
❑ 30600 [S]	Tonight/Maria	1959	3.75	7.50	15.00
—"Stereo Seven" single, small hole, plays at 33 1/3 rpm					
❑ 30601 [S]	Secret Love/And This Is My Beloved	1959	3.75	7.50	15.00
—"Stereo Seven" single, small hole, plays at 33 1/3 rpm					
❑ 30684 [S]	Maria/Hey Love	1960	3.75	7.50	15.00
—"Stereo Seven" single, small hole, plays at 33 1/3 rpm					
❑ 30764 [S]	My Love for You/Oh That Feeling	1960	3.75	7.50	15.00
—"Stereo Seven" single, small hole, plays at 33 1/3 rpm					
❑ 30828 [S]	Everything's Coming Up Roses/I Wish I Were in Love Again	1960	3.00	6.00	12.00
—Part of "JS7-9"; "Stereo Seven" single, small hole, plays at 33 1/3 rpm					
❑ 30829 [S]	You Do Something To Me/Let's Misbehave	1960	3.00	6.00	12.00
—Part of "JS7-9"; "Stereo Seven" single, small hole, plays at 33 1/3 rpm					
❑ 30830 [S]	I Could Have Danced All Night/A Cock-Eyed Optimist	1960	3.00	6.00	12.00
—Part of "JS7-9"; "Stereo Seven" single, small hole, plays at 33 1/3 rpm					
❑ 30831 [S]	I Just Found Out About Love/Let's Do It	1960	3.00	6.00	12.00
—Part of "JS7-9"; "Stereo Seven" single, small hole, plays at 33 1/3 rpm					
❑ 30832 [S]	I Am in Love/Love Eyes	1960	3.00	6.00	12.00
—Part of "JS7-9"; "Stereo Seven" single, small hole, plays at 33 1/3 rpm					
❑ 30866 [S]	How to Handle a Woman/While You're Young	1960	3.75	7.50	15.00
—"Stereo Seven" single, small hole, plays at 33 1/3 rpm					
❑ 30980 [S]	You Set My Heart to Music/Jenny	1961	3.75	7.50	15.00
—"Stereo Seven" single, small hole, plays at 33 1/3 rpm					
❑ 31048 [S]	Laurie, My Love/Should I Wait	1961	3.75	7.50	15.00
—"Stereo Seven" single, small hole, plays at 33 1/3 rpm					
❑ 31238 [S]	Christmas Eve/My Kind of Christmas	1961	6.25	12.50	25.00
—"Stereo Seven" single, small hole, plays at 33 1/3 rpm					
❑ 31261 [S]	Sweet Thursday/One Look	1962	5.00	10.00	20.00
—"Stereo Seven" single, small hole, plays at 33 1/3 rpm					
❑ 31344 [S]	Live It Up/Just Friends	1962	3.00	6.00	12.00
—Part of "JS7-47"; "Stereo Seven" single, small hole, plays at 33 1/3 rpm					
❑ 31345 [S]	Why Not/On a Cold and Rainy Day	1962	3.00	6.00	12.00
—Part of "JS7-47"; "Stereo Seven" single, small hole, plays at 33 1/3 rpm					
❑ 31346 [S]	I Won't Dance/Johnny One Note	1962	3.00	6.00	12.00
—Part of "JS7-47"; "Stereo Seven" single, small hole, plays at 33 1/3 rpm					
❑ 31347 [S]	Crazy in the Heart/Too Much Too Soon	1962	3.00	6.00	12.00
—Part of "JS7-47"; "Stereo Seven" single, small hole, plays at 33 1/3 rpm					
❑ 31348 [S]	Hey Look Me Over/Love	1962	3.00	6.00	12.00
—Part of "JS7-47"; "Stereo Seven" single, small hole, plays at 33 1/3 rpm					
❑ 31420 [S]	Marianna/Unaccustomed As I Am	1962	5.00	10.00	20.00
—"Stereo Seven" single, small hole, plays at 33 1/3 rpm					

Number	Title (A Side/B Side)	Yr	VG	VG+	NM
❑ 31509 [S]	That's the Way It Is/I'll Never Be Lonely Again	1962	5.00	10.00	20.00
—"Stereo Seven" single, small hole, plays at 33 1/3 rpm					
❑ 31582 [S]	Gina/I Love Her That's Why	1962	5.00	10.00	20.00
—"Stereo Seven" single, small hole, plays at 33 1/3 rpm					
❑ 31666 [S]	What Will Mary Say/Quiet Girl	1963	6.25	12.50	25.00
—"Stereo Seven" single, small hole, plays at 33 1/3 rpm					
❑ 31666 [S]	What Will My Mary Say/Quiet Girl	1963	6.25	12.50	25.00
—"Stereo Seven" single, small hole, plays at 33 1/3 rpm; revised A-side title					
❑ 31731 [S]	Rapture/Love Me As Though There Were No Tomorrow	1963	3.00	6.00	12.00
—Part of "JS7-78"; "Stereo Seven" single, small hole, plays at 33 1/3 rpm					
❑ 31732 [S]	Moments Like This/You've Come Home	1963	3.00	6.00	12.00
—Part of "JS7-78"; "Stereo Seven" single, small hole, plays at 33 1/3 rpm					
❑ 31733 [S]	Here I'll Stay/My Darling, My Darling	1963	3.00	6.00	12.00
—Part of "JS7-78"; "Stereo Seven" single, small hole, plays at 33 1/3 rpm					
❑ 31734 [S]	Stars Fell on Alabama/I Was Telling Her About You	1963	3.00	6.00	12.00
—Part of "JS7-78"; "Stereo Seven" single, small hole, plays at 33 1/3 rpm					
❑ 31735 [S]	Lost in Loveliness/Stella by Starlight	1963	3.00	6.00	12.00
—Part of "JS7-78"; "Stereo Seven" single, small hole, plays at 33 1/3 rpm					
❑ 31799 [S]	Every Step of the Way/No Man Can Stand Alone	1963	3.75	7.50	15.00
—"Stereo Seven" single, small hole, plays at 33 1/3 rpm					
❑ 31836 [S]	Sooner or Later/In Wisconsin	1963	3.75	7.50	15.00
—"Stereo Seven" single, small hole, plays at 33 1/3 rpm					
❑ 31916 [S]	I'll Search My Heart/All the Sad Young Men	1963	3.75	7.50	15.00
—"Stereo Seven" single, small hole, plays at 33 1/3 rpm					
❑ 33001	It's Not for Me to Say/Chances Are	196?	—	3.00	6.00
—Red label					
❑ 33001	It's Not for Me to Say/Chances Are	198?	—	—	3.00
—Gray label					
❑ 3-33001	It's Not for Me to Say/Chances Are	196?	3.75	7.50	15.00
—"Hall of Fame Series"; "Columbia Single 33"; small hole					
❑ 33042	Maria/Misty	196?	—	3.00	6.00
—Red label					
❑ 33042	Maria/Misty	198?	—	—	3.00
—Gray label					
❑ 33048	Wonderful, Wonderful/The Twelfth of Never	196?	—	3.00	6.00
—Red label					
❑ 33048	Wonderful, Wonderful/The Twelfth of Never	198?	—	—	3.00
—Gray label					
❑ 33056	Small World/A Certain Smile	196?	—	3.00	6.00
—Red label					
❑ 33056	Small World/A Certain Smile	198?	—	—	3.00
—Gray label					
❑ 33142	Venus/Gina	196?	—	3.00	6.00
—Red label					
❑ 33142	Venus/Gina	198?	—	—	3.00
—Gray label					
❑ 33174	I'll Never Fall in Love Again/A Time for Us	197?	—	2.00	4.00
—Red label					
❑ 33174	I'll Never Fall in Love Again/A Time for Us	198?	—	—	3.00
—Gray label					
❑ 33226	What Will My Mary Say/Call Me	197?	—	2.00	4.00
—Red label					
❑ 33226	What Will My Mary Say/Call Me	198?	—	—	3.00
—Gray label					
❑ 33253	Show and Tell/Soul and Inspiration-Just Once in My Life	197?	—	2.00	4.00
—Red label					
❑ 33253	Show and Tell/Soul and Inspiration-Just Once in My Life	198?	—	—	3.00
—Gray label					
❑ 33264	I'm Coming Home/I'm Stone in Love with You	197?	—	2.00	4.00
—Red label					
❑ 33264	I'm Coming Home/I'm Stone in Love with You	198?	—	—	3.00
—Gray label					
❑ JZSP 39330 [DJ]	In Other Words (Complete Version)/In Other Words (Short Version)	1956	6.25	12.50	25.00
—Promo only, possibly his first single. Came with a "Columbia Records Introduces" sleeve, the presence of which doubles the value					
❑ 40784	Wonderful! Wonderful!/When Sunny Gets Blue	1956	3.00	6.00	12.00
❑ 40851	It's Not for Me to Say/Warm and Tender	1957	3.00	6.00	12.00
❑ 40993	Chances Are/The Twelfth of Never	1957	2.50	5.00	10.00
❑ 40993 [PS]	Chances Are/The Twelfth of Never	1957	5.00	10.00	20.00
❑ 41060	No Love (But Your Love)/Wild Is the Wind	1957	2.50	5.00	10.00
❑ 41060 [PS]	No Love (But Your Love)/Wild Is the Wind	1957	3.75	7.50	15.00
❑ 41082	Come to Me/When I Am With You	1957	2.50	5.00	10.00
❑ 41152	All the Time/Teacher, Teacher	1958	2.50	5.00	10.00
❑ 41193	A Certain Smile/Let It Rain	1958	2.50	5.00	10.00
❑ 41193 [PS]	A Certain Smile/Let It Rain	1958	3.75	7.50	15.00
❑ 41253	Call Me/Stairway to the Sea	1958	2.50	5.00	10.00
❑ 41253 [PS]	Call Me/Stairway to the Sea	1958	3.75	7.50	15.00
❑ 41304	Let's Love/You Are Beautiful	1958	2.50	5.00	10.00
❑ 41355	Someone/Very Much in Love	1959	2.50	5.00	10.00
❑ 41410	Small World/You Are Everything to Me	1959	2.50	5.00	10.00
❑ 41483	Misty/The Story of Our Love	1959	2.50	5.00	10.00
❑ 41483 [PS]	Misty/The Story of Our Love	1959	3.75	7.50	15.00
❑ 41491	The Best of Everything/Cherie	1959	2.50	5.00	10.00
❑ 41491 [PS]	The Best of Everything/Cherie	1959	3.75	7.50	15.00
❑ 41583	Starbright/All Is Well	1960	2.00	4.00	8.00
❑ 41583 [PS]	Starbright/All Is Well	1960	3.00	6.00	12.00
❑ 41684	Maria/Hey Love	1960	2.00	4.00	8.00
—Reissued in 1961 with the same catalog number					
❑ 41764	My Love for You/Oh That Feeling	1960	2.00	4.00	8.00
❑ 3-41764	My Love for You/Oh That Feeling	1960	3.75	7.50	15.00
—"Columbia Single 33"; small hole					
❑ 41866	How to Handle a Woman/While You're Young	1960	2.00	4.00	8.00
❑ 41866 [PS]	How to Handle a Woman/While You're Young	1960	3.00	6.00	12.00
❑ 3-41866	How to Handle a Woman/While You're Young	1960	3.75	7.50	15.00
—"Columbia Single 33"; small hole					
❑ 41980	You Set My Heart to Music/Jenny	1961	2.00	4.00	8.00
❑ 41980 [PS]	You Set My Heart to Music/Jenny	1961	3.00	6.00	12.00
❑ 3-41980	You Set My Heart to Music/Jenny	1961	3.75	7.50	15.00
—"Columbia Single 33"; small hole					
❑ 42005	Should I Wait/Oh How I Try	1961	—	—	—
—Unreleased?					
❑ 3-42005	Should I Wait/Oh How I Try	1961	—	—	—
—Unreleased?					
❑ 42048	Laurie My Love/Should I Wait (Or Should I Run to Her)	1961	2.00	4.00	8.00
❑ 42048 [PS]	Laurie My Love/Should I Wait (Or Should I Run to Her)	1961	3.00	6.00	12.00
❑ 3-42048	Laurie My Love/Should I Wait (Or Should I Run to Her)	1961	3.75	7.50	15.00
—"Columbia Single 33"; small hole					
❑ 42156	Wasn't the Summer Short/There You Are	1961	2.00	4.00	8.00
❑ 42156 [PS]	Wasn't the Summer Short/There You Are	1961	3.00	6.00	12.00
❑ 3-42156	Wasn't the Summer Short/There You Are	1961	3.75	7.50	15.00
—"Columbia Single 33"; small hole					
❑ 42238	My Kind of Christmas/Christmas Eve	1961	3.00	6.00	12.00
❑ 42238 [PS]	My Kind of Christmas/Christmas Eve	1961	5.00	10.00	20.00
❑ 3-42238	My Kind of Christmas/Christmas Eve	1961	5.00	10.00	20.00
—"Columbia Single 33"; small hole					
❑ 42261	Sweet Thursday/One Look	1962	2.00	4.00	8.00
❑ 42261 [PS]	Sweet Thursday/One Look	1962	3.00	6.00	12.00
❑ 3-42261	Sweet Thursday/One Look	1962	3.75	7.50	15.00
—"Columbia Single 33"; small hole					
❑ 42420	Marianna/Unaccustomed As I Am	1962	2.00	4.00	8.00
❑ 42420 [PS]	Marianna/Unaccustomed As I Am	1962	3.00	6.00	12.00
❑ 3-42420	Marianna/Unaccustomed As I Am	1962	3.75	7.50	15.00
—"Columbia Single 33"; small hole					
❑ 42509	That's the Way It Is/I'll Never Be Lonely Again	1962	2.00	4.00	8.00
❑ 42509 [PS]	That's the Way It Is/I'll Never Be Lonely Again	1962	2.50	5.00	10.00
❑ 3-42509	That's the Way It Is/I'll Never Be Lonely Again	1962	3.75	7.50	15.00
—"Columbia Single 33"; small hole					
❑ 42582	Gina/I Love Her That's Why	1962	2.00	4.00	8.00
❑ 42582 [DJ]	Gina (same on both sides)	1962	5.00	10.00	20.00
—Promo only on red vinyl					
❑ 42582 [PS]	Gina/I Love Her That's Why	1962	2.50	5.00	10.00
❑ 3-42582	Gina/I Love Her That's Why	1962	3.75	7.50	15.00
—"Columbia Single 33"; small hole					
❑ 42666	What Will Mary Say/Quiet Girl	1963	2.50	5.00	10.00
❑ 42666	What Will My Mary Say/Quiet Girl	1963	2.00	4.00	8.00
—Revised A-side title					
❑ 42666 [DJ]	What Will My Mary Say (same on both sides)	1963	5.00	10.00	20.00
—Promo only on red vinyl					
❑ 42666 [PS]	What Will Mary Say/Quiet Girl	1963	3.00	6.00	12.00
❑ 3-42666	What Will Mary Say/Quiet Girl	1963	5.00	10.00	20.00
—"Columbia Single 33"; small hole					
❑ 3-42666	What Will My Mary Say/Quiet Girl	1963	3.75	7.50	15.00
—"Columbia Single 33"; small hole; revised A-side title					
❑ 42799	Every Step of the Way/No Man Can Stand Alone	1963	2.00	4.00	8.00
❑ 42799 [PS]	Every Step of the Way/No Man Can Stand Alone	1963	2.50	5.00	10.00
❑ 3-42799	Every Step of the Way/No Man Can Stand Alone	1963	5.00	10.00	20.00
—"Columbia Single 33"; small hole					
❑ 42836	Sooner or Later/In Wisconsin	1963	2.00	4.00	8.00
❑ 3-42836	Sooner or Later/In Wisconsin	1963	5.00	10.00	20.00
—"Columbia Single 33"; small hole					
❑ 42916	I'll Search My Heart/All the Sad Young Men	1963	2.00	4.00	8.00
❑ 42916 [DJ]	I'll Search My Heart (same on both sides)	1963	5.00	10.00	20.00
—Promo only on red vinyl					
❑ 44266	Misty Roses/Don't Talk to Me	1967	—	2.50	5.00
❑ 44357	Among the First to Know/Long Winter Nights	1967	—	2.50	5.00
❑ 44517	Venus/Don't Go Breakin' My Heart	1968	—	2.50	5.00
❑ 44637	You Make Me Think About You/Night Dreams	1968	—	2.50	5.00
❑ 44728	The End of the World/The 59th Street Bridge Song (Feelin' Groovy)	1968	—	2.50	5.00
❑ 44837	I'll Never Fall in Love Again/Whoever You Are, I Love You	1969	—	2.50	5.00
❑ 44915	Love Theme from Romeo and Juliet (A Time for Us)/The World I Threw Away	1969	—	2.50	5.00
❑ JZSP 44991 [DJ]	The Christmas Song (Merry Christmas to You)/What Child Is This?	1958	5.00	10.00	20.00
❑ 45022	Midnight Cowboy/We	1969	—	2.50	5.00
❑ 45035	Give Me Your Love for Christmas/Calypso Noel	1969	—	3.00	6.00
❑ 45035 [PS]	Give Me Your Love for Christmas/Calypso Noel	1969	2.00	4.00	8.00
❑ 45100 [DJ]	Give Me Your Love for Christmas/Calypso Noel	1969	2.00	4.00	8.00
❑ 45100 [PS]	Give Me Your Love for Christmas/Calypso Noel	1969	2.50	5.00	10.00
—The above sleeve and record were the 1969 Christmas Seals promo					
❑ 45104	For All We Know/Odds and Ends	1970	—	2.50	5.00
❑ 45183	The Last Time I Saw Her/Wherefore and Why	1970	—	2.50	5.00
❑ 45223	Darling Lili/Pieces of Dreams	1970	—	2.50	5.00
❑ 45263	Until It's Time for You to Go/Evil Ways	1970	—	2.50	5.00
❑ JZSP 45265 [DJ]	An Open Fire/I Concentrate on You	1959	5.00	10.00	20.00
❑ 45281	Christmas Is/Sign of the Dove	1970	—	2.50	5.00
❑ 45323	I Was There/Ten Times Forever More	1971	—	2.50	5.00
❑ 45371	Evie/Think About Things	1971	—	2.50	5.00
❑ 45415	Long Ago and Far Away/For All We Know	1971	—	2.50	5.00
❑ 45470	How Can You Mend a Broken Heart/If We Only Have Love	1971	—	2.50	5.00
❑ 45513	Christmas Is/Sign of the Dove	1971	—	2.50	5.00
❑ 45559	If We Only Have Love/This Way, Mary	1972	—	2.50	5.00
❑ 45635	Make It Easy on Yourself/Sometimes	1972	—	2.50	5.00
❑ 45729	Soul and Inspiration-Just Once in My Life/I	1972	—	2.50	5.00
❑ 45777	Walking Tall (Theme)/Take Good Care of Her	1973	—	2.50	5.00
❑ 45835	Show and Tell/Happy (Theme from Lady Sings the Blues)	1973	—	2.50	5.00
❑ 45908	I'm Coming Home/Stop, Look, and Listen to Your Heart	1973	—	2.50	5.00
❑ 45975	Life Is a Song Worth Singing/I Just Wanted to Be Me	1973	—	2.50	5.00
❑ 46048	I'm Stone in Love with You/Sweet Child	1974	—	2.50	5.00
❑ JZSP 55369 [DJ]	Maria/Tonight	1959	5.00	10.00	20.00

Number	Title (A Side/B Side)	Yr	VG	VG+	NM
❑ 69092	In the Still of the Night/True Love Ways	1989	—	2.00	4.00
—A-side with Take 6					
MERCURY					
❑ DJ-72 [DJ]	Chim Chim Cheree (same on both sides?)	1964	3.75	7.50	15.00
❑ 72184	Come Back/Your Teenage Dreams	1963	—	3.00	6.00
❑ 72184 [PS]	Come Back/Your Teenage Dreams	1963	2.50	5.00	10.00
❑ 72217	The Little Drummer Boy/Have Reindeer, Will Travel	1963	2.50	5.00	10.00
❑ 72217 [PS]	The Little Drummer Boy/Have Reindeer, Will Travel	1963	5.00	10.00	20.00
❑ 72229	Bye Bye Barbara/A Great Night for Cryin'	1964	—	3.00	6.00
❑ 72229 [PS]	Bye Bye Barbara/A Great Night for Cryin'	1964	2.50	5.00	10.00
❑ 72263	No More/The Fall of Love	1964	—	3.00	6.00
❑ 72287	Taste of Tears/White Roses from a Blue Valentine	1964	—	3.00	6.00
❑ 72339	Listen Lonely Girl/All I Wanted	1964	—	3.00	6.00
❑ 72339 [PS]	Listen Lonely Girl/All I Wanted	1964	2.50	5.00	10.00
❑ 72432	Dianacita/Take the Time	1965	—	3.00	6.00
❑ 72432 [PS]	Dianacita/Take the Time	1965	2.50	5.00	10.00
❑ 72464	Mirage/The Sweetheart Tree	1965	—	3.00	6.00
❑ 72464 [PS]	Mirage/The Sweetheart Tree	1965	2.50	5.00	10.00
❑ 72493	On a Clear Day You Can See Forever/Come Back to Me	1965	—	3.00	6.00
❑ 72539	Moment to Moment/Glass Mountain	1966	—	3.00	6.00
❑ 72568	The Shadow of Your Smile (Love Theme from "The Sandpiper")/The Sweetheart Tree	1966	—	3.00	6.00
❑ 72610	The Impossible Dream/So Nice	1966	—	3.00	6.00
❑ 72610 [PS]	The Impossible Dream/So Nice	1966	2.50	5.00	10.00
❑ 72653	Saturday Sunshine/Two Tickets and a Candy Heart	1967	—	3.00	6.00
❑ 72653 [PS]	Saturday Sunshine/Two Tickets and a Candy Heart	1967	2.50	5.00	10.00

7-Inch Extended Plays

Number	Title (A Side/B Side)	Yr	VG	VG+	NM
COLUMBIA					
❑ B-2129	*It's Not for Me to Say/Warm and Tender/Wonderful, Wonderful/Babalu	1957	3.75	7.50	15.00
❑ B-2129 [PS]	Songs from "Lizzie" and Other Favorites	1957	3.75	7.50	15.00
❑ B-2143	*Come to Me/Wild Is the Wind/No Love/When I Am with You	1957	3.75	7.50	15.00
❑ B-2143 [PS]	Johnny Mathis Sings	1957	3.75	7.50	15.00
❑ B-2537	The Twelfth of Never/Chances Are//Wonderful, Wonderful/It's Not for Me to Say	1959	3.00	6.00	12.00
❑ B-2537 [PS]	Johnny Mathis (Hall of Fame Series)	1959	3.00	6.00	12.00
❑ B-2626	*Call Me/A Certain Smile/All the Time/When Sunny Gets Blue	195?	3.00	6.00	12.00
❑ B-2626 [PS]	Johnny Mathis (Hall of Fame Series)	195?	3.00	6.00	12.00
❑ B-2640	*Come to Me/Wild Is the Wind/Someone/You Are Beautiful	195?	3.00	6.00	12.00
❑ B-2640 [PS]	Johnny Mathis (Hall of Fame Series)	195?	3.00	6.00	12.00
❑ B-8871	*Autumn in Rome/Love, Your Magic Spell Is Everywhere/Cabin in the Sky/In Other Words	1957	3.75	7.50	15.00
❑ B-8871 [PS]	Johnny Mathis, Vol. 1	1957	3.75	7.50	15.00
❑ B-8872	*Caravan/Star Eyes/It Might As Well Be Spring/Street of Dreams	1957	3.75	7.50	15.00
❑ B-8872 [PS]	Johnny Mathis, Vol. 2	1957	3.75	7.50	15.00
❑ B-8873	*Easy to Love/Prelude to a Kiss/Babalu/Angel Eyes	1957	3.75	7.50	15.00
❑ B-8873 [PS]	Johnny Mathis, Vol. 3	1957	3.75	7.50	15.00
❑ B-10281	*Will I Find My Love Today/Looking at You/Let Me Love You/All Through the Night	1957	3.00	6.00	12.00
❑ B-10281 [PS]	Will I Find My Love Today	1957	3.00	6.00	12.00
❑ B-10281 [PS]	Looking at You	1957	3.00	6.00	12.00
—Same contents, different title					
❑ B-10282	*It Could Happen to You/That Old Black Magic/Too Close for Comfort/In the Wee Small Hours of the Morning	1957	3.00	6.00	12.00
❑ B-10282 [PS]	Too Close for Comfort	1957	3.00	6.00	12.00
❑ B-10283	*Year After Year/Early Autumn/You Stepped Out of a Dream/Day In, Day Out	1957	3.00	6.00	12.00
❑ B-10283 [PS]	Day In, Day Out	1957	3.00	6.00	12.00
❑ B-10781	Warm/A Handful of Stars//My One and Only Love/While We're Young	1958	3.00	6.00	12.00
❑ B-10781 [PS]	Warm, Vol. 1	1958	3.00	6.00	12.00
❑ B-10782	*By Myself/I've Grown Accustomed to Her Face/Baby, Baby, Baby/What'll I Do	1958	3.00	6.00	12.00
❑ B-10782 [PS]	Warm, Vol. 2	1958	3.00	6.00	12.00
❑ B-10783	*I'm Glad There Is You/The Lovely Things You Do/There Goes My Heart/Then I'll Be Tired of You	1958	3.00	6.00	12.00
❑ B-10783 [PS]	Warm, Vol. 3	1958	3.00	6.00	12.00
❑ B-11191	*Good Night, Dear Lord/I Heard a Forest Praying/Deep River/Swing Low, Sweet Chariot	1958	2.50	5.00	10.00
❑ B-11191 [PS]	Good Night, Dear Lord	1958	2.50	5.00	10.00
❑ B-11192	*Eli Eli/Kol Nidre/Where Can I Go?/One God	1958	2.50	5.00	10.00
❑ B-11192 [PS]	Eli Eli	1958	2.50	5.00	10.00
❑ B-11193	*Ave Maria (Bach-Gounod)/The Rosary/May the Good Lord Bless and Keep You/Ave Maria (Schubert)	1958	2.50	5.00	10.00
❑ B-11193 [PS]	Ave Maria	1958	2.50	5.00	10.00
❑ B-11651	To Be in Love/You'd Be So Nice to Come Home To//It's De-Lovely/I've Got the World on a String	1958	3.00	6.00	12.00
❑ B-11651 [PS]	Swing Softly, Vol. 1	1958	3.00	6.00	12.00
❑ B-11652	*Sweet Lorraine/Can't Get Out of This Mood/You Hit the Spot/Get Me to the Church on Time	1958	3.00	6.00	12.00
❑ B-11652 [PS]	Swing Softly, Vol. 2	1958	3.00	6.00	12.00
❑ B-11653	*Love Walked In/Easy to Say/This Heart of Mine/Like Someone in Love	1958	3.00	6.00	12.00
❑ B-11653 [PS]	Swing Softly, Vol. 3	1958	3.00	6.00	12.00
❑ B-11951	Winter Wonderland/Blue Christmas//White Christmas/Sleigh Ride	1958	3.00	6.00	12.00
❑ B-11951 [PS]	Merry Christmas, Vol. 1	1958	3.00	6.00	12.00
❑ B-11952	I'll Be Home for Christmas/Oh Holy Night//The Christmas Song/Silver Bells	1958	3.00	6.00	12.00
❑ B-11952 [PS]	Merry Christmas, Vol. 2	1958	3.00	6.00	12.00
❑ B-11953	The First Noel/It Came Upon a Midnight Clear//What Child Is This?/Silent Night, Holy Night	1958	3.00	6.00	12.00
❑ B-11953 [PS]	Merry Christmas, Vol. 3	1958	3.00	6.00	12.00
❑ B-12701	*Open Fire/Please Be Kind/Bye Bye Blackbird/Tenderly	1959	2.50	5.00	10.00
❑ B-12701 [PS]	Open Fire, Two Guitars, Vol. 1	1959	2.50	5.00	10.00
❑ B-12702	*Embraceable You/My Funny Valentine/I'll Be Seeing You/I'm Just a Boy in Love	1959	2.50	5.00	10.00
❑ B-12702 [PS]	Open Fire, Two Guitars, Vol. 2	1959	2.50	5.00	10.00
❑ B-12703	*I Concentrate on You/You'll Never Know/When I Fall in Love/In the Still of the Night	1959	2.50	5.00	10.00
❑ B-12703 [PS]	Open Fire, Two Guitars, Vol. 3	1959	2.50	5.00	10.00
❑ B-13511	*Heavenly/Misty/Hello, Young Lovers/I'll Be Easy to Find	1959	2.50	5.00	10.00
❑ B-13511 [PS]	Heavenly, Vol. 1	1959	2.50	5.00	10.00
❑ B-13512	*Something I Dreamed Last Night/Moonlight Becomes You/They Say It's Wonderful/More Than You Know	1959	2.50	5.00	10.00
❑ B-13512 [PS]	Heavenly, Vol. 2	1959	2.50	5.00	10.00
❑ B-13513	A Lovely Way to Spend an Evening/That's All//A Ride on a Rainbow/Stranger in Paradise	1959	2.50	5.00	10.00
❑ B-13513 [PS]	Heavenly, Vol. 3	1959	2.50	5.00	10.00
❑ B-14221	Secret Love/Where Are You//Maria/Where Do You Think You're Going	1959	2.50	5.00	10.00
❑ B-14221 [PS]	Faithfully, Vol. 1	1959	2.50	5.00	10.00
❑ B-14222	*Faithfully/One Starry Night/Nobody Knows/You Better Go Now	1959	2.50	5.00	10.00
❑ B-14222 [PS]	Faithfully, Vol. 2	1959	2.50	5.00	10.00
❑ B-14223	And This Is My Beloved/Tonight//Follow Me/Blue Gardenia	1959	2.50	5.00	10.00
❑ B-14223 [PS]	Faithfully, Vol. 3	1959	2.50	5.00	10.00
❑ B-15261	Goodnight My Love/There's No You//Once/I'm So Lost	1960	2.50	5.00	10.00
❑ B-15261 [PS]	Johnny's Mood, Vol. 1	1960	2.50	5.00	10.00
❑ B-15262	*Corner to Corner/The Folks Who Live on the Hill/I'm in the Mood for Love/Stay Warm	1960	2.50	5.00	10.00
❑ B-15262 [PS]	Johnny's Mood, Vol. 2	1960	2.50	5.00	10.00
❑ B-15263	*I'm Gonna Laugh You Right Out of My Life/How High the Moon/April in Paris/In Return	1960	2.50	5.00	10.00
❑ B-15263 [PS]	Johnny's Mood, Vol. 3	1960	2.50	5.00	10.00

MATHIS, JOHNNY/DENIECE WILLIAMS

Number	Title (A Side/B Side)	Yr	VG	VG+	NM
COLUMBIA					
❑ 04379	Love Won't Let Me Wait/Lead Me to Your Love	1984	—	—	3.00
❑ 10693	Too Much, Too Little, Too Late/Emotion	1978	—	2.50	5.00
❑ 10693	Too Much, Too Little, Too Late/I Wrote a Symphony on My Guitar	1978	2.50	5.00	10.00
—B-side by Johnny Mathis solo					
❑ 10772	You're All I Need to Get By/You're a Special Part of My Life	1978	—	2.50	5.00
❑ 10772 [PS]	You're All I Need to Get By	1978	2.50	5.00	10.00
—Sleeve is promo only					
❑ 10826	That's What Friends Are For/I Just Can't Get Over You	1978	—	2.50	5.00
❑ 33360	Too Much, Too Little, Too Late/You're All I Need to Get By	198?	—	2.00	4.00
—Red label					
❑ 33360	Too Much, Too Little, Too Late/You're All I Need to Get By	198?	—	—	3.00
—Gray label					

MATHIS BROTHERS, THE

See DEAN AND MARK; THE NEWBEATS.

MATTHEWS, FAT MAN

Number	Title (A Side/B Side)	Yr	VG	VG+	NM
BAYOU					
❑ 016	I'm Thankful/Goin' Down	1952	37.50	75.00	150.00
IMPERIAL					
❑ 5211	When Boy Meets Girl/Later Baby	1952	1000.	1500.	2000.
❑ 5235	Down the Line/You Know It	1953	25.00	50.00	100.00

MATTY, JAY

Number	Title (A Side/B Side)	Yr	VG	VG+	NM
ERA					
❑ 3008	Janie My Lover/Tall Tale	1959	3.75	7.50	15.00
LUTE					
❑ 6021	Merry Twist Mas/Teenage Monster	1961	5.00	10.00	20.00

MAUDS, THE

Number	Title (A Side/B Side)	Yr	VG	VG+	NM
DUNWICH					
❑ 160	Hold On/C'mon and Move	1967	3.00	6.00	12.00
MERCURY					
❑ 72694	Hold On/C'mon and Move	1967	2.00	4.00	8.00
❑ 72720	When Something Is Wrong (With My Baby)/You Make Me Feel So Bad	1967	2.00	4.00	8.00
❑ 72760	He Will Break Your Heart/You Must Believe Me	1967	2.00	4.00	8.00
❑ 72832	Forever Gone/Soul Drippin'	1968	2.00	4.00	8.00
❑ 72877	Only Love Can Save You/Sergeant Sunshine	1968	2.00	4.00	8.00
❑ 72919	Brother Chickie/Satisfy My Hunger	1969	2.00	4.00	8.00
RCA VICTOR					
❑ 74-0377	Forget It, I've Got It/A Man Without a Dream	1970	—	3.00	6.00

MAXIMILLIAN

Organist/keyboard player on DEL SHANNON's biggest hit records of the early 1960s.

Number	Title (A Side/B Side)	Yr	VG	VG+	NM
BIG TOP					
❑ 3068	The Wanderer/The Snake	1961	5.00	10.00	20.00
❑ 3095	The Twistin' Ghost/The Breeze and I-Peter Gunn Theme	1961	5.00	10.00	20.00
CUB					
❑ 9046	Gee Baby, You're the Utmost/Blowing My Brains Out (Over You)	1959	6.25	12.50	25.00

MAXWELL, HOLLY

Number	Title (A Side/B Side)	Yr	VG	VG+	NM
CONSTELLATION					
❑ 152	One Thin Dime/It's Impossible	1965	6.25	12.50	25.00
❑ 162	Let Him Go for Himself/Only When You're Lonely	1965	6.25	12.50	25.00
CURTOM					
❑ 1942	No One Else/Suffer	1969	3.00	6.00	12.00

MAY, BRIAN, AND FRIENDS

Also see QUEEN.

Number	Title (A Side/B Side)	Yr	VG	VG+	NM
CAPITOL					
❑ B-5278	Star Fleet/Son of Star Fleet	1983	—	2.00	4.00

MAYALL, JOHN

Number	Title (A Side/B Side)	Yr	VG	VG+	NM
ABC					
❑ 12216	Sunshine/Turn Me Loose	1976	—	2.50	5.00
BLUE THUMB					
❑ 264	Step in the Sun/Al Goldstein Blues	1975	—	2.50	5.00
IMMEDIATE					
❑ 502	Telephone Blues/I'm Your Witch Doctor	1967	2.00	4.00	8.00
LONDON					
❑ 20016	Key to Love/Parchman Farm	1966	2.50	5.00	10.00
❑ 20024	All Your Love/Hideaway	1966	2.50	5.00	10.00
❑ 20035	Oh, Pretty Woman/Suspicions	1967	2.00	4.00	8.00
❑ 20037	Jenny/Picture on the Wall	1967	2.00	4.00	8.00
❑ 20039	Broken Wings/Sonny Boy Blue	1967	2.00	4.00	8.00
❑ 20042	Living Alone/Walking on Sunset	1968	2.00	4.00	8.00
POLYDOR					
❑ 14004	Don't Waste My Time/Don't Pick a Flower	1969	—	3.00	6.00
❑ 14010	Room to Move/Saw Mill Gulch Road	1969	—	3.00	6.00
❑ 14051	Nature's Disappearing/My Pretty Girl	1970	—	3.00	6.00
❑ 14117	Nobody Cares/Play the Harp	1972	—	3.00	6.00
❑ 14151	Moving On/Keep Our Country Green	1972	—	3.00	6.00
❑ 14243	The 1974 Gasoline Blues/Brand New Band	1974	—	3.00	6.00
❑ 14253	Let Me Give/Passing Through	1974	—	3.00	6.00

MAYE, LEE

Also recorded as "Arthur Lee Maye."

Number	Title (A Side/B Side)	Yr	VG	VG+	NM
ABC					
❑ 11028	If You Leave Me/The Greatest Love I've Ever Known	1967	2.00	4.00	8.00
BUDDAH					
❑ 141	He'll Have to Go/Jus' Lookin'	1969	—	3.00	6.00
CASH					
❑ 1063	Will You Be Mine/Honey Honey	1958	37.50	75.00	150.00
❑ 1065	All I Want Is Someone to Love/Pounding	1958	30.00	60.00	120.00
DIG					
❑ 124	This Is the Night for Love/(B-side unknown)	1956	62.50	125.00	250.00
❑ 133	A Fool's Prayer/(B-side unknown)	1957	37.50	75.00	150.00
FLIP					
❑ 330	Hey Pretty Baby/'Cause You're Mine Alone	1958	20.00	40.00	80.00
—As "Arthur Lee Maye"					
IMPERIAL					
❑ 5790	Will You Be Mine/Honey Honey	1961	5.00	10.00	20.00
JAMIE					
❑ 1272	Who Made You What You Are/Loving Fool	1964	2.50	5.00	10.00
❑ 1276	How's the World Treating You/Loving Fool	1964	2.50	5.00	10.00
❑ 1284	Only a Dream/The Breaks of Life	1964	2.50	5.00	10.00
❑ 1287	Even a Nobody/Who Made You What You Are	1964	2.50	5.00	10.00
❑ 1295	(Don't Pretend) Just Lay It on the Line/Careless Hands	1965	2.00	4.00	8.00
—With Barbara Lynn					
LENOX					
❑ 5566	Half Way (Out of Love with You)/I Can't Please You	1963	3.00	6.00	12.00
MODERN					
❑ 944	Set My Heart Free/I Wanna Love	1954	150.00	300.00	600.00
—As "Arthur Lee Maye and the Crowns"					
RPM					
❑ 424	Truly/Oochie Pachie	1955	50.00	100.00	200.00
—As "Arthur Lee Maye and the Crowns"					
❑ 429	Loop De Loop/Love Me Always	1955	30.00	60.00	120.00
—As "Arthur Lee Maye"					
❑ 438	Do the Bop/Please Don't Leave Me	1955	37.50	75.00	150.00
—As "Arthur Lee Maye and the Crowns"					
SPECIALTY					
❑ 573	Gloria/Oo-Rooba-Lee	1956	15.00	30.00	60.00
—As "Arthur Lee Maye and the Crowns"					
TOWER					
❑ 243	When My Heart Hurts No More/At the Party	1966	2.00	4.00	8.00

MAYER, NATHANIEL

Number	Title (A Side/B Side)	Yr	VG	VG+	NM
FORTUNE					
❑ 449	Village of Love/I Want a Woman	1962	6.25	12.50	25.00
❑ 487	Hurting Love/Leave Me Alone	1962	7.50	15.00	30.00
—Fortune 449 and 487 were part of the United Artists numbering system					
❑ 542	My Last Dance with You/My Little Darling	1962	5.00	10.00	20.00
❑ 545	Village of Love/I Want a Woman	1962	5.00	10.00	20.00
❑ 547	Hurting Love/Leave Me Alone	1962	5.00	10.00	20.00
❑ 550	Mr. Santa Claus/(B-side unknown)	1962	7.50	15.00	30.00
❑ 550	Work It Out/Well, I've Got News	1962	3.75	7.50	15.00
❑ 554	I Had a Dream/I'm Not Gonna Cry	1963	3.75	7.50	15.00
❑ 557	Going Back to the Village of Love/My Last Dance with You	1963	3.75	7.50	15.00
❑ 562	The Place I Know/Don't Come Back	196?	3.75	7.50	15.00
❑ 563	Village of Love/I Want a Woman	196?	3.00	6.00	12.00
❑ 567	From Now On/I Want Love and Affection	196?	3.00	6.00	12.00

MAYFIELD, CURTIS

Also see THE IMPRESSIONS.

Number	Title (A Side/B Side)	Yr	VG	VG+	NM
ARISTA					
❑ 9806	He's a Flyguy/(Instrumental)	1989	—	—	2.00
❑ 9806 [PS]	He's a Flyguy/(Instrumental)	1989	—	—	3.00
—With Fishbone					
BOARDWALK					
❑ NB7-11-122	She Don't Let Nobody (But Me)/You Get All My Love	1981	—	2.00	4.00
❑ NB7-11-132	Toot An'Toot An'Toot/Come Free Your People	1981	—	2.00	4.00
❑ NB7-11-155	Hey Baby (Give It All to Me)/Summer Hot	1982	—	2.00	4.00
❑ NB7-11-169	Dirty Laundry/Nobody But You	1982	—	2.00	4.00
COLUMBIA					
❑ 10147	Stash That Butt, Sucker/Zanzibar	1975	—	2.50	5.00
CRC					
❑ 001	Baby It's You/(B-side unknown)	1985	—	3.00	6.00
CURTOM					
❑ 0105	So in Love/Hard Times	1975	—	2.50	5.00
❑ 0118	Only You Babe/Love to the People	1976	—	2.50	5.00
❑ 0122	Party Night/P.S. I Love You	1976	—	2.50	5.00
❑ 0125	Show Me Love/Just Want to Be with You	1977	—	2.50	5.00
❑ 0131	Do Do Wap Is Strong in Here/Need Someone to Love	1977	—	2.50	5.00
❑ 0135	You Are, You Are/Get a Little Bit (Give, Get, Take and Have)	1978	—	2.50	5.00
❑ 0135 [PS]	You Are, You Are/Get a Little Bit (Give, Get, Take and Have)	1978	—	3.00	6.00
❑ 0141	Do It All Night/Party Party	1978	—	2.50	5.00
❑ 0142	In Love, In Love, In Love/Keeps Me Loving You	1978	—	2.50	5.00
❑ 1955	(Don't Worry) If There's a Hell Below We're All Going to Go/The Makings of You	1970	—	3.00	6.00
❑ 1960	Beautiful Brother of Mine/Give It Up	1971	—	3.00	6.00
❑ 1963	Mighty Mighty (Spade and Whitey)/(B-side unknown)	1971	—	3.00	6.00
❑ 1966	Get Down/We're a Winner	1971	—	3.00	6.00
❑ 1968	We Got to Have Peace/We're a Winner	1972	—	3.00	6.00
❑ 1968 [PS]	We Got to Have Peace/We're a Winner	1972	2.00	4.00	8.00
❑ 1972	Beautiful Brother of Mine/Love to Keep You In My Mind	1972	—	3.00	6.00
❑ 1974	Move On Up/Underground	1972	—	3.00	6.00
❑ 1975	Freddie's Dead (Theme from "Superfly")/ Underground	1972	—	3.00	6.00
❑ 1978	Superfly/Underground	1972	—	3.00	6.00
❑ 1978 [PS]	Superfly/Underground	1972	2.00	4.00	8.00
❑ 1987	Future Shock/The Other Side of Town	1973	—	3.00	6.00
❑ 1991	If I Were Only a Child Again/Think	1973	—	3.00	6.00
❑ 1993	Can't Say Nothin'/Future Song	1973	—	3.00	6.00
❑ 1999	Kung Fu/Right On for the Darkness	1974	—	3.00	6.00
❑ 1999 [PS]	Kung Fu/Right On for the Darkness	1974	2.00	4.00	8.00
❑ 2005	Sweet Exorcist/Suffer	1974	—	3.00	6.00
❑ 2006	Mother's Son/Love Me	1974	—	3.00	6.00
RSO/CURTOM					
❑ 919	This Year/(Instrumental)	1979	—	2.50	5.00
❑ 941	You're So Good to Me/Between You, Babe, and Me	1979	—	2.50	5.00
—With Linda Clifford					
❑ 1029	Love's Sweet Sensation/(Instrumental)	1980	—	2.50	5.00
—With Linda Clifford					
❑ 1036	Love Me, Love Me Now/It's Alright	1980	—	2.50	5.00
❑ 1046	Tripping Out/Never Stop Loving	1980	—	2.50	5.00

MAYFIELD, PERCY

Number	Title (A Side/B Side)	Yr	VG	VG+	NM
ATLANTIC					
❑ 3207	I Don't Want to Be President/Nothin' Stays the Same Forever	1974	—	2.50	5.00
BRUNSWICK					
❑ 55390	Walking on a Tightrope/P.M. Blues	1968	2.00	4.00	8.00
CHESS					
❑ 1599	Double Dealing/Are You Out There	1955	15.00	30.00	60.00
IMPERIAL					
❑ 5577	One Love/My Reward	1959	3.75	7.50	15.00
❑ 5620	My Heart Is a Prisoner/My Memories	1959	3.75	7.50	15.00
KING					
❑ 4480	Two Years of Torture/Half Awake	1951	15.00	30.00	60.00
RCA VICTOR					
❑ 74-0307	To Live the Past/Lying Woman (Not Trustworthy)	1970	—	3.00	6.00
❑ 74-0348	A Highway Is Like a Woman/You Wear Your Hair Too Long	1970	—	3.00	6.00
❑ 74-0379	Daddy Wants You to Come Home/Weakness Is a Thing Called Man	1970	—	3.00	6.00
❑ 74-0462	The Flirt/California Blues	1971	—	3.00	6.00
SPECIALTY					
❑ 375	Please Send Me Someone to Love/Strange Things Happening	1950	20.00	40.00	80.00
❑ 390	Lost Love/Life Is Suicide	1951	15.00	30.00	60.00
❑ 400	What a Fool I Was/Nightless Lover	1951	15.00	30.00	60.00
❑ 408	Prayin' For Your Return/My Blues	1951	15.00	30.00	60.00
❑ 416	Cry Baby/Hopeless	1952	10.00	20.00	40.00
❑ 425	The Big Question/The Hurt Is On	1952	10.00	20.00	40.00
❑ 432	Louisiana/Two Hearts Are Greater Than One	1952	10.00	20.00	40.00
❑ 439	Lonesome Highway/My Heart	1952	10.00	20.00	40.00
❑ 460	Lost Mind/Lonely One	1953	10.00	20.00	40.00
—Black vinyl					
❑ 460	Lost Mind/Lonely One	1953	20.00	40.00	80.00
—Colored vinyl					
❑ 473	The Bachelor Blues/How Deep Is the Well	1953	10.00	20.00	40.00
—Black vinyl					
❑ 473	The Bachelor Blues/How Deep Is the Well	1953	20.00	40.00	80.00
—Colored vinyl					
❑ 485	I Need Love So Bad/Loose Lips	1954	10.00	20.00	40.00

Number	Title (A Side/B Side)	Yr	VG	VG+	NM
❑ 499	You Don't Exist No More/Sugar Mama, Peach Papa	1954	10.00	20.00	40.00
❑ 537	My Heart Is Cryin'/You Were Lyin' to Me	1954	10.00	20.00	40.00
❑ 544	Baby You're Rich/The Voice Within	1955	7.50	15.00	30.00
❑ 607	Diggin' the Moonglow/Please Believe Me	1956	7.50	15.00	30.00
❑ 690	When Did You Leave Heaven/What Must I Do	1960	5.00	10.00	20.00
❑ 723	Lost Mind/River's Invitation	1973	—	3.00	6.00
TANGERINE					
❑ 923	Never No More/I Reached for a Tear	1962	3.00	6.00	12.00
❑ 927	Never Say Now/Life Is Suicide	1963	2.50	5.00	10.00
❑ 931	River's Invitation/Baby Please	1963	2.50	5.00	10.00
❑ 934	The Hunt Is On/Cookin' in Style	1963	2.50	5.00	10.00
❑ 935	You Don't Exist No More/Memory Pain	1964	2.50	5.00	10.00
❑ 941	Stranger in My Own Home Town/Maybe It's Because of Love	1964	2.50	5.00	10.00
❑ 950	Fading Love/Stand By	1965	2.00	4.00	8.00
❑ 957	Give Me Time to Explain/My Jug and I	1965	2.00	4.00	8.00
❑ 966	It's Time to Make a Change/We Both Must Cry	1966	2.00	4.00	8.00
❑ 973	My Love/My Bottle Is My Companion	1966	2.00	4.00	8.00
❑ 977	As Long As You're Mine/Ha Ha in the Daytime	1967	2.00	4.00	8.00
❑ 979	Don't Start Lyin' to Me/Pretty Eyed Baby	1967	2.00	4.00	8.00

MAYO, FRANKIE, AND THE FALCONS

RCA VICTOR

Number	Title (A Side/B Side)	Yr	VG	VG+	NM
❑ 47-7076	Stepping Stone/Jigsaw Puzzle	1957	6.25	12.50	25.00

MAYS, WILLIE

Number	Title (A Side/B Side)	Yr	VG	VG+	NM
DUKE					
❑ 350	My Sad Heart/If You Love Me	1962	2.50	5.00	10.00
❑ 418	My Sad Heart/If You Love Me	1967	2.00	4.00	8.00
EPIC					
❑ 9066	Say Hey (The Willie Mays Song)/Out of the Bushes	1954	6.25	12.50	25.00
—With the Treniers					

MC5

Number	Title (A Side/B Side)	Yr	VG	VG+	NM
A-SQUARE					
❑ 333	Looking at You/Borderline	1967	20.00	40.00	80.00
—500 copies of this record were pressed					
❑ 333 [PS]	Looking at You/Borderline	1967	10.00	20.00	40.00
ALIVE/TOTAL ENERGY					
❑ NER 3012	Looking at You/Borderline	1998	—	—	2.00
—30th anniversary reissue					
❑ NER 3012 [PS]	Looking at You/Borderline	1998	—	—	2.00
AMG					
❑ 1000 [DJ]	I Can Only Give You Everything (same on both sides)	1966	12.50	25.00	50.00
❑ 1001	I Can Only Give You Everything/One of the Guys	1969	12.50	25.00	50.00
—Yellow label					
❑ 1001	I Can Only Give You Everything/I Just Don't Know	1969	12.50	25.00	50.00
—Black label					
ATLANTIC					
❑ 2678	Tonight/Looking at You	1969	3.75	7.50	15.00
❑ 2724	The American Ruse/Shakin' Street	1970	3.75	7.50	15.00
ELEKTRA					
❑ MC5-1 [DJ]	Kick Out the Jams/Motor City Is Burning	1968	17.50	35.00	70.00
—Distributed free at Fillmore East concert 12/12/68; A-side is an alternate take					
❑ 45648	Kick Out the Jams/Motor City Is Burning	1969	5.00	10.00	20.00

MCCARTNEY, LINDA

See PAUL McCARTNEY; SUZY AND THE RED STRIPES.

MCCARTNEY, PAUL

Includes duets with Linda McCartney plus his work with Wings. Also see THE BEATLES; MICHAEL JACKSON AND PAUL McCARTNEY.

Number	Title (A Side/B Side)	Yr	VG	VG+	NM
APPLE					
❑ 1829	Another Day/Oh Woman, Oh Why	1971	3.00	6.00	12.00
—With star on A-side label					
❑ 1829	Another Day/Oh Woman, Oh Why	1971	2.00	4.00	8.00
❑ 1837	Uncle Albert/Admiral Halsey//Too Many People	1971	3.75	7.50	15.00
—Paul and Linda McCartney; with "Pual" misspelling on producer credit					
❑ 1837	Uncle Albert/Admiral Halsey//Too Many People	1971	2.00	4.00	8.00
—Paul and Linda McCartney; with no misspelling					
❑ 1837	Uncle Albert/Admiral Halsey//Too Many People	1971	12.50	25.00	50.00
—Paul and Linda McCartney; with unsliced apple on B-side label					
❑ 1837	Uncle Albert/Admiral Halsey//Too Many People	1975	7.50	15.00	30.00
—Paul and Linda McCartney; with "All rights reserved" on label					
❑ 1847	Give Ireland Back to the Irish/Give Ireland Back to the Irish (Version)	1972	2.50	5.00	10.00
—Wings					
❑ 1847 [PS]	Give Ireland Back to the Irish/Give Ireland Back to the Irish (Version)	1972	7.50	15.00	30.00
—Wings; title sleeve with large center hole					
❑ 1851	Mary Had a Little Lamb/Little Woman Love	1972	2.50	5.00	10.00
—Wings					
❑ 1851 [DJ]	Mary Had a Little Lamb/Little Woman Love	1972	75.00	150.00	300.00
—White label promo, lists artist as Paul McCartney					
❑ 1851 [PS]	Mary Had a Little Lamb/Little Woman Love	1972	6.25	12.50	25.00
—Wings; without "Little Woman Love" on sleeve					
❑ 1851 [PS]	Mary Had a Little Lamb/Little Woman Love	1972	10.00	20.00	40.00
—Wings; with "Little Woman Love" on sleeve					
❑ 1857	Hi Hi Hi/C Moon	1972	2.50	5.00	10.00
—Wings; red label					
❑ 1861	My Love/The Mess	1973	2.00	4.00	8.00
—Paul McCartney and Wings; custom "Red Rose Speedway" label					
❑ 1861 [DJ]	My Love/The Mess	1973	50.00	100.00	200.00
—Paul McCartney and Wings; white label					
❑ 1863	Live and Let Die/I Lie Around	1973	2.00	4.00	8.00
—Wings					
❑ 1869	Helen Wheels/Country Dreamer	1973	2.00	4.00	8.00
—Paul McCartney and Wings					
❑ 1871	Jet/Mamunia	1974	2.50	5.00	10.00
—Paul McCartney and Wings					
❑ 1871	Jet/Mamunia	1974	25.00	50.00	100.00
—Paul McCartney and Wings; A-side incorrectly listed as playing for 2:49					
❑ 1871	Jet/Let Me Roll It	1974	2.00	4.00	8.00
—Paul McCartney and Wings					
❑ P-1871 [DJ]	Jet (Edited Mono)/Jet (Stereo)	1974	12.50	25.00	50.00
—Paul McCartney and Wings					
❑ 1873	Band on the Run/Nineteen Hundred and Eighty-Five	1974	2.00	4.00	8.00
—Paul McCartney and Wings					
❑ P-1873 [DJ]	Band on the Run (Edited Mono)/Band on the Run (Full-length Stereo)	1974	10.00	20.00	40.00
—Paul McCartney and Wings					
❑ P-1873 [DJ]	Band on the Run (mono/stereo, both edits)	1974	25.00	50.00	100.00
—Paul McCartney and Wings					
❑ 1875	Junior's Farm/Sally G	1974	2.00	4.00	8.00
—Paul McCartney and Wings					
❑ 1875	Junior's Farm/Sally G	1975	20.00	40.00	80.00
—Paul McCartney and Wings; with "All Rights Reserved" on label					
❑ P-1875 [DJ]	Junior's Farm (Edited Mono)/Junior's Farm (Full-length Stereo)	1974	12.50	25.00	50.00
—Paul McCartney and Wings					
❑ P-1875 [DJ]	Sally G (mono/stereo)	1974	20.00	40.00	80.00
—Paul McCartney and Wings					
❑ PRO-6193/4 [DJ]	Another Day/Oh Woman, Oh Why	1971	20.00	40.00	80.00
❑ PRO-6786 [DJ]	Helen Wheels (mono/stereo)	1973	12.50	25.00	50.00
—Paul McCartney and Wings					
❑ PRO-6787 [DJ]	Country Dreamer (mono/stereo)	1973	100.00	200.00	400.00
—Paul McCartney and Wings					
CAPITOL					
❑ (no #) [DJ]	Figure of Eight (same on both sides)	1989	25.00	50.00	100.00
—Test pressings with blank label; most known copies come in a Capitol sleeve					
❑ 1829	Another Day/Oh Woman, Oh Why	1976	3.75	7.50	15.00
—Black label					
❑ 1837	Uncle Albert/Admiral Halsey//Too Many People	1976	3.75	7.50	15.00
—Black label					
❑ 1847	Give Ireland Back to the Irish/Give Ireland Back to the Irish	1976	5.00	10.00	20.00
—Wings; black label					
❑ 1851	Mary Had a Little Lamb/Little Woman Love	1976	3.00	6.00	12.00
—Wings; black label					
❑ 1857	Hi Hi Hi/C Moon	1976	3.75	7.50	15.00
—Wings; black label					
❑ 1861	My Love/The Mess	1976	5.00	10.00	20.00
—Paul McCartney and Wings; black label; "The Mess" plays too fast					
❑ 1861	My Love/The Mess	1976	5.00	10.00	20.00
—Paul McCartney and Wings; black label; "The Mess" plays normally					
❑ 1863	Live and Let Die/I Lie Around	1976	3.00	6.00	12.00
—Wings; black label					
❑ 1869	Helen Wheels/Country Dreamer	1976	3.75	7.50	15.00
—Paul McCartney and Wings; black label					
❑ 1871	Jet/Let Me Roll It	1976	3.75	7.50	15.00
—Paul McCartney and Wings; black label					
❑ 1873	Band on the Run/Nineteen Hundred and Eighty-Five	1976	3.75	7.50	15.00
—Paul McCartney and Wings; black label					
❑ 1875	Junior's Farm/Sally G	1976	3.75	7.50	15.00
—Paul McCartney and Wings; black label					
❑ 4091	Listen to What the Man Said/Love in Song	1975	—	2.50	5.00
❑ 4091 [PS]	Listen to What the Man Said/Love in Song	1975	3.00	6.00	12.00
—Wings					
❑ 4145	Letting Go/You Gave Me the Answer	1975	—	2.50	5.00
—Wings					
❑ 4175	Venus and Mars Rock Show/Magneto and Titanium Man	1975	—	2.50	5.00
—Wings					
❑ 4256	Silly Love Songs/Cook of the House	1976	2.00	4.00	8.00
—Wings; black label					
❑ 4256	Silly Love Songs/Cook of the House	1976	—	2.00	4.00
—Wings; "Speed of Sound" label (more common version)					
❑ 4293	Let 'Em In/Beware My Love	1976	—	3.00	6.00
—Wings; black label (more common version)					
❑ 4293	Let 'Em In/Beware My Love	1976	—	2.00	4.00
—Wings; "Speed of Sound" label					
❑ 4385	Maybe I'm Amazed/Soily	1976	—	2.00	4.00
—Wings; custom label (more common version)					
❑ 4385	Maybe I'm Amazed/Soily	1976	5.00	10.00	20.00
—Wings; black label					
❑ 4504	Girls' School/Mull of Kintyre	1977	—	2.50	5.00
—Wings; black label (more common version)					
❑ 4504	Girls' School/Mull of Kintyre	1978	30.00	60.00	120.00
—Wings; purple label, label has reeded edge					
❑ 4504 [PS]	Girls' School/Mull of Kintyre	1977	3.00	6.00	12.00
—Wings					
❑ 4559	With a Little Luck/Backwards Traveller-Cuff Link	1978	—	2.00	4.00
—Wings					
❑ 4594	I've Had Enough/Deliver Your Children	1978	—	2.00	4.00
—Wings					
❑ 4625	London Town/I'm Carrying	1978	—	2.00	4.00
—Wings					
❑ B-5537	Spies Like Us/My Carnival	1985	—	—	3.00
❑ B-5537 [PS]	Spies Like Us/My Carnival	1985	—	3.00	6.00
❑ B-5597	Press/It's Not True	1986	—	2.50	5.00
❑ B-5597 [PS]	Press/It's Not True	1986	—	2.50	5.00
❑ B-5636	Stranglehold/Angry	1986	—	2.50	5.00
❑ B-5636 [PS]	Stranglehold/Angry	1986	—	2.50	5.00
❑ B-5672	Only Love Remains/Tough on a Tightrope	1987	—	2.50	5.00
❑ B-5672 [PS]	Only Love Remains/Tough on a Tightrope	1987	—	2.50	5.00
❑ S7-17318	Off the Ground/Cosmically Conscious	1993	—	3.00	6.00
—White vinyl standard issue					

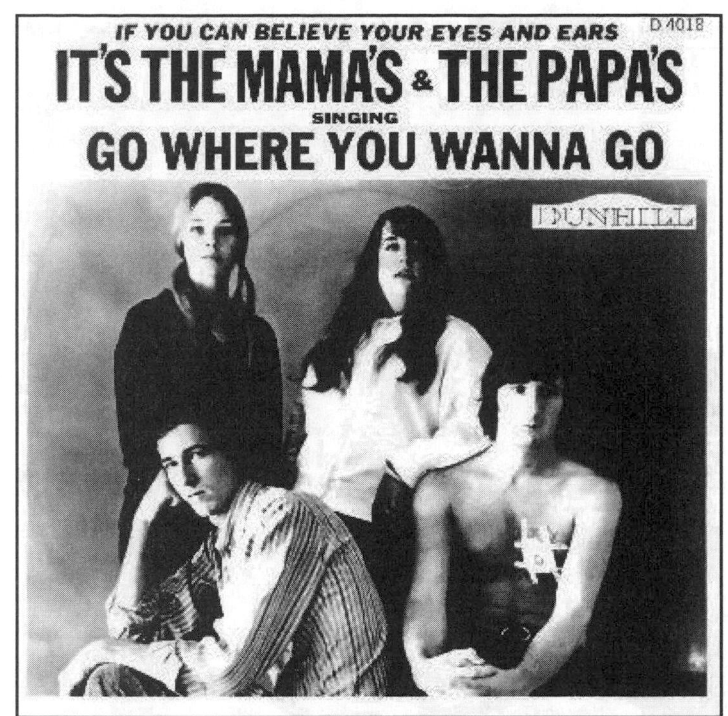

IF YOU CAN BELIEVE YOUR EYES AND EARS
D 4018
IT'S THE MAMA'S & THE PAPA'S
SINGING
GO WHERE YOU WANNA GO
DUNHILL

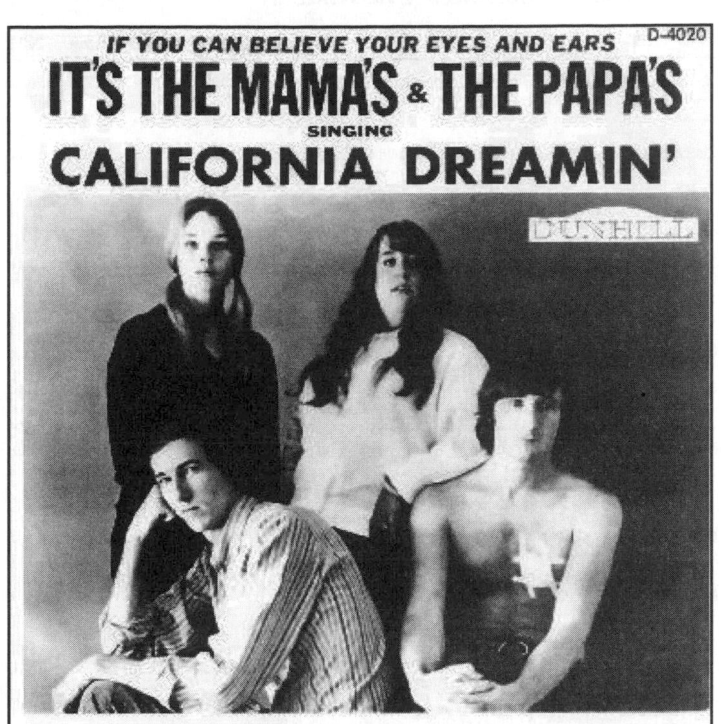

IF YOU CAN BELIEVE YOUR EYES AND EARS
D-4020
IT'S THE MAMA'S & THE PAPA'S
SINGING
CALIFORNIA DREAMIN'
DUNHILL

TAMLA
TAMLA RECORDS, DETROIT, MICHIGAN
AUDITION COPY
NOT FOR SALE
T-54091
Jobete BMI
DM W-067221
R4KM 3043
Produced by
Smokey
Time: 2:20
45 RPM
YES HE IS
(Wm. Robinson)
THE MARVELETTES

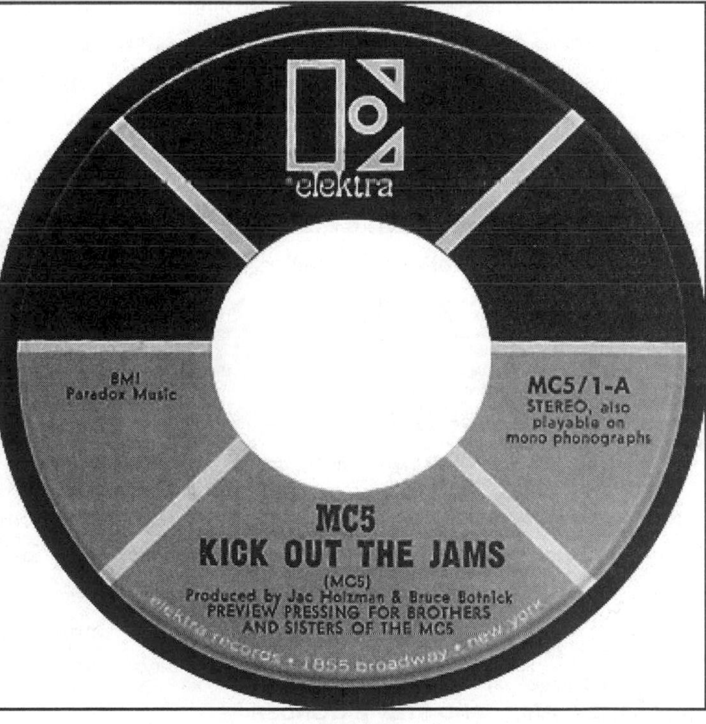

elektra
BMI
Paradox Music
MC5/1-A
STEREO, also
playable on
mono phonographs
MC5
KICK OUT THE JAMS
(MC5)
Produced by Jac Holzman & Bruce Botnick
PREVIEW PRESSING FOR BROTHERS
AND SISTERS OF THE MC5
elektra records • 1855 broadway • new york

(Top left) Not known to exist until recently, here is the promo-only picture sleeve for the Mamas and the Papas' first, unreleased, single, "Go Where You Wanna Go." The record never was issued except as a promotional copy, because the label decided to choose a different song as the first "official" single. (Top right) And that different song was "California Dreamin'." Here's the promo-only picture sleeve for that one, which was a monster hit. Notice that the two are almost identical, except for the song title and the catalog number of the record. (Bottom left) Another curious promo single is from the Marvelettes. This one-sided 1964 white label pressing used the title "Yes He Is," but when the song was issued commercially, the song had become "He's a Good Guy (Yes He Is)." (Bottom right) Before the song was issued to the general public, a different version of the MC5's "Kick Out the Jams," with a different catalog number, was given away to "brothers and sisters of the MC5" at a December 12, 1968 Fillmore East concert.

Number	Title (A Side/B Side)	Yr	VG	VG+	NM
❑ S7-17318	Off the Ground/Cosmically Conscious	1993	—	3.00	6.00
—Black vinyl "error" issue					
❑ S7-17319	Biker Like an Icon/Things We Said Today	1993	—	3.00	6.00
—Black vinyl "error" issue					
❑ S7-17319	Biker Like an Icon/Things We Said Today	1993	—	3.00	6.00
—White vinyl standard issue					
❑ S7-17489	C'mon People/Down to the River	1993	2.00	4.00	8.00
—All copies on white vinyl					
❑ S7-17643	Wonderful Christmastime/Rudolph, the Red-Nosed Reggae	1993	—	3.00	6.00
—Paul McCartney & Wings; red vinyl					
❑ B-44367	My Brave Face/Flying to My Home	1989	2.50	5.00	10.00
—Version 1: Both title and artist in block print, time of A-side is "3:17"					
❑ B-44367	My Brave Face/Flying to My Home	1989	2.00	4.00	8.00
—Version 2: Artist in custom print, title in block print, time of A-side is "3:17"					
❑ B-44367	My Brave Face/Flying to My Home	1989	—	2.50	5.00
—Version 3: Same as Version 2, time of A-side is "3:16"					
❑ B-44367 [PS]	My Brave Face/Flying to My Home	1989	—	2.50	5.00
❑ S7-56946	Hope of Deliverance/Long Leather Coat	1993	—	3.00	6.00
❑ 58823	No Other Baby/Try Not to Cry	1999	—	2.00	4.00
❑ 7PRO-79700 [DJ]	This One (same on both sides)	1989	100.00	200.00	400.00
—Vinyl is promo only					

COLUMBIA

Number	Title (A Side/B Side)	Yr	VG	VG+	NM
❑ 02171	Silly Love Songs/Cook of the House	1981	6.25	12.50	25.00
—Wings; despite label information, this has an edited version of A-side					
❑ 03018	Take It Away/I'll Give You a Ring	1982	—	—	3.00
❑ 03018 [PS]	Take It Away/I'll Give You a Ring	1982	—	—	3.00
❑ 03235	Tug of War/Get It	1982	3.00	6.00	12.00
❑ 04127	Wonderful Christmastime/Rudolph the Red-Nosed Reggae	1983	7.50	15.00	30.00
—Scarce reissue with B-side in stereo					
❑ 04296	So Bad/Pipes of Peace	1983	—	2.50	5.00
❑ 04296 [PS]	So Bad/Pipes of Peace	1983	—	2.50	5.00
❑ 04581	No More Lonely Nights/No More Lonely Nights (playout version)	1984	—	2.00	4.00
❑ 04581	No More Lonely Nights/No More Lonely Nights (Special Dance Version)	1984	10.00	20.00	40.00
❑ 04581 [PS]	No More Lonely Nights/No More Lonely Nights (playout version)	1984	7.50	15.00	30.00
—Title print in gray, credit print in white					
❑ 04581 [PS]	No More Lonely Nights/No More Lonely Nights (playout version)	1984	—	2.50	5.00
—Title print in white, credit print in gray					
❑ 10939	Goodnight Tonight/Daytime Nighttime Suffering	1979	—	3.00	6.00
—Wings					
❑ 11020	Getting Closer/Spin It On	1979	—	3.00	6.00
—Wings					
❑ 11020 [PS]	Getting Closer/Spin It On	1979	7.50	15.00	30.00
—Title sleeve with large center hole					
❑ 11070	Arrow Through Me/Old Siam, Sir	1979	—	3.00	6.00
—Wings					
❑ 11162	Wonderful Christmastime/Rudolph the Red-Nosed Reggae	1979	2.50	5.00	10.00
❑ 11162 [PS]	Wonderful Christmastime/Rudolph the Red-Nosed Reggae	1979	3.75	7.50	15.00
❑ 11263	Coming Up//Coming Up (Live at Glasgow)/Lunch Box-Odd Sox	1980	—	2.00	4.00
❑ 11263 [PS]	Coming Up//Coming Up (Live at Glasgow)/Lunch Box-Odd Sox	1980	—	2.50	5.00
❑ 11335	Waterfalls/Check My Machine	1980	—	3.00	6.00
❑ 11335 [PS]	Waterfalls/Check My Machine	1980	5.00	10.00	20.00
❑ 33405	Goodnight Tonight/Getting Closer	1980	2.50	5.00	10.00
—Wings; red label "Hall of Fame" series					
❑ 33407	My Love/Maybe I'm Amazed	1980	2.50	5.00	10.00
—Paul McCartney and Wings; red label "Hall of Fame" series					
❑ 33407	My Love/Maybe I'm Amazed	1985	7.50	15.00	30.00
—Paul McCartney and Wings; briefly available gray label reissue					
❑ 33408	Jet//Uncle Albert/Admiral Halsey	1980	2.50	5.00	10.00
—Paul McCartney and Wings; red label "Hall of Fame" series					
❑ 33408	Jet//Uncle Albert/Admiral Halsey	1985	7.50	15.00	30.00
—Paul McCartney and Wings; briefly available gray label reissue					
❑ 33409	Band on the Run/Helen Wheels	1980	2.50	5.00	10.00
—Paul McCartney and Wings; red label "Hall of Fame" series					
❑ 33409	Band on the Run/Helen Wheels	1985	7.50	15.00	30.00
—Paul McCartney and Wings; briefly available gray label reissue					

EMI

Number	Title (A Side/B Side)	Yr	VG	VG+	NM
❑ 3977	Walking in the Park with Eloise/Bridge on the River Suite	1974	15.00	30.00	60.00
❑ 3977 [PS]	Walking in the Park with Eloise/Bridge on the River Suite	1974	20.00	40.00	80.00
—As "The Country Hams"					

MCCARTNEY, PAUL, AND STEVIE WONDER

Also see each artist's individual listings.

COLUMBIA

Number	Title (A Side/B Side)	Yr	VG	VG+	NM
❑ 02860	Ebony and Ivory/Rainclouds	1982	—	2.00	4.00
❑ 02860 [PS]	Ebony and Ivory/Rainclouds	1982	—	2.00	4.00

MCCLAY, YUL, AND THE MONDELLOS

See THE MONDELLOS.

MCCLINTON, DELBERT

Also see TANYA TUCKER.

ABC

Number	Title (A Side/B Side)	Yr	VG	VG+	NM
❑ 12132	Object of My Affection/Two More Bottles of Wine	1975	—	2.50	5.00
❑ 12167	Victim of Life's Circumstances/(I Guess I Done Me Some) Honky Tonkin'	1976	—	2.50	5.00
❑ 12218	Blue Monday/Special Love Song	1976	—	2.50	5.00

BOBILL

Number	Title (A Side/B Side)	Yr	VG	VG+	NM
❑ 101	I Know She Knows/Please Help Me, I'm Falling	1967	2.50	5.00	10.00

BROWNFIELD

Number	Title (A Side/B Side)	Yr	VG	VG+	NM
❑ 303	I Know She Knows/Please Help Me, I'm Falling	1964	5.00	10.00	20.00

CAPITOL/MSS

Number	Title (A Side/B Side)	Yr	VG	VG+	NM
❑ 4948	Giving It Up for Your Love/My Sweet Baby	1980	—	2.00	4.00
❑ 4984	Shotgun Rider/Baby Ruth	1981	—	2.00	4.00
❑ 5003	Going Back to Louisiana/Jealous Kind	1981	—	2.00	4.00
❑ 5069	Sandy Beaches/I Wanna Thank You	1981	—	2.00	4.00

CAPRICORN

Number	Title (A Side/B Side)	Yr	VG	VG+	NM
❑ 0302	Take It Easy/Lovingest Man	1978	—	2.50	5.00
❑ 0328	Shot from the Saddle (mono/stereo)	1979	2.00	4.00	8.00
—Only released as a promo					

CURB

Number	Title (A Side/B Side)	Yr	VG	VG+	NM
❑ 76823	I'm with You/My Love Is Burnin'	1990	—	2.00	4.00
❑ 76839	My Baby's Lovin'/Who's Foolin' Who	1990	—	2.50	5.00
❑ 76847	I Want to Love You/That's the Way I Feel	1991	—	2.00	4.00

JUBILEE

Number	Title (A Side/B Side)	Yr	VG	VG+	NM
❑ 9012	I Know She Knows/Please Help Me, I'm Falling	1965	3.00	6.00	12.00

LONDON

Number	Title (A Side/B Side)	Yr	VG	VG+	NM
❑ 9544	Angel Eyes/Dunkirk	1962	5.00	10.00	20.00
—As "Del McClinton"					

MCA

Number	Title (A Side/B Side)	Yr	VG	VG+	NM
❑ 51124	Special Love Song/Let Love Come Between Us	1981	—	2.00	4.00

PARAMOUNT

Number	Title (A Side/B Side)	Yr	VG	VG+	NM
❑ 0016	Fannie Mae/I Know She Knows	1969	2.50	5.00	10.00

RISING TIDE

Number	Title (A Side/B Side)	Yr	VG	VG+	NM
❑ 56050	Sending Me Angels/Better Off with the Blues	1997	—	2.00	4.00

SOFT

Number	Title (A Side/B Side)	Yr	VG	VG+	NM
❑ 1041	100 Pounds of Honey/Zip-a-Dee-Doo-Dah	1970	2.50	5.00	10.00

MCCORMICK, GAYLE

Also see SMITH.

ABC DUNHILL

Number	Title (A Side/B Side)	Yr	VG	VG+	NM
❑ 4281	Gonna Be Alright Now/Save Me	1971	—	2.50	5.00
❑ 4288	It's a Cryin' Shame/If Only You Believe	1971	—	2.50	5.00
❑ 4298	You Really Got a Hold on Me/C'est La Vie	1972	—	2.50	5.00

DECCA

Number	Title (A Side/B Side)	Yr	VG	VG+	NM
❑ 33030	Near You/Take Me Back	1972	—	2.50	5.00

MCA

Number	Title (A Side/B Side)	Yr	VG	VG+	NM
❑ 40007	Sweet Feelings/Take Me Back	1973	—	2.00	4.00

SHADYBROOK

Number	Title (A Side/B Side)	Yr	VG	VG+	NM
❑ 45017	Coming In Out of the Rain/Simon Said	1977	2.50	5.00	10.00

MCCORMICK, MAUREEN

Also see THE BRADY BUNCH; CHRIS KNIGHT AND MAUREEN McCORMICK.

PARAMOUNT

Number	Title (A Side/B Side)	Yr	VG	VG+	NM
❑ 0292	Love's in the Roses/Harmonize	1974	3.75	7.50	15.00

MCCOYS, THE

Also see RICK DERRINGER.

BANG

Number	Title (A Side/B Side)	Yr	VG	VG+	NM
❑ 506	Hang On Sloopy/I Can't Explain It	1965	3.75	7.50	15.00
❑ 511	Fever/Sorrow	1965	2.50	5.00	10.00
❑ 516	Up and Down/If You Tell a Lie	1966	2.50	5.00	10.00
❑ 522	Come On Let's Go/Little People	1966	2.50	5.00	10.00
❑ 527	(You Make Me Feel) So Good/Runaway	1966	2.50	5.00	10.00
❑ 532	Don't Worry Mother, Your Son's Heart Is Pure/Ko-Ko	1966	2.50	5.00	10.00
❑ 538	I Got to Go Back (And Watch That Little Girl Dance)/Dynamite	1966	2.50	5.00	10.00
❑ 543	Beat the Clock/Like You Do to Me	1967	2.50	5.00	10.00
❑ 549	I Wonder If She Remembers Me/Say Those Magic Words	1967	2.50	5.00	10.00

MERCURY

Number	Title (A Side/B Side)	Yr	VG	VG+	NM
❑ 72843	Jesse Brady/Resurrection	1968	2.00	4.00	8.00
❑ 72897	Daybreak/Epilogue	1969	2.00	4.00	8.00
❑ 72967	Don't Fight It/Rosa Rodriguez	1969	3.75	7.50	15.00

PHILCO-FORD

Number	Title (A Side/B Side)	Yr	VG	VG+	NM
❑ HP-6	Fever/Hang On Sloopy	1967	5.00	10.00	20.00
—4-inch plastic "Hip Pocket Record" with color sleeve					

RCA VICTOR

Number	Title (A Side/B Side)	Yr	VG	VG+	NM
❑ 47-7204	Daddy's Geisha Girl/Our Love Goes On and On	1958	5.00	10.00	20.00
❑ 47-7354	Full Grown Cat/Throwing Kisses	1958	6.25	12.50	25.00

MCCRACKEN, HUGH

CONGRESS

Number	Title (A Side/B Side)	Yr	VG	VG+	NM
❑ 257	Buzz in My Head/You Blow My Mind	1965	6.25	12.50	25.00
❑ 261	Runnin', Runnin'/What I Gotta Do to Satisfy You	1966	6.25	12.50	25.00

MCCRACKLIN, JIMMY

ART-TONE

Number	Title (A Side/B Side)	Yr	VG	VG+	NM
❑ 825	Just Got to Know/The Drag	1961	3.00	6.00	12.00
❑ 826	Christmas Time (Part 1)/Christmas Time (Part 2)	1961	3.00	6.00	12.00
❑ 827	Shame, Shame, Shame/I'm the One	1962	3.00	6.00	12.00
❑ 831	That's No Big Thing/Susie and Pat	1962	3.00	6.00	12.00

CHECKER

Number	Title (A Side/B Side)	Yr	VG	VG+	NM
❑ 885	The Walk/I'm to Blame	1958	6.25	12.50	25.00
❑ 893	Everybody Rock/Get Tough	1958	3.75	7.50	15.00

CHESS

Number	Title (A Side/B Side)	Yr	VG	VG+	NM
❑ 1809	I Know/Later On	1961	2.50	5.00	10.00
❑ 1826	One Track Love/Trottin'	1962	2.50	5.00	10.00

HI

Number	Title (A Side/B Side)	Yr	VG	VG+	NM
❑ 2023	Things I Meant to Say/Here Today and Gone Tomorrow	1960	3.00	6.00	12.00

HOLLYWOOD

Number	Title (A Side/B Side)	Yr	VG	VG+	NM
❑ 1054	It's All Right/Fare You Well	1955	12.50	25.00	50.00

IMPERIAL

Number	Title (A Side/B Side)	Yr	VG	VG+	NM
❑ 5892	Bitter Pill/Head Over Flip	1962	2.50	5.00	10.00
❑ 5906	I Don't Care/Just Got to Know	1963	2.50	5.00	10.00
❑ 5911	Advice/No No	1963	2.50	5.00	10.00
❑ 5926	The Bitter and the Sweet/Just Pretending	1963	2.50	5.00	10.00
❑ 5955	That's the Way (It Goes)/I'll See It Through	1963	2.50	5.00	10.00
❑ 5977	Every Night/The Slightest Idea	1963	2.50	5.00	10.00

Number	Title (A Side/B Side)	Yr	VG	VG+	NM
❑ 5982	Sooner or Later/Looking for a Woman	1963	2.50	5.00	10.00
❑ 66010	I Did Wrong/Someone	1964	2.00	4.00	8.00
❑ 66035	Just Like It Is/Let's Do It All	1964	2.00	4.00	8.00
❑ 66067	Believe in Me/Set Six	1964	2.00	4.00	8.00
❑ 66094	Every Night, Every Day/Can't Raise Me	1965	2.00	4.00	8.00
❑ 66116	Arkansas (Part 1)/Arkansas (Part 2)	1965	2.00	4.00	8.00
❑ 66129	Think/Steppin' Up in Class	1965	2.00	4.00	8.00
❑ 66147	My Answer/Beulah	1966	2.00	4.00	8.00
❑ 66168	Come On Home (Back Where You Belong)/ Something That Belongs to Me	1966	2.00	4.00	8.00
❑ 66180	Just Let Me Cry/These Boots Are Made for Walkin'	1966	2.00	4.00	8.00
❑ 66207	It's Got to Be Love/Sorry	1966	2.00	4.00	8.00
IRMA					
❑ 102	You're the One/I Wanna Make Love to You	1956	7.50	15.00	30.00
❑ 103	Take a Chance/Fare Well	1956	7.50	15.00	30.00
❑ 107	I'm the One/Savoy's Jump	1957	7.50	15.00	30.00
❑ 109	Beer Tavern Girl/Love for You	1957	7.50	15.00	30.00
KENT					
❑ 369	I've Got Eyes for You/I'm Gonna Tell Your Mother	1962	2.50	5.00	10.00
LIBERTY					
❑ 56198	Believe Me/I Never Thought	1970	—	2.50	5.00
MERCURY					
❑ 71412	The Wobble/With Your Love	1959	3.75	7.50	15.00
❑ 71516	Let's Do It (The Chicken Scratch)/Georgia Slop	1959	3.75	7.50	15.00
❑ 71613	Doomed Lover/By Myself	1960	3.00	6.00	12.00
❑ 71666	You Rascal You/No One to Love Me	1960	3.00	6.00	12.00
❑ 71747	What's That (Part 1)/The Bridge	1961	3.00	6.00	12.00
❑ 71766	No One to Love Me/(B-side unknown)	1961	3.00	6.00	12.00
MINIT					
❑ 32018	Let the Door Hit You/This Thing	1967	—	3.00	6.00
❑ 32022	Dog (Part 1)/Dog (Part 2)	1967	—	3.00	6.00
❑ 32033	Get Together/How You Like Your Love	1967	—	3.00	6.00
❑ 32044	Pretty Little Sweet Thing/A & I	1968	—	3.00	6.00
❑ 32052	Love, Love, Love/Married Life	1968	—	3.00	6.00
❑ 32064	Drown in My Own Tears/What's Going On	1969	—	3.00	6.00
❑ 32086	I Had to Get With It/You Ain't Nothin' But a Devil	1969	—	3.00	6.00
❑ 32092	Stick to My Mind/I Just Live by the Rules	1970	—	3.00	6.00
MODERN					
❑ 926	Blues Blasters' Boogie/The Panic's On	1954	10.00	20.00	40.00
❑ 934	Darlin' Share Your Love/Give My Heart a Break	1954	10.00	20.00	40.00
❑ 951	Please Forgive Me Baby/Couldn't Be a Dream	1954	10.00	20.00	40.00
❑ 967	Gonna Tell Your Mother/That Ain't Right	1955	10.00	20.00	40.00
PEACOCK					
❑ 1605	My Days Are Limited/She's Gone	1952	15.00	30.00	60.00
❑ 1615	She Felt Too Good/Share and Share Alike	1953	15.00	30.00	60.00
❑ 1634	I Cried/The End	1953	15.00	30.00	60.00
❑ 1639	The Cheater/My Story	1954	15.00	30.00	60.00
❑ 1683	I Need Your Loving/The Swinging Thing	1958	6.25	12.50	25.00

MCCULLERS, MICKEY

Number	Title (A Side/B Side)	Yr	VG	VG+	NM
TAMI A					
❑ 54064	Same Old Story/I'll Cry a Million Tears	1962	10.00	20.00	40.00
V.I.P.					
❑ 25009	Same Old Story/Who You Gonna Run To	1964	12.50	25.00	50.00

MCDANIELS, GENE

Number	Title (A Side/B Side)	Yr	VG	VG+	NM
ATLANTIC					
❑ 2805	The Lord Is Back/Tell Me Mr. President	1971	—	3.00	6.00
—As "Eugene McDaniels"					
COLUMBIA					
❑ 43800	Something Blue/Cause I Love You So	1966	2.50	5.00	10.00
❑ 44010	Touch of Your Lips/Sweet Lover No More	1967	2.50	5.00	10.00
LIBERTY					
❑ 55231	In Times Like These/Once Before	1959	3.75	7.50	15.00
❑ 55265	The Green Door/Facts of Life	1960	3.75	7.50	15.00
❑ 55308	A Hundred Pounds of Clay/Take a Chance on Love	1961	4.00	8.00	16.00
❑ 55344	A Tear/She's Come Back	1961	3.75	7.50	15.00
❑ 55371	Tower of Strength/The Secret	1961	4.00	8.00	16.00
❑ 55405	Chip Chip/Another Tear Falls	1962	3.75	7.50	15.00
❑ 55444	Funny/Chapel of Tears	1962	3.75	7.50	15.00
❑ 55480	Point of No Return/Warmer Than a Whisper	1962	3.75	7.50	15.00
❑ 55510	Spanish Lace/Somebody's Waiting	1962	3.75	7.50	15.00
❑ 55541	The Puzzle/Cry Baby Cry	1963	3.00	6.00	12.00
❑ 55597	It's a Lonely Town/False Friends	1963	3.00	6.00	12.00
❑ 55637	Old Country/Anyone Else	1963	3.00	6.00	12.00
❑ 55723	Make Me a Present of You/In Times Like These	1964	3.00	6.00	12.00
❑ 55752	Emily/Forgotten Man	1964	3.00	6.00	12.00
❑ 55805	A Miracle/Walk with a Winner	1965	2.50	5.00	10.00
❑ 55834	Hang On/Will It Last Forever	1965	2.50	5.00	10.00
MGM					
❑ 14613	Ol' Heartbreak Top Ten/River	1973	—	2.50	5.00
ODE					
❑ 66107	Lady Fair/Natural Juices	1975	—	2.00	4.00
UNITED ARTISTS					
❑ 0053	A Hundred Pounds of Clay/Tower of Strength	1973	—	2.00	4.00
—"Silver Spotlight Series" reissue					
❑ 0054	Chip Chip/Point of No Return	1973	—	2.00	4.00
—"Silver Spotlight Series" reissue					

MCDEVITT, CHAS., AND HIS SKIFFLE GROUP

Number	Title (A Side/B Side)	Yr	VG	VG+	NM
CHIC					
❑ 1008	Freight Train/The Cotton Song	1957	3.75	7.50	15.00
EPIC					
❑ 9244	Face in the Rain/Sporting Life	1957	3.75	7.50	15.00
KAPP					
❑ 216	Sing, Sing, Sing/Johnny-O	1958	3.75	7.50	15.00
❑ 238	Stack-O-Lee/Real Love	1958	3.75	7.50	15.00

MCDONALD, COUNTRY JOE

See COUNTRY JOE AND THE FISH.

MCDONALD, KATHI

Number	Title (A Side/B Side)	Yr	VG	VG+	NM
CAPITOL					
❑ 3835	Freak Lover/Bogart to Bowie	1974	2.50	5.00	10.00
❑ 3880	Heat Wave/Bogart to Bowie	1974	2.50	5.00	10.00

MCDONALD, MICHAEL

Also see THE DOOBIE BROTHERS; THE REGENTS (5).

Number	Title (A Side/B Side)	Yr	VG	VG+	NM
BELL					
❑ 45182	Dear Me/I Think I Love You Again	1972	2.00	4.00	8.00
—All Bell records as "Mike McDonald"					
❑ 45219	Good Old Time Love Song/When I'm Home	1972	2.00	4.00	8.00
❑ 45259 [DJ]	Drivin' Wheel/(B-side unknown)	1972	2.00	4.00	8.00
—Stock copy may not exist					
❑ 45308 [DJ]	Where Do I Go from Here/(B-side unknown)	1973	2.00	4.00	8.00
—Stock copy may not exist					
MCA					
❑ 52857	Sweet Freedom/The Freedom Eights	1986	—	—	3.00
❑ 52857 [PS]	Sweet Freedom/The Freedom Eights	1986	—	—	3.00
QWEST					
❑ 29394	Yah Mo B There/Come in Da Machine	1983	—	2.00	4.00
—A-side with James Ingram; B-side: James Ingram solo					
RCA VICTOR					
❑ 74-0405	God Knows/If You Won't, I Will	1970	3.75	7.50	15.00
—As "Mike McDonald"					
REPRISE					
❑ 18469	I Stand for You/East of Eden	1993	—	—	3.00
WARNER BROS.					
❑ 28596	Our Love (Theme from "No Mercy")/Don't Let Me Down	1986	—	—	3.00
❑ 28847	Lost in the Parade/By Heart	1985	—	2.00	4.00
❑ 28960	No Lookin' Back/Don't Let Me Down	1985	—	—	3.00
❑ 28960 [PS]	No Lookin' Back/Don't Let Me Down	1985	—	—	3.00
❑ 29743	Believe in It/Playin' by the Rules	1983	—	2.00	4.00
❑ 29862	I Gotta Try/Believe in It	1982	—	2.00	4.00
❑ 29862 [PS]	I Gotta Try/Believe in It	1982	—	2.00	4.00
❑ 29933	I Keep Forgettin'/Losin' End	1982	—	2.50	5.00
—First pressing has no subtitle on A-side					
❑ 29933	I Keep Forgettin' (Every Time You're Near)/Losin' End	1982	—	2.00	4.00
—Second pressing has subtitle on A-side					
❑ 29933 [PS]	I Keep Forgettin'/Losin' End	1982	—	2.50	5.00
—First pressing has no subtitle on A-side					
❑ 29933 [PS]	I Keep Forgettin' (Every Time You're Near)/Losin' End	1982	—	2.00	4.00
—Second pressing has subtitle on A-side					

MCFADDEN, BOB

Number	Title (A Side/B Side)	Yr	VG	VG+	NM
BRUNSWICK					
❑ 55120	Frankie and Igor at a Rock and Roll Party/ Children Cross the Bridge	1959	6.25	12.50	25.00
❑ 55140	The Mummy/The Beat Generation	1959	6.25	12.50	25.00
—As "Bob McFadden and Dor"					
❑ 55140 [PS]	The Mummy/The Beat Generation	1959	10.00	20.00	40.00
—As "Bob McFadden and Dor"					
❑ 55156	Bingo/Shake, Rattle and Roll	1959	6.25	12.50	25.00
CORAL					
❑ 62209	Dracula Cha-Cha/Transylvania Polka	1959	7.50	5.00	30.00

MCGHEE, BROWNIE

Number	Title (A Side/B Side)	Yr	VG	VG+	NM
DOT					
❑ 1184	Cheatin' and Lyin'/Need Someone to Love	1954	62.50	125.00	250.00
HARLEM					
❑ 2323	Worrying Over You/Christina	1954	15.00	30.00	60.00
❑ 2329	My Confession (I Want to Thank You)/Bluebird, Bluebird	1954	15.00	30.00	60.00
JAX					
❑ 302	Smiling and Crying Blues/A Letter to Lightnin' Hopkins	1951	30.00	60.00	120.00
❑ 304	I Feel So Good/Key to the Highway	1952	30.00	60.00	120.00
❑ 307	Meet You in the Morning/Brownie's Blues	1952	30.00	60.00	120.00
❑ 310	Guitar Strangers Blues/Dissatisfied Woman	1952	30.00	60.00	120.00
❑ 312	I'm 10,000 Years Old/Cherry Red	1952	30.00	60.00	120.00
❑ 322	New Bad Blood Blues/Pawnshop Blues	1953	30.00	60.00	120.00
RED ROBIN					
❑ 111	Don't Dog Your Woman/Daisy	1953	62.50	125.00	250.00
SAVOY					
❑ 835	Diamond Ring/So Much Trouble	1952	7.50	15.00	30.00
❑ 872	Tell Me Baby/Bad Nerves	1952	7.50	15.00	30.00
❑ 899	Sweet Baby Blues/4 O'Clock in the Morning	1953	7.50	15.00	30.00
❑ 1177	I'd Love to Love You/Anna Mae	1955	5.00	10.00	20.00
❑ 1185	When It's Love Time/My Fault	1956	5.00	10.00	20.00
❑ 1564	Living with the Blues/Be My Friend	1959	3.75	7.50	15.00

MCGHEE, STICK

Number	Title (A Side/B Side)	Yr	VG	VG+	NM
ATLANTIC					
❑ 955	Wee Wee Hours (Part 1)/Wee Wee Hours (Part 2)	1952	25.00	50.00	100.00
—Note: Stick McGhee records on Atlantic before 955 are unconfirmed on 45 rpm					
❑ 991	New Found Love/Meet You in the Morning	1953	20.00	40.00	80.00
ATLANTIC CLASSICS					
❑ 873	Drinkin' Wine Spo-Dee-O-Dee/Blues Mixture (I'd Rather Drink Muddy Water)	1971	5.00	10.00	20.00
HERALD					
❑ 553	Money Fever/Sleep-In Job	1960	3.75	7.50	15.00
KING					
❑ 4610	Little Things We Used to Do/Head Happy with Wine	1953	25.00	50.00	100.00
❑ 4628	Whiskey, Women and Loaded Dice/Blues in My Heart and Tears in My Eyes	1953	25.00	50.00	100.00

Number	Title (A Side/B Side)	Yr	VG	VG+	NM
❑ 4672	Jungle Juice/Dealing from the Bottom	1953	25.00	50.00	100.00
❑ 4700	I'm Doin' All This Time/Wiggle Waggin' Woo	1954	25.00	50.00	100.00
❑ 4783	Double Crossin' Liquor/Six to Eight	1955	30.00	60.00	120.00
❑ 4800	Get Your Mind Out the Gutter/Sad, Bad, Glad	1955	25.00	50.00	100.00
LONDON					
❑ 978	You Gotta Have Something on the Ball/(B-side unknown)	1951	62.50	125.00	250.00
SAVOY					
❑ 1148	Things Have Changed/Help Me Baby	1955	7.50	15.00	30.00

MCGILL, JERRY

Number	Title (A Side/B Side)	Yr	VG	VG+	NM
SUN					
❑ 326	Love Struck/I Wanna Make Sweet Love	1959	7.50	15.00	30.00

MCGONNIGLE, MEL

Number	Title (A Side/B Side)	Yr	VG	VG+	NM
ROCKET					
❑ 101	Rattle Shakin' Mama/I Want You	1958	175.00	350.00	700.00

MCGUINN, ROGER

Also see THE BYRDS; McGUINN AND HILLMAN; McGUINN, CLARK AND HILLMAN.

Number	Title (A Side/B Side)	Yr	VG	VG+	NM
COLUMBIA					
❑ 10019	Gate of Horn/Same Old Sound	1974	—	3.00	6.00
❑ 10181	Somebody Loves You/Easy Does It	1975	—	3.00	6.00
❑ 10201	Lover of the Bayou/Easy Does It	1975	—	3.00	6.00
❑ 10385	Take Me Away/Friend	1976	—	3.00	6.00
❑ 10543	American Girl/I'm Not Lonely Anymore	1977	—	3.00	6.00
❑ 45931	Draggin'/Time Cube	1973	—	3.00	6.00

MCGUINN AND HILLMAN

Also see THE BYRDS; ROGER McGUINN.

Number	Title (A Side/B Side)	Yr	VG	VG+	NM
CAPITOL					
❑ 4952	Turn Your Radio On/Making Movies	1980	—	2.00	4.00
❑ 4965	Love Me Tonight/Two Lonely Nights	1981	—	2.00	4.00
UNIVERSAL					
❑ UVL-66006	You Ain't Going Nowhere/Don't You Hear Jerusalem Moan	1989	—	2.00	4.00
—As "Chris Hillman and Roger McGuinn"					

MCGUINN, CLARK, & HILLMAN

Also see THE BYRDS; GENE CLARK; ROGER McGUINN.

Number	Title (A Side/B Side)	Yr	VG	VG+	NM
CAPITOL					
❑ 4693	Don't You Write Her Off/Sad Boy	1979	—	2.50	5.00
❑ 4739	Surrender to Me/Little Mama	1979	—	2.00	4.00
❑ 4763	Bye Bye Baby/Backstage Pass	1979	—	2.00	4.00
❑ 4821	Street Talk/One More Chance	1980	—	2.00	4.00
❑ 4855	Deeper/City	1980	—	2.00	4.00

MCGUINNESS FLINT

Number	Title (A Side/B Side)	Yr	VG	VG+	NM
CAPITOL					
❑ 3014	When I'm Dead and Gone/Lazy Afternoon	1971	—	3.00	6.00
❑ 3139	Rock On/Malt and Barley Blues	1971	—	3.00	6.00
❑ 3186	Friends of Mine/Happy Birthday, Ruthy Baby	1971	—	3.00	6.00

MCGUIRE, BARRY

Number	Title (A Side/B Side)	Yr	VG	VG+	NM
DUNHILL					
❑ 4009	Eve of Destruction/What Exactly's the Matter with Me	1965	3.00	6.00	12.00
❑ 4014	Child of Our Times/Upon a Painted Ocean	1965	2.50	5.00	10.00
❑ 4014 [PS]	Child of Our Times/Upon a Painted Ocean	1965	3.75	7.50	15.00
❑ 4019	This Precious Time/Don't You Wonder Where It's At	1966	3.00	6.00	12.00
—A-side backing group: The Mamas and The Papas					
❑ 4028	Cloudy Summer Afternoon (Raindrops)/I'd Have to Be Outta My Mind	1966	2.50	5.00	10.00
❑ 4048	There's Nothing Else on My Mind/Why Not Stop and Dig It	1966	2.50	5.00	10.00
❑ 4098	Masters of War/Stop Now and Dig It While You Can	1967	2.00	4.00	8.00
❑ 4116	Lollipop Train/Inner-Manipulations	1968	2.00	4.00	8.00
❑ 4124	Grasshopper Song/Top o' the Hill	1968	2.50	5.00	10.00
❑ 4124 [PS]	Grasshopper Song/Top o' the Hill	1968	3.75	7.50	15.00
HORIZON					
❑ 4	One by One/Town and Country	1963	3.00	6.00	12.00
❑ 8	Oh, Miss Mary/So Long, Stay Well	1963	3.00	6.00	12.00
MIRA					
❑ 205	Greenback Dollar/Oh, Miss Mary	1965	2.50	5.00	10.00
MOSAIC					
❑ 1001	The Three/Theme from The Tree	1961	3.00	6.00	12.00
❑ 1004	I've Got a Secret/Cindy and Johnny	1962	3.00	6.00	12.00
MYRRH					
❑ 119	Love Is/David and Goliath	1973	—	2.50	5.00
ODE					
❑ 66010	Old Farm/South of the Border	1970	—	3.00	6.00
SPARROW					
❑ 1023	Cosmic Cowboy/What Good Would It Do	197?	—	3.00	6.00

MCGUIRE, BARRY, AND BARRY KANE

Number	Title (A Side/B Side)	Yr	VG	VG+	NM
HORIZON					
❑ 354	Another Man/Bull 'Gine Run	1962	3.00	6.00	12.00

MCGUIRE, PHYLLIS

Also see THE McGUIRE SISTERS.

Number	Title (A Side/B Side)	Yr	VG	VG+	NM
ABC-PARAMOUNT					
❑ 10826	My Happiness/Vaya Con Dios	1966	—	3.00	6.00
ORPHEUM					
❑ 4502	Just a Little Lovin'/You Don't Have the Heart to Tell Me	1968	—	3.00	6.00
REPRISE					
❑ 0310	I Don't Want to Walk Without You/That's Life	1964	—	3.00	6.00
❑ 0354	Run to My Arms/Someone Else Is Taking My Place	1965	—	3.00	6.00

MCGUIRE SISTERS, THE

Also see PHYLLIS McGUIRE.

Number	Title (A Side/B Side)	Yr	VG	VG+	NM
ABC-PARAMOUNT					
❑ 10776	Grazia/Truer Than You Are	1966	—	3.00	6.00
CORAL					
❑ 60917	Picking Sweethearts/One, Two, Three, Four	1953	3.00	6.00	12.00
❑ 60969	Miss You/Tootle-Ooh Siana	1953	3.00	6.00	12.00
❑ 61002	Hey, Mister Cotton Picker/Where Good Times Are	1954	3.00	6.00	12.00
❑ 61073	Are You Looking for a Sweetheart/You'll Never Know Till Monday	1953	3.00	6.00	12.00
❑ 61126	Cling to Me/Pine Tree, Pine Over Me	1954	3.00	6.00	12.00
—With Johnny Desmond and Eileen Barton					
❑ 61187	Goodnight, Sweetheart, Goodnight/Heavenly Feeling	1954	3.00	6.00	12.00
❑ 61239	Uno, Duo, Tre/Lonesome Polecat	1954	3.00	6.00	12.00
❑ 61258	Muskrat Ramble/Not as a Stranger	1954	3.00	6.00	12.00
❑ 61278	Muskrat Ramble/Lonesome Polecat	1954	3.00	6.00	12.00
❑ 61303	Christmas Alphabet/Give Me Your Heart for Christmas	1954	3.00	6.00	12.00
❑ 61323	Sincerely/No More	1954	3.00	6.00	12.00
❑ 61334	Open Up Your Heart (And Let the Sun Shine In)/Melody of Love	1955	3.00	6.00	12.00
❑ 61335	Hearts of Stone/The Naughty Lady of Shady Lane	1955	3.00	6.00	12.00
❑ 61369	It May Sound Silly/Doesn't Anybody Love Me?	1955	3.00	6.00	12.00
❑ 61423	Something's Gotta Give/Rhythm 'N' Blues (Mama's Got the Rhythm — Papa's Got the Blues)	1955	3.00	6.00	12.00
❑ 61494	Give Me Love/Sweet Song of India	1955	3.00	6.00	12.00
❑ 61501	He/If You Believe	1955	3.00	6.00	12.00
❑ 61531	The Littlest Angel/I'd Like to Trim a Tree with You	1955	3.00	6.00	12.00
❑ 61532	My Baby's Got Such Lovin' Ways/(Baby, Baby) Be Good to Me	1955	3.00	6.00	12.00
❑ 61587	Missing/Tell Me Now	1956	2.50	5.00	10.00
❑ 61627	Picnic/Delilah Jones	1956	2.50	5.00	10.00
❑ 61703	Every Day of My Life/Endless	1956	2.50	5.00	10.00
❑ 61748	Goodnight My Love, Pleasant Dreams/Mommy	1956	2.50	5.00	10.00
❑ 61771	Kid Stuff/Without Him	1957	2.50	5.00	10.00
❑ 61798	He's Got Time/Blue Skies	1957	2.50	5.00	10.00
❑ 61815	Drownin' in Memories/Please Don't Do That to Me	1957	2.50	5.00	10.00
❑ 61842	Rock Bottom/Beginning to Miss You	1957	2.50	5.00	10.00
❑ 61856	Around the World in 80 Days/Interlude	1957	2.50	5.00	10.00
❑ 61888	Forgive Me/Kiss Them for Me	1957	2.50	5.00	10.00
❑ 61911	Santa Claus Is Comin' to Town/Honorable Congratulations	1957	2.50	5.00	10.00
❑ 61924	Sugartime/Banana Split	1958	3.00	6.00	12.00
❑ 61991	Ding Dong/Since You Went Away to School	1958	2.50	5.00	10.00
❑ 62021	Volare (Nel Blu, Dipinto Di Blue)/Do You Love Me Like You Kiss Me	1958	2.50	5.00	10.00
❑ 62047	Sweetie Pie/I'll Think of You	1958	2.50	5.00	10.00
❑ 62059	May You Always/Achoo Cha Cha	1958	2.50	5.00	10.00
❑ 62106	Summer Dreams/Peace	1959	2.50	5.00	10.00
❑ 62135	Red River Valley/Compromise	1959	2.50	5.00	10.00
❑ 62155	Some of These Days/Have a Nice Weekend	1959	2.50	5.00	10.00
❑ 62162	Livin' Dangerously/Lover's Lullaby	1960	2.00	4.00	8.00
❑ 62162 [PS]	Livin' Dangerously/Lover's Lullaby	1960	2.50	5.00	10.00
❑ 62196	The Unforgiven/I Give Thanks	1960	2.00	4.00	8.00
❑ 62216	The Last Dance/Nine O'Clock	1960	2.00	4.00	8.00
❑ 62235	To Be Loved/I Don't Know Why	1960	2.00	4.00	8.00
❑ 62249	Just for Old Times' Sake/Really Neat	1961	2.00	4.00	8.00
❑ 62249 [PS]	Just for Old Times' Sake/Really Neat	1961	2.50	5.00	10.00
❑ 62276	Tears on My Pillow/Will There Be Room in the Space Ship	1961	2.00	4.00	8.00
❑ 62276 [PS]	Tears on My Pillow/Will There Be Room in the Space Ship	1961	2.50	5.00	10.00
❑ 62288	Just Because/I Do, I Do, I Do	1961	2.00	4.00	8.00
❑ 62296	I Can Dream, Can't I/I'm Just Taking My Time	1961	2.00	4.00	8.00
❑ 62305	Sugartime Twist/More Hearts Are Broken That Way	1962	2.00	4.00	8.00
❑ 62333	I Really Don't Want to Know/Mama's Gone, Goodbye	1962	2.00	4.00	8.00
REPRISE					
❑ 0256	Now and Forever/Never	1964	—	3.00	6.00
❑ 0330	Dear Heart/Candy Heart	1964	—	3.00	6.00
❑ 0338	I'll Walk Alone/Ticket to Anywhere	1965	—	3.00	6.00
❑ 20197	Summertime (The Time for Love)/Cordially Invited	1963	—	3.00	6.00

7-Inch Extended Plays

Number	Title (A Side/B Side)	Yr	VG	VG+	NM
CORAL					
❑ EC 81074	(contents unknown)	195?	3.75	7.50	15.00
❑ EC 81074 [PS]	The Three McGuire Sisters	195?	3.75	7.50	15.00
❑ EC 81082	(contents unknown)	195?	3.75	7.50	15.00
❑ EC 81082 [PS]	Sweethearts on Broadway	195?	3.75	7.50	15.00
❑ EC 81090	(contents unknown)	195?	3.75	7.50	15.00
❑ EC 81090 [PS]	TV Favorites	195?	3.75	7.50	15.00
❑ EC 81098	Melody of Love/Hearts of Stone//Open Up Your Heart/The Naughty Lady of Shady Lane	1955	3.75	7.50	15.00
❑ EC 81098 [PS]	By Request	1955	3.75	7.50	15.00
❑ EC 81127	(contents unknown)	195?	3.00	6.00	12.00
❑ EC 81127 [PS]	'S Wonderful	195?	3.00	6.00	12.00
❑ EC 81145	Sugartime/Banana Split//I Tried/Lullaby of Birdland	1958	3.00	6.00	12.00
❑ EC 81145 [PS]	The McGuire Sisters	1958	3.00	6.00	12.00
❑ EC 81165	(contents unknown)	1958	3.00	6.00	12.00
❑ EC 81165 [PS]	While the Lights Are Low	1958	3.00	6.00	12.00
❑ EC 81184 [M]	(contents unknown)	1959	3.00	6.00	12.00
❑ EC 81184 [PS]	I'll Think of You	1959	3.00	6.00	12.00
❑ EC 81507	(contents unknown)	1959	3.00	6.00	12.00
❑ EC 81507 [PS]	The McGuire Sisters	1959	3.00	6.00	12.00
❑ EC 82022	(contents unknown)	195?	3.00	6.00	12.00
❑ EC 82022 [PS]	Do You Remember When	195?	3.00	6.00	12.00
❑ EC 82031	(contents unknown)	195?	3.00	6.00	12.00

Number	Title (A Side/B Side)	Yr	VG	VG+	NM
❑ EC 82031 [PS]	Children's Holiday	195?	3.00	6.00	12.00
❑ EC 781184 [PS]	I'll Think of You	1959	5.00	10.00	20.00
❑ EC 781184 [S]	(contents unknown)	1959	5.00	10.00	20.00

MCKAY, SCOTTY

ACE

Number	Title (A Side/B Side)	Yr	VG	VG+	NM
❑ 603	Let the Good Times Roll/Little Liza Jane	1960	12.50	25.00	50.00
❑ 608	Brown Eyed Handsome Man/Cry Me a River	1960	15.00	30.00	60.00
❑ 623	Ole King Cole/Pull Down the Sky	1961	12.50	25.00	50.00
❑ 636	I've Got My Eyes on You/Shattered Dreams	1961	10.00	20.00	40.00
❑ 652	Olive Learned to Pop-Eye/Shame	1962	10.00	20.00	40.00
❑ 8003	Half a Heartache/Little Miss Blue	1962	7.50	15.00	30.00

CLARIDGE

Number	Title (A Side/B Side)	Yr	VG	VG+	NM
❑ 309	Batman/All Around the World	1966	6.25	12.50	25.00

EVENT

Number	Title (A Side/B Side)	Yr	VG	VG+	NM
❑ 4295	Rollin' Dynamite/Evenin' Time	1959	12.50	25.00	50.00

HANNA-BARBERA

Number	Title (A Side/B Side)	Yr	VG	VG+	NM
❑ 495	I'm Gonna Love Ya/Waikiki Beach	1966	6.25	12.50	25.00

LAWN

Number	Title (A Side/B Side)	Yr	VG	VG+	NM
❑ 102	I've Been Thinkin'/It's a Fun Thing	1960	6.25	12.50	25.00

PARKWAY

Number	Title (A Side/B Side)	Yr	VG	VG+	NM
❑ 806	Rollin' Dynamite/Evenin' Time	1959	10.00	20.00	40.00

PHILIPS

Number	Title (A Side/B Side)	Yr	VG	VG+	NM
❑ 40109	Mess Around/Sittin' Down and Cryin'	1963	5.00	10.00	20.00

SAVANNAH SOUND

Number	Title (A Side/B Side)	Yr	VG	VG+	NM
❑ 501	Here Comes Batman/All Around the World	196?	10.00	20.00	40.00

SWAN

Number	Title (A Side/B Side)	Yr	VG	VG+	NM
❑ 4049	Little Lump of Sugar/Midnight Cryin' Time	1960	15.00	30.00	60.00

UNI

Number	Title (A Side/B Side)	Yr	VG	VG+	NM
❑ 55205	High on Life/If You Really Want Me To, I'll Go	1970	3.00	6.00	12.00

MCKENNITT, LOREENA

QR/WARNER BROS.

Number	Title (A Side/B Side)	Yr	VG	VG+	NM
❑ 17241	The Mummers' Dance/The Mystic's Dream	1998	—	—	3.00

MCKENZIE, SCOTT

Also see THE JOURNEYMEN (1); THE SMOOTHIES.

CAPITOL

Number	Title (A Side/B Side)	Yr	VG	VG+	NM
❑ 5348	All I Want Is You/Look in Your Eyes	1965	2.50	5.00	10.00
❑ 5500	There Stands the Glass/Wipe the Tears (From Your Face)	1965	2.50	5.00	10.00
❑ 5961	All I Want Is You/Look in Your Eyes	1967	—	3.00	6.00

EPIC

Number	Title (A Side/B Side)	Yr	VG	VG+	NM
❑ 10124	No, No, No, No, No/I Want to Be Alone	1967	2.00	4.00	8.00

—B-side by McKenzie's Musicians

ODE

Number	Title (A Side/B Side)	Yr	VG	VG+	NM
❑ 103	San Francisco "Wear Some Flowers in Your Hair"/What's the Difference	1967	3.75	7.50	15.00

—Original title; also has a different mix (echoey bass drum in bridge) than the later, more common version

Number	Title (A Side/B Side)	Yr	VG	VG+	NM
❑ 103	San Francisco (Be Sure to Wear Flowers in Your Hair)/What's the Difference	1967	2.00	4.00	8.00

—Revised title

Number	Title (A Side/B Side)	Yr	VG	VG+	NM
❑ 105	Like and Old Time Movie/What's the Difference, Chapter II	1967	—	3.00	6.00
❑ 107	Holy Man/What's the Difference, Chapter III	1968	—	3.00	6.00
❑ 66012	Going Home Again/Take a Moment	1970	—	2.50	5.00

MCKINLEYS, THE

SWAN

Number	Title (A Side/B Side)	Yr	VG	VG+	NM
❑ 4185	A Million Miles Away/Someone Cares for Me	1964	3.75	7.50	15.00

MCKUEN, ROD

A&M

Number	Title (A Side/B Side)	Yr	VG	VG+	NM
❑ 712	Hi Lonesome/Ballad of Hollywood	1963	2.50	5.00	10.00

BUDDAH

Number	Title (A Side/B Side)	Yr	VG	VG+	NM
❑ 372	Cycles/I Have Loved You	1973	—	2.00	4.00
❑ 401	Seasons in the Sun/(B-side unknown)	1974	—	2.00	4.00

BUENA VISTA

Number	Title (A Side/B Side)	Yr	VG	VG+	NM
❑ 482	Pastures Green/Scandalous John	1971	—	2.50	5.00

DECCA

Number	Title (A Side/B Side)	Yr	VG	VG+	NM
❑ 30660	Two Brothers/Jump Up	1958	3.75	7.50	15.00
❑ 30840	Lonesome Boy/Time's A-Gettin' Hard	1959	3.75	7.50	15.00
❑ 30902	Sure/Take It Like a Man	1959	3.75	7.50	15.00

HORIZON

Number	Title (A Side/B Side)	Yr	VG	VG+	NM
❑ 3	Advice to Folk Singers/There's a Hoot Tonight	1963	2.50	5.00	10.00

JUBILEE

Number	Title (A Side/B Side)	Yr	VG	VG+	NM
❑ 5420	Oliver Twist Meets the Duke of Oil/Steel Men	1962	3.00	6.00	12.00

KAPP

Number	Title (A Side/B Side)	Yr	VG	VG+	NM
❑ 366	In a Lonely Place/Marie, Marie	1961	3.00	6.00	12.00

LIBERTY

Number	Title (A Side/B Side)	Yr	VG	VG+	NM
❑ 55019	Rock Island Line/Head Like a Rock	1956	3.00	6.00	12.00
❑ 55034	Happy Is a Boy Named Me/Repeat After Me	1956	3.00	6.00	12.00

RCA VICTOR

Number	Title (A Side/B Side)	Yr	VG	VG+	NM
❑ 47-8613	Summer in My Eye/So Many Others	1965	2.00	4.00	8.00
❑ 47-8772	So Long, San Francisco/Some Trust in Chariots	1965	2.00	4.00	8.00
❑ 47-9139	The Ever Constant Sea/Baby Be My Love	1967	2.00	4.00	8.00
❑ 47-9376	Listen to the Warm/A Cat Named Sloopy	1967	2.00	4.00	8.00
❑ 47-9478	The Importance of the Rose/The Single Man	1968	2.00	4.00	8.00

SPIRAL

Number	Title (A Side/B Side)	Yr	VG	VG+	NM
❑ 1407	Oliver Twist/Celebrity Twist	1962	3.75	7.50	15.00

STANYAN

Number	Title (A Side/B Side)	Yr	VG	VG+	NM
❑ 34	Simple Christmas/A Hand To Hold At Christmas	1974	—	2.50	5.00

—B-side by Glenn Yarbrough

WARNER BROS.

Number	Title (A Side/B Side)	Yr	VG	VG+	NM
❑ 7243	Seasons in the Sun/To Watch the Trains	1968	—	3.00	6.00
❑ 7259	Ivy That Clings to the Wall/Kaleidoscope	1969	—	3.00	6.00
❑ 7274	Boat Ride/I'll Catch the Sun	1969	—	3.00	6.00
❑ 7288	Look Away/Trashy	1969	—	3.00	6.00
❑ 7332	The Things Men Do/The Time It Takes to Love You	1969	—	3.00	6.00
❑ 7346	Bring Her a Rose/Mister Kelly-Kelly and Me	1969	—	3.00	6.00
❑ 7389	I Think It's Going to Rain Today/London	1970	—	2.50	5.00
❑ 7420	My Mother's Eyes/Soldiers Want to Be Heroes	1970	—	2.50	5.00
❑ 7454	Champion Charlie Brown/Something for Snoopy	1971	—	3.00	6.00
❑ 7533	Hit 'Em in the Head with Love/Soldiers Want to Be Heroes	1971	—	2.50	5.00
❑ 7542	The Carols of Christmas/So My Sheep May Safely Graze	1971	—	2.50	5.00
❑ 7542 [PS]	The Carols of Christmas/So My Sheep May Safely Graze	1971	—	3.00	6.00
❑ 7620	Time to Sing My Song/Minute-Thirty-Second Waltz	1972	—	2.50	5.00
❑ 7699	Good for Nothin' Bill/The World I Used to Know	1973	—	2.00	4.00

MCLACHLAN, SARAH

ARISTA

Number	Title (A Side/B Side)	Yr	VG	VG+	NM
❑ 9804	Vox/Touch	1989	—	2.50	5.00

MCLAIN, DENNY

CAPITOL

Number	Title (A Side/B Side)	Yr	VG	VG+	NM
❑ 2282	Extra Innings/Lonely Is the Name	1968	3.00	6.00	12.00

MCLAWLER, SARAH

KING

Number	Title (A Side/B Side)	Yr	VG	VG+	NM
❑ 4549	Please Try to Love Me/Ready, Willing, and Able	1952	25.00	50.00	100.00
❑ 4561	Romance in the Dark/I'm Just Another One	1952	25.00	50.00	100.00

VEE JAY

Number	Title (A Side/B Side)	Yr	VG	VG+	NM
❑ 199	Babe in the Woods/Flamingo	1956	7.50	15.00	30.00
❑ 239	Snowfall/Relax Miss Frisky	1957	7.50	15.00	30.00

—With Richard Otto

MCLEAN, DON

ARISTA

Number	Title (A Side/B Side)	Yr	VG	VG+	NM
❑ 0284	Prime Time/The Statue	1977	—	2.00	4.00
❑ 0379	It Doesn't Matter Anymore/If We Try	1978	—	2.00	4.00

CAPITOL

Number	Title (A Side/B Side)	Yr	VG	VG+	NM
❑ B-44098	Perfect Love/Can't Blame the Train	1987	—	—	3.00
❑ B-44186	Love in the Heart/Every Day's a Miracle	1988	—	—	3.00
❑ B-44258	Eventually/It's Not Your Fault	1988	—	—	3.00

EMI

Number	Title (A Side/B Side)	Yr	VG	VG+	NM
❑ 9100	American Pie/Vincent	1992	2.00	4.00	8.00

—Scarce reissue with entire 8:30 version of "American Pie" on one side

EMI AMERICA

Number	Title (A Side/B Side)	Yr	VG	VG+	NM
❑ 8375	He's Got You/To Have and To Hold	1987	—	—	3.00
❑ 43025	Superman's Ghost/(B-side unknown)	1987	—	—	3.00

MEDIARTS

Number	Title (A Side/B Side)	Yr	VG	VG+	NM
❑ 108	And I Love You So/Castles in the Air	1970	2.50	5.00	10.00

MILLENNIUM

Number	Title (A Side/B Side)	Yr	VG	VG+	NM
❑ YB-11799	Crying/Genesis (In the Beginning)	1980	—	2.00	4.00
❑ YB-11803	Lloras "Crying"/Genesis (In the Beginning)	1981	—	—	—

—Unreleased

Number	Title (A Side/B Side)	Yr	VG	VG+	NM
❑ YB-11804	Since I Don't Have You/Your Cheating Heart	1981	—	2.00	4.00
❑ YB-11809	It's Just the Sun/Words and Music	1981	—	2.00	4.00
❑ YB-11819	Castles in the Air/Crazy Eyes	1981	—	2.00	4.00
❑ YB-13106	Jerusalem/Left for Dead on the Road of Love	1982	—	2.00	4.00
❑ GB-13477	Crying/Since I Don't Have You	1983	—	—	3.00

—Gold Standard Series

UNITED ARTISTS

Number	Title (A Side/B Side)	Yr	VG	VG+	NM
❑ XW206	If We Try/The More You Pay	1973	—	2.00	4.00
❑ XW363	Fool's Paradise/Happy Trails	1973	—	2.00	4.00
❑ XW519	Vincent/Dreidel	1974	—	2.00	4.00

—Reissue

Number	Title (A Side/B Side)	Yr	VG	VG+	NM
❑ XW520	American Pie (Part 1)/American Pie (Part 2)	1974	—	2.00	4.00

—Reissue

Number	Title (A Side/B Side)	Yr	VG	VG+	NM
❑ XW541	Sitting on Top of the World/Mule Skinner Blues	1974	—	2.00	4.00
❑ XW579	Homeless Brothers/La La Love You	1974	—	2.00	4.00
❑ XW614	Wonderful Baby/Birthday Song	1975	—	2.00	4.00
❑ 50796	And I Love You So/Castles in the Air	1971	—	3.00	6.00
❑ 50856	American Pie/Empty Chairs	1971	—	—	—

—Unreleased?

Number	Title (A Side/B Side)	Yr	VG	VG+	NM
❑ 50856	American Pie — Part 1/American Pie — Part 2	1971	—	2.50	5.00
❑ 50856 [DJ]	American Pie (mono/stereo)	1971	2.00	4.00	8.00

—With a different edit than the Part 1/Part 2 stock copy

Number	Title (A Side/B Side)	Yr	VG	VG+	NM
❑ 50856 [PS]	American Pie	1971	2.50	5.00	10.00

—Comes with both promos and stock copies

Number	Title (A Side/B Side)	Yr	VG	VG+	NM
❑ 50887	Vincent/Castles in the Air	1972	—	2.50	5.00
❑ 50887 [PS]	Vincent/Castles in the Air	1972	2.50	5.00	10.00
❑ 51100	Dreidel/Bronco Bill's Lament	1973	—	2.00	4.00

MCLOLLIE, OSCAR

CLASS

Number	Title (A Side/B Side)	Yr	VG	VG+	NM
❑ 206	Here I Am/Say	1957	3.75	7.50	15.00
❑ 228	Hey Girl — Hey Boy/Let Me Know Let Me Know	1958	3.75	7.50	15.00

—With Jeanette Baker

Number	Title (A Side/B Side)	Yr	VG	VG+	NM
❑ 238	Let's Get Together/Rock-a-Cha	1958	3.75	7.50	15.00

—With Jeanette Baker

Number	Title (A Side/B Side)	Yr	VG	VG+	NM
❑ 243	Convicted/My Heart Speaks	1959	3.75	7.50	15.00
❑ 265	The Honey Jump/Call It Love	1960	3.75	7.50	15.00
❑ 503	Rain/Casino	1956	5.00	10.00	20.00

MERCURY

Number	Title (A Side/B Side)	Yr	VG	VG+	NM
❑ 70964	Blue Velvet/The Penalty	1956	6.25	12.50	25.00

MODERN

Number	Title (A Side/B Side)	Yr	VG	VG+	NM
❑ 902	The Honey Jump (Part 1)/The Honey Jump (Part 2)	1952	15.00	30.00	60.00
❑ 915	Be Cool My Heart/All the Oil in Texas	1952	12.50	25.00	50.00
❑ 920	Falling in Love with You/Lolly Pop	1953	12.50	25.00	50.00
❑ 938	Hot Banana/Wiggle Toe	1954	10.00	20.00	40.00
❑ 943	God Gave Us Christmas/Dig That Crazy Santa Claus	1954	10.00	20.00	40.00
❑ 950	Pretty Girl/Hey Lolly Lolly	1955	10.00	20.00	40.00

Number	Title (A Side/B Side)	Yr	VG	VG+	NM
❑ 955	Pagliacci (With a Broken Heart)/Eternal Love	1955	10.00	20.00	40.00
❑ 970	Roll, Hot Rod, Roll/Convicted	1955	10.00	20.00	40.00
❑ 976	God Gave Us Christmas/(B-side unknown)	1955	7.50	15.00	30.00

WING

Number	Title (A Side/B Side)	Yr	VG	VG+	NM
❑ 90083	God's Green Earth/Got Your Love in My Heart	1956	6.25	12.50	25.00

MCMANUS, ROSS

Father of ELVIS COSTELLO.

IMPERIAL

Number	Title (A Side/B Side)	Yr	VG	VG+	NM
❑ 66042	Patsy Girl/I'm the Greatest	1964	3.00	6.00	12.00

MCNABB, CECIL

KING

Number	Title (A Side/B Side)	Yr	VG	VG+	NM
❑ 5116	Clock Tickin' Rhythm/Nothing Like This	1958	62.50	125.00	250.00

MCNAIR, BARBARA

AUDIO FIDELITY

Number	Title (A Side/B Side)	Yr	VG	VG+	NM
❑ 153	Love Has a Way/(B-side unknown)	1969	2.50	5.00	10.00
❑ 162	After St. Francis/I Can Tell	1969	2.50	5.00	10.00

CORAL

Number	Title (A Side/B Side)	Yr	VG	VG+	NM
❑ 61923	Till There Was You/Bobby	1958	6.25	12.50	25.00
❑ 61972	He's Got the Whole World in His Hands/Flipped Over You	1958	7.50	15.00	30.00
❑ 61996	Indiscreet/Waltz Me Around	1958	6.25	12.50	25.00
❑ 62020	Too Late This Spring/See If I Care	1958	6.25	12.50	25.00
❑ 62071	Goin' Steady with the Moon/I Feel a Feeling	1959	6.25	12.50	25.00
❑ 62116	Lover's Prayer/Old Devil Moon	1959	6.25	12.50	25.00

KC

Number	Title (A Side/B Side)	Yr	VG	VG+	NM
❑ 109	Cross Over the Bridge/Gloryland	1962	12.50	25.00	50.00
❑ 112	A Little Bird Told Me/Nobody Rings My Bell	1963	10.00	20.00	40.00

MOTOWN

Number	Title (A Side/B Side)	Yr	VG	VG+	NM
❑ 1087	Touch of Time/You're Gonna Love My Baby	1965	6.25	12.50	25.00
❑ 1099	What a Day/Everything Is Good About You	1966	6.25	12.50	25.00
❑ 1106	Here I Am Baby/My World Is Empty Without You	1966	6.25	12.50	25.00
❑ 1112	Steal Away Tonight/For Once in My Life	1967	125.00	250.00	500.00
❑ 1123	Where Would I Be Without You/For Once in My Life	1968	6.25	12.50	25.00
❑ 1133	You Could Never Love Him/Fancy Passes	1968	6.25	12.50	25.00

SIGNATURE

Number	Title (A Side/B Side)	Yr	VG	VG+	NM
❑ 12024	He's a King/Murray, What's Your Hurry	1960	5.00	10.00	20.00
❑ 12033	All About Love/You Done Me Wrong	1960	5.00	10.00	20.00
❑ 12049	Kansas City/Love Talk	1960	5.00	10.00	20.00

WARNER BROS.

Number	Title (A Side/B Side)	Yr	VG	VG+	NM
❑ 5633	Wanted Me/It Was Never Like This	1965	7.50	15.00	30.00

MCNAUGHTON, BYRON, AND HIS ALL NEWS ORCHESTRA

JAMIE

Number	Title (A Side/B Side)	Yr	VG	VG+	NM
❑ 1427	Right from the Shark's Jaws (The Jaws Interview)/Jaws Jam	1975	2.50	5.00	10.00

MCNEELY, BIG JAY

BAYOU

Number	Title (A Side/B Side)	Yr	VG	VG+	NM
❑ 014	Hometown Jamboree/Teenage Hop	1953	20.00	40.00	80.00
❑ 018	Catastrophe/Calamity	1953	20.00	40.00	80.00

FEDERAL

Number	Title (A Side/B Side)	Yr	VG	VG+	NM
❑ 12102	The Goof/Big Jay Shuffle	1952	10.00	20.00	40.00
❑ 12111	Just Crazy/Penthouse Serenade	1952	10.00	20.00	40.00
❑ 12141	Nervous Man, Nervous/Rock Candy	1953	10.00	20.00	40.00
❑ 12151	3-D/Texas Turkey	1953	10.00	20.00	40.00
❑ 12168	Mule Walk/Ice Water	1954	10.00	20.00	40.00
❑ 12179	Hot Cinders/Whipped Cream	1954	10.00	20.00	40.00
❑ 12186	Let's Work/Hard Tack	1954	10.00	20.00	40.00
❑ 12191	Beachcomber/Strip Tease Swing	1954	10.00	20.00	40.00

IMPERIAL

Number	Title (A Side/B Side)	Yr	VG	VG+	NM
❑ 5219	Deacon's Express/Jet Fury	1953	12.50	25.00	50.00

—Note: Earlier Big Jay McNeely releases on Imperial are unknown on 45 rpm

SAVOY

Number	Title (A Side/B Side)	Yr	VG	VG+	NM
❑ 1143	Deacon Hop/The Hucklebuck	1955	7.50	15.00	30.00

—With Paul Williams

SWINGIN'

Number	Title (A Side/B Side)	Yr	VG	VG+	NM
❑ 614	There Is Something on Your Mind/Back...Shack...Track	1959	6.25	12.50	25.00
❑ 618	I Got the Message/Psycho Serenade	1959	3.75	7.50	15.00
❑ 622	Minnie/My Darling Dear	1960	3.75	7.50	15.00
❑ 627	I Love You, Oh Darling/Oh, What a Fool	1960	3.75	7.50	15.00
❑ 629	After Midnight/Before Midnight	1961	3.75	7.50	15.00
❑ 637	Without a Love/The Squat	1962	3.75	7.50	15.00

VEE JAY

Number	Title (A Side/B Side)	Yr	VG	VG+	NM
❑ 142	Big Jay's Hop/Three Blind Mice	1955	10.00	20.00	40.00
❑ 212	Jay's Rock/The Convention	1956	15.00	30.00	60.00

—B-side by the Delegates

WARNER BROS.

Number	Title (A Side/B Side)	Yr	VG	VG+	NM
❑ 5401	You Don't Have to Go/Big Jay's Count	1963	3.00	6.00	12.00

7-Inch Extended Plays

FEDERAL

Number	Title (A Side/B Side)	Yr	VG	VG+	NM
❑ 246	(contents unknown)	1953	75.00	150.00	300.00
❑ 246 [PS]	Go! Go! Go! With Big Jay McNeely	1953	75.00	150.00	300.00
❑ 301	(contents unknown)	1954	50.00	100.00	200.00
❑ 301 [PS]	Big Jay McNeely, Volume 2	1954	50.00	100.00	200.00
❑ 332	(contents unknown)	1954	50.00	100.00	200.00
❑ 332 [PS]	Wild Man of the Saxophone	1954	50.00	100.00	200.00
❑ 373	(contents unknown)	1955	25.00	50.00	100.00
❑ 373 [PS]	Just Crazy	1955	25.00	50.00	100.00

MCPHATTER, CLYDE

Also see THE DRIFTERS.

AMY

Number	Title (A Side/B Side)	Yr	VG	VG+	NM
❑ 941	Everybody's Somebody's Fool/I Belong to You	1965	3.75	7.50	15.00
❑ 950	Little Bit of Sunshine/Everybody Loves a Good Time	1966	3.00	6.00	12.00
❑ 968	A Shot of Rhythm and Blues/I'm Not Going to Work Today	1966	3.00	6.00	12.00
❑ 975	Sweet and Innocent/Lavender Lace	1967	3.00	6.00	12.00
❑ 993	I Dreamt I Died/Lonely People Can't Afford to Cry	1967	3.00	6.00	12.00

ATLANTIC

Number	Title (A Side/B Side)	Yr	VG	VG+	NM
❑ 1070	Everybody's Laughing/Hot Ziggity	1955	7.50	15.00	30.00
❑ 1077	Love Has Joined Us Together/I Gotta Have You	1955	7.50	15.00	30.00

—With Ruth Brown

Number	Title (A Side/B Side)	Yr	VG	VG+	NM
❑ 1081	Seven Days/I'm Not Worthy	1956	7.50	15.00	30.00
❑ 1092	Treasure of Love/When You're Sincere	1956	10.00	20.00	40.00
❑ 1106	Thirty Days/I'm Lonely Tonight	1956	7.50	15.00	30.00
❑ 1117	Without Love (There Is Nothing)/I Make Believe	1956	7.50	15.00	30.00
❑ 1133	No Matter What/Just to Hold My Hand	1957	6.25	12.50	25.00
❑ 1149	Long Lonely Nights/Heartaches	1957	6.25	12.50	25.00
❑ 1158	You'll Be There/Rock and Cry	1957	6.25	12.50	25.00
❑ 1170	That's Enough for Me/No Love Like Her Love	1958	6.25	12.50	25.00
❑ 1185	Come What May/Let Me Know	1958	6.25	12.50	25.00
❑ 1199	A Lover's Question/I Can't Stand Up Long	1958	6.25	12.50	25.00
❑ 2018	Lovey Dovey/My Island of Dreams	1959	5.00	10.00	20.00
❑ 2028	Since You've Been Gone/Try, Try Baby	1959	5.00	10.00	20.00

—B-side actually the "old" Drifters (uncredited)

Number	Title (A Side/B Side)	Yr	VG	VG+	NM
❑ 2038	You Went Back on Your Word/There You Go	1959	5.00	10.00	20.00

—B-side actually the "old" Drifters (uncredited)

Number	Title (A Side/B Side)	Yr	VG	VG+	NM
❑ 2049	Just Give Me a Ring/Don't Dog Me	1960	5.00	10.00	20.00

—B-side actually the "old" Drifters (uncredited)

Number	Title (A Side/B Side)	Yr	VG	VG+	NM
❑ 2060	Deep Sea Ball/Let the Boogie-Woogie Roll	1960	5.00	10.00	20.00

—B-side actually the "old" Drifters (uncredited)

Number	Title (A Side/B Side)	Yr	VG	VG+	NM
❑ 2082	If I Didn't Love You Like I Do/Go! Yes Go!	1960	5.00	10.00	20.00

—B-side actually the "old" Drifters (uncredited)

DECCA

Number	Title (A Side/B Side)	Yr	VG	VG+	NM
❑ 32719	Book of Memories/I'll Belong to You	1970	2.00	4.00	8.00
❑ 32753	Why Can't We Get Together/Mixed-Up Cup	1970	2.00	4.00	8.00

DERAM

Number	Title (A Side/B Side)	Yr	VG	VG+	NM
❑ 85032	Thank You Love/Only a Fool	1968	2.50	5.00	10.00
❑ 85039	Baby You've Got It/Baby I Could Be So Good at Loving You	1969	2.50	5.00	10.00

MERCURY

Number	Title (A Side/B Side)	Yr	VG	VG+	NM
❑ 71660	Ta Ta/I Ain't Givin' Up Nothin'	1960	3.75	7.50	15.00
❑ 71692	I Just Want to Love You/You're for Me	1960	3.75	7.50	15.00
❑ 71692 [PS]	I Just Want to Love You/You're for Me	1960	7.50	15.00	30.00
❑ 71740	One More Chance/Before I Fall in Love Again	1960	3.75	7.50	15.00
❑ 71740 [PS]	One More Chance/Before I Fall in Love Again	1960	7.50	15.00	30.00
❑ 71783	Tomorrow Is a-Comin'/I'll Love You Till the Cows Come Home	1961	3.75	7.50	15.00
❑ 71783 [PS]	Tomorrow Is a-Comin'/I'll Love You Till the Cows Come Home	1961	7.50	15.00	30.00
❑ 71809	A Whole Heap o'Love/You're Movin' Me	1961	3.75	7.50	15.00
❑ 71809 [PS]	A Whole Heap o'Love/You're Movin' Me	1961	7.50	15.00	30.00
❑ 71841	I Never Knew/Happiness	1961	3.75	7.50	15.00
❑ 71841 [PS]	I Never Knew/Happiness	1961	6.25	12.50	25.00
❑ 71868	Same Time, Same Place/Your Second Choice	1961	3.75	7.50	15.00
❑ 71868 [PS]	Same Time, Same Place/Your Second Choice	1961	7.50	15.00	30.00
❑ 71941	Lover Please/Let's Forget About the Past	1962	5.00	10.00	20.00
❑ 71941 [PS]	Lover Please/Let's Forget About the Past	1962	10.00	20.00	40.00
❑ 71987	Little Bitty Pretty One/Next to Me	1962	3.75	7.50	15.00
❑ 71987 [PS]	Little Bitty Pretty One/Next to Me	1962	10.00	20.00	40.00
❑ 72025	Maybe/I Do Believe	1962	3.75	7.50	15.00
❑ 72025 [PS]	Maybe/I Do Believe	1962	7.50	15.00	30.00
❑ 72051	The Best Man Cried/Stop	1962	3.75	7.50	15.00
❑ 72051 [PS]	The Best Man Cried/Stop	1962	7.50	15.00	30.00
❑ 72166	So Close to Being in Love/From One to One	1963	3.75	7.50	15.00
❑ 72166 [PS]	So Close to Being in Love/From One to One	1963	7.50	15.00	30.00
❑ 72220	Deep in the Heart of Harlem/Happy Good Times	1963	3.75	7.50	15.00
❑ 72220 [PS]	Deep in the Heart of Harlem/Happy Good Times	1963	7.50	15.00	30.00
❑ 72253	Second Window, Second Floor/In My Tenement	1964	3.75	7.50	15.00
❑ 72317	Lucille/Baby, Baby	1964	3.75	7.50	15.00
❑ 72407	Crying Won't Help You Now/I Found My Love	1965	3.75	7.50	15.00
❑ 72407 [PS]	Crying Won't Help You Now/I Found My Love	1965	7.50	15.00	30.00

MGM

Number	Title (A Side/B Side)	Yr	VG	VG+	NM
❑ 12780	I Told Myself a Lie/The Masquerade Is Over	1959	5.00	10.00	20.00
❑ 12816	Twice As Nice/Where Did I Make My Mistake	1959	5.00	10.00	20.00
❑ 12843 [M]	Let's Try Again/Bless You	1959	5.00	10.00	20.00
❑ 12877	Think Me a Kiss/When the Right Time Comes Along	1960	5.00	10.00	20.00
❑ 12949	One Right After Another/This Is Not Goodbye	1960	5.00	10.00	20.00
❑ 12988	The Glory of Love/Take a Step	1961	5.00	10.00	20.00
❑ SK-50134 [S]	Let's Try Again/Bless You	1959	10.00	20.00	40.00

7-Inch Extended Plays

ATLANTIC

Number	Title (A Side/B Side)	Yr	VG	VG+	NM
❑ 584	*Without Love (There Is Nothing)/Thirty Days/I Make Believe/Treasure of Love	1958	62.50	125.00	250.00
❑ 584 [PS]	Clyde McPhatter	1958	62.50	125.00	250.00
❑ 605	(contents unknown)	1958	62.50	125.00	250.00
❑ 605 [PS]	Rock with Clyde McPhatter	1958	62.50	125.00	250.00
❑ 618	A Lover's Question/I Can't Stand Up Alone//Lovey Dovey/My Island of Dreams	1959	62.50	125.00	250.00
❑ 618 [PS]	Clyde McPhatter	1959	62.50	125.00	250.00

MCVIE, CHRISTINE

Also see CHICKEN SHACK; FLEETWOOD MAC.

EPIC

Number	Title (A Side/B Side)	Yr	VG	VG+	NM
❑ 10536	I'd Rather Go Blind/Get Like You Used to Be	1969	3.00	6.00	12.00

—As "Christine Perfect"

SIRE

Number	Title (A Side/B Side)	Yr	VG	VG+	NM
❑ 732	I'd Rather Go Blind/Close to Me	1976	2.00	4.00	8.00

WARNER BROS.

Number	Title (A Side/B Side)	Yr	VG	VG+	NM
❑ GWB 0488	Got a Hold on Me/Love Will Show Us How	1986	—	—	3.00

—"Back to Back Hits" series

Number	Title (A Side/B Side)	Yr	VG	VG+	NM
❑ 29160	I'm the One/The Challenge	1984	—	—	3.00
❑ 29313	Love Will Show Us How/The Challenge	1984	—	—	3.00
❑ 29313 [PS]	Love Will Show Us How/The Challenge	1984	—	—	3.00

Number	Title (A Side/B Side)	Yr	VG	VG+	NM
❑ 29372	Got a Hold on Me/Who's Dreaming This Dream	1984	—	—	3.00
❑ 29372 [PS]	Got a Hold on Me/Who's Dreaming This Dream	1984	—	—	3.00
ME AND THEM					
U.S. SONGS					
❑ 601	Everything I Do Is Wrong/Show You Mean It Too	1964	3.75	7.50	15.00
ME & YOU					
PARKWAY					
❑ 121	Let the World In/I've Got My Time Baby	1966	5.00	10.00	20.00
MEAT LOAF					
Also see STONEY AND MEATLOAF.					
ATLANTIC					
❑ 89303	Rock 'N' Roll Mercenary/Execution Day	1987	—	—	3.00
—A-side with John Parr					
❑ 89340	Getting Away with Murder/Rock 'N' Roll Hero	1986	—	—	3.00
CLEVELAND INT'L.					
❑ 02490	I'm Gonna Love Her for Both of Us/Peel Out	1981	—	2.00	4.00
❑ 02607	Read 'Em and Weep/Peel Out	1981	—	2.00	4.00
❑ 04028	The Razor's Edge/You Never Can Be Too Sure About the Girl	1983	—	2.00	4.00
EPIC					
❑ 50467	You Took the Words Right Out of My Mouth/For Crying Out Loud	1977	2.00	4.00	8.00
❑ 50513	Two Out of Three Ain't Bad (3:50)/For Crying Out Loud	1978	—	2.50	5.00
❑ 50513	Two Out of Three Ain't Bad (5:12)/For Crying Out Loud	1978	—	3.00	6.00
❑ 50588	Paradise by the Dashboard Light/"Bat" Overture	1978	—	2.50	5.00
❑ 50634	You Took the Words Right Out of My Mouth/Paradise by the Dashboard Light	1978	—	2.50	5.00
MCA					
❑ 54626	I'd Do Anything for Love (But I Won't Do That) (Single Edit)/I'd Do Anything for Love (But I Won't Do That) (Edit)	1993	—	2.00	4.00
❑ 54757	Rock and Roll Dreams Come Through/I'd Do Anything for Love (But I Won't Do That) (Live)	1993	—	2.00	4.00
❑ 54848	Objects in the Rear View Mirror May Appear Closer Than They Are/Two Out of Three Ain't Bad (Live)	1994	—	2.00	4.00
RCA					
❑ PB-14101	(Give Me the Future with a) Modern Girl/Sailor to a Siren	1985	—	—	3.00
❑ PB-14149	Surf's Up/Jumpin' the Sun	1985	—	—	3.00
RSO					
❑ 407	More Than You Deserve/Presence of the Lord	1974	3.00	6.00	12.00
MEDALLIONS, THE (1)					
DOOTO					
❑ 419	For Better or For Worse/I Wonder, Wonder, Wonder	1957	7.50	15.00	30.00
—As "Vernon Green and the Medallions"					
❑ 425	A Lover's Prayer/Unseen	1957	7.50	15.00	30.00
—As "Vernon Green and the Medallions"					
❑ 446	Magic Mountain/59 Volvo	1959	6.25	12.50	25.00
—As "Vernon Green and the Medallions"					
❑ 454	Behind the Door/Rocket Ship	1959	6.25	12.50	25.00
—As "Vernon Green and the Medallions"					
DOOTONE					
❑ 347	The Letter/Buick 59	1955	50.00	100.00	200.00
—Red label					
❑ 347	The Letter/Buick 59	1955	15.00	30.00	60.00
—Black label					
❑ 357	The Telegram/Coupe de Ville Baby	1955	15.00	30.00	60.00
—Maroon label					
❑ 357	The Telegram/Coupe de Ville Baby	1955	37.50	75.00	150.00
—Blue label					
❑ 364	Edna/Speeding	1955	15.00	30.00	60.00
❑ 373	My Pretty Baby/I'll Never Love Again	1955	15.00	30.00	60.00
—As "Johnny Twovoice and the Medallions"					
❑ 379	Dear Darling/Don't Shoot Baby	1955	17.50	35.00	70.00
❑ 393	I Want a Love/Dance and Swing	1956	12.50	25.00	50.00
❑ 400	Shedding Tears for You/Push Button Automobile	1956	15.00	30.00	60.00
—As "Vernon Green and the Medallions"					
❑ 407	My Mary Lou/Did You Have Fun	1956	15.00	30.00	60.00
—As "Vernon Green and the Medallions"					
❑ 479	Can You Talk/You Don't Know	1964	3.75	7.50	15.00
MINIT					
❑ 32034	Look at Me, Look at Me/Am I Ever Gonna See My Baby	1968	5.00	10.00	20.00
—As "Vernon Green and the Medallions"					
PAN WORLD					
❑ 71	Dear Ann/Shimmy Shimmy Shake	1962	12.50	25.00	50.00
—As "Vernon Green and the Medallions"					
7-Inch Extended Plays					
DOOTONE					
❑ 202	(contents unknown)	1958	25.00	50.00	100.00
❑ 202 [PS]	Rhythm and Blues	1958	37.50	75.00	150.00
MEDALLIONS, THE (2)					
ESSEX					
❑ 901	I Know/Laki-Lani	1955	100.00	200.00	400.00
MEDALLIONS, THE (3)					
LENOX					
❑ 5556	You Are Irresistible/Why Do You Look at Me	1962	6.25	12.50	25.00
MEDALLIONS, THE (4)					
SINGULAR					
❑ 1002	A Broken Heart/Lolo Baby	1957	12.50	25.00	50.00

Number	Title (A Side/B Side)	Yr	VG	VG+	NM
SULTAN					
❑ 4004	Love That Girl/Carachi	1959	20.00	40.00	80.00
MEDALLIONS, THE (U)					
Could be group (1), (3) or (4), or a totally different group.					
SARG					
❑ 191	I Love You True/My Baby's Gone	1961	10.00	20.00	40.00
❑ 194	Lovin' Time/Home Town	1961	10.00	20.00	40.00
MEDLEY, BILL					
Also see THE RIGHTEOUS BROTHERS.					
A&M					
❑ 1285	A Song for You/We've Only Just Begun	1971	—	2.50	5.00
❑ 1309	You've Lost That Lovin' Feeling/We've Only Just Begun	1971	—	2.50	5.00
❑ 1311	A Song for You/We've Only Just Begun	1971	—	2.00	4.00
❑ 1336	Help Me Make It Through the Night/Hung on You	1972	—	2.00	4.00
❑ 1350	Freedom for the Stallion/Damn Good Friend	1972	—	2.00	4.00
❑ 1371	A Simple Man/Missing You Too Long	1972	—	2.00	4.00
❑ 1434	Put a Little Love Away/It's Not Easy	1973	—	2.00	4.00
COLUMBIA					
❑ 38-07938	He Ain't Heavy, He's My Brother/The Bridge	1988	—	—	3.00
—B-side by Georgio Moroder					
CURB					
❑ 10542	Most of All You/I'm Gonna Be Strong	1989	—	—	3.00
❑ 76890	Don't Let Go/Bridge Over Troubled Water	1990	—	—	3.00
ELEKTRA					
❑ 69281	Rude Awakening/Leave Love Behind	1989	—	—	3.00
—B-side by Jonathan Elias					
LIBERTY					
❑ 1402	Don't Know Much/Woman	1981	—	2.00	4.00
❑ 1412	Stay the Night/Grandma and Grandpa	1981	—	2.00	4.00
MCA					
❑ 53443	Brown Eyed Woman/You've Lost That Lovin' Feelin'	1988	—	—	3.00
MGM					
❑ 13931	I Can't Make It Alone/One Day Girl	1968	2.00	4.00	8.00
❑ 13959	Brown Eyed Woman/Let the Good Times Roll	1968	2.00	4.00	8.00
❑ 14000	Peace Brother Peace/Winter Won't Come This Year	1968	2.00	4.00	8.00
❑ 14025	Something's So Wrong/This Is a Love Song	1969	2.00	4.00	8.00
❑ 14081	Reaching Back/Someone Is Standing Outside	1969	2.00	4.00	8.00
❑ 14099	Evie/Let Me Love Again	1969	2.00	4.00	8.00
❑ 14119	Hold On, I'm Comin'/Makin' My Way	1970	—	3.00	6.00
❑ 14145	Nobody Knows/Something's So Wrong	1970	—	3.00	6.00
❑ 14179	Gone/What Have You Got to Lose	1970	—	3.00	6.00
❑ 14202	Wasn't It Easy/Gone	1970	—	3.00	6.00
PARAMOUNT					
❑ 0089	Swing Low, Sweet Chariot/(B-side unknown)	1971	—	3.00	6.00
PLANET					
❑ YB-13317	Right Here and Now/The Best of My Life	1982	—	2.00	4.00
❑ YB-13425	I'm No Angel/I Need You in My Life	1983	—	—	3.00
❑ YB-13474	For You/I Need You in My Life	1983	—	—	3.00
RCA					
❑ 5224-7-RX	(I've Had) The Time of My Life/Love Is Strange	1987	—	—	3.00
—A-side: With Jennifer Warnes; B-side by Mickey and Sylvia					
❑ 5224-7-RX [PS]	(I've Had) The Time of My Life/Love Is Strange	1987	—	2.00	4.00
—A-side: With Jennifer Warnes; B-side by Mickey and Sylvia					
❑ PB-13692	I've Got Dreams to Remember/Till Your Memory's Gone	1983	—	—	3.00
❑ PB-13753	I Still Do/I've Got Dreams to Remember	1984	—	—	3.00
❑ PB-13851	Turn It Loose/I've Always Got the Heart to Sing the Blues	1984	—	—	3.00
❑ PB-13962	She Keeps Me in One Piece/Old Friend	1984	—	—	—
—Unreleased					
❑ PB-14021	Is There Anything I Can Do/Old Friend	1985	—	—	3.00
❑ PB-14081	Women in Love/Stand Up	1985	—	—	3.00
REPRISE					
❑ 0413	I Surrender to Your Touch/Leavin' Town	1965	3.75	7.50	15.00
UNITED ARTISTS					
❑ XW1256	Lay a Little Lovin' On Me/Wasn't That You Last Night	1978	—	2.00	4.00
❑ XW1270	Statue of a Fool/Wasn't That You Last Night	1978	—	2.00	4.00
❑ 1349	Hello Rock & Roll/Still a Fool	1980	—	2.00	4.00
VERVE					
❑ 10569	That Lucky Old Sun/My Darling Clementine	1967	2.50	5.00	10.00
MEEK, JOE					
LONDON					
❑ 9634	Kennedy March/Theme of Freedom	1964	5.00	10.00	20.00
MEGADETH					
CAPITOL					
❑ S7-57798	Symphony of Destruction/Breakpoint	1992	2.00	4.00	8.00
—Label misspells band's name as "Megadeath"					
❑ 58852	Breadline/Crush 'Em	2000	—	2.00	4.00
MEGATRONS, THE					
ACOUSTICON					
❑ 101	Velvet Waters/The Merry Piper	1959	3.75	7.50	15.00
AUDICON					
❑ 101	Velvet Waters/The Merry Piper	1959	3.00	6.00	12.00
❑ 104	Whispering Winds/Tootie Flutie	1960	2.50	5.00	10.00
❑ 107	Dance of the Silhouettes/Ranchero	1960	2.50	5.00	10.00
❑ 110	Julienne/By the Waters of the Minnetonka	1960	2.50	5.00	10.00
LAURIE					
❑ 3291	Velvet Waters/The Merry Piper	1965	2.00	4.00	8.00
❑ 3310	A Love That Will Last Forever/The Detroit Sound	1965	2.00	4.00	8.00

MEISNER, RANDY

Also see EAGLES.

Number	Title (A Side/B Side)	Yr	VG	VG+	NM
ASYLUM					
❑ 45502	I Really Want You Here Tonight/Heart Song	1978	—	2.50	5.00
EPIC					
❑ 02059	Gotta Get Away/Trouble Ahead	1981	—	2.00	4.00
❑ 03032	Never Been in Love/Nothing Is Said ('Til the Artist Is Dead)	1982	—	2.00	4.00
❑ 03352	Strangers Still/Runnin'	1982	—	2.00	4.00
❑ 50939	Deep Inside My Heart/I Need You Bad	1980	—	2.00	4.00
❑ 50964	Hearts on Fire/Anyway Bye Bye	1981	—	2.00	4.00

MEL AND TIM

Number	Title (A Side/B Side)	Yr	VG	VG+	NM
BAMBOO					
❑ 106	I've Got Puredee/(Instrumental)	1969	—	3.00	6.00
❑ 107	Backfield in Motion/Do It Right Baby	1969	2.00	4.00	8.00
—White label, not a promo					
❑ 107	Backfield in Motion/Do It Right Baby	1969	—	3.00	6.00
—Multicolor label					
❑ 109	Good Guys Only Win in the Movies/I Found That I Was Wrong	1970	—	3.00	6.00
❑ 112	Feeling Bad/I've Got Puredee	1970	—	3.00	6.00
❑ 114	Mail Call Time/Forget It, I've Got It	1970	—	3.00	6.00
❑ 116	We've Got a Groove to Move On/Never on Time	1970	—	3.00	6.00
❑ 118	I'm the One/Put An Extra Plus to Your Love	1971	—	3.00	6.00
STAX					
❑ 0127	Starting All Over Again/It Hurts to Want It So Bad	1972	—	2.50	5.00
❑ 0154	I May Not Be What You Want/Too Much Wheelin' and Dealin'	1973	—	2.50	5.00
❑ 0160	Heaven Knows/Don't Mess with My Money, My Honey, Oh My Woman	1973	—	2.50	5.00
❑ 0202	Those Little Things That Count/The Same Folks	1974	—	2.50	5.00
❑ 0224	Forever and a Day/That's the Way I Want to Live My Life	1974	—	2.50	5.00

MEL-O-DOTS, THE

Number	Title (A Side/B Side)	Yr	VG	VG+	NM
APOLLO					
❑ 1192	One More Time/Just How Long	1952	750.00	1500.	3000.

MELA, DENNY

Number	Title (A Side/B Side)	Yr	VG	VG+	NM
PARKWAY					
❑ 802	Forget My Past/Blondie	1959	3.75	7.50	15.00

MELANIE

Number	Title (A Side/B Side)	Yr	VG	VG+	NM
AMHERST					
❑ 300	Who's Been Sleeping in My Bed (Edited)/Who's Been Sleeping in My Bed	1985	—	2.00	4.00
ATLANTIC					
❑ 3380	If I Needed You/Cyclone	1977	—	2.50	5.00
BLANCHE					
❑ 1	Imaginary Heroes/Detroit or Buffalo	1982	—	2.00	4.00
❑ 110	When You're Dead and Gone/Detroit or Buffalo	1982	—	2.00	4.00
BUDDAH					
❑ 113	Bo Bo's Party/I'm Back in Town	1969	—	3.00	6.00
❑ 135	Beautiful People/Any Guy	1969	—	3.00	6.00
❑ 161 [DJ]	Take Me Home (mono/stereo)	1970	—	3.00	6.00
—May be promo only					
❑ 167	Lay Down (Candles in the Rain)/Candles in the Rain	1970	—	3.00	6.00
❑ 167 [PS]	Lay Down (Candles in the Rain)/Candles in the Rain	1970	2.00	4.00	8.00
❑ 186	Peace Will Come (According to Plan)/Close to It All	1970	—	2.50	5.00
❑ 186	Peace Will Come (According to Plan)/Stop (I Don't Want to Hear It Anymore)	1970	—	2.50	5.00
❑ 186 [PS]	Peace Will Come (According to Plan)/Stop (I Don't Want to Hear It Anymore)	1970	—	3.00	6.00
❑ 202	Ruby Tuesday/Merry Christmas	1970	—	2.50	5.00
❑ 224	We Don't Know Where We're Going/The Good Book	1971	—	2.50	5.00
❑ 268	The Nickel Song/What Have They Done to My Song Ma	1971	—	2.50	5.00
❑ 268 [PS]	The Nickel Song/What Have They Done to My Song Ma	1971	—	3.00	6.00
❑ 304	I'm Back in Town/Johnny Boy	1972	—	2.50	5.00
COLUMBIA					
❑ 44349	My Beautiful People/God's Only Daughter	1967	2.50	5.00	10.00
❑ 44349 [PS]	My Beautiful People/God's Only Daughter	1967	5.00	10.00	20.00
❑ 44524	Garden in the City/Why Didn't My Mother Tell Me	1968	2.50	5.00	10.00
❑ 44524 [PS]	Garden in the City/Why Didn't My Mother Tell Me	1968	5.00	10.00	20.00
GORDIAN					
❑ 1947	Rag Doll/(B-side unknown)	1985	—	2.00	4.00
MIDSONG INT'L.					
❑ 40858	I'd Rather Leave While I'm in Love/Record People	1978	—	2.50	5.00
❑ 40903	Knock on Wood/Record People	1978	—	2.50	5.00
NEIGHBORHOOD					
❑ 4201	Brand New Key/Some Say (I Got Devil)	1971	—	3.00	6.00
—White label (not a promo)					
❑ 4201	Brand New Key/Some Say (I Got Devil)	1971	—	2.50	5.00
—Multicolor label					
❑ 4202	Ring the Living Bell/Railroad	1972	—	2.00	4.00
❑ 4202 [PS]	Ring the Living Bell/Railroad	1972	—	2.50	5.00
❑ 4204	Steppin'/Someday I'll Be a Farmer	1972	—	2.00	4.00
❑ 4207	Together Alone/Center of the Circle	1972	—	2.00	4.00
❑ 4207 [PS]	Together Alone/Center of the Circle	1972	—	2.50	5.00
❑ 4209	Stoneground Woman/Do You Believe	1972	—	2.00	4.00
❑ 4210	Bitter Bad/Do You Believe	1973	—	2.00	4.00
❑ 4212	Seeds/Some Say (I Got Devil)	1973	—	2.00	4.00
❑ 4213	Will You Love Me Tomorrow/Here I Am	1973	—	2.00	4.00
❑ 4213 [PS]	Will You Love Me Tomorrow/Here I Am	1973	—	2.50	5.00
❑ 4214	Love to Love Again/Fine and Feather	1974	—	2.00	4.00
❑ 4214 [PS]	Love to Love Again/Fine and Feather	1974	—	3.00	6.00
❑ 4215	Lover's Cross/Holding Out	1974	—	2.00	4.00
❑ 10000	You're Not a Bad Ghost, Just an Old Song/Eyes of Man	1975	—	2.00	4.00
❑ 10001	Sweet Misery/Record Machine	1975	—	2.00	4.00
PORTRAIT					
❑ 51001	One More Try/Apathy	1981	—	2.00	4.00
STORK					
❑ (no #)	Timothy Scott Bogart	1970	3.00	6.00	12.00
—One-sided promo of "Christopher Robin" to celebrate the birth of Neil Bogart's son					
TOMATO					
❑ 10007	Running After Love/Holding Out	1979	—	2.50	5.00
WORLD UNITED					
❑ 1947	Oh Boy/Brand New Key	1978	—	2.50	5.00
7-Inch Extended Plays					
BUDDAH					
❑ SP 2 [DJ]	Merry Christmas/Christopher Robin//I'm Back In Town/I Really Loved Harold	1971	2.50	5.00	10.00
❑ SP 2 [PS]	I'm Back in Town	1971	2.50	5.00	10.00

MELANIE C

Also see SPICE GIRLS.

Number	Title (A Side/B Side)	Yr	VG	VG+	NM
VIRGIN					
❑ 58883	I Turn to You/Never Be the Same Again	2000	—	2.00	4.00

MELCHER, TERRY

Also see BRUCE AND TERRY.

Number	Title (A Side/B Side)	Yr	VG	VG+	NM
COLUMBIA					
❑ 42427	I Waited Too Long/That's All I Want	1962	5.00	10.00	20.00
—As "Terry Day"					
❑ 42427 [PS]	I Waited Too Long/That's All I Want	1962	10.00	20.00	40.00
—As "Terry Day"					
❑ 42678	Be a Soldier/I Love You Betty	1963	5.00	10.00	20.00
—As "Terry Day"					
❑ 42678 [PS]	Be a Soldier/I Love You Betty	1963	10.00	20.00	40.00
RCA VICTOR					
❑ PB-10587	Fire in a Rainstorm/So Right Tonight	1976	2.50	5.00	10.00

MELLENCAMP, JOHN

Includes records as "Johnny Cougar," "John Cougar," and "John Cougar Mellencamp."

Number	Title (A Side/B Side)	Yr	VG	VG+	NM
ELEKTRA					
❑ 69370	Rave On/Tutti Frutti	1988	—	—	3.00
—B-side by Little Richard					
❑ 69370 [PS]	Rave On/Tutti Frutti	1988	—	2.00	4.00
MCA					
❑ 40634	American Dream/Oh, Pretty Woman	1976	2.50	5.00	10.00
—As "Johnny Cougar"					
MERCURY					
❑ 574244-7	Key West Intermezzo (I Saw You First)/Just Another Day	1997	—	—	3.00
❑ 856258-7	Dance Naked/R.O.C.K. in the U.S.A.	1994	—	2.00	4.00
❑ 858738-7	Wild Night/Brothers	1994	—	2.00	4.00
—With Me'Shell NgedeOcelo					
❑ 862702-7	Human Wheels/Human Wheels (Edit)	1993	—	2.00	4.00
❑ 866414-7	Again Tonight/Get a Leg Up (Live)	1992	—	2.00	4.00
❑ 867890-7	Get a Leg Up (Family Version)/Whenever We Wanted	1991	—	2.00	4.00
❑ 870126-7	Check It Out/We Are the People	1988	—	—	3.00
—Mercury releases starting with "870" and "888" are by "John Cougar Mellecamp"					
❑ 870126-7 [PS]	Check It Out/We Are the People	1988	—	—	3.00
❑ 870327-7	Rooty Toot Toot/Check It Out	1988	—	—	3.00
❑ 870327-7 [PS]	Rooty Toot Toot/Check It Out	1988	—	—	3.00
❑ 874012-7	Pop Singer/J.M.'s Question	1989	—	—	3.00
❑ 874012-7 [PS]	Pop Singer/J.M.'s Question	1989	—	—	3.00
❑ 874644-7	Jackie Brown/Jackie Brown (Acoustic Version)	1989	—	—	3.00
❑ 874644-7 [PS]	Jackie Brown/Jackie Brown (Acoustic Version)	1989	—	—	3.00
❑ 874932-7	Let It All Hang Out/Country Gentleman	1989	—	2.00	4.00
❑ 874932-7 [PS]	Let It All Hang Out/Country Gentleman	1989	—	2.00	4.00
❑ 888763-7	Paper in Fire/Never Too Old	1987	—	—	3.00
❑ 888763-7 [PS]	Paper in Fire/Never Too Old	1987	—	—	3.00
❑ 888934-7	Cherry Bomb/Shama Lama Ding Dong	1987	—	—	3.00
❑ 888934-7 [PS]	Cherry Bomb/Shama Lama Ding Dong	1987	—	—	3.00
RIVA					
❑ 202	I Need a Lover/Welcome to Chinatown	1979	—	2.00	4.00
—Riva 202-211 as "John Cougar"					
❑ 202 [PS]	I Need a Lover/Welcome to Chinatown	1979	2.50	5.00	10.00
❑ 203	Small Paradise/Sugar Marie	1980	—	2.00	4.00
❑ 204	A Little Night Dancin'/Pray for Me	1980	—	2.50	5.00
❑ 205	This Time/Don't Misunderstand Me	1980	—	2.00	4.00
❑ 207	Ain't Even Done with the Night/Make Me Feel	1981	—	2.00	4.00
❑ 209	Hurts So Good/Close Enough	1982	—	2.00	4.00
❑ 209 [PS]	Hurts So Good/Close Enough	1982	2.50	5.00	10.00
❑ 210	Jack and Diane/Can You Take It	1982	—	2.00	4.00
❑ 211	Hand to Hold On To/Small Paradise	1982	—	2.00	4.00
❑ 214	Crumblin' Down/Golden Gates	1983	—	2.00	4.00
—Riva 214 on as "John Cougar Mellencamp"					
❑ 214 [PS]	Crumblin' Down/Golden Gates	1983	—	2.50	5.00
❑ 215	Pink Houses/Serious Business	1983	—	2.00	4.00
❑ 215 [PS]	Pink Houses/Serious Business	1983	—	3.00	6.00
❑ 216	Authority Song/Pink Houses (Acoustic Version)	1984	—	2.00	4.00
❑ 216 [PS]	Authority Song/Pink Houses (Acoustic Version)	1984	—	2.50	5.00
❑ 880984-7	Lonely Ol' Night/The Kind of Fella I Am	1985	—	—	3.00
❑ 880984-7 [PS]	Lonely Ol' Night/The Kind of Fella I Am	1985	—	2.00	4.00
❑ 884202-7	Small Town/Small Town (Acoustic Version)	1985	—	—	3.00
❑ 884202-7 [PS]	Small Town/Small Town (Acoustic Version)	1985	—	2.00	4.00
❑ 884455-7	R.O.C.K. in the U.S.A. (A Salute to 60's Rock)/Under the Boardwalk	1986	—	—	3.00
❑ 884455-7 [PS]	R.O.C.K. in the U.S.A. (A Salute to 60's Rock)/Under the Boardwalk	1986	—	—	3.00
❑ 884635-7	Rain on the Scarecrow/Pretty Ballerina	1986	—	—	3.00
❑ 884635-7 [PS]	Rain on the Scarecrow/Pretty Ballerina	1986	—	—	3.00
❑ 884856-7	Rumbleseat/Cold Sweat	1986	—	—	3.00

Number	Title (A Side/B Side)	Yr	VG	VG+	NM
❑ 884856-7 [PS]	Rumbleseat/Cold Sweat	1986	—	—	3.00

MELLO-HARPS, THE

CASINO

Number	Title (A Side/B Side)	Yr	VG	VG+	NM
❑ 104	Gumma Gumma/No Good	1959	15.00	30.00	60.00

DO-RE-MI

Number	Title (A Side/B Side)	Yr	VG	VG+	NM
❑ 203	Love Is a Vow/Valerie	1956	4000.	6000.	8000.

TIN PAN ALLEY

Number	Title (A Side/B Side)	Yr	VG	VG+	NM
❑ 145/6	I Love Only You/Ain't Got the Money	1955	100.00	200.00	400.00
❑ 157/8	What Good Are My Dreams/Gone	1956	150.00	300.00	600.00
❑ 159	I Couldn't Believe/My Bleeding Heart	1956	150.00	300.00	600.00

MELLO-KINGS, THE

HERALD

Number	Title (A Side/B Side)	Yr	VG	VG+	NM
❑ 502	Tonite Tonite/Do Baby Do	1957	125.00	250.00	500.00
—First pressing credits "The Mellotones"					
❑ 502	Tonite Tonite/Do Baby Do	1957	12.50	25.00	50.00
—Label corrected to "The Mello-Kings"; script print inside flag					
❑ 502	Tonite Tonite/Do Baby Do	1961	6.50	12.50	25.00
—Reissue; block print inside flag					
❑ 507	Chapel on the Hill/Sassafras	1957	7.50	15.00	30.00
❑ 511	Baby Tell Me Why Why Why/The Only Girl I'll Ever Know	1958	7.50	15.00	30.00
❑ 518	Valerie/She's Real Cool	1958	7.50	15.00	30.00
❑ 536	Chip Chip/Running to You	1959	7.50	15.00	30.00
—Both sides play as labeled					
❑ 536	Chip Chip/Running to You	1959	37.50	75.00	150.00
—Mispressing; plays "Rockin' at the Bandstand"/"Down in Cuba" by the Royal Holidays					
❑ 548	Our Love Is Beautiful/Dear Mr. Jock	1960	6.25	12.50	25.00
❑ 554	Kid Stuff/I Promise	1960	6.25	12.50	25.00
❑ 561	Penny/Till There Were None	1961	6.25	12.50	25.00
❑ 567	Love at First Sight/She's Real Cool	1961	6.25	12.50	25.00

LESCAY

Number	Title (A Side/B Side)	Yr	VG	VG+	NM
❑ 3009	Walk Softly/But You Lied	1962	7.50	15.00	30.00

7-Inch Extended Plays

HERALD

Number	Title (A Side/B Side)	Yr	VG	VG+	NM
❑ 451	(contents unknown)	1957	75.00	150.00	300.00
❑ 451 [PS]	The Fabulous Mello-Kings	1957	100.00	200.00	400.00

MELLO-MOODS, THE

GAMBLE

Number	Title (A Side/B Side)	Yr	VG	VG+	NM
❑ 2512	Stop Taking My Love for Granted/Inspirational Pleasure	1972	2.50	5.00	10.00

HAMILTON

Number	Title (A Side/B Side)	Yr	VG	VG+	NM
❑ 143	I'm Lost/I Woke Up This Morning	1953	25.00	50.00	100.00

PRESTIGE

Number	Title (A Side/B Side)	Yr	VG	VG+	NM
❑ 799	Call on Me/I Tried and Tried and Tried	1953	175.00	350.00	700.00
❑ 856	I'm Lost/I Woke Up This Morning	1953	175.00	350.00	700.00

ROBIN

Number	Title (A Side/B Side)	Yr	VG	VG+	NM
❑ 104	I Couldn't Sleep a Wink Last Night/And You Just Can't Go Through Life Alone	1952	750.00	1500.	3000.
❑ 105	Where Are You (Now That I Need You)/How Could You	1952	1250.	2500.	5000.

MELLO-TONES, THE

More than one group.

COLUMBIA

Number	Title (A Side/B Side)	Yr	VG	VG+	NM
❑ 6-900 (?)	When The Rain Gates Unfold/What Are They Doing in Heaven	1950	100.00	200.00	400.00
—Probably originally released on Columbia's short-lived special numbering system for 7-inch records					
❑ 39051	When The Rain Gates Unfold/What Are They Doing in Heaven	1950	75.00	150.00	300.00
❑ 39215	Looking for a City/Flysing Saucers	1951	75.00	150.00	300.00

DECCA

Number	Title (A Side/B Side)	Yr	VG	VG+	NM
❑ 48318	Winos on Parade/Man Loves Woman	1954	100.00	200.00	400.00
❑ 48319	I'm Just Another One in Love with You/I'm Gonna Get	1954	100.00	200.00	400.00

FASCINATION

Number	Title (A Side/B Side)	Yr	VG	VG+	NM
❑ 1001	Rosie Lee/I'll Never Fall in Love Again	1957	37.50	75.00	150.00

GEE

Number	Title (A Side/B Side)	Yr	VG	VG+	NM
❑ 1037	Rosie Lee/I'll Never Fall in Love Again	1957	10.00	20.00	40.00
❑ 1040	Ca-Sandra/Rattle Shake Roll	1957	10.00	20.00	40.00

OKEH

Number	Title (A Side/B Side)	Yr	VG	VG+	NM
❑ 6828	Rough and Rocky Road/Cool by the River Banks	1951	75.00	150.00	300.00

MELLOW MOODS, THE

RONNIE

Number	Title (A Side/B Side)	Yr	VG	VG+	NM
❑ 202	The Christmas Song/Love Me	19??	2.50	5.00	10.00
—B-side by the Rainbows					

MELLOWLARKS, THE

ARGO

Number	Title (A Side/B Side)	Yr	VG	VG+	NM
❑ 5285	Sing a Silly Sing Song/Farewell to You, My Nancy	1958	6.25	12.50	25.00

MELLOWS, THE

CANDLELIGHT

Number	Title (A Side/B Side)	Yr	VG	VG+	NM
❑ 1011	Moon of Silver/You're Gone	1956	37.50	75.00	150.00
❑ 1012	Farewell Farewell/No More Loneliness	1956	37.50	75.00	150.00

CELESTE

Number	Title (A Side/B Side)	Yr	VG	VG+	NM
❑ 3002	Lucky Guy/My Darling	1956	30.00	60.00	120.00
❑ 3004	I'm Yours/Sweet Lorraine	1956	150.00	300.00	600.00

JAY DEE

Number	Title (A Side/B Side)	Yr	VG	VG+	NM
❑ 793	How Sentimental Can I Be/Nothin' to Do	1954	50.00	100.00	200.00
❑ 797	Smoke from Your Cigarette/Pretty Baby	1954	62.50	125.00	250.00
❑ 801	I Was a Fool to Let You Go/I Still Care	1955	50.00	100.00	200.00
❑ 807	Yesterday's Memories/Loveable Lilly	1955	37.50	75.00	150.00

MELO GENTS, THE

WARNER BROS.

Number	Title (A Side/B Side)	Yr	VG	VG+	NM
❑ 5056	Baby Be Mine/Get Off My Back	1959	12.50	25.00	50.00

MELODY MAKERS, THE

HOLLIS

Number	Title (A Side/B Side)	Yr	VG	VG+	NM
❑ 1001	Carolina Moon/Let's Make Love Worthwhile	1957	25.00	50.00	100.00
❑ 1002	The Nearnes of You/Gotta Go	1957	37.50	75.00	150.00

MELVIN, HAROLD, AND THE BLUE NOTES

Also see THE BLUE NOTES (1).

ABC

Number	Title (A Side/B Side)	Yr	VG	VG+	NM
❑ 12240	Reaching for the World/Stay Together	1976	—	2.50	5.00
❑ 12268	After You Love Me, Why Do You Leave Me/Big Singing Star	1977	—	2.50	5.00
—With Sharon Paige					
❑ 12327	Baby, You Got My Nose Open/Try to Live a Day	1978	—	2.50	5.00
❑ 12368	Power of Love/Now Is the Time	1978	—	2.50	5.00

ARCTIC

Number	Title (A Side/B Side)	Yr	VG	VG+	NM
❑ 135	Go Away/What Can a Man Do	1967	2.50	5.00	10.00

LANDA

Number	Title (A Side/B Side)	Yr	VG	VG+	NM
❑ 703	Get Out (And Let Me Cry)/You May Not Love Me	1964	4.00	8.00	16.00
—As "The Blue Notes"					

MCA

Number	Title (A Side/B Side)	Yr	VG	VG+	NM
❑ 41291	Tonight's the Night/If You're Looking for Someone to Love	1980	—	2.00	4.00
—With Sharon Paige					
❑ 51190	Hang On In There/If You Love Me, Really Love Me	1982	—	2.00	4.00

PHILADELPHIA INT'L.

Number	Title (A Side/B Side)	Yr	VG	VG+	NM
❑ 3516	I Miss You (Part I)/I Miss You (Part II)	1972	—	2.50	5.00
❑ 3520	If You Don't Know Me By Now/Let Me Into Your World	1972	—	2.50	5.00
❑ 3525	Yesterday I Had the Blues/Ebony Woman	1973	—	2.50	5.00
❑ 3525 [PS]	Yesterday I Had the Blues/Ebony Woman	1973	—	3.00	6.00
❑ 3533	The Love I Lost (Part 1)/The Love I Lost (Part 2)	1973	—	2.50	5.00
❑ 3543	Satisfaction Guaranteed (Or Take Your Love Back)/I'm Weak for You	1974	—	2.50	5.00
❑ 3552	Where Are All My Friends/Let It Be You	1974	—	2.50	5.00
❑ 3562	Bad Luck (Part 1)/Bad Luck (Part 2)	1975	—	2.50	5.00
❑ 3569	Hope That We Can Be Together Soon/Be for Real	1975	—	2.50	5.00
—With Sharon Paige					
❑ 3579	Wake Up Everybody (Part 1)/Wake Up Everybody (Part 2)	1975	—	2.50	5.00
❑ 3588	Tell the World How I Feel About 'Cha Baby/You Know How to Make Me Feel So Good	1976	—	2.50	5.00

PHILLY WORLD

Number	Title (A Side/B Side)	Yr	VG	VG+	NM
❑ 99709	I Really Love You/I Can't Let Go	1984	—	2.00	4.00
❑ 99735	Today's Your Lucky Day (Long)/Today's Your Lucky Day (Short)	1984	—	2.00	4.00
❑ 99761	Don't Give Me Up/(Instrumental)	1984	—	2.00	4.00

SOURCE

Number	Title (A Side/B Side)	Yr	VG	VG+	NM
❑ 41156	Prayin' (Part 1)/Prayin' (Part 2)	1979	—	2.00	4.00
❑ 41157	Tonight's the Night/Your Love Is Taking Me on a Journey	1979	—	2.00	4.00
❑ 41231	I Should Be Your Lover (Part 1)/I Should Be Your Lover (Part 2)	1980	—	2.00	4.00

MEMORIES, THE

WAY-LIN

Number	Title (A Side/B Side)	Yr	VG	VG+	NM
❑ 101	Love Bells/I Promise	1959	100.00	200.00	400.00

MEMPHIS MINNIE

CHECKER

Number	Title (A Side/B Side)	Yr	VG	VG+	NM
❑ 771	Broken Heart/Me and My Chauffeur	1953	1000.	2000.	3000.

J.O.B.

Number	Title (A Side/B Side)	Yr	VG	VG+	NM
❑ 1101	Kissing in the Dark/World of Trouble	1952	250.00	500.00	1000.

MEPHISTOPHELES

REPRISE

Number	Title (A Side/B Side)	Yr	VG	VG+	NM
❑ 0832	Cricket Song/Take a Jet	1969	3.00	6.00	12.00

MERCED BLUE NOTES, THE

ACCENT

Number	Title (A Side/B Side)	Yr	VG	VG+	NM
❑ 1069	Rufus/Your Tender Lips	1961	10.00	20.00	40.00

GALAXY

Number	Title (A Side/B Side)	Yr	VG	VG+	NM
❑ 738	Rufus Jr./Thumping	1965	7.50	15.00	30.00
❑ 744	Mama Rufus/Bad Bad Whiskey	1965	7.50	15.00	30.00

SOUL

Number	Title (A Side/B Side)	Yr	VG	VG+	NM
❑ 35007	Do the Pig/Thumping	1965	250.00	500.00	1000.

TRI-PHI

Number	Title (A Side/B Side)	Yr	VG	VG+	NM
❑ 1011	Midnight Sessions (Part 1)/Midnight Sessions (Part 2)	1962	12.50	25.00	50.00
❑ 1023	Whole Lotta Nothin'/Fragile	1963	10.00	20.00	40.00

MERCER, WILL

CONSTELLATION

Number	Title (A Side/B Side)	Yr	VG	VG+	NM
❑ 109	Penny Candy/Willowy Billowy Land	1963	3.75	7.50	15.00

SUN

Number	Title (A Side/B Side)	Yr	VG	VG+	NM
❑ 329	You're Just My Kind/Ballad of St. Mark's	1959	6.25	12.50	25.00

MERCURY, FREDDIE

Also see QUEEN.

ANTHEM

Number	Title (A Side/B Side)	Yr	VG	VG+	NM
❑ 104	I Can Hear Music/Going Back	1973	25.00	50.00	100.00
—As "Larry Lurex"; A-side matrix number on label is "A-0009-REMIX"					
❑ 104	I Can Hear Music/Going Back	1973	37.50	75.00	150.00
—As "Larry Lurex"; A-side matrix number on label is "A-0009"					

CAPITOL

Number	Title (A Side/B Side)	Yr	VG	VG+	NM
❑ B-5696	The Great Pretender/Exercises in Free Love	1987	—	—	3.00
❑ B-5696 [PS]	The Great Pretender/Exercises in Free Love	1987	—	2.00	4.00

COLUMBIA

Number	Title (A Side/B Side)	Yr	VG	VG+	NM
❑ 04606	Love Kills/Rotwang's Party (Robot Dance)	1984	—	2.00	4.00
❑ 04606 [PS]	Love Kills/Rotwang's Party (Robot Dance)	1984	—	2.00	4.00
❑ 04869	I Was Born to Love You/.Stop All the Fighting	1985	—	2.00	4.00
❑ 04869 [PS]	I Was Born to Love You/.Stop All the Fighting	1985	—	2.00	4.00
❑ 05455	Living on My Own/She Blows Hot and Cold	1985	—	2.00	4.00

Number	Title (A Side/B Side)	Yr	VG	VG+	NM

MERCY

Number	Title (A Side/B Side)	Yr	VG	VG+	NM
SUNDI					
❑ 6811	Love (Can Make You Happy)/Fire Ball	1969	2.00	4.00	8.00
WARNER BROS.					
❑ 7291	Love Can Make You Happy/Happy As Can Be, La La La	1969	3.75	7.50	15.00
—Pressed in U.S. for export only; A-side is a re-recording of the hit on Sundi					
❑ 7297	Forever/The Morning's Come	1969	—	3.00	6.00
❑ 7331	Hello Baby/Heard You Went Away	1969	—	3.00	6.00

MERRI-MEN, THE

Another group containing former members of BILL HALEY AND HIS COMETS.

Number	Title (A Side/B Side)	Yr	VG	VG+	NM
APT					
❑ 25051	Big Daddy/St, Louis Blues	1960	6.25	12.50	25.00

MERRY-GO-ROUND, THE

Also see EMMITT RHODES.

Number	Title (A Side/B Side)	Yr	VG	VG+	NM
A&M					
❑ 834	Live/Time Will Show the Wiser	1967	2.50	5.00	10.00
❑ 857	Gonna Fight the World/We're in Love	1967	2.50	5.00	10.00
❑ 863	You're a Very Lovely Woman/Where Have You Been All My Life	1967	2.50	5.00	10.00
❑ 886	Had to Run Around/She Laughed Loud	1967	2.50	5.00	10.00
❑ 920	Missing You/Listen, Listen	1968	2.50	5.00	10.00
❑ 957	Highway/'Til the Day After	1968	2.50	5.00	10.00

MERSEY LADS, THE

Number	Title (A Side/B Side)	Yr	VG	VG+	NM
MGM					
❑ 13481	Johnny No Love/What 'Cha Gonna Do Baby	1966	3.75	7.50	15.00

MERSEYBEATS, THE

Number	Title (A Side/B Side)	Yr	VG	VG+	NM
FONTANA					
❑ 1513	It Would Take a Long Time/Don't Let It Happen to Us	1965	3.75	7.50	15.00
❑ 1532	I Love You, Yes I Do/See Me Back	1965	3.75	7.50	15.00
❑ 1882	Mr. Moonlight/I Think of You	1964	3.75	7.50	15.00
❑ 1905	Don't Turn Around/Really Mystified	1964	3.75	7.50	15.00
❑ 1950	See Me Back/Last Night	1964	3.75	7.50	15.00

MERSEYS, THE

Number	Title (A Side/B Side)	Yr	VG	VG+	NM
MERCURY					
❑ 72582	Sorrow/Some Other Day	1966	5.00	10.00	20.00

MESSENGERS, THE (1)

Milwaukee-based rock group.

Number	Title (A Side/B Side)	Yr	VG	VG+	NM
RARE EARTH					
❑ 5032	That's the Way a Woman Is/In the Jungle	1971	—	2.50	5.00
SOUL					
❑ 35037	Window Shopping/California Soul	1967	2.50	5.00	10.00
U.S.A.					
❑ 866	Midnight Hour/Hard Hard Year	1967	3.75	7.50	15.00
—As "The Messengers"					
❑ 866	Midnight Hour/Up 'Til Now	1967	3.00	6.00	12.00
—As "Michael and the Messengers"					
❑ 874	Romeo and Juliet/Lies	1967	3.75	7.50	15.00
—As "Michael and the Messengers"					

MESSENGERS, THE (2)

Number	Title (A Side/B Side)	Yr	VG	VG+	NM
ERA					
❑ 3143	Let Me Be Your Man/You've Got Me Cryin'	1964	3.00	6.00	12.00

MESSENGERS, THE (3)

British group.

Number	Title (A Side/B Side)	Yr	VG	VG+	NM
MGM					
❑ 13293	I'm Stealin' Back/This Little Light of Mine	1964	3.00	6.00	12.00
❑ 13346	When Did You Leave Heaven/More Pretty Girls Than One	1965	3.00	6.00	12.00

MESSENGERS, THE (4)

Chicago group; after THE MESSENGERS (1) changed record labels, this group recorded as "Michael and the Messengers" on U.S.A.

Number	Title (A Side/B Side)	Yr	VG	VG+	NM
U.S.A.					
❑ 889	Run and Hide/She Was the Girl	1967	2.00	4.00	8.00
—As "Michael and the Messengers"					
❑ 897	Gotta Take It Easy/I Need Her Here	1968	2.00	4.00	8.00
—As "Michael and the Messengers"					

MESSINA, JIM

Also see BUFFALO SPRINGFIELD; LOGGINS AND MESSINA; POCO.

Number	Title (A Side/B Side)	Yr	VG	VG+	NM
AUDIO FIDELITY					
❑ 098	The Breeze and I/Straight Man	1964	7.50	15.00	30.00
COLUMBIA					
❑ 11094	New and Different Way/(Is This) Lovin' You Lady	1979	—	2.00	4.00
❑ 11182	Do You Want to Dance/Seeing You (For the First Time)	1980	—	2.00	4.00
FEATURE					
❑ 101	Panther Pounce/Tiger Tail	1964	7.50	15.00	30.00
ULTIMA					
❑ 705	Drag Bike Boogie/A-Rab	1964	7.50	15.00	30.00
VIV					
❑ 1000	Side Track/Sherrie	1965	6.25	12.50	25.00
WARNER BROS.					
❑ 29278	Big Tease/The Island	1984	—	2.00	4.00
❑ 29457	Forever My Love/One More Mile	1983	—	2.00	4.00
❑ 49784	Move Into Your Heart/Stay the Night	1981	—	2.00	4.00
—With Pauline Wilson					
❑ 49839	It's All Right Here/Move Into Your Heart	1981	—	2.00	4.00

METALLICA

Number	Title (A Side/B Side)	Yr	VG	VG+	NM
ELEKTRA					
❑ 69329	One/The Prince	1988	—	2.50	5.00
❑ 69329 [PS]	One/The Prince	1988	—	2.50	5.00
❑ 69357	Eye of the Beholder/Breadfan	1988	2.50	5.00	10.00
❑ 69357 [PS]	Eye of the Beholder/Breadfan	1988	2.50	5.00	10.00

METERS, THE

Also see AARON NEVILLE.

Number	Title (A Side/B Side)	Yr	VG	VG+	NM
JOSIE					
❑ 1001	Sophisticated Cissy/Sehorn's Farm	1968	2.50	5.00	10.00
❑ 1005	Cissy Strut/Here Comes the Meter Man	1969	2.50	5.00	10.00
❑ 1008	Ease Back/Ann	1969	2.50	5.00	10.00
❑ 1013	Dry Spell/Look-Ka Py Py	1969	2.50	5.00	10.00
❑ 1015	Look-Ka Py Py/This Is My Last Affair	1970	2.50	5.00	10.00
❑ 1018	Chicken Strut/Hey! Last Minute	1970	2.50	5.00	10.00
❑ 1021	Hand Clapping Song/Joog	1970	2.50	5.00	10.00
❑ 1024	A Message from the Meters/Zony Mash	1970	2.50	5.00	10.00
❑ 1026	Stretch Your Rubber Band/Groovy Lady	1971	2.50	5.00	10.00
❑ 1029	(The World Is a Bit Under the Weather) Doodle-Oop/I Need More Time	1971	2.50	5.00	10.00
❑ 1031	Good Old Funky Music/Sassy Lady	1971	2.50	5.00	10.00
REPRISE					
❑ 1086	Do the Dirt/Smiling	1972	2.00	4.00	8.00
❑ 1106	Cabbage Alley/The Flower Song	1972	2.00	4.00	8.00
❑ 1135	Chug Chug Chug-A-Lug (Part 1)/Chug Chug Chug-A-Lug (Part 2)	1972	2.00	4.00	8.00
❑ 1307	Hey Pocky A-Way/Africa	1974	—	3.00	6.00
❑ 1314	People Say/Loving You Is On My Mind	1974	—	3.00	6.00
❑ 1338	Running Fast/They All Ask'd for You	1975	—	3.00	6.00
❑ 1357	Disco Is the Thing Today/Mister Moon	1976	—	3.00	6.00
❑ 1372	Trick Bag/Find Yourself	1976	—	3.00	6.00
WARNER BROS.					
❑ 8434	Be My Lady/No More Okey Doke	1977	—	2.50	5.00

METRONOMES, THE (1)

Number	Title (A Side/B Side)	Yr	VG	VG+	NM
CADENCE					
❑ 1310	I Love My Girl/I'm Gonna Get Me a Girl Somehow	1957	25.00	50.00	100.00
❑ 1339	How Much I Love You/Dear Don	1957	30.00	60.00	120.00

METRONOMES, THE (2)

Number	Title (A Side/B Side)	Yr	VG	VG+	NM
CHALLENGE					
❑ 9157	Hot Time/Tears, Tears, Tears	1962	3.75	7.50	15.00
MAUREEN					
❑ 1000	My Dearest Darling/The Chickie-Goo	1962	12.50	25.00	50.00

METROS, THE (1)

Number	Title (A Side/B Side)	Yr	VG	VG+	NM
1-2-3					
❑ 1720	If You Can Feel/The Dampness from Your Kiss	1969	2.50	5.00	10.00
RCA VICTOR					
❑ 47-8994	Sweetest One/Time Changes Things	1966	3.75	7.50	15.00
❑ 47-9159	Since I Found My Baby/No Baby	1967	20.00	40.00	80.00
❑ 47-9331	Let's Groove/The Replacer	1967	6.25	12.50	25.00

METROS, THE (2)

Number	Title (A Side/B Side)	Yr	VG	VG+	NM
JUST					
❑ 1502	All of My Life/Lookin'	1959	100.00	200.00	400.00

METROS, THE (3)

Number	Title (A Side/B Side)	Yr	VG	VG+	NM
MTM					
❑ B-72070	After the Passion's Gone/Don't Let Our Love Go (Baby)	1986	—	2.00	4.00

METROTONES, THE

Number	Title (A Side/B Side)	Yr	VG	VG+	NM
COLUMBIA					
❑ 40420	A-Ting-a-Ling/Tonight	1955	5.00	10.00	20.00
❑ 40486	Write Me Baby/Even Though	1955	5.00	10.00	20.00
RESERVE					
❑ 116	Please Come Back/Skitter Skatter	1957	62.50	125.00	250.00
7-Inch Extended Plays					
COLUMBIA					
❑ B-2026	(contents unknown)	1955	5.00	10.00	20.00
❑ B-2026 [PS]	Tops in Rock and Roll, Vol. 1	1955	5.00	10.00	20.00
❑ B-2027	(contents unknown)	1955	5.00	10.00	20.00
❑ B-2027 [PS]	Tops in Rock and Roll, Vol. 2	1955	5.00	10.00	20.00

MEYERS, AUGIE

Number	Title (A Side/B Side)	Yr	VG	VG+	NM
ATLANTIC AMERICA					
❑ 99382	Kep Pa So/To Nothing at All	1988	—	—	3.00
AXBAR					
❑ 6020	Release Me/Deep in the Heart of Texas	198?	—	2.50	5.00
PARAMOUNT					
❑ 0192	Sugar Blu/Five Cent Bag	1973	2.00	4.00	8.00
TEXAS RE-CORD					
❑ 103	High Texas Rider/Memories	197?	2.00	4.00	8.00
❑ 106	Why Don't We Make Love Like We Used To/Just Because	197?	2.00	4.00	8.00
—With Domingo Saldivar					
❑ 107	Down in Mexico/The Sun Shines Down on Me in Texas	197?	2.00	4.00	8.00
❑ 121	I Want to See You Again/Wedding Blues	197?	2.00	4.00	8.00
V.O.L.					
❑ 135	If You Ever Go/I've Seen the Way	196?	2.50	5.00	10.00
—As "Augie"					

MICHAEL AND THE MESSENGERS

See THE MESSENGERS (1); THE MESSENGERS (4).

MICHAELS, MARILYN

Number	Title (A Side/B Side)	Yr	VG	VG+	NM
RCA VICTOR					
❑ 47-7771	Tell Tommy I Miss Him/Everyone Was There But You	1960	5.00	10.00	20.00
❑ 47-7831	Past the Age of Innocence/Danny	1961	3.75	7.50	15.00

MICKEY AND KITTY

MICKEY BAKER (ex-MICKEY AND SYLVIA) and Kitty Noble.

Number	Title (A Side/B Side)	Yr	VG	VG+	NM
ATLANTIC					
❑ 2024	Ooh-Sha-Lala/The Kid Brother	1959	3.75	7.50	15.00
❑ 2036	First Love/St. Louis Blues	1959	3.75	7.50	15.00
❑ 2046	My Reverie/Buttercup	1959	3.75	7.50	15.00

MICKEY AND SYLVIA

Also see MICKEY BAKER; SYLVIA (1).

Number	Title (A Side/B Side)	Yr	VG	VG+	NM
ALL PLATINUM					
❑ 2307	Lovedrops/Because You Do It to Me	1969	—	3.00	6.00
❑ 2310	Anytime/Souling with Mickey and Sylvia	1969	—	3.00	6.00
CAT					
❑ 102	Fine Love/Speedy Life	1954	10.00	20.00	40.00
—As "Little" Sylvia Vanderpool and Mickey Baker					
GROOVE					
❑ 0164	No Good Lover/Walkin' in the Rain	1956	7.50	15.00	30.00
❑ 0175	Love Is Strange/I'm Going Home	1956	7.50	15.00	30.00
KING					
❑ 5737	Baby, Let's Dance/Oh Yea, Ah Ah	1963	3.00	6.00	12.00
❑ 6006	Love Is Strange/Darling	1965	2.50	5.00	10.00
RAINBOW					
❑ 316	I'm So Glad/Se De Boom Run Dun	1955	7.50	15.00	30.00
❑ 318	Forever and a Day/Ride, Sally, Ride	1955	7.50	15.00	30.00
RCA					
❑ 5224-7-RX	Love Is Strange/(I've Had) The Time of My Life	1987	—	—	3.00
—B-side by Bill Medley and Jennifer Warnes					
RCA VICTOR					
❑ APAO-0080	Love Is Strange/Dearest	1973	—	3.00	6.00
❑ 37-7877	Love Is the Only Thing/Love Lesson	1961	12.50	25.00	50.00
—"Compact Single 33" (small hole, plays at LP speed)					
❑ 47-7403	To the Valley/Oh Yeah! Uh-Huh	1958	5.00	10.00	20.00
❑ 47-7774 [M]	Sweeter As the Days Go By/Mommy Out De Light	1960	3.75	7.50	15.00
❑ 47-7811 [M]	What Would I Do/This Is My Story	1960	5.00	10.00	20.00
❑ 47-7877	Love Is the Only Thing/Love Lesson	1961	3.75	7.50	15.00
❑ 47-8517	Let's Shake Some More/Gypsy	1965	3.00	6.00	12.00
❑ 47-8582	Fallin' in Love/From the Beginning of Time	1965	3.00	6.00	12.00
❑ 61-7774 [S]	Sweeter As the Days Go By/Mommy Out De Light	1960	10.00	20.00	40.00
—"Living Stereo" (large hole, plays at 45 rpm)					
❑ 61-7811 [S]	What Would I Do/This Is My Story	1960	10.00	20.00	40.00
—"Living Stereo" (large hole, plays at 45 rpm)					
STANG					
❑ 5004	Rocky Raccoon/Souling with Mickey and Sylvia	1969	2.00	4.00	8.00
❑ 5047	Baby You're So Fine/Anytime You Want To	1973	—	3.00	6.00
VIK					
❑ 0252	Love Is Strange/I'm Going Home	1957	7.50	15.00	30.00
❑ 0267	There Oughta Be a Law/Dearest	1957	6.25	12.50	25.00
❑ 0280	Two Shadows on Your Window/Love Will Make You Fail in School	1957	6.25	12.50	25.00
❑ 0290	Love Is a Treasure/Let's Have a Picnic	1957	6.25	12.50	25.00
❑ 0297	There'll Be No Backin' Out/Where Is My Honey	1957	6.25	12.50	25.00
❑ 0324	Rock and Stroll Room/Bewildered	1958	5.00	10.00	20.00
❑ 0334	It's You I Love/True, True Love	1958	5.00	10.00	20.00
WILLOW					
❑ 23000	Baby, You're So Fine/Lovedrops	1961	3.75	7.50	15.00
❑ 23002	Darling (I Miss You So)/I'm Guilty	1961	3.75	7.50	15.00
❑ 23004	Since I Fell for You/He Gave Me Everything	1962	3.75	7.50	15.00
❑ 23006	Love Is Strange/Walking in the Rain	1962	3.75	7.50	15.00

7-Inch Extended Plays

Number	Title (A Side/B Side)	Yr	VG	VG+	NM
GROOVE					
❑ 018	(contents unknown)	1957	37.50	75.00	150.00
❑ 018 [PS]	Mickey and Sylvia	1957	37.50	75.00	150.00
VIK					
❑ 262	(contents unknown)	1957	20.00	40.00	80.00
❑ 262 [PS]	Love Is Strange	1957	20.00	40.00	80.00

MIDDLETON, TONY

Also see THE WILLOWS.

Number	Title (A Side/B Side)	Yr	VG	VG+	NM
ABC-PARAMOUNT					
❑ 10695	You Spoiled My Reputation/If I Could Write a Song	1965	7.50	15.00	30.00
ALFA					
❑ 113	My Home Town/Please Take Me	1962	3.00	6.00	12.00
ALTO					
❑ 2001	Untouchable/I Need You	1960	3.00	6.00	12.00
A&M					
❑ 1084	Angela/Keep On Dancing	1969	5.00	10.00	20.00
❑ 1124	Harlem Lady/Sound of Goodbye	1969	3.75	7.50	15.00
BIG TOP					
❑ 3037	Unchained Melody/Sweet Baby of Mine	1960	7.50	15.00	30.00
ELDORADO					
❑ 508	First Taste of Love/Only My Heart	1957	7.50	15.00	30.00
GONE					
❑ 5015	Let's Fall in Love/Say Yeah	1957	15.00	30.00	60.00
MALA					
❑ 544	Out of This World/My Baby Likes to Boogaloo	1966	6.25	12.50	25.00
MGM					
❑ 13493	Don't Ever Leave Me/To the Ends of the Earth	1966	10.00	20.00	40.00
MR. G					
❑ 811	Let Me Down Easy (Part 1)/Let Me Down Easy (Part 2)	1968	3.00	6.00	12.00
❑ 815	Good Morning World/(B-side unknown)	1968	3.00	6.00	12.00
PHILIPS					
❑ 40151	I Need You Tonight/Send Me Away	1963	3.00	6.00	12.00
❑ 40184	Too Hot to Handle/I Just Couldn't Help Myself	1964	3.00	6.00	12.00
ROULETTE					
❑ 4345	Is It This or Is It That/I'm Gonna Try Love One More Time	1961	6.25	12.50	25.00
ROYAL FLUSH					
❑ 102	Lady Fingers/A Garden in the Ghetto	1976	—	3.00	6.00
SAXONY					
❑ 104	I'm On My Way/(B-side unknown)	1958	12.50	25.00	50.00
SCEPTER					
❑ 12290	Border Song (Holy Moses)/Silliest People	1970	2.50	5.00	10.00
TOY					
❑ 3803	Rock and Roll Lullaby/Sittin' in the Sunshine	1972	2.00	4.00	8.00
TRIUMPH					
❑ 600	Count Your Blessings (See What Love Has Done)/I Just Want Somebody	1959	6.25	12.50	25.00
❑ 605	The Universe/Blackjack	1959	6.25	12.50	25.00
UNITED ARTISTS					
❑ 410	Drifting/Memories Are Made of This	1962	3.75	7.50	15.00

MIDNIGHT ANGELS, THE

Number	Title (A Side/B Side)	Yr	VG	VG+	NM
APEX					
❑ 77073	I'm Sufferin'/In the Moonlight	1967	7.50	15.00	30.00
❑ 77073 [PS]	I'm Sufferin'/In the Moonlight	1967	10.00	20.00	40.00

MIDNIGHTERS, THE

Also see HANK BALLARD AND THE MIDNIGHTERS; THE ROYALS (1).

Number	Title (A Side/B Side)	Yr	VG	VG+	NM
FEDERAL					
❑ 12169	Work With Me Annie/Until I Die	1954	25.00	50.00	100.00
—Silver top label; as " The Midnighters (Formerly Known As the Royals)"					
❑ 12169	Work With Me Annie/Until I Die	1954	10.00	20.00	40.00
—All-green label; as "The Midnighters (Formerly Known As the Royals)"					
❑ 12177	Give It Up/That Woman	1954	20.00	40.00	80.00
—As "The Midnighters Formerly the Royals"					
❑ 12185	Sexy Ways/Don't Say Your Last Goodbye	1954	20.00	40.00	80.00
—As "The Midnighters Formerly the Royals"					
❑ 12195	Annie Had a Baby/She's the One	1954	15.00	30.00	60.00
❑ 12200	Annie's Aunt Fanny/Crazy Loving	1954	15.00	30.00	60.00
❑ 12202	Tell Them/Stingy Little Thing	1954	15.00	30.00	60.00
❑ 12205	She's the One/Moonrise	1955	15.00	30.00	60.00
❑ 12210	Ashamed of Myself/Ring-a-Ling-Ling	1955	15.00	30.00	60.00
❑ 12220	Why Are We Apart/Switchie, Witchie, Titchie	1955	15.00	30.00	60.00
❑ 12224	Henry's Got Flat Feet (Can't Dance No More)/Whatsoever You Do	1955	15.00	30.00	60.00
❑ 12227	It's Love Baby (24 Hours a Day)/Looka Here	1955	15.00	30.00	60.00
❑ 12230	Give It Up/That Woman	1955	15.00	30.00	60.00
❑ 12240	Rock and Roll Wedding/That House on the Hill	1955	15.00	30.00	60.00
❑ 12243	Don't Change Your Pretty Ways/We'll Never Meet Again	1955	15.00	30.00	60.00
❑ 12251	Partners for Life/Sweet Mama, Do Right	1956	15.00	30.00	60.00
❑ 12260	Rock Granny Roll/Open Up the Back Door	1956	15.00	30.00	60.00
❑ 12270	Tore Up Over You/Early One Morning	1956	12.50	25.00	50.00
❑ 12285	I'll Be Home Some Day/Come On and Get It	1957	12.50	25.00	50.00
❑ 12288	Let Me Hold Your Hand/Oh Bah Baby	1957	12.50	25.00	50.00
❑ 12293	E Basta Cosi/In the Doorway Crying	1957	12.50	25.00	50.00
❑ 12299	Oh, So Happy/Is Your Love for Real	1957	10.00	20.00	40.00
❑ 12305	Let 'Em Roll/What Made You Change Your Mind	1957	10.00	20.00	40.00
❑ 12317	Stay By My Side/Daddy's Little Baby	1958	10.00	20.00	40.00
❑ 12339	Baby Please/Ow-Wow-Oo-Wee	1958	10.00	20.00	40.00

7-Inch Extended Plays

Number	Title (A Side/B Side)	Yr	VG	VG+	NM
FEDERAL					
❑ 333	Work with Me Annie/Moonrise//Sexy Ways/Get It	1955	75.00	150.00	300.00
—Green label, silver top					
❑ 333	Work with Me Annie/Moonrise//Sexy Ways/Get It	1955	37.50	75.00	150.00
—All-green label					
❑ 333 [PS]	The Midnighters Sing Their Greatest Hits	1955	50.00	100.00	200.00
—Pink cover					
❑ 333 [PS]	The Midnighters Sing Their Greatest Hits	1955	50.00	100.00	200.00
—Purple cover					

MIDNIGHTERS, THE (2)

Number	Title (A Side/B Side)	Yr	VG	VG+	NM
20TH FOX					
❑ 182	The Road Home/Taco	1960	3.00	6.00	12.00

MIGHTY AVENGERS, THE

Number	Title (A Side/B Side)	Yr	VG	VG+	NM
PRESS					
❑ 9746	Blue Turns to Grey/I'm Lost Without You	1965	2.50	5.00	10.00

MIGHTY MARVELOWS, THE

See THE MARVELOWS.

MIGIL FIVE, THE

Number	Title (A Side/B Side)	Yr	VG	VG+	NM
CAMEO					
❑ 316	Mockin' Bird Hill/Long Ago (And Far Away)	1964	2.50	5.00	10.00
HICKORY					
❑ 1292	Your Cheatin' Heart/Boys and Girls	1965	2.50	5.00	10.00
❑ 1334	I'm in Love Again/One Hundred Years	1965	2.50	5.00	10.00
MERCURY					
❑ 72301	Near You/Don't Wanna Go On Shaking	1964	2.50	5.00	10.00

MIKE AND THE JAYS

Number	Title (A Side/B Side)	Yr	VG	VG+	NM
DOYL					
❑ 1001	My Only Girl/Dingle Dangle Doll	1960	20.00	40.00	80.00

MIKE AND THE MODIFIERS

Number	Title (A Side/B Side)	Yr	VG	VG+	NM
GORDY					
❑ 7006	I Found Myself a Brand New Baby/It's Too Bad	1962	15.00	30.00	60.00

MIKE AND THE UTOPIANS

Number	Title (A Side/B Side)	Yr	VG	VG+	NM
CEE JAY					
❑ 574	Erlene/I Wish	1958	75.00	150.00	300.00
❑ 574	Erlene/I Found a Penny	1958	37.50	75.00	150.00

MIKE, JOHN AND BILL

"Mike" is MICHAEL NESMITH, later of THE MONKEES.

Number	Title (A Side/B Side)	Yr	VG	VG+	NM
OMNIBUS					
❑ 239	How Can You Kiss Me/Just a Little Love	1963	50.00	100.00	200.00

Number	Title (A Side/B Side)	Yr	VG	VG+	NM
MILBURN, AMOS					
ALADDIN					
❑ 3014	Chicken Shack Boogie/It Took a Long, Long Time	1950	50.00	100.00	200.00
—78 originally released in 1948					
❑ 3018	Bewildered/A and M Blues	1950	30.00	60.00	120.00
—78 originally released in 1948					
❑ 3068	Bad, Bad Whiskey/I'm Going to Tell My Mama	1950	125.00	250.00	500.00
—Note: Amos Milburn singles on Aladdin before 3068 are unconfirmed on 45 rpm except those listed					
❑ 3080	Let's Rock a While/Tears, Tears, Tears	1951	20.00	40.00	80.00
❑ 3090	Everybody Clap Hands/That Was Your Last Mistake	1951	20.00	40.00	80.00
❑ 3093	Ain't Nothin' Shaking/Just One More Drink	1951	20.00	40.00	80.00
❑ 3105	She's Gone Again/Boogie Woogie	1951	20.00	40.00	80.00
❑ 3124	Thinking and Drinking/Trouble in Mind	1952	20.00	40.00	80.00
❑ 3125	Flying Home/Put Something in My Hand	1952	20.00	40.00	80.00
❑ 3133	I Won't Be Your Fool Anymore/Roll Mr. Jelly	1952	20.00	40.00	80.00
❑ 3146	Button Your Lip/Everything I Do Is Wrong	1952	20.00	40.00	80.00
❑ 3150	Kiss Me Again/Greyhound	1952	20.00	40.00	80.00
❑ 3159	Rock, Rock, Rock/Boo Hoo	1953	15.00	30.00	60.00
❑ 3164	Let Me Go Home, Whiskey/Three Times a Fool	1953	15.00	30.00	60.00
❑ 3168	Long, Long Day/Please Mr. Johnson	1953	15.00	30.00	60.00
❑ 3197	One Scotch, One Bourbon, One Beer/What Can I Do	1953	25.00	50.00	100.00
❑ 3218	Good, Good Whiskey/Let's Have a Party	1954	20.00	40.00	80.00
❑ 3226	How Could You Hurt Me So/Rocky Mountain	1954	15.00	30.00	60.00
❑ 3240	Milk and Water/I'm Still a Fool for You	1954	15.00	30.00	60.00
❑ 3248	Glory of Love/Baby, Baby All the Time	1954	15.00	30.00	60.00
❑ 3253	Vicious, Vicious Vodka/I Done Done It	1954	15.00	30.00	60.00
❑ 3269	That's It/One, Two, Three Everybody	1954	15.00	30.00	60.00
❑ 3281	Why Don't You Do Right/I Love You Anyway	1955	10.00	20.00	40.00
❑ 3293	All Is Well/My Happiness Depends on You	1955	10.00	20.00	40.00
❑ 3306	House Party/I Guess I'll Go	1955	10.00	20.00	40.00
❑ 3320	French Fried Potatoes and Ketchup/I Need Someone	1956	10.00	20.00	40.00
❑ 3332	Chicken Shack Boogie/Juice, Juice, Juice	1956	10.00	20.00	40.00
❑ 3340	Girl of My Dreams/Everyday of the Week	1956	10.00	20.00	40.00
❑ 3363	Rum and Coca-Cola/Soft Pollow	1957	7.50	15.00	30.00
❑ 3370	Greyhound/Dear Angel	1957	7.50	15.00	30.00
❑ 3383	Thinking of You Baby/If I Could Be with You	1957	7.50	15.00	30.00
IMPERIAL					
❑ 5831	I'm Still a Fool for You/Rocky Mountain	1962	3.00	6.00	12.00
KING					
❑ 5405	Christmas (Comes But Once a Year)/Please Come Home for Christmas	1960	3.00	6.00	12.00
—B-side by Charles Brown					
❑ 5464	I Wanna Go Back Home/My Little Baby	1961	3.00	6.00	12.00
—With Charles Brown					
❑ 5483	My Sweet Baby's Love/Heartaches That Make You Cry	1961	3.00	6.00	12.00
❑ 5529	Movin' Time/The Hammer	1961	3.00	6.00	12.00
❑ 6095	Whiz O Shoo Pepi/Same Old Thing	1967	2.50	5.00	10.00
MOTOWN					
❑ 1038	I'll Make It Up to You Somehow/My Baby Gave Me Another Chance	1963	7.50	15.00	30.00
❑ 1046	My Daily Prayer/(B-side unknown)	1963	7.50	15.00	30.00
UNITED ARTISTS					
❑ 0149	Chicken Shack Boogie/Revitalized	1973	—	2.00	4.00
—"Silver Spotlight Series" reissue					
MILBURN, BILL					
BONNIE					
❑ 527	(I Took a Little Ride on) Santa's Sleigh/Santa Comes on Christmas Eve	19??	—	2.50	5.00
MILES, BUDDY					
ATLANTIC					
❑ 3852 [DJ]	Can You Hold Me (same on both sides)	1981	—	2.00	4.00
—May be promo only					
❑ 4006 [DJ]	Sunshine of Your Love (same on both sides)	1982	—	2.00	4.00
—May be promo only					
CASABLANCA					
❑ 839	Rockin' and Rollin' on the Streets of Hollywood/Livin' in the Right Space	1975	—	2.00	4.00
❑ 849	Nasty Disposition/Do It to Me	1975	—	2.00	4.00
❑ 859	Reuben "The Hurricane"/Where You Gonna Run To Lady	1976	—	2.00	4.00
COLUMBIA					
❑ 10030	Pain/We Get Love	1974	—	2.50	5.00
❑ 10089	Pull Yourself Together/I'm Just a Kiss Away	1975	—	2.50	5.00
❑ 45826	Love Affair/Life Is What You Make It	1973	—	2.50	5.00
❑ 45876	Elvira/Hear No Evil	1973	—	2.50	5.00
❑ 45969	Crazy Love/Thinking of You	1973	—	2.50	5.00
MERCURY					
❑ 72860	The Train (Part 1)/The Train (Part 2)	1968	2.00	4.00	8.00
❑ 72903	This Lady/'69 Freedom Special	1969	2.00	4.00	8.00
❑ 72945	Memphis Train/My Chant	1969	—	3.00	6.00
❑ 73008	Them Changes/Spot on the Wall	1970	—	3.00	6.00
❑ 73086	Down By the River/Hearts Delight	1970	—	3.00	6.00
❑ 73119	Dreams/Your Feeling Is Mine	1970	—	3.00	6.00
❑ 73159	We Got to Live Together (Part 1)/We Got to Live Together (Part 2)	1970	—	3.00	6.00
❑ 73170	Runaway Child/(B-side unknown)	1970	—	3.00	6.00
❑ 73205	Wholesale Love/That's the Way Life Is	1971	—	2.50	5.00
❑ 73238	Them Changes/The Way I Feel Tonight	1971	—	2.50	5.00
❑ 73261	Give Away None of My Love/Take It Off Him and Put It On Me	1972	—	2.50	5.00
❑ 73277	Life Is What You Make It (Part 1)/Life Is What You Make It (Part 2)	1972	—	2.50	5.00
MILES, GARRY					
LIBERTY					
❑ 55261	Look for a Star/Afraid of Love	1960	3.75	7.50	15.00
❑ 55261 [PS]	Look for a Star/Afraid of Love	1960	7.50	15.00	30.00
❑ 55279	Wishing Well/Dream Girl	1960	3.00	6.00	12.00
❑ 55596	Candy/Do the Bug	1963	3.00	6.00	12.00
❑ 55685	What Kind of Girl Are You/What's New	1964	2.50	5.00	10.00
❑ 55714	Here Goes a Fool/Ecstasy	1964	2.50	5.00	10.00
❑ 55738	How Are Things in Paradise/Please Take the Time	1964	2.50	5.00	10.00
UNITED ARTISTS					
❑ 0099	Look for a Star/Look for a Star	1973	—	2.50	5.00
—"Silver Spotlight Series" reissue; B-side by Garry Mills					
7-Inch Extended Plays					
LIBERTY					
❑ LSX-1005	Look for a Star/Wishing Well//I Miss You So/Afraid of Love	1960	12.50	25.00	50.00
❑ LSX-1005 [PS]	Look for a Star	1960	12.50	25.00	50.00
MILLER, BOBBY					
CONSTELLATION					
❑ 103	The Big Question/I Don't Believe You	1963	5.00	10.00	20.00
❑ 111	The Big Question/Uncle Willie Time	1963	5.00	10.00	20.00
❑ 116	Whoa (She's All Mine)/Take It in Stride	1964	5.00	10.00	20.00
❑ 127	This Is My Dance/Simon Says	1964	5.00	10.00	20.00
❑ 134	I'm For the Girls/Love Take the Case	1964	7.50	15.00	30.00
MILLER, CHUCK					
CAPITOL					
❑ F2613	Am I to Blame/Count Your Blessings	1953	5.00	10.00	20.00
❑ F2700	The Pucker-Nut Free/After All	1954	5.00	10.00	20.00
❑ F2766	Idaho Red/The Joker (In the Card Game of Life)	1954	5.00	10.00	20.00
—With Dave Cavanaugh					
❑ F2841	Hopahula Boogie/I'll Know My Love	1954	5.00	10.00	20.00
❑ F3187	No Baby Like You/Rouge River Valley	1955	3.75	7.50	15.00
MERCURY					
❑ 70627	The House of Blue Lights/Can't Help Wonderin'	1955	5.00	10.00	20.00
❑ 70697	Hawk Eye/Something to Live For	1955	3.75	7.50	15.00
❑ 70767	Boogie Along/Lookout Mountain	1955	3.75	7.50	15.00
❑ 70842	Bright Red Convertible/Baltimore Jones	1956	3.75	7.50	15.00
❑ 70942	Vim Vam Vamoose/Cool It Baby!	1956	3.75	7.50	15.00
❑ 71001	The Auctioneer/Baby Doll	1956	3.75	7.50	15.00
❑ 71056	Me Head in De Barrel/Good Mornin' Darlin'	1957	3.00	6.00	12.00
❑ 71118	Rang Tang Ding Dong/Bye Bye Love	1957	3.00	6.00	12.00
❑ 71173	Plaything/After Yesterday	1957	3.00	6.00	12.00
❑ 71308	Down the Road Apiece/Mad About Her Blues	1958	3.00	6.00	12.00
MILLER, CLINT					
ABC-PARAMOUNT					
❑ 9878	Bertha Lou/Doggone It Baby, I'm in Love	1957	12.50	25.00	50.00
MILLER, HAL, AND THE RAYS					
"The Rays" actually are the future FOUR SEASONS.					
AMY					
❑ 909	I Still Care/On My Own Two Feet	1964	25.00	50.00	100.00
❑ 920	A Blessing in Disguise/Cry Like the Rain	1965	20.00	40.00	80.00
TOPIX					
❑ 6003	An Angel Cried/Faith, Hope, Dreams	1961	10.00	20.00	40.00
MILLER, NED					
CAPITOL					
❑ 2074	Endless/Only a Fool	1968	—	3.00	6.00
❑ 4607	My Heart Waits at the Door/Cold Gray Bars	1961	3.00	6.00	12.00
❑ 4652	Dark Moon/Go On Back, You Fool	1961	3.00	6.00	12.00
❑ 5431	Whistle Walkin'/Two Voices, Two Shadows, Two Faces	1965	2.00	4.00	8.00
❑ 5502	Fall of the King/Down the Street	1965	2.00	4.00	8.00
❑ 5568	Lovin' Pains/If the World Turned Into Ashes	1965	2.00	4.00	8.00
❑ 5661	Right Behind These Lips/Summer Roses	1966	2.00	4.00	8.00
❑ 5742	Lorraine/Teardrop Lane	1966	2.00	4.00	8.00
❑ 5868	The Hobo/Echo of the Pines	1967	2.00	4.00	8.00
DOT					
❑ 15601	From a Jack to a King/Parade of Broken Hearts	1957	10.00	20.00	40.00
❑ 15651	Turn Back/Lights in the Street	1957	3.75	7.50	15.00
FABOR					
❑ 114	From a Jack to a King/Parade of Broken Hearts	1962	3.00	6.00	12.00
❑ 116	One Among the Many/Man Behind the Gun	1963	2.50	5.00	10.00
❑ 121	Another Fool Like Me/Magic Moon	1963	2.50	5.00	10.00
❑ 125	Big Love/Sunday Morning Tears	1964	2.50	5.00	10.00
❑ 128	Invisible Tears/Old Restless Ocean	1964	2.50	5.00	10.00
❑ 137	Do What You Do Do Well/Dusty Guitar	1964	2.00	4.00	8.00
❑ 139	What I Know/Lights in the Street	1965	2.00	4.00	8.00
JACKPOT					
❑ 48020	Girl from the Second World/Ring the Bell for Johnny	1960	3.00	6.00	12.00
—With Jan Howard					
RADIO					
❑ 105	Gypsy/With Enough Love	1958	6.25	12.50	25.00
REPUBLIC					
❑ 1404	Autumn Winds/My Last Go-Round	1969	—	2.50	5.00
❑ 1410	Breakin'/Just Walkin' in the Rain	1970	—	2.50	5.00
❑ 1411	The Lover's Song/Cold Gray Bars	1970	—	2.50	5.00
❑ 1416	Back to Oklahoma/I Hang My Head and Cry	1970	—	2.50	5.00
MILLER, ROGER					
20TH CENTURY					
❑ 2421	The Hat/Pleasing the Crowd	1979	—	2.00	4.00
BUENA VISTA					
❑ 493	Whistle Stop/Not in Nottingham	1973	—	2.50	5.00
❑ 493 [PS]	Whistle Stop/Not in Nottingham	1973	—	2.50	5.00
COLUMBIA					
❑ 02681	Old Friends/When a House Is Not a Home	1982	—	2.00	4.00
—Roger Miller/Willie Nelson/Ray Price					
❑ 10052	Our Love/Yester Waltz	1974	—	2.50	5.00
❑ 10107	I Love a Rodeo/Lovin' You Is Always on My Mind	1975	—	2.50	5.00

Number	Title (A Side/B Side)	Yr	VG	VG+	NM
❑ 45873	Open Up Your Heart/Qua La Linta	1973	—	2.50	5.00
❑ 45948	I Believe in the Sunrise/Shannon's Song	1973	—	2.50	5.00
❑ 46000	Whistle Stop/The 4th of July	1974	—	2.50	5.00
DECCA					
❑ 30838	Wrong Kind of Girl/A Man Like Me	1959	3.75	7.50	15.00
❑ 30953	Sweet Ramona/Jason Fleming	1959	3.75	7.50	15.00
ELEKTRA					
❑ 47192	Everyone Gets Crazy Now and Then/Aladam Bama	1981	—	2.00	4.00
MCA					
❑ 52663	River in the Rain/Hand for the Hog	1985	—	—	3.00
❑ 52855	Some Hearts Get All the Breaks/Arkansas	1986	—	—	3.00
MERCURY					
❑ 71212	Poor Little John/My Fellow	1957	6.25	12.50	25.00
❑ 73102	South/Don't We All Have the Right	1970	—	2.50	5.00
❑ 73190	Tomorrow Night in Baltimore/A Million Years or So	1971	—	2.50	5.00
❑ 73230	Loving Her Was Easier (Than Anything I'll Ever Do Again)/Que La Linta	1971	—	2.50	5.00
❑ 73268	We Found It in Each Other's Arms/Sunny Side of My Life	1972	—	2.50	5.00
❑ 73321	Rings for Sale/Conversations	1972	—	2.50	5.00
❑ 73354	Hoppy's Gone/I Jumped from Uncle Harvey's Plane	1972	—	2.50	5.00
MUSICOR					
❑ 1102	Can't Stop Loving You/You're Forgetting Me	1965	2.50	5.00	10.00
RCA VICTOR					
❑ 47-7776	Footprints in the Snow/You Don't Want My Love	1960	3.75	7.50	15.00
❑ 47-7878	When Two Worlds Collide/Every Which-A-Way	1961	3.75	7.50	15.00
❑ 47-7958	Burma Shave/Fair Swiss Maiden	1961	3.75	7.50	15.00
❑ 47-8028	Sorry, Willie/Hitch-Hiker	1962	3.00	6.00	12.00
❑ 47-8091	Trouble on the Turnpike/Hey Little Star	1962	3.00	6.00	12.00
❑ 47-8175	Lock, Stock and Teardrops/I Know Who It Is	1963	3.00	6.00	12.00
❑ 47-8651	If You Want Me To/Hey Little Star	1965	2.50	5.00	10.00
SMASH					
❑ 1876	Less and Less/Got Two Again	1964	3.00	6.00	12.00
❑ 1881	Dang Me/Got Two Again	1964	2.50	5.00	10.00
❑ 1881 [PS]	Dang Me/Got Two Again	1964	3.75	7.50	15.00
—Red sleeve					
❑ 1881 [PS]	Dang Me/Got Two Again	1964	5.00	10.00	20.00
—Yellow sleeve					
❑ 1926	Chug-a-Lug/Reincarnation	1964	2.50	5.00	10.00
❑ 1947	Do-Wacka-Do/Love Is Not for Me	1964	2.50	5.00	10.00
❑ 1947 [PS]	Do-Wacka-Do/Love Is Not for Me	1964	3.75	7.50	15.00
❑ 1965	King of the Road/Atta Boy Girl	1965	3.00	6.00	12.00
❑ 1983	Engine, Engine #9/The Last Word in Lonesome Is Me	1965	2.00	4.00	8.00
❑ 1994	One Dyin' and a-Buryin'/It Happened Just That Way	1965	2.00	4.00	8.00
❑ 1994 [PS]	One Dyin' and a-Buryin'/It Happened Just That Way	1965	3.75	7.50	15.00
❑ 1998	Kansas City Star/Guess I'll Pack Up My Heart (And Go Home)	1965	2.00	4.00	8.00
❑ 2010	England Swings/Good Old Days	1965	2.00	4.00	8.00
❑ 2024	Husbands and Wives/I've Been a Long Time Leavin'	1966	2.00	4.00	8.00
❑ 2043	You Can't Roller Skate in a Buffalo Herd/Train of Life	1966	2.00	4.00	8.00
❑ 2055	My Uncle Used to Love Me But She Died/You're My Kingdom	1966	2.00	4.00	8.00
❑ 2066	Heartbreak Hotel/Less and Less	1966	2.00	4.00	8.00
❑ 2081	Walkin' in the Sunshine/Home	1967	2.00	4.00	8.00
❑ 2121	The Ballad of Waterhole #3 (Code of the West)/ Rainbow Valley	1967	2.00	4.00	8.00
❑ 2121 [PS]	The Ballad of Waterhole #3 (Code of the West)/ Rainbow Valley	1967	3.75	7.50	15.00
❑ 2130	Old Toy Trains/Silent Night	1967	2.50	5.00	10.00
❑ 2130 [PS]	Old Toy Trains/Silent Night	1967	3.00	6.00	12.00
❑ 2148	Little Green Apples/Our Little Love	1968	2.00	4.00	8.00
❑ 2148 [PS]	Little Green Apples/Our Little Love	1968	3.00	6.00	12.00
❑ 2183	What I'd Give (To Be the Wind)/Toliver	1968	2.00	4.00	8.00
❑ 2197	Vance/Little Children Run and Play	1968	2.00	4.00	8.00
❑ 2230	Me and Bobby McGee/I'm Gonna Teach My Heart to Bend (Instead of Break)	1969	—	3.00	6.00
❑ 2246	Where Have All the Average People Gone/ Boeing Boeing 707	1969	—	3.00	6.00
❑ 2258	The Tom Green County Fair/I Know Who It Is	1970	—	3.00	6.00
STARDAY					
❑ 356	Can't Stop Loving You/You're Forgetting Me	1958	5.00	10.00	20.00
❑ 718	Playboy/Poor Little John	1965	2.50	5.00	10.00
❑ 7029	Under Your Spell Again/I Ain't Never	197?	—	2.50	5.00
❑ 7032	Country Girl/Jimmy Brown, The Newsboy	197?	—	2.50	5.00
❑ 7038	Tip of My Fingers/I Wish I Could Fall in Love Today	197?	—	2.50	5.00
WINDSONG					
❑ CB-11072	Baby Me Baby/Dark Side of the Moon	1977	—	2.00	4.00
❑ CB-11166	Oklahoma Woman/There's Nobody Like You	1977	—	2.00	4.00

MILLER, STEVE, BAND

Also see THE GOLDBERG-MILLER BLUES BAND; BOZ SCAGGS.

Number	Title (A Side/B Side)	Yr	VG	VG+	NM
CAPITOL					
❑ 2156	Roll With It/Sittin' in Circles	1968	3.00	6.00	12.00
❑ 2156 [PS]	Roll With It/Sittin' in Circles	1968	6.25	12.50	25.00
❑ 2287	Living in the U.S.A./Quicksilver Girl	1968	3.00	6.00	12.00
❑ 2447	Rock Love/(B-side unknown)	1969	2.50	5.00	10.00
❑ 2520	My Dark Hour/Song for Our Ancestors	1969	2.00	4.00	8.00
❑ 2638	Don't Let Nobody Turn You Around/Little Girl	1969	2.00	4.00	8.00
❑ 2878	Going to the Country/Never Kill Another Man	1970	—	3.00	6.00
❑ 2945	Going to Mexico/Steve Miller's Midnight Tango	1970	—	3.00	6.00
❑ 3228	Rock Love/Let Me Serve You	1971	—	3.00	6.00
❑ 3344	Fandango/Love's Riddle	1972	—	3.00	6.00
❑ 3732	The Joker/Something to Believe In	1973	—	2.50	5.00
❑ 3837	Your Cash Ain't Nothin' But Trash/Evil	1974	—	2.50	5.00
❑ 3884	Living in the U.S.A./Kow Kow Calqulator	1974	—	2.50	5.00
❑ 4260	Take the Money and Run/Sweet Maree	1976	—	2.00	4.00
❑ 4323	Rock'n Me/Shu Ba Du Da Ma Ma Ma Ma	1976	—	2.00	4.00
❑ 4323	Rockin' Me/Living in the U.S.A.	1976	—	2.50	5.00
❑ 4372	Fly Like an Eagle/Lovin' Cup	1976	—	2.00	4.00
❑ 4424	Jet Airliner/Babes in the Wood	1977	—	2.00	4.00
❑ 4466	Jungle Love/Wish Upon a Star	1977	—	2.00	4.00
❑ 4496	Swingtown/Winter Time	1977	—	2.00	4.00
❑ A-5068	Heart Like a Wheel/True Fine Love	1981	—	—	3.00
❑ A-5068 [PS]	Heart Like a Wheel/True Fine Love	1981	—	2.00	4.00
❑ A-5086	Circle of Love/(B-side unknown)	1982	—	—	3.00
❑ B-5126	Abracadabra/Live It Up	1982	—	2.00	4.00
❑ B-5126	Abracadabra/Baby Wanna Dance	1982	—	—	3.00
❑ B-5126 [PS]	Abracadabra	1982	—	2.00	4.00
—Same sleeve has been found with record of either B-side					
❑ B-5162	Cool Magic/Young Girl's Heart	1982	—	—	3.00
❑ B-5162 [PS]	Cool Magic/Young Girl's Heart	1982	—	2.00	4.00
❑ B-5194	Live It Up/Heart Like a Wheel	1982	—	—	3.00
❑ B-5223	Buffalo's Serenade/Living in the U.S.A.	1983	—	—	3.00
❑ B-5407	Shangri-La/Circle of Love	1984	—	—	3.00
❑ B-5407 [PS]	Shangri-La/Circle of Love	1984	—	—	3.00
❑ B-5442	Get On Home/Bongo Bongo	1985	—	—	3.00
❑ B-5442 [PS]	Get On Home/Bongo Bongo	1985	—	—	3.00
❑ B-5476	Italian X-Rays/Who Do You Love	1985	—	—	3.00
❑ B-5646	I Want to Make the World Turn Around/Slinky	1986	—	—	3.00
❑ B-5646 [PS]	I Want to Make the World Turn Around/Slinky	1986	—	—	3.00
❑ B-5671	Nobody But You Baby/Maelstrom	1987	—	—	3.00
❑ B-5704	I Wanna Be Loved/I Wanna Be Loved	1987	—	—	3.00
❑ B-5704 [PS]	I Wanna Be Loved/I Wanna Be Loved	1987	—	—	3.00
❑ B-44222	Ya Ya/Filthy McNasty	1988	—	—	3.00
❑ B-44222 [PS]	Ya Ya/Filthy McNasty	1988	—	—	3.00

MILLER SISTERS, THE

Number	Title (A Side/B Side)	Yr	VG	VG+	NM
ACME					
❑ 111	Let's Start Anew/The Flip Skip	1957	12.50	25.00	50.00
❑ 717	You Made Me a Promise/Crazy Billboard Song	1957	10.00	20.00	40.00
❑ 721	Let's Start Anew/The Flip Skip	1958	10.00	20.00	40.00
EMBER					
❑ 1004	Guess Who/How Am I to Know	1956	7.50	15.00	30.00
FLIP					
❑ 504	Someday You Will Pay/I Knew You Would	1955	50.00	100.00	200.00
GLODIS					
❑ 1003	Pop Your Finger/You Got to Reap What You Sow	1961	3.75	7.50	15.00
GMC					
❑ 10006	I'm Telling It Like It Is/Until You Come Home I'll Walk Alone	1967	2.50	5.00	10.00
HERALD					
❑ 455	Hippity Ha/Until You're Mine	1955	12.50	25.00	50.00
❑ 527	Hippity Ha/Until You're Mine	1958	5.00	10.00	20.00
HULL					
❑ 718	Please Don't Leave/Do You Wanna Go	1956	10.00	20.00	40.00
❑ 736	Just Wait and See/Black Pepper	1960	6.25	12.50	25.00
—B-side by Leo Price and Band					
❑ 750	Roll Back the Rug (And Twist)/Don't You Forget	1962	6.25	12.50	25.00
❑ 752	I Cried All Night/Hully Gully Reel	1962	5.00	10.00	20.00
MILLER					
❑ 1140	Oh Lover/Remember That	1960	5.00	10.00	20.00
❑ 1141	Pony Dance/Give Me Some Old Fashioned Love	1960	5.00	10.00	20.00
❑ 1143	Please Mr. D.J./(B-side unknown)	1960	5.00	10.00	20.00
ONYX					
❑ 507	Sugar Candy/My Own	1957	12.50	25.00	50.00
RAYNA					
❑ 5001	I Miss You So/Dance Little Sister	1962	3.75	7.50	15.00
❑ 5004	Oh Why/Walk On	1962	3.75	7.50	15.00
RIVERSIDE					
❑ 4535	Dance Close/Tell Him	1962	5.00	10.00	20.00
ROULETTE					
❑ 4491	Baby Your Baby/Silly Girl	1963	3.00	6.00	12.00
STARDUST					
❑ 3001	Feel Good/Cooncha	1964	2.50	5.00	10.00
SUN					
❑ 230	There's No Right Way to Do Me Wrong/You Can Tell Me	1956	12.50	25.00	50.00
❑ 255	Finders Keepers/Ten Cats Down	1956	12.50	25.00	50.00
❑ 504	Someday You Will Pay/I Knew You Would	1955	37.50	75.00	150.00
YORKTOWN					
❑ 75	Looking Over My Life/Si Senor	1965	2.50	5.00	10.00

MILLINDER, LUCKY

Number	Title (A Side/B Side)	Yr	VG	VG+	NM
KING					
❑ 4449	Chew Tobacco Rag/Georgia Rose	1951	15.00	30.00	60.00
❑ 4453	I'm Waiting Just for You/Bongo Boogie	1951	15.00	30.00	60.00
❑ 4476	The Grape Vine/No One Else Could Be	1951	15.00	30.00	60.00
❑ 4496	The Right Kind of Love/It's Been a Long, Long Time	1951	15.00	30.00	60.00
❑ 4534	Ram-Bunk-Shush/Loaded with Love	1952	15.00	30.00	60.00
❑ 4545	When I Have You My Love/Please Be Careful	1952	25.00	50.00	100.00
❑ 4557	Lord Knows I Tried/Heavy Sugar	1952	25.00	50.00	100.00
❑ 4571	Backslider's Ball/Please Be Careful	1952	25.00	50.00	100.00
❑ 4792	It's a Sad, Sad Feeling/Ow	1955	20.00	40.00	80.00
—With the Admirals					
❑ 4803	Goody Good Love/I'm Here, Love	1955	7.50	15.00	30.00
❑ 5240	Heavy Sugar/Honeydripper	1959	3.00	6.00	12.00
RCA VICTOR					
❑ 47-2961	Tomorrow/I Ain't Got Nothin' to Lose	1949	12.50	25.00	50.00
❑ 47-3005	Awful Natural/In the Middle of the Night	1949	12.50	25.00	50.00
❑ 47-3128	I'll Never Be Free/Journey's End	1949	12.50	25.00	50.00

Number	Title (A Side/B Side)	Yr	VG	VG+	NM
❑ 50-0054	D Natural Blues/Little Girl, Don't Cry	1949	15.00	30.00	60.00

—Gray label, orange vinyl

Number	Title (A Side/B Side)	Yr	VG	VG+	NM
❑ 50-0088	Let It Be/(B-side unknown)	1950	12.50	25.00	50.00

WARWICK

Number	Title (A Side/B Side)	Yr	VG	VG+	NM
❑ 582	Big Fat Mama/Slide My Trombone	1960	3.00	6.00	12.00

MILLS, GARRY

IMPERIAL

Number	Title (A Side/B Side)	Yr	VG	VG+	NM
❑ 5674	Look for a Star — Part 1/Look for a Star — Part 2	1960	3.75	7.50	15.00

LONDON

Number	Title (A Side/B Side)	Yr	VG	VG+	NM
❑ 9504	I'll Step Down/Treasure Island	1962	3.75	7.50	15.00

TOP RANK

Number	Title (A Side/B Side)	Yr	VG	VG+	NM
❑ 2071	Top Teen Baby/Don't Forget	1960	3.75	7.50	15.00

UNITED ARTISTS

Number	Title (A Side/B Side)	Yr	VG	VG+	NM
❑ 0099	Look for a Star/Look for a Star	1973	—	2.50	5.00

—"Silver Spotlight Series" reissue; B-side by Gary Miles

MILLS, HAYLEY

BUENA VISTA

Number	Title (A Side/B Side)	Yr	VG	VG+	NM
❑ 385	Let's Get Together/Cobbler, Cobbler	1961	3.00	6.00	12.00
❑ 385 [PS]	Let's Get Together/Cobbler, Cobbler	1961	6.25	12.50	25.00
❑ 395	Johnny Jingo/Jeepers Creepers	1962	2.50	5.00	10.00
❑ 395 [PS]	Johnny Jingo/Jeepers Creepers	1962	6.25	12.50	25.00
❑ 401	Side by Side/Ching Ching and a Ring Ding Ding	1962	2.50	5.00	10.00
❑ 401 [PS]	Side by Side/Ching Ching and a Ring Ding Ding	1962	6.25	12.50	25.00
❑ 408	Castaway/Sweet River	1962	2.50	5.00	10.00
❑ 408 [PS]	Castaway/Sweet River	1962	6.25	12.50	25.00
❑ 409	Let's Climb/Enjoy It	1962	2.50	5.00	10.00

—With Maurice Chevalier

Number	Title (A Side/B Side)	Yr	VG	VG+	NM
❑ 409 [PS]	Let's Climb/Enjoy It	1962	6.25	12.50	25.00
❑ 420	Flitterin'/Beautiful Beulah	1963	2.50	5.00	10.00

—With Eddie Hodges

Number	Title (A Side/B Side)	Yr	VG	VG+	NM
❑ 420 [PS]	Flitterin'/Beautiful Beulah	1963	6.25	12.50	25.00

MAINSTREAM

Number	Title (A Side/B Side)	Yr	VG	VG+	NM
❑ 656	Gypsy Girl/Younger Than Seventeen	1966	2.00	4.00	8.00

MILLS BROTHERS, THE

DECCA

Number	Title (A Side/B Side)	Yr	VG	VG+	NM
❑ 23930	You Always Hurt the One You Love/Till Then	1950	5.00	10.00	20.00

—Reissue of 78 from 1944; black label with lines on either side of "Decca"

Number	Title (A Side/B Side)	Yr	VG	VG+	NM
❑ 23930	You Always Hurt the One You Love/Till Then	1955	3.00	6.00	12.00

—Black label with star under "Decca"

Number	Title (A Side/B Side)	Yr	VG	VG+	NM
❑ 23930	You Always Hurt the One You Love/Till Then	1960	2.00	4.00	8.00

—Black label with color bar

Number	Title (A Side/B Side)	Yr	VG	VG+	NM
❑ 24756	If I Had My Way/Sweet Genevieve	1950	5.00	10.00	20.00
❑ 24872	Daddy's Little Girl/If I Live to Be a Hundred	1950	5.00	10.00	20.00
❑ 25046	Lazy River/Cielito Lindo	1950	5.00	10.00	20.00
❑ 25516	Across the Alley from the Alamo/Don't Be a Baby, Baby	1961	2.00	4.00	8.00
❑ 27157	Paper Doll/I'll Be Around	1950	5.00	10.00	20.00

—Reissue of 78 from 1943; black label with lines on either side of "Decca"

Number	Title (A Side/B Side)	Yr	VG	VG+	NM
❑ 27157	Paper Doll/I'll Be Around	1955	3.00	6.00	12.00

—Black label with star under "Decca"

Number	Title (A Side/B Side)	Yr	VG	VG+	NM
❑ 27157	Paper Doll/I'll Be Around	1960	2.00	4.00	8.00

—Black label with color bar

Number	Title (A Side/B Side)	Yr	VG	VG+	NM
❑ 27184	A Star for Everyone/I'm Afraid to Love You	1950	5.00	10.00	20.00
❑ 27236	Daddy's Little Boy/I Still Love You	1950	5.00	10.00	20.00
❑ 27253	Nevertheless (I'm in Love with You)/Thirsty for Your Kisses	1950	5.00	10.00	20.00
❑ 27267	Funny Feelin'/I Don't Mind Being Alone	1950	5.00	10.00	20.00
❑ 27400	Around the World/You Don't Have to Drop a Heart to Break It	1951	3.75	7.50	15.00
❑ 27447	Please Don't Talk About Me When I'm Gone/You Know You Belong to Someone Else	1951	3.75	7.50	15.00

—With Tommy Dorsey

Number	Title (A Side/B Side)	Yr	VG	VG+	NM
❑ 27579	Mister and Mississippi/Wonderful, Wasn't It	1951	3.75	7.50	15.00
❑ 27615	Love Me/Who Knows Love	1951	3.75	7.50	15.00
❑ 27683	Lord Ups an' Downs/A Cottage with a Prayer	1951	5.00	10.00	20.00
❑ 27762	I Ran All the Way Home/Get Her Off My Hands	1951	3.75	7.50	15.00
❑ 27889	Be My Life's Companion/Love Lies	1951	3.75	7.50	15.00
❑ 28021	High and Dry/You're Not Worth My Tears	1952	3.75	7.50	15.00
❑ 28180	Pretty As a Picture/When You Come Back to Me	1952	3.75	7.50	15.00
❑ 28309	Just When We're Falling in Love/Blue and Sentimental	1952	3.75	7.50	15.00
❑ 28384	The Glow-Worm/After All	1952	3.75	7.50	15.00
❑ 28458	Lazy River/Wish Me Good Luck, Amigo	1952	3.75	7.50	15.00
❑ 28459	Someone Loved Someone/A Shoulder to Weep On	1952	3.75	7.50	15.00
❑ 28586	Twice As Much/I Want Someone to Care For	1953	3.00	6.00	12.00
❑ 28670	Say Si Si/I'm With You	1953	3.00	6.00	12.00
❑ 28736	Pretty Butterfly/Don't Let Me Dream	1953	3.00	6.00	12.00
❑ 28818	Who Put the Devil in Evelyn's Eyes/Beware	1953	3.00	6.00	12.00
❑ 28945	The Jones Boy/She Was Five and He Was Ten	1953	3.00	6.00	12.00
❑ 29019	I Had to Call You Up to Say I'm Sorry/You Didn't Want Me When You Had Me	1954	3.00	6.00	12.00
❑ 29115	A Carnival in Venice/Go In and Out the Window	1954	3.00	6.00	12.00
❑ 29185	How Blue/Why Do I Keep Lovin' You	1954	3.00	6.00	12.00
❑ 29276	You're Nobody 'Til Somebody Loves You/Every Second of Every Day	1954	3.00	6.00	12.00
❑ 29382	Paper Valentine/The Urge	1954	3.00	6.00	12.00
❑ 29496	Opus One/There You Are	1955	3.00	6.00	12.00
❑ 29511	Smack Dab in the Middle/Kiss Me and Kill Me with Love	1955	3.00	6.00	12.00
❑ 29564	Daddy's Little Girl/Daddy's Little Boy	1955	3.00	6.00	12.00
❑ 29686	Suddenly There's a Valley/Gum Drop	1955	3.00	6.00	12.00
❑ 29754	I Believe in Santa Claus/You Don't Have to Be a Santa Claus	1955	3.00	6.00	12.00
❑ 29781	All the Way 'Round the World/I've Changed My Mind a Thousand Times	1956	2.50	5.00	10.00
❑ 29853	Dream of You/In a Mellow Tone	1956	2.50	5.00	10.00
❑ 29897	Standing on the Corner/King Porter Stomp	1956	2.50	5.00	10.00
❑ 30024	Don't Get Caught (Short on Love)/That's Right	1956	2.50	5.00	10.00
❑ 30136	That's All I Need/Tell Me More	1956	2.50	5.00	10.00
❑ 30224	In De Banana Tree/Knocked-Out Nightingale	1957	2.50	5.00	10.00
❑ 30299	Queen of the Senior Prom/My Troubled Mind	1957	2.50	5.00	10.00
❑ 30430	Two Minute Tango/Change for a Penny	1957	2.50	5.00	10.00
❑ 30546	The Barbershop Quartet/You Only Told Me Half	1958	2.50	5.00	10.00

DOT

Number	Title (A Side/B Side)	Yr	VG	VG+	NM
❑ 15695	Get a Job/I Found a Million Dollar Baby	1958	3.75	7.50	15.00
❑ 15827	Me and My Shadow/Music, Maestro, Please	1958	2.50	5.00	10.00
❑ 15858	Yellow Bird/Baby Clementine	1958	2.00	4.00	8.00
❑ 15909	You Can't Be True Dear/Beaver	1959	2.50	5.00	10.00
❑ 15950	Lullaby in Ragtime/Te Quiero	1959	2.50	5.00	10.00
❑ 15987	You Always Hurt the One You Love/(B-side unknown)	1959	2.50	5.00	10.00
❑ 16037	Paper Doll/The Glow-Worm	1960	2.00	4.00	8.00
❑ 16049	I Miss You So/Oh Ma Ma	1960	2.00	4.00	8.00
❑ 16091	Highways Are Happy Ways/I Got You	1960	2.00	4.00	8.00
❑ 16234	Yellow Bird/Baby Clementine	1961	2.00	4.00	8.00
❑ 16258	I'll Take Care of Your Cares/Ballerina	1961	2.00	4.00	8.00
❑ 16360	I Found the Only Girl for Me/Queen of the Senior Prom	1961	2.00	4.00	8.00
❑ 16432	Tonight You Belong to Me/You Broke the Only Heart That Ever Loved You	1963	—	3.50	7.00
❑ 16451	The End of the World/Big City	1963	—	3.50	7.00
❑ 16579	Don't Blame Me/It Hurts Me More Than It Hurts You	1964	—	3.50	7.00
❑ 16703	Welcome Home/Chum Chum Chittilum Chum	1965	—	3.50	7.00
❑ 16733	Bye Bye Blackbird/Chum Chum Chittilum Chum	1965	—	3.50	7.00
❑ 16972	Smack Dab in the Middle/Honeysuckle Rose Blues Bossa Nova	1967	—	3.00	6.00
❑ 17041	Cab Driver/Fortuosity	1967	—	3.00	6.00
❑ 17096	My Shy Violet/Flower Road	1968	—	3.00	6.00
❑ 17162	The Ol' Race Track/But for Love	1968	—	3.00	6.00
❑ 17198	Dream/Jimtown Road	1969	—	3.00	6.00
❑ 17235	A Guy on the Go/What Have I Done for Her Lately	1969	—	3.00	6.00
❑ 17285	I'll Never Forgive Myself/Up to Maggie Jones	1969	—	3.00	6.00
❑ 17321	It Ain't No Big Thing/Help Yourself to Some Tomorrow	1969	—	3.00	6.00

PARAMOUNT

Number	Title (A Side/B Side)	Yr	VG	VG+	NM
❑ 0046	Smile Away Every Rainy Day/Between Winston-Salem and Nashville, Tennessee	1970	—	2.50	5.00
❑ 0095	Happy Songs of Love/I'm Sorry I Answered the Phone	1971	—	2.50	5.00
❑ 0117	L-O-V-E/Strollin'	1971	—	2.50	5.00
❑ 0147	Come Summer/Sally Sunshine	1972	—	2.50	5.00
❑ 0181	There's No Life on the Moon/A Donut and a Dream	1972	—	2.50	5.00

RANWOOD

Number	Title (A Side/B Side)	Yr	VG	VG+	NM
❑ 961	Truck Stop/He Gives Me Love	1973	—	2.00	4.00
❑ 1003	Tiger Rag/On a Chinese Honeymoon	1974	—	2.00	4.00
❑ 1020	You Are My Sunshine/Between Winston-Salem and Nashville, Tennessee	1974	—	2.00	4.00
❑ 1040	El Paso/Till Then	197?	—	2.00	4.00
❑ 1042	Daisies Never Tell/Sawdust Heart	197?	—	2.00	4.00
❑ 1054	Coney Island Washboard/Nevertheless	197?	—	2.00	4.00

7-Inch Extended Plays

DECCA

Number	Title (A Side/B Side)	Yr	VG	VG+	NM
❑ ED 2010	Lazy River/I'm Afraid to Love You//Blue and Sentimental/I've Got My Love to Keep Me Warm	195?	3.75	7.50	15.00
❑ ED 2010 [PS]	The Mills Brothers, Volume 1	195?	3.75	7.50	15.00
❑ ED 2044	*Caravan/Solitude/It Don't Mean a Thing/Georgia on My Mind	195?	3.75	7.50	15.00
❑ ED 2044 [PS]	The Mills Brothers, Vol. 2	195?	3.75	7.50	15.00
❑ ED 2742	Daddy's Little Girl/Daddy's Little Boy//You're Nobody 'Til Somebody Loves You/Queen of the Senior Prom	195?	3.00	6.00	12.00
❑ ED 2742 [PS]	The Mills Brothers	195?	3.00	6.00	12.00

DOT

Number	Title (A Side/B Side)	Yr	VG	VG+	NM
❑ DEP-1087	Glow Worm/Lazy River//Till Then/Paper Doll	195?	2.50	5.00	10.00
❑ DEP-1087 [PS]	Great Hits	195?	2.50	5.00	10.00

MIMMS, GARNET, AND THE ENCHANTERS

Includes Garnet Mimms credited alone. Also see THE ENCHANTERS (2).

ARISTA

Number	Title (A Side/B Side)	Yr	VG	VG+	NM
❑ 0239	What It Is (Part 1)/What It Is (Part 2)	1977	—	2.00	4.00
❑ 0289	Johnny Perter/Tail Snatcher	1977	—	2.00	4.00
❑ 0332	Right Here in the Palm of My Hand/Tail Snatcher	1978	—	2.00	4.00

GSF

Number	Title (A Side/B Side)	Yr	VG	VG+	NM
❑ 6874	Another Place/Stop and Check Yourself	1972	—	3.00	6.00
❑ 6887	I'll Keep On Loving/Somebody, Someplace	1972	—	3.00	6.00

UNITED ARTISTS

Number	Title (A Side/B Side)	Yr	VG	VG+	NM
❑ 0109	Cry Baby/For Your Precious Love	1973	—	2.00	4.00

—"Silver Spotlight Series" reissue

Number	Title (A Side/B Side)	Yr	VG	VG+	NM
❑ 629	Cry Baby/Don't Change Your Heart	1963	3.75	7.50	15.00
❑ 658	Baby Don't You Weep/For Your Precious Love	1963	3.00	6.00	12.00
❑ 658 [PS]	Baby Don't You Weep/For Your Precious Love	1963	15.00	30.00	60.00
❑ 694	Tell Me Baby/Anytime You Want Me	1964	3.00	6.00	12.00
❑ 715	One Girl/A Quiet Place	1964	3.00	6.00	12.00
❑ 773	One Woman Man/Look Away	1964	3.00	6.00	12.00
❑ 796	A Little Bit of Soap/I'll Make It Up to You	1964	3.00	6.00	12.00
❑ 848	So Close/It Was Easier to Hurt Her	1965	3.00	6.00	12.00
❑ 868	Welcome Home/The Adventures of Moll Flanders	1965	3.00	6.00	12.00
❑ 887	Everytime/That Goes to Show You	1965	3.00	6.00	12.00
❑ 951	Looking for You/More Than a Miracle	1965	3.00	6.00	12.00
❑ 995	Prove It to Me/I'll Take Good Care of You	1966	3.00	6.00	12.00
❑ 50058	My Baby/Keep On Smilin'	1966	—	—	—

—Unreleased

VEEP

Number	Title (A Side/B Side)	Yr	VG	VG+	NM
❑ 1232	Thinkin'/It's Been Such a Long Time Comin'	1966	2.00	4.00	8.00
❑ 1234	My Baby/Keep On Smilin'	1966	2.00	4.00	8.00
❑ 1252	All About Love/The Truth Hurts	1967	2.00	4.00	8.00

VERVE

Number	Title (A Side/B Side)	Yr	VG	VG+	NM
❑ 10596	Stop and Think It Over/I Can Hear My Baby Crying	1968	2.00	4.00	8.00
❑ 10624	Can You Top This/We Can Find That Love	1968	2.00	4.00	8.00
❑ 10642	Take Me/Happy Landing	1969	2.00	4.00	8.00
❑ 10650	Sad Song/Get It While You Can	1970	2.00	4.00	8.00

MINDBENDERS, THE

Also see WAYNE FONTANA AND THE MINDBENDERS.

FONTANA

Number	Title (A Side/B Side)	Yr	VG	VG+	NM
❑ 1541	A Groovy Kind of Love/Love Is Good	1966	3.00	6.00	12.00
❑ 1555	Ashes to Ashes/Don't Know About Love	1966	2.00	4.00	8.00
❑ 1571	I Want Her, She Wants Me/Morning After	1967	2.00	4.00	8.00
❑ 1595	It's Getting Harder All the Time/Off and Running	1967	2.00	4.00	8.00
❑ 1620	Yellow Brick Road/Blessed Are the Lonely	1968	2.00	4.00	8.00
❑ 1628	Uncle Joe the Ice Cream Man/The Man Who Loved Trees	1968	2.00	4.00	8.00

MINEO, SAL

DECCA

Number	Title (A Side/B Side)	Yr	VG	VG+	NM
❑ 31692	Why Don't You Love Me/A Girl Across the Way	1964	3.00	6.00	12.00

EPIC

Number	Title (A Side/B Side)	Yr	VG	VG+	NM
❑ 9216	Start Movin' (In My Direction)/Love Affair	1957	6.25	12.50	25.00
❑ 9216 [PS]	Start Movin' (In My Direction)/Love Affair	1957	10.00	20.00	40.00
❑ 9227	Lasting Love/You Shouldn't Do That	1957	5.00	10.00	20.00
❑ 9227 [PS]	Lasting Love/You Shouldn't Do That	1957	7.50	15.00	30.00
❑ 9246	Party Time/The Words That I Whisper	1957	5.00	10.00	20.00
❑ 9246 [PS]	Party Time/The Words That I Whisper	1957	7.50	15.00	30.00
❑ 9260	Little Pigeon/Cuttin' In	1958	5.00	10.00	20.00
❑ 9271	Seven Steps to Love/A Couple of Crazy Kids	1958	5.00	10.00	20.00
❑ 9287	Baby Face/Souvenirs of Summertime	1958	5.00	10.00	20.00
❑ 9327	Young As We Are/Make Believe Baby	1959	5.00	10.00	20.00
❑ 9327 [PS]	Young As We Are/Make Believe Baby	1959	7.50	15.00	30.00
❑ 9345	I'll Never Be Myself Again/The Words That I Whisper	1959	5.00	10.00	20.00

FONTANA

Number	Title (A Side/B Side)	Yr	VG	VG+	NM
❑ 1504	Save the Last Dance for Me/Take Me Back	1965	3.00	6.00	12.00

7-Inch Extended Plays

EPIC

Number	Title (A Side/B Side)	Yr	VG	VG+	NM
❑ EG-7187	(contents unknown)	1958	12.50	25.00	50.00
❑ EG-7187 [PS]	Sal Mineo	1958	12.50	25.00	50.00
❑ EG-7194	(contents unknown)	1958	10.00	20.00	40.00
❑ EG-7194 [PS]	Sal	1958	10.00	20.00	40.00
❑ EG-7195	(contents unknown)	1958	10.00	20.00	40.00
❑ EG-7195 [PS]	Sal	1958	10.00	20.00	40.00
❑ EG-7204	(contents unknown)	1959	12.50	25.00	50.00
❑ EG-7204 [PS]	Souvenirs of Summertime	1959	12.50	25.00	50.00
❑ ZTEP 27283/4	Too Young/Start Movin'//Baby Face/Little Pigeon	195?	15.00	30.00	60.00

—Special item for Scotch cellophane tape

Number	Title (A Side/B Side)	Yr	VG	VG+	NM
❑ ZTEP 27283/4 [PS]	(title unknown)	195?	20.00	40.00	80.00

MINORBOPS, THE

LAMP

Number	Title (A Side/B Side)	Yr	VG	VG+	NM
❑ 2012	Need You Tonight/Want You for My Own	1957	62.50	125.00	250.00

MINT JULEPS, THE

HERALD

Number	Title (A Side/B Side)	Yr	VG	VG+	NM
❑ 481	Bells of Love/Vip-a-Dip	1956	25.00	50.00	100.00

—With script logo inside flag

Number	Title (A Side/B Side)	Yr	VG	VG+	NM
❑ 481	Bells of Love/Vip-a-Dip	1956	6.25	12.50	25.00

—With block logo inside flag

MINT TATTOO

DOT

Number	Title (A Side/B Side)	Yr	VG	VG+	NM
❑ 17242	Mark of the Beast/When Talking About You	1969	2.50	5.00	10.00

MINTS, THE

See KEN COPELAND.

MINUTE MEN, THE

ARGO

Number	Title (A Side/B Side)	Yr	VG	VG+	NM
❑ 5469	Please Keep the Beatles in England/My Love Is Gone	1964	3.75	7.50	15.00

MIRACLES, THE

Includes records as "Smokey Robinson and the Miracles." Also see SMOKEY ROBINSON.

CHESS

Number	Title (A Side/B Side)	Yr	VG	VG+	NM
❑ 1734	Bad Girl/I Love Your Baby	1959	15.00	30.00	60.00

—Blue label with vertical Chess logo (original)

Number	Title (A Side/B Side)	Yr	VG	VG+	NM
❑ 1734	Bad Girl/I Love Your Baby	1963	6.25	12.50	25.00

—Black label

Number	Title (A Side/B Side)	Yr	VG	VG+	NM
❑ 1734	Bad Girl/I Love Your Baby	1966	5.00	10.00	20.00

—Blue label with "Chess" at top

Number	Title (A Side/B Side)	Yr	VG	VG+	NM
❑ 1768	I Need a Change/All I Want (Is You)	1960	10.00	20.00	40.00

COLUMBIA

Number	Title (A Side/B Side)	Yr	VG	VG+	NM
❑ 10464	Spy for Brotherhood/The Bird Must Fly Away	1976	—	2.50	5.00
❑ 10517	Women (Make the World Go 'Round)/I Can Touch the Sky	1977	—	2.50	5.00
❑ 10706	Mean Machine/The Magic of Your Eyes (Laura's Eyes)	1978	—	2.50	5.00

END

Number	Title (A Side/B Side)	Yr	VG	VG+	NM
❑ 1016	Got a Job/My Mama Done Told Me	1958	15.00	30.00	60.00
❑ 1029	Money/I Cry	1958	12.50	25.00	50.00

—Mostly gray-white label, no mention of Roulette Records

Number	Title (A Side/B Side)	Yr	VG	VG+	NM
❑ 1029	Money/I Cry	1958	10.00	20.00	40.00

—Multicolor label with "A Division of Roulette Records Inc." on label

Number	Title (A Side/B Side)	Yr	VG	VG+	NM
❑ 1084	Money/I Cry	1961	6.25	12.50	25.00

MOTOWN

Number	Title (A Side/B Side)	Yr	VG	VG+	NM
❑ G 1/G 2	Bad Girl/I Love Your Baby	1959	1250.	1875.	2500.
❑ TLX-2207	Bad Girl/I Love Your Baby	1959	1250.	1875.	2500.

STANDARD GROOVE

Number	Title (A Side/B Side)	Yr	VG	VG+	NM
❑ 13090 [DJ]	I Care About Detroit	1968	50.00	100.00	200.00

—With Tamla globe logo on label

Number	Title (A Side/B Side)	Yr	VG	VG+	NM
❑ 13090 [DJ]	I Care About Detroit	1968	37.50	75.00	150.00

—With no Tamla logo on label

TAMLA

Number	Title (A Side/B Side)	Yr	VG	VG+	NM
❑ EX-009 [DJ]	The Christmas Song/Christmas Everyday	1963	50.00	100.00	200.00
❑ 54028	The Feeling Is So Fine/You Can Depend On Me	1960	125.00	250.00	500.00

—With alternate take of B-side; matrix number followed by "A" in trail-off wax

Number	Title (A Side/B Side)	Yr	VG	VG+	NM
❑ 54028	The Feeling Is So Fine/You Can Depend On Me	1960	100.00	200.00	400.00
❑ 54028	Way Over There/Depend On Me	1960	15.00	30.00	60.00

—With overdubbed strings on A-side

Number	Title (A Side/B Side)	Yr	VG	VG+	NM
❑ 54028	Way Over There/Depend on Me	1960	37.50	75.00	150.00

—No strings on A-side recording

Number	Title (A Side/B Side)	Yr	VG	VG+	NM
❑ 54034	Shop Around/Who's Lovin' You	1960	45.00	90.00	180.00

—Original take, withdrawn shortly after release. In trail-off wax is "H55518A."

Number	Title (A Side/B Side)	Yr	VG	VG+	NM
❑ 54034	Shop Around/Who's Lovin' You	1960	7.50	15.00	30.00

—Hit take. In trail-off wax is "L-1." Horizontal lines label.

Number	Title (A Side/B Side)	Yr	VG	VG+	NM
❑ 54034	Shop Around/Who's Lovin' You	1960	3.00	6.00	12.00

—Hit take. In trail-off wax is "L-1." Globe label.

Number	Title (A Side/B Side)	Yr	VG	VG+	NM
❑ 54036	Ain't It Baby/The Only One I Love	1961	37.50	75.00	150.00
❑ 54044	Mighty Good Lovin'/Broken Hearted	1961	12.50	25.00	50.00
❑ 54044 [PS]	Mighty Good Lovin'/Broken Hearted	1961	37.50	75.00	150.00
❑ 54048	Everybody's Gotta Pay Some Dues/I Can't Believe	1961	12.50	25.00	50.00
❑ 54048	You Gotta Pay Some Dues/I Can't Believe	1961	25.00	50.00	100.00

—Alternate A-side title

Number	Title (A Side/B Side)	Yr	VG	VG+	NM
❑ 54048 [PS]	Everybody's Gotta Pay Some Dues/I Can't Believe	1961	50.00	100.00	200.00
❑ 54053	What's So Good About Good-By/I've Been Good to You	1962	7.50	15.00	30.00
❑ 54053 [PS]	What's So Good About Good-By/I've Been Good to You	1962	30.00	60.00	120.00
❑ 54059	I'll Try Something New/You Never Miss a Good Thing	1962	5.00	10.00	20.00
❑ 54059 [PS]	I'll Try Something New/You Never Miss a Good Thing	1962	30.00	60.00	120.00
❑ 54069	Way Over There/If Your Mother Only Knew	1962	5.00	10.00	20.00
❑ 54073	You've Really Got a Hold on Me/Happy Landing	1962	5.00	10.00	20.00
❑ 54078	A Love She Can Count On/I Can Take a Hint	1963	5.00	10.00	20.00
❑ 54083	Mickey's Monkey/Whatever Makes You Happy	1963	5.00	10.00	20.00
❑ 54089	I Gotta Dance to Keep from Crying/Such Is Love, Such Is Life	1963	3.75	7.50	15.00
❑ 54092	(You Can't Let the Boy Overpower) The Man in You/Heartbreak Road	1964	3.75	7.50	15.00
❑ 54098	I Like It Like That/You're So Fine and Sweet	1964	3.75	7.50	15.00
❑ 54098 [PS]	I Like It Like That/You're So Fine and Sweet	1964	30.00	60.00	120.00
❑ 54102	That's What Love Is Made Of/Would I Love You	1964	3.75	7.50	15.00
❑ 54109	Come On Do the Jerk/Baby Don't You Go	1964	3.75	7.50	15.00
❑ 54113	Ooo Baby Baby/All That's Good	1965	3.75	7.50	15.00
❑ 54118	The Tracks of My Tears/A Fork in the Road	1965	3.75	7.50	15.00
❑ 54123	My Girl Has Gone/Since You Won My Heart	1965	3.75	7.50	15.00
❑ 54127	Going to A-Go-Go/Choosey Beggar	1965	3.75	7.50	15.00
❑ 54127 [PS]	Going to A-Go-Go/Choosey Beggar	1966	25.00	50.00	100.00
❑ 54134	Whole Lot of Shakin' in My Heart (Since I Met You)/Oh Be My Lover	1966	2.50	5.00	10.00
❑ 54140	Come 'Round Here — I'm the One You Need/Save Me	1966	2.50	5.00	10.00
❑ 54140 [PS]	Come 'Round Here — I'm the One You Need/Save Me	1966	25.00	50.00	100.00
❑ 54145	The Love I Saw in You Was Just a Mirage/Come Spy with Me	1967	2.00	4.00	8.00

—Starting here, through Tamla 54225, as "Smokey Robinson and the Miracles"

Number	Title (A Side/B Side)	Yr	VG	VG+	NM
❑ 54152	More Love/Swept for You Baby	1967	2.00	4.00	8.00
❑ 54159	I Second That Emotion/You Must Be Love	1967	2.00	4.00	8.00
❑ 54162	If You Can Want/When the Words from Your Heart Get Caught Up in Your Throat	1968	2.00	4.00	8.00

—"Tamla" in box on label

Number	Title (A Side/B Side)	Yr	VG	VG+	NM
❑ 54162	If You Can Want/When the Words from Your Heart Get Caught Up in Your Throat	1968	3.75	7.50	15.00

—"Tamla" in globe on label

Number	Title (A Side/B Side)	Yr	VG	VG+	NM
❑ 54167	Yester Love/Much Better Off	1968	2.00	4.00	8.00
❑ 54172	Special Occasion/Give Her Up	1968	2.00	4.00	8.00
❑ 54178	Baby, Baby Don't Cry/Your Mother's Only Daughter	1968	2.00	4.00	8.00
❑ 54183	Here I Go Again/Doggone Right	1969	2.00	4.00	8.00
❑ 54184	Abraham, Martin, and John/Much Better Off	1969	2.00	4.00	8.00
❑ 54189	Point It Out/Darling Dear	1969	2.00	4.00	8.00
❑ 54194	Who's Gonna Take the Blame/I Gotta Thing For You	1970	2.00	4.00	8.00
❑ 54199	The Tears of a Clown/Promise Me	1970	—	3.00	6.00
❑ 54205	I Don't Blame You at All/That Girl	1971	—	3.00	6.00
❑ 54206	Crazy About the La La La/Oh Baby Baby I Love You	1971	—	3.00	6.00
❑ 54211	Satisfaction/Flower Girl	1971	—	3.00	6.00
❑ 54220	We've Come Too Far to End It Now/When Sundown Comes	1972	—	3.00	6.00
❑ 54225	I Can't Stand to See You Cry/With Your Love Came	1972	—	3.00	6.00
❑ 54237	Don't Let It End (Til You Let It Begin)/Wigs and Lashes	1973	—	2.50	5.00

—Starting here, name reverts to The Miracles

Number	Title (A Side/B Side)	Yr	VG	VG+	NM
❑ 54240	Give Me Just Another Day/I Wanna Be with You	1973	—	2.50	5.00
❑ 54248	Do It Baby/I Wanna Be with You	1974	—	2.50	5.00
❑ 54256	Don't Cha Love It/Up Again	1974	—	2.50	5.00
❑ 54259	You Are Love/Gemini	1975	—	2.50	5.00
❑ 54262	Love Machine (Part 1)/Love Machine (Part 2)	1975	—	2.50	5.00
❑ 54268	Night Life/Smog	1976	—	2.50	5.00

TOPPS/MOTOWN

Number	Title (A Side/B Side)	Yr	VG	VG+	NM
❑ 11	Shop Around	1967	18.75	37.50	75.00

—Cardboard record

MIRACLES, THE (2)

No relation to the more famous group above.

Number	Title (A Side/B Side)	Yr	VG	VG+	NM
BATON					
❑ 210	A Lover's Chant/Come Home with Me	1955	37.50	75.00	150.00
CASH					
❑ 1008	You're An Angel/A Gal Named Jo	1955	50.00	100.00	200.00

MIRANDA, BOB

Of THE HAPPENINGS.

Number	Title (A Side/B Side)	Yr	VG	VG+	NM
B.T. PUPPY					
❑ 544	Girl on a Swing/When I Lock My Door	1968	2.50	5.00	10.00
JUBILEE					
❑ 5709	Everybody Is a Star/Evergreen	1971	2.00	4.00	8.00

MIRETTES, THE

Also see THE IKETTES.

Number	Title (A Side/B Side)	Yr	VG	VG+	NM
MINIT					
❑ 32045	Help Wanted/Play Fair	1968	2.50	5.00	10.00
MIRWOOD					
❑ 5514	He's Alright with Me/Your Kind Ain't No Good	1966	3.00	6.00	12.00
❑ 5531	He's Alright with Me/Now That I Found You Baby	1967	2.50	5.00	10.00
REVUE					
❑ 11004	In the Midnight Hour/To Love Somebody	1968	2.50	5.00	10.00
❑ 11017	Take Me for a Little While/Real Thing	1968	2.00	4.00	8.00
❑ 11029	First Love/I'm a Whole New Thing	1968	2.00	4.00	8.00
UNI					
❑ 55110	Stand By Your Man/If Everybody'd Help Somebody	1969	—	3.00	6.00
❑ 55126	Heart Full of Gladness/You Ain't Trying to Cross Over	1969	—	3.00	6.00
❑ 55147	Whirlpool/You Ain't Trying to Cross Over	1969	—	3.00	6.00
❑ 55161	Rap Run It On Down/Sweet Soul Sister	1969	—	3.00	6.00
—A-side: Nate Turner and the Mirettes; B-side: Venetta Fields and the Mirettes					

MISFITS, THE

The famous punk band. Also see GLENN DANZIG; SAMHAIN.

Number	Title (A Side/B Side)	Yr	VG	VG+	NM
BLANK					
❑ A 101	Cough Cool/She	1977	50.00	100.00	200.00
—500 copies were pressed					
❑ A 101 [PS]	Cough Cool/She	1977	50.00	100.00	200.00
GEFFEN					
❑ PRO-S-1112 [DJ]	Dig Up Her Bones/Hate the Living, Love the Dead	1997	—	2.50	5.00
—All copies on blue vinyl					
❑ PRO-S-1112 [PS]	Dig Up Her Bones/Hate the Living, Love the Dead	1997	—	2.50	5.00
PLAN 9					
❑ PL 1001	Bullet/We Are 138/Attitude/Hollywood Babylon	1978	25.00	50.00	100.00
—Black vinyl					
❑ PL 1001	Bullet/We Are 138/Attitude/Hollywood Babylon	1978	31.25	62.50	125.00
—Red vinyl					
❑ PL 1001 [PS]	Bullet/We Are 138/Attitude/Hollywood Babylon	1978	10.00	20.00	125.00
—First edition with gatefold and lyric sheet					
❑ PL 1001 [PS]	Bullet/We Are 138/Attitude/Hollywood Babylon	1978	31.25	62.50	125.00
—Second edition with new back cover "Better Dead on Red"					
❑ PL 1009	Horror Business/Teenagers from Mars/Children in Heat	1979	15.00	30.00	60.00
—Yellow vinyl					
❑ PL 1009	Horror Business/Teenagers from Mars/Children in Heat	1979	500.00	1000.	2000.
—25 (!!) on black vinyl, no picture sleeve					
❑ PL 1009 [PS]	Horror Business/Teenagers from Mars/Children in Heat	1979	25.00	50.00	100.00
—With insert (deduct 40 percent if missing)					
❑ PL 1009 [PS]	Horror Business/Teenagers from Mars/Children in Heat	1979	75.00	150.00	300.00
—Withdrawn sleeve; these have a back cover with a group photo and were never used, but some have hit the collector's market					
❑ PL 1010	Night of the Living Dead/Where Eagles Dare/Ratt Fink	1979	15.00	30.00	60.00
❑ PL 1010 [PS]	Night of the Living Dead/Where Eagles Dare/Ratt Fink	1979	15.00	30.00	60.00
❑ PL 1013	London Dungeon/Horror Hotel/Ghouls Night Out	1981	12.50	25.00	50.00
—3,000 with gray label					
❑ PL 1013	London Dungeon/Horror Hotel/Ghouls Night Out	1981	12.50	25.00	50.00
—7,000 with orange label					
❑ PL 1013	London Dungeon/Horror Hotel/Ghouls Night Out	1981	12.50	25.00	50.00
—Second pressing: 400 on black vinyl, smal center hole					
❑ PL 1013	London Dungeon/Horror Hotel/Ghouls Night Out	1981	12.50	25.00	50.00
—Second pressing: 400 on white vinyl					
❑ PL 1013 [PS]	3 Hits from Hell: London Dungeon/Horror Hotel/Ghouls Night Out	1981	12.50	25.00	50.00
❑ PL 1017	Halloween I/Halloween II	1981	12.50	25.00	50.00
❑ PL 1017 [PS]	Halloween I/Halloween II	1981	15.00	30.00	60.00
—Orange sleeve with lyric sheet					
❑ PL 1017 [PS]	Halloween I/Halloween II	1981	100.00	200.00	400.00
—Black and white test sleeve; approximately 10 were made					

MISFITS, THE (2)

Completely different punk band than the above, they changed their name to The Tragics.

Number	Title (A Side/B Side)	Yr	VG	VG+	NM
BLACK & WHITE					
❑ (no #)	Pretty Boy/Laughing Lover/Mommi I'm a Misfit/When I Was Young	1982	12.50	25.00	50.00
❑ (no #) [PS]	Pretty Boy/Laughing Lover/Mommi I'm a Misfit/When I Was Young	1982	12.50	25.00	50.00
—Most picture sleeves have a sticker with the band's new name, The Tragics					

MISFITS, THE (U)

More than one group, but none of these are either of the above bands.

Number	Title (A Side/B Side)	Yr	VG	VG+	NM
ARIES					
❑ 3	Midnight Star/I Don't Know	1961	50.00	100.00	200.00
HUSH					
❑ 105	Give Me Your Heart/My Mother-in-Law	1960	100.00	200.00	400.00
IMPERIAL					
❑ 66054	This Little Piggy (I'm a Hog for You)/Lost Love	1964	6.25	12.50	25.00
JOEY					
❑ 117	Naughty Rooster/Chicago Confidential	1961	3.00	6.00	12.00
SOUND STAGE 7					
❑ 2538	It's Up to You/Skiing Time	1965	6.25	12.50	25.00
TROY					
❑ 227	The Uncle Willie/Big Bad Wolf	196?	6.25	12.50	25.00

MR. CLEAN

Number	Title (A Side/B Side)	Yr	VG	VG+	NM
ORIGINAL SOUND					
❑ 40	Mr. Clean/Jessie Lee	1964	37.50	75.00	150.00
—Written, produced and performed on by Frank Zappa					

MR. LUCKY AND THE GAMBLERS

Number	Title (A Side/B Side)	Yr	VG	VG+	NM
DOT					
❑ 16930	Take a Look at Me/I Told You (Once Before)	1966	5.00	10.00	20.00
PANORAMA					
❑ 37	Take a Look at Me/I Told You (Once Before)	1966	5.00	10.00	20.00
❑ 52	Alice Designs/You Don't Need Me	1967	3.75	7.50	15.00
UNITED INT'L.					
❑ 1001	New Orleans/Searching	1965	5.00	10.00	20.00
❑ 4404	Koko Joe/I Told You (Once Before)	1966	5.00	10.00	20.00

MITCHELL, BOBBY

Number	Title (A Side/B Side)	Yr	VG	VG+	NM
IMPERIAL					
❑ 5236	I'm Cryin'/Rack 'Em Back	1953	50.00	100.00	200.00
❑ 5250	One Friday Morning/Four-Eleven-Forty-Four	1953	50.00	100.00	200.00
❑ 5270	Baby's Gone/Sister Lucy	1954	30.00	60.00	120.00
❑ 5282	Angel Child/School Boy Blues	1954	30.00	60.00	120.00
❑ 5295	The Wedding Bells Are Ringing/Meant for Me	1954	30.00	60.00	120.00
❑ 5309	I'm a Young Man/She Couldn't Be Found	1954	30.00	60.00	120.00
❑ 5326	I Wish I Knew/Nothing Sweet As You	1955	20.00	40.00	80.00
❑ 5346	I Cried/I'm in Love	1955	15.00	30.00	60.00
❑ 5378	Try Rock and Roll/No, No, No	1956	12.50	25.00	50.00
❑ 5392	Goin' Round in Circles/I Try So Hard	1956	12.50	25.00	50.00
❑ 5412	You Are My Angel/I've Got My Fingers Crossed	1956	12.50	25.00	50.00
❑ 5440	You Always Hurt the One You Love/I Would Like to Know	1957	10.00	20.00	40.00
❑ 5475	I'm Gonna Be a Wheel Someday/You Better Go Home	1957	12.50	25.00	50.00
❑ 5511	I Love to Hold You/64 Hours	1958	10.00	20.00	40.00
❑ 5558	Hearts of Fire/You're Going to Be Sorry	1959	10.00	20.00	40.00
❑ 5882	My Southern Bell/When First We Met	1962	3.00	6.00	12.00
❑ 5923	I Don't Want to Be a Wheel No More/I Got to Call That Number	1963	3.00	6.00	12.00
RON					
❑ 337	Sand Me Your Picture/You're Doing Me Wrong	1961	3.00	6.00	12.00
❑ 342	Mama Don't Allow/There's Only One of You	1961	3.00	6.00	12.00

MITCHELL, CHAD

Also see THE CHAD MITCHELL TRIO.

Number	Title (A Side/B Side)	Yr	VG	VG+	NM
AMY					
❑ 11043	For What It's Worth/Follow	1968	—	2.50	5.00
❑ 11054	The Bus Song/What's That Got to Do with Me	1969	—	2.50	5.00
WARNER BROS.					
❑ 5880	Quiet Room/Violets of Dawn	1966	—	3.00	6.00
❑ 7043	Suzanne/Marieka	1967	—	3.00	6.00

MITCHELL, CHAD, TRIO

Also see CHAD MITCHELL; THE MITCHELL TRIO.

Number	Title (A Side/B Side)	Yr	VG	VG+	NM
COLPIX					
❑ 133	Sally Ann/Vaya Con Dios	1959	3.00	6.00	12.00
❑ 136	Up On the Mountain/Walkin' on the Green Grasses	1959	3.00	6.00	12.00
❑ 144	I Do Adore Her/The Gallows Tree	1960	3.00	6.00	12.00
❑ 154	The Ballad of Herbie Spear/Pretty Saro	1960	3.00	6.00	12.00
❑ 157	Devil Road/Paddy West	1960	3.00	6.00	12.00
❑ 610	Six Men/I'm Going Home	1961	2.50	5.00	10.00
—B-side by Eugene Lamarr					
KAPP					
❑ 439	Lizzie Borden/Super Skier	1961	3.00	6.00	12.00
❑ 439 [PS]	Lizzie Borden/Super Skier	1961	5.00	10.00	20.00
❑ 457	John Birch Society/Golden Vanity	1962	2.50	5.00	10.00
❑ 481	Alberta/Come Along Home	1962	2.50	5.00	10.00
❑ 485	You Can Tell the World/Hello, Susan Brown	1962	2.50	5.00	10.00
❑ 510	Blowing in the Wind/Adios, Mi Corazon	1963	2.50	5.00	10.00
❑ 518	Green Grow the Lilacs/Leave Me If You Want To	1963	2.50	5.00	10.00
MAY					
❑ 116	The Ballad of Herbie Spear/Sally Ann	1962	2.50	5.00	10.00
MERCURY					
❑ 72197	The Marvelous Toy/Bonny Streets of Fyve-10	1963	2.50	5.00	10.00
❑ 72197 [PS]	The Marvelous Toy/Bonny Streets of Fyve-10	1963	3.75	7.50	15.00
❑ 72234	The Tarrier's Song/Tell Old Billy	1964	2.00	4.00	8.00
❑ 72234 [PS]	The Tarrier's Song/Tell Old Billy	1964	3.75	7.50	15.00
❑ 72257	What Did You Learn in School Today/Barry's Boys	1964	2.00	4.00	8.00

MITCHELL, GUY

Number	Title (A Side/B Side)	Yr	VG	VG+	NM
CHALICE					
❑ 711	My Angel/Bit of Love	1963	7.50	15.00	30.00
❑ 711	My Angel/Mr. Hobo	1963	7.50	15.00	30.00
❑ 712	Take Your Time/(B-side unknown)	1963	7.50	15.00	30.00
❑ 713	Your Imagination/(B-side unknown)	1963	7.50	15.00	30.00
COLUMBIA					
❑ 1-640 (?)	Giddy Up/Where in the World	1950	7.50	15.00	30.00
—Microgroove 33 1/3 rpm 7-inch single					
❑ 1-680 (?)	Me and My Imagination/To Me You're a Song	1950	7.50	15.00	30.00
—Microgroove 33 1/3 rpm 7-inch single					

Number	Title (A Side/B Side)	Yr	VG	VG+	NM
❑ 1-760 (?)	Angels Cry/You're Not in My Arms Tonight	1950	7.50	15.00	30.00
—Microgroove 33 1/3 rpm 7-inch single					
❑ 6-760 (?)	Angels Cry/You're Not in My Arms Tonight	1950	6.25	12.50	25.00
❑ 1-918	My Heart Cries for You/The Roving Kind	1950	7.50	15.00	30.00
—Microgroove 33 1/3 rpm 7-inch single					
❑ 6-918	My Heart Cries for You/The Roving Kind	1950	6.25	12.50	25.00
❑ 39067	My Heart Cries for You/The Roving Kind	1950	3.75	7.50	15.00
❑ 39190	Sparrow in the Tree Top/Christopher Columbus	1951	3.70	7.50	15.00
❑ 3-39190	Sparrow in the Tree Top/Christopher Columbus	1951	7.50	15.00	30.00
—Microgroove 33 1/3 rpm 7-inch single					
❑ 39331	Unless/A Beggar in Love	1951	3.75	7.50	15.00
❑ 39415	My Truly, Truly Fair/Who Knows Love	1951	3.75	7.50	15.00
❑ 39512	Belle, Belle, My Liberty Belle/Sweetheart of Yesterday	1951	3.75	7.50	15.00
❑ 39595	There's Always Room at Our House/I Can't Help It (If I'm Still in Love with You)	1951	3.75	7.50	15.00
❑ 39639	Wimmin'/We Don't Live in a Castle	1952	5.00	10.00	20.00
❑ 39663	Pittsburgh, Pennsylvania/Doll with a Sawdust Heart	1952	3.75	7.50	15.00
❑ 39753	The Day of Jubilo/You'll Never Be Mine	1952	5.00	10.00	20.00
❑ 39822	Feet Up (Pat Him on the Po-Po)/Jenny Kissed Me	1952	3.75	7.50	15.00
❑ 39879	('Cause I Love You) That's-a Why/Train of Love	1952	3.75	7.50	15.00
—With Mindy Carson					
❑ 39886	Don't Rob Another Man's Castle/Why Should I Go Home	1952	3.75	7.50	15.00
❑ 39909	She Wears Red Feathers/Pretty Little Blackeyed Susie	1952	3.75	7.50	15.00
❑ 39950	I Want You for a Sunbeam/So Am I	1953	3.00	6.00	12.00
❑ 39992	There's Nothing As Sweet As My Baby/Tell Us Where the Good Times Are	1953	3.00	6.00	12.00
—With Mindy Carson					
❑ 40008	Hannah Lee/Look at That Girl	1953	3.00	6.00	12.00
❑ 40035	Cloud Lucky Seven/Chicka-Boom	1953	3.00	6.00	12.00
❑ 40077	Sippin' Soda/Strollin' Blues	1953	3.00	6.00	12.00
❑ 40128	Got a Hole in My Sweater/The Cuff of My Shirt	1953	3.00	6.00	12.00
❑ 40175	Tear Down the Mountains/A Dime and a Dollar	1954	3.00	6.00	12.00
❑ 40240	There Once Was a Man/My Heaven on Earth	1954	3.00	6.00	12.00
❑ 40278	What Am I Doin' in Kansas City/You've Ruined Me	1954	3.00	6.00	12.00
❑ 40389	I Met the Cutest Little Eyeful (At the Eiffel Tower)/Gee But You Gotta Come Home	1954	3.00	6.00	12.00
❑ 40468	Nobody Home/Zoo Baby	1955	2.50	5.00	10.00
❑ 40507	Otto's Gotta Go (Otto Drives Me Crazy)/Man Overboard	1955	3.00	6.00	12.00
❑ 40531	Let Us Be Sweethearts Again/Too Late	1955	2.50	5.00	10.00
❑ 40560	When Binky Blows/Belonging	1955	2.50	5.00	10.00
❑ 40631	Ninety Nine Years (Dead or Alive)/Perfume, Candy and Flowers	1955	2.50	5.00	10.00
❑ 40672	Solo/Green Grows the Grass	1956	2.50	5.00	10.00
❑ 40700	Give Me a Carriage with Eight White Horses/I Used to Hate Ya	1956	2.50	5.00	10.00
❑ 40724	Finders Keepers/I'd Like to Say a Few Words About Texas	1956	2.50	5.00	10.00
❑ 40769	Singing the Blues/Crazy with Love	1956	2.50	5.00	10.00
❑ 40769 [PS]	Singing the Blues/Crazy with Love	1956	5.00	10.00	20.00
❑ 40820	Knee Deep in the Blues/Take Me Back Baby	1957	2.50	5.00	10.00
❑ 40820 [PS]	Knee Deep in the Blues/Take Me Back Baby	1957	3.75	7.50	15.00
❑ 40877	Rock-a-Billy/Hoot Owl	1957	2.50	5.00	10.00
❑ 40877 [PS]	Rock-a-Billy/Hoot Owl	1957	3.75	7.50	15.00
❑ 40940	Sweet Stuff/In the Middle of a Dark, Dark Night	1957	2.50	5.00	10.00
❑ 40987	A Cure for the Blues/Call Rosie on the Phone	1957	2.50	5.00	10.00
❑ 41033	C'mon Let's Go/The Unbeliever	1957	2.50	5.00	10.00
❑ 41075	One Way Street/The Lord Made a Peanut	1957	2.50	5.00	10.00
❑ 41146	Hey, Madame/Till We're Engaged	1958	2.00	4.00	8.00
❑ 41177	Hangin' Around/Honey Brown Eyes	1958	2.00	4.00	8.00
❑ 41215	Let It Shine, Let It Shine/Butterfly Doll	1958	2.00	4.00	8.00
❑ 41274	My Heart Cries for You/Under the Rainbow	1958	2.00	4.00	8.00
❑ 41311	Guilty Heart/Half As Much	1958	2.00	4.00	8.00
❑ 41359	Alias Jesse James/Pride o' Dixie	1959	2.00	4.00	8.00
❑ 41397	Loosen Up, Lucy/I'm Gonna Leave You Now	1959	2.00	4.00	8.00
❑ 41476	Heartaches By the Number/Two	1959	2.50	5.00	10.00
❑ 41476 [PS]	Heartaches By the Number/Two	1959	3.75	7.50	15.00
❑ 41576	The Same Old Me/Build Up My Gallows High	1960	2.00	4.00	8.00
❑ 41653	Symphony of Spring/Cry Hurtin' Heart	1960	2.00	4.00	8.00
❑ 41725	My Shoes Keep Walking Back to You/Silver Moon Upon the Golden Sands	1960	2.00	4.00	8.00
❑ 41853	Sunshine Guitar/Ridin' Around in the Rain	1960	2.00	4.00	8.00
❑ 41853 [PS]	Sunshine Guitar/Ridin' Around in the Rain	1960	3.00	6.00	12.00
❑ 41970	Follow Me/Your Goodnight Kiss	1961	2.00	4.00	8.00
❑ 42143	Divorce/I'll Just Pretend	1961	2.00	4.00	8.00
❑ 42231	Soft Rain/Big Big Chance	1961	2.00	4.00	8.00
JOY					
❑ 264	Rusty Old Halo/Charlie's Shoes	1962	2.00	4.00	8.00
❑ 270	Go Tiger Go/If You Ever Go Away	1962	2.00	4.00	8.00
❑ 273	Have I Told You Lately That I Love You/Blue Violet	1963	2.00	4.00	8.00
REPRISE					
❑ 0477	Best Thing That Ever Happened to Me/If I Had My Life to Live Over	1966	—	3.00	6.00
❑ 0513	Run to the Door/Foreign Love Affair	1966	—	3.00	6.00
STARDAY					
❑ 819	Traveling Shoes/Every Night Is a Lifetime	1967	—	3.00	6.00
❑ 828	Alabam/Irene Good-By	1968	—	3.00	6.00
❑ 846	Frisco Line/Singing the Blues	1968	—	3.00	6.00
❑ 866	Get It Over/Just Wish You'd Change Your Mind	1969	—	3.00	6.00
❑ 878	Smokey Blue Eyes/Heartaches by the Number	1969	—	3.00	6.00

7-Inch Extended Plays

COLUMBIA

Number	Title (A Side/B Side)	Yr	VG	VG+	NM
❑ B-1585	My Truly, Truly Fair/The Roving Kind//Sparrow in the Treetop/My Heart Cries for You	195?	5.00	10.00	20.00
❑ B-1585 [PS]	Guy Mitchell Spotlite	195?	5.00	10.00	20.00
❑ B-2502	*My Heart Cries for You/The Roving Kind/My Truly, Truly Fair/Pittsburgh, Pennsylvania	1957	3.00	6.00	12.00
❑ B-2502 [PS]	Guy Mitchell (Hall of Fame Series)	1957	3.00	6.00	12.00

MITCHELL, GUY, AND ROSEMARY CLOONEY

COLUMBIA

Number	Title (A Side/B Side)	Yr	VG	VG+	NM
❑ 39052	You're Just in Love/Marrying for Love	1950	3.75	7.50	15.00

MITCHELL, JONI

ASYLUM

Number	Title (A Side/B Side)	Yr	VG	VG+	NM
❑ 11010	You Turn Me On, I'm a Radio/Urge for Going	1972	—	2.50	5.00
❑ 11029	Raised on Robbery/Court and Spark	1973	—	2.50	5.00
❑ 11034	Help Me/Just Like This Train	1974	—	2.50	5.00
❑ 11041	Free Man in Paris/People's Parties	1974	—	2.50	5.00
❑ 45221	Big Yellow Taxi/Rainy Night House	1974	—	2.00	4.00
❑ 45244	Jericho/Carey	1975	—	2.00	4.00
❑ 45298	In France They Kiss on Main Street/Boho Dance	1976	—	2.00	4.00
❑ 45377	Coyote/Blue Motel Room	1976	—	2.00	4.00
❑ 45467	Dreamland/Jericho	1978	—	2.00	4.00
❑ 46506	The Dry Cleaner from Des Moines/God Must Be a Boogie Man	1979	—	2.00	4.00
❑ 47038	Why Do Fools Fall in Love/Black Crow	1980	—	2.00	4.00
GEFFEN					
❑ 27887	My Secret Place/Lakota	1988	—	2.00	4.00
❑ 28675	Shiny Toys/Three Great Stimulants	1986	—	2.00	4.00
❑ 28840	Good Friends/Smokin' Empty (Try Another)	1985	—	2.00	4.00
❑ 28840 [PS]	Good Friends/Smokin' Empty (Try Another)	1985	—	2.50	5.00
❑ 29757	Underneath the Streetlight/Be Cool	1983	—	2.00	4.00
❑ 29849	(You're So Square) Baby I Don't Care/Love	1982	—	2.00	4.00
❑ 29849 [PS]	(You're So Square) Baby I Don't Care/Love	1982	—	2.50	5.00
REPRISE					
❑ 0694	I Had a King/Night in the City	1968	2.00	4.00	8.00
❑ 0906	Big Yellow Taxi/Woodstock	1970	2.00	4.00	8.00
❑ 1029	Carey/This Flight Tonight	1971	2.00	4.00	8.00
❑ 1049	Case of You/California	1971	—	3.00	6.00
❑ 1154	Both Sides Now/Chelsea Morning	1972	—	2.50	5.00
—"Back to Back Hits" series					
❑ 1155	Big Yellow Taxi/Carey	1972	—	2.50	5.00
—"Back to Back Hits" series					

MITCHELL, LEE

PHILLIPS INT'L.

Number	Title (A Side/B Side)	Yr	VG	VG+	NM
❑ 3530	The Frog/A Little Bird Told Me	1958	3.75	7.50	15.00
SHARP					
❑ 0862	Rootie Tootie Baby/Who's That Big Man	1959	75.00	150.00	300.00

MITCHELL, MARLON

VENA

Number	Title (A Side/B Side)	Yr	VG	VG+	NM
❑ 100	Ice Cold Baby/Bermuda Shorts	1957	30.00	60.00	120.00

MITCHELL, ROSE

IMPERIAL

Number	Title (A Side/B Side)	Yr	VG	VG+	NM
❑ 5243	Slipping In/I'm Searching	1953	15.00	30.00	60.00
❑ 5260	Live My Life/Baby Please Don't Go	1954	15.00	30.00	60.00

MITCHELL, STAN

GONE

Number	Title (A Side/B Side)	Yr	VG	VG+	NM
❑ 5106	Devil in Disguise/Lovin' Man	1961	7.50	15.00	30.00

MITCHELL TRIO, THE

Records issued after JOHN DENVER replaced CHAD MITCHELL in THE CHAD MITCHELL TRIO.

MERCURY

Number	Title (A Side/B Side)	Yr	VG	VG+	NM
❑ 72340	I Can't Help But Wonder/Stewball and Griselda	1964	2.00	4.00	8.00
❑ 72340 [PS]	I Can't Help But Wonder/Stewball and Griselda	1964	3.75	7.50	15.00
❑ 72400	You Were On My Mind/My Name Is Morgan	1965	2.00	4.00	8.00
❑ 72518	That's the Way It's Gonna Be/Violets of Dawn	1966	2.00	4.00	8.00
❑ 72544	Your Friendly, Liberal, Neighborhood Ku Klux Klan/Violets of Dawn	1966	2.00	4.00	8.00
❑ 72591	Dark Shadows and Empty Hallways/Stay with Me	1966	2.00	4.00	8.00
REPRISE					
❑ 0588	Leaving on a Jet Plane/Baby, That's Where It Is	1967	—	3.00	6.00
❑ 0630	She Loves You/Like to Deal with the Ladies	1967	—	3.00	6.00

MITCHUM, ROBERT

CAPITOL

Number	Title (A Side/B Side)	Yr	VG	VG+	NM
❑ F3672	What Is This Generation Coming To/Mama Looka Boo Boo	1957	3.75	7.50	15.00
❑ 3741	The Ballad of Thunder Road/My Baby's Lovin' Arms	1973	—	3.00	6.00
❑ 3986	The Ballad of Thunder Road/My Honey's Lovin' Arms	1962	2.00	4.00	8.00
—Orange and yellow swirl label, no "F" prefix					
❑ 3986	The Ballad of Thunder Road/My Honey's Lovin' Arms	1969	—	3.00	6.00
—Red and orange "target" label					
❑ 3986	The Ballad of Thunder Road/My Honey's Lovin' Arms	1973	—	2.00	4.00
—Orange label, "Capitol" at bottom					
❑ F3986	The Ballad of Thunder Road/My Honey's Lovin' Arms	1958	3.75	7.50	15.00
—Purple label with "F" prefix					
❑ F3986 [PS]	The Ballad of Thunder Road/My Honey's Lovin' Arms	1958	6.25	12.50	25.00
COLUMBIA					
❑ 03483	The Ballad of Thunder Road/That Little Ole Wine Drinker Me	1983	—	2.50	5.00
MONUMENT					
❑ 1006	Little Old Wine Drinker Me/Walker's Woods	1967	—	3.50	7.00
❑ 1025	You Deserve Each Other/That Man Right There	1967	—	3.50	7.00

MIZELL, HANK

AMAZON

Number	Title (A Side/B Side)	Yr	VG	VG+	NM
❑ 711	Jungle Rock/Then I'm In Your Arms	1963	12.50	25.00	50.00

EKO

Number	Title (A Side/B Side)	Yr	VG	VG+	NM
❑ 506	Jungle Rock/Then I'm In Your Arms	1958	150.00	300.00	600.00

—Issued as "Jim Bobo" on A-side and "Jim Bobo and Hank Mizell" on B-side

KING

Number	Title (A Side/B Side)	Yr	VG	VG+	NM
❑ 5236	Jungle Rock/Then I'm In Your Arms	1959	75.00	150.00	300.00

MOBY GRAPE

COLUMBIA

Number	Title (A Side/B Side)	Yr	VG	VG+	NM
❑ 44170	Changes/Fall on You	1967	2.00	4.00	8.00
❑ 44170 [PS]	Changes/Fall on You	1967	5.00	10.00	20.00
❑ 44171	Sitting by the Window/Indifference	1967	2.00	4.00	8.00
❑ 44171 [PS]	Sitting by the Window/Indifference	1967	5.00	10.00	20.00
❑ 44172	8:05/Mister Blues	1967	2.00	4.00	8.00
❑ 44172 [PS]	8:05/Mister Blues	1967	5.00	10.00	20.00
❑ 44173	Omaha/Someday	1967	2.00	4.00	8.00
❑ 44173 [PS]	Omaha/Someday	1967	5.00	10.00	20.00
❑ 44174	Hey Grandma/Come in the Morning	1967	2.00	4.00	8.00
❑ 44174 [PS]	Hey Grandma/Come in the Morning	1967	5.00	10.00	20.00
❑ 44567	Can't Be So Bad/Bitter Wind	1968	—	3.00	6.00
❑ 44789	If You Can't Learn From My Mistakes/Trucking Man	1969	—	3.00	6.00
❑ 44885	Ooh Mama Ooh/It's a Beautiful Day Today	1969	—	3.00	6.00
❑ JZSP 118972 [DJ]	Omaha/8:05	1967	3.00	6.00	12.00

—Yellow label promo; "Rush Reservice"

REPRISE

Number	Title (A Side/B Side)	Yr	VG	VG+	NM
❑ 1040	Gypsy Wedding/Apocalypse	1971	—	2.50	5.00
❑ 1055	Goin' Down to Texas/About Time	1971	—	2.50	5.00
❑ 1096	Gone Fishin'/Gypsy Wedding	1972	—	2.50	5.00

MOCKINGBIRDS, THE

With GRAHAM GOULDMAN and Kevin Godley, later of 10CC.

ABC-PARAMOUNT

Number	Title (A Side/B Side)	Yr	VG	VG+	NM
❑ 10653	That's How/I Never Should Have Kissed You	1965	3.75	7.50	15.00

MOGEN DAVID AND THE GRAPES OF WRATH

CHA CHA

Number	Title (A Side/B Side)	Yr	VG	VG+	NM
❑ 757	Little Girl Gone/Go Away Girl	1967	2000.	3000.	4000.

MOJO MEN, THE

AUTUMN

Number	Title (A Side/B Side)	Yr	VG	VG+	NM
❑ 11	Mama's Little Baby/Off the Hook	1965	3.75	7.50	15.00
❑ 19	Dance with Me/The Loneliest Boy in Town	1965	3.75	7.50	15.00
❑ 27	She's My Baby/Fire in My Heart	1966	3.75	7.50	15.00

GRT

Number	Title (A Side/B Side)	Yr	VG	VG+	NM
❑ 5	Flower of Love/I Can't Let Go	1969	2.50	5.00	10.00
❑ 8	Candle to Burn/Make You at Home	1969	2.50	5.00	10.00
❑ 16	Everyday Love/There Goes My Mind	1969	2.50	5.00	10.00

REPRISE

Number	Title (A Side/B Side)	Yr	VG	VG+	NM
❑ 0486	She's My Baby/Do the Hanky Panky	1966	5.00	10.00	20.00
❑ 0539	Sit Down, I Think I Love You/Don't Leave Me Crying Like Before	1966	2.50	5.00	10.00
❑ 0580	Me About You/When You're in Love	1967	2.50	5.00	10.00
❑ 0617	Whatever Happened to Happy/Make You at Home	1967	2.50	5.00	10.00
❑ 0661	Not Too Old to Start Crying/New York City	1968	2.50	5.00	10.00
❑ 0689	Should I Cry/You to Me	1968	2.50	5.00	10.00
❑ 0707	Sit Down, I Think I Love You/Me About You	1968	—	3.00	6.00

—"Back to Back Hits" series

Number	Title (A Side/B Side)	Yr	VG	VG+	NM
❑ 0759	Don't Be Cruel/Let It Be Him	1968	2.50	5.00	10.00

TIDE

Number	Title (A Side/B Side)	Yr	VG	VG+	NM
❑ 2000	Surfin' Fat Man/Paula	1964	10.00	20.00	40.00

MOJOS, THE

PARROT

Number	Title (A Side/B Side)	Yr	VG	VG+	NM
❑ 9707	Seven Daffodils/Nothin' at All	1964	2.50	5.00	10.00
❑ 45001	Everything's Alright/Give Your Loving to Me	1964	3.00	6.00	12.00
❑ 45002	Why Not Tonight/Don't Do It Anymore	1964	3.00	6.00	12.00

MOLES, GENE

CHALLENGE

Number	Title (A Side/B Side)	Yr	VG	VG+	NM
❑ 59249	Burning Rubber/Twin Pipes	1964	6.25	12.50	25.00

GARPAX

Number	Title (A Side/B Side)	Yr	VG	VG+	NM
❑ 44176	Kaha Huna (Goddess of Surfing)/Maria (The Wind)	1963	6.25	12.50	25.00

MOLLERN, RONNIE

KING

Number	Title (A Side/B Side)	Yr	VG	VG+	NM
❑ 5365	Rockin' Up/Fat Mama	1960	37.50	75.00	150.00

MOM'S APPLE PIE

BROWN BAG

Number	Title (A Side/B Side)	Yr	VG	VG+	NM
❑ XW192	Love Plays a Song/Can You Help Me	1973	2.50	5.00	10.00

MOMENTS, THE

R&B trio. For legal reasons, their records on EMI America, EMI Manhattan, Panoramic and Polydor were issued under the name "Ray, Goodman and Brown."

ALL PLATINUM

Number	Title (A Side/B Side)	Yr	VG	VG+	NM
❑ 2350	Sho Nuff Boogie (Part 1)/Sho Nuff Boogie (Part 2)	1974	—	2.50	5.00

—With Sylvia

EMI AMERICA

Number	Title (A Side/B Side)	Yr	VG	VG+	NM
❑ 8365	Take It to the Limit/(Instrumental)	1986	—	—	3.00
❑ 8365 [PS]	Take It to the Limit/(Instrumental)	1986	—	—	3.00
❑ 8378	Celebrate Our Love/(Instrumental)	1987	—	—	3.00
❑ 8378 [PS]	Celebrate Our Love/(Instrumental)	1987	—	—	3.00
❑ 43022	Tonight (Baby)/Good Love	1987	—	—	3.00

EMI MANHATTAN

Number	Title (A Side/B Side)	Yr	VG	VG+	NM
❑ 50155	Where Did You Get That Body, (Baby)?/Where Are You Now	1988	—	—	3.00
❑ 50155 [PS]	Where Did You Get That Body, (Baby)?/Where Are You Now	1988	—	—	3.00

PANORAMIC

Number	Title (A Side/B Side)	Yr	VG	VG+	NM
❑ 201	Who's Gonna Make the First Move/Look Like Lovers	1984	—	2.00	4.00

POLYDOR

Number	Title (A Side/B Side)	Yr	VG	VG+	NM
❑ 2033	Special Lady/Deja Vu	1979	—	2.50	5.00
❑ 2077	Inside of You/Treat Her Right	1980	—	2.00	4.00
❑ 2116	My Prayer/The Way It Should Be	1980	—	2.00	4.00
❑ 2135	Happy Anniversary/You	1980	—	2.00	4.00
❑ 2159	Shoestrings/Me	1981	—	2.00	4.00
❑ 2191	How Can Love Be So Right (Yet So Wrong)/Each Time Is Like the First Time	1981	—	2.00	4.00
❑ 2203	Stay/Good Ole Days	1982	—	2.00	4.00
❑ 2208	Till the Right One Comes Along/Heaven in the Rain	1982	—	2.00	4.00
❑ 2222	Gambled on Your Love/Pool of Love	1982	—	2.00	4.00
❑ 2227	After All/Love Minus One	1982	—	2.00	4.00
❑ 810056-7	Special Lady/My Prayer	1983	—	—	3.00

—Reissue

STANG

Number	Title (A Side/B Side)	Yr	VG	VG+	NM
❑ 5000	Not on the Outside/Understanding	1968	2.00	4.00	8.00
❑ 5003	Sunday/Everybody Loves My Baby	1969	—	3.00	6.00
❑ 5005	I Do/Pocketful of Heartbreaks	1969	—	3.00	6.00
❑ 5008	I'm So Lost/Where	1969	—	3.00	6.00
❑ 5009	Lovely Way She Loves/I've Got to Keep On Loving, Love	1969	—	3.00	6.00
❑ 5012	Love on a Two-Way Street/I Won't Do Anything	1970	2.00	4.00	8.00
❑ 5016	If I Didn't Care/You Make Me Feel Good	1970	—	3.00	6.00
❑ 5017	All I Have/The Hurt's On Me	1970	—	3.00	6.00
❑ 5020	I Can't Help It/To You with Love	1971	—	3.00	6.00
❑ 5024	That's How It Feels/That's How It Feels (Long)	1971	—	3.00	6.00
❑ 5031	Lucky Me/I Lost One Bird in the Hand (Reaching Out for Two in the Bush)	1971	—	3.00	6.00
❑ 5033	To You with Love/Key to My Happiness	1971	—	3.00	6.00
❑ 5036	Thanks a Lot/I Lost One Bird in the Hand (Reaching Out for Two in the Bush)	1972	—	3.00	6.00
❑ 5041	Just Because He Wants to Make Love (Doesn't Mean He Loves You)/So This Is Our Goodbye	1972	—	3.00	6.00
❑ 5045	My Thing/Thanks a Lot	1972	—	3.00	6.00
❑ 5048	Girl I'm Gonna Miss You/I Think So	1973	—	2.50	5.00
❑ 5050	Gotta Find a Way/Sweeter As the Days Go By	1973	—	2.50	5.00
❑ 5052	Sexy Mama/Where Can I Find Her	1973	—	3.00	6.00
❑ 5054	Sweet Sweet Lady/Next Time I See You	1974	—	2.50	5.00
❑ 5056	What's Your Name/Mama I Miss You	1974	—	2.50	5.00
❑ 5057	Girls (Part 1)/Girls (Part 2)	1974	—	2.50	5.00

—With the Whatnauts

Number	Title (A Side/B Side)	Yr	VG	VG+	NM
❑ 5060	Look at Me (I'm in Love)/You've Come a Long Way	1975	—	2.50	5.00
❑ 5064	Got to Get to Know You/I Feel So Bad	1975	—	2.50	5.00
❑ 5066	Nine Times/When the Morning Comes	1976	—	2.50	5.00
❑ 5068	With You/The Next Time I See You	1976	—	2.50	5.00
❑ 5071	We Don't Cry Out Loud/Come In Girl	1977	—	2.50	5.00
❑ 5073	I Don't Wanna Go/Oh I Could Have Loved You	1977	—	2.50	5.00
❑ 5075	I Could Have Loved You/Jack in the Box	1978	—	2.50	5.00
❑ 5076	Rain in My Backyard/Disco Man	1978	—	2.50	5.00

SUGAR HILL

Number	Title (A Side/B Side)	Yr	VG	VG+	NM
❑ 758	Baby Let's Rap Now (Part 1)/Baby Let's Rap Now (Part 2)	1980	—	2.50	5.00
❑ 769	Record Breakin' Love Affair/(B-side unknown)	1981	—	2.50	5.00

MOMENTS, THE (2)

California studio group.

ERA

Number	Title (A Side/B Side)	Yr	VG	VG+	NM
❑ 3099	Walk Right In/(Instrumental)	1963	2.50	5.00	10.00
❑ 3104	Homework/Big Bound Wheel	1963	2.50	5.00	10.00
❑ 3114	Surfin' Train/Mamu Zey	1963	3.00	6.00	12.00
❑ 3128	In the Phonograph Booth/Blues at Sandy Cove	1964	2.50	5.00	10.00

MOMENTS, THE (3)

Steve Marriott, later of SMALL FACES and HUMBLE PIE, was in this group.

WORLD ARTISTS

Number	Title (A Side/B Side)	Yr	VG	VG+	NM
❑ 1032	You Really Got Me/Money, Money	1964	2.50	5.00	10.00

MONARCHS, THE (1)

MONUMENT

Number	Title (A Side/B Side)	Yr	VG	VG+	NM
❑ 03484	Look Homeward, Angel/This Old Heart	1983	—	2.50	5.00

SOUND STAGE 7

Number	Title (A Side/B Side)	Yr	VG	VG+	NM
❑ 2502	This Old Heart/'Til I Hear It From You	1963	3.00	6.00	12.00
❑ 2516	Look Homeward, Angel/What Made You Change Your Mind	1964	3.00	6.00	12.00
❑ 2530	Climb Every Mountain/Take Me Home	1964	3.00	6.00	12.00

MONARCHS, THE (2)

DOT

Number	Title (A Side/B Side)	Yr	VG	VG+	NM
❑ 15228	Gravy/Caravan Mambo	1954	10.00	20.00	40.00

MONARCHS, THE (3)

MELBA

Number	Title (A Side/B Side)	Yr	VG	VG+	NM
❑ 101	Pretty Little Girl/In My Younger Days	1956	20.00	40.00	80.00

NEIL

Number	Title (A Side/B Side)	Yr	VG	VG+	NM
❑ 101	Pretty Little Girl/In My Younger Days	1956	37.50	75.00	150.00
❑ 103	Always Be Faithful/How Are You	1956	30.00	60.00	120.00

MONARCHS, THE (U)

Some of these could be by the above groups.

LIBAN

Number	Title (A Side/B Side)	Yr	VG	VG+	NM
❑ 1002	Love You That's Why/Coming Home	1959	500.00	1000.	2000.

WING

Number	Title (A Side/B Side)	Yr	VG	VG+	NM
❑ 90040	Angels in the Sky/Wanna Go Home	1955	20.00	40.00	80.00

YUCCA

Number	Title (A Side/B Side)	Yr	VG	VG+	NM
❑ 172	Forever Lost/Cuckoo	1964	12.50	25.00	50.00

ZONE

Number	Title (A Side/B Side)	Yr	VG	VG+	NM
❑ 1067	Friday Night/El Bandito	1963	3.75	7.50	15.00

MONDAY MORNING QUARTERBACK, THE

WARNER BROS

Number	Title (A Side/B Side)	Yr	VG	VG+	NM
❑ 7664 [PS]	The 12 Days of Christmas (The Game Plan to Beat Miami)/Santa Claus Medley	1972	3.75	7.50	15.00

WARNER BROS.

Number	Title (A Side/B Side)	Yr	VG	VG+	NM
❑ 7664	The 12 Days of Christmas (The Game Plan to Beat Miami)/Santa Claus Medley	1972	2.50	5.00	10.00

MONDELLOS, THE

RHYTHM

Number	Title (A Side/B Side)	Yr	VG	VG+	NM
❑ 102	Come Back Home/100 Years from Today	1956	50.00	100.00	200.00
—As "Alice Jean and the Mondellos"					
❑ 105	Over the Rainbow/Never Leave Me Alone	1956	37.50	75.00	150.00
—As "Yul McClay and the Mondellos"					
❑ 106	That's What I Call Love/Daylight Saving Time	1956	37.50	75.00	150.00
❑ 109	Hard to Please/Happiness Street	1957	37.50	75.00	150.00
❑ 114	My Heart/That's What I Call Love	1957	37.50	75.00	150.00
—As "Rudy Lambert and the Mondellos"					
❑ 128	That Old Feeling/Sunday Kind of Love	1957	37.50	75.00	150.00
—As "Rudy Lambert and the Mondellos"					

MONIQUES, THE

CENTAUR

Number	Title (A Side/B Side)	Yr	VG	VG+	NM
❑ 105	I'm With You All the Way/Rock Pretty Baby	1963	6.25	12.50	25.00

MONITORS, THE (1)

SOUL

Number	Title (A Side/B Side)	Yr	VG	VG+	NM
❑ 35049	Step by Step (Hand in Hand)/Time Is Passing By	1968	3.75	7.50	15.00

V.I.P.

Number	Title (A Side/B Side)	Yr	VG	VG+	NM
❑ 25028	Say You/All for Someone	1965	5.00	10.00	20.00
❑ 25032	Greetings (This Is Uncle Sam)/Number One in Your Heart	1965	5.00	10.00	20.00
❑ 25039	Since I Lost You Girl/Don't Put Off Till Tomorrow What You Can Do Today	1966	5.00	10.00	20.00
❑ 25046	Bring Back the Love/The Further You Look, The Less You See	1967	5.00	10.00	20.00
❑ 25049	Step by Step (Hand in Hand)/Time Is Passing By	1968	12.50	25.00	50.00

MONITORS, THE (2)

ALADDIN

Number	Title (A Side/B Side)	Yr	VG	VG+	NM
❑ 3309	Tonight's the Night/Candy Coated Kisses	1955	25.00	50.00	100.00

MONITORS, THE (U)

Some of these may be groups (1) or (2).

BUDDAH

Number	Title (A Side/B Side)	Yr	VG	VG+	NM
❑ 278	Fence Around Your Heart/Have You Seen Her	1972	—	2.50	5.00

CIRCUS

Number	Title (A Side/B Side)	Yr	VG	VG+	NM
❑ 219	A Boyfriend's Prayer/Nita	1957	37.50	75.00	150.00

SPECIALTY

Number	Title (A Side/B Side)	Yr	VG	VG+	NM
❑ 595	Our Schooldays/I've Got a Dream	1957	20.00	40.00	80.00
❑ 622	Closer to Heaven/Rock 'N' Roll Forever	1957	50.00	100.00	200.00
❑ 636	Mamma Linda/Hop Scotch	1958	15.00	30.00	60.00

MONKEES, THE

Also see DOLENZ, JONES & TORK; DOLENZ, JONES, BOYCE & HART; MICKEY DOLENZ; DAVY JONES; MICHAEL NESMITH.

ARISTA

Number	Title (A Side/B Side)	Yr	VG	VG+	NM
❑ 0201	Daydream Believer/Monkee's Theme	1976	2.50	5.00	10.00
❑ 9505	That Was Then, This Is Now/(Theme from) The Monkees	1986	2.50	5.00	10.00
—First pressings list both sides' artist as "The Monkees"					
❑ 9505	That Was Then, This Is Now/(Theme from) The Monkees	1986	—	—	3.00
—With A-side artist listed as " Mickey Dolenz and Peter Tork (of the Monkees)"					
❑ 9505 [PS]	That Was Then, This Is Now/(Theme from) The Monkees	1986	2.50	5.00	10.00
—Without "By Mickey Dolenz and Peter Tork (of the Monkees)" on sleeve					
❑ 9505 [PS]	That Was Then, This Is Now/(Theme from) The Monkees	1986	—	—	3.00
—With "By Mickey Dolenz and Peter Tork (of the Monkees)" on sleeve					
❑ 9532	Daydream Believer/Randy Scouse Git	1986	—	2.00	4.00
❑ 9532 [PS]	Daydream Believer/Randy Scouse Git	1986	—	2.00	4.00

COLGEMS

Number	Title (A Side/B Side)	Yr	VG	VG+	NM
❑ 66-1001	Last Train to Clarksville/Take a Giant Step	1966	3.75	7.50	15.00
❑ 66-1001 [PS]	Last Train to Clarksville/Take a Giant Step	1966	7.50	15.00	30.00
—Version 1: Black & white photo, no red strip at bottom					
❑ 66-1001 [PS]	Last Train to Clarksville/Take a Giant Step	1966	6.25	12.50	25.00
—Version 2: Black & white photo, red strip at bottom with "Ask For The Monkees LP Album" in white					
❑ 66-1001 [PS]	Last Train to Clarksville/Take a Giant Step	1966	5.00	10.00	20.00
—Version 3: Color photo, light blue strip at bottom of each side. Side 1 type reads "Ask For The Monkees LP Album"; Side 2 has "Write To Monkees"					
❑ 66-1002	I'm a Believer/(I'm Not Your) Steppin' Stone	1966	3.75	7.50	15.00
❑ 66-1002 [PS]	I'm a Believer/(I'm Not Your) Steppin' Stone	1966	7.50	15.00	30.00
❑ 66-1003	A Little Bit Me, A Little Bit You/She Hangs Out	1967	—	—	—
—Unreleased					
❑ 66-1003 [PS]	A Little Bit Me, A Little Bit You/She Hangs Out	1967	250.00	500.00	1000.
—Though the record does not exist, this picture sleeve does. It uses the same photo that appears on the "Pleasant Valley Sunday" sleeve.					
❑ 66-1004	A Little Bit Me, A Little Bit You/The Girl I Knew Somewhere	1967	3.75	7.50	15.00
❑ 66-1007	Pleasant Valley Sunday/Words	1967	3.75	7.50	15.00
❑ 66-1007 [PS]	Pleasant Valley Sunday/Words	1967	7.50	15.00	30.00
❑ 66-1012	Daydream Believer/Goin' Down	1967	3.75	7.50	15.00
❑ 66-1012 [PS]	Daydream Believer/Goin' Down	1967	7.50	15.00	30.00
❑ 66-1019	Valleri/Tapioca Tundra	1968	2.50	5.00	10.00
❑ 66-1023	D.W. Washburn/It's Nice to Be with You	1968	2.50	5.00	10.00
❑ 66-1023 [PS]	D.W. Washburn/It's Nice to Be with You	1968	7.50	15.00	30.00
❑ 66-1031	Porpoise Song/As We Go Along	1968	2.50	5.00	10.00
❑ 66-1031 [PS]	Porpoise Song/As We Go Along	1968	5.00	10.00	20.00
❑ 66-5000	Tear Drop City/A Man Without a Dream	1969	2.50	5.00	10.00
❑ 66-5000 [PS]	Tear Drop City/A Man Without a Dream	1969	6.25	12.50	25.00
❑ 66-5004	Listen to the Band/Someday Man	1969	2.50	5.00	10.00
❑ 66-5004 [PS]	Listen to the Band/Someday Man	1969	6.25	12.50	25.00
—"Listen to the Band" listed first					
❑ 66-5004 [PS]	Someday Man/Listen to the Band	1969	5.00	10.00	20.00
—"Someday Man" listed first					
❑ 66-5005	Good Clean Fun/Mommy and Daddy	1969	3.75	7.50	15.00
❑ 66-5005 [PS]	Good Clean Fun/Mommy and Daddy	1969	6.25	12.50	25.00
❑ 66-5011	Oh My My/I Love You Better	1970	3.75	7.50	15.00
❑ 66-5011 [PS]	Oh My My/I Love You Better	1970	7.50	15.00	30.00

RHINO

Number	Title (A Side/B Side)	Yr	VG	VG+	NM
❑ 74408	Heart and Soul/M.G.B.G.T.	1987	—	—	3.00
—Black vinyl					
❑ 74408	Heart and Soul/M.G.B.G.T.	1987	2.50	5.00	10.00
—Pink vinyl					
❑ 74408 [PS]	Heart and Soul/M.G.B.G.T.	1987	—	2.00	4.00
❑ 74410	Every Step of the Way/(I'll) Love You Forever	1987	—	—	3.00
❑ 74410 [PS]	Every Step of the Way/(I'll) Love You Forever	1987	—	2.00	4.00

7-Inch Extended Plays

COLGEMS

Number	Title (A Side/B Side)	Yr	VG	VG+	NM
❑ CGLP-101 [DJ]	Theme from The Monkees/I Wanna Be Free/Take a Giant Step//Last Train to Clarksville/Saturday's Child/Tomorrow's Gonna Be Another Day	1966	37.50	75.00	150.00
—Jukebox mini-LP, small hole, plays at 33 1/3 rpm					
❑ CGLP-101 [PS]	The Monkees	1966	37.50	75.00	150.00

MONORAYS, THE

More than one group?

20TH CENTURY FOX

Number	Title (A Side/B Side)	Yr	VG	VG+	NM
❑ 594	You're No Good/Love	1965	12.50	25.00	50.00

ASTRA

Number	Title (A Side/B Side)	Yr	VG	VG+	NM
❑ 1018	Face in the Crowd/Step Right Up	196?	3.75	7.50	15.00
—Yellow vinyl					

RED ROCKET

Number	Title (A Side/B Side)	Yr	VG	VG+	NM
❑ 476	Guardian Angel/Five Minutes to Love You	1959	10.00	20.00	40.00

TAMMY

Number	Title (A Side/B Side)	Yr	VG	VG+	NM
❑ 1005	Guardian Angel/Five Minutes to Love You	1959	50.00	100.00	200.00

MONOTONES, THE (1)

Male vocal group from New Jersey.

ARGO

Number	Title (A Side/B Side)	Yr	VG	VG+	NM
❑ 5290	Book of Love/You Never Loved Me	1958	7.50	15.00	30.00
❑ 5301	Tom Foolery/Zombi	1958	7.50	15.00	30.00
❑ 5321	The Legend of Sleepy Hollow/Soft Shadows	1958	7.50	15.00	30.00
❑ 5339	Tell It to the Judge/Fools Will Be Fools	1959	12.50	25.00	50.00

HULL

Number	Title (A Side/B Side)	Yr	VG	VG+	NM
❑ 735	Reading the Book of Love/Dream	1960	12.50	25.00	50.00
❑ 743	Daddy's Home, But Momma's Gone/Tattle Tale	1961	12.50	25.00	50.00

MASCOT

Number	Title (A Side/B Side)	Yr	VG	VG+	NM
❑ 124	Book of Love/You Never Loved Me	1957	200.00	400.00	800.00

MONOTONES, THE (2)

British group.

HICKORY

Number	Title (A Side/B Side)	Yr	VG	VG+	NM
❑ 1250	Is It Right/What Would You Do	1964	5.00	10.00	20.00
❑ 1306	When Will I Be Loved/If You Can't Give Me All	1965	5.00	10.00	20.00

MONOTONES, THE (U)

Could be group (2); it's doubtful that it's group (1).

ABC-PARAMOUNT

Number	Title (A Side/B Side)	Yr	VG	VG+	NM
❑ 10796	Crystal Ball/A Thousand Faces	1966	5.00	10.00	20.00

MONROE, MARILYN

20TH FOX

Number	Title (A Side/B Side)	Yr	VG	VG+	NM
❑ 311	River of No Return/One Silver Dollar	1962	5.00	10.00	20.00
❑ 311 [PS]	River of No Return/One Silver Dollar	1962	20.00	40.00	80.00

RCA VICTOR

Number	Title (A Side/B Side)	Yr	VG	VG+	NM
❑ 47-5745	River of No Return/I'm Gonna File My Claim	1954	12.50	25.00	50.00
❑ 47-5745 [DJ]	River of No Return/I'm Gonna File My Claim	1954	30.00	60.00	120.00
—Promo only with Marilyn Monroe's picture on label					
❑ 47-5745 [PS]	River of No Return/I'm Gonna File My Claim	1954	30.00	60.00	120.00
❑ 47-6033	Heat Wave/After You Get What You Want	1955	7.50	15.00	30.00
❑ 47-6033 [PS]	Heat Wave/After You Get What You Want	1955	30.00	60.00	120.00

UNITED ARTISTS

Number	Title (A Side/B Side)	Yr	VG	VG+	NM
❑ 161	I Wanna Be Loved By You/I'm Through with Love	1959	5.00	10.00	20.00

MONTCLAIRS, THE (1)

PAULA

Number	Title (A Side/B Side)	Yr	VG	VG+	NM
❑ 345	Is This for Real/All I Really Care About Is You	1971	—	2.50	5.00
❑ 363	Dreaming Out of Season/I Just Can't Get Away	1972	—	2.50	5.00
❑ 375	Beggin' Is Hard to Do/Unwanted Love	1973	—	2.50	5.00
❑ 381	Make Up for Lost Time/How Can One Man Live	1973	—	2.50	5.00
❑ 382	I Need You More Than Ever/Prelude to a Heartbreak	1973	—	2.50	5.00
❑ 390	I'm Calling You/Hung Up on Your Love	1973	—	2.50	5.00
❑ 409	Baby, You Know I'm Gonna Miss You (Part 1)/Baby, You Know I'm Gonna Miss You (Part 2)	1974	—	2.50	5.00

MONTCLAIRS, THE (2)

ABC-PARAMOUNT

Number	Title (A Side/B Side)	Yr	VG	VG+	NM
❑ 10463	I Believe (In Your Love)/No Baby	1963	3.75	7.50	15.00

MONTCLAIRS, THE (3)

AUDICON

Number	Title (A Side/B Side)	Yr	VG	VG+	NM
❑ 111	Goodnight, Well, It's Time to Go/A Broken Promise	1961	7.50	15.00	30.00

MONTCLAIRS, THE (4)

HI-Q

Number	Title (A Side/B Side)	Yr	VG	VG+	NM
❑ 5001	Golden Angel/Don Juan	1957	75.00	150.00	300.00

PREMIUM

Number	Title (A Side/B Side)	Yr	VG	VG+	NM
❑ 404	Give Me a Chance/My Every Dream	1956	100.00	200.00	400.00

Number	Title (A Side/B Side)	Yr	VG	VG+	NM
SONIC					
❑ 104	All I Want Is Love/I've Heard About You	1956	200.00	400.00	800.00

MONTCLAIRS, THE (U)

Some of these could be group (2) or (3).

Number	Title (A Side/B Side)	Yr	VG	VG+	NM
SUNBURST					
❑ 106	Wait for Me/Happy Feet Time	1965	3.00	6.00	12.00
❑ 115	Poopsie/Sore Feet	1965	3.00	6.00	12.00
UNITED INT'L.					
❑ 1007	Lisa/Tap Tap Daisy	1963	6.25	12.50	25.00
❑ 1013	Young Wings Can Fly/Come On and Hold Me	1964	5.00	10.00	20.00
WICKWIRE					
❑ 13009	It's Gonna Work Out Fine/If You Need Me	196?	3.00	6.00	12.00

MONTEREYS, THE

More than one group.

Number	Title (A Side/B Side)	Yr	VG	VG+	NM
ARWIN					
❑ 130	Goodbye My Love/It Hurts Me So	1961	10.00	20.00	40.00
BLAST					
❑ 219	Face in the Crowd/Step Right Up	1965	100.00	200.00	400.00
DOMINION					
❑ 1019	First Kiss/Just One More Kiss	1964	10.00	20.00	40.00
EASTWEST					
❑ 121	I'll Love You Again/The American Teens	1958	6.25	12.50	25.00
GNP CRESCENDO					
❑ 314	For Sentimental Reasons/I Still Love You	1964	6.25	12.50	25.00
IMPALA					
❑ 213	Without a Girl/So Deep	1959	30.00	60.00	120.00
MAJOR					
❑ 1009	A Crowded Room/You Said That You Loved Me	1959	17.50	35.00	70.00
PRINCE					
❑ 5060	Rita/Billy Bud	1960	3.75	7.50	15.00
ROSE					
❑ 109	You're the Girl for Me/Ape Shape	1958	25.00	50.00	100.00
SATURN					
❑ 1002	My Girl/With You	1956	10.00	20.00	40.00
TRANS AMERICAN					
❑ 1000/1	Darlin' Send Me a Letter/Late Darlin'	1960	150.00	300.00	600.00

MONTEZ, CHRIS

Number	Title (A Side/B Side)	Yr	VG	VG+	NM
A&M					
❑ 780	Call Me/Go Head On	1965	2.00	4.00	8.00
❑ 796	The More I See You/You, I Love You	1966	2.50	5.00	10.00
❑ 810	There Will Never Be Another You/You Can Hurt the One You Love	1966	2.00	4.00	8.00
❑ 822	Keep Talkin'/Time After Time	1966	2.00	4.00	8.00
❑ 839	Because of You/Elena	1967	2.00	4.00	8.00
❑ 852	Just Friends/Twiggy	1967	—	3.00	6.00
❑ 855	Foollin' Around/Dindi (Jin-Jee)	1967	—	3.00	6.00
❑ 906	Once in a While/The Face I Love	1968	—	3.00	6.00
❑ 958	Love Is Here to Stay/Nothing to Hide	1968	—	3.00	6.00
❑ 985	Where Are You Now/Watch What Happens	1968	—	3.00	6.00
JAMIE					
❑ 1410	Let's Dance/Somebody Loves You	1973	—	2.50	5.00
MONOGRAM					
❑ 500	All You Had to Do (Was Tell Me)/Love Me	1962	3.00	6.00	12.00
❑ 505	Let's Dance/You're the One	1962	5.00	10.00	20.00
❑ 507	Some Kinda Fun/Tell Me	1962	3.00	6.00	12.00
❑ 508	Rockin' Blues/(Let's Do the) Limbo	1963	3.75	7.50	15.00
❑ 513	In An English Towne/My Baby Loves to Dance	1963	3.00	6.00	12.00
❑ 516	No, No, No/Monkey Fever	1963	3.00	6.00	12.00
❑ 517	You're the One/All You Had to Do Was Tell Me	1964	3.00	6.00	12.00
—With Kathy Young					
❑ 520	It Takes Two/To Shoot the Curl	1964	3.00	6.00	12.00
—With Kathy Young					
❑ 522	(It's Not) Puppy Love/He's Been Leading You On	1964	3.00	6.00	12.00
PARAMOUNT					
❑ 0109	We Can Make the World a Whole Lot Brighter/ The End of the Line	1971	—	2.50	5.00

MONTGOMERY, BOB

Number	Title (A Side/B Side)	Yr	VG	VG+	NM
BRUNSWICK					
❑ 55157	Because I Love You/Taste of the Blues	1959	10.00	20.00	40.00

MONTGOMERY, CHRISTOPHER

Number	Title (A Side/B Side)	Yr	VG	VG+	NM
DOLTON					
❑ 84	My Paradise/Giants of Bombora	1963	7.50	15.00	30.00

MONTGOMERY, JACK

Number	Title (A Side/B Side)	Yr	VG	VG+	NM
SCEPTER					
❑ 12152	Do You Believe It/My Dearly Beloved	1966	12.50	25.00	50.00

MONTGOMERY, TAMMY

Later known as TAMMI TERRELL.

Number	Title (A Side/B Side)	Yr	VG	VG+	NM
CHECKER					
❑ 1072	If I Would Marry You/This Time Tomorrow	1964	10.00	20.00	40.00
—Maroon label					
❑ 1072	If I Would Marry You/This Time Tomorrow	1964	6.25	12.50	25.00
—Mostly blue label with red and black checkers					
SCEPTER					
❑ 1224	If You See Bill/It's Mine	1961	15.00	30.00	60.00
TRY ME					
❑ 28001	I Cried/If You Don't Think	1962	7.50	15.00	30.00
—As "Tana Montgomery"					
WAND					
❑ 123	Voice of Experience/Wancha To Be Sure	1962	7.50	15.00	30.00

MONTGOMERYS, THE

Number	Title (A Side/B Side)	Yr	VG	VG+	NM
AMY					
❑ 883	Promise of Love/Gotta Make a Hit Record	1963	62.50	125.00	250.00

MONTROSE

Also see SAMMY HAGAR.

Number	Title (A Side/B Side)	Yr	VG	VG+	NM
WARNER BROS.					
❑ 7776	Rock the Nation/One Thing on My Mind	1974	—	2.50	5.00
❑ 7814	Make It Last/Space Station No. 5	1974	—	2.50	5.00
❑ 8063	The Dreamer/Paper Money	1975	—	2.50	5.00
❑ 8080	Connection/We're Going Home	1975	—	2.50	5.00
❑ 8172	Clown Woman/Matriarch	1976	—	2.50	5.00
❑ 8281	Music Man/Tuft-Sedge	1976	—	2.50	5.00
❑ 8351	Let's Go/(B-side unknown)	1977	—	2.50	5.00

MONTY PYTHON

Number	Title (A Side/B Side)	Yr	VG	VG+	NM
ARISTA					
❑ 0130	The Single/(B-side unknown)	1975	2.00	4.00	8.00
❑ 0578	They Won't Play This Song on the Radio/Sit on My Face-Farewell to John Denver	1980	2.00	4.00	8.00
WARNER BROS.					
❑ 49112	Always Look on the Bright Side of Life/Brian	1979	2.50	5.00	10.00

MOODS, THE (1)

Number	Title (A Side/B Side)	Yr	VG	VG+	NM
BANG					
❑ 555	Gotta Figure Out/Genuine Jade	1968	2.00	4.00	8.00
WAND					
❑ 11224	Rainmaker/Lady Rain	1970	2.00	4.00	8.00

MOODS, THE (2)

Number	Title (A Side/B Side)	Yr	VG	VG+	NM
KOOL					
❑ 1024	High School Days/The Broken Hip	1964	2.50	5.00	10.00
❑ 1028	Oop-Sy-Do/Stay with Me	1965	2.50	5.00	10.00
❑ 1032	Only the Young/(B-side unknown)	1965	2.50	5.00	10.00

MOODS, THE (3)

Number	Title (A Side/B Side)	Yr	VG	VG+	NM
SARG					
❑ 162	Little Alice/Lady of the Sea	1959	20.00	40.00	80.00
❑ 176	Easy Going/Duck Walk	1959	10.00	20.00	40.00
❑ 179	Let Me Have Your Love/Broke Up	1959	12.50	25.00	50.00
❑ 184	Rockin' Santa Claus/Teenager's Past	1959	10.00	20.00	40.00
❑ 185	On the Move/Teenager's Past	1960	10.00	20.00	40.00

MOODY BLUES, THE

Also see GRAEME EDGE; JUSTIN HAYWARD; DENNY LAINE; JOHN LODGE; RAY THOMAS.

Number	Title (A Side/B Side)	Yr	VG	VG+	NM
DERAM					
❑ 85023	Nights in White Satin/Cities	1968	2.50	5.00	10.00
—Composer of "Nights in White Satin" listed as "Redwave"					
❑ 85023	Nights in White Satin/Cities	1968	2.00	4.00	8.00
—Composer of "Nights in White Satin" listed as "Justin Hayward"					
❑ 85028	Tuesday Afternoon (Forever Afternoon)/Another Morning	1968	2.00	4.00	8.00
❑ 85033	Ride My See-Saw/Voices in the Sky	1968	2.00	4.00	8.00
❑ 85044	Never Comes the Day/So Deep Within You	1969	2.00	4.00	8.00
LONDON					
❑ 270	Steppin' in a Slide Zone/I'll Be Level with You	1978	—	2.00	4.00
❑ 273	Driftwood/I'm Your Man	1978	—	2.50	5.00
❑ 1005	This Is My House (But Nobody Calls)/Boulevard de la Madelaine	1967	3.00	6.00	12.00
❑ 9726V [DJ]	Go Now!/It's Easy Child	1965	5.00	10.00	20.00
—Orange and brown swirl label; may be promo only					
❑ 9726	Go Now!/Lose Your Money	1965	5.00	10.00	20.00
—White, purple and blue label					
❑ 9726	Go Now!/Lose Your Money	1965	3.00	6.00	12.00
—Blue swirl label, "London" in white					
❑ 9726	Go Now!/Lose Your Money	1965	2.00	4.00	8.00
—Blue swirl label, "London" in black					
❑ 9764	From the Bottom of My Heart (I Love You)/And My Baby's Gone	1965	3.75	7.50	15.00
❑ 9799	Ev'ry Day/You Don't	1965	3.75	7.50	15.00
❑ 9810	Stop!/Bye Bye Bird	1966	3.75	7.50	15.00
❑ 20030	Fly Me High/I Really Haven't Got the Time	1967	3.00	6.00	12.00
POLYDOR					
❑ 870990-7	No More Lies/River of Endless Love	1988	—	—	3.00
❑ 870990-7 [PS]	No More Lies/River of Endless Love	1988	—	—	3.00
❑ 871270-7	Al Fin Voy a Encontrarte (I Know You're Out There Somewhere — Spanish Version)/I Know You're Out There Somewhere	1989	—	2.50	5.00
❑ 883906-7	Your Wildest Dreams/Talkin' Talkin'	1986	—	—	3.00
❑ 883906-7 [PS]	Your Wildest Dreams/Talkin' Talkin'	1986	—	—	3.00
❑ 885201-7	The Other Side of Life/The Spirit	1986	—	2.50	5.00
—Blue vinyl					
❑ 885201-7 [PS]	The Other Side of Life/The Spirit	1986	—	2.50	5.00
—Special sleeve for blue vinyl version					
❑ 885212-7	The Other Side of Life/The Spirit	1986	—	—	3.00
❑ 885212-7 [PS]	The Other Side of Life/The Spirit	1986	—	—	3.00
❑ 887600-7	I Know You're Out There Somewhere/Miracle	1988	—	—	3.00
❑ 887600-7 [PS]	I Know You're Out There Somewhere/Miracle	1988	—	—	3.00
❑ 887815-7	Here Comes the Weekend/River of Endless Love	1988	—	—	3.00
THRESHOLD					
❑ 601	Gemini Dream/Painted Smile	1981	—	2.00	4.00
❑ 602	The Voice/22,000 Days	1981	—	2.00	4.00
❑ 602 [PS]	The Voice/22,000 Days	1981	—	3.00	6.00
❑ 603	Talking Out of Turn/Veteran Cosmic Rocker	1981	—	2.00	4.00
❑ 604	Sitting at the Wheel/Going Nowhere	1983	—	2.00	4.00
❑ 604 [PS]	Sitting at the Wheel/Going Nowhere	1983	—	3.00	6.00
❑ 605	Blue World/Sorry	1983	—	2.00	4.00
❑ 606	Running Water/Under My Feet	1983	—	2.00	4.00
❑ 67004	Question/Candle of Life	1970	—	3.00	6.00
❑ 67006	The Story in Your Eyes/Melancholy Man	1971	—	3.00	6.00
❑ 67006 [PS]	The Story in Your Eyes/Melancholy Man	1971	3.00	6.00	12.00
❑ 67009	Isn't Life Strange/After You Came	1972	—	2.50	5.00
❑ 67012	I'm Just a Singer (In a Rock and Roll Band)/For My Lady	1973	—	2.50	5.00

Number	Title (A Side/B Side)	Yr	VG	VG+	NM

MOON, KEITH
Also see THE WHO.

TRACK

Number	Title (A Side/B Side)	Yr	VG	VG+	NM
❑ 40316	Teenage Idol/Don't Worry Baby	1974	3.75	7.50	15.00
❑ 40387	Solid Gold/Move Over Ms. L.	1975	3.75	7.50	15.00
❑ 40435	In My Life/Crazy Like a Fox	1975	3.75	7.50	15.00

MOON, THE
With David Marks, ex-BEACH BOYS.

IMPERIAL

Number	Title (A Side/B Side)	Yr	VG	VG+	NM
❑ 66285	Mothers and Fathers/Someday Girl	1968	7.50	15.00	30.00
❑ 66330	Faces/John Automaton	1968	6.25	12.50	25.00
❑ 66415	Not to Know/Pirate	1969	6.25	12.50	25.00

MOON BEAMS, THE
GRATE

Number	Title (A Side/B Side)	Yr	VG	VG+	NM
❑ 100	A Lover's Plea/Don't Go Away	1959	37.50	75.00	150.00

MOONGLOWS, THE
Also see HARVEY.

BIG P

Number	Title (A Side/B Side)	Yr	VG	VG+	NM
❑ 101	Sincerely '72/You've Chosen Me	1972	2.50	5.00	10.00

CHAMPAGNE

Number	Title (A Side/B Side)	Yr	VG	VG+	NM
❑ 7500	I Just Can't Tell No Lie/I've Been Your Dog (Ever Since I've Been Your Man)	1952	375.00	750.00	1500.

CHANCE

Number	Title (A Side/B Side)	Yr	VG	VG+	NM
❑ 1147	Baby Please/Whistle My Love	1953	250.00	500.00	1000.
—Black vinyl					
❑ 1147	Baby Please/Whistle My Love	1953	1500.	2250.	3000.
—Red vinyl					
❑ 1150	Just a Lonely Christmas/Hey, Santa Claus	1953	1500.	2250.	3000.
—Red vinyl (this may not exist legitimately on black vinyl)					
❑ 1152	Secret Love/Real Gone Mama	1954	375.00	750.00	1500.
—Silver and blue label					
❑ 1152	Secret Love/Real Gone Mama	1954	250.00	500.00	1000.
—Yellow and black label					
❑ 1156	I Was Wrong/Ooh Rockin' Daddy	1954	150.00	300.00	600.00
—Yellow and black label					
❑ 1156	I Was Wrong/Ooh Rockin' Daddy	1954	150.00	300.00	600.00
—Black and white label					
❑ 1161	My Gal/219 Train	1954	2500.	3750.	5000.

CHESS

Number	Title (A Side/B Side)	Yr	VG	VG+	NM
❑ 1581	Sincerely/Tempting	1954	15.00	30.00	60.00
—Blue label, silver top					
❑ 1589	Most of All/She's Gone	1955	15.00	30.00	60.00
—Blue label, silver top					
❑ 1598	Foolish Me/Slow Down	1955	15.00	30.00	60.00
—Blue label, silver top					
❑ 1605	Starlite/In Love	1955	15.00	30.00	60.00
—Blue label, silver top					
❑ 1611	In My Diary/Lover, Love Me	1955	15.00	30.00	60.00
—Blue label, silver top					
❑ 1619	We Go Together/Chickie Um Bah	1956	12.50	25.00	50.00
—Blue label, silver top					
❑ 1629	See Saw/When I'm With You	1956	12.50	25.00	50.00
—Blue label, silver top					
❑ 1646	Over and Over Again/I Knew from the Start	1957	15.00	30.00	60.00
—With slower version of A-side; "8189A" in in the run-off area					
❑ 1646	Over and Over Again/I Knew from the Start	1957	12.50	25.00	50.00
—With normal version of A-side; blue label, silver top					
❑ 1651	I'm Afraid the Masquerade Is Over/Don't Say Goodbye	1957	12.50	25.00	50.00
—Blue label, silver top					
❑ 1661	Please Send Me Someone to Love/Mr. Engineer (Bring Her Back to Me)	1957	12.50	25.00	50.00
—Blue label, silver top					
❑ 1669	The Beating of My Heart/Confess It to Your Heart	1957	12.50	25.00	50.00
—In general, for the above singles, the blue label with vertical "Chess" versions are 60% of the above values; yellow early-1960s label versions and black mid-1960s versions are 40% of above; and blue late-1960s versions, with "Chess" on top, are about 20%					
❑ 1681	Too Late/Here I Am	1958	7.50	15.00	30.00
❑ 1689	In the Middle of the Night/Soda Pop	1958	7.50	15.00	30.00
❑ 1701	This Love/Sweeter Than Words	1958	7.50	15.00	30.00
❑ 1705	Ten Commandments of Love/Mean Old Blues	1958	7.50	15.00	30.00
—As "Harvey and the Moonglows"					
❑ 1717	Love Is a River/I'll Never Stop Wanting You	1959	6.25	12.50	25.00
❑ 1738	Mama Loocie/Unemployment	1959	6.25	12.50	25.00
—As "Harvey and the Moonglows"					
❑ 1770	Beatnick/Junior	1960	6.25	12.50	25.00
❑ 1811	Blue Velvet/Penny Arcade	1962	6.25	12.50	25.00
—As "Bobby Lester and the Moonglows"					

CRIMSON

Number	Title (A Side/B Side)	Yr	VG	VG+	NM
❑ 1003	My Imagination/Gee	1964	5.00	10.00	20.00

LOST NITE

Number	Title (A Side/B Side)	Yr	VG	VG+	NM
❑ 275	Just a Lonely Christmas/Baby Please	196?	3.00	6.00	12.00
—Reissue					

MELLO

Number	Title (A Side/B Side)	Yr	VG	VG+	NM
❑ 69	Just a Lonely Christmas/Hey, Santa Claus	19??	2.00	4.00	8.00
—Reissue					

RCA VICTOR

Number	Title (A Side/B Side)	Yr	VG	VG+	NM
❑ 74-0759	Sincerely/I Was Wrong	1972	—	2.50	5.00
❑ 74-0839	When I'm With You/You've Chosen Me	1972	—	2.50	5.00

VEE JAY

Number	Title (A Side/B Side)	Yr	VG	VG+	NM
❑ 423	Secret Love/Real Gone Mama	1962	6.25	12.50	25.00

7-Inch Extended Plays

CHESS

Number	Title (A Side/B Side)	Yr	VG	VG+	NM
❑ 5122	(contents unknown)	1959	62.50	125.00	250.00
❑ 5122 [PS]	Look! It's the Moonglows	1959	62.50	125.00	250.00
❑ 5123	True Love/Penny Arcade//I'll Stop Waiting/Sweeter Than Words	1959	62.50	125.00	250.00
❑ 5123 [PS]	Look! It's the Moonglows, Vol. 2	1959	62.50	125.00	250.00

MOORE, HARV
AMERICAN ARTS

Number	Title (A Side/B Side)	Yr	VG	VG+	NM
❑ 20	Interview of the Fab Four/I Feel So Fine	1964	75.00	150.00	300.00

MOORE, LATTIE
ARC

Number	Title (A Side/B Side)	Yr	VG	VG+	NM
❑ 8005	Juke Joint Johnny/Pretty Woman Blues	1952	50.00	100.00	200.00

KING

Number	Title (A Side/B Side)	Yr	VG	VG+	NM
❑ 1194	Foolish Castles/I'm Gonna Tell You Something	1953	12.50	25.00	50.00
❑ 1250	I Gotta Go Home/A Brand New Case of Love	1953	12.50	25.00	50.00
❑ 1327	They're Not Worth the Paper They're Printed On/Under a Mexico Moon	1954	12.50	25.00	50.00
❑ 1350	Pull Down the Blinds/What Am I Supposed to Do	1954	12.50	25.00	50.00
❑ 4955	100,000 Women Can't Be Wrong/Lonesome Man Blues	1956	12.50	25.00	50.00
❑ 5370	Cajun Doll/Mine Again	1960	10.00	20.00	40.00
❑ 5413	Drunk Again/Driving Nails	1960	6.25	12.50	25.00
❑ 5526	Sundown and Sorrow/If the Good Lord's Willing	1961	5.00	10.00	20.00
❑ 5685	I Told You So/Heaven All Around Me	1962	3.75	7.50	15.00
❑ 5723	Out of Control/Just About Then	1963	3.75	7.50	15.00
❑ 5762	Honky Tonk Heaven/Lonesome Man Blues	1963	3.75	7.50	15.00

SPEED

Number	Title (A Side/B Side)	Yr	VG	VG+	NM
❑ 101	Juke Joint Johnny/(B-side unknown)	1952	100.00	200.00	400.00

STARDAY

Number	Title (A Side/B Side)	Yr	VG	VG+	NM
❑ 403	You Never Looked Sweeter/Why Did You Lie to Me	1958	7.50	15.00	30.00
❑ 441	Too Hot to Handle/Just a-Waitin'	1959	7.50	15.00	30.00

MOORE, MELVIN
KING

Number	Title (A Side/B Side)	Yr	VG	VG+	NM
❑ 4539	Possessed/Hold Me, Kiss Me, Squeeze Me	1952	25.00	50.00	100.00

MOORE, RUDY
FEDERAL

Number	Title (A Side/B Side)	Yr	VG	VG+	NM
❑ 12253	My Little Angel/I'm Mad with You	1956	12.50	25.00	50.00
❑ 12259	The Buggy Ride/Ring-a-Ling-Dong	1956	12.50	25.00	50.00
❑ 12276	Step It Up and Go/Let Me Come Home	1956	25.00	50.00	100.00
❑ 12280	Bobbie Dobbie/I'll Be Home to See You Tomorrow Night	1956	12.50	25.00	50.00

MOORE, SAM
Also see SAM AND DAVE.

ATLANTIC

Number	Title (A Side/B Side)	Yr	VG	VG+	NM
❑ 2762	Give You Plenty Lovin'/Tennessee Waltz	1970	—	3.00	6.00
❑ 2791	Keep On Sockin' It To Me/Stop	1971	—	3.00	6.00
❑ 2814	Shop Around/If I Should Lose Your Love	1971	—	3.00	6.00

MOORE, SCOTTY
Original guitarist in ELVIS PRESLEY's backup band.

FERNWOOD

Number	Title (A Side/B Side)	Yr	VG	VG+	NM
❑ 107	Have Guitar Will Travel/Rest	1958	7.50	15.00	30.00

MORGAN, LOUMELL
ATLANTIC

Number	Title (A Side/B Side)	Yr	VG	VG+	NM
❑ 953	Charmaine/Jock-O-Mo	1952	50.00	100.00	200.00

MORGAN TWINS, THE
RCA VICTOR

Number	Title (A Side/B Side)	Yr	VG	VG+	NM
❑ 47-7300	TV Hop/This Feeling's Bound to Be Love	1958	6.25	12.50	25.00
❑ 47-7373	Let's Get Goin'/While It Lasted	1958	6.25	12.50	25.00

MORISSETTE, ALANIS
LAMOR

Number	Title (A Side/B Side)	Yr	VG	VG+	NM
❑ LMR-10-12	Fate Stay With Me/Find the Right Man	1987	62.50	125.00	250.00
❑ LMR-10-12 [PS]	Fate Stay With Me/Find the Right Man	1987	62.50	125.00	250.00
—As "Alanis"; Canadian release only, this was her first record					

MAVERICK

Number	Title (A Side/B Side)	Yr	VG	VG+	NM
❑ 17644	You Learn/You Oughta Know	1996	—	2.00	4.00
—B-side is "Live Grammy Version"					
❑ 17698	Ironic/Forgiven (Live)	1996	—	2.00	4.00

MORLEY, COZY
ABC-PARAMOUNT

Number	Title (A Side/B Side)	Yr	VG	VG+	NM
❑ 9811	I Love My Girl/Why Don't You Fall in Love	1957	6.25	12.50	25.00

MORRIS, JOE
ATLANTIC

Number	Title (A Side/B Side)	Yr	VG	VG+	NM
❑ 914	Any Time, Any Place, Any Where/Come Back Daddy Daddy	1950	125.00	250.00	500.00
—With Laura Tate...Atlantic's earliest number on 45. Morris had numerous 78s on Atlantic before 914, which are not listed here.					
❑ 985	I'm Goin' to Leave You/That's What Makes My Baby Fat	1953	25.00	50.00	100.00
❑ 1160	Going, Going, Gone/Sinner Woman	1957	5.00	10.00	20.00

HERALD

Number	Title (A Side/B Side)	Yr	VG	VG+	NM
❑ 420	Travelin' Man/No, It Can't Be Done	1954	10.00	20.00	40.00
—Black vinyl					
❑ 420	Travelin' Man/No, It Can't Be Done	1954	20.00	40.00	80.00
—Red vinyl					
❑ 446	Be Careful/Way Down Yonder	1955	7.50	15.00	30.00

MORRISON, VAN
Also see THEM.

BANG

Number	Title (A Side/B Side)	Yr	VG	VG+	NM
❑ 545	Brown Eyed Girl/Goodbye, Baby	1967	3.00	6.00	12.00
❑ 552	Chick-a-Boom/Ro Ro Rosey	1967	2.50	5.00	10.00
❑ 585	Spanish Rose/Midnight Special	1971	2.00	4.00	8.00

MERCURY

Number	Title (A Side/B Side)	Yr	VG	VG+	NM
❑ 880669-7	Haunts of Ancient Peace/Tore Down A La Rimbaud	1985	—	2.00	4.00
❑ 884841-7	Ivory Tower/New Kind of Man	1986	—	2.00	4.00

PHILCO-FORD

Number	Title (A Side/B Side)	Yr	VG	VG+	NM
❑ HP-16	Brown Eyed Girl/Midnight Special	1968	5.00	10.00	20.00

—4-inch plastic "Hip Pocket Record" with color sleeve

POINTBLANK

Number	Title (A Side/B Side)	Yr	VG	VG+	NM
❑ 38655	Precious Time/Jackie Wilson Said (I'm in Heaven When You Smile) (Live)	1999	—	2.00	4.00

POINTBLANK/VIRGIN/EXILE

Number	Title (A Side/B Side)	Yr	VG	VG+	NM
❑ 38754	No Way Pedro/Let's Talk About Us	2000	—	2.00	4.00

—With Linda Gail Lewis

WARNER BROS.

Number	Title (A Side/B Side)	Yr	VG	VG+	NM
❑ 7383	Come Running/Crazy Love	1970	—	3.00	6.00
❑ 7434	Domino/Sweet Janine	1970	—	3.00	6.00
❑ 7462	Blue Money/Sweet Thing	1971	—	3.00	6.00
❑ 7488	Call Me Up in Dreamland/Street Choir	1971	—	3.00	6.00
❑ 7518	Wild Night/When That Evening Sun Goes Down	1971	—	3.00	6.00
❑ 7543	Tupelo Honey/Starting a New Life	1971	—	3.00	6.00
❑ 7573	Straight to My Heart Like a Cannonball/Old Old Woodstock	1972	—	2.50	5.00
❑ 7616	Jackie Wilson Said (I'm in Heaven When You Smile)/You've Got the Power	1972	—	2.50	5.00
❑ 7638	Redwood Tree/Saint Dominic's Preview	1972	—	2.50	5.00
❑ 7665	Gypsy/Saint Dominic's Preview	1972	—	2.50	5.00
❑ 7706	Warm Love/I Will Be There	1973	—	2.50	5.00
❑ 7744	Green/Wild Children	1973	—	2.50	5.00
❑ 7786	Gloria/(B-side unknown)	1973	—	2.50	5.00
❑ 7797	Ain't Nothin' You Can Do/Wild Children	1974	—	2.50	5.00
❑ 8029	Bulbs/Cul-De-Sac	1974	—	2.50	5.00
❑ 8411	Joyous Sound/Mechanical Bliss	1977	—	2.50	5.00
❑ 8450	Moondance/Cold Wind in August	1977	—	2.50	5.00
❑ 8661	Wavelength/Checkin' It Out	1978	—	2.50	5.00
❑ 8743	Lifetimes/Natalia	1979	—	2.00	4.00
❑ 8805	Checkin' It Out/Kingdom Hall	1979	—	2.00	4.00
❑ 49086	Rolling Hills/Bright Side of the Road	1979	—	2.00	4.00
❑ 49162	Full Force Gale/You Make Me Feel So Free	1980	—	2.00	4.00
❑ 50031	Scandinavia/Cleaning Windows	1982	—	2.00	4.00

MORRISSEY

Also see THE SMITHS.

SIRE

Number	Title (A Side/B Side)	Yr	VG	VG+	NM
❑ 27837	Everyday Is Like Sunday/Disappointed	1988	—	3.00	6.00
❑ 27907	Suedehead/I Know Very Well How I Got My Name	1988	—	3.00	6.00

MORTIMER

PHILIPS

Number	Title (A Side/B Side)	Yr	VG	VG+	NM
❑ 40524	Dedicated Music Man/To Understand Someone	1968	2.00	4.00	8.00
❑ 40524 [PS]	Dedicated Music Man/To Understand Someone	1968	3.00	6.00	12.00
❑ 40567	Ingenue's Theme/Slicker Beauty Hints	1968	2.00	4.00	8.00

MOSES, JOHNNY

IMPERIAL

Number	Title (A Side/B Side)	Yr	VG	VG+	NM
❑ 5329	You're Torturing Me/Do You Love Me? Do You?	1955	10.00	20.00	40.00

MOSS, ROY

FASCINATION

Number	Title (A Side/B Side)	Yr	VG	VG+	NM
❑ 1002	Wiggle Walkin' Baby/(B-side unknown)	1957	50.00	100.00	200.00

MERCURY

Number	Title (A Side/B Side)	Yr	VG	VG+	NM
❑ 70770	You're My Big Baby Now/You Nearly Lost Your Mind	1955	50.00	100.00	200.00
❑ 70858	Corinne, Corinna/You Don't Know My Mind	1956	50.00	100.00	200.00

MOST, MICKIE

LAWN

Number	Title (A Side/B Side)	Yr	VG	VG+	NM
❑ 236	Sea Cruise/It's a Little Bit Hot	1964	5.00	10.00	20.00

MOTHER EARTH

Also see TRACY NELSON.

MERCURY

Number	Title (A Side/B Side)	Yr	VG	VG+	NM
❑ 72878	Down So Long/Goodbye Nelda Greeby	1968	2.00	4.00	8.00
❑ 72909	Mother Earth/I Did My Part	1969	2.00	4.00	8.00
❑ 72943	Painted Girls and Wine/Your Time's Comin'	1969	2.00	4.00	8.00

REPRISE

Number	Title (A Side/B Side)	Yr	VG	VG+	NM
❑ 1019	Soul of Sadness/Temptation Took Control of Me and I Fell	1971	—	3.00	6.00
❑ 1041	I'll Be Long Gone/Bring Me Home	1971	—	3.00	6.00

UNITED ARTISTS

Number	Title (A Side/B Side)	Yr	VG	VG+	NM
❑ 50303	Revolution/Stranger in My Own Home	1968	2.50	5.00	10.00

MOTHERS OF INVENTION, THE

See FRANK ZAPPA.

MOTIONS, THE (1)

ABC-PARAMOUNT

Number	Title (A Side/B Side)	Yr	VG	VG+	NM
❑ 10529	Big Chief/Where Is Your Heart	1964	3.00	6.00	12.00

CONGRESS

Number	Title (A Side/B Side)	Yr	VG	VG+	NM
❑ 237	It's Gone/I've Got Money	1965	3.00	6.00	12.00

MERCURY

Number	Title (A Side/B Side)	Yr	VG	VG+	NM
❑ 72297	Beatle Drums/Long Hair	1964	6.25	12.50	25.00
❑ 72368	I Can Dance/Land Beyond the Moon	1964	5.00	10.00	20.00
❑ 72413	Bumble Bee '65/Motions	1965	5.00	10.00	20.00

MOTIONS, THE (2)

LAURIE

Number	Title (A Side/B Side)	Yr	VG	VG+	NM
❑ 3112	Make Me a Love/Mr. Night	1961	30.00	60.00	120.00

MOTIONS, THE (3)

PHILIPS

Number	Title (A Side/B Side)	Yr	VG	VG+	NM
❑ 40624	Freedom/What's Your Name	1969	2.00	4.00	8.00

MOTLEY CRUE

ELEKTRA

Number	Title (A Side/B Side)	Yr	VG	VG+	NM
❑ 64985	Without You/Slice of Your Pie	1990	—	—	3.00
❑ 69248	Kickstart My Heart/She Goes Down	1990	—	—	3.00
❑ 69271	Dr. Feelgood/Sticky Sweet	1989	—	—	3.00
❑ 69271 [PS]	Dr. Feelgood/Sticky Sweet	1989	—	—	3.00
❑ 69429	You're All I Need/All in the Name	1987	—	—	3.00
❑ 69449	Wild Side/Five Years Dead	1987	—	—	3.00
❑ 69449 [PS]	Wild Side/Five Years Dead	1987	—	—	3.00
❑ 69465	Girls, Girls, Girls/Sumthin' for Nuthin'	1987	—	—	3.00
❑ 69465 [PS]	Girls, Girls, Girls/Sumthin' for Nuthin'	1987	—	—	3.00
❑ 69591	Home Sweet Home/Red Hot	1985	—	2.00	4.00
❑ 69625	Smokin' in the Boys' Room/Use It or Lose It	1985	—	2.00	4.00
❑ 69625 [PS]	Smokin' in the Boys' Room/Use It or Lose It	1985	—	2.00	4.00
❑ 69732	Too Young to Fall in Love/Take Me to the Top	1984	—	2.50	5.00
❑ 69732 [PS]	Too Young to Fall in Love/Take Me to the Top	1984	—	2.50	5.00
❑ 69756	Looks That Kill/Piece of Your Action	1984	—	2.50	5.00
❑ 69756 [PS]	Looks That Kill/Piece of Your Action	1984	—	2.50	5.00

LEATHUR

Number	Title (A Side/B Side)	Yr	VG	VG+	NM
❑ 001	Stick to Your Guns/Toast of the Town	1981	20.00	40.00	80.00
❑ 001 [PS]	Stick to Your Guns/Toast of the Town	1981	37.50	75.00	150.00

MOTT THE HOOPLE

Also see IAN HUNTER.

ATLANTIC

Number	Title (A Side/B Side)	Yr	VG	VG+	NM
❑ 2749	Rock and Roll Queen/Backsliding Fearlessly	1970	2.00	4.00	8.00

COLUMBIA

Number	Title (A Side/B Side)	Yr	VG	VG+	NM
❑ 10091	All the Young Dudes/Rose	1975	—	2.50	5.00
❑ 45673	All the Young Dudes/One of the Boys	1972	—	3.00	6.00

—A-side has altered lyrics from LP version to avoid British airplay ban on brand names; matrix number in dead wax ends in "1" plus a letter

Number	Title (A Side/B Side)	Yr	VG	VG+	NM
❑ 45673	All the Young Dudes/One of the Boys	1972	2.00	4.00	8.00

—A-side is the LP version with "Marks and Sparks"; matrix number ends in the number "2" plus a letter

Number	Title (A Side/B Side)	Yr	VG	VG+	NM
❑ 45673 [PS]	All the Young Dudes/One of the Boys	1972	5.00	10.00	20.00
❑ 45754	One of the Boys/Sucker	1973	—	2.50	5.00
❑ 45784	Sweet Jane/Jerkin' Crocus	1973	—	2.50	5.00
❑ 45882	Honaloochie Boogie/Rose	1973	—	2.50	5.00
❑ 45920	All the Way from Memphis/I Wish I Was Your Mother	1973	—	2.50	5.00
❑ 46035	The Golden Age of Rock 'N' Roll/Rest in Peace	1974	—	2.50	5.00
❑ 46076	Roll Away the Stone/Looking Glass	1974	—	2.50	5.00
❑ 74712	All the Young Dudes/Hanoloochie Boogie	1992	—	—	3.00

—Reissue

MOULD, BOB

Also see HUSKER DU.

VIRGIN

Number	Title (A Side/B Side)	Yr	VG	VG+	NM
❑ 99190	See a Little Light/All Those People Know	1989	—	2.00	4.00
❑ 99190	See a Little Light/All Those People Know	1989	—	3.00	6.00

MOUNTAIN

Also see FELIX PAPPALARDI; LESLIE WEST; WEST, BRUCE AND LAING.

COLUMBIA

Number	Title (A Side/B Side)	Yr	VG	VG+	NM
❑ 74711	Mississippi Queen/The Animal Trainer and the Toad	1992	—	—	3.00

—Reissue

WINDFALL

Number	Title (A Side/B Side)	Yr	VG	VG+	NM
❑ 532	Mississippi Queen/The Laird	1970	—	3.00	6.00
❑ 533	For Yasgur's Farm/To My Friend	1970	—	2.50	5.00
❑ 534	The Animal Trainer and the Toad/Tired Angels	1971	—	2.50	5.00
❑ 535	Silver Paper/Travelin' in the Dark	1971	—	2.50	5.00
❑ 536	Roll Over Beethoven/Crossroader	1971	—	2.50	5.00
❑ 537	Waiting to Take You Away/(B-side unknown)	1972	—	2.50	5.00

MOURNING REIGN, THE

CONTOUR

Number	Title (A Side/B Side)	Yr	VG	VG+	NM
❑ 601	Evil Hearted You/Get Out of My Life, Woman	1967	6.25	12.50	25.00

LINK

Number	Title (A Side/B Side)	Yr	VG	VG+	NM
❑ 1	Satisfaction Guaranteed/Our Fate	1966	7.50	15.00	30.00
❑ 1 [PS]	Satisfaction Guaranteed/Our Fate	1966	150.00	300.00	600.00
❑ 2	Evil Hearted You/Get Out of My Life, Woman	1966	7.50	15.00	30.00

7-Inch Extended Plays

SUNDAZED

Number	Title (A Side/B Side)	Yr	VG	VG+	NM
❑ SEP 115	*Satisfaction Guaranteed/Our Fate/Light Switch/ Cut Back	199?	—	—	2.00
❑ SEP 115 [PS]	The Mourning Reign	199?	—	—	2.00

MOUSE AND THE TRAPS

CAPITOL

Number	Title (A Side/B Side)	Yr	VG	VG+	NM
❑ 2460	Streets of a Dusty Town/Mouse	1969	2.50	5.00	10.00

FRATERNITY

Number	Title (A Side/B Side)	Yr	VG	VG+	NM
❑ 956	A Public Execution/All for You	1966	5.00	10.00	20.00
❑ 966	Mad of Sugar/I Am the One	1966	3.75	7.50	15.00
❑ 971	Would You Believe/Like I Know You Do	1966	3.75	7.50	15.00
❑ 973	Promises, Promises/Do the Best You Can	1966	3.75	7.50	15.00
❑ 989	Ya Ya/Cryin' Inside	1967	3.75	7.50	15.00
❑ 1000	Beg, Borrow, and Steal/L.O.V.E. Love	1967	3.75	7.50	15.00
❑ 1005	Sometimes You Just Can't Win/Cryin' Inside	1968	3.75	7.50	15.00
❑ 1005 [PS]	Sometimes You Just Can't Win/Cryin' Inside	1968	20.00	40.00	80.00
❑ 1011	I Satisfy/Good Times	1968	3.75	7.50	15.00
❑ 1015	Look at the Sun/Requiem for Sarah	1968	3.75	7.50	15.00

SMUDGE

Number	Title (A Side/B Side)	Yr	VG	VG+	NM
❑ 0703	Bottom Line/Gypsy Girl	1981	3.00	6.00	12.00

MOVE, THE

Also see ELECTRIC LIGHT ORCHESTRA; ROY WOOD.

A&M

Number	Title (A Side/B Side)	Yr	VG	VG+	NM
❑ 884	Flowers in the Rain/(Here We Go Round the) Lemon Tree	1967	3.00	6.00	12.00
❑ 914	Walk Upon the Water/Fire Brigade	1968	3.75	7.50	15.00
❑ 966	Yellow Rainbow/Something	1968	3.00	6.00	12.00
❑ 1020	Blackberry Way/Something	1969	3.00	6.00	12.00
❑ 1119	This Time Tomorrow/Curly	1969	3.00	6.00	12.00
❑ 1197	Brontosaurus/Lightning Never Strikes Twice	1970	3.00	6.00	12.00
❑ 1239	When Alice Comes Back to the Farm/What?	1971	3.00	6.00	12.00
❑ 1546	Zing Went the Strings of My Heart/Wild Tiger Woman	1974	2.50	5.00	10.00

CAPITOL

Number	Title (A Side/B Side)	Yr	VG	VG+	NM
❑ 3126	Tonight/Don't Mess Me Up	1971	5.00	10.00	20.00

DERAM

Number	Title (A Side/B Side)	Yr	VG	VG+	NM
❑ 7504	The Disturbance/Night of Fear	1967	3.75	7.50	15.00
❑ 7506	I Can Hear the Grass Grow/Wave the Flag and Stop the Train	1967	3.75	7.50	15.00

MGM

Number	Title (A Side/B Side)	Yr	VG	VG+	NM
❑ 14332 [DJ]	Chinatown/Down by the Bay	1971	5.00	10.00	20.00
—Evidently not released as stock copy					

UNITED ARTISTS

Number	Title (A Side/B Side)	Yr	VG	VG+	NM
❑ XW202	Tonight/My Marge	1973	—	3.00	6.00
❑ 50876	Chinatown/Down on the Bay	1972	2.00	4.00	8.00
❑ 50928	Do Ya/California Man	1972	2.00	4.00	8.00

MOVING SIDEWALKS, THE

With Billy Gibbons, later of ZZ TOP.

TANTARA

Number	Title (A Side/B Side)	Yr	VG	VG+	NM
❑ 3101	99th Floor/What Are You Going to Do	1967	10.00	20.00	40.00
❑ 3103	I Want to Hold Your Hand/Joe Blues	1968	10.00	20.00	40.00
❑ 3113	Flashback/(B-side unknown)	1969	7.50	15.00	30.00

WAND

Number	Title (A Side/B Side)	Yr	VG	VG+	NM
❑ 1156	99th Floor/What Are You Going to Do	1967	6.25	12.50	25.00
❑ 1167	Need Me/Every Night a New Surprise	1968	6.25	12.50	25.00

MRS. MILLS

CAPITOL

Number	Title (A Side/B Side)	Yr	VG	VG+	NM
❑ 4758	Bobbikins/Popcorn	1962	3.00	6.00	12.00

MUDCRUTCH

Early TOM PETTY AND THE HEARTBREAKERS.

PEPPER

Number	Title (A Side/B Side)	Yr	VG	VG+	NM
❑ 9449	Up in Mississippi/Cause Is Understood	1971	100.00	200.00	400.00

SHELTER

Number	Title (A Side/B Side)	Yr	VG	VG+	NM
❑ 40357	Depot Street/Wild Eyes	1975	7.50	15.00	30.00

MUDHONEY

AMPHETAMINE REPTILE

Number	Title (A Side/B Side)	Yr	VG	VG+	NM
❑ Scale 36	She's Just Fifteen/Jagged Time Lapse	1991	6.75	13.75	27.50
—B-side by Halo of Flies; burgundy vinyl					
❑ Scale 36	She's Just Fifteen/Jagged Time Lapse	1991	—	3.75	7.50
—B-side by Halo of Flies; black vinyl					
❑ Scale 36 [PS]	She's Just Fifteen/Jagged Time Lapse	1991	—	3.75	7.50
❑ Scale 76	Goat Cheese/Porn Weasel	1995	—	2.50	5.00
—B-side by Strapping Fieldhands					
❑ Scale 76 [PS]	Porn #3: Goat Cheese/Porn Weasel	1995	—	2.50	5.00

EMPTY

Number	Title (A Side/B Side)	Yr	VG	VG+	NM
❑ MT-166	You Stupid Asshole/Knife Manual	1991	—	3.00	6.00
—B-side by Gas Huffer; green vinyl					
❑ MT-166	You Stupid Asshole/Knife Manual	1991	—	3.00	6.00
—B-side by Gas Huffer; blue vinyl					
❑ MT-166 [PS]	You Stupid Asshole/Knife Manual	1991	—	3.00	6.00

FOX

Number	Title (A Side/B Side)	Yr	VG	VG+	NM
❑ 10012	Pump It Up/Stomp	1994	—	2.50	5.00
—B-side by George Clinton/Parliament Funkadelic					
❑ 10012 [PS]	Pump It Up/Stomp	1994	—	2.50	5.00
—B-side by George Clinton/Parliament Funkadelic					

MAKE 'EM BLEED AND SUFFER

Number	Title (A Side/B Side)	Yr	VG	VG+	NM
❑ (no #)	Hate the Police (Live)/Symptom of the Universe	1988	6.25	12.50	25.00
—B-side by the Melvins					
❑ (no #) [PS]	Hate the Police (Live)/Symptom of the Universe	1988	6.25	12.50	25.00
—Actually a large envelope that contained this single, which was enclosed in a Japanese porno magazine					

REPRISE

Number	Title (A Side/B Side)	Yr	VG	VG+	NM
❑ PRO-S-5740 [DJ]	Suck You Dry/Deception Pass	1992	3.75	7.50	15.00
❑ PRO-S-6025 [DJ]	Blinding Sun/King Sandbox	1993	3.75	7.50	15.00

SUB POP

Number	Title (A Side/B Side)	Yr	VG	VG+	NM
❑ 18	Touch Me I'm Sick/Sweet Young Thing	1988	22.50	45.00	90.00
—First 800 were pressed on brown vinyl					
❑ 18	Touch Me I'm Sick/Sweet Young Thing	1988	25.00	50.00	100.00
—Standard black vinyl pressing, toilet label					
❑ 18	Touch Me I'm Sick/Sweet Young Thing	1988	50.00	100.00	200.00
—Any of accidental purple, red, yellow or blueish vinyl pressings					
❑ 18	Touch Me I'm Sick/Sweet Young Thing	1988	—	3.75	7.50
—Regular Sub Pop label, black vinyl					
❑ 18 [PS]	Touch Me I'm Sick/Sweet Young Thing	1988	—	3.75	7.50
—Only accompanied regular Sub Pop label pressings					
❑ 26	Halloween/Touch Me I'm Sick	1988	12.50	25.00	50.00
—B-side by Sonic Youth; first 500 on clear vinyl					
❑ 26	Halloween/Touch Me I'm Sick	1988	3.75	7.50	15.00
—B-side by Sonic Youth; last 2,500 on black vinyl					
❑ 26 [PS]	Halloween/Touch Me I'm Sick	1988	5.00	10.00	20.00
—#2 in Sub Pop Singles Club series					
❑ 33	You Got It/Burn It Clean	1989	2.50	5.00	10.00
❑ 33	You Got It/Burn It Clean	1989	3.75	7.50	15.00
—White vinyl					
❑ 33 [PS]	You Got It/Burn It Clean	1989	6.25	12.50	25.00
—Foldout poster sleeve					
❑ 33 [PS]	You Got It/Burn It Clean	1989	—	2.50	5.00
—Regular picture sleeve					
❑ 44a	This Gift/Baby Help Me Forget	1989	—	2.50	5.00
❑ 44a	This Gift/Baby Help Me Forget	1989	7.50	15.00	30.00
—Purple vinyl					
❑ 44a [PS]	This Gift/Baby Help Me Forget	1989	—	2.50	5.00
❑ 63	You're Gone//Thorn/You Make Me Die	1990	5.00	10.00	20.00
—First 3,000 on pink vinyl					
❑ 63	You're Gone//Thorn/You Make Me Die	1990	—	2.50	5.00
❑ 63 [PS]	You're Gone//Thorn/You Make Me Die	1990	—	2.50	5.00
❑ 95	Let It Slide//Ounce of Deception/Checkout Time	1991	6.25	12.50	25.00
—Clear chartreuse vinyl					
❑ 95	Let It Slide//Ounce of Deception/Checkout Time	1991	—	—	3.00
❑ 95 [PS]	Let It Slide//Ounce of Deception/Checkout Time	1991	—	2.50	5.00
❑ 248	Tonight I'm Gonna Go Downtown/Blinding Sun	1994	—	3.75	7.50
—B-side by Jimmie Dale Gilmore					
❑ 248 [PS]	Tonight I'm Gonna Go Downtown/Blinding Sun	1994	—	3.75	7.50
—B-side by Jimmie Dale Gilmore					

SUPER ELECTRO

Number	Title (A Side/B Side)	Yr	VG	VG+	NM
❑ SE 708	Into Your Shtik/You Give Me the Creeps	1995	—	—	3.00
❑ SE 708 [PS]	Into Your Shtik/You Give Me the Creeps	1995	—	—	3.00
❑ SE 716	Night of the Hunted/Brand New Face	1998	—	—	2.50
❑ SE 716 [PS]	Night of the Hunted/Brand New Face	1998	—	—	2.50

WARNER BROS.

Number	Title (A Side/B Side)	Yr	VG	VG+	NM
❑ PRO-S-5652 [DJ]	Who Is Who/Heat	1992	3.75	7.50	15.00
—Part of "Soil X Samples" series; orange vinyl; B-side by the Jesus and Mary Chain					

MUDLARKS, THE

ROULETTE

Number	Title (A Side/B Side)	Yr	VG	VG+	NM
❑ 4143	Love Game/My Grandfather's Clock	1959	3.00	6.00	12.00

MUDSLINGER, ROGER

RED BIRD

Number	Title (A Side/B Side)	Yr	VG	VG+	NM
❑ 10-013	The Election Year 1964 (Part 1)/The Election Year 1964 (Part 2)	1964	5.00	10.00	20.00

MUGWUMPS, THE

Also see DENNY DOHERTY; CASS ELLIOT; ZALMAN YANOVSKY.

SIDEWALK

Number	Title (A Side/B Side)	Yr	VG	VG+	NM
❑ 900	Bald Headed Woman/Jug Band Music	1966	6.25	12.50	25.00
❑ 909	Season of the Witch/My Gal	1967	5.00	10.00	20.00

WARNER BROS.

Number	Title (A Side/B Side)	Yr	VG	VG+	NM
❑ 5471	I'll Remember Tonight/I Don't Wanna Know	1964	3.75	7.50	15.00
❑ 7018	Searchin'/Here It Is, Another Day	1967	2.50	5.00	10.00

MULBERRY FRUIT BAND, THE

BUDDAH

Number	Title (A Side/B Side)	Yr	VG	VG+	NM
❑ 1	Yes, We Have No Bananas/The Audition	1967	3.00	6.00	12.00

MULL, MARTIN

ABC

Number	Title (A Side/B Side)	Yr	VG	VG+	NM
❑ 12251	Boogie Man/Bombed Away	1977	—	2.50	5.00
❑ 12304	Humming Song/Get Up, Get Down	1977	—	2.50	5.00

CAPRICORN

Number	Title (A Side/B Side)	Yr	VG	VG+	NM
❑ 0019	Dueling Tubas/2001 Polkas	1973	2.00	4.00	8.00
❑ 0024	In the Eyes of My Dog (Part 1)/In the Eyes of My Dog (Part 2)	1973	2.00	4.00	8.00
❑ 0037	Santafly/Santa Doesn't Cop Out On Dope	1973	3.00	6.00	12.00
❑ 0241	Do the Dog/Thousands of Girls	1975	2.00	4.00	8.00
❑ 0282	Santafly/Santa Doesn't Cop Out On Dope	1977	2.50	5.00	10.00

ELEKTRA

Number	Title (A Side/B Side)	Yr	VG	VG+	NM
❑ 46056	The Fruit Song/Pig in a Blanket	1979	—	2.50	5.00
❑ 46057	Bernie Don't Disco/Bun and Run Part 1 and 3	1979	—	2.50	5.00

MULLINS, SHAWN

COLUMBIA

Number	Title (A Side/B Side)	Yr	VG	VG+	NM
❑ 79080	Lullaby/The Gulf of Mexico	1998	—	—	3.00

MULTIPLICATION ROCK (SOUNDTRACK)

CAPITOL

Number	Title (A Side/B Side)	Yr	VG	VG+	NM
❑ 3693	Naughty Number Nine/I Got Six	1973	3.75	7.50	15.00

MUNGO JERRY

BELL

Number	Title (A Side/B Side)	Yr	VG	VG+	NM
❑ 45123	Lady Rose/Little Louis	1971	—	2.00	4.00
❑ 45383	Alright, Alright, Alright/Little Miss Hipshake	1973	—	2.00	4.00
❑ 45427	Wild Love/Glad I'm a Rocker	1973	—	2.00	4.00
❑ 45451	Long Legged Woman Dressed in Black/Gonna Bop Till I Drop	1974	—	2.00	4.00

JANUS

Number	Title (A Side/B Side)	Yr	VG	VG+	NM
❑ 125	In the Summertime/Mighty Man	1970	—	3.00	6.00
❑ 128	Johnny B. Badde/My Friend	1970	—	2.50	5.00
❑ 148	Baby Jump/The Man Beside the Piano	1971	—	2.50	5.00

PYE

Number	Title (A Side/B Side)	Yr	VG	VG+	NM
❑ 65003	You Don't Have to Be in the Army/O'Reilly	1972	—	2.00	4.00
❑ 65009	Going Back Home/Open Up	1972	—	2.00	4.00
❑ 71032	In the Summertime/(B-side unknown)	1975	—	2.00	4.00

MUNSTERS, THE

DECCA

Number	Title (A Side/B Side)	Yr	VG	VG+	NM
❑ 31670	Munster Creep/Make It Go Away	1964	5.00	10.00	20.00

MURMAIDS, THE

CHATTAHOOCHIE

Number	Title (A Side/B Side)	Yr	VG	VG+	NM
❑ 628	Popsicles and Icicles/Blue Dress	1963	5.00	10.00	20.00
❑ 628	Popsicles and Icicles/Huntington Flats	1963	3.75	7.50	15.00
❑ 628	Popsicles and Icicles/Bunny Stomp	1963	3.75	7.50	15.00
❑ 628	Popsicles and Icicles/Comedy and Tragedy	1963	3.75	7.50	15.00
❑ 636	Heartbreak Ahead/He's Good to Me	1964	2.50	5.00	10.00
❑ 641	Wild and Wonderful/Bull Talk	1964	2.50	5.00	10.00
❑ 668	Stuffed Animals/Little White Lies	1965	2.50	5.00	10.00
❑ 711	Little Boys/Go Away	1966	2.50	5.00	10.00

LIBERTY

Number	Title (A Side/B Side)	Yr	VG	VG+	NM
❑ 56069	Paper Sun/Song Through Perception	1968	—	—	—
—Unreleased					
❑ 56078	Paper Sun/Song Through Perception	1968	2.50	5.00	10.00

MURPHY, KEITH, AND THE DAZE

KING

Number	Title (A Side/B Side)	Yr	VG	VG+	NM
❑ 6171	Dirty Ol' Sam/Slightly Reminiscent of Her	1968	25.00	50.00	100.00

MURRAY, ANNE

CAPITOL

Number	Title (A Side/B Side)	Yr	VG	VG+	NM
❑ 2738	Snowbird/Just Bidin' My Time	1970	—	3.00	6.00
❑ 2988	Sing High — Sing Low/Days of the Looking Glass	1970	—	2.50	5.00
❑ 3059	A Stranger in My Place/Sycamore Slick	1971	—	2.50	5.00
❑ 3082	Put Your Hand in the Hand/It Takes Time	1971	—	2.50	5.00

Number	Title (A Side/B Side)	Yr	VG	VG+	NM
❑ 3159	Talk It Over in the Morning/Head Above the Water	1971	—	2.50	5.00
❑ 3260	Cotton Jenny/Destiny	1972	—	2.50	5.00
❑ 3352	Bobbie's Song for Jesus/You Can't Have a Hand on Me	1972	—	2.50	5.00
❑ 3481	Danny's Song/Drown Me	1972	—	2.00	4.00
❑ 3600	What About Me/Let Sunshine Have Its Day	1973	—	2.00	4.00
❑ 3648	Send a Little Love My Way/Head Above the Water	1973	—	2.00	4.00
❑ 3776	Love Song/You Can't Go Back	1973	—	2.00	4.00
❑ 3867	You Won't See Me/He Thinks I Still Care	1974	—	2.50	5.00
❑ 3955	Just One Look/Son of a Rotten Gambler	1974	—	2.00	4.00
❑ 4000	Day Tripper/Lullaby	1974	—	2.00	4.00
❑ 4025	Uproar/Lift Your Hearts to the Sun	1975	—	2.00	4.00
❑ 4072	A Stranger in My Place/Dream Lover	1975	—	2.00	4.00
❑ 4142	Sunday Sunrise/Out on the Road Again	1975	—	2.00	4.00
❑ 4207	The Call/Lady Bug	1976	—	2.00	4.00
❑ 4265	Golden Oldie/Together	1976	—	2.00	4.00
❑ 4329	Things/Caress Me Pretty Music	1976	—	2.00	4.00
❑ 4375	Sunday School to Broadway/Dancin' All Night Long	1976	—	2.00	4.00
❑ 4402	Canterbury Song/Shilo Song	1977	—	2.00	4.00
—With Gene MacLellan					
❑ 4527	Walk Right Back/A Million More	1978	—	2.00	4.00
❑ 4574	You Needed Me/I Still Wish the Very Best for You	1978	—	2.00	4.00
❑ 4675	I Just Fall in Love Again/Just to Feel This Love from You	1979	—	2.00	4.00
❑ 4675 [PS]	I Just Fall in Love Again/Just to Feel This Love from You	1979	—	2.50	5.00
❑ 4716	Shadows in the Moonlight/Yucatan Cafe	1979	—	2.00	4.00
❑ 4773	Broken Hearted Me/Why Don't You Stick Around	1979	—	2.00	4.00
❑ 4813	Daydream Believer/Do You Think of Me	1979	—	2.00	4.00
❑ 4848	Lucky Me/Somebody's Waiting	1980	—	2.00	4.00
❑ 4878	I'm Happy Just to Dance with You/What's Forever For	1980	—	2.00	4.00
❑ 4920	Could I Have This Dance/Somebody's Waiting	1980	—	2.00	4.00
❑ 4920 [PS]	Could I Have This Dance/Somebody's Waiting	1980	—	2.50	5.00
❑ 4987	Blessed Are the Believers/Only Love	1981	—	2.00	4.00
❑ 4987 [PS]	Blessed Are the Believers/Only Love	1981	—	2.50	5.00
❑ A-5013	We Don't Have to Hold Out/Call Me with the News	1981	—	2.00	4.00
❑ A-5023	It's All I Can Do/If a Heart Must Be Broken	1981	—	2.00	4.00
❑ A-5083	Another Sleepless Night/It Should Have Been Easy	1982	—	2.00	4.00
❑ B-5145	Hey! Baby!/Song for the Mira	1982	—	—	3.00
❑ B-5183	Somebody's Always Saying Goodbye/That'll Keep Me Dreamin'	1982	—	—	3.00
❑ B-5264	A Little Good News/I'm Not Afraid Anymore	1983	—	—	3.00
❑ B-5264 [PS]	A Little Good News/I'm Not Afraid Anymore	1983	—	2.50	5.00
❑ B-5305	That's Not the Way (It's S'posed to Be)/The More We Try	1983	—	—	3.00
❑ B-5344	Just Another Woman in Love/Heart Stealer	1984	—	—	3.00
❑ B-5384	Let Your Heart Do the Talking/I Don't Think I'm Ready for You	1984	—	—	3.00
❑ B-5401	Nobody Loves Me Like You Do/Love You Out of Your Mind	1984	—	—	3.00
—A-side: With Dave Loggins					
❑ B-5436	Time Don't Run Out on Me/Let Your Heart Do the Talking	1985	—	—	3.00
❑ B-5472	I Don't Think I'm Ready for You/Take Good Care of My Baby	1985	—	—	3.00
❑ B-5472 [PS]	I Don't Think I'm Ready for You/Take Good Care of My Baby	1985	—	2.00	4.00
❑ B-5536	Go Tell It On the Mountain/O Holy Night	1985	—	2.00	4.00
❑ B-5536 [PS]	Go Tell It On the Mountain/O Holy Night	1985	—	2.50	5.00
❑ B-5547	Now and Forever (You and Me)/I Don't Wanna Spend Another Night Without You	1986	—	—	3.00
❑ B-5547 [PS]	Now and Forever (You and Me)/I Don't Wanna Spend Another Night Without You	1986	—	2.00	4.00
❑ B-5576	Who's Leaving Who/Reach for Me	1986	—	—	3.00
❑ B-5610	My Life's a Dance/Call Us Fools	1986	—	—	3.00
❑ B-5655	On and On/Gotcha	1986	—	—	3.00
❑ SPRO-9723 [DJ]	Christmas Medley: Silver Bells/I'll Be Home for Christmas/Winter Wonderland (same on both sides)	1981	2.00	4.00	8.00
❑ B-44005	Are You Still in Love with Me/Give Me Your Love	1987	—	—	3.00
❑ B-44053	Anyone Can Do the Heartbreak/Without You	1987	—	—	3.00
❑ B-44134	Perfect Strangers/It Happens All the Time	1988	—	—	3.00
—With Doug Mallory					
❑ B-44219	Flying On Your Own/Slow All Night	1988	—	—	3.00
❑ B-44272	Slow Passin' Time/Flying on Your Own	1989	—	—	3.00
❑ B-44341	Who But You/You Make Me Curious	1989	—	—	3.00
❑ B-44432	If I Ever Fall in Love Again/Just Another Woman in Love	1989	—	—	3.00
—A-side: With Kenny Rogers					
❑ B-44495	I'd Fall in Love Tonight/Now and Forever (You and Me)	1989	—	—	3.00
❑ 7PRO-79189	Feed This Fire (same on both sides)	1990	2.00	4.00	8.00
—Vinyl is promo only					

SBK

Number	Title (A Side/B Side)	Yr	VG	VG+	NM
❑ S7-18912	Winter Wonderland/The Little Drummer Boy	1995	—	—	3.00

MURRAY, ANNE, AND GLEN CAMPBELL

Also see each artist's individual listings.

CAPITOL

Number	Title (A Side/B Side)	Yr	VG	VG+	NM
❑ 3200	I Say a Little Prayer-By the Time I Get to Phoenix/All Through the Night	1971	—	2.50	5.00
❑ 3287	United We Stand/Ease Your Pain	1972	—	2.50	5.00

MURRAY, JACK

LAURIE

Number	Title (A Side/B Side)	Yr	VG	VG+	NM
❑ 3199	Surfin' with Me/What Do You Think of Me Baby	1963	3.75	7.50	15.00

MURRAY, RAY, AND THE DYNAMICS

ARBO

Number	Title (A Side/B Side)	Yr	VG	VG+	NM
❑ 222	With All My Love/Baby, What You Want Me to Do	1960	25.00	50.00	100.00

MURRAY THE "K"

BRS

Number	Title (A Side/B Side)	Yr	VG	VG+	NM
❑ 1/2	Murray the "K" and The Beatles As It Happened	1964	10.00	20.00	40.00
❑ 1/2 [PS]	Murray the "K" and The Beatles As It Happened	1964	30.00	60.00	120.00

IBC

Number	Title (A Side/B Side)	Yr	VG	VG+	NM
❑ F4KM-0082/3	Murray the "K" and The Beatles As It Happened	1976	2.50	5.00	10.00
❑ F4KM-0082/3 [PS]	Murray the "K" and The Beatles As It Happened	1976	2.50	5.00	10.00

RED BIRD

Number	Title (A Side/B Side)	Yr	VG	VG+	NM
❑ 10-045	It's What's Happening, Baby/Sins of a Family	1966	3.75	7.50	15.00

MUSIC EXPLOSION, THE

ATTACK

Number	Title (A Side/B Side)	Yr	VG	VG+	NM
❑ 1404	The Little Black Egg/Stay By My Side	1966	6.25	12.50	25.00

LAURIE

Number	Title (A Side/B Side)	Yr	VG	VG+	NM
❑ 3380	Little Bit O'Soul/I See the Light	1967	3.00	6.00	12.00
❑ 3400	Can't Stop Now/Sunshine Games	1967	2.00	4.00	8.00
❑ 3414	We Gotta Go Home/Hearts and Flowers	1967	2.00	4.00	8.00
❑ 3429	What You Want/Road Runner	1968	2.00	4.00	8.00
❑ 3440	Where Are We Going/Flash	1968	2.00	4.00	8.00
❑ 3454	Yes Sir/Dazzling	1968	2.00	4.00	8.00
❑ 3466	Jack in the Box/Rewind	1968	2.00	4.00	8.00
❑ 3479	What's Your Name/Call Me Anything	1969	2.00	4.00	8.00
❑ 3500	The Little Black Egg/Stay By My Side	1969	2.00	4.00	8.00

MUSIC MACHINE, THE

Also see T.S. BONNIWELL.

BELL

Number	Title (A Side/B Side)	Yr	VG	VG+	NM
❑ 764	Mother Nature—Father Earth/Advise and Consent	1969	2.00	4.00	8.00

ORIGINAL SOUND

Number	Title (A Side/B Side)	Yr	VG	VG+	NM
❑ (no #)	The Music Machine	1967	2.50	5.00	10.00
—Custom sleeve, large center hole, not assigned to any one record, with pictures of band members on front and ads for "Oldies But Goodies" LPs on back					
❑ 61	Talk Talk/Come On In	1966	3.00	6.00	12.00
❑ 67	The People in Me/Masculine Institution	1967	2.50	5.00	10.00
❑ 71	Double Yellow Line/Absolutely Positive	1967	2.50	5.00	10.00
❑ 75	I've Loved You/The Eagle Never Hunts the Fly	1967	2.50	5.00	10.00
❑ 82	Hey Joe/Wrong	1968	2.50	5.00	10.00

SUNDAZED

Number	Title (A Side/B Side)	Yr	VG	VG+	NM
❑ 131	Point of No Return/King Mixer	199?	—	—	2.00
❑ 131 [PS]	Point of No Return/King Mixer	199?	—	—	2.00

WARNER BROS.

Number	Title (A Side/B Side)	Yr	VG	VG+	NM
❑ 7093	Bottom of the Soul/Astrologically Incompatible	1968	2.00	4.00	8.00
❑ 7093 [PS]	Bottom of the Soul/Astrologically Incompatible	1968	3.75	7.50	15.00
❑ 7199	To the Light/You'll Love Me Again	1968	2.00	4.00	8.00

MUSICAL CAST OF TOYS, THE

Featuring WENDY AND LISA, with a guest vocal by Seal.

GEFFEN

Number	Title (A Side/B Side)	Yr	VG	VG+	NM
❑ 19146	The Closing of the Year/(instrumental)	1992	—	2.00	4.00

MYDDLE CLASS, THE

BUDDAH

Number	Title (A Side/B Side)	Yr	VG	VG+	NM
❑ 150	I Happen to Love You/Don't Let Me Sleep Too Long	1969	2.50	5.00	10.00

TOMORROW

Number	Title (A Side/B Side)	Yr	VG	VG+	NM
❑ 912	Don't Look Back/Wind Chimes Laughter	1966	5.00	10.00	20.00
❑ 7501	Gates of Eden/Free As the Wind	1966	5.00	10.00	20.00
❑ 7503	I Happen to Love You/Don't Let Me Sleep Too Long	1966	6.25	12.50	25.00

MYLES, BILLY

DOT

Number	Title (A Side/B Side)	Yr	VG	VG+	NM
❑ 15809	King of Clowns/So In Need of You	1958	5.00	10.00	20.00

EMBER

Number	Title (A Side/B Side)	Yr	VG	VG+	NM
❑ 1026	The Joker (That's What They Call Me)/Honey Bee	1957	7.50	15.00	30.00
❑ 1040	Price of Your Love/I'm Too Sentimental	1958	6.25	12.50	25.00
❑ 1046	I'm Gonna Walk/Price of Your Love	1958	6.25	12.50	25.00

KING

Number	Title (A Side/B Side)	Yr	VG	VG+	NM
❑ 5395	Dance Little Girlie/Two Empty Arms	1960	3.75	7.50	15.00

MYSTERY TOUR, THE

MGM

Number	Title (A Side/B Side)	Yr	VG	VG+	NM
❑ 14097	The Ballad of Paul/The Ballad of Paul (Follow the Bouncing Ball)	1969	6.25	12.50	25.00

MYSTICS, THE

AMBIENT SOUND

Number	Title (A Side/B Side)	Yr	VG	VG+	NM
❑ 02871	Now That Summer Is Here/Prayer to An Angel	1982	—	2.50	5.00

BLACK CAT

Number	Title (A Side/B Side)	Yr	VG	VG+	NM
❑ 101	Snoopy/Ooh Poo Pah Doo	1966	10.00	20.00	40.00

CONSTELLATION

Number	Title (A Side/B Side)	Yr	VG	VG+	NM
❑ 138	She's Got Everything/Just a Loser	1964	3.00	6.00	12.00

DOT

Number	Title (A Side/B Side)	Yr	VG	VG+	NM
❑ 16862	Now and For Always/Didn't We Have a Good Time	1966	2.50	5.00	10.00

KING

Number	Title (A Side/B Side)	Yr	VG	VG+	NM
❑ 5678	Mashed Potatoes With Me/The Hoppy Hop	1962	3.75	7.50	15.00
❑ 5735	The Jumpin' Bean/Just For Your Love	1963	3.75	7.50	15.00

LAURIE

Number	Title (A Side/B Side)	Yr	VG	VG+	NM
❑ 3028 [M]	Hushabye/Adam and Eve	1959	7.50	15.00	30.00
❑ S-3028 [S]	Hushabye/Adam and Eve	1959	30.00	60.00	120.00
❑ 3038	Don't Take the Stars/So Tenderly	1959	6.25	12.50	25.00
❑ 3047	All Through the Night/To Think of You Again	1960	6.25	12.50	25.00
❑ 3058	White Cliffs of Dover/Blue Star	1960	6.25	12.50	25.00
❑ 3086	Star Crossed Lovers/Goodbye Mr. Blue	1961	6.25	12.50	25.00
❑ 3104	Sunday Kind of Love/Darling I Know How	1961	7.50	15.00	30.00

NOLTA

Number	Title (A Side/B Side)	Yr	VG	VG+	NM
❑ 353	The Fox/Dan	1963	3.75	7.50	15.00

N

'N SYNC

JIVE

Number	Title (A Side/B Side)	Yr	VG	VG+	NM
❑ 42694	Bye Bye Bye (same on both sides)	2000	—	2.00	4.00
❑ 42695	It's Gonna Be Me (same on both sides)	2000	—	2.00	4.00
❑ 42747	This I Promise You/Yo Te Voy A Amar (This I Promise You)	2000	—	—	3.00

RCA

Number	Title (A Side/B Side)	Yr	VG	VG+	NM
❑ 65469	I Want You Back/Tearin' Up My Heart	1998	—	—	3.00
❑ 65721	(God Must Have Spent) A Little More Time on You/Drive Myself Crazy	1999	—	—	3.00

NABAY

IMPACT

Number	Title (A Side/B Side)	Yr	VG	VG+	NM
❑ 1032	Believe It or Not/(Instrumental)	1967	100.00	200.00	400.00

NAPOLEON XIV

WARNER BROS.

Number	Title (A Side/B Side)	Yr	VG	VG+	NM
❑ 5831	They're Coming to Take Me Away, Ha-Haaa!/ !Aaah-Ah, Yawa Em Ekat ot Gnimoc Er'yeht	1966	3.00	6.00	12.00
❑ 5853	I'm in Love with My Little Red Tricycle/Doin' the Napoleon	1966	2.50	5.00	10.00
❑ 7726	They're Coming to Take Me Away, Ha-Haaa!/ !Aaah-Ah, Yawa Em Ekat ot Gnimoc Er'yeht	1973	2.00	4.00	8.00

NASH, GRAHAM

Also see CROSBY, STILLS AND NASH; CROSBY, STILLS, NASH & YOUNG; THE HOLLIES.

ATLANTIC

Number	Title (A Side/B Side)	Yr	VG	VG+	NM
❑ 2804	Chicago/Simple Man	1971	—	3.00	6.00
❑ 2827	Military Madness/Sleep Song	1971	—	2.50	5.00
❑ 2840	Used to Be a King/Wounded Bird	1971	—	2.50	5.00
❑ 2990	Prison Song/Hey You (Looking at the Moon)	1973	—	2.50	5.00
❑ 89373	Chippin' Away/Newday	1986	—	—	3.00
❑ 89396	Sad Eyes/Newday	1986	—	—	3.00
❑ 89434	Innocent Eyes/I Got a Rock	1986	—	—	3.00
❑ 89434 [PS]	Innocent Eyes/I Got a Rock	1986	—	2.00	4.00

CAPITOL

Number	Title (A Side/B Side)	Yr	VG	VG+	NM
❑ 4812	In the 80's/T.V. Guide	1979	—	2.00	4.00
❑ 4849	Helicopter Song/Out on the Island	1980	—	2.00	4.00
❑ 4879	Earth and Sky/Magical Child	1980	—	2.00	4.00

NASH, GRAHAM, AND DAVID CROSBY

Also see each artist's individual listings.

ABC

Number	Title (A Side/B Side)	Yr	VG	VG+	NM
❑ 12140	Carry Me/Mama Lion	1975	—	2.00	4.00
❑ 12165	Bittersweet/Take the Money and Run	1976	—	2.00	4.00
❑ 12185	Love Workout/Bittersweet	1976	—	2.00	4.00
❑ 12199	Out of the Darkness/Broken Bird	1976	—	2.00	4.00
❑ 12217	Foolish Man/Spotlight	1976	—	2.00	4.00

ATLANTIC

Number	Title (A Side/B Side)	Yr	VG	VG+	NM
❑ 2070	Immigration Man/Whole Cloth	1972		2.50	5.00
❑ 2892	Southbound Train/The Wall Song	1972	—	2.50	5.00

NASH, JOHNNY

Also see PAUL ANKA/GEORGE HAMILTON IV/JOHNNY NASH.

ABC-PARAMOUNT

Number	Title (A Side/B Side)	Yr	VG	VG+	NM
❑ 9743	Out of Town/A Teenager Sings the Blues	1956	5.00	10.00	20.00
❑ 9844	The Ladder of Love/I'll Walk Alone	1957	5.00	10.00	20.00
❑ 9874	A Very Special Love/Won't You Let Me Share My Love with You	1957	5.00	10.00	20.00
❑ 9894	My Pledge to You/It's So Easy to Say	1958	5.00	10.00	20.00
❑ 9927	Please Don't Go/I Lost My Love Last Night	1958	5.00	10.00	20.00
❑ 9942	Truly Love/You're Looking at Me	1958	5.00	10.00	20.00
❑ 9960	Almost in Your Arms/Midnight Moonlight	1958	5.00	10.00	20.00
❑ 9989	Roots of Heaven/Walk with Faith in Your Heart	1958	5.00	10.00	20.00
❑ 9996	As Time Goes By/The Voice of Love	1959	5.00	10.00	20.00
❑ 9996 [PS]	As Time Goes By/The Voice of Love	1959	10.00	20.00	40.00
❑ 10026	And the Angels Sing/Baby, Baby, Baby	1959	5.00	10.00	20.00
❑ 10046	Take a Giant Step/But Not for Me	1959	5.00	10.00	20.00
❑ 10060	The Wish/Too Proud	1959	5.00	10.00	20.00
❑ 10076	A Place in the Sun/Goodbye	1960	3.75	7.50	15.00
❑ 10095	Never My Love/(You've Got the) Love I Love	1960	3.75	7.50	15.00
❑ 10112	Let the Rest of the World Go By/Music of Love	1960	3.75	7.50	15.00
❑ 10137	(Looks Like) The End of the World/We Kissed	1960	3.75	7.50	15.00
❑ 10160	Kisses/Somebody	1960	3.75	7.50	15.00
❑ 10181	World of Tears/Some of Your Lovin'	1961	3.00	6.00	12.00
❑ 10205	I Need Someone to Stand By/A House on the Hill	1961	3.00	6.00	12.00
❑ 10212	A Thousand Miles Away/I Need Someone to Stand By Me	1961	3.00	6.00	12.00
❑ 10230	I'm Counting on You/I Lost My Baby	1961	3.00	6.00	12.00
❑ 10251	Too Much Love/Love's Young Dream	1961	3.00	6.00	12.00

ARGO

Number	Title (A Side/B Side)	Yr	VG	VG+	NM
❑ 5471	Talk to Me/Love Ain't Nothin'	1964	2.00	4.00	8.00
❑ 5479	Then You Can Tell Me Goodbye/Always	1964	2.00	4.00	8.00
❑ 5492	Spring Is Here/Strange Feeling	1965	2.00	4.00	8.00
❑ 5501	Teardrops in the Rain/I Know What I Want	1965	2.00	4.00	8.00

ATLANTIC

Number	Title (A Side/B Side)	Yr	VG	VG+	NM
❑ 2344	Big City/Somewhere	1966	2.00	4.00	8.00

CADET

Number	Title (A Side/B Side)	Yr	VG	VG+	NM
❑ 5528	Teardrops in the Rain/Get Myself Together	1966	5.00	10.00	20.00

EPIC

Number	Title (A Side/B Side)	Yr	VG	VG+	NM
❑ 10873	Stir It Up/Cream Puff	1972	—	3.50	7.00
❑ 10902	I Can See Clearly Now/How Good It Is	1972	—	3.00	6.00
❑ 10949	Stir It Up/Ooh Baby You've Been Good to Me	1973	—	3.00	6.00
❑ 11003	My Merry-Go-Round/We're Trying to Get Back to You	1973	—	2.50	5.00
❑ 11034	Ooh What a Feeling/Yellow House	1973	—	2.50	5.00
❑ 11070	Loving You/Gonna Open Up My Heart Again	1973	—	2.50	5.00
❑ 50021	You Can't Go Halfway/The Very First Time	1974	—	2.50	5.00
❑ 50051	Beautiful Baby/Celebrate Life	1974	—	2.50	5.00
❑ 50091	Good Vibrations/The Very First Time	1975	—	2.50	5.00
❑ 50138	Tears on My Pillow (I Can't Take It)/Beautiful Baby	1975	—	2.50	5.00
❑ 50219	(What a) Wonderful World/Rock It Baby (We've Got a Date)	1976	—	2.50	5.00
❑ 50386	Back in Time/That Woman	1977	—	2.00	4.00
❑ 50737	Closer/Mr. Sea	1979	—	2.00	4.00
❑ 50821	You're the One/Don't Forget	1980	—	2.00	4.00

GROOVE

Number	Title (A Side/B Side)	Yr	VG	VG+	NM
❑ 58-0018	Helpless/I've Got a Lot to Offer, Darling	1963	2.50	5.00	10.00
❑ 58-0018 [PS]	Helpless/I've Got a Lot to Offer, Darling	1963	7.50	15.00	30.00
❑ 58-0021	Deep in the Heart of Harlem/What Kind of Love Is This	1963	10.00	20.00	40.00
❑ 58-0021 [PS]	Deep in the Heart of Harlem/What Kind of Love Is This	1963	12.50	25.00	50.00
❑ 58-0026	It's No Good for Me/Town of Lonely Hearts	1963	2.50	5.00	10.00
❑ 58-0030	I'm Leaving/Oh Mary Don't You Weep	1964	2.50	5.00	10.00

JAD

Number	Title (A Side/B Side)	Yr	VG	VG+	NM
❑ 207	Hold Me Tight/Cupid	1968	2.00	4.00	8.00
—Mostly light green label with purple trim					
❑ 209	You Got Soul/Don't Cry	1968	2.00	4.00	8.00
❑ 214	Lovey Dovey/You Got Soul	1969	—	3.00	6.00
❑ 215	Sweet Charity/People in Love	1969	—	3.00	6.00
❑ 218	Love and Peace/People in Love	1969	—	3.00	6.00
❑ 220	Cupid/Hold Me Tight	1969	—	3.00	6.00
❑ 223	What a Groovy Feeling/You Got Soul (Part 1)	1970	—	3.00	6.00

JANUS

Number	Title (A Side/B Side)	Yr	VG	VG+	NM
❑ 136	Falling In and Out of Love/You've Got to Change Your Ways	1970	—	3.00	6.00

JODA

Number	Title (A Side/B Side)	Yr	VG	VG+	NM
❑ 102	Let's Move and Groove (Together)/ Understanding	1965	2.50	5.00	10.00
❑ 105	One More Time/Got to Find Her	1965	2.50	5.00	10.00
❑ 106	Somewhere/Big City	1966	2.50	5.00	10.00

MGM

Number	Title (A Side/B Side)	Yr	VG	VG+	NM
❑ 13637	Amen/Perfumed Flower	1966	2.00	4.00	8.00
❑ 13683	Good Goodness/You Never Know	1967	2.00	4.00	8.00
❑ 13805	Stormy/(I'm So) Glad You're My Baby	1967	2.00	4.00	8.00

WARNER BROS.

Number	Title (A Side/B Side)	Yr	VG	VG+	NM
❑ 5270	Don't Take Your Love Away/Moment of Weakness	1962	3.00	6.00	12.00
❑ 5301	Ol' Man River/My Dear Little Sweetheart	1962	3.00	6.00	12.00
❑ 5336	Cigarettes, Whiskey and Wild, Wild Women/I'm Movin' On	1963	3.00	6.00	12.00

NASHVILLE TEENS, THE

LONDON

Number	Title (A Side/B Side)	Yr	VG	VG+	NM
❑ 9689	Tobacco Road/I Like It Like That	1964	3.75	7.50	15.00
❑ 9712	T.N.T./Google Eyes	1964	3.00	6.00	12.00
❑ 9736	Devil-in-Law/Find My Way Back Home	1965	3.00	6.00	12.00

MGM

Number	Title (A Side/B Side)	Yr	VG	VG+	NM
❑ 13357	Little Bird/Whatcha Gonna Do	1965	2.50	5.00	10.00
❑ 13406	I Know How It Feels to Be Loved/Soon Forgotten	1965	2.50	5.00	10.00
❑ 13483	The Hard Way/Upside Down	1966	2.50	5.00	10.00
❑ 13678	That's My Woman/Words	1967	2.50	5.00	10.00

UNITED ARTISTS

Number	Title (A Side/B Side)	Yr	VG	VG+	NM
❑ 50880	Tennessee Woman/Ella James	1972	5.00	10.00	20.00

NATURAL FOUR, THE

ABC

Number	Title (A Side/B Side)	Yr	VG	VG+	NM
❑ 11205	Why Should We Stop Now/You Did This for Me	1969	2.00	4.00	8.00
❑ 11236	Same Thing in Mind/The Situation Needs No Explanation	1969	3.00	6.00	12.00
❑ 11253	Hurt/I Thought You Were Mine	1969	6.25	12.50	25.00
❑ 11257	Message from a Black Man/Stepping On Up	1970	3.00	6.00	12.00

CURTOM

Number	Title (A Side/B Side)	Yr	VG	VG+	NM
❑ 0101	Heaven Right Here on Earth/While We're Away	1975	—	2.50	5.00
❑ 0104	Love's So Wonderful/What's Happening Here	1975	—	2.50	5.00
❑ 0114	It's the Music/It's the Music (Disco Version)	1976	—	2.50	5.00
❑ 0119	Free/Nothing Beats a Failure (But a Try)	1976	—	2.50	5.00
❑ 1981	Things Will Be Better Tomorrow/Eddie, You Should Know Better	1973	—	2.50	5.00
❑ 1984	Try Love Again/Eddie, You Should Know Better	1973	—	2.50	5.00
❑ 1990	Can This Be Real/Try Love Again	1973	—	2.50	5.00
❑ 1995	Love That Really Counts/Love's Society	1974	—	2.50	5.00
❑ 2000	You Bring Out the Best in Me/You Can't Keep Running Away	1974	—	2.50	5.00

NATURALS, THE (1)

CALLA

Number	Title (A Side/B Side)	Yr	VG	VG+	NM
❑ 181	I Can't Share You/Young Generation	1972	—	3.00	6.00

MOTOWN

Number	Title (A Side/B Side)	Yr	VG	VG+	NM
❑ 1208	Good Things/Where Was I When Love Came By	1972	—	3.00	6.00

SHOUT

Number	Title (A Side/B Side)	Yr	VG	VG+	NM
❑ 307	Color Him Father/Crystal Blue Persuasion	197?	—	3.00	6.00
❑ 310	Cold Day in Hell/(B-side unknown)	197?	—	3.00	6.00

NATURALS, THE (2)

BEACON

Number	Title (A Side/B Side)	Yr	VG	VG+	NM
❑ 462	You Give Me So Much/What a Shape I'm In	1958	10.00	20.00	40.00

NATURALS, THE (3)

CHATTAHOOCHIE

Number	Title (A Side/B Side)	Yr	VG	VG+	NM
❑ 633	Just in Case You Change Your Mind/Why Don't They Understand	1963	3.00	6.00	12.00

NATURALS, THE (4)

ERA

Number	Title (A Side/B Side)	Yr	VG	VG+	NM
❑ 1089	The Mummy/Don't Send Me Away	1959	3.75	7.50	15.00

NATURALS, THE (5)

Also see THE FOUR NATURALS.

HUNT

Number	Title (A Side/B Side)	Yr	VG	VG+	NM
❑ 325	Blue Moon/How Strange	1959	3.75	7.50	15.00

RED TOP

Number	Title (A Side/B Side)	Yr	VG	VG+	NM
❑ 113	Blue Moon/How Strange	1959	7.50	15.00	30.00

NATURALS, THE (6)

British group.

LIBERTY

Number	Title (A Side/B Side)	Yr	VG	VG+	NM
❑ 55741	I Should Have Known Better/Didn't I	1964	3.00	6.00	12.00
❑ 55758	It Was You/Look at Me Now	1964	3.00	6.00	12.00

NATURALS, THE (7)

MGM

Number	Title (A Side/B Side)	Yr	VG	VG+	NM
❑ 12576	Patti Ann/Missing	1957	3.00	6.00	12.00
❑ 12576 [PS]	Patti Ann/Missing	1957	5.00	10.00	20.00

NATURALS, THE (8)

SMASH

Number	Title (A Side/B Side)	Yr	VG	VG+	NM
❑ 1925	Different Girls/Hey Fellas	1964	3.00	6.00	12.00

NATURALS, THE (U)

We're not sure if this is a ninth different group.

20TH CENTURY FOX

Number	Title (A Side/B Side)	Yr	VG	VG+	NM
❑ 545	Caravan/Whole Lotta Rockin'	1964	3.00	6.00	12.00

NATURE BOY & FRIENDS

BERTRAM INT'L.

Number	Title (A Side/B Side)	Yr	VG	VG+	NM
❑ 255	Surfer John/John John	1964	10.00	20.00	40.00

NAZZ (1)

Also see TODD RUNDGREN.

SGC

Number	Title (A Side/B Side)	Yr	VG	VG+	NM
❑ 001	Hello It's Me/Open My Eyes	1969	5.00	10.00	20.00
—First pressing: Light yellow label, no horizontal lines on label					
❑ 001	Hello It's Me/Open My Eyes	1969	3.00	6.00	12.00
—Second pressing: Darker yellow label with horizontal lines					
❑ 001	Hello It's Me/Open My Eyes	1969	2.00	4.00	8.00
—Third printing: Mostly green label with some yellow. Red vinyl copies on any label are bootlegs.					
❑ 001 [PS]	Hello It's Me/Open My Eyes	1969	5.00	10.00	20.00
—Legitimate sleeves are paper, not cardboard					
❑ 006	Not Wrong Long/Under the Ice	1969	3.00	6.00	12.00
❑ 006 [PS]	Not Wrong Long/Under the Ice	1969	5.00	10.00	20.00
❑ 009	Magic Me/Some People	1970	3.00	6.00	12.00
❑ 009	Magic Me/Kicks	1970	6.25	12.50	25.00

NAZZ (2)

Early ALICE COOPER.

VERY

Number	Title (A Side/B Side)	Yr	VG	VG+	NM
❑ 001	Lay Down and Die, Goodbye/Wonder Who's Loving Her Now	1967	1000.	1500.	2000.
—Warning! Reproductions of this record were made in the 1990s with white promo labels and picture sleeves. They are NOT the real thing.					

NEAL, JERRY

DOT

Number	Title (A Side/B Side)	Yr	VG	VG+	NM
❑ 15810	I Hates Rabbits/Scratchin'	1958	20.00	40.00	80.00
—With Eddie Cochran on guitar on B-side					

NED AND GARY

LIBERTY

Number	Title (A Side/B Side)	Yr	VG	VG+	NM
❑ 55160	Lovin'/I Bust My Seams	1958	15.00	30.00	60.00

NED AND NELDA

FRANK ZAPPA and Ray Collins.

VIGAH

Number	Title (A Side/B Side)	Yr	VG	VG+	NM
❑ 002	Hey Nelda/Surf Along	1963	37.50	75.00	150.00

NEIGHB'RHOOD CHILDREN

ACTA

Number	Title (A Side/B Side)	Yr	VG	VG+	NM
❑ 813	Maintain/Just No Way	1967	5.00	10.00	20.00
—As "Neighborhood"					
❑ 823	Happy Child/Please Leave Me Alone	1968	3.75	7.50	15.00
❑ 828	Behold the Lilies/I Want Action	1968	5.00	10.00	20.00

DOT

Number	Title (A Side/B Side)	Yr	VG	VG+	NM
❑ 17238	On Our Way/Woman Thing	1969	3.75	7.50	15.00

NAM

Number	Title (A Side/B Side)	Yr	VG	VG+	NM
❑ 2014	Dancing in the Street/(B-side unknown)	196?	3.75	7.50	15.00

NEIL AND JACK

NEIL DIAMOND and Jack Parker.

DUEL

Number	Title (A Side/B Side)	Yr	VG	VG+	NM
❑ 508	What Will I Do/You Are My Love at Last	1962	100.00	200.00	400.00
❑ 517	I'm Afraid/Till You've Tried Love	1962	100.00	200.00	400.00

NELSON

Gunnar and Matthew Nelson, twin sons of RICKY NELSON.

DGC

Number	Title (A Side/B Side)	Yr	VG	VG+	NM
❑ 19002	More Than Ever/Keep One Heart	1991	—	—	3.00
❑ 19014	Only Time Will Tell/(Can't Live Without Your) Love and Affection (Acoustic)	1991	—	—	3.00
❑ 19386	(You Got Me) All Shook Up/After the Rain '95	1995	—	—	3.00
❑ 19667	After the Rain/Fill You Up	1990	—	—	3.00
❑ 19689	(Can't Live Without Your) Love and Affection/Will You Love Me?	1990	—	2.00	4.00

NELSON, KATHY

LIBERTY

Number	Title (A Side/B Side)	Yr	VG	VG+	NM
❑ 55115	Santa Dear/Gimmie a Little Kiss, Will Ya Huh?	1957	5.00	10.00	20.00

NELSON, RICKY

Includes records as "Rick Nelson."

CAPITOL

Number	Title (A Side/B Side)	Yr	VG	VG+	NM
❑ 4962	Almost Saturday Night/The Loser Babe Is You	1981	—	2.50	5.00
❑ 4974	Call It What You Want/It Hasn't Happened Yet	1981	—	2.50	5.00
❑ 4988	Believe What You Say/The Loser Babe Is You	1981	—	2.50	5.00
❑ B-5178	No Fair Falling in Love/Give 'Em My Number	1982	—	2.50	5.00
❑ 89574	The Christmas Song (Chestnuts Roasting on an Open Fire)/Jingle Bells	2000	2.00	4.00	8.00
—Red vinyl					

DECCA

Number	Title (A Side/B Side)	Yr	VG	VG+	NM
❑ 31475	You Don't Love Me Anymore (And I Can Tell)/I Got a Woman	1963	3.75	7.50	15.00
❑ 31475 [PS]	You Don't Love Me Anymore (And I Can Tell)/I Got a Woman	1963	7.50	15.00	30.00
❑ 31495	String Along/Gypsy Woman	1963	3.75	7.50	15.00
❑ 31495 [PS]	String Along/Gypsy Woman	1963	7.50	15.00	30.00
❑ 31533	Fools Rush In/Down Home	1963	3.75	7.50	15.00
❑ 31533 [PS]	Fools Rush In/Down Home	1963	7.50	15.00	30.00
❑ 31574	For You/That's All She Wrote	1963	3.75	7.50	15.00
❑ 31574 [PS]	For You/That's All She Wrote	1963	7.50	15.00	30.00
❑ 31612	The Very Thought of You/I Wonder (If Your Love Will Ever Belong to Me)	1964	3.00	6.00	12.00
❑ 31612 [PS]	The Very Thought of You/I Wonder (If Your Love Will Ever Belong to Me)	1964	7.50	15.00	30.00
❑ 31656	There's Nothing I Can Say/Lonely Corner	1964	3.00	6.00	12.00
❑ 31656 [PS]	There's Nothing I Can Say/Lonely Corner	1964	7.50	15.00	30.00
❑ 31703	A Happy Guy/Don't Breathe a Word	1964	3.00	6.00	12.00
❑ 31703 [PS]	A Happy Guy/Don't Breathe a Word	1964	7.50	15.00	30.00
❑ 31756	Mean Old World/When the Chips Are Down	1965	3.00	6.00	12.00
❑ 31756 [PS]	Mean Old World/When the Chips Are Down	1965	7.50	15.00	30.00
❑ 31800	Yesterday's Love/Come Out Dancin'	1965	3.00	6.00	12.00
❑ 31845	Love and Kisses/Say You Love Me	1965	3.00	6.00	12.00
❑ 31845 [PS]	Love and Kisses/Say You Love Me	1965	10.00	20.00	40.00
❑ 31900	Your Kind of Lovin'/Fire Breathin' Dragon	1966	3.00	6.00	12.00
❑ 31900 [PS]	Your Kind of Lovin'/Fire Breathin' Dragon	1966	20.00	40.00	80.00
❑ 31956	Louisiana Man/You Jsut Can't Quit	1966	3.00	6.00	12.00
❑ 31956 [PS]	Louisiana Man/You Jsut Can't Quit	1966	15.00	30.00	60.00
❑ 32026	Alone/Things You Gave Me	1966	3.00	6.00	12.00
❑ 32026 [PS]	Alone/Things You Gave Me	1966	20.00	40.00	80.00
❑ 32055	They Don't Give Medals (To Yesterday's Heroes)/Take a Broken Heart	1966	3.00	6.00	12.00
❑ 32120	Take a City Bride/I'm Called Lonely	1967	2.50	5.00	10.00
❑ 32120 [PS]	Take a City Bride/I'm Called Lonely	1967	15.00	30.00	60.00
❑ 32176	Moonshine/Suzanne on a Sunday Morning	1967	2.50	5.00	10.00
❑ 32222	Dream Weaver/Baby Close Your Eyes	1967	2.50	5.00	10.00
❑ 32284	Don't Blame It on Your Wife/Promenade in Green	1968	2.50	5.00	10.00
❑ 32298	Barefoot Boy/Don't Make Promises	1968	2.50	5.00	10.00
❑ 32550	She Belongs to Me/Promises	1969	2.00	4.00	8.00
❑ 32635	Easy to Be Free/Come On In	1970	2.00	4.00	8.00
❑ 32635 [PS]	Easy to Be Free/Come On In	1970	3.75	7.50	15.00
❑ 32676	I Shall Be Released/If You Gotta Go, Go Now	1970	2.00	4.00	8.00
❑ 32711	Look at Mary/We Got Such a Long Way to Go	1970	2.00	4.00	8.00
❑ 32739	How Long/Down Along the Bayou Country	1970	2.00	4.00	8.00
❑ 32779	Life/California	1971	2.00	4.00	8.00
❑ 32860	Thank You Lord/Sing Me a Song	1971	2.00	4.00	8.00
❑ 32906	Love Minus Zero-No Limit/Gypsy Pilot	1971	2.00	4.00	8.00
❑ 32980	Garden Party/So Long Mama	1972	2.50	5.00	10.00
❑ 34193/7 [PS]	Envelope, bonus photo and intact jukebox title strips for below 5 singles	1963	25.00	50.00	100.00
❑ 34193 [S]	Gypsy Woman/For Your Sweet Love	1963	25.00	50.00	100.00
❑ 34194 [S]	Pick Up the Pieces/Every Time I See You Smilin'	1963	25.00	50.00	100.00
❑ 34195 [S]	One Boy Too Late/Everytime I Think About You	1963	25.00	50.00	100.00
❑ 34196 [S]	Let's Talk the Whole Thing Over/I Got a Woman	1963	25.00	50.00	100.00
❑ 34197 [S]	I Will Follow You/What Comes Next	1963	25.00	50.00	100.00
—34193-34197 are 33 1/3 rpm, small hole jukebox singles. The set came with a package, priced separately.					

EPIC

Number	Title (A Side/B Side)	Yr	VG	VG+	NM
❑ 06066	Dream Lover/Rave On	1986	—	2.00	4.00
❑ 06066 [PS]	Dream Lover/Rave On	1986	—	2.00	4.00
❑ 50458	It's Another Day/You Can't Dance	1977	—	2.50	5.00
❑ 50501	Gimme A Little Sign/Something You Can't Buy	1978	—	2.50	5.00
❑ 50674	Dream Lover/That Ain't the Way Love's Supposed to Be	1979	—	2.50	5.00

IMPERIAL

Number	Title (A Side/B Side)	Yr	VG	VG+	NM
❑ 5463	Be-Bop Baby/Have I Told You Lately That I Love You	1957	12.50	25.00	50.00
—Red label					
❑ 5463	Be-Bop Baby/Have I Told You Lately That I Love You	1957	6.25	12.50	25.00
—Black label					
❑ 5463 [PS]	Be-Bop Baby/Have I Told You Lately That I Love You	1957	20.00	40.00	80.00
❑ 5483	Stood Up/Waitin' in School	1957	10.00	20.00	40.00
—Red label					
❑ 5483	Stood Up/Waitin' in School	1957	6.25	12.50	25.00
—Black label					
❑ 5483 [PS]	Stood Up/Waitin' in School	1957	17.50	35.00	70.00
❑ 5503	Believe What You Say/My Bucket's Got a Hole in It	1958	7.50	15.00	30.00
❑ 5503 [PS]	Believe What You Say/My Bucket's Got a Hole in It	1958	17.50	35.00	70.00
❑ 5528	Poor Little Fool/Don't Leave Me This Way	1958	7.50	15.00	30.00
❑ 5545	Lonesome Town/I Got a Feeling	1958	7.50	15.00	30.00
❑ 5545	Lonesome Town/I Got a Feeling	1958	150.00	300.00	600.00
—Red vinyl					
❑ 5545 [PS]	Lonesome Town/I Got a Feeling	1958	17.50	35.00	70.00
❑ 5565	Never Be Anyone Else But You/It's Late	1959	6.25	12.50	25.00
—Black label					
❑ 5565	Never Be Anyone Else But You/It's Late	1959	10.00	20.00	40.00
—Red label					

Number	Title (A Side/B Side)	Yr	VG	VG+	NM
❑ 5565 [PS]	Never Be Anyone Else But You/It's Late	1959	20.00	40.00	80.00
❑ 5595	Just a Little Too Much/Sweeter Than You	1959	6.25	12.50	25.00
❑ 5595 [PS]	Just a Little Too Much/Sweeter Than You	1959	17.50	35.00	70.00
❑ 5614	I Wanna Be Loved/Mighty Good	1959	6.25	12.50	25.00
❑ 5614 [PS]	I Wanna Be Loved/Mighty Good	1959	17.50	35.00	70.00
❑ 5663	Young Emotions/Right By My Side	1960	6.25	12.50	25.00
❑ 5663 [PS]	Young Emotions/Right By My Side	1960	17.50	35.00	70.00
❑ 5685	I'm Not Afraid/Yes Sir, That's My Baby	1960	6.25	12.50	25.00
❑ 5685 [PS]	I'm Not Afraid/Yes Sir, That's My Baby	1960	17.50	35.00	70.00
❑ 5707	You Are the Only One/Milk Cow Blues	1960	6.25	12.50	25.00
❑ 5707 [PS]	You Are the Only One/Milk Cow Blues	1960	17.50	35.00	70.00
❑ 5741	Travelin' Man/Hello Mary Lou	1961	6.25	12.50	25.00
❑ 5741	Travelin' Man/Hello Mary Lou	1961	200.00	400.00	800.00
—Red vinyl					
❑ 5741 [PS]	Travelin' Man/Hello Mary Lou	1961	17.50	35.00	70.00
❑ 5770	A Wonder Like You/Everlovin'	1961	5.00	10.00	20.00
—Starting here, Imperial singles by "Rick Nelson"					
❑ 5770 [PS]	A Wonder Like You/Everlovin'	1961	10.00	20.00	40.00
❑ 5805	Young World/Summertime	1962	5.00	10.00	20.00
❑ 5805 [PS]	Young World/Summertime	1962	10.00	20.00	40.00
❑ 5864	Teen Age Idol/I've Got My Eyes on You	1962	5.00	10.00	20.00
❑ 5864 [PS]	Teen Age Idol/I've Got My Eyes on You	1962	10.00	20.00	40.00
❑ 5901	It's Up to You/I Need You	1962	5.00	10.00	20.00
❑ 5901 [PS]	It's Up to You/I Need You	1962	10.00	20.00	40.00
❑ 5910	That's All/I'm in Love Again	1963	6.25	12.50	25.00
❑ 5935	Old Enough to Love/If You Can't Rock Me	1963	5.00	10.00	20.00
❑ 5935 [PS]	Old Enough to Love/If You Can't Rock Me	1963	10.00	20.00	40.00
❑ 5958	A Long Vacation/Mad Mad World	1963	5.00	10.00	20.00
❑ 5958	A Long Vacation/Mad Mad World	1963	75.00	150.00	300.00
—Red vinyl					
❑ 5985	Time After Time/There's Not a Minute	1963	5.00	10.00	20.00
❑ 58896	Young World/A Wonder Like You	2000	—	2.50	5.00
—EMI-Capitol jukebox issue with Imperial logo at top					
❑ 66004	Today's Teardrops/Thank You Darlin'	1963	3.75	7.50	15.00
❑ 66004 [PS]	Today's Teardrops/Thank You Darlin'	1963	10.00	20.00	40.00
❑ 66017	Congratulations/One Minute to One	1964	3.75	7.50	15.00
❑ 66039	Everybody But Me/Lucky Star	1964	3.75	7.50	15.00
MCA					
❑ 40001	Palace Guard/A Flower Opens Gently By	1973	—	3.00	6.00
❑ 40130	Evil Woman Child/Lifestream	1973	—	3.00	6.00
❑ 40187	Windfall/Legacy	1974	—	3.00	6.00
❑ 40214	One Night Stand/Lifestream	1974	—	3.00	6.00
❑ 40392	Louisiana Belle/Try (Try to Fall in Love)	1975	—	3.00	6.00
❑ 40458	Rock and Roll Lady/Fadeaway	1975	—	3.00	6.00
❑ 52781	You Know What I Mean/Don't Leave Me This Way	1986	—	2.50	5.00
❑ 52781 [PS]	You Know What I Mean/Don't Leave Me This Way	1986	—	2.50	5.00
UNITED ARTISTS					
❑ 0071	Be-Bop Baby/Stood Up	1973	—	2.50	5.00
❑ 0072	Lonesome Town/It's Up to You	1973	—	2.50	5.00
❑ 0073	Poor Little Fool/My Bucket's Got a Hole in It	1973	—	2.50	5.00
❑ 0074	Travelin' Man/Believe What You Say	1973	—	2.50	5.00
❑ 0075	Teen Age Idol/Young Emotions	1973	—	2.50	5.00
❑ 0076	Never Be Anyone Else But You/That's All	1973	—	2.50	5.00
❑ 0077	Young World/It's Late	1973	—	2.50	5.00
❑ 0078	Just a Little Too Much/Waitin' in School	1973	—	2.50	5.00
❑ 0079	Hello Mary Lou/Sweeter Than You	1973	—	2.50	5.00
❑ 0080	A Wonder Like You/Everlovin'	1973	—	2.50	5.00
—0071 through 0080 are "Silver Spotlight Series" reissues					
VERVE					
❑ 10047	I'm Walkin'/A Teenager's Romance	1957	12.50	25.00	50.00
—Orange and yellow label					
❑ 10047	I'm Walkin'/A Teenager's Romance	1957	10.00	20.00	40.00
—Black and white label					
❑ 10070	You're My One and Only Love/Honey Rock	1957	10.00	20.00	40.00
—B-side by Barney Kessel					

7-Inch Extended Plays

Number	Title (A Side/B Side)	Yr	VG	VG+	NM
DECCA					
❑ ED 2760	I Will Follow You/Pick Up the Pieces//One Boy Too Late/Let's Talk the Whole Thing Over	1963	37.50	75.00	150.00
❑ ED 2760 [PS]	One Boy Too Late	1963	37.50	75.00	150.00
❑ 7-34319 [PS]	Best Always	1965	7.50	15.00	30.00
—With title strips					
❑ 7-34319 [S]	I'm Not Ready for You Yet/Lonely Corner/Mean Old World//I Know a Place/It's Beginning to Hurt/When the Chips Are Down	1965	7.50	15.00	30.00
—33 1/3 rpm, small hole jukebox edition					
IMPERIAL					
❑ IMP 153	Be-Bop Baby/Have I Told You Lately That I Love You//Honeycomb/Boppin' the Blues	1957	12.50	25.00	50.00
❑ IMP 153 [PS]	Ricky (Honeycomb)	1957	12.50	25.00	50.00
❑ IMP 154	Teenage Doll/If You Can't Rock Me//Whole Lotta Shakin' Goin' On/Baby I'm Sorry	1957	12.50	25.00	50.00
❑ IMP 154 [PS]	Ricky, Volume 2	1957	12.50	25.00	50.00
❑ IMP 155	Your True Love/True Love//Am I Blue/I'm Confessin'	1957	12.50	25.00	50.00
❑ IMP 155 [PS]	Ricky (True Love)	1957	12.50	25.00	50.00
❑ IMP 156	Shirley Lee/There's Good Rockin' Tonight//Someday/I'm Feelin' Sorry	1958	12.50	25.00	50.00
❑ IMP 156 [PS]	Ricky Nelson (Someday)	1958	12.50	25.00	50.00
❑ IMP 157	Down the Line/Don't Leave Me This Way//I'm in Love Again/My Babe	1958	12.50	25.00	50.00
❑ IMP 157 [PS]	Ricky Nelson (Down the Line)	1958	12.50	25.00	50.00
❑ IMP 158	Unchained Melody/I'll Walk Alone//There Goes My Baby/Poor Little Fool	1958	12.50	25.00	50.00
❑ IMP 158 [PS]	Ricky Nelson (Unchained Melody)	1958	12.50	25.00	50.00
❑ IMP 159	Be True to Me/One of These Mornings//Lonesome Town/It's Late	1959	12.50	25.00	50.00
❑ IMP 159 [PS]	Ricky Sings Again (Be True to Me)	1959	12.50	25.00	50.00
❑ IMP 160	Restless Kid/It's All in the Game//Believe What You Say/You Tear Me Up	1959	12.50	25.00	50.00
❑ IMP 160 [PS]	Ricky Sings Again (Restless Kid)	1959	12.50	25.00	50.00
❑ IMP 161	Old Enough to Love/Tryin' to Get to You//Never Be Anyone Else But You/I Can't Help It	1959	12.50	25.00	50.00
❑ IMP 161 [PS]	Ricky Sings Again (Old Enough to Love)	1959	12.50	25.00	50.00
❑ IMP 162	You'll Never Know What You're Missin'/I've Been Thinkin'//So Long/You're So Fine	1959	12.50	25.00	50.00
❑ IMP 162 [PS]	Songs by Ricky (You'll Never Know What You're Missin')	1959	12.50	25.00	50.00
❑ IMP 163	One Minute To One/Blood from a Stone//Half Breed/Just a Little Too Much	1959	12.50	25.00	50.00
❑ IMP 163 [PS]	Songs by Ricky (One Minute to One)	1959	12.50	25.00	50.00
❑ IMP 164	Don't Leave Me/That's All//Sweeter Than You/A Long Vacation	1959	12.50	25.00	50.00
❑ IMP 164 [PS]	Songs by Ricky (Don't Leave Me)	1959	12.50	25.00	50.00
❑ IMP 165	Glory Train/I Bowed My Head in Shame//March with the Band of the Lord/If You Believe It	1959	25.00	50.00	100.00
❑ IMP 165 [PS]	Ricky Sings Spirituals	1959	25.00	50.00	100.00
❑ LP 4-2232 [PS]	Million Sellers	1964	20.00	40.00	80.00
❑ LP 4-2232 [S]	Travelin' Man/Never Be Anyone Else But You/It's Late//Young Emotions/Hello Mary Lou/Yes Sir, That's My Baby	1964	20.00	40.00	80.00
—33 1/3 rpm, small hole, jukebox edition					
VERVE					
❑ 5048	I'm Walkin'/A Teenager's Romance//You're My One and Only Love/Honey Rock	1957	37.50	75.00	150.00
❑ 5048 [PS]	Ricky	1957	50.00	100.00	200.00

NELSON, SANDY

Also see THE GAMBLERS.

Number	Title (A Side/B Side)	Yr	VG	VG+	NM
IMPERIAL					
❑ 5630	Drum Party/Big Noise from Winnetka	1959	3.00	6.00	12.00
❑ 5648	Party Time/The Wiggle	1960	3.00	6.00	12.00
❑ 5672	Bouncy/Lost Dreams	1960	3.00	6.00	12.00
❑ 5708	Cool Operator/Jive Talk	1960	3.00	6.00	12.00
❑ 5745	Big Noise from the Jungle/Get With It	1961	3.00	6.00	12.00
❑ 5775	Let There Be Drums/Quite a Beat	1961	3.75	7.50	15.00
❑ 5809	Drums Are My Beat/The Birth of the Beat	1962	3.00	6.00	12.00
❑ 5829	Drummin' Up a Storm/Drum Stomp	1962	3.00	6.00	12.00
❑ 5860	All Night Long/Rompin' and Stompin'	1962	3.00	6.00	12.00
❑ 5870	And Then There Were Drums/Live It Up	1962	3.00	6.00	12.00
❑ 5884	Teenage House Party/Day Train	1962	3.00	6.00	12.00
❑ 5904	Be-Bop Baby/Let the Four Winds Blow	1962	3.00	6.00	12.00
❑ 5932	Ooh Poo Pah Doo/Feel So Good	1963	3.00	6.00	12.00
❑ 5940	You Name It/Alexis	1963	3.00	6.00	12.00
❑ 5965	Here We Go Again/Just Bill	1963	3.00	6.00	12.00
❑ 5988	Caravan/Sandy	1963	3.00	6.00	12.00
❑ 66019	Drum Shack/Kitty's Theme	1964	2.50	5.00	10.00
❑ 66034	Castle Rock/You Don't Say	1964	2.50	5.00	10.00
❑ 66060	Teen Beat '65/Kitty's Theme	1964	3.00	6.00	12.00
❑ 66093	Chop Chop/Reach for a Star	1965	2.50	5.00	10.00
❑ 66107	Land of 1000 Dances/Let There Be Drums	1965	2.50	5.00	10.00
❑ 66127	Drums A-Go-Go/Caesar	1965	2.50	5.00	10.00
❑ 66146	A Lover's Concerto/Treat Her Right	1965	2.50	5.00	10.00
❑ 66193	Rock It To 'Em J.B./The Charge	1966	2.50	5.00	10.00
❑ 66209	Let's Go Trippin'/Pipeline	1966	3.00	6.00	12.00
❑ 66246	The Drums Go On/Lawdy Miss Clawdy	1967	2.50	5.00	10.00
❑ 66253	Peter Gunn/You Got Me Hummin'	1967	2.50	5.00	10.00
❑ 66284	Alligator Boogaloo/Midnight Magic	1968	2.50	5.00	10.00
❑ 66350	Rebirth of the Beat/Lion in Winter	1969	2.50	5.00	10.00
❑ 66375	Manhattan Spiritual/The Stripper	1969	2.50	5.00	10.00
❑ 66402	Let There Be Drums and Brass/Leap Frog	1969	2.50	5.00	10.00
ORIGINAL SOUND					
❑ 5	Teen Beat/Big Jump	1959	6.25	12.50	25.00
UNITED ARTISTS					
❑ 0082	Teen Beat/Let There Be Drums	1973	—	2.50	5.00
—"Silver Spotlight Series" reissue					
❑ XW383	You Are the Sunshine of My Life/Dance with the Devil	1974	2.50	5.00	10.00
❑ 50830	Sapporo '72	1971	—	—	—
—Unreleased					
VEEBLETRONICS					
❑ 1	Drum Tunnel/Boogie #5	198?	—	2.50	5.00
❑ 2	Hunk of Drums/Witch Hunt	198?	—	2.50	5.00
❑ 3	A Drum Is a Woman/Boogie #5	198?	—	2.50	5.00

NELSON, TERI, GROUP

Number	Title (A Side/B Side)	Yr	VG	VG+	NM
KAMA SUTRA					
❑ 245	Sweet Talkin' Willie/Back Side	1968	2.50	5.00	10.00

NELSON, TRACY

Also see MOTHER EARTH; TRACY AND WILLIE NELSON.

Number	Title (A Side/B Side)	Yr	VG	VG+	NM
ATLANTIC					
❑ 3235	It Takes a Lot to Laugh, It Takes a Train to Cry/Lean On Me	1975	—	2.50	5.00
CAPITOL					
❑ 4442	Sad Situation/Let's Get Down to the Truth	1977	—	2.00	4.00
—With Larry Ballard					
MCA					
❑ 40479	Sweet Soul Music/Nothing I Can't Handle	1975	—	2.00	4.00
MERCURY					
❑ 72995	Sad Situation/Stay As Sweet As You Are	1970	2.00	4.00	8.00

NELSON, TRACY AND WILLIE

Also see each artist's individual listings.

Number	Title (A Side/B Side)	Yr	VG	VG+	NM
ATLANTIC					
❑ 4028	After the Fire Is Gone/Whiskey River	1976	—	2.50	5.00

NELSON, WILLIE

Also see HANK COCHRAN; MERLE HAGGARD AND WILLIE NELSON; TRACY AND WILLIE NELSON; WAYLON AND WILLIE.

Number	Title (A Side/B Side)	Yr	VG	VG+	NM
AMERICAN GOLD					
❑ 7601	Night Life/Rainy Day Blues	1976	—	2.50	5.00

Number	Title (A Side/B Side)	Yr	VG	VG+	NM
ATLANTIC					
❑ 2968	Shotgun Willie/Sad Songs and Waltzes	1973	—	2.50	5.00
❑ 2979	Devil in a Sleepin' Bag/Stay All Night	1973	—	2.50	5.00
❑ 3008	Heaven and Hell/I Still Can't Believe You're Gone	1974	—	2.50	5.00
❑ 3020	Phases and Stages/Bloody Mary Morning	1974	—	2.50	5.00
❑ 3228	Sister's Coming Home/Pick Up the Tempo	1974	—	2.50	5.00
❑ 3334	Heaven and Hell/I Still Can't Believe You're Gone	1976	—	2.50	5.00
BELLAIRE					
❑ 107	Night Life/Rainy Day Blues	1963	7.50	15.00	30.00
❑ 107	Night Life/Rainy Day Blues	1963	15.00	30.00	60.00
—Colored vinyl					
❑ 5000	Night Life '76/Man with the Blues	1976	—	2.50	5.00
BETTY					
❑ 5702	What a Way to Love/Misery Mansion	1964	5.00	10.00	20.00
❑ 5703	Man with the Blues/The Storm Has Just Begun	1964	5.00	10.00	20.00
CHALLENGE					
❑ 59280	I'm Talking About Love/I'm in Love with a Dancing Girl Working at Metropole	1965	3.75	7.50	15.00
COLUMBIA					
❑ AE7 1182 [DJ]	White Christmas/Blue Christmas	1979	6.25	12.50	25.00
—Green vinyl					
❑ AE7 1183 [DJ]	Pretty Paper/Rudolph the Red-Nosed Reindeer	1979	6.25	12.50	25.00
—Red vinyl					
❑ AE7 1775 [DJ]	Pretty Paper/White Christmas	1982	—	3.00	6.00
❑ 02000	Mona Lisa/Twinkle, Twinkle Little Star	1981	—	2.00	4.00
❑ 02166	On the Road Again/September Song	1981	—	—	3.00
—Reissue					
❑ 02187	I'm Gonna Sit Right Down and Write Myself a Letter/Over the Rainbow	1981	—	2.00	4.00
❑ 02558	Heartaches of a Fool/Uncloudy Day	1981	—	2.00	4.00
❑ 02741	Always on My Mind/The Party's Over	1982	—	2.00	4.00
❑ 03073	Let It Be Me/Permanently Lonely	1982	—	2.00	4.00
❑ 03123	Angel Flying Too Close to the Ground/Mona Lisa	1982	—	—	3.00
—Reissue					
❑ 03124	Heartache of a Fool/Midnight Rider	1982	—	—	3.00
—Reissue					
❑ 03385	Last Thing I Needed First Thing This Morning/Old Fords and a Natural Stone	1982	—	2.00	4.00
❑ 03476	Pretty Paper/White Christmas	1982	—	2.50	5.00
❑ 03674	Beer Barrel Polka/Little Old Fashioned Karma	1983	—	2.00	4.00
❑ 03965	Why Do I Have to Choose/Would You Lay with Me (In a Field of Stone)	1983	—	2.00	4.00
❑ 04217	To All the Girls I've Loved Before/I Don't Want to Wake You	1984	—	—	3.00
—Julio Iglesias & Willie Nelson; B-side by Julio Iglesias solo					
❑ 04217 [PS]	To All the Girls I've Loved Before/I Don't Want to Wake You	1984	—	2.50	5.00
—Julio Iglesias & Willie Nelson; first sleeve has artists' names in both capital and small letters					
❑ 04217 [PS]	To All the Girls I've Loved Before/I Don't Want to Wake You	1984	—	2.00	4.00
—Julio Iglesias & Willie Nelson; second sleeve has artists' names in all capital letters					
❑ 04263	Without a Song/I Can't Begin to Tell You	1983	—	—	3.00
❑ 04495	As Time Goes By/You'll Never Know	1984	6.25	12.50	25.00
—Willie Nelson and Julio Iglesias; withdrawn immediately upon release					
❑ 04495 [PS]	As Time Goes By/You'll Never Know	1984	6.25	12.50	25.00
—Willie Nelson and Julio Iglesias; withdrawn immediately upon release					
❑ 04568	City of New Orleans/Why Are You Pickin' On Me	1984	—	—	3.00
❑ 04568 [PS]	City of New Orleans/Why Are You Pickin' On Me	1984	—	2.00	4.00
❑ 04715	Seven Spanish Angels/Who Cares	1984	—	—	3.00
—A-side: Ray Charles and Willie Nelson; B-side: Ray Charles and Janie Frickie					
❑ 04847	Forgiving You Was Easy/You Wouldn't Cross the Street (To Say Goodbye)	1985	—	—	3.00
❑ 04881	Highwayman/The Human Condition	1985	—	—	3.00
—A-side: Willie Nelson/Waylon Jennings/Johnny Cash/Kris Kristofferson; B-side: Nelson, Cash					
❑ 04881 [PS]	Highwayman/The Human Condition	1985	—	2.00	4.00
—A-side: Willie Nelson/Waylon Jennings/Johnny Cash/Kris Kristofferson; B-side: Nelson, Cash					
❑ 05566	Are There Any More Real Cowboys/I'm a Memory	1985	—	—	3.00
—A-side with Neil Young					
❑ 05594	Desperadoes Waiting for a Train/The Twentieth Century Is Almost Over	1985	—	—	3.00
—A-side: Willie Nelson/Waylon Jennings/Johnny Cash/Kris Kristofferson; B-side: Nelson, Cash					
❑ 05597	Me and Paul/I Let My Mind Wander	1985	—	—	3.00
❑ 05677	Slow Movin' Outlaw/They All Went to Mexico	1985	—	—	3.00
—A-side with Lacy J. Dalton; B-side with Carlos Santana					
❑ 05749	I Told a Lie to My Heart/Slow Movin' Outlaw	1986	—	—	3.00
—A-side with Hank Williams, Jr.; B-side: with Lacy J. Dalton					
❑ 05834	Living in the Promiseland/Bach Minuet in G	1986	—	—	3.00
❑ 06246	I'm Not Trying to Forget You/I've Got the Craziest Feeling	1986	—	—	3.00
❑ 06530	Partners After All/Home Away from Home	1986	—	—	3.00
❑ 07007	Heart of Gold/So Much Like My Dad	1987	—	—	3.00
❑ 07202	Island in the Sun/There Is No Easy Way (But There Is a Way)	1987	—	—	3.00
❑ 07636	Nobody There But Me/Wake Me When It's Over	1987	—	—	3.00
❑ 08044	Spanish Eyes/Ole Buttermilk Sky	1988	—	—	3.00
—With Julio Iglesias					
❑ 08395	Living in the Promiseland/Forgiving You Was Easy	1988	—	—	3.00
—Reissue					
❑ 08406	Highwayman/Desperadoes Waiting for a Train	1988	—	—	3.00
—Waylon Jennings/Willie Nelson/Johnny Cash/Kris Kristofferson; reissue					
❑ 08541	Twilight Time/Ac-Cent-Tchu-Ate the Positive	1989	—	—	3.00
❑ 10176	Blue Eyes Cryin' in the Rain/Bandera	1975	—	2.50	5.00
❑ 10275	Remember Me/Time of the Preacher	1975	—	2.50	5.00
❑ 10327	I'd Have to Be Crazy/Amazing Grace	1976	—	2.50	5.00
❑ 10383	If You've Got the Money, I've Got the Time/The Sound in Your Mind	1976	—	2.50	5.00
❑ 10453	Uncloudy Day/Precious Memories	1976	—	2.50	5.00
❑ 10588	I Love You a Thousand Ways/Mom and Dad's Waltz	1977	—	2.50	5.00

Number	Title (A Side/B Side)	Yr	VG	VG+	NM
❑ 10644	Something to Brag About/Anybody's Darlin' (Anybody But Mine)	1977	—	2.50	5.00
—With Mary Kay Place					
❑ 10704	Georgia on My Mind/On the Sunny Side of the Street	1978	—	2.50	5.00
❑ 10784	Blue Skies/Moonlight in Vermont	1978	—	2.50	5.00
❑ 10834	All of Me/Unchained Melody	1978	—	2.50	5.00
❑ 10877	Whiskey River/Under the Double Eagle	1978	—	2.50	5.00
❑ 10929	September Song/Don't Get Around Much Anymore	1979	—	2.00	4.00
❑ 11126	Help Me Make It Through the Night/The Pilgrim: Chapter 33	1979	—	2.00	4.00
❑ 11186	My Heroes Have Always Been Cowboys/Rising Star (Love Theme)	1980	—	2.00	4.00
❑ 11257	Midnight Rider/Do You Think You're a Cowboy	1980	—	2.00	4.00
❑ 11351	On the Road Again/Jumpin' Cotton-Eyed Joe	1980	—	2.00	4.00
—B-side by Johnny Gimble					
❑ 11418	Angel Flying Too Close to the Ground/I Guess I've Come to Live Here in Your Eyes	1981	—	2.00	4.00
❑ 68923	Nothing I Can Do About It Now/If I Were a Painting	1989	—	—	3.00
❑ 73015	There You Are/Spirit	1989	—	—	3.00
❑ 73233	Silver Stallion/America Remains	1990	—	—	3.00
—Waylon Jennings/Willie Nelson/Johnny Cash/Kris Kristofferson					
❑ 73249	The Highway/Spirit	1990	—	—	3.00
❑ 73374	Is the Better Part Over/Mr. Record Man	1990	—	—	3.00
❑ 73381	Born and Raised in Black and White/Texas	1990	—	—	3.00
—The Highwaymen (Waylon Jennings/Willie Nelson/Johnny Cash/Kris Kristofferson)					
❑ 73518	It Ain't Necessarily So/I Never Cared for You	1990	—	—	3.00
❑ 73572	American Remains/Texas	1990	—	—	3.00
—The Highwaymen (Waylon Jennings/Willie Nelson/Johnny Cash/Kris Kristofferson)					
❑ 73655	The Piper Came Today/(I Don't Have a Reason) To Go to California Anymore	1991	—	—	3.00
❑ 73749	Ten with a Two/You Decide	1991	—	—	3.00
❑ 77184	Still Is Still Moving to Me/Valentine	1993	—	—	3.00
D					
❑ 1084	Man with the Blues/The Storm Has Just Begun	1959	7.50	15.00	30.00
❑ 1131	What a Way to Love/Misery Mansion	1960	7.50	15.00	30.00
ISLAND					
❑ 572414-7	The Maker/I Never Cared for You	1998	—	—	3.00
LIBERTY					
❑ S7-18486	It Is What It Is/The Devil's Right Hand	1995	—	—	3.00
—By The Highwaymen					
❑ S7-18584	One After 909/Yesterday	1995	—	—	3.00
—B-side by Billy Dean					
❑ 55155	Susie/No Dough	1958	6.25	12.50	25.00
❑ 55386	Mr. Record Man/The Part Where I Cry	1961	5.00	10.00	20.00
❑ 55403	Willingly/Chain of Love	1962	3.75	7.50	15.00
—A-side with Shirley Collie					
❑ 55439	Touch Me/Where My House Lives	1962	3.75	7.50	15.00
❑ 55468	You Dream About Me/Is This My Destiny	1962	3.75	7.50	15.00
—A-side with Shirley Collie					
❑ 55494	Wake Me When It's Over/There's Gonna Be Love in My House	1962	3.75	7.50	15.00
❑ 55532	Half a Man/The Last Letter	1963	3.00	6.00	12.00
❑ 55591	Take My Word/Feed It a Memory	1963	3.00	6.00	12.00
❑ 55638	How Long Is Forever/You Took My Happy Away	1963	3.00	6.00	12.00
❑ 55661	Am I Blue/There'll Be No Teardrops Tonight	1964	2.50	5.00	10.00
❑ 55697	River Boy/Opportunity to Cry	1964	2.50	5.00	10.00
❑ 56143	Right or Wrong/I Hope So	1969	—	3.00	6.00
LONE STAR					
❑ 703	The End of Understanding/Will You Remember Mine	1978	—	2.50	5.00
MONUMENT					
❑ 855	I Never Cared for You/You Left Me	1964	3.75	7.50	15.00
❑ 03408	Everything Is Beautiful (In Its Own Way)/Put It Off Until Tomorrow	1982	—	2.00	4.00
—A-side: Willie Nelson and Dolly Parton; B-side: Dolly Parton and Kris Kristofferson					
❑ 03781	You're Gonna Love Yourself (In the Morning)/What Do You Think About Lovin'	1983	—	2.00	4.00
—A-side: Willie Nelson and Brenda Lee; B-side: Dolly Parton and Brenda Lee					
PARADISE					
❑ 629	Wabash Cannonball/Tennessee Waltz	1984	—	2.00	4.00
—A-side with Hank Wilson (a.k.a. Leon Russell); B-side by Wilson solo					
RCA					
❑ PB-10969	I'm a Memory/It Should Be Easier Now	1977	—	2.50	5.00
—With Darrell McCall					
❑ PB-11061	You Ought to Hear Me Cry/One in a Row	1977	—	2.50	5.00
❑ PB-11235	If You Can Touch Her at All/Rainy Day Blues	1978	—	2.50	5.00
❑ PB-11465	Sweet Memories/Little Things	1979	—	2.50	5.00
❑ PB-11673	Crazy Arms/Hurricane Shirley	1979	—	2.50	5.00
—B-side by Bobby Bare					
❑ GB-11995	Sweet Memories/If You Can Touch Her At All	1980	—	—	3.00
—Gold Standard Series					
❑ PB-12254	Good Times/Where Do You Stand	1981	—	2.00	4.00
❑ PB-12254 [PS]	Good Times/Where Do You Stand	1981	—	2.50	5.00
❑ PB-12328	Mountain Dew/Laying My Burdens Down	1981	—	2.00	4.00
RCA VICTOR					
❑ PB-10429	I'm a Memory/Fire and Rain	1975	—	2.50	5.00
❑ PB-10461	Pretty Paper/What a Merry Christmas This Could Be	1975	2.00	4.00	8.00
❑ PB-10591	Summer of Roses/I Gotta Get Drunk	1976	—	2.50	5.00
❑ 47-8484	Pretty Paper/What a Merry Christmas This Could Be	1964	3.75	7.50	15.00
❑ 47-8519	She's Not for You/Permanently Lonely	1965	3.00	6.00	12.00
❑ 47-8594	Healing Hands of Time/One Day at a Time	1965	3.00	6.00	12.00
❑ 47-8682	I Just Can't Let You Say Goodbye/And So Will You, My Love	1965	3.00	6.00	12.00
❑ 47-8801	Columbus Stockade Blues/He Sits at My Table	1966	3.00	6.00	12.00
❑ 47-8852	I'm Still Not Over You/I Love You Because	1966	3.00	6.00	12.00
❑ 47-8933	One in a Row/San Antonio Rose	1966	3.00	6.00	12.00

Number	Title (A Side/B Side)	Yr	VG	VG+	NM
❑ 47-9029	Pretty Paper/What a Merry Christmas This Could Be	1966	3.00	6.00	12.00
❑ 47-9100	The Party's Over/Make Way for a Better Man	1967	2.50	5.00	10.00
❑ 47-9202	Blackjack County Chain/Some Other World	1967	2.50	5.00	10.00
❑ 47-9324	San Antonio/To Make a Long Story Short	1967	2.50	5.00	10.00
❑ 47-9427	Little Things/I'll Stay Around	1968	2.50	5.00	10.00
❑ 47-9536	Good Times/Don't You Ever Get Tired	1968	2.50	5.00	10.00
❑ 47-9605	Johnny One Time/She's Still Gone	1968	2.50	5.00	10.00
❑ 47-9684	Bring Me Sunshine/Don't Say Love or Nothing	1968	2.50	5.00	10.00
❑ 47-9778	Pretty Paper/What a Merry Christmas This Could Be	1969	—	—	—
—Unreleased					
❑ 47-9798	Who Do I Know in Dallas/Once More with Feeling	1969	2.00	4.00	8.00
❑ 47-9903	Laying My Burdens Down/Truth Number One	1970	2.00	4.00	8.00
❑ 47-9931	Pretty Paper/What a Merry Christmas This Could Be	1970	2.00	4.00	8.00
❑ 47-9951	I'm a Memory/I'm So Lonesome I Could Cry	1971	—	3.00	6.00
❑ 47-9984	Kneel at the Feet of Jesus/What Can You Do to Me Now	1971	—	3.00	6.00
❑ 74-0162	Jimmy's Road/Natural to Be Gone	1969	2.00	4.00	8.00
❑ 74-0542	Yesterday's Wine/Me and Paul	1971	—	3.00	6.00
❑ 74-0635	A Moment Isn't Very Long/Words Don't Fit the Picture	1972	—	3.00	6.00
❑ 74-0816	Mountain Dew/Phases, Stages, Circles, Cycles, and Scenes	1972	—	3.00	6.00
SARG					
❑ 260	A Storm Has Just Begun/When I Sang My Last Hillbilly Song	196?	12.50	25.00	50.00
—Some sources say this came out in 1955, but that doesn't coincide with this label's history					
SONGBIRD					
❑ 41313	Family Bible/In God's Eyes	1980	—	2.00	4.00
UNITED ARTISTS					
❑ 641	Night Life/Rainy Day Blues	1963	3.75	7.50	15.00
❑ XW771	The Last Letter/There Goes a Man	1976	—	2.50	5.00
❑ XW1165	Hello Walls/The Last Letter	1978	—	2.50	5.00
❑ XW1254	There'll Be Teardrops Tonight/Blue Must Be the Color of the Blues	1978	—	2.50	5.00
WILLIE NELSON					
❑ 628	No Place for Me/The Lumberjack	1957	75.00	150.00	300.00

NELSON, WILLIE, AND KRIS KRISTOFFERSON

Also see each artist's individual listings.

Number	Title (A Side/B Side)	Yr	VG	VG+	NM
COLUMBIA					
❑ 38-04652	How Do You Feel About Foolin' Around/Eye of the Storm	1984	—	—	3.00

NELSON, WILLIE, AND ROGER MILLER

Also see each artist's individual listings.

Number	Title (A Side/B Side)	Yr	VG	VG+	NM
COLUMBIA					
❑ 02681	Old Friends/When a House Is Not a Home	1982	—	2.00	4.00
—With Ray Price					

NELSON, WILLIE, AND WEBB PIERCE

Also see each artist's individual listings.

Number	Title (A Side/B Side)	Yr	VG	VG+	NM
COLUMBIA					
❑ 03231	In the Jailhouse Now/Back Street Affair	1982	—	2.00	4.00

NELSON, WILLIE, AND RAY PRICE

Also see each artist's individual listings.

Number	Title (A Side/B Side)	Yr	VG	VG+	NM
COLUMBIA					
❑ 11329	Faded Love/This Cold World with You	1980	—	2.00	4.00
❑ 11405	Don't You Ever Get Tired (Of Loving Me)/Funny How Time Slips Away	1980	—	2.00	4.00

NELSON, WILLIE, AND LEON RUSSELL

Also see each artist's individual listings.

Number	Title (A Side/B Side)	Yr	VG	VG+	NM
COLUMBIA					
❑ 11023	Heartbreak Hotel/Sioux City Sue	1979	—	2.00	4.00
❑ 11119	Trouble in Mind/One for My Baby (And One More for the Road)	1979	—	2.00	4.00

NEON PHILHARMONIC, THE

Number	Title (A Side/B Side)	Yr	VG	VG+	NM
MCA					
❑ 40518	So Glad You're a Woman/Making Out the Best You Can	1976	—	2.50	5.00
TRX					
❑ 5039	Annie Poor/Love Will Find a Way	1972	—	2.50	5.00
WARNER BROS.					
❑ 7261	Morning Girl/Brilliant Colors	1969	2.00	4.00	8.00
❑ 7311	No One Is Going to Hurt You/You Lied	1969	—	3.00	6.00
❑ 7355	Clouds/Snow	1969	—	3.00	6.00
❑ 7380	Don't Know the Way Around Soul/Highty-Ho, Princess	1970	—	3.00	6.00
❑ 7419	Flowers for Your Pillow/To Be Continued	1970	—	3.00	6.00
❑ 7457	Something to Believe In/A Little Love	1971	—	3.00	6.00
❑ 7497	Gotta Feeling in My Bones/Keep the Faith in Me	1971	—	3.00	6.00

NEONS, THE (1)

Number	Title (A Side/B Side)	Yr	VG	VG+	NM
CHALLENGE					
❑ 9147	Magic Moment/Fat Girls	1962	25.00	50.00	100.00
❑ 59147	Magic Moment/Fat Girls	1962	12.50	25.00	50.00

NEONS, THE (2)

Number	Title (A Side/B Side)	Yr	VG	VG+	NM
GONE					
❑ 5090	Angel Face/Golden Dreams	1960	10.00	20.00	40.00
TETRA					
❑ 4444	Angel Face/Kiss Me Quickly	1956	20.00	40.00	80.00
❑ 4449	Road of Romance/My Chickadee	1957	20.00	40.00	80.00
VINTAGE					
❑ 1016	Honey Bun/Golden Dreams	1974	—	2.50	5.00

NEONS, THE (3)

Number	Title (A Side/B Side)	Yr	VG	VG+	NM
WALDON					
❑ 1001	My Lover/Tucson	1961	175.00	350.00	700.00

NEPTUNES, THE

Several different groups.

Number	Title (A Side/B Side)	Yr	VG	VG+	NM
CHECKER					
❑ 967	She'll Understand/So Little Time	1960	3.00	6.00	12.00
GEM					
❑ 100	Turn Around/(B-side unknown)	196?	6.25	12.50	25.00
GLORY					
❑ 269	Fraidy Cat/As Long As	1959	5.00	10.00	20.00
INSTANT					
❑ 3255	Make a Memory/House of Heartaches	1963	6.25	12.50	25.00
PAYSON					
❑ 101/2	If You Care/She Went That-a-Way	1958	5.00	10.00	20.00
RCA VICTOR					
❑ 47-7931	Curiosity Killed the Cat/This Is Love	1961	3.00	6.00	12.00
VICTORIA					
❑ 102	I'm Coming Home/I Don't Cry Anymore	1964	6.25	12.50	25.00
WARNER BROS.					
❑ 5453	Shame Girl/I've Got Plans	1964	3.00	6.00	12.00

NERO, FRANCES

Number	Title (A Side/B Side)	Yr	VG	VG+	NM
SOUL					
❑ 35020	Keep On Lovin' Me/Fight Off Fire with Fire	1966	12.50	25.00	50.00

NERVOUS NORVUS

Number	Title (A Side/B Side)	Yr	VG	VG+	NM
DOT					
❑ 15470	Transfusion/Dig	1956	12.50	25.00	50.00
—Originals have maroon labels					
❑ 15470	Transfusion/Dig	1956	7.50	15.00	30.00
—Second pressings have black labels					
❑ 15485	Ape Call/Wild Dog of Kentucky	1956	7.50	15.00	30.00
—Originals have maroon labels					
❑ 15485	Ape Call/Wild Dog of Kentucky	1956	5.00	10.00	20.00
—Second pressings have black labels					
❑ 15500	The Fang/The Bullfrog	1956	7.50	15.00	30.00
—Originals have maroon labels					
❑ 15500	The Fang/The Bullfrog	1956	5.00	10.00	20.00
—Second pressings have black labels					
❑ 16765	Transfusion/Ape Call	1965	3.00	6.00	12.00
EMBEE					
❑ 117	I Like Girls/Stone Age Woo	1959	5.00	10.00	20.00

NESMITH, MICHAEL

Also see MIKE, JOHN AND BILL; THE MONKEES.

Number	Title (A Side/B Side)	Yr	VG	VG+	NM
COLPIX					
❑ 787	The New Recruit/A Journey	1965	37.50	75.00	150.00
—As "Michael Blessing"					
❑ 792	Until It's Time for You to Go/What's the Trouble, Officer	1965	37.50	75.00	150.00
—As "Michael Blessing"					
EDAN					
❑ 1001	Just a Little Love/Curson Terrace	1965	30.00	60.00	120.00
PACIFIC ARTS					
❑ 084	Life, the Unsuspecting Captive/Rio	1977	2.00	4.00	8.00
❑ 101	Roll with the Flow/I've Just Begun to Care	1978	—	3.00	6.00
❑ 104	Casablanca Moonlight/Rio	1978	—	3.00	6.00
❑ 104 [PS]	Casablanca Moonlight/Rio	1978	3.00	6.00	12.00
❑ 106	Magic (This Night Is Magic)/Dance	1979	—	3.00	6.00
❑ 108	Cruisin'/Horserace	1979	—	3.00	6.00
❑ 6373	Life, the Unsuspecting Captive/Rio	1976	2.50	5.00	10.00
❑ 6398	Navajo Trail/Love's First Kiss	1976	2.50	5.00	10.00
RCA VICTOR					
❑ 47-9853	Rose City Chimes/Little Red Rider	1970	2.50	5.00	10.00
❑ 74-0368	Joanne/One Rose	1970	3.00	6.00	12.00
❑ 74-0399	Silver Moon/Lady of the Valley	1970	2.50	5.00	10.00
❑ 74-0453	Nevada Fighter/Here I Am	1971	2.00	4.00	8.00
❑ 74-0453 [PS]	Nevada Fighter/Here I Am	1971	5.00	10.00	20.00
❑ 74-0491	Tumbling Tumbleweeds/Texas Morning	1971	2.00	4.00	8.00
❑ 74-0540	Only Bound/Propinquity	1971	2.00	4.00	8.00
❑ 74-0629	Lazy Lady/Mama Rocker	1971	2.00	4.00	8.00
❑ 74-0804	Roll with the Flow/Keep On	1972	2.00	4.00	8.00

NETTLES, BILL

Number	Title (A Side/B Side)	Yr	VG	VG+	NM
MERCURY					
❑ 6350	Smiles Won't Hide an Achin' Heart/Long Road to Travel	1951	7.50	15.00	30.00
STARDAY					
❑ 174	Wine-O Boogie/Gumbo Mumbo	1955	25.00	50.00	100.00

NEUMAN, ALFRED E., AND THE FURSHLUGGINER FIVE

Number	Title (A Side/B Side)	Yr	VG	VG+	NM
ABC-PARAMOUNT					
❑ 10013	What — Me Worry?/Potrzebie	1959	10.00	20.00	40.00
❑ 10013 [PS]	What — Me Worry?/Potrzebie	1959	15.00	30.00	60.00

NEVILLE, AARON

Also see THE METERS; LINDA RONSTADT.

Number	Title (A Side/B Side)	Yr	VG	VG+	NM
A&M					
❑ 31458 0312 7	The Grand Tour/Don't Take Away My Heaven	1993	—	2.00	4.00
❑ 31458 0442 7	Please Come Home for Christmas/Louisiana Christmas Day	1993	—	2.50	5.00
❑ 31458 1112 7	For the Good Times/Crying in the Chapel	1995	—	2.00	4.00
❑ 75021 1563 7	Everybody Plays the Fool/House on a Hill	1991	—	2.00	4.00
BELL					
❑ 746	You Can Give, But You Can't Take/Where Is My Baby	1968	2.00	4.00	8.00
❑ 781	Speak to Me/You Don't Love Me Anymore	1969	2.00	4.00	8.00
❑ 834	All These Things/She's On My Mind	1969	2.00	4.00	8.00

Number	Title (A Side/B Side)	Yr	VG	VG+	NM
MERCURY					
73310	Baby I'm-a Want You/Mojo Hannah	1972	—	3.00	6.00
73387	Hercules/Going Home	1973	—	3.00	6.00
MINIT					
612	Over You/Every Day	1960	3.75	7.50	15.00
—As "Arron Neville"					
618	Show Me the Way/Get Out of My Life	1960	3.00	6.00	12.00
624	Don't Cry/Reality	1961	3.00	6.00	12.00
631	Let's Live/I Found Another Love	1961	3.00	6.00	12.00
639	How Many Times/I'm Waitin' at the Station	1962	3.00	6.00	12.00
650	Humdinger/Sweet Little Mama	1962	3.00	6.00	12.00
657	Wrong Number/How Could I Help But Love You	1963	3.00	6.00	12.00
PAR-LO					
101	Tell It Like It Is/Why Worry	1966	5.00	10.00	20.00
—Black and white label					
101	Tell It Like It Is/Why Worry	1966	6.25	12.50	25.00
—Turquoise label, silver print					
103	She Took You for a Ride/Space Man	1967	2.00	4.00	8.00
POLYDOR					
14426	Greatest Love/Performance	1977	—	2.00	4.00
WHO DAT?					
VPAG-4476/7	Who Dat? (The History of the Saints)/(Extended Version)	1987	2.00	4.00	8.00

NEVILLE, AARON, AND TRISHA YEARWOOD

Also see each artist's individual listings.

Number	Title (A Side/B Side)	Yr	VG	VG+	NM
MCA					
54836	I Fall to Pieces/(Instrumental)	1994	—	2.00	4.00

NEW COLONY SIX, THE

Number	Title (A Side/B Side)	Yr	VG	VG+	NM
CENTAUR					
1201	I Confess/Dawn Is Breaking	1966	3.75	7.50	15.00
1202	I Like Awake/At the River's Edge	1966	3.75	7.50	15.00
MCA					
40215	Never Be Lonely/Long Time to Be Alone	1974	6.25	12.50	25.00
40288	I Really Don't Want to Go/Run	1974	7.50	15.00	30.00
MERCURY					
72737	Treat Her Groovy/Rap-a-Tap	1967	2.50	5.00	10.00
—Orange and red swirl label					
72737	Treat Her Groovy/Rap-a-Tap	1967	3.00	6.00	12.00
—Red label with "Mercury" logo in all capital letters					
72737 [PS]	Treat Her Groovy/Rap-a-Tap	1967	3.75	7.50	15.00
72775	I Will Always Think About You/Hold Me with Your Eyes	1968	2.50	5.00	10.00
—Orange and red swirl label					
72775	I Will Always Think About You/Hold Me with Your Eyes	1968	3.00	6.00	12.00
—Red label with "Mercury" logo in all capital letters					
72817	Can't You See Me Cry/Summertime's Another Name for Love	1968	2.00	4.00	8.00
72817 [PS]	Can't You See Me Cry/Summertime's Another Name for Love	1968	3.75	7.50	15.00
72858	Things I'd Like to Say/Come and Give Your Love to Me	1968	2.50	5.00	10.00
—Red label with "Mercury" logo in an oval					
72858	Things I'd Like to Say/Come and Give Your Love to Me	1968	3.00	6.00	12.00
—Orange and red swirl label					
72920	I Could Never Lie to You/Just Feel Worse	1969	2.00	4.00	8.00
72961	I Want You to Know/Free	1969	2.00	4.00	8.00
73004	Barbara, I Love You/Prairie Grey	1970	2.00	4.00	8.00
73063	People and Me/Ride the Wicked Wind	1970	3.75	7.50	15.00
73093	Close Your Eyes Little Girl/Love, That's the Best I Can Do	1970	5.00	10.00	20.00
—Promo copies go for less					
SENTAR					
1203	Cadillac/Sunshine	1966	3.75	7.50	15.00
1204	(Ballad of the) Wingbat Marmaduke/Power of Love	1966	3.75	7.50	15.00
1205	Love You So Much/Let Me Love You	1967	3.75	7.50	15.00
1206	You're Gonna Be Mine/Woman	1967	3.75	7.50	15.00
1207	I'm Just Waiting Anticipating for Her to Show Up/Hello Lonely	1967	3.75	7.50	15.00
SENTAUR					
1202	I Like Awake/At the River's Edge	1966	5.00	10.00	20.00
—Reissue of Centaur 1202, but harder to find					
SUNLIGHT					
1001	Roll On/If You Could See	1971	—	3.00	6.00
1004	Long Time to Be Alone/Never Be Lonely	1971	—	3.00	6.00
1005	Someone, Sometime/Come On Down	1972	2.00	4.00	8.00
TWILIGHT					
1004	Long Time to Be Alone/Never Be Lonely	1973	—	—	—
—The existence of this record as a US pressing has not been confirmed					

NEW DAWN, THE

Number	Title (A Side/B Side)	Yr	VG	VG+	NM
GARLAND					
2020	Why Did You Go/Tears	1970	6.25	12.50	25.00
IMPERIAL					
66397	Melody Fair/Sometimes in the Morning	1969	2.00	4.00	8.00
MAINSTREAM					
652	If I Can't Have Your Love/Loser	1966	6.25	12.50	25.00
664	Slave of Desire/Funny Feeling	1966	6.25	12.50	25.00
RCA VICTOR					
47-9569	Listen to the Music/Someday	1968	2.00	4.00	8.00

NEW HOPE

See THE KIT KATS.

NEW KINGSTON TRIO, THE

See THE KINGSTON TRIO.

NEW MARKETTS, THE

See THE MARKETTS.

NEW MONKEES

Number	Title (A Side/B Side)	Yr	VG	VG+	NM
WARNER BROS.					
28188	What I Want/Corner of My Eye	1987	—	—	3.00
28188 [PS]	What I Want/Corner of My Eye	1987	—	—	3.00

NEW ORDER

Also see JOY DIVISION.

Number	Title (A Side/B Side)	Yr	VG	VG+	NM
FACTORY					
FAC 53	Procession/Everything's Gone Green	1982	—	2.50	5.00
FAC 53 [PS]	Procession/Everything's Gone Green	1982	—	2.50	5.00
—American edition has a "Rough Trade" sticker added to UK cover (deduct 25% if missing)					
QWEST					
PRO-S-3464 [DJ]	Fine Time (7" Edit)/Round and Round (Edit)	1989	2.00	4.00	8.00
18586	Regret/Regret (New Order Mix)	1993	—	—	3.00
21887	True Faith/Blue Monday 1988	198?	—	—	3.00
—Reissue					
27524	Round & Round/Best and Marsh	1989	—	—	3.00
27524 [PS]	Round & Round/Best and Marsh	1989	—	—	3.00
27979	Blue Monday 1988/Touched by the Hand of God	1988	—	—	3.00
27979 [PS]	Blue Monday 1988/Touched by the Hand of God	1988	—	—	3.00
28271	True Faith/1963	1987	—	—	3.00
28271 [PS]	True Faith/1963	1987	—	—	3.00
28421	Bizarre Love Triangle/Every Little Bit Counts	1987	2.50	5.00	10.00
28421 [DJ]	Bizarre Love Triangle (same on both sides)	1987	—	2.50	5.00
28968	The Perfect Kiss/The Perfect Kiss (instrumental)	1985	—	3.00	6.00

NEW RIDERS OF THE PURPLE SAGE

JERRY GARCIA was briefly in this group.

Number	Title (A Side/B Side)	Yr	VG	VG+	NM
A&M					
2327	Fly Right/Night for Making Love	1981	—	2.00	4.00
2352	Full Moon at Midnite/No Other Love	1981	—	2.00	4.00
COLUMBIA					
10067	You Angel You/Parson Brown	1974	—	2.50	5.00
45469	Louisiana Lady/The Last Lonely Eagle	1971	—	3.00	6.00
45526	Garden of Eden/I Don't Know You	1972	—	2.50	5.00
45607	I Don't Need No Doctor/Runnin' Back to You	1972	—	2.50	5.00
45682	Rainbow/Dim Lights, Thick Smoke	1972	—	2.50	5.00
45763	Groupie/She's No Angel	1973	—	2.50	5.00
45976	Panama Red/Cement, Clay, and Glass	1973	—	3.00	6.00
MCA					
40564	Don't Put Her Down/Fifteen Days Under the Hood	1976	—	2.00	4.00
40591	Dead Flowers/She's Looking Better Every Beer	1976	—	2.00	4.00
40686	Red Hot Women and Ice Cold Beer/Love Has Strange Ways	1977	—	2.00	4.00
40715	(Just) Another Night in Reno/Home Grown	1977	—	2.00	4.00

NEW SEEKERS, THE

Number	Title (A Side/B Side)	Yr	VG	VG+	NM
COCA-COLA					
(no #) [DJ]	Buy the World a Coke//Bring a Little Sunshine/It's the Real Thing	1971	3.00	6.00	12.00
—All three songs are Coca-Coca jingles. The A-side became "I'd Like to Teach the World to Sing"					
COLUMBIA					
10559	You Never Can Tell/Give Me Love Your Way	1977	—	2.50	5.00
ELEKTRA					
45699	Look What They've Done to My Song, Ma/It's a Beautiful Day	1970	—	3.00	6.00
45710	Beautiful People/When There's No Love Left	1970	—	2.50	5.00
45719	The Nickel Song/Cincinnati	1971	—	2.50	5.00
45734	Never Ending Song of Love/All Right My Love	1971	—	—	—
—Unreleased					
45747	Tonight/Sweet Louise	1971	—	2.50	5.00
45762	I'd Like to Teach the World to Sing/Boom Town	1971	—	3.00	6.00
45780	Beg, Steal or Borrow/Mystic Queen	1972	—	2.50	5.00
45787	Circles/I Can Say You're Beautiful	1972	—	2.50	5.00
45805	Dance, Dance, Dance/I Can Say You're Beautiful	1972	—	2.50	5.00
MGM					
14586	The Greatest Song I've Ever Heard/Woman Grows	1973	—	2.50	5.00
14683	Reach Out I'll Be There/You Won't Find Another Fool Like Me	1973	—	2.50	5.00
14691	Song for You and Me/You Won't Find Another Fool Like Me	1974	—	2.50	5.00
VERVE					
10698	Come Softly to Me/Unwithered Rose	1972	—	2.50	5.00
10698 [PS]	Come Softly to Me/Unwithered Rose	1972	—	2.50	5.00
10709	Pinball Wizard-See Me, Feel Me/Come Softly to Me	1973	—	2.50	5.00

NEW THINGS, THE

Number	Title (A Side/B Side)	Yr	VG	VG+	NM
ACCENT					
1228	Dumbo/I Want You Back	1967	10.00	20.00	40.00

NEW TWEEDY BROTHERS, THE

Number	Title (A Side/B Side)	Yr	VG	VG+	NM
DOT					
16910	Good Time Car/Terms of You Love Me	1966	10.00	20.00	40.00

NEW VAUDEVILLE BAND, THE

Number	Title (A Side/B Side)	Yr	VG	VG+	NM
FONTANA					
1562	Winchester Cathedral/Wait for Me Baby	1966	2.00	4.00	8.00
1573	Peek-A-Boo/Amy	1967	—	3.00	6.00
1589	Finchley Central/Sadie Moonshine	1967	—	3.00	6.00
1589 [PS]	Finchley Central/Sadie Moonshine	1967	2.50	5.00	10.00
1598	Green Street Green/Fourteen Lovely Women	1967	—	3.00	6.00
1612	Bonnie and Clyde/Anniversary Song	1968	—	3.00	6.00

NEW WAVE, THE

Number	Title (A Side/B Side)	Yr	VG	VG+	NM
CANTERBURY					
❑ 503	Where Do We Go from Here/Not from You	1967	2.50	5.00	10.00
❑ 512	Little Dreams/Autre Fois	1967	2.50	5.00	10.00

NEW YORK DOLLS

Number	Title (A Side/B Side)	Yr	VG	VG+	NM
MERCURY					
❑ DJ-378 [DJ]	Trash (mono/stereo)	1973	3.75	7.50	15.00
❑ DJ-378 [PS]	Trash (mono/stereo)	1973	18.75	37.50	75.00
—Promo-only numbered sleeve					
❑ DJ-387 [DJ]	Personality Crisis (mono/stereo)	1973	3.75	7.50	15.00
❑ 73414	Trash/Personality Crisis	1973	15.00	30.00	60.00
❑ 73414 [PS]	Trash/Personality Crisis	1973	3.75	7.50	15.00
❑ 73478	Stranded in the Jungle/Who Are the Mystery Girls	1974	3.75	7.50	15.00
❑ 73615	Puss 'N' Boots/Showmen	1974	5.00	10.00	20.00

NEW YORK ROCK ENSEMBLE, THE

Includes records as "The New York Rock and Roll Ensemble."

Number	Title (A Side/B Side)	Yr	VG	VG+	NM
ATCO					
❑ 6467	Biji/Biji Rock	1967	2.50	5.00	10.00
❑ 6501	Kiss Her Once/Suddenly	1967	2.50	5.00	10.00
❑ 6584	The Thing to Do/Pick Up in the Morning	1968	2.50	5.00	10.00
❑ 6671	Wait Until Tomorrow/The Brandenburg	1969	2.50	5.00	10.00
COLUMBIA					
❑ 45242	Running Down the Highway/Law and Order	1970	—	2.50	5.00
❑ 45288	The King Is Dead/Beside You	1970	—	2.50	5.00
❑ 45367	Fields of Joy/Ride, Ride My Lady	1971	—	2.50	5.00
❑ 45574	Roll Over/A Whiter Shade of Pale	1972	—	2.50	5.00

NEW YORK SOUNDS, THE

Number	Title (A Side/B Side)	Yr	VG	VG+	NM
RED BIRD					
❑ 10-060	Drag Street/Good Lovin'	1966	5.00	10.00	20.00

NEW YORKERS, THE (1)

With FRED PARRIS of THE FIVE SATINS.

Number	Title (A Side/B Side)	Yr	VG	VG+	NM
WALL					
❑ 547	Miss Fine/Dream a Little Dream	1961	7.50	15.00	30.00
❑ 548	Tears in My Eyes/A Little Bit	1961	7.50	15.00	30.00

NEW YORKERS, THE (2)

Early version of THE HUDSON BROTHERS.

Number	Title (A Side/B Side)	Yr	VG	VG+	NM
DECCA					
❑ 32569	I Guess the Lord Must Be in New York City/Do Wah Diddy	1969	2.50	5.00	10.00
JERDEN					
❑ 906	Adrienne/Ice Cream World	1968	3.00	6.00	12.00
❑ 908	Land of Ur/Michael Glover	1969	3.00	6.00	12.00
SCEPTER					
❑ 12190	You're Not My Girl/When I'm Gone	1967	3.75	7.50	15.00
❑ 12199	Mr. Kirby/Seeds of Spring	1967	3.75	7.50	15.00
❑ 12207	Again/Show Me the Way to Love	1968	3.00	6.00	12.00
WARNER BROS.					
❑ 7318	Lonely/There'll Come a Time	1969	2.50	5.00	10.00

NEW YORKERS, THE (3)

Number	Title (A Side/B Side)	Yr	VG	VG+	NM
TAC-FUL					
❑ 101	You Should Have Told Me/Don't Want to Be Your Fool	1964	12.50	25.00	50.00

NEW YORKERS FIVE, THE

Number	Title (A Side/B Side)	Yr	VG	VG+	NM
DANICE					
❑ 801	Gloria My Darling/Cha Cha Baby	1955	100.00	200.00	400.00

NEWBAG, JOHNNY

Number	Title (A Side/B Side)	Yr	VG	VG+	NM
ATLANTIC					
❑ 2355	The Poorer the Man (The Higher His Love)/Got to Get You Back	1966	3.00	6.00	12.00
PORT					
❑ 3008	Sweet Thing/Little Samson	1965	6.25	12.50	25.00

NEWBEATS, THE

Also see DEAN AND MARC.

Number	Title (A Side/B Side)	Yr	VG	VG+	NM
BUDDAH					
❑ 390	The Way You Do the Things You Do/Does Your Body Need Lovin'	1973	2.00	4.00	8.00
HICKORY					
❑ 326	Bread and Butter/Tough Little Buggy	1974	—	3.00	6.00
❑ 1269	Bread and Butter/Tough Little Buggy	1964	3.75	7.50	15.00
❑ 1282	Everything's All Right/Pink Dally Rue	1964	3.00	6.00	12.00
❑ 1290	Break Away (From That Boy)/Hey-O Daddy-O	1965	2.50	5.00	10.00
❑ 1305	(The Bees Are For the Birds) The Birds Are For the Bees/Better Watch Your Step	1965	2.50	5.00	10.00
❑ 1320	Little Child/I Can't Hear You No More	1965	2.50	5.00	10.00
❑ 1332	Run, Baby, Run (Back Into My Arms)/Mean Wooly Willie	1965	3.00	6.00	12.00
❑ 1366	Shake Hands (And Come Out Crying)/Too Sweet to Be Forgotten	1966	2.50	5.00	10.00
❑ 1387	Short on Love/Crying My Heart Out	1966	2.00	4.00	8.00
❑ 1408	Bird Dog/Evil Eva	1966	2.00	4.00	8.00
❑ 1422	My Yesterday Love/Patent on Love	1966	2.00	4.00	8.00
❑ 1436	So Fine/Top Secret	1967	2.00	4.00	8.00
❑ 1467	Hide the Moon/It's Really Goodbye	1967	2.00	4.00	8.00
❑ 1485	Don't Turn Me Loose/You and Me and Happiness	1967	2.00	4.00	8.00
❑ 1496	Bad Dreams/Swinger	1968	2.00	4.00	8.00
❑ 1510	I've Been a Long Time Loving You/Michelle de Ann	1968	2.00	4.00	8.00
❑ 1522	Ain't That Lovin' You/The Girls and the Boys	1968	2.00	4.00	8.00
❑ 1539	Great Balls of Fire/Thou Shalt Not Steal	1969	2.00	4.00	8.00
❑ 1552	Groovin' (Out on Life)/Bread and Butter	1969	2.50	5.00	10.00
❑ 1562	Laura (What's He Got That I Ain't Got)/Break Away (From That Boy)	1970	—	3.00	6.00
❑ 1569	I'm a Teardrop/She Won't Hang Her Love (Out on the Line)	1970	—	3.00	6.00
❑ 1600	Am I Not My Brother's Keeper/Run, Baby, Run (Back Into My Arms)	1971	2.50	5.00	10.00
❑ 1624	Oh, Pretty Woman/Remember Love	1972	2.50	5.00	10.00
❑ 1637	Love Gets Sweeter/Eveything's All Right	1972	2.50	5.00	10.00
PLAYBOY					
❑ 6013	I Believe I'm in Love with You/I Know (You Don't Want Me No More)	1974	—	3.00	6.00

NEWLYWEDS, THE

Number	Title (A Side/B Side)	Yr	VG	VG+	NM
HOMOGENIZED SOUL					
❑ 601	Love Walked Out/The Quarrel	1961	1500.	2250.	3000.

NEWMAN, RANDY

Number	Title (A Side/B Side)	Yr	VG	VG+	NM
DOT					
❑ 16411	Golden Gridiron Boy/Country Boy	1962	12.50	25.00	50.00
—May be promo only					
REPRISE					
❑ 0692	I Think It's Going to Rain Today/The Beehive State	1968	3.75	7.50	15.00
❑ 0771	Last Night I Had a Dream/I Think He's Hiding	1968	6.25	12.50	25.00
—May be promo only					
❑ 0917	Have You Seen My Baby/Hold On	1970	3.75	7.50	15.00
❑ 0945	Gone Dead Train/Harry Flowers	1970	3.75	7.50	15.00
❑ 1102	Sail Away/Political Science	1972	—	3.00	6.00
❑ 1123	You Can Leave Your Hat On/Memo to My Son	1972	—	3.00	6.00
❑ 1324	Guilty/Naked Man	1975	—	2.50	5.00
❑ 1387	Louisiana 1927/Marie	1977	—	2.50	5.00
❑ 22798	I'd Love to See You Smile/End Title (I'd Love to See You Smile)	1989	—	—	3.00
❑ 27709	It's Money That Matters/Roll with the Punches	1988	—	—	3.00
❑ 27709 [PS]	It's Money That Matters/Roll with the Punches	1988	—	—	3.00
❑ 27856	Falling in Love/Bad News from Home	1989	—	—	3.00
WARNER BROS.					
❑ 8492	Short People/Old Man on the Farm	1977	—	2.50	5.00
❑ 8550	Baltimore/You Can't Fool the Fat Man	1978	—	2.00	4.00
❑ 8630	Rider in the Rain/Sigmund Freud's Impersonation of Albert Einstein in America	1978	—	2.00	4.00
❑ 29241	The Natural/The Natural (Final Game)	1984	—	2.00	4.00
❑ 29687	I Love L.A./Song for the Dead	1983	—	2.00	4.00
❑ 29803	The Blues/The Same Girl	1983	—	2.00	4.00
—A-side: With Paul Simon					
❑ 29803 [PS]	The Blues/The Same Girl	1983	—	2.00	4.00
❑ 49088	It's Money That I Love/Ghosts	1979	—	2.00	4.00
❑ 49149	Half a Man/The Story of a Rock and Roll Band	1979	—	2.00	4.00
❑ 49223	Spies/Political Science (Let's Drop the Big One)	1980	—	2.00	4.00

NEWPORTS, THE (1)

Number	Title (A Side/B Side)	Yr	VG	VG+	NM
CRYSTAL BALL					
❑ 129	Jingle Bells/My Juanita	1979	2.00	4.00	8.00
GUYDEN					
❑ 2067	If I Could Tonight/A Fellow Needs a Girl	1962	7.50	15.00	30.00
❑ 2116	Tears/Disillusioned Love	1964	7.50	15.00	30.00

NEWPORTS, THE (2)

Number	Title (A Side/B Side)	Yr	VG	VG+	NM
KENT					
❑ 380	The Wonder of Love/Dixie Women	1962	7.50	15.00	30.00

NEWPORTS, THE (3)

Number	Title (A Side/B Side)	Yr	VG	VG+	NM
LAURIE					
❑ 3327	The Trouble Is You/I Want You	1966	6.25	12.50	25.00

NEWPORTS, THE (U)

May be group (3), may be completely different.

Number	Title (A Side/B Side)	Yr	VG	VG+	NM
PARROT					
❑ 45008	Party Night/Listen to Your Big Brother	1966	3.75	7.50	15.00

NEWTON, WAYNE

Also see THE NEWTON BROTHERS.

Number	Title (A Side/B Side)	Yr	VG	VG+	NM
20TH CENTURY					
❑ 2393	Hold Me Like You Never Had Me/Housewife	1978	—	2.00	4.00
ARIES II					
❑ 101	You Stepped Into My Life/She Believes in Me	1979	—	2.00	4.00
❑ 108	Years/Rhythm Rhapsody	1980	—	2.00	4.00
CAPITOL					
❑ 2016	Love of the Common People/It's Still Loving You	1967	—	3.00	6.00
❑ 2917	Up Here in a Tree/Fallin'	1970	—	2.50	5.00
❑ 2980	For the Good Times/Little Dreamer	1970	—	2.50	5.00
❑ 3044	Apartment 21/Me and Bobby McGee	1971	—	2.50	5.00
❑ 3118	Remember the Good Times/Good Morning Dear	1971	—	2.50	5.00
❑ 3189	I Ain't That Easy to Love/Leavin' Ya Going My Way	1971	—	2.50	5.00
❑ 3241	Just a Memory/Higher Ground	1971	—	2.50	5.00
❑ 4920	Heart! (I Hear You Beating)/So Long Lucy	1963	2.50	5.00	10.00
❑ 4989	Danke Schoen/Better Now Than Later	1963	3.00	6.00	12.00
❑ 5058	Shirl Girl/Someone's Ahead of You	1963	2.50	5.00	10.00
❑ 5124	Dream Baby (How Long Must I Dream)/I'm Looking Over a Four-Leaf Clover	1964	2.50	5.00	10.00
❑ 5171	Bill Bailey/When the Saints Go Marching In	1964	2.50	5.00	10.00
❑ 5203	Only You/Too Late to Meet	1964	2.50	5.00	10.00
❑ 5338	Comin' On Too Strong/Lookin' Through a Tear	1965	6.24	12.50	25.00
—Bruce Johnston and Terry Melcher help out on this record					
❑ 5366	Red Roses for a Blue Lady/One More Memory	1965	2.00	4.00	8.00
❑ 5419	I'll Be With You in Apple Blossom Time/Laura Lee	1965	2.00	4.00	8.00
❑ 5470	Summer Wind/I'll Be Standing By	1965	2.00	4.00	8.00
❑ 5514	Keep the Lovin' Feelin'/Remember When	1965	2.00	4.00	8.00
❑ 5553	A Little Bit of Heaven/Some Sunday Morning	1965	2.00	4.00	8.00
❑ 5578	You Just Don't Know/After the Laughter	1966	2.00	4.00	8.00
❑ 5643	Somebody to Love/Stagecoach to Cheyenne	1966	2.00	4.00	8.00
❑ 5692	Excuse Me/How Loud a Sound	1966	2.00	4.00	8.00
❑ 5754	The Games That Lovers Play/Half a World Away	1966	2.00	4.00	8.00
❑ 5793	Happy Is Gone/How D'Ya Talk to a Girl	1966	2.00	4.00	8.00
❑ 5842	If I Only Had a Song to Sing/Sunny Day Girl	1967	—	3.00	6.00
❑ 5954	Dream Street Rose/Summer Colors	1967	—	3.00	6.00

Number	Title (A Side/B Side)	Yr	VG	VG+	NM
❑ 5993	Through the Eyes of Love/Just a Memory	1967	—	3.00	6.00

CHALLENGE

Number	Title (A Side/B Side)	Yr	VG	VG+	NM
❑ 59228	I Want to Mean Everything to You/I Still Love You	1964	2.50	5.00	10.00
❑ 59238	The Little White Cloud That Cried/Calorie Date	1964	2.50	5.00	10.00
❑ 59238	The Little White Cloud That Cried/Born When You Kissed Me	1964	2.50	5.00	10.00

CHELSEA

Number	Title (A Side/B Side)	Yr	VG	VG+	NM
❑ BCBO-0091	May the Road Rise to Meet You/Pour Me a Little More Wine	1973	—	2.00	4.00
❑ 78-0100	Daddy Don't You Walk So Fast/Echo Valley 2-6809	1972	—	3.00	6.00
—White label (not a promo)					
❑ 78-0100	Daddy Don't You Walk So Fast/Echo Valley 2-6809	1972	—	2.50	5.00
—Mostly pink label					
❑ 78-0105	Can't You Hear the Song?/You Don't Have to Ask	1972	—	2.00	4.00
❑ 78-0109	Anthem/Fool	1972	—	2.00	4.00
❑ 78-0116	Just Yesterday/While We're Still Young	1973	—	2.00	4.00
❑ 78-0124	Help Me Help You/We Didn't Know the Time of Day	1973	—	2.00	4.00
❑ 3003	Lay Lady Lay/Walking in the Sand	1974	—	2.00	4.00
❑ 3018	All Alone Am I/You Don't Have to Ask	1975	—	2.00	4.00
❑ 3028	Run to Me/Lady Lonely	1975	—	2.00	4.00
❑ 3041	The Hungry Years/In Dreams	1976	—	2.00	4.00
❑ 3058	It Could Have Been a Wonderful Christmas/Jingle Bell Hustle	1976	—	2.50	5.00

CURB

Number	Title (A Side/B Side)	Yr	VG	VG+	NM
❑ 10520	Cowboy's Christmas/(B-side unknown)	1988	—	—	3.00
❑ 10559	While the Feeling's Good/Our Wedding Band	1989	—	—	3.00
—A-side with Tammy Wynette					

ELEKTRA

Number	Title (A Side/B Side)	Yr	VG	VG+	NM
❑ 45528	Last Exit for Love/Too Good to Be True	1978	—	2.00	4.00

GEORGE

Number	Title (A Side/B Side)	Yr	VG	VG+	NM
❑ 7777	The Little White Cloud That Cried/(B-side unknown)	1962	5.00	10.00	20.00

MGM

Number	Title (A Side/B Side)	Yr	VG	VG+	NM
❑ 13891	All the Time/Like Everything Else	1968	—	2.50	5.00
❑ 13936	Remembering/Angelica	1968	—	2.50	5.00
❑ 13955	Dreams of the Everyday Housewife/The Tip of My Fingers	1968	—	2.50	5.00
❑ 13993	Silence Says/Town and Country	1968	—	2.50	5.00
❑ 14014	I Just Can't Help Believin'/Husbands and Wives	1968	—	2.50	5.00
❑ 14019	Christmas Prayer/Santa Claus Is Comin' to Town	1968	—	2.50	5.00
❑ 14046	Everything's in Love Today/The Silence Says	1969	—	2.50	5.00
❑ 14083	New York City/For the First Time	1969	—	2.50	5.00
❑ 14098	It's Such a Lonely Time of the Year/The Country	1969	—	2.50	5.00
❑ 14430	With Pen in Hand/Town and Country	1972	—	2.00	4.00

RCA VICTOR

Number	Title (A Side/B Side)	Yr	VG	VG+	NM
❑ AMBO-0126	Daddy Don't You Walk So Fast/Fool	1973	—	2.00	4.00
—Gold Standard Series reissue					

WARNER BROS.

Number	Title (A Side/B Side)	Yr	VG	VG+	NM
❑ 8415	I Want You with Me/Midnight Sun	1977	—	2.00	4.00

7-Inch Extended Plays

ARIES II

Number	Title (A Side/B Side)	Yr	VG	VG+	NM
❑ 102	White Christmas/It's the Season//I'll Be Home for Christmas/Blue Snow at Christmas	1979	—	2.00	4.00

NEWTON BROTHERS, THE

With WAYNE NEWTON.

CAPITOL

Number	Title (A Side/B Side)	Yr	VG	VG+	NM
❑ F-4236	The Real Thing/I Spy	1959	20.00	40.00	80.00

NEWTON-JOHN, OLIVIA

Also see JOHN TRAVOLTA AND OLIVIA NEWTON-JOHN.

ATLANTIC

Number	Title (A Side/B Side)	Yr	VG	VG+	NM
❑ 89420	The Best of Me/Sage	1986	—	—	3.00
—With David Foster					
❑ 89420 [PS]	The Best of Me/Sage	1986	—	—	3.00

MCA

Number	Title (A Side/B Side)	Yr	VG	VG+	NM
❑ 40043	Take Me Home, Country Roads/Sail Into Tomorrow	1973	—	—	—
—Unreleased?					
❑ 40043 [DJ]	Take Me Home, Country Roads (mono/stereo)	1973	5.00	10.00	20.00
❑ 40101	Let Me Be There/Maybe Then I'll Think of You	1973	—	2.50	5.00
❑ 40209	If You Love Me (Let Me Know)/Brotherly Love	1974	—	2.50	5.00
❑ 40280	I Honestly Love You/Home Ain't Home Anymore	1974	—	2.50	5.00
❑ 40349	Have You Never Been Mellow/Water Under the Bridge	1974	—	2.50	5.00
❑ 40418	Please Mr. Please/And In the Morning	1975	—	2.50	5.00
❑ 40418 [PS]	Please Mr. Please/And In the Morning	1975	2.50	5.00	10.00
❑ 40459	Something Better to Do/He's My Rock	1975	—	2.50	5.00
❑ 40459 [PS]	Something Better to Do/He's My Rock	1975	—	3.00	6.00
❑ 40495	Let It Shine/He Ain't Heavy, He's My Brother	1975	—	2.50	5.00
❑ 40525	Come On Over/Small Talk and Pride	1976	—	2.00	4.00
❑ 40600	Don't Stop Believin'/Greensleeves	1976	—	2.00	4.00
—A-side not a Christmas song					
❑ 40600 [PS]	Don't Stop Believin'/Greensleeves	1976	—	2.50	5.00
❑ 40642	Every Face Tells a Story/Love You Hold the Key	1976	—	2.00	4.00
❑ 40670	Sam/I'll Bet You a Kangaroo	1976	—	2.00	4.00
❑ 40737	Making a Good Thing Better/I Think I'll Say Goodbye	1977	—	2.00	4.00
❑ 40811	I Honestly Love You/Don't Cry for Me Argentina	1977	—	2.50	5.00
❑ 40811 [PS]	I Honestly Love You/Don't Cry for Me Argentina	1977	2.50	5.00	10.00
❑ 40975	A Little More Love/Borrowed Time	1978	—	2.00	4.00
❑ 40975 [PS]	A Little More Love/Borrowed Time	1978	—	2.50	5.00
❑ 41009	Deeper Than the Night/Please Don't Keep Me Waiting	1979	—	2.00	4.00
❑ 41074	Totally Hot/Dancing Round and Round	1979	—	2.00	4.00
❑ 41074 [PS]	Totally Hot/Dancing Round and Round	1979	—	2.50	5.00
❑ 41247	Magic/Fool Country	1980	—	2.50	5.00
—Custom pink "Xanadu" label					
❑ 41247	Magic/Fool Country	1980	—	2.00	4.00
—Standard blue rainbow label					
❑ 41247 [PS]	Magic/Fool Country	1980	—	2.50	5.00
❑ 41286	Xanadu/Whenever You're Away from Me	1980	—	2.00	4.00
—A-side with Electric Light Orchestra; B-side with Gene Kelly. Persistent rumors claim existence of a U.S. picture sleeve for this record, but we've never seen one.					
❑ 41287	Suddenly/You Made Me Love You	1980	—	2.50	5.00
—A-side with Cliff Richard					
❑ 51007	Suddenly/You Made Me Love You	1980	—	2.00	4.00
—A-side with Cliff Richard					
❑ 51007 [PS]	Suddenly/You Made Me Love You	1980	—	2.50	5.00
❑ 51182	Physical/The Promise (The Dolphin Song)	1981	—	—	3.00
❑ 51182 [PS]	Physical/The Promise (The Dolphin Song)	1981	—	2.00	4.00
❑ 52000	Make a Move on Me/Falling	1982	—	—	3.00
❑ 52000 [PS]	Make a Move on Me/Falling	1982	—	2.50	5.00
❑ 52069	Landslide/Recovery	1982	—	—	3.00
❑ 52069 [PS]	Landslide/Recovery	1982	—	2.00	4.00
❑ 52100	Heart Attack/Strangers Touch	1982	—	—	3.00
❑ 52100 [PS]	Heart Attack/Strangers Touch	1982	—	—	3.00
❑ 52155	Tied Up/Silvery Rain	1983	—	—	3.00
❑ 52155 [PS]	Tied Up/Silvery Rain	1983	—	—	3.00
❑ 52284	Twist of Fate/Take a Chance	1983	—	—	3.00
❑ 52284 [PS]	Twist of Fate/Take a Chance	1983	—	—	3.00
❑ 52341	Livin' in Desperate Times/Landslide	1984	—	—	3.00
❑ 52341 [PS]	Livin' in Desperate Times/Landslide	1984	—	—	3.00
❑ 52686	Soul Kiss/Electric	1985	—	—	3.00
❑ 52686 [PS]	Soul Kiss/Electric	1985	—	—	3.00
❑ 52757	Toughen Up/Driving Music	1986	—	—	3.00
❑ 52757 [PS]	Toughen Up/Driving Music	1986	—	—	3.00
❑ 53294	The Rumour/Winter Angel	1988	—	—	3.00
❑ 53294 [PS]	The Rumour/Winter Angel	1988	—	—	3.00
❑ 53438	Can't We Talk It Over in Bed/Get Out	1988	—	—	3.00
❑ 72053	I Honestly Love You/I Honestly Love You (Remix)	1998	—	—	3.00
—New recordings					

MCA NASHVILLE

Number	Title (A Side/B Side)	Yr	VG	VG+	NM
❑ 72074	Back with a Heart/Under My Skin	1998	—	—	3.00

RSO

Number	Title (A Side/B Side)	Yr	VG	VG+	NM
❑ 903	Hopelessly Devoted to You/Love Is a Many-Splendored Thing	1978	—	2.00	4.00

UNI

Number	Title (A Side/B Side)	Yr	VG	VG+	NM
❑ 55281	If Not for You/The Biggest Clown	1971	2.50	5.00	10.00
❑ 55304	Banks of the Ohio/It's So Hard to Say Goodbye	1971	2.00	4.00	8.00
❑ 55317	What Is Life/I'm a Small and Lonely Light	1972	2.00	4.00	8.00
❑ 55348	Just a Little Too Much/My Old Man's Gotta Gun	1972	3.00	6.00	12.00

NIC NACS, THE

RPM

Number	Title (A Side/B Side)	Yr	VG	VG+	NM
❑ 342	Gonna Have a Merry Christmas/Found Me a Sugar Daddy	1951	50.00	100.00	200.00

NICE, THE

Keith Emerson, later of EMERSON, LAKE AND PALMER, was in this group.

IMMEDIATE

Number	Title (A Side/B Side)	Yr	VG	VG+	NM
❑ 5004	Azrial (Angel of Death)/Thoughts of Emerlist Davjack	1968	3.00	6.00	12.00
❑ 5008	America/Diamnd Hard Apples of the Moon	1968	3.00	6.00	12.00

MERCURY

Number	Title (A Side/B Side)	Yr	VG	VG+	NM
❑ 73114	Country Pie/(B-side unknown)	1970	2.00	4.00	8.00
❑ 73272	Country Pie-Brandenburg Concerto No. 6 (Part 1)/Finale-5th Bridge	1972	—	3.00	6.00

NICK AND THE JAGUARS

TAMLA

Number	Title (A Side/B Side)	Yr	VG	VG+	NM
❑ 5501F	Ich-I-Bon #1/Cool and Crazy	1960	75.00	150.00	300.00

NICK AND THE NACKS

BARRY

Number	Title (A Side/B Side)	Yr	VG	VG+	NM
❑ 108	The Night/That Old Black Magic	1964	100.00	200.00	400.00

NICK AND THE STINGRAYS

MILL-MONT

Number	Title (A Side/B Side)	Yr	VG	VG+	NM
❑ 1628	You Are So Beautiful/Broken Hearted Baby	196?	50.00	100.00	200.00

NICKIE AND THE NITELITES

With Nick Massi, later of THE FOUR SEASONS.

BRUNSWICK

Number	Title (A Side/B Side)	Yr	VG	VG+	NM
❑ 55155	I'm Lonely/Tell Me You Care	1959	25.00	50.00	100.00

NICKS, STEVIE

Also see BUCKINGHAM NICKS; FLEETWOOD MAC.

ATLANTIC OLDIES SERIES

Number	Title (A Side/B Side)	Yr	VG	VG+	NM
❑ OS 13236	Stop Draggin' My Heart Around/Leather and Lace	1983	—	—	3.00
❑ OS 13258	Edge of Seventeen/Stand Back	1985	—	—	3.00
❑ 84964	Talk to Me/I Can't Wait	1987	—	—	3.00
❑ 84998	If Anyone Falls/Nightbird	1986	—	—	3.00

MODERN

Number	Title (A Side/B Side)	Yr	VG	VG+	NM
❑ 3836	Stop Draggin' My Heart Around/Kind of Woman	1981	—	—	—
—Canceled; reassigned to 7336 (Atco series)					
❑ 7336	Stop Draggin' My Heart Around/Kind of Woman	1981	—	2.00	4.00
—With Tom Petty and the Heartbreakers					
❑ 7336 [PS]	Stop Draggin' My Heart Around/Kind of Woman	1981	—	3.00	6.00
❑ 7341	Leather and Lace/Bella Donna	1981	—	2.50	5.00
—With Don Henley; first pressing states "Written for Waylon Jennings and Jessi Colter"					
❑ 7341	Leather and Lace/Bella Donna	1981	—	2.00	4.00
—With Don Henley; with no reference to Waylon Jennings and Jessi Colter on label					
❑ 7341 [PS]	Leather and Lace/Bella Donna	1981	2.50	5.00	10.00
❑ 7401	Edge of Seventeen (Just Like the White Winged Dove)/Edge of Seventeen (Live)	1982	—	2.00	4.00
❑ 7401 [PS]	Edge of Seventeen (Just Like the White Winged Dove)/Edge of Seventeen (Live)	1982	—	3.00	6.00
❑ 7405	After the Glitter Fades/Think About It	1982	—	3.00	6.00
❑ 7405 [PS]	After the Glitter Fades/Think About It	1982	2.00	4.00	8.00
❑ 99150	Whole Lotta Trouble/Ghosts	1989	—	—	3.00

Number	Title (A Side/B Side)	Yr	VG	VG+	NM
❑ 99150 [PS]	Whole Lotta Trouble/Ghosts	1989	2.50	5.00	10.00
❑ 99179	Two Kinds of Love/Real Tears	1989	—	—	3.00
❑ 99179 [PS]	Two Kinds of Love/Real Tears	1989	—	2.50	5.00
❑ 99216	Rooms on Fire/Alice	1989	—	—	3.00
❑ 99216 [PS]	Rooms on Fire/Alice	1989	—	—	3.00
❑ 99532	Has Anyone Ever Written Anything for You/ Imperial Hotel	1986	—	—	3.00
❑ 99532 [PS]	Has Anyone Ever Written Anything for You/ Imperial Hotel	1986	2.00	4.00	8.00
❑ 99565	I Can't Wait/The Nightmare	1986	—	—	3.00
❑ 99565 [DJ]	I Can't Wait (Remix)/I Can't Wait (Soft Intro)	1986	2.00	4.00	8.00
❑ 99565 [PS]	I Can't Wait/The Nightmare	1986	—	—	3.00
❑ 99565 [PS]	I Can't Wait (Remix)/I Can't Wait (Soft Intro)	1986	3.00	6.00	12.00
❑ 99582	Talk to Me/One More Big Time Rock and Roll Star	1985	—	—	3.00
❑ 99582 [PS]	Talk to Me/One More Big Time Rock and Roll Star	1985	—	—	3.00
❑ 99799	Nightbird/Gate and Garden	1984	—	—	3.00
❑ 99799 [PS]	Nightbird/Gate and Garden	1984	12.50	25.00	50.00
❑ 99832	If Anyone Falls/Wild Heart	1983	—	2.00	4.00
❑ 99832 [PS]	If Anyone Falls/Wild Heart	1983	—	2.50	5.00
❑ 99863	Stand Back/Garbo	1983	—	—	3.00
❑ 99863 [PS]	Stand Back/Garbo	1983	—	2.00	4.00
WARNER SUNSET					
❑ 17132	If You Ever Did Believe/Crystal	1998	—	2.00	4.00

NICKY AND THE NOBLES

Number	Title (A Side/B Side)	Yr	VG	VG+	NM
END					
❑ 1021	Schoolhouse Rock/A Way to Tell Her	1958	12.50	25.00	50.00
❑ 1098	School Bells/School Day Crush	1961	6.25	12.50	25.00
GONE					
❑ 5039	School Bells/School Day Crush	1958	15.00	30.00	60.00
—Black label					
❑ 5039	School Bells/School Day Crush	1958	6.25	12.50	25.00
—Multicolor label					
❑ 5039	School Bells/School Days	1958	25.00	50.00	100.00
—With B-side title variation					

NICOL, JIMMY

His 15 minutes of fame came from his brief stint filling in for an ailing Ringo Starr on a 1964 Beatles tour.

Number	Title (A Side/B Side)	Yr	VG	VG+	NM
ARGO					
❑ 5464	Night Train/Humpty Dumpty	1964	—	—	—
—Unreleased					
MAR MAR					
❑ 313	Night Train/Humpty Dumpty	1965	37.50	75.00	150.00
PARROT					
❑ 9752	Sweet Clementine/Roaring Blue	1965	6.25	12.50	25.00

NIGHT WATCH, THE

Number	Title (A Side/B Side)	Yr	VG	VG+	NM
ABC					
❑ 10862	Closed Time/Lips to Your Heart	1966	6.25	12.50	25.00

NIGHTCRAWLERS, THE

Number	Title (A Side/B Side)	Yr	VG	VG+	NM
KAPP					
❑ KE-110	The Little Black Egg/You're Running Wild	1966	2.50	5.00	10.00
❑ 709	The Little Black Egg/You're Running Wild	1965	3.75	7.50	15.00
❑ 746	A Basket of Flowers/Washboard	1966	3.75	7.50	15.00
❑ 826	My Butterfly/Today I'm Happy	1967	7.50	15.00	30.00
LEE					
❑ 101	Cry/Marie	1964	15.00	30.00	60.00
❑ 1012	The Little Black Egg/You're Running Wild	1965	12.50	25.00	50.00
MARLIN					
❑ 1904	A Basket of Flowers/Washboard	1966	5.00	10.00	20.00

NIGHTHAWK, ROBERT

Number	Title (A Side/B Side)	Yr	VG	VG+	NM
STATES					
❑ 131	The Moon Is Rising/Maggie Campbell	1954	75.00	150.00	300.00

NILSSON

Also see THE FOTO-FI FOUR; THE RIC-A-SHAYS.

Number	Title (A Side/B Side)	Yr	VG	VG+	NM
CRUSADER					
❑ 103	Baa Baa Black Sheep/Baa Baa Black Sheep (Part 2)	1964	7.50	15.00	30.00
—As "Bo Pete"					
MUSICOR					
❑ 6308	Please Mr. Music Man/Foolish Clock	1977	—	2.00	4.00
POLYDOR					
❑ 881177-7	Silver Horse/Loneliness	1984	—	2.00	4.00
RCA					
❑ PB-10759	Just One Look-Baby I'm Yours/That Is All	1976	—	2.00	4.00
—With Lynda Lawrence					
❑ PB-11059	Perfect Day/Who Done It	1977	—	2.00	4.00
❑ PB-11059 [PS]	Perfect Day/Who Done It	1977	—	2.50	5.00
❑ PB-11144	All I Think About Is You/I Never Thought I'd Get This Lonely	1977	—	2.00	4.00
❑ PB-11193	Ain't It Kinda Wonderful/I'm Bringing a Red, Red Rose	1978	—	2.00	4.00
❑ PB-11318	Spaceman/Me and My Arrow	1978	—	2.00	4.00
RCA VICTOR					
❑ APBO-0039	As Time Goes By/Lullabye in Ragtime	1973	—	3.00	6.00
❑ APBO-0246	Daybreak/Down	1974	—	2.00	4.00
❑ APBO-0246 [PS]	Daybreak/Down	1974	—	3.00	6.00
❑ SP-45-304 [DJ]	Jump Into the Fire (mono/stereo)	1972	2.50	5.00	10.00
—Promo-only number					
❑ PB-10001	Many Rivers to Cross/Don't Forget Me	1974	2.00	4.00	8.00
❑ PB-10078	Subterranean Homesick Blues/Mucho Mungo	1974	2.00	4.00	8.00
❑ PB-10130	Remember (Christmas)/The Lottery Song	1974	—	2.00	4.00
❑ PB-10139	Loop De Loop/Don't Forget Me	1974	—	2.00	4.00
❑ PB-10183	Kojak Columbo/Turn Out the Light	1975	—	2.00	4.00
❑ PB-10183 [PS]	Kojak Columbo/Turn Out the Light	1975	—	2.50	5.00
❑ PB-10634	Sail Away/Moonchino Bandit	1976	—	2.00	4.00
❑ 47-9206	Without Her/Freckles	1967	2.00	4.00	8.00
❑ 47-9298	You Can't Do That/Ten Little Indians	1967	2.50	5.00	10.00
❑ 47-9383	River Deep Mountain High/She Sang Hymns Out of Tune	1967	2.00	4.00	8.00
❑ 47-9442	One/Sister Marie	1968	2.00	4.00	8.00
❑ 47-9544	Everybody's Talkin'/Don't Leave Me	1968	3.00	6.00	12.00
❑ 47-9675	Rainmaker/I Will Take You There	1968	2.00	4.00	8.00
❑ 74-0161	Everybody's Talkin'/Rainmaker	1969	2.50	5.00	10.00
❑ 74-0207	Maybe/Marchin' Down Broadway	1969	2.00	4.00	8.00
❑ 74-0261	I Guess the Lord Must Be in New York City/Maybe	1969	2.00	4.00	8.00
❑ 74-0310	I'll Be Home/Waiting	1970	—	3.00	6.00
❑ 74-0336	Caroline/Yellow Man	1970	—	3.00	6.00
❑ 74-0362	Down to the Valley/Buy My Album	1970	—	3.00	6.00
❑ 74-0443	Me and My Arrow/Are You Sleeping	1971	—	3.00	6.00
❑ 74-0524	Without Her/Good Old Desk	1971	—	3.00	6.00
❑ 74-0604	Without You/Gotta Get Up	1971	—	2.50	5.00
❑ 74-0673	Jump Into the Fire/The Moonbeam Song	1972	—	2.50	5.00
❑ 74-0718	Coconut/Down	1972	—	2.50	5.00
❑ 74-0788	Spaceman/Turn On Your Radio	1972	—	2.50	5.00
❑ 74-0855	Remember (Christmas)/The Lottery Song	1972	—	2.50	5.00
TOWER					
❑ 103	Sixteen Tons/I'm Gonna Lose My Mind	1964	3.75	7.50	15.00
❑ 136	You Can't Take Your Love Away from Me/Born in Grenada	1965	3.75	7.50	15.00
❑ 244	She's Yours/Growing Up	1966	3.75	7.50	15.00
❑ 518	Good Time/Growin' Up	1969	3.75	7.50	15.00
TRY					
❑ 501	Do You Wanna/Groovy Little Suzie	1964	10.00	20.00	40.00
—As "Bo Pete"					

NIMBLE, JACK B. AND THE QUICKS

Number	Title (A Side/B Side)	Yr	VG	VG+	NM
DEL RIO					
❑ 2303/4	Like Keyed/Babes in Toyland	1962	6.25	12.50	25.00
❑ 2305	Nut Rocker/Never on Sunday	1962	7.50	15.00	30.00
DOT					
❑ 16319	Nut Rocker/Never on Sunday	1962	3.75	7.50	15.00

NIMOY, LEONARD

Number	Title (A Side/B Side)	Yr	VG	VG+	NM
DOT					
❑ 17028	The Ballad of Bilbo Baggins/Cotton Candy	1967	3.75	7.50	15.00
❑ 17038	Theme from "Star Trek"/Visit to a Sad Planet	1967	5.00	10.00	20.00
❑ 17125	I'd Love Making Love to You/Please Don't Try to Change My Mind	1968	3.75	7.50	15.00
❑ 17175	Consilium/Here We Go 'Round Again	1968	3.75	7.50	15.00
❑ 17330	The Sun Will Rise/Time to Get It Together	1969	3.75	7.50	15.00

NINE DAYS

Number	Title (A Side/B Side)	Yr	VG	VG+	NM
EPIC					
❑ 34 79532	Absolutely (Story of a Girl)/If I Am	2000	—	2.00	4.00

1910 FRUITGUM COMPANY

Number	Title (A Side/B Side)	Yr	VG	VG+	NM
ATTACK					
❑ 10293	Lawdy, Lawdy/The Clock	1970	3.00	6.00	12.00
BUDDAH					
❑ 24	Simon Says/Reflections from the Looking Glass	1968	2.50	5.00	10.00
❑ 39	May I Take a Giant Step (Into Your Heart)/(Poor Old) Mr. Jensen	1968	2.00	4.00	8.00
❑ 54	1,2,3, Red Light/Sticky, Sticky	1968	2.50	5.00	10.00
❑ 71	Goody Goody Gumdrops/Candy Kisses	1968	2.00	4.00	8.00
❑ 91	Indian Giver/Pow Wow	1969	2.50	5.00	10.00
❑ 114	Special Delivery/No Good Annie	1969	2.00	4.00	8.00
❑ 130	The Train/Eternal Light	1969	2.00	4.00	8.00
❑ 146	When We Get Married/Baby Sweet	1969	2.00	4.00	8.00
SUPER K					
❑ 115	Go Away/The Track	1970	3.00	6.00	12.00

94 EAST

Early band led by PRINCE.

Number	Title (A Side/B Side)	Yr	VG	VG+	NM
HOT PINK					
❑ 3223	Just Another Sucker/(B-side unknown)	1986	—	3.00	6.00
POLYDOR					
❑ 14414	Be My Fortune Teller/I Just Wanna Be	1977	—	—	—
—Unreleased?					

NINO AND THE EBB TIDES

Number	Title (A Side/B Side)	Yr	VG	VG+	NM
ACME					
❑ 720	Franny Franny/Darling I'll Love Only You	1958	75.00	150.00	300.00
MADISON					
❑ 162	Those Oldies But Goodies (Remind Me of You)/ Don't Run Away	1961	10.00	20.00	40.00
❑ 166	Juke Box Saturday Night/(Someday) I'll Fall in Love	1961	7.50	15.00	30.00
MALA					
❑ 480	Automatic Reaction/Linda Lou Garrett Like 24 Karat	1964	5.00	10.00	20.00
MARCO					
❑ 105	Little Miss Blue/Someday	1961	12.50	25.00	50.00
MR. PEACOCK					
❑ 102	Wished I Was Home/Happy Guy	1961	6.25	12.50	25.00
❑ 117	Lovin' Time/Stamps, Baby, Stamps	1962	6.25	12.50	25.00
MR. PEEKE					
❑ 123	Tonight I'll Be Lonely/Nursery Rhymes	1963	6.25	12.50	25.00
RECORTE					
❑ 405	Puppy Love/You Make Me Rock 'N' Roll	1958	12.50	25.00	50.00
❑ 408	The Real Meaning of Christmas/Two Purple Shadows in the Snow	1958	75.00	150.00	300.00
❑ 409	I'm Confessin'/Tell the World I Do	1959	12.50	25.00	50.00
❑ 413	Don't Look Around/I Love Girls	1959	25.00	50.00	100.00

NIRVANA

Two different groups. The records on Bell are by a different group than the rest.

Number	Title (A Side/B Side)	Yr	VG	VG+	NM
BELL					
❑ 715	We Can Help You/Pentecost Hotel	1968	2.50	5.00	10.00
❑ 730	You Are Just the One/Girl in the Park	1968	2.50	5.00	10.00

Number	Title (A Side/B Side)	Yr	VG	VG+	NM
❑ 739	Trapeze/The Touchables	1968	2.50	5.00	10.00
COMMUNION					
❑ 23	Here She Comes Now/Venus in Furs	1991	3.00	6.25	12.50
—B-side by The Melvins; blue vinyl					
❑ 23	Here She Comes Now/Venus in Furs	1991	3.00	6.25	12.50
—B-side by The Melvins; green vinyl					
❑ 23 [PS]	Here She Comes Now/Venus in Furs	1991	3.00	6.25	12.50
—B-side by The Melvins					
DGC					
❑ 19050	Smells Like Teen Spirit/Even In His Youth	1991	2.00	4.00	8.00
❑ 19120	Come As You Are/Drain You	1992	2.00	4.00	8.00
SUB POP					
❑ 23	Love Buzz/Big Cheese	1988	100.00	200.00	400.00
—#1 in Sub Pop Singles Club series					
❑ 23 [PS]	Love Buzz/Big Cheese	1988	100.00	200.00	400.00
—Hand-numbered edition of 1,000					
❑ 73	Sliver/Dive	1990	10.00	20.00	40.00
—First 3,000 on blue vinyl					
❑ 73	Sliver/Dive	1990	—	3.50	7.00
—Later issues on pale yellow vinyl with California address on label					
❑ 73	Sliver/Dive	1990	2.50	5.00	10.00
—Black vinyl, no California address on label					
❑ 73	Sliver/Dive	1990	—	—	3.00
—Still later issues on black vinyl with California address on label					
❑ 73	Sliver/Dive	1990	12.50	25.00	50.00
—Clear pink/lavender vinyl					
❑ 73 [PS]	Sliver/Dive	1990	2.50	5.00	10.00
—Original picture sleeves were fold-over, not seam sealed					
❑ 73 [PS]	Sliver/Dive	1990	—	—	3.00
—Later picture sleeves were seam sealed					
❑ 97	Molly's Lips (Live)/Candy	1991	8.75	17.50	35.00
—B-side by Fluid; green vinyl					
❑ 97	Molly's Lips (Live)/Candy	1991	2.50	5.00	10.00
—B-side by Fluid; black vinyl					
❑ 97 [PS]	Molly's Lips (Live)/Candy	1991	2.50	5.00	10.00
—B-side by Fluid; #27 in Sub Pop Singles Club series					

NITE RIDERS, THE

Possibly two different groups.

Number	Title (A Side/B Side)	Yr	VG	VG+	NM
MGM					
❑ 12487	Sippin' Coffee/Tank Town	1957	7.50	15.00	30.00
TEEN					
❑ 116	Starlight and You/I Know You're In There	1955	10.00	20.00	40.00
❑ 118	Got Me a Six-Button Benny/Don't Hang Up the Phone	1955	10.00	20.00	40.00
❑ 120	When a Man Cries/Waiting in the Schoolroom	1955	10.00	20.00	40.00

NITE ROCKERS, THE

Number	Title (A Side/B Side)	Yr	VG	VG+	NM
RCA VICTOR					
❑ 47-7323	Nite Rock/Oh! Baby	1958	7.50	15.00	30.00

NITTY GRITTY DIRT BAND

Includes The Dirt Band. Also see JOHN DENVER.

Number	Title (A Side/B Side)	Yr	VG	VG+	NM
DECCA					
❑ 55206	Maybe Baby/Crying, Waiting, Hoping	1996	—	—	3.00
—B-side by Marty Stuart and Steve Earle					
LIBERTY					
❑ 1389	High School Yearbook/Too Good to Be True	1980	—	2.00	4.00
—As "The Dirt Band"					
❑ 1398	Nazamas Nuestra Magic (Make a Little Magic)/Jas' Moon	1981	—	2.00	4.00
—As "The Dirt Band"					
❑ 1429	Fire in the Sky/EZ Slow	1981	—	2.00	4.00
—As "The Dirt Band"					
❑ 1449	Badlands/Jealousy	1982	—	2.00	4.00
—As "The Dirt Band"					
❑ 1467	Too Close for Comfort/Circular Man	1982	—	2.00	4.00
—As "The Dirt Band"					
❑ 1499	Let's Go/Shot Full of Love	1983	—	2.00	4.00
❑ 1507	Mary Anne/Dance Little Jean	1983	—	2.00	4.00
❑ 1513	Colorado Christmas/Mr. Bojangles	1983	—	3.00	6.00
❑ 55948	Buy for Me the Rain/Candy Man	1967	2.50	5.00	10.00
❑ 55982	The Teddy Bear's Picnic/Truly Right	1967	2.00	4.00	8.00
❑ 55982 [PS]	The Teddy Bear's Picnic/Truly Right	1967	3.75	7.50	15.00
❑ 56054	These Days/Collegiana	1968	2.00	4.00	8.00
❑ 56134	Some of Shelley's Blues/Yukon Railroad	1969	—	3.00	6.00
❑ 56159	Rave On/The Cure	1970	—	3.00	6.00
❑ 56197	Mr. Bojangles/Mr. Bojangles (Prelude: Uncle Charlie and His Dog Teddy)	1970	—	3.00	6.00
❑ 56197	Mr. Bojangles (Prelude: Uncle Charlie and His Dog Teddy)/Spanish Fandango	1970	2.00	4.00	8.00
❑ S7-57766	I Fought the Law/Mr. Bojangles	1992	—	2.00	4.00
MCA					
❑ 53795	One Step Over the Line/Riding Along	1990	—	—	3.00
—A-side: With Roseanne Cash; B-side: With Emmylou Harris					
❑ 53964	The Rest of the Dream/Snowballs	1990	—	—	3.00
❑ 55182	You Believed in Me/Atlanta Reel '96	1996	—	—	3.00
—A-side by Karla Bonoff and the Nitty Gritty Dirt Band; B-side by Michael Omartian					
❑ 79013	From Small Things (Big Things One Day Come)/Blues Berry Hill	1990	—	—	3.00
❑ 79075	You Make Life Good Again/Snowballs	1990	—	—	3.00
UNITED ARTISTS					
❑ 0061	Mr. Bojangles/Buy for Me the Rain	1973	—	2.00	4.00
—"Silver Spotlight Series" reissue					
❑ XW177	Will the Circle Be Unbroken/Honky Tonkin'	1973	—	2.50	5.00
❑ XW247	Grand Ole Opry Song/Orange Blossom Special	1973	—	2.50	5.00
❑ XW263	Cosmic Cowboy (Part 1)/Cosmic Cowboy (Part 2)	1973	—	2.50	5.00
❑ XW321	Tennessee Stud/Way Down Town	1973	—	2.50	5.00
—With Doc Watson					
❑ XW544	The Battle of New Orleans/Mountain Whipporwill	1974	—	2.50	5.00
❑ XW544 [PS]	The Battle of New Orleans/Mountain Whipporwill	1974	—	3.00	6.00
❑ XW655	(All I Have to Do Is) Dream/Raleigh-Durham Reel	1975	—	2.50	5.00
❑ XW741	Mother of Love/The Moon Just Turned Blue	1975	—	2.50	5.00
❑ XW830	Cosmic Cowboy/Stars and Stripes Forever	1976	—	2.00	4.00
—As "The Dirt Band"					
❑ XW889	Jamaica Lady/Bayou Jubilee-Sally Was a Goodun	1976	—	2.00	4.00
—As "The Dirt Band"					
❑ XW936	Buy for Me the Rain/Mother Earth (Provides for Me)	1976	—	2.00	4.00
—As "The Dirt Band"					
❑ XW1164	Orange Blossom Special/Will the Circle Be Unbroken	1978	—	2.00	4.00
❑ XW1228	Wild Nights/In for the Night	1978	—	2.00	4.00
—As "The Dirt Band"					
❑ XW1268	For a Little While/On the Loose	1978	—	2.00	4.00
—As "The Dirt Band"					
❑ 1312	In Her Eyes/Jas' Moon	1979	—	2.00	4.00
—As "The Dirt Band"					
❑ 1330	An American Dream/Take Me Back	1979	—	2.50	5.00
—As "The Dirt Band"					
❑ 1356	Make a Little Magic/Jas' Moon	1980	—	2.00	4.00
—As "The Dirt Band"					
❑ 1378	Badlands/Too Good to Be True	1980	—	2.00	4.00
—As "The Dirt Band"					
❑ 50769	House at Pooh Corner/Travelin' Mood	1971	—	3.00	6.00
❑ 50769 [PS]	House at Pooh Corner/Travelin' Mood	1971	2.00	4.00	8.00
❑ 50817	The Cure/Some of Shelly's Blues	1971	—	3.00	6.00
❑ 50849	Precious Jewel/I Saw the Light	1971	—	3.00	6.00
—With Roy Acuff					
❑ 50861	I Saw the Light/Sixteen Tracks	1971	—	3.00	6.00
❑ 50890	Jambalaya (On the Bayou)/Hoping to Say	1972	—	3.00	6.00
❑ 50890 [PS]	Jambalaya (On the Bayou)/Hoping to Say	1972	2.00	4.00	8.00
❑ 50921	Baltimore/Fish Song	1972	—	3.00	6.00
❑ 50965	Honky Tonkin'/Jamaica	1972	—	3.00	6.00
UNIVERSAL					
❑ UVL-66009	Turn of the Century/Blueberry Hill	1989	—	—	3.00
❑ UVL-66023	When It's Gone/I'm Sittin' on Top of the World	1989	—	2.00	4.00
WARNER BROS					
❑ PRO-S-2869 [DJ]	Colorado Christmas/The Cowboy's Christmas Ball	1987	—	3.00	6.00
—B-side by Michael Martin Murphey					
WARNER BROS.					
❑ 27679	Down That Road Tonight/A Lot Like Me	1989	—	—	3.00
❑ 27750	I've Been Lookin'/Must Be Love	1988	—	—	3.00
❑ 27940	Workin' Man/Brass Sky	1988	—	—	3.00
❑ 28173	Oh What a Love/America, My Sweetheart	1987	—	—	3.00
❑ 28311	Fishin' in the Dark/Keepin' the Road Hot	1987	—	—	3.00
❑ 28443	Baby's Got a Hold on Me/Oleanna	1987	—	—	3.00
❑ 28547	Cadillac Ranch/Fire in the Sky	1986	—	—	3.00
❑ 28690	Stand a Little Rain/Miner's Night Out	1986	—	—	3.00
❑ 28780	Partners, Brothers and Friends/Redneck Riviera	1986	—	—	3.00
❑ 28897	Home Again in My Heart/Telluride	1985	—	2.00	4.00
❑ 29027	Modern Day Romance/Queen of the Road	1985	—	2.00	4.00
❑ 29099	High Horse/Must Be Love	1985	—	2.00	4.00
❑ 29203	I Love Only You/Face on the Cutting Room Floor	1984	—	2.00	4.00
❑ 29282	Long Hard Road (The Sharecropper's Dream)/Video Tape	1984	—	2.00	4.00

NITZSCHE, JACK

Number	Title (A Side/B Side)	Yr	VG	VG+	NM
FANTASY					
❑ 760	One Flew Over the Cuckoo's Nest/The Last Dance	1976	—	3.00	6.00
❑ 760 [PS]	One Flew Over the Cuckoo's Nest/The Last Dance	1976	2.50	5.00	10.00
—Jack Nicholson is pictured on the sleeve					
MCA					
❑ 40897	Coke Machine/Hard Workin' Man	1978	—	2.00	4.00
REPRISE					
❑ 0262	The Last Race/Man with the Golden Arm	1964	5.00	10.00	20.00
❑ 0285	Theme from The Long Ships/Zapata	1964	5.00	10.00	20.00
❑ 0337	The Green Grass of Texas/Night Walker	1965	5.00	10.00	20.00
❑ 0364	Senorita from Detroit/Puerto Vallarta	1965	5.00	10.00	20.00
❑ 20202	The Lonely Surfer/Song for a Summer Night	1963	7.50	15.00	30.00
❑ 20202 [PS]	The Lonely Surfer/Song for a Summer Night	1963	25.00	50.00	100.00
❑ 20225	Rumble/Theme for a Broken Heart	1963	5.00	10.00	20.00

NIX, WILLIE

Number	Title (A Side/B Side)	Yr	VG	VG+	NM
CHANCE					
❑ 1163	Nervous Wreck/No More Love	1954	750.00	1500.	3000.
SABRE					
❑ 104	All By Myself/Just Can't Stay	1953	500.00	1000.	2000.

NO DOUBT

Number	Title (A Side/B Side)	Yr	VG	VG+	NM
TRAUMA/INTERSCOPE					
❑ 069 497403-7	Simple Kind of Life/Ex-Girlfriend	2000	—	2.00	4.00

NOBELLS, THE

Number	Title (A Side/B Side)	Yr	VG	VG+	NM
MAR					
❑ 101	Searchin' for My Love/Crying Over You	1962	25.00	50.00	100.00

NOBLES, CLIFF

Number	Title (A Side/B Side)	Yr	VG	VG+	NM
ATLANTIC					
❑ 2352	My Love Is Getting Stronger/Too Fond of You	1966	2.00	4.00	8.00
❑ 2380	Your Love Is All I Need/Everybody Is Weak for Somebody	1967	2.00	4.00	8.00
JAMIE					
❑ 1406	The Horse/If You Don't	1972	—	3.00	6.00
MOON SHOT					
❑ 6710	Pony the Horse/Little Claudie	1969	2.00	4.00	8.00
PHIL-L.A. OF SOUL					
❑ 310	The More I Do for You Baby/This Love Will Last	1968	2.00	4.00	8.00
❑ 313	The Horse/Love Is All Right	1968	2.50	5.00	10.00

Number	Title (A Side/B Side)	Yr	VG	VG+	NM
❑ 318	Horse Fever/Judge Baby, I'm Back	1968	2.00	4.00	8.00
❑ 324	Switch It On/Burning Desire	1969	2.00	4.00	8.00
❑ 329	The Camel/Goin' Away	1969	2.00	4.00	8.00
ROULETTE					
❑ 7142	This Feeling of Loneliness/We Got Our Thing Together	1973	—	3.00	6.00

NOBLES, THE

Number	Title (A Side/B Side)	Yr	VG	VG+	NM
COLUMBIA					
❑ 10642	Nobody But You/We Can Make the Difference	1977	—	2.50	5.00

NOBLES, THE (1)

Number	Title (A Side/B Side)	Yr	VG	VG+	NM
ABC-PARAMOUNT					
❑ 9984	Till the End of Time/Standing Loose	1958	6.25	12.50	25.00
❑ 10012	Just for Me/To Me	1959	6.25	12.50	25.00

NOBLES, THE (2)

Number	Title (A Side/B Side)	Yr	VG	VG+	NM
KLIK					
❑ 305	Poor Rock and Roll/Ting-a-Ling	1958	50.00	100.00	200.00
TIMES SQUARE					
❑ 1	Poor Rock and Roll/Ting-a-Ling	1963	7.50	15.00	30.00
—Blue vinyl					
❑ 1	Poor Rock and Roll/Ting-a-Ling	1963	6.25	12.50	25.00
—Green vinyl					
❑ 12	Crime Doesn't Pay/Darkness	1963	5.00	10.00	20.00
—All copies on blue vinyl					
❑ 33	Why Be a Fool/The Search	1964	5.00	10.00	20.00

NOBLES, THE (3)

Number	Title (A Side/B Side)	Yr	VG	VG+	NM
SELBON					
❑ 1005	Black Widow/Jaguar	1963	10.00	20.00	40.00

NOBLES, THE (4)

Number	Title (A Side/B Side)	Yr	VG	VG+	NM
STACY					
❑ 926	Serenade/You Ain't Right	1962	10.00	20.00	40.00

NOBLES, THE (5)

Number	Title (A Side/B Side)	Yr	VG	VG+	NM
U.S.A.					
❑ 788	Marlene/That Special One	1965	6.25	12.50	25.00

NOBLES, THE (U)

Number	Title (A Side/B Side)	Yr	VG	VG+	NM
TEE GEE					
❑ 101	Oops Oh Lawdy/Stop Crying	1958	12.50	25.00	50.00

NOCTURNES, THE

Number	Title (A Side/B Side)	Yr	VG	VG+	NM
CARLSON INT'L					
❑ 4105	My Christmas Star/(B-side unknown)	1964	15.00	30.00	60.00

NODAENS, THE

With Dave Nowlen, formerly of THE SURVIVORS.

Number	Title (A Side/B Side)	Yr	VG	VG+	NM
GOLD					
❑ 1001	Beach Girl/Gypsy	196?	20.00	40.00	80.00

NOEL, SID

Number	Title (A Side/B Side)	Yr	VG	VG+	NM
ALADDIN					
❑ 3331	The Flying Saucer (Part 1)/The Flying Saucer (Part 2)	1956	10.00	20.00	40.00
—Cover version of the Buchanan and Goodman break-in record					

NOLAN, FRANKIE

Number	Title (A Side/B Side)	Yr	VG	VG+	NM
ABC-PARAMOUNT					
❑ 10231	I Still Care/(I Wish It Were) Summer All Year Round	1961	10.00	20.00	40.00
—Frankie Valli also appears on this record					

NOLAND, TERRY

Number	Title (A Side/B Side)	Yr	VG	VG+	NM
APT					
❑ 25065	There Goes a Girl/Long Gone Baby	1962	3.75	7.50	15.00
BRUNSWICK					
❑ 55010	Hypnotized/Ten Little Women	1957	7.50	15.00	30.00
❑ 55036	Patti Baby/Don't Do Me This Way	1957	7.50	15.00	30.00
❑ 55054	Puppy Love/Oh Baby, Look at Me	1958	7.50	15.00	30.00
❑ 55069	Crazy Dream/Everyone But One	1958	7.50	15.00	30.00
❑ 55092	There Was a Fungus Among Us/Sugar Drop	1958	10.00	20.00	40.00
❑ 55122	Guess I'm Gonna Fall/Teenage Teardrops	1959	7.50	15.00	30.00
CORAL					
❑ 62274	There Was a Fungus Among Us/Sugar Drop	1961	5.00	10.00	20.00

NON-CONFORMISTS, THE

Number	Title (A Side/B Side)	Yr	VG	VG+	NM
SCEPTER					
❑ 12184	Two-Legged Big Eyed Yellow Haired Crying Canary/Bird Walk	1967	7.50	15.00	30.00

NOONE, PETER

Also see HERMAN'S HERMITS.

Number	Title (A Side/B Side)	Yr	VG	VG+	NM
BELL					
❑ 45131	Oh You Pretty Thing/Because You're There	1971	12.50	25.00	50.00
—Allegedly features David Bowie on A-side piano					
❑ 45266	Should I/(B-side unknown)	1972	2.00	4.00	8.00
CASABLANCA					
❑ 0017	Meet Me at the Corner Down at Joe's Cafe/(Blame It)On the Pony Express	1974	—	2.50	5.00
❑ 0106	Meet Me at the Corner Down at Joe's Cafe/(Blame It)On the Pony Express	1974	—	2.00	4.00
❑ 802	Meet Me at the Corner Down at Joe's Cafe/(Blame It)On the Pony Express	1974	—	2.00	4.00
❑ 823	Something Old, Something New/(B-side unknown)	1975	—	2.00	4.00
JOHNSTON					
❑ 02838	(I Don't Wanna Love You But) You Got Me Anyway/I'm One of the Glory Boys	1982	—	2.00	4.00
PHILIPS					
❑ 40730	All Sing Together/Getting Over You	1974	—	2.50	5.00

NORMAN, GENE, AND THE ROCKIN' ROCKETS

Number	Title (A Side/B Side)	Yr	VG	VG+	NM
SNAG					
❑ 101	Snaggle Tooth Ann/Long Gone Night Train	1958	250.00	500.00	1000.

NORMAN, LARRY

A founding father of Christian rock. Also see PEOPLE.

Number	Title (A Side/B Side)	Yr	VG	VG+	NM
CAPITOL					
❑ 2766	Sweet Sweet Song of Salvation/Walking Backwards Down the Stairs	1970	5.00	10.00	20.00
MGM					
❑ 14351	Righteous Rocker, Holy Rocker/Peace, Pollution, Revolution	1972	3.75	7.50	15.00
❑ 14676	Christmas Time/The Same Old Story	1973	3.75	7.50	15.00
❑ 14703	Nightmare/Baroquen Spirits	1974	3.75	7.50	15.00
SOLID ROCK					
❑ 202	Christmas Time/The Christmas Song	1976	2.00	4.00	8.00
VERVE					
❑ 10718	I've Got to Learn to Live Without You/Readers Digest	1973	5.00	10.00	20.00
❑ 10720	I've Got to Learn to Live Without You/The Outlaw	1973	5.00	10.00	20.00

NORMANAIRES, THE

Number	Title (A Side/B Side)	Yr	VG	VG+	NM
MGM					
❑ 11622	My Greatest Sin/Wrap It Up	1953	20.00	40.00	80.00

NORRIS, CHARLES

Number	Title (A Side/B Side)	Yr	VG	VG+	NM
ATLANTIC					
❑ 994	Messin' Up/Let Me Know	1953	15.00	30.00	60.00

NORTH, JAY

Number	Title (A Side/B Side)	Yr	VG	VG+	NM
KEM					
❑ 2756	The Cat And The Christmas Tree/Christmas For Tommy	1960	3.75	7.50	15.00

NORTHERN LIGHTS, THE

With Bjorn Ulvaeus, later of ABBA.

Number	Title (A Side/B Side)	Yr	VG	VG+	NM
UNITED ARTISTS					
❑ 991	Time to Move Along/No Time	1966	5.00	10.00	20.00

NOTE-TORIALS, THE

Number	Title (A Side/B Side)	Yr	VG	VG+	NM
IMPALA					
❑ 201	Valerie/Loved and Lost	1958	250.00	500.00	1000.
SUNBEAM					
❑ 119	Valerie/Loved and Lost	1958	50.00	100.00	200.00

NOTES, THE

Number	Title (A Side/B Side)	Yr	VG	VG+	NM
CAPITOL					
❑ F3332	Don't Leave Me Now/Cha Jezebel	1956	75.00	150.00	300.00
MGM					
❑ 12338	Trust in Me/Round and Round	1956	50.00	100.00	200.00
SARG					
❑ 177	Little Girl/G.I. Blues	1959	12.50	25.00	50.00

NOVA LOCAL, THE

Number	Title (A Side/B Side)	Yr	VG	VG+	NM
DECCA					
❑ 32138	Games/If You Only Had the Time	1967	5.00	10.00	20.00
❑ 32194	Other Girls/John Knight's Body (I Wanna Get Out)	1967	5.00	10.00	20.00

NOVAS, THE

Number	Title (A Side/B Side)	Yr	VG	VG+	NM
PARROT					
❑ 45005	The Crusher/Take 7	1964	20.00	40.00	80.00
TWIN TOWN					
❑ 713	Novas Coaster/On the Road Again	1965	10.00	20.00	40.00

NOWOTTNY, MARIANNE

Number	Title (A Side/B Side)	Yr	VG	VG+	NM
ABATON					
❑ 004	Jesus-in-a-Jiffy/Sequin Serenade	1999	—	—	3.00
—White vinyl					
❑ 004 [PS]	Jesus-in-a-Jiffy/Sequin Serenade	1999	—	—	3.00

NRBQ

Number	Title (A Side/B Side)	Yr	VG	VG+	NM
BEARSVILLE					
❑ 29588	Rain at the Drive-In/Shackaroo	1983	—	2.50	5.00
BUTTON					
❑ 037	Froggy Went a-Courtin'/Bless Your Beautiful Hide	1975	12.50	25.00	50.00
COLUMBIA					
❑ 44865	Stomp/I Didn't Know Myself	1969	—	3.00	6.00
❑ 44937	C'mon Everybody/Rocket No. 9	1969	—	3.00	6.00
❑ 45019	Sure to Fall (In Love With You)/Down in My Heart	1969	—	3.00	6.00
KAMA SUTRA					
❑ 544	Howard Johnson's Got His Hojo Workin'/Do You Feel It	1972	—	3.00	6.00
❑ 549	Only You/Magnet	1972	—	3.00	6.00
❑ 575	C'mon If You're Comin'/RC Cola and a Moon Pie	1973	—	3.00	6.00
❑ 586	Get That Gasoline Blues/Mona	1974	—	3.00	6.00
MERCURY					
❑ 73991	Green Lights/I Love Her, She Loves Me	1978	—	2.50	5.00
RED ROOSTER					
❑ 1001	Ridin' in My Car/Do the Bump	1977	2.50	5.00	10.00
❑ 1002	I Got a Rocket in My Pocket/Tapdancin' Bats	1977	—	3.00	6.00
❑ 1002 [PS]	I Got a Rocket in My Pocket/Tapdancin' Bats	1977	2.50	5.00	10.00
❑ 1006	Christmas Wish/Jolly Old St. Nicholas	1978	2.50	5.00	10.00
❑ 1006 [PS]	Christmas Wish/Jolly Old St. Nicholas	1978	2.50	5.00	10.00
ROUNDER					
❑ 1010	Captain Lou!/Boardin' House Pie	1982	—	2.00	4.00
❑ 1010 [PS]	Captain Lou!/Boardin' House Pie	1982	—	2.00	4.00
❑ 4521	Hot Biscuits and Sweet Marie/She Don't Look Good	1979	—	2.50	5.00
❑ 4522	Get That Gasoline Blues/Wacky Tobacky	1979	—	2.50	5.00
❑ 4525	Christmas Wish/Jolly Old St. Nicholas	1979	—	2.50	5.00
❑ 4525 [PS]	Christmas Wish/Jolly Old St. Nicholas	1979	—	3.00	6.00
❑ 4531	Me and the Boys/People	1980	—	2.50	5.00

Number	Title (A Side/B Side)	Yr	VG	VG+	NM
❑ 4531 [PS]	Me and the Boys/People	1980	2.50	5.00	10.00
❑ 4539	Never Take the Place of You/Captain Lou Albano for Tiddlywinks	1980	—	2.50	5.00
❑ 4556	Things to Do/I Can't Stop Loving You Now	1985	—	2.00	4.00
—With Skeeter Davis					
SCEPTER					
❑ 12322	Sho' Need Love/Don't Talk About My Music1	1971	12.50	25.00	50.00
—As "The Dickens"					
SELECT-O-HIT					
❑ 022	Sourpuss/Rumors	1974	12.50	25.00	50.00
VIRGIN					
❑ 99130	If I Don't Have You/Boozoo, That's Who	1989	—	2.00	4.00
❑ 99161 [DJ]	Wild Weekend/This Love Is True	1989	—	2.00	4.00
7-Inch Extended Plays					
RED ROOSTER					
❑ EP-1	Christmas Wish/Here Comes Santa Claus//God Rest Ye Merry Gentlemen/Message from the North Pole	1979	3.75	7.50	15.00
—Called "Merry Christmas from NRBQ"; not issued with cover					

NU-TONES, THE

Number	Title (A Side/B Side)	Yr	VG	VG+	NM
COMBO					
❑ 127	At Midnight/Beans 'N' Greens	1957	37.50	75.00	150.00
HOLLYWOOD STAR					
❑ 798	Annie Kicked the Bucket/Believe	1955	2000.	4000.	8000.
❑ 798	You're No Barking Dog/Believe	1955	150.00	300.00	600.00

NU TORNADOS, THE

Number	Title (A Side/B Side)	Yr	VG	VG+	NM
CARLTON					
❑ 492	Philadelphia, U.S.A./Magic Record	1959	6.25	12.50	25.00
❑ 497	The "Ole Mummers" Strut/Let's Have a Party	1959	5.00	10.00	20.00
FELSTED					
❑ 8577	Cry Baby Cry/Keep a Flower Growing in Your Heart	1959	5.00	10.00	20.00

NUGENT, TED

Also see THE AMBOY DUKES.

Number	Title (A Side/B Side)	Yr	VG	VG+	NM
ATLANTIC					
❑ 89436	Little Miss Dangerous/Angry Young Man	1986	—	—	3.00
❑ 89442	High Heels in Motion/Angry Young Man	1986	—	—	3.00
❑ 89661	Lean Mean R&R Machine/(Where Do You) Draw the Line	1984	—	—	3.00
❑ 89705 [DJ]	Tied Up in Love (same on both sides)	1984	—	2.00	4.00
—May be promo only					
❑ 89978	No, No, No/Habitual Offender	1982	—	—	3.00
❑ 89998	Bound and Gagged/Habitual Offender	1982	—	—	3.00
❑ 89998 [PS]	Bound and Gagged/Habitual Offender	1982	—	2.50	5.00
EPIC					
❑ 01046	Land of a Thousand Dances/The TNT Overture	1981	—	2.00	4.00
❑ 50172	Motor City Madness/Where Have You Been All My Life	1975	—	2.50	5.00
❑ 50197	Hey Baby/Stormtroopin'	1976	—	2.50	5.00
❑ 50301	Dog Eat Dog/Light My Way	1976	—	2.50	5.00
❑ 50363	Free-for-All/Street Rags	1977	—	2.00	4.00
❑ 50425	Cat Scratch Fever/Wang Dang Sweet Poontang	1977	—	2.50	5.00
❑ 50493	Death by Misadventure/Home Bound	1977	—	2.00	4.00
❑ 50533	Yank Me, Crank Me/Cat Scratch Fever	1978	—	2.00	4.00
❑ 50648	Need You Bad/I Got the Feelin'	1979	—	2.00	4.00
❑ 50713	Bite Down Hard/I Want to Tell You	1979	—	2.00	4.00
❑ 50907	Wango Tango/Scream Dream	1980	—	2.00	4.00

NUGGETS, THE (1)

Number	Title (A Side/B Side)	Yr	VG	VG+	NM
CAPITOL					
❑ F-2989	So Help Me I Love You/Quirl Up in My Arms	1954	5.00	10.00	20.00
❑ F-3052	Anxious Heart/Shtiggy Boom	1955	3.75	7.50	15.00

NUGGETS, THE (2)

Number	Title (A Side/B Side)	Yr	VG	VG+	NM
RCA VICTOR					
❑ 47-7930	Before We Say Goodnight/Angel on the Dance Floor	1961	7.50	5.00	30.00
❑ 47-8031	Just a Friend/Cat Snapper	1962	3.75	7.50	15.00

NUMBERS, THE

Number	Title (A Side/B Side)	Yr	VG	VG+	NM
BONNEVILLE					
❑ 101	Big Red/My Pillow	1962	50.00	100.00	200.00
DORE					
❑ 641	Big Red/My Pillow	1962	12.50	25.00	50.00

NUTMEGS, THE

Number	Title (A Side/B Side)	Yr	VG	VG+	NM
BABY GRAND					
❑ 800	Story Untold '72/Tell Me	1972	2.00	4.00	8.00
HERALD					
❑ 452	Story Untold/Make Me Lose My Mind	1955	17.50	35.00	70.00
❑ 459	Ship of Love/Rock Me	1955	10.00	20.00	40.00
❑ 466	Whispering Sorrows/Betty Lou	1955	12.50	25.00	50.00
❑ 475	Key to the Kingdom (Of Your Heart)/Gift O' Gabbin' Woman	1956	12.50	25.00	50.00
❑ 492	Love So True/Comin' Home	1956	10.00	20.00	40.00
❑ 538	My Sweet Dream/My Story	1959	10.00	20.00	40.00
❑ 574	Rip Van Winkle/Crazy 'Bout You	1962	6.25	12.50	25.00
NIGHTRAIN					
❑ 905	Shifting Sands/Take Me and Make Me	1973	2.00	4.00	8.00
TEL					
❑ 1014	A Dream of Love/Someone, Somewhere (Help Me)	1960	25.00	50.00	100.00
TIMES SQUARE					
❑ 6	Let Me Tell You/Hello	1963	6.25	12.50	25.00
—Blue vinyl					
❑ 14	The Way Love Should Be/Wide Hoop Skirts	1963	5.00	10.00	20.00
❑ 19	Down to Earth/Coo Coo Cuddle Coo	1963	5.00	10.00	20.00
—B-side by the Admirations					
❑ 22	Why Must We Go to School/Ink Dries Quicker Than Tears	1963	5.00	10.00	20.00
—B-side by the Volumes					
❑ 27	Down in Mexico/My Sweet Dreams	1964	5.00	10.00	20.00
❑ 103	You're Crying/Wa-Do-Wa	1964	5.00	10.00	20.00
7-Inch Extended Plays					
HERALD					
❑ 452	*Story Untold/Betty Lou/Comin' Home/Whispering Sorrows	1960	25.00	50.00	100.00
❑ 452 [PS]	Story Untold	1960	30.00	60.00	120.00

NUTTY SQUIRRELS, THE

Number	Title (A Side/B Side)	Yr	VG	VG+	NM
COLUMBIA					
❑ 41818	Please Don't Take Our Tree for Christmas/Nutty Noel	1960	5.00	10.00	20.00
❑ 41818 [PS]	Please Don't Take Our Tree for Christmas/Nutty Noel	1960	10.00	20.00	40.00
HANOVER					
❑ 4540	Uh! Oh! (Part 1)/Uh! Oh! (Part 2)	1959	6.25	12.50	25.00
❑ 4540 [PS]	Uh! Oh! (Part 1)/Uh! Oh! (Part 2)	1959	12.50	25.00	50.00
❑ 4551	Eager Beaver/Zowee	1960	5.00	10.00	20.00
RCA VICTOR					
❑ 47-8287	Hello Again/Bluesette	1963	3.75	7.50	15.00

NYRO, LAURA

Number	Title (A Side/B Side)	Yr	VG	VG+	NM
COLUMBIA					
❑ 44531	Sweet Blindness/Eli's Comin'	1968	2.00	4.00	8.00
❑ 44786	Once It Was Alright (Farmer Joe)/Lu	1969	—	3.00	6.00
❑ 45041	Time and Love/A Man Who Sends Me Home	1969	—	3.00	6.00
❑ 45089	Save the Country/New York Tendaberry	1970	—	3.00	6.00
❑ 45230	Up On the Roof/Captain Saint Lucifer	1970	—	3.00	6.00
❑ 45298	When I Was a Freeport and You Were the Main Drag/Been On a Train	1971	—	3.00	6.00
VERVE FOLKWAYS					
❑ 5024	Wedding Bell Blues/Stoney End	1966	2.50	5.00	10.00
❑ 5038	Billie's Blues/Goodbye Joe	1967	2.50	5.00	10.00
❑ 5051	And When I Die/Flim Flam Man	1967	2.50	5.00	10.00
VERVE FORECAST					
❑ 5095	Stoney End/Flim Flam Man	1968	2.00	4.00	8.00
❑ 5104	And When I Die/I Never Meant to Hurt You	1969	2.00	4.00	8.00
❑ 5112	Goodbye Joe/I Never Meant to Hurt You	1969	2.00	4.00	8.00

O

O'DELL, KENNY

Number	Title (A Side/B Side)	Yr	VG	VG+	NM
CAPRICORN					
❑ 0020	Rock and Roll Man/Ain't Gonna Study No More	1973	—	2.50	5.00
❑ 0038	You Bet Your Sweet. Sweet Love/Let's Go Find Some Country Music	1973	—	2.50	5.00
❑ 0203	I Take It On Home/I'll Find Another Way	1974	—	2.00	4.00
❑ 0219	Soulful Woman/Let's Get On the Road	1975	—	2.00	4.00
❑ 0233	My Honky Tonk Ways/Behind Closed Doors	1975	—	2.00	4.00
❑ 0247	Together This Christmas/I Can't Think When You're Doing That to Me	1975	—	2.00	4.00
❑ 0301	Let's Shake Hands and Come Out Lovin'/We Might Be All Night	1978	—	2.00	4.00
❑ 0309	As Long As I Can Wake Up in Your Arms/Soulful Woman	1978	—	2.00	4.00
❑ 0317	Medicine Woman/Who Do I Know in Denver	1979	—	2.00	4.00
EPIC					
❑ 10693	If I Was a Rambler/High on Life	1971	—	2.50	5.00
❑ 10730	I Was a Loser (But Now I've Got You)/Jubal	1971	—	2.50	5.00
❑ 10791	I Was a Loser (But Now I've Got You)/Jubal	1971	—	2.50	5.00
KAPP					
❑ 2169	Two for the Road/Why Don't We Go Somewhere and Love	1972	—	2.50	5.00
❑ 2178	Lizzie and the Rainman/Homecoming Queen	1972	—	2.50	5.00
MAR-KAY					
❑ 3696	Old Time Lovin'/Take Another Look	1966	2.50	5.00	10.00
VEGAS					
❑ 718	Beautiful People/Flower Girl	1967	2.00	4.00	8.00
❑ 722	Springfield Plane/I'm Gonna Take It	1968	—	3.00	6.00
❑ 724	Happy with You/Couldn't Love You	1968	—	3.00	6.00
WHITE WHALE					
❑ 319	No Obligation/(B-side unknown)	1969	—	3.00	6.00
❑ 331	Groovy Relationship/(B-side unknown)	1969	—	3.00	6.00

O'JAYS, THE

Number	Title (A Side/B Side)	Yr	VG	VG+	NM
APOLLO					
❑ 759	Miracles/Can't Take It	1961	7.50	15.00	30.00
ASTROSCOPE					
❑ 106	Wisdom of a Child/Peace	1974	2.00	4.00	8.00
❑ 110	Peace/Don't You Know a True Love (When You See Her)	1974	2.00	4.00	8.00
BELL					
❑ 691	I'll Be Sweeter Tomorrow (Than I Was Today)/I Dig Your Act	1967	2.50	5.00	10.00
❑ 704	Look Over Your Shoulder/I'm So Glad I Found You	1968	2.50	5.00	10.00
❑ 737	The Choice/Going, Going, Gone	1968	2.50	5.00	10.00
❑ 749	I Miss You/Now That I Found You	1968	2.50	5.00	10.00
❑ 770	Don't You Know a True Love/That's All Right	1969	2.00	4.00	8.00
❑ 45378	Look Over Your Shoulder/Four for the Price of One	1973	—	2.50	5.00
EMI					
❑ S7-17491	Somebody Else Will/Decisions	1993	—	2.00	4.00
❑ S7-18914	Have Yourself a Merry Little Christmas/I Can Hardly Wait 'Til Christmas	1995	—	—	3.00

Number	Title (A Side/B Side)	Yr	VG	VG+	NM
❑ 50180	Have You Had Your Love Today/The Pot Can't Call the Kettle Black	1989	—	—	3.00
❑ 50212	Out of My Mind (Radio Mix)/Out of My Mind (Soul 2 Mix)	1989	—	—	3.00
IMPERIAL					
❑ 5942	How Does It Feel/Crack Up Laughing	1963	3.75	7.50	15.00
❑ 5976	Lonely Drifter/That's Enough	1963	2.50	5.00	10.00
❑ 66007	Stand Tall/The Storm Is Over	1963	2.50	5.00	10.00
❑ 66025	I'll Never Stop Loving You/My Dearest Beloved	1964	2.50	5.00	10.00
❑ 66037	You're on Top/Lovely Dee	1964	2.50	5.00	10.00
❑ 66076	Girl Machine/Oh How You Hurt Me	1964	2.50	5.00	10.00
❑ 66102	Lipstick Traces/Think It Over, Baby	1965	2.50	5.00	10.00
❑ 66121	Whip It On Me Baby/I've Cried My Last Tear	1965	2.50	5.00	10.00
❑ 66131	You're the One (You're the Only One)/Let It All Come Out	1965	2.50	5.00	10.00
❑ 66145	I'll Never Let You Go/It Won't Hurt	1965	2.50	5.00	10.00
❑ 66162	I'll Never Forget You/Pretty Words	1966	10.00	20.00	40.00
❑ 66177	No Time for You/It's a Blowin' Wind	1966	2.50	5.00	10.00
❑ 66197	Friday Night/Stand In for Love	1966	2.50	5.00	10.00
❑ 66200	Lonely Drifter/That's Enough	1966	2.50	5.00	10.00
LITTLE STAR					
❑ 124	How Does It Feel/Crack Up Laughing	1963	6.25	12.50	25.00
❑ 125	Dream Girl/Joey St. Vincent	1963	6.25	12.50	25.00
❑ 1401	Now He's Home/Just to Be with You	1962	6.25	12.50	25.00
MINIT					
❑ 32015	Hold On/Working on Your Case	1967	2.50	5.00	10.00
NEPTUNE					
❑ 12	One Night Affair/There's Someone (Waiting Back Home)	1969	2.00	4.00	8.00
❑ 18	Branded Bad/You're the Best Thing Since Candy	1969	2.00	4.00	8.00
❑ 20	Christmas Ain't Christmas New Year's Ain't New Year's Without the One You Love/There's Someone Waiting	1969	2.50	5.00	10.00
❑ 22	Deeper (In Love with You)/I've Got the Groove	1970	2.00	4.00	8.00
❑ 31	Looky Looky (Look at Me Girl)/Let Me in Your World	1970	2.00	4.00	8.00
❑ 33	Christmas Ain't Christmas New Year's Ain't New Year's Without the One You Love/Just Can't Get Enough	1970	2.00	4.00	8.00
PHILADELPHIA INT'L.					
❑ 02096	Forever Mine/Girl, Don't Let It Get You Down	1981	—	—	3.00
—Reissue					
❑ 02834	Don't Walk Away Mad/I Just Want to Satisfy	1982	—	2.00	4.00
❑ 02982	One by One/My Favorite Person	1982	—	2.00	4.00
❑ 03009	Out in the Real World/Your Body's Here with Me	1982	—	2.00	4.00
❑ 3517	Back Stabbers/Sunshine	1972	—	2.50	5.00
❑ 3522	992 Arguments/Listen to the Clock on the Wall	1972	—	2.50	5.00
❑ 3524	Love Train/Who Am I	1973	—	2.50	5.00
❑ 3531	Time to Get Down/Shiftless, Shady, Jealous Kind of People	1973	—	2.50	5.00
❑ 3535	Put Your Hands Together/You Got Your Hooks in Me	1973	—	2.50	5.00
❑ 3537	Christmas Ain't Christmas New Year's Ain't New Year's Without the One You Love/Just Can't Get Enough	1973	—	3.00	6.00
❑ 3544	For the Love of Money/People Keep Tellin' Me	1974	—	2.50	5.00
❑ 3558	Sunshine (Part 1)/Sunshine (Part 2)	1974	—	2.50	5.00
❑ 3565	Give the People What They Want/What Am I Waiting For	1975	—	2.50	5.00
❑ 3573	Let Me Make Love to You/Survival	1975	—	2.50	5.00
❑ 3577	I Love Music (Part 1)/I Love Music (Part 2)	1975	—	2.50	5.00
❑ 3581	Christmas Ain't Christmas New Year's Ain't New Year's Without the One You Love/Just Can't Get Enough	1975	—	2.50	5.00
❑ 3587	Livin' for the Weekend/Stairway to Heaven	1976	—	2.50	5.00
❑ 3596	Family Reunion/Unity	1976	—	2.50	5.00
❑ 3601	Message in Our Music/She's Only a Woman	1976	—	2.50	5.00
❑ 3610	Darlin' Darlin' Baby (Sweet, Tender, Love)/A Prayer	1976	—	2.50	5.00
❑ 3631	Work On Me/Let's Spend Some Time Together	1977	—	2.50	5.00
❑ 3642	Use Ta Be My Girl/This Time Baby	1978	—	2.50	5.00
❑ 3652	Brandy/Take Me to the Stars	1978	—	2.50	5.00
❑ 3666	Cry Together/Strokety Stroke	1978	—	2.50	5.00
❑ 3707	Sing a Happy Song/One in a Million (Girl)	1979	—	2.50	5.00
❑ 3726	I Want You Here with Me/Get On Out and Party	1979	—	2.50	5.00
❑ 3727	Forever Mine/Get On Out and Party	1979	—	2.50	5.00
❑ 03892	A Letter to My Friends/I Can't Stand the Pain	1983	—	2.00	4.00
❑ 04069	Put Our Heads Together/Nice and Easy	1983	—	2.00	4.00
❑ 04437	I Really Need You Now/Extraordinary Girl	1984	—	2.00	4.00
❑ 04535	Let Me Show You (How Much I Really Love You)/Love You Direct	1984	—	2.00	4.00
❑ 50013	Just Another Lonely Night/What Good Are These Arms of Mine	1985	—	—	3.00
❑ 50021	What a Woman/I Love America	1985	—	—	3.00
❑ 50067	Don't Take Your Love Away/I Just Want Somebody to Love Me	1987	—	—	3.00
❑ 50084	Lovin' You/Don't Let the Dream Get Along	1987	—	—	3.00
❑ 50104	Let Me Touch You/Undercover Lover	1987	—	—	3.00
❑ 50122	I Just Want Someone to Love Me/Lovin' You	1988	—	—	3.00
SARU					
❑ 1220	Shattered Man/La De Da (Means I'm Out to Get You)	1971	—	3.00	6.00
TSOP					
❑ 3771	Christmas Ain't Christmas New Year's Ain't New Year's Without the One You Love/Just Can't Get Enough	1980	—	2.00	4.00
❑ 4790	Girl, Don't Let It Get You Down/You're the Girl of My Dreams	1980	—	2.00	4.00
❑ 4791	Once Is Not Enough/To Prove I Love You	1980	—	2.00	4.00
❑ 70050	You Won't Fall/You'll Never Know (All There Is to Know 'Bout Love)	1981	—	2.00	4.00

O'KAYSIONS, THE

Number	Title (A Side/B Side)	Yr	VG	VG+	NM
ABC					
❑ 11094	Girl Watcher/Deal Me In	1968	2.00	4.00	8.00
❑ 11153	Love Machine/Dedicated to the One I Love	1968	—	3.00	6.00
❑ 11207	Twenty-Four Hours from Tulsa/Colors	1969	—	3.00	6.00
COTILLION					
❑ 44089	Happiness/Watch Out Girl	1970	—	2.50	5.00
❑ 44134	Life and Things/Travelin' Life	1971	—	2.50	5.00
NORTH STATE					
❑ 1001	Girl Watcher/Deal Me In	1968	25.00	50.00	100.00
❑ 1001 [PS]	Girl Watcher/Deal Me In	1968	75.00	150.00	300.00

O'KEEFE, DANNY

Number	Title (A Side/B Side)	Yr	VG	VG+	NM
ATLANTIC					
❑ 2978	Angel, Spread Your Wings/Mad Ruth the Babe	1973	—	2.50	5.00
❑ 3267	The Delta Queen/Quits	1975	—	2.50	5.00
JERDEN					
❑ 806	Don't Wake Me in the Morning/That Old Sweet Song	1966	2.50	5.00	10.00
PICCADILLY					
❑ 228	Don't Wake Me in the Morning/That Old Sweet Song	1967	2.00	4.00	8.00
❑ 237	Today One Day Later/Baby	1967	2.00	4.00	8.00
SIGNPOST					
❑ 70004	Good Time Charlie's Got the Blues/The Valentine Pieces	1972	—	3.00	6.00
❑ 70012	The Road/I'm Sober Now	1972	—	2.50	5.00
WARNER BROS.					
❑ 8435	You Look Just Like a Girl Again/On Discovering a Missing Person	1977	—	2.50	5.00
❑ 8489	The Runaway/Just Jones	1977	—	2.50	5.00

O'KEEFE, JOHNNY

Number	Title (A Side/B Side)	Yr	VG	VG+	NM
BRUNSWICK					
❑ 55067	Real Wild Child/Shake Baby Shake	1958	50.00	100.00	200.00
LIBERTY					
❑ 55223	She's My Baby/Own True Self	1959	10.00	20.00	40.00
❑ 55228	She's My Baby/It's Too Late	1959	7.50	15.00	30.00
❑ 55228 [PS]	She's My Baby/It's Too Late	1959	12.50	25.00	50.00
❑ 55262	Come On and Take My Hand/Don't You Know Little Baby	1960	10.00	20.00	40.00
MR. PEACOCK					
❑ 111	I'm Counting on You/The Steady Game	1962	10.00	20.00	40.00
SIMS					
❑ 337	So Why/Cryin' Is the One Thing I Do Very Well	1968	2.00	4.00	8.00

O'SULLIVAN, GILBERT

Number	Title (A Side/B Side)	Yr	VG	VG+	NM
EPIC					
❑ 50415	You Got Me Going/Call On Me	1977	—	2.00	4.00
❑ 50967	What's in a Kiss/Down, Down, Down	1981	—	2.00	4.00
MAM					
❑ 3602	Nothing Rhymed/Everybody Knows	1971	—	0.00	6.00
❑ 3607	Underneath the Blanket Go/(B-side unknown)	1971	—	3.00	6.00
❑ 3613	We Will/I Didn't Know What to Do	1971	—	3.00	6.00
❑ 3617	No Matter How I Try/If I Don't Get You Back	1972	—	2.50	5.00
❑ 3619	Alone Again (Naturally)/Save It	1972	—	3.00	6.00
❑ 3626	Clair/Ooh Wakka Doo Wakka Day	1972	—	2.50	5.00
❑ 3626 [PS]	Clair/Ooh Wakka Doo Wakka Day	1972	—	3.00	6.00
❑ 3628	Out of the Question/Everybody Knows	1973	—	2.50	5.00
❑ 3629	Get Down/A Very Extraordinary Sort of Girl	1973	—	2.50	5.00
❑ 3633	Ooh Baby/Good Company	1973	—	2.00	4.00
❑ 3636	Happiness Is Me and You/Breakfast, Dinner and Tea	1974	—	2.00	4.00
❑ 3641	A Woman's Place/Too Bad	1974	—	2.00	4.00
❑ 3642	You Are You/To Cut a Long Story Short	1974	—	2.00	4.00
❑ 3643	Marriage Machine/Tell Me Why	1975	—	2.00	4.00
❑ 3644	I Don't Love You But I Think I Like You/That's a Fact	1975	—	2.00	4.00
❑ 3645	Christmas Song/Just As You Are	1975	—	2.50	5.00

O-TOWN

Number	Title (A Side/B Side)	Yr	VG	VG+	NM
J					
❑ 21006	Liquid Dreams/All for Love	2001	—	2.00	4.00

OCTAVES, THE

Number	Title (A Side/B Side)	Yr	VG	VG+	NM
VAL					
❑ 1001	You're Too Young/Mambo Carolyn	1958	18.75	37.50	75.00

ODDIS, RAY

Number	Title (A Side/B Side)	Yr	VG	VG+	NM
V.I.P.					
❑ 25012	Happy Ghoul Tide/Ray the Newspaper Boy	1964	5.00	10.00	20.00

ODDS AND ENDS

Number	Title (A Side/B Side)	Yr	VG	VG+	NM
RED BIRD					
❑ 10-083	Before You Go (Hey Little Girl)/Never Learn	1967	3.00	6.00	12.00

OERTLING, JIM

Number	Title (A Side/B Side)	Yr	VG	VG+	NM
HAMMOND					
❑ 267	Old Moss Back/A Wilde Rose	1959	100.00	200.00	400.00

OFF KEYS, THE

Number	Title (A Side/B Side)	Yr	VG	VG+	NM
ROWE					
❑ 003	Our Wedding Day/Singing Bells	1962	25.00	50.00	100.00
TECHNICHORD					
❑ 1001	Our Wedding Day/Singing Bells	1962	12.50	25.00	50.00
—Glossy red label					
❑ 1001	Our Wedding Day/Singing Bells	1962	6.25	12.50	25.00
—Flat maroon label					

OGNIR AND THE NIGHT PEOPLE

Number	Title (A Side/B Side)	Yr	VG	VG+	NM
SAMRON					
❑ 102	I Found a New Love/All My Heart	1965	10.00	20.00	40.00

WARNER BROS.

Number	Title (A Side/B Side)	Yr	VG	VG+	NM
❑ 5687	I Found a New Love/All My Heart	1965	6.25	12.50	25.00

OHIO EXPRESS, THE
Also see THE RARE BREED.

BUDDAH

Number	Title (A Side/B Side)	Yr	VG	VG+	NM
❑ 38	Yummy Yummy Yummy/Zig Zag	1968	2.50	5.00	10.00
❑ 56	Down at Lulu's/She's Not Coming Home	1968	2.00	4.00	8.00
❑ 70	Chewy Chewy/Firebird	1968	2.50	5.00	10.00
❑ 92	Sweeter Than Sugar/Bitter Than Lemon	1969	2.00	4.00	8.00
❑ 102	Mercy/Roll It Up	1969	2.00	4.00	8.00
❑ 117	Pinch Me (Baby, Convince Me)/Peanuts	1969	2.00	4.00	8.00
❑ 129	Sausalito (Is the Place to Go)/Make Love Not War	1969	2.00	4.00	8.00
—With Graham Gouldman, later of 10CC, on lead vocal					
❑ 147	Cowboy Convention/The Race (That Took Place)	1970	2.00	4.00	8.00
❑ 160	Love Equals Love/Peanuts	1970	2.00	4.00	8.00
❑ 386	Wham Bam/Slow and Steady	1973	3.75	7.50	15.00
—As "Ohio Ltd."					

CAMEO

Number	Title (A Side/B Side)	Yr	VG	VG+	NM
❑ 483	Beg, Borrow and Steal/Maybe	1967	3.00	6.00	12.00
❑ 2001	Try It/Soul Struttin'	1967	3.00	6.00	12.00

SUPER K

Number	Title (A Side/B Side)	Yr	VG	VG+	NM
❑ 114	Hot Dog/Ooh La La	1970	2.50	5.00	10.00

OHIO PLAYERS, THE
Also see THE OHIO UNTOUCHABLES.

AIR CITY

Number	Title (A Side/B Side)	Yr	VG	VG+	NM
❑ 402	Sight for Sore Eyes/(B-side unknown)	1984	—	2.00	4.00
❑ 402 [PS]	Sight for Sore Eyes/(B-side unknown)	1984	—	2.00	4.00

ARISTA

Number	Title (A Side/B Side)	Yr	VG	VG+	NM
❑ 0408	Everybody Up/Take De Funk Off, Fly	1979	—	2.00	4.00
❑ 0440	Don't Say Goodbye/Say It	1979	—	2.00	4.00

BOARDWALK

Number	Title (A Side/B Side)	Yr	VG	VG+	NM
❑ NB7-11-133	Star of the Party/I Better Take a Coffee Break	1981	—	2.00	4.00
❑ 02063	Skinny/Call Me	1981	—	2.00	4.00
❑ 5708	Try a Little Tenderness/Try to Be a Man	1981	—	2.00	4.00

CAPITOL

Number	Title (A Side/B Side)	Yr	VG	VG+	NM
❑ 2385	Bad Bargain/Here Today and Gone Tomorrow	1969	2.50	5.00	10.00
❑ 2523	Find Someone to Love/Over the Rainbow	1969	2.50	5.00	10.00

COMPASS

Number	Title (A Side/B Side)	Yr	VG	VG+	NM
❑ 7015	Tresspassin'/You Don't Mean It	1967	3.00	6.00	12.00
❑ 7018	It's a Crying Shame/I've Got to Hold On	1968	3.00	6.00	12.00

MERCURY

Number	Title (A Side/B Side)	Yr	VG	VG+	NM
❑ 73480	Jive Turkey (Part 1)/Streakin' Cheek to Cheek	1974	—	2.50	5.00
❑ 73609	Skin Tight/Heaven Must Be Like This	1974	—	2.50	5.00
❑ 73643	Fire/Together	1974	—	2.50	5.00
❑ 73675	I Want to Be Free/Smoke	1975	—	2.50	5.00
❑ 73713	Sweet Sticky Thing/Alone	1975	—	2.50	5.00
❑ 73734	Love Rollercoaster/It's All Over	1975	—	2.50	5.00
❑ 73753	Happy Holidays (Part 1)/Happy Holidays (Part 2)	1975	—	3.00	6.00
❑ 73775	Fopp/Let's Love	1976	—	2.50	5.00
❑ 73814	Who'd She Coo?/Bi-Centennial	1976	—	2.50	5.00
❑ 73860	Far East Mississippi/Only a Child Can Love	1976	—	2.50	5.00
❑ 73881	Feel the Beat (Everybody Disco)/Contradiction	1976	—	2.50	5.00
❑ 73913	Body Vibes/Don't Fight My Love	1977	—	2.50	5.00
❑ 73932	O-H-I-O/Can You Still Love Me	1977	—	2.50	5.00
❑ 73956	Merry Go Round/Angel	1977	—	2.50	5.00
❑ 73974	Good Luck Charm (Part 1)/Good Luck Charm (Part 2)	1977	—	2.50	5.00
❑ 73983	Magic Trick/Mr. Mean	1978	—	2.50	5.00
❑ 74014	Funk-O-Nots/Sleepwalkin'	1978	—	2.50	5.00
❑ 74031	Time Slips Away/Nott Enuff	1978	—	2.50	5.00

TANGERINE

Number	Title (A Side/B Side)	Yr	VG	VG+	NM
❑ 978	Neighbors/A Thing Called Love	1967	3.00	6.00	12.00

TRACK

Number	Title (A Side/B Side)	Yr	VG	VG+	NM
❑ 58812	Let's Play (From Now On)/(B-side unknown)	1988	—	—	3.00
❑ 58815	Sweat/Rock the House	1988	—	—	3.00

WESTBOUND

Number	Title (A Side/B Side)	Yr	VG	VG+	NM
❑ 188	Pain (Part 1)/Pain (Part 2)	1971	—	3.00	6.00
❑ 204	Pleasure/I Wanna Hear from You	1972	—	3.00	6.00
❑ 208	Walt's First Trip/Varce Is Love	1972	—	3.00	6.00
❑ 214	Funky Worm/Paint Me	1973	—	3.00	6.00
❑ 216	Ecstasy/Not So Sad and Lonely	1973	—	3.00	6.00
❑ 228	Sleep Talk/Food Stamps Y'All	1974	—	3.00	6.00
❑ 5018	Rattlesnake/Gone Forever	1976	—	3.00	6.00

OHIO UNTOUCHABLES, THE
Early version of THE OHIO PLAYERS.

LUPINE

Number	Title (A Side/B Side)	Yr	VG	VG+	NM
❑ 109	She's My Heart's Desire/What to Do	1962	12.50	25.00	50.00
❑ 110	Love Is Amazing/Forgive Me Darling	1962	12.50	25.00	50.00
❑ 116/7	I'm Tired/Uptown	1962	10.00	20.00	40.00
❑ 1009	She's My Heart's Desire/What to Do	1964	5.00	10.00	20.00
❑ 1010	Love Is Amazing/Forgive Me Darling	1964	5.00	10.00	20.00
❑ 1011	I'm Tired/Uptown	1964	3.75	7.50	15.00

OLDHAM, ANDREW

PARROT

Number	Title (A Side/B Side)	Yr	VG	VG+	NM
❑ 9684	Theme from The Dick Van Dyke Show/I'd Like to See Me on the "B" Side	1964	7.50	15.00	30.00
❑ 9745	I Get Around/Save It For Me	1965	7.50	15.00	30.00

OLIVER

CREWE

Number	Title (A Side/B Side)	Yr	VG	VG+	NM
❑ 334	Jean/The Arrangement	1969	2.00	4.00	8.00
❑ 334 [PS]	Jean/The Arrangement	1969	3.75	7.50	15.00
❑ 337	Sunday Mornin'/Let Me Kiss You with a Dream	1969	—	3.00	6.00
❑ 341	Angelica/Anna	1970	—	3.00	6.00
❑ 346	I Can Remember/Where There's a Heartache There Must Be a Heart	1970	—	3.00	6.00

JUBILEE

Number	Title (A Side/B Side)	Yr	VG	VG+	NM
❑ 5659	Good Morning Starshine/Can't You See	1969	2.00	4.00	8.00

MCA

Number	Title (A Side/B Side)	Yr	VG	VG+	NM
❑ 52063	Don't Take Your Love Away/Everybody Wants to Be the Boss	1982	—	—	3.00
❑ 52113	I Want Your Love, I Need Your Love/Make Up Your Mind	1982	—	—	3.00

PARAMOUNT

Number	Title (A Side/B Side)	Yr	VG	VG+	NM
❑ 0198	Everybody I Love You/I Am Reaching	1973	—	2.00	4.00

UNITED ARTISTS

Number	Title (A Side/B Side)	Yr	VG	VG+	NM
❑ 0130	Good Morning Starshine/Jean	1973	—	2.00	4.00
—"Silver Spotlight Series" reissue					
❑ 50735	Sweet Kindness/Light the Way	1970	—	2.50	5.00
❑ 50750	Dedicated to the One I Love/Light the Way	1971	—	—	—
—Unreleased					
❑ 50762	Early Morning Rain/Catch Me If You Can	1971	—	2.50	5.00
❑ 50814	Walkin' Down the Line/Firelight	1971	—	2.50	5.00
❑ 50862	Why You Been Gone So Long/Please	1971	—	2.50	5.00

OLIVER AND THE TWISTERS

COLPIX

Number	Title (A Side/B Side)	Yr	VG	VG+	NM
❑ 615	Mother Goose Twist/Locomotion Twist	1961	3.00	6.00	12.00
❑ 615 [PS]	Mother Goose Twist/Locomotion Twist	1961	6.25	12.50	25.00

OLIVERS, THE

PHALANX

Number	Title (A Side/B Side)	Yr	VG	VG+	NM
❑ 1022	Bleecker Street/I Saw What You Did	1967	15.00	30.00	60.00

RCA VICTOR

Number	Title (A Side/B Side)	Yr	VG	VG+	NM
❑ 47-9113	Bleecker Street/I Saw What You Did	1967	5.00	10.00	20.00

OLSSON, NIGEL
Drummer in ELTON JOHN's band.

BANG

Number	Title (A Side/B Side)	Yr	VG	VG+	NM
❑ 740	Dancin' Shoes/Living in a Fantasy	1978	—	2.50	5.00
❑ 4800	Little Bit of Soap/Thinking of You	1979	—	2.00	4.00
❑ 4803	All It Takes/Part of the Chosen Few	1979	—	2.00	4.00

COLUMBIA

Number	Title (A Side/B Side)	Yr	VG	VG+	NM
❑ 10733	Rainy Day/Right or Wrong	1978	—	2.50	5.00

ROCKET

Number	Title (A Side/B Side)	Yr	VG	VG+	NM
❑ 40337	Only One Woman/In Good Time	1974	—	2.50	5.00
❑ 40455	Songs I Sing/Something Lacking in Me	1975	—	2.50	5.00
❑ 40491	A Girl Like You/Girl, We've Got to Keep On	1975	—	2.50	5.00

UNI

Number	Title (A Side/B Side)	Yr	VG	VG+	NM
❑ 55291	Some Sweet Day/Weirdhouse	1971	—	3.00	6.00
—As "Nigel Olsson's Drum Orchestra"					
❑ 55308	And I Know in My Heart/Sunshine Looks Like Rain	1971	—	3.00	6.00

OLYMPICS, THE
Also see THE CHALLENGERS (3); WALTER WARD AND THE CHALLENGERS.

ARVEE

Number	Title (A Side/B Side)	Yr	VG	VG+	NM
❑ 562	(Baby) Hully Gully/Private Eye	1959	6.25	12.50	25.00
❑ 595	Big Boy Pete/The Slop	1960	6.25	12.50	25.00
❑ 5006	Shimmy Like Kate/Workin' Hard	1960	5.00	10.00	20.00
❑ 5020	Dance by the Light of the Moon/Dodge City	1960	5.00	10.00	20.00
❑ 5023	Little Pedro/The Bullfight	1961	5.00	10.00	20.00
❑ 5031	Stay Where You Are/Dooley	1961	10.00	20.00	40.00
❑ 5044	Mash Them 'Taters/The Stomp	1961	5.00	10.00	20.00
❑ 5051	Everybody Likes to Cha Cha Cha/The Twist	1962	3.75	7.50	15.00
❑ 5056	Baby It's Hot/The Scotch	1962	3.75	7.50	15.00
❑ 5073	What'd I Say (Part 1)/What'd I Say (Part 2)	1963	3.75	7.50	15.00
❑ 6501	Big Boy Pete '65/Stay Where You Are	1965	3.00	6.00	12.00

DEMON

Number	Title (A Side/B Side)	Yr	VG	VG+	NM
❑ 1508	Western Movies/Well!	1958	7.50	15.00	30.00
❑ 1512	Dance with the Teacher/Everybody Needs Love	1958	6.25	12.50	25.00
❑ 1514	Your Love/The Chicken	1959	6.25	12.50	25.00

DUO DISC

Number	Title (A Side/B Side)	Yr	VG	VG+	NM
❑ 104	The Boogler (Part 1)/The Boogler (Part 2)	1964	3.00	6.00	12.00
❑ 105	Return of Big Boy Pete/Return of the Watusi	1964	3.00	6.00	12.00

JUBILEE

Number	Title (A Side/B Side)	Yr	VG	VG+	NM
❑ 5674	The Cartoon Song/Things That Make Me Laugh	1969	2.00	4.00	8.00

LOMA

Number	Title (A Side/B Side)	Yr	VG	VG+	NM
❑ 2010	I'm Comin' Home/Rainin' in My Heart	1965	2.50	5.00	10.00
❑ 2013	Good Lovin'/Olympic Shuffle	1965	2.50	5.00	10.00
❑ 2017	Baby I'm Yours/No More Will I Cry	1965	2.50	5.00	10.00

MGM

Number	Title (A Side/B Side)	Yr	VG	VG+	NM
❑ 14505	Worm in Your Wheatgerm/The Apartment	1973	—	2.50	5.00

MIRWOOD

Number	Title (A Side/B Side)	Yr	VG	VG+	NM
❑ 5504	We Go Together (Pretty Baby)/Secret Agents	1966	2.00	4.00	8.00
❑ 5513	Mine Exclusively/Secret Agents	1966	2.00	4.00	8.00
❑ 5523	Baby Do the Philly Dog/Western Movies	1966	2.00	4.00	8.00
❑ 5525	The Bounce/The Duck	1966	2.00	4.00	8.00
❑ 5529	The Same Old Thing/I'll Do a Little Bit More	1967	2.00	4.00	8.00
❑ 5533	Big Boy Pete/(Baby) Hully Gully	1967	2.00	4.00	8.00

PARKWAY

Number	Title (A Side/B Side)	Yr	VG	VG+	NM
❑ 6003	Lookin' for a Love/Good Things	1968	2.00	4.00	8.00

TITAN

Number	Title (A Side/B Side)	Yr	VG	VG+	NM
❑ 1718	The Chicken/Cool Short	1961	6.25	12.50	25.00

TRI DISC

Number	Title (A Side/B Side)	Yr	VG	VG+	NM
❑ 105	Return of Big Boy Pete/Return of the Watusi	1962	3.75	7.50	15.00
❑ 106	The Bounce/Fireworks	1963	3.75	7.50	15.00
❑ 107	Dancin' Holiday/Do the Slauson Shuffle	1963	3.75	7.50	15.00
❑ 110	Bounce Again/A New Dancin' Partner	1963	3.75	7.50	15.00
❑ 112	The Broken Hip/So Goodbye	1963	3.75	7.50	15.00

WARNER BROS.

Number	Title (A Side/B Side)	Yr	VG	VG+	NM
❑ 7369	Girl, You're My Kind of People/Please, Please, Please	1970	—	3.00	6.00

7-Inch Extended Plays

ARVEE

Number	Title (A Side/B Side)	Yr	VG	VG+	NM
❑ 423	(contents unknown)	1960	50.00	100.00	200.00

Number	Title (A Side/B Side)	Yr	VG	VG+	NM
❑ 423 [PS]	Doin' the Hully Gully	1960	50.00	100.00	200.00

OMEGAS, THE (1)

DECCA

Number	Title (A Side/B Side)	Yr	VG	VG+	NM
❑ 31008	When You Touch Me/Froze	1959	5.00	10.00	20.00
❑ 31094	So How Come (No One Loves Me)/Study Hall	1960	5.00	10.00	20.00
❑ 31138	Falling in Love/No One Will Ever Know	1960	5.00	10.00	20.00

GROOVE

Number	Title (A Side/B Side)	Yr	VG	VG+	NM
❑ 4	I Wanna Go Home/Midnight Run	1961	3.75	7.50	15.00

OMEGAS, THE (2)

UNITED ARTISTS

Number	Title (A Side/B Side)	Yr	VG	VG+	NM
❑ 50247	I Can't Believe/Mr. Yates	1968	7.50	15.00	30.00

ONCOMERS, THE

GATEWAY CUSTOM

Number	Title (A Side/B Side)	Yr	VG	VG+	NM
❑ 103	Every Day Now/You Let Me Down	196?	10.00	20.00	40.00

100 PROOF AGED IN SOUL

HOT WAX

Number	Title (A Side/B Side)	Yr	VG	VG+	NM
❑ 6904	Too Many Cooks (Spoil the Soup)/Not Enough Love to Satisfy	1969	3.00	6.00	12.00
—First pressings as "Aged in Soul"					
❑ 6904	Too Many Cooks (Spoil the Soup)/Not Enough Love to Satisfy	1969	—	3.00	6.00
—Later pressings as "100 Proof Aged in Soul"					
❑ 7004	Somebody's Been Sleeping/I've Come to Save You	1970	—	3.00	6.00
❑ 7009	One Man's Leftovers (Is Another Man's Feast)/If I Could See the Light in the Window	1970	—	3.00	6.00
❑ 7104	Driveway/Love Is Sweeter	1971	—	3.00	6.00
❑ 7108	90 Day Freeze (On Her Love)/Not Enough Love to Satisfy	1971	—	3.00	6.00
❑ 7202	Everything Good Is Bad/I'd Rather Fight Than Switch	1972	—	3.00	6.00
❑ 7206	Don't Scratch/If I Could See the Light in the Window	1972	—	3.00	6.00
❑ 7211	Nothing Sweeter Than Love/Since You've Been Gone	1972	—	3.00	6.00

ONO, YOKO

Also see JOHN LENNON.

APPLE

Number	Title (A Side/B Side)	Yr	VG	VG+	NM
❑ GM/OYB-1 [DJ]	Greenfield Morning/Open Your Box	1971	200.00	400.00	800.00
—Exactly six copies made for the personal use of Yoko Ono.					
❑ 1839	Mrs. Lennon/Midsummer New York	1971	—	3.50	7.00
—As "Yoko Ono/Plastic Ono Band"					
❑ 1853	Now or Never/Move On Fast	1972	—	3.50	7.00
❑ 1853 [PS]	Now or Never/Move On Fast	1972	2.00	4.00	8.00
❑ 1859	Death of Samantha/Yang Yang	1973	—	3.50	7.00
❑ 1867	Woman Power/Men, Men, Men	1973	—	3.50	7.00

CAPITOL

Number	Title (A Side/B Side)	Yr	VG	VG+	NM
❑ S7-18550	Never Say Goodbye/We're All Water	1995	—	—	3.00

GEFFEN

Number	Title (A Side/B Side)	Yr	VG	VG+	NM
❑ PRO-S-935 [DJ]	Walking on Thin Ice (3:23)/Walking on Thin Ice (5:58)	1981	2.50	5.00	10.00
❑ 49683	Walking on Thin Ice/It Happened	1981	—	2.00	4.00
❑ 49683 [PS]	Walking on Thin Ice/It Happened	1981	—	2.00	4.00
—Includes picture sleeve and lyric insert					
❑ 49802	No, No, No/Will You Touch Me	1981	—	2.00	4.00
❑ 49802 [PS]	No, No, No/Will You Touch Me	1981	—	2.00	4.00
❑ 49849	Goodbye Sadness/I Don't Know Why	1981	—	2.00	4.00

POLYDOR

Number	Title (A Side/B Side)	Yr	VG	VG+	NM
❑ 2224	My Man/Let the Tears Dry	1982	—	—	3.00
❑ 2224 [PS]	My Man/Let the Tears Dry	1982	—	—	3.00
❑ 883455-7	Hell in Paradise/(Instrumental)	1985	—	—	3.00
❑ 883455-7 [PS]	Hell in Paradise/(Instrumental)	1985	—	—	3.00

OPALS, THE (1)

APOLLO

Number	Title (A Side/B Side)	Yr	VG	VG+	NM
❑ 462	My Heart's Desire/Oh But She Did	1954	50.00	100.00	200.00
—Original with flat (non-glossy) label					
❑ 462	My Heart's Desire/Oh But She Did	1958	10.00	20.00	40.00
—Reissue with glossy label					

OPALS, THE (2)

BELTONE

Number	Title (A Side/B Side)	Yr	VG	VG+	NM
❑ 2025	Love/Two-Sided Love	1962	6.25	12.50	25.00

OPALS, THE (3)

OKEH

Number	Title (A Side/B Side)	Yr	VG	VG+	NM
❑ 7188	Does It Matter/Tender Lover	1964	6.25	12.50	25.00
❑ 7202	You Can't Hurt Me No More/Rhythm	1964	6.25	12.50	25.00
❑ 7224	I'm So Afraid/Restless Lover	1965	6.25	12.50	25.00

OPALS, THE (U)

May be group (3); could be a different group.

LAURIE

Number	Title (A Side/B Side)	Yr	VG	VG+	NM
❑ 3288	No, No, Never Again/Just Like a Little Bitty Baby	1965	3.00	6.00	12.00

ORANGE COLORED SKY

UNI

Number	Title (A Side/B Side)	Yr	VG	VG+	NM
❑ 55088	Orange Colored Sky/The Shadow of Summer	1968	3.00	6.00	12.00
❑ 55115	Happiness Is/Another Sky	1969	3.00	6.00	12.00
❑ 55156	The Sun and I/Sweet Potato	1969	3.00	6.00	12.00

ORBISON, ROY

ASYLUM

Number	Title (A Side/B Side)	Yr	VG	VG+	NM
❑ 46048	Tears/Easy Way Out	1979	—	2.50	5.00
❑ 46541	Poor Baby/Lay It Down	1979	—	2.50	5.00

ERIC

Number	Title (A Side/B Side)	Yr	VG	VG+	NM
❑ 7101	Pretty Paper/Oh Pretty Woman	197?	—	2.00	4.00

JE-WEL

Number	Title (A Side/B Side)	Yr	VG	VG+	NM
❑ 101	Ooby Dooby/Tryin' to Get to You	1956	1500.	2750.	4000.
—As "The Teen Kings"; with "Vocal: Roy Orbison" credit (spelled correctly)					
❑ 101	Ooby Dooby/Tryin' to Get to You	1956	1500.	2750.	4000.
—As "The Teen Kings"; with "Vocal: Roy Oribson" credit (spelled incorrectly)					

MERCURY

Number	Title (A Side/B Side)	Yr	VG	VG+	NM
❑ 73610	Sweet Mama Blue/Heartache	1974	2.00	4.00	8.00
❑ 73652	Hung Up onYou/Spanish Nights	1975	—	3.00	6.00
❑ 73705	It's Lonely/Still	1975	—	3.00	6.00

MGM

Number	Title (A Side/B Side)	Yr	VG	VG+	NM
❑ CS9-5	Celebrity Scene: Roy Orbison	1967	25.00	50.00	100.00
—Box set of five singles (13756-13760). Price includes box, all 5 singles, jukebox title strips, bio. Records are sometimes found by themselves, so they are also listed separately.					
❑ 13386	Ride Away/Wonderin'	1965	2.50	5.00	10.00
❑ 13386 [PS]	Ride Away/Wonderin'	1965	5.00	10.00	20.00
❑ 13410	Crawling Back/If You Can't Say Something Nice	1965	2.50	5.00	10.00
❑ 13410 [PS]	Crawling Back/If You Can't Say Something Nice	1965	5.00	10.00	20.00
❑ 13446	Breakin' Up Is Breakin' My Heart/Wait	1966	2.50	5.00	10.00
❑ 13446 [PS]	Breakin' Up Is Breakin' My Heart/Wait	1966	5.00	10.00	20.00
❑ 13498	Twinkle Toes/Where Is Tomorrow	1966	2.50	5.00	10.00
❑ 13498 [PS]	Twinkle Toes/Where Is Tomorrow	1966	5.00	10.00	20.00
❑ 13549	Too Soon to Know/You'll Never Be Sixteen Again	1966	2.50	5.00	10.00
❑ 13549 [PS]	Too Soon to Know/You'll Never Be Sixteen Again	1966	25.00	50.00	100.00
❑ 13634	Communication Breakdown/Going Back to Gloria	1966	2.50	5.00	10.00
❑ 13685	So Good/Memories	1967	2.50	5.00	10.00
❑ 13756	Ride Away/Crawlin' Back	1967	3.75	7.50	15.00
—Part of Celebrity Scene CS9-5					
❑ 13757	Breakin' Up Is Breakin' My Heart/Too Soon to Know	1967	3.75	7.50	15.00
—Part of Celebrity Scene CS9-5					
❑ 13758	Twinkle Toes/Where Is Tomorrow?	1967	3.75	7.50	15.00
—Part of Celebrity Scene CS9-5					
❑ 13759	Sweet Dreams/Going Back to Gloria	1967	3.75	7.50	15.00
—Part of Celebrity Scene CS9-5					
❑ 13760	You'll Never Be Sixteen Again/There Won't Be Many Coming Home	1967	3.75	7.50	15.00
—Part of Celebrity Scene CS9-5					
❑ 13764	Cry Softly Lonely One/Pistolero	1967	2.50	5.00	10.00
❑ 13764 [PS]	Cry Softly Lonely One/Pistolero	1967	5.00	10.00	20.00
❑ 13817	She/Here Comes the Rain Baby	1967	2.50	5.00	10.00
❑ 13889	Shy Away/Born to Be Loved by You	1968	2.50	5.00	10.00
❑ 13950	Flowers/Walk On	1968	2.50	5.00	10.00
❑ 13991	Heartache/Sugar Man	1968	2.50	5.00	10.00
❑ 14039	Southbound Jericho Parkway/My Friend	1969	2.50	5.00	10.00
❑ 14079	Penny Arcade/Tennessee Own My Soul	1969	2.50	5.00	10.00
❑ 14105	How Do You Start Over/She Cheats on Me	1970	2.50	5.00	10.00
❑ 14121	So Young/If I Had a Woman Like You	1970	2.50	5.00	10.00
❑ 14293	Close Again/Last Night	1971	2.50	5.00	10.00
❑ 14358	Changes/God Loves You	1972	2.50	5.00	10.00
❑ 14413	Remember the Good/Harlem Woman	1972	2.50	5.00	10.00
❑ 14413	Remember the Good/If Only for a While	1972	2.50	5.00	10.00
❑ 14441	I Can Read Between the Lines/Memphis, Tennessee	1972	2.50	5.00	10.00
❑ 14552	Rain Rain (Coming Down)/Sooner or Later	1973	2.50	5.00	10.00
❑ 14626	I Wanna Live/You Lay So Easy on My Mind	1973	2.50	5.00	10.00

MONUMENT

Number	Title (A Side/B Side)	Yr	VG	VG+	NM
❑ 409	Paper Boy/With the Bug	1959	20.00	40.00	80.00
—White label with vertical lines					
❑ 412	Uptown/Pretty One	1959	7.50	15.00	30.00
❑ 421	Only the Lonely (Know the Way I Feel)/Here Comes That Song Again	1960	6.25	12.50	25.00
❑ 425	Blue Angel/Today's Teardrops	1960	5.00	10.00	20.00
❑ 433	I'm Hurtin'/I Can't Stop Loving You	1960	5.00	10.00	20.00
❑ 433 [PS]	I'm Hurtin'/I Can't Stop Loving You	1960	30.00	60.00	120.00
❑ 438	Running Scared/Love Hurts	1961	5.00	10.00	20.00
❑ 438 [PS]	Running Scared/Love Hurts	1961	10.00	20.00	40.00
❑ 447	Crying/Candy Man	1961	5.00	10.00	20.00
❑ 447 [PS]	Crying/Candy Man	1961	10.00	20.00	40.00
❑ 456	Dream Baby (How Long Must I Dream)/The Actress	1962	5.00	10.00	20.00
❑ 456 [PS]	Dream Baby (How Long Must I Dream)/The Actress	1962	10.00	20.00	40.00
❑ 461	The Crowd/Mama	1962	5.00	10.00	20.00
❑ 461 [PS]	The Crowd/Mama	1962	10.00	20.00	40.00
❑ 467	Leah/Workin' for the Man	1962	5.00	10.00	20.00
❑ 467 [PS]	Leah/Workin' for the Man	1962	10.00	20.00	40.00
❑ 806	In Dreams/Shahdaroba	1963	5.00	10.00	20.00
❑ 806 [PS]	In Dreams/Shahdaroba	1963	10.00	20.00	40.00
❑ 815	Falling/Distant Drums	1963	5.00	10.00	20.00
❑ 815 [PS]	Falling/Distant Drums	1963	12.50	25.00	50.00
❑ 824	Mean Woman Blues/Blue Bayou	1963	5.00	10.00	20.00
❑ 830	Pretty Paper/Beautiful Dreamer	1963	5.00	10.00	20.00
❑ 837	It's Over/Indian Wedding	1964	5.00	10.00	20.00
❑ 837 [PS]	It's Over/Indian Wedding	1964	10.00	20.00	40.00
❑ 851	Pretty Woman/Yo Te Amo Maria	1964	7.50	15.00	30.00
—Original title					
❑ 851	Oh Pretty Woman/Yo Te Amo Maria	1964	5.00	10.00	20.00
—Revised title					
❑ 873	Goodnight/Only with You	1965	3.75	7.50	15.00
❑ 891	(Say) You're My Girl/Sleepy Hollow	1965	3.75	7.50	15.00
❑ 906	Let the Good Times Roll/Distant Drums	1965	3.75	7.50	15.00
❑ 939	Lana/Our Summer Song	1966	3.75	7.50	15.00
❑ 1936	Pretty Paper/Beautiful Dreamer	1976	—	2.00	4.00
❑ 8690	Belinda/All These Chains	1976	—	2.50	5.00
❑ 45200	(I'm a) Southern Man/Born to Love Me	1976	—	2.50	5.00
❑ 45215	Drifting Away/Under Suspicion	1977	—	2.50	5.00

RCA VICTOR

Number	Title (A Side/B Side)	Yr	VG	VG+	NM
❑ 47-7381	Sweet and Innocent/Seems to Me	1958	10.00	20.00	40.00
❑ 47-7447	Almost Eighteen/Julie	1959	10.00	20.00	40.00

SUN

Number	Title (A Side/B Side)	Yr	VG	VG+	NM
❑ 242	Ooby Dooby/Go! Go! Go!	1956	25.00	50.00	100.00

Number	Title (A Side/B Side)	Yr	VG	VG+	NM
❑ 251	Rockhouse/You're My Baby	1956	15.00	30.00	60.00
❑ 265	Devil Doll/Sweet and Easy to Love	1957	20.00	40.00	80.00
❑ 284	Chicken Hearted/I Like Love	1958	12.50	25.00	50.00
❑ 353	Devil Doll/Sweet and Easy to Love	1960	62.50	125.00	250.00
VIRGIN					
❑ 99159	Oh Pretty Woman/Claudette	1989	—	—	3.00
❑ 99159 [PS]	Oh Pretty Woman/Claudette	1989	—	—	3.00
❑ 99202	California Blue/In Dreams	1989	—	—	3.00
❑ 99202 [PS]	California Blue/In Dreams	1989	—	—	3.00
❑ 99227	She's a Mystery to Me/Dream Baby	1989	—	—	3.00
❑ 99227 [PS]	She's a Mystery to Me/Dream Baby	1989	—	—	3.00
❑ 99245	You Got It/The Only One	1989	—	—	3.00
❑ 99245 [PS]	You Got It/The Only One	1989	—	—	3.00
❑ 99388	Crying/Falling	1988	—	—	3.00
—A-side with k.d. lang					
❑ 99388 [PS]	Crying/Falling	1988	—	—	3.00
❑ 99434	In Dreams/Leah	1987	—	—	3.00
❑ 99434 [PS]	In Dreams/Leah	1987	—	2.00	4.00
WARNER BROS.					
❑ 49262	That Lovin' You Feeling Again/Lola	1980	—	2.50	5.00
—A-side with Emmylou Harris; B-side by Craig Hundley					

ORBITS, THE

More than one group.

Number	Title (A Side/B Side)	Yr	VG	VG+	NM
ARGO					
❑ 5286	Who Are You/Mr. Bad Luck	1958	10.00	20.00	40.00
DOOTO					
❑ 601	Tell Me Baby/Two Crazy Scientists	196?	5.00	10.00	20.00
FLAIR-X					
❑ 5000	Message of Love/I Really Do	1956	7.50	15.00	30.00
NU-KAT					
❑ 116/7	Knock Her Down/My Love	1959	7.50	15.00	30.00

ORCHIDS, THE (1)

Number	Title (A Side/B Side)	Yr	VG	VG+	NM
COLUMBIA					
❑ 42913	That Boy Is Messin' Up My Mind/Harlem Tango	1963	5.00	10.00	20.00
❑ 43066	Tell Me a Story/From Bad to Worse	1964	5.00	10.00	20.00
❑ 43175	Christmas Is the Time to Be With Your Baby/It Doesn't Matter	1964	5.00	10.00	20.00

ORCHIDS, THE (2)

Number	Title (A Side/B Side)	Yr	VG	VG+	NM
HARLOW					
❑ 101	I Don't Think You Missed Me/We're in Love	1962	5.00	10.00	20.00

ORCHIDS, THE (3)

Number	Title (A Side/B Side)	Yr	VG	VG+	NM
KING					
❑ 4661	Oh Why/All Night Baby	1953	100.00	200.00	400.00
❑ 4663	I've Been a Fool from the Start/Beginning to Miss You	1953	100.00	200.00	400.00
PARROT					
❑ 815	Newly Wed/You're Everything to Me	1955	100.00	200.00	400.00
❑ 819	I Can't Refuse/You Said You Loved Me	1955	62.50	125.00	250.00

ORCHIDS, THE (U)

Some of these could be group (1) or (2).

Number	Title (A Side/B Side)	Yr	VG	VG+	NM
ROULETTE					
❑ 4412	Pony Walk/Good Time Stomp	1962	5.00	10.00	20.00
❑ 4633	Good Good Time/Love Is What You Make It	1965	3.00	6.00	12.00
UNITED ARTISTS					
❑ 375	You'll Never Know/Say Yes	1961	5.00	10.00	20.00
WALL					
❑ 549	Soft Shadows/Good Gully	1961	5.00	10.00	20.00

ORIENTS, THE

Number	Title (A Side/B Side)	Yr	VG	VG+	NM
LAURIE					
❑ 3232	Queen of the Angels/Shouldn't I	1964	10.00	20.00	40.00

ORIGINAL CADILLACS, THE

See THE CADILLACS.

ORIGINAL CASTE, THE

Number	Title (A Side/B Side)	Yr	VG	VG+	NM
DOT					
❑ 17071	Just Like Tom Thumb's Blues/I Can't Make It Anymore	1968	3.75	7.50	15.00
❑ 17138	Snakes and Ladders/I'm So Much in Love	1968	3.75	7.50	15.00
T-A					
❑ 186	One Tin Soldier/Live for Tomorrow	1969	3.00	6.00	12.00
❑ 186 [PS]	One Tin Soldier/Live for Tomorrow	1969	3.00	6.00	12.00
❑ 192	Mr. Monday/Highway	1970	2.50	5.00	10.00
❑ 197	Nothing Can Touch Me/Country Song	1970	2.50	5.00	10.00
❑ 204	Sweet Chicago/Ain't That Tellin' You People	1970	2.50	5.00	10.00
❑ 211	Sault Ste. Marie/When Love Is Near	1971	2.50	5.00	10.00

ORIGINAL CASUALS, THE

Number	Title (A Side/B Side)	Yr	VG	VG+	NM
BACK BEAT					
❑ 503	So Tough/I Love My Darling	1958	10.00	20.00	40.00
—Original pressings by "The Casuals"					
❑ 503	So Tough/I Love My Darling	1958	6.25	12.50	25.00
❑ 510	Ju-Judy/Don't Pass Me By	1958	6.25	12.50	25.00
❑ 514	Three Kisses Past Midnight/It's Been a Long Time	1958	6.25	12.50	25.00

ORIGINAL SURFARIS, THE

See THE SURFARIS (2).

ORIGINALS, THE (1)

Number	Title (A Side/B Side)	Yr	VG	VG+	NM
FANTASY					
❑ 820	Take This Love/Ladies (We Need You)	1978	—	2.50	5.00
❑ 847	Blue Moon/Ladies (We Need You)	1979	—	2.50	5.00
❑ 856	J-E-A-L-O-U-S (Means I Love You)/Jezebel (You've Got Me Under Your Spell)	1979	—	2.50	5.00
MOTOWN					
❑ PR-1 [DJ]	Young Train (same on both sides?)	1973	50.00	100.00	200.00
❑ 1355	Good Lovin' Is Just a Dime Away/Nothing Can Take the Place (Of Your Love)	1975	—	3.00	6.00
❑ 1370	50 Years/Financial Affair	1975	—	3.00	6.00
❑ 1379	Everybody's Got to Do Something/(Instrumental)	1975	—	3.00	6.00
PHASE II					
❑ 02061	Baby I'm for Real/Share Your Love with Me	1981	—	2.00	4.00
❑ 02147	The Magic Is You/Let Me Dance	1981	—	2.00	4.00
❑ 02724	Baby I'm for Real/The Magic Is You	1982	—	2.00	4.00
—As "Hank Dixon and the Originals"					
❑ 5653	Waitin' on a Letter-Mr. Postman/(B-side unknown)	1981	—	2.50	5.00
SOUL					
❑ 35029	Goodnight Irene/Need Your Loving (Want It Back)	1967	3.00	6.00	12.00
❑ 35056	We've Got a Way Out Love/You're the One	1969	3.00	6.00	12.00
❑ 35061	Green Grow the Lilacs/You're the One	1969	3.00	6.00	12.00
❑ 35066	Baby I'm for Real/The Moment of Truth	1969	2.00	4.00	8.00
❑ 35069	The Bells/I'll Wait for You	1970	2.00	4.00	8.00
❑ 35074	We Can Make It Baby/I Like Your Style	1970	2.00	4.00	8.00
❑ 35074	We Can Make It/I Like Your Style	1970	3.00	6.00	12.00
❑ 35079	God Bless Whoever Sent You/Desperate Young Man	1970	2.00	4.00	8.00
❑ 35085	Keep Me/A Man Without Love	1971	—	3.00	6.00
❑ 35093	I'm Someone Who Cares/Once I Have You	1972	—	3.00	6.00
❑ 35102	Be My Love/Endlessly Love	1973	—	3.00	6.00
❑ 35109	First Lady (Sweet Mother's Love)/There's a Chance When You Love, You Love	1973	—	3.00	6.00
❑ 35112	Supernatural Voodoo Woman (Part 1)/Supernatural Voodoo Woman (Part 2)	1974	—	3.00	6.00
❑ 35113	Game Called Love/Ooh You Put a Spell on Me	1974	—	3.00	6.00
❑ 35115	You're My Only World/So Near (And Yet So Far)	1974	—	3.00	6.00
❑ 35117	Touch/Ooh You Put a Spell on Me	1975	—	3.00	6.00
❑ 35119	Down to Love Town/Just to Be Closer to You	1976	—	3.00	6.00
❑ 35121 [DJ]	Call On Your Six Million Dollar Man (mono/stereo)	1977	—	3.00	6.00

ORIGINALS, THE (2)

Number	Title (A Side/B Side)	Yr	VG	VG+	NM
DIAMOND					
❑ 102	At Times Like These/Gimme a Little Kiss, Will Ya, Huh?	1961	10.00	20.00	40.00
❑ 116	Summer Schoo/You and I	1962	10.00	20.00	40.00

ORIGINALS, THE (3)

CHUCK RIO was in this group.

Number	Title (A Side/B Side)	Yr	VG	VG+	NM
JACKPOT					
❑ 48007	The Whip/The Blue Kat	1959	7.50	15.00	30.00
❑ 48012	Anna/Sleepless Nights	1959	7.50	15.00	30.00

ORIGINALS, THE (4)

TONY ALLEN was in this group.

Number	Title (A Side/B Side)	Yr	VG	VG+	NM
ORIGINAL SOUND					
❑ 10	Wishing Star/Let Me Hear You Say Yeah	1960	7.50	15.00	30.00
❑ 13	Little Lonely Girl/I Still Love You	1960	5.00	10.00	20.00
—As "Tony Allen and the Originals"					

ORIGINALS, THE (U)

7-Inch Extended Plays

Number	Title (A Side/B Side)	Yr	VG	VG+	NM
SOMERSET					
❑ EX-6000	Lazy Mary/Billy//(B-side unknown)	1958	5.00	10.00	20.00

ORIOLES, THE

Also see SONNY TIL.

Number	Title (A Side/B Side)	Yr	VG	VG+	NM
ABNER					
❑ 1016	Sugar Girl/Didn't I Say	1958	15.00	30.00	60.00
CHARLIE PARKER					
❑ 211	Secret Love/The Wobble	1962	5.00	10.00	20.00
❑ 212	In the Chapel in the Moonlight/Hey! Little Woman	1962	5.00	10.00	20.00
❑ 213	Back to the Chapel Again/(It's Gonna Be a) Lonely Christmas	1962	5.00	10.00	20.00
❑ 214	What Are You Doing New Year's Eve/Don't Mess Around with My Love	1962	5.00	10.00	20.00
❑ 215	It's Too Soon to Know/I Miss You So	1963	3.75	7.50	15.00
❑ 216	Write and Tell Me Why/Don't Tell Her What Happens to Me	1963	3.75	7.50	15.00
❑ 219	I Miss You So/Hey! Little Woman	1963	3.75	7.50	15.00
HARLEM SOUND					
❑ 1001	Lonely Christmas/What Are You Doing New Year's Eve	19??	—	2.50	5.00
JUBILEE					
❑ 5000	It's Too Soon to Know/Barbara Lee	1951	1000.	2000.	4000.
❑ 5005	Tell Me So/Deacon Jones	1951	500.00	1000.	2000.
❑ 5016	So Much/Forgive and Forget	1951	500.00	1000.	2000.
❑ 5017	What Are You Doing New Year's Eve/Lonely Christmas	1951	200.00	400.00	800.00
❑ 5017 [PS]	What Are You Doing New Year's Eve/Lonely Christmas	1954	250.00	500.00	1000.
❑ 5025	At Night/Every Dog-Gone Time	1951	250.00	500.00	1000.
❑ 5040	I Cross My Fingers/Can't Seem to Laugh Anymore	1951	500.00	1000.	2000.
❑ 5045	Oh Holy Night/The Lord's Prayer	1951	150.00	300.00	600.00
—Original on blue label					
❑ 5045	Oh Holy Night/The Lord's Prayer	196?	6.25	12.50	25.00
—Reissue on black label					
❑ 5045 [PS]	Oh Holy Night/The Lord's Prayer	1954	150.00	300.00	600.00
❑ 5051	I Miss You So/You Are My First Love	1951	1000.	1500.	2000.
—Red vinyl					
❑ 5051	I Miss You So/You Are My First Love	1951	200.00	400.00	800.00
❑ 5055	Pal of Mine/Happy Go Lucky Local Blues	1951	200.00	400.00	800.00
❑ 5061	I'm Just a Fool in Love/Hold Me, Squeeze Me	1951	200.00	400.00	800.00
❑ 5065	Baby, Please Don't Go/Don't Tell Her What's Happened to Me	1951	1000.	1500.	2000.
—Red vinyl					
❑ 5065	Baby, Please Don't Go/Don't Tell Her What's Happened to Me	1951	150.00	300.00	600.00
❑ 5071	When You're Not Around/How Blind Can You Be	1952	150.00	300.00	600.00

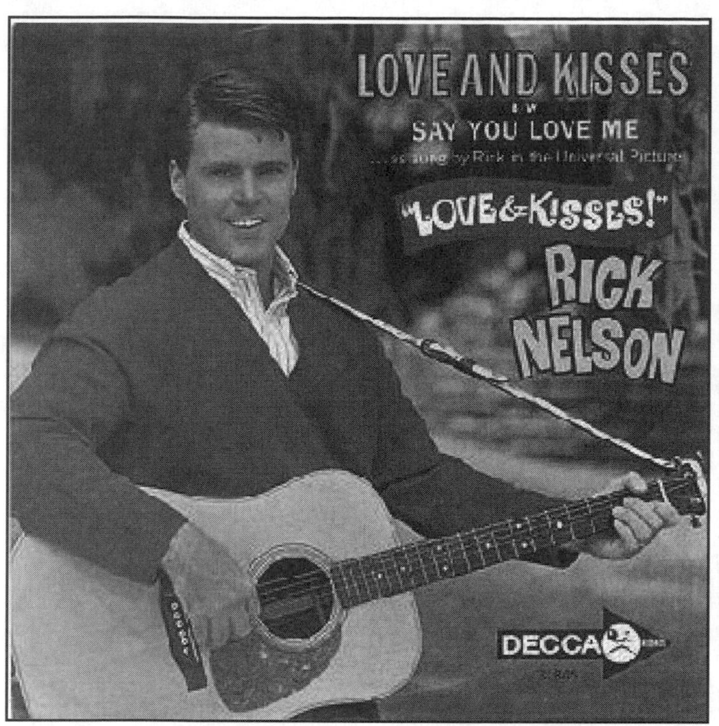

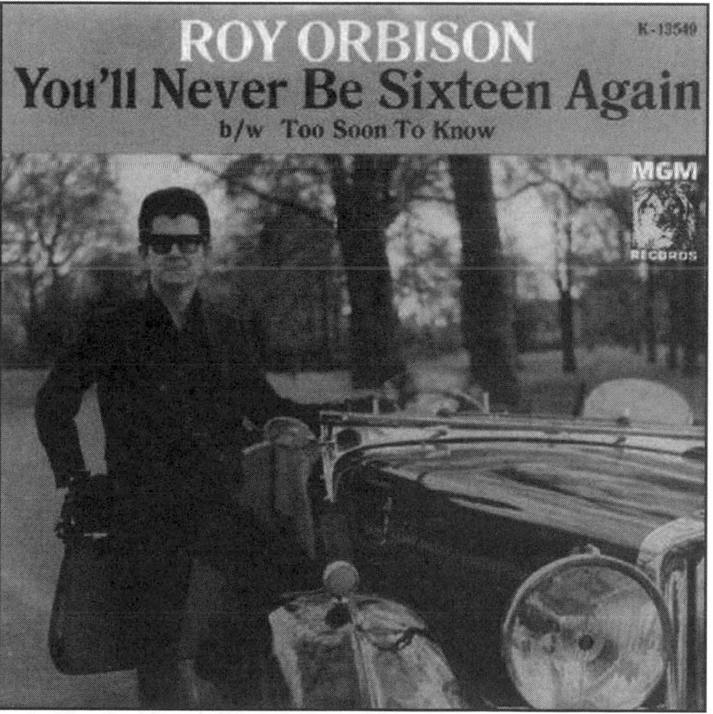

(Top left) Far more attention is paid to Rick Nelson's Imperial years, as that's when he was having most of his hits. But collectors are finding that the Decca material is just as rewarding — and by comparison, much more difficult to find. Here's a Decca picture sleeve from the 1965 single "Love and Kisses" that was not previously listed in our price guides. (Top right) When it was first issued in 1974, "I Honestly Love You" by Olivia Newton-John did not have a picture sleeve. But a 1976 re-release, in conjunction with a greatest-hits album, did have this picture sleeve. (Bottom left) I wonder how many people, who are probably seeing a photo of The O'Kaysions for the first time on this rare original picture sleeve of "Girl Watcher," thought the group was black? (Bottom right) Another artist with many tough-to-find picture sleeves after his peak of popularity is Roy Orbison. This one has been known to trade in the $100 range.

Number	Title (A Side/B Side)	Yr	VG	VG+	NM
❑ 5074	Trust in Me/Shrimp Boats	1952	125.00	250.00	500.00
❑ 5076	Proud of You/You Never Cared for Me	1952	125.00	250.00	500.00
❑ 5082	It's All Over Because We're Through/Waiting	1952	125.00	250.00	500.00
❑ 5084	Barfly/Getting Tired, Tired, Tired	1952	100.00	200.00	400.00
❑ 5092	Don't Cry Baby/See See Rider	1952	375.00	750.00	1500.
—Red vinyl					
❑ 5092	Don't Cry Baby/See See Rider	1952	100.00	200.00	400.00
❑ 5102	You Belong to Me/I Don't Want to Take a Chance	1952	125.00	250.00	500.00
❑ 5107	I Miss You So/Till Then	1952	375.00	750.00	1500.
—Red vinyl					
❑ 5107	I Miss You So/Till Then	1952	100.00	200.00	400.00
❑ 5107	I Miss You So/Till Then	1963	6.25	12.50	25.00
—Reissue, credited to "Sonny Til and the Orioles"					
❑ 5108	Teardrops on My Pillow/Hold Me, Thrill Me, Kiss Me	1953	375.00	750.00	1500.
—Red vinyl					
❑ 5108	Teardrops on My Pillow/Hold Me, Thrill Me, Kiss Me	1953	100.00	200.00	400.00
❑ 5115	Bad Little Girl/Dem Days	1953	100.00	200.00	400.00
❑ 5120	I Cover the Waterfront/One More Time	1953	300.00	600.00	1200.
—Red vinyl					
❑ 5120	I Cover the Waterfront/One More Time	1953	100.00	200.00	400.00
❑ 5122	Crying in the Chapel/Don't You Think I Ought to Know	1953	20.00	40.00	80.00
❑ 5127	In the Mission of St. Augustine/Write and Tell Me Why	1953	12.50	25.00	50.00
❑ 5134	There's No One But You/Rose of Calvary	1954	12.50	25.00	50.00
❑ 5137	Secret Love/Don't Go to Strangers	1954	12.50	25.00	50.00
❑ 5143	Maybe You'll Be There/Drowining Every Hope I Ever Had	1954	20.00	40.00	80.00
❑ 5154	In the Chapel in the Moonlight/Thank the Lord, Thank the Lord	1954	12.50	25.00	50.00
❑ 5161	If You Believe/Longing	1954	12.50	25.00	50.00
❑ 5172	Runaround/Count Your Blessings Instead of Sheep	1954	12.50	25.00	50.00
❑ 5177	I Love You Mostly/Fair Exchange	1955	10.00	20.00	40.00
❑ 5189	I Need You Baby/The Good Lord Will Smile	1955	10.00	20.00	40.00
❑ 5221	Please Sing My Blues Tonight/Moody Over You	1955	10.00	20.00	40.00
❑ 5231	Angel/Don't Go to Strangers	1956	15.00	30.00	60.00
❑ 5363	Tell Me So/At Night	1959	3.75	7.50	15.00
—As "Sonny Til and the Orioles"					
❑ 5384	Come On Home/The First of Summer	1960	3.75	7.50	15.00
—As "Sonny Til and the Orioles"					
❑ 6001	Crying in the Chapel/Forgive and Forget	1959	3.75	7.50	15.00
—As "Sonny Til and the Orioles"					
LANA					
❑ 109	What Are You Doing New Year's Eve/Crying in the Chapel	196?	—	3.00	6.00
VEE JAY					
❑ 196	I Just Got Lucky/Happy 'Til the Letter	1956	7.50	15.00	30.00
❑ 228	For All We Know/Never Leave Me Baby	1956	7.50	15.00	30.00
❑ 244	Sugar Girl/Didn't I Say	1957	10.00	20.00	40.00
VIRGO					
❑ 6017	What Are You Doing New Year's Eve/Crying in the Chapel	1972	—	2.00	4.00

7-Inch Extended Plays

Number	Title (A Side/B Side)	Yr	VG	VG+	NM
JUBILEE					
❑ 5000	Too Soon to Know/Forgive and Forget//Tell Me So/At Night	1954	250.00	500.00	1000.
❑ 5000 [PS]	The Orioles Sing	1954	250.00	500.00	1000.

ORION

Also see JIMMY ELLIS.

Number	Title (A Side/B Side)	Yr	VG	VG+	NM
KRISTAL					
❑ 2292/2308	I'm Saving Up My Pennies/I'm Starting Over	1985	—	2.00	4.00
❑ 2338	100 Pounds of Clay/Because He Lived	1986	—	2.00	4.00
RADIOACTIVE					
❑ 18772-1 [DJ]	Unchained Melody (same on both sides)	1987	—	2.50	5.00
STARGEM					
❑ 2465 [DJ]	Only a Woman Like You (same on both sides)	1990	—	2.50	5.00
❑ 2469	I Want You, I Need You, I Love You/Plastic Saddle	1990	—	2.50	5.00
❑ 2502	Love It Back Together/If That Isn't Love	1990	—	2.50	5.00
—Red vinyl					
❑ 2502 [PS]	Love It Back Together/If That Isn't Love	1990	—	2.50	5.00
SUN					
❑ 1142	Honey/Ebony Eyes	1979	—	2.00	4.00
❑ 1147	Before the Next Teardrop Falls/Washing Machine	1979	—	2.00	4.00
❑ 1148	Remember Bethlehem/Silent Night	1979	—	2.00	4.00
❑ 1148 [DJ]	Remember Bethlehem (same on both sides)	1979	2.50	5.00	10.00
—Yellow vinyl promo					
❑ 1151	Be-Bop-a-Lula/The Breakup	1980	—	2.00	4.00
—A-side with Jerry Lee Lewis; B-side with Charlie Rich					
❑ 1152	It Ain't No Mystery/Stranger in My Place	1980	—	2.00	4.00
❑ 1152 [DJ]	It Ain't No Mystery (same on both sides)	1980	2.50	5.00	10.00
—Yellow vinyl promo					
❑ 1153	Texas Tea/Faded Love	1980	—	2.00	4.00
❑ 1153 [DJ]	Texas Tea (same on both sides)	1980	2.50	5.00	10.00
—Yellow vinyl promo					
❑ 1156	Am I That Easy to Forget/Crazy Arms	1980	—	2.00	4.00
❑ 1156 [DJ]	Am I That Easy to Forget (same on both sides)	1980	2.50	5.00	10.00
—Yellow vinyl promo					
❑ 1159	Rockabilly Rebel/Memphis Sun	1980	—	2.00	4.00
❑ 1159 [DJ]	Rockabilly Rebel (same on both sides)	1980	2.50	5.00	10.00
—Yellow vinyl promo					
❑ 1162	Crazy Little Thing Called Love/Matchbox	1981	—	2.00	4.00
❑ 1165	Born/If I Can't Have You	1981	—	2.00	4.00
❑ 1165 [DJ]	Born (same on both sides)	1981	2.50	5.00	10.00
—Yellow vinyl promo					
❑ 1170	Some You Win, Some You Lose/Ain't No Good	1981	—	2.00	4.00
❑ 1170 [DJ]	Some You Win, Some You Lose (same on both sides)	1981	2.50	5.00	10.00
—Yellow vinyl promo					
❑ 1172	Baby Please Say Yes/Feelings	1982	—	2.00	4.00
❑ 1175	Honky Tonk Heaven/Morning, Noon and Night	1982	—	2.00	4.00
❑ 1175 [DJ]	Honky Tonk Heaven (same on both sides)	1982	2.50	5.00	10.00
—Yellow vinyl promo					

7-Inch Extended Plays

Number	Title (A Side/B Side)	Yr	VG	VG+	NM
SUN					
❑ 1152 [DJ]	Stranger in My Place Greetings: Wedding Anniversary/Good Music/Great Station//Favorite Station/Best Music/Birthday	1981	10.00	20.00	40.00
—Came with insert but no cover					

ORLANDO, TONY

Also see BERTELL DACHE; DAWN (1).

Number	Title (A Side/B Side)	Yr	VG	VG+	NM
ATCO					
❑ 6376	Think Before You Act/She Loves Me (For What I Am)	1965	2.50	5.00	10.00
CAMEO					
❑ 471	Sweet Sweet/Manuelito (Little Manuel	1967	2.50	5.00	10.00
CASABLANCA					
❑ 967	They're Playing Our Song (Medley)/Moonlight	1979	—	2.00	4.00
❑ 991	Sweets for My Sweet/High Steppin'	1979	—	2.00	4.00
❑ 2229	San Pedros Children/High Steppin'	1979	—	2.00	4.00
❑ 2249	Pullin' Together/She Always Knew	1980	—	2.00	4.00
EPIC					
❑ 9441	Halfway to Paradise/Lonely Tomorrows	1961	3.75	7.50	15.00
❑ 9441 [PS]	Halfway to Paradise/Lonely Tomorrows	1961	6.25	12.50	25.00
❑ 9452	Bless You/Am I the Guy	1961	3.75	7.50	15.00
❑ 9452 [PS]	Bless You/Am I the Guy	1961	6.25	12.50	25.00
❑ 9476	Hapy Times (Are Here to Stay)/Lonely Am I	1961	3.00	6.00	12.00
❑ 9476 [PS]	Hapy Times (Are Here to Stay)/Lonely Am I	1961	6.25	12.50	25.00
❑ 9491	My Baby's a Starnger/Talkin' About You	1962	3.00	6.00	12.00
❑ 9491 [PS]	My Baby's a Starnger/Talkin' About You	1962	6.25	12.50	25.00
❑ 9502	I'd Never Find Another You/Love on Your Lips	1962	3.00	6.00	12.00
❑ 9519	At the Edge of Tears/Chills	1962	3.00	6.00	12.00
❑ 9519 [PS]	At the Edge of Tears/Chills	1962	6.25	12.50	25.00
❑ 9562	Beautiful Dreamer/The Loneliest	1962	2.50	5.00	10.00
❑ 9570	Joanie/Shirley	1963	2.50	5.00	10.00
❑ 9622	I'll Be There/What Am I Gonna Do	1963	2.50	5.00	10.00
❑ 9668	She Doesn't Know It/Tell Me What I Can Do	1964	2.50	5.00	10.00
❑ 9715	To Wait for Love/Accept It	1964	2.50	5.00	10.00

ORLANDO, TONY (2)

This is not by the same singer as the rest.

Number	Title (A Side/B Side)	Yr	VG	VG+	NM
MILO					
❑ 101	Ding Dong/You and Only You	1959	25.00	50.00	100.00

ORLANDO, TONY, AND DAWN

See DAWN (1).

ORLONS, THE

Number	Title (A Side/B Side)	Yr	VG	VG+	NM
ABC					
❑ 10894	Everything/Keep Your Hands Off My Baby	1967	2.50	5.00	10.00
❑ 10948	Kissin' Time/Once Upon a Time	1967	2.50	5.00	10.00
CALLA					
❑ 113	Spinnin' Top/Anyone Who Had a Heart	1966	2.50	5.00	10.00
CAMEO					
❑ 105 [DJ]	Big Girls Don't Cry/Pop Pop Pop-Pie	1962	10.00	20.00	40.00
—Yellow label, black print, promo only					
❑ 198	I'll Be True/Heart Darling Angel	1961	12.50	25.00	50.00
❑ 211	Mr. 21/Please Let It Be Me	1961	12.50	25.00	50.00
❑ 218	The Wah-Watusi/Holiday Hill	1962	5.00	10.00	20.00
❑ 231	Don't Hang Up/The Conservative	1962	5.00	10.00	20.00
❑ 231 [PS]	Don't Hang Up/The Conservative	1962	10.00	20.00	40.00
❑ 243	South Street/Those Terrible Boots	1963	5.00	10.00	20.00
❑ 243 [PS]	South Street/Those Terrible Boots	1963	10.00	20.00	40.00
❑ 257	Not Me/My Best Friend	1963	5.00	10.00	20.00
❑ 257 [PS]	Not Me/My Best Friend	1963	7.50	15.00	30.00
❑ 273	Cross Fire!/It's No Big Thing	1963	5.00	10.00	20.00
❑ 273 [PS]	Cross Fire!/It's No Big Thing	1963	7.50	15.00	30.00
❑ 287	Bon-Doo-Wah/Don't Throw Your Love Away	1963	3.75	7.50	15.00
❑ 287 [PS]	Bon-Doo-Wah/Don't Throw Your Love Away	1963	7.50	15.00	30.00
❑ 295	Shimmy Shimmy/Everything Nice	1964	3.75	7.50	15.00
❑ 295 [PS]	Shimmy Shimmy/Everything Nice	1964	6.25	12.50	25.00
❑ 319	Rules of Love/Heartbreak Hotel	1964	3.75	7.50	15.00
❑ 319 [PS]	Rules of Love/Heartbreak Hotel	1964	6.25	12.50	25.00
❑ 332	Knock! Knock! (Who's There)/Goin' Places	1964	3.75	7.50	15.00
❑ 332 [PS]	Knock! Knock! (Who's There)/Goin' Places	1964	6.25	12.50	25.00
❑ 346	I Ain't Coming Back/Envy (In My Eyes)	1965	3.00	6.00	12.00
❑ 352	Come On Down Baby/I Ain't Coming Back	1965	3.00	6.00	12.00
❑ 372	Don't You Want My Lovin'/I Can't Take It	1965	3.00	6.00	12.00
❑ 384	No Love But Your Love/Envy (In My Eyes)	1965	10.00	20.00	40.00

ORPHEUS

Number	Title (A Side/B Side)	Yr	VG	VG+	NM
BELL					
❑ 45128	Big Green Pearl/Sweet Life	1971	—	2.50	5.00
MGM					
❑ 13882	Can't Find the Time/Lesley's Girl	1967	2.50	5.00	10.00
—Originals have black labels					
❑ 13882	Can't Find the Time/Lesley's Girl	1969	—	3.00	6.00
—Reissues (same number) have blue and gold labels					
❑ 13947	I ve Never Seen Love Like This/Congress Alley	1968	—	3.00	6.00
❑ 14022	Brown Arms in Houston/I Can Make the Sun Rise	1969	—	3.00	6.00
❑ 14022 [PS]	Brown Arms in Houston/I Can Make the Sun Rise	1969	2.50	5.00	10.00
❑ 14139	Joyful/By the Size of My Shoes	1970	—	3.00	6.00
RED BIRD					
❑ 10-041	My Life/Music Minus Orpheus	1965	3.75	7.50	15.00

ORR, J.D.

Number	Title (A Side/B Side)	Yr	VG	VG+	NM
SUMMIT					
❑ 105	Hula-Hoop Boogie/Lonesome Hearted Blues	1958	100.00	200.00	400.00

ORRELL, DAVID

Number	Title (A Side/B Side)	Yr	VG	VG+	NM
FELSTED					
❑ 8515	Be My Baby/You're the One	1958	20.00	40.00	80.00

ORSI, PHIL, AND THE LITTLE KINGS

Number	Title (A Side/B Side)	Yr	VG	VG+	NM
LUCKY					
❑ 1009	Come On Everybody/Oh My Darling	1963	18.75	37.50	75.00
❑ 1015	Don't You Just Know It/(B-side unknown)	1964	6.25	12.50	25.00
U.S.A.					
❑ 837	Stay/Whoever He May Be	1965	6.25	12.50	25.00
❑ 841	Sorry (I Ran All the Way Home)/Whoever He May Be	1965	6.25	12.50	25.00

OSBORNE, ARTHUR

Number	Title (A Side/B Side)	Yr	VG	VG+	NM
BRUNSWICK					
❑ 55068	Hey Ruby/Don't Give Me Heartaches	1958	15.00	30.00	60.00

OSBORNE, KELL, AND THE CHICKS

Number	Title (A Side/B Side)	Yr	VG	VG+	NM
CLASS					
❑ 302	Little Chick-A-Dee/Do You Mind	1962	3.75	7.50	15.00
LOMA					
❑ 2023	That's What's Happening/You Can't Outsmart a Woman	1965	2.50	5.00	10.00
TITANIC					
❑ 5008	Quicksand/Lonely Boy Song	1963	25.00	50.00	100.00
TREY					
❑ 3006	The Bells of St. Mary's/That's Alright, Baby	1960	6.25	12.50	25.00

OSBOURNE, OZZY

Also see BLACK SABBATH.

Number	Title (A Side/B Side)	Yr	VG	VG+	NM
CBS ASSOCIATED					
❑ 04318	Bark at the Moon/Spiders	1984	—	2.50	5.00
❑ 04383	So Tired/"B" Side	1984	—	2.50	5.00
❑ 05810	Shot in the Dark/You Said It All	1986	—	2.00	4.00
❑ 05810 [PS]	Shot in the Dark/You Said It All	1986	—	2.00	4.00
❑ 07168	Crazy Train (Live)/Crazy Train (Original)	1987	—	—	3.00
❑ 08463	Shot in the Dark/Crazy Train	1988	—	—	3.00
—Reissue					
❑ 08516	Miracle Man/Man You Said It All	1988	—	—	3.00
❑ 68534	Crazy Babies/Demon Alcohol	1989	—	—	3.00
EPIC					
❑ 74986	Changes/No More Tears	1993	—	—	3.00
EPIC ASSOCIATED					
❑ 73973	No More Tears/S.I.N.	1991	—	2.00	4.00
❑ 74093	Mama, I'm Coming Home/Don't Blame Me	1991	—	2.00	4.00
JET					
❑ 02079	Crazy Train/Steal Away (The Night)	1981	—	2.50	5.00
❑ 02582	Flying High Again/I Don't Know	1981	—	2.50	5.00
❑ 02707	Little Dolls/Tonight	1982	—	2.50	5.00
❑ 03392	Paranoid/Iron Man	1982	—	2.50	5.00
❑ 03534	Never Say Die/Paranoid	1983	—	2.50	5.00

OSHINS, MILT

Number	Title (A Side/B Side)	Yr	VG	VG+	NM
PELVIS					
❑ 169	All About Elvis/All About Elvis (Part 2)	1956	18.75	37.50	75.00

OSMOND, DONNY

Also see DONNY AND MARIE OSMOND; THE OSMONDS.

Number	Title (A Side/B Side)	Yr	VG	VG+	NM
CAPITOL					
❑ B-44369	Soldier of Love/My Secret Touch	1989	—	—	3.00
❑ B-44369 [PS]	Soldier of Love/My Secret Touch	1989	—	2.50	5.00
❑ B-44379	Sacred Emotion/Groove	1989	—	—	3.00
❑ 7PRO-79608	[DJ]Sacred Emotion (same on both sides)	1989	—	2.50	5.00
❑ 7PRO-79608	[PS]Sacred Emotion (same on both sides)	1989	—	2.50	5.00
—Picture sleeve appears to have been released only with promo copies					
❑ 7PRO-79683	[DJ]Hold On (same on both sides)	1989	—	2.50	5.00
—Vinyl is promo only					
❑ 7PRO-79913	[DJ]I'll Be Good to You (same on both sides)	1990	—	2.50	5.00
—Vinyl is promo only					
MGM					
❑ 14227	Sweet and Innocent/Flirtin'	1971	—	3.00	6.00
❑ 14227 [PS]	Sweet and Innocent/Flirtin'	1971	2.00	4.00	8.00
❑ 14285	Go Away Little Girl/Time to Ride	1971	—	3.00	6.00
❑ 14285	Go Away Little Girl/The Wild Rover (Time to Ride)	1971	—	2.50	5.00
—Altered B-side title					
❑ 14322	Hey Girl/I Knew You When	1971	—	3.00	6.00
❑ 14367	Puppy Love/Let My People Go	1972	—	3.00	6.00
❑ 14407	Too Young/Love Me	1972	—	3.00	6.00
❑ 14424	Lonely Boy/Why	1972	—	3.00	6.00
❑ 14503	The Twelfth of Never/Life Is Just What You Make It	1973	—	2.50	5.00
❑ 14503 [PS]	The Twelfth of Never/Life Is Just What You Make It	1973	2.00	4.00	8.00
❑ 14583	A Million to One/Young Love	1973	—	2.50	5.00
❑ 14677	Are You Lonesome Tonight/When I Fall in Love	1973	—	2.50	5.00
❑ 14781	I Have a Dream/I'm Dyin'	1975	—	2.00	4.00
POLYDOR					
❑ 14320	C'mon Marianne/Ol' Man Auctioneer	1976	—	2.00	4.00
❑ 14417	You Got Me Dangling on a String/I'm Sorry	1977	—	2.00	4.00

OSMOND, DONNY AND MARIE

Also see DONNY OSMOND; MARIE OSMOND; THE OSMONDS.

Number	Title (A Side/B Side)	Yr	VG	VG+	NM
MGM					
❑ 14735	I'm Leaving It (All) Up to You/The Umbrella Song	1974	—	2.50	5.00
❑ 14765	Morning Side of the Mountain/One of Those Days	1974	—	2.00	4.00
❑ 14807	Make the World Go Away/Living on My Suspicion	1975	—	2.00	4.00
❑ 14840	Deep Purple/Take Me Back Again	1975	—	2.00	4.00
POLYDOR					
❑ 14363	Ain't Nothin' Like the Real Thing/Sing	1976	—	2.00	4.00
❑ 14439	(You're My) Soul and Inspiration/Now We're Together	1977	—	2.00	4.00
❑ 14456	Baby, I'm Sold on You/Sure Would Be Nice	1978	—	2.00	4.00
❑ 14474	May Tomorrow Be a Perfect Day/I Want to Give You My Everything	1978	—	2.00	4.00
❑ 14510	On the Shelf/Certified Honey	1978	—	2.00	4.00

OSMOND, JIMMY

Youngest of the first generation of singing Osmonds.

Number	Title (A Side/B Side)	Yr	VG	VG+	NM
MERCURY					
❑ 74005	Life Is Just What You Make It/Theme from "The Great Brain"	1978	—	2.00	4.00
MGM					
❑ 14199	Santa, No Chimney/I Hope You Have a Merry Christmas	1970	—	3.00	6.00
❑ 14328	If Santa Were My Daddy/Silent Night	1971	—	3.00	6.00
—As "Little Jimmy Osmond"					
❑ 14328 [PS]	If Santa Were My Daddy/Silent Night	1971	2.00	4.00	8.00
❑ 14376	Long Haired Lover from Liverpool/Mother of Mine	1972	—	2.50	5.00
❑ 14468	Tweedlee Dee/Mama'd Know What to Do	1972	—	2.50	5.00
❑ 14687	I'm Gonna Knock on Your Door/Give Me a Good Old Mammy Song	1973	—	2.50	5.00
❑ 14770	Yes Virginia, There Is a Santa Claus/If Santa Were My Daddy	1974	—	3.00	6.00
❑ 14771	Don't You Remember/Little Arrows	1974	—	2.50	5.00

OSMOND, MARIE

Also see DONNY AND MARIE OSMOND.

Number	Title (A Side/B Side)	Yr	VG	VG+	NM
CAPITOL					
❑ B-5445	Until I Fall in Love Again/I Don't Want to Go Too Far	1985	—	—	3.00
❑ B-5478	Meet Me in Montana/What Do Lonely People Do	1985	—	—	3.00
—With Dan Seals					
❑ B-5478 [PS]	Meet Me in Montana/What Do Lonely People Do	1985	—	2.00	4.00
❑ B-5521	There's No Stopping Your Heart/Blue Sky Shinin'	1985	—	—	3.00
❑ B-5563	Read My Lips/That Old Devil Moon	1986	—	—	3.00
❑ B-5613	You're Still New to Me/New Love	1986	—	—	3.00
—With Paul Davis					
❑ B-5613 [PS]	You're Still New to Me/New Love	1986	—	2.00	4.00
❑ B-5663	I Only Wanted You/We're Gonna Need a Love Song	1986	—	—	3.00
❑ B-5703	Everybody's Crazy 'Bout My Baby/Making Music	1987	—	—	3.00
❑ B-44044	Cry Just a Little/More Than Dancing	1987	—	—	3.00
❑ B-44176	Without a Trace/Baby's Blue Eyes	1988	—	—	3.00
❑ B-44215	Sweet Life/My Home Town Boy	1988	—	—	3.00
—A-side: With Paul Davis					
❑ B-44269	I'm in Love and He's in Dallas/My Home Town Boy	1989	—	—	3.00
❑ B-44412	Steppin' Stone/What Would You Do About Me If You Were Me	1989	—	—	3.00
❑ B-44468	Slowly But Surely/What Would You Do About You	1989	—	2.00	4.00
❑ 7PRO-79808	Slowly But Surely (same on both sides)	1989	—	2.50	5.00
—Vinyl originally was promo only					
❑ 7PRO-(# unk)	[DJ]Let Me Be the First (same on both sides)	1990	—	2.50	5.00
—Vinyl is promo only					
CURB					
❑ 76840	Like a Hurricane/I'll Be Faithful to You	1990	—	2.00	4.00
❑ 76851	Paper Roses/Think with Your Heart	1990	—	2.00	4.00
ELEKTRA					
❑ 69882	I'm Learning/Look Who's Getting Over Who	1982	—	2.00	4.00
❑ 69995	Back to Believing Again/Look Who's Getting Over Who	1982	—	2.00	4.00
MGM					
❑ 14609	Paper Roses/Least of All You	1973	—	2.50	5.00
❑ 14609 [PS]	Paper Roses/Least of All You	1973	2.00	4.00	8.00
❑ 14694	My Little Corner of the World/It's Just the Other Way Around	1974	—	2.00	4.00
❑ 14786	Who's Sorry Now/This I Promise You	1975	—	2.00	4.00
POLYDOR					
❑ 14333	"A" My Name Is Alice/Weeping Willow	1976	—	2.00	4.00
❑ 14385	This Is the Way That I Feel/Play the Music Loud	1977	—	2.00	4.00
❑ 14385 [PS]	This Is the Way That I Feel/Play the Music Loud	1977	—	2.50	5.00
❑ 14405	Cry, Baby, Cry/Please Tell Him I Said Hello	1977	—	2.00	4.00
RCA					
❑ PB-13680	Who's Counting/'Til the Best Comes Along	1983	—	2.00	4.00

OSMONDS, THE

Includes records as "The Osmond Brothers." (Most of these were pre-1970, before Donny was a member of the group.) Also see DONNY OSMOND.

Number	Title (A Side/B Side)	Yr	VG	VG+	NM
BARNABY					
❑ 2002	Mary Elizabeth/Speak Like a Child	1968	2.50	5.00	10.00
❑ 2004	I've Got Loving on My Mind/Mollie-"A"	1968	2.50	5.00	10.00
❑ 2005	Taking a Chance on Love/Groove With What You Got	1969	2.50	5.00	10.00
ELEKTRA					
❑ 47438	I Think About Your Lovin'/Working Man's Blues	1982	—	2.00	4.00
❑ 69883	Never Ending Song of Love/You'll Be Seeing Me	1982	—	2.00	4.00
❑ 69969	It's Like Falling in Love/Your Leaving Was the Last Thing on My Mind	1982	—	2.00	4.00
EMI AMERICA					
❑ 8298	Baby When Your Heart Breaks Down/Love Burning Down	1985	—	—	3.00
❑ 8313	Baby Wants/Lovin' Proof	1986	—	—	3.00
❑ 8325	You Look Like the One I Love/It's Only a Heartache	1986	—	—	3.00
❑ 8360	Looking for Suzanne/Back in Your Arms	1986	—	—	3.00
❑ 43033	Slow Ride/Heartbreak Radio	1987	—	—	3.00
MERCURY					
❑ 74056	Love on the Line/You're Mine	1979	—	2.00	4.00
❑ 74079	Emily/Rainin'	1979	—	2.00	4.00

Number	Title (A Side/B Side)	Yr	VG	VG+	NM
MGM					
❑ 13162	Be My Little Baby Bumble Bee/I Wouldn't Trade the Silver in My Mother's Hair	1963	3.75	7.50	15.00
❑ 13174	Theme from "The Travels of Jamie McPheeters"/ Aura Lee	1963	3.75	7.50	15.00
❑ 13174 [PS]	Theme from "The Travels of Jamie McPheeters"/ Aura Lee	1963	7.50	15.00	30.00
❑ 13281	Mr. Sandman/My Mom	1964	5.00	10.00	20.00
❑ 13281 [PS]	Mr. Sandman/My Mom	1964	12.50	25.00	50.00
❑ 14159	Movin' Along/Open Up Your Heart	1970	2.00	4.00	8.00
❑ 14193	One Bad Apple/He Ain't Heavy, He's My Brother	1970	—	3.00	6.00
❑ 14259	Double Lovin'/Chilly Winds	1971	—	3.00	6.00
❑ 14295	Yo-Yo/Keep on My Side	1971	—	3.00	6.00
❑ 14324	Down by the Lazy River/He's the Light of the World	1971	—	3.00	6.00
❑ 14405	Hold Her Tight/Love Is	1972	—	2.50	5.00
❑ 14450	Crazy Horses/That's My Girl	1972	—	2.50	5.00
❑ 14562	Goin' Home/Are You Up There	1973	—	2.50	5.00
❑ 14617	Let Me In/One Way Ticket to Anywhere	1973	—	2.50	5.00
❑ 14617 [PS]	Let Me In/One Way Ticket to Anywhere	1973	2.00	4.00	8.00
❑ 14746	Love Me for a Reason/Fever	1974	—	2.50	5.00
❑ 14791	The Proud One/The Last Day Is Coming	1975	—	2.50	5.00
❑ 14831	Thank You/I'm Still Gonna Need You	1975	—	2.50	5.00
❑ 14831 [PS]	Thank You/I'm Still Gonna Need You	1975	—	3.00	6.00
POLYDOR					
❑ 14348	Check It Out/I Can't Live a Dream	1976	—	2.00	4.00
UNI					
❑ 55015	I Can't Stop/Flower Music	1967	2.50	5.00	10.00
❑ 55276	I Can't Stop/Flower Music	1971	—	3.00	6.00
WARNER BROS.					
❑ 28982	Any Time/Desperately	1985	—	—	3.00
❑ 29312	If Every Man Had a Woman Like You/Come Back to Me	1984	—	2.00	4.00
❑ 29387	Where Does An Angel Go When She Cries/One More for Lovers	1984	—	2.00	4.00
❑ 29594	She's Ready for Someone to Love Her/You Make the Long Road Shorter with Your Love	1983	—	2.00	4.00

OTHER HALF, THE (1)

Number	Title (A Side/B Side)	Yr	VG	VG+	NM
ACTA					
❑ 801	Flight of the Dragon Lady/Wonderful Day	1967	5.00	10.00	20.00
❑ 806	I Need You/No Doubt About It	1967	5.00	10.00	20.00
❑ 819	What Can I Do for You/Bad Day	1968	3.75	7.50	15.00
❑ 825	Morning Fire/Ozlee Eaves Drop	1968	3.75	7.50	15.00
GNP CRESCENDO					
❑ 378	I've Come So Far/Mr. Pharmacist	1966	5.00	10.00	20.00

OTHER ONES, THE

Number	Title (A Side/B Side)	Yr	VG	VG+	NM
ABC-PARAMOUNT					
❑ 10793	Stop/Dreaming Out Loud	1966	3.00	6.00	12.00

OTHER TIKIS, THE

See THE TIKIS.

OTHERS, THE (1)

British group.

Number	Title (A Side/B Side)	Yr	VG	VG+	NM
FONTANA					
❑ 1944	Oh Yeah!/I'm Taking Her Home	1964	7.50	15.00	30.00

OTHERS, THE (2)

Number	Title (A Side/B Side)	Yr	VG	VG+	NM
MERCURY					
❑ 72602	Revenge/I'm in Need	1966	7.50	15.00	30.00

OTHERS, THE (U)

Number	Title (A Side/B Side)	Yr	VG	VG+	NM
RCA VICTOR					
❑ 47-8669	I Can't Stand This Love, Goodbye/Until I Heard It From You	1965	7.50	15.00	30.00
❑ 47-8776	Lonely Street/(I Remember) The First Time I Saw You	1965	3.75	7.50	15.00

OTIS, JOHNNY

Number	Title (A Side/B Side)	Yr	VG	VG+	NM
ATLANTIC					
❑ 2409	Keep the Faith — Part I/Keep the Faith — Part II	1967	3.00	6.00	12.00
CAPITOL					
❑ F3799/3802	The Johnny Otis Show	1957	100.00	200.00	400.00
—Four-record set with four-pocket cover. Price is for entire set. Records alone are valued separately below.					
❑ F3799	Can't You Hear Me Callin'/My Ding-a-Ling	1957	12.50	25.00	50.00
❑ F3800	Ma, He's Makin' Eyes at Me/In the Dark	1957	12.50	25.00	50.00
❑ F3801	Stay with Me/Tell Me So	1957	12.50	25.00	50.00
❑ F3802	It's Too Soon to Know/Star of Love	1957	12.50	25.00	50.00
❑ F3852	Bye Bye Baby/Good Golly	1957	6.25	12.50	25.00
❑ F3889	Well, Well, Well/You Just Kissed Me Goodbye	1958	6.25	12.50	25.00
❑ F3966	Willie and the Hand Jive/Ring-a-Ling	1958	7.50	15.00	30.00
❑ F4060	Willie Did the Cha Cha/Crazy Country Hop	1958	6.25	12.50	25.00
❑ F4156	My Dear/You	1959	5.00	10.00	20.00
❑ F4168 [M]	Castin' My Spell/Telephone Baby	1959	5.00	10.00	20.00
❑ F4168 [S]	Castin' My Spell/Telephone Baby	1959	12.50	25.00	50.00
❑ F4226	Three Girls Named Molly (Doin' the Hully Gully)/ I'll Do the Same for You	1959	5.00	10.00	20.00
❑ F4260	Let the Sun Shine in My Life/Baby, Just You	1959	5.00	10.00	20.00
❑ 4326	Mumblin' Mosie/Hey Baby, Don't You Know	1960	3.75	7.50	15.00
DIG					
❑ 119	Hey! Hey! Hey! Hey!/Let the Sunshine in My Heart	1956	7.50	15.00	30.00
❑ 122	The Midnite Creeper (Part 1)/The Midnite Creeper (Part 2)	1956	7.50	15.00	30.00
❑ 132	My Eyes Are Full of Tears/Turtle Dove	1957	7.50	15.00	30.00
❑ 134	Wa Wa (Part 1)/Wa Wa (Part 2)	1957	7.50	15.00	30.00
❑ 139	Stop, Look and Love Me/The Night Is Young	1957	7.50	15.00	30.00
ELDO					
❑ 106	The New Bo Diddley/The Jelly Roll	1960	3.75	7.50	15.00
❑ 152	Keep the Faith (Part 1)/Keep the Faith (Part 2)	1968	2.00	4.00	8.00
❑ 153	Long Distance/Banana Peels	1968	2.00	4.00	8.00
EPIC					
❑ 10606	You Can Depend on Me/The Watts Breakaway	1970	—	3.00	6.00
❑ 10757	Willie and the Hand Jive/Goin' Back to L.A.	1971	—	3.00	6.00
—With Delmar Evans					
HAWK SOUND					
❑ 1003	Jaws/Good to the Last Drop	1975	—	2.50	5.00
KENT					
❑ 506	Country Girl/Bye Bye Baby	1969	2.00	4.00	8.00
❑ 4521	Shuggie's Blues/Cool Ade	1969	2.00	4.00	8.00
KING					
❑ 5581	Hand Jive One More Time/Baby I Got News for You	1961	3.75	7.50	15.00
❑ 5606	She's All Right/It Must Be Love	1962	3.75	7.50	15.00
❑ 5634	Queen of the Twist/I Know My Love Is True	1962	3.75	7.50	15.00
❑ 5690	The Hey Hey Hey Song/Early in the Morning Blues	1962	3.75	7.50	15.00
❑ 5707	Somebody Call the Station/Yes	1963	3.00	6.00	12.00
❑ 5790	Bye, Bye Baby/The Hash	1963	3.00	6.00	12.00
MERCURY					
❑ 8263	Oopy Doo/Stardust	1952	12.50	25.00	50.00
❑ 8273	One-Nighter Blues/Goomp Blues	1952	12.50	25.00	50.00
❑ 8289	Call Operator 210/Baby Baby Blues	1952	12.50	25.00	50.00
❑ 8295	Gypsy Blues/The Candle's Burning Low	1952	12.50	25.00	50.00
❑ 70038	Why Don't You Believe Me/Wishing Well	1953	12.50	25.00	50.00
❑ 70050	Love Bug Boogie/Brown Skin Butterball	1953	12.50	25.00	50.00
OKEH					
❑ 7332	Watts Breakaway/You Can Depend On Me	1969	—	3.00	6.00
PEACOCK					
❑ 1625	Young Girl/Rock Me Baby	1953	20.00	40.00	80.00
❑ 1636	Shake It/I Won't Be Your Fool No More	1954	12.50	25.00	50.00
❑ 1648	Sittin' Here Drinkin'/You Got Me Crying	1955	12.50	25.00	50.00
❑ 1675	Butter Ball/Dandy's Boogie	1957	12.50	25.00	50.00
SAVOY					
❑ 731	Double Crossing Blues/Ain't Nothin' Shakin'	1950	30.00	60.00	120.00
❑ 731	Double Crossing Blues/Back Alley Blues	1950	25.00	50.00	100.00
—B-side by the Beale Street Gang					
❑ 750	Cupid Boogie/Just Can't Get Free	1950	15.00	30.00	60.00
❑ 764	Wedding Blues/Far Away Blues (Xmas Blues)	1950	15.00	30.00	60.00
❑ 766	Rockin' Blues/My Heart Tells Me	1950	15.00	30.00	60.00
❑ 777	Gee Baby/Mambo Boogie	1951	12.50	25.00	50.00
❑ 780	Doggin' Blues/Living and Loving You	1951	12.50	25.00	50.00
❑ 787	I Dream/Hangover Blues	1951	12.50	25.00	50.00
❑ 788	All Nite Long/New Love	1951	12.50	25.00	50.00
❑ 812	Warning Blues/I'll Ask My Heart	1951	12.50	25.00	50.00
❑ 815	Harlem Nocturne/Midnight in the Barrelhouse	1951	12.50	25.00	50.00
❑ 824	Get Together Blues/Chittlin' Switch	1951	12.50	25.00	50.00
❑ 855	It Ain't the Beauty/Gonna Take a Train	1952	12.50	25.00	50.00

7-Inch Extended Plays

Number	Title (A Side/B Side)	Yr	VG	VG+	NM
CAPITOL					
❑ EAP 1-940	Hum Ding a Ling/It's Too Soon to Know//Stay with Me/Ma (He's Makin' Eyes at Me)	1958	37.50	75.00	150.00
❑ EAP 1-940 [PS]	The Johnny Otis Show	1958	37.50	75.00	150.00

OTIS AND CARLA

Number	Title (A Side/B Side)	Yr	VG	VG+	NM
ATCO					
❑ 6665	When Something Is Wrong with My Baby/Ooh Carla, Ooh Otis	1968	2.50	5.00	10.00
STAX					
❑ 216	Tramp/Tell It Like It Is	1967	2.50	5.00	10.00
❑ 228	Knock on Wood/Let Me Be Good to You	1967	2.50	5.00	10.00
❑ 244	Lovey Dovey/New Year's Resolution	1968	2.50	5.00	10.00

OTT, PAUL

Number	Title (A Side/B Side)	Yr	VG	VG+	NM
ELEKTRA					
❑ 46066	A Salute to the Duke/Listen to the Eagle	1979	—	2.50	5.00
MONUMENT					
❑ 45-291	Jody and the Kid/I Don't Want My Poor Heart to Remember	1980	—	2.50	5.00
❑ 45-293	Our First Night/Turn to Me	1980	—	2.50	5.00
❑ 8605	Ole Blue/Plant a Tree	1974	—	2.50	5.00
❑ 8655	I'm the South/Keep Me Comin' 'Round	1975	—	2.50	5.00
❑ 8691	Listen to the Eagle/Ole Blue	1976	—	2.50	5.00
SHOW BIZ					
❑ 502	Soldier's Prayer/Danny Boy	1972	—	3.00	6.00
❑ 503	The Twenty-Second Day/Danny Boy	1972	—	3.00	6.00
THUNDER INT'L.					
❑ 1022	Kitty Kat/(B-side unknown)	1960	25.00	50.00	100.00
❑ 1024	Times Have Changed/(B-side unknown)	1960	25.00	50.00	100.00

OUR GANG

Number	Title (A Side/B Side)	Yr	VG	VG+	NM
BR'ER BIRD					
❑ 001	Summertime Summertime/Theme from Leon's Garage	1966	50.00	100.00	200.00

OUTLAWS

"Southern rock" band; few, if any, of their releases used the word "The" before their name.

Number	Title (A Side/B Side)	Yr	VG	VG+	NM
ARISTA					
❑ 0150	There Goes Another Love Song/Keep Prayin'	1975	—	2.00	4.00
❑ 0188	Breaker-Breaker/South Carolina	1976	—	2.00	4.00
❑ 0213	Green Grass and High Tides/Prisoner	1976	—	2.50	5.00
❑ 0258	Hurry Sundown/So Afraid	1977	—	2.00	4.00
❑ 0282	Hearin' My Heart Talkin'/Holiday	1977	—	2.00	4.00
❑ 0338	Green Grass and High Tides/Holiday	1978	—	2.00	4.00
❑ 0378	Take It Anyway You Want It/Cry Some More	1978	—	2.00	4.00
❑ 0397	You Are the Show/If Dreams Came True	1979	—	2.00	4.00
❑ 0582	(Ghost) Riders in the Sky/Devil's Road	1981	—	2.00	4.00
❑ 0597	Wishing Well/I Can't Stop Loving You	1981	—	2.00	4.00
❑ 0678	Running/(B-side unknown)	1982	—	2.00	4.00
PASHA					
❑ 06550	Saved by the Bell/One Last Ride	1987	—	—	3.00

OUTLAWS, THE (2)

CRUSADE

Number	Title (A Side/B Side)	Yr	VG	VG+	NM
❑ 92765	Chains/(B-side unknown)	1965	7.50	15.00	30.00

OUTLAWS, THE (3)

DOT

Number	Title (A Side/B Side)	Yr	VG	VG+	NM
❑ 16512	Hold-Up/Somethin' Else	1963	10.00	20.00	40.00

OUTLAWS, THE (U)

Could be group (2); could be a completely different group.

SMASH

Number	Title (A Side/B Side)	Yr	VG	VG+	NM
❑ 2025	Don't Cry/Only for You	1966	3.00	6.00	12.00

OUTSIDERS, THE

Lead singer Sonny Geraci later sang with CLIMAX.

BELL

Number	Title (A Side/B Side)	Yr	VG	VG+	NM
❑ 904	Changes/Lost in My World	1970	—	3.00	6.00

CAPITOL

Number	Title (A Side/B Side)	Yr	VG	VG+	NM
❑ 2055	Little Bit of Lovin'/I Will Love You	1967	2.00	4.00	8.00
❑ 2216	Oh How It Hurts/We Ain't Gonna Make It	1968	2.00	4.00	8.00
❑ 5573	Time Won't Let Me/Was It Really Real	1966	3.00	6.00	12.00
❑ 5646	Girl in Love/What Makes You So Bad	1966	2.50	5.00	10.00
❑ 5646 [PS]	Girl in Love/What Makes You So Bad	1966	5.00	10.00	20.00
❑ 5701	Respectable/Lost in My World	1966	2.50	5.00	10.00
❑ 5759	Help Me Girl/You Gotta Look	1966	2.50	5.00	10.00
❑ 5759 [PS]	Help Me Girl/You Gotta Look	1966	5.00	10.00	20.00
❑ 5843	I'll Give You Time/I'm Not Trying to Hurt You	1967	2.00	4.00	8.00
❑ 5843 [PS]	I'll Give You Time/I'm Not Trying to Hurt You	1967	5.00	10.00	20.00
❑ 5892	I Just Can't See You Anymore/Gotta Leave Us Alone	1967	2.00	4.00	8.00
❑ 5955	I'll See You in the Summertime/And Now You Want My Sympathy	1967	2.00	4.00	8.00
❑ 5955 [PS]	I'll See You in the Summertime/And Now You Want My Sympathy	1967	5.00	10.00	20.00

ELLEN

Number	Title (A Side/B Side)	Yr	VG	VG+	NM
❑ 503	Rickity-Boom-Bal-Aye/The Bird Rattle	196?	3.75	7.50	15.00

KAPP

Number	Title (A Side/B Side)	Yr	VG	VG+	NM
❑ 2104	Tinker, Tailor/Oh You're Not So Pretty	1970	—	3.00	6.00

OUTSIDERS, THE (U)

Probably not the same group as above.

KARATE

Number	Title (A Side/B Side)	Yr	VG	VG+	NM
❑ 505	The Guy with the Long Liverpool Hair/Outsider	1964	5.00	10.00	20.00

OVATIONS, THE (1)

R&B vocal group. In essence this is two versions of the same group; the later records featured former members of OLLIE AND THE NIGHTINGALES.

GOLDWAX

Number	Title (A Side/B Side)	Yr	VG	VG+	NM
❑ 110	Pretty Little Angel/Won't You Call	1964	3.75	7.50	15.00
❑ 113	It's Wonderful to Be in Love/Dance Party	1965	3.75	7.50	15.00
❑ 117	I'm Living Good/Recipe for Love	1965	3.75	7.50	15.00
❑ 300	Don't Cry/I Need a Lot of Loving	1966	3.75	7.50	15.00
❑ 306	I Believe I'll Go Back Home/Qualifications	1966	3.75	7.50	15.00
❑ 314	Me and My Imagination/They Say	1967	3.75	7.50	15.00
❑ 322	I've Gotta Go/Kiss My Troubles and Blues Away	1967	3.75	7.50	15.00
❑ 341	Happiness/Rockin' Chair	1969	3.75	7.50	15.00
❑ 342	You Had Your Choice/I'm Living Good	1969	3.75	7.50	15.00

MGM

Number	Title (A Side/B Side)	Yr	VG	VG+	NM
❑ 14623	"Having a Party" Medley/Just Too Good to Be True	1973	2.00	4.00	8.00
❑ 14705	I'm in Love/Don't Say You Love Me	1974	2.00	4.00	8.00

—As "Louis Williams and the Ovations"

SOUNDS OF MEMPHIS

Number	Title (A Side/B Side)	Yr	VG	VG+	NM
❑ 708	Touching Me/Don't Break Your Promise	1972	2.00	4.00	8.00
❑ 712	Hooked on a Feeling/Take It From One Who Knows	1972	2.00	4.00	8.00
❑ 717	One in a Million/So Nice to Be Loved by You	1973	2.00	4.00	8.00

OVATIONS, THE (2)

ANDIE

Number	Title (A Side/B Side)	Yr	VG	VG+	NM
❑ 5017	My Lullaby/Whole Wide World	1960	10.00	20.00	40.00

BARRY

Number	Title (A Side/B Side)	Yr	VG	VG+	NM
❑ 101	My Lullaby/The Day We Fell in Love	1961	10.00	20.00	40.00

EPIC

Number	Title (A Side/B Side)	Yr	VG	VG+	NM
❑ 9470	Oh, What a Day/Real True Love	1961	10.00	20.00	40.00

OVATIONS, THE (3)

CAPITOL

Number	Title (A Side/B Side)	Yr	VG	VG+	NM
❑ 5082	I Don't Wanna Cry/Loneliness Never Entered My Mind	1963	7.50	15.00	30.00

OVATIONS, THE (U)

Each of these could be by one of the above groups.

HAWK

Number	Title (A Side/B Side)	Yr	VG	VG+	NM
❑ 153	I Still Love You/Runaround	1963	50.00	100.00	200.00

JOSIE

Number	Title (A Side/B Side)	Yr	VG	VG+	NM
❑ 916	Who Needs Love/Remembering	1964	6.25	12.50	25.00

OVERLANDERS, THE

HICKORY

Number	Title (A Side/B Side)	Yr	VG	VG+	NM
❑ 1258	Yesterday's Gone/Gone the Rainbow	1964	3.00	6.00	12.00
❑ 1275	Movin'/Don't It Make You Feel Good	1964	3.00	6.00	12.00
❑ 1295	January/Leaves Are Falling	1965	3.00	6.00	12.00
❑ 1327	Rainbow/Take the Bucket to the Well	1965	3.00	6.00	12.00
❑ 1362	Michelle/Cradle of Love	1965	3.00	6.00	12.00
❑ 1384	My Life/Girl from Indiana	1966	3.00	6.00	12.00
❑ 1427	Shanghai Rooster/Leaves Are Falling	1966	3.00	6.00	12.00

MERCURY

Number	Title (A Side/B Side)	Yr	VG	VG+	NM
❑ 72165	Call of the Wild/Summer Skies and Golden Sands	1963	3.75	7.50	15.00

OWEN, MACK

SUN

Number	Title (A Side/B Side)	Yr	VG	VG+	NM
❑ 336	Walkin' and Talkin'/Somebody Like You	1960	5.00	10.00	20.00

OWENS, BUCK

CAPITOL

Number	Title (A Side/B Side)	Yr	VG	VG+	NM
❑ 2001	It Takes People Like You (To Make People Like Me)/You Left Her Lonely Too Long	1967	2.00	4.00	8.00
❑ 2001 [PS]	It Takes People Like You (To Make People Like Me)/You Left Her Lonely Too Long	1967	3.00	6.00	12.00
❑ 2080	How Long Will My Baby Be Gone/Everybody Needs Somebody	1968	2.00	4.00	8.00
❑ 2080 [PS]	How Long Will My Baby Be Gone/Everybody Needs Somebody	1968	3.00	6.00	12.00
❑ 2142	Sweet Rosie Jones/Happy Times Are Here Again	1968	2.00	4.00	8.00
❑ 2142 [PS]	Sweet Rosie Jones/Happy Times Are Here Again	1968	3.00	6.00	12.00
❑ 2237	Let the World Keep On a-Turnin'/I'll Love You Forever and Ever	1968	2.00	4.00	8.00
—With Buddy Alan					
❑ 2237 [PS]	Let the World Keep On a-Turnin'/I'll Love You Forever and Ever	1968	3.00	6.00	12.00
—As "Buck Owens and Buddy Alan and the Buckaroos"					
❑ 2300	I've Got You on My Mind Again/That's All Right with Me (If It's All Right with You)	1968	2.00	4.00	8.00
❑ 2300 [PS]	I've Got You on My Mind Again/That's All Right with Me (If It's All Right with You)	1968	3.00	6.00	12.00
❑ 2328	Christmas Shopping/One of Everything You Got	1968	2.00	4.00	8.00
❑ 2330	Turkish Holiday/Things I Saw Happening at the Fountain	1968	2.00	4.00	8.00
❑ 2377	Who's Gonna Mow Your Grass/There's Gotta Be Some Chances Made	1969	2.00	4.00	8.00
❑ 2377 [PS]	Who's Gonna Mow Your Grass/There's Gotta Be Some Chances Made	1969	3.00	6.00	12.00
❑ 2485	Johnny B. Goode/Maybe If I Close My Eyes (It'll Go Away)	1969	2.00	4.00	8.00
❑ 2485 [PS]	Johnny B. Goode/Maybe If I Close My Eyes (It'll Go Away)	1969	3.00	6.00	12.00
❑ 2570	Tall Dark Stranger/Sing That Kind of Song	1969	2.00	4.00	8.00
❑ 2570 [PS]	Tall Dark Stranger/Sing That Kind of Song	1969	3.00	6.00	12.00
❑ 2646	Big in Vegas/White Satin Bed	1969	2.00	4.00	8.00
❑ 2646 [PS]	Big in Vegas/White Satin Bed	1969	3.00	6.00	12.00
❑ 2783	The Kansas City Song/I'd Love to Be Your Man	1970	2.00	4.00	8.00
❑ 2783 [PS]	The Kansas City Song/I'd Love to Be Your Man	1970	2.50	5.00	10.00
❑ 2947	I Wouldn't Live in New York City (If They Gave Me the Whole Dang Town)/No Milk and Honey in Baltimore	1970	2.00	4.00	8.00
❑ 2947 [PS]	I Wouldn't Live in New York City (If They Gave Me the Whole Dang Town)/No Milk and Honey in Baltimore	1970	2.50	5.00	10.00
❑ 2962	Buckaroo/Okie from Muskogee	1970	3.00	6.00	12.00
—As "Buck Owens' Bakersfield Brass"					
❑ 3011	Act Naturally/My Heart Skips a Beat	1971	3.00	6.00	12.00
—As "Buck Owens' Bakersfield Brass"					
❑ 3023	Bridge Over Troubled Water/(I'm Goin') Home	1971	—	3.00	6.00
❑ 3023 [PS]	Bridge Over Troubled Water/(I'm Goin') Home	1971	2.50	5.00	10.00
❑ 3066	Cajun Brass/Waitin' in Your Welfare Line	1971	2.50	5.00	10.00
—As "Buck Owens' Bakersfield Brass"					
❑ 3096	Ruby (Are You Mad)/Heartbreak Mountain	1971	—	3.00	6.00
❑ 3164	Rollin' in My Sweet Baby's Arms/Corn Likker	1971	—	3.00	6.00
❑ 3164 [PS]	Rollin' in My Sweet Baby's Arms/Corn Likker	1971	2.50	5.00	10.00
❑ 3215	Too Old to Cut the Mustard/Wham Bam	1971	—	3.00	6.00
—As "Buck and Buddy" (Buck Owens and BUDDY ALAN)					
❑ 3215 [PS]	Too Old to Cut the Mustard/Wham Bam	1971	2.50	5.00	10.00
❑ 3262	I'll Still Be Waiting for You/Full Time Daddy	1972	—	3.00	6.00
❑ 3314	Made in Japan/Black Texas Dirt	1972	—	3.00	6.00
❑ 3429	You Ain't Gonna Have Ol' Buck to Kick Around No More/I Love You So Much It Hurts	1972	—	3.00	6.00
❑ 3504	In the Palm of Your Hand/Get Out of Town Before Sundown	1972	—	3.00	6.00
❑ 3563	Ain't It Amazing, Gracie/The Good Old Days	1973	—	3.00	6.00
❑ 3688	Arms Full of Empty/Songwriter's Lament	1973	—	3.00	6.00
❑ 3769	Big Game Hunter/That Loving Feeling	1973	—	3.00	6.00
❑ F3824	Come Back/I Know What It Means	1957	5.00	10.00	20.00
❑ 3841	On the Cover of the Music City News/Stony Mountain, West Virginia	1974	—	3.00	6.00
❑ 3907	(It's a) Monsters' Holiday/Great Expectations	1974	—	3.00	6.00
❑ F3957	Sweet Thing/I Only Know That I Love You So	1957	5.00	10.00	20.00
❑ 3976	Great Expectations/Let the Fun Begin	1974	—	3.00	6.00
❑ 4043	41st Street Lonely Hearts Club/Weekend Daddy	1975	—	3.00	6.00
❑ F4090	I'll Take a Chance on Loving You/Walk the Floor	1958	5.00	10.00	20.00
❑ 4138	The Battle of New Orleans/Run Him to the Roundhouse Nellie	1975	—	3.00	6.00
❑ F4172	Second Fiddle/Everlasting Love	1959	5.00	10.00	20.00
❑ 4181	Meanwhile Back at the Ranch/Country Singer's Prayer	1976	—	3.00	6.00
❑ F4245	Under Your Spell Again/Tired of Livin'	1959	5.00	10.00	20.00
❑ 4337	Above and Beyond/Till These Dreams Come True	1960	3.75	7.50	15.00
❑ 4412	Excuse Me (I Think I've Got a Heartache)/I've Got a Right to Know	1960	3.75	7.50	15.00
❑ 4496	Foolin' Around/High As the Mountains	1961	3.75	7.50	15.00
❑ 4602	Under the Influence of Love/Bad Dreams	1961	3.75	7.50	15.00
❑ 4679	Nobody's Fool But Yours/Mirror Mirror on the Wall	1962	3.75	7.50	15.00
❑ 4765	Save the Last Dance for Me/King of Fools	1962	3.75	7.50	15.00
❑ 4826	Kickin' Our Hearts Around/I Can't Stop (My Lovin' You)	1962	3.75	7.50	15.00
❑ 4872	You're for Me/House Down the Block	1962	3.75	7.50	15.00
❑ 4937	Act Naturally/Over and Over Again	1963	3.75	7.50	15.00
❑ 5025	Love's Gonna Live Here/Getting Used to Losing You	1963	3.00	6.00	12.00
❑ 5136	My Heart Skips a Beat/Together Again	1964	3.00	6.00	12.00
❑ 5240	I Don't Care (Just As Long As You Love Me)/Don't Let Her Know	1964	3.00	6.00	12.00
❑ 5336	I've Got a Tiger by the Tail/Cryin' Time	1965	2.50	5.00	10.00
❑ 5336 [PS]	I've Got a Tiger by the Tail/Cryin' Time	1965	3.75	7.50	15.00
❑ 5410	Before You Go/No One But You	1965	2.50	5.00	10.00
❑ 5410 [PS]	Before You Go/No One But You	1965	3.75	7.50	15.00

Number	Title (A Side/B Side)	Yr	VG	VG+	NM
❑ 5465	Only You (Can Break My Heart)/Gonna Have Love	1965	2.50	5.00	10.00
❑ 5465 [PS]	Only You (Can Break My Heart)/Gonna Have Love	1965	3.75	7.50	15.00
❑ 5517	Buckaroo/If You Want a Love	1965	2.50	5.00	10.00
❑ 5537	Santa Looked a Lot Like Daddy/All I Want for Christmas Dear Is You	1965	2.50	5.00	10.00
❑ 5537	Santa Looked A Lot Like Daddy/All I Want For Christmas Dear Is You	1973	—	2.00	4.00

—Orange label, "Capitol" at bottom

Number	Title (A Side/B Side)	Yr	VG	VG+	NM
❑ 5537 [PS]	Santa Looked a Lot Like Daddy/All I Want for Christmas Dear Is You	1965	3.75	7.50	15.00
❑ 5566	Waitin' in Your Welfare Line/In the Palm of Your Hand	1965	2.50	5.00	10.00
❑ 5647	Think of Me/Heart of Glass	1966	2.50	5.00	10.00
❑ 5647 [PS]	Think of Me/Heart of Glass	1966	3.75	7.50	15.00
❑ 5705	Open Up Your Heart/No More Me and You	1966	2.50	5.00	10.00
❑ 5705 [PS]	Open Up Your Heart/No More Me and You	1966	3.75	7.50	15.00
❑ 5811	Where Does the Good Times Go/The Way That I Love You	1967	2.00	4.00	8.00
❑ 5811 [PS]	Where Does the Good Times Go/The Way That I Love You	1967	3.00	6.00	12.00
❑ 5865	Sam's Place/Don't Ever Tell Me Goodbye	1967	2.00	4.00	8.00
❑ 5865 [PS]	Sam's Place/Don't Ever Tell Me Goodbye	1967	3.00	6.00	12.00
❑ 5942	Your Tender Loving Care/What a Liar I Am	1967	2.00	4.00	8.00
❑ 5942 [PS]	Your Tender Loving Care/What a Liar I Am	1967	3.00	6.00	12.00
❑ B-44248	Hot Dog/Second Fiddle	1988	—	2.00	4.00
❑ B-44248 [PS]	Hot Dog/Second Fiddle	1988	—	2.50	5.00
❑ B-44295	A-11/Sweethearts in Heaven	1989	—	2.00	4.00
❑ B-44356	Put a Quarter in the Jukebox/Don't Let Her Know	1989	—	2.00	4.00
❑ B-44409	Act Naturally/The Key's in the Mailbox	1989	3.75	7.50	15.00

—A-side with Ringo Starr

Number	Title (A Side/B Side)	Yr	VG	VG+	NM
❑ 7PRO-79805 [DJ]	Gonna Have Love (same on both sides)	1989	2.50	5.00	10.00

—Vinyl is promo only

DIXIE

Number	Title (A Side/B Side)	Yr	VG	VG+	NM
❑ 505	Hot Dog/Rhythm and Booze	1956	100.00	200.00	400.00

—As "Corky Jones"

PEP

Number	Title (A Side/B Side)	Yr	VG	VG+	NM
❑ 105	It Don't Show on Me/Down on the Corner of Love	1956	12.50	25.00	50.00
❑ 106	The House Down the Block/Right After the Dance	1956	12.50	25.00	50.00
❑ 107	Hot Dog/Rhythm and Booze	1956	62.50	125.00	250.00

—As "Corky Jones"

Number	Title (A Side/B Side)	Yr	VG	VG+	NM
❑ 109	There Goes My Love/Sweethearts in Heaven	1957	12.50	25.00	50.00

REPRISE

Number	Title (A Side/B Side)	Yr	VG	VG+	NM
❑ 27964	Streets of Bakersfield/One More Name	1988	—	—	3.00

—With Dwight Yoakam

Number	Title (A Side/B Side)	Yr	VG	VG+	NM
❑ 27964 [PS]	Streets of Bakersfield/One More Name	1988	—	2.00	4.00

STARDAY

Number	Title (A Side/B Side)	Yr	VG	VG+	NM
❑ 571	There Goes My Love/It Don't Show on Me	1961	3.75	7.50	15.00
❑ 588	Down on the Corner of Love/Right After the Dance	1962	3.75	7.50	15.00
❑ 7010	Sweethearts in Heaven/Down on the Corner of Love	196?	—	2.50	5.00
❑ 8004	Sweethearts in Heaven/Down on the Corner of Love	197?	—	2.00	4.00

WARNER BROS.

Number	Title (A Side/B Side)	Yr	VG	VG+	NM
❑ 8223	Hollywood Waltz/Rain on Your Parade	1976	—	2.50	5.00
❑ 8255	California Okie/Child Support	1976	—	2.50	5.00
❑ 8316	World Famous Holiday Inn/He Don't Deserve You Anymore	1977	2.50	5.00	10.00
❑ 8316	World Famous Paradise Inn/He Don't Deserve You Anymore	1977	—	2.50	5.00
❑ 8395	It's Been a Long, Long Time/Rain on Your Parade	1977	—	2.50	5.00
❑ 8433	Our Old Mansion/How Come My God Don't Bark	1977	—	2.50	5.00
❑ 8486	Let the Good Times Roll/Texas Tornado	1977	—	2.50	5.00
❑ 8614	Nights Are Forever Without You/When I Need You	1978	—	2.00	4.00
❑ 8701	Do You Wanna Make Love/Seasons of My Heart	1978	—	2.00	4.00
❑ 8830	Play Together Again Again/He Don't Deserve You Anymore	1979	—	2.00	4.00

—A-side with Emmylou Harris

Number	Title (A Side/B Side)	Yr	VG	VG+	NM
❑ 49046	Hangin' In and Hangin' On/Sweet Molly Brown's	1979	—	2.00	4.00
❑ 49118	Let Jesse Rob the Train/Victim of Life's Circumstances	1979	—	2.00	4.00
❑ 49200	Love Is a Warm Cowboy/I Don't Want to Live in San Francisco	1980	—	2.00	4.00
❑ 49278	Moonlight and Magnolia/Nickels and Dimes	1980	—	2.00	4.00
❑ 49651	Without You/Love Don't Make the Bars	1981	—	2.00	4.00

7-Inch Extended Plays

CAPITOL

Number	Title (A Side/B Side)	Yr	VG	VG+	NM
❑ R-5446	Memphis/Let the Bad Times Roll On//Fallin' for You/If You Fall Out of Love	1965	3.75	7.50	15.00
❑ R-5446 [PS]	4-By Buck Owens	1965	6.25	12.50	25.00

OWENS, BUCK, AND ROSE MADDOX

CAPITOL

Number	Title (A Side/B Side)	Yr	VG	VG+	NM
❑ 4550	Mental Cruelty/Loose Talk	1961	3.75	7.50	15.00
❑ 4992	We're the Talk of the Town/Sweethearts in Heaven	1963	3.75	7.50	15.00

OWENS, BUCK, AND SUSAN RAYE

CAPITOL

Number	Title (A Side/B Side)	Yr	VG	VG+	NM
❑ 2731	We're Gonna Get Together/Everybody Needs Somebody	1970	2.00	4.00	8.00
❑ 2731 [PS]	We're Gonna Get Together/Everybody Needs Somebody	1970	2.50	5.00	10.00
❑ 2791	Togetherness/Fallin' for You	1970	2.00	4.00	8.00
❑ 2791 [PS]	Togetherness/Fallin' for You	1970	2.50	5.00	10.00
❑ 2871	The Great White Horse/Your Tender Loving Care	1970	2.00	4.00	8.00
❑ 2871 [PS]	The Great White Horse/Your Tender Loving Care	1970	2.50	5.00	10.00
❑ 3225	Santa's Gonna Come in a Stagecoach/One of Everything You Got	1971	2.00	4.00	8.00
❑ 3368	Looking Back to See/Cryin' Time	1972	—	3.00	6.00
❑ 3368 [PS]	Looking Back to See/Cryin' Time	1972	2.50	5.00	10.00
❑ 3601	The Good Old Days (Are Here Again)/When You Get to Heaven (I'll Be There)	1973	—	3.00	6.00
❑ 4100	Love Is Strange/Sweethearts in Heaven	1975	—	3.00	6.00

OWENS BROTHERS, THE

ABC-PARAMOUNT

Number	Title (A Side/B Side)	Yr	VG	VG+	NM
❑ 9775	Night Train/Don't Cry	1956	10.00	20.00	40.00

—Also released on Sheraton by the Four Chaps.

OXFORD CIRCLE, THE

WORLD UNITED

Number	Title (A Side/B Side)	Yr	VG	VG+	NM
❑ 002	Mind Destruction/Foolsih Woman	196?	12.50	25.00	50.00

OXFORD CIRCUS, THE

ZIG ZAG

Number	Title (A Side/B Side)	Yr	VG	VG+	NM
❑ 101	Tracy/4th Street Carnival	1967	10.00	20.00	40.00

P

P. FUNK ALL STARS

Also see PARLIAMENT; FUNKADELIC.

CBS ASSOCIATED

Number	Title (A Side/B Side)	Yr	VG	VG+	NM
❑ 04032	Generator Pop/Hydraulic Pump	1983	—	2.00	4.00

HUMP

Number	Title (A Side/B Side)	Yr	VG	VG+	NM
❑ 1	Hydraulic Pump (Part 1)/Hydraulic Pump (Part 2)	1981	—	2.50	5.00
❑ 3	One of Those Summers/It's Too Funky in Here	1982	—	2.50	5.00

UNCLE JAM

Number	Title (A Side/B Side)	Yr	VG	VG+	NM
❑ 04408	Pumpin' It Up/Pumpin' It Up (Special Mix)	1984	—	2.00	4.00

P.J.

TAMLA

Number	Title (A Side/B Side)	Yr	VG	VG+	NM
❑ 54215	T.L.C./It Takes a Man to Teach a Woman How to Love	1972	6.25	12.50	25.00

V.I.P.

Number	Title (A Side/B Side)	Yr	VG	VG+	NM
❑ 25062	It Takes a Man to Teach a Woman How to Love/ The Best Years of My Life	1970	10.00	20.00	40.00

PABLO CRUISE

A&M

Number	Title (A Side/B Side)	Yr	VG	VG+	NM
❑ 1695	Island Woman/Denny	1975	—	2.50	5.00
❑ 1742	What Does It Take/In My Own Quiet Way	1975	—	2.50	5.00
❑ 1815	(I Think) It's Finally Over/Look to the Sky	1976	—	2.50	5.00
❑ 1834	Don't Believe It/Look to the Sky	1976	—	2.50	5.00
❑ 1876	Crystal/Look to the Sky	1976	—	2.50	5.00
❑ 1910	A Place in the Sun/El Verano	1977	—	2.50	5.00
❑ 1920	Whatcha Gonna Do?/Atlanta June	1977	—	2.00	4.00
❑ 1920 [PS]	Whatcha Gonna Do?/Atlanta June	1977	—	3.00	6.00
❑ 1976	A Place in the Sun/El Verano	1977	—	2.00	4.00
❑ 1999	Atlanta June/Never Had a Love	1977	—	2.00	4.00
❑ 2048	Love Will Find a Way/Always Be Together	1978	—	2.00	4.00
❑ 2048 [PS]	Love Will Find a Way/Always Be Together	1978	—	2.50	5.00
❑ 2076	Don't Want to Live Without It/Raging Fire	1978	—	2.00	4.00
❑ 2112	I Go to Rio/Raging Fire	1979	—	2.00	4.00
❑ 2195	I Want You Tonight/Family Man	1979	—	2.00	4.00
❑ 2217 [DJ]	Part of the Game (mono/stereo)	1980	—	2.50	5.00

—No stock copies known

Number	Title (A Side/B Side)	Yr	VG	VG+	NM
❑ 2349	Cool Love/Jenny	1981	—	2.00	4.00
❑ 2373	Slip Away/That's When	1981	—	2.00	4.00
❑ 2373 [PS]	Slip Away/That's When	1981	—	2.00	4.00
❑ 2570	Another World/Will You, Won't You	1983	—	—	3.00

PACERS, THE

More than one group.

CALICO

Number	Title (A Side/B Side)	Yr	VG	VG+	NM
❑ 101/2	I Found a Dream/I Wanna Dance with You	1958	7.50	15.00	30.00

CORAL

Number	Title (A Side/B Side)	Yr	VG	VG+	NM
❑ 62398	Sassy Sue/You Got Me Bugged	1964	2.50	5.00	10.00

GUYDEN

Number	Title (A Side/B Side)	Yr	VG	VG+	NM
❑ 2064	How Sweet/No Wonder	1962	375.00	750.00	1500.

RAZORBACK

Number	Title (A Side/B Side)	Yr	VG	VG+	NM
❑ 103	Fright Street/Sooie	1958	6.25	12.50	25.00
❑ 108	Confound It/Skeeter Dape	1960	6.25	12.50	25.00
❑ 112	Don't Get Around Much/Sad Sad	1962	6.25	12.50	25.00
❑ 115	West Memphis/Dollar, Two Ninety-Eight	1963	6.25	12.50	25.00
❑ 118	Tennessee Stud/Beautiful Debbie	1964	5.00	10.00	20.00
❑ 123	The Pit/Pace Setter	1965	5.00	10.00	20.00
❑ 125	Batman/Gotham City	1966	5.00	10.00	20.00
❑ 137	Short Squashed Texan/Sock It To 'Em Soobey	1967	5.00	10.00	20.00

PACIFIC GAS & ELECTRIC

COLUMBIA

Number	Title (A Side/B Side)	Yr	VG	VG+	NM
❑ 45009	Redneck/Bluebuster	1969	—	3.00	6.00
❑ 45158	Are You Ready?/Staggolee	1970	—	3.00	6.00

—Available with at least three different label variations, all equal in value

Number	Title (A Side/B Side)	Yr	VG	VG+	NM
❑ 45221	Elvira/Father Come On Home	1970	—	2.50	5.00
❑ 45304	The Time Has Come/Death Row No. 172	1971	—	2.50	5.00
❑ 45444	One More River to Cross/Rocky Roller's Lament	1971	—	2.50	5.00
❑ 45519	Thank God for You Baby/See the Monkey Run	1971	—	2.50	5.00
❑ 45621	Heat Wave/We Did What We Could	1972	—	2.50	5.00

POWER

Number	Title (A Side/B Side)	Yr	VG	VG+	NM
❑ 1701	Wade in the Water/Live Love	1969	2.50	5.00	10.00

PACKARDS, THE

PARADISE

Number	Title (A Side/B Side)	Yr	VG	VG+	NM
❑ 105	Dream of Love/Ding Dong	1956	100.00	200.00	400.00

PLA-BAC

Number	Title (A Side/B Side)	Yr	VG	VG+	NM
❑ 106	Ladise/My Doctor of Love	1956	500.00	1000.	2000.

Number	Title (A Side/B Side)	Yr	VG	VG+	NM
PAGE, HOT LIPS					
KING					
❑ 1404	Cadillac Song/Ain't Nothing Wrong	1954	25.00	50.00	100.00
❑ 4584	Last Call for Alcohol/Old Parie	1952	75.00	150.00	300.00
❑ 4594	I Bongo You/Ruby	1953	50.00	100.00	200.00
❑ 4616	Jungle King/What Shall I Do	1953	37.50	75.00	150.00
RCA VICTOR					
❑ 50-0120	Let Me In/That's the One for Me	1951	25.00	50.00	100.00
❑ 50-0129	Strike While the Iron's Hot/I Wanna Ride Like the Cowboys Do	1951	25.00	50.00	100.00
PAGE, JIMMY					
Also see THE HONEYDRIPPERS; LED ZEPPELIN; THE YARDBIRDS.					
GEFFEN					
❑ 27821	Wasting My Time/Fires of Winter	1988	—	2.00	4.00
PAGE, LARRY, ORCHESTRA					
CALLA					
❑ 126	Jo Jo/Waltzing to Jazz	1966	3.00	6.00	12.00
❑ 144	Girl on a Swing/The Last Waltz	1967	2.50	5.00	10.00
LONDON					
❑ 259	I'm Hooked on You/Erotic Soul	1977	—	2.00	4.00
PAGE ONE					
❑ 21010	Hey Jude/Those Were the Days	1969	2.00	4.00	8.00
❑ 21018	Promises, Promises/Wichita Lineman	1969	2.00	4.00	8.00
PAGE BOYS, THE					
Probably more than one group.					
ABC-PARAMOUNT					
❑ 10323	Lonely Sea/Road of Life	1962	2.50	5.00	10.00
BIG B					
❑ 1017	Santa's Snowdeer/White Wonderland	19??	2.00	4.00	8.00
DECCA					
❑ 31505	If Tears Could Speak/Ole Buttermilk Skies	1963	3.00	6.00	12.00
HAMILTON					
❑ 50025	Barracuda/Peter Gunn	1960	3.00	6.00	12.00
PREP					
❑ 117	Waiting/This I Give to You	1957	6.25	12.50	25.00
PAGENTS, THE					
BAMBOO					
❑ 525	Pa-Cha/Sad and Lonely	1963	12.50	25.00	50.00
ERA					
❑ 3119	Enchanted/The Big Daddy	1963	7.50	15.00	30.00
❑ 3124	Glenda/Shake	1964	7.50	15.00	30.00
❑ 3134	Pa-Cha/Sad and Lonely	1964	6.25	12.50	25.00
IKE					
❑ 631	Enchanted Surf/The Big Daddy	1963	25.00	50.00	100.00
PAIGE, HAL					
ATLANTIC					
❑ 996	Drive It Home/Break of Day Blues	1953	37.50	75.00	150.00
❑ 1032	Big Foot May/Please Say You Do	1954	37.50	75.00	150.00
CHECKER					
❑ 873	Don't Have to Cry No More/Pour the Corn	1957	5.00	10.00	20.00
FURY					
❑ 1002	Don't Have to Cry No More/Pour the Corn	1957	20.00	40.00	80.00
❑ 1024	After Hours Blues/Going Back to My Home Town	1959	5.00	10.00	20.00
J&S					
❑ 1601	Thunderbird/Sugar Bare	1957	7.50	15.00	30.00
PALACE GUARD, THE					
ORANGE EMPIRE					
❑ 331	All Night Long/Playgirl	1965	3.75	7.50	15.00
❑ 332	A Girl You Can Depend On/If You Need Me	1965	3.75	7.50	15.00
❑ 400	Falling Sugar/Oh Blue	1965	3.75	7.50	15.00
PARKWAY					
❑ 111	Saturday's Child/Party Lights	1966	3.00	6.00	12.00
❑ 124	Calliope/Creed	1966	3.00	6.00	12.00
VERVE					
❑ 10410	Falling Sugar/Oh Blue	1966	2.50	5.00	10.00
PALISADES, THE					
More than one group.					
CALICO					
❑ 113	Close Your Eyes/I Can't Quit	1960	5.00	10.00	20.00
CHAIRMAN					
❑ 4401	Heaven Is Being with You/Make the Night a Little Longer	1963	6.25	12.50	25.00
—With Carole King					
DEBRA					
❑ 1003	Chapel Bells/She Can't Stop Dancing	1963	37.50	75.00	150.00
—Also released credited to "The Magics"					
DORE					
❑ 609	Hometown Girl/Oh My Love	1961	3.75	7.50	15.00
LEADER					
❑ 806	Dear Joan/The Shrine	1960	5.00	10.00	20.00
MEDIEVAL					
❑ 205	This Is the Night/Relic Rock	1962	5.00	10.00	20.00
PALMER, ROBERT					
Also see THE POWER STATION.					
EMI					
❑ 7PRO-04311 [DJ]	Tell Me I'm Not Dreaming/Tell Me I'm Not Dreaming (12" Edit)	1989	—	2.50	5.00
—Vinyl is promo only					
❑ S7-18129	Know By Now/In the Stars	1994	—	—	3.00
❑ 50183	She Makes My Day/Casting a Spell	1989	—	—	3.00
❑ 50183 [PS]	She Makes My Day/Casting a Spell	1989	—	—	3.00
EMI MANHATTAN					
❑ 50133	Simply Irresistible/Nova	1988	—	—	3.00
❑ 50133 [PS]	Simply Irresistible/Nova	1988	—	—	3.00
❑ 50157	Early in the Morning/Disturbing Behavior	1988	—	—	3.00
❑ 50157 [PS]	Early in the Morning/Disturbing Behavior	1988	—	—	3.00
ISLAND					
❑ 006	Sneakin' Sally Through the Alley/Epidemic	1974	—	2.50	5.00
❑ 015	Get Ta Steppin'/Get Right On Down	1975	—	2.50	5.00
❑ 042	Which One of Us Is the Fool/Get Outside	1975	—	2.50	5.00
❑ 049	Pressure Drop/Give Me an Inch Girl	1976	—	2.50	5.00
❑ 075	Man Smart, Woman Smarter/Keep in Touch	1976	—	2.50	5.00
❑ 081	One Last Look/Some People Can Do What They Want	1977	—	2.50	5.00
❑ 100	Every Kinda People/How Much Fun	1978	—	2.00	4.00
❑ 105	You Overwhelm Me/Come Over	1978	—	2.00	4.00
❑ 8697	Where Can It Go/You're Gonna Get What's Coming	1978	—	2.00	4.00
❑ 49016	Bad Case of Loving You (Doctor, Doctor)/Love Can Run Faster	1979	—	2.00	4.00
❑ 49094	In Walks Love Again/Jealous	1979	—	2.00	4.00
❑ 49137	Can We Still Be Friends/Remember to Remember	1979	—	2.00	4.00
❑ 49554	Style Kills/Johnny and Mary	1980	—	2.00	4.00
❑ 49620	Looking for Clues/Woke Up Laughing	1980	—	2.00	4.00
❑ 50042	Some Guys Have All the Luck/Too Good to Be True	1982	—	2.00	4.00
❑ 99139	Bad Case of Loving You/Sweet Lies	1989	—	—	3.00
❑ 99139 [PS]	Bad Case of Loving You/Sweet Lies	1989	—	2.00	4.00
❑ 99377	Sweet Lies/Want You More	1988	—	—	3.00
❑ 99377 [PS]	Sweet Lies/Want You More	1988	—	—	3.00
❑ 99537	I Didn't Mean to Turn You On/Get It Through Your Heart	1986	—	—	3.00
❑ 99537 [PS]	I Didn't Mean to Turn You On/Get It Through Your Heart	1986	—	—	3.00
❑ 99545	Hyperactive/Woke Up Laughing	1986	—	—	3.00
❑ 99570	Addicted to Love/Let's Fall in Love Tonight	1986	—	—	3.00
❑ 99570 [PS]	Addicted to Love/Let's Fall in Love Tonight	1986	—	2.00	4.00
—First version: Close-up photo of Robert Palmer					
❑ 99570 [PS]	Addicted to Love/Let's Fall in Love Tonight	1986	—	2.00	4.00
—Second version: Photo of "models" band from video					
❑ 99597	Discipline of Love (Why Did You Do It)/Dance for Me	1985	—	—	3.00
❑ 99597 [PS]	Discipline of Love (Why Did You Do It)/Dance for Me	1985	—	—	3.00
❑ 99835	Pride/(B-side unknown)	1983	—	—	3.00
❑ 99835 [PS]	Pride/(B-side unknown)	1983	—	2.00	4.00
❑ 99866	You Are In My System/Deadline	1983	—	—	3.00
❑ 99866 [PS]	You Are In My System/Deadline	1983	—	—	3.00
MCA					
❑ 52643	All Around the World/It's Not Difficult	1985	—	—	3.00
PALS, THE					
GUYDEN					
❑ 2019	My Baby Likes to Rock/Summer Is Here	1959	5.00	10.00	20.00
TURF					
❑ 1000	My Baby Likes to Rock/Summer Is Here	1958	10.00	20.00	40.00
PAPA DOO RUN RUN					
With BRUCE JOHNSTON.					
BLUE PACIFIC					
❑ 1-001	Lady Love/Slow Down	197?	—	2.00	4.00
❑ 1-001 [PS]	Lady Love/Slow Down	197?	—	2.00	4.00
EQUINOX					
❑ PB-10404	Disney Girls/Be True to Your School	1975	2.50	5.00	10.00
PAPPALARDI, FELIX					
Also see MOUNTAIN.					
COLUMBIA					
❑ 43773	Love Someday/You Lie to Me	1966	6.25	12.50	25.00
PARADE, THE					
A&M					
❑ 841	Sunshine Girl/This Old Melody	1967	2.50	5.00	10.00
❑ 867	She's Got the Magic/Welcome, You're in Love	1967	—	3.00	6.00
❑ 887	Frog Prince/Hallelujah Rocket	1967	—	3.00	6.00
❑ 904	I Can See Love/Radio Song	1968	—	3.00	6.00
❑ 950	A.C.-D.C./She Sleeps Alone	1968	—	3.00	6.00
❑ 970	Laughing Lady/Hallelujah Rocket	1968	—	3.00	6.00
PARADONS, THE					
MILESTONE					
❑ 2003	Diamonds and Pearls/I Want Love	1960	12.50	25.00	50.00
—Maroon label					
❑ 2003	Diamonds and Pearls/I Want Love	1960	7.50	15.00	30.00
—Red label					
❑ 2003	Diamonds and Pearls/I Want Love	1960	5.00	10.00	20.00
—Green label					
❑ 2005	Bells Ring/Please Tell Me	1960	7.50	15.00	30.00
❑ 2015	I Had a Dream/Never, Never	1962	10.00	20.00	40.00
TUFFEST					
❑ 102	Never Again/This Is Love	1961	37.50	75.00	150.00
WARNER BROS.					
❑ 5186	Take All of Me/So Fine, So Fine, So Fine	1960	5.00	10.00	20.00
PARAGONS, THE					
BUDDAH					
❑ 478	Oh Lovin' You/Con Me	1975	—	3.00	6.00
MUSIC CLEF					
❑ 3001/2	Time After Time/Baby, Take My Hand	1963	5.00	10.00	20.00
MUSICRAFT					
❑ 1102	Wedding Bells/Blue Velvet	1960	6.25	12.50	25.00

TAP

Number	Title (A Side/B Side)	Yr	VG	VG+	NM
❑ 500	If/Hey Baby	1961	12.50	25.00	50.00
❑ 503	In the Midst of the Night/Begin the Beguine	1961	10.00	20.00	40.00
❑ 504	These Are the Things I Love/If You Love Me	1961	10.00	20.00	40.00

TIMES SQUARE

Number	Title (A Side/B Side)	Yr	VG	VG+	NM
❑ 9	So You Will Know/Don't Cry Baby	1963	5.00	10.00	20.00

WINLEY

Number	Title (A Side/B Side)	Yr	VG	VG+	NM
❑ 215	Hey Little School Girl/Florence	1957	12.50	25.00	50.00
❑ 220	Let's Start All Over Again/Stick With Me Baby	1957	12.50	25.00	50.00
❑ 223	Two Hearts Are Better Than One/Give Me Love	1958	10.00	20.00	40.00
❑ 227	The Vows of Love/Twilight	1958	10.00	20.00	40.00
❑ 227	The Wows of Love/Twilight	1958	250.00	500.00	1000.

—With misspelled A-side title

Number	Title (A Side/B Side)	Yr	VG	VG+	NM
❑ 228	Don't Cry Baby/So You Will Know	1958	10.00	20.00	40.00
❑ 236	Darling, I Love You/Doll Baby	1959	10.00	20.00	40.00
❑ 240	So You Will Know/Doll Baby	1959	7.50	15.00	30.00
❑ 250	Kneel and Pray/Just a Moment	1961	7.50	15.00	30.00

PARAGONS, THE (2)

Not the same group as the others.

CENTURY CUSTOM

Number	Title (A Side/B Side)	Yr	VG	VG+	NM
❑ 19317	Surf Drums/Sunday Morning	196?	15.00	30.00	60.00

—B-side by the Samohi Serenaders

PARAKEETS, THE (1)

BIG TOP

Number	Title (A Side/B Side)	Yr	VG	VG+	NM
❑ 3130	I Love You Like I Do/I Want You Right Now	1962	5.00	10.00	20.00

JUBILEE

Number	Title (A Side/B Side)	Yr	VG	VG+	NM
❑ 5407	Come Back/Shangri-La	1961	6.25	12.50	25.00

PARAKEETS, THE (2)

GEM

Number	Title (A Side/B Side)	Yr	VG	VG+	NM
❑ 218	Give Me Time/I'm Losing My Mind Over You	1954	100.00	200.00	400.00

PARAMOUNTS, THE (1)

CARLTON

Number	Title (A Side/B Side)	Yr	VG	VG+	NM
❑ 524	Girl Friend/Trying	1960	10.00	20.00	40.00

PARAMOUNTS, THE (2)

CENTAUR

Number	Title (A Side/B Side)	Yr	VG	VG+	NM
❑ 103	When I Dream/Where's Carolyn Tonight	1963	15.00	30.00	60.00

PARAMOUNTS, THE (3)

ROBERT KNIGHT was in this group.

DOT

Number	Title (A Side/B Side)	Yr	VG	VG+	NM
❑ 16175	Why Do You Have to Go/Congratulations	1961	6.25	12.50	25.00
❑ 16201	When You Dance/Year 17	1961	6.25	12.50	25.00

PARAMOUNTS, THE (4)

British group; an early incarnation of PROCOL HARUM.

LIVERPOOL SOUND

Number	Title (A Side/B Side)	Yr	VG	VG+	NM
❑ 903	Poison Ivy/I Feel Good All Over	1964	12.50	25.00	50.00

PARAMOUNTS, THE (U)

Could be any of the above groups except (4), or they could be entirely different.

COMBO

Number	Title (A Side/B Side)	Yr	VG	VG+	NM
❑ 156	Take My Heart/Thunderbird Baby	1960	30.00	60.00	120.00

FLEETWOOD

Number	Title (A Side/B Side)	Yr	VG	VG+	NM
❑ 1014	I Know You'll Be My Love/Christopher Columbus	1960	25.00	50.00	100.00

LAURIE

Number	Title (A Side/B Side)	Yr	VG	VG+	NM
❑ 3201	Just to Be with You/One More for the Road	1963	7.50	15.00	30.00

MAGNUM

Number	Title (A Side/B Side)	Yr	VG	VG+	NM
❑ 722	Time Will Bring a Change/Under Your Spell	1964	7.50	15.00	30.00

MERCURY

Number	Title (A Side/B Side)	Yr	VG	VG+	NM
❑ 72429	Girl with the Big Black Boots/I Won't Share Your Love	1965	3.00	6.00	12.00

PARAMOURS, THE

BIL MEDLEY and BOBBY HATFIELD, later THE RIGHTEOUS BROTHERS.

MOONGLOW

Number	Title (A Side/B Side)	Yr	VG	VG+	NM
❑ 214	That's All I Want Tonight/There She Goes	1962	5.00	10.00	20.00
❑ 214	That's All I Want Tonight/There She Goes	1962	10.00	20.00	40.00

—Red vinyl

SMASH

Number	Title (A Side/B Side)	Yr	VG	VG+	NM
❑ 1701	That's the Way We Love/Prison Break	1961	5.00	10.00	20.00
❑ 1718	Cutie Cutie/Miss Social Climber	1961	5.00	10.00	20.00

PARFAYS, THE

FONTANA

Number	Title (A Side/B Side)	Yr	VG	VG+	NM
❑ 1526	You've Got a Good Thing Goin' Boy/In the Beginning	1965	7.50	15.00	30.00

PARIS

With BOB WELCH, ex-FLEETWOOD MAC.

CAPITOL

Number	Title (A Side/B Side)	Yr	VG	VG+	NM
❑ 4356	Blue Robin/Big Towne, 2061	1976	—	2.50	5.00

PARIS, FREDDIE

No relation to FRED PARRIS.

RCA VICTOR

Number	Title (A Side/B Side)	Yr	VG	VG+	NM
❑ 47-9232	Take Me As I Am/It's Okay to Cry Now	1967	2.50	5.00	10.00
❑ 47-9358	Little Things Can Make a Woman Cry/Face It, Boy, It's Over	1967	2.50	5.00	10.00
❑ 47-9571	There She Goes/Young Hearts, Young Hands	1968	5.00	10.00	20.00

PARIS BROTHERS, THE

BRUNSWICK

Number	Title (A Side/B Side)	Yr	VG	VG+	NM
❑ 55132	This Is It/Our Love Is Here to Stay	1959	7.50	15.00	30.00

CORAL

Number	Title (A Side/B Side)	Yr	VG	VG+	NM
❑ 62220	Funny Feeling/(B-side unknown)	1959	5.00	10.00	20.00

PARIS SISTERS, THE

CAPITOL

Number	Title (A Side/B Side)	Yr	VG	VG+	NM
❑ 2081	Golden Days/Greener Days	1968	2.00	4.00	8.00

CAVALIER

Number	Title (A Side/B Side)	Yr	VG	VG+	NM
❑ 828	Christmas in My Home Town/Man with the Mistletoe Moustache	197?	—	3.00	6.00

DECCA

Number	Title (A Side/B Side)	Yr	VG	VG+	NM
❑ 29372	Ooh La La/Whose Arms Are You Missing	1954	6.25	12.50	25.00
❑ 29488	Baby, Honey, Baby/Huckleberry Pie	1955	6.25	12.50	25.00
❑ 29527	His and Hers/Truly Do	1955	6.25	12.50	25.00

—With Gary Crosby

Number	Title (A Side/B Side)	Yr	VG	VG+	NM
❑ 29574	The Know How/I Wanna	1955	6.25	12.50	25.00
❑ 29744	Lover Boy/Oh Yes You Do	1955	6.25	12.50	25.00
❑ 29891	I Love You Dear/Mistaken	1956	6.25	12.50	25.00
❑ 29970	Daughter! Daughter!/So Much — So Very Much	1956	6.25	12.50	25.00
❑ 30554	Don't Tell Anybody/Mind Reader	1958	5.00	10.00	20.00

GNP CRESCENDO

Number	Title (A Side/B Side)	Yr	VG	VG+	NM
❑ 410	Stand Naked Clown/Ugliest Girl in Town	1968	2.00	4.00	8.00

GREGMARK

Number	Title (A Side/B Side)	Yr	VG	VG+	NM
❑ 2	Be My Boy/I'll Be Crying Tomorrow	1961	5.00	10.00	20.00
❑ 6	I Love How You Love Me/All Through the Night	1961	6.25	12.50	25.00
❑ 10	He Knows I Love Him Too Much/Lonely Girl's Prayer	1962	5.00	10.00	20.00
❑ 12	Let Me Be the One/What Am I to Do	1962	5.00	10.00	20.00
❑ 13	Yes I Love You/Once Upon a While Ago	1962	5.00	10.00	20.00

—All the Gregmark records were Phil Spector productions

IMPERIAL

Number	Title (A Side/B Side)	Yr	VG	VG+	NM
❑ 5465	Old Enough to Cry/Tell Me More	1957	5.00	10.00	20.00
❑ 5487	Some Day/My Original Love	1958	5.00	10.00	20.00

MERCURY

Number	Title (A Side/B Side)	Yr	VG	VG+	NM
❑ 72320	Once Upon a Time/When I Fall in Love	1964	2.50	5.00	10.00
❑ 72320 [PS]	Once Upon a Time/When I Fall in Love	1964	5.00	10.00	20.00
❑ 72468	Always Waitin'/Why Do I Take It from You	1965	2.50	5.00	10.00
❑ 72468 [PS]	Always Waitin'/Why Do I Take It from You	1965	5.00	10.00	20.00

MGM

Number	Title (A Side/B Side)	Yr	VG	VG+	NM
❑ 13236	Dream Lover/Lonely Girl	1964	3.75	7.50	15.00
❑ 13236 [PS]	Dream Lover/Lonely Girl	1964	6.25	12.50	25.00

REPRISE

Number	Title (A Side/B Side)	Yr	VG	VG+	NM
❑ 0440	Sincerely/Too Good to Be True	1965	2.50	5.00	10.00
❑ 0472	I'm Me/You	1966	2.50	5.00	10.00
❑ 0511	It's My Party/My Good Friend	1966	2.50	5.00	10.00
❑ 0548	Some of Your Lovin'/Long After Tonight Is All Over	1967	2.50	5.00	10.00

PARKER, FESS

BUENA VISTA

Number	Title (A Side/B Side)	Yr	VG	VG+	NM
❑ F-426	Ballad of Davy Crockett/Farewell	1963	3.00	6.00	12.00
❑ F-426 [PS]	Ballad of Davy Crockett/Farewell	1963	3.75	7.50	15.00

CASCADE

Number	Title (A Side/B Side)	Yr	VG	VG+	NM
❑ 5910	Eyes of an Angel/Strong Man	1959	3.75	7.50	15.00
❑ 5913	Lonely/Jayhawkers	1959	3.75	7.50	15.00

COLUMBIA

Number	Title (A Side/B Side)	Yr	VG	VG+	NM
❑ J4-242	Ballad of Davy Crockett/I Gave My Love (Riddle Song)	1955	5.00	10.00	20.00

—Yellow label "Children's Series" release

Number	Title (A Side/B Side)	Yr	VG	VG+	NM
❑ J4-242 [PS]	Ballad of Davy Crockett/I Gave My Love (Riddle Song)	1955	10.00	20.00	40.00

—Yellow label "Children's Series" release

Number	Title (A Side/B Side)	Yr	VG	VG+	NM
❑ 4-40449	Ballad of Davy Crockett/I Gave My Love (Riddle Song)	1955	3.75	7.50	15.00
❑ 4-40450	Farewell/I'm Lonely My Darlin'	1955	3.75	7.50	15.00
❑ 4-40568	Yaller Yaller Gold/King of the River	1955	6.25	12.50	25.00

DISNEYLAND

Number	Title (A Side/B Side)	Yr	VG	VG+	NM
❑ F-039	Wringle Wrangle/(Instrumental)	1957	7.50	15.00	30.00

—B-side by Camarata

Number	Title (A Side/B Side)	Yr	VG	VG+	NM
❑ F-043	Wringle Wrangle/The Ballad of John Coulter	1957	3.00	6.00	12.00
❑ F-043 [PS]	Wringle Wrangle/The Ballad of John Coulter	1957	6.25	12.50	25.00
❑ F-045	Pioneer's Prayer/The Ballad of John Coulter	1957	3.00	6.00	12.00
❑ F-045 [PS]	Pioneer's Prayer/The Ballad of John Coulter	1957	6.25	12.50	25.00
❑ F-049	A Hole in the Sky/Wedding Bell Calypso	1957	3.00	6.00	12.00
❑ F-049 [PS]	A Hole in the Sky/Wedding Bell Calypso	1957	6.25	12.50	25.00
❑ F-053	Gonna Find Me a Bluebird/Catch Me Fish	1957	6.25	12.50	25.00

GUSTO

Number	Title (A Side/B Side)	Yr	VG	VG+	NM
❑ 900	Ballad of Davy Crockett/Lonely	1963	2.50	5.00	10.00

RCA VICTOR

Number	Title (A Side/B Side)	Yr	VG	VG+	NM
❑ 47-8429	Daniel Boone/The Ballad of Davy Crockett	1964	3.00	6.00	12.00
❑ 47-8429 [PS]	Daniel Boone/The Ballad of Davy Crockett	1964	5.00	10.00	20.00
❑ 74-0249	Comin' After Jimmy/Sittin' Here Drinkin'	1969	2.50	5.00	10.00

PARKER, FESS, AND BUDDY EBSEN

COLUMBIA

Number	Title (A Side/B Side)	Yr	VG	VG+	NM
❑ B-2031	Davy Crockett, Indian Fighter	1955	10.00	20.00	40.00

—Cover for 40476 and 40477

Number	Title (A Side/B Side)	Yr	VG	VG+	NM
❑ B-2032	Davy Crockett Goes to Congress	1955	10.00	20.00	40.00

—Cover for 40478 and 40479

Number	Title (A Side/B Side)	Yr	VG	VG+	NM
❑ B-2033	Davy Crockett at the Alamo	1955	10.00	20.00	40.00

—Cover for 40480 and 40481

Number	Title (A Side/B Side)	Yr	VG	VG+	NM
❑ 4-40476	Davy Crockett, Indian Fighter (Part 1)/Davy Crockett, Indian Fighter (Part 4)	1955	5.00	10.00	20.00
❑ 4-40477	Davy Crockett, Indian Fighter (Part 2)/Davy Crockett, Indian Fighter (Part 3)	1955	5.00	10.00	20.00
❑ 4-40478	Davy Crockett Goes to Congress (Part 1)/Davy Crockett Goes to Congress (Part 4)	1955	5.00	10.00	20.00
❑ 4-40479	Davy Crockett Goes to Congress (Part 2)/Davy Crockett Goes to Congress (Part 3)	1955	5.00	10.00	20.00
❑ 4-40480	Davy Crockett at the Alamo (Part 1)/Davy Crockett at the Alamo (Part 4)	1955	5.00	10.00	20.00
❑ 4-40481	Davy Crockett at the Alamo (Part 2)/Davy Crockett at the Alamo (Part 3)	1955	5.00	10.00	20.00
❑ 4-40510	Be Sure You're Right (Then Go Ahead)/Old Betsy (Davy Crockett's Rifle)	1955	5.00	10.00	20.00

PARKER, GRAHAM

ARISTA

Number	Title (A Side/B Side)	Yr	VG	VG+	NM
❑ 0420	Local Girls/I Want You Back	1979	—	2.00	4.00
❑ 0420 [PS]	Local Girls/I Want You Back	1979	—	2.00	4.00
❑ 0439	Mercury Poisoning/I Want You Back (Alive)	1979	—	2.00	4.00
❑ 0523	Stupefaction/Women in Charge	1980	—	2.00	4.00
❑ 0523 [PS]	Stupefaction/Women in Charge	1980	—	2.00	4.00
❑ 0549	Endless Nights/No Holding Back	1980	—	2.00	4.00
—A-side: Guest vocals by Bruce Springsteen					
❑ 0652	Temporary Beauty/No More Excuses	1981	—	2.00	4.00
❑ 0687	You Hit the Spot/Habit Worth Forming	1982	—	—	3.00
❑ 9065	Life Gets Better/Beyond a Joke	1983	—	—	3.00

ELEKTRA

Number	Title (A Side/B Side)	Yr	VG	VG+	NM
❑ 69654	Wake Up (Next to You)/Bricks and Mortar	1985	—	2.00	4.00
❑ 69654 [PS]	Wake Up (Next to You)/Bricks and Mortar	1985	—	2.00	4.00

MERCURY

Number	Title (A Side/B Side)	Yr	VG	VG+	NM
❑ DJ-491 [DJ]	Hold Back the Night (same on both sides)	1977	3.00	6.00	12.00
❑ DJ-531 [DJ]	Stick to Me (same on both sides)	1977	3.00	6.00	12.00
❑ 73834	Soul Shoes/You've Got to Be Kidding	1976	2.00	4.00	8.00
❑ 73876	Heat Treatment/Back Door Love	1976	2.00	4.00	8.00
❑ 73970	Stick to Me/The Heat in Harlem	1977	2.00	4.00	8.00
❑ 74000	Hold Back the Night/(Let Me Get) Sweet on You//White Honey/Soul Shoes	1977	—	2.50	5.00
—Pink vinyl					
❑ 74000	Hold Back the Night/(Let Me Get) Sweet on You//White Honey/Soul Shoes	1977	—	3.50	7.00
—Also on black vinyl; scarcer than pink version					
❑ 74000 [PS]	"The Pink Parker": Hold Back the Night/(Let Me Get) Sweet on You//White Honey/Soul Shoes	1977	—	2.50	5.00

RCA

Number	Title (A Side/B Side)	Yr	VG	VG+	NM
❑ 8639-7-R	(Get Started) Start a Fire/Ordinary Girl	1988	—	—	3.00
❑ 8639-7-R [PS]	(Get Started) Start a Fire/Ordinary Girl	1988	—	—	3.00

PARKER, JUNIOR

Also includes records as "Little Junior Parker."

BLUE ROCK

Number	Title (A Side/B Side)	Yr	VG	VG+	NM
❑ 4064	I Got Money/Lover to Friend	1968	2.00	4.00	8.00
❑ 4067	Reconsider Baby/Lovin' Man on Your Hands	1968	2.00	4.00	8.00
❑ 4080	Ain't Gon' Be No Cuttin' Loose/I'm So Satisfied	1969	2.00	4.00	8.00
❑ 4088	Easy Lovin'/You Can't Keep a Good Woman Down	1969	2.00	4.00	8.00

CAPITOL

Number	Title (A Side/B Side)	Yr	VG	VG+	NM
❑ 2857	The Outside Man/Darling, Depend on Me	1970	—	3.00	6.00
❑ 2997	Drownin' on Dry Land/River's Invitation	1970	—	3.00	6.00

DUKE

Number	Title (A Side/B Side)	Yr	VG	VG+	NM
❑ 120	Dirty Friend Blues/Can't Understand	1954	15.00	30.00	60.00
❑ 127	Please Baby Please/Sittin', Drinkin' and Thinkin'	1954	15.00	30.00	60.00
❑ 137	Backtracking/I Wanna Ramble	1954	17.50	35.00	70.00
❑ 147	Driving Me/There Better Not Be No Feel	1956	12.50	25.00	50.00
❑ 157	Mother-in-Law Blues/That's My Baby	1956	12.50	25.00	50.00
❑ 164	Next Time You See Me/My Dolly Bee	1957	7.50	15.00	30.00
❑ 168	That's Alright/Pretty Baby	1957	7.50	15.00	30.00
❑ 177	Peaches/Pretty Little Doll	1957	7.50	15.00	30.00
❑ 184	Wondering/Sitting and Thinking	1958	6.25	12.50	25.00
❑ 193	Barefoot Rock/What Did I Do	1958	6.25	12.50	25.00
❑ 301	Sweet Home Chicago/Sometimes	1959	5.00	10.00	20.00
❑ 306	Five Long Years/I'm Holding On	1959	5.00	10.00	20.00
❑ 309	Stranded/Blue Letter	1959	5.00	10.00	20.00
❑ 315	Dangerous Woman/Belinda Marie	1960	3.75	7.50	15.00
❑ 317	The Next Time/You're On My Mind	1960	3.75	7.50	15.00
❑ 326	I'll Learn to Love Again/That's Just Alright	1960	3.75	7.50	15.00
❑ 330	Stand By Me/I'll Forget About You	1960	3.75	7.50	15.00
❑ 335	Driving Wheel/Seven Days	1961	6.25	12.50	25.00
❑ 341	In the Dark/How Long Can This Go On	1961	3.00	6.00	12.00
❑ 345	Annie Get Your Yo-Yo/Mary Jo	1961	3.00	6.00	12.00
❑ 351	I Feel Alright Again/Sweeter As the Days Go By	1962	3.00	6.00	12.00
❑ 357	Foxy Devil/Someone Somewhere	1962	3.00	6.00	12.00
❑ 362	It's a Pity/Last Night	1963	3.00	6.00	12.00
❑ 364	If You Don't Love Me/I Can't Forget About You	1963	3.00	6.00	12.00
❑ 367	The Tables Have Turned/Yonders Wall	1963	3.00	6.00	12.00
❑ 371	Strange Things Happening/I'm Gonna Stop	1964	3.00	6.00	12.00
❑ 376	Things I Used to Do/That's Why I'm Always Crying	1964	3.00	6.00	12.00
❑ 384	I'm in Love/Jivin' Woman	1964	3.00	6.00	12.00
❑ 389	Crying for My Baby/Guess You Don't Know (The Golden Rule)	1965	3.00	6.00	12.00
❑ 394	These Kind of Blues (Part 1)/These Kind of Blues (Part 2)	1966	3.00	6.00	12.00
❑ 398	Walking the Floor Over You/Goodbye Little Girl	1966	3.00	6.00	12.00
❑ 406	Get Away Blues/Why Do You Make Me Cry	1966	3.00	6.00	12.00
❑ 413	Man or Mouse/Wait for Another Day	1966	3.00	6.00	12.00

MERCURY

Number	Title (A Side/B Side)	Yr	VG	VG+	NM
❑ 72620	Baby Please/Just Like a Fish	1966	2.50	5.00	10.00
❑ 72651	You Can Make It If You Care/Ooh Wee Baby, That's the Way You Make Me Feel	1967	2.50	5.00	10.00
❑ 72672	Country Girl/Sometimes I Wonder	1967	2.50	5.00	10.00
❑ 72699	I Can't Put My Finger On It/If I Had Your Love	1967	2.50	5.00	10.00
❑ 72733	Hurtin' Inside/What a Fool I Was	1967	2.50	5.00	10.00
❑ 72793	It Must Be Love/Your Love's All Over	1968	2.00	4.00	8.00

MINIT

Number	Title (A Side/B Side)	Yr	VG	VG+	NM
❑ 32080	Worried Life Blues/Let the Good Times Roll	1969	—	3.00	6.00

SUN

Number	Title (A Side/B Side)	Yr	VG	VG+	NM
❑ 187	Feelin' Good/Fussin' and Fightin' Blues	1953	100.00	200.00	400.00
—As "Little Junior's Blue Flames"					
❑ 192	Mystery Train/Love My Baby	1954	75.00	150.00	300.00
—As "Little Junior's Blue Flames"					

PARKER, RAY, JR.

Includes records as "Raydio" and "Ray Parker Jr. and Raydio."

ARISTA

Number	Title (A Side/B Side)	Yr	VG	VG+	NM
❑ 0283	Jack and Jill/Get Down	1977	—	2.50	5.00
—As "Raydio"					
❑ 0283 [PS]	Jack and Jill/Get Down	1977	—	3.00	6.00
—As "Raydio"					
❑ 0328	Is This a Love Thing/Let's Go All the Way	1978	—	2.50	5.00
—As "Raydio"					
❑ 0353	Honey I'm Rich/Betcha You Can't Love Me Just Once	1978	—	2.50	5.00
—As "Raydio"					
❑ 0399	You Can't Change That/Rock On	1979	—	2.50	5.00
—As "Raydio"					
❑ 0441	More Than One Way to Love a Woman/Hot Stuff	1979	—	2.50	5.00
—As "Raydio"					
❑ 0494	Two Places at the Same Time/Everybody Makes Mistakes	1980	—	2.00	4.00
—As "Ray Parker Jr. and Raydio"					
❑ 0522	For Those Who Like to Groove/Can't Keep from Cryin'	1980	—	2.00	4.00
—As "Ray Parker Jr. and Raydio"					
❑ 0554	Can't Keep from Cryin'/It's Time to Party Now	1980	—	2.00	4.00
—As "Ray Parker Jr. and Raydio"					
❑ 0575	Little Bit of You/It's Time to Party Now	1980	—	2.00	4.00
—As "Ray Parker Jr. and Raydio"					
❑ 0592	A Woman Needs Love (Just Like You Do)/So Into You	1981	—	2.00	4.00
—As "Ray Parker Jr. and Raydio"					
❑ 0616	That Old Song/Old Pro	1981	—	2.00	4.00
—As "Ray Parker Jr. and Raydio"					
❑ 0616 [PS]	That Old Song/Old Pro	1981	—	2.00	4.00
—As "Ray Parker Jr. and Raydio"					
❑ 0641	It's Your Night/Old Pro	1981	—	2.00	4.00
—As "Ray Parker Jr. and Raydio"					
❑ 0669	The Other Woman/Stay the Night	1982	—	2.00	4.00
❑ 0695	Let Me Go/Stop, Look Before You Love	1982	—	2.00	4.00
❑ 1014	It's Our Own Affair/Just Havin' Fun	1982	—	2.00	4.00
❑ 1030	Bad Boy/Let's Get Off	1982	—	2.00	4.00
❑ 1035	Christmas Time Is Here/(Instrumental)	1982	—	2.50	5.00
❑ 1035 [PS]	Christmas Time Is Here/(Instrumental)	1982	—	3.00	6.00
❑ 1051	The People Next Door/Streetlove	1983	—	2.00	4.00
❑ 9048	Woman Out of Control/She Still Feels the Need	1983	—	2.00	4.00
❑ 9116	I Still Can't Get Over Losing You/She Still Feels the Need	1983	—	2.00	4.00
❑ 9198	In the Heat of the Night/N2 U2	1984	—	2.00	4.00
❑ 9212	Ghostbusters/(Instrumental)	1984	—	—	3.00
❑ 9293	Jamie/Christmas Time Is Here	1984	—	—	3.00
❑ 9352	Girls Are More Fun/I'm in Love	1985	—	—	3.00
❑ 9352 [PS]	Girls Are More Fun/I'm in Love	1985	—	—	3.00
❑ 9451	One Sided Love Affair/(B-side unknown)	1985	—	—	3.00

ATLANTIC

Number	Title (A Side/B Side)	Yr	VG	VG+	NM
❑ 89456	One Sunny Day/(B-side unknown)	1986	—	—	3.00
—With Helen Terry					
❑ 89456 [PS]	One Sunny Day/(B-side unknown)	1986	—	—	3.00

FLASHBACK

Number	Title (A Side/B Side)	Yr	VG	VG+	NM
❑ 9288	Christmas Time Is Here/(Instrumental)	1984	—	—	3.00
—Reissue					

GEFFEN

Number	Title (A Side/B Side)	Yr	VG	VG+	NM
❑ 28152	Over You/After Midnite	1987	—	—	3.00
❑ 28152 [PS]	Over You/After Midnite	1987	—	—	3.00
—With Natalie Cole					
❑ 28417	I Don't Think That Man Should Sleep Alone/After Midnight	1987	—	—	3.00
❑ 28417 [PS]	I Don't Think That Man Should Sleep Alone/After Midnight	1987	—	—	3.00

PARKER, ROBERT

IMPERIAL

Number	Title (A Side/B Side)	Yr	VG	VG+	NM
❑ 5842	Mash Potatoes All Night Long/Twistin' Out of Space	1962	3.00	6.00	12.00
❑ 5889	You're Lookin' Good/Little Things Mean a Lot	1962	3.00	6.00	12.00
❑ 5916	Please Forgive Me/You Got It	1963	3.00	6.00	12.00

ISLAND

Number	Title (A Side/B Side)	Yr	VG	VG+	NM
❑ 044	Give Me the Country Side of Life/It's Hard But It's Fair	1975	—	2.00	4.00
❑ 074	A Little Bit Something/Better Luck in the Summer	1976	—	2.00	4.00

NOLA

Number	Title (A Side/B Side)	Yr	VG	VG+	NM
❑ 721	Barefootin'/Let's Go Baby (Where the Action Is)	1966	5.00	10.00	20.00
❑ 724	Ring Around the Roses/She's Coming Home	1966	3.00	6.00	12.00
❑ 726	Happy Feet/The Scratch	1966	3.00	6.00	12.00
❑ 729	Tip Toe/Soul Kind of Loving	1966	3.00	6.00	12.00
❑ 730	A Letter To Santa/C.C. Rider	1966	3.00	6.00	12.00
❑ 733	Yak Yak Yak/Secret Agents	1967	3.00	6.00	12.00
❑ 735	Everybody's Hip-Hugging/Foxy Mama	1967	3.00	6.00	12.00
❑ 738	I Caught You in a Lie/Holdin' Out	1967	3.00	6.00	12.00

RON

Number	Title (A Side/B Side)	Yr	VG	VG+	NM
❑ 327	All Nite Long (Part 1)/All Nite Long (Part 2)	1959	3.75	7.50	15.00
❑ 331	Walkin'/Across the Track	1960	3.75	7.50	15.00

SILVER FOX

Number	Title (A Side/B Side)	Yr	VG	VG+	NM
❑ 12	You Shakin' Things Up/You See Me	1969	—	3.00	6.00

PARKS, GINO

CRAZY HORSE

Number	Title (A Side/B Side)	Yr	VG	VG+	NM
❑ 1303	Nerves of Steel/Help Me Somebody	1968	7.50	15.00	30.00

FORTUNE

Number	Title (A Side/B Side)	Yr	VG	VG+	NM
❑ 528	Last Night I Cried/Just Go	1957	20.00	40.00	80.00

GOLDEN WORLD

Number	Title (A Side/B Side)	Yr	VG	VG+	NM
❑ 32	My Sophisticated Lady/Talkin' About My Baby	1966	5.00	10.00	20.00

MIRACLE

Number	Title (A Side/B Side)	Yr	VG	VG+	NM
❑ 3	Don't Say Bye Bye/(B-side unknown)	1960	200.00	400.00	800.00

TAMLA

Number	Title (A Side/B Side)	Yr	VG	VG+	NM
❑ 54042	That's No Lie/Same Thing	1961	15.00	30.00	60.00
❑ 54066	For This I Thank You/Fire	1962	15.00	30.00	60.00

PARKS, MICHAEL

Number	Title (A Side/B Side)	Yr	VG	VG+	NM
MGM					
❑ 14092	Tie Me to Your Apron Strings Again/Won't You Ride in My Little Red Wagon	1969	—	2.50	5.00
❑ 14104	Long Lonesome Highway/Mountain High	1970	—	3.00	6.00
❑ 14154	Sally/Save a Little, Spend a Little	1970	—	2.50	5.00
❑ 14363	Won't You Ride in My Little Red Wagon/Big "T" Water	1972	—	2.50	5.00
VERVE					
❑ 10653	Drownin' on Dry Land/River's Invitation	1971	—	2.50	5.00

PARKS, RAY

Number	Title (A Side/B Side)	Yr	VG	VG+	NM
CAPITOL					
❑ F3580	You're Gonna Have to Bawl, That's All/Just a-Hangin' Around	1956	17.50	35.00	70.00

PARKS, VAN DYKE

Number	Title (A Side/B Side)	Yr	VG	VG+	NM
MGM					
❑ 13441	Do What You Wanta/Number Nine	1966	3.00	6.00	12.00
❑ 13570	Come to the Sunshine/Farther Along	1966	3.00	6.00	12.00
WARNER BROS.					
❑ 7026	Donovan's Colors Part 1/Part 2	1967	3.00	6.00	12.00
—As "George Washington Brown"					
❑ 7409	On the Rolling Sea When Jesus Speaks to Me/The Eagle and Me	1970	2.50	5.00	10.00
❑ 7609	Occapella/Ode to Tobago	1972	—	3.00	6.00
❑ 7632	Riverboat/John Jones	1972	—	3.00	6.00

PARLET

Female offshoot of PARLIAMENT.

Number	Title (A Side/B Side)	Yr	VG	VG+	NM
CASABLANCA					
❑ 919	Pleasure Principle/(Instrumental)	1978	—	2.50	5.00
❑ 932	Cookie Jar/Are You Dreaming	1978	—	2.50	5.00
❑ 975	Ridin' High (Part 1)/Ridin' High (Part 2)	1979	—	2.50	5.00
❑ 995	Don't Ever Stop/Huff-N-Puff	1979	—	2.50	5.00
❑ 2260	Wolf Tickets/(Instrumental)	1980	—	2.50	5.00
❑ 2293	Help from My Friends/Watch Me Do My Thang	1980	—	2.50	5.00

PARLIAMENT

Also see GEORGE CLINTON; FUNKADELIC; PARLET; THE PARLIAMENTS.

Number	Title (A Side/B Side)	Yr	VG	VG+	NM
CASABLANCA					
❑ 0003	The Goose (Part 1)/The Goose (Part 2)	1974	—	3.00	6.00
❑ 0013	Up for the Down Stroke/Presence of a Brain	1974	—	3.00	6.00
❑ 0104	Up for the Down Stroke/Presence of a Brain	1974	—	2.50	5.00
❑ 803	Up for the Down Stroke/Presence of a Brain	1974	—	2.50	5.00
❑ 811	Testify/I Can Move You	1974	—	2.50	5.00
❑ 831	Chocolate City/Chocolate City (Part 2)	1975	—	2.50	5.00
❑ 843	Ride On/Big Footin'	1975	—	2.50	5.00
❑ 852	P. Funk (Wants to Get Funked Up)/Night of the Tempasaurus Peoples	1976	—	2.50	5.00
❑ 856	Tear the Roof Off the Sucker (Give Up the Funk)/P-Funk	1976	—	2.50	5.00
—Blue label					
❑ 856	Tear the Roof Off the Sucker (Give Up the Funk)/P-Funk	1976	—	2.00	4.00
—Tan label					
❑ 864	Star Child (Mothership Connection)/Supergroovealistic	1976	—	2.50	5.00
❑ 871	Do That Stuff/Handcuffs	1976	—	2.50	5.00
❑ 875	Dr. Funkenstein/Children of Production	1977	—	2.50	5.00
❑ 892	Fantasy Is Reality/The Landing (Of the Mothership)	1977	—	2.50	5.00
❑ 900	Bop Gun (Endangered Species)/I've Been Watchin' You	1977	—	2.50	5.00
❑ 909	Flash Light/Swing Down, Sweet Chariot	1978	—	2.50	5.00
❑ 921	Funkentelechy/Funkentelechy (Part 2)	1978	—	2.50	5.00
❑ 950	Aqua Boogie (A Psychoalphadiscobetabioaquadoloop)/(You're a Fish and I'm a) Water Sign	1978	—	2.50	5.00
❑ 950 [PS]	Aqua Boogie (A Psychoalphadiscobetabioaquadoloop)/(You're a Fish and I'm a) Water Sign	1978	2.50	5.00	10.00
❑ 976	Rumpofsteelskin/Liquid Sunshine	1979	—	2.50	5.00
❑ 2222	Party People/Party People (Part 2)	1979	—	2.50	5.00
❑ 2235	Theme from The Black Hole/(You're a Fish and I'm a) Water Sign	1980	—	2.50	5.00
❑ 2250	The Big Bang Theory/The Big Bang Theory (Part 2)	1980	—	2.50	5.00
❑ 2317	Agony of DeFeet/The Freeze	1980	—	2.50	5.00
❑ 2330	Crush It/Body Language	1981	—	2.50	5.00
INVICTUS					
❑ 9077	I Call My Baby Pussy Cat/Little Ole Country Boy	1970	2.50	5.00	10.00
❑ 9091	Red Hot Mama/Little Ole Country Boy	1971	2.50	5.00	10.00
❑ 9095	Breakdown/Little Ole Country Boy	1971	2.50	5.00	10.00
❑ 9123	Come In Out of the Rain/Little Ole Country Boy	1972	2.00	4.00	8.00

PARLIAMENTS, THE

All of the below are probably the same group, a Detriot-based R&B group led by GEORGE CLINTON that evolved into PARLIAMENT and FUNKADELIC.

Number	Title (A Side/B Side)	Yr	VG	VG+	NM
APT					
❑ 25036	Poor Willie/Party Boys	1959	10.00	20.00	40.00
ATCO					
❑ 6675	A New Day Begins/I'll Wait	1969	5.00	10.00	20.00
FLIPP					
❑ 100/1	Lonely Island/You Make Me Wanna Cry	1960	10.00	20.00	40.00
—Red label					
❑ 100/1	Lonely Island/You Make Me Wanna Cry	1960	7.50	15.00	30.00
—Yellow label					
GOLDEN WORLD					
❑ 46	Heart Trouble/That Was My Girl	1966	12.50	25.00	50.00
LEN					
❑ 101	Don't Need You Anymore/Honey, Take Me Home with You	1958	20.00	40.00	80.00
REVILOT					
❑ 207	(I Wanna) Testify/I Can Feel the Ice Melting	1967	3.75	7.50	15.00
❑ 211	All Your Goodies Are Gone (The Loser's Seat)/Don't Be Sore at Me	1967	3.75	7.50	15.00
❑ 214	Little Man/The Goose (That Laid the Golden Egg)	1968	3.75	7.50	15.00
❑ 217	Look at What I Almost Missed/What You Been Growing	1968	3.75	7.50	15.00
❑ 223	Good Old Music/Time	1968	3.75	7.50	15.00
❑ 228	A New Day Begins/I'll Wait	1968	7.50	15.00	30.00
SYMBOL					
❑ 917	You're Cute/I'll Get You Yet	1962	6.25	12.50	25.00
U.S.A.					
❑ 719	My Only Love/To Be Alone	1961	5.00	10.00	20.00

PARRIS, FRED

Not to be confused with FREDDIE PARIS. Also see THE CHAMPLAINS; THE CHEROKEES (5); THE FIVE SATINS; THE NEW YORKERS (1).

Number	Title (A Side/B Side)	Yr	VG	VG+	NM
ATCO					
❑ 6439	Land of the Broken Hearts/Bring It Home to Daddy	1966	2.50	5.00	10.00
BIRTH					
❑ 101	Dark at the Top of My Heart/Benediction	196?	2.00	4.00	8.00
CHECKER					
❑ 1108	No Use in Crying/Walk a Little Faster	1965	2.50	5.00	10.00
GREEN SEA					
❑ 106	Blushing Bride/Giving My Love to You	1966	2.50	5.00	10.00
❑ 107	I'll Be Hangin' On/I Can Really Satisfy	1966	2.50	5.00	10.00
MAMA SADIE					
❑ 1001	In the Still of the Nite "67"/Heck No	1967	2.50	5.00	10.00

PARROTS, THE (1)

Number	Title (A Side/B Side)	Yr	VG	VG+	NM
CHECKER					
❑ 772	Don't Leave Me/Weep, Weep, Weep	1953	125.00	250.00	500.00

PARROTS, THE (2)

Number	Title (A Side/B Side)	Yr	VG	VG+	NM
MALA					
❑ 558	They All Got Carried Away/Hey, Put the Clock Back on the Wall	1967	3.00	6.00	12.00

PARSONS, ALAN, PROJECT

Number	Title (A Side/B Side)	Yr	VG	VG+	NM
20TH CENTURY					
❑ 2297	(The System of) Doctor Tarr and Professor Fether/Dream Within a Dream	1976	—	2.50	5.00
❑ 2308	The Raven/Prelude to Fall of the House of Usher	1976	—	2.50	5.00
❑ 2333	To One in Paradise/The Cask of Amontillado	1977	—	3.00	6.00
ARISTA					
❑ 0260	I Wouldn't Want to Be Like You/Nucleus	1977	—	2.00	4.00
❑ 0288	I Robot/Don't Let It Show	1977	—	2.00	4.00
❑ 0310	Day After Day/Breakdown	1978	—	2.00	4.00
❑ 0352	What Goes Up/In the Lap of the Gods	1978	—	2.00	4.00
❑ 0454	Damned If I Do/If I Could Change Your Mind	1979	—	2.00	4.00
❑ 0491	You Won't Be There/Secret Garden	1980	—	2.00	4.00
❑ 0502	You Lie Down with Dogs/Lucifer	1980	—	2.00	4.00
❑ 0573	Games People Play/Ace of Swords	1980	—	2.00	4.00
❑ 0598	Time/The Gold Bug	1981	—	2.00	4.00
❑ 0635	Snake Eyes/I Don't Wanna Go Home	1981	—	2.00	4.00
❑ 0696	Eye in the Sky/Gemini	1982	—	2.00	4.00
❑ 1029	Psychobabble/Children of the Moon	1982	—	2.00	4.00
❑ 1048	Old and Wise/You're Gonna Get Your Fingers Burned	1983	—	2.00	4.00
❑ 9108	You Don't Believe/Lucifer	1983	—	2.00	4.00
❑ 9160	Don't Answer Me/Don't Let It Show	1984	—	—	3.00
❑ 9160 [PS]	Don't Answer Me/Don't Let It Show	1984	—	—	3.00
❑ 9208	Prime Time/Gold Bug	1984	—	—	3.00
❑ 9282	Let's Talk About Me/Hawkeye	1984	—	—	3.00
❑ 9282 [PS]	Let's Talk About Me/Hawkeye	1984	—	—	3.00
❑ 9349	Days Are Numbers (The Traveller)/Somebody Out There	1985	—	—	3.00
❑ 9443	Stereotomy/Urbania	1985	—	—	3.00
❑ 9576	Standing on Higher Ground/Inside Looking Out	1987	—	—	3.00
❑ 9576 [PS]	Standing on Higher Ground/Inside Looking Out	1987	—	—	3.00

PARSONS, BILL

Also see BOBBY BARE.

Number	Title (A Side/B Side)	Yr	VG	VG+	NM
FRATERNITY					
❑ 835	The All American Boy/Rubber Dolly	1959	10.00	20.00	40.00
—This record is actually by Bobby Bare miscredited					
❑ 838	Educated Rock and Roll/Carefree Wanderer	1959	7.50	15.00	30.00
STARDAY					
❑ 526	Hod Rod Volkswagen/Guitar Blues	1960	7.50	15.00	30.00
❑ 544	The Price We Pay for Livin'/A-Waitin'	1960	5.00	10.00	20.00

PARSONS, GRAM

Also see THE BYRDS; THE FLYING BURRITO BROTHERS; THE INTERNATIONAL SUBMARINE BAND.

Number	Title (A Side/B Side)	Yr	VG	VG+	NM
REPRISE					
❑ 1139	That's All It Took/She	1972	—	3.00	6.00
❑ 1192	Love Hurts/In My Hour of Darkness	1974	—	3.00	6.00
SIERRA					
❑ 104	Medley (Bony Moronie/40 Days/Almost Grown)//Conversations/Hot Burrito #1	1982	—	2.50	5.00
—Second song on side 2 by Gene Parsons					
❑ 104 [PS]	Gram Parsons and the Fallen Angels	1982	—	2.50	5.00
❑ 105	Love Hurts/The New Soft Shoe	1982	—	2.50	5.00
WARNER BROS.					
❑ 50013	Return of the Grievous Angel/Hearts on Fire	1982	—	2.50	5.00

PARTON, DOLLY

Also see KENNY ROGERS AND DOLLY PARTON; PORTER WAGONER AND DOLLY PARTON.

COLUMBIA

Number	Title (A Side/B Side)	Yr	VG	VG+	NM
❑ 07665	The River Unbroken/More Than I Can Say	1988	—	—	3.00
❑ 07665 [PS]	The River Unbroken/More Than I Can Say	1988	—	—	3.00
❑ 07727	I Know You by Heart/Could I Have Your Autograph	1988	—	—	3.00
—With Smokey Robinson					
❑ 07727 [PS]	I Know You by Heart/Could I Have Your Autograph	1988	—	—	3.00
❑ 07995	Make Love Mine/Two Lovers	1988	—	—	3.00
❑ 68760	Why'd You Come In Here Lookin' Like That/Wait Til I Get You Home	1989	—	—	3.00
❑ 69040	Yellow Roses/Wait Til I Get You Home	1989	—	—	3.00
❑ 73200	He's Alive/What Is It We Love	1990	—	—	3.00
❑ 73226	Time for Me to Fly/The Moon, the Stars, and Me	1990	—	—	3.00
❑ 73341	White Limozeen/The Moon, the Stars, and Me	1990	—	—	3.00
❑ 73498	Slow Healin' Heart/Take Me Back to the Country	1990	—	—	3.00
❑ 73711	Rockin' Years/What a Heartache	1991	—	—	3.00
—A-side with Ricky Van Shelton					
❑ 73826	Silver and Gold/Runaway Feelin'	1991	—	—	3.00
❑ 74011	Eagle When She Flies/Wildest Dreams	1991	—	—	3.00
❑ 74183	The Best Woman Wins/Country Road	1992	—	—	3.00
—A-side with Lorrie Morgan					
❑ 74876	Romeo/The High and the Mighty	1993	—	—	3.00
—A-side: "Dolly Parton and Friends"					
❑ 74954	More Where That Came From/I'll Make Your Bed	1993	—	—	3.00
❑ 77083	Full Circle/What Will Baby Be	1993	—	—	3.00
❑ 77294	Silver Threads and Golden Needles/Let Her Fly	1993	—	—	3.00
—Dolly Parton/Tammy Wynette/Loretta Lynn					
❑ 77723	To Daddy/PMS Blues	1994	—	—	3.00
❑ 78079	I Will Always Love You/Speakin' of the Devil	1995	—	—	3.00
—A-side: "With Special Guest Vince Gill"					

DECCA

Number	Title (A Side/B Side)	Yr	VG	VG+	NM
❑ 72061	Honky Tonk Songs/Paradise Road	1998	—	—	3.00
❑ 72080	The Salt in My Tears/Hungry Again	1998	—	—	3.00

GOLD BAND

Number	Title (A Side/B Side)	Yr	VG	VG+	NM
❑ 1086	Puppy Love/Girl Left Alone	1959	150.00	300.00	600.00

MERCURY

Number	Title (A Side/B Side)	Yr	VG	VG+	NM
❑ 71982	It's Sure Gonna Hurt/The Love You Gave	1962	75.00	150.00	300.00

MONUMENT

Number	Title (A Side/B Side)	Yr	VG	VG+	NM
❑ 869	I Wasted My Tears/What Do You Think About Lovin'	1965	3.75	7.50	15.00
❑ 897	Old Enough to Know Better (Too Young to Resist)/Happy, Happy Birthday Baby	1965	3.75	7.50	15.00
❑ 913	Busy Signal/I Took Him for Granted	1965	3.75	7.50	15.00
❑ 922	Control Yourself/Don't Drop Out	1966	3.75	7.50	15.00
❑ 948	Little Things/I'll Put It Off Until Tomorrow	1966	3.75	7.50	15.00
❑ 982	Dumb Blonde/The Giving and the Taking	1967	2.50	5.00	10.00
❑ 1007	Something Fishy/I've Lived My Life	1967	2.50	5.00	10.00
❑ 1032	Why, Why, Why/I Couldn't Wait Forever	1967	2.50	5.00	10.00
❑ 1047	I'm Not Worth the Tears/Ping Pong	1968	2.00	4.00	8.00
❑ 03408	Everything Is Beautiful (In Its Own Way)/Put It Off Until Tomorrow	1982	—	2.00	4.00
—A-side with Willie Nelson; B-side with Kris Kristofferson					
❑ 03781	What Do You Think About Lovin'/You're Gonna Love Yourself (In the Morning)	1983	—	2.00	4.00
—A-side: Dolly Parton and Brenda Lee; B-side: Willie Nelson and Brenda Lee					

RCA

Number	Title (A Side/B Side)	Yr	VG	VG+	NM
❑ 5001-7-R	Do I Ever Cross Your Mind/We Had It All	1986	—	—	3.00
❑ PB-10935	Light of a Clear Blue Morning/There	1977	—	2.00	4.00
❑ PB-11123	Here You Come Again/Me and Little Andy	1977	—	2.00	4.00
❑ PB-11240	Two Doors Down/It's All Wrong, But It's All Right	1978	—	2.00	4.00
❑ JB-11296 [DJ]	Heartbreaker (same on both sides)	1978	2.50	5.00	10.00
—Promo only on red vinyl					
❑ PB-11296	Heartbreaker/Sure Thing	1978	—	2.00	4.00
❑ JB-11420 [DJ]	Baby I'm Burning (same on both sides)	1978	2.50	5.00	10.00
—Promo only on red vinyl					
❑ PB-11420	Baby I'm Burning/I Really Got the Feeling	1978	—	2.00	4.00
❑ GB-11505	Here You Come Again/Two Doors Down	1979	—	—	3.00
—Gold Standard Series					
❑ PB-11577	You're the Only One/Down	1979	—	2.00	4.00
❑ JB-11705 [DJ]	Great Balls of Fire (same on both sides)	1979	2.50	5.00	10.00
—Promo only on red vinyl					
❑ PB-11705	Sweet Summer Lovin'/Great Balls of Fire	1979	—	2.00	4.00
❑ JH-11926 [DJ]	Starting Over Again (same on both sides)	1980	3.00	6.00	12.00
—Promo only on green vinyl					
❑ PB-11926	Starting Over Again/Sweet Agony	1980	—	2.00	4.00
❑ GB-11993	Baby I'm Burnin'/Heartbreaker	1980	—	—	3.00
—Gold Standard Series					
❑ PB-12040	Old Flames Can't Hold a Candle to You/I Knew You When	1980	—	2.00	4.00
❑ JH-12133 [DJ]	9 to 5 (same on both sides)	1980	3.75	7.50	15.00
—Promo only on blue vinyl					
❑ PB-12133	9 to 5/Sing for the Common Man	1980	—	2.00	4.00
❑ PB-12133 [PS]	9 to 5/Sing for the Common Man	1980	—	2.50	5.00
❑ PB-12200	But You Know I Love You/Poor Folks' Town	1981	—	2.00	4.00
❑ PB-12282	The House of the Rising Sun/Working Girl	1981	—	2.00	4.00
❑ GB-12316	9 to 5/Old Flames Can't Hold a Candle to You	1981	—	—	3.00
—Gold Standard Series					
❑ JK-13057 [DJ]	Single Women (same on both sides)	1982	3.00	6.00	12.00
—Promo only on red vinyl					
❑ PB-13057	Single Women/Barbara on Your Mind	1982	—	2.00	4.00
❑ PB-13234	Heartbreak Express/Act Like a Fool	1982	—	2.00	4.00
❑ PB-13260	I Will Always Love You/Do I Ever Cross Your Mind	1982	—	2.00	4.00
—A-side is the same song, but a different recording than that on APBO-0234					
❑ PB-13260 [PS]	I Will Always Love You/Do I Ever Cross Your Mind	1982	—	2.50	5.00
❑ JK-13361 [DJ]	Hard Candy Christmas (same on both sides)	1982	3.00	6.00	12.00
—Promo only on red vinyl					
❑ PB-13361	Hard Candy Christmas/Me and Little Andy	1982	—	2.00	4.00
❑ JK-13514 [DJ]	Potential New Boyfriend (Short) (same on both sides)	1983	3.00	6.00	12.00
—Promo only on yellow vinyl					
❑ JK-13514 [DJ]	Potential New Boyfriend (same on both sides)	1983	3.00	6.00	12.00
—Promo only on blue vinyl					
❑ PB-13514	Potential New Boyfriend/One of Those Days	1983	—	—	3.00
❑ PB-13619	Tennessee Homesick Blues/Butterflies	1984	—	—	3.00
❑ JK-13703 [DJ]	Save the Last Dance for Me (same on both sides)	1983	2.50	5.00	10.00
—Promo only on green vinyl					
❑ PB-13703	Save the Last Dance for Me/Elusive Butterfly	1983	—	—	3.00
❑ PB-13756	The Great Pretender/Downtown	1984	—	—	3.00
❑ PB-13756 [PS]	The Great Pretender/Downtown	1984	—	—	3.00
❑ PB-13856	Sweet Lovin' Friends/Too Much Water	1984	—	—	—
—Unreleased					
❑ PB-13883	Sweet Lovin' Friends/God Won't Get You	1984	—	—	3.00
—With Sylvester Stallone					
❑ JK-13944 [DJ]	Medley: Winter Wonderland/Sleigh Ride (same on both sides)	1984	—	2.00	4.00
❑ PB-13944	Medley: Winter Wonderland-Sleigh Ride/The Christmas Song	1984	—	—	3.00
—B-side by Kenny Rogers					
❑ PB-13987	Don't Call It Love/We Got Too Much	1985	—	—	3.00
❑ GB-14070	Tennessee Homesick Blues/Hard Candy Christmas	1985	—	—	3.00
—Gold Standard Series					
❑ PB-14218	Think About Love/Come Back to Me	1985	—	—	3.00
❑ PB-14297	Tie Our Love (In a Double Knot)/I Hope You're Never Happy	1986	—	—	3.00
❑ GB-14346	Don't Call It Love/Real Love	1986	—	—	3.00
—Gold Standard Series					

RCA VICTOR

Number	Title (A Side/B Side)	Yr	VG	VG+	NM
❑ APBO-0145	Jolene/Love, You're So Beautiful Tonight	1973	—	2.50	5.00
❑ APBO-0234	I Will Always Love You/Lonely Comin' Down	1974	—	2.50	5.00
❑ PB-10031	Love Is Like a Butterfly/Sacred Memories	1974	—	2.00	4.00
❑ PB-10164	The Bargain Store/I'll Never Forget	1975	—	2.00	4.00
❑ GB-10165	Jolene/My Tennessee Mountain Home	1975	—	—	3.00
—Gold Standard Series					
❑ PB-10310	The Seeker/Love with Feeling	1975	—	2.00	4.00
❑ PB-10396	We Used To/My Heart Started Breaking	1975	—	2.00	4.00
❑ GB-10504	Love Is Like a Butterfly/Sacred Memories	1975	—	—	3.00
—Gold Standard Series					
❑ GB-10505	I Will Always Love You/Lovely Comin' Down	1975	—	—	3.00
—Gold Standard Series					
❑ PB-10564	Hey, Lucky Lady/Most of All, Why	1976	—	2.00	4.00
❑ GB-10676	The Bargain Store/The Seeker	1976	—	—	3.00
—Gold Standard Series					
❑ PB-10730	All I Can Do/Falling Out of Love with Me	1976	—	2.00	4.00
❑ 47-9548	Just Because I'm a Woman/I Wish I Felt This Way at Home	1968	2.00	4.00	8.00
❑ 47-9657	In the Good Old Days (When Times Were Bad)/Try Being Lonely	1968	2.00	4.00	8.00
❑ 47-9784	Daddy Come and Get Me/Chas	1969	—	3.00	6.00
❑ 47-9863	Mule Skinner Blues/More Than Their Share	1970	—	3.00	6.00
❑ 47-9928	Joshua/I'm Doing This for Your Sake	1970	—	3.00	6.00
❑ 47-9971	Comin' For to Carry Me Home/Golden Streets of Glory	1971	—	3.00	6.00
❑ 47-9999	My Blue Tears/The Mystery of the Mystery	1971	—	3.00	6.00
❑ 74-0132	Daddy/He's a Go-Getter	1969	—	3.00	6.00
❑ 74-0192	In the Ghetto/Bridge	1969	—	3.00	6.00
❑ 74-0243	My Blue Ridge Mountain Boy/'Til Death Do Us Part	1969	—	3.00	6.00
❑ 74-0538	Coat of Many Colors/Here I Am	1971	—	3.00	6.00
❑ 74-0538 [PS]	Coat of Many Colors/Here I Am	1971	2.50	5.00	10.00
❑ 74-0662	Touch Your Woman/Mission Chapel Memories	1972	—	2.50	5.00
❑ 74-0757	Washday Blues/Just As Good As Gone	1972	—	2.50	5.00
❑ 74-0797	Lord, Hold My Hand/When I Sing for Him	1972	—	2.50	5.00
❑ 74-0868	My Tennessee Mountain Home/Better Part of Life	1973	—	2.50	5.00
❑ 74-0950	Traveling Man/I Remember	1973	—	2.50	5.00

RISING TIDE

Number	Title (A Side/B Side)	Yr	VG	VG+	NM
❑ 56041	Just When I Needed You Most/For the Good Times	1996	—	—	3.00

PARTON, DOLLY/LINDA RONSTADT/EMMYLOU HARRIS

Also see each artist's individual listings.

WARNER BROS.

Number	Title (A Side/B Side)	Yr	VG	VG+	NM
❑ 27970	Wildflowers/Hobo's Meditation	1988	—	—	3.00
❑ 28248	Those Memories of You/My Dear Companion	1987	—	—	3.00
❑ 28248 [PS]	Those Memories of You/My Dear Companion	1987	—	2.00	4.00
❑ 28371	Telling Me Lies/Rosewood Casket	1987	—	—	3.00
❑ 28492	To Know Him Is to Love Him/Farther Along	1987	—	—	3.00
❑ 28492 [PS]	To Know Him Is to Love Him/Farther Along	1987	—	2.00	4.00

PARTRIDGE FAMILY, THE

Also see DANNY BONADUCE; DAVID CASSIDY.

BELL

Number	Title (A Side/B Side)	Yr	VG	VG+	NM
❑ 910	I Think I Love You/Somebody Wants to Love You	1970	—	2.50	5.00
❑ 910 [PS]	I Think I Love You/Somebody Wants to Love You	1970	—	3.00	6.00
❑ 963	Doesn't Somebody Want to Be Wanted/You Are Always on My Mind	1971	—	2.50	5.00
❑ 963 [PS]	Doesn't Somebody Want to Be Wanted/You Are Always on My Mind	1971	—	3.00	6.00
❑ 996	I'll Meet You Halfway/Morning Rider on the Road	1971	—	2.50	5.00
❑ 45130	I Woke Up in Love This Morning/Twenty-Four Hours a Day	1971	—	2.50	5.00
❑ 45160	It's One of Those Nights (Yes Love)/One Night Stand	1971	—	2.50	5.00
❑ 45200	Am I Losing You/If You Ever Go	1972	—	2.00	4.00
❑ 45235	Breaking Up Is Hard to Do/I'm Here, You're Here	1972	—	2.00	4.00
❑ 45301	Looking Through the Eyes of Love/Storybook Love	1972	—	2.00	4.00
❑ 45336	Friend and a Lover/Something's Wrong	1973	—	2.00	4.00
❑ 45414	Lookin' for a Good Time/Money Money	1973	—	2.00	4.00

Number	Title (A Side/B Side)	Yr	VG	VG+	NM
❑ 45414 [PS]	Lookin' for a Good Time/Money Money	1973	2.00	4.00	8.00

PASSIONS, THE (1)

Number	Title (A Side/B Side)	Yr	VG	VG+	NM
ABC-PARAMOUNT					
❑ 10436	The Bully/The Empty Seat	1963	6.25	12.50	25.00
AUDICON					
❑ 102	Just to Be with You/Oh Melancholy Me	1959	10.00	20.00	40.00
❑ 105	I Only Want You/This Is My Love	1960	7.50	15.00	30.00
—Red label					
❑ 105	I Only Want You/This Is My Love	1960	5.00	10.00	20.00
—Red, black and white label					
❑ 106	Gloria/Jungle Drums	1960	7.50	15.00	30.00
❑ 108	Beautiful Dreamer/One Look Is All It Took	1960	7.50	15.00	30.00
❑ 112	Made for Lovers/You Don't Have Me Anymore	1961	10.00	20.00	40.00
DIAMOND					
❑ 146	Sixteen Candles/The Third Floor	1963	10.00	20.00	40.00
JUBILEE					
❑ 5406	Lonely Road/One Look Is All It Took	1961	5.00	10.00	20.00
OCTAVIA					
❑ 8005	Aphrodite/I've Gotta Know	1962	200.00	400.00	800.00

PASSIONS, THE (2)

Number	Title (A Side/B Side)	Yr	VG	VG+	NM
BACK BEAT					
❑ 573	Baby I Do/Man About Town	1966	2.50	5.00	10.00
TOWER					
❑ 424	Without a Warning/Just Like a Rolling Seal	1968	2.00	4.00	8.00
❑ 443	I Can See My Way Through/Just Another Reason	1968	2.00	4.00	8.00
❑ 443	I Can See My Way Through/Without a Warning	1968	2.00	4.00	8.00
❑ 474	Just Like a Rolling Stone/Just Another	1969	2.00	4.00	8.00
❑ 485	Hijacked/Hijacked	1969	2.00	4.00	8.00

PASSIONS, THE (3)

Number	Title (A Side/B Side)	Yr	VG	VG+	NM
CAPITOL					
❑ F-3963	Jackie Brown/My Aching Heart	1958	7.50	15.00	30.00
ERA					
❑ 1063	Jackie Brown/My Aching Heart	1957	10.00	20.00	40.00

PASSIONS, THE (U)

Could be group (1) or (3), or a completely different group.

Number	Title (A Side/B Side)	Yr	VG	VG+	NM
DORE					
❑ 505	Nervous About Sally/Tango of Love	1958	7.50	15.00	30.00
TOPAZ					
❑ 1317	It Ain't Fair/I'm So Afraid	196?	2.50	5.00	10.00

PASTEL SIX, THE

Number	Title (A Side/B Side)	Yr	VG	VG+	NM
CHATTAHOOCHIE					
❑ 696	I Can't Dance/Red River Quetzal	1966	2.50	5.00	10.00
DOWNEY					
❑ 101	Twitchin'/Wino Stomp	1962	7.50	15.00	30.00
❑ 101	Twitchin'/Open House at the Cinder	1962	7.50	15.00	30.00
❑ 102	Braum's Nightmare/Open House at the Cinder	1962	6.25	12.50	25.00
ZEN					
❑ 102	The Cinnamon Cinder (It's a Very Nice Dance)/ Bandido	1962	6.25	12.50	25.00
❑ 105	Sing Along Song/The Strange Ghost	1963	6.25	12.50	25.00
❑ 108	The Milkshake/Parchman Farm	1963	6.25	12.50	25.00
❑ 111	Miss Sue/Baby Please Don't Go	1963	6.25	12.50	25.00

PASTELS, THE

Number	Title (A Side/B Side)	Yr	VG	VG+	NM
ARGO					
❑ 5287	Been So Long/My One and Only Dream	1958	6.25	12.50	25.00
❑ 5297	You Don't Love Me Anymore/Let's Go to the Rock 'N' Roll Ball	1958	7.50	15.00	30.00
❑ 5314	So Far Away/Don't Knock	1958	6.25	12.50	25.00
ARK					
❑ 298	Jungle Run/K-Nif	196?	12.50	25.00	50.00
JUBILEE					
❑ 5495	First Star/Tokyo Melody	1965	3.00	6.00	12.00
MASCOT					
❑ 123	Been So Long/My One and Only Dream	1957	75.00	150.00	300.00
UNITED					
❑ 196	Put Your Arms Around Me/Boom De De Boom	1957	20.00	40.00	80.00

PATIENCE AND PRUDENCE

Number	Title (A Side/B Side)	Yr	VG	VG+	NM
CHATATHOOCHIE					
❑ 665	Tonight You Belong to Me (New Version)/How Can I Tell Him	1965	2.50	5.00	10.00
LIBERTY					
❑ 55022	Tonight You Belong to Me/A Smile and a Ribbon	1956	7.50	15.00	30.00
❑ 55040	Gonna Get Along Without Ya Now/The Money Tree	1956	6.25	12.50	25.00
❑ 55058	Dreamer's Bay/We Can't Sing Rhythm and Blues	1957	6.25	12.50	25.00
❑ 55084	You Tattletale/Very Nice in Bali Bali	1957	6.25	12.50	25.00
❑ 55084 [PS]	You Tattletale/Very Nice in Bali Bali	1957	12.50	25.00	50.00
❑ 55107	Witchcraft/Over Here	1957	6.25	12.50	25.00
❑ 55125	Heavenly Angel/Little Wheel	1958	6.25	12.50	25.00
❑ 55154	All I Do Is Dream of You/Your Careless Love	1958	6.25	12.50	25.00
❑ 55169	Golly Oh Gee/Tom Thumb's Tune	1958	6.25	12.50	25.00
❑ 55207	Should I/Whisper Whisper	1959	3.75	7.50	15.00
—With Mike Clifford					
UNITED ARTISTS					
❑ 0012	Tonight You Belong to Me/Gonna Get Along Without You Now	1973	—	2.50	5.00
—"Silver Spotlight Series" reissue					

PATTON, JIMMY

Number	Title (A Side/B Side)	Yr	VG	VG+	NM
SAGE AND SAND					
❑ 261	Call Me/Forty-Nine Women	1958	30.00	60.00	120.00
❑ 282	Ocean Full of Tears/Twinklin' Teardrops	1959	10.00	20.00	40.00
SIMS					
❑ 103	Careful/Guilty	1955	12.50	25.00	50.00
—With Ann Jones					
❑ 104	Teenage Haert/Jalopy	1955	12.50	25.00	50.00
❑ 105	Ocean of Tears/I Don't Want It	1955	12.50	25.00	50.00
❑ 117	Okie's in the Pokie/Lonely Nights	1960	50.00	100.00	200.00
❑ 256	Can't Shake the Blues/(B-side unknown)	1965	3.00	6.00	12.00

PATTY AND THE EMBLEMS

Number	Title (A Side/B Side)	Yr	VG	VG+	NM
CONGRESS					
❑ 263	Easy Come, Easy Go/It's the Little Things	1966	5.00	10.00	20.00
HERALD					
❑ 590	Mixed-Up, Shook-Up, Girl/Ordinary Guy	1964	5.00	10.00	20.00
❑ 593	The Sound of Music Makes Me Want to Dance/ You Took Advantage of a Good Thing	1964	3.75	7.50	15.00
❑ 595	And We Danced/You Can't Get Away from Me	1964	3.75	7.50	15.00
KAPP					
❑ 791	Let Him Go Little Heart/Try It, You Won't Forget It	1966	5.00	10.00	20.00
❑ 850	Please Don't Ever Leave Me/All My Tomorrows Are Gone	1967	5.00	10.00	20.00
❑ 870	I'll Cry Later/One Man Woman	1967	5.00	10.00	20.00
❑ 897	I'm Gonna Love You a Long, Long Time/My Heart's So Full of You	1968	3.75	7.50	15.00

PATTY FLABBIE'S COUGHED ENGINE

Number	Title (A Side/B Side)	Yr	VG	VG+	NM
DIAMOND					
❑ 252	Billy Got a Goat/Tin Can Eater	1968	6.25	12.50	25.00

PAUL

See RAY HILDEBRAND.

PAUL, BILLY

Number	Title (A Side/B Side)	Yr	VG	VG+	NM
GAMBLE					
❑ 232	Somewhere/Bluesette	1968	3.00	6.00	12.00
JUBILEE					
❑ 5081	That's Why I Dream/Why Am I	1952	7.50	15.00	30.00
❑ 5086	You Didn't Know/The Stars Are Mine	1952	7.50	15.00	30.00
NEPTUNE					
❑ 30	Mrs. Robinson/Let's Fall in Love All Over	1970	2.50	5.00	10.00
PHILADELPHIA INT'L.					
❑ 3120	Jesus Boy (You Only Look Like a Man)/Love Buddies	1980	—	2.50	5.00
❑ 3509	Love Buddies/Magic Carpet Ride	1971	—	3.00	6.00
❑ 3515	This Is Your Life/I Wish It Were Yesterday	1972	—	3.00	6.00
❑ 3521	Me and Mrs. Jones/Your Song	1972	—	2.50	5.00
❑ 3526	Am I Black Enough for You/I'm Gonna Make It This Time	1973	—	2.50	5.00
❑ 3538	Thanks for Saving My Life/I Was Married	1974	—	2.50	5.00
❑ 3551	Be Truthful to Me/I Wish It Was Yesterday	1974	—	2.50	5.00
❑ 3563	Billy's Back Home/I've Got So Much to Live For	1975	—	2.50	5.00
❑ 3572	When It's Your Turn to Go/July, July, July, July	1975	—	2.50	5.00
❑ 3584	Let's Make a Baby/My Head's On Straight	1976	—	2.50	5.00
❑ 3593	People Power/I Want Cha Baby	1976	—	2.50	5.00
❑ 3613	How Good Is Your Game/I Think I'll Stay Home Today	1977	—	2.50	5.00
❑ 3621	Let 'Em In/We All Got a Mission	1977	—	2.50	5.00
❑ 3630	I Trust You/Love Won't Come Easy	1977	—	2.50	5.00
❑ 3635	Only the Strong Survive/Where I Belong	1977	—	2.50	5.00
❑ 3639	Everybody's Breakin' Up/Sooner or Later	1978	—	2.50	5.00
❑ 3645	One Man's Junk/Don't Give Up on Love	1978	—	2.50	5.00
❑ 3676	Bring the Family Back/It's Critical	1979	—	2.50	5.00
❑ 3699	False Faces/I Gotta Put This Life Down	1979	—	2.50	5.00
❑ 3736	You're My Sweetness/(B-side unknown)	1979	—	2.50	5.00

PAUL, BUNNY

Number	Title (A Side/B Side)	Yr	VG	VG+	NM
BRUNSWICK					
❑ 55003	Poor Joe/Buzz Me	1957	3.75	7.50	15.00
❑ 55022	Breedle-Lump-Bump/The One You Love	1957	3.75	7.50	15.00
DOT					
❑ 15107	Magic Guitar/Never Let Me Go	1953	6.25	12.50	25.00
ESSEX					
❑ 344	New Love/You'll Never Leave My Side	1954	25.00	50.00	100.00
❑ 352	Such a Night/I'm Gonna Have Some Fun	1954	15.00	30.00	60.00
❑ 359	Lovey Dovey/Answer the Call	1954	15.00	30.00	60.00
❑ 364	Honey Love/I'll Never Tell	1954	25.00	50.00	100.00
❑ 371	You Are Always in My Heart/You Came a Long Way from St. Louis	1954	15.00	30.00	60.00
❑ 385	Brown Jug/Pam-Poo-Dey	1955	15.00	30.00	60.00
GORDY					
❑ 7017	We're Only Young Once/I'm Hooked	1963	5.00	10.00	20.00
POINT					
❑ 5	Sweet Talk/History	1956	10.00	20.00	40.00
ROULETTE					
❑ 4186	Such a Night/A Million Miles from Nowhere	1959	3.75	7.50	15.00

PAUL, LES

See note under LES PAUL AND MARY FORD.

Number	Title (A Side/B Side)	Yr	VG	VG+	NM
DECCA					
❑ 27903	Blue Skies/Dark Eyes	1951	3.75	7.50	15.00
❑ 29013	Steel Guitar Rag/Guitar Boogie	1954	3.75	7.50	15.00
LONDON					
❑ 120	Los Angeles/The System	1969	—	3.00	6.00

PAUL, LES, AND MARY FORD

Included in the Capitol listings are LES PAUL solo works. Some of these appear on B-sides of duet hits.

Number	Title (A Side/B Side)	Yr	VG	VG+	NM
CAPITOL					
❑ F1014	Nola/Jealous	1950	5.00	10.00	20.00
❑ F1088	Dry My Tears/Cryin'	1950	5.00	10.00	20.00
❑ F1192	Goofus/Sugar Sweet	1950	5.00	10.00	20.00
❑ F1316	Tennessee Waltz/Little Rock Getaway	1950	5.00	10.00	20.00
❑ F1373	Mockin' Bird Hill/Chicken Reel	1951	5.00	10.00	20.00
❑ F1451	How High the Moon/Walkin' Whistlin' Blues	1951	6.25	12.50	25.00
❑ F1592	Josephine/I Wish I Had Never Seen Sunshine	1951	3.75	7.50	15.00

Number	Title (A Side/B Side)	Yr	VG	VG+	NM
❑ F1621	Nola/Jealous	1951	3.00	6.00	12.00
—Reissue					
❑ F1675	How High the Moon/Josephine	195?	3.00	6.00	12.00
—Reissue					
❑ F1676	Tennessee Waltz/Mockin' Bird Hill	195?	3.00	6.00	12.00
—Reissue					
❑ F1690	Meet Mister Callaghan/My Baby's Comin' Home	195?	3.00	6.00	12.00
—Reissue					
❑ F1748	The World Is Waiting for the Sunrise/Whispering	1951	3.75	7.50	15.00
❑ F1825	Just One More Chance/Jazz Me Blues	1951	3.75	7.50	15.00
❑ F1881	Jingle Bells/Silent Night	1951	3.75	7.50	15.00
❑ F1920	Tiger Rag/It's a Lonesome Old Town	1951	3.75	7.50	15.00
❑ F2080	I'm Confessin' (That I Love You)/Carioca	1952	3.75	7.50	15.00
❑ F2123	Smoke Rings/In the Good Old Summertime	1952	3.75	7.50	15.00
❑ F2193	Meet Mister Callaghan/Take Me in Your Arms and Hold Me	1952	3.75	7.50	15.00
❑ F2265	My Baby's Coming Home/Lady of Spain	1952	3.75	7.50	15.00
❑ F2316	Bye Bye Blues/Mammy's Boogie	1953	3.75	7.50	15.00
❑ F2400	I'm Sitting on Top of the World/Sleep	1953	3.75	7.50	15.00
❑ F2486	Vaya Con Dios (May God Be With You)/Johnny (Is the Boy for Me)	1953	3.75	7.50	15.00
❑ F2614	Don'cha Hear Them Bells/The Kangaroo	1953	3.75	7.50	15.00
❑ F2617	Jungle Bells (Dingo-Dango-Day)/White Christmas	1953	3.75	7.50	15.00
❑ F2735	I Really Don't Want to Know/South	1954	3.00	6.00	12.00
❑ F2839	I'm a Fool to Care/Auctioneer	1954	3.00	6.00	12.00
❑ F2928	Whither Thou Goest/Mandolino	1954	3.00	6.00	12.00
❑ F3015	Someday Sweetheart/Song in Blue	1955	3.00	6.00	12.00
❑ F3108	No Letter Today/Genuine Love	1955	3.00	6.00	12.00
❑ F3165	Hummingbird/Goodbye My Love	1955	3.00	6.00	12.00
❑ F3248	Amukiriki (The Lord Willing)/Magic Melody	1955	3.00	6.00	12.00
❑ F3301	Texas Lady/Alabamy Bound	1955	3.00	6.00	12.00
❑ F3302	Rudolph the Red-Nosed Reindeer/Santa Claus Is Comin' to Town	1955	3.00	6.00	12.00
❑ F3329	Moritat (Theme from Threepenny Opera)/Nuevo Laredo	1956	2.50	5.00	10.00
❑ F3389	Say the Words I Love to Hear/Send Me Some Money	1956	2.50	5.00	10.00
❑ F3444	Cimarron/San Antonio Rose	1956	2.50	5.00	10.00
❑ F3570	Blow the Smoke Away/Running Wild	1956	2.50	5.00	10.00
❑ F3612	Cinco Robles (Five Oaks)/Ro-Ro-Robinson	1957	2.50	5.00	10.00
❑ F3725	Tuxedos and Flowers/Hummin' and Waltzin'	1957	2.50	5.00	10.00
❑ F3776	I Don't Want You No More/Strollin' Blues	1957	2.50	5.00	10.00
❑ F3825	A Pair of Fools/Fire	1957	2.50	5.00	10.00
❑ F3858	Goodnight My Someone/The Night of the Fourth	1957	2.50	5.00	10.00
❑ F3934	More and More Each Day/A Small Island	1958	2.50	5.00	10.00

COLUMBIA

Number	Title (A Side/B Side)	Yr	VG	VG+	NM
❑ 31385 [S]	'Deed I Do/Makin' Whoopee!	1962	3.00	6.00	12.00
—"Stereo Seven" jukebox single, part of set JS7-52					
❑ 31386 [S]	A Cottage for Sale/Chasing Shadows	1962	3.00	6.00	12.00
—"Stereo Seven" jukebox single, part of set JS7-52					
❑ 31387 [S]	It's Been a Long, Long Time/After You've Gone	1962	3.00	6.00	12.00
—"Stereo Seven" jukebox single, part of set JS7-52					
❑ 31388 [S]	Am I Blue/You Brought a New Kind of Love to Me	1962	3.00	6.00	12.00
—"Stereo Seven" jukebox single, part of set JS7-52					
❑ 31389 [S]	(titles unknown)	1962	3.00	6.00	12.00
—"Stereo Seven" jukebox single, part of set JS7-52					
❑ 41222	Put a Ring on My Finger/Fantasy	1958	2.50	5.00	10.00
❑ 41222 [PS]	Put a Ring on My Finger/Fantasy	1958	3.75	7.50	15.00
❑ 41278	Jealous Heart/Big Eyed Gal	1958	2.50	5.00	10.00
❑ 41350	All I Need Is You/At the Save-a-Penny Super Store	1959	2.50	5.00	10.00
❑ 41592	The Poor People of Paris/All Night Long	1960	2.00	4.00	8.00
❑ 41660	Wonderful Rain/Take a Warning	1960	2.00	4.00	8.00
❑ 41994	Jura (I Swear I Love You)/It's Been a Long, Long Time	1961	2.00	4.00	8.00
❑ 41994 [PS]	Jura (I Swear I Love You)/It's Been a Long, Long Time	1961	3.00	6.00	12.00
❑ 42179	It's Too Late/Mountain Railroad	1961	2.00	4.00	8.00
❑ 42241	Goodnight Irene/Lonely Guitar	1961	2.00	4.00	8.00
❑ 42241 [PS]	Goodnight Irene/Lonely Guitar	1961	3.00	6.00	12.00
❑ 42419	Your Cheatin' Heart/Another Town, Another Time	1962	2.00	4.00	8.00
❑ 42419 [PS]	Your Cheatin' Heart/Another Town, Another Time	1962	3.00	6.00	12.00
❑ 42602	Playing Make Believe/I Just Don't Understand	1962	2.00	4.00	8.00
❑ 42602 [PS]	Playing Make Believe/I Just Don't Understand	1962	3.00	6.00	12.00
❑ 42754	Gentle Is Your Love/Move Along Baby (Don't Waste My Time)	1963	2.00	4.00	8.00
❑ 42754 [PS]	Gentle Is Your Love/Move Along Baby (Don't Waste My Time)	1963	3.00	6.00	12.00

7-Inch Extended Plays

CAPITOL

Number	Title (A Side/B Side)	Yr	VG	VG+	NM
❑ EAP 1-416	How High the Moon//Josephine//Mockin' Bird Hill//Whispering	195?	5.00	10.00	20.00
❑ EAP 1-416 [PS]	The Hit Makers, Volume 1	195?	5.00	10.00	20.00
❑ EAP 2-416	(contents unknown)	195?	5.00	10.00	20.00
❑ EAP 2-416 [PS]	The Hit Makers, Volume 2	195?	5.00	10.00	20.00
❑ EAP 3-416	(contents unknown)	195?	5.00	10.00	20.00
❑ EAP 3-416 [PS]	The Hit Makers, Volume 3	195?	5.00	10.00	20.00
❑ EAP 1-495	Vaya Con Dios (May God Be With You)/Sleep//Lady of Spain/My Baby's Comin' Home	195?	5.00	10.00	20.00
❑ EAP 1-495 [PS]	Vaya Con Dios	195?	5.00	10.00	20.00
❑ EAP 1-540	I'm Sitting on Top of the World/South//Smoke Rings/Jazz Me Blues	195?	5.00	10.00	20.00
❑ EAP 1-540 [PS]	Sitting on Top of the World	195?	5.00	10.00	20.00
❑ EAP 1-543	Jingle Bells/White Christmas//Santa Claus Is Comin' to Town/Silent Night	195?	5.00	10.00	20.00
❑ EAP 1-543 [PS]	Christmas Cheer	195?	5.00	10.00	20.00
❑ EAP 1-554	I'm a Fool to Care/I Really Don't Want to Know//Auctioneer/It's a Lonesome Old Town	1956	3.75	7.50	15.00
❑ EAP 1-554 [PS]	I'm a Fool to Care	1956	3.75	7.50	15.00
❑ EAP 1-559	Whither Thou Goest/Nola//Take Me in Your Arms and Hold Me/Mandolino	1955	5.00	10.00	20.00
❑ EAP 1-559 [PS]	Whither Thou Goest	1955	5.00	10.00	20.00
❑ EAP 1-577	(contents unknown)	195?	3.75	7.50	15.00
❑ EAP 1-577 [PS]	Les & Mary, Volume 1	195?	3.75	7.50	15.00
❑ EAP 2-577	(contents unknown)	195?	3.75	7.50	15.00
❑ EAP 2-577 [PS]	Les & Mary, Volume 2	195?	3.75	7.50	15.00
❑ EAP 3-577	(contents unknown)	195?	3.75	7.50	15.00
❑ EAP 3-577 [PS]	Les & Mary, Volume 3	195?	3.75	7.50	15.00
❑ EAP 1-599	(contents unknown)	195?	3.75	7.50	15.00
❑ EAP 1-599 [PS]	Whither Thou Goest	195?	3.75	7.50	15.00
❑ EAP 1-695	(contents unknown)	195?	3.75	7.50	15.00
❑ EAP 1-695 [PS]	Songs for Today	195?	3.75	7.50	15.00
❑ EAP 1-802	(contents unknown)	1956	3.75	7.50	15.00
❑ EAP 1-802 [PS]	Time to Dream, Volume 1	1956	3.75	7.50	15.00
❑ EAP 2-802	(contents unknown)	1956	3.75	7.50	15.00
❑ EAP 2-802 [PS]	Time to Dream, Volume 2	1956	3.75	7.50	15.00
❑ EAP 3-802	(contents unknown)	1956	3.75	7.50	15.00
❑ EAP 3-802 [PS]	Time to Dream, Volume 3	1956	3.75	7.50	15.00
❑ EAP 1-9121	Mister Sandman/That's What I Like//I Need You Now/The Things I Didn't Do	1955	3.75	7.50	15.00
❑ EAP 1-9121 [PS]	Les Paul and Mary Ford	1955	3.75	7.50	15.00

PAUL AND PAULA

Also see RAY HILDEBRAND; JILL JACKSON.

LE CAM

Number	Title (A Side/B Side)	Yr	VG	VG+	NM
❑ 99	The Beginning of Love/All I Want Is You	1963	5.00	10.00	20.00
❑ 305	From the Top of the World/All I Want Is You	197?	—	2.00	4.00
—As "Jill and Ray"					
❑ 315	Hey Paula ('77 Disco)/(Instrumental)	1977	—	2.00	4.00
❑ 321	Hey Paula/Paula (My Love)	1978	—	2.00	4.00
—Reissued in 1982 with the same catalog number					
❑ 354	Hey Paula/Elmer's Tune	198?	—	2.00	4.00
❑ 979	Hey Paula/Bobbie Is the One	1962	12.50	25.00	50.00
—As "Jill and Ray"					

PHILIPS

Number	Title (A Side/B Side)	Yr	VG	VG+	NM
❑ 40084	Hey Paula/Bobby Is the One	1962	3.75	7.50	15.00
❑ 40096	Young Lovers/Ba-Hey-Be	1963	3.00	6.00	12.00
❑ 40096 [PS]	Young Lovers/Ba-Hey-Be	1963	5.00	10.00	20.00
❑ 40114	First Quarrel/School Is Thru	1963	3.00	6.00	12.00
❑ 40114 [PS]	First Quarrel/School Is Thru	1963	5.00	10.00	20.00
❑ 40130	Something Old, Something New/Flipped Over You	1963	3.00	6.00	12.00
❑ 40142	First Day Back at School/A Perfect Pair	1963	3.00	6.00	12.00
❑ 40158	Holiday for Teens/Holiday Hootenanny	1963	3.00	6.00	12.00
❑ 40168	We'll Never Break Up for Good/Crazy Little Things	1964	2.50	5.00	10.00
❑ 40209	The Young Years/Darlin'	1964	2.50	5.00	10.00
❑ 40234	No Other Baby/Too Dark to See	1964	2.50	5.00	10.00
❑ 40268	True Love/Any Way You Want Me	1965	2.00	4.00	8.00
❑ 40296	Dear Paula/All the Love	1965	2.00	4.00	8.00
❑ 40352	All I Want Is You/The Beginning of Love	1966	2.50	5.00	10.00

UNI

Number	Title (A Side/B Side)	Yr	VG	VG+	NM
❑ 55052	All These Things/Wedding	1968	2.00	4.00	8.00

UNITED ARTISTS

Number	Title (A Side/B Side)	Yr	VG	VG+	NM
❑ 50712	Moments Like These/Mrs. Bean	1970	—	3.00	6.00

PAULA, MARLENA

REGENT

Number	Title (A Side/B Side)	Yr	VG	VG+	NM
❑ 7506	I Wanna Spend Christmas with Elvis/Once More It's Christmas	1956	12.50	25.00	50.00

PAULSON, BUTCH

VIRGELLE

Number	Title (A Side/B Side)	Yr	VG	VG+	NM
❑ 708	Man from Mars/My Own Brother	195?	25.00	50.00	100.00
❑ 718	Candy Lou/Today Was Blue Tomorrow	195?	12.50	25.00	50.00

PAVLOV'S DOG

ABC

Number	Title (A Side/B Side)	Yr	VG	VG+	NM
❑ 12086	Episode/Julia	1975	2.50	5.00	10.00

PAXTON, GARY

Also see THE HOLLYWOOD ARGYLES; THE PLEDGES; SKIP AND FLIP.

CAPITOL

Number	Title (A Side/B Side)	Yr	VG	VG+	NM
❑ 5467	My Heart Won't Let My Lips Say Goodbye/It's My Way (Of Lovin' You)	1965	3.75	7.50	15.00
❑ 5707	Goin' Through the Motions/You Got to Do the Best You Can	1966	3.75	7.50	15.00
❑ 5975	Mother-in-Law/Miles and Cities	1967	3.75	7.50	15.00

FELSTED

Number	Title (A Side/B Side)	Yr	VG	VG+	NM
❑ 8691	Sweet Senorita from Santa Fe/Kansas City	1964	5.00	10.00	20.00

GARPAX

Number	Title (A Side/B Side)	Yr	VG	VG+	NM
❑ 44172	It Had to Be You/We're Going Back Together	1963	5.00	10.00	20.00
❑ 44177	The Scavenger/How to Be a Fool (In Six Easy Lessons)	1963	5.00	10.00	20.00
❑ 44180	Two Duel Bump Camel Named Robert E. Lee/Your Past Is Back Again	1964	5.00	10.00	20.00

LIBERTY

Number	Title (A Side/B Side)	Yr	VG	VG+	NM
❑ 55407	Teen Age Crush/It's So Funny I Could Cry	1962	5.00	10.00	20.00
❑ 55485	Stop Twistin' Baby/Alley Oop Was a Two Dab Man	1962	5.00	10.00	20.00
❑ 55584	Spooky Movies (Part 1)/Spooky Movies (Part 2)	1963	5.00	10.00	20.00

LONDON

Number	Title (A Side/B Side)	Yr	VG	VG+	NM
❑ 5208	Super Torque/Cute Little Coly	1964	5.00	10.00	20.00

LUTE

Number	Title (A Side/B Side)	Yr	VG	VG+	NM
❑ 5801	You're Ruinin' My Gladness/The Way I See It	1960	5.00	10.00	20.00

MGM

Number	Title (A Side/B Side)	Yr	VG	VG+	NM
❑ 14306	Carin' for Karen/Out on a Limb	1971	—	3.00	6.00
❑ 14362	Rocky Top/Parchman Farm	1972	—	3.00	6.00

PAX

Number	Title (A Side/B Side)	Yr	VG	VG+	NM
❑ 2406	The Big A/The Big M	197?	—	3.00	6.00
—Red vinyl					

PRIVATE STOCK

Number	Title (A Side/B Side)	Yr	VG	VG+	NM
❑ 45007	The Clone Affair/(B-side unknown)	1975	—	2.50	5.00

Number	Title (A Side/B Side)	Yr	VG	VG+	NM
RCA VICTOR					
❑ APBO-0081	It's Hard to Be a Rock and Roll Star When You're Old and Fat/White Tornado Alias Gary S. Paxton	1973	—	2.50	5.00
❑ PB-10449	Too Far Gone (To Care What You Do to Me)/Freedom Lives in a Country Song	1975	—	2.50	5.00
❑ 74-0916	Shadow of Your Memory/This Little Light of Mine	1973	—	2.50	5.00

PAYCHECK, JOHNNY

Also includes records made under his original alter ego, "Donny Young." Also see GEORGE JONES.

Number	Title (A Side/B Side)	Yr	VG	VG+	NM
AMI					
❑ 1322	I Never Got Over You/Ole Pay Ain't Checked Out Yet	1984	—	2.50	5.00
❑ 1323	You're Every Step I Take/I Can't Stop Drinking	1985	—	2.50	5.00
❑ 1327	Everything Is Changing/Palimony	1985	—	2.50	5.00
CERTRON					
❑ 10003	Forever Ended Yesterday/It's For Sure I Can't Go On	1970	2.00	4.00	8.00
DAMASCUS					
❑ 2001	Scars/(B-side unknown)	1989	—	3.00	6.00
DECCA					
❑ 9-30763	On This Mountaintop/It's Been a Long, Long Time for Me	1958	7.50	15.00	30.00
—A-side as "Donny Young and Roger Miller"; B-side as "Donny Young"					
❑ 9-30881	The Old Man and the River/Pictures Can't Talk Back	1959	6.25	12.50	25.00
—As "Donny Young"					
❑ 31077	Shakin' the Blues/Miracle of Love	1960	10.00	20.00	40.00
—As "Donny Young"					
❑ 31283	Go Ring the Bells/I Guess I Had It Coming	1961	6.25	12.50	25.00
—As "Donny Young"					
DESPERADO					
❑ 1001	Out of Beer/Oklahoma Lady	1988	—	3.00	6.00
EPIC					
❑ 19-02144	Yesterday's News (Just Hit Home Today)/Someone Told My Story	1981	—	2.00	4.00
❑ 14-02684	The Highlight of '81/Sharon Rae	1982	—	2.00	4.00
❑ 14-02817	No Way Out/We've All Gone Crazy	1982	—	2.00	4.00
❑ 14-03052	D.O.A. (Drunk On Arrival)/Gonna Get Right (And Do Something Wrong)	1982	—	2.00	4.00
❑ 5-10783	She's All I Got/You Touched	1971	—	3.50	7.00
❑ 5-10836	Someone to Give My Love To/Love Sure Is Beautiful	1972	—	3.50	7.00
❑ 5-10876	Love Is a Good Thing/High on the Thought of You	1972	—	3.50	7.00
❑ 5-10912	Somebody Loves Me/Without You	1972	—	3.50	7.00
❑ 5-10947	Something About You I Love/Your Love Is the Key to It All	1973	—	3.00	6.00
❑ 5-10999	Mr. Lovemaker/Once You've Had the Best	1973	—	3.00	6.00
❑ 5-11046	Song and Dance Man/Love Is a Strange and Wonderful Thing	1973	—	3.00	6.00
❑ 5-11090	My Part of Forever/If Love Gets Any Better	1974	—	3.00	6.00
❑ 5-11142	Keep On Lovin' Me/The Ballad of Thunder Road	1974	—	3.00	6.00
❑ 8-50040	For a Minute There/She's All I Live For	1974	—	3.00	6.00
❑ 8-50073	Loving You Beats All I've Ever Seen/Touch of the Master's Hand	1975	—	3.00	6.00
❑ 8-50111	I Didn't Love Her Anymore/Loving Her Is All I Thought It Would Be	1975	—	3.00	6.00
❑ 8-50146	All-American Man/The Fool Strikes Again	1975	—	3.00	6.00
❑ 8-50193	The Feminine Touch/Rhythm Guitar	1976	—	3.00	6.00
❑ 8-50215	Gone at Last/Live with Me	1976	—	3.00	6.00
❑ 8-50249	11 Months and 29 Days/Live with Me (Till I Can Learn to Live Again)	1976	—	3.00	6.00
❑ 8-50291	I Can See Me Lovin' You Again/I Sleep with Her Memory Every Night	1976	—	3.00	6.00
❑ 8-50334	Slide Off of Your Satin Sheets/That's What the Outlaws in Texas Want to Hear	1977	—	3.00	6.00
❑ 8-50391	I'm the Only Hell (Mama Ever Raised)/She's Still Lookin' Good	1977	—	3.00	6.00
❑ 8-50469	Take This Job and Shove It/Colorado Kool-Aid	1977	2.00	4.00	8.00
❑ 8-50539	Georgia in a Jug/Me and the I.R.S.	1978	—	3.00	6.00
❑ 8-50621	Friend, Lover, Wife/Leave It to Me	1978	—	3.00	6.00
❑ 8-50655	The Outlaw's Prayer/Armed and Crazy	1979	—	3.00	6.00
❑ 9-50777	(Stay Away From) The Cocaine Train/Billy Bardo	1979	—	2.50	5.00
❑ 9-50818	Drinkin' and Drivin'/Just Makin' Love Don't Make It Love	1979	—	2.50	5.00
❑ 9-50863	Fifteen Beers/Who Was That Man Who Beat Me So	1980	—	2.50	5.00
❑ 9-50923	In Memory of a Memory/New York Town	1980	—	2.50	5.00
HILLTOP					
❑ 3002	Don't Start Countin' on Me/I'd Rather Be Your Fool	1964	5.00	10.00	20.00
❑ 3006	For Those Who Think Young/The Girl They Talk About	1965	3.75	7.50	15.00
❑ 3007	A-11/Where (In the World)	1965	3.75	7.50	15.00
❑ 3009	Heartbreak Tennessee/Help Me Hank, I'm Fallin'	1966	3.75	7.50	15.00
❑ 3015	I'm Barely Hangin' On to Me/The Real Mr. Heartache	1966	3.75	7.50	15.00
LITTLE DARLIN'					
❑ 008	The Lovin' Machine/Pride Covered Ears	1966	2.50	5.00	10.00
❑ 0011	The Ballad of the Green Berets/A Dying Hero	1966	2.50	5.00	10.00
❑ 0014	Right Back Where We Parted/The Way Things Were Going	1966	2.50	5.00	10.00
—With Micki Evans					
❑ 0016	Motel Time Again/If You Should Come Back Today	1966	2.50	5.00	10.00
❑ 0020	Jukebox Charlie/Something in Your World	1967	2.50	5.00	10.00
❑ 0032	The Cave/Then Love Dies	1967	2.50	5.00	10.00
❑ 0035	Don't Monkey with Another Monkey's Monkey/You'll Recover in Time	1967	2.50	5.00	10.00
❑ 0042	(It Won't Be Long) And I'll Be Hating You/Fools Hall of Fame	1968	2.50	5.00	10.00
❑ 0043	The Old Year Is Gone/According to the Bible	1968	2.50	5.00	10.00
❑ 0046	My Heart Keeps Running to You/Yesterday, Today and Tomorrow	1968	2.50	5.00	10.00
❑ 0052	If I'm Gonna Sink/The Loser	1968	2.50	5.00	10.00
❑ 0055	Jingle Bells/The Old Year Is Gone	1968	2.50	5.00	10.00
❑ 0057	My World of Memories/(B-side unknown)	1969	2.50	5.00	10.00
❑ 0060	Wherever You Are/I Can't Promise You Won't Get Lonely	1969	2.50	5.00	10.00
❑ 0072	Wildfire/Basin Street Mama	1969	2.50	5.00	10.00
❑ 7804	It Won't Be Long/If I'm Gonna Sink (Might As Well Go to the Bottom)	1978	—	3.00	6.00
❑ 7808	Down on the Corner at a Bar Named Kelly's/Something He'll Have to Learn	1978	—	3.00	6.00
❑ 7810	I'll Place My Order Early/The Old Year Is Gone	1978	—	3.00	6.00
❑ 7918	California Dreams/The Loser	1979	—	3.00	6.00
❑ 7923	Gentle on My Mind/Everything You Touch Turns to Hurt	1979	—	3.00	6.00
MERCURY					
❑ 71900	On Second Thought/One Day a Week	1962	5.00	10.00	20.00
—As "Donny Young"					
❑ 71981	Not Much I Don't/I'd Come Back to Me	1962	5.00	10.00	20.00
—As "Donny Young"					
❑ 884720-7	Old Violin/Comin' Home to Baby	1986	—	2.00	4.00
❑ 888088-7	Don't Bury Me 'Til I'm Ready/Ex-Wives and Lovers	1986	—	2.00	4.00
❑ 888341-7	Come to Me/Ragtime Redneck	1987	—	2.00	4.00
❑ 888651-7	I Grow Old Too Fast (And Smart Too Slow)/Caught Between a Rock and a Soft Place	1987	—	2.00	4.00
❑ 888925-7	Modern Times/She Don't Love Me All the Time	1987	—	2.00	4.00
TODD					
❑ 1098	Don't You Get Lonesome Without Me/I'm Glad to Have Her Back Again	1964	5.00	10.00	20.00
—As "Donny Young"					

PAYCHECK, JOHNNY, AND MERLE HAGGARD

Also see each artist's individual listings.

Number	Title (A Side/B Side)	Yr	VG	VG+	NM
EPIC					
❑ 19-51012	I Can't Hold Myself in Line/Carolyn	1981	—	2.00	4.00

PAYNE, FREDA

Number	Title (A Side/B Side)	Yr	VG	VG+	NM
ABC					
❑ 12079	Shadows on the Wall/I Get Carried Away	1975	—	2.50	5.00
❑ 12139	Lost in Love/You	1975	—	2.50	5.00
ABC-PARAMOUNT					
❑ 10366	Desafinado/He Who Laughs Last	1962	5.00	10.00	20.00
❑ 10437	Pretty Baby/Grin and Bear It	1963	5.00	10.00	20.00
ABC DUNHILL					
❑ 15018	It's Yours to Have/Run for Life	1974	—	2.50	5.00
CAPITOL					
❑ 4383	I Can't Live on a Memory/I Get High (On Your Memory)	1976	—	2.50	5.00
❑ 4431	Baby, You've Got What It Takes/Bring Back the Joy	1977	—	2.50	5.00
❑ 4494	Love Magnet/Loving You Means So Much to Me	1977	—	2.50	5.00
❑ 4537	Feed Me Your Love/Stares and Whispers	1978	—	2.50	5.00
❑ 4631	Happy Days Are Here Again-Happy Music (Dance the Night Away)/Falling in Love	1978	—	2.50	5.00
❑ 4695	I'll Do Anything for You (Part 1)/I'll Do Anything for You (Part 2)	1979	—	2.50	5.00
❑ 4775	Red Hot/Longest Night	1979	—	2.50	5.00
❑ 4805	Can't Wait/Longest Night	1979	—	2.50	5.00
IMPULSE!					
❑ 221	It's Time/Sweet September	1963	5.00	10.00	20.00
INVICTUS					
❑ 1255	Two Wrongs Don't Make a Right/We've Gotta Find a Way Back to Love	1973	—	3.00	6.00
❑ 1257	For No Reason/Mother Misery's Favorite Child	1973	—	3.00	6.00
❑ 9073	The Unhooked Generation/Easiest Way to Fall	1969	—	3.00	6.00
❑ 9075	Band of Gold/Easiest Way to Fall	1970	—	3.00	6.00
❑ 9080	Deeper and Deeper/The Unhooked Genration	1970	—	3.00	6.00
❑ 9085	Cherish What Is Dear to You (While It Is Near to You)/They Don't Owe Me a Thing	1971	—	3.00	6.00
❑ 9085 [PS]	Cherish What Is Dear to You (While It Is Near to You)/They Don't Owe Me a Thing	1971	2.50	5.00	10.00
❑ 9092	Bring the Boys Home/I Shall Not Be Moved	1971	—	3.00	6.00
❑ 9100	You Brought the Joy/Suddenly It's Yesterday	1971	—	3.00	6.00
❑ 9109	I'm Not Getting Any Better/The Road We Didn't Take	1972	—	3.00	6.00
❑ 9128	She's in My Life/Through the Memory of My Mind	1972	—	3.00	6.00
MGM					
❑ 13509	You've Lost That Lovin' Feelin'/Sad Sad September	1966	5.00	10.00	20.00
SUTRA					
❑ 117	In Motion/(Instrumental)	1982	—	2.50	5.00

PEACHEROOS, THE

Number	Title (A Side/B Side)	Yr	VG	VG+	NM
EXCELLO					
❑ 2044	Be-Bop Baby/Everyday My Love Is True	1954	100.00	200.00	400.00

PEACHES AND HERB

Herb Fame with at least three different female singers who were "Peaches."

Number	Title (A Side/B Side)	Yr	VG	VG+	NM
COLUMBIA					
❑ 03872	Remember/Come to Me	1983	—	2.00	4.00
❑ 04081	In My World/Keep On Smiling	1983	—	2.00	4.00
❑ 45386	The Sound of Silence/The Two of Us	1971	—	2.50	5.00
❑ 45554	God Save This World/I Can't Forget the One I Love	1972	—	2.50	5.00
DATE					
❑ 1523	Let's Fall in Love/We're In This Thing Together	1966	2.50	5.00	10.00
❑ 1549	Close Your Eyes/I Will Watch Over You	1967	2.50	5.00	10.00
❑ 1549 [PS]	Close Your Eyes/I Will Watch Over You	1967	3.75	7.50	15.00
❑ 1555	Cupid-Venus/Darling, How Long	1967	3.75	7.50	15.00
❑ 1563	For Your Love/I Need Your Love So Desperately	1967	2.50	5.00	10.00

Number	Title (A Side/B Side)	Yr	VG	VG+	NM
❑ 1563 [PS]	For Your Love/I Need Your Love So Desperately	1967	3.75	7.50	15.00
❑ 1574	Love Is Strange/It's True I Love You	1967	2.50	5.00	10.00
❑ 1574 [PS]	Love Is Strange/It's True I Love You	1967	3.75	7.50	15.00
❑ 1586	Two Little Kids/We've Got to Love One Another	1967	2.00	4.00	8.00
❑ 1592	The Ten Commandments of Love/What a Lovely Way (To Say Goodnight)	1968	2.00	4.00	8.00
❑ 1603	United/Thank You	1968	2.00	4.00	8.00
❑ 1603 [PS]	United/Thank You	1968	3.75	7.50	15.00
❑ 1623	Let's Make a Promise/Me and You	1968	2.00	4.00	8.00
❑ 1623 [PS]	Let's Make a Promise/Me and You	1968	3.75	7.50	15.00
❑ 1633	We've Got to Love One Another/So True	1968	2.50	5.00	10.00
❑ 1637	When He Touches Me (Nothing Else Matters)/Thank You	1969	2.00	4.00	8.00
❑ 1649	Let Me Be the One/I Need Your Love So Desperately	1969	2.00	4.00	8.00
❑ 1655	Cupid/Darling, How Long	1969	2.00	4.00	8.00
❑ 1669	It's Just a Game, Love/Satisfy My Hunger	1970	2.00	4.00	8.00
❑ 1676	Soothe Me with Your Love/We're So Much in Love	1970	2.00	4.00	8.00
MCA					
❑ 40701	We're Still Together/Love Is Here Beside Us	1977	—	2.50	5.00
❑ 40782	It Will Never Be the Same Again/I'm Counting on You	1977	—	2.50	5.00
MERCURY					
❑ 73350	Keep It Coming/I'm a-Hurtin' Inside	1973	—	2.50	5.00
❑ 73388	Can't It Wait/Thank Heaven for You	1973	—	2.50	5.00
POLYDOR					
❑ 2031	Roller-Skatin' Mate (Part 1)/Roller-Skatin' Mate (Part 2)	1979	—	2.00	4.00
❑ 2053	I Pledge My Love/(I Want Us) Back Together	1980	—	2.00	4.00
❑ 2115	Funtime (Part 1)/Funtime (Part 2)	1980	—	2.00	4.00
❑ 2140	One Child of Love/Hearsay	1980	—	2.00	4.00
❑ 2157	Surrender/Love Stealers	1981	—	2.00	4.00
❑ 2178	Freeway/Pickin' Up the Pieces	1981	—	2.00	4.00
❑ 2187	Bluer Than Blue/Go with the Flow	1981	—	2.00	4.00
❑ 14514	Shake Your Groove Thing/All Your Love (Get It Here)	1978	—	2.00	4.00
❑ 14547	Reunited/Easy as Pie	1979	—	2.00	4.00
❑ 14577	We've Got Love/Four's a Traffic Jam	1979	—	2.00	4.00
PEANUT BUTTER CONSPIRACY, THE					
CHALLENGE					
❑ 500	Back in L.A./Have a Little Faith	1969	2.00	4.00	8.00
❑ 500 [PS]	Back in L.A./Have a Little Faith	1969	12.50	25.00	50.00
COLUMBIA					
❑ 43985	It's a Happening Thing/Twice Is Life	1967	2.50	5.00	10.00
❑ 43985 [PS]	It's a Happening Thing/Twice Is Life	1967	10.00	20.00	40.00
❑ 44063	Then Came Love/Dark on You Now	1967	2.00	4.00	0.00
❑ 44356	Turn On a Friend (To the Good Life)/Captain Sandwich	1967	2.00	4.00	8.00
❑ 44667	I'm a Fool/It's So Hard	1968	2.00	4.00	8.00
VAULT					
❑ 933	Time Is After You/Floating Dream	1966	3.75	7.50	15.00
PEARL JAM					
EPIC					
❑ ES7 3857 [DJ]	Happy When I'm Crying/Live for Today	1997	2.50	5.00	10.00
—B-side by R.E.M.					
❑ ES7 3857 [PS]	Happy When I'm Crying/Live for Today	1997	2.50	5.00	10.00
—1997 fan club single					
❑ ZS7 4906 [DJ]	Sonic Reducer/Ramblings Continued	1992	5.00	10.00	20.00
❑ ZS7 4906 [PS]	Sonic Reducer/Ramblings Continued	1992	5.00	10.00	20.00
—Picture sleeve front states "Who Killed Rudolph?"; 1992 fan-club single					
❑ ZS7 5610 [DJ]	Angel/Ramblings	1993	5.00	10.00	20.00
❑ ZS7 5610 [PS]	Angel/Ramblings	1993	5.00	10.00	20.00
—1993 fan-club single					
❑ ZSS 7628-1 [DJ]	History Never Repeats/Sonic Reducer	1995	3.75	7.50	15.00
❑ ZSS 7628-2 [DJ]	Swallow My Pride/My Way	1995	3.75	7.50	15.00
—The above two were in the same sleeve (below)					
❑ ZSS 7628 [PS]	History Never Repeats/Sonic Reducer//Swallow My Pride/My Way	1995	3.75	7.50	15.00
—1995 fan club double single (there was no 1994 fan club release)					
❑ ES7 9358 [DJ]	Olympic Platinum/Smile	1996	3.75	7.50	15.00
❑ ES7 9358 [PS]	Olympic Platinum/Smile	1996	3.75	7.50	15.00
—1996 fan club single					
❑ ES7 16450 [DJ]	Crown of Thorns/Can't Help Falling in Love with You	2000	3.75	7.50	15.00
❑ ES7 16450 [PS]	Crown of Thorns/Can't Help Falling in Love with You	2000	3.75	7.50	15.00
—2000 fan club single					
❑ ES7 41700 [DJ]	Soldier of Love/Last Kiss	1998	3.75	7.50	15.00
❑ ES7 41700 [PS]	Soldier of Love/Last Kiss	1998	3.75	7.50	15.00
—1998 fan club single					
❑ ES7 49997 [DJ]	Strangest Tribe/Drifting	1999	2.50	5.00	10.00
❑ ES7 49997 [PS]	Strangest Tribe/Drifting	1999	2.50	5.00	10.00
—1999 fan club single					
❑ 74745	Jeremy/Alive	1995	—	2.00	4.00
—Gray-label reissue with Collectables logo					
❑ 74745	Jeremy/Alive	1997	—	—	3.00
—Dark-blue label reissue					
❑ 77771	Spin the Black Circle/Tremor Christ	1994	—	—	3.00
❑ 77771 [PS]	Spin the Black Circle/Tremor Christ	1994	—	—	3.00
❑ 77772	Not for You/Out of My Mind	1995	—	—	3.00
❑ 77772 [PS]	Not for You/Out of My Mind	1995	—	—	3.00
❑ 77873	Immortality/Rearviewmirror	1995	—	—	3.00
—B-side by The Frogs					
❑ 77873 [PS]	Immortality/Rearviewmirror	1995	—	—	3.00
❑ 78199	I Got ID/Long Road	1995	—	—	2.50
❑ 78199 [PS]	I Got ID/Long Road	1995	—	—	2.50
—"Merkinball" cardboard sleeve					
❑ 78389	Who You Are/Habit	1996	—	—	2.50
❑ 78389 [PS]	Who You Are/Habit	1996	—	—	2.50
❑ 78491	Off He Goes/Dead Man	1996	—	—	2.50
❑ 78491 [PS]	Off He Goes/Dead Man	1996	—	—	2.50
❑ 78797	Given to Fly//Pilate/Leatherman	1997	—	—	2.00
❑ 78797 [PS]	Given to Fly//Pilate/Leatherman	1997	—	—	2.00
❑ 78896	Wishlist//U/Brain of J	1998	—	—	2.00
❑ 78896 [PS]	Wishlist//U/Brain of J	1998	—	—	2.00
EPIC ASSOCIATED					
❑ ZS7 4354 [DJ]	Let Me Sleep (Christmas Time)/Ramblings	1991	12.50	25.00	50.00
—Small hole, plays at 33 1-3 RPM					
❑ ZS7 4354 [PS]	Let Me Sleep (Christmas Time)/Ramblings	1991	12.50	25.00	50.00
—1991 fan-club single and by far the rarest					
❑ 74745	Jeremy/Alive	1992	5.00	10.00	20.00
—White label; deleted upon release, then briefly available again in 1995					
R.E.M. FAN CLUB					
❑ REM 97 [DJ]	Happy When I'm Crying/Live for Today	1997	3.75	7.50	15.00
—B-side by R.E.M.					
❑ REM 97 [PS]	Happy When I'm Crying/Live for Today	1997	3.75	7.50	15.00
—1997 R.E.M. fan club single					
PEARLS, THE (1)					
AMBER					
❑ 2003	I Cried/It Must Be Love	1961	125.00	250.00	500.00
—Originals have matrix muber stamped into trail-off wax					
PEARLS, THE (2)					
ATCO					
❑ 6057	Shadows of Love/Yum Yummy	1956	7.50	15.00	30.00
❑ 6066	Bells of Love/Come On Home	1956	10.00	20.00	40.00
ON THE SQUARE					
❑ 320	Band of Angels/Ugly Face	1959	5.00	10.00	20.00
ONYX					
❑ 503	Let's You and I Go Steady/Zippidy Zippidy Zoom	1956	15.00	30.00	60.00
❑ 506	My Oh My/Tree in the Meadow	1956	37.50	75.00	150.00
❑ 510	Your Cheatin' Heart/I Sure Need You	1957	15.00	30.00	60.00
❑ 511	Ice Cream Baby/Yuz-a-Ma-Tuz	1957	15.00	30.00	60.00
❑ 516	The Wheel of Love/It's Love, Love, Love	1957	30.00	60.00	120.00
PEARLS, THE (3)					
BELL					
❑ 45342	You Came, You Saw, You Conquered/(B-side unknown)	1973	—	2.50	5.00
PEARLS, THE (4)					
WARNER BROS.					
❑ 5300	Happy Over You/If I Had a Choice	1962	5.00	10.00	20.00
PEARLS BEFORE SWINE					
ESP-DISK'					
❑ 4554	Morning Song/Drop Out	1967	10.00	20.00	40.00
❑ 4575	Images of April/There Was a Man	1968	10.00	20.00	40.00
❑ 4576	I Saw the World/(B-side unknown)	1968	10.00	20.00	40.00
REPRISE					
❑ 0873	If You Don't Want To/These Things Too	1969	3.00	6.00	12.00
❑ 0916	God Save the Child/Rocket Man	1970	3.00	6.00	12.00
❑ 0949	The Jeweler/Rocket Man	1970	3.00	6.00	12.00
PEBBLES AND BAMM BAMM					
HANNA-BARBERA					
❑ 449	Open Up Your Heart/The Lord Is Counting on You	1965	6.25	12.50	25.00
❑ 449 [PS]	Open Up Your Heart/The Lord Is Counting on You	1965	12.50	25.00	50.00
❑ 484	The World Is Full of Toys/Daddy	1966	6.25	12.50	25.00
7-Inch Extended Plays					
HANNA-BARBERA					
❑ CS 7044	Little Drummer Boy/We Three Kings//Silent Night/It Came Upon a Midnight Clear	1965	12.50	25.00	50.00
❑ CS 7044 [PS]	We Wish You a Merry Christmas	1965	25.00	50.00	100.00
PEDICIN, MIKE					
20TH CENTURY					
❑ 5006	My Heart Is Breaking/I'll Always Love You Some	195?	7.50	15.00	30.00
❑ 5009	Kiss, Kiss, Kiss/Love Every Moment	195?	7.50	15.00	30.00
❑ 5012	Never Mind/M-m-Boy	195?	7.50	15.00	30.00
❑ 5019	I've Got a Feeling It's Love/Is That What You Call Love	195?	7.50	15.00	30.00
❑ 5021	Disc Jockey's Boogie/Tiger Rag	195?	7.50	15.00	30.00
❑ 5023	It's My Heart to Give/Kiss Me Before You Say Goodbye	195?	7.50	15.00	30.00
❑ 5027	Shake a Hand/When We Meet	195?	10.00	20.00	40.00
❑ 5029	Not Somebody Else Just Me/Sweet Georgia Brown	195?	7.50	15.00	30.00
ABC-PARAMOUNT					
❑ 10303	Gotta Twist/When the Cats Come Twistin' In	1962	3.00	6.00	12.00
APOLLO					
❑ 534	Hey Pop, Give Me the Keys/St. James Infirmary	1959	10.00	20.00	40.00
CAMEO					
❑ 125	Shake a Hand/The Dickie Doo	1957	6.25	12.50	25.00
FEDERAL					
❑ 12417	Burnt Toast/You Gotta Go, You Gotta Go	1961	3.75	7.50	15.00
MALVERN					
❑ 101	The Dickie Doo/(B-side unknown)	1957	7.50	15.00	30.00
RCA VICTOR					
❑ 47-6043	I'm Hip/I Wanna Hug You, Kiss You, Squeeze You	1955	6.25	12.50	25.00
❑ 47-6051	Mambo Rock/D-E-V-I-L	1955	6.25	12.50	25.00
❑ 47-6150	Fe-Fi-Fo-Fum/The Hot Barcarolle	1955	6.25	12.50	25.00
❑ 47-6235	You Gotta Go/The Banjo Rock	1955	6.25	12.50	25.00
❑ 47-6285	Jackpot/When the Cats Come Marching In	1955	6.25	12.50	25.00
❑ 47-6369	The Large, Large House/Hotter Than a Pistol	1955	6.25	12.50	25.00
❑ 47-6546	The Beat/Save Us, Preacher Davis	1956	6.25	12.50	25.00
❑ 47-6676	Teenage Fairy Tales/Close All the Doors	1956	6.25	12.50	25.00
❑ 47-6847	The Hucklebuck/Calypso Rock	1957	6.25	12.50	25.00

PEEL, DAVID

Number	Title (A Side/B Side)	Yr	VG	VG+	NM
APPLE					
❑ PRO-6498/9 [DJ]	F Is Not a Dirty Word/The Ballad of New York City	1972	30.00	60.00	120.00
❑ PRO-6545/6 [DJ]	Hippie from New York City/The Ballad of New York City	1972	30.00	60.00	120.00
ORANGE					
❑ 1001	Bring Back the Beatles/Imagine	1977	2.50	5.00	10.00

PEELS, THE

Number	Title (A Side/B Side)	Yr	VG	VG+	NM
KARATE					
❑ 522	Juanita Banana/Fun	1966	3.00	6.00	12.00
❑ 527	Scrooey Mooey/Time Marches On	1966	2.00	4.00	8.00
❑ 533	Juanita Banana II/Rosita Tomato	1966	2.50	5.00	10.00

PEIL, DANNY, AND THE APOLLOS

Number	Title (A Side/B Side)	Yr	VG	VG+	NM
REYNARD					
❑ 602	Jingle Jump/Flip Side	1964	3.75	7.50	15.00

PEJOE, MORRIS

Number	Title (A Side/B Side)	Yr	VG	VG+	NM
CHECKER					
❑ 766	Tired of Crying Over You/Gonna Buy Me a Telephone	1953	125.00	250.00	500.00
—Black vinyl					
❑ 766	Tired of Crying Over You/Gonna Buy Me a Telephone	1953	1500.	2250.	3000.
—Red vinyl					
❑ 781	Can't Get Along/It'll Plumb Get It	1953	100.00	200.00	400.00
—Black vinyl					
❑ 781	Can't Get Along/It'll Plumb Get It	1953	250.00	500.00	1000.
—Red vinyl					
VEE JAY					
❑ 148	You're Gonna Need Me/Hurt My Feelings	1955	15.00	30.00	60.00

PELICANS, THE

Number	Title (A Side/B Side)	Yr	VG	VG+	NM
IMPERIAL					
❑ 5307	Chimes/Ain't Gonna Do It	1954	250.00	500.00	1000.
PARROT					
❑ 793	White Cliffs of Dover/Aurelia	1954	750.00	1500.	3000.
❑ 793	White Cliffs of Dover/Aurelia	1954	3000.	4500.	6000.
—Red vinyl					

PENDARVIS, TRACY

Number	Title (A Side/B Side)	Yr	VG	VG+	NM
SUN					
❑ 335	A Thousand Guitars/Is It Too Late	1960	5.00	10.00	20.00
❑ 345	Is It Me/South Bound Line	1960	6.25	12.50	25.00
❑ 359	Eternally/Belle of the Swanee	1961	5.00	10.00	20.00

PENDERGRASS, TEDDY

Also see HAROLD MELVIN AND THE BLUE NOTES.

Number	Title (A Side/B Side)	Yr	VG	VG+	NM
ASYLUM					
❑ 69401	Joy/Let Me Be Closer	1988	—	—	3.00
❑ 69422	2 A.M./(Instrumental)	1988	—	2.00	4.00
❑ 69538	Lert Me Be Closer/Love Emergency	1986	—	2.00	4.00
❑ 69568	Love 4/2//One of Us Feels in Love	1986	—	2.00	4.00
❑ 69595	Never Felt Like Dancin'/Love Emergency	1985	—	2.00	4.00
❑ 69628	Somewhere I Belong/Hot Love	1985	—	2.00	4.00
❑ 69628 [PS]	Somewhere I Belong/Hot Love	1985	—	2.00	4.00
❑ 69669	In My Time/Stay with Me	1985	—	2.00	4.00
❑ 69696	You're My Choice Tonight (Choose Me)/So Sad the Song	1984	—	2.00	4.00
❑ 69720	Hold Me/Love	1984	—	2.00	4.00
—With Whitney Houston					
❑ 69720 [PS]	Hold Me/Love	1984	—	2.00	4.00
ELEKTRA					
❑ 69312	The Last Time/(B-side unknown)	1989	—	—	3.00
❑ 69358	Love Is the Power/I'm Ready	1988	—	—	3.00
❑ 69358 [PS]	Love Is the Power/I'm Ready	1988	—	—	3.00
❑ 69422	2 A.M./(Instrumental)	1988	—	—	3.00
PHILADELPHIA INT'L.					
❑ 02095	Can't You Try/Love T.K.O.	1981	—	2.00	4.00
❑ 02462	I Can't Live Without Your Love/You Must Live On	1981	—	2.00	4.00
❑ 02619	You're My Latest, Greatest Inspiration/Keep On Lovin' Me	1981	—	2.00	4.00
❑ 02856	Nine Times Out of Ten/This Gift of Life	1982	—	2.00	4.00
❑ 3107	Can't We Try/Plenty Good Lovin'	1980	—	2.50	5.00
❑ 3116	Love T.K.O./I Just Called to Say	1980	—	2.50	5.00
❑ 03116	Love T.K.O./I Just Called to Say	1982	—	—	3.00
—Reissue					
❑ 03284	I Can't Win for Losing/Don't Lead Me Out Along the Road	1982	—	2.00	4.00
❑ 03325	I Can't Win for Losing	1982	—	3.00	6.00
—One-sided budget release					
❑ 3622	I Don't Love You Anymore/Somebody Told Me	1977	—	2.50	5.00
❑ 3633	The Whole Town's Laughing at Me/The More I Get, The More I Want	1977	—	2.50	5.00
❑ 3648	Close the Door/Get Up, Get Down, Get Funky, Get Loose	1978	—	2.50	5.00
❑ 3657	Only You/It Don't Hurt Now	1978	—	2.50	5.00
❑ 3669	Life Is a Song Worth Singing/Cold, Cold World	1978	—	2.50	5.00
❑ 3696	Turn Off the Lights/If You Know Like I Know	1979	—	2.50	5.00
❑ 3717	Come Go with Me/Do Me	1979	—	2.50	5.00
❑ 3733	Shout and Scream/Close the Door	1979	—	2.50	5.00
❑ 3742	It's You I Love/Where Did All the Lovin' Go	1980	—	2.50	5.00
❑ 04302	Life Is for the Living/I Want My Baby Back	1984	—	2.00	4.00
❑ 70062	Is It Still Good to You/Girl You Know	1981	—	2.00	4.00

PENDLETONS, THE

Number	Title (A Side/B Side)	Yr	VG	VG+	NM
DOT					
❑ 16511	Board Party/Barefoot Adventure	1963	25.00	50.00	100.00
RENDEZVOUS					
❑ 194	The Waddle/Itchy Bon Mash	1962	10.00	20.00	40.00

PENETRATIONS, THE

Number	Title (A Side/B Side)	Yr	VG	VG+	NM
ICON					
❑ 1002	Bring 'Em In/Fackin' Out	196?	15.00	30.00	60.00
—Blue vinyl					
❑ 1002	Bring 'Em Back Alive/Fackin' Out	196?	7.50	15.00	30.00
—Black vinyl; note slightly different A-side title					

PENGUINS, THE

Number	Title (A Side/B Side)	Yr	VG	VG+	NM
ATLANTIC					
❑ 1132	Pledge of Love/I Knew I'd Fall in Love	1957	7.50	15.00	30.00
DOOTO					
❑ 348	Earth Angel/Hey Senorita	1959	5.00	10.00	20.00
—Reissue on altered label name and yellow label					
❑ 428	That's How Much I Need You/Be My Lovin' Baby	1957	10.00	20.00	40.00
❑ 432	Sweet Love/Let Me Make Up Your Mind	1958	7.50	15.00	30.00
❑ 435	Do Not Pretend/If You're Mine	1958	7.50	15.00	30.00
DOOTONE					
❑ 345	No There Ain't No News Today/When I Am Gone	1954	75.00	150.00	300.00
—B-side by Dootsie Williams Orchestra					
❑ 348	Earth Angel/Hey Senorita	1954	37.50	75.00	150.00
—First pressings on glossy red labels					
❑ 348	Earth Angel/Hey Senorita	1955	12.50	25.00	50.00
—Maroon label					
❑ 348	Earth Angel/Hey Senorita	1955	10.00	20.00	40.00
—Blue label					
❑ 348	Earth Angel/Hey Senorita	1955	7.50	15.00	30.00
—Black label					
❑ 353	Love Will Make Your Mind Go Wild/Ookey Ook	1954	17.50	35.00	70.00
—First pressings on glossy red label					
❑ 353	Love Will Make Your Mind Go Wild/Ookey Ook	1955	12.50	25.00	50.00
—Maroon label					
❑ 353	Love Will Make Your Mind Go Wild/Ookey Ook	1955	10.00	20.00	40.00
—Blue label					
❑ 353	Love Will Make Your Mind Go Wild/Ookey Ook	1955	7.50	15.00	30.00
—Black label					
❑ 362	Baby, Let's Make Some Love/Kiss a Fool Goodbye	1955	12.50	25.00	50.00
ELDO					
❑ 119	Universal Twist/To Keep Our Love	1962	5.00	10.00	20.00
GLENVILLE					
❑ 101	Earth Angel/Hey Senorita	197?	—	3.00	6.00
—Reissue					
MERCURY					
❑ 70610	Don't Do It/Be Mine or Be a Fool	1955	12.50	25.00	50.00
—Black vinyl					
❑ 70610	Don't Do It/Be Mine or Be a Fool	1955	50.00	100.00	200.00
—Red vinyl					
❑ 70654	Walkin' Down Broadway/It Only Happens with You	1955	12.50	25.00	50.00
❑ 70703	Promises, Promises, Promises/The Devil That I See	1955	12.50	25.00	50.00
❑ 70762	A Christmas Prayer/Jingle Jangle	1955	20.00	40.00	80.00
❑ 70799	My Troubles Are Not At an End/She's Gone, Gone	1956	12.50	25.00	50.00
—Maroon label					
❑ 70799	My Troubles Are Not At an End/She's Gone, Gone	1956	6.25	12.50	25.00
—Black label					
❑ 70943	Earth Angel/Ice	1956	10.00	20.00	40.00
—Not the same recording as the hit on Dootone					
❑ 71033	Cool Baby Cool/Will You Be Mine	1957	10.00	20.00	40.00
ORIGINAL SOUND					
❑ 27	Memories of El Monte/Be Mine	1963	25.00	50.00	100.00
—Black and red label					
❑ 27	Memories of El Monte/Be Mine	1963	12.50	25.00	50.00
—Black and silver label; A-side written by Frank Zappa					
❑ 54	Heavenly Angel/Big Bobo's Party Train	1965	6.25	12.50	25.00
SUN STATE					
❑ 001	Believe Me/The Pony Rock	1962	6.25	12.50	25.00
WING					
❑ 90076	Dealer of Dreams/Peace of Mind	1956	7.50	15.00	30.00

7-Inch Extended Plays

Number	Title (A Side/B Side)	Yr	VG	VG+	NM
DOOTO					
❑ 241	Butterball/Heart of a Fool//Money Talks/Lover or Fool	1959	30.00	60.00	120.00
❑ 241 [PS]	The Cool, Cool Penguins Vol. 1	1959	30.00	60.00	120.00
❑ 243	(contents unknown)	1959	30.00	60.00	120.00
❑ 243 [PS]	The Cool, Cool Penguins, Vol. 2	1959	30.00	60.00	120.00
❑ 244	(contents unknown)	1959	30.00	60.00	120.00
❑ 244 [PS]	The Cool, Cool Penguins, Vol. 3	1959	30.00	60.00	120.00
DOOTONE					
❑ 201	(contents unknown)	1955	62.50	125.00	250.00
❑ 201 [PS]	The Penguins	1955	62.50	125.00	250.00
—Issued in "Dootone" jacket rather than custom jacket					

PENN, LITTLE "LAMBSIE"

Number	Title (A Side/B Side)	Yr	VG	VG+	NM
ATCO					
❑ 6082	I Wanna Spend Christmas With Elvis/Painted Lips and Pigtails	1956	12.50	25.00	50.00

PENN, WILLIAM, AND THE QUAKERS

Number	Title (A Side/B Side)	Yr	VG	VG+	NM
DUANE					
❑ 104	Coming Up My Way/Care Free	196?	10.00	20.00	40.00
HUSH					
❑ 230	Little Girl/Somebody's Dum Dum	196?	12.50	25.00	50.00
MELRON					
❑ 5013	California Sun/No More Love	1966	12.50	25.00	50.00
❑ 5024	Santa Needs Ear Muffs on His Nose/Philly	1966	15.00	30.00	60.00
❑ 5024	Santa Needs Ear Muffs on His Nose/Sweet Caroline	1966	15.00	30.00	60.00

Number	Title (A Side/B Side)	Yr	VG	VG+	NM
THUNDERBIRD					
❑ 502	Blow My Mind/Swami	1966	10.00	20.00	40.00
—As the "William Penn Fyve"					
TWILIGHT					
❑ 410	Ghost of the Monks/Goodbye My Love	1967	7.50	15.00	30.00
UPTOWN					
❑ 745	Chrome Dome Wheeler Dealer/Scrapped	1967	10.00	20.00	40.00

PENNANTS, THE

Number	Title (A Side/B Side)	Yr	VG	VG+	NM
WORLD					
❑ 102	Don't Go/Workin' Man	1961	25.00	50.00	100.00

PENNER, DICK

Number	Title (A Side/B Side)	Yr	VG	VG+	NM
SUN					
❑ 282	Cindy Lou/Your Honey Love	1958	12.50	25.00	50.00

PENNSYLVANIA PLAYERS, THE

See DICKIE GOODMAN.

PENNY, JOE

Number	Title (A Side/B Side)	Yr	VG	VG+	NM
FEDERAL					
❑ 12322	Mercy, Mercy Percy/Bip a Little, Bop a Little	1958	50.00	100.00	200.00
SIMS					
❑ 173	Frosty Window Pane/Hatty Fatty	1964	5.00	10.00	20.00

PENNY AND THE OVERTONES

Number	Title (A Side/B Side)	Yr	VG	VG+	NM
RIM					
❑ 2021	What Made You Forget/(B-side unknown)	1958	25.00	50.00	100.00

PENTAGONS, THE

Number	Title (A Side/B Side)	Yr	VG	VG+	NM
DONNA					
❑ 1337	To Be Loved/(B-side unknown)	1961	7.50	15.00	30.00
FLEET INT'L.					
❑ 100	To Be Loved/(B-side unknown)	1960	50.00	100.00	200.00

PENTANGLE, THE

Number	Title (A Side/B Side)	Yr	VG	VG+	NM
REPRISE					
❑ PRO 391 [DJ]	Light Flight/Sally Go 'Round the Roses	1969	2.50	5.00	10.00
❑ 0784	Let No Man Steal Your Throne/Way Behind the Sun	1968	2.00	4.00	8.00
❑ 0843	I Saw an Angel/Once I Had a Sweetheart	1969	2.00	4.00	8.00

PEOPLE

Also see LARRY NORMAN.

Number	Title (A Side/B Side)	Yr	VG	VG+	NM
CAPITOL					
❑ 2078	I Love You/Somebody Tell Me My Name	1968	3.00	6.00	12.00
❑ 2251	Apple Cider/Ashes of Me	1968	2.50	5.00	10.00
❑ 2499	Turnin' Me In/Ulla	1969	2.50	5.00	10.00
❑ 5920	Organ Grinder/Riding High	1967	2.50	5.00	10.00
PARAMOUNT					
❑ 0005	Love Will Take Us Higher and Higher/Livin' It Up	1969	—	3.00	6.00
❑ 0011	Sunshine Lady/Crosstown Bus	1969	—	3.00	6.00
❑ 0019	For What It's Worth/Maple Street	1970	—	3.00	6.00
❑ 0028	One Chain Don't Make No Prison/Keep It Alive	1970	—	3.00	6.00
POLYDOR					
❑ 14087	Chant for Peace/I Don't Carry No Guns	1971	—	3.00	6.00
ZEBRA					
❑ 102	Come Back Beatles (same on both sides)	1978	2.50	5.00	10.00

PEOPLE'S CHOICE

Number	Title (A Side/B Side)	Yr	VG	VG+	NM
CASABLANCA					
❑ 2322	My Feet Won't Move, But My Shoes Did the Boogie/You Ought to Be Dancin'	1980	—	2.00	4.00
PALMER					
❑ 5020	Easy to Be True/Savin' My Love for You	1967	62.50	125.00	250.00
PHIL-L.A. OF SOUL					
❑ 349	I Likes to Do It/Big Ladies Man	1971	—	3.00	6.00
❑ 352	Wootie-T-Woo/'Cause That's the Way I Know	1971	—	3.00	6.00
❑ 356	Magic/Oh How I Love It	1972	—	3.00	6.00
❑ 358	Let Me Do My Thing/On a Cloudy Day	1972	—	3.00	6.00
PHILADELPHIA INT'L.					
❑ 3649	Turn Me Loose/Soft and Tender	1978	—	2.00	4.00
❑ 3658	Rough-Ride/Stay with Me	1978	—	2.00	4.00
PHILIPS					
❑ 40653	Keep On Holding On/Just Look What You've Done	1969	3.00	6.00	12.00
TSOP					
❑ 4751	Love Shot/The Big Hurt	1973	—	2.50	5.00
❑ 4759	Party Is a Groovy Thing/Asking for Trouble	1974	—	2.50	5.00
❑ 4769	Do It Any Way You Wanna/The Big Hurt	1975	—	2.50	5.00
❑ 4773	Nursery Rhymes (Part 1)/Nursery Rhymes (Part 2)	1975	—	2.50	5.00
❑ 4781	Here We Go Again/Mickey D's	1976	—	2.50	5.00
❑ 4782	Movin' In All Directions/Mellow Hood	1976	—	2.50	5.00
❑ 4784	Cold Blooded & Down-Right Funky/Jam, Jam, Jam (All Night Long)	1976	—	2.50	5.00
❑ 4786	If You Gonna Do It (Put Your Mind To It) (Part I)/If You Gonna Do It (Put Your Mind To It) (Part II)	1977	—	2.50	5.00

PEPE AND THE ASTROS

Number	Title (A Side/B Side)	Yr	VG	VG+	NM
SWAMI					
❑ 553/4	Judy My Love/Now, Ain't That a Shame	1961	12.50	25.00	50.00

PEPPERMINT RAINBOW, THE

Number	Title (A Side/B Side)	Yr	VG	VG+	NM
DECCA					
❑ 32316	Pink Lemonade/Walking in Different Circles	1968	2.00	4.00	8.00
❑ 32410	Will You Be Staying After Sunday/And I'll Be There	1968	2.50	5.00	10.00
❑ 32498	Don't Wake Me Up in the Morning, Michael/Rosemary	1969	2.00	4.00	8.00
❑ 32498 [PS]	Don't Wake Me Up in the Morning, Michael/Rosemary	1969	3.00	6.00	12.00
❑ 32562	You're the Sound of Love/Jamais	1969	2.00	4.00	8.00
❑ 32601	Good Morning Means Goodbye/Don't Love Me Unless It's Forever	1969	2.00	4.00	8.00

PEPPERMINT TROLLEY COMPANY, THE

Number	Title (A Side/B Side)	Yr	VG	VG+	NM
ACTA					
❑ 807	She's the Kind of Girl/Little Miss Sunshine	1967	2.00	4.00	8.00
❑ 809	It's a Lazy Summer Day/Blue Eyes	1967	2.00	4.00	8.00
❑ 815	Baby You Come Rollin' Across My Mind/9 O'Clock Business Man	1968	2.50	5.00	10.00
❑ 829	Trust/I Remember Long Along	1968	2.00	4.00	8.00
❑ 834	The Last Thing on My Mind/Memphis City Letter	1969	2.00	4.00	8.00
❑ 835	Spinnin' 'n' Whirlin' Around/New York City	1969	2.00	4.00	8.00
VALIANT					
❑ 752	Lollipop Train/Bored to Tears	1966	3.75	7.50	15.00

PEPS, THE

See THE FABULOUS PEPS.

PERENNIALS, THE

Number	Title (A Side/B Side)	Yr	VG	VG+	NM
BALL					
❑ 1016	My Big Mistake/I'm Yours 'Til the End	1963	100.00	200.00	400.00

PERFECT, CHRISTINE

See CHRISTINE McVIE.

PERFECT CIRCLE, A

Number	Title (A Side/B Side)	Yr	VG	VG+	NM
VIRGIN					
❑ 38719	Judith/Orestes	2000	—	2.00	4.00
❑ 58888	3 Libras/The Hollow	2000	—	2.00	4.00

PERFIDIANS, THE

Number	Title (A Side/B Side)	Yr	VG	VG+	NM
HUSKY					
❑ 1	La Paz/Whiplash	1962	20.00	40.00	80.00
—Red vinyl					
❑ 1	La Paz/Whiplash	1962	10.00	20.00	40.00
—Black vinyl					

PERKINS, CARL

Number	Title (A Side/B Side)	Yr	VG	VG+	NM
COLUMBIA					
❑ 41131	Pink Pedal Pushers/Jive After Five	1958	7.50	15.00	30.00
❑ 41131 [PS]	Pink Pedal Pushers/Jive After Five	1958	30.00	60.00	120.00
❑ 41207	Levi Jacket/Pop, Let Me Have the Car	1958	6.25	12.50	25.00
❑ 41296	Y-O-U/This Life I Live	1958	6.25	12.50	25.00
❑ 41379	Pointed Toe Shoes/Highway of Love	1959	6.25	12.50	25.00
❑ 41449	One Ticket to Loneliness/I Don't See Me in Your Eyes Anymore	1959	6.25	12.50	25.00
❑ 41651	L-O-V-E-V-I-L-L-E/Too Much for a Man to Understand	1960	6.25	12.50	25.00
❑ 41825	Honey, 'Cause I Love You/Just for You	1960	6.25	12.50	25.00
❑ 42061	Anyway the Wind Blows/The Unhappy Girls	1961	6.25	12.50	25.00
❑ 42403	Hollywood City/Forget Me Next Time Around	1962	—	—	—
—Unreleased?					
❑ 42405	Hollywood City/The Fool I Used to Be	1962	6.25	12.50	25.00
❑ 42405 [PS]	Hollywood City/The Fool I Used to Be	1962	30.00	60.00	120.00
❑ 42514	Sister Twister/Hambone	1962	6.25	12.50	25.00
❑ 42514 [PS]	Sister Twister/Hambone	1962	100.00	200.00	400.00
❑ 42753	I Just Got Back from There/Forget Me Next Time Around	1963	6.25	12.50	25.00
❑ 44723	Restless/1143	1968	2.00	4.00	8.00
❑ 44883	For Your Love/Four Letter Word	1969	2.00	4.00	8.00
❑ 44993	C.C. Rider/Soul Beat	1969	2.00	4.00	8.00
❑ 45107	All Mama's Children/Step Aside	1970	2.00	4.00	8.00
—With NRBQ					
❑ 45132	State of Confusion/My Son, My Son	1970	—	3.00	6.00
❑ 45253	What Every Little Boy Ought to Know/Just As Long	1970	—	2.50	5.00
❑ 45347	Me Without You/Red Headed Woman	1971	—	2.50	5.00
❑ 45466	Cotton Top/About All I Can Give You Is My Love	1971	—	2.50	5.00
❑ 45582	High on Love/Take Me Back to Memphis	1972	—	2.50	5.00
❑ 45694	Someday/The Trip	1972	—	2.50	5.00
DECCA					
❑ 31548	Help Me Find My Baby/For a Little While	1963	3.75	7.50	15.00
❑ 31591	After Sundown/I Wouldn't Have Told You	1964	3.75	7.50	15.00
❑ 31709	The Monkeyshine/Let My Baby Be	1964	3.75	7.50	15.00
❑ 31786	One of These Days/Mama of My Song	1965	3.75	7.50	15.00
DOLLIE					
❑ 505	Country Boy's Dream/If I Could Come Back	1966	3.00	6.00	12.00
❑ 508	Shine, Shine, Shine/Almost Love	1967	3.00	6.00	12.00
❑ 512	Without You/You Can Take the Boy Out of the Country	1967	3.00	6.00	12.00
❑ 514	My Old Home Town/Back to Tennessee	1967	3.00	6.00	12.00
❑ 516	It's You/Lake County Cotton Country	1968	3.00	6.00	12.00
FLIP					
❑ 501	Movie Magg/Turn Around	1955	250.00	500.00	1000.
JET					
❑ 5054	Blue Suede Shoes/Rock Around the World	1979	—	2.00	4.00
MERCURY					
❑ 55009	The E.P. Express/Big Bad Blues	1977	—	2.00	4.00
❑ 73425	(Let's Get) Dixiefried/One More Loser Goin' Home	1973	—	3.00	6.00
❑ 73489	Ruby, Don't Take Your Love to Town/Sing My Song	1974	—	2.50	5.00
❑ 73653	You'll Always Be a Lady to Me/Low Class	1974	—	2.50	5.00
❑ 73690	The E.P. Express/Big Bad Blues	1975	—	2.50	5.00
❑ 73993	Help Me Dream/You Tore My Heaven All to Hell	1973	—	3.00	6.00
MMI					
❑ 1016	Don't Get Off Gettin' It On/Georgia Court Room	1977	—	2.00	4.00
❑ 1019	Standing in the Need of Love/Georgia Court Room	1977	—	2.00	4.00
MUSIC MILL					
❑ 1007	Born to Boogie/Take Me Back	1976	—	2.00	4.00

SMASH

Number	Title (A Side/B Side)	Yr	VG	VG+	NM
❑ 884760-7	Birth of Rock and Roll/Rock and Roll (Fais-Do-Do)	1986	—	2.00	4.00
—B-side with Jerry Lee Lewis, Roy Orbison and Johnny Cash					
❑ 884760-7 [PS]	Birth of Rock and Roll/Rock and Roll (Fais-Do-Do)	1986	—	2.00	4.00
—B-side with Jerry Lee Lewis, Roy Orbison and Johnny Cash					
❑ 884934-7	Sixteen Candles/Rock & Roll (Fais-Do-Do)	1986	—	2.00	4.00
—B-side with Jerry Lee Lewis, Roy Orbison and Johnny Cash; A-side by Jerry Lee Lewis					
❑ 888142-7	Class of '55/We Remember the King	1987	—	2.00	4.00
—B-side with Jerry Lee Lewis, Roy Orbison and Johnny Cash					

SUEDE

Number	Title (A Side/B Side)	Yr	VG	VG+	NM
❑ 101	I Don't Want to Fall in Love Again/We Did It in '54	1978	—	2.00	4.00
❑ 102	Rock-a-Billy Fever/Till You Get Through with Me	1978	—	2.00	4.00
❑ 6777	Little Teardrops/Green Grass of Home	1977	—	2.00	4.00

SUN

Number	Title (A Side/B Side)	Yr	VG	VG+	NM
❑ 224	Gone, Gone, Gone/Let the Jukebox Keep On Playing	1955	25.00	50.00	100.00
❑ 234	Blue Suede Shoes/Honey Don't	1956	15.00	30.00	60.00
❑ 235	Sure to Fall/Tennessee	1956	—	—	—
—Unreleased					
❑ 243	Boppin' the Blues/All Mama's Children	1956	10.00	20.00	40.00
❑ 249	Dixie Fried/I'm Sorry, I'm Not Sorry	1956	7.50	15.00	30.00
❑ 261	Matchbox/Your True Love	1957	7.50	15.00	30.00
❑ 274	That's Right/Forever Yours	1957	7.50	15.00	30.00
❑ 287	Glad All Over/Lend Me Your Comb	1958	7.50	15.00	30.00

UNIVERSAL

Number	Title (A Side/B Side)	Yr	VG	VG+	NM
❑ UVL-66002	Charlene/Love Makes Dreams Come True	1989	—	2.00	4.00
❑ UVL-66019	Hambone/Love Makes Dreams Come True	1989	—	2.00	4.00

7-Inch Extended Plays

COLUMBIA

Number	Title (A Side/B Side)	Yr	VG	VG+	NM
❑ B-12341	(contents unknown)	1958	50.00	100.00	200.00
❑ B-12341 [PS]	Whole Lotta Shakin'	1958	50.00	100.00	200.00

SUN

Number	Title (A Side/B Side)	Yr	VG	VG+	NM
❑ EPA-115	Blue Suede Shoes/Movie Magg//Sure to Fall/Gone, Gone, Gone	1958	100.00	200.00	400.00
❑ EPA-115 [PS]	Carl Perkins	1958	100.00	200.00	400.00

PERKINS, DAL

CHALLENGE

Number	Title (A Side/B Side)	Yr	VG	VG+	NM
❑ 59262	Last of the Lovers/It's So Nice to See You	1964	3.75	7.50	15.00
❑ 59288	If You Were Mine/Money Greases the Wheel	1965	3.75	7.50	15.00
❑ 59318	Second Choice/Standing in Your Shadow	1965	3.75	7.50	15.00

COLUMBIA

Number	Title (A Side/B Side)	Yr	VG	VG+	NM
❑ 4-44204	Here's to the Girls/One Day a Week	1967	2.50	5.00	10.00
❑ 4-44343	Helpless/Woman in the Darkness	1967	2.50	5.00	10.00

VIV

Number	Title (A Side/B Side)	Yr	VG	VG+	NM
❑ 102	Shy/Young Lovers	195?	6.25	12.50	25.00

PERKINS, LAURA LEE

IMPERIAL

Number	Title (A Side/B Side)	Yr	VG	VG+	NM
❑ 5493	Kiss Me Baby/I Just Don't Like This Kind of Lovin'	1958	10.00	20.00	40.00
❑ 5507	Don't Wait Up/Oh La Baby	1958	10.00	20.00	40.00

PERKINS, ROY

MELADEE

Number	Title (A Side/B Side)	Yr	VG	VG+	NM
❑ 111	Bye Bye Baby/You're on My Mind	1958	25.00	50.00	100.00
❑ 112	You're Gone/Here Am I	1958	150.00	300.00	600.00

MERCURY

Number	Title (A Side/B Side)	Yr	VG	VG+	NM
❑ 71278	Drop Top/That's What the Mailman Had to Say	1958	10.00	20.00	40.00

PERKINS, TONY

EPIC

Number	Title (A Side/B Side)	Yr	VG	VG+	NM
❑ 9165	If You'll Be Mine/A Little Love Can Go a Long Way	1956	5.00	10.00	20.00
—As "Anthony Perkins"					
❑ 9181	Friendly Persuasion/If You Were the Only Girl	1956	5.00	10.00	20.00
—As "Anthony Perkins"					
❑ 9201	A Fool in Love/Melody for Lovers	1957	5.00	10.00	20.00
—As "Anthony Perkins"					

RCA VICTOR

Number	Title (A Side/B Side)	Yr	VG	VG+	NM
❑ 47-7020	Moon-Light Swim/First Romance	1957	3.00	6.00	12.00
❑ 47-7078	When School Starts Again/Rocket to the Moon	1957	3.00	6.00	12.00
❑ 47-7155	Indian Giver/Just Being of Age	1958	3.00	6.00	12.00
❑ 47-7155 [PS]	Indian Giver/Just Being of Age	1958	6.25	12.50	25.00
❑ 47-7244	The Prettiest Girl in School/No, No, No	1958	3.00	6.00	12.00
❑ 47-7295	Moonlight Swim/She Used to Be My Girl	1958	3.00	6.00	12.00
❑ 47-7415	Treasure Island/Gonna Get Some Lovin'	1958	3.00	6.00	12.00

PERPETUAL MOTION

DIAL

Number	Title (A Side/B Side)	Yr	VG	VG+	NM
❑ 4078	Neckin' Don't Make It/Get Ready	1968	3.00	6.00	12.00

PERRY, JOE, PROJECT

Member of AEROSMITH who went solo for several years in the early 1980s.

COLUMBIA

Number	Title (A Side/B Side)	Yr	VG	VG+	NM
❑ 02497	Buzz Buzz/East Coast, West Coast	1981	—	2.00	4.00
❑ 11250	Let the Music Do the Talking/Bone to Bone	1980	—	2.00	4.00

PERRY, STEVE

Of JOURNEY.

COLUMBIA

Number	Title (A Side/B Side)	Yr	VG	VG+	NM
❑ 04391	Oh Sherrie/Don't Tell Me Why You're Leaving	1984	—	—	3.00
❑ 04391 [PS]	Oh Sherrie/Don't Tell Me Why You're Leaving	1984	—	—	3.00
❑ 04496	She's Mine/You Should Be Happy	1984	—	—	3.00
❑ 04496 [PS]	She's Mine/You Should Be Happy	1984	—	—	3.00
❑ 04598	Strung Out/Captured by the Moment	1984	—	—	3.00
❑ 04693	Foolish Heart/It's Only Love	1984	—	—	3.00

PERSIANS, THE (1)

ABC

Number	Title (A Side/B Side)	Yr	VG	VG+	NM
❑ 11087	Too Much Pride/That's If You Want Me To	1968	2.00	4.00	8.00
❑ 11145	I Only Have Eyes for You/The Sun's Gotta Shine in Your Heart	1968	2.00	4.00	8.00

CAPITOL

Number	Title (A Side/B Side)	Yr	VG	VG+	NM
❑ 3230	Your Love/Keep On Moving	1971	—	3.00	6.00
❑ 3333	I Want to Go Home/Baby Come Back Home	1972	—	3.00	6.00
❑ 3414	Give Me a Little Tune/I Won't Cry for You Anymore	1972	—	3.00	6.00

GWP

Number	Title (A Side/B Side)	Yr	VG	VG+	NM
❑ 509	I Don't Know How (To Fall Out of Love)/Here It Comes	1969	—	3.50	7.00

GWP'S GRAPEVINE

Number	Title (A Side/B Side)	Yr	VG	VG+	NM
❑ 201	Detour/(B-side unknown)	1970	—	3.50	7.00

PERSIANS, THE (2)

GOLDEN EAGLE

Number	Title (A Side/B Side)	Yr	VG	VG+	NM
❑ 1813	Love Me Tonight/Gee What a Girl	1962	6.25	12.50	25.00

GOLDISC

Number	Title (A Side/B Side)	Yr	VG	VG+	NM
❑ 1	Teardrops Are Falling/Vault of Memories	1963	15.00	30.00	60.00
❑ 17	Let's Monkey Again/When You Said Let's Get Married	1963	7.50	15.00	30.00

MUSIC WORLD

Number	Title (A Side/B Side)	Yr	VG	VG+	NM
❑ 102	Let's Monkey Again/When You Said Let's Get Married	1963	3.00	6.00	12.00

PAGEANT

Number	Title (A Side/B Side)	Yr	VG	VG+	NM
❑ 601	Get a Hold of Yourself/The Steady Kind	1963	3.75	7.50	15.00

RSVP

Number	Title (A Side/B Side)	Yr	VG	VG+	NM
❑ 114	Tears of Love/Dance Now	1962	7.50	15.00	30.00

RTO

Number	Title (A Side/B Side)	Yr	VG	VG+	NM
❑ 100	Sunday Kind of Love/When We Get Married	1963	3.75	7.50	15.00

PERSONALITIES, THE

SAFARI

Number	Title (A Side/B Side)	Yr	VG	VG+	NM
❑ 1002	Woe Woe Baby/Yours to Command	1957	50.00	100.00	200.00
—With giraffe on label					
❑ 1002	Woe Woe Baby/Yours to Command	1957	12.50	25.00	50.00
—No giraffe on label					

PERSUADERS, THE

More than one group?

ATCO

Number	Title (A Side/B Side)	Yr	VG	VG+	NM
❑ 6822	Thin Line Between Love and Hate/Thigh Spy	1971	2.50	5.00	10.00
❑ 6919	Bad, Bold and Beautiful Girl/Please Stay	1973	—	3.50	7.00
❑ 6943	Some Guys Have All the Luck/Love Attack	1973	2.00	4.00	8.00
❑ 6956	Best Thing That Ever Happened to Me/The Way She Is	1974	—	3.50	7.00
❑ 6964	All Strung Out on You/Once in a Lifetime Thing	1974	—	3.50	7.00
❑ 7012	I've Been Through This Before/Stay with Me	1975	—	3.50	7.00

BUM BUM

Number	Title (A Side/B Side)	Yr	VG	VG+	NM
❑ 701	Miserlou/World of Wonder	196?	7.50	15.00	30.00

CALLA

Number	Title (A Side/B Side)	Yr	VG	VG+	NM
❑ 3006	I Need Love/Sure Shot	1977	—	3.00	6.00
❑ 3007	Trying to Love Two Women/Quickest Way Out	1977	—	3.00	6.00

CARLTON

Number	Title (A Side/B Side)	Yr	VG	VG+	NM
❑ 568	Arabella/Viva El Matador	1962	3.75	7.50	15.00

SATURN

Number	Title (A Side/B Side)	Yr	VG	VG+	NM
❑ 404	Surfing Strip/Hanging Ten	1963	7.50	15.00	30.00
❑ 405	Caught in the Soup/Gremmie Bread	1963	7.50	15.00	30.00

WIN OR LOSE

Number	Title (A Side/B Side)	Yr	VG	VG+	NM
❑ 220	Love Gonna Pack Up (And Walk Out)/You Musta Put Something In Your Love	1971	2.00	4.00	8.00
❑ 222	If This Is What You Call Love (I Don't Want No Part of It)/Thanks for Loving Me	1972	2.00	4.00	8.00
❑ 225	Peace in the Valley of Love/What Is the Definition of Love	1972	2.00	4.00	8.00

WINLEY

Number	Title (A Side/B Side)	Yr	VG	VG+	NM
❑ 235	Tears/What Could It Be	1959	37.50	75.00	150.00

PET SHOP BOYS

EMI

Number	Title (A Side/B Side)	Yr	VG	VG+	NM
❑ S7-17492	Can You Forgive Her/I Want to Wake Up	1993	—	2.00	4.00
❑ S7-17708	Go West/Yesterday, When I Was Mad	1994	—	2.00	4.00
❑ S7-18736	Paninaro '95/Girls & Boys (Live in Rio)	1995	—	2.00	4.00
❑ S7-57696	Was It Worth It/Miserabilism	1992	—	2.00	4.00
—A-side is dub version, perhaps released in error					

EMI AMERICA

Number	Title (A Side/B Side)	Yr	VG	VG+	NM
❑ 8307	West End Girls/A Man Could Get Arrested	1986	—	2.00	4.00
❑ 8307 [PS]	West End Girls/A Man Could Get Arrested	1986	—	2.00	4.00
❑ 8321	Opportunities (Let's Make Lots of Money)/In the Night	1986	2.50	5.00	10.00
❑ 8321 [PS]	Opportunities (Let's Make Lots of Money)/In the Night	1986	2.50	5.00	10.00
—Withdrawn shortly after release					
❑ 8330	Opportunities (Let's Make Lots of Money)/Was That What It Was	1986	—	2.00	4.00
❑ 8330 [PS]	Opportunities (Let's Make Lots of Money)/Was That What It Was	1986	—	2.00	4.00
❑ 8338	Love Comes Quickly/That's My Impression	1986	—	2.00	4.00
❑ 8338 [PS]	Love Comes Quickly/That's My Impression	1986	—	2.00	4.00
❑ 8355	Suburbia/Jack the Lad	1986	—	2.00	4.00
❑ 8355 [PS]	Suburbia/Jack the Lad	1986	—	2.00	4.00
❑ 43027	It's a Sin/You Know Where You Went Wrong	1987	—	2.00	4.00
❑ 43027 [PS]	It's a Sin/You Know Where You Went Wrong	1987	—	2.00	4.00

EMI MANHATTAN

Number	Title (A Side/B Side)	Yr	VG	VG+	NM
❑ 50107	What Have I Done to Deserve This?/A New Life	1987	—	2.00	4.00
—Vocal guest: Dusty Springfield					
❑ 50107 [PS]	What Have I Done to Deserve This?/A New Life	1987	—	2.00	4.00
❑ 50123	Always on My Mind/Do I Have To?	1988	—	2.00	4.00
❑ 50161	Domino Dancing/Don Juan	1988	—	2.00	4.00
❑ 50161 [PS]	Domino Dancing/Don Juan	1988	—	2.00	4.00
❑ 50171	Left to My Own Devices/The Sound of the Atom Splitting	1988	—	2.00	4.00

Number	Title (A Side/B Side)	Yr	VG	VG+	NM
50171 [PS]	Left to My Own Devices/The Sound of the Atom Splitting	1988	2.00	4.00	8.00

PETER AND GORDON

Also see GORDON WALLER.

CAPITOL

Number	Title (A Side/B Side)	Yr	VG	VG+	NM
2071	Greener Days/Never Ever	1968	2.50	5.00	10.00
2214	You've Had Better Times/Sipping My Wine	1968	2.50	5.00	10.00
2544	I Can Remember (But Not Too Long Ago)/Hard Time, Rainy Day	1969	2.50	5.00	10.00
5175	A World Without Love/If I Were You	1964	3.00	6.00	12.00
5211	Nobody I Know/You Don't Have to Tell Me	1964	3.00	6.00	12.00
5211 [PS]	Nobody I Know/You Don't Have to Tell Me	1964	4.00	8.00	16.00
5272	I Don't Want to See You Again/I Would Buy You Presents	1964	3.00	6.00	12.00
5272 [PS]	I Don't Want to See You Again/I Would Buy You Presents	1964	4.00	8.00	16.00
5335	I Go to Pieces/Love Me, Baby	1965	3.00	6.00	12.00
5335 [PS]	I Go to Pieces/Love Me, Baby	1965	4.00	8.00	16.00
5406	True Love Ways/If You Wish	1965	3.00	6.00	12.00
5406 [PS]	True Love Ways/If You Wish	1965	4.00	8.00	16.00
5461	To Know You Is to Love You/I Told You So	1965	2.50	5.00	10.00
5461 [PS]	To Know You Is to Love You/I Told You So	1965	3.75	7.50	15.00
5532	Don't Pity Me/Crying in the Rain	1965	2.50	5.00	10.00
5579	Woman/Wrong from the Start	1966	3.00	6.00	12.00
—A-side composer listed as "Bernard Webb"					
5579	Woman/Wrong from the Start	1966	2.50	5.00	10.00
—A-side composer listed as "A. Smith"					
5650	There's No Living Without Your Loving/A Stranger with a Black Dove	1966	2.50	5.00	10.00
5650 [PS]	There's No Living Without Your Loving/A Stranger with a Black Dove	1966	3.75	7.50	15.00
5684	To Show I Love You/Start Trying Someone Else	1966	2.50	5.00	10.00
5684 [PS]	To Show I Love You/Start Trying Someone Else	1966	3.75	7.50	15.00
5740	Lady Godiva/Morning's Calling	1966	2.50	5.00	10.00
5740	Lady Godiva/The House I Live In	1966	3.75	7.50	15.00
5808	Knight in Rusty Armour/Flower Lady	1966	2.50	5.00	10.00
5808 [PS]	Knight in Rusty Armour/Flower Lady	1966	3.75	7.50	15.00
5864	Sunday for Tea/Hurtin' Is Lovin'	1967	2.50	5.00	10.00
5864 [PS]	Sunday for Tea/Hurtin' Is Lovin'	1967	3.75	7.50	15.00
5919	The Jokers/Red Cream and Velvet	1967	2.50	5.00	10.00

CAPITOL CREATIVE PRODUCTS

Number	Title (A Side/B Side)	Yr	VG	VG+	NM
51 [DJ]	Wrong from the Start/You've Lost That Lovin' Feelin'	1966	3.00	6.00	12.00
—B-side by the Lettermen					

CAPITOL STARLINE

Number	Title (A Side/B Side)	Yr	VG	VG+	NM
6076	A World Without Love/Nobody I Know	1965	2.00	4.00	8.00
—Green swirl label original					
6103	I Go to Pieces/Love Me Baby	1966	2.00	4.00	8.00
—Green swirl label original					
6104	There's No Living Without Your Loving/Stranger with a Black Dove	1966	2.00	4.00	8.00
—Green swirl label original					
6155	I Don't Want to See You Again/Woman	197?	—	3.00	6.00
—Red and white "bullseye" label original					
6156	Lady Godiva/You've Had Better Times	197?	—	3.00	6.00
—Red and white "bullseye" label original					

PETER, PAUL AND MARY

Also see PAUL STOOKEY; MARY TRAVERS; PETER YARROW.

WARNER BROS.

Number	Title (A Side/B Side)	Yr	VG	VG+	NM
(no #)	A-Soalin' (mono/stereo)	196?	3.00	6.00	12.00
—Green custom label					
(no #) [PS]	A-Soalin' (mono/stereo)	196?	5.00	10.00	20.00
—Illustrated book with lyrics					
PRO 149 [DJ]	Morning Train/(B-side unknown)	1963	3.75	7.50	15.00
—Promo-only 7-inch 33 1/3 rpm record with small hole					
5274	Lemon Tree/Early in the Morning	1962	2.50	5.00	10.00
5296	If I Had a Hammer/Gone the Rainbow	1962	2.50	5.00	10.00
5325	Big Boat/Tiny Sparrow	1962	2.50	5.00	10.00
5325 [PS]	Big Boat/Tiny Sparrow	1962	5.00	10.00	20.00
5334	Settle Down (Goin' Down That Highway)/500 Miles	1963	2.50	5.00	10.00
5348	Puff/Pretty Mary	1963	3.00	6.00	12.00
—First pressings have no subtitle on A-side					
5348	Puff (The Magic Dragon)/Pretty Mary	1963	2.50	5.00	10.00
—Later pressings add subtitle					
5368	Blowin' in the Wind/Flora	1963	2.50	5.00	10.00
5385	Don't Think Twice, It's All Right/Autumn to May	1963	2.50	5.00	10.00
5399	Stewball/The Cruel War	1963	2.50	5.00	10.00
5402	A-Soalin'/High-A-Bye	1963	3.00	6.00	12.00
5402 [PS]	A-Soalin'/High-A-Bye	1963	5.00	10.00	20.00
5418	Tell It on the Mountain/Old Coat	1964	2.50	5.00	10.00
5442	Oh, Rock My Soul (Part 1)/Oh, Rock My Soul (Part 2)	1964	2.50	5.00	10.00
5496	For Lovin' Me/Monday Morning	1965	2.00	4.00	8.00
5625	When the Ship Comes In/The Times They Are a-Changin'	1965	2.00	4.00	8.00
5659	Early Morning Rain/The Rising of the Moon	1965	2.00	4.00	8.00
5809	The Cruel War/Mon Vrai Destin	1966	2.00	4.00	8.00
5842	Hurry Sundown/Sometime Lover	1966	—	—	—
—Unreleased?					
5849	The Other Side of This Life/Sometime Lover	1966	2.00	4.00	8.00
5883	For Baby (For Bobbie)/Hurry Sundown	1967	2.00	4.00	8.00
7067	I Dig Rock and Roll Music/The Great Mandella (The Wheel of Life)	1967	2.50	5.00	10.00
7092	Too Much of Nothing/The House Song	1967	2.00	4.00	8.00
7232	Yesterday's Tomorrow/Love City (Postcards to Duluth)	1968	2.00	4.00	8.00
7279	Day Is Done/Make Believe Town	1969	2.00	4.00	8.00
7340	Leaving on a Jet Plane/The House Song	1969	2.50	5.00	10.00
7359	Christmas Dinner/The Marvelous Toy	1969	2.50	5.00	10.00
8684	Like the First Time/Best of Friends	1978	—	2.00	4.00
8728	Forever Young/Best of Friends	1978	—	2.00	4.00

(NO LABEL)

Number	Title (A Side/B Side)	Yr	VG	VG+	NM
(no #) [DJ]	Eugene McCarthy for President	1968	6.25	12.50	25.00

PETERIK, JIM

Also see THE IDES OF MARCH; SURVIVOR.

EPIC

Number	Title (A Side/B Side)	Yr	VG	VG+	NM
50272	Don't Fight the Feeling/Hard Day at the World	1976	—	2.50	5.00
50311	Last Tango/Lay Back	1976	—	2.50	5.00
50406	The Closest Thing to My Mind/Don't Fight the Feeling	1977	—	2.50	5.00

PETERSEN, PAUL

COLPIX

Number	Title (A Side/B Side)	Yr	VG	VG+	NM
620	She Can't Find Her Keys/Very Likely	1962	3.75	7.50	15.00
620 [PS]	She Can't Find Her Keys/Very Likely	1962	7.50	15.00	30.00
—Sleeve spells his last name "Peterson" in error					
631	What Did They Do Before Rock and Roll/Very Unlikely	1962	5.00	10.00	20.00
—With Shelly Fabares					
631 [PS]	What Did They Do Before Rock and Roll/Very Unlikely	1962	100.00	200.00	400.00
632	Keep Your Love Locked (Deep in Your Heart)/Be Everything to Anyone You Love	1962	3.00	6.00	12.00
632 [PS]	Keep Your Love Locked (Deep in Your Heart)/Be Everything to Anyone You Love	1962	7.50	15.00	30.00
649	Lollipops and Roses/Please Mr. Sun	1962	3.00	6.00	12.00
663	My Dad/Little Boy Sad	1962	3.75	7.50	15.00
663 [PS]	My Dad/Little Boy Sad	1962	7.50	15.00	30.00
676	Amy/Goody Goody	1963	3.00	6.00	12.00
676	Amy/I Only Have Eyes for You	1963	3.00	6.00	12.00
697	Girls in the Summertime/Mama, Your Little Boy Fell	1963	3.00	6.00	12.00
707	The Cheer Leader/Polka Dots and Moonbeams	1963	3.00	6.00	12.00
720	She Rides with Me/Poorest Boy in Town	1964	20.00	40.00	80.00
—A-side produced by Brian Wilson					
730	Where Is She/Hey There Beautiful	1964	3.00	6.00	12.00
763	Happy/Little Dreamer	1965	3.00	6.00	12.00
785	The Ring/You Don't Need Money	1965	3.00	6.00	12.00

MOTOWN

Number	Title (A Side/B Side)	Yr	VG	VG+	NM
1108	Chained/Don't Let It Happen	1967	5.00	10.00	20.00
1129	A Little Bit for Sandy/Your Love's Got Me Runnin'	1968	5.00	10.00	20.00

PETERSON, EARL

COLUMBIA

Number	Title (A Side/B Side)	Yr	VG	VG+	NM
21364	Boogie Blues/Believe Me	1955	12.50	25.00	50.00
21406	Be Careful of the Heart You're Going to Break/I'm Not Buying Baby	1955	12.50	25.00	50.00
21467	I Ain't Gonna Fall in Love/I'll Live My Life Alone	1955	12.50	25.00	50.00
21540	You Gotta Be My Baby/World of Make Believe	1956	10.00	20.00	40.00

SUN

Number	Title (A Side/B Side)	Yr	VG	VG+	NM
197	Boogie Blues/In the Dark	1954	125.00	250.00	500.00

PETERSON, RAY

CLOUD 9

Number	Title (A Side/B Side)	Yr	VG	VG+	NM
134	Nobody But Me/(B-side unknown)	1975	—	2.50	5.00

DECCA

Number	Title (A Side/B Side)	Yr	VG	VG+	NM
32861	Stamp Out Loneliness/There's a Better Way	1971	—	2.50	5.00

DUNES

Number	Title (A Side/B Side)	Yr	VG	VG+	NM
2002	Corrina, Corrina/Be My Girl	1960	6.25	12.50	25.00
—Produced by Phil Spector					
2002 [PS]	Corrina, Corrina/Be My Girl	1960	15.00	30.00	60.00
2004	Sweet Little Kathy/You Didn't Care	1961	3.75	7.50	15.00
2006	Missing You/You Thrill Me	1961	3.75	7.50	15.00
2009	I Could Have Loved You So Well/Why Don't You Write Me	1961	5.00	10.00	20.00
—Produced by Phil Spector					
2013	You Know Me Much Too Well/You Didn't Care	1962	3.75	7.50	15.00
2018	If Only Tomorrow/You Didn't Care	1962	3.75	7.50	15.00
2019	Is It Wrong/Slowly	1963	3.75	7.50	15.00
2022	A Love to Remember/I'm Not Jimmy	1963	3.75	7.50	15.00
2024	Where Are You/Deep Are the Roots	1963	3.75	7.50	15.00
2025	Give Us Your Blessing/Without Love (There Is Nothing)	1963	3.75	7.50	15.00
2027	I Forgot What It Was Like/Be My Girl	1963	3.75	7.50	15.00
2030	Promises/Sweet Little Kathy	1963	3.75	7.50	15.00

MGM

Number	Title (A Side/B Side)	Yr	VG	VG+	NM
13269	If You Were Here/Oh No	1964	2.50	5.00	10.00
13269 [PS]	If You Were Here/Oh No	1964	3.75	7.50	15.00
13299	Across the Street (Is a Million Miles Away)/When I Stop Dreaming	1964	2.50	5.00	10.00
13330	Unchained Melody/That's All	1965	2.00	4.00	8.00
13336	A House Without Windows/Wish I Could Say No to You	1965	2.00	4.00	8.00
13388	I'm Only Human/One Lonesome Rose	1965	2.00	4.00	8.00
13436	Love Hurts/Everybody	1966	2.00	4.00	8.00
13508	Amanda/I'm Gonna Change Everything	1966	2.00	4.00	8.00
13564	Just One Smile/The Whole World's Goin' Crazy	1966	2.00	4.00	8.00

RCA

Number	Title (A Side/B Side)	Yr	VG	VG+	NM
GB-11758	Tell Laura I Love Her/The Wonder of You	1979	—	—	3.00
—Gold Standard Series					

RCA VICTOR

Number	Title (A Side/B Side)	Yr	VG	VG+	NM
37-7845	My Blue Angel/I'm Tired	1961	12.50	25.00	50.00
—"Compact Single 33" (small hole, plays at LP speed)					
47-7087	Fever/We're Old Enough to Cry	1957	6.25	12.50	25.00
47-7165	Let's Try Romance/Shirley Purley	1958	5.00	10.00	20.00
47-7255	Suddenly/Tall Light	1958	5.00	10.00	20.00
47-7303	Patricia/The Blue-Eyed Baby	1958	5.00	10.00	20.00
47-7336	Dream Way/I'll Always Want You Near	1958	5.00	10.00	20.00
47-7404	Richer Than I/Love Is a Woman	1958	5.00	10.00	20.00
47-7513	The Wonder of You/I'm Gone	1959	6.25	12.50	25.00

Number	Title (A Side/B Side)	Yr	VG	VG+	NM
❑ 47-7578	My Blue Angel/Come and Get It	1959	5.00	10.00	20.00
❑ 47-7635	Goodnight My Love (Pleasant Dreams)/Till Then	1959	5.00	10.00	20.00
❑ 47-7635 [PS]	Goodnight My Love (Pleasant Dreams)/Till Then	1959	7.50	15.00	30.00
❑ 47-7703	Answer Me, My Love/What Do You Want to Make Those Eyes At Me For	1960	5.00	10.00	20.00
❑ 47-7745	Tell Laura I Love Her/Wedding Days	1960	6.25	12.50	25.00
❑ 47-7779	Teenage Heartache/I'll Always Want You Near	1960	5.00	10.00	20.00
❑ 47-7845	My Blue Angel/I'm Tired	1961	5.00	10.00	20.00
❑ 47-8333	The Wonder of You/Goodnight My Love	1964	2.50	5.00	10.00
❑ 61-7578 [S]	My Blue Angel/Come and Get It	1959	20.00	40.00	80.00

—"Living Stereo" (large hole, plays at 45 rpm)

Number	Title (A Side/B Side)	Yr	VG	VG+	NM
❑ 61-7745 [S]	Tell Laura I Love Her/Wedding Days	1960	25.00	50.00	100.00

—"Living Stereo" (large hole, plays at 45 rpm)

REPRISE

Number	Title (A Side/B Side)	Yr	VG	VG+	NM
❑ 0811	Love Rules the World/Together	1969	2.00	4.00	8.00

UNI

Number	Title (A Side/B Side)	Yr	VG	VG+	NM
❑ 55249	Love the Understanding Way/Oklahoma City Rimes	1970	2.00	4.00	8.00
❑ 55268	Tell Laura I Love Her/To Wait for Love	1971	—	3.00	6.00
❑ 55275	Fever/Changes	1971	—	3.00	6.00

7-Inch Extended Plays

RCA VICTOR

Number	Title (A Side/B Side)	Yr	VG	VG+	NM
❑ EPA-4367	*Tell Laura I Love Her/Suddenly/Fever/The Wonder of You	1960	30.00	60.00	120.00
❑ EPA-4367 [PS]	Tell Laura I Love Her	1960	30.00	60.00	120.00

PETRIFIED FOREST, THE

FONTANA

Number	Title (A Side/B Side)	Yr	VG	VG+	NM
❑ 1596	So Mystifying/She's the Only Thing That's Kept Me Going	1967	3.75	7.50	15.00

PETTICOATS, THE (1)

CHALLENGE

Number	Title (A Side/B Side)	Yr	VG	VG+	NM
❑ 9211	Surfin' Sally/Why Does Billy Play in Your Yard	1963	6.25	12.50	25.00

PETTICOATS, THE (2)

DOT

Number	Title (A Side/B Side)	Yr	VG	VG+	NM
❑ 16052	By the Light of the Silvery Moon/Troubadour	1960	5.00	10.00	20.00
❑ 16155	For Sentimental Reasons/Cincinnati	1960	5.00	10.00	20.00

PETTICOATS, THE (3)

PREP

Number	Title (A Side/B Side)	Yr	VG	VG+	NM
❑ 125	I Ain't Gonna Do It No More/Manhattan Mountains	1957	5.00	10.00	20.00

UNIQUE

Number	Title (A Side/B Side)	Yr	VG	VG+	NM
❑ 344	The Motorboat Song/The First One	1956	5.00	10.00	20.00
❑ 363	High Heels/I'll Go Along with You	1956	5.00	10.00	20.00

PETTIS, RAY

DREXEL

Number	Title (A Side/B Side)	Yr	VG	VG+	NM
❑ 911	Does It Have To Be Christmas/Christmas Here, Christmas There	1956	12.50	25.00	50.00

PETTY, NORMAN, TRIO

Also see THE PICKS.

ABC-PARAMOUNT

Number	Title (A Side/B Side)	Yr	VG	VG+	NM
❑ 9787	Almost Paradise/It's Been a Long, Long Time	1957	3.00	6.00	12.00

COLUMBIA

Number	Title (A Side/B Side)	Yr	VG	VG+	NM
❑ 40929	The First Kiss/(Instrumental)	1957	3.00	6.00	12.00
❑ 41039	Moondreams/Toy Boy	1957	25.00	50.00	100.00

—With Buddy Holly on guitar

JARO

Number	Title (A Side/B Side)	Yr	VG	VG+	NM
❑ 77027	Ditty Dum/Bring Your Heart	1960	3.00	6.00	12.00

"X"

Number	Title (A Side/B Side)	Yr	VG	VG+	NM
❑ 0040	Mood Indigo/Petty's Little Polka	1954	3.00	6.00	12.00
❑ 0071	On the Alamo/Echo Polka	1954	3.00	6.00	12.00
❑ 0104	I Wonder Why/Three Little Kisses	1955	3.00	6.00	12.00
❑ 0130	Oh! You Pretty Woman/Hey! Good Lookin'	1955	3.00	6.00	12.00
❑ 0167	Solitude/When It's Darkness on the Delta	1955	3.00	6.00	12.00

7-Inch Extended Plays

COLUMBIA

Number	Title (A Side/B Side)	Yr	VG	VG+	NM
❑ B-10921	(contents unknown)	1958	25.00	50.00	100.00
❑ B-10921 [PS]	Moondreams	1958	25.00	50.00	100.00

"X"

Number	Title (A Side/B Side)	Yr	VG	VG+	NM
❑ EXA-82	(contents unknown)	1955	5.00	10.00	20.00
❑ EXA-82 [PS]	The Norman Petty Trio In Full Fidelity	1955	5.00	10.00	20.00

PETTY, TOM, AND THE HEARTBREAKERS

Includes Tom Petty solo. Also see MUDCRUTCH.

BACKSTREET

Number	Title (A Side/B Side)	Yr	VG	VG+	NM
❑ 41138	Don't Do Me Like That/Casa Dega	1979	—	2.00	4.00
❑ 41138 [PS]	Don't Do Me Like That/Casa Dega	1979	—	2.50	5.00
❑ 41169	Refugee/It's Rainin' Again	1980	—	2.00	4.00
❑ 41169 [PS]	Refugee/It's Rainin' Again	1980	—	2.50	5.00
❑ 41227	Here Comes My Girl/Louisiana Rain	1980	—	2.00	4.00
❑ 41227 [PS]	Here Comes My Girl/Louisiana Rain	1980	—	2.50	5.00
❑ 51100	The Waiting/Nightwatchman	1981	—	2.00	4.00
❑ 51100 [PS]	The Waiting/Nightwatchman	1981	—	2.00	4.00
❑ 51136	A Woman in Love (It's Not Me)/Gator on the Lawn	1981	—	2.00	4.00
❑ 51136 [PS]	A Woman in Love (It's Not Me)/Gator on the Lawn	1981	—	2.00	4.00
❑ 52144	You Got Lucky/Between Two Worlds	1982	—	2.00	4.00
❑ 52144 [PS]	You Got Lucky/Between Two Worlds	1982	—	2.00	4.00
❑ 52181	Change of Heart/Heartbreakers Beach Party	1983	2.00	4.00	8.00

—Red vinyl in clear plastic sleeve with sticker

Number	Title (A Side/B Side)	Yr	VG	VG+	NM
❑ 52181	Change of Heart/Heartbreakers Beach Party	1983	—	—	3.00
❑ 52181 [PS]	Change of Heart/Heartbreakers Beach Party	1983	—	2.00	4.00

—Only issued with black-vinyl versions

MCA

Number	Title (A Side/B Side)	Yr	VG	VG+	NM
❑ 52496	Don't Come Around Here No More/Trailer	1985	—	2.00	4.00

—Original copies have a 4:19 version of the A-side

Number	Title (A Side/B Side)	Yr	VG	VG+	NM
❑ 52496	Don't Come Around Here No More/Trailer	1985	—	2.00	4.00

—Second pressings feature a 5-plus-minute version of the A-side

Number	Title (A Side/B Side)	Yr	VG	VG+	NM
❑ 52496 [PS]	Don't Come Around Here No More/Trailer	1985	—	2.00	4.00
❑ 52605	Make It Better (Forget About Me)/Crackin' Up	1985	—	—	3.00
❑ 52605 [PS]	Make It Better (Forget About Me)/Crackin' Up	1985	—	—	3.00
❑ 52658	Rebels/Southern Accents	1985	—	—	3.00
❑ 52658 [PS]	Rebels/Southern Accents	1985	—	—	3.00
❑ 52772	Needles and Pins/Spike	1985	—	—	3.00

—A-side: With Stevie Nicks

Number	Title (A Side/B Side)	Yr	VG	VG+	NM
❑ 52772 [PS]	Needles and Pins/Spike	1985	—	—	3.00
❑ 53065	Jammin' Me/Make That Connection	1987	—	—	3.00
❑ 53065 [PS]	Jammin' Me/Make That Connection	1987	—	—	3.00
❑ 53153	All Mixed Up/Let Me Up (I've Had Enough)	1987	—	—	3.00
❑ 53153 [PS]	All Mixed Up/Let Me Up (I've Had Enough)	1987	—	—	3.00
❑ 53669	I Won't Back Down/The Apartment Song	1989	—	2.00	4.00
❑ 53682	Runnin' Down a Dream/Alright for Now	1989	—	2.00	4.00
❑ 53748	Free Fallin'/Down the Line	1989	—	2.50	5.00
❑ 53781	A Face in the Crowd/A Mind with a Heart of Its Own	1990	—	2.00	4.00
❑ 54124	Learning to Fly/Too Good to Be True	1991	—	2.00	4.00
❑ 54131	Into the Great Wide Open/Makin' Some Noise	1991	—	2.00	4.00
❑ 54387	King's Highway/All or Nothin'	1992	—	2.00	4.00
❑ 54732	Mary Jane's Last Dance/The Waiting	1993	—	2.00	4.00
❑ 79030	Yer So Bad/Love Is a Long Road	1990	—	2.00	4.00

SHELTER

Number	Title (A Side/B Side)	Yr	VG	VG+	NM
❑ 62006	Breakdown/The Wild One, Forever	1976	—	—	—

—Unreleased?

Number	Title (A Side/B Side)	Yr	VG	VG+	NM
❑ 62006 [DJ]	Breakdown (Mono)/Breakdown (Stereo)	1976	2.50	5.00	10.00
❑ 62007	American Girl/Luna	1977	—	3.00	6.00
❑ 62008	Breakdown/Fooled Again (I Can't Take It)	1977	—	3.00	6.00
❑ 62010	I Need to Know/No Second Thoughts	1978	—	2.50	5.00
❑ 62011	Listen to Her Heart/I Don't Know What to Say to You	1978	—	2.50	5.00
❑ 62011 [PS]	Listen to Her Heart/I Don't Know What to Say to You	1978	—	2.50	5.00

WARNER BROS.

Number	Title (A Side/B Side)	Yr	VG	VG+	NM
❑ 17593	Walls (Circus)/Walls (No. 3)	1996	—	—	3.00
❑ 17925	It's Good to Be King/Cabin Down Below	1995	—	—	3.00
❑ 18026	A Higher Place/Only a Broken Heart	1995	—	—	3.00
❑ 18030	You Don't Know How It Feels/Girl on LSD	1994	—	—	3.00

PHAETONS, THE

HI-Q

Number	Title (A Side/B Side)	Yr	VG	VG+	NM
❑ 5012	Fling/Homemade	1959	5.00	10.00	20.00

SAHARA

Number	Title (A Side/B Side)	Yr	VG	VG+	NM
❑ 102	I'm So Lonely/Road of Blues	1963	5.00	10.00	20.00
❑ 103	The Beatle Walk/Frantic	1964	12.50	25.00	50.00

—B-side by the Premiers

VIN

Number	Title (A Side/B Side)	Yr	VG	VG+	NM
❑ 1015	I Love My Baby/As You Know	1959	15.00	30.00	60.00

WARNER BROS.

Number	Title (A Side/B Side)	Yr	VG	VG+	NM
❑ 7082	She Came Like the Rain/Three Weeks, Four Days and Fifteen Hours	1967	2.50	5.00	10.00
❑ 7205	Leave It to Me/You'd Better Come Home	1968	2.50	5.00	10.00

PHAIR, LIZ

MATADOR

Number	Title (A Side/B Side)	Yr	VG	VG+	NM
❑ OLE 103-7	Supernova/Combo Platter	1994	—	2.00	4.00

—Blue vinyl, small center hole

Number	Title (A Side/B Side)	Yr	VG	VG+	NM
❑ OLE 103-7 [PS]	Supernova/Combo Platter	1994	—	2.00	4.00
❑ 58719	Polyester Bride/Greased Lightning	1998	—	2.00	4.00

MINTY FRESH

Number	Title (A Side/B Side)	Yr	VG	VG+	NM
❑ MF-4	Carnivore/Carnivore (Raw Version)	1993	3.75	7.50	15.00

—First pressing: 1,000 on clear red vinyl

Number	Title (A Side/B Side)	Yr	VG	VG+	NM
❑ MF-4	Carnivore/Carnivore (Raw Version)	1993	3.75	7.50	15.00

—Second pressing: 1,000 on red/blue vinyl

Number	Title (A Side/B Side)	Yr	VG	VG+	NM
❑ MF-4 [PS]	Carnivore/Carnivore (Raw Version)	1993	3.75	7.50	15.00

PHANTOM, THE (1)

CAPITOL

Number	Title (A Side/B Side)	Yr	VG	VG+	NM
❑ 3857	Calm Before the Storm/Black Magic, White Magic	1974	3.00	6.00	12.00

HIDEOUT

Number	Title (A Side/B Side)	Yr	VG	VG+	NM
❑ 1080	Calm Before the Storm/Black Magic, White Magic	1974	5.00	10.00	20.00

PHANTOM, THE (2)

DOT

Number	Title (A Side/B Side)	Yr	VG	VG+	NM
❑ 16056	Love Me/Whisper Your Love	1960	37.50	75.00	150.00
❑ 16056 [PS]	Love Me/Whisper Your Love	1960	75.00	150.00	300.00

PHAPHNER

DRAGON

Number	Title (A Side/B Side)	Yr	VG	VG+	NM
❑ 1001	Overdrive/(B-side unknown)	1971	50.00	100.00	200.00

PHILIP AND STEPHAN

P.F. SLOAN and STEVE BARRI, again.

INTERPHON

Number	Title (A Side/B Side)	Yr	VG	VG+	NM
❑ 7711	Meet Me Tonight Little Girl/When You're Near, You're So Far Away	1964	3.75	7.50	15.00

PHILIPS, TERRY

CORAL

Number	Title (A Side/B Side)	Yr	VG	VG+	NM
❑ 62247	Fear/Find a Horseshoe	1961	3.75	7.50	15.00

UNITED ARTISTS

Number	Title (A Side/B Side)	Yr	VG	VG+	NM
❑ 351	My Foolish Ways/Hands of a Fool	1961	20.00	40.00	80.00

PHILLIPS, CHARLIE

COLUMBIA

Number	Title (A Side/B Side)	Yr	VG	VG+	NM
❑ 42035	No More Sugartime/Welcome to the Wedding	1961	3.00	6.00	12.00
❑ 42289	I Guess I'll Never Learn/Now That It's Over	1962	2.50	5.00	10.00
❑ 42526	Cancel the Call/You're Moving Away	1962	2.50	5.00	10.00
❑ 42691	No One to Love/Til Sunday	1963	2.50	5.00	10.00
❑ 42851	Later Tonight/This Is the House	1963	2.50	5.00	10.00
❑ 43014	Street of Loneliness/Please Help Me Believe	1964	2.50	5.00	10.00

CORAL

Number	Title (A Side/B Side)	Yr	VG	VG+	NM
❑ 61970	Be My Bride/Too Many Tears	1958	6.25	12.50	25.00

Number	Title (A Side/B Side)	Yr	VG	VG+	NM
K-ARK					
❑ 874	Your Going Is Coming/Just Let the Flowers Grow	197?	2.00	4.00	8.00
REPRISE					
❑ 0581	Be Careful, Go Easy, Go Slow/Souvenirs of Sorrow	1967	2.00	4.00	8.00

PHILLIPS, ESTHER

Includes records as "Little Esther" and "Little Esther Phillips."

Number	Title (A Side/B Side)	Yr	VG	VG+	NM
ATLANTIC					
❑ 2223	Hello Walls/Double Crossing Blues	1964	3.75	7.50	15.00
—With Jimmy Ricks					
❑ 2229	No Headstone on My Grave/Mo Jo Hannah	1964	3.75	7.50	15.00
❑ 2251	It's Too Soon to Know/You're the Reason I'm Living	1964	3.75	7.50	15.00
❑ 2265	Half a Heart/Some Things You Never Get Used To	1964	3.75	7.50	15.00
❑ 2281	And I Love Him/Shangri-La	1965	3.00	6.00	12.00
❑ 2294	Moonglow & Theme from Picnic/Makin' Whoopee	1965	3.00	6.00	12.00
❑ 2304	Let Me Know When It's Over/I Saw Me	1965	3.00	6.00	12.00
❑ 2324	Just Say Goodbye/I Could Have Told You	1966	3.00	6.00	12.00
❑ 2335	When a Woman Loves a Man/Ups and Downs	1966	3.00	6.00	12.00
❑ 2360	Somebody Else Is Taking My Place/When Love Comes to the Human Race	1966	3.00	6.00	12.00
❑ 2370	Fever/Try Me	1966	3.00	6.00	12.00
❑ 2411	Release Me/Don't Feel Rained	1967	2.50	5.00	10.00
❑ 2417	I'm Sorry/Cheater Man	1967	2.50	5.00	10.00
❑ 2745	Brand New Day/Set Me Free	1970	—	3.00	6.00
❑ 2775	Crazy Love/All God Has Is Us	1970	—	3.00	6.00
❑ 2783	Catch Me I'm Falling/Woman Will Do Wrong	1971	—	3.00	6.00
❑ 2800	Cry Me a River Blues/I'm Getting 'Long Alright	1971	—	3.00	6.00
DECCA					
❑ 28804	If You Want Me/Talkin' All Out of My Head	1953	10.00	20.00	40.00
❑ 48305	Please Don't Send Me/Stop Crying	1953	10.00	20.00	40.00
❑ 48314	Sit Back Down/He's a No Good Man	1954	15.00	30.00	60.00
FEDERAL					
❑ 12023	I'm a Bad, Bad Girl/Don't Make a Fool Out of Me	1951	20.00	40.00	80.00
❑ 12036	Heart to Heart/Looking for a Man to Satisfy My Soul	1951	125.00	250.00	500.00
—With the Dominoes					
❑ 12042	Cryin' and Singin' the Blues/Tell Him That I Need Him	1951	20.00	40.00	80.00
❑ 12055	Ring-a-Ding-Doo/The Crying Blues	1952	17.50	35.00	70.00
❑ 12063	Summertime/The Storm	1952	17.50	35.00	70.00
❑ 12065	Better Beware/I'll Be There	1952	17.50	35.00	70.00
❑ 12078	Aged and Mellow/Bring My Lovin' Back to Me	1952	17.50	35.00	70.00
❑ 12090	Somebody New/Ramblin' Blues	1952	17.50	35.00	70.00
❑ 12100	Saturday Night Daddy/Mainliner	1952	75.00	150.00	300.00
—With Bobby Nunn					
❑ 12108	Last Laugh Blues/Flesh, Blood and Bones	1952	17.50	35.00	70.00
—With Little Willie Littlefield					
❑ 12115	Hollerin' and Screamin'/Turn the Lamp Down Low	1953	17.50	35.00	70.00
—With Little Willie Littlefield					
❑ 12122	You Took My Love Too Fast/Street Lights	1953	75.00	150.00	300.00
—With Bobby Nunn					
❑ 12126	Hound Dog/Sweet Lips	1953	17.50	35.00	70.00
❑ 12142	Cherry Wine/Love Oh Love	1953	17.50	35.00	70.00
KUDU					
❑ 904	Home Is Where the Hatred Is/Til My Back Ain't Got No Bone	1972	—	2.50	5.00
❑ 906	Baby I'm for Real/That's All Right with Me	1972	—	2.50	5.00
❑ 910	I've Never Found a Man (To Love Me Like You Do)/Cherry Red	1972	—	2.50	5.00
❑ 915	Use Me/Let Me in Your Life	1973	—	2.50	5.00
❑ 917	Justified/Too Many Roads	1973	—	2.50	5.00
❑ 921	Such a Night/Can't Trust Your Neighbor	1974	—	2.50	5.00
❑ 922	Disposable Society/(B-side unknown)	1974	—	2.50	5.00
❑ 925	What a Difference a Day Makes/Turn Around, Look at Me	1975	—	2.50	5.00
❑ 929	For All We Know/Fever	1976	—	2.50	5.00
❑ 936	Boy I Really Tied One On/Magic's in the Air	1976	—	2.50	5.00
❑ 938	Higher and Higher/All the Way Down	1976	—	2.50	5.00
LENOX					
❑ 5555	Release Me/Don't Feel Rained On	1962	7.50	15.00	30.00
❑ 5560	Ain't That Easy to Forget/I Really Don't Want to Know	1963	5.00	10.00	20.00
❑ 5565	You Never Miss Your Water (Till the Well Runs Dry)/If You Want It (I Got It)	1963	5.00	10.00	20.00
—As "Little Esther Phillips and Big Al Downing"					
❑ 5570	Why Should We Try Anymore/While It Lasted	1963	5.00	10.00	20.00
❑ 5575	Don't Let Me Go/Why Was I Born	1963	5.00	10.00	20.00
❑ 5577	A Lover's Hymn/God Bless the Child Who's Got His Own	1963	5.00	10.00	20.00
MERCURY					
❑ 73967	Love Addict/I've Never Been a Woman Before	1977	—	2.00	4.00
❑ 74030	There You Go Again (There She Goes Again)/ Stormy Weather	1978	—	2.00	4.00
❑ 74060	Oo-Oop-Oo-Oop/I'll Close My Eyes	1979	—	2.00	4.00
❑ 74077	Our Day Will Come/Mr. Melody	1979	—	2.00	4.00
ROULETTE					
❑ 7031	Too Late to Worry, Too Blue to Cry/I'm in the Mood for Love	1969	—	3.50	7.00
❑ 7049	Tonight I'll Be Staying Here with You/Sweet Dreams	1969	—	3.50	7.00
❑ 7059	Nobody But You/Too Much of a Man	1969	—	3.50	7.00
SAVOY					
❑ 1193	You Can Bet Your Life/'Tain't Whatcha Say It's Whatcha Do	1956	6.25	12.50	25.00
❑ 1516	Longing in My Heart/If It's News to Me	1957	5.00	10.00	20.00
❑ 1563	It's So Good/Do You Ever Think of Me	1959	3.75	7.50	15.00
WARWICK					
❑ 610	Gee Baby/Wild Child	1961	3.75	7.50	15.00

Number	Title (A Side/B Side)	Yr	VG	VG+	NM
WINNING					
❑ 1001	Turn Me Out/(B-side unknown)	1983	—	2.50	5.00

PHILLIPS, JOHN

Also see THE JOURNEYMEN; THE MAMAS AND THE PAPAS; THE SMOOTHIES.

Number	Title (A Side/B Side)	Yr	VG	VG+	NM
ABC DUNHILL					
❑ 4236	Mississippi/April Anne	1970	—	3.00	6.00
ATCO					
❑ 6960	Green-Eyed Lady/Lion	1974	—	3.00	6.00
COLUMBIA					
❑ 45737	Cup of Tea/Revolution on Vacation	1972	—	2.50	5.00

PHILLIPS, MICHELLE

Also see THE MAMAS AND THE PAPAS.

Number	Title (A Side/B Side)	Yr	VG	VG+	NM
A&M					
❑ 1740	There She Goes/Aloha Louie	1975	—	2.50	5.00
❑ 1824	No Love Today/Aloha Louie	1976	—	2.00	4.00
❑ 1824 [PS]	No Love Today/Aloha Louie	1976	—	3.00	6.00
❑ 1996	The Aching Kind/Lady of Fantasy	1977	—	2.50	5.00
❑ 2021	There She Goes/Victim of Romance	1978	—	2.50	5.00

PHILLIPS, PHIL

Number	Title (A Side/B Side)	Yr	VG	VG+	NM
KHOURY'S					
❑ 711	Sea of Love/Juella	1959	375.00	750.00	1500.
MERCURY					
❑ 10021 [S]	Take This Heart/Verdie Mae	1959	12.50	25.00	50.00
❑ 71465	Sea of Love/Juella	1959	6.25	12.50	25.00
❑ 71531 [M]	Take This Heart/Verdie Mae	1959	5.00	10.00	20.00
❑ 71550	Providing/Don't Leave Me	1960	5.00	10.00	20.00
❑ 71611	What Will I Tell My Heart/Your True Love Once More	1960	5.00	10.00	20.00
❑ 71649	Stormy Weather/Don't Cry Baby	1960	5.00	10.00	20.00
❑ 71657	Come BackMy Darling/Nobody Knows-Nobody Cares	1960	5.00	10.00	20.00

PIANO RED

Also see DR. FEELGOOD AND THE INTERNS.

Number	Title (A Side/B Side)	Yr	VG	VG+	NM
CHECKER					
❑ 911	Get Up Mare/So Worried	1958	7.50	15.00	30.00
GROOVE					
❑ 0023	Decatur Street Blues/Big Rock Joe from Kokomo	1954	7.50	15.00	30.00
❑ 0101	Pay It No Mind/Jump, Man, Jump	1955	7.50	15.00	30.00
❑ 0118	Six O'Clock Bounce/Goodbye	1955	7.50	15.00	30.00
❑ 0126	Red's Blues/Gordy's Rock	1955	7.50	15.00	30.00
❑ 0136	Jumpin' with Daddy/She Knocks Me Out	1956	7.50	15.00	30.00
❑ 0145	I'm Nobody's Fool/That's My Desire	1956	7.50	15.00	30.00
❑ 0169	Woo-Ee/You Were Mine for Awhile	1956	7.50	15.00	30.00
JAX					
❑ 1000	This Old World/I Feel Good	1959	3.75	7.50	15.00
❑ 1006	Guitar Walk/I've Been Walkin'	1959	3.75	7.50	15.00
KING					
❑ 6330	I Want a Bowlegged Woman/Underground Atlanta	1970	—	2.50	5.00
RCA VICTOR					
❑ 47-4265	Diggin' the Boogie/Let's Have a Good Time Tonight	1951	15.00	30.00	60.00
❑ 47-4380	Hey Good Lookin'/It Makes No Difference Now	1951	15.00	30.00	60.00
❑ 47-4524	Bouncin' with Red/Count the Days I'm Gone	1952	15.00	30.00	60.00
❑ 47-4766	She Walks Right In/Sales Tax Boogie	1952	15.00	30.00	60.00
❑ 47-4957	Yoo Doopee Doo/Daybreak	1952	15.00	30.00	60.00
❑ 47-5101	I'm Gonna Rock Some More/Everybody's Boogie	1952	12.50	25.00	50.00
❑ 47-5224	She's Dynamite/I'm Gonna Tell Everybody	1953	10.00	20.00	40.00
❑ 47-5337	Decatur Street Boogie/Your Mouth's Got a Hole In It	1953	10.00	20.00	40.00
❑ 47-5544	Right and Read, Taxi, Taxi 6963	1953	10.00	20.00	40.00
❑ 47-6856	Wild Fire/Rock Baby	1957	5.00	10.00	20.00
❑ 47-6953	Peachtree Parade/Please Don't Talk About Me	1957	5.00	10.00	20.00
❑ 47-7065	South/Coo Cha	1957	5.00	10.00	20.00
❑ 47-7217	Comin' On/One Glimpse of Heaven	1958	5.00	10.00	20.00
❑ 50-0099	Rockin' with Red/Red's Boogie	1950	37.50	75.00	150.00
—Gray label, orange vinyl					
❑ 50-0106	The Wrong Yo-Yo/My Gal Jo	1951	15.00	30.00	60.00
❑ 50-0118	Jumpin' the Boogie/Just Right Bounce	1951	15.00	30.00	60.00
❑ 50-0130	Layin' the Boogie/Baby What's Wrong	1951	15.00	30.00	60.00

7-Inch Extended Plays

Number	Title (A Side/B Side)	Yr	VG	VG+	NM
GROOVE					
❑ EGA-3	(contents unknown)	1956	25.00	50.00	100.00
❑ EGA-3 [PS]	Jump, Man, Jump	1956	25.00	50.00	100.00
❑ EGA-26	(contents unknown)	1956	15.00	30.00	60.00
❑ EGA-26 [PS]	Piano Red In Concert, Vol. 1	1956	15.00	30.00	60.00
❑ EGA-27	(contents unknown)	1956	15.00	30.00	60.00
❑ EGA-27 [PS]	Piano Red In Concert, Vol. 2	1956	15.00	30.00	60.00
❑ EGA-28	(contents unknown)	1956	15.00	30.00	60.00
❑ EGA-28 [PS]	Piano Red In Concert, Vol. 3	1956	15.00	30.00	60.00
RCA VICTOR					
❑ EPA-587	(contents unknown)	1954	25.00	50.00	100.00
❑ EPA-587 [PS]	Rockin' with Red	1954	25.00	50.00	100.00
❑ EPA-5091	(contents unknown)	1959	25.00	50.00	100.00
—Maroon label					
❑ EPA-5091	(contents unknown)	1959	12.50	25.00	50.00
—Black label					
❑ EPA-5091 [PS]	Rockin' with Red	1959	12.50	25.00	50.00

PICKETT, BOBBY "BORIS"

Number	Title (A Side/B Side)	Yr	VG	VG+	NM
ANTHEM					
❑ 205	Monster Concert/Am I	1973	—	3.00	6.00
CAPITOL					
❑ 5063	Simon the Sensible Surfer/Simon Says So What	1963	6.25	12.50	25.00
GARPAX					
❑ P-1	Monster Mash/Monster's Mash Party	1962	7.50	15.00	30.00
—Orange label, first release of 44167?					

Number	Title (A Side/B Side)	Yr	VG	VG+	NM
❑ 724	I'm Down to My Last Heartbreak/I Can't Stop	1962	6.25	12.50	25.00
❑ 44167	Monster Mash/Monster's Mash Party	1962	6.25	12.50	25.00
❑ 44167 [PS]	Monster Mash/Monster's Mash Party	1962	15.00	30.00	60.00
❑ 44171	Monster's Holiday/Monster's Motion	1962	6.25	12.50	25.00
❑ 44171 [PS]	Monster's Holiday/Monster's Motion	1962	10.00	20.00	40.00
❑ 44175	Graduation Day/The Humpty Dumpty	1963	6.25	12.50	25.00
❑ 44175 [PS]	Graduation Day/The Humpty Dumpty	1963	10.00	20.00	40.00
❑ 44185	Blood Bank Blues/Me and My Mummy	1965	6.25	12.50	25.00
METROMEDIA					
❑ BMBO-0089	Me and My Mummy/It's Not the Same Without You	1973	2.50	5.00	10.00
—B-side by Pickett and Payne					
PARROT					
❑ 348	Monster Mash/Monster's Mash Party	1970	2.50	5.00	10.00
—Reissued in 1973 with the same number and label design					
❑ 366	Monster's Holiday/Monster Minuet	1971	2.50	5.00	10.00
PIZZERIA					
❑ 1	Star Drek/Mangy Old Sidewinder	1977	2.00	5.00	10.00
—With Peter Ferrara; originals are autographed on the label by both					
POLYDOR					
❑ 14361	King Kong (Your Song)/Disco Kong	1976	—	2.50	5.00
—With Peter Ferrara					
RCA VICTOR					
❑ 47-8312	Smoke! Smoke! Smoke! (That Cigarette)/Gotta Leave This Town	1964	3.75	7.50	15.00
❑ 47-8459	The Werewolf Watusi/Monster Swim	1964	3.75	7.50	15.00
WHITE WHALE					
❑ 363	Monster Man Jam/Am I	1970	6.25	12.50	25.00
—B-side by Bobby and Joan Pickett					
❑ 365	Monster Concert/(B-side unknown)	1970	6.25	12.50	25.00

PICKETT, WILSON

Also see THE FALCONS.

Number	Title (A Side/B Side)	Yr	VG	VG+	NM
ATLANTIC					
❑ 2233	I'm Gonna Cry/For Better or Worse	1964	3.75	7.50	15.00
❑ 2271	Come Home Baby/Take a Little Love	1965	3.75	7.50	15.00
❑ 2289	In the Midnight Hour/I'm Not Tired	1965	3.75	7.50	15.00
❑ 2306	Don't Fight It/It's All Over	1965	3.75	7.50	15.00
❑ 2320	634-5789 (Soulsville, U.S.A.)/That's a Man's Way	1966	3.75	7.50	15.00
❑ 2334	Ninety-Nine and a Half (Won't Do)/Danger Zone	1966	3.75	7.50	15.00
❑ 2348	Land of 1000 Dances/You're So Fine	1966	3.75	7.50	15.00
❑ 2365	Mustang Sally/Three Time Loser	1966	3.75	7.50	15.00
❑ 2381	Everybody Needs Somebody to Love/Nothing You Can Do	1967	3.00	6.00	12.00
❑ 2394	I Found a Love — Part I/I Found a Love — Part II	1967	3.00	6.00	12.00
❑ 2412	Soul Dance Number Three/You Can't Stand Alone	1967	3.00	6.00	12.00
❑ 2430	Funky Broadway/I'm Sorry About That	1967	3.00	6.00	12.00
❑ 2448	Stag-O-Lee/I'm In Love	1967	3.00	6.00	12.00
❑ 2484	Jealous Love/I've Come a Long Way	1968	2.50	5.00	10.00
❑ 2504	She's Lookin' Good/We've Got to Have Love	1968	2.50	5.00	10.00
❑ 2528	I'm a Midnight Mover/Deborah	1968	2.50	5.00	10.00
❑ 2558	I Found a True Love/For Better or Worse	1968	2.50	5.00	10.00
❑ 2575	A Man and a Half/People Make the World (What It Is)	1968	2.50	5.00	10.00
❑ 2591	Hey Jude/Search Your Heart	1968	2.50	5.00	10.00
❑ 2611	Mini-Skirt Minnie/Back in Your Arms	1969	2.00	4.00	8.00
❑ 2631	Born to Be Wild/Toe Hold	1969	2.00	4.00	8.00
❑ 2648	Hey Joe/Night Owl	1969	2.00	4.00	8.00
❑ 2682	You Keep Me Hangin' On/Now You See Me, Now You Don't	1969	2.00	4.00	8.00
❑ 2722	Sugar, Sugar/Cole, Cooke, and Redding	1970	2.00	4.00	8.00
❑ 2753	She Said Yes/It's Still Good	1970	—	3.00	6.00
❑ 2765	Engine Number Nine/International Playboy	1970	—	3.00	6.00
❑ 2781	Don't Let the Green Grass Fool You/Ain't No Doubt About It	1971	—	3.00	6.00
❑ 2797	Don't Knock My Love (Part 1)/Don't Knock My Love (Part 2)	1971	—	3.00	6.00
❑ 2824	Call My Name, I'll Be There/Woman Let Me Down Home	1971	—	3.00	6.00
❑ 2852	Fire and Water/Pledging My Love	1971	—	3.00	6.00
❑ 2878	Funk Factory/One Step Away	1972	—	3.00	6.00
❑ 2909	Mama Told Me Not to Come/Covering the Same Old Ground	1972	—	3.00	6.00
❑ 2961	Come Right Here/International Playboy	1973	—	3.00	6.00
BIG TREE					
❑ 16121	Who Turned You On/Dance You Down	1978	—	2.50	5.00
❑ 16129	Groovin'/Time to Let the Sun Shine In	1978	—	2.50	5.00
CORREC-TONE					
❑ 501	Let Me Be Your Boy/My Heart Belongs to You	1962	15.00	30.00	60.00
CUB					
❑ 9113	Let Me Be Your Boy/My Heart Belongs to You	1962	7.50	15.00	30.00
DOUBLE L					
❑ 713	If You Need Me/Baby Call on Me	1963	5.00	10.00	20.00
❑ 717	It's Too Late/I'm Gonna Love You	1963	5.00	10.00	20.00
❑ 724	I'm Down to My Last Heartbreak/I Can't Stop	1963	3.75	7.50	15.00
EMI AMERICA					
❑ 8027	I Want You/Love of My Life	1979	—	2.50	5.00
❑ 8034	Live with Me/Granny	1980	—	2.50	5.00
❑ 8070	Ain't Gonna Give You No More/Don't Underestimate the Power of Love	1981	—	2.50	5.00
❑ 8082	Back on the Right Track/It's You	1981	—	2.50	5.00
ERVA					
❑ 318	Love Dagger/Time to Let the Sun Shine on Me	1977	—	2.50	5.00
MOTOWN					
❑ 1898	Don't Turn Away/Can't Stop Now	1987	—	2.00	4.00
❑ 1916	In the Midnight Hour/Just Let Her Know	1987	—	2.00	4.00
❑ 1938	Love Never Let Me Down/Just Let Her Know	1988	—	2.00	4.00
❑ 53407	Love Never Let Me Down/Just Let Her Know	1988	—	2.00	4.00
PHILCO-FORD					
❑ HP-11	Land of a 1000 Dances/Midnight Hour	1967	3.75	7.50	15.00
—4-inch plastic "Hip Pocket Record" with color sleeve					
RCA VICTOR					
❑ APBO-0049	Take a Closer Look at the Woman You're With/Two Woman and a Wife	1973	—	3.00	6.00
❑ APBO-0174	Soft Soul Boogie Woogie/Take That Pollution Out of Your Throat	1973	—	3.00	6.00
❑ APBO-0309	Take Your Pleasure Where You FInd It/What Good Is a Lie	1974	—	3.00	6.00
❑ PB-10067	I Was Too Nice/Isn't That So	1974	—	3.00	6.00
❑ 74-0908	Mr. Magic Man/I Sho' Love You	1973	—	3.00	6.00
VERVE					
❑ 10378	Let Me Be Your Boy/My Heart Belongs to You	1966	5.00	10.00	20.00
WICKED					
❑ 8101	The Best Part of a Man/How Will I Ever Know	1975	—	3.00	6.00
❑ 8102	Love Will Keep Us Together/It's Gonna Be Good	1976	—	3.00	6.00

7-Inch Extended Plays

Number	Title (A Side/B Side)	Yr	VG	VG+	NM
ATLANTIC					
❑ SD 8129 [DJ]	Something You Got/Barefootin'/Land of 1000 Dances//In the Midnight Hour/Ninety-Nine and a Half (Won't Do)/I'm Drifting	1966	3.75	7.50	15.00
—Jukebox mini-LP, small hole, plays at 33 1/3 rpm					
❑ SD 8129 [PS]	The Exciting Wilson Pickett	1966	3.75	7.50	15.00

PICKS, THE

Also see NORMAN PETTY TRIO.

Number	Title (A Side/B Side)	Yr	VG	VG+	NM
COLUMBIA					
❑ 41096	Moondreams/Look to the Future	1958	12.50	25.00	50.00

PICKWICKS, THE

Number	Title (A Side/B Side)	Yr	VG	VG+	NM
PARROT					
❑ 9679	Apple Blossom Time/I Don't Want to Tell You Again	1964	3.75	7.50	15.00
WARNER BROS.					
❑ 5492	Little by Little/I Took My Baby Home	1965	3.75	7.50	15.00

PIERCE, WEBB

Also see WILLIE NELSON; RED SOVINE; MEL TILLIS; KITTY WELLS.

Number	Title (A Side/B Side)	Yr	VG	VG+	NM
4 STAR					
❑ 1601	Heebie Jeebie Blues/High Geared Daddy	1952	7.50	15.00	30.00
❑ 1610	Hawaiian Echoes/I Saw Your Face in the Moon	1952	7.50	15.00	30.00
❑ 1616	Georgia Rag/Lucky Lee	1952	7.50	15.00	30.00
❑ 1629	Jilted Love/I'm Happy You Hurt Me	1953	7.50	15.00	30.00
DECCA					
❑ 9-28091	That Heart Belongs to Me/So Used to Loving You	1952	6.25	12.50	25.00
❑ 9-28369	Back Street Affair/I'll Always Take Care of You	1952	6.25	12.50	25.00
❑ 9-28431	Bow Thy Head/The Country Church	1952	7.50	15.00	30.00
❑ 9-28534	I'll Go On Alone/That's Me Without You	1953	6.25	12.50	25.00
❑ 9-28594	The Last Waltz/I Haven't Got the Heart	1953	6.25	12.50	25.00
❑ 9-28725	It's Been So Long/Don't Throw Your Life Away	1953	6.25	12.50	25.00
❑ 9-28834	There Stands the Glass/I'm Walking the Dog	1953	6.25	12.50	25.00
❑ 9-28991	Slowly/You Just Can't Be True	1954	6.25	12.50	25.00
❑ 9-29107	Even Tho/Sparkling Blue Eyes	1954	6.25	12.50	25.00
❑ 9-29155	Mother Calling My Name in Prayer/Bugle Call from Heaven	1954	7.50	15.00	30.00
❑ 9-29252	More and More/You're Not Mine Anymore	1954	6.25	12.50	25.00
❑ 9-29391	In the Jailhouse Now/I'm Gonna Fall Out of Love with You	1955	5.00	10.00	20.00
❑ 9-29480	I Don't Care/Your Good for Nothing Heart	1955	5.00	10.00	20.00
❑ 9-29662	Love, Love, Love/If You Were Me	1955	5.00	10.00	20.00
❑ 9-29805	Yes, I Know Why/'Cause I Love You	1956	5.00	10.00	20.00
❑ 9-29974	Any Old Time/We'll Find a Way	1956	5.00	10.00	20.00
❑ 9-30045	Teenage Boogie/I'm Really Glad You Hurt Me	1956	10.00	20.00	40.00
❑ 9-30155	I'm Tired/It's My Way	1956	5.00	10.00	20.00
❑ 9-30255	Honky Tonk Song/Someday	1957	5.00	10.00	20.00
❑ 9-30321	Bye Bye, Love/Missing You	1957	3.75	7.50	15.00
❑ 9-30419	Holiday for Love/Don't Do It Darlin'	1957	3.75	7.50	15.00
❑ 9-30550	New Panhandle Rag/How Long?	1958	3.75	7.50	15.00
❑ 9-30623	Cryin' Over You/You'll Come Back	1958	3.75	7.50	15.00
❑ 9-30711	Tupelo County Jail/Falling Back to You	1958	3.75	7.50	15.00
❑ 9-30789	I'm Letting You Go/Sittin' Alone	1958	3.75	7.50	15.00
❑ 9-30858	A Thousand Miles Ago/What Goes On in Your Heart	1959	3.75	7.50	15.00
❑ 9-30923	I Ain't Never/Shanghaied	1959	3.75	7.50	15.00
❑ 9-31021	No Love Have I/Whirlpool of Love	1959	3.75	7.50	15.00
❑ 31058	Is It Wrong (For Loving You)/(Doin' the) Lovers Leap	1960	3.00	6.00	12.00
❑ 31118	Drifting Texas Sand/All I Need Is You	1960	3.00	6.00	12.00
❑ 31165	Fallen Angel/Truck Driver's Blues	1960	3.00	6.00	12.00
❑ 31197	Let Forgiveness In/There's More Pretty Girls Than One	1961	3.00	6.00	12.00
❑ 31249	Sweet Lips/Last Night	1961	3.00	6.00	12.00
❑ 31298	Walking the Streets/How Do You Talk to a Baby	1961	3.00	6.00	12.00
❑ 31347	Alla My Love/You Are My Life	1962	3.00	6.00	12.00
❑ 31380	Take Time/Crazy Wild Desire	1962	3.00	6.00	12.00
❑ 31421	Cow Town/Sooner or Later	1962	3.00	6.00	12.00
❑ 31451	Sawmill/If I Could Come Back	1963	2.50	5.00	10.00
❑ 31488	Sands of Gold/Nobody's Darlin'	1963	2.50	5.00	10.00
❑ 31544	Those Wonderful Years/If the Back Door Could Talk	1963	2.50	5.00	10.00
❑ 31582	Waiting a Lifetime/Love Come to Me	1964	2.50	5.00	10.00
❑ 31617	Memory No. 1/French Riviera	1964	2.50	5.00	10.00
❑ 31704	That's Where My Money Goes/Broken Engagement	1964	2.50	5.00	10.00
❑ 31737	Loving You Then Losing You/Let Me Live a Little	1965	2.50	5.00	10.00
❑ 31816	Who Do I Think I Am/Hobo and the Rose	1965	2.50	5.00	10.00
❑ 31867	Christmas at Home/Sweet Memories	1965	3.00	6.00	12.00
❑ 31924	You Ain't No Better Than Me/The Champ	1966	2.50	5.00	10.00
❑ 31982	Love's Something (I Can't Understand)/A Loner	1966	2.50	5.00	10.00
❑ 32033	Where'd Ya Stay Last Night/She's Twenty-One	1966	2.50	5.00	10.00

Number	Title (A Side/B Side)	Yr	VG	VG+	NM
❑ 32098	Goodbye City, Goodbye Girl/That Same Old Street	1967	2.00	4.00	8.00
❑ 32167	Fool Fool Fool/Bottles and Babies	1967	2.00	4.00	8.00
❑ 32246	Luzianna/Somebody Please Kiss My Sweet Thing	1967	2.00	4.00	8.00
❑ 32339	Stranger in a Strange, Strange City/In Another World	1968	2.00	4.00	8.00
❑ 32388	Saturday Night/I Tried Everything to Please	1968	2.00	4.00	8.00
❑ 32438	If I Had Last Night to Live Over/No Tears Tonight	1969	2.00	4.00	8.00
❑ 32508	This Thing/Does My Memory Ever Cross Your Mind	1969	2.00	4.00	8.00
❑ 32577	Love Ain't Never Gonna Be No Better/The Other Side of You	1969	2.00	4.00	8.00
❑ 32641	Merry-Go-Round World/Fools Night Out	1970	2.00	4.00	8.00
❑ 32694	The Man You Want Me to Be/Too Long	1970	2.00	4.00	8.00
❑ 32762	Showing His Dollar/The Way We Were Back Then	1970	2.00	4.00	8.00
❑ 32787	Tell Him That You Love Him/Heartaches Are for Lovers, Not for Friends	1971	2.00	4.00	8.00
❑ 32855	Someone Stepped In (And Stole Me Blind)/I Miss the Little Things	1971	2.00	4.00	8.00
❑ 32924	Hey Good Lookin'/Wonderful, Wonderful, Wonderful	1972	2.00	4.00	8.00
❑ 32973	I'm Gonna Be a Swinger/Someday	1972	2.00	4.00	8.00
❑ 33015	There Stands the Glass/Valentino of the Hobos	1972	2.00	4.00	8.00
❑ 33044	Let the Children Pick the Flowers/You're Letting Me Go	1973	2.00	4.00	8.00
❑ 7-34014 [S]	Hideaway Heart/(B-side unknown)	1962	3.75	7.50	15.00
—33 1/3 rpm jukebox single, small hole					
❑ 7-34015 [S]	Cow Town/(B-side unknown)	1962	3.75	7.50	15.00
—33 1/3 rpm jukebox single, small hole					
❑ 7-34016 [S]	First to Have a Second Chance/(B-side unknown)	1962	3.75	7.50	15.00
—33 1/3 rpm jukebox single, small hole					
❑ 7-34017 [S]	Tennessee Waltz/(B-side unknown)	1962	3.75	7.50	15.00
—33 1/3 rpm jukebox single, small hole					
❑ 7-34018 [S]	I'm Walking Behind You/(B-side unknown)	1962	3.75	7.50	15.00
—33 1/3 rpm jukebox single, small hole					
❑ 7-34135 [S]	I've Got a New Heartache/(B-side unknown)	1963	3.75	7.50	15.00
—33 1/3 rpm jukebox single, small hole					
❑ 7-34136 [S]	What Good Will It Do/(B-side unknown)	1963	3.75	7.50	15.00
—33 1/3 rpm jukebox single, small hole					
❑ 7-34137 [S]	Are You Sincere?/(B-side unknown)	1963	3.75	7.50	15.00
—33 1/3 rpm jukebox single, small hole					
❑ 7-34138 [S]	I Can't Stop Loving You/(B-side unknown)	1963	3.75	7.50	15.00
—33 1/3 rpm jukebox single, small hole					
❑ 7-34139 [S]	If I Lost Your Love/(B-side unknown)	1963	3.75	7.50	15.00
—33 1/3 rpm jukebox single, small hole					
❑ 9-46322	If Crying Would Make You Care/Drifting Texas Sand	1951	7.50	15.00	30.00
❑ 9-46332	California Blues/You Scared the Love Right Out of Me	1951	7.50	15.00	30.00
❑ 9-46364	Wondering/New Silver Bells	1951	6.25	12.50	25.00
❑ 9-46385	I'm Gonna See My Baby/You Know I'm Still in Love	1952	6.25	12.50	25.00

KING

Number	Title (A Side/B Side)	Yr	VG	VG+	NM
❑ 5366	New Panhandle Rag/It's All Between the Lines	1960	3.00	6.00	12.00
❑ 5429	Jilted Love/Georgia Rag	1960	3.00	6.00	12.00

MCA

Number	Title (A Side/B Side)	Yr	VG	VG+	NM
❑ 40128	Lo-Lenna/When You're Living in Hell	1973	—	3.00	6.00
❑ 40181	I'd Be Number One/You Better Treat Her Right	1974	—	3.00	6.00
❑ 40255	Honey (Open That Door)/Take the Time It Takes	1974	—	3.00	6.00
❑ 40310	I Know, I Know, I Know/I'm Ashamed to Be Here	1974	—	3.00	6.00

PLANTATION

Number	Title (A Side/B Side)	Yr	VG	VG+	NM
❑ 131	The Good Lord Giveth (And Uncle Sam Taketh Away)/Send My Love to Me	1975	—	3.00	6.00
❑ 136	I've Got Leaving on My Mind/Shame, Shame, Shame	1976	—	3.00	6.00
❑ 141	That's Me Without You/Appleton	1976	—	3.00	6.00
❑ 145	Christmas Time's a Coming/The Family Christmas Tree	1976	—	3.00	6.00
❑ 149	Got You on My Mind/Love Brought Us Together	1977	—	2.50	5.00
—With Carol Channing					
❑ 154	Rhinestone Cowboy Club/Sparkling Brown Eyes	1977	—	3.00	6.00

7-Inch Extended Plays

DECCA

Number	Title (A Side/B Side)	Yr	VG	VG+	NM
❑ ED 2144	Wondering/There Stands the Glass//That's Me Without You/Don't Throw Your Life Away	195?	5.00	10.00	20.00
❑ ED 2144	The Wondering Boy, Part 1	195?	5.00	10.00	20.00
❑ ED 2145	Back Street Affair/It's Been So Long//Slowly/That Heart Belongs to Me	195?	5.00	10.00	20.00
❑ ED 2145	The Wondering Boy, Part 2	195?	5.00	10.00	20.00
❑ ED 2241	(contents unknown)	195?	5.00	10.00	20.00
❑ ED 2241 [PS]	Webb Pierce, Vol. 1	195?	5.00	10.00	20.00
❑ ED 2242	(contents unknown)	195?	5.00	10.00	20.00
❑ ED 2242 [PS]	Webb Pierce, Vol. 2	195?	5.00	10.00	20.00
❑ ED 2243	(contents unknown)	195?	5.00	10.00	20.00
❑ ED 2243 [PS]	Webb Pierce, Vol. 3	195?	5.00	10.00	20.00
❑ ED 2355	(contents unknown)	1956	5.00	10.00	20.00
❑ ED 2355 [PS]	The Country Church	1956	5.00	10.00	20.00
❑ ED 2364	(contents unknown)	1956	5.00	10.00	20.00
❑ ED 2364 [PS]	The Wondering Boy, Vol. 3	1956	5.00	10.00	20.00
❑ ED 2581	*New Love Affair/I Care No More/Just Imagination/I Love	1958	5.00	10.00	20.00
❑ ED 2581 [PS]	Just Imagination	1958	5.00	10.00	20.00
❑ ED 2653 [M]	*After the Boy Gets the Girl/I Owe It to Myself/My Shoes Keep Walking Back to You/Life to Go	1959	5.00	10.00	20.00
❑ ED 2653 [PS]	Webb	1959	5.00	10.00	20.00
❑ ED 7-2653 [PS]	Webb	1959	7.50	15.00	30.00
❑ ED 7-2653 [S]	*After the Boy Gets the Girl/I Owe It to Myself/My Shoes Keep Walking Back to You/Life to Go	1959	7.50	15.00	30.00
❑ ED 2668 [M]	*I Ain't Never/Shanghaied/A Thousand Miles Ago/What Goes On in Your Heart	1959	5.00	10.00	20.00
❑ ED 2668 [PS]	I Ain't Never	1959	5.00	10.00	20.00
❑ ED 7-2668 [PS]	I Ain't Never	1959	7.50	15.00	30.00
❑ ED 7-2668 [S]	*I Ain't Never/Shanghaied/A Thousand Miles Ago/What Goes On in Your Heart	1959	7.50	15.00	30.00
❑ ED 2685	*Walking the Streets/All I Need Is You/Drifting Texas Sand/Drinking My Blues Away	1960	6.25	12.50	25.00
❑ ED 2685 [PS]	Walking the Streets	1960	6.25	12.50	25.00
❑ ED 2694	*Is It Wrong/Lover's Leap/No Love Have I/Whirlpool of Love	1961	6.25	12.50	25.00
❑ ED 2694 [PS]	Is It Wrong	1961	6.25	12.50	25.00
❑ ED 2709	*Hideaway Heart/Tender Years/Pictures on the Wall/First to Have a Second Chance	1962	6.25	12.50	25.00
❑ ED 2709 [PS]	Hideaway Heart	1962	6.25	12.50	25.00
❑ ED 2719	(contents unknown)	1962	6.25	12.50	25.00
❑ ED 2719 [PS]	Webb Pierce	1962	6.25	12.50	25.00
❑ ED 2734	*Crazy Wild Desire/Take Time/I'm Falling in Love with You/There's More Pretty Girls Than One	1962	6.25	12.50	25.00
❑ ED 2734 [PS]	Crazy Wild Desire	1962	6.25	12.50	25.00
❑ ED 2748	(contents unknown)	1963	7.50	15.00	30.00
❑ ED 2748 [PS]	Fallen Angel	1963	7.50	15.00	30.00
❑ ED 2761	*Cow Town/If I Could Come Back/Sooner or Later/Sawmill	1964	7.50	15.00	30.00
❑ ED 2761 [PS]	Cow Town	1964	7.50	15.00	30.00
❑ ED 2785	(contents unknown)	1965	10.00	20.00	40.00
❑ ED 2785 [PS]	Nobody's Darling But Mine	1965	10.00	20.00	40.00
❑ ED 2786	(contents unknown)	1965	10.00	20.00	40.00
❑ ED 2786 [PS]	Softly and Tenderly	1965	10.00	20.00	40.00
❑ ED 2799	(contents unknown)	1966	10.00	20.00	40.00
❑ ED 2799 [PS]	Loving You Then Losing You	1966	10.00	20.00	40.00

PIERCE, WEBB AND DEBBIE

MCA

Number	Title (A Side/B Side)	Yr	VG	VG+	NM
❑ 40048	Foreign Girl/What the People Say	1973	—	3.00	6.00

PLANTATION

Number	Title (A Side/B Side)	Yr	VG	VG+	NM
❑ 189	On My Way Out/I'm Coming Home Again	1980	—	2.50	5.00
❑ 191	Reality of Life/My Memory Remembers	1980	—	2.50	5.00
❑ 196	Happy Birthday Jesus/(B-side unknown)	1980	—	3.00	6.00

PIERCE, WEBB, AND NANCY DEE

DECCA

Number	Title (A Side/B Side)	Yr	VG	VG+	NM
❑ 32884	Above Suspicion/I Owe It to My Heart	1971	2.00	4.00	8.00

PILOT (1)

ARISTA

Number	Title (A Side/B Side)	Yr	VG	VG+	NM
❑ AS 0259	One Good Reason Why/Get Up and Go	1977	—	2.00	4.00

EMI

Number	Title (A Side/B Side)	Yr	VG	VG+	NM
❑ 3992	Magic/Just Let Me Be	1974	—	2.50	5.00
❑ 4135	Don't Speak Loudly/Just a Smile	1975	—	2.00	4.00
❑ 4202	January/Do Me Good	1975	—	2.00	4.00
❑ 4305	Canada/Mover	1976	—	2.00	4.00

PILOT (2)

RCA VICTOR

Number	Title (A Side/B Side)	Yr	VG	VG+	NM
❑ 74-0770	Rider/Miss Sandy	1972	—	3.00	6.00

PING PONGS, THE

CUB

Number	Title (A Side/B Side)	Yr	VG	VG+	NM
❑ 9062	Big Ben/In the Chapel in the Moonlight	1960	5.00	10.00	20.00

UNITED ARTISTS

Number	Title (A Side/B Side)	Yr	VG	VG+	NM
❑ 236	Zyzzle/Summer Reverie	1960	5.00	10.00	20.00

PINK CLOUD, THE

TOWER

Number	Title (A Side/B Side)	Yr	VG	VG+	NM
❑ 376	Midnight Sun (Vocal)/Midnight Sun (Instrumental)	1967	5.00	10.00	20.00

PINK FLOYD

Also see SYD BARRETT; DAVID GILMOUR; ROGER WATERS.

CAPITOL

Number	Title (A Side/B Side)	Yr	VG	VG+	NM
❑ 58884	Money (Single Edit)/Time (Single Edit)	2000	—	2.00	4.00
❑ 58885	Wish You Were Here/Have a Cigar	2000	—	2.00	4.00

COLUMBIA

Number	Title (A Side/B Side)	Yr	VG	VG+	NM
❑ AE7 1653 [DJ]	Not Now John (Obscured Version) (same on both sides)	1983	2.50	5.00	10.00
❑ AE7 1653 [PS]	Not Now John (Obscured Version) (same on both sides)	1983	2.50	5.00	10.00
❑ 02165	Run Like Hell/Comfortably Numb	1981	—	—	3.00
—Reissue					
❑ 03118	Another Brick in the Wall, Part 2/One of My Turns	1982	—	—	3.00
—Reissue					
❑ 03142	When the Tigers Broke Free/Bring the Boys Back Home	1982	—	2.00	4.00
❑ 03142 [PS]	When the Tigers Broke Free/Bring the Boys Back Home	1982	—	2.50	5.00
—Fold-open cardboard sleeve					
❑ X18-03176	When the Tigers Broke Free/Bring the Boys Back Home	1982	2.50	5.00	10.00
❑ X18-03176 [PS]	When the Tigers Broke Free/Bring the Boys Back Home	1982	2.50	5.00	10.00
—Fold-open cardboard sleeve					
❑ 03905	Not Now John (Obscured Version)/The Heroes Return	1983	—	2.00	4.00
❑ 03905 [PS]	Not Now John (Obscured Version)/The Heroes Return	1983	—	2.50	5.00
❑ 07363	Learning to Fly/Terminal Frost	1987	—	2.00	4.00
❑ 07363 [PS]	Learning to Fly/Terminal Frost	1987	—	2.00	4.00
❑ 07660	On the Turning Away/Run Like Hell	1987	—	2.00	4.00
❑ 07660 [PS]	On the Turning Away/Run Like Hell	1987	—	2.00	4.00
❑ 10248	Have a Cigar/Welcome to the Machine	1975	3.00	6.00	12.00
❑ 11187	Another Brick in the Wall (Part 2)/One of My Turns	1980	—	2.50	5.00
—Custom "wall" label					
❑ 11187	Another Brick in the Wall (Part 2)/One of My Turns	1980	—	2.00	4.00
—Regular Columbia orange label					
❑ 11187 [PS]	Another Brick in the Wall (Part 2)/One of My Turns	1980	2.00	4.00	8.00

Number	Title (A Side/B Side)	Yr	VG	VG+	NM
❑ 11265	Run Like Hell/Don't Leave Me Now	1980	—	2.00	4.00
❑ 11311	Comfortably Numb/Hey You	1980	—	2.00	4.00
❑ 77493	Take It Back/Astronomy Domine (Live)	1994	—	2.00	4.00
HARVEST					
❑ 3240	Fearless/One of These Days	1971	5.00	10.00	20.00
❑ 3391	Stay/Free Four	1972	5.00	10.00	20.00
❑ 3609	Money/Any Colour You Like	1973	3.75	7.50	15.00
❑ P-3609 [DJ]	Money (Edited Mono)/Money (Edited Stereo)	1973	5.00	10.00	20.00
❑ 3832	Time/Us and Them	1974	5.00	10.00	20.00
❑ SPRO-6669 [DJ]	Money (Censored Edited Mono)/Money (Censored Edited Stereo)	1973	3.75	7.50	15.00
—This promo was sent to radio stations with a frantic note telling them to disregard the first promo					
TOWER					
❑ 333	Arnold Layne/Candy and a Currant Bun	1967	50.00	100.00	200.00
❑ 333 [PS]	Arnold Layne/Candy and a Currant Bun	1967	175.00	350.00	700.00
—Only issued with promotional copies					
❑ 356	See Emily Play/Scarecrow	1967	50.00	100.00	200.00
❑ 356 [PS]	See Emily Play/Scarecrow	1967	175.00	350.00	700.00
—Title sleeve; only issued with some promotional copies					
❑ 356 [PS]	See Emily Play/Scarecrow	1967	200.00	400.00	800.00
—Photo sleeve; only issued with some promotional copies					
❑ 378	The Gnome/Flaming	1967	37.50	75.00	150.00
❑ 426	It Would Be So Nice/Julia Dream	1968	62.50	125.00	250.00
❑ 440	Let There Be More Light/Remember a Day	1968	75.00	150.00	300.00

PINKERTON'S ASSORTED COLOURS

Number	Title (A Side/B Side)	Yr	VG	VG+	NM
LONDON					
❑ 9820	Mirror, Mirror/She Don't Care	1966	5.00	10.00	20.00
PARROT					
❑ 40001	Don't Stop Loving Me Baby/Will You	1966	5.00	10.00	20.00

PINKNEY, BILL

Also see THE DRIFTERS.

Number	Title (A Side/B Side)	Yr	VG	VG+	NM
FONTANA					
❑ 1956	Don't Call Me/I Do the Jerk	1964	3.00	6.00	12.00
GAME					
❑ 394	Ol' Man River/Millionaire	196?	12.50	25.00	50.00
PHILLIPS INT'L.					
❑ 3524	After the Hop/Sally's Got a Sister	1958	5.00	10.00	20.00
—As "Bill Pinky"					
VEEP					
❑ 1264	I Found Some Lovin'/The Masquerade Is Over	1967	2.50	5.00	10.00

PIPES, THE (1)

Number	Title (A Side/B Side)	Yr	VG	VG+	NM
CARLTON					
❑ 575	Teamwork/Soon I Will Be Done	1962	5.00	10.00	20.00

PIPES, THE (2)

Number	Title (A Side/B Side)	Yr	VG	VG+	NM
DOOTO					
❑ 388	Be Fair/Let Me Give You Money	1958	6.25	12.50	25.00
❑ 401	You Are An Angel/I Love the Life I Live	1958	6.25	12.50	25.00
DOOTONE					
❑ 388	Be Fair/Let Me Give You Money	1956	75.00	150.00	300.00
❑ 401	You Are An Angel/I Love the Life I Live	1956	75.00	150.00	300.00

PIPKINS, THE

Number	Title (A Side/B Side)	Yr	VG	VG+	NM
CAPITOL					
❑ 2819	Gimme Dat Ding/To Love You	1970	—	3.00	6.00
❑ 2874	Sugra and Spice-Are You Cookin' Goose/Yakety Yak	1970	—	2.50	5.00

PIPS, THE

See GLADYS KNIGHT AND THE PIPS.

PIRATES, THE

Early version of THE TEMPTATIONS.

Number	Title (A Side/B Side)	Yr	VG	VG+	NM
MEL-O-DY					
❑ 105	Mind Over Matter (I'm Gonna Make You Mine)/I'll Love You Till I Die	1962	25.00	50.00	100.00

PISTILLI, GENE

Also see CASHMAN, PISTILLI & WEST.

Number	Title (A Side/B Side)	Yr	VG	VG+	NM
ATCO					
❑ 6850	Benn Down So Long It Looks Like Up to Me/Lettin' Down an Old Friend	1971	—	2.50	5.00
CAPITOL					
❑ 2627	Mr. Bojangles/Ruby Tuesday	1969	—	2.50	5.00

PITNEY, GENE

Also see JAMIE AND JANE.

Number	Title (A Side/B Side)	Yr	VG	VG+	NM
BLAZE					
❑ 351	Going Back to My Love/Cradle of My Arms	1958	7.50	15.00	30.00
—As "Billy Bryan"					
EPIC					
❑ 50332	Dedication AKA This Song I Want to Dedicate to You/Sandman	1977	—	2.50	5.00
❑ 50461	It's Over, It's Over/Walkin' in the Sun	1977	—	2.50	5.00
FESTIVAL					
❑ 25002	Please Come Back/I'll Find You	1960	7.50	15.00	30.00
MUSICOR					
❑ 1002	(I Wanna) Love My Life Away/I Laughed So Hard I Cried	1960	3.75	7.50	15.00
❑ 1002 [PS]	(I Wanna) Love My Life Away/I Laughed So Hard I Cried	1960	10.00	20.00	40.00
❑ 1006	Louisiana Mama/Take Me Tonight	1961	3.75	7.50	15.00
❑ 1006 [PS]	Louisiana Mama/Take Me Tonight	1961	7.50	15.00	30.00
❑ 1009	Town Without Pity/Air Mail Special Delivery	1961	3.75	7.50	15.00
❑ 1011	Every Breath I Take/Mr. Moon, Mr. Cupid and I	1961	5.00	10.00	20.00
—Produced by Phil Spector					
❑ 1011 [PS]	Every Breath I Take/Mr. Moon, Mr. Cupid and I	1961	6.25	12.50	25.00
❑ 1020	(The Man Who Shot) Liberty Valance/Take It Like a Man	1962	3.75	7.50	15.00
❑ 1022	Only Love Can Break a Heart/If I Didn't Have a Dime	1962	3.75	7.50	15.00
❑ 1026	Half Heaven-Half Heartache/Tower Tall	1962	3.75	7.50	15.00
❑ 1028	Mecca/Teardrop by Teardrop	1963	3.75	7.50	15.00
❑ 1028 [PS]	Mecca/Teardrop by Teardrop	1963	5.00	10.00	20.00
❑ 1032	True Love Never Runs Smooth/Donna Means Heartbreak	1963	3.75	7.50	15.00
❑ 1034	Twenty-Four Hours from Tulsa/Lonely Night Dream	1963	3.75	7.50	15.00
❑ 1034 [PS]	Twenty-Four Hours from Tulsa/Lonely Night Dream	1963	5.00	10.00	20.00
❑ 1036	That Girl Belongs to Yesterday/Who Needs It	1964	5.00	10.00	20.00
—A-side written by Mick Jagger and Keith Richards and produced by Andrew Oldham					
❑ 1036 [PS]	That Girl Belongs to Yesterday/Who Needs It	1964	6.25	12.50	25.00
❑ 1038	Yesterday's Hero/Cornflower Blue	1964	3.75	7.50	15.00
❑ 1039	I'm Gonna Find Myself a Girl/Lips Are Redder	1964	—	—	—
—Unreleased?					
❑ 1040	It Hurts to Be in Love/Hawaii	1964	3.75	7.50	15.00
❑ 1040 [PS]	It Hurts to Be in Love/Hawaii	1964	5.00	10.00	20.00
❑ 1045	I'm Gonna Be Strong/Aladdin's Lamp	1964	5.00	10.00	20.00
❑ 1045	I'm Gonna Be Strong/E Se Domani	1964	3.75	7.50	15.00
❑ 1045 [PS]	I'm Gonna Be Strong/E Se Domani	1964	5.00	10.00	20.00
❑ 1065	Amici Miri/I Tuoi Anni Piu Belli	1965	—	—	—
—Unreleased?					
❑ 1070	I Must Be Seeing Things/Marianne	1965	3.00	6.00	12.00
❑ 1070 [PS]	I Must Be Seeing Things/Marianne	1965	3.75	7.50	15.00
❑ 1093	Last Chance to Turn Around/Save Your Love	1965	3.00	6.00	12.00
❑ 1103	Looking Through the Eyes of Love/There's No Living Without Your Loving	1965	3.00	6.00	12.00
❑ 1130	Princess in Rags/Amore Mio	1965	3.00	6.00	12.00
❑ 1150	Me Voy Para El Compo/Hojas Muertas	1966	—	—	—
—Unreleased?					
❑ 1155	Lei Mi Aspetta/Nessuno Mi Puo' Guidcare	1966	3.75	7.50	15.00
❑ 1171	Backstage/Blue Color	1966	2.50	5.00	10.00
❑ 1171 [PS]	Backstage/Blue Color	1966	3.75	7.50	15.00
❑ 1200	(In the) Cold Light of Day/The Boss' Daughter	1966	2.50	5.00	10.00
❑ 1200 [PS]	(In the) Cold Light of Day/The Boss' Daughter	1966	3.75	7.50	15.00
❑ 1219	Just One Smile/Innamorato	1966	2.50	5.00	10.00
❑ 1233	For Me, This Is Happy/I'm Gonna Listen to Me	1967	2.50	5.00	10.00
❑ 1235	Don't Mean to Be a Preacher/Animal Crackers (In Cellophane Boxes)	1967	2.50	5.00	10.00
❑ 1245	Tremblin'/Where Did the Magic Go	1967	2.50	5.00	10.00
❑ 1252	Somethin' Gotten Hold of My Heart/Building Up My Dream World	1967	2.50	5.00	10.00
❑ 1299	The More I Saw of Her/Won't Take Long	1968	2.00	4.00	8.00
❑ 1306	She's a Heartbreaker/Conquistador	1968	2.50	5.00	10.00
❑ 1308	Somewhere in the Country/Lonely Drifter	1968	2.00	4.00	8.00
❑ 1331	Billy, You're My Friend/She Believes in Me	1968	2.00	4.00	8.00
❑ 1331	Billy, You're My Friend/Lonely Drifter	1968	2.00	4.00	8.00
❑ 1331 [PS]	Billy, You're My Friend/Lonely Drifter	1968	3.00	6.00	12.00
❑ 1348	Baby, You're My Kind of Woman/Hate	1969	2.00	4.00	8.00
❑ 1358	Maria Elena/The French Horn	1969	2.00	4.00	8.00
❑ 1361	Playing Games of Love/California	1969	2.00	4.00	8.00
❑ 1384	She Lets Her Hair Down (Early in the Morning)/I Remember	1969	2.00	4.00	8.00
❑ 1394	All the Young Women/I Remember	1970	—	3.00	6.00
❑ 1405	A Street Called Hope/Think of Us	1970	—	3.00	6.00
❑ 1419	Shady Lady/Billy, You're My Friend	1970	—	3.00	6.00
❑ 1439	Higher and Higher/Beautiful Sounds	1971	—	3.00	6.00
❑ 1442	A Thousand Arms (Five Hundred Hearts)/Gene, Are You There?	1971	—	3.00	6.00
❑ 1453	I Just Can't Help Myself/Beautiful Sounds	1972	—	3.00	6.00
❑ 1461	Summertime Dreaming/A Thousand Arms (Five Hundred Hearts)	1972	—	3.00	6.00
❑ 1474	Shady Lady/Run, Run Roadrunner	1973	—	3.00	6.00

PITNEY, GENE, AND GEORGE JONES

Also see each artist's individual listings.

Number	Title (A Side/B Side)	Yr	VG	VG+	NM
MUSICOR					
❑ 1066	I've Got Five Dollars and It's Saturday Night/Wreck on the Highway	1965	3.00	6.00	12.00
❑ 1071	I've Got a New Heartache/My Shoes Keep Walking Back to You	1965	—	—	—
—Unreleased?					
❑ 1097	I'm a Fool to Care/Louisiana Man	1965	3.00	6.00	12.00
❑ 1097 [PS]	I'm a Fool to Care/Louisiana Man	1965	3.75	7.50	15.00
❑ 1115	Your Old Standby/Big Job	1965	3.00	6.00	12.00
❑ 1115 [PS]	Your Old Standby/Big Job	1965	3.75	7.50	15.00
❑ 1165	Y'All Come/That's All It Took	1966	2.50	5.00	10.00

PITNEY, GENE, AND MELBA MONTGOMERY

Number	Title (A Side/B Side)	Yr	VG	VG+	NM
MUSICOR					
❑ 1135	Baby, Ain't That Fine/Everybody Knows But You and Me	1965	3.00	6.00	12.00
❑ 1173	King and Queen/Being Together	1966	2.50	5.00	10.00

PITTMAN, BARBARA

Number	Title (A Side/B Side)	Yr	VG	VG+	NM
PHILLIPS INT'L.					
❑ 3518	Two Young Fools in Love/I'm Getting Better All the Time	1957	10.00	20.00	40.00
❑ 3527	Cold, Cold Heart/Everlasting Love	1958	10.00	20.00	40.00
❑ 3553	Handsome Man/The Eleventh Commandment	1960	5.00	10.00	20.00
SUN					
❑ 253	I Need a Man/No Matter Who's to Blame	1956	37.50	75.00	150.00

PITTS, GLORIA JEAN

Number	Title (A Side/B Side)	Yr	VG	VG+	NM
IMPERIAL					
❑ 5406	I Don't Stand No Quittin'/Things You Should Know	1956	12.50	25.00	50.00

PIXIES THREE, THE

Number	Title (A Side/B Side)	Yr	VG	VG+	NM
MERCURY					
❑ 72130	Birthday Party/Our Love	1963	3.75	7.50	15.00
❑ 72130 [PS]	Birthday Party/Our Love	1963	6.25	12.50	25.00

Number	Title (A Side/B Side)	Yr	VG	VG+	NM
❑ 72208	Cold, Cold Winter/442 Glenwood Avenue	1963	3.75	7.50	15.00
❑ 72208 [PS]	Cold, Cold Winter/442 Glenwood Avenue	1963	6.25	12.50	25.00
❑ 72250	Gee/After the Party	1964	3.75	7.50	15.00
❑ 72250 [PS]	Gee/After the Party	1964	7.50	15.00	30.00
❑ 72288	It's Summertime U.S.A./The Hootch	1964	3.75	7.50	15.00
❑ 72288 [PS]	It's Summertime U.S.A./The Hootch	1964	6.25	12.50	25.00
❑ 72331	Love Walked In/Orphan Boy	1964	3.75	7.50	15.00
❑ 72357	Love Me, Love Me/Your Way	1964	3.75	7.50	15.00
PLAIDS, THE					
DARL					
❑ 1001	Keeper of My Heart/I Sing for You	1956	5.00	10.00	20.00
ERA					
❑ 3002	Around the Corner/He Stole Flo	1959	5.00	10.00	20.00
LIBERTY					
❑ 55167	Hungry for Your Love/Chit-Chat	1958	100.00	200.00	400.00
NASCO					
❑ 6011	Till the End of the Dance/My Pretty Baby	1958	5.00	10.00	20.00
PLANETS, THE (1)					
ALJON					
❑ 1244	Be Sure/Once Upon a Lifetime	1962	75.00	150.00	300.00
PLANETS, THE (2)					
ERA					
❑ 1038	Never Again/Stand There Mountain	1957	12.50	25.00	50.00
❑ 1049	Be Sure/Wild Leaves	1957	12.50	25.00	50.00
NU-CLEAR					
❑ 7422	I Need You So/Sharin' Lockers	1959	15.00	30.00	60.00
PLANETS, THE (3)					
ROULETTE					
❑ 4551	You Are My Sunshine/Mr. Moon	1964	3.75	7.50	15.00
PLANETS, THE (4)					
MOTOWN					
❑ 1485	Break It To Me Gently/Secret	1980	—	2.00	4.00
PLANT, ROBERT					
Also see THE HONEYDRIPPERS; LED ZEPPELIN; LISTEN.					
ES PARANZA					
❑ 99333	Ship of Fools/Billy's Revenge	1988	—	—	3.00
❑ 99333 [PS]	Ship of Fools/Billy's Revenge	1988	—	—	3.00
❑ 99348	Tall Cool One/White, Clean and Neat	1988	—	—	3.00
❑ 99348 [PS]	Tall Cool One/White, Clean and Neat	1988	2.50	5.00	10.00
❑ 99373	Heaven Knows/Walking Towards Paradise	1988	—	—	3.00
❑ 99373 [PS]	Heaven Knows/Walking Towards Paradise	1988	—	—	3.00
❑ 99622	Too Loud/Kallalou Kallalou	1985	—	—	3.00
❑ 99622 [PS]	Too Loud/Kallalou Kallalou	1985	—	2.00	4.00
❑ 99644	Little by Little/Trouble Your Money	1985	—	—	3.00
❑ 99644 [PS]	Little by Little/Trouble Your Money	1985	—	—	3.00
❑ 99820	In the Mood/Horizontal Departure	1983	—	—	3.00
❑ 99820 [PS]	In the Mood/Horizontal Departure	1983	—	—	3.00
❑ 99844	Big Log/Far Post	1983	—	—	3.00
❑ 99844 [PS]	Big Log/Far Post	1983	—	—	3.00
SWAN SONG					
❑ 99952	Pledge Pin/Fat Lip	1982	—	2.00	4.00
❑ 99952 [PS]	Pledge Pin/Fat Lip	1982	7.50	15.00	30.00
❑ 99979	Burning Down One Side/Moonlight in Samosa	1982	—	2.00	4.00
❑ 99979 [PS]	Burning Down One Side/Moonlight in Samosa	1982	—	3.00	6.00
PLANT LIFE					
DATE					
❑ 1572	Flower Girl/Say It Over Again	1967	2.50	5.00	10.00
PLANTS, THE					
J&S					
❑ 248/9	I Searched the Seven Seas/I Took a Trip Way Over the Sea	1956	100.00	200.00	400.00
❑ 1602	Dear, I Swear/It's You	1957	100.00	200.00	400.00
—Address under label name					
❑ 1602	Dear, I Swear/It's You	1957	10.00	20.00	40.00
—No address under label name					
PLASTIC COW, THE					
DOT					
❑ 17284	The Plastic Cow/Medicine Man	1969	2.50	5.00	10.00
❑ 17300	Lady Jane/One Many, One Vault	1969	2.50	5.00	10.00
PLASTIC ONO BAND					
See JOHN LENNON; YOKO ONO.					
PLATTERS, THE					
More than one group has used this name over the years, but all are related. Also see TONY WILLIAMS.					
ANTLER					
❑ 3000/1	I Do It All the Time/Shake What Your Mama Gave You	1982	—	3.00	6.00
AVALANCHE					
❑ XW224	Sunday with You/If the World Loved	1973	2.00	4.00	8.00
—As "The Buck Ram Platters"					
ENTREE					
❑ 107	Won't You Be My Friend/Run While It's Dark	1965	2.00	4.00	8.00
—As "The Platters 1965"					
FEDERAL					
❑ 12153	Give Thanks/Hey Now	1953	100.00	200.00	400.00
—As "Tony Williams and the Platters"					
❑ 12164	I'll Cry When You're Gone/I Need You All the Time	1954	250.00	500.00	1000.
❑ 12181	Roses of Picardy/Beer Barrel Polka	1954	75.00	150.00	300.00
❑ 12188	Tell the World/Love All Night	1954	50.00	100.00	200.00
❑ 12198	Voo-Vee-Ah-Bee/Shake It Up Mambo	1954	50.00	100.00	200.00
❑ 12204	Maggie Doesn't Work Here Anymore/Take Me Back, Take Me Back	1955	50.00	100.00	200.00
❑ 12244	Only You (And You Alone)/You Made Me Cry	1955	75.00	150.00	300.00

Number	Title (A Side/B Side)	Yr	VG	VG+	NM
❑ 12250	Tell the World/I Need You All the Time	1956	30.00	60.00	120.00
❑ 12271	Give Thanks/I Need You All the Time	1956	20.00	40.00	80.00
MERCURY					
❑ 10001 [S]	Smoke Gets In Your Eyes/No Matter What You Are	1959	12.50	25.00	50.00
❑ 10007 [S]	Remember When/Love of a Lifetime	1959	10.00	20.00	40.00
❑ 70633	Only You (And You Alone)/Bark, Battle and Ball	1955	12.50	25.00	50.00
—Earliest pressings have pink labels					
❑ 70633	Only You (And You Alone)/Bark, Battle and Ball	1955	10.00	20.00	40.00
—Black label					
❑ 70753	The Great Pretender/I'm Just a Dancing Partner	1955	10.00	20.00	40.00
—Maroon label					
❑ 70753	The Great Pretender/I'm Just a Dancing Partner	1955	5.00	10.00	20.00
—Black label					
❑ 70819	(You've Got) The Magic Touch/Winner Take All	1956	10.00	20.00	40.00
—Maroon label					
❑ 70819	(You've Got) The Magic Touch/Winner Take All	1956	5.00	10.00	20.00
—Black label					
❑ 70893	My Prayer/Heaven on Earth	1956	10.00	20.00	40.00
—Maroon label					
❑ 70893	My Prayer/Heaven on Earth	1956	5.00	10.00	20.00
—Black label					
❑ 70948	You'll Never Never Know/It Isn't Right	1956	7.50	15.00	30.00
—Maroon label					
❑ 70948	You'll Never Never Know/It Isn't Right	1956	5.00	10.00	20.00
—Black label					
❑ 71011	One in a Million/On My Word of Honor	1956	7.50	15.00	30.00
❑ 71032	I'm Sorry/He's Mine	1957	7.50	15.00	30.00
—Maroon label					
❑ 71032	I'm Sorry/He's Mine	1957	5.00	10.00	20.00
—Black label					
❑ 71093	My Dream/I Wanna	1957	7.50	15.00	30.00
—Maroon label					
❑ 71093	My Dream/I Wanna	1957	5.00	10.00	20.00
—Black label					
❑ 71184	Only Because/The Mystery of You	1957	6.25	12.50	25.00
❑ 71246	Helpless/Indifferent	1957	6.25	12.50	25.00
❑ 71289	Twilight Time/Out of My Mind	1958	6.25	12.50	25.00
❑ 71320	You're Making a Mistake/My Old Flame	1958	6.25	12.50	25.00
❑ 71353	I Wish/It's Raining Outside	1958	6.25	12.50	25.00
—Black label					
❑ 71353	I Wish/It's Raining Outside	1958	7.50	15.00	30.00
—Blue label					
❑ 71383	Smoke Gets In Your Eyes/No Matter What You Are	1958	6.25	12.50	25.00
—Black label					
❑ 71383	Smoke Gets In Your Eyes/No Matter What You Are	1958	7.50	15.00	30.00
—Blue label					
❑ 71427	Enchanted/The Sound and the Fury	1959	5.00	10.00	20.00
❑ 71467 [M]	Remember When/Love of a Lifetime	1959	5.00	10.00	20.00
❑ 71502	Where/Wish It Were Me	1959	5.00	10.00	20.00
❑ 71538	My Secret/What Does It Matter	1959	5.00	10.00	20.00
❑ 71563	Harbor Lights/Sleepy Lagoon	1960	5.00	10.00	20.00
❑ 71563 [PS]	Harbor Lights/Sleepy Lagoon	1960	10.00	20.00	40.00
❑ 71624	Ebb Tide/(I'll Be With You) In Apple Blossom Time	1960	5.00	10.00	20.00
❑ 71656	Red Sails in the Sunset/Sad River	1960	5.00	10.00	20.00
❑ 71656 [PS]	Red Sails in the Sunset/Sad River	1960	7.50	15.00	30.00
❑ 71697	To Each His Own/Down the River of Golden Dreams	1960	5.00	10.00	20.00
❑ 71697 [PS]	To Each His Own/Down the River of Golden Dreams	1960	7.50	15.00	30.00
❑ 71749	If I Didn't Care/True Lover	1961	3.75	7.50	15.00
❑ 71749 [PS]	If I Didn't Care/True Lover	1961	7.50	15.00	30.00
❑ 71791	Trees/Immortal Love	1961	3.75	7.50	15.00
❑ 71791 [PS]	Trees/Immortal Love	1961	7.50	15.00	30.00
❑ 71847	I'll Never Smile Again/You Don't Say	1961	3.75	7.50	15.00
❑ 71847 [PS]	I'll Never Smile Again/You Don't Say	1961	7.50	15.00	30.00
❑ 71904	Song for the Lonely/You'll Never Know	1961	3.75	7.50	15.00
❑ 71921	It's Magic/Reaching for a Star	1962	3.75	7.50	15.00
❑ 71921 [PS]	It's Magic/Reaching for a Star	1962	7.50	15.00	30.00
❑ 71986	More Than You Know/Every Little Moment	1962	3.00	6.00	12.00
❑ 72060	Memories/Heartbreak	1962	3.00	6.00	12.00
❑ 72107	Once in a While/I'll See You in My Dreams	1963	2.50	5.00	10.00
❑ 72129	Strangers/Here Comes Heaven Again	1963	2.50	5.00	10.00
❑ 72194	Viva Ju Joy/Quando Caliente El Sol	1963	2.50	5.00	10.00
❑ 72242	Java Jive/Michael Row the Boat Ashore	1964	2.50	5.00	10.00
❑ 72305	Sincerely/P.S. I Love You	1964	2.50	5.00	10.00
❑ 72359	Love Me Tender/Little Things Mean a Lot	1964	2.50	5.00	10.00
❑ 76160	Platterama Medley/Red Sails in the Sunset	1982	—	3.00	6.00
MUSICOR					
❑ 1166	I Love You 1000 Times/Don't Hear, Speak, See No Evil	1966	2.00	4.00	8.00
❑ 1195	Alone in the Light (Without You)/Devri	1966	2.00	4.00	8.00
❑ 1211	I'll Be Home/(You've Got) The Magic Touch	1966	2.00	4.00	8.00
❑ 1229	With This Ring/If I Had a Love	1967	2.50	5.00	10.00
❑ 1251	Washed Ashore (On a Lonely Island in the Sea)/What Name Shall I Give You, My Love	1967	2.00	4.00	8.00
❑ 1251	Washed Ashore (On a Lonely Island in the Sea)/One in a Million	1967	2.00	4.00	8.00
❑ 1262	On Top of My Mind/Shing-a-Ling-a-Loo	1967	2.00	4.00	8.00
❑ 1275	Sweet, Sweet Lovin'/Sonata	1967	2.00	4.00	8.00
❑ 1288	Love Must Go On/How Beautiful Our Love Is	1968	2.00	4.00	8.00
❑ 1302	So Many Tears/Think Before You Walk Away	1968	2.00	4.00	8.00
❑ 1322	Hard to Get a Thing Called Love/Why	1968	2.00	4.00	8.00
❑ 1341	Fear of Loving You/Sonata	1968	2.00	4.00	8.00
❑ 1443	Be My Love/Sweet Sweet Lovin'	1971	2.00	4.00	8.00
OWL					
❑ 320	Sixteen Tons/Are You Sincere	1973	2.00	4.00	8.00
RAM					
❑ 1002	Only You/Here Comes the Boogie Man	1977	2.00	4.00	8.00

Number	Title (A Side/B Side)	Yr	VG	VG+	NM
❑ 1004/5	My Ship Is Coming In/Guilty	1977	2.00	4.00	8.00
❑ 4852	Personality/Who's Sorry Now	1978	2.00	4.00	8.00

7-Inch Extended Plays

FEDERAL

Number	Title (A Side/B Side)	Yr	VG	VG+	NM
❑ 378	(contents unknown)	1956	100.00	200.00	400.00
❑ 378 [PS]	The Platters Sing for Only You	1956	100.00	200.00	400.00

KING

Number	Title (A Side/B Side)	Yr	VG	VG+	NM
❑ 378	(contents unknown)	1956	37.50	75.00	150.00
❑ 378 [PS]	The Platters	1956	37.50	75.00	150.00

—Reissue of Federal EP

Number	Title (A Side/B Side)	Yr	VG	VG+	NM
❑ 651	(contents unknown)	1956	40.00	80.00	160.00

—"Federal" 651 is a counterfeit; all originals are on King

Number	Title (A Side/B Side)	Yr	VG	VG+	NM
❑ 651 [PS]	The Platters	1956	40.00	80.00	160.00

MERCURY

Number	Title (A Side/B Side)	Yr	VG	VG+	NM
❑ EP 1-3336	My Prayer/Have Mercy//On My Word of Honor/I'm Sorry	1957	10.00	20.00	40.00
❑ EP 1-3336 [PS]	The Platters	1957	10.00	20.00	40.00
❑ EP 1-3343	Heart of Stone/I'd Climb the Highest Mountain//September in the Rain/You've Changed	1957	10.00	20.00	40.00
❑ EP 1-3343 [PS]	The Platters (Part 1)	1957	10.00	20.00	40.00
❑ EP 1-3344	I'll Get By/I'll Give You My Word//In the Still of the Night/Wagon Wheels	1957	10.00	20.00	40.00
❑ EP 1-3344 [PS]	The Platters (Part 2)	1957	10.00	20.00	40.00
❑ EP 1-3345	Take Me in Your Arms/You Can Depend on Me//Temptation/I Don't Know Why	1957	10.00	20.00	40.00
❑ EP 1-3345 [PS]	The Platters (Part 3)	1957	10.00	20.00	40.00
❑ EP 1-3353	(contents unknown)	1958	10.00	20.00	40.00
❑ EP 1-3353 [PS]	The Flying Platters (Part 1)	1958	10.00	20.00	40.00
❑ EP 1-3354	(contents unknown)	1958	10.00	20.00	40.00
❑ EP 1-3354 [PS]	The Flying Platters (Part 2)	1958	10.00	20.00	40.00
❑ EP 1-3355	Mean to Me/Oh Promise Me//Time and Tide/Don't Forget	1958	10.00	20.00	40.00
❑ EP 1-3355 [PS]	The Flying Platters	1958	10.00	20.00	40.00
❑ EP 1-3393	(contents unknown)	1958	10.00	20.00	40.00
❑ EP 1-3393 [PS]	Twilight Time	1958	10.00	20.00	40.00

PLAYBOYS, THE (1)

The only of the many Playboys groups to have a national hit (other than Gary Lewis' or John Fred's bands).

CAMEO

Number	Title (A Side/B Side)	Yr	VG	VG+	NM
❑ 142	Over the Weekend/Double Talk	1958	5.00	10.00	20.00

MARTINIQUE

Number	Title (A Side/B Side)	Yr	VG	VG+	NM
❑ 101	Over the Weekend/Double Talk	1958	12.50	25.00	50.00
❑ 400	Please Forgive Me/Sing Along	1959	10.00	20.00	40.00

PLAYBOYS, THE (2)

ABC-PARAMOUNT

Number	Title (A Side/B Side)	Yr	VG	VG+	NM
❑ 10070	You're All I See/Memories	1959	5.00	10.00	20.00

PLAYBOYS, THE (3)

ACE

Number	Title (A Side/B Side)	Yr	VG	VG+	NM
❑ 670	Gotta Feelin'/How Could You Forget	1963	3.00	6.00	12.00

PLAYBOYS, THE (4)

CAT

Number	Title (A Side/B Side)	Yr	VG	VG+	NM
❑ 108	Tell Me/Rock, Moan and Cry	1954	12.50	25.00	50.00
❑ 115	Good Golly Miss Molly/Honey Run	1955	12.50	25.00	50.00

PLAYBOYS, THE (5)

CATALINA

Number	Title (A Side/B Side)	Yr	VG	VG+	NM
❑ 1069	Shortnin' Bread/Cheater Stomp	1964	7.50	15.00	30.00

PLAYBOYS, THE (6)

TETRA

Number	Title (A Side/B Side)	Yr	VG	VG+	NM
❑ 4447	One Question/So Good	1956	37.50	75.00	150.00

PLAYBOYS, THE (U)

Many of these could be by the above groups; many probably are not.

CHANCELLOR

Number	Title (A Side/B Side)	Yr	VG	VG+	NM
❑ 1074	Boston Hop/What'd I Say	1961	3.75	7.50	15.00

—B-side by the Cousins

Number	Title (A Side/B Side)	Yr	VG	VG+	NM
❑ 1106	Duck Walk/If I Had My Way	1962	3.75	7.50	15.00

COTTON

Number	Title (A Side/B Side)	Yr	VG	VG+	NM
❑ 1008	Careful with My Heart/Girl of My Dreams	1962	6.25	12.50	25.00

DOLTON

Number	Title (A Side/B Side)	Yr	VG	VG+	NM
❑ 8	Party Ice/Icy Fingers	1959	5.00	10.00	20.00

HEARTBEAT

Number	Title (A Side/B Side)	Yr	VG	VG+	NM
❑ 60	Harlem Nocturne/Blue Moon	1963	5.00	10.00	20.00

IMPERIAL

Number	Title (A Side/B Side)	Yr	VG	VG+	NM
❑ 5586	Sweet Talk/Crazy Daisy	1959	5.00	10.00	20.00

LEGATO

Number	Title (A Side/B Side)	Yr	VG	VG+	NM
❑ 101	Mope De Mope/The Night Before Christmas	1963	7.50	15.00	30.00

MERCURY

Number	Title (A Side/B Side)	Yr	VG	VG+	NM
❑ 71228	Why Do I Love You, Why Do I Care/Don't Do Me Wrong	1957	6.25	12.50	25.00

RIK

Number	Title (A Side/B Side)	Yr	VG	VG+	NM
❑ 572	Jungle Fever/Shotgun	1959	6.25	12.50	25.00

SOUVENIR

Number	Title (A Side/B Side)	Yr	VG	VG+	NM
❑ 1001	Believe It or Not/Hawaiian War Chant	1959	3.75	7.50	15.00

TITAN

Number	Title (A Side/B Side)	Yr	VG	VG+	NM
❑ 1732	The Scramble/Cat Walk	1963	5.00	10.00	20.00

ZIPP

Number	Title (A Side/B Side)	Yr	VG	VG+	NM
❑ 101	Sweet Talk/Crazy Daisy	1959	10.00	20.00	40.00

PLAYER

CASABLANCA

Number	Title (A Side/B Side)	Yr	VG	VG+	NM
❑ 2265	It's for You/Tip of the Iceberg	1980	—	2.00	4.00
❑ 2295	Givin' It All/Tip of the Iceberg	1980	—	2.00	4.00

RCA

Number	Title (A Side/B Side)	Yr	VG	VG+	NM
❑ PB-13006	If Looks Could Kill/Born to Be with You	1981	—	2.00	4.00
❑ PB-13089	My Mind's Made Up/Thank You for the Use of Your Love	1982	—	2.00	4.00

RSO

Number	Title (A Side/B Side)	Yr	VG	VG+	NM
❑ 879	Baby Come Back/Love Is Where You Find It	1977	—	2.50	5.00
❑ 890	This Time I'm In It for Love/Every Which Way	1978	—	2.00	4.00
❑ 908	Prisoner of Your Love/Join In the Dance	1978	—	2.00	4.00
❑ 914	Silver Lining/Forever	1978	—	2.00	4.00
❑ 920	I Just Wanna Be with You/Let Me Down Easy	1979	—	2.00	4.00

PLAYMATES, THE

ABC-PARAMOUNT

Number	Title (A Side/B Side)	Yr	VG	VG+	NM
❑ 10422	"A" My Name Is Alice/Just a Little Bit	1963	2.50	5.00	10.00
❑ 10468	She Never Looked Better/But Not Through Tears	1963	2.50	5.00	10.00
❑ 10492	I Cross My Fingers/I'll Never Get Over You	1963	2.50	5.00	10.00
❑ 10522	Guy Behind the Wheel/One Guy Left on the Corner	1964	2.50	5.00	10.00

BELL

Number	Title (A Side/B Side)	Yr	VG	VG+	NM
❑ 45149	Foundation of Love/Davenu	1971	—	3.00	6.00

COLPIX

Number	Title (A Side/B Side)	Yr	VG	VG+	NM
❑ 760	Fiddler on the Roof/Piece of the Sky	1964	2.00	4.00	8.00
❑ 769	One by One the Roses Died/Spanish Perfume	1965	2.00	4.00	8.00

CONGRESS

Number	Title (A Side/B Side)	Yr	VG	VG+	NM
❑ 245	Ballad of Stanley the Lifeguard/Should I Ask Someone Else to Tell Her	1965	2.00	4.00	8.00

RAINBOW

Number	Title (A Side/B Side)	Yr	VG	VG+	NM
❑ 360	Nickelodeon Rag/I Have Only Myself to Blame	1956	7.50	15.00	30.00

ROULETTE

Number	Title (A Side/B Side)	Yr	VG	VG+	NM
❑ 4003	Barefoot Girl/Pretty Woman	1957	3.75	7.50	15.00
❑ 4022	Darling It's Wonderful/Magic Shoes	1957	3.75	7.50	15.00
❑ 4022	Darling It's Wonderful/Island Girl	1957	3.75	7.50	15.00
❑ 4037	Jo-Ann/You Can't Stop Me from Dreaming	1957	6.25	12.50	25.00
❑ 4056	Let's Be Lovers/Give Me Another Chance	1958	3.75	7.50	15.00
❑ 4072	Don't Go Home/Can't You Get It Through Your Head	1958	3.75	7.50	15.00
❑ 4100	The Day I Died/While the Record Goes Around	1958	3.75	7.50	15.00
❑ 4115	Beep Beep/Your Love	1958	6.25	12.50	25.00
❑ 4136	Star Love/The Thing-A-Ma-Jig	1959	3.00	6.00	12.00
❑ 4160	What Is Love/I Am	1959	3.00	6.00	12.00
❑ 4200	First Love/A-Ciu-E	1959	3.00	6.00	12.00
❑ 4211	On the Beach/The Song Everybody's Singing	1959	3.00	6.00	12.00
❑ 4227	Second Chance/These Things I Offer You	1960	3.00	6.00	12.00
❑ 4252	Parade of Pretty Girls/Our Wedding Day	1960	3.00	6.00	12.00
❑ 4276	Wait for Me/Eyes of Angel	1960	3.00	6.00	12.00
❑ 4322	Little Mis Stuck-Up/Real Life	1961	3.00	6.00	12.00
❑ 4370	Tell Me What She Said/Cowboys Never Cry	1961	3.00	6.00	12.00
❑ 4393	Wimoweh/One Little Kiss	1961	3.00	6.00	12.00
❑ 4417	A Rose and a Star/Bachelor Flat	1962	2.50	5.00	10.00
❑ 4432	Keep Your Hands in Your Pocket/The Cop on the Beat	1962	2.50	5.00	10.00
❑ 4464	What a Funny Way to Show It/Petticoats Fly	1962	2.50	5.00	10.00

PLEASURE FAIR, THE

With Robb Royer, later of BREAD.

UNI

Number	Title (A Side/B Side)	Yr	VG	VG+	NM
❑ 55016	Morning Glory Days/Fade In, Fade Out	1967	2.00	4.00	8.00
❑ 55078	Today/I'm Gonna Hafta Let You Go	1968	2.00	4.00	8.00

PLEASURE SEEKERS

SUZI QUATRO was in this group.

CAPITOL

Number	Title (A Side/B Side)	Yr	VG	VG+	NM
❑ 2050	(Theme from) Valley of the Dolls/If You Climb on the Tiger's Back	1967	5.00	10.00	20.00

HIDEOUT

Number	Title (A Side/B Side)	Yr	VG	VG+	NM
❑ 1006	Never Thought You'd Leave Me/What a Way to Die	1967	25.00	50.00	100.00

MERCURY

Number	Title (A Side/B Side)	Yr	VG	VG+	NM
❑ 72800	Good Kind of Hurt/Light of Love	1968	6.25	12.50	25.00

PLEBS, THE

MGM

Number	Title (A Side/B Side)	Yr	VG	VG+	NM
❑ 13320	Bad Blood/Babe I'm Gonna Leave You	1965	3.00	6.00	12.00

PLEDGES, THE

Actually Clyde Battin and GARY PAXTON, who recorded as SKIP AND FLIP.

REV

Number	Title (A Side/B Side)	Yr	VG	VG+	NM
❑ 3517	Betty Jean/Her Bermuda Shorts	1958	6.25	12.50	25.00

PLUMB, EVE

"Jan Brady" of THE BRADY BUNCH.

RCA VICTOR

Number	Title (A Side/B Side)	Yr	VG	VG+	NM
❑ 74-0409	How Will It Be/Fortune Cookie Song	1970	3.75	7.50	15.00
❑ 74-0409 [PS]	How Will It Be/Fortune Cookie Song	1970	5.00	10.00	20.00

PLUMMER, DAVE, AND THE PLUNGERS

MAYBROOK

Number	Title (A Side/B Side)	Yr	VG	VG+	NM
❑ 320	Surfin' Monster/King of the Road	196?	10.00	20.00	40.00

PO' BOYS, THE

Backing group for BILL ANDERSON.

DECCA

Number	Title (A Side/B Side)	Yr	VG	VG+	NM
❑ 31915	Dear Heart/Orange Blossom Special	1966	2.00	4.00	8.00
❑ 32170	Faded Love/Sunny-Gem	1967	2.00	4.00	8.00
❑ 32281	White Rabbit/Up & Atom	1968	2.00	4.00	8.00
❑ 32821	Louisiana Man/Sidewalkin'	1971	2.00	4.00	8.00
❑ 32944	Sunnyside Up/Guitar Boy	1972	2.00	4.00	8.00

MCA

Number	Title (A Side/B Side)	Yr	VG	VG+	NM
❑ 40117	Pass Me By/Fire Ball Mail	1973	—	3.00	6.00

POCO

Also see JIM MESSINA.

ABC

Number	Title (A Side/B Side)	Yr	VG	VG+	NM
❑ 12126	Keep On Tryin'/Georgia, Bind My Ties	1975	—	2.50	5.00
❑ 12159	Makin' Love/Flyin' Solo	1976	—	2.50	5.00
❑ 12204	Rose of Cimarron/Tulsa Turnaround	1976	—	2.50	5.00
❑ 12295	Indian Summer/Me and You	1977	—	2.50	5.00

Number	Title (A Side/B Side)	Yr	VG	VG+	NM
❑ 12439	Crazy Love/Barbados	1978	—	2.50	5.00
ATLANTIC					
❑ 89629 [DJ]	Save a Corner of Your Heart (same on both sides)	1984	—	—	3.00
—May be promo only					
❑ 89650	This Old Flame/The Storm	1984	—	—	3.00
❑ 89674	Days Gone By/Daylight	1984	—	—	3.00
❑ 89851 [DJ]	Break of Hearts (same on both sides)	1983	—	—	3.00
—May be promo only					
❑ 89919	Shoot for the Moon/The Midnight Rodeo	1982	—	—	3.00
❑ 89970	Ghostown/High Sierra	1982	—	—	3.00
❑ 89970 [PS]	Ghostown/High Sierra	1982	—	2.00	4.00
EPIC					
❑ 10501	Pickin' Up the Pieces/First Love	1969	2.50	5.00	10.00
❑ 10543	My Kind of Love/Hard Luck	1969	2.50	5.00	10.00
❑ 10636	You Better Think Twice/Anyway, Bye Bye	1970	2.00	4.00	8.00
❑ 10714	C'Mon/I Guess You Made It	1971	2.00	4.00	8.00
❑ 10804	Just for Me and You/Ol' Forgiver	1971	2.00	4.00	8.00
❑ 10816	You Are the One/Railroad Days	1971	2.00	4.00	8.00
❑ 10890	Good Feeling to Know/Early Times	1972	—	3.00	6.00
❑ 10958	I Can See Everything/Go and Say Goodbye	1973	—	3.00	6.00
❑ 11055	Here We Go Again/Fools Gold	1973	—	3.00	6.00
❑ 11092	Magnolia/Blue Water	1974	—	3.00	6.00
❑ 11141	Rocky Mountain Breakdown/Faith in the Families	1974	—	3.00	6.00
❑ 50076	Bitter Blue/High and Dry	1975	—	3.00	6.00
MCA					
❑ 41023	Heart of the Night/Last Goodbye	1979	—	2.00	4.00
❑ 41103	Legend/Indian Summer	1979	—	2.00	4.00
❑ 41269	Under the Gun/Reputation	1980	—	2.00	4.00
❑ 41269 [PS]	Under the Gun/Reputation	1980	—	3.00	6.00
❑ 41326	Midnight Rain/Fool's Paradise	1980	—	2.00	4.00
❑ 51034	Everlasting Kind/Friends in the Distance	1980	—	2.00	4.00
❑ 51172	Down on the River Again/Widowmaker	1981	—	2.00	4.00
❑ 52001	Seas of Heartbreals/Feudin'	1982	—	2.00	4.00
RCA					
❑ 9038-7-R	Call It Love/Lovin' You Every Minute	1989	—	—	3.00
❑ 9038-7-R [PS]	Call It Love/Lovin' You Every Minute	1989	—	—	3.00
❑ 9131-7-R	Nothin' to Hide/If It Wasn't for You	1989	—	—	3.00
❑ 9131-7-R [PS]	Nothin' to Hide/If It Wasn't for You	1989	—	—	3.00

POETS, THE (1)

Number	Title (A Side/B Side)	Yr	VG	VG+	NM
SYMBOL					
❑ 214	She Blew a Good Thing/Out to Lunch	1966	3.75	7.50	15.00
❑ 216	So Young (And So Innocent)/A Sure Thing	1966	3.00	6.00	12.00
❑ 219	I'm Particular/I've Only Two Hearts	1966	3.00	6.00	12.00
VEEP					
❑ 1286	The Hustler/Soul Brothers Holiday	1968	5.00	10.00	20.00

POETS, THE (2)

British group.

Number	Title (A Side/B Side)	Yr	VG	VG+	NM
DYNO VOX					
❑ 201	Now We're Thru/There Are Some	1965	2.50	5.00	10.00

POETS, THE (3)

Number	Title (A Side/B Side)	Yr	VG	VG+	NM
FLASH					
❑ 129	Vowels of Love/Dead	1958	50.00	100.00	200.00
—Black label					
❑ 129	Vowels of Love/Dead	1958	15.00	30.00	60.00
—Maroon label					

POETS, THE (4)

Number	Title (A Side/B Side)	Yr	VG	VG+	NM
IMPERIAL					
❑ 5664	Honey Chile/I'm in Love	1960	3.75	7.50	15.00

POETS, THE (U)

These could be group (1) or (2).

Number	Title (A Side/B Side)	Yr	VG	VG+	NM
CHAIRMAN					
❑ 4408	Coffee House/Number One (More Time)	1963	3.00	6.00	12.00
RED BIRD					
❑ 10-046	Merry Christmas Baby/I'm Stuck on You	1965	3.00	6.00	12.00

POINDEXTER, BUSTER

Actually David Johansen, ex-NEW YORK DOLLS member.

Number	Title (A Side/B Side)	Yr	VG	VG+	NM
RCA					
❑ 2572-7-R	Under the Sea/Debourge Yourself	1990	—	—	3.00
❑ 5357-7-R	Hot Hot Hot/Cannibal	1987	—	—	3.00
❑ 5357-7-R [PS]	Hot Hot Hot/Cannibal	1987	—	—	3.00
❑ 6893-7 [DJ]	Zat You Santa Claus/Hot Hot Hot	1987	3.75	7.50	15.00
❑ 7638-7-R	Oh Me Oh My (I'm a Fool for You Baby)/Cannibal	1988	—	—	3.00
❑ 7638-7-R [PS]	Oh Me Oh My (I'm a Fool for You Baby)/Cannibal	1988	—	—	3.00
❑ 8914-7-R	Hit the Road Jack/Heart of Gold	1989	—	—	3.00
❑ 8914-7-R [PS]	Hit the Road Jack/Heart of Gold	1989	—	—	3.00
❑ 9007-7-R	All Night Party (Hot Mix)/All Night Party (Power Mix)	1989	—	—	3.00
❑ 9007-7-R [PS]	All Night Party (Hot Mix)/All Night Party (Power Mix)	1989	—	—	3.00
❑ 9195-7-R	Under the Sea/Debourge Yourself	1990	—	—	3.00

POINDEXTER, DON, AND THE STARLITE WRANGLERS

Number	Title (A Side/B Side)	Yr	VG	VG+	NM
SUN					
❑ 202	Now She Cares No More for Me/My Kind of Love	1954	500.00	1000.	2000.

POINTER, ANITA

Also see THE POINTER SISTERS.

Number	Title (A Side/B Side)	Yr	VG	VG+	NM
RCA					
❑ 5291-7-R	Overnight Success/Love Me Like You Do	1987	—	—	3.00
❑ 6847-7-R	More Than a Memory/Have a Little Faith in Love	1987	—	—	3.00

POINTER, BONNIE

Also see THE POINTER SISTERS.

Number	Title (A Side/B Side)	Yr	VG	VG+	NM
MOTOWN					
❑ 1451	Free Me from My Freedom-Tie Me to a Tree (Handcuff Me)/(Instrumental)	1978	—	2.00	4.00
❑ 1451 [PS]	Free Me from My Freedom-Tie Me to a Tree (Handcuff Me)/(Instrumental)	1978	—	3.00	6.00
❑ 1451 [PS]	Free Me from My Freedom-Tie Me to a Tree (Handcuff Me)/(Instrumental)	1978	2.00	4.00	8.00
—Stock copy on red vinyl					
❑ 1459	Heaven Must Have Sent You/Heaven Must Have Sent You (LP Version)	1979	—	2.00	4.00
❑ 1478	I Can't Help Myself (Sugar Pie, Honey Bunch)/I Wanna Make It (In Your World)	1979	—	2.00	4.00
❑ 1484	Deep Inside My Soul/I Love to Sing to You	1980	—	2.00	4.00
PRIVATE I					
❑ 04449	Your Touch/There's Nobody Quite Like You	1984	—	—	3.00
❑ 04658	Premonition/Tight Blue Jeans	1984	—	—	3.00
❑ 04819	The Beast in Me/There's Nobody Quite Like You	1985	—	—	3.00
❑ 04819 [PS]	The Beast in Me/There's Nobody Quite Like You	1985	—	—	3.00

POINTER, JUNE

Also see THE POINTER SISTERS.

Number	Title (A Side/B Side)	Yr	VG	VG+	NM
COLUMBIA					
❑ 68748	Tight on Time (I'll Fit U In)/Fool for Love	1989	—	—	3.00
PLANET					
❑ YB-13522	Ready for Some Action/Always	1983	—	2.00	4.00
❑ YB-13592	Don't Mess With Bill/I Understand	1983	—	2.00	4.00

POINTER, RUTH

Also see THE POINTER SISTERS.

Number	Title (A Side/B Side)	Yr	VG	VG+	NM
EPIC					
❑ 08115	Enemies Like You and Me/I Need You	1988	—	—	3.00
—With Billy Vera					

POINTER SISTERS, THE

Also see ANITA POINTER; BONNIE POINTER; JUNE POINTER; RUTH POINTER.

Number	Title (A Side/B Side)	Yr	VG	VG+	NM
ATLANTIC					
❑ 2845	Don't Try to Take the Fifth/Tulsa County	1971	5.00	10.00	20.00
❑ 2893	Destination No More Heartaches/Send Him Back	1972	5.00	10.00	20.00
BLUE THUMB					
❑ 229	Yes We Can Can/Jada	1973	—	3.00	6.00
❑ 243	Wang Dang Doodle/Cloudburst	1973	—	3.00	6.00
❑ 248	Steam Heat/Shaky Flat Blues	1974	—	3.00	6.00
❑ 254	Fairytale/Love In Them Thar Hills	1974	2.50	5.00	10.00
—First pressing has a gray to white label and no reference to ABC					
❑ 254	Fairytale/Love In Them Thar Hills	1974	—	2.50	5.00
—Second pressing has a multicolor label with ABC logo					
❑ 262	Live Your Life Before You Die/Shaky Flat Blues	1975	—	2.50	5.00
❑ 265	How Long (Betcha' Got a Chick on the Side)/Easy Days	1975	—	2.50	5.00
❑ 268	Going Down Slowly/Sleeping Alone	1975	—	2.50	5.00
❑ 271	You Gotta Believe/Shaky Flat Blues	1976	—	2.50	5.00
❑ 275	Having a Party/Lonely Gal	1977	—	2.50	5.00
❑ 277	I Need a Man/I'll Get By Without You	1978	—	2.50	5.00
COLUMBIA					
❑ 08015	Power of Persuasion/(Instrumental)	1988	—	—	3.00
❑ 08015 [PS]	Power of Persuasion/(Instrumental)	1988	—	—	3.00
MCA					
❑ 53120	Be There/(Instrumental)	1987	—	—	3.00
❑ 53120 [PS]	Be There/(Instrumental)	1987	—	—	3.00
MOTOWN					
❑ 902	Friends' Advice (Don't Take It)/Friends' Advice (Don't Take It) (Dub)	1990	—	2.00	4.00
PLANET					
❑ YB-13254	American Music/I Want to Do It with You	1982	—	2.00	4.00
❑ YB-13327	I'm So Excited/Nothing But a Heartache (Live)	1982	—	2.00	4.00
❑ YB-13430	If You Wanna Get Back Your Lady/I'm So Excited	1983	—	2.00	4.00
❑ GB-13485	American Music/I'm So Excited	1983	—	—	3.00
—Gold Standard Series					
❑ YB-13639	I Need You/If You Wanna Get Back Your Lady	1983	—	2.00	4.00
❑ YB-13730	Automatic/Nightline	1984	—	2.00	4.00
❑ YB-13780	Jump (For My Love)/Heart Beat	1984	—	2.00	4.00
❑ GB-13795	I Need You/If You Wanna Get Back Your Lady	1984	—	—	3.00
—Gold Standard Series					
❑ YB-13857	I'm So Excited/Dance Electric	1984	—	2.00	4.00
❑ YB-13951	Neutron Dance/Telegraph Your Love	1984	—	2.00	4.00
❑ YB-14041	Baby Come and Get It/Operator	1985	—	2.00	4.00
❑ YB-14041 [PS]	Baby Come and Get It/Operator	1985	—	2.00	4.00
❑ GB-14072	Jump (For My Love)/Automatic	1985	—	—	3.00
—Gold Standard Series					
❑ GB-14076	Fire/He's So Shy	1985	—	—	3.00
—Gold Standard Series					
❑ GB-14077	Slow Hand/Should I Do It	1985	—	—	3.00
—Gold Standard Series					
❑ 45901	Fire/Love Is Like a Rolling Stone	1978	—	2.00	4.00
❑ 45901 [PS]	Fire/Love Is Like a Rolling Stone	1978	—	3.00	6.00
❑ 45902	Happiness/Too Late	1979	—	2.00	4.00
❑ 45906	Blind Faith/The Shape I'm In	1979	—	2.00	4.00
❑ 47916	He's So Shy/Movin' On	1980	—	2.00	4.00
❑ 47918	Es Tan Timido/Cosas Especiales	1980	—	3.00	6.00
❑ 47920	Could I Be Dreaming/Evil	1980	—	2.00	4.00
❑ 47925	Where Did the Time Go/Special Things	1981	—	2.00	4.00
❑ 47929	Slow Hand/Holdin' Out for Love	1981	—	2.00	4.00
❑ 47937	What a Surprise/Fall in Love Again	1981	—	2.00	4.00
❑ 47945	Sweet Lover Man/Got to Find Love	1981	—	2.00	4.00
❑ 47960	Should I Do It/We're Gonna Make It	1982	—	2.00	4.00
RCA					
❑ 5062-7-R	Goldmine/Sexual Power	1986	—	—	3.00
❑ 5062-7-R [PS]	Goldmine/Sexual Power	1986	—	—	3.00
❑ 5112-7-R	All I Know Is the Way I Feel/Translation	1987	—	—	3.00
❑ 5230-7-R	Mercury Rising/Say the Word	1987	—	—	3.00
❑ 6865-7-R	He Turned Me Out/Translation	1988	—	—	3.00
❑ 6865-7-R [PS]	He Turned Me Out/Translation	1988	—	—	3.00
❑ 8378-7-R	I'm in Love/Uh-Oh	1988	—	—	3.00
❑ PB-14126	Dare Me/I'll Be There	1985	—	—	3.00

Number	Title (A Side/B Side)	Yr	VG	VG+	NM
❑ PB-14126 [PS]	Dare Me/I'll Be There	1985	—	—	3.00
❑ PB-14197	Twist My Arm/Easy Persuasion	1986	—	—	3.00
❑ PB-14197 [PS]	Twist My Arm/Easy Persuasion	1986	—	—	3.00
❑ PB-14224	Freedom/Telegraph Your Love	1985	—	—	3.00
❑ PB-14224 [PS]	Freedom/Telegraph Your Love	1985	—	—	3.00
❑ GB-14354	Neutron Dance/Baby Come and Get It	1986	—	—	3.00
—Gold Standard Series					

SBK

Number	Title (A Side/B Side)	Yr	VG	VG+	NM
❑ S7-17637	Don't Walk Away/Tell It to My Heart	1993	—	2.00	4.00

POISON

CAPITOL

Number	Title (A Side/B Side)	Yr	VG	VG+	NM
❑ B-5686	Talk Dirty to Me/Want Some, Need Some	1987	—	—	3.00
—Originals have Capitol logo at top with colorband					
❑ B-5686 [PS]	Talk Dirty to Me/Want Some, Need Some	1987	—	2.00	4.00
❑ S7-56969	Stand/Until You Suffer Some (Fire and Ice)	1993	—	3.00	6.00
—Blue vinyl					
❑ S7-56969	Stand/Until You Suffer Some (Fire and Ice)	1993	—	2.00	4.00
—Black vinyl					
❑ 88643	Shut Up, Make Love/Every Rose Has Its Thorn	2000	—	—	3.00

ENIGMA

Number	Title (A Side/B Side)	Yr	VG	VG+	NM
❑ B-44004	I Want Action/Play Dirty	1987	—	—	3.00
❑ B-44004 [PS]	I Want Action/Play Dirty	1987	—	2.00	4.00
—Fold-out poster sleeve					
❑ B-44038	I Won't Forget You/Blame It on You	1987	—	—	3.00
❑ B-44038 [PS]	I Won't Forget You/Blame It on You	1987	—	—	3.00
❑ B-44145	Nothin' But a Good Time/Look But You Can't Touch	1988	—	—	3.00
❑ B-44145 [PS]	Nothin' But a Good Time/Look But You Can't Touch	1988	—	—	3.00
❑ B-44191	Fallen Angel/Bad to Be Good	1988	—	—	3.00
❑ B-44191 [PS]	Fallen Angel/Bad to Be Good	1988	—	—	3.00
❑ B-44203	Every Rose Has Its Thorn/Livin' for the Minute	1988	—	—	3.00
❑ B-44203 [PS]	Every Rose Has Its Thorn/Livin' for the Minute	1988	—	—	3.00
❑ B-44293	Your Mama Don't Dance/Look What the Cat Dragged In	1989	—	—	3.00
❑ B-44293 [PS]	Your Mama Don't Dance/Look What the Cat Dragged In	1989	—	—	3.00
❑ NR-44584	Swamp Juice (Soul-O)-Unskinny Bop/Valley of Lost Souls	1990	—	2.00	4.00

POLICE, THE

Also see KLARK KENT; STING; ANDY SUMMERS.

A&M

Number	Title (A Side/B Side)	Yr	VG	VG+	NM
❑ 2096	Roxanne/Dead End Job	1978	—	3.00	6.00
❑ 2147	Can't Stand Losing You/No Time This Time	1979	—	2.50	5.00
❑ 2147 [PS]	Can't Stand Losing You/No Time This Time	1979	2.50	5.00	10.00
❑ 2190	Message in a Bottle/Landlord	1979	—	2.50	5.00
❑ 2190 [PS]	Message in a Bottle/Landlord	1979	2.50	5.00	10.00
—Fold-out poster sleeve					
❑ 2218	Bring On the Night/Visions of the Night	1980	—	2.50	5.00
❑ 2275	De Do Do Do, De Da Da Da/Friends	1980	—	2.00	4.00
—Standard A&M late-1970s label					
❑ 2275	De Do Do Do, De Da Da Da/Friends	1980	—	—	3.00
—Yellowish custom label with blueish triangle (most common version)					
❑ 2275	De Do Do Do, De Da Da Da/Friends	1980	—	2.00	4.00
—Red custom label with silver triangle					
❑ 2275 [PS]	De Do Do Do, De Da Da Da/Friends	1980	—	3.00	6.00
—Actually a title sleeve with large center hole					
❑ 2301	Don't Stand So Close to Me/A Sermon	1981	—	—	3.00
❑ 2301 [PS]	Don't Stand So Close to Me/A Sermon	1981	—	—	3.00
❑ 2371	Every Little Thing She Does Is Magic/Shambelle	1981	—	—	3.00
❑ 2371 [PS]	Every Little Thing She Does Is Magic/Shambelle	1981	—	—	3.00
❑ 2390	Spirits in the Material World/Flexible Strategies	1982	—	—	3.00
❑ 2390 [PS]	Spirits in the Material World/Flexible Strategies	1982	—	—	3.00
❑ 2408	Secret Journey/Darkness	1982	—	—	3.00
❑ 2408 [PS]	Secret Journey/Darkness	1982	—	—	3.00
❑ 2542	Every Breath You Take/Murder by Numbers	1983	—	—	3.00
❑ 2542 [PS]	Every Breath You Take/Murder by Numbers	1983	—	—	3.00
❑ 2569	King of Pain/Someone to Talk To	1983	—	—	3.00
❑ 2569 [PS]	King of Pain/Someone to Talk To	1983	—	—	3.00
❑ 2571	Synchronicity II/Once Upon a Daydream	1983	—	—	3.00
❑ 2571 [PS]	Synchronicity II/Once Upon a Daydream	1983	—	—	3.00
❑ 2614	Wrapped Around Your Finger/Tea in the Sahara (Live)	1984	—	—	3.00
❑ 2614 [PS]	Wrapped Around Your Finger/Tea in the Sahara (Live)	1984	—	—	3.00
❑ 2879	Don't Stand So Close to Me '86/Don't Stand So Close to Me (Live)	1986	—	—	3.00
❑ 2879 [PS]	Don't Stand So Close to Me '86/Don't Stand So Close to Me (Live)	1986	—	—	3.00
❑ 2908	Walking on the Moon/Message in a Bottle	1986	—	2.50	5.00
❑ 2908 [PS]	Walking on the Moon/Message in a Bottle	1986	—	2.50	5.00
❑ PR-4400 [PD]	Message in a Bottle/Message in a Bottle (Live)	1980	2.50	5.00	10.00
—Star-shaped badge picture disc in folder; promo only					
❑ PR-4401 [PD]	Don't Stand So Close to Me/De Do Do Do, De Da Da Da	1981	2.50	5.00	10.00
—Star-shaped badge picture disc in folder; promo only					
❑ 8622	Roxanne/Can't Stand Losing You	198?	—	—	3.00
—Reissue					
❑ 8631	De Do Do Do, De Da Da Da/Don't Stand So Close to Me	198?	—	—	3.00
—Reissue					
❑ 8633	Every Little Thing She Does Is Magic/Spirits in the Material World	198?	—	—	3.00
—Reissue					
❑ 8640	Every Breath You Take/Wrapped Around Your Finger	198?	—	—	3.00
—Reissue					
❑ 8649	King of Pain/Synchronicity II	198?	—	—	3.00
—Reissue					
❑ 75021 8738 7	Canary in a Coal Mine/Message in a Bottle	1996	—	—	3.00
—Oldies reissue; first appearance of A-side on U.S. 45					
❑ 25000	De Do Do Do, De Da Da Da (Japanese)/De Do Do Do, De Da Da Da (Spanish)	1981	—	2.50	5.00
—Small center hole					
❑ 25000 [PS]	De Do Do Do, De Da Da Da (Japanese)/De Do Do Do, De Da Da Da (Spanish)	1981	—	2.50	5.00
❑ (no #) [(5) DJ]	The Police File	1985	12.50	25.00	50.00
—Boxed set of five "A&M Memories" singles released to radio. Price is mostly for the box.					
❑ (# unknown) [PD]	Roxanne/Can't Stand Losing You	1979	2.50	5.00	10.00
—Badge-shaped picture disc					

PONI-TAILS, THE

ABC-PARAMOUNT

Number	Title (A Side/B Side)	Yr	VG	VG+	NM
❑ 9846	Wild Eyes and Tender Lips/It's Just My Luck to Be Fifteen	1957	5.00	10.00	20.00
❑ 9934	Born Too Late/Come On Joey Dance With Me	1958	6.25	12.50	25.00
❑ 9969	Close Friends/Seven Minutes in Heaven	1958	5.00	10.00	20.00
❑ 9995	Early to Bed/Father Time	1959	5.00	10.00	20.00
❑ 10027	Moody/Ooh-Pah Polka	1959	5.00	10.00	20.00
❑ 10047	I'll Be Seeing You/I'll Keep Tryin'	1959	5.00	10.00	20.00
❑ 10077	Before We Say Goodnight/Come Be My Love	1960	5.00	10.00	20.00
❑ 10114	Who, When and Why/Oh My, You	1960	5.00	10.00	20.00

MARC

Number	Title (A Side/B Side)	Yr	VG	VG+	NM
❑ 1001	Can I Be Sure/Still in Your Teens	1957	6.25	12.50	25.00

POINT

Number	Title (A Side/B Side)	Yr	VG	VG+	NM
❑ 8	Your Wild Heart/Que La Bozena	1957	6.25	12.50	25.00

POOLE, BRIAN

Also see BRIAN POOLE AND THE TREMELOES.

DATE

Number	Title (A Side/B Side)	Yr	VG	VG+	NM
❑ 1539	Everything I Touch Turns to Tears/I Need Her Tonight	1966	2.50	5.00	10.00

POOLE, BRIAN, AND THE TREMELOES

Also see BRIAN POOLE; THE TREMELOES.

AUDIO FIDELITY

Number	Title (A Side/B Side)	Yr	VG	VG+	NM
❑ 112	I Go Crazy/Love Me Baby	1965	2.50	5.00	10.00
❑ 121	Good Lovin'/Could It Be You	1966	2.50	5.00	10.00

LONDON

Number	Title (A Side/B Side)	Yr	VG	VG+	NM
❑ 9600	Keep On Dancing/Blue	1963	3.75	7.50	15.00
❑ 9625	Do You Love Me/Why Can't You Love Me	1964	3.75	7.50	15.00

MONUMENT

Number	Title (A Side/B Side)	Yr	VG	VG+	NM
❑ 840	Candy Man/I Can Dream	1964	3.00	6.00	12.00
❑ 846	Someone, Someone/(Meet Me) Where We Used to Meet	1964	3.00	6.00	12.00
❑ 882	After a While/Don't Cry	1965	3.00	6.00	12.00

POPCORN AND THE MOHAWKS

MOTOWN

Number	Title (A Side/B Side)	Yr	VG	VG+	NM
❑ 1002	Custer's Last Man/Shimmy Gully	1960	15.00	30.00	60.00

POPE, RAYMOND, AND THE LOVETONES

SQUALOR

Number	Title (A Side/B Side)	Yr	VG	VG+	NM
❑ 1313	I Love Nadine/Star	1962	37.50	75.00	150.00

POPPIES, THE

Dorothy Moore of "Misty Blue" fame was in this group.

EPIC

Number	Title (A Side/B Side)	Yr	VG	VG+	NM
❑ 9893	I Wonder Why/Lullaby of Love	1966	2.50	5.00	10.00
❑ 10019	He's Ready/He's Got Real Love	1966	2.50	5.00	10.00
❑ 10019 [PS]	He's Ready/He's Got Real Love	1966	5.00	10.00	20.00
❑ 10059	Do It with Soul/He Means So Much to Me	1966	3.00	6.00	12.00
❑ 10086	There's a Pain in My Heart/My Love and I	1966	6.25	12.50	25.00

TUFF

Number	Title (A Side/B Side)	Yr	VG	VG+	NM
❑ 372	Johnny Don't Cry/(Instrumental)	1964	3.75	7.50	15.00

POPPY FAMILY, THE

LONDON

Number	Title (A Side/B Side)	Yr	VG	VG+	NM
❑ 129	Which Way You Goin' Billy/Endless Sleep	1970	—	3.00	6.00
❑ 139	That's When I Went Wrong/Shadows on My Wall	1970	—	2.50	5.00
❑ 148	I Was Wondering/Where Evil Grows	1971	—	2.50	5.00
❑ 164	No Good to Cry/I'll See You There	1971	—	2.50	5.00
❑ 172	Good Friends/Tryin'	1972	—	2.50	5.00

POPSICLES, THE (1)

GNP CRESCENDO

Number	Title (A Side/B Side)	Yr	VG	VG+	NM
❑ 336	I Don't Want to Be Your Baby Anymore/Baby I Miss You	1965	2.50	5.00	10.00

POPSICLES, THE (2)

KNIGHT

Number	Title (A Side/B Side)	Yr	VG	VG+	NM
❑ 2002	Thumb Print/This Is the End	1958	10.00	20.00	40.00

POPULAIRES, THE

MARVELLO

Number	Title (A Side/B Side)	Yr	VG	VG+	NM
❑ 5001	Island of Paradise/I Lost My Heart	1957	50.00	100.00	200.00

PORTER, ROYCE

D

Number	Title (A Side/B Side)	Yr	VG	VG+	NM
❑ 1026	Lookin'/I Still Belong to You	1958	25.00	50.00	100.00

LOOK

Number	Title (A Side/B Side)	Yr	VG	VG+	NM
❑ 1001	Yes I Do/(B-side unknown)	1957	62.50	125.00	250.00

MERCURY

Number	Title (A Side/B Side)	Yr	VG	VG+	NM
❑ 71314	Good Time/Beach of Love	1958	25.00	50.00	100.00

PORTRAITS, THE (1)

CAPITOL

Number	Title (A Side/B Side)	Yr	VG	VG+	NM
❑ F-4181	Close to You/Easy Cash	1959	7.50	15.00	30.00

PORTRAITS, THE (2)

SIDEWALK

Number	Title (A Side/B Side)	Yr	VG	VG+	NM
❑ 928	A Million to One/Let's Tell the World	1967	3.75	7.50	15.00
❑ 935	Over the Rainbow/Runaround Girl	1968	5.00	10.00	20.00

PORTRAITS, THE (3)
TRI-DISC

Number	Title (A Side/B Side)	Yr	VG	VG+	NM
❑ 109	We're Gonna Party/Three Blind Mice	1963	3.75	7.50	15.00

PORTRAITS, THE (U)
Could be group (1) or (3).

RCA VICTOR

Number	Title (A Side/B Side)	Yr	VG	VG+	NM
❑ 47-7900	Yo-Yo Girl/My Big Brother's Friend	1961	3.75	7.50	15.00

POSEY, SANDY
AUDIOGRAPH

Number	Title (A Side/B Side)	Yr	VG	VG+	NM
❑ 449	Can't Get Used to Sleeping Without You/(B-side unknown)	1983	—	2.00	4.00

COLUMBIA

Number	Title (A Side/B Side)	Yr	VG	VG+	NM
❑ 45360	Losing Out on You/You Say Beautiful Things to Me	1971	—	2.50	5.00
❑ 45458	Bring Him Safely Home To Me/A Man in Need of Love	1971	—	2.50	5.00
❑ 45596	Why Don't We Go Somewhere and Love/Together	1972	—	2.50	5.00
❑ 45703	Happy Happy Birthday Baby/Thank the Lord for New York City	1972	—	2.50	5.00
❑ 45828	Don't/Thank the Lord for New York City	1973	—	2.50	5.00
❑ 45828	Don't/Thank the Lord for New York City	1973	—	2.50	5.00

MGM

Number	Title (A Side/B Side)	Yr	VG	VG+	NM
❑ 13501	Born a Woman/Caution to the Wind	1967	2.00	4.00	8.00
❑ 13612	Single Girl/Blue Is My Best Color	1966	2.00	4.00	8.00
❑ 13612 [PS]	Single Girl/Blue Is My Best Color	1966	3.00	6.00	12.00
❑ 13702	What a Woman in Love Won't Do/Shattered	1967	2.00	4.00	8.00
❑ 13744	I Take It Back/The Boy I Love	1967	2.00	4.00	8.00
❑ 13744 [PS]	I Take It Back/The Boy I Love	1967	3.00	6.00	12.00
❑ 13824	Are You Never Coming Home/I Can Show You How to Live	1967	2.00	4.00	8.00
❑ 13892	Silly Girl, Silly Boy/Something I'll Remember	1968	—	3.00	6.00
❑ 13967	Ways of the World/Wonderful World of Summer	1968	—	3.00	6.00
❑ 14006	All Hung Up in Your Green Eyes/Your Conception of Love	1968	—	3.00	6.00

MONUMENT

Number	Title (A Side/B Side)	Yr	VG	VG+	NM
❑ 8698	Trying to Live Without You Kind of Days/Why Do We Carry On	1976	—	2.50	5.00

WARNER BROS.

Number	Title (A Side/B Side)	Yr	VG	VG+	NM
❑ 8289	It's Midnight (Do You Know Where Your Baby Is)/Long Distance Kissing	1976	—	2.00	4.00
❑ 8540	Born to Be with You/It's Not Too Late	1978	—	2.00	4.00
❑ 8610	Love, Love, Love-Chapel of Love/I Believe in Love	1978	—	2.00	4.00
❑ 8731	Love Is Sometimes Easy/I Believe In Love	1979	—	2.00	4.00
❑ 8852	Try Home/Love Is Sometimes Easy	1979	—	2.00	4.00
❑ 49104	Black Is the Night/Best Things in My Life	1979	—	2.00	4.00

POSITIVELY 13 O'CLOCK
HANNA-BARBERA

Number	Title (A Side/B Side)	Yr	VG	VG+	NM
❑ 500	Psychotic Reaction/13 O'Clock Theme for Psychotics	1966	10.00	20.00	40.00

POSSESSIONS, THE
BRITTON

Number	Title (A Side/B Side)	Yr	VG	VG+	NM
❑ 1003	No More Love/You and Your Lies	1964	10.00	20.00	40.00
❑ 1003	No More Love/You and Your Lies	1964	17.50	35.00	70.00

—Blue vinyl

PARKWAY

Number	Title (A Side/B Side)	Yr	VG	VG+	NM
❑ 930	No More Love/You and Your Lies	1964	5.00	10.00	20.00

POSSUM
HIGHLAND

Number	Title (A Side/B Side)	Yr	VG	VG+	NM
❑ 10	The Cockroach That Ate Cincinnati/Chula Vista	1966	3.75	7.50	15.00

POSTA, ADRIENNE
LONDON

Number	Title (A Side/B Side)	Yr	VG	VG+	NM
❑ 9782	When a Girl Really Loves You/Winds That Bloe	1966	2.50	5.00	10.00

POWDER PUFFS, THE
IMPERIAL

Number	Title (A Side/B Side)	Yr	VG	VG+	NM
❑ 66014	(You Can't Take) My Boyfriend's Woody/Woody Wagon	1964	6.25	12.50	25.00

POWELL, AUSTIN
ATLANTIC

Number	Title (A Side/B Side)	Yr	VG	VG+	NM
❑ 968	Wrong Again/What More Can I Ask	1952	50.00	100.00	200.00

DECCA

Number	Title (A Side/B Side)	Yr	VG	VG+	NM
❑ 48206	All This Can't Be True/Some Other Spring	1951	20.00	40.00	80.00

POWELL, CHRIS, AND THE FIVE BLUE FLAMES
COLUMBIA

Number	Title (A Side/B Side)	Yr	VG	VG+	NM
❑ 39272	Country Girl Blues/Man with a Horn	1951	37.50	75.00	150.00
❑ 39407	My Love Has Gone/In the Cool of the Evening	1951	125.00	250.00	500.00

GRAND

Number	Title (A Side/B Side)	Yr	VG	VG+	NM
❑ 108	Sweet Sue Mambo/Uh Uh Baby	1953	12.50	25.00	50.00
❑ 112	Secret Love Mambo/I Love Paris Mambo	1954	12.50	25.00	50.00
❑ 116	Dinah/Song of the Vagabond	1954	12.50	25.00	50.00
❑ 120	Mr. Sandman/Mambo Gunch	1954	12.50	25.00	50.00
❑ 124	Anniversary Waltz/Sweet Georgia Brown	1955	10.00	20.00	40.00
❑ 127	Mandolin Mambo/The Whiffenpoof Song	1955	10.00	20.00	40.00

GROOVE

Number	Title (A Side/B Side)	Yr	VG	VG+	NM
❑ 0105	Break It Up/Love Ya Like Crazy	1955	5.00	10.00	20.00
❑ 0111	Unchained Melody/Something's Gotta Give	1955	5.00	10.00	20.00
❑ 0128	Goodbye Little Girl/Chinatown	1955	5.00	10.00	20.00
❑ 0144	Moritat/The Poor People of Paris	1956	5.00	10.00	20.00

OKEH

Number	Title (A Side/B Side)	Yr	VG	VG+	NM
❑ 6818	The Masquerade Is Over/Talkin'	1951	75.00	150.00	300.00
❑ 6850	October Twilight/That's Right	1952	25.00	50.00	100.00
❑ 6875	Ida Red/Darn That Dream	1952	25.00	50.00	100.00
❑ 6900	Blue Boy/I Come from Jamaica	1952	25.00	50.00	100.00

POWELL, JIMMY
DECCA

Number	Title (A Side/B Side)	Yr	VG	VG+	NM
❑ 32685	Stranger on a Train/Sugar Man	1970	—	3.00	6.00

LONDON

Number	Title (A Side/B Side)	Yr	VG	VG+	NM
❑ 9545	I Love You/Dance Her By Me (One More Time)	1962	2.50	5.00	10.00

POWELL, SANDY
HERALD

Number	Title (A Side/B Side)	Yr	VG	VG+	NM
❑ 557	Bon Bon/Pistol-Packin' Mama	1961	25.00	50.00	100.00

IMPALA

Number	Title (A Side/B Side)	Yr	VG	VG+	NM
❑ 211	Bon Bon/Pistol-Packin' Mama	1961	75.00	150.00	300.00

SINGULAR

Number	Title (A Side/B Side)	Yr	VG	VG+	NM
❑ 714	My Jimmie/Next Thing to Paradise	1958	6.25	12.50	25.00

POWER, DUFFY
EPIC

Number	Title (A Side/B Side)	Yr	VG	VG+	NM
❑ 10650	Hellhound/Hummingbird	1970	—	3.00	6.00

VEEP

Number	Title (A Side/B Side)	Yr	VG	VG+	NM
❑ 1204	Where Am I/I Don't Care	1964	3.00	6.00	12.00

POWER STATION, THE
Also see DURAN DURAN; ROBERT PALMER.

CAPITOL

Number	Title (A Side/B Side)	Yr	VG	VG+	NM
❑ 5444	Some Like It Hot/The Heat Is On	1985	—	—	3.00
❑ 5444 [PS]	Some Like It Hot/The Heat Is On	1985	—	—	3.00
❑ 5479	Get It On/Go To Zero	1985	—	—	3.00
❑ 5479 [PS]	Get It On/Go To Zero	1985	—	—	3.00
❑ 5511	Communication/Murderess	1985	—	—	3.00
❑ 5511 [PS]	Communication/Murderess	1985	—	—	3.00

GUARDIAN

Number	Title (A Side/B Side)	Yr	VG	VG+	NM
❑ S7-19855	Taxman/Scared	1998	—	—	3.00

POWERS, JETT
See P.J. PROBY.

POWERS, JOEY
AMY

Number	Title (A Side/B Side)	Yr	VG	VG+	NM
❑ 892	Midnight Mary/Where Do You Want the World Delivered	1963	3.00	6.00	12.00
❑ 898	Billy Old Buddy/In the Morning Gloria	1964	2.50	5.00	10.00
❑ 903	Love Is a Season/You Comb Her Hair	1964	2.50	5.00	10.00
❑ 914	Tears Keep Falling/Where Did the Summer Go	1964	2.50	5.00	10.00
❑ 986	Gimmie Gimmie/Baila Maria	1967	2.00	4.00	8.00

MGM

Number	Title (A Side/B Side)	Yr	VG	VG+	NM
❑ 13421	I Love You/Leave Me Alone	1965	2.00	4.00	8.00

RCA VICTOR

Number	Title (A Side/B Side)	Yr	VG	VG+	NM
❑ 47-8039	Two Tickets and a Candy Heart/Jenny, Won't You Walk Up?	1962	2.50	5.00	10.00
❑ 47-8119	Don't Envy Me/Me, Myself and I	1962	2.50	5.00	10.00
❑ 47-9790	Hard to Be Without You/You're in a Bad Way	1969	—	2.50	5.00

—As "Joey Powers' Flower"

Number	Title (A Side/B Side)	Yr	VG	VG+	NM
❑ 74-0326	Land of the Midnight Sun/So Sing the Children on the Avenue	1970		2.50	5.00

—As "Joey Powers' Flower"

POWERS, JOHNNY
FORTUNE

Number	Title (A Side/B Side)	Yr	VG	VG+	NM
❑ 199	Honey Let's Go (To a Rock and Roll Show)/Your Love	1955	50.00	100.00	200.00

FOX

Number	Title (A Side/B Side)	Yr	VG	VG+	NM
❑ 916	Rock Rock/Long Blonde Hair, Red Rose Lips	1957	125.00	250.00	500.00

HI-Q

Number	Title (A Side/B Side)	Yr	VG	VG+	NM
❑ 5044	Rock the Universe/Honey Let's Go (To a Rock and Roll Show)	1958	25.00	50.00	100.00

SUN

Number	Title (A Side/B Side)	Yr	VG	VG+	NM
❑ 327	With Your Love, With Your Kiss/Be Mine, All Mine	1959	12.50	25.00	50.00

TRIODEX

Number	Title (A Side/B Side)	Yr	VG	VG+	NM
❑ 103	A Teenage Prayer/A Young Boy's Heart	1960	6.25	12.50	25.00

POWERSOURCE
POWERVISION

Number	Title (A Side/B Side)	Yr	VG	VG+	NM
❑ 8603	Dear Mr. Jesus/Love, Sharon	1987	3.00	6.00	12.00

PRECISIONS, THE (1)
ATCO

Number	Title (A Side/B Side)	Yr	VG	VG+	NM
❑ 6643	Don't Double (With Trouble)/Into My Life	1969	3.00	6.00	12.00
❑ 6669	New York City/You're the Best (That Ever Did It)	1969	3.00	6.00	12.00

D-TOWN

Number	Title (A Side/B Side)	Yr	VG	VG+	NM
❑ 1033	My Lover Come Back/I Wanna Tell My Baby	1965	50.00	100.00	200.00
❑ 1055	Mexican Love Song/You're Sweet	1965	6.25	12.50	25.00

DREW

Number	Title (A Side/B Side)	Yr	VG	VG+	NM
❑ 1001	Such Misery/Lover's Plea	1967	6.25	12.50	25.00
❑ 1002	Why Girl/What I Want	1967	3.75	7.50	15.00
❑ 1003	If This Is Love (I'd Rather Be Lonely)/You'll Soon Be Gone	1967	6.25	12.50	25.00
❑ 1004	Instant Heartbreak/Dream Girl	1968	3.75	7.50	15.00
❑ 1005	A Place/Never Let Her Go	1968	3.75	7.50	15.00

PRECISIONS, THE (2)
HIGHLAND

Number	Title (A Side/B Side)	Yr	VG	VG+	NM
❑ 300	Eight Reasons Why I Love You/(B-side unknown)	1962	100.00	200.00	400.00

PRECISIONS, THE (U)
May be group (2); could be someone else.

RAYNA

Number	Title (A Side/B Side)	Yr	VG	VG+	NM
❑ 1001	White Christmas/Silent Night	19??	25.00	50.00	100.00

PRELUDES, THE (1)
ARLISS

Number	Title (A Side/B Side)	Yr	VG	VG+	NM
❑ 1004	Lorraine/Oh Please, Genie	1961	20.00	40.00	80.00

OCTAVIA

Number	Title (A Side/B Side)	Yr	VG	VG+	NM
❑ 8008	A Place for You (In My Heart)/That Would Be So Good	1962	10.00	20.00	40.00

PRELUDES, THE (2)

CUB

Number	Title (A Side/B Side)	Yr	VG	VG+	NM
❑ 9005	Kingdom of Love/Vanishing Angel	1958	37.50	75.00	150.00

PRELUDES, THE (3)

EMPIRE

Number	Title (A Side/B Side)	Yr	VG	VG+	NM
❑ 103	Don't Fall in Love Too Soon/I Want Your Arms Around Me (All the Time)	1956	25.00	50.00	100.00

PRELUDES FIVE, THE

PIK

Number	Title (A Side/B Side)	Yr	VG	VG+	NM
❑ 231	Starlight/Don't You Know Love?	1961	6.25	12.50	25.00

PREMEERS, THE

HERALD

Number	Title (A Side/B Side)	Yr	VG	VG+	NM
❑ 577	Diary of Our Love/Gee Oh Gee	1963	7.50	15.00	30.00

PREMIERS, THE (1)

FARO

Number	Title (A Side/B Side)	Yr	VG	VG+	NM
❑ 615	Farmer John/Duffy's Blues	1964	7.50	15.00	30.00
❑ 621	Get Your Baby/Little Ways	1965	3.00	6.00	12.00
❑ 624	Come On and Dance/Get On the Plane	1966	3.00	6.00	12.00
❑ 627	Ring Around My Rosie (Part 1)/Ring Around My Rosie (Part 2)	1967	3.00	6.00	12.00

WARNER BROS.

Number	Title (A Side/B Side)	Yr	VG	VG+	NM
❑ 5443	Farmer John/Duffy's Blues	1964	3.75	7.50	15.00
❑ 5464	Annie Oakley/Blues for Arlene	1964	3.00	6.00	12.00

PREMIERS, THE (2)

ALERT

Number	Title (A Side/B Side)	Yr	VG	VG+	NM
❑ 706	Jolene/Oh, Theresa	1959	25.00	50.00	100.00

FURY

Number	Title (A Side/B Side)	Yr	VG	VG+	NM
❑ 1029	I Pray/Pigtails, Eyes Are Blue	1960	10.00	20.00	40.00

RUST

Number	Title (A Side/B Side)	Yr	VG	VG+	NM
❑ 5032	Falling Star/She Gives Me Fever	1961	25.00	50.00	100.00

PREMIERS, THE (3)

CINDY

Number	Title (A Side/B Side)	Yr	VG	VG+	NM
❑ 3008	China Doll/Life Is Grand	1958	20.00	40.00	80.00

DIG

Number	Title (A Side/B Side)	Yr	VG	VG+	NM
❑ 106	New Moon/Baby	1956	37.50	75.00	150.00
❑ 113	My Darling/Have a Heart	1956	62.50	125.00	250.00

FORTUNE

Number	Title (A Side/B Side)	Yr	VG	VG+	NM
❑ 527	When You Are in Love/The Trap of Love	1956	20.00	40.00	80.00

GONE

Number	Title (A Side/B Side)	Yr	VG	VG+	NM
❑ 5009	Is It a Dream/Valerie	1957	125.00	250.00	500.00
—With correct track on side 1					
❑ 5009	Is It a Dream/Valerie	1957	50.00	100.00	200.00
—With "Let Me Share Your Dream" by The Deltas (Gone 5010) on Side 1 by mistake					

RCA VICTOR

Number	Title (A Side/B Side)	Yr	VG	VG+	NM
❑ 47-6958	Run Along Baby/Hey Miss Fancy	1957	20.00	40.00	80.00

PREMIERS, THE (4)

KING

Number	Title (A Side/B Side)	Yr	VG	VG+	NM
❑ 6061	She's Always There/I'm Better Off Now	1966	5.00	10.00	20.00

STAX

Number	Title (A Side/B Side)	Yr	VG	VG+	NM
❑ 177	Make It Me/You Make a Strong Girl Weak	1965	7.50	15.00	30.00

PREMIERS, THE (5)

MINK

Number	Title (A Side/B Side)	Yr	VG	VG+	NM
❑ 21	Tonight/I Think I Love You	1959	25.00	50.00	100.00

PARKWAY

Number	Title (A Side/B Side)	Yr	VG	VG+	NM
❑ 807	Tonight/I Think I Love You	1959	5.00	10.00	20.00

PREMIERS, THE (6)

NU-PHI

Number	Title (A Side/B Side)	Yr	VG	VG+	NM
❑ 367/8	Cruisin'/(B-side unknown)	1959	7.50	15.00	30.00
❑ 701	Firewater/Younger Than You	1960	7.50	15.00	30.00

PREMIERS, THE (U)

Could be one of the above groups; could be a completely different group.

BOND

Number	Title (A Side/B Side)	Yr	VG	VG+	NM
❑ 5803/4	Hop and Skip/Uh-Huh	1958	5.00	10.00	20.00

PRESENT, THE

PHILIPS

Number	Title (A Side/B Side)	Yr	VG	VG+	NM
❑ 40466	I Know/Many's the Slip Twixt the Cup and the Lip	1966	7.50	15.00	30.00

PRESIDENTS, THE (1)

SUSSEX

Number	Title (A Side/B Side)	Yr	VG	VG+	NM
❑ 200	For You/Gotta Keep Movin'	1970	—	3.50	7.00
❑ 207	5-10-15-20 (25-30 Years of Love)/I'm Still Dancing	1970	2.00	4.00	8.00
❑ 212	Triangle of Love (Hey Diddle Diddle)/Sweet Magic	1971	—	3.50	7.00
❑ 217	The Sweetest Thing This Side of Heaven/It's All Over Now	1971	—	3.50	7.00

PRESIDENTS, THE (2)

Not the same as group (1). The Sussex group's success forced this group to change its name, as reflected in the label credit on their final DeLuxe 45.

DELUXE

Number	Title (A Side/B Side)	Yr	VG	VG+	NM
❑ 113	Gold Walk/I Want My Baby	1969	2.00	4.00	8.00
❑ 120	Snoopy/Stinky	1969	2.00	4.00	8.00
❑ 127	Which Way/Peter Rabbit	1970	2.00	4.00	8.00
❑ 134	Lover's Psalm/Our Meeting	1971	—	3.00	6.00
—As "The President's Band"					

PRESIDENTS, THE (3)

MERCURY

Number	Title (A Side/B Side)	Yr	VG	VG+	NM
❑ 72016	Pots 'n' Pans/The Toasts	1962	5.00	10.00	20.00

PRESIDENTS, THE (U)

The Hollywood record could be group (1) or (2); the Warner Bros. record could be group (3).

HOLLYWOOD

Number	Title (A Side/B Side)	Yr	VG	VG+	NM
❑ 1137	Shoeshine (Part 1)/Shoeshine (Part 2)	1968	2.50	5.00	10.00

WARNER BROS.

Number	Title (A Side/B Side)	Yr	VG	VG+	NM
❑ 5240	Hot Toddy March/I Do Love You (Do I Love You)	1961	3.75	7.50	15.00

PRESLEY, ELVIS

COLLECTABLES

Number	Title (A Side/B Side)	Yr	VG	VG+	NM
❑ COL-4500 *—Black vinyl*	Good Rockin' Tonight/I Don't Care If the Sun Don't Shine	1986	—	—	3.00
❑ COL-4500 *—Gold vinyl*	Good Rockin' Tonight/I Don't Care If the Sun Don't Shine	1992	—	2.00	4.00
❑ COL-4501 *—Black vinyl*	You're a Heartbreaker/Milkcow Blues Boogie	1986	—	—	3.00
❑ COL-4501 *—Gold vinyl*	You're a Heartbreaker/Milkcow Blues Boogie	1992	—	2.00	4.00
❑ COL-4502 *—Black vinyl*	Baby Let's Play House/I'm Left, You're Right, She's Gone	1986	—	—	3.00
❑ COL-4502 *—Gold vinyl*	Baby Let's Play House/I'm Left, You're Right, She's Gone	1992	—	2.00	4.00
❑ COL-4503 *—Black vinyl*	I Got a Woman/I'm Counting on You	1986	—	—	3.00
❑ COL-4503 *—Gold vinyl*	I Got a Woman/I'm Counting on You	1992	—	2.00	4.00
❑ COL-4504 *—Black vinyl*	I'll Never Let You Go (Little Darlin')/I'm Gonna Sit Right Down and Cry (Over You)	1986	—	—	3.00
❑ COL-4504 *—Gold vinyl*	I'll Never Let You Go (Little Darlin')/I'm Gonna Sit Right Down and Cry (Over You)	1992	—	2.00	4.00
❑ COL-4505 *—Black vinyl*	Tryin' to Get to You/I Love You Because	1986	—	—	3.00
❑ COL-4505 *—Gold vinyl*	Tryin' to Get to You/I Love You Because	1992	—	2.00	4.00
❑ COL-4506 *—Black vinyl*	Money Honey/One-Sided Love Affair	1986	—	—	3.00
❑ COL-4506 *—Gold vinyl*	Money Honey/One-Sided Love Affair	1992	—	2.00	4.00
❑ COL-4507 *—Black vinyl*	Too Much/Playing for Keeps	1986	—	—	3.00
❑ COL-4507 *—Gold vinyl*	Too Much/Playing for Keeps	1992	—	2.00	4.00
❑ COL-4508 *—Black vinyl*	A Big Hunk o'Love/My Wish Came True	1986	—	—	3.00
❑ COL-4508 *—Gold vinyl*	A Big Hunk o'Love/My Wish Came True	1992	—	2.00	4.00
❑ COL-4509 *—Black vinyl*	Stuck on You/Fame and Fortune	1986	—	—	3.00
❑ COL-4509 *—Gold vinyl*	Stuck on You/Fame and Fortune	1992	—	2.00	4.00
❑ COL-4510 *—Black vinyl*	I Feel So Bad/Wild in the Country	1986	—	—	3.00
❑ COL-4510 *—Gold vinyl*	I Feel So Bad/Wild in the Country	1992	—	2.00	4.00
❑ COL-4511 *—Black vinyl*	She's Not You/Jailhouse Rock	1986	—	—	3.00
❑ COL-4511 *—Gold vinyl*	She's Not You/Jailhouse Rock	1992	—	2.00	4.00
❑ COL-4512 *—Black vinyl*	One Broken Heart for Sale/Devil in Disguise	1986	—	—	3.00
❑ COL-4512 *—Gold vinyl*	One Broken Heart for Sale/Devil in Disguise	1992	—	2.00	4.00
❑ COL-4513 *—Black vinyl*	Bossa Nova Baby/Such a Night	1986	—	—	3.00
❑ COL-4513 *—Gold vinyl*	Bossa Nova Baby/Such a Night	1992	—	2.00	4.00
❑ COL-4514 *—Black vinyl*	Love Me/Flaming Star	1986	—	—	3.00
❑ COL-4514 *—Gold vinyl*	Love Me/Flaming Star	1992	—	2.00	4.00
❑ COL-4515 *—Black vinyl*	Follow That Dream/When My Blue Moon Turns to Gold Again	1986	—	—	3.00
❑ COL-4515 *—Gold vinyl*	Follow That Dream/When My Blue Moon Turns to Gold Again	1992	—	2.00	4.00
❑ COL-4516 *—Black vinyl*	Frankie and Johnny/Love Letters	1986	—	—	3.00
❑ COL-4516 *—Gold vinyl*	Frankie and Johnny/Love Letters	1992	—	2.00	4.00
❑ COL-4517 *—Black vinyl*	U.S. Male/Until It's Time for You to Go	1986	—	—	3.00
❑ COL-4517 *—Gold vinyl*	U.S. Male/Until It's Time for You to Go	1992	—	2.00	4.00
❑ COL-4518 *—Black vinyl*	Old Shep/You'll Never Walk Alone	1986	—	—	3.00
❑ COL-4518 *—Gold vinyl*	Old Shep/You'll Never Walk Alone	1992	—	2.00	4.00
❑ COL-4519 *—Black vinyl*	Poor Boy/An American Trilogy	1986	—	—	3.00
❑ COL-4519 *—Gold vinyl*	Poor Boy/An American Trilogy	1992	—	2.00	4.00
❑ COL-4520 *—Black vinyl*	How Great Thou Art/His Hand in Mine	1986	—	—	3.00
❑ COL-4520 *—Gold vinyl*	How Great Thou Art/His Hand in Mine	1992	—	2.00	4.00

Number	Title (A Side/B Side)	Yr	VG	VG+	NM
❑ COL-4521	Big Boss Man/Paralyzed	1986	—	—	3.00
—Black vinyl					
❑ COL-4521	Big Boss Man/Paralyzed	1992	—	2.00	4.00
—Gold vinyl					
❑ COL-4522	Fools Fall in Love/Blue Suede Shoes	1986	—	—	3.00
—Black vinyl					
❑ COL-4522	Fools Fall in Love/Blue Suede Shoes	1992	—	2.00	4.00
—Gold vinyl					
❑ COL-4564	The Elvis Medley/Always on My Mind	1986	—	—	3.00
❑ COL-4738	Ask Me/The Girl of My Best Friend	1997	—	—	3.00
❑ COL-4743	Girls! Girls! Girls!/Ain't That Loving You Baby	1997	—	—	3.00
❑ COL-4744	It's Only Love/Beyond the Reef	1997	—	—	3.00
❑ 04764	Witchcraft/Spinout	1997	—	—	3.00
❑ 80000	(Now and Then There's) A Fool Such As I/I Need Your Love Tonight	1997	—	2.00	4.00
—Gray marbled vinyl					
❑ 80001	Separate Ways/Always On My Mind	1997	—	2.00	4.00
—Gray marbled vinyl					
❑ 80002	An American Trilogy/Until It's Time for You to Go	1997	—	2.00	4.00
—Gray marbled vinyl					
❑ 80003	Crying in the Chapel/I Believe in the Man in the Sky	1997	—	2.00	4.00
—Gray marbled vinyl					
❑ 80004	Don't/I Beg of You	1997	—	2.00	4.00
—Gray marbled vinyl					
❑ 80005	Don't Cry Daddy/Rubberneckin'	1997	—	2.00	4.00
—Gray marbled vinyl					
❑ 80006	Good Luck Charm/Anything That's Part of You	1997	—	2.00	4.00
—Gray marbled vinyl					
❑ 80007	Guitar Man/Hi-Heel Sneakers	1997	—	2.00	4.00
—Gray marbled vinyl					
❑ 80008	Hard Headed Woman/Don't Ask Me Why	1997	—	2.00	4.00
—Gray marbled vinyl					
❑ 80009	Heartbreak Hotel/I Was the One	1997	—	2.00	4.00
—Gray marbled vinyl					
❑ 80010	Mystery Train/I Forgot to Remember to Forget	1997	—	2.00	4.00
—Gray marbled vinyl					
❑ 80011	One Night/I Got Stung	1997	—	2.00	4.00
—Gray marbled vinyl					
❑ 80012	I Really Don't Want to Know/There Goes My Everything	1997	—	2.00	4.00
—Gray marbled vinyl					
❑ 80013	I Want You, I Need You, I Love You/My Baby Left Me	1997	—	2.00	4.00
—Gray marbled vinyl					
❑ 80014	If I Can Dream/Edge of Reality	1997	—	2.00	4.00
—Gray marbled vinyl					
❑ 80015	Kentucky Rain/My Little Friend	1997	—	2.00	4.00
—Gray marbled vinyl					
❑ 80016	Kiss Me Quick/Suspicion	1997	—	2.00	4.00
—Gray marbled vinyl					
❑ 80017	Kissin' Cousins/It Hurts Me	1997	—	2.00	4.00
—Gray marbled vinyl					
❑ 80018	Marie's the Name His Latest Flame/Little Sister	1997	—	2.00	4.00
—Gray marbled vinyl					
❑ 80019	(Let Me Be You) Teddy Bear/Loving You	1997	—	2.00	4.00
—Gray marbled vinyl					
❑ 80020	The Wonder of You/Mama Liked the Roses	1997	—	2.00	4.00
—Gray marbled vinyl					
❑ 80021	Memories/Charro	1997	—	2.00	4.00
—Gray marbled vinyl					
❑ 80022	My Boy/Thinking About You	1997	—	2.00	4.00
—Gray marbled vinyl					
❑ 80023	Way Down/My Way	1997	—	2.00	4.00
—Gray marbled vinyl					
❑ 80024	Patch It Up/You Don't Have to Say You Love Me	1997	—	2.00	4.00
—Gray marbled vinyl					
❑ 80025	Surrender/Lonely Man	1997	—	2.00	4.00
—Gray marbled vinyl					
❑ 80026	That's All Right/Blue Moon of Kentucky	1997	—	2.00	4.00
—Gray marbled vinyl					
❑ 80027	Wear My Ring Around Your Neck/Doncha' Think It's Time	1997	—	2.00	4.00
—Gray marbled vinyl					
❑ 80028	Puppet on a String/Wooden Heart	1997	—	2.00	4.00
—Gray marbled vinyl					
RCA					
❑ DME1-1803R	King of the Whole Wide World/King Creole	1997	3.75	7.50	15.00
—Red vinyl, marked as a promotional copy (about 3,000 pressed)					
❑ DME1-1803	King of the Whole Wide World/King Creole	1997	2.00	4.00	8.00
—Gold vinyl (about 7,000 pressed)					
❑ DME1-1803 [DJ]	King of the Whole Wide World/King Creole	1997	100.00	200.00	400.00
—Test pressings of above on green, blue, white and clear vinyl. Value is for any of them.					
❑ DME1-1803 [PS]	King of the Whole Wide World/King Creole	1997	2.00	4.00	8.00
—Same picture sleeve with either edition					
❑ 8760-7-R	Heartbreak Hotel/Heartbreak Hotel	1988	—	2.50	5.00
—B-side by David Keith					
❑ 8760-7-R [PS]	Heartbreak Hotel/Heartbreak Hotel	1988	—	3.00	6.00
—"Pink Cadillac" sleeve					
❑ 8760-7-R [PS]	Heartbreak Hotel/Heartbreak Hotel	1988	20.00	40.00	80.00
—Promo-only sleeve of RCA executive Butch Waugh dressed as Elvis					
❑ GB-10485	Take Good Care of Her/I've Got a Thing About You, Baby	1977	—	2.00	4.00
—Gold Standard Series; black label					
❑ GB-10486	Separate Ways/Always on My Mind	1977	—	2.00	4.00
—Gold Standard Series; black label					
❑ GB-10487	T-R-O-U-B-L-E/Mr. Songman	1977	—	2.00	4.00
—Gold Standard Series; black label					
❑ GB-10488	Promised Land/It's Midnight	1977	—	2.00	4.00
—Gold Standard Series; black label					
❑ GB-10489	My Boy/Thinking About You	1977	—	2.00	4.00
—Gold Standard Series; black label					
❑ PB-10601	Hurt/For the Heart	1976	25.00	50.00	100.00
—Second pressings (very rare) on the 1976-88 "dog near top" black label					
❑ JB-10857 [DJ]	Moody Blue/She Thinks I Still Care	1976	250.00	500.00	1000.
—Colored vinyl pressings exist in five different colors -- red, white, gold, blue green. Value is for any of them.					
❑ PB-10857	Moody Blue/She Thinks I Still Care	1976	—	2.50	5.00
❑ PB-10857 [PS]	Moody Blue/She Thinks I Still Care	1976	2.50	5.00	10.00
❑ JH-10951 [DJ]	Let Me Be There (mono/stereo)	1977	50.00	100.00	200.00
—Promo only					
❑ PB-10998	Way Down/Pledging My Love	1977	—	2.50	5.00
❑ PB-10998 [PS]	Way Down/Pledging My Love	1977	2.50	5.00	10.00
❑ PB-11099	Hound Dog/Don't Be Cruel	1977	—	2.00	4.00
❑ PB-11099 [PS]	Hound Dog/Don't Be Cruel	1977	—	2.00	4.00
—From boxes "15 Golden Records, 30 Golden Hits" and "20 Golden Hits in Full Color Sleeves"					
❑ PB-11100	In the Ghetto/Any Day Now	1977	—	2.00	4.00
❑ PB-11100 [PS]	In the Ghetto/Any Day Now	1977	—	2.00	4.00
—From boxes "15 Golden Records, 30 Golden Hits" and "20 Golden Hits in Full Color Sleeves"					
❑ PB-11101	Jailhouse Rock/Treat Me Nice	1977	—	2.00	4.00
❑ PB-11101 [PS]	Jailhouse Rock/Treat Me Nice	1977	—	2.00	4.00
—From box "15 Golden Records, 30 Golden Hits"					
❑ PB-11102	Can't Help Falling in Love/Rock-a-Hula Baby	1977	—	2.00	4.00
❑ PB-11102 [PS]	Can't Help Falling in Love/Rock-a-Hula Baby	1977	—	2.00	4.00
—From boxes "15 Golden Records, 30 Golden Hits" and "20 Golden Hits in Full Color Sleeves"					
❑ PB-11103	Suspicious Minds/You'll Think of Me	1977	—	2.00	4.00
❑ PB-11103 [PS]	Suspicious Minds/You'll Think of Me	1977	—	2.00	4.00
—From box "15 Golden Records, 30 Golden Hits"					
❑ PB-11104	Are You Lonesome To-Night?/I Gotta Know	1977	—	2.00	4.00
❑ PB-11104 [PS]	Are You Lonesome To-Night?/I Gotta Know	1977	—	2.00	4.00
—From boxes "15 Golden Records, 30 Golden Hits" and "20 Golden Hits in Full Color Sleeves"					
❑ PB-11105	Heartbreak Hotel/I Was the One	1977	—	2.00	4.00
❑ PB-11105 [PS]	Heartbreak Hotel/I Was the One	1977	—	2.00	4.00
—From boxes "15 Golden Records, 30 Golden Hits" and "20 Golden Hits in Full Color Sleeves"					
❑ PB-11106	All Shook Up/That's When Your Heartaches Begin	1977	—	2.00	4.00
❑ PB-11106 [PS]	All Shook Up/That's When Your Heartaches Begin	1977	—	2.00	4.00
—From boxes "15 Golden Records, 30 Golden Hits" and "20 Golden Hits in Full Color Sleeves"					
❑ PB-11107	Blue Suede Shoes/Tutti Frutti	1977	—	2.00	4.00
❑ PB-11107 [PS]	Blue Suede Shoes/Tutti Frutti	1977	—	2.00	4.00
—From boxes "15 Golden Records, 30 Golden Hits" and "20 Golden Hits in Full Color Sleeves"					
❑ PB-11108	Love Me Tender/Any Way You Want Me (That's How I Will Be)	1977	—	2.00	4.00
❑ PB-11108 [PS]	Love Me Tender/Any Way You Want Me (That's How I Will Be)	1977	—	2.00	4.00
—From boxes "15 Golden Records, 30 Golden Hits" and "20 Golden Hits in Full Color Sleeves"					
❑ PB-11109	(Let Me Be Your) Teddy Bear/Loving You	1977	—	2.00	4.00
❑ PB-11109 [PS]	(Let Me Be Your) Teddy Bear/Loving You	1977	—	2.00	4.00
—From boxes "15 Golden Records, 30 Golden Hits" and "20 Golden Hits in Full Color Sleeves"					
❑ PB-11110	It's Now or Never/A Mess of Blues	1977	—	2.00	4.00
❑ PB-11110 [PS]	It's Now or Never/A Mess of Blues	1977	—	2.00	4.00
—From box "15 Golden Records, 30 Golden Hits"					
❑ PB-11111	Return to Sender/Where Do You Come From	1977	—	2.00	4.00
❑ PB-11111 [PS]	Return to Sender/Where Do You Come From	1977	—	2.00	4.00
—From boxes "15 Golden Records, 30 Golden Hits" and "20 Golden Hits in Full Color Sleeves"					
❑ PB-11112	One Night/I Got Stung	1977	—	2.00	4.00
❑ PB-11112 [PS]	One Night/I Got Stung	1977	—	2.00	4.00
—From box "15 Golden Records, 30 Golden Hits"					
❑ PB-11113	Crying in the Chapel/I Believe in the Man in the Sky	1977	—	2.00	4.00
❑ PB-11113 [PS]	Crying in the Chapel/I Believe in the Man in the Sky	1977	—	2.00	4.00
—From box "15 Golden Records, 30 Golden Hits"					
❑ PB-11165	My Way/America	1977	—	2.50	5.00
❑ PB-11165	My Way/America the Beautiful	1977	5.00	10.00	20.00
❑ PB-11165 [PS]	My Way/America	1977	2.50	5.00	10.00
❑ PB-11165 [PS]	My Way/America the Beautiful	1977	6.25	12.50	25.00
❑ PB-11212	Unchained Melody/Softly, As I Leave You	1978	2.50	5.00	10.00
—Erroneously states "Vocal Accompaniment by Sherrill Nielsen" on "Unchained Melody" side					
❑ PB-11212	Unchained Melody/Softly, As I Leave You	1978	—	2.50	5.00
—No credit to Sherrill Nielsen on the "Unchained Melody" side					
❑ PB-11212 [PS]	Unchained Melody/Softly, As I Leave You	1978	2.50	5.00	10.00
❑ PP-11301	15 Golden Records, 30 Golden Hits	1977	15.00	30.00	60.00
—Includes 15 records (11099-11113) and outer box					
❑ PB-11320	(Let Me Be Your) Teddy Bear/Puppet on a String	1978	—	2.50	5.00
❑ PB-11320 [PS]	(Let Me Be Your) Teddy Bear/Puppet on a String	1978	2.50	5.00	10.00
❑ GB-11326	Moody Blue/For the Heart	1978	—	2.00	4.00
—Gold Standard Series					
❑ PP-11340	20 Golden Hits in Full Color Sleeves	1977	20.00	40.00	80.00
—Includes 10 records (11099, 11100, 11102, 11104-11109, 11111) and outer box					
❑ GB-11504	Way Down/My Way	1979	—	2.00	4.00
—Gold Standard Series					
❑ PB-11533	Are You Sincere/Solitaire	1979	—	2.50	5.00
❑ PB-11533 [PS]	Are You Sincere/Solitaire	1979	2.50	5.00	10.00
❑ PB-11679	There's a Honky Tonk Angel (Who Will Take Me Back In)/I Got a Feelin' in My Body	1979	3.75	7.50	15.00
—Has full production credits (background vocals, strings) listed in error on both sides					
❑ PB-11679	There's a Honky Tonk Angel (Who Will Take Me Back In)/I Got a Feelin' in My Body	1979	—	2.50	5.00
—Has production credits removed; only producers are listed					
❑ PB-11679 [PS]	There's a Honky Tonk Angel (Who Will Take Me Back In)/I Got a Feelin' in My Body	1979	2.50	5.00	10.00
❑ GB-11988	Unchained Melody/Are You Sincere	1980	—	2.00	4.00
—Gold Standard Series					
❑ JH-12158 [DJ]	Guitar Man (mono/stereo)	1981	75.00	150.00	300.00
—Promo only on red vinyl					
❑ PB-12158	Guitar Man/Faded Love	1981	—	2.50	5.00
❑ PB-12158 [PS]	Guitar Man/Faded Love	1981	2.50	5.00	10.00
❑ JB-12205 [DJ]	Lovin' Arms/You Asked Me To	1981	75.00	150.00	300.00
—Promo only on green vinyl					

Number	Title (A Side/B Side)	Yr	VG	VG+	NM
❑ PB-12205	Lovin' Arms/You Asked Me To	1981	—	3.00	6.00
—Not issued with picture sleeve (bootlegs exist)					
❑ PB-13058	There Goes My Everything/You'll Never Walk Alone	1982	—	2.50	5.00
❑ PB-13058 [PS]	There Goes My Everything/You'll Never Walk Alone	1982	2.50	5.00	10.00
❑ GB-13275	Suspicious Minds/You'll Think of Me	1982	—	2.00	4.00
—Gold Standard Series					
❑ JH-13302	The Impossible Dream (The Quest)/An American Trilogy	1982	25.00	50.00	100.00
❑ JH-13302 [PS]	The Impossible Dream (The Quest)/An American Trilogy	1982	25.00	50.00	100.00
—Promo only, distributed to visitors to Elvis' birthplace in Tupelo, Mississippi, in 1982.					
❑ JB-13351 [DJ]	The Elvis Medley (Long Version)/The Elvis Medley (Short Version)	1982	75.00	150.00	300.00
—Promo only on gold vinyl					
❑ PB-13351	The Elvis Medley/Always on My Mind	1982	—	2.50	5.00
❑ PB-13351 [PS]	The Elvis Medley/Always on My Mind	1982	2.50	5.00	10.00
❑ JB-13500 [DJ]	I Was the One/Wear My Ring Around Your Neck	1983	75.00	150.00	300.00
—Promo only on gold vinyl					
❑ PB-13500	I Was the One/Wear My Ring Around Your Neck	1983	—	2.50	5.00
❑ PB-13500 [PS]	I Was the One/Wear My Ring Around Your Neck	1983	2.50	5.00	10.00
❑ JB-13547 [DJ]	Little Sister/Paralyzed	1983	75.00	150.00	300.00
—Promo only on blue vinyl					
❑ PB-13547	Little Sister/Paralyzed	1983	—	2.50	5.00
❑ PB-13547 [PS]	Little Sister/Paralyzed	1983	2.50	5.00	10.00
❑ JB-13875 [DJ]	Baby Let's Play House/Hound Dog	1984	50.00	100.00	200.00
—Gold vinyl, custom label					
❑ PB-13875	Baby Let's Play House/Hound Dog	1984	10.00	20.00	40.00
—Gold vinyl, custom label					
❑ PB-13875 [PS]	Baby Let's Play House/Hound Dog	1984	10.00	20.00	40.00
❑ PB-13885	Blue Suede Shoes/Tutti Frutti	1984	—	2.00	4.00
—From box "Elvis' Greatest Hits, Golden Singles, Volume 1"; gold vinyl					
❑ PB-13885 [PS]	Blue Suede Shoes/Tutti Frutti	1984	—	2.00	4.00
❑ PB-13886	Don't Be Cruel/Hound Dog	1984	—	2.00	4.00
—From box "Elvis' Greatest Hits, Golden Singles, Volume 1"; gold vinyl					
❑ PB-13886 [PS]	Don't Be Cruel/Hound Dog	1984	—	2.00	4.00
❑ PB-13887	I Want You, I Need You, I Love You/Love Me	1984	—	2.00	4.00
—From box "Elvis' Greatest Hits, Golden Singles, Volume 1"; gold vinyl					
❑ PB-13887 [PS]	I Want You, I Need You, I Love You/Love Me	1984	—	2.00	4.00
❑ PB-13888	All Shook Up/(Let Me Be Your) Teddy Bear	1984	—	2.00	4.00
—From box "Elvis' Greatest Hits, Golden Singles, Volume 1"; gold vinyl					
❑ PB-13888 [PS]	All Shook Up/(Let Me Be Your) Teddy Bear	1984	—	2.00	4.00
❑ PB-13889	It's Now or Never/Surrender	1984	—	2.00	4.00
—From box "Elvis' Greatest Hits, Golden Singles, Volume 1"; gold vinyl					
❑ PB-13889 [PS]	It's Now or Never/Surrender	1984	—	2.00	4.00
❑ PB-13890	In the Ghetto/If I Can Dream	1984	—	2.00	4.00
—From box "Elvis' Greatest Hits, Golden Singles, Volume 1"; gold vinyl					
❑ PB-13890 [PS]	In the Ghetto/If I Can Dream	1984	—	2.00	4.00
❑ PB-13891	That's All Right/Blue Moon of Kentucky	1984	—	2.00	4.00
—From box "Elvis' Greatest Hits, Golden Singles, Volume 2"; gold vinyl					
❑ PB-13891 [PS]	That's All Right/Blue Moon of Kentucky	1984	—	2.00	4.00
❑ PB-13892	Heartbreak Hotel/Jailhouse Rock	1984	—	2.00	4.00
—From box "Elvis' Greatest Hits, Golden Singles, Volume 2"; gold vinyl					
❑ PB-13892 [PS]	Heartbreak Hotel/Jailhouse Rock	1984	—	2.00	4.00
❑ PB-13893	Love Me Tender/Loving You	1984	—	2.00	4.00
—From box "Elvis' Greatest Hits, Golden Singles, Volume 2"; gold vinyl					
❑ PB-13893 [PS]	Love Me Tender/Loving You	1984	—	2.00	4.00
❑ PB-13894	(Marie's the Name) His Latest Flame/Little Sister	1984	—	2.00	4.00
—From box "Elvis' Greatest Hits, Golden Singles, Volume 2"; gold vinyl					
❑ PB-13894 [PS]	(Marie's the Name) His Latest Flame/Little Sister	1984	—	2.00	4.00
❑ PB-13895	Are You Lonesome Tonight/Can't Help Falling in Love	1984	—	2.00	4.00
—From box "Elvis' Greatest Hits, Golden Singles, Volume 2"; gold vinyl					
❑ PB-13895 [PS]	Are You Lonesome Tonight/Can't Help Falling in Love	1984	—	2.00	4.00
❑ PB-13896	Suspicious Minds/Burning Love	1984	—	2.00	4.00
—From box "Elvis' Greatest Hits, Golden Singles, Volume 2"; gold vinyl					
❑ PB-13896 [PS]	Suspicious Minds/Burning Love	1984	—	2.00	4.00
❑ PB-13897	Elvis' Greatest Hits, Golden Singles, Volume 1	1984	3.75	7.50	15.00
—Box set of six 45s with sleeves (13885-13890) with box					
❑ PB-13898	Elvis' Greatest Hits, Golden Singles, Volume 2	1984	3.75	7.50	15.00
—Box set of six 45s with sleeves (13891-13896) with box					
❑ PB-13929	Blue Suede Shoes/Promised Land	1984	3.75	7.50	15.00
—Blue vinyl; incorrect label -- "Blue Suede Shoes" side says "Stereo" and "Promised Land" side says "Mono"					
❑ PB-13929	Blue Suede Shoes/Promised Land	1984	3.00	6.00	12.00
—Blue vinyl; correct label -- "Blue Suede Shoes" side says "Mono" and "Promised Land" side says "Stereo"					
❑ PB-13929 [PS]	Blue Suede Shoes/Promised Land	1984	2.50	5.00	10.00
❑ PB-14090	Always on My Mind/My Boy	1985	2.50	5.00	10.00
—Purple vinyl					
❑ PB-14090 [PS]	Always on My Mind/My Boy	1985	2.50	5.00	10.00
❑ PB-14237	Merry Christmas Baby/Santa Claus Is Back in Town	1985	3.75	7.50	15.00
—"Elvis 50th Anniversary" label					
❑ PB-14237	Merry Christmas Baby/Santa Claus Is Back in Town	1985	—	2.50	5.00
—Normal black RCA label					
❑ PB-14237	Merry Christmas Baby/Santa Claus Is Back in Town	1985	3.75	7.50	15.00
—Green vinyl					
❑ PB-14237 [PS]	Merry Christmas Baby/Santa Claus Is Back in Town	1985	3.00	6.00	12.00
❑ 62402	Don't Be Cruel/Ain't That Lovin' You Baby (Fast Version)	1992	—	2.50	5.00
❑ 62402 [PS]	Don't Be Cruel/Ain't That Lovin' You Baby (Fast Version)	1992	—	2.50	5.00
—Generic white sleeve with "Elvis -- The King of Rock 'n' Roll" sticker					
❑ 62403	Blue Christmas/Love Me Tender	1992	—	2.50	5.00
❑ 62403 [PS]	Blue Christmas/Love Me Tender	1992	—	2.50	5.00
—Generic white sleeve with "Elvis -- The King of Rock 'n' Roll" sticker					
❑ 62411	Silver Bells (Unreleased Version)/Silver Bells	1993	—	2.50	5.00
❑ 62449	Heartbreak Hotel/Hound Dog	1992	—	2.50	5.00
❑ 64476	Heartbreak Hotel/I Was the One//Heartbreak Hotel (Alternate Take 5)/I Was the One (Alternate Take 2)	1996	—	—	3.00
❑ 64476 [PS]	Heartbreak Hotel/I Was the One//Heartbreak Hotel (Alternate Take 5)/I Was the One (Alternate Take 2)	1996	—	—	3.00
❑ 447-0600	I Forgot to Remember to Forget/Mystery Train	1977	—	2.00	4.00
—Note: All RCA releases with a "447" prefix are from the Gold Standard Series and are black label, dog on side					
❑ 447-0601	That's All Right/Blue Moon of Kentucky	1977	—	2.00	4.00
❑ 447-0602	Good Rockin' Tonight/I Don't Care If the Sun Don't Shine	1977	—	2.00	4.00
❑ 447-0603	Milkcow Blues Boogie/You're a Heartbreaker	1977	—	2.00	4.00
❑ 447-0604	Baby Let's Play House/I'm Left, You're Right, She's Gone	1977	—	2.00	4.00
❑ 447-0605	Heartbreak Hotel/I Was the One	1977	—	2.00	4.00
❑ 447-0607	I Want You, I Need You, I Love You/My Baby Left Me	1977	—	2.00	4.00
❑ 447-0608	Hound Dog/Don't Be Cruel	1977	—	2.00	4.00
❑ 447-0609	Blue Suede Shoes/Tutti Frutti	1977	—	2.00	4.00
❑ 447-0613	Blue Moon/Just Because	1977	—	2.00	4.00
❑ 447-0614	Money Honey/One-Sided Love Affair	1977	—	2.00	4.00
❑ 447-0615	Lawdy Miss Clawdy/Shake, Rattle, and Roll	1977	—	2.00	4.00
❑ 447-0616	Love Me Tender/Anyway You Want Me (That's How I Will Be)	1977	—	2.00	4.00
❑ 447-0617	Too Much/Playing for Keeps	1977	—	2.00	4.00
❑ 447-0618	All Shook Up/That's When Your Heartaches Begin	1977	—	2.00	4.00
❑ 447-0619	Jailhouse Rock/Treat Me Nice	1977	—	2.00	4.00
❑ 447-0620	(Let Me Be Your) Teddy Bear/Loving You	1977	—	2.00	4.00
❑ 447-0621	Don't/I Beg of You	1977	—	2.00	4.00
❑ 447-0622	Wear My Ring Around Your Neck/Don'tcha Think It's Time	1977	—	2.00	4.00
❑ 447-0623	Hard Headed Woman/Don't Ask Me Why	1977	—	2.00	4.00
❑ 447-0624	One Night/I Got Stung	1977	—	2.00	4.00
❑ 447-0625	(Now and Then There's) A Fool Such As I/I Need Your Love Tonight	1977	—	2.00	4.00
❑ 447-0626	A Big Hunk o'Love/My Wish Came True	1977	—	2.00	4.00
❑ 447-0627	Stuck on You/Fame and Fortune	1977	—	2.00	4.00
❑ 447-0628	It's Now or Never/A Mess of Blues	1977	—	2.00	4.00
❑ 447-0629	Are You Lonesome To-Night?/I Gotta Know	1977	—	2.00	4.00
❑ 447-0630	Surrender/Lonely Man	1977	—	2.00	4.00
❑ 447-0631	I Feel So Bad/Wild in the Country	1977	—	2.00	4.00
❑ 447-0634	(Marie's the Name) His Latest Flame/Little Sister	1977	—	2.00	4.00
❑ 447-0635	Can't Help Falling in Love/Rock-a-Hula Baby	1977	—	2.00	4.00
❑ 447-0636	Good Luck Charm/Anything That's Part of You	1977	—	2.00	4.00
❑ 447-0637	She's Not You/Just Tell Her Jim Said Hello	1977	—	2.00	4.00
❑ 447-0638	Return to Sender/Where Do You Come From	1977	—	2.00	4.00
❑ 447-0639	Kiss Me Quick/Suspicion	1977	—	2.00	4.00
❑ 447-0640	One Broken Heart for Sale/They Remind Me Too Much of You	1977	—	2.00	4.00
❑ 447-0641	(You're the) Devil in Disguise/Please Don't Drag That String Around	1977	—	2.00	4.00
❑ 447-0642	Bossa Nova Baby/Witchcraft	1977	—	2.00	4.00
❑ 447-0643	Crying in the Chapel/I Believe in the Man in the Sky	1977	—	2.00	4.00
❑ 447-0644	Kissin' Cousins/It Hurts Me	1977	—	2.00	4.00
❑ 447-0645	Such a Night/Never Ending	1977	—	2.00	4.00
❑ 447-0646	Viva Las Vegas/What'd I Say	1977	—	2.00	4.00
❑ 447-0647	Blue Christmas/Santa Claus Is Back in Town	1977	—	2.00	4.00
❑ 447-0647 [PS]	Blue Christmas/Santa Claus Is Back in Town	1977	2.50	5.00	10.00
—Does not mention "Gold Standard Series" on sleeve					
❑ 447-0648	Do the Clam/You'll Be Gone	1977	—	2.00	4.00
❑ 447-0649	Ain't That Loving You Baby/Ask Me	1977	—	2.00	4.00
❑ 447-0650	Puppet on a String/Wooden Heart	1977	—	2.00	4.00
❑ 447-0651	Joshua Fit the Battle/Known Only to Him	1977	—	2.00	4.00
❑ 447-0653	(Such An) Easy Question/It Feels So Right	1977	—	2.00	4.00
❑ 447-0654	I'm Yours/(It's a) Long, Lonely Highway	1977	—	2.00	4.00
❑ 447-0655	Tell Me Why/Blue River	1977	—	2.00	4.00
❑ 447-0656	Frankie and Johnny/Please Don't Stop Loving Me	1977	—	2.00	4.00
❑ 447-0657	Love Letters/Come What May	1977	—	2.00	4.00
❑ 447-0658	Spinout/All That I Do	1977	—	2.00	4.00
❑ 447-0659	Indescribably Blue/Fools Fall in Love	1977	—	2.00	4.00
❑ 447-0661	There's Always Me/Judy	1977	—	2.00	4.00
❑ 447-0662	Big Boss Man/You Don't Know Me	1977	—	2.00	4.00
❑ 447-0663	Guitar Man/High Heel Sneakers	1977	—	2.00	4.00
❑ 447-0664	U.S. Male/Stay Away	1977	—	2.50	5.00
❑ 447-0665	You'll Never Walk Alone/We Call on Him	1977	—	2.00	4.00
❑ 447-0666	Let Yourself Go/Your Time Hasn't Come Yet, Baby	1977	—	2.00	4.00
❑ 447-0667	A Little Less Conversation/Almost in Love	1977	—	2.00	4.00
❑ 447-0668	If I Can Dream/Edge of Reality	1977	—	2.00	4.00
❑ 447-0669	Memories/Charro	1977	—	2.00	4.00
❑ 447-0670	How Great Thou Art/His Hand in Mine	1977	—	2.00	4.00
❑ 447-0671	In the Ghetto/Any Day Now	1977	—	2.00	4.00
❑ 447-0672	Clean Up Your Own Back Yard/The Fair Is Moving On	1977	—	2.00	4.00
❑ 447-0673	Suspicious Minds/You'll Think of Me	1977	—	2.00	4.00
❑ 447-0674	Don't Cry Daddy/Rubberneckin'	1977	—	2.00	4.00
❑ 447-0675	Kentucky Rain/My Little Friend	1977	—	2.00	4.00
❑ 447-0676	The Wonder of You/Mama Liked the Roses	1977	—	2.00	4.00
❑ 447-0677	I've Lost You/The Next Step Is Love	1977	—	2.00	4.00
❑ 447-0678	You Don't Have to Say You Love Me/Patch It Up	1977	—	2.00	4.00
❑ 447-0679	I Really Don't Want to Know/There Goes My Everything	1977	—	2.00	4.00
❑ 447-0680	Where Did They Go, Lord/Rags to Riches	1977	—	2.00	4.00
❑ 447-0681	If Every Day Was Like Christmas/How Would You Like to Be	1977	—	2.00	4.00
❑ 447-0682	Life/Only Believe	1977	—	2.00	4.00

Number	Title (A Side/B Side)	Yr	VG	VG+	NM
❑ 447-0683	I'm Leavin'/Heart of Rome	1977	—	2.00	4.00
❑ 447-0684	It's Only Love/The Sound of Your Cry	1977	—	2.00	4.00
❑ 447-0685	An American Trilogy/Until It's Time for You to Go	1977	—	2.00	4.00
RCA VICTOR					
❑ CR-15 [DJ]	Old Shep	1956	250.00	500.00	1000.
—One-sided promo					
❑ SP-45-76 [DJ]	Don't/Wear My Ring Around Your Neck	1960	200.00	400.00	800.00
❑ SP-45-76 [PS]	Don't/Wear My Ring Around Your Neck	1960	1000.	1500.	2000.
❑ APBO-0088	Raised on Rock/For Ol' Times Sake	1973	—	3.00	6.00
❑ APBO-0088 [PS]	Raised on Rock/For Ol' Times Sake	1973	3.75	7.50	15.00
❑ 4-834-115 [DJ]	I'll Be Back	1966	4000.	6000.	8000.
—One-sided promo with designation "For Special Academy Consideration Only"					
❑ SP-45-118 [DJ]	King of the Whole Wide World/Home Is Where the Heart Is	1962	50.00	100.00	200.00
❑ SP-45-118 [PS]	King of the Whole Wide World/Home Is Where the Heart Is	1962	75.00	150.00	300.00
❑ SP-45-139 [DJ]	Roustabout/One Track Heart	1964	75.00	150.00	300.00
❑ SP-45-162 [DJ]	How Great Thou Art/So High	1967	37.50	75.00	150.00
❑ SP-45-162 [PS]	How Great Thou Art/So High	1967	50.00	100.00	200.00
❑ APBO-0196	Take Good Care of Her/I've Got a Thing About You, Baby	1973	—	3.00	6.00
❑ APBO-0196 [PS]	Take Good Care of Her/I've Got a Thing About You, Baby	1973	3.75	7.50	15.00
❑ APBO-0280	If You Talk in Your Sleep/Help Me	1974	3.00	6.00	12.00
—On label, the title "If You Talk in Your Sleep" is all on one line					
❑ APBO-0280	If You Talk in Your Sleep/Help Me	1974	—	3.00	6.00
—On label, the title "If You Talk" is on one line and "In Your Sleep" is on another line					
❑ APBO-0280 [PS]	If You Talk in Your Sleep/Help Me	1974	3.75	7.50	15.00
❑ HO7W-0808 [DJ]	Blue Christmas (same on both sides)	1957	375.00	750.00	1500.
❑ PB-10074	Promised Land/It's Midnight	1974	—	2.50	5.00
—Orange label (available at the same time as gray label)					
❑ PB-10074	Promised Land/It's Midnight	1974	—	2.50	5.00
—Gray label (available at the same time as orange label)					
❑ PB-10074	Promised Land/It's Midnight	1975	6.25	12.50	25.00
—Tan label (reissue)					
❑ PB-10074 [PS]	Promised Land/It's Midnight	1975	2.50	5.00	10.00
❑ GB-10156	Burning Love/Steamroller Blues	1975	2.00	4.00	8.00
—Gold Standard Series; red label					
❑ GB-10156	Burning Love/Steamroller Blues	1977	—	2.00	4.00
—Gold Standard Series; black label					
❑ GB-10157	Raised on Rock/If You Talk in Your Sleep	1975	2.00	4.00	8.00
—Gold Standard Series; red label					
❑ GB-10157	Raised on Rock/If You Talk in Your Sleep	1977	—	2.00	4.00
—Gold Standard Series; black label					
❑ PB-10191	My Boy/Thinking About You	1975	—	2.50	5.00
—Orange label					
❑ PB-10191	My Boy/Thinking About You	1975	—	2.50	5.00
—Tan label					
❑ PB-10191 [PS]	My Boy/Thinking About You	1975	2.50	5.00	10.00
❑ PB-10278	T-R-O-U-B-L-E/Mr. Songman	1975	—	2.50	5.00
—Orange label					
❑ PB-10278	T-R-O-U-B-L-E/Mr. Songman	1975	25.00	50.00	100.00
—Gray label					
❑ PB-10278	T-R-O-U-B-L-E/Mr. Songman	1975	2.50	5.00	10.00
—Tan label					
❑ PB-10278 [PS]	T-R-O-U-B-L-E/Mr. Songman	1975	2.50	5.00	10.00
❑ PB-10401	Bringing It Back/Pieces of My Life	1975	50.00	100.00	200.00
—Orange label					
❑ PB-10401	Bringing It Back/Pieces of My Life	1975	—	2.50	5.00
—Tan label					
❑ PB-10401 [PS]	Bringing It Back/Pieces of My Life	1975	2.50	5.00	10.00
❑ GB-10485	Take Good Care of Her/I've Got a Thing About You, Baby	1975	2.00	4.00	8.00
—Gold Standard Series; red label					
❑ GB-10486	Separate Ways/Always on My Mind	1975	2.00	4.00	8.00
—Gold Standard Series; red label					
❑ GB-10487	T-R-O-U-B-L-E/Mr. Songman	1975	2.00	4.00	8.00
—Gold Standard Series; red label					
❑ GB-10488	Promised Land/It's Midnight	1975	2.00	4.00	8.00
—Gold Standard Series; red label					
❑ GB-10489	My Boy/Thinking About You	1975	2.00	4.00	8.00
—Gold Standard Series; red label					
❑ PB-10601	Hurt/For the Heart	1976	—	2.50	5.00
—Originals on tan labels					
❑ PB-10601 [PS]	Hurt/For the Heart	1976	2.50	5.00	10.00
❑ 37-7850	Surrender/Lonely Man	1961	150.00	300.00	600.00
—"Compact Single 33" (small hole, plays at LP speed)					
❑ 37-7850 [PS]	Surrender/Lonely Man	1961	250.00	500.00	1000.
—Special picture sleeve for above record					
❑ 37-7880	I Feel So Bad/Wild in the Country	1961	250.00	500.00	1000.
—"Compact Single 33" (small hole, plays at LP speed)					
❑ 37-7880 [PS]	I Feel So Bad/Wild in the Country	1961	300.00	600.00	1200.
—Special picture sleeve for above record					
❑ 37-7908	(Marie's the Name) His Latest Flame/Little Sister	1961	375.00	750.00	1500.
—"Compact Single 33" (small hole, plays at LP speed)					
❑ 37-7908 [PS]	(Marie's the Name) His Latest Flame/Little Sister	1961	1000.	1500.	2000.
—Special picture sleeve for above record					
❑ 37-7908 [PS]	(Marie's the Name) His Latest Flame/Little Sister	1961	1125.	1688.	2250.
—Special picture sleeve for above record; says "Stereo-Orthophonic" on sleeve in error					
❑ 37-7968	Can't Help Falling in Love/Rock-a-Hula Baby	1961	1000.	1500.	2000.
—"Compact Single 33" (small hole, plays at LP speed)					
❑ 37-7968 [PS]	Can't Help Falling in Love/Rock-a-Hula Baby	1961	2000.	3000.	4000.
—Special picture sleeve for above record					
❑ 37-7992	Good Luck Charm/Anything That's Part of You	1962	1250.	1875.	2500.
—"Compact Single 33" (small hole, plays at LP speed)					
❑ 37-7992 [PS]	Good Luck Charm/Anything That's Part of You	1962	2500.	3750.	5000.
—Special picture sleeve for above record					
❑ 47-6357	I Forgot to Remember to Forget/Mystery Train	1955	15.00	30.00	60.00
—No horizontal line on label					
❑ 47-6357	I Forgot to Remember to Forget/Mystery Train	1955	15.00	30.00	60.00
—With horizontal line on label					
❑ 47-6357 [PS]	This Is His Life: Elvis Presley	1955	375.00	750.00	1500.
—Promo-only sleeve issued with above single; no stock picture sleeve was issued. This was formerly listed under "I Want You, I Need You, I Love You," as the sleeve does not have a number. Consensus opinion now places it with "Mystery Train."					
❑ 47-6380	That's All Right/Blue Moon of Kentucky	1955	15.00	30.00	60.00
—No horizontal line on label					
❑ 47-6380	That's All Right/Blue Moon of Kentucky	1955	15.00	30.00	60.00
—With horizontal line on label					
❑ 47-6381	Good Rockin' Tonight/I Don't Care If the Sun Don't Shine	1955	15.00	30.00	60.00
—With horizontal line on label					
❑ 47-6381	Good Rockin' Tonight/I Don't Care If the Sun Don't Shine	1955	15.00	30.00	60.00
—No horizontal line on label					
❑ 47-6382	Milkcow Blues Boogie/You're a Heartbreaker	1955	15.00	30.00	60.00
—No horizontal line on label					
❑ 47-6382	Milkcow Blues Boogie/You're a Heartbreaker	1955	15.00	30.00	60.00
—With horizontal line on label					
❑ 47-6383	Baby Let's Play House/I'm Left, You're Right, She's Gone	1955	15.00	30.00	60.00
—With horizontal line on label					
❑ 47-6383	Baby Let's Play House/I'm Left, You're Right, She's Gone	1955	15.00	30.00	60.00
—No horizontal line on label					
❑ 47-6420	Heartbreak Hotel/I Was the One	1956	10.00	20.00	40.00
—No horizontal line on label					
❑ 47-6420	Heartbreak Hotel/I Was the One	1956	10.00	20.00	40.00
—With horizontal line on label					
❑ 47-6540	I Want You, I Need You, I Love You/My Baby Left Me	1956	10.00	20.00	40.00
—No horizontal line on label					
❑ 47-6540	I Want You, I Need You, I Love You/My Baby Left Me	1956	10.00	20.00	40.00
—With horizontal line on label					
❑ 47-6604	Don't Be Cruel/Hound Dog	1956	7.50	15.00	30.00
—No horizontal line on label					
❑ 47-6604	Don't Be Cruel/Hound Dog	1956	7.50	15.00	30.00
—With horizontal line on label					
❑ 47-6604 [PS]	Don't Be Cruel/Hound Dog	1956	50.00	100.00	200.00
—"Don't Be Cruel" listed on top of "Hound Dog!"					
❑ 47-6604 [PS]	Don't Be Cruel/Hound Dog	1956	30.00	60.00	120.00
—"Hound Dog!" listed on top of "Don't Be Cruel"					
❑ 47-6636	Blue Suede Shoes/Tutti Frutti	1956	20.00	40.00	80.00
—No horizontal line on label					
❑ 47-6636	Blue Suede Shoes/Tutti Frutti	1956	20.00	40.00	80.00
—With horizontal line on label					
❑ 47-6637	I Got a Woman/I'm Countin' On You	1956	20.00	40.00	80.00
—With horizontal line on label					
❑ 47-6637	I Got a Woman/I'm Countin' On You	1956	20.00	40.00	80.00
—No horizontal line on label					
❑ 47-6638	I'm Gonna Sit Right Down and Cry (Over You)/I'll Never Let You Go (Little Darlin')	1956	17.50	35.00	70.00
—No horizontal line on label					
❑ 47-6638	I'm Gonna Sit Right Down and Cry (Over You)/I'll Never Let You Go (Little Darlin')	1956	17.50	35.00	70.00
—With horizontal line on label					
❑ 47-6639	Tryin' to Get to You/I Love You Because	1956	17.50	35.00	70.00
—With horizontal line on label					
❑ 47-6639	Tryin' to Get to You/I Love You Because	1956	17.50	35.00	70.00
—No horizontal line on label					
❑ 47-6640	Blue Moon/Just Because	1956	15.00	30.00	60.00
—No horizontal line on label					
❑ 47-6640	Blue Moon/Just Because	1956	15.00	30.00	60.00
—With horizontal line on label					
❑ 47-6641	Money Honey/One-Sided Love Affair	1956	12.50	25.00	50.00
—With horizontal line on label					
❑ 47-6641	Money Honey/One-Sided Love Affair	1956	12.50	25.00	50.00
—No horizontal line on label					
❑ 47-6642	Lawdy Miss Clawdy/Shake, Rattle, and Roll	1956	10.00	20.00	40.00
—No horizontal line on label					
❑ 47-6642	Lawdy Miss Clawdy/Shake, Rattle, and Roll	1956	50.00	100.00	200.00
—With horizontal line on label, but with no dog					
❑ 47-6642	Lawdy Miss Clawdy/Shake, Rattle, and Roll	1956	10.00	20.00	40.00
—With horizontal line on label, dog on label as usual					
❑ 47-6643	Love Me Tender/Anyway You Want Me (That's How I Will Be)	1956	7.50	15.00	30.00
—No horizontal line on label					
❑ 47-6643	Love Me Tender/Anyway You Want Me (That's How I Will Be)	1956	7.50	15.00	30.00
—With horizontal line on label					
❑ 47-6643	Love Me Tender/Anyway You Want Me (That's How I Will Be)	1956	10.00	20.00	40.00
—No reference to the movie "Love Me Tender" on label					
❑ 47-6643 [PS]	Love Me Tender/Anyway You Want Me (That's How I Will Be)	1956	45.00	90.00	180.00
—Black and white sleeve					
❑ 47-6643 [PS]	Love Me Tender/Anyway You Want Me (That's How I Will Be)	1956	18.75	37.50	75.00
—Black and green sleeve					
❑ 47-6643 [PS]	Love Me Tender/Anyway You Want Me (That's How I Will Be)	1956	10.00	20.00	40.00
—Black and dark pink sleeve					
❑ 47-6643 [PS]	Love Me Tender/Anyway You Want Me (That's How I Will Be)	1956	7.50	15.00	30.00
—Black and light pink sleeve					
❑ 47-6800	Too Much/Playing for Keeps	1957	7.50	15.00	30.00
—No horizontal line on label					
❑ 47-6800	Too Much/Playing for Keeps	1957	50.00	100.00	200.00
—With horizontal line on label, but with no dog					
❑ 47-6800	Too Much/Playing for Keeps	1957	7.50	15.00	30.00
—With horizontal line on label, dog on label as normal					

Number	Title (A Side/B Side)	Yr	VG	VG+	NM
❑ 47-6800 [PS]	Too Much/Playing for Keeps	1957	22.50	45.00	90.00
❑ 47-6870	All Shook Up/That's When Your Heartaches Begin	1957	7.50	15.00	30.00
—No horizontal line on label					
❑ 47-6870	All Shook Up/That's When Your Heartaches Begin	1957	7.50	15.00	30.00
—With horizontal line on label					
❑ 47-6870 [PS]	All Shook Up/That's When Your Heartaches Begin	1957	22.50	45.00	90.00
❑ 47-7000	(Let Me Be Your) Teddy Bear/Loving You	1957	10.00	20.00	40.00
—Label says "Let Me Be Your TEDDY BEAR" (no parentheses)					
❑ 47-7000	(Let Me Be Your) Teddy Bear/Loving You	1957	7.50	15.00	30.00
—Parentheses around "Let Me Be Your", no horizontal line on label					
❑ 47-7000	(Let Me Be Your) Teddy Bear/Loving You	1957	7.50	15.00	30.00
—Parentheses around "Let Me Be Your", with horizontal line on label					
❑ 47-7000 [PS]	(Let Me Be Your) Teddy Bear/Loving You	1957	30.00	60.00	120.00
❑ 47-7035	Jailhouse Rock/Treat Me Nice	1957	7.50	15.00	30.00
—No horizontal line on label					
❑ 47-7035	Jailhouse Rock/Treat Me Nice	1957	7.50	15.00	30.00
—With horizontal line on label					
❑ 47-7035	Jailhouse Rock/Treat Me Nice	1957	5000.	7500.	10000.
—Gold label; gold vinyl					
❑ 47-7035 [PS]	Jailhouse Rock/Treat Me Nice	1957	25.00	50.00	100.00
❑ 47-7150	Don't/I Beg of You	1958	6.25	12.50	25.00
—No horizontal line on label					
❑ 47-7150	Don't/I Beg of You	1958	6.25	12.50	25.00
—With horizontal line on label					
❑ 47-7150 [PS]	Don't/I Beg of You	1958	22.50	45.00	90.00
❑ 47-7240	Wear My Ring Around Your Neck/Don'tcha Think It's Time	1958	6.25	12.50	25.00
❑ 47-7240 [PS]	Wear My Ring Around Your Neck/Don'tcha Think It's Time	1958	22.50	45.00	90.00
❑ 47-7280	Hard Headed Woman/Don't Ask Me Why	1958	6.25	12.50	25.00
❑ 47-7280 [PS]	Hard Headed Woman/Don't Ask Me Why	1958	17.50	35.00	70.00
❑ 47-7410	One Night/I Got Stung	1958	6.25	12.50	25.00
❑ 47-7410 [PS]	One Night/I Got Stung	1958	17.50	35.00	70.00
❑ 47-7506	(Now and Then There's) A Fool Such As I/I Need Your Love Tonight	1959	6.25	12.50	25.00
❑ 47-7506 [PS]	(Now and Then There's) A Fool Such As I/I Need Your Love Tonight	1959	250.00	500.00	1000.
—Sleeve promotes the "Elvis Sails" EP					
❑ 47-7506 [PS]	(Now and Then There's) A Fool Such As I/I Need Your Love Tonight	1959	15.00	30.00	60.00
—Sleeve lists Elvis' EPs and Gold Standard singles					
❑ 47-7600	A Big Hunk o'Love/My Wish Came True	1959	6.25	12.50	25.00
❑ 47-7600 [PS]	A Big Hunk o'Love/My Wish Came True	1959	17.50	35.00	70.00
❑ 47-7740	Stuck on You/Fame and Fortune	1960	5.00	10.00	20.00
❑ 47-7740 [PS]	Stuck on You/Fame and Fortune	1960	15.00	30.00	60.00
❑ 47-7777	It's Now or Never/A Mess of Blues	1960	250.00	500.00	1000.
—An early mispress is missing the piano part on the A-side. Has the number "L2WW-0100-3S" or "L2WW-0100-4S" in trail-off wax.					
❑ 47-7777	It's Now or Never/A Mess of Blues	1960	5.00	10.00	20.00
—All other pressings with overdubbed piano					
❑ 47-7777 [PS]	It's Now or Never/A Mess of Blues	1960	15.00	30.00	60.00
❑ 47-7810	Are You Lonesome To-Night?/I Gotta Know	1960	5.00	10.00	20.00
❑ 47-7810 [PS]	Are You Lonesome To-Night?/I Gotta Know	1960	15.00	30.00	60.00
❑ 47-7850	Surrender/Lonely Man	1961	5.00	10.00	20.00
❑ 47-7850 [PS]	Surrender/Lonely Man	1961	15.00	30.00	60.00
❑ 47-7880	I Feel So Bad/Wild in the Country	1961	5.00	10.00	20.00
❑ 47-7880 [PS]	I Feel So Bad/Wild in the Country	1961	12.50	25.00	50.00
❑ 47-7908	(Marie's the Name) His Latest Flame/Little Sister	1961	5.00	10.00	20.00
—All copies of this record actually read "Marie's the Name HIS LATEST FLAME" (no parentheses)					
❑ 47-7908 [PS]	(Marie's the Name) His Latest Flame/Little Sister	1961	12.50	25.00	50.00
❑ 47-7968	Can't Help Falling in Love/Rock-a-Hula Baby	1961	5.00	10.00	20.00
❑ 47-7968 [PS]	Can't Help Falling in Love/Rock-a-Hula Baby	1961	10.00	20.00	40.00
❑ 47-7992	Good Luck Charm/Anything That's Part of You	1962	5.00	10.00	20.00
❑ 47-7992 [PS]	Good Luck Charm/Anything That's Part of You	1962	10.00	20.00	40.00
—Titles in blue and pink letters					
❑ 47-7992 [PS]	Good Luck Charm/Anything That's Part of You	1962	10.00	20.00	40.00
—Titles in rust and lavender letters					
❑ 47-8041	She's Not You/Just Tell Her Jim Said Hello	1962	5.00	10.00	20.00
❑ 47-8041 [PS]	She's Not You/Just Tell Her Jim Said Hello	1962	10.00	20.00	40.00
❑ 47-8100	Return to Sender/Where Do You Come From	1962	5.00	10.00	20.00
❑ 47-8100 [PS]	Return to Sender/Where Do You Come From	1962	10.00	20.00	40.00
❑ 47-8134	One Broken Heart for Sale/They Remind Me Too Much of You	1963	3.00	6.00	12.00
❑ 47-8134 [PS]	One Broken Heart for Sale/They Remind Me Too Much of You	1963	7.50	15.00	30.00
❑ 47-8188	(You're the) Devil in Disguise/Please Don't Drag That String Along	1963	50.00	100.00	200.00
—First pressing with incorrect B-side title					
❑ 47-8188	(You're the) Devil in Disguise/Please Don't Drag That String Around	1963	3.00	6.00	12.00
—Second pressing with correct B-side title					
❑ 47-8188 [PS]	(You're the) Devil in Disguise/Please Don't Drag That String Around	1963	7.50	15.00	30.00
—All sleeves have correct B-side title					
❑ 47-8243	Bossa Nova Baby/Witchcraft	1963	3.00	6.00	12.00
❑ 47-8243 [PS]	Bossa Nova Baby/Witchcraft	1963	7.50	15.00	30.00
—"Coming Soon" on sleeve					
❑ 47-8243 [PS]	Bossa Nova Baby/Witchcraft	1963	7.50	15.00	30.00
—"Ask For" on sleeve					
❑ 47-8243 [PS]	Bossa Nova Baby/Witchcraft	1963	7.50	15.00	30.00
—No reference to another album on sleeve					
❑ 47-8307	Kissin' Cousins/It Hurts Me	1964	3.00	6.00	12.00
❑ 47-8307 [PS]	Kissin' Cousins/It Hurts Me	1964	6.25	12.50	25.00
❑ 47-8360	Viva Las Vegas/What'd I Say	1964	3.00	6.00	12.00
❑ 47-8360 [PS]	Viva Las Vegas/What'd I Say	1964	6.25	12.50	25.00
—"Coming Soon" on sleeve					
❑ 47-8360 [PS]	Viva Las Vegas/What'd I Say	1964	12.50	25.00	50.00
—"Ask For" on sleeve					
❑ 47-8400	Such a Night/Never Ending	1964	3.00	6.00	12.00
❑ 47-8400 [DJ]	Such a Night/Never Ending	1964	2500.	3750.	5000.
—An inexplicably rare regular white label promo					
❑ 47-8400 [PS]	Such a Night/Never Ending	1964	6.25	12.50	25.00
❑ 47-8440	Ain't That Loving You Baby/Ask Me	1964	2.50	5.00	10.00
❑ 47-8440 [PS]	Ain't That Loving You Baby/Ask Me	1964	6.25	12.50	25.00
—"Coming Soon" on sleeve					
❑ 47-8440 [PS]	Ain't That Loving You Baby/Ask Me	1964	6.25	12.50	25.00
—"Ask For" on sleeve					
❑ 47-8500	Do the Clam/You'll Be Gone	1965	2.50	5.00	10.00
❑ 47-8500 [PS]	Do the Clam/You'll Be Gone	1965	6.25	12.50	25.00
❑ 47-8585	(Such An) Easy Question/It Feels So Right	1965	2.50	5.00	10.00
❑ 47-8585 [PS]	(Such An) Easy Question/It Feels So Right	1965	6.25	12.50	25.00
—"Coming Soon" on sleeve					
❑ 47-8585 [PS]	(Such An) Easy Question/It Feels So Right	1965	6.25	12.50	25.00
—"Ask For" on sleeve					
❑ 47-8657	I'm Yours/(It's a) Long, Lonely Highway	1965	2.50	5.00	10.00
❑ 47-8657 [PS]	I'm Yours/(It's a) Long, Lonely Highway	1965	6.25	12.50	25.00
❑ 47-8740	Tell Me Why/Blue River	1965	2.50	5.00	10.00
❑ 47-8740 [PS]	Tell Me Why/Blue River	1965	6.25	12.50	25.00
❑ 47-8780	Frankie and Johnny/Please Don't Stop Loving Me	1966	2.50	5.00	10.00
❑ 47-8780 [PS]	Frankie and Johnny/Please Don't Stop Loving Me	1966	6.25	12.50	25.00
❑ 47-8870	Love Letters/Come What May	1966	2.50	5.00	10.00
❑ 47-8870 [PS]	Love Letters/Come What May	1966	6.25	12.50	25.00
—"Coming Soon" on sleeve					
❑ 47-8870 [PS]	Love Letters/Come What May	1966	6.25	12.50	25.00
—"Ask For" on sleeve					
❑ 47-8941	Spinout/All That I Do	1966	2.50	5.00	10.00
❑ 47-8941 [PS]	Spinout/All That I Do	1966	6.25	12.50	25.00
—"Watch For" on sleeve					
❑ 47-8941 [PS]	Spinout/All That I Do	1966	6.25	12.50	25.00
—"Ask For" on sleeve					
❑ 47-8950	If Every Day Was Like Christmas/How Would You Like to Be	1966	5.00	10.00	20.00
❑ 47-8950 [PS]	If Every Day Was Like Christmas/How Would You Like to Be	1966	10.00	20.00	40.00
❑ 47-9056	Indescribably Blue/Fools Fall in Love	1966	2.50	5.00	10.00
❑ 47-9056 [PS]	Indescribably Blue/Fools Fall in Love	1966	6.25	12.50	25.00
❑ 47-9115	Long Legged Girl (With the Short Dress On)/That's Someone You Never Forget	1967	2.50	5.00	10.00
❑ 47-9115 [PS]	Long Legged Girl (With the Short Dress On)/That's Someone You Never Forget	1967	6.25	12.50	25.00
—"Coming Soon" on sleeve					
❑ 47-9115 [PS]	Long Legged Girl (With the Short Dress On)/That's Someone You Never Forget	1967	6.25	12.50	25.00
—"Ask For" on sleeve					
❑ 47-9287	There's Always Me/Judy	1967	2.50	5.00	10.00
❑ 47-9287 [PS]	There's Always Me/Judy	1967	6.25	12.50	25.00
❑ 47-9341	Big Boss Man/You Don't Know Me	1967	2.50	5.00	10.00
❑ 47-9341 [PS]	Big Boss Man/You Don't Know Me	1967	6.25	12.50	25.00
❑ 47-9425	Guitar Man/High Heel Sneakers	1968	2.50	5.00	10.00
❑ 47-9425 [PS]	Guitar Man/High Heel Sneakers	1968	6.25	12.50	25.00
—"Coming Soon" on sleeve					
❑ 47-9425 [PS]	Guitar Man/High Heel Sneakers	1968	6.25	12.50	25.00
—"Ask For" on sleeve					
❑ 47-9465	U.S. Male/Stay Away	1968	2.50	5.00	10.00
❑ 47-9465 [PS]	U.S. Male/Stay Away	1968	6.25	12.50	25.00
❑ 47-9547	Let Yourself Go/Your Time Hasn't Come Yet, Baby	1968	2.50	5.00	10.00
❑ 47-9547 [PS]	Let Yourself Go/Your Time Hasn't Come Yet, Baby	1968	6.25	12.50	25.00
—"Coming Soon" on sleeve					
❑ 47-9547 [PS]	Let Yourself Go/Your Time Hasn't Come Yet, Baby	1968	6.25	12.50	25.00
—"Ask For" on sleeve					
❑ 47-9600	You'll Never Walk Alone/We Call on Him	1968	3.00	6.00	12.00
❑ 47-9600 [PS]	You'll Never Walk Alone/We Call on Him	1968	25.00	50.00	100.00
❑ 47-9610	A Little Less Conversation/Almost in Love	1968	2.50	5.00	10.00
❑ 47-9610 [PS]	A Little Less Conversation/Almost in Love	1968	6.25	12.50	25.00
❑ 47-9670	If I Can Dream/Edge of Reality	1968	2.00	4.00	8.00
—First Elvis single on orange label					
❑ 47-9670 [PS]	If I Can Dream/Edge of Reality	1968	5.00	10.00	20.00
—Mentions his NBC-TV special on sleeve					
❑ 47-9670 [PS]	If I Can Dream/Edge of Reality	1968	5.00	10.00	20.00
—Does not mention his NBC-TV special on sleeve					
❑ 47-9731	Memories/Charro	1969	2.00	4.00	8.00
❑ 47-9731 [PS]	Memories/Charro	1969	5.00	10.00	20.00
❑ 47-9741	In the Ghetto/Any Day Now	1969	2.00	4.00	8.00
❑ 47-9741 [PS]	In the Ghetto/Any Day Now	1969	5.00	10.00	20.00
—"Coming Soon" on sleeve					
❑ 47-9741 [PS]	In the Ghetto/Any Day Now	1969	5.00	10.00	20.00
—"Ask For" on sleeve					
❑ 47-9747	Clean Up Your Own Back Yard/The Fair Is Moving On	1969	2.00	4.00	8.00
❑ 47-9747 [PS]	Clean Up Your Own Back Yard/The Fair Is Moving On	1969	5.00	10.00	20.00
❑ 47-9764	Suspicious Minds/You'll Think of Me	1969	2.00	4.00	8.00
❑ 47-9764 [PS]	Suspicious Minds/You'll Think of Me	1969	5.00	10.00	20.00
❑ 47-9768	Don't Cry Daddy/Rubberneckin'	1969	2.00	4.00	8.00
❑ 47-9768 [PS]	Don't Cry Daddy/Rubberneckin'	1969	3.75	7.50	15.00
❑ 47-9791	Kentucky Rain/My Little Friend	1969	2.00	4.00	8.00
❑ 47-9791 [PS]	Kentucky Rain/My Little Friend	1969	3.75	7.50	15.00
❑ 47-9835	The Wonder of You/Mama Liked the Roses	1970	2.00	4.00	8.00
❑ 47-9835 [PS]	The Wonder of You/Mama Liked the Roses	1970	3.75	7.50	15.00
❑ 47-9873	I've Lost You/The Next Step Is Love	1970	—	3.00	6.00
❑ 47-9873 [PS]	I've Lost You/The Next Step Is Love	1970	3.75	7.50	15.00
❑ 47-9916	You Don't Have to Say You Love Me/Patch It Up	1970	—	3.00	6.00
❑ 47-9916 [PS]	You Don't Have to Say You Love Me/Patch It Up	1970	3.75	7.50	15.00
❑ 47-9960	I Really Don't Want to Know/There Goes My Everything	1971	—	3.00	6.00
❑ 47-9960 [PS]	I Really Don't Want to Know/There Goes My Everything	1971	3.75	7.50	15.00
—"Coming Soon" on sleeve					

Number	Title (A Side/B Side)	Yr	VG	VG+	NM
❑ 47-9960 [PS]	I Really Don't Want to Know/There Goes My Everything	1971	3.75	7.50	15.00
—"Ask For" on sleeve					
❑ 47-9980	Where Did They Go, Lord/Rags to Riches	1971	—	3.00	6.00
❑ 47-9980 [PS]	Where Did They Go, Lord/Rags to Riches	1971	5.00	10.00	20.00
❑ 47-9985	Life/Only Believe	1971	—	3.00	6.00
❑ 47-9985 [PS]	Life/Only Believe	1971	7.50	15.00	30.00
❑ 47-9998	I'm Leavin'/Heart of Rome	1971	—	3.00	6.00
❑ 47-9998 [PS]	I'm Leavin'/Heart of Rome	1971	5.00	10.00	20.00
❑ 48-1017	It's Only Love/The Sound of Your Cry	1971	—	3.00	6.00
❑ 48-1017 [PS]	It's Only Love/The Sound of Your Cry	1971	3.75	7.50	15.00
❑ 61-7740 [S]	Stuck on You/Fame and Fortune	1960	100.00	200.00	400.00
—"Living Stereo" (large hole, plays at 45 rpm)					
❑ 61-7777 [S]	It's Now or Never/A Mess of Blues	1960	100.00	200.00	400.00
—"Living Stereo" (large hole, plays at 45 rpm)					
❑ 61-7810 [S]	Are You Lonesome To-Night?/I Gotta Know	1960	150.00	300.00	600.00
—"Living Stereo" (large hole, plays at 45 rpm)					
❑ 61-7850 [S]	Surrender/Lonely Man	1961	200.00	400.00	800.00
—"Living Stereo" (large hole, plays at 45 rpm)					
❑ 68-7850 [S]	Surrender/Lonely Man	1961	1000.	1500.	2000.
—"Compact Stereo 33" in "Living Stereo"					
❑ 74-0130	How Great Thou Art/His Hand in Mine	1969	6.25	12.50	25.00
❑ 74-0130 [PS]	How Great Thou Art/His Hand in Mine	1969	37.50	75.00	150.00
❑ 74-0572	Merry Christmas Baby/O Come All Ye Faithful	1971	3.75	7.50	15.00
❑ 74-0572 [PS]	Merry Christmas Baby/O Come All Ye Faithful	1971	10.00	20.00	40.00
❑ 74-0619	Until It's Time for You to Go/We Can Make the Morning	1971	—	3.00	6.00
❑ 74-0619 [PS]	Until It's Time for You to Go/We Can Make the Morning	1971	3.75	7.50	15.00
❑ 74-0651	He Touched Me/The Bosom of Abraham	1972	37.50	75.00	150.00
—"He Touched Me" actually plays at about 35 rpm in error. A-side has "AWKS-1277" stamped in trail-off wax.					
❑ 74-0651	He Touched Me/The Bosom of Abraham	1972	2.00	4.00	8.00
—"He Touched Me" plays correctly. A-side has "APKS-1277" stamped in trail-off wax.					
❑ 74-0651 [PS]	He Touched Me/The Bosom of Abraham	1972	30.00	60.00	120.00
❑ 74-0672	An American Trilogy/The First Time Ever I Saw Your Face	1972	5.00	10.00	20.00
❑ 74-0672 [PS]	An American Trilogy/The First Time Ever I Saw Your Face	1972	10.00	20.00	40.00
❑ 74-0769	Burning Love/It's a Matter of Time	1972	—	3.00	6.00
—Originals have orange labels					
❑ 74-0769	Burning Love/It's a Matter of Time	1974	37.50	75.00	150.00
—Very rare reissues have gray labels					
❑ 74-0769 [PS]	Burning Love/It's a Matter of Time	1972	3.75	7.50	15.00
❑ 74-0815	Separate Ways/Always on My Mind	1972	—	3.00	6.00
❑ 74-0815 [PS]	Separate Ways/Always on My Mind	1972	3.75	7.50	15.00
❑ 74-0910	Steamroller Blues/Fool	1973	—	3.00	6.00
❑ 74-0910 [PS]	Steamroller Blues/Fool	1973	3.75	7.50	15.00
❑ 447-0600	I Forgot to Remember to Forget/Mystery Train	1959	3.75	7.50	15.00
—Note: All RCA Victor releases with a "447" prefix are from the Gold Standard Series. Black label, dog on top					
❑ 447-0600	I Forgot to Remember to Forget/Mystery Train	1965	2.50	5.00	10.00
—Black label, dog on left					
❑ 447-0600	I Forgot to Remember to Forget/Mystery Train	1969	6.25	12.50	25.00
—Orange label					
❑ 447-0600	I Forgot to Remember to Forget/Mystery Train	1970	2.00	4.00	8.00
—Red label					
❑ 447-0601	That's All Right/Blue Moon of Kentucky	1959	3.75	7.50	15.00
—Black label, dog on top					
❑ 447-0601	That's All Right/Blue Moon of Kentucky	1965	2.50	5.00	10.00
—Black label, dog on left					
❑ 447-0601	That's All Right/Blue Moon of Kentucky	1969	2.00	4.00	8.00
—Red label; B-side artist credit is misspelled "Elvis Presely"					
❑ 447-0601 [DJ]	That's All Right/Blue Moon of Kentucky	1964	25.00	50.00	100.00
❑ 447-0601 [PS]	That's All Right/Blue Moon of Kentucky	1964	50.00	100.00	200.00
❑ 447-0602	Good Rockin' Tonight/I Don't Care If the Sun Don't Shine	1959	3.75	7.50	15.00
—Black label, dog on top					
❑ 447-0602	Good Rockin' Tonight/I Don't Care If the Sun Don't Shine	1965	2.50	5.00	10.00
—Black label, dog on left					
❑ 447-0602	Good Rockin' Tonight/I Don't Care If the Sun Don't Shine	1970	2.00	4.00	8.00
—Red label					
❑ 447-0602 [DJ]	Good Rockin' Tonight/I Don't Care If the Sun Don't Shine	1964	25.00	50.00	100.00
❑ 447-0602 [PS]	Good Rockin' Tonight/I Don't Care If the Sun Don't Shine	1964	50.00	100.00	200.00
❑ 447-0603	Milkcow Blues Boogie/You're a Heartbreaker	1959	3.75	7.50	15.00
—Black label, dog on top					
❑ 447-0603	Milkcow Blues Boogie/You're a Heartbreaker	1965	2.50	5.00	10.00
—Black label, dog on left					
❑ 447-0603	Milkcow Blues Boogie/You're a Heartbreaker	1969	6.25	12.50	25.00
—Orange label					
❑ 447-0603	Milkcow Blues Boogie/You're a Heartbreaker	1970	2.00	4.00	8.00
—Red label					
❑ 447-0604	Baby Let's Play House/I'm Left, You're Right, She's Gone	1959	3.75	7.50	15.00
—Black label, dog on top					
❑ 447-0604	Baby Let's Play House/I'm Left, You're Right, She's Gone	1965	2.50	5.00	10.00
—Black label, dog on left					
❑ 447-0604	Baby Let's Play House/I'm Left, You're Right, She's Gone	1970	2.00	4.00	8.00
—Red label					
❑ 447-0605	Heartbreak Hotel/I Was the One	1959	3.75	7.50	15.00
—Black label, dog on top					
❑ 447-0605	Heartbreak Hotel/I Was the One	1965	2.50	5.00	10.00
—Black label, dog on left					
❑ 447-0605	Heartbreak Hotel/I Was the One	1969	6.25	12.50	25.00
—Orange label					
❑ 447-0605	Heartbreak Hotel/I Was the One	1970	2.00	4.00	8.00
—Red label					
❑ 447-0605 [DJ]	Heartbreak Hotel/I Was the One	1964	25.00	50.00	100.00
❑ 447-0605 [PS]	Heartbreak Hotel/I Was the One	1964	50.00	100.00	200.00
❑ 447-0607	I Want You, I Need You, I Love You/My Baby Left Me	1959	3.75	7.50	15.00
—Black label, dog on top					
❑ 447-0607	I Want You, I Need You, I Love You/My Baby Left Me	1965	2.50	5.00	10.00
—Black label, dog on left					
❑ 447-0607	I Want You, I Need You, I Love You/My Baby Left Me	1969	6.25	12.50	25.00
—Orange label					
❑ 447-0607	I Want You, I Need You, I Love You/My Baby Left Me	1970	2.00	4.00	8.00
—Red label					
❑ 447-0608	Hound Dog/Don't Be Cruel	1959	3.75	7.50	15.00
—Black label, dog on top					
❑ 447-0608	Hound Dog/Don't Be Cruel	1965	2.50	5.00	10.00
—Black label, dog on left					
❑ 447-0608	Hound Dog/Don't Be Cruel	1969	6.25	12.50	25.00
—Orange label					
❑ 447-0608	Hound Dog/Don't Be Cruel	1970	2.00	4.00	8.00
—Red label					
❑ 447-0608 [DJ]	Hound Dog/Don't Be Cruel	1964	25.00	50.00	100.00
❑ 447-0608 [PS]	Hound Dog/Don't Be Cruel	1964	50.00	100.00	200.00
❑ 447-0609	Blue Suede Shoes/Tutti Frutti	1959	3.75	7.50	15.00
—Black label, dog on top					
❑ 447-0609	Blue Suede Shoes/Tutti Frutti	1965	2.50	5.00	10.00
—Black label, dog on left					
❑ 447-0609	Blue Suede Shoes/Tutti Frutti	1969	6.25	12.50	25.00
—Orange label					
❑ 447-0609	Blue Suede Shoes/Tutti Frutti	1970	2.00	4.00	8.00
—Red label					
❑ 447-0610	I Got a Woman/I'm Countin' On You	1959	3.75	7.50	15.00
—Black label, dog on top					
❑ 447-0611	I'm Gonna Sit Right Down and Cry (Over You)/I'll Never Let You Go (Little Darlin')	1959	3.75	7.50	15.00
—Black label, dog on top					
❑ 447-0612	Tryin' to Get to You/I Love You Because	1959	3.75	7.50	15.00
—Black label, dog on top					
❑ 447-0613	Blue Moon/Just Because	1959	3.75	7.50	15.00
—Black label, dog on top					
❑ 447-0613	Blue Moon/Just Because	1965	2.50	5.00	10.00
—Black label, dog on left					
❑ 447-0613	Blue Moon/Just Because	1969	6.25	12.50	25.00
—Orange label					
❑ 447-0613	Blue Moon/Just Because	1970	2.00	4.00	8.00
—Red label					
❑ 447-0614	Money Honey/One-Sided Love Affair	1959	3.75	7.50	15.00
—Black label, dog on top					
❑ 447-0614	Money Honey/One-Sided Love Affair	1965	2.50	5.00	10.00
—Black label, dog on left					
❑ 447-0614	Money Honey/One-Sided Love Affair	1969	6.25	12.50	25.00
—Orange label					
❑ 447-0614	Money Honey/One-Sided Love Affair	1970	2.00	4.00	8.00
—Red label					
❑ 447-0615	Lawdy Miss Clawdy/Shake, Rattle, and Roll	1959	3.75	7.50	15.00
—Black label, dog on top					
❑ 447-0615	Lawdy Miss Clawdy/Shake, Rattle, and Roll	1965	2.50	5.00	10.00
—Black label, dog on left					
❑ 447-0615	Lawdy Miss Clawdy/Shake, Rattle, and Roll	1969	6.25	12.50	25.00
—Orange label					
❑ 447-0615	Lawdy Miss Clawdy/Shake, Rattle, and Roll	1970	2.00	4.00	8.00
—Red label					
❑ 447-0616	Love Me Tender/Anyway You Want Me (That's How I Will Be)	1959	3.75	7.50	15.00
—Black label, dog on top					
❑ 447-0616	Love Me Tender/Anyway You Want Me (That's How I Will Be)	1965	2.50	5.00	10.00
—Black label, dog on left					
❑ 447-0616	Love Me Tender/Anyway You Want Me (That's How I Will Be)	1969	6.25	12.50	25.00
—Orange label					
❑ 447-0616	Love Me Tender/Anyway You Want Me (That's How I Will Be)	1970	2.00	4.00	8.00
—Red label					
❑ 447-0617	Too Much/Playing for Keeps	1959	3.75	7.50	15.00
—Black label, dog on top					
❑ 447-0617	Too Much/Playing for Keeps	1965	2.50	5.00	10.00
—Black label, dog on left					
❑ 447-0617	Too Much/Playing for Keeps	1969	6.25	12.50	25.00
—Orange label					
❑ 447-0617	Too Much/Playing for Keeps	1970	2.00	4.00	8.00
—Red label					
❑ 447-0618	All Shook Up/That's When Your Heartaches Begin	1959	3.75	7.50	15.00
—Black label, dog on top					
❑ 447-0618	All Shook Up/That's When Your Heartaches Begin	1965	2.50	5.00	10.00
—Black label, dog on left					
❑ 447-0618	All Shook Up/That's When Your Heartaches Begin	1969	6.25	12.50	25.00
—Orange label					
❑ 447-0618	All Shook Up/That's When Your Heartaches Begin	1970	2.00	4.00	8.00
—Red label					
❑ 447-0618 [DJ]	All Shook Up/That's When Your Heartaches Begin	1964	25.00	50.00	100.00
❑ 447-0618 [PS]	All Shook Up/That's When Your Heartaches Begin	1964	50.00	100.00	200.00

Number	Title (A Side/B Side)	Yr	VG	VG+	NM
❑ 447-0619	Jailhouse Rock/Treat Me Nice —*Black label, dog on top*	1959	3.75	7.50	15.00
❑ 447-0619	Jailhouse Rock/Treat Me Nice —*Black label, dog on left*	1965	2.50	5.00	10.00
❑ 447-0619	Jailhouse Rock/Treat Me Nice —*Orange label*	1969	6.25	12.50	25.00
❑ 447-0619	Jailhouse Rock/Treat Me Nice —*Red label*	1970	2.00	4.00	8.00
❑ 447-0620	(Let Me Be Your) Teddy Bear/Loving You —*Black label, dog on top*	1959	3.75	7.50	15.00
❑ 447-0620	(Let Me Be Your) Teddy Bear/Loving You —*Black label, dog on left*	1965	2.50	5.00	10.00
❑ 447-0620	(Let Me Be Your) Teddy Bear/Loving You —*Orange label*	1969	6.25	12.50	25.00
❑ 447-0620	(Let Me Be Your) Teddy Bear/Loving You —*Red label*	1970	2.00	4.00	8.00
❑ 447-0621	Don't/I Beg of You —*Black label, dog on top*	1961	3.00	6.00	12.00
❑ 447-0621	Don't/I Beg of You —*Black label, dog on left*	1965	2.50	5.00	10.00
❑ 447-0621	Don't/I Beg of You —*Orange label*	1969	6.25	12.50	25.00
❑ 447-0621	Don't/I Beg of You —*Red label*	1970	2.00	4.00	8.00
❑ 447-0622	Wear My Ring Around Your Neck/Don'tcha Think It's Time —*Black label, dog on top*	1961	3.00	6.00	12.00
❑ 447-0622	Wear My Ring Around Your Neck/Don'tcha Think It's Time —*Black label, dog on left*	1965	2.50	5.00	10.00
❑ 447-0622	Wear My Ring Around Your Neck/Don'tcha Think It's Time —*Orange label*	1969	6.25	12.50	25.00
❑ 447-0622	Wear My Ring Around Your Neck/Don'tcha Think It's Time —*Red label*	1970	2.00	4.00	8.00
❑ 447-0623	Hard Headed Woman/Don't Ask Me Why —*Black label, dog on top*	1961	3.75	7.50	15.00
❑ 447-0623	Hard Headed Woman/Don't Ask Me Why —*Black label, dog on left*	1965	2.50	5.00	10.00
❑ 447-0623	Hard Headed Woman/Don't Ask Me Why —*Orange label*	1969	6.25	12.50	25.00
❑ 447-0623	Hard Headed Woman/Don't Ask Me Why —*Red label*	1970	2.00	4.00	8.00
❑ 447-0624	One Night/I Got Stung —*Black label, dog on top*	1961	3.00	6.00	12.00
❑ 447-0624	One Night/I Got Stung —*Black label, dog on left*	1965	2.50	5.00	10.00
❑ 447-0624	One Night/I Got Stung —*Orange label*	1969	6.25	12.50	25.00
❑ 447-0624	One Night/I Got Stung —*Red label*	1970	2.00	4.00	8.00
❑ 447-0625	(Now and Then There's) A Fool Such As I/I Need Your Love Tonight —*Black label, dog on top*	1961	3.75	7.50	15.00
❑ 447-0625	(Now and Then There's) A Fool Such As I/I Need Your Love Tonight —*Black label, dog on left*	1965	2.50	5.00	10.00
❑ 447-0625	(Now and Then There's) A Fool Such As I/I Need Your Love Tonight —*Orange label*	1969	6.25	12.50	25.00
❑ 447-0625	(Now and Then There's) A Fool Such As I/I Need Your Love Tonight —*Red label*	1970	2.00	4.00	8.00
❑ 447-0626	A Big Hunk o'Love/My Wish Came True —*Black label, dog on top*	1962	3.75	7.50	15.00
❑ 447-0626	A Big Hunk o'Love/My Wish Came True —*Black label, dog on left*	1965	2.50	5.00	10.00
❑ 447-0626	A Big Hunk o'Love/My Wish Came True —*Orange label*	1969	6.25	12.50	25.00
❑ 447-0626	A Big Hunk o'Love/My Wish Came True —*Red label*	1970	2.00	4.00	8.00
❑ 447-0627	Stuck on You/Fame and Fortune —*Black label, dog on top*	1962	3.00	6.00	12.00
❑ 447-0627	Stuck on You/Fame and Fortune —*Black label, dog on left*	1965	2.50	5.00	10.00
❑ 447-0627	Stuck on You/Fame and Fortune —*Orange label*	1969	6.25	12.50	25.00
❑ 447-0627	Stuck on You/Fame and Fortune —*Red label*	1970	2.00	4.00	8.00
❑ 447-0628	It's Now or Never/A Mess of Blues —*Black label, dog on top*	1962	3.00	6.00	12.00
❑ 447-0628	It's Now or Never/A Mess of Blues —*Black label, dog on left*	1965	2.50	5.00	10.00
❑ 447-0628	It's Now or Never/A Mess of Blues —*Orange label*	1969	6.25	12.50	25.00
❑ 447-0628	It's Now or Never/A Mess of Blues —*Red label*	1970	2.00	4.00	8.00
❑ 447-0629	Are You Lonesome To-Night?/I Gotta Know —*Black label, dog on top*	1962	3.75	7.50	15.00
❑ 447-0629	Are You Lonesome To-Night?/I Gotta Know —*Black label, dog on left*	1965	2.50	5.00	10.00
❑ 447-0629	Are You Lonesome To-Night?/I Gotta Know —*Orange label*	1969	6.25	12.50	25.00
❑ 447-0629	Are You Lonesome To-Night?/I Gotta Know —*Red label*	1970	2.00	4.00	8.00
❑ 447-0630	Surrender/Lonely Man —*Black label, dog on top*	1962	6.25	12.50	25.00
❑ 447-0630	Surrender/Lonely Man —*Black label, dog on left*	1965	2.50	5.00	10.00
❑ 447-0630	Surrender/Lonely Man —*Orange label*	1969	6.25	12.50	25.00
❑ 447-0630	Surrender/Lonely Man —*Red label*	1970	2.00	4.00	8.00
❑ 447-0631	I Feel So Bad/Wild in the Country —*Black label, dog on top*	1962	3.00	6.00	12.00
❑ 447-0631	I Feel So Bad/Wild in the Country —*Black label, dog on left*	1965	2.50	5.00	10.00
❑ 447-0631	I Feel So Bad/Wild in the Country —*Red label*	1970	2.00	4.00	8.00
❑ 447-0634	(Marie's the Name) His Latest Flame/Little Sister —*Black label, dog on top*	1962	3.00	6.00	12.00
❑ 447-0634	(Marie's the Name) His Latest Flame/Little Sister —*Black label, dog on left*	1965	2.50	5.00	10.00
❑ 447-0634	(Marie's the Name) His Latest Flame/Little Sister —*Orange label*	1969	6.25	12.50	25.00
❑ 447-0634	(Marie's the Name) His Latest Flame/Little Sister —*Red label*	1970	2.00	4.00	8.00
❑ 447-0635	Can't Help Falling in Love/Rock-a-Hula Baby —*Black label, dog on top*	1962	3.00	6.00	12.00
❑ 447-0635	Can't Help Falling in Love/Rock-a-Hula Baby —*Black label, dog on left*	1965	2.50	5.00	10.00
❑ 447-0635	Can't Help Falling in Love/Rock-a-Hula Baby —*Orange label*	1969	6.25	12.50	25.00
❑ 447-0635	Can't Help Falling in Love/Rock-a-Hula Baby —*Red label*	1970	2.00	4.00	8.00
❑ 447-0636	Good Luck Charm/Anything That's Part of You —*Black label, dog on top*	1962	3.00	6.00	12.00
❑ 447-0636	Good Luck Charm/Anything That's Part of You —*Black label, dog on left*	1965	2.50	5.00	10.00
❑ 447-0636	Good Luck Charm/Anything That's Part of You —*Orange label*	1969	6.25	12.50	25.00
❑ 447-0636	Good Luck Charm/Anything That's Part of You —*Red label*	1970	2.00	4.00	8.00
❑ 447-0637	She's Not You/Just Tell Her Jim Said Hello —*Black label, dog on top*	1963	3.00	6.00	12.00
❑ 447-0637	She's Not You/Just Tell Her Jim Said Hello —*Black label, dog on left*	1965	2.50	5.00	10.00
❑ 447-0637	She's Not You/Just Tell Her Jim Said Hello —*Orange label*	1969	6.25	12.50	25.00
❑ 447-0637	She's Not You/Just Tell Her Jim Said Hello —*Red label*	1970	2.00	4.00	8.00
❑ 447-0638	Return to Sender/Where Do You Come From —*Black label, dog on top*	1963	3.00	6.00	12.00
❑ 447-0638	Return to Sender/Where Do You Come From —*Black label, dog on left*	1965	2.50	5.00	10.00
❑ 447-0638	Return to Sender/Where Do You Come From —*Orange label*	1969	6.25	12.50	25.00
❑ 447-0638	Return to Sender/Where Do You Come From —*Red label*	1970	2.00	4.00	8.00
❑ 447-0639	Kiss Me Quick/Suspicion —*Black label, dog on top*	1964	2.50	5.00	10.00
❑ 447-0639	Kiss Me Quick/Suspicion —*Orange label*	1969	6.25	12.50	25.00
❑ 447-0639	Kiss Me Quick/Suspicion —*Red label*	1970	2.00	4.00	8.00
❑ 447-0639 [PS]	Kiss Me Quick/Suspicion	1964	10.00	20.00	40.00
❑ 447-0640	One Broken Heart for Sale/They Remind Me Too Much of You —*Black label, dog on top*	1964	6.25	12.50	25.00
❑ 447-0640	One Broken Heart for Sale/They Remind Me Too Much of You —*Black label, dog on left*	1965	2.50	5.00	10.00
❑ 447-0640	One Broken Heart for Sale/They Remind Me Too Much of You —*Orange label*	1969	6.25	12.50	25.00
❑ 447-0640	One Broken Heart for Sale/They Remind Me Too Much of You —*Red label*	1970	2.00	4.00	8.00
❑ 447-0641	(You're the) Devil in Disguise/Please Don't Drag That String Around —*Black label, dog on top*	1964	6.25	12.50	25.00
❑ 447-0641	(You're the) Devil in Disguise/Please Don't Drag That String Around —*Black label, dog on left*	1965	2.50	5.00	10.00
❑ 447-0641	(You're the) Devil in Disguise/Please Don't Drag That String Around —*Red label*	1970	2.00	4.00	8.00
❑ 447-0642	Bossa Nova Baby/Witchcraft —*Black label, dog on top*	1964	6.25	12.50	25.00
❑ 447-0642	Bossa Nova Baby/Witchcraft —*Black label, dog on left*	1965	2.50	5.00	10.00
❑ 447-0642	Bossa Nova Baby/Witchcraft —*Orange label*	1969	6.25	12.50	25.00
❑ 447-0642	Bossa Nova Baby/Witchcraft —*Red label*	1970	2.00	4.00	8.00
❑ 447-0643	Crying in the Chapel/I Believe in the Man in the Sky —*Black label, dog on left*	1965	2.50	5.00	10.00
❑ 447-0643	Crying in the Chapel/I Believe in the Man in the Sky —*Red label*	1970	2.00	4.00	8.00
❑ 447-0643 [PS]	Crying in the Chapel/I Believe in the Man in the Sky	1965	7.50	15.00	30.00
❑ 447-0644	Kissin' Cousins/It Hurts Me —*Black label, dog on left*	1965	2.50	5.00	10.00
❑ 447-0644	Kissin' Cousins/It Hurts Me —*Orange label*	1969	6.25	12.50	25.00
❑ 447-0644	Kissin' Cousins/It Hurts Me —*Red label*	1970	2.00	4.00	8.00

Number	Title (A Side/B Side)	Yr	VG	VG+	NM
❑ 447-0645	Such a Night/Never Ending	1965	10.00	20.00	40.00
—Black label, dog on top					
❑ 447-0645	Such a Night/Never Ending	1965	2.50	5.00	10.00
—Black label, dog on left					
❑ 447-0645	Such a Night/Never Ending	1969	6.25	12.50	25.00
—Orange label					
❑ 447-0645	Such a Night/Never Ending	1970	2.00	4.00	8.00
—Red label					
❑ 447-0646	Viva Las Vegas/What'd I Say	1965	6.25	12.50	25.00
—Black label, dog on top					
❑ 447-0646	Viva Las Vegas/What'd I Say	1965	2.50	5.00	10.00
—Black label, dog on left					
❑ 447-0646	Viva Las Vegas/What'd I Say	1969	6.25	12.50	25.00
—Orange label					
❑ 447-0646	Viva Las Vegas/What'd I Say	1970	2.00	4.00	8.00
—Red label					
❑ 447-0647	Blue Christmas/Santa Claus Is Back in Town	1965	3.00	6.00	12.00
—Black label, dog on side					
❑ 447-0647	Blue Christmas/Santa Claus Is Back in Town	1969	6.25	12.50	25.00
—Orange label					
❑ 447-0647	Blue Christmas/Santa Claus Is Back in Town	1970	2.00	4.00	8.00
—Red label					
❑ 447-0647 [PS]	Blue Christmas/Santa Claus Is Back in Town	1965	7.50	15.00	30.00
—Has "Gold Standard Series" on sleeve					
❑ 447-0648	Do the Clam/You'll Be Gone	1965	2.50	5.00	10.00
—Black label, dog on left					
❑ 447-0648	Do the Clam/You'll Be Gone	1970	2.50	5.00	10.00
—Red label					
❑ 447-0649	Ain't That Loving You Baby/Ask Me	1965	2.50	5.00	10.00
—Black label, dog on left					
❑ 447-0649	Ain't That Loving You Baby/Ask Me	1970	2.00	4.00	8.00
—Red label					
❑ 447-0650	Puppet on a String/Wooden Heart	1965	2.50	5.00	10.00
—Black label, dog on left					
❑ 447-0650	Puppet on a String/Wooden Heart	1970	2.00	4.00	8.00
—Red label					
❑ 447-0650 [PS]	Puppet on a String/Wooden Heart	1965	7.50	15.00	30.00
❑ 447-0651	Joshua Fit the Battle/Known Only to Him	1966	3.75	7.50	15.00
—Black label, dog on left					
❑ 447-0651	Joshua Fit the Battle/Known Only to Him	1970	2.00	4.00	8.00
—Red label					
❑ 447-0651 [PS]	Joshua Fit the Battle/Known Only to Him	1966	50.00	100.00	200.00
❑ 447-0652	Milky White Way/Swing Down Sweet Chariot	1966	3.75	7.50	15.00
—Black label, dog on left					
❑ 447-0652	Milky White Way/Swing Down Sweet Chariot	1970	2.00	4.00	8.00
—Red label					
❑ 447-0652 [PS]	Milky White Way/Swing Down Sweet Chariot	1966	50.00	100.00	200.00
❑ 447-0653	(Such An) Easy Question/It Feels So Right	1966	2.50	5.00	10.00
—Black label, dog on left					
❑ 447-0653	(Such An) Easy Question/It Feels So Right	1970	2.00	4.00	8.00
—Red label					
❑ 447-0654	I'm Yours/(It's a) Long, Lonely Highway	1966	2.50	5.00	10.00
—Black label, dog on left					
❑ 447-0654	I'm Yours/(It's a) Long, Lonely Highway	1970	2.00	4.00	8.00
—Red label					
❑ 447-0655	Tell Me Why/Blue River	1968	2.50	5.00	10.00
—Black label, dog on left					
❑ 447-0655	Tell Me Why/Blue River	1970	2.00	4.00	8.00
—Red label					
❑ 447-0656	Frankie and Johnny/Please Don't Stop Loving Me	1968	2.50	5.00	10.00
—Black label, dog on left					
❑ 447-0656	Frankie and Johnny/Please Don't Stop Loving Me	1969	6.25	12.50	25.00
—Orange label					
❑ 447-0656	Frankie and Johnny/Please Don't Stop Loving Me	1970	2.00	4.00	8.00
—Red label					
❑ 447-0657	Love Letters/Come What May	1968	2.50	5.00	10.00
—Black label, dog on left					
❑ 447-0657	Love Letters/Come What May	1970	2.00	4.00	8.00
—Red label					
❑ 447-0658	Spinout/All That I Do	1968	2.50	5.00	10.00
—Black label, dog on left					
❑ 447-0658	Spinout/All That I Do	1970	2.00	4.00	8.00
—Red label					
❑ 447-0659	Indescribably Blue/Fools Fall in Love	1969	6.25	12.50	25.00
—Orange label					
❑ 447-0659	Indescribably Blue/Fools Fall in Love	1970	2.00	4.00	8.00
—Red label					
❑ 447-0660	Long Legged Girl (With the Short Dress On)/ That's Someone You Never Forget	1970	10.00	20.00	40.00
❑ 447-0661	There's Always Me/Judy	1970	3.75	7.50	15.00
❑ 447-0662	Big Boss Man/You Don't Know Me	1970	2.50	5.00	10.00
❑ 447-0663	Guitar Man/High Heel Sneakers	1970	2.00	4.00	8.00
❑ 447-0664	U.S. Male/Stay Away	1970	2.00	4.00	8.00
❑ 447-0665	You'll Never Walk Alone/We Call on Him	1970	2.50	5.00	10.00
❑ 447-0666	Let Yourself Go/Your Time Hasn't Come Yet, Baby	1970	2.00	4.00	8.00
❑ 447-0667	A Little Less Conversation/Almost in Love	1970	2.00	4.00	8.00
❑ 447-0668	If I Can Dream/Edge of Reality	1970	2.00	4.00	8.00
❑ 447-0669	Memories/Charro	1970	2.00	4.00	8.00
❑ 447-0670	How Great Thou Art/His Hand in Mine	1970	2.50	5.00	10.00
❑ 447-0671	In the Ghetto/Any Day Now	1970	2.00	4.00	8.00
❑ 447-0672	Clean Up Your Own Back Yard/The Fair Is Moving On	1970	2.00	4.00	8.00
❑ 447-0673	Suspicious Minds/You'll Think of Me	1970	2.00	4.00	8.00
❑ 447-0674	Don't Cry Daddy/Rubberneckin'	1970	2.00	4.00	8.00
❑ 447-0675	Kentucky Rain/My Little Friend	1971	2.00	4.00	8.00
❑ 447-0676	The Wonder of You/Mama Liked the Roses	1971	2.00	4.00	8.00
❑ 447-0677	I've Lost You/The Next Step Is Love	1971	2.00	4.00	8.00
❑ 447-0678	You Don't Have to Say You Love Me/Patch It Up	1972	2.00	4.00	8.00
❑ 447-0679	I Really Don't Want to Know/There Goes My Everything	1972	2.00	4.00	8.00
❑ 447-0680	Where Did They Go, Lord/Rags to Riches	1972	2.00	4.00	8.00
❑ 447-0681	If Every Day Was Like Christmas/How Would You Like to Be	1972	2.00	4.00	8.00
❑ 447-0682	Life/Only Believe	1972	2.50	5.00	8.00
❑ 447-0683	I'm Leavin'/Heart of Rome	1972	2.00	4.00	8.00
❑ 447-0684	It's Only Love/The Sound of Your Cry	1972	2.00	4.00	8.00
❑ 447-0685	An American Trilogy/Until It's Time for You to Go	1973	2.00	4.00	8.00
❑ 447-0720	Blue Christmas/Wooden Heart	1964	3.75	7.50	15.00
❑ 447-0720 [PS]	Blue Christmas/Wooden Heart	1964	15.00	30.00	60.00

SUN

Number	Title (A Side/B Side)	Yr	VG	VG+	NM
❑ 209	That's All Right/Blue Moon of Kentucky	1954	2000.	4000.	6000.
—A mint copy of this has sold for over $17,000, but so far that is an aberration					
❑ 210	Good Rockin' Tonight/I Don't Care If the Sun Don't Shine	1954	1500.	2500.	3500.
❑ 215	Milkcow Blues Boogie/You're a Heartbreaker	1955	2000.	3500.	5000.
❑ 217	Baby Let's Play House/I'm Left, You're Right, She's Gone	1955	1000.	2000.	3000.
❑ 223	I Forgot to Remember to Forget/Mystery Train	1955	625.00	1250.	2500.

7-Inch Extended Plays

RCA VICTOR

Number	Title (A Side/B Side)	Yr	VG	VG+	NM
❑ SPD-22 [PS]	Elvis Presley	1956	100.00	200.00	400.00
—Bonus given to buyers of a Victrola					
❑ SPD-22 [(2)]	Elvis Presley	1956	100.00	200.00	400.00
—Value is for both discs together					
❑ SPD-23 [PS]	Elvis Presley	1956	1000.	2000.	3000.
—Bonus given to buyers of a more expensive Victrola					
❑ SPD-23 [(3)]	Elvis Presley	1956	1000.	2000.	3000.
—Value is for all three discs together					
❑ SPA-7-37 [DJ]	Perfect for Parties	1956	15.00	30.00	60.00
—Without horizontal line on label					
❑ SPA-7-37 [DJ]	Perfect for Parties	1956	15.00	30.00	60.00
—With horizontal line on label					
❑ SPA-7-37 [PS]	Perfect for Parties	1956	15.00	30.00	60.00
❑ LPC-126	Flaming Star/Summer Kisses, Winter Tears//Are You Lonesome To-Night?/It's Now or Never	1961	10.00	20.00	40.00
—"Compact 33 Double" with small hole					
❑ LPC-126 [PS]	Elvis By Request	1961	10.00	20.00	40.00
❑ EPA-747	Blue Suede Shoes/Tutti Frutti//I Got a Woman/ Just Because	1956	12.50	25.00	50.00
—Without horizontal line on label					
❑ EPA-747	Blue Suede Shoes/Tutti Frutti//I Got a Woman/ Just Because	1956	12.50	25.00	50.00
—With horizontal line on label					
❑ EPA-747	Blue Suede Shoes/Tutti Frutti//I Got a Woman/ Just Because	1956	50.00	100.00	200.00
—With horizontal line on label, but with no dog					
❑ EPA-747	Blue Suede Shoes/Tutti Frutti//I Got a Woman/ Just Because	1956	50.00	100.00	200.00
—With incorrect label on Side 1 that lists, as song 3, "I'm Gonna Sit Right Down and Cry (Over You)," which does not appear on this record. Known copies of this version do not have horizontal line on label.					
❑ EPA-747	Blue Suede Shoes/Tutti Frutti//I Got a Woman/ Just Because	1965	7.50	15.00	30.00
—Black label, dog on left					
❑ EPA-747	Blue Suede Shoes/Tutti Frutti//I Got a Woman/ Just Because	1969	20.00	40.00	80.00
—Orange label					
❑ EPA-747 [PS]	Elvis Presley	1956	250.00	500.00	1000.
—Temporary envelope sleeve with dark blue print, "Blue Suede Shoes by Elvis Presley" in big letters					
❑ EPA-747 [PS]	Elvis Presley	1956	150.00	300.00	600.00
—Temporary envelope sleeve with black print, "Blue Suede Shoes by Elvis Presley" in big letters					
❑ EPA-747 [PS]	Elvis Presley	1956	12.50	25.00	50.00
—Five different back covers exist, all with titles on front cover; any are of equal value					
❑ EPA-747 [PS]	Elvis Presley	1965	7.50	15.00	30.00
—No titles at top of front cover					
❑ EPA-821	Heartbreak Hotel/I Was the One//Money Honey/ I Forgot to Remember to Forget	1956	12.50	25.00	50.00
—Without horizontal line on label					
❑ EPA-821	Heartbreak Hotel/I Was the One//Money Honey/ I Forgot to Remember to Forget	1956	12.50	25.00	50.00
—With horizontal line on label					
❑ EPA-821	Heartbreak Hotel/I Was the One//Money Honey/ I Forgot to Remember to Forget	1956	50.00	100.00	200.00
—With horizontal line on label, but with no dog					
❑ EPA-821	Heartbreak Hotel/I Was the One//Money Honey/ I Forgot to Remember to Forget	1965	7.50	15.00	30.00
—Black label, dog on left					
❑ EPA-821	Heartbreak Hotel/I Was the One//Money Honey/ I Forgot to Remember to Forget	1969	20.00	40.00	80.00
—Orange label					
❑ EPA-821 [PS]	Heartbreak Hotel	1956	12.50	25.00	50.00
❑ EPA-830	Shake, Rattle and Roll/I Love You Because//Blue Moon/Lawdy, Miss Clawdy	1956	12.50	25.00	50.00
—Without horizontal line on label					
❑ EPA-830	Shake, Rattle and Roll/I Love You Because//Blue Moon/Lawdy, Miss Clawdy	1956	12.50	25.00	50.00
—With horizontal line on label					
❑ EPA-830	Shake, Rattle and Roll/I Love You Because//Blue Moon/Lawdy, Miss Clawdy	1956	50.00	100.00	200.00
—With horizontal line on label, but with no dog					
❑ EPA-830	Shake, Rattle and Roll/I Love You Because//Blue Moon/Lawdy, Miss Clawdy	1965	7.50	15.00	30.00
—Black label, dog on left					
❑ EPA-830	Shake, Rattle and Roll/I Love You Because//Blue Moon/Lawdy, Miss Clawdy	1969	20.00	40.00	80.00
—Orange label					
❑ EPA-830 [PS]	Elvis Presley	1956	12.50	25.00	50.00
❑ EPA-940	Don't Be Cruel/I Want You, I Need You, I Love You//Hound Dog/My Baby Left Me	1956	12.50	25.00	50.00
—Without horizontal line on label					

Number	Title (A Side/B Side)	Yr	VG	VG+	NM
❑ EPA-940	Don't Be Cruel/I Want You, I Need You, I Love You//Hound Dog/My Baby Left Me	1956	12.50	25.00	50.00
—With horizontal line on label					
❑ EPA-940	Don't Be Cruel/I Want You, I Need You, I Love You//Hound Dog/My Baby Left Me	1956	50.00	100.00	200.00
—With horizontal line on label, but with no dog					
❑ EPA-940 [PS]	The Real Elvis	1956	12.50	25.00	50.00
❑ EPA-965	Anyway You Want Me (That's How I Will Be)/I'm Left, You're Right, She's Gone//I Don't Care If the Sun Don't Shine/Mystery Train	1956	10.00	20.00	40.00
—Without horizontal line on label					
❑ EPA-965	Anyway You Want Me (That's How I Will Be)/I'm Left, You're Right, She's Gone//I Don't Care If the Sun Don't Shine/Mystery Train	1956	10.00	20.00	40.00
—With horizontal line on label					
❑ EPA-965	Anyway You Want Me (That's How I Will Be)/I'm Left, You're Right, She's Gone//I Don't Care If the Sun Don't Shine/Mystery Train	1956	50.00	100.00	200.00
—With horizontal line on label, but with no dog					
❑ EPA-965	Anyway You Want Me (That's How I Will Be)/I'm Left, You're Right, She's Gone//I Don't Care If the Sun Don't Shine/Mystery Train	1965	7.50	15.00	30.00
—Black label, dog on left					
❑ EPA-965	Anyway You Want Me (That's How I Will Be)/I'm Left, You're Right, She's Gone//I Don't Care If the Sun Don't Shine/Mystery Train	1969	20.00	40.00	80.00
—Orange label					
❑ EPA-965 [PS]	Anyway You Want Me	1956	12.50	25.00	50.00
—With song titles and catalog number on front					
❑ EPA-965 [PS]	Anyway You Want Me	196?	10.00	20.00	40.00
—Without song titles and catalog number on front					
❑ EPA-992	Rip It Up/Love Me//When My Blue Moon Turns to Gold Again/Paralyzed	1956	10.00	20.00	40.00
—Without horizontal line on label					
❑ EPA-992	Rip It Up/Love Me//When My Blue Moon Turns to Gold Again/Paralyzed	1956	10.00	20.00	40.00
—With horizontal line on label					
❑ EPA-992	Rip It Up/Love Me//When My Blue Moon Turns to Gold Again/Paralyzed	1956	50.00	100.00	200.00
—With horizontal line on label; bot with no dog					
❑ EPA-992	Rip It Up/Love Me//When My Blue Moon Turns to Gold Again/Paralyzed	1965	7.50	15.00	30.00
—Black label, dog on left					
❑ EPA-992	Rip It Up/Love Me//When My Blue Moon Turns to Gold Again/Paralyzed	1969	20.00	40.00	80.00
—Orange label					
❑ EPA-992 [PS]	Elvis (Volume 1)	1956	12.50	25.00	50.00
❑ EPA-993	So Glad You're Mine/Old Shep//Ready Teddy/ Anyplace Is Paradise	1956	10.00	20.00	40.00
—Without horizontal line on label					
❑ EPA-993	So Glad You're Mine/Old Shep//Ready Teddy/ Anyplace Is Paradise	1956	10.00	20.00	40.00
—With horizontal line on label					
❑ EPA-993	So Glad You're Mine/Old Shep//Ready Teddy/ Anyplace Is Paradise	1956	50.00	100.00	200.00
—With horizontal line on label, but with no dog					
❑ EPA-993	So Glad You're Mine/Old Shep//Ready Teddy/ Anyplace Is Paradise	1965	7.50	15.00	30.00
—Black label, dog on left					
❑ EPA-993	So Glad You're Mine/Old Shep//Ready Teddy/ Anyplace Is Paradise	1969	20.00	40.00	80.00
—Orange label					
❑ EPA-993 [PS]	Elvis (Volume 2)	1956	12.50	25.00	50.00
—Titles at top of front cover					
❑ EPA-993 [PS]	Elvis (Volume 2)	1965	7.50	15.00	30.00
—No titles at top of front cover					
❑ EPA-994	Long Tall Sally/First in Line//How Do You Think I Feel/How's the World Treating You	1956	12.50	25.00	50.00
—Without horizontal line on label					
❑ EPA-994	Long Tall Sally/First in Line//How Do You Think I Feel/How's the World Treating You	1956	12.50	25.00	50.00
—With horizontal line on label					
❑ EPA-994	Long Tall Sally/First in Line//How Do You Think I Feel/How's the World Treating You	1956	50.00	100.00	200.00
—With horizontal line on label, but with no dog					
❑ EPA-994	Long Tall Sally/First in Line//How Do You Think I Feel/How's the World Treating You	1965	7.50	15.00	30.00
—Black label, dog on left					
❑ EPA-994	Long Tall Sally/First in Line//How Do You Think I Feel/How's the World Treating You	1969	20.00	40.00	80.00
—Orange label					
❑ EPA-994 [PS]	Strictly Elvis (Elvis, Vol. 3)	1956	12.50	25.00	50.00
—With titles listed on front cover					
❑ EPA-994 [PS]	Strictly Elvis (Elvis, Vol. 3)	1965	7.50	15.00	30.00
—No titles listed on front cover					
❑ EPB-1254 [PS]	Elvis Presley	1956	50.00	100.00	200.00
—Three different back covers exist hyping other non-Elvis RCA Victor releases; any are of equal value					
❑ EPB-1254 [PS]	Elvis Presley	1956	37.50	75.00	150.00
—With no hype of other non-Elvis releases on back					
❑ EPB-1254 [PS]	Elvis Presley... the most talked-about new personality in the last ten years of recorded music	1956	375.00	750.00	1500.
❑ EPB-1254 [(2)]	Elvis Presley	1956	50.00	100.00	200.00
—Without horizontal line on label; eight songs on two discs; value is for both discs together					
❑ EPB-1254 [(2)]	Elvis Presley	1956	50.00	100.00	200.00
—With horizontal line on label; eight songs on two discs; value is for both discs together					
❑ EPB-1254 [(2)]	Elvis Presley	1956	375.00	750.00	1500.
—Two records have three songs on each side (12 total), as opposed to the two of the standard release					

Number	Title (A Side/B Side)	Yr	VG	VG+	NM
❑ EPA-1-1515	Loving You/Party//(Let Me Be Your) Teddy Bear/ True Love	1957	10.00	20.00	40.00
—Without horizontal line on label					
❑ EPA-1-1515	Loving You/Party//(Let Me Be Your) Teddy Bear/ True Love	1957	10.00	20.00	40.00
—With horizontal line on label					
❑ EPA-1-1515	Loving You/Party//(Let Me Be Your) Teddy Bear/ True Love	1965	7.50	15.00	30.00
—Black label, dog on left					
❑ EPA-1-1515	Loving You/Party//(Let Me Be Your) Teddy Bear/ True Love	1969	20.00	40.00	80.00
—Orange label					
❑ EPA-1-1515 [PS]	Loving You, Vol. I	1957	10.00	20.00	40.00
❑ EPA-2-1515	Lonesome Cowboy/Hot Dog//Mean Woman Blues/Got a Lot of Livin' to Do	1957	10.00	20.00	40.00
—Without horizontal line on label					
❑ EPA-2-1515	Lonesome Cowboy/Hot Dog//Mean Woman Blues/Got a Lot of Livin' to Do	1957	10.00	20.00	40.00
—With horizontal line on label					
❑ EPA-2-1515	Lonesome Cowboy/Hot Dog//Mean Woman Blues/Got a Lot of Livin' to Do	1965	7.50	15.00	30.00
—Black label, dog on left					
❑ EPA-2-1515	Lonesome Cowboy/Hot Dog//Mean Woman Blues/Got a Lot of Livin' to Do	1969	20.00	40.00	80.00
—Orange label					
❑ EPA-2-1515 [PS]	Loving You, Vol. II	1957	10.00	20.00	40.00
—With song titles on top of front cover					
❑ EPA-2-1515 [PS]	Loving You, Vol. II	1965	7.50	15.00	30.00
—No song titles on top of front cover					
❑ EPA-4006	Love Me Tender/Let Me//Poor Boy/We're Gonna Move	1956	12.50	25.00	50.00
—Without horizontal line on label					
❑ EPA-4006	Love Me Tender/Let Me//Poor Boy/We're Gonna Move	1956	12.50	25.00	50.00
—With horizontal line on label					
❑ EPA-4006	Love Me Tender/Let Me//Poor Boy/We're Gonna Move	1956	50.00	100.00	200.00
—With horizontal line on label, but with no dog					
❑ EPA-4006	Love Me Tender/Let Me//Poor Boy/We're Gonna Move	1965	7.50	15.00	30.00
—Black label, dog on left					
❑ EPA-4006	Love Me Tender/Let Me//Poor Boy/We're Gonna Move	1969	20.00	40.00	80.00
—Orange label					
❑ EPA-4006 [PS]	Love Me Tender	1956	12.50	25.00	50.00
—With song titles on top of front cover					
❑ EPA-4006 [PS]	Love Me Tender	1965	7.50	15.00	30.00
—No song titles on top of front cover					
❑ EPA-4041	I Need You So/Have I Told You Lately//Blueberry Hill/Is It So Strange	1957	12.50	25.00	50.00
—Without horizontal line on label					
❑ EPA-4041	I Need You So/Have I Told You Lately//Blueberry Hill/Is It So Strange	1957	12.50	25.00	50.00
—With horizontal line on label					
❑ EPA-4041	I Need You So/Have I Told You Lately//Blueberry Hill/Is It So Strange	1957	50.00	100.00	200.00
—With horizontal line on label, but with no dog					
❑ EPA-4041	I Need You So/Have I Told You Lately//Blueberry Hill/Is It So Strange	1965	7.50	15.00	30.00
—Black label, dog on left					
❑ EPA-4041	I Need You So/Have I Told You Lately//Blueberry Hill/Is It So Strange	1969	20.00	40.00	80.00
—Orange label					
❑ EPA-4041 [PS]	Just for You (Elvis Presley)	1957	12.50	25.00	50.00
❑ EPA-4054	(There'll Be) Peace in the Valley (For Me)/It Is No Secret (What God Can Do)//I Believe/Take My Hand, Precious Lord	1957	10.00	20.00	40.00
—Without horizontal line on label					
❑ EPA-4054	(There'll Be) Peace in the Valley (For Me)/It Is No Secret (What God Can Do)//I Believe/Take My Hand, Precious Lord	1957	10.00	20.00	40.00
—With horizontal line on label					
❑ EPA-4054 [PS]	Peace in the Valley	1957	10.00	20.00	40.00
❑ EPA-4108	Santa Bring My Baby Back (To Me)/Blue Christmas//Santa Claus Is Back in Town/I'll Be Home for Christmas	1957	10.00	20.00	40.00
—Black label, dog on top					
❑ EPA-4108	Santa Bring My Baby Back (To Me)/Blue Christmas//Santa Claus Is Back in Town/I'll Be Home for Christmas	1965	7.50	15.00	30.00
—Black label, dog on left					
❑ EPA-4108	Santa Bring My Baby Back (To Me)/Blue Christmas//Santa Claus Is Back in Town/I'll Be Home for Christmas	1969	20.00	40.00	80.00
—Orange label					
❑ EPA-4108 [PS]	Elvis Sings Christmas Songs	1957	10.00	20.00	40.00
❑ EPA-4114	Jailhouse Rock/Young and Beautiful//I Want to Be Free/Don't Leave Me Now/(You're So Square) Baby I Don't Care	1957	10.00	20.00	40.00
—Black label, dog on top					
❑ EPA-4114	Jailhouse Rock/Young and Beautiful//I Want to Be Free/Don't Leave Me Now/(You're So Square) Baby I Don't Care	1965	7.50	15.00	30.00
—Black label, dog on left					
❑ EPA-4114	Jailhouse Rock/Young and Beautiful//I Want to Be Free/Don't Leave Me Now/(You're So Square) Baby I Don't Care	1969	20.00	40.00	80.00
—Orange label					
❑ EPA-4114 [PS]	Jailhouse Rock	1957	10.00	20.00	40.00
❑ EPA-4319	King Creole/New Orleans//As Long As I Have You/Lover Doll	1958	10.00	20.00	40.00

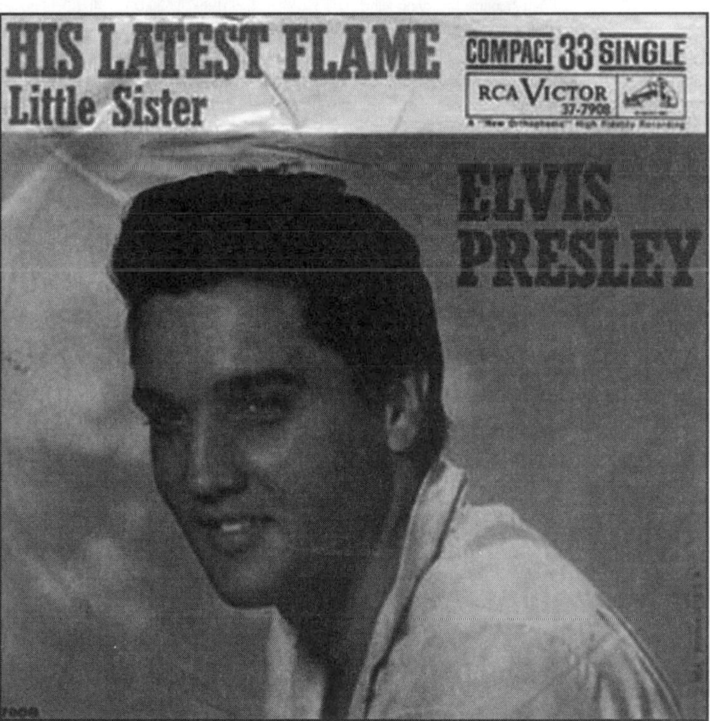

Of all the Elvis Presley singles released commercially by RCA Victor, the greatest demand lies in some odd pressings from the early 1960s. RCA tried to issue both "Living Stereo" 45 rpm singles and "Compact 33" singles that played at the same speed as LPs. Both were colossal failures, and thus any Elvis record in those formats is highly collectible. (Top left) "Stuck on You," his first post-Army single, was issued in "Living Stereo" with a 61 prefix, in addition to the normal release with a 47 prefix. (Top right) RCA introduced the "Compact 33" in 1961 and discontinued them in 1962. The records are rare enough; the custom picture sleeves are even more rare. The first Elvis single to get this treatment was "Surrender." (Bottom left) RCA's next attempt was "Wild in the Country" backed with "I Feel So Bad." (Bottom right) Each later "Compact 33" is harder to find than the one before it. Still tougher than the first two is the third, "His Latest Flame" backed with "Little Sister."

Number	Title (A Side/B Side)	Yr	VG	VG+	NM
❑ EPA-4319 [PS]	King Creole	1958	12.50	25.00	50.00
—With copyright notice on front cover					
❑ EPA-4319 [PS]	King Creole	1958	10.00	20.00	40.00
—Without copyright notice on front cover					
❑ EPA-4321	Trouble/Young Dreams//Crawfish/Dixieland Rock	1958	10.00	20.00	40.00
—Black label, dog on top					
❑ EPA-4321	Trouble/Young Dreams//Crawfish/Dixieland Rock	1965	7.50	15.00	30.00
—Black label, dog on left					
❑ EPA-4321	Trouble/Young Dreams//Crawfish/Dixieland Rock	1969	20.00	40.00	80.00
—Orange label					
❑ EPA-4321 [PS]	King Creole, Vol. 2	1958	10.00	20.00	40.00
❑ EPA-4325	Press Interview with Elvis Presley//Elvis Presley's Newsreel Interview/Pat Hernon Interviews Elvis...	1958	20.00	40.00	80.00
❑ EPA-4325 [PS]	Elvis Sails	1958	20.00	40.00	80.00
—With 1959 calendar and a hole to make it suitable for hanging					
❑ EPA-4340	White Christmas/Here Comes Santa Claus//Oh Little Town of Bethlehem/Silent Night	1958	17.50	35.00	70.00
—Black label, dog on top					
❑ EPA-4340	White Christmas/Here Comes Santa Claus//Oh Little Town of Bethlehem/Silent Night	1965	10.00	20.00	40.00
—Black label, dog on left					
❑ EPA-4340	White Christmas/Here Comes Santa Claus//Oh Little Town of Bethlehem/Silent Night	1969	10.00	40.00	80.00
—Orange label					
❑ EPA-4340 [PS]	Christmas with Elvis	1958	20.00	40.00	80.00
—With copyright notice and "Printed in U.S.A." at lower right					
❑ EPA-4340 [PS]	Christmas with Elvis	1965	10.00	20.00	40.00
—Without copyright notice and "Printed in U.S.A." at lower right					
❑ EPA-4368	Follow That Dream/Angel//What a Wonderful Life/I'm Not the Marrying Kind	1962	7.50	15.00	30.00
—Black label, dog on top, no playing times on label					
❑ EPA-4368	Follow That Dream/Angel//What a Wonderful Life/I'm Not the Marrying Kind	1962	10.00	20.00	40.00
—Black label, dog on top, with playing times on label					
❑ EPA-4368	Follow That Dream/Angel//What a Wonderful Life/I'm Not the Marrying Kind	1965	6.25	12.50	25.00
—Black label, dog on left					
❑ EPA-4368	Follow That Dream/Angel//What a Wonderful Life/I'm Not the Marrying Kind	1969	20.00	40.00	80.00
—Orange label					
❑ EPA-4368 [PS]	Follow That Dream	1962	37.50	75.00	150.00
—Paper sleeve with "Coin Operator -- DJ Prevue" at top; print is in red					
❑ EPA-4368 [PS]	Follow That Dream	1962	10.00	20.00	40.00
—Incorrect playing times on back cover; "Follow That Dream" is listed as 1:35 but is actually 1:38, and two others are wrong also					
❑ EPA-4368 [PS]	Follow That Dream	1965	6.25	12.50	25.00
—Correct playing times on back cover					
❑ EPA-4371	King of the Whole Wide World/This Is Living/ Riding the Rainbow//Home Is Where the Heart Is/I Got Lucky/A Whistling Tune	1962	10.00	20.00	40.00
—Black label, dog on top					
❑ EPA-4371	King of the Whole Wide World/This Is Living/ Riding the Rainbow//Home Is Where the Heart Is/I Got Lucky/A Whistling Tune	1965	7.50	15.00	30.00
—Black label, dog on left					
❑ EPA-4371	King of the Whole Wide World/This Is Living/ Riding the Rainbow//Home Is Where the Heart Is/I Got Lucky/A Whistling Tune	1969	20.00	40.00	80.00
—Orange label					
❑ EPA-4371 [PS]	Kid Galahad	1962	10.00	20.00	40.00
❑ EPA-4382	If You Think I Don't Need You/I Need Somebody to Lean On//C'mon Everybody/Today, Tomorrow and Forever	1964	10.00	20.00	40.00
—Black label, dog on top					
❑ EPA-4382	If You Think I Don't Need You/I Need Somebody to Lean On//C'mon Everybody/Today, Tomorrow and Forever	1965	7.50	15.00	30.00
—Black label, dog on left					
❑ EPA-4382	If You Think I Don't Need You/I Need Somebody to Lean On//C'mon Everybody/Today, Tomorrow and Forever	1969	20.00	40.00	80.00
—Orange label					
❑ EPA-4382 [PS]	Viva Las Vegas	1964	10.00	20.00	40.00
❑ EPA-4383	I Feel That I've Known You Forever/Slowly But Surely//Night Rider/Dirty Feeling	1965	7.50	15.00	30.00
—Black label, dog on left					
❑ EPA-4383	I Feel That I've Known You Forever/Slowly But Surely//Night Rider/Dirty Feeling	1969	20.00	40.00	80.00
—Orange label					
❑ EPA-4383 [PS]	Tickle Me	1965	7.50	15.00	30.00
—"Coming Soon" on front cover					
❑ EPA-4383 [PS]	Tickle Me	1965	7.50	15.00	30.00
—"Ask For" on front cover					
❑ EPA-4383 [PS]	Tickle Me	1969	8.75	17.50	35.00
—No blurb for new album on front cover					
❑ EPA-4387	Easy Come, Easy Go/The Love Machine/Yoga Is As Yoga Does//You Gotta Shop/Sing You Children/I'll Take Love	1967	7.50	15.00	30.00
—All copies appear to be black label, dog on left					
❑ EPA-4387 [PS]	Easy Come, Easy Go	1967	7.50	15.00	30.00
❑ EPA-5088	Hard Headed Woman/Good Rockin' Tonight// Don't/I Beg of You	1959	15.00	30.00	60.00
—Black label, dog on top					
❑ EPA-5088	Hard Headed Woman/Good Rockin' Tonight// Don't/I Beg of You	1959	100.00	200.00	400.00
—Maroon label					
❑ EPA-5088	Hard Headed Woman/Good Rockin' Tonight// Don't/I Beg of You	1965	7.50	15.00	30.00
—Black label, dog on left					
❑ EPA-5088	Hard Headed Woman/Good Rockin' Tonight// Don't/I Beg of You	1969	20.00	40.00	80.00
—Orange label					
❑ EPA-5088 [PS]	A Touch of Gold	1959	15.00	30.00	60.00
❑ EPA-5101	Wear My Ring Around Your Neck/Treat Me Nice/ /One Night/That's All Right	1959	15.00	30.00	60.00
—Black label, dog on top					
❑ EPA-5101	Wear My Ring Around Your Neck/Treat Me Nice/ /One Night/That's All Right	1959	100.00	200.00	400.00
—Maroon label					
❑ EPA-5101	Wear My Ring Around Your Neck/Treat Me Nice/ /One Night/That's All Right	1965	7.50	15.00	30.00
—Black label, dog on left					
❑ EPA-5101	Wear My Ring Around Your Neck/Treat Me Nice/ /One Night/That's All Right	1969	20.00	40.00	80.00
—Orange label					
❑ EPA-5101 [PS]	A Touch of Gold, Volume II	1959	15.00	30.00	60.00
❑ EPA-5120	Don't Be Cruel/I Want You, I Need You, I Love You//Hound Dog/My Baby Left Me	1959	15.00	30.00	60.00
—Black label, dog on top					
❑ EPA-5120	Don't Be Cruel/I Want You, I Need You, I Love You//Hound Dog/My Baby Left Me	1959	150.00	300.00	600.00
—Maroon label					
❑ EPA-5120	Don't Be Cruel/I Want You, I Need You, I Love You//Hound Dog/My Baby Left Me	1965	6.25	12.50	25.00
—Black label, dog on left					
❑ EPA-5120	Don't Be Cruel/I Want You, I Need You, I Love You//Hound Dog/My Baby Left Me	1969	20.00	40.00	80.00
—Orange label					
❑ EPA-5120 [PS]	The Real Elvis	1959	15.00	30.00	60.00
❑ EPA-5121	(There'll Be) Peace in the Valley (For Me)/It Is No Secret (What God Can Do)//I Believe/Take My Hand, Precious Lord	1959	7.50	15.00	30.00
—Black label, dog on top					
❑ EPA-5121	(There'll Be) Peace in the Valley (For Me)/It Is No Secret (What God Can Do)//I Believe/Take My Hand, Precious Lord	1959	100.00	200.00	400.00
—Maroon label					
❑ EPA-5121	(There'll Be) Peace in the Valley (For Me)/It Is No Secret (What God Can Do)//I Believe/Take My Hand, Precious Lord	1965	6.25	12.50	25.00
—Black label, dog on left					
❑ EPA-5121	(There'll Be) Peace in the Valley (For Me)/It Is No Secret (What God Can Do)//I Believe/Take My Hand, Precious Lord	1969	20.00	40.00	80.00
—Orange label					
❑ EPA-5121 [PS]	Peace in the Valley	1959	10.00	20.00	40.00
—Three slightly different cover variations with no difference in value					
❑ EPA-5122	King Creole/New Orleans//As Long As I Have You/Lover Doll	1959	7.50	15.00	30.00
—Black label, dog on top					
❑ EPA-5122	King Creole/New Orleans//As Long As I Have You/Lover Doll	1959	1000.	1500.	2000.
—Maroon label					
❑ EPA-5122	King Creole/New Orleans//As Long As I Have You/Lover Doll	1965	6.25	12.50	25.00
—Black label, dog on left					
❑ EPA-5122	King Creole/New Orleans//As Long As I Have You/Lover Doll	1969	20.00	40.00	80.00
—Orange label					
❑ EPA-5122 [PS]	King Creole	1959	10.00	20.00	40.00
—With "Gold Standard Series" on front cover					
❑ EPA-5122 [PS]	King Creole	1965	7.50	15.00	30.00
—Without "Gold Standard Series" on front cover					
❑ EPA-5141	All Shook Up/Don't Ask Me Why//Too Much/Blue Moon of Kentucky	1959	17.50	35.00	70.00
—Black label, dog on top					
❑ EPA-5141	All Shook Up/Don't Ask Me Why//Too Much/Blue Moon of Kentucky	1959	100.00	200.00	400.00
—Maroon label					
❑ EPA-5141	All Shook Up/Don't Ask Me Why//Too Much/Blue Moon of Kentucky	1959	7.50	15.00	30.00
—Black label, dog on left					
❑ EPA-5141	All Shook Up/Don't Ask Me Why//Too Much/Blue Moon of Kentucky	1959	20.00	40.00	80.00
—Orange label					
❑ EPA-5141 [PS]	A Touch of Gold, Volume 3	1959	17.50	35.00	70.00
❑ EPA-5157	Press Interview with Elvis Presley//Elvis Presley's Newsreel Interview/Pat Hernon Interviews Elvis...	1965	7.50	15.00	30.00
—Black label, dog on top					
❑ EPA-5157	Press Interview with Elvis Presley//Elvis Presley's Newsreel Interview/Pat Hernon Interviews Elvis...	1969	20.00	40.00	80.00
—Orange label					
❑ EPA-5157 [PS]	Elvis Sails	1965	7.50	15.00	30.00
❑ G8-MW-8705 [DJ]	TV Guide Presents Elvis Presley	1956	300.00	600.00	1200.
—Blue label, locked grooves (needle has to be lifted to play each of the four excerpts)					

PRESLEY, ELVIS (2)

CIN KAY

Number	Title (A Side/B Side)	Yr	VG	VG+	NM
❑ 064	Tell Me Pretty Baby (same on both sides)	1978	—	—	2.50
❑ 064 [PS]	Tell Me Pretty Baby (same on both sides)	1978	—	—	2.50

ELVIS CLASSIC

Number	Title (A Side/B Side)	Yr	VG	VG+	NM
❑ EC-5478	Tell Me Pretty Baby (same on both sides)	1978	—	—	2.50
❑ EC-5478 [PS]	Tell Me Pretty Baby (same on both sides)	1978	—	—	2.50

—The above are two different issues of a record that purported to be the "real" Elvis' first studio recording, but turned out to be an utter fake

PRESTON, BILLY

Number	Title (A Side/B Side)	Yr	VG	VG+	NM
APPLE					
❑ 1808	That's the Way God Planned It/What About You	1969	2.00	4.00	8.00
❑ 1808	That's the Way God Planned It/What About You	1972	2.00	4.00	8.00
—With "Mono" on both sides of record and reference to LP					
❑ 1808 [PS]	That's the Way God Planned It/What About You	1969	2.50	5.00	10.00
❑ P-1808/PRO 6555 [DJ]	That's the Way God Planned It (Parts 1 & 2) (mono/stereo)	1969	15.00	30.00	60.00
❑ 1814	Everything's All Right/I Want to Thank You	1969	2.00	4.00	8.00
❑ 1817	All That I've Got (I'm Gonna Give It to You)/As I Get Older	1970	2.00	4.00	8.00
❑ 1817 [PS]	All That I've Got (I'm Gonna Give It to You)/As I Get Older	1970	3.75	7.50	15.00
❑ 1826	My Sweet Lord/Little Girl	1970	2.00	4.00	8.00
❑ 1826	My Sweet Lord/Little Girl	1970	3.00	6.00	12.00
—With star on A-side label					
APPLE/AMERICOM					
❑ 1808P/M-433	That's the Way God Planned It (Edit)/What About You	1969	100.00	200.00	400.00
—Four-inch flexi-disc sold from vending machines					
A&M					
❑ 1320	Outa-Space/I Wrote a Simple Song	1972	—	2.50	5.00
❑ 1340	Should Have Known Better/The Bus	1972	—	2.50	5.00
❑ 1380	Slaughter/God Loves You	1972	—	2.50	5.00
❑ 1380 [PS]	Slaughter/God Loves You	1972	—	3.00	6.00
❑ 1411	Will It Go Round in Circles/Blackbird	1973	—	2.00	4.00
❑ 1463	Space Race/We're Gonna Make It	1973	—	2.00	4.00
❑ 1463 [PS]	Space Race/We're Gonna Make It	1973	—	3.00	6.00
❑ 1492	You're So Unique/How Long Has the Train Been Gone	1973	—	2.00	4.00
❑ 1536	Creature Feature/My Soul Is a Witness	1974	—	2.00	4.00
❑ 1544	Nothing from Nothing/My Soul Is a Witness	1974	—	2.00	4.00
❑ 1544 [PS]	Nothing from Nothing/My Soul Is a Witness	1974	—	3.00	6.00
❑ 1644	Struttin'/You Are So Beautiful	1974	—	2.00	4.00
❑ 1735	Fancy Lady/Song of Joy	1975	—	2.00	4.00
❑ 1735 [PS]	Fancy Lady/Song of Joy	1975	—	3.00	6.00
❑ 1768	Do It While You Can/Song of Joy	1975	—	2.00	4.00
❑ 1892	Do What You Want/I've Got the Spirit	1976	—	2.00	4.00
❑ 1925	Girl/Ecstasy	1977	—	2.00	4.00
❑ 1954	Wide Stride/When You Are Mine	1977	—	2.00	4.00
❑ 1980	A Whole New Thing/Wide Stride	1977	—	2.00	4.00
❑ 2012	I Really Miss You/Attitudes	1978	—	2.00	4.00
❑ 2071	Get Back/Space Race	1978	—	2.00	4.00
CAPITOL					
❑ 2309	Hey Brother (Part 1)/Hey Brother (Part 2)	1968	2.00	4.00	8.00
❑ 5611	The Girl's Got "It"/The Night	1966	2.00	4.00	8.00
❑ 5660	In the Midnight Hour/Advice	1966	2.00	4.00	8.00
❑ 5730	Sunny/Let the Music Play	1966	2.00	4.00	8.00
❑ 5797	Phony Friends/Can't She Tell	1966	2.00	4.00	8.00
MGM					
❑ 14001	The Split/It's Just a Love Game	1968	2.00	4.00	8.00
MOTOWN					
❑ 1470	It Will Come In Time/All I Wanted Was You	1979	—	2.00	4.00
❑ 1505	Sock-It Rocket/Hope	1981	—	2.00	4.00
❑ 1511	A Change Is Gonna Come/You	1981	—	2.00	4.00
❑ 1625	I'm Never Gonna Say Goodbye/Love You So	1982	—	2.00	4.00
VEE JAY					
❑ 646	Don't Let the Sun Catch You Cryin'/(B-side unknown)	1965	—	—	—
—Canceled?					
❑ 653	Don't Let the Sun Catch You Cryin'/Billy's Bag	1965	2.50	5.00	10.00
❑ 692	Log Cabin/Drown in My Own Tears	1965	2.50	5.00	10.00

PRESTON, BILLY, AND SYREETA

Also see each artist's individual listings.

Number	Title (A Side/B Side)	Yr	VG	VG+	NM
MOTOWN					
❑ 1460	With You I'm Born Again/Go For It	1979	—	2.50	5.00
❑ 1477	With You I'm Born Again/All I Wanted Was You	1979	—	2.00	4.00
❑ 1520	Searchin'/Hey You	1981	—	2.00	4.00
❑ 1522	Just for You (Put the Boogie in Your Body)/Hey You	1981	—	2.00	4.00
TAMLA					
❑ 54312	Dance For Me Children/One More Time for Love	1980	—	2.00	4.00
❑ 54319	Please Stay/Signed, Sealed, Delivered (I'm Yours)	1980	—	2.00	4.00

PRESTON, JOHNNY

Number	Title (A Side/B Side)	Yr	VG	VG+	NM
ABC					
❑ 11085	I'm Only Human/There's No One Like You	1968	2.50	5.00	10.00
❑ 11187	Kick the Can/I've Just Been Wasting My Time	1969	2.50	5.00	10.00
HALLWAY					
❑ 1201	All Around the World/Just Plain Hurt	1964	3.75	7.50	15.00
❑ 1204	Willie and the Hand Jive/I've Got My Eyes on You	1964	3.75	7.50	15.00
❑ 1927	Running Bear '65/Dedicated to the One I Love	1965	3.75	7.50	15.00
IMPERIAL					
❑ 5924	This Little Bitty Tear/The Day the World Stood Still	1963	2.50	5.00	10.00
❑ 5947	I've Got My Eyes on You/I Couldn't Take It Again	1963	2.50	5.00	10.00
MERCURY					
❑ 10027 [S]	Cradle of Love/City of Tears	1960	12.50	25.00	50.00
❑ 10036 [S]	Feel So Fine/I'm Starting to Go Steady	1960	15.00	30.00	60.00
❑ 71474	Running Bear/My Heart Knows	1959	6.25	12.50	25.00
❑ 71598 [M]	Cradle of Love/City of Tears	1960	5.00	10.00	20.00
❑ 71598 [PS]	Cradle of Love/City of Tears	1960	7.50	15.00	30.00
❑ 71651 [M]	Feel So Fine/I'm Starting to Go Steady	1960	5.00	10.00	20.00
❑ 71651 [PS]	Feel So Fine/I'm Starting to Go Steady	1960	7.50	15.00	30.00
❑ 71691	Charming Billy/Up in the Air	1960	5.00	10.00	20.00
❑ 71728	New Baby for Christmas/(I Want a) Rock and Roll Guitar	1960	5.00	10.00	20.00
❑ 71761	Leave My Kitten Alone/Token of Love	1961	5.00	10.00	20.00
❑ 71761 [PS]	Leave My Kitten Alone/Token of Love	1961	7.50	15.00	30.00
❑ 71803	I Feel Good/Willy Walk	1961	5.00	10.00	20.00
❑ 71865	Let Them Talk/She Once Belonged to Me	1961	5.00	10.00	20.00
❑ 71908	Free Me/Kissin' Tree	1961	5.00	10.00	20.00
❑ 71908 [PS]	Free Me/Kissin' Tree	1961	7.50	15.00	30.00
❑ 71951	Let's Leave It That Way/Broken Hearts Anonymous	1962	3.75	7.50	15.00
❑ 72049	Let the Big Boss Man (Pull You Through)/The Day After Forever	1962	3.75	7.50	15.00
TCF HALL					
❑ 101	Running Bear '65/Dedicated to the One I Love	1965	2.50	5.00	10.00
❑ 110	Sounds Like Trouble/You Can Make It If You Try	1965	3.75	7.50	15.00
❑ 120	I'm Askin' Forgiveness/Good Good Lovin'	1965	2.50	5.00	10.00

PRESTON, MIKE

Number	Title (A Side/B Side)	Yr	VG	VG+	NM
LONDON					
❑ 1834	A House, a Car and a Wedding Ring/My Lucky Love	1958	3.00	6.00	12.00
❑ 1865	Girl Without a Heart/In Surabaya	1959	2.50	5.00	10.00
❑ 1903	'Till Tomorrow/An Ordinary Couple	1960	2.50	5.00	10.00
❑ 1981	Girl Without a Heart/Marry Me	1960	2.50	5.00	10.00
❑ 9601	Careless Love/Little Grain of Sand	1963	2.50	5.00	10.00

PRETENDERS

Anglo-American group led by Chrissie Hynde.

Number	Title (A Side/B Side)	Yr	VG	VG+	NM
AMERICAN PIE					
❑ 9014	Stop Your Sobbing/Talk of the Town	198?	—	—	3.00
—Reissue label; first appearance of B-side on U.S. stock 45					
MCA					
❑ 54615	I'm Not in Love/I'm Not in Love (instrumental)	1993	—	—	3.00
POLYDOR					
❑ 887816-7	Window of the World/1969	1988	—	—	3.00
❑ 887816-7 [PS]	Window of the World/1969	1988	—	—	3.00
SIRE					
❑ GSRE 0448	Back on the Chain Gang/My City Was Gone	198?	—	—	3.00
—"Back to Back Hits" reissue					
❑ GSRE 0474	Brass in Pocket/Middle of the Road	198?	—	—	3.00
—"Back to Back Hits" reissue					
❑ GSRE 0496	Show Me/Thin Line Between Love and Hate	198?	—	—	3.00
—"Back to Back Hits" reissue					
❑ PRO-S-942 [DJ]	Message of Love/Talk of the Town	1981	2.50	5.00	10.00
❑ 18160	I'll Stand By You/Rebel Rock Me	1994	—	—	3.00
❑ 18163	Night in My Veins/Angel of the Morning	1994	—	—	3.00
❑ 28354	Hymn to Her (She Will Always Carry On)/Tradition of Love	1987	—	—	3.00
❑ 28354 [PS]	Hymn to Her (She Will Always Carry On)/Tradition of Love	1987	—	—	3.00
❑ 28496	My Baby/Room Full of Mirrors	1987	—	—	3.00
❑ 28496 [PS]	My Baby/Room Full of Mirrors	1987	—	—	3.00
❑ 28630	Don't Get Me Wrong/Dance!	1986	—	—	3.00
❑ 28630 [PS]	Don't Get Me Wrong/Dance!	1986	—	—	3.00
❑ 29249	Thin Line Between Love and Hate/Time the Avenger	1984	—	—	3.00
❑ 29249 [PS]	Thin Line Between Love and Hate/Time the Avenger	1984	—	—	3.00
❑ 29317	Show Me/Fast or Slow (The Law Is The Law)	1984	—	—	3.00
❑ 29317 [PS]	Show Me/Fast or Slow (The Law Is The Law)	1984	—	—	3.00
❑ 29444	Middle of the Road/2000 Miles	1983	—	—	3.00
—A-side is not a Christmas song					
❑ 29444 [PS]	Middle of the Road/2000 Miles	1983	—	—	3.00
❑ 29840	Back on the Chain Gang/My City Was Gone	1982	—	—	3.00
❑ 29840 [PS]	Back on the Chain Gang/My City Was Gone	1982	—	—	3.00
❑ 49181	Brass in Pocket (I'm Special)/Space Invader	1980	—	2.00	4.00
—Not issued with picture sleeve in U.S.					
❑ 49506	Stop Your Sobbing/Phone Call	1980	2.00	4.00	8.00
❑ 49506 [PS]	Stop Your Sobbing/Phone Call	1980	—	2.00	4.00
❑ 49533	Kid/Tattooed Love Boys	1980	—	2.00	4.00
❑ 49819	Louie Louie/In the Sticks	1981	—	2.00	4.00
❑ 49819 [PS]	Louie Louie/In the Sticks	1981	—	2.00	4.00
❑ 49861	I Go to Sleep/Waste Not Want Not	1981	—	2.00	4.00
WARNER BROS.					
❑ 28259	If There Was a Man/Into Vienna	1987	—	—	3.00
—B-side by John Barry					
❑ 28259 [PS]	If There Was a Man/Into Vienna	1987	—	—	3.00
—B-side by John Barry					

PRETENDERS, THE (2)

Number	Title (A Side/B Side)	Yr	VG	VG+	NM
APT					
❑ 25026	Blue and Lonely/Daddy Needs Baby	1959	125.00	250.00	500.00
CENTRAL					
❑ 2605	Blue and Lonely/Daddy Needs Baby	1958	375.00	750.00	1500.

PRETENDERS, THE (3)

Number	Title (A Side/B Side)	Yr	VG	VG+	NM
BETHLEHEM					
❑ 3050	The Day You Are Mine/Ding Dong Bells	1962	50.00	100.00	200.00

PRETENDERS, THE (4)

Number	Title (A Side/B Side)	Yr	VG	VG+	NM
CHATTAHOOCHIE					
❑ 685	Pepita's Theme/Tijuana Taxi	1965	5.00	10.00	20.00

PRETENDERS, THE (U)

The Rama and Whirlin' Disc records could be by group (1).

Number	Title (A Side/B Side)	Yr	VG	VG+	NM
POWER-MARTIN					
❑ 1001	Smile/I'm So Happy	1961	25.00	50.00	100.00
RAMA					
❑ 198	Possessive Love/I've Got to Have You Baby	1956	30.00	60.00	120.00
WHIRLIN' DISC					
❑ 106	Close Your Eyes/Part-Time Sweetheart	1957	62.50	125.00	250.00

PRETTY BOY

See DON COVAY.

PRETTY THINGS, THE

Number	Title (A Side/B Side)	Yr	VG	VG+	NM
FONTANA					
❑ 1508	I Can Never Say/Honey, I Need	1965	3.75	7.50	15.00

Number	Title (A Side/B Side)	Yr	VG	VG+	NM
❑ 1518	Cry to Me/I Can Never Say	1965	3.75	7.50	15.00
❑ 1518	Cry to Me/Judgment Day	1965	3.75	7.50	15.00
❑ 1540	Midnight to Six Man/Can't Stand Pain	1966	3.75	7.50	15.00
❑ 1550	Come See Me/Judgment Day	1966	3.75	7.50	15.00
❑ 1550	Come See Me/Progress	1966	3.75	7.50	15.00
❑ 1916	Big Boss Man/Rosalyn	1964	3.75	7.50	15.00
❑ 1941	Don't Bring Me Down/We'll Be Together	1964	3.75	7.50	15.00
LAURIE					
❑ 3458	Talkin' About the Good Times/Walking Through My Dreams	1968	7.50	15.00	30.00
NORTON					
❑ PT 109	All Light Up/Pretty Beat	1999	—	2.00	4.00
—Red vinyl, small hole, called "The Pretty Things U.S. Tour 45"					
RARE EARTH					
❑ 5005	Private Sorrow/Balloon Burning	1969	3.75	7.50	15.00
SWAN SONG					
❑ 70104	Come Home Momma/Joey	1975	—	2.50	5.00
❑ 70107	It Isn't Rock & Roll/Remember That Boy	1975	—	2.50	5.00
7-Inch Extended Plays					
NORTON					
❑ EP-501	Rosalyn/Judgement Day//Roadrunner/Don't Bring Me Down	1999	—	—	2.00
❑ EP-501 [PS]	Rosalyn	1999	—	—	2.00
❑ EP-502	Big City/I Can Never Say//Get Yourself Home/Honey I Need	1999	—	—	2.00
❑ EP-502 [PS]	Big City	1999	—	—	2.00
❑ EP-503	You Don't Believe Me/Buzz the Jerk//You'll Never Do It Baby/Come See Me	1999	—	—	2.00
❑ EP-503 [PS]	Buzz the Jerk	1999	—	—	2.00
❑ EP-504	Midnight to Six Man/Can't Stand the Pain//LSD/Me Needing You	1999	—	—	2.00
❑ EP-504 [PS]	Midnight to Six Man	1999	—	—	2.00
❑ EP-505	A House in the Country/Progress//Tripping/Photographer	1999	—	—	2.00
❑ EP-505 [PS]	A House in the Country	1999	—	—	2.00

PRICE, ALAN

Also see THE ANIMALS.

Number	Title (A Side/B Side)	Yr	VG	VG+	NM
COTILLION					
❑ 44044	Falling in Love Again/Sly Sadie	1969	—	3.00	6.00
EPIC					
❑ 04319	I Don't Feel No Pain No More (Time and Tide)/Rowf and Snitter Run to Sea	1984	—	2.00	4.00
JET					
❑ XW1119	I Wanna Dance/Just for You	1978	—	2.00	4.00
❑ 5056	This Is Your Lucky Day/Mama Don't Go Home	1979	—	2.00	4.00
PARROT					
❑ 3001	I Put a Spell on You/Iechyd-Da	1966	2.50	5.00	10.00
❑ 3007	Hi-Lili, Hi-Lo/Take Me Home	1966	2.50	5.00	10.00
❑ 3009	Tickle Me/Simon Smith and His Amazing Dancing Bears	1966	2.50	5.00	10.00
❑ 3013	Who Cares/The House That Jack Built	1967	2.00	4.00	8.00
❑ 3014	Shame/Don't Do That Again	1967	2.00	4.00	8.00
❑ 3019	Not Born to Follow/To Ramona	1968	2.00	4.00	8.00
WARNER BROS.					
❑ 7717	Poor People/O Lucky Man	1973	—	2.50	5.00

PRICE, LLOYD

Number	Title (A Side/B Side)	Yr	VG	VG+	NM
ABC					
❑ 1237	Stagger Lee/Personality	1969	—	3.00	6.00
—"Golden Treasure Chest" reissue; contains the "samitized" version of "Stagger Lee" with Mr. Lee and Billy arguing over a woman					
❑ 11016	Personality/Just Because	1967	2.00	4.00	8.00
ABC-PARAMOUNT					
❑ 9792	Just Because/Why	1957	5.00	10.00	20.00
❑ 9972 [M]	Stagger Lee/You Need Love	1958	5.00	10.00	20.00
—Most, if not all, copies contain the "raunchy" version of "Stagger Lee" with Mr. Lee and Billy playing cards					
❑ S-9972 [S]	Stagger Lee/You Need Love	1958	10.00	20.00	40.00
❑ 9997 [M]	Where Were You (On Our Wedding Day)?/Is It Really Love	1959	5.00	10.00	20.00
❑ S-9997 [S]	Where Were You (On Our Wedding Day)?/Is It Really Love	1959	10.00	20.00	40.00
❑ 10018 [M]	Personality/Have You Ever Had the Blues	1959	5.00	10.00	20.00
❑ 10018 [M]	(You've Got) Personality/Have You Ever Had the Blues	1959	5.00	10.00	20.00
—Note longer title					
❑ S-10018 [S]	Personality/Have You Ever Had the Blues	1959	12.50	25.00	50.00
❑ 10032 [M]	I'm Gonna Get Married/Three Little Pigs	1959	5.00	10.00	20.00
❑ S-10032 [S]	I'm Gonna Get Married/Three Little Pigs	1959	12.50	25.00	50.00
❑ 10062	Come Into My Heart/Won't Cha Come Home	1959	3.75	7.50	15.00
❑ S-10062 [S]	Come Into My Heart/Won't Cha Come Home	1959	12.50	25.00	50.00
❑ 10075	Lady Luck/Never Let Me Go	1960	3.75	7.50	15.00
❑ 10102	No If's — No And's/For Love	1960	3.75	7.50	15.00
❑ 10123	Question/If I Look a Little Blue	1960	3.75	7.50	15.00
❑ 10139	Just Call Me (And I'll Understand)/Who Could've Told You	1960	3.75	7.50	15.00
❑ 10162	(You Better) Know What You're Doin'/That's Why Tears Come and Go	1960	3.75	7.50	15.00
❑ 10177	Boo Hoo/I Made You Cry	1961	3.75	7.50	15.00
❑ 10197	One Hundred Percent/Say I'm the One	1961	3.75	7.50	15.00
❑ 10206	String of Pearls/Chantilly Lace	1961	3.75	7.50	15.00
❑ 10221	Mary and Man-O/I Ain't Givin' Up Nothin'	1961	3.75	7.50	15.00
❑ 10229	Talk to Me/I Cover the Waterfront	1961	3.75	7.50	15.00
❑ 10288	Be a Leader/'Nother Fairy Tale	1962	3.75	7.50	15.00
❑ 10299	Twistin' the Blues/Pop Eye's Irresistable You	1962	3.75	7.50	15.00
❑ 10342	Counterfeit Friends/Your Picture	1962	3.75	7.50	15.00
❑ 10372	Under Your Spell Again/Happy Birthday Mama	1962	3.75	7.50	15.00
❑ 10412	Who's Sorry Now/Hello Bill	1963	3.75	7.50	15.00
DOUBLE-L					
❑ 714	Pistol Packin' Mama/Tennessee Waltz	1963	2.50	5.00	10.00
❑ 722	Misty/Cry On	1963	2.50	5.00	10.00
❑ 728	Merry Christmas Mama/Auld Lang Syne	1963	3.00	6.00	12.00
❑ 729	Billie Baby/Try a Little Bit of Tenderness	1964	2.50	5.00	10.00
❑ 729 [PS]	Billie Baby/Try a Little Bit of Tenderness	1964	6.25	12.50	25.00
❑ 730	I'll Be a Fool for You/You're Nobody Till Somebody Loves You	1964	2.50	5.00	10.00
❑ 736	Go On Little Girl/You're Reading Me	1965	2.50	5.00	10.00
❑ 739	Every Night/Peeping and Hiding	1966	2.50	5.00	10.00
❑ 740	Send Me Some Loving/Somewhere Along the Way	1966	2.50	5.00	10.00
GSF					
❑ 6882	Sing a Song/(B-side unknown)	1972	—	3.00	6.00
❑ 6894	Love Music/Just for Baby	1973	—	3.00	6.00
❑ 6904	Trying to Slip (Away)/They Get Down	1973	—	3.00	6.00
HURD					
❑ 82	Misty '66/Saturday Night	1966	2.00	4.00	8.00
JAD					
❑ 208	Luv, Luv, Luv/Take All	1968	2.00	4.00	8.00
❑ 212	Don't Stop Now/The Truth	1968	2.00	4.00	8.00
KRC					
❑ 301	Lonely Chair/The Chicken and the Bop	1957	12.50	25.00	50.00
❑ 303	Hello Little Girl/Georgianna	1957	6.25	12.50	25.00
❑ 305	How Many Times/To Love and Be Loved	1957	6.25	12.50	25.00
❑ 587	Just Because/Why	1957	20.00	40.00	80.00
❑ 5000	No Limit to Love/Such a Mess	195?	6.25	12.50	25.00
❑ 5002	Gonna Let You Come Back Home/Down by the River	195?	6.25	12.50	25.00
LPG					
❑ 111	What Did You Do with My Love/Love Music	1976	—	3.00	6.00
LUDIX					
❑ 4747	Feelin' Good/Cupid's Bandwagon	197?	—	3.00	6.00
MONUMENT					
❑ 856	Don't Cry/I Love You, I Just Love You	1964	2.50	5.00	10.00
❑ 865	Amen/I'd Fight the World	1964	2.50	5.00	10.00
❑ 877	Oh, Lady Luck/Woman	1965	2.50	5.00	10.00
❑ 887	If I Had My Life to Live Over/Two for Love	1965	2.50	5.00	10.00
PARAMOUNT					
❑ 0168	In the Eyes of God/The Legend of Nigger Charley	1972	—	3.00	6.00
REPRISE					
❑ 0499	I Won't Cry Anymore/The Man Who Took the Valise Off the Floor at Grand Central Station at Noon	1966	2.00	4.00	8.00
SCEPTER					
❑ 12310	Hooked on a Feeling/If You Really Love Him	1971	—	3.00	6.00
❑ 12327	Mr. and Mrs. Untrue/Natural SInner	1971	—	3.00	6.00
SPECIALTY					
❑ 428	Lawdy Miss Clawdy/Mailman Blues	1952	62.50	125.00	250.00
❑ 428	Lawdy Miss Clawdy/Mailman Blues	1952	375.00	750.00	1500.
—Red vinyl					
❑ 440	Oooh-Oooh-Oooh/Restless Heart	1952	25.00	50.00	100.00
❑ 452	Ain't It a Shame?/Tell Me Pretty Baby	1953	25.00	50.00	100.00
❑ 452	Ain't It a Shame?/Tell Me Pretty Baby	1953	50.00	100.00	200.00
—Red vinyl					
❑ 457	What's the Matter Now/So Long	1953	25.00	50.00	100.00
❑ 457	What's the Matter Now/So Long	1953	50.00	100.00	200.00
—Red vinyl					
❑ 463	Where You At?/Baby Don't Turn Your Back on Me	1953	25.00	50.00	100.00
❑ 463	Where You At?/Baby Don't Turn Your Back on Me	1953	50.00	100.00	200.00
—Red vinyl					
❑ 471	I Wish Your Picture Was You/Frog Legs	1953	25.00	50.00	100.00
❑ 483	Let Me Come Home, Baby/Too Late for Tears	1954	20.00	40.00	80.00
❑ 483	Let Me Come Home, Baby/Too Late for Tears	1954	50.00	100.00	200.00
—Red vinyl					
❑ 494	Walkin' the Track/Jimmie Lee	1954	20.00	40.00	80.00
❑ 535	Oo-Ee Baby/Chee-Koo Baby	1954	10.00	20.00	40.00
❑ 540	Trying to Find Someone to Love/Lord, Lord, Amen!	1955	10.00	20.00	40.00
❑ 571	Woe Ho Ho/I Yi Yi Gomen-a-Sai (I'm Sorry)	1956	10.00	20.00	40.00
❑ 578	Country Boy Rock/Rock 'N' Dance	1956	12.50	25.00	50.00
❑ 582	Forgive Me, Clawdy/I'm Glad	1956	7.50	15.00	30.00
❑ 602	Baby Please Come Home/Breaking My Heart (All Over Again)	1957	7.50	15.00	30.00
❑ 661	Lawdy Miss Clawdy/Mailman Blues	1959	5.00	10.00	20.00
TURNTABLE					
❑ 501	I Understand/The Grass Will Sing (For You)	1969	2.00	4.00	8.00
❑ 502	I Heard It Through the Grapevine/It's Your Thing	1969	2.00	4.00	8.00
❑ 506	Bad Conditions/The Truth	1969	2.00	4.00	8.00
❑ 509	Lawdy Miss Clawdy/Little Volcano	1969	2.00	4.00	8.00
7-Inch Extended Plays					
ABC-PARAMOUNT					
❑ 277	(contents unknown)	1959	25.00	50.00	100.00
❑ 277 [PS]	The Exciting Lloyd Price	1959	25.00	50.00	100.00
❑ 315	(contents unknown)	1960	25.00	50.00	100.00
❑ 315 [PS]	Mr. Personality Sings the Blues	1960	25.00	50.00	100.00
❑ A-324	Lady Luck/Personality//Stagger Lee/I'm Gonna Get Married	1960	25.00	50.00	100.00
❑ A-324 [PS]	Mr. Personality's Big Hits	1960	25.00	50.00	100.00

PRICE, RAY

Also see WILLIE NELSON.

Number	Title (A Side/B Side)	Yr	VG	VG+	NM
ABC					
❑ 12084	Roses and Love Songs/The Closest Thing to Love	1975	—	2.00	4.00
❑ 12095	Farthest Thing from My Mind/All That Keeps Me Going	1975	—	2.00	4.00
ABC DOT					
❑ 17588	Say I Do/I'll Still Love You	1975	—	2.00	4.00
❑ 17616	That's All She Wrote/I Didn't Feel Nothing	1976	—	2.00	4.00
❑ 17637	To Make a Long Story Short/We're Getting There	1976	—	2.00	4.00
❑ 17666	A Mansion on the Hill/Hey, Good Lookin'	1976	—	2.00	4.00

Number	Title (A Side/B Side)	Yr	VG	VG+	NM
❑ 17690	Different Kind of Flower/Don't Let the Stars Get in Your Eyes	1977	—	2.00	4.00
❑ 17718	Born to Love Me/The Only Way to Say Good Morning	1977	—	2.00	4.00

COLUMBIA

Number	Title (A Side/B Side)	Yr	VG	VG+	NM
❑ 10006	Like a First Time Thing/You Are the Song	1974	—	2.50	5.00
❑ 10150	If You Ever Change Your Mind/Just Enough to Make Me Stay	1975	—	2.00	4.00
❑ 10503	Help Me/Nobody Wins	1977	—	2.00	4.00
❑ 10631	Born to Love Me/I'm Sorry for the Hateful Things I Did	1977	—	2.00	4.00
❑ 20810	You've Got My Troubles Now/If You're Ever Lonely Darling	1951	7.50	15.00	30.00
❑ 20833	I Saw My Castles Fall Today/Hey Lala	1951	7.50	15.00	30.00
❑ 20863	Heart Aching Blues/Till Death Do Us Part	1951	7.50	15.00	30.00
❑ 20883	I Made a Mistake and I'm Sorry/Weary Blues	1952	6.25	12.50	25.00
❑ 20913	Talk to Your Heart/I've Got to Hurry, Hurry, Hurry	1952	6.25	12.50	25.00
❑ 20943	Hot Diggity Dog/I've Got to Hurry, Hurry, Hurry	1952	5.00	10.00	20.00

—With Jimmy Dickens

Number	Title (A Side/B Side)	Yr	VG	VG+	NM
❑ 20963	Road of No Return/I Know I'll Never Win Your Love Again	1952	5.00	10.00	20.00
❑ 21015	I Can't Escape from You/Won't You Please Be Mine	1952	5.00	10.00	20.00
❑ 21025	Don't Let the Stars Get In Your Eyes/I Lost the Only Love I Know	1952	5.00	10.00	20.00
❑ 21053	You're Under Arrest/My Old Scrapbook	1953	5.00	10.00	20.00
❑ 21089	Price for Loving You/That's What I Got for Loving You	1953	5.00	10.00	20.00
❑ 21117	Cold Shoulder/You Weren't Ashamed to Kiss Me	1953	5.00	10.00	20.00
❑ 21149	Wrong Side of Town/Who Stole That Train	1953	5.00	10.00	20.00
❑ 21173	Leave Her Alone/You Always Get By	1953	5.00	10.00	20.00
❑ 21214	I'll Be There (If You Ever Want Me)/Release Me	1954	5.00	10.00	20.00
❑ 21249	Much Too Young to Die/I Love You So Much	1954	5.00	10.00	20.00
❑ 21299	I Could Love You More/What If He Don't Love You	1954	5.00	10.00	20.00
❑ 21315	If You Don't, Somebody Else Will/Oh Yes Darling	1954	5.00	10.00	20.00
❑ 21354	One Broken Heart/I'm Alone Because I Love You	1955	3.75	7.50	15.00
❑ 21402	Sweet Little Miss Blue Eyes/Let Me Talk to You	1955	3.75	7.50	15.00
❑ 21404	A Man Called Peter/Call the Lord and He'll Be There	1955	5.00	10.00	20.00
❑ 21442	I Can't Go On Like This/I Don't Want It on My Conscience	1955	3.75	7.50	15.00
❑ 21474	Run Boy/You Never Will Be True	1955	3.75	7.50	15.00
❑ 21510	Crazy Arms/You Done Me Wrong	1956	3.75	7.50	15.00
❑ 21562	I've Got a New Heartache/Wasted Words	1956	3.75	7.50	15.00
❑ 31428 [S]	(titles unknown)	1962	3.75	7.50	15.00
❑ 31429 [S]	(titles unknown)	1962	3.75	7.50	15.00
❑ 31430 [S]	(titles unknown)	1962	3.75	7.50	15.00
❑ 31431 [S]	(titles unknown)	1962	3.75	7.50	15.00
❑ 31432 [S]	(titles unknown)	1962	3.75	7.50	15.00

—Anyone who can fill in these gaps -- the above 5 all are Columbia "Stereo 7" singles -- please let us know.

Number	Title (A Side/B Side)	Yr	VG	VG+	NM
❑ 40889	I'll Be There (When You Get Lonely)/Please Don't Leave Me	1957	3.75	7.50	15.00
❑ 40951	My Shoes Keep Walking Back to You/Don't Do This to Me	1957	3.75	7.50	15.00
❑ 41105	Curtain in the Window/It's All Your Fault	1958	3.00	6.00	12.00
❑ 41191	City Lights/Invitation to the Blues	1958	3.00	6.00	12.00
❑ 41309	That's What It's Like to Be Lonesome/Kissing Your Picture	1958	3.00	6.00	12.00
❑ 41374	Heartaches By the Number/Wall of Tears	1959	3.00	6.00	12.00
❑ 41477	The Same Old Me/Under Your Spell Again	1959	3.00	6.00	12.00
❑ 41590	One More Time/Who'll Be the First	1960	3.00	6.00	12.00
❑ 41767	I Wish I Could Fall in Love Today/I Can't Run Away from Myself	1960	3.00	6.00	12.00
❑ 41947	Heart Over Mind/The Twenty-Fourth Hour	1961	2.50	5.00	10.00
❑ 42132	Soft Rain/Here We Are Again	1961	2.50	5.00	10.00
❑ 42310	I've Just Destroyed the World (I'm Living In)/Big Shoes	1962	2.50	5.00	10.00
❑ 42518	Pride/I'm Walking Slow	1962	2.50	5.00	10.00
❑ 42658	Walk Me to the Door/You Took Her Off My Hands (Now Please Take Her Off My Mind)	1963	2.50	5.00	10.00
❑ 42827	Make the World Go Away/Night Life	1963	2.50	5.00	10.00
❑ 42971	Burning Memories/That's All That Matters	1964	2.50	5.00	10.00
❑ 43086	Please Talk to My Heart/I Don't Know Why	1964	2.50	5.00	10.00
❑ 43162	A Thing Called Sadness/Here Comes My Baby Back Again	1964	2.50	5.00	10.00
❑ 43264	The Other Woman/Tearful Earful	1965	2.00	4.00	8.00
❑ 43427	Don't You Ever Get Tired of Hurting Me/Unloved, Unwanted	1965	2.00	4.00	8.00
❑ 43560	A Way to Survive/I'm Not Crazy Yet	1966	2.00	4.00	8.00
❑ 43795	Touch My Heart/It Should Be Easier Now	1966	2.00	4.00	8.00
❑ 44042	Danny Boy/I'll Let My Mind Wander	1967	2.00	4.00	8.00
❑ 44042 [PS]	Danny Boy/I'll Let My Mind Wander	1967	3.00	6.00	12.00
❑ 44195	I'm Still Not Over You/Crazy	1967	2.00	4.00	8.00
❑ 44374	Take Me As I Am (Or Let Me Go)/In the Summer of My Life	1967	2.00	4.00	8.00
❑ 44505	I've Been There Before/Night Life	1968	2.00	4.00	8.00
❑ 44628	She Wears My Ring/Goin' Away	1968	2.00	4.00	8.00
❑ 44747	Set Me Free/Trouble	1969	—	3.00	6.00
❑ 44761	Sweetheart of the Year/How Can I Write on Paper (What I Feel in My Heart)	1969	—	3.00	6.00
❑ 44931	Raining in My Heart/I Know Love	1969	—	3.00	6.00
❑ 45005	April's Fool/Make It Rain	1969	—	3.00	6.00
❑ 45046	Jingle Bells/Happy Birthday to You, Our Lord	1969	—	3.00	6.00
❑ 45095	You Wouldn't Know Love/Everybody Wants to Get to Heaven	1970	—	3.00	6.00
❑ 45178	For the Good Times/Grazin' in Greener Pastures	1970	—	3.00	6.00
❑ 45329	I Won't Mention It Again/Kiss the World Goodbye	1971	—	2.50	5.00
❑ 45425	I'd Rather Be Sorry/When I Loved Her	1971	—	2.50	5.00
❑ 45583	The Lonesomest Lonesome/That's What Leaving's About	1972	—	2.50	5.00
❑ 45724	She's Got to Be a Saint/Oh Lonesome Me	1972	—	2.50	5.00
❑ 45889	You're the Best Thing That Ever Happened to Me/What Kind of Love Is This	1973	—	2.50	5.00
❑ 46015	Storms of Troubled Times/Some Things Never Change	1974	—	2.50	5.00

DIMENSION

Number	Title (A Side/B Side)	Yr	VG	VG+	NM
❑ 1018	Getting Over You Again/Circle Driveway	1981	—	2.00	4.00
❑ 1021	It Don't Hurt Me Half As Bad/She's the Right Kind of Woman (Loving the Wrong Kind of Man)	1981	—	2.00	4.00
❑ 1024	Diamonds in the Stars/Grazing in Greener Pastures	1981	—	2.00	4.00
❑ 1031	Forty and Fadin'/Something to Forget You By	1982	—	2.00	4.00
❑ 1035	Will Till Those Bridges Are Gone/Angel in My Heart (Devil in My Mind)	1982	—	2.00	4.00
❑ 1038	Somewhere in Texas/Getting Down and Getting High	1982	—	2.00	4.00

MONUMENT

Number	Title (A Side/B Side)	Yr	VG	VG+	NM
❑ 45267	Feet/Let's Make a Nice Memory (Today)	1978	—	2.00	4.00
❑ 45277	There's Always Me/If It All the Same to You (I'll Be Leaving in the Morning)	1979	—	2.00	4.00
❑ 45283	That's the Only Way to Say Good Morning/All the Good Things Are Gone	1979	—	2.00	4.00
❑ 45290	Misty Morning Rain/We Can't Build a Fire in the Rain	1979	—	2.00	4.00

MYRRH

Number	Title (A Side/B Side)	Yr	VG	VG+	NM
❑ 146	Like Old Times Again/My First Day Without Her	1974	—	2.50	5.00
❑ 150	Roses and Love Songs/The Closest Thing to Love	1975	—	2.50	5.00

STEP ONE

Number	Title (A Side/B Side)	Yr	VG	VG+	NM
❑ 341	(She Got a Hold of Me Where It Hurts) She Won't Let Go/Memories to Burn	1985	—	2.00	4.00
❑ 344	I'm Not Leaving (I'm Just Getting Out of Your Way)/Why Don't Love Just Go Away	1985	—	2.00	4.00
❑ 350	Five Fingers/Lonely Like a Rose	1985	—	2.00	4.00
❑ 352	You're Nobody Till Somebody Loves You/I'm In the Mood for Love	1986	—	2.00	4.00
❑ 355	All the Way/Bummin' Around	1986	—	2.00	4.00
❑ 361	Please Don't Talk About Me When I'm Gone/For the Good Times	1986	—	2.00	4.00
❑ 366	When You Gave Your Love to Me/Forty and Fadin'	1986	—	2.00	4.00
❑ 370	Sentimental Journey/Better Class of Loser	1987	—	2.00	4.00
❑ 378	Just Enough Love/Why Don't Love Just Go Away	1987	—	2.00	4.00
❑ 381	For Christmas/With Christmas Near	1987	—	2.00	4.00
❑ 383	Big Ole Teardrops/The Season for Missing You	1988	—	2.00	4.00
❑ 388	Don't the Morning Always Come Too Soon/All You Have to Do Is Come Back	1988	—	2.00	4.00
❑ 393	I'd Do It All Over Again/Wind Beneath My Wings	1988	—	2.00	4.00
❑ 410	Love Me Down to Size/(B-side unknown)	1989	—	2.00	4.00
❑ 436	Memories That Last/A Whole Lot of You	1991	—	2.00	4.00

—With Faron Young

VIVA

Number	Title (A Side/B Side)	Yr	VG	VG+	NM
❑ 29147	What Am I Gonna Do Without You/You've Been Leaving Me for Years	1984	—	—	3.00
❑ 29217	Better Class of Loser/Everytime I Sing a Love Song	1984	—	—	3.00
❑ 29277	A New Place to Begin/Everyone Gets Crazy Now and Then	1984	—	—	3.00
❑ 29458	Coors in Colorado/Living Her Life in a Song	1983	—	2.00	4.00
❑ 29543	Scotch and Soda/I Love You Eyes	1983	—	—	3.00

WARNER BROS.

Number	Title (A Side/B Side)	Yr	VG	VG+	NM
❑ 29691	Willie, Write Me a Song/I Love You Eyes	1983	—	—	3.00
❑ 29830	One Fiddle, Two Fiddle/San Antonio Rose	1982	—	2.00	4.00

7-Inch Extended Plays

COLUMBIA

Number	Title (A Side/B Side)	Yr	VG	VG+	NM
❑ B-1786	(contents unknown)	195?	7.50	15.00	30.00
❑ B-1786 [PS]	Ray Price	195?	7.50	15.00	30.00
❑ B-2809	*I'll Be There/Release Me/Don't Let the Stars Get In Your Eyes/I Lost the Only Love I Knew	195?	3.75	7.50	15.00
❑ B-2809 [PS]	Ray Price (Hall of Fame Series)	195?	3.75	7.50	15.00
❑ B-2812	The Last Letter/My Shoes Keep Walking Back to You//Crazy Arms/I'm Alone Because I Love You	195?	3.75	7.50	15.00
❑ B-2812 [PS]	Ray Price (Hall of Fame Series)	195?	3.75	7.50	15.00

PRIESMAN, MAGEL

SUN

Number	Title (A Side/B Side)	Yr	VG	VG+	NM
❑ 294	Memories of You/I Feel So Blue	1958	6.25	12.50	25.00

PRIMA, LOUIS

ABC

Number	Title (A Side/B Side)	Yr	VG	VG+	NM
❑ 11093	Almost Persuaded/Waitin' in Your Welfare Line	1968	—	3.00	6.00
❑ 11122	Joanna/You Can't Take the Country Out of the Boy	1968	—	3.00	6.00
❑ 11166	Flooby Dooby Doo/I Never Opened My Eyes	1969	—	3.00	6.00
❑ 12047	Time Heals Everything/When Hazel Comes in the Room	1974	—	2.00	4.00

BRUNSWICK

Number	Title (A Side/B Side)	Yr	VG	VG+	NM
❑ 55485	I Left My Heart in San Francisco/I Never Promised You a Rose Garden	1972	—	3.00	6.00

BUENA VISTA

Number	Title (A Side/B Side)	Yr	VG	VG+	NM
❑ 446	Jolly Holiday/Supercalifragilisticexpialidocious	1965	3.75	7.50	15.00

—With Gia Maione

Number	Title (A Side/B Side)	Yr	VG	VG+	NM
❑ 454	Santa, How Come Your Eyes Are Green When Last Year They Were Blue/Senor Santa Claus	1966	3.00	6.00	12.00

CAPITOL

Number	Title (A Side/B Side)	Yr	VG	VG+	NM
❑ F3566	A Banana Spilt for My Baby/Five Months, Two Weeks, Two Days	1956	3.00	6.00	12.00

—With Sam Butera

Number	Title (A Side/B Side)	Yr	VG	VG+	NM
❑ F3615	Whistle Stop/Be Mine	1957	3.00	6.00	12.00

—With Sam Butera

Number	Title (A Side/B Side)	Yr	VG	VG+	NM
❑ F3667	Midnight Melody/The Wild Ones	1957	3.00	6.00	12.00

—With Sam Butera

Number	Title (A Side/B Side)	Yr	VG	VG+	NM
❑ F3856	Beep Beep/Buona Sera	1957	3.00	6.00	12.00

Number	Title (A Side/B Side)	Yr	VG	VG+	NM
❑ 4732	Twist All Night/Everybody Knows	1962	2.50	5.00	10.00
❑ 4805	Big Daddy/Ooh, Look What You've Done to Me	1962	2.50	5.00	10.00
—With Gia Maione					
❑ 58572	Jump, Jive, An' Wail/Just a Gigolo-I Ain't Got Nobody (Medley)	1998	—	—	3.00
❑ 58804	Buona Sera/Oh Marie	1999	—	—	3.00

COLUMBIA

Number	Title (A Side/B Side)	Yr	VG	VG+	NM
❑ 39614	Shake Hands with Santa/Eleanor	1951	5.00	10.00	20.00
❑ 39692	Basta/Ooh Dah Dilly Dah	1952	5.00	10.00	20.00
❑ 39735	The Bigger the Figure/Boney Bones	1952	5.00	10.00	20.00
❑ 39823	Chili Sauce/One Mint Julep	1952	5.00	10.00	20.00
❑ 39969	Oh Marie/Luigi	1953	5.00	10.00	20.00
❑ 40015	Paul Revere/It's As Good As New	1953	5.00	10.00	20.00
❑ 40064	Barncale Bill the Sailor/Shepherd Boy	1953	5.00	10.00	20.00

DECCA

Number	Title (A Side/B Side)	Yr	VG	VG+	NM
❑ 29162	Paper Doll/The Dummy Song	1954	3.75	7.50	15.00

DOT

Number	Title (A Side/B Side)	Yr	VG	VG+	NM
❑ 15978	Confessin'/Night and Day	1959	2.50	5.00	10.00
❑ 16009	Hey Ba-Ba-Re-Bop/My Cucuzza	1959	2.50	5.00	10.00
❑ 16060	When My Baby Smiles at Me/Paradise	1960	2.50	5.00	10.00
❑ 16108	Don't You Know/Brooklyn Bridge	1960	2.50	5.00	10.00
❑ 16151	Wonderland by Night/Ol' Man Moses	1960	2.50	5.00	10.00
❑ 16193	Enchantment/Chapel by the Sea	1961	2.50	5.00	10.00
❑ 16211	My Prayer/You Can Depend on Me	1961	2.50	5.00	10.00
❑ 16273	Mod Indigo/Come Back to Sorrento	1961	2.50	5.00	10.00
❑ 16301	Continental Twist/Oh Ma Ma Twist	1962	2.50	5.00	10.00
❑ 16401	Josephine, Please No Lean on the Bell/Brooklyn Bridge	1962	2.50	5.00	10.00

HANNA-BARBERA

Number	Title (A Side/B Side)	Yr	VG	VG+	NM
❑ 467	I'm Gonna Sit Right Down and Write Myself a Letter/Civilization (Bongo, Bongo, Bongo)	1966	2.50	5.00	10.00

KAMA SUTRA

Number	Title (A Side/B Side)	Yr	VG	VG+	NM
❑ 213	Jug Band Music/Bald-Headed Girl	1966	2.00	4.00	8.00

MERCURY

Number	Title (A Side/B Side)	Yr	VG	VG+	NM
❑ 5386	Over the Rainbow/Tears on My Tie	1950	7.50	15.00	30.00
—Note: Earlier Louis Prima 45s on Mercury may exist.					
❑ 5406	Francis, the Talking Mule/A Good Time Was Had By All	1950	7.50	15.00	30.00
❑ 5451	Here, Pretty Kitty/Buona Sera	1950	7.50	15.00	30.00

RCA VICTOR

Number	Title (A Side/B Side)	Yr	VG	VG+	NM
❑ 47-2960	Five Foot Two, Eyes of Blue/For Mari-Yooten	1949	5.00	10.00	20.00

ROBIN HOOD

Number	Title (A Side/B Side)	Yr	VG	VG+	NM
❑ 101	Oh Babe!/Piccolina Lena	1950	7.50	15.00	30.00

SAVOY

Number	Title (A Side/B Side)	Yr	VG	VG+	NM
❑ 1111	Robin Hood/Brooklyn Boogie	1953	5.00	10.00	20.00

UNITED ARTISTS

Number	Title (A Side/B Side)	Yr	VG	VG+	NM
❑ 50175	Illya Darling/I Believe in You	1967	—	3.00	6.00
❑ 50200	My Cup Runneth Over/Cabaret	1967	—	3.00	6.00
❑ 50223	The Impossible Dream/Poor Old Marat	1967	—	3.00	6.00

7-Inch Extended Plays

CAPITOL

Number	Title (A Side/B Side)	Yr	VG	VG+	NM
❑ EAP 1-908	*On the Sunny Side of the Street/Exactly Like You/Robin Hood/Oh Babe	1957	3.75	7.50	15.00
❑ EAP 1-908 [PS]	The Wildest Show at Tahoe, Part 1	1957	3.75	7.50	15.00
❑ EAP 2-908	(contents unknown)	1957	3.75	7.50	15.00
❑ EAP 2-908 [PS]	The Wildest Show at Tahoe, Part 2	1957	3.75	7.50	15.00

PRIMA, LOUIS, AND KEELY SMITH

Also see each artist's individual listings.

CAPITOL

Number	Title (A Side/B Side)	Yr	VG	VG+	NM
❑ F4063	That Old Black Magic/You Are My Love	1958	3.00	6.00	12.00
❑ F4140	I've Got You Under My Skin/Don't Take Your Love from Me	1959	2.50	5.00	10.00

DOT

Number	Title (A Side/B Side)	Yr	VG	VG+	NM
❑ 15956	Bei Mir Bist Du Schoen/I Don't Know Why	1959	2.50	5.00	10.00
❑ 16042	Nyot! Nyot! Nyot! (The Pussycat Song)/Moshiya	1960	2.50	5.00	10.00
❑ 16192	Begin the Beguine/Surprise Package	1961	2.50	5.00	10.00
❑ 16221	Mustapha/The Shepard Man	1961	2.50	5.00	10.00
❑ 16249	Because of You/Absent Minded Lover	1961	2.50	5.00	10.00

TOD

Number	Title (A Side/B Side)	Yr	VG	VG+	NM
❑ 123	Oh Babe!/(B-side unknown)	196?	2.00	4.00	8.00

PRIMETTES, THE

Early version of THE SUPREMES.

LUPINE

Number	Title (A Side/B Side)	Yr	VG	VG+	NM
❑ 120	Tears of Sorrow/Pretty	1962	75.00	150.00	300.00

PRIMITIVES, THE (1)

PARKWAY

Number	Title (A Side/B Side)	Yr	VG	VG+	NM
❑ 940	Help Me/Let Them Fall	1965	5.00	10.00	20.00

PRIMITIVES, THE (2)

LOU REED was in this group.

PICKWICK

Number	Title (A Side/B Side)	Yr	VG	VG+	NM
❑ 1001	The Ostrich/Sneaky Pete	1964	75.00	150.00	300.00

PRINCE

Includes records as "Prince and the Revolution," "Prince and the N.P.G." (or New Power Generation); plus later releases as an unpronounceable glyph. Also see 94 EAST.

PAISLEY PARK

Number	Title (A Side/B Side)	Yr	VG	VG+	NM
❑ GWB 0528	Purple Rain/Raspberry Beret	1986	—	—	3.00
—"Back to Back Hits" reissue					
❑ GWB 0529	Pop Life/America	1986	—	—	3.00
—"Back to Back Hits" reissue					
❑ PRO-S-3371 [DJ]	I Wish U Heaven (Radio Edit of Remix)/I Wish U Heaven (Single Edit of Remix)	1988	3.75	7.50	15.00
❑ 18583	The Morning Papers/Live 4 Love	1993	—	—	3.00
❑ 18700	Damn U/2 Whom It May Concern	1993	—	—	3.00
❑ 18707	My Name Is Prince/Sexy Mutha	1992	—	—	3.00
❑ 18817	Sexy M.F./Strollin'	1992	—	—	3.00
❑ 18824	7/7 (Acoustic Version)	1992	—	—	3.00
❑ 19020	Money Don't Matter 2 Night/Call the Law	1992	—	—	3.00
❑ 19083	Diamonds and Pearls/X-Cerpts	1991	—	—	3.00
❑ 19090	Insatiable/I Love U in Me	1991	—	—	3.00
❑ 19175	Cream/Horny Pony	1991	—	—	3.00
❑ 19225	Gett Off/Horny Pony	1991	—	—	3.00
❑ 19525	New Power Generation/New Power Generation	1990	—	—	3.00
❑ 19751	Thieves in the Temple/Thieves in the Temple	1990	—	—	3.00
❑ 27745	I Wish U Heaven/Scarlet Pussy	1988	—	—	3.00
❑ 27745 [PS]	I Wish U Heaven/Scarlet Pussy	1988	—	—	3.00
❑ 27806	Glam Slam/Escape	1988	—	—	3.00
❑ 27806 [PS]	Glam Slam/Escape	1988	—	—	3.00
—Heavy plastic sleeve with title sticker					
❑ 27900	Alphabet St./Alphabet St. Part 2	1988	—	—	3.00
❑ 27900 [PS]	Alphabet St./Alphabet St. Part 2	1988	—	—	3.00
—Heavy plastic sleeve with title sticker					
❑ 28288	I Could Never Take the Place of Your Man/Hot Thing	1987	—	—	3.00
❑ 28288 [PS]	I Could Never Take the Place of Your Man/Hot Thing	1987	—	—	3.00
❑ 28289	U Got the Look/Housequake	1987	—	—	3.00
❑ 28289 [PS]	U Got the Look/Housequake	1987	—	—	3.00
❑ 28334	If I Was Your Girlfriend/Shockadelica	1987	—	—	3.00
❑ 28334 [PS]	If I Was Your Girlfriend/Shockadelica	1987	—	—	3.00
❑ 28399	Sign "O" the Times/La, La, La, Hee, Hee, Hee	1987	—	—	3.00
❑ 28399 [PS]	Sign "O" the Times/La, La, La, Hee, Hee, Hee	1987	—	—	3.00
❑ 28620	Anotherloverholenyohead/Girls and Boys	1986	—	—	3.00
❑ 28620 [PS]	Anotherloverholenyohead/Girls and Boys	1986	—	—	3.00
❑ 28711	Mountains/Alexa de Paris	1986	—	—	3.00
❑ 28711 [PS]	Mountains/Alexa de Paris	1986	—	—	3.00
❑ 28751	Kiss/Love or $	1986	—	—	3.00
❑ 28751 [PS]	Kiss/Love or $	1986	—	—	3.00
❑ 28972	Raspberry Beret/She's Always In My Hair	1985	—	—	3.00
❑ 28972 [PS]	Raspberry Beret/She's Always In My Hair	1985	—	—	3.00
❑ 28998	Pop Life/Hello	1985	—	—	3.00
❑ 28998 [PS]	Pop Life/Hello	1985	—	—	3.00
❑ 28999	America/Girl	1985	—	—	3.00
❑ 28999 [PS]	America/Girl	1985	—	—	3.00
❑ 29052	Paisley Park/She's Always In My Hair	1985	—	—	—
—Unreleased					
❑ 29052 [PS]	Paisley Park/She's Always In My Hair	1985	125.00	250.00	500.00

WARNER BROS.

Number	Title (A Side/B Side)	Yr	VG	VG+	NM
❑ GWB 0392	I Wanna Be Your Lover/Why You Wanna Treat Me So Bad?	1982	—	2.00	4.00
—"Back to Back Hits" reissue					
❑ GWB 0468	1999/Little Red Corvette	1984	—	—	3.00
—"Back to Back Hits" reissue					
❑ GWB 0476	Delirious/Let's Pretend We're Married	1984	—	—	3.00
—"Back to Back Hits" reissue					
❑ GWB 0516	When Doves Cry/Let's Go Crazy	1985	—	—	3.00
—"Back to Back Hits" reissue					
❑ GWB 0517	I Would Die 4 U/Take Me With U	1985	—	—	3.00
—"Back to Back Hits" reissue					
❑ 8619	Soft and Wet/So Blue	1978	7.50	15.00	30.00
❑ 8619 [DJ]	Soft and Wet (mono/stereo)	1978	3.75	7.50	15.00
❑ 8713	Just As Long As We're Together/In Love	1978	7.50	15.00	30.00
❑ 8713 [DJ]	Just As Long As We're Together (mono/stereo)	1978	3.75	7.50	15.00
❑ 17715	Gold/Rock 'N' Roll Is Alive! (and it lives in Minneapolis)	1995	—	—	3.00
❑ 17811	I Hate U/I Hate U	1995	—	—	3.00
❑ 17903	Purple Medley/Kirk J's B Sides Remix	1995	—	—	3.00
❑ 18012	Space (Radio Remix)/Space (Album Version)	1994	—	—	3.00
❑ 18074	Letitgo/Solo	1994	—	—	3.00
❑ 18371	Pink Cashmere/Soft and Wet	1993	—	—	3.00
❑ 18372	Peach/Nothing Compares 2 U (Live)	1993	—	—	3.00
❑ 21858	I Could Never Take the Place of Your Man/Alphabet St.	1989	—	—	3.00
—"Back to Back Hits" series					
❑ 21859	Batdance/Partyman	1989	—	—	3.00
—"Back to Back Hits" series					
❑ 21938	Sign "O" the Times/U Got the Look	1988	—	—	3.00
—"Back to Back Hits" series					
❑ 21980	Anotherloverholenyohead/Mountains	1987	—	—	3.00
—"Back to Back Hits" series					
❑ 21981	Uptown/Controversy	1987	—	—	3.00
—"Back to Back Hits" series					
❑ 21982	Kiss/Soft and Wet	1987	—	—	3.00
—"Back to Back Hits" series					
❑ 22757	The Arms of Orion/I Love U in Me	1989	—	—	3.00
❑ 22757 [PS]	The Arms of Orion/I Love U in Me	1989	—	—	3.00
—With Sheena Easton					
❑ 22814	Partyman/Feel U Up	1989	—	—	3.00
❑ 22814 [PS]	Partyman/Feel U Up	1989	—	—	3.00
❑ 22824	Scandalous/When 2 R In Love	1989	—	—	3.00
❑ 22824 [PS]	Scandalous/When 2 R In Love	1989	—	—	3.00
❑ 22924	Batdance/200 Balloons	1989	—	—	3.00
❑ 22924 [PS]	Batdance/200 Balloons	1989	—	—	3.00
❑ 29079	Take Me With U/Baby I'm a Star	1985	—	2.00	4.00
❑ 29079 [PS]	Take Me With U/Baby I'm a Star	1985	—	2.00	4.00
❑ 29121	I Would Die 4 U/Another Lonely Christmas	1984	—	2.00	4.00
❑ 29121 [PS]	I Would Die 4 U/Another Lonely Christmas	1984	—	2.00	4.00
❑ 29174	Purple Rain/God	1984	—	2.00	4.00
—Purple vinyl					
❑ 29174	Purple Rain/God	1984	2.00	4.00	8.00
—Black vinyl					
❑ 29174 [PS]	Purple Rain/God	1984	2.00	4.00	8.00
—Plastic semi-transparent sleeve					
❑ 29216	Let's Go Crazy/Erotic City	1984	—	2.00	4.00
❑ 29216 [PS]	Let's Go Crazy/Erotic City	1984	2.00	4.00	8.00
❑ 29286	When Doves Cry/17 Days	1984	5.00	10.00	20.00
—Purple vinyl					

Number	Title (A Side/B Side)	Yr	VG	VG+	NM
❑ 29286	When Doves Cry/17 Days	1984	—	—	3.00
—Black vinyl					
❑ 29286 [DJ]	When Doves Cry (same on both sides)	1984	2.50	5.00	10.00
❑ 29286 [PS]	When Doves Cry/17 Days	1984	—	—	3.00
❑ 29503	Delirious/Horny Toad	1983	—	3.00	6.00
—Label erroneously lists A-side time at 3:56					
❑ 29503	Delirious/Horny Toad	1983	—	—	5.00
—Label lists correct A-side time of 2:36					
❑ 29503 [PS]	Delirious/Horny Toad	1983	12.50	25.00	50.00
—Fold-out poster sleeve					
❑ 29548	Let's Pretend We're Married/Irresistible Bitch	1983	—	2.50	5.00
❑ 29548 [PS]	Let's Pretend We're Married/Irresistible Bitch	1983	2.50	5.00	10.00
❑ 29746	Little Red Corvette/All the Critics Love U in New York	1983	—	2.50	5.00
—Not issued with picture sleeve in U.S.					
❑ 29896	1999/How Come U Don't Call Me Anymore?	1982	—	2.50	5.00
❑ 29896 [PS]	1999/How Come U Don't Call Me Anymore?	1982	2.50	5.00	10.00
❑ 29942	Do Me, Baby/Private Joy	1982	3.75	7.50	15.00
❑ 29942 [DJ]	Do Me, Baby (same on both sides)	1982	—	3.75	7.50
❑ 49050	I Wanna Be Your Lover/My Love Is Forever	1979	2.50	5.00	10.00
❑ 49050 [DJ]	I Wanna Be Your Lover (mono/stereo)	1979	3.75	7.50	15.00
❑ 49050 [DJ]	My Love Is Forever (mono/stereo)	1979	3.75	7.50	15.00
❑ 49050 [PS]	My Love Is Forever	1979	18.75	37.50	75.00
—Promo-only sleeve; withdrawn when "I Wanna Be Your Lover" was pushed as the A-side					
❑ 49178	Why You Wanna Treat Me So Bad/Baby	1980	7.50	15.00	30.00
❑ 49178 [DJ]	Why You Wanna Treat Me So Bad (mono/stereo)	1980	3.75	7.50	15.00
❑ 49178 [PS]	Why You Wanna Treat Me So Bad/Baby	1980	15.00	30.00	60.00
❑ 49226	Still Waiting/Bambi	1980	3.75	7.50	15.00
❑ 49226 [DJ]	Still Waiting (mono/stereo)	1980	—	3.75	7.50
❑ 49559	Uptown/Crazy You	1980	3.75	7.50	15.00
❑ 49559 [DJ]	Uptown (mono/stereo)	1980	—	3.75	7.50
❑ 49559 [PS]	Uptown/Crazy You	1980	3.75	7.50	15.00
❑ 49638	Dirty Mind/When We're Dancing Close and Slow	1980	3.75	7.50	15.00
❑ 49638 [DJ]	Dirty Mind (same on both sides)	1980	—	3.75	7.50
❑ 49808	Controversy/When You Were Mine	1981	3.75	7.50	15.00
❑ 49808 [DJ]	Controversy (same on both sides)	1981	—	3.75	7.50
❑ 50002	Let's Work/Ronnie Talk to Russia	1982	3.75	7.50	15.00
❑ 50002 [DJ]	Let's Work (same on both sides)	1982	—	3.75	7.50

PRINCE, BOBBY

Number	Title (A Side/B Side)	Yr	VG	VG+	NM
CHANCE					
❑ 1128	Tell Me Why, Why, Why/I Want to Hold You	1953	125.00	250.00	500.00
❑ 1158	Better Think It Over/If You Only Knew	1954	100.00	200.00	400.00
EXCELLO					
❑ 2039	Too Many Keys/Please Give Me Your Love	1954	20.00	40.00	80.00

PRINCE BUSTER

Number	Title (A Side/B Side)	Yr	VG	VG+	NM
AMY					
❑ 906	Everybody Ska/30 Pieces of Silver	1964	3.75	7.50	15.00
ATLANTIC					
❑ 2231	Don't Make Me Cry/That Lucky Old Sun	1964	3.75	7.50	15.00
PHILIPS					
❑ 40427	Ten Commandments/Don't Make Me Cry	1967	3.00	6.00	12.00
RCA VICTOR					
❑ 47-9114	Ten Commandments from Woman to Man/Ain't That Saying a Lot	1967	3.00	6.00	12.00

PRISONAIRES, THE

Number	Title (A Side/B Side)	Yr	VG	VG+	NM
SUN					
❑ 186	Just Walking in the Rain/Baby Please	1953	125.00	250.00	500.00
❑ 186	Just Walking in the Rain/Baby Please	1953	2500.	3750.	5000.
—Red vinyl					
❑ 189	Softly and Tenderly/My God Is Real	1953	175.00	350.00	700.00
❑ 191	A Prisoner's Prayer/I Know	1953	125.00	250.00	500.00
❑ 207	There Is Love in You/What'll You Do Next	1954	5000.	8500.	12000.

PROBY, P.J.

Number	Title (A Side/B Side)	Yr	VG	VG+	NM
BETA					
❑ 1008	Loud Perfume/(B-side unknown)	1958	50.00	100.00	200.00
—As "Jett Powers"					
DESIGN					
❑ 811	Go Girl Go/(B-side unknown)	1957	75.00	150.00	300.00
—As "Jett Powers"					
IMPERIAL					
❑ 66079	Rocking Pneumonia/Just Call, I'll Be There	1964	3.75	7.50	15.00
❑ 66084	Somewhere/Just Like Him	1965	—	—	—
—Unreleased					
LIBERTY					
❑ 55367	There Stands the One/Try to Forget Her	1961	3.75	7.50	15.00
❑ 55505	The Other Side of Town/Watch Me Walk Away	1962	3.75	7.50	15.00
❑ 55588	So Do I/I Can't Take It Like You Can	1963	3.75	7.50	15.00
❑ 55757	Somewhere/Just Like Him	1964	3.00	6.00	12.00
❑ 55777	Rocking Pneumonia/I Apologize	1965	3.00	6.00	12.00
❑ 55791	Stagger Lee/Mission Bell	1965	3.00	6.00	12.00
❑ 55806	That Means a Lot/Let the Water Run Down	1965	3.75	7.50	15.00
—The A-side is a Lennon-McCartney song; the Beatles' own version was not released until 1996					
❑ 55850	Good Things Are Coming My Way/Maria	1965	3.00	6.00	12.00
❑ 55875	My Prayer/Wicked Woman	1966	3.00	6.00	12.00
❑ 55915	I Can't Make It Alone/If I Ruled the World	1966	3.00	6.00	12.00
❑ 55915 [PS]	I Can't Make It Alone/If I Ruled the World	1966	3.75	7.50	15.00
❑ 55936	Niki-Hoeky/Good Things Are Coming My Way	1966	2.50	5.00	10.00
❑ 55974	Work with Me Annie/You Can't Come Home Again (If You Leave Me Now)	1967	2.50	5.00	10.00
❑ 55974 [PS]	Work with Me Annie/You Can't Come Home Again (If You Leave Me Now)	1967	3.75	7.50	15.00
❑ 55989	Butterfly High/Just Holding On	1967	2.50	5.00	10.00
❑ 56031	It's Your Day Today/I Apologize	1968	2.00	4.00	8.00
❑ 56051	What's Wrong with My World/Turn Her Away	1968	2.00	4.00	8.00
LONDON					
❑ 9648	Hold Me/The Tip of My Fingers	1964	3.75	7.50	15.00
❑ 9688	Hold Me/The Tip of My Fingers	1964	3.75	7.50	15.00
❑ 9705	Sweet and Tender Romance/Together	1964	3.75	7.50	15.00
SURFSIDE					
❑ 714	You Got Me Crying/I Need Love	1965	5.00	10.00	20.00
UNITED ARTISTS					
❑ 0070	Niki-Hoeky/Let the Water Run Down	1973	—	2.00	4.00
—"Silver Spotlight Series" reissue					

PROCOL HARUM

Also see THE PARAMOUNTS (4); ROBIN TROWER.

Number	Title (A Side/B Side)	Yr	VG	VG+	NM
A&M					
❑ 885	Homburg/Good Captain Clack	1967	3.00	6.00	12.00
❑ 927	In the Wee Small Hours of Sixpence/Quite Rightly So	1968	3.00	6.00	12.00
❑ 1069	A Salty Dog/Long Gone Geek	1969	2.00	4.00	8.00
❑ 1111	The Devil Came from Kansas/Boredom	1969	2.00	4.00	8.00
❑ 1218	Whiskey Train/About to Die	1970	—	3.00	6.00
❑ 1264	Power Failure/Broken Barricades	1971	—	3.00	6.00
❑ 1287	Song for a Dreamer/Simple Sister	1971	—	3.00	6.00
❑ 1287 [PS]	Song for a Dreamer/Simple Sister	1971	2.50	5.00	10.00
❑ 1347	Conquistador/A Salty Dog	1972	—	2.50	5.00
❑ 1347 [PS]	Conquistador/A Salty Dog	1972	2.00	4.00	8.00
❑ 1389	A Whiter Shade of Pale/Lime Street Blues	1972	—	2.50	5.00
❑ 1389 [PS]	A Whiter Shade of Pale/Lime Street Blues	1972	—	2.50	5.00
CHRYSALIS					
❑ 2011 [DJ]	Bringing Home the Bacon (mono/stereo)	1973	2.00	4.00	8.00
—May be promo only					
❑ 2013	Grand Hotel/Fires	1973	—	2.50	5.00
❑ 2013 [PS]	Grand Hotel/Fires	1973	2.50	5.00	10.00
❑ 2032	Nothing But the Truth/Drunk Again	1973	—	2.50	5.00
❑ 2109	Pandora's Box/Piper's Tune	1975	—	2.50	5.00
DERAM					
❑ 7507	A Whiter Shade of Pale/Lime Street Blues	1967	3.75	7.50	15.00
WARNER BROS.					
❑ CRS 2115	Wizard Man/Something Magic	1977	—	3.00	6.00
—Warner Bros. label with Chrysalis number; possible factory mispress?					

PROCTOR, BILLY

Number	Title (A Side/B Side)	Yr	VG	VG+	NM
EPIC					
❑ 50160	(I'm Gonna) Chop Down That Oak Tree/Keeping Up with the Joneses	1975	—	2.50	5.00
SOUL					
❑ 35099	What Is Black/I Can Take It All	1972	5.00	10.00	20.00

PROFESSOR MORRISON'S LOLLIPOP

Number	Title (A Side/B Side)	Yr	VG	VG+	NM
WHITE WHALE					
❑ 275	Gypsy Lady/You Got the Love	1968	2.50	5.00	10.00
❑ 288	Angela/Duba Duba Doo	1968	2.50	5.00	10.00
❑ 293	Oo Poo Pah Susie/You Can Take It	1969	2.50	5.00	10.00

PROFFITT, RANDY, AND THE BEACHCOMBERS

Number	Title (A Side/B Side)	Yr	VG	VG+	NM
BETT-COE					
❑ 103	Check That Baby Out One Time/Young Love in Spring	1967	12.50	25.00	50.00

PROFILES, THE (1)

Number	Title (A Side/B Side)	Yr	VG	VG+	NM
BAMBOO					
❑ 104	Got to Be Love (Something Stupid)/You Don't Care About Me	1969	2.00	4.00	8.00
❑ 108	Be Careful/I Still Love You	1969	2.00	4.00	8.00
❑ 115	A Little Misunderstanding/Got to Be Love	1970	2.00	4.00	8.00
DUO					
❑ 7449	If I Didn't Love You/(B-side unknown)	1968	2.50	5.00	10.00

PROFILES, THE (2)

Number	Title (A Side/B Side)	Yr	VG	VG+	NM
GAIT					
❑ 1444	Never/Right By Her Side	1962	50.00	100.00	200.00

PROGRESSIVES, THE

Number	Title (A Side/B Side)	Yr	VG	VG+	NM
DOT					
❑ 16514	Hot Cinders/Man of Mystery	1963	5.00	10.00	20.00

PROW, JIMMY LEE

Number	Title (A Side/B Side)	Yr	VG	VG+	NM
KING					
❑ 4929	Shopping List/You Tell Her, I Stutter	1956	7.50	15.00	30.00

PRYOR, SNOOKY

Number	Title (A Side/B Side)	Yr	VG	VG+	NM
J.O.B.					
❑ 1014	Cryin' Shame/Eight, Nine, Ten	1953	100.00	200.00	400.00
❑ 1126	Uncle Sam, Don't Take My Man/Boogie Twist	1963	50.00	100.00	200.00
PARROTLL					
❑ 807	Crosstown Blues/I Want You for Myself	1954	375.00	750.00	1500.
—Black vinyl					
❑ 807	Crosstown Blues/I Want You for Myself	1954	625.00	1250.	2500.
—Red vinyl					
VEE JAY					
❑ 215	Judgment Day/Someone to Love Me	1956	30.00	60.00	120.00

PUCKETT, GARY, AND THE UNION GAP

Includes Gary Puckett solo and records credited to "The Union Gap Featuring Gary Puckett."

Number	Title (A Side/B Side)	Yr	VG	VG+	NM
COLUMBIA					
❑ 44297	Woman, Woman/Don't Make Promises	1967	2.00	4.00	8.00
❑ 44297 [PS]	Woman, Woman/Don't Make Promises	1967	3.00	6.00	12.00
—As "The Union Gap"					
❑ 44450	Young Girl/I'm Losing You	1968	2.00	4.00	8.00
❑ 44450 [PS]	Young Girl/I'm Losing You	1968	3.00	6.00	12.00
—As "The Union Gap"					
❑ 44547	Lady Willpower/Daylight Strangers	1968	2.00	4.00	8.00
❑ 44547 [PS]	Lady Willpower/Daylight Strangers	1968	3.00	6.00	12.00
—As "The Union Gap"					
❑ 44644	Over You/If the Day Would Come	1968	—	3.00	6.00
❑ 44644 [PS]	Over You/If the Day Would Come	1968	3.00	6.00	12.00
❑ 44788	Don't Give In to Him/Could I	1969	—	3.00	6.00

Number	Title (A Side/B Side)	Yr	VG	VG+	NM
❑ 44967	This Girl Is a Woman Now/His Other Woman	1969	—	3.00	6.00
❑ 45097	Let's Give Adam and Eve Another Chance/The Beggar	1970	—	3.00	6.00
❑ 45097 [PS]	Let's Give Adam and Eve Another Chance/The Beggar	1970	2.00	4.00	8.00
❑ 45249	I Just Don't Know What to Do With Myself/All That Matters	1970	—	2.50	5.00
❑ 45303	Keep the Customer Satisfied/No One Really Knows	1971	—	2.50	5.00
❑ 45358	Life Has Its Little Ups and Downs/Shimmering Eyes	1971	—	2.50	5.00
❑ 45438	Hello Morning/Gentle Woman	1971	—	2.50	5.00
❑ 45509	Hello Morning/I Can't Hold On	1971	—	2.50	5.00
❑ 45678	Bless the Child/Leavin' in the Morning	1972	—	2.50	5.00

PUFNSTUF
DECCA

Number	Title (A Side/B Side)	Yr	VG	VG+	NM
❑ 32702	Pufnstuf/Nonsense	1970	3.75	7.50	15.00

PULLEN, DWIGHT
CARLTON

Number	Title (A Side/B Side)	Yr	VG	VG+	NM
❑ 455	Sunglasses After Dark/Teenage Bug	1958	75.00	150.00	300.00

SAGE AND SAND

Number	Title (A Side/B Side)	Yr	VG	VG+	NM
❑ 279	By You, By the Bayou/It's Over With	1959	7.50	15.00	30.00
❑ 283	I Live a Lifetime Last Night/You'll Get Yours Some Day	1959	7.50	15.00	30.00

PULLEN, WHITEY
SAGE AND SAND

Number	Title (A Side/B Side)	Yr	VG	VG+	NM
❑ 274	Walk My Way Back Home/Don't Make Me Cry	1958	62.50	125.00	250.00
❑ 294	Let's All Go Wild Tonight/Gently	1959	37.50	75.00	150.00
❑ 303	I'm Beggin' Your Pardon/Let Your Left Hand Know	1960	25.00	50.00	100.00
❑ 313	Tuscaloosa Lucy/Waltz of the Steel Guitar	1960	30.00	60.00	120.00
❑ 372	Crazy in Love/I Won the Day I Lost You	1962	10.00	20.00	40.00

PURIFY, JAMES AND BOBBY
BELL

Number	Title (A Side/B Side)	Yr	VG	VG+	NM
❑ 648	I'm Your Puppet/So Many Reasons	1966	3.75	7.50	15.00
❑ 660	Wish You Didn't Have to Go/You Can't Keep a Good Man Down	1967	2.00	4.00	8.00
❑ 669	Shake a Tail Feather/Goodness Gracious	1967	3.00	6.00	12.00
❑ 680	I Take What I Want/Sixteen Tons	1967	2.00	4.00	8.00
❑ 685	Let Love Come Between Us/I Don't Want to Have to Go	1967	2.00	4.00	8.00
❑ 700	Do Unto Me/Everybody Needs Somebody	1967	2.00	4.00	8.00
❑ 721	I Can Remember/I Was Born to Lose Out	1968	2.00	4.00	8.00
❑ 735	Help Yourself (To All of My Lovin')/Last Piece of Love	1968	2.00	4.00	8.00
❑ 751	Untie Me/We're Finally Gonna Make It	1968	2.00	4.00	8.00
❑ 774	I Don't Know What It Is You Got/Section C	1969	2.00	4.00	8.00

CASABLANCA

Number	Title (A Side/B Side)	Yr	VG	VG+	NM
❑ 812	Do Your Thing/Why Love	1974	—	2.50	5.00
❑ 827	Man Can't Be a Man Without a Woman/You and Me Together Forever	1975	—	2.50	5.00
❑ 830	All the Love I Got/(B-side unknown)	1975	—	2.50	5.00

MERCURY

Number	Title (A Side/B Side)	Yr	VG	VG+	NM
❑ 73767	I'm Your Puppet/Lay Me Down Easy	1976	—	2.50	5.00
❑ 73806	Morning Glory/Turning Back the Pages	1976	—	2.50	5.00
❑ 73884	I Ain't Got to Love Nobody Else/What's Better Than Love	1977	—	2.50	5.00
❑ 73893	Get Closer/What's Better Than Love	1977	—	2.50	5.00

PHILCO-FORD

Number	Title (A Side/B Side)	Yr	VG	VG+	NM
❑ HP-28	I'm Your Puppet/Goodnight Gracious	1968	3.75	7.50	15.00

—4-inch plastic "Hip Pocket Record" with color sleeve

SPHERE SOUND

Number	Title (A Side/B Side)	Yr	VG	VG+	NM
❑ 77004	I'm Your Puppet/Everybody Needs Somebody	196?	2.00	4.00	8.00

PYRAMIDS, THE
More than one group.

BEST

Number	Title (A Side/B Side)	Yr	VG	VG+	NM
❑ 1	Pyramid's Stomp/Paul	1963	7.50	15.00	30.00
❑ 102	Penetration/Here Comes Marsha	1963	10.00	20.00	40.00
❑ 13001	Pyramid's Stomp/Paul	1963	5.00	10.00	20.00
❑ 13002	Penetration/Here Comes Marsha	1964	5.00	10.00	20.00
—No mention of London Records on label					
❑ 13002	Penetration/Here Comes Marsha	1964	3.75	7.50	15.00
—With "Dist. by London" or similar wording on label					
❑ 13002 [PS]	Penetration/Here Comes Marsha	1964	10.00	20.00	40.00
—Red sleeve					
❑ 13002 [PS]	Penetration/Here Comes Marsha	1964	10.00	20.00	40.00
—Black sleeve					

CEDWICKE

Number	Title (A Side/B Side)	Yr	VG	VG+	NM
❑ 13005	Midnight Run/Custom Caravan	1964	10.00	20.00	40.00
❑ 13006	Contact/Pressure	1964	10.00	20.00	40.00

CUB

Number	Title (A Side/B Side)	Yr	VG	VG+	NM
❑ 9112	I'm the Playboy/Cryin'	1962	5.00	10.00	20.00

DAVIS

Number	Title (A Side/B Side)	Yr	VG	VG+	NM
❑ 453	At Any Cost/Okay, Baby!	1956	12.50	25.00	50.00
❑ 457	Why Did You Go/Before It's Too Late	1957	12.50	25.00	50.00

FEDERAL

Number	Title (A Side/B Side)	Yr	VG	VG+	NM
❑ 12233	Deep in My Heart for You/And I Need You	1955	100.00	200.00	400.00

HOLLYWOOD

Number	Title (A Side/B Side)	Yr	VG	VG+	NM
❑ 1047	Someday/Bow Wow	1955	125.00	250.00	500.00

RCA VICTOR

Number	Title (A Side/B Side)	Yr	VG	VG+	NM
❑ 47-7556	Long Long Time/Oh No You Won't (Oh Yes You Will)	1959	3.75	7.50	15.00

SHELL

Number	Title (A Side/B Side)	Yr	VG	VG+	NM
❑ 304	Ankle Bracelet/Hot Dog Dooly Wah	1961	6.25	12.50	25.00
—As "The Original Pyramids"					
❑ 711	Ankle Bracelet/Hot Dog Dooly Wah	1958	12.50	25.00	50.00

SONBERT

Number	Title (A Side/B Side)	Yr	VG	VG+	NM
❑ 82861	I'm the Playboy/Cryin'	1962	10.00	20.00	40.00

VEE JAY

Number	Title (A Side/B Side)	Yr	VG	VG+	NM
❑ 489	What Is Love/Shakin' Fit	1963	6.25	12.50	25.00

PYTHON LEE JACKSON
With ROD STEWART on vocals.

GNP CRESCENDO

Number	Title (A Side/B Side)	Yr	VG	VG+	NM
❑ 449	In a Broken Dream/Doin' Fine	1972	—	3.00	6.00
❑ 449	In a Broken Dream/Turn the Music Down	1972	—	3.00	6.00
❑ 462	Cloud Nine/Rod's Blues	1973	—	3.00	6.00

Q

QUADRANGLE, THE
PHILIPS

Number	Title (A Side/B Side)	Yr	VG	VG+	NM
❑ 40408	She's Too Familiar Now/No More Time	1966	7.50	15.00	30.00

QUADRELLS, THE
WHIRLIN' DISC

Number	Title (A Side/B Side)	Yr	VG	VG+	NM
❑ 103	What Can the Matter Be/Come to Me	1957	17.50	35.00	70.00

QUADS, THE
VAULT

Number	Title (A Side/B Side)	Yr	VG	VG+	NM
❑ 907	Surfin' Hearse/Little Queenie	1963	10.00	20.00	40.00

QUAILS, THE (1)
See BILL ROBINSON AND THE QUAILS.

QUAILS, THE (2)
HARVEY

Number	Title (A Side/B Side)	Yr	VG	VG+	NM
❑ 116	My Love/Never Felt Like This Before	1961	12.50	25.00	50.00
❑ 120	I Thought/Over the Hump	1963	12.50	25.00	50.00

QUAITE, CHRISTINE
WORLD ARTISTS

Number	Title (A Side/B Side)	Yr	VG	VG+	NM
❑ 1022	Tell Me Mamma/In the Middle of the Floor	1964	3.00	6.00	12.00
❑ 1028	Mr. Stuck Up/Will You Be the Same Tomorrow	1964	3.00	6.00	12.00

QUARTER NOTES, THE (1)
BISON

Number	Title (A Side/B Side)	Yr	VG	VG+	NM
❑ 757	Frantic Flip/Canadian Sunset	1960	7.50	15.00	30.00

IMPERIAL

Number	Title (A Side/B Side)	Yr	VG	VG+	NM
❑ 5647	Frantic Flip/Canadian Sunset	1960	3.75	7.50	15.00

WIZZ

Number	Title (A Side/B Side)	Yr	VG	VG+	NM
❑ 715	Record Hop Blues/Suki-Yaki-Rocki	1959	6.25	12.50	25.00

QUARTER NOTES, THE (2)
BOOM

Number	Title (A Side/B Side)	Yr	VG	VG+	NM
❑ 60018	Hey Little Girl/I've Been Loved	1966	3.75	7.50	15.00

QUARTER NOTES, THE (3)
DELUXE

Number	Title (A Side/B Side)	Yr	VG	VG+	NM
❑ 6116	Loneliness/Come De Nite	1957	6.25	12.50	25.00
❑ 6129	My Fantasy/Ten Minutes to Midnight	1957	6.25	12.50	25.00

QUARTER NOTES, THE (U)
Some of these could be group (1) or (3).

DOT

Number	Title (A Side/B Side)	Yr	VG	VG+	NM
❑ 15685	Please Come Home/Like You Bug Me	1958	6.25	12.50	25.00

GUYDEN

Number	Title (A Side/B Side)	Yr	VG	VG+	NM
❑ 2083	Pretty Pretty Eyes/I Don't Wanna Go Home	1963	5.00	10.00	20.00

RCA VICTOR

Number	Title (A Side/B Side)	Yr	VG	VG+	NM
❑ 47-7327	The Interview/Punkanilla	1958	3.75	7.50	15.00

QUARTERFLASH
Also see SEAFOOD MAMA.

GEFFEN

Number	Title (A Side/B Side)	Yr	VG	VG+	NM
❑ 28894	Walking on Ice/Come to Me	1985	—	—	3.00
❑ 28894 [PS]	Walking on Ice/Come to Me	1985	—	—	3.00
❑ 28908	Talk to Me/Grace Under Fire	1985	—	—	3.00
❑ 28908 [PS]	Talk to Me/Grace Under Fire	1985	—	—	3.00
❑ 29523	Take Another Picture/One More Round to Go	1983	—	2.00	4.00
❑ 29523 [PS]	Take Another Picture/One More Round to Go	1983	—	2.00	4.00
❑ 29603	Take Me to Heart/Nowhere Left to Hide	1983	—	2.00	4.00
❑ 29603 [PS]	Take Me to Heart/Nowhere Left to Hide	1983	—	2.00	4.00
❑ 29882	Try to Make It True/Critical Times	1982	—	2.00	4.00
❑ 29994	Right Kind of Love/You're Holdin' Me Back	1982	—	2.00	4.00
❑ 29994 [PS]	Right Kind of Love/You're Holdin' Me Back	1982	—	2.00	4.00
❑ 49824	Harden My Heart/Don't Be Lonely	1981	—	2.00	4.00
❑ 50006	Find Another Fool/Cruisin' with the Deuce	1982	—	2.00	4.00
❑ 50006 [PS]	Find Another Fool/Cruisin' with the Deuce	1982	—	2.00	4.00

WARNER BROS.

Number	Title (A Side/B Side)	Yr	VG	VG+	NM
❑ 29932	Night Shift/Love Should Be So Kind	1982	—	2.00	4.00

QUATRO, SUZI
Also see THE PLEASURE SEEKERS.

ARISTA

Number	Title (A Side/B Side)	Yr	VG	VG+	NM
❑ 0106	Your Mama Won't Like Me/Peter Peter	1975	—	2.50	5.00

BELL

Number	Title (A Side/B Side)	Yr	VG	VG+	NM
❑ 45401	48 Crash/Little Bitch Blue	1973	—	2.50	5.00
❑ 45416	Can the Can/48 Crash	1973	—	2.50	5.00
❑ 45477	All Shook Up/Glycerine Queen	1974	—	2.50	5.00
❑ 45609	Devil Gate Drive/In the Morning	1974	—	2.50	5.00
❑ 45615	Keep a-Knockin'/Cat Size	1974	—	2.50	5.00

BIG TREE

Number	Title (A Side/B Side)	Yr	VG	VG+	NM
❑ 16053	Can the Can/Don't Mess Around	1975	—	2.50	5.00

DREAMLAND

Number	Title (A Side/B Side)	Yr	VG	VG+	NM
❑ 104	Rock Hard/State of Mind	1980	—	2.00	4.00
❑ 104 [PS]	Rock Hard/State of Mind	1980	—	2.00	4.00
❑ 107	Lipstick/Woman Cry	1980	—	2.00	4.00

Number	Title (A Side/B Side)	Yr	VG	VG+	NM
RAK					
❑ 4512	Brain Confusion (For All the Lonely People)/ Rolling Stone	1972	2.50	5.00	10.00
RSO					
❑ 917	Stumblin' In/A Stranger to Paradise	1979	—	2.00	4.00
—With Chris Norman (lead singer of Smokie)					
❑ 929	If You Can't Give Me Love/Non-Citizen	1979	—	2.00	4.00
❑ 1001	I've Never Been in Love/Space Cadets	1979	—	2.00	4.00
❑ 1014	Starlight Lady/She's in Love with You	1979	—	2.00	4.00

QUEEN

Also see BRIAN MAY AND FRIENDS; FREDDIE MERCURY; ROGER TAYLOR.

Number	Title (A Side/B Side)	Yr	VG	VG+	NM
CAPITOL					
❑ B-5317	Radio Ga Ga/I Go Crazy	1984	—	2.00	4.00
❑ B-5317 [PS]	Radio Ga Ga/I Go Crazy	1984	—	2.00	4.00
❑ B-5350	I Want to Break Free/Machines (Or Back to Humans)	1984	—	2.00	4.00
❑ B-5350 [PS]	I Want to Break Free/Machines (Or Back to Humans)	1984	—	2.50	5.00
—With Freddie Mercury in center					
❑ B-5350 [PS]	I Want to Break Free/Machines (Or Back to Humans)	1984	—	2.50	5.00
—With Brian May in center					
❑ B-5350 [PS]	I Want to Break Free/Machines (Or Back to Humans)	1984	—	2.50	5.00
—With Roger Taylor in center					
❑ B-5350 [PS]	I Want to Break Free/Machines (Or Back to Humans)	1984	—	2.50	5.00
—With John Deacon in center					
❑ B-5372	It's a Hard Life/Is This the World We Created?	1984	—	2.50	5.00
❑ B-5372 [PS]	It's a Hard Life/Is This the World We Created?	1984	—	2.50	5.00
❑ B-5424	Hammer to Fall/Tear It Up	1984	—	2.50	5.00
❑ B-5424 [PS]	Hammer to Fall/Tear It Up	1984	—	2.50	5.00
❑ B-5530	One Vision/Blurred Vision	1985	—	2.00	4.00
❑ B-5530 [PS]	One Vision/Blurred Vision	1985	—	2.00	4.00
❑ B-5568	Princes of the Universe/A Dozen Red Roses for My Darling	1985	—	2.00	4.00
❑ B-5568 [PS]	Princes of the Universe/A Dozen Red Roses for My Darling	1985	—	2.00	4.00
❑ B-5590	A Kind of Magic/A Dozen Red Roses for My Darling	1986	—	2.00	4.00
❑ B-5590 [PS]	A Kind of Magic/A Dozen Red Roses for My Darling	1986	—	2.00	4.00
❑ B-5633	Pain Is So Close to Pleasure/Don't Lose Your Head	1986	—	2.00	4.00
❑ B-5633 [PS]	Pain Is So Close to Pleasure/Don't Lose Your Head	1986	—	2.00	4.00
❑ 7PRO-9114 [DJ]	I Want to Break Free	1984	3.00	6.00	12.00
—No song title or name of group on label					
❑ 7PRO-9546/7 [DJ]	One Vision (4:00)/One Vision (3:46)	1985	3.00	6.00	12.00
❑ B-44372	I Want It All/Hang On In There	1989	—	2.50	5.00
❑ B-44372 [PS]	I Want It All/Hang On In There	1989	—	2.50	5.00
❑ 7PRO-79685 [DJ]	Breakthru (same on both sides)	1989	3.00	6.00	12.00
—Vinyl is promo only					
ELEKTRA					
❑ 45226	Killer Queen/Flick of the Wrist	1975	2.00	4.00	8.00
❑ 45268	Keep Yourself Alive//Lily of the Valley/God Save the Queen	1975	2.00	4.00	8.00
❑ 45297	Bohemian Rhapsody/I'm in Love with My Car	1975	2.00	4.00	8.00
—Butterfly label					
❑ 45297	Bohemian Rhapsody/I'm in Love with My Car	1976	2.50	5.00	10.00
—Red label, much scarcer than butterfly label					
❑ 45318	You're My Best Friend/'39	1976	—	3.00	6.00
—Butterfly label					
❑ 45318	You're My Best Friend/'39	1976	2.50	5.00	10.00
—Red label, much scarcer than butterfly label					
❑ 45362	Somebody to Love/White Man	1976	—	3.00	6.00
—Butterfly label					
❑ 45362	Somebody to Love/White Man	1976	2.50	5.00	10.00
—Red label, much scarcer than butterfly label					
❑ 45385	Tie Your Mother Down/Drowse	1977	—	3.00	6.00
❑ 45412	Long Way/You and I	1977	2.00	4.00	8.00
❑ 45441	We Are the Champions/We Will Rock You	1977	—	3.00	6.00
❑ 45441 [PS]	We Are the Champions/We Will Rock You	1977	2.50	5.00	10.00
❑ 45478	It's Late/Sheer Heart Attack	1978	—	3.00	6.00
❑ 45478 [PS]	It's Late/Sheer Heart Attack	1978	2.50	5.00	10.00
❑ 45541	Bicycle Race/Fat Bottomed Girls	1978	—	3.00	6.00
❑ 45541 [PS]	Bicycle Race/Fat Bottomed Girls	1978	3.00	6.00	12.00
❑ 45863	Keep Yourself Alive/Son and Daughter	1973	3.75	7.50	15.00
❑ 45884	Liar/Doing All Right	1974	3.00	6.00	12.00
❑ 45891	Seven Seas of Rhye/See What a Fool I've Been	1974	3.00	6.00	12.00
❑ 46008	Don't Stop Me Now/More of That Jazz	1979	—	3.00	6.00
❑ 46039	Jealousy/Fun It	1979	—	3.00	6.00
❑ 46532	We Will Rock You (Live)/Let Me Entertain You	1979	2.00	4.00	8.00
❑ 46579	Crazy Little Thing Called Love/Spread Your Wings	1979	—	2.00	4.00
❑ 46652	Play the Game/A Human Body	1980	—	2.00	4.00
❑ 46652 [PS]	Play the Game/A Human Body	1980	—	2.50	5.00
❑ 47031	Another One Bites the Dust/Don't Try Suicide	1980	—	2.00	4.00
❑ 47086	Need Your Loving Tonight/Rock It (prime jive)	1980	—	2.00	4.00
❑ 47092	Flash's Theme AKA Flash/Football Fight	1980	—	2.00	4.00
❑ 47092 [PS]	Flash's Theme AKA Flash/Football Fight	1980	—	2.50	5.00
❑ 47235	Under Pressure/Soul Brother	1981	—	2.00	4.00
—A-side with David Bowie					
❑ 47235 [PS]	Under Pressure/Soul Brother	1981	—	3.00	6.00
❑ 47452	Body Language/Life Is Real (Song for Lennon)	1981	—	2.00	4.00
—Most copies of this did not come with picture sleeves					
❑ 47452 [PS]	Body Language/Life Is Real (Song for Lennon)	1981	3.75	7.50	15.00
—Nude bodies sleeve					
❑ 47452 [PS]	Body Language/Life Is Real (Song for Lennon)	1981	2.50	5.00	10.00
—All-white sleeve					
❑ 69941	Back Chat/Staying Power	1982	—	2.00	4.00
❑ 69941 [PS]	Back Chat/Staying Power	1982	—	2.50	5.00
❑ 69981	Calling All Girls/Put Out the Fire	1981	—	2.00	4.00
❑ 69981 [PS]	Calling All Girls/Put Out the Fire	1981	—	2.50	5.00
HOLLYWOOD					
❑ 64725	We Are the Champions/These Are the Days of Our Lives	1992	—	2.00	4.00
❑ 64794	Bohemian Rhapsody/The Show Must Go On	1992	—	2.00	4.00

QUEEN, THE

Number	Title (A Side/B Side)	Yr	VG	VG+	NM
MERCURY					
❑ 71389	Honky Tonky/Somewhere Along the Line	1958	5.00	10.00	20.00

QUEEN'S NECTORINE MACHINE, THE

Number	Title (A Side/B Side)	Yr	VG	VG+	NM
ABC					
❑ 11172	I Got Trouble/Gypsy Lady	1969	3.75	7.50	15.00

QUEENSRYCHE

Number	Title (A Side/B Side)	Yr	VG	VG+	NM
EMI					
❑ 7PRO-04345 [DJ]	I Don't Believe in Love (same on both sides)	1989	2.50	5.00	10.00
❑ S7-18305	Bridge/I Am I	1995	—	2.00	4.00
❑ S7-18553	Disconnected/Bridge	1995	—	2.00	4.00
❑ 50201	Eyes of a Stranger/(B-side unknown)	1989	2.50	5.00	10.00
❑ S7-57752	Anybody Listening?/Silent Lucidity	1992	2.50	5.00	10.00

? (QUESTION MARK) AND THE MYSTERIANS

Number	Title (A Side/B Side)	Yr	VG	VG+	NM
ABKCO					
❑ 4020	96 Tears/Can't Get Enough of You, Baby	1973	3.00	6.00	12.00
—Reissue; contains full-length version of A-side (Cameo single is edited)					
❑ 4033	I Need Somebody/Girl (You Captivate Me)	1973	3.00	6.00	12.00
—Reissue					
CAMEO					
❑ 428	96 Tears/Midnight Hour	1966	5.00	10.00	20.00
❑ 441	I Need Somebody/"8" Teen	1966	3.75	7.50	15.00
❑ 467	Can't Get Enough of You, Baby/Smokes	1967	3.75	7.50	15.00
❑ 479	Girl (You Captivate Me)/Got To	1967	3.75	7.50	15.00
❑ 496	Do Something to Me/Love Me, Baby	1967	3.75	7.50	15.00
CAPITOL					
❑ 2162	Make You Mine/I Love You, Baby (Like Nobody's Business)	1968	5.00	10.00	20.00
CHICORY					
❑ 410	Talk Is Cheap/She Goes to Church on Sunday	1968	7.50	15.00	30.00
COLLECTABLES					
❑ 4050	96 Tears/Midnight Hour	1997	—	2.00	4.00
—Yellow-orange vinyl; new recordings by the original group					
LUV					
❑ 159	Funky Lady/Hot N' Groovin'	1975	3.75	7.50	15.00
PA-GO-GO					
❑ 102	96 Tears/Midnight Hour	1965	175.00	350.00	700.00
SUPER K					
❑ 102	Hang In/Sha La La	1969	3.75	7.50	15.00
TANGERINE					
❑ 989	Ain't It a Shame/Turn Around Baby (Don't Ever Look Back)	1970	3.75	7.50	15.00

QUICK, THE

Featuring ERIC CARMEN.

Number	Title (A Side/B Side)	Yr	VG	VG+	NM
EPIC					
❑ 10516	Ain't Nothing Gonna Stop Me/Southern Comfort	1969	6.25	12.50	25.00

QUICKLY, TOMMY

Number	Title (A Side/B Side)	Yr	VG	VG+	NM
LIBERTY					
❑ 55732	It's As Simple As That/You Might As Well Forget Him	1964	2.50	5.00	10.00
❑ 55753	Wild Side of Life/Forget the Other Guy	1964	2.50	5.00	10.00

QUICKSILVER MESSENGER SERVICE

Number	Title (A Side/B Side)	Yr	VG	VG+	NM
CAPITOL					
❑ 2194	Pride of Man/Dino's Song	1968	3.00	6.00	12.00
❑ 2320	Stand By Me/Bears	1968	3.00	6.00	12.00
❑ 2557	Who Do You Love/Which Do You Love	1969	3.00	6.00	12.00
❑ 2670	Words Can't Say/Holy Holy	1969	3.00	6.00	12.00
❑ 2800	Shady Grove/Three or Four Feet from Home	1970	2.50	5.00	10.00
❑ 2920	Fresh Air/Freeway Flyer	1970	2.50	5.00	10.00
❑ 3046	Good Old Rock and Roll/What About Me	1971	2.00	4.00	8.00
❑ 3233	Hope/I Found Love	1971	2.00	4.00	8.00
❑ 3349	Doin' Time in the U.S.A./Changes	1972	2.00	4.00	8.00
❑ 3417	Fresh Air/Freeway Flyer	1972	2.00	4.00	8.00
❑ 4206	Gypsy Lights/Witches' Moon	1976	—	3.00	6.00

QUIN-TONES, THE

Number	Title (A Side/B Side)	Yr	VG	VG+	NM
HUNT					
❑ 321	Down the Aisle of Love/Please Dear	1958	12.50	25.00	50.00
❑ 322	There'll Be No Sorrow/What Am I to Do	1958	15.00	30.00	60.00
RED TOP					
❑ 108	Down the Aisle of Love/Please Dear	1958	30.00	60.00	120.00
—Red label					
❑ 108	Down the Aisle of Love/Please Dear	1958	10.00	20.00	40.00
❑ 116	Heavenly Father/I Watch the Stars	1959	25.00	50.00	100.00

QUINTEROS, EDDIE

Number	Title (A Side/B Side)	Yr	VG	VG+	NM
BRENT					
❑ 7009	Come Dance with Me/Vivian	1960	7.50	15.00	30.00
❑ 7012	Please Don't Go/Lookin' for My Baby	1960	8.75	17.50	35.00
❑ 7014	Slow Down Sandy/Lindy Lou	1960	12.50	25.00	50.00

QUINTONES, THE (1)

Number	Title (A Side/B Side)	Yr	VG	VG+	NM
CHESS					
❑ 1685	I Try So Hard/Ding Dong	1957	10.00	20.00	40.00

QUINTONES, THE (2)

Number	Title (A Side/B Side)	Yr	VG	VG+	NM
GEE					
❑ 1009	I'm Willing/Strange As It Seems	1956	250.00	500.00	1000.

QUINTONES, THE (3)

PHILLIPS INT'L.

Number	Title (A Side/B Side)	Yr	VG	VG+	NM
❑ 3586	Times Sho' Gettin' Ruff/Softie	1963	5.00	10.00	20.00

QUINTONES, THE (U)

JORDAN

Number	Title (A Side/B Side)	Yr	VG	VG+	NM
❑ 1601	The Lonely Telephone/Just a Little Loving	196?	75.00	150.00	300.00

PARK

Number	Title (A Side/B Side)	Yr	VG	VG+	NM
❑ 111/2	South Sea Island/More Than a Notion	1957	100.00	200.00	400.00

QUOTATIONS, THE

Several different groups.

ADMIRAL

Number	Title (A Side/B Side)	Yr	VG	VG+	NM
❑ 753	In the Night/Oh No, I Still Love Her	1964	5.00	10.00	20.00

DEVENUS

Number	Title (A Side/B Side)	Yr	VG	VG+	NM
❑ 107	It Can Happen to You/You Don't Have to Worry	1968	3.00	6.00	12.00

DOWNSTAIRS

Number	Title (A Side/B Side)	Yr	VG	VG+	NM
❑ 1003	Night/Why Do You Do Me Like You Do	1970	2.00	4.00	8.00

IMPERIAL

Number	Title (A Side/B Side)	Yr	VG	VG+	NM
❑ 66338	Havin' a Good Time/Can I Have Someone	1968	2.50	5.00	10.00
❑ 66368	Havin' a Good Time (With My Baby)/Can I Have Someone (For Once)	1969	2.50	5.00	10.00

LIBERTY

Number	Title (A Side/B Side)	Yr	VG	VG+	NM
❑ 55527	Listen, My Children, And You Shall Hear/Speak Softly and Carry a Big Horn	1962	6.25	12.50	25.00

VERVE

Number	Title (A Side/B Side)	Yr	VG	VG+	NM
❑ 10245	Imagination/Ala-Men-Say	1961	7.50	15.00	30.00
❑ 10252	This Love of Mine/We'll Reach Heaven Together	1962	7.50	15.00	30.00
❑ 10261	See You in September/Sumemrtime Goodbye	1962	12.50	25.00	50.00

R

R.E.M.

Also see HINDU LOVE GODS.

EPIC

Number	Title (A Side/B Side)	Yr	VG	VG+	NM
❑ ES7 3857 [DJ]	Live for Today/Happy When I'm Crying	1997	2.50	5.00	10.00
—B-side by Pearl Jam					
❑ ES7 3857 [PS]	Live for Today/Happy When I'm Crying	1997	2.50	5.00	10.00
—1997 Pearl Jam fan club single					

EVATONE

Number	Title (A Side/B Side)	Yr	VG	VG+	NM
❑ 105900-15	Dark Globe (one-sided)	1989	—	3.00	6.00
—5-inch black flexi-disc included in issue of Sassy magazine (double value if record is still attached to magazine)					

FAN CLUB

Number	Title (A Side/B Side)	Yr	VG	VG+	NM
❑ REM 92 [DJ]	Where's Captain Kirk?/Toyland	1992	6.25	12.50	25.00
❑ REM 92 [PS]	Where's Captain Kirk?/Toyland	1992	6.25	12.50	25.00
—Any of three variations of a gray sleeve					
❑ REM 92 [PS]	Where's Captain Kirk?/Toyland	1992	6.25	12.50	25.00
—White sleeve					
❑ REM 94 [DJ]	Sex Bomb/Christmas in Tunisia	1994	6.25	12.50	25.00
❑ REM 94 [PS]	Sex Bomb/Christmas in Tunisia	1994	6.25	12.50	25.00
—Picture sleeve also included a magnet, stamps and sticker					
❑ REM 95 [DJ]	Wicked Game/Java	1995	3.75	7.50	15.00
❑ REM 95 [PS]	Wicked Game/Java	1995	3.75	7.50	15.00
❑ REM 96 [DJ]	Only in America/I Will Survive	1996	3.75	7.50	15.00
❑ REM 96 [PS]	Only in America/I Will Survive	1996	3.75	7.50	15.00
❑ REM 97 [DJ]	Live for Today/Happy When I'm Crying	1997	3.75	7.50	15.00
—B-side by Pearl Jam					
❑ REM 97 [PS]	Live for Today/Happy When I'm Crying	1997	3.75	7.50	15.00
❑ REM 1993 [DJ]	Silver Bells/Christmas Time Is Here	1993	6.25	12.50	25.00
❑ REM 1993 [PS]	Silver Bells/Christmas Time Is Here	1993	6.25	12.50	25.00
❑ 2000 [DJ]	Christmas Time (Is Here Again)//Hastings and Main/Take Seven	2000	2.50	5.00	10.00
—Blue vinyl, small hole					
❑ 2000 [PS]	Christmas Time (Is Here Again)//Hastings and Main/Take Seven	2000	2.50	5.00	10.00
—Die-cut sleeve					
❑ U-23518M [DJ]	Parade of the Wooden Soldiers/See No Evil	1988	15.00	30.00	60.00
—Green vinyl					
❑ U-23518M [PS]	Parade of the Wooden Soldiers/See No Evil	1988	15.00	30.00	60.00
❑ 122589 [DJ]	Good King Wenceslas/Academy Fight Song	1989	12.50	25.00	50.00
❑ 122589 [PS]	Good King Wenceslas/Academy Fight Song	1989	12.50	25.00	50.00
—Fold-out poster sleeve					
❑ 122590 [DJ]	Ghost Reindeer in the Sky/Summertime	1990	10.00	20.00	40.00
❑ 122590 [PS]	Ghost Reindeer in the Sky/Summertime	1990	10.00	20.00	40.00
❑ 122591 [DJ]	Baby Baby/Christmas Griping	1991	10.00	20.00	40.00
❑ 122591 [PS]	Baby Baby/Christmas Griping	1991	10.00	20.00	40.00

HIB-TONE

Number	Title (A Side/B Side)	Yr	VG	VG+	NM
❑ HT-0001	Radio Free Europe/Sitting Still	1981	18.75	37.50	75.00
—First pressing, with no address for Hib-Tone Records on label					
❑ HT-0001	Radio Free Europe/Sitting Still	1981	12.50	25.00	50.00
—Second pressing, with Hib-Tone address					
❑ HT-0001 [PS]	Radio Free Europe/Sitting Still	1981	18.75	37.50	75.00

I.R.S.

Number	Title (A Side/B Side)	Yr	VG	VG+	NM
❑ 9916	Radio Free Europe/There She Goes Again	1983	2.50	5.00	10.00
❑ 9916 [PS]	Radio Free Europe/There She Goes Again	1983	7.50	15.00	30.00
❑ 9927	So. Central Rain (I'm Sorry)/King of the Road	1984	—	3.00	6.00
❑ 9927 [PS]	So. Central Rain (I'm Sorry)/King of the Road	1984	3.75	7.50	15.00
❑ 9931	(Don't Go Back to) Rockville/Catapult (Live)	1984	2.50	5.00	10.00
❑ 9931 [PS]	(Don't Go Back to) Rockville/Catapult (Live)	1984	3.75	7.50	15.00
❑ 52642	Can't Get There from Here/Bandwagon	1985	—	3.00	6.00
❑ 52642 [PS]	Can't Get There from Here/Bandwagon	1985	—	3.00	6.00
❑ 52678	Driver 8/Crazy	1985	—	3.00	6.00
❑ 52678 [PS]	Driver 8/Crazy	1985	—	3.00	6.00
❑ 52883	Fall on Me/Rotary Ten	1986	—	2.50	5.00
❑ 52883 [PS]	Fall on Me/Rotary Ten	1986	—	2.50	5.00
❑ 52971	Superman/White Tornado	1986	—	2.50	5.00
❑ 52971 [PS]	Superman/White Tornado	1986	—	2.50	5.00
❑ 53171	The One I Love/Maps and Legends	1987	—	—	3.00
❑ 53171 [PS]	The One I Love/Maps and Legends	1987	—	—	3.00
❑ 53220	It's the End of the World As We Know It (And I Feel Fine)/Last Date	1987	—	—	3.00
❑ 53220 [PS]	It's the End of the World As We Know It (And I Feel Fine)/Last Date	1987	—	—	3.00

THE BOB

Number	Title (A Side/B Side)	Yr	VG	VG+	NM
❑ 5	Tighten Up (one-sided)	198?	4.50	9.00	18.00
❑ 20	Femme Fatale (one-sided)	1986	3.75	7.50	15.00
—Flexi-disc included with The Bob magazine; black					
❑ 20	Femme Fatale (one-sided)	1986	3.75	7.50	15.00
—Flexi-disc included with The Bob magazine; red					
❑ 20 [PS]	Femme Fatale (one-sided)	1986	10.00	20.00	40.00
—Picture sleeve sent to The Bob subscribers only					

WARNER BROS.

Number	Title (A Side/B Side)	Yr	VG	VG+	NM
❑ W-2960	Orange Crush/Ghost Riders	1989	—	—	—
—Import, issued in U.S. with some copies of Warner Bros. 22780					
❑ W-2960 [PS]	Orange Crush/Ghost Riders	1989	—	—	—
—Import, issued in U.S. with some copies of Warner Bros. 22780					
❑ 16888	The Great Beyond/Man on the Moon (Live)	2000	—	2.00	4.00
❑ 17129	Daysleeper/Emphysema	1998	—	—	3.00
❑ 17446	Electrolite/The Wake-Up Bomb-Live	1997	—	—	3.00
❑ 17490	Bittersweet Me/Undertow	1996	—	—	3.00
❑ 17529	E-Bow the Letter/Tricycle	1996	—	—	3.00
❑ 17737	Tongue/Tongue (Live)	1995	—	—	3.00
❑ 17900	Strange Currencies/(Instrumental)	1995	—	—	3.00
❑ 17994	Bang and Blame/(Instrumental)	1995	—	—	3.00
❑ 18050	What's the Frequency, Kenneth?/(Instrumental)	1994	—	—	3.00
❑ 18523	The Sidewinder Sleeps Tonite/The Lion Sleeps Tonight	1993	—	—	3.00
❑ 18638	Everybody Hurts/Mandolin Strum	1993	—	—	3.00
❑ 18642	Man on the Moon/New Orleans Instrumental #2	1992	—	—	3.00
❑ 18729	Drive/Winged Mammal Theme	1992	—	—	3.00
❑ 19242	Shiny Happy People/Forty Second Song	1991	—	—	3.00
❑ 19246	Radio Song/Love Is All Around	1991	—	—	3.00
❑ 19392	Losing My Religion/Rotary Eleven	1991	—	—	3.00
❑ 21864	Stand/Pop Song 89	1989	—	—	3.00
—"Back to Back Hits" series					
❑ 22780	Singleactiongreen	1989	6.25	12.50	25.00
—Box set of 4 7-inch 45s, each with picture sleeve, plus poster. All have WB 27688, 27640 and 22791; all also are supposed to have W2960, but some contain 927 652 in error. No difference in value.					
❑ 22791	Get Up/Funtime	1989	—	—	3.00
❑ 22791 [PS]	Get Up/Funtime	1989	—	—	3.00
❑ 27640	Pop Song 89/Pop Song 89 (Acoustic Version)	1989	—	—	3.00
❑ 27640 [PS]	Pop Song 89/Pop Song 89 (Acoustic Version)	1989	—	—	—
—Only issued as part of Warner Bros. 22780; not available otherwise					
❑ 27688	Stand/Memphis Train Blues	1988	—	—	3.00
❑ 27688 [PS]	Stand/Memphis Train Blues	1988	—	—	3.00
❑ 927652	Orange Crush/Memphis Train Blues	1989	—	—	—
—Import with large hole, issued in U.S. with some copies of Warner Bros. 22780					
❑ 927652 [PS]	Orange Crush/Memphis Train Blues	1989	—	—	—
—Import, issued in U.S. with some copies of Warner Bros. 22780					

RABBITT, EDDIE

20TH FOX

Number	Title (A Side/B Side)	Yr	VG	VG+	NM
❑ 474	Six Nights and Seven Days/Next to the Note	1964	5.00	10.00	20.00

CAPITOL

Number	Title (A Side/B Side)	Yr	VG	VG+	NM
❑ NR-44527	On Second Thought/Only One Love in My Life	1990	—	—	—
—Reissue of Universal 66025; unreleased on vinyl?					
❑ NR-44538	Runnin' with the Wind/Feel Like a Stranger	1990	—	2.00	4.00
❑ 7PRO-79999	Runnin' with the Wind (same on both sides)	1990	—	3.00	6.00
—White label promo number					

CAPITOL NASHVILLE

Number	Title (A Side/B Side)	Yr	VG	VG+	NM
❑ S7-19347	Rockin' Around the Christmas Tree/Have Yourself a Merry Little Christmas	1996	—	—	3.00

DATE

Number	Title (A Side/B Side)	Yr	VG	VG+	NM
❑ 1599	The Bed/Holding On	1968	3.00	6.00	12.00

ELEKTRA

Number	Title (A Side/B Side)	Yr	VG	VG+	NM
❑ 378 [DJ]	Song of Ireland (same on both sides)	1978	3.75	7.50	15.00
—Promo only on green vinyl; small center hole					
❑ 45237	Forgive and Forget/Pure Love	1975	—	2.50	5.00
❑ 45269	I Should Have Married You/Sweet Janine	1975	—	2.50	5.00
❑ 45301	Drinkin' My Baby (Off My Mind)/When I Was Young	1976	—	2.50	5.00
❑ 45315	Rocky Mountian Music/Do You Right Tonight	1976	—	2.50	5.00
—Butterfly label; most, if not all, copies misspell "Mountain" as above					
❑ 45315	Rocky Mountian Music/Do You Right Tonight	1976	—	3.00	6.00
—Red label; most, if not all, copies misspell "Mountain" as above					
❑ 45357	Two Dollars in the Jukebox/Don't Wanna Make Love	1976	—	2.50	5.00
—Butterfly label					
❑ 45357	Two Dollars in the Jukebox/Don't Wanna Make Love	1976	—	3.00	6.00
—Red label					
❑ 45381	Could You Love a Poor Boy, Dolly/There's Someone She Lies To (To Lie Here with Me)	1977	—	3.00	6.00
❑ 45390	I Can't Help Myself/She Loves Me Like She Means It	1977	—	2.00	4.00
❑ 45418	We Can't Go On Living Like This/We Made Love Beautiful	1977	—	2.00	4.00
❑ 45461	Hearts on Fire/Girl on My Mind	1978	—	2.00	4.00
❑ 45488	You Don't Love Me Anymore/Caroline	1978	—	2.00	4.00
❑ 45531	I Just Want to Love You/Crossin' the Mississippi	1978	—	2.00	4.00
❑ 45554	Every Which Way But Loose/Under the Double Eagle	1978	—	2.00	4.00
❑ 45895	You Get to Me/Que Pasa	1974	—	2.50	5.00
❑ 46053	Suspicions/I Don't Want to Make Love (With Anyone But You)	1979	—	2.00	4.00
❑ 46558	Pour Me Another Tequila/I Will Never Let You Go	1979	—	2.00	4.00
❑ 46613	Gone Too Far/Loveline	1980	—	2.00	4.00

Number	Title (A Side/B Side)	Yr	VG	VG+	NM
❑ 46656	Drivin' My Life Away/Pretty Lady	1980	—	2.00	4.00
❑ 47066	I Love a Rainy Night/Short Road to Love	1980	—	2.00	4.00
❑ 47174	Step By Step/My Only Wish	1981	—	2.00	4.00
❑ 47174 [PS]	Step By Step/My Only Wish	1981	—	3.00	6.00
❑ 47239	Someone Could Lose a Heart Tonight/Nobody Loves Me Like My Baby	1981	—	2.00	4.00
❑ 47435	I Don't Know Where to Start/Skip-A-Beat	1982	—	2.00	4.00
❑ 69936	You and I/All My Life, All My Love	1982	—	2.00	4.00
—A-side: With Crystal Gayle					
RCA					
❑ 5012-7-R	Gotta Have You/Singing in the Subway	1986	—	—	3.00
❑ 5093-7-R	When We Make Love/(B-side unknown)	1987	—	—	3.00
❑ 5238-7-R	Wanna Dance with You/Gotta Have You	1987	—	—	3.00
❑ 8306-7-R	The Wanderer/Workin' Out	1988	—	—	3.00
❑ 8716-7-R	We Must Be Doing Something Right/He's a Cheater	1988	—	—	3.00
❑ 8819-7-R	That's Why I Fell in Love with You/She's An Old Cadillac	1988	—	—	3.00
❑ PB-14192	A World Without Love/1-2-3, You Really Got a Hold on Me (The Wrestling Song)	1985	—	—	3.00
❑ PB-14317	Repetitive Love/Letter from Home	1986	—	—	3.00
❑ PB-14377	Both to Each Other (Friends and Lovers)/A World Without Love	1986	—	—	3.00
—With Juice Newton					
❑ PB-14377 [PS]	Both to Each Other (Friends and Lovers)/A World Without Love	1986	—	2.50	5.00
UNIVERSAL					
❑ UVL-66025	On Second Thought/Only One Love in My Life	1989	—	2.00	4.00
WARNER BROS.					
❑ 28976	She's Comin' Back to Say Goodbye/Dial That Telephone	1985	—	2.00	4.00
❑ 29089	Warning Sign/Go to Sleep, Big Bertha	1985	—	2.00	4.00
❑ 29186	The Best Year of My Life/Over There	1984	—	2.00	4.00
❑ 29279	B-B-B-Burnin' Up with Love/747	1984	—	2.00	4.00
❑ 29431	Nothing Like Falling in Love/Gone Too Far	1983	—	2.00	4.00
❑ 29512	Our Love Will Survive/You Put the Beat in My Heart	1983	—	2.00	4.00
❑ 29712	You Can't Run from Love/You Got Me Now	1983	—	2.00	4.00

RABIN, MIKE, AND THE DEMONS

Number	Title (A Side/B Side)	Yr	VG	VG+	NM
TOWER					
❑ 109	Head Over Heels/I'm Leaving You	1964	3.75	7.50	15.00

RACE MARBLES, THE

Number	Title (A Side/B Side)	Yr	VG	VG+	NM
TOWER					
❑ 194	Like a Dribbling Fram/Someday	1965	7.50	15.00	30.00

RACHEL AND THE REVOLVERS

Number	Title (A Side/B Side)	Yr	VG	VG+	NM
DOT					
❑ 16392	The Revo-Lution/Number One	1962	125.00	250.00	500.00
—Produced by Brian Wilson					

RACKET SQUAD, THE

Number	Title (A Side/B Side)	Yr	VG	VG+	NM
JUBILEE					
❑ 5591	Hung Up/Higher Than High	1967	7.50	15.00	30.00
❑ 5601	Little Red Wagon/(Just Like) Romeo and Juliet	1967	5.00	10.00	20.00
❑ 5613	The Loser/No Fair at All	1968	5.00	10.00	20.00
❑ 5623	Let's Dance to the Beat of My Heart/Higher Than High	1968	5.00	10.00	20.00
❑ 5628	That's How Much I Love My Baby/(B-side unknown)	1968	5.00	10.00	20.00
❑ 5638	Suburban Life/The Loser	1968	5.00	10.00	20.00
❑ 5657	I'll Never Forget Your Love/(B-side unknown)	1969	5.00	10.00	20.00
❑ 5682	In Your Arms/(B-side unknown)	1969	7.50	15.00	30.00
❑ 5694	Roller Coaster Ride/Coal Town	1970	7.50	15.00	30.00

RADHA KRISHNA TEMPLE

Number	Title (A Side/B Side)	Yr	VG	VG+	NM
APPLE					
❑ 1810	Hare Krishna Mantra/Prayer to the Spiritual Masters	1969	2.00	4.00	8.00
❑ 1810 [PS]	Hare Krishna Mantra/Prayer to the Spiritual Masters	1969	100.00	200.00	400.00
—Only one copy is known to exist. The price is highly speculative.					
❑ 1821	Govinda/Govinda Jai Jai	1970	2.00	4.00	8.00
❑ 1821	Govinda/Govinda Jai Jai	1970	2.50	5.00	10.00
—With Capitol logo on B-side label bottom					
❑ 1821 [PS]	Govinda/Govinda Jai Jai	1970	2.50	5.00	10.00
❑ PRO-5013/4 [DJ]	Govinda/Govinda Jai Jai	1970	6.25	12.50	25.00
—With an edit of the A-side					
❑ SPRO-5067/8 [DJ]	Govinda (Edit)/Govinda	1970	10.00	20.00	40.00

RADIANTS, THE

Number	Title (A Side/B Side)	Yr	VG	VG+	NM
ABC					
❑ 12394	I Need a Vacation/Just Like You	1978	—	2.50	5.00
CHESS					
❑ 1832	Father Knows Best/One Day I'll SHow You	1962	3.75	7.50	15.00
❑ 1849	Please Don't Leave Me/Heartbreak Society	1963	3.75	7.50	15.00
❑ 1872	I'm in Love/Shy Guy	1963	3.75	7.50	15.00
❑ 1887	Noble the Bargain Man/I Got to Dance to Keep My Baby	1964	3.75	7.50	15.00
❑ 1904	Voice Your Choice/If I Only Had You	1964	3.00	6.00	12.00
❑ 1925	It Ain't No Big Thing/I Got a Girl	1965	3.00	6.00	12.00
❑ 1939	Whole Lot of Love/Tomorrow	1965	3.00	6.00	12.00
❑ 1954	I Want to Thank You, Baby/Baby You've Got It	1966	3.00	6.00	12.00
—As "Maurice and the Radiants"					
❑ 1986	(Don't It Make You) Feel Kind of Bad/Anything You Do Is Alright	1967	3.00	6.00	12.00
❑ 2021	Don't Take Your Love/The Clown Is Clever	1967	3.00	6.00	12.00
❑ 2037	Hold On/I'm Glad I'm the Loser	1968	3.00	6.00	12.00
❑ 2057	Tears of a Clown/I'm Just a Man	1968	3.00	6.00	12.00
❑ 2066	Choo Choo/Ida Mae Foster	1969	2.50	5.00	10.00
❑ 2078	Book of Love/Another Mule Is Kicking In Your Stall	1969	2.50	5.00	10.00
❑ 2083	I'm So Glad I'm the Loser/Shadow of a Doubt	1970	2.50	5.00	10.00
TWINIGHT					
❑ 153	My Sunshine Girl/Don't Wanna Face the Truth	1971	2.00	4.00	8.00

RAFFERTY, GERRY

Also see THE HUMBLEBUMS; STEALERS WHEEL

Number	Title (A Side/B Side)	Yr	VG	VG+	NM
BLUE THUMB					
❑ 231	Can I Have My Money Back/Sign on the Dotted Line	1973	2.00	4.00	8.00
LIBERTY					
❑ 1482	Good Intentions/Standing at the Gates	1982	—	2.00	4.00
SIGNPOST					
❑ 70001	Make You, Break You/Mary Skeffington	1972	2.50	5.00	10.00
UNITED ARTISTS					
❑ XW1098	Mattie's Rag/City to City	1977	—	2.50	5.00
❑ XW1192	Baker Street/Big Change in the Weather	1978	2.00	4.00	8.00
—Mispress with the full-length album version of "Baker Street" on A-side There is no "E" in the trail-off wax.					
❑ XW1192	Baker Street/Big Change in the Weather	1978	—	2.00	4.00
—Regular press with the edited, slightly sped-up version of "Baker Street" on A-side					
❑ XW1233	Right Down the Line/Waiting for the Day	1978	—	2.00	4.00
❑ XW1233 [PS]	Right Down the Line/Waiting for the Day	1978	—	2.50	5.00
❑ XW1266	Home and Dry/Mattie's Rag	1978	—	2.00	4.00
❑ XW1298	Days Gone Down (Still Got That Light in Your Eyes)/Why Won't You Talk to Me	1979	—	2.00	4.00
❑ 1316	Get It Right Next Time/It's Gonna Be a Long Night	1979	—	2.00	4.00
❑ 1366	The Royal Mile/In Transit	1980	—	2.00	4.00

RAG DOLLS, THE

Number	Title (A Side/B Side)	Yr	VG	VG+	NM
MALA					
❑ 493	Dusty/Hey Hoagy	1964	2.50	5.00	10.00
❑ 499	Baby's Gone/We Almost Made It	1965	2.50	5.00	10.00
❑ 506	Little Girl Tears/Put a Ring on My Finger	1965	2.50	5.00	10.00
PARKWAY					
❑ 921	Society Girl/Ragen (Society Girl Bossa Nova)	1964	3.00	6.00	12.00

RAGLAND, LOU

Number	Title (A Side/B Side)	Yr	VG	VG+	NM
AMY					
❑ 988	Travel Alone/Big Wheel	1967	50.00	100.00	200.00

RAIDERS, THE (1)

See PAUL REVERE AND THE RAIDERS.

RAIDERS, THE (2)

Number	Title (A Side/B Side)	Yr	VG	VG+	NM
ANDEX					
❑ 4015	Yoo Hoo/Hocus Pocus	1958	30.00	60.00	120.00
ATCO					
❑ 6125	Raiders from Outer Space/The Castle of Love	1958	20.00	40.00	80.00
BRUNSWICK					
❑ 55090	Walking Through the Jungle/My Steady Girl	1958	10.00	20.00	40.00

RAIDERS, THE (3)

Number	Title (A Side/B Side)	Yr	VG	VG+	NM
LIBERTY					
❑ 55393	Dardanella/What Time Is It	1961	7.50	15.00	30.00

RAIDERS, THE (4)

Number	Title (A Side/B Side)	Yr	VG	VG+	NM
SPRING-DALE					
❑ 102	Raiders' Rhythm/Tall Texas Women	1964	12.50	25.00	50.00

RAIDERS, THE (5)

Number	Title (A Side/B Side)	Yr	VG	VG+	NM
VAN					
❑ 00262	Stick Shift/Skipping Around	1962	12.50	25.00	50.00
❑ 00663	On a Straight Away/It's Motivation	1963	5.00	10.00	20.00
❑ 00763	Supercharger/Cruisin' Low	1963	5.00	10.00	20.00
❑ 01064	Raisin' Cain/Repetition	1964	5.00	10.00	20.00
VEE JAY					
❑ 504	Stick Shift/Skipping Around	1963	5.00	10.00	20.00

RAIN

At least two different groups.

Number	Title (A Side/B Side)	Yr	VG	VG+	NM
A.P.I.					
❑ 336	Outta My Life/E.S.P.	1967	10.00	20.00	40.00
❑ 337	Substitute/Hear You Cry	1967	10.00	20.00	40.00
BELL					
❑ 45206	Caught in the Middle of It/Stop Me from Believing in You	1972	—	2.50	5.00
LONDON					
❑ 107	Outta My Life/E.S.P.	1967	6.25	12.50	25.00
❑ 111	Substitute/Hear You Cry	1967	7.50	15.00	30.00
MGM					
❑ 13622	Take It Away/City Lovin'	1966	6.25	12.50	25.00
PARAMOUNT					
❑ 0087	Show Me the Road Home/Funky Junky Blues	1971	5.00	10.00	20.00

RAINBO

Sissy Spacek is on this record.

Number	Title (A Side/B Side)	Yr	VG	VG+	NM
ROULETTE					
❑ 7030	John You Went Too Far This Time/C'mon Teach Me to Live	1969	5.00	10.00	20.00

RAINBOW PRESS, THE

Number	Title (A Side/B Side)	Yr	VG	VG+	NM
MR. G					
❑ 817	There's a War On/Better Way	1968	3.75	7.50	15.00
❑ 821	Great White Whale/The Last Platoon	1969	3.75	7.50	15.00

RAINBOWS, THE (1)

Number	Title (A Side/B Side)	Yr	VG	VG+	NM
ARGYLE					
❑ 1012	Shirley/Stay	1962	6.25	12.50	25.00
FIRE					
❑ 1012	Mary Lee/Evening	1960	5.00	10.00	20.00
PILGRIM					
❑ 703	Mary Lee/Evening	1956	12.50	25.00	50.00
❑ 711	Shirley/Stay	1956	50.00	100.00	200.00

Number	Title (A Side/B Side)	Yr	VG	VG+	NM
RAMA					
❑ 209	Minnie/They Say	1956	150.00	300.00	600.00
RED ROBIN					
❑ 134	Mary Lee/Evening	1955	150.00	300.00	600.00
—Note: Red Robin 141 is a bootleg					

RAINBOWS, THE (2)

Number	Title (A Side/B Side)	Yr	VG	VG+	NM
DAVE					
❑ 908	I Know/Only a Picture	1963	7.50	15.00	30.00
❑ 909	It Wouldn't Be Right/Family Monkey	1963	7.50	15.00	30.00

RAINBOWS, THE (3)

Number	Title (A Side/B Side)	Yr	VG	VG+	NM
DOT					
❑ 16612	My Ringo/He's Hooked on J's	1964	3.75	7.50	15.00
❑ 16920	Color of Love/Down the Block	1966	2.50	5.00	10.00

RAINBOWS, THE (4)

Number	Title (A Side/B Side)	Yr	VG	VG+	NM
EPIC					
❑ 9900	Balla Balla/Ju Ju Hand	1966	2.50	5.00	10.00
JAMIE					
❑ 1339	Balla Balla/Ju Ju Hand	1967	2.00	4.00	8.00

RAINBOWS, THE (U)

Some of these could be by groups (2), (3) or (4).

Number	Title (A Side/B Side)	Yr	VG	VG+	NM
GRAMO					
❑ 5508	Till Tomorrow/Mama, Take Your Daughter Back	196?	5.00	10.00	20.00
MERCURY					
❑ 72068	Gonna Go Down/Dreamwalk	1962	3.75	7.50	15.00
MGM					
❑ 13058	Old Man's Twist/Straight Ahead	1962	5.00	10.00	20.00
RONNIE					
❑ 202	The Christmas Song/Love Me	19??	2.50	5.00	10.00
—B-side by the Mellow Moods					

RAINDROPS, THE (1)

JEFF BARRY and ELLIE GREENWICH.

Number	Title (A Side/B Side)	Yr	VG	VG+	NM
JUBILEE					
❑ 5444	What a Guy/It's So Wonderful	1963	5.00	10.00	20.00
❑ 5455	The Kind of Boy You Can't Forget/Even Though You Can't Dance	1963	6.25	12.50	25.00
❑ 5466	That Boy John/Hanky Panky	1963	6.25	12.50	25.00
❑ 5469	Book of Love/I Won't Cry	1964	5.00	10.00	20.00
❑ 5475	Let;s Go Together/You Got What I Like	1964	5.00	10.00	20.00
❑ 5487	One More Tear/Another Boy Like Mine	1964	5.00	10.00	20.00
❑ 5497	Don't Let Go/My Mama Don't Like Him	1965	5.00	10.00	20.00

RAINDROPS, THE (2)

Number	Title (A Side/B Side)	Yr	VG	VG+	NM
CAPITOL					
❑ F-4136	Rockababy Rock/Rain	1959	7.50	15.00	30.00

RAINDROPS, THE (3)

Number	Title (A Side/B Side)	Yr	VG	VG+	NM
CORSAIR					
❑ 104	Maybe/Love Is Like a Mountain	1960	20.00	40.00	80.00
DORE					
❑ 561	Maybe/Love Is Like a Mountain	1960	6.25	12.50	25.00

RAINDROPS, THE (4)

Number	Title (A Side/B Side)	Yr	VG	VG+	NM
IMPERIAL					
❑ 5785	I Remember in the Still of the Night/Sweet Song	1961	7.50	15.00	30.00

RAINDROPS, THE (5)

Number	Title (A Side/B Side)	Yr	VG	VG+	NM
SPIN-IT					
❑ 104	(I Found) Heaven in Love/I Prayed for Gold	1956	50.00	100.00	200.00
❑ 106	Little One/Rockin' on the Farm	1956	50.00	100.00	200.00

RAINDROPS, THE (U)

Not sure which group this is.

Number	Title (A Side/B Side)	Yr	VG	VG+	NM
HAMILTON					
❑ 50021	Oh Why/Without Love, Love, Love	1960	5.00	10.00	20.00

RAINWATER, MARVIN

Also see CONNIE FRANCIS AND MARVIN RAINWATER.

Number	Title (A Side/B Side)	Yr	VG	VG+	NM
BRAVE					
❑ 1001	Part Time Lover/That Aching Heart	1963	2.50	5.00	10.00
—With Bill Guess					
❑ 1003	Love's Prison/These Thoughts of You	196?	2.50	5.00	10.00
—With Bill Guess					
❑ 1004	Bad Girl/I Saw Your New Love Today	196?	2.50	5.00	10.00
—With Bill Guess					
❑ 1017	The Old Gang's Gone/Run for Your Life Boy	196?	2.00	4.00	8.00
❑ 1028	Oklahoma Hills/Wedding Rings	196?	2.00	4.00	8.00
CORAL					
❑ 9-61342	I Gotta Go Get My Baby/Daddy's Glad You Came Home	1955	5.00	10.00	20.00
MGM					
❑ 12071	Sticks and Stones/Albino Stallion	1955	5.00	10.00	20.00
❑ 12090	Tennessee Houn' Dog Yodel/Tea Bag Romeo	1955	5.00	10.00	20.00
❑ 12152	Where Do We Go from Here/Dem Low Down Blues	1955	5.00	10.00	20.00
❑ 12240	Hot and Cold/Mr. Blues	1956	10.00	20.00	40.00
❑ 12313	Why Did You Have to Go and Leave Me/What Am I Supposed to Do	1956	5.00	10.00	20.00
❑ 12370	Get Off the Stool/(Sometimes) I Feel Like Leaving Town	1956	7.50	15.00	30.00
❑ 12412	Gonna Find Me a Bluebird/So You Think You've Got Troubles	1957	5.00	10.00	20.00
❑ 12511	My Brand of Blues/My Love Is Real	1957	5.00	10.00	20.00
❑ 12586	Lucky Star/Look for Me	1957	5.00	10.00	20.00
❑ 12609	Whole Lotta Woman/Baby Don't Go	1958	5.00	10.00	20.00
❑ 12653	Moanin' the Blues/Gamblin' Man	1958	6.25	12.50	25.00
❑ 12665	I Dig You Baby/Moanin' the Blues	1958	5.00	10.00	20.00
❑ 12701	Nothin' Needs Nothin' (Like I Need You)/(There's Always) A Need for Love	1958	5.00	10.00	20.00
❑ 12739	Lonely Island/Born to Be Lonesome	1958	5.00	10.00	20.00
❑ 12773	Love Me Baby (Like There's No Tomorrow)/That's When I'll Stop Loving You	1959	5.00	10.00	20.00
❑ 12803	Half-Breed/A Song of Love	1959	5.00	10.00	20.00
❑ 12829	Young Girls/Valley of the Moon	1959	5.00	10.00	20.00
❑ 12865	Pale Faced Indian/Wayward Angel	1960	3.75	7.50	15.00
❑ 12891	Hard Luck Blues/She's Gone	1960	3.75	7.50	15.00
❑ 12938	You're Not Happy ('Til I'm Cryin')/Yesterday's Kisses	1960	3.75	7.50	15.00
NU TRAYL					
❑ 902	Haircut/Looking Good	1976	—	3.00	6.00
RALPH HIMSELF					
❑ 17094	Little Ralph the Robot (Poem)/Little Ralph the Robot (Song)	197?	—	2.50	5.00
UNITED ARTISTS					
❑ 837	It Wasn't Enough/My Old Home Town	1965	2.50	5.00	10.00
❑ 917	Black Sheet/Indian Burial Ground	1965	2.50	5.00	10.00
❑ 50023	Sorrow Brings a Good Man Down/The Troubles My Little Boy Had	1966	2.50	5.00	10.00
WARNER BROS.					
❑ 7373	Let Me Live Again/I Love My Country	1970	—	3.50	7.00
WARWICK					
❑ 666	Boo Hoo/I Can't Forget	1961	10.00	20.00	40.00
❑ 674	Tough Top Cat/(There's a) Honky Tonk in Your Heart	1962	6.25	12.50	25.00
(NO LABEL)					
❑ MR 1 [DJ]	Hearts Hall of Fame//Gotta Go Get My Baby/Albino Stallion	195?	25.00	50.00	100.00
—Called "Especially for Friends by Marvin Rainwater"; white label					

7-Inch Extended Plays

Number	Title (A Side/B Side)	Yr	VG	VG+	NM
MGM					
❑ X1464	(contents unknown)	1957	6.25	12.50	25.00
❑ X1464 [PS]	Songs by Marvin Rainwater, Vol. 1	1957	6.25	12.50	25.00
❑ X1465	Tennessee Houn' Dog Yodel/What Am I Supposed to Do//Why Did You Have to Go and Leave Me/Mr. Blues	1957	6.25	12.50	25.00
❑ X1465 [PS]	Songs by Marvin Rainwater Vol. 2	1957	6.25	12.50	25.00
❑ X1466	(contents unknown)	1957	6.25	12.50	25.00
❑ X1466 [PS]	Songs by Marvin Rainwater, Vol. 3	1957	6.25	12.50	25.00

RAINY DAYS, THE

Number	Title (A Side/B Side)	Yr	VG	VG+	NM
JUBILEE					
❑ 5517	He Was a Friend of Mine/Don't Want No Fool	1965	3.00	6.00	12.00
PANIK					
❑ 7542	Turn on Your Lovelight/Go On and Cry	1966	6.25	12.50	25.00
❑ 7566	I Can Only Give You Anything/(B-side unknown)	1966	6.25	12.50	25.00

RAINY DAZE, THE

Number	Title (A Side/B Side)	Yr	VG	VG+	NM
CHICORY					
❑ 404	That Acapulco Gold/In My Mind Lives a Forest	1967	3.75	7.50	15.00
UNI					
❑ 55002	That Acapulco Gold/In My Mind Lives a Forest	1967	2.50	5.00	10.00
❑ 55011	Discount City/Good Morning, Mr. Smith	1967	2.50	5.00	10.00
❑ 55026	Stop Sign/Blood of Oblivion	1967	2.50	5.00	10.00
WHITE WHALE					
❑ 279	My Door Is Always Open/Make Me Laugh	1968	2.50	5.00	10.00

RAITT, BONNIE

Number	Title (A Side/B Side)	Yr	VG	VG+	NM
ARISTA					
❑ 12795	You Got It/Feeling of Falling	1995	—	—	3.00
A&M					
❑ 1249	Baby Mine/Mickey Mouse March	1988	—	2.00	4.00
—A-side with Was (Not Was); B-side by Aaron Neville					
❑ 1249 [PS]	Baby Mine/Mickey Mouse March	1988	—	2.00	4.00
CAPITOL					
❑ S7-17818	Love Sneakin' Up on You/Hell to Pay	1994	—	—	3.00
❑ S7-18039	You/Feeling of Falling	1994	—	2.00	4.00
—Red vinyl					
❑ S7-18299	Storm Warning/Longing in Their Hearts	1995	—	—	3.00
❑ B-44364	Nick of Time/The Road's My Middle Name	1989	—	2.00	4.00
❑ B-44365	Thing Called Love/The Road's My Middle Name	1989	—	2.00	4.00
❑ B-44365 [PS]	Thing Called Love/The Road's My Middle Name	1989	—	2.00	4.00
❑ NR-44729	I Can't Make You Love Me/Come to Me	1991	—	2.00	4.00
—White label, but not a promo					
❑ S7-56799	All at Once/Come to Me	1992	—	2.00	4.00
❑ S7-57698	Not the Only One/All at Once	1992	—	2.00	4.00
❑ S7-57741	I Can't Make You Love Me/Something to Talk About	1992	—	2.00	4.00
❑ S7-57879	Good Man, Good Woman/Nick of Time	1992	—	2.00	4.00
—A-side: Duet with Delbert McClinton					
❑ 58844	The Fundamental Things/Cold, Cold, Cold	2000	—	—	3.00
❑ 7PRO-79940 [DJ]	Have a Heart (same on both sides)	1990	2.00	4.00	8.00
—Vinyl is promo only					
FULL MOON					
❑ 49612	Once in a Lifetime/You're Only Lonely	1980	—	2.00	4.00
—B-side by J.D. Souther					
FULL MOON/ASYLUM					
❑ 47033	Don't It Make You Wanna Dance/Orange Blossom Special	1980	—	2.50	5.00
—B-side by Gilley's Urban Cowboy Band					
❑ 47033 [PS]	Don't It Make You Wanna Dance/Orange Blossom Special	1980	—	3.00	6.00
REPRISE					
❑ 1370	When You Touch Me This Way/Since I've Been With You Babe	1976	—	2.50	5.00
—By Geoff Muldaur and Bonnie Raitt					
WARNER BROS.					
❑ 7554	Bluebird/Women Be Wise	1972	2.00	4.00	8.00
❑ 7645	Too Long at the Fair/Under the Falling Sky	1972	2.00	4.00	8.00

Number	Title (A Side/B Side)	Yr	VG	VG+	NM
❑ 7758	Everybody's Cryin' Mercy/You've Been in Love Too Long	1973	—	3.00	6.00
❑ 8044	I Got Plenty/You Got to Be Ready for Love	1974	—	3.00	6.00
❑ 8166	Good Enough/My First Night Alone Without You	1975	—	3.00	6.00
❑ 8189	Run Like a Thief/Walk Out the Front Door	1976	—	2.50	5.00
❑ 8382	Runaway/Louise	1977	—	2.50	5.00
❑ 8430	Two Lives/Three Time Loser	1977	—	2.50	5.00
❑ 8485	Gamblin' Man/About to Make Me Leave Home	1977	—	2.50	5.00
❑ 28450	Crimes of Passion/Stand Up to the Night	1987	—	2.00	4.00
❑ 28615	No Way to Treat a Lady/Stand Up to the Night	1986	—	2.00	4.00
❑ 29992	River of Tears/Me and the Boys	1982	—	2.00	4.00
❑ 49116	You're Gonna Get What's Comin'/The Glow	1979	—	2.00	4.00
❑ 49116 [PS]	You're Gonna Get What's Comin'/The Glow	1979	2.00	4.00	8.00
❑ 49185	Wild for You Baby/(I Could Have Been Your) Best Old Friend	1980	—	2.00	4.00
❑ 50022	Can't Get Enough/Keep This Heart in Mind	1982	—	2.00	4.00

RAJAHS, THE
KLIK

Number	Title (A Side/B Side)	Yr	VG	VG+	NM
❑ 7805	I Fell in Love/Shifting Sands	1957	75.00	150.00	300.00

RALLY PACKS, THE
STEVE BARRI and P.F. SLOAN with JAN AND DEAN.

IMPERIAL

Number	Title (A Side/B Side)	Yr	VG	VG+	NM
❑ 66036	Move Out Little Mustang/Bucket Seats	1964	15.00	30.00	60.00

RAMAL, BILL

Number	Title (A Side/B Side)	Yr	VG	VG+	NM
20TH CENTURY FOX					
❑ 432	Exodus/Theme from "Dr. No"	1963	2.50	5.00	10.00
MGM					
❑ 13123	Hard Times/Sax Fifth Ave.	1963	2.50	5.00	10.00

RAMBLERS, THE (1)
ADDIT

Number	Title (A Side/B Side)	Yr	VG	VG+	NM
❑ 1257	Rambling/Devil Train	1960	7.50	15.00	30.00

RAMBLERS, THE (2)
ALMONT

Number	Title (A Side/B Side)	Yr	VG	VG+	NM
❑ 311	Father Sebastian/Barbara (I Loved You)	1964	6.25	12.50	25.00
❑ 313	School Girl/Birdland Baby	1964	5.00	10.00	20.00
❑ 315	Surfin' Santa/Silly Little Boy	1964	6.25	12.50	25.00

RAMBLERS, THE (3)
FEDERAL

Number	Title (A Side/B Side)	Yr	VG	VG+	NM
❑ 12286	Don't You Know?/The Heaven and Earth	1957	37.50	75.00	150.00

RAMBLERS, THE (4)
JAX

Number	Title (A Side/B Side)	Yr	VG	VG+	NM
❑ 319	Search My Heart/50-50 Love	1953	125.00	250.00	500.00
—Red vinyl					

RAMBLERS, THE (5)
MGM

Number	Title (A Side/B Side)	Yr	VG	VG+	NM
❑ 11850	Vadunt-Un-Va-Da Song (Oui Oui Baby)/Please Bring Yourself Back Home	1954	75.00	150.00	300.00
❑ 55006	Bad Girl/Rickey-Do, Rickey-Do	1955	37.50	75.00	150.00

RAMBLERS, THE (6)
TRUMPET

Number	Title (A Side/B Side)	Yr	VG	VG+	NM
❑ 102	Come On Back/So Sad	1963	100.00	200.00	400.00

RAMBLERS, THE (U)
Some of these could be by some of the above groups.

Number	Title (A Side/B Side)	Yr	VG	VG+	NM
IMPACT					
❑ 10	Yaba Daba Ah Doo/Funny Papers	1961	6.25	12.50	25.00
RCA VICTOR					
❑ 47-5240	Mama He Treats Your Daughter Mean/And the Bull Walked Around Olay	1953	100.00	200.00	400.00
SIDEWINDER					
❑ 101	Ticonderoga/Mozart Stomp	1964	10.00	20.00	40.00

RAMISTELLA, JOHNNY
See JOHNNY RIVERS.

RAMONES, THE

Number	Title (A Side/B Side)	Yr	VG	VG+	NM
NORTON					
❑ 45-065	I Wanna Be Your Boyfriend/Judy Is a Punk	1997	—	—	2.00
—1975 demo versions					
❑ 45-065 [PS]	I Wanna Be Your Boyfriend/Judy Is a Punk	1997	—	—	2.00
RSO					
❑ 1055	I Wanna Be Sedated/The Return of Jackie and Judy	1980	—	2.50	5.00
SIRE					
❑ 725	Blitzkrieg Bop/Havana Affair	1976	10.00	20.00	40.00
—Promo copies worth slightly less					
❑ 734	I Wanna Be Your Boyfriend//California Sun/I Don't Wanna Walk Around with You	1976	—	3.00	6.00
❑ 734 [PS]	I Wanna Be Your Boyfriend//California Sun/I Don't Wanna Walk Around with You	1976	3.50	7.00	14.00
❑ 738	Swallow My Pride/Pinhead	1977	—	3.00	6.00
❑ 738 [PS]	Swallow My Pride/Pinhead	1977	3.00	6.00	12.00
❑ 746	Sheena Is a Punk Rocker/I Don't Care	1977	—	3.00	6.00
❑ 746 [PS]	Sheena Is a Punk Rocker/I Don't Care	1977	3.00	6.00	12.00
❑ 1006	Sheena Is a Punk Rocker/I Don't Care	1977	—	2.00	4.00
❑ 1006 [PS]	Sheena Is a Punk Rocker/I Don't Care	1977	2.00	4.00	8.00
❑ 1008	Rockaway Beach/Locket Love	1977	—	2.00	4.00
❑ 1008 [PS]	Rockaway Beach/Locket Love	1977	2.00	4.00	8.00
❑ 1017	Do You Wanna Dance?/Baby Sitter	1978	2.50	5.00	10.00
❑ 1017 [PS]	Do You Wanna Dance?/Baby Sitter	1978	7.50	15.00	30.00
❑ 1025	Don't Come Close/I Don't Want You	1978	—	3.00	6.00
❑ 1045	Needles and Pins/I Wanted Everything	1979	—	2.50	5.00
❑ 1051	Rock 'N' Roll High School/Do You Wanna Dance	1979	—	2.00	4.00
❑ 1051 [PS]	Rock 'N' Roll High School/Do You Wanna Dance	1979	2.00	4.00	8.00
❑ 22911	Pet Sematary/Sheena Is a Punk Rocker	1989	—	2.50	5.00
❑ 22911 [PS]	Pet Sematary/Sheena Is a Punk Rocker	1989	—	2.50	5.00
❑ 27663	I Wanna Be Sedated/I Wanna Be Sedated (Ramones On 45 Mega-Mix)	1988	—	2.00	4.00
❑ 27663 [PS]	I Wanna Be Sedated/I Wanna Be Sedated (Ramones On 45 Mega-Mix)	1988	—	3.00	6.00
❑ 28599	Something to Believe In/Animal Boy	1986	2.00	4.00	8.00
❑ 29107	Howling at the Moon (Sha La La)/Wart Hog	1985	2.00	4.00	8.00
❑ 29606	The Time Has Come Today/Psycho Therapy	1983	—	3.00	6.00
❑ 49182	Baby I Love You/High Risk Insurance	1980	—	2.50	5.00
❑ 49261	Do You Remember Rock & Roll Radio/Let's Go	1980	2.00	4.00	8.00
❑ 49812	We Want the Airwaves/All's Quiet on the Western Front	1981	2.00	4.00	8.00

RAMRODS

Number	Title (A Side/B Side)	Yr	VG	VG+	NM
AMY					
❑ 813	(Ghost) Riders in the Sky/Zig Zag	1961	6.25	12.50	25.00
❑ 817	Loch Lomond Rock/Take Me Back to My Boots and Saddle	1961	5.00	10.00	20.00
❑ 846	War Cry/Boing!	1962	5.00	10.00	20.00
QUEEN					
❑ 240145	Slee-Zee/Slouchee	1962	5.00	10.00	20.00
R&H					
❑ 1001	Moonlight Surf/Night Ride	1963	12.50	25.00	50.00

RAMS, THE
FLAIR

Number	Title (A Side/B Side)	Yr	VG	VG+	NM
❑ 1066	Sweet Thing/Rock Bottom	1955	37.50	75.00	150.00

RAN-DELLS, THE

Number	Title (A Side/B Side)	Yr	VG	VG+	NM
CHAIRMAN					
❑ 4403	Martian Hop/Forgive Me, Darling (I Have Lied)	1963	5.00	10.00	20.00
❑ 4403 [PS]	Martian Hop/Forgive Me, Darling (I Have Lied)	1963	12.50	25.00	50.00
❑ 4407	Sound of the Sun/Come On and Love Me	1964	3.75	7.50	15.00
R.S.V.P.					
❑ 1104	Beyond the Stars/Wintertime	1964	3.75	7.50	15.00

RANCHEROS, THE

Number	Title (A Side/B Side)	Yr	VG	VG+	NM
DOT					
❑ 16572	Linda's Tune/Little Linda	1964	6.25	12.50	25.00
LONNIE					
❑ 5005	Linda's Tune/Little Linda	1963	12.50	25.00	50.00

RANDELL, LYNNE

Number	Title (A Side/B Side)	Yr	VG	VG+	NM
ABC					
❑ 11112	Open Letter/Right to Cry	1968	5.00	10.00	20.00
EPIC					
❑ 10147	Stranger in My Arms/Ciao Baby	1967	7.50	15.00	30.00
❑ 10197	I Need You Boy/That's a Hoe-Down	1967	7.50	15.00	30.00

RANDOLPH, BARBARA
SOUL

Number	Title (A Side/B Side)	Yr	VG	VG+	NM
❑ 35038	I Got a Feeling/You Got Me Hurtin' All Over	1967	5.00	10.00	20.00
❑ 35050	Can I Get a Witness/You Got Me Hurtin' All Over	1968	5.00	10.00	20.00

RANDY AND THE RADIANTS
SUN

Number	Title (A Side/B Side)	Yr	VG	VG+	NM
❑ 395	The Mountain's High/Peek-a-Boo	1965	6.25	12.50	25.00
❑ 398	My Way of Thinking/Truth from My Eyes	1966	6.25	12.50	25.00

RANDY AND THE RAINBOWS

Number	Title (A Side/B Side)	Yr	VG	VG+	NM
AMBIENT SOUND					
❑ 02872	Debbie/Try the Impossible	1982	—	2.50	5.00
B.T. PUPPY					
❑ 535	I'll Be Seeing You/Oh to Get Away	1967	2.50	5.00	10.00
MIKE					
❑ 4001	Lovely Lies/I'll Forget Her Tomorrow	1966	3.00	6.00	12.00
❑ 4004	Quarter to Three/He's a Fugitive	1966	3.00	6.00	12.00
❑ 4008	Bonnie's Part of Town/Can It Be	1966	3.00	6.00	12.00
RUST					
❑ 5059	Denise/Come Back	1963	7.50	15.00	30.00
—Blue label					
❑ 5059	Denise/Come Back	1963	5.00	10.00	20.00
—Mostly white label					
❑ 5073	She's My Angel/Why Do Kids Grow Up	1964	3.75	7.50	15.00
❑ 5080	Happy Teenager/Dry Your Eyes	1964	3.75	7.50	15.00
❑ 5091	Little Star/Sharin'	1964	3.75	7.50	15.00
❑ 5101	Joy Ride/Little Hot Rod Suzie	1965	3.75	7.50	15.00

RANGERS, THE

Number	Title (A Side/B Side)	Yr	VG	VG+	NM
CHALLENGE					
❑ 59229	Snow Skiing/Mogul Monster	1964	5.00	10.00	20.00
❑ 59239	Justine/Reputation	1964	5.00	10.00	20.00
FTP					
❑ 404	Four on the Floor/Riders in the Sky	1961	7.50	15.00	30.00

RANGLIN, ERNEST
STUDIO

Number	Title (A Side/B Side)	Yr	VG	VG+	NM
❑ 1	Surfing (Part 1)/Surfing (Part 2)	196?	12.50	25.00	50.00

RANK, KEN
FENTON

Number	Title (A Side/B Side)	Yr	VG	VG+	NM
❑ 2194	Twin City Saucer/Ken's Thing	1968	7.50	15.00	30.00

RARE BREED, THE
Later known as THE OHIO EXPRESS.

ATTACK

Number	Title (A Side/B Side)	Yr	VG	VG+	NM
❑ 1401	Beg, Borrow and Steal/Jeri's Theme	1966	7.50	15.00	30.00
❑ 1403	Come and Take a Ride in My Boat/Take Me to This World of Yours	1966	5.00	10.00	20.00

RARE EARTH
PRODIGAL

Number	Title (A Side/B Side)	Yr	VG	VG+	NM
❑ 0637	Crazy Love/Is Your Teacher Cool	1977	—	2.50	5.00
❑ 0640	Warm Ride/Would You Like to Come Along	1978	—	2.50	5.00

Number	Title (A Side/B Side)	Yr	VG	VG+	NM
❑ 0643	I Can Feel My Love Risin'/S.O.S. (Stop Her On Sight)	1978	—	2.50	5.00
RARE EARTH					
❑ 960/961 [DJ]	What'd I Say (stereo/mono)	1972	6.25	12.50	25.00
—Blue vinyl, promo only, white label					
❑ 5010	Generation (Light of the Sky)/Magic Key	1969	3.00	6.00	12.00
❑ 5012	Get Ready/Magic Key	1970	—	3.00	6.00
❑ 5017	(I Know) I'm Losing You/When Joanie Smiles	1970	—	3.00	6.00
❑ 5021	Born to Wander/Here Comes the Night	1970	—	3.00	6.00
❑ 5031	I Just Want to Celebrate/The Seed	1971	—	3.00	6.00
❑ 5031 [PS]	I Just Want to Celebrate/The Seed	1971	2.50	5.00	10.00
❑ 5038	Hey Big Brother/Under God's Light	1971	—	3.00	6.00
❑ 5043	What'd I Say/Nice to Be with You	1972	—	3.00	6.00
❑ 5048	Good Time Sally/Love Shines Down	1972	—	3.00	6.00
❑ 5052	We're Gonna Have a Good Time/Would You Like to Come Along	1973	—	3.00	6.00
❑ 5053	Ma/(Instrumental)	1973	—	3.00	6.00
❑ 5054	Hum Along and Dance/Come with Me	1973	—	3.00	6.00
❑ 5056	Big John Is My Name/Ma	1974	—	3.00	6.00
❑ 5057	Chained/Fresh from the Can	1974	—	3.00	6.00
❑ 5058	It Makes You Happy (But It Ain't Gonna Last Too Long)/Boogie with Me Children	1975	—	3.00	6.00
❑ 5059	Let Me Be Your Sunshine/Keep Me Out of the Storm	1976	—	3.00	6.00
❑ 5060	Midnight Lady/Walking Shtick	1976	—	3.00	6.00
RCA					
❑ PB-13076	Howzabout Some Love/Let Me Take You Out	1982	—	—	—
—Unreleased					
VERVE					
❑ 10622	Stop-Where Did Our Love Go/Mother's Oats	1968	3.00	6.00	12.00

RASCALS, THE

Includes "The Young Rascals." Also see FELIX CAVALIERE; GENE CORNISH; FELIX AND THE ESCORTS.

Number	Title (A Side/B Side)	Yr	VG	VG+	NM
ATLANTIC					
❑ 2312	I Ain't Gonna Eat Out My Heart Anymore/Slow Down	1965	3.75	7.50	15.00
—From here through Atlantic 2463, as "The Young Rascals"					
❑ 2321	Good Lovin'/Mustang Sally	1966	3.75	7.50	15.00
❑ 2338	You Better Run/Love Is a Beautiful Thing	1966	2.50	5.00	10.00
❑ 2338 [PS]	You Better Run/Love Is a Beautiful Thing	1966	5.00	10.00	20.00
❑ 2353	Come On Up/What Is the Reason	1966	2.50	5.00	10.00
❑ 2377	I've Been Lonely Too Long/If You Knew	1967	2.50	5.00	10.00
❑ 2377 [PS]	I've Been Lonely Too Long/If You Knew	1967	5.00	10.00	20.00
❑ 2401	Groovin'/Sueno	1967	2.00	4.00	8.00
❑ 2401 [PS]	Groovin'/Sueno	1967	5.00	10.00	20.00
❑ 2424	A Girl Like You/It's Love	1967	2.00	4.00	8.00
❑ 2424 [PS]	A Girl Like You/It's Love	1967	5.00	10.00	20.00
❑ 2428	Groovin' (Spanish)/Groovin' (Italian)	1967	5.00	10.00	20.00
❑ 2438	How Can I Be Sure/I'm So Happy Now	1967	2.00	4.00	8.00
❑ 2463	It's Wonderful/Of Course	1967	2.00	4.00	8.00
❑ 2493	A Beautiful Morning/Rainy Day	1968	—	3.00	6.00
—First record as "The Rascals"					
❑ 2493 [PS]	A Beautiful Morning/Rainy Day	1968	5.00	10.00	20.00
❑ 2537	People Got to Be Free/My World	1968	—	3.00	6.00
❑ 2537 [PS]	People Got to Be Free/My World	1968	3.00	6.00	12.00
❑ 2584	A Ray of Hope/Any Dance'll Do	1968	—	3.00	6.00
❑ 2584 [PS]	A Ray of Hope/Any Dance'll Do	1968	3.00	6.00	12.00
❑ 2599	Heaven/Baby I'm Blue	1969	—	3.00	6.00
❑ 2634	See/Away Away	1969	—	3.00	6.00
❑ 2634 [PS]	See/Away Away	1969	3.00	6.00	12.00
❑ 2664	Carry Me Back/Real Thing	1969	—	3.00	6.00
❑ 2664 [PS]	Carry Me Back/Real Thing	1969	3.00	6.00	12.00
❑ 2695	Hold On/I Believe	1969	—	3.00	6.00
❑ 2695 [PS]	Hold On/I Believe	1969	3.00	6.00	12.00
❑ 2743	Glory Glory/You Don't Know	1970	—	3.00	6.00
❑ 2743 [PS]	Glory Glory/You Don't Know	1970	3.00	6.00	12.00
❑ 2773	Right On/Almost Home	1970	—	3.00	6.00
COLUMBIA					
❑ 45400	Love Me/Happy Song	1971	—	3.00	6.00
❑ 45491	Lucky Day/Love Letter	1971	—	3.00	6.00
❑ 45568	Brother Tree/Saga of New York	1972	—	3.00	6.00
❑ 45600	Echoes/Hummin' Song	1972	—	3.00	6.00
❑ 45649	Jungle Walk/Saga of New York	1972	2.50	5.00	10.00
PHILCO					
❑ HP-18	A Girl Like You/I've Been Lonely Too Long	1967	3.75	7.50	15.00
—4-inch plastic "Hip Pocket Record" with color sleeve					

RASPBERRIES

Also see ERIC CARMEN; THE CHOIR.

Number	Title (A Side/B Side)	Yr	VG	VG+	NM
CAPITOL					
❑ 3280	Don't Want to Say Goodbye/Rock and Roll Mama	1972	2.00	4.00	8.00
❑ 3280 [PS]	Don't Want to Say Goodbye/Rock and Roll Mama	1972	6.25	12.50	25.00
❑ 3348	Go All the Way/With You in My Life	1972	—	3.00	6.00
❑ 3473	I Wanna Be with You/Goin' Nowhere Tonight	1972	—	3.00	6.00
❑ 3546	Let's Pretend/Every Way I Can	1973	—	3.00	6.00
❑ 3546 [PS]	Let's Pretend/Every Way I Can	1973	3.00	6.00	12.00
❑ 3610	Tonight/Had to Get Over a Heartbreak	1973	—	3.00	6.00
❑ 3765	I'm a Rocker/Money Down	1973	—	3.00	6.00
❑ 3826	Don't Want to Say Goodbye/Ecstasy	1974	—	3.00	6.00
❑ 3885	Drivin' Around/Might As Well	1974	—	3.00	6.00
❑ 3946	Overnight Sensation (Hit Record)/Hands on You	1974	—	3.00	6.00
❑ 4001	The Party's Over/Cruisin' Music	1974	—	3.00	6.00

RATIONALS, THE

Number	Title (A Side/B Side)	Yr	VG	VG+	NM
A-SQUARE					
❑ 101	Look What You're Doin'/Gave My Love	1966	6.25	12.50	25.00
❑ 103	Feelin' Lost/Little Girls Cry	1966	5.00	10.00	20.00
❑ 104/3	Leavin' Here/Feelin' Lost	1966	6.25	12.50	25.00
❑ 104	Leavin' Here/Respect	1966	7.50	15.00	30.00
—This is the original issue of this single					
❑ 107	I Need You/Out in the Streets	1968	5.00	10.00	20.00
❑ 402	I Need You/Get the Picture	1967	6.25	12.50	25.00
—B-side by SRC (Scott Richard Case)					
CAMEO					
❑ 437	Respect/Feelin' Lost	1966	3.00	6.00	12.00
❑ 455	Hold On Baby/Sing	1967	3.75	7.50	15.00
❑ 481	Leavin' Here/Not Like It Is	1967	3.75	7.50	15.00
CAPITOL					
❑ 2124	I Need You/Out in the Streets	1968	3.00	6.00	12.00
CREWE					
❑ 340	Handbags and Gladrags/Guitar Army	1969	2.50	5.00	10.00
DANBY'S					
❑ (no #)	Turn On/Irrational	1966	12.50	25.00	50.00
—Made for Danby's clothiers					
GENESIS					
❑ 1	Guitar Army/Sunset	1969	3.75	7.50	15.00

RAVEN, PAUL

See GARY GLITTER.

RAVENAIRS, THE

Number	Title (A Side/B Side)	Yr	VG	VG+	NM
ALGONQUIN					
❑ 718	A Night to Remember/Together Forever	1958	25.00	50.00	100.00
—Originally released as "The Rivieras"					

RAVENS, THE

Also see JIMMY RICKS.

Number	Title (A Side/B Side)	Yr	VG	VG+	NM
ARGO					
❑ 5255	Kneel and Pray/I Can't Believe	1956	10.00	20.00	40.00
❑ 5261	A Simple Prayer/Water Boy	1956	20.00	40.00	80.00
❑ 5276	That'll Be the Day/Dear One	1957	7.50	15.00	30.00
❑ 5284	Here Is My Heart/Lazy Mule	1957	7.50	15.00	30.00
CHECKER					
❑ 871	That'll Be the Day/Dear One	1957	5.00	10.00	20.00
COLUMBIA					
❑ 1-903	Don't Look Now/Time Takes Care of Everything	1950	375.00	750.00	1500.
—Microgroove 33 1/3 single					
❑ 6-903	Don't Look Now/Time Takes Care of Everything	1950	175.00	350.00	700.00
❑ 1-925	My Baby's Gone/I'm So Crazy for Love	1950	375.00	750.00	1500.
—Microgroove 33 1/3 single					
❑ 6-925	My Baby's Gone/I'm So Crazy for Love	1950	150.00	300.00	600.00
❑ 39112	You Don't Have to Drop a Heart/Midnight Blues	1950	500.00	1000.	2000.
❑ 39194	You're Always in My Dreams/Gotta Find My Baby	1951	500.00	1000.	2000.
❑ 39408	You Foolish Thing/Honey I Don't Want You	1951	500.00	1000.	2000.
JUBILEE					
❑ 5184	Bye Bye Baby Blues/Happy Go Lucky Baby	1955	7.50	15.00	30.00
❑ 5203	Green Eyes/The Bells of San Rafael	1955	7.50	15.00	30.00
—As "Jimmy Ricks and the Ravens"					
❑ 5217	On Chapel Hill/We'll Raise a Ruckus Tonight	1955	7.50	15.00	30.00
❑ 5237	I'll Always Be in Love with You/(Take Me Back To My) Boots and Saddles	1956	7.50	15.00	30.00
—As "Jimmy Ricks and the Ravens"					
MERCURY					
❑ 5764	There's No Use Pretending/Wagon Wheels	1951	75.00	150.00	300.00
❑ 5800	Begin the Beguine/Looking for My Baby	1952	62.50	125.00	250.00
❑ 5853	Why Did You Leave Me/Chloe	1952	62.50	125.00	250.00
❑ 8291	Rock Me All Night Long/One Sweet Letter	1952	37.50	75.00	150.00
❑ 70060	I'll Be Back/Don't Mention My Name	1953	50.00	100.00	200.00
❑ 70119	Come a Little Bit Closer/She's Got to Go	1953	37.50	75.00	150.00
❑ 70213	Who'll Be the Fool/Rough Ridin'	1953	37.50	75.00	150.00
❑ 70240	Without a Song/Walkin' My Blues Away	1953	37.50	75.00	150.00
❑ 70307	September Song/Escortin' Or Courtin'	1954	37.50	75.00	150.00
❑ 70330	Going Home/Lonesome Road	1954	37.50	75.00	150.00
❑ 70413	I've Got You Under My Skin/Love Is No Dream	1954	62.50	125.00	250.00
—Pink label					
❑ 70413	I've Got You Under My Skin/Love Is No Dream	1954	25.00	50.00	100.00
—Black label					
❑ 70505	White Christmas/Silent Night	1954	50.00	100.00	200.00
—Pink label					
❑ 70505	White Christmas/Silent Night	1954	25.00	50.00	100.00
—Black label					
❑ 70554	Ol' Man River/Write Me a Letter	1955	50.00	100.00	200.00
—Pink label					
❑ 70554	Ol' Man River/Write Me a Letter	1955	25.00	50.00	100.00
—Black label					
NATIONAL					
❑ 9111	Count Every Star/I'm Gonna Paper All My Walls with Your Love	1950	1500.	2250.	3000.
—The only known Ravens single on a National 45; 20 other Ravens singles exist on National 78s					
OKEH					
❑ 6825	The Whiffenpoof Song/I Get All My Lovin' on a Saturday Night	1951	125.00	250.00	500.00
❑ 6843	That Old Gang of Mine/Everything But You	1951	125.00	250.00	500.00
❑ 6888	Mam'selle/Calypso Song	1952	100.00	200.00	400.00
SAVOY					
❑ 1540	White Christmas/Silent Night	1958	5.00	10.00	20.00
TOP RANK					
❑ 2003	Into the Shadows/The Rising Sun	1959	6.25	12.50	25.00
❑ 2016	Solitude/Hole in the Middle of the Moon	1959	6.25	12.50	25.00

7-Inch Extended Plays

Number	Title (A Side/B Side)	Yr	VG	VG+	NM
KING					
❑ 310	(contents unknown)	1954	125.00	250.00	500.00
❑ 310 [PS]	The Ravens Featuring Jimmy Ricks	1954	125.00	250.00	500.00
RENDITION					
❑ 104	(contents unknown)	195?	375.00	750.00	1500.
❑ 104 [PS]	Ol' Man River	195?	500.00	1000.	2000.

RAWLS, LOU

Number	Title (A Side/B Side)	Yr	VG	VG+	NM
ARISTA					
❑ 0103	Baby You Don't Know How Good You Are/Hour Glass	1975	—	3.00	6.00

Number	Title (A Side/B Side)	Yr	VG	VG+	NM
BELL					
❑ 45608	She's Gone/Hour Glass	1974	—	3.00	6.00
❑ 45616	Who Can Tell Us Why?/Now You're Coming Back Michelle	1974	—	3.00	6.00
CANDIX					
❑ 305	In My Little Black Book/Just Thought You'd Like to Know	1960	5.00	10.00	20.00
❑ 312	When We Get Old/Eighty Ways	1961	5.00	10.00	20.00
CAPITOL					
❑ 2026	Little Drummer Boy/A Child with a Toy	1967	2.00	4.00	8.00
❑ 2084	Evil Woman/My Ancestors	1968	2.00	4.00	8.00
❑ 2172	Soul Serenade/You're Good for Me	1968	2.00	4.00	8.00
❑ 2252	Down Here on the Ground/I'm Satisfied (The Duffy Theme)	1968	2.00	4.00	8.00
❑ 2348	The Split/Why Can't I Speak	1968	2.00	4.00	8.00
❑ 2408	It's You/Sweet Charity	1969	2.00	4.00	8.00
❑ 2550	Your Good Thing (Is About to End)/Season of the Witch	1969	2.00	4.00	8.00
❑ 2668	I Can't Make It Alone/Make the World Go Away	1969	2.00	4.00	8.00
❑ 2734	You've Made Me So Very Happy/Let's Burn Down the Cornfield	1970	2.00	4.00	8.00
❑ 2856	Bring It On Home/Can You Dig It-Take Me for What I Am	1970	2.00	4.00	8.00
❑ 2942	Win Your Love for Me/Coppin' a Plea	1970	2.00	4.00	8.00
❑ 4622	That Lucky Old Sun/In My Heart	1961	3.75	7.50	15.00
❑ 4669	Nine-Pound Hammer/Above My Head	1961	3.75	7.50	15.00
❑ 4695	The Wedding (The Bride)/The Biggest Lover in Town	1962	3.00	6.00	12.00
❑ 4743	Trust Me/Please Let Me Be the First to Know	1962	3.00	6.00	12.00
❑ 4761	Save Your Love for Me/Trust Me	1962	3.00	6.00	12.00
❑ 4803	Stormy Monday/Sweet Lover	1962	3.00	6.00	12.00
—With Les McCann					
❑ 5049	Tobacco Road/Blues for Four-String Guitar	1963	3.00	6.00	12.00
❑ 5160	The House Next Door/Come On In, Mr. Blues	1964	3.00	6.00	12.00
❑ 5227	Love Is Blind/I Fell in Love	1964	3.00	6.00	12.00
❑ 5424	Three O'Clock in the Morning/Nothing Really Feels the Same	1965	3.00	6.00	12.00
❑ 5505	What'll I Do/Can I Please	1965	3.00	6.00	12.00
❑ 5655	The Shadow of Your Smile/Southside Blues	1966	2.50	5.00	10.00
❑ 5709	Love Is a Hurtin' Thing/Memory Lane	1966	2.50	5.00	10.00
❑ 5790	You Can Bring Me All Your Heartaches/A Woman Who's a Woman	1966	2.50	5.00	10.00
❑ 5824	Trouble Down Here Below/The Life That I Lead	1967	2.50	5.00	10.00
❑ 5824 [PS]	Trouble Down Here Below/The Life That I Lead	1967	2.50	5.00	10.00
❑ 5869	Dead End Street/Yes It Hurts, Doesn't It	1967	2.50	5.00	10.00
❑ 5941	Show Business/When Love Goes Wrong	1967	2.50	5.00	10.00
❑ S7-18908	What Are You Doing New Year's Eve?/Have Yourself a Merry Little Christmas	1995	—	—	3.00
EPIC					
❑ 02999	Now Is the Time for Love/Will You Kiss Me One More Time	1982	—	2.00	4.00
❑ 03299	Together Again/Here Comes Garfield	1982	—	2.00	4.00
—Lou Rawls and Desiree Goyette					
❑ 03357	Let Me Show You How/Watch Your Back	1982	—	2.00	4.00
❑ 03758	Wind Beneath My Wings/Midnight Sun	1983	—	2.00	4.00
❑ 03944	Couple More Years/Upside Down	1983	—	2.00	4.00
❑ 04079	The One I Sing My Love Songs To/You Can't Take It With You	1983	—	2.00	4.00
❑ 04550	All-Time Lover/When We Were Young	1984	—	2.00	4.00
❑ 04677	Close Company/The Lady in My Life	1984	—	2.00	4.00
❑ 04773	Close Company/Forever I Do	1985	—	2.00	4.00
❑ 05714	Learn to Love Again/Ready or Not	1985	—	2.00	4.00
❑ 05831	Are You With Me/(Instrumental)	1986	—	2.00	4.00
❑ 05831 [PS]	Are You With Me/(Instrumental)	1986	—	2.00	4.00
❑ 06145	Stop Me from Starting This Feeling/Never Entered My Mind	1986	—	2.00	4.00
GAMBLE & HUFF					
❑ 310	I Wish You Belonged to Me/(B-side unknown)	1987	—	2.50	5.00
MGM					
❑ 14262	A Natural Man/You Can't Hold On	1971	—	3.00	6.00
❑ 14349	His Song Shall Be Sung/I'm Waiting	1972	—	3.00	6.00
❑ 14428	Politician/Walk On In	1972	—	3.00	6.00
❑ 14489	Man of Value/Learning Cup	1973	—	3.00	6.00
❑ 14527	Star Spangled Banner/Just a Closer Walk with Thee	1973	—	3.00	6.00
❑ 14574	Send for Me/Morning Comes Around	1973	—	3.00	6.00
❑ 14652	Dead End Street/Love Is a Hurtin' Thing	1973	—	3.00	6.00
PHILADELPHIA INT'L.					
❑ 3102	Ain't That Loving You (For More Reasons Than One)/(B-side unknown)	1980	—	2.50	5.00
❑ 3114	I Go Crazy/Be Anything (But Be Mine)	1980	—	2.50	5.00
❑ 3592	You'll Never Find Another Love Like Mine/Let's Fall in Love All Over Again	1976	—	2.50	5.00
❑ 3604	Groovy People/This Song Will Last Forever	1976	—	2.50	5.00
❑ 3623	See You When I Git There/Spring Again	1977	—	2.50	5.00
❑ 3634	Lady Love/Not the Staying Kind	1977	—	2.50	5.00
❑ 3643	One Life to Live/If I Coulda, Woulda, Shoulda	1978	—	2.50	5.00
❑ 3653	There Will Be Love/Unforgettable	1978	—	2.50	5.00
❑ 3672	Send In the Clowns/This Song Will Last Forever	1978	—	2.50	5.00
❑ 3684	Let Me Be Good to You/Lover's Holiday	1979	—	2.50	5.00
❑ 3738	Sit Down and Talk to Me/(B-side unknown)	1979	—	2.50	5.00
❑ 70051	Hoochie Coochie Man/You've Lost That Lovin' Feelin'	1981	—	2.50	5.00

RAY, DANNY

Number	Title (A Side/B Side)	Yr	VG	VG+	NM
VIN					
❑ 1025	Love Me/Gone	1960	25.00	50.00	100.00

RAY, DIANE

Number	Title (A Side/B Side)	Yr	VG	VG+	NM
MERCURY					
❑ 72117	Please Don't Talk to the Lifeguard/That's All I Want from You	1963	3.75	7.50	15.00
❑ 72117 [PS]	Please Don't Talk to the Lifeguard/That's All I Want from You	1963	25.00	50.00	100.00
❑ 72195	My Summer Love/Where Is the Boy	1963	3.75	7.50	15.00
❑ 72195 [PS]	My Summer Love/Where Is the Boy	1963	15.00	30.00	60.00
❑ 72223	Snow Man/Just So Bobby Can See	1963	3.75	7.50	15.00
❑ 72223 [PS]	Snow Man/Just So Bobby Can See	1963	15.00	30.00	60.00
❑ 72248	No Arms Can Ever Hold You/Tied Up with Mary	1964	3.75	7.50	15.00
❑ 72276	Happy Happy Birthday Baby/That Boy's Gonna Be Mine	1964	3.75	7.50	15.00

RAY, JAMES

Number	Title (A Side/B Side)	Yr	VG	VG+	NM
CAPRICE					
❑ 110	If You Gotta Make a Fool of Somebody/It's Been a Drag	1961	7.50	15.00	30.00
❑ 114	Itty Bitty Pieces/You Remember the Face	1962	6.25	12.50	25.00
❑ 117	Things Are Gonna Be Different/A Miracle	1962	6.25	12.50	25.00
CONGRESS					
❑ 109	Marie/The Old Man and the Mule	1963	5.00	10.00	20.00
❑ 201	Do the Monkey/Put Me in Your Diary	1963	5.00	10.00	20.00
❑ 203	The Masquerade Is Over/One by One	1963	5.00	10.00	20.00
❑ 218	We Got a Thing Goin' On/On That Day	1964	5.00	10.00	20.00
DYNAMIC SOUND					
❑ 503	I've Got My Mind Set on You/Always	1963	10.00	20.00	40.00
—The A-side was remade by George Harrison in 1987 as "Got My Mind Set on You"					

7-Inch Extended Plays

Number	Title (A Side/B Side)	Yr	VG	VG+	NM
CAPRICE					
❑ 1002	(contents unknown)	1962	12.50	25.00	50.00
❑ 1002 [PS]	James Ray	1962	12.50	25.00	50.00

RAY, JOHNNIE

Also see DORIS DAY/JOHNNIE RAY.

Number	Title (A Side/B Side)	Yr	VG	VG+	NM
CADENCE					
❑ 1387	In the Heart of a Fool/Let's Forget It Now	1960	3.00	6.00	12.00
COLUMBIA					
❑ 39636	Please Mr. Sun/Here Am I — Broken Hearted	1952	3.75	7.50	15.00
❑ 39659	Cry/Because of You	1952	3.00	6.00	12.00
—B-side by Tony Bennett; early reissue					
❑ 39698	What's the Use?/Mountains in Moonlight	1952	3.75	7.50	15.00
❑ 39700	Coffee and Cigarettes/Don't Blame Me	1952	3.00	6.00	12.00
❑ 39701	Walking My Baby Back Home/Out in the Cold Again	1952	3.00	6.00	12.00
❑ 39702	Don't Take Your Love from Me/The Lady Drinks Champagne	1952	3.00	6.00	12.00
❑ 39703	All of Me/Give Me Time	1952	3.00	6.00	12.00
—The above four comprise a box set					
❑ 39720	What's the Use?/A Guy Is a Guy	1952	2.50	5.00	10.00
—B-side by Doris Day					
❑ 39750	Walkin' My Baby Back Home/Give Me Time	1952	3.75	7.50	15.00
❑ 39788	All of Me/A Sinner Am I	1952	3.75	7.50	15.00
❑ 39814	Gee But I'm Lonesome/Don't Say Love Has Ended	1952	3.75	7.50	15.00
❑ 39837	Love Me (Baby Can't You Love Me)/Faith Can Move Mountains	1952	3.75	7.50	15.00
❑ 39897	The Thing I Might Have Been/The Commandments of Love	1952	3.75	7.50	15.00
❑ 39908	A Touch of God's Hand/I'm Gonna Walk and Talk with the Lord	1952	3.75	7.50	15.00
❑ 39939	Mr. Midnight/Oh, What a Sad, Sad Day	1953	3.00	6.00	12.00
❑ 39961	Somebody Stole My Gal/Glad Rag Doll	1953	3.00	6.00	12.00
❑ 40006	Satisfied/With These Hands	1953	3.00	6.00	12.00
❑ 40046	All I Do Is Dream of You/Tell the Lady I Said Goodbye	1953	3.00	6.00	12.00
❑ 40090	Please Don't Talk About Me When I'm Gone/An Orchid for the Lady	1953	3.00	6.00	12.00
❑ 40154	Why Should I Be Sorry?/You'd Be Surprised	1954	3.00	6.00	12.00
❑ 40200	Such a Night/Destiny	1954	3.75	7.50	15.00
❑ 40224	Hernando's Hideaway/Hey There	1954	3.00	6.00	12.00
❑ 40252	Going-Going-Gone/To Ev'ry Girl-To Ev'ry Boy	1954	3.00	6.00	12.00
❑ 40324	Papa Loves Mambo/The Only Girl I'll Ever Love	1954	3.00	6.00	12.00
❑ 40391	Alexander's Ragtime Band/If You Believe	1954	3.00	6.00	12.00
❑ 40392	As Time Goes By/Nobody's Sweetheart	1954	3.00	6.00	12.00
❑ 40435	Parade of Broken Hearts/Paths of Paradise	1955	3.00	6.00	12.00
❑ 40471	Flip, Flop and Fly/Thine Eyes Are As the Eyes of a Dove	1955	3.00	6.00	12.00
❑ 40528	Song of the Dreamer/I've Got So Many Million Miles	1955	3.00	6.00	12.00
❑ 40578	Johnnie's Comin' Home/Love, Love, Love	1955	3.00	6.00	12.00
❑ 40613	Who's Sorry Now/A Heart Comes In Handy	1955	3.00	6.00	12.00
❑ 40649	Ain't Misbehavin'/Walk Along with Kings	1956	3.00	6.00	12.00
❑ 40695	Because I Love You/Goodbye, Au Revoir, Adios	1956	3.00	6.00	12.00
❑ 40729	Just Walking in the Rain/In the Candlelight	1956	2.50	5.00	10.00
❑ 40803	You Don't Owe Me a Thing/Look Homeward, Angel	1956	2.50	5.00	10.00
❑ 40893	Yes Tonight, Josephine/No Wedding Today	1957	2.50	5.00	10.00
❑ 40942	Build Your Love (On a Strong Foundation)/Street of Memories	1957	2.50	5.00	10.00
❑ 41002	Pink Sweater Angel/Texas Tambourine	1957	2.50	5.00	10.00
❑ 41069	Miss Me Just a Little/Soliloquy of a Fool	1957	2.50	5.00	10.00
❑ 41124	Plant a Little Seed/Strollin' Girl	1958	2.50	5.00	10.00
❑ 41162	Endlessly/Lonely for a Letter	1958	2.50	5.00	10.00
❑ 41213	Up Until Now/No Regrets	1958	2.50	5.00	10.00
❑ 41327	One Man's Love Song Is Another Man's Blues/When's Your Birthday, Baby	1959	2.50	5.00	10.00
❑ 41372	Call Me Yours/Here and Now	1959	2.50	5.00	10.00
❑ 41438	I'll Never Fall in Love Again/You're All That I Live For	1959	2.50	5.00	10.00
❑ 41528	When It's Springtime in the Rockies/An Ordinary Couple	1959	2.50	5.00	10.00
❑ 41626	I'll Make You Mine/Before You	1959	2.50	5.00	10.00
❑ 41705	Don't Leave Me Now/Tell Me	1960	2.50	5.00	10.00

Number	Title (A Side/B Side)	Yr	VG	VG+	NM
DECCA					
❑ 31459	After My Laughter Came Tears/Lookout Chattanooga	1963	2.00	4.00	8.00
❑ 31507	Lonely Wine/I Can't Stop Crying for You	1963	2.00	4.00	8.00
❑ 31601	Can't I/Break My Heartbreak	1964	2.00	4.00	8.00
GROOVE					
❑ 58-0044	One Life/Sometime Love	1964	2.00	4.00	8.00
LIBERTY					
❑ 55400	I Believe/A Mother's Love	1961	2.50	5.00	10.00
—With Timi Yuro					
❑ 55404	A Lover's Question/Nothing Goes Up Without Coming Down	1962	2.00	4.00	8.00
❑ 55431	Cry/Scotch and Soda	1962	2.00	4.00	8.00
OKEH					
❑ 6809	Whiskey and Gin/Tell the Lady I Said Goodbye	1951	6.25	12.50	25.00
❑ 6840	Cry/The Little White Cloud That Cried	1951	5.00	10.00	20.00
UNITED ARTISTS					
❑ 341	How Many Nights, How Many Days/I'll Bring Along My Banjo	1961	2.50	5.00	10.00

7-Inch Extended Plays

Number	Title (A Side/B Side)	Yr	VG	VG+	NM
COLUMBIA					
❑ B-2115	Just Walking in the Rain/All of Me//In the Candlelight/Weaker Than Wise	195?	5.00	10.00	20.00
❑ B-2115 [PS]	(title unknown)	195?	5.00	10.00	20.00
❑ B-2536	*Walkin' My Baby Back Home/Somebody Stole My Gal/Nobody's Sweetheart/Please Don't Talk About Me When I'm Gone	195?	5.00	10.00	20.00
❑ B-2536 [PS]	Johnnie Ray (Hall of Fame Series)	195?	5.00	10.00	20.00
❑ B-2566	*Just Walking in the Rain/Please, Mr. Sun/All of Me/Tell the Lady I Said Goodbye	195?	5.00	10.00	20.00
❑ B-2566 [PS]	Johnnie Ray (Hall of Fame Series)	195?	5.00	10.00	20.00
❑ B-9611	Pretty-Eyed Baby/Lotus Blossom//Shake a Hand/I'll Never Be Free	1957	5.00	10.00	20.00
❑ B-9611 [PS]	The Big Beat, Part 1	1957	5.00	10.00	20.00
❑ B-9612	(contents unknown)	1957	5.00	10.00	20.00
❑ B-9612 [PS]	The Big Beat, Part 2	1957	5.00	10.00	20.00
EPIC					
❑ EG-7021	Cry/The Little White Cloud That Cried//Whiskey and Gin/Tell the Lady I Said Goodbye	1957	6.25	12.50	25.00
❑ EG-7021 [PS]	Johnnie Ray's Greatest	1957	6.25	12.50	25.00

RAY AND THE DARCHAES

Number	Title (A Side/B Side)	Yr	VG	VG+	NM
ALJON					
❑ 1249	Carol/Little Girl So Fine	1962	30.00	60.00	120.00
BUZZY					
❑ 202	Darling Forever/There Will Always Be	1962	25.00	50.00	100.00

RAY-O-VACS, THE

Number	Title (A Side/B Side)	Yr	VG	VG+	NM
ATCO					
❑ 6085	Party Time/Crying All Alone	1957	6.25	12.50	25.00
DECCA					
❑ 48162	Besame Mucho/You Gotta Love My Baby Too	1950	6.25	12.50	25.00
❑ 48181	A Kiss in the Dark/Got Two Arms	1950	6.25	12.50	25.00
❑ 48197	Goodnight My Love/Take Me Back to My Boots and Saddle	1951	6.25	12.50	25.00
❑ 48211	You Can Depend on Me/If You Ever Should Leave Me	1951	6.25	12.50	25.00
❑ 48221	My Baby's Gone/Let's	1951	6.25	12.50	25.00
❑ 48234	What's Mine Is Mine/I Still Love You Baby	1951	6.25	12.50	25.00
❑ 48260	Charmaine/Hands Across the Table	1951	6.25	12.50	25.00
❑ 48274	When the Swallows Come Back to Capistrano/She's a Real Lovin' Baby	1952	6.25	12.50	25.00
JOSIE					
❑ 763	Darling/Ridin' High	1954	7.50	15.00	30.00
❑ 781	I Still Love You/Daddy	1955	7.50	15.00	30.00
JUBILEE					
❑ 5098	What Can I Say/Start Lovin' Me	1952	7.50	15.00	30.00
❑ 5124	Outside of Paradise/You Know	1953	7.50	15.00	30.00
KAISER					
❑ 384	Crying All Alone/Party Time	1956	7.50	15.00	30.00
❑ 389	Wine-O/Hong Kong	1956	7.50	15.00	30.00
SHARP					
❑ 103	I'll Always Be in Love with You/Little Boy	1960	5.00	10.00	20.00

RAY-VONS, THE

Number	Title (A Side/B Side)	Yr	VG	VG+	NM
LAURIE					
❑ 3248	Judy/Regina	1964	20.00	40.00	80.00

RAYDIO

See RAY PARKER JR.

RAYS, THE

Number	Title (A Side/B Side)	Yr	VG	VG+	NM
AMY					
❑ 900	Love Another Girl/Sad Saturday	1964	2.00	4.00	8.00
CAMEO					
❑ 117	Silhouettes/Daddy Cool	1957	6.25	12.50	25.00
❑ 128	Rendezvous/Triangle	1958	7.50	15.00	30.00
❑ 133	Rags to Riches/The Man Above	1958	7.50	15.00	30.00
CHESS					
❑ 1613	Tippity Top/Moo-Goo-Gai-Pan	1956	6.25	12.50	25.00
❑ 1678	How Long Must I Wait/Second Fiddle	1957	6.25	12.50	25.00
UNART					
❑ 2001	Souvenirs of Summertime/Elevator Operator	1958	10.00	20.00	40.00
XYZ					
❑ 100	My Steady Girl/No One Loves You Like I Do	1957	15.00	30.00	60.00
❑ 102	Silhouettes/Daddy Cool	1957	50.00	100.00	200.00
—Gray label					
❑ 102	Silhouettes/Daddy Cool	1957	15.00	30.00	60.00
—Blue label					
❑ 106	Souvenirs of Summertime/Elevator Operator	1958	12.50	25.00	50.00
❑ 600	Why Do You Look the Other Way/Zimbo Lula	1959	12.50	25.00	50.00
❑ 605	It's a Cryin' Shame/Mediterranean Moon	1959	10.00	20.00	40.00
❑ 607	Magic Moon/Louie Hoo Hoo	1960	10.00	20.00	40.00
—Blue label					
❑ 607	Magic Moon/Louie Hoo Hoo	1960	6.25	12.50	25.00
—Red label					
❑ 608	Old Devil Moon/Silver Starlight	1960	6.25	12.50	25.00

7-Inch Extended Plays

Number	Title (A Side/B Side)	Yr	VG	VG+	NM
CHESS					
❑ 5120	(contents unknown)	1958	100.00	200.00	400.00
❑ 5120 [PS]	The Rays	1958	100.00	200.00	400.00

RAYS, THE (2)

Number	Title (A Side/B Side)	Yr	VG	VG+	NM
PERRI					
❑ 1004	Are You Happy Now/Bright Brown Eyes	1962	7.50	15.00	30.00
—Frankie Valli performed on this record					

RE'VELLS, THE

Number	Title (A Side/B Side)	Yr	VG	VG+	NM
ROMAN PRESS					
❑ 201	Let It Please Be You/Love Walked In	1962	25.00	50.00	100.00

RE-VELS, THE

Number	Title (A Side/B Side)	Yr	VG	VG+	NM
ATLAS					
❑ 1035	My Lost Love/Love Me, Baby	1954	100.00	200.00	400.00
—As "The Re-Vels Quartette"					
CHESS					
❑ 1708	False Alarm/When You Come Back to Me	1958	37.50	75.00	150.00
SOUND					
❑ 129	You Lied to Me/Later, Later Baby	1956	37.50	75.00	150.00
❑ 135	Dream, My Darlin', Dream/Cha Cha Toni	1956	37.50	75.00	150.00
TEEN					
❑ 122	So in Love/It Happened to Me	1955	200.00	400.00	600.00

REAL ORIGINAL BEATLES, THE

Yeah, right.

Number	Title (A Side/B Side)	Yr	VG	VG+	NM
DOT					
❑ 16655	The Beatle Story (Part 1)/The Beatle Story (Part 2)	1964	5.00	10.00	20.00

REBELS, THE (1)

See ROCKIN' REBELS.

REBELS, THE (2)

Number	Title (A Side/B Side)	Yr	VG	VG+	NM
KING'S X					
❑ 3362	In the Park/In My Heart	1959	250.00	500.00	1000.

REBELS, THE (3)

Number	Title (A Side/B Side)	Yr	VG	VG+	NM
PEACOCK					
❑ 1909	The Donkey Step/Just Give Me Your Heart	1962	5.00	10.00	20.00

REBENACK, MAC

See DR. JOHN.

REBOUNDS, THE

This is not the group that became the Stampeders, according to a former member of the band.

Number	Title (A Side/B Side)	Yr	VG	VG+	NM
TOWER					
❑ 288	Since I Fell for You/I'm Not Your Steppin' Stone	1966	3.75	7.50	15.00

RECALLS, THE

Number	Title (A Side/B Side)	Yr	VG	VG+	NM
ARROW					
❑ 2002	No Reason/Nobody's Guy	196?	20.00	40.00	80.00

RECORD, EUGENE

Also see THE CHI-LITES.

Number	Title (A Side/B Side)	Yr	VG	VG+	NM
WARNER BROS.					
❑ 8322	Laying Beside You/Love Don't Live by Sex Alone	1977	—	2.50	5.00
❑ 8386	Mother of Love/Overdose of Joy	1977	—	2.50	5.00
❑ 8570	You Are the Star of My Show/Trying to Get to You	1978	—	2.00	4.00
❑ 8836	I Don't Mind/Take Everything	1979	—	2.00	4.00
❑ 8890	Sweet Insanity/Where Are You	1979	—	2.00	4.00
❑ 49060	Sweet Insanity/Where Are You	1979	—	2.00	4.00
❑ 49126	Help Yourself to Love/Fan the Fire	1979	—	2.00	4.00

RED HOT CHILI PEPPERS

Number	Title (A Side/B Side)	Yr	VG	VG+	NM
EMI					
❑ S7-18210	Deck the Halls/Knock Me Down	1994	—	2.50	5.00
—Red vinyl					
❑ S7-56949	Behind the Sun/Fire	1993	—	2.00	4.00
❑ S7-57992	Higher Ground/If You Want Me to Stay	1992	—	2.00	4.00
EMI AMERICA					
❑ B-8280	Hollywood (Africa)/Nevermind	198?	2.50	5.00	10.00
WARNER BROS.					
❑ 15993	Under the Bridge/Give It Away	1992	—	—	3.00
—Reissue; first release of B-side on U.S. 45					
❑ 7-16875	Otherside/How Strong	2000	—	—	3.00
❑ 16913	Scar Tissue/Gong Li	1999	—	—	3.00
❑ 18401	Soul to Squeeze/Nobody Weird Like Me	1993	—	—	3.00
❑ 18978	Under the Bridge/The Righteous and the Wicked	1992	—	2.00	4.00
WTG					
❑ 68678	Taste the Rain/All for Love	1989	—	2.00	4.00
—B-side by Nancy Wilson (of Heart)					

REDBONE

Also see PAT AND LOLLY VEGAS.

Number	Title (A Side/B Side)	Yr	VG	VG+	NM
EPIC					
❑ 10597	Crazy Cajun Cade Walk Band/Night Come Down	1970	—	3.00	6.00
❑ 10670	Maggie/New Blue Sermonette	1970	—	3.00	6.00
❑ 10712	Who Can Say/Light as a Feather	1971	—	3.00	6.00
❑ 10749	The Witch Queen of New Orleans/Chant: 13th Hour	1971	—	3.00	6.00
❑ 10839	When You Got Trouble/(B-side unknown)	1972	—	2.50	5.00
❑ 10866	One Monkey (Don't Stop No Show)/Message from a Drum	1972	—	2.50	5.00
❑ 10910	Already Here/Fais-Do	1972	—	2.50	5.00
❑ 10946	Poison Ivy/Condition Your Condition	1973	—	2.50	5.00

Number	Title (A Side/B Side)	Yr	VG	VG+	NM
❑ 10979	We Were All Wounded at Wounded Knee/Speakeasy	1973	—	2.50	5.00
❑ 11035	Come and Get Your Love/Your Miserable Face	1973	—	2.50	5.00
❑ 11035	Come and Get Your Love/Day to Day Life	1973	—	2.50	5.00
❑ 11131	Wovoka/Clouds in My Sunshine	1974	—	2.00	4.00
❑ 50015	Suzie Girl/Interstate Highway 101	1974	—	2.00	4.00
❑ 50043	One More Time/Blood, Sweat and Tears	1974	—	2.00	4.00
❑ 50074	Only You and Rock and Roll/Interstate Highway 101	1975	—	2.00	4.00
❑ 50107	Physical Attraction/I've Got to Find the Right Woman	1975	—	2.00	4.00
RCA					
❑ PB-11096	Give Our Love Another Try/Funny Silk	1977	—	2.00	4.00
❑ PB-11182	Checkin' It Out/Funky Silk	1977	—	2.00	4.00

REDCOATS, THE

Also see STEVE ALAIMO.

Number	Title (A Side/B Side)	Yr	VG	VG+	NM
KITE					
❑ 2003	Perkin/Hi Ho	1957	12.50	25.00	50.00
❑ 2003	Perkins/Hi Ho	1957	12.50	25.00	50.00
—Note slight variation in A-side title					

REDDING, OTIS

Also see OTIS AND CARLA; THE SHOOTERS.

Number	Title (A Side/B Side)	Yr	VG	VG+	NM
ATCO					
❑ 6592	Hard to Handle/Amen	1968	2.50	5.00	10.00
❑ 6612	I've Got Dreams to Remember/Nobody's Fault But Mine	1968	2.50	5.00	10.00
❑ 6631	White Christmas/Merry Christmas, Baby	1968	2.50	5.00	10.00
❑ 6636	Papa's Got a Brand New Bag/Direct Me	1968	2.50	5.00	10.00
❑ 6654	A Lover's Question/You Made a Man Out of Me	1969	2.50	5.00	10.00
❑ 6677	Love Man/I Can't Turn You Loose	1969	2.50	5.00	10.00
❑ 6700	Free Me/Higher and Higher	1969	2.50	5.00	10.00
❑ 6723	Look at the Girl/That's a Good Idea	1969	2.50	5.00	10.00
❑ 6742	Demonstration/Johnny's Heartbreak	1970	2.00	4.00	8.00
❑ 6766	Giving Away None of My Love/Snatch a Little Piece	1970	2.00	4.00	8.00
❑ 6802	Try a Little Tenderness/I've Been Loving You Too Long (To Stop Now)	1971	—	3.00	6.00
❑ 6907	My Girl/Good to Me	1972	—	2.50	5.00
❑ 7069	White Christmas/Merry Christmas, Baby	1976	—	2.50	5.00
❑ 7321	White Christmas/Merry Christmas, Baby	1980	—	2.00	4.00
❑ 99955	White Christmas/Merry Christmas, Baby	1982	—	2.00	4.00
BETHLEHEM					
❑ 3083	Shout Bamalama/Fat Girl	1964	5.00	10.00	20.00
CONFEDERATE					
❑ 135	Shout Bamalama/Fat Girl	1962	12.50	25.00	50.00
FINER ARTS					
❑ 2016	She's Alright/Tough Enuff	1961	12.50	25.00	50.00
—Originally released on Trans World by "The Shooters"					
KING					
❑ 6149	Shout Bamalama/Fat Girl	1968	2.50	5.00	10.00
ORBIT					
❑ 135	Shout Bamalama/Fat Girl	1961	75.00	150.00	300.00
PHILCO-FORD					
❑ HP-13	Shake/Fa-Fa-Fa-Fa-Fa	1967	5.00	10.00	20.00
—4-inch plastic "Hip Pocket Record" with color sleeve					
STONE					
❑ 209	You Left the Water Running/The Otis Jam	1976	3.00	6.00	12.00
—B-side by the Memphis Studio Band					
VOLT					
❑ 103	These Arms of Mine/Hey, Hey Baby	1962	5.00	10.00	20.00
❑ 109	That's What My Heart Needs/Mary's Little Lamb	1963	5.00	10.00	20.00
❑ 112	Pain in My Heart/Something Is Worrying Me	1963	5.00	10.00	20.00
❑ 116	Come to Me/Don't Leave Me This Way	1964	3.75	7.50	15.00
❑ 117	Security/I Want to Thank You	1964	3.75	7.50	15.00
❑ 121	Chained and Bound/Your One and Only Man	1964	3.75	7.50	15.00
❑ 124	Mr. Pitiful/That's How Strong My Love Is	1965	3.75	7.50	15.00
❑ 126	I've Been Loving You Too Long (To Stop Now)/I'm Depending on You	1965	3.75	7.50	15.00
❑ 128	Respect/Ole Man Trouble	1965	3.75	7.50	15.00
❑ 130	I Can't Turn You Loose/Just One More Day	1965	3.75	7.50	15.00
❑ 132	Satisfaction/Any Ole Way	1966	3.75	7.50	15.00
❑ 136	My Lover's Prayer/Don't Mess with Cupid	1966	3.75	7.50	15.00
❑ 138	Fa-Fa-Fa-Fa-Fa (Sad Song)/Good to Me	1966	3.75	7.50	15.00
❑ 141	Try a Little Tenderness/I'm Sick Y'All	1966	3.75	7.50	15.00
❑ 146	I Love You More Than Words Can Say/Let Me Come On Home	1967	3.00	6.00	12.00
❑ 149	Shake/You Don't Miss Your Water	1967	3.00	6.00	12.00
❑ 152	Glory of Love/I'm Coming Home	1967	3.00	6.00	12.00
❑ 157	(Sittin' On) The Dock of the Bay/Sweet Lorene	1968	3.00	6.00	12.00
—Black and red label					
❑ 157	(Sittin' On) The Dock of the Bay/Sweet Lorene	1968	2.50	5.00	10.00
—Multicolor (mostly brown) label					
❑ 163	The Happy Song (Dum-Dum)/Open That Door	1968	2.50	5.00	10.00

REDELL, TEDDY

Number	Title (A Side/B Side)	Yr	VG	VG+	NM
ATCO					
❑ 6162	Judy/Can't You See	1960	5.00	10.00	20.00
HI					
❑ 2024	Pipeliner/I Want to Hold You	1960	5.00	10.00	20.00
VADEN					
❑ 110	Knockin' on the Backside/Before It Began	1960	30.00	60.00	120.00
❑ 115	Goldust/Corrine, Corrina	1960	30.00	60.00	120.00
❑ 116	Judy/Can't You See	1960	30.00	60.00	120.00
❑ 117	Pipeliner/I Want to Hold You	1960	30.00	60.00	120.00
❑ 301	Pipeliner/I Want to Hold You	1961	20.00	40.00	80.00
❑ 305	I'll Sail My Ship Alone/Don't Grow Old Alone	1961	20.00	40.00	80.00

REDJACKS, THE

Number	Title (A Side/B Side)	Yr	VG	VG+	NM
APT					
❑ 25006	Big Brown Eyes/To Make You Mine	1958	5.00	10.00	20.00
OKLAHOMA					
❑ 5005	Big Brown Eyes/To Make You Mine	1958	12.50	25.00	50.00

REDNOW, EIVETS

See STEVIE WONDER.

REDWOODS, THE

JEFF BARRY was involved with this group.

Number	Title (A Side/B Side)	Yr	VG	VG+	NM
EPIC					
❑ 9447	Shake, Shake Sherry/The Memory Lingers On	1961	10.00	20.00	40.00
—As "The Flairs"					
❑ 9447	Shake, Shake Sherry/The Memory Lingers On	1961	7.50	15.00	30.00
—As "The Redwoods"					
❑ 9473	Never Take It Away/Unemployment Insurance	1961	7.50	15.00	30.00
❑ 9505	Please, Mr. Scientist/Where You Need to Be	1962	10.00	20.00	40.00

REED, JAMES

Number	Title (A Side/B Side)	Yr	VG	VG+	NM
BIG TOWN					
❑ 117	Things Ain't What They Used to Be/You Better Hold Me	1954	37.50	75.00	150.00
FLAIR					
❑ 1034	My Mama Told Me/This Is the End	1954	50.00	100.00	200.00
❑ 1042	Dr. Brown/You Better Hold Me	1954	50.00	100.00	200.00
MONEY					
❑ 201	Oh People/My Love Is Real	1954	50.00	100.00	200.00
RHYTHM					
❑ 1775	Tin Pan Alley/Biggest Place in Town	1954	125.00	250.00	500.00

REED, JIMMY

Number	Title (A Side/B Side)	Yr	VG	VG+	NM
ABC					
❑ 10887	Got Nowhere to Go/Two Ways to Skin (A Cat)	1966	2.00	4.00	8.00
BLUESWAY					
❑ 61003	I Wanna Know/Two Heads Are Better Than One	1967	2.00	4.00	8.00
❑ 61006	Don't Press Your Luck Woman/Feel Like I Want to Ramble	1967	2.00	4.00	8.00
❑ 61013	Buy Me a Hound Dog/Crazy About Oklahoma	1968	2.00	4.00	8.00
❑ 61020	Peepin' and Hidin'/My Baby Told Me	1968	2.00	4.00	8.00
❑ 61025	Don't Light My Fire/The Judge Should Know	1969	2.00	4.00	8.00
CANYON					
❑ 38	Hard Walkin' Hannah (Part 1)/Hard Walkin' Hannah (Part 2)	196?	2.00	4.00	8.00
CHANCE					
❑ 1142	High and Lonesome/Roll and Rhumba	1953	700.00	1400.	2100.
EXODUS					
❑ 2005	Knockin' At Your Door/Dedication to Sonny	1966	2.50	5.00	10.00
❑ 2008	Cousin Peaches/Crazy 'Bout Oklahoma	1966	2.50	5.00	10.00
RRG					
❑ 44001	Christmas Present Blues/Crying Blind	19??	2.00	4.00	8.00
VEE JAY					
❑ 100	High and Lonesome/Roll and Rumba	1953	300.00	600.00	1200.
—Red vinyl					
❑ 100	High and Lonesome/Roll and Rumba	1953	150.00	300.00	600.00
❑ 105	I Found My Baby/Jimmy's Boogie	1953	100.00	200.00	400.00
—Red vinyl					
❑ 105	I Found My Baby/Jimmy's Boogie	1953	50.00	100.00	200.00
❑ 119	You Don't Have to Go/Boogie in the Dark	1954	75.00	150.00	300.00
—Red vinyl					
❑ 119	You Don't Have to Go/Boogie in the Dark	1954	20.00	40.00	80.00
❑ 132	Pretty Thing/I'm Gonna Ruin You	1955	25.00	50.00	100.00
❑ 153	I Don't Go for That/She Don't Want Me No More	1955	12.50	25.00	50.00
❑ 168	Ain't That Lovin' You Baby/Baby, Don't Say That No More	1956	10.00	20.00	40.00
❑ 186	Can't Stand to See You Go/Rockin' with Reed	1956	10.00	20.00	40.00
❑ 203	I Love You Baby/My First Plea	1956	7.50	15.00	30.00
❑ 226	You've Got Me Dizzy/Honey, Don't Let Me Go	1956	7.50	15.00	30.00
❑ 237	Honey, Where You Going/Little Rain	1957	7.50	15.00	30.00
❑ 248	The Sun Is Shining/Baby, What's On Your Mind	1957	7.50	15.00	30.00
❑ 253	Honest I Do/Signals of Love	1957	7.50	15.00	30.00
❑ 270	You're Something Else/A String to My Heart	1958	7.50	15.00	30.00
❑ 275	You Got Me Crying/Go On to School	1958	7.50	15.00	30.00
❑ 287	I Know It's a Sin/Down in Virginia	1958	7.50	15.00	30.00
❑ 298	I'm Gonna Get My Baby/Odds and Ends	1958	7.50	15.00	30.00
❑ 304	I Told You Baby/Ends and Odds (Instrumental)	1958	7.50	15.00	30.00
❑ 314	Take Out Some Insurance/You Know I Love You	1959	7.50	15.00	30.00
❑ 326	I Wanna Be Loved/Going to New York	1959	7.50	15.00	30.00
❑ 333	Baby What You Want Me to Do/Caress Me, Baby	1959	7.50	15.00	30.00
❑ 347	Found Love/Where Can You Be	1960	6.25	12.50	25.00
❑ 357	Hush Hush/Going to the River, Part 2	1960	6.25	12.50	25.00
❑ 373	Laughing at the Blues/Close Together	1961	6.25	12.50	25.00
❑ 380	Big Boss Man/I'm a Love You	1961	6.25	12.50	25.00
❑ 398	Bright Lights, Big City/I'm Mr. Luck	1961	6.25	12.50	25.00
❑ 425	Aw, Shucks, Hush Your Mouth/Baby, What's Wrong	1962	5.00	10.00	20.00
❑ 449	Tell Me You Love Me/Good Lover	1962	5.00	10.00	20.00
❑ 459	I'll Change My Style/Too Much	1962	5.00	10.00	20.00
❑ 473	Let's Get Together/Oh, John	1962	5.00	10.00	20.00
❑ 509	There'll Be a Day/Shame, Shame, Shame	1963	3.75	7.50	15.00
❑ 552	Mary Mary/I'm Gonna Help You	1963	3.75	7.50	15.00
❑ 570	Outskirts of Town/St. Louis Blues	1963	3.75	7.50	15.00
❑ 584	See See Rider/Wee Wee Baby Blues	1964	3.75	7.50	15.00
❑ 593	Help Yourself/Heading for a Fall	1964	3.75	7.50	15.00
❑ 616	Oh John/Down in Mississippi	1964	3.75	7.50	15.00
❑ 622	I'm Going Upside Your Head/The Devil's Shoestring	1964	3.75	7.50	15.00
❑ 642	I Wanna Be Loved/A New Leaf	1965	3.75	7.50	15.00
❑ 702	I'm the Man Down There/Left Handed Woman	1965	3.75	7.50	15.00
❑ 709	Don't Think I'm Through/When Girls Do It	1966	3.75	7.50	15.00

REED, LOU

Also see THE PRMITIVES; THE VELVET UNDERGROUND.

ARISTA

Number	Title (A Side/B Side)	Yr	VG	VG+	NM
❑ 215	I Believe in Love/Senselessly Cruel	1976	—	2.00	4.00
❑ 431	City Lights/I Want to Boogie with You	1979	—	2.00	4.00
❑ 535	Growing Up in Public/The Power of Positive Drinking	1980	—	2.00	4.00

ATLANTIC

Number	Title (A Side/B Side)	Yr	VG	VG+	NM
❑ 89468	My Love Is Chemical/People Have Got to Move	1985	—	—	3.00
—B-side by Jenny Burton					
❑ 89468 [PS]	My Love Is Chemical/People Have Got to Move	1985	—	—	3.00

A&M

Number	Title (A Side/B Side)	Yr	VG	VG+	NM
❑ 2781	September Song/Oh Heavenly Salvation	1985	—	2.00	4.00
—B-side by Mark Bingham/Johnny Adams/Aaron Neville					
❑ 2883	Soul Man/Sweet Sarah	1986	—	—	3.00
—With Sam Moore					

RCA

Number	Title (A Side/B Side)	Yr	VG	VG+	NM
❑ JB-13558	Martial Law/Don't Talk to Me About Work	1983	—	—	3.00
❑ PB-13841	I Love You Suzanne/My Friend George	1984	—	—	3.00
❑ PB-14368	No Money Down/Don't Hurt a Woman	1986	—	—	3.00

RCA VICTOR

Number	Title (A Side/B Side)	Yr	VG	VG+	NM
❑ APBO-0054	Vicious/Good Night Ladies	1973	—	2.50	5.00
❑ APBO-0172	Lady Day/How Do You Think It Feels	1973	—	2.50	5.00
❑ APBO-0238	Sweet Jane/Lady Day	1974	7.50	15.00	30.00
—Part of U.S. numbering system, but pressed for export.					
❑ PB-10053	Sally Can't Dance/Vicious	1974	—	2.00	4.00
❑ PB-10081	Sally Can't Dance/Ennui	1974	—	2.00	4.00
❑ GB-10162	Walk on the Wild Side/Vicious	1975	—	—	3.00
—Gold Standard Series reissue					
❑ PB-10573	Charley's Girl/Nowhere At All	1976	—	2.00	4.00
❑ PB-10648	Crazy Feeling/Nowhere At All	1976	—	2.00	4.00
❑ 74-0727	I Can't Stand It/Going Down	1972	—	3.00	6.00
❑ 74-0784	Walk and Talk It/Wild Child	1972	—	3.00	6.00
❑ 74-0887	Walk on the Wild Side/Perfect Day	1973	—	3.00	6.00
❑ 74-0964	Satellite of Love/Walk and Talk It	1973	—	3.00	6.00

SIRE

Number	Title (A Side/B Side)	Yr	VG	VG+	NM
❑ 22876	Romeo Had Juliette/Busload of Faith	1989	—	—	3.00
❑ 22876 [PS]	Romeo Had Juliette/Busload of Faith	1989	—	—	3.00

REED, TAWNEY

CONGRESS

Number	Title (A Side/B Side)	Yr	VG	VG+	NM
❑ 270	My Heart Cried/Can't Take It Away	1966	3.00	6.00	12.00

RED BIRD

Number	Title (A Side/B Side)	Yr	VG	VG+	NM
❑ 10-044	Needle in a Haystack/I Got a Feeling	1965	10.00	20.00	40.00

REED, URSULA

OLD TOWN

Number	Title (A Side/B Side)	Yr	VG	VG+	NM
❑ 1001	Your're Laffin' "Cause I'm Cryin'/Ursula's Blues	1954	100.00	200.00	400.00

REEDER, BILL

FERNWOOD

Number	Title (A Side/B Side)	Yr	VG	VG+	NM
❑ 121	You're My Baby/Where Were You Last Night	1960	20.00	40.00	80.00

HI

Number	Title (A Side/B Side)	Yr	VG	VG+	NM
❑ 2037	Till I Waltz Again with You/There Was a Time	1961	20.00	40.00	80.00
❑ 2041	Secret Love/Judy	1961	5.00	10.00	20.00

VOLL

Number	Title (A Side/B Side)	Yr	VG	VG+	NM
❑ 100	Till I Waltz Again with You/There Was a Time	1961	50.00	100.00	200.00

REEKERS, THE

RY-JAC

Number	Title (A Side/B Side)	Yr	VG	VG+	NM
❑ 13	Grindin'/Don't Call Me Flyface	1964	12.50	25.00	50.00

REESE, DELLA

ABC

Number	Title (A Side/B Side)	Yr	VG	VG+	NM
❑ 10815	Stranger on Earth/If It's the Last Thing I Do	1966	2.00	4.00	8.00
❑ 10841	It Was a Very Good Year/Solitary Woman	1966	2.00	4.00	8.00
❑ 10876	Sunny/That's Life	1966	2.00	4.00	8.00
❑ 10931	Soon/Every Other Day	1967	—	3.00	6.00
❑ 10962	I Heard You Cried Last Night/On the South Side of Chicago	1967	—	3.00	6.00
❑ 11017	Let's Make the Most of a Beautiful Thing/Sorry Baby	1967	—	3.00	6.00
❑ 11051	I Gotta Be Me/Never My Love	1968	—	3.00	6.00

ABC-PARAMOUNT

Number	Title (A Side/B Side)	Yr	VG	VG+	NM
❑ 10691	After Loving You/How Do You Keep from Crying	1965	2.00	4.00	8.00
❑ 10721	And That Reminds Me/I Only Want a Buddy, Not a Sweetheart	1965	2.00	4.00	8.00
❑ 10759	'T'Ain't Nobody's Bizness If I Do/I Ain't Ready for That	1965	2.00	4.00	8.00

AVCO

Number	Title (A Side/B Side)	Yr	VG	VG+	NM
❑ 4586	If It Feels Good Do It/Good Lovin' Makes It Right	1972	—	2.50	5.00

AVCO EMBASSY

Number	Title (A Side/B Side)	Yr	VG	VG+	NM
❑ 4515	Games People Play/Compared to What	1969	—	3.00	6.00
❑ 4545	Billy My Love/(B-side unknown)	1970	—	3.00	6.00
❑ 4566	The Troublemaker/The Love I've Been Looking For	1971	—	3.00	6.00

CHI-SOUND

Number	Title (A Side/B Side)	Yr	VG	VG+	NM
❑ XW978	I'll Be Your Sunshine/Nothing But a True Love	1977	—	2.00	4.00

JUBILEE

Number	Title (A Side/B Side)	Yr	VG	VG+	NM
❑ 5198	In the Still of the Night/Kiss My Love Goodbye	1955	3.75	7.50	15.00
❑ 5214	Time After Time/Fine Sugar	1955	3.75	7.50	15.00
❑ 5233	I've Got My Love to Keep Me Warm/Years from Now	1956	3.75	7.50	15.00
❑ 5247	Headin' Home/Daybreak Serenade	1956	3.75	7.50	15.00
❑ 5251	My Melancholy Baby/One for My Baby	1956	3.75	7.50	15.00
❑ 5263	In the Meantime/The More I See You	1956	3.75	7.50	15.00
❑ 5278	How About You/How Can You Not Believe	1957	3.75	7.50	15.00
❑ 5292	And That Reminds Me/I Cried for You	1957	3.00	6.00	12.00
❑ 5307	I Only Want to Love You/By Love Possessed	1957	3.00	6.00	12.00
❑ 5317	How Can You Lose (What You Never Had)/If Not for You	1958	3.00	6.00	12.00
❑ 5323	I've Got a Feelin' You're Foolin'/C'mon, C'mon	1958	3.00	6.00	12.00
❑ 5332	I Wish/You Gotta Love Everybody	1958	3.00	6.00	12.00
❑ 5345	Sermonette/Dreams End at Dawn	1958	3.00	6.00	12.00
❑ 5346	When I Grow Too Old to Dream/You're Just in Love	1958	3.00	6.00	12.00
—Della Reese and Kirk Stuart					
❑ 5369	Time Was/Once Upon a Dream	1959	3.00	6.00	12.00
❑ 5375	I Don't Want to Walk Without You/I'm Nobody's Baby	1959	3.00	6.00	12.00
❑ 5453	Sermonette/You Gotta Love Somebody	1963	2.50	5.00	10.00

RCA VICTOR

Number	Title (A Side/B Side)	Yr	VG	VG+	NM
❑ 47-7591	Don't You Know/Soldier Won't You Marry Me	1959	2.50	5.00	10.00
❑ 47-7644	Not One Minute More/You're My Love	1959	2.50	5.00	10.00
❑ 47-7683	Someday/The Lady Is a Tramp	1960	2.50	5.00	10.00
❑ 47-7706	Someday You'll Want Me to Want You/Faraway Boy	1960	2.50	5.00	10.00
❑ 47-7750	Everyday/There's No Two Ways About It	1960	2.50	5.00	10.00
❑ 47-7750 [PS]	Everyday/There's No Two Ways About It	1960	5.00	10.00	20.00
❑ 47-7784	And Now/There's Nothin' Like a Boy	1960	2.50	5.00	10.00
❑ 47-7784 [PS]	And Now/There's Nothin' Like a Boy	1960	5.00	10.00	20.00
❑ 47-7833	The Most Beautiful Words/You Mean All the World to Me	1961	2.50	5.00	10.00
❑ 47-7867	The Touch of Your Lips/Won'cha Come Home, Bill Bailey	1961	2.50	5.00	10.00
❑ 47-7884	I Possess/A Far, Far Better Thing	1961	2.50	5.00	10.00
❑ 47-7961	One/What Do You Think, Joe	1961	2.50	5.00	10.00
❑ 47-7996	Ninety-Nine and a Half Won't Do/You Don't Know How Blessed You Are	1962	2.50	5.00	10.00
❑ 47-8021	Rome Adventure/Here's That Rainy Day	1962	2.50	5.00	10.00
❑ 47-8070	I Love You So Much It Hurts/Blow Out the Sun	1962	2.50	5.00	10.00
❑ 47-8093	As Long As He Needs Me/It Makes No Difference Now	1962	2.50	5.00	10.00
❑ 47-8093 [PS]	As Long As He Needs Me/It Makes No Difference Now	1962	3.75	7.50	15.00
❑ 47-8145	Be My Love/I Behold You	1963	2.50	5.00	10.00
❑ 47-8187	More/Serenade	1963	2.50	5.00	10.00
❑ 47-8260	Angel D'Amore/Forbidden Games	1963	2.50	5.00	10.00
❑ 47-8337	The Bottom of Old Smokey/A Clock That's Got No Hands	1964	2.00	4.00	8.00
❑ 47-8394	If I Didn't Care/Wind in the Willows	1964	2.00	4.00	8.00
❑ 48-1018	Ninety-Nine and a Half Won't Do/And Now	1971	—	2.00	4.00
❑ 74-0558	You Came a Long Way from St. Louis/Nobody's Sweetheart	1971	—	2.00	4.00

7-Inch Extended Plays

RCA VICTOR

Number	Title (A Side/B Side)	Yr	VG	VG+	NM
❑ EPA-4349	Don't You Know/Soldier, Won't You Marry Me// Not One Minute More/You're My Love	1959	3.75	7.50	15.00
❑ EPA-4349 [PS]	Don't You Know	1959	3.75	7.50	15.00

REEVES, JIM

ABBOTT

Number	Title (A Side/B Side)	Yr	VG	VG+	NM
❑ 115	Wagon Load of Love/What Were You Doing Last Nite	1953	6.25	12.50	25.00
❑ 115	Wagon Load of Love/What Were You Doing Last Nite	1953	15.00	30.00	60.00
—Red vinyl					
❑ 116	Mexican Joe/I Could Cry	1953	6.25	12.50	25.00
❑ 116	Mexican Joe/I Could Cry	1953	15.00	30.00	60.00
—Red vinyl					
❑ 137	Let Me Love You Just a Little/Butterfly Love	1953	6.25	12.50	25.00
❑ 137	Let Me Love You Just a Little/Butterfly Love	1953	15.00	30.00	60.00
—Red vinyl					
❑ 143	El Rancho Del Rio/It's Hard to Love Just One	1953	6.25	12.50	25.00
❑ 143	El Rancho Del Rio/It's Hard to Love Just One	1953	15.00	30.00	60.00
—Red vinyl					
❑ 148	Bimbo/Gypsy Heart	1953	6.25	12.50	25.00
❑ 148	Bimbo/Gypsy Heart	1953	15.00	30.00	60.00
—Red vinyl					
❑ 160	Echo Bonita/Then I'll Stop Loving You	1954	5.00	10.00	20.00
❑ 164	Ramblin' Heart/Beatin' on the Ding Dong	1954	5.00	10.00	20.00
❑ 168	Padre of Old San Antone/Mother Went A-Walkin'	1954	5.00	10.00	20.00
❑ 170	Penny Candy/I'll Follow You	1954	5.00	10.00	20.00
❑ 174	Where Does a Broken Heart Go/The Wilder Your Heart Beats, The Sweeter You Love	1954	5.00	10.00	20.00
❑ 180	Drinking Tequila/Red Eyed and Rowdy	1955	5.00	10.00	20.00
❑ 182	Give Me One More Kiss/Tahiti	1955	5.00	10.00	20.00
❑ 184	Are You the One/How Many	1955	5.00	10.00	20.00
—With Alvadean Coker					
❑ 186	Let Me Remember/Hillbilly Waltz	1956	5.00	10.00	20.00

RCA

Number	Title (A Side/B Side)	Yr	VG	VG+	NM
❑ PB-10956	It's Nothin' to Me/I Won't Forget You	1977	—	2.00	4.00
❑ PB-11060	Little Ole Dime/A Letter to My Heart	1977	—	2.00	4.00
❑ PB-11187	You're the Only Good Thing (That's Happened to Me)/When You Are Gone	1978	—	2.00	4.00
❑ PB-11564	Don't Let Me Cross Over/I've Enjoyed As Much of This As I Can Stand	1979	—	2.00	4.00
❑ PB-11737	Oh, How I Miss You Tonight/The Talking Walls	1979	—	2.00	4.00
❑ PB-11946	Take Me in Your Arms and Hold Me/Missing Angel	1980	—	2.00	4.00
—With Deborah Allen (overdubbed)					
❑ PB-12118	There's Always Me/Somewhere Along the Line	1980	—	2.00	4.00
❑ PB-13410	The Jim Reeves Medley/He'll Have to Go	1982	—	2.00	4.00
❑ PB-13693	The Image of Me/Won't Come In While He's There	1983	—	2.00	4.00

RCA VICTOR

Number	Title (A Side/B Side)	Yr	VG	VG+	NM
❑ APBO-0255	I'd Fight the World/What's In It for Me	1974	—	2.00	4.00
❑ EP-10133	He Will/We Thank Thee	1974	—	2.00	4.00
❑ PB-10299	You Belong to Me/Maureen	1975	—	2.00	4.00
❑ PB-10418	You'll Never Know/There's That Smile Again	1975	—	2.00	4.00
❑ GB-10511	Missing You/I'd Fight the World	1975	—	2.00	4.00
—Gold Standard Series					
❑ 47-6200	Yonder Comes a Sucker/I'm Hurtin' Inside	1955	5.00	10.00	20.00

Number	Title (A Side/B Side)	Yr	VG	VG+	NM
❑ 47-6274	I've Lived a Lot in My Time/Jimbo Jenkins	1955	5.00	10.00	20.00
❑ 47-6401	If You Were Mine/That's a Sad Affair	1956	5.00	10.00	20.00
❑ 47-6517	My Lips Are Sealed/Pickin' a Chicken	1956	5.00	10.00	20.00
❑ 47-6620	According to My Heart/The Mother of a Honky Tonk Girl	1956	5.00	10.00	20.00
—With Carol Johnson					
❑ 47-6625	Bimbo/Penny Candy	1956	5.00	10.00	20.00
❑ 47-6626	Mexican Joe/How Many	1956	5.00	10.00	20.00
❑ 47-6627	Then I'll Stop Loving You/Drinking Tequila	1956	5.00	10.00	20.00
❑ 47-6749	Am I Losing You/Waitin' for a Train	1956	5.00	10.00	20.00
❑ 47-6874	Four Walls/I Know and You Know	1957	3.75	7.50	15.00
❑ 47-6973	Young Hearts/Two Shadows on Your Window	1957	3.75	7.50	15.00
❑ 47-7070	Anna Marie/Everywhere You Go	1957	3.75	7.50	15.00
❑ 47-7171	I Love You More/Overnight	1958	3.75	7.50	15.00
❑ 47-7266	Blue Boy/Theme of Love (I Love to Say I Love You)	1958	3.75	7.50	15.00
❑ 47-7380	Billy Bayou/I'd Like to Be	1958	3.75	7.50	15.00
❑ 47-7479	Home/If Heartache Is the Fashion	1959	3.75	7.50	15.00
❑ 47-7557	Partners/I'm Beginning to Forget You	1959	3.75	7.50	15.00
❑ 47-7643	He'll Have to Go/In a Mansion Stands My Love	1959	3.00	6.00	12.00
❑ 47-7756	I'm Gettin' Better/I Know One	1960	3.00	6.00	12.00
❑ 47-7756 [PS]	I'm Gettin' Better/I Know One	1960	5.00	10.00	20.00
❑ 47-7800	Am I Losing You/I Missed Me	1960	3.00	6.00	12.00
❑ 47-7800 [PS]	Am I Losing You/I Missed Me	1960	5.00	10.00	20.00
❑ 47-7855	The Blizzard/Danny Boy	1961	3.00	6.00	12.00
❑ 47-7905	What Would You Do?/Stand At Your Window	1961	3.00	6.00	12.00
❑ 47-7950	Losing Your Love/(How Can I Write on Paper) What I Feel in My Heart	1961	3.00	6.00	12.00
❑ 47-8019	Adios Amigos/A Letter to My Heart	1962	2.50	5.00	10.00
❑ 47-8080	I'm Gonna Change Everything/Pride Goes Before a Fall	1962	2.50	5.00	10.00
❑ 47-8127	Is This Me?/Missing Angel	1963	2.50	5.00	10.00
❑ 47-8193	Guilty/Little Ole You	1963	2.50	5.00	10.00
❑ 47-8193 [PS]	Guilty/Little Ole You	1963	3.75	7.50	15.00
❑ 47-8252	An Old Christmas Card/Senor Santa Claus	1963	3.75	7.50	15.00
❑ 47-8252 [PS]	An Old Christmas Card/Senor Santa Claus	1963	10.00	20.00	40.00
❑ 47-8289	Welcome to My World/Good Morning Self	1963	2.50	5.00	10.00
❑ 47-8324	Love Is No Excuse/Look Who's Talking	1964	2.50	5.00	10.00
—With Dottie West					
❑ 47-8383	I Guess I'm Crazy/Not Until the Next Time	1964	2.50	5.00	10.00
❑ 47-8461	I Won't Forget You/Highway to Nowhere	1964	2.50	5.00	10.00
❑ 47-8508	This Is It/There's That Smile Again	1965	2.00	4.00	8.00
❑ 47-8625	Is It Really Over?/Rosa Rio	1965	2.00	4.00	8.00
❑ 47-8625 [PS]	Is It Really Over?/Rosa Rio	1965	3.00	6.00	12.00
❑ 47-8719	Snowflake/Take My Hand, Precious Lord	1965	2.00	4.00	8.00
❑ 47-8789	Distant Drums/Old Tige	1966	2.00	4.00	8.00
❑ 47-8902	Blue Side of Lonesome/It Hurts So Much (To See You Go)	1966	2.00	4.00	8.00
❑ 47-9057	I Won't Come In While He's There/Maureen	1966	2.00	4.00	8.00
❑ 47-9238	The Storm/Trying to Forget	1967	2.00	4.00	8.00
❑ 47-9343	I Heard a Heart Break Last Night/Golden Memories and Silver Tears	1967	2.00	4.00	8.00
❑ 47-9455	That's When I See the Blues (In Your Pretty Brown Eyes)/I've Lived a Lot in My Time	1968	2.00	4.00	8.00
❑ 47-9614	When You Are Gone/How Can I Write on Paper	1968	2.00	4.00	8.00
❑ 47-9880	Angels Don't Lie/You Kept Me Awake Last Night	1970	—	3.00	6.00
❑ 47-9969	Gypsy Feet/He Will	1971	—	3.00	6.00
❑ 74-0135	When Two Worlds Collide/Could I Be Falling in Love	1969	—	3.00	6.00
❑ 74-0286	Why Do I Love You (Melody of Love)/Nobody's Fool	1969	—	3.00	6.00
❑ 74-0626	The Writing on the Wall/You're Free to Go	1971	—	3.00	6.00
❑ 74-0744	Missing You/The Tie That Binds	1972	—	2.50	5.00
❑ 74-0859	Blue Christmas/Snowflake	1972	—	2.50	5.00
❑ 74-0963	Am I That Easy to Forget/Rosa Rio	1973	—	2.00	4.00
❑ 447-0884	An Old Christmas Card/Senor Santa Claus	1972	—	2.00	4.00
—Gold Standard Series					
❑ 447-0885	Snowflake/Take My Hand, Precious Lord	1972	—	2.00	4.00
—Gold Standard Series					

7-Inch Extended Plays

RCA VICTOR

Number	Title (A Side/B Side)	Yr	VG	VG+	NM
❑ EPA-4357	*He'll Have to Go/Wishful Thinking/Please Come Home/After Awhile	1960	5.00	10.00	20.00
❑ EPA-4357 [PS]	He'll Have to Go	1960	5.00	10.00	20.00

REEVES, JIM, AND PATSY CLINE

Also see each artist's individual listings. Their duets were created electronically; they never actually recorded together.

MCA

Number	Title (A Side/B Side)	Yr	VG	VG+	NM
❑ 52052	So Wrong/I Fall to Pieces	1982	—	2.00	4.00

RCA

Number	Title (A Side/B Side)	Yr	VG	VG+	NM
❑ PB-12346	Have You Ever Been Lonely (Have You Ever Been Blue)/Welcome to My World	1981	—	2.00	4.00

REEVES, MARTHA

Also see MARTHA AND THE VANDELLAS.

ARISTA

Number	Title (A Side/B Side)	Yr	VG	VG+	NM
❑ 0124	Love Blind/This Time I'll Be Sweeter	1975	—	2.50	5.00
—Also see "Martha and the Vandellas"					
❑ 0160	Now That We Found Love/Higher and Higher	1975	—	2.00	4.00
❑ 0211	The Rest of My Life/Thank You	1976	—	2.00	4.00
❑ 0228	You've Lost That Lovin' Feelin'/Now That We Found Love	1977	—	2.00	4.00

FANTASY

Number	Title (A Side/B Side)	Yr	VG	VG+	NM
❑ 825	Love Don't Come No Stronger/You're Like Sunshine	1978	—	2.00	4.00
❑ 868	Dancin' in the Streets (Skatin' in the Streets)/When You Came	1979	—	2.00	4.00
❑ 887	Really Like Your Rap/That's What I Want	1979	—	2.00	4.00

MCA

Number	Title (A Side/B Side)	Yr	VG	VG+	NM
❑ 40194	Power of Love/Stand By Me	1974	—	2.50	5.00
❑ 40274	Stand By Me/Wild Night	1974	—	2.50	5.00
❑ 40329	My Man/Facsimile	1974	—	2.50	5.00

REFLECTIONS, THE (1)

Detroit-based rock group.

ABC

Number	Title (A Side/B Side)	Yr	VG	VG+	NM
❑ 10794	Like Adam and Eve/Vito's House	1966	6.25	12.50	25.00
❑ 10822	You're Gonna Find Out (You Love Me)/Long Cigarette	1966	7.50	15.00	30.00

GOLDEN WORLD

Number	Title (A Side/B Side)	Yr	VG	VG+	NM
❑ 9	(Just Like) Romeo and Juliet/Can't You Tell By the Look in His Eyes	1964	5.00	10.00	20.00
❑ 12	Like Columbus Did/Lonely Girl	1964	3.75	7.50	15.00
❑ 15	Oowee Now/Talkin' Bout My Girl	1964	3.75	7.50	15.00
❑ 16	Henpecked Guy/Don't Do That to Me	1964	3.75	7.50	15.00
❑ 19	You're My Baby/Shabby Little Hut	1964	3.75	7.50	15.00
❑ 20	Poor Man's Son/Comin' At You	1965	3.75	7.50	15.00
❑ 22	Wheelin' and Dealin'/Deborah Ann	1965	3.75	7.50	15.00
❑ 24	June Bride/Out of the Picture	1965	3.75	7.50	15.00
❑ 29	Girl in the Candy Store/Your Kind of Love	1965	3.75	7.50	15.00

LANA

Number	Title (A Side/B Side)	Yr	VG	VG+	NM
❑ 140	(Just Like) Romeo and Juliet/(B-side unknown)	196?	—	3.00	6.00
—Early reissue					

REFLECTIONS, THE (2)

R&B group from New York.

CAPITOL

Number	Title (A Side/B Side)	Yr	VG	VG+	NM
❑ 4078	Three Steps from True Love/How Could We Let the Love Get Away	1975	—	3.00	6.00
❑ 4137	Love on Delivery/One Into One	1975	—	2.50	5.00
❑ 4222	Are You Ready (Here I Am)/Day After Day (Night After Night)	1976	—	2.50	5.00
❑ 4358	Gift Wrap My Love/She's My Summer Breeze	1976	—	2.50	5.00

RCA

Number	Title (A Side/B Side)	Yr	VG	VG+	NM
❑ PB-11408	Boogie City/I'm Gonna Let You Go This Time	1978	—	2.50	5.00

REFLECTIONS, THE (3)

CROSSROADS

Number	Title (A Side/B Side)	Yr	VG	VG+	NM
❑ 401	I Really Must Know/Maybe Tomorrow	1961	15.00	30.00	60.00
❑ 402	Rocket to the Moon/Because of You	1962	20.00	40.00	80.00

REFLECTIONS, THE (U)

These could be either group (1) or (3).

KAY-KO

Number	Title (A Side/B Side)	Yr	VG	VG+	NM
❑ 1003	Helpless/You Said Goodbye	1963	50.00	100.00	200.00

TIGRE

Number	Title (A Side/B Side)	Yr	VG	VG+	NM
❑ 602	In the Still of the Night/Tic Toc	1962	10.00	20.00	40.00

REGALS, THE (1)

ALADDIN

Number	Title (A Side/B Side)	Yr	VG	VG+	NM
❑ 3266	Run Pretty Baby/May the Good Lord Bless and Keep You	1954	30.00	60.00	120.00

ATLANTIC

Number	Title (A Side/B Side)	Yr	VG	VG+	NM
❑ 1062	I'm So Lonely/Got the Water Boiling	1955	15.00	30.00	60.00

MGM

Number	Title (A Side/B Side)	Yr	VG	VG+	NM
❑ 11869	There'll Always Be a Christmas/When You're Home with the Ones You Love	1954	10.00	20.00	40.00

REGALS, THE (2)

LAST CHANCE

Number	Title (A Side/B Side)	Yr	VG	VG+	NM
❑ 109	See You in the Morning/Yes My Love	1961	2.50	5.00	10.00

LAVENDER

Number	Title (A Side/B Side)	Yr	VG	VG+	NM
❑ 1452	See You in the Morning/Yes My Love	1960	7.50	15.00	30.00

UNITED ARTISTS

Number	Title (A Side/B Side)	Yr	VG	VG+	NM
❑ 380	Icy Fingers/Tiger Tears	1961	7.50	15.00	30.00

REGAN, EDDIE

ABC

Number	Title (A Side/B Side)	Yr	VG	VG+	NM
❑ 10795	Playin' Hide and Seek/Talk About Heartaches	1966	7.50	15.00	30.00

REGAN, RUSS

ABC-PARAMOUNT

Number	Title (A Side/B Side)	Yr	VG	VG+	NM
❑ 9949	Junior, Junior, Junior/I Never Knew	1958	5.00	10.00	20.00

CAPITOL

Number	Title (A Side/B Side)	Yr	VG	VG+	NM
❑ F4169	Joan of Love/That's When I Ran	1959	3.00	6.00	12.00
❑ F4280	Adults Only/Just the Two of Us	1959	3.00	6.00	12.00

REGAN, TOMMY

COLPIX

Number	Title (A Side/B Side)	Yr	VG	VG+	NM
❑ 725	I'll Never Stop Loving You/This Time I'm Losing You	1964	25.00	50.00	100.00

TELL STAR

Number	Title (A Side/B Side)	Yr	VG	VG+	NM
❑ 5001	Santa Twist/(B-side unknown)	1962	3.00	6.00	12.00

WORLD ARTISTS

Number	Title (A Side/B Side)	Yr	VG	VG+	NM
❑ 1049	I Adore You/9 to 5	1965	3.75	7.50	15.00

REGENTS, THE (1)

COUSINS

Number	Title (A Side/B Side)	Yr	VG	VG+	NM
❑ 1002	Barbara-Ann/I'm So Lonely	1961	300.00	600.00	1200.

GEE

Number	Title (A Side/B Side)	Yr	VG	VG+	NM
❑ 1065	Barbara-Ann/I'm So Lonely	1961	7.50	15.00	30.00
❑ 1071	Runaround/Laura My Darling	1961	6.25	12.50	25.00
❑ 1073	Don't Be a Fool/Liar	1961	6.25	12.50	25.00
❑ 1075	Lonesome Boy/Oh Baby	1961	6.25	12.50	25.00

REGENTS, THE (2)

ARGO

Number	Title (A Side/B Side)	Yr	VG	VG+	NM
❑ 5268	Isle of Trinidad/Bamboo Tree	1957	6.25	12.50	25.00

REGENTS, THE (3)

BLUE CAT

Number	Title (A Side/B Side)	Yr	VG	VG+	NM
❑ 110	Playmates/Me and You	1965	2.50	5.00	10.00

DOT

Number	Title (A Side/B Side)	Yr	VG	VG+	NM
❑ 16970	The Russian Spy and I/Bald Headed Woman	1966	2.50	5.00	10.00

Number	Title (A Side/B Side)	Yr	VG	VG+	NM
PENTHOUSE					
❑ 502	Words/Worryin' Kind	1966	2.50	5.00	10.00

REGENTS, THE (4)

Number	Title (A Side/B Side)	Yr	VG	VG+	NM
KAYO					
❑ 101	(That's What I Call) A Real Good Time/No Hard Feelings	1960	6.25	12.50	25.00
PEORIA					
❑ 8	Summertime Blues/(B-side unknown)	196?	3.75	7.50	15.00

REGENTS, THE (5)

MICHAEL McDONALD, later of THE DOOBIE BROTHERS, was in this group.

Number	Title (A Side/B Side)	Yr	VG	VG+	NM
REPRISE					
❑ 0430	She's Got Her Own Way of Lovin'/When I Die, Don't You Cry	1965	7.50	15.00	30.00

REID, CLARENCE

Number	Title (A Side/B Side)	Yr	VG	VG+	NM
ALSTON					
❑ 3717	Baptize Me in Your Love/Whatever It Takes	1975	—	2.50	5.00
❑ 3720	Come On With It/Mr. Smith's Wife	1976	—	2.50	5.00
❑ 3723	Shake Your Butt/Caution! Love Ahead	1976	—	2.50	5.00
❑ 3733	Just Another Guy in the Band/I'm Excited	1977	—	2.50	5.00
❑ 3748	You Get Me Up/It's Hell Trying to Get to Heaven	1979	—	2.50	5.00
❑ 4572	Fools Are Not Born (They Are Made)/Part-Time Lover	1969	2.00	4.00	8.00
❑ 4574	Nobody But You Babe	1969	2.00	4.00	8.00
❑ 4578	I'm a Man of My Word/I'm Gonna Tear You a New Heart	1969	2.00	4.00	8.00
❑ 4582	I've Been Trying/Don't Look Too Hard	1970	—	3.00	6.00
❑ 4584	Chicken Hawk/That's How It Is	1970	—	3.00	6.00
❑ 4588	Masterpiece/Down the Road of Love	1970	—	3.00	6.00
❑ 4592	Direct Me/You Knock Me Out	1971	—	3.00	6.00
❑ 4597	You Got to Fight/Three Is a Crowd	1971	—	3.00	6.00
❑ 4598	I Get My Kicks/Gotta Take It Home to Mother	1971	—	3.00	6.00
❑ 4602	Love Every Woman You Can/Ten Tons of Dynamite	1971	—	3.00	6.00
❑ 4603	Good Old Days/Ten Tons of Dynamite	1972	—	3.00	6.00
❑ 4608	I'm Gonna Do Something Good to You/Real Woman	1972	—	3.00	6.00
❑ 4613	Ruby/Two People in Love	1972	—	3.00	6.00
❑ 4616	Till I Get My Share/With Friends Like These	1973	—	3.00	6.00
❑ 4621	Funky Party/Winter Man	1974	—	3.00	6.00
DIAL					
❑ 3018	I Got My Shake/There'll Come a Day	1964	3.75	7.50	15.00
❑ 4019	I Refuse to Give Up/Somebody Will	1965	3.00	6.00	12.00
❑ 4040	Gimmie a Try/Part of Your Love	1966	3.00	6.00	12.00
PHIL-L.A. OF SOUL					
❑ 301	Cadillac Annie/Tired Blood	1967	2.50	5.00	10.00
WAND					
❑ 1106	Somebody Will/I Refuse to Give Up	1966	6.25	12.50	25.00
❑ 1121	I'm Your Yes Man/Your Love Is All the Help I Need	1966	10.00	20.00	40.00

REID, MATTHEW

Number	Title (A Side/B Side)	Yr	VG	VG+	NM
ABC-PARAMOUNT					
❑ 10259	Jane/Why Start	1961	6.25	12.50	25.00
❑ 10305	Tarzan Twist (Bwana Ungava)/Through My Tears	1962	6.25	12.50	25.00
DECCA					
❑ 31662	One More Minute/Hurt Me	1964	3.00	6.00	12.00
PHILIPS					
❑ 40634	Outward Bound/Hey There Sweet Sue	1969	2.50	5.00	10.00
SCEPTER					
❑ 1238	Faded Roses/Tomorrow	1962	6.25	12.50	25.00
TOPIX					
❑ 6006	Cry Myself to Sleep/Lollipops Went Out of Style	1961	10.00	20.00	40.00

RELATIVES, THE

Number	Title (A Side/B Side)	Yr	VG	VG+	NM
ALMONT					
❑ 306	Never Will I Love You Again/I'm Just Looking for Love	1964	10.00	20.00	40.00
MUSICOR					
❑ 1063	Eternally/Hadn't Been for Baby	1965	2.50	5.00	10.00

RELF, KEITH

Also see THE YARDBIRDS.

Number	Title (A Side/B Side)	Yr	VG	VG+	NM
EPIC					
❑ 10044	Mr. Zero/Knowing	1966	12.50	25.00	50.00
❑ 10044 [DJ]	Mr. Zero/Knowing	1966	37.50	75.00	150.00
—Promo on red vinyl... Reportedly, two promos were released for this single; the second, a different mix, was accompanied by a note telling the radio people not to play the first one, but to use the second one instead. This has not been confirmed.					
❑ 10110	Shapes in My Mind/Blue Sands	1966	12.50	25.00	50.00
❑ 10110 [DJ]	Shapes in My Mind (same on both sides)	1966	37.50	75.00	150.00
—Promo on red vinyl					
❑ 10110 [PS]	Shapes in My Mind/Blue Sands	1966	25.00	50.00	100.00
MCCM					
❑ 002	Together Now/All the Falling Angels	1989	—	2.50	5.00
—Purple marbled vinyl					
❑ 002 [PS]	Together Now/All the Falling Angels	1989	—	2.50	5.00

REMAINS, THE

Number	Title (A Side/B Side)	Yr	VG	VG+	NM
EPIC					
❑ 9777	You Say You're Sorry/I'm Talking About You	1965	20.00	40.00	80.00
❑ 9783	My Babe/Why Do I Cry	1965	20.00	40.00	80.00
❑ 9872	But I Ain't Got You/I Can't Get Away from You	1965	20.00	40.00	80.00
❑ 10001	Diddy Wah Diddy/Once Before	1966	20.00	40.00	80.00
❑ 10001 [DJ]	Diddy Wah Diddy/Once Before	1966	27.50	75.00	150.00
—Promo on red vinyl					
❑ 10001 [PS]	To Be Seen and Heard: Diddy Wah Diddy	1966	25.00	50.00	100.00
—Promo-only sleeve					
❑ 10060	Don't Look Back/Me Right Now	1966	20.00	40.00	80.00

REMBRANDTS, THE

Also see GREAT BUILDINGS.

Number	Title (A Side/B Side)	Yr	VG	VG+	NM
EASTWEST					
❑ 64429	I'll Be There for You/Album Snippets	1995	—	2.00	4.00

REMINISCENTS, THE

Number	Title (A Side/B Side)	Yr	VG	VG+	NM
DAY					
❑ 1000	Zoom Zoom Zoom/Oh Let Me Dream	1963	12.50	25.00	50.00
—Blue vinyl					
MARCEL					
❑ 1000	Cards of Love/Flames	1962	30.00	60.00	120.00

REMUS, EUGENE

Number	Title (A Side/B Side)	Yr	VG	VG+	NM
MOTOWN					
❑ 1001	You Never Miss a Good Thing/Hold Me Tight	1960	150.00	300.00	600.00
❑ 1001	You Never Miss a Good Thing/Gotta Have Your Lovin'	1960	125.00	250.00	500.00

RENAISSANCE

Also see ANNIE HASLAM.

Number	Title (A Side/B Side)	Yr	VG	VG+	NM
CAPITOL					
❑ 3487	Prologue/Spare Some Love	1972	2.00	4.00	8.00
❑ 3715	Carpet of the Sun/Bound for Infinity	1973	2.00	4.00	8.00
I.R.S.					
❑ 9904	Remember/Bon Jour Swan Song	1982	—	2.50	5.00
❑ 9914	Richard IX/(B-side unknown)	1982	—	2.50	5.00
SIRE					
❑ 714	Mother Russia/I Think of You	1974	—	3.00	6.00
❑ 728	Carpet of the Sun/Kiev	1976	—	3.00	6.00
❑ 740	Midas Man/Captive Heart	1977	—	3.00	6.00
❑ 1022	Northern Lights/Opening Out	1978	—	2.50	5.00
❑ 1041	Northern Lights/Opening Out	1979	—	2.50	5.00
❑ 49041	Forever Changing/Jekyll and Hyde	1979	—	2.50	5.00

RENAY, DIANE

Number	Title (A Side/B Side)	Yr	VG	VG+	NM
20TH CENTURY FOX					
❑ 456	Navy Blue/Unbelievable Boy	1964	3.75	7.50	15.00
❑ 477	Kiss Me Sailor/Soft Spoken Guy	1964	2.50	5.00	10.00
❑ 514	Growin' Up Too Fast/Waitin' for Joey	1964	2.50	5.00	10.00
❑ 533	It's In Your Tears/Present from Eddie	1964	2.50	5.00	10.00
ATCO					
❑ 6240	Falling Star/Little White Lies	1962	3.00	6.00	12.00
❑ 6262	Dime a Dozen/Tender	1963	3.00	6.00	12.00
FONTANA					
❑ 1679	Hold Me, Thrill Me, Kiss Me/Yesterday	1969	2.50	5.00	10.00
MGM					
❑ 13296	Billy Blue Eyes/Watch Out Sally	1964	2.50	5.00	10.00
❑ 13335	I Had a Dream/Troublemaker	1965	5.00	10.00	20.00
NEW VOICE					
❑ 800	Words/The Company You Keep	1965	2.50	5.00	10.00
❑ 803	Cross My Heart, Hope to Die/Happy Birthday, Broken Heart	1965	2.50	5.00	10.00
UNITED ARTISTS					
❑ 50048	Dynamite/Please Gypsy	1966	3.75	7.50	15.00

RENDEZVOUS

Number	Title (A Side/B Side)	Yr	VG	VG+	NM
REPRISE					
❑ 20089	Congratulations Baby/Faithfully	1962	7.50	15.00	30.00
RUST					
❑ 5041	It Breaks My Heart/Take a Break	1961	10.00	20.00	40.00

RENEGADES, THE (1)

Number	Title (A Side/B Side)	Yr	VG	VG+	NM
AMERICAN INT'L.					
❑ 537	Charge/Geronimo	1959	12.50	25.00	50.00

RENEGADES, THE (2)

Number	Title (A Side/B Side)	Yr	VG	VG+	NM
CONGRESS					
❑ 241	Cadillac/Matelot (Sailor Boy)	1965	7.50	15.00	30.00

RENEGADES, THE (3)

Number	Title (A Side/B Side)	Yr	VG	VG+	NM
DORSET					
❑ 5007	Stolen Angel/Keep Laughin'	1961	12.50	25.00	50.00

RENEGADES, THE (U)

If these are any of the above, they are most likely group (2).

Number	Title (A Side/B Side)	Yr	VG	VG+	NM
GARLAND					
❑ 2036	I'm a Loner/Travelin' Through This Countryside	196?	2.50	5.00	10.00
KARATE					
❑ 519	Take a Heart/If It Gets Lonesome	1966	3.75	7.50	15.00

RENO, AL

Number	Title (A Side/B Side)	Yr	VG	VG+	NM
KAPP					
❑ 432	Cheryl/Congratulations	1961	10.00	20.00	40.00

RENO, MIKE, AND ANN WILSON

Of Loverboy and HEART, respectively.

Number	Title (A Side/B Side)	Yr	VG	VG+	NM
COLUMBIA					
❑ 04418	Almost Paradise...Love Theme from Footloose/Strike Zone	1984	—	—	3.00
❑ 04418 [PS]	Almost Paradise...Love Theme from Footloose/Strike Zone	1984	—	2.00	4.00

REO SPEEDWAGON

Number	Title (A Side/B Side)	Yr	VG	VG+	NM
EPIC					
❑ 01054	Take It on the Run/Someone Tonight	1981	—	2.00	4.00
❑ 02127	Don't Let Him Go/I Wish You Were There	1981	—	2.00	4.00
❑ 02127 [PS]	Don't Let Him Go/I Wish You Were There	1981	—	2.50	5.00
❑ 02153	Keep On Loving You/Time for Me to Fly	1981	—	—	3.00
—Reissue					
❑ 02457	In Your Letter/Shakin' It Loose	1981	—	2.00	4.00
❑ 02967	Keep the Fire Burnin'/I'll Follow You	1982	—	2.00	4.00
❑ 03175	Sweet Time/Stillness of the Night	1982	—	2.00	4.00
❑ 03175 [PS]	Sweet Time/Stillness of the Night	1982	—	2.50	5.00

Number	Title (A Side/B Side)	Yr	VG	VG+	NM
❑ ENR-03264	Sweet Time	1982	—	2.50	5.00
—One-sided budget release					
❑ 03400	Let's Be-Bop/The Key	1982	—	2.00	4.00
❑ 03846	Keep the Fire Burnin'/Take It on the Run	1983	—	—	3.00
—Reissue					
❑ 03847	In Your Letter/Don't Let Him Go	1983	—	—	3.00
—Reissue					
❑ 04659	I Do'Wanna Know/Rock 'N Roll Star	1984	—	—	3.00
❑ 04659 [PS]	I Do'Wanna Know/Rock 'N Roll Star	1984	—	2.00	4.00
❑ 04713	Can't Fight This Feeling/Break His Spell	1984	—	—	3.00
❑ 04713 [PS]	Can't Fight This Feeling/Break His Spell	1984	—	3.00	6.00
❑ 04848	One Lonely Night/Wheels Are Turnin'	1985	—	—	3.00
❑ 04848 [PS]	One Lonely Night/Wheels Are Turnin'	1985	—	2.00	4.00
❑ 05412	Live Every Moment/Gotta Feel More	1985	—	—	3.00
❑ 06656	That Ain't Love/Accidents Can Happen	1987	—	—	3.00
❑ 06656 [PS]	That Ain't Love/Accidents Can Happen	1987	—	—	3.00
❑ 07055	Variety Tonight/Tired of Gettin' Nowhere	1987	—	—	3.00
❑ 07055 [PS]	Variety Tonight/Tired of Gettin' Nowhere	1987	—	—	3.00
❑ 07255	In My Dreams/Over the Edge	1987	—	—	3.00
❑ 07255 [PS]	In My Dreams/Over the Edge	1987	—	—	3.00
❑ 07901	Here with Me/Wherever You're Goin' (It's Alright)	1988	—	—	3.00
❑ 07901 [PS]	Here with Me/Wherever You're Goin' (It's Alright)	1988	—	—	3.00
❑ 08030	I Don't Want to Lose You/On the Road Again	1988	—	—	3.00
❑ 10827	Sophisticated Lady/Prison Women	1972	3.00	6.00	12.00
❑ 10847	157 Riverside Avenue/Five Men Were Killed Today	1972	3.00	6.00	12.00
❑ 10892	Lay Me Down/Gypsy Woman's Passion	1972	3.00	6.00	12.00
❑ 10975	Golden Country/Little Queenie	1973	3.00	6.00	12.00
❑ 11078	Ridin' the Storm Out/Whiskey Night	1974	3.00	6.00	12.00
❑ 11132	Start a New Life/Open Up	1974	2.50	5.00	10.00
❑ 50059	Sky Blues/Throw the Chains Away	1975	2.00	4.00	8.00
❑ 50120	Out of Control/Running Blind	1975	2.00	4.00	8.00
❑ 50180	Reelin'/Headed for a Fall	1975	2.00	4.00	8.00
❑ 50254	Tonight/Keep Pushin'	1976	—	3.00	6.00
❑ 50288	Flying Turkey Trot/Keep Pushin'	1976	—	3.00	6.00
❑ 50367	Ridin' the Storm Out/Being Kind	1977	—	3.00	6.00
❑ 50459	Flying Turkey Trot/Keep Pushin'	1977	—	3.00	6.00
❑ 50545	Roll with the Changes/Unidentified Flying Tuna Trot	1978	—	2.50	5.00
❑ 50582	Time for Me to Fly/Runnin' Blind	1978	—	2.50	5.00
❑ 50764	I Need You Tonight/Easy Money	1979	—	2.50	5.00
❑ 50790	Only the Strong Survive/Drop It (An Old Disguise)	1979	—	2.50	5.00
❑ 50858	Time for Me to Fly/Lightning	1980	—	2.00	4.00
❑ 50953	Keep On Loving You/Follow My Heart	1980	—	2.00	4.00
❑ 51006	Take It on the Run/Someone Tonight	1981	—	—	—
—Unreleased?					
❑ 73499	Live It Up/All Heaven Broke Loose	1990	—	—	3.00
❑ 73540	Love Is a Rock/Go for Broke	1990	—	—	3.00

REPARATA AND THE DELRONS

BIG TREE

Number	Title (A Side/B Side)	Yr	VG	VG+	NM
❑ 114	Just You/There's So Little Time	1971	—	2.50	5.00

KAPP

Number	Title (A Side/B Side)	Yr	VG	VG+	NM
❑ 989	(That's What Sends Men to) The Bowery/I've Got an Awful Lot of Losing to Do	1969	—	3.00	6.00
❑ 2010	San Juan/We're Gonna Hold the Night	1969	—	3.00	6.00
❑ 2050	Waking in the Rain/Got Fear of Losing You	1969	—	3.00	6.00

LAURIE

Number	Title (A Side/B Side)	Yr	VG	VG+	NM
❑ 3252	Your Big Mistake/Leave Us Alone	1964	7.50	15.00	30.00
—As "The Delrons"					
❑ 3589	Octopus' Garden/Your Life Is Gone	1972	—	2.50	5.00
—As "Reparata"					

MALA

Number	Title (A Side/B Side)	Yr	VG	VG+	NM
❑ 573	I Believe/It's Waiting There for You	1967	—	3.00	6.00
❑ 589	Captain of Your Ship/Toom Toom Is a Little Boy	1968	3.00	6.00	12.00
❑ 12000	Saturday Night Didn't Happen/Panic	1968	—	3.00	6.00
❑ 12016	You Can't Change a Young Boy's Mind/Weather Forecast	1968	—	3.00	6.00
❑ 12026	Heaven Only Knows/Summer Laughter	1968	—	3.00	6.00

POLYDOR

Number	Title (A Side/B Side)	Yr	VG	VG+	NM
❑ 14271	Shoes/Song for All	1975	—	2.00	4.00
—As "Reparata"					
❑ 14298	Jezebee Lancer the Belly Dancer/We Need You	1975	—	—	—
—Unreleased					

RCA VICTOR

Number	Title (A Side/B Side)	Yr	VG	VG+	NM
❑ 47-8721	I Can Tell/Take a Look Around You	1965	2.50	5.00	10.00
❑ 47-8820	I'm Nobody's Baby Now/The Loneliest Girl in Town	1966	3.75	7.50	15.00
❑ 47-8921	Mama's Little Girl/He Don't Want You	1966	2.50	5.00	10.00
❑ 47-9123	Boys and Girls/That Kind of Trouble That I Love	1967	2.50	5.00	10.00
❑ 47-9185	I Can Hear the Rain/Always Waitin'	1967	2.50	5.00	10.00

WORLD ARTISTS

Number	Title (A Side/B Side)	Yr	VG	VG+	NM
❑ 1036	Whenever a Teenager Cries/He's My Guy	1964	3.00	6.00	12.00
❑ 1051	Tommy/Mama Don't Allow	1965	3.00	6.00	12.00
❑ 1057	He's the Greatest/A Summer Thought	1965	3.00	6.00	12.00
❑ 1062	The Boy I Love/I Found My Place	1965	3.00	6.00	12.00

REPLACEMENTS, THE

SIRE

Number	Title (A Side/B Side)	Yr	VG	VG+	NM
❑ 22992	I'll Be You/Date to Church	1989	—	2.00	4.00
❑ 22992 [PS]	I'll Be You/Date to Church	1989	—	2.00	4.00
❑ 28151	Can't Hardly Wait/Cool Water	1987	—	2.00	4.00

TWIN/TONE

Number	Title (A Side/B Side)	Yr	VG	VG+	NM
❑ TTR 8120	I'm in Trouble/If Only You Were Lonely	1981	3.75	7.50	15.00
❑ TTR 8120 [PS]	I'm in Trouble/If Only You Were Lonely	1981	3.75	7.50	15.00

RESIDENTS, THE

CRYPTIC

Number	Title (A Side/B Side)	Yr	VG	VG+	NM
❑ RZ-SP-1SP 1	Earth Vs. the Flying Saucers	1986	5.00	10.00	20.00
—Green vinyl, one-sided, bonus with collector's edition of book "The Cryptic Guide to the Residents"					

EVA-TONE

Number	Title (A Side/B Side)	Yr	VG	VG+	NM
❑ 10371900-1	Diskomo (Live)	1988	—	2.50	5.00
—Flexi-disc included with April 1988 issue of Reflex					

RALPH

Number	Title (A Side/B Side)	Yr	VG	VG+	NM
❑ RR 0577	Beyond the Valley of A Day in the Life/Flying	1977	37.50	75.00	150.00
❑ RR 0577 [PS]	Beyond the Valley of A Day in the Life/Flying	1977	37.50	75.00	150.00
—Also known as "The Residents Meet the Beatles and The Beatles Meet the Residents"					
❑ RR 0776	Satisfaction/Loser Is Congruent to Weed	1976	37.50	75.00	150.00
❑ RR 0776 [PS]	Satisfaction/Loser Is Congruent to Weed	1976	37.50	75.00	150.00
❑ RR 1272	Fire/Aircraft Damage	1972	25.00	50.00	100.00
—Part of "Santa Dog" two-7" single set					
❑ RR 1272	Lightning/Explosion	1972	25.00	50.00	100.00
—Part of "Santa Dog" two-7" single set					
❑ RR 1272 [PS]	Santa Dog: Fire/Aircraft Damage; Lightning/Explosion	1972	100.00	200.00	400.00
—Signed, intentionally misnumbered sleeve for above two records					
❑ RR 7803	Satisfaction/Loser Is Congruent to Weed	1978	—	2.00	4.00
❑ RR 7803 [PS]	Satisfaction/Loser Is Congruent to Weed	1978	—	2.00	4.00
❑ RR 7812	Santa Dog '78/Fire	1978	5.00	10.00	20.00
❑ RR 7812 [PS]	Santa Dog '78/Fire	1978	5.00	10.00	20.00
❑ RZ 8422	It's a Man's Man's Man's World/Safety Is a Cootie Wootie	1984	2.50	5.00	10.00
—White vinyl picture disc					
❑ RZ 8422	It's a Man's Man's Man's World/Safety Is a Cootie Wootie	1984	—	—	3.00
❑ RZ 8422	It's a Man's Man's Man's World/Safety Is a Cootie Wootie	1984	3.75	7.50	15.00
—White vinyl picture disc; first pressing was mislabeled					
❑ RZ 8422 [PS]	It's a Man's Man's Man's World/Safety Is a Cootie Wootie	1984	—	—	3.00
❑ RZ 8621	Kaw-Liga/Stars and Stripes Forever	1986	2.50	5.00	10.00
—Picture disc					
❑ RZ 8622	Kaw-Liga/Stars and Stripes Forever	1986	2.00	4.00	8.00
—White vinyl					
❑ RZ 8622	Kaw-Liga/Stars and Stripes Forever	1986	—	—	3.00
❑ RZ 8622 [PS]	Kaw-Liga/Stars and Stripes Forever	1986	—	—	3.00
❑ RR 8722	Hit the Road Jack/For Elsie (Excerpt)	1987	—	—	3.00
❑ RR 8722 [PD]	Hit the Road Jack/For Elsie (Excerpt)	1987	2.50	5.00	10.00
—Picture disc					
❑ RR 8722 [PS]	Hit the Road Jack/For Elsie (Excerpt)	1987	—	—	3.00

7-Inch Extended Plays

RALPH

Number	Title (A Side/B Side)	Yr	VG	VG+	NM
❑ WEIRD 1	Babyfingers	1981	5.00	10.00	20.00
—Pink vinyl on labels left over from fan club issue					
❑ WEIRD 1 [PS]	Babyfingers	1981	5.00	10.00	20.00
❑ RR 0377	Babyfingers	1979	18.75	37.50	75.00
❑ RR 0377 [PS]	Babyfingers	1979	18.75	37.50	75.00
❑ RR 1177	Duck Stab	1978	—	2.50	5.00
—Red label					
❑ RR 1177 [PS]	Duck Stab	1978	—	2.50	5.00
—Matte cover					
❑ RR 1177 [PS]	Duck Stab	1978	11.25	22.50	45.00
—Shiny cover					

W.E.I.R.D.

Number	Title (A Side/B Side)	Yr	VG	VG+	NM
❑ WEIRD 1	Babyfingers	1981	5.00	10.00	20.00
—Fan club reissue					
❑ WEIRD 1 [PS]	Babyfingers	1981	5.00	10.00	20.00

RESTIVO, JOHNNY

20TH FOX

Number	Title (A Side/B Side)	Yr	VG	VG+	NM
❑ 260	Sweet Lovin'/Looka Here Now	1961	3.75	7.50	15.00
❑ 279	Doctor Love/The Magic Age Is Seventeen	1961	3.75	7.50	15.00
❑ 279 [PS]	Doctor Love/The Magic Age Is Seventeen	1961	7.50	15.00	30.00

EPIC

Number	Title (A Side/B Side)	Yr	VG	VG+	NM
❑ 9537	My Reputation/You Can't Turn Back the Clock	1962	3.75	7.50	15.00

RCA VICTOR

Number	Title (A Side/B Side)	Yr	VG	VG+	NM
❑ 47-7559 [M]	The Shape I'm In/Ya Ya	1959	5.00	10.00	20.00
❑ 47-7559 [PS]	The Shape I'm In/Ya Ya	1959	12.50	25.00	50.00
❑ 47-7601	Dear Someone/I Like Girls	1959	3.75	7.50	15.00
❑ 47-7601 [PS]	Dear Someone/I Like Girls	1959	7.50	15.00	30.00
❑ 47-7636	Our Wedding Day/Come Closer	1959	5.00	10.00	20.00
❑ 47-7697	High School Play/But I Love You	1960	3.75	7.50	15.00
❑ 47-7758	That's Good That's Bad/I Can't Take It	1960	3.75	7.50	15.00
❑ 47-7818	Two Crazy Kids/Give Me a Little Whistle (And I'll Be There)	1960	3.75	7.50	15.00
❑ 61-7559 [S]	The Shape I'm In/Ya Ya	1959	12.50	25.00	50.00
—"Living Stereo" issue with large hole					

REUNION

A&M

Number	Title (A Side/B Side)	Yr	VG	VG+	NM
❑ 1308	City Song/No Good Alone	1971	—	2.00	4.00

BELL

Number	Title (A Side/B Side)	Yr	VG	VG+	NM
❑ 45222	Smile (Theme from Modern Times)/Turn Back the Hands of Time (Gotta Have You Back)	1972	—	2.00	4.00
❑ 45287	Living Together, Growing Together/Just Say Goodbye	1974	—	2.00	4.00

RCA VICTOR

Number	Title (A Side/B Side)	Yr	VG	VG+	NM
❑ PB-10056	Life Is a Rock (But the Radio Rolled Me)/Are You Ready to Believe	1974	—	2.50	5.00
❑ PB-10150	Disco-Tekin/Goodstuff	1975	—	2.00	4.00
❑ PB-10252	They Don't Make 'Em Like That Anymore/Goodstuff	1975	—	2.00	4.00
❑ GB-10491	Life Is a Rock (But the Radio Rolled Me)/Are You Ready to Believe	1975	—	—	3.00
—Gold Standard Series					

REV-LONS, THE

GARPAX

Number	Title (A Side/B Side)	Yr	VG	VG+	NM
❑ 44168	Boy Trouble/Give Me One More Chance	1962	3.75	7.50	15.00

REPRISE

Number	Title (A Side/B Side)	Yr	VG	VG+	NM
❑ 0251	After Last Night/It's Gonna Happen Someday	1964	3.00	6.00	12.00

Number	Title (A Side/B Side)	Yr	VG	VG+	NM
❑ 20200	I Can't Forget About You/Love Can't Be a One-Way Deal	1963	3.00	6.00	12.00

REVALONS, THE

Number	Title (A Side/B Side)	Yr	VG	VG+	NM
PET					
❑ 802	Dreams Are for Fools/This Is the Moment	1958	30.00	60.00	120.00

REVELS, THE (1)

Number	Title (A Side/B Side)	Yr	VG	VG+	NM
NORGOLDE					
❑ 103	Dead Man's Stroll/Talking to My Heart	1959	30.00	60.00	120.00
❑ 103	Midnight Stroll/Talking to My Heart	1959	6.25	12.50	25.00
—Same A-side as above, but with revised title					
❑ 104	Tweedlee Dee/Foo Man Choo	1959	5.00	10.00	20.00

REVELS, THE (2)

Number	Title (A Side/B Side)	Yr	VG	VG+	NM
CT					
❑ 1	Church Key/Vesuvius	1960	25.00	50.00	100.00
DOWNEY					
❑ 123	Intoxica/Comanche	1964	6.25	12.50	25.00
IMPACT					
❑ 1	Church Key/Vesuvius	1960	6.25	12.50	25.00
—Black vinyl					
❑ 1	Church Key/Vesuvius	1960	12.50	25.00	50.00
—Red vinyl					
❑ 3	Intoxica/Tequila	1961	6.25	12.50	25.00
❑ 7	Comanche/Rampage	1961	6.25	12.50	25.00
—Black vinyl					
❑ 7	Comanche/Rampage	1961	12.50	25.00	50.00
—Yellow vinyl					
❑ 13	Party Time/Soft Top	1961	6.25	12.50	25.00
❑ 22	The Monkey Bird/Revellion	1962	6.25	12.50	25.00
—Black vinyl					
❑ 22	The Monkey Bird/Revellion	1962	12.50	25.00	50.00
—Yellow vinyl					
❑ 22	Conga Twist/Revellion	1962	6.25	12.50	25.00
—Black vinyl					
❑ 22	Conga Twist/Revellion	1962	12.50	25.00	50.00
—Yellow vinyl; Both A-sides of Impact 22 are the same song					
LYNN					
❑ 1302	Six Pak/Good Grief	1960	15.00	30.00	60.00
SWINGIN'					
❑ 620	Six Pak/Good Grief	1960	10.00	20.00	40.00
WESTCO					
❑ 3/4	Party Time/Soft Top	1963	12.50	25.00	50.00
—Red and yellow vinyl					

REVELS, THE (3)

Number	Title (A Side/B Side)	Yr	VG	VG+	NM
DIAMOND					
❑ 143	Lots of Luck/Gonna Have Some Fun	1963	3.75	7.50	15.00

REVELS, THE (4)

Number	Title (A Side/B Side)	Yr	VG	VG+	NM
JAMIE					
❑ 1318	True Love/Everybody Can Do the New Dog But Me	1966	2.50	5.00	10.00

REVELS, THE (U)

It's doubtful that any of these are group (2), and they probably aren't group (1), either. Group (3) and (4) are not out of the question, though.

Number	Title (A Side/B Side)	Yr	VG	VG+	NM
ANDIE					
❑ 5077	Please/Two Little Monkeys (In a Banana Tree)	1960	5.00	10.00	20.00
KAPP					
❑ 621	Downtown/Dollar Sign	1964	7.50	15.00	30.00
PALETTE					
❑ 5074	O How I Love You/I Met My Lost Love	1961	5.00	10.00	20.00

REVERE, PAUL, AND THE RAIDERS

Includes records as "Raiders" in the early 1970s. Also see MARK LINDSAY; JIM VALLEY.

Number	Title (A Side/B Side)	Yr	VG	VG+	NM
20TH CENTURY					
❑ 2283	The British Are Coming/Surrender at Appomattox	1976	—	2.50	5.00
—B-side by Susie Allanson					
COLUMBIA					
❑ CSP-262	SS 396/Corvair Baby	1965	6.25	12.50	25.00
❑ CSM-466	SS 396/Camaro	1967	6.25	12.50	25.00
—B-side by The Cyrcle					
❑ CSM-466 [PS]	SS 396/Camaro	1967	12.50	25.00	50.00
—B-side by The Cyrcle					
❑ 10126	Gonna Have a Good Time/Your Love (Is the Only Love)	1975	2.50	5.00	10.00
❑ 42814	Louie Louie/Night Train	1963	10.00	20.00	40.00
❑ 43008	Louie Go Home/Have Love Will Travel	1964	3.75	7.50	15.00
❑ 43114	Over You/Swim	1964	3.75	7.50	15.00
❑ 43273	Ooh Poo Pah Doo/Sometimes	1965	3.75	7.50	15.00
❑ 43375	Steppin' Out/Blue Fox	1965	2.50	5.00	10.00
❑ 43375 [DJ]	Steppin' Out (same on both sides)	1965	12.50	25.00	50.00
—Red vinyl promo					
❑ 43461	Just Like Me/B.F.R.D.F. Blues	1965	2.50	5.00	10.00
❑ 43461 [DJ]	Just Like Me (same on both sides)	1965	12.50	25.00	50.00
—Red vinyl promo					
❑ 43556	Kicks/Shake It Up	1966	2.50	5.00	10.00
❑ 43556 [DJ]	Kicks (same on both sides)	1966	12.50	25.00	50.00
—Red vinyl promo					
❑ 43678	Hungry/There She Goes	1966	2.50	5.00	10.00
❑ 43678 [DJ]	Hungry (same on both sides)	1966	12.50	25.00	50.00
—Red vinyl promo					
❑ 43678 [PS]	Hungry/There She Goes	1966	5.00	10.00	20.00
❑ 43810	The Great Airplane Strike/In My Community	1966	2.50	5.00	10.00
❑ 43810 [DJ]	The Great Airplane Strike (same on both sides)	1966	12.50	25.00	50.00
—Red vinyl promo					
❑ 43810 [PS]	The Great Airplane Strike/In My Community	1966	3.75	7.50	15.00
❑ 43907	Good Thing/Undecided Man	1966	2.50	5.00	10.00
❑ 43907 [PS]	Good Thing/Undecided Man	1966	5.00	10.00	20.00
❑ 44018	Ups and Downs/Leslie	1967	2.50	5.00	10.00
❑ 44018 [PS]	Ups and Downs/Leslie	1967	3.75	7.50	15.00
❑ 44094	Him or Me — What's It Gonna Be?/Legend of Paul Revere	1967	2.50	5.00	10.00
❑ 44094 [PS]	Him or Me — What's It Gonna Be?/Legend of Paul Revere	1967	3.75	7.50	15.00
❑ 44227	I Had a Dream/Upon Your Leaving	1967	2.00	4.00	8.00
❑ 44227 [PS]	I Had a Dream/Upon Your Leaving	1967	2.50	5.00	10.00
❑ 44335	Peace of Mind/Do Unto Others	1967	2.00	4.00	8.00
❑ 44335 [PS]	Peace of Mind/Do Unto Others	1967	2.50	5.00	10.00
❑ 44444	Too Much Talk/Happening '68	1968	2.00	4.00	8.00
❑ 44444 [PS]	Too Much Talk/Happening '68	1968	2.50	5.00	10.00
❑ 44553	Don't Take It Too Hard/Observation from Flight 285 (In 3/4 Time)	1968	—	3.00	6.00
❑ 44553 [PS]	Don't Take It Too Hard/Observation from Flight 285 (In 3/4 Time)	1968	2.50	5.00	10.00
❑ 44655	Cinderella Sunshine/It's Happening	1968	2.00	4.00	8.00
❑ 44744	Mr. Sun, Mr. Moon/Without You	1969	—	3.00	6.00
❑ 44744 [PS]	Mr. Sun, Mr. Moon/Without You	1969	2.50	5.00	10.00
❑ 44854	Let Me/I Don't Know	1969	—	3.00	6.00
❑ 44970	We Gotta All Get Together/Frankfort Side Street	1969	—	3.00	6.00
❑ 45082	Just Seventeen/Sorceress with Blue Eyes	1970	—	3.00	6.00
—As "Raiders"					
❑ 45150	Gone Movin' On/Interlude (To Be Forgotten)	1970	—	3.00	6.00
—As "Raiders"					
❑ 45332	Indian Reservation (The Lament of the Cherokee Reservation Indian)/Terry's Tune	1971	2.00	4.00	8.00
—As "Raiders"; red label, black print					
❑ 45332	Indian Reservation (The Lament of the Cherokee Reservation Indian)/Terry's Tune	1971	—	3.00	6.00
—As "Raiders"; orange label with "Columbia" background print					
❑ 45453	Birds of a Feather/The Turkey	1971	—	3.00	6.00
—As "Raiders"					
❑ 45535	Country Wine/It's So Hard Getting Up Today	1972	—	3.00	6.00
—As "Raiders"					
❑ 45601	Powder Blue Mercedes Queen/Golden Girls Sometimes	1972	2.00	4.00	8.00
—As "Raiders"					
❑ 45688	Song Seller/A Simple Song	1972	2.00	4.00	8.00
—As "Raiders"					
❑ 45759	Love Music/Goodbye, No. 9	1973	2.00	4.00	8.00
—As "Raiders"					
❑ 45898	All Over You/Seaboard Line Boogie	1973	2.00	4.00	8.00
—As "Raiders"					
DRIVE					
❑ 6248	Ain't Nothing Wrong/You're Really Saying Something	1976	—	2.50	5.00
GARDENA					
❑ 106	Beatnik Sticks/Orbit (The Spy)	1960	7.50	15.00	30.00
❑ 115	Paul Revere's Ride/Unfinished Fifth	1960	10.00	20.00	40.00
❑ 116	Like, Long Hair/Sharon	1961	7.50	15.00	30.00
❑ 118	Like, Charleston/Midnite Ride	1961	6.25	12.50	25.00
❑ 124	All Night Long/Groovey	1962	10.00	20.00	40.00
❑ 127	Like, Bluegrass/Leatherneck	1962	10.00	20.00	40.00
❑ 131	Shake It Up (Part 1)/Shake It Up (Part 2)	1962	10.00	20.00	40.00
❑ 137	Tall Cool One/Road Runner	1963	12.50	25.00	50.00
HITBOUND					
❑ X-2	Jingle Bell Rock/Jingle Bells	1983	3.00	6.00	12.00
—B-side by Mike Love and Dean Torrence					
❑ X-2 [PS]	Jingle Bell Rock/Jingle Bells	1983	5.00	10.00	20.00
—B-side by Mike Love and Dean Torrence					
JERDEN					
❑ 807	So Fine/Blues Stay Away	1966	6.25	12.50	25.00
SANDE					
❑ 101	Louie Louie/Night Train	1963	62.50	125.00	250.00

REVERES, THE (1)

Number	Title (A Side/B Side)	Yr	VG	VG+	NM
GLORY					
❑ 272	Leonore/Honeystroller	1958	5.00	10.00	20.00
—B-side by the Honeystrollers					

REVERES, THE (2)

Number	Title (A Side/B Side)	Yr	VG	VG+	NM
JUBILEE					
❑ 5463	Beyond the Sea/The Show Must Go On	1963	6.25	12.50	25.00

REVERES, THE (3)

BRUCE JOHNSTON appears on this record.

Number	Title (A Side/B Side)	Yr	VG	VG+	NM
VALIANT					
❑ 6041	Big "T"/Me and My Spider	1964	12.50	25.00	50.00

REVLONS, THE

More than one group.

Number	Title (A Side/B Side)	Yr	VG	VG+	NM
CAPITOL					
❑ 4739	Dry Your Eyes/She'll Come to Me	1962	7.50	15.00	30.00
PARKWAY					
❑ 107	Ya Ya/It Could Happen to You	1966	3.00	6.00	12.00
RAE COX					
❑ 105	This Restless Heart/I Promise Love	1961	7.50	15.00	30.00
TIMES SQUARE					
❑ 15	Ride Awy/Betty	1963	6.25	12.50	25.00
—B-side by the Centuries					
TOY					
❑ 101	What a Love This Is/Did I Make a Mistake	1962	5.00	10.00	20.00

REYNOLDS, JODY

Number	Title (A Side/B Side)	Yr	VG	VG+	NM
BRENT					
❑ 7042	Raggedy Ann/The Girl from King Marie	1963	2.50	5.00	10.00
DEMON					
❑ 1507	Endless Sleep/Tight Capris	1958	7.50	15.00	30.00
❑ 1509	Fire of Love/Daisy Mae	1958	6.25	12.50	25.00
❑ 1511	Closin' In/Elope with Me	1958	6.25	12.50	25.00
❑ 1515	Golden Idol/Beulah Lee	1959	6.25	12.50	25.00

Number	Title (A Side/B Side)	Yr	VG	VG+	NM
❑ 1519	The Storm/Please Remember	1959	6.25	12.50	25.00
❑ 1523	Whipping Post/I Wanna Be with You Tonight	1960	6.25	12.50	25.00
❑ 1524	Stone Cold/(The Girl with) The Raven Hair	1960	6.25	12.50	25.00
INDIGO					
❑ 127	Tarantula/Thunder	1961	12.50	25.00	50.00
PULSAR					
❑ 2419	Endless Sleep/My Baby's Eyes	1969	—	3.00	6.00
SMASH					
❑ 1810	Don't Jmp/Stormy	1963	3.00	6.00	12.00
TITAN					
❑ 1734	Devil Girl/A Tear for Hesse	1963	3.75	7.50	15.00
❑ 1736	Requiem for Love/Stranger in the Mirror	1963	3.75	7.50	15.00
—With Bobbie Gentry					

RHODES, EMITT

Also see THE MERRY-GO-ROUND.

Number	Title (A Side/B Side)	Yr	VG	VG+	NM
ABC DUNHILL					
❑ 4267	Fresh as a Daisy/You Take the Dark Out of the Night	1970	—	3.00	6.00
❑ 4274	Live Till You Die/Promises I've Made	1971	—	2.50	5.00
❑ 4280	A Lullaby/With My Face on the Floor	1971	—	2.50	5.00
❑ 4295	Really Wanted You/Love Will Stone You	1971	—	2.50	5.00
❑ 4303	Take You Far Away/Golden Child of God	1972	—	2.50	5.00
❑ 4315	Tame the Lion/Golden Child of God	1972	—	2.50	5.00
A&M					
❑ 1254	Till the Day After/You're a Very Lovely Woman	1971	—	3.00	6.00
—As "Emitt Rhodes with the Merry-Go-Round"					

RHODES, SLIM

Number	Title (A Side/B Side)	Yr	VG	VG+	NM
RHODES					
❑ 101	Brothers Frank and Jesse James/(B-side unknown)	195?	12.50	25.00	50.00
SUN					
❑ 216	Don't Believe/Uncertain Blues	1955	25.00	50.00	100.00
❑ 225	Are You Ashamed of Me/The House of Sin	1955	75.00	150.00	300.00
❑ 238	Bad Girl/Gonna Romp and Stomp	1956	25.00	50.00	100.00
❑ 256	Do What I Do/Take and Give	1956	12.50	25.00	50.00

RHODES, TODD

Number	Title (A Side/B Side)	Yr	VG	VG+	NM
KING					
❑ 4469	Gin, Gin, Gin/I Shouldn't Cry But I Do	1951	25.00	50.00	100.00
❑ 4486	Good Man/Evening Breeze	1951	15.00	30.00	60.00
❑ 4509	Your Daddy's Doggin' Around/Red Boy Is Back	1952	15.00	30.00	60.00
❑ 4528	Rocket 69/Possessed	1952	12.50	25.00	50.00
❑ 4556	Snuff Dipper/Trying	1952	12.50	25.00	50.00
—B-side by La Vern Baker					
❑ 4566	Pig Latin Blues/Blue Autumn	1952	12.50	25.00	50.00
❑ 4583	Hog Maw and Cabbage Slaw/Must I Cry Again	1952	12.50	25.00	50.00
—B-side by La Vern Baker					
❑ 4601	Thunderbolt Boogie/Lost Child	1953	12.50	25.00	50.00
—B-side by La Vern Baker					
❑ 4648	Your Mouth Got a Hole In It/Feathers	1953	10.00	20.00	40.00
❑ 4666	Let Down Blues/Beet Patch	1953	10.00	20.00	40.00
❑ 4736	Silver Sunset/Specks	1954	7.50	15.00	30.00
❑ 4755	Chicken Strut/Echoes	1954	7.50	15.00	30.00

RHYTHM, JOHNNY

Number	Title (A Side/B Side)	Yr	VG	VG+	NM
MGM					
❑ 13043	This Is It/Wouldn't It Be Nice	1961	10.00	20.00	40.00

RHYTHM ACES, THE (1)

Number	Title (A Side/B Side)	Yr	VG	VG+	NM
ACE					
❑ 518	Rock and Roll March/Look What You've Done	1956	10.00	20.00	40.00
—B-side by Bob Douglas					
VEE JAY					
❑ 124	I Wonder Why/Get Lost	1954	500.00	1000.	2000.
—Red vinyl					
❑ 124	I Wonder Why/Get Lost	1954	50.00	100.00	200.00
—Black vinyl					
❑ 138	Whisper to Me/Olly, Olly, Oxsen Free	1955	500.00	1000.	2000.
—Red vinyl					
❑ 138	Whisper to Me/Olly, Olly, Oxsen Free	1955	50.00	100.00	200.00
—Black vinyl					
❑ 160	That's My Sugar/Flippety Flop	1955	30.00	60.00	120.00

RHYTHM ACES, THE (2)

Number	Title (A Side/B Side)	Yr	VG	VG+	NM
MARK-X					
❑ 8004	Boppin' Sloppin' Baby/Crazy Jealousy	1960	7.50	15.00	30.00

RHYTHM ACES, THE (3)

Number	Title (A Side/B Side)	Yr	VG	VG+	NM
ROULETTE					
❑ 4268	Mohawk Rock/It'll Do	1960	3.75	7.50	15.00
❑ 4426	Raunchy Twist/Mockin' Bird Twist	1962	3.75	7.50	15.00
SIOUX					
❑ 82260	Allan's Rock/Go Get It	1960	7.50	15.00	30.00
❑ 102261	Yahma/What'd I Say Twist	1961	7.50	15.00	30.00
UNIVERSAL ARTISTS					
❑ 3160	Mohawk Rock/It'll Do	1960	10.00	20.00	40.00

RHYTHM CADETS, THE

Number	Title (A Side/B Side)	Yr	VG	VG+	NM
VESTA					
❑ 501/2	Dearest Doryce/Rocking Jimmy	1957	200.00	400.00	800.00

RHYTHM MASTERS, THE (1)

Number	Title (A Side/B Side)	Yr	VG	VG+	NM
ACE					
❑ 610	The Devil and His Old Suitcase/Holding My Savior's Hand	1961	5.00	10.00	20.00

RHYTHM MASTERS, THE (2)

Number	Title (A Side/B Side)	Yr	VG	VG+	NM
FLIP					
❑ 314	Baby We Two/Patricia	1956	75.00	150.00	300.00

RHYTHM ROCKERS (1)

Number	Title (A Side/B Side)	Yr	VG	VG+	NM
CHALLENGE					
❑ 9196	Rendezvous Stomp/The Slide	1963	6.25	12.50	25.00

RHYTHM ROCKERS (2)

Number	Title (A Side/B Side)	Yr	VG	VG+	NM
SATIN					
❑ 921	Oh Boy/We Belong Together	1960	15.00	30.00	60.00
❑ 921 [PS]	Oh Boy/We Belong Together	1960	25.00	50.00	100.00

RHYTHM ROCKERS (3)

Number	Title (A Side/B Side)	Yr	VG	VG+	NM
SUN					
❑ 248	Fiddle Bop/Juke Box, Help Me Find My Baby	1956	25.00	50.00	100.00

RHYTHM ROCKERS (U)

These could be by group (1) or (2).

Number	Title (A Side/B Side)	Yr	VG	VG+	NM
FENTON					
❑ 944	Surf Around/Three Strikes	1962	12.50	25.00	50.00
WIPE OUT					
❑ 1001	Foot Cruising/Get It On	1962	10.00	20.00	40.00

RIA AND THE REASONS

Number	Title (A Side/B Side)	Yr	VG	VG+	NM
AMY					
❑ 888	Memories Linger On/Sorry I Lied	1963	6.25	12.50	25.00
❑ 888	Memories Linger On/Sorry I Lied	1963	20.00	40.00	80.00
—Blue vinyl					
RSVP					
❑ 1110	He's Not There/She Fell in Love	1965	5.00	10.00	20.00
—As "Ria and the Revellons"					

RIALTOS, THE

Number	Title (A Side/B Side)	Yr	VG	VG+	NM
CB					
❑ 5009	Let Me In/It Hurts	1962	75.00	150.00	300.00

RIC-A-SHAYS, THE

Harry NILSSON was in this group.

Number	Title (A Side/B Side)	Yr	VG	VG+	NM
LOLA					
❑ 002	Groovy/Turn On	1964	6.25	12.50	25.00

RICARDOS, THE

Number	Title (A Side/B Side)	Yr	VG	VG+	NM
STAR-X					
❑ 512	Mary's Little Lamb/I Mean Really	1958	40.00	80.00	160.00

RICE, JIMMY

Number	Title (A Side/B Side)	Yr	VG	VG+	NM
RED BIRD					
❑ 10-022	The Grass Is Always Greener/Spanish Perfume	1965	5.00	10.00	20.00
❑ 10-027	Nobody But You/Or Not at All	1965	5.00	10.00	20.00

RICE, TONY

Number	Title (A Side/B Side)	Yr	VG	VG+	NM
ACTION					
❑ 100	My Darling Y-O-U/I Thank You Baby	1961	7.50	15.00	30.00
PRINCETON					
❑ 101	Summer's Love/Please Don't	1960	15.00	30.00	60.00
RAE COX					
❑ 106	Little School Girl/Blue Bird of Happiness	1961	5.00	10.00	20.00

RICH, CHARLIE

Number	Title (A Side/B Side)	Yr	VG	VG+	NM
ELEKTRA					
❑ 45553	I'll Wake You Up When I Get Home/Salty Dog Blues	1978	—	2.00	4.00
❑ 47047	A Man Just Doesn't Know What a Woman Goes Through/Marie	1980	—	2.00	4.00
❑ 47104	Are We Dreamin' the Same Dream/Angelina	1981	—	2.00	4.00
EPIC					
❑ 02058	You Made It Beautiful/How Good It Used to Be	1981	—	2.00	4.00
❑ 03165	Try a Little Tenderness/As Time Goes By	1982	—	2.00	4.00
❑ 10287	Set Me Free/I'll Just Go Away	1968	—	3.00	6.00
❑ 10358	Raggedy Ann/Nothing in the World	1968	—	3.00	6.00
❑ 10492	Life's Little Ups and Downs/It Takes Time	1969	—	3.00	6.00
❑ 10585	July 12, 1939/I'm Flying to Nashville Tonight	1970	—	3.00	6.00
❑ 10662	Nice 'N' Easy/I Can't Even Drink It Away	1970	—	3.00	6.00
❑ 10745	A Woman Left Lonely/Have a Heart	1971	—	2.50	5.00
❑ 10809	A Part of Your Life/A Sunday Kind of Woman	1971	—	2.50	5.00
❑ 10867	I Take It On Home/Peace on You	1972	—	2.50	5.00
❑ 10950	Behind Closed Doors/A Sunday Kind of Woman	1973	—	2.50	5.00
—Originals have yellow labels					
❑ 10950	Behind Closed Doors/A Sunday Kind of Woman	1973	—	2.00	4.00
—Repressings have orange labels					
❑ 11040	The Most Beautiful Girl/I Feel Like Going Home	1973	—	2.00	4.00
❑ 11091	A Very Special Love Song/I Can't Even Drink It Away	1974	—	2.00	4.00
❑ 20006	I Love My Friend/Why Oh Why	1974	—	2.00	4.00
❑ 50064	My Elusive Dreams/Whatever Happened	1975	—	2.00	4.00
❑ 50103	Every Time You Touch Me (I Get High)/Pass On By	1975	—	2.00	4.00
❑ 50142	All Over Me/You & I	1975	—	2.00	4.00
❑ 50182	Since I Fell for You/She	1975	—	2.00	4.00
❑ 50222	America the Beautiful (1976)/Down By the Riverside	1976	—	2.00	4.00
❑ 50268	Road Song/The Grass Is Always Greener	1976	—	2.00	4.00
❑ 50328	Easy Look/My Lady	1976	—	2.00	4.00
❑ 50392	Rollin' with the Flow/To Sing a Love Song	1977	—	2.00	4.00
❑ 50562	Beautiful Woman/Everybody Wrote That Song for Me	1978	—	2.00	4.00
❑ 50616	On My Knees/Mellow Melody	1978	—	2.00	4.00
❑ 50701	Spanish Eyes/I Do My Swingin' at Home	1979	—	2.00	4.00
❑ 50869	Even a Fool Would Let Go/Pretty People	1980	—	2.00	4.00
GROOVE					
❑ 58-0020	The Grass Is Always Greener/She Loved Everybody But Me	1963	3.75	7.50	15.00
❑ 58-0020 [PS]	The Grass Is Always Greener/She Loved Everybody But Me	1963	7.50	15.00	30.00
❑ 58-0025	Big Boss Man/Let Me Go My Merry Way	1963	3.75	7.50	15.00
❑ 58-0032	Lady Love/Why, Oh Why	1964	3.75	7.50	15.00

Number	Title (A Side/B Side)	Yr	VG	VG+	NM
❑ 58-0035	The Ways of a Woman in Love/My Mountain Dew	1964	3.75	7.50	15.00
❑ 58-0041	Nice 'N' Easy/Turn Around and Face Me	1964	3.75	7.50	15.00
HI					
❑ 2116	Love Is After Me/Pass On By	1966	2.50	5.00	10.00
❑ 2123	My Heart Would Know/Nobody's Lonesome for Me	1967	2.50	5.00	10.00
❑ 2134	Hurry Up Freight Train/Only Me	1967	2.50	5.00	10.00
MERCURY					
❑ 73466	I Washed My Hands in Muddy Water/No Home	1974	—	2.50	5.00
❑ 73498	A Field of Yellow Daisies/Party Girl	1974	—	2.50	5.00
❑ 73646	Something Just Came Over Me/Best Years	1974	—	2.50	5.00
PHILLIPS INT'L.					
❑ 3532	Whirlwind/Philadelphia Baby	1959	6.25	12.50	25.00
❑ 3542	Rebound/Big Man	1959	6.25	12.50	25.00
❑ 3552	Lonely Weekends/Everything I Do Is Wrong	1960	6.25	12.50	25.00
❑ 3560	School Days/Gonna Be Waiting	1960	6.25	12.50	25.00
❑ 3562	On My Knees/Stay	1960	6.25	12.50	25.00
❑ 3566	Who Will the Next Fool Be/Caught in the Middle	1961	6.25	12.50	25.00
❑ 3572	Just a Little Sweet/It's Too Late	1962	5.00	10.00	20.00
❑ 3576	Easy Money/Midnight Blues	1962	5.00	10.00	20.00
❑ 3582	Sittin' and Thinkin'/Finally Found Out	1962	5.00	10.00	20.00
❑ 3584	There's Another Place I Can't Go/I Need Your Love	1963	5.00	10.00	20.00
RCA					
❑ PB-10859	My Mountain Dew/Nice 'N Easy	1976	—	2.00	4.00
❑ PB-10966	Nice 'N Easy/It's All Over Now	1977	—	2.00	4.00
RCA VICTOR					
❑ APBO-0195	There Won't Be Anymore/It's All Over Now	1973	—	2.50	5.00
❑ APBO-0260	I Don't See Me in Your Eyes Anymore/No Room to Dance	1974	—	2.00	4.00
❑ PB-10062	She Called Me Baby/$10 and a Clean White Shirt	1974	—	2.00	4.00
❑ GB-10159	There Won't Be Anymore/Tomorrow Night	1975	—	—	3.00
—Gold Standard Series					
❑ PB-10256	It's All Over Now/Big Jack	1975	—	2.00	4.00
❑ PB-10458	Not Everybody Knows/I've Got You Under My Skin	1975	—	2.00	4.00
❑ GB-10512	She Called Me Baby/$10 And a Clean White Shirt	1975	—	—	3.00
—Gold Standard Series					
❑ 47-8468	It's All Over Now/Too Many Teardrops	1964	3.75	7.50	15.00
❑ 47-8536	There Won't Be Anymore/Gentleman Jim	1965	5.00	10.00	20.00
❑ 47-8817	Nice 'N' Easy/Ol' Man River	1966	3.00	6.00	12.00
❑ 74-0983	Tomorrow Night/The Ways of a Woman in Love	1973	—	2.00	4.00
SMASH					
❑ 1993	Mohair Sam/I Washed My Hands in Muddy Water	1965	5.00	10.00	20.00
❑ 2012	Dance of Love/I Can't Go On	1965	3.75	7.50	15.00
❑ 2022	Hawg Jaw/Something Just Came Over Me	1966	3.75	7.50	15.00
❑ 2038	No Home/Tears a-Go-Go	1966	3.75	7.50	15.00
❑ 2060	That's the Way/When My Baby Comes Home	1966	3.75	7.50	15.00
SUN					
❑ 1110	Who Will the Next Fool Be/Stay	1970	—	2.50	5.00
❑ 1151	The Breakup/Be-Bop-a-Lula	1980	—	2.00	4.00
—B-side by Jerry Lee Lewis; both sides are duets with Orion					
UNITED ARTISTS					
❑ XW1193	Puttin' In Overtime at Home/Ghost of Another Man	1978	—	2.00	4.00
❑ XW1223	I Still Believe in Love/Wishful Thinking	1978	—	2.00	4.00
❑ XW1269	The Fool Strikes Again/I Loved You All the Way	1978	—	2.00	4.00
❑ XW1280	I Lost My Head/She Knows Just How to Touch Me	1979	—	2.00	4.00
❑ XW1307	Life Goes On/Standing Tall	1979	—	2.00	4.00
❑ 1325	You're Gonna Love Yourself in the Morning/Top of the Stairs	1979	—	2.00	4.00
❑ 1340	I'd Build a Bridge/All You Ever Have to Do Is Touch Me	1980	—	2.00	4.00

RICH, DAVE

Number	Title (A Side/B Side)	Yr	VG	VG+	NM
RCA VICTOR					
❑ 47-6327	I Forgot/I Think I'm Gonna Die	1955	7.50	15.00	30.00
❑ 47-6435	I'm Glad/Darling, I'm Lonesome	1956	7.50	15.00	30.00
❑ 47-6595	Your Pretty Blue Eyes/Ain't It Fine	1956	10.00	20.00	40.00
❑ 47-6687	I'm Sorry, Goodbye/I Love 'Em All	1956	7.50	15.00	30.00
❑ 47-6753	Lonely Street/Didn't Work Out, Did It	1956	7.50	15.00	30.00
❑ 47-6824	Tuggin' on My Heart Strings/Our Last Night Together	1957	7.50	15.00	30.00
❑ 47-6926	The Key to My Heart/Red Sweater	1957	7.50	15.00	30.00
❑ 47-7045	Chicken House/I've Learned	1957	7.50	15.00	30.00
❑ 47-7141	School Blues/I've Thought It Over	1958	7.50	15.00	30.00
❑ 47-7247	City Lights/Burn On Love Fire	1958	7.50	15.00	30.00
❑ 47-7334	Rosie Let's Get Cozy/Sunshine in My Heart	1958	7.50	15.00	30.00
REPUBLIC					
❑ 390	Because You're Gone/(B-side unknown)	1977	—	2.50	5.00
STOP					
❑ 122	When I've Learned/I Don't Need Nobody Else	196?	2.00	4.00	8.00
❑ 132	I Never Gave Up/On the Battlefield	196?	2.00	4.00	8.00
❑ 171	I Believe/Peace On Earth Begins Today	196?	2.00	4.00	8.00

RICHARD, CLIFF

Also see THE SHADOWS.

Number	Title (A Side/B Side)	Yr	VG	VG+	NM
ABC-PARAMOUNT					
❑ 10042	Living Doll/Apron Strings	1959	6.25	12.50	25.00
❑ 10066	Travellin' Light/Dynamite	1959	5.00	10.00	20.00
❑ 10093	Voice in the Wilderness/Don't Be Mad at Me	1960	5.00	10.00	20.00
❑ 10109	Fall in Love with You/Choppin' 'N' Changin'	1960	5.00	10.00	20.00
❑ 10136	Please Don't Tease/Where Is My Heart	1960	5.00	10.00	20.00
❑ 10175	Catch Me, I'm Falling/"D" in Love	1961	5.00	10.00	20.00
❑ 10195	Theme for a Dream/Mumblin' Mosie	1961	10.00	20.00	40.00
BIG TOP					
❑ 3101	The Young Ones/We Say Yeah	1962	5.00	10.00	20.00
CAPITOL					
❑ F4096	Move It/High Class Baby	1958	10.00	20.00	40.00
❑ F4154	Livin' Lovin' Doll/Steady with You	1959	10.00	20.00	40.00
DOT					
❑ 16399	Wonderful to Be Young/Got a Funny Feeling	1962	5.00	10.00	20.00
EMI					
❑ S7-19767	Mistletoe and Wine/Have Yourself a Merry Little Christmas	1997	—	2.00	4.00
EMI AMERICA					
❑ 8025	We Don't Talk Anymore/Count Me Out	1979	—	2.00	4.00
❑ 8035	Carrie/Language of Love	1980	—	2.00	4.00
❑ 8057	Dreaming/Dynamite	1980	—	2.50	5.00
—Green label					
❑ 8057	Dreaming/Dynamite	1980	—	2.00	4.00
—Gray label					
❑ 8068	A Little in Love/Everyman	1980	—	2.00	4.00
❑ 8076	Give a Little Bit More/Keep Lookin'	1981	—	2.00	4.00
❑ 8076 [PS]	Give a Little Bit More/Keep Lookin'	1981	—	2.50	5.00
❑ 8095	Wired for Sound/Hold On	1981	—	2.00	4.00
❑ 8103	Daddy's Home/Summer Rain	1982	—	2.00	4.00
❑ 8135	The Only Way Out/Be in My Heart	1982	—	2.00	4.00
❑ 8149	Little Town/Be in My Heart	1982	—	2.00	4.00
❑ 8180	Never Say Die (Give a Little Bit More)/Front Page	1983	—	2.00	4.00
❑ 8193	Donna/Ocean Deep	1984	—	2.00	4.00
EPIC					
❑ 9597	Lucky Lips/Next Time	1963	5.00	10.00	20.00
❑ 9597 [PS]	Lucky Lips/Next Time	1963	6.25	12.50	25.00
❑ 9633	It's All in the Game/I'm Looking Out the Window	1963	5.00	10.00	20.00
❑ 9670	I'm the Lonely One/I Only Have Eyes for You	1964	5.00	10.00	20.00
❑ 9670 [PS]	I'm the Lonely One/I Only Have Eyes for You	1964	6.25	12.50	25.00
❑ 9691	Bachelor Boy/True, True Lovin'	1964	5.00	10.00	20.00
❑ 9737	I Don't Wanna Love You/Look in My Eyes Maria	1964	3.75	7.50	15.00
❑ 9757	Again/The Minute You're Gone	1965	3.75	7.50	15.00
❑ 9810	I Could Easily Fall (In Love with You)/On My Word	1965	3.75	7.50	15.00
❑ 9839	The Twelfth of Never/Paradise Lost	1965	3.75	7.50	15.00
❑ 9866	Wind Me Up (and Let Me Go)/Eye of a Needle	1965	3.75	7.50	15.00
❑ 10018	Blue Turns to Grey/I'll Walk Alone	1966	3.75	7.50	15.00
❑ 10070	Visions/Quando, Quando, Quando	1966	3.75	7.50	15.00
❑ 10101	Time Drags By/The La La La Song	1966	3.75	7.50	15.00
❑ 10178	It's All Over/Heartbeat	1967	3.75	7.50	15.00
MONUMENT					
❑ 1211	Goodbye Sam, Hello Samantha/You Never Can Tell	1970	—	3.00	6.00
❑ 1229	I Ain't Got Time Anymore/Morning Comes Too Soon	1970	—	3.00	6.00
POLYDOR					
❑ 885336-7	All I Ask of You/Phantom of the Opera Overture, Act 2	1987	—	—	3.00
—With Sarah Brightman					
❑ 885336-7 [PS]	All I Ask of You/Phantom of the Opera Overture, Act 2	1987	—	—	3.00
ROCKET					
❑ YB-11463	Green Light/Needing a Friend	1979	—	2.00	4.00
❑ 40531	Miss You Nights/Love Enough	1976	—	2.00	4.00
❑ 40574	Devil Woman/Love On (Shine On)	1976	—	2.50	5.00
❑ 40652	Junior Cowboy/I Can't Ask for Anymore Than You	1976	—	2.00	4.00
❑ 40724	Don't Turn the Light Out/Nothing Left for Me to Say	1977	—	2.00	4.00
❑ 40771	You've Got Me Wondering/Try a Smile	1977	—	2.00	4.00
SIRE					
❑ 703	Living in Harmony/Jesus	1973	—	2.50	5.00
❑ 707	Power to All Our Friends/Come Back Billie Joe	1973	—	2.50	5.00
STRIPED HORSE					
❑ 7008	My Pretty One/Love Ya	1988	—	—	3.00
❑ 7008 [PS]	My Pretty One/Love Ya	1988	—	—	3.00
❑ 7011	Some People/Love Ya	1988	—	—	3.00
❑ 7011 [PS]	Some People/Love Ya	1988	—	—	3.00
UNI					
❑ 55061	All My Love/Our Story Book	1968	2.50	5.00	10.00
❑ 55069	Congratulations/High 'N' Dry	1968	2.50	5.00	10.00
❑ 55145	The Day I Met Marie/Sweet Little Jesus Boy	1969	3.00	6.00	12.00
WARNER BROS.					
❑ 7344	Throw Down a Line/Reflections	1969	2.00	4.00	8.00
—A-side by Cliff and Hank (Marvin)					

RICHARD AND THE YOUNG LIONS

Number	Title (A Side/B Side)	Yr	VG	VG+	NM
PHILIPS					
❑ 40381	Open Up Your Door/Once Upon Your Smile	1966	2.50	5.00	10.00
❑ 40381 [PS]	Open Up Your Door/Once Upon Your Smile	1966	5.00	10.00	20.00
❑ 40414	Nasty/Lost and Found	1966	2.00	4.00	8.00
❑ 40438	To Have and to Hold/You Can Make It	1967	2.00	4.00	8.00

RICHARDS, DICK

Number	Title (A Side/B Side)	Yr	VG	VG+	NM
COLUMBIA					
❑ 4-21532	Just Walkin' in the Rain/Born to Lose	1956	5.00	10.00	20.00
❑ 4-40957	Blue Jean Baby/We've Got a Right to Love	1957	10.00	20.00	40.00
❑ 4-41035	I Love You So Much It Hurts/Not Until I Pray for You	1957	6.25	12.50	25.00

RICHARDS, KEITH

Also see THE ROLLING STONES.

Number	Title (A Side/B Side)	Yr	VG	VG+	NM
ROLLING STONES					
❑ 19311	Run Rudolph Run/The Harder They Come	1978	5.00	10.00	20.00
❑ 19311 [DJ]	Run Rudolph Run (same on both sides)	1978	2.50	5.00	10.00
VIRGIN					
❑ S7-56955	Eileen/Wicked As It Seems	1993	—	2.00	4.00
❑ 99240	Make No Mistake/It Means a Lot	1988	—	—	3.00
❑ 99240 [PS]	Make No Mistake/It Means a Lot	1988	—	—	3.00
❑ 99297	Take It So Hard/I Could Have Stood You Up	1988	—	—	3.00
❑ 99297 [PS]	Take It So Hard/I Could Have Stood You Up	1988	—	—	3.00

Number	Title (A Side/B Side)	Yr	VG	VG+	NM
RICHARDSON, JAPE					
See THE BIG BOPPER.					
RICHARDSON, RUDI					
SUN					
❑ 271	Fools Hall of Fame/Why Should I Cry	1957	7.50	15.00	30.00
RICHIE, LIONEL					
Also see COMMODORES.					
MERCURY					
❑ 852856-7	Don't Wanna Lose You (Radio Version)/Don't Wanna Lose You (Album Version)	1996	—	—	3.00
MOTOWN					
❑ 1519	Endless Love/(Instrumental)	1981	—	2.00	4.00
—With Diana Ross					
❑ 1644	Truly/Just Put Some Love in Your Heart	1982	—	2.00	4.00
❑ 1657	You Are/You Mean More to Me	1983	—	2.00	4.00
❑ 1657 [PS]	You Are/You Mean More to Me	1983	—	2.50	5.00
❑ 1677	My Love/Round and Round	1983	—	2.00	4.00
❑ 1677 [PS]	My Love/Round and Round	1983	—	2.50	5.00
❑ 1698	All Night Long (All Night)/Wandering Stranger	1983	—	2.00	4.00
❑ 1710	Running with the Night/Serves You Right	1983	—	2.00	4.00
❑ 1722	Hello/You Mean More to Me	1984	—	2.00	4.00
❑ 1746	Stuck on You/Round and Round	1984	—	2.00	4.00
❑ 1746 [PS]	Stuck on You/Round and Round	1984	—	2.00	4.00
❑ 1762	Penny Lover/Tell Me	1984	—	2.00	4.00
❑ 1762 [PS]	Penny Lover/Tell Me	1984	—	2.50	5.00
❑ 1819	Say You, Say Me/Can't Slow Down	1985	—	—	3.00
❑ 1819 [PS]	Say You, Say Me/Can't Slow Down	1985	—	2.00	4.00
—Two different sleeves were released, each of equal value					
❑ 1843	Dancing on the Ceiling/Love Will Find a Way	1986	—	—	3.00
❑ 1843 [PS]	Dancing on the Ceiling/Love Will Find a Way	1986	—	—	3.00
❑ 1866	Love Will Conquer All/The Only One	1986	—	—	3.00
❑ 1866 [PS]	Love Will Conquer All/The Only One	1986	—	—	3.00
❑ 1873	Ballerina Girl/Deep River Woman	1986	—	—	3.00
—B-side with Alabama					
❑ 1873 [PS]	Ballerina Girl/Deep River Woman	1986	—	2.00	4.00
❑ 1883	Se La/Serves You Right	1987	—	—	3.00
❑ 1883 [PS]	Se La/Serves You Right	1987	—	—	3.00
❑ 2160	Do It To Me (Edit)/Do It To Me (LP Version)	1992	—	2.00	4.00
RICHIE AND THE ROYALS					
GOLDEN CREST					
❑ 573	Be My Girl/We're Strollin'	1962	12.50	25.00	50.00
RELLO					
❑ 1	And When I'm Near You/Goody Goody	1961	20.00	40.00	80.00
❑ 3	Be My Girl/We're Strollin'	1962	50.00	100.00	200.00
RICHIE AND THE SAXONS					
TIP					
❑ 1020	Bottom of the Barrel/Easy Now	196?	12.50	25.00	50.00
RICHY, PAUL					
SUN					
❑ 338	The Legend of the Big Steeple/Broken Hearted Willie	1960	5.00	10.00	20.00
RICK AND THE KEENS					
AUSTIN					
❑ 303	Peanuts/I'll Be Home	1961	12.50	25.00	50.00
JAMIE					
❑ 1219	Your Turn ot Cry/Tender Years	1962	5.00	10.00	20.00
LE CAM					
❑ 133	Darla/Someone New	1964	7.50	15.00	30.00
❑ 721	Peanuts/I'll Be Home	1961	12.50	25.00	50.00
SMASH					
❑ 1705	Peanuts/I'll Be Home	1961	5.00	10.00	20.00
❑ 1722	Maybe/Popcorn	1961	5.00	10.00	20.00
TOLLIE					
❑ 9016	Darla/Someone New	1964	5.00	10.00	20.00
RICK AND THE MASTERS					
CAMEO					
❑ 226	Flame of Love/Here Come Nancy	1962	12.50	25.00	50.00
❑ 247	Let It Please Be You/I Don't Want Your Love	1963	12.50	25.00	50.00
HARAL					
❑ 776	Bewitched, Bothered and Bewildered/A Kissin' Friend	1962	15.00	30.00	60.00
TABA					
❑ 101	Flame of Love/Here Come Nancy	1962	37.50	75.00	150.00
RICK AND THE RANDELLS					
ABC-PARAMOUNT					
❑ 10055	Let It Be You/Honey Doll	1959	10.00	20.00	40.00
RICK AND THE RAVENS					
With RAY MANZAREK, later of THE DOORS.					
AURA					
❑ 4506	Henrietta/Just for Me	1965	15.00	30.00	60.00
❑ 4511	Soul Train/Geraldine	1965	12.50	25.00	50.00
POSAE					
❑ 101	Big Bucket "T"/Rampage	196?	20.00	40.00	80.00
RICK, ROBIN & HIM					
V.I.P.					
❑ 25035	Three Choruses of Despair/Cause You Know Me	1965	6.25	12.50	25.00
RICKIE AND THE HALLMARKS					
AMY					
❑ 877	Wherever You Are/Joanie Don't You Cry	1963	10.00	20.00	40.00

Number	Title (A Side/B Side)	Yr	VG	VG+	NM
RICKS, JIMMY					
Also see THE RAVENS.					
ARNOLD					
❑ 1011	Canadian Sunset/Change of Heart	1961	3.75	7.50	15.00
ATCO					
❑ 6220	Daddy Rolling Stone/Homesick	1962	5.00	10.00	20.00
ATLANTIC					
❑ 2246	Trouble in Mind/Romance in the Dark	1964	3.75	7.50	15.00
BATON					
❑ 236	I'm a Fool to Want You/Bad Man of Missouri	1957	10.00	20.00	40.00
DECCA					
❑ 30443	What Have I Done/Lazy Mule	1957	6.25	12.50	25.00
FELSTED					
❑ 8560	Secret Love/If It Didn't Hurt So Much	1959	6.25	12.50	25.00
❑ 8582	Leaning On Your Love/Here Come the Tears Again	1959	6.25	12.50	25.00
FURY					
❑ 1070	I Wonder/Let Me Down Easy	1962	5.00	10.00	20.00
JOSIE					
❑ 796	She's Fine, She's Mine/The Unbeliever	1956	10.00	20.00	40.00
JUBILEE					
❑ 5559	Lonely Man/If You Ever Loved Someone	1967	3.00	6.00	12.00
❑ 5561	Wigglin' and Gigglin'/Long, Long Arm of Love	1967	3.00	6.00	12.00
❑ 5579	Don't Go to Strangers/Lonely Man	1967	3.00	6.00	12.00
❑ 5608	It's All in the Game/Baby Don't Leave Me	1967	3.00	6.00	12.00
❑ 5619	Snap Your Fingers/Wigglin' and Gigglin'	1968	3.00	6.00	12.00
MAINSTREAM					
❑ 625	Girl of My Dreams/Glow Worm	1965	3.75	7.50	15.00
MERCURY					
❑ 8296	Love Is the Thing/Too Soon	1952	20.00	40.00	80.00
PARIS					
❑ 504	Do You Promise/The Sugar Man Song	1957	7.50	15.00	30.00
SIGNATURE					
❑ 12040	I Needed Your Love/Timber	1960	5.00	10.00	20.00
❑ 12051	The Christmas Song/Love Is the Thing	1960	5.00	10.00	20.00
RICKY AND THE VACELS					
EXPRESS					
❑ 711	Lorraine/Bubble Gum	1962	7.50	15.00	30.00
FARGO					
❑ 1050	His Girl/Don't Want Your Love No More	1963	7.50	15.00	30.00
❑ 1050	His Girl/Don't Want Your Love No More	1963	20.00	40.00	80.00
—Blue vinyl					
RICO AND THE RAVENS					
AUTUMN					
❑ 6	Don't You Know/In My Heart	1965	3.75	7.50	15.00
RALLY					
❑ 1601	Don't You Know/In My Heart	1965	10.00	20.00	40.00
RIFFS, THE					
JAMIE					
❑ 1296	Tell Her/I Been Thinkin'	1965	3.00	6.00	12.00
OLD TOWN					
❑ 1179	Tell Tale Friends/Why Are the Nights So Cold	1965	12.50	25.00	50.00
SUNNY					
❑ 22	Little Girl/Why Are the Nights So Cold	1964	50.00	100.00	200.00
RIGHTEOUS BROTHERS, THE					
Also see BOBBY HATFIELD; BILL MEDLEY; THE PARAMOURS; PHIL SPECTOR.					
HAVEN					
❑ 800	Hold On to What You Got/Let Me Make the Music	1976	—	2.00	4.00
❑ 7002	Rock and Roll Heaven/I Just Wanna Be Me	1974	—	2.50	5.00
❑ 7004	Give It to the People/Love Is Not a Dirty Word	1974	—	2.00	4.00
❑ 7006	Dream On/Dr. Rock and Roll	1974	—	2.00	4.00
❑ 7011	High Blood Pressure/Never Say I Love You	1975	—	2.00	4.00
❑ 7014	Young Blood/Substitute	1975	—	2.00	4.00
MOONGLOW					
❑ 215	Little Latin Lupe Lu/I'm So Lonely	1963	5.00	10.00	20.00
❑ 215 [DJ]	Little Latin Lupe Lu (same on both sides)	1963	12.50	25.00	50.00
—Red vinyl promo					
❑ 221	Gotta Tell You How I Feel/If You're Lying, You'll Be Crying	1963	5.00	10.00	20.00
❑ 223	My Babe/Fee-Fi-Fidily-I-Oh	1963	5.00	10.00	20.00
❑ 224	Ko Ko Joe/B-Flat Blues	1963	5.00	10.00	20.00
❑ 231	Try to Find Another Man/I Still Love You	1964	5.00	10.00	20.00
❑ 234	Bring Your Love to Me/If You're Lying, You'll Be Crying	1964	5.00	10.00	20.00
❑ 235	This Little Girl of Mine/If You're Lying, You'll Be Crying	1964	3.75	7.50	15.00
❑ 238	Bring Your Love to Me/Fannie Mae	1965	3.75	7.50	15.00
❑ 239	You Can Have Her/Love or Magic	1965	3.75	7.50	15.00
❑ 242	Justine/In That Great Gettin' Up Morning	1965	3.75	7.50	15.00
❑ 243	For Your Love/Gotta Tell You How I Feel	1965	3.75	7.50	15.00
❑ 244	Georgia on My Mind/My Tears Will Go Away	1966	3.75	7.50	15.00
❑ 245	I Need a Girl/Bring Your Love to Me	1966	3.75	7.50	15.00
PHILLES					
❑ 124	You've Lost That Lovin' Feelin'/There's a Woman	1964	3.75	7.50	15.00
❑ 127	Just Once in My Life/The Blues	1965	3.75	7.50	15.00
❑ 127 [PS]	Just Once in My Life/The Blues	1965	7.50	15.00	30.00
❑ 129	Unchained Melody/Hung on You	1965	3.75	7.50	15.00
❑ 130	Ebb Tide/(I Love You) For Sentimental Reasons	1965	3.75	7.50	15.00
❑ 130 [PS]	Ebb Tide/(I Love You) For Sentimental Reasons	1965	7.50	15.00	30.00
❑ 132	The White Cliffs of Dover/She's Mine, All Mine	1966	5.00	10.00	20.00
VERVE					
❑ CS8-5	Celebrity Scene: The Righteous Brothers	1967	15.00	30.00	60.00
—Box set of five singles (10520-10524). Price includes box, all 5 singles, jukebox title strips, bio. Records are sometimes found by themselves, so they are also listed separately.					
❑ 10383	(You're My) Soul and Inspiration/B Side Blues	1966	3.75	7.50	15.00
❑ 10383 [PS]	(You're My) Soul and Inspiration/B Side Blues	1966	7.50	15.00	30.00

Number	Title (A Side/B Side)	Yr	VG	VG+	NM
❑ 10403	Rat Race/Green Onions	1966	3.75	7.50	15.00
❑ 10406	He/He Will Break Your Heart	1966	2.50	5.00	10.00
❑ 10406 [PS]	He/He Will Break Your Heart	1966	5.00	10.00	20.00
❑ 10430	Go Ahead and Cry/Things Didn't Go Your Way	1966	2.50	5.00	10.00
❑ 10449	On This Side of Goodbye/A Man Without a Dream	1966	2.50	5.00	10.00
❑ 10479	Along Came Jones/Jimmy's Blues	1967	2.00	4.00	8.00
❑ 10507	Melancholy Music Man/Don't Give Up on Me	1967	2.00	4.00	8.00
❑ 10520	(You're My) Soul and Inspiration/Go Ahead and Cry	1967	2.50	5.00	10.00
❑ 10521	Hold On, I'm Coming/He Will Break Your Heart	1967	2.50	5.00	10.00
❑ 10522	Melancholy Music Man/I Believe	1967	2.50	5.00	10.00
❑ 10523	I (Who Have Nothing)/Island in the Sun	1967	2.50	5.00	10.00
❑ 10524	My Girl/Something You Got	1967	2.50	5.00	10.00
❑ 10551	Stranded in the Middle of No Place/Been So Nice	1967	2.00	4.00	8.00
❑ 10551 [PS]	Stranded in the Middle of No Place/Been So Nice	1967	3.75	7.50	15.00
❑ 10577	Here I Am/So Many Lonely Nights Ahead	1968	2.00	4.00	8.00
❑ 10637	Let the Good Times Roll/You've Lost That Lovin' Feelin'	1968	2.00	4.00	8.00
❑ 10648	And the Party Goes On/Woman, Man Needs Ya	1968	2.00	4.00	8.00
❑ 10649	Good N' Nuff/Po' Folks	1968	2.00	4.00	8.00
❑ 871882-7	Unchained Melody/Hung on You	1989	—	2.00	4.00

RILEY, BILLY LEE

ATLANTIC

Number	Title (A Side/B Side)	Yr	VG	VG+	NM
❑ 2525	Sittin' and a Waitin'/Happy Man	1968	2.00	4.00	8.00

BRUNSWICK

Number	Title (A Side/B Side)	Yr	VG	VG+	NM
❑ 55085	Rockin' on the Moon/Is That All to the Ball	1958	50.00	100.00	200.00

ENTRANCE

Number	Title (A Side/B Side)	Yr	VG	VG+	NM
❑ 7508	I Got a Thing About You Baby/You Don't Love Me	1972	—	2.50	5.00

GNP CRESCENDO

Number	Title (A Side/B Side)	Yr	VG	VG+	NM
❑ 371	Gonna Find a Cave/That's the Bag I'm In	1966	2.50	5.00	10.00
❑ 377	The Way I Feel/St. James Infirmary	1966	2.50	5.00	10.00

HIP

Number	Title (A Side/B Side)	Yr	VG	VG+	NM
❑ 8006	Family Portrait/Going Back to Memphis	1968	2.00	4.00	8.00
❑ 8011	Show Me Your Soul/Midnight Hour	1968	2.00	4.00	8.00

HOME OF THE BLUES

Number	Title (A Side/B Side)	Yr	VG	VG+	NM
❑ 233	Flip, Flop, and Fly/Teenage Letter	1961	7.50	15.00	30.00

MERCURY

Number	Title (A Side/B Side)	Yr	VG	VG+	NM
❑ 72314	Bo Diddley/Memphis	1964	3.75	7.50	15.00
❑ 72385	Mojo Workout/Charlene	1965	3.00	6.00	12.00

MOJO

Number	Title (A Side/B Side)	Yr	VG	VG+	NM
❑ 1933	Southern Soul/Midnight Hour	1967	2.50	5.00	10.00

SUN

Number	Title (A Side/B Side)	Yr	VG	VG+	NM
❑ 245	Trouble Bound/Rock with Me, Baby	1956	30.00	60.00	120.00
❑ 260	Flying Saucers Rock and Roll/I Want You Baby	1957	25.00	50.00	100.00
❑ 277	Red Hot/Pearly Lee	1957	15.00	30.00	60.00
❑ 289	Baby Please Don't Go/Wouldn't You Know	1958	12.50	25.00	50.00
❑ 313	Down by the Riverside/No Name Girl	1959	6.25	12.50	25.00
❑ 322	One More Time/Got the Water Boilin'	1959	12.50	25.00	50.00
❑ 1100	Kay/Looking for Her Heart	1969	—	3.00	6.00
❑ 1105	Pilot Town L.A./Workin' on the River	1969	—	3.00	6.00
❑ 1116	Tallahassee/Old Home Place	1970	—	2.50	5.00

RILEY, BOB

CORAL

Number	Title (A Side/B Side)	Yr	VG	VG+	NM
❑ 62125	I Think It's a Shame/Blue Guitar Waltz	1959	5.00	10.00	20.00

DOT

Number	Title (A Side/B Side)	Yr	VG	VG+	NM
❑ 15625	Baby Sittin'/Without Your Love	1957	6.25	12.50	25.00

MGM

Number	Title (A Side/B Side)	Yr	VG	VG+	NM
❑ 12612	Wanda Jean/The Midnight Line	1958	37.50	75.00	150.00

RILEY, JEANNIE C.

CAPITOL

Number	Title (A Side/B Side)	Yr	VG	VG+	NM
❑ 2378	The Price I Pay to Stay/How Can Anything So Right Be So Wrong	1969	—	2.50	5.00
❑ 2449	I Don't Know What I'm Doing Here/You've Got Me Singing Nursery Rhymes	1969	—	2.50	5.00

LITTLE DARLIN'

Number	Title (A Side/B Side)	Yr	VG	VG+	NM
❑ 0031	What About Them/You Write the Music	1967	3.75	7.50	15.00

—As "Jean Riley"

Number	Title (A Side/B Side)	Yr	VG	VG+	NM
❑ 0048	I Don't Know What I'm Doing Here/I'll Be a Woman of the World	1968	—	3.00	6.00

MCA

Number	Title (A Side/B Side)	Yr	VG	VG+	NM
❑ 52018	From Harper Valley to the Mountain/I Don't Have to Die to Get Into Heaven	1982	—	—	3.00

MERCURY

Number	Title (A Side/B Side)	Yr	VG	VG+	NM
❑ 73616	Plain Vanilla/Country Girl	1974	—	2.00	4.00

MGM

Number	Title (A Side/B Side)	Yr	VG	VG+	NM
❑ 14310	Houston Blues/How Hard I'm Trying	1971	—	2.00	4.00
❑ 14341	Give Myself a Party/Why You Been Gone So Long	1972	—	2.00	4.00
❑ 14382	Good Morning Country Rain/This Is for You	1972	—	2.00	4.00
❑ 14427	One Night/Without You	1972	—	2.00	4.00
❑ 14495	When Love Has Gone Away/Thou Shalt Not Kill	1973	—	2.00	4.00
❑ 14554	Hush/Not Looking Back	1973	—	2.00	4.00
❑ 14666	Another Football Year/Mother America	1973	—	2.00	4.00
❑ 14696	Missouri/Sing Jeannie Sing	1974	—	2.00	4.00

PLANTATION

Number	Title (A Side/B Side)	Yr	VG	VG+	NM
❑ 3	Harper Valley P.T.A./Yesterday All Day Long Today	1968	2.00	4.00	8.00

—Yellow label

Number	Title (A Side/B Side)	Yr	VG	VG+	NM
❑ 3	Harper Valley P.T.A./Yesterday All Day Long Today	1968	—	3.00	6.00

—Green and white label

Number	Title (A Side/B Side)	Yr	VG	VG+	NM
❑ 7	The Girl Most Likely/My Scrapbook	1968	—	2.50	5.00
❑ 16	There Never Was a Time/Back to School	1969	—	2.50	5.00
❑ 22	The Rib/I'm the Woman	1969	—	2.50	5.00
❑ 29	The Back Side of Dallas/Things Go Better with Love	1969	—	2.50	5.00
❑ 44	Country Girl/We Were Raised on Love	1970	—	2.50	5.00
❑ 59	Duty Not Desire/Holdin' On	1970	—	2.50	5.00
❑ 65	My Man/The Generation Gap	1970	—	2.50	5.00
❑ 72	Oh, Singer/I'll Take What's Left of You	1971	—	2.50	5.00
❑ 75	Good Enough to Be Your Wife/Light Your Light	1971	—	2.50	5.00
❑ 79	Roses and Thorns/Shed Me No Tears	1971	—	2.50	5.00
❑ 85	The Lion's Club/Tell the Truth and Shame the Devil	1972	—	2.50	5.00
❑ 93	If You Could Read My Mind/Will the Real Jesus Please Stand Up	1972	—	2.50	5.00
❑ 173	Harper Valley P.T.A. (Soundtrack Version)/I've Done a Lot of Living Since Then	1979	—	3.00	6.00

PLAYBACK

Number	Title (A Side/B Side)	Yr	VG	VG+	NM
❑ 1350	Here's to the Cowboys/Free	1989	—	3.00	6.00

WARNER BROS.

Number	Title (A Side/B Side)	Yr	VG	VG+	NM
❑ 8226	The Best I've Ever Had/Thank You for Forgiving	1976	—	2.00	4.00
❑ 8290	Pure Gold/Take Time	1976	—	2.00	4.00

RIMES, LEANN

CAPITOL

Number	Title (A Side/B Side)	Yr	VG	VG+	NM
❑ 88644	I Need You/Jesus, Theme from the Original Soundtrack	2000	—	2.00	4.00

—B-side by Patrick Williams

CURB

Number	Title (A Side/B Side)	Yr	VG	VG+	NM
❑ D7-73022	How Do I Live/How Do I Live (Extended Mix)	1997	—	2.00	4.00
❑ D7-73027	You Light Up My Life/I Believe	1997	—	2.00	4.00
❑ D7-73055	Looking Through Your Eyes/Commitment	1998	—	2.00	4.00
❑ D7-73086	Big Deal/Leaving's Not Leaving	1999	—	2.00	4.00
❑ D7-76959	Blue/The Light in Your Eyes	1996	—	2.00	4.00

RINGO, JIMMY

DOT

Number	Title (A Side/B Side)	Yr	VG	VG+	NM
❑ 15787	I Like This Kind of Music/No One Else	1958	7.50	15.00	30.00
❑ 15997	I Like This Kind of Music/No One Else	1959	5.00	10.00	20.00

RINKY-DINKS, THE

See BOBBY DARIN.

RIO, BOBBY

ABC-PARAMOUNT

Number	Title (A Side/B Side)	Yr	VG	VG+	NM
❑ 10656	Boy Meets Girl/Don't Break My Heart and Run Away	1965	3.75	7.50	15.00

LENOX

Number	Title (A Side/B Side)	Yr	VG	VG+	NM
❑ 5569	Don Diddley/I Got You	1963	3.75	7.50	15.00

RIO, CHUCK

Also see THE CHAMPS; THE ORIGINALS (3).

CHALLENGE

Number	Title (A Side/B Side)	Yr	VG	VG+	NM
❑ 59019	Bad Boy/Denise	1958	5.00	10.00	20.00
❑ 59073	Ramblin' Through Dixie/Akiko	1960	5.00	10.00	20.00

FLAIR

Number	Title (A Side/B Side)	Yr	VG	VG+	NM
❑ 103	You Don't Have to Be a Baby to Cry/Big Boy	1962	10.00	20.00	40.00

JACKPOT

Number	Title (A Side/B Side)	Yr	VG	VG+	NM
❑ 48016	Margarita/C'est La Vie	1960	7.50	15.00	30.00

KENT

Number	Title (A Side/B Side)	Yr	VG	VG+	NM
❑ 308	Bye Bye Baby/No Matter What You Do	1958	5.00	10.00	20.00

SATURN

Number	Title (A Side/B Side)	Yr	VG	VG+	NM
❑ 402	Kreschendo Stomp/Rock-A-Nova	1962	12.50	25.00	50.00

TEQUILA

Number	Title (A Side/B Side)	Yr	VG	VG+	NM
❑ 100	Caravan/El Bracero	1961	5.00	10.00	20.00
❑ 103	La Cha Cha Twist/If You Were the Only Girl in the World	1961	5.00	10.00	20.00

RIOS, AUGIE

METRO

Number	Title (A Side/B Side)	Yr	VG	VG+	NM
❑ 20010	Donde Esta Santa Claus?/Ol' Fatso	1958	10.00	20.00	40.00
❑ 20016	Run Rattler Run/Hop, Skip and Jump	1959	7.50	15.00	30.00
❑ 20027	Trip to the Island/Teacher Walked Out of the Room	1959	7.50	15.00	30.00

MGM

Number	Title (A Side/B Side)	Yr	VG	VG+	NM
❑ 12966	Feliz Navidades/Gypsy Boy	1960	5.00	10.00	20.00
❑ 13292	Donde Esta Santa Claus?/Ol' Fatso	1964	3.00	6.00	12.00

SHELLEY

Number	Title (A Side/B Side)	Yr	VG	VG+	NM
❑ 181	I've Got a Girl/There's a Girl Down the Way	1963	10.00	20.00	40.00
❑ 186	When You Dance/No One	1963	7.50	15.00	30.00
❑ 192	Teach Me Tonight/Linda Lou	1964	5.00	10.00	20.00

RIOT SQUAD, THE

HANNA-BARBERA

Number	Title (A Side/B Side)	Yr	VG	VG+	NM
❑ 485	I Take It That We're Through/Working Man	1966	3.00	6.00	12.00

REPRISE

Number	Title (A Side/B Side)	Yr	VG	VG+	NM
❑ 0457	Cry, Cry, Cry/How Is It Done?	1966	2.50	5.00	10.00

ROULETTE

Number	Title (A Side/B Side)	Yr	VG	VG+	NM
❑ 4621	Gonna Make You Mine/I Wanna Talk About My Baby	1965	3.00	6.00	12.00

RIP CHORDS, THE

COLUMBIA

Number	Title (A Side/B Side)	Yr	VG	VG+	NM
❑ 42687	Here I Stand/Karen	1963	3.75	7.50	15.00
❑ 42687 [DJ]	Here I Stand (same on both sides)	1963	12.50	25.00	50.00

—Green vinyl promo

Number	Title (A Side/B Side)	Yr	VG	VG+	NM
❑ 42687 [PS]	Here I Stand (same on both sides)	1963	12.50	25.00	50.00

—Sleeve is promo only

Number	Title (A Side/B Side)	Yr	VG	VG+	NM
❑ 42812	Gone/She Thinks I Still Care	1963	3.75	7.50	15.00
❑ 42812 [DJ]	Gone (same on both sides)	1963	12.50	25.00	50.00

—Blue vinyl promo

Number	Title (A Side/B Side)	Yr	VG	VG+	NM
❑ 42812 [PS]	Gone (same on both sides)	1963	12.50	25.00	50.00

—Sleeve is promo only

Number	Title (A Side/B Side)	Yr	VG	VG+	NM
❑ 42921	Hey, Little Cobra/The Queen	1963	5.00	10.00	20.00
❑ 42921 [DJ]	Hey, Little Cobra (same on both sides)	1963	12.50	25.00	50.00

—Yellow vinyl promo

Number	Title (A Side/B Side)	Yr	VG	VG+	NM
❑ 43035	Three Window Coupe/Hot Rod U.S.A.	1964	3.75	7.50	15.00
❑ 43035 [DJ]	Three Window Coupe (same on both sides)	1964	12.50	25.00	50.00

—Red vinyl promo

Number	Title (A Side/B Side)	Yr	VG	VG+	NM
❑ 43093	One Piece Topless Bathing Suit/Wah-Wahini	1964	3.75	7.50	15.00
❑ 43221	Don't Be Scared/Bunny Hill	1965	3.75	7.50	15.00

RIP-CHORDS, THE

Number	Title (A Side/B Side)	Yr	VG	VG+	NM
ABCO					
❑ 105	I Love You the Most/Let's Do the Razzle Dazzle	1956	150.00	300.00	600.00
—Black vinyl					
❑ 105	I Love You the Most/Let's Do the Razzle Dazzle	1956	375.00	750.00	1500.
—Red vinyl					

RIPERTON, MINNIE

Also see ROTARY CONNECTION.

Number	Title (A Side/B Side)	Yr	VG	VG+	NM
CAPITOL					
❑ 4706	Memory Lane/I'm a Woman	1979	—	2.00	4.00
❑ 4761	Lover and Friend/Return to Forever	1979	—	2.00	4.00
❑ 4902	Here We Go/Return to Forever	1980	—	2.00	4.00
❑ 4955	Give Me Time/Island in the Sun	1980	—	2.00	4.00
CHESS					
❑ 1980	Lonely Girl/You Gave Me Soul	1966	2.50	5.00	10.00
—As "Andrea Davis"					
EPIC					
❑ 11139	Every Time He Comes Around/Reasons	1974	—	2.50	5.00
❑ 50020	Edge of a Dream/Seeing You This Way	1974	—	2.50	5.00
❑ 50057	Lovin' You/Edge of a Dream	1974	—	2.50	5.00
❑ 50128	Don't Let Anyone Bring You Down/Inside My Love	1975	—	2.50	5.00
❑ 50155	When It Comes Down To It/Minnie's Lament	1975	—	2.50	5.00
❑ 50166	Simple Things/Minnie's Lament	1975	—	2.50	5.00
❑ 50190	Adventures in Paradise/When It Comes Down To It	1976	—	2.50	5.00
❑ 50337	Stick Together (Part One)/Stick Together (Part Two)	1977	—	2.50	5.00
❑ 50351	Young, Willing and Able/Stick Together	1977	—	2.50	5.00
❑ 50394	Wouldn't Matter Where You Are	1977	—	2.50	5.00
❑ 50427	How Could I Love You More/Young, Willing and Able	1977	—	2.50	5.00
GRT					
❑ 42	Oh! By the Way/Le Fleur	1972	—	3.00	6.00

RIPPLES AND WAVES PLUS MICHAEL, THE

See THE JACKSONS.

RISING SUNS, THE

Among the members of this group were RY COODER and Taj Mahal.

Number	Title (A Side/B Side)	Yr	VG	VG+	NM
COLUMBIA					
❑ 43534	Candy Man/The Devil's Got My Woman	1966	10.00	20.00	40.00

RITA MARIE

Number	Title (A Side/B Side)	Yr	VG	VG+	NM
SUN					
❑ 1106	Lottie's Lament/Trouble	1969	—	2.50	5.00

RITES, THE

Number	Title (A Side/B Side)	Yr	VG	VG+	NM
DECCA					
❑ 32218	Things/Hour Glass	1967	6.25	12.50	25.00

RITES OF SPRING, THE

Number	Title (A Side/B Side)	Yr	VG	VG+	NM
PARKWAY					
❑ 109	Why/Comin' On to Me	1966	7.50	15.00	30.00

RITUALS, THE

Featuring Arnie Ginsburg, formerly of JAN AND ARNIE.

Number	Title (A Side/B Side)	Yr	VG	VG+	NM
ARWIN					
❑ 120	Girl in Zanzibar/Guitarro	1963	7.50	15.00	30.00
❑ 127	This Is Paradise/Gone	1964	7.50	15.00	30.00
❑ 128	Surfers Rule/Gone	1964	10.00	20.00	40.00

RIVERS, JOHNNY

Number	Title (A Side/B Side)	Yr	VG	VG+	NM
ATLANTIC					
❑ 3011	Sitting in Limbo/Artists and Poets	1974	—	2.50	5.00
❑ 3028	Six Days on the Road/Artists and Poets	1974	—	2.50	5.00
❑ 3230	John Lee Hooker '74/Get It Up for Love	1974	—	2.50	5.00
BIG TREE					
❑ 16094	Swayin' to the Music (Slow Dancin')/Outside Help	1977	—	2.00	4.00
❑ 16106	Curious Mind (Um, Um, Um, Um, Um, Um)/Ashes and Sand	1977	—	2.00	4.00
CAPITOL					
❑ 4850	Long Black Veil/This Could Be the One	1962	3.75	7.50	15.00
❑ 4913	If You Want It, I've Got It/My Heart Is In Your Hands	1963	3.75	7.50	15.00
❑ 5232	Long Black Veil/Don't Look Now	1964	3.75	7.50	15.00
CHANCELLOR					
❑ 1070	I Get So Doggone Lonesome/Knock Three Times	1961	5.00	10.00	20.00
❑ 1108	To Be Loved/Too Good to Last	1962	5.00	10.00	20.00
CORAL					
❑ 62425	That's My Baby/Your First and Last Love	1964	3.75	7.50	15.00
CUB					
❑ 9047	Everyday/Darling Talk to Me	1959	6.25	12.50	25.00
❑ 9058	Answer Me My Love/The Customary Thing	1960	5.00	10.00	20.00
DEE DEE					
❑ 239	The White Cliffs of Dover/Your First and Last Love	1959	5.00	10.00	20.00
EPIC					
❑ 50121	Help Me Rhonda/New Lovers and Old Friends	1975	—	2.50	5.00
—A-side features Brian Wilson on backing vocals					
❑ 50150	Can I Change My Mind/John Lee Hooker	1975	—	2.00	4.00
❑ 50208	Welcome Home/Outside Help	1976	—	2.00	4.00
❑ 50248	Linda Lue/Outside Help	1976	—	2.00	4.00
ERA					
❑ 3037	Call Me/Andersonville	1961	5.00	10.00	20.00
GONE					
❑ 5026	Baby Come Back/Long Long Walk	1958	10.00	20.00	40.00
GUYDEN					
❑ 2003	You're the One/A Hole in the Ground	1958	6.25	12.50	25.00
❑ 2110	You're the One/A Hole in the Ground	1964	3.75	7.50	15.00
IMPERIAL					
❑ 66032	Memphis/It Wouldn't Happen with Me	1964	3.00	6.00	12.00
❑ 66056	Maybelline/Walk Myself On Home	1964	2.50	5.00	10.00
❑ 66056 [PS]	Maybelline/Walk Myself On Home	1964	3.75	7.50	15.00
❑ 66075	Mountain of Love/Moody River	1964	2.50	5.00	10.00
❑ 66087	Midnight Special/Cupid	1965	2.50	5.00	10.00
❑ 66112	Seventh Son/Unsquare Dance	1965	2.50	5.00	10.00
❑ 66112 [PS]	Seventh Son/Unsquare Dance	1965	3.75	7.50	15.00
❑ 66133	Where Have All the Flowers Gone/Love Me While You Can	1965	2.50	5.00	10.00
❑ 66144	Under Your Spell Again/Long Time Man	1965	2.50	5.00	10.00
❑ 66144 [PS]	Under Your Spell Again/Long Time Man	1965	3.75	7.50	15.00
❑ 66159	Secret Agent Man/You Dig	1966	3.00	6.00	12.00
❑ 66159 [PS]	Secret Agent Man/You Dig	1966	3.75	7.50	15.00
❑ 66175	(I Washed My Hands In) Muddy Water/Roogalator	1966	2.50	5.00	10.00
❑ 66205	Poor Side of Town/A Man Can Cry	1966	3.00	6.00	12.00
❑ 66205 [PS]	Poor Side of Town/A Man Can Cry	1966	3.75	7.50	15.00
❑ 66227	Baby I Need Your Lovin'/Gettin' Ready for Tomorrow	1967	2.50	5.00	10.00
❑ 66227 [PS]	Baby I Need Your Lovin'/Gettin' Ready for Tomorrow	1967	3.75	7.50	15.00
❑ 66244	The Tracks of My Tears/Rewind Medley	1967	2.50	5.00	10.00
❑ 66244 [PS]	The Tracks of My Tears/Rewind Medley	1967	3.75	7.50	15.00
❑ 66267	Summer Rain/Memory of the Coming Good	1967	2.50	5.00	10.00
❑ 66286	Look To Your Soul/Something's Strange	1968	2.00	4.00	8.00
❑ 66286 [PS]	Look To Your Soul/Something's Strange	1968	3.00	6.00	12.00
❑ 66314	Everybody's Talkin'/The Way We Live	1968	—	—	—
—Unreleased					
❑ 66335	Right Relations/Better Life	1968	2.00	4.00	8.00
❑ 66335 [PS]	Right Relations/Better Life	1968	3.00	6.00	12.00
❑ 66360	These Are Not My People/Going Back to Big Sur	1969	2.00	4.00	8.00
❑ 66386	Muddy River/Resurrection	1969	2.00	4.00	8.00
❑ 66386 [PS]	Muddy River/Resurrection	1969	3.00	6.00	12.00
❑ 66418	One Woman/Ode to John Lee	1969	2.00	4.00	8.00
❑ 66448	Into the Mystic/Jesus Is a Soul Man	1970	2.00	4.00	8.00
❑ 66453	Fire and Rain/Apple Tree	1970	2.00	4.00	8.00
MCA					
❑ 52502	Heartbreak Love/Why Can't We Communicate	1984	—	2.00	4.00
MGM					
❑ 13266	Answer Me, My Love/Customary Thing	1964	3.75	7.50	15.00
RIVERAIRE					
❑ 1001	Don't Bug Me Baby/Haunting Black Eyes	1959	7.50	15.00	30.00
ROULETTE					
❑ 4565	Baby Come Back/Long Long Walk	1964	5.00	10.00	20.00
RSO					
❑ 1030	Romance (Give Me a Chance)/Don't Need No Other Now	1980	—	2.00	4.00
❑ 1045	China/The Price	1980	—	2.00	4.00
SOUL CITY					
❑ 007	Ashes and Sand/Outside Help	1977	—	2.50	5.00
❑ 008	Swayin' to the Music (Slow Dancin')/Outside Help	1977	2.00	4.00	8.00
❑ 010	Little White Lie/Be My Baby	1980	—	2.50	5.00
❑ 014	RSVP/The Price	1982	—	2.50	5.00
SUEDE					
❑ 1401	Little Girl/Two by Two	1957	25.00	50.00	100.00
—As "Johnny Ramistella"					
UNITED ARTISTS					
❑ 0101	Memphis/Secret Agent Man	1973	—	2.00	4.00
❑ 0102	Mountain of Love/Maybellene	1973	—	2.00	4.00
❑ 0103	Seventh Son/Midnight Special	1973	—	2.00	4.00
❑ 0104	Poor Side of Town/Baby I Need Your Lovin'	1973	—	2.00	4.00
❑ 0105	Summer Rain/The Tracks of My Tears	1973	—	2.00	4.00
—0101 through 0105 are "Silver Spotlight Series" reissues					
❑ XW198	Blue Suede Shoes/Stories to a Child	1973	—	2.50	5.00
❑ XW226	Searchin'-So Fine/New York City Dues	1973	—	2.50	5.00
❑ XW310	I'll Feel a Whole Lot Better/Over the Line	1973	—	2.50	5.00
❑ XW522	Rockin' Pneumonia-Boogie Woogie Flu/Blue Suede Shoes	1974	—	2.00	4.00
—Reissue					
❑ XW523	Where Have All the Flowers Gone/(I Washed My Hands in) Muddy Water	1974	—	2.00	4.00
—Reissue					
❑ 741	Oh What a Kiss/Knock Three Times	1964	3.00	6.00	12.00
❑ 769	Dream Doll/To Be Loved	1964	3.00	6.00	12.00
❑ 50778	Sea Cruise/Our Lady of the Well	1971	—	3.00	6.00
❑ 50822	Think His Name/Permanent Change	1971	—	3.00	6.00
❑ 50948	On the Borderline/Come Home America	1972	—	2.50	5.00
❑ 50960	Rockin' Pneumonia-Boogie Woogie Flu/Come Home America	1972	—	3.00	6.00
—On some pressings, the intro of the A-side is not repeated (lasts about 20 seconds)					
❑ 50960	Rockin' Pneumonia-Boogie Woogie Flu/Come Home America	1972	—	3.00	6.00
—On most pressings, the intro of the A-side lasts about 35 seconds					

RIVERS, TONY, AND THE CASTAWAYS

Number	Title (A Side/B Side)	Yr	VG	VG+	NM
CONSTELLATION					
❑ 128	I Love the Way You Walk/I Love You	1964	3.75	7.50	15.00

RIVIERAS, THE (1)

R&B vocal group from northern New Jersey.

Number	Title (A Side/B Side)	Yr	VG	VG+	NM
COED					
❑ 503	Count Every Star/True Love Is Hard to Find	1958	12.50	25.00	50.00
❑ 508	Moonlight Serenade/Neither Rain Nor Snow	1959	10.00	20.00	40.00
❑ 513	Our Love/True Love Is Hard to Find	1959	7.50	15.00	30.00
❑ 513	Our Love/Midnight Flyer	1959	7.50	15.00	30.00
❑ 522	Since I Made You Cry/11th Hour Melody	1959	7.50	15.00	30.00
❑ 529	Blessing of Love/Moonlight Cocktails	1960	6.25	12.50	25.00
❑ 538	My Friend/Great Big Eyes	1960	6.25	12.50	25.00
❑ 542	Easy to Remember/Stay in My Heart	1960	6.25	12.50	25.00
❑ 551	El Doraado/Refrigerator	1961	6.25	12.50	25.00

Number	Title (A Side/B Side)	Yr	VG	VG+	NM
❑ 592	Moonlight Cocktails/Midnight Flyer	1964	3.75	7.50	15.00

RIVIERAS, THE (2)

Surf-garage rock band from South Bend, Indiana.

RIVIERA

Number	Title (A Side/B Side)	Yr	VG	VG+	NM
❑ 1401	California Sun/H.B. Goose Step	1964	5.00	10.00	20.00
❑ 1401	California Sun/Played On	1964	10.00	20.00	40.00
—Possibly as few as 1,000 were pressed with this B-side					
❑ 1402	Little Donna/Let's Have a Party	1964	3.75	7.50	15.00
❑ 1403	Rockin' Robin/Battle Line	1964	3.75	7.50	15.00
❑ 1405	Whole Lotta Shakin'/Rip It Up	1965	3.75	7.50	15.00
❑ 1405	Whole Lotta Shakin'/Lakeview Lane	1965	5.00	10.00	20.00
❑ 1406	Let's Go to Hawaii/Lakeview Lane	1965	3.75	7.50	15.00
❑ 1407	Somebody Asked Me/Somebody New	1965	3.75	7.50	15.00
—Credited to the Rivieras, but actually by Bobby Whiteside					
❑ 1409	Bug Juice/Never Feel the Pain	1965	5.00	10.00	20.00

RIVIERAS, THE (3)

ALGONQUIN

Number	Title (A Side/B Side)	Yr	VG	VG+	NM
❑ 718	Together Forever/A Night to Remember	1958	50.00	100.00	200.00
—Reissued as "The Ravenairs"					

RIVILEERS, THE

BATON

Number	Title (A Side/B Side)	Yr	VG	VG+	NM
❑ 200	A Thousand Stars/Hey Chiquita	1953	50.00	100.00	200.00
❑ 201	Forever/Darling Farewell	1954	30.00	60.00	120.00
❑ 205	Carolyn/Eternal Love	1954	30.00	60.00	120.00
❑ 207	(I Love You) For Sentimental Reasons/I Want to See My Baby	1955	15.00	30.00	60.00
❑ 209	Little Girl/Don't Ever Leave Me	1955	15.00	30.00	60.00
❑ 241	A Thousand Stars/Who Is the Girl	1957	10.00	20.00	40.00

RIVINGTONS, THE

Number	Title (A Side/B Side)	Yr	VG	VG+	NM
AGC					
❑ 5	I Lost the Love/Mind Your Man	1968	2.00	4.00	8.00
A.R.E. AMERICAN					
❑ 100	All That Glitters/You Move Me Baby	1964	3.75	7.50	15.00
BATON MASTER					
❑ 202	Teach Me Tonight/Reach Our Goal	1967	2.00	4.00	8.00
COLUMBIA					
❑ 43581	A Rose Growing in the Ruins/Tend to Business	1966	3.00	6.00	12.00
❑ 43772	Yadi Yadi Yum Yum/Yadi Yadi Revisited	1966	3.00	6.00	12.00
J.D.					
❑ 122	Don't Hate Your Father (Part 1)/Don't Hate Your Father (Part 2)	1976	—	2.50	5.00
LIBERTY					
❑ 1484 [DJ]	Papa-Oom-Mow-Mow (same on both sides)	1982	—	3.00	6.00
—Reissue; promo only					
❑ 55427	Papa-Oom-Mow-Mow/Deep Water	1962	6.25	12.50	25.00
❑ 55513	Kickapoo Joy Juice/My Reward	1962	3.75	7.50	15.00
❑ 55528	Mama-Oom-Mow-Mow/Waiting	1962	3.75	7.50	15.00
❑ 55553	The Bird's the Word/I'm Losing My Grip	1963	5.00	10.00	20.00
❑ 55585	The Shaky Bird (Part 1)/The Shaky Bird (Part 2)	1963	3.75	7.50	15.00
❑ 55610	Little Sally Walker/Cherry	1963	7.50	15.00	30.00
❑ 55671	Fairy Tales/Wee Jee Walk	1964	3.75	7.50	15.00
QUAN					
❑ 1379	I Don't Want a New Baby/You're Gonna Pay	1967	2.50	5.00	10.00
RCA VICTOR					
❑ 74-0301	Pop Your Corn (Part 1)/Pop Your Corn (Part 2)	1969	2.00	4.00	8.00
REPRISE					
❑ 0293	I Tried/One Monkey Don't Stop No Show	1964	3.00	6.00	12.00
UNITED ARTISTS					
❑ 0096	Papa-Oom-Mow-Mow/The Bird's the Word	1973	—	2.00	4.00
—"Silver Spotlight Series" reissue					
VEE JAY					
❑ 634	All That Glitters/You Move Me Baby	1964	3.00	6.00	12.00
❑ 649	I Love You Always/Years of Tears	1965	3.00	6.00	12.00
❑ 677	The Willy/Just Got to Be Mine	1965	3.00	6.00	12.00
WAND					
❑ 11253	Papa-Oom-Mow-Mow/I Don't Want a New Baby	1973	—	2.50	5.00

ROAD RUNNERS, THE

More than one group. Also see GARY PAXTON.

Number	Title (A Side/B Side)	Yr	VG	VG+	NM
CHALLENGE					
❑ 9197	Dead Man/Pretty Girls	1963	5.00	10.00	20.00
FELSTED					
❑ 8692	Quasimoto/Road Runnah	1964	10.00	20.00	40.00
MIRAMAR					
❑ 116	Take Me/I'll Make It Up to You	1965	3.75	7.50	15.00
MOROCCO					
❑ 001	Goodbye/Tell Her You Love Her	1966	5.00	10.00	20.00
REPRISE					
❑ 0418	Take Me/I'll Make It Up to You	1965	3.75	7.50	15.00

ROBB, DEE

Later of THE ROBBS.

Number	Title (A Side/B Side)	Yr	VG	VG+	NM
ARGO					
❑ 5439	Bye Bye Baby/The Prom	1963	3.00	6.00	12.00
SCORE					
❑ 1006	He's Got the Whole World in His Hands/Say That Thing	1964	3.75	7.50	15.00

ROBBINS, EDDIE

Number	Title (A Side/B Side)	Yr	VG	VG+	NM
DAVID					
❑ 1001	Janice/It Was Fun	196?	6.25	12.50	25.00
DOT					
❑ 15702	A Girl Like You/Dear Parents	1958	10.00	20.00	40.00
POWER					
❑ 214	A Girl Like You/Dear Parents	1958	30.00	60.00	120.00

ROBBINS, MARTY

COLUMBIA

Number	Title (A Side/B Side)	Yr	VG	VG+	NM
❑ 02444	Jumper Cable Man/Good Hearted Woman	1981	—	2.00	4.00
❑ 02575	Teardrops on My Heart/Honeycomb	1981	—	2.00	4.00
❑ 02854	Lover, Lover/Some Memories Just Won't Die	1982	—	2.00	4.00
❑ 03236	Tie Your Dream to Mine/That's All She Wrote	1982	—	2.00	4.00
❑ 03789	Change of Heart/Devil in a Cowboy Hat	1983	—	2.00	4.00
❑ 03927	Baby That's Love/What If I Said I Love You	1983	—	2.00	4.00
❑ 10305	El Paso City/When I'm Gone	1976	—	2.50	5.00
❑ 10396	Among My Souvenirs/She's Just a Drifter	1976	—	2.50	5.00
❑ 10472	Adios Amigo/Helen	1977	—	2.50	5.00
❑ 10536	I Don't Know Why (I Just Do)/Inspiration for a Song	1977	—	2.50	5.00
❑ 10629	Don't Let Me Touch You/Tomorrow, Tomorrow, Tomorrow	1977	—	2.50	5.00
❑ 10673	Return to Me/More Than Anything, I Miss You	1978	—	2.50	5.00
❑ 10821	Please Don't Play a Love Song/Jenny	1978	—	2.50	5.00
❑ 10905	Touch Me with Magic/Confused and Lonely	1979	—	2.50	5.00
❑ 11016	All Around Cowboy/The Dreamer	1979	—	2.50	5.00
❑ 11102	Buenos Dias Argentina/Ballad of a Small Man	1979	—	2.50	5.00
❑ 11240	She's Made of Faith/Misery in My Soul	1980	—	2.00	4.00
❑ 11291	One Man's Trash (Is Another Man's Treasure)/I Can't Wait Until Tomorrow	1980	—	2.00	4.00
❑ 11372	An Occasional Rose/Holding On to You	1980	—	2.00	4.00
❑ 11425	Completely Out of Love/Another Cup of Coffee	1981	—	2.00	4.00
❑ 20925	Tomorrow You'll Be Gone/Love Me or Leave Me Alone	1952	7.50	15.00	30.00
❑ 20965	Crying 'Cause I Love You/I Wish Somebody Loved Me	1952	7.50	15.00	30.00
❑ 21022	I'll Go On Alone/You're Breaking My Heart	1952	7.50	15.00	30.00
❑ 21032	My Isle of Golden Dreams/Sweet Hawaiian Dream	1952	—	—	—
—Unreleased					
❑ 21075	I Couldn't Keep from Crying/After You Leave	1953	7.50	15.00	30.00
❑ 21111	A Castle in the Sky/A Half-Way Chance with You	1953	7.50	15.00	30.00
❑ 21145	Sing Me Something Sentimental/At the End of Long, Lonely Days	1953	7.50	15.00	30.00
❑ 21172	Blessed Jesus Should I Fall Don't Let Me Lay/Kneel and Let the Lord Take Your Load	1953	7.50	15.00	30.00
❑ 21176	Don't Make Me Ashamed/It's a Long, Long Ride	1953	7.50	15.00	30.00
❑ 21213	My Isle of Golden Dreams/Aloha Oe	1954	7.50	15.00	30.00
❑ 21246	Pretty Words/Your Heart's Turn to Break	1954	7.50	15.00	30.00
❑ 21291	Call Me Up (And I'll Come Calling on You)/I'm Too Big to Cry	1954	7.50	15.00	30.00
❑ 21324	Time Goes By/It's a Pity What Money Can Do	1954	7.50	15.00	30.00
❑ 21351	That's All Right/Gossip	1955	12.50	25.00	50.00
❑ 21352	God Understands/Have Thine Own Way, Lord	1955	6.25	12.50	25.00
❑ 21388	Daddy Loves You/Pray for Me, Mother of Mine	1955	6.25	12.50	25.00
❑ 21414	It Looks Like I'm Just in the Way/I'll Love You Till the Day I Die	1955	6.25	12.50	25.00
❑ 21446	Maybellene/This Broken Heart of Mine	1955	12.50	25.00	50.00
❑ 21461	Pretty Mama/Don't Let Me Hang Around	1955	12.50	25.00	50.00
❑ 21477	Tennessee Toddy/Mean Mama Blues	1955	12.50	25.00	50.00
❑ 21508	Singing the Blues/I Can't Quit (I've Gone Too Far)	1956	10.00	20.00	40.00
❑ 21525	I'll Know You're Gone/How Long Will It Be	1956	6.25	12.50	25.00
—With Lee Emerson					
❑ 21545	Singing the Blues/I Can't Quit (I've Gone Too Far)	1956	7.50	15.00	30.00
❑ 30511 [S]	El Paso/Running Gun	1959	7.50	15.00	30.00
—"Stereo Seven" (small hole, plays at 33 1/3 rpm)					
❑ 30589 [S]	Big Iron/Saddle Tramp	1960	7.50	15.00	30.00
—"Stereo Seven" single (small hole, plays at 33 1/3 rpm)					
❑ 30771 [S]	Five Brothers/Ride, Cowboy, Ride	1960	7.50	15.00	30.00
—"Stereo Seven" single (small hole, plays at 33 1/3 rpm)					
❑ 30809 [S]	Ballad of the Alamo/A Time and a Place for Everything	1960	7.50	15.00	30.00
—"Stereo Seven" single (small hole, plays at 33 1/3 rpm)					
❑ 31124 [S]	To Each His Own/I Can't Help It	1961	5.00	10.00	20.00
—"Stereo Seven" single, small hole, plays at 33 1/3 rpm					
❑ 31125 [S]	Answer Me My Love/Clara	1961	5.00	10.00	20.00
—"Stereo Seven" single, small hole, plays at 33 1/3 rpm					
❑ 31126 [S]	Half As Much/Unchained Melody	1961	5.00	10.00	20.00
—"Stereo Seven" single, small hole, plays at 33 1/3 rpm					
❑ 31127 [S]	Are You Sincere?/Guess I'll Be Going	1961	5.00	10.00	20.00
—"Stereo Seven" single, small hole, plays at 33 1/3 rpm					
❑ 31128 [S]	To Think You've Chosen Me/Too Young	1961	5.00	10.00	20.00
—"Stereo Seven" single, small hole, plays at 33 1/3 rpm; the above five comprise set JS7-32, "Just a Little Sentimental"					
❑ 31190 [S]	Just a Little Sentimental/Hurt	1961	5.00	10.00	20.00
—"Stereo Seven" single, small hole, plays at 33 1/3 rpm					
❑ 31191 [S]	To Each His Own/I Can't Help It	1961	5.00	10.00	20.00
—"Stereo Seven" single, small hole, plays at 33 1/3 rpm					
❑ 31192 [S]	Answer Me My Love/Half As Much	1961	5.00	10.00	20.00
—"Stereo Seven" single, small hole, plays at 33 1/3 rpm					
❑ 31193 [S]	Unchained Melody/Are You Sincere?	1961	5.00	10.00	20.00
—"Stereo Seven" single, small hole, plays at 33 1/3 rpm					
❑ 31194 [S]	To Think You've Chosen Me/Too Young	1961	5.00	10.00	20.00
—"Stereo Seven" single, small hole, plays at 33 1/3 rpm; the above five comprise set JS7-37, an alternate compilation of "Just a Little Sentimental"					
❑ 31747 [S]	Devil Woman/Time Can't Make Me Forget	1963	5.00	10.00	20.00
—"Stereo Seven" single, small hole, plays at 33 1/3 rpm					
❑ 31748 [S]	In the Ashes of an Old Love Affair/The Hands You're Holding Now	1963	5.00	10.00	20.00
—"Stereo Seven" single, small hole, plays at 33 1/3 rpm					
❑ 31749 [S]	Worried/Little Rich Girl	1963	5.00	10.00	20.00
—"Stereo Seven" single, small hole, plays at 33 1/3 rpm					
❑ 31750 [S]	Progressive Love/Love Is a Hurting Thing	1963	5.00	10.00	20.00
—"Stereo Seven" single, small hole, plays at 33 1/3 rpm					
❑ 31751 [S]	Kinda Halfway Feel/The Wine Flowed Freely	1963	5.00	10.00	20.00
—"Stereo Seven" single, small hole, plays at 33 1/3 rpm; the above five comprise set JS7-78, "Devil Woman"					
❑ 40679	Long Tall Sally/Mr. Teardrop	1956	12.50	25.00	50.00

Number	Title (A Side/B Side)	Yr	VG	VG+	NM
❑ 40706	Respectfully Miss Brooks/You Don't Owe Me a Thing	1956	12.50	25.00	50.00
❑ 40815	Knee Deep in the Blues/The Same Two Lips	1957	6.25	12.50	25.00
❑ 40864	A White Sport Coat (And a Pink Carnation)/Grown Up Tears	1957	6.25	12.50	25.00
❑ 40864 [PS]	A White Sport Coat (And a Pink Carnation)/Grown Up Tears	1957	10.00	20.00	40.00
❑ 40868	I Cried Like a Baby/Where D'Ja Go	1957	6.25	12.50	25.00
—With Lee Emerson					
❑ 40969	Please Don't Blame Me/Teen-Age Dream	1957	6.25	12.50	25.00
❑ 41013	The Story of My Life/Once-a-Week Date	1957	6.25	12.50	25.00
❑ 41013 [PS]	The Story of My Life/Once-a-Week Date	1957	10.00	20.00	40.00
❑ 41143	Just Married/Stairway of Love	1958	5.00	10.00	20.00
❑ 41208	She Was Only Seventeen (He Was One Year More)/Sittin' in a Tree House	1958	5.00	10.00	20.00
❑ 41208 [PS]	She Was Only Seventeen (He Was One Year More)/Sittin' in a Tree House	1958	10.00	20.00	40.00
❑ 41282	Ain't I the Lucky One/The Last Time I Saw My Heart	1958	5.00	10.00	20.00
❑ 41325	The Hanging Tree/The Blues, Country Style	1959	5.00	10.00	20.00
❑ 41325 [PS]	The Hanging Tree/The Blues, Country Style	1959	10.00	20.00	40.00
❑ 41408	Cap and Gown/Last Night About This Time	1959	5.00	10.00	20.00
❑ 41511 [M]	El Paso/Running Gun	1959	5.00	10.00	20.00
❑ 41511 [PS]	El Paso/Running Gun	1959	7.50	15.00	30.00
❑ 41589 [M]	Big Iron/Saddle Tramp	1960	3.75	7.50	15.00
❑ 41686	Is There Any Chance/I Told My Heart	1960	3.75	7.50	15.00
❑ 41766	Don't Worry/A Time and a Place for Everything	1960	—	—	—
—Unreleased					
❑ 41771 [M]	Five Brothers/Ride, Cowboy, Ride	1960	3.75	7.50	15.00
❑ 41809 [M]	Ballad of the Alamo/A Time and a Place for Everything	1960	3.75	7.50	15.00
❑ 41809 [PS]	Ballad of the Alamo/A Time and a Place for Everything	1960	7.50	15.00	30.00
❑ 41922	Don't Worry/Like All the Other Times	1961	3.75	7.50	15.00
❑ 41922 [PS]	Don't Worry/Like All the Other Times	1961	6.25	12.50	25.00
❑ 42008	Jimmy Martinez/Ghost Train	1961	3.75	7.50	15.00
❑ 42008 [PS]	Jimmy Martinez/Ghost Train	1961	6.25	12.50	25.00
❑ 42065	It's Your World/You Told Me So	1961	3.75	7.50	15.00
❑ 42065 [PS]	It's Your World/You Told Me So	1961	6.25	12.50	25.00
❑ 42246	I Told the Brook/Sometimes I'm Tempted	1961	3.75	7.50	15.00
❑ 42246 [PS]	I Told the Brook/Sometimes I'm Tempted	1961	6.25	12.50	25.00
❑ 42375	Love Can't Wait/Too Far Gone	1962	3.75	7.50	15.00
❑ 42375 [PS]	Love Can't Wait/Too Far Gone	1962	6.25	12.50	25.00
❑ 42486	Devil Woman/April Fool's Day	1962	3.75	7.50	15.00
❑ 42486 [PS]	Devil Woman/April Fool's Day	1962	6.25	12.50	25.00
❑ 42614	Ruby Ann/Won't You Forgive	1962	3.75	7.50	15.00
❑ 42614 [PS]	Ruby Ann/Won't You Forgive	1962	6.25	12.50	25.00
❑ 42672	Hawaii's Calling Me/Ka-Lu-A	1963	3.00	6.00	12.00
❑ 42701	Cigarettes and Coffee Blues/Teenager's Dad	1963	3.00	6.00	12.00
❑ 42701 [PS]	Cigarettes and Coffee Blues/Teenager's Dad	1963	6.25	12.50	25.00
❑ 42781	No Sign of Loneliness Here/I'm Not Ready Yet	1963	3.00	6.00	12.00
❑ 42781 [PS]	No Sign of Loneliness Here/I'm Not Ready Yet	1963	6.25	12.50	25.00
❑ 42831	Not So Long Ago/I Hope You Learn a Lot	1963	3.00	6.00	12.00
❑ 42890	Begging to You/Over High Mountain	1963	3.00	6.00	12.00
❑ 42968	Girl from Spanish Town/Kingston Girl	1964	2.50	5.00	10.00
❑ 43049	The Cowboy in the Continental Suit/Man Walks Among Us	1964	2.50	5.00	10.00
❑ 43134	One of These Days/Up in the Air	1964	2.50	5.00	10.00
❑ 43196	I Eish-Tay-Mah-Su (I Love You)/A Whole Lot Easier	1964	2.50	5.00	10.00
❑ 43258	Ribbon of Darkness/Little Robin	1965	2.50	5.00	10.00
❑ 43377	Old Red/Matilda	1965	2.00	4.00	8.00
❑ 43428	While You're Dancing/Lonely Too Long	1965	2.00	4.00	8.00
❑ 43500	Count Me Out/Private Wilson White	1965	2.00	4.00	8.00
❑ 43651	Ain't I Right/My Own Native Land	1966	—	—	—
—Unreleased					
❑ 43680	The Shoe Goes On the Other Foot Tonight/It Kind of Reminds Me of You	1966	2.00	4.00	8.00
❑ 43845	No Tears Milady/Fly Butterfly Fly	1966	2.00	4.00	8.00
❑ 43870	Mr. Shorty/Tall Handsome Strangers	1966	2.00	4.00	8.00
❑ 44128	Tonight Carmen/Waiting in Reno	1967	—	3.00	6.00
❑ 44271	Gardenias in Her Hair/In the Valley of the Rio Grande	1967	—	3.00	6.00
❑ 44509	Love Is In the Air/I've Been Leaving Everyday	1968	—	3.00	6.00
❑ 44633	I Walk Alone/Lily of the Valley	1968	—	3.00	6.00
❑ 44641	It Finally Happened/Big Mouthin' Around	1968	—	3.00	6.00
—By "Marty Robbins Jr. and Sr."					
❑ 44739	It's a Sin/I Feel Another Heartache Coming On	1969	—	2.50	5.00
❑ 44895	I Can't Say Goodbye/Hello Daily News	1969	—	2.50	5.00
❑ 44968	Girl from Spanish Town/Kingston Girl	1969	2.00	4.00	8.00
❑ 45024	Camelia/Virginia	1969	—	2.50	5.00
❑ 45091	My Woman, My Woman, My Wife/Martha Ellen Jenkins	1970	—	2.50	5.00
❑ 45215	Jolie Girl/The City	1970	—	2.50	5.00
❑ 45273	Padre/At Times	1970	—	3.00	6.00
❑ 45346	Little Spot in Heaven/Wait a Little Longer Please, Jesus	1971	—	3.00	6.00
❑ 45377	The Chair/Seventeen Years	1971	—	2.50	5.00
❑ 45442	Early Morning Sunshine/Another Day Has Gone By	1971	—	2.50	5.00
❑ 45520	The Best Part of Living/Gone with the Wind	1971	—	2.50	5.00
❑ 45668	I've Got a Woman's Love/A Little Spot in Heaven	1972	—	2.50	5.00
❑ 45775	Laura (What's He Got That I Ain't Got)/It Kind of Reminds Me of You	1973	—	2.50	5.00
❑ JZSP 49158/48863 [DJ]	El Paso (2:58)/El Paso (4:37)	1959	10.00	20.00	40.00

DECCA

Number	Title (A Side/B Side)	Yr	VG	VG+	NM
❑ 33006	This Much a Man/Guess I'll Stand Here Looking Dumb	1972	—	3.50	7.00

MCA

Number	Title (A Side/B Side)	Yr	VG	VG+	NM
❑ 40012	Franklin, Tennessee/Walking Piece of Heaven	1973	—	2.50	5.00
❑ 40067	A Man and a Train/Las Vegas, Nevada	1973	—	2.50	5.00
❑ 40134	Love Me/Crawling on My Knees	1973	—	2.50	5.00
❑ 40172	I'm Wanting To/Twentieth Century Drifter	1973	—	2.50	5.00
❑ 40236	Don't You Think/I Couldn't Believe It Was True	1974	—	2.50	5.00
❑ 40296	Two-Gun Daddy/Queen of the Big Rodeo	1974	—	2.50	5.00
❑ 40342	Life/It Takes Faith	1974	—	2.50	5.00
❑ 40425	These Are My Souvenirs/Shotgun Rider	1975	—	2.50	5.00
❑ 52197	Two Gun Daddy/Life	1983	—	2.50	5.00

WARNER BROS.

Number	Title (A Side/B Side)	Yr	VG	VG+	NM
❑ 29847	Honkytonk Man/Shotgun Rag	1982	—	2.00	4.00
—B-side by Johnny Gimble and the Texas Swing Band					

7-Inch Extended Plays

COLUMBIA

Number	Title (A Side/B Side)	Yr	VG	VG+	NM
❑ H-1785	I'll Go On Alone/Crying 'Cause I Love You//I Couldn't Keep from Crying/A Half-Way Chance with You	1953	15.00	30.00	60.00
❑ H-1785 [PS]	Marty Robbins	1953	15.00	30.00	60.00
❑ B-2116	*Singing the Blues/I Can't Quit/Long Gone Lonesome Blues/Lorelei	1956	12.50	25.00	50.00
❑ B-2116 [PS]	Singing the Blues	1956	12.50	25.00	50.00
❑ B-2134	*A White Sport Coat/Mean Mama Blues/Grown-Up Tears/Long Tall Sally	1957	10.00	20.00	40.00
❑ B-2134 [PS]	A White Sport Coat	1957	10.00	20.00	40.00
❑ B-2153	The Letter Edged in Black/The Little Rosewood Casket//The Dream of the Miner's Child/The Convict and the Rose	1957	7.50	15.00	30.00
❑ B-2153 [PS]	Marty Robbins	1957	7.50	15.00	30.00
❑ B-2808	I Couldn't Keep from Crying/Sing Me Something Sentimental//Tennessee Toddy/You Don't Owe Me a Thing	1957	12.50	25.00	50.00
❑ B-2808 [PS]	Marty Robbins	1957	12.50	25.00	50.00
❑ B-2814	*A White Sport Coat/The Story of My Life/Singing the Blues/I'm So Lonesome I Could Cry	1958	3.00	6.00	12.00
❑ B-2814 [PS]	Marty Robbins	1958	3.00	6.00	12.00
❑ B-9761	Lovesick Blues/I'm So Lonesome I Could Cry//It's Too Late Now/Rose of Ol' Pawnee	1957	3.75	7.50	15.00
❑ B-9761 [PS]	The Song of Robbins Vol. I	1957	3.75	7.50	15.00
❑ B-9762	I Never Let You Cross My Mind/I Hang My Head and Cry//You Only Want Me When You're Lonely/Moanin' the Blues	1957	3.75	7.50	15.00
❑ B-9762 [PS]	The Song of Robbins Vol. II	1957	3.75	7.50	15.00
❑ B-9763	I'll Step Aside/All the World Is Lonely Now//Bouquet of Roses/Have I Told You Lately That I Love You?	1957	3.75	7.50	15.00
❑ B-9763 [PS]	The Song of Robbins, Vol. III	1957	3.75	7.50	15.00
❑ B-10871	*Song of the Islands/Now Is the Hour/Sweet Leilani/Aloha Oe	1957	3.75	7.50	15.00
❑ B-10871 [PS]	Song of the Islands	1957	3.75	7.50	15.00
❑ B-11891	Kaw-Liga/Waltz of the Wind//Then I Turned and Walked Slowly Away/A House with Everything But Love	1958	3.75	7.50	15.00
❑ B-11891 [PS]	Marty Robbins	1958	3.75	7.50	15.00
❑ B-13491	El Paso/A Hundred and Sixty Acres//They're Hanging Me Tonight/The Strawberry Roan	1959	3.00	6.00	12.00
❑ B-13491 [PS]	Gunfighter Ballads and Trail Songs, Vol. I	1959	3.00	6.00	12.00
❑ B-13492	Big Iron/In the Valley//Running Gun/Utah Carol	1959	3.00	6.00	12.00
❑ B-13492 [PS]	Gunfighter Ballads and Trail Songs, Vol. II	1959	3.00	6.00	12.00
❑ B-13493	Cool Water/The Master's Call//Billy the Kid/The Little Green Valley	1959	3.75	7.50	15.00
❑ B-13493 [PS]	Gunfighter Ballads and Trail Songs, Vol. III	1959	3.75	7.50	15.00
❑ B-14811	*San Angelo/Prairie Fire/Streets of Laredo	1960	3.00	6.00	12.00
❑ B-14811 [PS]	More Gunfighter Ballads and Trail Songs, Vol. I	1960	3.00	6.00	12.00
❑ B-14812	*Five Brothers/Little Joe the Wrangler/Song of the Bandit/I've Got No Use for the Woman	1960	3.00	6.00	12.00
❑ B-14812 [PS]	More Gunfighter Ballads and Trail Songs, Vol. II	1960	3.00	6.00	12.00
❑ B-14813	*She Was Young and She Was Pretty/My Love/Ride Cowboy Ride/This Peaceful Sod	1960	3.00	6.00	12.00
❑ B-14813 [PS]	More Gunfighter Ballads and Trail Songs, Vol. III	1960	3.00	6.00	12.00

ROBBINS, MEL

ARGO

Number	Title (A Side/B Side)	Yr	VG	VG+	NM
❑ 5340	Save It/To Know You	1959	25.00	50.00	100.00

ROBBS, THE

Also see DEE ROBB.

ABC

Number	Title (A Side/B Side)	Yr	VG	VG+	NM
❑ 11270	I'll Never Get Enough/It All Comes Back	1970	—	3.00	6.00

ABC DUNHILL

Number	Title (A Side/B Side)	Yr	VG	VG+	NM
❑ 4208	Write to You/Movin'	1969	2.50	5.00	10.00
❑ 4233	Written in the Dust/Last of the Wine	1970	2.00	4.00	8.00

ATLANTIC

Number	Title (A Side/B Side)	Yr	VG	VG+	NM
❑ 2511	Castles in the Air/I Don't Want to Discuss It	1968	2.50	5.00	10.00
❑ 2578	A Good Time Song/Changin' Winds	1968	2.50	5.00	10.00

MERCURY

Number	Title (A Side/B Side)	Yr	VG	VG+	NM
❑ 72579	Race with the Wind/In a Funny Sort of Way	1966	2.50	5.00	10.00
❑ 72616	I Don't Feel Alone/Next Time You Call Me	1966	2.50	5.00	10.00
❑ 72641	Bittersweet/End of the Week	1966	2.50	5.00	10.00
❑ 72641 [PS]	Bittersweet/End of the Week	1966	3.75	7.50	15.00
❑ 72678	Rapid Transit/Cynthia Loves	1967	2.50	5.00	10.00
❑ 72730	Girls, Girls/Violets of Dawn	1967	2.50	5.00	10.00

ROBBY AND THE ROBBINS

TODD

Number	Title (A Side/B Side)	Yr	VG	VG+	NM
❑ 1089	Surfer's Life/She Cried	1963	10.00	20.00	40.00

ROBERT AND JOHNNY

OLD TOWN

Number	Title (A Side/B Side)	Yr	VG	VG+	NM
❑ 1021	I Believe You/Train to Paradise	1956	12.50	25.00	50.00
❑ 1029	You're Mine/Million Dollar Bills	1956	10.00	20.00	40.00
❑ 1038	Don't Do It/Baby Come Home	1957	10.00	20.00	40.00
❑ 1043	Broken Hearted Man/Indian Marriage	1957	10.00	20.00	40.00
❑ 1047	We Belong Together/In the Rain	1958	12.50	25.00	50.00
❑ 1052	I Know/Marry Me	1958	10.00	20.00	40.00
❑ 1052	I Believe in You/Marry Me	1958	10.00	20.00	40.00
❑ 1058	Eternity with You/I'm Truly, Truly Yours	1958	7.50	15.00	30.00

Number	Title (A Side/B Side)	Yr	VG	VG+	NM
❑ 1065	Give Me the Key to Your Heart/Truly in Love	1959	7.50	15.00	30.00
❑ 1068	Dream Girl/Oh My Love	1959	7.50	15.00	30.00
❑ 1072	Wear This Ring/Bad Dan	1959	7.50	15.00	30.00
❑ 1078	Hear My Heartbeat/Try Me Pretty Baby	1960	6.25	12.50	25.00
❑ 1086	We Belong Together/In the Rain	1960	6.25	12.50	25.00
❑ 1100	You're Mine/Please Me Please	1961	5.00	10.00	20.00
❑ 1108	Togetherness/I Got You	1961	5.00	10.00	20.00
❑ 1117	Wear This Ring/Broken Hearted Man	1962	5.00	10.00	20.00
SUE					
❑ 792	A Perfect Wife/Brown, Pretty Brown Eyes	1963	6.25	12.50	25.00

ROBERTS, AUSTIN

Number	Title (A Side/B Side)	Yr	VG	VG+	NM
ABC					
❑ 11289	Live Is for Living/I Can Make It Better	1971	—	3.00	6.00
ARISTA					
❑ 0335	Don't Stop Me Baby/Question of Love	1978	—	2.00	4.00
CHELSEA					
❑ BCBO-0053	Baby Don't You Walk Out on Me/One Word	1973	—	2.00	4.00
❑ 78-0101	Something's Wrong wtih Me/My Song	1972	—	2.50	5.00
❑ 78-0110	Keep On Singing/Take Away the Sunshine	1973	—	2.50	5.00
❑ 78-0123	The Last Thing on My Mind/Losing You Is More Than I Can Stand	1973	—	2.50	5.00
❑ AMBO-0129	Something's Wrong with Me/Keep On Singing	1973	—	2.00	4.00
—Gold Standard Series reissue					
❑ BCBO-0219	Somethin' to Believe In/Nothing Seems the Same When You're Not Here	1974	—	2.00	4.00
PHILIPS					
❑ 40560	I'll Smiule/Mary and Me	1968	—	3.00	6.00
❑ 40586	Ricky Ticky Ta Ta Ta/No Last Goodbyes	1969	—	3.00	6.00
❑ 40638	Runaway-Just a Little (Medley)/Sarah	1969	—	3.00	6.00
❑ 40649	Baltimore/Sarah	1969	—	3.00	6.00
❑ 40660	One Night Ann/The Other Side	1970	—	3.00	6.00
PRIVATE STOCK					
❑ 45020	Rocky/You Got the Power	1975	—	2.00	4.00
❑ 45051	Fool/Children of the Rain	1975	—	2.00	4.00
❑ 45061	Is There Somethin' Goin' On/Just to Make You Mine	1975	—	2.00	4.00
❑ 45080	This Time I'm In It for Love/Susannah	1976	—	2.00	4.00

ROBERTS, LANCE

Number	Title (A Side/B Side)	Yr	VG	VG+	NM
SUN					
❑ 348	The Good Guy Always Wins/The Time Is Right	1960	5.00	10.00	20.00

ROBERTS, LOU

Number	Title (A Side/B Side)	Yr	VG	VG+	NM
GENIE					
❑ 101	Rattle Snake Shake/(B-side unknown)	1965	20.00	40.00	80.00
MGM					
❑ 13347	Gettin' Ready/You Fooled Me	1965	7.50	15.00	30.00
❑ 13387	Don't Count on Me/Ten to One	1965	6.25	12.50	25.00

ROBERTS, WAYNE

Actually Neil Bogart, later owner of the Buddah, Casablanca and Boardwalk record labels.

Number	Title (A Side/B Side)	Yr	VG	VG+	NM
20TH CENTURY FOX					
❑ 644	Little Girl/One Piece Bathing Suit	1966	6.25	12.50	25.00

ROBERTSON, ROBBIE

Formerly of THE BAND.

Number	Title (A Side/B Side)	Yr	VG	VG+	NM
GEFFEN					
❑ 28111	Somewhere Down the Crazy River/Hell's Half Acre	1988	—	2.00	4.00
❑ 28175	Showdown at Big Sky/Hell's Half Acre	1987	—	2.00	4.00
❑ 28175 [PS]	Showdown at Big Sky/Hell's Half Acre	1987	—	2.00	4.00

ROBIN, RICHIE

Number	Title (A Side/B Side)	Yr	VG	VG+	NM
GOLDISC					
❑ 3002	Sugar Love/Bonnie Come Home	1960	3.75	7.50	15.00
❑ 3008	This Little Girl of Mine/A Little Bit Is Better Than Nothing	1960	3.75	7.50	15.00
GONE					
❑ 5077	Mama, I Wanna Dance/Jiving with the Saints	1959	5.00	10.00	20.00
❑ 5083	Branded/Strange Dreams	1959	5.00	10.00	20.00

ROBINS, THE (1)

Vocal group from Los Angeles. Part of the group splintered off and became the core of THE COASTERS.

Number	Title (A Side/B Side)	Yr	VG	VG+	NM
ATCO					
❑ 6059	Smokey Joe's Cafe/Just Like a Fool	1956	12.50	25.00	50.00
CROWN					
❑ 106	I Made a Vow/Double Crossing Baby	1954	100.00	200.00	400.00
❑ 120	Key to My Heart/All I Do Is Rock	1954	75.00	150.00	300.00
KNIGHT					
❑ 2001	Quarter to Twelve/Pretty Little Dolly	1958	12.50	25.00	50.00
❑ 2008	It's Never Too Late/A Little Bird Told Me	1958	20.00	40.00	80.00
RCA VICTOR					
❑ 47-5175	(Now and Then There's) A Fool Such As I/My Heart's the Biggest Fool	1953	125.00	250.00	500.00
❑ 47-5271	Oh Why/All Night Baby	1953	100.00	200.00	400.00
❑ 47-5434	How Would You Know/Let's Go to the Dance	1953	100.00	200.00	400.00
❑ 47-5486	My Baby Done Told Me/I'll Do It	1953	75.00	150.00	300.00
❑ 47-5489	Ten Days in Jail/Empty Bottles	1953	50.00	100.00	200.00
❑ 47-5564	Get It Off Your Mind/Don't Stop Now	1953	50.00	100.00	200.00
SPARK					
❑ 103	Riot in Cell Block #9/Wrap It Up	1954	75.00	150.00	300.00
—Copies on yellow labels are bootlegs					
❑ 107	Loop De Loop Mambo/Framed	1954	75.00	150.00	300.00
—Silver top label					
❑ 107	Loop De Loop Mambo/Framed	1954	25.00	50.00	100.00
—Red label					
❑ 110	If Teardrops Were Kisses/Whadaya Want	1955	75.00	150.00	300.00
—Red label					
❑ 110	If Teardrops Were Kisses/Whadaya Want	1955	25.00	50.00	100.00
—Blue label					
❑ 113	One Kiss/I Love Paris	1955	75.00	150.00	300.00
❑ 116	I Must Be Dreamin'/The Hatchet Man	1955	50.00	100.00	200.00
—Red label					
❑ 116	I Must Be Dreamin'/The Hatchet Man	1955	12.50	25.00	50.00
—Yellow label					
❑ 122	Smokey Joe's Cafe/Just Like a Fool	1955	87.50	175.00	350.00
WHIPPET					
❑ 200	Cherry Lips/Out of the Picture	1956	20.00	40.00	80.00
❑ 201	Hurt Me/Merry-Go-Rock	1956	17.50	35.00	70.00
❑ 203	That Old Black Magic/Since I First Met You	1956	17.50	35.00	70.00
❑ 206	A Fool in Love/All of a Sudden My Heart Sings	1957	17.50	35.00	70.00
❑ 208	Every Night/Where's the Fire	1957	17.50	35.00	70.00
❑ 211	In My Dreams/Keep Your Mind on Me	1957	17.50	35.00	70.00
❑ 212	Snowball/You Wanted Fun	1958	17.50	35.00	70.00

ROBINS, THE (2)

Number	Title (A Side/B Side)	Yr	VG	VG+	NM
ARDENT					
❑ 106	Batman/Batarang	1966	7.50	15.00	30.00

ROBINS, THE (3)

Number	Title (A Side/B Side)	Yr	VG	VG+	NM
LAVENDER					
❑ 001	The White Cliffs of Dover/How Many More Times	1961	10.00	20.00	40.00
❑ 002	Magic of a Dream/Mary Lou Loves to Hootchy Kootchy Koo	1961	10.00	20.00	40.00

ROBINS, THE (4)

Number	Title (A Side/B Side)	Yr	VG	VG+	NM
NEW HIT					
❑ 3010	Johnny/Doing the Popeye	1963	3.75	7.50	15.00
SWEET TAFFY					
❑ 400	Johnny/Doing the Popeye	1963	7.50	15.00	30.00

ROBINS, THE (U)

These could be by any of the above, or none of the above.

Number	Title (A Side/B Side)	Yr	VG	VG+	NM
ARVEE					
❑ 5001	Just Like That/Whole Lot of Imagination	1960	6.25	12.50	25.00
❑ 5013	Live Wire Suzie/Oh No	1960	6.25	12.50	25.00
DOT					
❑ 16519	Blue Grass Blues/Top 40 Blues	1963	3.00	6.00	12.00
GONE					
❑ 5101	Baby Love/We Loved	1961	7.50	15.00	30.00
MUSICOR					
❑ 1050	Cry Over You/Lucy Watusi	1964	3.75	7.50	15.00

ROBINSON, BILL, AND THE QUAILS

Number	Title (A Side/B Side)	Yr	VG	VG+	NM
DATE					
❑ 1620	Do I Love You/Lay My Head on Your Shoulder	1969	2.50	5.00	10.00
DELUXE					
❑ 6030	Lonely Star/Quit Pushin'	1954	50.00	100.00	200.00
❑ 6047	I Know She's Gone/Baby Don't Want Me No More	1954	75.00	150.00	300.00
❑ 6057	A Little Bit of Love/Somewhere Somebody Cares	1954	50.00	100.00	200.00
❑ 6059	Why Do I Wait/Heaven Is the Place	1954	50.00	100.00	200.00
❑ 6074	Love of My Life/Oh Sugar	1955	37.50	75.00	150.00
❑ 6085	The Things She Used to Do/Pretty Huggin' Baby	1955	17.50	35.00	70.00
—As "The Quails"					

ROBINSON, JOHNNY

Number	Title (A Side/B Side)	Yr	VG	VG+	NM
EPIC					
❑ 10578	God Is Love/Kansas City	1970	2.50	5.00	10.00
❑ 10607	Person to Person/Lady Doctor	1970	2.50	5.00	10.00
MERCURY					
❑ 72434	I Gotta Kick the Habit (Part 1)/I Gotta Kick the Habit (Part 2)	1965	5.00	10.00	20.00
OKEH					
❑ 7307	Gone But Not Forgotten/I Need Your Love So Bad	1968	25.00	50.00	100.00
❑ 7317	Poor Man/When a Man Cries	1968	5.00	10.00	20.00
❑ 7328	Green Green Grass of Home/You've Been With Him	1969	5.00	10.00	20.00

ROBINSON, MARK

Number	Title (A Side/B Side)	Yr	VG	VG+	NM
JAMIE					
❑ 1103	Pretty Jane/Want Me	1958	6.25	12.50	25.00
TEE GEE					
❑ 104	Pretty Jane/Want Me	1958	10.00	20.00	40.00

ROBINSON, SMOKEY

Also see THE MIRACLES; RON AND BILL.

Number	Title (A Side/B Side)	Yr	VG	VG+	NM
COLUMBIA					
❑ 07727	I Know You by Heart/Could I Have Your Autograph	1988	—	—	3.00
—With Dolly Parton					
MOTOWN					
❑ 914	(It's the) Same Old Love/(Instrumental)	1990	—	2.00	4.00
❑ 1877	Just to See Her/I'm Gonna Love You Like There's No Tomorrow	1987	—	—	3.00
❑ 1877 [PS]	Just to See Her/I'm Gonna Love You Like There's No Tomorrow	1987	2.00	4.00	8.00
❑ 1897	One Heartbeat/Love Will Set You Free (Theme from Solarbabies)	1987	—	—	3.00
❑ 1897 [PS]	One Heartbeat/Love Will Set You Free (Theme from Solarbabies)	1987	—	3.00	6.00
❑ 1911	What's Too Much/I've Made Love to You a Thousand Times	1987	—	—	3.00
❑ 1911 [PS]	What's Too Much/I've Made Love to You a Thousand Times	1987	—	2.50	5.00
❑ 1925	Love Don't Give No Reason/Hanging On by a Thread	1988	—	—	3.00
❑ 1925 [PS]	Love Don't Give No Reason/Hanging On by a Thread	1988	—	2.50	5.00
SBK					
❑ 07379	Double Good Everything/Guess What I Got for You	1991	—	2.00	4.00

TAMLA

Number	Title (A Side/B Side)	Yr	VG	VG+	NM
❑ 1601	Tell Me Tomorrow (Part 1)/Tell Me Tomorrow (Part 2)	1982	—	2.00	4.00
❑ 1615	Old Fashioned Love/Destiny	1982	—	2.00	4.00
❑ 1630	Are You Still Here/Yes It's You Lady	1982	—	2.00	4.00
❑ 1655	I've Made Love to You a Thousand Times/Into Each Rain Some Life Must Fall	1983	—	2.00	4.00
❑ 1678	Touch the Sky/All My Life's a Lie	1983	—	2.00	4.00
❑ 1684	Blame It on Love/Even Tho'	1983	—	2.00	4.00
—With Barbara Mitchell					
❑ 1700	Don't Play Another Love Song/Wouldn't You Like to Know	1983	—	2.00	4.00
❑ 1735	And I Don't Love You/Dynamite	1984	—	2.00	4.00
❑ 1756	I Can't Find/Gimme What You Want	1984	—	2.00	4.00
❑ 1786	First Time on a Ferris Wheel/Train of Thought	1985	—	2.00	4.00
❑ 1828	Hold On to Your Love/Train of Thought	1985	—	2.00	4.00
❑ 1828 [PS]	Hold On to Your Love/Train of Thought	1985	—	3.00	6.00
❑ 1839	Sleepless Nights/Close Encounters of the First Kind	1986	—	2.00	4.00
❑ 1839 [PS]	Sleepless Nights/Close Encounters of the First Kind	1986	—	2.50	5.00
❑ 1855	Girl I'm Standing There/Because of You (It's the Best It's Ever Been)	1986	—	2.00	4.00
❑ 1868	Love Will Set You Free (Theme from Solarbabies) (Parts 1 & 2)	1986	—	2.00	4.00
❑ 54233	Sweet Harmony/Want to Know My Mind	1973	—	2.50	5.00
❑ 54239	Baby Come Close/A Silent Partner in a Three-Way Love Affair	1973	—	2.50	5.00
❑ 54246	It's Her Turn to Live/Just My Soul Responding	1974	—	2.50	5.00
❑ 54250	Virgin Man/Fulfill Your Need	1974	—	2.50	5.00
❑ 54251	I Am, I Am/The Family Song	1974	—	2.50	5.00
❑ 54258	Baby That's Backatcha/Just Passing Through	1975	—	2.50	5.00
❑ 54261	The Agony and the Ecstasy/Wedding Song	1975	—	2.50	5.00
❑ 54265	Quiet Storm/Asleep on My Love	1975	—	2.50	5.00
❑ 54267	Open/Coincidentally	1976	—	2.50	5.00
❑ 54269	When You Came/Coincidentally	1976	3.00	6.00	12.00
—Released only in Canada					
❑ 54272	An Old Fashioned Man/(B-side unassigned)	1976	—	—	—
—Unreleased					
❑ 54276	An Old Fashioned Man/Just Passing Through	1976	—	2.50	5.00
❑ 54279	There Will Come a Day (I'm Gonna Happen to You)/Humming Song	1977	—	2.50	5.00
❑ 54284	Vitamin U/Holly	1977	—	2.50	5.00
❑ 54288	Theme from Big Time (Part 1)/Theme from Big Time (Part 2)	1977	—	2.50	5.00
❑ 54293	Daylight and Darkness/Why You Wanna See My Bad Side	1978	—	2.50	5.00
❑ 54296	I'm Loving You Softly/Shoe Soul	1978	—	2.50	5.00
❑ 54301	Get Ready/Ever Had a Dream	1979	—	2.00	4.00
❑ 54306	Cruisin'/Ever Had a Dream	1979	—	2.00	4.00
❑ 54311	Let Me Be the Clock/Travelin' Through	1980	—	2.00	4.00
❑ 54313	Heavy on Pride/I Love the Nearness of You	1980	—	2.00	4.00
❑ 54318	I Want to Be Your Love/Wine, Women and Song	1980	—	2.00	4.00
❑ 54321	Being with You/What's In Your Life for Me	1981	—	2.00	4.00
❑ 54325	Aquicontigo/Being with You (Aquicontigo)	1981	—	2.00	4.00
❑ 54327	You Are Forever/I Hear the Children Singing	1981	—	2.00	4.00
❑ 54332	Who's Sad/Food for Thought	1981	—	2.00	4.00

ROCCO, LENNY

DELSEY

Number	Title (A Side/B Side)	Yr	VG	VG+	NM
❑ 301	Sugar Girl/Rochelle	1961	75.00	150.00	300.00

ROCHELL AND THE CANDLES

CHALLENGE

Number	Title (A Side/B Side)	Yr	VG	VG+	NM
❑ 9158	Turn Her Down/Each Night	1962	10.00	20.00	40.00
❑ 9191	Annie's Not an Orphan Anymore/Let's Run Away and Get Married	1963	5.00	10.00	20.00

SWINGIN'

Number	Title (A Side/B Side)	Yr	VG	VG+	NM
❑ 623	Once Upon a Time/When My Baby Is Gone	1960	5.00	10.00	20.00
❑ 634	So Far Away/Hey, Pretty Baby	1961	5.00	10.00	20.00
❑ 640	Peg of My Heart/Squat with Me, Baby	1962	5.00	10.00	20.00
❑ 652	Big Boy Pete/A Long Time Ago	1963	5.00	10.00	20.00

ROCK-A-FELLAS, THE

ABC-PARAMOUNT

Number	Title (A Side/B Side)	Yr	VG	VG+	NM
❑ 9923	Don't Torment Me/Red Lips	1958	5.00	10.00	20.00

DEVERE

Number	Title (A Side/B Side)	Yr	VG	VG+	NM
❑ 313	Don't Torment Me/Red Lips	1958	12.50	25.00	50.00

ROCK-A-TEENS, THE

DORAN

Number	Title (A Side/B Side)	Yr	VG	VG+	NM
❑ 3515	Woo Hoo/Untrue	1959	37.50	75.00	150.00

ROULETTE

Number	Title (A Side/B Side)	Yr	VG	VG+	NM
❑ 4192	Woo Hoo/Untrue	1959	7.50	15.00	30.00
❑ 4217	Twangy/Doggone It, Baby	1959	6.25	12.50	25.00

ROCK BROTHERS, THE

KING

Number	Title (A Side/B Side)	Yr	VG	VG+	NM
❑ 4851	Dungaree Doll/Livin' It Up	1955	7.50	15.00	30.00
❑ 4882	Oh, Didn't I Ramble/I Gotta Get Back	1956	6.25	12.50	25.00

ROCKA, BILLY

BRUNSWICK

Number	Title (A Side/B Side)	Yr	VG	VG+	NM
❑ 55049	Listen Pretty Baby/I'm Gonna Sit Right Down and Cry	1958	15.00	30.00	60.00

ROCKAWAYS, THE

RED BIRD

Number	Title (A Side/B Side)	Yr	VG	VG+	NM
❑ 10-005	Top Down Time/Don't Cry	1964	6.25	12.50	25.00

ROCKERS, THE

CARTER

Number	Title (A Side/B Side)	Yr	VG	VG+	NM
❑ 3029	Tell Me Why/Count Every Star	1955	200.00	400.00	800.00

FEDERAL

Number	Title (A Side/B Side)	Yr	VG	VG+	NM
❑ 12267	What Am I to Do/I'll Die in Love with You	1956	50.00	100.00	200.00
❑ 12273	Down in the Bottom/Why Don't You Believe Me	1956	25.00	50.00	100.00

ROCKETEERS, THE (1)

GLAD HAMP

Number	Title (A Side/B Side)	Yr	VG	VG+	NM
❑ 2017	Drag Strip/Summertime	1963	10.00	20.00	40.00

ROCKETEERS, THE (2)

HERALD

Number	Title (A Side/B Side)	Yr	VG	VG+	NM
❑ 415	Foolish One/Gonna Feed My Baby Poison	1953	175.00	350.00	700.00
—Black vinyl					
❑ 415	Foolish One/Gonna Feed My Baby Poison	1953	500.00	1000.	2000.
—Red vinyl					

ROCKETEERS, THE (3)

MODERN

Number	Title (A Side/B Side)	Yr	VG	VG+	NM
❑ 999	Talk It Over Baby/Hey Rube	1956	12.50	25.00	50.00

ROCKETEERS, THE (4)

M.J.C.

Number	Title (A Side/B Side)	Yr	VG	VG+	NM
❑ 501	My Reckless Heart/They Turned the Party Out Down at Bessie's House	1958	500.00	1000.	2000.

ROCKETEERS, THE (U)

VAL-UE

Number	Title (A Side/B Side)	Yr	VG	VG+	NM
❑ 102	Rippin' and Rockin'/Downtown	1960	7.50	15.00	30.00

ROCKETONES, THE

MELBA

Number	Title (A Side/B Side)	Yr	VG	VG+	NM
❑ 113	Mexico/I Do	1957	15.00	30.00	60.00
❑ 113	Mexico/Dee I	1957	12.50	25.00	50.00

ROCKETS

With former members of MITCH RYDER AND THE DETROIT WHEELS.

CAPITOL

Number	Title (A Side/B Side)	Yr	VG	VG+	NM
❑ 5262	Turn Up the Radio/Can't Sleep	1983	—	—	3.00
❑ 5262 [PS]	Turn Up the Radio/Can't Sleep	1983	—	—	3.00

ELEKTRA

Number	Title (A Side/B Side)	Yr	VG	VG+	NM
❑ 47212	Lift You Up/Tired of Wearing Black	1981	—	—	3.00
❑ 69985	Rollin' By the Record Machine	1982	—	—	3.00

RSO

Number	Title (A Side/B Side)	Yr	VG	VG+	NM
❑ 926	Can't Sleep/Something Ain't Right	1979	—	2.00	4.00
❑ 935	Oh Well/Love Me Once More	1979	—	2.00	4.00
❑ 1022	Desire/Troublemaker	1980	—	2.00	4.00
❑ 1028	Sad Song/Takin' It Back	1980	—	2.00	4.00

TORTOISE INT'L.

Number	Title (A Side/B Side)	Yr	VG	VG+	NM
❑ TB-11207	She's a Pretty One/I've Got to Move	1978	—	2.00	4.00

ROCKETS, THE (2)

ATLANTIC

Number	Title (A Side/B Side)	Yr	VG	VG+	NM
❑ 988	Open the Door/Big Leg Mama	1953	25.00	50.00	100.00

ROCKETS, THE (3)

COLUMBIA

Number	Title (A Side/B Side)	Yr	VG	VG+	NM
❑ 41512	Gibraltar Rock/Walkin' Home	1959	6.25	12.50	25.00

ROCKETS, THE (4)

MODERN

Number	Title (A Side/B Side)	Yr	VG	VG+	NM
❑ 992	You Are the First One/Be Lovey Dovey	1956	10.00	20.00	40.00

ROCKETS, THE (5)

Features three future members of CRAZY HORSE.

WHITE WHALE

Number	Title (A Side/B Side)	Yr	VG	VG+	NM
❑ 270	Hole in My Pocket/Let Me Go	1968	3.75	7.50	15.00

ROCKETTES, THE

PARROT

Number	Title (A Side/B Side)	Yr	VG	VG+	NM
❑ 789	I Can't Forget/Love Nobody	1954	1000.	2000.	3000.

ROCKIN' BERRIES, THE

REPRISE

Number	Title (A Side/B Side)	Yr	VG	VG+	NM
❑ 0329	He's in Town/Flashbook	1964	3.00	6.00	12.00
❑ 0355	What in the World's Come Over You/You Don't Know What to Do	1965	2.50	5.00	10.00
❑ 0377	Poor Man's Son/Follow Me	1965	2.50	5.00	10.00
❑ 0400	You're My Girl/Brother Bill (Last Clean Shirt)	1965	2.50	5.00	10.00
❑ 0442	Doesn't Time Fly/The Water Is Over My Head	1965	2.50	5.00	10.00

ROCKIN' CHAIRS, THE

RECORTE

Number	Title (A Side/B Side)	Yr	VG	VG+	NM
❑ 402	Rockin' Chair Boogie/A Kiss Is a Kiss	1958	25.00	50.00	100.00
❑ 404	Please Mary/Come On Baby	1958	12.50	25.00	50.00
❑ 412	Memories of Love/(B-side unknown)	1959	12.50	25.00	50.00

ROCKIN' DUKES, THE

O.J.

Number	Title (A Side/B Side)	Yr	VG	VG+	NM
❑ 1007	Angel and a Rose/My Baby Left Me	1957	75.00	150.00	300.00

ROCKIN' KIDS, THE

DOT

Number	Title (A Side/B Side)	Yr	VG	VG+	NM
❑ 15749	Black Stockings/Yea Yea (I'm in the Mood)	1958	7.50	15.00	30.00

ROCKIN' R'S, THE

STEPHENY

Number	Title (A Side/B Side)	Yr	VG	VG+	NM
❑ 1842	Walkin' You to School/Bewitched (Bothered and Bewildered)	1960	6.25	12.50	25.00

TEMPUS

Number	Title (A Side/B Side)	Yr	VG	VG+	NM
❑ 1507	Nameless/Heat	1959	7.50	15.00	30.00
❑ 1515	Mustang/I'm Still in Love with You	1959	7.50	15.00	30.00
❑ 7541	Crazy Baby/The Beat	1959	10.00	20.00	40.00

VEE JAY

Number	Title (A Side/B Side)	Yr	VG	VG+	NM
❑ 334	Mustang/I'm Still in Love with You	1959	5.00	10.00	20.00
❑ 346	Hum Bug/The Mix	1960	5.00	10.00	20.00

ROCKIN' RAMRODS, THE

Number	Title (A Side/B Side)	Yr	VG	VG+	NM
BON-BON					
❑ 1315	She Lies/The Girl Can't Help It	1964	10.00	20.00	40.00
CLARIDGE					
❑ 301	Don't Fool with Fu Manchu/Tears	1965	5.00	10.00	20.00
❑ 317	Play It/Got My Mojo Workin'	1966	7.50	15.00	30.00
PLYMOUTH					
❑ 2961	I Wanna Be Your Man/I'll Be On My Way	1964	7.50	15.00	30.00
❑ 2963	Mister Wind/Bright Lit Blue Skies	1966	6.25	12.50	25.00
—As "The Ramrods"					
❑ 2965	Flowers in My Mind/Mary, Mary	1967	7.50	15.00	30.00
—As "The Ramrods"					

ROCKIN' REBELS, THE

Number	Title (A Side/B Side)	Yr	VG	VG+	NM
CORSICAN					
❑ 0056	Rockin' Crickets/Shakin' and Stompin'	1959	10.00	20.00	40.00
—As "The Hot-Toddys"					
ITZY					
❑ 8	Wild Weekend/Wild Weekend Cha Cha	1963	5.00	10.00	20.00
MAR-LEE					
❑ 0094	Wild Weekend/Wild Weekend Cha Cha	1960	25.00	50.00	100.00
—As "The Rebels"					
❑ 0095	Buffalo Blues/Donkey Walk	1961	7.50	15.00	30.00
—As "The Buffalo Rebels"					
❑ 0096	Theme from Rebel/Any Way You Want Me	1961	7.50	15.00	30.00
—As "The Buffalo Rebels"					
SHAN-TODD					
❑ 0056	Rockin' Crickets/Shakin' and Stompin'	1959	20.00	40.00	80.00
—As "The Hot-Toddys"					
STORK					
❑ 3	Bongo Blue Beat/Burn Baby Burn	1964	6.25	12.50	25.00
SWAN					
❑ 4125	Wild Weekend/Wild Weekend Cha Cha	1962	10.00	20.00	40.00
—First pressings credit "The Rebels"					
❑ 4125	Wild Weekend/Wild Weekend Cha Cha	1962	7.50	15.00	30.00
—Second pressings credit "Rockin' Rebels" and do not have "Don't Drop Out" on the label					
❑ 4125	Wild Weekend/Wild Weekend Cha Cha	1963	5.00	10.00	20.00
—Later pressings credit "Rockin' Rebels" and have "Don't Drop Out" on the label					
❑ 4140	Rockin' Crickets/Hully Gully Rock	1963	6.25	12.50	25.00
—A-side is the same recording as on Corsican and Shan-Todd					
❑ 4150	Another Wild Weekend/Happy Popcorn	1963	6.25	12.50	25.00
❑ 4161	Monday Morning/Flibbity Jibbit	1963	6.25	12.50	25.00
❑ 4248	Wild Weekend/Dockey Twine	1966	5.00	10.00	20.00

ROCKIN' SAINTS, THE

Number	Title (A Side/B Side)	Yr	VG	VG+	NM
DECCA					
❑ 30990	Saints Rock/Alright Baby	1959	7.50	15.00	30.00
❑ 31144	Cheat on Me, Baby/Half and Half	1960	20.00	40.00	80.00

ROCKIN' SIDNEY

Number	Title (A Side/B Side)	Yr	VG	VG+	NM
EPIC					
❑ 34-05430	My Toot Toot/Jalapeno Lena	1985	—	2.00	4.00
GOLDBAND					
❑ 1158	Actions Speak Louder Than Words/Lais Per La Patate	196?	3.00	6.00	12.00
❑ 1159	My Poor Heart/Something Working Baby	196?	3.00	6.00	12.00
❑ 1163	Deedle Didie Da/Life Without Love	196?	2.50	5.00	10.00
❑ 1170	Gonna Be Looking/Shed So Many Tears	196?	2.50	5.00	10.00
❑ 1177	Corpus Christi/(B-side unknown)	196?	3.00	6.00	12.00
❑ 1178	Trust/Put On It	196?	2.50	5.00	10.00
❑ 1183	Soul Christmas (Part 1)/Soul Christmas (Part 2)	1966	3.00	6.00	12.00
❑ 1186	The Grandpa/Feel Delicious	1967	2.50	5.00	10.00
JIN					
❑ 110	My Little Girl/Don't Say Goodbye	1959	12.50	25.00	50.00
❑ 141	Walking Out on You/Rocky	1960	7.50	15.00	30.00
❑ 156	No Good Woman/You Ain't Nothin' But Fine	1960	7.50	15.00	30.00
❑ 164	Send Me Some Lovin'/Past Bedtime	196?	7.50	15.00	30.00
❑ 168	No Good Man/If I Could, I Win	196?	7.50	15.00	30.00
❑ 170	Don't Let Me Cross Over/You Don't Have to Go	196?	7.50	15.00	30.00
❑ 174	Something's Wrong/It Really Is a Hurtin' Thing	196?	7.50	15.00	30.00
❑ 177	Ya Ya/Wasted Days and Wasted Nights	196?	7.50	15.00	30.00
MAISON DE SOUL					
❑ 1017	Good Time Woman/You Ain't Nothin' But Fine	198?	—	3.00	6.00
❑ 1020	Dance and Show Off/Relax and Go Slow	198?	—	3.00	6.00
❑ 1021	Boogie for Me/Sweet Li'l Woman	198?	—	3.00	6.00
❑ 1024	My Toot Toot/Zydeco Shoes	1984	2.00	4.00	8.00
❑ 1025	Party This Christmas/Christmas Without You	1984	—	3.00	6.00

ROCKIN' STOCKIN', THE

Number	Title (A Side/B Side)	Yr	VG	VG+	NM
SUN					
❑ 350	Rockin' Lang Syne/Yuleville U.S.A.	1960	7.50	15.00	30.00
❑ 1960	Rockin' Lang Syne/Yuleville U.S.A.	197?	3.75	7.50	15.00
—Reissue with green and red print on a white label with original Sun logo					

ROCKIN' VICKERS

Number	Title (A Side/B Side)	Yr	VG	VG+	NM
COLUMBIA					
❑ 43818	Dandy/I Don't Need Your Love	1966	3.00	6.00	12.00

ROCKING BROTHERS, THE

Number	Title (A Side/B Side)	Yr	VG	VG+	NM
IMPERIAL					
❑ 5333	Rock It/Behind the Sun	1955	7.50	15.00	30.00
❑ 5341	Blow Torch/Evening Shadows	1955	7.50	15.00	30.00
SAVOY					
❑ 1144	Play Boy Hop/The Grinder	1955	12.50	25.00	50.00
WHIPPET					
❑ 207	Yeah! Yeah!/Little Mike	1957	5.00	10.00	20.00

ROCKPILE

Also see DAVE EDMUNDS; NICK LOWE.

Number	Title (A Side/B Side)	Yr	VG	VG+	NM
COLUMBIA					
❑ 11388	Teacher Teacher/Fool Too Long	1980	—	2.00	4.00
❑ 11388 [PS]	Teacher Teacher/Fool Too Long	1980	2.50	5.00	10.00
—Promo-only sleeve detailing the history of Rockpile					
❑ 60503	Heart/Take a Message to Mary	1981	—	2.00	4.00
—B-side by Dave Edmunds and Nick Lowe					

ROCKY FELLERS, THE

Number	Title (A Side/B Side)	Yr	VG	VG+	NM
DONNA					
❑ 1383	Don't Sit Down/The Beachcomber Song	1963	3.00	6.00	12.00
PARKWAY					
❑ 836	Long Tall Sally/South Pacific Twist	1962	3.00	6.00	12.00
SCEPTER					
❑ 1245	Santa Santa/Great Big World	1962	5.00	10.00	20.00
—A-side is a very early Neil Diamond composition					
❑ 1245 [DJ]	Santa Santa/Santa's Grove	1963	3.00	6.00	12.00
—Promo reissue with new B-side. All-white label (no black oval)					
❑ 1245 [DJ]	Santa Santa (same on both sides)	196?	2.00	4.00	8.00
—Promo reissue; white label with mid-1960s Scepter Records logo (black oval)					
❑ 1246	Killer Joe/Lonely Teardrops	1963	3.75	7.50	15.00
❑ 1254	Like the Big Guys Do/Great Big World	1963	3.00	6.00	12.00
❑ 1254 [PS]	Like the Big Guys Do/Great Big World	1963	5.00	10.00	20.00
❑ 1258	Ching-a-Ling Baby/Hey Little Donkey	1963	3.00	6.00	12.00
❑ 1263	Bye Bye Baby/She Makes Me Wanna Dance	1963	3.00	6.00	12.00
❑ 1271	My Prayer/Two Guys from Trinidad	1964	3.00	6.00	12.00
VALMOR					
❑ 2004	Opus/Orange Peel	1962	3.75	7.50	15.00
WARNER BROS.					
❑ 5440	(Everybody Wants to Be a) Tiger/Jeannie Memsoh	1964	2.50	5.00	10.00
❑ 5459	Better Let Her Go/Nina	1964	2.50	5.00	10.00
❑ 5497	Man with the Blue Guitar/Don't Throw My Toys Away	1965	2.50	5.00	10.00
❑ 5613	Rented Tuxedo/Two Steps Downstairs in the Basement	1965	2.50	5.00	10.00

RODGERS, JIMMIE (1)

Legendary country & western singer known as "The Singing Brakeman."

Number	Title (A Side/B Side)	Yr	VG	VG+	NM
RCA VICTOR					
❑ WPT 21 [PS]	Yodelingly Yours, Jimmie Rodgers, Volume 1	1950	5.00	10.00	20.00
—Box for 27-0098, 27-0099 and 27-0100					
❑ AMAO-0130	Mule Skinner Blues/Waiting for a Train	1973	2.00	4.00	8.00
—Gold Standard Series reissue					
❑ 27-0098	Blue Yodel (T for Texas)/Away Out on the Mountain	1950	5.00	10.00	20.00
❑ 27-0099	Never No Mo' Blues/Daddy and Home	1950	5.00	10.00	20.00
❑ 27-0100	Frankie and Johnny/The Brakeman's Blues	1950	5.00	10.00	20.00
—The above three comprise box set WPT 21					
❑ 47-6092	In the Jailhouse Now No. 2/Peach Pickin' Time Down in Georgia	1955	5.00	10.00	20.00
❑ 47-6205	Mule Skinner Blues/Mother, the Queen of My Heart	1955	5.00	10.00	20.00
❑ 47-6408	Never No Mo' Blues/Daddy and Home	1955	5.00	10.00	20.00

7-Inch Extended Plays

Number	Title (A Side/B Side)	Yr	VG	VG+	NM
RCA VICTOR					
❑ EPAT 23	*My Carolina Sunshine Girl/Sleep, Baby, Sleep/Blue Yodel No. 2/Tuck Away My Lonesome Blues	1952	5.00	10.00	20.00
❑ EPAT 23 [PS]	Yodelingly Yours, Jimmie Rodgers, Volume 3	1952	5.00	10.00	20.00
❑ EPAT 409	(contents unknown)	195?	5.00	10.00	20.00
❑ EPAT 409 [PS]	Yodelingly Yours, Jimmie Rodgers, Volume 4	195?	5.00	10.00	20.00
❑ EPAT 410	(contents unknown)	195?	5.00	10.00	20.00
❑ EPAT 410 [PS]	Yodelingly Yours, Jimmie Rodgers, Volume 5	195?	5.00	10.00	20.00
❑ EPAT 411	*You and My Old Guitar/Prairie Lullaby/Old Pal of My Heart/My Little Lady	195?	5.00	10.00	20.00
❑ EPAT 411 [PS]	Yodelingly Yours, Jimmie Rodgers, Volume 6	195?	5.00	10.00	20.00

RODGERS, JIMMIE (2)

Pop-country vocalist, no relation to the above.

Number	Title (A Side/B Side)	Yr	VG	VG+	NM
A&M					
❑ 842	I'll Say Goodbye/Shadows	1967	—	3.00	6.00
❑ 871	Child of Clay/Turnaround	1967	—	3.00	6.00
❑ 898	If I Were the Man/What a Strange Town	1967	—	3.00	6.00
❑ 902	I Believe It All/You Pass Me By	1968	—	3.00	6.00
❑ 930	How Do You Say Goodbye/I Wanna Be Free	1968	—	3.00	6.00
❑ 976	Today/The Lovers	1968	—	3.00	6.00
❑ 1055	The Windmills of Your Mind/L.A. Break Down (And Take Me Back In)	1969	—	3.00	6.00
❑ 1120	Father Paul/Me About You	1969	—	3.00	6.00
❑ 1152	Cycles/Tomorrow My Friends	1969	—	3.00	6.00
❑ 1213	Troubled Times/The Dum Dum Song	1970	—	2.50	5.00
DOT					
❑ 16378	No One Will Ever Know/Because	1962	2.50	5.00	10.00
❑ 16378 [PS]	No One Will Ever Know/Because	1962	3.75	7.50	15.00
❑ 16407	Rainbow at Midnight/Rhumba Boogie	1962	2.50	5.00	10.00
❑ 16428	I'll Never Stand in Your Way/Afraid	1963	2.50	5.00	10.00
❑ 16450	Lonely Tears/A Face in the Crowd	1963	2.50	5.00	10.00
❑ 16467	(I Don't Know Why) I Just Do/Load 'Em Up (And Keep a Steppin')	1963	2.50	5.00	10.00
❑ 16490	Poor Little Raggedy Ann/I'm Gonna Be the Winner	1963	2.50	5.00	10.00
❑ 16527	Two-Ten Six-Eighteen (Doesn't Anybody Know My Name)/The Banana Boat Song	1963	2.50	5.00	10.00
❑ 16561	Together/Mama Was a Cotton Picker	1963	2.50	5.00	10.00
❑ 16595	The World I Used to Know/I Forgot More Than You'll Ever Know	1964	2.50	5.00	10.00
❑ 16653	Water Boy/Someplace Green	1964	2.50	5.00	10.00
❑ 16673	Two Tickets/I Forgot More Than You'll Ever Know	1964	2.50	5.00	10.00
❑ 16694	(All My Friends Are Gonna Be) Strangers/Bon Soir Mademoiselle	1965	2.00	4.00	8.00
❑ 16720	Careless Love/When I'm Right You Don't Remember	1965	2.00	4.00	8.00
❑ 16749	Are You Going My Way (Little Beachcomber)/Little Schoolgirl	1965	2.00	4.00	8.00

Number	Title (A Side/B Side)	Yr	VG	VG+	NM
16781	Bye Bye Love/Hollow Words	1965	2.00	4.00	8.00
16795	The Chipmunk Song (Christmas Don't Be Late)/ In the Snow	1965	2.00	4.00	8.00
16826	A Falen Star/Brother, Where Are You	1966	2.00	4.00	8.00
16861	It's Over/Anita, You're Dreaming	1966	2.50	5.00	10.00
16916	Morning Means Tomorrow/New Ideas	1966	2.00	4.00	8.00
16973	Love Me, Please Love Me/Wonderful You	1966	2.00	4.00	8.00
17040	Time/Yours and Mine	1967	2.00	4.00	8.00

EPIC

Number	Title (A Side/B Side)	Yr	VG	VG+	NM
10828	Froggy's Fable/Daylight Lights the Dawning	1972	—	2.50	5.00
10857	Kick the Can/Go On By	1972	—	2.50	5.00

MGM

Number	Title (A Side/B Side)	Yr	VG	VG+	NM
11732	Mama, Don't Cry at My Wedding/You Don't Live Here No More	1954	6.25	12.50	25.00

ROULETTE

Number	Title (A Side/B Side)	Yr	VG	VG+	NM
4015	Honeycomb/Their Hearts Were Full of Spring	1957	5.00	10.00	20.00
4031	Kisses Sweeter Than Wine/Better Loved You'll Never Be	1957	5.00	10.00	20.00
4045	Oh-Oh, I'm Falling in Love Again/The Long Hot Summer	1958	5.00	10.00	20.00
—Red label					
4045	Oh-Oh, I'm Falling in Love Again/The Long Hot Summer	1958	3.75	7.50	15.00
—White label with colored spokes					
4070	Secretly/Make Me a Miracle	1958	5.00	10.00	20.00
4070 [PS]	Secretly/Make Me a Miracle	1958	10.00	20.00	40.00
4090	Are You Really Mine/The Wizard	1958	3.75	7.50	15.00
4090 [PS]	Are You Really Mine/The Wizard	1958	10.00	20.00	40.00
4116	Bimbombey/You Understand Me	1958	3.75	7.50	15.00
4129	I'm Never Gonna Tell/Because You're Young	1959	3.75	7.50	15.00
4158 [M]	Ring-a-Ling-a-Lario/Wonderful You	1959	3.75	7.50	15.00
4158 [PS]	Ring-a-Ling-a-Lario/Wonderful You	1959	6.25	12.50	25.00
SSR-4158 [S]	Ring-a-Ling-a-Lario/Wonderful You	1959	7.50	15.00	30.00
4191	Tucumcari/That Night You Became Seventeen	1959	3.75	7.50	15.00
4205	It's Christmas Once Again/Wistful Willie	1959	5.00	10.00	20.00
4218 [M]	T.L.C. Tender Love and Care/Waltzing Matilda	1960	3.00	6.00	12.00
SSR-4218 [S]	T.L.C. Tender Love and Care/Waltzing Matilda	1960	7.50	15.00	30.00
4234	Just a Closer Walk with Thee/Joshua Fit the Battle of Jericho	1960	3.00	6.00	12.00
4260	The Wreck of the John B/Four Little Girls in Boston	1960	3.00	6.00	12.00
4293	Woman from Liberia/Come Along Julie	1960	3.00	6.00	12.00
4293 [PS]	Woman from Liberia/Come Along Julie	1960	5.00	10.00	20.00
4318	When Love Is Young/The Little Shepherd of Kingdom Come	1960	3.00	6.00	12.00
4349	Everytime My Heart Sings/I'm On My Way	1961	3.00	6.00	12.00
4371	John Brown's Baby/I'm Going Home	1961	3.00	6.00	12.00
4384	A Little Dog Cried/Englidh Country Garden	1961	3.00	6.00	12.00
4439	You Are Everything to Me/Wanderin' Eyes	1962	3.00	6.00	12.00
SSR-8001 [S]	Bo Diddley/Soldier Won't You Marry Me	1959	7.50	15.00	30.00
SSR-8007 [S]	Froggy Went a-Courtin'/Lisa	1959	7.50	15.00	30.00
SSR-8010 [S]	St. James Infirmary/Just a Wearyin' for You	1959	7.50	15.00	30.00

SCRIMSHAW

Number	Title (A Side/B Side)	Yr	VG	VG+	NM
1313	A Good Woman Likes to Drink with the Boys/ Dancing on the Moon	1977	—	2.00	4.00
1314	Everytime I Sing a Love Song/Just a Little Time	1978	—	2.00	4.00
1316	When Our Love Began (Cowboys and Indians)/ (B-side unknown)	1978	—	2.00	4.00
1318	Secretly/Shovelin' Coal	1978	—	2.00	4.00
1319/20	Easy to Love/Easy	1979	—	2.00	4.00
—With Michele					

7-Inch Extended Plays

ROULETTE

Number	Title (A Side/B Side)	Yr	VG	VG+	NM
EPR-1-303	Woman from Liberia/The Mating Call//Hey Little Baby/Water Boy	1957	12.50	25.00	50.00
EPR-1-303 [PS]	Jimmie Rodgers	1957	12.50	25.00	50.00
EPR-1-312	*Honeycomb/Oh-Oh, I'm Falling in Love Again/ The Preacher/Better Loved You'll Never Be	195?	12.50	25.00	50.00
EPR-1-312 [PS]	Jimmie Rodgers Sings	195?	12.50	25.00	50.00
EPR-1-313	*Tammy/The Song from Moulin Rouge/Love Letters in the Sand/Hey There	195?	12.50	25.00	50.00
EPR-1-313 [PS]	The Number One Ballads, Part 1	195?	12.50	25.00	50.00
EPR-1-315	Bo Diddley/Riddle Song//The Fox and the Goose/ Black Is the Color	1960	12.50	25.00	50.00
EPR-1-315 [PS]	Jimmie Rodgers Sings Folk Songs, Part I	1960	12.50	25.00	50.00
EPR-1-316	Waltzing Matilda/The Crocodile//Lord Randal/ Gotta Lotta Tunes in My Guitar	195?	12.50	25.00	50.00
EPR-1-316 [PS]	Jimmie Rodgers Sings Folk Songs, Part II	195?	12.50	25.00	50.00
EPR-1-317	Soldier, Won't You Marry Me?/Lassie O'Mine// Liza/Froggy Went a-Courtin'	1960	12.50	25.00	50.00
EPR-1-317 [PS]	Jimmie Rodgers Sings Folk Songs, Part III	1960	12.50	25.00	50.00

RODGERS, PAUL

Also see BAD COMPANY; FREE.

ATLANTIC

Number	Title (A Side/B Side)	Yr	VG	VG+	NM
89709	The Morning After the Night Before/Northwinds	1984	—	2.00	4.00
89749	Cut Loose/Talking Guitar Blues	1983	—	2.00	4.00
89749 [PS]	Cut Loose/Talking Guitar Blues	1983	—	2.00	4.00

ROE, TOMMY

ABC

Number	Title (A Side/B Side)	Yr	VG	VG+	NM
10762	Sweet Pea/Much More Love	1966	2.50	5.00	10.00
—Reissue; this was the common version when this song was a hit; earliest copies have "ABC Records" standing alone (not in a circle)					
10852	Hooray for Hazel/Need Your Love	1966	2.50	5.00	10.00
10888	It's Now Winters Day/Kick Me Charlie	1966	2.00	4.00	8.00
10888 [PS]	It's Now Winters Day/Kick Me Charlie	1966	3.75	7.50	15.00
10908	Sing Along with Me/Night Time	1967	2.00	4.00	8.00
10933	Moon Talk/Sweet Sounds	1967	2.00	4.00	8.00
10945	Little Miss Sunshine/You I Need	1967	2.00	4.00	8.00
10989	Melancholy Mood/Paisley Dreams	1967	2.00	4.00	8.00
11039	Dottie I Like It/Soft Words	1968	2.00	4.00	8.00
11076	An Oldie But a Goodie/Sugar Cane	1968	2.00	4.00	8.00
11140	It's Gonna Hurt Me/Gotta Keep Rolling Along	1968	2.00	4.00	8.00
11164	Dizzy/The You I Need	1969	2.50	5.00	10.00
11211	Heather Honey/Money Is My Pay	1969	—	3.00	6.00
11229	Jack and Jill/Tip Toe Tina	1969	—	3.00	6.00
11247	Jam Up Jelly Tight/Moontalk	1969	2.00	4.00	8.00
11247 [PS]	Jam Up Jelly Tight/Moontalk	1969	3.00	6.00	12.00
11258	Stir It Up and Serve It/Fire Fly	1970	—	3.00	6.00
11266	Pearl/A Dollar's Worth of Pennies	1970	—	3.00	6.00
11273	We Can Make Music/Gotta Keep Rolling Along	1970	—	3.00	6.00
11273 [PS]	We Can Make Music/Gotta Keep Rolling Along	1970	—	3.00	6.00
11281	King of Fools/Brush a Little Sunshine	1970	—	3.00	6.00
11287	Little Miss Goodie Two Shoes/Traffic Jam	1971	—	3.00	6.00
11293	King of Fools/Pistol-Legged Mama	1971	—	3.00	6.00
11307	Stagger Lee/Back Streets and Alleys	1971	—	3.00	6.00

ABC-PARAMOUNT

Number	Title (A Side/B Side)	Yr	VG	VG+	NM
10329	Sheila/Save Your Kisses	1962	3.75	7.50	15.00
10362	Susie Darlin'/Piddle De Pat	1962	3.00	6.00	12.00
10362 [PS]	Susie Darlin'/Piddle De Pat	1962	6.25	12.50	25.00
10379	Town Crier/Rainbow	1962	3.00	6.00	12.00
10389	Don't Cry Donna/Gonna Take a Chance	1962	3.00	6.00	12.00
10423	The Folk Singer/Count on Me	1963	2.50	5.00	10.00
10454	Kiss and Run/What Makes the Blues	1963	2.50	5.00	10.00
10478	Everybody/Sorry I'm Late, Lisa	1963	3.75	7.50	15.00
10515	Come On/There Will Be Better Years	1964	2.50	5.00	10.00
10543	Carol/Be a Good Little Girl	1964	2.50	5.00	10.00
10555	Dance with Me/Wild Water Skiing Weekend	1964	5.00	10.00	20.00
10579	Oh So Right/I Think I Love You	1964	3.00	6.00	12.00
10604	Party Girl/Oh How I Could Love You	1964	2.50	5.00	10.00
10623	Love Me, Love Me/Diane from Manchester Square	1965	3.00	6.00	12.00
10665	Fourteen Pair of Shoes/Combo Music	1965	2.50	5.00	10.00
10696	The Gunfighter/I'm a Rambler, I'm a Gambler	1965	5.00	10.00	20.00
10706	I Keep Remembering (Things I Forgot)/Wish You Didn't Have to Go	1965	2.50	5.00	10.00
10738	Doesn't Anybody Know My Name/Everytime a Bluebird Cries	1965	2.50	5.00	10.00
10762	Sweet Pea/Much More Love	1966	6.25	12.50	25.00

AWESOME

Number	Title (A Side/B Side)	Yr	VG	VG+	NM
104	First Things First/(B-side unknown)	1984	—	3.00	6.00
108	Sittin' on a Mood/(B-side unknown)	1984	—	3.00	6.00

BGO

Number	Title (A Side/B Side)	Yr	VG	VG+	NM
1003	She Do Run Run/(B-side unknown)	1982	2.50	5.00	10.00

JUDD

Number	Title (A Side/B Side)	Yr	VG	VG+	NM
1018	Caveman/I Gotta Girl	1960	12.50	25.00	50.00
1022	Sheila/Pretty Girl	1960	37.50	75.00	150.00

MARK IV

Number	Title (A Side/B Side)	Yr	VG	VG+	NM
001	Caveman/I Gotta Girl	1960	25.00	50.00	100.00

MCA CURB

Number	Title (A Side/B Side)	Yr	VG	VG+	NM
52711	Some Such Foolishness/Barbara Lou	1985	—	2.00	4.00
52778	Radio Romance/Barbara Lou	1986	—	2.00	4.00

MERCURY

Number	Title (A Side/B Side)	Yr	VG	VG+	NM
888206-7	Let's Be Fools Like That Again/Barbara Lou	1986	—	—	3.00
888497-7	Back When It Really Mattered/Radio Romance	1987	—	—	3.00

MGM SOUTH

Number	Title (A Side/B Side)	Yr	VG	VG+	NM
7001	Mean Little Woman, Rosalie/Skyline	1972	—	2.50	5.00
7008	Sarah My Love/Chewing on Sugar Cane	1972	—	2.50	5.00
7013	Working Class Hero/Sun in My Eyes	1973	—	2.50	5.00
7025	Silver Eyes/Memphis Me	1973	—	3.00	6.00

MONUMENT

Number	Title (A Side/B Side)	Yr	VG	VG+	NM
8644	Glitter and Gleam/Bad News	1975	—	2.50	5.00
8662	Snowing Me Under/Rita and Her Band	1975	—	2.50	5.00
8684	Slow Dancing/Burn On Love Light	1976	—	2.50	5.00
8705	Everybody/Energy	1976	—	2.50	5.00
45205	Early in the Morning/Bad News	1976	—	2.50	5.00
45228	Your Love Will See Me Through/Working Class Hero	1977	—	2.50	5.00

TRUMPET

Number	Title (A Side/B Side)	Yr	VG	VG+	NM
1401	Caveman/I Gotta Girl	1960	50.00	100.00	200.00

WARNER BROS.

Number	Title (A Side/B Side)	Yr	VG	VG+	NM
8660	Dreamin' Again/Love the Way You Love Me Up	1978	—	2.00	4.00
8720	Just Look at Me/Love the Way You Love Me Up	1978	—	2.50	5.00
8800	Massachusetts/Just Look at Me	1979	—	2.50	5.00
49085	You Better Move On/Just Look at Me	1979	—	2.00	4.00
49235	Charlie, I Love Your Wife/There Is No Sun on Sunset Boulevard	1980	—	2.00	4.00

ROEMANS, THE

TOMMY ROE's backing group.

ABC

Number	Title (A Side/B Side)	Yr	VG	VG+	NM
10814	When the Sun Shines in the Mornin'/Love (That's All I Want)	1966	3.75	7.50	15.00
10871	All the Good Things/Pleasing You Pleases Me	1966	3.75	7.50	15.00

ABC-PARAMOUNT

Number	Title (A Side/B Side)	Yr	VG	VG+	NM
10583	Give Me a Chance/Your Friend	1964	5.00	10.00	20.00
10671	Miserlou/Don't	1965	5.00	10.00	20.00
10723	Universal Soldier/Lost Little Girl	1965	5.00	10.00	20.00
10757	Listen to Me/You Make Me Feel Good	1965	5.00	10.00	20.00

ROGER AND THE TRAVELERS

EMBER

Number	Title (A Side/B Side)	Yr	VG	VG+	NM
1079	You're Daddy's Little Girl/Just Gonna Be That Way	1961	25.00	50.00	100.00

ROGERS, JIMMY

CHESS

Number	Title (A Side/B Side)	Yr	VG	VG+	NM
1506	I Used to Love a Woman/Back Door Friend	1952	50.00	100.00	200.00
—Earlier Jimmy Rogers 45s on Chess are not known to exist					
1519	The Last Time/Out on the Road	1952	50.00	100.00	200.00
1543	Left Me with a Broken Heart/Act Like You Love Me	1953	50.00	100.00	200.00
1574	Chicago Bound/Sloppy Drunk	1954	75.00	150.00	300.00

Number	Title (A Side/B Side)	Yr	VG	VG+	NM
❑ 1616	You're the One/Blues All Day Long	1956	12.50	25.00	50.00
❑ 1643	Walking By Myself/If It Ain't Me	1956	12.50	25.00	50.00
❑ 1659	One Kiss/I Can't Believe	1957	12.50	25.00	50.00
❑ 1687	What Have I Done/Trace of You	1958	10.00	20.00	40.00
❑ 1721	Rock This House/My Last Meal	1959	7.50	15.00	30.00

ROGERS, JULIE

MEGA

Number	Title (A Side/B Side)	Yr	VG	VG+	NM
❑ 0075	Almost Close to You/Where Do You Go	1972	—	2.50	5.00

MERCURY

Number	Title (A Side/B Side)	Yr	VG	VG+	NM
❑ 72332	The Wedding/Without Your Love	1964	2.50	5.00	10.00
—Black label					
❑ 72332	The Wedding/Without Your Love	1964	2.00	4.00	8.00
—Red label					
❑ 72380	Like a Child/The Love of a Boy	1965	2.00	4.00	8.00
❑ 72380 [PS]	Like a Child/The Love of a Boy	1965	3.00	6.00	12.00
❑ 72426	Hawaiian Wedding Song/Turn Around, Look at Me	1965	2.00	4.00	8.00
❑ 72535	Another Year, Another Love, Another Heartache/Don't Waste Your Young Years on Him	1966	2.00	4.00	8.00
❑ 72646	Climb Ev'ry Mountain/While the Angelus Was Ringing	1966	2.00	4.00	8.00

ROGERS, KENNY

Also see THE FIRST EDITION; THE SCHOLARS (1).

CARLTON

Number	Title (A Side/B Side)	Yr	VG	VG+	NM
❑ 454	That Crazy Feeling/We'll Always Have Each Other	1958	25.00	50.00	100.00
—As "Kenneth Rogers"					
❑ 454	That Crazy Feeling/We'll Always Have Each Other	1958	25.00	50.00	100.00
—As "Kenny Rogers"					
❑ 468	For You Alone/I've Got a Lot to Learn	1958	15.00	30.00	60.00

KEN-LEE

Number	Title (A Side/B Side)	Yr	VG	VG+	NM
❑ 102	Jole Blon/Lonely	195?	25.00	50.00	100.00

LIBERTY

Number	Title (A Side/B Side)	Yr	VG	VG+	NM
❑ 1380	Lady/Sweet Music Man	1980	—	2.00	4.00
❑ 1380 [PS]	Lady/Sweet Music Man	1980	—	2.50	5.00
❑ 1391	Long Arm of the Law/You Were a Good Friend	1980	—	2.00	4.00
❑ 1415	I Don't Need You/Without You in My Life	1981	—	—	3.00
❑ 1415 [PS]	I Don't Need You/Without You in My Life	1981	—	2.00	4.00
❑ 1430	Share Your Love with Me/Greybeard	1981	—	—	3.00
❑ 1430 [PS]	Share Your Love with Me/Greybeard	1981	—	2.00	4.00
❑ 1438	Kentucky Homemade Christmas/Carol of the Bells	1981	—	2.50	5.00
❑ 1438 [PS]	Kentucky Homemade Christmas/Carol of the Bells	1981	—	3.00	6.00
❑ 1441	Blaze of Glory/The Good Life	1981	—	—	3.00
❑ 1444	Through the Years/So In Love with You	1981	—	—	3.00
❑ 1471	Love Will Turn You Around/I Want a Son	1982	—	—	3.00
❑ 1471 [PS]	Love Will Turn You Around/I Want a Son	1982	—	2.50	5.00
❑ 1485	A Love Song/Fool in Me	1982	—	—	3.00
❑ 1492	We've Got Tonight/You Are So Beautiful	1983	—	2.00	4.00
—A-side with Sheena Easton					
❑ 1492 [PS]	We've Got Tonight/You Are So Beautiful	1983	—	2.50	5.00
❑ 1495	All My Life/The Farther I Go	1983	—	—	3.00
❑ 1495 [PS]	All My Life/The Farther I Go	1983	—	2.00	4.00
❑ 1503	Scarlet Fever/What I Learned from Loving You	1983	—	—	3.00
❑ 1511	Sweet Music Man/You Were a Good Friend	1983	—	—	3.00
❑ 1524	A Stranger in My Place/Love Is What We Make It	1985	—	—	3.00
❑ 1525	Twentieth Century Fool/It Turns Me Inside Out	1985	—	—	3.00
❑ 1526	Abraham, Martin and John/Goodbye Marie	1985	—	—	3.00
❑ 4065 [DJ]	Christmas Everyday//Kentucky Homemade Christmas/Carol Of The Bells	198?	—	3.00	6.00

MERCURY

Number	Title (A Side/B Side)	Yr	VG	VG+	NM
❑ 72545	Here's That Rainy Day/Take Life in Stride	1966	6.25	12.50	25.00

RCA

Number	Title (A Side/B Side)	Yr	VG	VG+	NM
❑ 5016-7-R	They Don't Make Them Like They Used To/Just the Thought of Losing You	1986	—	—	3.00
❑ 5016-7-R [PS]	They Don't Make Them Like They Used To/Just the Thought of Losing You	1986	—	—	3.00
❑ 5078-7-R	Twenty Years Ago/The Heart of the Matter	1986	—	—	3.00
❑ 5209-7-R	Make No Mistake, She's Mine/You're My Love	1987	—	—	3.00
—With Ronnie Milsap					
❑ 5258-7-R	I Prefer the Moonlight/We're Doin' Alright	1987	—	—	3.00
❑ 6832-7-R	The Factory/One More Day	1987	—	—	3.00
❑ 8381-7-R	I Prefer the Moonlight/Make No Mistake, She's Mine	1988	—	—	3.00
—Gold Standard Series; B-side with Ronnie Milsap					
❑ 8390-7-R	I Don't Call Him Daddy/We're Doin' Alright	1988	—	—	3.00
❑ PB-13710	This Woman/Buried Treasure	1984	—	—	3.00
❑ PB-13710 [PS]	This Woman/Buried Treasure	1984	—	2.00	4.00
❑ JK-13713 [DJ]	Buried Treasure (same on both sides)	1984	—	2.50	5.00
❑ PB-13774	Eyes That See in the Dark/Hold Me	1984	—	—	3.00
❑ PB-13832	Evening Star/Midsummer Nights	1984	—	—	3.00
❑ PB-13899	What About Me/The Rest of Last Night	1984	—	—	3.00
—With Kim Carnes and James Ingram					
❑ PB-13899 [PS]	What About Me/The Rest of Last Night	1984	—	2.00	4.00
❑ PB-13944	The Christmas Song/Medley: Winter Wonderland-Sleigh Ride	1984	—	2.00	4.00
—B-side by Dolly Parton					
❑ PB-13975	Crazy/The Stranger	1984	—	—	3.00
❑ PB-13975 [PS]	Crazy/The Stranger	1984	—	2.00	4.00
❑ GB-14074	This Woman/What About Me	1985	—	—	3.00
—Gold Standard Series; B-side by Kenny Rogers, Kim Carnes and James Ingram					
❑ PB-14194	Morning Desire/People in Love	1985	—	—	3.00
❑ PB-14194 [PS]	Morning Desire/People in Love	1985	—	2.00	4.00
—Fold-out poster sleeve					
❑ PB-14298	Tomb of the Unknown Love/Our Perfect Song	1986	—	—	3.00
❑ PB-14298 [PS]	Tomb of the Unknown Love/Our Perfect Song	1986	—	2.00	4.00
❑ GB-14353	Crazy/Morning Desire	1986	—	—	3.00
—Gold Standard Series					
❑ PB-14384	The Pride Is Back/Didn't We?	1986	—	2.00	4.00
—A-side: With Nickie Ryder					
❑ PB-14384 [PS]	The Pride Is Back/Didn't We?	1986	—	2.00	4.00

REPRISE

Number	Title (A Side/B Side)	Yr	VG	VG+	NM
❑ PRO-S-3904 [DJ]	Maybe (same on both sides)	1990	—	3.00	6.00
—With Holly Dunn					
❑ 18835	Bed of Roses/I'll Be There for You	1992	—	—	3.00
❑ 18967	Someone Must Feel Like a Fool Tonight/Sunshine	1992	—	—	3.00
❑ 19080	If You Want to Find Love/Sunshine	1991	—	—	3.00
❑ 19324	Walk Away/What I Did for Love	1991	—	—	3.00
❑ 19504	Lay My Body Down/Crazy in Love	1991	—	—	3.00
❑ 19972	Maybe/If I Knew Then What I Know Now	1990	—	—	3.00
—A-side with Holly Dunn; B-side with Gladys Knight					
❑ 22750	Christmas in America/Joy to the World	1989	—	—	3.00
❑ 22750 [PS]	Christmas in America/Joy to the World	1989	—	—	3.00
❑ 22828	The Vows Go Unbroken (Always True to You)/One Night	1989	—	—	3.00
❑ 22853	(Something Inside) So Strong/When You Put Your Heart In It	1989	—	—	3.00
❑ 27690	Planet Texas/When You Put Your Heart in It	1988	—	—	3.00
❑ 27690 [PS]	Planet Texas/When You Put Your Heart in It	1988	—	—	3.00
❑ 27812	When You Put Your Heart In It/(Instrumental)	1988	—	—	3.00
❑ 27812 [PS]	When You Put Your Heart In It/(Instrumental)	1988	—	—	3.00

UNITED ARTISTS

Number	Title (A Side/B Side)	Yr	VG	VG+	NM
❑ XW746	Love Lifted Me/Home-Made Love	1975	—	2.00	4.00
❑ XW798	There's an Old Man in Our Town/Home-Made Love	1976	—	2.00	4.00
❑ XW812	I Would Like to See You Again/While the Feeling's Good	1976	—	2.00	4.00
❑ XW868	Laura (What's He Got That I Ain't Got)/I Wasn't Mad Enough	1976	—	2.00	4.00
❑ XW929	Lucille/Till I Get It Right	1976	—	2.00	4.00
❑ XW1027	Daytime Friends/We Don't Make Love Anymore	1977	—	2.00	4.00
❑ XW1095	Sweet Music Man/Lying Again	1977	—	2.00	4.00
❑ XW1151	Love Lifted Me/Reuben James	1978	—	2.00	4.00
❑ XW1152	Today I Started Loving You Again/Just Dropped In (To See What Condition My Condition Was In)	1978	—	2.00	4.00
❑ XW1153	Daytime Friends/But You Know I Love You	1978	—	2.00	4.00
❑ XW1154	Lucille/Something's Burning	1978	—	2.00	4.00
❑ XW1155	Sweet Music Man/Ruby, Don't Take Your Love to Town	1978	—	2.00	4.00
—B-sides of the above five singles are re-recordings of First Edition hits paired with early United Artists country hits					
❑ XW1210	Love Or Something Like It/Starting Again	1978	—	2.00	4.00
❑ XW1250	The Gambler/Momma's Waiting	1978	—	2.00	4.00
❑ XW1273	She Believes in Me/Morgana Jones	1979	—	2.00	4.00
❑ XW1273 [PS]	She Believes in Me/Morgana Jones	1979	—	2.50	5.00
❑ 1315	You Decorated My Life/One Man's Woman	1979	—	2.00	4.00
❑ 1315 [PS]	You Decorated My Life/One Man's Woman	1979	—	2.50	5.00
❑ 1327	Coward of the County/I Wanna Make You Smile	1979	—	2.00	4.00
❑ 1345	Don't Fall in Love with a Dreamer/Intro: Goin' Home to the Rock-Gideon Tanner	1980	—	2.00	4.00
—A-side: With Kim Carnes					
❑ 1345 [PS]	Don't Fall in Love with a Dreamer/Intro: Goin' Home to the Rock-Gideon Tanner	1980	—	2.50	5.00
❑ 1359	Love the World Away/Sayin' Goodbye-Requiem	1980	—	2.00	4.00

ROGERS, KENNY, AND DOLLY PARTON

Also see each artist's individual listings.

RCA

Number	Title (A Side/B Side)	Yr	VG	VG+	NM
❑ 5352-7-R	Christmas Without You/I Believe in Santa Claus	1987	—	—	3.00
—B-side by Dolly Parton					
❑ 9070-7-R	Christmas Without You/Medley: Winter Wonderland-Sleigh Ride	1989	—	—	3.00
—B-side by Dolly Parton					
❑ PB-13615	Islands in the Stream/I Will Always Love You	1983	—	—	3.00
❑ PB-13615 [PS]	Islands in the Stream/I Will Always Love You	1983	—	2.50	5.00
—Version 1: With "(Duet with Dolly Parton)" in small letters					
❑ PB-13615 [PS]	Islands in the Stream/I Will Always Love You	1983	—	2.00	4.00
—Version 2: With Dolly Parton's name the same size as Kenny Rogers'					
❑ PB-13945	The Greatest Gift of All/White Christmas	1984	—	2.00	4.00
❑ PB-14058	Real Love/I Can't Be True	1985	—	—	3.00
❑ GB-14073	Islands in the Stream/Eyes That See in the Dark	1985	—	—	3.00
—Gold Standard Series; B-side by Kenny Rogers					
❑ PB-14261	Christmas Without You/A Christmas to Remember	1985	—	—	3.00
❑ PB-14261 [PS]	Christmas Without You/A Christmas to Remember	1985	—	2.00	4.00

REPRISE

Number	Title (A Side/B Side)	Yr	VG	VG+	NM
❑ 19760	Love Is Strange/Walk Away	1990	—	—	3.00

ROGERS, KENNY, AND THE FIRST EDITION

See THE FIRST EDITION.

ROGERS, KENNY, AND DOTTIE WEST

Also see each artist's individual listings.

LIBERTY

Number	Title (A Side/B Side)	Yr	VG	VG+	NM
❑ 1516	Baby I'm-a Want You/Together Again	1984	—	—	3.00

UNITED ARTISTS

Number	Title (A Side/B Side)	Yr	VG	VG+	NM
❑ XW1137	Every Time Two Fools Collide/We Love Each Other	1978	—	2.00	4.00
❑ XW1234	Anyone Who Isn't Me Tonight/You and Me	1978	—	2.00	4.00
❑ XW1276	All I Ever Need Is You/Another Somebody Done Somebody Wrong Song	1979	—	2.00	4.00
❑ XW1299	Till I Can Make It on My Own/Midnight Flyer	1979	—	2.00	4.00

ROGERS, MORRIS, AND THE CONTINENTALS

DELTA

Number	Title (A Side/B Side)	Yr	VG	VG+	NM
❑ 601/2	The Leg/Wonders of Love	1963	50.00	100.00	200.00

ROGERS, ROY

Number	Title (A Side/B Side)	Yr	VG	VG+	NM
20TH CENTURY					
❑ 2154	Hoppy, Gene & Me/Good News, Bad News	1974	—	3.00	6.00
❑ 2173	Happy Trails/Don't Cry, Baby	1975	—	3.00	6.00
❑ 2209	Cowboy Heaven/Don't Ever Wear It for Him	1975	—	3.00	6.00
CAPITOL					
❑ 2895	Money Can't Buy Love/You and Me Against the World	1970	2.00	4.00	8.00
❑ 3016	Lovenworth/Vision at the Peace Table	1971	2.00	4.00	8.00
❑ 3117	Happy Anniversary/If I Ever Get That Close Again	1971	2.00	4.00	8.00
❑ 3263	These Are the Good Old Days/Pass It On	1972	2.00	4.00	8.00
❑ 3338	Homemade Love/Love Rides a Big White Horse	1972	2.00	4.00	8.00
❑ 3490	Talkin' About Love/In Another Lifetime	1972	2.00	4.00	8.00
MCA					
❑ 41294	Ride Concrete Cowboy Ride/Deliverance of the Wildwood Flower	1980	—	2.50	5.00
—With the Sons of the Pioneers; B-side by the Bandit Band					
RCA VICTOR					
❑ 47-0200	Pecos Bill — Part 1/Pecos Bill — Part 4	1949	10.00	20.00	40.00
—Blue label, yellow vinyl					
❑ 47-0201	Pecos Bill — Part 2/Pecos Bill — Part 3	1949	10.00	20.00	40.00
—Blue label, yellow vinyl; the above two records comprise set "WY 389"					
❑ 47-0228	Roy Rogers' Rodeo — Part 1/Roy Rogers' Rodeo — Part 4	1950	10.00	20.00	40.00
—Blue label, yellow vinyl					
❑ 47-0229	Roy Rogers' Rodeo — Part 2/Roy Rogers' Rodeo — Part 3	1950	10.00	20.00	40.00
—Blue label, yellow vinyl; the above two comprise album "WY 413"					
❑ 47-0255	Frosty the Snowman/Gabby the Gobbler	1950	10.00	20.00	40.00
—Blue label, yellow vinyl					
❑ 47-0306	Egbert the Easter Egg/Peter Cottontail	1951	10.00	20.00	40.00
—Blue label, yellow vinyl					
❑ 47-0306 [PS]	Egbert the Easter Egg/Peter Cottontail	1951	20.00	40.00	80.00
—Blue label, yellow vinyl					
❑ 47-2806	Don't Fence Me In/Roll On Texas Moon	1949	10.00	20.00	40.00
❑ 47-2807	The Yellow Rose of Texas/On the Old Spanish Trail	1949	10.00	20.00	40.00
❑ 47-2808	San Fernando Valley/Along the Navajo Trail	1949	10.00	20.00	40.00
❑ 47-2809	Home in Oklahoma/A Gay Ranchero	1949	10.00	20.00	40.00
❑ 47-4237	Punky Punkin/The Kiwi Bird	1951	7.50	15.00	30.00
❑ 47-4242	I'm Gonna Lock You Out/Put All Your Kisses in an Envelope	1951	7.50	15.00	30.00
❑ 47-4301	Daddy's Cowboy/The Three Little Dwarfs	1951	7.50	15.00	30.00
❑ 47-4424	Horseshoe Moon/Home Sweet Oklahoma	1951	7.50	15.00	30.00
❑ 47-4520	Egbert the Easter Egg/Peter Cottontail	1952	7.50	15.00	30.00
❑ 47-4634	Four Legged Friend/There's a Cloud in My Valley of Sunshine	1952	7.50	15.00	30.00
❑ 47-4664	The Little White Duck/The Kiwi Bird	1952	7.50	15.00	30.00
❑ 47-4709	Happy Trails/California Rose	1952	10.00	20.00	40.00
❑ 47-4732	Peace in the Valley/Precious Memories	1952	7.50	15.00	30.00
❑ 47-4950	Hazy Mountains/You've Got a Rope Around My Heart	1952	7.50	15.00	30.00
❑ 48-0008	Don't Fence Me In/Roll On Texas Moon	1949	10.00	20.00	40.00
—Originals on green vinyl					
❑ 48-0009	The Yellow Rose of Texas/On the Old Spanish Trail	1949	10.00	20.00	40.00
—Originals on green vinyl					
❑ 48-0010	San Fernando Valley/Along the Navajo Trail	1949	10.00	20.00	40.00
—Originals on green vinyl					
❑ 48-0011	Home in Oklahoma/A Gay Ranchero	1949	10.00	20.00	40.00
—Originals on green vinyl					
❑ 48-0028	My Heart Went That-a-Way/No Children Allowed	1949	12.50	25.00	50.00
—Originals on green vinyl					
❑ 48-0034	The Kid with the Rip in His Pants/Dusty	1949	12.50	25.00	50.00
—Originals on green vinyl					
❑ 48-0035	Blue Shadows on the Trail/(There'll Never Be Another) Pecos Bill	1949	12.50	25.00	50.00
—Originals on green vinyl					
❑ 48-0074	Home on the Range/That Palomino Pal of Mine	1949	12.50	25.00	50.00
—Originals on green vinyl					
❑ 48-0115	My Chickashay Gal/A Little White Cross on the Hill	1949	10.00	20.00	40.00
—Originals on green vinyl					
❑ 48-0116	No Children Allowed/I Wish I Had Never Met Sunshine	1949	10.00	20.00	40.00
—Originals on green vinyl					
❑ 48-0117	My Heart Went That-a-Way/Dusty	1949	10.00	20.00	40.00
—Originals on green vinyl					
❑ 48-0152	Little Hula Honey/Mommy Can I Take My Doll to Heaven	1950	10.00	20.00	40.00
—Originals on green vinyl					
❑ 48-0161	Stampede/Church Music	1950	10.00	20.00	40.00
—Originals on green vinyl					
❑ 48-0207	Next to the X in Texas/Peter Cottontail	1950	10.00	20.00	40.00
—Originals on green vinyl					
❑ 48-0331	Buffalo Billy/Me and My Teddy Bear	1950	10.00	20.00	40.00
—Originals on green vinyl					
❑ 48-0374	Frosty the Snowman/Gabby the Gobbler	1950	10.00	20.00	40.00
—Originals on green vinyl					
❑ 48-0414	The Story of Bucky 'n' Dan/Ride, Son, Ride	1951	7.50	15.00	30.00
❑ 48-0423	Easter Parade/Peter Cottontail	1951	7.50	15.00	30.00
❑ 48-0438	Katy/Yogy the Doggie	1951	7.50	15.00	30.00
❑ 48-0458	Pliney Jane/Cowboy's Heaven	1951	7.50	15.00	30.00
❑ 48-0479	Buckeye Cowboy/I Wish I Wuz	1951	7.50	15.00	30.00
❑ 48-0496	The Lamp of Faith/Good Luck, Good Health	1951	7.50	15.00	30.00

ROGERS, ROY, AND CLINT BLACK

Number	Title (A Side/B Side)	Yr	VG	VG+	NM
RCA					
❑ 62061	Hold On Partner/Alive and Kickin'	1991	—	2.50	5.00

ROGERS, ROY, AND SPADE COOLEY

Number	Title (A Side/B Side)	Yr	VG	VG+	NM
RCA VICTOR					
❑ 48-0130	Skip to My Lou/Rickett's Reel	1949	10.00	20.00	40.00
—Originals on green vinyl					
❑ 48-0131	Old Joe Clark/Sycamore Reel	1949	10.00	20.00	40.00
—Originals on green vinyl					
❑ 48-0132	Oh Dem Golden Slippers/Lucky Leather Breeches	1949	10.00	20.00	40.00
—Originals on green vinyl					

ROGERS, ROY, AND DALE EVANS

Number	Title (A Side/B Side)	Yr	VG	VG+	NM
CAPITOL					
❑ 2022	Merry Christmas My Darling/Sleigh Ride-Jingle Bells	1967	2.50	5.00	10.00
RCA VICTOR					
❑ WBY-43	Happy Trails/The Yellow Rose of Texas	195?	10.00	20.00	40.00
❑ WBY-43 [PS]	Happy Trails/The Yellow Rose of Texas	195?	20.00	40.00	80.00
❑ 47-0373	May the Good Lord Bless and Keep You/Smiles Are Made Out of Sunshine	1950	10.00	20.00	40.00
—Originals on green vinyl					
❑ 48-0128	Christmas on the Plains/Wonderful Christmas Night	1949	12.50	25.00	50.00
—Originals on green vinyl					
❑ 48-0336	What a Friend We Have in Jesus/I Love to Tell the Story	1950	10.00	20.00	40.00
—Originals on green vinyl					
❑ 48-0337	He Is So Precious to Me/When Jesus Came Into My Heart	1950	10.00	20.00	40.00
—Originals on green vinyl					
❑ 48-0338	Where He Leads Me/Love Lifted Me	1950	10.00	20.00	40.00
—Originals on green vinyl					
❑ 48-0344	The Old Rugged Cross/In the Garden	1950	10.00	20.00	40.00
—Originals on green vinyl					
❑ 48-0399	Yellow Bonnets and Polka Dot Shoes/No Bed of Roses	1950	10.00	20.00	40.00
—Originals on green vinyl					
❑ 48-0490	Snow on the Mountain/Strawberry Tears	1951	7.50	15.00	30.00

ROGERS, TIMMIE

Number	Title (A Side/B Side)	Yr	VG	VG+	NM
CADET					
❑ 5685	Super Soul Brothers/It Rolls Through Everything	1971	—	2.50	5.00
CAMEO					
❑ 116	Back to School Again/I've Got a Dog Who Loves Me	1957	7.50	15.00	30.00
❑ 131	Take Me to Your Leader/Fla-Ga-La-Pa	1958	6.25	12.50	25.00
CAPITOL					
❑ F2406	Saturday Night/If I Were You, Baby	1953	6.25	12.50	25.00
❑ F2509	Oh Yeah/Nothin' Wrong with Nothin'	1953	6.25	12.50	25.00
EPIC					
❑ 9813	If You Can't Smile and Say Yes (Please Don't Cry and Say No)/Chum Goy Tum Toy Fricasee (Soy Soy Soo)	1965	2.00	4.00	8.00
❑ 9899	Everybody Wants to Go to Heaven, But Nobody Wants to Die/Too Young to Go Steady	1966	2.00	4.00	8.00
MERCURY					
❑ 70451	If I Give My Heart to You/Teedle-Dee Teedle-Dum	1954	10.00	20.00	40.00
PAR-TEE					
❑ 1303	Watergate/Snake Hips	1973	—	2.50	5.00
PARKWAY					
❑ 814	I Love Ya, I Love Ya, I Love Ya/Tee-Hee	1960	3.75	7.50	15.00
PHILIPS					
❑ 40074	Oh Yeah/Fla-Ga-La-Pa	1962	2.50	5.00	10.00
SIGNATURE					
❑ 12037	First Proposal/Underwater Cha Cha Cha	1960	3.75	7.50	15.00

ROGERS, WELDON

Number	Title (A Side/B Side)	Yr	VG	VG+	NM
IMPERIAL					
❑ 5451	So Long, Good Luck and Goodbye/Trying to Get to You	1957	50.00	100.00	200.00
—B-side is actually The Teen Kings' version rather than Rogers'; by mistake, the wrong recording left Norman Petty's studio for Imperial.					
JE-WEL					
❑ 103	Everybody Wants You/This Song's Just for You	1956	250.00	500.00	1000.

ROLIE, GREGG

Formerly of SANTANA and Journey.

Number	Title (A Side/B Side)	Yr	VG	VG+	NM
COLUMBIA					
❑ 05581	Young Love/Deep Blue Sea	1985	—	—	3.00
❑ 07351	The Hands of Time/I Will Get to You	1987	—	—	3.00

ROLLERS, THE

Number	Title (A Side/B Side)	Yr	VG	VG+	NM
LIBERTY					
❑ 55303	Bonneville/Got My Eye on You	1961	5.00	10.00	20.00
❑ 55320	The Continental Walk/I Want You So	1961	5.00	10.00	20.00
❑ 55357	The Bounce/Teenager's Waltz	1961	5.00	10.00	20.00

ROLLETTES, THE

Number	Title (A Side/B Side)	Yr	VG	VG+	NM
CLASS					
❑ 201	Sad Fool/Wham Bam	1957	10.00	20.00	40.00
❑ 203	Kiss Me Benny/More Than You Realize	1957	10.00	20.00	40.00
MELKER					
❑ 103	An Understanding/I'm Trying (To Make You Love Me)	1960	500.00	1000.	2000.

ROLLING STONES, THE

Also see MICK JAGGER; KEITH RICHARDS; MICK TAYLOR; RONNIE WOOD; BILL WYMAN.

Number	Title (A Side/B Side)	Yr	VG	VG+	NM
ABKCO					
❑ 4701	I Don't Know Why/Try a Little Harder	1975	—	2.50	5.00
—With A-side writing credits of "Wonder, Riser, Hunter, Hardaway"					
❑ 4701	I Don't Know Why/Try a Little Harder	1975	2.50	5.00	10.00
—With A-side writing credits of "Jagger, Richards, Taylor"					

Number	Title (A Side/B Side)	Yr	VG	VG+	NM
❑ 4701 [DJ]	I Don't Know Why (same on both sides)	1975	5.00	10.00	25.00
❑ 4702	Out of Time/Jiving Sister Fanny	1975	—	3.00	6.00
❑ 4702 [DJ]	Out of Time/Jiving Sister Fanny	1975	5.00	10.00	25.00
LONDON					
❑ 901	Paint It, Black/Stupid Girl	1966	3.75	7.50	15.00
❑ 901 [DJ]	Paint It, Black/Stupid Girl	1966	25.00	50.00	75.00
—Orange swirl label					
❑ 901 [PS]	Paint It, Black/Stupid Girl	1966	15.00	30.00	60.00
❑ 902	Mothers Little Helper/Lady Jane	1966	3.75	7.50	15.00
❑ 902 [DJ]	Mothers Little Helper/Lady Jane	1966	25.00	50.00	75.00
—Orange swirl label					
❑ 902 [PS]	Mothers Little Helper/Lady Jane	1966	15.00	30.00	60.00
❑ 903	Have You Seen Your Mother, Baby, Standing in the Shadow?/Who's Driving My Plane	1966	3.75	7.50	15.00
❑ 903 [DJ]	Have You Seen Your Mother, Baby, Standing in the Shadow?/Who's Driving My Plane	1966	25.00	50.00	75.00
—Orange swirl label					
❑ 903 [PS]	Have You Seen Your Mother, Baby, Standing in the Shadow?/Who's Driving My Plane	1966	15.00	30.00	60.00
❑ 904	Ruby Tuesday/Let's Spend the Night Together	1967	3.75	7.50	15.00
❑ 904 [DJ]	Ruby Tuesday/Let's Spend the Night Together	1967	25.00	50.00	75.00
—Orange swirl label					
❑ 904 [PS]	Let's Spend the Night Together/Ruby Tuesday	1967	15.00	30.00	60.00
❑ 905	Dandelion/We Love You	1967	5.00	10.00	20.00
❑ 905 [DJ]	Dandelion/We Love You	1967	25.00	50.00	75.00
—With full-length version of "We Love You"; orange swirl label					
❑ 905 [DJ]	Dandelion/We Love You	1967	50.00	100.00	150.00
—With 3:10 edited version of "We Love You"; orange swirl label					
❑ 905 [PS]	We Love You/Dandelion	1967	100.00	300.00	600.00
❑ 906	She's a Rainbow/2000 Light Years from Home	1967	5.00	10.00	20.00
❑ 906 [DJ]	She's a Rainbow/2000 Light Years from Home	1967	25.00	50.00	75.00
—Orange swirl label					
❑ 906 [PS]	She's a Rainbow/2000 Light Years from Home	1967	12.50	25.00	50.00
❑ 907	In Another Land/The Lantern	1967	6.25	12.50	25.00
—A-side credited to Bill Wyman, though taken from "Their Satanic Majesties Request"					
❑ 907 [DJ]	In Another Land/The Lantern	1967	25.00	50.00	75.00
—A-side credited to Bill Wyman; orange swirl label					
❑ 907 [PS]	In Another Land/The Lantern	1967	12.00	30.00	75.00
❑ 908	Jumpin' Jack Flash/Child of the Moon	1968	3.75	7.50	15.00
❑ 908 [DJ]	Jumpin' Jack Flash/Child of the Moon	1968	25.00	50.00	75.00
—Orange swirl label					
❑ 908 [PS]	Jumpin' Jack Flash/Child of the Moon	1968	10.00	20.00	40.00
❑ 909	Street Fighting Man/No Expectations	1968	5.00	10.00	20.00
❑ 909 [DJ]	Street Fighting Man/No Expectations	1968	25.00	50.00	75.00
—Orange swirl label					
❑ 909 [PS]	Street Fighting Man/No Expectations	1968	4000.	8000.	10000.
❑ 910	Honky Tonk Women/You Can't Always Get What You Want	1969	3.75	7.50	15.00
❑ 910 [PS]	Honky Tonk Women/You Can't Always Get What You Want	1969	7.50	15.00	30.00
❑ 9641	I Wanna Be Your Man/Stoned	1964	3000.	6000.	9000.
❑ 9641 [DJ]	I Wanna Be Your Man/Stoned	1964	300.00	600.00	1000.
—With similar label to stock copy, except in white, black and gray					
❑ 9641 [DJ]	I Wanna Be Your Man/Stoned	1964	200.00	500.00	1500.
—White label, black print, script "London" at top					
❑ 9657	Not Fade Away/I Wanna Be Your Man	1964	10.00	20.00	40.00
—White, purple and blue label					
❑ 9657	Not Fade Away/I Wanna Be Your Man	1964	2.00	4.00	8.00
—Blue swirl label					
❑ 9657 [DJ]	Not Fade Away/I Wanna Be Your Man	1964	200.00	400.00	900.00
—With similar label to original stock copy, except in white, black and gray					
❑ 9657 [DJ]	Not Fade Away/I Wanna Be Your Man	1964	300.00	600.00	1000.
—White label, black print, script "London" at top					
❑ 9657 [PS]	Not Fade Away/I Wanna Be Your Man	1964	75.00	300.00	450.00
❑ 9682	Tell Me (You're Coming Back)/I Just Want to Make Love to You	1964	10.00	20.00	40.00
—White, purple and blue label					
❑ 9682	Tell Me (You're Coming Back)/I Just Want to Make Love to You	1964	2.50	5.00	10.00
—Blue swirl label					
❑ 9682 [DJ]	Tell Me (You're Coming Back)/I Just Want to Make Love to You	1964	25.00	50.00	75.00
—Orange swirl label					
❑ 9682 [PS]	Tell Me (You're Coming Back)/I Just Want to Make Love to You	1964	50.00	125.00	175.00
❑ 9687	It's All Over Now/Good Times, Bad Times	1964	10.00	20.00	40.00
—White, purple and blue label					
❑ 9687	It's All Over Now/Good Times Bad Times	1964	2.50	5.00	10.00
—Blue swirl label					
❑ 9687 [DJ]	It's All Over Now/Good Times, Bad Times	1964	25.00	50.00	75.00
—Orange swirl label					
❑ 9687 [PS]	It's All Over Now/Good Times, Bad Times	1964	50.00	85.00	125.00
❑ 9708	Time Is On My Side/Congratulations	1964	7.50	15.00	30.00
—White, purple and blue label					
❑ 9708	Time Is On My Side/Congratulations	1964	2.50	5.00	10.00
—Blue swirl label					
❑ 9708 [DJ]	Time Is On My Side/Congratulations	1964	25.00	50.00	75.00
—Orange swirl label					
❑ 9708 [PS]	Time Is On My Side/Congratulations	1964	25.00	50.00	100.00
❑ 9725	Heart of Stone/What a Shame	1964	7.50	15.00	30.00
—White, purple and blue label					
❑ 9725	Heart of Stone/What a Shame	1964	2.50	5.00	10.00
—Blue swirl label					
❑ 9725 [DJ]	Heart of Stone/What a Shame	1964	25.00	50.00	75.00
—Orange swirl label					
❑ 9725 [PS]	Heart of Stone/What a Shame	1964	200.00	400.00	800.00
❑ 9741	The Last Time/Play with Fire	1965	2.50	5.00	10.00
—Blue swirl label, "London" in black letters					
❑ 9741	The Last Time/Play with Fire	1965	3.75	7.50	15.00
—Blue swirl label, "London" in white letters					
❑ 9741	The Last Time/Play with Fire	1965	6.25	12.50	25.00
—White, purple and blue label					
❑ 9741 [DJ]	The Last Time/Play with Fire	1965	25.00	50.00	75.00
—Orange swirl label					
❑ 9741 [PS]	The Last Time/Play with Fire	1965	37.50	75.00	150.00
❑ 9766	(I Can't Get No) Satisfaction/The Under Assistant West Coast Promotion Man	1965	5.00	10.00	20.00
❑ 9766 [DJ]	(I Can't Get No) Satisfaction/The Under Assistant West Coast Promotion Man	1965	25.00	50.00	75.00
—Orange swirl label					
❑ 9766 [PS]	(I Can't Get No) Satisfaction/The Under Assistant West Coast Promotion Man	1965	100.00	200.00	500.00
❑ 5N-9766 [DJ]	(I Can't Get No) Satisfaction/The Under Assistant West Coast Promotion Man	1975	20.00	40.00	60.00
—Promo reissue; orange swirl label					
❑ 9792	Get Off of My Cloud/I'm Free	1965	5.00	10.00	20.00
❑ 9792 [DJ]	Get Off of My Cloud/I'm Free	1965	25.00	50.00	75.00
—Orange swirl label					
❑ 9792 [PS]	Get Off of My Cloud/I'm Free	1965	15.00	30.00	60.00
❑ 9808	As Tears Go By/Gotta Get Away	1965	3.75	7.50	15.00
❑ 9808 [DJ]	As Tears Go By/Gotta Get Away	1965	25.00	50.00	75.00
—Orange swirl label					
❑ 9808 [PS]	As Tears Go By/Gotta Get Away	1965	15.00	30.00	60.00
❑ 9823	19th Nervous Breakdown/Sad Day	1966	3.75	7.50	15.00
❑ 9823 [DJ]	19th Nervous Breakdown/Sad Day	1966	25.00	50.00	75.00
—Orange swirl label					
❑ 9823 [PS]	19th Nervous Breakdown/Sad Day	1966	15.00	30.00	60.00
ROLLING STONES					
❑ PR 228 [DJ]	Time Waits for No One (mono/stereo)	1974	15.00	50.00	75.00
❑ PR 228 [PS]	Time Waits for No One (mono/stereo)	1974	75.00	125.00	175.00
❑ PR 316 [DJ]	Before They Make Me Run (mono/stereo)	1978	6.25	12.50	25.00
❑ PR 316 [PS]	Before They Make Me Run (mono/stereo)	1978	10.00	20.00	50.00
❑ 05802	Harlem Shuffle/Had It with You	1986	—	—	3.00
❑ 05802 [DJ]	Harlem Shuffle (same on both sides)	1986	5.00	10.00	20.00
❑ 05802 [PS]	Harlem Shuffle/Had It with You	1986	—	—	3.00
❑ 05802 [PS]	Harlem Shuffle	1986	5.00	10.00	20.00
—"Demonstration Not for Sale" on sleeve, and no B-side listed					
❑ 05906	One Hit (To the Body)/Fight	1986	—	—	3.00
❑ 05906 [DJ]	One Hit (To the Body) (same on both sides)	1986	5.00	10.00	20.00
❑ 05906 [PS]	One Hit (To the Body)/Fight	1986	—	—	3.00
❑ 05906 [PS]	One Hit (To the Body)	1986	5.00	10.00	20.00
—"Demonstration Not for Sale" on sleeve, and no B-side listed					
❑ 19100	Brown Sugar/Bitch	1971	—	2.50	5.00
❑ 19100 [DJ]	Brown Sugar (mono/stereo)	1971	10.00	20.00	30.00
❑ 19101	Wild Horses/Sway	1971	—	2.50	5.00
❑ 19101 [DJ]	Wild Horses (mono/stereo, both full length)	1971	10.00	20.00	30.00
❑ 19101 [DJ]	Wild Horses (long version/short version)	1971	20.00	30.00	50.00
❑ 19103	Tumbling Dice/Sweet Black Angel	1972	—	2.50	5.00
❑ 19103 [DJ]	Tumbling Dice (mono/stereo)	1972	10.00	20.00	30.00
❑ 19104	Happy/All Down the Line	1972	—	2.50	5.00
❑ 19104 [DJ]	Happy/All Down the Line	1972	10.00	20.00	30.00
❑ 19105	Silver Train/Angie	1973	3.00	6.00	12.00
—With "Silver Train" listed as "Side One" and "Angie" listed as "Side Two"					
❑ 19105	Angie/Silver Train	1973	—	2.50	5.00
—With "Angie" listed as "Side One" and "Silver Train" listed as "Side Two", or with no reference at all to "Side One" and "Side Two"					
❑ 19105 [DJ]	Angie (mono/stereo)	1973	10.00	20.00	30.00
❑ 19109	Doo Doo Doo Doo Doo (Heartbreaker)/Dancing with Mr. D.	1973	—	2.50	5.00
❑ 19109 [DJ]	Doo Doo Doo Doo Doo (Heartbreaker) (mono/stereo)	1973	10.00	20.00	30.00
❑ 19301	It's Only Rock 'N' Roll (But I Like It)/Through the Lonely Nights	1974	—	2.50	5.00
❑ 19301 [DJ]	It's Only Rock 'N' Roll (But I Like It) (Edit/Long Version)	1974	10.00	20.00	30.00
❑ 19302	Ain't Too Proud to Beg/Dance Little Sister	1974	—	2.50	5.00
❑ 19302 [DJ]	Ain't Too Proud to Beg (mono/stereo)	1974	10.00	20.00	30.00
❑ 19304	Fool to Cry/Hot Stuff	1976	—	2.00	4.00
❑ 19304	Fool to Cry/Crazy Mama	1976	—	—	—
—Promotional 12-inch singles exist with this coupling, but do U.S. 45s? Please advise.					
❑ 19304 [DJ]	Fool to Cry/Hot Stuff	1976	50.00	100.00	200.00
❑ 19304 [DJ]	Fool to Cry (same on both sides)	1976	10.00	20.00	30.00
❑ 19304 [DJ]	Fool to Cry (long/short versions)	1976	15.00	25.00	35.00
❑ 19304 [DJ]	Hot Stuff (same on both sides)	1976	10.00	20.00	30.00
❑ 19304 [DJ]	Hot Stuff (long/short versions)	1976	15.00	25.00	35.00
❑ 19307	Miss You/Far Away Eyes	1978	—	2.00	4.00
❑ 19307 [DJ]	Miss You (same on both sides)	1978	10.00	20.00	30.00
❑ 19307 [DJ]	Far Away Eyes (same on both sides)	1978	50.00	100.00	250.00
❑ 19307 [PS]	Miss You/Far Away Eyes	1978	—	2.00	4.00
❑ 19309	Beast of Burden/When the Whip Comes Down	1978	—	2.00	4.00
❑ 19309 [DJ]	Beast of Burden (long/short versions)	1978	10.00	20.00	30.00
❑ 19309 [PS]	Beast of Burden/When the Whip Comes Down	1978	1000.	1500.	2000.
—Beware of counterfeits! Original copies have a 1/2-inch inner fold on the inside of the picture sleeve (counterfeits have a much smaller fold). Also, the originals are a light lavender, almost pink, color (counterfeits are a grape or purple color).					
❑ 19310	Shattered/Everything Is Turning to Gold	1978	—	2.00	4.00
❑ 19310 [DJ]	Shattered (same on both sides)	1978	5.00	10.00	20.00
❑ 19310 [PS]	Shattered/Everything Is Turning to Gold	1978	—	3.00	6.00
❑ 20001	Emotional Rescue/Down in the Hole	1980	—	2.00	4.00
❑ 20001 [DJ]	Emotional Rescue (edit/LP versions)	1980	5.00	10.00	20.00
❑ 20001 [PS]	Emotional Rescue/Down in the Hole	1980	—	2.00	4.00
❑ 21001	She's So Cold/Send It to Me	1980	—	2.00	4.00
❑ 21001 [DJ]	She's So Cold (edit/LP versions)	1980	5.00	10.00	20.00
❑ 21001 [PS]	She's So Cold/Send It to Me	1980	—	3.00	6.00
❑ 21003	Start Me Up/No Use in Crying	1981	—	2.00	4.00
❑ 21003 [DJ]	Start Me Up (same on both sides)	1981	5.00	10.00	20.00
❑ 21003 [PS]	Start Me Up/No Use in Crying	1981	—	2.00	4.00
❑ 21004	Waiting on a Friend/Little T & A	1981	—	2.00	4.00
❑ 21004 [DJ]	Waiting on a Friend (same on both sides)	1981	5.00	10.00	20.00
❑ 21004 [PS]	Waiting on a Friend/Little T & A	1981	—	2.00	4.00
❑ 21300	Hang Fire/Neighbours	1982	—	2.00	4.00
❑ 21300 [DJ]	Hang Fire (same on both sides)	1982	5.00	10.00	20.00

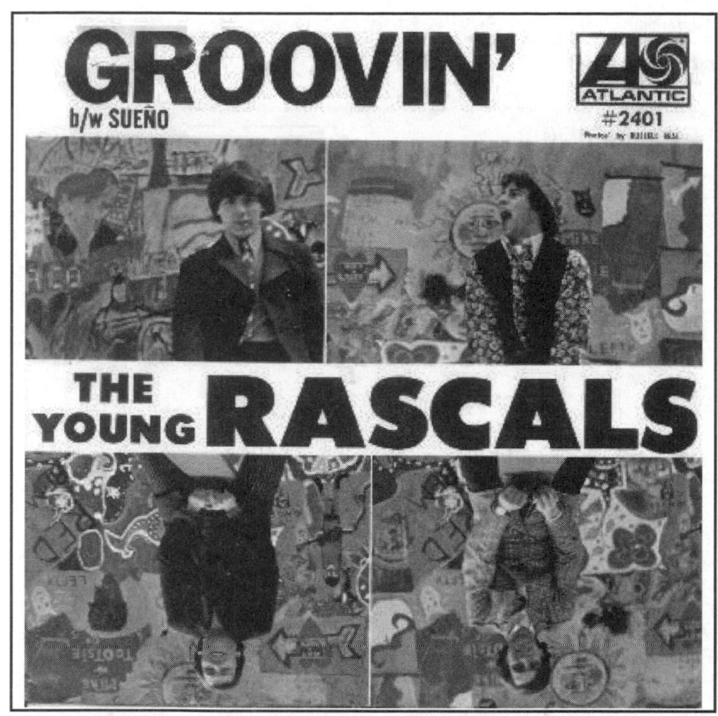

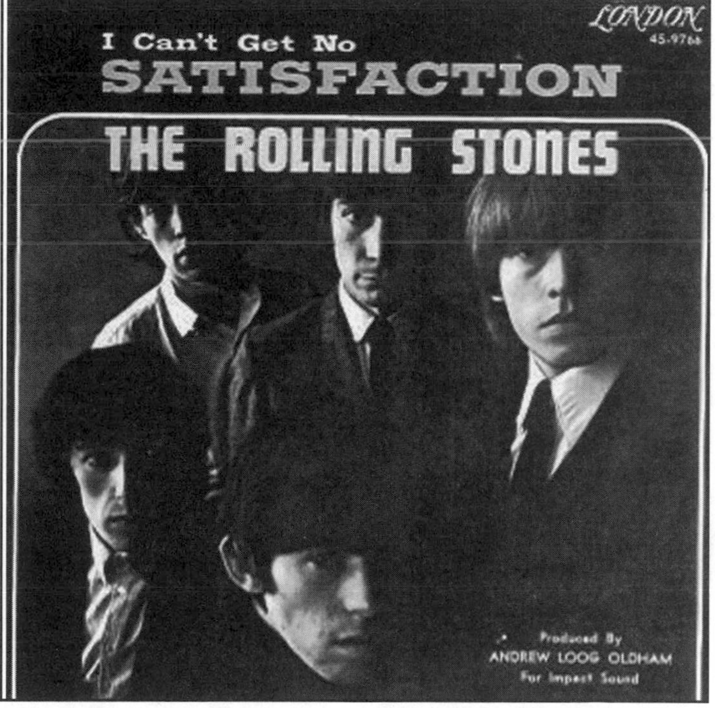

(Top left) Already, by 1967 the "Young" part of the "Young Rascals" name was being de-emphasized, as is evident on the picture sleeve for "Groovin'," one of their biggest hits. (Top right) The very first Rolling Stones single in America with a picture sleeve was their top 40 hit, "Not Fade Away." As with other early Stones sleeves, this one is rising in demand. (Bottom left) Other than "Street Fighting Man" and "Beast of Burden," the most in-demand Rolling Stones sleeve is the one for "Heart of Stone." Although listed in this book at $800 for a near-mint copy, it's been known to sell for more than that. (Bottom right) Not far behind "Heart of Stone" in the value category is the sleeve for the Stones' anthem, "(I Can't Get No) Satisfaction." It's listed at $500 for a near-mint copy. Because of the darkness of the sleeve, most copies are found with white ring wear near the middle.

Number	Title (A Side/B Side)	Yr	VG	VG+	NM
❑ 21301	Going to A-Go-Go/Beast of Burden	1982	—	2.00	4.00
❑ 21301 [DJ]	Going to A-Go-Go/Beast of Burden	1982	5.00	10.00	20.00
❑ 21301 [PS]	Going to A-Go-Go/Beast of Burden	1982	—	2.00	4.00
❑ 69008	Mixed Emotions/Fancy Man Blues	1989	—	—	3.00
❑ 69008 [DJ]	Mixed Emotions (same on both sides)	1989	10.00	20.00	45.00
❑ 73057	Rock and a Hard Place/Cook Cook Blues	1989	—	—	3.00
❑ 73093	Almost Hear You Sigh/Break the Spell	1989	—	—	3.00
❑ 73742	Highwire/2000 Light Years from Home	1991	—	2.50	5.00
❑ 73789	Sexdrive/Undercover of the Night	1991	2.00	4.00	8.00
❑ 99724	Too Tough/Miss You	1984	10.00	20.00	40.00
❑ 99724 [DJ]	Miss You (same on both sides)	1984	10.00	20.00	30.00
❑ 99788	She Was Hot/Think I'm Going Mad	1984	—	—	3.00
❑ 99788 [DJ]	She Was Hot (long/short versions)	1984	10.00	20.00	30.00
❑ 99788 [PS]	She Was Hot/Think I'm Going Mad	1984	—	—	3.00
❑ 99813	Undercover of the Night/All the Way Down	1983	—	—	3.00
❑ 99813 [DJ]	Undercover of the Night (same on both sides)	1983	5.00	10.00	20.00
❑ 99813 [PS]	Undercover of the Night/All the Way Down	1983	—	—	3.00
❑ 99978	Time Is On My Side (Live)/Twenty Flight Rock	1982	—	2.50	5.00
❑ 99978 [DJ]	Time Is On My Side (Live) (same on both sides)	1982	5.00	10.00	20.00
❑ 99978 [PS]	Time Is On My Side (Live)/Twenty Flight Rock	1982	—	2.50	5.00
VIRGIN					
❑ 38446	Love Is Strong//The Storm/Love Is Strong (Teddy Riley Remix)	1994	—	2.50	5.00
❑ 38446 [PS]	Love Is Strong//The Storm/Love Is Strong (Teddy Riley Remix)	1994	—	2.50	5.00
❑ 38459	Out of Tears//Out of Tears (Bob Clearmountain Remix Edit)/I'm Gonna Drive	1994	—	2.50	5.00
❑ 38459 [PS]	Out of Tears//Out of Tears (Bob Clearmountain Remix Edit)/I'm Gonna Drive	1994	—	2.50	5.00
❑ NR-38626	Saint of Me/Anyway You Look At It	1998	—	—	2.00
❑ NR-38626 [PS]	Saint of Me/Anyway You Look At It	1998	—	—	2.00

7-Inch Extended Plays

ROLLING STONES

Number	Title (A Side/B Side)	Yr	VG	VG+	NM
❑ PR 287 [DJ]	If You Can't Rock Me/Get Off of My Cloud/Brown Sugar//Jumpin' Jack Flash/Hot Stuff	1977	7.50	15.00	30.00
—Large hole; promo-only sampler from "Love You Live"					
❑ PR 287 [PS]	Love You Live	1977	12.50	25.00	50.00

ROMAN NUMERALS, THE

COLUMBIA

Number	Title (A Side/B Side)	Yr	VG	VG+	NM
❑ 44314	The Come-On/Matchstick in a Whirlpool	1967	5.00	10.00	20.00
❑ 44314 [PS]	The Come-On/Matchstick in a Whirlpool	1967	7.50	15.00	30.00

ROMANTICS, THE

BOMP!

Number	Title (A Side/B Side)	Yr	VG	VG+	NM
❑ 120	Tell It to Carrie/First in Line	1978	—	—	3.00
❑ 120 [PS]	Tell It to Carrie/First in Line	1978	—	—	3.00
COLUMBIA					
❑ 06445	Talking in Your Sleep/Mystified	198?	—	—	3.00
—Reissue					
❑ 07527	What I Like About You/First in Line	198?	—	—	3.00
—Reissue					
NEMPEROR					
❑ 02581	No One Like You/She's Hot	1981	—	2.00	4.00
❑ 04135	Talking in Your Sleep/I'm Hip	1983	—	—	3.00
❑ 04373	One in a Million/Do Me Anyway You Wanna	1984	—	—	3.00
❑ 04373 [PS]	One in a Million/Do Me Anyway You Wanna	1984	—	—	3.00
❑ 05587	Test of Time/Better Make a Move	1985	—	—	3.00
❑ 05587 [PS]	Test of Time/Better Make a Move	1985	—	—	3.00
❑ 05587 [PS]	Test of Time	1985	—	2.50	5.00
—"Demonstration -- Not for Sale" on back					
❑ 05684	Mystified/Make It Last	1985	—	—	3.00
❑ 05684 [PS]	Mystified/Make It Last	1985	—	2.00	4.00
❑ 7527	What I Like About You/First in Line	1979	—	2.50	5.00
❑ 7527 [PS]	What I Like About You/First in Line	1979	2.50	5.00	10.00
❑ 7530	When I Look in Your Eyes/Little White Lies	1980	—	—	3.00
❑ 7531	Tell It to Carrie/Hung on You	1980	—	—	3.00
❑ 7537	Forever Yours/New Cover Story	1981	—	2.00	4.00
❑ 70063	A Night Like This/I Ain't Got You	1981	—	2.00	4.00
SPIDER					
❑ SPDR-101	Little White Lies/I Can't Tell You Anything	1977	—	2.00	4.00
❑ SPDR-101 [PS]	Little White Lies/I Can't Tell You Anything	1977	—	2.00	4.00

ROMEOS, THE (1)

Featuring Philly Soul producers KENNY GAMBLE and Leon Huff.

MARK II

Number	Title (A Side/B Side)	Yr	VG	VG+	NM
❑ 101	Precious Memories/Juicy Lucy	1967	3.75	7.50	15.00
❑ 103	A Tear and a Smile/Seaching	1967	3.75	7.50	15.00

ROMEOS, THE (2)

AMY

Number	Title (A Side/B Side)	Yr	VG	VG+	NM
❑ 840	The Tiger's Wide Awake (The Lion Sleeps Tonight)/Hitch-Hikin'	1962	3.75	7.50	15.00

ROMEOS, THE (3)

APOLLO

Number	Title (A Side/B Side)	Yr	VG	VG+	NM
❑ 461	Love Me/I Beg You Please	1954	150.00	300.00	600.00

ROMEOS, THE (4)

ATCO

Number	Title (A Side/B Side)	Yr	VG	VG+	NM
❑ 6107	Moments to Remember You By/Fine, Fine Baby	1958	15.00	30.00	60.00
FOX					
❑ 749	Gone, Gone, Get Away/Let's Be Partners	1957	75.00	150.00	300.00
—Cream label					
❑ 749	Gone, Gone, Get Away/Let's Be Partners	1957	30.00	60.00	120.00
—Yellow label					
❑ 846	Moments to Remember You By/Fine, Fine Baby	1957	125.00	250.00	500.00
—Cream label					
❑ 846	Moments to Remember You By/Fine, Fine Baby	1957	30.00	60.00	120.00
—Yellow label					

ROMEOS, THE (5)

COLUMBIA

Number	Title (A Side/B Side)	Yr	VG	VG+	NM
❑ 43074	Baby Stay in Line/Two of the Chosen Few	1964	2.50	5.00	10.00

ROMEOS, THE (U)

If these are any of the above groups, the most likely contenders are groups (1), (2) or (5).

FELSTED

Number	Title (A Side/B Side)	Yr	VG	VG+	NM
❑ 8528	Two Innocent Loves/Love-Mobile	1958	7.50	15.00	30.00
❑ 8672	Julie/I'm Gonna Rebuild This World	1963	5.00	10.00	20.00
LOMA					
❑ 2028	Mucho Soul/Are You Ready for That	1966	3.00	6.00	12.00
❑ 2041	Calypso Chili/Mon Petite Chow	1966	3.00	6.00	12.00

ROMERO, CHAN

CHALLENGE

Number	Title (A Side/B Side)	Yr	VG	VG+	NM
❑ 59285	The Funniest Things/It's Not Fine	1965	3.75	7.50	15.00
DEL-FI					
❑ 4119	The Hippy Hippy Shake/If I Had My Way	1959	25.00	50.00	100.00
❑ 4126	I Don't Care Now/My Little Rudy	1959	15.00	30.00	60.00
PHILIPS					
❑ 40391	Humpy Bumpy/Man Can't Dog a Woman	1966	2.50	5.00	10.00

RON AND BILL

Ron White and Bill "SMOKEY" ROBINSON.

ARGO

Number	Title (A Side/B Side)	Yr	VG	VG+	NM
❑ 5350	It/Don't Say Bye Bye	1959	12.50	25.00	50.00
TAMLA					
❑ 54025	It/Don't Say Bye Bye	1960	30.00	60.00	120.00

RON-DELLS, THE

ARLEN

Number	Title (A Side/B Side)	Yr	VG	VG+	NM
❑ 723	I'll Be Gone/Slow Down	1963	3.75	7.50	15.00

RON-DELS, THE

Delbert McClinton was in this group.

BROWNFIELD

Number	Title (A Side/B Side)	Yr	VG	VG+	NM
❑ 18	If You Really Want Me To, I'll Go/Walk About	1965	6.25	12.50	25.00
SMASH					
❑ 1986	If You Really Want Me To, I'll Go/Walk About	1965	2.50	5.00	10.00
❑ 2002	She's My Girl/Over	1965	2.00	4.00	8.00
❑ 2014	A Picture of You/Lose Your Money	1965	2.00	4.00	8.00

RONDELLS, THE

More than one group.

ABC-PARAMOUNT

Number	Title (A Side/B Side)	Yr	VG	VG+	NM
❑ 10690	Don't Say That You Love Me/Parking in the Ko Ko Mo	1965	3.75	7.50	15.00
CARLTON					
❑ 467	Good Good/Dreamy	1958	5.00	10.00	20.00
DOT					
❑ 16593	Far Horizons/On the Run	1964	6.25	12.50	25.00
❑ 17323	Matilda/Tina	1970	2.50	5.00	10.00
—As "The Ron-Dels"					
SHALIMAR					
❑ 104	Matilda/Tina	1963	3.75	7.50	15.00

RONDELS, THE

AMY

Number	Title (A Side/B Side)	Yr	VG	VG+	NM
❑ 825	Back Beat #1/Shades of Green	1961	6.25	12.50	25.00
❑ 830	My Prayer/Satan's Theme	1961	6.25	12.50	25.00
❑ 839	Caldonia/110 Lbs. of Drums	1962	6.25	12.50	25.00
❑ 844	Red Peppers/Flute Salad	1962	6.25	12.50	25.00
❑ 857	Meet Us at the Peppermint Lounge/Cover Charge	1962	6.25	12.50	25.00

RONETTES, THE

Also see RONNIE SPECTOR.

A&M

Number	Title (A Side/B Side)	Yr	VG	VG+	NM
❑ 1040	You Came, You Saw, You Conquered/Oh, I Love You	1969	4.00	8.00	16.00
BUDDAH					
❑ 384	Go Out and Get It/Lover, Lover	1973	5.00	10.00	20.00
—As "Ronnie Spector and the Ronettes"					
❑ 408	I Wish I Never Saw the Sunshine/I Wonder What He's Doing	1974	5.00	10.00	20.00
COLPIX					
❑ 601	I Want a Boy/Sweet Sixteen	1961	25.00	50.00	100.00
—As "Ronnie and the Relatives"					
❑ 646	I'm Gonna Quit While I'm Ahead/I'm On the Wagon	1962	15.00	30.00	60.00
DIMENSION					
❑ 1046	He Did It/Recipe for Love	1965	12.50	25.00	50.00
MAY					
❑ 111	My Darling Angel/I'm Gonna Quit While I'm Ahead	1961	37.50	75.00	150.00
—As "Ronnie and the Relatives"					
❑ 114	Silhouettes/You Bet I Would	1962	12.50	25.00	50.00
❑ 138	Memory/Good Girls	1963	12.50	25.00	50.00
PAVILLION					
❑ 03333	I Saw Mommy Kissing Santa Claus/Rudolph the Red-Nosed Reindeer	1982	—	2.50	5.00
—B-side by The Crystals					
PHILLES					
❑ 116	Be My Baby/Tedesco and Pittman	1963	7.50	15.00	30.00
❑ 118	Baby I Love You/Miss Joan and Mr. Sam	1963	7.50	15.00	30.00
❑ 120	(The Best Part of) Breakin' Up/Big Red	1964	7.50	15.00	30.00
❑ 121	Do I Love You?/Bebe and Susu	1964	7.50	15.00	30.00
❑ 123	Walkin' in the Rain/How Does It Feel	1964	10.00	20.00	40.00
❑ 123 [PS]	Walkin' in the Rain/How Does It Feel	1964	37.50	75.00	150.00
❑ 126	Born to Be Together/Blues for Baby	1965	6.25	12.50	25.00
❑ 126 [PS]	Born to Be Together/Blues for Baby	1965	37.50	75.00	150.00
❑ 128	Is This What I Get for Loving You?/Oh, I Love You	1965	6.25	12.50	25.00
❑ 128 [PS]	Is This What I Get for Loving You?/Oh, I Love You	1965	37.50	75.00	150.00

Number	Title (A Side/B Side)	Yr	VG	VG+	NM
❑ 133	I Can Hear Music/When I Saw You	1966	7.50	15.00	30.00

RONNIE AND THE DEL-AIRES
See THE DEL-AIRES.

RONNIE AND THE HI-LITES

Number	Title (A Side/B Side)	Yr	VG	VG+	NM
ABC-PARAMOUNT					
❑ 10685	High School Romance/Too Young	1965	5.00	10.00	20.00
JOY					
❑ 260	I Wish That We Were Married/Twistin' and Kissin'	1962	6.25	12.50	25.00
❑ 265	Be Kind/Send My Love (Special Delivery)	1962	5.00	10.00	20.00
RAVEN					
❑ 8000	Valerie/The Fact of the Matter	1963	5.00	10.00	20.00
WIN					
❑ 250	A Slow Dance/What the Next Day May Bring	1963	5.00	10.00	20.00
❑ 251	The Fact of the Matter/You Keep Me Guessin'	1963	5.00	10.00	20.00
❑ 252	High School Romance/Uptown-Downtown	1963	6.25	12.50	25.00

RONNIE AND THE RELATIVES
See THE RONETTES.

RONNIE AND THE ROCKIN' KINGS

Number	Title (A Side/B Side)	Yr	VG	VG+	NM
RCA VICTOR					
❑ 47-7248	Rock and Roll Sal/You Know	1958	10.00	20.00	40.00

RONNY AND THE DAYTONAS

Number	Title (A Side/B Side)	Yr	VG	VG+	NM
MALA					
❑ 481	G.T.O./Hot Rod Baby	1964	6.25	12.50	25.00
❑ 490	California Bound/Hey Little Girl	1964	5.00	10.00	20.00
❑ 492	Bucket "T"/Little Rail Job	1964	5.00	10.00	20.00
❑ 497	Little Scrambler/Teenage Years	1965	5.00	10.00	20.00
❑ 503	Beach Boy/No Wheels	1965	6.25	12.50	25.00
❑ 513	Sandy/(Instrumental)	1965	5.00	10.00	20.00
❑ 525	Goodbye Baby/Somebody to Love Me	1966	5.00	10.00	20.00
❑ 531	Antique '32 Studebaker Dictator Coupe/Then the Rains Came	1966	5.00	10.00	20.00
❑ 542	I'll Think of Summer/Little Scrambler	1966	3.75	7.50	15.00
RCA VICTOR					
❑ 47-8896	All American Girl/Dianne, Dianne	1966	3.00	6.00	12.00
❑ 47-8896 [PS]	All American Girl/Dianne, Dianne	1966	6.25	12.50	25.00
❑ 47-9022	Winter Weather/Young	1966	3.00	6.00	12.00
❑ 47-9107	Walk with the Sun/The Last Letter	1967	3.00	6.00	12.00
❑ 47-9253	Brave New World/Hold Onto Your Heart	1968	3.00	6.00	12.00
❑ 47-9435	The Girls and the Boys/Alfie	1968	3.00	6.00	12.00
SHOW BIZ					
❑ 21207 [DJ]	4-Cast She'll Love Me Again	1968	5.00	10.00	20.00
—One-sided promo					

RONSON, MICK

Number	Title (A Side/B Side)	Yr	VG	VG+	NM
RCA VICTOR					
❑ APBO-0212	Love Me Tender/Only After Dark	1974	—	3.00	6.00
❑ APBO-0291	Slaughter on Tenth Avenue/Leave My Heart Alone	1974	—	3.00	6.00
❑ PB-10237	Easy Days/Billy Porter	1975	—	3.00	6.00

7-Inch Extended Plays

Number	Title (A Side/B Side)	Yr	VG	VG+	NM
RCA VICTOR					
❑ DJEO-0259 [DJ]	Slaughter on 10th Avenue/Growing Up and I'm Fine//All Cut Up on You/Andy Warhol	1974	3.00	6.00	12.00
—Promo-only EP with B-side by Dana Gillespie					

RONSTADT, LINDA
Also see CHRISTMAS SPIRIT; STONE PONEYS.

Number	Title (A Side/B Side)	Yr	VG	VG+	NM
ASYLUM					
❑ 11026	Love Has No Pride/I Can Almost See It	1973	—	2.50	5.00
❑ 11032	Silver Threads and Golden Needles/Don't Cry Now	1974	—	2.50	5.00
❑ 11039	Desperado/Colorado	1974	—	2.50	5.00
❑ 45271	Love Is a Rose/Silver Blue	1975	—	3.00	6.00
❑ 45282	Heat Wave/Love Is a Rose	1975	—	2.00	4.00
❑ 45295	Tracks of My Tears/The Sweetest Gift	1975	—	2.00	4.00
—B-side with Emmylou Harris					
❑ 45340	That'll Be the Day/Try Me Again	1976	—	2.00	4.00
—Clouds label					
❑ 45340	That'll Be the Day/Try Me Again	1976	—	2.50	5.00
—All-blue label					
❑ 45361	Someone to Lay Down Beside Me/Crazy	1976	—	2.00	4.00
❑ 45402	Lose Again/Lo Siento Mi Vida	1977	2.00	4.00	8.00
❑ 45431	Blue Bayou/Old Paint	1977	—	2.00	4.00
❑ 45438	It's So Easy/Lo Siento Mi Vida	1977	—	2.00	4.00
❑ 45462	Poor Poor Pitiful Me/Simple Man, Simple Dream	1978	—	2.00	4.00
❑ 45464	Lago Azul/Lo Siento Mi Vida	1978	2.00	4.00	8.00
❑ 45479	Tumbling Dice/I Never Will Marry	1978	—	2.00	4.00
❑ 45519	Back in the U.S.A./White Rhythm and Blues	1978	—	2.00	4.00
❑ 45519 [PS]	Back in the U.S.A./White Rhythm and Blues	1978	—	3.00	6.00
❑ 45546	Ooh Baby Baby/Blowing Away	1978	—	2.00	4.00
❑ 46011	Just One Look/Love Me Tender	1979	—	2.00	4.00
❑ 46034	Alison/Mohammed's Radio	1979	—	2.00	4.00
❑ 46602	How Do I Make You/Rambler Gambler	1980	—	2.00	4.00
❑ 46602 [PS]	How Do I Make You/Rambler Gambler	1980	—	2.50	5.00
❑ 46624	Hurt So Bad/Justine	1980	—	2.00	4.00
❑ 46654	I Can't Let Go/Look Out for My Love	1980	—	2.00	4.00
❑ 69476	(I Love You) For Sentimental Reasons/Straighten Up and Fly Right	1987	—	2.00	4.00
❑ 69507	When You Wish Upon a Star/Little Girl Blue	1986	—	2.00	4.00
❑ 69507 [PS]	When You Wish Upon a Star/Little Girl Blue	1986	—	2.00	4.00
❑ 69653	When I Fall in Love/It Never Entered My Mind	1985	—	2.00	4.00
❑ 69671	Lush Life/Skylark	1985	—	2.00	4.00
❑ 69725	Someone to Watch Over Me/What'll I Do	1984	—	2.00	4.00
❑ 69752	I've Got a Crush on You/Lover Man	1984	—	2.00	4.00
❑ 69780	What's New/Crazy He Calls Me	1983	—	2.00	4.00
❑ 69838	Easy for You to Say/Mr. Radio	1983	—	2.00	4.00
❑ 69853	I Knew You When/Talk to Me of Mendocino	1982	—	2.00	4.00
❑ 69853 [PS]	I Knew You When/Talk to Me of Mendocino	1982	—	2.50	5.00
❑ 69948	Get Closer/Sometimes You Just Can't Win	1982	—	2.00	4.00
❑ 69948 [PS]	Get Closer/Sometimes You Just Can't Win	1982	—	2.50	5.00
CAPITOL					
❑ 2438	Dolphins/The Long Way Around	1969	3.00	6.00	12.00
❑ 2767	Lovesick Blues/Will You Love Me Tomorrow	1970	2.00	4.00	8.00
❑ 2846	Long Long Time/Nobody's	1970	2.00	4.00	8.00
❑ 3021	The Long Way Around/(She's a) Very Lovely Woman	1971	—	3.00	6.00
❑ 3210	I Fall to Pieces/Can It Be True	1971	—	3.00	6.00
❑ 3273	Rock Me on the Water/Crazy Arms	1972	—	3.00	6.00
❑ 3990	You're No Good/I Can't Help It (If I'm Still in Love with You)	1974	—	2.00	4.00
❑ 4050	When Will I Be Loved/It Doesn't Matter Anymore	1975	—	2.00	4.00
ELEKTRA					
❑ 64427	The Waiting/Walk On	1995	—	—	3.00
❑ 64987	All My Life/Shattered	1990	—	—	3.00
—With Aaron Neville					
❑ 69261	Don't Know Much/Cry Like a Rainstorm	1989	—	—	3.00
—With Aaron Neville					
MCA					
❑ 52973	Somewhere Out There/(Instrumental)	1986	—	—	3.00
—With James Ingram					
❑ 52973 [PS]	Somewhere Out There/(Instrumental)	1986	—	2.00	4.00

ROOFTOP SINGERS, THE

Number	Title (A Side/B Side)	Yr	VG	VG+	NM
ATCO					
❑ 6526	My Life Is My Own/Kites	1967	—	3.00	6.00
PHILCO-FORD					
❑ HP-37	Walk Right In/Tom Cat	1969	3.75	7.50	15.00
—4-inch plastic "Hip Pocket Record" with color sleeve					
VANGUARD					
❑ 35017	Walk Right In/Cool Water	1962	2.50	5.00	10.00
❑ 35019	Tom Cat/Shoes	1963	2.00	4.00	8.00
❑ 35019 [PS]	Tom Cat/Shoes	1963	3.00	6.00	12.00
❑ 35020	Mama Don't Allow/It Don't Mean a Thing	1963	2.00	4.00	8.00
❑ 35020 [PS]	Mama Don't Allow/It Don't Mean a Thing	1963	3.00	6.00	12.00
❑ 35024	Sail Away Ladies/Twelve String	1964	2.00	4.00	8.00
❑ 35029	Rainy Day/Buddy Won't You Roll Down the Line	1964	2.00	4.00	8.00
❑ 35034	Ham and Eggs/Somebody Came Home	1965	2.00	4.00	8.00

ROOMATES, THE
Also see CATHY JEAN AND THE ROOMATES.

Number	Title (A Side/B Side)	Yr	VG	VG+	NM
BAN					
❑ 691	A Place Called Love/Knowing You	1985	—	2.50	5.00
CAMEO					
❑ 233	Sunday Kind of Love/A Lovely Way to Spend An Evening	1962	7.50	15.00	30.00
CANADIAN AMERICAN					
❑ 166	My Heart/Just for Tonight	1964	10.00	20.00	40.00
PHILIPS					
❑ 40105	Gee/Answer Me, My Love	1963	6.25	12.50	25.00
❑ 40153	The Nearness of You/Don't Cheat on Me	1963	6.25	12.50	25.00
PROMO					
❑ 2211	I Want a Little Girl/Making Believe	196?	5.00	10.00	20.00
—Sources conflict as to date (1960 or 1964)					
VALMOR					
❑ 008	Glory of Love/Never Know	1961	5.00	10.00	20.00
❑ 010	Band of Gold/O Baby Love	1961	5.00	10.00	20.00
❑ 013	My Foolish Heart/My Kisses for Your Thoughts	1962	5.00	10.00	20.00

ROONEY, TEDDY

Number	Title (A Side/B Side)	Yr	VG	VG+	NM
IMPERIAL					
❑ 5644	Bite Your Tongue/After the Dance	1960	10.00	20.00	40.00

ROOSTERS, THE
More than one group.

Number	Title (A Side/B Side)	Yr	VG	VG+	NM
A&M					
❑ 746	Shake a Tail Feather/Rooster Walk	1964	3.00	6.00	12.00
EPIC					
❑ 9487	Let's Try Again/Pretty Girl	1962	3.75	7.50	15.00
FELSTED					
❑ 8642	Chicken Hop/Fun House	1962	3.75	7.50	15.00
PHILIPS					
❑ 40504	Love Machine/I'm Suspectin'	1968	2.50	5.00	10.00
❑ 40559	Good Good Lovin'/Home Down Right	1968	2.00	4.00	8.00
SHAR-DEE					
❑ 704	Chicken Hop/Fun House	1959	5.00	10.00	20.00

ROSE GARDEN, THE

Number	Title (A Side/B Side)	Yr	VG	VG+	NM
ATCO					
❑ 6510	Next Plane to London/Flower Town	1967	3.00	6.00	12.00
❑ 6564	Here's Today/If My World Falls Through	1968	2.50	5.00	10.00

ROSE ROYCE

Number	Title (A Side/B Side)	Yr	VG	VG+	NM
ATLANTIC					
❑ 88942	Perfect Lover/You Get Right Down To It	1989	—	—	3.00
C&R					
❑ 7684	Magic Touch/(B-side unknown)	1984	—	2.50	5.00
EPIC					
❑ 02818	Best Love/Dance with Me	1982	—	2.00	4.00
❑ 02996	Fire in the Funk/Still in Love	1982	—	2.00	4.00
❑ 03319	Somehow We Made It Through the Rain/You Blew It	1982	—	2.00	4.00
MCA					
❑ 40615	Car Wash/Water	1976	—	2.50	5.00
—With Rose Royce's name prominent on label					
❑ 40615	Car Wash/Water	1976	2.00	4.00	8.00
—With "Music Composed and Produced by Norman Whitfield" and no mention of Rose Royce on either side					
❑ 40662	I Wanna Get Next to You/Sunrise	1976	—	2.50	5.00
❑ 40721	I'm Going Down/Yo Yo	1977	—	2.50	5.00

Number	Title (A Side/B Side)	Yr	VG	VG+	NM
❑ 40814	Put Your Money Where Your Mouth Is/You're On My Mind	1977	—	2.50	5.00

OMNI

Number	Title (A Side/B Side)	Yr	VG	VG+	NM
❑ 99476	Lonely Road/I Found Someone	1987	—	—	3.00
❑ 99488	Doesn't Have to Be That Way/You're My Peace of Mind	1986	—	—	3.00

WHITFIELD

Number	Title (A Side/B Side)	Yr	VG	VG+	NM
❑ 8440	Do Your Dance — Part 1/Do Your Dance — Part 2	1977	—	2.50	5.00
❑ 8491	Ooh Boy/You Can't Please Everybody	1977	—	2.50	5.00
❑ 8531	Wishing on a Star/Love, More Love	1978	—	2.50	5.00
❑ 8629	I'm in Love (And I Love the Feeling)/Get Up Off Your Fat	1978	—	2.50	5.00
❑ 8712	Love Don't Live Here Anymore/That's What's Wrong with Me	1978	—	2.50	5.00
❑ 8789	First Come, First Serve/Let Me Be the First to Know	1979	—	2.50	5.00
❑ 49049	Is It Love You're After/You Can't Run from Yourself	1979	—	2.50	5.00
❑ 49127	What You Waitin' For/Shine Your Light	1979	—	2.50	5.00
❑ 49274	Pop Your Fingers/I Wonder Where You Are Tonight	1980	—	2.50	5.00
❑ 49583	You're a Winner/Pazazz	1980	—	2.50	5.00
❑ 49624	Funkin' Around/Help Yourself	1980	—	2.50	5.00
❑ 49681	Golden Touch/Love Is In the Air	1981	—	2.50	5.00
❑ 49735	I Wanna Make It with You/Love Is in the Air	1981	—	2.50	5.00
❑ 49830	Fight It/R.R. Express	1981	—	2.50	5.00

ROSEBUDS, THE (1)

GEE

Number	Title (A Side/B Side)	Yr	VG	VG+	NM
❑ 1033	Dearest Darling/Unconditional Surrender	1957	12.50	25.00	50.00

LANCER

Number	Title (A Side/B Side)	Yr	VG	VG+	NM
❑ 102	Kiss Me Goodnight/Joey	1959	15.00	30.00	60.00

ROSEBUDS, THE (2)

TOWER

Number	Title (A Side/B Side)	Yr	VG	VG+	NM
❑ 104	Say You'll Be Mine/Mama Said	1964	3.00	6.00	12.00

ROSELLA, CARMELA

NANCY

Number	Title (A Side/B Side)	Yr	VG	VG+	NM
❑ 1004	Oh, It Was Elvis/Where?	1961	10.00	20.00	40.00

ROSES, THE

DOT

Number	Title (A Side/B Side)	Yr	VG	VG+	NM
❑ 15816	Almost Paradise/I Kissed An Angel	1958	6.25	12.50	25.00

ROSIE

RCA

Number	Title (A Side/B Side)	Yr	VG	VG+	NM
❑ PB-11090	Mississippi Baby/Words Don't Matter	1977	—	2.00	4.00

RCA VICTOR

Number	Title (A Side/B Side)	Yr	VG	VG+	NM
❑ PB-10610	Roll Me Through the Rushes/Denny's Ditty	1976	—	2.00	4.00

ROSIE AND THE ORIGINALS

BRUNSWICK

Number	Title (A Side/B Side)	Yr	VG	VG+	NM
❑ 55205	Lonely Blue Nights/We'll Have a Chance	1961	6.25	12.50	25.00

—By "Rosie, formerly with the Originals"

Number	Title (A Side/B Side)	Yr	VG	VG+	NM
❑ 55212	My Darling Forever/The Time Is Near	1961	6.25	12.50	25.00

—By "Rosie, formerly with the Originals"

ERA BACK TO BACK HITS

Number	Title (A Side/B Side)	Yr	VG	VG+	NM
❑ 038	Angel Baby/Bumble Boogie	197?	—	3.00	6.00

—B-side by B. Bumble and the Stingers

HIGHLAND

Number	Title (A Side/B Side)	Yr	VG	VG+	NM
❑ 1011	Angel Baby/Give Me Love	1960	6.25	12.50	25.00
❑ 1032	Lonely Blue Nights/We'll Have a Chance	196?	6.25	12.50	25.00

—Actually a reissue of Brunswick 55205, but harder to find

ROSS, DIANA

Also see THE SUPREMES.

COLUMBIA

Number	Title (A Side/B Side)	Yr	VG	VG+	NM
❑ 04507	All of You/The Last Time	1984	—	—	3.00

—A-side: Diana Ross and Julio Iglesias; B-side: Iglesias solo

Number	Title (A Side/B Side)	Yr	VG	VG+	NM
❑ 04507 [PS]	All of You/The Last Time	1984	—	—	3.00

MCA

Number	Title (A Side/B Side)	Yr	VG	VG+	NM
❑ 40947	Ease On Down the Road/Poppy Girls	1978	—	2.50	5.00

—With Michael Jackson

Number	Title (A Side/B Side)	Yr	VG	VG+	NM
❑ 40947 [PS]	Ease On Down the Road/Poppy Girls	1978	—	2.50	5.00

—With Michael Jackson

Number	Title (A Side/B Side)	Yr	VG	VG+	NM
❑ 53448	If We Hold On Together/(Instrumental)	1988	—	—	3.00
❑ 53448 [PS]	If We Hold On Together/(Instrumental)	1988	—	—	3.00

MOTOWN

Number	Title (A Side/B Side)	Yr	VG	VG+	NM
❑ (no #) [PS]	Diana Ross TV Special 4/8/71	1971	2.00	4.00	8.00

—Special sleeve issued with some Motown (usually Diana Ross) 45s in March and April 1971

Number	Title (A Side/B Side)	Yr	VG	VG+	NM
❑ 1165	Reach Out and Touch (Somebody's Hand)/Dark Side of the World	1970	—	2.50	5.00
❑ 1165 [PS]	Reach Out and Touch (Somebody's Hand)/Dark Side of the World	1970	3.00	6.00	12.00
❑ 1169	Ain't No Mountain High Enough/Can't It Wait Until Tomorrow	1970	—	2.50	5.00
❑ 1169 [PS]	Ain't No Mountain High Enough/Can't It Wait Until Tomorrow	1970	3.00	6.00	12.00
❑ 1176	Remember Me/What About You	1971	—	2.50	5.00
❑ 1176 [PS]	Remember Me/What About You	1971	3.00	6.00	12.00
❑ 1184	Reach Out I'll Be There/Close to You	1971	—	2.50	5.00
❑ 1188	Surrender/I'm a Winner	1971	—	2.50	5.00
❑ 1192	I'm Still Waiting/A Simple Thing Like Cry	1971	—	2.50	5.00
❑ 1211	Good Morning Heartache/God Bless the Child	1972	—	2.50	5.00
❑ 1211 [PS]	Good Morning Heartache/God Bless the Child	1972	2.50	5.00	10.00
❑ 1239	Touch Me in the Morning/I Won't Last a Day Without You	1973	—	2.50	5.00
❑ 1278	Last Time I Saw Him/Save the Children	1973	—	2.50	5.00
❑ 1295	Sleepin'/You	1974	—	2.50	5.00
❑ 1335	Sorry Doesn't Always Make It Right/Together	1975	—	2.50	5.00
❑ 1335 [PS]	Sorry Doesn't Always Make It Right/Together	1975	3.00	6.00	12.00
❑ 1377	Do You Know Where You're Going To/No One's Gonna Be a Fool Forever	1975	3.00	6.00	12.00

—Possibly Canadian release only, with different A-side title

Number	Title (A Side/B Side)	Yr	VG	VG+	NM
❑ 1377	Theme from Mahogany (Do You Know Where You're Going To)/No One's Gonna Be a Fool Forever	1975	—	2.50	5.00
❑ 1377 [PS]	Theme from Mahogany (Do You Know Where You're Going To)/No One's Gonna Be a Fool Forever	1975	5.00	10.00	20.00
❑ 1387	I Thought It Took a Little Time (But Today I Fell in Love)/After You	1976	—	2.50	5.00
❑ 1387 [PS]	I Thought It Took a Little Time (But Today I Fell in Love)/After You	1976	2.50	5.00	10.00
❑ 1392	Love Hangover/Kiss Me Now	1976	—	2.50	5.00
❑ 1398	One Love in My Lifetime/Smile	1976	—	2.50	5.00
❑ 1427	Gettin' Ready for Love/Confide in Me	1977	—	2.50	5.00
❑ 1436	Your Love Is So Good for Me/Baby It's Me	1978	—	2.50	5.00
❑ 1442	You Got It/Too Shy to Say	1978	—	2.50	5.00
❑ 1449 [DJ]	Top of the World (same on both sides)	1978	12.50	25.00	50.00

—Promo only; withdrawn before stock copies were pressed

Number	Title (A Side/B Side)	Yr	VG	VG+	NM
❑ 1450	Lovin' Livin' and Givin'/Baby It's Me	1978	—	—	—

—Unreleased

Number	Title (A Side/B Side)	Yr	VG	VG+	NM
❑ 1456	What You Gave Me/Together	1979	—	2.00	4.00
❑ 1462	The Boss/I'm in the World	1979	—	2.00	4.00
❑ 1471	It's My House/Sparkle	1979	—	2.00	4.00
❑ 1491	I'm Coming Out/Give Up	1980	—	2.00	4.00
❑ 1494	Upside Down/Friend to Friend	1980	—	2.00	4.00
❑ 1496	It's My Turn/Together	1980	—	2.00	4.00
❑ 1496 [PS]	It's My Turn/Together	1980	3.00	6.00	12.00
❑ 1508	One More Chance/After You	1981	—	2.00	4.00
❑ 1513	To Love Again/Crying My Heart Out for You	1981	—	2.00	4.00
❑ 1519	Endless Love/(Instrumental)	1981	—	2.00	4.00

—With Lionel Richie

Number	Title (A Side/B Side)	Yr	VG	VG+	NM
❑ 1531	My Old Piano/Now That You're Gone	1981	—	2.00	4.00
❑ 1626	We Can Never Light That Old Flame Again/Old Funky Rolls	1982	—	2.00	4.00
❑ 1964	Workin' Overtime/(Instrumental)	1989	—	—	3.00
❑ 1964 [PS]	Workin' Overtime/(Instrumental)	1989	—	—	3.00
❑ 1998	This House/Paradise	1989	—	—	3.00
❑ 2003	Bottom Line/(Instrumental)	1989	—	—	3.00
❑ 2139	When You Tell Me That You Love Me/You and I	1991	—	2.00	4.00

RCA

Number	Title (A Side/B Side)	Yr	VG	VG+	NM
❑ 5172-7-R	Dirty Looks/So Close	1987	—	—	3.00
❑ 5172-7-R [PS]	Dirty Looks/So Close	1987	—	—	3.00
❑ 5297-7-R	Tell Me Again/I Am Me	1987	—	—	3.00
❑ 5297-7-R [PS]	Tell Me Again/I Am Me	1987	—	—	3.00
❑ PB-12349	Why Do Fools Fall in Love/Think I'm in Love	1981	—	2.00	4.00
❑ JB-13013 [DJ]	Endless Love (Long)/Endless Love (Short)	1981	2.50	5.00	10.00

—Promo only

Number	Title (A Side/B Side)	Yr	VG	VG+	NM
❑ PB-13021	Mirror, Mirror/Sweet Nothings	1981	—	2.00	4.00
❑ PB-13201	Work That Body/You Can Make It	1982	—	2.00	4.00
❑ PB-13348	Muscles/I Am Me	1982	—	2.00	4.00
❑ PB-13348 [PS]	Muscles/I Am Me	1982	—	2.00	4.00
❑ PB-13424	So Close/Fool for Your Love	1983	—	2.00	4.00
❑ GB-13479	Why Do Fools Fall in Love/Mirror, Mirror	1983	—	—	3.00

—Gold Standard Series

Number	Title (A Side/B Side)	Yr	VG	VG+	NM
❑ PB-13549	Pieces of Ice/Still in Love	1983	—	2.00	4.00
❑ PB-13549 [PS]	Pieces of Ice/Still in Love	1983	—	2.00	4.00
❑ PB-13624	Up Front/Love or Loneliness	1983	—	2.00	4.00
❑ PB-13671	Let's Go Up/Girls	1983	—	2.00	4.00
❑ GB-13798	Muscles/Pieces of Ice	1984	—	—	3.00

—Gold Standard Series

Number	Title (A Side/B Side)	Yr	VG	VG+	NM
❑ PB-13864	Swept Away/Fight for It	1984	—	—	3.00
❑ PB-13864 [PS]	Swept Away/Fight for It	1984	—	—	3.00
❑ PB-13966	Missing You/We Are the Children of the World	1984	—	—	3.00
❑ PB-13966 [PS]	Missing You/We Are the Children of the World	1984	—	—	3.00
❑ PB-14032	Telephone/Fool for Your Love	1985	—	—	3.00
❑ PB-14032 [PS]	Telephone/Fool for Your Love	1985	—	—	3.00
❑ PB-14181	Eaten Alive/(Instrumental)	1985	—	—	3.00
❑ PB-14181 [PS]	Eaten Alive/(Instrumental)	1985	—	—	3.00
❑ PB-14244	Chain Reaction/More and More	1985	—	2.00	4.00
❑ PB-14244	Chain Reaction (Remix)/More and More	1986	—	—	3.00
❑ PB-14244 [PS]	Chain Reaction/More and More	1985	—	—	3.00
❑ GB-14342	Missing You/Swept Away	1986	—	—	3.00

—Gold Standard Series

7-Inch Extended Plays

MOTOWN

Number	Title (A Side/B Side)	Yr	VG	VG+	NM
❑ LLP-133 [DJ]	My Place/Baby It's Love/The Long and Winding Road//How About You/I'm Still Waiting/Everything Is Everything	1971	3.00	6.00	12.00

—Jukebox issue, small hole, plays at 33 1/3 rpm

Number	Title (A Side/B Side)	Yr	VG	VG+	NM
❑ LLP-133 [PS]	Everything Is Everything	1971	3.00	6.00	12.00

—Part of "Little LP" series

ROSS, DIANA, AND MARVIN GAYE

Also see each artist's individual listings.

MOTOWN

Number	Title (A Side/B Side)	Yr	VG	VG+	NM
❑ 1269	My Mistake (Was to Love You)/Include Me in Your Life	1973	—	2.50	5.00
❑ 1280	You're a Special Part of Me/I'm Falling in Love with You	1973	—	2.50	5.00
❑ 1296	Don't Knock My Love/Just Say Just Say	1974	—	2.50	5.00

ROSS, DIANA; MARVIN GAYE; SMOKEY ROBINSON; AND STEVIE WONDER

Also see each artist's individual listings.

MOTOWN

Number	Title (A Side/B Side)	Yr	VG	VG+	NM
❑ 1455	Pops, We Love You/(Instrumental)	1979	—	2.00	4.00

ROSS, DIANA, AND THE SUPREMES
See THE SUPREMES.

ROSS, JACKIE

Number	Title (A Side/B Side)	Yr	VG	VG+	NM
BRUNSWICK					
❑ 55325	Keep Your Chin Up/Love Is Easy to Lose	1967	2.00	4.00	8.00
❑ 55361	Mr. Sunshine/Walk on My Side	1968	2.00	4.00	8.00
CAPITOL					
❑ 4308	I Can't Stand to See You Go/Ain't No Fun to Me	1976	—	2.00	4.00
CHESS					
❑ 1903	Selfish One/Everything But Love	1964	2.00	4.00	8.00
❑ 1913	I've Got the Skill/Change Your Ways	1964	2.00	4.00	8.00
❑ 1915	Haste Makes Waste/Wasting Time	1964	2.00	4.00	8.00
❑ 1920	Jerk and Twine/New Lover	1965	2.00	4.00	8.00
❑ 1929	You Really Know How to Hurt a Girl/Dynamite Lovin'	1965	2.00	4.00	8.00
❑ 1938	Take Me for a Little While/Honey Dear	1965	2.00	4.00	8.00
❑ 1940	We Can Do It/Honey Dear	1965	2.00	4.00	8.00
GSF					
❑ 6886	Woman Get Nothing from Love/Do I	1972	—	2.50	5.00
❑ 6895	A One Woman Man/Take the Weight Off Me	1973	—	2.50	5.00
MERCURY					
❑ 73041	Angel of the Morning/Showcase	1970	—	3.00	6.00
❑ 73185	Glory Be/I Must Give You Time	1971	—	3.00	6.00
SAR					
❑ 129	Hard Times/Hold Me	1962	3.75	7.50	15.00
—As "Jacki Ross"					
SCEPTER					
❑ 12345	The World's in a Hell of a Shape/What Would You Give	1972	—	2.50	5.00

ROSSINGTON
Successor to ROSSINGTON-COLLINS BAND.

Number	Title (A Side/B Side)	Yr	VG	VG+	NM
ATLANTIC					
❑ 89364	Turn It Up/The Path Less Chosen	1986	—	—	3.00

ROSSINGTON-COLLINS BAND
Surviving members of LYNYRD SKYNYRD (Gary Rossington and Allen Collins) with lead singer Dale Krantz. Also see ROSSINGTON.

Number	Title (A Side/B Side)	Yr	VG	VG+	NM
MCA					
❑ 41284	Don't Misunderstand Me/Winners and Losers	1980	—	2.00	4.00
❑ 51023	Getaway/Sometimes You Can Put It Out	1980	—	2.00	4.00
❑ 51218	Don't Stop Me Now/Gotta Get It Straight	1981	—	2.00	4.00

ROSSINI, TONI

Number	Title (A Side/B Side)	Yr	VG	VG+	NM
SUN					
❑ 349	I Gotta Know/Is It Too Late	1960	5.00	10.00	20.00
❑ 366	Well I Ask Ya/Darlena	1961	5.00	10.00	20.00
❑ 378	Meet Me After School/Just Around the Corner	1962	5.00	10.00	20.00
❑ 380	New Girl in Town/You Made It Sound So Easy	1962	5.00	10.00	20.00
❑ 387	Nobody/Moved to Kansas City	1964	5.00	10.00	20.00

ROTARY CONNECTION
Also see MINNIE RIPERTON.

Number	Title (A Side/B Side)	Yr	VG	VG+	NM
CADET CONCEPT					
❑ DJ-1 [DJ]	Lady Jane/Amen	1968	3.75	7.50	15.00
❑ 7000	Like a Rollin' Stone/Turn Me On	1967	2.50	5.00	10.00
❑ 7002	Ruby Tuesday/Soul Man	1968	2.50	5.00	10.00
❑ 7007	Paper Castle/Teach Me How to Fly	1968	2.50	5.00	10.00
❑ 7008	Aladdin/Magical World	1968	2.50	5.00	10.00
❑ 7009	Silent Night Chant/Peace At Least	1968	3.00	6.00	12.00
❑ 7014	The Weight/Respect	1969	2.50	5.00	10.00
❑ 7018	Want You to Know/Memory Band	1969	2.50	5.00	10.00
❑ 7021	Love Me Now/May Our Amens Be True	1970	2.50	5.00	10.00
❑ 7027	Stormy Monday Blues/Teach Me How to Fly	1970	2.50	5.00	10.00
❑ 7028	Hey Love/If I Sing My Song	1971	2.50	5.00	10.00
—As "New Rotary Connection"					
JANUS					
❑ 249	Living Alone/Magical World	1975	—	2.50	5.00
—As "Minnie Riperton and Rotary Connection"					

ROTATIONS, THE (1)

Number	Title (A Side/B Side)	Yr	VG	VG+	NM
FRANTIC					
❑ 200	Put a Nickel on D-9 (Pt. 1)/Put a Nickel on D-9 (Pt. 2)	1965	37.50	75.00	150.00
❑ 202	Changed Man/Heartaches	1967	25.00	50.00	100.00
MALA					
❑ 576	Misty Roses/Trying to Make You My Own	1967	7.50	15.00	30.00

ROTATIONS, THE (2)

Number	Title (A Side/B Side)	Yr	VG	VG+	NM
ORIGINAL SOUND					
❑ 41	The Crusher/Heavies	1964	25.00	50.00	100.00
—Produced by FRANK ZAPPA					

ROTH, DAVID LEE
Also see VAN HALEN.

Number	Title (A Side/B Side)	Yr	VG	VG+	NM
WARNER BROS.					
❑ 27825	Skyscraper/Damn Good	1988	—	—	3.00
❑ 27825 [PS]	Skyscraper/Damn Good	1988	—	—	3.00
❑ 28108	Stand Up/Knucklebones	1988	—	—	3.00
❑ 28108 [PS]	Stand Up/Knucklebones	1988	—	—	3.00
❑ 28119	Just Like Paradise/Bottom Line	1988	—	—	3.00
❑ 28119 [PS]	Just Like Paradise/Bottom Line	1988	—	—	3.00
❑ 28511	That's Life/Bump and Grind	1986	—	—	3.00
❑ 28511 [PS]	That's Life/Bump and Grind	1986	—	—	3.00
❑ 28584	Goin' Crazy!/Occo Deo Calor!	1986	—	—	3.00
❑ 28584 [PS]	Goin' Crazy!/Occo Deo Calor!	1986	—	—	3.00
❑ 28656	Yankee Rose/Shyboy	1986	—	—	3.00
❑ 28656 [PS]	Yankee Rose/Shyboy	1986	—	—	3.00
❑ 29040	Just a Gigolo-I Ain't Got Nobody/Just a Gigolo-I Ain't Got Nobody	1985	—	—	3.00
❑ 29040 [PS]	Just a Gigolo-I Ain't Got Nobody/Just a Gigolo-I Ain't Got Nobody	1985	—	—	3.00
❑ 29102	California Girls/California Girls (Remix)	1985	—	—	3.00
❑ 29102 [PS]	California Girls/California Girls (Remix)	1985	—	—	3.00

ROULETTES, THE
More than one group.

Number	Title (A Side/B Side)	Yr	VG	VG+	NM
ANGLE					
❑ 1001	Surfer's Charge/Archibald II (Duke of Nothing)	1963	12.50	25.00	50.00
CHAMP					
❑ 102	I See a Star/Come On, Baby	1958	20.00	40.00	80.00
EBB					
❑ 124	The Way You Carry On/You Don't Care Anymore	1957	7.50	15.00	30.00
SCEPTER					
❑ 1204	Hasten Jason/Wouldn't It Be Goin' Steady	1959	150.00	300.00	600.00
UNITED ARTISTS					
❑ 718	Can You Go/Soon You'll Be Leaving Me	1964	2.50	5.00	10.00
❑ 990	Long Cigarette/Junk	1966	2.50	5.00	10.00

ROUND, JONATHAN

Number	Title (A Side/B Side)	Yr	VG	VG+	NM
WESTBOUND					
❑ 186	Don't It Make You Want to Go Home/Train a-Comin'	1971	2.00	4.00	8.00
❑ 199	Sympathy for the Devil/Travelin' Mama Blues	1972	2.50	5.00	10.00

ROUTERS, THE

Number	Title (A Side/B Side)	Yr	VG	VG+	NM
MERCURY					
❑ 73418	Superbird/Sack of Woe	1973	—	3.00	6.00
WARNER BROS.					
❑ 5283	Let's Go (pony)/Mashy	1962	3.75	7.50	15.00
❑ 5332	Half Time/Make It Snappy	1963	3.00	6.00	12.00
❑ 5349	Sting Ray/Snap Happy	1963	3.00	6.00	12.00
❑ 5379	A-Ooga/Big Band	1963	3.00	6.00	12.00
❑ 5403	Snap, Crackle and Pop/Amoeba	1963	3.00	6.00	12.00
❑ 5444	Crack Up/Let's Dance	1964	3.00	6.00	12.00
❑ 5467	Stamp and Shake/Ah-Ya	1964	3.00	6.00	12.00
❑ 7117	Let's Go (pony)/Mashy	1967	2.50	5.00	10.00

ROVER BOYS, THE

Number	Title (A Side/B Side)	Yr	VG	VG+	NM
ABC-PARAMOUNT					
❑ 9659	Come to Me/Love Me Again	1955	3.75	7.50	15.00
❑ 9678	My Queen/Sixteen Teens	1956	3.75	7.50	15.00
❑ 9700	Graduation Day/I Hear Music	1956	3.75	7.50	15.00
❑ 9732	From a School Ring to a Wedding Ring/Young Love	1956	3.75	7.50	15.00
❑ 9760	The Piano Tuner/Whoop Doodly Baby	1956	3.75	7.50	15.00
❑ 9779	Little Did I Know/Again and Again	1957	3.75	7.50	15.00
CORAL					
❑ 61271	Show Me/You've Got It	1954	5.00	10.00	20.00
DECCA					
❑ 31485	Shalom/I Hear Havana	1963	2.00	4.00	8.00
RCA VICTOR					
❑ 47-7432	Magic Lamp/Little Darlin'	1959	3.00	6.00	12.00
❑ 47-7482	Sweet Violets/Julia	1959	3.00	6.00	12.00
UNITED ARTISTS					
❑ 288	Is It Me/Marry Young	1961	2.50	5.00	10.00
❑ 331	For Every Boy or Girl/If You Plant a Little Kiss	1961	2.50	5.00	10.00
VIK					
❑ 0283	Soft Sands/My Baby's Steppin' Out	1957	5.00	10.00	20.00
❑ 0302	What Can I Do for a Heartache/I Got to You	1957	5.00	10.00	20.00
❑ 0313	Blue Willow/You're My Everything	1958	5.00	10.00	20.00
❑ 0317	Blind Date/Make Room for Me	1958	5.00	10.00	20.00
❑ 0338	S'Agapo/Ask Me Who Loves You	1958	5.00	10.00	20.00

ROVERS, THE (1)

Number	Title (A Side/B Side)	Yr	VG	VG+	NM
CAPITOL					
❑ F3078	Why Oh-h/Ichi-Bon Tami Dachi	1955	12.50	25.00	50.00
MUSIC CITY					
❑ 750	Why Oh-h/Ichi-Bon Tami Dachi	1954	20.00	40.00	80.00
—Black vinyl					
❑ 750	Why Oh-h/Ichi-Bon Tami Dachi	1954	62.50	125.00	250.00
—Red vinyl					
❑ 780	Salute to Johnny Ace/Jadda	1955	20.00	40.00	80.00
—Black vinyl					
❑ 780	Salute to Johnny Ace/Jadda	1955	62.50	125.00	250.00
—Red vinyl					

ROVERS, THE (2)

Number	Title (A Side/B Side)	Yr	VG	VG+	NM
CHATTAHOOCHIE					
❑ 653	The Web/Can't Be the First	1964	2.50	5.00	10.00

ROVERS, THE (3)

Number	Title (A Side/B Side)	Yr	VG	VG+	NM
KAPP					
❑ 278	Delia's Gone/I Know Where I'm Goin'	1959	3.00	6.00	12.00

ROVERS, THE (4)
Also see THE IRISH ROVERS.

Number	Title (A Side/B Side)	Yr	VG	VG+	NM
CLEVELAND INT'L.					
❑ 02148	Mexican Girl/Pheasant Pluckers Son	1981	—	2.00	4.00
❑ 02728	Pain in My Past/Daddies (Bobby's Song)	1982	—	2.00	4.00
❑ 02911	People Who Read People Magazine/Roly Poly Ladies	1982	—	2.00	4.00
❑ 51007	Wasn't That a Party/Matchstalk Men and Matchstalk Cats & Dogs	1981	—	2.50	5.00
EPIC					
❑ 03089	Wasn't That a Party/Pain in My Past	1982	—	—	3.00
—Reissue					

ROVIN' KIND, THE

Number	Title (A Side/B Side)	Yr	VG	VG+	NM
DUNWICH					
❑ 146	My Generation/Girl	1967	5.00	10.00	20.00
❑ 154	She/Didn't Want to Have to Do It	1967	5.00	10.00	20.00

Number	Title (A Side/B Side)	Yr	VG	VG+	NM
ROULETTE					
❑ 4687	Right on Time/Night People	1966	3.75	7.50	15.00

ROXETTE

Number	Title (A Side/B Side)	Yr	VG	VG+	NM
CAPITOL					
❑ B-5380	Teaser Japanese/Can You Touch Me	1984	—	3.00	6.00
❑ S7-17400	Almost Unreal/The Heart Shaped Sea	1993	—	2.00	4.00
EMI					
❑ 7PRO-04409 [DJ]	Listen to Your Heart (same on both sides)	1989	2.00	4.00	8.00
—Vinyl originally was promo only					
❑ S7-18044	Sleeping in My Car/The Look (Unplugged)	1994	—	2.00	4.00
—Yellow vinyl					
❑ S7-18128	Crash! Boom! Bang!/Joyride (Unplugged)	1994	—	2.00	4.00
—Yellow vinyl					
❑ 50190	The Look/Silver Blue	1989	—	2.00	4.00
❑ 50204	Dressed for Success/The Look	1989	—	2.00	4.00
❑ 50223	Listen to Your Heart/Half a Woman, Half a Shadow	1990	2.50	5.00	10.00
❑ 50233	Dangerous/Dangerous (12" Version)	1990	2.50	5.00	10.00
❑ 50283	It Must Have Been Love/Chances	1990	2.50	5.00	10.00
❑ S7-57697	Church of Your Heart/I Call Your Name	1992	—	2.00	4.00
❑ S7-57991	How Do You Do!/Fading Like a Flower (Live)	1992	—	2.00	4.00

ROXY MUSIC

Also see BRYAN FERRY.

Number	Title (A Side/B Side)	Yr	VG	VG+	NM
ATCO					
❑ 7018	The Thrill of It All/The Application Failed	1975	—	2.00	4.00
❑ 7042	Love Is the Drug/Both Ends Burning	1975	—	2.00	4.00
❑ 7100	Dance Away/Trash 2	1979	—	2.00	4.00
❑ 7204	Angel Eyes/My Little Girl	1979	—	2.00	4.00
❑ 7301	Over You/My Only Love	1980	—	2.00	4.00
❑ 7310	Oh Yeah (On the Radio)/Rain, Rain, Rain	1980	—	2.00	4.00
❑ 7315	In the Midnight Hour/(B-side unknown)	1980	—	2.00	4.00
❑ 7329	Jealous Guy/To Turn You On	1981	—	2.00	4.00
❑ 7329 [PS]	Jealous Guy/To Turn You On	1981	—	2.00	4.00
ATLANTIC					
❑ 13269	Love Is the Drug/Dance Away	198?	—	—	3.00
—Oldies Series reissue					
REPRISE					
❑ 1124	Virginia Plan/The Numberer	1972	—	2.50	5.00
WARNER BROS.					
❑ GWB 0316	Do the Strand/Virginia Plain	197?	—	—	3.00
—"Back to Back Hits" series					
❑ 7719	Do the Strand/Editions of You	1973	—	2.50	5.00
❑ 29912	More Than This/Always Unknowing	1982	—	—	3.00
❑ 29978	Take a Chance with Me/India	1982	—	—	3.00
❑ 29978 [PS]	Take a Chance with Me/India	1982	—	—	3.00

ROYAL, BILLY JOE

Number	Title (A Side/B Side)	Yr	VG	VG+	NM
ALL WOOD					
❑ 401	Wait for Me Baby/If It Wasn't for a Woman	1962	5.00	10.00	20.00
ATLANTIC					
❑ 2328	Never in a Hundred Years/We Haven't a Moment to Lose	1966	2.50	5.00	10.00
❑ 87770	If the Jukebox Took Teardrops/How Could You	1991	—	2.00	4.00
❑ 87867	Ring Where a Ring Used to Be/We Need to Walk	1990	—	2.00	4.00
❑ 87933	Searchin' for Some Kind of Clue/This Too Shall Pass	1990	—	2.00	4.00
❑ 88815	Till I Can't Take It Anymore/He Don't Know	1990	—	2.00	4.00
ATLANTIC AMERICA					
❑ 99217	Love Has No Right/Cross My Heart and Hope to Try	1989	—	—	3.00
❑ 99217 [PS]	Love Has No Right/Cross My Heart and Hope to Try	1989	—	2.00	4.00
❑ 99242	Tell It Like It Is/Losing You	1989	—	—	3.00
❑ 99242 [PS]	Tell It Like It Is/Losing You	1989	—	2.00	4.00
❑ 99295	It Keeps Right On Hurtin'/Let It Rain	1988	—	—	3.00
❑ 99295 [PS]	It Keeps Right On Hurtin'/Let It Rain	1988	—	—	3.00
❑ 99364	Out of Sight and On My Mind/She Don't Cry Like She Used To	1988	—	—	3.00
❑ 99364 [PS]	Out of Sight and On My Mind/She Don't Cry Like She Used To	1988	—	—	3.00
❑ 99404	I'll Pin a Note on Your Pillow/A Place for a Heartache	1987	—	—	3.00
❑ 99404 [PS]	I'll Pin a Note on Your Pillow/A Place for a Heartache	1987	—	—	3.00
❑ 99485	Old Bridges Burn Slow/We've Both Got a Lot to Learn	1987	—	—	3.00
❑ 99485 [PS]	Old Bridges Burn Slow/We've Both Got a Lot to Learn	1987	—	—	3.00
❑ 99519	I Miss You Already/Another Endless Night	1986	—	—	3.00
❑ 99555	Boardwalk Angel/Out of Sight and On My Mind	1986	—	—	3.00
❑ 99599	Burned Like a Rocket/Lonely Loving You	1985	—	—	3.00
COLUMBIA					
❑ 43305	Down in the Boondocks/Oh, What a Night	1965	2.50	5.00	10.00
❑ 43305 [DJ]	Down in the Boondocks (same on both sides)	1965	10.00	20.00	40.00
—Red vinyl promo					
❑ 43390	I Knew You When/Steal Away	1965	2.50	5.00	10.00
❑ 43390 [DJ]	I Knew You When (same on both sides)	1965	10.00	20.00	40.00
—Red vinyl promo					
❑ 43465	I've Got to Be Somebody/You Make Me Feel Like a Man	1965	2.00	4.00	8.00
❑ 43465 [DJ]	I've Got to Be Somebody (same on both sides)	1965	7.50	15.00	30.00
—Red vinyl promo					
❑ 43538	It's a Good Time/Don't Wait Up for Me Mama	1966	2.00	4.00	8.00
❑ 43622	Heart's Desire/Keep Inside Me	1966	2.00	4.00	8.00
❑ 43740	Campfire Girls/Should I Come Back	1966	2.00	4.00	8.00
❑ 43883	Yo-Yo/We Tried	1966	2.00	4.00	8.00
❑ 44003	Wisdom of a Fool/Everything Turned Blue	1967	2.00	4.00	8.00
❑ 44103	These Are Not My People/The Greatest Love	1967	2.00	4.00	8.00
❑ 44277	Hush/Watching from the Bandstand	1967	2.00	4.00	8.00
❑ 44468	Don't You Be Ashamed (To Call My Name)/Don't You Think It's Time	1968	2.00	4.00	8.00
❑ 44574	Storybook Children/Just Between You and Me	1968	2.00	4.00	8.00
❑ 44677	Movies in My Mind/Gabriel	1968	—	3.00	6.00
❑ 44743	Bed of Roses/The Greatest Love	1969	—	3.00	6.00
❑ 44814	Nobody Loves You But Me/Baby I'm Thinking of You	1969	—	2.50	5.00
❑ 44902	Cherry Hill Park/Helping Hand	1969	2.00	4.00	8.00
❑ 45085	Mama's Song/Me Without You	1970	—	2.50	5.00
❑ 45220	Burning a Hole/Every Night	1970	—	2.50	5.00
❑ 45289	Tulsa/Pick Up the Pieces	1970	—	2.50	5.00
❑ 45406	Poor Little Pearl/Lady Lives to Love	1971	—	2.50	5.00
❑ 45495	Colorado Rain/We Go Back	1971	—	2.50	5.00
❑ 45557	Later/The Family	1972	—	3.00	6.00
❑ 45620	Child of Mine/Natchez Trace	1972	—	3.00	6.00
FAIRLANE					
❑ 21009	Never in a Hundred Years/We Haven't a Moment to Lose	1961	7.50	15.00	30.00
❑ 21013	Dark Glasses/Perhaps	1962	7.50	15.00	30.00
KAT FAMILY					
❑ 01044	(Who is Like You) Sweet America/No Love Like a First Love	1981	—	2.00	4.00
❑ 02074	You Really Got a Hold on Me/No Love Like a First Love	1981	—	2.00	4.00
❑ 02297	Wasted Time/Outrun the Sun	1981	—	2.00	4.00
MERCURY					
❑ 76069	Mr. Kool/Let's Talk It Over	1980	—	2.00	4.00
MGM SOUTH					
❑ 7011	This Magic Moment/Mountain Woman	1973	—	2.50	5.00
❑ 7018	Summertime Skies/Look What I Found	1973	—	2.50	5.00
❑ 7022	If This Is the Last Time/Perfect Harmony	1973	—	2.50	5.00
❑ 7032	Star Again/Sugar Blue	1974	—	2.50	5.00
PLAYER'S					
❑ 1	I'm Specialized/Really You	1965	5.00	10.00	20.00
PRIVATE STOCK					
❑ 45192	Under the Boardwalk/Precious Time	1978	—	2.50	5.00
❑ 45212 [DJ]	Anchors Aweigh (mono/stereo)	1979	—	2.50	5.00
SCEPTER					
❑ 12419	All Night Rain/Time Don't Pass By Here	1976	—	2.00	4.00
TOLLIE					
❑ 9011	Mama Didn't Raise No Fools/Get Behind Me, Devil	1964	3.75	7.50	15.00

ROYAL DEBS, THE

Number	Title (A Side/B Side)	Yr	VG	VG+	NM
TIFCO					
❑ 826	I Do/Jerry	1962	6.25	12.50	25.00

ROYAL DRIFTERS, THE

Number	Title (A Side/B Side)	Yr	VG	VG+	NM
TEEN					
❑ 506	S'Why Hard/Little Linda	1959	25.00	50.00	100.00
❑ 508	To Each His Own/Da Kind	1959	37.50	75.00	150.00

ROYAL GUARDSMEN, THE

Number	Title (A Side/B Side)	Yr	VG	VG+	NM
LAURIE					
❑ 112	Snoopy's Christmas/The Smallest Astronaut	197?	—	2.00	4.00
—B-side by Barry Winslow; reissue					
❑ 3359	Baby Let's Wait/Leaving Me	1966	2.50	5.00	10.00
❑ 3366	Snoopy vs. the Red Baron/I Needed You	1966	3.00	6.00	12.00
❑ 3379	The Return of the Red Baron/Sweetmeats Slide	1967	2.50	5.00	10.00
❑ 3391	Airplane Song (My Airplane)/Om	1967	2.00	4.00	8.00
❑ 3397	Wednesday/So Right (To Be in Love)	1967	2.00	4.00	8.00
❑ 3416	Snoopy's Christmas/It Kinda Looks Like Christmas	1967	2.50	5.00	10.00
❑ 3416 [PS]	Snoopy's Christmas/It Kinda Looks Like Christmas	1967	5.00	10.00	20.00
❑ 3428	I Say Love/I'm Not Gonna Stay	1968	2.00	4.00	8.00
❑ 3451	Snoopy for President/Down Behind the Lines	1968	2.00	4.00	8.00
❑ 3461	Baby Let's Wait/Biplane "Evermore"	1968	2.00	4.00	8.00
❑ 3461	Baby Let's Wait/So Right (To Be in Love)	1968	2.00	4.00	8.00
❑ 3494	Magic Window/Mother, Where's Your Daughter	1969	2.50	5.00	8.00
❑ 3590	Snoopy for President/Down Behind the Lines	1972	—	3.00	6.00
❑ 3646	Snoopy for President/Sweetmeats Slide	1976	—	2.50	5.00

ROYAL HALOS, THE

Number	Title (A Side/B Side)	Yr	VG	VG+	NM
ALADDIN					
❑ 3460	My Love Is True/Nobody But Me and My Girl	1959	10.00	20.00	40.00

ROYAL HOLIDAYS, THE

Number	Title (A Side/B Side)	Yr	VG	VG+	NM
CARLTON					
❑ 472	Margaret/I'm Sorry	1958	6.25	12.50	25.00
HERALD					
❑ 536	Rockin' at the Bandstand/Down in Cuba	1959	37.50	75.00	150.00
—Most, and perhaps all, copies were labeled "Chip Chip"/"Running to You" by the Mello-Kings					
PENTHOUSE					
❑ 9357	Margaret/I'm Sorry	1958	37.50	75.00	150.00

ROYAL ROBINS, THE

Number	Title (A Side/B Side)	Yr	VG	VG+	NM
ABC-PARAMOUNT					
❑ 10504	Turn Me Loose/Country Fool	1963	7.50	15.00	30.00
❑ 10542	How High the Moon/Something You've Got, Baby	1964	7.50	15.00	30.00

ROYAL TEENS, THE

Bob Gaudio, later of THE FOUR SEASONS, was in this group.

Number	Title (A Side/B Side)	Yr	VG	VG+	NM
ABC-PARAMOUNT					
❑ 9882	Short Shorts/Planet Rock	1958	7.50	15.00	30.00
❑ 9918	Big Name Button/Sham Rock	1958	6.25	12.50	25.00
❑ 9945	Harvey's Got a Girl Friend/Hangin' Around	1958	6.25	12.50	25.00
❑ 9955	Open the Door/My Kind of Dream	1958	6.25	12.50	25.00
ALLNEW					
❑ 1415	Short Short Twist/Royal Twist	1962	5.00	10.00	20.00
ASTRA					
❑ 1012	Mad Gass/Sittin' with My Baby	196?	3.75	7.50	15.00

Number	Title (A Side/B Side)	Yr	VG	VG+	NM
CAPITOL					
❑ F4261	Believe Me/Little Cricket	1959	7.50	15.00	30.00
❑ 4335	The Moon's Not Meant for Lovers/Was It a Dream	1960	7.50	15.00	30.00
❑ 4402	With You/It's the Talk of the Town	1960	7.50	15.00	30.00
JUBILEE					
❑ 5418	Short Short Twist/Royal Twist	1962	3.75	7.50	15.00
MIGHTY					
❑ 111	Leotards/Royal Blues	1959	6.25	12.50	25.00
❑ 112	Cave Man/Wounded Heart	1959	7.50	15.00	30.00
❑ 200	My Memories of You/Little Trixie	1961	10.00	20.00	40.00
MUSICOR					
❑ 1398	Smile a Little Smile for Me/Hey Jude	1969	2.50	5.00	10.00
POWER					
❑ 113	Mad Gass/Sittin' with My Baby	1959	10.00	20.00	40.00
❑ 215	Short Shorts/Planet Rock	1957	37.50	75.00	150.00
SWAN					
❑ 4200	I'll Love You ('Til the End of Time)/(Instrumental)	1965	25.00	50.00	100.00
TCF HALL					
❑ 117	Bad Girl/Do the Montoona	1965	3.75	7.50	15.00

ROYAL TONES, THE

Number	Title (A Side/B Side)	Yr	VG	VG+	NM
TITANIC					
❑ 5014	Black Lightnin'/Surfer's Junction	1964	15.00	30.00	60.00

ROYALETTES, THE

Number	Title (A Side/B Side)	Yr	VG	VG+	NM
CHANCELLOR					
❑ 1133	No Big Thing/Yesterday's Lovers	1963	5.00	10.00	20.00
❑ 1140	Willie the Wolf/Blue Summer	1963	3.75	7.50	15.00
MGM					
❑ 13283	He's Gone/Don't You Cry	1964	3.00	6.00	12.00
❑ 13327	Poor Boy/Watch What Happens	1965	3.00	6.00	12.00
❑ 13366	It's Gonna Take a Miracle/Out of Sight, Out of Mind	1965	3.75	7.50	15.00
❑ 13405	I Want to Meet Him/Never Again	1965	3.00	6.00	12.00
❑ 13451	You Bring Me Down/Only When You're Lonely	1966	3.00	6.00	12.00
❑ 13507	It's a Big Mistake/It's Better Not to Know	1966	3.00	6.00	12.00
❑ 13544	I Don't Want to Be the One/An Affair to Remember	1966	3.00	6.00	12.00
❑ 13588	Love Without An End/When Summer's Gone	1966	3.00	6.00	12.00
❑ 13627	My Man/Take My Love	1966	3.00	6.00	12.00
ROULETTE					
❑ 4768	River of Ters/Something Wonderful	1967	2.50	5.00	10.00
WARNER BROS.					
❑ 5439	There He Goes/Come to Me	1964	3.75	7.50	15.00

ROYALS, THE (1)

Later known as THE MIDNIGHTERS. Also see HANK BALLARD AND THE MIDNIGHTERS.

Number	Title (A Side/B Side)	Yr	VG	VG+	NM
FEDERAL					
❑ 12064AA	Every Beat of My Heart/All Night Long	1952	1000.	2000.	3000.
—Blue vinyl					
❑ 12064	Every Beat of My Heart/All Night Long	1952	375.00	750.00	1500.
❑ 12077	I Know I Love You So/Starting From Tonight	1952	625.00	1250.	2500.
❑ 12088	Moonrise/Fifth Street Blues	1952	500.00	1000.	2000.
❑ 12088	Moonrise/Fifth Street Blues	1952	1000.	2000.	3000.
—Blue vinyl					
❑ 12098	A Love in My Heart/I'll Never Let You Go	1952	250.00	500.00	1000.
❑ 12113	Are You Forgetting?/What Did I Do	1952	150.00	300.00	600.00
❑ 12121	The Shrine of St. Cecelia/I Feel So Blue	1953	200.00	400.00	800.00
❑ 12133	Get It/No It Ain't	1953	50.00	100.00	200.00
❑ 12150	Hello Miss Fine/I Feel That-A-Way	1953	50.00	100.00	200.00
❑ 12160	That's It/Someone Like You	1953	62.50	125.00	250.00
❑ 12169	Work With Me Annie/Until I Die	1954	62.50	125.00	250.00
—Original pressing; for reissues, see "Midnighters, The"					
❑ 12177 [DJ]	Give It Up/That Woman	1954	75.00	150.00	300.00
—Evidently, some promos exist crediting The Royals					

ROYALS, THE (2)

Also see CHUCK WILLIS.

Number	Title (A Side/B Side)	Yr	VG	VG+	NM
OKEH					
❑ 6832	If You Love Me/Dreams of You	1951	250.00	500.00	1000.

ROYALS, THE (3)

Number	Title (A Side/B Side)	Yr	VG	VG+	NM
PENGUIN					
❑ 1008	Thunder Wagon/Teen Beat	1959	7.50	15.00	30.00

ROYALS, THE (4)

Number	Title (A Side/B Side)	Yr	VG	VG+	NM
VAGABOND					
❑ 134	Surfin' Lagoon/Wild Safari	1962	12.50	25.00	50.00
❑ 444	Christmas Party/White Christmas	1963	12.50	25.00	50.00
—Black vinyl					
❑ 444	Christmas Party/White Christmas	1963	25.00	50.00	100.00
—Red vinyl					

ROYALS, THE (5)

This Royals later became The Scooters.

Number	Title (A Side/B Side)	Yr	VG	VG+	NM
VENUS					
❑ 103	Someday We'll Meet Again/I Want You to Be My Mambo Baby	1954	100.00	200.00	400.00

ROYALTONES, THE

Number	Title (A Side/B Side)	Yr	VG	VG+	NM
GOLDISC					
❑ 3004	Short Line/Big Wheel	1960	2.50	5.00	10.00
❑ 3011	Flamingo Express/Tacos	1960	2.50	5.00	10.00
❑ 3011	Flamingo Express/Secret Love	1960	2.50	5.00	10.00
❑ 3016	Butterscotch/Dixie Cup	1961	2.00	4.00	8.00
❑ 3017	Royal Whirl/Dixie Rock	1961	2.00	4.00	8.00
❑ 3026	Peppermint Twist/Scotch and Soda	1962	2.00	4.00	8.00
❑ 3028	Do the Early Bird/Scotch and Soda	1962	2.00	4.00	8.00
JUBILEE					
❑ 5338	Poor Boy/Wail!	1958	3.75	7.50	15.00
❑ 5362	Seesaw/Little Bo	1959	3.00	6.00	12.00
MALA					
❑ 473	Holy Smokes/Our Faded Love	1964	2.00	4.00	8.00
❑ 482	El Toro/Lonely World	1964	2.00	4.00	8.00
❑ 487	The Yea Yea Song/Misty Sea	1964	2.00	4.00	8.00
OLD TOWN					
❑ 1018	Crazy Love/Never Let Me Go	1956	25.00	50.00	100.00
PORT					
❑ 70037	Poor Boy/See Saw	1963	3.00	6.00	12.00

ROYCE, EARL, AND THE OLYMPICS

British group; no relation to other Olympics groups.

Number	Title (A Side/B Side)	Yr	VG	VG+	NM
TOWER					
❑ 137	Que Sera Sera Sera/I Really Do	1965	2.00	4.00	8.00

ROZZI, LITTLE SAMMY

Number	Title (A Side/B Side)	Yr	VG	VG+	NM
PELHAM					
❑ 722	Christine/Over the Rainbow	1961	50.00	100.00	200.00

RUBEN AND THE JETS

Also see FRANK ZAPPA.

Number	Title (A Side/B Side)	Yr	VG	VG+	NM
MERCURY					
❑ 73381	If I Could Be Your Love Again/Wedding Bells	1973	—	3.00	6.00
❑ 73411	Charlena/Mah Man Flash	1973	—	3.00	6.00

RUBIN

Number	Title (A Side/B Side)	Yr	VG	VG+	NM
KAPP					
❑ 869	You've Been Away/Baby, You're My Everything	1967	15.00	30.00	60.00

RUBY AND THE ROMANTICS

Number	Title (A Side/B Side)	Yr	VG	VG+	NM
ABC					
❑ 10911	Twilight Time/Una Bella Brazilian Melody	1967	2.50	5.00	10.00
❑ 10941	Only Heaven Knows/This Is No Laughing Matter	1967	2.50	5.00	10.00
❑ 11065	On a Clear Day You Can See Forever/More Than Yesterday, Less Than Tomorrow	1968	2.50	5.00	10.00
A&M					
❑ 1042	Hurting Each Other/Baby, I Could Be So Good at Loving You	1969	2.00	4.00	8.00
KAPP					
❑ 501	Our Day Will Come/Moonlight and Music	1963	3.75	7.50	15.00
❑ 525	My Summer Love/Sweet Love and Sweet Forgiveness	1963	3.00	6.00	12.00
❑ 544	Hey There Lonely Boy/Not a Moment Too Soon	1963	3.00	6.00	12.00
❑ 544 [PS]	Hey There Lonely Boy/Not a Moment Too Soon	1963	3.75	7.50	15.00
❑ 557	Young Wings Can Fly (Higher Than You Know)/Day Dreaming	1963	3.00	6.00	12.00
❑ 557 [PS]	Young Wings Can Fly (Higher Than You Know)/Day Dreaming	1963	3.75	7.50	15.00
❑ 578	Our Everlasting Love/Much Better Off Than I've Ever Been	1964	3.00	6.00	12.00
❑ 601	Baby Come Home/Every Day's a Holiday	1964	3.00	6.00	12.00
❑ 615	When You're Young and In Love/I Cry Alone	1964	3.00	6.00	12.00
❑ 646	Does He Really Care for Me/Nevertheless (I'm in Love with You)	1965	3.00	6.00	12.00
❑ 665	We'll Meet Again/Your Baby Doesn't Love You Anymore	1965	3.00	6.00	12.00
❑ 702	Nobody But My Baby/Imagination	1965	3.00	6.00	12.00
❑ 759	We Can Make It/Remember Me	1966	2.50	5.00	10.00
❑ 773	Hey There Lonely Boy/Think	1966	2.50	5.00	10.00
❑ 839	I Know/We'll Love Again	1967	2.50	5.00	10.00

RUFFIN, DAVID

Also see DARYL HALL AND JOHN OATES; JIMMY AND DAVID RUFFIN; THE TEMPTATIONS.

Number	Title (A Side/B Side)	Yr	VG	VG+	NM
ANNA					
❑ 1127	I'm in Love/One of These Days	1961	15.00	30.00	60.00
CHECK MATE					
❑ 1003	You Can Get What I Got/Action Speaks Louder Than Words	1961	15.00	30.00	60.00
❑ 1010	Mr. Bus Driver — Hurry!/Knock You Out (With Love)	1962	15.00	30.00	60.00
MOTOWN					
❑ 1140	My Whole World Ended (The Moment You Left Me)/I've Got to Find Myself a Brand New Baby	1968	—	3.00	6.00
❑ 1149	I've Lost Everything I've Ever Loved/We'll Have a Good Thing Going On	1969	—	3.00	6.00
❑ 1158	I'm So Glad I Fell for You/I Pray Every Day You Won't Regret Loving Me	1969	—	3.00	6.00
❑ 1178	Each Day Is a Lifetime/Don't Stop Loving Me	1971	—	3.00	6.00
❑ 1187	You Can Come Right Back to Me/Dinah	1971	—	3.00	6.00
❑ 1204	A Day in the Life of a Working Man/A Little More Trust	1972	—	3.00	6.00
❑ 1223	Blood Donors Needed/Go On with Your Bad Self	1973	—	3.00	6.00
❑ 1259	Common Man/I'm Just a Mortal Man	1973	—	3.00	6.00
❑ 1327	Me and Rock and Roll (Are Here to Stay)/Smiling Faces Sometimes	1974	—	3.00	6.00
❑ 1332	Take Me Clear from Here/I Just Want to Celebrate	1975	—	—	—
—Unreleased					
❑ 1336	Superstar/No Matter Where	1975	—	2.50	5.00
❑ 1376	Walk Away from Love/Love Can Be Hazardous to Your Health	1975	—	2.50	5.00
❑ 1388	Heavy Love/Love Can Be Hazardous To Your Health	1976	—	2.50	5.00
❑ 1393	Everything's Coming Up Love/No Matter Where	1976	—	2.50	5.00
❑ 1405	On and Off/Statue of a Fool	1976	—	2.50	5.00
❑ 1420	Just Let Me Hold You for a Night/Rode by the Place (Where We Used to Stay)	1977	—	2.50	5.00
❑ 1435	You're My Peace of Mind/Rose By the Place (Where We Used to Stay)	1978	—	2.50	5.00
WARNER BROS.					
❑ 49030	Sexy Dancer/Break My Heart	1979	—	2.00	4.00
❑ 49123	I Get Excited/Chain on the Brain	1979	—	2.00	4.00
❑ 49277	Slow Dance/Don't You Go Home	1980	—	2.00	4.00
❑ 49577	Still in Love with You/I Wanna Be with You	1980	—	2.00	4.00

RUFFIN, DAVID, AND EDDIE KENDRICK

Also see each artist's individual listings; DARYL HALL AND JOHN OATES; THE TEMPTATIONS.

Number	Title (A Side/B Side)	Yr	VG	VG+	NM
RCA					
❑ 5313-7-R	I Couldn't Believe It/Don't Know Why You're Dreamin'	1987	—	—	3.00
❑ 6925-7-R	One More for the Lonely Hearts Club/Don't Know Why You're Dreaming	1988	—	—	3.00

RUFFIN, JIMMY

Number	Title (A Side/B Side)	Yr	VG	VG+	NM
CHESS					
❑ 2160	Tell Me What You Want/Do You Know Me	1974	—	2.50	5.00
❑ 2168	What You See (Ain't Always What You Get)/Boy from Mississippi	1975	—	2.50	5.00
EPIC					
❑ 50339	Fallin' in Love with You/Fallin' in Love with You	1977	—	2.50	5.00
❑ 50384	Fallin' in Love with You/Fallin' in Love with You	1977	—	2.50	5.00
MIRACLE					
❑ 1	Don't Feel Sorry for Me/Heart	1961	50.00	100.00	200.00
RSO					
❑ 1021	Hold On to My Love/(Instrumental)	1980	—	2.50	5.00
❑ 1042	Night of Love/Searchin'	1980	—	2.50	5.00
SOUL					
❑ 35002	Since I've Lost You/I Want Her Love	1964	10.00	20.00	40.00
❑ 35016	As Long As There Is L-O-V-E/How Can I Say I'm Sorry	1965	2.50	5.00	10.00
❑ 35022	What Becomes of the Brokenhearted/Baby I've Got It	1966	3.75	7.50	15.00
❑ 35027	I've Passed This Way Before/Tomorrow's Tears	1966	2.50	5.00	10.00
❑ 35032	Gonna Give Her All the Love I've Got/World So Wide (Nowhere to Hide from Your Heart)	1967	2.00	4.00	8.00
❑ 35035	Don't You Miss Me A Little Bit Baby/I Want Her Love	1967	2.00	4.00	8.00
❑ 35043	I'll Say Forever My Love/Everybody Needs Love	1968	2.00	4.00	8.00
❑ 35046	Don't Let Him Take Your Love from Me/Lonely, Lonely Man Am I	1968	2.00	4.00	8.00
❑ 35053	Sad and Lonesome Feeling/Gonna Keep On Trying Till I Win Your Love	1968	2.00	4.00	8.00
❑ 35060	Farewell Is a Lonely Sound/If You Will Let Me, I Know I Can	1969	2.00	4.00	8.00
❑ 35077	Maria (You Were the Only One)/Living in a World I Created For Myself	1970	2.00	4.00	8.00
❑ 35092	Our Favorite Melody/You Gave Me Love	1972	—	3.00	6.00

RUFFIN, JIMMY AND DAVID

Also see DAVID RUFFIN; JIMMY RUFFIN.

Number	Title (A Side/B Side)	Yr	VG	VG+	NM
SOUL					
❑ 35076	Stand By Me/Your Love Was Worth Waiting For	1970	—	2.50	5.00
❑ 35082	When My Love Hand Comes Do Down/Steppin' On a Dream	1971	—	2.50	5.00
❑ 35086	Lo and Behold/The Things We Have to Do	1971	—	2.50	5.00

RUFUS

Includes records as "Rufus Featuring Chaka Khan" and "Rufus and Chaka." Also see THE AMERICAN BREED.

Number	Title (A Side/B Side)	Yr	VG	VG+	NM
ABC					
❑ 11356	Slip 'N Slide/I Finally Found You	1973	2.00	4.00	8.00
❑ 11376	Whoever's Thrilling You (Is Killing Me)/I Finally Found You	1973	—	3.00	6.00
❑ 11394	Feel Good/Keep It Coming	1973	—	3.00	6.00
❑ 11427	Tell Me Something Good/Smokin' Room	1974	—	3.00	6.00
❑ 12010	Tell Me Something Good/Smokin' Room	1974	—	2.50	5.00
❑ 12032	You Got the Love/Rags to Rufus	1974	—	2.50	5.00
❑ 12066	Once You Get Started/Rufusized	1975	—	2.50	5.00
❑ 12099	Please Pardon Me (You Remind Me of a Friend)/Somebody's Watching You	1975	—	2.50	5.00
❑ 12149	Sweet Thing/Circles	1975	—	2.50	5.00
❑ 12179	Dance Wit' Me/Everybody's Got an Aura	1976	—	2.50	5.00
❑ 12197	Jive Talkin'/On Time	1976	—	2.50	5.00
❑ 12239	At Midnight (My Love Will Lift You Up)/Better Days	1976	—	2.50	5.00
❑ 12269	Holywood/Earth Song	1977	—	2.50	5.00
❑ 12296	Everlasting Love/Close the Door	1977	—	2.50	5.00
❑ 12349	Stay/My Ship Will Sail	1978	—	2.50	5.00
❑ 12390	Blue Love/Turn	1978	—	2.50	5.00
❑ 12444	Keep It Together (Declaration of Love)/Red Hot Poker	1979	—	2.50	5.00
EPIC					
❑ 10691	Read All About It/Brand New Day	1971	3.00	6.00	12.00
❑ 10691 [PS]	Read All About It/Brand New Day	1971	5.00	10.00	20.00
❑ 10726	Follow the Lamb/Fire One, Fire Two, Fire Three	1971	3.00	6.00	12.00
MCA					
❑ 41025	Ain't Nobody Like You/You're to Blame	1979	—	2.00	4.00
❑ 41131	Do You Love What You Feel/Dancin' Mood	1979	—	2.00	4.00
❑ 41191	What Am I Missing/Any Love	1980	—	2.00	4.00
❑ 41230	I'm Dancing for Your Love/Walk the Rockway	1980	—	2.00	4.00
❑ 51070	Tonight We Love/Afterwards	1981	—	2.00	4.00
❑ 51125	Party 'Til You're Broke/Hold On to a Friend	1981	—	2.00	4.00
❑ 51203	Sharing the Love/We Got the Way	1981	—	2.00	4.00
❑ 52002	True Love/Better Together	1982	—	2.00	4.00
WARNER BROS.					
❑ 29406	One Million Kisses/Stay	1983	—	2.00	4.00
❑ 29555	Ain't Nobody/Sweet Thing	1983	—	2.00	4.00
❑ 29675	Blinded by the Boogie/You're Really Out of Line	1983	—	2.00	4.00
❑ 29790	Take It to the Hop/Distant Lover	1983	—	2.00	4.00

RUFUS AND CARLA

Also see CARLA THOMAS; RUFUS THOMAS.

Number	Title (A Side/B Side)	Yr	VG	VG+	NM
ATCO					
❑ 6177	Cause I Love You/Deep Down Inside	1960	6.25	12.50	25.00
—As "Carla and Rufus"					
❑ 6199	I Didn't Believe/Yeah, Yea-Ah	1961	6.25	12.50	25.00
—As "Rufus and Friend"					
SATELLITE					
❑ 102	Cause I Love You/Deep Down Inside	1960	10.00	20.00	40.00
STAX					
❑ 151	That's Really Some Good/Night Time Is the Right Time	1964	3.00	6.00	12.00
❑ 176	When You Move You Lose/We're Tight	1965	3.00	6.00	12.00
❑ 184	Birds and Bees/Never Let You Go	1966	3.00	6.00	12.00

RUGBYS, THE

Number	Title (A Side/B Side)	Yr	VG	VG+	NM
AMAZON					
❑ 1	You, I/Stay with Me	1969	2.00	4.00	8.00
—Black vinyl					
❑ 1 [DJ]	You, I/Stay with Me	1969	5.00	10.00	20.00
—Colored vinyl					
❑ 4	The Light/Wendegahl Warlock	1970	2.00	4.00	8.00
❑ 6	Rockin' All Over/(B-side unknown)	1970	2.00	4.00	8.00
SMASH					
❑ 1997	James Is the Name/'Til the Day I Die	1965	3.00	6.00	12.00

RUMBLERS, THE

Number	Title (A Side/B Side)	Yr	VG	VG+	NM
DOT					
❑ 16421	Boss/I Don't Need You No More	1963	3.75	7.50	15.00
❑ 16455	Boss Strikes Back/Sorry	1963	3.75	7.50	15.00
❑ 16480	Angry Sea (Walmea)/Bugged	1963	3.75	7.50	15.00
❑ 16521	It's a Gas/Tootananny	1963	3.75	7.50	15.00
DOWNEY					
❑ 103	Boss/I Don't Need You No More	1962	7.50	15.00	30.00
❑ 106	Boss Strikes Back/Sorry	1963	7.50	15.00	30.00
❑ 107	Angry Sea (Walmea)/Bugged	1963	7.50	15.00	30.00
❑ 111	It's a Gas/Tootananny	1963	7.50	15.00	30.00
❑ 114	High Octane/Night Scene	1964	6.25	12.50	25.00
❑ 119	The Hustler/Riot in Cell Block #9	1964	6.25	12.50	25.00
❑ 127	Soulful Jerk/Hey-Did-a-Da-Do	1964	6.25	12.50	25.00
❑ 133	Boss Soul/Till Always	1965	6.25	12.50	25.00
HIGHLAND					
❑ 1026	Intersection/Stomping Theme	1962	12.50	25.00	50.00

RUN-D.M.C.

Number	Title (A Side/B Side)	Yr	VG	VG+	NM
MCA					
❑ 53680	Ghost Busters/Ghost Busters (Ghost Power Instrumental)	1989	—	3.50	7.00
PROFILE					
❑ 5019	It's Like That/It's Like That (instrumental)	1983	—	2.50	5.00
❑ 5036	Hard Times-Jam Master Jay/Hard Times-Jam Master Jay (instrumental)	1983	—	2.50	5.00
❑ 5045	Rock Box/Rock Box (Dub Version)	1984	—	2.50	5.00
❑ 5051	30 Days/30 Days (instrumental)	1984	—	2.50	5.00
❑ 5058	Hollis Crew/Hollis Crew (instrumental)	1984	—	2.50	5.00
❑ 5064	King of Rock/King of Rock (instrumental)	1985	—	2.50	5.00
❑ 5069	You Talk Too Much/Daryll and Joe (Krush Groove)	1985	—	2.50	5.00
❑ 5080	Jam-Master Jammin'/Jam-Master Jammin' (instrumental)	1985	—	2.50	5.00
❑ 5088	Can You Rock Like This/Together Forever	1986	—	2.50	5.00
❑ 5102	My Adidas/Peter Piper	1986	—	2.00	4.00
❑ 5102 [PS]	My Adidas/Peter Piper	1986	—	2.00	4.00
❑ 5112	Walk This Way/King of Rock	1986	—	2.00	4.00
—A-side: With Steven Tyler and Joe Perry of Aerosmith					
❑ 5112 [PS]	Walk This Way/King of Rock	1986	—	2.00	4.00
❑ 5119	You Be Illin'/Hit It Run	1986	—	2.00	4.00
❑ 5119 [PS]	You Be Illin'/Hit It Run	1986	—	2.00	4.00
❑ 5131	It's Tricky/Proud to Be Black	1987	—	2.00	4.00
❑ 5131 [PS]	It's Tricky/Proud to Be Black	1987	—	2.00	4.00
❑ 5202	Run's House/Beats to the Rhyme	1988	—	2.00	4.00
❑ 5202 [PS]	Run's House/Beats to the Rhyme	1988	—	2.00	4.00
❑ 5211	Mary, Mary/Rock Box	1988	—	2.00	4.00
❑ 5211 [PS]	Mary, Mary/Rock Box	1988	—	2.00	4.00
❑ 5224	I'm Not Going Out Like That/How'd Ya Do It Dee	1988	—	2.00	4.00
❑ 5224 [PS]	I'm Not Going Out Like That/How'd Ya Do It Dee	1988	—	2.00	4.00
❑ 5235	Christmas in Hollis/Let the Jingle Bells Rock	1988	—	2.00	4.00
—B-side by Sweet Tee; red vinyl					

RUNAROUNDS, THE

Probably more than one group.

Number	Title (A Side/B Side)	Yr	VG	VG+	NM
CAPITOL					
❑ 5644	Perfect Woman/You're a Drag	1966	6.25	12.50	25.00
COUSINS					
❑ 1004	Mashed Potato Mary/I'm All Alone	1964	5.00	10.00	20.00
FELSTED					
❑ 8704	Send Her Back/Carrie, You're An Angel	1964	7.50	15.00	30.00
KC					
❑ 116	Unbelievable/Hurray for Love	1963	6.25	12.50	25.00
❑ 116	Unbelievable/Hurray for Love	1963	10.00	20.00	40.00
—Brown vinyl					
MGM					
❑ 13763	My Little Girl/You Lied	1967	3.75	7.50	15.00
PIO					
❑ 107	The Nearest Thing to Heaven/Lover's Lane	1961	37.50	75.00	150.00
TARHEEL					
❑ 065	Are You Looking for a Sweetheart/Let Them Talk	1963	5.00	10.00	20.00

RUNAWAYS, THE

Also see JOAN JETT AND THE BLACKHEARTS.

Number	Title (A Side/B Side)	Yr	VG	VG+	NM
MERCURY					
❑ 73819	Cherry Bomb/Blackmail	1976	2.50	5.00	10.00
❑ 73890	Heartbeat/Neon Angels on the Road to Ruin	1977	2.50	5.00	10.00

RUNDGREN, TODD
Also see NAZZ (1); UTOPIA.

Number	Title (A Side/B Side)	Yr	VG	VG+	NM
AMPEX					
❑ 31001	We Gotta Get You a Woman/Medley	1970	2.50	5.00	10.00
—As "Runt"					
BEARSVILLE					
❑ 0003	I Saw the Light/Marlene	1972	3.00	6.00	12.00
—Blue vinyl					
❑ 0003	I Saw the Light/Marlene	1972	3.00	6.00	12.00
❑ 0007	Couldn't I Just Tell You/Wolfman Jack	1972	—	3.00	6.00
❑ 0009	Hello It's Me/Cold Morning Light	1973	—	3.00	6.00
❑ 0020	A Dream Goes On Forever/Heavy Metal Kids	1974	—	3.00	6.00
❑ 0030	We Gotta Get You a Woman/I Saw the Light	1973	—	2.00	4.00
—"Back to Back Hits" series					
❑ 0301	Breathless/Wolfman Jack	1974	—	3.00	6.00
❑ 0304	Real Man/Prana	1975	—	2.50	5.00
❑ 0309	Good Vibrations/When I Pray	1976	—	2.50	5.00
❑ 0310	Love of the Common Man/Black and White	1976	—	2.50	5.00
❑ 0324	Can We Still Be Friends/Determination	1978	—	2.50	5.00
❑ 0326	Can We Still Be Friends/Out of Control	1978	—	2.50	5.00
❑ 0330	You Cried Wolf/Onomatopoeia	1978	—	2.50	5.00
❑ 0335	It Wouldn't Have Made Any Difference/Did You Ever Learn	1979	—	2.50	5.00
❑ 29686	Bang the Drum All Day/Chant	1983	—	3.00	6.00
❑ 29759	Emperor of the Highway/Hideaway	1983	—	2.00	4.00
❑ 31002	Be Nice to Me/Broke Down and Busted	1971	2.00	4.00	8.00
—As "Runt-Todd Rundgren"					
❑ 31004	A Long Time, A Long Way to Go/Parole	1971	2.00	4.00	8.00
—As "Runt-Todd Rundgren"					
❑ 49696	Time Heals/Tiny Demon	1981	—	2.00	4.00
❑ 49771	Compassion/Pulse	1981	—	2.50	5.00
COLUMBIA					
❑ 6151	Loving You's a Dirty Job (But Somebody's Gotta Do It)/(B-side unknown)	1986	—	2.00	4.00
—With Bonnie Tyler					
GUARDIAN					
❑ S7-19726	Can We Still Be Friends/I Saw the Light	1997	—	—	3.00
RHINO					
❑ 74426	Bang the Drum All Day/Can We Still Be Friends	1987	—	2.00	4.00
WARNER BROS.					
❑ 22868	I Love My Life/Parallel Lines	1989	—	—	3.00
❑ 28821	Something to Fall Back On/Lockjaw	1986	—	2.00	4.00

RUSH

Number	Title (A Side/B Side)	Yr	VG	VG+	NM
MERCURY					
❑ 73623	Finding My Way/Need Some Love	1974	12.50	25.00	50.00
❑ 73623 [DJ]	Finding My Way (mono/stereo)	1974	10.00	20.00	40.00
❑ 73647	In the Mood/What You're Doing	1974	6.25	12.50	25.00
❑ 73681	Anthem/Fly by Night	1975	2.50	5.00	10.00
❑ 73737	Bastille Day/Lakeside Park	1975	2.50	5.00	10.00
❑ 73803	Lessons/Twilight Zone	1976	2.50	5.00	10.00
❑ 73873	Fly by Night-In the Mood/Something for Nothing	1976	2.50	5.00	10.00
❑ 73912	Making Memories/Temples of Syrinx	1977	2.50	5.00	10.00
❑ 73958	Closer to the Heart/Madrigal	1977	2.50	5.00	10.00
❑ 73990	Anthem/Fly by Night	1978	2.50	5.00	10.00
❑ 74051	The Trees/Circumstances	1979	2.50	5.00	10.00
❑ 76044	The Spirit of Radio/Circumstances	1980	2.50	5.00	10.00
❑ 76060	Entre Nous/Different Strings	1980	2.50	5.00	10.00
❑ 76095	Limelight/XYZ	1981	2.50	5.00	10.00
❑ 76109	Tom Sawyer/Witch Hunt	1981	2.50	5.00	10.00
❑ 76109 [PS]	Tom Sawyer/Witch Hunt	1981	6.25	12.50	25.00
❑ 76124	Closer to the Heart/Freewill	1981	2.00	4.00	8.00
❑ 76179	New World Man/Vital Signs	1982	2.00	4.00	8.00
❑ 76179 [PS]	New World Man/Vital Signs	1982	3.75	7.50	15.00
❑ 76196	Countdown/Subdivision	1982	2.50	5.00	10.00
❑ 880050-7	Body Electric/Between the Wheels	1984	2.00	4.00	8.00
❑ 884191-7	The Big Money/Red Sector A	1985	2.00	4.00	8.00
❑ 884191-7 [PS]	The Big Money/Red Sector A	1985	3.75	7.50	15.00
❑ 888891-7	Time Stand Still/High Water	1987	—	3.00	6.00
❑ 888891-7 [PS]	Time Stand Still/High Water	1987	2.50	5.00	10.00
MOON					
❑ 001	Not Fade Away/You Can't Fight It	1973	125.00	250.00	500.00
—Canada-only release					

RUSH, MERRILEE

Number	Title (A Side/B Side)	Yr	VG	VG+	NM
AGP					
❑ 107	Reach Out/Love Street	1969	—	3.00	6.00
❑ 112	Your Loving Eyes Are Blind/Everyday Livin' Days	1969	—	3.00	6.00
❑ 121	Sign On for the Good Times/Robin McCarver	1969	—	3.00	6.00
❑ 126	Angel of the Morning/It's Worth It All	1970	—	3.00	6.00
BELL					
❑ 705	Angel of the Morning/Reap What You Sow	1968	2.00	4.00	8.00
❑ 738	Sunshine and Roses/That Kind of Woman	1968	2.00	4.00	8.00
SCEPTER					
❑ 12329	Child of Mine/Everything Has Got to Be Free	1971	—	3.00	6.00
UNITED ARTISTS					
❑ XW930	Could It Be Love I Found Tonight/Be True to You	1976	—	2.00	4.00
❑ XW993	Save Me/Easy, Soft and Slow	1977	—	2.00	4.00
❑ XW1103	Mama/Rainstorm	1977	—	2.00	4.00
❑ XW1181	Angel of the Morning/Save	1978	—	2.00	4.00

RUSSELL, LEE
See LEON RUSSELL.

RUSSELL, LEON
Includes records by his country-western alter ego, "Hank Wilson" and "Hank and Mary Wilson." Also see WILLIE NELSON.

Number	Title (A Side/B Side)	Yr	VG	VG+	NM
ARK 21					
❑ S7-58714	Daddy Sang Bass/He Stopped Loving Her Today	1998	—	—	3.00
A&M					
❑ 734	Cindy/Misty	1964	5.00	10.00	20.00
DOT					
❑ 16771	Everybody's Talkin' 'Bout the Young/It's Alright with Me	1965	3.75	7.50	15.00
PARADISE					
❑ 628	Good Time Charlie's Got the Blues/Ain't No Love in the City	1984	—	2.00	4.00
❑ 629	Wabash Cannonball/Tennessee Waltz	1984	—	2.00	4.00
—As "Hank Wilson"; A-side with Willie Nelson					
❑ 631	Rescue My Heart/Lost Love	1985	—	2.00	4.00
❑ 631 [PS]	Rescue My Heart/Lost Love	1985	2.50	5.00	10.00
❑ 8208	Rainbow in Your Eyes/Love's Supposed to Be That Way	1976	—	2.00	4.00
—As "Leon and Mary Russell"					
❑ 8274	Satisfy You/Windsong	1976	—	2.00	4.00
—As "Leon and Mary Russell"					
❑ 8369	Love Crazy/Say You Will	1977	—	2.00	4.00
—As "Leon and Mary Russell"					
❑ 8438	Easy Love/Hold On to This Feeling	1977	—	2.00	4.00
—As "Leon and Mary Russell"					
❑ 8667	Elvis and Marilyn/Anita Bryant	1978	—	2.50	5.00
❑ 8667 [PS]	Elvis and Marilyn/Anita Bryant	1978	—	2.50	5.00
❑ 8719	Midnight Lover/From Maine to Mexico	1978	—	2.50	5.00
❑ 49662	Over the Rainbow/I've Just Seen a Face	1981	—	2.00	4.00
RCA VICTOR					
❑ 47-6884	(I Tasted) Tears on Your Lips/A Catchy Tune	1957	7.50	15.00	30.00
—As "Lee Russell"					
ROULETTE					
❑ 4049	Honky Tonk Woman/Rainbow at Midnight	1958	6.25	12.50	25.00
—As "Lee Russell"					
SHELTER					
❑ 301	Roll Away the Stone/Hummingbird	1970	—	3.00	6.00
❑ 7302	It Takes a Lot to Laugh, It Takes a Train to Cry/Home Sweet Oklahoma	1970	—	3.00	6.00
❑ 7305	A Hard Rain's A-Gonna Fall/Me and Baby Jane	1971	—	3.00	6.00
❑ 7316	A Song for You/A Hard Rain's A-Gonna Fall	1971	—	3.00	6.00
❑ 7325	Tight Rope/This Masquerade	1972	—	2.50	5.00
❑ 7328	Slipping Into Christmas/Christmas in Chicago	1972	—	2.50	5.00
❑ 7328 [PS]	Slipping Into Christmas/Christmas In Chicago	1972	6.25	12.50	25.00
❑ 7336	Roll in My Sweet Baby's Arms/I'm So Lonesome I Could Cry	1973	—	2.50	5.00
—As "Hank Wilson"					
❑ 7337	Queen of the Roller Derby/Roll Away the Stone	1973	—	2.50	5.00
❑ 7338	A Six Pack to Go/Uncle Pen	1973	—	2.50	5.00
—As "Hank Wilson"					
❑ 40210	If I Were a Carpenter/Wild Horses	1974	—	2.00	4.00
❑ 40210 [PS]	If I Were a Carpenter/Wild Horses	1974	2.00	4.00	8.00
❑ 40277	Time for Love/Leaving Whipporwhill	1974	—	2.00	4.00
❑ 40378	Lady Blue/Laying Right Here in Heaven	1975	—	2.00	4.00
❑ 40483	Back to the Island/Little Hideaway	1975	—	2.00	4.00
❑ 62004	Bluebird/Back to the Island	1976	—	2.00	4.00
❑ 65033	Slipping Into Christmas/Christmas in Chicago	1975	—	2.50	5.00
—Reissue of 7328					

RUSSELL, LEON, AND MARC BENNO
Also see LEON RUSSELL.

Number	Title (A Side/B Side)	Yr	VG	VG+	NM
SHELTER					
❑ 7313	Straight Brother/Tryin' to Stay Alive	1971	2.00	4.00	8.00
SMASH					
❑ 2186	Soul Food/Welcome to Hollywood	1968	2.00	4.00	8.00
—As "Asylum Choir"					
❑ 2204	Indian Style/Icicle Star Tree	1969	2.00	4.00	8.00
—As "Asylum Choir"					

RUSTY AND DOUG
See RUSTY AND DOUG KERSHAW.

RUTHERFORD, MIKE
Also see GENESIS.

Number	Title (A Side/B Side)	Yr	VG	VG+	NM
ATLANTIC					
❑ 89976	Halfway There/A Day to Remember	1982	—	2.00	4.00
❑ 89981	Maxine/A Day to Remember	1982	—	2.00	4.00
PASSPORT					
❑ 7919	Moonshine/Working in Line	1980	—	2.50	5.00

RUTLES, THE

Number	Title (A Side/B Side)	Yr	VG	VG+	NM
WARNER BROS.					
❑ 8560	I Must Be in Love/Doubleback Alley	1978	3.00	6.00	12.00

RYAN, CATHY

Number	Title (A Side/B Side)	Yr	VG	VG+	NM
KING					
❑ 4848	Come Home/The Cricket, the Dove, and the Goldfish	1955	7.50	15.00	30.00
❑ 4890	Only a Dream/High Falutin' Heart	1956	7.50	15.00	30.00
❑ 4916	Lazy River/Love You with All My Might	1956	7.50	15.00	30.00

RYAN, CHARLIE

Number	Title (A Side/B Side)	Yr	VG	VG+	NM
4 STAR					
❑ 1733	Hot Rod Lincoln/Thru the Mill	1959	5.00	10.00	20.00
❑ 1745	Side Car Cycle/Steel Rock	1960	5.00	10.00	20.00
❑ 1749	Hot Rod Hades/Hot Rod Guitar	1961	5.00	10.00	20.00
❑ 1761	Hot Rod Race/Hot Rod Lincoln	1963	5.00	10.00	20.00
SOUVENIR					
❑ 101	Hot Rod Lincoln/(B-side unknown)	1955	15.00	30.00	60.00

RYAN, PAUL AND BARRY

Number	Title (A Side/B Side)	Yr	VG	VG+	NM
MGM					
❑ 13442	Don't Bring Me Your Heartaches/To Remind You of Our Love	1966	2.50	5.00	10.00
❑ 13472	Have Pity on the Boy/There You Go	1966	2.50	5.00	10.00
❑ 13546	Silent Street/'Twas on a Night Like This	1966	2.50	5.00	10.00
❑ 13609	Have You Ever Loved Somebody/I'll Tell You Later	1966	2.50	5.00	10.00

Number	Title (A Side/B Side)	Yr	VG	VG+	NM
❑ 13719	Keep It Out of Sight/Who Told You	1967	2.00	4.00	8.00
❑ 13911	Madrigal/Pictures of Today	1968	2.00	4.00	8.00

RYDELL, BOBBY

CAMEO

Number	Title (A Side/B Side)	Yr	VG	VG+	NM
❑ (no #) [DJ]	Steel Pier	1963	6.25	12.50	25.00

—One-sided "Steel Pier Promotion"

Number	Title (A Side/B Side)	Yr	VG	VG+	NM
❑ 160	Please Don't Be Mad/Makin' Time	1959	12.50	25.00	50.00
❑ 164	All I Want Is You/For You, For You	1959	5.00	10.00	20.00
❑ 167	Kissin' Time/You'll Never Tame Me	1959	3.75	7.50	15.00
❑ 167 [PS]	Kissin' Time/You'll Never Tame Me	1959	6.25	12.50	25.00
❑ 169	We Got Love/I Dig Girls	1959	3.75	7.50	15.00
❑ 169 [PS]	We Got Love/I Dig Girls	1959	6.25	12.50	25.00
❑ 171	Wild One/Little Bitty Girl	1960	3.75	7.50	15.00
❑ 171 [PS]	Wild One/Little Bitty Girl	1960	6.25	12.50	25.00
❑ 175	Swingin' School/Ding-a-Ling	1960	3.75	7.50	15.00
❑ 175 [PS]	Swingin' School/Ding-a-Ling	1960	6.25	12.50	25.00
❑ 179	Volare/I'd Do It Again	1960	3.75	7.50	15.00
❑ 179 [PS]	Volare/I'd Do It Again	1960	6.25	12.50	25.00
❑ 182	Sway/Groovy Tonight	1961	3.75	7.50	15.00
❑ 182 [PS]	Sway/Groovy Tonight	1961	6.25	12.50	25.00
❑ 186	Good Time Baby/Cherie	1961	3.75	7.50	15.00
❑ 186 [PS]	Good Time Baby/Cherie	1961	6.25	12.50	25.00
❑ 190	That Old Black Magic/Don't Be Afraid (To Fall in Love)	1961	3.75	7.50	15.00
❑ 190 [PS]	That Old Black Magic/Don't Be Afraid (To Fall in Love)	1961	6.25	12.50	25.00
❑ 192	The Fish/The Third House	1961	3.75	7.50	15.00
❑ 192 [PS]	The Fish/The Third House	1961	6.25	12.50	25.00
❑ 201	I Wanna Thank You/The Door to Paradise	1961	3.75	7.50	15.00
❑ 201 [PS]	I Wanna Thank You/The Door to Paradise	1961	6.25	12.50	25.00
❑ 209	I've Got Bonnie/Lose Her	1962	3.00	6.00	12.00
❑ 209 [PS]	I've Got Bonnie/Lose Her	1962	5.00	10.00	20.00
❑ 217	I'll Never Dance Again/Gee It's Wonderful	1962	3.00	6.00	12.00
❑ 217 [PS]	I'll Never Dance Again/Gee It's Wonderful	1962	5.00	10.00	20.00
❑ 228	The Cha-Cha-Cha/The Best Man Cried	1962	3.75	7.50	15.00
❑ 228 [PS]	The Cha-Cha-Cha/The Best Man Cried	1962	6.25	12.50	25.00
❑ 242	Butterfly Baby/Love Is Blind	1963	3.75	7.50	15.00
❑ 242 [PS]	Butterfly Baby/Love Is Blind	1963	6.25	12.50	25.00
❑ 252	Wildwood Days/Will You Be My Baby	1963	3.00	6.00	12.00
❑ 252 [PS]	Wildwood Days/Will You Be My Baby	1963	5.00	10.00	20.00
❑ 265	Little Queenie/The Woodpecker Song	1963	3.75	7.50	15.00
❑ 265 [PS]	Little Queenie/The Woodpecker Song	1963	6.25	12.50	25.00
❑ 272	Let's Make Love Tonight/Childhood Sweetheart	1963	3.00	6.00	12.00
❑ 272 [PS]	Let's Make Love Tonight/Childhood Sweetheart	1963	5.00	10.00	20.00
❑ 280	Forget Him/Love, Love Go Away	1963	3.00	6.00	12.00
❑ 280 [PS]	Forget Him/Love, Love Go Away	1963	5.00	10.00	20.00
❑ 309	Make Me Forget/Little Girl, You've Had a Busy Day	1964	3.00	6.00	12.00
❑ 309 [PS]	Make Me Forget/Little Girl, You've Had a Busy Day	1964	5.00	10.00	20.00
❑ 320	A World Without Love/Our Faded Love	1964	3.75	7.50	15.00
❑ 320 [PS]	A World Without Love/Our Faded Love	1964	6.25	12.50	25.00
❑ 361	Ciao, Ciao Bambino/Voce de la Notte	1965	3.75	7.50	15.00
❑ 1070	Forget Him/A Message from Bobby	1963	5.00	10.00	20.00

—Bonus single with Cameo LP C-1070, "Top Hits of 1963"

CAPITOL

Number	Title (A Side/B Side)	Yr	VG	VG+	NM
❑ 5305	I Just Can't Say Goodbye/Two Is the Loneliest Number	1964	2.50	5.00	10.00
❑ 5305 [PS]	I Just Can't Say Goodbye/Two Is the Loneliest Number	1964	3.75	7.50	15.00
❑ 5352	Diana/Stranger in the World	1965	2.50	5.00	10.00
❑ 5436	The Joker/Side Show	1965	2.50	5.00	10.00
❑ 5513	When I See That Girl of Mine/It Takes Two	1965	2.50	5.00	10.00
❑ 5556	Roses in the Snow/A Word for Today	1965	2.50	5.00	10.00
❑ 5696	She Was the Girl/Not You	1966	2.50	5.00	10.00
❑ 5780	Open for Business As Usual/You Gotta Enjoy Joy	1966	2.50	5.00	10.00

PERCEPTION

Number	Title (A Side/B Side)	Yr	VG	VG+	NM
❑ 519	California Sunshine/Honey Buns	1973	—	2.50	5.00
❑ 552	Everything Seemed Better (When I Was Younger)/Sunday Son	1974	—	2.50	5.00

P.I.P.

Number	Title (A Side/B Side)	Yr	VG	VG+	NM
❑ 6515	Sway/Feels Good	1976	—	2.50	5.00
❑ 6521	You're Not the Only Girl for Me/Give Me Your Answer	1976	—	2.00	4.00
❑ 6531	It's Getting Better/The Singles Scene	1976	—	2.00	4.00

RCA VICTOR

Number	Title (A Side/B Side)	Yr	VG	VG+	NM
❑ 47-9892	Chapel on the Hill/It Must Be Love	1970	—	3.00	6.00

REPRISE

Number	Title (A Side/B Side)	Yr	VG	VG+	NM
❑ 0656	The Lovin' Thing/It's Getting Better	1968	2.00	4.00	8.00
❑ 0684	The River Is Wide/Absence Makes the Heart Grow Fonder	1968	2.00	4.00	8.00
❑ 0751	Every Little Bit Hurts/Time and Changes	1968	2.00	4.00	8.00

VEKO

Number	Title (A Side/B Side)	Yr	VG	VG+	NM
❑ 730/1	Dream Age/Fatty Fatty	1958	30.00	60.00	120.00

VENISE

Number	Title (A Side/B Side)	Yr	VG	VG+	NM
❑ 201	Fatty, Fatty/Happy Happy	1961	7.50	15.00	30.00

RYDELL, BOBBY/CHUBBY CHECKER

Also see each artist's individual listings.

CAMEO

Number	Title (A Side/B Side)	Yr	VG	VG+	NM
❑ 12E [DJ]	Chubby Sings Bobby-Bobby Sings Chubby	1962	10.00	20.00	40.00

—B-side blank, promo only

Number	Title (A Side/B Side)	Yr	VG	VG+	NM
❑ 13E [DJ]	What Are You Doing New Year's Eve?	1962	10.00	20.00	40.00

—B-side blank, promo only

Number	Title (A Side/B Side)	Yr	VG	VG+	NM
❑ 205	Jingle Bell Rock/Jingle Bell Imitations	1961	3.75	7.50	15.00
❑ 205 [PS]	Jingle Bell Rock/Jingle Bell Imitations	1961	6.25	12.50	25.00
❑ 214	Teach Me to Twist/Swingin' Together	1962	3.75	7.50	15.00
❑ 214 [PS]	Teach Me to Twist/Swingin' Together	1962	6.25	12.50	25.00

RYDER, MITCH

Also see DETROIT; MITCH RYDER AND THE DETROIT WHEELS.

AVCO EMBASSY

Number	Title (A Side/B Side)	Yr	VG	VG+	NM
❑ 4550	Jenny Take a Ride/I Never Had It Better	1970	2.50	5.00	10.00

DOT

Number	Title (A Side/B Side)	Yr	VG	VG+	NM
❑ 17290	I Believe (There Must Be Someone)/Sugar Bee (We Three)	1970	—	3.00	6.00
❑ 17325	It's Been a Long, Long, Long Time/Direct Me	1970	—	3.00	6.00

DYNOVOICE

Number	Title (A Side/B Side)	Yr	VG	VG+	NM
❑ 901	What Now My Love/Blessing in Disguise	1967	2.00	4.00	8.00
❑ 905	Personality-Chantilly Lace/I Make a Fool of Myself	1968	2.00	4.00	8.00
❑ 916	Lights of the Night/I Need Loving You	1968	2.00	4.00	8.00
❑ 934	Baby I Need Your Loving/Ring Your Bell	1969	2.00	4.00	8.00

NEW VOICE

Number	Title (A Side/B Side)	Yr	VG	VG+	NM
❑ 824	Joy/I'd Rather Go to Jail	1967	2.00	4.00	8.00
❑ 826	You Are My Sunshine/Wild Child	1967	2.00	4.00	8.00
❑ 828	Come See About Me/A Face in the Crowd	1968	2.00	4.00	8.00
❑ 830	Ruby Baby/You Get Your Kicks	1968	2.00	4.00	8.00

RIVA

Number	Title (A Side/B Side)	Yr	VG	VG+	NM
❑ 213	When You Were Mine/Stand	1983	—	2.50	5.00

RYDER, MITCH, AND THE DETROIT WHEELS

Also see DETROIT; THE DETROIT WHEELS; BILLY LEE AND THE RIVIERAS; ROCKETS; MITCH RYDER.

NEW VOICE

Number	Title (A Side/B Side)	Yr	VG	VG+	NM
❑ 801	I Need Help/I Hope	1965	2.50	5.00	10.00
❑ 806	Jenny Takes a Ride!/Baby Jane (Mo-Mo Jane)	1965	6.25	12.50	25.00

—Note slightly different A-side title

Number	Title (A Side/B Side)	Yr	VG	VG+	NM
❑ 806	Jenny Take a Ride!/Baby Jane (Mo-Mo Jane)	1965	3.00	6.00	12.00

—Actual A-side title

Number	Title (A Side/B Side)	Yr	VG	VG+	NM
❑ 808	Little Latin Lupe Lu/I Hope	1966	2.50	5.00	10.00
❑ 811	Break Out/I Need Help	1966	2.50	5.00	10.00
❑ 814	Takin' All I Can Get/You Get Your Kicks	1966	2.50	5.00	10.00
❑ 817	Devil with a Blue Dress On & Good Golly Miss Molly/I Had It Made	1966	3.00	6.00	12.00
❑ 820	Sock It To Me — Baby!/I Never Had It Better	1967	6.25	12.50	25.00

—Version 1: With lyric "Feels like a punch," mumbled to the point that it sounds obscene. The copy of this we've seen has a multicolor, concentric circle label, but we can't yet say that ALL copies with this label are this version.

Number	Title (A Side/B Side)	Yr	VG	VG+	NM
❑ 820	Sock It To Me — Baby!/I Never Had It Better	1967	2.50	5.00	10.00

—Version 2: With lyric "Hits me like a PUNCH!" with no doubt about the last word. The copies of this we've seen have a blue label, both "painted on" and not "painted on," but we can't say yet that ALL copies with that label have this version.

Number	Title (A Side/B Side)	Yr	VG	VG+	NM
❑ 820 [PS]	Sock It To Me — Baby!/I Never Had It Better	1967	5.00	10.00	20.00
❑ 822	Too Many Fish in the Sea & Three Little Fishes/One Grain of Sand	1967	2.50	5.00	10.00
❑ 822 [PS]	Too Many Fish in the Sea & Three Little Fishes/One Grain of Sand	1967	5.00	10.00	20.00

PHILCO-FORD

Number	Title (A Side/B Side)	Yr	VG	VG+	NM
❑ HP-4	Jenny Take a Ride/Sock It To Me Baby	1967	3.75	7.50	15.00

—4-inch plastic "Hip Pocket Record" with color sleeve

S

SA-SHAYS, THE

ALFI

Number	Title (A Side/B Side)	Yr	VG	VG+	NM
❑ 1	Boo Hoo Hoo/You Got Love	1961	6.25	12.50	25.00

ZEN

Number	Title (A Side/B Side)	Yr	VG	VG+	NM
❑ 110	Boo Hoo Hoo/You Got Love	1961	3.00	6.00	12.00

SABERS, THE

BULLSEYE

Number	Title (A Side/B Side)	Yr	VG	VG+	NM
❑ 101	You Can Depend on Me/Calypso Baby	1955	62.50	125.00	250.00

CAL-WEST

Number	Title (A Side/B Side)	Yr	VG	VG+	NM
❑ 847	Cool, Cool Christmas/Always and Forever	1955	100.00	200.00	400.00

SABRE, JOHNNY, AND THE PASSIONS

ADONIS

Number	Title (A Side/B Side)	Yr	VG	VG+	NM
❑ 103	Wish It Could Be Me/Dolly in a Toy Shop	1959	50.00	100.00	200.00

SACCO

See LOU CHRISTIE.

SAD SACKS, THE

IMPERIAL

Number	Title (A Side/B Side)	Yr	VG	VG+	NM
❑ 5517	Sack Dresses/Guard Your Heart	1958	3.75	7.50	15.00

SADLER, SSGT. BARRY

RCA VICTOR

Number	Title (A Side/B Side)	Yr	VG	VG+	NM
❑ 47-8739	The Ballad of the Green Berets/Letter from Vietnam	1966	—	3.00	6.00
❑ 47-8739 [PS]	The Ballad of the Green Berets/Letter from Vietnam	1966	2.00	4.00	8.00
❑ 47-8804	The "A" Team/An Empty Glass	1966	—	3.00	6.00
❑ 47-8804 [PS]	The "A" Team/An Empty Glass	1966	2.00	4.00	8.00
❑ 47-8966	Not Just Lonely/One Day Nearer Home	1966	—	3.00	6.00
❑ 47-9008	I Won't Be Home This Christmas/A Woman Is a Weepin' Willow Tree	1966	2.00	4.00	8.00

SAFARIS, THE

ELDO

Number	Title (A Side/B Side)	Yr	VG	VG+	NM
❑ 101	Image of a Girl/Four Steps to Love	1960	6.25	12.50	25.00
❑ 105	The Girl with the Story in Her Eyes/Summer Nights	1960	6.25	12.50	25.00
❑ 110	In the Still of the Night/Shadows	1960	7.50	15.00	30.00
❑ 113	Garden of Love/Soldier of Fortune	1961	7.50	15.00	30.00

VALIANT

Number	Title (A Side/B Side)	Yr	VG	VG+	NM
❑ 6036	Kick Out/Lonely Surf Guitar	1963	7.50	15.00	30.00

Number	Title (A Side/B Side)	Yr	VG	VG+	NM
SAGES, THE					
RCA VICTOR					
❑ 47-8760	In the Beginning/I'm Not Going to Cry	1965	6.25	12.50	25.00
SAHM, DOUG					
Also see SIR DOUGLAS QUINTET.					
ABC DOT					
❑ 17656	Cowboy Peyton Place/I Love the Way You Love (The Way I Love You)	1976	—	3.00	6.00
❑ 17674	Crying Inside Sometimes/I'm Missing You	1976	—	3.00	6.00
ATLANTIC					
❑ 2946	Is Anybody Going to San Antone/Don't Turn Around	1973	2.00	4.00	8.00
COBRA					
❑ 116	Just a Moment/Sapphire	1961	12.50	25.00	50.00
CRAZY CAJUN					
❑ 2004	If You Really Want/Not Tomato Man	1974	—	2.50	5.00
HARLEM					
❑ 108	Baby Tell Me/Sapphire	1960	12.50	25.00	50.00
❑ 108 [DJ]	Baby Tell Me/Sapphire	1960	25.00	50.00	100.00
—Gold vinyl promo					
❑ 113	More and More/Slow Down	1960	12.50	25.00	50.00
MERCURY					
❑ 73098	Be Real/I Don't Want to Go Home	1970	5.00	10.00	20.00
—As "Wayne Douglas"					
PERSONALITY					
❑ 260	Baby, What's On Your Mind/Crazy, Crazy Feeling	1962	12.50	25.00	50.00
RENNER					
❑ 212	Big Hat/Makes No Difference	1961	10.00	20.00	40.00
❑ 212 [DJ]	Big Hat/Makes No Difference	1961	25.00	50.00	100.00
—Red vinyl promo					
❑ 215	Baby, What's On Your Mind/Crazy, Crazy Feeling	1961	10.00	20.00	40.00
❑ 215 [DJ]	Baby, What's On Your Mind/Crazy, Crazy Feeling	1961	25.00	50.00	100.00
—Red vinyl promo					
❑ 226	Two Hearts in Love/Just Because	1962	10.00	20.00	40.00
❑ 232	Little Angel/Cry	1963	10.00	20.00	40.00
❑ 240	Lucky Me/A Year Ago Tonight	1963	10.00	20.00	40.00
❑ 247	Mr. Kool/Bill Beatty	1964	12.50	25.00	50.00
SARG					
❑ 113	A Real American Joe/Rolling Rolling	1958	25.00	50.00	100.00
—As "Little Doug"					
SATIN					
❑ 100	Crazy Daisy/I Can't Believe You Wanna Leave	1959	12.50	25.00	50.00
SOFT					
❑ 1031	Cry/Down the Pike	1965	7.50	15.00	30.00
SWINGIN'					
❑ 625	Why, Why, Why/If You Ever Need Me	1960	6.25	12.50	25.00
TEAR DROP					
❑ 3074	It's a Man Down There/4 A.M.	1966	6.25	12.50	25.00
—As "Him"					
TEARDROP					
❑ 3479	Who Were You Thinking Of/Velma	1982	—	2.00	4.00
—With Augie Myers					
❑ 3481	I'm Not a Fool Anymore/Don't Fight It	1982	—	2.00	4.00
—With Augie Myers					
WARNER BROS.					
❑ 7819	Girls Today/Groover's Paradise	1974	—	2.50	5.00
WARRIOR					
❑ 507	Crazy Daisy/If I Ever Need You	1958	20.00	40.00	80.00
SAIGONS, THE					
DOOTONE					
❑ 375	You're Heavenly/Honey Gee	1955	100.00	200.00	400.00
SAINT, CATHY					
DAISY					
❑ 501	Big Bad World/Mr. Heartbreak	1963	12.50	25.00	50.00
ST. CLOUD, ENDLE					
INTERNATIONAL ARTISTS					
❑ 129	Tell Me One More Time/(B-side unknown)	1969	5.00	10.00	20.00
❑ 139	She Wears It Like a Badge/Laughter	1970	5.00	10.00	20.00
ST. JAMES, HOLLY					
ABC					
❑ 10996	That's Not Love/Two Good Reasons	1967	15.00	30.00	60.00
❑ 11042	Waiting for My Friend/Magic Moments	1968	5.00	10.00	20.00
ST. JOHN, BARRY					
GRT					
❑ 2	Cry Like a Baby/Long and Lonely Nights	1969	—	3.00	6.00
ST. JOHN, DICK					
Also see DICK AND DEEDEE; SANDY AND DICK.					
DOT					
❑ 17080	Childhood/Lady of the Burning Green Jade	1968	2.00	4.00	8.00
—Of Dick and Deedee					
❑ 17140	Leaving on a Jet Plane/Brand New Season	1968	2.00	4.00	8.00
LIBERTY					
❑ 55380	Gonna Stick By You/Sha-Ta	1961	3.00	6.00	12.00
PHILIPS					
❑ 40256	Love's a Funny Little Game/Believe Me Baby	1965	2.50	5.00	10.00
❑ 40325	Swanee River/You Know What I Mean	1965	2.50	5.00	10.00
POM POM					
❑ 4156	Gonna Stick By You/Sha-Ta	1961	6.25	12.50	25.00
ROMA					
❑ 1001	Hey, Little Gal/Boogie Man (I Ain't Afraid of You)	1961	3.75	7.50	15.00
ST. JOHN, TAMMY					
CONGRESS					
❑ 236	He's the One for Me/I'm Tired Just Lookin' at You	1965	2.50	5.00	10.00
❑ 258	Dark Shadows and Empty Hallways/I Mustn't Cry	1965	2.50	5.00	10.00
ST. JOHN, TOMMY					
RCA					
❑ PB-13405	The Light of My Life (Has Gone Out Tonight)/Waitin' In Your Welfare Line	1982	—	2.00	4.00
❑ PB-13475	Where'd Ya Stay Last Night/She Can't Make Me What I Ain't	1983	—	2.00	4.00
❑ PB-13561	Stars on the Water/Wallflower	1983	—	2.00	4.00
ST. LOUIS JIMMY					
DUKE					
❑ 110	Drinkin' Woman/Why Work	1953	30.00	60.00	120.00
HERALD					
❑ 407	Hard Luck Boogie/Good Book Blues	1953	50.00	100.00	200.00
❑ 408	Your Evil Ways/Whiskey Drinkin' Woman	1953	50.00	100.00	200.00
PARROT					
❑ 823	Going Down Slow/Murder in the First Degree	1955	50.00	100.00	200.00
ST. LOUIS UNION					
PARROT					
❑ 9812	Girl/Respect	1966	2.00	4.00	8.00
ST. PETERS, CRISPIAN					
JAMIE					
❑ 1302	At This Moment/You'll Forget Me, Goodbye	1965	3.75	7.50	15.00
❑ 1309	At This Moment/No No No	1966	2.50	5.00	10.00
❑ 1310	You Were On My Mind/What I'm Gonna Be	1966	2.50	5.00	10.00
❑ 1320	The Pied Piper/Sweet Dawn My True Love	1966	3.00	6.00	12.00
❑ 1324	Changes/My Little Brown Eyes	1966	2.50	5.00	10.00
❑ 1328	Your Ever Changin' Mind/But She's Untrue	1966	2.50	5.00	10.00
❑ 1334	Almost Persuaded/You Are Gone	1967	2.50	5.00	10.00
❑ 1344	Free Spirit/I'm Always Crying	1967	2.50	5.00	10.00
❑ 1359	Please Take Me Back/Look Into My Teardrops	1968	2.00	4.00	8.00
SAKAMOTO, KYU					
CAPITOL					
❑ 4945	Sukiyaka/Anoko No Namaewa Nantenkana	1963	3.75	7.50	15.00
—First pressing: Misspelled A-side					
❑ 4945	Sukiyaki/Anoko No Namaewa Nantenkana	1963	2.50	5.00	10.00
—Second pressing: A-side spelled correctly, subtittled "Music of 'Ue O Muite Aruko' "					
❑ 4945	Sukiyaki/Anoko No Namaewa Nantenkana	1963	2.00	4.00	8.00
—Third pressing: A-side spelled correctly with no subtitle					
❑ 5016	China Nights (Shina No Yoru)/Benkyo No Cha Cha Cha	1963	2.00	4.00	8.00
❑ 5080	The Olympics Song/Tankobushi	1963	2.00	4.00	8.00
❑ 5262	Sayonara Tokyo/I Like You	1964	2.00	4.00	8.00
EMI					
❑ 4150	Why/Elimo	1975	—	2.50	5.00
SALEMS, THE					
EPIC					
❑ 9480	Ol' Man River/Maria	1961	3.75	7.50	15.00
MERCURY					
❑ 71754	My Precious Love/I'll Still Go On Loving You	1961	3.75	7.50	15.00
SALES, SOUPY					
ABC-PARAMOUNT					
❑ 10646	The Mouse/Pachalafaka	1965	3.00	6.00	12.00
❑ 10681	Speedy Gonzales/Hey, Pearl	1965	2.50	5.00	10.00
❑ 10747	I'm a Bird Watching Man/Where the Blue Folks Go	1965	2.50	5.00	10.00
BRUNSWICK					
❑ 55472	Break Your Back/Tom Jones (Push and Pull)	1972	2.50	5.00	10.00
CAPITOL					
❑ 5752	Spanish Flea/That Wasn't No Girl	1966	2.50	5.00	10.00
❑ 5766	Backwards Alphabet/Use Your Noggin	1966	2.50	5.00	10.00
MOTOWN					
❑ 1141	Muck-Arty Park/Green Grow the Lilacs	1968	10.00	20.00	40.00
REPRISE					
❑ 244	Santa Claus Is Surfin' to Town/Santa Claus Is Comin' to Town	1963	7.50	15.00	30.00
❑ 0368	Pie in the Face/Soupy Sez	1965	3.75	7.50	15.00
❑ 20041	Hippy's Cha Cha Hips/White Fang	1961	3.75	7.50	15.00
❑ 20064	Because of Black Tooth/Soupy's Theme	1962	3.75	7.50	15.00
❑ 20108	My Baby's Got a Crush on Frankenstein/Doggone Doggie	1962	3.75	7.50	15.00
❑ 20189	And That's a Shame/Hilly Billy Ding Dong Choo Choo	1963	3.75	7.50	15.00
SAM AND DAVE					
Also see SAM MOORE.					
ALSTON					
❑ 777	Never, Never/Lotta Lovin'	1964	5.00	10.00	20.00
ATLANTIC					
❑ 2517	You Don't Know What You Mean to Me/This Is Your World	1968	—	3.00	6.00
❑ 2540	Can't You Find Another Way (Of Doing It)/Still Is the Night	1968	—	3.00	6.00
❑ 2568	Everybody Got to Believe in Somebody/If I Didn't Have a Girl Like You	1968	—	3.00	6.00
❑ 2590	Soul Sister, Brown Sugar/Come On In	1968	—	3.00	6.00
❑ 2608	Born Again/Get It	1969	—	3.00	6.00
❑ 2668	Holdin' On/Ooh Ooh Ooh	1969	—	3.00	6.00
❑ 2714	I'm Not an Indian Giver/Baby-Baby Don't Stop Now	1970	—	3.00	6.00
❑ 2728	One Part Love, Two Parts Pain/When You Steal from Me	1970	—	3.00	6.00
❑ 2733	When You Steal from Me (You're Only Hurting Yourself)/You Easily Excite Me	1970	—	3.00	6.00
❑ 2839	Don't Pull Your Love/Jody Ryder Got Killed	1971	—	3.00	6.00
CONTEMPO					
❑ 7004	We Can Work It Out/Why Did You Do It	1977	—	2.50	5.00

Number	Title (A Side/B Side)	Yr	VG	VG+	NM
MARLIN					
❑ 6100	I Need Love/Keep a-Walkin'	1961	10.00	20.00	40.00
❑ 6104	No More Pain/My Love Belongs to You	1961	10.00	20.00	40.00
ROULETTE					
❑ 4419	I Need Love/Keep a-Walkin'	1962	3.00	6.00	12.00
❑ 4445	No More Pain/My Love Belongs to You	1962	3.00	6.00	12.00
❑ 4461	She's Alright/It Feels So Nice	1962	3.00	6.00	12.00
❑ 4480	It Was So Nice While It Lasted/You Ain't No Big Thing, Baby	1963	3.00	6.00	12.00
❑ 4508	If She'll Still Have Me/Listening for My Name	1963	3.00	6.00	12.00
❑ 4533	I Found Out/I Got a Thing Going On	1963	3.00	6.00	12.00
❑ 4671	It Feels So Nice/It Was So Nice While It Lasted	1966	2.00	4.00	8.00
STAX					
❑ 168	Goodnight Baby/A Place Nobody Can Find	1965	3.75	7.50	15.00
❑ 175	I Take What I Want/Sweet Home	1965	3.00	6.00	12.00
❑ 180	You Don't Know Like I Know/Blame Me (Don't Blame My Heart)	1965	3.00	6.00	12.00
❑ 189	Hold On! I'm a-Comin'/I Got Everything I Need	1966	3.75	7.50	15.00
❑ 198	Said I Wasn't Gonna Tell Nobody/If You Got the Loving	1966	2.50	5.00	10.00
❑ 204	You Got Me Hummin'/Sleep Good Tonight	1967	2.50	5.00	10.00
❑ 210	When Something Is Wrong with My Baby/Small Portion of Your Love	1967	2.50	5.00	10.00
❑ 218	Soothe Me/I Can't Stand Up for Falling Down	1967	2.50	5.00	10.00
❑ 231	Soul Man/May I Baby	1967	3.00	6.00	12.00
❑ 242	I Thank You/Wrap It Up	1968	3.00	6.00	12.00
UNITED ARTISTS					
❑ XW438	A Little Bit of Good (Cures a Whole Lot of Bad)/Blinded by Love	1974	—	3.00	6.00
❑ XW531	Under the Boardwalk/Give It What You Can	1974	—	3.00	6.00

SAM THE SHAM AND THE PHARAOHS

Number	Title (A Side/B Side)	Yr	VG	VG+	NM
ATLANTIC					
❑ 2767	Me and Bobby McGee/Key to the Highway	1970	—	2.50	5.00
—As "Sam Samudio"					
DINGO					
❑ 001	Haunted House/How Does a Cheating Woman Feel	1964	50.00	100.00	200.00
FRETONE					
❑ 048	Wookie (Part 1)/Wookie (Part 2)	1977	2.50	5.00	10.00
—As "Sam the Sham"					
❑ 049	Ain't No Lie/Baby You Got It	1977	2.50	5.00	10.00
—As "Sam the Sham"					
MGM					
❑ 13322	Wooly Bully/Ain't Gonna Move	1965	3.75	7.50	15.00
❑ 13364	Ju Ju Hand/Big City Lights	1965	3.00	6.00	12.00
❑ 13364 [PS]	Ju Ju Hand/Big City Lights	1965	5.00	10.00	20.00
❑ 13397	Ring Dang Doo/Don't Try It Again	1965	3.00	6.00	12.00
❑ 13397 [PS]	Ring Dang Doo/Don't Try It Again	1965	5.00	10.00	20.00
❑ 13452	Red Hot/Long Long Way	1966	3.00	6.00	12.00
❑ 13506	Lil' Red Riding Hood/Love Me Like Before	1966	3.75	7.50	15.00
❑ 13581	The Hair on My Chinny Chin Chin/(I'm In with the) Out Crowd	1966	3.00	6.00	12.00
❑ 13581 [PS]	The Hair on My Chinny Chin Chin/(I'm In with the) Out Crowd	1966	5.00	10.00	20.00
❑ 13649	How Do You Catch a Girl/Love You Left Behind	1966	3.00	6.00	12.00
❑ 13649 [PS]	How Do You Catch a Girl/Love You Left Behind	1966	5.00	10.00	20.00
❑ 13713	Oh That's Good, No That's Bad/Take What You Can Get	1967	2.50	5.00	10.00
❑ 13747	Black Sheep/My Day's Gonna Come	1967	2.50	5.00	10.00
❑ 13803	Banned in Boston/Money's My Problem	1967	2.50	5.00	10.00
—As "The Sam the Sham Revue"					
❑ 13863	Yakety Yak/Let Our Love Light Shine	1967	2.50	5.00	10.00
—As "The Sam the Sham Revue"					
❑ 13920	Old Mac Donald Has a Boogaloo Farm/I Never Was No One	1968	2.50	5.00	10.00
❑ 13972	I Couldn't Spell !!@!/Down Home Strut	1968	3.75	7.50	15.00
❑ 14021	Wolly Bully/Ain't Gonna Move	1968	2.50	5.00	10.00
❑ 14642	Fate/Oh Lo	1973	2.50	5.00	10.00
PHILCO-FORD					
❑ HP-3	Ju Ju Hand/Wooly Bully	1967	7.50	15.00	30.00
—4-inch plastic "Hip Pocket Record" with color sleeve					
TUPELO					
❑ 2982	Betty and Dupree/Manchild	1963	15.00	30.00	60.00
XL					
❑ 905	The Signifyin' Monkey/Juimonos	1964	12.50	25.00	50.00
❑ 906	Wooly Bully/Ain't Gonna Move	1965	75.00	150.00	300.00

SAMHAIN

Also see THE MISFITS.

7-Inch Extended Plays

Number	Title (A Side/B Side)	Yr	VG	VG+	NM
PLAN 9					
❑ PL9-05	Unholy Passion	1985	15.00	30.00	60.00
—White vinyl					
❑ PL9-05	Unholy Passion	1985	12.50	25.00	50.00
—Red vinyl					
❑ PL9-05 [PS]	Unholy Passion	1985	15.00	30.00	60.00
—Tan cover					
❑ PL9-05 [PS]	Unholy Passion	1985	12.50	25.00	50.00
—Maroon cover					

SAMMY AND THE DEL-LARKS

Number	Title (A Side/B Side)	Yr	VG	VG+	NM
EA-JAY					
❑ 100	Baby Come On/I Never Will Forget	1961	50.00	100.00	200.00

SAMUDIO, SAM

See SAM THE SHAM AND THE PHARAOHS.

SAN REMO GOLDEN STRINGS

Number	Title (A Side/B Side)	Yr	VG	VG+	NM
GORDY					
❑ 7060	Festival Time/Joy Road	1967	6.25	12.50	25.00
RIC-TIC					
❑ 104	Hungry for Love/All Turned On	1965	3.00	6.00	12.00
❑ 108	I'm Satisfied/Blueberry Hill	1965	3.00	6.00	12.00
❑ 112	Festival Time/Joy Road	1966	3.00	6.00	12.00
❑ 116	International Love Theme/Quanto Si Bella	1966	3.00	6.00	12.00

SANDALS, THE

Number	Title (A Side/B Side)	Yr	VG	VG+	NM
AURA					
❑ 4501	School's Out/Wild As the Sea	1964	6.25	12.50	25.00
—As "The Sandells"					
WORLD PACIFIC					
❑ 405	Scrambler/Out Front	1964	6.25	12.50	25.00
—As "The Sandells"					
❑ 415	Endless Summer/6-Pak	1964	6.25	12.50	25.00
❑ 421	All Over Again/Always	1965	3.75	7.50	15.00
❑ 77840	Theme from Endless Summer/6-Pak	1966	3.75	7.50	15.00
❑ 77852	Tell Us Dylan/Why Should I Cry	1966	3.75	7.50	15.00
❑ 77867	Cloudy/House of Painted Glass	1967	3.75	7.50	15.00

SANDERS, BOBBY

Number	Title (A Side/B Side)	Yr	VG	VG+	NM
KAYBO					
❑ 618	It Was You/I'm On My Way	1961	25.00	50.00	100.00
KENT					
❑ 382	Maybe I'm Wrong/You've Forgotten Me	1962	75.00	150.00	300.00
PICK-A-HIT					
❑ 100	Lover/The Way I Feel	196?	2.50	5.00	10.00

SANDERS, RAY

Number	Title (A Side/B Side)	Yr	VG	VG+	NM
CONCEPT					
❑ 897	Dynamite/(B-side unknown)	1957	25.00	50.00	100.00
—As "Curly Sanders"					
❑ 898	This Time/(B-side unknown)	1957	15.00	30.00	60.00
—As "Curly Sanders"					
GNP CRESCENDO					
❑ 397	Soldier's Last Letter/Two People	1967	2.00	4.00	8.00
❑ 409	I Always Do the Best with What I've Got/Come Back to Me	1968	2.00	4.00	8.00
HILLSIDE					
❑ 7901	It Was Always Our Song/Mountain of Love	1979	—	3.00	6.00
❑ 7904	Loose Talk/Silver Wings	1979	—	3.00	6.00
❑ 8005	You're a Pretty Lady, Lady/My Special Angel	1980	—	3.00	6.00
❑ 8103	Don't You Believe Her/Walk On By	1981	—	3.00	6.00
❑ 8105	There's a Little Bit of Everything in Texas/Another Place, Another Time	1981	—	3.00	6.00
IMPERIAL					
❑ 66366	Beer Drinking Music/Gotta Find a Way	1969	—	3.50	7.00
❑ 66408	Three Tears (For the Sad, Hurt and Blue)/Lucille	1969	—	3.50	7.00
❑ 66433	Holly Would/So Softly and Tenderly	1970	—	3.50	7.00
JAMBOREE					
❑ 590	Brand New Rock and Roll/(B-side unknown)	1956	25.00	50.00	100.00
—As "Curly Sanders"					
LIBERTY					
❑ 55267	A World So Full of Love/A Little Bitty Tear	1960	2.50	5.00	10.00
❑ 55304	Lonelyville/I Haven't Gone Far Enough Yet	1961	2.50	5.00	10.00
❑ 55348	Walk Slow/Two Hearts Are Broken	1961	2.50	5.00	10.00
❑ 55373	Don't Tell Nell/When Love Forgets to Die	1961	2.50	5.00	10.00
❑ 55406	Punish Me Tomorrow/You're Welcome Anytime	1962	2.50	5.00	10.00
❑ 55486	If I Can Slip Away/See One Broken Heart	1962	2.50	5.00	10.00
❑ 55568	Rich Living Woman/It's Not Funny	1963	2.50	5.00	10.00
REPUBLIC					
❑ 003	I Don't Want to Be Alone Tonight/The Power of Positive Drinkin'	1977	—	2.50	5.00
❑ 008	She Was Alone/(B-side unknown)	1977	—	2.50	5.00
❑ 013	Tennessee/You Keep Right On Walking	1978	—	2.50	5.00
❑ 016	Here Comes That Feelin'/(B-side unknown)	1978	—	2.50	5.00
STADIUM					
❑ 1115	Christmas Letter/Missing Christmas Card	1964	2.50	5.00	10.00
TOWER					
❑ 232	My World Is Upside Down/Graveyard Dance	1966	2.00	4.00	8.00
❑ 270	The Only Way to Fly/Don't Let Our Love Grow Cold	1966	2.00	4.00	8.00
❑ 330	City of Sin/I'll Try to Work You In	1967	2.00	4.00	8.00
UNITED ARTISTS					
❑ XW201	Another Way to Say Goodbye/(B-side unknown)	1973	—	3.00	6.00
❑ 50689	Blame It on Rosey/Waikiki Sand	1970	—	3.00	6.00
❑ 50732	Judy/Wild Side of Life	1970	—	3.00	6.00
❑ 50774	Walk All Over Georgia/Tonight She'll Make You Happy	1971	—	3.00	6.00
❑ 50827	All I Ever Need Is You/Before I Met You	1971	—	3.00	6.00
❑ 50886	A Rose By Any Other Name (Is Still a Rose)/We've Gotta Learn to Help Each Other	1972	—	3.00	6.00
❑ 50933	Lucius Grinder/You Let My Love Live	1972	—	3.00	6.00

SANDFORD, CHRIS

Number	Title (A Side/B Side)	Yr	VG	VG+	NM
FONTANA					
❑ 1534	(I Wish They Wouldn't Always Say) I Sound Like the Guy from USA Blues/Little Man-Nobody Cares	1965	3.00	6.00	12.00

SANDMEN, THE (1)

Number	Title (A Side/B Side)	Yr	VG	VG+	NM
BLUE JAY					
❑ 5002	If You Want Me/Searching for a New Love	1965	6.25	12.50	25.00

SANDMEN, THE (2)

BROOK BENTON was in this group.

Number	Title (A Side/B Side)	Yr	VG	VG+	NM
OKEH					
❑ 7052	When I Grow Too Old to Dream/Somebody to Love	1955	12.50	25.00	50.00

SANDS, JODIE

Number	Title (A Side/B Side)	Yr	VG	VG+	NM
ABC-PARAMOUNT					
❑ 10337	We Had Words/Uno Momento	1962	3.00	6.00	12.00

Number	Title (A Side/B Side)	Yr	VG	VG+	NM
10376	Hello, Heartache/This Little Fool	1962	3.00	6.00	12.00
10451	Time to Love/Charming Little Barefoot	1963	3.00	6.00	12.00

BERNLO

Number	Title (A Side/B Side)	Yr	VG	VG+	NM
1003	Love Me Always/Everybody Needs Somebody	1957	6.25	12.50	25.00

CHANCELLOR

Number	Title (A Side/B Side)	Yr	VG	VG+	NM
1003	With All My Heart/More Than Only Friends	1957	6.25	12.50	25.00
1005	If You're Not Completely Satisfied/Sayonara	1957	5.00	10.00	20.00
1009	The Way I Love You/Tantalizin' Love	1957	5.00	10.00	20.00
1015	Love Me Again/All I Ask of You	1958	5.00	10.00	20.00
1023	Someday/Always in My Heart	1958	5.00	10.00	20.00

PARIS

Number	Title (A Side/B Side)	Yr	VG	VG+	NM
543	I'd Cry No Tears/Kiss By Kiss	1960	3.75	7.50	15.00
551	Love Me Forever/Give Me a Break	1960	3.75	7.50	15.00

SIGNATURE

Number	Title (A Side/B Side)	Yr	VG	VG+	NM
12015	Turnabout Heart/Solo A Te Mio Amor	1959	3.75	7.50	15.00

TEEN

Number	Title (A Side/B Side)	Yr	VG	VG+	NM
109	Love Me Always/Everybody Needs Somebody	1955	10.00	20.00	40.00

THOR

Number	Title (A Side/B Side)	Yr	VG	VG+	NM
101	Hold Me/What Does It Mean	1959	5.00	10.00	20.00

SANDS, TOMMY

ABC-PARAMOUNT

Number	Title (A Side/B Side)	Yr	VG	VG+	NM
10466	Connie/Young Man's Fancy	1963	2.50	5.00	10.00
10480	Cinderella/Only 'Cause I'm Lonely	1963	2.50	5.00	10.00
10539	Won't You Be My Girl/Ten Dollars and a Clean White Shirt	1964	2.50	5.00	10.00
10591	Something More/Kisses (Love Theme)	1964	2.50	5.00	10.00

CAPITOL

Number	Title (A Side/B Side)	Yr	VG	VG+	NM
F3639	Teen-Age Crush/Hep Dee Hootie	1957	6.25	12.50	25.00
F3690	Ring-A-Ding-A-Ding/My Love Song	1957	6.25	12.50	25.00
F3723	Goin' Steady/Ring My Phone	1957	6.25	12.50	25.00
F3743	Let Me Be Loved/Fantastically Foolish	1957	5.00	10.00	20.00
F3810	A Swingin' Romance/Man, Like Wow!	1957	5.00	10.00	20.00
F3867	Sing, Boy, Sing/Crazy 'Cause I Love You	1957	5.00	10.00	20.00
F3953	Teenage Doll/Hawaiian Rock	1958	5.00	10.00	20.00
F3985	Big Date/After the Senior Prom	1958	5.00	10.00	20.00
F4036	Blue Ribbon Baby/I Love You Because	1958	5.00	10.00	20.00
F4082	Bigger Than Texas/The Worryin' Kind	1958	5.00	10.00	20.00
F4160	Is It Ever Gonna Happen/I Ain't Gittin' Rid of You	1959	3.75	7.50	15.00
F4231	Sinner Man/Bring Me Your Love	1959	3.75	7.50	15.00
F4259	I'll Be Seeing You/That's the Way I Am	1959	3.75	7.50	15.00
F4259 [PS]	I'll Be Seeing You/That's the Way I Am	1959	7.50	15.00	30.00
4316	You Hold the Future/I Gotta Have You	1959	3.75	7.50	15.00
4366	That's Love/Crossroads	1960	3.75	7.50	15.00
4405	The Old Oaken Bucket/These Are the Things You Are	1960	3.75	7.50	15.00
4470	Doctor Heartache/On and On	1960	3.75	7.50	15.00
4580	Love in a Goldfish Bowl/I Love My Baby	1961	3.00	6.00	12.00
4611	Rainbow/Remember Me to Jennie	1961	3.00	6.00	12.00
4660	Wrong Side of Love/Jimmy's Song	1961	3.00	6.00	12.00

IMPERIAL

Number	Title (A Side/B Side)	Yr	VG	VG+	NM
66174	As Long As I'm Travelin'/It's the Only One I've Got	1966	2.00	4.00	8.00
66229	Second Star to the Left/Candy Store Prophet	1967	2.00	4.00	8.00

LIBERTY

Number	Title (A Side/B Side)	Yr	VG	VG+	NM
55807	Love's Funny/One Rose Today, One Rose Tomorrow	1965	2.00	4.00	8.00
55842	The Statue/Little Rosita	1965	2.00	4.00	8.00
55864	Waitin' in Your Welfare Line/Don't Do It Darlin'	1966	—	—	—

—Unreleased

RCA VICTOR

Number	Title (A Side/B Side)	Yr	VG	VG+	NM
47-5435	Love Pains/Transfer	1953	7.50	15.00	30.00
47-5510	Roses Speak Louder Than Words/Spanish Coquita	1953	7.50	15.00	30.00
47-5628	A Dime and a Dollar/Life Is So Lonesome	1954	7.50	15.00	30.00
47-5697	Never Let Me Go/I Know About the Bees	1954	7.50	15.00	30.00
47-5800	Don't Drop It/A Place for Girls Like You	1954	7.50	15.00	30.00
47-6007	Kissin' Ain't No Fun/Something's Bound to Go Wrong	1955	7.50	15.00	30.00
47-6868	Don't Drop It/Love Pains	1957	5.00	10.00	20.00

SUPERSCOPE

Number	Title (A Side/B Side)	Yr	VG	VG+	NM
007	Seasons in the Sun/Ain't No Big Thing	1969	—	3.00	6.00

(NO LABEL)

Number	Title (A Side/B Side)	Yr	VG	VG+	NM
T 929 [DJ]	People in Love/That's All I Want from You	1957	12.50	25.00	50.00

—"Promotion Record" with no label name; used to promote the movie "Sing Boy Sing"; T 929 is catalog number of LP and the most prominent number on label

7-Inch Extended Plays

CAPITOL

Number	Title (A Side/B Side)	Yr	VG	VG+	NM
PRO 351 [DJ]	Goin' Steady/I Don't Know Why (I Just Do)//Graduation Day/A-You're Adorable (The Alphabet Song)	1957	10.00	20.00	40.00

—Promotional sampler from "Steady Date" album

Number	Title (A Side/B Side)	Yr	VG	VG+	NM
EAP 1-848	*Goin' Steady/Teach Me Tonight/Gonna Get a Girl/Somewhere Along the Way	1957	7.50	15.00	30.00
EAP 1-848 [PS]	Steady Date with Tommy Sands, Part 1	1957	7.50	15.00	30.00
EAP 2-848	Walkin' My Baby Back Home/Too Young to Go Steady//A-You're Adorable (The Alphabet Song)/Graduation Day	1957	7.50	15.00	30.00
EAP 2-848 [PS]	Steady Date with Tommy Sands, Part 2	1957	7.50	15.00	30.00
EAP 3-848	Ring My Phone/I Don't Know Why//Too Young/I Don't Care Who Knows It	1957	7.50	15.00	30.00
EAP 3-848 [PS]	Steady Date with Tommy Sands, Part 3	1957	7.50	15.00	30.00
EAP 1-851	*Teen-Age Crush/My Love Song/Hep Dee Hootie (Cutie Wootie)/Ring-a-Ding-a-Ding	1957	7.50	15.00	30.00
EAP 1-851 [PS]	Teen-Age Crush	1957	7.50	15.00	30.00
EAP 1-929	*I'm Gonna Walk and Talk with My Lord/Who Baby/Rock of Ages/Sing Boy Sing	1958	7.50	15.00	30.00
EAP 1-929 [PS]	Sing Boy Sing, Part 1	1958	7.50	15.00	30.00
EAP 2-929	(contents unknown)	1958	7.50	15.00	30.00
EAP 2-929 [PS]	Sing Boy Sing, Part 2	1958	7.50	15.00	30.00
EAP 3-929	People in Love/Crazy Cause I Love You//Your Daddy Wants to Do Right/That's All I Want from You	1958	7.50	15.00	30.00
EAP 3-929 [PS]	Sing Boy Sing, Part 3	1958	7.50	15.00	30.00

SANDY, FRANK

MARK

Number	Title (A Side/B Side)	Yr	VG	VG+	NM
138	Shamrock/Here She Comes	1959	10.00	20.00	40.00

MGM

Number	Title (A Side/B Side)	Yr	VG	VG+	NM
12626	Somebody Loves Me/Tarantella Rock	1958	12.50	25.00	50.00
12678	Let's Go Rock 'N' Roll/Midnight Stomp	1958	25.00	50.00	100.00

SANDY AND DICK

Also see DICK ST. JOHN.

CONGRESS

Number	Title (A Side/B Side)	Yr	VG	VG+	NM
6015	Groove With What You Got/Sing Along with Groove With What You Got	1970	2.00	4.00	8.00
6021	Sweet Sweet Lovin'/Quick Like a Bunny	1970	2.00	4.00	8.00

SANTANA

Also see GREGG ROLIE; CARLOS SANTANA.

ARISTA

Number	Title (A Side/B Side)	Yr	VG	VG+	NM
13773	Maria Maria (featuring The Product G&B)/Smooth (featuring Rob Thomas)	2000	—	2.50	5.00

COLUMBIA

Number	Title (A Side/B Side)	Yr	VG	VG+	NM
01050	Winning/The Brightest Star	1981	—	2.00	4.00
AE7 1064 [DJ]	All the Love of the Universe/Just in Time to See the Sun	1972	2.50	5.00	10.00
02178	The Sensitive Kind/American Gypsy	1981	—	2.00	4.00
02178 [PS]	The Sensitive Kind/American Gypsy	1981	—	2.50	5.00
02519	Searchin'/Tales of Kilimanjaro	1981	—	2.00	4.00
03160	Hold On/Oxun	1982	—	2.00	4.00
03268	Hold On	1982	—	3.00	6.00

—One-sided budget release

Number	Title (A Side/B Side)	Yr	VG	VG+	NM
03376	Nowhere to Run/Nueva York	1982	—	2.00	4.00
04034	Havana Moon/Lightnin'	1983	—	2.00	4.00
04758	Say It Again/Touchdown Raiders	1985	—	—	3.00
04758 [PS]	Say It Again/Touchdown Raiders	1985	—	2.00	4.00
04912	I'm the One Who Loves You/Right Now	1985	—	—	3.00
05677	They All Went to Mexico/Slow Movin' Outlaw	1985	—	—	3.00

—A-side: Willie Nelson and Carlos Santana; B-side: Willie and Lacy J. Dalton

Number	Title (A Side/B Side)	Yr	VG	VG+	NM
06654	Vera Cruz/Manuela	1987	—	2.00	4.00
07038	Vera Cruz (Remix)/Manuela	1987	—	—	3.00
07140	Praise/Love Is You	1987	—	—	3.00
10073	Mirage/Flor de Canela	1974	—	2.50	5.00
10088	Give and Take/Love Is Anew	1975	—	2.50	5.00
10336	Let It Shine/Tell Me Are You Tired	1976	—	2.50	5.00
10353	Dance Sister Dance (Baila Mi Hermana)/Let Me	1976	—	2.50	5.00
10421	Take Me with You/Europa (Earth's Cry Heaven's Smile)	1976	—	2.50	5.00
10481	Let the Children Play/Carnival	1977	—	2.50	5.00
10524	Give Me Love/Revelations	1977	—	2.50	5.00
10616	She's Not There/Zulu	1977	—	2.50	5.00
10677	Black Magic Woman/I'll Be Waiting	1977	—	2.50	5.00
10839	Well, All Right/Jericho	1978	—	2.50	5.00
10873	Stormy/Move On	1978	—	2.50	5.00
10938	One Chain (Don't Make a Prison)/Life Is a Lady-Holiday	1979	—	2.00	4.00
11144	You Know That I Love You/Aqua Marine	1979	—	2.00	4.00
11218	All I Ever Wanted/Lightning in the Sky	1980	—	2.00	4.00
45010	Jingo/Persuasion	1969	—	3.00	6.00
45010	Jin-Go-Lo-Ba/Persuasion	1969	—	3.00	6.00

—Same song, different A-side title

Number	Title (A Side/B Side)	Yr	VG	VG+	NM
45069	Evil Ways/Waiting	1970	—	3.00	6.00
45270	Black Magic Woman/Hope You're Feeling Better	1970	—	3.00	6.00
45270 [PS]	Black Magic Woman/Hope You're Feeling Better	1970	3.00	6.00	12.00
45330	Oye Como Va/Samba Pa Ti	1971	—	2.50	5.00
45330 [PS]	Oye Como Va/Samba Pa Ti	1971	2.00	4.00	8.00
45472	Everybody's Everything/Guajira	1971	—	2.50	5.00
45552	No One to Depend On/Taboo	1972	—	2.50	5.00
45552 [PS]	No One to Depend On/Taboo	1972	2.00	4.00	8.00
45753	Look Up/All the Love of the Universe	1973	—	2.50	5.00
45999	When I Look Into Your Eyes/Samba De Sausalito	1974	—	2.50	5.00
46067	Incident at Neshabur/Samba Pa Ti	1974	—	2.50	5.00

SANTANA, CARLOS

Also see SANTANA.

COLUMBIA

Number	Title (A Side/B Side)	Yr	VG	VG+	NM
03925	Tales of Kilimanjaro/Watch Your Step	1983	—	2.00	4.00

SANTANA, CARLOS, AND BUDDY MILES

Also see each artist's individual listings.

COLUMBIA

Number	Title (A Side/B Side)	Yr	VG	VG+	NM
45666	Them Changes/Evil Ways	1972	—	2.50	5.00

SANTO AND JOHNNY

CANADIAN AMERICAN

Number	Title (A Side/B Side)	Yr	VG	VG+	NM
103	Sleep Walk/All Night Diner	1959	6.25	12.50	25.00
107	Tear Drop/The Long Walk Home	1959	3.75	7.50	15.00
111	Caravan/Summertime	1960	3.75	7.50	15.00
115	The Breeze and I/Lazy Day	1960	3.75	7.50	15.00
118	Love Lost/Annie	1960	3.75	7.50	15.00
120	Twistin' Bells/Bullseye!	1960	4.00	8.00	16.00
120 [PS]	Twistin' Bells/Bullseye!	1960	10.00	20.00	40.00
124	Hop Scotch/Sea Shells	1961	3.75	7.50	15.00
128	Theme from Come September/The Long Walk Home	1961	3.75	7.50	15.00
131	The Mouse/Birmingham	1961	3.75	7.50	15.00
132	Twistin' Bells/Christmas Day	1961	5.00	10.00	20.00

—B-side by Linda Scott

Number	Title (A Side/B Side)	Yr	VG	VG+	NM
137	Spanish Harlem/Stage to Cimarron	1962	3.00	6.00	12.00
141	Three Caballeros/Step Aside	1962	3.00	6.00	12.00
144	Misirlou/Tokyo Twilight	1962	3.00	6.00	12.00

Number	Title (A Side/B Side)	Yr	VG	VG+	NM
❑ 148	Twistin' Bells/Manhattan	1962	3.00	6.00	12.00
❑ 151	On Your Mark/Manhattan	1963	3.00	6.00	12.00
❑ 155	The Wandering Sea/Manhattan Spiritual	1963	3.00	6.00	12.00
❑ 161	Love Letters in the Sand/Lido Beach	1963	3.00	6.00	12.00
❑ 164	I'll Remember (In the Still of the Night)/Song for Rosemary	1964	3.00	6.00	12.00
❑ 164 [PS]	I'll Remember (In the Still of the Night)/Song for Rosemary	1964	6.25	12.50	25.00
❑ 167	A Thousand Miles Away/Road Block	1964	3.00	6.00	12.00
❑ 167 [PS]	A Thousand Miles Away/Road Block	1964	6.25	12.50	25.00
❑ 174	Sugar Stroll/Rattler	1964	3.00	6.00	12.00
❑ 177	A Hard Day's Night/And I Love Her	1964	3.75	7.50	15.00
❑ 182	Goldfinger/Sleep Walk	1964	3.00	6.00	12.00
❑ 182 [PS]	Goldfinger/Sleep Walk	1964	6.25	12.50	25.00
❑ 189	Brazilian Summer/Off Tempo	1965	3.00	6.00	12.00
❑ 194	Watermelon Man/Return to Naples	1965	3.00	6.00	12.00
❑ 204	Come with Me/The Young World	1967	2.50	5.00	10.00
IMPERIAL					
❑ 66269	Live for Life/See You in September	1968	2.50	5.00	10.00
❑ 66292	Sleep Walk '68/It Must Be Him	1968	2.50	5.00	10.00
PAUSA					
❑ 703	Come Back Soldier/Flamingo	1976	—	2.50	5.00
UNITED ARTISTS					
❑ 970	Thunderball/Mister Kiss Kiss Bang Bang	1966	2.50	5.00	10.00
7-Inch Extended Plays					
CANADIAN AMERICAN					
❑ 1001	(contents unknown)	1959	20.00	40.00	80.00
❑ 1001 [PS]	Santo and Johnny	1959	20.00	40.00	80.00

SANTOS, LARRY

Number	Title (A Side/B Side)	Yr	VG	VG+	NM
ATLANTIC					
❑ 2250	Someday (When I'm Gone)/True	1964	5.00	10.00	20.00
—With the Four Seasons on backup					
BIG TREE					
❑ 136	Life Is Beautiful/Touchin' You	1972	—	2.50	5.00
CASABLANCA					
❑ 844	Can't Get You Off My Mind/We Can't Hide It Anymore	1975	—	3.00	6.00
—With "Can't Get You Off My Mind" listed as "Side A"					
❑ 844	We Can't Hide It Anymore/Can't Get You Off My Mind	1976	—	2.00	4.00
—With "We Can't Hide It Anymore" listed as "Side A"					
❑ 869	You Are Everything I Need/Long, Long Time	1976	—	2.00	4.00
❑ 881	Magic Mountain/Don't Let the Music Stop	1977	—	2.00	4.00
EVOLUTION					
❑ 1007	Tomorrow Without Love/You Got Me Where You Want Me	1969	—	3.00	6.00
❑ 1010	Subway Man/Woman-Child	1969	—	3.00	6.00
❑ 1018	Great Divide/Paper Chase	1970	—	3.00	6.00
❑ 1024	Mornin' Sun/Wandering Man	1970	—	3.00	6.00
❑ 1029	Now That I Have Found You/Wandering Man	1970	—	3.00	6.00
❑ 1039	Let It End/Little Bit of You	1971	—	3.00	6.00
❑ 1043	I Love You More Than Everything/Let It End	1971	—	3.00	6.00

SAPPHIRES, THE (1)

Number	Title (A Side/B Side)	Yr	VG	VG+	NM
ABC-PARAMOUNT					
❑ 10559	Hearts Are Made to Be Broken/Let's Break Up for Awhile	1964	3.75	7.50	15.00
❑ 10590	Thank You for Loving Me/Our Love Is Everywhere	1964	3.75	7.50	15.00
❑ 10639	Gee I'm Sorry, Baby/Gotta Have Your Love	1965	3.75	7.50	15.00
❑ 10693	Evil One/How Could I Say Goodbye	1965	3.75	7.50	15.00
❑ 10753	You'll Never Stop Me from Loving You/Gonna Be a Big Thing	1965	3.75	7.50	15.00
❑ 10778	Our Love Is Everywhere/Slow Fizz	1966	3.75	7.50	15.00
ITZY					
❑ 8	Who Do You Love/Oh So Soon	1963	10.00	20.00	40.00
SWAN					
❑ 4143	Your True Love/Where Is Johnny Now	1963	3.75	7.50	15.00
❑ 4162	Who Do You Love/Oh So Soon	1963	3.75	7.50	15.00
❑ 4177	I Found Out Too Late/I've Got Mine, You Better Get Yours	1964	3.75	7.50	15.00
❑ 4184	Gotta Be More Than Friends/Moulin Rouge	1964	3.75	7.50	15.00

SAPPHIRES, THE (2)

Number	Title (A Side/B Side)	Yr	VG	VG+	NM
RCA VICTOR					
❑ 47-7357	Everyone Knows/So Glad	1958	5.00	10.00	20.00

SARATOGAS, THE

Number	Title (A Side/B Side)	Yr	VG	VG+	NM
IMPERIAL					
❑ 5738	I'll Be Loving You/Get It in a Minute	1961	7.50	15.00	30.00

SARDO, FRANKIE

Number	Title (A Side/B Side)	Yr	VG	VG+	NM
20TH FOX					
❑ 208	I Know Why and So Do You/When the Bells Stop Ringing	1960	5.00	10.00	20.00
❑ 221	Dream Lover/Bonnie, Bonnie	1960	6.25	12.50	25.00
ABC-PARAMOUNT					
❑ 9963	Class Room/Fake Out	1958	5.00	10.00	20.00
❑ 10003	No Love Like Mine/Oh Linda	1959	5.00	10.00	20.00
LIDO					
❑ 602	Kiss and Make Up/The Girl I'm Gonna Dream About	1959	5.00	10.00	20.00
MGM					
❑ 12621	May I/My Story of Love	1958	5.00	10.00	20.00
NEWTOWN					
❑ 5005	I Got You Where I Want You/Mr. Make Believe	1962	6.25	12.50	25.00
RAYNA					
❑ 5005	Ring of Love/She Taught Me How to Cry	1962	3.75	7.50	15.00
STUDIO					
❑ 9910	Just You Watch Me/I'm Sittin' at Home	1961	12.50	25.00	50.00

SARDO, JOHNNY

Number	Title (A Side/B Side)	Yr	VG	VG+	NM
CHOCK FULL-O-HITS					
❑ 104	(Hip Hop) Take a Ride with Me/Hollywood Sign	1958	25.00	50.00	100.00
WARNER BROS.					
❑ 5014	I Wanna Rock/Used Heart	1958	6.25	12.50	25.00
❑ 5044	Late, Late, Late to School/New Kid in Town	1959	6.25	12.50	25.00

SARNE, MIKE

Number	Title (A Side/B Side)	Yr	VG	VG+	NM
ASCOT					
❑ 2213	An Englishman Sings "America Swings"/Can't Wait for Spring	1966	2.50	5.00	10.00
CAMEO					
❑ 220	Come On Outside/Fountain of Love	1962	3.00	6.00	12.00
STELLAR					
❑ 1506	Come Outside/Fountain of Love	1962	3.00	6.00	12.00

SARSTEDT, PETER

Number	Title (A Side/B Side)	Yr	VG	VG+	NM
SIRE					
❑ 1028	Beirut/The Hollywood Sign	1978	—	2.00	4.00
UNITED ARTISTS					
❑ 50923	You're a Lady/What Makes One Man Feel	1972	—	2.50	5.00
WORLD PACIFIC					
❑ 77906	I Am a Cathedral/Blagged	1969	—	3.00	6.00
❑ 77911	Where Do You Go To (My Lovely)/Morning Mountain	1969	2.00	4.00	8.00
❑ 77919	Frozen Orange Juice/Aretuza Loser	1969	—	3.00	6.00
❑ 77919 [PS]	Frozen Orange Juice/Aretuza Loser	1969	2.50	5.00	10.00
❑ 77933	Step Into the Battlefield/I Thought It Was	1970	—	3.00	6.00

SATAN AND THE DISCIPLES

Allegedly, this is FREDDY FENDER.

Number	Title (A Side/B Side)	Yr	VG	VG+	NM
GOLDBAND					
❑ 1188	Mummies Curse/Cat's Meow	1969	6.25	12.50	25.00

SATAN'S FOUR

Number	Title (A Side/B Side)	Yr	VG	VG+	NM
B.T. PUPPY					
❑ 515	I Can't Find the Girl on My Mind/Oh Cathy	1966	3.75	7.50	15.00

SATELLITES, THE

More than one group.

Number	Title (A Side/B Side)	Yr	VG	VG+	NM
ABC-PARAMOUNT					
❑ 10038	Linda Jean/Rockateen	1959	10.00	20.00	40.00
CLASS					
❑ 234	Heavenly Angel/You Ain't Sayin' Nothin'	1958	7.50	15.00	30.00
CUPID					
❑ (no #)	Linda Jean/Rockateen	1959	20.00	40.00	80.00
D-M-G					
❑ 4001	Each Night/Darktown Strutters Ball	1960	7.50	15.00	30.00
MALYNN					
❑ 231	Heavenly Angel/You Ain't Sayin' Nothin'	1958	6.25	12.50	25.00
PALACE					
❑ 102	Buzz Buzz/We Like Birdland	1960	5.00	10.00	20.00
PARROT					
❑ 313	Bodacious/El San Juan	1966	6.25	12.50	25.00
UNITED ARTISTS					
❑ 141	I Found a Girl/My Piggie's Gotta Dance	1958	10.00	20.00	40.00

SATINTONES, THE

Number	Title (A Side/B Side)	Yr	VG	VG+	NM
MOTOWN					
❑ 1000	Sugar Daddy/My Beloved	1960	100.00	200.00	400.00
—Without strings. Matrix number of A-side is "MNT 12345"					
❑ 1000	Sugar Daddy/My Beloved	1960	100.00	200.00	400.00
—With strings. Matrix number of A-side is "1000 G-3"					
❑ 1006	Tomorrow and Always/A Love That Can Never Be	1961	62.50	125.00	250.00
—Without strings					
❑ 1006	Angel/A Love That Can Never Be	1961	375.00	750.00	1500.
❑ 1006	Tomorrow and Always/A Love That Can Never Be	1961	62.50	125.00	250.00
—With strings					
❑ 1010	I Know How It Feels/My Kind of Love	1961	50.00	100.00	200.00
❑ 1020	Zing Went the Strings of My Heart/Faded Letter	1962	50.00	100.00	200.00
TAMLA					
❑ 54026	Motor City/Going to the Hop	1960	200.00	400.00	800.00

SATISFACTIONS, THE (1)

Number	Title (A Side/B Side)	Yr	VG	VG+	NM
LIONEL					
❑ 3201	This Bitter Earth/Ol' Man River	1970	3.00	6.00	12.00
❑ 3205	One Light Two Lights/Turn Back the Tears	1970	3.00	6.00	12.00
❑ 3214	God I'm Losing My Baby/O-o-o La La	1971	3.75	7.50	15.00

SATISFACTIONS, THE (2)

Number	Title (A Side/B Side)	Yr	VG	VG+	NM
CHESAPEKE					
❑ 610	We Will Walk Together/Oh Why	1962	7.50	15.00	30.00

SATISFACTIONS, THE (3)

Number	Title (A Side/B Side)	Yr	VG	VG+	NM
IMPERIAL					
❑ 66170	Bring It All Down/Daddy, You Just Gotta Let Him In	1966	5.00	10.00	20.00
SMASH					
❑ 2059	Give Me Your Love/Stop Following Me	1966	3.75	7.50	15.00
❑ 2098	Take It or Leave It/You Got to Share	1967	7.50	15.00	30.00

SATISFACTIONS, THE (U)

These could be group (1) or (3).

Number	Title (A Side/B Side)	Yr	VG	VG+	NM
1-2-3					
❑ 1716	Gonna Get Right Tonight/Living on a Prayer, a Hope and a Hand-Me-Down	1969	3.00	6.00	12.00
TWIN TOWN					
❑ 714	Bad Times/Don't Tell Me	1966	6.25	12.50	25.00

SATISFIERS, THE

Number	Title (A Side/B Side)	Yr	VG	VG+	NM
CORAL					
❑ 61727	Come Away, Love/Where'll I Be Tomorrow Night	1956	3.75	7.50	15.00

Number	Title (A Side/B Side)	Yr	VG	VG+	NM
❑ 61788	Over the Rainbow/Solitude	1957	3.75	7.50	15.00
❑ 61945	Will o' the Wisp/Remember That Crazy Rock and Roll	1958	3.75	7.50	15.00
JUBILEE					
❑ 5205	All or Nothing at All/Lies, Nothing But Lies	1955	5.00	10.00	20.00
VEGAS					
❑ 626	Ghost of a Chance/Fair Exchange	1960	3.00	6.00	12.00

SATURDAY, PATTY

Number	Title (A Side/B Side)	Yr	VG	VG+	NM
SWAN					
❑ 4022	Ladies Choice/Love Is a Beautiful Thing	1959	6.25	12.50	25.00

SATURDAY KNIGHTS, THE

Number	Title (A Side/B Side)	Yr	VG	VG+	NM
NOCTURNE					
❑ 1030	Sea Mist/Queen of the Nile	1963	12.50	25.00	50.00
SWAN					
❑ 4075	Ticonderoga/Tiger Lily	1961	5.00	10.00	20.00
❑ 4081	Hawaiian Tears/Texas Tommy	1961	5.00	10.00	20.00

SATURDAY'S CHILDREN

Number	Title (A Side/B Side)	Yr	VG	VG+	NM
ABC-PARAMOUNT					
❑ 10505	Raindrops/Cry Wind	1963	2.50	5.00	10.00
DUNWICH					
❑ 139	Born on Saturday/You Don't Know Better	1966	3.75	7.50	15.00
❑ 144	The Christmas Song/Deck Five	1967	3.75	7.50	15.00
❑ 156	Leave That Baby Alone/I Hardly Know Her	1967	3.75	7.50	15.00

SAUNDERS, LITTLE BUTCHIE

Number	Title (A Side/B Side)	Yr	VG	VG+	NM
HERALD					
❑ 485	Lindy Lou/Rock 'N' Roll Indian Dance	1956	12.50	25.00	50.00
❑ 491	Great Big Heart/I Wanna Holler	1956	12.50	25.00	50.00

SAVAGE, BOB

Number	Title (A Side/B Side)	Yr	VG	VG+	NM
ABC-PARAMOUNT					
❑ 9915	Rock Around the World/Butterfingers	1958	5.00	10.00	20.00

SAVAGE, DUKE, AND THE ARRIBINS

Number	Title (A Side/B Side)	Yr	VG	VG+	NM
ARGO					
❑ 5346	Your Love/Hey Baby	1959	10.00	20.00	40.00

SAVAGE GARDEN

Number	Title (A Side/B Side)	Yr	VG	VG+	NM
COLUMBIA					
❑ 78576	To the Moon & Back/Memories Are Designed to Fade	1997	—	—	3.00
❑ 78723	Truly Madly Deeply/I'll Bet He Was Cool	1997	—	—	3.00
❑ 79236	I Knew I Loved You/I Knew I Loved You (Acoustic)	1999	—	—	3.00

SAVAGE RESURRECTION

Number	Title (A Side/B Side)	Yr	VG	VG+	NM
MERCURY					
❑ 72778	Thing in "E"/The Fox Is Sick	1968	3.00	6.00	12.00

SAVOY BROWN

Number	Title (A Side/B Side)	Yr	VG	VG+	NM
LONDON					
❑ 206	Everybody Loves a Drinkin' Man/Ride On Babe	1974	—	2.50	5.00
❑ 234	Walkin' 'n' Talkin'/Stranger Blues	1976	—	2.50	5.00
PARROT					
❑ 40034	Shake 'Em On Down/(B-side unknown)	1968	3.75	7.50	15.00
❑ 40037	Grits Ain't Groceries/She's Got a Ring in His Nose and a Ring on Her Hand	1969	2.00	4.00	8.00
❑ 40039	Train to Nowhere/Made Up My Mind	1969	2.00	4.00	8.00
❑ 40042	I'm Tired/Stay with Me Baby	1969	2.00	4.00	8.00
❑ 40046	Hard Way to Go/The Incredible Gnome Meets Jaxman	1970	—	3.00	6.00
❑ 40057	Poor Girl/Mr. Hare	1970	—	3.00	6.00
❑ 40060	Sitting and Thinking/(B-side unknown)	1971	—	3.00	6.00
❑ 40066	Tell Mama/Rock and Roll on the Radio	1971	—	3.00	6.00
❑ 40075	Coming Down Your Way/Can't Find You	1973	—	3.00	6.00
TOWN HOUSE					
❑ 1055	Run to Me/Georgie	1981	—	2.00	4.00

SAWYER, RAY

Also see DR. HOOK.

Number	Title (A Side/B Side)	Yr	VG	VG+	NM
CAPITOL					
❑ 4344	(One More Year of) Daddy's Little Girl/I Need That High (But I Can't Stand the Taste)	1976	—	2.00	4.00
❑ 4386	Red-Winged Blackbird/The One I'm Holding Now	1977	—	2.00	4.00
❑ 4416	Walls and Doors/I Need That High (But I Can't Stand the Taste)	1977	—	2.00	4.00
❑ 4592	Dancing Fool/Rhythm Guitar	1978	—	2.00	4.00
❑ 4747	What I'm Holding/I Want Johnny's Job	1979	—	2.00	4.00
❑ 4820	Drinking Wine Alone/I Don't Feel Like Smilin'	1980	—	2.00	4.00
SANDY					
❑ 1030	Rockin' Satellite/Bells in My Heart	1961	10.00	20.00	40.00
❑ 1037	I'm Gonna Leave/You Gave Me the Right	1961	6.25	12.50	25.00

SAXON, EDDIE, AND THE PARAMOUNTS

Number	Title (A Side/B Side)	Yr	VG	VG+	NM
EMPRESS					
❑ 106	Blues No More/If It's Meant to Be	1962	37.50	75.00	150.00
❑ 106 [DJ]	Blues No More	1962	50.00	100.00	200.00
—Single-sided promo					

SAXON, SKY

Later recorded with THE SEEDS. Also see RITCHIE MARSH.

Number	Title (A Side/B Side)	Yr	VG	VG+	NM
CONQUEST					
❑ 777	They Say/Go Ahead and Cry	1964	7.50	15.00	30.00

SAYER, LEO

Number	Title (A Side/B Side)	Yr	VG	VG+	NM
WARNER BROS.					
❑ 7768	The Show Must Go On/Innocent Bystander	1974	2.00	4.00	8.00
❑ 7824	One Man Band/Drop Back	1974	—	3.00	6.00
❑ 8043	Long Tall Glasses/In My Life	1974	—	3.00	6.00
—First pressings have no A-side subtitle					
❑ 8043	Long Tall Glasses (I Can Dance)/In My Life	1975	—	2.50	5.00
—Later pressings add subtitle to A-side					
❑ 8097	One Man Band/Telepath	1975	—	2.50	5.00
❑ 8153	Moonlighting/Streets of Your Town	1975	—	2.50	5.00
❑ 8283	You Make Me Feel Like Dancing/Magdalena	1976	—	2.50	5.00
❑ 8319	How Much Love/I Hear the Laughter	1977	—	2.50	5.00
❑ 8332	When I Need You/I Think We Fell in Love Too Fast	1977	—	2.50	5.00
❑ 8465	Thunder in My Heart/Get the Girl	1977	—	2.50	5.00
❑ 8502	Easy to Love/Haunting Me	1977	—	2.50	5.00
❑ 8682	Raining in My Heart/No Looking Back	1978	—	2.00	4.00
❑ 8738	Don't Look Back/No Looking Back	1979	—	2.00	4.00
❑ 29904	Paris Dies in the Morning/We've Got Ourselves in Love	1982	—	2.00	4.00
❑ 29960	End of the Game/Heart	1982	—	2.00	4.00
❑ 49134	Oh Girl/Englishman in the U.S.A.	1979	—	2.00	4.00
❑ 49565	More Than I Can Say/Millionaire	1980	—	2.00	4.00
❑ 49657	Living in a Fantasy/Only Foolin'	1981	—	2.00	4.00
❑ 49714	Where Did We Go Wrong/She's Not Coming Back	1981	—	2.00	4.00
❑ 50060	Have You Ever Been in Love/I Don't Need Dreaming Anymore	1982	—	2.00	4.00

SCAFFOLD, THE

With Mike McGear, Paul McCartney's brother.

Number	Title (A Side/B Side)	Yr	VG	VG+	NM
BELL					
❑ 701	Thank U Very Much/Ide B the First	1968	4.00	8.00	16.00
❑ 724	Do You Remember/Carry On Krow	1968	4.00	8.00	16.00
❑ 747	Lily the Pink/Buttons of Your Mind	1968	4.00	8.00	16.00
❑ 821	Charity Bubbles/Goose	1969	4.00	8.00	16.00
❑ 849	Jelly Covered Cloud/Liver Birds	1969	3.00	6.00	12.00
WARNER BROS.					
❑ 8001	Liverpool Lou/Ten Years After on Strawberry Jam	1974	—	3.00	6.00

SCAGGS, BOZ

Also see STEVE MILLER BAND.

Number	Title (A Side/B Side)	Yr	VG	VG+	NM
ATLANTIC					
❑ 2692	I'm Easy/I'll Be Long Gone	1969	2.50	5.00	10.00
COLUMBIA					
❑ 01023	You Can Have Me Anytime/Georgia	1981	—	2.00	4.00
❑ 02423	Jojo/Miss Sun	1981	—	—	3.00
—Reissue					
❑ 02424	Breakdown Dead Ahead/Look What You've Done to Me	1981	—	—	3.00
—Reissue					
❑ 07780	Heart of Mine/You'll Never Know	1988	—	—	3.00
❑ 07780 [PS]	Heart of Mine/You'll Never Know	1988	—	2.00	4.00
❑ 07981	Cool Running/You'll Never Know	1988	—	—	3.00
❑ 08068	What's Number 1/Claudia	1988	—	—	3.00
❑ 10027	Slow Dancer/Pain of Love	1974	—	3.00	6.00
❑ 10124	You Make It So Hard (To Say Goodbye)/There Is Something Else	1975	—	2.50	5.00
❑ 10319	It's Over/Harbor Lights	1976	—	2.50	5.00
❑ 10367	Lowdown/Harbor Lights	1976	—	2.50	5.00
❑ 10440	What Can I Say/We're All Alone	1976	—	2.50	5.00
❑ 10491	Lido Shuffle/We're All Alone	1977	—	2.50	5.00
❑ 10606	Hard Times/We're Waiting	1977	—	2.50	5.00
❑ 10606 [PS]	Hard Times/We're Waiting	1977	2.50	5.00	10.00
❑ 10679	Hollywood/A Clue	1978	—	2.50	5.00
❑ 11241	Breakdown Dead Ahead/Isn't It Time	1980	—	2.00	4.00
❑ 11281	Jojo/Do Like You Do in New York	1980	—	2.00	4.00
❑ 11349	Look What You've Done to Me/Simone	1980	—	2.00	4.00
❑ 11406	Miss Sun/Dinah Flo	1980	—	2.00	4.00
❑ 45353	We Were Always Sweethearts/Painted Bells	1971	—	3.00	6.00
❑ 45408	Near You/Downright Woman	1971	—	3.00	6.00
❑ 45540	Here to Stay/Runnin' Blue	1972	—	3.00	6.00
❑ 45670	Dinah Flo/He's a Fool for You	1972	—	3.00	6.00
❑ 46025	You Make It So Hard (To Say Goodbye)/There Is Someone Else	1974	—	3.00	6.00
FULL MOON					
❑ 49676	You Make It So Hard (To Say Goodbye)/Something's Missing in My Life	1981	—	2.00	4.00
—B-side by Lady Sylvia					
VIRGIN					
❑ S7-18048	I'll Be the One/Time Change	1994	—	2.00	4.00
❑ S7-19529	It All Went Down the Drain/I've Got Your Love	1997	—	—	3.00
❑ S7-19651	Fly Like a Bird/Sick and Tired	1997	—	—	3.00

SCARLETS, THE (1)

Number	Title (A Side/B Side)	Yr	VG	VG+	NM
DOT					
❑ 16004	Stampede/Park Avenue	1959	6.25	12.50	25.00
PRINCE					
❑ 1207	Stampede/Park Avenue	1959	12.50	25.00	50.00

SCARLETS, THE (2)

Number	Title (A Side/B Side)	Yr	VG	VG+	NM
EVENT					
❑ 4287	Dear One/I've Lost	1958	10.00	20.00	40.00
RED ROBIN					
❑ 128	Dear One/I've Lost	1954	125.00	250.00	500.00
❑ 133	Darling, I'm Yours/Love Doll	1954	125.00	250.00	500.00
❑ 135	True Love/Cry Baby	1955	125.00	250.00	500.00
❑ 138	Kiss Me/Indian Fever	1955	150.00	300.00	600.00

SCARLETS, THE (3)

Number	Title (A Side/B Side)	Yr	VG	VG+	NM
TOWER					
❑ 144	I've Had It/You Don't Love Me	1965	2.50	5.00	10.00

SCARLETS, THE (U)

Could be group (1).

Number	Title (A Side/B Side)	Yr	VG	VG+	NM
FURY					
❑ 1036	Truly Yours/East of the Sun	1960	7.50	15.00	30.00

SCAVENGERS, THE

Number	Title (A Side/B Side)	Yr	VG	VG+	NM
FENTON					
❑ 987	Curfew/Oasis	1964	12.50	25.00	50.00
MOBILE FIDELITY					
❑ 1005	The Angels Listened In/My Love Waits for Me	1963	7.50	15.00	30.00

Number	Title (A Side/B Side)	Yr	VG	VG+	NM
❑ 1212	Devil's Reef/Little Annie	1963	7.50	15.00	30.00

STARS OF HOLLYWOOD

Number	Title (A Side/B Side)	Yr	VG	VG+	NM
❑ 1210	Shot Gun/Cream Puff	1963	12.50	25.00	50.00
❑ 1211	Shot Gun/Zip Code	1963	12.50	25.00	50.00

—"Cream Puff" and "Zip Code" are different titles for the same recording

Number	Title (A Side/B Side)	Yr	VG	VG+	NM
❑ 1212	Devil's Reef/Little Annie	1963	12.50	25.00	50.00

SUEMI

Number	Title (A Side/B Side)	Yr	VG	VG+	NM
❑ 4552	Bogus/Ghost Riders '65	1965	6.25	12.50	25.00

SCHAFF, MURRAY, AND THE ARISTOCRATS

JOSIE

Number	Title (A Side/B Side)	Yr	VG	VG+	NM
❑ 788	The Unfinished Rock/Ooh How I Love Ya	1956	7.50	15.00	30.00

KING

Number	Title (A Side/B Side)	Yr	VG	VG+	NM
❑ 4977	How Many Miles/Tombstone Number 9	1956	7.50	15.00	30.00

SCHILLING, JOHNNY, AND THE SHERWOODS

C&A

Number	Title (A Side/B Side)	Yr	VG	VG+	NM
❑ 507	King of the World/Marcelle	1963	25.00	50.00	100.00

SCHMIT, TIMOTHY B.

Also see EAGLES; POCO.

ASYLUM

Number	Title (A Side/B Side)	Yr	VG	VG+	NM
❑ 69600	Playin' It Cool/Wrong Number	1984	—	—	3.00
❑ 69939	So Much in Love/She's My Baby and She's Outta Control	1982	—	2.00	4.00

—B-side by Palmer/Jost

Number	Title (A Side/B Side)	Yr	VG	VG+	NM
❑ 69939 [PS]	So Much in Love/She's My Baby and She's Outta Control	1982	—	2.50	5.00

MCA

Number	Title (A Side/B Side)	Yr	VG	VG+	NM
❑ 53137	Boys Night Out/Into the Night	1987	—	—	3.00
❑ 53137 [PS]	Boys Night Out/Into the Night	1987	—	—	3.00
❑ 53233	Don't Give Up/Jazz Street	1987	—	—	3.00
❑ 53284	Everybody Needs a Lover/Into the Night	1988	—	—	3.00
❑ 53284 [PS]	Everybody Needs a Lover/Into the Night	1988	—	—	3.00

SCHOLARS, THE (1)

Featuring a young KENNY ROGERS.

IMPERIAL

Number	Title (A Side/B Side)	Yr	VG	VG+	NM
❑ 5449	I Didn't Want to Do It/Beloved	1957	6.25	12.50	25.00
❑ 5459	Eternally Yours/Kan-Gu-Wa	1957	6.25	12.50	25.00

SCHOLARS, THE (U)

May or may not be group (1).

CUE

Number	Title (A Side/B Side)	Yr	VG	VG+	NM
❑ 7927	What Did I Do Wrong/(B-side unknown)	1956	10.00	20.00	40.00

DOT

Number	Title (A Side/B Side)	Yr	VG	VG+	NM
❑ 15498	Rock Road/Spin the Wheel	1956	5.00	10.00	20.00
❑ 15519	If You Listen with Your Heart/Poor Little Doggie	1956	5.00	10.00	20.00

SCHOOLBOYS, THE

JUANITA

Number	Title (A Side/B Side)	Yr	VG	VG+	NM
❑ 103	Angel of Love/The Slide	1958	37.50	75.00	150.00

OKEH

Number	Title (A Side/B Side)	Yr	VG	VG+	NM
❑ 7076	Shirley/Please Say You Want Me	1957	7.50	15.00	30.00

—"Shirley" was the hit, but "Please Say You Want Me" is the side that has lived on

Number	Title (A Side/B Side)	Yr	VG	VG+	NM
❑ 7085	I Am Old Enough/Mary	1957	6.25	12.50	25.00
❑ 7090	Pearl/Carol	1957	6.25	12.50	25.00

SCHUMACHER, CHRISTINE, SINGS WITH THE SUPREMES

Also see THE SUPREMES.

MOTOWN

Number	Title (A Side/B Side)	Yr	VG	VG+	NM
❑ L-294-MO5 [DJ]	Mother You, Smother You (same on both sides)	1968	75.00	150.00	300.00

—Schumacher won a "Record a Record with the Supremes" contest on WKNR of Detroit. This is the rare result.

SCOTT, BILLY

CAMEO

Number	Title (A Side/B Side)	Yr	VG	VG+	NM
❑ 121	You're the Greatest/That's Why I Was Born	1957	6.25	12.50	25.00
❑ 143	A Million Boys/The Town of Never Worry	1958	5.00	10.00	20.00

EVEREST

Number	Title (A Side/B Side)	Yr	VG	VG+	NM
❑ 19315	Carole/Stairway to the Stars	1959	3.75	7.50	15.00

LAMON

Number	Title (A Side/B Side)	Yr	VG	VG+	NM
❑ 10114	Merry Christmas/A Night To Remember	1983	—	2.00	4.00

SCOTT, FREDDIE

Also see THE SYMPHONICS (2).

COLPIX

Number	Title (A Side/B Side)	Yr	VG	VG+	NM
❑ 692	Hey Girl/The Slide	1963	3.00	6.00	12.00
❑ 709	I Got a Woman/Brand New World	1963	2.50	5.00	10.00
❑ 724	Where Does Love Go/Where Have All the Flowers Gone	1964	2.50	5.00	10.00
❑ 752	On Broadway/If I Had a Hammer	1964	2.50	5.00	10.00

COLUMBIA

Number	Title (A Side/B Side)	Yr	VG	VG+	NM
❑ 43112	Mr. Heartache/One Heartache Too Many	1964	2.50	5.00	10.00
❑ 43199	Lonely Man/I'll Try Again	1964	2.50	5.00	10.00
❑ 43316	Don't Let It End/Come Up Singing	1965	2.50	5.00	10.00
❑ 43623	One Iddy Biddy Needle/Forget Me If You Can	1966	2.50	5.00	10.00

JOY

Number	Title (A Side/B Side)	Yr	VG	VG+	NM
❑ 250	Baby, You're a Long Time Dead/Lost the Right	1961	3.00	6.00	12.00
❑ 255	I Gotta Stand Tall/When the Wind Changes	1961	3.00	6.00	12.00
❑ 280	I Gotta Stand Tall/When the Wind Changes	1963	2.50	5.00	10.00

PROBE

Number	Title (A Side/B Side)	Yr	VG	VG+	NM
❑ 481	I Shall Be Released/Girl I Love You	1970	—	3.00	6.00

P.I.P.

Number	Title (A Side/B Side)	Yr	VG	VG+	NM
❑ 8932	Deep Is the Night/The Great If	1972	—	2.50	5.00

SHOUT

Number	Title (A Side/B Side)	Yr	VG	VG+	NM
❑ 207	Are You Lonely for Me/Where Were You	1966	2.00	4.00	8.00
❑ 211	Cry to Me/No One Could Ever Love You	1967	2.00	4.00	8.00
❑ 212	Am I Grooving You/Never You Mind	1967	2.00	4.00	8.00
❑ 216	He Will Break Your Heart/I'll Be Gone	1967	2.00	4.00	8.00
❑ 220	He Ain't Give You None/Run Joy	1967	2.00	4.00	8.00
❑ 227	Just Like a Flower/Spanish Harlem	1968	2.00	4.00	8.00
❑ 233	(You) Got What I Need/Powerful Love	1968	2.50	5.00	10.00
❑ 238	Loving You Is Killing Me/Eileen	1968	2.00	4.00	8.00
❑ 245	Forever My Darling/(You) Got What I Need	1969	2.50	5.00	10.00

VANGUARD

Number	Title (A Side/B Side)	Yr	VG	VG+	NM
❑ 35137	I Guess God Wants It This Way/Please Listen	1971	—	2.50	5.00

SCOTT, FREDDIE, AND THE CHIMES

ARROW

Number	Title (A Side/B Side)	Yr	VG	VG+	NM
❑ 724	Please Call/A Letter Came This Morning	1958	10.00	20.00	40.00
❑ 726	Lovin' Baby/A Faded Memory	1958	10.00	20.00	40.00

SCOTT, JACK

ABC

Number	Title (A Side/B Side)	Yr	VG	VG+	NM
❑ 10843	Before the Bird Flies/Insane	1966	5.00	10.00	20.00

ABC-PARAMOUNT

Number	Title (A Side/B Side)	Yr	VG	VG+	NM
❑ 9818	Baby She's Gone/You Can Bet Your Bottom Dollar	1957	37.50	75.00	150.00
❑ 9860	Two Timin' Woman/I Need Your Love	1957	37.50	75.00	150.00

CAPITOL

Number	Title (A Side/B Side)	Yr	VG	VG+	NM
❑ 4554	A Little Feeling (Called Love)/Now That I	1961	6.25	12.50	25.00
❑ 4554 [PS]	A Little Feeling (Called Love)/Now That I	1961	12.50	25.00	50.00
❑ 4597	My Dream Came True/Strange Desire	1961	5.00	10.00	20.00
❑ 4597 [PS]	My Dream Came True/Strange Desire	1961	12.50	25.00	50.00
❑ 4637	Steps 1 and 2/One of These Days	1961	5.00	10.00	20.00
❑ 4637 [PS]	Steps 1 and 2/One of These Days	1961	12.50	25.00	50.00
❑ 4689	Cry, Cry, Cry/Grizzly Bear	1962	5.00	10.00	20.00
❑ 4689 [PS]	Cry, Cry, Cry/Grizzly Bear	1962	12.50	25.00	50.00
❑ 4738	The Part Where I Cry/You Only See What You Wanna See	1962	5.00	10.00	20.00
❑ 4796	Sad Story/I Can't Hold Your Letters	1962	5.00	10.00	20.00
❑ 4855	If Only/Green, Green Valley	1962	5.00	10.00	20.00
❑ 4903	Strangers/Laugh and the World Laughs With You	1963	5.00	10.00	20.00
❑ 4955	All I See Is Blue/Meo Myo	1963	5.00	10.00	20.00

CARLTON

Number	Title (A Side/B Side)	Yr	VG	VG+	NM
❑ 462	My True Love/Leroy	1958	7.50	15.00	30.00
❑ 483	With Your Love/Geraldine	1958	7.50	15.00	30.00
❑ 483 [PS]	With Your Love/Geraldine	1958	15.00	30.00	60.00
❑ 493	Goodbye Baby/Save My Soul	1959	7.50	15.00	30.00
❑ 493 [PS]	Goodbye Baby/Save My Soul	1959	15.00	30.00	60.00
❑ 504	I Never Felt Like This/Bella	1959	7.50	15.00	30.00
❑ 514	The Way I Walk/Midgie	1959	7.50	15.00	30.00
❑ 519 [M]	There Comes a Time/Baby Marie	1959	5.00	10.00	20.00
❑ ST-519 [S]	There Comes a Time/Baby Marie	1959	10.00	20.00	40.00

DOT

Number	Title (A Side/B Side)	Yr	VG	VG+	NM
❑ 17475	May You Never Be Alone/Face to the Wall	1973	—	2.50	5.00
❑ 17504	You're Just Getting Better/Walk Through My Mind	1974	—	2.50	5.00

GROOVE

Number	Title (A Side/B Side)	Yr	VG	VG+	NM
❑ 58-0027	There's Trouble Brewin'/Jingle Bell Slide	1963	5.00	10.00	20.00
❑ 58-0031	Blue Skies (Moving In on Me)/I Knew You First	1964	3.75	7.50	15.00
❑ 58-0037	Wiggle On Out/What a Wonderful Night Out	1964	5.00	10.00	20.00
❑ 58-0042	Thou Shalt Not Steal/I Prayed for an Angel	1964	3.75	7.50	15.00
❑ 58-0049	Flakey John/Tall Tales	1964	5.00	10.00	20.00

GRT

Number	Title (A Side/B Side)	Yr	VG	VG+	NM
❑ 35	Billy Jack/Mary, Marry Me	1971	—	2.50	5.00

GUARANTEED

Number	Title (A Side/B Side)	Yr	VG	VG+	NM
❑ 209	What Am I Living For/Indiana Waltz	1960	7.50	15.00	30.00
❑ 211	No One Will Ever Know/Go Wild Little Sadie	1960	7.50	15.00	30.00

JUBILEE

Number	Title (A Side/B Side)	Yr	VG	VG+	NM
❑ 5606	My Special Angel/I Keep Changin' My Mind	1967	5.00	10.00	20.00

PONIE

Number	Title (A Side/B Side)	Yr	VG	VG+	NM
❑ 7021-10	Geraldine/Midgie	197?	—	2.00	4.00
❑ 7021-11	There's Trouble Brewin'/Jingle Bell Slide	197?	—	2.00	4.00
❑ 7021-12	Flakey John/Wiggle On Out	197?	—	2.00	4.00
❑ 5121-15	Baby She's Gone/Two Timin' Woman	197?	—	2.00	4.00
❑ 6063-20	Leroy/Go Wild Little Sadie	197?	—	2.00	4.00
❑ 6083-20	Country Witch/Blues, Stay Away from Me-Stones	197?	—	2.00	4.00
❑ 4104-30	Spirit of '76/(Instrumental)	1976	—	2.00	4.00

RCA VICTOR

Number	Title (A Side/B Side)	Yr	VG	VG+	NM
❑ 47-8505	Separation's Now Granted/I Don't Believe in Tea Leaves	1965	3.75	7.50	15.00
❑ 47-8685	Looking for Linda/I Hope I Think I Wish	1965	3.75	7.50	15.00
❑ 47-8724	Don't Hush the Laughter/Let's Learn to Live and Love Again	1965	3.75	7.50	15.00

TOP RANK

Number	Title (A Side/B Side)	Yr	VG	VG+	NM
❑ 2028 [M]	What in the World's Come Over You/Baby Baby	1959	7.50	15.00	30.00
❑ 2028 [S]	What in the World's Come Over You/Baby Baby	1959	10.00	20.00	40.00
❑ 2041 [M]	Burning Bridges/Oh Little One	1960	6.25	12.50	25.00
❑ 2041 [PS]	Burning Bridges/Oh Little One	1960	15.00	30.00	60.00
❑ 2041 [S]	Burning Bridges/Oh Little One	1960	15.00	30.00	60.00
❑ 2055	It Only Happened Yesterday/Cool Water	1960	5.00	10.00	20.00
❑ 2075	Patsy/Old Time Religion	1960	5.00	10.00	20.00
❑ 2093	Is There Something on Your Mind/Found a Woman	1960	5.00	10.00	20.00
❑ 2093 [PS]	Is There Something on Your Mind/Found a Woman	1960	15.00	30.00	60.00

7-Inch Extended Plays

CARLTON

Number	Title (A Side/B Side)	Yr	VG	VG+	NM
❑ EP 7/1070	Save My Soul/I Can't Help It//Geraldine/With Your Love	1959	50.00	100.00	200.00
❑ EP 7/1070 [PS]	Presenting Jack Scott (Volume 1)	1959	50.00	100.00	200.00
❑ EP 7/1071	Indiana Waltz,/Midgie//My True Love/Leroy	1959	50.00	100.00	200.00
❑ EP 7/1071 [PS]	Presenting Jack Scott (Volume 2)	1959	50.00	100.00	200.00
❑ EP 7/1072	No One Will Ever Know/Goodbye Baby//I'm Dreaming Of You/The Way I Walk	1959	50.00	100.00	200.00
❑ EP 7/1072 [PS]	Jack Scott Sings	1959	50.00	100.00	200.00

TOP RANK

Number	Title (A Side/B Side)	Yr	VG	VG+	NM
❑ 1001	(contents unknown)	1960	50.00	100.00	200.00
❑ 1001 [PS]	What in the World's Come Over You	1960	50.00	100.00	200.00

SCOTT, JOEL

PHILLES

Number	Title (A Side/B Side)	Yr	VG	VG+	NM
101	Here I Stand/You're My Only Love	1962	6.25	12.50	25.00

SCOTT, LINDA

CANADIAN AMERICAN

Number	Title (A Side/B Side)	Yr	VG	VG+	NM
123	I've Told Every Little Star/Three Guesses	1961	5.00	10.00	20.00
127	Don't Bet Money Honey/Starlight, Starbright	1961	5.00	10.00	20.00
129	I Don't Know Why/It's All Because	1961	5.00	10.00	20.00
132	Christmas Day/Twistin' Bells	1961	5.00	10.00	20.00
—B-side by Santo and Johnny					
133	Count Every Star/Land of Stars	1962	3.75	7.50	15.00
134	Bermuda/Lonely for You	1962	3.75	7.50	15.00

CONGRESS

Number	Title (A Side/B Side)	Yr	VG	VG+	NM
101	Yessiree/Town Crier	1962	3.75	7.50	15.00
103	Never in a Million Years/Through the Summer	1962	3.75	7.50	15.00
106	I Left My Heart in the Balcony/Lopsided Love Affair	1962	3.75	7.50	15.00
108	I'm So Afraid of Losing You/The Loneliest Girl in Town	1962	3.75	7.50	15.00
110	I'm Gonna Sit Right Down and Write Myself a Letter/Ain't That Fun	1963	3.75	7.50	15.00
200	Let's Fall in Love/I Know It, You Know It	1963	3.75	7.50	15.00
204	Who's Been Sleeping in My Bed/My Baby	1963	3.75	7.50	15.00
206	Let's Fall in Love/I Know It, You Know It	1964	3.75	7.50	15.00
209	I Envy You/Everybody Stopped Laughing at Jane	1964	3.75	7.50	15.00

KAPP

Number	Title (A Side/B Side)	Yr	VG	VG+	NM
610	That Old Feeling/This Is My Prayer	1964	2.50	5.00	10.00
641	If I Love Again/Patch It Up	1965	2.50	5.00	10.00
677	Don't Lose Your Head/I'll See You in My Dreams	1965	2.50	5.00	10.00
713	You Baby/I Can't Get Through to You	1965	2.50	5.00	10.00
762	Toys/Take a Walk Bobby	1966	2.50	5.00	10.00

RCA VICTOR

Number	Title (A Side/B Side)	Yr	VG	VG+	NM
47-9424	They Don't Know You/Three Miles High	1967	2.50	5.00	10.00

7-Inch Extended Plays

CANADIAN AMERICAN

Number	Title (A Side/B Side)	Yr	VG	VG+	NM
CAEP 1005	Count Every Star/Catch a Falling Star//Stars Fell on Alabama/Blue Star	196?	12.50	25.00	50.00
CAEP 1005 [PS]	(title unknown)	196?	12.50	25.00	50.00

SCOTT, RICKY

CUB

Number	Title (A Side/B Side)	Yr	VG	VG+	NM
9079	I Didn't Mean It/Darlin' Darlin'	1960	5.00	10.00	20.00

X-CLUSIVE

Number	Title (A Side/B Side)	Yr	VG	VG+	NM
1001	I Didn't Mean It/Darlin' Darlin'	1960	20.00	40.00	80.00

SCOTT, RODNEY

CANON

Number	Title (A Side/B Side)	Yr	VG	VG+	NM
225	Granny Went Rockin'/Bitter Tears	1961	50.00	100.00	200.00
231	You're So Square (Baby I Don't Care)/He'll Be There	1961	50.00	100.00	200.00

MR. PEEKE

Number	Title (A Side/B Side)	Yr	VG	VG+	NM
110	You're So Square (Baby I Don't Care)/He'll Be There	1962	20.00	40.00	80.00
126	That's the Way It Goes/Bitter Tears	1963	7.50	15.00	30.00

SCOTT, SHERREE

ROBBINS

Number	Title (A Side/B Side)	Yr	VG	VG+	NM
105	Twinkle Toes (The Littlest Reindeer)/Our Christmas Day	1959	10.00	20.00	40.00
1036	Fascinating Baby/You and I	1957	37.50	75.00	150.00

ROCKET

Number	Title (A Side/B Side)	Yr	VG	VG+	NM
101	Whole Lotta Shakin' Goin' On/Unhappy Birthday	1958	37.50	75.00	150.00
101 [PS]	Whole Lotta Shakin' Goin' On/Unhappy Birthday	1958	50.00	100.00	200.00

SCOTT, SIMON

IMPERIAL

Number	Title (A Side/B Side)	Yr	VG	VG+	NM
66066	Move It Baby/What Kind of a Woman	1964	3.75	7.50	15.00
66089	My Baby's Got Soul/Midnight	1965	3.75	7.50	15.00

SCOTT, TERRY

VALIANT

Number	Title (A Side/B Side)	Yr	VG	VG+	NM
6016	Little Angel/Love Only Me	1962	3.00	6.00	12.00

SCOTT, TOMMY

LONDON

Number	Title (A Side/B Side)	Yr	VG	VG+	NM
9694	Wrap Your Troubles in Dreams/Blueberry Hill	1964	3.00	6.00	12.00

SCOTT, WALTER

Lead singer with BOB KUBAN AND THE IN-MEN.

MUSICLAND U.S.A.

Number	Title (A Side/B Side)	Yr	VG	VG+	NM
111	Just You Wait/Silly Girl	1967	5.00	10.00	20.00
20009	Watch Out/My Shadow Is Gone	1966	3.75	7.50	15.00
20014	It's Been a Long Time/Proud	1966	3.75	7.50	15.00

PZAZZ

Number	Title (A Side/B Side)	Yr	VG	VG+	NM
026	Soul Stew Recipe/Feeling Something New Inside	1969	2.50	5.00	10.00

WHITE WHALE

Number	Title (A Side/B Side)	Yr	VG	VG+	NM
259	Just You Wait/Silly Girl	1967	5.00	10.00	20.00

SCOTT RICHARD CASE

See SRC.

SCRAMBLERS, THE

ARVEE

Number	Title (A Side/B Side)	Yr	VG	VG+	NM
6502	Super Surfer U.S.A./Go Getera Go	1963	6.25	12.50	25.00

DEL-FI

Number	Title (A Side/B Side)	Yr	VG	VG+	NM
4237	The Beatle Walk/The Beatle Blues	1964	6.25	12.50	25.00

SEA, JOHNNY

CAPITOL

Number	Title (A Side/B Side)	Yr	VG	VG+	NM
4585	The Torch and the Flame/No Tears Tonight	1961	2.50	5.00	10.00
4646	Livin' Is Lovin'/The Wayward Wind	1961	2.50	5.00	10.00

COLUMBIA

Number	Title (A Side/B Side)	Yr	VG	VG+	NM
44423	Going Out to Tulsa/There's a Shadow Bar	1968	—	2.50	5.00
44542	Mama When I'm Gone Don't Cry for Me/Song Number 9 1/2 on the Album	1968	—	2.50	5.00
44634	Three Six-Packs, Two Arms and a Juke Box/Loved Her Fine for a Time	1968	—	2.50	5.00
44717	I've Learned a Lot Today/A Poor Boy Just Trying to Get Along	1968	—	2.50	5.00
44805	Cryin' Gray Tombstone/Everybody's Friend	1969	—	2.50	5.00

NRC

Number	Title (A Side/B Side)	Yr	VG	VG+	NM
006	It Won't Be Easy to Forget/I Love You	1958	3.00	6.00	12.00
019	Frankie's Man, Johnny/Loneliness	1959	3.00	6.00	12.00
026	Stranger/Judy and Johnny	1959	3.00	6.00	12.00
049	Nobody's Darling But Mine/My Time to Cry	1959	3.00	6.00	12.00
060	Ghost Riders in the Sky/Mr. and Mrs. Sippi	1960	3.00	6.00	12.00

PHILIPS

Number	Title (A Side/B Side)	Yr	VG	VG+	NM
40164	My Baby Walks All Over Me/There's Another Man	1964	2.00	4.00	8.00
40214	All Mixed Up/Standing Room Only	1964	2.00	4.00	8.00
40267	My Old Faded Rose/It's a Shame	1965	2.00	4.00	8.00
40307	If It Wasn't for Hard Luck/Hitchin' and Hikin'	1965	2.00	4.00	8.00

VIKING

Number	Title (A Side/B Side)	Yr	VG	VG+	NM
1011	Fort Worth Girl/Willie's Drunk and Willie's Dying	1970	—	2.50	5.00
1017	Annie's Going to Sing Her Song/(B-side unknown)	1971	—	3.00	6.00

WARNER BROS.

Number	Title (A Side/B Side)	Yr	VG	VG+	NM
5820	Day for Decision/Mary Rocks Him to Sleep	1966	—	3.00	6.00
5861	Things You Gave Me/Wheels on the Highway	1966	—	3.00	6.00
5889	Nothin's Bad As Bein' Lonely/Ain't That Right	1967	—	3.00	6.00

SEA SHELLS, THE

GOLIATH

Number	Title (A Side/B Side)	Yr	VG	VG+	NM
1357	Love Those Beach Boys/Close to Jimmy	1964	10.00	20.00	40.00

JUBILEE

Number	Title (A Side/B Side)	Yr	VG	VG+	NM
5587	Hit the Surf/Barefoot in the Sand	1967	5.00	10.00	20.00

SEAFOOD MAMA

Early version of QUARTERFLASH.

WHITEFIRE

Number	Title (A Side/B Side)	Yr	VG	VG+	NM
(no #)	Harden My Heart/City of Roses	1980	6.25	12.50	25.00
(no #) [PS]	Harden My Heart/City of Roses	1980	6.25	12.50	25.00

SEALS, JIMMY

Also see THE CHAMPS; SEALS AND CROFTS.

CARLTON

Number	Title (A Side/B Side)	Yr	VG	VG+	NM
470	Sneaky Pete/Benguela	1958	7.50	15.00	30.00

CHALLENGE

Number	Title (A Side/B Side)	Yr	VG	VG+	NM
9153	Wish for You, Want for You, Wait for You/Runaway Heart	1962	7.50	15.00	30.00
9200	Lady Heartbreak/Grounded	1963	7.50	15.00	30.00
59270	Everybody's Doing the Jerk/Wa-Hoo	1965	5.00	10.00	20.00
59299	She's Not a Bad Girl/The Yesterday of Our Love	1965	5.00	10.00	20.00

WINSTON

Number	Title (A Side/B Side)	Yr	VG	VG+	NM
1021	Sneaky Pete/Benguela	1958	10.00	20.00	50.00
1027	Biscayne Bay/Juarez	1958	10.00	20.00	50.00

SEALS AND CROFTS

Also see THE CHAMPS; JIMMY SEALS.

T-A

Number	Title (A Side/B Side)	Yr	VG	VG+	NM
188	In Tune/Seldom's Sister	1969	2.00	4.00	8.00
191	See My Life/(B-side unknown)	1969	2.00	4.00	8.00
206	See My Life/In Tune//Hollow Reed/Leave	1970	2.50	5.00	10.00
208	Ridin' Thumb/Leave	1970	2.00	4.00	8.00
210	Gabriel Go On Home/Robin	1971	2.00	4.00	8.00

WARNER BROS.

Number	Title (A Side/B Side)	Yr	VG	VG+	NM
7536	When I Meet Them/Irish Linen	1971	—	3.00	6.00
7565	Sudan Village/High on a Mountain	1972	—	3.00	6.00
7606	Summer Breeze/East of Ginger Trees	1972	—	2.50	5.00
7671	Hummingbird/Say	1972	—	2.50	5.00
7697	We May Never Pass This Way (Again)/Intone My Servant	1973	—	—	—
—Unreleased?					
7708	Diamond Girl/Wisdom	1973	—	2.50	5.00
7740	We May Never Pass This Way (Again)/Jessica	1973	—	2.50	5.00
7771	Unborn Child/Ledges	1974	—	2.00	4.00
7810	King of Nothing/Follow Me	1974	—	2.00	4.00
8075	I'll Play for You/Truth Is But a Woman	1975	—	2.00	4.00
8130	Castles in the Sand/Golden Rainbow	1975	—	2.00	4.00
8190	Get Closer/Don't Fail	1976	—	2.00	4.00
8190 [PS]	Get Closer/Don't Fail	1976	—	2.50	5.00
8277	Baby, I'll Give It to You/Advance Guards	1976	—	2.00	4.00
8405	My Fair Share/East of Ginger Trees	1977	—	2.00	4.00
8405 [PS]	My Fair Share/East of Ginger Trees	1977	—	3.00	6.00
8551	You're the Love/Midnight Blue	1978	—	2.00	4.00
8639	Magnolia Moon/Takin' It Easy	1978	—	2.00	4.00
49522	First Love/Kite Dreams	1980	—	2.00	4.00

7-Inch Extended Plays

WARNER BROS.

Number	Title (A Side/B Side)	Yr	VG	VG+	NM
S 2761 [DJ]	Rachel/King of Nothing/Desert People//The Story of Her Love/Dance by the Light of the Moon	1974	2.00	4.00	8.00
—33 1/3 rpm, small hole jukebox edition					
S 2761 [PS]	Unborn Child	1974	2.50	5.00	10.00

SEAN AND THE BRANDYWINES

DECCA

Number	Title (A Side/B Side)	Yr	VG	VG+	NM
31910	She Ain't No Good/Cod'ine	1966	5.00	10.00	20.00
—Produced by Gary Usher					

SEARCHERS, THE

KAPP

Number	Title (A Side/B Side)	Yr	VG	VG+	NM
KJB-22	Needles and Pins/Ain't That Just Like Me	1964	2.00	4.00	8.00
—Orange label "Winners Circle Series"					

Number	Title (A Side/B Side)	Yr	VG	VG+	NM
❑ KJB-27	Love Potion Number Nine/Hi-Heel Sneakers	1964	2.50	5.00	10.00
—Orange label "Winners Circle Series"; no black label counterpart					
❑ KJB-29	Bumble Bee/Everything You Do	1964	2.50	5.00	10.00
—Orange label "Winners Circle Series"; no black label counterpart					
❑ KJB-29	Bumble Bee/A Tear Fell	1965	2.50	5.00	10.00
—Orange label "Winners Circle Series"; no black label counterpart					
❑ 577	Needles and Pins/Ain't That Just Like Me	1964	3.00	6.00	12.00
❑ 577	Needles and Pins/Saturday Night Out	1964	2.50	5.00	10.00
❑ 577 [PS]	Needles and Pins/Ain't That Just Like Me	1964	7.50	15.00	30.00
❑ 577 [PS]	Needles and Pins (promo-only version)	1964	12.50	25.00	50.00
❑ 584	Ain't That Just Like Me/Ain't Gonna Kiss You	1964	2.50	5.00	10.00
❑ 584 [PS]	Ain't That Just Like Me (special promo sleeve)	1964	12.50	25.00	50.00
❑ 593	Don't Throw Your Love Away/I'll Pretend I'm with You	1964	2.50	5.00	10.00
❑ 609	Someday We're Gonna Love Again/No One Else Could Love Me	1964	2.50	5.00	10.00
❑ 609 [PS]	Someday We're Gonna Love Again/No One Else Could Love Me	1964	7.50	15.00	30.00
❑ 618	When You Walk in the Room/I'll Be Missing You	1964	2.50	5.00	10.00
❑ 644	What Have They Done to the Rain/This Feeling Inside	1965	2.50	5.00	10.00
❑ 658	Goodbye My Lover Goodbye/'Til I Met You	1965	2.50	5.00	10.00
❑ 686	He's Got No Love/So Far Away	1965	2.50	5.00	10.00
❑ 706	Don't You Know Why/You Can't Lie to a Liar	1965	2.50	5.00	10.00
❑ 729	Take Me for What I'm Worth/Too Many Miles	1966	2.50	5.00	10.00
❑ 783	Have You Ever Loved Somebody/It's Just the Way	1966	2.50	5.00	10.00
❑ 811	Lovers/Popcorn Double Feature	1966	2.50	5.00	10.00
LIBERTY					
❑ 55646	Sugar and Spice/Saints and Sinners	1963	6.25	12.50	25.00
❑ 55689	Sugar and Spice/Saints and Sinners	1964	3.75	7.50	15.00
MERCURY					
❑ 72172	Sweets for My Sweet/It's All Been a Dream	1963	6.25	12.50	25.00
❑ 72390	(Ain't That) Just Like Me/I Can Tell	1964	3.75	7.50	15.00
RCA VICTOR					
❑ 74-0484	Desdemona/The World Is Waiting for Tomorrow	1971	—	3.00	6.00
❑ 74-0652	Love Is Everywhere/And the Button	1972	—	3.00	6.00
SIRE					
❑ 49175	It's Too Late/Don't Hang On	1980	—	2.00	4.00
❑ 49665	Love's Melody/Little Bit of Heaven	1981	—	2.00	4.00
WORLD PACIFIC					
❑ 77908	Umbrella Man/Over the Weekend	1969	2.00	4.00	8.00

SEBASTIAN, JOHN

Also see THE LOVIN' SPOONFUL.

Number	Title (A Side/B Side)	Yr	VG	VG+	NM
KAMA SUTRA					
❑ 254	She's a Lady/The Room Nobody Lives In	1968	2.50	5.00	10.00
❑ 254 [PS]	She's a Lady/The Room Nobody Lives In	1968	3.75	7.50	15.00
❑ 505	Younger Generation/Boredom	1970	2.00	4.00	8.00
MGM					
❑ 14122	Rainbows All Over Your Blues/You're a Big Boy Now	1970	—	3.00	6.00
REPRISE					
❑ 0902	Fa-Fana-Fa/Magical Connection	1970	—	3.00	6.00
❑ 0918	What She Thinks About/Red-Eye Express	1970	—	3.00	6.00
❑ 1026	I Don't Want Nobody Else/Sweet Muse	1971	—	3.00	6.00
❑ 1050	We'll See/Well, Well, Well	1971	—	3.00	6.00
❑ 1074	Give Us a Break/Music for People Who Don't Speak English	1972	—	3.00	6.00
❑ 1349	Welcome Back Kotter/Warm Baby	1976	2.00	4.00	8.00
—Original A-side title					
❑ 1349	Welcome Back/Warm Baby	1976	—	2.00	4.00
—Revised A-side title					
❑ 1355	Hideaway/One Step Forward, Two Steps Back	1976	—	2.00	4.00

SECRETS, THE (1)

Girl group.

Number	Title (A Side/B Side)	Yr	VG	VG+	NM
OMEN					
❑ 15	Here I Am/I Feel a Thrill Coming On	1966	3.00	6.00	12.00
PHILIPS					
❑ 40146	The Boy Next Door/Learnin' to Forget	1963	3.75	7.50	15.00
❑ 40173	Hey Big Boy/The Other Side of Town	1964	3.00	6.00	12.00
❑ 40173 [PS]	Hey Big Boy/The Other Side of Town	1964	5.00	10.00	20.00
❑ 40196	Here He Comes Now!/Oh Donnie	1964	3.00	6.00	12.00
❑ 40222	He's the Boy/He Doesn't Want You	1964	3.00	6.00	12.00

SECRETS, THE (2)

Number	Title (A Side/B Side)	Yr	VG	VG+	NM
SWAN					
❑ 4097	Hot Toddy/Twin Exhaust	1962	6.25	12.50	25.00
❑ 4097 [PS]	Hot Toddy/Twin Exhaust	1962	12.50	25.00	50.00

SECRETS, THE (3)

Number	Title (A Side/B Side)	Yr	VG	VG+	NM
HARMONY					
❑ 6958	Hot Night in the City/Don't Say Goodbye	1982	—	2.00	4.00
❑ 6958 [PS]	Hot Night in the City/Don't Say Goodbye	1982	—	2.50	5.00

SECRETS, THE (U)

Could be group (1).

Number	Title (A Side/B Side)	Yr	VG	VG+	NM
RED BIRD					
❑ 10-076	Every Day/A Smile Upside Down	1966	2.50	5.00	10.00

SEDAKA, NEIL

Also see THE TOKENS.

Number	Title (A Side/B Side)	Yr	VG	VG+	NM
DECCA					
❑ 30520	Laura Lee/Snowtime	1957	15.00	30.00	60.00
ELEKTRA					
❑ 45406	Amarillo/The Leaving Game	1977	—	2.00	4.00
❑ 45421	Alone at Last/Sleazy Love	1977	—	2.00	4.00
❑ 45525	Candy Kisses/All You Need Is the Music	1978	—	2.00	4.00
❑ 46017	Sad, Sad Story/Tillie the Twirler	1979	—	2.00	4.00
❑ 46615	Should've Never Let You Go/You're So Good for Me	1980	—	2.00	4.00
—With Dara Sedaka					
❑ 47017	Letting Go/It's Good to Be Alive Again	1980	—	3.00	6.00
❑ 47184	My World Keeps Slipping Away/Love Is Spreading Over the World	1981	—	2.00	4.00
GUYDEN					
❑ 2004	Ring-a-Rockin'/Fly, Don't Fly on Me	1958	12.50	25.00	50.00
KIRSHNER					
❑ SP-45-291 [DJ]	I'm a Song (Sing Me)/Silent Movies	1971	2.00	4.00	8.00
—Promo only number (mono versions)					
❑ SP-45-370 [DJ]	Beautiful You (Long)/Beautiful You (Short)	1972	2.00	4.00	8.00
—Promo only number					
❑ 63-5017	I'm a Song (Sing Me)/Silent Movies	1971	—	2.50	5.00
—As "Sedaka"					
❑ 63-5020	Superbird/Rosemary Blue	1972	—	2.50	5.00
❑ 63-5024	Beautiful You/Anywhere You're Gonna Be (Leba's Song)	1972	—	3.00	6.00
LEGION					
❑ 133	Ring-a-Rockin'/Fly, Don't Fly on Me	1958	25.00	50.00	100.00
MCA					
❑ 60189	Laughter in the Rain/The Immigrant	197?	—	—	3.00
—Reissue					
MCA CURB					
❑ 52307	Your Precious Love/Searchin'	1983	—	2.00	4.00
—With Dara Sedaka					
❑ 52400	New Orleans/Rhythm of the Rain	1984	—	2.00	4.00
—With Gary U.S. Bonds					
MGM					
❑ 14564	Standing on the Inside/Let Daddy Know	1973	—	2.50	5.00
❑ 14661	Alone in New York in the Rain/Suspicions	1973	—	2.50	5.00
PYRAMID					
❑ 623	Oh Delilah/Neil's Twist	1962	7.50	15.00	30.00
—B-side is an instrumental version of the A-side credited to The Marvels					
RCA VICTOR					
❑ SP-45-96 [DJ]	RCA Victor Special DJ Spots	196?	12.50	25.00	50.00
—Promo only; Sedaka introduces six songs and promotes his current release					
❑ 37-7829	Calendar Girl/The Same Old Fool	1960	12.50	25.00	50.00
—"Compact Single 33" (small hole, plays at LP speed)					
❑ 37-7874	Little Devil/I Must Be Dreaming	1961	12.50	25.00	50.00
—"Compact Single 33" (small hole, plays at LP speed)					
❑ 37-7922	Sweet Little You/I Found My World in You	1961	12.50	25.00	50.00
—"Compact Single 33" (small hole, plays at LP speed)					
❑ 37-7957	Happy Birthday Sweet Sixteen/Don't Lead Me On	1961	12.50	25.00	50.00
—"Compact Single 33" (small hole, plays at LP speed)					
❑ 47-7408	The Diary/No Vacancy	1958	5.00	10.00	20.00
❑ 47-7408 [DJ]	The Diary/No Vacancy	1958	10.00	20.00	40.00
—White label promo with Sedaka's photo on label					
❑ 47-7473	I Go Ape/Moon of Gold	1959	5.00	10.00	20.00
❑ 47-7530	You Gotta Learn Your Rhythm and Blues/Crying My Heart Out for You	1959	6.25	12.50	25.00
❑ 47-7595	Oh! Carol/One Way Ticket (To the Blues)	1959	5.00	10.00	20.00
❑ 47-7709	Stairway to Heaven/Forty Winks Away	1960	3.75	7.50	15.00
❑ 47-7781	You Mean Everything to Me/Run Samson Run	1960	3.75	7.50	15.00
❑ 47-7781 [PS]	You Mean Everything to Me/Run Samson Run	1960	6.25	12.50	25.00
❑ 47-7829	Calendar Girl/The Same Old Fool	1960	3.75	7.50	15.00
❑ 47-7829 [PS]	Calendar Girl/The Same Old Fool	1960	6.25	12.50	25.00
❑ 47-7874	Little Devil/I Must Be Dreaming	1961	3.75	7.50	15.00
❑ 47-7874 [PS]	Little Devil/I Must Be Dreaming	1961	6.25	12.50	25.00
❑ 47-7922	Sweet Little You/I Found My World in You	1961	3.75	7.50	15.00
❑ 47-7922 [PS]	Sweet Little You/I Found My World in You	1961	6.25	12.50	25.00
❑ 47-7957	Happy Birthday Sweet Sixteen/Don't Lead Me On	1961	3.75	7.50	15.00
❑ 47-8007	King of Clowns/Walk with Me	1962	3.75	7.50	15.00
❑ 47-8007 [PS]	King of Clowns/Walk with Me	1962	6.25	12.50	25.00
❑ 47-8046	Breaking Up Is Hard to Do/As Long As I Live	1962	3.75	7.50	15.00
❑ 47-8046 [PS]	Breaking Up Is Hard to Do/As Long As I Live	1962	6.25	12.50	25.00
❑ 47-8086	Next Door to An Angel/I Belong to You	1962	3.75	7.50	15.00
❑ 47-8086 [PS]	Next Door to An Angel/I Belong to You	1962	6.25	12.50	25.00
❑ 47-8137	Alice in Wonderland/Circulate	1963	3.00	6.00	12.00
❑ 47-8137 [PS]	Alice in Wonderland/Circulate	1963	6.25	12.50	25.00
❑ 47-8169	Let's Go Steady Again/Waiting for Never	1963	3.00	6.00	12.00
❑ 47-8169 [PS]	Let's Go Steady Again/Waiting for Never	1963	6.25	12.50	25.00
❑ 47-8209	The Dreamer/Look Inside Your Heart	1963	3.00	6.00	12.00
❑ 47-8209 [PS]	The Dreamer/Look Inside Your Heart	1963	6.25	12.50	25.00
❑ 47-8254	Bad Girl/Wait 'Til You See My Baby	1963	3.00	6.00	12.00
❑ 47-8341	The Closest Thing to Heaven/Without a Song	1964	2.50	5.00	10.00
❑ 47-8341 [PS]	The Closest Thing to Heaven/Without a Song	1964	5.00	10.00	20.00
❑ 47-8382	Sunny/She'll Never Be You	1964	2.50	5.00	10.00
❑ 47-8453	I Hope He Breaks Your Heart/Too Late	1964	2.50	5.00	10.00
❑ 47-8511	Let the People Talk/In the Chapel with You	1965	2.50	5.00	10.00
❑ 47-8511 [PS]	Let the People Talk/In the Chapel with You	1965	5.00	10.00	20.00
❑ 47-8637	The World Through a Tear/High On a Mountain	1965	2.50	5.00	10.00
❑ 47-8637 [PS]	The World Through a Tear/High On a Mountain	1965	5.00	10.00	20.00
❑ 47-8737	The Answer to My Prayer/Blue Boy	1965	2.50	5.00	10.00
❑ 47-8844	The Answer Lies Within/Grown-Up Games	1966	2.50	5.00	10.00
❑ 47-9004	We Can Make It If We Try/Too Late	1966	2.50	5.00	10.00
❑ 61-7595 [S]	Oh! Carol/One Way Ticket (To the Blues)	1959	12.50	25.00	50.00
—"Living Stereo" (large hole, plays at 45 rpm)					
❑ 61-7709 [S]	Stairway to Heaven/Forty Winks Away	1960	12.50	25.00	50.00
—"Living Stereo" (large hole, plays at 45 rpm)					
❑ 61-7781 [S]	You Mean Everything to Me/Run Samson Run	1960	12.50	25.00	50.00
—"Living Stereo" (large hole, plays at 45 rpm)					
❑ 61-7829 [S]	Calendar Girl/The Same Old Fool	1960	12.50	25.00	50.00
—"Living Stereo" (large hole, plays at 45 rpm)					
❑ 447-0575	Oh! Carol/Calendar Girl	196?	—	3.00	6.00
—Gold Standard Series; black label					
❑ 447-0575	Oh! Carol/Calendar Girl	197?	—	2.00	4.00
—Gold Standard Series; red label					
❑ 447-0597	The Diary/Happy Birthday Sweet Sixteen	196?	—	3.00	6.00
—Gold Standard Series; black label					

Number	Title (A Side/B Side)	Yr	VG	VG+	NM
❑ 447-0597	The Diary/Happy Birthday Sweet Sixteen	197?	—	2.00	4.00
—Gold Standard Series; red label					
❑ 447-0701	Breaking Up Is Hard to Do/Next Door to An Angel	196?	—	3.00	6.00
—Gold Standard Series; black label					
❑ 447-0701	Breaking Up Is Hard to Do/Next Door to An Angel	197?	—	2.00	4.00
—Gold Standard Series; red label					
❑ 447-0939	Little Devil/Stairway to Heaven	196?	—	3.00	6.00
—Gold Standard Series; black label					
ROCKET					
❑ 40313	Laughter in the Rain/Endlessly	1974	—	2.00	4.00
❑ 40370	The Immigrant/Hey Mister Sunshine	1975	—	2.00	4.00
—No mention of John Lennon on label					
❑ 40370	The Immigrant/Hey Mister Sunshine	1975	2.50	5.00	10.00
—With "Dedicated to John Lennon" under title in bold					
❑ 40426	That's When the Music Takes Me/Standing on the Inside	1975	—	2.00	4.00
❑ 40460	Bad Blood/Your Favorite Entertainer	1975	—	2.00	4.00
❑ 40500	Breaking Up Is Hard to Do/Nana's Song	1975	—	2.00	4.00
❑ 40543	Love in the Shadows/Baby Don't Let It Mess Your Mind	1976	—	2.00	4.00
❑ 40582	Steppin' Out/I Let You Walk Away	1976	—	2.00	4.00
❑ 40614	You Gotta Make Your Own Sunshine/Perfect Strangers	1976	—	2.00	4.00
SGC					
❑ 005	Star-Crossed Lovers/We Had a Good Thing Going	1969	—	3.00	6.00
❑ 008	Rainy Jane/Jeannine	1970	—	3.00	6.00

7-Inch Extended Plays

Number	Title (A Side/B Side)	Yr	VG	VG+	NM
RCA VICTOR					
❑ LPC-105	Oh! Carol/Stairway to Heaven//The Diary/Run Samson Run	1961	12.50	25.00	50.00
—"Compact Double 33" with small hole					
❑ LPC-105 [PS]	Neil's Best	1961	12.50	25.00	50.00
❑ LPC-135	Little Devil/Circulate//Calendar Girl/We Kiss in a Shadow	1961	12.50	25.00	50.00
—"Compact Double 33" with small hole					
❑ LPC-135 [PS]	Little Devil	1961	12.50	25.00	50.00
❑ EPA-4334	I Go Ape/All I Need Is You//Stop! You're Knocking Me Out/I Belong to You	1959	15.00	30.00	60.00
❑ EPA-4334 [PS]	I Go Ape	1959	15.00	30.00	60.00
❑ EPA-4353	Oh! Carol/Going Home to Mary Lou//The Girl for Me/I Ain't Hurtin' No More	1959	15.00	30.00	60.00
❑ EPA-4353 [PS]	Oh! Carol	1959	15.00	30.00	60.00

SEEDS, THE

Also see RITCHIE MARSH; SKY SAXON.

Number	Title (A Side/B Side)	Yr	VG	VG+	NM
GNP CRESCENDO					
❑ 354	Can't Seem to Make You Mine/Daisy Mae	1965	3.75	7.50	15.00
❑ 354	Can't Seem to Make You Mine/I Tell Myself	1967	2.50	5.00	10.00
❑ 354 [PS]	Can't Seem to Make You Mine/I Tell Myself	1967	12.50	25.00	50.00
❑ 364	You're Pushing Too Hard/Out of the Question	1965	3.75	7.50	15.00
❑ 370	The Other Place/Try to Understand	1966	3.75	7.50	15.00
❑ 372	Pushin' Too Hard/Try to Understand	1966	3.75	7.50	15.00
—With "GNP Crescendo" standing alone at top of label (no box)					
❑ 372	Pushin' Too Hard/Try to Understand	1966	3.00	6.00	12.00
—With "GNP Crescendo" in box at top of label					
❑ 383	Mr. Farmer/No Escape	1967	2.00	4.00	8.00
❑ 383	Mr. Farmer/Up in Her Room	1967	2.00	4.00	8.00
❑ 383 [PS]	Mr. Farmer/Up in Her Room	1967	12.50	25.00	50.00
❑ 394	A Thousand Shadows/March of the Flower Children	1967	2.00	4.00	8.00
❑ 394 [PS]	A Thousand Shadows/March of the Flower Children	1967	5.00	10.00	20.00
❑ 398	The Wind Blows Your Hair/Six Dreams	1967	2.00	4.00	8.00
❑ 408	Satisfy You/900 Million People Daily	1968	2.00	4.00	8.00
❑ 422	Fallin' Off the Edge of My Mind/Wild Blood	1969	2.50	5.00	10.00
MGM					
❑ 14163	Wish Me Up/Bad Part of Town	1970	5.00	10.00	20.00
❑ 14190	Did He Die/Love in a Summer Blanket	1970	5.00	10.00	20.00
PHILCO-FORD					
❑ HP-26	Pushin' Too Hard/Can't Seem to Make You Mine	1968	6.25	12.50	25.00
—4-inch plastic "Hip Pocket Record" with color sleeve					

SEEKERS, THE

Number	Title (A Side/B Side)	Yr	VG	VG+	NM
CAPITOL					
❑ 2013	When the Good Apples Fall/Myra (Shake Up the Party)	1967	2.50	5.00	10.00
❑ 2122	Love Is Kind, Love Is Wine/All I Can Remember	1968	2.50	5.00	10.00
❑ 5383	I'll Never Find Another You/Open Up Them Pearly Gates	1965	3.00	6.00	12.00
❑ 5430	A World of Our Own/Sinner Man	1965	3.00	6.00	12.00
❑ 5430 [PS]	A World of Our Own/Sinner Man	1965	5.00	10.00	20.00
❑ 5531	The Carnival Is Over/We Shall Not Be Moved	1965	2.50	5.00	10.00
❑ 5622	Some Day, One Day/Nobody Knows the Trouble I've Seen	1966	2.50	5.00	10.00
❑ 5756	Georgy Girl/When the Stars Begin to Fall	1966	3.00	6.00	12.00
❑ 5787	Morningtown Ride/Walk with Me	1967	2.50	5.00	10.00
❑ 5974	I Wish You Could Be Here/On the Other Side	1967	2.50	5.00	10.00
CAPITOL CREATIVE PRODUCTS					
❑ 50 [DJ]	Island of Dreams/Breaking My Back — Instead of Using My Mind	1966	3.75	7.50	15.00
—B-side by Lou Rawls					
❑ 50 [PS]	Island of Dreams/Breaking My Back — Instead of Using My Mind	1966	5.00	10.00	20.00
—Custom sleeve; no titles or artist, but "#50" is at right and "Capitol has specially produced this record for Frito-Lay" is under the center hole					
MARVEL					
❑ 1060	Chilly Winds/The Light from the Lighthouse	1965	3.75	7.50	15.00

SEGER, BOB

Includes records with The Last Heard, The Bob Seger System and The Silver Bullet Band. Also see THE BEACH BUMS.

Number	Title (A Side/B Side)	Yr	VG	VG+	NM
ABKCO					
❑ 4015	East Side Story/East Side Sound	1973	—	3.00	6.00
❑ 4016	Chain Smokin'/Persecution Smith	1973	—	3.00	6.00
❑ 4017	Heavy Music - Pt. I/Heavy Music - Pt. II	1973	—	3.00	6.00
❑ 4031	Heavy Music - Pt. I/Heavy Music - Pt. II	1973	—	2.50	5.00
CAMEO					
❑ 438	East Side Story/East Side Sound	1966	6.25	12.50	25.00
❑ 444	Sock It To Me, Santa/Florida Time	1966	7.50	15.00	30.00
❑ 465	Chain Smokin'/Persecution Smith	1967	6.25	12.50	25.00
❑ 473	Vagrant Winter/Very Few	1967	6.25	12.50	25.00
❑ 494	Heavy Music/Heavy Music (Part 2)	1967	5.00	10.00	20.00
CAPITOL					
❑ 2143	2 + 2 = ?/Death Row	1968	3.75	7.50	15.00
❑ 2297	Ramblin' Gamblin' Man/Tales of Lucy Blue	1968	3.00	6.00	12.00
❑ 2480	Ivory/The Lost Song (Love Needs to Be Loved)	1969	2.00	4.00	8.00
❑ 2576	Noah/Lennie Johnson	1969	2.00	4.00	8.00
❑ 2640	Lonely Man/Innervenus Eyes	1970	2.00	4.00	8.00
❑ 2748	Lucifer/Big River	1970	2.00	4.00	8.00
❑ 3187	Lookin' Back/Highway Child	1971	2.00	4.00	8.00
❑ 4062	Beautiful Loser/Fine Memory	1975	—	2.50	5.00
❑ 4116	Katmandu/Black Night	1975	—	2.50	5.00
❑ 4183	Nutbush City Limits/Travelin' Man	1975	—	2.50	5.00
❑ 4269	Nutbush City Limits/Lookin' Back	1976	—	2.50	5.00
❑ 4300	Beautiful Loser/Travelin' Man	1976	—	2.50	5.00
❑ 4369	Night Moves/Ship of Fools	1976	—	2.00	4.00
❑ 4422	Mainstreet/Jody Girl	1977	—	2.00	4.00
❑ 4449	Rock and Roll Never Forgets/Fire Down Below	1977	—	2.00	4.00
❑ 4581	Still the Same/Feel Like a Number	1978	—	2.00	4.00
❑ 4618	Hollywood Nights/Brave Strangers	1978	—	2.00	4.00
❑ 4653	We've Got Tonite/Ain't Got No Money	1978	—	2.00	4.00
❑ 4653 [DJ]	We've Got Tonite (mono/stereo)	1978	2.50	5.00	10.00
—Silver vinyl					
❑ 4653 [PS]	We've Got Tonite/Ain't Got No Money	1978	—	3.00	6.00
❑ 4702	Old Time Rock and Roll/Sunspot Baby	1979	—	2.00	4.00
❑ 4702 [PS]	Old Time Rock and Roll/Sunspot Baby	1979	—	3.00	6.00
❑ 4836	Fire Lake/Long Twin Silver Line	1980	—	2.00	4.00
❑ 4836 [PS]	Fire Lake/Long Twin Silver Line	1980	—	3.00	6.00
❑ 4863	Against the Wind/No Man's Land	1980	—	2.00	4.00
❑ 4863 [PS]	Against the Wind/No Man's Land	1980	—	3.00	6.00
❑ 4904	You'll Accomp'ny Me/Betty Lou's Gettin' Out Tonight	1980	—	2.50	5.00
❑ 4904 [PS]	You'll Accomp'ny Me/Betty Lou's Gettin' Out Tonight	1980	—	3.00	6.00
❑ 4951	The Horizontal Bop/Her Strut	1980	—	2.50	5.00
❑ 4951 [PS]	The Horizontal Bop/Her Strut	1980	25.00	50.00	100.00
❑ A-5042	Tryin' to Live My Life Without You/Brave Strangers	1981	—	—	3.00
❑ A-5042 [PS]	Tryin' to Live My Life Without You/Brave Strangers	1981	—	2.00	4.00
❑ A-5077	Feel Like a Number/Hollywood Nights	1981	—	2.00	4.00
❑ A-5077 [PS]	Feel Like a Number/Hollywood Nights	1981	—	2.50	5.00
❑ B-5187	Shame on the Moon/House Behind a House	1982	—	—	3.00
❑ B-5187 [PS]	Shame on the Moon/House Behind a House	1982	—	2.00	4.00
❑ B-5213	Even Now/Little Victories	1983	—	—	3.00
❑ B-5213 [PS]	Even Now/Little Victories	1983	—	2.00	4.00
❑ B-5235	Roll Me Away/Boomtown Blues	1983	—	—	3.00
❑ B-5235 [PS]	Roll Me Away/Boomtown Blues	1983	—	2.00	4.00
❑ B-5276	Old Time Rock and Roll/Till It Shines	1983	—	—	3.00
❑ B-5276 [PS]	Old Time Rock and Roll/Till It Shines	1983	—	2.50	5.00
❑ B-5413	Understanding/East L.A.	1984	—	—	3.00
❑ B-5413 [PS]	Understanding/East L.A.	1984	—	2.00	4.00
❑ B-5532	American Storm/Fortunate Son	1986	—	—	3.00
❑ B-5532 [PS]	American Storm/Fortunate Son	1986	—	—	3.00
❑ B-5592	Like a Rock/Livin' Inside My Heart	1986	—	—	3.00
❑ B-5592 [PS]	Like a Rock/Livin' Inside My Heart	1986	—	—	3.00
❑ B-5623	It's You/The Aftermath (12" Remix)	1986	—	—	3.00
❑ B-5623 [PS]	It's You/The Aftermath (12" Remix)	1986	—	—	3.00
❑ B-5658	Miami/Somewhere Tonight	1986	—	—	3.00
❑ B-5658 [PS]	Miami/Somewhere Tonight	1986	6.25	12.50	25.00
—May only have been released in the New York metro area, as it quotes reviewers from four different New York newspapers					
❑ SPRO 8433 [DJ]	Travelin' Man/Beautiful Loser	1976	2.50	5.00	10.00
❑ S7-18298	C'est La Vie/Night Moves	1995	—	2.00	4.00
❑ NR-44761	The Real Love/Roll Me Away	1991	—	2.00	4.00
❑ NR-44793	The Fire Inside/New Coat of Paint	1991	—	2.00	4.00
❑ S7-56784	Like a Rock/Sunspot Baby	1992	—	2.00	4.00
❑ S7-57732	New Coat of Paint/Blind Love	1992	—	2.00	4.00
❑ S7-57742	Night Moves/Her Strut	1992	—	2.00	4.00
❑ S7-57797	Old TIme Rock and Roll/Turn the Page	1992	—	2.00	4.00
HIDEOUT					
❑ 1013	East Side Story/East Side Sound	1966	12.50	25.00	50.00
❑ 1014	Chain Smokin'/Persecution Smith	1966	12.50	25.00	50.00
MCA					
❑ 53094	Shakedown/The Aftermath	1987	—	—	3.00
❑ 53094 [PS]	Shakedown/The Aftermath	1987	—	2.00	4.00
—Picture of Bob Seger on front cover					
❑ 53094 [PS]	Shakedown/The Aftermath	1987	3.75	7.50	15.00
—Picture of Eddie Murphy as Axel Foley on front cover					
PALLADIUM					
❑ 1079	If I Were a Carpenter/Jesse James	1972	2.50	5.00	10.00
❑ 1117	Turn On Your Love Light/Who Do You Love?	1972	2.50	5.00	10.00
❑ 1143	Rosalie/Neon Sky	1972	2.50	5.00	10.00
❑ 1171	Need Ya/Seen a Lot of Floors	1973	2.50	5.00	10.00
❑ 1205	Get Out of Denver/Long Song Comin'	1974	2.50	5.00	10.00
❑ 1316	This Ole House/U.M.C.	1974	3.75	7.50	15.00
REPRISE					
❑ PRO 571 [DJ]	Midnight Rider (same on both sides)	1972	3.75	7.50	15.00

Number	Title (A Side/B Side)	Yr	VG	VG+	NM

SEGER, GARY
TAX RECORDS

Number	Title (A Side/B Side)	Yr	VG	VG+	NM
❑ 319	The Christmas Equalization Act/The British Are Coming	1976	—	3.00	6.00

SELECTIONS, THE
ANTONE

Number	Title (A Side/B Side)	Yr	VG	VG+	NM
❑ 101	Guardian Angel/Soft and Sweet	1958	62.50	125.00	250.00

MONA LEE

Number	Title (A Side/B Side)	Yr	VG	VG+	NM
❑ 129	Guardian Angel/Soft and Sweet	1959	15.00	30.00	60.00

SPECIALTY

Number	Title (A Side/B Side)	Yr	VG	VG+	NM
❑ 751	Guardian Angel/Soft and Sweet	197?	2.50	5.00	10.00

SELF, MACK
PHILLIPS INT'L.

Number	Title (A Side/B Side)	Yr	VG	VG+	NM
❑ 3548	Mad at You/Willie Brown	1959	6.25	12.50	25.00

SUN

Number	Title (A Side/B Side)	Yr	VG	VG+	NM
❑ 273	Easy to Love/Every Day	1957	7.50	15.00	30.00

SELF, RONNIE
ABC-PARAMOUNT

Number	Title (A Side/B Side)	Yr	VG	VG+	NM
❑ 9714	Pretty Bad Blues/Three Hearts Later	1956	25.00	50.00	100.00
❑ 9768	Alone/Sweet Love	1956	25.00	50.00	100.00

AMY

Number	Title (A Side/B Side)	Yr	VG	VG+	NM
❑ 11009	High on Life/The Road Keeps Winding	1968	2.50	5.00	10.00

COLUMBIA

Number	Title (A Side/B Side)	Yr	VG	VG+	NM
❑ 40875	Big Fool/Flame of Love	1957	10.00	20.00	40.00
❑ 40989	Ain't I'm a Dog/Rocky Road Blues	1957	10.00	20.00	40.00
❑ 41101	Bop-A-Lena/I Ain't Going Nowhere	1958	7.50	15.00	30.00
❑ 41166	Big Blon' Baby/Date Bait	1958	7.50	15.00	30.00
❑ 41241	Petrified/You're So Right for Me	1958	20.00	40.00	80.00

DECCA

Number	Title (A Side/B Side)	Yr	VG	VG+	NM
❑ 30958	Big Town/This Must Be the Place	1959	6.25	12.50	25.00
❑ 31131	I've Been There/So High	1960	6.25	12.50	25.00
❑ 31351	Instant Man/Some Things You Can't Change	1962	6.25	12.50	25.00
❑ 31431	Oh Me, Oh My/Past, Present and Future	1962	6.25	12.50	25.00

KAPP

Number	Title (A Side/B Side)	Yr	VG	VG+	NM
❑ 546	Houdini/Bless My Broken Heart	1963	5.00	10.00	20.00

7-Inch Extended Plays

COLUMBIA

Number	Title (A Side/B Side)	Yr	VG	VG+	NM
❑ B-2149	(contents unknown)	1957	50.00	100.00	200.00
❑ B-2149 [PS]	Ain't I'm a Dog	1957	50.00	100.00	200.00

SELF, TED
PLAID

Number	Title (A Side/B Side)	Yr	VG	VG+	NM
❑ 1000	Little Angel (Come Rock Me to Sleep)/Walk Her Down the Aisle	1960	5.00	10.00	20.00

—Number also listed as "115"; we're not sure which is correct, or if perhaps both are correct!

SELLERS, PETER
CAPITOL

Number	Title (A Side/B Side)	Yr	VG	VG+	NM
❑ F4159	I'm So Ashamed/A Drop of the Hard Stuff	1959	3.00	6.00	12.00
❑ 5580	A Hard Day's Night/Help	1966	3.75	7.50	15.00

UNITED ARTISTS

Number	Title (A Side/B Side)	Yr	VG	VG+	NM
❑ X1221	Thank Heaven for Little Girls/Singin' in the Rain	1978	2.50	5.00	10.00

—As "Inspector Clouseau"

SELLERS, PETER, AND SOPHIA LOREN
CAPITOL

Number	Title (A Side/B Side)	Yr	VG	VG+	NM
❑ 4505	Bangers and Mash/Goodness Gracious Me	1961	3.00	6.00	12.00

SENATOR BOBBY
PARKWAY

Number	Title (A Side/B Side)	Yr	VG	VG+	NM
❑ 127	Wild Thing/Wild Thing	1966	3.00	6.00	12.00

—B-side by "Senator McKinley"

Number	Title (A Side/B Side)	Yr	VG	VG+	NM
❑ 137	Mellow Yellow/White Christmas	1967	2.50	5.00	10.00

—A-side by "Senator Bobby & Senator McKinley"; B-side by "Bobby the Poet" (Dylan impersonation)

Number	Title (A Side/B Side)	Yr	VG	VG+	NM
❑ 150	The Congressional Record/The Hardly Worthit Melody	1967	2.50	5.00	10.00

—By The Hardly Worthit Players

RCA VICTOR

Number	Title (A Side/B Side)	Yr	VG	VG+	NM
❑ 47-9522	Sock It To Me, Bobby/Sock It To Me, Baby	1968	2.50	5.00	10.00

—B-side by the Bobby Sockers

SENATORS, THE (1)
ABC-PARAMOUNT

Number	Title (A Side/B Side)	Yr	VG	VG+	NM
❑ 10178	There's a New Man in the White House/A Sing-Along Song	1961	3.75	7.50	15.00

SENATORS, THE (2)
ABNER

Number	Title (A Side/B Side)	Yr	VG	VG+	NM
❑ 1031	Julie/It Doesn't Matter	1959	30.00	60.00	120.00

GOLDEN CREST

Number	Title (A Side/B Side)	Yr	VG	VG+	NM
❑ 514	Loretta/Poor Little Puppet	1958	37.50	75.00	150.00

SENATORS, THE (3)
BRISTOL

Number	Title (A Side/B Side)	Yr	VG	VG+	NM
❑ 1916	Scheming/Tafu	1959	100.00	200.00	400.00

WINN

Number	Title (A Side/B Side)	Yr	VG	VG+	NM
❑ 1917	Wedding Bells/I Shouldn't Care	1962	62.50	125.00	250.00

SENIORS, THE (1)
ABC-PARAMOUNT

Number	Title (A Side/B Side)	Yr	VG	VG+	NM
❑ 10736	No Surfin' 'Round Here/Cindy	1965	7.50	15.00	30.00

SENIORS, THE (2)
DECCA

Number	Title (A Side/B Side)	Yr	VG	VG+	NM
❑ 31112	I've Lived Before/Hello Mr. Robin	1960	5.00	10.00	20.00
❑ 31244	When I Fall in Love/Baby, Say the Word	1961	5.00	10.00	20.00

SENIORS, THE (3)
EXCELLO

Number	Title (A Side/B Side)	Yr	VG	VG+	NM
❑ 2130	Why Did You Leave Me/Sloo Foot Soo	1958	10.00	20.00	40.00

TETRA

Number	Title (A Side/B Side)	Yr	VG	VG+	NM
❑ 4446	Evening Shadows Falling (I Think of You)/I've Got Plenty of Love	1956	50.00	100.00	200.00

SENIORS, THE (U)
ESV

Number	Title (A Side/B Side)	Yr	VG	VG+	NM
❑ 1016	Ah Sweet Mystery of Love/Rock and Rolly	1960	6.25	12.50	25.00

KENT

Number	Title (A Side/B Side)	Yr	VG	VG+	NM
❑ 342	Hully Gully Fever/Pitter Patter Heart	1960	5.00	10.00	20.00

TAMPA

Number	Title (A Side/B Side)	Yr	VG	VG+	NM
❑ 163	Who's Gonna Know/It's Been a Long Time	1959	10.00	20.00	40.00

SENORS, THE
Allegedly THE ISLEY BROTHERS in disguise.

SUE

Number	Title (A Side/B Side)	Yr	VG	VG+	NM
❑ 756	May I Have This Dance/Searching for Olive Oil	1962	12.50	25.00	50.00

SENSATIONS, THE
Also see YVONNE BAKER.

ARGO

Number	Title (A Side/B Side)	Yr	VG	VG+	NM
❑ 5391	Music, Music, Music/A Part of Me	1961	2.50	5.00	10.00
❑ 5405	Let Me In/Oh Yes I'll Be True	1961	3.00	6.00	12.00

—Brown label

Number	Title (A Side/B Side)	Yr	VG	VG+	NM
❑ 5405	Let Me In/Oh Yes I'll Be True	1961	5.00	10.00	20.00

—Black label

Number	Title (A Side/B Side)	Yr	VG	VG+	NM
❑ 5412	That's My Desire/Eyes	1962	2.50	5.00	10.00

—By "Yvonne Baker and the Sensations"

Number	Title (A Side/B Side)	Yr	VG	VG+	NM
❑ 5420	Party Across the Hall/No Changes	1962	2.50	5.00	10.00

—By "Yvonne Baker and the Sensations"

Number	Title (A Side/B Side)	Yr	VG	VG+	NM
❑ 5446	When My Lover Comes Home/Father Dear	1963	2.50	5.00	10.00

—By "Yvonne Baker and the Sensations"

ATCO

Number	Title (A Side/B Side)	Yr	VG	VG+	NM
❑ 6056	Yes Sir, That's My Baby/Sympathy	1955	10.00	20.00	40.00
❑ 6067	Please Mr. Disc Jockey/Ain't He Sweet	1956	10.00	20.00	40.00
❑ 6075	Cry Baby Cry/My Heart Cries for You	1956	10.00	20.00	40.00
❑ 6083	Little Wallflower/Such a Love	1957	10.00	20.00	40.00
❑ 6090	My Debut to Love/You Made Me Love You	1957	10.00	20.00	40.00
❑ 6115	Kiddy Car Love/Romance in the Dark	1958	10.00	20.00	40.00

JUNIOR

Number	Title (A Side/B Side)	Yr	VG	VG+	NM
❑ 1002	We Were Meant to Be/It's Good Enough for Me	1963	3.00	6.00	12.00
❑ 1005	You Made a Fool of Me/That's What You've Gotta Do	1963	5.00	10.00	20.00
❑ 1010	I Can't Change/Mend the Torn Pieces	1964	3.00	6.00	12.00
❑ 1021	We Were Meant to Be/It's Good Enough for Me	1964	3.00	6.00	12.00

TOLLIE

Number	Title (A Side/B Side)	Yr	VG	VG+	NM
❑ 9009	You Made a Fool of Me/That's What You've Gotta Do	1964	2.50	5.00	10.00

SENSATIONS OF LONDON, THE
YORK

Number	Title (A Side/B Side)	Yr	VG	VG+	NM
❑ 406	Look at My Baby/What a Wonderful Feeling	1966	3.75	7.50	15.00

SENTIMENTALS, THE
CHECKER

Number	Title (A Side/B Side)	Yr	VG	VG+	NM
❑ 875	I Want to Love You/Tommie Teenager	1957	10.00	20.00	40.00

CORAL

Number	Title (A Side/B Side)	Yr	VG	VG+	NM
❑ 62100	We Three/Understanding Love	1959	6.25	12.50	25.00
❑ 62172	Deep Down in My Heart/Two Different Worlds	1960	6.25	12.50	25.00

MINT

Number	Title (A Side/B Side)	Yr	VG	VG+	NM
❑ 801	I Want to Love You/Tommie Teenager	1957	12.50	25.00	50.00
❑ 802	Sunday Kind of Love/Wedding Bells	1957	10.00	20.00	40.00
❑ 803	I'm Your Fool, Always/Rock Me, Mama	1958	10.00	20.00	40.00
❑ 805	You're Mine/Danny Boy	1958	10.00	20.00	40.00
❑ 807	Found a New Baby/I'll Miss These Things	196?	3.00	6.00	12.00
❑ 808	This Time/I Want to Love You	196?	3.00	6.00	12.00

VANITY

Number	Title (A Side/B Side)	Yr	VG	VG+	NM
❑ 589	Love Is a Gamble/If It Isn't for You	1959	6.25	12.50	25.00

SENTINALS, THE
ADMIRAL

Number	Title (A Side/B Side)	Yr	VG	VG+	NM
❑ 900	Roughshod/Copy Cat Walk	1961	12.50	25.00	50.00

DEL-FI

Number	Title (A Side/B Side)	Yr	VG	VG+	NM
❑ 4197	Big Surf/Sunset Beach	1963	7.50	15.00	30.00

ERA

Number	Title (A Side/B Side)	Yr	VG	VG+	NM
❑ 3082	Torchula/Latin'ia	1962	7.50	15.00	30.00
❑ 3097	Christmas Eve/Latin Soul	1962	7.50	15.00	30.00
❑ 3117	Infinity/Encinada	1963	7.50	15.00	30.00

—As "The Sentinal Six"

POINT

Number	Title (A Side/B Side)	Yr	VG	VG+	NM
❑ 5100	The Bee/Over You	1963	12.50	25.00	50.00
❑ 5101	Blue Booze/Bony Moronie	1962	12.50	25.00	50.00

WCEB

Number	Title (A Side/B Side)	Yr	VG	VG+	NM
❑ 23	Torchula/Latin'ia	1962	12.50	25.00	50.00

WESTCO

Number	Title (A Side/B Side)	Yr	VG	VG+	NM
❑ 12	I've Been Blue/Hit the Road	1964	7.50	15.00	30.00
❑ 14	Tell Me/Hit the Road	1964	7.50	15.00	30.00

SEQUINS, THE
More than one group.

ASCOT

Number	Title (A Side/B Side)	Yr	VG	VG+	NM
❑ 2140	You Can't Sit Still/Mr. Leader of the Band	1963	3.75	7.50	15.00

A&M

Number	Title (A Side/B Side)	Yr	VG	VG+	NM
❑ 761	I'll Be Satisfied/Who Says You Can't Jerk to the Old Time Music	1965	3.00	6.00	12.00

CAMEO

Number	Title (A Side/B Side)	Yr	VG	VG+	NM
❑ 161	To Be Young/The Mountains	1959	5.00	10.00	20.00

GOLD STAR

Number	Title (A Side/B Side)	Yr	VG	VG+	NM
❑ 101	Hey Romeo/I've Got to Overcome	1970	—	3.00	6.00

RED ROBIN

Number	Title (A Side/B Side)	Yr	VG	VG+	NM
❑ 140	Why Can't You Treat Me Right/Don't Fall in Love	1956	100.00	200.00	400.00

Number	Title (A Side/B Side)	Yr	VG	VG+	NM
TERRACE					
❑ 7511	Love Me Forever/You're Dancing Now	1962	3.75	7.50	15.00
❑ 7515	Hideaway/I Ain't Gonna Cry (No More)	1963	3.75	7.50	15.00

SERENADERS, THE (1)

Number	Title (A Side/B Side)	Yr	VG	VG+	NM
CHOCK FULL O' HITS					
❑ 101	I Wrote a Letter/Never Let Me Go	1957	75.00	150.00	300.00
❑ 102	Dance Darling, Dance/Give Me a Girl	1957	50.00	100.00	200.00
MGM					
❑ 12623	I Wrote a Letter/Never Let Me Go	1958	25.00	50.00	100.00
❑ 12666	Dance Darling, Dance/Give Me a Girl	1958	30.00	60.00	120.00
MOTOWN					
❑ 1046	If Your Heart Says Yes/I'll Cry Tomorrow	1963	1000.	1500.	2000.
RAE COX					
❑ 101	Gotta Go to School/My Girl Flip-Flop	1959	15.00	30.00	60.00
RIVERSIDE					
❑ 4549	Adios, My Love/Two Lovers Make One Fool	1963	25.00	50.00	100.00
V.I.P.					
❑ 25002	If Your Heart Says Yes/I'll Cry Tomorrow	1964	25.00	50.00	100.00

SERENADERS, THE (2)

Number	Title (A Side/B Side)	Yr	VG	VG+	NM
CORAL					
❑ 60720	It's Funny/Confession Is Good for the Soul	1952	75.00	150.00	300.00
❑ 65093	Misery/But I Forgive You	1952	75.00	150.00	300.00
DELUXE					
❑ 6022	Please, Please Forgive Me/Baby	1953	125.00	250.00	500.00
JVB					
❑ 2001	Tomorrow Night/Why Don't You Do Right	1952	100.00	200.00	400.00
RED ROBIN					
❑ 115	Will She Know?/I Want to Love You Baby	1953	375.00	750.00	1500.
SWING TIME					
❑ 347	M-A-Y-B-E-L-L/Ain't Gonna Cry No More	1954	300.00	600.00	1200.

SERENADERS, THE (3)

Number	Title (A Side/B Side)	Yr	VG	VG+	NM
HANOVER					
❑ 4507	Honolulu/Summer Job	1959	3.75	7.50	15.00
❑ 4514	Alaska/Where Did You Go	1959	3.75	7.50	15.00

SERENADERS, THE (U)

Could be group (1) or (2).

Number	Title (A Side/B Side)	Yr	VG	VG+	NM
STARFIRE					
❑ 115	Nite Owl/I'm Gonna Love You	1980	—	3.00	6.00
TEEN LIFE					
❑ 9	Love Me Now/Gates of Gold	1958	175.00	350.00	700.00

SERENADETTS, THE

Number	Title (A Side/B Side)	Yr	VG	VG+	NM
ENRICA					
❑ 1008	Boyfriend/The Big Night	1961	3.00	6.00	12.00

SERRATT, HOWARD

Number	Title (A Side/B Side)	Yr	VG	VG+	NM
SUN					
❑ 198	I Must Be Saved/Troublesome Waters	1954	500.00	1000.	2000.

SETTLERS, THE

Number	Title (A Side/B Side)	Yr	VG	VG+	NM
HICKORY					
❑ 1451	Early Morning Rain/Do You Wanna Know the Reason	1967	2.00	4.00	8.00

SEVEN OF US

Number	Title (A Side/B Side)	Yr	VG	VG+	NM
RED BIRD					
❑ 10-069	The Way to Your Heart/How Could You	1966	7.50	15.00	30.00
❑ 10-080	Jamboree/It's Not Easy to Forget	1966	7.50	15.00	30.00

7TH AVENUE AVIATORS, THE

Number	Title (A Side/B Side)	Yr	VG	VG+	NM
CONGRESS					
❑ 255	You Should 'A Held On/The Boy Next Door	1965	30.00	60.00	120.00

SEVILLE, DAVID

Also see ROSS BAGDASARIAN; THE CHIPMUNKS.

Number	Title (A Side/B Side)	Yr	VG	VG+	NM
LIBERTY					
❑ 55041	Armen's Theme/Carousel in Rome	1956	6.25	12.50	25.00
❑ 55055	The Donkey and the Schoolboy/The Gift	1957	6.25	12.50	25.00
❑ 55079	Camel Rock/Gotta Get to Your House	1957	6.25	12.50	25.00
❑ 55079 [PS]	Camel Rock/Gotta Get to Your House	1957	12.50	25.00	50.00
❑ 55105	Pretty Dark Eyes/Cecelia	1957	6.25	12.50	25.00
❑ 55113	Bagdad Express/Starlight, Starbright	1957	6.25	12.50	25.00
❑ 55124	Bonjour Tristesse/Dance from Bonjour Tristesse	1958	6.25	12.50	25.00
❑ 55132	Witch Doctor/Don't Whistle at Me Baby	1958	7.50	15.00	30.00
❑ 55140	The Bird on My Head/Hey There Moon	1958	6.25	12.50	25.00
❑ 55153	Little Brass Band/Take Five	1958	6.25	12.50	25.00
❑ 55163	The Mountain/Mr. Grape	1958	6.25	12.50	25.00
❑ 55272	Witch Doctor/Swanee River	1960	5.00	10.00	20.00
❑ 55314	Oh Judge, Your Honor, Dear Sir, Sweetheart/ Freddy, Freddy	1961	6.25	12.50	25.00
UNITED ARTISTS					
❑ 0063	Witch Doctor/The Bird on My Head	1973	—	2.00	4.00
—"Silver Spotlight Series" reissue					

7-Inch Extended Plays

Number	Title (A Side/B Side)	Yr	VG	VG+	NM
LIBERTY					
❑ LSX-1003	(contents unknown)	1958	10.00	20.00	40.00
❑ LSX-1003 [PS]	Witch Doctor	1958	10.00	20.00	40.00

SEVILLE, DAVID, AND THE CHIPMUNKS

See THE CHIPMUNKS.

SEX PISTOLS, THE

Number	Title (A Side/B Side)	Yr	VG	VG+	NM
WARNER BROS.					
❑ 8516	Pretty Vacant/Sub-Mission	1978	5.00	10.00	20.00
❑ 8516 [DJ]	Pretty Vacant (mono/stereo)	1978	2.50	5.00	10.00
❑ 8516 [PS]	Pretty Vacant/Sub-Mission	1978	2.50	5.00	10.00

SEYMOUR, PHIL

Also see DWIGHT TWILLEY BAND.

Number	Title (A Side/B Side)	Yr	VG	VG+	NM
BOARDWALK					
❑ NB7-11-116	I Really Love You/We Don't Get Along	1981	—	2.50	5.00
❑ NB7-11-145	Better to Me Than You/Surrender	1982	—	2.50	5.00
❑ NB7-11-154	Talk to Me/Better to Me Than You	1982	—	2.50	5.00
❑ 02056	Let Her Dance/We Don't Get Along	1981	—	2.50	5.00
❑ 5703	Precious to Me/Baby It's You	1981	—	2.50	5.00
❑ 5703	Precious to Me/Suzy Glider	1981	—	3.00	6.00
❑ 5703 [PS]	Precious to Me/Baby It's You	1981	—	2.50	5.00

SH-BOOMS, THE

See THE CHORDS.

SHA NA NA

Number	Title (A Side/B Side)	Yr	VG	VG+	NM
KAMA SUTRA					
❑ 503	Lovers Never Say Goodbye/Remember Then	1970	—	3.00	6.00
❑ 507	Pay Day/Rock and Roll Is Here to Stay	1970	—	3.00	6.00
❑ 522	Only One Song/Yakety Yak	1971	—	3.00	6.00
❑ 528	Top Forty of the Lord/I Wonder Why	1971	—	3.00	6.00
❑ 528 [PS]	Top Forty of the Lord/I Wonder Why	1971	2.50	5.00	10.00
❑ 555	Bounce in Your Buggy/Bless My Soul	1972	—	3.00	6.00
❑ 555 [PS]	Bounce in Your Buggy/Bless My Soul	1972	2.50	5.00	10.00
❑ 560	In the Still of the Night/Sea Cruise	1972	—	2.50	5.00
❑ 578 [DJ]	In the Still of the Night (mono/stereo)	1973	3.75	7.50	15.00
—As "Eddie and the Evergreens"; may be promo only					
❑ 592	Maybe I'm Old Fashioned/Stroll All Night	1974	—	2.50	5.00
❑ 596	Too Chubby to Boogie/(B-side unknown)	1974	—	2.50	5.00
❑ 602	Just Like Romeo and Juliet/Circles of Love	1975	—	2.50	5.00
❑ 603	You're the Only Light on My Horizon Now	1975	—	2.50	5.00
❑ 604	Shanghied/Chills in My Spine	1975	—	2.50	5.00
RSO					
❑ 909	Rock and Roll Is Here to Stay/Greased Lightnin'	1978	—	2.00	4.00
—B-side by John Travolta					
❑ 930	Blue Moon/Sandy	1979	—	2.00	4.00
—B-side by John Travolta					

SHA-WEES, THE

Number	Title (A Side/B Side)	Yr	VG	VG+	NM
ALADDIN					
❑ 3170	No One to Love Me/Early Sunday Morning	1953	1000.	2000.	4000.

SHADES, THE

More than one group.

Number	Title (A Side/B Side)	Yr	VG	VG+	NM
ALADDIN					
❑ 3453	Dear Lori/One Touch of Heaven	1959	75.00	150.00	300.00
AOK					
❑ 1028	Ginger Bread Man/The Hip	1967	7.50	15.00	30.00
BIG TOP					
❑ 3003	Sun Glasses/Undivided Attention	1958	25.00	50.00	100.00
—B-side by The Knott Sisters					

SHADES OF BLUE

Number	Title (A Side/B Side)	Yr	VG	VG+	NM
IMPACT					
❑ 1007	Oh, How Happy/Little Orphan Boy	1966	5.00	10.00	20.00
❑ 1014	Lonely Summer/With This Ring	1966	5.00	10.00	20.00
❑ 1015	Happiness/The Night	1966	5.00	10.00	20.00
❑ 1026	All I Want Is Love/How Do You Save a Dying Love	1967	5.00	10.00	20.00
❑ 1028	Penny Arcade/Funny Kind of Love	1967	5.00	10.00	20.00

SHADOWS, THE (1)

Backing group for CLIFF RICHARD. Includes early records as "The Drifters" and "The Four Jets." Also see JET HARRIS AND TONY MEEHAN.

Number	Title (A Side/B Side)	Yr	VG	VG+	NM
ABC-PARAMOUNT					
❑ 10073	Saturday Dance/Lonesome Fella	1960	7.50	15.00	30.00
❑ 10138	Apache/Quartermaster's Stores	1960	7.50	15.00	30.00
ATLANTIC					
❑ 2111	FBI/The Frightened City	1961	5.00	10.00	20.00
❑ 2135	Kon-Tiki/Man of Mystery	1962	5.00	10.00	20.00
❑ 2146	Wonderful Land/Stars Fell on Stockton	1962	5.00	10.00	20.00
❑ 2166	Guitar Tango/What a Lovely Thing	1962	5.00	10.00	20.00
❑ 2177	Dance On/The Rumble	1963	5.00	10.00	20.00
❑ 2235	Theme for Young Lovers/The Rise and Fall of Flingel Bunt	1964	5.00	10.00	20.00
❑ 2257	Rhythm and Greens/The Miracle	1964	5.00	10.00	20.00
CAPITOL					
❑ F-4220	Feelin' Fine/Don't Be a Fool	1959	10.00	20.00	40.00
—As "The Drifters"					
❑ F-4270	Driftin'/Jet Black	1959	10.00	20.00	40.00
—As "The Four Jets"					
EPIC					
❑ 9793	Mary Anne/Chu Chi	1965	5.00	10.00	20.00
❑ 9826	Stingray/Alice in Sunderland	1965	5.00	10.00	20.00
❑ 9848	Don't Make My Baby Blue/My Grandfather's Clock	1965	5.00	10.00	20.00
❑ 10020	I Met a Girl/Last Night Set	1966	5.00	10.00	20.00

SHADOWS, THE (2)

Number	Title (A Side/B Side)	Yr	VG	VG+	NM
DECCA					
❑ 28765	No Use/Stay	1953	62.50	125.00	250.00
❑ 48307	Tell Her/Don't Be Bashful	1954	75.00	150.00	300.00
❑ 48322	Big Mouth Mama/Better Than Gold	1954	75.00	150.00	300.00

SHADOWS, THE (3)

Number	Title (A Side/B Side)	Yr	VG	VG+	NM
DEL-FI					
❑ 4109	Under the Stars of Love/Jungle Fever	1958	15.00	30.00	60.00

SHADOWS, THE (4)

Number	Title (A Side/B Side)	Yr	VG	VG+	NM
DOTTIE					
❑ 1006	I Wonder Why/Tell This Lonely Heart Goodbye	1961	5.00	10.00	20.00

SHADOWS, THE (U)

Could be group (3) or an entirely different group.

DELTA

Number	Title (A Side/B Side)	Yr	VG	VG+	NM
❑ 1509	Bop-A-Lena/There Stands the Glass	1958	50.00	100.00	200.00

SHADOWS OF KNIGHT, THE

ATCO

Number	Title (A Side/B Side)	Yr	VG	VG+	NM
❑ 6634	Gloria '69/A Spaniard at My Door	1968	4.00	8.00	16.00
❑ 6776	I Am the Hunter/Warwick County Affair	1970	4.00	8.00	16.00

AURAVISION

Number	Title (A Side/B Side)	Yr	VG	VG+	NM
❑ (no #)	Potato Chip	196?	15.00	30.00	60.00

—One-sided cardboard disc, 5 inches wide with small hole

DUNWICH

Number	Title (A Side/B Side)	Yr	VG	VG+	NM
❑ 116	Gloria/Dark Side	1966	6.25	12.50	25.00
—Gold label, no mention of Atco Records					
❑ 116	Gloria/Dark Side	1966	5.00	10.00	20.00
—Yellow label, "Distributed by Atco Record Sales Co."					
❑ 116	Gloria/Dark Side	1966	3.75	7.50	15.00
—Dark pink and yellow label; other label variations may exist					
❑ 122	Oh Yeah/Light Bulb Blues	1966	5.00	10.00	20.00
❑ 122 [PS]	Oh Yeah/Light Bulb Blues	1966	7.50	15.00	30.00
❑ 128	Bad Little Woman/Gospel Zone	1966	3.75	7.50	15.00
❑ 128 [PS]	Bad Little Woman/Gospel Zone	1966	12.50	25.00	50.00
❑ 141	I'm Gonna Make You Mine/I'll Make You Sorry	1966	6.25	12.50	25.00
❑ 151	The Behemoth/Willie Jean	1967	5.00	10.00	20.00
❑ 167	Someone Like Me/There for Love	1967	5.00	10.00	20.00

SUPER K

Number	Title (A Side/B Side)	Yr	VG	VG+	NM
❑ 108	Taurus/My Fire Department Needs a Fireman	1969	2.50	5.00	10.00
❑ 110	Run, Run, Billy Porter/My Fire Department Needs a Fireman	1969	2.50	5.00	10.00

TEAM

Number	Title (A Side/B Side)	Yr	VG	VG+	NM
❑ 520	Shake/From Way Out to Way In	1968	4.00	8.00	16.00

SHAFTO, BOBBY

RUST

Number	Title (A Side/B Side)	Yr	VG	VG+	NM
❑ 5082	She's My Girl/Wonderful You	1964	2.50	5.00	10.00
❑ 5092	I'll Never Get Over You/Who Wouldn't Love a Girl Like That	1964	2.50	5.00	10.00
❑ 5096	Baby Then/How Could You Do a Thing Like That to Me	1965	2.50	5.00	10.00
❑ 5108	Lonely Is As Lonely Does/The Same Old Room	1966	3.00	6.00	12.00
❑ 5110	See Me Cry/A Little Like You	1966	2.50	5.00	10.00

SHAG, THE

CAPITOL

Number	Title (A Side/B Side)	Yr	VG	VG+	NM
❑ 5995	Stop and Listen/Melissa	1967	5.00	10.00	20.00

SHALAMAR

COLUMBIA

Number	Title (A Side/B Side)	Yr	VG	VG+	NM
❑ 04372	Dancing in the Sheets/(Instrumental)	1984	—	2.00	4.00
❑ 04372 [PS]	Dancing in the Sheets/(Instrumental)	1984	—	2.00	4.00
❑ 08421	Dancing in the Sheets/(Instrumental)	1988	—	—	3.00
—Reissue					

MCA

Number	Title (A Side/B Side)	Yr	VG	VG+	NM
❑ 52335	Deadline U.S.A./One More Time Around the Block Ophelia	1984	—	2.00	4.00
—B-side by Gary U.S. Bonds					
❑ 52345	Deadline U.S.A./Knock Me On My Feet	1984	—	2.00	4.00
❑ 52594	Don't Get Stopped in Beverly Hills/The Discovery	1985	—	—	3.00
—B-side by Harold Faltermeyer					
❑ 52594 [PS]	Don't Get Stopped in Beverly Hills/The Discovery	1985	—	—	3.00

SOLAR

Number	Title (A Side/B Side)	Yr	VG	VG+	NM
❑ YB-11379	Take That to the Bank/Shalamar Disco Gardens	1978	—	2.00	4.00
❑ YB-11542	Stay Close to Love/Cindy, Cindy	1979	—	2.00	4.00
❑ YB-11709	The Second Time Around/Leave It All Up to Love	1979	—	2.00	4.00
❑ YB-11929	Right in the Socket/Girl	1980	—	2.00	4.00
❑ GB-11979	Uptown Festival (Part 1)/Take That to the Bank	1980	—	—	3.00
—Gold Standard Series					
❑ YB-12049	I Owe You One/Right Time for Us	1980	—	2.00	4.00
❑ YB-12152	Full of Fire/Let's Find the Time for Love	1981	—	2.00	4.00
❑ GB-12231	The Second Time Around/Right in the Socket	1981	—	—	3.00
—Gold Standard Series					
❑ YB-12250	This Is For the Lover in You/Some Things Never Change	1981	—	2.00	4.00
❑ YB-12329	Sweeter As the Days Go By/The Final Analysis	1981	—	2.00	4.00
❑ YB-13033	Talk to Me/Appeal	1981	—	2.00	4.00
❑ YB-13262	Attention to My Baby/Somewhere There's a Love	1982	—	—	—
—Unreleased					
❑ GB-13486	Make That Move/It's a Love Thing	1983	—	—	3.00
—Gold Standard Series; B-side by the Whispers					
❑ 48005	A Night to Remember/On Top of the World	1982	—	2.00	4.00
❑ 48013	I Can Make You Feel Good/I Just Stopped By Because I Had To	1982	—	2.00	4.00
❑ 69635	Just One of the Guys/Hard Way	1985	—	2.00	4.00
❑ 69660	My Girl Loves Me/Right Here	1985	—	2.00	4.00
❑ 69765	You Can Count on Me/The Look	1984	—	2.00	4.00
❑ 69787	Over and Over/You Won't Miss Love (Until It's Gone)	1983	—	2.00	4.00
❑ 69819	Dead Giveaway/I Don't Wanna Be the Last to Know	1983	—	2.00	4.00
❑ 69819 [PS]	Dead Giveaway/I Don't Wanna Be the Last to Know	1983	—	2.50	5.00
❑ 69958	There It Is/(B-side unknown)	1982	—	2.00	4.00
❑ 70008	Circumstantial Evidence/(Instrumental)	1987	—	—	3.00
❑ 70013	Games/(Instrumental)	1987	—	—	3.00
❑ 70021	I Want You (To Be My Playthang)/(Instrumental)	1988	—	—	3.00

SOUL TRAIN

Number	Title (A Side/B Side)	Yr	VG	VG+	NM
❑ SB-10885	Uptown Festival (Part 1)/Uptown Festival (Part 2)	1977	—	2.50	5.00
❑ SB-11045	Ooh, Baby, Baby/You Know	1977	—	2.50	5.00

SHAM-ETTES, THE

MGM

Number	Title (A Side/B Side)	Yr	VG	VG+	NM
❑ 13618	Big Bad Wolf (Hey There)/I'd Rather Have You	1966	3.75	7.50	15.00
❑ 13798	He'll Come Back/You're Welcome Back	1967	3.00	6.00	12.00

SHANE, BOB

Also see THE KINGSTON TRIO.

DECCA

Number	Title (A Side/B Side)	Yr	VG	VG+	NM
❑ 32239	Simple Gifts/Weeping Annaleah	1967	2.50	5.00	10.00
❑ 32275	Honey/I Don't Think of You Anymore	1968	2.50	5.00	10.00

SHANGRI-LAS, THE

MERCURY

Number	Title (A Side/B Side)	Yr	VG	VG+	NM
❑ 72645	I'll Never Learn/Sweet Sounds of Summer	1966	5.00	10.00	20.00
❑ 72670	Footsteps on the Roof/Take the Time	1967	5.00	10.00	20.00

RED BIRD

Number	Title (A Side/B Side)	Yr	VG	VG+	NM
❑ 10-008	Remember (Walkin' in the Sand)/It's Easier to Cry	1964	6.25	12.50	25.00
❑ 10-014	Leader of the Pack/What Is Love	1964	6.25	12.50	25.00
❑ 10-018	Give Him a Great Big Kiss/Twist and Shout	1964	6.25	12.50	25.00
❑ 10-019	Maybe/Shout	1964	5.00	10.00	20.00
❑ 10-025	Out in the Streets/The Boy	1965	5.00	10.00	20.00
❑ 10-030	Give Us Your Blessings/Heaven Only Knows	1965	5.00	10.00	20.00
❑ 10-036	Right Now and Not Later/The Train from Kansas City	1965	5.00	10.00	20.00
❑ 10-043	I Can Never Go Home Anymore/Bull Dog	1965	5.00	10.00	20.00
❑ 10-043	I Can Never Go Home Anymore/Sophisticated Boom Boom	1965	7.50	15.00	30.00
❑ 10-048	Long Live Our Love/Sophisticated Boom Boom	1966	5.00	10.00	20.00
❑ 10-048	Long Live Our Love/Bull Dog	1966	5.00	10.00	20.00
❑ 10-053	He Cried/Dressed in Black	1966	5.00	10.00	20.00
❑ 10-068	Past, Present and Future/Love You More Than Yesterday	1966	5.00	10.00	20.00
❑ 10-068	Past, Present and Future/Paradise	1966	5.00	10.00	20.00

SCEPTER

Number	Title (A Side/B Side)	Yr	VG	VG+	NM
❑ 1291	Wishing Well/Hate to Say I Told You So	1964	5.00	10.00	20.00

SMASH

Number	Title (A Side/B Side)	Yr	VG	VG+	NM
❑ 1866	Simon Says/Simon Speaks	1963	10.00	20.00	40.00

SPOKANE

Number	Title (A Side/B Side)	Yr	VG	VG+	NM
❑ 4006	Wishing Well/Hate to Say I Told You So	1964	7.50	15.00	30.00

SHANKAR, RAVI

APPLE

Number	Title (A Side/B Side)	Yr	VG	VG+	NM
❑ 1838	Joi Bangla-Oh Bhaugowan/Raga Mishra-Jhinjhoti	1971	2.00	4.00	8.00
—By Ravi Shankar & Ali Akbar with Alla Rakah					
❑ 1838 [PS]	Joi Bangla-Oh Bhaugowan/Raga Mishra-Jhinjhoti	1971	5.00	10.00	20.00

DARK HORSE

Number	Title (A Side/B Side)	Yr	VG	VG+	NM
❑ 10001	I Am Missing You/Lost	1974	—	2.50	5.00

WORLD PACIFIC

Number	Title (A Side/B Side)	Yr	VG	VG+	NM
❑ 77871	Pather Panchali/Gat Kirawani	1967	2.00	4.00	8.00
❑ 77898	Charly Theme/Love Montage	1968	2.00	4.00	8.00

SHANNON

See MARTY WILDE.

SHANNON, DEL

ABC DUNHILL

Number	Title (A Side/B Side)	Yr	VG	VG+	NM
❑ 4193	Sweet Mary Lou/Comin' Back to me	1969	3.75	7.50	15.00
❑ 4224	Sister Isabelle/Colorado Rain	1970	3.75	7.50	15.00

AMY

Number	Title (A Side/B Side)	Yr	VG	VG+	NM
❑ 897	Mary Jane/Stains on My Letter	1964	6.25	12.50	25.00
❑ 905	Handy Man/Give Her Lots of Lovin'	1964	3.75	7.50	15.00
❑ 911	Do You Want to Dance/This Is All I Have to Give	1964	3.75	7.50	15.00
❑ 915	Keep Searchin' (We'll Follow the Sun)/Broken Promises	1964	4.00	8.00	16.00
❑ 919	Stranger in Town/Over You	1965	4.00	8.00	16.00
❑ 925	Why Don't You Tell Him/Break Up	1965	3.75	7.50	15.00
❑ 937	Move It On Over/She Still Remembers Tony	1965	3.75	7.50	15.00
❑ 947	I Can't Believe My Ears/I Wish I Wasn't Me Tonight	1966	10.00	20.00	40.00
—Withdrawn shortly after release; promos worth about half these values					

BERLEE

Number	Title (A Side/B Side)	Yr	VG	VG+	NM
❑ 501	Sue's Gotta Be Mine/Now She's Gone	1963	3.75	7.50	15.00
❑ 502	That's the Way Love Is/Time of the Day	1964	3.75	7.50	15.00

BIG TOP

Number	Title (A Side/B Side)	Yr	VG	VG+	NM
❑ 3067	Runaway/Jody	1961	7.50	15.00	30.00
❑ 3075	Hats Off to Larry/Don't Gild the Lily, Lily	1961	6.25	12.50	25.00
❑ 3083	So Long Baby/The Answer to Everything	1961	6.25	12.50	25.00
❑ 3091	Hey! Little Girl/I Don't Care Anymore	1961	6.25	12.50	25.00
❑ 3098	Ginny in the Mirror/I Won't Be There	1962	6.25	12.50	25.00
❑ 3112	Cry Myself to Sleep/I'm Gonna Move On	1962	6.25	12.50	25.00
❑ 3117	The Swiss Maid/You Never Talked About Me	1962	6.25	12.50	25.00
❑ 3131	Little Town Flirt/The Wamboo	1962	6.25	12.50	25.00
❑ 3143	Two Kinds of Teardrops/Kelly	1963	6.25	12.50	25.00
❑ 3152	From Me to You/Two Silhouettes	1963	15.00	30.00	60.00
—A-side is the first American version of a Beatles song					

ERIC

Number	Title (A Side/B Side)	Yr	VG	VG+	NM
❑ 189 [S]	Runaway/Hats Off to Larry	1972	—	3.00	6.00
—Both sides of this reissue are the original recordings in true stereo!					

ISLAND

Number	Title (A Side/B Side)	Yr	VG	VG+	NM
❑ 021	Tell Her No/Restless	1975	3.75	7.50	15.00
❑ 038	Cry Baby Cry/In My Arms Again	1975	3.75	7.50	15.00

LIBERTY

Number	Title (A Side/B Side)	Yr	VG	VG+	NM
❑ 55866	The Big Hurt/I Got It Bad	1966	3.00	6.00	12.00
❑ 55889	Hey Little Star/For a Little While	1966	3.00	6.00	12.00
❑ 55894	Show Me/Never Thought I Could	1966	3.00	6.00	12.00
❑ 55904	Under My Thumb/She Was Mine	1966	3.00	6.00	12.00
❑ 55939	She/What Makes You Run	1967	3.00	6.00	12.00
❑ 55961	Led Along/I Can't Be True	1967	3.00	6.00	12.00
❑ 55993	Runaway '67/He Cheated	1967	3.75	7.50	15.00

Number	Title (A Side/B Side)	Yr	VG	VG+	NM
❑ 56018	Runnin' On Back/Thinkin' It Over	1968	2.50	5.00	10.00
❑ 56018 [PS]	Runnin' On Back/Thinkin' It Over	1968	7.50	15.00	30.00
❑ 56036	Magical Musical Box/Gemini	1968	2.50	5.00	10.00
❑ 56070	Raindrops/You Don't Love Me	1968	2.50	5.00	10.00
NETWORK					
❑ 47951	Sea of Love/Midnight Train	1981	—	2.50	5.00
❑ 48006	To Love Someone/Liar	1982	—	2.50	5.00
TWIRL					
❑ 4001	Runaway/Hey Little Girl	196?	—	3.00	6.00
❑ 4002	Hats Off to Larry/Little Town Flirt	196?	—	3.00	6.00
WARNER BROS.					
❑ 28853	Stranger on the Run/What You Gonna Do with That	1985	—	2.50	5.00
❑ 29098	In My Arms Again/You Can't Forgive Me	1985	—	2.50	5.00

SHANNON, PAT

Number	Title (A Side/B Side)	Yr	VG	VG+	NM
AMOS					
❑ 152	I Ain't Got Time Anymore/(B-side unknown)	1970	—	2.50	5.00
❑ 163	Liar/Something's Coming My Way	1971	—	2.50	5.00
CAPITOL					
❑ 3802	Eleanor Jones/102 Times a Day	1973	—	2.00	4.00
DECCA					
❑ 30545	Maybelle/Knock, Knock, Who's There	1958	3.00	6.00	12.00
❑ 30666	You're So Wild/Awaiting Love	1958	7.50	15.00	30.00
❑ 30751	Summer's Over/We Found Love	1958	3.00	6.00	12.00
❑ 30905	Summertime's Comin'/The Snake and the Bookworm	1959	3.00	6.00	12.00
❑ 31072	Everything But You/So Happy Now	1960	3.00	6.00	12.00
UNI					
❑ 55191	Back to Dreamin' Again/Moody	1969	—	2.50	5.00
❑ 55229	It's So Easy/The Story of Your Life	1970	—	2.50	5.00
❑ 55229	It's So Easy/102 Times a Day	1970	—	2.50	5.00
WARNER BROS.					
❑ 7210	Candy Apple, Cotton Candy/She Sleeps Alone	1968	—	3.00	6.00
❑ 7237	Here They Come Again/Run to Home	1968	—	3.00	6.00

SHANTONS, THE

Number	Title (A Side/B Side)	Yr	VG	VG+	NM
JAY-MAR					
❑ 241	To Be in Love with You/Lucille	1959	200.00	400.00	800.00
❑ 1292	The Christmas Song/Santa Claus Is Coming To Town	1960	50.00	100.00	200.00
❑ (# unknown)	Triangle Love/Lover's March	1959	100.00	200.00	400.00

SHAPIRO, HELEN

Number	Title (A Side/B Side)	Yr	VG	VG+	NM
CAPITOL					
❑ 4561	Don't Treat Me Like a Child/When I'm With You	1961	3.00	6.00	12.00
❑ 4627	You Don't Know/A Marvelous Lie	1961	3.00	6.00	12.00
❑ 4662	Walkin' Back to Happiness/Kiss 'N' Run	1961	3.00	6.00	12.00
❑ 4735	Tell Me What He Said/I Apologize	1962	3.00	6.00	12.00
EPIC					
❑ 9549	Little Miss Lonely/Keep Away from Other Girls	1962	3.00	6.00	12.00
❑ 9599	Woe Is Me/No Trespassing	1963	3.00	6.00	12.00
JANUS					
❑ 120	A Glass of Wine/Waiting on the Shores of Nowhere	1970	—	3.00	6.00
MUSICOR					
❑ 1075	It Might As Well Rain Until September/Shop Around	1965	2.50	5.00	10.00
TOWER					
❑ 346	Make Me Belong to You/The Way of the World	1967	2.00	4.00	8.00

SHARMEERS, THE

Number	Title (A Side/B Side)	Yr	VG	VG+	NM
RED TOP					
❑ 109	A School Girl in Love/You're My Love	1958	37.50	75.00	150.00

SHARMETTES, THE

Number	Title (A Side/B Side)	Yr	VG	VG+	NM
KING					
❑ 5648	Answer Me/My Dream	1962	3.75	7.50	15.00
❑ 5686	I Want to Be Loved/Tell Me	1962	3.75	7.50	15.00

SHARON MARIE

Number	Title (A Side/B Side)	Yr	VG	VG+	NM
CAPITOL					
❑ 5064	Run-Around Lover/Summertime	1963	62.50	125.00	250.00
❑ 5195	The Story of My Life/Thinkin' 'Bout You Baby	1964	50.00	100.00	200.00
—Both these records were produced by Brian Wilson					

SHARP, DEE DEE

Number	Title (A Side/B Side)	Yr	VG	VG+	NM
ATCO					
❑ 6445	Bye Bye Baby/My Best Friend's Man	1966	2.50	5.00	10.00
❑ 6502	Baby I Love You/What Am I Gonna Do	1967	2.00	4.00	8.00
❑ 6557	We Got a Thing Goin' On/What 'Cha Gonna Do About It	1968	2.00	4.00	8.00
—With Ben E. King					
❑ 6576	Woman Will Do Wrong/You're Just a Fool in Love	1968	2.00	4.00	8.00
❑ 6587	This Love Won't Run Out/Help Me Find My Glove	1968	2.00	4.00	8.00
CAMEO					
❑ 212	Mashed Potato Time/Set My Heart at Ease	1962	5.00	10.00	20.00
❑ 219	Gravy (For My Mashed Potatoes)/Baby Cakes	1962	3.75	7.50	15.00
❑ 219 [PS]	Gravy (For My Mashed Potatoes)/Baby Cakes	1962	6.25	12.50	25.00
❑ 230	Ride!/The Night	1962	3.75	7.50	15.00
❑ 230 [PS]	Ride!/The Night	1962	6.25	12.50	25.00
❑ 244	Do the Bird/Lover Boy	1963	3.75	7.50	15.00
❑ 244 [PS]	Do the Bird/Lover Boy	1963	6.25	12.50	25.00
❑ 260	Rock Me in the Cradle of Love/You'll Never Be Mine	1963	3.75	7.50	15.00
❑ 260 [PS]	Rock Me in the Cradle of Love/You'll Never Be Mine	1963	6.25	12.50	25.00
❑ 274	Wild!/Why Doncha Ask Me	1963	3.75	7.50	15.00
❑ 274 [PS]	Wild!/Why Doncha Ask Me	1963	6.25	12.50	25.00
❑ 296	Where Did I Go Wrong/Willyam, Willyam	1964	3.00	6.00	12.00
❑ 296 [PS]	Where Did I Go Wrong/Willyam, Willyam	1964	5.00	10.00	20.00
❑ 329	Never Pick a Pretty Boy/He's No Ordinary Guy	1964	3.00	6.00	12.00
❑ 335	Deep Dark Secret/Good	1964	3.00	6.00	12.00
❑ 347	To Know Him Is to Love Him/There Ain't Nothin' I Wouldn't Do for You	1965	2.50	5.00	10.00
❑ 357	Let's Twine/That's What My Mama Said	1965	2.50	5.00	10.00
❑ 375	I Really Love You/Standing in the Need of Love	1965	2.50	5.00	10.00
❑ 375 [PS]	I Really Love You/Standing in the Need of Love	1965	3.75	7.50	15.00
❑ 382	It's a Funny Situation/There Ain't Nothin' I Wouldn't Do for You	1965	2.50	5.00	10.00
FAIRMOUNT					
❑ 1004	(It's Wonderful) The Love I Feel for You/Willyam, Wilyam	1966	2.50	5.00	10.00
GAMBLE					
❑ 219	What Kind of Lady/You're Gonna Miss Me (When I'm Gone)	1968	5.00	10.00	20.00
❑ 4005	The Bottle or Me/You're Gonna Miss Me (When I'm Gone)	1969	3.75	7.50	15.00
PHILADELPHIA INT'L.					
❑ 02041	Breaking and Entering/I Love You Anyway	1981	—	2.00	4.00
❑ 3512	Conquer the World Together/We Gotta Good Thing Goin'	1971	—	3.00	6.00
—With Bunny Sigler					
❑ 3625	Flashback/Nobody Can Take Your Place	1977	—	2.50	5.00
❑ 3636	I'd Really Love to See You Tonight/What Color Is Love	1977	—	2.50	5.00
❑ 3638	I Believe in Love/Just As Long As I Know You're Mine	1978	—	2.50	5.00
❑ 3644	Tryin' to Get the Feeling Again/I Wanna Be Your Woman	1978	—	2.50	5.00
❑ 70058	I Love You Anyway/Easy Money	1981	—	2.00	4.00
—Philadelphia International records as "Dee Dee Sharp Gamble"					
TSOP					
❑ 4776	Happy 'Bout the Whole Thing/Touch My Life	1976	—	2.50	5.00
❑ 4778	I'm Not in Love/Make It Till Tomorrow	1976	—	2.50	5.00

SHARP, DEE DEE, AND CHUBBY CHECKER

Also see each artist's individual listings.

Number	Title (A Side/B Side)	Yr	VG	VG+	NM
CAMEO					
❑ 103 [DJ]	Do You Love Me?/One More Time	1962	10.00	20.00	40.00
—Yellow label, black print, promo only					

SHARPE, RAY

Number	Title (A Side/B Side)	Yr	VG	VG+	NM
ATCO					
❑ 6402	Help Me (Get the Feeling) Part 1/Help Me (Get the Feeling) Part 2	1966	2.50	5.00	10.00
❑ 6437	I Can't Take It/Mary Jane	1966	2.50	5.00	10.00
A&M					
❑ 1297	Dream On, Donna/Another Piece of the Puzzle	1971	—	2.50	5.00
DOT					
❑ 15788	Oh, My Baby's Gone/That's the Way I Feel	1958	3.75	7.50	15.00
❑ 15974	Oh, My Baby's Gone/That's the Way I Feel	1959	3.00	6.00	12.00
GREGMARK					
❑ 14	(The New) Linda Lu/The Bus Song	1963	3.00	6.00	12.00
HAMILTON					
❑ 50002	Oh, My Baby's Gone/That's the Way I Feel	1959	2.50	5.00	10.00
JAMIE					
❑ 1128	Linda Lu/Monkey's Uncle	1959	6.25	12.50	25.00
❑ 1128	Linda Lu/Red Sails in the Sunset	1959	3.75	7.50	15.00
❑ 1138	Long John/T.A. Blues	1959	3.75	7.50	15.00
❑ 1149	Bermuda/Gonna Let It Go This Time	1960	3.75	7.50	15.00
❑ 1155	For You My Love/Red Sails in the Sunset	1960	3.75	7.50	15.00
❑ 1164	Give'n Up/Kewpie Doll	1960	3.75	7.50	15.00
LHI					
❑ 1215	Linda Lu/Monkey's Uncle	1967	2.00	4.00	8.00
MONUMENT					
❑ 874	Let's Go, Let's Go, Let's Go/It's Too Cold	1965	2.50	5.00	10.00
PARK AVE.					
❑ 4904	Do the Thaxton/Baby Ora	196?	2.50	5.00	10.00
❑ 4906	Almost Grown/(B-side unknown)	196?	2.50	5.00	10.00
TREY					
❑ 3011	Justine/On the Street Where You Live	1961	3.00	6.00	12.00

SHARPS, THE

Possibly more than one group.

Number	Title (A Side/B Side)	Yr	VG	VG+	NM
ALADDIN					
❑ 3401	What Will I Gain/Shufflin'	1957	12.50	25.00	50.00
❑ 3401	What Will I Gain/Shufflin'	1957	100.00	200.00	400.00
—Purple vinyl					
CHESS					
❑ 1690	6 Months, 3 Weeks, 2 Days/Cha-Cho Bop	1958	7.50	15.00	30.00
—B-side by Jack McVea					
COMBO					
❑ 146	All My Love/Look What You've Done to Me	1958	12.50	25.00	50.00
DOT					
❑ 15806	All My Love/Look What You've Done to Me	1958	3.75	7.50	15.00
JAMIE					
❑ 1040	Sweet Sweetheart/Come On	1957	10.00	20.00	40.00
❑ 1108	Have Love, Will Travel/Look at Me	1958	12.50	25.00	50.00
❑ 1114	Here's My Heart/Gig-A-Lene	1958	7.50	15.00	30.00
LAMP					
❑ 2007	Our Love Is Here to Stay/Lock My Heart	1957	7.50	15.00	30.00
STAR-HI					
❑ 10406	Double Clutch/If Love Is What You Want	1960	7.50	15.00	30.00
TAG					
❑ 2200	6 Months, 3 Weeks, 2 Days/Cha-Cho Bop	1957	25.00	50.00	100.00
—B-side by Jack McVea					
VIK					
❑ 0264	Sweet Sweetheart/Come On	1957	6.25	12.50	25.00
WIN					
❑ 702	Teenage Girl/We Three	1958	12.50	25.00	50.00

SHARPTONES, THE
POST

Number	Title (A Side/B Side)	Yr	VG	VG+	NM
❑ 2009	Since I Fell for You/Made to Love	1955	100.00	200.00	400.00

SHATNER, WILLIAM
DECCA

Number	Title (A Side/B Side)	Yr	VG	VG+	NM
❑ 32399	How Insensitive/Transformed Man	1969	5.00	10.00	20.00

SHAW, JIMMY
IMPERIAL

Number	Title (A Side/B Side)	Yr	VG	VG+	NM
❑ 5603	Take a Chance on Me/Big Chief Hug-Um An' Kiss-Um	1959	5.00	10.00	20.00

SHAW, JOHN, AND THE DELL-OS
U-C

Number	Title (A Side/B Side)	Yr	VG	VG+	NM
❑ 5002	Why Did You Leave Me/Why Does It Have to Be Her	1957	2000.	3000.	4000.

SHAW, SANDIE
MERCURY

Number	Title (A Side/B Side)	Yr	VG	VG+	NM
❑ 72315	Ya, Ya, Da, Da/As Long As You're Happy	1964	3.75	7.50	15.00

RCA VICTOR

Number	Title (A Side/B Side)	Yr	VG	VG+	NM
❑ 47-9594	Together/One More Lie	1968	2.00	4.00	8.00
❑ 74-0118	Voice in the Crowd/Monsieur Dupont	1969	2.00	4.00	8.00
❑ 74-0370	Love Is For the Two of Us/Wight Is Wight	1970	2.00	4.00	8.00

REPRISE

Number	Title (A Side/B Side)	Yr	VG	VG+	NM
❑ 0320	(There's) Always Something There to Remind Me/Don't You Know	1964	3.00	6.00	12.00
❑ 0342	Girl Don't Come/I'd Be Far Better Off Without You	1965	2.50	5.00	10.00
❑ 0365	I'll Stop at Nothing/You Can't Blame Him	1965	2.50	5.00	10.00
❑ 0375	Long Live Love/I've Heard About Him	1965	2.50	5.00	10.00
❑ 0394	Stop Feeling Sorry for Yourself/I'll Stop at Nothing	1965	2.50	5.00	10.00
❑ 0427	If Ever You Need Me/How Can You Tell	1965	2.50	5.00	10.00
❑ 0449	Tomorrow/Hurting You	1966	2.50	5.00	10.00
❑ 0488	Nothing Comes Easy/Stop Before You Start	1966	2.50	5.00	10.00
❑ 0546	Think Sometime About Me/Hide All Emotion	1967	2.50	5.00	10.00
❑ 0575	Puppet on a String/I Had a Dream Last Night	1967	2.50	5.00	10.00
❑ 20191	Me/Now	1963	3.75	7.50	15.00
—B-side by Bob Candee					

SHAW, TOMMY
Also see STYX.

ATLANTIC

Number	Title (A Side/B Side)	Yr	VG	VG+	NM
❑ 89138	Ever Since the World Began/The Outsider	1988	—	—	3.00
❑ 89138 [PS]	Ever Since the World Began/The Outsider	1988	—	—	3.00
❑ 89183	No Such Thing/The Outsider	1987	—	—	3.00

A&M

Number	Title (A Side/B Side)	Yr	VG	VG+	NM
❑ 2676	Girls with Guns/Heads Up	1984	—	—	3.00
❑ 2676 [PS]	Girls with Guns/Heads Up	1984	—	2.00	4.00
❑ 2696	Lonely School/Come In and Explain	1984	—	—	3.00
❑ 2715	Free to Love You/Come In and Explain	1985	—	—	3.00
❑ 2773	Remo's Theme (What If)/Kiss Me Hello	1985	—	—	3.00
❑ 2773 [PS]	Remo's Theme (What If)/Kiss Me Hello	1985	—	—	3.00
❑ 2800	Jealousy/This Is Not a Test	1985	—	—	3.00

SHEAN AND JENKYNS
GNP CRESCENDO

Number	Title (A Side/B Side)	Yr	VG	VG+	NM
❑ 198	Goofy-Footer Ho-Dad/Do the Commercial	1963	6.25	12.50	25.00

SHEEP, THE
By the same people who gave us THE STRANGELOVES.

BOOM

Number	Title (A Side/B Side)	Yr	VG	VG+	NM
❑ 60000	Hide and Seek/Twelve Months Later	1966	5.00	10.00	20.00
❑ 60007	Dynamite/I Feel Good	1966	5.00	10.00	20.00

SHEFFIELDS, THE
DESTINATION

Number	Title (A Side/B Side)	Yr	VG	VG+	NM
❑ 613	My Loving Days Are Through/Please Come Back	1966	3.00	6.00	12.00
❑ 621	Do You Still Love Me/Nothing I Can Do	1966	3.00	6.00	12.00

DOT

Number	Title (A Side/B Side)	Yr	VG	VG+	NM
❑ 16722	Plenty of Love/Bags Groove	1965	3.75	7.50	15.00

SHEIKS, THE
More than one group. Some of these were labeled "The Shieks."

AMY

Number	Title (A Side/B Side)	Yr	VG	VG+	NM
❑ 807	Come On Back/Please Don't Take Away the Girl I Love	1960	50.00	100.00	200.00

CAT

Number	Title (A Side/B Side)	Yr	VG	VG+	NM
❑ 116	Walk That Walk/The Kissing Song (Sweetie Lover)	1955	10.00	20.00	40.00

EF-N-DE

Number	Title (A Side/B Side)	Yr	VG	VG+	NM
❑ 1000	Give Me Another Chance/Baby Don't You Cry	1955	200.00	400.00	600.00

FEDERAL

Number	Title (A Side/B Side)	Yr	VG	VG+	NM
❑ 12237	So Fine/Sentimental Heart	1955	37.50	75.00	150.00

JAMIE

Number	Title (A Side/B Side)	Yr	VG	VG+	NM
❑ 1147	Candlelight Cafe/The Song of Old Paree	1959	5.00	10.00	20.00

LEGRAND

Number	Title (A Side/B Side)	Yr	VG	VG+	NM
❑ 1013	What I'd Do for Your Love/Why Should I Dance	1961	25.00	50.00	100.00
❑ 1016	Cocoanut Woman/Twist That Twist	1962	6.25	12.50	25.00

MGM

Number	Title (A Side/B Side)	Yr	VG	VG+	NM
❑ 12876	Baghdad Rock (Part 1)/Baghdad Rock (Part 2)	1960	5.00	10.00	20.00

SHELDON, DOUG
CONGRESS

Number	Title (A Side/B Side)	Yr	VG	VG+	NM
❑ 266	How Can I Tell Her/It's Because of You	1966	2.50	5.00	10.00

MGM

Number	Title (A Side/B Side)	Yr	VG	VG+	NM
❑ 13261	Lonely Boy/Hello There Lonely Baby	1964	3.00	6.00	12.00

SHELLS, THE
END

Number	Title (A Side/B Side)	Yr	VG	VG+	NM
❑ 1022	Pretty Little Girl/Sippin' Soda	1958	37.50	75.00	150.00
❑ 1050	Whispering Wings/Shooma Dom Dom	1959	12.50	25.00	50.00

GONE

Number	Title (A Side/B Side)	Yr	VG	VG+	NM
❑ 5103	Pretty Little Girl/Sippin' Soda	1961	6.25	12.50	25.00

JOHNSON

Number	Title (A Side/B Side)	Yr	VG	VG+	NM
❑ 099	My Cherie/Explain It to Me	1972	—	3.00	6.00
❑ 104	Baby Oh Baby/Angel Eyes	1957	10.00	20.00	40.00
❑ 104	Baby Oh Baby/What's in An Angel's Eyes	1960	3.75	7.50	15.00
—Note lengthened B-side title					
❑ 106	Don't Say Goodbye/Pleading	1958	25.00	50.00	100.00
❑ 107	Explain It to Me/An Island Unknown	1961	6.25	12.50	25.00
❑ 109	Better Forget Him/Can't Take It	1961	6.25	12.50	25.00
❑ 110	In the Dim Light of the Dark/O-Mi Yum-Mi Yum-Mi	1961	6.25	12.50	25.00
❑ 112	Sweetest One/Baby Walk On In	1961	7.50	15.00	30.00
❑ 119	Deep in My Heart/(It's a) Happy Holiday	1962	7.50	15.00	30.00
❑ 120	The Drive/A Toast to Your Birthday	1962	7.50	15.00	30.00
❑ 127	On My Honor/My Royal Love	1963	12.50	25.00	50.00
❑ 332	Explain It to Me/An Island Unknown	1961	3.75	7.50	15.00

JOSIE

Number	Title (A Side/B Side)	Yr	VG	VG+	NM
❑ 912	Deep in My Heart/Our Wedding Day	1963	5.00	10.00	20.00

ROULETTE

Number	Title (A Side/B Side)	Yr	VG	VG+	NM
❑ 4156	The Thief/She Wasn't Meant for Me	1959	7.50	15.00	30.00

SHELTON, GARY
ALPINE

Number	Title (A Side/B Side)	Yr	VG	VG+	NM
❑ 56	Honey Bee/Till the End of the Line	1960	7.50	15.00	30.00

MARK

Number	Title (A Side/B Side)	Yr	VG	VG+	NM
❑ 145	Goodbye Little Darlin' Goodbye/Stop the World	1960	50.00	100.00	200.00

MERCURY

Number	Title (A Side/B Side)	Yr	VG	VG+	NM
❑ 71310	Kissin' at the Drive-In/Yours Till I Die	1958	7.50	15.00	30.00

SHEP AND THE LIMELITES
Also see THE HEARTBEATS; SHANE SHEPPARD.

HULL

Number	Title (A Side/B Side)	Yr	VG	VG+	NM
❑ 740	Daddy's Home/This I Know	1961	10.00	20.00	40.00
—Pink label					
❑ 740	Daddy's Home/This I Know	1961	6.25	12.50	25.00
—Red label					
❑ 740	Daddy's Home/This I Know	1961	5.00	10.00	20.00
—Tan label. Note: Any colored vinyl version is a counterfeit.					
❑ 742	Ready for Your Love/You'll Be Sorry	1961	5.00	10.00	20.00
❑ 747	Three Steps from the Altar/Oh What a Feeling	1961	5.00	10.00	20.00
❑ 748	Our Anniversary/Who Told the Sandman	1962	5.00	10.00	20.00
❑ 751	What Did Daddy Do/Teach Me, Teach Me How to Twist	1962	5.00	10.00	20.00
❑ 753	Gee Baby, What About You/Everything Is Going to Be Alright	1962	5.00	10.00	20.00
❑ 756	Remember Baby/The Monkey	1963	5.00	10.00	20.00
❑ 757	Stick By Me (And I'll Stick By You)/It's All Over Now	1963	5.00	10.00	20.00
❑ 759	Steal Away (With Your Baby)/For All My Love	1963	5.00	10.00	20.00
❑ 761	Easy to Remember (When You Want to Forget)/ Why, Why Won't You Believe Me	1964	5.00	10.00	20.00
❑ 767	I'm All Alone/Why Did You Fall for Me	1964	5.00	10.00	20.00
❑ 770	Party for Two/You Better Believe	1965	7.50	15.00	30.00
❑ 772	In Case I Forget/I'm a-Hurting Inside	1965	5.00	10.00	20.00

SHEPARDS, THE
ABC-PARAMOUNT

Number	Title (A Side/B Side)	Yr	VG	VG+	NM
❑ 10758	Little Girl Lost/Let Yourself Go	1965	6.25	12.50	25.00

SHEPHERD, CYBILL
PARAMOUNT

Number	Title (A Side/B Side)	Yr	VG	VG+	NM
❑ 0299	My Heart Belongs to Daddy/Anything Goes	1974	2.50	5.00	10.00

SHEPHERD SISTERS
Some of these spelled the name "Shepard," others "Sheppard," but they are all the same group.

20TH CENTURY FOX

Number	Title (A Side/B Side)	Yr	VG	VG+	NM
❑ 468	I've Got a Secret/Finders Keepers	1964	2.50	5.00	10.00

ATLANTIC

Number	Title (A Side/B Side)	Yr	VG	VG+	NM
❑ 2176	What Makes Little Girls Cry/Don't Mention My Name	1963	2.50	5.00	10.00
❑ 2195	Talk Is Cheap/The Greatest Lover	1963	2.50	5.00	10.00

BIG TOP

Number	Title (A Side/B Side)	Yr	VG	VG+	NM
❑ 3066	Hapsburg Serenade/Schoen-A, Schoen-A	1961	3.75	7.50	15.00

LANCE

Number	Title (A Side/B Side)	Yr	VG	VG+	NM
❑ 125	Alone (Why Must I Be Alone)/Congratulations to Someone	1957	6.25	12.50	25.00

MELBA

Number	Title (A Side/B Side)	Yr	VG	VG+	NM
❑ 100	Gone with the Wind/Rock and Roll, Cha Cha	1956	6.25	12.50	25.00
❑ 108	Remember That Crazy Rock and Roll Turf/I Walked Beside the Sea	1957	6.25	12.50	25.00

MERCURY

Number	Title (A Side/B Side)	Yr	VG	VG+	NM
❑ 71244	Gettin' Ready for Freddie/The Best Thing There Is	1957	6.25	12.50	25.00
❑ 71306	Eatin' Pizza/A Boy and a Girl	1958	5.00	10.00	20.00
❑ 71350	Dancing Baby/Is It a Crime	1958	5.00	10.00	20.00

MGM

Number	Title (A Side/B Side)	Yr	VG	VG+	NM
❑ 12766	Heart and Soul/(It's No) Sin	1959	5.00	10.00	20.00

PRIVATE STOCK

Number	Title (A Side/B Side)	Yr	VG	VG+	NM
❑ 45063	Our Town/(B-side unknown)	1975	—	3.00	6.00

UNITED ARTISTS

Number	Title (A Side/B Side)	Yr	VG	VG+	NM
❑ 350	Deeply/I'm Still Dancin'	1961	3.00	6.00	12.00
❑ 456	Lolita Ya Ya/Marvin	1962	3.00	6.00	12.00

WARWICK

Number	Title (A Side/B Side)	Yr	VG	VG+	NM
❑ 511	Here Comes Heaven Again/I Think It's Time	1959	3.75	7.50	15.00
❑ 530	Alone/Rocky	1960	3.75	7.50	15.00
❑ 548	Yea Yea Dixie/How Softly a Heart Breaks	1960	3.75	7.50	15.00

YORK

Number	Title (A Side/B Side)	Yr	VG	VG+	NM
❑ 50002	Alone (New Version)/Alone (Original Version)	1965	2.50	5.00	10.00

SHEPPARD, BUDDY, AND THE HOLIDAYS
THE BELMONTS in disguise.

Number	Title (A Side/B Side)	Yr	VG	VG+	NM
SABINA					
❑ 506	My Love Is Real/Brahms' Lullaby (Time to Dream)	1962	12.50	25.00	50.00
❑ 510	Now It's All Over/That Background Sound	1963	12.50	25.00	50.00

SHEPPARD, NEIL

Number	Title (A Side/B Side)	Yr	VG	VG+	NM
ALMONT					
❑ 314	You Can't Go Far Without a Guitar (Unless You're Ringo Starr)/Betty Is the Girl for You	1964	7.50	15.00	30.00

SHEPPARD, SHANE
Also see SHEP AND THE LIMELITES.

Number	Title (A Side/B Side)	Yr	VG	VG+	NM
APT					
❑ 25039	Too Young to Wed/Two Loving Hearts	1960	12.50	25.00	50.00
❑ 25046	One Week from Today/I'm So Lonely (What Can I Do)	1960	10.00	20.00	40.00

SHEPPARDS, THE
More than one group?

Number	Title (A Side/B Side)	Yr	VG	VG+	NM
ABNER					
❑ 7006	Elevator Operator/Loving You	1961	3.00	6.00	12.00
APEX					
❑ 7750	Loving You/Island of Love	1959	10.00	20.00	40.00
❑ 7752	Just Like You/Feel Like Lovin'	1959	6.25	12.50	25.00
❑ 7755	It's Crazy/Meant to Be	1960	6.25	12.50	25.00
❑ 7759	Just When I Need You Most/Society Gal	1960	6.25	12.50	25.00
❑ 7760	Come Home, Come Home/Just Like You	1960	6.25	12.50	25.00
❑ 7762	Tragic/Feel Like Lovin'	1961	6.25	12.50	25.00
BUNKY					
❑ 7764	Island of Love/Steal Away	1969	—	3.00	6.00
❑ 7766	I'm Not Wanted/Your Love (Has a Hole in It)	1969	—	3.00	6.00
CONSTELLATION					
❑ 123	Island of Love/Give a Hug to Me	1964	2.50	5.00	10.00
❑ 176	Island of Love/Give a Hug to Me	1966	2.00	4.00	8.00
IMPACT					
❑ 1018	Poor Man's Thing/When Johnny Comes Marching Home	1967	7.50	15.00	30.00
OKEH					
❑ 7173	Walkin'/Pretend You're Still Mine	1963	2.50	5.00	10.00
PAM					
❑ 1001	Never Let Me Go/Give a Hug to Me	1961	3.00	6.00	12.00
SHARP					
❑ 6039	What's the Name of the Game/Glitter in Your Eyes	1961	3.00	6.00	12.00
UNITED					
❑ 198	Sherry/Mozelle	1957	62.50	125.00	250.00
VEE JAY					
❑ 406	Every Now and Then/Glitter in Your Eyes	1961	3.00	6.00	12.00
❑ 441	Tragic/Come to Me	1962	5.00	10.00	20.00

SHERIDAN, BOBBY

Number	Title (A Side/B Side)	Yr	VG	VG+	NM
SUN					
❑ 354	Red Man/Sad News	1961	7.50	15.00	30.00

SHERIDAN, MIKE, AND THE NIGHTRIDERS

Number	Title (A Side/B Side)	Yr	VG	VG+	NM
LIVERPOOL SOUND					
❑ 902	Please Mr. Postman/In Love	1964	30.00	60.00	120.00

SHERIDAN, TONY, AND THE BEAT BROTHERS
See THE BEATLES.

SHERIFF AND THE RAVELS

Number	Title (A Side/B Side)	Yr	VG	VG+	NM
VEE JAY					
❑ 306	Shombalor/Lonely One	1959	10.00	20.00	40.00

SHERLOCKS, THE

Number	Title (A Side/B Side)	Yr	VG	VG+	NM
DOT					
❑ 16890	Skin of My Teeth/Turn Her Down	1966	5.00	10.00	20.00
❑ 16953	Shades of Blue/Too Good to Be True	1966	3.00	6.00	12.00

SHERMAN, ALLAN

Number	Title (A Side/B Side)	Yr	VG	VG+	NM
RCA VICTOR					
❑ 47-8412	The End of a Symphony (Part 1)/The End of a Symphony (Part 2)	1964	2.50	5.00	10.00
❑ 47-9693	Fig Leaves Are Falling/Juggling	1968	—	3.00	6.00
WARNER BROS.					
❑ 5378	Hello Mudduh! Hello Fadduh! (A Letter from Camp)/Here's to the Crabgrass	1963	3.75	7.50	15.00
❑ 5378	Hello Mudduh! Hello Fadduh! (A Letter from Camp)/Rat Fink	1963	3.00	6.00	12.00
❑ 5378 [PS]	Hello Mudduh! Hello Fadduh! (A Letter from Camp)/Rat Fink	1963	5.00	10.00	20.00
❑ 5406	The Twelve Gifts of Christmas/You Went the Wrong Way, Old King Louie	1963	6.25	12.50	25.00
❑ 5419	My Son the Vampire/I Can't Dance	1964	3.00	6.00	12.00
❑ 5435	Skin (Heart)/The Drop-Outs March	1964	2.50	5.00	10.00
❑ 5449	Hello Mudduh! Hello Fadduh! New 1964 Version/Hello Mudduh! Hello Fadduh! Original Version	1964	3.00	6.00	12.00
❑ 5449 [PS]	Hello Mudduh! Hello Fadduh! New 1964 Version/Hello Mudduh! Hello Fadduh! Original Version	1964	5.00	10.00	20.00
❑ 5490	Pop Hates the Beatles/Grow Mrs. Goldfarb	1964	3.75	7.50	15.00
❑ 5614	Crazy Downtown/The Drop-Outs March	1965	2.50	5.00	10.00
❑ 5672	The Drinking Man's Diet/The Laarge Daark Aardvark Song	1965	2.50	5.00	10.00
❑ 5806	His Own Little Island/Odd Ball	1966	2.50	5.00	10.00
❑ 5896	Westchester Hadassah/Strange Things in My Soup	1967	2.50	5.00	10.00
❑ 7112	Hello Mudduh! Hello Fadduh! (A Letter from Camp)/Sarah Jackman	1968	—	3.00	6.00

—"Back to Back Hits" series -- originals have green "W7" labels

SHERMAN, BOBBY

Number	Title (A Side/B Side)	Yr	VG	VG+	NM
CAMEO					
❑ 403	Happiness Is/Can't Get Used to Loving You	1966	2.50	5.00	10.00
❑ 403 [DJ]	Happiness Is	1966	5.00	10.00	20.00
—One-sided promo					
CONDOR					
❑ 1002	I'll Never Tell You/Telegram	1969	2.50	5.00	10.00
DECCA					
❑ 31672	Man Overboard/You Make Me Happy	1964	3.75	7.50	15.00
❑ 31741	It Hurts Me/Give Me Your Word	1965	3.75	7.50	15.00
❑ 31741 [PS]	It Hurts Me/Give Me Your Word	1965	12.50	25.00	50.00
❑ 31779	Hey Little Girl/Well All Right	1965	3.75	7.50	15.00
DOT					
❑ 16566	I Want to Hear It From Her/Nobody's Sweetheart	1963	3.75	7.50	15.00
EPIC					
❑ 10181	Cold Girl/Think of Rain	1967	2.50	5.00	10.00
❑ 10181 [PS]	Cold Girl/Think of Rain	1967	5.00	10.00	20.00
JANUS					
❑ 246	Runaway/Mr. Success	1975	—	2.00	4.00
❑ 254	Our Last Song Together/Sunshine Rose	1975	—	2.00	4.00
METROMEDIA					
❑ 68-0100	Early in the Morning/Unborn Lullaby	1973	—	2.50	5.00
❑ 121	Little Woman/One Too Many Mornings	1969	—	2.50	5.00
❑ 121 [PS]	Little Woman/One Too Many Mornings	1969	—	2.50	5.00
❑ 150	La La La (If I Had You)/Time	1969	—	2.50	5.00
❑ 150 [PS]	La La La (If I Had You)/Time	1969	—	2.50	5.00
❑ 177	Easy Come, Easy Go/July Seventeen	1970	—	2.50	5.00
❑ 177	Easy Come, Easy Go/Sounds Along the Way	1970	—	2.50	5.00
❑ 177 [PS]	Easy Come, Easy Go/July Seventeen	1970	—	2.50	5.00
❑ 188	Hey, Mister Sun/Two Blind Mice	1970	—	2.50	5.00
❑ 188 [PS]	Hey, Mister Sun/Two Blind Mice	1970	—	2.50	5.00
❑ 194	Julie, Do Ya Love Me/Spend Some Time Lovin' Me	1970	—	2.50	5.00
❑ 194 [PS]	Julie, Do Ya Love Me/Spend Some Time Lovin' Me	1970	—	2.50	5.00
❑ 204	Goin' Home (Sing a Song of Christmas Cheer)/Love's What You're Gettin' for Christmas	1970	—	3.00	6.00
❑ 204 [PS]	Goin' Home (Sing a Song of Christmas Cheer)/Love's What You're Gettin' for Christmas	1970	2.00	4.00	8.00
❑ 206	Cried Like a Baby/Is Anybody There	1971	—	2.50	5.00
❑ 206 [PS]	Cried Like a Baby/Is Anybody There	1971	—	2.50	5.00
❑ 217	The Drum/Free Now to Roam	1971	—	2.50	5.00
❑ 217 [PS]	The Drum/Free Now to Roam	1971	—	2.50	5.00
❑ 222	Waiting at the Bus Stop/Run Away	1971	—	2.50	5.00
❑ 222 [PS]	Waiting at the Bus Stop/Run Away	1971	—	2.50	5.00
❑ 227	Jennifer/Getting Together	1971	—	2.50	5.00
❑ 227 [PS]	Jennifer/Getting Together	1971	—	2.50	5.00
❑ 240	Together Again/Picture a Little Girl	1972	—	2.50	5.00
❑ 240 [PS]	Together Again/Picture a Little Girl	1972	—	2.50	5.00
❑ 249	I Don't Believe in Magic/Just a Little While Longer	1972	—	2.50	5.00
PARKWAY					
❑ 967	Goody Galumshus/Anything Your Little Heart Desires	1966	2.50	5.00	10.00
STARCREST					
❑ 100	Judy, You'll Never Know/Telegram	1962	5.00	10.00	20.00

SHERRYS, THE

Number	Title (A Side/B Side)	Yr	VG	VG+	NM
GUYDEN					
❑ 2068	Pop-Pop-Pop-Eye/Your Hand in Mine	1962	3.75	7.50	15.00
❑ 2077	Slop Time/Let's Stomp Again	1963	3.75	7.50	15.00
❑ 2084	Saturday Night/I've Got No One	1963	3.75	7.50	15.00
❑ 2094	Monk, Monk, Monkey/That Boy of Mine	1963	3.75	7.50	15.00
MERCURY					
❑ 72256	No No Baby/That Guy of Mine	1964	3.00	6.00	12.00
ROBERTS					
❑ 701	Slow Jerk/Confusion	1965	3.00	6.00	12.00

SHEVELLES, THE

Number	Title (A Side/B Side)	Yr	VG	VG+	NM
WORLD ARTISTS					
❑ 1023	Oo Poo Pa Doo/Like I Love You	1964	3.00	6.00	12.00
❑ 1025	How Would You Like Me to Love You/I Could Conquer the World	1964	3.00	6.00	12.00

SHEVETON, TONY

Number	Title (A Side/B Side)	Yr	VG	VG+	NM
PARROT					
❑ 10616	Dance with Me/A Million Drums	1964	3.75	7.50	15.00

SHIBLEY, ARKIE

Number	Title (A Side/B Side)	Yr	VG	VG+	NM
4 STAR					
❑ 1737	Pick Pick Pickin' (My Guitar)/I'm a Poor Oakie	1959	7.50	15.00	30.00
❑ 1746	The House Next Door/In My Travels	1960	—	—	—
—Canceled					
GILT EDGE					
❑ 5021	Hot Rod Race/I'm Living Alone with an Old Love	1950	25.00	50.00	100.00
❑ 5030	Hot Rod Race No. 2/I Wish I Was Somebody's Rose	1951	25.00	50.00	100.00
❑ 5036	Arkie Meets the Judge (Hot Rod Race No. 3)/Uncle Sam Has Called My Number	1951	25.00	50.00	100.00
❑ 5047	Hot Rod Race No. 4 (The Guy in the Mercury)/This Feeling You Brought Over Me	1951	25.00	50.00	100.00
❑ 5054	Hot Rod Race No. 5 (The Kid in the Model-A)/My Beautiful Washington Rose	1951	25.00	50.00	100.00
❑ 5059	Shore Leave/Guitar Hoedown	1952	15.00	30.00	60.00
❑ 5065	Arkie's Letter from Home/Five String Banjo March	1952	15.00	30.00	60.00
❑ 5072	Three Day Pass/Hot Woodpecker Rag	1953	12.50	25.00	50.00
❑ 5078	Arkie's Talking Blues/Blue Guitar Ramble	1953	12.50	25.00	50.00
❑ 5089	Hard Times in Arkansas/Dusty Blossom Boogie	1954	12.50	25.00	50.00

SHIELDS, BILLY
Pseudonym of TONY ORLANDO.

Number	Title (A Side/B Side)	Yr	VG	VG+	NM
HARBOUR					
❑ 304	I Was a Boy/Moments from Now	1969	6.25	12.50	25.00

SHIELDS, BOBBY

MELBA

Number	Title (A Side/B Side)	Yr	VG	VG+	NM
❑ 105	Land of Rock and Roll/I Wouldn't Change You for the World	1956	15.00	30.00	60.00

SHIELDS, THE

ATCO

Number	Title (A Side/B Side)	Yr	VG	VG+	NM
❑ 7071	The Way I Feel Tonight/All Right by Me	1977	—	2.50	5.00

CONTINENTAL

Number	Title (A Side/B Side)	Yr	VG	VG+	NM
❑ 4072	You Told Another Lie/Barnyard Dance	1961	100.00	200.00	400.00

DOT

Number	Title (A Side/B Side)	Yr	VG	VG+	NM
❑ 136	You Cheated/Nature Boy	196?	2.50	5.00	10.00
—Reissue; black label					
❑ 15805	You Cheated/That's the Way It's Gonna Be	1958	6.25	12.50	25.00
❑ 15856	I'm Sorry Now/Nature Boy	1958	7.50	15.00	30.00
❑ 15940	Fare Thee Well/Play the Game Fair	1959	6.25	12.50	25.00

TENDER

Number	Title (A Side/B Side)	Yr	VG	VG+	NM
❑ 513	You Cheated/That's the Way It's Gonna Be	1958	37.50	75.00	150.00
—No reference to Dot Records on label					
❑ 513	You Cheated/That's the Way It's Gonna Be	1958	10.00	20.00	40.00
—With reference to Dot Records on label					
❑ 518	I'm Sorry Now/Nature Boy	1958	15.00	30.00	60.00
❑ 521	Fare Thee Well/Play the Game Fair	1959	15.00	30.00	60.00

TRANSCONTINENTAL

Number	Title (A Side/B Side)	Yr	VG	VG+	NM
❑ 1013	The Girl Around the Corner/Fare Thee Well, My Love	1960	25.00	50.00	100.00

SHILOH

DON HENLEY was in this group.

AMOS

Number	Title (A Side/B Side)	Yr	VG	VG+	NM
❑ 140	Jennifer/Tell Her to Get Out of Your Life	1970	3.00	6.00	12.00
❑ 162	Down on the Farm/Simple Little Down Home Rock & Roll Love Song for Rosie	1971	3.00	6.00	12.00

SHINDIGS, THE

Also known as THE BOBBY FULLER FOUR.

MUSTANG

Number	Title (A Side/B Side)	Yr	VG	VG+	NM
❑ 3003	Thunder Reef/Wolfman	1965	10.00	20.00	40.00

SHINES, JOHNNY

J.O.B.

Number	Title (A Side/B Side)	Yr	VG	VG+	NM
❑ 1010	Evening Sun/Brutal Hearted Woman	1953	500.00	1000.	2000.

SHIRELLES, THE

BELL

Number	Title (A Side/B Side)	Yr	VG	VG+	NM
❑ 760	A Most Unusual Boy/Look What You've Done to My Heart	1969	2.50	5.00	10.00
❑ 787	Looking Glass/Playthings	1969	2.50	5.00	10.00
❑ 815	Never Give You Up/Go Away and Find Yourself	1969	2.50	5.00	10.00

BLUE ROCK

Number	Title (A Side/B Side)	Yr	VG	VG+	NM
❑ 4051	Don't Mess with Cupid/Sweet Sweet Lovin'	1968	2.50	5.00	10.00
❑ 4066	Call Me/There's a Storm Goin' Home in My Heart	1968	2.50	5.00	10.00

DECCA

Number	Title (A Side/B Side)	Yr	VG	VG+	NM
❑ 25506	I Met Him on a Sunday/My Love Is a Charm	196?	3.75	7.50	15.00
—Early reissue					
❑ 30588	I Met Him on a Sunday/I Want You to Be My Boyfriend	1958	6.25	12.50	25.00
❑ 30669	My Love Is a Charm/Slop Time	1958	10.00	20.00	40.00
❑ 30761	Stop Me/I Got the Message	1958	10.00	20.00	40.00

PHILCO-FORD

Number	Title (A Side/B Side)	Yr	VG	VG+	NM
❑ HP-30	Soldier Boy/My Heart Belongs to You	1968	5.00	10.00	20.00
—4-inch plastic "Hip Pocket Record" with color sleeve					

RCA VICTOR

Number	Title (A Side/B Side)	Yr	VG	VG+	NM
❑ APBO-0192	Touch the Wind (Eres Tu)/Do What You've a Mind To	1973	2.00	4.00	8.00
❑ 47-0902	Let's Give Each Other Love/Deep in the Night	1973	2.00	4.00	8.00
❑ 48-1019	No Sugar Tonight/Strange, I Still Love You	1971	2.50	5.00	10.00
❑ 48-1032	Brother, Brother/Sunday Dreaming	1972	2.50	5.00	10.00

SCEPTER

Number	Title (A Side/B Side)	Yr	VG	VG+	NM
❑ 1203	Dedicated to the One I Love/Look A Here Baby	1958	10.00	20.00	40.00
—White label					
❑ 1203	Dedicated to the One I Love/Look A Here Baby	1958	5.00	10.00	20.00
—Red label					
❑ 1205	A Teardrop and a Lollipop/Doin' the Ronde	1959	7.50	15.00	30.00
—White label					
❑ 1205	A Teardrop and a Lollipop/Doin' the Ronde	1959	5.00	10.00	20.00
—Red label					
❑ 1207	Please Be My Boyfriend/I Saw a Tear	1960	7.50	15.00	30.00
—White label					
❑ 1207	Please Be My Boyfriend/I Saw a Tear	1960	5.00	10.00	20.00
—Red label					
❑ 1208	Tonight's the Night/The Dance Is Over	1960	7.50	15.00	30.00
—White label					
❑ 1208	Tonight's the Night/The Dance Is Over	1960	5.00	10.00	20.00
—Red label					
❑ 1208	Tonight's the Night/The Dance Is Over	1960	6.25	12.50	25.00
—Pink label					
❑ 1211	Tomorrow/Boys	1960	10.00	20.00	40.00
—Original A-side title					
❑ 1211	Will You Love Me Tomorrow/Boys	1960	7.50	15.00	30.00
—Revised A-side title					
❑ 1217	Mama Said/Blue Holiday	1961	5.00	10.00	20.00
❑ 1220	A Thing of the Past/What a Sweet Thing That Was	1961	5.00	10.00	20.00
❑ 1223	Big John/Twenty-One	1961	5.00	10.00	20.00
❑ 1227	Baby It's You/Things I Want to Hear (Pretty Words)	1961	5.00	10.00	20.00
❑ 1228	Soldier Boy/Love Is a Swingin' Thing	1962	3.75	7.50	15.00
❑ 1234	Welcome Home Baby/Mama, Here Comes the Bride	1962	3.75	7.50	15.00
❑ 1237	Stop the Music/It's Love That Really Counts	1962	3.75	7.50	15.00
❑ 1243	Everybody Loves a Lover/I Don't Think So	1962	3.75	7.50	15.00
❑ 1248	Foolish Little Girl/Not for All the Money in the World	1963	3.75	7.50	15.00
❑ 1248 [PS]	Foolish Little Girl/Not for All the Money in the World	1963	10.00	20.00	40.00
❑ 1255	Don't Say Goodnight and Mean Goodbye/I Didn't Mean to Hurt You	1963	3.00	6.00	12.00
❑ 1255 [PS]	Don't Say Goodnight and Mean Goodbye/I Didn't Mean to Hurt You	1963	10.00	20.00	40.00
❑ 1259	What Does a Girl Do?/Don't Let It Happen to You	1963	3.00	6.00	12.00
❑ 1260	It's a Mad, Mad, Mad, Mad World/31 Flavors	1963	3.00	6.00	12.00
❑ 1264	Tonight You're Gonna Fall in Love with Me/20th Century Rock and Roll	1963	3.00	6.00	12.00
❑ 1267	Sha-La-La/His Lips Get In the Way	1964	3.00	6.00	12.00
❑ 1278	Thank You Baby/Doomsday	1964	3.00	6.00	12.00
❑ 1284	Maybe Tonight/Lost Love	1964	3.00	6.00	12.00
❑ 1292	Are You Still My Baby/I Saw a Tear	1964	3.00	6.00	12.00
❑ 1296	Shh, I'm Watching the Movies/A Plus B	1965	3.00	6.00	12.00
❑ 12101	March (You'll Be Sorry)/Everybody's Goin' Mad	1965	2.50	5.00	10.00
❑ 12114	My Heart Belongs to You/Love That Man	1965	2.50	5.00	10.00
❑ 12123	(Mama) My Soldier Boy Is Coming Home/Soldier Boy	1965	2.50	5.00	10.00
❑ 12132	I Met Him on a Sunday — '66/Love That Man	1966	2.50	5.00	10.00
❑ 12150	Till My Baby Comes Home/Que Sera, Sera	1966	2.50	5.00	10.00
❑ 12162	Shades of Blue/Looking Around	1966	2.50	5.00	10.00
❑ 12162	Shades of Blue/After Midnight	1966	2.50	5.00	10.00
❑ 12178	Teasin' Me/Look Away	1966	2.50	5.00	10.00
❑ 12185	Don't Go Home (My Little Baby)/Nobody Baby After You	1967	2.50	5.00	10.00
❑ 12192	Too Much of a Good Thing/Bright Shiny Colors	1967	2.50	5.00	10.00
❑ 12198	Last Minute Miracle/No Doubt About It	1967	2.50	5.00	10.00
❑ 12209	Wild and Sweet/Wait Till I Give the Signal	1968	2.50	5.00	10.00
❑ 12217	Hippie Walk (Part 1)/Hippie Walk (Part 2)	1968	2.50	5.00	10.00

TIARA

Number	Title (A Side/B Side)	Yr	VG	VG+	NM
❑ 6112	I Met Him on a Sunday/I Want You to Be My Boyfriend	1958	200.00	400.00	800.00

UNITED ARTISTS

Number	Title (A Side/B Side)	Yr	VG	VG+	NM
❑ 50648	There Goes My Baby-Be My Baby/Strange, I Still Love You	1970	2.00	4.00	8.00
❑ 50693	It's Gonna Take a Miracle/Lost	1970	2.00	4.00	8.00
❑ 50740	Take Me for a Little While/Dedicated to the One I Love	1971	2.00	4.00	8.00

SHIRLEY (AND COMPANY)

Shirley Goodman, earlier of SHIRLEY AND LEE.

VIBRATION

Number	Title (A Side/B Side)	Yr	VG	VG+	NM
❑ 532	Shame, Shame, Shame/(Instrumental)	1974	—	2.50	5.00
❑ 535	Cry, Cry, Cry/(Instrumental)	1975	—	2.50	5.00
❑ 539	Disco Shirley/Keep On Rolling On	1975	—	2.50	5.00
❑ 542	I Like to Dance/Jim Doc C'ain	1976	—	2.50	5.00
❑ 579	Revelations True/(Instrumental)	1978	—	2.50	5.00

SHIRLEY AND LEE

Also see SHIRLEY (AND COMPANY).

ALADDIN

Number	Title (A Side/B Side)	Yr	VG	VG+	NM
❑ 3153	I'm Gone/Sweethearts	1952	25.00	50.00	100.00
❑ 3173	Baby/Shirley Come Back to Me	1953	30.00	60.00	120.00
❑ 3192	Shirley's Back/So In Love	1953	15.00	30.00	60.00
❑ 3205	Two Happy People/The Proposal	1953	12.50	25.00	50.00
❑ 3222	Why Did I/Lee Goofed	1954	12.50	25.00	50.00
❑ 3244	Confessin'/Keep On	1954	12.50	25.00	50.00
❑ 3258	Comin' Over/Takes Money	1954	12.50	25.00	50.00
❑ 3289	Feel So Good/You'd Be Thinking of Me	1955	10.00	20.00	40.00
❑ 3302	Let's Dream/I'll Do It	1955	10.00	20.00	40.00
❑ 3325	Let the Good Times Roll/Do You Mean to Hurt Me So	1956	15.00	30.00	60.00
❑ 3338	I Feel Good/Now That It's Over	1956	6.25	12.50	25.00
❑ 3362	When I Saw You/That's What I Want to Do	1957	5.00	10.00	20.00
❑ 3369	I Want to Dance/Marry Me	1957	5.00	10.00	20.00
❑ 3380	Rock All Night/Don't You Know I Love You	1957	5.00	10.00	20.00
❑ 3390	Rockin' with the Clock/The Flirt	1957	5.00	10.00	20.00
❑ 3405	Love No One But You (I Love You So)/I'll Thrill You	1958	5.00	10.00	20.00
❑ 3418	Everybody's Rocking/Don't Leave Me Here to Cry	1958	5.00	10.00	20.00
❑ 3432	Come On and Have Your Fun/All I Want to Do Is Cry	1958	5.00	10.00	20.00
❑ 3455	True Love/When Day Is Done	1959	5.00	10.00	20.00

IMPERIAL

Number	Title (A Side/B Side)	Yr	VG	VG+	NM
❑ 5818	Together We Stand (Divided We Fall)/The Joker	1962	2.50	5.00	10.00
❑ 5854	My Last Letter/I'm Early Enough	1962	2.50	5.00	10.00
❑ 5868	Don't Stop Now/A Little Thing	1962	2.50	5.00	10.00
❑ 5922	The Golden Rule/Hey Little Boy	1963	2.50	5.00	10.00
❑ 5970	Dancing World/I'm Gone	1963	2.50	5.00	10.00
❑ 5979	Paper Doll/The Brink of Disaster	1963	2.50	5.00	10.00
❑ 66000	Somebody Put a Jukebox in the Study Hall/Never Let Me Go	1963	2.50	5.00	10.00

UNITED ARTISTS

Number	Title (A Side/B Side)	Yr	VG	VG+	NM
❑ 0087	Let the Good Times Roll/Feel So Good	1973	—	2.00	4.00
—"Silver Spotlight Series" reissue					
❑ XW274	Let the Good Times Roll/That's What I Wanna Do	1973	—	2.50	5.00

WARWICK

Number	Title (A Side/B Side)	Yr	VG	VG+	NM
❑ 581	Let the Good Times Roll/Keep Loving Me	1960	3.00	6.00	12.00
❑ 609	Two Peas in a Pod/Your Love Makes the Difference	1961	3.00	6.00	12.00
❑ 664	Well-a, Well-a/Our Kids	1961	3.00	6.00	12.00
❑ 679	Let's Live It Up/Girl, You're Married Now	1962	3.00	6.00	12.00

SHOCKING BLUE, THE

21 RECORDS

Number	Title (A Side/B Side)	Yr	VG	VG+	NM
❑ 99517	Venus/Mighty Joe	1986	—	2.00	4.00

BUDDAH

Number	Title (A Side/B Side)	Yr	VG	VG+	NM
❑ 258	Sleepless at Midnight/Serenade	1971	—	3.00	6.00

Number	Title (A Side/B Side)	Yr	VG	VG+	NM
COLOSSUS					
❑ 108	Venus/Hot Sand	1969	2.50	5.00	10.00
❑ 108 [PS]	Venus/Hot Sand	1969	3.75	7.50	15.00
❑ 111	Mighty Joe/I'm a Woman	1970	2.00	4.00	8.00
❑ 111 [PS]	Mighty Joe/I'm a Woman	1970	3.00	6.00	12.00
❑ 116	Long and Lonesome Road/Ackaragh	1970	2.00	4.00	8.00
❑ 123	Never Love a Railroad Man/Never Marry	1970	2.00	4.00	8.00
❑ 141	Boll Weevil/Long and Lonesome Road	1971	—	3.00	6.00
MGM					
❑ 14481	When I Was a Girl/Eve and the Apple	1973	—	3.00	6.00
❑ 14543	Oh Love/Inkpot	1973	—	3.00	6.00

SHONDELL, TROY

Number	Title (A Side/B Side)	Yr	VG	VG+	NM
AVM					
❑ 14	(I'm Looking for Some) New Blue Jeans/(B-side unknown)	1988	—	3.50	7.00
BEAR					
❑ 2002	No One Knows/Sweet Enough	1989	—	3.00	6.00
BRITE STAR					
❑ 2453	This Time/You're Nobody's Child	1973	2.00	4.00	8.00
❑ 2459	Still Loving You/Rip It Up	1973	2.00	4.00	8.00
❑ 4691	Deeper and Deeper in Love/Love Stuff	1974	2.00	4.00	8.00
DECCA					
❑ 31712	You Can't Catch Me/Walkin' in a Memory	1964	2.50	5.00	10.00
EVEREST					
❑ 2015	Gone/Some People Never Learn	1963	2.50	5.00	10.00
❑ 2018	I've Got a Woman/No Fool Like an Old Fool	1963	2.50	5.00	10.00
❑ 2041	Trouble/Little Miss Tease	1964	2.50	5.00	10.00
GAYE					
❑ 2010	This Time/I Catch Myself Crying	1961	20.00	40.00	80.00
GOLDCREST					
❑ 161-A	This Time/Girl After Girl	1961	7.50	15.00	30.00
—With no "Distributed by Liberty" on label					
❑ 161-A	This Time/Girl After Girl	1961	6.25	12.50	25.00
—With "Distributed by Liberty Record Sales" on label					
ITCO					
❑ 105	And We Made Love/Imitation Woman	198?	—	2.50	5.00
LIBERTY					
❑ 55353	This Time/Girl After Girl	1961	5.00	10.00	20.00
❑ 55392	Tears from an Angel/Island in the Sky	1961	4.00	8.00	16.00
❑ 55445	Just Because/Na-No-No	1962	4.00	8.00	16.00
RIC					
❑ 174	Just a Dream/Just Like Me	1965	2.50	5.00	10.00
❑ 184	Big Windy City/I Thought That You Were Mine	1966	2.50	5.00	10.00
STAR-FOX					
❑ 77	Still Loving You/Doctor Love	1979	2.00	4.00	8.00
TELESONIC					
❑ 804	(Sittin' Here) Lovin' You/(Here I Am) Single Again	1980	2.00	4.00	8.00
TRX					
❑ 5001	A Rose and a Baby Ruth/Here It Comes Again	1967	2.00	4.00	8.00
❑ 5003	Head Man/She's Got Everything She Needs	1967	2.00	4.00	8.00
❑ 5015	Let's Go All the Way/Let Me Love You	1968	2.00	4.00	8.00
❑ 5019	Something's Wrong in Indiana/A Rose and a Baby Ruth	1969	2.00	4.00	8.00

SHONDELLES, THE

Number	Title (A Side/B Side)	Yr	VG	VG+	NM
KING					
❑ 5597	Don't Cry My Soldier Boy/My Love	1962	5.00	10.00	20.00
❑ 5656	Wonderful One/I Gotta Tell It	1962	5.00	10.00	20.00
❑ 5705	Muscle Bound/Special Delivery	1963	5.00	10.00	20.00
❑ 5755	Watusi, One More/Ooo, Sometimes	1963	5.00	10.00	20.00

SHOOTERS, THE

With OTIS REDDING.

Number	Title (A Side/B Side)	Yr	VG	VG+	NM
TRANS WORLD					
❑ 6908	Tuff Enuff/She's All Right	1960	25.00	50.00	100.00

SHOTGUN EXPRESS

With ROD STEWART.

Number	Title (A Side/B Side)	Yr	VG	VG+	NM
UPTOWN					
❑ 747	I Could Feel the Whole World Turn/Curtains	1967	7.50	15.00	30.00

SHOWMEN, THE

With General Johnson, later of CHAIRMEN OF THE BOARD.

Number	Title (A Side/B Side)	Yr	VG	VG+	NM
AMY					
❑ 11036	Action/What Would It Take	1968	2.00	4.00	8.00
IMPERIAL					
❑ 66033	It Will Stand/Country Fool	1964	3.00	6.00	12.00
❑ 66071	Country Fool/Somebody Help Me	1964	3.00	6.00	12.00
LIBERTY					
❑ 56166	It Will Stand/Country Fool	1970	—	3.00	6.00
MINIT					
❑ 632	It Will Stand/Country Fool	1961	7.50	15.00	30.00
—Orange label					
❑ 632	It Will Stand/Country Fool	1961	5.00	10.00	20.00
—Black label					
❑ 643	The Wrong Girl/Fate Planned It This Way	1962	12.50	25.00	50.00
❑ 647	Com'n Home/I Love You, Can't You See	1962	6.25	12.50	25.00
❑ 654	True Fine Mama/The Owl Sees You	1962	6.25	12.50	25.00
❑ 662	39-21-46/Swish Fish	1963	6.25	12.50	25.00
❑ 32007	39-21-46/Swish Fish	1966	2.50	5.00	10.00
SWAN					
❑ 4213	In Paradise/Take It Baby	1965	2.50	5.00	10.00
❑ 4219	Our Love Will Grow/You're Everything	1965	2.50	5.00	10.00
❑ 4241	Please Try and Understand/Honey House	1966	2.50	5.00	10.00
UNITED ARTISTS					
❑ 0100	It Will Stand/I'm a Happy Man	1973	—	2.50	5.00
—"Silver Spotlight Series" reissue; B-side by the Jive Five					

SHUFFLES, THE

Number	Title (A Side/B Side)	Yr	VG	VG+	NM
RAYCO					
❑ 508	Do You Remember My Darling/Dancin' Little Girl	1963	50.00	100.00	200.00

SHUT DOWNS, THE

Number	Title (A Side/B Side)	Yr	VG	VG+	NM
DIMENSION					
❑ 1016	Four on the Floor/Beach Buggy	1963	6.25	12.50	25.00
KARSONG					
❑ 501	Four on the Floor/Straightaway	1963	12.50	25.00	50.00

SICKNICKS, THE

Number	Title (A Side/B Side)	Yr	VG	VG+	NM
AMY					
❑ 824	The Presidential Press Conference (Part 1)/The Presidential Press Conference (Part 2)	1961	3.75	7.50	15.00
❑ 824 [PS]	The Presidential Press Conference (Part 1)/The Presidential Press Conference (Part 2)	1961	6.25	12.50	25.00
❑ 831	Wadja Say Mr. K (Part 1)/Wadja Say Mr. K (Part 2)	1961	3.75	7.50	15.00

SIDEWALK SURFERS, THE

Number	Title (A Side/B Side)	Yr	VG	VG+	NM
JUBILEE					
❑ 5496	Skate Board/Fun Last Summer	1965	12.50	25.00	50.00

SIERRAS, THE

Number	Title (A Side/B Side)	Yr	VG	VG+	NM
DOT					
❑ 16569	Plan for Love/Then I'll Still Love You	1963	3.00	6.00	12.00
GOLDISC					
❑ G-4	I Should Have Loved You/I'll Believe It When I See It	1963	7.50	15.00	30.00
KNOX					
❑ 102	So Many Sleepless Nights/Nearer My Heart	1962	25.00	50.00	100.00
MAIL CALL					
❑ 2333/4	Stormy Weather/Chance	1963	50.00	100.00	200.00

SIGLER, BUNNY

Number	Title (A Side/B Side)	Yr	VG	VG+	NM
CRAIG					
❑ 501	I Won't Cry/Come On Home	1961	7.50	15.00	30.00
—As Bunny "Mr. Emotions" Sigler					
DECCA					
❑ 31880	Everything's Gonna Be All Right/For Cryin' Out Loud	1965	6.25	12.50	25.00
❑ 31947	Will You Love Me Tomorrow/Comparatively Speaking	1966	3.00	6.00	12.00
❑ 32183	Will You Love Me Tomorrow/Let Them Talk	1967	2.50	5.00	10.00
GOLD MIND					
❑ 4008	Let Me Party with You (Part 1) (Party, Party, Party)/Let Me Party with You (Part 2) (Party, Party, Party)	1977	—	2.50	5.00
❑ 4010	I Got What You Need/It's Time to Twist	1978	—	2.50	5.00
❑ 4012	Only You/Good Good Feeling	1978	—	3.00	6.00
—A-side with Loleatta Holloway; B-side is Holloway solo					
❑ 4014	Don't Even Try (Give It Up)/I'm a Fool	1978	—	2.50	5.00
❑ 4018	By the Way You Dance (I Knew It Was You)/Glad to Be Your Lover	1979	—	2.50	5.00
❑ 4020	I'm Funking You Tonight with My Music/Glad to Be Your Lover	1979	—	2.50	5.00
NEPTUNE					
❑ 14	Where Do the Lonely Go/Great Big Liar	1969	2.00	4.00	8.00
❑ 15	We're Only Human/Sure Didn't Take Long	1969	2.00	4.00	8.00
—With Cindy Scott					
❑ 24	Conquer the World Together/We're Only Human	1970	2.00	4.00	8.00
—With Cindy Scott					
❑ 25	Don't Stop Doing What You're Doing/Where Do the Lonely Go	1970	2.00	4.00	8.00
PARKWAY					
❑ 123	Girl Don't Make Me Wait/Always in the Wrong Place (At the Wrong Time)	1966	2.50	5.00	10.00
❑ 153	Let the Good Times Roll & Feel So Good/There's No Love Left (In This Old Heart of Mine)	1967	3.00	6.00	12.00
❑ 6000	Lovey Dovey & You're So Fine/Sunny Sunday	1967	2.50	5.00	10.00
❑ 6001	Follow Your Heart/Can You Dig It	1967	2.50	5.00	10.00
PHILADELPHIA INT'L.					
❑ 3505	Everybody Needs Good Lovin' (Part 1)/Everybody Needs Good Lovin' (Part 2)	1971	—	3.00	6.00
❑ 3512	Conquer the World Together/We Gotta Good Thing Goin'	1971	—	3.00	6.00
—With Dee Dee Sharp					
❑ 3519	Heaven Knows I've Changed/Regina	1972	—	3.00	6.00
❑ 3523	Tossin' and Turnin'/Picture Us	1972	—	3.00	6.00
❑ 3532	Theme from "Five Fingers of Death"/Regina	1973	—	3.00	6.00
❑ 3536	That's How Long I'll Be Loving You/Heaven Knows I've Changed	1973	—	3.00	6.00
❑ 3545	Love Train (Part 1)/Love Train (Part 2)	1974	—	3.00	6.00
❑ 3554	Keep Smilin'/Somebody Free	1974	—	3.00	6.00
❑ 3560	Shake Your Booty/Your Love Is Good	1975	—	3.00	6.00
❑ 3575	Somebody Free/That's How Long I'll Be Loving You	1975	—	3.00	6.00
❑ 3582	Jingle Bells (Part 1)/Jingle Bells (Part 2)	1975	—	2.50	5.00
❑ 3597	My Music/Can't Believe That You Love Me	1976	—	3.00	6.00
❑ 3608	Somebody Loves You/Woman, Woman	1976	—	3.00	6.00
SALSOUL					
❑ 2114	How Can I Tell Her (It's Over)/Since the Day I First Saw You	1980	—	2.00	4.00
❑ 2125	Super Duper Duper Superman/Kool Aid	1980	—	2.00	4.00
V-TONE					
❑ 500	Family Dance/Hold On	196?	5.00	10.00	20.00

SIGNATURES, THE

Number	Title (A Side/B Side)	Yr	VG	VG+	NM
NORMAN					
❑ 210	Julie Is Her Name/Someone in Love	1957	75.00	150.00	300.00
WHIPPET					
❑ 210	Julie Is Her Name/Someone in Love	1957	12.50	25.00	50.00

SILHOUETTES, THE

Number	Title (A Side/B Side)	Yr	VG	VG+	NM
ACE					
❑ 552	I Sold My Heart to the Junkman/What Would You Do	1958	5.00	10.00	20.00
❑ 562	Evelyn/Never Will Part	1959	5.00	10.00	20.00
—As "Bill Horton and the Silhouettes"					
EMBER					
❑ 1029	Get a Job/I Am Lonely	1958	7.50	15.00	30.00
—Red label					
❑ 1029	Get a Job/I Am Lonely	1960	5.00	10.00	20.00
—Black label					
❑ 1032	Headin' for the Poorhouse/Miss Thing	1958	5.00	10.00	20.00
❑ 1037	Bing Bong/Voodoo Eyes	1958	5.00	10.00	20.00
GOODWAY					
❑ 101	Not Me Baby/Gaucho Serenade	1966	50.00	100.00	200.00
—As "The New Silhouettes"					
GRAND					
❑ 142	Wish I Could Be There/Move On Over	1956	50.00	100.00	200.00
IMPERIAL					
❑ 5899	The Push/Which Way Did She Go	1962	3.00	6.00	12.00
JUNIOR					
❑ 391	Get a Job/I Am Lonely	1957	200.00	400.00	800.00
—Brown label (first press)					
❑ 391	Get a Job/I Am Lonely	1957	150.00	300.00	600.00
—Blue label (second press)					
❑ 396	I Sold My Heart to the Junkman/What Would You Do	1958	25.00	50.00	100.00
❑ 400	Evelyn/Never Will Part	1959	50.00	100.00	200.00
❑ 993	Your Love/Rent Man	1963	7.50	15.00	30.00
UNITED ARTISTS					
❑ 147	I Sold My Heart to the Junkman/What Would You Do	1958	—	—	—
—Canceled					

SILKIE, THE

Number	Title (A Side/B Side)	Yr	VG	VG+	NM
FONTANA					
❑ 1525	You've Got to Hide Your Love Away/City Winds	1965	3.75	7.50	15.00
—Light blue label; A-side was produced by John Lennon and Paul McCartney, with the two and George Harrison playing along					
❑ 1525	You've Got to Hide Your Love Away/City Wind	1965	5.00	10.00	20.00
—Dark blue label					
❑ 1536	The Keys to My Soul/Leave Me to Cry	1965	2.50	5.00	10.00
❑ 1551	Born to Be With You/I'm So Sorry	1966	2.50	5.00	10.00

SILVA TONES, THE

Number	Title (A Side/B Side)	Yr	VG	VG+	NM
ARGO					
❑ 5281	Chi-Wa-Wa (That's All I Want from You)/Roses Are Blooming	1957	6.25	12.50	25.00
❑ 5281	That's All I Want from You/Roses Are Blooming	1957	7.50	15.00	30.00
MONARCH					
❑ 615	That's All I Want from You/Weepin' and a-Wailin'	1957	12.50	25.00	50.00
—Yellow label					
❑ 615	That's All I Want from You/Roses Are Blooming	1957	7.50	15.00	30.00
—Black label					

SILVER

With Brent Mydland, later of THE GRATEFUL DEAD.

Number	Title (A Side/B Side)	Yr	VG	VG+	NM
ARISTA					
❑ 0189	Wham Bam Shang-a-Lang/Right on Time	1976	—	2.50	5.00
—Originals on white labels with pale blue logo					
❑ 0189	Wham Bam Shang-a-Lang/Right on Time	1976	—	2.50	5.00
—Second pressings on pale blue labels with white logo					
❑ 0189	Wham Bam/Right on Time	1976	—	2.00	4.00
—Third pressings: Same label as second pressings with altered title					
❑ 0210	Memory/So Much for the Past	1976	—	2.00	4.00
❑ 0227	Musician (It's Not An Easy Life)/Goodbye, So Long	1977	—	2.00	4.00

SILVER DUST

Number	Title (A Side/B Side)	Yr	VG	VG+	NM
SUN					
❑ 1124	Father and Son/Castle in the Sun	1971	—	2.50	5.00

SILVER FLEET

A precursor to 10CC.

Number	Title (A Side/B Side)	Yr	VG	VG+	NM
UNI					
❑ 55271	Look Out World/C'mon Plane	1971	6.25	12.50	25.00

SILVERCHAIR

Number	Title (A Side/B Side)	Yr	VG	VG+	NM
EPIC					
❑ ES7 9355 [DJ]	Freak//Punk Song II/New Race	1997	—	2.00	4.00
❑ ES7 9355 [PS]	Freak//Punk Song II/New Race	1997	—	2.00	4.00

SIMMONS, GENE

Also see KISS.

Number	Title (A Side/B Side)	Yr	VG	VG+	NM
CASABLANCA					
❑ 951	Radioactive/See You in Your Dreams	1978	—	3.00	6.00

SIMMONS, PATRICK

Also see THE DOOBIE BROTHERS.

Number	Title (A Side/B Side)	Yr	VG	VG+	NM
ELEKTRA					
❑ 69817	Don't Make Me Do It/Sue Sad	1983	—	2.00	4.00
❑ 69839	So Wrong/If You Want a Little Love	1983	—	2.00	4.00

SIMMONS, "JUMPIN'" GENE

Also includes records as "Gene Simmons."

Number	Title (A Side/B Side)	Yr	VG	VG+	NM
AGP					
❑ 119	Back Home Again/Don't Worry About Me	1969	2.00	4.00	8.00
CHECKER					
❑ 948	Bad Boy Willie/Goin' Back to Memphis	1960	3.00	6.00	12.00
DELTUNE					
❑ 1201	Why Didn't I Think of That/Tennessee Party Time	1977	2.00	4.00	8.00
—As "Gene Simmons"					
EPIC					
❑ 10601	She's There When I Come Home/Magnolia Street	1970	—	3.00	6.00
HI					
❑ 2034	Teddy Bear/Your True Love	1961	2.50	5.00	10.00
❑ 2050	Caldonia/Be Her Number One	1962	2.50	5.00	10.00
❑ 2076	Haunted House/Hey, Hey Little Girl	1964	3.75	7.50	15.00
—As "Gene Simmons"					
❑ 2076	Haunted House/Hey, Hey Little Girl	1964	3.75	7.50	15.00
—As "Jumpin' Gene Simmons"					
❑ 2080	The Dodo/The Jump	1964	2.50	5.00	10.00
❑ 2086	Skinnie Minnie/I'm a Ramblin' Man	1965	2.50	5.00	10.00
❑ 2092	Mattie Rae/Folsom Prison Blues	1965	2.50	5.00	10.00
❑ 2102	The Batman/Bossy Boss	1966	3.75	7.50	15.00
❑ 2113	Go On Shoes/Keep That Meat in the Pan	1966	2.50	5.00	10.00
MALA					
❑ 12012	I'm Just a Loser/Lila	1968	2.50	5.00	10.00
SANDY					
❑ 1027	The Waiting Game/Shenandoah Waltz	1959	5.00	10.00	20.00
—As "Morris Gene Simmons"					
SUN					
❑ 299	Drinkin' Wine/I Done Told You	1958	37.50	75.00	150.00
—As "Gene Simmons"					

SIMON, CARLY

Also see THE SIMON SISTERS.

Number	Title (A Side/B Side)	Yr	VG	VG+	NM
ARISTA					
❑ 2083	Better Not Tell Her/Happy Birthday	1990	—	—	3.00
❑ 2164	Life Is Eternal/We Just Got Here	1990	—	—	3.00
❑ 9525	Coming Around Again/Itsy Bitsy Spider	1986	—	—	3.00
❑ 9525 [PS]	Coming Around Again/Itsy Bitsy Spider	1986	2.00	4.00	8.00
—With "Heartburn" movie scenes					
❑ 9525 [PS]	Coming Around Again/Itsy Bitsy Spider	1986	—	2.00	4.00
—Black and white photo of Carly Simon					
❑ 9525 [PS]	Coming Around Again/Itsy Bitsy Spider	1986	—	2.00	4.00
—Color photo of Carly Simon					
❑ 9587	Give Me All Night/Sleight of Hand	1987	—	—	3.00
❑ 9587 [PS]	Give Me All Night/Sleight of Hand	1987	—	—	3.00
❑ 9619	The Stuff That Dreams Are Made Of/As Time Goes By	1987	—	—	3.00
❑ 9619 [PS]	The Stuff That Dreams Are Made Of/As Time Goes By	1987	—	—	3.00
❑ 9653	All I Want Is You/On a Hot Summer Night	1987	—	—	3.00
❑ 9653 [PS]	All I Want Is You/On a Hot Summer Night	1987	—	—	3.00
❑ 9732 [DJ]	Do the Walls Come Down (same on both sides)	1988	—	2.50	5.00
—Not released as stock copy on this number					
❑ 9732 [PS]	Do the Walls Come Down (same on both sides)	1988	—	2.50	5.00
—Promo-only picture sleeve					
❑ 9754	You're So Vain/Do the Walls Come Down	1988	—	—	3.00
❑ 9754 [PS]	You're So Vain/Do the Walls Come Down	1988	—	—	3.00
❑ 9793	Let the River Run/The Turn of the Tide	1988	—	—	3.00
❑ 9793 [PS]	Let the River Run/The Turn of the Tide	1988	—	—	3.00
ELEKTRA					
❑ 45246	Attitude Dancing/Are You Ticklish	1975	—	2.50	5.00
❑ 45248	Slave/Look Me in the Eyes	1975	—	—	—
—Unreleased?					
❑ 45263	Waterfall/After the Storm	1975	—	2.50	5.00
❑ 45278	More and More/Love Out in the Street	1975	—	2.50	5.00
❑ 45325	It Keeps You Runnin'/Look Me in the Eyes	1976	—	2.00	4.00
❑ 45341	Half a Chance/Libby	1976	—	2.00	4.00
—Butterfly label					
❑ 45341	Half a Chance/Libby	1976	—	2.50	5.00
—Red label					
❑ 45413	Nobody Does It Better/After the Storm	1977	—	2.00	4.00
❑ 45477	You Belong to Me/In a Small Moment	1978	—	2.00	4.00
❑ 45477 [PS]	You Belong to Me/In a Small Moment	1978	—	3.00	6.00
❑ 45506	Devoted to You/Boys in the Trees	1978	—	2.00	4.00
—A-side with James Taylor					
❑ 45544	Tranquillo (Melt My Heart)/Back Down to Earth	1978	—	2.00	4.00
❑ 45724	That's the Way I've Always Heard It Should Be/Alone	1971	—	3.00	6.00
❑ 45748	Our First Day Together/Share the Land	1971	—	—	—
—Unreleased					
❑ 45759	Anticipation/The Garden	1971	—	3.00	6.00
❑ 45774	Legend in Your Own Time/Julie Through the Glass	1972	—	3.00	6.00
❑ 45796	The Girl You Think You Are/Share the Land	1972	—	3.00	6.00
❑ 45824	You're So Vain/His Friends Are More Than Fond of Robin	1972	—	3.00	6.00
❑ 45843	The Right Thing to Do/We Have No Secrets	1973	—	2.50	5.00
❑ 45880	Mockingbird/Grownup	1974	—	2.50	5.00
—A-side with James Taylor					
❑ 45887	Haven't Got Time for the Pain/Mind on My Man	1974	—	2.50	5.00
❑ 46051	Vengeance/Love You by Heart	1979	—	2.00	4.00
❑ 46051 [PS]	Vengeance/Love You by Heart	1979	—	2.50	5.00
❑ 46514	Spy/Pure Sin	1979	—	2.00	4.00
❑ 69953	Hidin' Away/Fight for It	1982	—	2.00	4.00
—With Jesse Colin Young					
❑ 69953 [PS]	Hidin' Away/Fight for It	1982	—	3.00	6.00
—With Jesse Colin Young					
EPIC					
❑ 05419	Tired of Being Blonde/Black Honeymoon	1985	—	—	3.00
❑ 05419 [PS]	Tired of Being Blonde/Black Honeymoon	1985	—	2.00	4.00
❑ 05596	My New Boyfriend/The Wives Are in Connecticut	1985	—	—	3.00
MIRAGE					
❑ 4051	Why/Why	1982	—	2.00	4.00
—B-side by Chic					
❑ 99963	Why/(Instrumental)	1982	—	2.00	4.00
PLANET					
❑ YB-13779	Someone Waits for You/(B-side unknown)	1984	—	2.00	4.00

WARNER BROS.

Number	Title (A Side/B Side)	Yr	VG	VG+	NM
❑ 29428	Hello Big Man/Dawn You Get to Me	1983	—	2.00	4.00
❑ 29484	You Know What to Do/Orpheus	1983	—	2.00	4.00
❑ 29484 [PS]	You Know What to Do/Orpheus	1983	—	2.50	5.00
❑ 49518	Jesse/Stardust	1980	—	2.00	4.00
❑ 49518 [PS]	Jesse/Stardust	1980	—	2.50	5.00
❑ 49630	Take Me As I Am/James	1980	—	2.00	4.00
❑ 49689	Come Upstairs/Them	1981	—	2.00	4.00
❑ 49880	From the Heart/Hurt	1981	—	2.00	4.00
❑ 50027	Body and Soul/Get Along Without You Very Well	1982	—	2.00	4.00

SIMON, JOE

COMPLEAT

Number	Title (A Side/B Side)	Yr	VG	VG+	NM
❑ 140	It Turns Me Inside Out/Morning, Noon and Night	1985	—	2.00	4.00
❑ 146	Mr. Right or Mr. Right Now/Let Me Have My Way with You	1985	—	2.00	4.00

DOT

Number	Title (A Side/B Side)	Yr	VG	VG+	NM
❑ 16570	Just Like Yesterday/Only a Dream	1964	2.00	4.00	8.00

HUSH

Number	Title (A Side/B Side)	Yr	VG	VG+	NM
❑ 103	It's a Miracle/Land of Love	1960	3.00	6.00	12.00
❑ 104	Call My Name/Everybody Needs Somebody	1961	3.00	6.00	12.00
❑ 106	Pledge of Love/It's All Over	1961	3.00	6.00	12.00
❑ 107	I See Your Face/Troubles	1961	3.00	6.00	12.00
❑ 108	Land of Love/I Keep Remembering	1962	3.00	6.00	12.00

POSSE

Number	Title (A Side/B Side)	Yr	VG	VG+	NM
❑ 5001	Baby, When Love Is In Your Heart (It's In Your Eyes)/Are We Breaking Up	1980	—	2.50	5.00
❑ 5005	Glad You Came My Way/I Don't Wanna Make Love	1980	—	2.50	5.00
❑ 5010	Are We Breaking Up/We're Together	1981	—	2.50	5.00
❑ 5014	Fallin' in Love with You/Magnolia	1981	—	2.50	5.00
❑ 5018	You Give Life to Me/(Instrumental)	1982	—	2.50	5.00
—With Clare Bathe					
❑ 5019	Go Sam/(Instrumental)	1982	—	2.50	5.00
❑ 5021	Get Down, Get Down "82"/It Be's That Way Sometime	1982	—	2.50	5.00
❑ 5038	Deeper Than Love/Step by Step	198?	—	2.50	5.00

SOUND STAGE 7

Number	Title (A Side/B Side)	Yr	VG	VG+	NM
❑ 1508	Misty Blue/That's the Way I Want Our Love	1972	—	2.50	5.00
❑ 1512	Who's Julie/The Girl's Alright with Me	1973	—	2.50	5.00
❑ 1514	Someone to Lean On/I Got a Whole Lotta Lovin'	1974	—	2.50	5.00
❑ 1521	Funny How Time Slips Away/Message from Maria	1976	—	2.50	5.00
❑ 2564	Teenager's Prayer/Long Hot Summer	1966	2.00	4.00	8.00
❑ 2569	Too Many Teardrops/What Makes a Man Fool Good	1966	2.00	4.00	8.00
❑ 2577	My Special Prayer/Travelin' Man	1966	2.00	4.00	8.00
❑ 2583	Put Your Trust in Me (Depend on Me)/Just a Dream	1967	2.00	4.00	8.00
❑ 2589	Nine Pound Steel/The Girl's Alright with Me	1967	2.00	4.00	8.00
❑ 2602	No Sad Songs/Come On and Get It	1967	2.00	4.00	8.00
❑ 2608	(You Keep Me) Hangin' On/Long Hot Summer	1968	2.00	4.00	8.00
❑ 2617	Message from Maria/I Worry About You	1968	2.00	4.00	8.00
❑ 2622	Looking Back/Standing in the Safety Zone	1968	2.00	4.00	8.00
❑ 2628	The Chokin' Kind/Come On and Get It	1969	—	3.00	6.00
❑ 2634	Baby, Don't Be Looking in My Mind/Don't Let Me Lose the Feeling	1969	—	3.00	6.00
❑ 2637	Oon-Guela (Part 1)/Oon-Guela (Part 2)	1969	2.00	4.00	8.00
❑ 2641	It's Hard to Get Along/San Francisco Is a Lonely Town	1969	—	3.00	6.00
❑ 2651	Moon Walk Part 1/Moon Walk Part 2	1969	—	3.00	6.00
❑ 2656	Farther On Down the Road/Wounded Man	1970	—	3.00	6.00
❑ 2664	Yours Love/I Got a Whole Lotta Lovin'	1970	—	3.00	6.00
❑ 2667	That's the Way I Want Our Love/When	1970	—	3.00	6.00

SPRING

Number	Title (A Side/B Side)	Yr	VG	VG+	NM
❑ 108	Your Time to Cry/I Love You More (Than Anything)	1970	—	2.50	5.00
❑ 113	Help Me Make It Through the Night/To Lay Down Beside You	1971	—	2.50	5.00
❑ 113 [PS]	Help Me Make It Through the Night/To Lay Down Beside You	1971	—	3.00	6.00
❑ 115	You're the One for Me/I Ain't Givin' Up	1971	—	2.50	5.00
❑ 118	Georgia Blues/All My Hard Times	1971	—	2.50	5.00
❑ 120	Drowning in the Sea of Love/Let Me Be the One	1971	—	2.50	5.00
❑ 124	Pool of Bad Luck/Glad to Be Your Lover	1972	—	2.50	5.00
❑ 128	Power of Love/The Mirror Don't Lie	1972	—	2.50	5.00
❑ 130	Trouble in My Home/I Found My Dad	1972	—	2.50	5.00
❑ 133	Step by Step/Talk Don't Bother Me	1973	—	2.50	5.00
❑ 138	Theme from Cleopatra Jones/Who Is That Lady	1973	—	2.50	5.00
❑ 138 [PS]	Theme from Cleopatra Jones/Who Is That Lady	1973	—	3.00	6.00
❑ 141	River/Love Never Hurt Nobody	1973	—	2.50	5.00
❑ 145	Carry Me/Do You Know What It's Like to Be Lonesome	1974	—	2.50	5.00
❑ 149	The Best Time of My Life/What We Gonna Do Now	1974	—	2.50	5.00
❑ 156	Get Down, Get Down (Get On the Floor)/In My Baby's Arms	1975	—	2.50	5.00
❑ 159	Music in My Bones/Fire Burning	1975	—	2.50	5.00
❑ 163	I Need You, You Need Me/I'll Take Care (Of You)	1975	—	2.50	5.00
❑ 166	Come Get to This/Let the Good Times Roll	1976	—	2.50	5.00
❑ 169	Easy to Love/Can't Stand the Pain	1976	—	2.50	5.00
❑ 172	You Didn't Have to Play No Games/What's Left to Do	1977	—	2.50	5.00
❑ 176	One Step at a Time/Track of Your Love	1977	—	2.50	5.00
❑ 178	For Your Love, Love, Love/I've Got a Jones on You Baby	1977	—	2.50	5.00
❑ 184	I.O.U./It Must Be Love	1978	—	2.50	5.00
❑ 190	Love Vibration/(Instrumental)	1978	—	2.50	5.00
❑ 194	Going Through These Changes/I Can't Stand a Liar	1979	—	2.50	5.00
❑ 3003	I Wanna Taste Your Love/Make Every Moment Count	1979	—	2.50	5.00
❑ 3006	Hooked on Disco Music/I Still Love You	1980	—	2.50	5.00

VEE JAY

Number	Title (A Side/B Side)	Yr	VG	VG+	NM
❑ 609	My Adorable One/Say (That My Love Is True)	1964	2.00	4.00	8.00
❑ 663	When You're Near/When I'm Gone	1965	2.00	4.00	8.00
❑ 694	Let's Do It Over/The Whoo Pee	1965	2.00	4.00	8.00

SIMON, PAUL

Includes records under various pseudonyms, such as "Paul Kane," "Jerry Landis" and "True Taylor." Also see SIMON AND GARFUNKEL; TICO AND THE TRIUMPHS; TOM AND JERRY (1).

AMY

Number	Title (A Side/B Side)	Yr	VG	VG+	NM
❑ 875	The Lone Teen Ranger/Lisa	1962	15.00	30.00	60.00
—As "Jerry Landis"					

BIG

Number	Title (A Side/B Side)	Yr	VG	VG+	NM
❑ 614	True or False/Teenage Fool	1958	25.00	50.00	100.00
—As "True Taylor"					

CANADIAN AMERICAN

Number	Title (A Side/B Side)	Yr	VG	VG+	NM
❑ 130	I'm Lonely/I Wish I Weren't in Love	1961	25.00	50.00	100.00
—As "Jerry Landis"; the rarest of his pre-Columbia solo singles					

COLUMBIA

Number	Title (A Side/B Side)	Yr	VG	VG+	NM
❑ 10197	Gone at Last/Take Me to the Mardi Gras	1975	—	2.50	5.00
—A-side with Phoebe Snow and the Jesse Dixon Singers					
❑ 10270	50 Ways to Leave Your Lover/Some Folks Lives Roll Easy	1975	—	2.50	5.00
❑ 10332	Still Crazy After All These Years/I Do It for Your Love (Live)	1976	—	2.50	5.00
❑ 10630	Slip Slidin' Away/Something So Right	1977	—	3.00	6.00
—First pressings claim the A-side came from the LP "Blatant Greatest Hits." The Oak Ridge Boys are not mentioned.					
❑ 10630	Slip Slidin' Away/Something So Right	1977	—	2.50	5.00
—Later pressings correct the LP title to "Greatest Hits, Etc." The Oak Ridge Boys are credited in the fine print.					
❑ 10711	Stranded in a Limousine/Have a Good Time	1978	—	3.00	6.00
❑ 45547	Mother and Child Reunion/Paranoia Blues	1972	—	2.50	5.00
—Orange label					
❑ 45547	Mother and Child Reunion/Paranoia Blues	1972	—	2.00	4.00
—Gray label					
❑ 45585	Me and Julio Down by the Schoolyard/Congratulations	1972	—	2.50	5.00
—Orange label					
❑ 45585	Me and Julio Down by the Schoolyard/Congratulations	1972	—	2.00	4.00
—Gray label					
❑ 45638	Duncan/Run That Body Down.	1972	—	2.50	5.00
❑ 45859	Kodachrome/Tenderness.	1973	—	3.00	6.00
—With no trademark disclaimer on label					
❑ 45859	Kodachrome/Tenderness.	1973	—	3.00	6.00
—With sticker on label: "Kodachrome is a registered trademark for color film."					
❑ 45859	Kodachrome/Tenderness.	1973	—	2.50	5.00
—With printing on label: "Kodachrome is a registered trademark for color film."					
❑ 45900	American Tune/One Man's Ceiling Is Another Man's Floor.	1973	—	2.50	5.00
❑ 45900 [PS]	American Tune/One Man's Ceiling Is Another Man's Floor.	1973	2.50	5.00	10.00
❑ 45907	Loves Me Like a Rock/Learn How to Fall.	1973	—	2.50	5.00
—With the Dixie Hummingbirds					
❑ 46038	The Sound of Silence/Mother and Child Reunion.	1974	2.00	4.00	8.00

MGM

Number	Title (A Side/B Side)	Yr	VG	VG+	NM
❑ 12822	Anna Belle/Loneliness	1959	12.50	25.00	50.00
—As "Jerry Landis"					

TRIBUTE

Number	Title (A Side/B Side)	Yr	VG	VG+	NM
❑ 128	Carlos Dominguez/He Was My Brother	1963	15.00	30.00	60.00
—As "Paul Kane"; authentic copies make no mention of Paul Simon on the label					

WARNER BROS.

Number	Title (A Side/B Side)	Yr	VG	VG+	NM
❑ 19464	Proof/The Coast	1991	—	—	3.00
❑ 27903	Graceland/Hearts and Bones	1988	—	2.50	5.00
❑ 28221	Under African Skies/I Know What I Know	1987	—	—	3.00
—A-side with Linda Ronstadt					
❑ 28221 [PS]	Under African Skies/I Know What I Know	1987	—	—	3.00
❑ 28389	Diamonds on the Soles of Her Shoes/All Around the World Or the Myth of Fingerprints	1987	—	—	3.00
❑ 28389 [PS]	Diamonds on the Soles of Her Shoes/All Around the World Or the Myth of Fingerprints	1987	—	—	3.00
❑ 28460	The Boy in the Bubble/Crazy Love, Part 2	1987	—	—	3.00
❑ 28460 [PS]	The Boy in the Bubble/Crazy Love, Part 2	1987	—	—	3.00
❑ 28522	Graceland/Hearts and Bones	1986	—	—	3.00
❑ 28522 [PS]	Graceland/Hearts and Bones	1986	—	—	3.00
❑ 28667	You Can Call Me Al/Gumboots	1986	—	—	3.00
❑ 28667 [PS]	You Can Call Me Al/Gumboots	1986	—	—	3.00
❑ 29333	Think Too Much/Song About the Moon	1984	—	2.00	4.00
❑ 29453	Allergies/Think Too Much (ii)	1983	—	2.00	4.00
❑ 29453 [PS]	Allergies/Think Too Much (II)	1983	—	2.00	4.00
❑ 49511	Late in the Evening/How the Heart Approaches What It Yearns	1980	—	2.00	4.00
❑ 49511 [PS]	Late in the Evening/How the Heart Approaches What It Yearns	1980	—	2.50	5.00
❑ 49601	One-Trick Pony/Long, Long Day	1980	—	2.00	4.00
❑ 49675	Oh, Marion/God Bless the Absentee	1981	—	2.00	4.00

WARWICK

Number	Title (A Side/B Side)	Yr	VG	VG+	NM
❑ 522	Swanee/Toot, Toot, Tootsie Goodbye.	1960	12.50	25.00	50.00
—As "Jerry Landis"					
❑ 552	Shy/Just a Boy.	1960	12.50	25.00	50.00
—As "Jerry Landis"					
❑ 588	I'd Like to Be/Just a Boy.	1960	12.50	25.00	50.00
—As "Jerry Landis"					
❑ 619	Play Me a Sad Song/It Means a Lot to Them.	1961	12.50	25.00	50.00
—As "Jerry Landis"					

SIMON AND GARFUNKEL

Also see ART GARFUNKEL; PAUL SIMON; TOM AND JERRY (1).

Number	Title (A Side/B Side)	Yr	VG	VG+	NM
ABC-PARAMOUNT					
❑ 10788	That's My Story/Tia-Juana Blues	1966	5.00	10.00	20.00
—Outtakes from Tom and Jerry days					
COLUMBIA					
❑ AS 43 [DJ]	America/Keep the Customer Satisfied	1972	3.00	6.00	12.00
❑ 10230	My Little Town//Art Garfunkel: Rag Doll/Paul Simon: You're Kind	1975	—	2.50	5.00
❑ 10230 [PS]	My Little Town//Art Garfunkel: Rag Doll/Paul Simon: You're Kind	1975	—	2.50	5.00
❑ 43396	The Sounds of Silence/We've Got a Groovey Thing Goin'	1965	2.50	5.00	10.00
❑ 43396 [DJ]	The Sounds of Silence (same on both sides)	1965	12.50	25.00	50.00
—Red vinyl promo					
❑ 43511	Homeward Bound/Leaves That Are Green	1966	2.50	5.00	10.00
❑ 43511 [DJ]	Homeward Bound (same on both sides)	1966	12.50	25.00	50.00
—Red vinyl promo					
❑ 43617	I Am a Rock/Flowers Never Bend with the Rainfall	1966	2.50	5.00	10.00
❑ 43617 [DJ]	I Am a Rock (same on both sides)	1966	12.50	25.00	50.00
—Red vinyl promo					
❑ 43728	The Dangling Conversation/The Big Bright Green Pleasure Machine	1966	2.50	5.00	10.00
❑ 43728 [DJ]	The Dangling Conversation (same on both sides)	1966	12.50	25.00	50.00
—Red vinyl promo					
❑ 43728 [PS]	The Dangling Conversation/The Big Bright Green Pleasure Machine	1966	5.00	10.00	20.00
❑ 43873	A Hazy Shade of Winter/For Emily, Wherever I May Find Her	1966	2.50	5.00	10.00
❑ 44046	At the Zoo/The 59th Street Bridge Song (Feelin' Groovy)	1967	2.50	5.00	10.00
❑ 44046 [PS]	At the Zoo/The 59th Street Bridge Song (Feelin' Groovy)	1967	10.00	20.00	40.00
❑ 44232	Fakin' It/You Don't Know Where Your Interest Lies	1967	2.50	5.00	10.00
❑ 44465	Scarborough Fair (/Canticle)/April Come She Will	1968	2.50	5.00	10.00
❑ 44511	Mrs. Robinson/Old Friends-Bookends	1968	2.50	5.00	10.00
—Label says "From the Motion Picture 'The Graduate'"					
❑ 44511	Mrs. Robinson/Old Friends-Bookends	1968	2.00	4.00	8.00
—Label says "From the Columbia Lp BOOKENDS," etc. with no reference to "The Graduate"					
❑ 44785	The Boxer/Baby Driver	1969	—	3.00	6.00
—B-side mix (mono) is different than stereo LP version, especially near the end of the song					
❑ 44785 [PS]	The Boxer/Baby Driver	1969	2.00	4.00	8.00
❑ 45079	Bridge Over Troubled Water/Keep the Customer Satisfied	1970	—	3.00	6.00
❑ 45079 [PS]	Bridge Over Troubled Water/Keep the Customer Satisfied	1970	2.00	4.00	8.00
❑ 45133	Cecilia/The Only Living Boy in New York	1970	—	3.00	6.00
—Red label, "Columbia" in black at top					
❑ 45133	Cecilia/The Only Living Boy in New York	1970	2.50	5.00	10.00
—Red label, continuous "Columbia Records" in white along outer edge					
❑ 45133 [PS]	Cecilia/The Only Living Boy in New York	1970	2.00	4.00	8.00
❑ 45237	El Condor Pasa/Why Don't You Write Me	1970	—	3.00	6.00
❑ 45663	America/For Emily, Whenever I May Find Her	1972	—	3.00	6.00
❑ JZSP 116469 [DJ]	7 O'Clock News-Silent Night (same on both sides)	1966	6.25	12.50	25.00
—Promo-only Christmas release for radio stations					
WARNER BROS.					
❑ 50053	Wake Up Little Susie/Me and Julio Down by the Schoolyard	1982	—	2.00	4.00

SIMON SISTERS, THE

CARLY SIMON and her sister Lucy.

Number	Title (A Side/B Side)	Yr	VG	VG+	NM
CHILDREN'S RECORDS OF AMERICA					
❑ 100	My Love Is Like a Red, Red Rose/The Lamb	1968	5.00	10.00	20.00
COLUMBIA					
❑ 02675	Maryanne/(B-side unknown)	1982	—	2.00	4.00
—As "Carly and Lucy Simon"					
❑ 45840	Red, Red Rose/Lobster Quadrille	1973	—	3.00	6.00
—As "Carly and Lucy Simon"					
KAPP					
❑ 586	Winkin', Blinkin' and Nod/So Glad I'm Here	1964	3.75	7.50	15.00
❑ 624	Cuddlebug/No One to Talk My Troubles To	1964	3.75	7.50	15.00

SIMPSON, VALERIE

Number	Title (A Side/B Side)	Yr	VG	VG+	NM
TAMLA					
❑ 54204	Back to Nowhere/Can't It Wait Until Tomorrow	1971	—	2.50	5.00
❑ 54224	Silly Wasn't I/I Believe I'm Gonna Take This Ride	1972	—	2.50	5.00
❑ 54231	Genius/One More Baby Child Born	1973	—	2.50	5.00

SIMS, FRANKIE LEE

Number	Title (A Side/B Side)	Yr	VG	VG+	NM
ACE					
❑ 524	What Will Lucy Do/Misery Blues	1957	10.00	20.00	40.00
❑ 527	Hey Little Girl/Walking with Frankie	1957	10.00	20.00	40.00
❑ 539	I Warned You Baby/My Talk Didn't Do No Good	1957	10.00	20.00	40.00
SPECIALTY					
❑ 459	Lucky Man Blues/Don't Take It Out on Me	1953	12.50	25.00	50.00
❑ 478	I'm Long, Long Gone/Yeh Baby	1953	10.00	20.00	40.00
❑ 487	I'll Get Along Somehow/Rhumba My Boogie	1954	10.00	20.00	40.00
VIN					
❑ 1006	She Likes to Boogie Low/Well Goodbye Baby	1958	7.50	15.00	30.00

SIMS TWINS, THE

Number	Title (A Side/B Side)	Yr	VG	VG+	NM
KENT					
❑ 4556	Bring It On Home Where You Belong/Under the Double Eagle	1971	—	3.00	6.00
PARKWAY					
❑ 6002	Together/Baby It's Real	1968	2.50	5.00	10.00
SAR					
❑ 117	Soothe Me/I'll Never Come Running Back to You	1961	3.75	7.50	15.00
❑ 125	The Smile/Right to Love	1962	3.00	6.00	12.00
❑ 130	Double Portion of Love/You're Pickin' in the Right Cotton Patch	1962	3.00	6.00	12.00
❑ 136	I Gopher You/Good Good Lovin'	1963	3.00	6.00	12.00
❑ 138	That's Where It's At/Movin' and a Groovin'	1963	3.00	6.00	12.00
SPECIALTY					
❑ 731	Make It On Up/Something Hanging on Your Mind	197?	—	3.00	6.00

SINATRA, FRANK

Number	Title (A Side/B Side)	Yr	VG	VG+	NM
CAPITOL					
❑ X1-1069 [S]	titles unknown	196?	5.00	10.00	20.00
—Stereo jukebox single, 33 1/3 rpm, small hole					
❑ X2-1069 [S]	titles unknown	196?	5.00	10.00	20.00
—Stereo jukebox single, 33 1/3 rpm, small hole					
❑ X3-1069 [S]	Day In — Day Out/Saturday Night	196?	5.00	10.00	20.00
—Stereo jukebox single, 33 1/3 rpm, small hole					
❑ X1-1417 [S]	titles unknown	1960	5.00	10.00	20.00
—Stereo jukebox single, 33 1/3 rpm, small hole					
❑ X2-1417 [S]	Fools Rush In/I've Got a Crush on You	1960	5.00	10.00	20.00
—Stereo jukebox single, 33 1/3 rpm, small hole					
❑ X1-1491 [S]	When You're Smiling/It All Depends on You	1961	5.00	10.00	20.00
—Stereo jukebox single, 33 1/3 rpm, small hole					
❑ X2-1491 [S]	S'posin'/Blue Moon	1961	5.00	10.00	20.00
—Stereo jukebox single, 33 1/3 rpm, small hole					
❑ X3-1491 [S]	titles unknown	1961	5.00	10.00	20.00
—Stereo jukebox single, 33 1/3 rpm, small hole					
❑ X4-1491 [S]	I Concentrate on You/Should I	1961	5.00	10.00	20.00
—Stereo jukebox single, 33 1/3 rpm, small hole					
❑ X5-1491 [S]	September in the Rain/You Do Something to Me	1961	5.00	10.00	20.00
—Stereo jukebox single, 33 1/3 rpm, small hole					
❑ X1-1594 [S]	titles unknown	1961	5.00	10.00	20.00
—Stereo jukebox single, 33 1/3 rpm, small hole					
❑ X2-1594 [S]	Five Minutes More/Almost Like Being in Love	1961	5.00	10.00	20.00
—Stereo jukebox single, 33 1/3 rpm, small hole					
❑ X3-1594 [S]	Yes Indeed/American Beauty Rose	1961	5.00	10.00	20.00
—Stereo jukebox single, 33 1/3 rpm, small hole					
❑ F1699	Young at Heart/I've Got the World on a String	1955	25.00	50.00	100.00
—Early reissue					
❑ PRO 1707/8 [DJ]	Mistletoe and Holly (with spoken intro)/Mistletoe and Holly	1960	25.00	50.00	100.00
—Christmas Seals record for 1960, with Sinatra introducing the song					
❑ XE-1729 [S]	They Came to Cordura/I Gotta Right to Sing the Blues	1962	5.00	10.00	20.00
—Stereo jukebox single, 33 1/3 rpm, small hole					
❑ F2450	I'm Walking Behind You/Lean Baby	1953	6.25	12.50	25.00
—Add 50% for intact center					
❑ F2505	My One and Only Love/I've Got the World on a String	1953	5.00	10.00	20.00
—Add 50% for intact center					
❑ F2560	Anytime, Anywhere/From Here to Eternity	1953	5.00	10.00	20.00
❑ F2638	I Love You/South of the Border	1953	5.00	10.00	20.00
❑ F2703	Young at Heart/Take a Chance	1953	5.00	10.00	20.00
❑ F2787	Don't Worry 'Bout Me/I Could Have Told You	1954	5.00	10.00	20.00
❑ F2816	Three Coins in the Fountain/Rain	1954	5.00	10.00	20.00
❑ F2864	The Girl That Got Away/Half as Lovely	1954	5.00	10.00	20.00
❑ F2922	It Worries Me/When I Stop Loving You	1954	5.00	10.00	20.00
❑ 2954	White Christmas/The Christmas Waltz	1962	2.50	5.00	10.00
—Reissue without the "F" prefix on orange and yellow swirl label					
❑ F2954	White Christmas/The Christmas Waltz	1954	5.00	10.00	20.00
❑ F2993	You My Love/Someone to Watch Over Me	1954	5.00	10.00	20.00
❑ F3018	Melody of Love/I'm Gonna Live Till I Die	1954	5.00	10.00	20.00
❑ F3050	Why Should I Cry Over You?/Don't Change Your Mind About Me	1954	5.00	10.00	20.00
❑ F3084	Two Hearts, Two Kisses/From the Bottom to the Top	1955	3.75	7.50	15.00
❑ F3102	Learnin' the Blues/If I Had Three Wishes	1955	3.75	7.50	15.00
❑ F3130	Not as a Stranger/How Could You Do a Thing Like That to Me?	1955	3.75	7.50	15.00
❑ F3218	Same Old Saturday Night/Fairy Tale	1955	3.75	7.50	15.00
❑ F3260	Love and Marriage/The Impatient Years	1955	5.00	10.00	20.00
❑ F3290	(Love Is) The Tender Trap/Weep They Will	1955	3.75	7.50	15.00
❑ F3350	Flowers Mean Forgiveness/You'll Get Yours	1956	3.75	7.50	15.00
❑ F3423	(How Little It Maters) How Little We Know/Five Hundred Guys	1956	3.75	7.50	15.00
❑ F3469	You're Sensational/Johnny Concho Theme (Wait for Me)	1956	3.75	7.50	15.00
❑ F3507	Well, Did You Evah?/True Love	1956	3.75	7.50	15.00
—A-side by Bing Crosby and Frank Sinatra; B-side by Bing Crosby and Grace Kelly					
❑ F3508	Who Wants to Be a Millionaire/Mind If I Make Love to You?	1956	3.75	7.50	15.00
❑ F3552	Jealous Lover/You Forgot All the Words	1956	6.25	12.50	25.00
—Original pressings contain this title					
❑ F3552	Hey! Jealous Lover/You Forgot All the Words	1956	3.75	7.50	15.00
❑ F3608	Can I Steal a Little Love/Your Love for Me	1956	3.75	7.50	15.00
❑ F3703	Crazy Love/So Long, My Love	1957	3.00	6.00	12.00
❑ F3744	You're Cheatin' Yourself (If You're Cheatin' On Me)/Something Wonderful Happens in Summer	1957	3.00	6.00	12.00
❑ F3793	All the Way/Chicago	1957	3.00	6.00	12.00
❑ F3859	Witchcraft/Tell Her You Love Her	1957	3.00	6.00	12.00
❑ F3900	Mistletoe and Holly/The Christmas Waltz	1957	3.75	7.50	15.00
—"The Christmas Waltz" here is a different version than that on Capitol 2954.					
❑ F3952	How Are Ya' Fixed for Love?/Nothin' in Common	1958	3.00	6.00	12.00
—By Frank Sinatra and Keely Smith					
❑ F4003	Same Old Song and Dance/Monique (Song from Kings Go Forth)	1958	3.00	6.00	12.00
❑ F4070	Mr. Success/Sleep Warm	1958	3.00	6.00	12.00
❑ F4103	To Love and Be Loved/No One Ever Tells You	1958	3.00	6.00	12.00
❑ F4103 [PS]	To Love and Be Loved/No One Ever Tells You	1958	25.00	50.00	100.00
—Promo-only sleeve					
❑ F4155	French Foreign Legion/Time After Time	1959	3.00	6.00	12.00
❑ F4214	High Hopes/All My Tomorrows	1959	3.75	7.50	15.00
❑ F4214 [PS]	High Hopes/All My Tomorrows	1959	50.00	100.00	200.00
❑ F4284	Talk to Me/They Came to Cordura	1959	3.00	6.00	12.00

Number	Title (A Side/B Side)	Yr	VG	VG+	NM
❑ 4376	River, Stay 'Way from My Door/It's Over, It's Over, It's Over	1960	3.00	6.00	12.00
❑ 4408	Nice 'N' Easy/This Was My Love	1960	3.00	6.00	12.00
❑ 4466	Ol' MacDonald/You'll Always Be the One I Love	1960	3.00	6.00	12.00
❑ 4546	My Blue Heaven/Sentimental Baby	1960	3.00	6.00	12.00
❑ 4615	American Beauty Rose/Sentimental Journey	1961	3.00	6.00	12.00
❑ 4677	The Moon Was Yellow/I've Heard That Song Before	1962	3.00	6.00	12.00
❑ 4729	Five Minutes More/I'll Remember April	1962	3.00	6.00	12.00
❑ 4815	I Love Paris/Hidden Persuasion	1962	3.00	6.00	12.00
❑ 6019	Young at Heart/Learnin' the Blues	196?	—	3.00	6.00
—Starline reissue label					
❑ 6027	All the Way/High Hopes	196?	—	3.00	6.00
—Starline reissue label					
❑ 6078	Witchcraft/Chicago	1966	—	3.00	6.00
—Starline reissue label					
❑ 6193	One for My Baby/I've Got You Under My Skin	197?	—	3.00	6.00
❑ 6195	In the Wee Small Hours of the Morning/Night and Day	197?	—	3.00	6.00
❑ S7-17704	I've Got You Under My Skin/Come Rain or Come Shine	1994	—	—	—
—A-side with Bono, B-side with Gloria Estefan; canceled					
❑ S7-18204	Jingle Bells/I'll Be Home for Christmas	1994	—	2.50	5.00
—Red vinyl					
❑ 58741	Mistletoe and Holly/The Christmas Waltz	1998	—	—	3.00
COLUMBIA					
❑ 1-106	Sunflower/Once in Love with Amy	1948	15.00	30.00	60.00
—All records with a "1-" prefix are Microgroove 33 1/3 rpm 7-inch singles					
❑ 1-112	Why Can't You Behave/No Orchids for My Lady	1948	15.00	30.00	60.00
❑ B-112 [(4)]	The Voice of Frank Sinatra	1950	37.50	75.00	150.00
—Includes records 36918, 36919, 36920 and 36921 plus box					
❑ 1-130	Comme Ci, Comme Ca/While the Angelus Was Ringing	1948	15.00	30.00	60.00
❑ 1-144	When Is Sometime/If You Stub Your Toe on the Moon	1949	15.00	30.00	60.00
❑ 1-154	Where Is the One/Bop Goes My Heart	1949	15.00	30.00	60.00
❑ B-167 [(4)]	Christmas Songs by Sinatra	1950	37.50	75.00	150.00
—Includes records 38256, 38257, 38258 and 38259 plus box					
❑ 1-174	Bali Ha'i/Some Enchanted Evening	1949	15.00	30.00	60.00
❑ 1-191	The Right Girl for Me/Night After Night	1949	15.00	30.00	60.00
❑ B-197 [(4)]	Dedicated to You	1950	37.50	75.00	150.00
—Includes records 38683, 38684, 38685 and 38686 plus box					
❑ B-218 [(4)]	Sing and Dance with Frank Sinatra	1950	37.50	75.00	150.00
—Includes records 38996, 38997, 38998 and 38999 plus box					
❑ 1-222	It Happens Every Spring/The Hucklebuck	1949	15.00	30.00	60.00
❑ 1-260	Let's Take an Old-Fashioned Walk/Just One Way to Say I Love You	1949	15.00	30.00	60.00
—With Doris Day					
❑ 1-307	I Only Have Eyes for You/It All Depends on You	1949	15.00	30.00	60.00
❑ 1-315	Don't Cry Joe/The Wedding of Lili Marlene	1949	15.00	30.00	60.00
❑ 1-316	Just a Kiss Apart/Bye Bye Baby	1949	15.00	30.00	60.00
❑ 1-326	If I Ever Love Again/Every Man Should Marry	1949	15.00	30.00	60.00
❑ 1-372	Could'ja/That Lucky Old Sun	1949	15.00	30.00	60.00
❑ 1-380	On the Island of Stromboli/Mad About You	1949	15.00	30.00	60.00
❑ 1-427	The Old Master Painter/Lost in the Stars	1949	15.00	30.00	60.00
❑ 1-440	Sorry/Why Remind Me	1949	15.00	30.00	60.00
❑ 1-491	Sunshine Cake/We've Got a Sure Thing	1949	15.00	30.00	60.00
❑ 1-496	Chattanoogie Shoe Shine Boy/God's Country	1950	15.00	30.00	60.00
❑ 1-508	You'll Never Walk Alone/Begin the Beguine	1950	15.00	30.00	60.00
❑ 1-511	Among My Souvenirs/September Song	1950	15.00	30.00	60.00
❑ 1-611	Kisses and Tears/When the Sun Goes Down	1950	15.00	30.00	60.00
❑ 1-624	American Beauty Rose/Just An Old Stone House	1950	15.00	30.00	60.00
❑ 1-650	Poinciana/There's No Business Like Show Business	1950	15.00	30.00	60.00
❑ 1-669	Peachtree Street/This Is the Night	1950	15.00	30.00	60.00
❑ 1-718	Goodnight Irene/My Blue Heaven	1950	15.00	30.00	60.00
❑ 6-718	Goodnight Irene/My Blue Heaven	1950	7.50	15.00	30.00
❑ 1-780	Life Is So Peculiar/Dear Little Boy of Mine	1950	15.00	30.00	60.00
❑ 1-845	One Finger Melody/Accidents Will Happen	1950	15.00	30.00	60.00
❑ 1-888	Nevertheless/I Guess I'll Have to Dream the Rest	1950	15.00	30.00	60.00
❑ 6-888	Nevertheless/I Guess I'll Have to Dream the Rest	1950	7.50	15.00	30.00
❑ 1-924	Remember Me in Your Dreams/Let It Snow, Let It Snow, Let It Snow	1950	15.00	30.00	60.00
❑ 6-924	Remember Me in Your Dreams/Let It Snow, Let It Snow, Let It Snow	1950	7.50	15.00	30.00
❑ 1-936	I Am Loved/You Don't Remind Me	1950	15.00	30.00	60.00
❑ 6-936	I Am Loved/You Don't Remind Me	1950	7.50	15.00	30.00
❑ 13-33011	Nancy/Ol' Man River	1975	—	3.00	6.00
—Hall of Fame series; new prefix					
❑ 3-33011	Nancy/Ol' Man River	1961	12.50	25.00	50.00
—Hall of Fame series; Compact Single 33					
❑ 4-33011	Nancy/Ol' Man River	1960	2.50	5.00	10.00
❑ 33306	I've Got a Crush on You/The Birth of the Blues	1977	—	3.00	6.00
—Hall of Fame series					
❑ 33319	Among My Souvenirs/September Song	1977	—	3.00	6.00
—Hall of Fame series					
❑ 36814	If You Are But a Dream/Put Your Dreams Away	1950	5.00	10.00	20.00
—Most Columbia 45s from 36000-39000 are reissues of titles that first appeared on 78s					
❑ 36825	You'll Never Walk Alone/If I Loved You	1950	5.00	10.00	20.00
❑ 36918	You Go to My Head/I Don't Know Why	1950	5.00	10.00	20.00
❑ 36919	These Foolish Things/A Ghost of a Chance	1950	5.00	10.00	20.00
❑ 36920	Why Shouldn't I?/Try a Little Tenderness	1950	5.00	10.00	20.00
❑ 36921	Paradise/Someone to Watch Over Me	1950	5.00	10.00	20.00
—The above four comprise the box set The Voice of Frank Sinatra, B-112					
❑ 37161	Among My Souvenirs/September Song	1950	5.00	10.00	20.00
❑ 37257	That Old Black Magic/How Deep Is the Ocean?	1950	5.00	10.00	20.00
❑ 37259	She's Funny That Way/Embraceable You	1950	5.00	10.00	20.00
❑ 38151	I've Got a Crush on You/Ever Homeward	1950	5.00	10.00	20.00
❑ 38163	All of Me/I Went Down to Virginia	1950	5.00	10.00	20.00
❑ 38256	Silent Night/Adeste Fideles	1950	5.00	10.00	20.00
❑ 38257	Jingle Bells/White Christmas	1950	5.00	10.00	20.00

Number	Title (A Side/B Side)	Yr	VG	VG+	NM
❑ 38258	O Little Town of Bethlehem/It Came Upon a Midnight Clear	1950	5.00	10.00	20.00
❑ 38259	Have Yourself a Merry Little Christmas/Santa Claus Is Comin' to Town	1950	5.00	10.00	20.00
—The above four comprise the box set Christmas Songs by Sinatra, B-167					
❑ 38446	Bali Ha'i/Some Enchanted Evening	1950	5.00	10.00	20.00
❑ 38683	The Moon Was Yellow/The Music Stopped	1950	5.00	10.00	20.00
❑ 38684	Strange Music/I Love You	1950	5.00	10.00	20.00
❑ 38685	Where or When/None But the Lonely Heart	1950	5.00	10.00	20.00
❑ 38686	Always/Why Was I Born?	1950	5.00	10.00	20.00
—The above four comprise the box set Dedicated to You, B-197					
❑ 38829	Poinciana/There's No Business Like Show Business	1950	5.00	10.00	20.00
❑ 38892	Goodnight Irene/My Blue Heaven	1950	3.75	7.50	15.00
—Reissue of Columbia 6-718					
❑ 38996	Lover/When You're Smiling	1950	5.00	10.00	20.00
❑ 38997	The Continental/It's Only a Paper Moon	1950	5.00	10.00	20.00
❑ 38998	Should I?/My Blue Heaven	1950	5.00	10.00	20.00
❑ 38999	It All Depends on You/You Do Something to Me	1950	5.00	10.00	20.00
—The above four comprise the box set Sing and Dance with Frank Sinatra, B-218					
❑ 39044	Nevertheless/I Guess I'll Have to Dream the Rest	1950	3.75	7.50	15.00
—Reissue of Columbia 6-888					
❑ 39069	Remember Me in Your Dreams/Let It Snow, Let It Snow, Let It Snow	1950	3.75	7.50	15.00
—Reissue of Columbia 6-924					
❑ 39079	I Am Loved/You Don't Remind Me	1950	3.75	7.50	15.00
—Reissue of Columbia 6-936					
❑ 39118	Take My Love/Come Back to Sorrento	1950	3.75	7.50	15.00
❑ 3-39118	Take My Love/Come Back to Sorrento	1950	50.00	100.00	150.00
—Microgroove 33 1/3 rpm, 7-inch single					
❑ 39141	Love Means Love/Cherry Pies Ought to Be You	1951	6.25	12.50	25.00
❑ 3-39141	Love Means Love/Cherry Pies Ought to Be You	1951	200.00	400.00	600.00
—Microgroove 33 1/3 rpm, 7-inch single					
❑ 39213	Faithful/You're the One	1951	5.00	10.00	20.00
❑ 3-39213	Faithful/You're the One	1951	50.00	100.00	150.00
—Microgroove 33 1/3 rpm, 7-inch single					
❑ 39294	Hello, Young Lovers/We Kissed in a Shadow	1951	3.75	7.50	15.00
❑ 39346	I Whistle a Happy Tune/Love Me	1951	3.75	7.50	15.00
❑ 39425	Mama Will Bark/I'm a Fool to Want You	1951	10.00	20.00	40.00
—"Frank Sinatra & Dagmar"; the record Ol' Blue Eyes called his worst					
❑ 39493	I Fall in Love with You Everyday/It's a Long Way from Your House	1951	5.00	10.00	20.00
❑ 39498	It Never Entered My Mind/Try a Little Tenderness	1951	3.75	7.50	15.00
❑ 39527	Castle Rock/Deep Night	1951	5.00	10.00	20.00
❑ 39592	April in Paris/London by Night	1951	3.75	7.50	15.00
❑ 39652	I Hear a Rhapsody/I Could Write a Book	1952	3.75	7.50	15.00
❑ 39687	Feet of Clay/Don't Ever Be Afraid to Go Home	1952	5.00	10.00	20.00
❑ 39726	My Girl/Walkin' in the Sunshine	1952	5.00	10.00	20.00
❑ 39787	Luna Rosa/Tennessee Newsboy	1952	5.00	10.00	20.00
❑ 39819	Azure-Te/Bim Bam Baby	1952	3.75	7.50	15.00
❑ 39882	The Birth of the Blues/Why Try to Change Me Now?	1952	3.75	7.50	15.00
❑ 40229	I'm Glad There Is You/You Can Take My Word For It Baby	1954	5.00	10.00	20.00
❑ 40522	Dream/American Beauty Rose	1955	3.75	7.50	15.00
❑ 40565	Sheila/Day by Day	1955	7.50	15.00	30.00
❑ 41133	I'm a Fool to Want You/If I Forget You	1958	3.75	7.50	15.00
❑ 50003	Among My Souvenirs/September Song	1954	2.50	5.00	10.00
—Hall of Fame series					
❑ 50028	I've Got a Crush on You/The Birth of the Blues	1954	2.50	5.00	10.00
—Hall of Fame series					
❑ 50053	Nancy/The Girl That I Marry	1955	2.50	5.00	10.00
—Hall of Fame series					
❑ 50066	You'll Never Walk Alone/If I Loved You	1955	2.50	5.00	10.00
—Hall of Fame series					
❑ 50069	Saturday Night/Five Minutes More	1955	2.50	5.00	10.00
—Hall of Fame series					
❑ 50079	Silent Night/Adeste Fideles	1955	2.50	5.00	10.00
—Hall of Fame series					
❑ JZSP 116427/8 [DJ]	White Christmas/Have Yourself A Merry Little Christmas	1966	12.50	25.00	50.00
ISLAND/CAPITOL					
❑ 858076-7	I've Got You Under My Skin/Stay (Faraway, So Close!)	1994	—	2.00	4.00
—A-side: Frank Sinatra and Bono; B-side: U2					
❑ 858076-7 [PS]	I've Got You Under My Skin/Stay (Faraway, So Close!)	1994	—	2.00	4.00
—A-side: Frank Sinatra and Bono; B-side: U2					
MCA					
❑ 55127	Fly Me to the Moon/Check Yes or No	1995	—	2.00	4.00
—A-side with George Strait; B-side is George Strait solo					
QWEST					
❑ 28844	The Best of Everything/Teach Me Tonight	1985	—	2.00	4.00
❑ 29139	Mack the Knife/It's All Right with Me	1984	—	2.50	5.00
❑ 29223	L.A. Is My Lady/Until the Real Thing Comes Along	1984	—	2.50	5.00
❑ 29223 [PS]	L.A. Is My Lady/Until the Real Thing Comes Along	1984	3.75	7.50	15.00
RCA VICTOR					
❑ DTAO-3001	Street of Dreams/Whispering	1973	3.00	6.00	12.00
❑ DTBO-3012	The One I Love/This Love of Mine	1973	3.00	6.00	12.00
❑ 27-0012	Night and Day/The Lamplighter's Serenade	1948	3.75	7.50	15.00
—All RCA and 45s are reissues of material first issued on 78s. Part of WPT-5					
❑ 27-0076	Stardust/(B-side unknown)	1949	3.75	7.50	15.00
—From WDT 15					
❑ 27-0077	I'll Never Smile Again/(B-side unknown)	1949	3.75	7.50	15.00
—From WDT 15					
❑ 27-0095	Somewhere A Voice Is Calling/(B-side unknown)	1949	3.75	7.50	15.00
—From WDT 20					
❑ 27-0151	Daybreak/There Are Such Things	1948	3.75	7.50	15.00
❑ 447-0116	I'll Never Smile Again/I'll Be Seeing You	1950	3.00	6.00	12.00
❑ 447-0123	Stardust/There Are Such Things	1950	3.00	6.00	12.00
❑ 447-0408	Night and Day/The Lamplighter's Serenade	1952	3.00	6.00	12.00

Number	Title (A Side/B Side)	Yr	VG	VG+	NM
❑ 447-0445	Street of Dreams/East of the Sun	1952	3.00	6.00	12.00
❑ 447-0928	Night and Day/The Night We Called It a Day	1972	—	3.00	6.00
❑ 447-0929	The Song Is You/The Lamplighter's Serenade	1972	—	3.00	6.00
REPRISE					
❑ 0053	I'll Be Seeing You/Without a Song	1962	50.00	100.00	200.00
—Released in Great Britain as 20,053; pressed in the United States later					
❑ GRE 0113	Bad, Bad Leroy Brown/Let Me Try Again	1975	5.00	10.00	20.00
—"Back to Back Hits" series					
❑ GRE 0122	Theme from New York, New York/You and Me (We Wanted It All)	1981	—	2.00	4.00
—"Back to Back Hits" series					
❑ S 168 [S]	Moon River/Days of Wine and Roses	1964	5.00	10.00	20.00
❑ S 169 [S]	Three Coins in the Fountain/The Way You Look Tonight	1964	5.00	10.00	20.00
❑ S 170 [S]	Secret Love/In the Cool, Cool, Cool of the Evening	1964	5.00	10.00	20.00
❑ S 171 [S]	It Might As Well Be Spring/Swinging on a Star	1964	5.00	10.00	20.00
❑ S 172 [S]	All the Way/The Continental	1964	5.00	10.00	20.00
—The above five are 33 1/3 rpm, small hole jukebox singles					
❑ 243	Have Yourself a Merry Little Christmas/How Shall I Send Thee?	1963	5.00	10.00	20.00
—B-side by Les Baxter					
❑ 0249	Stay with Me/Talk to Me Baby	1963	2.50	5.00	10.00
❑ 0279	My Kind of Town/I Like to Lead When I Dance	1964	2.50	5.00	10.00
❑ 0279 [PS]	My Kind of Town/I Like to Lead When I Dance	1964	37.50	75.00	150.00
—Sleeve issued with promo copies only					
❑ 0301	Softly, As I Leave You/Then Suddenly Love	1964	2.50	5.00	10.00
❑ 0314	I Heard the Bells on Christmas Day/The Little Drummer Boy	1964	5.00	10.00	20.00
❑ 0314 [PS]	I Heard the Bells on Christmas Day/The Little Drummer Boy	1964	12.50	25.00	50.00
❑ 0317	We Wish You the Merriest/Go Tell It on the Mountain	1964	10.00	20.00	40.00
—By Frank Sinatra/Bing Crosby/Fred Waring					
❑ 0317 [PS]	We Wish You the Merriest/Go Tell It on the Mountain	1964	15.00	30.00	60.00
—By Frank Sinatra/Bing Crosby/Fred Waring					
❑ 0332	Somewhere in Your Heart/Emily	1964	2.00	4.00	8.00
—From here through 0677, originals on dark brown & orange label					
❑ 0350	Anytime at All/Available	1964	2.00	4.00	8.00
❑ 0373	Tell Her (You Love Her Each Day)/Here's to the Losers	1965	2.00	4.00	8.00
❑ 0380	Forget Domani/I Can't Believe I'm Losing You	1965	2.00	4.00	8.00
❑ 0398	When Somebody Loves You/When I'm Not Near the Girl I Love	1965	2.00	4.00	8.00
❑ 0410	Everybody Has the Right to Be Wrong/I'll Only Miss Her When I Think of Her	1965	2.00	4.00	8.00
❑ 0429	It Was a Very Good Year/Moment to Moment	1965	2.00	4.00	8.00
❑ 0429 [PS]	It Was a Very Good Year/Moment to Moment	1965	6.25	12.50	25.00
❑ 0470	Strangers in the Night/Oh, You Crazy Moon	1966	2.50	5.00	10.00
❑ 0493	Frank Sinatra Reads from Gunga Din	1966	125.00	250.00	500.00
—300 pressed and given away to friends; no stock copies					
❑ 0509	Summer Wind/You Make Me Feel So Young	1966	2.50	5.00	10.00
❑ 0531	That's Life/The September of My Years	1966	2.50	5.00	10.00
❑ 0531 [PS]	That's Life/The September of My Years	1966	6.25	12.50	25.00
❑ 0561	Somethin' Stupid/Give Her Love	1967	2.50	5.00	10.00
—A-side: Nancy Sinatra and Frank Sinatra					
❑ 0561	Somethin' Stupid/I Will Wait for You	1967	2.00	4.00	8.00
—A-side: Nancy Sinatra and Frank Sinatra					
❑ 0610	The World We Knew (Over and Over)/You Are There	1967	2.00	4.00	8.00
❑ 0631	This Town/This Is My Love	1967	2.00	4.00	8.00
❑ 0677	I Can't Believe I'm Losing You/How Old Am I?	1967	2.00	4.00	8.00
❑ 0702	My Kind of Town/That's Life	1968	—	2.50	5.00
—"Back to Back Hits" series					
❑ 0706	September of My Years/Softly, As I Leave You	1968	—	2.50	5.00
—"Back to Back Hits" series					
❑ 0710	Strangers in the Night/Summer Wind	1968	—	2.50	5.00
—"Back to Back Hits" series					
❑ 0713	It Was a Very Good Year/Stay with Me	1968	—	2.50	5.00
—"Back to Back Hits" series					
❑ 0727	Somethin' Stupid/The World We Knew (Over and Over)	1968	—	2.50	5.00
—"Back to Back Hits" series; A-side with Nancy Sinatra					
❑ 0734	My Way/Cycles	1970	—	2.50	5.00
—"Back to Back Hits" series					
❑ 0764	Cycles/My Way of Life	1968	—	3.00	6.00
—From here though 0865, orange/tan label with "W7/:r" logo					
❑ 0790	Whatever Happened to Christmas?/I Wouldn't Trade Christmas	1968	3.00	6.00	12.00
—B-side by The Sinatra Family					
❑ 0798	Rain in My Heart/Star	1968	—	3.00	6.00
❑ 0817	My Way/Blue Lace	1969	2.50	5.00	10.00
❑ 0852	Love's Been Good to Me/A Man Alone	1969	2.00	4.00	8.00
❑ 0865	Goin' Out of My Head/Forget to Remember	1969	2.00	4.00	8.00
❑ 0895	I Would Be in Love (Anyway)/Watertown	1970	2.00	4.00	8.00
—From here through 29903, orange (or tan) label with ":r" logo in square					
❑ 0920	The Train/What's Now Is Now	1969	2.00	4.00	8.00
❑ 0970	Lady Day/Song of the Sabia	1970	2.00	4.00	8.00
❑ 0980	Feelin' Kinda Sunday/Kids	1970	2.00	4.00	8.00
—A-side by Nancy Sinatra and Frank Sinatra; B-side by Nancy Sinatra					
❑ 0981	Something/Bein' Green	1970	2.00	4.00	8.00
❑ PRO-S-1007	To Love a Child (mono/stereo)	1982	75.00	150.00	300.00
—Special pressing of 500 with small hole, given to Nancy Reagan for distributuion at a White House function.					
❑ 1010	Witchcraft/Young at Heart	1971	2.00	4.00	8.00
❑ 1011	Life's a Trippy Thing/I'm Not Afraid	1971	2.00	4.00	8.00
—A-side by Nancy Sinatra and Frank Sinatra					
❑ 1181	Let Me Try Again/Send In the Clowns	1973	2.00	4.00	8.00
❑ 1190	You Will Be My Music/Winners	1973	2.00	4.00	8.00
❑ 1196	Bad, Bad Leroy Brown/I'm Gonna Make It All the Way	1974	2.00	4.00	8.00
❑ 1208	You Turned My World Around/Satisfy Me One More Time	1974	2.00	4.00	8.00
❑ 1327	Anytime (I'll Be There)/The Hurt Doesn't Go Away	1975	2.00	4.00	8.00
❑ 1335	I Believe I'm Gonna Love You/The Only Couple on the Floor	1975	2.00	4.00	8.00
❑ 1335 [PS]	I Believe I'm Gonna Love You	1975	10.00	20.00	40.00
—Issued with promo copies only					
❑ 1342	A Baby Just Like You/Christmas Mem'ries	1975	2.50	5.00	10.00
❑ 1342 [PS]	A Baby Just Like You/Christmas Mem'ries	1975	10.00	20.00	40.00
—Blue printing, released with promo copies only					
❑ 1342 [PS]	A Baby Just Like You/Christmas Mem'ries	1975	5.00	10.00	20.00
—Red and black printing, released with stock copies					
❑ 1343	Empty Tables/The Saddest Thing of All	1976	2.00	4.00	8.00
❑ 1347	I Sing the Songs (I Write the Songs)/Empty Tables	1976	2.50	5.00	10.00
❑ 1364	Stargazer/The Best I Ever Had	1976	2.00	4.00	8.00
❑ 1364 [PS]	Stargazer/The Best I Ever Had	1976	3.75	7.50	15.00
—Special sleeve: "New Sinatra Single"					
❑ 1377	Dry Your Eyes/Like a Sad Song	1976	2.00	4.00	8.00
❑ 1382	I Love My Wife/Send In the Clowns	1976	2.50	5.00	10.00
❑ 1386	Night and Day/Everybody Ought to Be in Love	1977	2.00	4.00	8.00
❑ 15999	My Way/Cycles	199?	—	—	3.00
—"Back to Back Hits" series					
❑ 19355	Fly Me to the Moon/The Last Dance	1991	—	2.00	4.00
❑ 20001	The Second Time Around/Tina	1961	6.25	12.50	25.00
—Originals on light blue label					
❑ 20010	Granada/The Curse of an Aching Heart	1961	3.75	7.50	15.00
—From here through 0317, originals on peach label					
❑ 20010 [PS]	Granada/The Curse of an Aching Heart	1961	6.25	12.50	25.00
❑ 20023	I'll Be Seeing You/The One I Love	1961	3.75	7.50	15.00
❑ 20024	Imagination/It's Always You	1961	3.75	7.50	15.00
❑ 20025	I'm Getting Sentimental Over You/East of the Sun (And West of the Moon)	1961	3.75	7.50	15.00
❑ 20026	There Are Such Things/Polkadots and Moonbeams	1961	3.75	7.50	15.00
❑ 20027	Without a Song/It Started All Over Again	1961	3.75	7.50	15.00
❑ 20028	Take Me/Daybreak	1961	3.75	7.50	15.00
❑ 20040	Pocketful of Miracles/Name It and It's Yours	1961	3.75	7.50	15.00
❑ 20040 [PS]	Pocketful of Miracles/Name It and It's Yours	1961	15.00	30.00	60.00
❑ 20059	Stardust/Come Rain or Come Shine	1962	3.75	7.50	15.00
❑ 20063	Everybody's Twistin'/Nothin' But the Best	1962	3.75	7.50	15.00
❑ 20063 [PS]	Everybody's Twistin'/Nothin' But the Best	1962	7.50	15.00	30.00
❑ 20092	Goody, Goody/Love Is Just Around the Corner	1962	3.00	6.00	12.00
❑ 20107	The Look of Love/I Left My Heart in San Francisco	1962	12.50	25.00	50.00
❑ 20107	The Look of Love/Indiscreet	1962	12.50	25.00	50.00
❑ 20128	Me and My Shadow/Sam's Song	1962	3.75	7.50	15.00
—A-side by Frank Sinatra and Sammy Davis, Jr.; B-side by Sammy Davis Jr. and Dean Martin					
❑ 20128 [PS]	Me and My Shadow/Sam's Song	1962	12.50	25.00	50.00
—A-side by Frank Sinatra and Sammy Davis, Jr.; B-side by Sammy Davis Jr. and Dean Martin					
❑ 20151	Call Me Irresponsible/Tina	1963	2.50	5.00	10.00
—B-side changed for commercial release					
❑ 20151	Call Me Irresponsible/Come Blow Your Horn	1963	125.00	250.00	500.00
—One stock copy is known to exist!					
❑ 20151 [DJ]	Call Me Irresponsible/Come Blow Your Horn	1963	25.00	50.00	100.00
❑ 20151 [PS]	Call Me Irresponsible/Come Blow Your Horn	1963	50.00	100.00	200.00
—Sleeve accompanies promo copies only					
❑ 20157 [DJ]	California/America the Beautiful	1963	62.50	125.00	250.00
—No stock copies isssued					
❑ 20157 [DJ]	California/America the Beautiful	1978	50.00	100.00	200.00
—Private pressing of 1,000 for Sinatra's personal use					
❑ 20157 [PS]	California/America the Beautiful	1963	187.50	375.00	750.00
—No stock copies isssued					
❑ 20184	I Have Dreamed/Come Blow Your Horn	1963	2.50	5.00	10.00
❑ 20209	Love Isn't Just for the Young/You Brought a New Kind of Love to Me	1963	3.00	6.00	12.00
❑ 20209 [PS]	Love Isn't Just for the Young/You Brought a New Kind of Love to Me	1963	12.50	25.00	50.00
❑ 20217	Fugue for Tinhorns/The Oldest Established (Permanent Floating Crap Game in New York)	1963	3.75	7.50	15.00
—By Frank Sinatra/Bing Crosby/Dean Martin					
❑ 20217 [PS]	Fugue for Tinhorns/The Oldest Established (Permanent Floating Crap Game in New York)	1963	18.75	37.50	75.00
—By Frank Sinatra/Bing Crosby/Dean Martin					
❑ 20235	Tangerine/A New Kind of Love	1963	—	—	—
—Unreleased					
❑ 29677	Here's to the Band/It's Sunday	1983	2.00	4.00	8.00
❑ 29903	To Love a Child/That's What God Looks Like to Me	1982	2.00	4.00	8.00
❑ 29903 [PS]	To Love a Child/That's What God Looks Like to Me	1982	3.75	7.50	15.00
❑ 40003	I Never Knew/Don't Be That Way	196?	5.00	10.00	20.00
—Jukebox 33 1/3 rpm, small hole single					
❑ 40009	It Started All Over Again/Without a Song	196?	5.00	10.00	20.00
—Jukebox 33 1/3 rpm, small hole single					
❑ 40013	Come Rain or Come Shine/It Might As Well Be Spring	196?	5.00	10.00	20.00
—Jukebox 33 1/3 rpm, small hole single					
❑ 40036	Pennies from Heaven/Please Be Kind	1963	5.00	10.00	20.00
—Jukebox 33 1/3 rpm, small hole single					
❑ 40037	The Tender Trap/Looking at the World Thru Rose Colored Glasses	1963	5.00	10.00	20.00
—Jukebox 33 1/3 rpm, small hole single					
❑ 40038	My Kind of Girl/I Only Have Eyes for You	1963	5.00	10.00	20.00
—Jukebox 33 1/3 rpm, small hole single					
❑ 40039	Nice Work If You Can Get It/Learnin' the Blues	1963	5.00	10.00	20.00
—Jukebox 33 1/3 rpm, small hole single					
❑ 40040	I'm Gonna Sit Right Down and Write Myself a Letter/I Won't Dance	1963	5.00	10.00	20.00
—Jukebox 33 1/3 rpm, small hole single					
❑ 40050	Please Be Kind/My Kind of Girl	1963	5.00	10.00	20.00
—Jukebox 33 1/3 rpm, small hole single					

Number	Title (A Side/B Side)	Yr	VG	VG+	NM
❑ 49233	Theme from New York, New York/That's What God Looks Like to Me	1980	2.50	5.00	10.00
❑ 49233 [PS]	Theme from New York, New York/That's What God Looks Like to Me	1980	3.75	7.50	15.00
❑ 49517	You and Me (We Wanted It All)/I've Been There	1980	2.00	4.00	8.00
❑ 49827	Say Hello/Good Thing Going	1981	2.00	4.00	8.00
—B-side listed on label as "RE-1"					
❑ 49827	Say Hello/Good Thing Going	1981	2.00	4.00	8.00
—B-side listed on label as "RE-2"					

(NO LABEL)

Number	Title (A Side/B Side)	Yr	VG	VG+	NM
❑ KB-2077/8	High Hopes with Jack Kennedy/Jack Kennedy All the Way	1960	75.00	150.00	300.00
—No artist or label shown, but Sinatra does sing the A-side					

7-Inch Extended Plays

CAPITOL

Number	Title (A Side/B Side)	Yr	VG	VG+	NM
❑ EAP 488 [PS]	Songs for Young Lovers	1954	12.50	25.00	50.00
—Both of above EPs in gatefold sleeve					
❑ EAP 1-488	My Funny Valentine/The Girl Next Door//They Can't Take That Away from Me/Violets for Your Furs	1954	5.00	10.00	20.00
❑ EAP 1-488 [PS]	Songs for Young Lovers, Vol. 1	1954	5.00	10.00	20.00
❑ EAP 2-488	A Foggy Day/Like Someone I Love//I Get a Kick Out of You/Little Girl Blue	1954	5.00	10.00	20.00
❑ EAP 2-488 [PS]	Songs for Young Lovers, Vol. 2	1954	5.00	10.00	20.00
❑ EAP 1-510	Young at Heart/I've Got the World on a String// From Here to Eternity/South of the Border	1954	6.25	12.50	25.00
❑ EAP 1-510 [PS]	Young at Heart	1954	6.25	12.50	25.00
❑ EAP 1-528	Just One of Those Things/I'm Gonna Sit Right Down and Write Myself a Letter//Sunday/Wrap Your Troubles in Dreams	1954	5.00	10.00	20.00
❑ EAP 1-528 [PS]	Swing Easy, Part I	1954	5.00	10.00	20.00
❑ EAP 2-528	Taking a Chance on Love/Jeepers Creepers//Get Happy/All of Me	1954	5.00	10.00	20.00
❑ EAP 2-528 [PS]	Swing Easy, Part II	1954	5.00	10.00	20.00
❑ EBF 528 [PS]	Swing Easy	1954	12.50	25.00	50.00
—Both 1-528 and 2-528 EPs in gatefold sleeve					
❑ EAP 1-542	Three Coins in the Fountain/My One and Only Love//Don't Worry 'Bout Me/I Love You	1954	6.25	12.50	25.00
❑ EAP 1-542 [PS]	3 Coins in the Fountain	1954	6.25	12.50	25.00
❑ EAP 1-571	Young at Heart/Someone to Watch Over Me//Just One of Those Things/You, My Love	1954	6.25	12.50	25.00
❑ EAP 1-571 [PS]	Frank Sinatra Sings Songs from His Warner Bros. Picture "Young at Heart"	1954	6.25	12.50	25.00
❑ EAP 1-581	In the Wee Small Hours of the Morning/I See Your Face Before Me//I'll Never Be the Same/This Love of Mine	1954	5.00	10.00	20.00
❑ EAP 1-581 [PS]	In the Wee Small Hours, Part 1	1955	5.00	10.00	20.00
❑ EAP 2-581	I'll Be Around/I Get Along Without You Very Well/ /It Never Entered My Mind/Dancing on the Ceiling	1955	5.00	10.00	20.00
❑ EAP 2-581 [PS]	In the Wee Small Hours, Part 2	1955	5.00	10.00	20.00
❑ EAP 3-581	Deep in a Dream/Mood Indigo//Glad to Be Unhappy/Ill Wind	1955	5.00	10.00	20.00
❑ EAP 3-581 [PS]	In the Wee Small Hours, Part 3	1955	5.00	10.00	20.00
❑ EAP 4-581	Can't We Be Friends/When Your Lover Has Gone//What Is This Thing Called Love/Last Night When We Were Young	1955	5.00	10.00	20.00
❑ EAP 4-581 [PS]	In the Wee Small Hours, Part 4	1955	5.00	10.00	20.00
❑ EBF 1-581 [PS]	In the Wee Small Hours, Parts 1 and 2	1955	12.50	25.00	50.00
—Gatefold sleeve for some editions of EAP 1-581 and 2-581					
❑ EBF 2-581 [PS]	In the Wee Small Hours, Parts 3 and 4	1955	12.50	25.00	50.00
—Gatefold sleeve for some editions of EAP 3-581 and 4-581					
❑ EAP 1-590	I'm Gonna Live Till I Die/Day In — Day Out// Melody of Love/Ever Since You Went Away	1955	6.25	12.50	25.00
—Second song on B-side by The Skyliners with Ray Anthony (no Sinatra involvement)					
❑ EAP 1-590 [PS]	Melody of Love	1955	6.25	12.50	25.00
❑ EAP 1-629	Two Hearts, Two Kisses (Make One Love)/Don't Change Your Mind About Me//Learnin' the Blues/Why Should I Cry Over You?	1955	6.25	12.50	25.00
❑ EAP 1-629 [PS]	Session with Sinatra	1955	6.25	12.50	25.00
❑ DU-653	It Happened in Monterey/Too Marvelous for Words/Anything Goes//You Make Me Feel So Young/I've Got You Under My Skin	196?	6.25	12.50	25.00
—Jukebox EP, plays at 33 1/3 rpm, small hole					
❑ DU-653 [PS]	Songs for Swinging Lovers	196?	6.25	12.50	25.00
❑ EAP 1-653	You Make Me Feel So Young/It Happened in Monterey//Anything Goes/How About You	1956	5.00	10.00	20.00
❑ EAP 1-653 [PS]	Songs for Swingin' Lovers, Part 1	1956	6.25	12.50	25.00
—With Sinatra facing away from the embracing couple					
❑ EAP 1-653 [PS]	Songs for Swingin' Lovers, Part 1	1957	5.00	10.00	20.00
—With Sinatra facing toward the embracing couple					
❑ EAP 2-653	You're Getting to Be a Habit with Me/You Brought a New Kind of Love to Me//Makin' Whoopee/ Swingin' Down the Lane	1956	5.00	10.00	20.00
❑ EAP 2-653 [PS]	Songs for Swingin' Lovers, Part 2	1956	6.25	12.50	25.00
—With Sinatra facing away from the embracing couple					
❑ EAP 2-653 [PS]	Songs for Swingin' Lovers, Part 2	1957	5.00	10.00	20.00
—With Sinatra facing toward the embracing couple					
❑ EAP 3-653	Too Marvelous for Words/Old Devil Moon//We'll Be Together Again	1956	5.00	10.00	20.00
❑ EAP 3-653 [PS]	Songs for Swingin' Lovers, Part 3	1956	6.25	12.50	25.00
—With Sinatra facing away from the embracing couple					
❑ EAP 3-653 [PS]	Songs for Swingin' Lovers, Part 3	1957	5.00	10.00	20.00
—With Sinatra facing toward the embracing couple					
❑ EAP 4-653	Pennies from Heaven/Love Is Here to Stay//I've Got You Under My Skin/I Thought About You	1956	5.00	10.00	20.00
❑ EAP 4-653 [PS]	Songs for Swingin' Lovers, Part 4	1956	6.25	12.50	25.00
—With Sinatra facing away from the embracing couple					
❑ EAP 4-653 [PS]	Songs for Swingin' Lovers, Part 4	1957	5.00	10.00	20.00
—With Sinatra facing toward the embracing couple					

Number	Title (A Side/B Side)	Yr	VG	VG+	NM
❑ EBF 1-653 [PS]	Songs for Swingin' Lovers, Parts 1 and 2	1956	15.00	30.00	60.00
—Gatefold sleeve for some editions of EAP 1-653 and 2-653; with Sinatra facing away from the embracing couple					
❑ EBF 1-653 [PS]	Songs for Swingin' Lovers, Parts 1 and 2	1957	12.50	25.00	50.00
—Gatefold sleeve for some editions of EAP 1-653 and 2-653; with Sinatra facing toward the embracing couple					
❑ EBF 2-653 [PS]	Songs for Swingin' Lovers, Parts 3 and 4	1956	15.00	30.00	60.00
—Gatefold sleeve for some editions of EAP 3-653 and 4-653; with Sinatra facing away from the embracing couple					
❑ EBF 2-653 [PS]	Songs for Swingin' Lovers, Parts 3 and 4	1957	12.50	25.00	50.00
—Gatefold sleeve for some editions of EAP 3-653 and 4-653; with Sinatra facing toward the embracing couple					
❑ EAP 1-673	Our Town/The Impatient Years//Love and Marriage/Look to Your Heart	1956	12.50	25.00	50.00
❑ EAP 1-673 [PS]	Our Town	1956	12.50	25.00	50.00
❑ DU-768	I've Got the World on a String/Three Coins in the Fountain/Love and Marriage//South of the Border/Young at Heart/The Tender Trap	196?	6.25	12.50	25.00
—Jukebox EP, plays at 33 1/3 rpm, small hole					
❑ DU-768 [PS]	This Is Sinatra	196?	6.25	12.50	25.00
❑ EAP 1-789	Close to You/Love Locked Out//The End of a Love Affair	1956	5.00	10.00	20.00
❑ EAP 1-789 [PS]	Close to You, Part 1	1956	5.00	10.00	20.00
❑ EAP 2-789	P.S. I Love You//With Every Breath I Take/I Couldn't Sleep a Wink Last Night	1956	5.00	10.00	20.00
❑ EAP 2-789 [PS]	Close to You, Part 2	1956	5.00	10.00	20.00
❑ EAP 3-789	Everything Happens to Me/It Could Happen to You//I've Had My Moments	1956	5.00	10.00	20.00
❑ EAP 3-789 [PS]	Close to You, Part 3	1956	5.00	10.00	20.00
❑ EAP 4-789	Don't Like Goodbyes//It's Easy to Remember/ Blame It on My Youth	1956	5.00	10.00	20.00
❑ EAP 4-789 [PS]	Close to You, Part 4	1956	5.00	10.00	20.00
❑ EBF 1-789 [PS]	Close to You, Parts 1 and 2	1956	12.50	25.00	50.00
—Gatefold sleeve for some editions of EAP 1-789 and 2-789					
❑ EBF 2-789 [PS]	Close to You, Parts 3 and 4	1956	12.50	25.00	50.00
—Gatefold sleeve for some editions of EAP 3-789 and 4-789					
❑ EAP 1-800	How Little We Know/Flowers Mean Forgiveness/ /You Forgot All the Words/Hey! Jealous Lover	1956	7.50	15.00	30.00
❑ EAP 1-800 [PS]	Hey! Jealous Lover	1956	7.50	15.00	30.00
❑ EAP 1-803	The Lonesome Road/You'd Be So Nice to Come Home To//From This Moment On/Nice Work If You Can Get It	1957	5.00	10.00	20.00
❑ EAP 1-803 [PS]	A Swingin' Affair, Part 1	1957	5.00	10.00	20.00
❑ EAP 2-803	I Won't Dance/At Long Last Love//I Got It Bad and That Ain't Good/I Guess I'll Have to Change My Plan	1957	5.00	10.00	20.00
❑ EAP 2-803 [PS]	A Swingin' Affair, Part 2	1957	5.00	10.00	20.00
❑ EAP 3-803	No One Ever Tells You/If I Had You//I Wish I Were in Love Again/I Got Plenty o' Nuttin'	1957	5.00	10.00	20.00
❑ EAP 3-803 [PS]	A Swingin' Affair, Part 3	1957	5.00	10.00	20.00
❑ EAP 4-803	Oh! Look at Me Now/Stars Fell on Alabama//Night and Day	1957	5.00	10.00	20.00
❑ EAP 4-803 [PS]	A Swingin' Affair, Part 4	1957	5.00	10.00	20.00
❑ EBF 1-803 [PS]	A Swingin' Affair, Parts 1 and 2	1957	12.50	25.00	50.00
—Gatefold sleeve for some editions of EAP 1-803 and 2-803					
❑ EBF 2-803 [PS]	A Swingin' Affair, Parts 3 and 4	1957	12.50	25.00	50.00
—Gatefold sleeve for some editions of EAP 3-803 and 4-803					
❑ EAP 1-855	Where Are You?/Where Is the One//Baby Won't You Please Come Home	1957	5.00	10.00	20.00
❑ EAP 1-855 [PS]	Where Are You? Part 1	1957	5.00	10.00	20.00
❑ EAP 2-855	I'm a Fool to Want You//I Cover the Waterfront/ Laura	1957	5.00	10.00	20.00
❑ EAP 2-855 [PS]	Where Are You? Part 2	1957	5.00	10.00	20.00
❑ EAP 3-855	Lonely Town//The Night We Called It a Day/ Autumn Leaves	1957	5.00	10.00	20.00
❑ EAP 3-855 [PS]	Where Are You? Part 3	1957	5.00	10.00	20.00
❑ EAP 4-855	There's No You//I Think of You/Maybe You'll Be There	1957	5.00	10.00	20.00
❑ EAP 4-855 [PS]	Where Are You? Part 4	1957	5.00	10.00	20.00
❑ EBF 1-855 [PS]	Where Are You? Parts 1 and 2	1957	12.50	25.00	50.00
—Gatefold sleeve for some editions of EAP 1-855 and 2-855					
❑ EBF 2-855 [PS]	Where Are You? Parts 3 and 4	1957	12.50	25.00	50.00
—Gatefold sleeve for some editions of EAP 3-855 and 4-855					
❑ EAP 1-894	Jingle Bells/The Christmas Song//Mistletoe and Holly/I'll Be Home for Christmas	1957	3.00	6.00	12.00
❑ EAP 1-894 [PS]	A Jolly Christmas from Frank Sinatra, Part 1	1957	3.00	6.00	12.00
❑ EAP 2-894	The Christmas Waltz/Have Yourself a Merry Little Christmas//The First Noel/Hark the Herald Angels Sing	1957	3.00	6.00	12.00
❑ EAP 2-894 [PS]	A Jolly Christmas from Frank Sinatra, Part 2	1957	3.00	6.00	12.00
❑ EAP 3-894	O Little Town of Bethlehem/Adeste Fideles//It Came Upon a Midnight Clear/Silent Night	1957	3.00	6.00	12.00
❑ EAP 3-894 [PS]	A Jolly Christmas from Frank Sinatra, Part 3	1957	3.00	6.00	12.00
❑ EAP 1-920	Come Fly with Me/Isle of Capri//It's Nice to Go Trav'ling	1958	3.75	7.50	15.00
❑ EAP 1-920 [PS]	Come Fly with Me, Part 1	1958	3.75	7.50	15.00
❑ EAP 2-920	Autumn in New York//April in Paris/Around the World	1958	3.75	7.50	15.00
❑ EAP 2-920 [PS]	Come Fly with Me, Part 2	1958	3.75	7.50	15.00
❑ EAP 3-920	Moonlight in Vermont//London by Night/Let's Get Away from It All	1958	3.75	7.50	15.00
❑ EAP 3-920 [PS]	Come Fly with Me, Part 3	1958	3.75	7.50	15.00
❑ EAP 4-920	On the Road to Mandalay//Blue Hawaii/Brazil	1958	3.75	7.50	15.00
❑ EAP 4-920 [PS]	Come Fly with Me, Part 4	1958	3.75	7.50	15.00
❑ SU-920	Come Fly with Me/Moonlight in Vermont//April in Paris/On the Road to Mandalay	196?	6.25	12.50	25.00
—Jukebox EP, plays at 33 1/3 rpm, small hole					
❑ SU-920 [PS]	Come Fly with Me	196?	6.25	12.50	25.00
❑ EAP 1-982	Hey! Jealous Lover/Everybody Loves Somebody//I Believe/Put Your Dreams Away	1958	5.00	10.00	20.00
❑ EAP 1-982 [PS]	This Is Sinatra, Volume Two, Part 1	1958	5.00	10.00	20.00

Number	Title (A Side/B Side)	Yr	VG	VG+	NM
❑ EAP 2-982	Something Wonderful Happens in Summer/Half As Lovely//So Long My Love/It's the Same Old Dreams	1958	5.00	10.00	20.00
❑ EAP 2-982 [PS]	This Is Sinatra, Volume Two, Part 2	1958	5.00	10.00	20.00
❑ EAP 3-982	You're Cheatin' Yourself/You'll Always Be the One I Love//Johnny Concho Theme (Wait for Me)/If You Are But a Dream	1958	5.00	10.00	20.00
❑ EAP 3-982 [PS]	This Is Sinatra, Volume Two, Part 3	1958	5.00	10.00	20.00
❑ EAP 4-982	You Forgot All the Words/How Little We Know// Time After Time/Crazy Love	1958	5.00	10.00	20.00
❑ EAP 4-982 [PS]	This Is Sinatra, Volume 2, Part 4	1958	5.00	10.00	20.00
❑ EAP 1-1013	The Lady Is a Tramp/Witchcraft//Come Fly with Me/Tell Her You Love Her	1958	7.50	15.00	30.00
❑ EAP 1-1013 [PS]	Frank Sinatra!	1958	7.50	15.00	30.00
❑ EAP 1-1053	(contents unknown)	1958	5.00	10.00	20.00
❑ EAP 1-1053 [PS]	Frank Sinatra Sings for Only the Lonely	1958	5.00	10.00	20.00
❑ EAP 1-1069	Come Dance with Me/Something's Gotta Give// The Song Is You/The Last Dance	1958	3.75	7.50	15.00
❑ EAP 1-1069 [PS]	Come Dance with Me, Part 1	1958	3.75	7.50	15.00
❑ EAP 2-1069	Just in Time/Dancing in the Dark//Cheek to Cheek/Baubles, Bangles and Beads	1958	3.75	7.50	15.00
❑ EAP 2-1069 [PS]	Come Dance with Me, Part 2	1958	3.75	7.50	15.00
❑ EAP 3-1069	Saturday Night/Day In — Day Out//Too Close for Comfort/I Could Have Danced All Night	1958	3.75	7.50	15.00
❑ EAP 3-1069 [PS]	Come Dance with Me, Part 3	1958	3.75	7.50	15.00
❑ EAP 1-1159	Angel Eyes/Willow Weep for Me	1958	7.50	15.00	30.00
❑ EAP 1-1159 [PS]	Frank Sinatra Sings Angel Eyes	1958	7.50	15.00	30.00
❑ EAP 1-1221	When No One Cares/I'll Never Smile Again//A Cottage for Sale/None But the Lonely Heart	1959	3.75	7.50	15.00
❑ EAP 1-1221 [PS]	No One Cares, Part 1	1959	3.75	7.50	15.00
❑ EAP 2-1221	I Don't Stand a Ghost of a Chance with You/Here's That Rainy Day//I Can't Get Started	1959	3.75	7.50	15.00
❑ EAP 2-1221 [PS]	No One Cares, Part 2	1959	3.75	7.50	15.00
❑ EAP 3-1221	*Stormy Weather/Where Do You Go/Why Try to Change Me Now/Just Friends	1959	3.75	7.50	15.00
❑ EAP 3-1221 [PS]	No One Cares, Part 3	1959	3.75	7.50	15.00
❑ EAP 1-1224	High Hopes/All My Tomorrows//French Foreign Legion/Mr. Success	1959	7.50	15.00	30.00
❑ EAP 1-1224 [PS]	High Hopes	1959	7.50	15.00	30.00
❑ SEP 1-1233 [PS]	French Foreign Legion	1959	12.50	25.00	50.00
❑ SEP 1-1233 [S]	French Foreign Legion/Mr. Success//Come Dance with Me/The Last Dance	1959	12.50	25.00	50.00
❑ EAP 1-1348	Talk to Me/They Came to Cordura//When No One Cares/Where Do You Go?	1959	7.50	15.00	30.00
❑ EAP 1-1348 [PS]	Talk to Me	1959	7.50	15.00	30.00
❑ EAP 1-1417	*Nice 'n' Easy/That Old Feeling/She's Funny That Way/Dream	1960	5.00	10.00	20.00
❑ EAP 1-1417 [PS]	Nice 'n' Easy, Part 1	1960	5.00	10.00	20.00
❑ EAP 2-1417	How Deep Is the Ocean/Mam'selle//Try a Little Tenderness/Embraceable You	1960	5.00	10.00	20.00
❑ EAP 2-1417 [PS]	Nice 'n' Easy, Part 2	1960	5.00	10.00	20.00
❑ EAP 3-1417	You Go to My Head/I've Got a Crush on You// Fools Rush In/Nevertheless	1960	5.00	10.00	20.00
❑ EAP 3-1417 [PS]	Nice 'n' Easy, Part 3	1960	5.00	10.00	20.00
❑ EAP 1-1491	When You're Smiling (The Whole World Smiles With You)/Blue Moon//S'Posin'/It All Depends on You	1961	6.25	12.50	25.00
❑ EAP 1-1491 [PS]	Sinatra's Swingin' Session, Part 1	1961	6.25	12.50	25.00
❑ EAP 2-1491	Always/I Can't Believe You're in Love with Me// It's Only a Paper Moon/My Blue Heaven	1961	6.25	12.50	25.00
❑ EAP 2-1491 [PS]	Sinatra's Swingin' Session, Part 2	1961	6.25	12.50	25.00
❑ EAP 3-1491	Should I/September in the Rain//I Concentrate on You/You Do Something to Me	1961	6.25	12.50	25.00
❑ EAP 3-1491 [PS]	Sinatra's Swingin' Session, Part 3	1961	6.25	12.50	25.00
❑ EAP 1-1594	(contents unknown)	1961	6.25	12.50	25.00
❑ EAP 1-1594 [PS]	Come Swing with Me, Part 1	1961	6.25	12.50	25.00
❑ EAP 2-1594	(contents unknown)	1961	6.25	12.50	25.00
❑ EAP 2-1594 [PS]	Come Swing with Me, Part 2	1961	6.25	12.50	25.00
❑ EAP 3-1594	(contents unknown)	1961	6.25	12.50	25.00
❑ EAP 3-1594 [PS]	Come Swing with Me, Part 3	1961	6.25	12.50	25.00
❑ SU-1762	All the Way/Hey Jealous Lover/Lean Baby// Witchcraft/One for My Baby	196?	6.25	12.50	25.00
—Jukebox EP, plays at 33 1/3 rpm, small hole					
❑ SU-1762 [PS]	All the Way/Hey Jealous Lover/Lean Baby// Witchcraft/One for My Baby	196?	6.25	12.50	25.00

COLUMBIA

Number	Title (A Side/B Side)	Yr	VG	VG+	NM
❑ B-112 [PS]	The Voice of Frank Sinatra	1950	12.50	25.00	50.00
—Gatefold cover for 2-EP set (1115 and 1116)					
❑ B-167 [PS]	Christmas Songs by Sinatra	1952	12.50	25.00	50.00
—Gatefold cover for 2-EP set (1322 and 1323)					
❑ B-218 [PS]	Sing and Dance with Frank Sinatra	1950	12.50	25.00	50.00
—Gatefold sleeve for 2-EP set (1129 and 1130)					
❑ B-419 [PS]	I've Got a Crush on You	1952	12.50	25.00	50.00
—Gatefold cover for 2-EP set (1907 and 1908)					
❑ 5-1115	You Go to My Head/Someone to Watch Over Me/ /A Ghost of a Chance/Paradise	1952	6.25	12.50	25.00
—One record of 2-EP version of B-112					
❑ 5-1116	These Foolish Things/Why Shouldn't I//I Don't Know Why/Try a Little Tenderness	1952	6.25	12.50	25.00
—One record of 2-EP version of B-112					
❑ 5-1129	Lover/It's Only a Paper Moon//The Continental/ When You're Smiling	1952	6.25	12.50	25.00
—One record of 2-EP version of B-218					
❑ 5-1130	My Blue Heaven/It All Depends on You//You Do Something to Me/Should I	1952	6.25	12.50	25.00
—One record of 2-EP version of B-218					
❑ 5-1193	Always/Blue Skies//How Deep Is the Ocean/They Say It's Wonderful	1952	6.25	12.50	25.00
—Record that goes with cover B-1524					
❑ 5-1322	White Christmas/Jingle Bells//Have Yourself a Merry Little Christmas/Have Yourself a Merry Little Christmas	1952	6.25	12.50	25.00
—One record of 2-EP version of B-167					
❑ 5-1323	Silent Night, Holy Night/Adeste Fideles//O Little Town of Bethlehem/It Came Upon a Midnight Clear	1952	6.25	12.50	25.00
—One record of 2-EP version of B-167					
❑ 5-1355	Some Enchanted Evening/Bali Ha'i//People Will Say We're in Love/Oh, What a Beautiful Morning	1952	7.50	15.00	30.00
—Record that goes with cover B-1608					
❑ 5-1389	Soliloquy//If I Loved You/You'll Never Walk Alone	1952	7.50	15.00	30.00
—Record that goes with cover B-1673					
❑ B-1524 [PS]	Frank Sinatra Sings Irving Berlin	1952	6.25	12.50	25.00
❑ 5-1555	Embraceable You/I've Got a Crush on You// Someone to Watch Over Me/Where Is My Bess?	1953	6.25	12.50	25.00
—Record that goes with cover B-1673					
❑ B-1608 [PS]	Frank Sinatra Sings Hits from South Pacific and Oklahoma	1952	7.50	15.00	30.00
❑ B-1620 [PS]	Carousel Sung by Frank Sinatra	1952	7.50	15.00	30.00
❑ B-1673 [PS]	Frank Sinatra Sings George Gershwin	1953	6.25	12.50	25.00
❑ B-1702	Ol' Man River/All the Things You Are//Why Was I Born/The Song Is You	1953	6.25	12.50	25.00
❑ B-1702 [PS]	Frank Sinatra Sings Jerome Kern	1953	6.25	12.50	25.00
❑ B-1815	I Concentrate on You/Why Can't You Behave// Why Shouldn't I/You Do Something to Me	1954	6.25	12.50	25.00
❑ B-1815 [PS]	Frank Sinatra Sings Cole Porter	1954	6.25	12.50	25.00
❑ B-1872	(contents unknown)	1954	6.25	12.50	25.00
❑ B-1872 [PS]	Frank Sinatra Sings Rodgers and Hart	1954	6.25	12.50	25.00
❑ 5-1907	I've Got a Crush on You/They Say It's Wonderful/ /If I Loved You/You Do Something to Me	1952	6.25	12.50	25.00
—One record of 2-EP set B-419					
❑ 5-1908	I Only Have Eyes for You/The Girl That I Marry// I Hear a Rhapsody/April in Paris	1952	6.25	12.50	25.00
—One record of 2-EP set B-419					
❑ B-1984	Hello Young Lovers/I Only Have Eyes for You// Falling in Love with Love/You'll Never Know	1955	6.25	12.50	25.00
❑ B-1984 [PS]	Frankie, Vol. 1	1955	6.25	12.50	25.00
❑ B-1985	It All Depends on You/S'posin//All of Me/Time After Time	1955	6.25	12.50	25.00
❑ B-1985 [PS]	Frankie, Vol. 2	1955	6.25	12.50	25.00
❑ B-1986	How Cute Can You Be/Almost Like Being in Love/ /Nancy/Oh! What It Seemed to Be	1955	6.25	12.50	25.00
❑ B-1986 [PS]	Frankie, Vol. 3	1955	6.25	12.50	25.00
❑ B-2515	I Couldn't Sleep a Wink Last Night/A Lovely Way to Spend an Evening//People Will Say We're in Love/Oh, What a Beautiful Mornin'	1957	6.25	12.50	25.00
❑ B-2515 [PS]	Frank Sinatra (Hall of Fame Series)	1957	6.25	12.50	25.00
❑ B-2516	Nancy (With the Laughing Face)/Day by Day// They Say It's Wonderful/The Girl That I Marry	1957	6.25	12.50	25.00
❑ B-2516 [PS]	Frank Sinatra (Hall of Fame Series)	1957	6.25	12.50	25.00
❑ B-2517	The Birth of the Blues/I've Got a Crush on You// Five Minutes More/Someone to Watch Over Me	1957	6.25	12.50	25.00
❑ B-2517 [PS]	Frank Sinatra (Hall of Fame Series)	1957	6.25	12.50	25.00
❑ B-2542	Castle Rock/Farewell, Farewell to Love//A Little Learnin' Is a Dangerous Thing	1957	12.50	25.00	50.00
❑ B-2542 [PS]	Frank Sinatra with Harry James and Pearl Bailey	1957	12.50	25.00	50.00
❑ B-2559	I Could Write a Book/If You Are But a Dream//I'm a Fool to Want You/I Should Care	1958	6.25	12.50	25.00
❑ B-2559 [PS]	Frank Sinatra (Hall of Fame Series)	1958	6.25	12.50	25.00
❑ B-2564	Ol' Man River/You'll Never Walk Alone//Soliloquy	1958	6.25	12.50	25.00
❑ B-2564 [PS]	Frank Sinatra (Hall of Fame Series)	1958	6.25	12.50	25.00
❑ B-2589	September Song/Among My Souvenirs//The Things We Did Last Summer/Oh! What It Seemed to Be	1958	6.25	12.50	25.00
❑ B-2589 [PS]	Frank Sinatra (Hall of Fame Series)	1958	6.25	12.50	25.00
❑ B-2614	One for My Baby/If I Loved You//Put Your Dreams Away/You'll Never Know	1958	6.25	12.50	25.00
❑ B-2614 [PS]	Frank Sinatra (Hall of Fame Series)	1958	6.25	12.50	25.00
❑ B-2626	Close to You/Embraceable You//The Charm of You/I Dream of You	1958	6.25	12.50	25.00
❑ B-2626 [PS]	Frank Sinatra (Hall of Fame Series)	1958	6.25	12.50	25.00
❑ B-2638	Stormy Weather/Why Was I Born//The House I Live In/How Deep Is the Ocean	1958	6.25	12.50	25.00
❑ B-2638 [PS]	Frank Sinatra (Hall of Fame Series)	1958	6.25	12.50	25.00
❑ B-2641	All or Nothing at All/You Go to My Head//Why Try to Change Me Now/I Concentrate on You	1958	6.25	12.50	25.00
❑ B-2641 [PS]	Frank Sinatra (Hall of Fame Series)	1958	6.25	12.50	25.00
❑ B-7431	I Don't Know Why (I Just Do)/Try a Little Tenderness//(I Don't Stand) A Ghost of a Chance/Paradise	1955	6.25	12.50	25.00
❑ B-7431 [PS]	The Voice, Vol. I	1955	6.25	12.50	25.00
❑ B-7432	(contents unknown)	1955	6.25	12.50	25.00
❑ B-7432 [PS]	The Voice, Vol. II	1955	6.25	12.50	25.00
❑ B-7433	Over the Rainbow/That Old Black Magic//Spring Is Here/Lover	1955	6.25	12.50	25.00
❑ B-7433 [PS]	The Voice, Vol. III	1955	6.25	12.50	25.00
❑ B-9021	That Old Feeling/Blue Skies//Autumn in New York/Don't Cry Joe	1956	6.25	12.50	25.00
❑ B-9021 [PS]	That Old Feeling	1956	6.25	12.50	25.00
❑ B-9022	The Nearness of You/That Lucky Old Sun//Full Moon and Empty Arms/Once in Love with Amy	1956	6.25	12.50	25.00
❑ B-9022 [PS]	The Nearness of You	1956	6.25	12.50	25.00
❑ B-9023	A Fellow Needs a Girl/Poinciana (Song of the Tree)//For Every Man There's a Woman/Mean to Me	1956	6.25	12.50	25.00
❑ B-9023 [PS]	A Fellow Needs a Girl	1956	6.25	12.50	25.00
❑ B-9531	I Guess I'll Have to Dream the Rest/If Only She'd Look My Way//Love Me/Nevertheless	1957	6.25	12.50	25.00
❑ B-9531 [PS]	Adventures of the Heart, Vol. I	1957	6.25	12.50	25.00
❑ B-9532	We Kiss in a Shadow/I Am Loved//Take My Love/ I Could Write a Book	1957	6.25	12.50	25.00
❑ B-9532 [PS]	Adventures of the Heart, Vol. II	1957	6.25	12.50	25.00
❑ B-9533	Mad About You/Sorry//On the Island of Stromboli/ It's Only a Paper Moon	1957	6.25	12.50	25.00
❑ B-9533 [PS]	Adventures of the Heart, Vol. III	1957	6.25	12.50	25.00

Number	Title (A Side/B Side)	Yr	VG	VG+	NM
B-10321	White Christmas/Jingle Bells//Have Yourself a Merry Little Christmas/Santa Claus Is Coming to Town	1957	7.50	15.00	30.00
B-10321 [PS]	Christmas Dreaming, Vol. 1	1957	10.00	20.00	40.00
B-10322	Silent Night, Holy Night/Adeste Fideles//O Little Town of Bethlehem/It Came Upon the Midnight Clear	1957	7.50	15.00	30.00
B-10322 [PS]	Christmas Dreaming, Vol. 2	1957	10.00	20.00	40.00
ZTEP 28595/6	[DJ]Nancy/I'm a Fool to Want You//Full Moon and Empty Arms/The Birth of the Blues	1958	12.50	25.00	50.00
ZTEP 28595/6	[PS]Nancy	1958	12.50	25.00	50.00

—Limited edition EP for the B.T. Babbit Soap Co.

RCA VICTOR

Number	Title (A Side/B Side)	Yr	VG	VG+	NM
947-0176	Night and Day/East of the Sun//Fools Rush In/The Lamplighter's Serenade	1954	7.50	15.00	30.00
—Part 1 of EPBT 3063					
947-0177	Everything Happens to Me/I'll Be Seeing You//This Is the Beginning of the End/Street of Dreams	1954	7.50	15.00	30.00
—Part 2 of EPBT 3063					
EPBT-3063	[PS]Fabulous Frankie	1954	10.00	20.00	40.00
—Cover for 947-0176 and 947-0177					
EPA-5014	Oh! Look at Me Now/This Love of Mine//I Guess I'll Have to Dream the Rest/How Do You Do Without Me	1958	5.00	10.00	20.00
EPA-5014	[PS]Frankie and Tommy	1958	5.00	10.00	20.00
EPA-5147	The Lamplighter's Serenade/The Night We Called It a Day//The Song Is You/Night and Day	1960	6.25	12.50	25.00
EPA-5147	[PS]Frank Sinatra	1960	6.25	12.50	25.00

REPRISE

Number	Title (A Side/B Side)	Yr	VG	VG+	NM
SR 1012 [PS]	It Might As Well Be Swing	1965	5.00	10.00	20.00
SR 1012 [S]	Fly Me to the Moon/I Wanna Be Around/More//I Can't Stop Loving You/The Good Life/I Wish You Love	1965	5.00	10.00	20.00

—33 1/3 rpm, small hole, "Promotion"

SINATRA, NANCY

Includes duets with Lee Hazlewood. Also see MEL TILLIS.

ELEKTRA

Number	Title (A Side/B Side)	Yr	VG	VG+	NM
46659	Let's Keep It That Way/One Jump Ahead of the Storm	1979	—	2.50	5.00

PRIVATE STOCK

Number	Title (A Side/B Side)	Yr	VG	VG+	NM
45022	Annabel of Mobile/(B-side unknown)	1975	—	2.50	5.00
45075	Kinky Love/She Played the Piano and He Beat the Drum	1976	—	2.50	5.00
45108	Indian Summer/Holly and Hawkeye	1976	—	2.50	5.00
—With Lee Hazelwood					
45158	It's For My Dad/A Gentle Man Like You	1977	—	2.50	5.00

RCA VICTOR

Number	Title (A Side/B Side)	Yr	VG	VG+	NM
APBO-0029	Ain't No Sunshine/Sugar Me	1973	—	2.50	5.00
47-0864	It's the Love/Kind of a Woman	1973	2.00	4.00	8.00
74-0614	Paris Summer/Down from Dover	1971	2.00	4.00	8.00
—With Lee Hazlewood					

REPRISE

Number	Title (A Side/B Side)	Yr	VG	VG+	NM
0238	Tammy/Thanks to You	1963	5.00	10.00	20.00
0263	Where Do the Lonely Go/Just Think About the Good Times	1964	5.00	10.00	20.00
0292	This Love of Mine/There Goes the Bride	1964	5.00	10.00	20.00
0335	The Answer to Everything/True Love	1965	3.75	7.50	15.00
0407	So Long Babe/If He'd Love Me	1965	3.75	7.50	15.00
0432	These Boots Are Made for Walkin'/The City Never Sleeps at Night	1965	3.00	6.00	12.00
0461	How Does That Grab You, Darlin'?/The Last of the Secret Agents	1966	2.50	5.00	10.00
0491	Friday's Child/Hutchinson Jail	1966	2.50	5.00	10.00
0514	In Our Time/Leave My Dog Alone	1966	2.50	5.00	10.00
0527	Sugar Town/Summer Wine	1966	3.00	6.00	12.00
0559	Love Eyes/Coastin'	1967	2.50	5.00	10.00
0561	Somethin' Stupid/Give Her Love	1967	2.50	5.00	10.00
—A-side: Nancy Sinatra and Frank Sinatra; B-side: Frank Sinatra					
0561	Somethin' Stupid/I Will Wait for You	1967	2.00	4.00	8.00
—A-side: Nancy Sinatra and Frank Sinatra; B-side: Frank Sinatra					
0595	Jackson/You Only Live Twice	1967	2.50	5.00	10.00
—A-side: With Lee Hazlewood					
0620	Lightning's Girl/Until It's Time for You to Go	1967	2.50	5.00	10.00
0620 [PS]	Lightning's Girl/Until It's Time for You to Go	1967	5.00	10.00	20.00
0629	Lady Bird/Sand	1967	2.00	4.00	8.00
—With Lee Hazlewood					
0636	Tony Rome/This Town	1967	2.00	4.00	8.00
0651	Some Velvet Morning/Oh Lonesome Me	1967	2.00	4.00	8.00
—With Lee Hazlewood					
0670	100 Years/See the Little Children	1968	2.00	4.00	8.00
0701	These Boots Are Made for Walkin'/Love Eyes	1968	—	2.50	5.00
—"Back to Back Hits" series					
0721	Sugar Town/Summer Wine	1968	—	2.50	5.00
—"Back to Back Hits" series					
0726	Jackson/Summer Wine	1968	—	2.50	5.00
—With Lee Hazlewood; "Back to Back Hits" series					
0729	Lightning's Girl/One Velvet Morning	1968	—	2.50	5.00
—B-side with Lee Hazlewood; "Back to Back Hits" series					
0756	Happy/Nice 'N' Easy	1968	2.00	4.00	8.00
0789	Good Time Girl/Old Devil Moon	1968	2.00	4.00	8.00
0813	God Knows I Love You/Just Plain Old Me	1969	2.00	4.00	8.00
0821	Here We Go Again/Memories	1969	2.00	4.00	8.00
0851	Drummer Man/Home	1969	2.00	4.00	8.00
0869	Highway Song/(B-side unknown)	1969	5.00	10.00	20.00
—Released only in England					
0880	It's Such a Lonely Time of the Year/Kids	1969	2.50	5.00	10.00
0890	I Love Them All/Home	1970	2.00	4.00	8.00
0932	Hello L.A., Bye Bye Birmingham/White Tattoo	1970	2.00	4.00	8.00
0968	I'm Not a Girl Anymore/How Are Things in California	1970	2.00	4.00	8.00
0980	Feelin' Kinda Sunday/Kids	1970	2.00	4.00	8.00
—A-side by Nancy Sinatra and Frank Sinatra					
0991	Is Anybody Goin' to San Antone/Hook and Ladder	1971	2.00	4.00	8.00
0991 [PS]	Is Anybody Goin' to San Antone/Hook and Ladder	1971	3.75	7.50	15.00
1011	Life's a Trippy Thing/I'm Not Afraid	1971	2.00	4.00	8.00
—A-side by Nancy Sinatra and Frank Sinatra; B-side by Frank Sinatra solo					
1021	Did You Ever/Back on the Road	1971	2.00	4.00	8.00
—As "Nancy and Lee" (Hazlewood)					
1034	Glory Road/Is Anybody Goin' to San Antone	1971	2.00	4.00	8.00
20017	Not Just Your Friend/Cuff Links and a Tie Clip	1961	5.00	10.00	20.00
20017 [PS]	Not Just Your Friend/Cuff Links and a Tie Clip	1961	15.00	30.00	60.00
20045	To Know Him Is to Love Him/Like I Do	1962	5.00	10.00	20.00
20097	June, July and August/Think of Me	1962	5.00	10.00	20.00
20127	Tonight You Belong to Me/You Can Have Any Boy	1962	5.00	10.00	20.00
20144	Put Your Head on My Shoulder/I See the Moon	1963	5.00	10.00	20.00
20188	The Cruel War/One Way	1963	5.00	10.00	20.00

SINCERES, THE (1)

COLUMBIA

Number	Title (A Side/B Side)	Yr	VG	VG+	NM
43110	Sincerely/Snap Your Fingers	1964	3.75	7.50	15.00

EPIC

Number	Title (A Side/B Side)	Yr	VG	VG+	NM
9583	Kookie Ookie/Our Winter Love	1963	3.75	7.50	15.00

TAURUS

Number	Title (A Side/B Side)	Yr	VG	VG+	NM
377	The Magic of Love/Tell Her	1966	7.50	15.00	30.00

SINCERES, THE (2)

JORDAN

Number	Title (A Side/B Side)	Yr	VG	VG+	NM
117	You're Too Young/Forbidden Love	1960	62.50	125.00	250.00

RICHIE

Number	Title (A Side/B Side)	Yr	VG	VG+	NM
545	Please Don't Cheat on Me/If You Should Leave Me	1961	175.00	350.00	700.00
—No mention of Roulette Records on label					
545	Please Don't Cheat on Me/If You Should Leave Me	1961	25.00	50.00	100.00
—With Roulette Records distribution mentioned on label					

SIGMA

Number	Title (A Side/B Side)	Yr	VG	VG+	NM
1003/4	Darling/Do You Remember	1960	100.00	200.00	400.00

SINGING DOGS, THE, DON CHARLES PRESENTS

RCA

Number	Title (A Side/B Side)	Yr	VG	VG+	NM
PA-10129	Jingle Bells/Oh! Susanna	1976	—	2.00	4.00
—Black label, dog near top					

RCA VICTOR

Number	Title (A Side/B Side)	Yr	VG	VG+	NM
F2NW-7846/7	[DJ]Pearl's Jingle Bells/Caesar's Pat-A-Cake/King's Three Blind Mice//Dolly's Oh! Susanna (Fast)/ Dolly's Oh! Susanna (Slow)	1955	10.00	20.00	40.00
—Banded version for radio use ("Jingle Bells" is 1:15)					
PA-10129	Jingle Bells/Oh! Susannah	1974	2.00	4.00	8.00
—First issue of PA-10129 has tan or brown (also possibly orange) labels					
47-6344	Oh! Susannah//Pat-a-Cake/Three Blind Mice/Jingle Bells	1955	3.75	7.50	15.00
—"Jingle Bells" is part of a medley and lasts 1:15					
47-6344 [PS]	Oh! Susannah//Pat-a-Cake/Three Blind Mice/Jingle Bells	1955	6.25	12.50	25.00
47-6432	Hot Dog Rock and Roll/Hot Dog Boogie	1956	3.00	6.00	12.00
48-1020	Jingle Bells/Oh! Susannah	1971	—	2.50	5.00
—First reissue; "Jingle Bells" lengthened to 1:47 on this and future issues					
48-1021	Hot Dog Rock and Roll/Hot Dog Boogie	1971	—	2.50	5.00

SINGING MCENTIRES, THE (PAKE, REBA AND SUSIE)

BOSS

Number	Title (A Side/B Side)	Yr	VG	VG+	NM
SPS-194	The Ballad of John McEntire/Interview by the Grandchildren	1969	125.00	250.00	500.00
—Supposedly only 25 copies were pressed					

SINGLETON, SHANA STACEY

SUN

Number	Title (A Side/B Side)	Yr	VG	VG+	NM
1177	Listen to Daddy (I'll Sing You What to Dream)/Remember Bethlehem	1982	—	2.00	4.00

SIOUXSIE AND THE BANSHEES

GEFFEN

Number	Title (A Side/B Side)	Yr	VG	VG+	NM
27760	Peek-A-Boo/False Face	1988	—	—	3.00
28813	Cities in Dust/An Execution	1986	—	—	3.00
28813 [PS]	Cities in Dust/An Execution	1986	—	—	3.00
29358	Dear Prudence/Tattoo	1984	—	—	3.00
29358 [PS]	Dear Prudence/Tattoo	1984	—	—	3.00

POLYDOR

Number	Title (A Side/B Side)	Yr	VG	VG+	NM
14561	Hong Kong Garden/Overground	1979	10.00	20.00	40.00

PVC

Number	Title (A Side/B Side)	Yr	VG	VG+	NM
1001	Israel/Red Over White	1980	—	2.50	5.00
1001 [PS]	Israel/Red Over White	1980	—	2.50	5.00

SIR DOUGLAS QUINTET

Also see THE DEVONS; DOUG SAHM.

ATLANTIC

Number	Title (A Side/B Side)	Yr	VG	VG+	NM
2965	The Nitty Gritty/I'm Just Tired of Getting Burned	1973	2.00	4.00	8.00
2985	Texas Tornado/Blue Horizon	1973	2.00	4.00	8.00
—As "Sir Douglas Band"					

CASABLANCA

Number	Title (A Side/B Side)	Yr	VG	VG+	NM
828	Roll With the Punches/I'm Not That Kat Anymore	1975	6.25	12.50	25.00

MERCURY

Number	Title (A Side/B Side)	Yr	VG	VG+	NM
73257	Michoacan/Westside Blues Again	1971	—	3.00	6.00

PACEMAKER

Number	Title (A Side/B Side)	Yr	VG	VG+	NM
280	Sugar Bee/Blue Norther	1964	5.00	10.00	20.00

PHILIPS

Number	Title (A Side/B Side)	Yr	VG	VG+	NM
40676	What About Tomorrow/A Nice Song	1970	2.00	4.00	8.00
40676 [PS]	What About Tomorrow/A Nice Song	1970	3.75	7.50	15.00
40687	Pretty Flower/Catch the Man on the Fly	1970	2.00	4.00	8.00
40708	Wasted Days, Wasted Nights/Me and My Destiny	1971	2.00	4.00	8.00

Number	Title (A Side/B Side)	Yr	VG	VG+	NM
SMASH					
❑ 2169	Are Inlaws Really Outlaws/Sell a Song	1968	2.00	4.00	8.00
❑ 2191	Mendocino/I Wanna Be Your Mama Again	1968	2.00	4.00	8.00
❑ 2222	Lawd, I'm Just a Country Boy in This Great Big Freaky City/It Didn't Even Bring Me Down	1969	2.00	4.00	8.00
❑ 2233	Dynamite Woman/Too Many Dociled Minds	1969	2.00	4.00	8.00
❑ 2253	At the Crossroads/Texas Me	1969	2.00	4.00	8.00
❑ 2259	Nuevo Laredo/I Don't Wanna Go Home	1970	2.00	4.00	8.00
TRIBE					
❑ 8308	She's About a Mover/We'll Take Our Last Walk Tonight	1965	3.00	6.00	12.00
❑ 8310	The Tracker/Blue Brother	1965	2.50	5.00	10.00
❑ 8312	In Time/The Story of John Hardy	1965	2.50	5.00	10.00
❑ 8314	The Rains Came/Bacon Fat	1966	2.50	5.00	10.00
❑ 8317	She's Gotta Be Boss/Quarter to Three	1966	2.50	5.00	10.00
❑ 8318	Beginning of the End/Love Don't Treat Me Fair	1966	2.50	5.00	10.00
❑ 8321	She Digs My Love/When I Sing the Blues	1966	2.50	5.00	10.00
❑ 8323	Hang Loose/I'm Sorry	1967	2.50	5.00	10.00
SISTER HAZEL					
UNIVERSAL					
❑ US7-56190	All for You/Happy	1998	—	2.00	4.00
❑ 012 158218-7	Change Your Mind/All for You	2000	—	2.00	4.00
SIX PENTZ, THE					
BRENT					
❑ 7062	Imitation Situation/Please Come Home	1967	5.00	10.00	20.00
❑ 7064	Don't Say You're Sorry/Tinkle Talk	1967	5.00	10.00	20.00
SIX TEENS, THE					
FLIP					
❑ 315	A Casual Look/Teenage Promise	1956	5.00	10.00	20.00
❑ 317	Send Me Flowers/Afar Into the Night	1956	3.75	7.50	15.00
❑ 320	My Special Guy/Only Jim	1956	3.75	7.50	15.00
❑ 322	Arrow of Love/Was It a Dream of Mine	1957	3.75	7.50	15.00
❑ 326	Baby You're Dynamite/My Surprise	1957	3.75	7.50	15.00
❑ 329	My Secret/Stop Playing Ping Pong	1958	3.75	7.50	15.00
❑ 333	Danny/Love's Funny That Way	1958	3.75	7.50	15.00
❑ 338	Baby-O/Oh, It's Crazy	1958	5.00	10.00	20.00
❑ 346	Why Do I Go to School/Heaven Knows I Love You	1959	6.25	12.50	25.00
❑ 350	So Happy/That Wonderful Secret of Love	1960	3.75	7.50	15.00
❑ 351	A Little Prayer/Suddenly in Love	1960	3.75	7.50	15.00
SIXPENCE, THE					
ALL AMERICAN					
❑ 313	Fortune Teller/My Flash on You	1966	10.00	20.00	40.00
❑ 333	Hey Joe/(B-side unknown)	1967	7.50	15.00	30.00
❑ 353	Fortune Teller/My Flash on You	1967	7.50	15.00	30.00
DOT					
❑ 16959	Fortune Teller/My Flash on You	1966	6.25	12.50	25.00
IMPACT					
❑ 1025	What to Do/You're the Love	1967	6.25	12.50	25.00
SKARLETTONES, THE					
EMBER					
❑ 1053	Do You Remember/Will You Dream	1959	30.00	60.00	120.00
SKEE BROTHERS, THE					
EPIC					
❑ 9275	Big Deal/While I'm Away	1958	25.00	50.00	100.00
OKEH					
❑ 7108	That's All She Wrote/Four Aces	1959	12.50	25.00	50.00
ROULETTE					
❑ 4164	Romeo Joe/Lu Ann	1959	5.00	10.00	20.00
SKELTON, EDDIE					
DIXIE					
❑ 2011	Keep It Swinging/Without You	1958	500.00	1000.	1500.
STARDAY					
❑ 294	My Heart Gets Lonely/Let Me Be With You Forever	1957	37.50	75.00	150.00
SKIP AND FLIP					
Also see GARY PAXTON.					
BRENT					
❑ 7002	It Was I/Lunch Hour	1959	6.25	12.50	25.00
❑ 7005	Fancy Nancy/It Could Be	1959	6.25	12.50	25.00
❑ 7010	Cherry Pie/I'll Quit Cryin' Over You	1960	6.25	12.50	25.00
❑ 7013	Teenage Honeymoon/Hully Gully Cha Cha Cha	1960	5.00	10.00	20.00
❑ 7017	The Green Door/Willow Tree	1960	5.00	10.00	20.00
❑ 7028	Over the Mountain/One More Drink for Julie	1962	5.00	10.00	20.00
CALIFORNIA					
❑ 2325	Tossin' and Turnin'/Everyday I Have to Cry	1963	3.75	7.50	15.00
REV					
❑ 3523	Why Not Confess/Johnny Risk	1959	6.25	12.50	25.00
—As "Gary and Clyde"					
TIME					
❑ 1007	Why Not Confess/Johnny Risk	1959	5.00	10.00	20.00
—As "Gary and Clyde"					
❑ 1031	Betty Jean/Doubt	1961	5.00	10.00	20.00
SKYLARKS, THE (1)					
ADMIRAL					
❑ 500	I'll Surf Around the World/How Many Times	1963	7.50	15.00	30.00
SKYLARKS, THE (2)					
DECCA					
❑ 48241	The Glory of Love/You and I	1951	125.00	250.00	500.00
SKYLARKS, THE (3)					
EVERLAST					
❑ 5022	Everybody's Got Somebody/Jeannie	1963	7.50	15.00	30.00

Number	Title (A Side/B Side)	Yr	VG	VG+	NM
SKYLARKS, THE (4)					
RCA VICTOR					
❑ 47-5257	Home in Pasadena/I Had the Craziest Dream	1953	6.25	12.50	25.00
SKYLARKS, THE (5)					
VERVE					
❑ 10082	Ol' Man River/There's a Boat Dat's Leavin' for New York	1957	5.00	10.00	20.00
SKYLARKS, THE (U)					
THUNDERBIRD					
❑ 102	Do You Know?/Here Comes the Fool	196?	3.00	6.00	12.00
SKYLINERS, THE					
Also see JIMMY BEAUMONT.					
ATCO					
❑ 6270	Since I Fell for You/I'd Die	1963	10.00	20.00	40.00
CALICO					
❑ 103/4	Since I Don't Have You/One Night, One Night	1959	12.50	25.00	50.00
❑ 106	This I Swear/Tomorrow	1959	7.50	15.00	30.00
❑ 109	It Happened Today/Lonely Way	1959	7.50	15.00	30.00
❑ 114	How Much/Lorraine from Spain	1960	6.25	12.50	25.00
❑ 117	Pennies from Heaven/I'll Be Seeing You	1960	6.25	12.50	25.00
❑ 120	Believe Me/Happy Time	1960	6.25	12.50	25.00
CAMEO					
❑ 215	Three Coins in the Fountain/Everyone But You	1962	10.00	20.00	40.00
CAPITOL					
❑ 3979	Where Have They Gone/I Could Have Loved You So Well	1974	6.25	12.50	25.00
—As "Jimmy Beaumont and the Skyliners"					
CLASSIC ARTISTS					
❑ 123	You're My Christmas Present/Another Lonely New Year's Eve	1990	—	2.50	5.00
COLPIX					
❑ 188	I'll Close My Eyes/The Door Is Still Open	1961	10.00	20.00	40.00
❑ 607	Ba'ion Rhythms/The End of a Story	196?	10.00	20.00	40.00
—As "Jimmy Beaumont and the Skyliners"					
❑ 613	Close Your Eyes/Our Love Will Last	1961	10.00	20.00	40.00
DRIVE					
❑ 6250	Our Day Is Here/The Day the Clown Cried	1976	2.00	4.00	8.00
JUBILEE					
❑ 5506	The Loser/Everything Is Fine	1965	3.75	7.50	15.00
❑ 5512	Who Do You Love/Get Yourself a Baby	1965	3.75	7.50	15.00
❑ 5520	I Run to You/Don't Hurt Me Baby	1965	3.75	7.50	15.00
MOTOWN					
❑ 1046 [DJ]	Since I Fell for You/I'd Die	1963	1000.	1500.	2000.
—Record never got beyond the test pressing stage (2 known copies)					
ORIGINAL SOUND					
❑ 35	Since I Don't Have You/One Night, One Night	1963	3.75	7.50	15.00
❑ 36	Pennies from Heaven/I'll Be Seeing You	1963	3.75	7.50	15.00
❑ 37	This I Swear/It Happened Today	1963	3.75	7.50	15.00
TORTOISE INT'L.					
❑ PB-11243	Oh How Happy/We've Got Love on Our Side	1978	2.00	4.00	8.00
❑ PB-11312	Smile On Me/Love Bug (Done Bit Me Again)	1978	2.00	4.00	8.00
VISCOUNT					
❑ 104	Comes Love/Tell Me	1962	5.00	10.00	20.00
SLADE					
Also see THE IN-BE-TWEENS.					
CBS ASSOCIATED					
❑ 04398	Run Runaway/Don't Take a Hurricane	1984	—	2.00	4.00
❑ 04528	My Oh My/High and Dry	1984	—	2.00	4.00
❑ 04865	Little Sheila/Lock Up Your Daughters	1985	—	2.00	4.00
COTILLION					
❑ 44128	Get Down and Get With It/The Gospel According to Rasputin	1971	6.25	12.50	25.00
❑ 44139	Cos I Love You/Gotta Keep a-Rockin'	1971	6.25	12.50	25.00
❑ 44150	Look Wot You Dun/Candidate	1972	6.25	12.50	25.00
POLYDOR					
❑ 15041	Look Wot You Dun/Candidate	1972	2.50	5.00	10.00
❑ 15044	Cuz I Love You/My Life Is Natural	1972	2.50	5.00	10.00
❑ 15046	Take Me Back 'Ome/Wondering Why	1972	2.50	5.00	10.00
❑ 15053	Mama Weer All Crazee Now/Man Who Speeks Evil	1972	2.50	5.00	10.00
❑ 15060	Gudbuy T' Jane/I Won't Let It 'Appen Again	1973	2.50	5.00	10.00
❑ 15069	Cum On Feel the Noize/I'm Mee, I'm Now, An' That's Orl	1973	3.75	7.50	15.00
❑ 15080	Let the Good Times Roll/Feel So Fine-I Don' Mind	1973	2.50	5.00	10.00
REPRISE					
❑ 1182	Skweeze Me Pleeze Me/My Town	1973	2.00	4.00	8.00
WARNER BROS.					
❑ 7759	Merry Christmas Everybody/Don't Blame Me	1973	2.50	5.00	10.00
❑ 7777	Good Time Gals/We're Really Gonna Raise the Roof	1974	2.00	4.00	8.00
❑ 7808	How Can It Be/When the Lights Are Out	1974	2.00	4.00	8.00
❑ 8134	How Does It Feel/OK, Yesterday Was Yesterday	1975	2.00	4.00	8.00
❑ 8185	Nobody's Fool/When the Chips Are Down	1976	2.00	4.00	8.00
SLADES, THE					
DOMINO					
❑ 500	You Cheated/The Waddle	1958	10.00	20.00	40.00
❑ 800	You Gambled/No Time	1959	10.00	20.00	40.00
❑ 901	Just You/It's Better to Love	1959	7.50	15.00	30.00
❑ 906	It's Your Turn/Take My Heart	1961	10.00	20.00	40.00
❑ 1000	Summertime/You Must Try	1961	7.50	15.00	30.00
LIBERTY					
❑ 55118	Baby/You Mean Everything to Me	1957	12.50	25.00	50.00
—As "The Spades," in error					
❑ 55118	Baby/You Mean Everything to Me	1957	6.25	12.50	25.00

SLAVIN, SLICK

Number	Title (A Side/B Side)	Yr	VG	VG+	NM
IMPERIAL					
❑ 5540	Speed Crazy/She Says She's Mine	1958	7.50	15.00	30.00

SLED, BOB, AND THE TOBOGGANS

Number	Title (A Side/B Side)	Yr	VG	VG+	NM
CAMEO					
❑ 400	Here We Go (Surfer Boys Are Going Skiing)/Sea and Ski	1966	12.50	25.00	50.00

SLEDGE, PERCY

Number	Title (A Side/B Side)	Yr	VG	VG+	NM
ATLANTIC					
❑ 2326	When a Man Loves a Woman/Love Me Like You Mean It	1966	5.00	10.00	20.00
❑ 2342	Warm and Tender Love/Sugar Puddin'	1966	2.50	5.00	10.00
❑ 2358	It Tears Me Up/Heart of a Child	1966	2.50	5.00	10.00
❑ 2383	Baby, Help Me/You Got That Something Wonderful	1967	2.50	5.00	10.00
❑ 2396	Out of Left Field/It Can't Be Stopped	1967	2.50	5.00	10.00
❑ 2414	Love Me Tender/What Am I Living For	1967	2.50	5.00	10.00
❑ 2434	Just Out of Reach (Of My Two Empty Arms)/Hard to Believe	1967	2.50	5.00	10.00
❑ 2453	Cover Me/Behind Every Great Man There Is a Woman	1967	2.50	5.00	10.00
❑ 2490	Take Time to Know Her/It's All Wrong But It's Alright	1968	3.00	6.00	12.00
❑ 2539	Sudden Stop/Between These Arms	1968	2.50	5.00	10.00
❑ 2563	You're All Around Me/Self-Preservation	1968	2.50	5.00	10.00
❑ 2594	My Special Prayer/Bless Your Little Sweet Soul	1969	2.00	4.00	8.00
❑ 2616	Any Day Now/The Angels Listened In	1969	2.50	5.00	10.00
❑ 2646	Woman of the Night/Kind Woman	1969	2.00	4.00	8.00
❑ 2679	Faithful and True/True Love Travels on a Gravel Road	1969	2.00	4.00	8.00
❑ 2719	Too Many Rivers to Cross/Push Mr. Pride Aside	1970	2.00	4.00	8.00
❑ 2754	Help Me Make It Through the Night/Thief in the Night	1970	2.00	4.00	8.00
❑ 2826	Stop the World Tonight/That's the Way I Want to Live	1971	—	3.00	6.00
❑ 2848	Rainbow Road/Standing on the Mountain	1971	—	3.00	6.00
❑ 2886	Sunday Brother/Everything You'll Ever Need	1972	—	3.00	6.00
❑ 2963	Sunshine/Unchanging Love	1973	—	3.00	6.00
❑ 89262	When a Man Loves a Woman/Cover Me	1987	—	—	3.00
❑ 89262 [PS]	When a Man Loves a Woman/Cover Me	1987	—	2.00	4.00
CAPRICORN					
❑ 0209	I'll Be Your Everything/Blue Water	1974	—	2.50	5.00
❑ 0220	If This Is the Last Time/Behind Closed Doors	1975	—	2.50	5.00
❑ 0273	When a Boy Becomes a Man/When She Touches Me	1977	—	2.50	5.00
MONUMENT					
❑ 03612	You Had to Be There/Hard Lovin' Woman	1983	—	2.00	4.00
❑ 03878	She's Too Pretty to Cry/Home Type Thing	1983	—	2.00	4.00
PHILCO-FORD					
❑ HP-12	When a Man Loves a Woman/Baby Help Me	1967	6.25	12.50	25.00
—4-inch plastic "Hip Pocket Record" with color sleeve					

SLICK, GRACE

Also see THE GREAT SOCIETY; JEFFERSON AIRPLANE; JEFFERSON STARSHIP; PAUL KANTNER AND GRACE SLICK; STARSHIP.

Number	Title (A Side/B Side)	Yr	VG	VG+	NM
GRUNT					
❑ BFBO-0183	Theme from "Manhole"/Come Again, Toucan	1973	—	3.00	6.00
RCA					
❑ PB-11939	Seasons/Angel of Night	1980	—	2.00	4.00
❑ PB-11939 [PS]	Seasons/Angel of Night	1980	—	2.50	5.00
❑ PB-12041	Dreams/Do It the Hard Way	1980	—	2.00	4.00
❑ PB-12171	Sea of Love/Full Moon Man	1981	—	2.00	4.00
❑ PB-12172	Mistreater/Full Moon Man	1981	—	—	—
—Canceled					
❑ PB-12186	Round and Round/Full Moon Man	1981	—	—	—
—Canceled					
❑ PB-13764	Through the Window/Habits	1984	—	2.00	4.00

SLLEDNATS, THE

See THE STANDELLS.

SLOAN, P.F.

Cohort of STEVE BARRI. Also see THE FANTASTIC BAGGYS; THE GRASS ROOTS; THE IMAGINATIONS (2); THE INNER CIRCLE; THE LIFEGUARDS (2); PHILIP AND STEPHAN; THE RALLY PACKS; THE STREET CLEANERS; THEMES INC.; WILLIE AND THE WHEELS.

Number	Title (A Side/B Side)	Yr	VG	VG+	NM
ALADDIN					
❑ 3461	All I Want Is Lovin'/Little Girl in the Cabin	1959	6.25	12.50	25.00
—As "Flip Sloan"					
ATCO					
❑ 6663	Star Gazin'/New Design	1969	5.00	10.00	20.00
DUNHILL					
❑ 4007	Sins of the Family/This Mornin'	1965	3.75	7.50	15.00
❑ 4016	Halloween Mary/I'd Have to Be Out of My Mind	1965	3.75	7.50	15.00
❑ 4016 [PS]	Halloween Mary/I'd Have to Be Out of My Mind	1965	6.25	12.50	25.00
—Sleeve is promo only					
❑ 4024	From a Distance/Patterns	1966	6.25	12.50	25.00
❑ 4037	City Women/Top of a Fence	1966	3.75	7.50	15.00
❑ 4054	I Found a Girl/A Melody for You	1966	3.75	7.50	15.00
❑ 4064	Sunflower, Sunflower/The Man Behind the Red Balloon	1967	6.25	12.50	25.00
❑ 4064 [PS]	Sunflower, Sunflower/The Man Behind the Red Balloon	1967	7.50	15.00	30.00
❑ 4106	Karma (Study of Divination)/I Can't Help But Wonder, Elizabeth	1967	6.25	12.50	25.00
—As "Philip Sloan"					
MART					
❑ 802	She's My Girl/If You Believe in Me	1960	20.00	40.00	80.00
MUMS					
❑ 6010	Let Me Be/Springtime	1972	5.00	10.00	20.00

SLY

See SLY STEWART.

SLY AND THE FAMILY STONE

Also see SLY STEWART.

Number	Title (A Side/B Side)	Yr	VG	VG+	NM
EPIC					
❑ 10229	Higher/Underdog	1967	2.50	5.00	10.00
❑ 10256	Dance to the Music/Let Me Hear It from You	1967	2.50	5.00	10.00
❑ 10353	Life/M'Lady	1968	2.00	4.00	8.00
❑ 10407	Everyday People/Sing a Simple Song	1968	2.50	5.00	10.00
❑ 10407 [PS]	Everyday People/Sing a Simple Song	1968	3.00	6.00	12.00
❑ 10450	Stand!/I Want to Take You Higher	1969	2.50	5.00	10.00
❑ 10450 [PS]	Stand!/I Want to Take You Higher	1969	3.00	6.00	12.00
❑ 10497	Hot Fun in the Summertime/Fun	1969	2.50	5.00	10.00
❑ 10555	Thank You Falettinme Be Mice Elf Agin/Everybody Is a Star	1969	—	3.00	6.00
❑ 10555 [PS]	Thank You Falettinme Be Mice Elf Agin/Everybody Is a Star	1969	2.50	5.00	10.00
❑ 10805	Family Affair/Luv N' Haight	1971	—	3.00	6.00
❑ 10829	Runnin' Away/Brave & Strong	1972	—	3.00	6.00
❑ 10850	Smilin'/Luv N' Haight	1972	—	3.00	6.00
❑ 11017	If You Want Me to Stay/Thankful N' Thoughtful	1973	—	3.00	6.00
❑ 11017	If You Want Me to Stay/Babies Makin' Babies	1973	—	3.00	6.00
❑ 11060	Frisky/If It Were Left Up to Me	1973	—	3.00	6.00
❑ 11140	Time for Livin'/Small Talk	1974	—	3.00	6.00
❑ 50035	Loose Booty/Can't Strain My Brain	1974	—	3.00	6.00
❑ 50119	Hot Fun in the Summertime/Fun	1975	2.00	4.00	8.00
❑ 50135	I Get High on You/That's Lovin' You	1975	—	2.50	5.00
❑ 50175	Li Lo Li/Who Do You Love	1975	—	2.50	5.00
❑ 50201	Greed/Crossword Puzzle	1976	—	2.50	5.00
❑ 50331	Family Again/Nothing Less Than Happiness	1977	—	2.50	5.00
LOADSTONE					
❑ 3951	I Ain't Got Nobody/I Can't Turn You Loose	1967	5.00	10.00	20.00
WARNER BROS.					
❑ 29682	High Y'All/Ha Ha He He	1983	—	2.00	4.00
❑ 49062	Sheer Energy/Remember Who You Are	1979	—	2.00	4.00
❑ 49132	Who's to Say/Same Thing	1979	—	2.00	4.00

SMALL, MILLIE

Number	Title (A Side/B Side)	Yr	VG	VG+	NM
ATCO					
❑ 6384	Tongue Tied/Blood Shot Eyes	1965	2.50	5.00	10.00
ATLANTIC					
❑ 2266	Bring It On Home to Me/I've Fallen in Love with a Snowman	1965	2.50	5.00	10.00
BRIT					
❑ 7002	My Street/Mixed-Up, Lonely, Self-Centered, Spoiled Kind of Boy	1965	3.00	6.00	12.00
SMASH					
❑ 1893	My Boy Lollipop/Something's Gotta Be Done	1964	3.75	7.50	15.00
❑ 1920	Sweet William/What Am I Living For	1964	3.00	6.00	12.00
❑ 1940	I Love the Way You Love/Bring It On Home to Me	1964	3.00	6.00	12.00
❑ 1946	Don't You Know/Tom Hark	1964	3.00	6.00	12.00

SMALL FACES

Also see FACES.

Number	Title (A Side/B Side)	Yr	VG	VG+	NM
IMMEDIATE					
❑ 501	Itchykoo Park/I'm Only Dreaming	1967	3.00	6.00	12.00
❑ 1902	Here Come the Nice/Talk to You	1967	2.50	5.00	10.00
❑ 5003	Tin Soldier/I Feel Much Better	1968	2.50	5.00	10.00
❑ 5003 [PS]	Tin Soldier/I Feel Much Better	1968	6.25	12.50	25.00
❑ 5007	Lazy Sunday/Rollin' Over	1968	2.50	5.00	10.00
❑ 5009	The Universal/Donkey Rides A Penny A Glass	1968	3.75	7.50	15.00
❑ 5012	Mad John/The Journey	1969	3.75	7.50	15.00
❑ 5014	Afterglow of Your Love/Wham, Bam, Thank You Ma'am	1969	3.75	7.50	15.00
PRESS					
❑ 5007	Almost Grown/Hey Girl	1969	5.00	10.00	20.00
❑ 9794	What 'Cha Gonna Do About It/What's a Matter	1965	6.25	12.50	25.00
❑ 9826	Sha-La-La-La-Lee/Grow Your Own	1966	3.75	7.50	15.00
PRIDE					
❑ 1006	Runaway/Shake	1972	3.00	6.00	12.00
RCA VICTOR					
❑ 47-8949	Understanding/All or Nothing	1966	5.00	10.00	20.00
❑ 47-8949 [PS]	Understanding/All or Nothing	1966	7.50	15.00	30.00
❑ 47-9055	My Mind's Eye/I Can't Dance with You	1966	5.00	10.00	20.00

SMART, JIMMY

Number	Title (A Side/B Side)	Yr	VG	VG+	NM
ALLSTAR					
❑ 7211	Broken Dream/It's Too Late for Me	1960	6.25	12.50	25.00
PLAID					
❑ 1004	Shorty/In My Dreams	1961	5.00	10.00	20.00

SMART TONES, THE

Number	Title (A Side/B Side)	Yr	VG	VG+	NM
HERALD					
❑ 529	Bob-O-Link/Ginny	1958	25.00	50.00	100.00

SMASH MOUTH

Number	Title (A Side/B Side)	Yr	VG	VG+	NM
INTERSCOPE					
❑ 069 497100 7	All Star/Then the Morning Comes	1999	—	—	3.00

SMASHING PUMPKINS

Number	Title (A Side/B Side)	Yr	VG	VG+	NM
LIMITED POTENTIAL					
❑ LIMP 006	I Am One/Not Worth Asking	1990	30.00	60.00	120.00
❑ LIMP 006 [PS]	I Am One/Not Worth Asking	1990	30.00	60.00	120.00
SUB POP					
❑ 90	Tristessa/La Dolly Vita	1991	6.25	12.50	25.00
—Pink vinyl (4,000 pressed)					
❑ 90	Tristessa/La Dolly Vita	1991	7.50	15.00	30.00
—Black vinyl (3,000 pressed)					
❑ 90	Tristessa/La Dolly Vita	1991	125.00	250.00	500.00
—Red vinyl (5 pressed)					

Number	Title (A Side/B Side)	Yr	VG	VG+	NM
❑ 90	Tristessa/La Dolly Vita	1991	30.00	60.00	120.00
—Gray vinyl (50 pressed)					
❑ 90 [PS]	Tristessa/La Dolly Vita	1991	6.25	12.50	25.00
VIRGIN					
❑ 38522	1979/Bullet with Butterfly Wings	1996	—	2.50	5.00
❑ 38522 [PS]	1979/Bullet with Butterfly Wings	1996	—	2.50	5.00

SMILE (1)

Brian May and Roger Taylor, later of QUEEN, were in this group.

Number	Title (A Side/B Side)	Yr	VG	VG+	NM
MERCURY					
❑ 72977	Earth/Step on Me	1968	50.00	100.00	200.00

SMILE (2)

Number	Title (A Side/B Side)	Yr	VG	VG+	NM
UNI					
❑ 55313	A Year Every Night/Southbound	1972	—	3.00	6.00
❑ 55336	Tonight/One Night Stand	1972	—	3.00	6.00

SMITH

Also see GAYLE McCORMACK.

Number	Title (A Side/B Side)	Yr	VG	VG+	NM
ABC DUNHILL					
❑ 4206	Baby It's You/I Don't Believe (I Believe)	1969	2.00	4.00	8.00
❑ 4206 [PS]	Baby It's You/I Don't Believe (I Believe)	1969	3.00	6.00	12.00
❑ 4228	Take a Look Around/Mojalesky Ridge	1970	—	3.00	6.00
❑ 4238	What Am I Gonna Do/Born in Boston	1970	—	3.00	6.00
❑ 4238 [PS]	What Am I Gonna Do/Born in Boston	1970	2.50	5.00	10.00
❑ 4246	Comin' Back to Me Baby/Minus-Plus	1970	—	3.00	6.00

SMITH, ARLENE

Also see THE CHANTELS.

Number	Title (A Side/B Side)	Yr	VG	VG+	NM
BIG TOP					
❑ 3073	Love, Love, Love/He Knows I Love Him Too Much	1961	7.50	15.00	30.00
SPECTOROUS					
❑ 150	Good Girls/Everything	196?	25.00	50.00	100.00

SMITH, ARTHUR "GUITAR BOOGIE"

Number	Title (A Side/B Side)	Yr	VG	VG+	NM
CHOICE					
❑ 6101	Shhh (With Dialogue)/Shhh (Without Dialogue)	1960	3.75	7.50	15.00
❑ 6102	I'm Afraid of Wimmin/Fishin' Fever	1961	3.75	7.50	15.00
DOT					
❑ 16695	The Billy Malone Story/I Look Up	1965	2.50	5.00	10.00
❑ 16852	Jet Set/New River Train	1966	2.50	5.00	10.00
❑ 17013	Today/Whitepoint	1967	2.50	5.00	10.00
MGM					
❑ K10516	Mountain Be-Bop/Don't Look for Trouble	1949	10.00	20.00	40.00
❑ K10551	Be-Bop Rag/I Never See Maggie Alone	1949	10.00	20.00	40.00
❑ K10577	Mule Train/Banjo Rag	1949	10.00	20.00	40.00
❑ K10608	Guitar and Piano Boogie/I'm Only Tellin' You	1950	7.50	15.00	30.00
❑ K10714	I.H. Boogie/I'm Afraid of Women	1950	7.50	15.00	30.00
❑ K10791	Mandolin Boogie/Conversation with a Mule	1950	7.50	15.00	30.00
❑ K10807	Memphis Blues/Beer Barrel Polka	1950	7.50	15.00	30.00
❑ K10829	Mr. Stalin, You're Eatin' Too High/Banjo Buster	1950	7.50	15.00	30.00
❑ K10847	Merry Christmas, Everyone/Guitar Jingle Bells	1950	7.50	15.00	30.00
❑ K10881	Hot Rod Race/Rhumba Boogie	1951	10.00	20.00	40.00
❑ K10914	Beautiful Brown Eyes (Vocal)/(Instrumental)	1951	7.50	15.00	30.00
❑ K10945	Chew Tobacco Rag/Big Mountain Shuffle	1951	7.50	15.00	30.00
❑ K10991	Who Shot Willie/Express Train Boogie	1951	7.50	15.00	30.00
❑ K11040	Fence Jumper/Tears Don't Always Mean a Broken Heart	1951	7.50	15.00	30.00
❑ K11096	Listen to the Mockingbird/BLue Moon Waltz	1951	7.50	15.00	30.00
❑ K11137	R.S.V.P. Uncle Sam/Shortnin' Bread	1952	6.25	12.50	25.00
❑ K11191	Just Lookin'/Fiddle Faddle	1952	6.25	12.50	25.00
❑ K11262	River Rag/Someone Left Another Young'un at Our House	1952	6.25	12.50	25.00
❑ K11317	Somebody's Knocking/I Know There's a Crown for Me	1952	6.25	12.50	25.00
❑ K11324	Make Me Know It/Five Foot Two, Eyes of Blue	1952	6.25	12.50	25.00
❑ K11361	Five String Banjo Boogie/Guitar Jamboree	1952	6.25	12.50	25.00
❑ K11379	The South/Lady of Spain	1952	6.25	12.50	25.00
❑ K11413	Indian Boogie/Cherokee Strut	1953	6.25	12.50	25.00
❑ K11433	In Memory of Hank Williams/I'm Richer Than You	1953	10.00	20.00	40.00
❑ K11503	Because You Love Me/Rainbow Waltz	1953	6.25	12.50	25.00
❑ K11558	He Went That-a-Way/Three "D" Boogie	1953	6.25	12.50	25.00
❑ K11605	Oklahoma Polka/You're Off Limits	1953	6.25	12.50	25.00
❑ K11657	The Honeymoon Is Over/Cotton Patch Rag	1954	6.25	12.50	25.00
❑ K11704	I Get So Lonely/Outboard	1954	6.25	12.50	25.00
❑ K11784	Red Headed Stranger/Sobbin' Women	1954	6.25	12.50	25.00
❑ K11817	Lonesome/Half-Moon	1954	6.25	12.50	25.00
❑ K11879	Hi-Lo Boogie/Truck Stop Grill	1954	6.25	12.50	25.00
❑ K11945	Midnight Rag/You're Hooked	1955	5.00	10.00	20.00
❑ K12006	Feudin' Banjos/'Bye 'Bye Back Smoke Choo Choo	1955	7.50	15.00	30.00
—With Don Reno					
❑ K12064	Your Way/Yes Sir, That's My Baby	1955	5.00	10.00	20.00
❑ K12135	Number One Street (Part 1)/Number One Street (Part 2)	1955	5.00	10.00	20.00
❑ K12176	Nobody, Somebody, Nobody/All Night Blues	1956	5.00	10.00	20.00
❑ K12224	The Gal with the Yaller Shoes/Buzz Saw	1956	5.00	10.00	20.00
❑ K12330	Blue Rock/More Foolish Questions	1956	5.00	10.00	20.00
❑ K12436	Freeze It Boogie/I Thought It Couldn't Happen to Me	1957	5.00	10.00	20.00
❑ K12458	Two Theme Calypso/Stamps	1957	5.00	10.00	20.00
❑ K12544	Teen-Age Rebel/Easy Rock	1957	6.25	12.50	25.00
❑ K12618	Rockin' the News/Guitar Bustin'	1958	5.00	10.00	20.00
❑ K12791	Banjo Boogie/Hard Boiled Boogie	1959	5.00	10.00	20.00
MONUMENT					
❑ 8572	Ringing Banjos/Battling Banjos Polka	1973	—	3.00	6.00
❑ 8583	Just Joshin'/Banjo Bustin'	1973	—	3.00	6.00
❑ 8604	Guitar Boogie/Right On	1974	—	3.00	6.00
❑ 8676	Theme from "Death Driver"/Moods from "Death Driver"	1975	—	3.00	6.00
STARDAY					
❑ 576	Guitar Boogie Twist/Napoleon's Retreat	1962	3.75	7.50	15.00
❑ 590	Heartaches/Foolish Questions — Silly Answers	1962	3.75	7.50	15.00
❑ 615	Philadelphia Guitar/Hospitality Blues	1962	3.75	7.50	15.00
❑ 634	Master of the Game/Travelin' Blues	1963	3.75	7.50	15.00
❑ 642	Tie My Hunting Dogs Down. Jed/Guitar Hop	1963	3.75	7.50	15.00
❑ 656	The Stuttering Song/Back to His Hole He Went	1963	3.75	7.50	15.00
❑ 701	I Like Lasses/Flat Top Hari Kari	1964	3.75	7.50	15.00
❑ 824	British Backbeat/Lynn's Gone	1968	2.00	4.00	8.00
❑ 861	What Is an American?/Psychoanalysis	1969	2.00	4.00	8.00
❑ 868	Guitar Unlimited/Summer Theme	1969	2.00	4.00	8.00
❑ 7007	Guitar Boogie Twist/Under the Double Eagle	197?	—	3.00	6.00
❑ 7018	The South/Memphis South	197?	—	3.00	6.00
❑ 8013	Guitar Boogie/Under the Double Eagle	197?	—	3.00	6.00

SMITH, BETTY, GROUP

Number	Title (A Side/B Side)	Yr	VG	VG+	NM
LONDON					
❑ 1763	Virginia/Double Shuffle	1958	3.00	6.00	12.00
❑ 1787	Bewitched/Hand Jive	1958	3.00	6.00	12.00
❑ 1819	My Foolsih Heart/Betty's Blues	1958	3.00	6.00	12.00

SMITH, BOBBIE, AND THE DREAM GIRLS

See THE DREAM GIRLS.

SMITH, HUEY "PIANO"

Number	Title (A Side/B Side)	Yr	VG	VG+	NM
ACE					
❑ 521	Everybody's Wailin'/Little Liza Jane	1956	6.25	12.50	25.00
❑ 530	Rockin' Pneumonia and the Boogie Woogie Flu (Part 1/Part 2)	1957	7.50	15.00	30.00
❑ 538	Free, Single and Disengaged/Just a Lonely Clown	1957	6.25	12.50	25.00
❑ 545	Don't You Just Know It/High Blood Pressure	1958	6.25	12.50	25.00
❑ 548	Havin' a Good Time/We Like Birdland	1958	6.25	12.50	25.00
❑ 553	Don't You Know Yockomo/Well, I'll Be John Brown	1958	6.25	12.50	25.00
❑ 562	Would You Believe It (I Have a Cold)/Genevieve	1959	5.00	10.00	20.00
❑ 571	Tu-Ber-Cu-Lucas and the Sinus Blues/Dearest Darling	1959	5.00	10.00	20.00
❑ 584	Beatnik Blues/For Cryin' Out Loud	1960	3.75	7.50	15.00
❑ 638	She Got Low Down/Mean, Mean, Mean	1961	3.75	7.50	15.00
❑ 639	She Got Low Down/Mean, Mean, Mean//Little Liza Jane/Rockin' Pnuemonia	1961	6.25	12.50	25.00
❑ 649	Pop-Eye/Scald Dog	1962	3.75	7.50	15.00
❑ 672	Every Once in a While/Somebody Told It	1962	3.00	6.00	12.00
❑ 8002	Talk to Me Baby/If It Ain't One Thing, It's Another	1962	3.00	6.00	12.00
❑ 8008	Let's Bring 'Em Back Again/Quiet as It's Kept	1963	3.75	7.50	15.00
CONSTELLATION					
❑ 102	He's Back Again/Quiet As It's Kept	1963	2.50	5.00	10.00
COTILLION					
❑ 44142	Rockin' Pneumonia and the Boogie Woogie Flu (Part 1/Part 2)	1971	—	3.00	6.00
IMPERIAL					
❑ 5721	The Little Moron/Someone to Love	1961	3.00	6.00	12.00
❑ 5747	Behind the Wheel — Part 1/Behind the Wheel — Part 2	1961	3.00	6.00	12.00
❑ 5772	More Girls/Sassy Sara	1961	3.00	6.00	12.00
❑ 5789	Don't Knock It/Shag-a-Tooth	1961	3.00	6.00	12.00
INSTANT					
❑ 3287	I'll Never Forget/Bury Me Dead	1967	2.00	4.00	8.00
❑ 3297	Two Way Pockaway (Part 1)/Two Way Pockaway (Part 2)	1969	2.00	4.00	8.00
❑ 3301	Epitaph of Uncle Tom/Eight Bars of Amen	1969	2.00	4.00	8.00
❑ 3303	You Got Too (Part 1)/You Got Too (Part 2)	1969	2.00	4.00	8.00
❑ 3305	Ballad of a Black Man/The Whatcha Call 'Em	1970	2.00	4.00	8.00
SAVOY					
❑ 1113	You Made Me Cry/You're Down with Me	1953	25.00	50.00	100.00
VIN					
❑ 1024	I Didn't Do It/They Kept On	1960	3.75	7.50	15.00

SMITH, HURRICANE

Number	Title (A Side/B Side)	Yr	VG	VG+	NM
CAPITOL					
❑ 3148	Don't Let It Die/The Writer Sings His Song	1971	—	2.50	5.00
❑ 3383	Oh Babe, What Would You Say?/Getting to Know You	1972	—	3.00	6.00
—Red and orange "target" label					
❑ 3383	Oh Babe, What Would You Say?/Getting to Know You	1972	—	2.00	4.00
—Orange label with "Capitol" at bottom					
❑ 3455	Who Was It?/Take Suki Home	1972	—	2.00	4.00
EMI					
❑ 3809	Beautiful Day-Beautiful Night/Sam	1973	—	2.00	4.00

SMITH, KEELY

Also see LOUIS PRIMA AND KEELY SMITH.

Number	Title (A Side/B Side)	Yr	VG	VG+	NM
ATLANTIC					
❑ 2429	One Less Bell to Answer/Begin the Beguine	1967	—	3.00	6.00
❑ 2457	Open Your Heart/All Fall Down	1967	—	3.00	6.00
CAPITOL					
❑ F3445	I Wish You Love/Shy	1956	3.75	7.50	15.00
❑ F3545	High School Affair/Hurt Me	1956	3.00	6.00	12.00
❑ F3663	Sentimental Journey/Baby, Won't You Please Come Home	1957	3.00	6.00	12.00
❑ F3698	Young and In Love/You Better Go Now	1957	3.00	6.00	12.00
❑ F3740	You'll Never Know/Good Behavior	1957	3.00	6.00	12.00
❑ F3820	Autumn Leaves/I Keep Forgetting	1957	3.00	6.00	12.00
❑ F3952	How Are Ya' Fixed for Love?/Nothin' in Common	1958	3.00	6.00	12.00
—By Frank Sinatra and Keely Smith					
❑ F3975	The Whippoorwill/Sometimes	1958	3.00	6.00	12.00
DOT					
❑ 15989	Don't Let the Stars Get In Your Eyes/I'd Climb the Highest Mountain	1959	3.00	6.00	12.00
❑ 16089	Close/Tea Leaves	1960	3.00	6.00	12.00
❑ 16146	Here in My Heart/Clearance Sale	1960	3.00	6.00	12.00
❑ 16147	Christmas Island/Silent Night	1960	3.75	7.50	15.00

Number	Title (A Side/B Side)	Yr	VG	VG+	NM
❑ 16182	La-Bou-Lay-A/Young in Years	1961	2.50	5.00	10.00
❑ 16228	I Keep Coming Back for More/Little Lover Boy	1961	2.50	5.00	10.00
❑ 16257	Prisoner of Love/The Loveliest Night of the Year	1961	2.50	5.00	10.00
❑ 16298	Can't Help Falling in Love/You'll Never Walk Alone	1961	2.50	5.00	10.00
❑ 16338	Confidential/How Deep Is the Ocean	1962	2.50	5.00	10.00
❑ 16386	What Kind of Fool Am I/If I Should Lose You	1962	2.50	5.00	10.00
RCA VICTOR					
❑ 74-0543	Your Love/Loving Gift	1971	—	2.50	5.00
REPRISE					
❑ 0294	Let Me Call You Sweetheart/Sunday Mornin'	1964	2.00	4.00	8.00
❑ 0303	I'll Always Love You/I Can't Get You Out of My Heart	1964	2.00	4.00	8.00
❑ 0346	You're Breaking My Heart/Crazy	1965	—	3.00	6.00
❑ 0374	Have You Ever Been Lonely/Something Wonderful Happened	1965	—	3.00	6.00
❑ 0396	Someday (You'll Want Me to Love You)/Standing in the Ruins	1965	—	3.00	6.00
❑ 0402	That Old Black Magic/Standing in the Ruins	1965	—	3.00	6.00
❑ 0428	It's All in the Way You Look at Life/I'll Bring You Water	1965	—	3.00	6.00
❑ 0452	Good-Bye My Love/Where Are You	1966	—	3.00	6.00
❑ 0482	The Wonder of You/Who's Afraid	1966	—	3.00	6.00
❑ 20149	Going Through the Motions/When You Cry	1963	2.00	4.00	8.00
❑ 20211	Love Again/No One Ever Tells You	1963	2.00	4.00	8.00

SMITH, LENDON, AND THE JESTERS

Number	Title (A Side/B Side)	Yr	VG	VG+	NM
METEOR					
❑ 5030	Women/Lost Love	1956	37.50	75.00	150.00

SMITH, LEON

Number	Title (A Side/B Side)	Yr	VG	VG+	NM
EPIC					
❑ 9326	Little 40 Ford/Cry All the Time	1959	10.00	20.00	40.00
LAVENDER					
❑ 1851	Basic Surf/Jailer, Bring Me Water	196?	7.50	15.00	30.00
WILLIAMETTE					
❑ 101	Little 40 Ford/Once I Had a Heart	1959	30.00	60.00	120.00
❑ 105	Honey Honey/That's the Way	1959	7.50	15.00	30.00
❑ 109	Flip, Flop and Fly/Sweet Love	1960	7.50	15.00	30.00

SMITH, O.C.

Number	Title (A Side/B Side)	Yr	VG	VG+	NM
BIG TOP					
❑ 3039	You Are My Sunshine/Well I'm Dancin'	1960	3.00	6.00	12.00
—As "Ocie Smith"					
CADENCE					
❑ 1304	Slow Walk/Forbidden Fruit	1956	3.75	7.50	15.00
—As "Ocie Smith"					
❑ 1312	If You Don't Love Me/Bad Man of Missouri	1957	3.75	7.50	15.00
—As "Ocie Smith"					
❑ 1329	Lighthouse/Too Many	1957	3.75	7.50	15.00
—As "Ocie Smith"					
CARIBOU					
❑ 9017	Together/Just Couldn't Help Myself	1976	—	2.50	5.00
❑ 9021	Simple Wife/Come with Me	1977	—	2.50	5.00
COLUMBIA					
❑ 10031	La La Peace Song/When Morning Comes	1974	—	2.50	5.00
❑ 43525	That's Life/I'm Your Man	1966	2.00	4.00	8.00
❑ 43809	Beyond the Next Hill/On Easy Street	1966	2.00	4.00	8.00
❑ 44151	Double Life/The Season	1967	2.00	4.00	8.00
❑ 44425	The Son of Hickory Holler's Tramp/The Best Man	1968	2.00	4.00	8.00
❑ 44555	Main Street Mission/Gas Food Lodging	1968	2.00	4.00	8.00
❑ 44616	Little Green Apples/Long Black Limousine	1968	2.00	4.00	8.00
❑ 44705	Isn't It Lonely Together/I Ain't the Worryin' Kind	1968	—	3.00	6.00
❑ 44751	Honey (I Miss You)/Keep On Keepin' On	1969	—	3.00	6.00
❑ 44859	Friend, Lover, Woman, Wife/I Taught Her Everything She Knows	1969	—	3.00	6.00
❑ 44948	Daddy's Little Man/If I Leave You Now	1969	—	3.00	6.00
❑ 44948 [PS]	Daddy's Little Man/If I Leave You Now	1969	2.00	4.00	8.00
❑ 45038	Me and You/Can't Take My Eyes Off You	1969	—	3.00	6.00
❑ 45098	Isn't Life Beautiful/Moody	1970	—	3.00	6.00
❑ 45160	Primrose Lane/Melodee	1970	—	3.00	6.00
❑ 45206	Baby I Need Your Loving/San Francisco Is a Lonely Town	1970	—	3.00	6.00
❑ 45301	Downtown U.S.A./That's What Life Is All About	1971	—	3.00	6.00
❑ 45343	Clean Up Your Own Back Yard/I've Been There	1971	—	3.00	6.00
❑ 45435	Help Me Make It Through the Night/Diamond in the Rough	1971	—	3.00	6.00
❑ 45655	Don't Misunderstand/If You Touch Me	1972	—	3.00	6.00
❑ 45863	La La Peace Song/When Morning Comes	1973	—	3.00	6.00
FAMILY					
❑ 5000	Dreams Come True/(B-side unknown)	1980	—	2.50	5.00
MGM					
❑ 12321	Just Kiss Me/At Last My Baby's Coming Home	1956	3.75	7.50	15.00
—As "Ocie Smith"					
MOTOWN					
❑ 1623	Love Changes/Got to Know	1982	—	2.50	5.00
❑ 1636	I Betcha/That's One for Love	1982	—	2.50	5.00
RENDEZVOUS					
❑ 101	What'cha Gonna Do/(B-side unknown)	1986	—	2.00	4.00
❑ 102	You're the First, the Last, My Everything/(B-side unknown)	1986	—	2.00	4.00
❑ 103	Brenda/(B-side unknown)	1986	—	2.00	4.00
SHADY BROOK					
❑ 1045	Love to Burn/Give Me Time	1978	—	2.50	5.00
❑ 1049	Living Without Your Love/Can't Be the One to Say It's Over	1978	—	2.50	5.00
❑ 45012	Love Is Forever/(B-side unknown)	197?	—	2.50	5.00
SOUTH BAY					
❑ 1003	Love Changes/Got to Know	1982	—	3.00	6.00

SMITH, OCIE

See O.C. SMITH.

SMITH, PATTI, GROUP

Number	Title (A Side/B Side)	Yr	VG	VG+	NM
ARISTA					
❑ SP-2 [DJ]	Pissing in the River (mono/stereo)	1976	6.25	12.50	25.00
❑ SP-4 [DJ]	Ask the Angels (mono/stereo)	1977	6.25	12.50	25.00
—With lyric insert (deduct 20% if missing)					
❑ 0171	Gloria/My Generation	1976	2.50	5.00	10.00
❑ 0171 [PS]	Gloria/My Generation	1976	2.50	5.00	10.00
❑ 0318	Because the Night/God Speed	1978	—	2.00	4.00
—A-side co-written by Bruce Springsteen					
❑ 0318 [PS]	Because the Night/God Speed	1978	2.00	4.00	8.00
❑ 0427	Frederick/Frederick (Live)	1979	—	2.00	4.00
❑ 0427 [PS]	Frederick/Frederick (Live)	1979	2.00	4.00	8.00
❑ 0453	So You Want to Be a Rock and Roll Star//5-4-3-2-1/A Fire of Unknown Origin	1979	—	2.00	4.00
❑ 0453 [PS]	So You Want to Be a Rock and Roll Star//5-4-3-2-1/A Fire of Unknown Origin	1979	5.00	10.00	20.00
❑ 9173	Because the Night/So You Want to Be a Rock 'n' Roll Star	198?	—	—	3.00
—"Flashback" reissue					
❑ 9689	People Have the Power/Wild Leaves	1988	—	—	3.00
❑ 9689 [PS]	People Have the Power/Wild Leaves	1988	—	—	3.00
❑ 9762	I Was (Looking for You)/Up There Down There	1988	—	—	3.00
MER					
❑ 601	Hey Joe/Piss Factory	1974	20.00	40.00	80.00
SIRE					
❑ 1009	Hey Joe/Piss Factory	1977	2.00	4.00	8.00
❑ 1009	Hey Joe/Piss Factory	1977	2.00	4.00	8.00

SMITH, RAY

Number	Title (A Side/B Side)	Yr	VG	VG+	NM
CELEBRITY CIRCLE					
❑ 6901	I Walk the Line/Fool #1	1964	3.75	7.50	15.00
CINNAMON					
❑ 755	Tiilted Cup of Love/I'd Traded Better for Worse	1973	—	2.50	5.00
❑ 760	It Wasn't Easy/It's Just Not the Same	1973	—	2.50	5.00
❑ 773	The First Lonely Weekend/A Handful of Friends	1973	—	2.50	5.00
❑ 795	Ten Steps Out in Front/Because of Losing You	1974	—	2.50	5.00
COLUMBIA					
❑ 2-225 (?)	Rainbow/Waltz of the Alamo	1949	10.00	20.00	40.00
—Microgroove 33 1/3 rpm single, small hole					
❑ 2-290 (?)	Snowdeer/Roll Along Kentucky Moon	1949	10.00	20.00	40.00
—Microgroove 33 1/3 rpm single, small hole					
❑ 2-300 (?)	An Old Christmas Card/Jolly Old St. Nicholas	1949	10.00	20.00	40.00
—Microgroove 33 1/3 rpm single, small hole					
❑ 2-305 (?)	Wedding Bells/I'm Throwing Rice (At the Girl I Love)	1949	10.00	20.00	40.00
—Microgroove 33 1/3 rpm single, small hole					
❑ 2-310 (?)	Pretty Little Eyes of Blue/Tennessee Polka	1949	10.00	20.00	40.00
—Microgroove 33 1/3 rpm single, small hole					
❑ 2-530 (?)	Unfaithful One/Daddy's Little Girl	1950	10.00	20.00	40.00
—Microgroove 33 1/3 rpm single, small hole					
❑ 2-535 (?)	I'm Saving Mother's Wedding Ring for You/Mommy Can I Take My Doll	1950	10.00	20.00	40.00
—Microgroove 33 1/3 rpm single, small hole					
❑ 2-590 (?)	No Trespassing/The Sun Has Gone Down	1950	10.00	20.00	40.00
—Microgroove 33 1/3 rpm single, small hole					
DIAMOND					
❑ 193	Everybody's Goin' Somewhere/Au-Go-Go-Go	1965	3.75	7.50	15.00
ERA BACK TO BACK HITS					
❑ 048	Rockin' Little Angel/Robbin' the Cradle	197?	—	2.50	5.00
—B-side by Tony Bellus					
HEART					
❑ 250	Gone, Baby, Gone/(B-side unknown)	195?	1000.	1500.	2000.
INFINITY					
❑ 003	After This Night Is Through/Turn On the Moonlight	1961	3.75	7.50	15.00
❑ 007	Let Yourself Go/Johnny the Hummer	1961	3.75	7.50	15.00
JUDD					
❑ 1016	Rockin' Little Angel/That's All Right	1959	7.50	15.00	30.00
❑ 1017	Maria Elena/Put Your Arms Around Me Honey	1960	7.50	15.00	30.00
❑ 1019	One Wonderful Love/Makes Me Feel Good	1960	7.50	15.00	30.00
❑ 1021	Blonde Hair, Blue Eyes/You Don't Want Me	1960	7.50	15.00	30.00
NU-TONE					
❑ 1182	Deep in My Heart/She's Mine	1964	3.75	7.50	15.00
SHI-RAY					
❑ 101	Sleepy Eyed Woman/Pretty Juke Box	197?	—	3.00	6.00
SMASH					
❑ 1787	Room 503/These Four Precious Years	1962	3.75	7.50	15.00
SUN					
❑ 298	So Right/Right Behind You Baby	1958	7.50	15.00	30.00
❑ 308	Why, Why, Why/You Made a Hit	1958	7.50	15.00	30.00
❑ 319	Rockin' Bandit/Sail Away	1959	7.50	15.00	30.00
❑ 372	Travelin' Salesman/I Won't Miss You ('Til You're Gone)	1961	7.50	15.00	30.00
❑ 375	Hey Boss Man/Candy Doll	1962	7.50	15.00	30.00
TOLLIE					
❑ 9029	There Comes My Baby Back Again/Did We Have a Party	1964	5.00	10.00	20.00
TOPPA					
❑ 1071	Almost Alone/A Place Within My Heart	1962	5.00	10.00	20.00
VEE JAY					
❑ 579	Rockin' Robin/Robbin' the Cradle	1964	3.75	7.50	15.00
WARNER BROS.					
❑ 5371	I'm Snowed/Turn Over a New Leaf	1963	3.75	7.50	15.00
ZIRKON					
❑ 1055	After This Night Is Through/Turn On the Moonlight	1961	5.00	10.00	20.00

Number	Title (A Side/B Side)	Yr	VG	VG+	NM
SMITH, RONNIE					
BRUNSWICK					
❑ 55137	Lookie, Lookie, Lookie/Tiny Kisses	1959	10.00	20.00	40.00
HAMILTON					
❑ 50003	My Babe/I've Got a Love	1959	6.25	12.50	25.00
IMPERIAL					
❑ 5667	It Hurts Me So/Long Time No Love	1960	7.50	15.00	30.00
❑ 5679	I Hear You Knocking/I Started Out Walkin'	1960	7.50	15.00	30.00
SMITH, SHELBY					
REBEL					
❑ 728	Rockin' Mama/Since My Baby Said Goodbye	1962	100.00	200.00	400.00
SMITH, WARREN					
LIBERTY					
❑ 55248	I Don't Believe I'll Fall in Love Today/Cave-In	1960	5.00	10.00	20.00
❑ 55302	Odds and Ends (Bits and Pieces)/A Whole Lot of Nothin'	1961	5.00	10.00	20.00
❑ 55336	Call of the Wild/Old Lonesome Feeling	1961	5.00	10.00	20.00
❑ 55361	Why Baby Why/Why I'm Walking	1961	5.00	10.00	20.00
—With Shirley Collie					
❑ 55409	Bad News Gets Around/Five Minutes of the Latest Blues	1962	5.00	10.00	20.00
❑ 55475	Book of Broken Hearts/160 Pounds of Hurt	1962	5.00	10.00	20.00
❑ 55615	Big City Ways/That's Why I Sing in a Honky Tonk	1963	3.75	7.50	15.00
❑ 55699	Blue Smoke/Judge and Jury	1964	3.75	7.50	15.00
MERCURY					
❑ 72825	Lie to Me/When the Heartaches Get to Me	1968	2.50	5.00	10.00
SUN					
❑ 239	Rock and Roll Ruby/I'd Rather Be Safe Than Sorry	1956	20.00	40.00	80.00
❑ 250	Ubangi Stomp/Black Jack David	1956	15.00	30.00	60.00
❑ 268	Miss Froggie/So Long, I'm Gone	1957	10.00	20.00	40.00
❑ 286	I Fell in Love/I've Got Love If You Want It	1958	7.50	15.00	30.00
❑ 314	Goodbye Mr. Love/Sweet Sweet Girl	1959	10.00	20.00	40.00
WARNER BROS.					
❑ 5125	Dear Santa/The Meaning of Christmas	1959	6.25	12.50	25.00
SMITH, WHISTLING JACK					
DERAM					
❑ 85005	I Was Kaiser Bill's Batman/The British Grin 'N' Bear	1967	2.00	4.00	8.00
❑ 85041	Only When I Laff/Early One Morning	1969	—	3.00	6.00
SMITHS, THE					
Also see MORRISSEY.					
SIRE					
❑ 28136	Stop Me If You Think You've Heard This One Before/I Keep Mine Hidden	1987	—	2.50	5.00
❑ 28136 [PS]	Stop Me If You Think You've Heard This One Before/I Keep Mine Hidden	1987	2.50	5.00	10.00
❑ 29007	How Soon Is Now?/Shakespear's Sister/Headmaster Ritual	1985	3.75	7.50	15.00
❑ 29007 [PS]	How Soon Is Now?/Shakespear's Sister/Headmaster Ritual	1985	5.00	10.00	20.00
❑ 29239	What Difference Does It Make/Back to the Old Home	1984	2.50	5.00	10.00
❑ 29239 [PS]	What Difference Does It Make/Back to the Old Home	1984	5.00	10.00	20.00
SMOKE RINGS, THE					
DOT					
❑ 16975	Love's the Thing/She Gives Me Love	1966	5.00	10.00	20.00
PROSPECT					
❑ 101	Love's the Thing/She Gives Me Love	1966	10.00	20.00	40.00
SMOKEY JOE					
FLIP					
❑ 228	The Signifying Monkey/Listen to Me Baby	1955	125.00	250.00	500.00
SUN					
❑ 228	The Signifying Monkey/Listen to Me Baby	1956	75.00	150.00	300.00
❑ 393	The Signifying Monkey/Listen to Me Baby	1964	50.00	100.00	200.00
SMOOTHIES, THE					
With JOHN PHILLIPS and SCOTT McKENZIE.					
DECCA					
❑ 31105	Softly/Joanie	1960	5.00	10.00	20.00
❑ 31159	Ride, Ride, Ride/Lonely Boy and Pretty Girl	1960	5.00	10.00	20.00
SNOW, EDDIE					
SUN					
❑ 226	Ain't That Right/Bring Your Love Back Home	1955	50.00	100.00	200.00
SNOW, HANK					
RCA					
❑ 2721-7-R	I've Been Everywhere/Ancient History	1990	—	—	3.00
—"Gold Standard Series" reissue					
❑ PB-10804	You're Wondering Why/Somewhere Someone Is Waiting for You	1976	—	2.50	5.00
❑ PB-11021	Trouble in Mind/Trying to Get My Baby Off My Mind	1977	—	2.50	5.00
❑ PB-11080	I'm Still Movin' On/I'm Gonna Bid My Blues Goodbye	1977	—	2.50	5.00
❑ PB-11153	Breakfast with the Blues/I've Done At Least One Thing	1977	—	2.50	5.00
❑ PB-11192	That Heart Belongs to Me/Love Is So Elusive	1978	—	2.50	5.00
❑ PB-11276	Nevertheless/Don't Rock the Boat	1978	—	2.50	5.00
❑ PB-11377	Ramblin' Rose/Red Roses	1978	—	2.50	5.00
❑ PB-11487	The Mysterious Lady from St. Martinique/Get On My Love Train	1979	—	2.50	5.00
❑ PB-11622	A Good Gal Is Hard to Find/I Wish My Heart Could Talk	1979	—	2.50	5.00
❑ PB-11734	It Takes Too Long/6 String Tennessee Flattop	1979	—	2.50	5.00
RCA VICTOR					
❑ APBO-0215	Hello Love/Until the End of Time	1974	—	3.50	7.00
❑ APBO-0307	That's You and Me/Brand on My Heart	1974	—	3.50	7.00
❑ PB-10108	Easy to Love/Just a Faded Petal from a Beautiful Bouquet	1974	—	3.00	6.00
❑ PB-10136	A Letter to Santa Claus/Christmas Roses	1974	—	3.50	7.00
❑ PB-10225	Merry-Go-Round of Love/My Filipino Love	1975	—	3.00	6.00
❑ PB-10338	Hijack/The Last Ride	1975	—	3.00	6.00
❑ PB-10439	Colorado Country Morning/I Keep Dreaming of You All the Time	1975	—	3.00	6.00
❑ PB-10459	Blue Christmas/Nestor, The Long Eared Christmas Donkey	1975	—	3.50	7.00
❑ GB-10513	Hello Love/Until the End of Time	1976	—	2.00	4.00
—"Gold Standard Series" reissue					
❑ PB-10681	Who's Been Here Since I've Been Gone/That's When He Dropped the World in My Hands	1976	—	3.00	6.00
❑ 37-7869	Beggar to a King/Poor Little Jimmie	1961	6.25	12.50	25.00
—"Compact Single 33" with small hole					
❑ 47-4095	Hobo Bill's Last Ride/Wreck of the Old 97	1951	5.00	10.00	20.00
❑ 47-4096	Ben Dewberry's Final Run/Engineer's Child	1951	5.00	10.00	20.00
❑ 47-4097	The Mystery of Number Five/One More Ride	1951	5.00	10.00	20.00
—The above three comprise a box set					
❑ 47-4346	Music Makin' Mama from Memphis/The Highest Bidder	1951	6.25	12.50	25.00
❑ 47-4398	Pray/These Things Shall Pass	1951	6.25	12.50	25.00
❑ 47-4522	The Gold Rush Is Over/Why Do You Promise Me	1952	6.25	12.50	25.00
❑ 47-4593	I'm Movin' On/Marriage Vow	1952	5.00	10.00	20.00
❑ 47-4594	Music Makin' Mama from Memphis/Down the Trail of Aching Hearts	1952	5.00	10.00	20.00
❑ 47-4595	Unwanted Sign Upon Your Heart/The Rhumba Boogie	1952	5.00	10.00	20.00
❑ 47-4596	The Golden Rocket/Bluebird Island	1952	5.00	10.00	20.00
—The above four comprise a box set					
❑ 47-4632	My Mother/I Just Telephone Upstairs	1952	6.25	12.50	25.00
❑ 47-4733	Lady's Man/Married by the Bible, Divorced by the Law	1952	6.25	12.50	25.00
❑ 47-4856	Jesus Wept/I'm in the Mood for Love	1952	6.25	12.50	25.00
❑ 47-4909	I Went to Your Wedding/Boogie Woogie Flying Cloud	1952	6.25	12.50	25.00
❑ 47-4973	Zeb Turney's Gal/Golden River	1952	5.00	10.00	20.00
❑ 47-4974	Moanin'/I Knew That We'd Meet Again	1952	5.00	10.00	20.00
❑ 47-4975	My Little Golden Horseshoe/The Yodeling Cowboy	1952	5.00	10.00	20.00
❑ 47-4976	Confused with the Blues/On That Old Hawaiian Shore	1952	5.00	10.00	20.00
—The above four comprise a box set					
❑ 47-5006	Broken Hearted/I Wonder Where You Are Tonight	1952	5.00	10.00	20.00
❑ 47-5026	Love Entered the Iron Door/I Cried But My Tears Were Too Late	1952	5.00	10.00	20.00
❑ 47-5034	(Now and Then, There's) A Fool Such As I/The Gal Who Invented Kissin'	1952	5.00	10.00	20.00
❑ 47-5155	Honeymoon on a Rocket Ship/There Wasn't an Organ at Our Wedding	1953	5.00	10.00	20.00
❑ 47-5220	Jimmie the Kid/My Blue Eyed Jane	1953	3.75	7.50	15.00
❑ 47-5221	When Jimmie Rodgers Said Goodbye/Treasure Untold	1953	3.75	7.50	15.00
❑ 47-5222	Southern Cannonball/Anniversary Blue Yodel	1953	3.75	7.50	15.00
❑ 47-5223	Why Did You Give Me Your Love/Mississippi River Blues	1953	3.75	7.50	15.00
—The above four comprise a box set					
❑ 47-5249	Glory Land March/In Daddy's Footsteps	1953	5.00	10.00	20.00
❑ 47-5296	Spanish Fire Ball/Between Fire and Water	1953	5.00	10.00	20.00
❑ 47-5340	Christmas Roses/Reindeer Boogie	1953	6.25	12.50	25.00
❑ 47-5380	For Now and Always/A Message from the Tradewinds	1953	5.00	10.00	20.00
❑ 47-5490	When Mexican Joe Met Jole Blon/No Longer a Prisoner	1953	5.00	10.00	20.00
❑ 47-5548	I'm Glad I'm On the Inside/Invisible Hands	1953	5.00	10.00	20.00
❑ 47-5592	Panamama/Act 1, Act 2, Act 3	1954	5.00	10.00	20.00
❑ 47-5648	My Religion's Not Old Fashioned/Old Rattler	1954	6.25	12.50	25.00
—With Grandpa Jones					
❑ 47-5698	I Don't Hurt Anymore/My Arabian Baby	1954	5.00	10.00	20.00
❑ 47-5794	The Alphabet/My Religion's Not Old Fashioned	1954	5.00	10.00	20.00
❑ 47-5912	That Crazy Mambo Thing/The Next Voice You Hear	1954	5.00	10.00	20.00
❑ 47-5960	Let Me Go, Lover!/I've Forgotten You	1954	5.00	10.00	20.00
❑ 47-6057	Yellow Roses/Would You Mind	1955	3.75	7.50	15.00
❑ 47-6154	Cryin', Prayin', Waitin', Hopin'/I'm Glad I Got to See You Once Again	1955	3.75	7.50	15.00
❑ 47-6269	Born to Be Happy/Mainliner (The Hawk with Silver Wings)	1955	3.75	7.50	15.00
❑ 47-6326	In an Eighteenth Century Drawing Room/La Cucaracha	1955	3.75	7.50	15.00
❑ 47-6379	These Hands/I'm Moving In	1956	3.75	7.50	15.00
❑ 47-6578	Conscience I'm Guilty/Hula Rock	1956	6.25	12.50	25.00
❑ 47-6715	Stolen Moments/Two Won't Care	1956	3.75	7.50	15.00
❑ 47-6772	Oh, Wonderful World/Carnival of Venice	1957	3.75	7.50	15.00
❑ 47-6831	Calypso Sweethearts/Marriage and Divorce	1957	3.75	7.50	15.00
❑ 47-6955	Tangled Mind/My Arms Are a House	1957	3.75	7.50	15.00
❑ 47-7060	Unfaithful/Intro to Listeners-Squid Giggin' Ground	1957	3.75	7.50	15.00
❑ 47-7121	The Blue Danube Waltz/Under the Double Eagle	1957	3.75	7.50	15.00
❑ 47-7154	Whispering Rain/I Wish I Was the Moon	1958	3.75	7.50	15.00
❑ 47-7233	Big Wheels/I'm Hurting All Over	1958	3.75	7.50	15.00
❑ 47-7325	A Woman Captured Me/My Lucky Friend	1958	3.75	7.50	15.00
❑ 47-7448	Doggone That Train/Father Time and Mother Love	1959	3.75	7.50	15.00
❑ 47-7524	Chasin' a Rainbow/I Heard My Heart Break Last Night	1959	3.75	7.50	15.00
❑ 47-7586	The Last Ride/The Party of the Second Part	1959	3.75	7.50	15.00
❑ 47-7702	Rockin', Rollin' Ocean/Walkin' and Talkin'	1960	3.75	7.50	15.00
❑ 47-7748	Miller's Cave/The Change of the Tide	1960	3.75	7.50	15.00

Number	Title (A Side/B Side)	Yr	VG	VG+	NM
❑ 47-7803	The Man Behind the Gun/I'm Asking for a Friend	1960	3.75	7.50	15.00
❑ 47-7869	Beggar to a King/Poor Little Jimmie	1961	3.00	6.00	12.00
❑ 47-7933	The Restless One/I Know	1961	3.00	6.00	12.00
❑ 47-8009	You Take the Future (And I'll Take the Past)/Dog Bone	1962	3.00	6.00	12.00
❑ 47-8072	I've Been Everywhere/Ancient History	1962	3.00	6.00	12.00
❑ 47-8151	The Man Who Robbed the Bank at Santa Fe/ You're Losing Your Baby	1963	3.00	6.00	12.00
❑ 47-8151 [PS]	The Man Who Robbed the Bank at Santa Fe/ You're Losing Your Baby	1963	6.25	12.50	25.00
❑ 47-8239	Ninety Miles an Hour (Down a Dead End Street)/ Blue Roses	1963	3.00	6.00	12.00
❑ 47-8334	Breakfast with the Blues/I Stepped Over the Line	1964	3.00	6.00	12.00
❑ 47-8437	My Memory of You/Ninety Days	1964	3.00	6.00	12.00
❑ 47-8488	The Wishing Well (Down in the Well)/Human	1964	3.00	6.00	12.00
❑ 47-8548	Trouble in Mind/In the Misty Moonlight	1965	2.50	5.00	10.00
❑ 47-8655	The Queen of Draw Poker Town/Tears in the Trade Winds	1965	2.50	5.00	10.00
❑ 47-8713	I've Cried a Mile/Crazy Little Train (Of Love)	1965	2.50	5.00	10.00
❑ 47-8808	The Count Down/Isle of Sicily	1966	2.50	5.00	10.00
❑ 47-9012	Hula Love/Letter from Vietnam	1966	2.50	5.00	10.00
❑ 47-9030	Christmas Cannonball/God Is My Santa Claus	1966	3.00	6.00	12.00
❑ 47-9188	Down at the Pawn Shop/Listen	1967	2.50	5.00	10.00
❑ 47-9300	Learnin' a New Way of Life/Wild Flower	1967	2.50	5.00	10.00
❑ 47-9433	Who Will Answer? (Aleluya No. 1)/I Just Wanted to Know (How the Wind Was Blowing)	1968	2.50	5.00	10.00
❑ 47-9523	The Late and Great Love (Of My Life)/Born for You	1968	2.50	5.00	10.00
❑ 47-9685	The Name of the Game Was Love/The Gypsy and Me	1968	2.00	4.00	8.00
❑ 47-9856	Vanishing Breed/What More Can I Say	1970	2.00	4.00	8.00
❑ 47-9907	Come the Morning/Francesca	1970	2.00	4.00	8.00
❑ 47-9964	Duquesne, Pennsylvania/So Goes My Heart	1971	2.00	4.00	8.00
❑ 48-0056	Marriage Vow/The Star Spangled Waltz	1949	10.00	20.00	40.00
—Originals on green vinyl					
❑ 48-0056	Marriage Vow/The Star Spangled Waltz	195?	6.25	12.50	25.00
—Reissues on black vinyl					
❑ 48-0088	The Blind Boy's Dog/Anniversary of My Broken Heart	1949	10.00	20.00	40.00
—Originals on green vinyl					
❑ 48-0104	My Filipino Rose/The Law of Love	1949	10.00	20.00	40.00
—Originals on green vinyl					
❑ 48-0147	Nobody's Child/The Only Rose	1950	10.00	20.00	40.00
—Originals on green vinyl					
❑ 48-0214	Blue Ranger/Only a Rose from My Mother's Grave	1950	7.50	15.00	30.00
—Originals on green vinyl					
❑ 48-0224	Brand on My Heart/I'll Not Forget My Mother's Prayers	1950	7.50	15.00	30.00
—Originals on green vinyl					
❑ 48-0303	The Drunkard's Son/I Wonder Where You Are Tonight	1950	7.50	15.00	30.00
—Originals on green vinyl					
❑ 48-0328	I'm Movin' On/With This Ring I Thee Wed	1950	10.00	20.00	40.00
—Originals on green vinyl					
❑ 48-0328	I'm Movin' On/With This Ring I Thee Wed	1950	5.00	10.00	20.00
—Reissues on black vinyl					
❑ 48-0356	The Night I Stole Sammy Morgan's Gin/I Cried But My Tears Were Too Late	1950	7.50	15.00	30.00
—Originals on green vinyl					
❑ 48-0362	No Golden Tomorrow Ahead/You Broke the Chain That Held Our Hearts	1950	6.25	12.50	25.00
—Originals on green vinyl					
❑ 48-0363	Wasted Love/My Two Timin' Woman	1950	6.25	12.50	25.00
—Originals on green vinyl					
❑ 48-0364	Somewhere Along Life's Highway/Within This Broken Heart of Mine	1950	6.25	12.50	25.00
—Originals on green vinyl					
❑ 48-0400	The Golden Rocket/Paving the Highway with Tears	1950	7.50	15.00	30.00
—Originals on green vinyl					
❑ 48-0431	The Rhumba Boogie/You Pass Me By	1951	6.25	12.50	25.00
❑ 48-0498	Unwanted Sign Upon Your Heart/Your Locket Is My Broken Heart	1951	6.25	12.50	25.00
❑ 74-0151	Rome Wasn't Built in a Day/Like a Bird	1969	2.00	4.00	8.00
❑ 74-0251	That's When the Hurtin' Sets In/I'm Movin'	1969	2.00	4.00	8.00
❑ 74-0459	Blue Christmas/Nestor, The Long Eared Christmas Donkey	1971	—	—	—
—Unreleased					
❑ 74-0544	No One Will Ever Know/Seashores of Old Mexico	1971	2.00	4.00	8.00
❑ 74-0676	Canadian Pacific/My Way	1972	—	3.50	7.00
❑ 74-0818	The Governor's Hand/Rolling Thunder in My Mind	1972	—	3.50	7.00
❑ 74-0915	North to Chicago/Friend	1973	—	3.50	7.00

7-Inch Extended Plays

RCA VICTOR

Number	Title (A Side/B Side)	Yr	VG	VG+	NM
❑ 547-0097	I'm Movin' On/Down the Trail of Achin' Hearts// The Rhumba Boogie/Bluebird Island	195?	5.00	10.00	20.00
—One record of 2-EP set EPB 3026					
❑ 547-0098	The Golden Rocket/Unwanted Sign Upon Your Heart//Music Makin' Mama from Memphis/ Marriage Vow	195?	5.00	10.00	20.00
—One record of 2-EP set EPB 3026					
❑ EPA 472	Frosty the Snowman/Silent Night//Christmas Roses/The Reindeer Boogie	1953	5.00	10.00	20.00
❑ EPA 472 [PS]	A Country Christmas with Hank Snow	1953	5.00	10.00	20.00
❑ 547-0606	Just Keep a-Movin'/The Bill Is Falling Due// Caribbean/Blue Sea Blues	1955	5.00	10.00	20.00
—One record of 2-EP set EPB-1113					
❑ 547-0607	Can't Have You Blues/A Scale to Measure Love/ /Cuba Rhumba/Blossoms in the Springtime	1955	5.00	10.00	20.00
—One record of 2-EP set EPB-1113					
❑ EPB-1113 [PS]	Just Keep a-Movin'	1955	5.00	10.00	20.00
—Gatefold cover for 547-0606 and 547-0607					
❑ EPB 3026 [PS]	Country Classics	195?	5.00	10.00	20.00
—Gatefold cover for 547-0097 and 547-0098					

SNOW, HANK, AND ANITA CARTER

RCA VICTOR

Number	Title (A Side/B Side)	Yr	VG	VG+	NM
❑ 47-6500	Keep Your Promise, Willie Thomas/It's You, Only You, That I Love	1956	3.75	7.50	15.00
❑ 48-0441	Down the Trail of Achin' Hearts/Bluebird Island	1951	6.25	12.50	25.00

SNOW, HANK, AND KELLY FOXTON

RCA

Number	Title (A Side/B Side)	Yr	VG	VG+	NM
❑ PB-11891	Hasn't It Been Good Together/It Was Love	1980	—	2.50	5.00
❑ PB-11967	There's Something About You/All I Want to Do Is Touch You	1980	—	2.50	5.00
❑ PB-12102	Pain Didn't Shout/Check	1980	—	2.50	5.00
❑ PB-12235	Things/Forbidden Lovers	1981	—	2.50	5.00

SNOW, PHOEBE

Number	Title (A Side/B Side)	Yr	VG	VG+	NM
COLUMBIA					
❑ 10315	Two Fisted Love/Inspired Insanity	1976	—	2.50	5.00
❑ 10351	All Over/No Regrets	1976	—	2.50	5.00
❑ 10463	Shakey Ground/Don't Sleep with Your Eyes Closed	1976	—	2.50	5.00
❑ 10504	Teach Me Tonight/Autobiography (Shine, Shine, Shine)	1977	—	2.50	5.00
❑ 10626	Never Letting Go/The Middle of the Night	1977	—	2.50	5.00
❑ 10654	Love Makes a Woman/Electra	1977	—	2.50	5.00
❑ 10856	Every Night/Random Time	1978	—	2.50	5.00
ELEKTRA					
❑ 69290	Something Real/Best of My Love	1989	—	—	3.00
❑ 69305	If I Can Just Get Through the Night/Soothin'	1989	—	—	3.00
MIRAGE					
❑ 3800	Games/Down in the Basement	1981	—	2.00	4.00
❑ 3818	Mercy, Mercy, Mercy/Something Good	1981	—	2.00	4.00
❑ 3843	Rock Away/Baby Please	1981	—	2.00	4.00
SHELTER					
❑ 40278	Harpo's Blues/Let the Good Times Roll	1974	—	2.50	5.00
❑ 40353	Poetry Man/Either or Both	1974	—	3.00	6.00
❑ 40400	Easy Street/Harpo's Blues	1975	—	2.50	5.00

SNOW, WHITNEY

TOWER

Number	Title (A Side/B Side)	Yr	VG	VG+	NM
❑ 380	The Christmas Angels Sing/Whitey, the Snow White Lamb	1967	2.50	5.00	10.00
—B-side by Justin Wilson					

SNOW MEN, THE

Early version of THE SUNRAYS.

CHALLENGE

Number	Title (A Side/B Side)	Yr	VG	VG+	NM
❑ 59227	Ski Storm (Part 1)/Ski Storm (Part 2)	1964	7.50	15.00	30.00

SOCIETY'S CHILDREN

ATCO

Number	Title (A Side/B Side)	Yr	VG	VG+	NM
❑ 6538	White Christmas/I'll Let You Know	1967	3.00	6.00	12.00
❑ 6553	Count the Ways/Golden Child	1968	2.50	5.00	10.00
❑ 6597	Live for Today/I'll Let You Know	1968	2.50	5.00	10.00
❑ 6618	A Tribute to the Four Seasons/Golden Child	1968	5.00	10.00	20.00

SOF-TONES, THE

CEE BEE

Number	Title (A Side/B Side)	Yr	VG	VG+	NM
❑ 1062	Oh Why/(B-side unknown)	195?	4000.	6000.	8000.

SOFT MACHINE, THE

PROBE

Number	Title (A Side/B Side)	Yr	VG	VG+	NM
❑ 452	Joy of a Toy/Why Are We Sleeping	1969	2.50	5.00	10.00

SOLDIER BOYS, THE

Also see DON COVAY.

SCEPTER

Number	Title (A Side/B Side)	Yr	VG	VG+	NM
❑ 1230	I'm Your Soldier Boy/You Picked Me	1962	15.00	30.00	60.00

SOLITAIRES, THE

Probably more than one group.

Number	Title (A Side/B Side)	Yr	VG	VG+	NM
ARGO					
❑ 5316	Walking Along/Please Kiss This Letter	1958	7.50	15.00	30.00
MGM					
❑ 13221	Fool That I Am/Fair Weather Lover	1964	7.50	15.00	30.00
OLD TOWN					
❑ 1000	Blue Valentine/Wonder Boy	1954	100.00	200.00	400.00
—Black vinyl					
❑ 1000	Blue Valentine/Wonder Boy	1954	375.00	750.00	1500.
—Red vinyl					
❑ 1003	Chapel of St. Clair/If I Loved You	1954	—	—	—
—Unreleased?					
❑ 1006/7	Please Remember My Heart/South of the Border	1954	175.00	350.00	700.00
—Black vinyl					
❑ 1006/7	Please Remember My Heart/South of the Border	1954	1000.	2000.	3000.
—Red vinyl					
❑ 1006/8	Please Remember My Heart/Chances I've Taken	1954	37.50	75.00	150.00
❑ 1008	Chances I've Taken/Lonely	1954	175.00	350.00	700.00
❑ 1008	Please Remember My Heart/Chances I've Taken	196?	6.25	12.50	25.00
—Blue label					
❑ 1010	I Don't Stand a Ghost of a Chance/Girl of Mine	1955	125.00	250.00	500.00
❑ 1012	My Dear/What Did She Say	1955	100.00	200.00	400.00
—Logo in Old English style					
❑ 1012	My Dear/What Did She Say	1956	18.75	37.50	75.00
—Logo in block letters					
❑ 1014	The Wedding/Don't Fall in Love	1955	25.00	50.00	100.00
❑ 1015	Magic Rose/Later for You Baby	1955	25.00	50.00	100.00
❑ 1019	The Honeymoon/Fine Little Girl	1956	25.00	50.00	100.00
❑ 1026	You've Sinned/The Angels Sang	1956	25.00	50.00	100.00

Number	Title (A Side/B Side)	Yr	VG	VG+	NM
❑ 1026	You've Sinned/You're Back with Me	1956	75.00	150.00	300.00
❑ 1032	Give Me One More Chance/Nothing Like a Little Love	1956	50.00	100.00	200.00
❑ 1034	Walking Along/Please Kiss This Letter	1957	18.75	37.50	75.00
—Yellow label					
❑ 1034	Walking Along/Please Kiss This Letter	196?	6.25	12.50	25.00
—Blue label					
❑ 1044	I Really Love You So/Thrill of Love	1957	100.00	200.00	400.00
❑ 1049	Walkin' and Talkin'/No More Sorrows	1958	25.00	50.00	100.00
❑ 1059	Please Remember My Heart/Big Mary's House	1958	10.00	20.00	40.00
❑ 1066	Embraceable You/Round Goes My Heart	1959	10.00	20.00	40.00
❑ 1071	Light a Candle in the Chapel/Helpless	1959	10.00	20.00	40.00
❑ 1096	Lonesome Lover/Pretty Thing	1961	10.00	20.00	40.00
❑ 1139	The Time Is Here/Honey Babe	1963	7.50	15.00	30.00

SOMETHING WILD

Number	Title (A Side/B Side)	Yr	VG	VG+	NM
PSYCHEDELIC					
❑ 1691	Trippin' Out/She's Kinda Weird	1966	12.50	25.00	50.00

SOMETHING YOUNG

Number	Title (A Side/B Side)	Yr	VG	VG+	NM
FONTANA					
❑ 1556	Oh, Don't Come Crying/The Words I'm Seeking	1966	6.25	12.50	25.00

SOMMERS, JOANIE

Number	Title (A Side/B Side)	Yr	VG	VG+	NM
ABC					
❑ 12323	Peppermint Choo Choo/Peppermint Engineer	1978	—	2.50	5.00
CAPITOL					
❑ 5936	Trains and Boats and Planes/Yesterday's Morning	1967	2.00	4.00	8.00
COLUMBIA					
❑ 43567	You've Got Possibilities/Never Throw Your Dreams	1966	2.00	4.00	8.00
❑ 43731	Alfie/You Take What Comes Along	1966	2.00	4.00	8.00
❑ 43950	It Doesn't Matter Anymore/Take a Broken Heart	1966	2.00	4.00	8.00
HAPPY TIGER					
❑ 522	Step Inside Love/Little Girl from Greenwood, Ga.	1970	—	3.00	6.00
❑ 537	Sunshine After the Rain/Tell Him	1970	—	3.00	6.00
WARNER BROS.					
❑ 5157	One Boy/I'll Never Be Free	1960	3.75	7.50	15.00
❑ 5177	Be My Love/Why Don't You Do Right	1960	3.75	7.50	15.00
❑ 5183	Ruby Duby Du/Bob White	1960	3.75	7.50	15.00
❑ 5201	I Don't Want to Walk Without You/Seems Like Long, Long Ago	1961	3.75	7.50	15.00
❑ 5226	Piano Boy/Serenade of the Bells	1961	3.75	7.50	15.00
❑ 5241	Makin' Whoopee/What's Wrong with Me	1961	3.75	7.50	15.00
❑ 5275	Johnny Get Angry/Theme from "A Summer Place"	1962	5.00	10.00	20.00
❑ 5308	When the Boys Get Together/Passing Strangers	1962	3.00	6.00	12.00
❑ 5324	Goodbye Joey/Bobby's Hobbies	1962	3.00	6.00	12.00
❑ 5339	Memories, Memories/Since Randy Moved Away	1963	3.00	6.00	12.00
❑ 5350	Little Bit of Everything/Henny Penny	1963	3.00	6.00	12.00
❑ 5361	One Boy/June Is Bustin' Out All Over	1963	3.00	6.00	12.00
❑ 5374	Little Girl Bad/Wishing Well	1963	3.00	6.00	12.00
❑ 5390	Goodbye Summer/Big Man	1963	3.00	6.00	12.00
❑ 5437	I'd Be So Good for You/I'm Gonna Know He's Mine	1964	2.50	5.00	10.00
❑ 5454	If You Love Him/I Think I'm Gonna Cry Now	1964	2.50	5.00	10.00
❑ 5507	Makin' Whoopee/What's Wrong with Me + 2	1961	6.25	12.50	25.00
—Part of Warner Bros. "+2" series, with two new songs and excerpts of two prior hits					
❑ 5507 [PS]	Makin' Whoopee/What's Wrong with Me + 2	1961	7.50	15.00	30.00
❑ 5629	Don't Pity Me/My Block	1965	2.50	5.00	10.00
❑ 7129	Johnny Get Angry/One Boy	1968	—	3.00	6.00
—"Back to Back Hits" series -- originals have green labels with "W7" logo					
❑ 7251	Great Divide/Talk Until Midnight	1968	2.00	4.00	8.00

SOMMERS, RONNY

See SONNY.

SONIC YOUTH

Number	Title (A Side/B Side)	Yr	VG	VG+	NM
DGC					
❑ 19664	Personality Crisis/Dirty Boots	1990	3.75	7.50	15.00
—Given away with copies of Sassy magazine					
❑ 106610 [DJ]	Goo	1990	2.50	5.00	10.00
—Promo flexi-disc with backing card					
FORCED EXPOSURE					
❑ 001	Making the Nature Scene/I Killed Christgau with My Big Fuckin' Dick	1984	12.50	25.00	50.00
❑ 001	Making the Nature Scene/I Killed Christgau with My Big Fuckin' Dick	1984	37.50	75.00	150.00
—Test pressing (25 made with special sleeve)					
❑ 001 [PS]	Making the Nature Scene/I Killed Christgau with My Big Fuckin' Dick	1984	12.50	25.00	50.00
—Black and white sleeve					
❑ 001 [PS]	Making the Nature Scene/I Killed Christgau with My Big Fuckin' Dick	1984	37.50	75.00	150.00
—Special multi-color sleeve with live band shot on rear; only released with test pressings (25 made)					
❑ 012	Silver Rocket/You Pose You Lose/Non-Metal Dude Wearing Metal Tee	1988	6.25	12.50	25.00
❑ 012 [PS]	Silver Rocket/You Pose You Lose/Non-Metal Dude Wearing Metal Tee	1988	6.25	12.50	25.00
IRIDESCENCE					
❑ 12	Death Valley 69/Brave Men Run	1984	3.00	6.25	12.50
—With Lydia Lunch					
❑ 12 [PS]	Death Valley 69/Brave Men Run	1984	3.00	6.25	12.50
SUB POP					
❑ 26	Touch Me I'm Sick/Halloween	1988	7.50	15.00	30.00
—B-side by Mudhoney; clear vinyl					
❑ 26	Touch Me I'm Sick/Halloween	1988	3.75	7.50	15.00
—B-side by Mudhoney; black vinyl					
❑ 26 [PS]	Touch Me I'm Sick/Halloween	1988	5.00	10.00	20.00
—#2 in Sub Pop Singles Club series					

SONICS, THE (1)

Male vocal group.

Number	Title (A Side/B Side)	Yr	VG	VG+	NM
AMCO					
❑ 001	It's You/Preacher Man	1962	50.00	100.00	200.00
CHECKER					
❑ 922	This Broken Heart/You Made Me Cry	1959	6.25	12.50	25.00
HARVARD					
❑ 801	This Broken Heart/You Made Me Cry	1959	100.00	200.00	400.00
❑ 922	This Broken Heart/You Made Me Cry	1959	12.50	25.00	50.00
JAMIE					
❑ 1235	Sugaree/Beautiful Brown Eyes	1962	5.00	10.00	20.00
X-TRA					
❑ 107	Once in a Lifetime/It Ain't True	1958	500.00	1000.	2000.

SONICS, THE (2)

Rock band from the Pacific Northwest.

Number	Title (A Side/B Side)	Yr	VG	VG+	NM
BURDETTE					
❑ 106	Dirty Old Man/Bama Lama Bama Loo	1975	2.00	4.00	8.00
ETIQUETTE					
❑ 11	Keep a-Knockin'/The Witch	1965	7.50	15.00	30.00
❑ 16	The Hustler/Boss Hoss	1965	7.50	15.00	30.00
❑ 18	Don't Be Afraid of the Dark/Shot Down	1965	7.50	15.00	30.00
❑ 22	Don't Believe in Christmas/Christmas Spirit	1965	7.50	15.00	30.00
—B-side by the Wailers					
❑ 23	Louie Louie/Cinderella	1966	7.50	15.00	30.00
GREAT NORTHWEST					
❑ 702	The Witch/Bama Lama Bama Loo	1979	—	2.50	5.00
JERDEN					
❑ 809	Love Lights/You Got Your Head On Backwards	1966	3.75	7.50	15.00
❑ 810	The Witch/Like No Other	1966	3.75	7.50	15.00
❑ 811	Psycho/Maintaining My Cool	1966	3.75	7.50	15.00
NORTON					
❑ 45-066	Don't Believe in Christmas/Santa Claus	1997	—	—	2.00
—A-side is reissue of Etiquette 22					
❑ 45-066 [PS]	Don't Believe in Christmas/Santa Claus	1997	—	—	2.00
PICCADILLY					
❑ 244	Anyway the Wind Blows/Lost Love	1967	5.00	10.00	20.00
—A-side written by Frank Zappa					
UNI					
❑ 55039	Anyway the Wind Blows/Lost Love	1967	3.75	7.50	15.00
—A-side written by Frank Zappa					

SONICS, THE (U)

Some of these could be group (1); none of these are group (2).

Number	Title (A Side/B Side)	Yr	VG	VG+	NM
ARMONIA					
❑ 102	Funny/I Get That Feeling	1962	37.50	75.00	150.00
GAITY					
❑ 114	Marlene/(B-side unknown)	1959	1000.	1500.	2000.
GROOVE					
❑ 0112	Bumble Bee/As I Live On	1955	50.00	100.00	200.00
NOCTURNE					
❑ 110	Triangle Love/Evil Eye	1959	20.00	40.00	80.00
RKO UNIQUE					
❑ 411	Triangle Love/Evil Eye	1957	15.00	30.00	60.00

SONNETS, THE

Number	Title (A Side/B Side)	Yr	VG	VG+	NM
GUYDEN					
❑ 2112	I Can't Get Sentimental/Forever for You	1964	3.75	7.50	15.00
HERALD					
❑ 477	Please Won't You Call Me/Why Should We Break Up	1956	15.00	30.00	60.00

SONNY

Contains many records he made under aliases. Also see SONNY AND CHER.

Number	Title (A Side/B Side)	Yr	VG	VG+	NM
ATCO					
❑ 6369	Laugh at Me/Gip Pony	1965	3.00	6.00	12.00
❑ 6386	The Revolution Kind/Georgia and John Quetzal	1965	3.00	6.00	12.00
❑ 6505	Misty Roses/I Told My Girl to Go Away	1967	2.50	5.00	10.00
❑ 6531	Pammie's on a Bummer/My Best Friend's Girl Is Out of Sight	1967	2.50	5.00	10.00
FIDELITY					
❑ 3020	Wearing Black/Don't Have to Tell Me	1960	6.25	12.50	25.00
—As "Don Christy"					
GO					
❑ 1001	As Long As You Love Me/I'll Always Be Grateful	1960	6.25	12.50	25.00
—As "Don Christy"					
HIGHLAND					
❑ 1160	I'll Change/Try It Out on Me	1963	7.50	15.00	30.00
—As "Sonny Bono"					
MCA					
❑ 40139	Laugh at Me/Rub Your Nose	1973	—	2.00	4.00
—As "Sonny Bono"					
❑ 40271	Classified 1A/Our Last Show	1974	—	2.00	4.00
—As "Sonny Bono"					
NAME					
❑ 3	As Long As You Love Me/I'll Always Be Grateful	1960	6.25	12.50	25.00
—As "Don Christy"					
SPECIALTY					
❑ 672	Wearing Black/One Little Answer	1959	6.25	12.50	25.00
—As "Don Christy"					
❑ 733	One Little Answer/Comin' Down the Chimney	1974	—	3.00	6.00
—As "Sonny Bono and Little Tootsie"					
SWAMI					
❑ 1001	Don't Shake My Tree/(Mama) Come Get Your Baby Boy	1961	6.25	12.50	25.00
—As "Ronny Sommers"					
VEE JAY					
❑ 710	Midnight Surf/Ride the Wild Quetzal	1966	6.25	12.50	25.00
—As "Sonny Bono"					

SONNY AND CHER

Includes early records as "Caesar and Cleo." Also see CHER; SONNY.

ATCO

Number	Title (A Side/B Side)	Yr	VG	VG+	NM
❑ 6345	Just You/Sing C'est La Vie	1965	2.50	5.00	10.00
❑ 6359	I Got You Babe/It's Gonna Rain	1965	3.00	6.00	12.00
❑ 6381	But You're Mine/Hello	1965	3.00	6.00	12.00
❑ 6395	What Now My Love/I Look for You	1965	3.00	6.00	12.00
❑ 6420	Have I Stayed Too Long/Leave Me Be	1966	2.50	5.00	10.00
❑ 6440	Little Man/Monday	1966	2.50	5.00	10.00
❑ 6449	Living for You/Love Don't Come	1966	2.50	5.00	10.00
❑ 6461	The Beat Goes On/Love Don't Come	1967	3.00	6.00	12.00
❑ 6480	A Beautiful Story/Podunk	1967	2.50	5.00	10.00
❑ 6486	Plastic Man/It's the Little Things	1967	2.50	5.00	10.00
❑ 6507	It's the Little Things/Don't Talk to Strangers	1967	2.50	5.00	10.00
❑ 6541	Good Combination/You and Me	1968	2.50	5.00	10.00
❑ 6555	Circus/I Would Marry You Today	1968	2.50	5.00	10.00
❑ 6605	You Gotta Have a Thing of Your Own/I Got You Babe	1968	2.50	5.00	10.00
❑ 6684	You're a Friend of Mine/I Would Marry You Today	1969	2.50	5.00	10.00
❑ 6758	Get It Together/Hold Me Tighter	1970	2.00	4.00	8.00

KAPP

Number	Title (A Side/B Side)	Yr	VG	VG+	NM
❑ 2141	Real People/Somebody	1971	—	2.00	4.00
❑ 2151	All I Ever Need Is You/I Got You Babe	1971	—	2.50	5.00
❑ 2163	A Cowboy's Work Is Never Done/Somebody	1972	—	2.50	5.00
❑ 2176	When You Say Love/Crystal Clear and Muddy Waters	1972	—	2.00	4.00

MCA

Number	Title (A Side/B Side)	Yr	VG	VG+	NM
❑ 40026	Mama Was a Rock and Roll Singer, Papa Used to Write All Her Songs (Parts 1 & 2)	1973	—	2.00	4.00
❑ 40083	The Greatest Show on Earth/You Know Darn Well	1973	—	2.00	4.00

PHILCO-FORD

Number	Title (A Side/B Side)	Yr	VG	VG+	NM
❑ HP-8	I Got You Babe/The Beat Goes On	1967	6.25	12.50	25.00
—4-inch plastic "Hip Pocket Record" with color sleeve					

REPRISE

Number	Title (A Side/B Side)	Yr	VG	VG+	NM
❑ 0308	Love Is Strange/Do You Want to Dance	1964	5.00	10.00	20.00
—As "Caesar and Cleo"					
❑ 0309	Baby Don't Go/Walkin' the Quetzal	1964	5.00	10.00	20.00
❑ 0392	Baby Don't Go/Walkin' the Quetzal	1965	3.75	7.50	15.00
❑ 0419	Love Is Strange/Let the Good Times Roll	1965	5.00	10.00	20.00
—As "Caesar and Cleo"					
❑ 0419 [PS]	Love Is Strange/Let the Good Times Roll	1965	10.00	20.00	40.00
—As "Caesar and Cleo"					
❑ 0723	Baby Don't Go/Love Is Strange	1968	—	2.50	5.00
—"Back to Back Hits" series -- originals have both "r:" and "W7" logos					

VAULT

Number	Title (A Side/B Side)	Yr	VG	VG+	NM
❑ 909	The Letter/Spring Fever	1964	7.50	15.00	30.00
—As "Caesar and Cleo"					
❑ 916	The Letter/Spring Fever	1965	3.00	6.00	12.00
❑ 916 [PS]	The Letter/Spring Fever	1965	12.50	25.00	50.00

WARNER BROS.

Number	Title (A Side/B Side)	Yr	VG	VG+	NM
❑ 8341	You're Not Right for Me/Wrong Number	1977	—	2.50	5.00

7-Inch Extended Plays

ATCO

Number	Title (A Side/B Side)	Yr	VG	VG+	NM
❑ LSD 33-177 [DJ]	It's Gonna Rain/You've Really Got a Hold on Me//I Got You Babe/The Letter/Why Don't They Let Us Fall in Love	1965	6.25	12.50	25.00
—Jukebox mini-LP					
❑ LSD 33-177 [PS]	Look at Us	1965	6.25	12.50	25.00

SONS OF CHAMPLIN, THE

With Bill Champlin, later of CHICAGO.

ARIOLA AMERICA

Number	Title (A Side/B Side)	Yr	VG	VG+	NM
❑ 7606	Look Out/Queen of the Rain	1975	—	2.00	4.00
❑ 7627	Hold On/Still in Love with You	1976	—	2.00	4.00
❑ 7633	You/Imagination's Sake	1976	—	2.00	4.00
❑ 7653	Follow Your Heart/Here Is Where Your Love Belongs	1976	—	2.00	4.00
❑ 7664	Saved by the Grace of Your Love/West End	1977	—	2.00	4.00

CAPITOL

Number	Title (A Side/B Side)	Yr	VG	VG+	NM
❑ 2437	1982-A/Black and Blue Rainbow	1969	2.00	4.00	8.00
❑ 2534	Freedom/Hello Sunlight	1969	2.00	4.00	8.00
❑ 2663	It's Time/Why Do People Run	1969	2.00	4.00	8.00
❑ 2786	You Can Fly/Terry's Tune	1970	—	3.00	6.00

COLUMBIA

Number	Title (A Side/B Side)	Yr	VG	VG+	NM
❑ 45872	Welcome to the Dance/Swim	1973	—	2.50	5.00

GOLDMINE

Number	Title (A Side/B Side)	Yr	VG	VG+	NM
❑ 101	Look Out/Queen of the Rain	1975	—	2.50	5.00

VERVE

Number	Title (A Side/B Side)	Yr	VG	VG+	NM
❑ 10500	Sing Me a Lullaby/Fat City	1967	2.50	5.00	10.00

SONS OF HERCULES, THE

GET HIP

Number	Title (A Side/B Side)	Yr	VG	VG+	NM
❑ SH-208	Surfin' in the Bars/Outta Your Head	1997	—	—	2.00
❑ SH-208 [PS]	Surfin' in the Bars/Outta Your Head	1997	—	—	2.00

SONS OF THE PIONEERS

CORAL

Number	Title (A Side/B Side)	Yr	VG	VG+	NM
❑ 9-61186	River of No Return/The Lilies Grow High	1954	5.00	10.00	20.00
❑ 9-61316	Montana/Lonely Little Room	1954	5.00	10.00	20.00
❑ 9-64172	Sierra Nevada/If You Would Only Be Mine	1954	5.00	10.00	20.00

DECCA

Number	Title (A Side/B Side)	Yr	VG	VG+	NM
❑ 9-29814	Cool Water/Tumbling Tumbleweeds	1956	3.75	7.50	15.00

GRANITE

Number	Title (A Side/B Side)	Yr	VG	VG+	NM
❑ 550	Cool Water/Pretty Painted Ladies	1976	—	3.00	6.00
❑ 551	Indian Woman/(B-side unknown)	1977	—	3.00	6.00

RCA VICTOR

Number	Title (A Side/B Side)	Yr	VG	VG+	NM
❑ WBY-25	The Ballad of Davy Crockett/The Graveyard Filler of the West	1955	7.50	15.00	30.00
❑ WBY-25 [PS]	The Ballad of Davy Crockett/The Graveyard Filler of the West	1955	12.50	25.00	50.00
❑ WBY-27	A Whale of a Tale/Old Betsy	1955	6.25	12.50	25.00
❑ WBY-46	Home on the Range/Cheyenne	1957	5.00	10.00	20.00
❑ WBY-46 [PS]	Home on the Range/Cheyenne	1957	7.50	15.00	30.00
❑ WBY-68	Wagon Train/Lie Low Little Doggies	195?	5.00	10.00	20.00
❑ 47-2836	Cool Water/Chant of the Wanderer	1949	7.50	15.00	30.00
❑ 47-2837	Tumbling Tumbleweeds/The Everlasting Hills of Oklahoma	1949	7.50	15.00	30.00
❑ 47-2838	Trees/The Timber Trail	1949	7.50	15.00	30.00
—The above three comprise a box set; quickly reissued as 48-0004, 0005 and 0006					
❑ 47-3983	America Forever/Little White Cross	1950	6.25	12.50	25.00
❑ 47-4071	Roses/Mexicali Rose	1951	5.00	10.00	20.00
❑ 47-4072	Moonlight and Roses/Bring Your Roses to Her Now	1951	5.00	10.00	20.00
❑ 47-4073	San Antonio Rose/Room Full of Roses	1951	5.00	10.00	20.00
—The above three comprise a box set					
❑ 47-4131	Daddy's Little Cowboy/Baby I Ain't Gonna Cry No More	1951	5.00	10.00	20.00
❑ 47-4264	Heart Break Hill/The Wind	1951	5.00	10.00	20.00
❑ 47-4347	The Lord's Prayer/Resurectus	1951	5.00	10.00	20.00
❑ 47-4431	Outlaws/I Still Do	1951	5.00	10.00	20.00
❑ 47-4459	I Told Them All About You/Ho-Le-O	1952	5.00	10.00	20.00
❑ 47-4571	Land Beyond the Sun/Waltz of the Roses	1952	5.00	10.00	20.00
❑ 47-4639	Diesel Smoke/Almost	1952	5.00	10.00	20.00
❑ 47-4937	Let's Pretend/The Everlasting Hills of Oklahoma	1952	5.00	10.00	20.00
❑ 47-6055	The Ballad of Davy Crockett/Graveyard Filler of the West	1955	6.25	12.50	25.00
❑ 47-6109	I Wonder When We'll Ever Know/The King's Highway	1955	3.75	7.50	15.00
❑ 47-6123	The Tennessee Rock 'n' Roll/The Three of Us	1955	6.25	12.50	25.00
❑ 47-6184	Be What You Want to Be/Epidemic	1955	3.75	7.50	15.00
❑ 47-6276	Yaller Yaller Gold/King of the River	1955	5.00	10.00	20.00
❑ 47-6376	How Great Thou Art/The Last Frontier	1956	3.75	7.50	15.00
❑ 47-6507	The Searchers/Song of the Prodigal Son	1956	3.75	7.50	15.00
❑ 47-6655	For the Love of You/Timmy's Tune	1956	3.75	7.50	15.00
❑ 47-6890	One More Time/Hasta La Vista	1957	3.75	7.50	15.00
❑ 47-7024	Ballad of the Cowboy Sailor/The Piney Woods	1957	3.75	7.50	15.00
❑ 47-7079	High Ridin' Woman/God Has His Arms Around Me	1957	3.75	7.50	15.00
❑ 47-7392	A Fiddle, a Rifle, an Ax and a Bible/My Last Goodbye	1958	3.00	6.00	12.00
❑ 47-8310	Crazy Arms/Cattle Call Rondolet	1963	2.50	5.00	10.00
❑ 47-8575	Destiny/Green Ice and Mountain Men	1965	2.50	5.00	10.00
❑ 47-9509	Gringo's Guitar/Margretta	1968	2.00	4.00	8.00
❑ 48-0004	Cool Water/Chant of the Wanderer	1949	7.50	15.00	30.00
—Green vinyl original					
❑ 48-0004	Cool Water/Chant of the Wanderer	1951	5.00	10.00	20.00
—Black vinyl reissue					
❑ 48-0005	Tumbling Tumbleweeds/Everlasting Hills of Oklahoma	1949	7.50	15.00	30.00
—Green vinyl original					
❑ 48-0005	Tumbling Tumbleweeds/Everlasting Hills of Oklahoma	1949	5.00	10.00	20.00
—Black vinyl reissue					
❑ 48-0006	Trees/The Timber Trail	1949	7.50	15.00	30.00
—Green vinyl original					
❑ 48-0006	Trees/The Timber Trail	1949	5.00	10.00	20.00
—Black vinyl reissue					
❑ 48-0007	Blue Prairie/Cowboy Camp Meetin'	1949	7.50	15.00	30.00
—Green vinyl original					
❑ 48-0007	Blue Prairie/Cowboy Camp Meetin'	1949	5.00	10.00	20.00
—Black vinyl reissue					
❑ 48-0060	Room Full of Roses/Riders in the Sky	1949	7.50	15.00	30.00
—Green vinyl original					
❑ 48-0094	Rounded Up in Glory/Too High, Too Wide, Too Low	1949	7.50	15.00	30.00
—Green vinyl original					
❑ 48-0095	Lead Me Gently Home Father/Power in the Blood	1949	7.50	15.00	30.00
—Green vinyl original					
❑ 48-0096	The Old Rugged Cross/Read the Bible Every Day	1949	7.50	15.00	30.00
—Green vinyl original					
❑ 48-0101	Lie Low Little Doggies/Bar None Ranch	1949	7.50	15.00	30.00
—Green vinyl original					
❑ 48-0141	Red River Valley/Santa Fe, New Mexico	1950	7.50	15.00	30.00
—Green vinyl original					
❑ 48-0171	Wedding Bells/Love at the County Fair	1950	7.50	15.00	30.00
—With Dale Evans; green vinyl original					
❑ 48-0183	Cigareets, Whusky and Wild, Wild Women/My Best to You	1950	7.50	15.00	30.00
—Green vinyl; reissue of hit 78 rpm from 1947					
❑ 48-0184	Let's Go West Again/Let Me Share Your Name	1950	7.50	15.00	30.00
—Green vinyl original					
❑ 48-0220	Teardrops in My Heart/You Don't Know What Lonesome Is	1950	7.50	15.00	30.00
—Green vinyl; reissue of hit 78 from 1947					
❑ 48-0221	The Sea Walker/The Touch of God's Hand	1950	7.50	15.00	30.00
—Green vinyl original					
❑ 48-0306	Roses/The Eagle's Heart	1950	6.25	12.50	25.00
—Green vinyl original					
❑ 48-0315	Rollin' Dust/Wagons West	1950	6.25	12.50	25.00
—Green vinyl original					
❑ 48-0345	Song of the Wagonmaster/Chuckawalla Swing	1950	6.25	12.50	25.00
—Green vinyl original					
❑ 48-0366	Land Beyond the Sun/I Told Them All About You	1950	6.25	12.50	25.00
—Green vinyl original					
❑ 48-0368	Old Man Atom/What This Country Needs	1950	6.25	12.50	25.00
—Green vinyl original					
❑ 48-0388	Where Are You/What This Country Needs	1950	6.25	12.50	25.00
—Green vinyl original					
❑ 48-0486	Lonesome/The Wondrous Word	1951	5.00	10.00	20.00
❑ 74-0199	Talli Wind/Hawaiian Lullaby	1969	2.00	4.00	8.00

7-Inch Extended Plays

RCA VICTOR

Number	Title (A Side/B Side)	Yr	VG	VG+	NM
❑ 547-0029	Cool Water/Chant of the Wanderer//Tumbling Tumbleweeds/The Everlasting Hills of Oklahoma	195?	5.00	10.00	20.00
	—One record of 2-EP set EPB 3032				
❑ 547-0030	Cowboy Camp Meetin'/Blue Prairie//The Timber Trail/Trees	195?	5.00	10.00	20.00
	—One record of 2-EP set EPB 3032				
❑ EPB 3032 [PS]	Cowboy Classics	195?	5.00	10.00	20.00
	—Gatefold cover for 547-0029 and 547-0030				

SOOTZ, MANNY

PIRATE

Number	Title (A Side/B Side)	Yr	VG	VG+	NM
❑ 841	Cape Canaveral (Part 1)/Cape Canaveral (Part 2)	1957	6.25	12.50	25.00

SOPHISTICATES, THE

VIVA

Number	Title (A Side/B Side)	Yr	VG	VG+	NM
❑ 61	When Elvis Comes Marching Home/Woody's Place	1960	12.50	25.00	50.00

SOPHOMORES, THE (1)

CHORD

Number	Title (A Side/B Side)	Yr	VG	VG+	NM
❑ 1302	Charades/What Can I Do	1957	10.00	20.00	40.00

DAWN

Number	Title (A Side/B Side)	Yr	VG	VG+	NM
❑ 216	Cool, Cool Baby/Every Night About This Time	1956	6.25	12.50	25.00
❑ 218	Linda/I Get a Thrill	1956	6.25	12.50	25.00
❑ 223	Ocean Blue/I Left My Sugar	1956	6.25	12.50	25.00
❑ 225	Is There Someone for Me/Everybody Loves Me	1957	6.25	12.50	25.00
❑ 228	I Just Can't Keep the Tears from Tumblin' Down/If I Should Lose Your Love	1957	6.25	12.50	25.00
❑ 237	Checkers/Each Time I Hold You	1958	6.25	12.50	25.00

EPIC

Number	Title (A Side/B Side)	Yr	VG	VG+	NM
❑ 9259	Charades/What Can I Do	1957	5.00	10.00	20.00

SOPHOMORES, THE (2)

SOUND STAGE 7

Number	Title (A Side/B Side)	Yr	VG	VG+	NM
❑ 2533	Summer of '64/I Know I Should (Every Night)	1964	2.50	5.00	10.00

SOPWITH "CAMEL", THE

KAMA SUTRA

Number	Title (A Side/B Side)	Yr	VG	VG+	NM
❑ 217	Hello Hello/Treadin'	1966	3.00	6.00	12.00
❑ 224	Postcard from Jamaica/Little Orphan Annie	1967	3.00	6.00	12.00
❑ 224 [PS]	Postcard from Jamaica/Little Orphan Annie	1967	5.00	10.00	20.00
❑ 236	Great Morpheum/Saga of the Lowdown Letdown	1967	3.00	6.00	12.00

REPRISE

Number	Title (A Side/B Side)	Yr	VG	VG+	NM
❑ 1179	Sleazy Love/Fazon	1973	2.00	4.00	8.00

SORENSON BROTHERS, THE

MARLINDA

Number	Title (A Side/B Side)	Yr	VG	VG+	NM
❑ 7507/8	They've Landed/Stowaway	196?	12.50	25.00	50.00

SORROWS, THE

WARNER BROS.

Number	Title (A Side/B Side)	Yr	VG	VG+	NM
❑ 5662	Take a Heart/We Should Get Along Fine	1965	3.00	6.00	12.00

SOUL, JIMMY

20TH FOX

Number	Title (A Side/B Side)	Yr	VG	VG+	NM
❑ 413	Respectable/I Wish I Could Dance	1963	2.50	5.00	10.00

SPQR

Number	Title (A Side/B Side)	Yr	VG	VG+	NM
❑ 3221	My Little Room/Ella Is Yella	1964	2.50	5.00	10.00
❑ 3300	Twistin' Matilda/I Can't Hold Out Any Longer	1962	3.00	6.00	12.00
❑ 3302	When Matilda Comes Back/Some Kinda Nut	1962	3.00	6.00	12.00
❑ 3304	Guess Things Happen That Way/My Baby Loves to Bowl	1963	3.00	6.00	12.00
❑ 3305	If You Wanna Be Happy/Don't Release Me	1963	3.75	7.50	15.00
❑ 3305 [PS]	If You Wanna Be Happy/Don't Release Me	1963	7.50	15.00	30.00
❑ 3310	Treat 'Em Tough/Church Street in the Summertime	1963	3.00	6.00	12.00
❑ 3312	Go 'Way Christina/Everybody's Gone Ape	1963	3.00	6.00	12.00
❑ 3314	Change Partners/I Hate You Baby	1963	3.00	6.00	12.00
❑ 3315	My Girl-She Sure Can Cook/A Woman Is Smarter in Every Kinda Way	1964	2.50	5.00	10.00
❑ 3318	You Can't Have Your Cake/Take Me to Los Angeles	1964	2.50	5.00	10.00
❑ 3319	Twistin' Matilda/Treat 'Em Tough	1964	2.50	5.00	10.00

SOUL AGENTS, THE

CAMEO

Number	Title (A Side/B Side)	Yr	VG	VG+	NM
❑ 350	Let's Make It Pretty Baby/The Seventh Son	1965	5.00	10.00	20.00

INTERPHON

Number	Title (A Side/B Side)	Yr	VG	VG+	NM
❑ 7702	I Just Want to Make Love to You/Mean Woman Blues	1964	5.00	10.00	20.00

SOUL ASYLUM

COLUMBIA

Number	Title (A Side/B Side)	Yr	VG	VG+	NM
❑ 77959	Misery/Hope	1995	—	—	3.00
❑ 77959 [PS]	Misery/Hope	1995	—	—	3.00
❑ 78215	Promises Broken/Can't Even Tell (Live)	1996	—	—	2.00
❑ 78215 [PS]	Promises Broken/Can't Even Tell (Live)	1996	—	—	2.00

TWIN/TONE

Number	Title (A Side/B Side)	Yr	VG	VG+	NM
❑ TTR 8560	Tied to the Tracks/Long Way Home	1985	3.00	6.25	12.50
❑ TTR 8560 [PS]	Tied to the Tracks/Long Way Home	1985	3.00	6.25	12.50

SOUL BROTHERS SIX

ATLANTIC

Number	Title (A Side/B Side)	Yr	VG	VG+	NM
❑ 2406	Some Kind of Wonderful/I'll Be Loving You	1967	3.75	7.50	15.00
❑ 2456	You Better Check Yourself/What Can You Do When You Ain't Got Nobody	1967	3.00	6.00	12.00
❑ 2535	Your Love Is Such a Wonderful Love/I Can't Live Without You	1968	3.00	6.00	12.00
❑ 2592	Somebody Else Is Loving My Baby/Thank You Baby for Loving Me	1969	3.00	6.00	12.00
❑ 2645	What You Got (Is So Good for Me)/Drive	1969	3.00	6.00	12.00

PHIL-L.A. OF SOUL

Number	Title (A Side/B Side)	Yr	VG	VG+	NM
❑ 355	Funky Funky Way of Making Love/Let Me Be the One	1972	—	3.00	6.00
❑ 360	You're My World/You Gotta Come a Little Closer	1973	—	3.00	6.00
❑ 365	Let Me Do What We Ain't Doin'/Lost the Will to Live	1974	—	3.00	6.00

SOUL CHILDREN, THE

EPIC

Number	Title (A Side/B Side)	Yr	VG	VG+	NM
❑ 50178	Finders Keepers/Midnight Sunshine	1976	—	2.50	5.00
❑ 50236	If You Move I'll Fall/Little Understanding	1976	—	2.50	5.00
❑ 50345	Where Is Your Woman Tonight?/Merry-Go-Round	1977	—	2.50	5.00
❑ 50405	There Always/You Don't Need a Ring	1977	—	2.50	5.00

STAX

Number	Title (A Side/B Side)	Yr	VG	VG+	NM
❑ 0008	Give 'Em Love/Move Over	1968	2.00	4.00	8.00
❑ 0018	I'll Understand/Doin' Our Thing	1969	2.00	4.00	8.00
❑ 0030	Tighten Up My Thang/Take Up the Slack	1969	2.00	4.00	8.00
❑ 0050	The Sweeter He Is — Part 1/The Sweeter He Is — Part 2	1969	2.00	4.00	8.00
❑ 0062	Hold On, I'm Coming/Make It Good	1970	—	3.50	7.00
❑ 0075	Give Me One Good Reason Why/Finish Me Off	1970	—	3.50	7.00
❑ 0086	Let's Make a Sweet Thing Sweeter/Finish Me Off	1971	—	3.50	7.00
❑ 0119	Hearsay/Don't Take My Sunshine	1972	—	3.50	7.00
❑ 0132	Don't Take My Kindness for Weakness/Just the One	1972	—	3.50	7.00
❑ 0152	It Ain't Always What You Do (It's Who You Let See You Do It)/All That Shines Ain't Gold	1973	—	3.50	7.00
❑ 0170	Love Is a Hurtin' Thing/Poem on the School House Door	1973	—	3.50	7.00
❑ 0182	I'll Be the Other Woman/Come Back Kind of Love	1973	—	3.00	6.00
❑ 0218	Love Makes It Right/Love Makes It Right — Part 2	1974	—	3.00	6.00
❑ 0230	What's Happening Baby/What's Happening Baby — Part 2	1974	—	3.00	6.00
❑ 3206	Can't Give Up a Good Thing/Signed, Sealed and Delivered	1978	—	2.50	5.00
❑ 3211	Summer in the Shade/Hard Living with a Woman	1978	—	2.50	5.00
❑ 3214	Who You Used to Be/Believing	1978	—	2.50	5.00

SOUL CLAN, THE

SOLOMON BURKE, ARTHUR CONLEY, DON COVAY, BEN E. KING and JOE TEX.

ATLANTIC

Number	Title (A Side/B Side)	Yr	VG	VG+	NM
❑ 2530	Soul Meeting/That's How It Feels	1968	2.50	5.00	10.00
❑ 2530 [PS]	Soul Meeting/That's How It Feels	1968	3.75	7.50	15.00

SOUL COMFORTERS, THE

HOLLYWOOD

Number	Title (A Side/B Side)	Yr	VG	VG+	NM
❑ 1042	White Christmas/Silent Night	1955	7.50	15.00	30.00

SOUL SURFERS, THE

CHALLENGE

Number	Title (A Side/B Side)	Yr	VG	VG+	NM
❑ 9209	Cannonball/Home from Camp	1963	10.00	20.00	40.00
❑ 59249	Cannonball/In the Misty Moonlight	1964	3.75	7.50	15.00
	—B-side by Jerry Wallace				

SOUL SURVIVORS

ATCO

Number	Title (A Side/B Side)	Yr	VG	VG+	NM
❑ 6627	Turn Out the Fire/Go Out Walking	1968	2.00	4.00	8.00
❑ 6650	Tell Daddy/Mama Soul	1969	2.00	4.00	8.00
❑ 6735	Still Got My Head/Tempting 'Bout to Get Me	1970	2.00	4.00	8.00

CRIMSON

Number	Title (A Side/B Side)	Yr	VG	VG+	NM
❑ 1010	Expressway to Your Heart/Hey Gyp	1967	3.00	6.00	12.00
❑ 1012	Explosion (In Your Soul)/Dathon's Theme	1967	2.50	5.00	10.00
❑ 1016	Poor Man's Dream/Impossible Mission	1968	2.50	5.00	10.00

DECCA

Number	Title (A Side/B Side)	Yr	VG	VG+	NM
❑ 32080	Devil with a Blue Dress On/Shakin' with Linda	1967	3.75	7.50	15.00

DOT

Number	Title (A Side/B Side)	Yr	VG	VG+	NM
❑ 16793	Look at Me/Can't Stand to Be in Love with You	1965	5.00	10.00	20.00
❑ 16830	Hung Up on Losin'/Snow Man	1966	3.00	6.00	12.00

PHILADELPHIA INT'L.

Number	Title (A Side/B Side)	Yr	VG	VG+	NM
❑ 3595	Happy Birthday America (Part 1)/Happy Birthday America (Part 2)	1976	—	2.50	5.00
❑ 3595 [PS]	Happy Birthday America (Part 1)/Happy Birthday America (Part 2)	1976	2.00	4.00	8.00

TSOP

Number	Title (A Side/B Side)	Yr	VG	VG+	NM
❑ 4756	City of Brotherly Love/The Best Time Was the Last Time	1974	—	3.00	6.00
❑ 4760	What It Takes/Virgin Girl	1974	—	3.00	6.00
❑ 4768	Your Love/Lover to Me	1975	—	3.00	6.00

SOUNDGARDEN

A&M

Number	Title (A Side/B Side)	Yr	VG	VG+	NM
❑ 31458 0766 7	Black Hole Sun/Spoonman	1994	—	2.00	4.00
❑ 31458 0974 7	Fell On Black Days/My Wave	1995	—	2.00	4.00

SUB POP

Number	Title (A Side/B Side)	Yr	VG	VG+	NM
❑ 12a	Hunted Down/Nothing to Say	1987	12.50	25.00	50.00
	—500 copies pressed, all on blue vinyl				
❑ 12a [PS]	Hunted Down/Nothing to Say	1987	12.50	25.00	50.00
	—Special blue sleeve (not a PS) with above				
❑ 83	Room a Thousand Years Wide/H.I.V. Baby	1990	7.50	15.00	30.00
	—Grape vinyl				
❑ 83	Room a Thousand Years Wide/H.I.V. Baby	1990	3.75	7.50	15.00
	—Black vinyl; bonus in Sub Pop Singles Club series				
❑ 83 [PS]	Room a Thousand Years Wide/H.I.V. Baby	1990	5.00	10.00	20.00

SOUNDS, INC.

LIBERTY

Number	Title (A Side/B Side)	Yr	VG	VG+	NM
❑ 55709	The Spartans/Detroit	1964	2.00	4.00	8.00
❑ 55729	Rinky Dink/Spanish Harlem	1964	2.00	4.00	8.00
❑ 55789	In the Hall of the Mountain King/Time for You	1965	2.00	4.00	8.00
❑ 55844	On the Brink/I Am Comin' Thru	1965	2.00	4.00	8.00

Number	Title (A Side/B Side)	Yr	VG	VG+	NM

SOUNDS LIKE US

FONTANA

Number	Title (A Side/B Side)	Yr	VG	VG+	NM
❑ 1570	Outside Chance/Clock on the Wall	1967	6.25	12.50	25.00

JILL ANN

Number	Title (A Side/B Side)	Yr	VG	VG+	NM
❑ 101	Outside Chance/Clock on the Wall	1966	12.50	25.00	50.00

SOMA

Number	Title (A Side/B Side)	Yr	VG	VG+	NM
❑ 8108	It Was a Very Good Year/The Other Side of the Record	1967	5.00	10.00	20.00

SOUNDS ORCHESTRAL

JANUS

Number	Title (A Side/B Side)	Yr	VG	VG+	NM
❑ 124	Love in the Shadows/Louie, Louie	1970	—	3.00	6.00

PARKWAY

Number	Title (A Side/B Side)	Yr	VG	VG+	NM
❑ 120	Pretty Flamingo/Sounds Like Jacques	1966	2.00	4.00	8.00
❑ 155	A Man and a Woman/West of Carnaby	1967	2.00	4.00	8.00
❑ 942	Cast Your Fate to the Wind/To Wendy With Love	1965	2.50	5.00	10.00
❑ 958	Canadian Sunset/Have Faith in Your Love	1965	2.00	4.00	8.00
❑ 968	A Boy and a Girl/Go Home Girl	1966	2.00	4.00	8.00
❑ 973	Thunderball/Mr. Kiss Kiss Bang Bang	1966	2.00	4.00	8.00

SOUNDS UNLIMITED

ABC

Number	Title (A Side/B Side)	Yr	VG	VG+	NM
❑ 10803	Nobody But Me/Why Doesn't She Believe Me	1966	5.00	10.00	20.00

DUNWICH

Number	Title (A Side/B Side)	Yr	VG	VG+	NM
❑ 157	A Girl As Sweet As You/Little Brother	1967	6.25	12.50	25.00

SOUTH, JOE

ALLWOOD

Number	Title (A Side/B Side)	Yr	VG	VG+	NM
❑ 402	Just Remember You're Mine/Silly Me	1962	3.00	6.00	12.00

APT

Number	Title (A Side/B Side)	Yr	VG	VG+	NM
❑ 25084	Deep Inside Me/I Want to Be Somebody	1965	2.50	5.00	10.00

CAPITOL

Number	Title (A Side/B Side)	Yr	VG	VG+	NM
❑ 2060	Birds of a Feather/It Got Away	1967	2.00	4.00	8.00
❑ 2169	How Can I Unlove You/She's Almost You	1968	2.00	4.00	8.00
❑ 2248	Games People Play/Mirror of Your Mind	1968	2.00	4.00	8.00
❑ 2284	Redneck/Don't Throw Your Love to the Wind	1968	2.00	4.00	8.00
❑ 2491	Leanin' On You/Don't You Be Ashamed	1969	—	3.00	6.00
❑ 2532	Birds of a Feather/These Are Not My People	1969	—	3.00	6.00
❑ 2592	Don't It Make You Want to Go Home/Heart's Desire	1969	—	3.00	6.00
❑ 2704	Walk a Mile in My Shoes/Sheltered	1969	—	3.00	6.00
❑ 2755	Children/The Clock Up On the Wall	1970	—	2.50	5.00
❑ 2916	Why Does a Man Do What He Has to Do/Be a Believer	1970	—	2.50	5.00
❑ 3008	Rose Garden/Mirror of Your Mind	1971	—	3.00	6.00
❑ 3053	United We Stand/So the Seeds Are Growing	1971	—	2.50	5.00
❑ 3204	Fool Me/Devil May Care	1971	—	2.50	5.00
❑ 3450	One Man Band/Coming Down All Alone	1972	—	2.50	5.00
❑ 3487	I'm a Star/Misunderstanding	1972	—	2.50	5.00
❑ 3554	Real Thing/Save Your Best	1973	—	2.50	5.00
❑ 3717	Riverdog/It Hurts Me Too	1973	—	2.50	5.00

COLUMBIA

Number	Title (A Side/B Side)	Yr	VG	VG+	NM
❑ 43983	Backfield in Motion/I'll Come Back to You	1967	3.00	6.00	12.00
❑ 44218	A Fool in Love/Great Day	1967	3.00	6.00	12.00

FAIRLANE

Number	Title (A Side/B Side)	Yr	VG	VG+	NM
❑ 21006	You're the Reason/Jukebox	1961	5.00	10.00	20.00
❑ 21010	Masquerade/I'm Sorry for You	1961	3.75	7.50	15.00
❑ 21015	Slippin' Around/Just to Be with You Again	1962	3.75	7.50	15.00

ISLAND

Number	Title (A Side/B Side)	Yr	VG	VG+	NM
❑ 034	To Have, to Hold and Let Go/Midnight Rainbows	1975	—	2.00	4.00

MGM

Number	Title (A Side/B Side)	Yr	VG	VG+	NM
❑ 13145	Same Old Song/Standing Invitation	1963	2.50	5.00	10.00
❑ 13196	Concrete Jungle/The Last One to Know	1963	2.50	5.00	10.00
❑ 13276	Naughty Claudie/Little Queenie	1964	2.50	5.00	10.00

NRC

Number	Title (A Side/B Side)	Yr	VG	VG+	NM
❑ 002	I'm Snowed/It's Only You	1958	10.00	20.00	40.00
❑ 022	Chills/What a Night	1959	3.75	7.50	15.00
❑ 041	Little Bluebird/Play It Cool	1959	3.75	7.50	15.00
❑ 053	Tell the Truth/If You Only Knew Her	1960	3.75	7.50	15.00
❑ 065	Let's Talk It Over/Formality	1961	3.75	7.50	15.00
❑ 5000	The Purple People Eater Meets the Witch Doctor/My Fondest Memories	1958	3.75	7.50	15.00
❑ 5001	One Fool to Another/Texas Ain't the Biggest Anymore	1958	3.75	7.50	15.00

SOUTH 40

METROBEAT

Number	Title (A Side/B Side)	Yr	VG	VG+	NM
❑ 4450	The Penny Song/Good Lovin'	1967	3.00	6.00	12.00
❑ 4457	I Want Sunshine/Goin' Someplace Else	1968	3.00	6.00	12.00

SOUTHER, J.D.

Includes records as "John David Souther." Also see THE SOUTHER, HILLMAN, FURAY BAND.

ASYLUM

Number	Title (A Side/B Side)	Yr	VG	VG+	NM
❑ 11009	How Long/The Fast One	1972	—	2.50	5.00
❑ 45332	Silver Blue/Black Rose	1976	—	2.00	4.00
—As "John David Souther"					
❑ 45364	Faithless Love/Midnight Prowl	1976	—	2.00	4.00
—As "John David Souther"					

COLUMBIA

Number	Title (A Side/B Side)	Yr	VG	VG+	NM
❑ 02422	You're Only Lonely/If You Don't Want My Love	1981	—	—	3.00
—Reissue					
❑ 11079	You're Only Lonely/Songs of Love	1979	—	2.00	4.00
❑ 11196	White Rhythm and Blues/The Last in Love	1980	—	2.00	4.00
❑ 11302	'Til the Bar Burns Down/If You Don't Want My Love	1980	—	2.00	4.00
—With Johnny Duncan					

FULL MOON

Number	Title (A Side/B Side)	Yr	VG	VG+	NM
❑ 49612	You're Only Lonely/Once in a Lifetime	1980	—	2.00	4.00
—B-side by Bonnie Raitt					

WARNER BROS.

Number	Title (A Side/B Side)	Yr	VG	VG+	NM
❑ 29289	Go Ahead and Rain/All I Want	1984	—	—	3.00

SOUTHER, HILLMAN, FURAY BAND, THE

Also see J.D. SOUTHER.

ASYLUM

Number	Title (A Side/B Side)	Yr	VG	VG+	NM
❑ 45201	Fallin' in Love/Heavenly Fire	1974	—	2.00	4.00
❑ 45217	Border Town/Safe at Home	1974	—	2.00	4.00
❑ 45251	Mexico/Move Me Real Slow	1975	—	2.00	4.00
❑ 45267	Trouble in Paradise/On the Line	1975	—	2.00	4.00
❑ 45280	For Someone I Love/Move Me Real Slow	1975	—	2.00	4.00

SOUTHWEST F.O.B.

"England" Dan Seals and John Ford Coley were in this group.

GPC

Number	Title (A Side/B Side)	Yr	VG	VG+	NM
❑ 1945	Smell of Incense/Green Skies	1968	3.75	7.50	15.00

HIP

Number	Title (A Side/B Side)	Yr	VG	VG+	NM
❑ 8002	Smell of Incense/Green Skies	1968	2.00	4.00	8.00
❑ 8009	Nadine/All One Big Game	1969	2.00	4.00	8.00
❑ 8015	Independent Me/As I Look at You	1969	2.00	4.00	8.00
❑ 8022	Feelin' Groovy/Beggar Man	1969	2.00	4.00	8.00

SOUVENIRS, THE

May be three different groups.

DOOTO

Number	Title (A Side/B Side)	Yr	VG	VG+	NM
❑ 412	So Long Daddy/Arlene, Sweet Little Texas Queen	1957	12.50	25.00	50.00

INFERNO

Number	Title (A Side/B Side)	Yr	VG	VG+	NM
❑ 2001	I Could Have Danced All Night/It's Too Bad	1967	12.50	25.00	50.00

REPRISE

Number	Title (A Side/B Side)	Yr	VG	VG+	NM
❑ 20065	The Worm/The Bump	1962	3.75	7.50	15.00
❑ 20066	The Real McCoy/The Watusi	1962	3.75	7.50	15.00

SOVINE, RED

CHART

Number	Title (A Side/B Side)	Yr	VG	VG+	NM
❑ 5142	Old Pine Tree/Two Hearts on a Post Card	1971	—	2.50	5.00
❑ 5152	Six Broken Hearts/The Greatest Grand Ol' Opry	1972	—	2.50	5.00
❑ 5161	Down Through the Years/Petunia	1972	—	2.50	5.00
❑ 5176	The Guilty One/The Day the Preacher Came	1973	—	2.50	5.00
❑ 5207	Midnight Rider/Why the Grass Is Green	1974	—	2.50	5.00
❑ 5216	From Champagne to Beer/Mama's Birthday	1974	—	2.50	5.00
❑ 5220	It'll Come Back/Down Through the Years	1974	—	2.50	5.00
❑ 5230	Can I Keep Him Daddy/Red's So Fine	1974	—	2.50	5.00
❑ 5231	Santa Claus Is a Texas Cowboy/The Legend of the Christmas Rose	1974	—	2.50	5.00
❑ 7507	Daddy's Girl/(B-side unknown)	1975	—	2.50	5.00

DECCA

Number	Title (A Side/B Side)	Yr	VG	VG+	NM
❑ 29068	My New Love Affair/How Do You Think I Feel	1954	3.75	7.50	15.00
❑ 29211	Don't Drop It/Don't Be the One	1954	3.75	7.50	15.00
❑ 29335	Outlaw/Which One Should I Choose	1954	3.75	7.50	15.00
❑ 29411	Are You Mine/Ko Ko Mo	1955	3.75	7.50	15.00
—With Goldie Hill					
❑ 29529	I Hope You Don't Care/I'm Glad You Found a Place for Me	1955	3.75	7.50	15.00
❑ 29739	Why Baby Why/Sixteen Tons	1955	5.00	10.00	20.00
—A-side with Webb Pierce					
❑ 29755	Why Baby Why/Missing You	1955	3.75	7.50	15.00
—A-side with Webb Pierce					
❑ 29825	If Jesus Came to Your House/I Got Religion	1956	3.75	7.50	15.00
❑ 29876	Little Rosa/Hold Everything (Till I Get Home)	1956	3.75	7.50	15.00
—A-side with Webb Pierce					
❑ 30018	The Best Years of Your Life/My Little Rat	1956	3.00	6.00	12.00
❑ 30162	A Poor Man's Riches/Down on the Corner of Love	1956	3.00	6.00	12.00
❑ 30239	Juke Joint Johnny/No Thanks, Bartender	1957	7.50	15.00	30.00
❑ 30458	Wrong/Who Knows Better Than You and I	1957	3.00	6.00	12.00
❑ 30595	Once More/For Arms	1958	3.00	6.00	12.00
❑ 30715	Courtin' Time in Tennessee/Where Will Mommie Go	1958	3.00	6.00	12.00
❑ 30814	You Used to Be My Baby/Leave Me Alone	1959	2.50	5.00	10.00
❑ 30920	Cold Hands of Fate/One Sided Love Affair	1959	2.50	5.00	10.00
❑ 31028	A Lot Like You/Ooooh How I Love You	1959	2.50	5.00	10.00
❑ 31903	You Used to Be My Baby/Leave Me Alone	1966	2.00	4.00	8.00

GUSTO

Number	Title (A Side/B Side)	Yr	VG	VG+	NM
❑ 169	Woman Behind the Man Behind the Wheel/Jealous Heart	1977	—	2.00	4.00
❑ 175	Lay Down Sally/The Farmers and the Miners	1978	—	2.00	4.00
❑ 180	Lay Down Sally/The King's Last Concert	1978	—	3.00	6.00
❑ 188	The Days of Me and You/I'd Love to Make Love	1978	—	2.00	4.00
❑ 9005	A Place for Mama's Roses/Does Steppin' Out Mean Daddy Took a Walk	1978	—	2.00	4.00
❑ 9015	Christmas Is For Kids/What Does Christmas Look Like	1978	—	2.00	4.00
❑ 9016	The Waylon and Willie Machine/Colorado Cool-Aid	1979	—	2.50	5.00
❑ 9017	Mr. F.C.C./Flesh and Blood	1979	—	2.00	4.00
❑ 9019	The Prettiest Dress/Flesh and Blood	1979	—	2.00	4.00
❑ 9021	The Hero/Flesh and Blood	1979	—	2.00	4.00
❑ 9026	The First Time I Saw Her/18 Wheels a-Hummin' Home Sweet Home	1980	—	2.00	4.00
❑ 9028	The Little Family Soldier/She Was Loving Me Goodbye	1980	—	2.00	4.00
❑ 9030	It'll Come Back/Love Is	1980	—	2.00	4.00

MGM

Number	Title (A Side/B Side)	Yr	VG	VG+	NM
❑ 10717	When I Get Rich/You're Barking Up the Wrong Tree	1950	6.25	12.50	25.00
❑ 10782	Christmas Alone/Dear Mister Santa Claus	1950	6.25	12.50	25.00
❑ 10887	Billy Goat Boogie/Big Dipper	1951	5.00	10.00	20.00
❑ 10981	Four Flusher/Farewell, So Long	1951	5.00	10.00	20.00
❑ 11090	Don't Worry/Sundown Sue	1951	5.00	10.00	20.00
❑ 11214	It'd Surprise You/Loveless Marriage	1952	5.00	10.00	20.00
❑ 11323	Okey Dokey/Till Today	1952	5.00	10.00	20.00
❑ 11402	A Quarter's Worth of Heartaches/I'm Gonna Lock My Heart	1953	5.00	10.00	20.00
❑ 11567	You Taught Me How/If You'll Be a Baby	1953	5.00	10.00	20.00

Number	Title (A Side/B Side)	Yr	VG	VG+	NM
RCA VICTOR					
❑ 47-7981	The Cajun Queen/Big Dreams	1962	3.00	6.00	12.00
RIC					
❑ 131	Big Ol' Ugly Fool/Hiding Out	1964	2.00	4.00	8.00
❑ 154	Losing My Grip/Star of the Show	1965	2.00	4.00	8.00
❑ 168	I Wish I Had Seen Sunshine/Salt on My Eggs	1965	2.00	4.00	8.00
STARDAY					
❑ 101	Phantom 309/(B-side unknown)	1975	—	2.00	4.00
❑ 137	Giddyup Go/Tonight My Lady Learns to Love	1976	—	2.00	4.00
❑ 142	Teddy Bear/Daddy	1976	—	2.50	5.00
❑ 144	Little Joe/Cold Love to Go	1976	—	2.00	4.00
❑ 147	Last Goodbye/Lonely Arms of Mine	1976	—	2.00	4.00
❑ 148	Just Gettin' By/I'm Gonna Move	1977	—	2.00	4.00
❑ 152	I'm Only Seventeen/No One's Too Big to Cry	1977	—	2.00	4.00
❑ 158	Daddy's Girl/Love Is All She Ever Wants from Me	1977	—	2.00	4.00
❑ 510	Burn the School/One Is a Lonely Number	1960	2.50	5.00	10.00
❑ 521	No Money in This Deal/If I Could Come Back	1960	2.50	5.00	10.00
❑ 540	Why Baby Why/Little Rosa	1961	2.50	5.00	10.00
❑ 553	Heart of a Man/Brand New Low	1961	2.50	5.00	10.00
❑ 567	Color of the Blues/Hold Everything	1961	2.50	5.00	10.00
❑ 579	East of West Berlin/Thanks for Nothing	1962	2.50	5.00	10.00
❑ 598	Rose of Love/She Can't Read My Writing	1962	2.50	5.00	10.00
❑ 616	Sittin' and Thinkin'/A Million to One	1962	2.50	5.00	10.00
❑ 632	Waltzing with Sin/I Forgot to Keep Her with Me	1963	2.50	5.00	10.00
❑ 650	Dream House for Sale/King of the Open Road	1963	2.50	5.00	10.00
❑ 672	Old Pipeliner/Peace of Mind	1964	2.50	5.00	10.00
❑ 737	Giddyup Go/A Kiss and the Keys	1965	2.00	4.00	8.00
❑ 757	Long Night/Too Much	1966	2.00	4.00	8.00
❑ 766	I'm the Man/I Think I Can Sleep Tonight	1966	2.00	4.00	8.00
❑ 774	Alabam/Nobody's Business	1966	2.00	4.00	8.00
—With Minnie Pearl					
❑ 779	Class of '49/I Hope My Wife Don't Find Out	1966	2.00	4.00	8.00
❑ 794	I Didn't Jump the Fence/Don't Let My Glass Run Dry	1967	2.00	4.00	8.00
❑ 811	Phantom 309/In Your Heart	1967	2.50	5.00	10.00
❑ 823	Tell Maude I Slipped/Not Like It Was with You	1967	2.00	4.00	8.00
❑ 831	Twenty-One/Sparkling Wine	1968	2.00	4.00	8.00
❑ 842	Loser Making Good/Good Enough for Nothing	1968	2.00	4.00	8.00
❑ 852	Normally, Norma Loves Me/Live and Let Live and Be Happy	1968	2.00	4.00	8.00
❑ 857	Between Closing Time and Dawn/The Father of Judy Ann	1968	2.00	4.00	8.00
❑ 864	Blues Stay Away from Me/Whiskey Flavored Kisses	1969	—	3.00	6.00
❑ 872	Who Am I/Three Hearts in a Tangle	1969	—	3.00	6.00
❑ 882	Truck Drivers Prayer/Chairman of the Board	1969	2.00	4.00	8.00
❑ 885	Castle of Shame/Why Don't You Haul Off and Love Me	1969	—	3.00	6.00
—With Lois Williams					
❑ 889	I Know You're Married But I Love You Still/Money, Marbles and Chalk	1970	—	3.00	6.00
❑ 896	Freightliner Fever/Mr. Sunday Sun	1970	—	3.00	6.00
❑ 915	Enough to Take the Me Out of Men/I'm Waiting Just for You	1970	—	3.00	6.00
❑ 918	Unfinished Letter/The Thought of Losing You	1970	—	3.00	6.00
❑ 926	Get in Touch/Violets Blue	1971	—	3.00	6.00
❑ 933	Happy Birthday, My Darlin'/I'll Sail My Ship Alone	1971	—	3.00	6.00
❑ 934	I Am a Pilgrim/Beautiful Life	1971	—	3.00	6.00
❑ 960	Go Hide John/Tear Stained Guitar	1973	—	2.50	5.00
❑ 977	Take Time to Remember/(B-side unknown)	1973	—	2.50	5.00
❑ 7004	Why Baby Why/Little Rosa	197?	—	2.00	4.00
—Reissue of 540					
❑ 7022	Six Days on the Road/Truck Drivin' Man	197?	—	2.00	4.00
❑ 7037	He'll Have to Go/I'll Step Aside	197?	—	2.00	4.00
❑ 8000	Giddyup Go/Phantom 309	197?	—	2.00	4.00
❑ 8023	Little Rosa/Ruby, Don't Take Your Love to Town	197?	—	2.00	4.00
❑ 8033	Truck Driving Son-of-a-Gun/Radar Blues	197?	—	2.00	4.00
—B-side by Coleman Wilson					

SPADES, THE (1)

For records on Liberty, see THE SLADES.

SPADES, THE (2)

Number	Title (A Side/B Side)	Yr	VG	VG+	NM
MAJOR					
❑ 1007	Close to You/I'm on Fire	1959	15.00	30.00	60.00

SPADES, THE (3)

Evolved into THE THIRTEENTH FLOOR ELEVATORS. Zero 10001 was recorded before Roky Erickson joined the group.

Number	Title (A Side/B Side)	Yr	VG	VG+	NM
ZERO					
❑ 10001	I Need a Girl/Do You Want to Dance	1965	15.00	30.00	60.00
❑ 10002	You're Gonna Miss Me/We Sell Soul	1966	100.00	200.00	400.00

SPANIELS, THE

Number	Title (A Side/B Side)	Yr	VG	VG+	NM
BUDDAH					
❑ 153	Goodnight Sweetheart/Maybe	1969	2.00	4.00	8.00
CALLA					
❑ 172	Fairy Tales/Jealous Heart	1970	—	3.00	6.00
CANTERBURY					
❑ 101	Peace of Mind/She Sang to Me/Danny Boy	1974	—	2.50	5.00
CHANCE					
❑ 1141	Baby It's You/Bounce	1953	125.00	250.00	500.00
❑ 1141	Baby It's You/Bounce	1953	375.00	750.00	1500.
—Red vinyl					
LOST-NITE					
❑ 262	Baby It's You/Bounce	197?	—	2.00	4.00
❑ 265	The Bells Ring Out/House Cleaning	197?	—	2.00	4.00
❑ 268	Goodnite, Sweetheart, Goodnite/You Don't Move Me	197?	—	2.00	4.00
❑ 271	Do-Wah/Don'cha Go	197?	—	2.00	4.00
❑ 274	Play It Cool/Let's Make Up	197?	—	2.00	4.00
❑ 277	False Love/Do You Really	197?	—	2.00	4.00
❑ 280	You Painted Pictures/Hey, SIster Lizzie	197?	—	2.00	4.00
❑ 283	Dear Heart/Why Won't You Dance	197?	—	2.00	4.00
❑ 286	Everyone's Laughing/I.O.U.	197?	—	2.00	4.00
❑ 289	I Lost You/Crazy Baby	197?	—	2.00	4.00
❑ 292	You Gave Me Peace of Mind/Please Don't Tease	197?	—	2.00	4.00
❑ 295	You're Gonna Cry/I Like It Like That	197?	—	2.00	4.00
❑ 298	Stormy Weather/Here Is Why I Love You	197?	—	2.00	4.00
❑ 301	Tina/Great Googley Moo	197?	—	2.00	4.00
❑ 304	Since I Fell for You/Baby Come Along with Me	197?	—	2.00	4.00
❑ 307	This Is a Lovely Way to Spend an Evening/Red Sails in the Sunset	197?	—	2.00	4.00
❑ 446	I Know/Bus Fare Home	197?	—	2.00	4.00
NEPTUNE					
❑ 124	I Love You For Sentimental Reasons/Meek Man	1961	5.00	10.00	20.00
—As "Pookie Hudson and the Spaniels"					
NORTH AMERICAN					
❑ 001	Fairy Tales/Jealous Heart	1970	—	2.50	5.00
❑ 002	Stand in Line/Lonely Man	1970	—	2.50	5.00
❑ 1114	Come Back to These Arms/Money Blues	1970	—	2.50	5.00
OWL					
❑ 328	Little Goe/The Posse	1973	—	2.50	5.00
VEE JAY					
❑ 101	Baby It's You/Bounce	1953	1125.	2250.	4500.
—Red vinyl					
❑ 101	Baby It's You/Bounce	1953	200.00	400.00	800.00
—Black vinyl, maroon label					
❑ 101	Baby It's You/Bounce	1961	10.00	20.00	40.00
—Black vinyl, black label					
❑ 103	The Bells Ring Out/House Cleaning	1953	150.00	300.00	600.00
—Red vinyl					
❑ 103	The Bells Ring Out/House Cleaning	1953	75.00	150.00	300.00
❑ 107	Goodnite, Sweetheart, Goodnite/You Don't Move Me	1953	200.00	400.00	800.00
—Red vinyl; no "Trade Mark Reg" on label					
❑ 107	Goodnite, Sweetheart, Goodnite/You Don't Move Me	1953	75.00	150.00	300.00
—Black vinyl; as "Spanials"					
❑ 107	Goodnite, Sweetheart, Goodnite/You Don't Move Me	1953	50.00	100.00	200.00
—Black vinyl, correct spelling					
❑ 107	Goodnite, Sweetheart, Goodnite/You Don't Move Me	1993	2.00	4.00	8.00
—Red vinyl; "Trade Mark Reg" on label; included in Vee-Jay CD box set					
❑ 116	Play It Cool/Let's Make Up	1954	125.00	250.00	500.00
—Red vinyl					
❑ 116	Play It Cool/Let's Make Up	1954	25.00	50.00	100.00
❑ 131	Do-Wah/Don'cha Go	1955	125.00	250.00	500.00
—Red vinyl					
❑ 131	Do-Wah/Don'cha Go	1955	20.00	40.00	80.00
❑ 154	You Painted Pictures/Hey, Sister Lizzie	1955	15.00	30.00	60.00
❑ 154	You Painted Pictures/Hey, Sister Lizzie	1955	12.50	25.00	50.00
—As "Spanials"					
❑ 178	False Love/Do You Really	1956	37.50	75.00	150.00
❑ 189	Dear Heart/Why Won't You Dance	1956	37.50	75.00	150.00
❑ 202	Since I Fell for You/Baby Come Along with Me	1956	37.50	75.00	150.00
❑ 229	Please Don't Tease/You Gave Me Peace of Mind	1956	15.00	30.00	60.00
❑ 246	Everyone's Laughing/I.O.U.	1957	15.00	30.00	60.00
❑ 257	You're Gonna Cry/I Need Your Kisses	1957	15.00	30.00	60.00
❑ 264	I Love You/Crazee Babee	1958	15.00	30.00	60.00
❑ 278	Tina/Great Googly Moo	1958	15.00	30.00	60.00
❑ 290	Stormy Weather/Here Is Why I Love You	1958	15.00	30.00	60.00
❑ 301	Baby It's You/Heart and Soul	1958	15.00	30.00	60.00
❑ 310	Trees/I Like It Like That	1959	15.00	30.00	60.00
❑ 328	These Three Words/100 Years from Today	1959	15.00	30.00	60.00
❑ 342	People Will Say We're in Love/The Bells Ring Out	1960	25.00	50.00	100.00
❑ 350	I Know/Bus Fare Home	1960	10.00	20.00	40.00

SPANKY AND OUR GANG

Number	Title (A Side/B Side)	Yr	VG	VG+	NM
EPIC					
❑ 50170	When I Wanna/I Won't Brand You	1975	—	2.50	5.00
❑ 50206	L.A. Freeway/Standing Room Only	1976	—	2.50	5.00
MERCURY					
❑ DJ-101 [DJ]	Give a Damn (mono/stereo)	1968	3.00	6.00	12.00
—Special promo for the New York Urban Coalition					
❑ DJ-101 [PS]	Give a Damn (mono/stereo)	1968	5.00	10.00	20.00
—Fold-open sleeve with insert letter					
❑ 72598	And Your Bird Can Sing/Sealed with a Kiss	1966	5.00	10.00	20.00
❑ 72679	Sunday Will Never Be the Same/Distance	1967	2.00	4.00	8.00
❑ 72714	Making Every Minute Count/If You Could Only Be Me	1967	2.00	4.00	8.00
❑ 72714 [PS]	Making Every Minute Count/If You Could Only Be Me	1967	2.50	5.00	10.00
❑ 72732	Lazy Day/(It Ain't Necessarily) Byrd Avenue	1967	2.00	4.00	8.00
❑ 72732 [PS]	Lazy Day/(It Ain't Necessarily) Byrd Avenue	1967	2.50	5.00	10.00
❑ 72765	Sunday Morning/Echoes	1968	2.00	4.00	8.00
❑ 72765 [PS]	Sunday Morning/Echoes	1968	2.50	5.00	10.00
❑ 72795	Like to Get to Know You/Three Ways from Tomorrow	1968	2.00	4.00	8.00
—Orange and tan swirl label					
❑ 72795	Like to Get to Know You/Three Ways from Tomorrow	1968	2.50	5.00	10.00
—Red label with white "Mercury" in all caps across top of label					
❑ 72795 [PS]	Like to Get to Know You/Three Ways from Tomorrow	1968	2.50	5.00	10.00
❑ 72831	Give a Damn/Swinging Gate	1968	2.00	4.00	8.00
❑ 72871	Yesterday's Rain/Without Rhyme or Reason	1968	2.00	4.00	8.00
❑ 72890	Anything You Choose/Mecca Flat Blues	1969	2.00	4.00	8.00
❑ 72926	And She's Mine/Leopard Skinned Phones	1969	2.00	4.00	8.00
❑ 72982	Everybody's Talkin'/(B-side unknown)	1969	2.00	4.00	8.00

Number	Title (A Side/B Side)	Yr	VG	VG+	NM
PHILCO-FORD					
❑ HP-19	Making Every Minute Count/Byrd Avenue	1968	3.75	7.50	15.00
—4-inch plastic "Hip Pocket Record" with color sleeve					

SPANN, OTIS

Number	Title (A Side/B Side)	Yr	VG	VG+	NM
CHECKER					
❑ 807	It Must Have Been the Devil/Five Spot	1954	300.00	600.00	1200.

SPARKLETONES, THE

Also see JOE BENNETT AND THE SPARKLETONES.

Number	Title (A Side/B Side)	Yr	VG	VG+	NM
ABC-PARAMOUNT					
❑ 10659	Run Rabbit Run/Well Dressed Man	1965	3.75	7.50	15.00

SPARKS

This group did not use the article "The" before its name.

Number	Title (A Side/B Side)	Yr	VG	VG+	NM
ATLANTIC					
❑ 4030	I Predict/Moustache	1982	—	—	3.00
❑ 4030 [PS]	I Predict/Moustache	1982	—	2.00	4.00
❑ 4065	Eaten by the Monster of Love/Mickey Mouse	1982	—	—	3.00
❑ 89616	Pretending to Be Drunk/Kiss Me Quick	1984	—	—	3.00
❑ 89797	All You Ever Think About Is Sex/I Wish I Looked a Little Better	1983	—	—	3.00
❑ 89866	Cool Places/Sports	1983	—	—	3.00
—A-side: Sparks and Jane Wiedlin					
❑ 89866 [PS]	Cool Places/Sports	1983	—	2.00	4.00
BEARSVILLE					
❑ 0006	Wonder Girl/(No More) Mr. Nice Guys	1972	2.50	5.00	10.00
COLUMBIA					
❑ 10579	Forever Young/Over the Summer	1977	3.75	7.50	15.00
ELEKTRA					
❑ 46045	Tryouts for the Human Race/No. 1 in Heaven	1979	—	2.50	5.00
ISLAND					
❑ 001	Barbecutie/This Town Ain't Big Enough for Both of Us	1974	—	2.50	5.00
❑ 009	Lost and Found/Talent Is an Asset	1974	—	2.50	5.00
❑ 023	Something for the Girl with Everything/Achoo	1975	—	2.50	5.00
❑ 043	Looks, Looks, Looks/The Wedding of Jackie	1975	3.75	7.50	15.00
MCA CURB					
❑ 52879	Shopping Mall of Love/Music That You Can Dance To	1986	—	—	3.00
PRIVATE I					
❑ 05627	Armies of the Night/Give It Up	1985	—	—	3.00
—B-side by Evelyn "Champagne" King					
RCA					
❑ PD-12252	Tips for Teens/Don't Shoot Me	1981	—	—	—
—Unreleased					

SPARKS, THE

Possibly more than one group.

Number	Title (A Side/B Side)	Yr	VG	VG+	NM
ARWIN					
❑ 114	Something's Happened/Robin Redbreast	1958	5.00	10.00	20.00
CARLTON					
❑ 522	The Genie/Gee, That's Bad	1959	5.00	10.00	20.00
CUB					
❑ 9151	Woe, Woe/Cool It	1967	2.50	5.00	10.00
DECCA					
❑ 30378	Ol' Man River/Merry, Merry Lou	1957	3.00	6.00	12.00
❑ 30509	Roamin' Candle/A Cuddle and a Kiss	1957	3.00	6.00	12.00
❑ 30974	Why Did You Leave/La Macerena	1959	2.50	5.00	10.00
HULL					
❑ 723	Danny Boy/Run Run Run	1957	100.00	200.00	400.00
❑ 724	Adreann/Finger	1957	37.50	75.00	150.00

SPARKS OF RHYTHM, THE

Number	Title (A Side/B Side)	Yr	VG	VG+	NM
APOLLO					
❑ 479	Women, Women, Women/Don't Love You Anymore	1955	75.00	150.00	300.00
❑ 481	Hurry Home/Stars Are in the Sky	1955	75.00	150.00	300.00
❑ 541	Handy Man/Everybody Rock and Roll	1959	12.50	25.00	50.00

SPARROW, THE

Evolved into STEPPENWOLF. Also see MARS BONFIRE.

Number	Title (A Side/B Side)	Yr	VG	VG+	NM
COLUMBIA					
❑ 10234	Eli's Coming/Oh Doctor	1975	2.50	5.00	10.00
❑ 43755	Tomorrow's Ship/Isn't It Strange	1966	6.25	12.50	25.00
—As "The Sparrows"					
❑ 43755 [PS]	Tomorrow's Ship/Isn't It Strange	1966	25.00	50.00	100.00
—As "The Sparrows"					
❑ 43960	Green Bottle Lover/Down Goes Your Love Life	1967	6.25	12.50	25.00
—As "The Sparrows"					

SPARROWS, THE

Probably two different groups.

Number	Title (A Side/B Side)	Yr	VG	VG+	NM
DAVIS					
❑ 456	Love Me Tender/Come Back to Me	1957	75.00	150.00	300.00
JAY DEE					
❑ 783	Tell Me Baby/Why Did You Leave Me	1953	125.00	250.00	500.00
❑ 790	I'll Be Loving You/Hey!	1954	125.00	250.00	500.00

SPATS, THE

Number	Title (A Side/B Side)	Yr	VG	VG+	NM
ABC-PARAMOUNT					
❑ 10585	Gator Tails and Monkey Ribs/The Roach	1964	2.50	5.00	10.00
❑ 10600	She Kissed Me Last Night/There's a Party in the Pad Down Below	1964	2.50	5.00	10.00
❑ 10640	Billy, the Blue Grasshoper/Gotta Tell Ya All About It, Baby	1965	2.50	5.00	10.00
❑ 10711	Go Go Yamaha/Have You Ever Seen Me Crying	1965	2.50	5.00	10.00
❑ 10790	Scoobee Doo/She Done Moved	1966	2.50	5.00	10.00
ENITH					
❑ 1268	Gator Tails and Monkey Ribs/The Roach	1964	6.25	12.50	25.00

SPEARS, BRITNEY

Number	Title (A Side/B Side)	Yr	VG	VG+	NM
JIVE					
❑ 42545	...Baby One More Time (same on both sides)	1999	—	2.50	5.00
❑ 42576	Sometimes (same on both sides)	1999	—	2.00	4.00
❑ 42653	From the Bottom of My Broken Heart/(You Drive Me) Crazy	2000	—	2.00	4.00
❑ 42696	Oops!...I Did It Again (same on both sides)	2000	—	2.00	4.00
❑ 42745	Lucky (same on both sides)	2000	—	2.00	4.00
❑ 42762	Stronger (same on both sides)	2000	—	2.00	4.00

SPECTOR, PHIL

Also see PHIL HARVEY; THE TEDDY BEARS.

Number	Title (A Side/B Side)	Yr	VG	VG+	NM
PAVILLION					
❑ AE7 1354 [DJ]	Phil Spector's Christmas Medley (same on both sides)	1981	3.75	7.50	15.00
—Promo-only sampler from the Pavillion reissue of Phil Spector's Christmas Album					
PHILLES					
❑ (no #) [DJ]	Thanks for Giving Me the Right Time! (same on both sides)	1965	250.00	500.00	1000.
—Has Phil's picture on label; actually plays "Ebb Tide" by the Righteous Brothers					

SPECTOR, RONNIE

Also see THE RONETTES; VERONICA.

Number	Title (A Side/B Side)	Yr	VG	VG+	NM
ALSTON					
❑ 3738	It's a Heartache/I Wanna Come Over	1978	2.00	4.00	8.00
APPLE					
❑ 1832	Try Some, Buy Some/Tandoori Chicken	1971	—	3.50	7.00
❑ 1832	Try Some, Buy Some/Tandoori Chicken	1971	2.00	4.00	8.00
—With star on A-side label					
❑ 1832 [PS]	Try Some, Buy Some/Tandoori Chicken	1971	2.50	5.00	10.00
COLUMBIA					
❑ 07082	Who Can Sleep/When We Danced	1987	—	2.00	4.00
❑ 07082 [PS]	Who Can Sleep/When We Danced	1987	—	2.00	4.00
❑ 07300	Love on a Rooftop/Good Love Is Hard to Find	1987	—	2.00	4.00
EPIC					
❑ 50374	Say Goodbye to Hollywood/Baby Please Don't Go	1977	2.50	5.00	10.00
❑ 50374 [PS]	Say Goodbye to Hollywood/Baby Please Don't Go	1977	6.25	12.50	25.00
POLISH					
❑ 202	Darlin'/Tonight	1980	—	2.50	5.00
TOM CAT					
❑ JB-10380 [DJ]	You'd Be Good for Me/Something Tells Me	1975	2.50	5.00	10.00
—Promo only on blue vinyl					
❑ PB-10380	You'd Be Good for Me/Something Tells Me	1975	—	2.50	5.00
WARNER/SPECTOR					
❑ 0409	Paradise/When I Saw You	1976	2.50	5.00	10.00

SPECTORS THREE, THE

Number	Title (A Side/B Side)	Yr	VG	VG+	NM
TREY					
❑ 3001	I Really Do/I Know Why	1959	6.25	12.50	25.00
❑ 3005	My Heart Stood Still/Mr. Robin	1960	6.25	12.50	25.00

SPEEDO AND THE IMPALAS

See THE IMPALAS.

SPEEDY AND THE REVERBS

Number	Title (A Side/B Side)	Yr	VG	VG+	NM
REVERB					
❑ 51	100 Proof/Gas Chamber	196?	12.50	25.00	50.00

SPELLMAN, BENNY

Number	Title (A Side/B Side)	Yr	VG	VG+	NM
ACE					
❑ 630	That's All I Ask of You/Roll On Big Wheel	1961	5.00	10.00	20.00
ALON					
❑ 9018	Tain't the Truth/No Don't Stop	1965	2.50	5.00	10.00
❑ 9024	The Word Game/I Feel Good	1965	5.00	10.00	20.00
❑ 9027	It Must Be Love/Spirit of Loneliness	1965	2.50	5.00	10.00
❑ 9031	It's for You/This Is My Love	1966	2.50	5.00	10.00
ATLANTIC					
❑ 2291	The Word Game/I Feel Good	1965	2.50	5.00	10.00
MINIT					
❑ 606	Life Is Too Short/Ammerette	1960	3.75	7.50	15.00
❑ 613	Darling No Matter Where/I Didn't Know	1960	3.75	7.50	15.00
❑ 644	Lipstick Traces (On a Cigarette)/Fortune Teller	1962	3.00	6.00	12.00
❑ 652	Every Now and Then/I'm in Love	1962	3.00	6.00	12.00
❑ 659	Stickin' Whicha' Baby/You Got to Get It	1963	3.00	6.00	12.00
❑ 664	Ammerette/Talk About Love	1963	3.00	6.00	12.00
SANSU					
❑ 462	But If You Love Her/Sinner Girl	1967	2.00	4.00	8.00
WATCH					
❑ 6336	Slow Down Baby (You Drive Too Fast)/Someday They'll Understand	1964	2.50	5.00	10.00

SPELLMAN, JIMMY

Number	Title (A Side/B Side)	Yr	VG	VG+	NM
DOT					
❑ 15564	Here I Am/Make Up Your Mind	1957	7.50	15.00	30.00
❑ 15607	Doggonit/I'll Never Smile Again	1957	7.50	15.00	30.00

SPENCER, JEREMY

Also see FLEETWOOD MAC.

Number	Title (A Side/B Side)	Yr	VG	VG+	NM
ATLANTIC					
❑ 3588	Cool Breeze/You Got the Right	1979	—	2.50	5.00
❑ 3601	Cool Breeze/You Got the Right	1979	—	2.50	5.00
❑ 3624 [DJ]	Travelin' (same on both sides)	1979	—	2.50	5.00
—May be promo-only					
COLUMBIA					
❑ 45854	Can You Hear the Song/The World in Her Heart	1973	—	2.50	5.00

SPENCER AND SPENCER

DICKIE GOODMAN and Mickey Shorr.

Number	Title (A Side/B Side)	Yr	VG	VG+	NM
ARGO					
❑ 5331	Russian Bandstand/Brass Wail	1959	6.25	12.50	25.00

GONE

Number	Title (A Side/B Side)	Yr	VG	VG+	NM
❑ 5053	Stagger Lawrence/Strogonoff Cha Cha	1959	6.25	12.50	25.00

SPICE GIRLS
Also see GERI HALLIWELL; MELANIE C.

VIRGIN

Number	Title (A Side/B Side)	Yr	VG	VG+	NM
❑ S7-19489	Wannbe/Bumper to Bumper	1997	—	2.00	4.00

SPIDELLS, THE
CORAL

Number	Title (A Side/B Side)	Yr	VG	VG+	NM
❑ 62508	Pushed Out of the Picture/With You in Mind	1966	12.50	25.00	50.00
❑ 62531	Don't You Forget That You're My Baby/If It Ain't One Thing (It's Another)	1967	5.00	10.00	20.00

SPIDERS, THE (1)
Also see CHUCK CARBO.

IMPERIAL

Number	Title (A Side/B Side)	Yr	VG	VG+	NM
❑ 5265	I Didn't Want to Do It/You're the One	1954	25.00	50.00	100.00
❑ 5280	Tears Begin to Flow/I'll Stop Cryin'	1954	25.00	50.00	100.00
❑ 5291	I'm Searching/I'm Slippin' In	1954	62.50	125.00	250.00
❑ 5305	The Real Thing/Mm Mm Baby	1954	25.00	50.00	100.00
❑ 5318	She Keeps Me Wondering/(3 x 7) = "21"	1954	25.00	50.00	100.00
❑ 5331	That's Enough/Lost and Bewildered	1955	18.75	37.50	75.00
❑ 5344	Am I the One/Sukey, Sukey, Sukey	1955	18.75	37.50	75.00
❑ 5354	Bells in My Heart/For a Thrill	1955	25.00	50.00	100.00
—Red label					
❑ 5354	Bells in My Heart/For a Thrill	1957	7.50	15.00	30.00
—Black label					
❑ 5366	Is It True/Witchcraft	1955	25.00	50.00	100.00
—Blue label					
❑ 5366	Is It True/Witchcraft	1955	10.00	20.00	40.00
—Red label					
❑ 5376	Don't Pity Me/How I Feel	1956	10.00	20.00	40.00
—Featuring Chuck Carbo					
❑ 5393	A-1 in My Heart/Dear Mary	1956	7.50	15.00	30.00
—As "The Spiders with Chuck Carbo"					
❑ 5618	I Didn't Want to Do It/You're the One	1959	7.50	15.00	30.00
❑ 5714	You're the One/Tennessee Slim	1960	7.50	15.00	30.00
❑ 5739	Witchcraft/(True) You Don't Love Me	1961	7.50	15.00	30.00

SPIDERS, THE (2)
Early ALICE COOPER.

MASCOT

Number	Title (A Side/B Side)	Yr	VG	VG+	NM
❑ 112	Why Don't You Love Me/Hitch Hike	1965	375.00	750.00	1500.

SANTA CRUZ

Number	Title (A Side/B Side)	Yr	VG	VG+	NM
❑ 003	Don't Blow Your Mind/No Price Tag	1966	250.00	500.00	1000.

SPIDERS, THE (U)
Definitely not group (2); could be group (1).

LAWN

Number	Title (A Side/B Side)	Yr	VG	VG+	NM
❑ 234	Run Boy Run/Baby Doll	1964	3.00	6.00	12.00

PHILIPS

Number	Title (A Side/B Side)	Yr	VG	VG+	NM
❑ 40363	No No Boy/How Could I Fall in Love	1966	2.00	4.00	8.00

SPIKE DRIVERS, THE
OM 1000

Number	Title (A Side/B Side)	Yr	VG	VG+	NM
❑ 1676	High Time/Baby Won't You Let Me Tell You How I Lost My Mind	1966	7.50	15.00	30.00

REPRISE

Number	Title (A Side/B Side)	Yr	VG	VG+	NM
❑ 0535	High Time/Baby Won't You Let Me Tell You How I Lost My Mind	1966	5.00	10.00	20.00
❑ 0558	Strange Mysterious Sounds/Break Out the Wine	1967	5.00	10.00	20.00

SPINDLES, THE
ABC

Number	Title (A Side/B Side)	Yr	VG	VG+	NM
❑ 10802	To Make You Mine/And the Band Played On	1966	5.00	10.00	20.00
❑ 10850	No One Loves You (The Way I Do)/Ten Shades of Blue	1966	6.25	12.50	25.00

SPINDRIFTS, THE
ABC-PARAMOUNT

Number	Title (A Side/B Side)	Yr	VG	VG+	NM
❑ 9904	Belinda/Cha Cha Doo	1958	6.25	12.50	25.00

SPINNERS
Many, though not all, of these did not use the article "The" before the name. These are all by the group known as "The Detroit Spinners" in the U.K.

ATLANTIC

Number	Title (A Side/B Side)	Yr	VG	VG+	NM
❑ 2904	I'll Be Around/How Could I Let You Get Away	1972	—	2.50	5.00
❑ 2927	Could It Be I'm Falling in Love/Just You and Me Baby	1972	—	2.50	5.00
❑ 2962	One of a Kind (Love Affair)/Don't Let the Green Grass Fool You	1973	—	2.50	5.00
❑ 2973	Ghetto Child/We Belong Together	1973	—	2.50	5.00
❑ 3006	Mighty Love — Pt. 1/Mighty Love — Pt. 2	1974	—	2.50	5.00
❑ 3027	I'm Coming Home/He'll Never Love You Like I Do	1974	—	2.50	5.00
❑ 3029	Then Came You/Just As Long As We Have Love	1974	—	3.00	6.00
—With Dionne Warwicke					
❑ 3202	Then Came You/Just As Long As We Have Love	1974	—	2.50	5.00
—With Dionne Warwicke					
❑ 3206	Love Don't Love Nobody (Part 1)/Love Don't Love Nobody (Part 2)	1974	—	2.50	5.00
❑ 3252	Living a Little, Loving a Little/Smile, We Have Each Other	1975	—	2.50	5.00
❑ 3268	Sadie/Lazy Susan	1975	—	2.50	5.00
❑ 3284	Games People Play/I Don't Want to Lose You	1975	2.50	5.00	10.00
❑ 3284	They Just Can't Stop it the (Games People Play)/I Don't Want to Lose You	1975	—	2.50	5.00
—Same A-side, altered title					
❑ 3309	Love Or Leave/You Made a Promise to Me	1975	—	2.50	5.00
❑ 3341	Wake Up Susan/If You Can't Be in Love	1976	—	2.50	5.00
❑ 3355	The Rubberband Man/Now That We're Together	1976	—	2.50	5.00
❑ 3382	You're Throwing a Good Love Away/You're All I Need in Life	1977	—	2.50	5.00
❑ 3400	Me and My Music/I'm Riding Your Shadow	1977	—	2.50	5.00
❑ 3425	Heaven on Earth (So Fine)/I'm Tired of Giving	1977	—	2.50	5.00
❑ 3462	Easy Come, Easy Go/Love Is One Step Away	1978	—	2.50	5.00
❑ 3483	If You Wanna Do a Dance/One in a Life Proposal	1978	—	2.50	5.00
❑ 3546	Are You Ready for Love/Once You Fall in Love	1978	—	2.50	5.00
❑ 3590	Don't Let the Man Get You/I Love the Music	1979	—	2.50	5.00
❑ 3619	Body Language/With My Eyes	1979	—	2.50	5.00
❑ 3637	Working My Way Back to You/Disco Ride	1979	2.00	4.00	8.00
—Original pressings mention only one song on the A-side					
❑ 3637	Working My Way Back to You-Forgive Me, Girl/Disco Ride	1979	—	2.00	4.00
❑ 3664	Cupid-I've Loved You for a Long Time/Pipedreams	1980	—	2.00	4.00
❑ 3757	Love Trippin'/Now That You're Mine Again	1980	—	2.00	4.00
❑ 3765	I Just Want to Fall in Love/Heavy on the Sunshine	1980	—	2.00	4.00
❑ 3798	Yesterday Once More-Nothing Remains the Same/Be My Love	1981	—	2.00	4.00
❑ 3814	Long Live Soul Music/Give Your Lady What She Wants	1981	—	2.00	4.00
❑ 3827	Winter of Our Love/The Deacon	1981	—	2.00	4.00
❑ 3848	What You Feel Is Real/Street Talk	1981	—	2.00	4.00
—With Gino Soccio					
❑ 3865	You Go Your Way (I'll Go Mine)/Got to Be Love	1981	—	2.00	4.00
❑ 3882 [DJ]	Love Connection (same on both sides)	1981	—	2.50	5.00
—May be promo only					
❑ 4007	Never Thought I'd Fall in Love/Send a Little Love	1982	—	2.00	4.00
❑ 89226	Spaceballs/Spaceballs (Dub Version)	1987	—	—	3.00
❑ 89648	(We Have Come Into) Our Time for All/All Your Love	1984	—	2.00	4.00
❑ 89689	Right or Wrong/Love Is In Season	1984	—	2.00	4.00
❑ 89862	City Full of Memories/No Other Love	1983	—	2.00	4.00
❑ 89922	Funny How Time Slips Away/I'm Calling You Now	1982	—	2.00	4.00
❑ 89962	Magic in the Moonlight/So Far Away	1982	—	2.00	4.00

MIRAGE

Number	Title (A Side/B Side)	Yr	VG	VG+	NM
❑ 99580	She Does/(B-side unknown)	1986	—	—	3.00
❑ 99604	Put Us Together Again/Show Us Your Magic	1985	—	—	3.00

MOTOWN

Number	Title (A Side/B Side)	Yr	VG	VG+	NM
❑ 1067	Sweet Thing/How Can I	1964	3.75	7.50	15.00
❑ 1078	I'll Always Love You/Tomorrow May Never Come	1965	3.75	7.50	15.00
❑ 1093	Truly Yours/Where Is That Girl	1966	3.75	7.50	15.00
❑ 1109	For All We Know/Cross My Heart	1967	3.75	7.50	15.00
❑ 1136	I Just Can't Help But Feel the Pain/Bad, Bad Weather	1968	3.75	7.50	15.00
❑ 1155	In My Diary/(She's Gonna Love Me) At Sundown	1969	375.00	750.00	1500.
❑ 1235	Together We Can Make Such Sweet Music/Bad, Bad Weather	1973	2.00	4.00	8.00

TRI-PHI

Number	Title (A Side/B Side)	Yr	VG	VG+	NM
❑ 1001	That's What Girls Are Made For/Heebie-Jeebies	1961	6.25	12.50	25.00
❑ 1004	Love (I'm So Glad I Found You)/Sudbuster	1961	6.25	12.50	25.00
❑ 1007	What Did She Use/Itching for My Baby, I Know Where to Scratch	1962	6.25	12.50	25.00
❑ 1010	She Loves Me So/Whistling About You	1962	6.25	12.50	25.00
❑ 1013	I've Been Hurt/I Got Your Water Boiling Baby (I'm Gonna Cook Your Goose)	1962	6.25	12.50	25.00
❑ 1018	She Don't Love Me/Too Young, Too Much, Too Soon	1962	7.50	15.00	30.00

V.I.P.

Number	Title (A Side/B Side)	Yr	VG	VG+	NM
❑ 25050	In My Diary/(She's Gonna Love Me) At Sundown	1969	6.25	12.50	25.00
❑ 25054	Message from a Black Man/(She's Gonna Love Me) At Sundown	1970	3.00	6.00	12.00
❑ 25057	It's a Shame/Together We Can Make Such Sweet Music	1970	3.00	6.00	12.00
❑ 25060	We'll Have It Made/My Whole World Ended (The Moment You Left Me)	1971	3.00	6.00	12.00

SPINNERS, THE
None of these are the popular soul group. Also see THE LIVERPOOL SPINNERS.

CAPITOL

Number	Title (A Side/B Side)	Yr	VG	VG+	NM
❑ F3955	Love's Prayer/Goofin'	1958	10.00	20.00	40.00

CRYSTALETTE

Number	Title (A Side/B Side)	Yr	VG	VG+	NM
❑ 736	Boomerang/Slave Chain	1960	12.50	25.00	50.00
—Reissued under different titles and on different labels credited to the Crestriders and Duke Mitchell					

END

Number	Title (A Side/B Side)	Yr	VG	VG+	NM
❑ 1045	Bird Watcher/Richard Pry, Private Eye	1959	25.00	50.00	100.00
—Gray label					
❑ 1045	Bird Watcher/Richard Pry, Private Eye	1959	10.00	20.00	40.00
—Multicolor label					

LAWSON

Number	Title (A Side/B Side)	Yr	VG	VG+	NM
❑ 324	Surfing Monkey/Beatle Mania	1964	7.50	15.00	30.00

LIBERTY

Number	Title (A Side/B Side)	Yr	VG	VG+	NM
❑ 55339	Till the End of Time/Dream	1961	2.50	5.00	10.00

RCA VICTOR

Number	Title (A Side/B Side)	Yr	VG	VG+	NM
❑ 47-8427	All I Want/It Must Be Love	1964	2.50	5.00	10.00

RHYTHM

Number	Title (A Side/B Side)	Yr	VG	VG+	NM
❑ 125	Marvella/My Love and Your Love	1958	100.00	200.00	400.00

SMASH

Number	Title (A Side/B Side)	Yr	VG	VG+	NM
❑ 1845	Happy Hootenanny/Nothin'	1963	2.50	5.00	10.00

WARNER BROS.

Number	Title (A Side/B Side)	Yr	VG	VG+	NM
❑ 5084	Little Otis/Rag Mop	1959	3.00	6.00	12.00

SPIRAL STARECASE
COLUMBIA

Number	Title (A Side/B Side)	Yr	VG	VG+	NM
❑ 44442	Makin' My Mind Up/Baby What I Mean	1968	—	3.00	6.00
❑ 44566	Inside, Outside, Upside Down/I'll Run	1968	—	3.00	6.00
❑ 44741	More Today Than Yesterday/Broken Hearted Man	1969	2.00	4.00	8.00
❑ 44924	Sweet Little Thing/No One for Me to Turn To	1969	—	2.50	5.00
❑ 45048	She's Ready/Judas to the Love We Know	1969	—	2.50	5.00

SPIRALS, THE

Number	Title (A Side/B Side)	Yr	VG	VG+	NM
CAPITOL					
❑ F4084	Rockin' Cow/Everybody Knows	1958	12.50	25.00	50.00
SMASH					
❑ 1719	Please Be My Love/Forever and a Day	1961	25.00	50.00	100.00

SPIRES, BIG BOY

Number	Title (A Side/B Side)	Yr	VG	VG+	NM
CHANCE					
❑ 1137	About to Lose My Mind/Which One Do I Love	1953	625.00	1250.	2500.

SPIRIT

Also see RANDY CALIFORNIA.

Number	Title (A Side/B Side)	Yr	VG	VG+	NM
EPIC					
❑ 10648	Animal Zoo/Red Light Roll On	1970	—	3.00	6.00
❑ 10685	Soldier/Mr. Skin	1970	—	3.00	6.00
❑ 10701	Mr. Skin/Nature's Way	1971	—	2.50	5.00
❑ 10849	Darkness/Cadillac Cowboys	1972	—	2.50	5.00
❑ 11020	Mr. Skin/Nature's Way	1973	—	2.00	4.00
MERCURY					
❑ 73697	America the Beautiful-The Times They Are a-Changin'/Lady of the Lakes	1975	—	2.50	5.00
❑ 73722	Holy Man/Looking Into Darkness	1975	—	2.50	5.00
❑ 73837	Atomic Boogie/Farther Along	1976	—	2.00	4.00
ODE					
❑ 108	Mechanical World/Uncle Jack	1967	2.50	5.00	10.00
❑ 115	I Got a Line on You/She Smiles	1968	2.50	5.00	10.00
❑ 122	Dark Eyed Woman/New Dope in Town	1969	2.00	4.00	8.00
❑ 128	1984/Sweet Stella Baby	1969	2.00	4.00	8.00
POTATO					
❑ 1722	Nature's Way/Rock and Roll Planet	1978	—	2.50	5.00
❑ 1722 [PS]	Nature's Way/Rock and Roll Planet	1978	—	2.50	5.00
RHINO					
❑ 008	Turn to the Right/Potato Land Theme Song	1980	—	2.50	5.00

SPIRITS AND WORM

Number	Title (A Side/B Side)	Yr	VG	VG+	NM
A&M					
❑ 1104	Fanny Firecracker/You and I Together	1969	10.00	20.00	40.00

SPLINTER

Also see BILL ELLIOTT AND THE ELASTIC OZ BAND.

Number	Title (A Side/B Side)	Yr	VG	VG+	NM
DARK HORSE					
❑ 8439	Round and Round/I'll Bend for You	1977	—	2.00	4.00
❑ 8523	I Need Your Love/Motions of Love	1978	—	2.00	4.00
❑ 10002	Costafine Town/Elly-Mae	1974	—	3.00	6.00
❑ 10002 [PS]	Costafine Town/Elly-Mae	1974	2.00	4.00	8.00
❑ 10003	China Light/Haven't Got Time	1975	—	3.00	6.00
❑ 10007	Which Way Will I Get Home/What Is It (If You Never Tried It Yourself)	1975	—	3.00	6.00
❑ 10010	After Five Years/Halfway There	1976	—	2.50	5.00

SPOKESMEN, THE

Number	Title (A Side/B Side)	Yr	VG	VG+	NM
DECCA					
❑ 31844	The Dawn of Correction/For You Babe	1965	3.00	6.00	12.00
❑ 31874	It Ain't Fair/Have Courage, Be Careful	1965	2.50	5.00	10.00
❑ 31895	Michelle/Better Days Are Yet to Come	1966	2.50	5.00	10.00
❑ 31949	Today's the Day/Enchante	1966	2.50	5.00	10.00
❑ 32049	I Love How You Love Me/Beautiful Girl	1966	2.50	5.00	10.00
WINCHESTER					
❑ 1001	Mary Jane/Flashback	1967	3.00	6.00	12.00

SPOOKY TOOTH

Also see GARY WRIGHT.

Number	Title (A Side/B Side)	Yr	VG	VG+	NM
A&M					
❑ 1144	That Was Only Yesterday/Waitin' for the Wind	1969	2.00	4.00	8.00
ISLAND					
❑ 004	The Mirror/Hell or High Water	1974	—	2.50	5.00
❑ 1219	All Sewn Up/Things Change	1973	—	3.00	6.00
MALA					
❑ 12013	Love Really Changed Me/Spooky Blow	1968	2.50	5.00	10.00
❑ 12022	The Weight/Do Right People	1968	2.50	5.00	10.00

SPORTONES, THE

Number	Title (A Side/B Side)	Yr	VG	VG+	NM
MUNICH					
❑ 101	In My Dreams/So Sincere	1959	125.00	250.00	500.00

SPOTLIGHTERS, THE

Two different groups?

Number	Title (A Side/B Side)	Yr	VG	VG+	NM
ALADDIN					
❑ 3436	Please Be My Girlfriend/Whisper	1958	25.00	50.00	100.00
❑ 3441	This Is My Story/Preaching	1959	25.00	50.00	100.00
IMPERIAL					
❑ 5342	It's Cold/Bam Jingle Jingle	1955	31.25	62.50	125.00
❑ 5342	It's Cold/Bam Jingle Jingle	1955	62.50	125.00	250.00
—Red vinyl					

SPOTNICKS, THE

Number	Title (A Side/B Side)	Yr	VG	VG+	NM
ATCO					
❑ 6261	Orange Blossom Special/Hava Nagila	1963	3.00	6.00	12.00
FELSTED					
❑ 8649	Spotnick/Old Spinning Wheel	1962	3.00	6.00	12.00
LAURIE					
❑ 3241	I'm Goin' Home/Orange Blossom Special	1964	2.50	5.00	10.00
❑ 3260	Summer in Sweden/Endless Sleep	1964	2.50	5.00	10.00
❑ 3297	Just Listen to My Heart/Pony Express	1965	2.50	5.00	10.00
❑ 3333	Drum Didley/Orange Blossom Special	1966	2.50	5.00	10.00

SPRING

Also see AMERICAN SPRING.

Number	Title (A Side/B Side)	Yr	VG	VG+	NM
UNITED ARTISTS					
❑ 50848	Now Everything's Been Said/Awake	1971	7.50	15.00	30.00
❑ 50907	Good Times/Sweet Mountain	1972	20.00	40.00	80.00

SPRINGFIELD, DUSTY

Also see THE SPRINGFIELDS.

Number	Title (A Side/B Side)	Yr	VG	VG+	NM
20TH CENTURY					
❑ 2457	It Goes Like It Goes/I Wish That Love Would Last	1980	—	2.50	5.00
ABC DUNHILL					
❑ 4341	Who Gets Your Love/Of All the Things	1973	—	3.00	6.00
❑ 4344	Mama's Little Girl/Learn to Say Goodbye	1973	—	3.00	6.00
❑ 4357	Mama's Little Girl/Learn to Say Goodbye	1973	2.00	4.00	8.00
ATLANTIC					
❑ 2580	Son-of-a-Preacher-Man/Just a Little Lovin'	1968	2.50	5.00	10.00
❑ 2580 [PS]	Son-of-a-Preacher-Man/Just a Little Lovin'	1968	3.75	7.50	15.00
❑ 2606	Breakfast in Bed/Don't Forget About Me	1969	2.00	4.00	8.00
❑ 2623	The Windmills of Your Mind/I Don't Want to Hear It Anymore	1969	2.00	4.00	8.00
❑ 2647	Willie & Laura May Jones/That Old Sweet Roll	1969	—	3.00	6.00
❑ 2673	In the Land of Make Believe/So Much Love	1969	—	3.00	6.00
❑ 2685	A Brand New Me/Bad Case of the Blues	1969	—	3.00	6.00
❑ 2705	Silly, Silly, Fool/Joe	1970	—	3.00	6.00
❑ 2729	I Wanna Be a Free Girl/Let Me In Your Way	1970	—	3.00	6.00
❑ 2739	Never Love Again/Lost	1970	—	3.00	6.00
❑ 2771	What Good Is I Love You/What Do You Do When Love Dies	1970	—	3.00	6.00
❑ 2825	Nothing Is Forever/Haunted	1971	—	3.00	6.00
❑ 2841	I Believe in You/Someone Who Cared	1971	—	3.00	6.00
CASABLANCA					
❑ 2356	I Am Curious/Donnez-Moi	1981	—	2.00	4.00
ENIGMA					
❑ 75042	Nothing Has Been Proved/(Instrumental)	1989	—	2.50	5.00
PHILIPS					
❑ 40162	I Only Want to Be with You/Once Upon a Time	1963	3.00	6.00	12.00
❑ 40180	Stay Awhile/Something Special	1964	2.50	5.00	10.00
❑ 40180 [PS]	Stay Awhile/Something Special	1964	5.00	10.00	20.00
❑ 40207	Wishin' and Hopin'/Do Re Mi (Forget About the Do and Think About Me)	1964	3.00	6.00	12.00
❑ 40229	All Cried Out/I Wish I'd Never Loved You	1964	2.50	5.00	10.00
❑ 40229 [PS]	All Cried Out/I Wish I'd Never Loved You	1964	5.00	10.00	20.00
❑ 40245	Guess Who/Live It Up	1964	2.50	5.00	10.00
❑ 40245 [PS]	Guess Who/Live It Up	1964	5.00	10.00	20.00
❑ 40270	Losing You/Here She Comes	1965	2.50	5.00	10.00
❑ 40270 [PS]	Losing You/Here She Comes	1965	5.00	10.00	20.00
❑ 40303	In the Middle of Nowhere/Baby, Don't You Know	1965	2.50	5.00	10.00
❑ 40303 [PS]	In the Middle of Nowhere/Baby, Don't You Know	1965	5.00	10.00	20.00
❑ 40319	I Just Don't Know What to Do with Myself/Some of Your Lovin'	1965	2.50	5.00	10.00
❑ 40319 [PS]	I Just Don't Know What to Do with Myself/Some of Your Lovin'	1965	5.00	10.00	20.00
❑ 40371	You Don't Have to Say You Love Me/Little by Little	1966	2.50	5.00	10.00
❑ 40371 [PS]	You Don't Have to Say You Love Me/Little by Little	1966	5.00	10.00	20.00
❑ 40396	All I See Is You/I'm Gonna Leave You	1966	2.50	5.00	10.00
❑ 40396 [PS]	All I See Is You/I'm Gonna Leave You	1966	5.00	10.00	20.00
❑ 40439	I'll Try Anything/The Corrupt Ones	1967	2.50	5.00	10.00
❑ 40439 [PS]	I'll Try Anything/The Corrupt Ones	1967	5.00	10.00	20.00
❑ 40465	The Look of Love/Give Me Time	1967	2.50	5.00	10.00
❑ 40498	What's It Gonna Be/Small Town Girl	1967	2.50	5.00	10.00
❑ 40498 [PS]	What's It Gonna Be/Small Town Girl	1967	4.00	8.00	16.00
❑ 40547	Sweet Ride/No Stranger Am I	1968	2.50	5.00	10.00
❑ 40553	La Bamba/I Close My Eyes and Count to Ten	1968	2.50	5.00	10.00
UNITED ARTISTS					
❑ XW1006	Let Me Love You Once Before You Go/I'm Your Child	1977	—	2.50	5.00
❑ XW1205	Checkmate/Sandra	1978	—	2.50	5.00
❑ XW1225	Give Me the Night/Checkmate	1978	—	2.50	5.00
❑ XW1255	Living Without Your Love/Get Yourself to Love	1978	—	2.50	5.00

SPRINGFIELD, RICK

Number	Title (A Side/B Side)	Yr	VG	VG+	NM
CAPITOL					
❑ 3340	Speak to the Sky/Why	1972	2.00	4.00	8.00
❑ 3340 [PS]	Speak to the Sky/Why	1972	3.75	7.50	15.00
❑ 3466	What Would the Children Think/Come On Everybody	1972	2.00	4.00	8.00
❑ 3466 [PS]	What Would the Children Think/Come On Everybody	1972	3.75	7.50	15.00
❑ 3637	I'm Your Superman/Why Are You Waiting	1973	2.00	4.00	8.00
❑ 3713	Believe in Me/The Liar	1973	3.00	6.00	12.00
CHELSEA					
❑ 3051	Take a Hand/Archangel	1976	—	2.50	5.00
❑ 3055	Million Dollar Face/(B-side unknown)	1976	—	2.50	5.00
❑ 3056	Jessica/(B-side unknown)	1976	—	2.50	5.00
COLUMBIA					
❑ 45935	Believe in Me/The Liar	1973	—	3.00	6.00
❑ 46032	Streakin' Across the U.S.A./Music to Streak By	1974	—	3.00	6.00
❑ 46057	American Girls/Weep No More	1974	—	2.50	5.00
MERCURY					
❑ 880405-7	Bruce/Guenevere	1984	—	2.00	4.00
❑ 880405-7 [PS]	Bruce/Guenevere	1984	—	2.50	5.00
RCA					
❑ 6853-7-R	Rock of Life/The Language of Love	1988	—	—	3.00
❑ 6853-7-R [PS]	Rock of Life/The Language of Love	1988	—	—	3.00
❑ 8391-7-R	Honeymoon in Beirut/My Father's Chair	1988	—	—	3.00
❑ 8391-7-R [PS]	Honeymoon in Beirut/My Father's Chair	1988	—	—	3.00
❑ PB-12166	I've Done Everything for You/Red Hot and Blue Love	1981	—	2.00	4.00
❑ PB-12166 [PS]	I've Done Everything for You/Red Hot and Blue Love	1981	—	2.00	4.00
❑ PB-12201	Jessie's Girl/Carry Me Away	1981	—	2.00	4.00
❑ PB-12201 [PS]	Jessie's Girl/Carry Me Away	1981	—	2.50	5.00
❑ PB-13008	Love Is Alright Tonite/Everybody's Girl	1981	—	2.00	4.00
❑ PB-13008 [PS]	Love Is Alright Tonite/Everybody's Girl	1981	—	2.00	4.00
❑ PB-13070	Don't Talk to Strangers/Tonight	1982	—	2.00	4.00
❑ PB-13070 [PS]	Don't Talk to Strangers/Tonight	1982	—	2.00	4.00
❑ PB-13245	What Kind of Fool Am I/How Do You Talk to Girls	1982	—	2.00	4.00

Number	Title (A Side/B Side)	Yr	VG	VG+	NM
❑ PB-13303	I Get Excited/Kristina	1982	—	2.00	4.00
❑ PB-13303 [PS]	I Get Excited/Kristina	1982	—	2.00	4.00
❑ GB-13482	Jessie's Girl/I've Done Everything for You	1983	—	—	3.00
—Gold Standard Series					
❑ GB-13483	Don't Talk to Strangers/What Kind of Fool Am I	1983	—	—	3.00
—Gold Standard Series					
❑ PB-13497	Affair of the Heart/Like Father, Like Son	1983	—	—	3.00
❑ PB-13497 [PS]	Affair of the Heart/Like Father, Like Son	1983	—	2.00	4.00
❑ PB-13576	Human Touch/Alyson	1983	—	—	3.00
❑ PB-13650	Souls/Souls (Live)	1983	—	—	3.00
❑ PB-13650 [PS]	Souls/Souls (Live)	1983	—	2.00	4.00
❑ PB-13738	Love Somebody/The Great Lost Art of Conversation	1984	—	—	3.00
❑ PB-13738 [PS]	Love Somebody/The Great Lost Art of Conversation	1984	—	—	3.00
❑ GB-13794	Affair of the Heart/Human Touch	1984	—	—	3.00
—Gold Standard Series					
❑ PB-13813	Don't Walk Away/S.F.O.	1984	—	—	3.00
❑ PB-13813 [PS]	Don't Walk Away/S.F.O.	1984	—	—	3.00
❑ PB-13861	Bop 'Til You Drop/Taxi Dancing	1984	—	—	3.00
—B-side: With Randy Crawford					
❑ PB-13861 [PS]	Bop 'Til You Drop/Taxi Dancing	1984	—	—	3.00
❑ PB-14047	Celebrate Youth/Stranger in the House	1985	—	—	3.00
❑ PB-14047 [PS]	Celebrate Youth/Stranger in the House	1985	—	—	3.00
❑ PB-14120	State of the Heart/The Power of Love (The Tao of Love)	1985	—	—	3.00
❑ PB-14120 [PS]	State of the Heart/The Power of Love (The Tao of Love)	1985	—	—	3.00

SPRINGFIELD RIFLE, THE

ABC

Number	Title (A Side/B Side)	Yr	VG	VG+	NM
❑ 10878	The Bears/There Is Life on Mars	1966	2.50	5.00	10.00

JERDEN

Number	Title (A Side/B Side)	Yr	VG	VG+	NM
❑ 812	Stop and Take a Look Around/100 or Two	1967	3.00	6.00	12.00
❑ 815	All She Said/It Ain't Happened	1967	3.00	6.00	12.00
❑ 901	I'll Be Standing There/Will You Love Me Tomorrow	196?	3.00	6.00	12.00
❑ 902	Left of Nowhere/I Must Go for a Walk	196?	3.00	6.00	12.00
❑ 905	I Love You/That's All I Really Need	196?	3.00	6.00	12.00

TOWER

Number	Title (A Side/B Side)	Yr	VG	VG+	NM
❑ 455	I Love Her/That's All I Really Need	1968	2.50	5.00	10.00

SPRINGFIELDS, THE

Also see DUSTY SPRINGFIELD.

PHILIPS

Number	Title (A Side/B Side)	Yr	VG	VG+	NM
❑ 40038	Silver Threads and Golden Needles/Aunt Rhody	1962	3.75	7.50	15.00
❑ 40072	Dear Hearts and Gentle People/Gotta Travel On	1962	3.00	6.00	12.00
❑ 40092	Little By Little/Waf-Woof	1963	3.00	6.00	12.00
❑ 40099	Foggy Mountain Top/Island of Dreams	1963	3.00	6.00	12.00
❑ 40121	Say I Won't Be There/Little Boat	1963	3.00	6.00	12.00

SPRINGSTEEN, BRUCE

COLUMBIA

Number	Title (A Side/B Side)	Yr	VG	VG+	NM
❑ AE7 1088 [DJ]	Rosalita (Come Out Tonight)//Spirit in the Night/Growin' Up	1974	75.00	150.00	300.00
—Small hole, plays at 33 1/3 RPM					
❑ AE7 1332 [DJ]	Santa Claus Is Coming to Town (same on both sides)	1981	5.00	10.00	20.00
❑ AE7 1332 [PS]	Santa Claus Is Coming to Town (same on both sides)	1981	6.25	12.50	25.00
❑ 03243	Hungry Heart/Fade Away	1983	—	2.00	4.00
—"Columbia Hall of Fame" series; red label					
❑ 03243	Hungry Heart/Fade Away	198?	—	—	3.00
—"Columbia Hall of Fame" series; gray label					
❑ 04463	Dancing in the Dark/Pink Cadillac	1984	—	2.00	4.00
❑ 04463 [PS]	Dancing in the Dark/Pink Cadillac	1984	—	2.50	5.00
❑ 04561	Cover Me/Jersey Girl	1984	2.50	5.00	10.00
—First pressings have a spoken intro to "Jersey Girl." Dead wax has matrix number followed by "-1" and a letter.					
❑ 04561	Cover Me/Jersey Girl	1984	—	2.00	4.00
—Spoken intro to "Jersey Girl" is deleted. Dead wax has matrix number followed by "-2" and a letter.					
❑ 04561 [PS]	Cover Me/Jersey Girl	1984	—	2.50	5.00
❑ 04680	Born in the U.S.A./Shut Out the Light	1984	—	2.00	4.00
❑ 04680 [PS]	Born in the U.S.A./Shut Out the Light	1984	—	2.50	5.00
❑ 04772	I'm on Fire/Johnny Bye Bye	1985	—	2.00	4.00
❑ 04772 [PS]	I'm on Fire/Johnny Bye Bye	1985	—	2.50	5.00
❑ 04924	Glory Days/Stand On It	1985	—	2.00	4.00
❑ 04924 [PS]	Glory Days/Stand On It	1985	—	2.50	5.00
❑ 05603	I'm Goin' Down/Janey, Don't You Lose Heart	1985	—	2.00	4.00
❑ 05603 [PS]	I'm Goin' Down/Janey, Don't You Lose Heart	1985	—	2.50	5.00
❑ 05728	My Hometown/Santa Claus Is Coming to Town	1985	—	2.00	4.00
❑ 05728 [PS]	My Hometown/Santa Claus Is Coming to Town	1985	—	2.00	4.00
❑ 06432	War/Merry Christmas Baby	1986	—	2.00	4.00
❑ 06432 [PS]	War/Merry Christmas Baby	1986	—	2.00	4.00
❑ 06657	Fire/Incident on 57th Street	1987	—	2.50	5.00
❑ 06657 [PS]	Fire/Incident on 57th Street	1987	—	2.50	5.00
❑ 07595	Brilliant Disguise/Lucky Man	1987	—	2.00	4.00
❑ 07595 [PS]	Brilliant Disguise/Lucky Man	1987	—	2.00	4.00
❑ 07663	Tunnel of Love/Two for the Road	1987	—	2.00	4.00
❑ 07663 [PS]	Tunnel of Love/Two for the Road	1987	—	2.00	4.00
❑ 07726	One Step Up/Roulette	1988	—	2.00	4.00
❑ 07726 [PS]	One Step Up/Roulette	1988	—	2.00	4.00
❑ 08408	Dancing in the Dark/Pink Cadillac	1984	—	—	3.00
—Gray label reissue					
❑ 08409	Cover Me/Jersey Girl	1984	—	—	3.00
—Gray label reissue					
❑ 08410	Born in the U.S.A./Shut Out the Light	1984	—	—	3.00
—Gray label reissue					
❑ 08411	I'm on Fire/Johnny Bye Bye	1985	—	—	3.00
—Gray label reissue					
❑ 08412	Glory Days/Stand On It	1985	—	—	3.00
—Gray label reissue					
❑ 08413	I'm Goin' Down/Janey, Don't You Lose Heart	1985	—	—	3.00
—Gray label reissue					
❑ 08414	My Hometown/Santa Claus Is Coming to Town	1985	—	—	3.00
—Gray label reissue; many copies of this were issued with Columbia 05728 picture sleeves					
❑ 10209	Born to Run/Meeting Across the River	1975	5.00	10.00	20.00
❑ 10274	Tenth Avenue Freeze-Out/She's the One	1976	3.75	7.50	15.00
❑ 10763	Prove It All Night/Factory	1978	3.00	6.00	12.00
❑ 10801	Badlands/Streets of Fire	1978	3.00	6.00	12.00
❑ 11391	Hungry Heart/Held Up Without a Gun	1980	—	2.00	4.00
❑ 11391 [PS]	Hungry Heart/Held Up Without a Gun	1980	—	3.00	6.00
❑ 11431	Fade Away/To Be True	1981	6.25	12.50	25.00
—Erroneous first pressing					
❑ 11431	Fade Away/Be True	1981	—	2.00	4.00
—Corrected second pressing					
❑ 11431 [PS]	Fade Away/Be True	1981	—	3.00	6.00
❑ 33323	Born to Run/Spirit in the Night	1976	—	2.00	4.00
—"Columbia Hall of Fame" series; red label					
❑ 33323	Born to Run/Spirit in the Night	198?	—	—	3.00
—"Columbia Hall of Fame" series; gray label					
❑ 45805	Blinded by the Light/The Angel	1972	125.00	250.00	500.00
❑ 45805 [DJ]	Blinded by the Light (mono/stereo)	1972	12.50	25.00	50.00
❑ 45805 [PS]	Blinded by the Light/The Angel	1972	100.00	200.00	400.00
❑ 45864	Spirit in the Night/For You	1973	375.00	750.00	1500.
❑ 45864 [DJ]	Spirit in the Night (mono/stereo)	1973	12.50	25.00	50.00
❑ 73796	Tunnel of Love/Two for the Road	1991	—	—	3.00
—Reissue					
❑ 73943	One Step Up/Roulette	1991	—	—	3.00
—Reissue					
❑ 74273	Human Touch/Better Days	1992	—	2.00	4.00
❑ 74354	57 Channels (And Nothin' On)/Part Man Part Monkey	1992	—	2.00	4.00
❑ 77384	Streets of Philadelphia/If I Should Fall Behind	1994	—	2.00	4.00
❑ 77847	Secret Garden/Thunder Road (Live)	1995	—	—	3.00
❑ 77847 [PS]	Secret Garden/Thunder Road (Live)	1995	—	—	3.00

SPUTNIKS, THE

CLASS

Number	Title (A Side/B Side)	Yr	VG	VG+	NM
❑ 217	My Love Is Gone/Hey Maryann	1958	12.50	25.00	50.00
❑ 222	Wait a Little While/Johnny's Little Lamb	1958	10.00	20.00	40.00

PAM MAR

Number	Title (A Side/B Side)	Yr	VG	VG+	NM
❑ 601	My Love Is Gone/Hey Maryann	1957	62.50	125.00	250.00

SQUIER, BILLY

CAPITOL

Number	Title (A Side/B Side)	Yr	VG	VG+	NM
❑ 4877	You Should Be High Love/Like I'm Lovin' You	1980	—	2.50	5.00
❑ 4877 [PS]	You Should Be High Love/Like I'm Lovin' You	1980	—	2.50	5.00
❑ 4901	The Music's All Right/Big Beat	1980	—	2.50	5.00
❑ A-5005	The Stroke/Too Daze Gone	1981	—	2.00	4.00
❑ A-5005 [PS]	The Stroke/Too Daze Gone	1981	—	2.50	5.00
❑ A-5037	My Kinda Lover/Christmas Is the Time to Say "I Love You"	1981	—	2.00	4.00
❑ A-5037 [PS]	My Kinda Lover/Christmas Is the Time to Say "I Love You"	1981	—	2.50	5.00
❑ A-5040	In the Dark/Whadda You Want from Me	1981	—	2.00	4.00
❑ A-5040 [PS]	In the Dark/Whadda You Want from Me	1981	—	2.50	5.00
❑ B-5135	Emotions in Motion/It Keeps You Rockin'	1982	—	2.00	4.00
❑ B-5135 [PS]	Emotions in Motion/It Keeps You Rockin'	1982	—	2.50	5.00
❑ B-5163	Everybody Wants You/Keep Me Satisfied	1982	—	2.00	4.00
❑ B-5163 [PS]	Everybody Wants You/Keep Me Satisfied	1982	—	2.50	5.00
❑ B-5202	She's a Runner/In Your Eyes	1983	—	2.00	4.00
❑ B-5202 [PS]	She's a Runner/In Your Eyes	1983	—	2.50	5.00
❑ B-5303	Christmas Is the Time to Say "I Love You"/White Christmas	1983	—	2.50	5.00
❑ B-5303 [PS]	Christmas Is the Time to Say "I Love You"/White Christmas	1983	—	3.00	6.00
❑ B-5370	Rock Me Tonite/Can't Get Next to You	1984	—	—	3.00
❑ B-5370 [PS]	Rock Me Tonite/Can't Get Next to You	1984	—	2.00	4.00
❑ B-5416	Eye on You/Calley Oh	1984	—	—	3.00
❑ B-5416 [PS]	Eye on You/Calley Oh	1984	—	2.00	4.00
❑ B-5422	All Night Long/Calley Oh	1984	—	—	3.00
❑ B-5422 [PS]	All Night Long/Calley Oh	1984	—	2.00	4.00
❑ B-5619	Love Is the Hero/Learn How to Live (Live)	1986	—	—	3.00
❑ B-5619 [PS]	Love Is the Hero/Learn How to Live (Live)	1986	—	—	3.00
❑ B-5657	Shot O' Love/One Good Woman	1986	—	—	3.00
❑ B-5657 [PS]	Shot O' Love/One Good Woman	1986	—	—	3.00
❑ SPRO 9870 [DJ]	Christmas Is The Time To Say I Love You/White Christmas	1983	2.00	4.00	8.00
—Has the same picture sleeve as B-5303					
❑ S7-17395	Rhythm (A Bridge So Far)/Lovin' You Ain't So Hard	1993	—	2.00	4.00
❑ S7-18207	Christmas Is the Time to Say "I Love You"/Everybody Wants You	1994	—	2.00	4.00
—Green vinyl					
❑ S7-57890	Christmas Is the Time to Say "I Love You"/Christmas Blues	1992	—	2.50	5.00
—B-side by Canned Heat					
❑ 58749	Christmas Is the Time to Say "I Love You"/White Christmas	1998	—	—	3.00
❑ 7PRO-79694 [DJ]	Don't Say You Love Me (same on both sides)	1989	2.50	5.00	10.00
—Vinyl is promo only					

SQUIRE, CHRIS

Also see YES.

ATLANTIC

Number	Title (A Side/B Side)	Yr	VG	VG+	NM
❑ 3317	Lucky Seven/Silently Falling	1976	—	2.50	5.00

SQUIRE, CHRIS, AND ALAN WHITE

Members of YES.

ATLANTIC

Number	Title (A Side/B Side)	Yr	VG	VG+	NM
❑ 3886	Run with the Fox/Return of the Fox	1982	—	2.50	5.00

SQUIRES, THE (1)

Number	Title (A Side/B Side)	Yr	VG	VG+	NM
ALADDIN					
❑ 3360	Dreamy Eyes/Danglin' with My Heart	1957	25.00	50.00	100.00
KICKS					
❑ 1	Dream Come True/Lucy Lou	1954	200.00	400.00	800.00
MAMBO					
❑ 105	Sindy/Do-Be-Do-Be-Wop-Wop	1955	37.50	75.00	150.00
VITA					
❑ 105	Sindy/Do-Be-Do-Be-Wop-Wop	1960	25.00	50.00	100.00
❑ 113	Sweet Girl/Me and My Deal	1955	25.00	50.00	100.00
❑ 116	Heavenly Angel/Sweet Girl	1955	25.00	50.00	100.00

SQUIRES, THE (2)

Number	Title (A Side/B Side)	Yr	VG	VG+	NM
ATCO					
❑ 6442	Go Ahead/Going All the Way	1966	10.00	20.00	40.00

SQUIRES, THE (3)

Number	Title (A Side/B Side)	Yr	VG	VG+	NM
CHAN					
❑ 102	Movin' Out/Our Theme	1961	7.50	15.00	30.00
❑ 105	Mean Misery/Chattanooga Choo Choo	1962	7.50	15.00	30.00
MGM					
❑ 13044	Movin' Out/Our Theme	1961	3.75	7.50	15.00

SQUIRES, THE (4)

Number	Title (A Side/B Side)	Yr	VG	VG+	NM
COMBO					
❑ 35	Let's Give Love a Try/Whop	1952	125.00	250.00	500.00
❑ 42	Oh Darling/My Little Girl	1953	150.00	300.00	600.00

SQUIRES, THE (U)

We can't conclusively place any of these with the above groups. Of course, they may not be any of the above groups.

Number	Title (A Side/B Side)	Yr	VG	VG+	NM
CONGRESS					
❑ 223	Joyce/Can't Believe That You've Grown Up	1964	15.00	30.00	60.00
FLAIR					
❑ 1030	Sayonara/Mia Bella Donna	1954	7.50	15.00	30.00
GEE					
❑ 1082	Don't Accuse Me/So Many Tears Ago	1962	12.50	25.00	50.00
HERALD					
❑ 580	Why Should I Suffer/Walkin'	1963	7.50	15.00	30.00
STARLITE					
❑ 1/2	Movin'/Night Road	1964	12.50	25.00	50.00
V					
❑ 109	The Sultan/Aurora	1961	250.00	500.00	1000.
—Canadian release only; with a very early Neil Young					

SQUIRRELS, THE

Number	Title (A Side/B Side)	Yr	VG	VG+	NM
CAMEO					
❑ 284	Grandma's House/The Girl That I'll Adore	1963	2.50	5.00	10.00
—B-side by the Philadelphia Minstrels					

STACY, CLYDE

Number	Title (A Side/B Side)	Yr	VG	VG+	NM
G&H					
❑ 101	You Want Love/Once in a While	1958	6.25	12.50	25.00

STAFFORD, TERRY

Number	Title (A Side/B Side)	Yr	VG	VG+	NM
ATLANTIC					
❑ 4006	Amarillo by Morning/Say, Has Anybody Seen My Sweet Gypsy Rose	1973	2.00	4.00	8.00
❑ 4015	Captured/It Sure Is Bad to Love Her	1974	—	3.00	6.00
❑ 4026	Stop If You Love Me/We've Grown Close	1974	—	3.00	6.00
A&M					
❑ 707	Heartaches on the Way/You Left Me Here to Cry	1963	3.00	6.00	12.00
CASINO					
❑ 113	It Sure Is Bad to Love Her/(B-side unknown)	1977	—	3.00	6.00
CRUSADER					
❑ 101	Suspicion/Judy	1964	3.75	7.50	15.00
❑ 105	I'll Touch a Star/Playing with Fire	1964	3.00	6.00	12.00
❑ 109	Follow the Rainbow/Are You a Fool Like Me	1964	3.00	6.00	12.00
❑ 110	A Little Bit Better/Hoping	1964	3.00	6.00	12.00
EASTLAND					
❑ 101	Back Together/Life's Railway to Heaven	198?	—	2.50	5.00
MELODYLAND					
❑ 6009	Darling, Think It Over/I Can't Find It	1975	—	2.50	5.00
MERCURY					
❑ 72538	Out of the Picture/Forbidden	1966	2.50	5.00	10.00
MGM					
❑ 14232	Mean Woman Blues-Candy Man/Chilly Chicago	1971	—	3.00	6.00
❑ 14271	California Dancer/The Walk	1971	—	3.00	6.00
PLAYER					
❑ 134	Lonestar Lonesome/(B-side unknown)	1989	—	3.00	6.00
SIDEWALK					
❑ 902	Soldier Boy/When Sin Stops, Love Begins	1966	2.50	5.00	10.00
❑ 914	A Step or Two Behind You/The Joke's on Me	1967	2.50	5.00	10.00
WARNER BROS.					
❑ 7286	Big in Dallas/Will a Man Ever Learn	1969	—	3.00	6.00

STAIRSTEPS, THE

See THE FIVE STAIRSTEPS.

STALK-FORREST GROUP, THE

Early version of BLUE OYSTER CULT.

Number	Title (A Side/B Side)	Yr	VG	VG+	NM
ELEKTRA					
❑ 45693	What Is Quicksand/Arthur Comics	1970	12.50	25.00	50.00

STAMPEDERS

Number	Title (A Side/B Side)	Yr	VG	VG+	NM
BELL					
❑ 45120	Sweet City Woman/Gator Road	1971	—	3.00	6.00
❑ 45154	Devil You/Giant in the Streets	1971	—	2.50	5.00
❑ 45188	Monday Morning Choo-Choo/Then Came the White Man	1972	—	3.00	6.00
❑ 45226	Wild Eyes/Carryin' On	1972	—	3.00	6.00
❑ 45331	Oh My Lady/No Destination	1973	—	3.00	6.00
CAPITOL					
❑ 3868	Goodbye Goodbye/Me and My Stone	1974	—	2.00	4.00
❑ 3964	Running Out of Time/Ramona	1974	—	2.00	4.00
MGM					
❑ 13970	Be a Woman/I Don't Believe	1968	3.00	6.00	12.00
POLYDOR					
❑ 14060	Carry Me/I Didn't Need You Anyhow	1970	2.50	5.00	10.00
QUALITY					
❑ 501	Hard Lovin' Woman/Hit the Road Jack	1976	—	2.00	4.00
❑ 505	Sweet Love Bandit/Let It Begin	1976	—	2.00	4.00

STANDARDS, THE

The record on Amos may be by a different group than the others.

Number	Title (A Side/B Side)	Yr	VG	VG+	NM
AMOS					
❑ 134	When You Wish Upon a Star/(Instrumental)	1969	2.50	5.00	10.00
CHESS					
❑ 1869	My Heart Belongs to You/Hello Love	1963	10.00	20.00	40.00
DEBRO					
❑ 3178	Tears Bring Heartaches/No, No, No	1963	50.00	100.00	200.00
GLENDEN					
❑ 1315	It Isn't Fair/Everybody Knows	1964	5.00	10.00	20.00
MAGNA					
❑ 1314	My Heart Belongs to You/Hello Love	1963	20.00	40.00	80.00
❑ 1315	It Isn't Fair/Everybody Knows	1963	12.50	25.00	50.00
ROULETTE					
❑ 4487	Tears Bring Heartaches/No, No, No	1963	7.50	15.00	30.00

STANDELLS, THE

Also see DICK DODD.

Number	Title (A Side/B Side)	Yr	VG	VG+	NM
LIBERTY					
❑ 55680	The Peppermint Beatle/The Shake	1964	6.25	12.50	25.00
❑ 55722	Help Yourself/I'll Go Crazy	1964	5.00	10.00	20.00
❑ 55743	So Fine/Linda Lou	1964	5.00	10.00	20.00
MGM					
❑ 13350	Someday You'll Cry/Zebra in the Kitchen	1965	7.50	15.00	30.00
SUNSET					
❑ 61000	Ooh Poo Pah Doo/Help Yourself	1966	5.00	10.00	20.00
TOWER					
❑ 185	Dirty Water/Rari	1966	5.00	10.00	20.00
❑ 257	Sometimes Good Guys Don't Wear White/Why Did You Hurt Me	1966	3.75	7.50	15.00
❑ 282	Why Pick on Me/Mr. Nobody	1966	3.75	7.50	15.00
❑ 310	Try It/Poor Shell of a Man	1967	3.75	7.50	15.00
❑ 310 [PS]	Try It/Poor Shell of a Man	1967	12.50	25.00	50.00
❑ 312	Don't Tell Me What to Do/When I Was a Cowboy	1967	5.00	10.00	20.00
—By "The Sllednats" (Standells backwards)					
❑ 314	Riot on Sunset Strip/Black Hearted Woman	1967	3.75	7.50	15.00
❑ 314 [PS]	Riot on Sunset Strip/Black Hearted Woman	1967	20.00	40.00	80.00
❑ 348	Can't Help But Love You/Ninety-Nine and One Half	1967	3.75	7.50	15.00
❑ 398	Animal Girl/Soul Drippin'	1968	3.75	7.50	15.00
VEE JAY					
❑ 643	The Boy Next Door/B.J. Quetzal	1965	5.00	10.00	20.00
❑ 643 [PS]	The Boy Next Door/B.J. Quetzal	1965	50.00	100.00	200.00
❑ 679	Big Boss Man/Don't Say Goodbye	1965	5.00	10.00	20.00

STANLEY, PAUL

Also see KISS.

Number	Title (A Side/B Side)	Yr	VG	VG+	NM
CASABLANCA					
❑ 940	Goodbye/Hold Me, Touch Me	1978	—	3.00	6.00

STAPLE SINGERS, THE

Also see MAVIS STAPLES.

Number	Title (A Side/B Side)	Yr	VG	VG+	NM
20TH CENTURY					
❑ 2508	Hold On to Your Dreams/Cold and Windy Night	1981	—	2.00	4.00
CURTOM					
❑ 0109	Let's Do It Again/After Sex	1975	—	2.00	4.00
❑ 0113	New Orleans/A Whole Lot of Love	1976	—	2.00	4.00
EPIC					
❑ 9748	Be Careful of Stones That You Throw/More Than a Hammer and Nail	1964	2.50	5.00	10.00
❑ 9776	Do Something for Yourself/Samson and Delilah	1965	2.50	5.00	10.00
❑ 9825	Freedom Highway/The Funeral	1965	2.50	5.00	10.00
❑ 9880	Why/What Are They Doing	1965	2.50	5.00	10.00
❑ 10054	King of Kings/Step Aside	1966	2.50	5.00	10.00
❑ 10104	Pray On/It's Been a Change	1966	2.50	5.00	10.00
❑ 10158	Why (Am I Treated So Bad)/What Are They Doing (In Heaven Today)	1967	2.00	4.00	8.00
❑ 10220	For What It's Worth/Are You Sure	1967	2.00	4.00	8.00
❑ 10264	Deliver Me/He	1967	2.00	4.00	8.00
❑ 10294	Let's Get Together/Power of Love	1968	2.00	4.00	8.00
❑ 10339	Crying in the Chapel/Nothing Lasts Forever	1968	2.00	4.00	8.00
❑ 10742	For What It's Worth/Why	1971	—	3.00	6.00
PRIVATE I					
❑ 04384	H-A-T-E (Don't Live Here Anymore)/Can You Hang	1984	—	2.00	4.00
❑ 04583	Slippery People/On My Own Again	1984	—	2.00	4.00
❑ 04711	This Is Our Night/Turning Point	1984	—	2.00	4.00
❑ 05565	Are You Ready/Love Wowks in Strange Ways	1985	—	2.00	4.00
❑ 05565 [PS]	Are You Ready/Love Wowks in Strange Ways	1985	—	3.00	6.00
❑ 05727	Nobody Can Make It on Their Own/Reasons to Love	1985	—	2.00	4.00
RIVERSIDE					
❑ 4518	Gloryland/Hammer and Nails	1962	3.00	6.00	12.00
❑ 4531	Gambling Man/Use What You Got	1962	3.00	6.00	12.00
❑ 4540	There Was a Star/The Virgin Mary Had One Son	1962	3.00	6.00	12.00
❑ 4553	I Can't Help from Cryin'/Let That Liar Again	1963	3.00	6.00	12.00
❑ 4563	Cotton Fields/This Land	1963	3.00	6.00	12.00
❑ 4568	Blowing in the Wind/Wish I Had Answered	1963	3.00	6.00	12.00

Number	Title (A Side/B Side)	Yr	VG	VG+	NM
SHARP					
❑ 603	This May Be the Last Time/This Same Jesus	1960	3.75	7.50	15.00
STAX					
❑ 0007	Long Walk to D.C./Stay with Us	1968	—	3.00	6.00
❑ 0019	The Ghetto/Got to Be Some Changes Made	1968	—	3.00	6.00
❑ 0031	(Sittin' On) The Dock of the Bay/Top of the Mountain	1969	—	3.00	6.00
❑ 0039	The Gardener/The Challenge	1969	—	3.00	6.00
❑ 0052	When Will We Be Paid/Tend to Your Own Business	1969	—	3.00	6.00
❑ 0066	Give a Damn/God Bless the Children	1970	—	3.00	6.00
❑ 0074	Brand New Day/God Bless the Children	1970	—	3.00	6.00
❑ 0083	Heavy Makes You Happy (Sha-Na-Boom-Boom)/Love Is Plentiful	1970	—	3.00	6.00
❑ 0084	Who Took the Merry Out of Christmas/(Instrumental)	1970	2.00	4.00	8.00
❑ 0093	You've Got to Earn It/I'm a Lover	1971	—	2.50	5.00
❑ 0104	Respect Yourself/You're Gonna Make Me Cry	1971	—	2.50	5.00
❑ 0125	I'll Take You There/I'm Just Another Soldier	1972	—	2.50	5.00
❑ 0137	This World/Are You Sure	1972	—	2.50	5.00
❑ 0156	Oh La De Da/We the People	1973	—	2.50	5.00
❑ 0164	Be What You Are/I Like the Things About Me	1973	—	2.50	5.00
—B-side by Cal Starr					
❑ 0179	If You're Ready (Come Go with Me)/Love Comes in All Colors	1973	—	2.50	5.00
❑ 0196	Touch a Hand, Make a Friend/Tellin' Lies	1974	—	2.50	5.00
❑ 0213	What's Your Thing/Whicha Way Did It Go	1974	—	2.50	5.00
—B-side by Pops Staples					
❑ 0215	City in the Sky/That's What Friends Are For	1974	—	2.50	5.00
❑ 0227	My Main Man/Who Made the Man	1974	—	2.50	5.00
❑ 0248	Back Road Into Town/My Main Man	1975	—	2.50	5.00
UNITED					
❑ 165	It Rained Children/Won't You Sit Down	1955	100.00	200.00	400.00
VEE JAY					
❑ 169	God's Wonderful Love/If I Could Hear My Mother	1956	5.00	10.00	20.00
❑ 224	Uncloudy Day/I Know I Got Religion	1956	5.00	10.00	20.00
❑ 846	Let Me Ride/I'm Coming Home	1957	5.00	10.00	20.00
❑ 856	I Had a Dream/Help Me Jesus	1958	3.75	7.50	15.00
❑ 866	Love Is the Way/On My Way to Heaven	1959	3.75	7.50	15.00
❑ 870	I'm Leaving/Going Away	1959	3.75	7.50	15.00
❑ 881	Downward Road/So Soon	1959	3.75	7.50	15.00
❑ 893	Pray On/Too Close	1960	3.00	6.00	12.00
❑ 902	I've Been Scorned/Don't Knock	1961	3.00	6.00	12.00
❑ 912	Sit Down Servant/Swing Low	1962	3.00	6.00	12.00
❑ 930	Swing Low Sweet Chariot/I'm So Glad	1963	3.00	6.00	12.00
WARNER BROS.					
❑ 8279	Love Me, Love Me, Love Me/Pass It On	1976	—	2.00	4.00
❑ 8317	Sweeter Than the Sweet/Making Love	1977	—	2.00	4.00
❑ 8460	See a Little Further (Than My Bed)/Let's Go to the Disco	1977	—	2.00	4.00
❑ 8510	I Honestly Love You/Family Tree	1978	—	2.00	4.00
❑ 8669	Unlock Your Mind/Mystery Train	1978	—	2.00	4.00
❑ 8748	Chica Boom/Handwriting on the Wall	1979	—	2.00	4.00
❑ 49598	God Can/Unlock Your Mind	1980	—	2.00	4.00
—Warner Bros. titles as "The Staples"					

STAPLES, GORDON, AND THE MOTOWN STRINGS

Number	Title (A Side/B Side)	Yr	VG	VG+	NM
MOTOWN					
❑ 1180	Strung Out/Sounds of the Zodiac	1971	7.50	15.00	30.00
❑ 1180 [DJ]	Strung Out (same on both sides)	1971	7.50	15.00	30.00
—Red vinyl promo					

STAPLES, MAVIS

Also see THE STAPLE SINGERS.

Number	Title (A Side/B Side)	Yr	VG	VG+	NM
CURTOM					
❑ 0132	A Piece of the Action/Till Blossoms Bloom	1977	—	2.00	4.00
PAISLEY PARK					
❑ 22968	20th Century Express/All the Discomforts of Home	1989	—	—	3.00
PHONO					
❑ 1051	Love Gone Bad/(B-side unknown)	1984	—	2.50	5.00
VOLT					
❑ 4044	I Have Learned to Do Without You/Since I Fell for You	1970	—	2.50	5.00
❑ 4086	Endlessly/Don't Change Me Now	1972	—	2.50	5.00
WARNER BROS.					
❑ PRO-S-3878 [DJ]	Christmas Vacation (same on both sides)	1989	—	2.50	5.00
❑ 8838	Tonight I Feel Like Dancing/If I Can't Have You	1979	—	2.00	4.00
❑ 28765	Show Me How It Works/Half Time	1986	—	—	3.00
❑ 49054	Oh What a Feeling/If I Can't Have You	1979	—	2.00	4.00

STAR FIRES, THE

Number	Title (A Side/B Side)	Yr	VG	VG+	NM
HARAL					
❑ 777	Each Night at Nine/What Good Is Money	1962	25.00	50.00	100.00
LAURIE					
❑ 3332	You Done Me Wrong/Like Socks and Shoes	1966	5.00	10.00	20.00

STARFIRES, THE (1)

Number	Title (A Side/B Side)	Yr	VG	VG+	NM
APT					
❑ 25030	Fender Bender/Camel Walk	1959	5.00	10.00	20.00
PACE					
❑ 101	Fender Bender/Camel Walk	1959	10.00	20.00	40.00

STARFIRES, THE (2)

Number	Title (A Side/B Side)	Yr	VG	VG+	NM
BARGAIN					
❑ 5001	You're the One/So Much	1961	15.00	30.00	60.00
❑ 5003	Love Will Break Your Heart/The Dances	1961	15.00	30.00	60.00
D&H					
❑ 200	These Foolish Things/Let's Do the Pony	1961	30.00	60.00	120.00

STARFIRES, THE (3)

Number	Title (A Side/B Side)	Yr	VG	VG+	NM
BERNICE					
❑ 201	Yearning for You/Do-Ko-Icki-No	1958	37.50	75.00	150.00
DECCA					
❑ 30730	Three Roses/I Have Someone	1958	10.00	20.00	40.00
❑ 30916	Love Is Here to Stay/Tomorrow	1959	12.50	25.00	50.00

STARFIRES, THE (4)

Number	Title (A Side/B Side)	Yr	VG	VG+	NM
DUEL					
❑ 518	Fools Fall in Love/Under the Stars	1962	12.50	25.00	50.00
TRIUMPH					
❑ 61	Fink/Work Out Fine	1965	5.00	10.00	20.00

STARFIRES, THE (5)

Number	Title (A Side/B Side)	Yr	VG	VG+	NM
G.I.					
❑ 4001	I Never Loved Her/Linda	1965	625.00	1250.	2500.
❑ 4002	Rockin' Dixie/(B-side unknown)	1965	25.00	50.00	100.00
❑ 4004	Cry for Freedom/(B-side unknown)	1965	25.00	50.00	100.00

STARFIRES, THE (6)

Early version of THE OUTSIDERS.

Number	Title (A Side/B Side)	Yr	VG	VG+	NM
PAMA					
❑ 115	Ring of Love/Cheating Game	196?	10.00	20.00	40.00
❑ 117	Chartreuse Caboose/Billy's Blues	196?	10.00	20.00	40.00

STARFIRES, THE (7)

Number	Title (A Side/B Side)	Yr	VG	VG+	NM
ROUND					
❑ 1016	Space Needle/The Jordan Stomp	1962	10.00	20.00	40.00
❑ 1016 [PS]	Space Needle/The Jordan Stomp	1962	15.00	30.00	60.00

STARFIRES, THE (8)

Number	Title (A Side/B Side)	Yr	VG	VG+	NM
SONIC					
❑ 7163	Re-Entry/Hand Full of Blood	1963	7.50	15.00	30.00

STARLETS, THE (1)

Later recorded as THE ANGELS (1).

Number	Title (A Side/B Side)	Yr	VG	VG+	NM
ASTRO					
❑ 202/3	P.S. I Love You/Where Is My Love Tonight	1960	7.50	15.00	30.00
❑ 204	Romeo and Juliet/Listen for a Lonely Tambourine	1960	6.25	12.50	25.00

STARLETS, THE (2)

Number	Title (A Side/B Side)	Yr	VG	VG+	NM
CHESS					
❑ 1997	My Baby's Real/Loving You Is Something New	1967	6.25	12.50	25.00
❑ 2038	I Wanna Be Good to You/Watered Down	1968	5.00	10.00	20.00

STARLETS, THE (3)

This is the same group that, as THE BLUE-BELLES, recorded "I Sold My Heart to the Junkman."

Number	Title (A Side/B Side)	Yr	VG	VG+	NM
LUTE					
❑ 5909	I'm So Young/He's Got It	1960	6.25	12.50	25.00
PAM					
❑ 1003	Better Tell Him No/You Are the One	1961	5.00	10.00	20.00
❑ 1004	My Last Cry/Money Hungry	1961	5.00	10.00	20.00

STARLETTES, THE

Number	Title (A Side/B Side)	Yr	VG	VG+	NM
CHECKER					
❑ 895	Please Ring My Phone/Jungle Love	1958	37.50	75.00	150.00

STARLIGHTERS, THE

At least two different groups.

Number	Title (A Side/B Side)	Yr	VG	VG+	NM
CAPITOL					
❑ F844	Rag Mop/It's Not Bad	1950	7.50	15.00	30.00
CRYSTALETTE					
❑ 661	Sweetheart of Sigma Chi/Don't Call Me Coach, Call Me George	1952	6.25	12.50	25.00
❑ 662	Christmas Won't Be the Same (With You Away)/La Pinata (Mexican Christmas Song)	1952	7.50	15.00	30.00
END					
❑ 1031	It's Twelve O'Clock/The Birdland	1958	125.00	250.00	500.00
❑ 1049	I Cried/You're the One to Blame	1959	20.00	40.00	80.00
❑ 1072	A Story of Love/Let's Take a Stroll	1960	30.00	60.00	120.00
IRMA					
❑ 101	Love Cry/Last Night	1956	100.00	200.00	400.00
LAMP					
❑ 2014	Slipping Out/Rocking Too Much	1958	12.50	25.00	50.00
SUN COAST					
❑ 1001	Until You Return/Whomp, Whomp	1956	62.50	125.00	250.00
WHEEL					
❑ 1004	Hot Licks/Creepin'	1960	3.75	7.50	15.00

STARLINGS, THE (1)

Number	Title (A Side/B Side)	Yr	VG	VG+	NM
DAWN					
❑ 212	I'm Just a Crying Fool/Hokey-Smokey Mama	1955	150.00	300.00	600.00
❑ 213	A-Loo, A-Loo/I Gotta Go Now	1955	100.00	200.00	400.00
JOSIE					
❑ 760	My Plea for Love/Music, Maestro, Please	1954	125.00	250.00	500.00

STARLINGS, THE (2)

Number	Title (A Side/B Side)	Yr	VG	VG+	NM
WORLD PACIFIC					
❑ 809	All I Want/That's Me	1959	10.00	20.00	40.00

STARLITES, THE

Number	Title (A Side/B Side)	Yr	VG	VG+	NM
PEAK					
❑ 5000	Missing You/(B-side unknown)	1957	50.00	100.00	200.00

STARR, ANDY

Number	Title (A Side/B Side)	Yr	VG	VG+	NM
KAPP					
❑ 190	Do It Right Now/I Waited for You to Remember	1957	6.25	12.50	25.00
MGM					
❑ 12263	Rockin' Rollin' Stone/I Wanna Go South	1956	37.50	75.00	150.00
❑ 12315	She's a-Going, Jessie/Old Deacon Jones	1956	37.50	75.00	150.00
❑ 12364	Round and Round/Give Me a Woman	1957	37.50	75.00	150.00
❑ 12421	No Room for Your Kind/One More Time	1957	37.50	75.00	150.00

STARR, EDWIN

20TH CENTURY

Number	Title (A Side/B Side)	Yr	VG	VG+	NM
❑ 2338	I Just Wanna Do My Thing/Mr. Davenport and Mr. James	1977	—	2.00	4.00
❑ 2389	I'm So Into You/Don't Waste Your Time	1978	—	2.00	4.00
❑ 2396	Contact/Don't Waste Your Time	1978	—	2.00	4.00
❑ 2408	H.A.P.P.Y. Radio/My Friend	1979	—	2.00	4.00
❑ 2420	It's Called the Rock/Patiently	1979	—	2.00	4.00
❑ 2423	It's Called the Rock/H.A.P.P.Y. Radio	1979	—	2.00	4.00
❑ 2441	It's Called the Rock/H.A.P.P.Y. Radio	1980	—	2.00	4.00
❑ 2445	Stronger Than You Think I Am/(Instrumental)	1980	—	2.00	4.00
❑ 2450	Tell-A-Star/Boop Boop Song	1980	—	2.00	4.00
❑ 2455	Get Up-Whirlpool/Better and Better	1980	—	2.00	4.00
❑ 2477	Twenty-Five Miles/Never Turn My Back on You	1980	—	2.00	4.00
❑ 2496	Real Live #10/Sweat	1981	—	2.00	4.00

GORDY

Number	Title (A Side/B Side)	Yr	VG	VG+	NM
❑ 7066	Gonna Keep On Tryin' Til I Win Your Love/I Want My Baby Back	1967	—	3.00	6.00
❑ 7071	I Am the Man for You Baby/My Weakness Is You	1968	—	3.00	6.00
❑ 7078	Way Over There/If My Heart Could Tell the Story	1968	—	3.00	6.00
❑ 7083	Twenty-Five Miles/Love Is the Destination	1969	—	3.00	6.00
❑ 7087	I'm Still a Struggling Man/Pretty Little Angel	1969	—	3.00	6.00
❑ 7090	Oh How Happy/Ooh Baby Baby	1969	—	3.00	6.00
—With Blinky					
❑ 7097	Time/Running Back and Forth	1970	—	3.00	6.00
❑ 7101	War/He Who Picks a Rose	1970	—	3.00	6.00
❑ 7104	Stop the War Now/Gonna Keep On Tryin' Til I Win Your Love	1970	—	3.00	6.00
❑ 7107	Funky Music Sho Nuff Turns Me On/Cloud Nine	1971	—	3.00	6.00

GRANITE

Number	Title (A Side/B Side)	Yr	VG	VG+	NM
❑ 522	Pain/I'll Never Forget You	1975	—	2.50	5.00
❑ 528	Stay with Me/Party	1975	—	2.50	5.00
❑ 532	Abyssinia Jones/Beginning	1975	—	2.50	5.00

MONTAGE

Number	Title (A Side/B Side)	Yr	VG	VG+	NM
❑ 1216	Tired of It/(B-side unknown)	1982	—	2.00	4.00

MOTOWN

Number	Title (A Side/B Side)	Yr	VG	VG+	NM
❑ 1276	You've Got My Soul on Fire/Love (The Lonely People's Prayer)	1973	—	2.50	5.00
❑ 1284	Ain't It Hell Up in Harlem/Don't It Feel Good to Be Free	1973	—	2.50	5.00
❑ 1300	Big Papa/Like We Used to Do	1974	—	2.50	5.00
❑ 1326	Who's Right or Wrong/Lonely Rainy Days in San Diego	1974	—	2.50	5.00

RIC-TIC

Number	Title (A Side/B Side)	Yr	VG	VG+	NM
❑ 103	Agent Double-O-Soul/(Instrumental)	1965	3.75	7.50	15.00
❑ 107	Back Street/(Instrumental)	1965	3.75	7.50	15.00
❑ 109X [DJ]	Scott's On Swingers (S.O.S.)/I Have Faith in You	1966	12.50	25.00	50.00
❑ 109	Stop Her on Sight (S.O.S.)/I Have Faith in You	1966	3.75	7.50	15.00
❑ 114	Headline News/Harlem	1966	3.75	7.50	15.00
❑ 118	It's My Turn Now/Girls Are Getting Prettier	1967	3.75	7.50	15.00
❑ 120	You're My Mellow/My Kind of Woman	1967	15.00	30.00	60.00

SOUL

Number	Title (A Side/B Side)	Yr	VG	VG+	NM
❑ 35096	Take Me Clear from Here/Ball of Confusion	1972	—	3.00	6.00
❑ 35100	Who Is the Leader of the People/Don't Tell Me I'm Crazy	1972	—	3.00	6.00
❑ 35103	There You Go/(Instrumental)	1973	—	3.00	6.00

STARR, KAY

ABC

Number	Title (A Side/B Side)	Yr	VG	VG+	NM
❑ 11013	When the Lights Go On Again (All Over the World)/Only When You're Lonely	1967	—	2.50	5.00
❑ 11049	My Melancholy Baby/Some Sweet Tomorrow	1968	—	2.50	5.00

CAPITOL

Number	Title (A Side/B Side)	Yr	VG	VG+	NM
❑ F936	Bonaparte's Retreat/Someday Sweetheart	1950	5.00	10.00	20.00
❑ F980	Hoop-Dee-Doo/A Woman Likes to Be Told	1950	5.00	10.00	20.00
❑ F1072	Mississippi/He's a Good Man to Have Around	1950	5.00	10.00	20.00
❑ F1124	I'll Never Be Free/Ain't Nobody's Business But My Own	1950	6.25	12.50	25.00
—With Tennessee Ernie Ford					
❑ F1152	When You're a Long Way from Home/Is There Anything Wrong with Texas (The Texas Song)	1950	3.75	7.50	15.00
❑ F1194	Nobody's Sweetheart/The Honeymoon	1950	3.75	7.50	15.00
❑ F1205	Mama Goes Everywhere Papa Goes/Please Love Me	1950	3.75	7.50	15.00
—With Tennessee Ernie Ford					
❑ F1256	Christopher Robin/The Man with the Bag	1950	3.75	7.50	15.00
❑ F1278	Oh Babe/Everybody's Somebody's Fool	1950	3.75	7.50	15.00
❑ F1357	Lovesick Blues/Evenin'	1951	3.75	7.50	15.00
❑ F1492	Come Back Darling/Then You've Never Been Blue	1951	3.75	7.50	15.00
❑ F1567	Oceans of Tears/You're My Sugar	1951	3.75	7.50	15.00
—With Tennessee Ernie Ford					
❑ F1615	You Were Only Fooling (While I Was Falling in Love)/If I Could Be with You	1951	3.00	6.00	12.00
—Reissue of 78 from 1948					
❑ F1649	I'm the Lonesomest Gal in Town/You've Got to See Mama Every Night	1951	3.00	6.00	12.00
—Reissue					
❑ F1652	Bonaparte's Retreat/The Honeymoon	1951	3.00	6.00	12.00
—Reissue					
❑ F1677	Wheel of Fortune/Angry	195?	2.50	5.00	10.00
—Reissue					
❑ F1688	Side by Side/Breeze	1954	2.50	5.00	10.00
—Reissue					
❑ F1710	Come On-a My House/Hold Me, Hold Me	1951	3.75	7.50	15.00
❑ F1796	Don't Tell Him What's Happened to Me/Angry	1951	3.75	7.50	15.00
❑ F1856	Two Brothers/Oh Honky Tonk Hardwood Floor	1951	3.75	7.50	15.00
❑ F1902	So Help Me/Hold Me, Hold Me	1951	3.75	7.50	15.00
❑ F1964	Wheel of Fortune/I Wanna Love You	1952	3.75	7.50	15.00
❑ F2062	I Waited a Little Too Long/Me Too	1952	3.00	6.00	12.00
❑ F2151	Fool, Fool, Fool/Kay's Lament	1952	3.00	6.00	12.00
❑ F2213	Comes A-Long A-Love/Three Letters	1952	3.00	6.00	12.00
❑ F2334	Side by Side/Noah	1953	3.00	6.00	12.00
❑ F2464	Half a Photograph/Allez-Vous-En	1953	3.00	6.00	12.00
❑ F2595	When My Dreamboat Comes Home/Swamp Fire	1953	3.75	7.50	15.00
❑ F2657	Changing Partners/I'll Always Be in Love with You	1953	3.00	6.00	12.00
❑ F2769	If You Love Me (Really Love Me)/The Man Upstairs	1954	3.00	6.00	12.00
❑ F2887	Fortune in Dreams/Am I a Toy or Treasure	1954	3.00	6.00	12.00
❑ F4295	Riders in the Sky/Night Train	1959	2.00	4.00	8.00
❑ 4419	Out in the Cold Again/Just for a Thrill	1960	2.00	4.00	8.00
❑ 4542	Foolin' Around/Kay's Lament	1961	2.00	4.00	8.00
❑ 4583	I'll Never Be Free/Nobody	1961	2.00	4.00	8.00
❑ 4620	Well I Ask Ya/Rough Riders	1961	2.00	4.00	8.00
❑ 4835	Four Walls/Oh Lonesome Me	1962	2.00	4.00	8.00
❑ 4835 [PS]	Four Walls/Oh Lonesome Me	1962	3.00	6.00	12.00
❑ 4894	Bossa Nova Casanova/Swingin' at the Hungry-O	1962	2.00	4.00	8.00
❑ 4983	No Regrets/Cherche La Rose	1963	2.00	4.00	8.00
❑ 5046	To Each His Own/Make a Circle	1963	2.00	4.00	8.00
❑ 5194	It's Happening All Over Again/Dancing on My Tears	1964	—	3.00	6.00
❑ 5259	Together Again/Friends	1964	—	3.00	6.00
❑ 5328	Look on the Brighter Side/Lorna's Here	1965	—	3.00	6.00
❑ 5386	Happy/I Forgot to Forget	1965	—	3.00	6.00
❑ 5492	I Never Dreamed I Could Love You/I Know That You Know That We…	1965	—	3.00	6.00
❑ 5601	Old Records/Tears and Photographs	1966	—	3.00	6.00

DOT

Number	Title (A Side/B Side)	Yr	VG	VG+	NM
❑ 17183	Something Happened to Me/12th Street Marching Band	1968	—	2.50	5.00

GNP CRESCENDO

Number	Title (A Side/B Side)	Yr	VG	VG+	NM
❑ 468	The Ranger's Waltz/Saturday Night	1973	—	2.00	4.00
❑ 476	The New Frankie and Johnny/(B-side unknown)	1974	—	2.00	4.00
❑ 488	Tie a Yellow Ribbon Round the Ole Oak Tree/Something's Missing	1974	—	2.00	4.00
❑ 493	What Can I Say After I Say I'm Sorry/What Is This Thing Called Love	1975	—	2.00	4.00

HAPPY TIGER

Number	Title (A Side/B Side)	Yr	VG	VG+	NM
❑ 553	Knock, Knock (Who's There)/Sweet Blindness	1970	—	2.50	5.00

RCA VICTOR

Number	Title (A Side/B Side)	Yr	VG	VG+	NM
❑ AMBO-0131	Rock and Roll Waltz/Down by the Riverside	1973	—	2.00	4.00
—"Gold Standard Series" reissue					
❑ 47-5999	Turn Right/If Anyone Finds This, I Love You	1955	2.50	5.00	10.00
❑ 47-6079	For Better or Worse/Foolishly Yours	1955	2.50	5.00	10.00
❑ 47-6146	Good and Lonesome/Where, What or When	1955	2.50	5.00	10.00
❑ 47-6247	Home Sweet Home on the Range/Without a Song	1955	2.50	5.00	10.00
❑ 47-6359	Rock and Roll Waltz/I've Changed My Mind a Thousand Times	1955	2.50	5.00	10.00
❑ 47-6541	Second Fiddle/Love Ain't Right	1956	2.50	5.00	10.00
❑ 47-6617	The Good Book/The Things I Never Had	1956	2.50	5.00	10.00
❑ 47-6748	The Brass Ring/Touch and Go	1956	2.50	5.00	10.00
❑ 47-6864	Jamie Boy/A Little Loneliness	1957	2.50	5.00	10.00
❑ 47-6981	My Heart Reminds Me/Flim Flam Floo	1957	2.50	5.00	10.00
❑ 47-7114	The Last Song and Dance/Help Me	1957	2.50	5.00	10.00
❑ 47-7218	Stroll Me/Rockin' Chair	1958	2.50	5.00	10.00
❑ 47-7338	Voodoo Man/Bridge of Sighs	1958	2.50	5.00	10.00
❑ 47-7414	He Cha-Cha'd Me/Oh How I Miss You Tonight	1958	2.50	5.00	10.00
❑ 47-7521	I Couldn't Care Less/Only Love Me	1959	2.50	5.00	10.00

STARR, RINGO

Also see THE BEATLES.

APPLE

Number	Title (A Side/B Side)	Yr	VG	VG+	NM
❑ 1826 [PS]	Beaucoups of Blues/Coochy-Coochy	1970	10.00	20.00	40.00
—Sleeve with wrong catalog number (actually 2969)					
❑ 1831	It Don't Come Easy/Early 1970	1971	2.00	4.00	8.00
❑ 1831	It Don't Come Easy/Early 1970	1971	3.00	6.00	12.00
—With star on A-side label					
❑ 1831	It Don't Come Easy/Early 1970	1975	7.50	15.00	30.00
—With "All rights reserved" on label					
❑ 1831 [PS]	It Don't Come Easy/Early 1970	1971	7.50	15.00	30.00
❑ 1849	Back Off Boogaloo/Blindman	1972	2.00	4.00	8.00
—Green-background label					
❑ 1849	Back Off Boogaloo/Blindman	1972	18.75	37.50	75.00
—Blue-background label					
❑ 1849 [DJ]	Back Off Boogaloo/Blindman	1972	37.50	75.00	150.00
—White label					
❑ 1849 [PS]	Back Off Boogaloo/Blindman	1972	3.75	7.50	15.00
—Black paper with flat finish					
❑ 1849 [PS]	Back Off Boogaloo/Blindman	1972	10.00	20.00	40.00
—Glossy black paper on both sides					
❑ 1849 [PS]	Back Off Boogaloo/Blindman	1972	10.00	20.00	40.00
—Glossy black on one side, gray on the other					
❑ 1865	Photograph/Down and Out	1973	—	3.00	6.00
—Custom star label					
❑ 1865 [PS]	Photograph/Down and Out	1973	5.00	10.00	20.00
❑ P-1865 [DJ]	Photograph (mono/stereo)	1973	12.50	25.00	50.00
❑ 1870	You're Sixteen/Devil Woman	1973	—	3.00	6.00
—Custom star label					
❑ 1870	You're Sixteen/Devil Woman	1973	6.25	12.50	25.00
—Regular Apple label					
❑ 1870 [PS]	You're Sixteen/Devil Woman	1973	6.25	12.50	25.00
❑ P-1870 [DJ]	You're Sixteen (mono/stereo)	1973	12.50	25.00	50.00
❑ 1872	Oh My My/Step Lightly	1974	—	3.00	6.00
—Custom star label					
❑ 1872	Oh My My/Step Lightly	1974	2.00	4.00	8.00
—Regular Apple label					
❑ P-1872 [DJ]	Oh My My (Edited Mono)/Oh My My (Long Stereo)	1974	12.50	25.00	50.00
❑ 1876	Only You/Call Me	1974	—	3.00	6.00
—Custom nebula label					
❑ 1876	Only You/Call Me	1974	2.00	4.00	8.00
—Regular Apple label					

Number	Title (A Side/B Side)	Yr	VG	VG+	NM
❑ 1876 [PS]	Only You/Call Me	1974	5.00	10.00	20.00
❑ P-1876 [DJ]	Only You (mono/stereo)	1974	10.00	20.00	40.00
❑ 1880	No No Song/Snookeroo	1975	—	3.00	6.00
—Custom nebula label					
❑ P-1880 [DJ]	No No Song/Snookeroo (both mono)	1975	10.00	20.00	40.00
❑ P-1880 [DJ]	No No Song/Snookeroo (both stereo)	1975	10.00	20.00	40.00
❑ 1882	It's All Down to Goodnight Vienna/Oo-Wee	1975	—	3.00	6.00
—Custom nebula label					
❑ 1882 [PS]	It's All Down to Goodnight Vienna/Oo-Wee	1975	5.00	10.00	20.00
❑ P-1882 [DJ]	It's All Down to Goodnight Vienna (mono/stereo)	1975	10.00	20.00	40.00
❑ P-1882 [DJ]	Oo-Wee/Oo-Wee	1975	17.50	35.00	70.00
❑ 2969	Beaucoups of Blues/Coochy-Coochy	1970	6.25	12.50	25.00
—With small Capitol logo on bottom of B-side label and star on A-side label					
❑ 2969	Beaucoups of Blues/Coochy-Coochy	1970	10.00	20.00	40.00
—With "Mfd. by Apple" on label and star on A-side label					
❑ 2969	Beaucoups of Blues/Coochy-Coochy	1970	2.00	4.00	8.00
—With "Mfd. by Apple" on label and no star on A-side label					
❑ 2969 [PS]	Beaucoups of Blues/Coochy-Coochy	1970	12.50	25.00	50.00
—Sleeve with correct catalog number					

ATLANTIC

Number	Title (A Side/B Side)	Yr	VG	VG+	NM
❑ 3361	A Dose of Rock 'N' Roll/Cryin'	1976	2.50	5.00	10.00
❑ 3371	Hey Baby/Lady Gaye	1976	7.50	15.00	30.00
❑ 3412	Drowning in the Sea of Love/Just a Dream	1977	30.00	60.00	120.00
❑ 3429	Wings/Just a Dream	1977	7.50	15.00	30.00

BOARDWALK

Number	Title (A Side/B Side)	Yr	VG	VG+	NM
❑ NB7-11-130	Wrack My Brain/Drumming Is My Madness	1981	—	2.50	5.00
❑ NB7-11-130 [PS]	Wrack My Brain/Drumming Is My Madness	1981	—	2.50	5.00
❑ NB7-11-134	Private Property/Stop and Take the Time to Smell the Roses	1982	3.00	6.00	12.00

CAPITOL

Number	Title (A Side/B Side)	Yr	VG	VG+	NM
❑ 1831	It Don't Come Easy/Early 1970	1976	6.25	12.50	25.00
—Orange label					
❑ 1831	It Don't Come Easy/Early 1970	1978	—	3.00	6.00
—Purple late-1970s label					
❑ 1831	It Don't Come Easy/Early 1970	1983	—	3.00	6.00
—Black colorband label					
❑ 1831	It Don't Come Easy/Early 1970	1988	—	2.50	5.00
—Purple late-1980s label (wider)					
❑ 1849	Back Off Boogaloo/Blindman	1976	7.50	15.00	30.00
—Orange label					
❑ 1849	Back Off Boogaloo/Blindman	1978	2.00	4.00	8.00
—Purple late-1970s label					
❑ 1865	Photograph/Down and Out	1978	2.00	4.00	8.00
—Purple late-1970s label					
❑ 1865	Photograph/Down and Out	1983	2.00	4.00	8.00
—Black colorband label					
❑ 1865	Photograph/Down and Out	1988	—	3.00	6.00
—Purple late-1980s label (wider)					
❑ 1870	You're Sixteen/Devil Woman	1976	15.00	30.00	60.00
—Orange label					
❑ 1870	You're Sixteen/Devil Woman	1978	2.00	4.00	8.00
—Purple late-1970s label					
❑ 1870	You're Sixteen/Devil Woman	1983	2.00	4.00	8.00
—Black colorband label					
❑ 1870	You're Sixteen/Devil Woman	1988	—	2.50	5.00
—Purple late-1980s label (wider)					
❑ 1876	Only You/Call Me	1978	2.00	4.00	8.00
—Purple late-1970s label					
❑ 1876	Only You/Call Me	1983	25.00	50.00	100.00
—Black colorband label					
❑ 1880	No No Song/Snookeroo	1978	2.00	4.00	8.00
—Purple late-1970s label					
❑ 1880	No No Song/Snookeroo	1983	2.00	4.00	8.00
—Black colorband label					
❑ 1880	No No Song/Snookeroo	1988	7.50	15.00	30.00
—Purple late-1980s label (wider)					
❑ 1882	It's All Down to Goodnight Vienna/Oo-Wee	1978	2.00	4.00	8.00
—Purple late-1970s label					
❑ 2969	Beaucoups of Blues/Coochy-Coochy	1976	10.00	20.00	40.00
—Orange label					
❑ B-44409	Act Naturally/Key's in the Mailbox	1989	3.75	7.50	15.00
—A-side with Buck Owens; B-side is Owens solo					

MERCURY

Number	Title (A Side/B Side)	Yr	VG	VG+	NM
❑ MELP-195 [DJ]	La De Da/Everyday	1998	3.75	7.50	15.00
—Number only in the dead wax					
❑ MELP-195 [PS]	La De Da/Everyday	1998	3.75	7.50	15.00
—The above record and sleeve were a giveaway from Beatlefest and J&R's Music World with advance purchase of the CD "Vertical Man" and later from Beatlefest with any Ringo Starr Mercury CD.					

PORTRAIT

Number	Title (A Side/B Side)	Yr	VG	VG+	NM
❑ 70015	Lipstick Traces (On a Cigarette)/Old Time Relovin'	1978	3.75	7.50	15.00
❑ 70018	Heart on My Sleeve/Who Needs a Heart	1978	3.75	7.50	15.00

THE RIGHT STUFF

Number	Title (A Side/B Side)	Yr	VG	VG+	NM
❑ S7-18178	In My Car/She's About a Mover	1994	2.00	4.00	8.00
—Gold/orange vinyl					
❑ S7-18179	Wrack My Brain/Private Property	1994	2.00	4.00	8.00
—Red vinyl					

STARR, SALLY

Philadelphia TV star backed by members of BILL HALEY AND HIS COMETS.

ARCADE

Number	Title (A Side/B Side)	Yr	VG	VG+	NM
❑ 157	Rocky the Rockin' Rabbit/Sing a Song of Happiness	1960	7.50	15.00	30.00

CLYMAX

Number	Title (A Side/B Side)	Yr	VG	VG+	NM
❑ 301	Rockin' in the Nursery/Little Pedro	1959	10.00	20.00	40.00

7-Inch Extended Plays

CLYMAX

Number	Title (A Side/B Side)	Yr	VG	VG+	NM
❑ EP-1001/2/3 [PS]	Our Gal Sal	1959	10.00	20.00	40.00
—Triple gatefold cover for all three EP-1001 records (despite what the cover says, the records are each numbered 1001)					
❑ EP-1001	Rockin' in the Nursery/Little Pedro//Rockin' Horse Cowgirl/Good Night Dear Lord	1959	7.50	15.00	30.00
—Third record of 3-EP set; master numbers are JB-144/JB-145					
❑ EP-1001	Toy Shop in the Town/Happy Birthday//Candy Red/Blue Ranger	1959	7.50	15.00	30.00
—First record of 3-EP set; master numbers are JB-140/JB-141					
❑ EP-1001	Cuckoo in the Clock/Sing a Song of Happiness//TV Pal/A.B.C. Rock	1959	7.50	15.00	30.00
—Second record of 3-EP set; master numbers are JB 142/JB 143					

STARSHIP

Also see JEFFERSON AIRPLANE; JEFFERSON STARSHIP; GRACE SLICK; MICKEY THOMAS.

ELEKTRA

Number	Title (A Side/B Side)	Yr	VG	VG+	NM
❑ 69349	Wild Again/Laying It on the Line	1988	—	—	3.00

GRUNT

Number	Title (A Side/B Side)	Yr	VG	VG+	NM
❑ 5109-7-R	Nothing's Gonna Stop Us Now/Layin' It on the Line	1987	—	—	3.00
❑ 5109-7-R [PS]	Nothing's Gonna Stop Us Now/Layin' It on the Line	1987	—	—	3.00
❑ 5225-7-R	It's Not Over ('Til It's Over)/Babylon	1987	—	—	3.00
❑ 5225-7-R [PS]	It's Not Over ('Til It's Over)/Babylon	1987	—	—	3.00
❑ 5308-7-R	Beat Patrol/Girls Like You	1987	—	—	3.00
❑ 5308-7-R [PS]	Beat Patrol/Girls Like You	1987	—	—	3.00
❑ JK-14170 [DJ]	We Built This City (Short)/We Built This City (Long)	1985	2.00	4.00	8.00
❑ PB-14170	We Built This City/Private Room	1985	—	—	3.00
❑ PB-14170 [PS]	We Built This City/Private Room	1985	—	2.50	5.00
❑ JB-14200 [DJ]	We Built This City (Special Non-DJ Rock Radio Version)/We Built This City	1985	2.50	5.00	10.00
❑ PB-14253	Sara/Hearts of the World (Will Understand)	1985	2.00	4.00	8.00
—Originals on blue vinyl					
❑ PB-14253	Sara/Hearts of the World (Will Understand)	1985	—	—	3.00
❑ PB-14253 [PS]	Sara/Hearts of the World (Will Understand)	1985	—	2.50	5.00
❑ PB-14332	Tomorrow Doesn't Matter Tonight/Love Rusts	1986	—	—	3.00
❑ PB-14332 [PS]	Tomorrow Doesn't Matter Tonight/Love Rusts	1986	12.50	25.00	50.00
❑ PB-14393	Before I Go/Cut You Down to Size	1986	—	—	3.00
❑ PB-14393 [PS]	Before I Go/Cut You Down to Size	1986	—	2.50	5.00

RCA

Number	Title (A Side/B Side)	Yr	VG	VG+	NM
❑ 6964-7-R	Set the Night to Music/I Don't Know Why	1988	—	2.00	4.00
❑ 8377-7-R	Nothing's Gonna Stop Us Now/Beat Patrol	1988	—	—	3.00
—Gold Standard Series					
❑ 9032-7-R	It's Not Enough/Love Among the Cannibals	1989	—	—	3.00
❑ 9032-7-R [PS]	It's Not Enough/Love Among the Cannibals	1989	—	—	3.00

STARSHIP (2)

No relation to the 1980s Starship, this features MICKEY DOLENZ.

LION

Number	Title (A Side/B Side)	Yr	VG	VG+	NM
❑ 132	Johnny B. Goode/It's Amazing to Me	1973	6.25	12.50	25.00

STARZ

CAPITOL

Number	Title (A Side/B Side)	Yr	VG	VG+	NM
❑ 4343	Monkey Business/(She's Just A) Fallen Angel	1976	—	2.50	5.00
❑ 4343 [PS]	Monkey Business/(She's Just A) Fallen Angel	1976	—	3.50	7.00
❑ 4399	Cherry Baby/Rock Six Times	1977	3.00	6.00	12.00
—Originals on yellow vinyl					
❑ 4399	Cherry Baby/Rock Six Times	1977	—	2.00	4.00
❑ 4399 [PS]	Cherry Baby/Rock Six Times	1977	—	3.00	6.00
❑ 4434	Sing It, Shout It/Subway Terror	1977	3.00	6.00	12.00
—Originals on yellow vinyl					
❑ 4434	Sing It, Shout It/Subway Terror	1977	—	2.00	4.00
❑ 4434 [PS]	Sing It, Shout It/Subway Terror	1977	—	3.00	6.00
❑ 4546	(Any Way That You Want It) I'll Be There/Texas	1978	—	2.00	4.00
❑ 4546 [PS]	(Any Way That You Want It) I'll Be There/Texas	1978	—	2.50	5.00
❑ 4566	Hold On to the Night/Texas	1978	—	2.00	4.00
❑ 4637	So Young, So Bad/Coliseum Rock	1978	—	2.00	4.00
❑ 4637 [PS]	So Young, So Bad/Coliseum Rock	1978	—	2.50	5.00
❑ 4671	Last Night I Wrote a Letter/Coliseum Rock	1979	—	2.00	4.00

STATENS, THE

MARK-X

Number	Title (A Side/B Side)	Yr	VG	VG+	NM
❑ 8011	Summertime Is the Time for Love/That Certain Kind	1961	20.00	40.00	80.00

STATLER BROTHERS, THE

COLUMBIA

Number	Title (A Side/B Side)	Yr	VG	VG+	NM
❑ 43069	The Wreck of the Old 97/Hammer and Nails	1964	3.00	6.00	12.00
❑ 43146	I Still Miss Someone/You're a Foolish Game	1964	3.00	6.00	12.00
❑ 43315	Flowers on the Wall/Billy Christian	1965	2.50	5.00	10.00
❑ 43315 [DJ]	Flowers on the Wall (same on both sides)	1965	5.00	10.00	20.00
—Promo only on red vinyl					
❑ 43526	The Doodlin' Song/My Darling Hildegarde	1966	2.00	4.00	8.00
❑ 43624	The Right One/Is That What You'd Have Me Do	1966	2.00	4.00	8.00
❑ 43868	That'll Be the Day/Makin' Rounds	1966	2.00	4.00	8.00
❑ 44070	Ruthless/Do You Love Me Tonight	1967	2.00	4.00	8.00
❑ 44245	You Can't Have Your Kate and Edith, Too/Walking in the Sunshine	1967	2.00	4.00	8.00
❑ 44480	Jump for Joy/Take a Bow, Rufus Humfry	1968	2.00	4.00	8.00
❑ 44608	Sissy/I Am the Boy	1968	2.00	4.00	8.00
❑ 44899	Oh Happy Day/How Great Thou Art	1969	2.00	4.00	8.00

MERCURY

Number	Title (A Side/B Side)	Yr	VG	VG+	NM
❑ DJ 557 [DJ]	Star Spangled Banner (With Spoken Intro)/Star Spangled Banner (Without Spoken Intro)	197?	2.00	4.00	8.00
❑ PRO 790-7 [DJ]	Don't Wait on Me (Live Edited Version/Live with Intro)	1989	2.00	4.00	8.00
—"US 99 10-In-a-Row Country Commemorative Edition" at top (other similar pressings may exist)					
❑ 55000	Silver Medals and Sweet Memories/The Regular Saturday Night Setback Card Game	1977	—	2.00	4.00

Number	Title (A Side/B Side)	Yr	VG	VG+	NM
❑ 55013	Some I Wrote/Carried Away	1977	—	2.00	4.00
❑ 55022	Do You Know You Are My Sunshine/You're the First	1978	—	2.00	4.00
❑ 55037	Who Am I to Say/I Dreamed About You	1978	—	2.00	4.00
❑ 55046	I Believe in Santa's Cause/Who Do You Think	1978	—	2.00	4.00
❑ 55048	The Official Historian on Shirley Jean Berrell/The Best That I Can Do	1978	—	2.00	4.00
❑ 55057	How to Be a Country Star/A Little Farther Down the Road	1979	—	2.00	4.00
❑ 55066	Here We Are Again/Mr. Autry	1979	—	2.00	4.00
❑ 57007	Nothing As Original As You/Counting My Memories	1979	—	2.00	4.00
❑ 57012	(I'll Even Love You) Better Than I Did Then/ Almost in Love	1980	—	2.00	4.00
❑ 57031	Charlotte's Web/One Less Day to Go	1980	—	2.00	4.00
❑ 57037	Don't Forget Yourself/We Got Paid by Cash	1980	—	2.00	4.00
❑ 57048	In the Garden/How Are Things in Clay, Kentucky	1981	—	2.00	4.00
❑ 57051	Don't Wait on Me/Chet Atkins' Band	1981	—	2.00	4.00
❑ 57059	Years Ago/Dad	1981	—	2.00	4.00
❑ 73141	Bed of Rose's/The Last Goodbye	1970	—	2.50	5.00
❑ 73194	New York City/This Part of the World	1971	—	2.50	5.00
❑ 73229	Pictures/Making Memories	1971	—	2.50	5.00
❑ 73253	You Can't Go Home/Second Thoughts	1971	—	2.50	5.00
❑ 73275	Do You Remember These/Since Then	1972	—	2.50	5.00
❑ 73315	The Class of '57/Every Time I Trust a Gal	1972	—	2.50	5.00
❑ 73360	Monday Morning Secretary/Special Song for Wanda	1973	—	2.50	5.00
❑ 73392	Woman Without a Home/I'll Be Your Baby Tonight	1973	—	2.50	5.00
❑ 73415	Carry Me Back/I Wish I Could Be	1973	—	2.50	5.00
❑ 73448	Whatever Happened to Randolph Scott/The Strand	1974	—	2.50	5.00
❑ 73485	Thank You World/The Blackwood Brothers by the Statler Brothers	1974	—	2.50	5.00
❑ 73625	Susan When She Tried/She's Too Good	1974	—	2.50	5.00
❑ 73665	All American Girl/A Few Old Memories	1975	—	2.50	5.00
❑ 73687	I'll Go to My Grave Loving You/You've Been Like a Mother to Me	1975	—	2.50	5.00
❑ 73732	How Great Thou Art/Noah Found Grace in the Eyes of the Lord	1975	—	2.50	5.00
❑ 73785	Your Picture in the Paper/All the Times	1976	—	2.50	5.00
❑ 73846	Thank God I've Got You/Hat and Boots	1976	—	2.50	5.00
❑ 73877	The Movies/You Could Be Coming to Me	1976	—	2.50	5.00
❑ 73906	I Was There/Somebody New Will Be Coming Along	1977	—	2.50	5.00
❑ 76130	I Never Spend A Christmas That I Don't Think Of You/Who Do You Think?	1981	—	2.00	4.00
❑ 76142	You'll Be Back (Every Night in My Dreams)/We Ain't Even Started Yet	1982	—	—	3.00
❑ 76162	Whatever/Do You Know You Are My Sunshine	1982	—	—	3.00
❑ 76184	A Child of the Fifties/I'll Love You All Over Again	1982	—	—	3.00
❑ 811488-7	Oh Baby Mine (I Get So Lonely)/I'm Dyin' a Little Each Day	1983	—	—	3.00
❑ 812988-7	Guilty/I Never Want to Kiss You Goodbye	1983	—	—	3.00
❑ 814881-7	Elizabeth/Class of '57	1983	—	—	3.00
❑ 818700-7	Atlanta Blue/If It Makes Any Difference	1984	—	—	3.00
❑ 818700-7 [PS]	Atlanta Blue/If It Makes Any Difference	1984	—	2.00	4.00
❑ 866302-7	Atlanta Blue/Put It on the Card	1991	—	2.00	4.00
❑ 868140-7	Remember Me/My Music, My Memories and You	1991	—	—	3.00
❑ 868484-7	You've Been Like a Mother to Me/Jesus Is the Answer	1991	—	2.00	4.00
❑ 868892-7	There's Still Times/Elizabeth	1991	—	—	3.00
❑ 870164-7	The Best I Know How/I Lost My Heart to You	1988	—	—	3.00
❑ 870442-7	Am I Crazy?/Beyond Romance	1988	—	—	3.00
❑ 870681-7	Let's Get Started If We're Gonna Break My Heart/ Guilty	1988	—	—	3.00
❑ 872604-7	Moon Pretty Moon/I'll Be the One	1989	—	—	3.00
❑ 874196-7	More Than a Name on the Wall/Atlanta Blue	1989	—	—	3.00
❑ 875498-7	Small Small World/My Music, My Memories and You	1990	—	—	3.00
❑ 876112-7	Don't Wait on Me/A Hurt I Can't Handle	1989	—	—	3.00
❑ 876876-7	Walkin' Heartache in Disguise/The Official Historian on Shirley Jean Berrell	1990	—	—	3.00
❑ 878386-7	He Is There/Nobody Else	1991	—	2.00	4.00
❑ 880130-7	One Takes the Blame/Give It Your Best	1984	—	—	3.00
❑ 880411-7	My Only Love/Let's Just Take One Night at a Time	1984	—	—	3.00
❑ 880685-7	Hello Mary Lou/Remembering You	1985	—	—	3.00
❑ 884016-7	Too Much on My Heart/Her Heart or Mine	1985	—	—	3.00
❑ 884317-7	Sweeter and Sweeter/Amazing Grace	1985	—	—	3.00
❑ 884320-7	Christmas Eve (Kodia's Theme)/Mary's Sweet Smile	1985	—	—	3.00
❑ 884721-7	Count On Me/Will You Be There?	1986	—	—	3.00
❑ 888042-7	Only You/We Got the Mem'ries	1986	—	—	3.00
❑ 888219-7	Forever/More Like Daddy Than Me	1986	—	—	3.00
❑ 888650-7	I'll Be the One/Deja Vu	1987	—	—	3.00
❑ 888920-7	Maple Street Mem'ries/Jesus Showed Me So	1987	—	—	3.00

7-Inch Extended Plays

MERCURY

Number	Title (A Side/B Side)	Yr	VG	VG+	NM
❑ DJ 577 [DJ]	I Never Spend a Christmas That I Don't Think of You/Jingle Bells//Away in a Manger/The Carols Those Kids Used to Sing	1978	—	3.00	6.00
❑ DJ 577 [PS]	A Very Merry Christmas from the Statler Brothers	1978	2.00	4.00	8.00

STATLERS, THE

LITTLE STAR

Number	Title (A Side/B Side)	Yr	VG	VG+	NM
❑ 108	Vicky/Gone	1962	37.50	75.00	150.00

STATON, CANDI

FAME

Number	Title (A Side/B Side)	Yr	VG	VG+	NM
❑ XW256	Something's Burning/It's Not Love	1973	—	2.50	5.00
❑ XW328	Love Chain/I'm Gonna Hold On	1973	—	2.50	5.00
❑ 1456	I'd Rather Be an Old Man's Sweetheart (Than a Young Man's Fool)/For You	1969	—	3.00	6.00
❑ 1459	Never in Public/You Don't Love Me No More	1969	—	3.00	6.00
❑ 1460	I'm Just a Prisoner (Of Your Good Lovin')/Heart on a String	1969	—	3.00	6.00
❑ 1466	Sweet Feeling/Evidence	1970	—	3.00	6.00
❑ 1472	Stand By Your Man/How Can I Put Out the Flame (When You Keep the Fire Burning)	1970	—	3.00	6.00
❑ 1476	He Called Me Baby/What Would Become of Me	1970	—	3.00	6.00
❑ 1478	Mr. and Mrs. Untrue/Too Hurt to Cry	1971	—	3.00	6.00
❑ 91000	In the Ghetto/Sure As Sin	1972	—	2.50	5.00
❑ 91005	Lovin' You, Lovin' Me/You Don't Love Me No More	1972	—	2.50	5.00
❑ 91009	Do It in the Name of Love/The Thanks I Get for Loving You	1972	—	2.50	5.00

LA

Number	Title (A Side/B Side)	Yr	VG	VG+	NM
❑ 0080	Without You I Cry/(B-side unknown)	1981	—	2.50	5.00

SUGAR HILL

Number	Title (A Side/B Side)	Yr	VG	VG+	NM
❑ 770	Count on Me/(B-side unknown)	1981	—	2.50	5.00
❑ 776	Suspicious Minds/(B-side unknown)	1982	—	2.50	5.00
❑ 784	Hurry Sundown/Count on Me	1982	—	2.50	5.00

UNITY

Number	Title (A Side/B Side)	Yr	VG	VG+	NM
❑ 711	Now That You Have the Upper Hand/(B-side unknown)	196?	37.50	75.00	150.00

WARNER BROS.

Number	Title (A Side/B Side)	Yr	VG	VG+	NM
❑ 8038	As Long As He Takes Care of Business/Little Taste of Love	1974	—	2.00	4.00
❑ 8078	Here I Am Again/Your Opening Night	1975	—	2.00	4.00
❑ 8112	Six Nights and a Day/We Can Work It Out	1975	—	2.00	4.00
❑ 8181	Young Hearts Run Free/I Know	1976	—	2.00	4.00
❑ 8249	Run to Me/What a Feeling	1976	—	2.00	4.00
❑ 8320	A Dreamer of a Dream/When You Want Love	1977	—	2.00	4.00
❑ 8387	Nights on Broadway/You Are	1977	—	2.00	4.00
❑ 8461	Music Speaks Louder Than Words/Cotton Candi	1977	—	2.00	4.00
❑ 8477	Listen to the Music/Music Speaks Louder Than Words	1977	—	2.00	4.00
❑ 8582	Victim/So Blue	1978	—	2.00	4.00
❑ 8691	Honest I Do Love You/I'm Gonna Make Me Love You	1978	—	2.00	4.00
❑ 8821	When You Wake Up Tomorrow/Rough Times	1979	—	2.00	4.00
❑ 49061	Chance/I Live	1979	—	2.00	4.00
❑ 49240	Looking for Love/It's Real	1980	—	2.00	4.00
❑ 49240 [PS]	Looking for Love/It's Real	1980	—	3.00	6.00
❑ 49536	The Hunter Gets Captured by the Game/If You Feel the Need	1980	—	2.00	4.00

STATUES, THE

HOLIDAY

Number	Title (A Side/B Side)	Yr	VG	VG+	NM
❑ 1026 [DJ]	White Christmas/Get Off My Roof	197?	3.00	6.00	12.00

—B-side by Jerry and the Landsliders

LIBERTY

Number	Title (A Side/B Side)	Yr	VG	VG+	NM
❑ 55245	Blue Velvet/Keep the Hall Light Burning	1959	5.00	10.00	20.00
❑ 55292	White Christmas/Jeannie with the Light Brown Hair	1960	6.25	12.50	25.00
❑ 55363	Ten Commandments of Love/Love at First Sight	1961	5.00	10.00	20.00

STATUS QUO

A&M

Number	Title (A Side/B Side)	Yr	VG	VG+	NM
❑ 1425	Don't Waste My TIme/All the Reasons	1973	—	2.50	5.00
❑ 1445	Paper Plane/All the Reasons	1973	—	2.50	5.00
❑ 1510	Carolina/Softer Ride	1974	—	2.50	5.00

BELL

Number	Title (A Side/B Side)	Yr	VG	VG+	NM
❑ 45417	Gerdundula/(B-side unknown)	1973	—	2.50	5.00

CADET CONCEPT

Number	Title (A Side/B Side)	Yr	VG	VG+	NM
❑ 7001	Pictures of Matchstick Men/Gentleman Joe's Sidewalk Café	1968	2.50	5.00	10.00
❑ 7006	Ice in the Sun/When My Mind Is Not Live	1968	2.00	4.00	8.00
❑ 7010	Technicolor Dreams/Spicks and Specks	1969	2.00	4.00	8.00
❑ 7015	Black Veils of Melancholy/To Be Free	1969	2.00	4.00	8.00
❑ 7017	The Price of Love/Little Miss Nothing	1969	2.00	4.00	8.00

CAPITOL

Number	Title (A Side/B Side)	Yr	VG	VG+	NM
❑ 4039	Nightride/Down Down	1975	—	2.00	4.00
❑ 4125	Bye Bye Johnny/Down Down	1975	—	2.00	4.00
❑ 4407	Wild Side of Life/All Through the Night	1977	—	2.00	4.00

JANUS

Number	Title (A Side/B Side)	Yr	VG	VG+	NM
❑ 127	Down the Dustpipe/Face Without a Soul	1970	—	3.00	6.00
❑ 141	Gerdundula/In My Chair	1970	—	3.00	6.00

PYE

Number	Title (A Side/B Side)	Yr	VG	VG+	NM
❑ 65000	Good Thinking/Tuned to the Music	1971	—	3.00	6.00
❑ 65017	Mean Girl/Everything	1971	—	3.00	6.00

RIVA

Number	Title (A Side/B Side)	Yr	VG	VG+	NM
❑ 206	Living on an Island/(B-side unknown)	1980	—	2.50	5.00

STEALERS WHEEL

Also see GERRY RAFFERTY.

A&M

Number	Title (A Side/B Side)	Yr	VG	VG+	NM
❑ 1416	Stuck in the Middle with You/Jose	1973	—	2.50	5.00
❑ 1450	Everyone's Agreed That Everything Will Turn Out Fine/Next to Me	1973	—	2.00	4.00
❑ 1483	Star/What More Could You Want	1973	—	2.00	4.00
❑ 1483 [PS]	Star/What More Could You Want	1973	—	3.00	6.00
❑ 1529	You Put Something Better Inside of Me/Wheelin'	1974	—	2.00	4.00
❑ 1675	This Morning/Found My Way to You	1975	—	2.00	4.00
❑ 2075	(Everyone's Agreed That) Everything Will Turn Out Fine/Who Cares	1978	—	2.50	5.00

STEAM

FONTANA

Number	Title (A Side/B Side)	Yr	VG	VG+	NM
❑ 1667	Na Na Hey Hey Kiss Him Goodbye/It's the Magic in You Girl	1969	2.00	4.00	8.00

MERCURY

Number	Title (A Side/B Side)	Yr	VG	VG+	NM
❑ 30160	Na Na Hey Hey Kiss Him Goodbye/Don't Stop Lovin' Me	1976	—	2.00	4.00

—Reissue

Number	Title (A Side/B Side)	Yr	VG	VG+	NM
❑ 30160 [PS]	Na Na Hey Hey Kiss Him Goodbye/Don't Stop Lovin' Me	1976	5.00	10.00	20.00

—Special Chicago White Sox sleeve, available only in that area

Number	Title (A Side/B Side)	Yr	VG	VG+	NM
❑ 73020	I've Gotta Make You Love Me/One Good Woman	1970	—	3.00	6.00
❑ 73053	What I'm Saying Is True/I'm the One Who Loves You	1970	—	3.00	6.00
❑ 73117	Don't Stop Lovin' Me/Do Unto Others	1970	—	3.00	6.00

STEELE, TOMMY

BUENA VISTA

Number	Title (A Side/B Side)	Yr	VG	VG+	NM
❑ 457	Fortuosity/I'm a Brass Band Today	1967	2.00	4.00	8.00

LONDON

Number	Title (A Side/B Side)	Yr	VG	VG+	NM
❑ 1706	Doomsday Rock/Elevator Rock	1957	3.75	7.50	15.00
❑ 1735	Butterfingers/Teenage Party	1957	3.75	7.50	15.00
❑ 1760	Water, Water/A Handful of Songs	1958	3.75	7.50	15.00
❑ 1795	Nairobi/Neon Sign	1958	3.75	7.50	15.00
❑ 1824	Swaller Tail Coat/The Only Man Across the Way	1959	3.75	7.50	15.00
❑ 1838	Hey You/Number 22 Across the Way	1959	3.75	7.50	15.00
❑ 1878	The Trail/Give, Give, Give	1959	3.75	7.50	15.00
❑ 1950	She's My Baby/Happy-Go-Lucky Blues	1960	3.75	7.50	15.00

RCA VICTOR

Number	Title (A Side/B Side)	Yr	VG	VG+	NM
❑ 47-8602	Half a Sixpence/If the Rain's Got to Fall	1965	2.50	5.00	10.00
❑ 47-9458	Half a Sixpence/If the Rain's Got to Fall	1968	2.00	4.00	8.00

STEELY DAN

Also see DONALD FAGEN.

ABC

Number	Title (A Side/B Side)	Yr	VG	VG+	NM
❑ 11323	Dallas/Sail the Waterway	1972	7.50	15.00	30.00

—Neither of these songs has appeared on a U.S. Steely Dan album -- not even the "complete" CD box set!

Number	Title (A Side/B Side)	Yr	VG	VG+	NM
❑ 11338	Do It Again/Fire in the Hole	1972	—	2.00	4.00
❑ 11352	Reeling In the Years/Only a Fool Would Say That	1973	—	2.00	4.00
❑ 11382	Show Biz Kids/Razor Boy	1973	—	2.00	4.00
❑ 11396	My Old School/Pearl of the Quarter	1973	—	2.00	4.00
❑ 11439	Rikki Don't Lose That Number/Any Major Dude Will Tell You	1974	—	2.00	4.00
❑ 12014	Rikki Don't Lose That Number/Any Major Dude Will Tell You	1974	—	3.00	6.00
❑ 12033	Pretzel Logic/Through with Buzz	1974	—	2.00	4.00
❑ 12101	Black Friday/Throw Back the Little Ones	1975	—	2.00	4.00
❑ 12128	Chain Lightning/Bad Sneakers	1975	—	2.00	4.00
❑ 12195	Kid Charlemagne/Green Earrings	1976	—	2.00	4.00
❑ 12222	The Fez/Sign In Stranger	1976	—	2.00	4.00
❑ 12320	Peg/I Got the News	1977	—	2.00	4.00
❑ 12355	Deacon Blues/Home at Last	1978	—	2.00	4.00
❑ 12404	Josie/Black Cow	1978	—	2.00	4.00

MCA

Number	Title (A Side/B Side)	Yr	VG	VG+	NM
❑ 40894	FM (No Static at All)/(Instrumental)	1978	—	2.00	4.00
❑ 51036	Hey Nineteen/Bodhisattva	1980	—	2.00	4.00
❑ 51082	Time Out of Mind/Bodhisattva	1981	—	2.00	4.00

STEIN, FRANK N., AND THE TOMBSTONES

MARCO

Number	Title (A Side/B Side)	Yr	VG	VG+	NM
❑ 003	Mess Around/Graveyard Giggle	1962	10.00	20.00	40.00

STEIN, FRANKIE, AND THE GHOULS

KING

Number	Title (A Side/B Side)	Yr	VG	VG+	NM
❑ 6414	Franken Boogie/All She Wants to Do Is Boogie	1972	2.50	5.00	10.00

POWER

Number	Title (A Side/B Side)	Yr	VG	VG+	NM
❑ 338	Goon River/Weerdo the Wolf	1964	6.25	12.50	25.00
❑ 338 [PS]	Goon River/Weerdo the Wolf	1964	7.50	15.00	30.00

STEPPENWOLF

Also see JOHN KAY; SPARROW.

ABC

Number	Title (A Side/B Side)	Yr	VG	VG+	NM
❑ 1436	The Pusher/Born to Be Wild	1970	—	2.00	4.00

—"Goldies 45" series

Number	Title (A Side/B Side)	Yr	VG	VG+	NM
❑ 1436 [PS]	The Pusher/Born to Be Wild	1970	—	3.00	6.00

ABC DUNHILL

Number	Title (A Side/B Side)	Yr	VG	VG+	NM
❑ 4138	Born to Be Wild/Everybody's Next One	1968	2.00	4.00	8.00
❑ 4161	Magic Carpet Ride/Sookie Sookie	1968	2.00	4.00	8.00
❑ 4182	Rock Me/Jupiter Child	1969	2.00	4.00	8.00
❑ 4192	It's Never Too Late/Happy Birthday	1969	—	3.00	6.00
❑ 4205	Move Over/Power Play	1969	—	3.00	6.00
❑ 4221	Monster/Berry Rides Again	1969	—	3.00	6.00
❑ 4234	Hey Lawdy Mama/Twisted	1970	—	3.00	6.00
❑ 4248	Screaming Night Hog/Spiritual Fantasy	1970	—	3.00	6.00
❑ 4261	Who Needs Ya/Earschplittenloudenboomer	1970	—	3.00	6.00
❑ 4269	Snow Blind Friend/Hippo Stomp	1971	—	2.50	5.00
❑ 4283	Ride with Me/Black Pit	1971	—	2.50	5.00
❑ 4283	Ride with Me/For Madmen Only	1971	—	2.50	5.00
❑ 4283 [PS]	Ride with Me/For Madmen Only	1971	—	3.00	6.00
❑ 4292	For Ladies Only/Sparkle Eyes	1971	—	2.50	5.00

ALLEGIANCE

Number	Title (A Side/B Side)	Yr	VG	VG+	NM
❑ 3909	Hot Night in a Cold Town/Every Man for Himself	1983	—	2.00	4.00

—As "John Kay and Steppenwolf"

DUNHILL

Number	Title (A Side/B Side)	Yr	VG	VG+	NM
❑ 4109	The Ostrich/A Girl I Know	1967	2.50	5.00	10.00
❑ 4123	Sookie Sookie/Take What You Need	1968	2.50	5.00	10.00

MUMS

Number	Title (A Side/B Side)	Yr	VG	VG+	NM
❑ 6031	Straight Shootin' Woman/Justice, Don't Be Slow	1974	—	2.00	4.00
❑ 6031 [PS]	Straight Shootin' Woman/Justice, Don't Be Slow	1974	—	3.00	6.00
❑ 6034	Get Into the Wind/Morning Blue	1974	—	2.00	4.00
❑ 6036	Fool's Fantasy/Smokey Factory Blues	1975	—	2.00	4.00
❑ 6040	Caroline (Are You Ready for the Outlaw)/Angel Drawers	1975	—	2.00	4.00

STEVENS, APRIL

Also see NINO TEMPO AND APRIL STEVENS.

ATCO

Number	Title (A Side/B Side)	Yr	VG	VG+	NM
❑ 6346	Teach Me Tiger 1965/Morning Till Midnight	1965	2.00	4.00	8.00
❑ 6380	Lovin' Valentine/No Hair Say	1965	2.00	4.00	8.00

A&M

Number	Title (A Side/B Side)	Yr	VG	VG+	NM
❑ 1636	Marry Me Again/Gotta Leave You Baby	1974	—	2.00	4.00

CONTRACT

Number	Title (A Side/B Side)	Yr	VG	VG+	NM
❑ 429	You and Only You/Love Kitten	1961	3.75	7.50	15.00

IMPERIAL

Number	Title (A Side/B Side)	Yr	VG	VG+	NM
❑ 5626	Teach Me, Tiger/That Warm Afternoon	1959	5.00	10.00	20.00
❑ 5666	In Other Words/Jonny	1960	3.75	7.50	15.00
❑ 5761	You and Only You/Love Kitten	1961	3.75	7.50	15.00
❑ 5907	Fly Me to the Moon/That's My Name	1963	3.75	7.50	15.00

KING

Number	Title (A Side/B Side)	Yr	VG	VG+	NM
❑ 5826	Soft Warm Lips/How Could Red Riding Hood	1963	2.50	5.00	10.00

RCA VICTOR

Number	Title (A Side/B Side)	Yr	VG	VG+	NM
❑ 47-4148	I'm in Love Again/Roller Coaster	1951	5.00	10.00	20.00

—With Henri Rene

Number	Title (A Side/B Side)	Yr	VG	VG+	NM
❑ 47-4208	Gimme a Little Kiss, Will Ya, Huh?/Dreamy Melody	1951	5.00	10.00	20.00

—With Henri Rene

Number	Title (A Side/B Side)	Yr	VG	VG+	NM
❑ 47-4283	And So to Sleep Again/Aw, C'mon	1951	5.00	10.00	20.00
❑ 47-4381	Put Me in Your Pocket/The Tricks of the Trade	1951	5.00	10.00	20.00
❑ 47-4567	I Love the Way You're Breaking My Heart/Meant to Tell You	1952	5.00	10.00	20.00
❑ 47-4876	I Like to Talk to Myself/That Naughty Waltz	1952	5.00	10.00	20.00

STEVENS, CAT

A&M

Number	Title (A Side/B Side)	Yr	VG	VG+	NM
❑ 1211	Lady D'Arbanville/Time — Fill My Eyes	1970	—	2.50	5.00
❑ 1231	Wild World/Miles from Nowhere	1970	—	2.50	5.00
❑ 1265	Moon Shadow/I Think I See the Light	1971	—	2.00	4.00
❑ 1265 [PS]	Moon Shadow/I Think I See the Light	1971	—	3.00	6.00
❑ 1291	Peace Train/Where Do the Children Play	1971	—	2.00	4.00
❑ 1291 [PS]	Peace Train/Where Do the Children Play	1971	—	3.00	6.00
❑ 1335	Morning Has Broken/I Want to Live in a Wigwam	1972	—	2.00	4.00
❑ 1335 [PS]	Morning Has Broken/I Want to Live in a Wigwam	1972	—	3.00	6.00
❑ 1396	Sitting/Crab Dance	1972	—	2.00	4.00
❑ 1396 [PS]	Sitting/Crab Dance	1972	—	3.00	6.00
❑ 1418	The Hurt/Silent Sunlight	1973	—	2.00	4.00
❑ 1418 [PS]	The Hurt/Silent Sunlight	1973	—	3.00	6.00
❑ 1503	Oh Very Young/100 I Dream	1974	—	2.00	4.00
❑ 1503 [PS]	Oh Very Young/100 I Dream	1974	—	3.00	6.00
❑ 1549	Another Saturday Night/Home in the Sky	1974	—	—	—

—Unreleased?

Number	Title (A Side/B Side)	Yr	VG	VG+	NM
❑ 1602	Another Saturday Night/Home in the Sky	1974	—	2.00	4.00
❑ 1602 [PS]	Another Saturday Night/Home in the Sky	1974	—	3.00	6.00
❑ 1645	Ready/I Think I See the Light	1974	—	2.00	4.00
❑ 1700	Two Fine People/Bad Penny	1975	—	2.00	4.00
❑ 1785	Banapple Gas/Ghost Town	1976	—	2.00	4.00
❑ 1785 [PS]	Banapple Gas/Ghost Town	1976	—	3.00	6.00
❑ 1924	(I Never Wanted) To Be a Star/Land O' Freelove and Goodbye	1977	—	2.00	4.00
❑ 1948	(Remember the Days of the) Old School Yard/Land O' Freelove and Goodbye	1977	—	2.00	4.00
❑ 1948 [PS]	(Remember the Days of the) Old School Yard/Land O' Freelove and Goodbye	1977	—	3.00	6.00
❑ 1971	Was Dog a Doughnut/Sweet Jamaica	1977	—	2.00	4.00
❑ 2109	Bad Brakes/Nascimento	1979	—	2.00	4.00
❑ 2126	Randy/Nascimento	1979	—	2.00	4.00
❑ 2683	If You Want to Sing Out, Sing Out/I Want to Live in a Wigwam	1984	—	2.00	4.00
❑ 2711 [DJ]	Father and Son (same on both sides)	1985	2.50	5.00	10.00

—No stock copies issued

DERAM

Number	Title (A Side/B Side)	Yr	VG	VG+	NM
❑ 7501	I Love My Dog/Portobello Road	1966	2.50	5.00	10.00
❑ 7505	Matthew and Son/Granny	1967	2.50	5.00	10.00
❑ 7518	Kitty/The Blackness of the Night	1968	2.00	4.00	8.00
❑ 85006	I'm Gonna Get Me a Gun/School Is Out	1967	2.50	5.00	10.00
❑ 85015	Laughing Apple/Bad Night	1967	2.50	5.00	10.00
❑ 85079	Kitty/Where Are You	1972	—	3.00	6.00

STEVENS, CONNIE

Also see EDD BYRNES.

BELL

Number	Title (A Side/B Side)	Yr	VG	VG+	NM
❑ 866	She'll Never Understand Him/5:30 Plane	1970	—	2.50	5.00
❑ 922	Keep Growing Strong/Tick-Tock	1970	—	2.50	5.00
❑ 992	Keep Growing Strong/(B-side unknown)	1971	—	2.50	5.00
❑ 45234	Simple Girl/(B-side unknown)	1972	—	2.50	5.00

MGM

Number	Title (A Side/B Side)	Yr	VG	VG+	NM
❑ 13906	Cinderella Could Have Saved Us All/Wouldn't It Be Nice (To Have Wings and Fly)	1968	—	3.00	6.00

WARNER BROS.

Number	Title (A Side/B Side)	Yr	VG	VG+	NM
❑ 5092	Apollo/Why Do I Cry for Joey	1959	5.00	10.00	20.00
❑ 5137	Sixteen Reasons/Little Sister	1960	3.75	7.50	15.00

—First pressing has pink labels

Number	Title (A Side/B Side)	Yr	VG	VG+	NM
❑ 5137	Sixteen Reasons/Little Sister	1960	3.00	6.00	12.00

—Second pressing has red label with arrows

Number	Title (A Side/B Side)	Yr	VG	VG+	NM
❑ 5159	Too Young to Go Steady/A Little Kiss Is a Kiss Is a Kiss	1960	3.00	6.00	12.00
❑ 5159 [PS]	Too Young to Go Steady/A Little Kiss Is a Kiss Is a Kiss	1960	7.50	15.00	30.00
❑ 5217	Make Believe Lover/And This Is Mine	1961	3.00	6.00	12.00
❑ 5232	If You Don't, Somebody Else Will/Greenwood Tree	1961	3.00	6.00	12.00
❑ 5238	Man Soil Such So Schwell Nicht Uberliebe/La Le Lu	1961	7.50	15.00	30.00

—German release only

Number	Title (A Side/B Side)	Yr	VG	VG+	NM
❑ 5265	Why'd You Wanna Make Me Cry/Just One Kiss	1962	3.00	6.00	12.00
❑ 5289	Mr. Songwriter/I Couldn't Say No	1962	3.00	6.00	12.00
❑ 5318	Hey, Good Lookin'/Nobody's Lonesome for Me	1962	3.00	6.00	12.00
❑ 5380	Little Miss Understood/There Goes Your Guy	1963	2.50	5.00	10.00
❑ 5425	A Girl Never Knows/They're Jealous of Me	1964	2.50	5.00	10.00
❑ 5610	Now That You've Gone/Lost in Wonderland	1965	3.00	6.00	12.00
❑ 5656	In the Deep of Night/Something Beautiful	1965	2.50	5.00	10.00

Number	Title (A Side/B Side)	Yr	VG	VG+	NM
❑ 5691	Don't You Want to Love Me/In My Room (El Amor)	1966	2.50	5.00	10.00
❑ 5804	All of My Life/That's All I Want from You	1966	2.50	5.00	10.00
❑ 5834	How Bitter the Taste of Love/Most of All	1966	2.50	5.00	10.00
❑ 5872	It'll Never Happen Again/What Will I Tell Him	1966	2.50	5.00	10.00
❑ 7128	Sixteen Reasons/Make Believe Lover	1968	—	2.50	5.00

—"Back to Back Hits" series -- originals have green labels with "W7" logo

STEVENS, DEBBIE

ABC-PARAMOUNT

Number	Title (A Side/B Side)	Yr	VG	VG+	NM
❑ 10034	Billy Boy's Theme/I Sit and Cry	1959	3.75	7.50	15.00

APT

Number	Title (A Side/B Side)	Yr	VG	VG+	NM
❑ 25027	If You Can't Rock Me/What Will I Tell My Heart	1959	6.25	12.50	25.00

STEVENS, DODIE

Also see GERALDINE STEVENS.

CRYSTALETTE

Number	Title (A Side/B Side)	Yr	VG	VG+	NM
❑ 724	Pink Shoe Laces/Coming of Age	1959	5.00	10.00	20.00
❑ 728	Yes-Sir-Ee/The Five Pennies	1959	5.00	10.00	20.00

DOLTON

Number	Title (A Side/B Side)	Yr	VG	VG+	NM
❑ 83	You Don't Have to Prove a Thing to Me/I Wore Out Our Record	1963	3.00	6.00	12.00
❑ 88	Sailor Boy/Does Goodnight Mean Goodbye	1964	3.00	6.00	12.00

DOT

Number	Title (A Side/B Side)	Yr	VG	VG+	NM
❑ 15975	Miss Lonely Heart/Poor Butterfly	1959	5.00	10.00	20.00
❑ 16002	Steady Date/Mairzy Doats	1959	5.00	10.00	20.00
❑ 16067	Candy Store Blues/Gringo's Guitar	1960	3.75	7.50	15.00
❑ 16103	No/A Tisket, A Tasket	1960	3.75	7.50	15.00
❑ 16139	Am I Too Young/So Let's Dance	1960	3.75	7.50	15.00
❑ 16166	Merry Christmas Baby/Jingle Bells	1960	5.00	10.00	20.00
❑ 16167	Yes, I'm Lonesome Tonight/Too Young	1960	5.00	10.00	20.00
❑ 16200	I Fall to Pieces/Turn Around	1961	3.75	7.50	15.00
❑ 16259	Let Me Tell You About Johnny/You Are the Only One	1961	3.75	7.50	15.00
❑ 16279	The In-Between Years/Trade Winds	1961	3.75	7.50	15.00
❑ 16339	I Cried/Dancing on My Ceiling	1962	3.75	7.50	15.00
❑ 16389	Pink Shoelaces/Yes-Sir-Ee	1962	3.75	7.50	15.00

IMPERIAL

Number	Title (A Side/B Side)	Yr	VG	VG+	NM
❑ 5908	Don't Send Me No Roses/Daddy Could Get Me One of These	1963	3.75	7.50	15.00
❑ 5930	Hello Stranger/For a Little While	1963	3.75	7.50	15.00

STEVENS, GERALDINE

Also see DODIE STEVENS.

WORLD PACIFIC

Number	Title (A Side/B Side)	Yr	VG	VG+	NM
❑ 77927	Billy, I've Got to Go to Town/It's Not Their Heartache, It's Mine	1969	2.00	4.00	8.00
❑ 77930	Play Me a Song/I've Got to Have More	1969	2.00	4.00	8.00
❑ 77934	Love Is Gonna Get You/You Ain't Goin' Nowhere	1970	2.00	4.00	8.00

STEVENS, JOHNNY

FORD

Number	Title (A Side/B Side)	Yr	VG	VG+	NM
❑ 123	Oh Yeah/Last Chicken in the Shack	1963	7.50	15.00	30.00

PARKWAY

Number	Title (A Side/B Side)	Yr	VG	VG+	NM
❑ 805	Apple Taffy/Mm, Baby, Mm	1959	6.25	12.50	25.00

STEVENS, MARK, AND THE CHARMERS

ALLISON

Number	Title (A Side/B Side)	Yr	VG	VG+	NM
❑ 921	Magic Rose/Come Back to My Heart	1962	15.00	30.00	60.00

STEVENS, NEIL

BRUNSWICK

Number	Title (A Side/B Side)	Yr	VG	VG+	NM
❑ 55095	More and More/What Could Be Better	1958	7.50	15.00	30.00

—With the Dee-Vines

GOLDISC

Number	Title (A Side/B Side)	Yr	VG	VG+	NM
❑ 3019	Ballad of Love/Tonight My Heart She Is Crying	1961	5.00	10.00	20.00

—With the Temptations

GONE

Number	Title (A Side/B Side)	Yr	VG	VG+	NM
❑ 5067	Ballad of Love/Gambler's Game	1959	12.50	25.00	50.00

STEVENS, RAY

BARNABY

Number	Title (A Side/B Side)	Yr	VG	VG+	NM
❑ 514	Gitarzan/Unwind	197?	—	2.00	4.00
❑ 515	Everything Is Beautiful/Turn Your Radio On	197?	—	2.00	4.00
❑ 516	Mr. Businessman/Sunday Morning Comin' Down	197?	—	2.00	4.00
❑ 517	Ahab the Arab/Along Came Jones	197?	—	2.00	4.00
❑ 518	Freddie Feelgood (And His Funky Little Five Piece Band)/Isn't It Lonely Together	197?	—	2.00	4.00
❑ 519	Have a Little Talk with Myself/Bridget the Midget (The Queen of the Blues)	197?	—	2.00	4.00

—Barnaby releases in the 500 series are reissues; some may be re-recordings

Number	Title (A Side/B Side)	Yr	VG	VG+	NM
❑ 600	The Streak/You've Got the Music Inside	1974	—	2.50	5.00

—White label (not a promo)

Number	Title (A Side/B Side)	Yr	VG	VG+	NM
❑ 600	The Streak/You've Got the Music Inside	1974	—	2.00	4.00

—Multicolor label

Number	Title (A Side/B Side)	Yr	VG	VG+	NM
❑ 605	Moonlight Special/Just So Proud to Be Here	1974	—	2.00	4.00
❑ 610	Everybody Needs a Rainbow/Inside	1974	—	2.00	4.00
❑ 614	Misty/Sunshine	1975	—	2.00	4.00
❑ 616	Indian Love Call/Piece of Paradise	1975	—	2.00	4.00
❑ 618	Young Love/Deep Purple	1975	—	2.00	4.00
❑ 619	Lady of Spain/Mockingbird Hill	1976	—	2.00	4.00
❑ 2011	Everything Is Beautiful/A Brighter Day	1970	—	3.00	6.00
❑ 2016	America, Communicate with Me/Monkey See, Monkey Do	1970	—	2.50	5.00
❑ 2021	Sunset Strip/Islands	1970	—	2.50	5.00
❑ 2024	Bridget the Midget (The Queen of the Blues)/Night People	1970	—	2.50	5.00
❑ 2024 [PS]	Bridget the Midget (The Queen of the Blues)/Night People	1970	2.50	5.00	10.00
❑ 2029	A Mama and a Papa/Melt	1971	—	2.50	5.00
❑ 2039	All My Trials/Have a Little Talk with Myself	1971	—	2.50	5.00
❑ 2048	Turn Your Radio On/Loving You on Paper	1971	—	2.50	5.00
❑ 2058	Love Lifted Me/Glory Special	1972	—	2.50	5.00
❑ 2058	Love Lifted Me/Monkey See, Monkey Do	1972	—	2.50	5.00
❑ 2065	Losing Streak/Inside	1972	—	2.50	5.00
❑ 5020	Golden Age/Nashville	1973	—	2.00	4.00
❑ 5028	Love Me Longer/Float	1973	—	2.00	4.00

CAPITOL

Number	Title (A Side/B Side)	Yr	VG	VG+	NM
❑ F3967	Chickie Chickie Wah Wah/Crying Goodbye	1958	6.25	12.50	25.00
❑ F4030	Cat Pants/Love Goes On Forever	1958	7.50	15.00	30.00
❑ F4101	The School/The Clown	1958	6.25	12.50	25.00
❑ 7PRO-79430 [DJ]	Help Me Make It Through the Night (same on both sides)	1991	—	2.50	5.00

—Vinyl is promo only

MCA

Number	Title (A Side/B Side)	Yr	VG	VG+	NM
❑ 52451	Joggin'/I'm Kissin' You Goodbye	1984	—	2.00	4.00
❑ 52492	Mississippi Squirrel Revival/Ned Nostril	1984	—	2.00	4.00
❑ 52548	It's Me Again, Margaret/Joggin'	1985	—	—	3.00
❑ 52657	The Haircut Song/Punk Country Love	1985	—	—	3.00
❑ 52738	Santa Claus Is Watching You/Armchair Quarterback	1985	—	2.00	4.00
❑ 52738 [PS]	Santa Claus Is Watching You/Armchair Quarterback	1985	—	2.00	4.00
❑ 52771	Vacation Bible School/The Ballad of the Blue Cyclone	1986	—	—	3.00
❑ 52906	The Camping Trip/Southern Air	1986	—	—	3.00
❑ 52924	People's Court/Dudley Doright (Of the Highway Patrol)	1986	—	—	3.00
❑ 53007	Can He Love You Half As Much As I Do/Dudley Doright (Of the Highway Patrol)	1987	—	—	3.00
❑ 53007 [DJ]	Can He Love You Half As Much As I Do (same on both sides)	1987	2.50	5.00	10.00

—Blue vinyl promo

Number	Title (A Side/B Side)	Yr	VG	VG+	NM
❑ 53101	Would Jesus Wear a Rolex?/Cool Down Willard	1987	—	2.00	4.00
❑ 53178	Three-Legged Man/Doctor, Doctor (Have Mercy on Me)	1987	—	—	3.00
❑ 53232	Sex Symbols/The Ballad of Cactus Pete and Lefty	1987	—	—	3.00
❑ 53372	Surfin' U.S.S.R./Language, Nudity, Violence & Sex	1988	—	—	3.00
❑ 53423	The Day I Tried to Teach Charlene MacKenzie How to Drive/I Don't Need None of That	1988	—	—	3.00
❑ 53661	I Saw Elvis in a U.F.O./I Used to Be Crazy	1989	2.50	5.00	10.00

MERCURY

Number	Title (A Side/B Side)	Yr	VG	VG+	NM
❑ 71843	Jeremiah Peabody's Poly Unsaturated Quick Dissolving Fast Acting Pleasant Tasting Green and Purple Pills/Teen Years	1961	3.75	7.50	15.00
❑ 71843 [PS]	Jeremiah Peabody's Poly Unsaturated Quick Dissolving Fast Acting Pleasant Tasting Green and Purple Pills/Teen Years	1961	6.25	12.50	25.00
❑ 71888	Scratch My Back/When You Wish Upon a Star	1961	3.75	7.50	15.00
❑ 71966	Ahab, the Arab/It's Been So Long	1962	3.75	7.50	15.00
❑ 71966 [PS]	Ahab, the Arab/It's Been So Long	1962	7.50	15.00	30.00
❑ 72039	Further More/Saturday Night at the Movies	1962	3.75	7.50	15.00
❑ 72058	Santa Claus Is Watching You/Loved and Lost	1962	3.75	7.50	15.00
❑ 72058 [PS]	Santa Claus Is Watching You/Loved and Lost	1962	6.25	12.50	25.00
❑ 72098	Funny Man/Just One of Life's Little Tragedies	1963	3.75	7.50	15.00
❑ 72125	Harry the Hairy Ape/Little Stone Statue	1963	3.75	7.50	15.00
❑ 72125 [PS]	Harry the Hairy Ape/Little Stone Statue	1963	6.25	12.50	25.00
❑ 72189	Speed Ball/It's Party Time	1963	3.75	7.50	15.00
❑ 72255	Butch Barbarian (Sure Footed Mountain Climber World Famous Yodeling Champion)/Don't Say Anything	1963	3.75	7.50	15.00
❑ 72307	Bubble Gum the Bubble Dancer/Laughing Over My Grave	1964	3.75	7.50	15.00
❑ 72382	Rockin' Teenage Mummies/It Only Hurts When I Love	1965	5.00	10.00	20.00
❑ 72430	Mr. Baker the Undertaker/Old English Surfer	1965	5.00	10.00	20.00
❑ 72816	Funny Man/Just One of Life's Little Tragedies	1968	3.00	6.00	12.00
❑ 812496-7	Pice of Paradise Called Tennessee/Mary Lou Nights	1983	—	2.00	4.00
❑ 812906-7	My Dad/Game Show Love	1983	—	2.50	5.00
❑ 814196-7	Love Will Beat Your Brains Out/Game Show Love	1983	—	2.00	4.00
❑ 818057-7	My Dad/Me	1984	—	2.00	4.00

MONUMENT

Number	Title (A Side/B Side)	Yr	VG	VG+	NM
❑ 911	A-B-C/Party People	1966	2.50	5.00	10.00
❑ 927	Devil-May-Care/Make a Few Memories	1966	2.50	5.00	10.00
❑ 946	Freddy Feelgood (And His Funky Little Five Piece Band)/There's One in Every Crowd	1966	2.50	5.00	10.00
❑ 1001	Mary, My Secretary/Answer Me, My Love	1967	2.00	4.00	8.00
❑ 1048	Unwind/For He's a Jolly Good Fellow	1968	2.00	4.00	8.00
❑ 1083	Mr. Businessman/Face the Music	1968	2.00	4.00	8.00
❑ 1099	Isn't It Lonely Together/The Great Escape	1968	2.00	4.00	8.00
❑ 1131	Gitarzan/Bagpipes-That's My Bag	1969	2.00	4.00	8.00
❑ 1150	Along Came Jones/Yakety Yak	1969	2.00	4.00	8.00
❑ 1163	Sunday Mornin' Comin' Down/The Minority	1969	—	3.00	6.00
❑ 1171	Have a Little Talk with Myself/Little Woman	1969	—	3.00	6.00
❑ 1187	I'll Be Your Baby Tonight/Fool on the Hill	1970	—	3.00	6.00

NRC

Number	Title (A Side/B Side)	Yr	VG	VG+	NM
❑ 031	High School Yearbook (Deck of Cards)/Truly True	1959	6.25	12.50	25.00
❑ 042	What Would I Do Without You/My Heart Cries for You	1959	6.25	12.50	25.00
❑ 057	Sergeant Preston of the Yukon/Who Do You Love	1960	6.25	12.50	25.00
❑ 063	Happy Blue Year/White Christmas	1960	6.25	12.50	25.00

PREP

Number	Title (A Side/B Side)	Yr	VG	VG+	NM
❑ 108	Rang Tang Ding Dong (I'm the Japanese Sandman)/Silver Bracelet	1957	6.25	12.50	25.00
❑ 122	Five More Steps/Tingle	1957	6.25	12.50	25.00

RCA

Number	Title (A Side/B Side)	Yr	VG	VG+	NM
❑ PB-11911	Shriner's Convention/You're Never Goin' to Tampa With Me	1980	—	2.00	4.00
❑ PB-12069	Night Games/Let's Do It Right This Time	1980	—	2.00	4.00
❑ PB-12170	One More Last Chance/I Believe You Love Me	1981	—	2.00	4.00
❑ PB-12185	The Streak/Misty	1981	—	2.00	4.00
❑ GB-12368	Everything Is Beautiful/Gitarzan	1981	—	—	3.00

—Gold Standard Series

Number	Title (A Side/B Side)	Yr	VG	VG+	NM
❑ GB-12370	Shriner's Convention/You're Never Goin' to Tampa with Me	1981	—	—	3.00
—Gold Standard Series					
❑ PB-13038	Written Down in My Heart/Country Boy, Country Club Girl	1981	—	2.00	4.00
❑ PB-13207	Where the Sun Don't Shine/Why Don't We Go Somewhere and Love	1982	—	2.00	4.00
WARNER BROS.					
❑ 8198	You Are So Beautiful/One Man Band	1976	—	2.00	4.00
❑ 8237	Honky Tonk Waltz/Om	1976	—	2.00	4.00
❑ 8301	In the Mood/Classical Cluck	1976	—	3.00	6.00
—As "Henhouse Five Plus Too"					
❑ 8318	Get Crazy with Me/Dixie Hummingbird	1977	—	2.00	4.00
❑ 8393	Dixie Hummingbird/Feel the Music	1977	—	2.00	4.00
❑ 8603	Be Your Own Best Friend/With a Smile	1978	—	2.00	4.00
❑ 8785	I Need Your Help Barry Manilow/Daydream Romance	1979	—	2.00	4.00
❑ 8785 [PS]	I Need Your Help Barry Manilow/Daydream Romance	1979	—	3.00	6.00
❑ 8849	The Feeling's Not Right Again/Get Crazy with Me	1979	—	2.00	4.00

STEVENSON, B.W.

Number	Title (A Side/B Side)	Yr	VG	VG+	NM
MCA					
❑ 41151	A Special Wish/Holding a Special Place for You	1979	—	2.00	4.00
❑ 41166	Headin' Home/Holding a Special Place for You	1980	—	2.00	4.00
PRIVATE STOCK					
❑ 45208	Holdin' On for Dear Love/I'm a Better Man for Lovin' You	1979	—	2.00	4.00
RCA VICTOR					
❑ APBO-0030	My Maria/August Evening Lady	1973	—	3.00	6.00
❑ APBO-0171	River of Love/Lucky Touch	1973	—	2.50	5.00
❑ APBO-0242	Song for Katy/Look for the Light	1974	—	2.00	4.00
❑ APBO-0279	Remember Me/Roll On	1974	—	2.00	4.00
❑ PB-10012	Here We Go Again/Little Bit of Understanding	1974	—	2.00	4.00
❑ GB-10158	My Maria/Shambala	1975	—	—	3.00
—Gold Standard Series					
❑ 47-0728	Say What I Feel/Lonesome Song	1972	—	2.50	5.00
❑ 47-0778	On My Own/Highway One	1972	—	2.50	5.00
❑ 47-0840	Minuet for My Lady/Don't Go to Mexico	1972	—	2.50	5.00
❑ 47-0952	Shambala/My Feet Are So Weary	1973	—	3.00	6.00
WARNER BROS.					
❑ 8184	Jerrry's Bar and Grill/Way Down by the Ocean	1976	—	2.00	4.00
❑ 8247	Dream Baby/Wastin' Time	1976	—	2.00	4.00
❑ 8343	Down to the Station/May You Find Yourself in Heaven	1977	—	2.00	4.00

STEWART, AL

Number	Title (A Side/B Side)	Yr	VG	VG+	NM
ARISTA					
❑ 0362	Time Passages/Almost Lucy	1978	—	2.00	4.00
❑ 0389	Song on the Radio/A Man for All Seasons	1979	—	2.00	4.00
❑ 0552	Midnight Rocks/Constantinople	1980	—	2.00	4.00
❑ 0576	Paint by Numbers/Optical Illusion	1980	—	2.00	4.00
❑ 0585	Running Man/Merlin's Theme	1981	—	2.00	4.00
❑ 0639	Indian Summer/Soko (Needless to Say)	1981	—	2.00	4.00
JANUS					
❑ 243	Nostradamus/Terminal Eyes	1974	—	2.50	5.00
❑ 250	Carol/Sirens of Titan	1975	—	2.50	5.00
❑ 266	Year of the Cat/Broadway Hotel	1976	—	2.50	5.00
❑ 267	On the Border/Flying Sorcery	1977	—	2.50	5.00

STEWART, AMII

Number	Title (A Side/B Side)	Yr	VG	VG+	NM
ARIOLA AMERICA					
❑ 7736	Knock on Wood/When You Are Beautiful	1979	—	2.50	5.00
❑ 7753	Light My Fire-137 Disco Heaven/Am I Losing	1979	—	2.00	4.00
❑ 7771	Jealousy/Step Into the Love Line	1979	—	2.00	4.00
EMERGENCY					
❑ 4548	Friends/Picture	1985	—	2.00	4.00
HANDSHAKE					
❑ 02441	Why'd You Have to Be So Sexy/Where Did Our Love Go	1981	—	2.00	4.00
❑ 02591	I'm Gonna Get Your Love/Premier	1981	—	2.00	4.00
❑ 02844	Digital Love/Tonight	1982	—	2.00	4.00
❑ 5300	My Guy-My Girl/(B-side unknown)	1980	—	2.00	4.00
—With Johnny Bristol					

STEWART, ANDY

Number	Title (A Side/B Side)	Yr	VG	VG+	NM
CAPITOL					
❑ 4809	The Road and the Miles to Dundee/Take Me Back	1962	2.50	5.00	10.00
WARWICK					
❑ 627	The Scottish Soldier/The Muckin' O' Georgie's Brye	1961	3.00	6.00	12.00
❑ 665	Donald Where's Your Troosers?/The Battle's Over	1961	3.00	6.00	12.00
❑ 676	The Road and the Miles to Dundee/Take Me Back	1962	3.00	6.00	12.00

STEWART, BILLY

Number	Title (A Side/B Side)	Yr	VG	VG+	NM
ARGO					
❑ 5256	Billy's Blues (Part 1)/Billy's Blues (Part 2)	1956	10.00	20.00	40.00
CHESS					
❑ 1625	Billy's Blues (Part 1)/Billy's Blues (Part 2)	1956	15.00	30.00	60.00
❑ 1820	Reap What You Sow/Fat Boy	1962	3.00	6.00	12.00
❑ 1835	True Fine Lovin'/Wedding Bells	1962	3.00	6.00	12.00
❑ 1852	Scramble/Oh What Can the Matter Be	1963	3.00	6.00	12.00
❑ 1868	Strange Feeling/Sugar and Spice	1963	3.00	6.00	12.00
❑ 1888	Count Me Out/A Fat Boy Can Cry	1964	2.50	5.00	10.00
❑ 1905	Tell It Like It Is/My Sweet Senorita	1964	2.50	5.00	10.00
❑ 1922	I Do Love You/Keep Loving	1965	2.50	5.00	10.00
❑ 1932	Sitting in the Park/Once Again	1965	2.50	5.00	10.00
❑ 1941	How Nice It Is/No Girl	1965	2.50	5.00	10.00
❑ 1948	Because I Love You/Mountain of Love	1965	2.50	5.00	10.00
❑ 1960	Love Me/Why Am I Lonely	1966	2.50	5.00	10.00
❑ 1966	Summertime/To Love, To Love	1966	3.75	7.50	15.00
—Black label					
❑ 1966	Summertime/To Love, To Love	1966	3.00	6.00	12.00
—Blueish label					
❑ 1978	Secret Love/Look Back and Smile	1966	2.50	5.00	10.00
❑ 1991	Every Day I Have the Blues/Ol' Man River	1967	2.50	5.00	10.00
❑ 2002	Cross My Heart/Why (Do I Love You So)	1967	2.50	5.00	10.00
❑ 2053	Tell Me the Truth/What Have I Done	1968	2.50	5.00	10.00
❑ 2063	I'm in Love (Oh Yes I Am)/Crazy 'Bout You Baby	1969	2.50	5.00	10.00
❑ 2080	By the Time I Get to Phoenix/We'll Always Be Together	1969	2.50	5.00	10.00
OKEH					
❑ 7095	Baby, You're My Only Love/Billy's Heartache	1957	75.00	150.00	300.00
UNITED ARTISTS					
❑ 340	This Is a Fine Time/Young in Years	1961	3.75	7.50	15.00

STEWART, DANNY

See SLY STEWART.

STEWART, JOHN

Also see THE KINGSTON TRIO.

Number	Title (A Side/B Side)	Yr	VG	VG+	NM
ALLEGIANCE					
❑ 3900	The Queen of Hollywood High/Judy in G Major	198?	—	2.00	4.00
CAPITOL					
❑ 2469	Mother Country/Shackles and Chains	1969	—	3.00	6.00
❑ 2538	July, You're a Woman/She Believes in Me	1969	—	3.00	6.00
❑ 2605	Armstrong/Anna on a Memory	1969	—	3.00	6.00
❑ 2711	Earth Rider/The Lady and the Outlaw	1969	—	3.00	6.00
❑ 2712	World of No Return/Wild Is Love	1969	2.00	4.00	8.00
—B-side by Patti Drew					
❑ 2842	Clack Clack/Marshall Wind	1970	—	3.00	6.00
RCA VICTOR					
❑ APBO-0109	Anna on a Memory/Wheatfield	1973	—	2.50	5.00
❑ PB-10003	July, You're a Woman/Runaway Fool of Love	1974	—	2.50	5.00
❑ PB-10227	Survivors/Josie	1975	—	2.50	5.00
❑ PB-10268	Survivors/Josie	1975	—	2.50	5.00
❑ 74-0970	Chilly Winds/Durango	1973	—	2.50	5.00
RSO					
❑ 894	Promise the Wind/Morning Thunder	1978	—	2.00	4.00
❑ 931	Gold/Comin' Out of Nowhere	1979	—	2.00	4.00
❑ 1000	Midnight Wind/Somewhere Down the Line	1979	—	2.00	4.00
❑ 1016	Lost Her in the Sun/Heart of the Dream	1979	—	2.00	4.00
❑ 1031	(Odin) Spirit of the Water/Love Has Tied My Wings	1980	—	2.00	4.00
VITA					
❑ 169	Rockin' Anna/Lorraine	1958	62.50	125.00	250.00
—As "Johnny Stewart"					
WARNER BROS.					
❑ 7525	Daydream Believer/Sweet Lizard	1971	—	2.50	5.00
❑ 7552	Light Come Shine/A Little Road and a Stone to Roll	1972	—	2.50	5.00
❑ 7592	An Accent of Halley's Comet/Arkansas Breakout	1972	—	2.50	5.00

STEWART, ROD

Also see JEFF BECK; FACES; PYTHON LEE JACKSON; SHOTGUN EXPRESS.

Number	Title (A Side/B Side)	Yr	VG	VG+	NM
GEFFEN					
❑ 28303	Twistin' the Night Away/Let's Get Small	1987	—	2.00	4.00
—B-side by Steve Martin					
❑ 28303 [PS]	Twistin' the Night Away/Let's Get Small	1987	—	2.00	4.00
MERCURY					
❑ 73009	Handbags and Gladrags/An Old Raincoat Won't Ever Let You Down	1970	2.50	5.00	10.00
❑ 73031	Handbags and Gladrags/Man of Constant Sorrow	1970	2.00	4.00	8.00
❑ 73095	It's All Over Now/Joe's Lament	1970	2.50	5.00	10.00
❑ 73115	Only a Hero/Gasoline Alley	1970	2.50	5.00	10.00
❑ 73156	Cut Across Shorty/Gasoline Alley	1970	2.50	5.00	10.00
❑ 73175	My Way of Giving/Lady Day	1971	—	3.00	6.00
❑ 73196	Country Comfort/Gasoline Alley	1971	—	3.00	6.00
❑ 73224	Maggie May/Reason to Believe	1971	—	3.00	6.00
❑ 73244	(I Know) I'm Losing You/Mandolin Wind	1971	—	2.50	5.00
❑ 73330	You Wear It Well/True Blue	1972	—	2.50	5.00
❑ 73330 [PS]	You Wear It Well/True Blue	1972	3.75	7.50	15.00
❑ 73344	Angel/Lost Paraguayos	1972	—	2.50	5.00
❑ 73412	Twistin' the Night Away//True Blue-Lady Day	1973	—	2.50	5.00
❑ 73412 [PS]	Twistin' the Night Away//True Blue-Lady Day	1973	—	3.00	6.00
❑ 73426	Oh No Not My Baby/Jodie	1973	—	2.50	5.00
❑ 73426 [PS]	Oh No Not My Baby/Jodie	1973	—	3.00	6.00
❑ 73636	Mine for Me/Farewell	1974	—	2.50	5.00
❑ 73660	Let Me Be Your Car/Sailor	1974	—	3.00	6.00
❑ 73802	Every Picture Tells a Story/What's Made Milwaukee Famous (Has Made a Loser Out of Me)	1976	—	2.50	5.00
PRESS					
❑ 9722	Good Morning Little Schoolgirl/I'm Gonna Move to the Outskirts of Town	1965	10.00	20.00	40.00
PRIVATE STOCK					
❑ 45130	Shake/Bright Lights, Big City	1976	—	3.00	6.00
WARNER BROS.					
❑ 8066	As Long As You Tell Him/You Can Make Me Dance, Sing or Anything	1975	—	2.50	5.00
—As "Rod Stewart and Faces"					
❑ 8102	As Long As You Tell Him/You Can Make Me Dance, Sing or Anything	1975	—	2.00	4.00
—As "Rod Stewart and Faces"					
❑ 8146	Sailing/All in the Name of Rock and Roll	1975	—	2.00	4.00
❑ 8170	This Old Heart of Mine/Still Love Again	1975	—	2.50	5.00
❑ 8262	Tonight's the Night (Gonna Be Alright)/Fool for You	1976	—	2.00	4.00
❑ 8321	The First Cut Is the Deepest/Ball Trap	1977	—	2.00	4.00
❑ 8396	The Killing of Georgie (Part 1 and 2)/Rosie	1977	—	2.00	4.00

Number	Title (A Side/B Side)	Yr	VG	VG+	NM
❑ 8475	You're In My Heart (The Final Acclaim)/You Got a Nerve	1977	—	2.00	4.00
❑ 8535	Hot Legs/You're Insane	1978	—	2.00	4.00
❑ 8535 [PS]	Hot Legs/You're Insane	1978	—	2.50	5.00
❑ 8568	I Was Only Joking/Born Loose	1978	—	2.00	4.00
❑ 8568 [PS]	I Was Only Joking/Born Loose	1978	—	2.50	5.00
❑ 8724	Da Ya Think I'm Sexy?/Scarred and Scared	1978	—	2.00	4.00
❑ 8724 [PS]	Da Ya Think I'm Sexy?/Scarred and Scared	1978	—	2.50	5.00
❑ 8810	Ain't Love a Bitch/Last Summer	1979	—	2.00	4.00
❑ 8810 [PS]	Ain't Love a Bitch/Last Summer	1979	—	2.50	5.00
❑ 15995	Broken Arrow/Downtown Train	1993	—	—	3.00
—"Back to Back Hits" series; only 45 release of A-side					
❑ 17195	Ooh La La/A Night Like This	1998	—	—	3.00
❑ 17459	If We Fall in Love Tonight/Tom Traubert's Blues (Waltzing Matilda)	1996	—	—	3.00
❑ 17847	Leave Virginia Alone/Shock to the System	1995	—	—	3.00
❑ 17854	This/The Groom's Still Waiting at the Altar	1995	—	—	3.00
❑ 18424	Having a Party/Sweet Little Rock and Roller	1993	—	—	3.00
❑ 18427	Reason to Believe/It's All Over Now	1993	—	—	3.00
❑ 18511	Have I Told You Lately/Gasoline Alley	1993	—	2.00	4.00
❑ 19322	The Motown Song/Sweet Soul Marie	1991	—	—	3.00
❑ 19366	Rhythm of My Heart/Moment of Glory	1991	—	—	3.00
❑ 19983	This Old Heart of Mine/You're In My Heart	1990	—	—	3.00
❑ 22685	Downtown Train/The Killing of Georgie (Part 1 and 2)	1989	—	—	3.00
❑ 22685 [PS]	Downtown Train/The Killing of Georgie (Part 1 and 2)	1989	—	3.00	6.00
❑ 27657	Crazy About Her/Dynamite	1989	—	—	3.00
❑ 27729	My Heart Can't Tell You No/The Wild Horse	1988	—	—	3.00
❑ 27729 [PS]	My Heart Can't Tell You No/The Wild Horse	1988	—	—	3.00
❑ 27796	Forever Young/Days of Rage	1988	—	—	3.00
❑ 27796 [PS]	Forever Young/Days of Rage	1988	—	—	3.00
❑ 27927	Lost in You/Almost Illegal	1988	—	—	3.00
❑ 27927 [PS]	Lost in You/Almost Illegal	1988	—	—	3.00
❑ 28625	Every Beat of My Heart/Trouble	1986	—	—	3.00
❑ 28625 [PS]	Every Beat of My Heart/Trouble	1986	—	—	3.00
❑ 28631	Another Heartache/You're In My Heart (The Final Acclaim)	1986	—	—	3.00
❑ 28631 [PS]	Another Heartache/You're In My Heart (The Final Acclaim)	1986	—	—	3.00
❑ 28668	Love Touch (Love Theme from Legal Eagles)/Heart Is on the Line	1986	—	—	3.00
❑ 28668 [PS]	Love Touch (Love Theme from Legal Eagles)/Heart Is on the Line	1986	—	—	3.00
❑ 29122	All Right Now/Dancin' Alone	1984	—	2.00	4.00
❑ 29215	Some Guys Have All the Luck/I Was Only Joking	1984	—	2.00	4.00
❑ 29215 [PS]	Some Guys Have All the Luck/I Was Only Joking	1984	—	2.00	4.00
❑ 29256	Infatuation/She Won't Dance with Me	1984	—	2.00	4.00
❑ 29256 [PS]	Infatuation/She Won't Dance with Me	1984	—	2.00	4.00
❑ 29564	What Am I Gonna Do (I'm So in Love with You)/Dancin' Alone	1983	—	2.00	4.00
❑ 29564 [PS]	What Am I Gonna Do (I'm So in Love with You)/Dancin' Alone	1983	—	2.00	4.00
❑ 29608	Baby Jane/Ready Now	1983	—	2.00	4.00
❑ 29874	Guess I'll Always Love You/Rock My Plimsoul	1982	—	2.00	4.00
❑ 29874 [PS]	Guess I'll Always Love You/Rock My Plimsoul	1982	—	2.50	5.00
❑ 49138	I Don't Want to Talk About It/Best Days of My Life	1979	—	2.00	4.00
❑ 49138 [PS]	I Don't Want to Talk About It/Best Days of My Life	1979	—	2.50	5.00
❑ 49617	Passion/Better Off Dead	1980	—	2.00	4.00
❑ 49617 [PS]	Passion/Better Off Dead	1980	—	2.50	5.00
❑ 49686	Somebody Special/She Won't Dance with Me	1981	—	2.00	4.00
❑ 49843	Young Turks/Sonny	1981	—	2.00	4.00
❑ 49843 [PS]	Young Turks/Sonny	1981	—	2.50	5.00
❑ 49886	Tonight I'm Yours (Don't Hurt Me)/Tora, Tora, Tora	1981	—	2.00	4.00
❑ 49886 [PS]	Tonight I'm Yours (Don't Hurt Me)/Tora, Tora, Tora	1981	—	2.50	5.00
❑ 50051	How Long/Jealous	1982	—	2.00	4.00
❑ 50051 [PS]	How Long/Jealous	1982	—	2.50	5.00

7-Inch Extended Plays

MERCURY

Number	Title (A Side/B Side)	Yr	VG	VG+	NM
❑ MEPL-28 [DJ]	I'd Rather Go Blind/What's Made Milwaukee Famous//Italian Girls/Twistin' the Night Away	1972	2.50	5.00	10.00
❑ MEPL-28 [PS]	(title unknown)	1972	2.50	5.00	10.00

STEWART, SLY

Sylvester Stewart, later "Sly" of SLY AND THE FAMILY STONE.

Number	Title (A Side/B Side)	Yr	VG	VG+	NM
AUTUMN					
❑ 3	I Just Learned How to Swim/Scat Swim	1964	5.00	10.00	20.00
—Sylvester Stewart, later "Sly" of The Family Stone					
❑ 14	Buttermilk — Part 1/Buttermilk — Part 2	1965	5.00	10.00	20.00
—As "Sly"					
❑ 26	Temptation Walk/Temptation Walk — Part 2	1966	5.00	10.00	20.00
A&M					
❑ 2890	Eek-Ah-Bo-Static Automatic/Black Girls	1986	—	—	3.00
—B-side by Rae Dawn Chong					
❑ 2896	Love and Affection/Black Girls	1986	—	—	3.00
—A-side as "Sly Stone and Martha Davis"; B-side by Rae Dawn Chong					
EPIC					
❑ 50795	Dance to the Music/Sing a Simple Song	1979	—	2.50	5.00
—As "Sly Stone"					
G&P					
❑ 901	Help Me With My Heart/A Long Time Away	1962	62.50	125.00	250.00
—As "Sylvester Stewart"					
LUKE					
❑ 1008	A Long Time Alone/I'm Just a Fool	1961	62.50	125.00	250.00
—As "Danny Stewart"					

STEWART, VERNON

Number	Title (A Side/B Side)	Yr	VG	VG+	NM
BLU-J					
❑ 304	Christmas Tree in Heaven/Down to the Blues	196?	2.50	5.00	10.00
CHART					
❑ 501	The Way It Feels to Die/You're Not All Here	1962	3.75	7.50	15.00
PEACH					
❑ 740	I'm Tired of Make Believe/I'll Still Love You	1961	6.25	12.50	25.00
❑ 751	Mean, Mean Baby/Heal This Old Heart	1961	15.00	30.00	60.00

STEWART BROTHERS, THE

Number	Title (A Side/B Side)	Yr	VG	VG+	NM
ENSIGN					
❑ 4032	The Rat/Ra Ra Roo	1959	25.00	50.00	100.00
KEEN					
❑ 2113	Sleep on the Porch/Yum Yum	1960	25.00	50.00	100.00

STILLROVEN, THE

Number	Title (A Side/B Side)	Yr	VG	VG+	NM
AUGUST					
❑ 101	Little Picture Playhouse/Cast Thy Burden Upon the Stone	1968	6.25	12.50	25.00
❑ 102	Necessary Person/Come in the Morning	1968	25.00	50.00	100.00
❑ 102	Necessary Person/Have You Ever Seen Me	1968	6.25	12.50	25.00
FALCON					
❑ 69	Hey Joe/Sunny Day	1967	12.50	25.00	50.00
❑ 7296	She's Your Woman/I'm Not Your Steppin' Stone	1966	50.00	100.00	200.00
ROULETTE					
❑ 4748	Hey Joe/Sunny Day	1967	3.75	7.50	15.00

STILLS, STEPHEN

Also see BUFFALO SPRINGFIELD; CROSBY, STILLS AND NASH; CROSBY, STILLS, NASH AND YOUNG; THE STILLS-YOUNG BAND.

Number	Title (A Side/B Side)	Yr	VG	VG+	NM
ATLANTIC					
❑ 2778	Love the One You're With/To a Flame	1970	—	3.00	6.00
❑ 2790	Sit Yourself Down/We Are Not Helpless	1971	—	2.50	5.00
❑ 2806	Change Partners/Relaxing Town	1971	—	2.50	5.00
❑ 2806 [PS]	Change Partners/Relaxing Town	1971	—	3.00	6.00
❑ 2820	Marianne/Nothin' to Do But Today	1971	—	2.50	5.00
❑ 2876	It Doesn't Matter/Rock & Roll's Crazy Medley	1972	—	2.50	5.00
❑ 2888	Rock and Roll Crazies/Colorado	1972	—	2.50	5.00
—With Manassas					
❑ 2917	Down the Road/Guaguanco De Vero	1972	—	2.50	5.00
—With Manassas					
❑ 2959	So Many Times/Isn't It About Time	1973	—	2.50	5.00
❑ 89597	Only Love Can Break Your Heart/Love Again	1984	—	2.00	4.00
❑ 89611	Can't Let Go/Grey to Green	1984	—	2.00	4.00
—With Walter Finnegan					
❑ 89633	Stranger/No Hiding Place	1984	—	2.00	4.00
❑ 89633 [PS]	Stranger/No Hiding Place	1984	—	2.00	4.00
COLUMBIA					
❑ 10179	Turn Back the Pages/Shuffle Just as Bad	1975	—	2.50	5.00
❑ 10369	Buyin' Time/Soldier	1976	—	2.50	5.00
❑ 10804	Lowdown/Can't Get No Booty	1978	—	2.50	5.00
❑ 10872	Thoroughfare Gap/Lowdown	1978	—	2.50	5.00

STILLS-YOUNG BAND, THE

STEPHEN STILLS and NEIL YOUNG.

Number	Title (A Side/B Side)	Yr	VG	VG+	NM
REPRISE					
❑ 1365	Long May You Run//12/8 Blues (All the Same)	1976	—	3.00	6.00
❑ 1378	Midnight on the Bay/Black Coral	1976	—	2.50	5.00

STING

Also see THE POLICE.

Number	Title (A Side/B Side)	Yr	VG	VG+	NM
ARK 21					
❑ S7-19939	This Was Never Meant to Be/This Was Never Meant to Be (Shellac Mix)	1998	—	2.00	4.00
—B-side by Anne Dudley					
A&M					
❑ 31458 0530 7	Shape of My Heart/If I Ever Lose My Faith in You	1994	—	—	3.00
❑ 31458 0838 7	When We Dance/Fields of Gold	1994	—	—	3.00
❑ 1200	Englishman in New York/If You're There	1988	—	—	3.00
❑ 1200 [PS]	Englishman in New York/If You're There	1988	—	—	3.00
❑ 1211	Fragile/Gragilidad	1988	—	—	3.00
❑ 1242	They Dance Alone (Gueca Solo)/They Dance Alone (Gueca Solo)	1988	—	—	3.00
❑ 75021 1541 7	All This Time/I Miss You Kate	1991	—	2.00	4.00
❑ 31458 1582 7	You Still Touch Me/Let Your Soul Be Your Pilot	1996	—	—	2.00
❑ 31458 1582 7 [PS]	You Still Touch Me/Let Your Soul Be Your Pilot	1996	—	—	2.00
❑ 31458 1982 7	I'm So Happy I Can't Stop Crying/This Was Never Meant to Be	1996	—	—	3.00
❑ 2501	Spread a Little Happiness/Only You	1982	—	2.00	4.00
❑ 2738	If You Love Somebody Set Them Free/Another Day	1985	—	2.00	4.00
—Blue custom label					
❑ 2738	If You Love Somebody Set Them Free/Another Day	1985	—	—	3.00
—Normal red and black label					
❑ 2738 [PS]	If You Love Somebody Set Them Free/Another Day	1985	—	—	3.00
❑ 2765	If You Love Somebody Set Them Free/Another Day	1985	—	2.50	5.00
❑ 2765 [PS]	If You Love Somebody Set Them Free/Another Day	1985	—	2.50	5.00
❑ 2767	Fortress Around Your Heart/Consider Me Gone	1985	—	—	3.00
❑ 2767 [PS]	Fortress Around Your Heart/Consider Me Gone	1985	—	—	3.00
❑ 2787	Love Is the Seventh Wave/The Dream of the Blue Turtles	1985	—	—	3.00
❑ 2787 [PS]	Love Is the Seventh Wave/The Dream of the Blue Turtles	1985	—	—	3.00
❑ 2799	Russians/Gabriel's Message	1985	—	—	3.00
❑ 2799 [PS]	Russians/Gabriel's Message	1985	—	—	3.00
❑ 2983	We'll Be Together/Conversation with a Dog	1987	—	—	3.00
❑ 2983 [PS]	We'll Be Together/Conversation with a Dog	1987	—	—	3.00
❑ 2992	Be Still My Beating Heart/Ghost in the Strand	1987	—	—	3.00
❑ 2992 [PS]	Be Still My Beating Heart/Ghost in the Strand	1987	—	—	3.00

Number	Title (A Side/B Side)	Yr	VG	VG+	NM
❑ 8655	If You Love Somebody Set Them Free/Fortress Around Your Heart	198?	—	—	3.00
—Reissue					
❑ 8656	Love Is the Seventh Wave/Russians	198?	—	—	3.00
—Reissue					
❑ 8722	All This Time/Be Still My Beating Heart	199?	—	—	3.00
—Reissue					
❑ 8723	The Soul Cages/Why Should I Cry for You?	199?	—	—	3.00
—Reissue series; first appearance on U.S. 45 for both sides					
❑ 8740	Shape of My Heart/If I Ever Lose My Faith in You	1996	—	—	3.00
—Reissue					
❑ 069 497214 7	Brand New Day/I'm So Happy I Can't Stop Crying	1999	—	—	3.00
❑ 069 497404 7	Desert Rose/After the Rain Has Fallen	2000	—	—	3.00

STINIT, DANE

SUN

Number	Title (A Side/B Side)	Yr	VG	VG+	NM
❑ 402	Always on the Go/Don't Knock What You Don't Understand	1966	3.75	7.50	15.00
❑ 405	Sweet Country Girl/That Muddy Ole River	1967	3.75	7.50	15.00

STITES, GARY

CARLTON

Number	Title (A Side/B Side)	Yr	VG	VG+	NM
❑ 508	Lonely for You/Shine That Ring	1959	5.00	10.00	20.00
❑ 516	A Girl Like You/Hey Little Girl	1959	5.00	10.00	20.00
❑ 521	Starry Eyed/Without Your Love	1959	5.00	10.00	20.00
❑ 525	Lawdy Miss Clawdy/Don't Wanna Say Goodbye	1960	5.00	10.00	20.00
❑ 529	Gloria Lee/Hey, Hey	1960	5.00	10.00	20.00

EPIC

Number	Title (A Side/B Side)	Yr	VG	VG+	NM
❑ 10064	Hurting/Thinking of You	1966	3.00	6.00	12.00

MADISON

Number	Title (A Side/B Side)	Yr	VG	VG+	NM
❑ 138	Young Love/Little Tear	1960	3.75	7.50	15.00
❑ 155	Honey Girl/Little Lonely One	1961	3.75	7.50	15.00

MR. PEEKE

Number	Title (A Side/B Side)	Yr	VG	VG+	NM
❑ 122	You Doubted Me/Only a Fool Would Say	1962	3.75	7.50	15.00

STOECKLEIN, VAL

DOT

Number	Title (A Side/B Side)	Yr	VG	VG+	NM
❑ 17200	Sounds of Yesterday/Say It's Not Over	1969	3.75	7.50	15.00
❑ 17234	All the Way Home/I Wonder Who I'll Be Tomorrow	1969	3.75	7.50	15.00

STOMPERS, THE

GONE

Number	Title (A Side/B Side)	Yr	VG	VG+	NM
❑ 5120	Stompin' Round the Christmas Tree/Forgive Me	1961	37.50	75.00	150.00

LANDA

Number	Title (A Side/B Side)	Yr	VG	VG+	NM
❑ 684	Foolish One/Quarter to Four Stomp	1962	6.25	12.50	25.00
❑ 684	Foolish One/Surf Stompin'	1962	6.25	12.50	25.00

MERCURY

Number	Title (A Side/B Side)	Yr	VG	VG+	NM
❑ 72111	Frump/Blacksmith Blues	1963	3.75	7.50	15.00
—As "The Ski Stompers"					

SOUVENIR

Number	Title (A Side/B Side)	Yr	VG	VG+	NM
❑ 1003	I Miss You So/Blue Moon of Kentucky	1960	25.00	50.00	100.00

STONE, JIMMY

CROSS COUNTRY

Number	Title (A Side/B Side)	Yr	VG	VG+	NM
❑ 523	Found/Mine	1956	75.00	150.00	300.00

GONE

Number	Title (A Side/B Side)	Yr	VG	VG+	NM
❑ 5001	Found/Mine	1957	50.00	100.00	200.00

STONE, SLY

See SLY STEWART.

STONE PONEYS

Also see LINDA RONSTADT.

CAPITOL

Number	Title (A Side/B Side)	Yr	VG	VG+	NM
❑ 2004	Different Drum/I've Got to Know	1967	3.75	7.50	15.00
❑ 2110	Up to My Neck in High Muddy Water/Carnival Bear	1968	2.50	5.00	10.00
❑ 2110 [PS]	Up to My Neck in High Muddy Water/Carnival Bear	1968	10.00	20.00	40.00
—By "Linda Ronstadt and the Stone Poneys"					
❑ 2195	Hobo (Mornin' Glory)/Some of Shelly's Blues	1968	2.50	5.00	10.00
❑ 5838	All the Beautiful Things/Sweet Summer Blue and Gold	1967	2.50	5.00	10.00
❑ 5910	One for One/Evergreen	1967	2.50	5.00	10.00

SIDEWALK

Number	Title (A Side/B Side)	Yr	VG	VG+	NM
❑ 937	So Fine/Everyone Has Their Own Ideas	1968	50.00	100.00	200.00

STONES, THE

SOLLY

Number	Title (A Side/B Side)	Yr	VG	VG+	NM
❑ 928	She Said Yeah/Watch Me	1966	6.25	12.50	25.00
—Reissued with group renamed "The Tracers"					

STONEY AND MEATLOAF

Also see MEAT LOAF.

RARE EARTH

Number	Title (A Side/B Side)	Yr	VG	VG+	NM
❑ 5027	What You See Is What You Get/Lady Be Mine	1971	—	3.00	6.00
❑ 5033	The Way You Do the Things You Do/It Takes All Kinds of People	1971	—	3.00	6.00

STOOKEY, PAUL

Also see PETER, PAUL AND MARY.

BENSON

Number	Title (A Side/B Side)	Yr	VG	VG+	NM
❑ 5616 [DJ]	For Christmas (same on both sides)	198?	—	2.00	4.00
—As "Noel Paul Stookey and the Bodyworks Band"					
❑ 5616 [PS]	For Christmas (same on both sides)	198?	—	2.00	4.00

WARNER BROS.

Number	Title (A Side/B Side)	Yr	VG	VG+	NM
❑ 7511	Wedding Song (There Is Love)/Give a Damn	1971	—	3.00	6.00
—Of Peter, Paul and Mary					
❑ 7602	Hey, Sad Sack/Sebastian	1972	—	2.50	5.00
❑ 7683	Funky Monkey (Part 1)/Blessed	1973	—	2.50	5.00
—As "Noel Paul Stookey"					

STORIES

KAMA SUTRA

Number	Title (A Side/B Side)	Yr	VG	VG+	NM
❑ 545	I'm Coming Home/You Told Me	1972	—	2.00	4.00
❑ 558	Top of the City/Stepback	1972	—	2.00	4.00
❑ 566	Darling/Take Cover	1972	—	2.00	4.00
❑ 574	Love in Motion/Changes Have Begun	1973	—	2.00	4.00
❑ 577	Brother Louie/Changes Have Begun	1973	—	3.00	6.00
❑ 577	Brother Louie/What Comes After	1973	—	2.50	5.00
❑ 584	Mammy Blue/Travelling Underground	1973	—	2.00	4.00
❑ 588	Circles/If It Feels Good	1974	—	2.00	4.00
❑ 594	Another Love/Love Is In Motion	1974	—	2.00	4.00

STORM, GALE

DOT

Number	Title (A Side/B Side)	Yr	VG	VG+	NM
❑ 15412	I Hear You Knocking/Never Leave Me	1955	5.00	10.00	20.00
❑ 15436	Teen-Age Prayer/Memories Are Made of This	1955	3.75	7.50	15.00
❑ 15448	Why Do Fools Fall in Love/I Walk Alone	1956	3.75	7.50	15.00
❑ 15458	Ivory Tower/I Ain't Gonna Worry	1956	3.75	7.50	15.00
❑ 15474	Tell Me Why/Don't Be That Way	1956	3.75	7.50	15.00
❑ 15492	Now Is the Hour/A Heart Without a Sweetheart	1956	3.75	7.50	15.00
—Originals have maroon labels					
❑ 15492	Now Is the Hour/A Heart Without a Sweetheart	1956	2.50	5.00	10.00
—Second pressings have black labels					
❑ 15515	My Heart Belongs to You/Orange Blossoms	1956	2.50	5.00	10.00
❑ 15528	I Need You So/On Treasure Island	1957	2.50	5.00	10.00
❑ 15539	On Treasure Island/Lucky Lips	1957	2.50	5.00	10.00
❑ 15558	Dark Moon/A Little Too Late	1957	2.50	5.00	10.00
❑ 15606	On My Mind Again/Love by the Jukebox Light	1957	2.50	5.00	10.00
❑ 15666	Go 'Way from My Window/Winter Warm	1957	2.50	5.00	10.00
❑ 15691	A Farewell to Arms/I Get That Feeling	1958	2.50	5.00	10.00
❑ 15734	Angry/You	1958	2.50	5.00	10.00
❑ 15783	South of the Border/Soon I'll Wed My Love	1958	2.50	5.00	10.00
❑ 15861	Oh, Lonely Crowd/Happiness Left Yesterday	1958	2.50	5.00	10.00
❑ 16031	I Hear You Knocking/Ivory Tower	1960	2.00	4.00	8.00
❑ 16032	Dark Moon/Memories Are Made of This	1960	2.00	4.00	8.00
❑ 16057	On Treasure Island/I Need You So	1960	2.00	4.00	8.00
❑ 16111	Please Help Me, I'm Falling/He's There	1960	2.00	4.00	8.00

STORM, RORY, AND THE HURRICANES

The group that Ringo Starr drummed for before joining the Beatles. He is not on this record.

COLUMBIA

Number	Title (A Side/B Side)	Yr	VG	VG+	NM
❑ 43018	I Can Tell/Let's Stomp	1964	6.25	12.50	25.00
—B-side by Faron's Flamingos					

STORM, TOM, AND THE PEPS

GE GE

Number	Title (A Side/B Side)	Yr	VG	VG+	NM
❑ 501	I Love You/That's the Way Love Is	1965	7.50	15.00	30.00

STORME, ROBB

AURORA

Number	Title (A Side/B Side)	Yr	VG	VG+	NM
❑ 162	Here Today/Don't Cry	1966	3.00	6.00	12.00

CAPITOL

Number	Title (A Side/B Side)	Yr	VG	VG+	NM
❑ 5452	Love Is Strange/Shy Guy	1965	2.50	5.00	10.00

STORMS, THE

Also see JODY REYNOLDS.

SUNDOWN

Number	Title (A Side/B Side)	Yr	VG	VG+	NM
❑ 114	Thunder/Tarantula	1959	12.50	25.00	50.00
—This was re-recorded on Indigo 127					

STORYTELLERS, THE

CAPITOL

Number	Title (A Side/B Side)	Yr	VG	VG+	NM
❑ 5042	I Don't Want an Angel/Down in the Valley	1964	6.25	12.50	25.00

CLASSIC ARTISTS

Number	Title (A Side/B Side)	Yr	VG	VG+	NM
❑ 137	Christmas Time Is Coming/White Christmas	1990	—	2.50	5.00
—B-side by The Storytellers and Vicky Tafoya					

DIMENSION

Number	Title (A Side/B Side)	Yr	VG	VG+	NM
❑ 1014	When Two People/Time Will Tell	1963	5.00	10.00	20.00

RAMARCA

Number	Title (A Side/B Side)	Yr	VG	VG+	NM
❑ 501	When Two People/Time Will Tell	1963	7.50	15.00	30.00

STACK

Number	Title (A Side/B Side)	Yr	VG	VG+	NM
❑ 500	Hey Baby/You Played Me for a Fool	1959	50.00	100.00	200.00

STRAIT, GEORGE

MCA

Number	Title (A Side/B Side)	Yr	VG	VG+	NM
❑ S45-17234 [DJ]	Merry Christmas Strait to You/White Christmas	1986	5.00	10.00	20.00
—Promo only on red vinyl					
❑ S45-17451 [DJ]	For Christ's Sake, It's Christmas/When It's Christmas Time in Texas	1987	3.75	7.50	15.00
—Promo only on white vinyl					
❑ 51104	Unwound/She's Playing Hell Trying to Get Me to Heaven	1981	—	2.00	4.00
❑ 51170	Down and Out/Blame It on Mexico	1981	—	2.00	4.00
❑ 51228	If You're Thinking You Want a Stranger (There's One Coming Home)/Her Goodbye Hit Me in the Heart	1982	—	2.00	4.00
❑ 52066	Fool Hearted Memory/Steal of the Night	1982	—	2.00	4.00
❑ 52120	Marina Del Rey/I Can't See Texas from Here	1982	—	2.00	4.00
❑ 52162	Amarillo by Morning/Lover in Disguise	1983	—	2.00	4.00
❑ 52225	A Fire I Can't Put Out/Honky Tonk Crazy	1983	—	2.00	4.00
❑ 52279	You Look So Good in Love/A Little Heaven's Rubbing Off on Me	1983	—	2.00	4.00
❑ 52337	Right or Wrong/Fifteen Years Going Up (And One Night Going Down)	1984	—	—	3.00
❑ 52392	Let's Fall to Pieces Together/You're the Cloud I'm On (When I'm High)	1984	—	—	3.00
❑ 52458	Does Fort Worth Ever Cross Your Mind/Love Comes from the Other Side of Town	1984	—	—	3.00
❑ 52526	The Cowboy Rides Away/Any Old Time	1985	—	—	3.00
❑ 52586	The Fireman/What Did You Expect Me to Do	1985	—	—	3.00
❑ 52667	The Chair/In Too Deep	1985	—	—	3.00
❑ 52667 [DJ]	The Chair (same on both sides)	1985	3.75	7.50	15.00
—Promo only on blue vinyl					

Number	Title (A Side/B Side)	Yr	VG	VG+	NM
❑ 52667 [PS]	The Chair/In Too Deep	1985	—	2.50	5.00
❑ 52764	You're Something Special to Me/Dance Time in Texas	1986	—	—	3.00
❑ 52817	Nobody in His Right Mind Would've Left Her/You Still Get to Me	1986	—	—	3.00
❑ 52914	It Ain't Cool to Be Crazy About You/Rhythm of the Road	1986	—	—	3.00
❑ 53021	Ocean Front Property/My Heart Won't Wander Very Far from You	1987	—	2.00	4.00
❑ 53021 [DJ]	Ocean Front Property (same on both sides)	1987	3.75	7.50	15.00
—Promo only on yellow vinyl					
❑ 53087	All My Ex's Live in Texas/I'm All Behind You Now	1987	—	2.00	4.00
❑ 53087 [DJ]	All My Ex's Live in Texas (same on both sides)	1987	3.75	7.50	15.00
—Promo only on yellow vinyl					
❑ 53165	Am I Blue/Someone's Walkin' Around Upstairs	1987	—	—	3.00
❑ 53165 [DJ]	Am I Blue (same on both sides)	1987	3.75	7.50	15.00
—Promo only on blue vinyl					
❑ 53248	Famous Last Words of a Fool/It's Too Late Now	1988	—	—	3.00
❑ 53340	Baby Blue/Back to Bein' Me	1988	—	—	3.00
❑ 53400	If You Ain't Lovin' (You Ain't Livin')/Is It That Time Again	1988	—	—	3.00
❑ 53486	Baby's Gotten Good at Goodbye/Bigger Man Than Me	1988	—	—	3.00
❑ 53648	What's Going On in Your World/Let's Get Down to It	1989	—	—	3.00
❑ 53693	Ace in the Hole/Oh Me, Oh My Sweet Baby	1989	—	2.50	5.00
❑ 53755	Overnight Success/Hollywood Squares	1989	—	2.00	4.00
❑ 53969	I've Come to Expect It from You/Stranger in My Arms	1990	—	2.00	4.00
❑ 54052	If I Know Me/Home in San Antone	1991	—	2.00	4.00
❑ 54127	You Know Me Better Than That/Baby Blue	1991	—	2.00	4.00
❑ 54180	The Chill of an Early Fall/Her Only Bad Habit Is Me	1991	—	2.00	4.00
❑ 54277	Drinking Champagne (A Toast to the Battlin' Bucs)/(B-side unknown)	1991	—	—	3.00
—Reissue of 79070 with new subtitle					
❑ 54318	Lovesick Blues/Is It Already Time	1992	—	—	3.00
❑ 54379	Gone as a Girl Can Get/Faults and All	1992	—	2.00	4.00
❑ 54439	So Much Like My Dad/Wonderland of Love	1992	—	2.00	4.00
❑ 54478	I Cross My Heart/You're Right I'm Wrong	1992	—	2.50	5.00
❑ 54563	Heartland/Baby Your Baby	1993	—	2.00	4.00
❑ 54642	When Did You Stop Loving Me/Where the Sidewalk Ends	1993	—	2.00	4.00
❑ 54717	Easy Come, Easy Go/She Lays It All on the Line	1993	—	2.00	4.00
❑ 54767	I'd Like to Have That One Back/That's Where My Baby Feels at Home	1993	—	2.00	4.00
❑ 54819	Love Bug/Just Look at Me	1994	—	2.00	4.00
❑ 54854	The Man in Love with You/We Must Be Loving Right	1994	—	2.00	4.00
❑ 54938	The Big One/No One But You	1994	—	2.00	4.00
❑ 54964	You Can't Make a Heart Love Somebody/What Am I Waiting For	1994	—	2.00	4.00
❑ 55019	Adalida/Down Louisiana Way	1995	—	2.00	4.00
❑ 55064	Lead On/I Met a Friend of Yours Today	1995	—	2.00	4.00
❑ 55127	Check Yes or No/Fly Me to the Moon	1995	—	2.00	4.00
—B-side with Frank Sinatra					
❑ 55163	I Know She Still Loves Me/Unwound	1995	—	2.00	4.00
—B-side with Frank Sinatra					
❑ 55187	Blue Clear Sky/I Ain't Never Seen No One Like You	1996	—	2.00	4.00
❑ 55204	Carried Away/Do the Right Thing	1996	—	2.00	4.00
❑ 55248	I Can Still Make Cheyenne/Need I Say More	1996	—	—	3.00
❑ 55288	King of the Mountain/I'd Just As Soon Go	1996	—	—	3.00
❑ 55321	One Night at a Time/Won't You Come Home (And Talk to a Stranger)	1997	—	—	3.00
❑ 72007	Carrying Your Love with Me/I've Got a Funny Feeling	1997	—	—	3.00
❑ 72019	Today My World Slipped Away/Round About Way	1997	—	—	3.00
❑ 72028	Round About Way/She'll Leave You with a Smile	1997	—	—	3.00
❑ 72046	I Just Want to Dance with You/Neon Row	1998	—	—	3.00
❑ 79015	Love Without End, Amen/Too Much of Too Little	1990	—	2.50	5.00
❑ 79070	Drinking Champagne/We're Supposed to Do That Now and Then	1990	—	2.50	5.00
MCA NASHVILLE					
❑ 72063	True/Remember the Alamo	1998	—	—	3.00
❑ 72071	We Really Shouldn't Be Doing This/Maria	1998	—	—	3.00
❑ 72084	Meanwhile/You Haven't Left Me Yet	1999	—	—	3.00
❑ 72095	Write This Down/4 Minus 3 Equals Zero	1999	—	—	3.00
❑ 72108	What Do You Say to That/4 Minus 3 Equals Zero	1999	—	—	3.00
❑ 088 172147 7	The Best Day/I Can Still Make Cheyenne	2000	—	—	3.00
❑ 088 172169 7	Go On/Murder on Music Row (a Duet with Alan Jackson)	2000	—	—	3.00
❑ 088 172194 7	Don't Make Me Come Over There and Love You/You're Stronger Than Me	2000	—	—	3.00
STRANGE, TOMMY					
ERA					
❑ 3157	Don't Bug Me Baby/Two Steps Forward	1965	2.00	4.00	8.00
RAMCO					
❑ 1986	Piano Man from Louisiana/My Mind Just Don't Fit My Head	1967	2.00	4.00	8.00
❑ 1995	She Was Never Mine to Lose/One More Time	1967	2.00	4.00	8.00
ROCKO					
❑ 504	Nervous and Shakin' All Over/What Am I to Do	1958	50.00	100.00	200.00
STRANGEBREW					
ABC					
❑ 11217	Union Man/I Can Hardly Wait to Live	1969	3.00	6.00	12.00
STRANGELOVES, THE					
Also see THE SHEEP.					
BANG					
❑ 501	I Want Candy/It's About My Baby	1965	3.75	7.50	15.00
❑ 508	Cara-Lin/(Roll On) Mississippi	1965	3.00	6.00	12.00

Number	Title (A Side/B Side)	Yr	VG	VG+	NM
❑ 514	Night Time/Rhythm of Love	1965	3.00	6.00	12.00
❑ 524	Hand Jive/I Gotta Dance	1966	3.00	6.00	12.00
❑ 544	Just the Way You Are/Quarter to Three	1967	3.00	6.00	12.00
SIRE					
❑ 4102	I Wanna Do It/Honey Do	1968	2.50	5.00	10.00
SWAN					
❑ 4192	Love Love (That's All I Want from You)/I'm on Fire	1964	5.00	10.00	20.00
STRANGERS, THE (1)					
Instrumental group; the only Strangers that made the charts.					
TITAN					
❑ 1701	The Caterpillar Crawl/Rockin' Rebel	1959	7.50	15.00	30.00
❑ 1702	Hill Stomp/A Lost Soul	1959	6.25	12.50	25.00
❑ 1704	Boogie Man/Young Maggie	1960	6.25	12.50	25.00
❑ 1711	Navajo/Dance of the Ants	1960	6.25	12.50	25.00
STRANGERS, THE (2)					
CHATTAHOOCHIE					
❑ 710	Like a Stranger/Can't Get the Water from My Eye	1966	3.00	6.00	12.00
JUBILEE					
❑ 5514	Plan On Someone New/What's the Matter Baby	1965	3.00	6.00	12.00
STRANGERS, THE (3)					
CHECKER					
❑ 1010	Darlin'/Pa and Billie	1962	3.75	7.50	15.00
STRANGERS, THE (4)					
CHOICE					
❑ 5	"Bart" Maverick/"Bret" Maverick	1960	5.00	10.00	20.00
STRANGERS, THE (5)					
CHRISTY					
❑ 107	We're in Love, We're in Love, We're in Love/Crab Louie	1959	7.50	15.00	30.00
❑ 108	J-U-D-Y/The Lord Will Welcome You	1959	6.25	12.50	25.00
STRANGERS, THE (6)					
Group that backed BOBBY VEE on some of his later records, most notably "Come Back When You Grow Up."					
CUCA					
❑ 1172	Runaway/John Henry	1960	50.00	100.00	200.00
LIBERTY					
❑ 55481	Toy Soldier/Loco	1962	5.00	10.00	20.00
❑ 55550	Card Shark/Mindreader	1963	5.00	10.00	20.00
STRANGERS, THE (7)					
KING					
❑ 4697	My Friends/I've Got Eyes	1954	100.00	200.00	400.00
❑ 4709	Blue Flowers/Beg and Steal	1954	125.00	250.00	500.00
❑ 4728	Hoping You'll Understand/Just Don't Care	1954	100.00	200.00	400.00
❑ 4745	Drop Down to My Place/Get It One More Time	1954	75.00	150.00	300.00
❑ 4766	How Long Must I Wait/Dreams Came True	1955	62.50	125.00	250.00
❑ 4821	Without a Friend/Think Again	1955	15.00	30.00	60.00
—With "High Fidelity" on label					
❑ 4821	Without a Friend/Think Again	1955	62.50	125.00	250.00
—Without "High Fidelity" on label (original)					
STRANGERS, THE (8)					
LINDA					
❑ 118	Easy Livin'/Tell Me	1965	7.50	15.00	30.00
WARNER BROS.					
❑ 5438	Night Winds/These Are the Things I Love	1964	5.00	10.00	20.00
STRANGERS, THE (9)					
MGM					
❑ 11980	Strange Lady in Town/North Dakota	1955	10.00	20.00	40.00
STRASSMAN, MARCIA					
UNI					
❑ 55006	The Flower Children/Out of the Picture	1967	2.50	5.00	10.00
❑ 55023	The Groovy World of Jack and Jill/The Flower Shop	1967	2.50	5.00	10.00
❑ 55023 [PS]	The Groovy World of Jack and Jill/The Flower Shop	1967	3.75	7.50	15.00
❑ 55056	Star Gazer/Self-Analysis	1968	2.50	5.00	10.00
STRAWBERRY ALARM CLOCK					
ALL AMERICAN					
❑ 373	Incense and Peppermints/The Birdman of Alcatrash	1967	50.00	100.00	200.00
UNI					
❑ 55018	Incense and Peppermints/The Birdman of Alcatrash	1967	3.00	6.00	12.00
❑ 55046	Tomorrow/Birds in My Tree	1967	2.50	5.00	10.00
❑ 55055	Pretty Song from Psych-Out/Sit with the Guru	1968	2.50	5.00	10.00
❑ 55076	Barefoot in Baltimore/Angry Young Man	1968	2.50	5.00	10.00
❑ 55093	Paxton's Back Street Carnival/Sea Shell	1968	2.50	5.00	10.00
❑ 55113	Stand By/Miss Attraction	1969	2.00	4.00	8.00
❑ 55125	Good Morning Starshine/Me and the Township	1969	2.00	4.00	8.00
❑ 55158	Desiree/Changes	1969	2.00	4.00	8.00
❑ 55185	Small Package/Starting Out the Day	1969	2.00	4.00	8.00
❑ 55190	I Climbed the Mountain/Three	1969	2.00	4.00	8.00
❑ 55218	California Day/Three	1970	5.00	10.00	20.00
❑ 55241	Girl from the City/Three	1970	5.00	10.00	20.00
STRAWBS, THE					
ARISTA					
❑ 0327	I Don't Want to Talk About It/Words of Wisdom	1978	—	2.00	4.00
A&M					
❑ 944	Oh How She Changed/Or Am I Dreaming	1968	—	2.50	5.00
❑ 998	Poor Jimmy Wilson/The Man Who Called Himself Jesus	1968	—	2.50	5.00

Number	Title (A Side/B Side)	Yr	VG	VG+	NM
❑ 1242 [DJ]	Where Is This Dream of Your Youth (mono/ stereo)	1971	—	3.00	6.00

—No stock copies known

Number	Title (A Side/B Side)	Yr	VG	VG+	NM
❑ 1364	Heavy Disguise/Benedictus	1972	—	2.50	5.00
❑ 1419	Part of the Union/Tomorrow	1973	—	2.50	5.00
❑ 1451	Lay Down/The Winter and the Summer	1973	—	2.50	5.00
❑ 1476	Shine On Silver Sun/And Wherefore	1973	—	2.50	5.00
❑ 1519	Round and Round/The Heroine's Theme	1974	—	2.50	5.00
❑ 1687	Where Do You Go/Lemon Pie	1975	—	2.00	4.00
❑ 1747	Little Sleepy/Golden Salamander	1975	—	2.00	4.00

OYSTER

Number	Title (A Side/B Side)	Yr	VG	VG+	NM
❑ 702	I Only Want My Love to Grow on You/(Wasting My Time) Thinking of You	1976	—	2.00	4.00
❑ 704	So Close and Yet So Far Away/(B-side unknown)	1977	—	2.00	4.00
❑ 705	Burning for Me/Heartbreaker	1977	—	2.00	4.00

STRAY CATS

EMI AMERICA

Number	Title (A Side/B Side)	Yr	VG	VG+	NM
❑ 8122	Stray Cat Strut/You Don't Believe Me	1982	—	—	3.00
❑ 8122 [PS]	Stray Cat Strut/You Don't Believe Me	1982	—	3.00	6.00
❑ 8132	Rock This Town/You Can't Hurry Love	1982	—	—	3.00
❑ 8132 [PS]	Rock This Town/You Can't Hurry Love	1982	—	—	3.00
❑ 8168	(She's) Sexy + 17/Lookin' Better Every Beer	1983	—	—	3.00
❑ 8168 [PS]	(She's) Sexy + 17/Lookin' Better Every Beer	1983	—	—	3.00
❑ 8169-1	(She's) Sexy + 17/Lookin' Better Every Beer	1983	—	2.50	5.00

—Paired with 8169-2

Number	Title (A Side/B Side)	Yr	VG	VG+	NM
❑ 8169-1/2 [PS]	(She's) Sexy + 17/Lookin' Better Every Beer/ Cruisin'/Lucky Charm	1983	—	2.50	5.00

—Gatefold sleeve for two-record set

Number	Title (A Side/B Side)	Yr	VG	VG+	NM
❑ 8169-2	Cruisin'/Lucky Charm	1983	—	2.50	5.00

—Paired with 8169-1

Number	Title (A Side/B Side)	Yr	VG	VG+	NM
❑ 8185	I Won't Stand In Your Way/I Won't Stand In Your Way (Acapella Version)	1983	—	—	3.00
❑ 8194	Look at That Cadillac/Lucky Charm	1984	—	—	3.00
❑ 8194 [PS]	Look at That Cadillac/Lucky Charm	1984	—	—	3.00

STREAMERS, THE

DOT

Number	Title (A Side/B Side)	Yr	VG	VG+	NM
❑ 16648	Slip-Stream/Blue Mountain	1964	7.50	15.00	30.00

STREET CLEANERS, THE

Yet another incarnation of P.F. SLOAN and STEVE BARRI.

AMY

Number	Title (A Side/B Side)	Yr	VG	VG+	NM
❑ 914	Garbage City/That's Cool, That's Trash	1964	7.50	15.00	30.00

STREISAND, BARBRA

Also see BARBRA AND NEIL.

ARISTA

Number	Title (A Side/B Side)	Yr	VG	VG+	NM
❑ 0123	How Lucky Can You Get/More Than You Know	1975	—	3.00	6.00

COLUMBIA

Number	Title (A Side/B Side)	Yr	VG	VG+	NM
❑ 02065	Promises/Make It Like a Memory	1981	—	2.00	4.00
❑ 02621	Comin' In and Out of Your Life/Lost Inside of You	1981	—	2.00	4.00
❑ 02717	Memory/Love Theme from "A Star Is Born"	1982	—	2.00	4.00
❑ 04177	The Way He Makes Me Feel (Studio)/The Way He Makes Me Feel (Film Version)	1983	—	—	3.00
❑ 04177 [PS]	The Way He Makes Me Feel (Studio)/The Way He Makes Me Feel (Film Version)	1983	—	2.00	4.00
❑ 04357	Papa Can You Hear Me?/Will Someone Ever Look at Me That Way	1984	—	—	3.00
❑ 04357 [PS]	Papa Can You Hear Me?/Will Someone Ever Look at Me That Way	1984	—	2.00	4.00
❑ 04605	Left in the Dark/Here We Are at Last	1984	—	—	3.00
❑ 04605 [PS]	Left in the Dark/Here We Are at Last	1984	—	2.00	4.00
❑ 04695	Make No Mistake, He's Mine/Clear Sailing	1984	—	—	3.00

—A-side with Kim Carnes

Number	Title (A Side/B Side)	Yr	VG	VG+	NM
❑ 04695 [PS]	Make No Mistake, He's Mine/Clear Sailing	1984	—	2.00	4.00
❑ 04707	Emotion/Here We Are at Last	1984	—	—	3.00
❑ 04707 [PS]	Emotion/Here We Are at Last	1984	—	2.00	4.00
❑ 05680	Somewhere/Not While I'm Around	1985	—	—	3.00
❑ 05680 [PS]	Somewhere/Not While I'm Around	1985	—	2.00	4.00
❑ 05837	Send In the Clowns/Being Alive	1986	—	—	3.00
❑ 05837 [PS]	Send In the Clowns/Being Alive	1986	2.00	4.00	8.00
❑ 08026	All I Ask of You/On My Way to You	1988	—	2.00	4.00
❑ 08026 [PS]	All I Ask of You/On My Way to You	1988	—	2.00	4.00
❑ 08062	Till I Loved You/Two People	1988	—	—	3.00

—A-side with Don Johnson

Number	Title (A Side/B Side)	Yr	VG	VG+	NM
❑ 08062 [PS]	Till I Loved You/Two People	1988	—	2.00	4.00
❑ 10075	Love in the Afternoon/Guava Jelly	1974	—	2.50	5.00
❑ 10130	Let the Good Times Roll/Jubilation	1975	—	2.50	5.00
❑ 10198	My Father's Song/By the Way	1975	—	2.50	5.00
❑ 10272	Shake Me, Wake Me, When It's Over/Widescreen	1975	—	2.50	5.00
❑ 10450	Love Theme from "A Star Is Born" (Evergreen)/I Believe in Love	1976	—	2.50	5.00
❑ 10450 [PS]	Love Theme from "A Star Is Born" (Evergreen)/I Believe in Love	1976	—	3.00	6.00
❑ 10555	My Heart Belongs to Me/Answer Me	1977	—	2.50	5.00
❑ 10756	Songbird/Honey Can I Put On Your Clothes	1978	—	2.00	4.00
❑ 10777	Love Theme from "Eyes of Laura Mars" (Prisoner)/Laura and Nevil	1978	—	2.00	4.00
❑ 10931	Superman/A Man I Loved	1979	—	2.00	4.00
❑ 11008	The Main Event/Fight//(Instrumental)	1979	—	2.00	4.00
❑ 11125	No More Tears (Enough Is Enough)/Wet	1979	—	2.00	4.00

—A-side with Donna Summer

Number	Title (A Side/B Side)	Yr	VG	VG+	NM
❑ 11125 [PS]	No More Tears (Enough Is Enough)/Wet	1979	—	2.50	5.00
❑ 11179	Kiss Me in the Rain/I Ain't Gonna Cry Tonight	1980	—	2.00	4.00
❑ 11364	Woman in Love/Run Wild	1980	—	2.00	4.00
❑ 11390	Guilty/Life Story	1980	—	2.00	4.00

—A-side with Barry Gibb

Number	Title (A Side/B Side)	Yr	VG	VG+	NM
❑ 11430	What Kind of Fool/The Lovin' Side	1981	—	2.00	4.00

—A-side with Barry Gibb

Number	Title (A Side/B Side)	Yr	VG	VG+	NM
❑ 42631	Happy Days Are Here Again/When the Sun Comes Out	1962	5.00	10.00	20.00
❑ 42648	My Coloring Book/Lover Come Back to Me	1962	3.75	7.50	15.00
❑ 42937	Gotta Move/Make Believe	1964	3.75	7.50	15.00
❑ 42965	People/I Am Woman	1964	2.50	5.00	10.00
❑ 43127	Funny Girl/Absent Minded Me	1964	2.50	5.00	10.00
❑ 43248	Why Did I Choose You/My Love	1965	2.00	4.00	8.00
❑ 43323	My Man/Where Is the Wonder	1965	2.00	4.00	8.00
❑ 43403	He Touched Me/I Like Him	1965	2.00	4.00	8.00
❑ 43469	Second Hand Rose/The Kind of Man a Woman Needs	1965	2.00	4.00	8.00
❑ 43518	Where Am I Going?/You Wanna Bet	1966	—	3.00	6.00
❑ 43612	Sam, You Made the Pants Too Long/The Minute Waltz	1966	—	3.00	6.00
❑ 43739	La Mer/C'est Rien	1966	2.00	4.00	8.00
❑ 43808	Free Again/I've Been Here	1966	—	3.00	6.00
❑ 43896	Sleep in Heavenly Peace (Silent Night)/Gounod's Ave Maria	1966	2.50	5.00	10.00
❑ 43896 [PS]	Sleep in Heavenly Peace (Silent Night)/Gounod's Ave Maria	1966	5.00	10.00	20.00
❑ 44225	Stout-Hearted Men/Look	1967	—	3.00	6.00
❑ 44331	Lover Man (Oh, Where Can You Be)/My Funny Valentine	1967	—	3.00	6.00
❑ 44350	Jingle Bells?/White Christmas	1967	7.50	15.00	30.00
❑ 44350 [PS]	Jingle Bells?/White Christmas	1967	10.00	20.00	40.00
❑ 44351	Have Yourself a Merry Little Christmas/The Best Gift	1967	2.50	5.00	10.00
❑ 44351 [PS]	Have Yourself a Merry Little Christmas/The Best Gift	1967	5.00	10.00	20.00
❑ 44352	My Favorite Things/The Christmas Song	1967	7.50	15.00	30.00
❑ 44352 [PS]	My Favorite Things/The Christmas Song	1967	10.00	20.00	40.00
❑ 44354	I Wonder As I Wander/The Lord's Prayer	1967	7.50	15.00	30.00
❑ 44476	Our Corner of the Night/He Could Show Me	1968	—	2.50	5.00
❑ 44532	Morning After/Where Is the Wonder	1968	—	2.50	5.00
❑ 44622	Funny Girl/I'd Rather Be Blue Over You	1968	—	2.50	5.00
❑ 44704	Don't Rain on My Parade/My Man	1968	—	3.00	6.00
❑ 44775	Punky's Dilemma/Frank Mills	1969	—	2.50	5.00
❑ 44921	Honey Pie/Little Tin Soldier	1969	—	2.50	5.00
❑ 45040	What About Today/What Are You Doing the Rest of Your Life	1969	—	2.50	5.00
❑ 45072	Love Is Only Love/Before the Parade Passes By	1970	—	2.50	5.00
❑ 45147	The Best Thing You've Ever Done/Summer Me, Winter Me	1970	—	2.50	5.00
❑ 45236	Stoney End/I'll Be Home	1970	—	2.50	5.00
❑ 45341	Time and Love/No Easy Way Down	1971	—	2.50	5.00
❑ 45384	Flim Flam Man/Maybe	1971	—	2.50	5.00
❑ 45414	Where You Lead/Since I Fell for You	1971	—	2.50	5.00
❑ 45471	Mother/The Summer Knows	1971	—	2.50	5.00
❑ 45511	One Less Bell to Answer-A House Is Not a Home/ Space Captain	1971	—	2.50	5.00
❑ 45626	Sweet Inspiration-Where You Lead/Didn't We	1972	—	2.50	5.00
❑ 45686	Sing a Song-Make Your Own Kind of Music/ Starting Here-Starting Now	1972	—	2.50	5.00
❑ 45739	Didn't We/On a Clear Day	1972	—	2.50	5.00
❑ 45780	If I Close My Eyes/(Instrumental)	1973	—	2.50	5.00
❑ 45944	The Way We Were/What Are You Doing the Rest of Your Life	1973	—	2.50	5.00

—A-side contains a different vocal than most of the album versions

Number	Title (A Side/B Side)	Yr	VG	VG+	NM
❑ 46024	All in Love Is Fair/My Buddy-How About Me	1974	—	2.50	5.00
❑ 68691	What Were We Thinking Of/Why Let It Go	1989	—	—	3.00
❑ 73016	We're Not Makin' Love Anymore/Here We Are at Last	1989	—	—	3.00
❑ 73794	Till I Loved You/Two People	1991	—	—	3.00

—Reissue

Number	Title (A Side/B Side)	Yr	VG	VG+	NM
❑ 73944	All I Ask of You/On My Way to You	1991	—	—	3.00

—Reissue

Number	Title (A Side/B Side)	Yr	VG	VG+	NM
❑ 77533	Ordinary Miracles/Ordinary Miracles (Live)	1994	—	2.00	4.00
❑ JZSP 79183/4 [DJ]	I'm All Smiles/Autumn	1964	7.50	15.00	30.00

—White label promo only

STRENGTH, "TEXAS" BILL

BRITE STAR

Number	Title (A Side/B Side)	Yr	VG	VG+	NM
❑ 2448	Nothing Is Sweeter Than You/Somehow, Someday, Someway	197?	3.00	6.00	12.00

CAPITOL

Number	Title (A Side/B Side)	Yr	VG	VG+	NM
❑ F3217	Yellow Rose of Texas/Cry, Cry, Cry	1955	5.00	10.00	20.00
❑ F3282	When Love Comes Knockin'/Turn Around	1955	5.00	10.00	20.00
❑ F3394	It Ain't Much, But It's Home/When the Bright Lights Grow Dim	1956	3.75	7.50	15.00
❑ F3477	Where Did My Heart Go/Gotta Lotta Love	1956	3.75	7.50	15.00
❑ F3568	North Wind/But Do You Think I'm Happy	1956	3.75	7.50	15.00
❑ F3701	Six Fools/I Wanna Ride On Your Merry-Go-Round	1957	3.75	7.50	15.00

CORAL

Number	Title (A Side/B Side)	Yr	VG	VG+	NM
❑ 9-61284	Nice to Be Living/Nobody Knows This More	1954	5.00	10.00	20.00
❑ 9-64117	Cherry Pie/Is Someone Else the Lucky One Tonight	1952	6.25	12.50	25.00
❑ 9-64133	Paper Boy Boogie/I Was Only Teasin' You	1952	6.25	12.50	25.00
❑ 9-64139	I Found My Love/It's a Shame	1952	6.25	12.50	25.00
❑ 9-64152	Rain or Shine/Heart, Don't Complain	1953	6.25	12.50	25.00
❑ 9-64171	Alone/Country Love	1954	5.00	10.00	20.00
❑ 9-64177	Let's Make Love or Go Home/You Can't Have My Love	1954	5.00	10.00	20.00

—With Tabby West

SUN

Number	Title (A Side/B Side)	Yr	VG	VG+	NM
❑ 346	Guess I'd Better Go/Senorita	1960	6.25	12.50	25.00

—As "Bill Strength"

STRIDERS, THE (1)

APOLLO

Number	Title (A Side/B Side)	Yr	VG	VG+	NM
❑ 480	I Wonder/Hesitating Fool	1955	75.00	150.00	300.00

DERBY

Number	Title (A Side/B Side)	Yr	VG	VG+	NM
❑ 857	Come Back to Me Tomorrow/Rollin'	1954	50.00	100.00	200.00

STRIDERS, THE (2)

Number	Title (A Side/B Side)	Yr	VG	VG+	NM
COLUMBIA					
❑ 43738	Sorrow/Say You Love Me	1966	5.00	10.00	20.00
❑ 43948	Am I On Your Mind/There's a Storm Comin'	1966	5.00	10.00	20.00
❑ 44143	When You Walk In the Room/Do It Now	1967	3.75	7.50	15.00

STRIKES, THE

Number	Title (A Side/B Side)	Yr	VG	VG+	NM
IMPERIAL					
❑ 5433	Baby I'm Sorry/If You Can't Rock Me	1957	12.50	25.00	50.00
❑ 5446	Rockin'/I Don't Want to Cry Over You	1957	12.50	25.00	50.00
LIN					
❑ 5006	Baby I'm Sorry/If You Can't Rock Me	1957	18.75	37.50	75.00

STRING-A-LONGS, THE

Number	Title (A Side/B Side)	Yr	VG	VG+	NM
7 ARTS					
❑ 700	Tell the World/For My Angel	1961	3.75	7.50	15.00
—As "Mickey Boyd and the Plain Viewers"					
ATCO					
❑ 6694	Popi/Places I Remember	1969	2.00	4.00	8.00
DOT					
❑ 16331	Twistwatch/Sunday	1962	2.50	5.00	10.00
❑ 16379	Spinnin' My Wheels/My Blue Heaven	1962	2.50	5.00	10.00
❑ 16393	Matilda/Replica	1962	2.50	5.00	10.00
❑ 16448	Heartaches/Happy Melody	1963	2.50	5.00	10.00
❑ 16575	Myna Bird/My Babe	1964	2.50	5.00	10.00
❑ 16592	Beatles, You Bug Me/Bloomin' Bird	1964	4.00	8.00	16.00
—As "The Bug Men"					
❑ 16708	Caravan/Mathilda	1965	2.50	5.00	10.00
WARWICK					
❑ 603	Wheels/Am I Asking Too Much	1960	3.75	7.50	15.00
❑ 603	Wheels/Tell the World	1960	5.00	10.00	20.00
—Red label					
❑ 603	Wheels/Tell the World	1960	6.25	12.50	25.00
—White label (not marked as a promo)					
❑ 606	Tell the World/For an Angel	1960	3.75	7.50	15.00
❑ 625	Brass Buttons/Panic Button	1961	3.75	7.50	15.00
❑ 654	Take a Minute/Should I	1961	3.75	7.50	15.00
❑ 668	Myna Bird/Scottie	1961	3.75	7.50	15.00
❑ 675	Theme for Twisters/Nearly Sunrise	1962	3.75	7.50	15.00

STRONG, BARRETT

Number	Title (A Side/B Side)	Yr	VG	VG+	NM
ANNA					
❑ 1111	Money (That's What I Want)/Oh I Apologize	1960	7.50	15.00	30.00
❑ 1116	You Know What to Do/Yes, No, Maybe So	1960	6.25	12.50	25.00
ATCO					
❑ 6225	Seven Sins/What Went Wrong	1962	10.00	20.00	40.00
CAPITOL					
❑ 4052	Is It True/Anywhere	1975	—	2.50	5.00
❑ 4120	Surrender/There's Something About You	1975	—	2.50	5.00
❑ 4223	Gonna Make It Right/The Man Up in the Sky	1976	—	2.50	5.00
EPIC					
❑ 11011	Stand Up and Cheer for the Preacher (Part 1)/ Stand Up and Cheer for the Preacher (Part 2)	1973	—	2.50	5.00
PHASE II					
❑ 02048	Rock It Easy/Love Will Make It Right	1981	—	2.00	4.00
TAMLA					
❑ 54022	Let's Rock/(B-side unknown)	1960	1000.	1500.	2000.
❑ 54027	Money (That's What I Want)/Oh I Apologize	1960	30.00	60.00	120.00
—Horizontal lines label					
❑ 54027	Money (That's What I Want)/Oh I Apologize	1960	12.50	25.00	50.00
—Globe label					
❑ 54029	You Know What to Do/Yes, No, Maybe So	1960	12.50	25.00	50.00
❑ 54033	I'm Gonna Cry/Whirl Wind	1960	12.50	25.00	50.00
❑ 54035	You Got What It Takes/Money and Me	1961	12.50	25.00	50.00
❑ 54043	Two Wrongs Don't Make a Right/Misery	1961	12.50	25.00	50.00
TOLLIE					
❑ 9023	Make Up Your Mind/I Better Run	1964	7.50	15.00	30.00

STRONG, NOLAN, AND THE DIABLOS

Some of these refer only to "The Diablos," others only to "Nolan Strong."

Number	Title (A Side/B Side)	Yr	VG	VG+	NM
FORTUNE					
❑ 509/10	Adios, My Desert Love/(I Want) An Old Fashioned Girl	1954	25.00	50.00	100.00
❑ 511	The Wind/Baby, Be Mine	1954	25.00	50.00	100.00
❑ 511	The Wind/Baby, Be Mine	196?	5.00	10.00	20.00
—Later pressing adds reference to LP on which it appears					
❑ 514	Hold Me Until Eternity/Route 16	1955	25.00	50.00	100.00
❑ 516	Daddy Rockin' Strong/Do You Remember What You Did Last Night	1955	25.00	50.00	100.00
❑ 518	The Way You Dog Me Around/Jump, Shake and Move	1955	25.00	50.00	100.00
❑ 519	You're the Only Girl, Dolores/You Are	1956	20.00	40.00	80.00
❑ 522	Teardrop from Heaven/Try Me One More Time	1956	20.00	40.00	80.00
❑ 525	Can't We Talk This Over/The Mambo of Love	1957	20.00	40.00	80.00
❑ 529	For Old Times' Sake/My Heart Will Always Belong to You	1959	10.00	20.00	40.00
❑ 531	I Am With You/Goodbye Matilda	1959	10.00	20.00	40.00
❑ 532	If I Could Be with You Tonite/I Wanna Know	1959	10.00	20.00	40.00
❑ 536	Since You're Gone/What You Gonna Do	1960	7.50	15.00	30.00
❑ 544	Blue Moon/I Don't Care	1962	5.00	10.00	20.00
❑ 546	Mind Over Matter (I'm Gonna Make You Mine)/ Beside You	1962	5.00	10.00	20.00
❑ 553	I Really Love You/You're My Love	1963	5.00	10.00	20.00
❑ 556	(Yeah, Baby) It's Because of You/You're Every Beat of My Heart	1963	5.00	10.00	20.00
❑ 564	Are You Making a Fool Out of Me/You're My Happiness	1964	3.75	7.50	15.00
❑ 569	(What Did That Genie Mean When He Said) Ali-Coochie/(You're Not Good Looking But) You're Presentable	1964	3.75	7.50	15.00
❑ 574	The Way You Dog Me Around/Jump with Me	1980	3.75	7.50	15.00

Number	Title (A Side/B Side)	Yr	VG	VG+	NM
PYRAMID					
❑ 159	White Christmas/Danny Boy	19??	3.75	7.50	15.00

STUART, CHAD

Also see CHAD AND JEREMY.

Number	Title (A Side/B Side)	Yr	VG	VG+	NM
SIDEWALK					
❑ 944	Good Morning Sunrise/Paxton's Song	1968	2.00	4.00	8.00
❑ 944 [PS]	Good Morning Sunrise/Paxton's Song	1968	3.75	7.50	15.00

STUART, CHAD AND JILL

Also see CHAD STUART.

Number	Title (A Side/B Side)	Yr	VG	VG+	NM
COLUMBIA					
❑ 43467	The Cruel War/I Can't Talk to You	1965	2.00	4.00	8.00
❑ 43467 [PS]	The Cruel War/I Can't Talk to You	1965	3.75	7.50	15.00

STUART, CHAD, AND JEREMY CLYDE

See CHAD AND JEREMY.

STUBBS, JOE

Number	Title (A Side/B Side)	Yr	VG	VG+	NM
LU-PINE					
❑ 120	Keep On Loving Me/What's My Destiny	1964	50.00	100.00	200.00

STUDENT NURSES, THE

Number	Title (A Side/B Side)	Yr	VG	VG+	NM
RCA VICTOR					
❑ 47-8482	Kiss Me Goodnight/Simply	1964	6.25	12.50	25.00

STUDENTS, THE

Number	Title (A Side/B Side)	Yr	VG	VG+	NM
ARGO					
❑ 5386	I'm So Young/Every Day of the Week	1961	5.00	10.00	20.00
CHECKER					
❑ 902	I'm So Young/Every Day of the Week	1958	10.00	20.00	40.00
❑ 1004	My Vow to You/That's How I Feel	1962	3.75	7.50	15.00
NOTE					
❑ 10012	I'm So Young/Every Day of the Week	1958	125.00	250.00	500.00
❑ 10019	My Vow to You/That's How I Feel	1959	100.00	200.00	400.00
RED TOP					
❑ 100	My Heart Is an Open Door/Mommy and Daddy	1958	50.00	100.00	200.00
—Blue label					
❑ 100	My Heart Is an Open Door/Mommy and Daddy	1958	10.00	20.00	40.00
—Red label					

STYLERS, THE (1)

Number	Title (A Side/B Side)	Yr	VG	VG+	NM
GOLDEN CREST					
❑ 117	You Tell Me/Blues in the Night	1957	10.00	20.00	40.00
❑ 117 [PS]	You Tell Me/Blues in the Night	1957	25.00	50.00	100.00
❑ 129	Kiss and Run Lover/Girlie, Girlie, Girlie	1957	10.00	20.00	40.00
JUBILEE					
❑ 5168	Believe It or Not/The World Is Yours	1954	10.00	20.00	40.00
❑ 5188	Shoo Shoo Sha La La/I Love Ya Like Crazy	1955	10.00	20.00	40.00
❑ 5246	Lost John/Huffin' and Puffin'	1956	10.00	20.00	40.00
❑ 5253	Confession of a Sinner/Gonna Tell 'Em	1956	10.00	20.00	40.00
❑ 5279	Breaker of Hearts/Miracle in Milan	1957	7.50	15.00	30.00

STYLERS, THE (U)

These could both be by group (1), or they may be different groups.

Number	Title (A Side/B Side)	Yr	VG	VG+	NM
GORDY					
❑ 7018	Going Steady Anniversary/Pushing Up Daisies	1963	15.00	30.00	60.00
KICKS					
❑ 2	Gentle as a Teardrop/There Were Others	1954	125.00	250.00	500.00

STYLES, THE (1)

Number	Title (A Side/B Side)	Yr	VG	VG+	NM
JOSIE					
❑ 920	I Love You for Sentimental Reasons/School Bells to Chapel Bells	1964	15.00	30.00	60.00
SERENE					
❑ 1501	Scarlet Angel/Gotta Go, Go, Go	1961	37.50	75.00	150.00

STYLES, THE (2)

Number	Title (A Side/B Side)	Yr	VG	VG+	NM
MODERN					
❑ 1048	I Know You Know That I Know/Baby You're Alive	1967	3.00	6.00	12.00
SWAN					
❑ 4258	I Do Love You/Hush Little Girl	1966	3.00	6.00	12.00

STYLISTICS, THE

Number	Title (A Side/B Side)	Yr	VG	VG+	NM
AMHERST					
❑ 301	Because I Love You Girl/My Love, Come Live With Me	1985	—	2.00	4.00
AVCO					
❑ 4581	You Are Everything/Country Living	1971	—	2.50	5.00
❑ 4591	Betcha by Golly, Wow/Ebony Eyes	1972	—	2.50	5.00
❑ 4595	People Make the World Go Round/Point of No Return	1972	—	2.50	5.00
❑ 4603	I'm Stone in Love with You/Make It Last	1972	—	2.50	5.00
❑ 4611	Break Up to Make Up/You and Me	1973	—	2.50	5.00
❑ 4618	You'll Never Get to Heaven (If You Break My Heart)/If You Don't Watch Out	1973	—	2.50	5.00
❑ 4625	Rockin' Roll Baby/Pieces	1973	—	2.50	5.00
❑ 4634	You Make Me Feel Brand New/Only for the Children	1974	—	2.50	5.00
❑ 4640	Let's Put It All Together/I Take It Out on You	1974	—	2.50	5.00
❑ 4647	Heavy Fallin' Out/Go Now	1974	—	2.50	5.00
❑ 4649	Star on a TV Show/Hey Girl, Come and Get It	1975	—	2.50	5.00
❑ 4652	Thank You Baby/Sing, Baby, Sing	1975	—	2.50	5.00
❑ 4656	Can't Give You Anything (But My Love)/I'd Rather Be Hurt by You	1975	—	2.50	5.00
❑ 4661	Funky Weekend/If You Are There	1975	—	2.50	5.00
❑ 4664	You Are Beautiful/Michael and Me	1976	—	2.50	5.00
❑ 4664 [PS]	You Are Beautiful/Michael and Me	1976	2.50	5.00	10.00
AVCO EMBASSY					
❑ 4555	You're a Big Girl Now/Let the Junkie Beat the Pusher	1970	—	3.00	6.00
❑ 4572	Stop, Look, Listen (To Your Heart)/If I Love You	1971	—	3.00	6.00

Number	Title (A Side/B Side)	Yr	VG	VG+	NM
H&L					
❑ 4669	Can't Help Falling in Love/Jenny	1976	—	2.00	4.00
❑ 4674	Because I Love You, Girl/You Are	1976	—	2.00	4.00
❑ 4676	Only You/What Goes Around Comes Around	1976	—	2.00	4.00
❑ 4678	I Got a Letter/Satin Doll	1977	—	2.00	4.00
❑ 4681	Shame and Scandal in the Family/That Don't Shake Me	1977	—	2.00	4.00
❑ 4686	I'm Coming Home/I Run to You	1977	—	2.00	4.00
❑ 4695	Fool of the Year/Good Thing Goin'	1978	—	2.00	4.00
MERCURY					
❑ 74005	First Impressions/Your Love's Too Good to Be Forgotten	1978	—	2.00	4.00
❑ 74022	I Can't Stop Livin'/You're the Best Thing in My Life	1978	—	2.00	4.00
❑ 74042	Love at First Sight/Broken Wing	1979	—	2.00	4.00
❑ 74057	Don't Know Where I'm Going/You Make Me Feel So Doggone Good	1979	—	2.00	4.00
PHILADELPHIA INT'L.					
❑ 02901	Callin' You/Don't Come Telling Me Lies	1982	—	2.00	4.00
❑ 03085	Lighten Up/We Should Be Lovers	1982	—	2.00	4.00
SEBRING					
❑ 8370	You're a Big Girl Now/Let the Junkie Beat the Pusher	1970	7.50	15.00	30.00
STREETWISE					
❑ 1136	Give a Little Love/Give a Little Love (Sing Along Version)	1984	—	2.00	4.00
❑ 1137	Some Things Never Change/Row Your Love	1985	—	2.00	4.00
❑ 1138	Special/(B-side unknown)	1985	—	2.00	4.00
TSOP					
❑ 02195	What's Your Name/Almost There	1981	—	2.00	4.00
❑ 02588	Mine All Mine/Closer Than Close	1981	—	2.00	4.00
❑ 02702	Habit/I've Got This Feeling	1982	—	2.00	4.00
❑ 4789	Hurry Up This Way Again/It Started Out	1980	—	2.00	4.00
❑ 4798	And I'll See You No More/Driving Me Wild	1980	—	2.00	4.00

STYLISTS, THE

Number	Title (A Side/B Side)	Yr	VG	VG+	NM
V.I.P.					
❑ 25066	What Is Love/Where Did the Children Go	1970	6.25	12.50	25.00

STYX

Also see DENNIS DeYOUNG; TOMMY SHAW.

Number	Title (A Side/B Side)	Yr	VG	VG+	NM
A&M					
❑ 1786	Lorelei/Midnight Ride	1976	—	2.00	4.00
❑ 1818	Born for Adventure/Light Up	1976	—	2.50	5.00
❑ 1877	Mademoiselle/Light Up	1976	—	2.50	5.00
❑ 1900	Jennifer/Shooz	1976	—	2.50	5.00
❑ 1931	Crystal Ball/Put Me On	1977	—	2.50	5.00
❑ 1977	Come Sail Away/Put Me On	1977	—	2.00	4.00
❑ 1977 [PS]	Come Sail Away/Put Me On	1977	—	3.00	6.00
❑ 2007	Fooling Yourself (The Angry Young Man)/The Grand Finale	1978	—	2.00	4.00
❑ 2007 [PS]	Fooling Yourself (The Angry Young Man)/The Grand Finale	1978	—	3.00	6.00
❑ 2087	Blue Collar Man (Long Nights)/Superstars	1978	—	2.00	4.00
❑ 2087 [PS]	Blue Collar Man (Long Nights)/Superstars	1978	—	3.00	6.00
❑ 2110	Sing for the Day/Queen of Spades	1979	—	2.50	5.00
❑ 2110	Renegade/Sing for the Day	1979	—	2.00	4.00
❑ 2110 [PS]	Renegade/Sing for the Day	1979	—	2.50	5.00
❑ 2188	Babe/I'm O.K.	1979	—	2.00	4.00
❑ 2206	Why Me/Lights	1979	—	2.00	4.00
❑ 2228	Borrowed Time/Eddie	1980	—	2.00	4.00
❑ 2294	The Best of Times/Lights	1980	—	—	—
—Unreleased?					
❑ 2300	The Best of Times/Lights	1981	—	2.00	4.00
❑ 2300 [PS]	The Best of Times/Lights	1981	—	2.00	4.00
❑ 2323	Too Much Time on My Hands/Queen of Spades	1981	—	2.00	4.00
❑ 2348	Nothing Ever Goes As Planned/Never Say Never	1981	—	2.00	4.00
❑ 2525	Mr. Roboto/Snowblind	1983	—	—	3.00
❑ 2525 [PS]	Mr. Roboto/Snowblind	1983	—	—	3.00
❑ 2543	Don't Let It End/Rockin' the Paradise	1983	—	—	3.00
❑ 2543 [PS]	Don't Let It End/Rockin' the Paradise	1983	—	—	3.00
❑ 2560	Double Life/Haven't We Been Here Before	1983	—	—	3.00
❑ 2568	High Time/Double Life	1983	—	—	3.00
❑ 2625	Music Time/Heavy Metal Poisoning	1984	—	—	3.00
❑ 2625 [PS]	Music Time/Heavy Metal Poisoning	1984	—	—	3.00
❑ 8696	Show Me the Way/Love at First Sight	1993	—	2.00	4.00
—Reissue series; both songs were unreleased on 45 until this record					
WOODEN NICKEL					
❑ BWBO-0065	You Need Love/Winner Take All	1973	—	2.50	5.00
❑ 65-0106	Best Thing/What Has Come Between	1972	—	2.50	5.00
❑ 65-0111	I'm Gonna Make You Feel It/Quick Is the Beat of My Heart	1972	—	2.50	5.00
❑ 65-0116	Lady/You Better Ask	1973	2.50	5.00	10.00
❑ BWBO-0252	Young Man/Unfinished Song	1974	—	2.50	5.00
❑ WB-10027	Lies/22 Years	1974	—	2.50	5.00
❑ WB-10102	Lady/Children of the Land	1974	—	2.50	5.00
❑ WB-10272	You Need Love/You Better Ask	1975	—	2.50	5.00
❑ WB-10329	Best Thing/Havin' a Ball	1975	—	2.50	5.00
❑ GB-10492	Lady/Children of the Land	1975	—	2.00	4.00
—Gold Standard Series					
❑ WB-11205	Winner Take All/Best Thing	1978	—	2.50	5.00

STYX (2)

Number	Title (A Side/B Side)	Yr	VG	VG+	NM
ABC					
❑ 10848	Don't Bring Me Down/MacDougal Street	1966	3.00	6.00	12.00

STYX (U)

Definitely not the more famous Styx; could be group (2), though.

Number	Title (A Side/B Side)	Yr	VG	VG+	NM
ONYX					
❑ 2200	Puppetmaster/Hey, I'm Lost	1966	6.25	12.50	25.00
PARAMOUNT					
❑ 0104	Promised Land/Soul Flow	1971	—	3.00	6.00

SUDDENS, THE

Also recorded as THE SAFARIS.

Number	Title (A Side/B Side)	Yr	VG	VG+	NM
SUDDEN					
❑ 103	Garden of Love/Childish Ways	1961	25.00	50.00	100.00

SUGAR BEARS, THE

Kim Carnes was in this group.

Number	Title (A Side/B Side)	Yr	VG	VG+	NM
BIG TREE					
❑ 122	Someone Like You/You Are the One	1971	—	3.00	6.00
❑ 143	Right On/Happiness Train	1972	—	3.00	6.00
❑ 151	Some Kind of a Summer/Put Some Love Into It	1972	—	3.00	6.00

SUGAR CANES, THE

Number	Title (A Side/B Side)	Yr	VG	VG+	NM
KING					
❑ 5157	Poor Boy/Sioux Rock	1958	6.25	12.50	25.00

SUGAR RAY

Number	Title (A Side/B Side)	Yr	VG	VG+	NM
ATLANTIC					
❑ 84462	Every Morning/Even Though	1999	—	—	3.00

SUGARLOAF

Number	Title (A Side/B Side)	Yr	VG	VG+	NM
BRUT					
❑ 805	Round and Round/Colorado Jones	1973	—	2.50	5.00
❑ 815	I Got a Song/Myra, Myra	1973	—	2.50	5.00
❑ 815 [PS]	I Got a Song/Myra, Myra	1973	—	3.00	6.00
CLARIDGE					
❑ 402	Don't Call Us, We'll Call You/Texas Two-Lane	1974	—	2.50	5.00
❑ 405	Stars in My Eyes/Myra, Myra	1975	—	2.50	5.00
❑ 408	Boogie Man/I Got a Song	1975	—	2.50	5.00
❑ 415	Have a Good Time/You Set My Dreams to Music	1976	—	2.50	5.00
❑ 422	Last Dance, Take a Chance/Satisfaction Guaranteed	1976	—	2.50	5.00
LIBERTY					
❑ 56183	Green-Eyed Lady/West of Tomorrow	1970	—	3.00	6.00
❑ 56218	Tongue in Cheek/Woman	1970	—	2.50	5.00
❑ 56218 [PS]	Tongue in Cheek/Woman	1970	2.50	5.00	10.00
UNITED ARTISTS					
❑ 0062	Green-Eyed Lady/Tongue in Cheek	1973	—	2.00	4.00
—"Silver Spotlight Series" reissue					
❑ 50757	Woman/Tongue in Cheek	1971	—	—	—
—Unreleased					
❑ 50784	Chest Fever/Mother Nature's Wine	1971	—	2.50	5.00

SUGGS, BRAD

Number	Title (A Side/B Side)	Yr	VG	VG+	NM
METEOR					
❑ 5034	Charcoal Suit/Bop Baby Bop	1956	100.00	200.00	400.00
PHILLIPS INT'L.					
❑ 3545	Low Outside/706 Union	1959	6.25	12.50	25.00
❑ 3549	I Walk the Line/Ooh-Wee	1959	6.25	12.50	25.00
❑ 3554	Cloudy/Partly Cloudy	1960	6.25	12.50	25.00
❑ 3563	My Gypsy/Sam's Tune	1960	6.25	12.50	25.00
❑ 3571	Elephant Walk/Catching Up	1961	6.25	12.50	25.00

SULLIVAN, JIM

Number	Title (A Side/B Side)	Yr	VG	VG+	NM
LONDON					
❑ 9585	Back and Forth/Toad Stool	1963	3.00	6.00	12.00

SULLIVAN, NIKI

Also see THE CRICKETS (1).

Number	Title (A Side/B Side)	Yr	VG	VG+	NM
DOT					
❑ 15751	Three Steps to Heaven/It's All Over	1958	25.00	50.00	100.00
JOLI					
❑ 073	Do the Dive/My Lost Dream	196?	15.00	30.00	60.00
❑ 075	It Really Doesn't Matter/You Better Get a Move On	196?	18.75	37.50	75.00

SULTANS, THE (1)

Number	Title (A Side/B Side)	Yr	VG	VG+	NM
ASCOT					
❑ 2228	I Wanna Know/Gloria	1967	5.00	10.00	20.00

SULTANS, THE (2)

Number	Title (A Side/B Side)	Yr	VG	VG+	NM
DUKE					
❑ 125	Good Thing Baby/How Deep Is the Ocean	1954	25.00	50.00	100.00
❑ 133	I Cried My Heart Out/Baby Don't Put Me Down	1954	25.00	50.00	100.00
❑ 135	Boppin' with the Mambo/What Makes Me Feel This Way	1954	25.00	50.00	100.00
❑ 178	My Love Is So High/If I Could Tell	1957	12.50	25.00	50.00

SULTANS, THE (3)

Number	Title (A Side/B Side)	Yr	VG	VG+	NM
GUYDEN					
❑ 2079	Someone You Can Trust/Christina	1963	3.75	7.50	15.00
JAM					
❑ 103	Toss in My Sleep/I Feel Your Love Growing Cold	1962	7.50	15.00	30.00
❑ 107	Mary, Mary/How Far Does a Friendship Go	1963	7.50	15.00	30.00
❑ 113	Poor Boy/Don't Tie Me Down	1964	7.50	15.00	30.00
TILT					
❑ 782	It'll Be Easy/You Got Me Goin'	1961	25.00	50.00	100.00
—Yellow label					
❑ 782	It'll Be Easy/You Got Me Goin'	1961	10.00	20.00	40.00
—Black label					

SULTANS, THE (4)

Number	Title (A Side/B Side)	Yr	VG	VG+	NM
JUBILEE					
❑ 5054	Lemon Squeezing Daddy/You Captured My Heart	1951	62.50	125.00	250.00
❑ 5077	Blues at Dawn/Don't Be Angry	1952	200.00	400.00	800.00

SUMAC, YMA

Number	Title (A Side/B Side)	Yr	VG	VG+	NM
CAPITOL					
❑ CDF 244 [PS]	Voice of the Xtabay	195?	3.75	7.50	15.00
—Box for 15647, 15648, 15649 and 19650 (listed separately)					
❑ F1717	Virgin of the Sun God/Lure of the Unknown Love	1951	5.00	10.00	20.00
❑ F1819	Birds/Najalas Lament	1951	5.00	10.00	20.00

Number	Title (A Side/B Side)	Yr	VG	VG+	NM
❑ F1819 [PS]	Birds/Najalas Lament	1951	10.00	20.00	40.00
❑ F2079	Babalu/Wimoweh	1952	5.00	10.00	20.00
❑ F15647	Virgin of the Sun God/Lure of the Unknown Love	195?	3.75	7.50	15.00
❑ F15648	Monkeys/High Andes	195?	3.75	7.50	15.00
❑ F15649	Dance of the Winds/Chant of the Chosen Maidens	195?	3.75	7.50	15.00
❑ F15650	Dance of the Moon Festival/Earthquake	195?	3.75	7.50	15.00

—The above four comprise box set CDF-244, "Voice of the Xtabay"

CORAL

Number	Title (A Side/B Side)	Yr	VG	VG+	NM
❑ 60741	The Sun Maidens/Beautiful Eyes	1952	5.00	10.00	20.00
❑ 60742	Cholitas Punenas/The Hummingbird	1952	5.00	10.00	20.00
❑ 60743	One Love/Indian Love	1952	5.00	10.00	20.00
❑ 60744	La Benita/I Love Only You	1952	5.00	10.00	20.00

—The above four comprise a box set

7-Inch Extended Plays

CAPITOL

Number	Title (A Side/B Side)	Yr	VG	VG+	NM
❑ EAP 1-299	(contents unknown)	1955	6.25	12.50	25.00
❑ EAP 1-299 [PS]	Legend of the Sun Virgin, Part 1	1955	6.25	12.50	25.00
❑ EAP 2-299	(contents unknown)	1955	6.25	12.50	25.00
❑ EAP 2-299 [PS]	Legend of the Sun Virgin, Part 2	1955	6.25	12.50	25.00
❑ EAP 1-564	(contents unknown)	1955	6.25	12.50	25.00
❑ EAP 1-564 [PS]	Mambo!	1955	6.25	12.50	25.00
❑ EAP 2-564	(contents unknown)	1955	6.25	12.50	25.00
❑ EAP 2-564 [PS]	Mambo!	1955	6.25	12.50	25.00
❑ EAP 1-770	(contents unknown)	1956	5.00	10.00	20.00
❑ EAP 1-770 [PS]	Legend of the Jivaro, Part 1	1956	5.00	10.00	20.00
❑ EAP 2-770	(contents unknown)	1956	5.00	10.00	20.00
❑ EAP 2-770 [PS]	Legend of the Jivaro, Part 2	1956	5.00	10.00	20.00
❑ EAP 3-770	(contents unknown)	1956	5.00	10.00	20.00
❑ EAP 3-770 [PS]	Legend of the Jivaro, Part 3	1956	5.00	10.00	20.00

CORAL

Number	Title (A Side/B Side)	Yr	VG	VG+	NM
❑ EC 81050	(contents unknown)	1954	12.50	25.00	50.00
❑ EC 81050 [PS]	Presenting Yma Sumac	1954	12.50	25.00	50.00
❑ EC 81051	(contents unknown)	1954	12.50	25.00	50.00
❑ EC 81051 [PS]	Presenting Yma Sumac	1954	12.50	25.00	50.00

SUMMER, DONNA

ATLANTIC

Number	Title (A Side/B Side)	Yr	VG	VG+	NM
❑ 88792	Breakaway/Thinkin' Bout My Baby	1989	—	—	3.00
❑ 88840	Love's About to Change My Heart/Love's About to Change My Heart	1989	—	—	3.00
❑ 88899	This Time I Know It's for Real/If It Makes You Feel Good	1989	—	—	3.00
❑ 88899 [PS]	This Time I Know It's for Real/If It Makes You Feel Good	1989		2.00	4.00

CASABLANCA

Number	Title (A Side/B Side)	Yr	VG	VG+	NM
❑ 872	Spring Affair/The Landing	1976	—	2.50	5.00
❑ 874	Winter Melody/Spring Affair	1977	—	2.50	5.00
❑ 884	Can't We Just Sit Down (And Talk It Over)/I Feel Love	1977	—	3.00	6.00

Original copies have "I Feel Love" listed as "Side B"

Number	Title (A Side/B Side)	Yr	VG	VG+	NM
❑ 884	I Feel Love/Can't We Just Sit Down (And Talk It Over)	1977	—	2.50	5.00

—Second pressings have "I Feel Love" listed as "Side A"

Number	Title (A Side/B Side)	Yr	VG	VG+	NM
❑ 907	I Love You/Once Upon a Time	1977	—	2.50	5.00
❑ 916	Rumour Has It/Once Upon a Time	1978	—	2.50	5.00
❑ 926	Last Dance/With Your Love	1978	—	2.00	4.00
❑ 939	Mac Arthur Park/Once Upon a Time	1978	—	2.00	4.00
❑ 959	Heaven Knows/Only One Love	1979	—	2.00	4.00

—A-side with Brooklyn Dreams

Number	Title (A Side/B Side)	Yr	VG	VG+	NM
❑ 978	Hot Stuff/Journey to the Center of Your Heart	1979	—	2.00	4.00
❑ 988	Bad Girls/On My Honor	1979	—	2.00	4.00
❑ 2201	Dim All the Lights/There Will Always Be a You	1979	—	2.00	4.00
❑ 2236	On the Radio/There Will Always Be a You	1980	—	2.00	4.00
❑ 2273	Our Love/Sunset People	1980	—	2.50	5.00
❑ 2300	Walk Away/Could It Be Magic	1980	—	2.00	4.00
❑ 858366-7	Melody of Love/The Christmas Song	1994	—	—	3.00
❑ 858366-7 [PS]	Melody of Love/The Christmas Song	1994	—	—	3.00

EPIC

Number	Title (A Side/B Side)	Yr	VG	VG+	NM
❑ 79201	I Will Go with You (Con Te Partiro)/Love On & On	1999	—	—	3.00

GEFFEN

Number	Title (A Side/B Side)	Yr	VG	VG+	NM
❑ 27939	Fascination/All Systems Go	1988	—	2.00	4.00
❑ 28165	Only the Fool Survives/Love Shock	1987	—	2.00	4.00

—A-side with Mickey Thomas

Number	Title (A Side/B Side)	Yr	VG	VG+	NM
❑ 28165 [PS]	Only the Fool Survives/Love Shock	1987	—	2.00	4.00

—A-side with Mickey Thomas

Number	Title (A Side/B Side)	Yr	VG	VG+	NM
❑ 28418	Dinner with Gershwin/(Instrumental)	1987	—	2.00	4.00
❑ 28418 [PS]	Dinner with Gershwin/(Instrumental)	1987	—	2.00	4.00
❑ 29142	Supernatural Love/Face the Music	1984	—	2.00	4.00
❑ 29142 [PS]	Supernatural Love/Face the Music	1984	—	2.00	4.00
❑ 29291	There Goes My Baby/Maybe It's Over	1984	—	2.00	4.00
❑ 29291 [PS]	There Goes My Baby/Maybe It's Over	1984	—	2.00	4.00
❑ 29805	The Woman in Me/Livin' in America	1982	—	2.00	4.00
❑ 29805 [PS]	The Woman in Me/Livin' in America	1982	—	2.00	4.00
❑ 29895	State of Independence/Love Is Just a Breath Away	1982	—	2.00	4.00
❑ 29895 [PS]	State of Independence/Love Is Just a Breath Away	1982	—	2.00	4.00
❑ 29982	Love Is In Control (Finger on the Trigger)/Sometimes Like Butterflies	1982	—	2.00	4.00
❑ 29982 [PS]	Love Is In Control (Finger on the Trigger)/Sometimes Like Butterflies	1982	—	2.50	5.00
❑ 49563	The Wanderer/Stop Me	1980	—	2.00	4.00

—Second pressings have WB logo replaced by Geffen logo

Number	Title (A Side/B Side)	Yr	VG	VG+	NM
❑ 49563 [PS]	The Wanderer/Stop Me	1980	—	2.50	5.00
❑ 49634	Cold Love/Grand Illusion	1980	—	2.00	4.00
❑ 49634 [PS]	Cold Love/Grand Illusion	1980	—	2.50	5.00
❑ 49664	Who Do You Think You're Foolin'/Runnin' for Cover	1981	—	2.00	4.00

MERCURY

Number	Title (A Side/B Side)	Yr	VG	VG+	NM
❑ 812370-7	She Works Hard for the Money/I Do Believe (I'll Fall in Love)	1983	—	2.00	4.00
❑ 812370-7 [PS]	She Works Hard for the Money/I Do Believe (I'll Fall in Love)	1983	—	2.50	5.00
❑ 814088-7	Unconditional Love/People, People	1983	—	2.00	4.00
❑ 814088-7 [PS]	Unconditional Love/People, People	1983	—	2.50	5.00
❑ 814922-7	Love Has a Mind of Its Own/Stop, Look and Listen	1983	—	2.00	4.00

OASIS

Number	Title (A Side/B Side)	Yr	VG	VG+	NM
❑ 401 A /B	Love to Love You Baby/Need-A-Man Blues	1975	3.00	6.00	12.00

—"Love to Love You Baby" has a radically different mix on the above first pressing

Number	Title (A Side/B Side)	Yr	VG	VG+	NM
❑ 401 AA/BB	Love to Love You Baby (4:55)/Love to Love You Baby (3:24)	1975	—	3.00	6.00
❑ 405	Could It Be Magic/Whispering Waves	1976	—	3.00	6.00
❑ 406	Try Me, I Know We Can Make It/Wasted	1976	—	3.00	6.00
❑ 406 [PS]	Try Me, I Know We Can Make It/Wasted	1976	2.00	4.00	8.00

WARNER BROS./GEFFEN

Number	Title (A Side/B Side)	Yr	VG	VG+	NM
❑ 49563	The Wanderer/Stop Me	1980	—	3.00	6.00

—Original pressings have a WB logo on the left side and "Geffen Records" in a box at the top of the label

SUMMERS, ANDY

Also see THE POLICE.

A&M

Number	Title (A Side/B Side)	Yr	VG	VG+	NM
❑ 2513 [DJ]	I Advance Masked (same on both sides)	1982	—	2.00	4.00

—With Robert Fripp; no stock copy was issued

Number	Title (A Side/B Side)	Yr	VG	VG+	NM
❑ 2699	Parade/Train	1984	—	—	3.00

—With Robert Fripp

Number	Title (A Side/B Side)	Yr	VG	VG+	NM
❑ 2704	2010/To Hal and Back	1984	—	—	3.00
❑ 2704 [PS]	2010/To Hal and Back	1984	—	—	3.00

MCA

Number	Title (A Side/B Side)	Yr	VG	VG+	NM
❑ 53112	Love Is the Strangest Way/XYZ	1987	—	—	3.00

SUMMERS, DAVEY, AND THE SINGING ANTS

DORE

Number	Title (A Side/B Side)	Yr	VG	VG+	NM
❑ 684	Gonna Climb That Big Ole Hill/Doin' the Davey Drag	1963	10.00	20.00	40.00

SUMMERS, GENE

CAPRI

Number	Title (A Side/B Side)	Yr	VG	VG+	NM
❑ 502	Blue Diamond/You Said You Loved Me	196?	5.00	10.00	20.00
❑ 507	Alabama Shake/Just Because	1964	15.00	30.00	60.00

JAMIE

Number	Title (A Side/B Side)	Yr	VG	VG+	NM
❑ 1273	Blue Diamond/You Said You Loved Me	1964	3.75	7.50	15.00

JAN

Number	Title (A Side/B Side)	Yr	VG	VG+	NM
❑ 100	School of Rock 'N' Roll/Straight Skirt	1958	15.00	30.00	60.00
❑ 102	Nervous/Gotta Love That	1959	15.00	30.00	60.00
❑ 106	Twixteen/I'll Never Be Lonely	1959	15.00	30.00	60.00

MERCURY

Number	Title (A Side/B Side)	Yr	VG	VG+	NM
❑ 72606	Green-Eyed Monster/The Clown	1966	3.75	7.50	15.00

TEARDROP

Number	Title (A Side/B Side)	Yr	VG	VG+	NM
❑ 3405	Goodbye Priscilla (Bye Bye Baby Blue)/Down on the Farm	1977	2.00	4.00	8.00
❑ 3405 [DJ]	Goodbye Priscilla (Bye Bye Blue Baby)	1977	3.00	6.00	12.00

—Single-sided promo copies have erroneous subtitle

SUN-RAYS, THE

SUN

Number	Title (A Side/B Side)	Yr	VG	VG+	NM
❑ 293	Love Is a Stranger/The Lonely Hours	1958	10.00	20.00	40.00

SUNBEAMS, THE (1)

ACME

Number	Title (A Side/B Side)	Yr	VG	VG+	NM
❑ 109	Please Say You'll Be Mine/You've Got to Rock and Roll	1957	750.00	1500.	3000.

HERALD

Number	Title (A Side/B Side)	Yr	VG	VG+	NM
❑ 451	Tell Me Why/Come Back Baby	1955	75.00	150.00	300.00

SUNBEAMS, THE (2)

DOT

Number	Title (A Side/B Side)	Yr	VG	VG+	NM
❑ 1271	I'm Gonna Go Home to Mama/Blue Mountain Waltz	1955	7.50	15.00	30.00
❑ 1280	How About It/Wrap It Up and Save It	1956	7.50	15.00	30.00

SUNBEAMS, THE (3)

TOLLIE

Number	Title (A Side/B Side)	Yr	VG	VG+	NM
❑ 9022	Sing a Song/Good Old Days	1964	3.00	6.00	12.00

SUNDAY FUNNIES, THE

CAPITOL

Number	Title (A Side/B Side)	Yr	VG	VG+	NM
❑ 5614	Another Time, Another Place/Headlines	1966	3.00	6.00	12.00

HIDEOUT

Number	Title (A Side/B Side)	Yr	VG	VG+	NM
❑ 1070	Heavy Music/Path of Freedom	196?	7.50	15.00	30.00

MERCURY

Number	Title (A Side/B Side)	Yr	VG	VG+	NM
❑ 72571	Wonder Woman/She's Not at All Like You	1966	3.00	6.00	12.00

RARE EARTH

Number	Title (A Side/B Side)	Yr	VG	VG+	NM
❑ 5035	Walk Down the Path of Freedom/It's Just a Dream	1971	2.00	4.00	8.00

UNI

Number	Title (A Side/B Side)	Yr	VG	VG+	NM
❑ 55157	Baby, I Could Be So Good at Loving You/See Things My Way	1969	2.50	5.00	10.00

SUNDOWN PLAYBOYS, THE

APPLE

Number	Title (A Side/B Side)	Yr	VG	VG+	NM
❑ 1852	Saturday Night Special/Valse De Soleil Coucher	1972	3.75	7.50	15.00

GOLDBAND

Number	Title (A Side/B Side)	Yr	VG	VG+	NM
❑ 1073	Sundown Waltz/River Two Step	195?	7.50	15.00	30.00

SUNDOWNERS, THE

JAMIE

Number	Title (A Side/B Side)	Yr	VG	VG+	NM
❑ 1271	A Shot of Rhythm 'N' Blues/Come On In	1964	3.00	6.00	12.00

Number	Title (A Side/B Side)	Yr	VG	VG+	NM
SUNGLOWS, THE					
See SUNNY AND THE SUNLINERS.					
SUNLINERS, THE					
GOLDEN WORLD					
❑ 31	The Swingin' Kind/All Alone	1965	7.50	15.00	30.00
MGM					
❑ 13809	Land of Nod/Well One	1967	6.25	12.50	25.00
SUNNY AND THE HORIZONS					
LUXOR					
❑ 1013	Nature's Creation/Because They Tell Me	1962	50.00	100.00	200.00
—Yellow label					
❑ 1013	Nature's Creation/Because They Tell Me	1962	18.75	37.50	75.00
—Red label					
SUNNY AND THE SUNGLOWS					
See SUNNY AND THE SUNLINERS.					
SUNNY AND THE SUNLINERS					
DISCO GRANDE					
❑ 1021	Peanuts (La Cacahuata)/The Happy Hippo	1965	5.00	10.00	20.00
KEY-LOC					
❑ 1010	I Want To Come Home For Christmas/(B-side unknown)	1966	2.00	4.00	8.00
OKEH					
❑ 7143	Golly Gee/Touring	1962	3.00	6.00	12.00
—As "Sunny and the Sunglows"					
SUNGLOW					
❑ 102	Sylvia/(B-side unknown)	1961	3.75	7.50	15.00
❑ 103	A Dream/The Lasso	1961	3.75	7.50	15.00
❑ 104	Golly Gee/Touring	1961	3.75	7.50	15.00
❑ 105	Once in a While/Ho Ho Ha Ha	1962	3.75	7.50	15.00
❑ 106	Won't You Tell Me/(B-side unknown)	1962	3.75	7.50	15.00
❑ 107	Peanuts (La Cacahuata)/The Happy Hippo	1962	3.75	7.50	15.00
❑ 107	Peanuts (La Cacahuata)/Falasette Corazon	1962	3.75	7.50	15.00
❑ 109	Close Your Eyes/Ooo Poo Pa Doo	1963	3.75	7.50	15.00
❑ 110	Talk to Me/Pony Time	1963	5.00	10.00	20.00
❑ 111	Rags to Riches/It Won't Be Me	1963	4.50	9.00	18.00
❑ 112	The Dog/You Can Make It If You Try	1963	3.75	7.50	15.00
❑ 115	Till the End of Time/La Bamba	1964	3.75	7.50	15.00
❑ 116	Guess Who/Just as I Thought	1964	3.75	7.50	15.00
❑ 117	Love Me/Honey Child	1964	3.75	7.50	15.00
❑ 118	Popcorn/The Circus	1964	3.75	7.50	15.00
❑ 118	Popcorn/All Night Worker	1965	3.75	7.50	15.00
❑ 119	Baby I Apologize/Cut Across Shorty	1965	3.75	7.50	15.00
❑ 120	Oh Heart/Latin Trumpet	1965	3.75	7.50	15.00
❑ 122	Fly Me to the Moon/La Macarena	1966	3.75	7.50	15.00
❑ 123	If You Don't Love Me/(B-side unknown)	1966	3.75	7.50	15.00
❑ 124	Just a Game/Maria Elena	1966	3.75	7.50	15.00
❑ 125	Again/Roly Poly	1967	3.75	7.50	15.00
❑ 127	It's Okay/99 + 1	1968	3.75	7.50	15.00
—All Sunglow releases as "The Sunglows"					
TEAR DROP					
❑ 3014	Talk to Me/Every Week, Every Month, Every Year	1963	2.50	5.00	10.00
—As "Sunny and the Sunglows"					
❑ 3016	Carino Nuevo/(B-side unknown)	1963	3.00	6.00	12.00
❑ 3022	Rags to Riches/Not Even Judgment Day	1963	2.50	5.00	10.00
❑ 3025	Cuando El Destino/(B-side unknown)	1963	3.00	6.00	12.00
❑ 3027	Out of Sight, Out of Mind/No One Else Will Do	1964	2.50	5.00	10.00
❑ 3031	Pa Que Sientas, Lo Que Sientex Que Tal Te Sientes/De Mi Nada Mas, Usted	1964	3.00	6.00	12.00
—As "Sunny Ozuna"					
❑ 3035	It's Too Late/You Gave Me a True Love	1964	2.50	5.00	10.00
❑ 3037	Tu Nueva Viva/Dime Como Le Haces	1964	3.00	6.00	12.00
❑ 3040	You Send Me/His Greatest Creation	1964	2.50	5.00	10.00
❑ 3045	Something's Got a Hold on Me/Teenage Promise-I'm Not a Fool Anymore	1964	2.50	5.00	10.00
❑ 3056	Token of Love/Little Dancing Girl	1965	2.50	5.00	10.00
—As "Sunny Ozuna"					
❑ 3066	El Ta Conazo/La Diudades	1965	3.00	6.00	12.00
❑ 3067	Hitch Hike/That Night in San Antonio	1965	2.50	5.00	10.00
❑ 3071	Too Young/The Very Thought of You	1965	2.50	5.00	10.00
❑ 3079	Trick Bag/Cheatin' Traces	1965	2.50	5.00	10.00
❑ 3094	Fly Me to the Moon/Short Short Shorty	1966	2.00	4.00	8.00
❑ 3096	Tristie Y Lastimado/(B-side unknown)	1966	3.00	6.00	12.00
❑ 3123	No One Else Will Do/Cheatin' Traces	1966	2.00	4.00	8.00
❑ 3183	Wonderful Girl/Talk That Trash	1966	2.00	4.00	8.00
WHITE WHALE					
❑ 324	It's Okay/99 + 1	1969	2.00	4.00	8.00
—As "The Sunglows"					
SUNRAYS, THE					
Also see THE SNOW MEN.					
TOWER					
❑ 101	Outta Gas/Car Party	1964	5.00	10.00	20.00
❑ 148	I Live for the Sun/Bye Baby Bye	1965	3.00	6.00	12.00
❑ 191	Andrea/You Don't Phase Me	1966	3.00	6.00	12.00
❑ 224	Still/When You're Not There	1966	3.00	6.00	12.00
❑ 256	Don't Take Yourself Too Seriously/I Look Baby, I Can't See	1966	3.00	6.00	12.00
❑ 256 [PS]	Don't Take Yourself Too Seriously/I Look Baby, I Can't See	1966	6.25	12.50	25.00
❑ 290	Hi, How Are You/Just 'Round the River Bend	1966	3.75	7.50	15.00
❑ 340	Loaded with Love/Time (A Special Thing)	1967	3.75	7.50	15.00
WARNER BROS.					
❑ 5253	Talk to Him/Gideon	1962	3.75	7.50	15.00
SUNSETS, THE (1)					
CHALLENGE					
❑ 9186	C.C. Rider/The Chug-a-Lug	1963	10.00	20.00	40.00
❑ 9198	Lonely Surfer Boy/Playmate of the Year	1963	10.00	20.00	40.00
❑ 9208	My Little Beach Bunny/My Little Surfin' Woody	1963	12.50	25.00	50.00
PETAL					
❑ 1040	Lydia/Only You, Only Me	1963	12.50	25.00	50.00
SUNSETS, THE (2)					
RAE COX					
❑ 102	How Will I Remember/Sittin' and Cryin'	1959	10.00	20.00	40.00
SUNSHINE COMPANY, THE					
IMPERIAL					
❑ 66241	Up Up and Away/Blue May	1967	—	—	—
—Unreleased					
❑ 66247	Happy/Blue May	1967	2.50	5.00	10.00
❑ 66260	Back on the Street Again/I Just Want to Be Your Friend	1967	2.50	5.00	10.00
❑ 66278	Reflections on an Angel/It's Sunday	1968	—	—	—
—Unreleased					
❑ 66280	Look, Here Comes the Sun/It's Sunday	1968	2.50	5.00	10.00
❑ 66298	Let's Get Together/Sunday Brought the Rain	1968	2.50	5.00	10.00
❑ 66308	On a Beautiful Day/Darcy Farrow	1968	2.50	5.00	10.00
❑ 66324	Love Poem/Willie Jean	1968	2.50	5.00	10.00
❑ 66399	The Only Thing That Matters/Bolaro	1969	2.50	5.00	10.00
UNITED ARTISTS					
❑ 0132	Happy/Back on the Street Again	1973	—	2.00	4.00
—"Silver Spotlight Series" reissue					
SUPER K GENERATION, THE					
LAURIE					
❑ 3413	Heartful O'Soul (Part 1)/Heartful O'Soul (Part 2)	1967	2.50	5.00	10.00
SUPER STOCKS, THE					
CAPITOL					
❑ 5153	Thunder Road/Wheel Stands	1964	6.25	12.50	25.00
SUPERFINE DANDELION, THE					
MAINSTREAM					
❑ 672	People in the Street/(B-side unknown)	1967	3.00	6.00	12.00
❑ 673	Crazy Town/Janie's Tomb	1967	3.00	6.00	12.00
SUPERIORS, THE (1)					
ATCO					
❑ 6106	Lost Love/Don't Say Goodbye	1957	17.50	35.00	70.00
MAIN LINE					
❑ 104	Lost Love/Don't Say Goodbye	1958	150.00	300.00	600.00
—With Fairmount Ave., Philadelphia street address on label					
❑ 104	Lost Love/Don't Say Goodbye	1962	10.00	20.00	40.00
—No address on label or only "Philadelphia, Pennsylvania" address on label					
SUPERIORS, THE (2)					
FAL					
❑ 301	What Is Love/Flee the Scene	1961	20.00	40.00	80.00
FEDERAL					
❑ 12436	I'm Sorry Baby (I Didn't Mean to Do You Wrong)/Dance of Love	1961	7.50	15.00	30.00
SUPERIORS, THE (3)					
MGM					
❑ 13503	Can't Make It Without You/Let Me Make You Happy	1966	3.00	6.00	12.00
SUE					
❑ 12	Heavenly Angel/I'd Rather Die	1969	2.00	4.00	8.00
VERVE					
❑ 10370	Tell Me to Go/What Would I Do	1965	5.00	10.00	20.00
SUPERTRAMP					
A&M					
❑ 1305	Forever/Your Poppa Don't Mind	1971	—	3.00	6.00
❑ 1660	Bloody Well Right/Dreamer	1975	—	2.50	5.00
❑ 1766	Lady/You Started Laughing When I Held You in My Arms	1975	—	—	—
—Unreleased?					
❑ 1793	Lady/You Started Laughing When I Held You in My Arms	1976	—	2.50	5.00
❑ 1814	Sister Moonshine/Ain't Nobody But Me	1976	—	2.50	5.00
❑ 1938	Give a Little Bit/Downstream	1977	—	2.00	4.00
❑ 1938 [PS]	Give a Little Bit/Downstream	1977	—	3.00	6.00
❑ 1981	Dreamer/From Now On	1977	—	2.50	5.00
❑ 1981 [PS]	Dreamer/From Now On	1977	—	3.00	6.00
❑ 2128	The Logical Song/Just Another Nervous Wreck	1979	—	2.00	4.00
❑ 2128 [PS]	The Logical Song/Just Another Nervous Wreck	1979	—	2.50	5.00
❑ 2162	Goodbye Stranger/Even in the Quietest Moments	1979	—	2.00	4.00
❑ 2162 [PS]	Goodbye Stranger/Even in the Quietest Moments	1979	—	2.50	5.00
❑ 2193	Take the Long Way Home/Ruby	1979	—	2.00	4.00
❑ 2193 [PS]	Take the Long Way Home/Ruby	1979	—	2.00	4.00
—With yellow maze					
❑ 2193 [PS]	Take the Long Way Home/Ruby	1979	—	2.50	5.00
—With green maze					
❑ 2193 [PS]	Take the Long Way Home/Ruby	1979	—	2.50	5.00
—With red maze. Other colors may exist as well.					
❑ 2269	Dreamer/From Now On	1980	—	2.00	4.00
❑ 2269 [PS]	Dreamer/From Now On	1980	—	2.50	5.00
❑ 2292	Breakfast in America/You Started Laughing	1980	—	2.00	4.00
❑ 2502	It's Raining Again/Monnie	1982	—	2.00	4.00
❑ 2502 [PS]	It's Raining Again/Monnie	1982	—	2.00	4.00
❑ 2517	My Kind of Lady/Know Who You Are	1983	—	2.00	4.00
❑ 2517 [PS]	My Kind of Lady/Know Who You Are	1983	—	2.00	4.00
❑ 2720 [DJ]	Still in Love with You (same on both sides)	1985	—	—	—
—Unreleased?					
❑ 2731	Cannonball/Every Open Door	1985	—	—	3.00
❑ 2731 [PS]	Cannonball/Every Open Door	1985	—	—	3.00
❑ 2760	Better Days/No In-Between	1985	—	—	3.00
❑ 2985	I'm Beggin' You/No Inbetween	1987	—	—	3.00
❑ 2985 [PS]	I'm Beggin' You/No Inbetween	1987	—	—	3.00

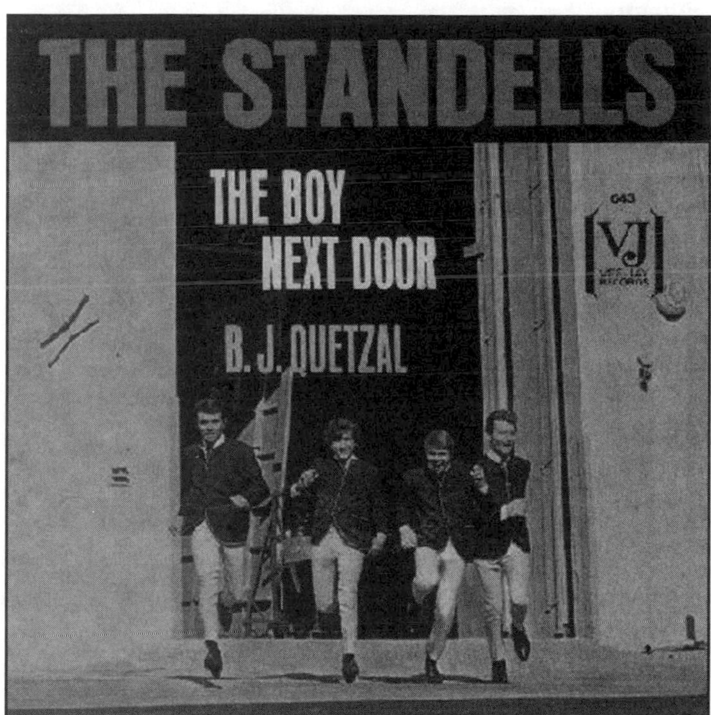

(Top left) After many years of recording under various names, both real and imagined, Sylvester Stewart finally found success with Sly and the Family Stone. But their first record, "I Ain't Got Nobody," was only issued on the Loadstone label in the San Francisco area. That first big hit was still a couple years away. (Top right) The group Smith was more or less a one-hit wonder, but what a hit it was. The band, with Gayle McCormick singing lead, did quite the number on the old Shirelles hit "Baby It's You." This picture sleeve is rather obscure today. (Bottom left) Hey, hey, we're the - Standells? Their picture sleeve for their 1965 single on Vee Jay, "The Boy Next Door," features a street scene the likes of which, except for the outfits, would not have been out of place for The Monkees. The sleeve also is quite rare. (Bottom right) Before the Supremes had ever had a hit single, Motown put out this picture sleeve with their second release on the label. Today, it's one of the most collectible commercially available Motown items.

Number	Title (A Side/B Side)	Yr	VG	VG+	NM
❑ 2996	Free as a Bird/Thing for You	1987	—	—	3.00

SUPREMES, THE

Motown girl group. Also see FLORENCE BALLARD; THE PRIMETTES; DIANA ROSS.

EEOC

Number	Title (A Side/B Side)	Yr	VG	VG+	NM
❑ SL4M-3114 [DJ]	Things Are Changing (same on both sides)	1965	37.50	75.00	150.00
❑ SL4M-3114 [PS]	Things Are Changing (same on both sides)	1965	37.50	75.00	150.00

—Promotional item for the Equal Employment Opportunity Commission (number not on sleeve)

GEORGE ALEXANDER INC.

Number	Title (A Side/B Side)	Yr	VG	VG+	NM
❑ 1079 [DJ]	The Only Time I'm Happy/Supremes Interview	1965	15.00	30.00	60.00

MOTOWN

Number	Title (A Side/B Side)	Yr	VG	VG+	NM
❑ 1008	I Want a Guy/Never Again	1961	75.00	150.00	300.00
❑ 1027	Your Heart Belongs to Me/(He's) Seventeen	1962	6.25	12.50	25.00
❑ 1027 [PS]	Your Heart Belongs to Me/(He's) Seventeen	1962	100.00	200.00	400.00
❑ 1034	Let Me Go the Right Way/Time Changes Things	1962	12.50	25.00	50.00
❑ 1040	My Heart Can't Take It No More/You Bring Back Memories	1963	10.00	20.00	40.00
❑ 1044	A Breath Taking, First Sight Soul Shaking, One Night Love Making, Next Day Heart Breaking Guy/Rock and Roll Banjo Band	1963	25.00	50.00	100.00
—Original pressing with long title. This does exist on stock copies as well as on promos.					
❑ 1044	A Breath Taking Guy/Rock and Roll Banjo Band	1963	6.25	12.50	25.00
❑ 1051	When the Lovelight Starts Shining Through His Eyes/Standing at the Crossroads of Love	1963	5.00	10.00	20.00
❑ 1054	Run, Run, Run/I'm Giving You Your Freedom	1964	6.25	12.50	25.00
❑ 1060	Where Did Our Love Go/He Means the World to Me	1964	5.00	10.00	20.00
❑ 1060 [PS]	Where Did Our Love Go/He Means the World to Me	1964	7.50	15.00	30.00
❑ 1066	Baby Love/Ask Any Girl	1964	5.00	10.00	20.00
❑ 1066 [PS]	Baby Love/Ask Any Girl	1964	7.50	15.00	30.00
❑ 1068	Come See About Me/Always in My Heart	1964	5.00	10.00	20.00
❑ 1074	Stop! In the Name of Love/I'm in Love Again	1965	3.75	7.50	15.00
❑ 1074 [PS]	Stop! In the Name of Love/I'm in Love Again	1965	7.50	15.00	30.00
❑ 1075	Back in My Arms Again/Whisper You Love Me Boy	1965	3.75	7.50	15.00
❑ 1075 [PS]	Back in My Arms Again/Whisper You Love Me Boy	1965	7.50	15.00	30.00
❑ 1080	Nothing But Heartaches/He Holds His Own	1965	3.75	7.50	15.00
❑ 1080 [PS]	Nothing But Heartaches/He Holds His Own	1965	7.50	15.00	30.00
❑ 1083	I Hear a Symphony/Who Could Ever Doubt My Love	1965	3.75	7.50	15.00
❑ 1085	Children's Christmas Song/Twinkle, Twinkle Little Me	1965	5.00	10.00	20.00
❑ 1085 [DJ]	Children's Christmas Song/Twinkle, Twinkle Little Me	1965	6.25	12.50	25.00
—Promo only on red vinyl					
❑ 1085 [PS]	Children's Christmas Song/Twinkle, Twinkle Little Me	1965	8.75	17.50	35.00
❑ 1089	My World Is Empty Without You/Everything Is Good About You	1966	3.75	7.50	15.00
❑ 1094	Love Is Like an Itching in My Heart/He's All I Got	1966	3.75	7.50	15.00
❑ 1097	You Can't Hurry Love/Put Yourself in My Place	1966	3.75	7.50	15.00
❑ 1097 [PS]	You Can't Hurry Love/Put Yourself in My Place	1966	7.50	15.00	30.00
❑ 1101	You Keep Me Hangin' On/Remove This Doubt	1966	3.75	7.50	15.00
❑ 1101 [PS]	You Keep Me Hangin' On/Remove This Doubt	1966	7.50	15.00	30.00
❑ 1103	Love Is Here and Now You're Gone/There's No Stopping Us Now	1967	3.00	6.00	12.00
❑ 1107	The Happening/All I Know About You	1967	3.00	6.00	12.00
❑ 1111	Reflections/Going Down for the Third Time	1967	2.00	4.00	8.00
—Starting here, through 1156, as "Diana Ross and the Supremes"					
❑ 1116	In and Out of Love/I Guess I'll Always Love You	1967	2.00	4.00	8.00
❑ 1122	Forever Came Today/Time Changes Things	1968	2.00	4.00	8.00
❑ 1125	What the World Needs Now/Your Kiss of Fire	1968	—	—	—
—Unreleased					
❑ 1126	Some Things You Never Get Used To/You've Been So Wonderful to Me	1968	2.00	4.00	8.00
❑ 1135	Love Child/Will This Be the Day	1968	2.00	4.00	8.00
❑ 1139	I'm Livin' in Shame/I'm So Glad I Got Somebody	1969	2.00	4.00	8.00
❑ 1146	The Composer/The Beginning of the End	1969	2.00	4.00	8.00
❑ 1148	No Matter What Sign You Are/The Young Folks	1969	2.00	4.00	8.00
❑ 1156	Someday We'll Be Together/He's My Sunny Boy	1969	2.00	4.00	8.00
❑ 1162	Up the Ladder to the Roof/Bill, When Are You Coming Home	1970	—	3.00	6.00
—Starting here, name reverts to "The Supremes" (unless noted)					
❑ 1167	Everybody's Got the Right to Love/But I Love You More	1970	—	3.00	6.00
❑ 1172	Stoned Love/Shine on Me	1970	—	3.00	6.00
❑ 1182	Nathan Jones/Happy (Is a Bumpy Road)	1971	—	3.00	6.00
❑ 1190	Touch/It's So Hard for Me to Say Goodbye	1971	—	3.00	6.00
❑ 1195	Floy Joy/This Is the Story	1972	—	2.50	5.00
❑ 1200	Automatically Sunshine/Precious Little Things	1972	—	2.50	5.00
❑ 1206	Your Wonderful, Sweet Sweet Love/The Wisdom of Time	1972	—	2.50	5.00
❑ 1213	I Guess I'll Miss the Man/Over and Over	1972	—	2.50	5.00
❑ 1225	Bad Weather/Oh Be My Love	1973	—	2.50	5.00
❑ 1350	It's All Been Said Before/(B-side unassigned)	1975	—	—	—
—Unreleased					
❑ 1357	He's My Man/Give Out But Don't Give Up	1975	—	2.50	5.00
❑ 1374	Where Do I Go from Here/Give Out But Don't Give Up	1975	—	2.50	5.00
❑ 1391	I'm Gonna Let My Heart Do the Walking/Early Morning Love	1976	—	2.50	5.00
❑ 1407	You're My Driving Wheel/You're What's Missing in My Life	1976	—	2.50	5.00
❑ 1415	Let Yourself Go/You Are the Heart of Me	1977	—	2.50	5.00
❑ 1488	Medley of Hits/Where Did We Go Wrong	1980	—	2.00	4.00
—As "Diana Ross and the Supremes"					
❑ 1523	Medley of Hits/Where Did We Go Wrong	1981	—	2.00	4.00
—As "Diana Ross and the Supremes"					

TAMLA

Number	Title (A Side/B Side)	Yr	VG	VG+	NM
❑ 54038	I Want a Guy/Never Again	1961	31.25	62.50	125.00
—Lines label					
❑ 54038	I Want a Guy/Never Again	1961	15.00	30.00	60.00
—Globes label					
❑ 54045	Buttered Popcorn/Who's Lovin' You	1961	15.00	30.00	60.00
—Globes label					
❑ 54045	Buttered Popcorn/Who's Lovin' You	1961	31.25	62.50	125.00
—Lines label					

TOPPS/MOTOWN

Number	Title (A Side/B Side)	Yr	VG	VG+	NM
❑ 1	Baby Love	1967	18.75	37.50	75.00
—Cardboard record					
❑ 2	Stop in the Name of Love	1967	18.75	37.50	75.00
—Cardboard record					
❑ 3	Where Did Our Love Go	1967	18.75	37.50	75.00
—Cardboard record					
❑ 15	Come See About Me	1967	18.75	37.50	75.00
—Cardboard record					
❑ 16	My World Is Empty Without You	1967	18.75	37.50	75.00
—Cardboard record					

7-Inch Extended Plays

MOTOWN

Number	Title (A Side/B Side)	Yr	VG	VG+	NM
❑ S 621 [PS]	Where Did Our Love Go	1965	6.25	12.50	25.00
❑ S 621 [S]	He Means the World to Me/Baby Love/Ask Any Girl//Where Did Our Love Go/Come See About Me/Run, Run, Run	1965	6.25	12.50	25.00

—33 1/3 rpm, small hole

SUPREMES, THE (2)

ACE

Number	Title (A Side/B Side)	Yr	VG	VG+	NM
❑ 534	Just for You and I/Don't Leave Me Here to Cry	1957	20.00	40.00	80.00

SUPREMES, THE (3)

APT

Number	Title (A Side/B Side)	Yr	VG	VG+	NM
❑ 25055	Another Chance to Love/Fidgety	1961	10.00	20.00	40.00

SUPREMES, THE (4)

KITTEN

Number	Title (A Side/B Side)	Yr	VG	VG+	NM
❑ 6969	Could This Be You/Margie	1956	125.00	250.00	500.00

SUPREMES, THE (5)

MARK

Number	Title (A Side/B Side)	Yr	VG	VG+	NM
❑ 129	Nobody Can Love You/Snap, Crackle and Pop	1958	200.00	400.00	800.00

SUPREMES, THE (6)

MASCOT

Number	Title (A Side/B Side)	Yr	VG	VG+	NM
❑ 126	Little Sally Walker/Just Yell	1960	25.00	50.00	100.00

SUPREMES, THE (7)

OLD TOWN

Number	Title (A Side/B Side)	Yr	VG	VG+	NM
❑ 1024	Tonight/My Babe	1956	25.00	50.00	100.00
❑ 1024	Tonight/She Don't Want Me No More	1956	37.50	75.00	150.00

SUPREMES, THE, AND THE FOUR TOPS

Also see each artist's individual listings.

MOTOWN

Number	Title (A Side/B Side)	Yr	VG	VG+	NM
❑ 1173	River Deep-Mountain High/Together We Can Make Such Sweet Music	1970	—	3.00	6.00
❑ 1181	You Gotta Have Love in Your Heart/I'm Glad About It	1971	—	3.00	6.00

SUPREMES, THE, DIANA ROSS AND, AND THE TEMPTATIONS

Also see each artist's individual listings.

MOTOWN

Number	Title (A Side/B Side)	Yr	VG	VG+	NM
❑ 1137	I'm Gonna Make You Love Me/A Place in the Sun	1968	—	3.50	7.00
❑ 1137 [PS]	I'm Gonna Make You Love Me/A Place in the Sun	1968	5.00	10.00	20.00
❑ 1142	I'll Try Something New/The Way You Do the Things You Do	1969	—	3.50	7.00
❑ 1150	Stubborn Kind of Fellow/Try It Baby	1969	—	3.50	7.00
❑ 1153	The Weight/For Better or Worse	1969	—	3.50	7.00

SUPREMES FOUR, THE

SARA

Number	Title (A Side/B Side)	Yr	VG	VG+	NM
❑ 1032	I Lost My Job/I Love You Patricia	1958	500.00	1000.	2000.

SURF BOYS, THE

KARATE

Number	Title (A Side/B Side)	Yr	VG	VG+	NM
❑ 526	Da Doo Ron Ron/Hurt	1966	6.25	12.50	25.00

SCEPTER

Number	Title (A Side/B Side)	Yr	VG	VG+	NM
❑ 12180	Stuck in the Chimney/I Told Santa Claus I Want You	1966	6.25	12.50	25.00

SURF BREAKERS, THE

MERCURY

Number	Title (A Side/B Side)	Yr	VG	VG+	NM
❑ 72174	Hang Ten/Ridin' In #9	1963	12.50	25.00	50.00

SURF BUNNIES, THE

DOT

Number	Title (A Side/B Side)	Yr	VG	VG+	NM
❑ 16523	Our Surfer Boys/Surf Bunny Beach	1963	7.50	15.00	30.00

GOLIATH

Number	Title (A Side/B Side)	Yr	VG	VG+	NM
❑ 1352	Our Surfer Boys/Surf Bunny Beach	1963	12.50	25.00	50.00
❑ 1353	Surf City High/Met the Boy I Adore	1963	12.50	25.00	50.00

SURF RIDERS, THE

DECCA

Number	Title (A Side/B Side)	Yr	VG	VG+	NM
❑ 31477	The Birds/Blues for the Birds	1963	7.50	15.00	30.00

NASCO

Number	Title (A Side/B Side)	Yr	VG	VG+	NM
❑ 6008	I'm Out/Rocko Socko	1958	15.00	30.00	60.00

SURF STOMPERS, THE

See BRUCE JOHNSTON.

SURFARIS, THE (1)

DECCA

Number	Title (A Side/B Side)	Yr	VG	VG+	NM
❑ 31538	Point Panic/Waikiki Run	1963	3.75	7.50	15.00

Number	Title (A Side/B Side)	Yr	VG	VG+	NM
❑ 31561	A Surfer's Christmas List/Santa's Speed Shop	1963	7.50	15.00	30.00
❑ 31581	I Wanna Take a trip to the Islands/Scatter Shield	1964	5.00	10.00	20.00
❑ 31605	Murphy the Surfie/Go Go Go For Louie's Place	1964	3.75	7.50	15.00
❑ 31641	Bossa Barracuda/Dune Buggy	1964	3.75	7.50	15.00
❑ 31682	Hot Rod High/Karen	1964	3.75	7.50	15.00
❑ 31731	Beat '65/Black Denim	1965	5.00	10.00	20.00
❑ 31784	Theme of the Battle Maiden/Somethin' Else	1965	5.00	10.00	20.00
❑ 31835	Catch a Little Ride with Me/Don't Hurt My Little Sister	1965	5.00	10.00	20.00
❑ 31954	Hey Joe Where Are You Going/So Get Out	1966	5.00	10.00	20.00
❑ 32003	Wipe Out/I'm a Hog for You	1966	2.50	5.00	10.00
DFS					
❑ 11/12	Wipe Out/Surfer Joe	1963	1500.	2250.	3000.
DOT					
❑ 144	Wipe Out/Surfer Joe	1966	2.50	5.00	10.00
—Black label, script "Dot" in multicolor letters					
❑ 144	Wipe Out/Surfer Joe	1969	—	3.00	6.00
—Multicolor label, "DOT" in all capital letters in box at top					
❑ 144 [DJ]	Wipe Out (same on both sides)	1966	25.00	50.00	100.00
—Red vinyl					
❑ 144 [DJ]	Wipe Out (same on both sides)	1966	37.50	75.00	150.00
—Red vinyl; error pressing with "Surfer Joe" on both sides					
❑ 16479	Wipe Out/Surfer Joe	1963	3.75	7.50	15.00
❑ 16757	Surfer Joe/Can't Sit Down	1965	7.50	15.00	30.00
—B-side by the Challengers, but credited to the Surfaris					
❑ 16757	Surfer Joe/Can't Sit Down	1965	12.50	25.00	50.00
—B-side by the Challengers, and credited correctly					
❑ 16966	Show Biz/Chicago Green	1966	2.50	5.00	10.00
❑ 17008	Shake/The Search	1967	2.50	5.00	10.00
PRINCESS					
❑ 50	Wipe Out/Surfer Joe	1963	100.00	200.00	400.00
—With long versions of both songs. No "RE-1" is in the trail-off area.					
❑ 50	Wipe Out/Surfer Joe	1963	37.50	75.00	150.00
—With short versions of both songs. "RE-1" is in the trail-off area.					

SURFARIS, THE (2)

This group was forced to change its name to "The Original Surfaris."

Number	Title (A Side/B Side)	Yr	VG	VG+	NM
CHANCELLOR					
❑ 1142	The Midnight Surf/Psyche-Out	1963	12.50	25.00	50.00
DEL-FI					
❑ 4219	Surfari/Bombora	1963	25.00	50.00	100.00
FELSTED					
❑ 8688	Tor-Chula/Psyche-Out	1964	12.50	25.00	50.00
NORTHRIDGE					
❑ 1001	Moment of Truth/Church Key	1963	15.00	30.00	60.00
—B-side by the Biscaynes					
REGANO					
❑ 1062	Surfin' '63/Boss Beat	1963	12.50	25.00	50.00
—As "The Original Surfaris"					
REPRISE					
❑ 20180	Moment of Truth/Church Key	1963	7.50	15.00	30.00
—B-side by the Biscaynes					
SURFARI					
❑ 301	Gum Dipped Slicks/High Time	1964	25.00	50.00	100.00
—As "The Original Surfaris"					

SURVIVOR

Also see JIM PETERIK.

Number	Title (A Side/B Side)	Yr	VG	VG+	NM
CASABLANCA					
❑ 880053-7	Moment of Truth/It Doesn't Have to Be That Way	1984	—	2.00	4.00
SCOTTI BROS.					
❑ 511	Somwhere in America/Freelance	1980	—	2.50	5.00
❑ 517	Rebel Girl/Freelance	1980	—	2.50	5.00
❑ 02434	Memphis/Love Isn't Easy	1981	—	2.00	4.00
❑ 02560	Poor Man's Son/Love Is On My Side	1981	—	2.00	4.00
❑ 02700	Summer Nights/Take You on a Saturday	1982	—	2.00	4.00
❑ 02912	Eye of the Tiger/Take You on a Saturday	1982	—	2.00	4.00
❑ 02912 [PS]	Eye of the Tiger/Take You on a Saturday	1982	—	3.00	6.00
❑ 03213	American Heartbeat/Silver Girl	1982	—	2.00	4.00
❑ 03213 [PS]	American Heartbeat/Silver Girl	1982	—	2.50	5.00
❑ 03485	The One That Really Matters/Hesitation Dance	1983	—	2.00	4.00
❑ 04074	Caught in the Game/Slander	1983	—	2.00	4.00
❑ 04074 [PS]	Caught in the Game/Slander	1983	—	2.50	5.00
❑ 04347	I Never Stopped Loving You/Ready for the Real Thing	1984	—	2.00	4.00
❑ 04603	I Can't Hold Back/I See You in Everyone	1984	—	—	3.00
❑ 04603 [PS]	I Can't Hold Back/I See You in Everyone	1984	—	2.00	4.00
❑ 04685	High on You/Broken Promises	1984	—	—	3.00
❑ 04685 [PS]	High on You/Broken Promises	1984	—	2.00	4.00
❑ 04871	The Search Is Over/It's the Singer, Not the Song	1985	—	—	3.00
❑ 04871 [PS]	The Search Is Over/It's the Singer, Not the Song	1985	—	2.00	4.00
❑ 05579	First Night/Feels Like Love	1985	—	—	3.00
❑ 05579 [PS]	First Night/Feels Like Love	1985	—	2.00	4.00
❑ 05663	Burning Heart/Feels Like Love	1985	—	—	3.00
❑ 05663 [PS]	Burning Heart/Feels Like Love	1985	—	2.00	4.00
❑ 06381	Is This Love/Can't Let You Go	1986	—	—	3.00
❑ 06381 [PS]	Is This Love/Can't Let You Go	1986	—	2.00	4.00
❑ 06705	How Much Love/Backstreet Love Affair	1987	—	—	3.00
❑ 07070	Man Against the World/Oceans	1987	—	—	3.00
❑ 07070 [PS]	Man Against the World/Oceans	1987	—	2.00	4.00
❑ 08067	Didn't Know It Was Love/Rhythm of the City	1988	—	—	3.00
❑ 68526	Across the Miles/Burning Bridges	1989	—	—	3.00

SURVIVORS, THE

Dave Nowlen, Bob Norberg and friends with help from BRIAN WILSON. This record is NOT by the Beach Boys.

Number	Title (A Side/B Side)	Yr	VG	VG+	NM
CAPITOL					
❑ 5102	Pamela Jean/After the Game	1963	250.00	500.00	1000.

SUSIE AND THE FOUR TRUMPETS

Number	Title (A Side/B Side)	Yr	VG	VG+	NM
UNITED ARTISTS					
❑ 471	Starry Eyes/Blue Little Girl	1962	15.00	30.00	60.00

SUTCH, SCREAMING LORD

Number	Title (A Side/B Side)	Yr	VG	VG+	NM
CAMEO					
❑ 341	She's Fallen in Love with the Monster Man/Bye Bye Baby	1964	3.75	7.50	15.00
COTILLION					
❑ 44149	Gotta Keep a-Rocking/Country Club	1972	2.50	5.00	10.00
—As "Lord Sutch"					

SUZY AND THE RED STRIPES

Actually Linda McCartney with Wings. Also see PAUL McCARTNEY.

Number	Title (A Side/B Side)	Yr	VG	VG+	NM
CAPITOL					
❑ B-5608	Seaside Woman/B-Side to Seaside	1986	7.50	15.00	30.00
EPIC					
❑ 50403	Seaside Woman/B-Side to Seaside	1977	2.50	5.00	10.00
❑ 50403 [DJ]	Seaside Woman (mono/stereo)	1977	25.00	50.00	100.00
—"Advance Promotion" label, black vinyl					
❑ 50403 [DJ]	Seaside Woman (mono/stereo)	1977	6.25	12.50	25.00
—Red vinyl, orange label on one side, white on the other					
❑ 50403 [DJ]	Seaside Woman (mono/stereo)	1977	25.00	50.00	100.00
—Black vinyl, orange label on one side, white on the other					

SWALLOWS, THE

Number	Title (A Side/B Side)	Yr	VG	VG+	NM
AFTER HOURS					
❑ 104	My Baby/Good Time Girls	1954	800.00	1600.	2400.
FEDERAL					
❑ 12319	Oh Lonesome Me/Angel Baby	1958	10.00	20.00	40.00
❑ 12328	We Want to Rock/Rock-a-Bye-Baby Rock	1958	10.00	20.00	40.00
❑ 12329	Beside You/Laughing Boy	1958	10.00	20.00	40.00
❑ 12333	Itchy Twitchy Feeling/Who Knows, Do You?	1958	10.00	20.00	40.00
KING					
❑ 4458	Will You Be Mine/Dearest	1951	500.00	1000.	1500.
❑ 4501	Eternally/It Ain't the Meat	1952	200.00	400.00	800.00
—Black vinyl					
❑ 4501	Eternally/It Ain't the Meat	1952	625.00	1250.	2500.
—Blue vinyl					
❑ 4501	Eternally/It Ain't the Meat	1952	625.00	1250.	2500.
—Green vinyl					
❑ 4515	Tell Me Why/Roll, Roll, Pretty Baby	1952	1000.	1500.	2000.
❑ 4525	Beside You/You Left Me	1952	100.00	200.00	400.00
❑ 4533	You Walked In/I Only Have Eyes for You	1952	200.00	400.00	800.00
❑ 4579	Where Do I Go from Here/Please, Baby, Please	1952	200.00	400.00	800.00
❑ 4612	Laugh (Though You Want to Cry)/Our Love Is Dying	1953	125.00	250.00	500.00
❑ 4632	Nobody's Lovin' Me/Bicycle Tillie	1953	125.00	250.00	500.00
❑ 4656	Trust Me/Pleading Blues	1953	100.00	200.00	400.00
❑ 4676	I'll Be Waiting/It Feels So Good	1953	100.00	200.00	400.00

SWALLOWS, THE (2)

Number	Title (A Side/B Side)	Yr	VG	VG+	NM
GUYDEN					
❑ 2023	How Long Must a Fool Go On/You Must Try	1959	12.50	25.00	50.00
—Reissued credited to "The Guides"					

SWAMP RATS, THE

Number	Title (A Side/B Side)	Yr	VG	VG+	NM
CO & CE					
❑ 245	In the Midnight Hour/It's Not Easy	1967	5.00	10.00	20.00
ST. CLAIR					
❑ 69	Louie Louie/Hey Joe	1966	12.50	25.00	50.00
❑ 2222	Psycho/Here, There and Everywhere	1966	50.00	100.00	200.00
❑ 3333	Two Tymes Two/(B-side unknown)	1966	12.50	25.00	50.00
❑ 711711	It's Not Easy/No Friend of Mine	1966	12.50	25.00	50.00

SWANS, THE (1)

Number	Title (A Side/B Side)	Yr	VG	VG+	NM
BALLAD					
❑ 1003/6	It's a Must/Night Train	1954	150.00	300.00	600.00
❑ 1007	Happy/The Santa Claus Boogie	1955	150.00	300.00	600.00
FORTUNE					
❑ 822	I'll Forever Love You/Mister Cool Breeze	1955	200.00	400.00	800.00
RAINBOW					
❑ 233	No More/My True Love	1954	375.00	750.00	1500.
—Red vinyl					
STEAMBOAT					
❑ 101	Believe in Me/In the Morning	1956	625.00	1250.	2500.

SWANS, THE (2)

Number	Title (A Side/B Side)	Yr	VG	VG+	NM
CAMEO					
❑ 302	The Boy with the Beatle Hair/Please Hurry Home	1964	10.00	20.00	40.00
PARKWAY					
❑ 881	Daydreamin' of You/The Promise	1963	7.50	15.00	30.00
SWAN					
❑ 4151	He's Mine/You Better Be a Good Girl Now	1963	7.50	15.00	30.00

SWANS, THE (3)

Number	Title (A Side/B Side)	Yr	VG	VG+	NM
ROULETTE					
❑ 4213	He Wasn't On the Air Again Today/If I Could Stop Every Clock	1959	6.25	12.50	25.00

SWANSON, BOBBY

Number	Title (A Side/B Side)	Yr	VG	VG+	NM
DONNA					
❑ 1326	Tom and Susie/China Doll	1960	6.25	12.50	25.00
❑ 1336	Janie's Face/Peggy's Last Birthday	1961	6.25	12.50	25.00
❑ 1356	Twisting at the Top/Hello There Lover Doll	1962	6.25	12.50	25.00
IGLOO					
❑ 1003	Rockin' Little Eskimo/Ballad of an Angel	1959	100.00	200.00	400.00

SWATLEY, HANK

Number	Title (A Side/B Side)	Yr	VG	VG+	NM
AARON					
❑ 101	Oakie Boogie/I Can't Help It	1957	125.00	250.00	500.00

SWEET, THE (1)
British pop-rock band.

20TH CENTURY

Number	Title (A Side/B Side)	Yr	VG	VG+	NM
❑ 2033	It's Lonely Out There/I'm On My Way	1973	2.50	5.00	10.00

—U.S. issue of 1968 material that was on Fontana in the U.K.

BELL

Number	Title (A Side/B Side)	Yr	VG	VG+	NM
❑ 45106	Funny, Funny/You're Not Wrong for Loving Me	1971	2.00	4.00	8.00
❑ 45126	Co-Co/You're Not Wrong for Loving Me	1971	—	3.00	6.00
❑ 45184	Poppa Joe/Jeanie	1972	—	3.00	6.00
❑ 45251	Little Willy/Man from Mecca	1972	—	3.00	6.00
❑ 45361	Blockbuster/Need a Lot of Lovin'	1973	—	2.50	5.00
❑ 45408	Wig-Wam Bam/New York Connection	1973	—	2.50	5.00

CAPITOL

Number	Title (A Side/B Side)	Yr	VG	VG+	NM
❑ 4055	Ballroom Blitz/Restless	1975	—	2.50	5.00
❑ 4157	Fox on the Run/Burn On the Flame	1975	—	2.50	5.00
❑ 4220	Action/Medussa	1976	—	2.50	5.00
❑ 4429	Fever of Love/Heartbreak Today	1977	—	2.50	5.00
❑ 4454	Funk It Up (David's Song)/Stairway to the Stars	1977	—	2.50	5.00
❑ 4549	Love Is Like Oxygen/Cover Girl	1978	—	2.50	5.00
❑ 4610	California Nights/Dream On	1978	—	2.50	5.00
❑ 4730	Mother Earth/Why Don't You	1979	—	2.00	4.00
❑ 4908	Sixties Man/Water's Edge	1980	—	2.00	4.00

PARAMOUNT

Number	Title (A Side/B Side)	Yr	VG	VG+	NM
❑ 0044	All You'll Ever Get from Me/The Juicer	1970	5.00	10.00	20.00

SWEET, THE (2)

SMASH

Number	Title (A Side/B Side)	Yr	VG	VG+	NM
❑ 2116	Got to Have More Love/You Can't Win at Love	1967	3.75	7.50	15.00
❑ 2136	Broken Heart Attack/Don't Do It	1967	3.75	7.50	15.00

SWEET INSPIRATIONS, THE
Also see CISSY HOUSTON.

ATLANTIC

Number	Title (A Side/B Side)	Yr	VG	VG+	NM
❑ 2410	Why (Am I Treated So Bad)/I Don't Want to Go On Without You	1967	2.00	4.00	8.00
❑ 2418	Let It Be Me/When Something Is Wrong with My Baby	1967	2.00	4.00	8.00
❑ 2436	I've Been Loving You Too Long (To Stop Now)/That's How Strong My Love Is	1967	2.00	4.00	8.00
❑ 2449	O' What a Fool I've Been/Don't Fight It	1967	2.00	4.00	8.00
❑ 2465	Reach Out for Me/Do Right Woman — Do Right Man	1967	2.00	4.00	8.00
❑ 2476	Sweet Inspiration/I'm Blue	1968	2.00	4.00	8.00
❑ 2529	To Love Somebody/Where Did It Go	1968	2.00	4.00	8.00
❑ 2551	Unchained Melody/Am I Ever Gonna See My Baby Again	1968	2.00	4.00	8.00
❑ 2571	What the World Needs Now Is Love/You Really Didn't Mean It	1968	2.00	4.00	8.00
❑ 2620	Crying in the Rain/Everyday WIll Be Like a Holiday	1969	2.00	4.00	8.00
❑ 2638	Sweets for My Sweet/Get a Little Order	1969	2.00	4.00	8.00
❑ 2653	Don't Go/Chained	1969	2.00	4.00	8.00
❑ 2686	(Gotta Find) A Brand New Lover — Part I/(Gotta Find) A Brand New Lover — Part II	1969	2.00	4.00	8.00
❑ 2720	At Last I Found a Love/That's the Way My Baby Is	1970	—	3.00	6.00
❑ 2732	Them Boys/Flash in the Pan	1970	—	3.00	6.00
❑ 2750	This World/A Light Sings	1970	—	3.00	6.00
❑ 2779	Evidence/Change Me Not	1970	—	3.00	6.00

CARIBOU

Number	Title (A Side/B Side)	Yr	VG	VG+	NM
❑ 9022	Black Sunday/(Instrumental)	1977	—	2.00	4.00

RSO

Number	Title (A Side/B Side)	Yr	VG	VG+	NM
❑ 932	Love Is On the Way/(Instrumental)	1979	—	2.50	5.00
❑ 1013	Love Is On the Way/(Instrumental)	1979	—	2.00	4.00

STAX

Number	Title (A Side/B Side)	Yr	VG	VG+	NM
❑ 0178	Emercury/Slipped and Tripped	1973	—	2.50	5.00
❑ 0203	Try a Little Tenderness/Dirty Tricks	1974	—	2.50	5.00

SWEET MARQUEES, THE

APACHE

Number	Title (A Side/B Side)	Yr	VG	VG+	NM
❑ 1516	You Lied/I Love My Baby	1961	75.00	150.00	300.00

SWEET SICK TEENS, THE

RCA VICTOR

Number	Title (A Side/B Side)	Yr	VG	VG+	NM
❑ 37-7940	The Pretzel/Agnes, the Teenage Russian Spy	1961	20.00	40.00	80.00

—"Compact Single 33" (small hole, plays at LP speed)

Number	Title (A Side/B Side)	Yr	VG	VG+	NM
❑ 47-7940	The Pretzel/Agnes, the Teenage Russian Spy	1961	10.00	20.00	40.00

SWEET TEENS, THE

FLIP

Number	Title (A Side/B Side)	Yr	VG	VG+	NM
❑ 311	Forever More/Don't Worry About a Thing	1955	15.00	30.00	60.00

GEE

Number	Title (A Side/B Side)	Yr	VG	VG+	NM
❑ 1030	My Valentine/With This Ring	1957	15.00	30.00	60.00

SWEETIES, THE

END

Number	Title (A Side/B Side)	Yr	VG	VG+	NM
❑ 1110	After You/Paul's Love	1962	5.00	10.00	20.00

SWENSONS, THE

X-TRA

Number	Title (A Side/B Side)	Yr	VG	VG+	NM
❑ 100	Remember Me to My Darling/Golly Boo	1957	50.00	100.00	200.00

SWIFT, BASIL, AND THE SEEGRAMS
Also see DANNY HUTTON.

MERCURY

Number	Title (A Side/B Side)	Yr	VG	VG+	NM
❑ 72386	Farmer's Daughter/Shambles	1965	50.00	100.00	200.00

SWINGIN' MEDALLIONS

1-2-3

Number	Title (A Side/B Side)	Yr	VG	VG+	NM
❑ 1723	We're Gonna Hate Ourselves in the Morning/It's Alright	1970	2.00	4.00	8.00
❑ 1732	Rollin' Rovin' River/Don't Let Your Feet Touch the Ground	1971	2.00	4.00	8.00

4 SALE

Number	Title (A Side/B Side)	Yr	VG	VG+	NM
❑ 002	Double Shot (Of My Baby's Love)/Here It Comes Again	1966	25.00	50.00	100.00

CAPITOL

Number	Title (A Side/B Side)	Yr	VG	VG+	NM
❑ 2338	Sun, Sand and Sea/Hey, Hey Baby	1968	2.00	4.00	8.00

DOT

Number	Title (A Side/B Side)	Yr	VG	VG+	NM
❑ 16721	Bye Bye, Silly Girl/I Want to Be Your Guy	1965	3.00	6.00	12.00

SMASH

Number	Title (A Side/B Side)	Yr	VG	VG+	NM
❑ 2033	Double Shot (Of My Baby's Love)/Here It Comes Again	1966	3.75	7.50	15.00
❑ 2050	She Drives Me Out of My Mind/You Gotta Have Faith	1966	3.00	6.00	12.00
❑ 2075	I Don't Want to Lose It for You Baby/Night Owl	1966	3.00	6.00	12.00
❑ 2084	Don't Cry No More/I Found a Rainbow	1967	2.50	5.00	10.00
❑ 2107	Turn On the Music/Summer's Not the Same This Year	1967	2.50	5.00	10.00
❑ 2129	Bow and Arrow/Where Can I Go to Get Soul	1967	2.50	5.00	10.00

SWINGING BLUE JEANS, THE
Also see TERRY SYLVESTER.

IMPERIAL

Number	Title (A Side/B Side)	Yr	VG	VG+	NM
❑ 66021	Hippy Hippy Shake/Now I Must Go	1964	3.75	7.50	15.00
❑ 66030	Good Golly Miss Molly/Shaking Feeling	1964	3.00	6.00	12.00
❑ 66049	Shake, Rattle and Roll/You're No Good	1964	3.00	6.00	12.00
❑ 66059	Tutti Frutti/Promise You'll Tell Her	1964	3.00	6.00	12.00
❑ 66090	It Isn't There/One of These Days	1965	3.00	6.00	12.00
❑ 66154	Don't Make Me Over/What Can I Do Today	1966	3.00	6.00	12.00
❑ 66225	Now the Summer's Gone/Rumors, Gossip, Words Untrue	1967	2.50	5.00	10.00
❑ 66255	Something's Coming Along/Tremblin'	1967	2.50	5.00	10.00

SWINGING EMBERS, THE

ACE

Number	Title (A Side/B Side)	Yr	VG	VG+	NM
❑ 644	Winter Wonderland/I'm So Lonely	1961	3.75	7.50	15.00

SWINGING HEARTS, THE

620

Number	Title (A Side/B Side)	Yr	VG	VG+	NM
❑ 1002	How Can I Love You/(B-side unknown)	1963	50.00	100.00	200.00

NRM

Number	Title (A Side/B Side)	Yr	VG	VG+	NM
❑ 1002	How Can I Love You/(B-side unknown)	1963	75.00	150.00	300.00

SWINGING TIGERS

TAMLA

Number	Title (A Side/B Side)	Yr	VG	VG+	NM
❑ 54024	Snake Walk (Part 1)/Snake Walk (Part 2)	1960	75.00	150.00	300.00

SYCAMORES, THE

GROOVE

Number	Title (A Side/B Side)	Yr	VG	VG+	NM
❑ 0121	I'll Be Waiting/Darling, Is It True	1955	50.00	100.00	200.00

SYLVESTER, TERRY
Also see THE HOLLIES; THE SWINGING BLUE JEANS.

EPIC

Number	Title (A Side/B Side)	Yr	VG	VG+	NM
❑ 20002	It's Better Off This Way/For the Peace of All Mankind	1974	—	2.00	4.00
❑ 20002 [PS]	It's Better Off This Way/For the Peace of All Mankind	1974	—	2.50	5.00
❑ 50017	It's Better Off This Way/For the Peace of All Mankind	1974	—	2.00	4.00
❑ 50532	Silver and Gold/Realistic Situation	1978	—	2.00	4.00

SYLVIA, MARGO
See TUNE WEAVERS.

SYLVIA (1)
R&B singer and record company mogul (All Platinum/Stang/Vibration, Sugar Hill). Also see MICKEY AND SYLVIA.

ALL PLATINUM

Number	Title (A Side/B Side)	Yr	VG	VG+	NM
❑ 2303	I Can't Help It/It's a Good Life	1969	2.00	4.00	8.00
❑ 2350	Sho Nuff Boogie (Part 1)/Sho Nuff Boogie (Part 2)	1974	—	2.50	5.00

—With the Moments

JUBILEE

Number	Title (A Side/B Side)	Yr	VG	VG+	NM
❑ 5093	Drive, Daddy, Drive/I Found Somebody to Love	1952	12.50	25.00	50.00

—As "Little Sylvia"

STANG

Number	Title (A Side/B Side)	Yr	VG	VG+	NM
❑ 5015	Have You Had Any Lately/Anytime	1970	—	3.00	6.00

SUGAR HILL

Number	Title (A Side/B Side)	Yr	VG	VG+	NM
❑ 781	It's Good to Be the Queen/(B-side unknown)	1982	—	2.00	4.00

VIBRATION

Number	Title (A Side/B Side)	Yr	VG	VG+	NM
❑ 512	Next Time I See You/Gimme a Little Action	1972	—	3.00	6.00
❑ 521	Pillow Talk/My Thing	1973	—	3.00	6.00
❑ 524	Didn't I/Had Any Lately	1973	—	2.50	5.00
❑ 525	Soul Je T'Aime/Sunday	1973	—	2.50	5.00

—With Ralfi Pagan

Number	Title (A Side/B Side)	Yr	VG	VG+	NM
❑ 527	Alfredo/Lay It On Me	1973	—	2.50	5.00
❑ 528	Private Performance/If You Get the Notion	1974	—	2.50	5.00
❑ 529	Sweet Stuff/Had Any Lately	1974	—	2.50	5.00
❑ 530	Easy Evil/Give It Up in Vain	1974	—	2.50	5.00
❑ 536	Pussy Cat (Part 1)/Pussy Cat (Part 2)	1975	—	2.50	5.00
❑ 567	L.A. Sunshine/Taxi	1976	—	2.50	5.00
❑ 570	Lay It On Me (Vocal)/(Instrumental)	1977	—	2.50	5.00
❑ 572	Lollipop Man/Lay It On Me	1977	—	2.50	5.00
❑ 576	Automatic Lover/Stop Boy	1978	—	2.50	5.00

SYMBOLS, THE (1)

DORE

Number	Title (A Side/B Side)	Yr	VG	VG+	NM
❑ 666	Last Year About This Time/Better Get Your Own One Buddy	1963	3.75	7.50	15.00

SYMBOLS, THE (2)

IMPERIAL

Number	Title (A Side/B Side)	Yr	VG	VG+	NM
❑ 66382	I Will Still Be There/The Wrong Girl	1969	2.00	4.00	8.00

Number	Title (A Side/B Side)	Yr	VG	VG+	NM

SYMBOLS, THE (3)

Number	Title (A Side/B Side)	Yr	VG	VG+	NM
MGM					
❑ 13348	One Fine Girl/Don't Go	1965	2.50	5.00	10.00
❑ 13463	Don't Go/Oo Wee Baby	1966	2.50	5.00	10.00

SYMBOLS, THE (4)

Number	Title (A Side/B Side)	Yr	VG	VG+	NM
VINTAGE					
❑ 1007	Bye Bye/I Love You	1973	—	2.50	5.00

SYMBOLS, THE (U)

Number	Title (A Side/B Side)	Yr	VG	VG+	NM
LAURIE					
❑ 3401	Bye Bye Baby/The Things You Do to Me	1967	2.50	5.00	10.00
❑ 3435	The Best Part of Breaking Up/Again	1968	2.50	5.00	10.00
PRESIDENT					
❑ 102	Canadian Sunset/The Gentle Art of Loving	1966	2.50	5.00	10.00

SYNDICATE, THE

Number	Title (A Side/B Side)	Yr	VG	VG+	NM
DORE					
❑ 743	My Baby Is Barefoot/Love Will Take Away	1965	10.00	20.00	40.00
DOT					
❑ 16807	Egyptian Thing/She Haunts You	1965	10.00	20.00	40.00

SYNDICATE OF SOUND

Number	Title (A Side/B Side)	Yr	VG	VG+	NM
BELL					
❑ 640	Little Girl/You	1966	5.00	10.00	20.00
❑ 646	Rumors/Upper Hand	1966	3.75	7.50	15.00
❑ 655	Goodtime Music/Keep It Up	1966	3.75	7.50	15.00
❑ 666	Mary/That Kind of Man	1967	3.75	7.50	15.00
BUDDAH					
❑ 156	Brown Paper Bag/Reverb Beat	1970	2.50	5.00	10.00
❑ 183	Mexico/First to Love You	1970	2.50	5.00	10.00
CAPITOL					
❑ 2426	You're Looking Fine/Change the World	1969	2.50	5.00	10.00
DEL-FI					
❑ 4304	Prepare for Love/Tell the World	1965	5.00	10.00	20.00
HUSH					
❑ 228	Little Girl/You	1966	12.50	25.00	50.00
PHILCO-FORD					
❑ HP-29	Little Girl/Rumors	1968	5.00	10.00	20.00
—4-inch plastic "Hip Pocket Record" with color sleeve					
SCARLET					
❑ 503	Prepare for Love/Tell the World	1965	7.50	15.00	30.00

SYNERGY

Number	Title (A Side/B Side)	Yr	VG	VG+	NM
PASSPORT					
❑ 7907	Classical Gas/Cybersports	1976	2.00	4.00	8.00

SYREETA

Also see BILLY PRESTON AND SYREETA.

Number	Title (A Side/B Side)	Yr	VG	VG+	NM
MOTOWN					
❑ 1297	Come and Get This Stuff/Black Maybe	1974	—	2.50	5.00
❑ 1317	I'm Goin' Left/Heavy day	1974	—	2.50	5.00
❑ 1328	Your Kiss Is Sweeter/Spinnin' and Spinnin'	1975	—	2.50	5.00
❑ 1353	Harmour Love/Cause We've Ended As Lovers	1975	—	2.50	5.00
❑ 1353 [DJ]	Harmour Love (same on both sides?)	1975	2.50	5.00	10.00
—Promo only on red vinyl					
MOWEST					
❑ 5016	I Love Every Little Thing About You/Black Maybe	1972	—	3.00	6.00
❑ 5021	Happiness/To Know You Is to Love You	1972	—	3.00	6.00
TAMLA					
❑ 1610	I Must Be in Love/Wish Upon a Star	1982	—	2.00	4.00
❑ 1675	Forever Is Not Enough/She's Leaving Home	1983	—	2.00	4.00
❑ 54333	Quick Slick/I Don't Know	1981	—	2.00	4.00

SZIGETI, SANDY

Number	Title (A Side/B Side)	Yr	VG	VG+	NM
DECCA					
❑ 32862	America's Sweetheart/My Steady Diet	1971	2.50	5.00	10.00
—Produced by Rick Nelson					

T

T-BIRDS, THE

Number	Title (A Side/B Side)	Yr	VG	VG+	NM
CHESS					
❑ 1778	Green Stamps/Come On Dance with Me	1961	6.25	12.50	25.00
❑ 1792	Hog Wild/Taco Harry	1961	6.25	12.50	25.00
GONE					
❑ 5141	Wild Stomp/Soft Smoke	1962	5.00	10.00	20.00
T-BIRD					
❑ 101	Green Stamps/Come On Dance with Me	1961	10.00	20.00	40.00
VEGAS					
❑ 720	Nobody But You/Have You Ever Been in Love Before	1968	15.00	30.00	60.00

T-BONES, THE

Members of this group later formed HAMILTON, JOE FRANK AND REYNOLDS.

Number	Title (A Side/B Side)	Yr	VG	VG+	NM
LIBERTY					
❑ 55677	Draggin'/Rail-Vette	1964	5.00	10.00	20.00
❑ 55814	That's Where It's At/Pearlin'	1965	3.75	7.50	15.00
❑ 55836	No Matter What Shape (Your Stomach's In)/ Feelin' Fine	1965	3.00	6.00	12.00
❑ 55867	Sippin' & Chippin'/Moment of Softness	1966	2.50	5.00	10.00
❑ 55885	Underwater/Wherever You Look, Wherever You Go	1966	2.50	5.00	10.00
❑ 55906	Let's Go Get Stoned/Farre Thee Well	1966	2.50	5.00	10.00
❑ 55925	Balboa Blues/Walkin' My Cat Named Dog	1966	2.50	5.00	10.00
❑ 55951	Tee Hee Hee (My Life Seems Different Now)/ Proper Thing to Do	1967	2.50	5.00	10.00
UNITED ARTISTS					
❑ 0068	No Matter What Shape (Your Stomach's In)/ Sippin' N Chippin'	1973	—	2.50	5.00
—"Silver Spotlight Series" reissue					

T.C. ATLANTIC

Number	Title (A Side/B Side)	Yr	VG	VG+	NM
AESOP'S LABEL					
❑ 6044	Once Upon a Melody/I Love You So, Little Girl	1965	10.00	20.00	40.00
B. SHARP					
❑ 272	Mona/My Babe	1966	7.50	15.00	30.00
CANDY FLOSS					
❑ 101	I'm So Glad/Twenty Years Ago	1968	10.00	20.00	40.00
PARAMOUNT					
❑ 0098	Judgment Train/Shine the Light	1971	3.75	7.50	15.00
PARROT					
❑ 330	I'm So Glad/Twenty Years Ago	1968	5.00	10.00	20.00
❑ 338	Love Is Just/Faces	1969	5.00	10.00	20.00
TURTLE					
❑ 1103	Faces/Baby, Please Don't Go	1966	25.00	50.00	100.00
❑ 1105	Shake/Spanish Harlem	1967	10.00	20.00	40.00

T.I.M.E.

Number	Title (A Side/B Side)	Yr	VG	VG+	NM
LIBERTY					
❑ 56020	Take Me Along/Make It Right	1968	2.50	5.00	10.00
❑ 56020 [PS]	Take Me Along/Make It Right	1968	3.75	7.50	15.00
❑ 56060	Tripping Into Sunshine/What Would Life Be Without You	1968	2.50	5.00	10.00

T. REX

Number	Title (A Side/B Side)	Yr	VG	VG+	NM
A&M					
❑ 955	Child Star/Debora	1968	3.00	6.00	12.00
—As "Tyrannosaurus Rex"					
BLUE THUMB					
❑ 212	By the Light of the Magical Moon/Fina a Little Wood	1971	—	3.00	6.00
❑ SP-6115/6 [DJ]	Ride a White Swan/Is It Love	1970	3.00	6.00	12.00
—As "Tyrannosaurus Rex"					
❑ 7121	Ride a White Swan/Summertime Blues	1970	2.00	4.00	8.00
—As "Tyrannosaurus Rex"					
CASABLANCA					
❑ 810	Precious Star/(B-side unknown)	1974	—	3.00	6.00
REPRISE					
❑ 1006	Hot Love//One Inch Rock/Seagull Woman	1971	—	3.00	6.00
❑ 1032	Bang a Gong (Get It On)/Raw Ramp	1971	2.00	4.00	8.00
❑ 1056	Jeepster/Rip Off	1971	—	3.00	6.00
❑ 1078	Telegram Sam/Cadillac	1972	—	3.00	6.00
❑ 1095	Metal Guru/Lady	1972	—	3.00	6.00
❑ 1122	The Slider/Rock On	1972	—	3.00	6.00
❑ 1150	Bang a Gong (Get It On)/Telegram Sam	1972	—	2.00	4.00
—"Back to Back Hits" series					
❑ 1151	Jeepster/Metal Guru	1972	—	2.00	4.00
—"Back to Back Hits" series					
❑ 1161	Born to Boogie/The Groover	1973	—	2.50	5.00
❑ 1161 [PS]	Born to Boogie/The Groover	1973	6.25	12.50	25.00
❑ 1170	Hot Love/Rip Off	1973	—	2.50	5.00

T.S.U. TORONADOES, THE

Number	Title (A Side/B Side)	Yr	VG	VG+	NM
ATLANTIC					
❑ 2579	Getting the Corners/What Good Am I!	1968	2.00	4.00	8.00
❑ 2614	Got to Get Through to You/The Goose	1969	2.00	4.00	8.00
VOLT					
❑ 4030	My Thing Is a Moving Thing/Still Love You	1969	—	3.00	6.00
❑ 4038	One Flight Too Many/Play the Music Toronadoes	1970	—	3.00	6.00

TABBYS, THE

Number	Title (A Side/B Side)	Yr	VG	VG+	NM
TIME					
❑ 1008	Yes I Do/My Darling	1959	12.50	25.00	50.00
—Blue label					
❑ 1008	Yes I Do/My Darling	1959	6.25	12.50	25.00
—Red label					

TABS, THE

Number	Title (A Side/B Side)	Yr	VG	VG+	NM
DOT					
❑ 15887	Avenue of Tears/The First Star	1959	7.50	15.00	30.00
GARDENA					
❑ 110	Never Forget/Rock and Roll Holiday	1960	12.50	25.00	50.00
NASCO					
❑ 6016	Will We Meet Again/Still Love You Baby	1958	7.50	15.00	30.00
NOBLE					
❑ 719	Never Forget/Rock and Roll Holiday	1959	37.50	75.00	150.00
❑ 720	Oops/My Girl Is Gone	1959	100.00	200.00	400.00
VEE JAY					
❑ 418	Dance All By Myself/Dance Party	1961	5.00	10.00	20.00
❑ 446	Mash Dem Taters/But You're My Baby	1962	5.00	10.00	20.00
WAND					
❑ 130	Two Stupid Feet/Footsteps	1962	3.75	7.50	15.00
❑ 139	I'm with You/Take My Love Along with You	1963	3.75	7.50	15.00

TADS, THE

Number	Title (A Side/B Side)	Yr	VG	VG+	NM
DOT					
❑ 15518	Your Reason/The Pink Panther	1956	6.25	12.50	25.00
LIBERTY BELL					
❑ 9010	Your Reason/The Pink Panther	1956	12.50	25.00	50.00
REV					
❑ 3513	Wolf Call/She Is My Dream	1958	12.50	25.00	50.00

TAGES, THE

With PETER FRAMPTON.

Number	Title (A Side/B Side)	Yr	VG	VG+	NM
VERVE					
❑ 10626	Halcyon Days/I Read You Like an Open Book	1968	5.00	10.00	20.00

TAKERS, THE
INTERPHON

Number	Title (A Side/B Side)	Yr	VG	VG+	NM
❑ 7709	Think/If You Don't Come Back	1964	2.50	5.00	10.00

TALKING HEADS
Also see JERRY HARRISON.

SIRE

Number	Title (A Side/B Side)	Yr	VG	VG+	NM
❑ GSRE 0452	Take Me to the River/Life During Wartime	198?	—	—	3.00
—"Back to Back Hits" reissue					
❑ GSRE 0479	Burning Down the House/This Must Be the Place	198?	—	—	3.00
—"Back to Back Hits" reissue					
❑ 737	Love Goes to Bulding on Fire/New Feeling	1977	2.00	4.00	8.00
❑ 737 [PS]	Love Goes to Bulding on Fire/New Feeling	1977	2.00	4.00	8.00
❑ 1002	Uh-Oh, Love Comes to Town/I Wish You Wouldn't Say That	1977	—	3.00	6.00
❑ 1002 [PS]	Uh-Oh, Love Comes to Town/I Wish You Wouldn't Say That	1977	—	3.00	6.00
❑ 1013	Psycho Killer/Psycho Killer (Acoustic)	1978	2.00	4.00	8.00
❑ 1013 [PS]	Psycho Killer/Psycho Killer (Acoustic)	1978	2.00	4.00	8.00
❑ 1032	Take Me to the River/Thank You for Sending Me an Angel (Version)	1978	—	2.00	4.00
❑ 1032 [PS]	Take Me to the River/Thank You for Sending Me an Angel (Version)	1978	—	2.00	4.00
❑ 21975	Wild, Wild Life/And She Was	198?	—	—	3.00
—"Back to Back Hits" reissue					
❑ 27948	Blind/Still	1988	—	—	2.00
❑ 27948 [PS]	Blind/Still	1988	—	—	2.00
❑ 27992	(Nothing But) Flowers/Ruby Dear	1988	—	—	2.00
❑ 27992 [PS]	(Nothing But) Flowers/Ruby Dear	1988	—	—	2.00
❑ 28497	Love for Sale/Hey Now	1987	—	—	2.00
❑ 28497 [PS]	Love for Sale/Hey Now	1987	—	—	2.00
❑ 28629	Wild Wild Life/People Like Us (Movie Version)	1986	—	—	2.00
❑ 28629 [PS]	Wild Wild Life/People Like Us (Movie Version)	1986	—	—	2.00
❑ 28917	And She Was/And She Was (Dub)	1985	—	—	2.00
❑ 28917 [PS]	And She Was/And She Was (Dub)	1985	—	—	2.00
❑ 28987	Road to Nowhere/Give Me Back My Name	1985	—	—	3.00
❑ 28987 [PS]	Road to Nowhere/Give Me Back My Name	1985	—	—	3.00
❑ 29080	Stop Making Sense (Girlfriend Is Better)/Heaven	1985	—	—	3.00
❑ 29080 [PS]	Stop Making Sense (Girlfriend Is Better)/Heaven	1985	—	2.00	4.00
❑ 29163	Once in a Lifetime/This Must Be the Place (Naive Melody)	1984	—	—	3.00
❑ 29163 [PS]	Once in a Lifetime/This Must Be the Place (Naive Melody)	1984	—	—	3.00
❑ 29451	This Must Be the Place (Naive Melody)/Moon Rocks	1983	—	—	3.00
❑ 29451 [PS]	This Must Be the Place (Naive Melody)/Moon Rocks	1983	—	—	3.00
❑ 29565	Burning Down the House/I Get Wild-Wild Gravity	1983	—	—	3.00
❑ 29565 [PS]	Burning Down the House/I Get Wild-Wild Gravity	1983	—	—	3.00
❑ 49075	Life During Wartime (This Ain't No Party...This Ain't No Disco...This Ain't No Foolin' Around)/ Electric Guitar	1979	—	2.00	4.00
❑ 49649	Once in a Lifetime/Seen and Not Seen	1981	—	2.00	4.00
❑ 49734	Houses in Motion/The Overload	1981	—	2.00	4.00

TALLEY, JOHNNY T.
MERCURY

Number	Title (A Side/B Side)	Yr	VG	VG+	NM
❑ 70902	Lonesome Train/(I've Changed My) Wild Mind	1956	75.00	150.00	300.00

TALLYSMEN, THE
TALLY

Number	Title (A Side/B Side)	Yr	VG	VG+	NM
❑ 200688	Little By Little/You Don't Care About Me	1966	15.00	30.00	60.00

TAMANEERS, THE
BRAMLEY

Number	Title (A Side/B Side)	Yr	VG	VG+	NM
❑ 102	Searching/Be Anything (But Be Mine)	1960	100.00	200.00	400.00

TAMBLYN, LARRY
FARO

Number	Title (A Side/B Side)	Yr	VG	VG+	NM
❑ 601	Patty Ann/Dearest	1960	5.00	10.00	20.00
❑ 603	The Lie/My Bride-to-Be	1960	5.00	10.00	20.00
❑ 612	This Is the Night/Destiny	1961	6.25	12.50	25.00

LINDA

Number	Title (A Side/B Side)	Yr	VG	VG+	NM
❑ 112	You'll Be Mine Someday/The Girl in My Heart	1963	5.00	10.00	20.00
—With the Standells					

TAMMI AND THE BACHELORS
BANGAR

Number	Title (A Side/B Side)	Yr	VG	VG+	NM
❑ 00610	My Summer Love/My Love	1964	6.25	12.50	25.00

TAMMYS, THE
UNITED ARTISTS

Number	Title (A Side/B Side)	Yr	VG	VG+	NM
❑ 632	Take Back Your Ring/Part of Growing Up	1963	3.00	6.00	12.00
❑ 678	Egyptian Shamba/What's So Sweet About Sweet Sixteen	1963	3.00	6.00	12.00

VEEP

Number	Title (A Side/B Side)	Yr	VG	VG+	NM
❑ 1210	Gypsy/Hold Back the Light of Dawn	1965	3.00	6.00	12.00
❑ 1220	His Actions Speak Louder Than Words/Blues Sixteen	1965	3.00	6.00	12.00

TAMPA RED
RCA VICTOR

Number	Title (A Side/B Side)	Yr	VG	VG+	NM
❑ 47-4275	Boogie Woogie Women/I Won't Let Her Do It	1951	12.50	25.00	50.00
❑ 47-4399	She's a Cool Operator/Green and Lucky Blues	1951	12.50	25.00	50.00
❑ 47-4722	But I Forgive You/I'm Gonna Put You Down	1952	12.50	25.00	50.00
❑ 47-4898	True Love/Look-a There, Look-a There	1952	12.50	25.00	50.00
❑ 47-5134	All Mixed Up Over You/Too Late Too Long	1953	10.00	20.00	40.00
❑ 47-5273	I'll Never Let You Go/Got a Mind to Leave This Town	1953	10.00	20.00	40.00
❑ 47-5523	So Craazy About You Baby/So Much Trouble	1953	10.00	20.00	40.00
❑ 47-5594	If She Don't Come Back/Big Stars Falling	1954	10.00	20.00	40.00
❑ 50-0002	If You Ever Change Your Ways/Chicago Breakdown	1949	30.00	60.00	120.00
—Gray label, orange vinyl; With Big Maceo					
❑ 50-0019	Come On If You're Coming/When Things Go Wrong with You	1950	30.00	60.00	120.00
—Gray label, orange vinyl					
❑ 50-0027	It's a Brand New Boogie/Put Your Money Where Your Mouth Is	1950	30.00	60.00	120.00
—Gray label, orange vinyl					
❑ 50-0041	I'll Find My Way/That's Her Own Business	1950	30.00	60.00	120.00
—Gray label, orange vinyl					
❑ 50-0071	It's Too Late Now/Please Try to See It My Way	1950	25.00	50.00	100.00
—Gray label, orange vinyl					
❑ 50-0084	1950 Blues/Love Her with a Feelin'	1950	25.00	50.00	100.00
—Gray label, orange vinyl					
❑ 50-0094	It's Good Like That/New Deal Blues	1950	25.00	50.00	100.00
—Gray label, orange vinyl					
❑ 50-0107	Sweet Little Angel/Don't Blame Shorty for That	1951	20.00	40.00	80.00
❑ 50-0112	Midnight Boogie/I Miss My Lovin' Blues	1951	20.00	40.00	80.00
❑ 50-0123	She's Dynamite/Early in the Morning	1951	20.00	40.00	80.00
❑ 50-0136	Pretty Baby Blues/Since My Baby's Been Gone	1951	20.00	40.00	80.00

TAMS, THE
1-2-3

Number	Title (A Side/B Side)	Yr	VG	VG+	NM
❑ 1726	How Long Love/Too Much Foolin' Around	1970	—	3.00	6.00

ABC

Number	Title (A Side/B Side)	Yr	VG	VG+	NM
❑ 10825	Holding On/Is It Better to Have Loved a Little	1966	2.00	4.00	8.00
❑ 10885	Shelter/Get Away (Leave Me Alone)	1966	2.00	4.00	8.00
❑ 10929	Breaking Up/How 'Bout It	1967	2.00	4.00	8.00
❑ 10956	Everything Else Is Gone/Mary, Mary, Row Your Boat	1967	2.00	4.00	8.00
❑ 11019	All My Heard Times/A Little More Soul	1967	2.00	4.00	8.00
❑ 11066	Be Young, Be Foolish, Be Happy/That Same Old Song	1968	2.00	4.00	8.00
❑ 11128	Laugh at the World/Trouble Maker	1968	2.00	4.00	8.00
❑ 11183	Sunshine, Rainbow, Blue Sky, Brown Eyed Girl/ There's a Great Big Change in Me	1969	2.00	4.00	8.00
❑ 11228	Be Young, Be Foolish, Be Happy/Love, Love, Love	1969	2.00	4.00	8.00
❑ 11358	Don't You Just Know It/Making Music	1973	—	2.50	5.00

ABC-PARAMOUNT

Number	Title (A Side/B Side)	Yr	VG	VG+	NM
❑ 10502	What Kind of Fool (Do You Think I Am)/Laugh It Off	1963	3.75	7.50	15.00
❑ 10533	It's All Right (You're Just in Love)/You Lied to Your Daddy	1964	3.00	6.00	12.00
❑ 10573	Hey Girl Don't Bother Me/Take Away	1964	3.00	6.00	12.00
❑ 10601	Silly Little Girl/Weep Little Girl	1964	3.00	6.00	12.00
❑ 10614	The Truth Hurts/Why Did My Little Girl Cry	1965	2.50	5.00	10.00
❑ 10635	What Do You Do/Unlove You	1965	2.50	5.00	10.00
❑ 10702	Concrete Jungle/Till the End of Time	1965	2.50	5.00	10.00
❑ 10741	Carryin' On/I've Been Hurt	1965	2.50	5.00	10.00
❑ 10779	Got to Get Used to a Broken Heart/Riding for a Fall	1966	2.50	5.00	10.00

ABC DUNHILL

Number	Title (A Side/B Side)	Yr	VG	VG+	NM
❑ 4290	Hey Girl Don't Bother Me/Weep Little Girl	1971	—	3.00	6.00
❑ 4290 [PS]	Hey Girl Don't Bother Me/Weep Little Girl	1971	2.50	5.00	10.00
—Title sleeve with "#1 in England"					

APT

Number	Title (A Side/B Side)	Yr	VG	VG+	NM
❑ 26010	Long Distance Operator/Numbers	1970	—	3.00	6.00

ARLEN

Number	Title (A Side/B Side)	Yr	VG	VG+	NM
❑ 711	Untie Me/Disillusioned	1962	3.00	6.00	12.00
❑ 717	Deep Inside Me/If You're So Smart (Why Do You Have a Broken Heart)	1962	3.00	6.00	12.00
❑ 720	You'll Never Know/Blue Shadows	1963	3.00	6.00	12.00
❑ 729	Don't Ever Go/Find Another Love	1963	3.00	6.00	12.00

CAPITOL

Number	Title (A Side/B Side)	Yr	VG	VG+	NM
❑ 3050	The Tams Medley/Wire Help	1971	—	3.00	6.00

COMPLEAT

Number	Title (A Side/B Side)	Yr	VG	VG+	NM
❑ 109	My Baby Sure Can Shag/Making True Love	1983	—	2.00	4.00

GENERAL AMERICAN

Number	Title (A Side/B Side)	Yr	VG	VG+	NM
❑ 714	My Baby Loves Me/Find Another Love	1962	3.75	7.50	15.00

HERITAGE

Number	Title (A Side/B Side)	Yr	VG	VG+	NM
❑ 101	Vacation Time/If Love Were Like Rivers	1961	75.00	150.00	300.00

KING

Number	Title (A Side/B Side)	Yr	VG	VG+	NM
❑ 6012	Untie Me/Find Another Love	1965	2.50	5.00	10.00

SWAN

Number	Title (A Side/B Side)	Yr	VG	VG+	NM
❑ 4055	Sorry/Valley of Love	1960	3.75	7.50	15.00

TAMS, THE (2)
MINK

Number	Title (A Side/B Side)	Yr	VG	VG+	NM
❑ 22	Memory Lane/Teenage Kids	1959	10.00	20.00	40.00
—Originally issued as "The Stereos"					

PARKWAY

Number	Title (A Side/B Side)	Yr	VG	VG+	NM
❑ 863	Memory Lane/A Lovely Piano	1963	5.00	10.00	20.00
—The same record was reissued as "The Hippies"					

TANEGA, NORMA
NEW VOICE

Number	Title (A Side/B Side)	Yr	VG	VG+	NM
❑ 807	Walkin' My Cat Named Dog/I'm the Sky	1966	3.00	6.00	12.00
❑ 810	A Street That Rhymes at 6 A.M./Treat Me Right	1966	2.50	5.00	10.00
❑ 815	Bread/Waves	1966	2.50	5.00	10.00
❑ 821	No Stranger Am I/Run on the Run	1967	2.50	5.00	10.00

TANGEERS, THE
OKEH

Number	Title (A Side/B Side)	Yr	VG	VG+	NM
❑ 7319	Let My Heart and Soul Be Free/What's the Use of Me Trying	1968	10.00	20.00	40.00

TANGERINE ZOO, THE
MAINSTREAM

Number	Title (A Side/B Side)	Yr	VG	VG+	NM
❑ 682	A Trip to the Zoo/One More Heartache	1968	5.00	10.00	20.00
❑ 690	Like People/(B-side unknown)	1968	5.00	10.00	20.00

TANGIERS, THE

Possibly more than one group. Also see THE HOLLYWOOD FLAMES.

Number	Title (A Side/B Side)	Yr	VG	VG+	NM
A-J					
❑ 905	The Plea/The Waddle	1962	6.25	12.50	25.00
CLASS					
❑ 224	School Days Will Be Over/Don't Try	1958	7.50	15.00	30.00
DECCA					
❑ 29603	I Won't Be Around/Tabarin	1955	37.50	75.00	150.00
❑ 29971	Remember Me/Oh, Baby!	1956	37.50	75.00	150.00
STRAND					
❑ 25039	Ping Pong/Don't Stop the Music	1961	7.50	15.00	30.00

TANTONES, THE

Number	Title (A Side/B Side)	Yr	VG	VG+	NM
LAMP					
❑ 2002	No Matter/I Love You, Really I Do	1957	37.50	75.00	150.00
❑ 2008	So Afraid/Tell Me	1957	37.50	75.00	150.00

TARANTULAS, THE

Number	Title (A Side/B Side)	Yr	VG	VG+	NM
ATLANTIC					
❑ 2102	Tarantula/Black Widow	1961	6.25	12.50	25.00
STOP					
❑ 102	Herky Jerky/Vera Brown	1964	2.50	5.00	10.00

TARGETS, THE

Number	Title (A Side/B Side)	Yr	VG	VG+	NM
KING					
❑ 5538	It Doesn't Matter/Girls, Girls, Girls	1961	10.00	20.00	40.00

TARRIERS, THE

Number	Title (A Side/B Side)	Yr	VG	VG+	NM
DECCA					
❑ 31387	Last Night I Had the Strangest Dream/Lonesome Traveler	1962	2.50	5.00	10.00
❑ 31470	Casey Jones/Mary Ann	1963	2.50	5.00	10.00
❑ 31524	Lonesome Traveller/Seven Daffodils	1963	2.50	5.00	10.00
❑ 31631	San Francisco Bay Blues/Guantanamera	1964	2.50	5.00	10.00
GLORY					
❑ 246	Wishing Well Song/East Virginia	1956	3.75	7.50	15.00
❑ 249	The Banana Boat Song/No Hidin' Place	1956	5.00	10.00	20.00
❑ 254	Those Brown Eyes/Chaucon	1957	3.75	7.50	15.00
❑ 255	I Know Where I'm Going/Pretty Boy	1957	3.75	7.50	15.00
❑ 264	Dunya/Quinto	1957	3.75	7.50	15.00
❑ 271	Lonesome Traveler/East Virginia	1958	3.75	7.50	15.00
❑ 286	Tom Dooley/Everybody Loves Saturday Night	1958	3.75	7.50	15.00
UNITED ARTISTS					
❑ 168	Hard Travelin'/Times Are Getting Hard	1959	3.00	6.00	12.00

TARRYTONS, THE

Number	Title (A Side/B Side)	Yr	VG	VG+	NM
DOT					
❑ 16537	Rough Surfin'/Mansion on the Hill	1963	6.25	12.50	25.00
EXCLUSIVE					
❑ 2270	Rough Surfin'/Mansion on the Hill	1963	10.00	20.00	40.00

TASSELS, THE

Number	Title (A Side/B Side)	Yr	VG	VG+	NM
AMY					
❑ 946	To a Soldier Boy/The Boy for Me	1966	2.50	5.00	10.00
MADISON					
❑ 117	To a Soldier Boy/The Boy for Me	1959	6.25	12.50	25.00
❑ 121	To a Young Lover/My Guy and I	1959	5.00	10.00	20.00

TASTE OF HONEY, A

Number	Title (A Side/B Side)	Yr	VG	VG+	NM
CAPITOL					
❑ 4565	Boogie Oogie Oogie/World Spin	1978	—	2.00	4.00
❑ 4565 [PS]	Boogie Oogie Oogie/World Spin	1978	—	2.50	5.00
❑ 4655	Distant/You're in Good Hands	1978	—	2.00	4.00
❑ 4668	Disco Dancin'/Sky High	1978	—	2.00	4.00
❑ 4744	Do It Good/I Love You	1979	—	2.00	4.00
❑ 4776	Let's Begin/Race	1979	—	2.00	4.00
❑ 4888	Rescue Me/Say That You'll Stay	1980	—	2.00	4.00
❑ 4932	I'm Talkin' 'Bout You/Don't You Lead Me On	1980	—	2.00	4.00
❑ 4953	Sukiyaki/Don't You Lead Me On	1980	—	2.00	4.00
❑ 4953 [PS]	Sukiyaki/Don't You Lead Me On	1980	—	2.50	5.00
❑ B-5099	I'll Try Something New/Good-Bye Baby	1982	—	2.00	4.00
❑ B-5099 [PS]	I'll Try Something New/Good-Bye Baby	1982	—	2.50	5.00
❑ B-5132	We've Got the Groove/This Love of Ours	1982	—	2.00	4.00

TATE, BILLY

Number	Title (A Side/B Side)	Yr	VG	VG+	NM
IMPERIAL					
❑ 5337	Single Life/You Told Me	1955	50.00	100.00	200.00
—Script logo					
PEACOCK					
❑ 1671	Don't Call My Name/Right from Wrong	1957	7.50	15.00	30.00

TATE, LAURIE

Number	Title (A Side/B Side)	Yr	VG	VG+	NM
ATLANTIC					
❑ 965	Rock Me Daddy/You Can't Stop My Crying	1952	25.00	50.00	100.00

TATE, TOMMY

Number	Title (A Side/B Side)	Yr	VG	VG+	NM
ABC-PARAMOUNT					
❑ 10626	What's the Matter/Ordinarily	1965	6.25	12.50	25.00
KOKO					
❑ 722	Hardtimes S.O.S./Always	1976	—	3.00	6.00
❑ 723	If You Ain't Man Enough/Revelations	1976	—	3.00	6.00
❑ 727	I'm So Satisfied/If You Ain't Man Enough	1977	—	3.00	6.00
❑ 2109	I Remember/Help Me Love	1971	—	3.00	6.00
❑ 2112	School of Life/I Remember	1972	—	3.00	6.00
❑ 2114	I Ain't Gonna Worry/More Power To You	1972	—	3.00	6.00
OKEH					
❑ 7242	Are You From Heaven/I'm Taking On Pain	1966	5.00	10.00	20.00
❑ 7253	Big Blue Diamonds/Lover's Reward	1967	5.00	10.00	20.00

TAUPIN, BERNIE

ELTON JOHN's songwriting partner.

Number	Title (A Side/B Side)	Yr	VG	VG+	NM
RCA					
❑ 5162-7-R	Friend of the Flag/Backbone	1987	—	—	3.00
❑ 5162-7-R [PS]	Friend of the Flag/Backbone	1987	—	—	3.00
❑ 5216-7-R	Citizen Jane/White Boys in Chains	1987	—	—	3.00
❑ 5216-7-R [PS]	Citizen Jane/White Boys in Chains	1987	—	—	3.00

TAVARES

Also see CHUBBY AND THE TURNPIKES.

Number	Title (A Side/B Side)	Yr	VG	VG+	NM
CAPITOL					
❑ 3674	Check It Out/The Judgment Day	1973	—	2.50	5.00
❑ 3794	That's the Sound That Lonely Makes/Little Girl	1973	—	2.50	5.00
❑ 3882	Too Late/Leave It Up to the Lady	1974	—	2.50	5.00
❑ 3957	She's Gone/To Love You	1974	—	2.50	5.00
❑ 4010	Remember What I Told You to Forget/My Ship	1974	—	2.50	5.00
❑ 4111	It Only Takes a Minute/I Hope She Chooses Me	1975	—	2.50	5.00
❑ 4184	Free Ride/In the Eyes of Love	1975	—	2.50	5.00
❑ 4221	The Love I Never Had/In the City	1976	—	2.50	5.00
❑ 4270	Heaven Must Be Missing An Angel (Part 1)/Heaven Must Be Missing An Angel (Part 2)	1976	—	2.50	5.00
❑ 4348	Don't Take Away the Music/Guiding Star	1976	—	2.50	5.00
❑ 4398	Whodunit/Fool of the Year	1977	—	2.50	5.00
❑ 4453	Goodnight My Love/Watchin' the Woman's Movement	1977	—	2.50	5.00
❑ 4500	More Than a Woman/Keep in Touch	1977	—	2.00	4.00
❑ 4544	The Ghost of Love (Part 1)/The Ghost of Love (Part 2)	1978	—	2.00	4.00
❑ 4583	Timber/Feel So Good	1978	—	2.00	4.00
❑ 4658	Never Had a Love Like This Before/Positive Forces	1978	—	2.00	4.00
❑ 4703	Straight from the Heart/I'm Back for Me	1979	—	2.00	4.00
❑ 4738	One Telephone Call Away/Let Me Heal the Bruises	1979	—	2.00	4.00
❑ 4781	Hard Core Poetry/Stabilize	1979	—	2.00	4.00
❑ 4811	Bad Times/Got to Have Your Love	1979	—	2.00	4.00
❑ 4846	I Can't Go On Living Without You/Why Can't We Fall in Love	1980	—	2.00	4.00
❑ 4880	I Don't Want You Anymore/Paradise	1980	—	2.00	4.00
❑ 4933	Love Uprising/Not Love	1980	—	2.00	4.00
❑ 4969	Loneliness/Break Down for Love	1981	—	2.00	4.00
❑ A-5019	Turn Out the Nightlight/House of Music	1981	—	2.00	4.00
❑ A-5043	Loveline/Right On Time	1981	—	2.00	4.00
RCA					
❑ PB-13292	A Penny for Your Thoughts/The Skin You're In	1982	—	2.00	4.00
❑ PB-13433	Got to Find My Way Back to You/I Hope You Will Be Very Unhappy Without Me	1983	—	2.00	4.00
❑ PB-13530	Abra-Ca-Dabra Love You Too/Mystery Lady	1983	—	2.00	4.00
❑ PB-13611	Deeper in Love/I Really Miss You Baby	1983	—	2.00	4.00
❑ PB-13684	Words and Music/I'll Send Love (We Go Together)	1983	—	2.00	4.00
❑ GB-13799	A Penny for Your Thoughts/Got to Find My Way Back to You	1984	—	—	3.00
—Gold Standard Series					

TAVARES, ERNIE, TRIO

Number	Title (A Side/B Side)	Yr	VG	VG+	NM
DOOTONE					
❑ 325	I'm Alone Tonight/It's Christmas	1953	37.50	75.00	150.00
—B-side by the Bonairs					

TAYLOR, ANDREW

Number	Title (A Side/B Side)	Yr	VG	VG+	NM
GONE					
❑ 5109	That's How I Feel About You/Never Bite Off More Than You Could Chew	1961	50.00	100.00	200.00

TAYLOR, ANDY

Also see DURAN DURAN.

Number	Title (A Side/B Side)	Yr	VG	VG+	NM
ATLANTIC					
❑ 89414	Take It Easy/Angel Eyes	1986	—	—	3.00
❑ 89414 [PS]	Take It Easy/Angel Eyes	1986	—	—	3.00
MCA					
❑ 52946	When the Rain Comes Down/Broken Window	1986	—	—	3.00
❑ 52946 [PS]	When the Rain Comes Down/Broken Window	1986	—	—	3.00
❑ 52999	Life Goes On/Broken Window	1987	—	—	3.00
❑ 52999 [PS]	Life Goes On/Broken Window	1987	—	—	3.00
❑ 53063	I Might Lie/Broken Window	1987	—	—	3.00
❑ 53063 [PS]	I Might Lie/Broken Window	1987	—	—	3.00
❑ 53085	Don't Let Me Die Young/Broken Window	1987	—	—	3.00
❑ 53085 [PS]	Don't Let Me Die Young/Broken Window	1987	—	—	3.00

TAYLOR, BILL, AND SMOKEY JO

Number	Title (A Side/B Side)	Yr	VG	VG+	NM
FLIP					
❑ 502	Split Personality/Lonely Sweetheart	1955	375.00	750.00	1500.

TAYLOR, BILLY

Number	Title (A Side/B Side)	Yr	VG	VG+	NM
CITATION					
❑ 5002	Income Taxes and You/Lullaby to Carolyn	1962	3.75	7.50	15.00
FAME					
❑ 502	Little Jewel/Study Hall Romance	196?	75.00	150.00	300.00
FELCO					
❑ 101	Wombie Zombie/I'm Young	1959	5.00	10.00	20.00
FELSTED					
❑ 8564	Bandstand Baby/Cat with No Future	1959	5.00	10.00	20.00
TOWER					
❑ 421	Sunny/I Wish I Knew How I Would Feel to Be Free	1968	2.00	4.00	8.00

TAYLOR, BOBBY, AND THE VANCOUVERS

Number	Title (A Side/B Side)	Yr	VG	VG+	NM
GORDY					
❑ 7069	Does Your Mama Know About Me/Fading Away	1968	5.00	10.00	20.00
❑ 7073	I Am Your Man/If You Love Her	1968	5.00	10.00	20.00
❑ 7079	Malinda/It's Growing	1968	5.00	10.00	20.00
❑ 7088	Oh I've Been Blessed/It Should Have Been Me Loving Her	1969	150.00	300.00	600.00
❑ 7092	My Girl Is Gone/It Should Have Been Me Loving Her	1969	5.00	10.00	20.00
INTEGRA					
❑ 103	This Is My Woman/(B-side unknown)	1968	25.00	50.00	100.00

Number	Title (A Side/B Side)	Yr	VG	VG+	NM
MOWEST					
❑ 5006	Hey Lordy/Just a Little Bit Closer	1971	3.75	7.50	15.00
PLAYBOY					
❑ 6046	Why Play Games/Don't Wonder Why	1975	—	2.50	5.00
SUNFLOWER					
❑ 126	There Are Roses Somewhere in the World/It Was a Good Time	1972	6.25	12.50	25.00
V.I.P.					
❑ 25053	Oh I've Been Blessed/Blackmail	1969	6.25	12.50	25.00

TAYLOR, CARMEN

Number	Title (A Side/B Side)	Yr	VG	VG+	NM
APOLLO					
❑ 489	Oh Please/Teen Age Ball	1956	15.00	30.00	60.00
ATLANTIC					
❑ 1002	Lovin' Daddy/Ding Dong	1953	12.50	25.00	50.00
❑ 1015	Big Mamou Daddy/Mamma Me and Johnny Free	1953	12.50	25.00	50.00
❑ 1041	Freddie/Ooh I	1954	30.00	60.00	120.00
GUYDEN					
❑ 100	Let Me Go Lover/No More, No Less	1954	10.00	20.00	40.00
KAMA SUTRA					
❑ 206	My Son/You're Puttin' Me On	1966	3.00	6.00	12.00
KING					
❑ 5085	So What/Why Did You Leave Me Alone	1957	12.50	25.00	50.00

TAYLOR, CHIP

Number	Title (A Side/B Side)	Yr	VG	VG+	NM
BUDDAH					
❑ 325	Angel of the Morning/(B-side unknown)	1972	—	3.00	6.00
❑ 344	Londonderry Company/(B-side unknown)	1973	—	3.00	6.00
CAPITOL					
❑ 4692	Saint Sebastian/One Night Out with the Boys	1979	—	2.00	4.00
❑ 4840	Stealin' Each Other Blind/He Ain't Makin' Music Anymore	1980	—	2.00	4.00
COLUMBIA					
❑ 10446	Hello Atlanta/Farmer's Daughter	1976	—	2.00	4.00
❑ 10520	Three Younger Bandits/Nothing Like You Girl	1977	—	2.00	4.00
❑ 44736	It's Such a Lonely Time of the Year/(B-side unknown)	1968	3.00	6.00	12.00
EPIC					
❑ 10567	It's Such a Lonely Time of Year/(Instrumental)	1969	2.50	5.00	10.00
MALA					
❑ 476	On My World/Joanie's Blues	1964	3.00	6.00	12.00
❑ 489	Suzannah (Comin' Home to Louisiana)/(B-side unknown)	1964	3.00	6.00	12.00
❑ 507	Young Love/Betty Ann	1965	2.50	5.00	10.00
MGM					
❑ 12993	Foolin' Around/Innocent Eyes	1961	5.00	10.00	20.00
❑ 13040	If You Don't Want Me Now/Sad Songs	1961	5.00	10.00	20.00
WARNER BROS.					
❑ 5314	Here I Am/I Love You But I Know	1962	3.75	7.50	15.00
❑ 5333	Lucky Star/A Guy Don't Need a Lot of Time	1963	3.75	7.50	15.00
❑ 8050	Me As I Am/Comin' From Behind	1974	—	2.00	4.00
❑ 8090	Early Sunday Morning/Shickshinny	1975	—	2.00	4.00
❑ 8128	Big River/John Tucker's On the Wagon Again	1975	—	2.00	4.00
❑ 8159	Circle of Tears/You're Alright, Charlie	1975	—	2.00	4.00

TAYLOR, EDDIE

Number	Title (A Side/B Side)	Yr	VG	VG+	NM
VEE JAY					
❑ 149	Bad Boy/E.T. Blues	1955	30.00	60.00	120.00
❑ 185	Big Town Playboy/Ride 'Em On Down	1956	20.00	40.00	80.00
❑ 206	You'll Always Have a Home/Don't Knock at My Door	1956	15.00	30.00	60.00
❑ 267	I'm Gonna Love You/Looking for Trouble	1958	10.00	20.00	40.00
VIVID					
❑ 104	I'm Sitting Here/Do You Want Me to Cry	1964	5.00	10.00	20.00

TAYLOR, FAITH, AND THE SWEET TEENS

Number	Title (A Side/B Side)	Yr	VG	VG+	NM
BEA & BABY					
❑ 104	I Need Him to Love Me/I Love You Darling	1959	12.50	25.00	50.00
FEDERAL					
❑ 12334	Your Candy Kisses/Won't Someone Tell Me Why?	1958	12.50	25.00	50.00

TAYLOR, JAMES

Also see CARLY SIMON.

Number	Title (A Side/B Side)	Yr	VG	VG+	NM
APPLE					
❑ 1805	Carolina in My Mind/Taking It In	1969	75.00	150.00	300.00
❑ 1805	Carolina in My Mind/Something's Wrong	1970	2.50	5.00	10.00
—With star on A-side label					
❑ 1805	Carolina in My Mind/Something's Wrong	1970	2.00	4.00	8.00
—Without star on A-side label					
❑ 1805 [DJ]	Carolina on My Mind/Something's Wrong	1970	7.50	15.00	30.00
—Promo with error in title on A-side					
COLUMBIA					
❑ 02093	Hard Times/Summer's Here	1981	—	—	3.00
❑ 02093 [PS]	Hard Times/Summer's Here	1981	—	2.00	4.00
❑ 05681	Everyday/Limousine Driver	1985	—	—	3.00
❑ 05681 [PS]	Everyday/Limousine Driver	1985	—	2.00	4.00
❑ 05785	Only One/Mona	1986	—	—	3.00
❑ 05785 [PS]	Only One/Mona	1986	—	—	3.00
❑ 05884	That's Why I'm Here/Going Around One More Time	1986	—	—	3.00
❑ 06278	Only a Dream in Rio/Turn Away	1986	—	—	3.00
❑ 07616	Never Die Young/Valentine's Day	1987	—	—	3.00
❑ 07616 [PS]	Never Die Young/Valentine's Day	1987	—	2.00	4.00
❑ 07948	Baby Boom Baby/Letter in the Mail	1988	—	—	3.00
❑ 08493	Sweet Potato Pie/First of May	1988	—	—	3.00
❑ 10557	Handy Man/Bartender's Blues	1977	—	2.00	4.00
❑ 10602	Your Smiling Face/If I Keep My Heart Out of Sight	1977	—	2.00	4.00
❑ 10676	(What a) Wonderful World/Wooden Planes	1978	—	3.00	6.00
—By Art Garfunkel with Paul Simon and James Taylor; B-side is Garfunkel solo					
❑ 10689	Honey Don't Leave L.A./Another Grey Morning	1978	—	2.00	4.00
❑ 11005	Up on the Roof/Chanson Francaise	1979	—	2.00	4.00
❑ 60514	Her Town Too/Believe It or Not	1981	—	2.00	4.00
—A-side: James Taylor and J.D. Souther					
WARNER BROS.					
❑ 7387	Sweet Baby James/Suite for 20G	1970	2.00	4.00	8.00
❑ 7423	Fire and Rain/Anywhere Like Heaven	1970	2.00	4.00	8.00
❑ 7460	Country Road/Sunny Skies	1970	—	3.00	6.00
❑ 7498	You've Got a Friend/You Can Close Your Eyes	1971	—	3.00	6.00
❑ 7521	Long Ago and Far Away/Let Me Ride	1971	—	2.50	5.00
❑ 7655	Don't Let Me Be Lonely Tonight/Wow, Don't You Know	1972	—	2.50	5.00
❑ 7682	One Man Parade/Nobody But You	1973	—	2.50	5.00
❑ 7695	Hymn/Fanfare	1973	—	2.50	5.00
❑ 8015	Let It All Fall Down/Daddy's Baby	1974	—	2.50	5.00
❑ 8028	Walking Man/Daddy's Baby	1974	—	2.50	5.00
❑ 8109	How Sweet It Is (To Be Loved By You)/Sarah Maria	1975	—	2.50	5.00
❑ 8137	Mexico/Gorilla	1975	—	2.50	5.00
❑ 8222	Shower the People/I Can Dream of You	1976	—	2.50	5.00
❑ 8278	Woman's Gotta Have It/You Make It Easy	1976	—	2.50	5.00

TAYLOR, JOHN

Also see DURAN DURAN.

Number	Title (A Side/B Side)	Yr	VG	VG+	NM
CAPITOL					
❑ 5551	I Do What I Do...(Theme for 9 1/2 Weeks)/Jazz	1986	—	—	3.00
❑ 5551 [PS]	I Do What I Do...(Theme for 9 1/2 Weeks)/Jazz	1986	—	—	3.00

TAYLOR, JOHNNIE

Number	Title (A Side/B Side)	Yr	VG	VG+	NM
BEVERLY GLEN					
❑ 2003	What About My Love/Reaganomics	1982	—	2.00	4.00
❑ 2004	I'm So Proud/I Need a Freak	1982	—	2.00	4.00
❑ 2007	Just Ain't Good Enough/Don't Wait	1983	—	2.00	4.00
❑ 2016	Seconds of Your Love/Shoot for the Stars	1983	—	2.00	4.00
COLUMBIA					
❑ AE7 1153 [DJ]	God Is Standing By/God Is Amazing	1977	2.00	4.00	8.00
—B-side by Deniece Williams; promo with "Suggested Christmas Programming" on label					
❑ 10281	Disco Lady/You're the Best in the World	1976	—	2.50	5.00
❑ 10334	Somebody's Gettin' It/Please Don't Stop (That Song from Playing)	1976	—	2.50	5.00
❑ 10478	Love Is Better in the A.M. (Part 1)/Love Is Better in the A.M. (Part 2)	1977	—	2.50	5.00
❑ 10541	Your Love Is Rated X/Here I Go (Through These Chains Again)	1977	—	2.50	5.00
❑ 10610	Disco 9000/Right Now	1977	—	2.00	4.00
❑ 10709	Keep On Dancing/I Love to Make Love When It's Raining	1978	—	2.00	4.00
❑ 10776	Give Me My Baby/Ever Ready	1978	—	2.00	4.00
❑ 11084	(Ooh-Wee) She's Killing Me/Play Something Pretty	1979	—	2.00	4.00
❑ 11315	I Got This Thing for Your Love/Signing Off with Love	1980	—	2.00	4.00
❑ 11373	I Wanna Get Into You/Baby Don't Hesitate	1980	—	2.00	4.00
DERBY					
❑ 101	Shine, Shine, Shine/Dance What You Wanna	1963	3.75	7.50	15.00
❑ 1006	Baby, We've Got Love/In Love with You	1963	3.75	7.50	15.00
❑ 1010	I Need Lots of Love/Getting Married Soon	1964	3.75	7.50	15.00
MALACO					
❑ 2107	Lady, My Whole World Is You/L-O-V-E	1984	—	—	3.00
❑ 2111	Good with My Hips/This Is Your Night	1985	—	—	3.00
❑ 2118	Still Called the Blues/She's Cheatin' on Me	1985	—	—	3.00
❑ 2125	Wall to Wall/(B-side unknown)	1986	—	—	3.00
❑ 2128	Can I Love You/There's Nothing I Wouldn't Do	1986	—	—	3.00
❑ 2132	Just Because/When She Stops Asking	1987	—	—	3.00
❑ 2135	Don't Make Me Late/Happy Time	1987	—	—	3.00
❑ 2140	If I Lose Your Love/Something Is Going Wrong	1987	—	—	3.00
❑ 2143	Everything's Out in the Open/Got to Leave This Woman	1988	—	—	3.00
❑ 2153	In Control/I Found a Love	1989	—	—	3.00
❑ 2159	Still Crazy for You/(B-side unknown)	1989	—	—	3.00
RCA					
❑ PB-11137	I Want You Back Again/Heaven Bless This Home	1977	—	2.50	5.00
SAR					
❑ 114	A Whole Lotta Woman/Why Oh Why	1961	5.00	10.00	20.00
❑ 131	Never Never/Rome (Wasn't Built in a Day)	1962	10.00	20.00	40.00
❑ 156	Oh, How I Love You/Run, But You Can't Hide	1964	3.75	7.50	15.00
STAX					
❑ 0009	Who's Making Love/I'm Trying	1968	2.00	4.00	8.00
❑ 0023	Take Care of Your Homework/Hold On This Time	1969	2.00	4.00	8.00
❑ 0033	Testify (I Wanna)/I Had a Fight with Love	1969	2.00	4.00	8.00
❑ 0042	Just Keep On Loving Me/My Life	1969	2.00	4.00	8.00
—With Carla Thomas					
❑ 0046	I Could Never Be President/It's Amazing	1969	2.00	4.00	8.00
❑ 0055	Love Bones/Mr. Nobody Is Somebody	1969	2.00	4.00	8.00
❑ 0068	Steal Away/Friday Night	1970	—	3.00	6.00
❑ 0078	I Am Somebody (Part 1)/I Am Somebody (Part 2)	1970	—	3.00	6.00
❑ 0085	Jody's Got Your Girl and Gone/A Fool Like Me	1970	—	3.00	6.00
❑ 0089	I Don't Wanna Lose You/Party Life	1971	—	3.00	6.00
❑ 0096	Hijackin' Love/Love in the Streets	1971	—	3.00	6.00
❑ 0114	Standing In for Jody/Shackin' Up	1972	—	3.00	6.00
❑ 0122	Doing My Own Thing (Part 1)/Doing My Own Thing (Part 2)	1972	—	3.00	6.00
❑ 0142	Stop Doggin' Me/Stop Teasin' Me	1972	—	3.00	6.00
❑ 0155	Don't You Fool with My Soul (Part 1)/Don't You Fool with My Soul (Part 2)	1973	—	3.00	6.00
❑ 0161	I Believe in You (You Believe in Me)/Love Depression	1973	—	3.00	6.00
—With A-side time listed at 4:37					
❑ 0161	I Believe in You (You Believe in Me)/Love Depression	1973	—	3.00	6.00
—With A-side time listed at 3:58					
❑ 0176	Cheaper to Keep Her/I Can Read Between the Lines	1973	—	3.00	6.00

Number	Title (A Side/B Side)	Yr	VG	VG+	NM
❑ 186	I Had a Dream/Changes	1966	2.50	5.00	10.00
❑ 193	I Got to Love Somebody's Baby/Just the One I've Been Looking For	1966	2.50	5.00	10.00
❑ 0193	We're Getting Careless with Our Love/Poor Make Believer	1974	—	3.00	6.00
❑ 202	Little Bluebird/Toe Hold	1967	2.50	5.00	10.00
❑ 0208	I've Been Born Again/At Night Time	1974	—	3.00	6.00
❑ 209	Ain't That Loving You/Outside Love	1967	2.50	5.00	10.00
❑ 226	If I Had It to Do Over/You Can't Get Away from It	1967	2.50	5.00	10.00
❑ 0226	It's September/Just One Moment	1974	—	3.00	6.00
❑ 235	Somebody's Sleeping in My Bed/Strange Thing	1967	2.50	5.00	10.00
❑ 0241	Try Me Tonight/Free	1975	—	3.00	6.00
❑ 247	Next Time/Sundown	1968	2.50	5.00	10.00
❑ 253	I Ain't Particular/Where There's Smoke There's Fire	1968	2.50	5.00	10.00
❑ 3201	It Don't Pay to Get Up in the Mornin'/Just Keep On Loving Me	1977	—	2.50	5.00

TAYLOR, LITTLE JOHNNY

GALAXY

Number	Title (A Side/B Side)	Yr	VG	VG+	NM
❑ 718	You'll Need Another Favor/What You Need Is a Ball	1963	3.00	6.00	12.00
❑ 722	Part Time Love/Somewhere Down the Line	1963	5.00	10.00	20.00
❑ 725	Since I Found a New Love/My Heart Is Filled with Pain	1963	3.00	6.00	12.00
❑ 729	First Class Love/If You Love Me	1964	2.50	5.00	10.00
❑ 731	You Win, I Lose/Nightingale Melody	1964	2.50	5.00	10.00
❑ 733	True Love/I Smell Trouble	1964	2.50	5.00	10.00
❑ 735	For Your Precious Love/I've Never Had a Woman Like You Before	1965	2.00	4.00	8.00
❑ 736	Help Yourself/Somebody's Got to Pay	1965	2.00	4.00	8.00
❑ 739	One More Chance/Looking at the Future	1965	2.00	4.00	8.00
❑ 743	Please Come Home For Christmas/Miracle Maker	1965	2.00	4.00	8.00
❑ 745	My Love Is Real/All I Want Is You	1966	2.00	4.00	8.00
❑ 748	Zig Zag Lightning/The Things I Used to Do	1966	2.00	4.00	8.00
❑ 752	I Know You Hear Me Calling/Big Blue Diamonds	1967	2.00	4.00	8.00
❑ 756	Driving Wheel/Darling Believe in Me	1967	2.00	4.00	8.00
❑ 764	Double or Nothing/Sometimey Woman	1968	2.00	4.00	8.00

ICHIBAN

Number	Title (A Side/B Side)	Yr	VG	VG+	NM
❑ 169	Christmas Is Here Again/Ugly Man	1988	—	3.00	6.00
❑ 174	Christmas Is Here Again/I Enjoy You	1989	—	3.00	6.00

RONN

Number	Title (A Side/B Side)	Yr	VG	VG+	NM
❑ 43	Make Love to Me Baby/Sweet Soul Woman	1970	—	3.00	6.00
❑ 48	How Can a Broke Man Survive/Make Love to Me Baby	1970	—	3.00	6.00
❑ 51	How Are You Fixed for Love/Keep On Keepin' On	1971	—	3.00	6.00
❑ 55	Everybody Knows About My Good Thing Pt. 1/Pt. 2	1971	—	3.00	6.00
❑ 59	It's My Fault Darling/There Is Something On Your Mind	1972	—	3.00	6.00
❑ 64	Open House at My House (Part 1)/Open House at My House (Part 2)	1972	—	3.00	6.00
❑ 66	As Long As I Don't See You/Strange Bed with a Bad Head	1972	—	3.00	6.00
❑ 69	I'll Make It Worth Your While/You're Not the Only One	1973	—	3.00	6.00
❑ 73	My Special Rose/A Thousand Miles Away	1973	—	3.00	6.00
❑ 78	You're Savin' Your Best Lovin' for Me/What Would I Do Without You	1974	—	3.00	6.00
❑ 80	I Don't Want It All/I Can't See Myself As a One-Woman Man	1974	—	3.00	6.00
❑ 85	Found a New Love/Oh, How I Love My Baby	1975	—	3.00	6.00
❑ 87	True Love/When Are You Coming Home	1975	—	3.00	6.00
❑ 88	A Hard Head Makes a Sore Behind/The Future	1976	—	3.00	6.00
❑ 92	L.J.T./I Should Have Known	197?	—	3.00	6.00
❑ 98	Just One More Chance/New Song	197?	—	3.00	6.00

TAYLOR, LITTLE JOHNNY, AND TED TAYLOR

RONN

Number	Title (A Side/B Side)	Yr	VG	VG+	NM
❑ 75	Walking the Floor/Cry It Out Baby	1973	—	3.00	6.00
❑ 89	Pretending Love/Funky Ghetto	1976	—	3.00	6.00

TAYLOR, MAD MAN

EASTWEST

Number	Title (A Side/B Side)	Yr	VG	VG+	NM
❑ 117	Rumble Tumble/Rock and Roll Espanola	1958	18.75	37.50	75.00

TAYLOR, MICK

Also see THE ROLLING STONES.

COLUMBIA

Number	Title (A Side/B Side)	Yr	VG	VG+	NM
❑ 11065	Leather Jacket/Show Blues	1979	—	2.50	5.00

TAYLOR, R. DEAN

20TH CENTURY

Number	Title (A Side/B Side)	Yr	VG	VG+	NM
❑ 2510	Let's Talk It Over/Add Up the Score	1981	—	2.00	4.00

AUDIO MASTER

Number	Title (A Side/B Side)	Yr	VG	VG+	NM
❑ 1	At the High School Dance/How Wrong Can You Be?	1960	50.00	100.00	200.00

FARR

Number	Title (A Side/B Side)	Yr	VG	VG+	NM
❑ 001	We'll Show Them All/Magdalena	1976	—	2.50	5.00

MALA

Number	Title (A Side/B Side)	Yr	VG	VG+	NM
❑ 444	I'll Remember/It's a Long Way to St. Louis	1962	25.00	50.00	100.00

RARE EARTH

Number	Title (A Side/B Side)	Yr	VG	VG+	NM
❑ 5013	Indiana Wants Me/Love's Your Name	1970	—	3.00	6.00
❑ 5023	Ain't It a Sad Thing/Back Street	1970	—	2.50	5.00
❑ 5023 [PS]	Ain't It a Sad Thing/Back Street	1970	2.50	5.00	10.00
❑ 5026	Gotta See Jane/Back Street	1971	—	2.50	5.00
❑ 5030	Candy Apple Red/Woman Alive	1971	—	2.50	5.00
❑ 5041	Taos New Mexico/Shadow	1972	—	2.50	5.00

STRUMMER

Number	Title (A Side/B Side)	Yr	VG	VG+	NM
❑ 3748	Let's Talk It Over/(B-side unknown)	1982	—	3.00	6.00

V.I.P.

Number	Title (A Side/B Side)	Yr	VG	VG+	NM
❑ 25027	Let's Go Somewhere/Poor Girl	1965	6.25	12.50	25.00
❑ 25042	Don't Fool Around/There's a Ghost in My House	1966	6.25	12.50	25.00
❑ 25045	Gotta See Jane/Don't Fool Around	1967	6.25	12.50	25.00

TAYLOR, ROGER

Also see QUEEN.

CAPITOL

Number	Title (A Side/B Side)	Yr	VG	VG+	NM
❑ B-5364	Man on Fire/Killing Time	1984	—	2.00	4.00
❑ B-5364 [PS]	Man on Fire/Killing Time	1984	—	2.50	5.00
❑ B-5420	Strange Frontier/I Cry for You (Love, Hope and Confusion)	1984	—	2.00	4.00

ELEKTRA

Number	Title (A Side/B Side)	Yr	VG	VG+	NM
❑ 47151	Let's Get Crazy/Laugh Or Cry	1981	—	2.50	5.00

TAYLOR, SHEILA

MELODYLAND

Number	Title (A Side/B Side)	Yr	VG	VG+	NM
❑ 6013	How Important Can It Be/She Satisfies	1975	—	2.50	5.00

TAYLOR, SHERRI

GLORECO

Number	Title (A Side/B Side)	Yr	VG	VG+	NM
❑ 1002	I've Got a Crush/(B-side unknown)	196?	15.00	30.00	60.00

MOTOWN

Number	Title (A Side/B Side)	Yr	VG	VG+	NM
❑ 1004	Lover/That's Why I Love You So Much	1960	10.00	20.00	40.00

—With Singin' Sammy Ward

TAYLOR, TRUE

See PAUL SIMON.

TAYLOR, VERNON

DOT

Number	Title (A Side/B Side)	Yr	VG	VG+	NM
❑ 15632	I've Got the Blues/The Losing Game	1957	25.00	50.00	100.00
❑ 15697	Satisfaction Guaranteed/Why Must You Leave Me	1958	12.50	25.00	50.00

SUN

Number	Title (A Side/B Side)	Yr	VG	VG+	NM
❑ 310	Breeze/Today Is a Blue Day	1958	6.25	12.50	25.00
❑ 325	Sweet and Easy to Love/Mystery Train	1959	8.75	17.50	35.00

TAYLOR, VINCE

PALETTE

Number	Title (A Side/B Side)	Yr	VG	VG+	NM
❑ 5065	I'll Be Your Hero/Jet Black Machine	1960	3.00	6.00	12.00
❑ 5084	Move Over Tiger/What Cha Gonna Do	1961	3.00	6.00	12.00

TAYLOR, ZOLA

RPM

Number	Title (A Side/B Side)	Yr	VG	VG+	NM
❑ 405	Make Love to Me/Oh My Dear	1954	75.00	150.00	300.00

TAZMEN, THE

ABC-PARAMOUNT

Number	Title (A Side/B Side)	Yr	VG	VG+	NM
❑ 9812	Easy Pickin'/The Chicken	1957	3.75	7.50	15.00

TEA COMPANY, THE

SMASH

Number	Title (A Side/B Side)	Yr	VG	VG+	NM
❑ 2176	Come and Have Some Tea with Me/Flowers	1968	3.75	7.50	15.00

TEAM MATES, THE

ABC-PARAMOUNT

Number	Title (A Side/B Side)	Yr	VG	VG+	NM
❑ 10760	If Only I Had Known/You Must Pay	1965	3.00	6.00	12.00

LE CAM

Number	Title (A Side/B Side)	Yr	VG	VG+	NM
❑ 701	I Just Might/Sooner or Later	196?	6.25	12.50	25.00
❑ 706	If Only I Had Known/You Must Pay	196?	6.25	12.50	25.00
❑ 707	Once There Was a Time/Come On Baby	1962	6.25	12.50	25.00

PAULA

Number	Title (A Side/B Side)	Yr	VG	VG+	NM
❑ 220	Most of All/Please Believe Me	1965	7.50	15.00	30.00

PHILIPS

Number	Title (A Side/B Side)	Yr	VG	VG+	NM
❑ 40029	Once There Was a Time/Never Believed in Love	1962	3.00	6.00	12.00

TEARDROPS, THE (1)

DORE

Number	Title (A Side/B Side)	Yr	VG	VG+	NM
❑ 679	Little Orphan Boy/(Instrumental)	1963	3.00	6.00	12.00

TEARDROPS, THE (2)

DOT

Number	Title (A Side/B Side)	Yr	VG	VG+	NM
❑ 15669	Bridge of Love/Jellyfish	1957	6.25	12.50	25.00

RENDEZVOUS

Number	Title (A Side/B Side)	Yr	VG	VG+	NM
❑ 102	Catch Me, I'm Falling Again/Sugar Baby	1958	7.50	15.00	30.00

TEARDROPS, THE (3)

JOSIE

Number	Title (A Side/B Side)	Yr	VG	VG+	NM
❑ 766	The Stars Are Out Tonight/Oh Stop It	1954	75.00	150.00	300.00
❑ 771	My Heart/Ooh Baby	1954	125.00	250.00	500.00

PORT

Number	Title (A Side/B Side)	Yr	VG	VG+	NM
❑ 70019	The Stars Are Out Tonight/Oh Stop It	1960	6.25	12.50	25.00

TEARDROPS, THE (4)

Even though on the same label as group (3), this is a different group.

JOSIE

Number	Title (A Side/B Side)	Yr	VG	VG+	NM
❑ 856	We Won't Tell/Al Chiar Di Luna (Porto Fortuna)	1959	6.25	12.50	25.00
❑ 862	Cry No More/You're My Hollywood Star	1959	6.25	12.50	25.00
❑ 873	Daddy's Little Girl/Always You	1960	6.25	12.50	25.00

TEARDROPS, THE (5)

KING

Number	Title (A Side/B Side)	Yr	VG	VG+	NM
❑ 5004	My Inspiration/I Prayed for Love	1956	6.25	12.50	25.00
❑ 5037	After School/Don't Be Afraid to Love	1957	6.25	12.50	25.00

TEARDROPS, THE (6)

Girl group.

MUSICOR

Number	Title (A Side/B Side)	Yr	VG	VG+	NM
❑ 1139	Tears Come Tumbling/You Won't Be There	1965	3.75	7.50	15.00
❑ 1218	I Will Love You Dear Forever/Bubblegummers	1966	3.75	7.50	15.00

SAXONY

Number	Title (A Side/B Side)	Yr	VG	VG+	NM
❑ 1007	Tonight I'm Gonna Fall in Love Again/That's Why I'll Get By	1964	20.00	40.00	80.00
❑ 1008	I'm Gonna Steal Your Boyfriend/Call Me and I'll Be Happy	1965	6.25	12.50	25.00
❑ 1009	Tears Come Tumbling/You Won't Be There	1965	5.00	10.00	20.00

TEARDROPS, THE (7)

Number	Title (A Side/B Side)	Yr	VG	VG+	NM
SAMPSON					
❑ 634	Come Back to Me/Sweet Lovin' Daddy-O	1952	100.00	200.00	400.00

TEARDROPS, THE (8)

Number	Title (A Side/B Side)	Yr	VG	VG+	NM
LAURIE					
❑ 3642	Welcome Back Kotter/Champagne Lady	1976	2.00	4.00	8.00
❑ 3660	Goodnight Elvis/Hey Gingerbread	1977	2.00	4.00	8.00

TEARS FOR FEARS

Number	Title (A Side/B Side)	Yr	VG	VG+	NM
FONTANA					
❑ 874710-7	Sowing the Seeds of Love/Tears Roll Down	1989	—	—	3.00
❑ 874710-7 [PS]	Sowing the Seeds of Love/Tears Roll Down	1989	—	—	3.00
❑ 876248-7	Woman in Chains/Always in the Past	1990	—	—	3.00
❑ 876248-7 [PS]	Woman in Chains/Always in the Past	1990	—	—	3.00
MERCURY					
❑ PRO 392-7 DJ	[DJ]Head Over Heels (Live) (same on both sides)	1985	2.50	5.00	10.00
❑ 812213-7	Mad World/Ideas As Opiates	1983	—	2.00	4.00
❑ 812213-7 [PS]	Mad World/Ideas As Opiates	1983	—	2.00	4.00
❑ 812677-7	Change/The Conflict	1983	—	2.00	4.00
❑ 862240-7	Break It Down Again/Bloodletting Go	1993	—	—	3.00
❑ 862804-7	Goodnight Song/New Star	1993	—	—	3.00
❑ 880294-7	Shout/The Big Chair	1985	—	—	3.00
❑ 880294-7 [PS]	Shout/The Big Chair	1985	—	—	3.00
❑ 880659-7	Everybody Wants to Rule the World/Pharaohs	1985	—	—	3.00
❑ 880899-7	Head Over Heels/When in Love with a Blind Man	1985	—	—	3.00
❑ 880899-7 [PS]	Head Over Heels/When in Love with a Blind Man	1985	—	—	3.00
❑ 884636-7	Mothers Talk/Sea Song	1986	—	—	3.00
❑ 884636-7 [PS]	Mothers Talk/Sea Song	1986	—	—	3.00

TEASERS, THE

Number	Title (A Side/B Side)	Yr	VG	VG+	NM
CHECKER					
❑ 800	I Was a Fool to Love You/How Could You Hurt One So	1954	150.00	300.00	600.00
❑ 800	I Was a Fool to Love You/How Could You Hurt One So	1954	300.00	600.00	1200.
—Red vinyl					

TECHNICS, THE

Number	Title (A Side/B Side)	Yr	VG	VG+	NM
CHEX					
❑ 1010	Has He Told You/Workout With a Pretty Girl	1963	7.50	15.00	30.00
—As "Tony and the Technics"					
❑ 1012	Because I Really Love You/A Man's Confusion	1963	7.50	15.00	30.00
❑ 1013	Hey Girl Don't Leave Me/I Met Her on the First of September	1963	10.00	20.00	40.00

TECHNIQUES, THE

Number	Title (A Side/B Side)	Yr	VG	VG+	NM
ROULETTE					
❑ 4030	Hey! Little Girl/In a Round-About Way	1957	6.25	12.50	25.00
❑ 4048	(Why Did I Ever) Let Her Go/Marindy	1958	6.25	12.50	25.00
❑ 4097	The Wisest Man You Know/Moon Tan	1958	6.25	12.50	25.00
STARS					
❑ 551	Hey Little Girl/In a Round-About Way	1957	10.00	20.00	40.00

TEDDY AND HIS PATCHES

Number	Title (A Side/B Side)	Yr	VG	VG+	NM
CHANCE					
❑ 100	Suzy Creamcheese/From Day to Day	1967	25.00	50.00	100.00
❑ 668	Suzy Creamcheese/It Ain't Nothin'	1967	25.00	50.00	100.00
❑ 669	Haight Ashbury/It Ain't Nothin'	1967	25.00	50.00	100.00

TEDDY AND THE CONTINENTALS

Number	Title (A Side/B Side)	Yr	VG	VG+	NM
PIK					
❑ 235	Tick Tick Tock/Everybody Pony	1961	6.25	12.50	25.00
RAGO					
❑ 201	Tick Tick Tock/Wild Christening Party	1962	6.25	12.50	25.00
—B-side by the Teen Kings					
RICHIE					
❑ 445	Do You/Tighten Up	1961	25.00	50.00	100.00
—With no mention of Roulette distribution on label					
❑ 445	Do You/Tighten Up	1961	10.00	20.00	40.00
—With Roulette Records distribution mentioned on label					
❑ 453	Crying Over You/Crossfire With Me Baby	1963	12.50	25.00	50.00
❑ 1001	Tick Tick Tock/Everybody Pony	1961	15.00	30.00	60.00

TEDDY BEARS, THE

With PHIL SPECTOR and Annette Kleinbard (a.k.a. Carol Connors).

Number	Title (A Side/B Side)	Yr	VG	VG+	NM
DORE					
❑ 503	To Know Him, Is to Love Him/Don't You Worry My Little Pet	1958	7.50	15.00	30.00
❑ 520	Wonderful Loveable You/Till You'll Be Mine	1959	5.00	10.00	20.00
IMPERIAL					
❑ 5562	Oh Why/I Don't Need You Anymore	1959	7.50	15.00	30.00
❑ 5581	You Said Goodbye/If You Only Knew	1959	7.50	15.00	30.00
❑ 5594	Seven Lonely Days/Don't Go Away	1959	7.50	15.00	30.00

TEDDY BOYS, THE

Number	Title (A Side/B Side)	Yr	VG	VG+	NM
CAMEO					
❑ 433	Where Have All the Good Times Gone/La La	1966	5.00	10.00	20.00
❑ 448	Mona/Good Morning Blues	1966	5.00	10.00	20.00
MGM					
❑ 13515	Jezebel/It's You	1966	5.00	10.00	20.00

TEE SET, THE

Number	Title (A Side/B Side)	Yr	VG	VG+	NM
COLOSSUS					
❑ 107	Ma Belle Amie/Angels Coming in the Holy Night	1969	—	2.50	5.00
❑ 107 [PS]	Ma Belle Amie/Angels Coming in the Holy Night	1969	—	3.00	6.00
❑ 114	If You Do Believe in Love/Charmaine	1970	—	2.00	4.00
❑ 139	She Likes Weeds/(B-side unknown)	1971	—	2.00	4.00

TEEGARDEN AND VAN WINKLE

Number	Title (A Side/B Side)	Yr	VG	VG+	NM
PLUMM					
❑ 68102	God, Love, and Rock & Roll (We Believe)/Work Me Tomorrow	1970	3.75	7.50	15.00
WESTBOUND					
❑ 170	God, Love and Rock & Roll/Work Me Tomorrow	1970	—	2.50	5.00
❑ 170 [PS]	God, Love and Rock & Roll/Work Me Tomorrow	1970	—	3.00	6.00
❑ 171	Everything Is Going to Be All Right/You Do	1970	—	2.50	5.00
❑ 187	Stoned on the Love for Jesus/I Need You	1971	—	2.50	5.00
❑ 200	Passing Gas/Ride Away with Me	1971	—	2.50	5.00
❑ 210	Carry On/Ride Away with Me	1972	—	2.50	5.00

TEEMATES, THE

Number	Title (A Side/B Side)	Yr	VG	VG+	NM
AUDIO FIDELITY					
❑ 104	Dream On Little Girl/Moving Out	1964	3.75	7.50	15.00
❑ 105	Night Fall/No More Tomorrows	1964	3.75	7.50	15.00

TEEN ANGELS, THE

Number	Title (A Side/B Side)	Yr	VG	VG+	NM
SUN					
❑ 388	Ain't Gonna Let You (Break My Heart)/Tell Me My Love	1964	7.50	15.00	30.00

TEEN CLEFS, THE

Number	Title (A Side/B Side)	Yr	VG	VG+	NM
DICE					
❑ 98/99	Sputnik/Hiding My Tears with a Smile	1959	37.50	75.00	150.00

TEEN KINGS, THE

See ROY ORBISON.

TEEN-KINGS, THE

Number	Title (A Side/B Side)	Yr	VG	VG+	NM
BEE					
❑ 1114/5	That's a Teen-Age Love/Tell Me If You Know	1959	500.00	1000.	1500.
—Legitimate original copies are on black vinyl					
WILLETT					
❑ 118	Don't Just Stand There/My Greatest Wish	1959	62.50	125.00	250.00

TEEN QUEENS, THE

Number	Title (A Side/B Side)	Yr	VG	VG+	NM
ANTLER					
❑ 4014	There's Nothing on My Mind (Part 1)/There's Nothing on My Mind (Part 2)	1959	3.75	7.50	15.00
❑ 4015	Politician/I'm a Fool	1959	3.75	7.50	15.00
❑ 4016	Donny (Part 1)/Donny (Part 2)	1960	3.75	7.50	15.00
❑ 4017	I Hear Violins/Magoo Can See	1960	3.75	7.50	15.00
KENT					
❑ 359	Eddie My Love/Just Goofed	1961	3.00	6.00	12.00
RCA VICTOR					
❑ 47-7206	Dear Tommy/You Good Boy-You Get Cookie	1958	4.00	8.00	16.00
❑ 47-7396	Movie Star/First Crush	1958	4.00	8.00	16.00
RPM					
❑ 453	Eddie My Love/Just Goofed	1956	7.50	15.00	30.00
—Black label					
❑ 453	Eddie My Love/Just Goofed	1956	30.00	60.00	120.00
—Red label					
❑ 460	So All Alone/Baby Mine	1956	6.25	12.50	25.00
❑ 464	Billy Boy/Until the Day I Die	1956	6.25	12.50	25.00
❑ 470	Red Top/Love Sweet Love	1956	6.25	12.50	25.00
❑ 480	My First Love/(B-side unknown)	1956	6.25	12.50	25.00
❑ 484	Rock Everybody/My Heart's Desire	1957	5.00	10.00	20.00
❑ 500	I Miss You/Two Loves and Two Lives	1957	5.00	10.00	20.00

TEEN TONES, THE

More than one group. Some may be listed as "Teen-Tones."

Number	Title (A Side/B Side)	Yr	VG	VG+	NM
DANDY DAN					
❑ 2	Darling I Love You/My Sweet	1958	20.00	40.00	80.00
DECCA					
❑ 30895	Don't Call Me Baby, I'll Call You/Yes You May	1959	7.50	15.00	30.00
GONE					
❑ 5061	The Rockin' Rumble/Latino Part 2	1959	7.50	15.00	30.00
SWAN					
❑ 4040	My Little Baby/Head Strong Baby	1959	7.50	15.00	30.00
TRI-DISC					
❑ 102	I'm So Happy/Shoutin' Twist	1961	3.75	7.50	15.00
WYNNE					
❑ 107	Faded Love/Gypsy Boogie	1958	6.25	12.50	25.00

TEENA MARIE

Number	Title (A Side/B Side)	Yr	VG	VG+	NM
EPIC					
❑ 04124	Fix It/(Instrumental)	1983	—	—	3.00
❑ 04124 [PS]	Fix It/(Instrumental)	1983	—	2.00	4.00
❑ 04271	Midnight Magnet/(Instrumental)	1983	—	—	3.00
❑ 04415	Dear Lover/Playboy	1984	—	—	3.00
❑ 04619	Lovergirl/(Instrumental)	1984	—	—	3.00
❑ 04619 [PS]	Lovergirl/(Instrumental)	1984	—	3.00	6.00
❑ 04738	Jammin'/(Instrumental)	1985	—	—	3.00
❑ 04738 [PS]	Jammin'/(Instrumental)	1985	—	2.00	4.00
❑ 04943	Out on a Limb/Starchild	1985	—	—	3.00
❑ 04943 [PS]	Out on a Limb/Starchild	1985	—	—	3.00
❑ 05599	14K/(Instrumental)	1985	—	—	3.00
❑ 05599 [PS]	14K/(Instrumental)	1985	—	—	3.00
❑ 05872	Lips to Find You/(Instrumental)	1986	—	—	3.00
❑ 05872 [PS]	Lips to Find You/(Instrumental)	1986	—	—	3.00
❑ 06292	Love Me Down Easy/(Instrumental)	1986	—	—	3.00
❑ 06292 [PS]	Love Me Down Easy/(Instrumental)	1986	—	—	3.00
❑ 06535	Lead Me On/(Instrumental)	1986	—	—	3.00
❑ 07708	Ooh La La La/Sing One to Your Love	1988	—	—	3.00
❑ 07708 [PS]	Ooh La La La/Sing One to Your Love	1988	—	—	3.00
❑ 07902	Work It/(Instrumental)	1988	—	—	3.00
❑ 07902 [PS]	Work It/(Instrumental)	1988	—	—	3.00
❑ 08040	Surrealistic Pillow/(Instrumental)	1988	—	—	3.00
❑ 08444	Lovergirl/Out on a Limb	1988	—	—	3.00
—Reissue					
❑ 68591	Bad Boy/Trick Bag	1989	—	—	3.00
GORDY					
❑ 7169	I'm a Sucker for Your Love/Deja Vu (I've Been There Before)	1979	—	2.00	4.00
❑ 7173	Don't Look Back/I'm Gonna Have My Cake (And Eat It Too)	1979	—	2.00	4.00

Number	Title (A Side/B Side)	Yr	VG	VG+	NM
❑ 7180	Can It Be Love/Too Many Colors	1980	—	2.00	4.00
❑ 7184	Behind the Groove/You're All the Boogie I Need	1980	—	2.00	4.00
❑ 7189	I Need Your Lovin'/Irons in the Fire	1980	—	2.00	4.00
❑ 7194	First Class Love/Young Love	1981	—	2.00	4.00
❑ 7202	Square Biz/Opus III (Does Anybody Care)	1981	—	2.00	4.00
❑ 7212	It Must Be Magic/Yes I Need	1981	—	2.00	4.00
❑ 7216	Portuguese Love/The Ballad of Cradle Rob and Me	1981	—	2.00	4.00

TEENAGE MOONLIGHTERS

MARK

Number	Title (A Side/B Side)	Yr	VG	VG+	NM
❑ 134	Sorry Sorry/I Want to Cry	1960	1000.	1500.	2000.

TEENAGERS, THE

These are records by the original group without FRANKIE LYMON. Also see FRANKIE LYMON AND THE TEENAGERS.

Number	Title (A Side/B Side)	Yr	VG	VG+	NM
END					
❑ 1071	Crying/Tonight's the Night	1960	15.00	30.00	60.00
❑ 1076	Can You Tell Me/A Little Wiser Now	1960	10.00	20.00	40.00
GEE					
❑ 1046	Flip Flop/Everything to Me	1957	7.50	15.00	30.00
ROULETTE					
❑ 4086	My Broken Heart/Momma Wanna Rock	1958	20.00	40.00	80.00

TEENBEATS, THE

TEENBEAT

Number	Title (A Side/B Side)	Yr	VG	VG+	NM
❑ (No #)	Surfbound/Mr. Moto	1963	20.00	40.00	80.00

TEENETTES, THE

Number	Title (A Side/B Side)	Yr	VG	VG+	NM
BRUNSWICK					
❑ 55125	I Want a Boy with a Hi-Fi Supersonic Stereophonic Bloop Bleep/From the Word Go	1959	6.25	12.50	25.00
JOSIE					
❑ 830	My Lucky Star/Too Young to Fall in Love	1958	15.00	30.00	60.00

TELSTARS, THE

Number	Title (A Side/B Side)	Yr	VG	VG+	NM
COLUMBIA					
❑ 44141	Keep On Running/Hold Tight	1967	5.00	10.00	20.00
IMPERIAL					
❑ 5903	Continental Mash/Stomp Happy	1962	6.25	12.50	25.00
TEEN					
❑ 510	Continental Mash/Stomp Happy	1962	10.00	20.00	40.00
❑ 513	Pow Wow/Lovina	1963	8.75	17.50	35.00
❑ 516	Topless/Spaghetti Strap	1964	8.75	17.50	35.00
❑ 517	Tough George/'Cause I Really Do	1964	8.75	17.50	35.00

TEMPLE, BOB

KING

Number	Title (A Side/B Side)	Yr	VG	VG+	NM
❑ 4958	Come Back, Come Back/Vam Vam Vamoose	1956	7.50	15.00	30.00

TEMPO, NINO

Also see NINO TEMPO AND APRIL STEVENS.

Number	Title (A Side/B Side)	Yr	VG	VG+	NM
A&M					
❑ 1461	Sister James/Clair De Lune (In Jazz)	1973	—	2.00	4.00
❑ 1499	Roll It/Hawkeye	1974	—	2.00	4.00
❑ 1532	High on the Music/Come See Me 'Round Midnight	1974	—	2.00	4.00
❑ 1625	Gettin' Off/Don't Stop Now	1974	—	2.00	4.00
❑ 2131	Hooked on Young Stuff/Ronan's Road	1979	—	2.00	4.00
RCA VICTOR					
❑ 47-7424	15 Girl Friends/Lonnie 'Bout Junie	1958	3.00	6.00	12.00
❑ 47-7647	Ding-a-Ling/When You Were Sweet Sixteen	1959	3.00	6.00	12.00
❑ 47-7694	Jack the Ripper/Main Theme from "Jack the Ripper"	1960	2.50	5.00	10.00
—B-side by Pete Rugolo					
TOWER					
❑ 369	Boys Town/Boys Town (Sing Along)	1967	—	3.00	6.00
UNITED ARTISTS					
❑ 256	What Is Love to a Teenager/Lipstick on Your Lips	1960	2.50	5.00	10.00

TEMPO, NINO, AND APRIL STEVENS

Also see each artist's individual listings.

Number	Title (A Side/B Side)	Yr	VG	VG+	NM
ATCO					
❑ 6224	Sweet and Lovely/True Love	1962	2.50	5.00	10.00
❑ 6248	Indian Love Call/Paradise	1962	2.50	5.00	10.00
❑ 6263	Together We'll Always Be/Baby Weemus	1963	2.50	5.00	10.00
❑ 6273	Deep Purple/I've Been Carrying a Torch for You So Long That I Burned a Great Big Hole in My Heart	1963	3.00	6.00	12.00
❑ 6281	Whispering/Tweedledee	1963	2.50	5.00	10.00
❑ 6286	Stardust/I-45	1964	2.00	4.00	8.00
❑ 6294	Tea for Two/I'm Confessin' (That I Love You)	1964	2.00	4.00	8.00
❑ 6306	I Surrender Dear/Who	1964	2.00	4.00	8.00
❑ 6314	Melancholy Baby/Ooh La La	1964	2.00	4.00	8.00
❑ 6325	Our Love/Honeywell Rose	1964	2.00	4.00	8.00
❑ 6337	These Arms of Mine/The Coldest Night of the Year	1965	2.00	4.00	8.00
❑ 6350	Swing Me/Tomorrow Is Soon a Memory	1965	2.00	4.00	8.00
❑ 6360	Think of You/I'm Sweet on You	1965	2.00	4.00	8.00
❑ 6368	That's My Desire/King Kong	1965	2.00	4.00	8.00
❑ 6375	I Love How You Love Me/Tears of Sorrow	1965	2.00	4.00	8.00
❑ 6391	Hey Baby/The Poison of Your Kisses	1965	2.00	4.00	8.00
❑ 6410	Bye Bye Blues/King Kong	1966	2.00	4.00	8.00
❑ 6897	She's My Baby/Tomorrow Is Soon a Memory	1972	—	3.00	6.00
A&M					
❑ 1394	Love Story/Hoochy Coochy — Wing Dang Doo	1972	—	2.00	4.00
❑ 1443	Put It Where You Want It/I Can't Get Over You Baby	1973	—	2.00	4.00
❑ 1674	Never Had a Lover/You Turn Me On	1975	—	2.00	4.00
BELL					
❑ 769	Did I or Didn't I/Yesterday I Heard the Rain	1969	2.00	4.00	8.00
❑ 823	Seas of Love-Dock of the Bay/Twilight	1969	2.00	4.00	8.00
CHELSEA					
❑ 3052	What Kind of Fool Am I/(B-side unknown)	1976	—	2.00	4.00
MGM					
❑ 13825	Falling in Love Again/Wanting You	1967	2.00	4.00	8.00
❑ 14266	How About Me/Makin' Love to Rainbow Colors	1971	—	3.00	6.00
UNITED ARTISTS					
❑ 272	Ooeah (That's What You Do to Me)/High School Sweetheart	1960	2.50	5.00	10.00
WHITE WHALE					
❑ 236	All Strung Out/I Can't Go On Living (Baby Without You)	1966	2.00	4.00	8.00
❑ 241	You'll Be Needing Me Baby/Habit of Lovin' You Baby	1966	2.00	4.00	8.00
❑ 246	Wings of Love/My Old Flame	1967	2.00	4.00	8.00
❑ 252	I Can't Go On Living Baby Without You/Little Child	1967	2.00	4.00	8.00
❑ 268	Let It Be Me/Words of Love	1968	2.00	4.00	8.00
❑ 271	Ooh Poo Pa Doo/Let It Be Me	1968	2.00	4.00	8.00

TEMPO-TONES, THE

ACME

Number	Title (A Side/B Side)	Yr	VG	VG+	NM
❑ 713	Get Yourself Another Fool/Ride Along	1957	37.50	75.00	150.00
❑ 715	In My Dreams/My Boy Sleep Pete	1957	125.00	250.00	500.00
❑ 718	Come Into My Heart/Somewhere There Is Sunshine	1957	125.00	250.00	500.00
❑ 722	The Day I Met You/Wishing All the Time	1957	100.00	200.00	400.00

TEMPOS, THE

Probably more than one group.

Number	Title (A Side/B Side)	Yr	VG	VG+	NM
ASCOT					
❑ 2167	When You Loved Me/My Barbara Ann	1965	6.25	12.50	25.00
❑ 2173	I Wish It Were Summer/My Barbara Ann	1965	6.25	12.50	25.00
CANTERBURY					
❑ 504	Here I Come (Countdown) Part 1/Here I Come (Countdown) Part 2	1967	3.75	7.50	15.00
CLIMAX					
❑ 102	See You in September/Bless You My Love	1959	5.00	10.00	20.00
❑ 105	The Crossroads of Love/Whatever Happens	1959	5.00	10.00	20.00
FAIRMOUNT					
❑ 611	Oh Play That Thing/Monkey Doo	1963	3.00	6.00	12.00
HI-Q					
❑ 100	It's Tough/Sham-Rock	1959	10.00	20.00	40.00
KAPP					
❑ 178	Kingdom of Love/That's What You Do to Me	1957	6.25	12.50	25.00
❑ 199	Prettiest Girl in School/Never You Mind	1957	6.25	12.50	25.00
❑ 213	I Got a Job/Strollin' with My Baby	1958	6.25	12.50	25.00
MONTEL					
❑ 955	I Gotta Make a Move/It Was You	1966	3.75	7.50	15.00
PARIS					
❑ 550	Look Homeward, Angel/Under Ten Flags	1960	5.00	10.00	20.00
RHYTHM					
❑ 121	Promise Me/Never Let Me Go	1958	125.00	250.00	500.00
RILEY'S					
❑ 8781	Don't Leave Me/I Need You	1966	7.50	15.00	30.00
U.S.A.					
❑ 810	Why Don't You Write Me/A Thief in the Night	1965	6.25	12.50	25.00

TEMPREES

Number	Title (A Side/B Side)	Yr	VG	VG+	NM
EPIC					
❑ 50192	I Found Love on a Disco Floor/There Ain't a Dream Been Dreamed	1976	—	2.50	5.00
WE PRODUCE					
❑ 1801	I'm for You, You for Me/Rules and Regulations	1971	2.00	4.00	8.00
❑ 1803	(Girl) I Love You/I Love You, You Love Me	1971	2.00	4.00	8.00
❑ 1805	My Baby Love/If I Could Say What's On My Mind	1972	2.00	4.00	8.00
❑ 1807	Explain It to Her Mama/Love Can Be So Wonderful	1972	2.00	4.00	8.00
❑ 1808	Dedicated to the One I Love/I Love You, You Love Me	1972	2.00	4.00	8.00
❑ 1810	A Thousand Miles Away/Chalk It Up to Experience	1973	2.00	4.00	8.00
❑ 1811	Love's Maze/Wrap Me in Love	1973	2.00	4.00	8.00
❑ 1812	At Last/Love Can Be So Wonderful	1974	—	3.50	7.00
❑ 1813	You Make Me Love You/You Make the Sunshine	1974	—	3.50	7.00
❑ 1814	Mr. Cool That Ain't Cool/Lovin' You Is So Easy	1974	—	3.50	7.00
❑ 1815	I Love, I Love/Your Love	1975	—	3.50	7.00
❑ 1816	Come and Get Your Love/I'll Live Her Life	1975	—	3.50	7.00

TEMPTATIONS, THE

The famous Detroit/Motown male vocal group. Also see EDDIE KENDRICKS; DAVID RUFFIN; THE SUPREMES AND THE TEMPTATIONS.

Number	Title (A Side/B Side)	Yr	VG	VG+	NM
ATLANTIC					
❑ 3436	In a Lifetime/I Could Never Stop Loving You	1977	—	2.00	4.00
❑ 3461	Think for Yourself/Let's Live in Place	1978	—	2.00	4.00
❑ 3517	Bare Back/I See My Child	1978	—	2.00	4.00
❑ 3538	Ever Ready Love/Touch Me Again	1978	—	2.00	4.00
❑ 3567	Mystic Woman/I Just Don't Know How to Let You Go	1979	—	2.00	4.00
GORDY					
❑ 1616	Standing on the Top-Part 1/Standing on the Top-Part 2	1982	—	2.00	4.00
—With Rick James					
❑ 1631	More on the Inside/Money's Hard to Get	1982	—	2.00	4.00
❑ 1654	Silent Night/Everything for Christmas	1982	—	3.00	6.00
❑ 1666	Love on My Mind Tonight/Bring Your Body Here	1983	—	2.00	4.00
❑ 1683	Made in America/Surface Thrills	1983	—	2.00	4.00
❑ 1707	Miss Busy Body (Get Your Body Busy)/(Instrumental)	1983	—	2.00	4.00
❑ 1713	Silent Night/Everything for Christmas	1983	—	2.50	5.00
❑ 1720	Sail Away/Isn't the Night Fantastic	1984	—	2.00	4.00
❑ 1765	Treat Her Like a Lady/Isn't the Night Fantastic	1984	—	2.00	4.00

Number	Title (A Side/B Side)	Yr	VG	VG+	NM
❑ 1781	My Love Is True (Truly for You)/Set Your Love Right	1985	—	2.00	4.00
❑ 1789	How Can You Say That It's Over/I'll Keep My Light in My Window	1985	—	2.00	4.00
❑ 1818	Do You Really Love Your Baby/I'll Keep My Light in My Window	1985	—	2.00	4.00
❑ 1834	Touch Me/Set Your Love Right	1986	—	2.00	4.00
❑ 1856	Lady Soul/Put Us Together Again	1986	—	2.00	4.00
❑ 1871	To Be Continued/You're the One	1986	—	2.00	4.00
❑ 1871 [PS]	To Be Continued/You're the One	1986	—	3.00	6.00
❑ 1881	Someone/Love Me Right	1987	—	2.00	4.00
❑ 7001	Dream Come True/Isn't She Pretty	1962	10.00	20.00	40.00
❑ 7010	Paradise/Slow Down Heart	1962	7.50	15.00	30.00
❑ 7015	I Want a Love I Can See/The Further You Look, The Less You See	1963	6.25	12.50	25.00
❑ 7020	May I Have This Dance?/Farewell, My Love	1963	6.25	12.50	25.00
❑ 7028	The Way You Do the Things You Do/Just Let Me Know	1964	3.75	7.50	15.00
❑ 7032	I'll Be in Trouble/The Girl's Alright with Me	1964	3.75	7.50	15.00
❑ 7035	Girl (Why You Wanna Make Me Blue)/Baby, Baby I Need You	1964	3.75	7.50	15.00
❑ 7038	My Girl/Nobody But My Baby	1965	3.75	7.50	15.00
❑ 7038 [PS]	My Girl/Nobody But My Baby	1965	30.00	60.00	120.00
❑ 7040	It's Growing/What Love Has Joined Together	1965	3.75	7.50	15.00
❑ 7043	Since I Lost My Baby/You've Got to Earn It	1965	3.75	7.50	15.00
❑ 7047	My Baby/Don't Look Back	1965	3.75	7.50	15.00
❑ 7049	Get Ready/Fading Away	1966	3.75	7.50	15.00
❑ 7054	Ain't Too Proud to Beg/You'll Lose a Precious Love	1966	3.75	7.50	15.00
❑ 7055	Beauty Is Only Skin Deep/You're Not an Ordinary Girl	1966	3.75	7.50	15.00
❑ 7055 [PS]	Beauty Is Only Skin Deep/You're Not an Ordinary Girl	1966	10.00	20.00	40.00
❑ 7057	(I Know) I'm Losing You/I Couldn't Cry If I Wanted To	1966	3.75	7.50	15.00
❑ 7061	All I Need/Sorry Is a Sorry Word	1967	2.50	5.00	10.00
❑ 7063	You're My Everything/I've Been Good to You	1967	2.50	5.00	10.00
—"Gordy" on left					
❑ 7063	You're My Everything/I've Been Good to You	1967	3.75	7.50	15.00
—"Gordy" on top					
❑ 7065	(Loneliness Made Me Realize) It's You That I Need/Don't Send Me Away	1967	2.50	5.00	10.00
❑ 7068	I Wish It Would Rain/I Truly, Truly Believe	1967	2.50	5.00	10.00
❑ 7072	I Could Never Love Another (After Loving You)/ Gonna Give Her All the Love I've Got	1968	2.50	5.00	10.00
❑ 7074	Please Return Your Love to Me/How Can I Forget	1968	2.50	5.00	10.00
❑ 7081	Cloud Nine/Why Did She Have to Leave Me	1968	2.00	4.00	8.00
❑ 7082	Silent Night/Rudolph, the Red-Nosed Reindeer	1968	3.00	6.00	12.00
❑ 7084	Run Away Child, Running Wild/I Need Your Love	1969	2.00	4.00	8.00
❑ 7086	Don't Let the Joneses Get You Down/Since I've Lost You	1969	2.00	4.00	8.00
❑ 7093	I Can't Get Next to You/Running Away (Ain't Gonna Help You)	1969	2.00	4.00	8.00
❑ 7096	Psychedelic Shack/That's the Way Love Is	1970	—	3.00	6.00
❑ 7099	Ball of Confusion (That's What the World Is Today)/It's Summer	1970	—	3.00	6.00
❑ 7099 [PS]	Ball of Confusion (That's What the World Is Today)/It's Summer	1970	5.00	10.00	20.00
❑ 7102	Ungena Za Ulimwengu (Unite the World)/Hum Along and Dance	1970	—	3.00	6.00
❑ 7105	Just My Imagination (Running Away with Me)/ You Make Your Own Heaven and Hell Right Here on Earth	1971	—	3.00	6.00
❑ 7109	It's Summer/I'm the Exception to the Rule	1971	—	3.00	6.00
❑ 7111	Superstar (Remember How You Got Where You Are)/Gonna Keep On Tryin' Till I Win Your Love	1971	—	3.00	6.00
❑ 7115	Take a Look Around/Smooth Sailing (From Now On)	1972	—	3.00	6.00
❑ 7119	Mother Nature/Funky Music Sho Nuff Turns Me On	1972	—	3.00	6.00
❑ 7121	Papa Was a Rollin' Stone/(Instrumental)	1972	—	3.00	6.00
❑ 7126	Masterpiece/(Instrumental)	1973	—	3.00	6.00
❑ 7129	Plastic Man/Hurry Tomorrow	1973	—	3.00	6.00
❑ 7131	Hey Girl (I Like Your Style)/Ma	1973	—	3.00	6.00
❑ 7133	Let Your Hair Down/Ain't No Justice	1973	—	3.00	6.00
❑ 7135	Heavenly/Zoom	1974	—	3.00	6.00
❑ 7136	You've Got My Soul on Fire/I Need You	1974	—	3.00	6.00
❑ 7138	Happy People/(Instrumental)	1974	—	3.00	6.00
❑ 7142	Shakey Ground/I'm a Bachelor	1975	—	3.00	6.00
❑ 7144	Glasshouse/The Prophet	1975	—	3.00	6.00
❑ 7146	Keep Holding On/What You Need Most (I Do Best of All)	1975	—	3.00	6.00
❑ 7150	Up the Creek (Without a Paddle)/Darling Stand By Me (Song for a Woman)	1976	—	3.00	6.00
❑ 7151	Who Are You (And What Are You Doing the Rest of Your Life)/Darling Stand By Me (Song for a Woman)	1976	—	—	—
—Unreleased					
❑ 7152	Let Me Count the Ways (I Love You)/Who Are You (And What Are You Doing the Rest of Your Life)	1976	—	3.00	6.00
❑ 7183	Power/Power (Part 2)	1980	—	2.00	4.00
❑ 7183 [DJ]	Power (same on both sides)	1980	2.50	5.00	10.00
—Promo only on red vinyl					
❑ 7188	Struck by Lightning Twice/I'm Coming Home	1980	—	2.00	4.00
❑ 7208	Aiming at Your Heart/Life of a Cowboy	1981	—	2.00	4.00
❑ 7213	Oh What a Night/Isn't the Night Fantastic	1981	—	2.00	4.00

MIRACLE

Number	Title (A Side/B Side)	Yr	VG	VG+	NM
❑ 5	Oh, Mother of Mine/Romance Without Finance	1961	25.00	50.00	100.00
❑ 12	Check Yourself/Your Wonderful Love	1961	25.00	50.00	100.00

MOTOWN

Number	Title (A Side/B Side)	Yr	VG	VG+	NM
❑ 903	One Step at a Time/(Instrumental)	1990	—	—	3.00
❑ 1501	Take Me Away/There's More Where That Came From	1980	—	2.00	4.00
❑ 1837	A Fine Mess/Wishful Thinking	1986	—	2.00	4.00
❑ 1837 [PS]	A Fine Mess/Wishful Thinking	1986	—	3.00	6.00
❑ 1908	I Wonder Who She's Seeing Now/Girls (They Like It)	1987	—	—	3.00
❑ 1908 [PS]	I Wonder Who She's Seeing Now/Girls (They Like It)	1987	—	2.00	4.00
❑ 1920	Look What You Started/More Love, Your Love	1987	—	—	3.00
❑ 1933	Do You Wanna Go with Me/Put Your Foot Down	1988	—	—	3.00
❑ 1974	All I Want from You/(Instrumental)	1989	—	—	3.00
❑ 860862-7	Stay/My Girl	1998	—	—	3.00

MOTOWN YESTERYEAR

Number	Title (A Side/B Side)	Yr	VG	VG+	NM
❑ 690	Silent Night/Everything For Christmas	198?	—	2.00	4.00

TOPPS/MOTOWN

Number	Title (A Side/B Side)	Yr	VG	VG+	NM
❑ 4	My Girl	1967	18.75	37.50	75.00
—Cardboard record					
❑ 13	The Way You Do the Things You Do	1967	18.75	37.50	75.00
—Cardboard record					

TEMPTATIONS, THE (2)

White doo-wop group.

GOLDISC

Number	Title (A Side/B Side)	Yr	VG	VG+	NM
❑ 3001	Barbara/Someday	1960	7.50	15.00	30.00
—All-black label					
❑ 3001	Barbara/Someday	1960	5.00	10.00	20.00
—Multicolor (black, red, gold) label					
❑ 3007	Letter of Devotion/Fickle Little Girl	1960	6.25	12.50	25.00

TEMPTATIONS, THE (3)

KING

Number	Title (A Side/B Side)	Yr	VG	VG+	NM
❑ 5118	Standing Alone/Roaches Rock	1958	75.00	150.00	300.00

TEMPTATIONS, THE (4)

PARKWAY

Number	Title (A Side/B Side)	Yr	VG	VG+	NM
❑ 803	Temptations/Birds N' Bees	1959	7.50	15.00	30.00

TEMPTATIONS, THE (5)

P&L

Number	Title (A Side/B Side)	Yr	VG	VG+	NM
❑ 1001	Blue Surf/Egyptian Surf	1963	15.00	30.00	60.00

TEMPTATIONS, THE (6)

SAVOY

Number	Title (A Side/B Side)	Yr	VG	VG+	NM
❑ 1532	Mister Juke Box/Mad at Love	1958	5.00	10.00	20.00
❑ 1550	I Love You/Don't You Know	1958	5.00	10.00	20.00

TEMPTONES, THE

DARYL HALL was in this group.

ARCTIC

Number	Title (A Side/B Side)	Yr	VG	VG+	NM
❑ 130	Girl, I Love You/Good-Bye	1967	10.00	20.00	40.00
❑ 136	Say These Words of Love/This Could Be the Start of Something Good	1967	10.00	20.00	40.00

TEN BROKEN HEARTS

Allegedly, NEIL DIAMOND appears on this record.

DIAMOND

Number	Title (A Side/B Side)	Yr	VG	VG+	NM
❑ 123	Ten Lonely Guys/Shining Star	1962	10.00	20.00	40.00

10CC

Also see GODLEY AND CREME; GRAHAM GOULDMAN; HOTLEGS; THE MOCKINGBIRDS; SILVER FLEET.

MERCURY

Number	Title (A Side/B Side)	Yr	VG	VG+	NM
❑ 73678	I'm Not in Love/Channel Swimmer	1975	—	2.50	5.00
❑ 73725	Art for Art's Sake/Get It While You Can	1975	—	2.50	5.00
❑ 73725 [PS]	Art for Art's Sake/Get It While You Can	1975	2.00	4.00	8.00
❑ 73779	I'm Mandy Fly Me/How Dare You	1976	—	2.50	5.00
❑ 73875	The Things We Do for Love/Hot to Trot	1976	—	2.50	5.00
❑ 73917	People in Love/Don't Squeeze Me Like Toothpaste	1977	—	2.50	5.00
❑ 73943	Good Morning Judge/I'm So Laid Back I'm Laid Out	1977	—	2.50	5.00
❑ 73980	You've Got a Cold/The Wall Street Shuffle	1977	—	2.50	5.00

POLYDOR

Number	Title (A Side/B Side)	Yr	VG	VG+	NM
❑ 14511	Dreadlock Holiday/Nothing Can Move Me	1978	—	2.50	5.00
❑ 14528	For You and I/Take These Chains	1978	—	2.50	5.00

UK

Number	Title (A Side/B Side)	Yr	VG	VG+	NM
❑ 49005	Donna/Hot Sun Rock	1972	—	3.00	6.00
❑ 49015	Ruber Bullets/Waterfall	1973	—	3.00	6.00
❑ 49019	Headline Hustler/Speed Kills	1973	—	3.00	6.00
❑ 49023	The Wall Street Shuffle/Gismo My Way	1974	—	3.00	6.00

WARNER BROS.

Number	Title (A Side/B Side)	Yr	VG	VG+	NM
❑ 29973	Power of Love/Action Man in Motown Suit	1982	—	2.50	5.00
❑ 49266	It Doesn't Matter Anymore/Strange Lover	1980	—	2.50	5.00

10,000 MANIACS

ELEKTRA

Number	Title (A Side/B Side)	Yr	VG	VG+	NM
❑ 64595	Because the Night/Eat for Two	1993	—	2.00	4.00
❑ 65962	Like the Weather/Peace Train	198?	—	—	3.00
—"Spun Gold" reissue					
❑ 69253	You Happy Puppet/Gunshy	1989	—	2.00	4.00
❑ 69298	Trouble Me/The Lion's Share	1989	—	2.00	4.00
❑ 69298 [PS]	Trouble Me/The Lion's Share	1989	—	2.00	4.00
❑ 69388	What's the Matter Here?/Cherry Tree	1988	—	2.00	4.00
❑ 69388 [PS]	What's the Matter Here?/Cherry Tree	1988	—	2.00	4.00
❑ 69418	Like the Weather/A Campfire Song	1988	—	2.00	4.00
❑ 69418 [PS]	Like the Weather/A Campfire Song	1988	—	2.00	4.00
❑ 69439	Don't Talk/City of Angels	1987	—	2.00	4.00
❑ 69439 [PS]	Don't Talk/City of Angels	1987	—	2.00	4.00
❑ 69457	Peace Train/Painted Desert	1987	—	2.00	4.00
❑ 69457 [PS]	Peace Train/Painted Desert	1987	—	2.00	4.00

TEN YEARS AFTER

COLUMBIA

Number	Title (A Side/B Side)	Yr	VG	VG+	NM
❑ 45457	I'd Love to Change the World/Let the Sky Fall	1971	—	2.50	5.00

Number	Title (A Side/B Side)	Yr	VG	VG+	NM
❑ 45530	Baby Won't You Let Me Rock 'N' Roll You/Once There Was a Time	1972	—	2.50	5.00
❑ 45736	You Can't Win Them All/Choo Choo Mama	1972	—	2.50	5.00
❑ 45787	Tomorrow, I'll Be Out of Town/Convention Prevention	1973	—	2.50	5.00
❑ 45915	I'm Going Home/You Give Me Loving	1973	—	2.50	5.00
❑ 46061	It's Getting Harder/I Wanted to Boogie	1974	—	2.50	5.00
DERAM					
❑ 7529	If You Should Love Me/Love Like a Man	1970	2.00	4.00	8.00
❑ 85027	Portable People/The Sounds	1968	2.00	4.00	8.00
❑ 85035	Hear Me Calling/I'm Going Home	1968	2.00	4.00	8.00

TENDER TONES, THE

Number	Title (A Side/B Side)	Yr	VG	VG+	NM
DUCKY					
❑ 713	I Love You So/Just for a Little While	1959	200.00	400.00	800.00

TENDERFOOTS, THE

Number	Title (A Side/B Side)	Yr	VG	VG+	NM
FEDERAL					
❑ 12214	Kissing Bug/Watussi Wussi Wo	1955	15.00	30.00	60.00
❑ 12219	My Confession/Save Me Some Kisses	1955	15.00	30.00	60.00
❑ 12225	Those Golden Bells/I'm Yours Anyhow	1955	20.00	40.00	80.00
❑ 12228	Sindy/Sugar Ways	1955	30.00	60.00	120.00

TENNESSEE DRIFTERS, THE

Number	Title (A Side/B Side)	Yr	VG	VG+	NM
DOT					
❑ 1166	Boogie Woogie Baby/Drive Those Blues Away	1953	7.50	15.00	30.00
❑ 1187	Corrine, Corrina/Somebody Loves You	1954	7.50	15.00	30.00

TENNESSEE GUITARS, THE

Number	Title (A Side/B Side)	Yr	VG	VG+	NM
SUN					
❑ 1102	Tennessee Toddy/Trophy Run	1969	—	3.00	6.00

TENNILLE, TONI

Also see CAPTAIN AND TENNILLE.

Number	Title (A Side/B Side)	Yr	VG	VG+	NM
MIRAGE					
❑ 99733	More Than You Know/Let's Do It	1984	—	—	3.00

TERMITES, THE

Number	Title (A Side/B Side)	Yr	VG	VG+	NM
BEE					
❑ 1825	Give Me Your Heart/Carrie Lou	1964	12.50	25.00	50.00

TERRACETONES, THE

Number	Title (A Side/B Side)	Yr	VG	VG+	NM
APT					
❑ 25016	Words of Wisdom/Ride of Paul Revere	1958	25.00	50.00	100.00

TERRELL, ERNIE

Number	Title (A Side/B Side)	Yr	VG	VG+	NM
ARGO					
❑ 5511	Dear Abbie/I Can't Wait	1965	3.00	6.00	12.00

TERRELL, TAMMI

Also see MARVIN GAYE AND TAMMI TERRELL; TAMMY MONTGOMERY.

Number	Title (A Side/B Side)	Yr	VG	VG+	NM
MOTOWN					
❑ 1086	I Can't Believe You Love Me/Hold Me Oh My Darling	1965	2.50	5.00	10.00
❑ 1095	Come On and See Me/Baby Don'tcha Worry	1966	2.50	5.00	10.00
❑ 1115	What a Good Man He Is/There Are Things	1967	2.50	5.00	10.00
❑ 1138	This Old Heart of Mine (Is Weak for You)/Just Too Much to Hope For	1968	2.50	5.00	10.00

TERRI AND THE KITTENS

Number	Title (A Side/B Side)	Yr	VG	VG+	NM
IMPERIAL					
❑ 5728	Wedding Bells/You Cheated	1961	5.00	10.00	20.00

TERRI AND THE VELVETEENS

Number	Title (A Side/B Side)	Yr	VG	VG+	NM
KERWOOD					
❑ 711	Bells of Love/You've Broken My Heart	1962	10.00	20.00	40.00

TERRI-TONES, THE

Number	Title (A Side/B Side)	Yr	VG	VG+	NM
CORTLAND					
❑ 105	Go/The Sinner	1962	12.50	25.00	50.00
REGENCY					
❑ 929	Go/The Sinner	1962	7.50	15.00	30.00

TERRY, AL

Number	Title (A Side/B Side)	Yr	VG	VG+	NM
FEATURE					
❑ 1061	I Wonder If I Can Lose the Blues This Way/Walking and Crying with the Blues	1953	12.50	25.00	50.00
❑ 1075	Say a Prayer for Me/I Nearly Made a Fool of My Heart	1953	12.50	25.00	50.00
❑ 1079	Will Christmas Be a Happy Day for Me/Santa Claus Is On His Way	1953	12.50	25.00	50.00
❑ 2000	You're Worse Than a Tramp/Please Think of Me	1954	12.50	25.00	50.00
HICKORY					
❑ 1003	Good Deal, Lucille/Say a Prayer for Me	1954	10.00	20.00	40.00
❑ 1012	House of Glass/Show Me That You Love Me	1954	7.50	15.00	30.00
❑ 1017	Hey Whatta Y'Say/Let's Postpone Our Wedding	1954	10.00	20.00	40.00
❑ 1022	The Wall Around My Heart/Hate Me Not	1955	7.50	15.00	30.00
❑ 1029	Gone Again/No No John	1955	7.50	15.00	30.00
❑ 1037	Goodbye Mr. Sunshine/I Love Her So	1955	7.50	15.00	30.00
❑ 1041	Not Anymore/We Make a Lovely Couple	1956	7.50	15.00	30.00
—With Wilma Lee (Cooper)					
❑ 1045	Follow Me/Lesson of Love	1956	7.50	15.00	30.00
❑ 1049	No Shrimp Today/Without You	1956	7.50	15.00	30.00
❑ 1056	Am I Seeing Things/Roughneck Blues	1956	7.50	15.00	30.00
❑ 1061	Money/If I Win, I Win	1957	7.50	15.00	30.00
—B-side by Rusty & Doug (Kershaw)					
❑ 1066	It's What You Are to Me/Last Date	1957	7.50	15.00	30.00
❑ 1071	Coconut Girl/Bring Me Some Rain	1957	7.50	15.00	30.00
❑ 1075	Good Deal, Lucille/Because I'm Yours	1958	7.50	15.00	30.00
❑ 1082	I'm Not the Girl/It's Just As Well	1958	7.50	15.00	30.00
—With Wilma Lee (Cooper)					
❑ 1088	My Baby Knows/Your Sweet Lies	1958	7.50	15.00	30.00
❑ 1093	It's Better Late Than Never/Then You're Living Just Like Me	1958	7.50	15.00	30.00
❑ 1111	Watch Dog/Passing the Blues Around	1960	6.25	12.50	25.00

Number	Title (A Side/B Side)	Yr	VG	VG+	NM
INDEX					
❑ 5025	I've Been Losing You/I Saw the Enemy Today	196?	2.50	5.00	10.00
❑ 5026	Today's Another Day (Like Tomorrow)/Bourbon Street Parade	196?	2.50	5.00	10.00
❑ 5027	Only the Hangman (Gold in the Mountain)/Not Anymore	196?	2.50	5.00	10.00
—A-side with Bob Terry					
❑ 5029	I'm Beginning to Forget You/Hurricane Party	196?	2.50	5.00	10.00

TERRY, DON

Number	Title (A Side/B Side)	Yr	VG	VG+	NM
LIN					
❑ 5018	Knees Shakin'/She Giggles	1959	37.50	75.00	150.00

TERRY, DOSSIE

Number	Title (A Side/B Side)	Yr	VG	VG+	NM
KING					
❑ 5072	Thunderbird/I Got a Watch Dog	1957	12.50	25.00	50.00
❑ 5890	Thunderbird/Be-Bop Wino	1964	3.75	7.50	15.00
—B-side by the Lamplighters					
RCA VICTOR					
❑ 47-4474	Didn't Satisfy You/24 Years	1952	15.00	30.00	60.00
❑ 47-4648	When I Hit the Number/My Love Is Gone	1952	15.00	30.00	60.00
❑ 47-4864	Lost My Head/Sad, Sad Affair	1952	15.00	30.00	60.00

TERRY, GENE

Number	Title (A Side/B Side)	Yr	VG	VG+	NM
GOLDBAND					
❑ 1066	Cindy Lou/Teardrops in My Eyes	1958	30.00	60.00	120.00
❑ 1081	Never Let Her Go/No Mail Today	1958	10.00	20.00	40.00
❑ 1088	Cinderella, Cinderella/Guy with a Million Dreams	1959	7.50	15.00	30.00
SAVOY					
❑ 1559	This Should Go On Forever/Fine, Fine, Fine	1959	5.00	10.00	20.00

TERRY, GORDON

Number	Title (A Side/B Side)	Yr	VG	VG+	NM
CADENCE					
❑ 1316	Service with a Smile/Johnson's Old Gray Mule	1957	5.00	10.00	20.00
❑ 1317	Orange Blossom Special/Black Mountain Rag	1957	5.00	10.00	20.00
❑ 1334	Wild Honey/Run Little Joey	1957	5.00	10.00	20.00
❑ 1343	If You Don't Know It/I Lost Her	1958	5.00	10.00	20.00
CAPITOL					
❑ 2792	The Ballad of J.C./Untanglin' My Mind	1970	—	3.50	7.00
❑ 3092	The Hole/He'll Have to Go	1971	—	3.50	7.00
CHART					
❑ 1014	Easy Way Out/Togetherness	1967	2.50	5.00	10.00
❑ 1030	Baby Gets All Her Lovin' from Me/That's What Tears Me Up	1968	2.50	5.00	10.00
❑ 1049	Holding Trouble/A Little Bit	1968	2.50	5.00	10.00
❑ 5005	Charlie's Pride/Vision of Blindness	1969	2.00	4.00	8.00
❑ 5028	The Ballad of Biggersville/Day of the Gun	1969	2.00	4.00	8.00
COLUMBIA					
❑ 4-21484	You'll Regret/Hook, Line and Sinker	1956	5.00	10.00	20.00
❑ 4-21544	Keep Right On Talking/Maybe	1956	5.00	10.00	20.00
LIBERTY					
❑ 55500	Wild Honey/For Old Times' Sake	1962	3.00	6.00	12.00
❑ 55533	I Wish I'd Said That/In a Moment	1963	3.00	6.00	12.00
❑ 55558	Most of All/We've Got a Lot in Common	1963	3.00	6.00	12.00
❑ 55630	Sitting Just One Car from You/Almost Gone	1963	3.00	6.00	12.00
PLANTATION					
❑ 146	Orange Blossom Special/Smoking Violin	1977	—	2.50	5.00
❑ 156	Disco Mule/Tennessee Waltz	1977	—	2.50	5.00
RCA VICTOR					
❑ 47-7428	It Ain't Right/The Saddest Day	1958	5.00	10.00	20.00
❑ 47-7632	A Lotta Lotta Woman/Lonely Road	1959	10.00	20.00	40.00
❑ 47-7741	Trouble on the Turnpike/Almost Alone	1960	3.75	7.50	15.00
❑ 47-7788	Gonna Go Down to the River/When They Ring Those Wedding Bells	1960	3.75	7.50	15.00
❑ 47-7875	And Then I Heard the Bad News/I Had a Talk with Me	1961	3.75	7.50	15.00
❑ 47-7944	You Remembered Me/How My Baby Can Love	1961	3.75	7.50	15.00
❑ 47-7989	Long Black Limousine/Wild Desire	1962	3.75	7.50	15.00

TERRY, LARRY

Number	Title (A Side/B Side)	Yr	VG	VG+	NM
TESTA					
❑ 006	Hep Cat/Why Did She Go	1960	300.00	600.00	1200.

TERRY, NAT

Number	Title (A Side/B Side)	Yr	VG	VG+	NM
IMPERIAL					
❑ 5150	Take It Easy/I Don't Know Why	1951	25.00	50.00	100.00

TERRY, SONNY

Number	Title (A Side/B Side)	Yr	VG	VG+	NM
CAPITOL					
❑ F931	Telephone Blues/Dirty Mistreater Don't You Know	1950	30.00	60.00	120.00
CHESS					
❑ 1860	Dangerous Woman/Hootenanny Blues	1963	5.00	10.00	20.00
CHOICE					
❑ 15	Hootin'/Dupre	1961	5.00	10.00	20.00
GOTHAM					
❑ 517	Baby Let's Have Some Fun/Four O'Clock Blues	1951	10.00	20.00	40.00
❑ 518	Harmonica Rhumba/Lonesome Room	1951	10.00	20.00	40.00
GRAMERCY					
❑ 1004	Hootin' Blues/(B-side unknown)	1952	12.50	25.00	50.00
—Black vinyl					
❑ 1004	Hootin' Blues/(B-side unknown)	1952	25.00	50.00	100.00
—Colored vinyl					
GROOVE					
❑ 0015	Lost Jawbone/Louise	1954	7.50	15.00	30.00
❑ 0135	Ride and Roll/Hootin' Blues #2	1956	7.50	15.00	30.00
HARLEM					
❑ 2327	Dangerous Woman/I Love You Baby	1954	75.00	150.00	300.00
JAX					
❑ 305	I Don't Worry (Sittin' on Top of the World)/Man Ain't Nothin' But a Fool	195?	100.00	200.00	400.00
—Colored vinyl					

OLD TOWN

Number	Title (A Side/B Side)	Yr	VG	VG+	NM
❑ 1023	Uncle Bud/Climbing on Top of the Hill	1956	6.25	12.50	25.00

RCA VICTOR

Number	Title (A Side/B Side)	Yr	VG	VG+	NM
❑ 47-5492	Hootin' and Jumpin'/Hooray, Hooray	1953	25.00	50.00	100.00
❑ 47-5577	Sonny Is Drinking/I'm Gonna Rock My Wig	1954	25.00	50.00	100.00

RED ROBIN

Number	Title (A Side/B Side)	Yr	VG	VG+	NM
❑ 110	Harmonica Hop/Doggin' My Heart Around	1952	75.00	150.00	300.00

TERRY, SONNY, AND BROWNIE MCGHEE

BLUESVILLE

Number	Title (A Side/B Side)	Yr	VG	VG+	NM
❑ 802	Let Me Be Your Big Dig/Stranger Here	196?	5.00	10.00	20.00
❑ 809	Pawnshop/Too Nicey Mama	196?	5.00	10.00	20.00
❑ 818	Freight Train/Beggin' and Tryin'	196?	5.00	10.00	20.00

CHOICE

Number	Title (A Side/B Side)	Yr	VG	VG+	NM
❑ 1	John Henry/Oh Lawdy Pick a Bale of Cotton	196?	5.00	10.00	20.00
—As "Brownie & Sonny"					
❑ 7	Study War No More/I'm Gonna Tell God	196?	5.00	10.00	20.00
—As "Brownie & Sonny"					

TERRY AND THE MACS

ABC-PARAMOUNT

Number	Title (A Side/B Side)	Yr	VG	VG+	NM
❑ 9668	Baby-O-Mine/Love Is a Beautiful Thing	1956	5.00	10.00	20.00
❑ 9721	You Don't Have to Explain/Spinning, Spinning, Spinning	1956	5.00	10.00	20.00
❑ 9753	Please Don't Tease/The Mystery of Love	1956	5.00	10.00	20.00

TERRY AND THE PIRATES

CHESS

Number	Title (A Side/B Side)	Yr	VG	VG+	NM
❑ 1696	Talk About the Girl/What Did He Say	1958	10.00	20.00	40.00

TERRY AND THE TAGS

SYLVESTER

Number	Title (A Side/B Side)	Yr	VG	VG+	NM
❑ 100	Rampage/The Twomp	1962	12.50	25.00	50.00

TEX, JOE

ACE

Number	Title (A Side/B Side)	Yr	VG	VG+	NM
❑ 544	Cut It Out/Just for You and Me	1958	15.00	30.00	60.00
❑ 550	Mother's Advice/You Little Baby Face Thing	1958	20.00	40.00	80.00
❑ 559	Charlie Brown Got Expelled/Blessed Are These Tears	1959	15.00	30.00	60.00
❑ 572	Don't Hold It Against Me/Yum, Yum, Yum	1959	15.00	30.00	60.00
❑ 591	Boys Will Be Boys/Grannie Stole the Show	1960	10.00	20.00	40.00
❑ 674	Boys Will Be Boys/Baby You're Right	1963	3.75	7.50	15.00

ANNA

Number	Title (A Side/B Side)	Yr	VG	VG+	NM
❑ 1119	All I Could Do Was Cry (Part 1)/All I Could Do Was Cry (Part 2)	1960	10.00	20.00	40.00
❑ 1124	I'll Never Break Your Heart (Part 1)/I'll Never Break Your Heart (Part 2)	1960	10.00	20.00	40.00
❑ 1128	Baby, You're Right/Ain't It a Mess	1961	10.00	20.00	40.00

ATLANTIC

Number	Title (A Side/B Side)	Yr	VG	VG+	NM
❑ 2874	I'll Never Fall in Love Again (Part 1)/I'll Never Fall in Love Again (Part 2)	1972	—	3.00	6.00

CHECKER

Number	Title (A Side/B Side)	Yr	VG	VG+	NM
❑ 1104	Baby, You're Right/All I Could Do Was Cry (Part 2)	1965	3.00	6.00	12.00

DIAL

Number	Title (A Side/B Side)	Yr	VG	VG+	NM
❑ 1001	Bad Feet/I Know Him	1971	—	3.00	6.00
❑ 1003	Papa's Dream/I'm Comin' Home	1971	—	3.00	6.00
❑ 1006 [DJ]	King Thaddeus (mono/stereo)	1971	—	3.50	7.00
—May be promo only					
❑ 1008	Give the Baby Anything the Baby Wants/Takin' a Chance	1971	—	3.00	6.00
❑ 1010	I Gotcha/A Mother's Prayer	1972	—	3.00	6.00
❑ 1012	You Said a Bad Word/It Ain't Gonna Work Baby	1972	—	3.00	6.00
❑ 1018	Rain Go Away/King Thaddeus	1973	—	3.00	6.00
❑ 1020	Woman Stealer/Cat's Got Her Tongue	1973	—	3.00	6.00
❑ 1020 [PS]	Woman Stealer/Cat's Got Her Tongue	1973	2.00	4.00	8.00
❑ 1021	All the Heaven a Man Really Needs/Let's Go Somewhere and Talk	1973	—	3.00	6.00
❑ 1024	Trying to Win Your Love/I've Seen Enough	1973	—	3.00	6.00
❑ 1154	Sassy Sexy Wiggle/Under Your Powerful Love	1975	—	3.00	6.00
❑ 1155	I'm Goin' Back Again/My Body Wants You	1975	—	3.00	6.00
❑ 1156	Baby, It's Rainin'/Have You Ever	1975	—	3.00	6.00
❑ 1157	Mama Red/Love Shortage	1975	—	3.00	6.00
❑ 2800	Loose Caboose/Music Ain't Got No Color	1979	—	2.50	5.00
❑ 2801	Who Gave Birth to the Funk/If You Don't Want the Man	1979	—	2.50	5.00
❑ 2802	Discomania/Fat People	1979	—	2.50	5.00
❑ 3000	What Should I Do/The Only Girl I've Ever Loved	1961	3.00	6.00	12.00
❑ 3002	One Giant Step/The Rib	1961	3.00	6.00	12.00
❑ 3003	Popeye Johnny/Hand Shakin', Love Makin', Girl Talkin', Son-of-a-Gun From Next Door	1962	3.00	6.00	12.00
❑ 3007	Meet Me in Church/Be Your Own Judge	1962	3.00	6.00	12.00
❑ 3009	I Let Her Get Away/The Peck	1963	3.00	6.00	12.00
❑ 3013	Someone to Take Your Place/I Should Have Kissed You More	1963	3.00	6.00	12.00
❑ 3016	I Wanna Be Free/Blood's Thicker Than Water	1963	3.00	6.00	12.00
❑ 3019	Looking for My Pig/Say Thank You	1964	3.00	6.00	12.00
❑ 3020	I'd Rather Have You/Old Time Lover	1964	3.00	6.00	12.00
❑ 3023	I Had a Good Thing But I Left (Part 1)/I Had a Good Thing But I Left (Part 2)	1964	3.00	6.00	12.00
❑ 4001	Hold What You've Got/Fresh Out of Tears	1964	3.75	7.50	15.00
❑ 4003	You Better Get It/You Got What It Takes	1965	2.50	5.00	10.00
❑ 4006	A Woman Can Change a Man/Don't Let Your Left Hand Know	1965	2.50	5.00	10.00
❑ 4011	One Monkey Don't Stop No Show/Build Your Love on a Solid Foundation	1965	2.50	5.00	10.00
❑ 4016	I Want To (Do Everything For You)/Funny Bone	1965	2.50	5.00	10.00
❑ 4022	A Sweet Woman Like You/Close the Door	1965	2.50	5.00	10.00
❑ 4026	The Love You Save (May Be Your Own)/If Sugar Was As Sweet As You	1966	2.50	5.00	10.00
❑ 4028	S.Y.S.L.J.F.M. (Letter Song)/I'm a Man	1966	2.50	5.00	10.00
❑ 4033	I Believe I'm Gonna Make It/Better Believe It, Baby	1966	2.50	5.00	10.00
❑ 4045	I've Got to Do a Little Bit Better/What in the World	1966	2.50	5.00	10.00
❑ 4051	Papa Was Too/Truest Woman in the World	1966	2.50	5.00	10.00
❑ 4055	Show Me/A Woman Sees a Hard Time (When Her Man Is Gone)	1967	2.00	4.00	8.00
❑ 4059	Woman Like That, Yeah/I'm Going and Get It	1967	2.00	4.00	8.00
❑ 4061	A Woman's Hands/See See Rider	1967	2.00	4.00	8.00
❑ 4063	Skinny Legs and All/Watch the One	1967	2.50	5.00	10.00
❑ 4068	I'll Make Everyday Christmas (For My Woman)/Don't Give Up	1967	3.00	6.00	12.00
❑ 4069	Men Are Gettin' Scarce/You're Gonna Thank Me, Woman	1968	2.00	4.00	8.00
❑ 4076	I'll Never Do You Wrong/Wooden Spoon	1968	2.00	4.00	8.00
❑ 4079	Chocolate Cherry/Betwixt and Between	1968	2.00	4.00	8.00
❑ 4083	Keep the One You Got/Go Home and Do It	1968	2.00	4.00	8.00
❑ 4086	You Need Me, Baby/Baby, Be Good	1968	2.00	4.00	8.00
❑ 4089	That's Your Baby/Sweet, Sweet Woman	1968	2.00	4.00	8.00
❑ 4090	Buying a Book/Chicken Crazy	1969	2.00	4.00	8.00
❑ 4093	That's the Way/Anything You Wanna Know	1969	2.00	4.00	8.00
❑ 4094	We Can't Sit Down Now/It Ain't Sanitary	1969	2.00	4.00	8.00
❑ 4095	I Can't See You No More (When Johnny Comes Marching Home Again)/Sure Is Good	1969	2.00	4.00	8.00
❑ 4096	Everything Happens on Time/You're Right, Ray Charles	1970	2.00	4.00	8.00
❑ 4098	I'll Never Fall in Love Again/The Only Way I Know to Love You	1970	2.00	4.00	8.00

EPIC

Number	Title (A Side/B Side)	Yr	VG	VG+	NM
❑ 50313	Ain't Gonna Bump No More (With No Big Fat Woman)/I Mess Up Everything I Get My Hands On	1976	—	2.50	5.00
❑ 50426	Hungry for Your Love/I Almost Got to Heaven Once	1977	—	2.50	5.00
❑ 50494	Rub Down/Be Kind to Old People	1977	—	2.50	5.00
❑ 50530	Get Back, Leroy/You Can Be My Star	1978	—	2.50	5.00

HANDSHAKE

Number	Title (A Side/B Side)	Yr	VG	VG+	NM
❑ 02565	Don't Do Da Do/Here Comes No. 34 (Do the Earl Campbell)	1981	—	2.00	4.00

KING

Number	Title (A Side/B Side)	Yr	VG	VG+	NM
❑ 4840	Come In This House/Baby, You Upset My Home	1955	15.00	30.00	60.00
❑ 4884	My Biggest Mistake/Right Back to My Arms	1956	12.50	25.00	50.00
❑ 4911	She's Mine/I Had to Come Back to You	1956	12.50	25.00	50.00
❑ 4980	Get Way Back/Pneumonia	1956	12.50	25.00	50.00
❑ 5064	I Want to Have a Talk with You/Ain't Nobody's Business	1957	12.50	25.00	50.00
❑ 5981	Come In This House/I Want to Have a Talk with You	1965	2.50	5.00	10.00

TEX AND THE CHEX

20TH FOX

Number	Title (A Side/B Side)	Yr	VG	VG+	NM
❑ 411	Beach Party/Now (Love Me)	1963	7.50	15.00	30.00

ATLANTIC

Number	Title (A Side/B Side)	Yr	VG	VG+	NM
❑ 2116	I Do Love You/My Love	1961	15.00	30.00	60.00

NEWTOWN

Number	Title (A Side/B Side)	Yr	VG	VG+	NM
❑ 5010	Watching Willie Wobble/Be on the Lookout for My Girl	1963	5.00	10.00	20.00

TEXANS, THE

Also see JOHNNY AND DORSEY BURNETTE.

GOTHIC

Number	Title (A Side/B Side)	Yr	VG	VG+	NM
❑ 001	Old Reb/Rockin' Johnny Home	1961	7.50	15.00	30.00

INFINITY

Number	Title (A Side/B Side)	Yr	VG	VG+	NM
❑ 001	Green Grass of Texas/Bloody River	1961	7.50	15.00	30.00

JOX

Number	Title (A Side/B Side)	Yr	VG	VG+	NM
❑ 001	Old Reb/Rockin' Johnny Home	1965	7.50	15.00	30.00

VEE JAY

Number	Title (A Side/B Side)	Yr	VG	VG+	NM
❑ 658	Green Grass of Texas/Bloody River	1965	5.00	10.00	20.00

TEXAS TORNADOS, THE

Also see FREDDY FENDER; DOUG SAHM.

REPRISE

Number	Title (A Side/B Side)	Yr	VG	VG+	NM
❑ 7-17587	Little Bit Is Better Than Nada/Amor	1996	—	2.00	4.00
❑ 7-18571	Guacamole/Hangin' On by a Thread	1993	—	2.50	5.00
❑ 7-19155	Is Anybody Goin' to San Antone/La Mucura	1992	—	2.50	5.00
❑ 7-19244	Adios Mexico/Rosa de Amor	1992	—	2.50	5.00
❑ 7-19516	A Man Can Cry/(Hey Baby) Que Paso	1990	—	2.50	5.00
❑ 7-19787	Who Were You Thinkin' Of/Soy de San Luis	1990	—	2.50	5.00

TEXAS TROUBADOURS, THE

Backing group for ERNEST TUBB.

DECCA

Number	Title (A Side/B Side)	Yr	VG	VG+	NM
❑ 31627	Honey Love/Last Letter	1964	2.50	5.00	10.00
❑ 31699	Pan Handle Rag/Rhodes-Bud Boogie	1964	2.50	5.00	10.00
❑ 31770	Cain's Corner/Honky Tonks and You	1965	2.50	5.00	10.00
❑ 31837	Highway Man/Leon's Guitar Boogie	1965	2.50	5.00	10.00
❑ 32065	E.T. Blues/Walking the Floor Over You	1966	2.50	5.00	10.00
❑ 32121	Gardenia Waltz/Honey Fingers	1967	2.50	5.00	10.00
❑ 32185	Almost to Tulsa/Oklahoma Hills	1967	2.50	5.00	10.00
❑ 32587	Ridgetop Stomp/Jamming with C & C	1969	2.50	5.00	10.00

THARP, CHUCK, AND THE FIREBALLS

See THE FIREBALLS.

THEE MIDNITERS

CHATTAHOOCHIE

Number	Title (A Side/B Side)	Yr	VG	VG+	NM
❑ 666-2	Land of a Thousand Dances (Part 1)/Ball O' Twine	1965	3.75	7.50	15.00
❑ 666	Land of a Thousand Dances (Part 1)/Land of a Thousand Dances (Part 2)	1965	3.75	7.50	15.00
❑ 674	Sad Girl/Heat Wave	1965	4.00	8.00	16.00
❑ 675	Sad Girl/Heat Wave	1965	3.75	7.50	15.00
❑ 684	Whittier Blvd./Evil Love	1965	3.75	7.50	15.00
❑ 693	I Need Someone/Empty Heart	1965	5.00	10.00	20.00
❑ 695	Brother, Where Are You/Heat Wave	1966	3.75	7.50	15.00
❑ 706	Are You Angry/I Found a Peanut	1966	3.75	7.50	15.00

(continued)

UNI

Number	Title (A Side/B Side)	Yr	VG	VG+	NM
❑ 55170	She Only Wants What She Can't Get/I've Come Alive	1969	2.50	5.00	10.00

WHITTIER

Number	Title (A Side/B Side)	Yr	VG	VG+	NM
❑ 201	That's All/To Be with You	196?	3.00	6.00	12.00
❑ 500	Love, Special Delivery/Don't Go Away	1966	5.00	10.00	20.00
❑ 501	The Midnite Feeling/It'll Never Be Over for Me	1966	5.00	10.00	20.00
❑ 503	Dragon Fly/The Big Ranch	1966	5.00	10.00	20.00
❑ 504	Never Knew I Had It So Bad/The Walking Song	1967	5.00	10.00	20.00
❑ 504	Never Knew I Had It So Bad/Everybody Needs Somebody	1967	7.50	15.00	30.00
❑ 507	Jump Five and Harmonize/Looking Out a Window	1967	5.00	10.00	20.00
❑ 508	Chile Con Soul/Tu Despedida	1967	5.00	10.00	20.00
❑ 509	Breakfast on the Grass/Dreaming Casually	1967	5.00	10.00	20.00
❑ 511	You're Gonna Make Me Cry/Make Ends Meet	1968	50.00	100.00	200.00
❑ 512	The Ballad of Cesar Chavez/The Ballad of Cesar Chavez (Spanish)	1968	5.00	10.00	20.00
❑ 513	Chicano Power/Never Goin' to Give You Up	1968	5.00	10.00	20.00
❑ 674	Sad Girl/Heat Wave	1968	3.00	6.00	12.00
❑ 694	It's Not Unusual/It's Not Unusual	1969	3.00	6.00	12.00

THEM

Also see BELFAST GYPSIES; VAN MORRISON.

A&M

Number	Title (A Side/B Side)	Yr	VG	VG+	NM
❑ 1201	Baby Please Don't Go/Danger Heartbreak Dead Ahead	1988	—	2.00	4.00
—B-side by the Marvelettes					
❑ 1201 [PS]	Danger Heartbreak Dead Ahead/Baby Please Don't Go	1988	—	2.00	4.00
—"Good Morning Vietnam" sleeve					

HAPPY TIGER

Number	Title (A Side/B Side)	Yr	VG	VG+	NM
❑ 525	Lonely Weekends/I Am Waiting	1969	3.75	7.50	15.00
❑ 534	Memphis Lady/Nobody Cares	1970	3.00	6.00	12.00

PARROT

Number	Title (A Side/B Side)	Yr	VG	VG+	NM
❑ 365	Gloria/Bring 'Em On In	1971	2.50	5.00	10.00
❑ 3003	Richard Cory/Don't You Know	1966	3.75	7.50	15.00
❑ 3006	Don't Start Crying Now/I Can Only Give You Everything	1966	3.75	7.50	15.00
❑ 9702	Don't Start Crying Now/One, Two Brown Eyes	1964	5.00	10.00	20.00
❑ 9727	Gloria/Baby, Please Don't Go	1965	4.00	8.00	16.00
❑ 9749	Here Comes the Night/All By Myself	1965	3.75	7.50	15.00
❑ 9784	Gonna Dress in Black/Half As Much	1965	3.75	7.50	15.00
❑ 9796	Mystic Eyes/If You and I Could Be As Two	1965	3.75	7.50	15.00
❑ 9819	Call My Name/Bring 'Em On In	1966	3.75	7.50	15.00

RUFF

Number	Title (A Side/B Side)	Yr	VG	VG+	NM
❑ 1088	Walking in the Queen's Garden/I Happen to Love You	1967	6.25	12.50	25.00

TOWER

Number	Title (A Side/B Side)	Yr	VG	VG+	NM
❑ 384	Walking in the Queen's Garden/I Happen to Love You	1967	3.00	6.00	12.00
❑ 384 [PS]	Walking in the Queen's Garden/I Happen to Love You	1967	7.50	15.00	30.00
❑ 407	But It's Alright/Square Room	1968	3.00	6.00	12.00
❑ 461	Waltz of the Flies/We All Agreed to Help	1969	3.00	6.00	12.00
❑ 493	Corina/Dark Are the Shadows	1969	3.00	6.00	12.00

THEM (2)

KING

Number	Title (A Side/B Side)	Yr	VG	VG+	NM
❑ 5967	Don't Look Now/A Girl Like You	1964	3.75	7.50	15.00

THEMES, INC.

Yet another creation of STEVE BARRI and P.F. SLOAN.

VEE JAY

Number	Title (A Side/B Side)	Yr	VG	VG+	NM
❑ 635	Theme from Petyon Place/Paula's Percussion	1964	3.75	7.50	15.00

THERRIEN, JOE, JR.

BRUNSWICK

Number	Title (A Side/B Side)	Yr	VG	VG+	NM
❑ 9-55005	Hey Babe, Let's Go Downtown/Come Back to Me Darling	1957	10.00	20.00	40.00
❑ 9-55017	Wheels/You're Long Gone	1957	20.00	40.00	80.00

JAT

Number	Title (A Side/B Side)	Yr	VG	VG+	NM
❑ 101	I Ain't Gonna Be Around/Play Me a Blue Song	1958	20.00	40.00	80.00

LIDO

Number	Title (A Side/B Side)	Yr	VG	VG+	NM
❑ 505	Hey Babe, Let's Go Downtown/Come Back to Me Darling	1957	30.00	60.00	120.00

THIN LIZZY

Also see PHILIP LYNOTT.

LONDON

Number	Title (A Side/B Side)	Yr	VG	VG+	NM
❑ 20076	Whiskey in the Jar/Black Boys on the Corner	1972	2.00	4.00	8.00
❑ 20078	Broken Dreams/Randolph's Tango	1973	2.00	4.00	8.00
❑ 20082	Little Darling/The Rocket	1973	2.00	4.00	8.00

MERCURY

Number	Title (A Side/B Side)	Yr	VG	VG+	NM
❑ 73786	The Boys Are Back in Town/Jailbreak	1976	—	2.50	5.00
❑ 73841	Cowboy Song/Angel from the Coast	1976	—	2.50	5.00
❑ 73867	Rocky/Half-Caste	1976	—	2.50	5.00
❑ 73882	Old Flame/Johnny the Fox Meets Jimmy the Weed	1977	—	2.50	5.00
❑ 73892	Don't Believe a Word/Boogie Woogie Dance	1977	—	2.50	5.00
❑ 73945	Bad Reputation/Dancing in the Moonlight (It's Caught Me in the Spotlight)	1977	—	2.50	5.00

VERTIGO

Number	Title (A Side/B Side)	Yr	VG	VG+	NM
❑ 202	Night Life/Showdown	1974	—	3.00	6.00
❑ 205	Wild One/Freedom Song	1975	—	3.00	6.00

WARNER BROS.

Number	Title (A Side/B Side)	Yr	VG	VG+	NM
❑ 8648	Cowboy Song/Johnny the Fox Meets Jimmy the Weed	1978	—	2.50	5.00
❑ 49019	S & M/Do Anything You Want To	1979	—	2.50	5.00
❑ 49078	Got to Give It Up/With Love	1979	—	2.50	5.00
❑ 49643	Killer on the Loose/Sugar Blues	1980	—	2.00	4.00
❑ 49679	We Will Be Strong/Sweetheart	1981	—	2.00	4.00
❑ 50056	Hollywood/Pressure Will Blow	1982	—	2.00	4.00

THINGS TO COME

DUNWICH

Number	Title (A Side/B Side)	Yr	VG	VG+	NM
❑ 124	I'm Not Talkin'/'Til the End	1966	12.50	25.00	50.00

STARFIRE

Number	Title (A Side/B Side)	Yr	VG	VG+	NM
❑ 103	Sweet Gina/(B-side unknown)	1966	10.00	20.00	40.00

WARNER BROS.

Number	Title (A Side/B Side)	Yr	VG	VG+	NM
❑ 7164	Come Alive/Dancer	1968	3.75	7.50	15.00
❑ 7228	Cool Day/Hello	1968	3.75	7.50	15.00

THINK

BIG TREE

Number	Title (A Side/B Side)	Yr	VG	VG+	NM
❑ 15000	Once You Understand/Gather	1974	—	2.00	4.00

COLUMBIA

Number	Title (A Side/B Side)	Yr	VG	VG+	NM
❑ 44627	Faster Faster/Stop Runnin' Away	1968	—	3.00	6.00
❑ 44848	California (Is Getting So Heavy)/It's a Good Thing	1969	—	3.00	6.00

LAURIE

Number	Title (A Side/B Side)	Yr	VG	VG+	NM
❑ 3583	Once You Understand/Gather	1972	—	2.50	5.00
❑ 3594	It's Not the World — It's the People/Who Are You to Tell Me What to Do?	1972	—	2.50	5.00

THIRD EYE BLIND

ELEKTRA

Number	Title (A Side/B Side)	Yr	VG	VG+	NM
❑ 64058	Jumper/Graduate	1999	—	—	3.00

THIRD RAIL, THE

CAMEO

Number	Title (A Side/B Side)	Yr	VG	VG+	NM
❑ 445	The Subway Train That Came to Life/Train Rush Hour Stomp	1966	3.75	7.50	15.00

EPIC

Number	Title (A Side/B Side)	Yr	VG	VG+	NM
❑ 10191	Run, Run, Run/No Return	1967	2.50	5.00	10.00
❑ 10240	Boppa Do Down Down/Invisible Man	1967	2.00	4.00	8.00
❑ 10285	Overdose of Love/It's Time to Say Goodbye	1968	2.00	4.00	8.00
❑ 10323	Shape of Things to Come/She Ain't No Choir Girl	1968	2.00	4.00	8.00
❑ 10457	The Ballad of General Humpty/Beggin' Me to Stay	1969	2.00	4.00	8.00

THIRTEENTH FLOOR ELEVATORS, THE

Also see THE SPADES (3).

CONTACT

Number	Title (A Side/B Side)	Yr	VG	VG+	NM
❑ 5269	You're Gonna Miss Me/Tried to Hide	1966	25.00	50.00	100.00

HANNA-BARBERA

Number	Title (A Side/B Side)	Yr	VG	VG+	NM
❑ 492	You're Gonna Miss Me/Tried to Hide	1966	50.00	100.00	200.00

INTERNATIONAL ARTISTS

Number	Title (A Side/B Side)	Yr	VG	VG+	NM
❑ 107	You're Gonna Miss Me/Tried to Hide	1967	7.50	15.00	30.00
—Blue label					
❑ 107	You're Gonna Miss Me/Tried to Hide	1967	5.00	10.00	20.00
—Yellow label					
❑ 111	Reverberation (Doubt)/Fire Engine	1967	5.00	10.00	20.00
❑ 113	Before You Accuse Me/Levitation	1968	5.00	10.00	20.00
❑ 121	Baby Blue/She Lives	1968	5.00	10.00	20.00
❑ 122	Slip Inside This House/Splash 1	1968	5.00	10.00	20.00
❑ 126	May the Circle Remain Unbroken/I'm Gonna Love You Too	1968	5.00	10.00	20.00
❑ 130	Livin' On/Scarlet and Gold	1969	10.00	20.00	40.00

31ST OF FEBRUARY, THE

VANGUARD

Number	Title (A Side/B Side)	Yr	VG	VG+	NM
❑ 35066	Sandcastles/Pick a Gripe	1968	2.50	5.00	10.00
❑ 35087	In the Morning When I'm Real/Porcelain Mirrors	1969	2.50	5.00	10.00

.38 SPECIAL

A&M

Number	Title (A Side/B Side)	Yr	VG	VG+	NM
❑ 1246	Rock and Roll Strategy/Love Strikes	1988	—	—	3.00
❑ 1246 [PS]	Rock and Roll Strategy/Love Strikes	1988	—	—	3.00
❑ 1273	Second Chance/Comin' Down Tonight	1989	—	—	3.00
❑ 1424	Comin' Down Tonight/Chauahoocie	1989	—	—	3.00
❑ 1946	Long Time Gone/Four Wheels	1977	—	2.00	4.00
❑ 1964	Tell Everybody/Play a Simple Song	1977	—	2.00	4.00
❑ 2051	I'm a Fool for You/Travelin' Man	1978	—	2.00	4.00
❑ 2205	Rockin' Into the Night/Robin Hood	1979	—	2.00	4.00
❑ 2242	Stone Cold Believer/Stone Cold Believer (Part 2)	1980	—	2.00	4.00
❑ 2316	Hold On Loosely/Throw Out the Line	1981	—	2.00	4.00
❑ 2330	Fantasy Girl/Honky Tonk Dancer	1981	—	2.00	4.00
❑ 2330 [PS]	Fantasy Girl/Honky Tonk Dancer	1981	—	2.00	4.00
❑ 2412	Caught Up in You/Firestarter	1982	—	2.00	4.00
❑ 2412 [PS]	Caught Up in You/Firestarter	1982	—	2.00	4.00
❑ 2431	You Keep Runnin' Away/Prisoners of Rock and Roll	1982	—	2.00	4.00
❑ 2431 [PS]	You Keep Runnin' Away/Prisoners of Rock and Roll	1982	—	2.00	4.00
❑ 2505	Chain Lightnin'/Back on the Track	1982	—	2.00	4.00
❑ 2594	If I'd Been the One/Twentieth Century Fox	1983	—	—	3.00
❑ 2594 [PS]	If I'd Been the One/Twentieth Century Fox	1983	—	—	3.00
❑ 2615	Back Where You Belong/Undercover Lover	1984	—	—	3.00
❑ 2615 [PS]	Back Where You Belong/Undercover Lover	1984	—	—	3.00
❑ 2633	Long Distance Affair/One Time for Old Times	1984	—	—	3.00
❑ 2831	Like No Other Night/Hearts on Fire	1986	—	—	3.00
❑ 2831 [PS]	Like No Other Night/Hearts on Fire	1986	—	—	3.00
❑ 2854	Somebody Like You/Against the Night	1986	—	—	3.00
❑ 2854 [PS]	Somebody Like You/Against the Night	1986	—	—	3.00
❑ 2873	One in a Million/Last Time	1986	—	—	3.00
❑ 2955	Back to Paradise/Hold On Loosely	1987	—	—	3.00
❑ 2955 [PS]	Back to Paradise/Hold On Loosely	1987	—	—	3.00

CAPITOL

Number	Title (A Side/B Side)	Yr	VG	VG+	NM
❑ B-5405	Teacher Teacher/Twentieth Century Fox	1984	—	—	3.00
❑ B-5405 [PS]	Teacher Teacher/Twentieth Century Fox	1984	—	—	3.00

THOMAS, B.J.

ABC

Number	Title (A Side/B Side)	Yr	VG	VG+	NM
❑ 12054	(Hey, Won't You Play) Another Somebody Done Somebody Wrong Song/City Blues	1974	—	2.00	4.00
❑ 12121	We Are Happy Together/Help Me Make It (To My Rockin' Chair)	1975	—	2.00	4.00

Number	Title (A Side/B Side)	Yr	VG	VG+	NM
BRAGG					
❑ 103	Billy and Sue/Never Tell	1964	5.00	10.00	20.00
CLEVELAND INT'L.					
❑ 03492	Whatever Happened to Old Fashioned Love/I Just Sing	1983	—	2.00	4.00
❑ 04608	From This Moment On/The Girl Most Likely To	1984	—	2.00	4.00
COLUMBIA					
❑ 03985	New Looks from an Old Lover/You Keep the Man in Me Happy	1983	—	2.00	4.00
❑ 04237	Two Car Garage/Beautiful World	1983	—	2.00	4.00
❑ 04431	The Whole World's in Love When You're Lonely/We're Here to Love	1984	—	—	3.00
❑ 04531	Rock and Roll Shoes/Then I'll Be Over You	1984	—	—	3.00
—Ray Charles and B.J. Thomas					
❑ 05647	A Part of Me That Needs You Most/Northern Lights	1985	—	—	3.00
❑ 05771	America Is/Broken Toys	1986	—	—	3.00
❑ 05771 [PS]	America Is/Broken Toys	1986	—	2.00	4.00
❑ 06314	Night Life/Make the World Go Away	1986	—	—	3.00
HICKORY					
❑ 1395	Billy and Sue/Never Tell	1966	2.50	5.00	10.00
LORI					
❑ 9547	I've Got a Feeling/Hey Judy	1963	6.25	12.50	25.00
❑ 9561	For Your Precious Love/Here I Am Again	1964	6.25	12.50	25.00
MCA					
❑ 40735	Don't Worry Baby/My Love	1977	—	2.00	4.00
❑ 40812	Still the Lovin' Is Fun/Play Me a Little Traveling Music	1977	—	2.00	4.00
❑ 40854	Everybody Loves a Rain Song/Dusty Roads	1978	—	2.00	4.00
❑ 40914	Sweet Young America/Aloha	1978	—	2.00	4.00
❑ 40986	We Could Have Been the Closest of Friends/In My Heart	1979	—	2.00	4.00
❑ 41134	God Bless the Children/On This Christmas Night	1979	—	2.00	4.00
❑ 41134 [PS]	God Bless the Children/On This Christmas Night	1979	—	2.50	5.00
❑ 41207	Nothin' Could Be Better/Walkin' on a Cloud	1980	—	2.00	4.00
❑ 41281	Everything Always Works Out for the Best/No Limit	1980	—	2.00	4.00
❑ 51087	Some Love Songs Never Die/There Ain't No Love	1981	—	2.00	4.00
❑ 51151	The Lovin' Kind/I Recall a Gypsy Woman	1981	—	2.00	4.00
❑ 52053	I Really Got the Feeling/But Love Me	1982	—	2.00	4.00
MYRRH					
❑ 166	Home Where I Belong/Hallelujah	1977	—	2.50	5.00
❑ 176	Without a Doubt/(B-side unknown)	1977	—	2.50	5.00
❑ 234	Uncloudy Day/(B-side unknown)	1981	—	2.50	5.00
PACEMAKER					
❑ 227	I'm So Lonesome I Could Cry/Candy Baby	1964	5.00	10.00	20.00
❑ 231	Mama/Wendy	1965	3.75	7.50	15.00
❑ 234	Bring Back the Time/I Don't Have a Mind of My Own	1965	3.75	7.50	15.00
❑ 239	Tomorrow Never Comes/Your Tears Leave Me Cold	1965	3.75	7.50	15.00
❑ 247	Plain Jane/My Home Town	1965	3.75	7.50	15.00
❑ 253	I'm Not a Fool Anymore/Baby Cried	1965	3.75	7.50	15.00
❑ 256	I Can't Help It (If I'm Still in Love with You)/Baby Cried	1965	3.75	7.50	15.00
❑ 259	Pretty Country Girl/Houston Town	1965	3.75	7.50	15.00
PARAMOUNT					
❑ 0218	Songs/Goodbye's a Long, Long Time	1973	—	2.50	5.00
❑ 0218 [PS]	Songs/Goodbye's a Long, Long Time	1973	—	3.00	6.00
❑ 0239	Sunday Sunrise/Talkin' Confidentially	1973	—	2.50	5.00
❑ 0239	Sunday Sunrise/Early Morning Rush	1973	—	2.50	5.00
❑ 0277	Play Something Sweet (Brickyard Blues)/Talkin' Confidentially	1974	—	2.50	5.00
REPRISE					
❑ 22837	Don't Leave Love (Out There All Alone)/One Woman	1989	—	—	3.00
SCEPTER					
❑ 12129	I'm So Lonesome I Could Cry/Candy Baby	1966	2.50	5.00	10.00
❑ 12139	Mama/Wendy	1966	2.00	4.00	8.00
❑ 12154	Bring Back the Time/I Don't Have a Mind of My Own	1966	2.00	4.00	8.00
❑ 12165	Tomorrow Never Comes/Your Tears Leave Me Cold	1966	2.00	4.00	8.00
❑ 12179	Plain Jane/My Home Town	1966	2.00	4.00	8.00
❑ 12194	I Can't Help It (If I'm Still in Love with You)/Baby Cried	1967	2.00	4.00	8.00
❑ 12200	Just the Wisdom of a Fool/Treasure of Love	1967	2.00	4.00	8.00
❑ 12201	Wisdom of a Fool/Human	1967	2.00	4.00	8.00
❑ 12205	The Girl Can't Help It/Walkin' Back	1967	2.00	4.00	8.00
❑ 12219	The Eyes of a New York Woman/I May Never Get to Heaven	1968	2.00	4.00	8.00
❑ 12230	Hooked on a Feeling/I've Been Down This Road Before	1968	2.00	4.00	8.00
❑ 12244	It's Only Love/You Don't Love Me Anymore	1969	—	3.00	6.00
❑ 12255	Pass the Apple Eve/Fairy Tale of Time	1969	—	3.00	6.00
❑ 12259	You Don't Love Me Anymore/Skip a Rope	1969	—	3.00	6.00
❑ 12265	Raindrops Keep Fallin' on My Head/Never Had It So Good	1969	—	3.50	7.00
❑ 12277	Everybody's Out of Town/Living Again	1970	—	3.00	6.00
❑ 12283	I Just Can't Help Believing/Send My Picture to Scranton, Pa.	1970	—	3.00	6.00
❑ 12299	Most of All/The Mask	1970	—	2.50	5.00
❑ 12307	No Love at All/Have a Heart	1971	—	2.50	5.00
❑ 12320	Mighty Clouds of Joy/Life	1971	—	2.50	5.00
❑ 12335	Long Ago Tomorrow/Burnin' a Hole in My Mind	1971	—	2.50	5.00
❑ 12344	Rock and Roll Lullaby/Are We Losing Touch	1972	—	3.00	6.00
❑ 12354	That's What Friends Are For/I Get Enthused	1972	—	2.50	5.00
❑ 12364	Happier Than the Morning Sun/We Have Got to Get Out Ship Together	1972	—	2.50	5.00
❑ 12379	Sweet Cherry Wine/Roads	1973	—	2.50	5.00

Number	Title (A Side/B Side)	Yr	VG	VG+	NM
VALERIE					
❑ 226	I've Got a Feeling/Hey Judy	1963	5.00	10.00	20.00
WARNER BROS.					
❑ 5491	Billy and Sue/Never Tell	1964	5.00	10.00	20.00

THOMAS, CARLA

Also see OTIS AND CARLA; RUFUS AND CARLA.

Number	Title (A Side/B Side)	Yr	VG	VG+	NM
ATLANTIC					
❑ 2086	Gee Whiz (Look at His Eyes)/For You	1960	3.75	7.50	15.00
❑ 2101	A Love of My Own/Promises	1961	3.00	6.00	12.00
❑ 2113	Wish Me Good Luck/In Your Spare Time	1961	3.00	6.00	12.00
❑ 2132	The Masquerade Is Over/I Kinda Think He Does	1962	3.00	6.00	12.00
❑ 2163	I'll Bring It On Home to You/I Can't Take It	1962	3.00	6.00	12.00
❑ 2189	What a Fool I've Been/The Life I Live	1963	3.00	6.00	12.00
❑ 2212	Gee Whiz, It's Christmas/All I Want for Christmas Is You	1963	3.75	7.50	15.00
❑ 2238	I've Got No Time to Lose/A Boy Named Tom	1964	3.00	6.00	12.00
❑ 2258	A Woman's Love/Don't Let the Love Light Leave	1964	3.00	6.00	12.00
❑ 2272	How Do You Quit (Someone You Love)/The Puppet	1965	3.00	6.00	12.00
GUSTO					
❑ 816	All I Want For Christmas Is You/Gee Whiz, It's Christmas	1979	2.50	5.00	10.00
—A Canadian import ($5) from 1986 exists on King					
SATELLITE					
❑ 104	Gee Whiz (Look at His Eyes)/For You	1960	125.00	250.00	500.00
STAX					
❑ 0011	I've Fallen in Love/Where Do I Go	1968	2.00	4.00	8.00
❑ 0024	I Like What You're Doing (To Me)/Strung Out	1969	2.00	4.00	8.00
❑ 0042	Just Keep On Loving Me/My Love	1969	2.00	4.00	8.00
—With Johnnie Taylor					
❑ 0044	I Can't Stop/I Need You Woman	1969	—	2.50	5.00
—With William Bell					
❑ 0056	Guide Me Well/Some Other Man (Is Beating Your Time)	1970	2.00	4.00	8.00
❑ 0061	The Time for Love Is Anytime/Living in the City	1970	—	3.00	6.00
❑ 0067	All I Have to Do Is Dream/Leave the Girl Alone	1970	—	2.50	5.00
—With William Bell					
❑ 0080	Hi De Ho (That Old Sweet Roll)/I Loved You Like I Love My Very Life	1970	—	3.00	6.00
❑ 0113	You've Got a Cushion to Fall On/Love Means (You Never Have to Say You're Sorry)	1972	—	3.00	6.00
❑ 0133	Sugar/You've Got a Cushion to Fall On	1972	—	3.00	6.00
❑ 0149	I May Not Be All You Want/Sugar	1972	—	3.00	6.00
❑ 172	Stop! Look What You're Doing/Every Ounce of Strength	1965	3.00	6.00	12.00
❑ 0173	I Have a God Who Loves/Love Among People	1973	—	3.00	6.00
❑ 183	Comfort Me/I'm for You	1966	3.00	6.00	12.00
❑ 188	Let Me Be Good to You/Another Night Without My Man	1966	3.00	6.00	12.00
❑ 195	B-A-B-Y/What Have You Got to Offer Me	1966	3.75	7.50	15.00
❑ 206	All I Want for Christmas Is You/Winter Snow	1966	3.00	6.00	12.00
❑ 207	Something Good (Is Going to Happen to You)/It's Starting to Grow	1967	2.50	5.00	10.00
❑ 214	Unchanging Love/When Tomorrow Comes	1967	2.50	5.00	10.00
❑ 222	I'll Always Have Faith in You/Stop Thief	1967	2.50	5.00	10.00
❑ 239	Pick Up the Pieces/Separation	1967	2.50	5.00	10.00
❑ 251	A Dime a Dozen/I Want You Back	1968	2.50	5.00	10.00

THOMAS, IRMA

Number	Title (A Side/B Side)	Yr	VG	VG+	NM
CANYON					
❑ 21	Save a Little Bit for Me/That's How I Feel About You	1970	—	3.00	6.00
❑ 31	I'll Do It All Over You/We Won't Be In Your Way Anymore	1970	—	3.00	6.00
CHESS					
❑ 2010	Cheater Man/Somewhere Crying	1967	2.00	4.00	8.00
❑ 2017	A Woman Will Do Wrong/I Gave You Everything	1967	2.00	4.00	8.00
❑ 2036	Good to Me/We Got Something Good	1968	2.00	4.00	8.00
COTILLION					
❑ 44144	Full Time Woman/She's Taken My Part	1972	—	3.00	6.00
IMPERIAL					
❑ 66013	Wish Someone Would Care/Break-A-Way	1964	3.00	6.00	12.00
❑ 66041	Time Is On My Side/Anyone Who Knows What Love Is (Will Understand)	1964	3.00	6.00	12.00
❑ 66069	Times Have Changed/Moments to Remember	1964	2.50	5.00	10.00
❑ 66080	He's My Guy/(I Want a) True, True Love	1964	2.50	5.00	10.00
❑ 66095	Some Things You Better Get Used To/You Don't Miss a Good Thing	1965	2.50	5.00	10.00
❑ 66106	Nobody Wants to Hear Nobody's Troubles/I'm Gonna Cry Till My Tears Run Dry	1965	2.50	5.00	10.00
❑ 66120	Hurts All Over/It's Starting to Get Me Now	1965	2.50	5.00	10.00
❑ 66137	Take a Look/What Are You Trying to Do	1965	2.50	5.00	10.00
❑ 66178	It's a Man-Woman's World (Part 1)/It's a Man-Woman's World (Part 2)	1966	2.50	5.00	10.00
MINIT					
❑ 625	Cry On/Girl Needs Boy	1961	3.00	6.00	12.00
❑ 633	It's Too Soon to Know/That's All I Ask	1961	3.00	6.00	12.00
❑ 642	Gone/Done Got Over It	1962	3.00	6.00	12.00
❑ 653	It's Raining/I Did My Part	1962	3.00	6.00	12.00
❑ 660	Somebody Told Me/Two Winters Long	1963	3.00	6.00	12.00
❑ 666	Ruler of My Heart/Hitting on Nothing	1963	3.00	6.00	12.00
RON					
❑ 328	Don't Mess with My Man/Set Me Free	1960	3.75	7.50	15.00
❑ 330	Good Man/I May Be Wrong	1960	3.75	7.50	15.00
UNITED ARTISTS					
❑ 0088	Wish Someone Would Care/Take a Look	1973	—	2.00	4.00
—"Silver Spotlight Series" reissue					

THOMAS, JON

ABC-PARAMOUNT

Number	Title (A Side/B Side)	Yr	VG	VG+	NM
❑ 10122	Heartbreak (It's Hurtin' Me)/Tearin'	1960	3.75	7.50	15.00
❑ 10140	Hey Hey Baby/Buffalo Blues	1960	3.75	7.50	15.00
❑ 10190	The Snake/Story Telling	1961	3.00	6.00	12.00
❑ 10238	Boss Hoss/Flip, Flop, Fly	1961	3.00	6.00	12.00
❑ 10274	The Thomas Twist/So Good	1961	3.00	6.00	12.00

CHECKER

Number	Title (A Side/B Side)	Yr	VG	VG+	NM
❑ 809	Rib Tips/Hi-Fi	1955	7.50	15.00	30.00

MERCURY

Number	Title (A Side/B Side)	Yr	VG	VG+	NM
❑ 71078	Hard Head (Part 1)/Hard Head (Part 2)	1957	7.50	15.00	30.00
❑ 71151	St. Louis Blues/Fat Back	1957	6.25	12.50	25.00

NOTE

Number	Title (A Side/B Side)	Yr	VG	VG+	NM
❑ 10001	Rib Tips/Hi-Fi	1954	10.00	20.00	40.00

THOMAS, MICKEY

Lead singer for ELVIN BISHOP; later with JEFFERSON STARSHIP and STARSHIP.

MCA

Number	Title (A Side/B Side)	Yr	VG	VG+	NM
❑ 40732	Can You Fool/Where Are We	1977	—	2.00	4.00
❑ 40767	Somebody to Love/Where Are We	1977	—	2.00	4.00

RCA

Number	Title (A Side/B Side)	Yr	VG	VG+	NM
❑ PB-11244	The Theme from Skateboard/(Instrumental)	1978	—	2.00	4.00
❑ PB-14273	Stand in the Fire/Opening Score	1986	—	—	3.00
❑ PB-14273 [PS]	Stand in the Fire/Opening Score	1986	—	2.00	4.00

THOMAS, RAY

Also see THE MOODY BLUES.

THRESHOLD

Number	Title (A Side/B Side)	Yr	VG	VG+	NM
❑ 67020	High Above My Head/Love Is the Key	1975	—	2.50	5.00
❑ 67023	One Night Stand/Carousel	1975	—	2.50	5.00

THOMAS, RUFUS

Also see RUFUS AND CARLA.

ARTISTS OF AMERICA

Number	Title (A Side/B Side)	Yr	VG	VG+	NM
❑ 126	If There Were No Music/Blues in the Basement	1976	—	2.50	5.00

AVI

Number	Title (A Side/B Side)	Yr	VG	VG+	NM
❑ 149	Who's Makin' Love to Your Old Lady/Hot Grits	1977	—	2.00	4.00
❑ 178	I Ain't Gettin' Older, I'm Gettin' Better (Part 1)/I Ain't Gettin' Older, I'm Gettin' Better (Part 2)	1977	—	2.00	4.00

HI

Number	Title (A Side/B Side)	Yr	VG	VG+	NM
❑ 78520	Fried Chicken/I Ain't Got Time	1978	—	2.00	4.00

HIGH STACKS

Number	Title (A Side/B Side)	Yr	VG	VG+	NM
❑ 9801	Hey Rufus!/Body Fine	1999	—	—	3.00

—B-side by the Barkays

ICHIBAN

Number	Title (A Side/B Side)	Yr	VG	VG+	NM
❑ 85-103	Rappin' Rufus/(Instrumental)	1985	—	2.00	4.00

METEOR

Number	Title (A Side/B Side)	Yr	VG	VG+	NM
❑ 5039	I'm Steady Holdin' On/The Easy Livin' Plan	1956	37.50	75.00	150.00

STAX

Number	Title (A Side/B Side)	Yr	VG	VG+	NM
❑ 0010	Funky Mississippi/So Hard to Get Along With	1968	—	3.00	6.00
❑ 0022	Funky Way/I Want to Hold You	1969	—	3.00	6.00
❑ 0059	Do the Funky Chicken/Turn Your Damper Down	1969	—	3.00	6.00
❑ 0071	Sixty Minute Man/The Preacher and the Bear	1970	—	3.00	6.00
❑ 0079	(Do the) Push and Pull Part I/(Do the) Push and Pull Part II	1970	—	3.00	6.00
❑ 0090	The World Is Round/(I Love You) For Sentimental Reasons	1971	—	3.00	6.00
❑ 0098	The Breakdown (Part 1)/The Breakdown (Part 2)	1971	—	3.00	6.00
❑ 0112	Do the Funky Penguin (Part 1)/Do the Funky Penguin (Part 2)	1971	—	3.00	6.00
❑ 126	It's Aw-Rite/Can't Ever Let You Go	1962	3.75	7.50	15.00
❑ 0129	Love Trap/6-3-8	1972	—	3.00	6.00
❑ 130	The Dog/Did You Ever Love a Woman	1963	3.75	7.50	15.00
❑ 140	Walking the Dog/You Said	1963	3.00	6.00	12.00
❑ 140	Walking the Dog/Fine and Mellow	1963	7.50	15.00	30.00
❑ 0140	Itch and Scratch (Part 1)/Itch and Scratch (Part 2)	1972	—	3.00	6.00
❑ 144	Can Your Monkey Do the Dog/I Want to Get Married	1964	3.00	6.00	12.00
❑ 149	Somebody Stole My Dog/I Want to Be Loved	1964	3.00	6.00	12.00
❑ 0153	Funky Robot (Part 1)/Funky Robot (Part 2)	1973	—	3.00	6.00
❑ 157	Jump Back/All Night Worker	1964	3.00	6.00	12.00
❑ 167	Baby Walk/Little Sally Walker	1965	2.00	4.00	8.00
❑ 173	Willy Nilly/Sho' Gonna Mess Him Up	1965	2.00	4.00	8.00
❑ 0177	I Know You Don't Want Me No More/I'm Still in Love with You	1973	—	3.00	6.00
❑ 178	Chicken Scratch/The World Is Round	1965	2.00	4.00	8.00
❑ 0187	That Makes Christmas Day/I'll Be Your Santa Baby	1973	—	3.00	6.00
❑ 0192	The Funky Bird/Steal a Little	1974	—	3.00	6.00
❑ 200	Talkin' 'Bout True Love/Sister's Got a Boyfriend	1967	2.00	4.00	8.00
❑ 0219	Boogie Ain't Nothin' (But Gettin' Down) (Part 1)/Boogie Ain't Nothin' (But Gettin' Down) (Part 2)	1974	—	3.00	6.00
❑ 221	Sophisticated Sissy/Grasy Spoon	1967	2.00	4.00	8.00
❑ 0236	Do the Double Bump/Do the Double Bump	1975	—	3.00	6.00
❑ 240	Down Ta My House/Steady Holding On	1968	2.00	4.00	8.00
❑ 250	The Memphis Train/I Think I Made a Boo-Boo	1968	2.00	4.00	8.00
❑ 0254	Jump Back '75 (Part 1)/Jump Back '75 (Part 2)	1975	—	3.00	6.00
❑ 1073	I'll Be Your Santa Claus/Christmas Comes Once A Year	197?	—	2.50	5.00

—B-side by Albert King; reissue

SUN

Number	Title (A Side/B Side)	Yr	VG	VG+	NM
❑ 181	Bear Cat (The Answer to Hound Dog)/Walking in the Rain	1953	87.50	175.00	350.00

—With subtitle on A-side

Number	Title (A Side/B Side)	Yr	VG	VG+	NM
❑ 181	Bear Cat/Walking in the Rain	1953	50.00	100.00	200.00

—No subtitle on A-side

Number	Title (A Side/B Side)	Yr	VG	VG+	NM
❑ 188	Tiger Man (King of the Jungle)/Save Your Money	1953	125.00	250.00	500.00

THOMAS, TIMMY

GLADES

Number	Title (A Side/B Side)	Yr	VG	VG+	NM
❑ 1703	Why Can't We Live Together/Funky Me	1972	—	3.00	6.00
❑ 1709	People Are Changin'/Rainbow Power	1973	—	3.00	6.00
❑ 1712	Let Me Be Your Eyes/Cold Cold People	1973	—	3.00	6.00
❑ 1717	What Can I Tell Her/Opportunity	1973	—	3.00	6.00
❑ 1719	One Brief Moment/Rio Girl	1974	—	3.00	6.00
❑ 1721	Deep in You/Spread Us Around	1974	—	2.50	5.00
❑ 1723	I've Got to See You Tonight/You're the Song (I've Always Wanted to Sing)	1974	—	2.50	5.00
❑ 1727	Sexy Woman/Sweet Brown Sugar	1975	—	2.50	5.00
❑ 1730	Ebony Affair/It's What They Can't See	1975	—	2.50	5.00
❑ 1735	Love Shine/Running Out of Time	1976	—	2.50	5.00
❑ 1740	Stone to the Bone/Watch It! Watch It!	1977	—	2.50	5.00
❑ 1748	Touch to Touch/When a House Got Music	1978	—	2.50	5.00
❑ 1749	Freak In, Freak Out/Say Love, Can You Chase	1978	—	2.50	5.00
❑ 1758	Drown in My Own Tears (Part 1)/Drown in My Own Tears (Part 2)	1980	—	2.50	5.00

GOLD MOUNTAIN

Number	Title (A Side/B Side)	Yr	VG	VG+	NM
❑ 82004	Gotta Give a Little Love (Ten Years After)/Same Old Song	1984	—	2.00	4.00
❑ 82008	Love Is Never Too Late/Let It Flow	1984	—	2.00	4.00

GOLDWAX

Number	Title (A Side/B Side)	Yr	VG	VG+	NM
❑ 320	Have Some Boogaloo/Liquid Mood	1967	3.75	7.50	15.00
❑ 327	It's My Life/Whole Lotta Shakin' Goin' On	1967	3.75	7.50	15.00

MARLIN

Number	Title (A Side/B Side)	Yr	VG	VG+	NM
❑ 3348	Are You Crazy??? (Pt. 1)/Are You Crazy??? (Pt. 2)	1981	—	2.00	4.00

THOMAS, VIC

PHILIPS

Number	Title (A Side/B Side)	Yr	VG	VG+	NM
❑ 40183	Napoleon Bonaparte/Marianne	1964	18.75	37.50	75.00
❑ 40228	Village of Love/There Stands An Empty Man	1964	18.75	37.50	75.00

THOMPSON, BILLY

COLUMBUS

Number	Title (A Side/B Side)	Yr	VG	VG+	NM
❑ 1043	Black Eyed Girl/Kiss Tomorrow Goodbye	1965	50.00	100.00	200.00

WAND

Number	Title (A Side/B Side)	Yr	VG	VG+	NM
❑ 1108	Black Eyed Girl/Kiss Tomorrow Goodbye	1966	15.00	30.00	60.00

THOMPSON, CHRIS

Also see MANFRED MANN'S EARTH BAND.

PLANET

Number	Title (A Side/B Side)	Yr	VG	VG+	NM
❑ 45904	If You Remember Me/Theme from "The Champ"	1979	—	3.00	6.00
❑ 45909	If You Remember Me/You Ain't Pretty Enough	1979	—	2.00	4.00

—As "Chris Thompson and Night"

THOMPSON, HANK

ABC

Number	Title (A Side/B Side)	Yr	VG	VG+	NM
❑ 12409	I'm Just Gettin' By/I Hear the South Callin' Me	1978	—	2.50	5.00
❑ 12447	Dance with Me Molly/Point of No Return	1979	—	2.50	5.00

ABC DOT

Number	Title (A Side/B Side)	Yr	VG	VG+	NM
❑ 17535	Mama Don't 'Low/Wait a Little Longer Baby	1974	—	3.00	6.00
❑ 17556	That's Just My Truckin' Luck/After You Have Made Me Over	1975	—	3.00	6.00
❑ 17583	Mona Lisa/Too Young	1975	—	3.00	6.00
❑ 17612	Asphalt Cowboy/Fifteen Miles to Clarksville	1976	—	3.00	6.00
❑ 17649	Big Band Days/Forgive Me	1976	—	3.00	6.00
❑ 17673	Honky Tonk Girl/Another Shot of Today	1976	—	3.00	6.00
❑ 17695	Just an Old Flame/Don't Get Around Much Anymore	1977	—	3.00	6.00

CAPITOL

Number	Title (A Side/B Side)	Yr	VG	VG+	NM
❑ F876	All That Goes Up Must Come Down/Standing on the Outside	1950	7.50	15.00	30.00
❑ F1016	Take a Look at This Broken Heart/She's a Girl Without a Sweetheart	1950	7.50	15.00	30.00
❑ F1113	Humpty Dumpty Heart/California Women	1950	6.25	12.50	25.00
❑ F1114	Soft Lips/Give a Little, Take a Little	1950	6.25	12.50	25.00
❑ F1115	Whoa Sailor/Today	1950	6.25	12.50	25.00
❑ F1116	Swing Wide/Tomorrow Night	1950	6.25	12.50	25.00
❑ F1117	Second Hand Gal/Don't Flirt with Me	1950	6.25	12.50	25.00
❑ F1118	Green Light/Mary Had a Little Lamb	1950	6.25	12.50	25.00
❑ F1119	The Grass Looks Greener/Rock in the Ocean	1950	6.25	12.50	25.00
❑ F1120	My Front Door Is Open/A Cat Has Nine Lives	1950	6.25	12.50	25.00
❑ F1121	I Find You Cheatin' on Me/You Remembered Me	1950	6.25	12.50	25.00
❑ F1163	When God Calls His Children Home/I Can't Feel at Home	1950	7.50	15.00	30.00
❑ F1198	Humpty Dumpty Boogie/Daddy Blues	1950	7.50	15.00	30.00
❑ F1327	A Broken Heart and a Glass of Beer/If I Cry	1950	7.50	15.00	30.00
❑ F1379	New Roving Gambler/Playin' Possum	1951	6.25	12.50	25.00
❑ F1444	Where Is Your Heart Tonight/Those Things Money Can't Buy	1951	6.25	12.50	25.00
❑ F1528	I Ain't Crying Over You/Hangover Heart	1951	6.25	12.50	25.00
❑ F1632	Humpty Dumpty Heart/Green Light	1951	5.00	10.00	20.00

—Reissue of hit A-sides from 1948

Number	Title (A Side/B Side)	Yr	VG	VG+	NM
❑ F1745	Love Thief/How Do You Feel	1951	6.25	12.50	25.00
❑ F1870	Teardrops on the Tea Leaves/I'll Be Your Sweetheart	1951	6.25	12.50	25.00
❑ F1942	The Wild Side of Life/Cryin' in the Deep Blue Sea	1952	6.25	12.50	25.00
❑ F2063	Waiting in the Lobby of Your Heart/Don't Make Me Cry Again	1952	6.25	12.50	25.00
❑ F2169	How Cold Hearted Can You Get/It's Better to Have Loved a Little	1952	6.25	12.50	25.00
❑ F2178	Whoa Sailor/Mary Had a Little Lamb	1952	5.00	10.00	20.00
❑ F2269	The New Wears Off Too Fast/You're Walking on My Heart	1952	6.25	12.50	25.00
❑ F2377	No Help Wanted/I'd Have Never Found Somebody New	1953	6.25	12.50	25.00
❑ F2445	Rub-a-Dub-Dub/I'll Sign My Heart Away	1953	6.25	12.50	25.00
❑ F2553	Yesterday's Girl/John Henry	1953	6.25	12.50	25.00
❑ F2646	Wake Up, Irene/Go Cry Your Heart Out	1953	6.25	12.50	25.00
❑ F2758	A Fooler, a Faker/Breakin' the Rules	1954	5.00	10.00	20.00
❑ F2792	Jersey Bounce/Sunrise Serenade	1954	6.25	12.50	25.00
❑ F2823	Honky-Tonk Girl/We've Gone Too Far	1954	5.00	10.00	20.00
❑ F2920	The New Green Light/A Lonely Heart Knows	1954	5.00	10.00	20.00
❑ F2998	Dardanelle/Johnson Rag	1954	5.00	10.00	20.00

Number	Title (A Side/B Side)	Yr	VG	VG+	NM
❑ F3030	If Lovin' You Is Wrong/Annie Over	1955	5.00	10.00	20.00
❑ F3106	Wildwood Flower/Breakin' In Another Heart	1955	5.00	10.00	20.00
—A-side with Merle Travis					
❑ F3188	Most of All/Simple Simon	1955	5.00	10.00	20.00
❑ F3235	Westphalia Waltz/Red Skin Gal	1955	5.00	10.00	20.00
❑ F3275	Don't Take It Out on Me/Honey, Honey Bee Ball	1955	5.00	10.00	20.00
❑ F3347	The Blackboard of My Heart/I'm Not Mad, Just Hurt	1956	5.00	10.00	20.00
❑ F3440	Weeping Willow/You Can Give Me Back My Heart	1956	5.00	10.00	20.00
❑ F3536	It Makes No Difference Now/Taking My Chances	1956	5.00	10.00	20.00
❑ F3623	Rockin' in the Congo/I Was the First One	1957	10.00	20.00	40.00
❑ F3709	Girl in the Night/Quicksand	1957	5.00	10.00	20.00
❑ F3781	Tears Are Only Rain/Under the Double Eagle	1957	5.00	10.00	20.00
❑ F3850	Just an Old Flame/If I'm Not Too Late	1957	5.00	10.00	20.00
❑ F3950	How Do You Hold a Memory/Li'l Liza Jane	1958	5.00	10.00	20.00
❑ F4017	Squaws Along the Yukon/Gathering Flowers	1958	5.00	10.00	20.00
❑ F4085	I've Run Out of Tomorrows/You're Going Back to Your Old Ways Again	1958	5.00	10.00	20.00
❑ F4138	Tuxedo Junction/The Cocoanut Grove	1959	5.00	10.00	20.00
❑ F4182	Anybody's Girl/Total Strangers	1959	5.00	10.00	20.00
❑ F4269	I Didn't Mean to Fall in Love/I Guess I'm Gettin' Over You	1959	5.00	10.00	20.00
❑ 4334	A Six Pack to Go/What Made Her Change	1960	5.00	10.00	20.00
❑ 4386	She's Just a Whole Lot Like You/There My Future Goes	1960	5.00	10.00	20.00
❑ 4454	It's Got to Be a Habit/Will We Start It All Over Again	1960	5.00	10.00	20.00
❑ 4502	Just One Step Away/Two Hearts Deep in the Blues	1961	5.00	10.00	20.00
❑ 4556	Oklahoma Hills/Teach Me How to Lie	1961	5.00	10.00	20.00
❑ 4605	Hangover Tavern/Give the World a Smile	1961	5.00	10.00	20.00
❑ 4649	Lost John/I've Convinced Everyone But Myself	1961	5.00	10.00	20.00
❑ 4649 [PS]	Lost John/I've Convinced Everyone But Myself	1961	7.50	15.00	30.00
❑ 4694	That's the Recipe for a Heartache/Drop Me Gently	1962	3.75	7.50	15.00
❑ 4722	Blue Skirt Waltz/Westphalia Waltz	1962	3.75	7.50	15.00
❑ 4786	How Many Teardrops Will It Take/I Cast a Lonesome Shadow	1962	3.75	7.50	15.00
❑ 4871	Honky Tonk Town/I'd Look Forward to Tomorrow	1963	3.75	7.50	15.00
❑ 4912	Yesterday's Girl/The Wild Side of Life	1963	3.75	7.50	15.00
❑ 4968	I Wasn't Even in the Running/The More in Love Your Heart Is	1963	3.75	7.50	15.00
❑ 5008	Too in Love/Blackboard of My Heart	1963	3.75	7.50	15.00
❑ 5071	Twice As Much/Reaching for the Moon	1964	3.75	7.50	15.00
❑ 5123	Just to Ease the Pain/Stirring Up the Ashes	1964	3.75	7.50	15.00
❑ 5217	Whatever Happened to Mary/Luckiest Heartache in Town	1964	3.75	7.50	15.00
❑ 5310	Mr. and Mrs. Snowman/I'd Like to Have an Elephant for Christmas	1964	3.75	7.50	15.00
❑ 5344	I'm Gonna Practice Freedom/Life's Sweetest Moment	1965	3.75	7.50	15.00
❑ 5422	Then I'll Start Believing in You/In the Back of Your Mind	1965	3.75	7.50	15.00
❑ 5507	Paper Doll/You Only Hurt the One You Love	1965	3.75	7.50	15.00
❑ 5535	Little Christmas/Gonna Wrap My Heart in Angel Ribbons	1965	3.75	7.50	15.00
❑ 5599	Pick Me Up on Your Way Down/You Nearly Lose Your Mind	1966	3.00	6.00	12.00
❑ F40264	Give a Little, Take a Little/A Cat Has Nine Lives	1949	7.50	15.00	30.00

CHURCHILL

Number	Title (A Side/B Side)	Yr	VG	VG+	NM
❑ 7779	Rockin' in the Congo/The Convict and the Rose	1981	2.00	4.00	8.00
❑ 7779 [PS]	Rockin' in the Congo/The Convict and the Rose	1981	2.50	5.00	10.00
❑ 94003	Cocaine Blues/Drop Me Gently	1982	—	2.50	5.00
❑ 94009	Driving Nails in My Coffin/What Ever Happened to Mary	1982	—	2.50	5.00
❑ 94026	Once in a Blue Moon/Let's Stop What We Started	1983	—	2.50	5.00
❑ 94026 [PS]	Once in a Blue Moon/Let's Stop What We Started	1983	—	3.00	6.00

CURB

Number	Title (A Side/B Side)	Yr	VG	VG+	NM
❑ D7-73035	Gotta Sell Them Chickens/Total Stranger	1997	—	2.00	4.00
—A-side with Junior Brown; B-side with Lyle Lovett					

DOT

Number	Title (A Side/B Side)	Yr	VG	VG+	NM
❑ 17108	On Tap, In the Can, or In the Bottle	1968	2.00	4.00	8.00
❑ 17163	Smoky the Bar/Clubs, Spades, Diamonds and Hearts	1968	2.00	4.00	8.00
❑ 17207	I See Them Everywhere/Today	1969	2.00	4.00	8.00
❑ 17262	The Pathway of My Life/At Certain Times	1969	2.00	4.00	8.00
❑ 17307	Oklahoma Home Brew/Let's Get Drunk and Be Somebody	1969	2.00	4.00	8.00
❑ 17347	But That's All Right/Take It All Away	1970	2.00	4.00	8.00
❑ 17354	One of the Fortunate Few/I'm Afraid I Lied	1970	2.00	4.00	8.00
❑ 17365	Next Time I Fall in Love (I Won't)/Big Boat Across Oklahoma	1971	—	3.50	7.00
❑ 17385	The Mark of a Heel/Promise Her Anything	1971	—	3.50	7.00
❑ 17390	Oklahoma Stomp/Maiden's Prayer	1971	—	3.50	7.00
❑ 17399	I've Come Awful Close/Teardrops on the Rocks	1971	—	3.50	7.00
❑ 17410	Cab Driver/Gloria	1972	—	3.50	7.00
❑ 17430	Glow Worm/You're Nobody Till Somebody Loves You	1972	—	3.50	7.00
❑ 17447	Roses in the Wine/That's Why I Sing	1973	—	3.50	7.00
❑ 17470	Kindly Keep It Country/Jill's Jack in the Box	1973	—	3.50	7.00
❑ 17490	The Older the Violin, the Sweeter the Music/A Six Pack to Go	1974	—	3.50	7.00
❑ 17512	Who Left the Door to Heaven Open/When My Blue Moon Turns to Gold Again	1974	—	3.50	7.00

MCA

Number	Title (A Side/B Side)	Yr	VG	VG+	NM
❑ 41079	I Hear the South Callin' Me/Through the Bottom of the Glass	1979	—	2.00	4.00
❑ 41176	Tony's Tank-Up, Drive-In Cafe/Point of No Return	1980	—	2.00	4.00
❑ 41274	You're Poppin' Tops/Rollin' in Your Sweet Sunshine	1980	—	2.00	4.00
❑ 51030	King of Western Swing/Take Me Back to Tulsa	1980	—	2.00	4.00

STEP ONE

Number	Title (A Side/B Side)	Yr	VG	VG+	NM
❑ 382	Here's to Country Music/The Hand I'm Holding Now	1988	—	2.00	4.00
❑ 394	If I Were You I'd Fall in Love with Me/(B-side unknown)	1988	—	2.00	4.00

WARNER BROS.

Number	Title (A Side/B Side)	Yr	VG	VG+	NM
❑ 5858	Where Is the Circus/Love Walked Out Long Before She Did	1966	2.50	5.00	10.00
❑ 5886	He's Got a Way with Women/Let the Four Winds Choose	1967	2.50	5.00	10.00

7-Inch Extended Plays

CAPITOL

Number	Title (A Side/B Side)	Yr	VG	VG+	NM
❑ EAP 1-418	(contents unknown)	195?	5.00	10.00	20.00
❑ EAP 1-418 [PS]	Songs of the Brazos Valley, Part 1	195?	5.00	10.00	20.00
❑ EAP 2-418	(contents unknown)	195?	5.00	10.00	20.00
❑ EAP 2-418 [PS]	Songs of the Brazos Valley, Part 2	195?	5.00	10.00	20.00
❑ EAP 3-418	(contents unknown)	195?	5.00	10.00	20.00
❑ EAP 3-418 [PS]	Songs of the Brazos Valley, Part 3	195?	5.00	10.00	20.00
❑ EAP 1-601	(contents unknown)	195?	6.25	12.50	25.00
❑ EAP 1-601 [PS]	Hank Thompson	195?	6.25	12.50	25.00
❑ EAP 1-618	(contents unknown)	195?	5.00	10.00	20.00
❑ EAP 1-618 [PS]	North of the Rio Grande, Part 1	195?	5.00	10.00	20.00
❑ EAP 2-618	(contents unknown)	195?	5.00	10.00	20.00
❑ EAP 2-618 [PS]	North of the Rio Grande, Part 2	195?	5.00	10.00	20.00
❑ EAP 3-618	(contents unknown)	195?	5.00	10.00	20.00
❑ EAP 3-618 [PS]	North of the Rio Grande, Part 3	195?	5.00	10.00	20.00
❑ EAP 1-705	(contents unknown)	195?	6.25	12.50	25.00
❑ EAP 1-705 [PS]	Dancing Western Style	195?	6.25	12.50	25.00
❑ EAP 1-729	Humpty Dumpty Heart/Today//You Remembered Me/I'll Be Your Sweetheart for a Day	1957	3.75	7.50	15.00
❑ EAP 1-729 [PS]	New Recordings of Hank Thompson's All-Time Hits, Part 1	1957	3.75	7.50	15.00
❑ EAP 2-729	Don't Flirt with Me/The Grass Looks Greener//Swing Wide Your Gate of Love/I Find You Cheatin' on Me	1957	3.75	7.50	15.00
❑ EAP 2-729 [PS]	New Recordings of Hank Thompson's All-Time Hits, Part 2	1957	3.75	7.50	15.00
❑ EAP 3-729	My Front Door Is Open/Standing on the Outside//Whoa Sailor/Tomorrow Night	1957	3.75	7.50	15.00
❑ EAP 3-729 [PS]	New Recordings of Hank Thompson's All-Time Hits, Part 3	1957	3.75	7.50	15.00
❑ EAP 1-826	(contents unknown)	1957	3.75	7.50	15.00
❑ EAP 1-826 [PS]	Hank! Part 1	1957	3.75	7.50	15.00
❑ EAP 2-826	(contents unknown)	1957	3.75	7.50	15.00
❑ EAP 2-826 [PS]	Hank! Part 2	1957	3.75	7.50	15.00
❑ EAP 3-826	(contents unknown)	1957	3.75	7.50	15.00
❑ EAP 3-826 [PS]	Hank! Part 3	1957	3.75	7.50	15.00
❑ EAP 1-975	(contents unknown)	1958	3.75	7.50	15.00
❑ EAP 1-975 [PS]	Dance Ranch, Part 1	1958	3.75	7.50	15.00
❑ EAP 2-975	(contents unknown)	1958	3.75	7.50	15.00
❑ EAP 2-975 [PS]	Dance Ranch, Part 2	1958	3.75	7.50	15.00
❑ EAP 3-975	(contents unknown)	1958	3.75	7.50	15.00
❑ EAP 3-975 [PS]	Dance Ranch, Part 3	1958	3.75	7.50	15.00
❑ EAP 1-1111	Shenandoah Waltz/Wednesday Night Waltz//(B-side unknown)	1959	3.75	7.50	15.00
❑ EAP 1-1111 [PS]	Favorite Waltzes by Hank Thompson, Part 1	1959	3.75	7.50	15.00
❑ EAP 2-1111	(contents unknown)	1959	3.75	7.50	15.00
❑ EAP 2-1111 [PS]	Favorite Waltzes by Hank Thompson, Part 2	1959	3.75	7.50	15.00
❑ EAP 3-1111	(contents unknown)	1959	3.75	7.50	15.00
❑ EAP 3-1111 [PS]	Favorite Waltzes by Hank Thompson, Part 3	1959	3.75	7.50	15.00
❑ EAP 1-1246	(contents unknown)	1960	3.75	7.50	15.00
❑ EAP 1-1246 [PS]	Songs for Rounders, Part 1	1960	3.75	7.50	15.00
❑ EAP 2-1246	(contents unknown)	1960	3.75	7.50	15.00
❑ EAP 2-1246 [PS]	Songs for Rounders, Part 2	1960	3.75	7.50	15.00
❑ EAP 3-1246	(contents unknown)	1960	3.75	7.50	15.00
❑ EAP 3-1246 [PS]	Songs for Rounders, Part 3	1960	3.75	7.50	15.00

THOMPSON, JUNIOR

ATCO

Number	Title (A Side/B Side)	Yr	VG	VG+	NM
❑ 6500	You're the One/Jungle Girl	1967	3.00	6.00	12.00

METEOR

Number	Title (A Side/B Side)	Yr	VG	VG+	NM
❑ 5029	Mama's Little Baby/Raw Deal	1956	100.00	200.00	400.00

THOMPSON, LORETTA

SKOOP

Number	Title (A Side/B Side)	Yr	VG	VG+	NM
❑ 1050	Buddy-Big Bopper-Ritchie/Square from Nowhere	1959	12.50	25.00	50.00

UNITED

Number	Title (A Side/B Side)	Yr	VG	VG+	NM
❑ 214	He Do Ho Rock 'N' Roll/Let's Change the Alphabet	1958	10.00	20.00	40.00

THOMPSON, SUE

Also see DON GIBSON AND SUE THOMPSON.

DECCA

Number	Title (A Side/B Side)	Yr	VG	VG+	NM
❑ 29314	Walkin' in the Snow/Come a Little Bit Closer	1954	6.25	12.50	25.00
—With Hank Penny					
❑ 29545	Day Dreaming/Your Mommie and Your Daddy	1955	6.25	12.50	25.00
❑ 30435	Walkin' to Missouri/Red Hot Honey Brown	1957	6.25	12.50	25.00

HICKORY

Number	Title (A Side/B Side)	Yr	VG	VG+	NM
❑ 308	Just Plain Country/Oh Johnny, Oh Johnny, Oh	1973	—	2.50	5.00
❑ 313	Find Out/Stay Another Day	1974	—	2.50	5.00
❑ 320	Making Love to You Is Just Like Eating Peanuts/Sweet Memories	1974	—	2.50	5.00
❑ 330	Trains/And Love Me	1974	—	2.50	5.00
❑ 339	The Thought of Losing You/Tennessee Waltz	1975	—	2.00	4.00
❑ 346	I Can't Stop Loving You/Any Other Morning	1975	—	2.00	4.00
❑ 354	Big Mabel Murphy/Big Daddy	1975	—	2.00	4.00
❑ 364	Never Naughty Rosie/He Cheats on Me	1976	—	2.00	4.00
❑ 370	Baby's Not Home/I Want It All	1976	—	2.00	4.00
❑ 1144	Throwin' Kisses/Angel, Angel	1961	5.00	10.00	20.00
❑ 1153	Sad Movies (Make Me Cry)/Nine Little Teardrops	1961	5.00	10.00	20.00
❑ 1159	Norman/Never Love Again	1961	5.00	10.00	20.00
❑ 1166	Two of a Kind/It Has to Be	1962	3.75	7.50	15.00

Number	Title (A Side/B Side)	Yr	VG	VG+	NM
❑ 1174	Have a Good Time/If the Boy Only Knew	1962	3.75	7.50	15.00
❑ 1183	James (Hold the Ladder Steady)/My Hero	1962	3.75	7.50	15.00
❑ 1196	Willie Can/Too Much in Love	1962	3.75	7.50	15.00
❑ 1204	What's Wrong Bill/I Need a Harbor	1963	3.75	7.50	15.00
❑ 1204 [PS]	What's Wrong Bill/I Need a Harbor	1963	5.00	10.00	20.00
❑ 1217	True Confession/Suzie	1963	3.75	7.50	15.00
❑ 1217 [PS]	True Confession/Suzie	1963	5.00	10.00	20.00
❑ 1221	Too Hot to Dance/I Like Your Kind of Love	1963	3.00	6.00	12.00
—With Bob Luman					
❑ 1234	'Cause I Ask You To/It's 12:35	1963	3.00	6.00	12.00
❑ 1240	Big Daddy/I'd Like to Know You Better	1964	3.00	6.00	12.00
❑ 1255	Bad Boy/Toys	1964	3.00	6.00	12.00
❑ 1270	Big Hearted Me/Looking for a Good Boy	1964	3.00	6.00	12.00
❑ 1284	Paper Tiger/Mama, Don't Cry at My Wedding	1964	3.75	7.50	15.00
❑ 1308	Stop Th' Music/What I'm Needin' Is You	1965	3.00	6.00	12.00
❑ 1328	Afraid/It's Break-Up Time	1965	3.00	6.00	12.00
❑ 1340	Just Kiss Me/Sweet Hunk of Misery	1965	3.00	6.00	12.00
❑ 1359	Walkin' My Baby/I'm Lookin' (For a World)	1965	3.00	6.00	12.00
❑ 1381	What Should I Do/After the Heartache	1966	2.50	5.00	10.00
❑ 1403	I Can't Help It/Put It Back	1966	2.50	5.00	10.00
❑ 1423	Someone/From My Balcony	1966	2.50	5.00	10.00
❑ 1431	Language of Love/Let Me Down Hard	1967	2.50	5.00	10.00
❑ 1457	Don't Forget to Cry/Ferris Wheel	1967	2.50	5.00	10.00
❑ 1469	That's Just Too Much/Straight to Helen	1967	2.50	5.00	10.00
❑ 1488	Dear Boy/Love Has Come My Way	1967	2.50	5.00	10.00
❑ 1493	How Do You Start Over/Why Not	1968	2.00	4.00	8.00
❑ 1512	You Deserve Each Other/Doin' Nothing	1968	2.00	4.00	8.00
❑ 1524	Don't Try to Change Me/The Real Me	1968	2.00	4.00	8.00
❑ 1534	Tennessee Waltz/Who's Gonna Mow Your Grass	1969	2.00	4.00	8.00
❑ 1547	Pair of Broken Hearts/You Two-Timed Me One Time Too Often	1969	2.00	4.00	8.00
❑ 1560	I Just Keep Hangin' On/Lost Highway	1970	—	3.00	6.00
❑ 1577	Whole Lot of Walkin'/Guess Who's Coming to Dinner Tonight	1970	—	3.00	6.00
❑ 1587	Because You Love Me/Take a Little Time	1971	—	3.00	6.00
❑ 1596	Here's To Forever/What You See Is What You Get	1971	—	3.00	6.00
❑ 1612	Swiss Cottage Place/Thanks to Rumors	1971	—	3.00	6.00
❑ 1622	Let Your Thoughts Be Sweet/What a Woman in Love Won't Do	1972	—	3.00	6.00
❑ 1641	Sweet Memories/Take Me As I Am	1972	—	3.00	6.00
❑ 1652	Candy and Roses/Full Time Job	1972	—	3.00	6.00
❑ 1669	How I Love Them Old Songs/Just Two Young People	1973	—	2.50	5.00

MERCURY

Number	Title (A Side/B Side)	Yr	VG	VG+	NM
❑ 6325	You're Getting a Good Girl (When You Get Me)/What've You Got (That Makes Me Love You So)	1951	10.00	20.00	40.00
❑ 6377	Just Walking Out the Door/I'll Hate Myself in the Morning	1952	7.50	15.00	30.00
❑ 6390	Junior's a Big Boy Now/Tadpole	1952	7.50	15.00	30.00
❑ 6407	You Belong to Me/You're an Angel on the Outside	1952	7.50	15.00	30.00
❑ 6416	Red Hot Henrietta Brown/Last Night I Heard Somebody Cry	1952	7.50	15.00	30.00
❑ 70066	How Many Tears/If You Should Change	1953	6.25	12.50	25.00
❑ 70084	Take Care My Love/Things I Might Have Been	1953	6.25	12.50	25.00
❑ 70089	You and Me/Say It with Your Heart	1953	6.25	12.50	25.00
❑ 70152	I'm Not That Kind of Girl/I Long to Tell You	1953	6.25	12.50	25.00
❑ 70309	Donna Wanna/Gee But I Hate to Go Home Alone	1954	6.25	12.50	25.00

THOMPSON TWINS

ARISTA

Number	Title (A Side/B Side)	Yr	VG	VG+	NM
❑ 0671	In the Name of Love/Coastline	1982	—	2.00	4.00
❑ 1024	Lies/Beach Culture	1982	—	2.00	4.00
❑ 1056	Love On Your Side/Love On Your Back	1983	—	2.00	4.00
❑ 1056 [PS]	Love On Your Side/Love On Your Back	1983	—	2.00	4.00
❑ 9013	Love On Your Side/Love On Your Back	1983	—	—	3.00
❑ 9013 [PS]	Love On Your Side/Love On Your Back	1983	—	—	3.00
❑ 9164	Hold Me Now/Let Loving Start	1984	—	—	3.00
❑ 9164 [PS]	Hold Me Now/Let Loving Start	1984	—	—	3.00
❑ 9209	Doctor! Doctor!/Nurse Shark	1984	—	—	3.00
❑ 9209 [PS]	Doctor! Doctor!/Nurse Shark	1984	—	—	3.00
❑ 9237	Lies/Love on Your Side	1984	—	—	3.00
—"Flashback" reissue					
❑ 9238	In the Name of Love/Coastline	1984	—	—	3.00
—"Flashback" reissue					
❑ 9244	You Take Me Up/Passion Planet	1984	—	—	3.00
❑ 9244 [PS]	You Take Me Up/Passion Planet	1984	—	—	3.00
❑ 9290	The Gap/Out of the Gap	1984	—	—	3.00
❑ 9347	Hold Me Now/Doctor! Doctor!	1985	—	—	3.00
—Reissue					
❑ 9396	Lay Your Hands on Me/The Lewis Carroll (Adventures in Wonderland)	1985	—	—	3.00
❑ 9396 [PS]	Lay Your Hands on Me/The Lewis Carroll (Adventures in Wonderland)	1985	—	—	3.00
❑ 9450	King for a Day/Rollunder	1985	—	—	3.00
❑ 9450 [PS]	King for a Day/Rollunder	1985	—	—	3.00
❑ 9485	Lay Your Hands on Me/King for a Day	1986	—	—	3.00
—Reissue					
❑ 9511	Nothing in Common/Nothing to Lose	1986	—	—	3.00
❑ 9511 [PS]	Nothing in Common/Nothing to Lose	1986	—	—	3.00
❑ 9577	Get That Love/Perfect Day	1987	—	—	3.00
❑ 9577 [PS]	Get That Love/Perfect Day	1987	—	—	3.00
❑ 9609	Long Goodbye/Dancin' in Your Shoes	1987	—	—	3.00
❑ 9609 [PS]	Long Goodbye/Dancin' in Your Shoes	1987	—	—	3.00
❑ 9622	Follow Your Heart/Bush Baby	1987	—	—	3.00

WARNER BROS.

Number	Title (A Side/B Side)	Yr	VG	VG+	NM
❑ 22819	Sugar Daddy/Monkey Man	1989	—	—	3.00
❑ 22819 [PS]	Sugar Daddy/Monkey Man	1989	—	—	3.00

THOR-ABLES, THE

TITANIC

Number	Title (A Side/B Side)	Yr	VG	VG+	NM
❑ 1001	Our Love Song/Get That Bread	1962	75.00	150.00	300.00
❑ 1002	My Reckless Heart/Batman and Robin	1962	75.00	150.00	300.00

THORNE, WOODY

GNP

Number	Title (A Side/B Side)	Yr	VG	VG+	NM
❑ 169	Teenagers in Love/Sadie Lou	1961	5.00	10.00	20.00

THORNTON, BIG MAMA

ARHOOLIE

Number	Title (A Side/B Side)	Yr	VG	VG+	NM
❑ 512	Swing It On Home/My Heavy Load	1968	2.00	4.00	8.00
❑ 520	Ball and Chain/Wade in the Water	1968	2.00	4.00	8.00

BAYTONE

Number	Title (A Side/B Side)	Yr	VG	VG+	NM
❑ 107	You Did Me Wrong/Big Mama's Blues	1961	3.75	7.50	15.00

GALAXY

Number	Title (A Side/B Side)	Yr	VG	VG+	NM
❑ 749	Life Goes On/Because It's Love	1966	2.50	5.00	10.00

KENT

Number	Title (A Side/B Side)	Yr	VG	VG+	NM
❑ 424	Before Day/Me and My Chauffeur	1965	2.50	5.00	10.00

MERCURY

Number	Title (A Side/B Side)	Yr	VG	VG+	NM
❑ 72981	Hound Dog/Let's Go Get Started	1969	2.00	4.00	8.00

PEACOCK

Number	Title (A Side/B Side)	Yr	VG	VG+	NM
❑ 1603	Everytime I Think of You/Mischievous Boogie	1952	25.00	50.00	100.00
❑ 1612	Hound Dog/Rock-a-Bye Baby	1953	50.00	100.00	200.00
❑ 1612	Hound Dog/Nightmare	1953	45.00	90.00	180.00
❑ 1621	They Call Me Big Mama/Cotton Pickin' Blues	1953	25.00	50.00	100.00
❑ 1626	Big Change/I Ain't No Fool Either	1953	25.00	50.00	100.00
❑ 1632	I've Searched the Whole World/I Smell a Rat	1954	15.00	30.00	60.00
❑ 1642	Stop Hoppin' on Me/Story of My Blues	1954	15.00	30.00	60.00
❑ 1647	Walking Blues/Rock-a-Bye Baby	1955	15.00	30.00	60.00
❑ 1650	The Fish/Laugh, Laugh, Laugh	1955	15.00	30.00	60.00
❑ 1681	Just Like a Dog/My Man Called Me	1957	10.00	20.00	40.00

THORNTON, FRADKIN AND UNGER

ESP-DISK

Number	Title (A Side/B Side)	Yr	VG	VG+	NM
❑ 63019	God Bless California/Sometimes	1972	3.75	7.50	15.00
—Paul McCartney appears on this record					

THREE BELLS, THE

LAWN

Number	Title (A Side/B Side)	Yr	VG	VG+	NM
❑ 251	He Doesn't Love Me/Softly in the Night	1965	3.00	6.00	12.00

THREE BLONDE MICE

ATCO

Number	Title (A Side/B Side)	Yr	VG	VG+	NM
❑ 6324	Ringo Bells/The 12 Days of Christmas	1964	7.50	15.00	30.00
❑ 6353	Alley Cat/What Did I Say	1965	2.50	5.00	10.00

THREE CHUCKLES, THE

BOULEVARD

Number	Title (A Side/B Side)	Yr	VG	VG+	NM
❑ 100	Runaround/At Last You Understand	1954	20.00	40.00	80.00

VIK

Number	Title (A Side/B Side)	Yr	VG	VG+	NM
❑ 0186	Anyway/The Funny Little Things We Used to Do	1956	5.00	10.00	20.00
❑ 0194	Tell Me/And the Angels Sing	1956	5.00	10.00	20.00
❑ 0216	Gypsy in My Soul/We're Still Holding Hands	1956	5.00	10.00	20.00
❑ 0232	Fallen Out of Love/Midnight 'Til Dawn	1956	5.00	10.00	20.00
❑ 0244	Won't You Give Me a Chance/We're Gonna Rock Tonight	1956	5.00	10.00	20.00

"X"

Number	Title (A Side/B Side)	Yr	VG	VG+	NM
❑ 0066	Runaround/At Last You Understand	1954	6.25	12.50	25.00
❑ 0095	Foolishly/If I Should Love Again	1955	6.25	12.50	25.00
❑ 0134	So Long/You Should Have Told Me	1955	6.25	12.50	25.00
❑ 0150	Blue Lover/Realize	1955	6.25	12.50	25.00
❑ 0162	Times Two, I Love You/Still Thinking of You	1955	6.25	12.50	25.00
❑ 0186	Anyway/The Funny Little Things We Used to Do	1956	6.25	12.50	25.00
❑ 0194	Tell Me/And the Angels Sing	1956	6.25	12.50	25.00
❑ 0216	Gypsy in My Soul/We're Still Holding Hands	1956	6.25	12.50	25.00

7-Inch Extended Plays

"X"

Number	Title (A Side/B Side)	Yr	VG	VG+	NM
❑ EXA-192	(contents unknown)	1955	10.00	20.00	40.00
❑ EXA-192 [PS]	The Three Chuckles (Vol. 1)	1955	10.00	20.00	40.00
❑ EXA-193	(contents unknown)	1955	10.00	20.00	40.00
❑ EXA-193 [PS]	The Three Chuckles (Vol. 2)	1955	10.00	20.00	40.00
❑ EXA-194	(contents unknown)	1955	10.00	20.00	40.00
❑ EXA-194 [PS]	The Three Chuckles (Vol. 3)	1955	10.00	20.00	40.00

THREE D'S, THE (1)

BRUNSWICK

Number	Title (A Side/B Side)	Yr	VG	VG+	NM
❑ 55152	Nothing to Wear/The Happiest Boy and Girl	1959	6.25	12.50	25.00

PARIS

Number	Title (A Side/B Side)	Yr	VG	VG+	NM
❑ 503	Little Billy Boy/Let Me Know	1957	5.00	10.00	20.00
❑ 508	Never Let You Go/Birth of An Angel	1957	5.00	10.00	20.00
❑ 511	Baby Doll/Crazy Little Woman	1958	5.00	10.00	20.00
❑ 514	Jumpin' Jack/I Never Saw My Pretty Little Baby Alone	1958	5.00	10.00	20.00

PILGRIM

Number	Title (A Side/B Side)	Yr	VG	VG+	NM
❑ 719	Broken Dreams/Tell Me That You Love Me	1956	6.25	12.50	25.00

SQUARE

Number	Title (A Side/B Side)	Yr	VG	VG+	NM
❑ 502	Squeeze/Graveyard Cha-Cha	1959	20.00	40.00	80.00

THREE D'S, THE (2)

CAPITOL

Number	Title (A Side/B Side)	Yr	VG	VG+	NM
❑ 5188	Sinner Man/Give, Said the Little Stream	1964	2.50	5.00	10.00
❑ 5249	Chim Chim Cheree/Crayon Box	1964	2.50	5.00	10.00

THREE D'S, THE (U)

DEAN

Number	Title (A Side/B Side)	Yr	VG	VG+	NM
❑ 521	Broken Hearted/I Love You So	1961	5.00	10.00	20.00

THREE DEGREES, THE

ARIOLA AMERICA

Number	Title (A Side/B Side)	Yr	VG	VG+	NM
❑ 801	My Simple Heart/Hot Summer Night	1980	—	2.00	4.00
❑ 7721	Giving Up, Giving In/Woman in Love	1978	—	2.00	4.00
❑ 7742	Woman in Love/Out of Love Again	1979	—	2.00	4.00
❑ 7746	The Runner/Out of Love Again	1979	—	2.00	4.00

EPIC

Number	Title (A Side/B Side)	Yr	VG	VG+	NM
❑ 50283	What I Did for Love/Macaronie Man	1976	—	2.00	4.00

Number	Title (A Side/B Side)	Yr	VG	VG+	NM
❑ 50330	In Love We Grow/Standing Up for Love	1977	—	2.00	4.00
ICHIBAN					
❑ 89-167	Tie U Up/(B-side unknown)	1989	—	2.50	5.00
METROMEDIA					
❑ 109	Down in the Boondocks/Warm Weather Music	1969	2.00	4.00	8.00
❑ 128	Feeling of Love/Warm Weather Music	1969	2.00	4.00	8.00
NEPTUNE					
❑ 23	Reflections of Yesterday/What I See	1970	—	3.00	6.00
PHILADELPHIA INT'L.					
❑ 3534	Dirty Ol Man/Can't You See What You're Doing to Me	1973	—	3.00	6.00
❑ 3539	Year of Decision/A Woman Needs a Good Man	1974	—	2.50	5.00
❑ 3550	When Will I See You Again/Year of Decision	1974	—	2.50	5.00
❑ 3561	I Didn't Know/Dirty Ol Man	1975	—	2.50	5.00
❑ 3568	Take Good Care of Yourself/Here I Am	1975	—	2.50	5.00
❑ 3585	Free Ride/Loving Cup	1976	—	2.50	5.00
ROULETTE					
❑ 7072	Melting Pot/The Grass Will Sing for You	1970	—	3.00	6.00
❑ 7079	Maybe/Collage	1970	—	3.00	6.00
❑ 7088	I Do Take You/You're the Fool	1970	—	3.00	6.00
❑ 7097	You're the One/Stardust	1971	—	3.00	6.00
❑ 7102	There's So Much Love All Around/Yours	1971	—	3.00	6.00
❑ 7105	Ebb Tide/Low Down	1971	—	3.00	6.00
❑ 7117	Trade Winds/I Turn to You	1972	—	3.00	6.00
❑ 7125	Find My Way/I Wanna Be Your Baby	1972	—	3.00	6.00
❑ 7137	I Won't Let You Go/Through Misty Eyes	1972	—	3.00	6.00
SWAN					
❑ 4197	Gee Baby (I'm Sorry)/Do What You're Supposed to Do	1965	3.00	6.00	12.00
❑ 4214	I'm Gonna Need You/Just Right for Love	1965	3.00	6.00	12.00
❑ 4224	Close Your Eyes/Gotta Draw the Line	1965	3.00	6.00	12.00
❑ 4235	Look in My Eyes/Drivin' Me Mad	1965	3.00	6.00	12.00
❑ 4245	Maybe/Yours	1966	3.00	6.00	12.00
❑ 4253	I Wanna Be Your Baby/Tales Are True	1966	3.00	6.00	12.00
❑ 4267	Love of My Life/Are You Satisfied	1967	3.00	6.00	12.00
WARNER BROS.					
❑ 7198	Contact/Oh No Not Again	1968	2.50	5.00	10.00

THREE DOG NIGHT

Also see DANNY HUTTON; CORY WELLS AND THE ENEMYS.

Number	Title (A Side/B Side)	Yr	VG	VG+	NM
ABC					
❑ 12114	'Til the World Ends/Yo Te Quiero Hablo (Take You Down)	1975	—	2.00	4.00
❑ 12192	Everybody Is a Masterpiece/Drive On, Ride On	1976	—	2.00	4.00
ABC DUNHILL					
❑ 4168	Nobody/It's for You	1968	3.00	6.00	12.00
❑ 4168 [PS]	Nobody/It's for You	1968	7.50	15.00	30.00
—Sleeve is promo only					
❑ 4177	Try a Little Tenderness/That No One Ever Hurt So Bad	1969	2.00	4.00	8.00
❑ 4191	One/Chest Fever	1969	2.00	4.00	8.00
❑ 4203	Easy to Be Hard/Dreaming Isn't Good for You	1969	2.00	4.00	8.00
❑ 4215	Eli's Coming/Circle for a Landing	1969	2.00	4.00	8.00
❑ 4229	Celebrate/Feeling Alright	1970	—	3.00	6.00
❑ 4239	Mama Told Me (Not to Come)/Rock and Roll Widow	1970	—	3.00	6.00
❑ 4239 [PS]	Mama Told Me (Not to Come)/Rock and Roll Widow	1970	3.00	6.00	12.00
❑ 4250	Out in the Country/Good Time Living	1970	—	3.00	6.00
❑ 4262	One Man Band/It Ain't Easy	1970	—	3.00	6.00
❑ 4272	Joy to the World/I Can Hear You Calling	1971	—	2.50	5.00
❑ 4282	Liar/Can't Get Enough of It	1971	—	2.50	5.00
❑ 4294	An Old Fashioned Love Song/Jam	1971	—	2.50	5.00
❑ 4299	Never Been to Spain/Peace of Mind	1972	—	2.50	5.00
❑ 4306	The Family of Man/Going in Circles	1972	—	2.50	5.00
❑ 4317	Black and White/Freedom for the Stallion	1972	—	2.50	5.00
❑ 4331	Pieces of April/The Writings on the Wall	1972	—	2.50	5.00
❑ 4352	Shambala/Our "B" Side	1973	—	2.50	5.00
—First pressings have "Dunhill" spelled out in children's blocks					
❑ 4352	Shambala/Our "B" Side	1973	—	2.50	5.00
—Transitional pressings have "Dunhill" in children's blocks on one label and "Dunhill" in a box on the other label					
❑ 4352	Shambala/Our "B" Side	1973	—	2.00	4.00
—Later pressings have "Dunhill" in a box on both labels (1968-72 style)					
❑ 4370	Let Me Serenade You/Storybook Feeling	1973	—	2.00	4.00
❑ 4382	The Show Must Go On/On the Way Back Home	1974	—	2.00	4.00
❑ 15001	Sure As I'm Sittin' Here/Anytime Babe	1974	—	2.00	4.00
❑ 15010	The Show Must Go On/On the Way Back Home	1974	2.00	4.00	8.00
❑ 15013	Play Something Sweet (Brickyard Blues)/I'd Be So Happy	1974	—	2.00	4.00
PASSPORT					
❑ 7921	It's a Jungle Out There/Somebody's Gonna Get Hurt	1983	—	2.50	5.00

THREE DOTS AND A DASH

With JESSE BELVIN.

Number	Title (A Side/B Side)	Yr	VG	VG+	NM
IMPERIAL					
❑ 5164	I'll Never Love Again/Let's Do It	1951	125.00	250.00	500.00

THREE FRIENDS, THE (1)

Number	Title (A Side/B Side)	Yr	VG	VG+	NM
CAL-GOLD					
❑ 169	Walkin' Shoes/Blue Ribbon Baby	1961	50.00	100.00	200.00
IMPERIAL					
❑ 5763	Dedicated (To the Songs I Love)/Happy as a Man Can Be	1961	7.50	15.00	30.00
❑ 5773	You're a Square/Go On to School	1961	5.00	10.00	20.00

THREE FRIENDS, THE (2)

Number	Title (A Side/B Side)	Yr	VG	VG+	NM
BRUNSWICK					
❑ 55032	Jinx/Chinese Tearoom	1957	7.50	15.00	30.00
LIDO					
❑ 500	Baby I'll Cry/Blanche	1956	15.00	30.00	60.00
—Gray label					
❑ 500	Baby I'll Cry/Blanche	1956	10.00	20.00	40.00
—Blue label					
❑ 502	I'm Only a Boy/Jinx	1957	12.50	25.00	50.00
❑ 504	Now That You've Gone/Chinese Tea Room	1957	12.50	25.00	50.00

THREE VALES, THE

Number	Title (A Side/B Side)	Yr	VG	VG+	NM
CINDY					
❑ 3007	Blue Lights/Ay, Ay, Ay	1957	30.00	60.00	120.00

THREETEENS, THE

Number	Title (A Side/B Side)	Yr	VG	VG+	NM
REV					
❑ 3516	Dear 53310761/Doowaddie	1958	10.00	20.00	40.00
❑ 3522	X + Y = Z/For the Love of Mike	1959	6.25	12.50	25.00
TODD					
❑ 1021	X + Y = Z/For the Love of Mike	1959	5.00	10.00	20.00

THRILLERS, THE (1)

Number	Title (A Side/B Side)	Yr	VG	VG+	NM
BIG TOWN					
❑ 109	The Drunkard/Mattie, Leave Me Alone	1953	100.00	200.00	400.00
HERALD					
❑ 432	Lizabeth/Please Talk to Me	1954	100.00	200.00	400.00
THRILLER					
❑ 3530	Lessie Mae/I'm Going to Live My Life Alone	1953	250.00	500.00	1000.

THRILLERS, THE (2)

Number	Title (A Side/B Side)	Yr	VG	VG+	NM
UPTOWN					
❑ 715	Come What May/This I Know Little Girl	1965	3.00	6.00	12.00

THRILLS, THE

Number	Title (A Side/B Side)	Yr	VG	VG+	NM
CAPITOL					
❑ 5631	What Can Go Wrong/No One	1966	5.00	10.00	20.00
❑ 5719	Here's a Heart/Bring It On Home to Me	1966	5.00	10.00	20.00
❑ 5871	Show the World Where It's At/Underneath My Make-Up	1967	5.00	10.00	20.00

THUDPUCKER, JIMMY

Fictional singing star from Garry Trudeau's "Doonesbury" comic strip.

Number	Title (A Side/B Side)	Yr	VG	VG+	NM
WARNER BROS.					
❑ 8245	Ginny's Song (Part 1)/Ginny's Song (Part 2)	1976	—	3.00	6.00
❑ 8245 [PS]	Ginny's Song (Part 1)/Ginny's Song (Part 2)	1976	—	3.00	6.00
WINDSONG					
❑ CB-11230	You Can't Fight It/Take Your Life	1978	—	2.50	5.00
❑ CB-11230 [PS]	You Can't Fight It/Take Your Life	1978	—	2.50	5.00

THUNDER, JOHNNY

Number	Title (A Side/B Side)	Yr	VG	VG+	NM
CALLA					
❑ 161	I'm Alive/Verbal Expressions of T.V.	1969	—	3.00	6.00
DIAMOND					
❑ 129	Loop De Loop/Don't Be Ashamed	1962	3.75	7.50	15.00
❑ 132	Rock-a-Bye My Darling/The Rosy Dance	1963	2.50	5.00	10.00
❑ 132 [PS]	Rock-a-Bye My Darling/The Rosy Dance	1963	5.00	10.00	20.00
❑ 137	The Outlaw/Jailer, Bring Me Water	1963	2.50	5.00	10.00
❑ 148	Hey Child/Darling Je Vous Aime Beaucoup	1963	2.50	5.00	10.00
❑ 152	Constitution of Love/Good Morning Sadness	1964	2.00	4.00	8.00
❑ 155	Everybody Likes to Dance with Johnny/Zoo-Lee-Oh	1964	2.00	4.00	8.00
❑ 169	More, More More Love, Love, Love/Shout It to the World	1964	2.00	4.00	8.00
❑ 175	Send Her to Me/Shout It to the World	1964	2.00	4.00	8.00
❑ 185	Suzie-Q/Dear John, I'm Going to Leave You	1965	2.00	4.00	8.00
❑ 192	Everybody Do the Sloopy/Beautiful	1965	2.00	4.00	8.00
❑ 196	My Prayer/A Broken Heart	1966	2.00	4.00	8.00
❑ 206	Bewildered/Just Me and You	1966	2.00	4.00	8.00
❑ 218	Make Love to Me/Teach Me Tonight	1967	2.00	4.00	8.00
—With Ruby Winters					
❑ 222	Am I Right or Am I Wrong/You Send Me	1967	2.00	4.00	8.00
❑ 238	We Only Have One Life (Let's Live It Together)/Teach Me Tonight	1968	2.00	4.00	8.00
—With Ruby Winters					
❑ 246	Put It in Motion/Groovy Two Shoes	1968	2.00	4.00	8.00
EPIC					
❑ 9329	Ever Your Man/Horror Show	1959	3.75	7.50	15.00
UNITED ARTISTS					
❑ 50736	Power to the People/Love Trip	1971	—	3.00	6.00

THUNDER AND ROSES

Number	Title (A Side/B Side)	Yr	VG	VG+	NM
UNITED ARTISTS					
❑ 50536	Country Life/I Love a Woman	1969	3.00	6.00	12.00

THUNDER BOLTS, THE

Number	Title (A Side/B Side)	Yr	VG	VG+	NM
RONDACK					
❑ 7546	Thunder Head/Blending	196?	12.50	25.00	50.00

THUNDER HEADS, THE

Number	Title (A Side/B Side)	Yr	VG	VG+	NM
CARTWHEEL					
❑ 100	Thunder Head/Unemployment	1966	7.50	15.00	30.00

THUNDERBOLTS, THE

Number	Title (A Side/B Side)	Yr	VG	VG+	NM
DOT					
❑ 16496	Lost Planets/March of the Spacemen	1963	5.00	10.00	20.00

THUNDERCLAP NEWMAN

Jimmy McCulloch, later of WINGS, was in this group.

Number	Title (A Side/B Side)	Yr	VG	VG+	NM
TRACK					
❑ 2656	Something in the Air/Wilhelmina	1969	2.50	5.00	10.00
❑ 2769	Something in the Air/Wilhelmina	1970	—	3.00	6.00

THUNDERGRIN

Number	Title (A Side/B Side)	Yr	VG	VG+	NM
EPIC					
❑ 10215	Women in the Street/Mr. Simms	1967	2.50	5.00	10.00

THUNDERTONES, THE

DONNA

Number	Title (A Side/B Side)	Yr	VG	VG+	NM
❑ 1343	Thunder Rhythm/Pay Day	1961	7.50	15.00	30.00

DOT

Number	Title (A Side/B Side)	Yr	VG	VG+	NM
❑ 16137	Jungle Fever/Hot Ice	1960	7.50	15.00	30.00
❑ 16177	The Street Beat/Happy Little Jug	1961	7.50	15.00	30.00

—As "Lenny and the Thundertones"

THURSDAY'S CHILDREN

INTERNATIONAL ARTISTS

Number	Title (A Side/B Side)	Yr	VG	VG+	NM
❑ 110	Air Conditioned Man/Sominoes	1967	37.50	75.00	150.00
❑ 115	Help, Murder, Police/You Can't Forget About That	1967	37.50	75.00	150.00

N-JOY

Number	Title (A Side/B Side)	Yr	VG	VG+	NM
❑ 1019	Running Around on Me/I Don't Need Your Love	1967	3.75	7.50	15.00

THYME

A-SQUARE

Number	Title (A Side/B Side)	Yr	VG	VG+	NM
❑ 201	Somehow/Shame, Shame	1969	10.00	20.00	40.00
❑ 202	Time of the Season/I Found a Love	1969	10.00	20.00	40.00

BANG

Number	Title (A Side/B Side)	Yr	VG	VG+	NM
❑ 546	Love to Love/Very Last Day	1967	5.00	10.00	20.00

TIATT, LYNN, AND THE COMETS

PUSSYCAT

Number	Title (A Side/B Side)	Yr	VG	VG+	NM
❑ 1	Dad Is Home/Vilma's Jump-Up	195?	75.00	150.00	300.00

TICO AND THE TRIUMPHS

PAUL SIMON was a member.

AMY

Number	Title (A Side/B Side)	Yr	VG	VG+	NM
❑ 835	Motorcycle/I Don't Believe Them	1961	25.00	50.00	100.00
❑ 845	Wildflower/Express Train	1962	25.00	50.00	100.00
❑ 860	Cry, Lil' Boy, Cry/Get Up and Do the Wobble	1962	25.00	50.00	100.00
❑ 876	Cards of Love/Noise	1963	50.00	100.00	200.00

MADISON

Number	Title (A Side/B Side)	Yr	VG	VG+	NM
❑ 169	Motorcycle/I Don't Believe Them	1961	50.00	100.00	200.00

TIFFANY SHADE, THE

MAINSTREAM

Number	Title (A Side/B Side)	Yr	VG	VG+	NM
❑ 677	One Good Reason/Would You Take My Mind Out for a Walk	1968	3.75	7.50	15.00
❑ 680	An Older Man/Sam	1968	3.75	7.50	15.00

TIFFANYS, THE

Probably not all the same group.

ARCTIC

Number	Title (A Side/B Side)	Yr	VG	VG+	NM
❑ 101	Love Me/Happiest Girl in the World	1964	5.00	10.00	20.00

ATLANTIC

Number	Title (A Side/B Side)	Yr	VG	VG+	NM
❑ 2240	Please Tell Me/Gossip	1964	5.00	10.00	20.00

JOSIE

Number	Title (A Side/B Side)	Yr	VG	VG+	NM
❑ 942	I Feel the Same Way Too/I Just Wanna Be a Girl	1965	3.00	6.00	12.00
❑ 952	Heaven on Earth/Take Another Look at Me	1966	3.00	6.00	12.00

KR

Number	Title (A Side/B Side)	Yr	VG	VG+	NM
❑ 120	He's Good for Me/It's Got to Be a Great Song	1967	5.00	10.00	20.00

—As "The Tiffanies"

MRS

Number	Title (A Side/B Side)	Yr	VG	VG+	NM
❑ 777	Please Tell Me/Gossip	1964	20.00	40.00	80.00

RKO

Number	Title (A Side/B Side)	Yr	VG	VG+	NM
❑ 120	He's Good for Me/It's Got to Be a Great Song	1967	2.50	5.00	10.00

—Are the KR and RKO releases one and the same? We don't know

ROCKIN' ROBIN

Number	Title (A Side/B Side)	Yr	VG	VG+	NM
❑ 1	I've Got a Girl/I Don't Dig Western Movies	1963	75.00	150.00	300.00

SWAN

Number	Title (A Side/B Side)	Yr	VG	VG+	NM
❑ 4104	Atlanta/The Pleasure of Love	1962	5.00	10.00	20.00

TIGERS, THE

COLPIX

Number	Title (A Side/B Side)	Yr	VG	VG+	NM
❑ 773	GeeTO Tiger/The Prowl	1965	12.50	25.00	50.00
❑ SPEC-773	GeeTO Tiger/The Big Sounds of the GeeTO Tiger	1965	20.00	40.00	80.00
—Special promotional issue					
❑ SPEC-773 [PS]	GeeTO Tiger/The Big Sounds of the GeeTO Tiger	1965	50.00	100.00	200.00

—Sleeve appears to have been available only with the promotional B-side

TIKIS, THE

ASCOT

Number	Title (A Side/B Side)	Yr	VG	VG+	NM
❑ 2186	Stop-Look-Listen/Cream in My Coffee	1965	2.50	5.00	10.00
❑ 2204	High School Dropout Blues/Whole Lotta Soul	1966	2.50	5.00	10.00

AUTUMN

Number	Title (A Side/B Side)	Yr	VG	VG+	NM
❑ 18	If I've Been Dreaming/Pay Attention to Me	1965	2.50	5.00	10.00
—As "The Other Tikis"					
❑ 28	Bye Bye Bye/Lost My Love Today	1966	2.50	5.00	10.00

—As "The Other Tikis"

DIAL

Number	Title (A Side/B Side)	Yr	VG	VG+	NM
❑ 4048	Somebody's Sun/Little Miss Lovelight	1966	2.50	5.00	10.00

MINARET

Number	Title (A Side/B Side)	Yr	VG	VG+	NM
❑ 115	Big Feet/One More Chance	196?	3.00	6.00	12.00
❑ 116	Popsicle/All That Talk	196?	3.00	6.00	12.00
❑ 118	Traveling Shoes/Valley of Tears	196?	3.00	6.00	12.00

WARNER BROS.

Number	Title (A Side/B Side)	Yr	VG	VG+	NM
❑ 5818	Bye Bye Bye/Lost My Love Today	1966	2.50	5.00	10.00

TIKIS, THE, AND THE FABULONS

PANORAMA

Number	Title (A Side/B Side)	Yr	VG	VG+	NM
❑ 13	Take a Look/For Your Love	1965	5.00	10.00	20.00

TOWER

Number	Title (A Side/B Side)	Yr	VG	VG+	NM
❑ 181	Take a Look/Cherry Pie	1965	3.00	6.00	12.00

TIL, SONNY

Also see THE ORIOLES.

JUBILEE

Number	Title (A Side/B Side)	Yr	VG	VG+	NM
❑ 5060	I Never Knew (I Could Love Anybody)/My Prayer	1951	75.00	150.00	300.00
❑ 5066	Fool's World/For All We Know	1951	75.00	150.00	300.00
—Black vinyl					
❑ 5066	Fool's World/For All We Know	1951	200.00	400.00	800.00
—Red vinyl					
❑ 5090	Once in Awhile/I Only Have Eyes for You	1952	12.50	25.00	50.00
—With Edna McGriff					
❑ 5099	Good/Picadilly	1952	20.00	40.00	80.00
—With Edna McGriff					
❑ 5112	Have You Heard/Lonely Wine	1953	50.00	100.00	200.00
❑ 5118	(Danger) Soft Shoulders/Congratulations to Someone	1953	50.00	100.00	200.00
❑ 5394	Night and Day/Shimmy Time	1960	5.00	10.00	20.00

RCA VICTOR

Number	Title (A Side/B Side)	Yr	VG	VG+	NM
❑ 47-9733	You're All I Need/After You	1969	2.00	4.00	8.00
❑ 47-9759	Tears and Misery/I Better Leave Love Alone	1969	2.00	4.00	8.00
❑ 74-0390	Don't Feel No Pain/One Big Happy Family	1970	2.00	4.00	8.00
❑ 74-0432	Colours/Love Is What It's All About	1971	2.00	4.00	8.00
❑ 74-0529	'Til Then/Love or Desire	1971	2.00	4.00	8.00
❑ 74-0606	Crying in the Chapel/What Are You Doing New Year's Eve	1971	2.00	4.00	8.00

ROULETTE

Number	Title (A Side/B Side)	Yr	VG	VG+	NM
❑ 4079	Shy/First Blush	1958	5.00	10.00	20.00

'TIL TUESDAY

EPIC

Number	Title (A Side/B Side)	Yr	VG	VG+	NM
❑ 04795	Voices Carry/Are You Serious	1985	—	—	3.00
❑ 04795 [PS]	Voices Carry/Are You Serious	1985	—	—	3.00
❑ 04795 [PS]	Voices Carry	1985	—	2.50	5.00
—"Demonstration -- Not for Sale" on back					
❑ 04935	Looking Over My Shoulder (Single Mix)/Don't Watch Me Bleed	1985	—	—	3.00
❑ 04935 [PS]	Looking Over My Shoulder (Single Mix)/Don't Watch Me Bleed	1985	—	—	3.00
❑ 05673	Love in a Vacuum/No More Crying	1985	—	—	3.00
❑ 05673 [PS]	Love in a Vacuum/No More Crying	1985	—	2.00	4.00
❑ 06289	What About Love/Will She Just Fall Down	1986	—	—	3.00
❑ 06289 [PS]	What About Love/Will She Just Fall Down	1986	—	—	3.00
❑ 06450	Voices Carry/Love in a Vacuum	1986	—	—	3.00
—Reissue					
❑ 06571	Coming Up Close/Angels Never Call	1986	—	—	3.00
❑ 06571 [PS]	Coming Up Close/Angels Never Call	1986	—	3.00	6.00
❑ 08059	(Believed You Were) Lucky/Limits to Love	1988	—	—	3.00
❑ 08059 [PS]	(Believed You Were) Lucky/Limits to Love	1988	—	—	3.00
❑ 68622	Rip in Heaven/How Can You Give Up	1989	—	—	3.00

TILLIS, MEL

COLUMBIA

Number	Title (A Side/B Side)	Yr	VG	VG+	NM
❑ 4-40845	It Takes a Worried Man to Sing a Worried Song/Honky Tonk Song	1957	5.00	10.00	20.00
❑ 4-40904	Case of the Blues/It's My Life	1957	5.00	10.00	20.00
❑ 4-40944	Juke Box Man/If You'll Be My Love	1957	6.25	12.50	25.00
❑ 4-41038	This Heart/Take My Hand	1957	5.00	10.00	20.00
❑ 4-41115	Teen Age Wedding/Lonely Street	1958	7.50	15.00	30.00
❑ 4-41189	The Violet and a Rose/No Song to Sing	1958	3.75	7.50	15.00
❑ 4-41277	Finally/The Brooklyn Bridge	1958	3.75	7.50	15.00
❑ 4-41602	It's So Easy/Loco Weed	1960	3.75	7.50	15.00
❑ 4-41863	Say/Walk On, Boy	1960	3.75	7.50	15.00
❑ 4-41986	Hearts of Stone/That's Where the Hurt Comes In	1961	5.00	10.00	20.00
❑ 4-42262	Party Girl/If I Lost Your Love	1962	5.00	10.00	20.00

DECCA

Number	Title (A Side/B Side)	Yr	VG	VG+	NM
❑ 31474	Don't Tell Mama/Half Laughing, Half Crying	1963	2.50	5.00	10.00
❑ 31528	Couldn't See the Forest for the Trees/It's No Surprise	1963	2.50	5.00	10.00
❑ 31623	It'll Be Easy/I'm Gonna Act Right	1964	2.50	5.00	10.00

ELEKTRA

Number	Title (A Side/B Side)	Yr	VG	VG+	NM
❑ 46536	Blind in Love/Blackjack, Arizona	1979	—	2.00	4.00
❑ 46583	Lying Time Again/Fooled Around and Fell in Love	1980	—	2.00	4.00
❑ 46628	Your Body Is an Outlaw/Rain on My Parade	1980	—	2.00	4.00
❑ 47015	Steppin' Out/Whiskey Chasin'	1980	—	2.00	4.00
❑ 47082	Southern Rains/Forgive Me for Giving You the Blues	1980	—	2.00	4.00
❑ 47116	A Million Old Goodbyes/Louisiana Lonely	1981	—	2.00	4.00
❑ 47178	One-Night Fever/Time Has Treated You Well	1981	—	2.00	4.00
❑ 47233 [DJ]	White Christmas/Blue Christmas	1981	—	3.00	6.00
—B-side by Eddy Raven					
❑ 47412	It's a Long Way to Daytona/Always You, Always Me	1982	—	2.00	4.00
❑ 47453	The One That Got Away/Why Ain't Life the Way It's S'posed to Be	1982	—	2.00	4.00
❑ 69963	Stay a Little Longer/Dream of Me	1982	—	2.00	4.00

KAPP

Number	Title (A Side/B Side)	Yr	VG	VG+	NM
❑ 764	Mental Revenge/Guide Me Home My Georgia Moon	1966	2.50	5.00	10.00
❑ 772	Stateside/Home Is Where the Hurt Is	1966	2.00	4.00	8.00
❑ 804	Life Turned Her That Way/If I Could Only Start Over	1967	2.00	4.00	8.00
❑ 804 [PS]	Life Turned Her That Way/If I Could Only Start Over	1967	3.75	7.50	15.00
❑ 837	Goodbye Wheeling/At the Sight of You	1967	2.00	4.00	8.00
❑ 867	Survival of the Fittest/The Old Gang's Gone	1967	2.00	4.00	8.00
❑ 881	All Right (I'll Sign the Papers)/Helpless, Hopeless Fool	1968	2.00	4.00	8.00
❑ 905	Something Special/You Name It	1968	2.00	4.00	8.00
❑ 941	Destroyed by Man/I Haven't Seen Mary in Years	1968	2.00	4.00	8.00
❑ 959	Who's Julie/Give Me One More Day	1968	2.00	4.00	8.00
❑ 986	Old Faithful/Sorrow Overtakes the Wine	1969	2.00	4.00	8.00
❑ 2031	These Lonely Hands of Mine/Cover Mama's Flowers	1969	—	3.50	7.00
❑ 2072	She'll Be Hanging 'Round Somewhere/Where Love Has Died	1970	—	3.50	7.00
❑ 2086	Heart Over Mind/Lingering Memories	1970	—	3.50	7.00

Number	Title (A Side/B Side)	Yr	VG	VG+	NM
❑ 2103	Too Lonely, Too Long/Memories Made This House	1970	—	3.50	7.00
❑ 2121	One More Drink/I Could Never Be Ashamed by You	1971	—	3.50	7.00

MCA

Number	Title (A Side/B Side)	Yr	VG	VG+	NM
❑ KFC-001 [DJ]	There's No Turning Back/(B-side unknown)	1977	3.00	6.00	12.00
—Promo only; "America's Country Good Music from Kentucky Fried Chicken" on label					
❑ 40559	Love Revival/Gator Bar	1976	—	2.50	5.00
❑ 40627	Good Woman Blues/You Can't Trust a Crazy Man	1976	—	2.50	5.00
❑ 40667	Heart Healer/It's Just Not That Easy to Say	1976	—	2.50	5.00
❑ 40710	Burning Memories/Golden Nugget Gambling Casino	1977	—	2.50	5.00
❑ 40764	I Got the Hoss/It's Been a Long Time	1977	—	2.50	5.00
❑ 40836	What Did I Promise Her Last Night/Woman, You Should Be in the Movies	1977	—	2.50	5.00
❑ 40900	I Believe in You/She Don't Trust You Daddy	1978	—	2.50	5.00
❑ 40946	Ain't No California/What Comes Natural to a Fool	1978	—	2.50	5.00
❑ 40983	Send Me Down to Tucson/Charlie's Angel	1978	—	2.50	5.00
❑ 41041	Coca Cola Cowboy/Cottonmouth	1979	—	2.50	5.00
❑ 52182	In the Middle of the Night/Even at Her Worst (She's Still the Best)	1983	—	—	3.00
❑ 52247	A Cowboy's Dream/After All This Time	1983	—	—	3.00
❑ 52285	She Meant Forever When She Said Goodbye/Try It Again	1983	—	—	3.00
❑ 52373	New Patches/Almost Like You Never Went Away	1984	—	—	3.00

MERCURY

Number	Title (A Side/B Side)	Yr	VG	VG+	NM
❑ 870192-7	You'll Come Back (You Always Do)/Try It Again	1988	—	—	3.00

MGM

Number	Title (A Side/B Side)	Yr	VG	VG+	NM
❑ 14148	Heaven Everyday/How Do You Drink the Wine	1970	—	3.00	6.00
❑ 14176	Commercial Affection/I Thought About You	1970	—	3.00	6.00
❑ 14211	The Arms of a Fool/Veil of White Lace	1971	—	3.00	6.00
❑ 14275	Brand New Mister Me/Brand New Wrapper	1971	—	3.00	6.00
❑ 14329	Untouched/I Went a Ramblin'	1971	—	3.00	6.00
❑ 14372	Would You Want the World to End/Things Have Changed a Lot	1972	—	3.00	6.00
❑ 14418	I Ain't Never/Border of Love	1972	—	3.00	6.00
❑ 14454	Neon Rose/It's My Love	1972	—	3.00	6.00
❑ 14522	Thank You for Being You/Over the Hill	1973	—	3.00	6.00
❑ 14585	Sawmill/Mama's Gonna Pray	1973	—	3.00	6.00
❑ 14689	Midnight, Me and the Blues/Modern Home Magazine	1974	—	3.00	6.00
❑ 14720	Stomp Them Grapes/Hang My Pictures in Your Heart	1974	—	3.00	6.00
❑ 14744	Memory Maker/Second Best	1974	—	3.00	6.00
❑ 14782	Best Way I Know How/Honey Dew Melon	1975	—	3.00	6.00
❑ 14804	Woman in the Back of My Mind/Kissing Your Picture (Is So Cold)	1975	—	3.00	6.00
❑ 14835	Lookin' for Tomorrow (And Findin' Yesterdays)/Tennessee Banjo Man	1975	—	3.00	6.00
❑ 14846	Mental Revenge/My Bad Girl	1976	—	3.00	6.00
❑ 14850	Always Just a Memory Away/Come On Home	1976	—	3.00	6.00

RADIO

Number	Title (A Side/B Side)	Yr	VG	VG+	NM
❑ 001	City Lights/Who's Julie	1989	—	3.00	6.00

RCA

Number	Title (A Side/B Side)	Yr	VG	VG+	NM
❑ PB-14061	You Done Me Wrong/Another Heart Down	1985	—	—	3.00
❑ PB-14175	California Road/One More Time	1985	—	—	3.00

RIC

Number	Title (A Side/B Side)	Yr	VG	VG+	NM
❑ 150	Ode to the Little Brown Shack Out Back/Not in Front of the Kids	1965	3.00	6.00	12.00
❑ 158	Wine/Buried Alive	1965	3.00	6.00	12.00
❑ 178	Bring On the Blues/Mr. Dropout	1965	3.00	6.00	12.00

STARDAY

Number	Title (A Side/B Side)	Yr	VG	VG+	NM
❑ 8036	Wine/Stateside	197?	—	2.50	5.00

TILLIS, MEL, AND SHERRY BRYCE

MGM

Number	Title (A Side/B Side)	Yr	VG	VG+	NM
❑ 14255	Take My Hand/Life's Little Surprises	1971	—	3.00	6.00
❑ 14303	Living and Learning/Tangled Vines	1971	—	3.00	6.00
❑ 14365	Anything's Better Than Nothing/Then It Will Be All Over	1972	—	3.00	6.00
❑ 14472	Back to Life/Happyville	1972	—	3.00	6.00
❑ 14660	Let's Go All the Way Tonight/In the Vine	1973	—	3.00	6.00
❑ 14714	Don't Let Go/Why Not Do the Things (They Think We've Done)	1974	—	3.00	6.00
❑ 14776	You Are the One/I Saw Heaven in You	1974	—	3.00	6.00
❑ 14803	Mr. Right and Mrs. Wrong/Just Two Strangers Passing in the Night	1975	—	3.00	6.00

TILLIS, MEL, WITH GLEN CAMPBELL

Also see each artist's individual listings.

MCA

Number	Title (A Side/B Side)	Yr	VG	VG+	NM
❑ 52474	Slow Nights/Midnight Love	1984	—	—	3.00

TILLIS, MEL, AND BILL PHILLIPS

COLUMBIA

Number	Title (A Side/B Side)	Yr	VG	VG+	NM
❑ 4-41416	Sawmill/You Are the Reason	1959	3.75	7.50	15.00
❑ 4-41530	Georgia Town Blues/Till I Get Enough of These Blues	1959	3.75	7.50	15.00

TILLIS, MEL, AND WEBB PIERCE

Also see each artist's individual listings.

DECCA

Number	Title (A Side/B Side)	Yr	VG	VG+	NM
❑ 31445	How Come Your Dog Don't Bite Nobody But Me/So Soon	1962	2.50	5.00	10.00

TILLIS, MEL, AND NANCY SINATRA

Also see each artist's individual listings.

ELEKTRA

Number	Title (A Side/B Side)	Yr	VG	VG+	NM
❑ 47157	Texas Cowboy Night/After the Lovin'	1981	—	2.50	5.00
❑ 47234 [DJ]	Rudolph the Red-Nosed Reindeer/Winter Wonderland	1981	2.00	4.00	8.00
—As "Mel and Nancy"; B-side by Dave Rowland and Sugar					
❑ 47247	Play Me or Trade Me/Where Would I Be	1981	—	2.50	5.00

TILLOTSON, JOHNNY

AMOS

Number	Title (A Side/B Side)	Yr	VG	VG+	NM
❑ 117	Tears on My Pillow/Remember When	1969	—	3.00	6.00
❑ 125	What Am I Living For/Joy to the World	1969	—	3.00	6.00
❑ 128	Raining in My Heart/Today I Started Loving You Again	1969	—	3.00	6.00
❑ 136	Susan/Love Waits for Me	1970	—	3.00	6.00
❑ 146	I Don't Believe In It Anymore/Kansas City, Kansas	1970	—	3.00	6.00

ATLANTIC

Number	Title (A Side/B Side)	Yr	VG	VG+	NM
❑ 87978	Bim Bam Boom/(B-side unknown)	1990	—	2.00	4.00

BUDDAH

Number	Title (A Side/B Side)	Yr	VG	VG+	NM
❑ 232	Star Spangled Bus/Apple Bend	1971	—	2.50	5.00
❑ 256	Welfare Hero/The Flower Kissed the Shoes That Jesus Wore	1971	—	2.50	5.00
❑ 279	Make Me Believe/The Flower Kissed the Shoes That Jesus Wore	1972	—	2.50	5.00
❑ 311	Your Love's Been a Long Time Comin'/Apple Bend	1972	—	2.50	5.00

CADENCE

Number	Title (A Side/B Side)	Yr	VG	VG+	NM
❑ 1353	Dreamy Eyes/Well, I'm Your Man	1958	5.00	10.00	20.00
❑ 1354	I'm Never Gonna Kiss You/Cherie, Cherie	1958	6.25	12.50	25.00
—With Genevieve					
❑ 1365	True True Happiness/Love Is Blind	1959	5.00	10.00	20.00
❑ 1372	Why Do I Love You So/Never Let Me Go	1959	5.00	10.00	20.00
❑ 1377	Earth Angel/Pledging My Love	1960	5.00	10.00	20.00
❑ 1377 [PS]	Earth Angel/Pledging My Love	1960	7.50	15.00	30.00
❑ 1384	Poetry in Motion/Princess, Princess	1960	5.00	10.00	20.00
❑ 1391	Jimmy's Girl/His True Love Said Godbye	1960	3.75	7.50	15.00
❑ 1391 [PS]	Jimmy's Girl/His True Love Said Godbye	1960	7.50	15.00	30.00
❑ 1404	Without You/Cutie Pie	1961	3.75	7.50	15.00
❑ 1409	Dreamy Eyes/Well, I'm Your Man	1961	3.75	7.50	15.00
❑ 1418	It Keeps Right On a-Hurtin'/She Gave Sweet Love to Me	1962	3.75	7.50	15.00
❑ 1424	Send Me the Pillow You Dream On/What'll I Do	1962	3.75	7.50	15.00
❑ 1432	I Can't Help It (If I'm Still in Love with You)/I'm So Lonesome I Could Cry	1962	3.75	7.50	15.00
❑ 1434	Out of My Mind/Empty Feelin'	1963	3.75	7.50	15.00
❑ 1437	You Can Never Stop Me Loving You/Judy, Judy, Judy	1963	3.75	7.50	15.00
❑ 1441	Funny How Time Slips Away/A Very Good Year for Girls	1963	3.75	7.50	15.00

COLUMBIA

Number	Title (A Side/B Side)	Yr	VG	VG+	NM
❑ 10125	Big Ole Jean/Mississippi Lady	1975	—	2.50	5.00
❑ 10199	Right Here in Your Arms/Willow County Request Live	1975	—	2.50	5.00
❑ 45842	Sunshine of My Life/If You Wouldn't Be My Lady	1973	—	2.50	5.00
❑ 45984	So Much of My Life/I Love How She Needs Me	1973	—	2.50	5.00
❑ 46065	Till I Can't Take It Anymore/Sunday Kind of Woman	1974	—	2.50	5.00

MGM

Number	Title (A Side/B Side)	Yr	VG	VG+	NM
❑ 13181	Talk Back Trembling Lips/Another You	1963	3.00	6.00	12.00
❑ 13181 [PS]	Talk Back Trembling Lips/Another You	1963	5.00	10.00	20.00
❑ 13193	Worried Guy/Please Don't Go Away	1963	2.50	5.00	10.00
❑ 13193 [PS]	Worried Guy/Please Don't Go Away	1963	5.00	10.00	20.00
❑ 13232	I Rise, I Fall/I'm Watching My Watch	1964	2.50	5.00	10.00
❑ 13232 [PS]	I Rise, I Fall/I'm Watching My Watch	1964	5.00	10.00	20.00
❑ 13255	Worry/Sufferin' from a Heartache	1964	2.50	5.00	10.00
❑ 13255 [PS]	Worry/Sufferin' from a Heartache	1964	5.00	10.00	20.00
❑ 13284	She Understands Me/Tomorrow	1964	2.50	5.00	10.00
❑ 13284 [PS]	She Understands Me/Tomorrow	1964	5.00	10.00	20.00
❑ 13316	Angel/Little Boy	1965	2.50	5.00	10.00
❑ 13316 [PS]	Angel/Little Boy	1965	5.00	10.00	20.00
❑ 13344	Then I'll Count Again/One's Yours, One's Mine	1965	2.50	5.00	10.00
❑ 13344 [PS]	Then I'll Count Again/One's Yours, One's Mine	1965	5.00	10.00	20.00
❑ 13376	Heartaches by the Number/Your Mem'ry Comes Along	1965	2.50	5.00	10.00
❑ 13376 [PS]	Heartaches by the Number/Your Mem'ry Comes Along	1965	5.00	10.00	20.00
❑ 13408	Our World/(Wait 'Till You See) My Gidget	1965	2.50	5.00	10.00
❑ 13445	Hello Enemy/I Never Loved You Anyway	1966	2.50	5.00	10.00
❑ 13499	Me, Myself and I/Country Boy, Country Boy	1966	2.50	5.00	10.00
❑ 13519	No Love at All/What Am I Gonna Do	1966	2.50	5.00	10.00
❑ 13598	More Than Before/Baby's Gone	1966	2.50	5.00	10.00
❑ 13598	More Than Before/Open Up Your Heart	1966	2.50	5.00	10.00
❑ 13633	Christmas Country Style/Christmas Is the Best of All	1966	2.50	5.00	10.00
❑ 13684	Strange Things Happen/Tommy Jones	1967	2.50	5.00	10.00
❑ 13738	Don't Tell Me It's Raining/Takin' It Easy	1967	2.50	5.00	10.00
❑ 13829	You're the Reason/Countin' My Teardrops	1967	2.50	5.00	10.00
❑ 13888	I Can Spot a Cheater/It Keeps Right On a-Hurtin'	1968	2.00	4.00	8.00
❑ 13924	I Haven't Begun to Love You Yet/Why So Lonely	1968	2.00	4.00	8.00
❑ 13977	Letter to Emily/Your Mem'ry Comes Along	1968	2.00	4.00	8.00

REWARD

Number	Title (A Side/B Side)	Yr	VG	VG+	NM
❑ 03327	Baby You Do It for Me (And I'll Do It for You)/She's Not As Married As She Used to Be	1982	—	2.00	4.00
❑ 03901	Crying/You're a Beautiful Place to Be	1983	—	2.00	4.00
❑ 04123	Burnin'/What's Another Year	1983	—	2.00	4.00
❑ 04346	Lay Back (In the Arms of Somebody)/What's Another Year	1984	—	2.00	4.00

SCEPTER

Number	Title (A Side/B Side)	Yr	VG	VG+	NM
❑ 12389	Song for Hank Williams (mono/stereo)	1973	2.00	4.00	8.00
—With John Edward Beland; may be promo-only					

UNITED ARTISTS

Number	Title (A Side/B Side)	Yr	VG	VG+	NM
❑ XW860	It Could've Been Nashville/Summertime Lovin'	1976	—	2.50	5.00
❑ XW986	Toy Hearts/Just An Ordinary Man	1977	—	2.50	5.00

7-Inch Extended Plays

CADENCE

Number	Title (A Side/B Side)	Yr	VG	VG+	NM
❑ CEP-114	True True Happiness/Love Is Blind//Dreamy Eyes/Well I'm Your Man	1960	6.25	12.50	25.00
❑ CEP-114 [PS]	Johnny Tillotson	1960	6.25	12.50	25.00

Number	Title (A Side/B Side)	Yr	VG	VG+	NM
TIM TAM AND THE TURN-ONS					
PALMER					
❑ 5002	Wait a Minute/Ophelia	1965	6.25	12.50	25.00
❑ 5003	Cheryl Ann/Sealed with a Kiss	1966	7.50	15.00	30.00
❑ 5006	Kimberly/I Leave You in Tears	1966	10.00	20.00	40.00
❑ 5014	Don't Say Hi/(Instrumental)	1967	6.25	12.50	25.00
TIMERS, THE					
With GARY USHER and BRIAN WILSON.					
REPRISE					
❑ 20231	No-Go Showboat/Competition Coupe	1963	25.00	50.00	100.00
TIMETONES, THE					
ATCO					
❑ 6201	I've Got a Feeling/(B-side unknown)	1961	6.25	12.50	25.00
TIMES SQUARE					
❑ 421	Here in My Heart/(B-side unknown)	1961	7.50	15.00	30.00
❑ 421	In My Heart/(B-side unknown)	1961	5.00	10.00	20.00
TIN TIN					
ATCO					
❑ 6794	Toast and Marmalade for Tea/Manhattan Woman	1971	2.00	4.00	8.00
❑ 6821	Is That the Way/Swans on the Canal	1971	—	3.00	6.00
❑ 6853	Set Sail for England/The Cavalry Is Coming	1971	—	3.00	6.00
POLYDOR					
❑ 15055	Talking Turkey/The Cavalry Is Coming	1972	—	3.00	6.00
SIRE					
❑ 29750	Kiss Me/Kiss Me	1983	—	2.50	5.00
TINGLING MOTHER'S CIRCUS					
MUSICOR					
❑ 1335	Positively Negative/Sunday Kind of Feeling	1968	2.50	5.00	10.00
❑ 1359	I Found a New Love/Happy Bubble	1969	2.50	5.00	10.00
ROULETTE					
❑ 4758	Face in My Mind/Isn't It Strange	1967	3.75	7.50	15.00
TINY TIM					
BLUE CAT					
❑ 127	April Showers/Little Girl	1966	3.00	6.00	12.00
CLOUDS					
❑ 17	Tip Toe to the Gas Pumps/Hickey on Your Neck	1979	2.50	5.00	10.00
NLT					
❑ 1993	Leave Me Satisfied/I Wanna' Get Crazy with You	1988	2.00	4.00	8.00
REPRISE					
❑ 0679	Tip-Toe Thru' the Tulips with Me/Fill Your Heart	1968	2.00	4.00	8.00
❑ 0740	Tip-Toe Thru' the Tulips with Me/Don't Bite the Hand That's Feeding You	1971	—	2.00	4.00
—"Back to Back Hits" series					
❑ 0760	Bring Back Those Rock-A-Bye Baby Days/Hello, Hello	1968	—	3.00	6.00
❑ 0760	Bring Back Those Rock-A-Bye Baby Days/This Is All I Ask	1968	—	3.00	6.00
❑ 0769	Be My Love/This Is All I Ask	1968	—	3.00	6.00
❑ 0802	Great Balls of Fire/As Time Goes By	1969	—	3.00	6.00
❑ 0837	On the Good Ship Lollipop/America I Love You	1969	—	3.00	6.00
❑ 0855	Mickey the Monkey/Neighborhood Children	1969	—	3.00	6.00
❑ 0867	I'm a Lonesome Little Raindrop/What the World Needs Now Is Love	1969	—	3.00	6.00
❑ 0939	Don't Bite the Hand That's Feeding You/What Kind of American Are You	1970	—	3.00	6.00
❑ 0985	Why/Spaceship Song	1971	—	3.00	6.00
—With Miss Vicky					
❑ 20174	Bring Back Rockabye Baby Days/Just Say I Love Her	1963	3.00	6.00	12.00
—B-side by Johnny Prophet					
SCEPTER					
❑ 12351	Am I Just Another Pretty Face/The Movies	1972	—	3.00	6.00
VICTIM					
❑ 1001	Rudolph The Red-Nosed Reindeer/White Christmas	198?	3.00	6.00	12.00
TINY TIM AND THE HITS					
ROULETTE					
❑ 4123	Wedding Bells/Doll Baby	1958	12.50	25.00	50.00
TITANS, THE					
More than one group.					
BANGAR					
❑ 00611	Surfer's Lullaby/Motivation	1964	6.25	12.50	25.00
CLASS					
❑ 244	No Time/The Tootin' Tutor	1959	6.25	12.50	25.00
DUFF'S					
❑ 111	Little Girl/Pretty Young Thing	1969	3.00	6.00	12.00
❑ 112	Ode to Billy Martin/Please Don't Be Angry	1970	3.00	6.00	12.00
FIDELITY					
❑ 3016	What Have I Done/Everybody Happy?	1960	7.50	15.00	30.00
METROBEAT					
❑ 4452	To Covet the Turf/Mountain of Love	196?	5.00	10.00	20.00
MGM					
❑ 13207	Yojimbo/Midnight in Tokyo	1964	3.00	6.00	12.00
—B-side by the Tokyo Boys					
NOLTA					
❑ 351	A-Rab/Marquette	1961	6.25	12.50	25.00
SOMA					
❑ 1402	A Summer Place/Tchaikovsky Rides Again	1963	5.00	10.00	20.00
❑ 1411	The No Place Special/Reveille Rock	1964	5.00	10.00	20.00
SOUND OF MUSIC					
❑ 12186	Need You/Fun Seekers	196?	3.00	6.00	12.00
❑ 12186 [PS]	Need You/Fun Seekers	196?	12.50	25.00	50.00
SPECIALTY					
❑ 614	Sweet Peach/Free and Easy	1957	6.25	12.50	25.00
❑ 625	Don't You Just Know It/Can It Be	1958	6.25	12.50	25.00
❑ 632	Arlene/Love Is a Wonderful Thing	1958	6.25	12.50	25.00
STUDIO CITY					
❑ 1008	The No Place Special/Reveille Rock	1964	10.00	20.00	40.00
VITA					
❑ 148	Rhythm and Blues/So Hard to Laugh, So Easy to Cry	1957	18.75	37.50	75.00
❑ 158	G'Wan Home Calypso/Look What You're Doing Baby	1957	15.00	30.00	60.00
TITONES, THE					
SCEPTER					
❑ 1206	Symbol of Love/The Movies	1960	12.50	25.00	50.00
—White label					
❑ 1206	Symbol of Love/The Movies	1960	6.25	12.50	25.00
—Red label					
WAND					
❑ 105	Symbol of Love/My Movie Queen	1960	5.00	10.00	20.00
TOBY BEAU					
RCA					
❑ PB-11250	My Angel Baby/California	1978	—	2.50	5.00
❑ PB-11388	Into the Night/Wink of an Eye	1978	—	2.00	4.00
❑ PB-11670	Then You Can Tell Me Goodbye/Boogie Woogie Melody	1979	—	2.00	4.00
❑ PB-11964	If I Were You/If You Believe	1980	—	2.00	4.00
❑ PB-12098	Ships in the Night/Little Miss American Dream	1980	—	2.00	4.00
TODAY AND TOMORROW					
NOOSE					
❑ 812	Dooley Swings (Part 1)/Dooley Swings (Part 2)	1959	10.00	20.00	40.00
TODD, ART AND DOTTY					
ABBOTT					
❑ 3006	Busy Signal/Oh Honey Why Don't Cha	1955	5.00	10.00	20.00
CAPITOL					
❑ 4778	Sweet Someone/Ring-a-Ding	1962	2.00	4.00	8.00
DART					
❑ 404	Wait for Me/Joie de Vivre	1956	3.00	6.00	12.00
❑ 405	Chop Chop/Say You	1956	3.00	6.00	12.00
❑ 51986	Blueberry Hill/Wonderful, Loveable You	1959	2.50	5.00	10.00
DECCA					
❑ 31227	Ca C'est La Vie/Drifting and Dreaming	1961	2.50	5.00	10.00
❑ 31329	Your Cheatin' Heart/Sweet Cha Cha Chariot	1961	2.50	5.00	10.00
DOT					
❑ 16939	I'll Take Care of Your Cares/Bodie Tree	1966	—	3.00	6.00
ERA					
❑ 1064	Chanson D'Amour (Song of Love)/Along the Trail with You	1957	3.00	6.00	12.00
❑ 1076	Au Revoir Amour/Der Glockenspiel	1958	2.50	5.00	10.00
❑ 1087	Pray/Don't You Worry My Little Pet	1958	2.50	5.00	10.00
❑ 1088	Straight as an Arrow/Stand There Mountain	1959	2.50	5.00	10.00
❑ 3001	Paradise/Ayuh Ayuh	1959	2.50	5.00	10.00
RCA VICTOR					
❑ 47-5029	Heavenly Heavenly/Broken Wings	1952	3.75	7.50	15.00
SIGNET					
❑ 2020	Bernadette Soubirous/Bodie Tree	1965	2.00	4.00	8.00
TODD, DYLAN					
RCA VICTOR					
❑ 47-6463	The Ballad of James Dean/More Precious Than Gold	1956	7.50	15.00	30.00
❑ 47-6463 [PS]	The Ballad of James Dean/More Precious Than Gold	1956	12.50	25.00	50.00
❑ 47-6711	Timber/Golden Spurs and a Silver Saddle	1956	5.00	10.00	20.00
TODD, FULLER					
KING					
❑ 5048	Old Fashioned/Proud Lady Heart Stealer	1957	6.25	12.50	25.00
❑ 5075	Real True Love/Young Hearts Are True	1957	6.25	12.50	25.00
❑ 5111	Top Ten Rock/Jeannie Marie	1958	6.25	12.50	25.00
TODD, JOHNNY					
MODERN					
❑ 1003	Pink Cadillac/What's Up	1956	30.00	60.00	120.00
TODD, NICK					
DOT					
❑ 15643	Plaything/The Honey Song	1957	5.00	10.00	20.00
❑ 15675	At the Hop/I Do	1957	5.00	10.00	20.00
❑ 15688	Teen-Age Cutie/Ever Since I Met Lucy	1958	5.00	10.00	20.00
❑ 15772	Forever and a Day/Too Much Rosita	1958	5.00	10.00	20.00
❑ 15860	My Little Girl/Does Your Heart Beat for Me?	1958	5.00	10.00	20.00
❑ 15893	Red Roses for a Blue Lady/Little Rosey Red	1959	3.75	7.50	15.00
❑ 15951	Tiger/Twice As Nice	1959	3.75	7.50	15.00
❑ 15981	Invisible Man/Sayin' Something	1959	3.75	7.50	15.00
❑ 16109	Each Moment/Your Love's Gotta Grip on Me	1960	3.75	7.50	15.00
TOGGERY FIVE, THE					
TOWER					
❑ 119	I'm Gonna Jump/Bye Bye Bird	1965	3.75	7.50	15.00
TOKAYS, THE					
BONNIE					
❑ 102	Lost and Found/Fatty-Boom Bi Laddy	1962	25.00	50.00	100.00
BRUTE					
❑ 001	Hey Senorita/Baby Baby Baby	1967	30.00	60.00	120.00
SCORPIO					
❑ 403	Now/Ask Me No Questions	1966	5.00	10.00	20.00

TOKENS, THE

NEIL SEDAKA was (very) briefly a member. Also see THE COEDS; CROSS COUNTRY; THE FOUR WINDS (1); JOHNNY AND THE TOKENS; UNITED STATES DOUBLE QUARTET.

Number	Title (A Side/B Side)	Yr	VG	VG+	NM
ATCO					
❑ 7009	The Lord Can't Sing a Solo/Penny Whistle Band	1974	—	3.00	6.00
BELL					
❑ 45190	You and Me/I Like to Throw My Head Back and Sing	1972	—	3.00	6.00
BUDDAH					
❑ 151	She Lets Her Hair Down (Early in the Morning)/Oh to Get Away	1970	—	3.00	6.00
❑ 159	Don't Worry Baby/If the Shoe Fits Ya Baby	1970	—	2.50	5.00
❑ 159	Don't Worry Baby/Some People Sleep	1970	—	2.50	5.00
❑ 174	Both Sides Now/I Could See Me (Dancin' with You)	1970	—	2.50	5.00
❑ 187	Listen to the Words (Listen to the Music)/Groovin' On the Sunshine	1970	—	2.50	5.00
B.T. PUPPY					
❑ 500	A Girl Named Arlene/Swing	1964	3.00	6.00	12.00
❑ 502	He's in Town/Oh Cathy	1964	3.00	6.00	12.00
❑ 504	You're My Girl/Havin' Fun	1964	3.00	6.00	12.00
❑ 505	Nobody But You/Mr. Cupid	1965	2.50	5.00	10.00
❑ 507	A Message to the World/Sylvie Sleepin'	1965	2.50	5.00	10.00
❑ 512	Only My Friend/Cattle Call	1965	2.50	5.00	10.00
❑ 513	The Bells of St. Mary/Just One Smile	1966	2.50	5.00	10.00
❑ 515	The Three Bells/Message to the World	1966	2.50	5.00	10.00
❑ 518	I Hear Trumpets Blow/Don't Cry, Sing Along with the Music	1966	2.50	5.00	10.00
❑ 519	Breezy/Greatest Moments of a Girl's Life	1966	2.50	5.00	10.00
❑ 519 [PS]	Breezy/Greatest Moments of a Girl's Life	1966	6.25	12.50	25.00
❑ 525	Green Plant/Saloogy	1967	2.50	5.00	10.00
❑ 552	Please Say You Want Me/Get a Job	1969	2.50	5.00	10.00
DATE					
❑ 2737	Oh What a Night/(Hey Hey) Juanita	1961	12.50	25.00	50.00
GARY					
❑ 1006	Doom-Lang/Come Dance with Me	1961	25.00	50.00	100.00
LAURIE					
❑ 3180	I'll Always Love You/Please Write	1963	5.00	10.00	20.00
MELBA					
❑ 104	While I Dream/I Love My Baby	1956	12.50	25.00	50.00
RCA					
❑ 8749-7-R	Re-Doo-Wopp/I'm Through with You	1988	—	2.00	4.00
❑ 8836-7-R	Re-Doo-Wopp (Edit)/I'm Through with You	1988	—	2.00	4.00
RCA VICTOR					
❑ 37-7896	When I Go to Sleep at Night/Dry Your Eyes	1961	10.00	20.00	40.00
—"Compact Single 33" (small hole, plays at LP speed)					
❑ 37-7925	Sincerely/When the Summer Is Through	1961	10.00	20.00	40.00
—"Compact Single 33" (small hole, plays at LP speed)					
❑ 37-7954	The Lion Sleeps Tonight/Tina	1961	12.50	25.00	50.00
—"Compact Single 33" (small hole, plays at LP speed)					
❑ 37-7991	B'wa Nina/Weeping River	1962	10.00	20.00	40.00
—"Compact Single 33" (small hole, plays at LP speed)					
❑ 37-8018	The Riddle/Big Boat	1962	10.00	20.00	40.00
—"Compact Single 33" (small hole, plays at LP speed)					
❑ 47-7896	When I Go to Sleep at Night/Dry Your Eyes	1961	5.00	10.00	20.00
❑ 47-7896 [PS]	When I Go to Sleep at Night/Dry Your Eyes	1961	10.00	20.00	40.00
❑ 47-7925	Sincerely/When the Summer Is Through	1961	5.00	10.00	20.00
❑ 47-7954	The Lion Sleeps Tonight/Tina	1961	6.25	12.50	25.00
❑ 47-7991	B'wa Nina/Weeping River	1962	5.00	10.00	20.00
❑ 47-7991 [PS]	B'wa Nina/Weeping River	1962	12.50	25.00	50.00
—No mention of "The Lion Sleeps Tonight" LP on sleeve					
❑ 47-7991 [PS]	B'wa Nina/Weeping River	1962	7.50	15.00	30.00
—"The Lion Sleeps Tonight" LP mentioned on sleeve					
❑ 47-8018	The Riddle/Big Boat	1962	5.00	10.00	20.00
❑ 47-8018 [PS]	The Riddle/Big Boat	1962	10.00	20.00	40.00
❑ 47-8052	La Bomba/A Token of Love	1962	5.00	10.00	20.00
❑ 47-8052 [PS]	La Bomba/A Token of Love	1962	10.00	20.00	40.00
❑ 47-8089	I'll Do My Crying Tomorrow/Dream Angel Goodnight	1962	5.00	10.00	20.00
❑ 47-8089 [PS]	I'll Do My Crying Tomorrow/Dream Angel Goodnight	1962	10.00	20.00	40.00
❑ 47-8114	A Bird Flies Out of Sight/Wishing	1962	5.00	10.00	20.00
❑ 47-8114 [PS]	A Bird Flies Out of Sight/Wishing	1962	10.00	20.00	40.00
❑ 47-8148	Tonight I Met An Angel/Hindi Lullabye	1963	3.75	7.50	15.00
❑ 47-8148 [PS]	Tonight I Met An Angel/Hindi Lullabye	1963	7.50	15.00	30.00
❑ 47-8210	Hear the Bells/ABC 1-2-3	1963	3.75	7.50	15.00
❑ 47-8210 [PS]	Hear the Bells/ABC 1-2-3	1963	7.50	15.00	30.00
❑ 47-8309	Two Cars/Let's Go to the Drag Strip	1963	3.75	7.50	15.00
❑ 47-8309 [PS]	Two Cars/Let's Go to the Drag Strip	1963	20.00	40.00	80.00
ROULETTE					
❑ 4174	Roses Are Red/Pictures in My Wallet	1959	7.50	15.00	30.00
—As "Darrell and the Oxfords"					
❑ 4230	Can't You Tell/Your Mother Said So	1960	7.50	15.00	30.00
—As "Darrell and the Oxfords"					
RUST					
❑ 5094	Arlene/Rumble in the Park	1965	2.50	5.00	10.00
WARNER BROS.					
❑ 5900	Portrait of My Love/She Comes and Goes	1967	2.00	4.00	8.00
❑ 5900 [PS]	Portrait of My Love/She Comes and Goes	1967	5.00	10.00	20.00
❑ 7056	It's a Happening World/How Nice	1967	—	3.00	6.00
❑ 7099	Ain't That Peculiar/Bye, Bye, Bye	1967	—	3.00	6.00
❑ 7118	Portrait of My Love/It's a Happening World	1968	—	2.50	5.00
—"Back to Back Hits" series -- originals have green labels with "W7" logo					
❑ 7169	Till/Poor Man	1968	—	3.00	6.00
❑ 7183	Mister Snail/Needles of Evergreen	1968	2.50	5.00	10.00
—As "Margo, Margo, Medress and Siegel"					
❑ 7202	Animal/Bathroom Wall	1968	—	3.00	6.00
❑ 7233	Grandfather/The Banana Boat Song	1968	—	3.00	6.00
❑ 7255	The World Is Full of Wonderful Things/Some People Sleep	1968	—	3.00	6.00
❑ 7280	Go Away Little Girl-Young Girl/I Want to Make Love to You	1969	—	3.00	6.00
❑ 7323	I Could Be/End of the World	1969	—	3.00	6.00
WARWICK					
❑ 615	Tonight I Fell in Love/I'll Always Love You	1961	7.50	15.00	30.00

TOLLIVER, MICKEY, AND THE CAPITOLS

Number	Title (A Side/B Side)	Yr	VG	VG+	NM
CINDY					
❑ 3002	Rose Marie/Millie	1957	50.00	100.00	200.00

TOM AND JERRIO

Number	Title (A Side/B Side)	Yr	VG	VG+	NM
ABC-PARAMOUNT					
❑ 10638	Boo-Ga-Loo/Boomerang	1965	3.00	6.00	12.00
❑ 10704	Great Goo-Ga Moo-Ga/Come On and Love Me	1965	3.00	6.00	12.00
❑ 10787	Oolya-Coo/Bacardi	1966	3.00	6.00	12.00

TOM AND JERRY (1)

"Tommy Graph" and "Jerry Landis," i.e., ART GARFUNKEL and PAUL SIMON. Also see SIMON AND GARFUNKEL.

Number	Title (A Side/B Side)	Yr	VG	VG+	NM
ABC-PARAMOUNT					
❑ 10363	Surrender, Please Surrender/Fightin' Mad	1962	10.00	20.00	40.00
❑ 10788	That's My Story/Tia-Juana Blues	1966	5.00	10.00	20.00
—As "Simon and Garfunkel" (may have been reissued as "Tom and Jerry", but we don't know)					
BELL					
❑ 120	Baby Talk/I'm Gonna Get Married	1959	12.50	25.00	50.00
—B-side by Ronnie Lawrence					
❑ 120 [PS]	Baby Talk/I'm Gonna Get Married	1959	25.00	50.00	100.00
BIG					
❑ 613	Hey, Schoolgirl/Dancin' Wild	1957	12.50	25.00	50.00
—With songwriting credits as "Tommy Graph-Jerry Landis"					
❑ 613	Hey, Schoolgirl/Dancin' Wild	1957	12.50	25.00	50.00
—With songwriting credits as "Paul Simon-Art Garfunkel"					
❑ 616	Our Song/Two Teen Agers	1958	12.50	25.00	50.00
❑ 618	That's My Story/Don't Say Goodbye	1958	12.50	25.00	50.00
❑ 621	Baby Talk/Two Teen Agers	1959	—	—	—
—Unreleased?					
EMBER					
❑ 1094	I'm Lonesome/Looking at You	1959	12.50	25.00	50.00
HUNT					
❑ 319	That's My Story/Don't Say Goodbye	1959	12.50	25.00	50.00
KING					
❑ 5167	Hey, Schoolgirl/Dancin' Wild	1958	20.00	40.00	80.00

TOM AND JERRY (2)

Tommy Tomlinson and Jerry Kennedy, a country instrumental duo.

Number	Title (A Side/B Side)	Yr	VG	VG+	NM
MERCURY					
❑ 71753	Golden Wildwood Flower/South	1961	5.00	10.00	20.00
❑ 71827	Swing Low/Sungarfoot Rag	1961	5.00	10.00	20.00
❑ 71930	I'll Drown in My Tears/French Twist	1961	5.00	10.00	20.00

TOMMY AND THE HUSTLERS

Number	Title (A Side/B Side)	Yr	VG	VG+	NM
FANTASY					
❑ 573	Diggin' Out/The Right Size	1963	10.00	20.00	40.00
—Green vinyl					
❑ 573	Diggin' Out/The Right Size	1963	6.25	12.50	25.00

TONETTES, THE

Two different groups?

Number	Title (A Side/B Side)	Yr	VG	VG+	NM
ABC-PARAMOUNT					
❑ 9905	Oh What a Baby/Howie	1958	5.00	10.00	20.00
DOE					
❑ 101	Oh What a Baby/Howie	1958	20.00	40.00	80.00
❑ 103	Uh Oh/He Loves Me, He Loves Me Not	1958	15.00	30.00	60.00
MODERN					
❑ 997	Tonight You Belong to Me/Don't Fall in Love Too Soon	1956	6.25	12.50	25.00
VOLT					
❑ 101	Please Don't Go/No Tears	1962	5.00	10.00	20.00
❑ 104	Stolen Angel/Teardrop Sea	1963	5.00	10.00	20.00

TONY AND THE DAYDREAMS

Number	Title (A Side/B Side)	Yr	VG	VG+	NM
PLANET					
❑ 1008	Why Don't You Be Nice/I'll Never Tell	1958	25.00	50.00	100.00
❑ 1054	Christmas Lullaby/Handin' Hand	1961	50.00	100.00	200.00

TONY AND THE HOLIDAYS

Number	Title (A Side/B Side)	Yr	VG	VG+	NM
ABC-PARAMOUNT					
❑ 10295	There Goes My Heart Again/My Love Is Real	1962	50.00	100.00	200.00

TONY AND THE MASQUINS

Number	Title (A Side/B Side)	Yr	VG	VG+	NM
RUTHIE					
❑ 1000	My Angel Eyes/Fugi Womma	1961	25.00	50.00	100.00

TONY AND THE RAINDROPS

Number	Title (A Side/B Side)	Yr	VG	VG+	NM
CHESAPEKE					
❑ 609	While Walking/Our Love Is Over	1961	15.00	30.00	60.00
CROSLEY					
❑ 340	Tina/My Heart Cried	1962	50.00	100.00	200.00

TONY AND THE TECHNICS

See THE TECHNICS.

TONY AND THE TWILIGHTERS

Early version of ANTHONY AND THE SOPHOMORES.

Number	Title (A Side/B Side)	Yr	VG	VG+	NM
JALYNNE					
❑ 106	Be My Girl/Did You Make Up Your Mind	1960	20.00	40.00	80.00
RED TOP					
❑ 127	Key to My Heart/Yes or No	1960	50.00	100.00	200.00

TONY AND TYRONE

Number	Title (A Side/B Side)	Yr	VG	VG+	NM
ATLANTIC					
❑ 2458	Please Operator/Apple of My Eye	1967	7.50	15.00	30.00

Number	Title (A Side/B Side)	Yr	VG	VG+	NM
COLUMBIA					
❑ 43432	Turn It On/Talkin' About the People	1965	3.75	7.50	15.00

TOOMORROW
OLIVIA NEWTON-JOHN was in this group.

Number	Title (A Side/B Side)	Yr	VG	VG+	NM
KIRSHNER					
❑ 63-5005	Goin' Back/You're My Baby Now	1970	15.00	30.00	60.00

TOONE, GENE

Number	Title (A Side/B Side)	Yr	VG	VG+	NM
ANNETTE					
❑ 1001	You're My Baby/Jose	1964	50.00	100.00	200.00
—Produced by Phil Spector					
WAND					
❑ 11293	Baby Boy (Part 1)/Baby Boy (Part 2)	1975	—	3.00	6.00

TOOTIE AND THE BOUQUETS

Number	Title (A Side/B Side)	Yr	VG	VG+	NM
PARKWAY					
❑ 887	The Conqueror/You Done Me Wrong	1963	6.25	12.50	25.00

TOP HITS, THE

Number	Title (A Side/B Side)	Yr	VG	VG+	NM
NORMAN					
❑ 504	Love No One/Thum-A-Lum-A	1961	50.00	100.00	200.00

TOP NOTES, THE

Number	Title (A Side/B Side)	Yr	VG	VG+	NM
ABC-PARAMOUNT					
❑ 10399	I Love You So Much/It's Alright	1963	2.50	5.00	10.00
ATLANTIC					
❑ 2066	A Wonderful Time/Walkin' with Love	1960	3.75	7.50	15.00
❑ 2080	Say Man/Warm Your Heart	1960	3.75	7.50	15.00
❑ 2097	Hearts of Stone/The Basic Things	1961	3.75	7.50	15.00
❑ 2115	Twist and Shout/Always Late (Why Lead Me On)	1961	6.25	12.50	25.00

TOPICS, THE
Also see THE FOUR SEASONS.

Number	Title (A Side/B Side)	Yr	VG	VG+	NM
PERRI					
❑ 1007	The Girl in My Dreams	1961	37.50	75.00	150.00
—One-sided record					

TOPPERS, THE
More than one group.

Number	Title (A Side/B Side)	Yr	VG	VG+	NM
ABC-PARAMOUNT					
❑ 9667	George Washington/Honey, Honey	1956	5.00	10.00	20.00
❑ 9699	God Bless Kids and Little Animals/Tornado	1956	5.00	10.00	20.00
❑ 9759	Three Roads/Lonely	1956	5.00	10.00	20.00
AVALON					
❑ 63707	I Love You, I Love You/Bow-Legged Boy	1954	10.00	20.00	40.00
DECCA					
❑ 30209	The Purple Hills/Stashu Pandowski	1957	3.75	7.50	15.00
❑ 30297	Pots and Pans/It Was Twice As Big As I Thought It Was	1957	3.75	7.50	15.00
JUBILEE					
❑ 5136	Let Me Bang Your Box/You're Laughing 'Cause I'm Crying	1954	37.50	75.00	150.00
STACY					
❑ 927	Tell Me Why/All Around	1962	3.00	6.00	12.00

TOPPS, THE

Number	Title (A Side/B Side)	Yr	VG	VG+	NM
RED ROBIN					
❑ 126	What Do You Do (To Make Me Love You So)/Tippin'	1954	75.00	150.00	300.00
❑ 131	I've Got a Feeling/Won't You Come Home Baby	1954	75.00	150.00	300.00

TOPS, THE

Number	Title (A Side/B Side)	Yr	VG	VG+	NM
SINGULAR					
❑ 712	An Innocent Kiss/Walkin' with My Baby	1957	30.00	60.00	120.00

TORNADOES, THE (1)
British band.

Number	Title (A Side/B Side)	Yr	VG	VG+	NM
DATE					
❑ 1519	Hey Baby!/Next Stop Kansas City	1966	3.00	6.00	12.00
LONDON					
❑ 9561	Telstar/Jungle Fever	1962	6.25	12.50	25.00
❑ 9579	Globetrottin'/Like Locomotion	1963	5.00	10.00	20.00
❑ 9581	Ridin' the Wind/The Breeze and I	1963	5.00	10.00	20.00
❑ 9599	Life on Venus (Telstar II)/Robot	1963	5.00	10.00	20.00
❑ 9614	Theme from "The Scales of Justice"/The Ice Cream Man	1963	5.00	10.00	20.00
❑ 11003	Telestar/Jungle Fever	1964	5.00	10.00	20.00
—Gold label "Demand Performance" with misspelled A-side					
TOWER					
❑ 152	Stompin' Through the Rye/Early Bird	1965	3.75	7.50	15.00
❑ 171	Stingray/Aqua Marina	1965	3.75	7.50	15.00

TORNADOES, THE (2)
California surf band, also called "Hollywood Tornadoes."

Number	Title (A Side/B Side)	Yr	VG	VG+	NM
AERTAUN					
❑ 100	Bustin' Surfboards/Beyond the Surf	1962	10.00	20.00	40.00
❑ 101	The Gremmie (Part 1)/The Gremmie (Part 2)	1963	6.25	12.50	25.00
—As "The Hollywood Tornadoes"					
❑ 102	Inebriated Surfer/Moon Dawg	1963	7.50	15.00	30.00
—As "The Hollywood Tornadoes"					
❑ 103	Phantom Surfer/Shootin' Beavers	1963	7.50	15.00	30.00
❑ 103	Phantom Surfer/Lightnin'	1964	6.25	12.50	25.00
—B-side is same recording as "Shootin' Beavers" but retitled					

TORNADOES, THE (3)

Number	Title (A Side/B Side)	Yr	VG	VG+	NM
ABC-PARAMOUNT					
❑ 10174	Cora/Like a Frog	1960	5.00	10.00	20.00

TORNADOES, THE (4)

Number	Title (A Side/B Side)	Yr	VG	VG+	NM
CUCA					
❑ 1092	Scalping Party/7-0-7	1962	10.00	20.00	40.00
❑ 1099	Loneliest Guy in the World/It Always Makes Me Cry	1962	7.50	15.00	30.00
❑ 1104	Hey There/Standing Watch	1963	7.50	15.00	30.00

TOROK, MITCHELL

Number	Title (A Side/B Side)	Yr	VG	VG+	NM
ABBOTT					
❑ 136	Little Hoo-Wee/Judalina	1953	6.25	12.50	25.00
❑ 140	Caribbean/Weep Away	1953	7.50	15.00	30.00
❑ 150	Hootchy Kootchy Henry (From Hawaii)/Gigolo	1953	6.25	12.50	25.00
❑ 156	Edgar the Eager Easter Bunny/Living on Love	1954	6.25	12.50	25.00
❑ 162	Dancerette/Haunting Waterfall	1954	6.25	12.50	25.00
CAPITOL					
❑ 4846	Rio Grande/Fools Disguise	1962	2.00	4.00	8.00
❑ 4946	Mighty Mighty Man/For Someone Who's Supposed to Be Hurtin'	1963	2.00	4.00	8.00
DECCA					
❑ 29326	Roulette/Havana Huddle	1954	5.00	10.00	20.00
❑ 29408	Peasant's Guitar/The World Keeps Turning Around	1955	3.75	7.50	15.00
❑ 29576	Too Late Now/Smooth Talk	1955	3.75	7.50	15.00
❑ 29661	Marching My Blues Away/Country and Western	1955	3.75	7.50	15.00
❑ 29863	No Money Down/Red Light, Green Light	1956	3.75	7.50	15.00
❑ 29986	I Wish I Was a Little Bit Younger/When Mexico Gave Up Rhumba	1956	3.75	7.50	15.00
❑ 30134	Take This Heart/Drink Up and Go Home	1956	3.75	7.50	15.00
❑ 30230	Pledge of Love/What's Behind That Strange Door	1957	3.75	7.50	15.00
❑ 30424	Two Words/You're Tempting Me	1957	3.75	7.50	15.00
❑ 30599	Be Kind to Me/How Much Do I Love You	1958	3.00	6.00	12.00
❑ 30661	Sweet Revenge/Love Me Like You Mean It	1958	3.00	6.00	12.00
❑ 30742	Date with a Teardrop/These Things I Hold Dear	1958	3.00	6.00	12.00
❑ 30859	Go Ahead and Be a Fool/Memories of You Haunting Me Night and Day	1959	3.00	6.00	12.00
❑ 30901	PTA Rock and Roll/Teenie Weenie Bikini	1959	5.00	10.00	20.00
GUYDEN					
❑ 2018	Caribbean/Hootchy Kootchy Henry (From Hawaii)	1959	3.00	6.00	12.00
❑ 2028	You Are the One/Mexican Joe	1959	2.50	5.00	10.00
❑ 2032	Guardian Angel/I Want to Know Everything	1960	2.50	5.00	10.00
❑ 2034	Pink Chiffon/What You Don't Know	1960	2.50	5.00	10.00
❑ 2034 [PS]	Pink Chiffon/What You Don't Know	1960	5.00	10.00	20.00
❑ 2040	Happy Street/Little Boy in Love	1960	2.50	5.00	10.00
MERCURY					
❑ 71826	El Tigre/Eating My Heart Out	1961	2.50	5.00	10.00
RCA VICTOR					
❑ 47-8646	I Needed All the Help I Can Get/Man with a Golden Hand	1965	2.00	4.00	8.00
❑ 47-8703	Caribbean/Witch Woman	1965	2.00	4.00	8.00
REPRISE					
❑ 0541	Instant Love/Put Me in the Driver's Seat	1966	—	3.00	6.00
❑ 0568	Falling in Love Again/Baby, Baby, Baby	1967	—	3.00	6.00

TORQUAYS, THE

Number	Title (A Side/B Side)	Yr	VG	VG+	NM
AERTAUN					
❑ 1020	Turmoil/Crying in the Chapel	1964	7.50	15.00	30.00
COLPIX					
❑ 782	Image of a Girl/Stolen Moments	1965	5.00	10.00	20.00
GEE CEE					
❑ 8163	Escondido/Surfer's City	1963	12.50	25.00	50.00
GYPSY					
❑ 265	Busting Point/The Other Side	1965	12.50	25.00	50.00
ORIGINAL SOUND					
❑ 66	Harmonica Man/Our Teenage Love	1967	5.00	10.00	20.00
PUNCH					
❑ 1007	Shake a Tail Feather/Temptation	196?	5.00	10.00	20.00
ROCK-IT					
❑ 1004	Image of a Girl/Stolen Moments	1965	7.50	15.00	30.00
❑ 1005	Hooked on Her/Harmonica Man	1965	7.50	15.00	30.00

TORQUES, THE

Number	Title (A Side/B Side)	Yr	VG	VG+	NM
DIAL					
❑ 4060	Merry Maker/You Make Me Feel So Good	1967	5.00	10.00	20.00
LEMCO					
❑ 880	Tidal Wave/Harlem Nocturne	1965	7.50	15.00	30.00
❑ 890	Mercy Mercy/Bumpin'	1966	7.50	15.00	30.00
❑ 1001	Linden Walk/Deep Blue, At Dusk	196?	7.50	15.00	30.00
❑ 1007	I've Been Hurt/Bumpin'	1966	6.25	12.50	25.00

TORQUETTS, THE

Number	Title (A Side/B Side)	Yr	VG	VG+	NM
SANTA CRUZ					
❑ 10002	Any More/(Who's Got The) Tortillas	196?	12.50	25.00	50.00
TORQUETT					
❑ 005/6	Feedback/Bacardi	196?	12.50	25.00	50.00
❑ 007/8	Side Swiped/Blue Corral	196?	6.25	12.50	25.00

TORRENCE, JOHNNY

Number	Title (A Side/B Side)	Yr	VG	VG+	NM
IMPERIAL					
❑ 5230	Sad Day/Bad Habit	1953	30.00	60.00	120.00
❑ 5897	Rat Race/Your Lover Man	1962	3.75	7.50	15.00
R&B					
❑ 1306	Rosalie/Living from Day to Day	1954	50.00	100.00	200.00
—With the Jewels					

TOTO

Number	Title (A Side/B Side)	Yr	VG	VG+	NM
COLUMBIA					
❑ 01056	It's the Last Night/Turn Back	1981	—	2.00	4.00
❑ 02811	Rosanna/It's a Feeling	1982	—	2.00	4.00
❑ 03143	Make Believe/We Made It	1982	—	2.00	4.00
❑ 03143 [PS]	Make Believe/We Made It	1982	—	2.50	5.00
❑ 03267	Make Believe	1982	—	3.00	6.00
—One-sided budget release					
❑ 03335	Africa/Good for You	1982	—	2.00	4.00

Number	Title (A Side/B Side)	Yr	VG	VG+	NM
❑ 03399	Africa	1982	—	3.00	6.00
—One-sided budget release					
❑ 03597	I Won't Hold You Back/Afraid of Love	1983	—	—	3.00
❑ 03597 [PS]	I Won't Hold You Back/Afraid of Love	1983	—	2.00	4.00
❑ 03981	Waiting for Your Love/Lovers in the Night	1983	—	—	3.00
❑ 04672	Stranger in Town/Change of Heart	1984	—	—	3.00
❑ 04672 [PS]	Stranger in Town/Change of Heart	1984	—	2.00	4.00
❑ 04752	Holyanna/Mr. Friendly	1985	—	—	3.00
❑ 04752 [PS]	Holyanna/Mr. Friendly	1985	—	2.00	4.00
❑ 04844	How Does It Feel/Mr. Friendly	1985	—	—	3.00
❑ 06280	I'll Be Over You/In a Word	1986	—	—	3.00
❑ 06280 [PS]	I'll Be Over You/In a Word	1986	—	—	3.00
❑ 06570	Without Your Love/Can't Stand It Any Longer	1987	—	—	3.00
❑ 06570 [PS]	Without Your Love/Can't Stand It Any Longer	1987	—	—	3.00
❑ 07030	Till the End/Don't Stop Me Now	1987	—	—	3.00
❑ 07715	Pamela/The Seventh One	1988	—	—	3.00
❑ 07715 [PS]	Pamela/The Seventh One	1988	—	—	3.00
❑ 07945	Straight for the Heart/The Seventh One	1988	—	—	3.00
❑ 07945 [PS]	Straight for the Heart/The Seventh One	1988	—	—	3.00
❑ 08010	Anna/The Seventh One	1988	—	—	3.00
❑ 10830	Hold the Line/Takin' It Back	1978	—	2.50	5.00
❑ 10898	I'll Supply the Love/You Are the Flower	1979	—	2.00	4.00
❑ 10944	Georgy Porgy/Child's Anthem	1979	—	2.50	5.00
❑ 11040	Georgy Porgy/Child's Anthem	1979	—	2.00	4.00
❑ 11173	99/Hydra	1980	—	2.00	4.00
❑ 11238	All Us Boys/Hydra	1980	—	2.00	4.00
❑ 11437	Goodbye Eleanore/Turn Back	1981	—	2.00	4.00
POLYDOR					
❑ 881628-7	Dune (Desert Theme)/Theme from Dune	1985	—	2.00	4.00

TOUSAN, AL

See ALLEN TOUSSAINT.

TOUSSAINT, ALLEN

Number	Title (A Side/B Side)	Yr	VG	VG+	NM
ALON					
❑ 9021	Go Back Home/Poor Boy, Got to Move	1965	2.50	5.00	10.00
BELL					
❑ 732	Get Out of My Life, Woman/Gotta Travel On	1968	2.00	4.00	8.00
❑ 748	Hans Christian Anderson/I've Got That Feeling Now	1968	2.00	4.00	8.00
❑ 782	Tequila/We the People	1969	2.00	4.00	8.00
RCA VICTOR					
❑ 47-7192	Whirlaway/Happy Times	1958	6.25	12.50	25.00
—As "Al Tousan"					
REPRISE					
❑ 1109	Soul Sister/She Once Belonged to Me	1972	—	2.50	5.00
❑ 1132	Am I Expecting Too Much/Out of the City	1972	—	2.50	5.00
❑ 1334	Country John/When the Party's Over	1975	—	2.00	4.00
SCEPTER					
❑ 12317	From a Whisper to a Scream/Secret Touch of Love	1971	—	3.00	6.00
❑ 12334	Working in a Coal Mine/What Is Success	1971	—	3.00	6.00
SEVILLE					
❑ 103	Chico/Sweetie-Pie	1960	3.75	7.50	15.00
—All Seville releases as "Al Tousan"					
❑ 110	Back Home in Indiana/Naomi	1960	3.75	7.50	15.00
❑ 113	A Blue Mood/Moo Moo	1961	3.75	7.50	15.00
❑ 124	Twenty Years Later/Real Churchy	1962	3.75	7.50	15.00
WARNER BROS.					
❑ 8561	Night People/Optimism Blues	1978	—	2.00	4.00
❑ 8609	Happiness/Lover of Love	1978	—	2.00	4.00

TOWNSEND, ED

Number	Title (A Side/B Side)	Yr	VG	VG+	NM
ALADDIN					
❑ 3373	Every Night/Love Never Dies	1957	6.25	12.50	25.00
CAPITOL					
❑ F3926	For Your Love/Over and Over Again	1958	3.75	7.50	15.00
❑ F3994	What Shall I Do/Please Never Change	1958	3.00	6.00	12.00
❑ F4048	When I Grow Too Old to Dream/You Are My Everything	1958	3.00	6.00	12.00
❑ F4104	Richer Than I/Getting By Without You	1958	3.00	6.00	12.00
❑ F4171	Don't Ever Leave Me/Lover Come Back to Me	1959	3.00	6.00	12.00
❑ F4240	This Little Love of Mine/Hold On	1959	3.00	6.00	12.00
❑ 4314	Be My Love/With No One to Love	1959	3.00	6.00	12.00
CHALLENGE					
❑ 9118	Ed Townsend's Boogie Woogie (Part 1)/Ed Townsend's Boogie Woogie (Part 2)	1961	3.00	6.00	12.00
❑ 9129	And Then Came Love/Little Bitty Dave	1961	3.00	6.00	12.00
❑ 9144	You Walked In/I Love to Hear That Best	1962	3.00	6.00	12.00
DOT					
❑ 15596	Tall Grows the Sycamore/My Need for You	1957	5.00	10.00	20.00
LIBERTY					
❑ 55516	Tell Her/Down Home	1962	3.00	6.00	12.00
❑ 55516	Tell Her/Hard Way to Go	1962	3.00	6.00	12.00
❑ 55542	That's What I Get for Loving You/There's No End	1963	3.00	6.00	12.00
MAXX					
❑ 325	I Love You/I Might Like It	1964	2.50	5.00	10.00
MGM					
❑ 13784	Mommy's Never Comin' Back Again/Who Would Deny Me	1967	2.50	5.00	10.00
POLYDOR					
❑ 14021	No/Color Me Human	1970	—	3.00	6.00
WARNER BROS.					
❑ 5174	Stay with Me/I Love Everything About You	1960	3.00	6.00	12.00
❑ 5200	Cherrigale/Dream World	1961	3.00	6.00	12.00

TOWNSEND, SHERRELL

Number	Title (A Side/B Side)	Yr	VG	VG+	NM
GONE					
❑ 5135	He Thinks I Still Care/Glass of Tears	1962	5.00	10.00	20.00
LITTLE STAR					
❑ 115	I Love You Alone/Summer Days Are Here	1962	10.00	20.00	40.00
LUTE					
❑ 6015	I Love You Alone/Summer Days Are Here	1961	7.50	15.00	30.00

TOWNSHEND, PETE

Also see THE WHO.

Number	Title (A Side/B Side)	Yr	VG	VG+	NM
ATCO					
❑ 7217	Let My Love Open the Door/And I Moved	1980	—	2.00	4.00
❑ 7312	A Little Is Enough/Cat's in a Cupboard	1980	—	2.00	4.00
❑ 7318	Rough Boys/Jools and Jim	1980	—	2.00	4.00
❑ 99499	Barefootin'/Behind Blue Eyes	1986	—	—	3.00
❑ 99499 [PS]	Barefootin'/Behind Blue Eyes	1986	—	2.00	4.00
❑ 99553	Secondhand Love/White City Fighting	1986	—	—	3.00
❑ 99577	Give Blood/Magic Bus	1986	—	—	3.00
❑ 99577 [PS]	Give Blood/Magic Bus	1986	—	—	3.00
❑ 99590	Face the Face/Hiding Out	1985	—	—	3.00
❑ 99590 [PS]	Face the Face/Hiding Out	1985	—	—	3.00
❑ 99884	Bargain/Dirty Water	1983	—	2.00	4.00
❑ 99884 [PS]	Bargain/Dirty Water	1983	—	2.00	4.00
❑ 99973	Slit Skirts/Uniforms	1982	—	2.00	4.00
❑ 99989	Face Dances Part Two/Man Watching	1982	—	2.00	4.00
❑ 99989 [PS]	Face Dances Part Two/Man Watching	1982	—	2.00	4.00
ATLANTIC					
❑ 88875	A Friend Is a Friend/Man Machines	1989	—	—	3.00
❑ 88875 [PS]	A Friend Is a Friend/Man Machines	1989	—	—	3.00

TOWNSHEND, PETE, AND RONNIE LANE

Also see each artist's individual listings.

Number	Title (A Side/B Side)	Yr	VG	VG+	NM
MCA					
❑ 40818	My Baby Gives It Away/April Fool	1977	—	2.00	4.00
❑ 40878	Nowhere to Run/Keep Me Turning	1978	—	2.00	4.00

TOWNSMEN, THE

More than one group?

Number	Title (A Side/B Side)	Yr	VG	VG+	NM
CARDINAL					
❑ 1022	Pretty Patricia/(B-side unknown)	195?	3.75	7.50	15.00
COLUMBIA					
❑ 43207	Please Don't Say Goodbye/Gotta Get Moving	1965	2.50	5.00	10.00
HERALD					
❑ 585	Is It All Over/Just a Little Bit	1963	3.75	7.50	15.00
JOEY					
❑ 6202	Moonlight Was Made for Lovers/I'm in the Mood for Love	1963	6.25	12.50	25.00
PJ					
❑ 1341	That's All I'll Ever Need/I Can't Let Go	1963	50.00	100.00	200.00
VANITY					
❑ 579/80	It's Time/Little Jeanie	1960	5.00	10.00	20.00
WARNER BROS.					
❑ 5190	You're Having the Last Dance with Me/Gloria's Theme from "Butterfield-8"	1960	3.00	6.00	12.00

TOYS, THE

Number	Title (A Side/B Side)	Yr	VG	VG+	NM
DYNO VOICE					
❑ 209	A Lover's Concerto/This Night	1965	3.00	6.00	12.00
❑ 214	Attack/See How They Run	1965	2.50	5.00	10.00
❑ 218	My My Heart Be Cast Into Stone/On Backstreet	1966	2.50	5.00	10.00
❑ 219	Can't Get Enough of You Baby/Silver Spoon	1966	2.50	5.00	10.00
❑ 222	Baby Toys/Happy Birthday Broken Heart	1966	2.50	5.00	10.00
MUSICOR					
❑ 1300	You Got It Baby/You've Got to Give Her Love	1968	2.00	4.00	8.00
❑ 1319	Sealed with a Kiss/I Got My Heart Set on You	1968	2.00	4.00	8.00
PHILIPS					
❑ 40432	Ciao Baby/I Got Carried Away	1967	2.50	5.00	10.00
❑ 40456	My Love Sonata/I Close My Eyes	1967	2.50	5.00	10.00

TRACERS, THE

Number	Title (A Side/B Side)	Yr	VG	VG+	NM
SULLY					
❑ 928	She Said Yeah/Watch Me	1966	6.25	12.50	25.00
—Originally released under the name "The Stones"					

TRACEY, WREG

Number	Title (A Side/B Side)	Yr	VG	VG+	NM
ANNA					
❑ 1105	All I Want Is You/Take Me Back	1959	10.00	20.00	40.00
❑ 1126	All I Want for Christmas (Is Your Love)/Take Me Back	1960	10.00	20.00	40.00

TRACEY TWINS, THE

Number	Title (A Side/B Side)	Yr	VG	VG+	NM
EASTWEST					
❑ 108	Heartbreak Hill/Don't Mean Maybe Baby	1958	5.00	10.00	20.00
EPIC					
❑ 9230	Kissin' Diploma/Because We Are Young	1957	5.00	10.00	20.00
RESERVE					
❑ 110	Tonight You Belong to Me/(B-side unknown)	1956	6.25	12.50	25.00
❑ 114	Do You Ever Think of Me/(B-side unknown)	195?	6.25	12.50	25.00

TRACY, BILL

Number	Title (A Side/B Side)	Yr	VG	VG+	NM
DEL-FI					
❑ 4124	You're My Girl/Tops to Summer	1959	5.00	10.00	20.00
❑ 4132	I'm So Happy/January Love	1959	5.00	10.00	20.00
DOT					
❑ 15797	One Chance/Hold Me, Thrill Me, Kiss Me	1958	15.00	30.00	60.00
❑ 15868	Flame Out/Disappointed	1958	10.00	20.00	40.00
RADIANT					
❑ 1504	High School Hero/Lost Love	1961	3.75	7.50	15.00
RPM					
❑ 489	Kiss at Daybreak/No One But You	1957	10.00	20.00	40.00

TRADE WINDS, THE

Number	Title (A Side/B Side)	Yr	VG	VG+	NM
KAMA SUTRA					
❑ 212	Mind Excursion/Little Susan's Dreamin'	1966	3.00	6.00	12.00
❑ 218	I Believe in Her/Catch Me in the Meadow	1966	3.00	6.00	12.00
❑ 234	Mind Excursion/Only When I'm Dreamin'	1967	3.00	6.00	12.00

Number	Title (A Side/B Side)	Yr	VG	VG+	NM
RED BIRD					
❑ 10-020	New York's a Lonely Town/Club Seventeen	1965	5.00	10.00	20.00
❑ 10-028	Girl from Greenwich Village/There's a Rock and Roll Show in Town	1965	5.00	10.00	20.00
❑ 10-033	Summertime Girl/The Party Starts at Nine	1965	10.00	20.00	40.00

TRADEWINDS, THE

Number	Title (A Side/B Side)	Yr	VG	VG+	NM
DAWN CORY					
❑ 1005	Surfin' Thunder/Gotcha	196?	20.00	40.00	80.00
RCA VICTOR					
❑ 47-7511	Toni/Twins	1959	5.00	10.00	20.00
❑ 47-7553	Crossroads/Furry Murry	1959	5.00	10.00	20.00

TRAFFIC

Also see JIM CAPALDI; DAVE MASON; STEVE WINWOOD.

Number	Title (A Side/B Side)	Yr	VG	VG+	NM
ASYLUM					
❑ 45207	Walking in the Wind/(Instrumental)	1974	—	2.50	5.00
ISLAND					
❑ 1201	Rock and Roll Stew (Part 1)/Rock and Roll Stew (Part 2)	1972	—	2.50	5.00
UNITED ARTISTS					
❑ 0129	Paper Sun/Empty Pages	1973	—	2.00	4.00
—"Silver Spotlight Series" reissue					
❑ 1694	Feelin' Alright?/You Can All Join In	197?	—	2.50	5.00
—"Silver Spotlight Series" reissue					
❑ 50195	Paper Sun/Giving to You	1967	2.50	5.00	10.00
❑ 50218	Hole in My Shoe/Smiling Phases	1967	2.50	5.00	10.00
❑ 50232	Here We Go 'Round the Mulberry Bush/Coloured Rain	1967	2.50	5.00	10.00
❑ 50261	Heaven Is In Your Mind/No Face, No Name and No Number	1968	2.00	4.00	8.00
❑ 50460	Feelin' Alright?/Withering Tree	1968	2.00	4.00	8.00
❑ 50500	Medicated Goo/Pearly Queen	1969	—	3.00	6.00
❑ 50692	Empty Pages/Stranger to Himself	1970	—	3.00	6.00
❑ 50841	Gimme Some Lovin' (Part 1)/Gimme Some Lovin' (Part 2)	1971	—	3.00	6.00
—By "Traffic, Etc."					
❑ 50883	Glad (Part 1)/Glad (Part 2)	1972	—	3.00	6.00
VIRGIN					
❑ S7-17971	Here Comes a Man (Rock Mix)/Glad (Live)	1994	—	2.00	4.00
❑ S7-18134	Some Kinda Woman/Forty Thousand Headmen (Live)	1994	—	2.00	4.00

TRAITS, THE

Also see ROY HEAD.

Number	Title (A Side/B Side)	Yr	VG	VG+	NM
ASCOT					
❑ 2108	Linda Lou/Little Mama	1962	7.50	15.00	30.00
PACEMAKER					
❑ 254	Too Good to Be True/Gotta Keep Cool	1967	5.00	10.00	20.00
RENNER					
❑ 221	Linda Lou/Little Mama	1962	10.00	20.00	40.00
❑ 229	Got My Mojo Working/Woe Woe	1962	6.25	12.50	25.00
—Black vinyl					
❑ 229 [DJ]	Got My Mojo Working/Woe Woe	1962	10.00	20.00	40.00
—Promo only on colored vinyl					
SCEPTER					
❑ 12169	Harlem Shuffle/Strange Lips Start Old Memories	1966	2.00	4.00	8.00
TNT					
❑ 164	One More Time/Don't Be Blue	1959	5.00	10.00	20.00
—Later reissued on TNT 194 credited to "Roy Head"					
❑ 175	Live It Up/Yes I Do	1960	5.00	10.00	20.00
❑ 177	My Baby's Fine/Here I Am in Love Again	1960	5.00	10.00	20.00
❑ 181	Summer Time Love/Your Turn to Cry	1960	5.00	10.00	20.00
❑ 185	Night Time Blues/Walking All Day	1961	5.00	10.00	20.00
UNIVERSAL					
❑ 30494	Harlem Shuffle/Strange Lips Start Old Memories	1966	7.50	15.00	30.00

TRAMMELL, BOBBY LEE

Number	Title (A Side/B Side)	Yr	VG	VG+	NM
ABC-PARAMOUNT					
❑ 9890	Shirley Lee/I Sure Do Love You Baby	1958	20.00	40.00	80.00
ALLEY					
❑ 1001	It's All Your Fault/Arkansas Twist	1962	6.25	12.50	25.00
❑ 1004	Come On Baby/I Tried Not to Cry	1963	6.25	12.50	25.00
ATLANTA					
❑ 1101	Just Let Me Love You One More Time/Tator	196?	6.25	12.50	25.00
❑ 1501	Carolyn/Sally Twist	196?	6.25	12.50	25.00
❑ 1502	Come On/I Love 'Em All	196?	6.25	12.50	25.00
❑ 1503	Give Me That Good Lovin'/New Dance in France	196?	6.25	12.50	25.00
❑ 3001	I'll Step Aside/Mary Ann	196?	6.25	12.50	25.00
ATLANTIC					
❑ 2332	Shimmy Loo/You Make Me Feel So Fine	1966	3.00	6.00	12.00
CAPITOL					
❑ 3718	Love Don't Let Me Down/I Couldn't Believe My Eyes	1973	2.00	4.00	8.00
❑ 3801	You Mostest Girl/You Stand a Chance of Losing What You've Got	1973	2.00	4.00	8.00
CINNAMON					
❑ 797	The Warmth of Your Love/Marion County Tradition	1974	—	3.00	6.00
CONFEDERATE					
❑ 125	Shake Me Baby/Run Fool Run	195?	250.00	500.00	1000.
FABOR					
❑ 127	You Mostest Girl/Uh Oh	1964	3.00	6.00	12.00
❑ 4038	Shirley Lee/I Sure Do Love You Baby	1957	37.50	75.00	150.00
HOT					
❑ 101	Shimmy Lou/(B-side unknown)	1959	10.00	20.00	40.00
❑ 102	Betty Jean/(B-side unknown)	1959	10.00	20.00	40.00
RADIO					
❑ 102	You Mostest Girl/Uh Oh	1958	12.50	25.00	50.00
❑ 114	My Susie Jane/Should I Make Amends	1958	10.00	20.00	40.00
SANTO					
❑ 9052	Hi-O Silver/Don't You Know I Love You	196?	5.00	10.00	20.00
SIMS					
❑ 183	Good Lovin'/New Dance in France	1964	3.00	6.00	12.00
❑ 195	Come On and Love Me/If You Don't Wanna, You Don't Have To	1964	3.00	6.00	12.00
❑ 225	Twenty-Four Hours/Just Let Me Move You One More Time	1965	3.00	6.00	12.00
❑ 241	I Tried/Am I Satisfying You	1965	3.00	6.00	12.00
❑ 254	Long Tall Sally/The Saints Go Marchin' In	1965	3.00	6.00	12.00
SKYLA					
❑ 1307	You Mostest Girl/Uh Oh	1961	3.75	7.50	15.00
SOUNCOT					
❑ 1100	I Dare America to Be Great/A Gift from God	1970	—	3.00	6.00
❑ 1104	24 Hours a Day/I Lost the Girl I Love Tonight	1970	—	3.00	6.00
❑ 1113	You Mostest Girl/Whole Lotta Shakin' Goin' On	1971	—	3.00	6.00
❑ 1119	My Shoes Keep Walkin' Back to You/Let's Wash the World and Make It Clean	1971	—	3.00	6.00
❑ 1128	Don't Let the Stars Get In Your Eyes/Sheila	1971	—	3.00	6.00
❑ 1130	You Were Worth the Wait/Wadin' in the Water	1972	—	3.00	6.00
❑ 1135	Love Isn't Love (Till You Give It Away)/Tell Me That You Want Me	1972	—	3.00	6.00
❑ 1143	I Believe in You/My Love Keeps Growing	1972	—	3.00	6.00
❑ 1145	You Put Love Back in My Heart/I Lost the Girl I Love Tonight	1972	—	3.00	6.00
SUN					
❑ 1135	Jenny Lee/It's All Your Fault	1977	—	3.00	6.00
WARRIOR					
❑ 1554	Woe Is Me/(B-side unknown)	1959	20.00	40.00	80.00

TRAMMPS, THE

Also see THE VOLCANOS.

Number	Title (A Side/B Side)	Yr	VG	VG+	NM
ATLANTIC					
❑ 3286	Hooked for Life/I'm Alright	1975	—	2.50	5.00
❑ 3306	That's Where the Happy People Go (Short)/ That's Where the Happy People Go (Long)	1975	—	2.50	5.00
❑ 3345	Soul Searchin' Time/Love Is a Funky Thing	1976	—	2.50	5.00
❑ 3365	Ninety-Nine and a Half (Won't Do)/Can We Come Together	1976	—	2.50	5.00
❑ 3389	Disco Inferno/You Touch My Hot Line	1977	—	3.00	6.00
❑ 3389	Disco Inferno/That's Where the Happy People Go	1978	—	2.50	5.00
—Reissue in conjunction with the success of "Saturday Night Fever"					
❑ 3389 [PS]	Disco Inferno/You Touch My Hot Line	1977	2.00	4.00	8.00
❑ 3403	I Feel Like I've Been Livin' (On the Dark Side of the Moon)/Don't Burn Bridges	1977	—	2.50	5.00
❑ 3442	The Night the Lights Went Out/I'm So Glad You Came Along	1977	—	2.50	5.00
❑ 3460	Seasons for Girls/Love Ain't Been Easy	1978	—	2.50	5.00
❑ 3460	Seasons for Girls/Body Contact Contract	1978	—	2.50	5.00
❑ 3537	Soul Bones/Love Magnet	1978	—	2.50	5.00
❑ 3573	More Good Times to Remember/Teaser	1979	—	2.50	5.00
❑ 3654	Dance Contest/Hard Rock and Disco	1980	—	2.00	4.00
❑ 3669	Music Freek/V.I.P.	1980	—	2.00	4.00
❑ 3777	Mellow Out/Looking for You	1980	—	2.00	4.00
❑ 3797	I Don't Want to Ever Lose Your Love/Breathtaking View	1981	—	2.00	4.00
BUDDAH					
❑ 306	Zing Went the Strings of My Heart/Penguin at the Big Apple	1972	2.50	5.00	10.00
—As "Tramps"					
❑ 306	Zing Went the Strings of My Heart/Penguin at the Big Apple	1972	—	3.00	6.00
—As "Trammps"					
❑ 321	Sixty Minute Man/Scrub Board	1972	—	3.00	6.00
❑ 339	Rubber Band/Pray All You Sinners	1973	—	3.00	6.00
❑ 507	Hold Back the Night/Tom's Song	1975	—	2.50	5.00
GOLDEN FLEECE					
❑ 3251	Love Epidemic/I Know That Feeling	1973	—	3.00	6.00
❑ 3253	Where Do We Go from Here/Shout	1974	—	3.00	6.00
❑ 3255	Trusting Heart/Down These Dark Streets	1974	—	3.00	6.00

TRANQUILS, THE

Number	Title (A Side/B Side)	Yr	VG	VG+	NM
HAMILTON					
❑ 50005	You're Such a Much/One Billion, Seven Million and Thirty-Three	1959	7.50	15.00	30.00

TRAPEZE

Number	Title (A Side/B Side)	Yr	VG	VG+	NM
THRESHOLD					
❑ 67001	Send Me No More Letters/Another Day	1970	2.00	4.00	8.00
❑ 67005 [DJ]	Black Cloud (mono/stereo)	1971	2.50	5.00	10.00
❑ 67011	Coast to Coast/Your Love Is Alright	1972	2.00	4.00	8.00

TRASH

Number	Title (A Side/B Side)	Yr	VG	VG+	NM
APPLE					
❑ 1804	Road to Nowhere/Illusions	1969	25.00	50.00	100.00
—With star on A-side label					
❑ 1804	Road to Nowhere/Illusions	1969	12.50	25.00	50.00
—Without star on A-side label					
❑ 1811	Golden Slumbers-Carry That Weight/Trash Can	1969	3.75	7.50	15.00
—A-side listed as "Golden Slumbers/Carry That Weight"					
❑ 1811	Golden Slumbers-Carry That Weight/Trash Can	1969	5.00	10.00	20.00
—A-side listed as "Golden Slumbers and Carry That Weight"					
❑ 1811	Golden Slumbers-Carry That Weight/Trash Can	1969	5.00	10.00	20.00
—A-side listed as "Golden Slumbers Carry That Weight"					
❑ PRO-4671/2	Road to Nowhere (Edit)/Road to Nowhere	1969	20.00	40.00	80.00

TRASHMEN, THE

Number	Title (A Side/B Side)	Yr	VG	VG+	NM
ARGO					
❑ 5516	Bird '65/Ubangi Stomp	1965	12.50	25.00	50.00
BEAR					
❑ 1966	Keep Your Hands Off My Baby/Lost Angel	1965	5.00	10.00	20.00

Number	Title (A Side/B Side)	Yr	VG	VG+	NM
ERA BACK TO BACK HITS					
❑ 016	Liar, Liar/Surfin' Bird	197?	—	2.50	5.00
—B-side by the Castaways					
ERIC					
❑ 247	Surfin' Bird/Liar, Liar	197?	—	2.50	5.00
—B-side by the Castaways; reissue					
GARRETT					
❑ 4002	Surfin' Bird/King of the Surf	1963	7.50	15.00	30.00
❑ 4003	Bird Dance Beat/A-Bone	1964	5.00	10.00	20.00
❑ 4005	Bad News/On the Move	1964	5.00	10.00	20.00
❑ 4010	Peppermint Man/New Generation	1964	5.00	10.00	20.00
❑ 4012	Whoa Dad/Walkin' My Baby	1964	5.00	10.00	20.00
❑ 4012 [PS]	Whoa Dad/Walkin' My Baby	1964	62.50	125.00	250.00
❑ 4013	Dancing with Santa/Real Live Doll	1964	6.25	12.50	25.00
❑ 4013 [PS]	Dancing with Santa/Real Live Doll	1964	62.50	125.00	250.00
GET HIP					
❑ 2	Well All Right/That's What They Say	1994	—	2.00	4.00
METROBEAT					
❑ 7927	Green, Green Backs of Home/Address Enclosed	1968	3.75	7.50	15.00
OLDIES 45					
❑ 301	Surfin' Bird/King of the Surf	1965	3.00	6.00	12.00
—Early reissue					
SOMA					
❑ 1469	Surfin' Bird/Liar, Liar	1966	3.00	6.00	12.00
—B-side by the Castaways					
SUNDAZED					
❑ 102	Henrietta/Rumble	1995	—	—	2.00
❑ 102 [PS]	Henrietta/Rumble	1995	—	—	2.00
❑ 103	Lucille/Green Onions	1995	—	—	2.00
❑ 103 [PS]	Lucille/Green Onions	1995	—	—	2.00
❑ 104	Roll Over Beethoven/Betty Jean	1995	—	—	2.00
❑ 104 [PS]	Roll Over Beethoven/Betty Jean	1995	—	—	2.00
❑ 112	Dancing with Santa/Real Live Doll	1996	—	—	2.00
—Red vinyl					
❑ 112 [PS]	Dancing with Santa/Real Live Doll	1996	—	—	2.00
TERRIFIC					
❑ 5003	Surfin' Bird/Bird Dance Beat	196?	2.50	5.00	10.00
—Early reissue					
TRIBE					
❑ 8315	Hanging On Me/Some Lies	1966	6.25	12.50	25.00

TRAVELERS, THE

Probably more than one group.

Number	Title (A Side/B Side)	Yr	VG	VG+	NM
ABC-PARAMOUNT					
❑ 10119	June, July, August and September/What a Weekend	1960	5.00	10.00	20.00
ANDEX					
❑ 2011	I'll Be Home for Christmas/Katie the Kangaroo	1958	7.50	15.00	30.00
❑ 4033	I Go for You/I'll Always Be in Love with You	1959	7.50	15.00	30.00
❑ 34006	Why/Teenage Machine Age	1957	7.50	15.00	30.00
❑ 34012	He's Got the Whole World in His Hands/Green Town Girl	1957	7.50	15.00	30.00
DECCA					
❑ 31215	Ivy on the Old School Wall/Cadwallader 0002	1961	10.00	20.00	40.00
❑ 31282	White Rose/Oh My Love (Love Me)	1961	10.00	20.00	40.00
DON RAY					
❑ 5965	Traveler/Seven Minutes Till Four	1963	12.50	25.00	50.00
MAGIC LAMP					
❑ 516	Big House/Goin' Home	1964	3.00	6.00	12.00
VAULT					
❑ 911	Spanish Moon/She's Got the Blues	1964	3.75	7.50	15.00
YELLOW SAND					
❑ 2	Windy and Warm/Last Date	1963	12.50	25.00	50.00
❑ 451	Groovy/(B-side unknown)	1965	7.50	15.00	30.00
❑ 452	Malibu Sunset/Hang On	1965	7.50	15.00	30.00

TRAVELING WILBURYS

Also see BOB DYLAN; GEORGE HARRISON; JEFF LYNNE; ROY ORBISON; TOM PETTY AND THE HEARTBREAKERS.

Number	Title (A Side/B Side)	Yr	VG	VG+	NM
WILBURY					
❑ 21867	Handle with Care/End of the Line	1990	3.75	7.50	15.00
—"Back to Back Hits" series					
❑ 27637	End of the Line/Congratulations	1989	3.75	7.50	15.00
❑ 27637 [DJ]	End of the Line (same on both sides)	1989	5.00	10.00	20.00
❑ 27637 [PS]	End of the Line/Congratulations	1989	5.00	10.00	20.00
❑ 27732	Handle with Care/Margarita	1988	2.00	4.00	8.00
❑ 27732 [DJ]	Handle with Care (same on both sides)	1988	3.75	7.50	15.00
❑ 27732 [PS]	Handle with Care/Margarita	1988	2.00	4.00	8.00

TRAVELLERS, THE

Number	Title (A Side/B Side)	Yr	VG	VG+	NM
GASS					
❑ 1000	Tie Me Surfer Board Down, Sport/In the Pines	1963	10.00	20.00	40.00

TRAVERS, MARY

Also see PETER, PAUL AND MARY.

Number	Title (A Side/B Side)	Yr	VG	VG+	NM
CHRYSALIS					
❑ 2202	The Air That I Breathe/You Turn Me Around	1977	—	2.50	5.00
❑ 2367	Freedom/(B-side unknown)	1979	—	2.00	4.00
WARNER BROS.					
❑ 7481	Follow Me/I Guess He'd Rather Be in Colorado	1971	—	2.50	5.00
❑ 7517	The Song Is Love/Ericka with the Windy Yellow Hair	1971	—	2.50	5.00
❑ 7588	Morning Glory/That's Enough for Me	1972	—	2.50	5.00
❑ 7675	Too Many Mondays/That Year There Was No Winter	1972	—	2.50	5.00
❑ 7731	Five Hundred Miles/Oh, What a Feeling	1973	—	2.50	5.00
❑ 7790	Circles/I'll Have to Say I Love You in a Song	1974	—	2.50	5.00

TRAVIS, RANDY

Number	Title (A Side/B Side)	Yr	VG	VG+	NM
DREAMWORKS					
❑ 59007	Out of My Bones/Brinks Truck	1998	—	2.00	4.00
PAULA					
❑ 429	Dreamin'/I'll Take Any Willing Woman	1978	6.25	12.50	25.00
—As "Randy Traywick"					
❑ 431	She's My Woman/(Instrumental)	1978	6.25	12.50	25.00
—As "Randy Traywick"					
WARNER BROS.					
❑ PRO-S-2842 [DJ]	White Christmas Makes Me Blue/Sleigh Ride	1987	—	3.00	6.00
—B-side by Mark O'Connor					
❑ 7-17382	Price to Pay/I Wish It Would Rain	1997	—	—	3.00
❑ 7-17494	Would I/Don't Take Your Love Away from Me	1996	—	—	3.00
❑ 7-17619	Are We in Trouble Now/Nobody's Home	1996	—	—	3.00
❑ 7-17970	The Box/Honky Tonk Side of Town	1995	—	2.00	4.00
❑ 7-18062	This Is Me/Gonna Walk That Line	1994	—	—	3.00
❑ 7-18153	Whisper My Name/Oscar the Angel	1994	—	2.00	4.00
❑ 7-18208	Before You Kill Us All/The Box	1994	—	—	3.00
❑ 7-18274	Wind in the Wire/Down in the Old Corral	1994	—	—	3.00
❑ 18616	An Old Pair of Shoes/Promises	1993	—	—	3.00
❑ 18709	Look Heart, No Hands/The Heart to Climb the Mountain	1992	—	2.00	4.00
❑ 18792	If I Didn't Have You/I Told You So	1992	—	2.00	4.00
❑ 18943	I'd Surrender All/Let Me Try	1992	—	—	3.00
❑ 19067	Better Class of Losers/I'm Gonna Have a Little Talk	1991	—	2.00	4.00
❑ 19158	Forever Together/This Day Was Made for Me and You	1991	—	2.00	4.00
❑ 19283	Point of Light/Waiting on the Light to Change	1991	—	—	3.00
—B-side with B.B. King					
❑ 19469	Heroes and Friends/Shopping for Dresses	1991	—	2.00	4.00
—B-side with Loretta Lynn					
❑ 19586	A Few Ole Country Boys/Smokin' the Hive	1990	—	2.00	4.00
—A-side with George Jones; B-side with Clint Eastwood					
❑ 19878	He Walked on Water/Card Carryin' Fool	1990	—	—	3.00
❑ 19935	Hard Rock Bottom of Your Heart/When Your World Was Turning for Me	1990	—	2.00	4.00
❑ 22766	Oh, What a Silent Night/Winter Wonderland	1989	—	2.00	4.00
❑ 22841	It's Just a Matter of Time/This Day Was Made for You and Me	1989	—	2.00	4.00
❑ 22841 [PS]	It's Just a Matter of Time/This Day Was Made for You and Me	1989	2.00	4.00	8.00
❑ 22917	Promises/Written in Stone	1989	—	—	3.00
❑ 27551	Is It Still Over?/Here in My Heart	1989	—	2.00	4.00
❑ 27689	Deeper Than the Holler/It's Out of My Hands	1988	—	2.00	4.00
❑ 27689 [PS]	Deeper Than the Holler/It's Out of My Hands	1988	—	2.50	5.00
❑ 27707	An Old Time Christmas/How Do I Wrap My Heart Up for Christmas	1988	—	2.50	5.00
❑ 27707 [PS]	An Old Time Christmas/How Do I Wrap My Heart Up for Christmas	1988	—	2.50	5.00
❑ 27833	Honky Tonk Moon/Young Guns	1988	—	—	3.00
❑ 27833 [PS]	Honky Tonk Moon/Young Guns	1988	—	2.50	5.00
❑ 27969	I Told You So/Good Intentions	1988	—	—	3.00
❑ 27969 [PS]	I Told You So/Good Intentions	1988	—	2.50	5.00
❑ 28246	I Won't Need You Anymore (Always and Forever)/Tonight I'm Walking Out on the Blues	1987	—	2.00	4.00
❑ 28286	Too Gone Too Long/My House	1987	—	2.00	4.00
❑ 28286 [PS]	Too Gone Too Long/My House	1987	—	2.50	5.00
❑ 28384	Forever and Ever, Amen/Promises	1987	—	2.50	5.00
❑ 28384 [PS]	Forever and Ever, Amen/Promises	1987	—	2.50	5.00
❑ 28525	No Place Like Home/Send My Body	1986	—	2.00	4.00
❑ 28556	White Christmas Makes Me Blue/Pretty Paper	1986	—	2.50	5.00
❑ 28649	Diggin' Up Bones/There'll Always Be a Honky Tonk Somewhere	1986	—	2.00	4.00
❑ 28828	1982/Reasons I Quit	1985	—	2.00	4.00
❑ 28962	On the Other Hand/Can't Stop Now	1985	—	2.00	4.00
—Reissued in 1986 with the same label and number					

TRAVIS AND BOB

Number	Title (A Side/B Side)	Yr	VG	VG+	NM
BIG TOP					
❑ 3054	Pocahontas/Day Dreams	1960	3.75	7.50	15.00
MERCURY					
❑ 71797	Give Your Love to Me/Stay Close to Me	1961	3.75	7.50	15.00
❑ 71866	The Spider and the Fly/What a Change	1961	3.75	7.50	15.00
SANDY					
❑ 1017	Tell Him No/We're Too Young	1959	6.25	12.50	25.00
—With no mention of Dot Records on label					
❑ 1017	Tell Him No/We're Too Young	1959	5.00	10.00	20.00
—With Dot Records distribution mentioned on label					
❑ 1019	Teenage Vision/Little Bitty Johnny	1959	5.00	10.00	20.00
❑ 1024	Lover's Rendezvous/Oh Yeah	1959	5.00	10.00	20.00
❑ 1029	That's How Long/Wake Up and Cry	1960	5.00	10.00	20.00

TRAVOLTA, JOHN

Number	Title (A Side/B Side)	Yr	VG	VG+	NM
MIDLAND INT'L.					
❑ JB-10623 [PS]	Let Her In/Big Trouble	1976	3.75	7.50	15.00
—Picture sleeve with promo copies, completely different from stock sleeve					
❑ MB-10623	Let Her In/Big Trouble	1976	—	2.50	5.00
❑ MB-10623 [PS]	Let Her In/Big Trouble	1976	2.00	4.00	8.00
—Picture sleeve with stock copies, has "RE" in lower left corner					
❑ MB-10780	Whenever I'm Away from You/Razzamatazz	1976	—	2.50	5.00
❑ MB-10780 [PS]	Whenever I'm Away from You/Razzamatazz	1976	—	3.00	6.00
❑ MB-10907	All Strung Out on You/Easy Evil	1977	—	2.50	5.00
❑ MB-10907 [PS]	All Strung Out on You/Easy Evil	1977	—	3.00	6.00
MIDSONG INT'L.					
❑ 1000	Big Trouble/Can't Let You Go	1978	—	2.50	5.00
❑ MB-10977	Slow Dancin'/Moonlight	1977	—	2.50	5.00
❑ MB-10977 [PS]	Slow Dancin'/Moonlight	1977	—	3.00	6.00
❑ MB-11206	What Would They Say/Razzamatazz	1978	—	2.50	5.00
❑ MB-11206 [PS]	What Would They Say/Razzamatazz	1978	—	3.00	6.00
❑ 72007	You Set My Dreams to Music/It Had to Be You	1980	—	2.50	5.00

Number	Title (A Side/B Side)	Yr	VG	VG+	NM
RCA					
❑ GB-10945	Let Her In/Whenever I'm Away from You	1977	—	2.00	4.00
—Gold Standard Series					
RSO					
❑ 909	Greased Lightnin'/Rock and Roll Is Here to Stay	1978	—	2.00	4.00
—B-side by Sha Na Na					
❑ 909 [PS]	Greased Lightnin'/Rock and Roll Is Here to Stay	1978	—	2.50	5.00
❑ 930	Sandy/Blue Moon	1979	—	2.00	4.00
—B-side by Sha Na Na					

TRAVOLTA, JOHN, AND OLIVIA NEWTON-JOHN

Also see each artist's individual listings.

Number	Title (A Side/B Side)	Yr	VG	VG+	NM
RSO					
❑ 891	You're the One That I Want/Alone at a Drive-In Movie	1978	—	2.00	4.00
❑ 891 [PS]	You're the One That I Want/Alone at a Drive-In Movie	1978	—	2.50	5.00
❑ 906	Summer Nights/Rock 'N' Roll Party Queen	1978	—	2.00	4.00
—B-side by Louis St. Louis					

TRAYNOR, JAY

Also see JAY AND THE AMERICANS.

Number	Title (A Side/B Side)	Yr	VG	VG+	NM
ABC					
❑ 10809	Come On/The Merry-Go-Round Is Slowing You Down	1966	3.75	7.50	15.00
❑ 10845	Up and Over/Don't Let the End Begin	1966	7.50	15.00	30.00
CORAL					
❑ 62396	How Sweet It Is/I Rise, I Fall	1964	3.00	6.00	12.00
❑ 62420	I've Known You All My Life/Little Sister	1964	3.00	6.00	12.00

TREADWELL, IRENE

Number	Title (A Side/B Side)	Yr	VG	VG+	NM
JAY DEE					
❑ 782	Church Bells Are Ringing on Christmas Morning/Dear Santa Bring Back My Daddy to Me	1953	5.00	10.00	20.00

TREASURERS, THE

Number	Title (A Side/B Side)	Yr	VG	VG+	NM
CROWN					
❑ 005	Story of Love/I Walk with An Angel	1961	75.00	150.00	300.00

TREASURES, THE

Number	Title (A Side/B Side)	Yr	VG	VG+	NM
SHIRLEY					
❑ 500	Hold Me Tight/Pete Meets Vinnie	1964	7.50	15.00	30.00
VALOR					
❑ (# unknown)	Minor Chaos/Valley of the Broken Hearts	1964	100.00	200.00	400.00
—Marbled vinyl					
❑ (# unknown)	Minor Chaos/Valley of the Broken Hearts	1964	50.00	100.00	200.00
—Green vinyl					
❑ (# unknown)	Minor Chaos/Valley of the Broken Hearts	1964	25.00	50.00	100.00
—Sources differ as to what the number of this record is, and we've never seen a copy, so we haven't listed one.					

TREBELAIRES, THE

Number	Title (A Side/B Side)	Yr	VG	VG+	NM
NESTOR					
❑ 16	There Goes That Train/I Gotta	1954	25.00	50.00	100.00

TREBLE CHORDS, THE

Number	Title (A Side/B Side)	Yr	VG	VG+	NM
DECCA					
❑ 31015	Teresa/My Little Girl	1959	25.00	50.00	100.00

TREMAINES, THE

Number	Title (A Side/B Side)	Yr	VG	VG+	NM
CASH					
❑ 100/1	Jingle, Jingle/Moon Shining Bright	1958	100.00	200.00	400.00
KANE					
❑ 008	Heavenly/Wonderful, Marvelous	1959	12.50	25.00	50.00
OLD TOWN					
❑ 1051	Jingle, Jingle/Moon Shining Bright	1958	12.50	25.00	50.00
V-TONE					
❑ 507	Heavenly/Wonderful, Marvelous	1959	6.25	12.50	25.00
VAL					
❑ 100/1	Jingle, Jingle/Moon Shining Bright	1958	62.50	125.00	250.00

TREMELOES, THE

Also see BRIAN POOLE AND THE TREMELOES.

Number	Title (A Side/B Side)	Yr	VG	VG+	NM
DJM					
❑ 1008	Hard Woman/My Friend Delaney	1976	—	2.50	5.00
❑ 1016	September, November, December/(B-side unknown)	1976	—	2.50	5.00
EPIC					
❑ 10075	Good Day Sunshine/What a State I'm In	1966	3.00	6.00	12.00
❑ 10139	Here Comes My Baby/Gentlemen of Pleasure	1967	2.50	5.00	10.00
❑ 10184	Silence Is Golden/Let Your Hair Hang Down	1967	2.50	5.00	10.00
❑ 10184 [PS]	Silence Is Golden/Let Your Hair Hang Down	1967	3.75	7.50	15.00
❑ 10233	Even the Bad Times Are Good/Jenny's All Right	1967	2.00	4.00	8.00
❑ 10233 [PS]	Even the Bad Times Are Good/Jenny's All Right	1967	3.75	7.50	15.00
❑ 10293	Suddenly You Love Me/Suddenly Winter	1968	2.00	4.00	8.00
❑ 10328	Girl from Nowhere/Helule, Helule	1968	2.00	4.00	8.00
❑ 10376	My Little Lady/All the World to Me	1968	2.00	4.00	8.00
❑ 10437	I Shall Be Released/I Miss My Baby	1969	2.00	4.00	8.00
❑ 10467	Up, Down, All Around/Hello World	1969	2.00	4.00	8.00
❑ 10548	(Call Me) Number One/Instant Whip	1969	2.00	4.00	8.00
❑ 10621	Breakheart Motel/By the Way	1970	2.50	5.00	10.00
❑ 10682	Try Me/Me and My Life	1970	2.00	4.00	8.00
❑ 10807	My Woman/Hello Buddy	1971	—	3.00	6.00
❑ 10996	Yodelay/Blue Suede Tie	1973	—	3.00	6.00

TREMELOES, THE/THE HOLLIES

Also see each artist's individual listings.

Number	Title (A Side/B Side)	Yr	VG	VG+	NM
EPIC					
❑ 10184/0 [DJ]	Silence Is Golden/Carrie-Anne	1967	25.00	50.00	100.00
—Promo only on red vinyl					
❑ 10184/0 [PS]	Silence Is Golden/Carrie-Anne	1967	75.00	150.00	300.00
—"There's Room for Two at the Top!" across top of sleeve; has photos of both bands; all the print is in red					

TREMELOS, THE

Number	Title (A Side/B Side)	Yr	VG	VG+	NM
ROCKLAND					
❑ 102	Jaguar/Fly	196?	12.50	25.00	50.00

TREMONTS, THE

Number	Title (A Side/B Side)	Yr	VG	VG+	NM
BRUNSWICK					
❑ 55217	Believe My Heart/Legend of Love	1961	7.50	15.00	30.00
PAT RICCIO					
❑ 101	Believe My Heart/Legend of Love	1961	25.00	50.00	100.00

TREN-DELLS, THE

Number	Title (A Side/B Side)	Yr	VG	VG+	NM
CAPITOL					
❑ 4852	Nite Owl/Hully Gully Jones	1962	3.00	6.00	12.00
JAM					
❑ 101	Nite Owl/Hully Gully Jones	1962	6.25	12.50	25.00
❑ 111	Hey Da-Da Dow/Tough Little Buggy	1962	6.25	12.50	25.00
SOUND STAGE 7					
❑ 2508	Mr. Doughnut Man/Ain't That Funny	1963	3.00	6.00	12.00
TILT					
❑ 779	I'm So Young/Don't You Hear Me Calling Baby	1961	7.50	15.00	30.00
—As "The Trend-Els"					
❑ 788	Moments Like This/I Miss You So	1962	7.50	15.00	30.00

TREN-TEENS, THE

Number	Title (A Side/B Side)	Yr	VG	VG+	NM
CARNIVAL					
❑ 501	My Baby's Gone/Your Yah Yah Is Gone	1964	25.00	50.00	100.00

TRENDS, THE (1)

Number	Title (A Side/B Side)	Yr	VG	VG+	NM
ABC					
❑ 10817	A Night for Love/Gonna Have to Show You	1966	6.25	12.50	25.00
❑ 10881	No One There/That's How I Like It	1966	6.25	12.50	25.00
❑ 10944	Check My Tears/Don't Drop Out of School	1967	5.00	10.00	20.00
❑ 10993	Thanks for a Little Lovin'/I Never Knew How Good I Had It	1967	5.00	10.00	20.00
❑ 11091	Soul Clap/Big Parade	1968	5.00	10.00	20.00
❑ 11150	Not Another Day/You Sure Know How to Hurt a Guy	1968	10.00	20.00	40.00
ABC-PARAMOUNT					
❑ 10731	Not Too Old to Cry/If You Don't Dig the Blues	1965	10.00	20.00	40.00
SMASH					
❑ 1914	Dance with My Baby/To Be Happy Enough	1964	6.25	12.50	25.00
❑ 1933	Get Something Going/That's the Way the Story Goes	1964	6.25	12.50	25.00

TRENDS, THE (2)

Number	Title (A Side/B Side)	Yr	VG	VG+	NM
ARGO					
❑ 5341	I'll Be True/Class Ring	1959	7.50	15.00	30.00
SCOPE					
❑ 102	Gone Again/Silly Grin	1959	20.00	40.00	80.00

TRENDS, THE (U)

Definitely not group (1), but it may not be group (2), either.

Number	Title (A Side/B Side)	Yr	VG	VG+	NM
RCA VICTOR					
❑ 47-7733	The Beard/Chug-a-Lug	1960	3.75	7.50	15.00

TRENIERS, THE

Number	Title (A Side/B Side)	Yr	VG	VG+	NM
BRUNSWICK					
❑ 55014	Holy Mackerel Andy/Rock Calypso Joe	1957	5.00	10.00	20.00
❑ 55033	Pennies from Heaven/Ooh-La-La	1957	5.00	10.00	20.00
❑ 55047	Goodnight Irene/Rubbing Noses in the Midnight Sun	1958	5.00	10.00	20.00
DOM					
❑ 410	Gotta Travel On/Let It All Hang Out	1968	2.00	4.00	8.00
DOT					
❑ 15882	Never Never/When Your Hair Has Turned to Silver	1958	5.00	10.00	20.00
EPIC					
❑ 9127	Go! Go! Go!/Doin' 'Em Up	1955	6.25	12.50	25.00
❑ 9144	Rock'n Roll Call/Day-Old Bread and Canned Beans	1956	6.25	12.50	25.00
❑ 9162	Boodie Green/Good Rockin' Tonight	1956	6.25	12.50	25.00
OKEH					
❑ 6804	Go! Go! Go!/Plenty of Money	1951	12.50	25.00	50.00
❑ 6826	Hey, Little Girl/Old Woman Blues	1951	10.00	20.00	40.00
❑ 6853	It Rocks, It Rolls, It Swings/Taxi Blues	1952	10.00	20.00	40.00
❑ 6876	Hadacol, That's All/Long Distance Blues	1952	10.00	20.00	40.00
❑ 6904	Rockin' on Sunday Night/Cheatin' On Me	1952	10.00	20.00	40.00
❑ 6932	Hi-Yo Silver/Poon-Tang!	1953	10.00	20.00	40.00
❑ 6937	The Moondog/Poon-Tang!	1953	12.50	25.00	50.00
❑ 6960	Rockin' Is Our Bizness/Sugar Doo	1953	10.00	20.00	40.00
❑ 6984	I'd Do Nothin' But Grieve/This Is It	1953	10.00	20.00	40.00
❑ 7012	You Know, Yeah! Tiger/Bug Dance	1953	10.00	20.00	40.00
❑ 7023	Rock-a-Beatin' Boogie/Trapped	1954	10.00	20.00	40.00
❑ 7035	Bald Head/Come On Let's Face It	1954	10.00	20.00	40.00
❑ 7050	Who Put the "Ungh" in the Mambo/Get Out of the Car	1955	7.50	15.00	30.00
❑ 7057	Devil's Mambo/Do, Do, Do (Do-Be-Oo-Be-Oo)	1955	7.50	15.00	30.00
VIK					
❑ 0214	Lover Come Back to Me/Sorrento	1956	6.25	12.50	25.00
❑ 0227	Rock and Roll President/Cool It Baby	1956	6.25	12.50	25.00
7-Inch Extended Plays					
EPIC					
❑ EG-7014	(contents unknown)	1955	12.50	25.00	50.00
❑ EG-7014 [PS]	Go! Go! Go!	1955	12.50	25.00	50.00
❑ EG-7114	(contents unknown)	195?	12.50	25.00	50.00
❑ EG-7114 [PS]	Those Crazy Treniers	195?	12.50	25.00	50.00

TRENT, JACKIE

The record on Nasco may be by a different singer than the others.

Number	Title (A Side/B Side)	Yr	VG	VG+	NM
A&M					
❑ 1022	Hollywood/Don't Send Me Away	1969	—	3.00	6.00

Number	Title (A Side/B Side)	Yr	VG	VG+	NM
KAPP					
❑ 583	Only One Such As You/If You Love Me, Really Love Me	1964	3.00	6.00	12.00
❑ 630	Somewhere in the World/I Heard Someone Say	1964	3.00	6.00	12.00
NASCO					
❑ 6012	Little Andy/What's He Got	1958	6.25	12.50	25.00
PARKWAY					
❑ 941	Don't Stand in My Way/How Soon	1965	3.00	6.00	12.00
❑ 955	Where Are You Now My Love/On the Other Side of the Tracks	1965	3.00	6.00	12.00
❑ 963	To Show I Love Him/When Summertime Is Over	1965	3.00	6.00	12.00
WARNER BROS.					
❑ 5683	It's All in the Way You Look at Life/Time After Time	1965	2.50	5.00	10.00
❑ 5865	If You Ever Leave Me/Take Me Away	1966	2.50	5.00	10.00
❑ 7022	Hummingbird/I'll Be with You	1967	2.00	4.00	8.00
❑ 7070	It's Not Easy Loving You/Your Love Is Everywhere	1967	2.00	4.00	8.00
❑ 7178	7:10 to Suburbia/Stop Me and Buy One	1968	2.00	4.00	8.00
❑ 7189	I'll Be With You/Two of Us	1968	2.00	4.00	8.00

TRENTONS, THE

Number	Title (A Side/B Side)	Yr	VG	VG+	NM
SHEPHERD					
❑ 2204	All Alone/Star Bright	1962	20.00	40.00	80.00

TRIANGLES, THE

Number	Title (A Side/B Side)	Yr	VG	VG+	NM
FARGO					
❑ 1023	Dance the Magoo/Step-Up-and-Go	1962	3.75	7.50	15.00
FIFO					
❑ 107	My Oh My/Really I Do	1964	50.00	100.00	200.00
HERALD					
❑ 549	Savin' My Love/'Tis a Pity	1960	10.00	20.00	40.00

TRIBULATIONS, THE

Number	Title (A Side/B Side)	Yr	VG	VG+	NM
IMPERIAL					
❑ 66416	Mama's Love/You Gave Me Up for Promises	1969	7.50	15.00	30.00

TRICKELS, THE

Number	Title (A Side/B Side)	Yr	VG	VG+	NM
GONE					
❑ 5078	With Each Step a Tear/Outside the Chapel Door	1959	25.00	50.00	100.00
POWER					
❑ 250	With Each Step a Tear/When I Fall in Love	1958	50.00	100.00	200.00

TRIDELS, THE

Number	Title (A Side/B Side)	Yr	VG	VG+	NM
SAN-DEE					
❑ 1009	Land of Love/Image of My Love	1963	12.50	25.00	50.00

TRINIDADS, THE

Number	Title (A Side/B Side)	Yr	VG	VG+	NM
FORMAL					
❑ 1005	Don't Say Goodbye/On My Happy Way	1959	50.00	100.00	200.00
❑ 1006	One Lonely Night/When We're Together	1959	50.00	100.00	200.00

TRIOLO, FRANK

Number	Title (A Side/B Side)	Yr	VG	VG+	NM
FLAGSHIP					
❑ 106	Ice Cream Baby/Pretty Little Woman	1958	100.00	200.00	400.00

TROGGS, THE

Number	Title (A Side/B Side)	Yr	VG	VG+	NM
ATCO					
❑ 6415	Wild Thing/With a Girl Like You	1966	6.25	12.50	25.00
—"Wild Thing" writer is incorrectly credited as "Presley."					
❑ 6415	Wild Thing/With a Girl Like You	1966	5.00	10.00	20.00
—"Wild Thing" writer is correctly credited as "Taylor."					
❑ 6415	Wild Thing/I Want You	1966	5.00	10.00	20.00
❑ 6444	I Can't Control Myself/Gonna Make You	1966	3.75	7.50	15.00
BELL					
❑ 45405	Listen to the Man/Queen of Sorrow	1973	2.00	4.00	8.00
❑ 45426	Strange Movies/I'm on Fire	1973	2.00	4.00	8.00
FONTANA					
❑ 1548	Wild Thing/From Home	1966	2.50	5.00	10.00
❑ 1552	With a Girl Like You/I Want You	1966	2.50	5.00	10.00
❑ 1557	I Can't Control Myself/Gonna Make You	1966	2.50	5.00	10.00
❑ 1576	You're Lying/Give It To Me	1967	2.00	4.00	8.00
❑ 1585	6-5-4-3-2-1/Anyway That You Want Me	1967	2.00	4.00	8.00
❑ 1593	Night of the Long Grass/Girl in Black	1967	2.00	4.00	8.00
❑ 1607	Love Is All Around/When Will the Rain Come	1967	2.50	5.00	10.00
❑ 1622	You Can Cry If You Want To/There's Something About You	1968	2.00	4.00	8.00
❑ 1630	Surprise, Surprise/Cousin Jane	1968	2.00	4.00	8.00
❑ 1634	Hip Hip Hooray/Say Darlin'	1968	2.00	4.00	8.00
PAGE ONE					
❑ 21026	Evil Woman/Heads Or Tails	1969	—	3.00	6.00
❑ 21030	Easy Lovin'/Give Me Something	1970	—	3.00	6.00
❑ 21032	Come Now/Lover	1970	—	3.00	6.00
❑ 21035	The Raver/You	1970	—	3.00	6.00
PRIVATE STOCK					
❑ 45102	Rolling Stone/(B-side unknown)	1976	—	2.50	5.00
PYE					
❑ 65011	Feels Like a Woman/Everything's Funny	1972	2.00	4.00	8.00
❑ 71015	Good Vibrations/Push It Up to Me	1975	—	2.50	5.00
❑ 71035	Summertime/Jerry Come Down	1975	—	2.50	5.00
❑ 71054	Satisfaction/(B-side unknown)	1975	—	2.50	5.00

TROLL, THE

Number	Title (A Side/B Side)	Yr	VG	VG+	NM
SMASH					
❑ 2208	Satin City News/Professor Potts' Pornographic Projector	1969	3.00	6.00	12.00

TROLLS, THE

Number	Title (A Side/B Side)	Yr	VG	VG+	NM
ABC					
❑ 10823	Every Day and Every Night/Are You the One	1966	3.00	6.00	12.00
❑ 10884	Laughing All the Way/Someone Here Inside	1966	2.50	5.00	10.00
❑ 10916	They Don't Know/There Was a Time	1967	2.50	5.00	10.00
❑ 10952	Baby. What You Ain't Got (I Ain't in Need)/Who Was That Boy	1967	2.50	5.00	10.00

Number	Title (A Side/B Side)	Yr	VG	VG+	NM
RUFF					
❑ 1010	Into My Arms/That's the Way My Love Is	1966	10.00	20.00	40.00
U.S.A.					
❑ 905	I Got to Have You/Don't Come Around	1968	6.25	12.50	25.00
WARRIOR					
❑ 173	Stupid Girl/I Don't Recall	1967	3.00	6.00	12.00
❑ 173 [PS]	Stupid Girl/I Don't Recall	1967	5.00	10.00	20.00

TROPHIES, THE

More than one group?

Number	Title (A Side/B Side)	Yr	VG	VG+	NM
CHALLENGE					
❑ 9133	Desire/Doggone It	1962	15.00	30.00	60.00
❑ 9149	Peg O' My Heart/I Laughed So Hard I Cried	1962	3.75	7.50	15.00
❑ 9170	That's All I Want from You/Felicia	1962	3.75	7.50	15.00
KAPP					
❑ 714	Everywhere I Go/Baby Don't Live Here Anymore	1965	3.75	7.50	15.00
❑ 750	Leave My Girl Alone/You're the Queen	1966	3.75	7.50	15.00
NORK					
❑ 79907	Walkin' the Dog/Somethin' Blue	196?	5.00	10.00	20.00

TROWER, ROBIN

Also see JACK BRUCE/ROBIN TROWER; PROCOL HARUM.

Number	Title (A Side/B Side)	Yr	VG	VG+	NM
CHRYSALIS					
❑ 2009	Man of the World/Take a Fast Train	1973	—	3.00	6.00
❑ 2113	Too Rolling Stoned (Part 1)/Too Rolling Stoned (Part 2)	1976	—	3.00	6.00
❑ 2122	Caledonia/Messin' the Blues	1976	—	3.00	6.00
❑ 2172	Sweet Wine of Love/In City Dreams	1977	—	2.50	5.00
❑ 2206	Somebody Calling/Bluebird	1978	—	2.50	5.00
❑ 2238	My Love (Burning Love)/(B-side unknown)	1978	—	2.50	5.00
❑ 2272	It's for You/Birthday Boy	1979	—	2.50	5.00

TROY, DORIS

Number	Title (A Side/B Side)	Yr	VG	VG+	NM
APPLE					
❑ 1820	Ain't That Cute/Vaya Con Dios	1970	2.00	4.00	8.00
❑ 1824	Jacob's Ladder/Get Back	1970	2.00	4.00	8.00
ATLANTIC					
❑ 2188	Just One Look/Bossa Nova Blues	1963	5.00	10.00	20.00
❑ 2206	Tomorrow Is Another Day/What'cha Gonna Do About It	1963	3.00	6.00	12.00
❑ 2222	One More Chance/Please Little Angel	1964	3.00	6.00	12.00
❑ 2269	Hurry/He Don't Belong to Me	1965	3.00	6.00	12.00
CALLA					
❑ 114	Heartaches/I'll Do Anything	1966	5.00	10.00	20.00
CAPITOL					
❑ 2043	Face Up to the Truth/He's Qualified	1967	2.00	4.00	8.00
MIDLAND INT'L.					
❑ MB-10806	Lyin' Eyes/Give God Glory	1976	—	2.50	5.00
❑ MB-11082	Can't Hold On/Another Look	1977	—	2.50	5.00

TRU-TONES, THE

Number	Title (A Side/B Side)	Yr	VG	VG+	NM
CHART					
❑ 634	Tears in My Eyes/Magic	1957	200.00	400.00	800.00
DEN RIC					
❑ 4527	I'm the Guy/(B-side unknown)	196?	10.00	20.00	40.00
KEB					
❑ 6037	Soldier's Last Letter/(B-side unknown)	196?	10.00	20.00	40.00

TUBB, ERNEST

Also see THE TEXAS TROUBADOURS.

Number	Title (A Side/B Side)	Yr	VG	VG+	NM
CACHET					
❑ 4501	Waltz Across Texas/Jealous Loving Heart	1979	—	3.00	6.00
❑ 4507	Walking the Floor Over You/Let's Say Goodbye	1979	—	3.00	6.00
DECCA					
❑ 9-28067	Somebody's Stolen My Honey/My Mother Must Have Been a Girl Like You	1952	5.00	10.00	20.00
❑ 9-28310	Fortunes in Memories/So Many Times	1952	5.00	10.00	20.00
❑ 9-28448	Somebody Loves You/Don't Trifle on Your Sweetheart	1952	5.00	10.00	20.00
❑ 9-28453	Merry Texas Christmas, You All/Blue Snowflakes	1952	6.25	12.50	25.00
❑ 9-28550	Dear Judge/I Will Miss You When You Go	1953	5.00	10.00	20.00
❑ 9-28630	Hank It Will Never Be the Same/Beyond the Sunset	1953	7.50	15.00	30.00
❑ 9-28696	Jimmie Rodgers' Last Thoughts/When Jimmie Said Goodbye	1953	6.25	12.50	25.00
❑ 9-28777	Don't Brush Them on Me/My Wasted Past	1953	5.00	10.00	20.00
❑ 9-28837	A Dear John Letter/The Mean Age, In Between Age Blues	1953	5.00	10.00	20.00
—As "Bill and Ernest Tubb"					
❑ 9-28869	Divorce Granted/Counterfeit Kisses	1953	5.00	10.00	20.00
❑ 9-28946	I'm Trimming My Christmas Tree with Teardrops/We Need God for Christmas	1953	5.00	10.00	20.00
❑ 9-29011	Honky Tonk Heart/I'm Not Looking for an Angel	1954	5.00	10.00	20.00
❑ 9-29020	Jealous Loving Heart/Till We Two Are One	1954	5.00	10.00	20.00
❑ 9-29103	Baby Your Mother (Like She Babies You)/Your Mother, Your Darling, Your Friend	1954	6.25	12.50	25.00
❑ 9-29220	Two Glasses, Joe/Journey's End	1954	5.00	10.00	20.00
❑ 9-29350	I'll Be Walkin' the Floor This Christmas/Lonely Christmas Eve	1954	5.00	10.00	20.00
❑ 9-29415	Kansas City Blues/The Woman's Touch	1955	3.75	7.50	15.00
❑ 9-29520	It's a Lonely World/Have You Seen	1955	3.75	7.50	15.00
❑ 9-29624	I Met a Friend/When Jesus Calls	1955	3.75	7.50	15.00
❑ 9-29633	The Yellow Rose of Texas/A Million Miles from Here	1955	3.75	7.50	15.00
❑ 9-29731	Thirty Days (To Come Back Home)/Answer the Phone	1955	5.00	10.00	20.00
❑ 9-29836	So Doggone Lonesome/If I Never Have Anything Else	1956	3.75	7.50	15.00
❑ 9-29934	Jimmie Rodgers' Last Blue Yodel/Will You Be Satisfied That Way	1956	3.75	7.50	15.00
❑ 9-30098	Treat Her Right/Loving You Is My Weakness	1956	3.75	7.50	15.00
❑ 9-30219	Don't Forbid Me/God's Eye	1957	3.75	7.50	15.00

Number	Title (A Side/B Side)	Yr	VG	VG+	NM
9-30305	Mister Love/Leave Me	1957	3.75	7.50	15.00
9-30422	My Treasure/Go Home	1957	3.75	7.50	15.00
9-30526	Geisha Girl/I Found My Girl in the U.S.A.	1957	3.75	7.50	15.00
9-30549	House of Glass/Heaven Help Me	1958	3.75	7.50	15.00
9-30610	Hey, Mr. Bluebird/How Do We Know	1958	3.75	7.50	15.00
9- 30685	Half a Mind/The Blues	1958	3.75	7.50	15.00
9-30759	What Am I Living For/Goodbye Sunshine, Hello Blues	1958	3.75	7.50	15.00
9-30872	I Cried a Tear/I'd Rather Be	1959	3.75	7.50	15.00
9-30952	Next Time/What I Know About Her	1959	3.75	7.50	15.00
9-31082	Live It Up/Accidentally on Purpose	1960	3.00	6.00	12.00
9-31119	Ev'rybody's Somebody's Fool/Let the Little Girl Dance	1960	3.00	6.00	12.00
31161	White Silver Sands/A Guy Named Joe	1960	3.00	6.00	12.00
31196	Girl from Abilene/Little Old Band of Gold	1961	3.00	6.00	12.00
31241	Thoughts of a Fool/Don't Just Stand There	1961	3.00	6.00	12.00
31300	Through That Door/What Will You Tell Them	1961	3.00	6.00	12.00
31334	Christmas Is Just Another Day for Me/Rudolph the Red-Nosed Reindeer	1961	3.00	6.00	12.00
31357	Go to Sleep Conscience (Don't Hurt Me This Time)/I Could Never Say No	1962	3.00	6.00	12.00
31399	I'm Looking High and Low for My Baby/Show Her Lots of Gold	1962	3.00	6.00	12.00
31428	House of Sorrow/No Letter Today	1962	3.00	6.00	12.00
31476	Mr. Juke Box/Walking the Floor Over You	1963	3.00	6.00	12.00
31526	Thanks a Lot/The Way That You're Living	1963	3.00	6.00	12.00
31614	Be Better to Your Baby/Think of Me, Thinking of You	1964	2.50	5.00	10.00
31706	Pass the Booze/(A Memory) That's All You'll Ever Be to Me	1964	2.50	5.00	10.00
31742	Do What You Do Well/Turn Around, Walk Away	1965	2.50	5.00	10.00
31824	Waltz Across Texas/Lots of Luck	1965	2.50	5.00	10.00
31861	It's for God, and Country, and You Mom (That's Why I'm Fighting in Viet Nam)/After the Boy Gets the Girl	1965	2.50	5.00	10.00
31866	Who's Gonna Be Your Santa Claus/Blue Christmas Tree	1965	2.50	5.00	10.00
31908	Till Me Getup Has Gotup and Gone/Just One More	1966	2.50	5.00	10.00
32022	Another Story/There's No Room in My Heart (For the Blues)	1966	2.50	5.00	10.00
32131	In the Jailhouse Now/Yesterday's Winner Is a Loser Today	1967	2.50	5.00	10.00
32237	Too Much of Not Enough/Nothing Is Better Than You	1968	2.00	4.00	8.00
32315	I'm Gonna Make Like a Snake/Mama, Who Was That Man	1968	2.00	4.00	8.00
32377	Just Pack and Go/It Sure Helps a Lot	1968	2.00	4.00	8.00
32448	Saturday Satan Sunday Saint/Tommy's Doll	1969	2.00	4.00	8.00
32532	Just a Drink Away/One More Memory	1969	2.00	4.00	8.00
32632	It's America/Somebody Better Than Me	1970	2.00	4.00	8.00
32690	Dear Judge/A Good Year for the Wine	1970	2.00	4.00	8.00
32800	One Sweet Hello/Once Ole Going Gets a-Goin'	1971	2.00	4.00	8.00
32849	Don't Back a Man in a Corner/Shenandoah Waltz	1971	2.00	4.00	8.00
32943	Say Something Nice to Sarah/Teach My Daddy How to Pray	1972	2.00	4.00	8.00
33014	Baby, It's So Hard to Be Good/In This Corner	1972	2.00	4.00	8.00
9-46018	Rainbow at Midnight/I Don't Blame You	1950	10.00	20.00	40.00
—78 first issued in 1946					
9-46186	White Christmas/Blue Christmas	1950	7.50	15.00	30.00
—78 first issued in 1949; black label, lines on either side of "Decca"					
9-46243	Throw Your Love My Way/Give Me a Little Old Fashioned Love	1950	10.00	20.00	40.00
9-46257	You Don't Have to Be a Baby to Cry/G-I-R-L Spells Trouble	1950	7.50	15.00	30.00
9-46268	Christmas Island/Christmas	1950	7.50	15.00	30.00
—Black label, lines on either side of "Decca"					
9-46269	(Remember Me) I'm the One Who Loves You/I Need Attention Bad	1950	7.50	15.00	30.00
9-46289	Tomorrow Never Comes/Are You Waiting Just for Me	1951	6.25	12.50	25.00
9-46295	When It's Prayer Meetin' Time in the Hollow/May the Good Lord Bless and Keep You	1951	6.25	12.50	25.00
9-46296	Don't Stay Too Long/If You Want Some Lovin'	1951	6.25	12.50	25.00
9-46306	Mother, Queen of My Heart/I'm Lonely and Blue	1951	5.00	10.00	20.00
9-46307	Why Did You Give Me Your Love/I'm Free from the Blues	1951	5.00	10.00	20.00
9-46308	Hobo's Meditation/Why Should I Be Lonely	1951	5.00	10.00	20.00
9-46309	Any Old Time/A Drunkard's Child	1951	5.00	10.00	20.00
—The above four comprise a box set					
9-46338	Hey La La/Precious Little Baby	1951	6.25	12.50	25.00
9-46343	Rose of the Mountain/I'm With the Crowd, But So Alone	1951	6.25	12.50	25.00
9-46377	Driftwood on the River/I'm Stepping Out of the Picture	1951	6.25	12.50	25.00
9-46389	Missing in Action/A Heartsick Soldier on Heartbreak Ridge	1952	6.25	12.50	25.00
FIRST GENERATION					
001	Sometimes I Do/Half My Heart's in Texas	1977	—	3.50	7.00
MCA					
40056	I've Got All the Heartaches I Can Handle/The Texas Troubadour	1973	—	3.00	6.00
40222	Anything But This/Don't Water Down the Bad News	1974	—	3.00	6.00
40436	If You Don't Quit Checkin' on Me (I'm Checkin' Out on You)/I'd Like to Live It Again	1975	—	3.00	6.00
65024	White Christmas/Blue Christmas	1973	—	2.00	4.00
—Black label with rainbow					
65024	White Christmas/Blue Christmas	1980	—	—	3.00
—Blue label with rainbow					
RHINO					
74415	Walking the Floor Over You/(B-side unknown)	1991	3.00	6.00	12.00
—Black vinyl					
74415	Walking the Floor Over You/(B-side unknown)	1991	—	3.00	6.00
—Red vinyl					
74415	Walking the Floor Over You/(B-side unknown)	1991	—	3.50	7.00
—Blue vinyl					
74415 [PS]	Walking the Floor Over You/(B-side unknown)	1991	—	3.00	6.00
7-Inch Extended Plays					
DECCA					
ED 2026	(contents unknown)	195?	6.25	12.50	25.00
ED 2026 [PS]	Ernest Tubb Sings	195?	6.25	12.50	25.00
ED 2089	(contents unknown)	195?	6.25	12.50	25.00
ED 2089 [PS]	White Christmas	195?	6.25	12.50	25.00
ED 2356	(contents unknown)	1956	5.00	10.00	20.00
ED 2356 [PS]	Ernest Tubb Favorites, Vol. 1	1956	5.00	10.00	20.00
ED 2357	(contents unknown)	1956	5.00	10.00	20.00
ED 2357 [PS]	Ernest Tubb Favorites, Vol. 2	1956	5.00	10.00	20.00
ED 2521	*You're Breaking My Heart/I Know My Baby Loves Me in Her Own Peculiar Way/I've Got the Blues for Mammy/This Troubled Mind o' Mine	1957	5.00	10.00	20.00
ED 2521 [PS]	The Daddy of 'Em All	1957	5.00	10.00	20.00
ED 2522	*I Dreamed of an Old Love Affair/Mississippi Gal/When a Soldier Knocks and Finds Nobody Home/Daisy Mae	1957	5.00	10.00	20.00
ED 2522 [PS]	Encores	1957	5.00	10.00	20.00
ED 2523	*I Knew the Moment I Lost You/You're the Only Good Thing/My Hillbilly Baby/There's No Fool Like a Young Fool	1957	5.00	10.00	20.00
ED 2523 [PS]	My Hillbilly Baby	1957	5.00	10.00	20.00
ED 2563	*Geisha Girl/I Found My Girl in the U.S.A./Home of the Blues/Tangled Mind	1958	5.00	10.00	20.00
ED 2563 [PS]	Ernest Tubb Sings the Hits	1958	5.00	10.00	20.00
ED 2626	*House of Glass/My Treasure/Treat Her Right/Don't Forbid Me	1959	5.00	10.00	20.00
ED 2626 [PS]	Ernest Tubb	1959	5.00	10.00	20.00
ED 2627	*Mister Love/Leave Me/Hey Mr. Bluebird/How Do I Know	1959	5.00	10.00	20.00
ED 2627 [PS]	Ernest Tubb and the Wilburn Brothers	1959	5.00	10.00	20.00
ED 2643	*I'm a Long Gone Daddy/San Antonio Rose/Your Cheatin' Heart/It Makes No Difference Now	1959	5.00	10.00	20.00
ED 2643	The Importance of Being Ernest	1959	5.00	10.00	20.00
ED 2655 [M]	*Have You Ever Been Lonely/Rainbow at Midnight/Careless Darlin'/You Nearly Lost Your Mind	1959	5.00	10.00	20.00
ED 2655 [PS]	The Ernest Tubb Story	1959	5.00	10.00	20.00
ED 7-2655 [PS]	The Ernest Tubb Story	1959	7.50	15.00	30.00
ED 7-2655 [S]	*Have You Ever Been Lonely/Rainbow at Midnight/Careless Darlin'/You Nearly Lost Your Mind	1959	7.50	15.00	30.00
ED 2680	*He'll Have to Go/White Silver Sands/Am I That Easy to Forget/Guy Named Joe	1960	5.00	10.00	20.00
ED 2680 [PS]	The Ernest Tubb Record Shop	1960	5.00	10.00	20.00
ED 2691	*Ev'rybody's Somebody's Fool/Let the Little Girl Dance/Live It Up/Accidentally on Purpose	1960	5.00	10.00	20.00
ED 2691 [PS]	Ernest Tubb	1960	5.00	10.00	20.00
ED 2706	(contents unknown)	1962	5.00	10.00	20.00
ED 2706 [PS]	Ernest Tubb	1962	5.00	10.00	20.00
ED 2718	*What Will You Tell Them/Thoughts of a Fool/Go to Sleep Conscience/I Never Could Say No	1961	5.00	10.00	20.00
ED 2718 [PS]	Ernest Tubb	1961	5.00	10.00	20.00
ED 2728	*Show Her Lots of Gold/I'm Looking High and Low for My Baby/I Walk the Line/Crazy Arms	1962	6.25	12.50	25.00
ED 2728 [PS]	Show Her Lots of Gold	1962	6.25	12.50	25.00
ED 2739	*No Letter Today/Women Make a Fool Out of Me/House of Sorrow/Go On Home	1963	6.25	12.50	25.00
ED 2739 [PS]	Ernest Tubb	1963	6.25	12.50	25.00
ED 2769	(contents unknown)	1964	6.25	12.50	25.00
ED 2769 [PS]	Ernest Tubb	1964	6.25	12.50	25.00
ED 2774	*Thanks a Lot/Mr. Juke Box/Last Letter/Just Call Me Lonesome	1964	6.25	12.50	25.00
ED 2774 [PS]	Thanks a Lot	1964	6.25	12.50	25.00
ED 2787	(contents unknown)	1965	7.50	15.00	30.00
ED 2787 [PS]	Be Better to Your Baby	1965	7.50	15.00	30.00
ED 2797	(contents unknown)	1965	7.50	15.00	30.00
ED 2797 [PS]	Pass the Booze	1965	7.50	15.00	30.00
7-4518 [PS]	Blue Christmas	1964	3.75	7.50	15.00
7-4518 [S]	(contents unknown)	1964	3.75	7.50	15.00
—33 1/3 rpm, small hole jukebox edition					

TUBB, ERNEST, AND LORETTA LYNN

Also see LORETTA LYNN.

Number	Title (A Side/B Side)	Yr	VG	VG+	NM
DECCA					
31643	Mr. and Mrs. Used to Be/Love Was Right Here All the Time	1964	2.50	5.00	10.00
31793	Our Hearts Are Holding Hands/We're Not Kids Anymore	1965	2.50	5.00	10.00
32091	Sweet Thang/Beautiful, Unhappy Home	1967	2.50	5.00	10.00
32496	Who's Gonna Take the Garbage Out/Somewhere Between	1969	2.00	4.00	8.00
32570	I Chased You Till You Caught Me/If We Put Our Heads Together	1969	2.00	4.00	8.00

TUBES, THE

Number	Title (A Side/B Side)	Yr	VG	VG+	NM
A&M					
1733	White Punks on Dope (Part 1)/White Punks on Dope (Part 2)	1975	—	2.50	5.00
1733 [PS]	White Punks on Dope (Part 1)/White Punks on Dope (Part 2)	1975	2.00	4.00	8.00
1755	What Do You Want from Life/Space Baby	1975	—	2.50	5.00
1826	Don't Touch Me There/Proud to Be an American	1976	—	2.50	5.00
1956	This Town/I'm Just a Mess	1977	—	2.50	5.00
2037	Show Me a Reason/I Saw Her Standing There	1978	—	2.50	5.00

Number	Title (A Side/B Side)	Yr	VG	VG+	NM
❑ 2120	Prime Time/No Way Out	1979	—	2.50	5.00
❑ 2149	Love's a Mystery (I Don't Understand)/Telecide	1979	—	2.50	5.00
❑ 8591	White Punks on Dope/What Do You Want from Life?	198?	—	—	3.00

—Reissue

CAPIROL

Number	Title (A Side/B Side)	Yr	VG	VG+	NM
❑ SPRO-9740 [DJ]	Sports Fans (same on both sides)	1982	—	2.50	5.00

CAPITOL

Number	Title (A Side/B Side)	Yr	VG	VG+	NM
❑ 5007	Don't Want to Wait Anymore/Think About Me	1981	—	—	3.00
❑ 5007 [PS]	Don't Want to Wait Anymore/Think About Me	1981	—	—	3.00
❑ 5016	Talk To Ya Later/Power Tools	1981	—	2.00	4.00
❑ 5091	Gonna Get It Next Time/Sports Fans	1982	—	2.00	4.00
❑ B-5217	She's a Beauty/When You're Ready to Come	1983	—	2.00	4.00

—First pressing: Purple label

Number	Title (A Side/B Side)	Yr	VG	VG+	NM
❑ B-5217	She's a Beauty/When You're Ready to Come	1983	—	—	3.00

—Second pressing: Black label with multi-colored ring

Number	Title (A Side/B Side)	Yr	VG	VG+	NM
❑ B-5217 [PS]	She's a Beauty/When You're Ready to Come	1983	—	2.00	4.00

—Sleeve only came with first pressing, and then not with all of them

Number	Title (A Side/B Side)	Yr	VG	VG+	NM
❑ B-5254	The Monkey Time/Sports Fans	1983	—	—	3.00
❑ B-5254 [PS]	The Monkey Time/Sports Fans	1983	—	—	3.00
❑ B-5258	Tip of My Tongue/Keyboard Kids	1983	—	—	3.00
❑ B-5443	Piece by Piece/Night People	1985	—	—	3.00
❑ B-5443 [PS]	Piece by Piece/Night People	1985	—	2.00	4.00

TUBES

Number	Title (A Side/B Side)	Yr	VG	VG+	NM
❑ 12682XS	Tubular Holiday	1982	12.50	25.00	50.00

—Fan club flexidisc

Number	Title (A Side/B Side)	Yr	VG	VG+	NM
❑ 833502XS	Happy Holidaze	1983	12.50	25.00	50.00

—Fan club flexidisc

TUCKER, BILLY JOE

DOT

Number	Title (A Side/B Side)	Yr	VG	VG+	NM
❑ 16240	Boogie Woogie Bill/Mail Train	1961	25.00	50.00	100.00

MAHA

Number	Title (A Side/B Side)	Yr	VG	VG+	NM
❑ 103	Boogie Woogie Bill/Mail Train	1961	75.00	150.00	300.00

TUCKER, LITTLE TOMMY

See LITTLE TOMMY.

TUCKER, TANYA

ARISTA

Number	Title (A Side/B Side)	Yr	VG	VG+	NM
❑ 0677	Feel Right/Cry	1982	—	2.00	4.00
❑ 1053	Changes/Too Long	1983	—	2.00	4.00
❑ 9006	Changes/Too Long	1983	—	—	3.00
❑ 9046	Baby I'm Yours/I Don't Want You to Go	1983	—	—	3.00

CAPITOL

Number	Title (A Side/B Side)	Yr	VG	VG+	NM
❑ 4986	Why Don't We Just Sleep on It Tonight/It's Your World	1981	—	2.00	4.00

—With Glen Campbell

Number	Title (A Side/B Side)	Yr	VG	VG+	NM
❑ B-5533	One Love at a Time/(B-side unknown)	1985	—	—	3.00
❑ B-5533 [PS]	One Love at a Time/(B-side unknown)	1985	—	—	3.00
❑ B-5604	Just Another Love/You Could Change My Mind	1986	—	—	3.00
❑ B-5604 [PS]	Just Another Love/You Could Change My Mind	1986	—	—	3.00
❑ B-5652	I'll Come Back As Another Woman/Somebody to Care	1986	—	—	3.00
❑ B-5694	It's Only for You/Girls Like Me	1987	—	2.50	5.00

—First pressing had erroneous A-side title

Number	Title (A Side/B Side)	Yr	VG	VG+	NM
❑ B-5694	It's Only Over for You/Girls Like Me	1987	—	—	3.00
❑ B-44036	Love Me Like You Used To/If I Didn't Love You	1987	—	—	3.00
❑ B-44036 [PS]	Love Me Like You Used To/If I Didn't Love You	1987	—	—	3.00
❑ B-44100	I Won't Take Less Than Your Love/Heartbreaker	1987	—	—	3.00

—With Paul Davis and Paul Overstreet

Number	Title (A Side/B Side)	Yr	VG	VG+	NM
❑ B-44142	If It Don't Come Easy/I'll Tennessee You in My Dreams	1988	—	—	3.00
❑ B-44188	Strong Enough to Bend/Back on My Feet	1988	—	—	3.00
❑ B-44271	Highway Robbery/Lonesome Town	1989	—	—	3.00
❑ B-44348	Call on Me/Daddy and Home	1989	—	—	3.00
❑ B-44401	Daddy and Home/Playing for Keeps	1989	—	—	3.00
❑ B-44469	My Arms Stay Open All Night/Love Me Like You Used To	1989	—	—	3.00
❑ NR-44520	Walking Shoes/This Heart of Mine	1990	—	2.00	4.00
❑ NR-44586	Don't Go Out/(B-side unknown)	1990	—	2.50	5.00

—With T. Graham Brown; may only have been released on cassette single

Number	Title (A Side/B Side)	Yr	VG	VG+	NM
❑ 7PRO-79810	My Arms Stay Open All Night (same on both sides)	1989	—	2.50	5.00

—Originally promo only; stock copy on 44469

CAPITOL NASHVILLE

Number	Title (A Side/B Side)	Yr	VG	VG+	NM
❑ S7-19515	Little Things/You Don't Do It	1997	—	—	3.00
❑ S7-19628	Ridin' Out the Heartache/I Don't Believe That's How You Feel	1997	—	—	3.00
❑ NR-44774	(Without You) What Do I Do with Me/Oh What It Did to Me	1991	—	2.50	5.00
❑ 7PRO-79149	Don't Go Out (same on both sides)	1990	—	2.50	5.00

—With T. Graham Brown; vinyl may be promo only

Number	Title (A Side/B Side)	Yr	VG	VG+	NM
❑ 7PRO-79338	It Won't Be Me (same on both sides)	1990	—	3.00	6.00

—Vinyl is promo only

Number	Title (A Side/B Side)	Yr	VG	VG+	NM
❑ 7PRO-79535	Oh What It Did to Me (same on both sides)	1991	—	3.00	6.00

—Vinyl is promo only

Number	Title (A Side/B Side)	Yr	VG	VG+	NM
❑ 7PRO-79711	Down to My Last Teardrop (same on both sides)	1991	—	3.00	6.00

—Vinyl is promo only

COLUMBIA

Number	Title (A Side/B Side)	Yr	VG	VG+	NM
❑ 10069	I Believe the South Is Gonna Rise Again/Old Dan Tucker's Daughter	1974	—	2.50	5.00
❑ 10127	Spring/Bed of Roses	1975	—	2.50	5.00
❑ 10236	Greener Than the Grass (We Laid On)/Guess I'll Have to Love Him More	1975	—	2.50	5.00
❑ 10577	You Are So Beautiful/Almost Persuaded	1977	—	2.00	4.00
❑ 45588	Delta Dawn/I Love the Way He Loves Me	1972	—	2.50	5.00
❑ 45588 [PS]	Delta Dawn/I Love the Way He Loves Me	1972	2.50	5.00	10.00
❑ 45721	Love's the Answer/The Jamestown Ferry	1972	—	2.50	5.00
❑ 45799	What's Your Mama's Name/Rainy Girl	1973	—	2.50	5.00
❑ 45892	Blood Red and Goin' Down/Missing Piece of Puzzle	1973	—	2.50	5.00
❑ 45991	Would You Lay with Me (In a Field of Stone)/No Man's Land	1974	—	2.50	5.00
❑ 46047	The Man That Turned My Mama On/Satisfied with Missing You	1974	—	2.50	5.00

LIBERTY

Number	Title (A Side/B Side)	Yr	VG	VG+	NM
❑ S7-17594	Soon/Sneaky Moon	1993	—	2.00	4.00
❑ S7-17803	We Don't Have to Do This/Silence Is King	1994	—	2.00	4.00
❑ S7-17908	Hangin' In/Let the Good Times Roll	1994	—	2.00	4.00
❑ S7-18135	You Just Watch Me/I Love You Anyway	1994	—	2.00	4.00
❑ S7-18485	Between the Two of Them/Love Will	1995	—	2.00	4.00
❑ S7-18583	Something/All My Loving	1995	—	2.00	4.00

—B-side by Suzy Bogguss and Chet Atkins

Number	Title (A Side/B Side)	Yr	VG	VG+	NM
❑ S7-56825	Two Sparrows in a Hurricane/Danger Ahead	1992	—	2.00	4.00
❑ S7-56953	It's a Little Too Late/Rainbow Rider	1993	—	2.00	4.00
❑ S7-56985	Tell Me About It/What Do They Know	1993	—	2.00	4.00

—A-side with Delbert McClinton

Number	Title (A Side/B Side)	Yr	VG	VG+	NM
❑ S7-57703	Some Kind of Trouble/Oh What It Did to Me	1992	—	2.50	5.00
❑ S7-57768	If Your Heart Ain't Busy Tonight/Down to My Last Teardrop	1992	—	2.50	5.00
❑ S7-57895	Winter Wonderland/What Child Is This	1992	—	2.00	4.00

MCA

Number	Title (A Side/B Side)	Yr	VG	VG+	NM
❑ 40402	Lizzie and the Rainman/Traveling Salesman	1975	—	2.00	4.00
❑ 40444	San Antonio Stroll/The Serenade That We Played	1975	—	2.00	4.00
❑ 40497	Don't Believe My Heart Can Stand Another You/Depend on You	1975	—	2.00	4.00
❑ 40540	You've Got Me to Hold On To/Ain't That a Shame	1976	—	2.00	4.00
❑ 40598	Here's Some Love/The Pride of Franklin County	1976	—	2.00	4.00
❑ 40650	Ridin' Rainbows/Short Cut	1976	—	2.00	4.00
❑ 40708	It's a Cowboy Lovin' Night/Morning Comes	1977	—	2.00	4.00
❑ 40755	Dancing the Night Away/Let's Keep It That Way	1977	—	2.00	4.00
❑ 40902	Save Me/Slippin' Away	1978	—	2.00	4.00
❑ 40902 [PS]	Save Me/Slippin' Away	1978	—	3.00	6.00
❑ 40976	Texas (When I Die)/Not Fade Away	1978	—	2.00	4.00
❑ 40976 [PS]	Texas (When I Die)/Not Fade Away	1978	—	3.00	6.00
❑ 41005	I'm the Singer, You're the Song/Lover Goodbye	1979	—	2.00	4.00
❑ 41144	Lay Back in the Arms of Someone/By Day By Day	1979	—	2.00	4.00
❑ 41194	Tear Me Apart/Better Late Than Never	1980	—	2.00	4.00
❑ 41305	Pecos Promenade/King of Country Music	1980	—	2.00	4.00
❑ 41323	Dream Lover/Bronco	1980	—	2.00	4.00

—A-side with Glen Campbell

Number	Title (A Side/B Side)	Yr	VG	VG+	NM
❑ 51037	Can I See You Tonight/Let Me Count the Ways	1980	—	2.00	4.00
❑ 51096	Love Knows We Tried/Somebody (Trying to Tell You Something)	1981	—	2.00	4.00
❑ 51131	Should I Do It/Lucky Enough for Two	1981	—	2.00	4.00
❑ 51184	Rodeo Girls/Halfway to Heaven	1981	—	2.00	4.00
❑ 52017	Somebody Buy This Cowgirl a Beer/Delta Dawn	1982	—	2.00	4.00

TUCKER, TOMMY

May be two different performers.

CHECKER

Number	Title (A Side/B Side)	Yr	VG	VG+	NM
❑ 1067	Hi-Heel Sneakers/I Don't Want 'Cha	1964	6.25	12.50	25.00
❑ 1075	Long Tall Shorty/Mo' Shorty	1964	3.75	7.50	15.00
❑ 1112	Alimony/All About Melanie	1965	3.75	7.50	15.00
❑ 1133	Chewing Gun/I've Been a Fool	1966	2.50	5.00	10.00
❑ 1178	I'm Shorty/Sitting Home Alone	1967	2.00	4.00	8.00
❑ 1186	A Whole Lot of Fun Before the Weekend Is Done/Real True Love	1967	2.00	4.00	8.00

HI

Number	Title (A Side/B Side)	Yr	VG	VG+	NM
❑ 2014	Loving Lil/A Man in Love	1959	7.50	15.00	30.00
❑ 2020	Miller's Cave/The Strangers	1960	6.25	12.50	25.00

MGM

Number	Title (A Side/B Side)	Yr	VG	VG+	NM
❑ 10854	Christmas In Killarney/Jing-A-Ling	1950	3.75	7.50	15.00

RCA VICTOR

Number	Title (A Side/B Side)	Yr	VG	VG+	NM
❑ 37-7838	The Return of the Teenage Queen/Since You Have Gone	1961	6.25	12.50	25.00

—"Compact Single 33" (small hole, plays at LP speed)

Number	Title (A Side/B Side)	Yr	VG	VG+	NM
❑ 47-7838	The Return of the Teenage Queen/Since You Have Gone	1961	3.75	7.50	15.00
❑ 68-7838	The Return of the Teenage Queen/Since You Have Gone	1961	7.50	15.00	30.00

—"Compact Single 33" in "Living Stereo"

SUNBEAM

Number	Title (A Side/B Side)	Yr	VG	VG+	NM
❑ 128	My Blue Heaven/That Man Comes Around	1959	3.75	7.50	15.00

TUDOR MINSTRELS, THE

LONDON

Number	Title (A Side/B Side)	Yr	VG	VG+	NM
❑ 1012	Love in the Open Air/A Theme from "The Family Way"	1966	12.50	25.00	50.00

TUFFS, THE

DORE

Number	Title (A Side/B Side)	Yr	VG	VG+	NM
❑ 757	I Only Cry Once a Day Now/The Moon Out There	1966	6.25	12.50	25.00

DOT

Number	Title (A Side/B Side)	Yr	VG	VG+	NM
❑ 16304	Surfer Stomp (Part 1)/Surfer Stomp (Part 2)	1962	6.25	12.50	25.00

TULLY, LEE, AND MILT MOSS

FLAIR-X

Number	Title (A Side/B Side)	Yr	VG	VG+	NM
❑ 3007	Around the World with Elwood Pretzel (Part 1)/Around the World with Elwood Pretzel (Part 2)	1956	12.50	25.00	50.00

TUNE ROCKERS, THE

UNITED ARTISTS

Number	Title (A Side/B Side)	Yr	VG	VG+	NM
❑ 139	The Green Mosquito/Warm Up	1958	5.00	10.00	20.00
❑ 0145	The Green Mosquito/Bust Out	1973	—	2.00	4.00

—"Silver Spotlight Series" reissue; B-side by the Busters

TUNE WEAVERS, THE

CASA GRANDE

Number	Title (A Side/B Side)	Yr	VG	VG+	NM
❑ 101	Little Boy/Look Down That Lonesome Road	1959	10.00	20.00	40.00
❑ 3038	My Congratulations Baby/This Can't Be Love	1960	7.50	15.00	30.00
❑ 4037	Happy, Happy Birthday Baby/Ol' Man River	1957	37.50	75.00	150.00
❑ 4038	I Remember Dear/Pamela Jean	1957	7.50	15.00	30.00
❑ 4040	There Stands My Love/I'm Cold	1958	10.00	20.00	40.00

Number	Title (A Side/B Side)	Yr	VG	VG+	NM
CHECKER					
❑ 872	Happy, Happy Birthday Baby/Ol' Man River	1957	6.25	12.50	25.00
❑ 872	Happy, Happy Birthday Baby/Yo Yo Walk	1957	6.25	12.50	25.00
—B-side by Paul Gayten					
❑ 880	Ol' Man River/Tough Enough	1957	6.25	12.50	25.00
—B-side by Paul Gayten					
❑ 1007	Congratulations on Your Wedding/Your Skies of Blue	1962	6.25	12.50	25.00
CLASSIC ARTISTS					
❑ 104	Come Back to Me/I've Tried	1988	—	2.00	4.00
—As "Margo Sylvia and Tune Weavers"					
❑ 107	Merry, Merry Christmas Baby/What Are You Doing New Year's Eve	1988	—	2.00	4.00
—As "Margo Sylvia and Tune Weavers"					

TUNEDROPS, THE

Number	Title (A Side/B Side)	Yr	VG	VG+	NM
GONE					
❑ 5003	Rosie Lee/Speak for Yourself	1957	10.00	20.00	40.00
❑ 5072	Smoothie/Jumpin' Jellybeans	1959	6.25	12.50	25.00
METRO					
❑ 20028	Smoothie/Jumpin' Jelly Beans	1959	10.00	20.00	40.00

TUNEMASTERS, THE

Number	Title (A Side/B Side)	Yr	VG	VG+	NM
MARK					
❑ 7002	Sending This Letter/It's All Over	1957	75.00	150.00	300.00

TURBANS, THE

Also see THE TURKS/THE TURBANS.

Number	Title (A Side/B Side)	Yr	VG	VG+	NM
HERALD					
❑ 458	When You Dance/Let Me Show You (Around My Heart)	1955	12.50	25.00	50.00
—Yellow label, script print inside flag					
❑ 458	When You Dance/Let Me Show You (Around My Heart)	195?	5.00	10.00	20.00
—Yellow label, block print inside flag					
❑ 469	Sister Sookey/I'll Always Watch Over You	1956	7.50	15.00	30.00
❑ 478	B-I-N-G-O (Bingo)/I'm Nobody's	1956	7.50	15.00	30.00
❑ 486	It Was a Nite Like This/All of My Love	1956	7.50	15.00	30.00
❑ 495	Valley of Love/Bye and Bye	1957	7.50	15.00	30.00
❑ 510	Congratulations/The Wadda-Do	1957	6.25	12.50	25.00
IMPERIAL					
❑ 5807	Six Questions/The Lament of Silver Gulch	1962	10.00	20.00	40.00
❑ 5828	This Is My Story/Clicky Clicky Clack	1962	6.25	12.50	25.00
❑ 5847	I Wonder (I Wanna Know)/The Damage Is Done	1962	5.00	10.00	20.00
MONEY					
❑ 209	Tick Tock Awoo/No No Cherry	1955	50.00	100.00	200.00
❑ 209	Tick Tock Awoo/Nest Is Warm	1955	50.00	100.00	200.00
PARKWAY					
❑ 820	When You Dance/Golden Rings	1961	6.25	12.50	25.00
RED TOP					
❑ 115	I Promise You Love/Curfew Time	1959	12.50	25.00	50.00
ROULETTE					
❑ 4281	Diamonds and Pearls/Bad Man	1960	5.00	10.00	20.00
❑ 4326	Three Friends (Two Lovers)/I'm Not Your Fool Anymore	1961	5.00	10.00	20.00

TURKS, THE

More than one group.

Number	Title (A Side/B Side)	Yr	VG	VG+	NM
BALLY					
❑ 1017	This Heart of Mine/Why Did You	1956	7.50	15.00	30.00
CASH					
❑ 1042	It Can't Be True/Wagon Wheels	1956	7.50	15.00	30.00
—As "The Original Turks"					
CLASS					
❑ 256	Hully Gully/Rockville U.S.A.	1959	5.00	10.00	20.00
IMPERIAL					
❑ 5783	I'm a Fool/It Can't Be True	1961	3.00	6.00	12.00
KEEN					
❑ 3-4016	Father Time/Okay	1958	5.00	10.00	20.00
KNIGHT					
❑ 2005	I'm a Fool/It Can't Be True	1958	5.00	10.00	20.00
MONEY					
❑ 215	I'm a Fool/I've Been Accused	1956	10.00	20.00	40.00
P.B.D.					
❑ 112	Baja/Dianne	196?	7.50	15.00	30.00
❑ 113	Wipeout/Hideaway	196?	7.50	15.00	30.00

TURKS, THE / THE TURBANS

Also see each artist's individual listings.

Number	Title (A Side/B Side)	Yr	VG	VG+	NM
MONEY					
❑ 211	Emily/When I Return	1955	15.00	30.00	60.00

TURLEY, RICHARD

Number	Title (A Side/B Side)	Yr	VG	VG+	NM
DOT					
❑ 16231	I Wanna Dance/Since I Met You	1961	10.00	20.00	40.00
FRATERNITY					
❑ 845	Makin' Love with My Baby/All About Ann	1959	10.00	20.00	40.00

TURNER, IKE

Also see IKE AND TINA TURNER.

Number	Title (A Side/B Side)	Yr	VG	VG+	NM
ARTISTIC					
❑ 1504	(I Know) You Don't Love Me/Down and Out	1958	7.50	15.00	30.00
COBRA					
❑ 5033	Box Top/Walking Down the Aisle	1959	7.50	15.00	30.00
FEDERAL					
❑ 12297	Do You Mean It/She Made My Blood Run Cold	1957	25.00	50.00	100.00
❑ 12304	Rock a Bucket/The Big Question	1957	12.50	25.00	50.00
❑ 12307	You've Changed My Love/Trail Blazer	1957	10.00	20.00	40.00
FLAIR					
❑ 1040	Cubano Jump/Loosely	1954	15.00	30.00	60.00
❑ 1059	Cuban Getaway/Go To It	1955	15.00	30.00	60.00
KING					
❑ 5553	The Big Question/She Made My Blood Run Cold	1961	3.75	7.50	15.00
LIBERTY					
❑ 56194	Takin' Back My Name/Love Is a Game	1970	—	2.50	5.00
RPM					
❑ 356	You're Driving Me Insane/Trouble and Heartaches	1952	100.00	200.00	400.00
❑ 362	My Heart Belongs to You/Lookin' for My Baby	1952	15.00	30.00	60.00
—As "Bonnie and Ike Turner"					
❑ 446	As Long As I Have You/I Wanna Make Love to You	1955	10.00	20.00	40.00
SUE					
❑ 722	My Love/That's All I Need	1959	5.00	10.00	20.00
UNITED ARTISTS					
❑ XW460	Take My Hand, Precious Lord/Father Alone	1974	—	2.50	5.00
❑ 50865	River Deep Mountain High/Na Na	1971	—	2.50	5.00
❑ 50900	Right On/Tacks in My Shoes	1972	—	2.50	5.00
❑ 50930	Lawdy Miss Clawdy/Tacks in My Shoes	1972	—	2.50	5.00
❑ 51102	Dust My Broom/You Won't Let Me Go	1973	—	2.50	5.00

TURNER, IKE AND TINA

Also see IKE TURNER; TINA TURNER.

Number	Title (A Side/B Side)	Yr	VG	VG+	NM
A&M					
❑ 1118	River Deep, Mountain High/I'll Keep You Happy	1969	2.50	5.00	10.00
❑ 1170	A Love Like Yours/Save the Last Dance for Me	1970	2.50	5.00	10.00
BLUE THUMB					
❑ 101	I've Been Loving You Too Long/Grumbling	1969	—	3.00	6.00
❑ 102	The Hunter/Crazy 'Bout You Baby	1969	—	3.00	6.00
❑ 104	Bold Soul Sister/I Know	1969	—	3.00	6.00
❑ 202	I've Been Loving You Too Long/Crazy 'Bout You Baby	1971	—	2.50	5.00
CENCO					
❑ 112	Get It-Get It/You Weren't Ready (For My Love)	1967	3.75	7.50	15.00
INNIS					
❑ 6666	Betcha Can't Kiss Me/Don't Lie to Me	1968	2.50	5.00	10.00
❑ 6667	So Fine/So Blue Over You	1968	2.50	5.00	10.00
KENT					
❑ 402	I Can't Believe What You Say (For Seeing What You Do)/My Baby Now	1964	2.50	5.00	10.00
❑ 409	Am I a Fool in Love/Please, Please, Please	1964	2.50	5.00	10.00
❑ 418	Chicken Shack/He's the One	1965	2.50	5.00	10.00
❑ 4514	Plaese, Please, Please (Part 1)/Please, Please, Please (Part 2)	1970	—	3.00	6.00
LIBERTY					
❑ 56177	I Want to Take You Higher/Contact High	1970	—	3.00	6.00
❑ 56207	Workin' Together/The Way You Love Me	1970	—	3.00	6.00
❑ 56216	Proud Mary/Funkier Than a Mosquito's Tweeter	1970	—	3.00	6.00
LOMA					
❑ 2011	I'm Thru with Love/Tell Her I'm Not Home	1965	2.50	5.00	10.00
❑ 2015	Somebody Needs You/Just to Be with You	1965	2.50	5.00	10.00
MINIT					
❑ 32060	I'm Gonna Do All I Can (To Do Right By My Man)/You've Got Too Many Ties That Bind	1969	—	3.00	6.00
❑ 32068	I Wish It Would Rain/With a Little Help from My Friends	1969	—	3.00	6.00
❑ 32077	I Wanna Jump/Treating Us Funky	1969	—	3.00	6.00
❑ 32087	Come Together/Honky Tonk Women	1970	—	3.00	6.00
MODERN					
❑ 1007	Good Bye, So Long/Hurt Is All You Gave Me	1965	2.50	5.00	10.00
❑ 1012	I Don't Need/Gonna Have Fun	1965	2.50	5.00	10.00
PHILLES					
❑ 131	River Deep — Mountain High/I'll Keep You Happy	1966	5.00	10.00	20.00
❑ 134	Two to Tango/A Man Is a Man Is a Man	1966	3.75	7.50	15.00
❑ 135	I'll Never Need More Love Than This/The Cash Box Blues Or (Oops We Printed the Wrong Story Again)	1967	3.75	7.50	15.00
❑ 136	I Idolize You/A Love Like Yours	1967	3.75	7.50	15.00
POMPEII					
❑ 7003	Betcha Can't Kiss Me/Cussin', Cryin', and Carryin' On	1969	2.00	4.00	8.00
❑ 66675	It Sho' Ain't Me/We Need An Understanding	1968	2.00	4.00	8.00
❑ 66700	Shake a Tail Feather/Cussin', Cryin', and Carryin' On	1969	2.00	4.00	8.00
SONJA					
❑ 2005	You Can't Miss Nothing That You Never Had/(B-side unknown)	1968	3.00	6.00	12.00
SUE					
❑ 135	Two Is a Couple/Tin Top House	1965	3.75	7.50	15.00
❑ 138	The New Breed (Part 1)/The New Breed (Part 2)	1965	3.75	7.50	15.00
❑ 139	Stagger Lee and Billy/Can't Chance a Breakup	1965	3.75	7.50	15.00
❑ 146	Dear John/I Made a Promise Up Above	1966	3.00	6.00	12.00
❑ 730	A Fool in Love/The Way You Love Me	1960	7.50	15.00	30.00
❑ 734	You're My Baby/A Fool Too Long	1960	6.25	12.50	25.00
❑ 735	I Idolize You/Letter from Tina	1960	6.25	12.50	25.00
❑ 740	I'm Jealous/You're My Baby	1961	6.25	12.50	25.00
❑ 749	It's Gonna Work Out Fine/Won't You Forgive Me	1961	7.50	15.00	30.00
❑ 753	Poor Fool/You Can't Blame Me	1961	5.00	10.00	20.00
❑ 757	Tra La La La La/Puppy Love	1962	3.75	7.50	15.00
❑ 760	Prancing/It's Gonna Work Out Fine	1962	3.75	7.50	15.00
❑ 765	You Shoulda Treated Me Right/Sleepless	1962	3.75	7.50	15.00
❑ 768	Tina's Dilemma/I Idolize You	1962	3.75	7.50	15.00
❑ 772	The Argument/Mind in a Whirl	1962	3.75	7.50	15.00
❑ 774	Please Don't Hurt Me/Worried and Hurtin' Inside	1962	3.75	7.50	15.00
❑ 784	Don't Play Me Cheap/Wake Up	1963	3.75	7.50	15.00
TANGERINE					
❑ 963	Beauty Is Only Skin Deep/Anything You Wasn't Born With	1966	2.50	5.00	10.00
❑ 967	Dust My Broom/I'm Hooked	1966	2.50	5.00	10.00
UNITED ARTISTS					
❑ SP-48 [DJ]	I Want to Take You Higher/Ooh Poo Pah Doo	1971	2.50	5.00	10.00

Number	Title (A Side/B Side)	Yr	VG	VG+	NM
❑ 0119	A Fool in Love/I Idolize You	1973	—	2.00	4.00
❑ 0120	It's Gonna Work Out Fine/Poor Fool	1973	—	2.00	4.00
❑ 0121	I Want to Take You Higher/Come Together	1973	—	2.00	4.00
❑ 0122	Proud Mary/Tra La La La La	1973	—	2.00	4.00
—0119 through 0122 are "Silver Spotlight Series" reissues					
❑ XW174	With a Little Help from My Friends/Early One Morning	1973	—	2.50	5.00
❑ XW257	Work On Me/Born Free	1973	—	2.50	5.00
❑ XW298	Nutbosh City Limits/Help Him	1973	—	3.00	6.00
❑ XW409	Get it Out of Your Mind/Sweet Rhode Island Red	1974	—	2.50	5.00
❑ XW524	Nutbush City Limits/Ooh Poo Pah Doo	1974	—	2.00	4.00
—Reissue					
❑ XW528	Sexy Ida (Part 1)/Sexy Ida (Part 2)	1974	—	2.50	5.00
❑ XW598X	Baby, Get It On/Baby, Get It On (Disco Version)	1975	—	2.50	5.00
❑ 50782	Ooh Poo Pah Doo/I Wanna Jump	1971	—	2.50	5.00
❑ 50837	I'm Yours/Doin' It	1971	—	2.50	5.00
❑ 50881	Do Wah Ditty (Got to Get Ya)/Up in Heah	1972	—	2.50	5.00
❑ 50913	Outrageous/Feel Good	1972	—	2.50	5.00
❑ 50939	Games People Play/Pick Me Up	1972	—	2.50	5.00
❑ 50955	Let Me Touch Your Mind/Chopper	1972	—	2.50	5.00

WARNER BROS.

Number	Title (A Side/B Side)	Yr	VG	VG+	NM
❑ 5433	A Fool for a Fool/No Tears to Cry	1964	3.00	6.00	12.00
❑ 5433 [PS]	A Fool for a Fool/No Tears to Cry	1964	10.00	20.00	40.00
❑ 5461	It's All Over/Finger Poppin'	1964	3.00	6.00	12.00
❑ 5493	Ooh Poop A Doo/Merry Christmas Baby	1964	3.00	6.00	12.00

TURNER, JACK

HICKORY

Number	Title (A Side/B Side)	Yr	VG	VG+	NM
❑ 1050	Everybody's Rockin' But Me/I'm Gonna Get You If I Can	1956	6.25	12.50	25.00
❑ 1057	It's My Foolish Pride/Looking for Love	1956	5.00	10.00	20.00

RCA VICTOR

Number	Title (A Side/B Side)	Yr	VG	VG+	NM
❑ 47-5267	Hound Dog/(B-side unknown)	1953	7.50	15.00	30.00
❑ 47-5384	Gambler's Guitar/Butterfly Love	1953	7.50	15.00	30.00
❑ 47-5682	Walkin' a Chalk Line/Honey, I Reckon I Love You	1954	6.25	12.50	25.00
❑ 47-5815	If I Could Only Win Your Love/I'm Getting Married Tonight	1954	6.25	12.50	25.00
❑ 47-5901	I'm Not Jealous/Put It Down on Paper	1954	6.25	12.50	25.00
❑ 47-5997	Model T Baby/Hitchhikin' a Ride	1955	7.50	15.00	30.00
❑ 47-6163	Bama Bamboo Boy/The Story of the Smokey Mountain	1955	6.25	12.50	25.00
❑ 47-6305	Nightmare/Little Boy Why Do You Weep	1955	6.25	12.50	25.00

TURNER, JESSE LEE

CARLTON

Number	Title (A Side/B Side)	Yr	VG	VG+	NM
❑ 496	The Little Space Girl/Shake, Baby, Shake	1959	5.00	10.00	20.00
❑ 509	Baby Please Don't Tease/Thinkin'	1959	5.00	10.00	20.00
❑ 509 [PS]	Baby Please Don't Tease/Thinkin'	1959	10.00	20.00	40.00

FRATERNITY

Number	Title (A Side/B Side)	Yr	VG	VG+	NM
❑ 855	Teen-Age Misery/That's My Girl	1959	5.00	10.00	20.00
❑ 855 [PS]	Teen-Age Misery/That's My Girl	1959	10.00	20.00	40.00

GNP CRESCENDO

Number	Title (A Side/B Side)	Yr	VG	VG+	NM
❑ 184	All You Gotta Do (Is Ask Me To)/Voice Changing Song	1962	3.00	6.00	12.00
❑ 188	Shotgun Boogie/Ballad of Billy Sol Estes	1962	15.00	30.00	60.00

IMPERIAL

Number	Title (A Side/B Side)	Yr	VG	VG+	NM
❑ 5635	Slippin' Around/Early in the Morning	1960	3.75	7.50	15.00
❑ 5649	I'm the Little Space Girl's Father/Valley of Lost Soldiers	1960	5.00	10.00	20.00

TOP RANK

Number	Title (A Side/B Side)	Yr	VG	VG+	NM
❑ 2064	Do I Worry/All Right, Be That Way	1960	5.00	10.00	20.00

TURNER, JOE

ATLANTIC

Number	Title (A Side/B Side)	Yr	VG	VG+	NM
❑ 939	Chains of Love/After My Laughter Came Tears	1951	125.00	250.00	500.00
❑ 949	The Chill Is On/Bump Miss Suzie	1951	200.00	400.00	800.00
❑ 960	Sweet Sixteen/I'll Never Stop Loving You	1952	30.00	60.00	120.00
❑ 970	Don't You Cry/Poor Lover's Blues	1952	25.00	50.00	100.00
❑ 982	Still in Love/Baby I Still Want You	1953	25.00	50.00	100.00
❑ 1001	Honey Hush/Crawdad Hole	1953	50.00	100.00	200.00
❑ 1016	TV Mama/Oke-She-Moke-She-Pop	1954	30.00	60.00	120.00
❑ 1026	Shake, Rattle, and Roll/You Know I Love You	1954	20.00	40.00	80.00
❑ 1040	Well All Right/Married Woman	1954	17.50	35.00	70.00
❑ 1053	Flip, Flop, and Fly/Ti-Ri-Lee	1955	12.50	25.00	50.00
❑ 1069	Hide and Seek/Midnight Cannonball	1955	12.50	25.00	50.00
❑ 1080	Morning, Noon and Night/The Chicken and the Hawk	1956	12.50	25.00	50.00
❑ 1088	Corinne, Corinna/Boogie Woogie Country Girl	1956	7.50	15.00	30.00
❑ 1100	Rock a While/Lipstick, Powder, and Paint	1956	7.50	15.00	30.00
❑ 1122	Midnight Special Train/Feeling Happy	1957	7.50	15.00	30.00
❑ 1131	Red Sails in the Sunset/After a While	1957	7.50	15.00	30.00
❑ 1146	Love Roller Coaster/A World of Trouble	1957	7.50	15.00	30.00
❑ 1155	I Need a Girl/Trouble in Mind	1957	7.50	15.00	30.00
❑ 1167	Teen-Age Letter/Wee Baby Blues	1957	7.50	15.00	30.00
❑ 1184	Blues in the Night/Jump for Joy	1958	7.50	15.00	30.00
❑ 2034	Got You On My Mind/Love, Oh Careless Love	1959	5.00	10.00	20.00
❑ 2044	Tomorrow Night/Honey Hush	1959	5.00	10.00	20.00
❑ 2054	Chains of Love/My Little Honey Dripper	1960	5.00	10.00	20.00
❑ 2072	My Reason for Living/Sweet Sue	1960	5.00	10.00	20.00

BAYOU

Number	Title (A Side/B Side)	Yr	VG	VG+	NM
❑ 015	The Blues Jumped the Rabbit/The Sun Is Shining	1951	75.00	150.00	300.00

BLUESTIME

Number	Title (A Side/B Side)	Yr	VG	VG+	NM
❑ 45001	Two Loves Have I/Shake, Rattle and Roll	195?	10.00	20.00	40.00

BLUESWAY

Number	Title (A Side/B Side)	Yr	VG	VG+	NM
❑ 61009	Big Wheel/Bluer Than Blue	1967	2.00	4.00	8.00

CORAL

Number	Title (A Side/B Side)	Yr	VG	VG+	NM
❑ 62408	I Walk a Lonely Mile/I'm Packin' Up	1964	3.75	7.50	15.00
❑ 62429	Shake, Rattle and Roll/There'll Be Some Tears Falling	1964	3.75	7.50	15.00

DECCA

Number	Title (A Side/B Side)	Yr	VG	VG+	NM
❑ 29711	Piney Brown Blues/I Got a Gal for Every Day of the Week	1955	10.00	20.00	40.00
❑ 29924	Corrine, Corrina/It's the Same Old Story	1956	10.00	20.00	40.00

KENT

Number	Title (A Side/B Side)	Yr	VG	VG+	NM
❑ 512	Love Ain't Nothin'/10-20-25-30	1969	—	3.00	6.00
❑ 4561	Chains of Love/Battle Hymn of the Republic	1971	—	3.00	6.00
❑ 4569	One Hour in Your Garden/You've Been Squeezin' My Lemons	1972	—	3.00	6.00

MGM

Number	Title (A Side/B Side)	Yr	VG	VG+	NM
❑ 10719	Moody Baby/Feeling So Sad	1951	75.00	150.00	300.00

OKEH

Number	Title (A Side/B Side)	Yr	VG	VG+	NM
❑ 6829	Cherry Red/Joe Turner Blues	1951	50.00	100.00	200.00

RONN

Number	Title (A Side/B Side)	Yr	VG	VG+	NM
❑ 28	Up on the Mountain/I Love You Baby	1969	—	3.00	6.00
❑ 35	Morning Glory/Night-Time Is the Right Time	1969	—	3.00	6.00

RPM

Number	Title (A Side/B Side)	Yr	VG	VG+	NM
❑ 345	Riding Blues/Playful Baby	1952	50.00	100.00	200.00
—With Pete Johnson					

7-Inch Extended Plays

ATLANTIC

Number	Title (A Side/B Side)	Yr	VG	VG+	NM
❑ 536	(contents unknown)	1955	37.50	75.00	150.00
❑ 536 [PS]	Joe Turner Sings	1955	37.50	75.00	150.00
❑ 565	(contents unknown)	1956	37.50	75.00	150.00
❑ 565 [PS]	Joe Turner	1956	37.50	75.00	150.00
❑ 586	*Corrine Corrina/The Chicken and the Hawk/Feeling Happy/Hide and Seek	195?	37.50	75.00	150.00
❑ 586 [PS]	Joe Turner	195?	37.50	75.00	150.00

EMARCY

Number	Title (A Side/B Side)	Yr	VG	VG+	NM
❑ EP-1-6132	(contents unknown)	195?	25.00	50.00	100.00
❑ EP-1-6132 [PS]	Joe Turner	195?	25.00	50.00	100.00

TURNER, ODELLE

ATLANTIC

Number	Title (A Side/B Side)	Yr	VG	VG+	NM
❑ 964	Alarm Clock Boogie/Draggin' Hours	1952	37.50	75.00	150.00

TURNER, SAMMY

20TH FOX

Number	Title (A Side/B Side)	Yr	VG	VG+	NM
❑ 6610	For Your Love I'll Die/The House I Live In	1965	2.50	5.00	10.00

BIG TOP

Number	Title (A Side/B Side)	Yr	VG	VG+	NM
❑ 3007	Thunderbolt/Sweet Annie Laurie	1959	6.25	12.50	25.00
❑ 3016 [M]	Lavender-Blue/Wrapped Up in a Dream	1959	5.00	10.00	20.00
❑ 3016 [S]	Lavender-Blue/Wrapped Up in a Dream	1959	15.00	30.00	60.00
❑ 3029 [M]	Always/Symphony	1959	5.00	10.00	20.00
❑ 3029 [S]	Always/Symphony	1959	12.50	25.00	50.00
❑ 3032	Paradise/I'd Be a Fool Again	1960	5.00	10.00	20.00
❑ 3038	Goodnight Irene/I Want to Be Loved	1960	5.00	10.00	20.00
❑ 3049	Fools Fall in Love/Stay My Love	1960	5.00	10.00	20.00
❑ 3061	Falling/The Things I Do	1961	3.75	7.50	15.00
❑ 3065	Little Sir Echo/Love Keeps Calling	1961	3.75	7.50	15.00
❑ 3070	Starlight, Starbright/Let's Donkey On Down	1961	3.75	7.50	15.00
❑ 3082	Pour It On/The Fool of the Year	1961	3.75	7.50	15.00
❑ 3089	Falling/Raincoat in the River	1961	6.25	12.50	25.00
—B-side produced by Phil Spector					

MILLENNIUM

Number	Title (A Side/B Side)	Yr	VG	VG+	NM
❑ 616	Do You Know (What Life Is All About)/Nothing Can Separate Me (From Your Love)	1978	—	2.50	5.00

MOTOWN

Number	Title (A Side/B Side)	Yr	VG	VG+	NM
❑ 1055	Only You/Right Now	1964	7.50	15.00	30.00

PACIFIC

Number	Title (A Side/B Side)	Yr	VG	VG+	NM
❑ 3016	Lavender-Blue/Wrapped Up in a Dream	1959	10.00	20.00	40.00
—Despite label name, Pacific Records was in North Carolina!					

VERVE

Number	Title (A Side/B Side)	Yr	VG	VG+	NM
❑ 10465	A Child Was Born/Come to Me Comf'tably	1966	7.50	15.00	30.00

TURNER, SPYDER

KWANZA

Number	Title (A Side/B Side)	Yr	VG	VG+	NM
❑ 7688	Since I Don't Have You/Happy Days	1973	—	3.00	6.00

MGM

Number	Title (A Side/B Side)	Yr	VG	VG+	NM
❑ 13617	Stand By Me/You're Good Enough for Me	1966	2.50	5.00	10.00
❑ 13692	Don't Hold Back/I Can't Take It Anymore	1967	2.00	4.00	8.00
❑ 13739	For Your Precious Love/I Can't Wait to See My Baby's Face	1967	2.00	4.00	8.00
❑ 14263	I Can't Make It Anymore/I'm Alive with a Lovin' Feeling	1971	—	3.00	6.00

WHITFIELD

Number	Title (A Side/B Side)	Yr	VG	VG+	NM
❑ 8526	I've Been Waiting/Tomorrow's Only Yesterday	1978	—	2.00	4.00
❑ 8596	Get Down/Is It Love You're After	1978	—	2.00	4.00
❑ 49190	You're So Fine/Only Love	1980	—	2.00	4.00

TURNER, TINA

Also see IKE AND TINA TURNER.

CAPITOL

Number	Title (A Side/B Side)	Yr	VG	VG+	NM
❑ B-5322	Let's Stay Together/I Wrote a Letter	1984	—	—	3.00
❑ B-5322 [PS]	Let's Stay Together/I Wrote a Letter	1984	—	2.50	5.00
❑ B-5354	What's Love Got to Do with It/Rock 'N' Roll Widow	1984	—	—	3.00
❑ B-5354 [PS]	What's Love Got to Do with It/Rock 'N' Roll Widow	1984	—	2.00	4.00
❑ B-5387	Better Be Good to Me/When I Was Young	1984	—	—	3.00
❑ B-5387 [PS]	Better Be Good to Me/When I Was Young	1984	—	2.00	4.00
❑ B-5433	Private Dancer/Nutbush City Limits	1984	—	—	3.00
❑ B-5433 [PS]	Private Dancer/Nutbush City Limits	1984	—	2.00	4.00
❑ B-5461	Show Some Respect/Let's Pretend We're Married	1985	—	—	3.00
❑ B-5461 [PS]	Show Some Respect/Let's Pretend We're Married	1985	—	2.00	4.00
❑ B-5491	We Don't Need Another Hero (Thunderdome)/(Instrumental)	1985	—	—	3.00
❑ B-5491 [PS]	We Don't Need Another Hero (Thunderdome)/(Instrumental)	1985	—	2.00	4.00
❑ B-5518	One of the Living/One of the Living (Dub)	1985	—	—	3.00
❑ B-5518 [PS]	One of the Living/One of the Living (Dub)	1985	—	2.00	4.00

Number	Title (A Side/B Side)	Yr	VG	VG+	NM
❑ B-5615	Typical Male/Don't Turn Around	1986	—	—	3.00
❑ B-5615 [PS]	Typical Male/Don't Turn Around	1986	—	—	3.00
❑ B-5644	Two People/Havin' a Party	1986	—	—	3.00
❑ B-5644 [PS]	Two People/Havin' a Party	1986	—	—	3.00
❑ B-5668	What You Get Is What You See/What You Get Is What You See (Live)	1987	—	—	3.00
❑ B-5668 [PS]	What You Get Is What You See/What You Get Is What You See (Live)	1987	—	—	3.00
❑ B-44003	Break Every Rule/Take Me to the River	1987	—	—	3.00
❑ B-44003 [PS]	Break Every Rule/Take Me to the River	1987	—	—	3.00
❑ B-44111	Afterglow/Afterglow	1987	—	—	3.00
❑ B-44442	The Best/Undercover Agent for the Blues	1989	—	—	3.00
❑ B-44442 [PS]	The Best/Undercover Agent for the Blues	1989	—	—	3.00
❑ B-44473	Steamy Windows/The Best	1989	—	—	3.00
❑ B-44473 [PS]	Steamy Windows/The Best	1989	—	—	3.00
❑ NR-44510	Look Me in the Heart/Stronger Than the Wind	1990	—	—	3.00
❑ S7-57702	Way of the World/You Know Who	1992	—	—	3.00
FANTASY					
❑ 948	Lean On Me/Shame, Shame, Shame	1984	—	2.00	4.00
POLYDOR					
❑ PRO-002 [DJ]	Acid Queen/Pinball Wizard	1975	10.00	20.00	40.00
—B-side by Elton John; promo-only					
POMPEII					
❑ 66682	Too Hot to Hold/You Got What You Wanted	1968	2.50	5.00	10.00
UNITED ARTISTS					
❑ XW 724	Whole Lotta Love/Rockin' 'N' Rollin'	1975	—	3.00	6.00
❑ XW 730	Delilah's Power/That's My Power	1975	—	3.00	6.00
❑ XW 920	Come Together/I Want to Take You Higher	1977	—	3.00	6.00
❑ XW 1265	Fire Down Below/Viva La Money	1979	—	2.50	5.00
VIRGIN					
❑ S7-17401	I Don't Wanna Fight/Tina's Wish	1993	—	—	3.00
❑ S7-17498	Why Must We Wait Until Tomorrow/Shake a Tail Feather	1993	—	—	3.00
❑ S7-18047	Proud Mary (Edit Live Version)/The Best (Live)	1994	—	2.50	5.00
—Red vinyl					
❑ S7-19217	Missing You/Do Something	1996	—	—	3.00
❑ 38691	When the Heartache Is Over/On Silent Wings	2000	—	—	3.00

TURNER, TITUS

Number	Title (A Side/B Side)	Yr	VG	VG+	NM
ATCO					
❑ 6310	Baby Girl (Part 1)/Baby Girl (Part 2)	1964	2.00	4.00	8.00
ATLANTIC					
❑ 1127	A-Knockin' at My Baby's Door/Hungry Man	1957	5.00	10.00	20.00
COLUMBIA					
❑ 42873	Young Wings Can Fly/Goodbye Rose	1963	2.50	5.00	10.00
❑ 42947	Make Someone Love You/I'm a Fool About My Mama	1964	2.50	5.00	10.00
ENJOY					
❑ 1005	People Sure Act Funny/My Darkest Hour	1962	2.50	5.00	10.00
❑ 1015	Soulville/My Darkest Hour	1963	2.50	5.00	10.00
❑ 2010	Bow Wow/I Love You Baby	1963	2.50	5.00	10.00
GLOVER					
❑ 201	We Told You Not to Marry/Taking Care of Business	1959	6.25	12.50	25.00
❑ 202	When the Sergeant Comes Marching Home/(B-side unknown)	1960	6.25	12.50	25.00
JAMIE					
❑ 1177	Pony Train/Bla, Bla, Cha Cha Cha	1961	3.00	6.00	12.00
❑ 1184	Hey Doll Baby/I Want a Steady Girl	1961	3.00	6.00	12.00
❑ 1189	Horsin' Around/Chances Go Around	1961	3.00	6.00	12.00
❑ 1202	Shake the Hand of a Fool/Beautiful Stranger	1961	3.00	6.00	12.00
❑ 1213	Walk on the Wild Twist/Twistin' Train	1962	2.50	5.00	10.00
JOSIE					
❑ 990	I Just Can't Keep It to Myself/People Sure Are Funny	1968	—	3.00	6.00
❑ 1012	His Funeral, My Trial/Do You Dig It	1969	—	3.00	6.00
KING					
❑ 5067	Have Mercy Baby/You Turned Lamps Too	1957	3.00	6.00	12.00
❑ 5095	Hold Your Loving/Stop the Rain	1957	3.00	6.00	12.00
❑ 5129	Follow Me/Way Down Yonder	1958	3.00	6.00	12.00
❑ 5140	Coralee/Tears of Joy Fill My Eyes	1958	3.00	6.00	12.00
❑ 5186	The Return of Staggolee/Answer Me	1959	3.00	6.00	12.00
❑ 5213 [M]	Tarzan/Fall Guy	1959	3.00	6.00	12.00
❑ S-5213 [S]	Tarzan/Fall Guy	1959	7.50	15.00	30.00
❑ 5243	Bonnie Baby/Miss Rubberneck Jones	1959	3.00	6.00	12.00
❑ 5465	Way Down Yonder/Miss Rubberneck Jones	1961	2.50	5.00	10.00
MURBO					
❑ 1001	Huckle Buckle Beanstalk/Hoop Hoop Hoop a Hoopa Doo	1965	2.00	4.00	8.00
OKEH					
❑ 6844	Same Old Feeling/Don't Take Everybody to Be Your Friend	1951	7.50	15.00	30.00
❑ 6883	What'cha Gonna Do for Me/Got So Much Trouble	1952	6.25	12.50	25.00
❑ 6907	Jambalaya/Please Baby	1952	6.25	12.50	25.00
❑ 6929	Christmas Morning/Be Sure You Know	1952	7.50	15.00	30.00
❑ 6938	My Plea/It's Too Late Now	1953	6.25	12.50	25.00
❑ 6961	Big Mary's/Living in Misery	1953	6.25	12.50	25.00
❑ 7027	Over the Rainbow/My Lonely Room	1954	6.25	12.50	25.00
❑ 7038	Hello Stranger/Devilish Woman	1954	6.25	12.50	25.00
❑ 7244	Eye to Eye/What Kinda Deal Is This	1966	2.00	4.00	8.00
PHILIPS					
❑ 40445	(I'm Afraid the) Masquerade Is Over/Mary Mack	1967	2.00	4.00	8.00
WING					
❑ 90006	All Around the World/Do You Know	1955	5.00	10.00	20.00
❑ 90033	Sweet and Low/Big John	1955	5.00	10.00	20.00
❑ 90058	Get on the Right Track, Baby/I'll Wait Forever	1956	5.00	10.00	20.00

TURNPIKES, THE

Number	Title (A Side/B Side)	Yr	VG	VG+	NM
CAPITOL					
❑ 2234	Cast a Spell/Nothing But Promises	1968	6.25	12.50	25.00

TURTLES, THE

Also see FLO AND EDDIE.

Number	Title (A Side/B Side)	Yr	VG	VG+	NM
WHITE WHALE					
❑ 222	It Ain't Me, Babe/Almost There	1965	3.00	6.00	12.00
❑ 224	Let Me Be/Your Maw Said You Cried	1965	2.50	5.00	10.00
❑ 227	You Baby/Wanderin' Kind	1966	2.50	5.00	10.00
❑ 231	Grim Reaper of Love/Come Back	1966	5.00	10.00	20.00
❑ 234	We'll Meet Again/Outside Chance	1966	3.75	7.50	15.00
❑ 237	Outside Chance/Making My Mind Up	1966	2.50	5.00	10.00
❑ 238	Can I Get to Know You Better?/Like the Seasons	1966	2.50	5.00	10.00
❑ 244	Happy Together/Like the Seasons	1967	2.00	4.00	8.00
❑ 244 [PS]	Happy Together/Like the Seasons	1967	10.00	20.00	40.00
❑ 249	She'd Rather Be with Me/The Walking Song	1967	2.00	4.00	8.00
❑ 249 [PS]	She'd Rather Be with Me/The Walking Song	1967	6.25	12.50	25.00
❑ 251	Guide for the Married Man/Think I'll Run Away	1967	10.00	20.00	40.00
—Withdrawn shortly after release					
❑ 254	You Know What I Mean/Rugs of Woods and Flowers	1967	2.00	4.00	8.00
❑ 254 [PS]	You Know What I Mean/Rugs of Woods and Flowers	1967	3.75	7.50	15.00
❑ 260	She's My Girl/Chicken Little Was Right	1967	2.00	4.00	8.00
—White concentric circles on mostly blue label					
❑ 260	She's My Girl/Chicken Little Was Right	1967	2.50	5.00	10.00
—All-blue label					
❑ 260 [PS]	She's My Girl/Chicken Little Was Right	1967	5.00	10.00	20.00
❑ 264	Sound Asleep/Umbassa the Dragon	1968	2.00	4.00	8.00
❑ 264 [PS]	Sound Asleep/Umbassa the Dragon	1968	3.75	7.50	15.00
❑ 273	The Story of Rock and Roll/Can't You Hear the Cows	1968	2.00	4.00	8.00
❑ 273 [PS]	The Story of Rock and Roll/Can't You Hear the Cows	1968	12.50	25.00	50.00
❑ 276	Elenore/Surfer Dan	1968	2.00	4.00	8.00
❑ 276 [PS]	Elenore/Surfer Dan	1968	3.00	6.00	12.00
❑ 292	You Showed Me/Buzz Saw	1969	2.00	4.00	8.00
❑ 292 [PS]	You Showed Me/Buzz Saw	1969	3.00	6.00	12.00
❑ 306	House on the Hill/Come Over	1969	5.00	10.00	20.00
❑ 308	You Don't Have to Walk in the Rain/Come Over	1969	2.00	4.00	8.00
❑ 308 [PS]	You Don't Have to Walk in the Rain/Come Over	1969	2.50	5.00	10.00
❑ 326	Love in the City/Bachelor Mother	1969	2.00	4.00	8.00
❑ 326 [PS]	Love in the City/Bachelor Mother	1969	2.50	5.00	10.00
❑ 334	Lady-O/Somewhere Friday Nite	1969	2.00	4.00	8.00
❑ 341	Who Would Ever Think That I Would Marry Margaret?/We Ain't Gonna Party No More	1970	3.75	7.50	15.00
❑ 350	Is It Any Wonder?/Wanderin' Kind	1970	2.00	4.00	8.00
❑ 355	Eve of Destruction/Wanderin' Kind	1970	2.00	4.00	8.00
❑ 364	Me About You/Think I'll Run Away	1970	2.00	4.00	8.00

TURTLES, THE (2)

Number	Title (A Side/B Side)	Yr	VG	VG+	NM
RCA VICTOR					
❑ 47-6356	Mystery Train/Say You Care	1955	6.25	12.50	25.00

TUXEDOS, THE

Number	Title (A Side/B Side)	Yr	VG	VG+	NM
FORTE					
❑ 1414	Yes It's True/(B-side unknown)	1960	37.50	75.00	150.00
—Gold label					
❑ 1414	Yes It's True/(B-side unknown)	1960	7.50	15.00	30.00
—Yellow label					

TWAIN, SHANIA

Number	Title (A Side/B Side)	Yr	VG	VG+	NM
MERCURY					
❑ 172123-7	Come On Over/Man! I Feel Like a Woman!	1999	—	2.00	4.00
❑ 562582-7	Rock This Country!/I'm Holdin' On to Love (To Save My Life)	2000	—	2.00	4.00
❑ 566220-7	Honey, I'm Home/That Don't Impress Me Much	1998	—	2.00	4.00
❑ 566450-7	From This Moment On (Pop Radio Mix)/From This Moment On (Single Remix)	1998	—	2.50	5.00
❑ 568062-7	Love Gets Me Every Time/Love Gets Me Every Time (Dance Mix)	1997	—	2.50	5.00
❑ 568242-7	Don't Be Stupid (You Know I Love You)/If It Don't Take Two	1997	—	2.50	5.00
❑ 568452-7	You're Still the One/Don't Be Stupid (You Know I Love You) (Remix)	1998	—	2.50	5.00
❑ 578384-7	Home Ain't Where His Heart Is (Anymore)/Whose Bed Have Your Boots Been Under?	1996	—	2.50	5.00
❑ 578748-7	God Bless the Child/(If You're Not In It for Love) I'm Outta Here! (Remix)	1996	—	3.00	6.00
❑ 852138-7	You Win My Love/Home Ain't Where His Heart Is (Anymore)	1996	—	2.50	5.00
❑ 852206-7	The Woman in Me (Needs the Man in You)/Any Man of Mine	1995	—	2.50	5.00
❑ 852498-7	(If You're Not In It for Love) I'm Outta Here!/The Woman in Me (Needs the Man in You)	1995	—	2.50	5.00
❑ 852986-7	No One Needs to Know/Leaving Is the Only Way Out	1996	—	2.50	5.00
❑ 856448-7	Whose Bed Have Your Boots Been Under?/Any Man of Mine	1995	2.50	5.00	10.00
❑ 862346-7	Dance with the One That Brought You/When He Leaves You	1993	—	3.00	6.00
❑ 862806-7	You Lay a Whole Lot of Love on Me/God Ain't Gonna Getcha for That	1993	—	3.00	6.00
❑ 864992-7	What Made You Say That/Crime of the Century	1993	—	3.00	6.00

TWEETERS, THE

Number	Title (A Side/B Side)	Yr	VG	VG+	NM
DECCA					
❑ 30725	Mascara Mama/The Campus Rock	1958	7.50	15.00	30.00

TWENTIETH CENTURY ZOO, THE

Number	Title (A Side/B Side)	Yr	VG	VG+	NM
CAZ					
❑ 103	You Don't Remember/Love in Your Face	1967	6.25	12.50	25.00
VAULT					
❑ 948	Rainbow/Bullfrog	1969	3.00	6.00	12.00
❑ 961	Only Thing That's Wrong/Stallion of Fate	1969	3.00	6.00	12.00

Number	Title (A Side/B Side)	Yr	VG	VG+	NM
7-Inch Extended Plays					
SUNDAZED					
❑ SEP 145	You Don't Remember//Love in Your Face/Tossin' and Turnin'	1999	—	—	2.00
❑ SEP 145 [PS]	You Don't Remember	1999	—	—	2.00

TWICE AS MUCH

Number	Title (A Side/B Side)	Yr	VG	VG+	NM
MGM					
❑ 13530	Sittin' on a Fence/Baby I Want You	1966	3.75	7.50	15.00
—A-side is a Mick Jagger-Keith Richards song that only later was released by the Rolling Stones.					
❑ 13530 [PS]	Sittin' on a Fence/Baby I Want You	1966	7.50	15.00	30.00
❑ 13600	Step Out of Line/Simplified	1966	2.50	5.00	10.00

TWIGGY

Number	Title (A Side/B Side)	Yr	VG	VG+	NM
CAPITOL					
❑ 5903	Over and Over/When I Think of You	1967	2.50	5.00	10.00
❑ 5903 [PS]	Over and Over/When I Think of You	1967	7.50	15.00	30.00
MERCURY					
❑ 73863	Rain on the Roof/Vanilla Olay	1976	—	3.00	6.00
❑ 73923	I Lie Awake and Dream of You/Woman in Love	1977	—	3.00	6.00

TWILIGHTERS, THE (1)

Number	Title (A Side/B Side)	Yr	VG	VG+	NM
BELL					
❑ 624	Be Faithful/Thumper	1965	5.00	10.00	20.00

TWILIGHTERS, THE (2)

Number	Title (A Side/B Side)	Yr	VG	VG+	NM
BUBBLE					
❑ 1334	My Silent Prayer/Little Bitty Bed Bug	1962	10.00	20.00	40.00
CHESS					
❑ 1803	Scratchin'/Tears	1961	6.25	12.50	25.00
CHOLLY					
❑ 712	Let There Be Love/Eternally	1957	250.00	500.00	1000.
DOT					
❑ 15526	Eternally/I Believe	1957	10.00	20.00	40.00
EBB					
❑ 117	Pride and Joy/Live Like a King	1957	10.00	20.00	40.00
ELDO					
❑ 115	Nothin'/Do You Believe	1961	6.25	12.50	25.00
IMPERIAL					
❑ 66201	Shake a Tail Feather/Road to Fortune	1966	3.00	6.00	12.00
❑ 66238	I Still Love You/Meat Ball	1967	3.00	6.00	12.00
JVB					
❑ 83	How Many Times/Water-Water	1957	200.00	400.00	800.00
MGM					
❑ 55011	Little Did I Dream/Gotta Get On the Train	1955	75.00	150.00	300.00
❑ 55014	Lovely Lady/Half Angel	1955	100.00	200.00	400.00
PICO					
❑ 2801	Eternally/I Believe	1957	20.00	40.00	80.00

TWILIGHTERS, THE (3)

Number	Title (A Side/B Side)	Yr	VG	VG+	NM
CADDY					
❑ 103	Eternally/I Believe	1955	62.50	125.00	250.00

TWILIGHTERS, THE (4)

Number	Title (A Side/B Side)	Yr	VG	VG+	NM
FRATERNITY					
❑ 889	To Love in Vain/The Beginning of Love	1961	6.25	12.50	25.00
—As "The Twi-Lighters"					

TWILIGHTERS, THE (5)

Number	Title (A Side/B Side)	Yr	VG	VG+	NM
MARSHALL					
❑ 702	Please Tell Me You're Mine/Wondering	1953	50.00	100.00	200.00
—Black vinyl					
❑ 702	Please Tell Me You're Mine/Wondering	1953	250.00	500.00	1000.
—Red vinyl					

TWILIGHTERS, THE (6)

Number	Title (A Side/B Side)	Yr	VG	VG+	NM
SPECIALTY					
❑ 548	It's True/Wha-Bop-Sh-Wah	1955	15.00	30.00	60.00

TWILIGHTERS, THE (7)

Number	Title (A Side/B Side)	Yr	VG	VG+	NM
SPIN					
❑ 0001	Yes You Are/A Possibility	1960	50.00	100.00	200.00

TWILIGHTERS, THE (U)

Number	Title (A Side/B Side)	Yr	VG	VG+	NM
GROOVE					
❑ 0154	Sittin' in a Corner/It's a Cold, Cold, Rainy Day	1956	15.00	30.00	60.00
—As "The Twi-Lighters"					
RICKI					
❑ 907	Help Me/Rockin' Mule	1961	10.00	20.00	40.00
SARA					
❑ 1048	Restless Love/Can't You Stay a Little Longer	1961	15.00	30.00	60.00
VANCO					
❑ 204	Out of My Mind/I Need Your Lovin'	1968	2.50	5.00	10.00

TWILLEY, DWIGHT

Includes the Dwight Twilley Band. Also see PHIL SEYMOUR.

Number	Title (A Side/B Side)	Yr	VG	VG+	NM
ARISTA					
❑ 0278	Rock and Roll 47/Twilley Don't Mind	1977	—	2.50	5.00
❑ 0299	Trying to Find My Baby/Here She Comes	1977	—	2.50	5.00
❑ 0311	Looking for the Magic/Invasion	1978	—	2.50	5.00
❑ 0415	Out of My Hands/Nothing's Ever Gonna Change So Fast	1979	—	2.00	4.00
❑ 0433	Runaway/Burnin' Sand	1979	—	2.00	4.00
❑ 0478	Somebody to Love/Money (That's What I Want)	1979	—	2.00	4.00
CBS ASSOCIATED					
❑ 06050	Sexual/Wild Dogs	1986	—	—	3.00
EMI AMERICA					
❑ 8109	Later That Night/Somebody to Love	1982	—	2.00	4.00
❑ 8115	I Found the Magic/I'm Back Again	1982	—	2.00	4.00
❑ 8196	Girls/To Get to You	1984	—	—	3.00
❑ 8196 [PS]	Girls/To Get to You	1984	—	2.00	4.00
❑ 8206	Little Bit of Love/Mad Dog	1984	—	—	3.00
❑ 8206 [PS]	Little Bit of Love/Mad Dog	1984	—	2.00	4.00
❑ 8235	Why You Wanna Break My Heart/Chilly D's Theme	1984	—	—	3.00
❑ 8235 [PS]	Why You Wanna Break My Heart/Chilly D's Theme	1984	—	—	3.00
PRIVATE I					
❑ 04820	Keep On Working/(Instrumental)	1985	—	—	3.00
SHELTER					
❑ 40380	I'm on Fire/Did You See What Happened	1975	—	2.50	5.00
❑ 40380 [PS]	I'm on Fire/Did You See What Happened	1975	2.50	5.00	10.00
❑ 40450	Sincerely/You Were So Warm	1975	—	2.50	5.00
❑ 62003	Could Be Love/Feeling in the Dark	1976	—	2.50	5.00
❑ 62003 [PS]	Could Be Love/Feeling in the Dark	1976	2.00	4.00	8.00
THE RIGHT STUFF					
❑ S7-19563	I'm on Fire/Looking for the Magic	1997	—	—	3.00

TWIN-TONES, THE

See THE TWINS.

TWINKLE

Number	Title (A Side/B Side)	Yr	VG	VG+	NM
AURORA					
❑ 163	The End of the World/What Am I Doing Here with You	1966	2.50	5.00	10.00
TOLLIE					
❑ 9040	The Boy of My Dreams/Terry	1965	3.00	6.00	12.00
❑ 9047	Ain't Nobody Home But Me/Golden Lights	1965	3.00	6.00	12.00

TWINS, THE

Number	Title (A Side/B Side)	Yr	VG	VG+	NM
LANCER					
❑ 106	Heart of Gold/Buttercup	1959	3.75	7.50	15.00
RCA VICTOR					
❑ 47-7148	My Dear/The Flip Skip	1958	5.00	10.00	20.00
—As "The Twin-Tones"					
❑ 47-7235	Jo-Ann's Sister/Who Knows the Secret	1958	5.00	10.00	20.00
❑ 47-7382	Classroom Rock/Gee Whiz	1958	5.00	10.00	20.00
7-Inch Extended Plays					
RCA VICTOR					
❑ EPA-4107	Jo-Ann/Before You Go//My Dancing Lady/One Mail a Day	1957	5.00	10.00	20.00
—As "The Twin-Tones"					
❑ EPA-4107 [PS]	Jim and John The Twin-Tones	1957	5.00	10.00	20.00
❑ EPA-4237	My Dear/The Flip Skip//I Want a Girl/Together Forever	1958	5.00	10.00	20.00
❑ EPA-4237 [PS]	Teenagers Love the Twins	1958	5.00	10.00	20.00

TWISTERS, THE

Number	Title (A Side/B Side)	Yr	VG	VG+	NM
APT					
❑ 25045	Come Go with Me/Pretty Little Girl Next Door	1960	5.00	10.00	20.00
CAMPUS					
❑ 125	Elvis Leaves Sorrento/Street Dance	1961	7.50	15.00	30.00
CAPITOL					
❑ 4451	Turn the Page/Dancing Little Clown	1960	5.00	10.00	20.00
DUAL					
❑ 502	Silly Chilli/Peppermint Twist Time	1962	3.00	6.00	12.00
FELCO					
❑ 103	Count Down 1-2-3/Speed Limit	1959	6.25	12.50	25.00
SUN-SET					
❑ 501	Please Come Back/This Is the End	1961	150.00	300.00	600.00

TWISTIN' KINGS

Number	Title (A Side/B Side)	Yr	VG	VG+	NM
MOTOWN					
❑ 1022	Xmas Twist/White House Twist	1961	10.00	20.00	40.00
❑ 1023	Congo (Part 1)/Congo (Part 2)	1962	10.00	20.00	40.00

TWITTY, CONWAY

Also see CONWAY TWITTY AND LORETTA LYNN.

Number	Title (A Side/B Side)	Yr	VG	VG+	NM
ABC-PARAMOUNT					
❑ 10507	Go On and Cry/She Loves Me	1963	3.75	7.50	15.00
❑ 10550	Such a Night/My Baby Left Me	1964	6.25	12.50	25.00
DECCA					
❑ 31833	Together Forever/That Kind of Girl	1965	2.50	5.00	10.00
❑ 31897	Guess My Eyes Were Bigger Than Her Heart/Honky Tonk Man	1966	2.00	4.00	8.00
❑ 31983	Look Into My Teardrops/If You Were Mine to Lose	1966	2.00	4.00	8.00
❑ 32081	I Don't Want to Be with Me/Before I'll Set Her Free	1967	2.00	4.00	8.00
❑ 32147	Don't Put Your Hurt in My Heart/Walk Me to the Door	1967	2.00	4.00	8.00
❑ 32208	Funny (But I'm Not Laughing)/Working Girl	1967	2.00	4.00	8.00
❑ 32272	The Image of Me/Dim Lights, Truck Smoke (And Loud, Loud Music)	1968	2.00	4.00	8.00
❑ 32361	Next in Line/I'm Checking Out	1968	2.00	4.00	8.00
❑ 32424	Darling, You Know I Wouldn't Lie/Table in the Corner	1968	2.00	4.00	8.00
❑ 32481	I Love You More Today/Bad Girl	1969	2.00	4.00	8.00
❑ 32546	To See My Angel Cry/I Did the Best I Could	1969	2.00	4.00	8.00
❑ 32599	That's When She Started to Stop Loving You/I'll Get Over Losing You	1969	2.00	4.00	8.00
❑ 32661	Hello Darlin'/Girl at the Bar	1970	—	3.50	7.00
❑ 32742	Fifteen Years Ago/Up Comes the Bottle	1970	—	3.50	7.00
❑ 32801	How Much More Can She Stand/Just Like a Stranger	1971	—	3.50	7.00
❑ 32842	I Wonder What She'll Think About Me Leaving/A Heartache Just Walked In	1971	—	3.50	7.00
❑ 32895	I Can't See Me Without You/I Didn't Lose Her	1971	—	3.50	7.00
❑ 32945	(Lost Her Love) On Our Last Date/I'll Never Make It Home Tonight	1972	—	3.50	7.00
❑ 32988	I Can't Stop Loving You/She Needs Someone to Hold Her (When She Cries)	1972	—	3.50	7.00
❑ 32988	I Can't Stop Loving You/Since She's Not with the One She Loves	1972	—	3.50	7.00
❑ 33033	She Needs Someone to Hold Her (When She Cries)/This Road That I Walk	1972	—	3.50	7.00

ELEKTRA

Number	Title (A Side/B Side)	Yr	VG	VG+	NM
❑ 47302	The Clown/The Boy Next Door	1982	—	2.00	4.00
❑ 47302 [PS]	The Clown/The Boy Next Door	1982	—	2.50	5.00
❑ 47443	Slow Hand/When Love Was Something Else	1982	—	2.00	4.00
❑ 69854	The Rose/It's Only Make Believe	1982	—	2.00	4.00
❑ 69854 [PS]	The Rose/It's Only Make Believe	1982	—	2.50	5.00
❑ 69964	We Did But Now You Don't/(B-side unknown)	1982	—	2.00	4.00

MCA

Number	Title (A Side/B Side)	Yr	VG	VG+	NM
❑ 40027	Baby's Gone/Dim Lovely Places	1973	—	2.50	5.00
❑ 40094	You've Never Been This Far Before/You Make It Hard	1973	—	2.50	5.00
❑ 40173	There's a Honky Tonk Angel (Who'll Take Me Back In)/Don't Let It Go to Your Heart	1973	—	2.50	5.00
❑ 40224	I'm Not Through Loving You Yet/Before Your Time	1974	—	2.50	5.00
❑ 40282	I See the Want To in Your Eyes/Girl from Tupelo	1974	—	2.50	5.00
❑ 40339	Linda on My Mind/She's Just Not Over You Yet	1974	—	2.50	5.00
❑ 40407	Touch the Hand/Don't Cry Joni	1975	—	2.50	5.00
❑ 40492	This Time I've Hurt Her More Than She Loves Me/She Did, It Did, I Didn't	1975	—	2.50	5.00
❑ 40534	After All the Good Is Gone/I Got a Good Thing Going	1976	—	2.50	5.00
❑ 40601	The Games That Daddies Play/There's More Love in the Arms You're Leaving	1976	—	2.50	5.00
❑ 40649	I Can't Believe She Gives It All to Me/I Can't Help It If She Can't Stop Loving Me	1976	—	2.50	5.00
❑ 40682	Play, Guitar, Play/One in a Million	1977	—	2.50	5.00
❑ 40754	I've Already Loved You in My Mind/I Changed My Mind	1977	—	2.50	5.00
❑ 40805	Talkin' 'Bout You/Georgia Keeps Pulling on My Ring	1977	—	2.50	5.00
❑ 40857	I'm Used to Losing You/The Grandest Lady of Them All	1978	—	2.50	5.00
❑ 40929	That's All She Wrote/Boogie Grass Band	1978	—	2.50	5.00
❑ 40963	Your Love Had Taken Me That High/My Woman Knows	1978	—	2.50	5.00
❑ 41002	Don't Take It Away/Draggin' Chains	1979	—	2.00	4.00
❑ 41059	I May Never Get to Heaven/Grand Ole Blues	1979	—	2.00	4.00
❑ 41135	Happy Birthday Darlin'/Heavy Tears	1979	—	2.00	4.00
❑ 41174	I'd Just Love to Lay You Down/She Thinks I Still Care	1980	—	2.00	4.00
❑ 41174	I'd Love to Lay You Down/She Thinks I Still Care	1980	—	2.50	5.00

—Note slightly different A-side title

Number	Title (A Side/B Side)	Yr	VG	VG+	NM
❑ 41271	I've Never Seen the Likes of You/Soulful Woman	1980	—	2.00	4.00
❑ 51011	A Bridge That Just Won't Burn/You'll Be Back	1980	—	2.00	4.00
❑ 51059	Rest Your Love on Me/I Am the Dreamer (You Are the Dream)	1981	—	2.00	4.00
❑ 51137	Tight Fittin' Jeans/I Made You a Woman	1981	—	2.00	4.00
❑ 51199	Red Neckin' Love Makin' Night/Hearts	1981	—	2.00	4.00
❑ 52032	Over Thirty (Not Over the Hill)/Love Salvation	1982	—	2.00	4.00
❑ 52154	We Had It All/Cheatin' Fire	1983	—	2.00	4.00
❑ 53034	Julia/Everybody Needs a Hero	1987	—	2.00	4.00
❑ 53134	I Want to Know You Before We Make Love/Snake Boots	1987	—	2.00	4.00
❑ 53200	That's My Job/Lonely Town	1987	—	2.00	4.00
❑ 53276	Goodbye Time/Your Loving Side	1988	—	2.00	4.00
❑ 53373	Saturday Night Special/If You Were Mine to Lose	1988	—	2.00	4.00
❑ 53456	I Wish I Was Still in Your Dreams/If You Were Mine to Lose	1988	—	2.00	4.00
❑ 53633	She's Got a Single Thing In Mind/Too White to Sing the Blues	1989	—	2.00	4.00
❑ 53688	The House on Old Lonesome Road/Nobody Can Fill Your Shoes	1989	—	2.00	4.00
❑ 53759	Who's Gonna Know/Private Part of My Heart	1989	—	2.00	4.00
❑ 53983	I Couldn't See You Leavin'/Just the Thought of Losing You	1991	—	2.00	4.00
❑ 54077	One Bridge I Didn't Burn/I'm Tired of Being Something	1991	—	2.00	4.00
❑ 54186	She's Got a Man on Her Mind/You Put It There	1991	—	2.00	4.00
❑ 54281	Who Did They Think He Was/Let the Pretty Lady Dance	1991	—	2.00	4.00
❑ 54717	I'm the Only Thing (I'll Hold Against You)/Final Touches	1993	—	2.00	4.00
❑ 54766	Don't It Make You Lonely/I Don't Love You	1993	—	2.00	4.00
❑ 79000	Fit to Be Tied Down/When You're Cool (The Sun Shines All the Time)	1990	—	2.00	4.00
❑ 79067	Crazy in Love/Hearts Breakin' All Over Town	1990	—	2.00	4.00

MERCURY

Number	Title (A Side/B Side)	Yr	VG	VG+	NM
❑ 71086	I Need Your Lovin'/Born to Sing the Blues	1957	10.00	20.00	40.00
❑ 71148	Maybe Baby/Shake It Up	1957	10.00	20.00	40.00
❑ 71384	Why Can't I Get Through to You/Double Talk Baby	1958	10.00	20.00	40.00

MGM

Number	Title (A Side/B Side)	Yr	VG	VG+	NM
❑ 12677 [M]	It's Only Make Believe/I'll Try	1958	6.25	12.50	25.00
❑ 12748	The Story of My Love/Make Me Know You're Mine	1959	6.25	12.50	25.00
❑ 12785	Hey Little Lucy! (Don'tcha Put No Lipstick On)/When I'm Not with You	1959	6.25	12.50	25.00
❑ 12804	Mona Lisa/Heavenly	1959	6.25	12.50	25.00
❑ 12826 [M]	Danny Boy/Halfway to Heaven	1959	6.25	12.50	25.00

—First pressings on yellow labels

Number	Title (A Side/B Side)	Yr	VG	VG+	NM
❑ 12826 [M]	Danny Boy/Halfway to Heaven	1959	5.00	10.00	20.00

—Second pressings on black labels

Number	Title (A Side/B Side)	Yr	VG	VG+	NM
❑ 12857	Lonely Blue Boy/Star Spangled Heaven	1959	5.00	10.00	20.00
❑ 12886	What Am I Living For/The Hurt in My Heart	1960	5.00	10.00	20.00
❑ 12886 [PS]	What Am I Living For/The Hurt in My Heart	1960	12.50	25.00	50.00
❑ 12911	Is a Blue Bird Blue/She's Mine	1960	5.00	10.00	20.00
❑ 12911 [PS]	Is a Blue Bird Blue/She's Mine	1960	12.50	25.00	50.00
❑ 12918	What a Dream/Tell Me One More Time	1960	3.75	7.50	15.00
❑ 12943	Teasin'/I Need You So	1960	3.75	7.50	15.00
❑ 12962	Whole Lot of Shakin' Going On/The Flame	1960	3.75	7.50	15.00
❑ 12969	C'est Si Bon (It's So Good)/Don't You Dare Let Me Down	1960	3.75	7.50	15.00
❑ 12969 [PS]	C'est Si Bon (It's So Good)/Don't You Dare Let Me Down	1960	12.50	25.00	50.00
❑ 12998	The Next Kiss (Is the Last Goodbye)/A Man Alone	1961	3.75	7.50	15.00
❑ 12998 [PS]	The Next Kiss (Is the Last Goodbye)/A Man Alone	1961	12.50	25.00	50.00
❑ 13011	I'm in a Blue, Blue Mood/A Million Teardrops	1961	3.75	7.50	15.00
❑ 13034	It's Drivin' Me Wild/Sweet Sorrow	1961	3.75	7.50	15.00
❑ 13034 [PS]	It's Drivin' Me Wild/Sweet Sorrow	1961	10.00	20.00	40.00
❑ 13050	Portrait of a Fool/Tower of Tears	1961	3.75	7.50	15.00
❑ 13072	Little Piece of My Heart/Comfy N' Cozy	1962	3.75	7.50	15.00
❑ 13089	There's Something on Your Mind/Unchained Melody	1962	3.75	7.50	15.00
❑ 13112	I Hope, I Think, I Wish/The Pickup	1962	3.75	7.50	15.00
❑ 13149	I Got My Mojo Working/She Ain't No Angel	1963	3.75	7.50	15.00
❑ 14172	It's Only Make Believe/Lonely Blue Boy	1970	—	2.50	5.00
❑ 14205	What Am I Living For/I'll Try	1970	—	2.50	5.00
❑ 14274	What a Dream/Long Black Train	1971	—	2.50	5.00
❑ 14355	It's Too Late/I Hope, I Think, I Wish	1972	—	2.50	5.00
❑ 14408	Walk On By/Hey Miss Ruby	1972	—	2.50	5.00
❑ 14447	Boss Man/Fever	1972	—	2.50	5.00
❑ 14582	Danny Boy/The Pickup	1973	—	2.50	5.00
❑ SK-50107 [S]	It's Only Make Believe/I'll Try	1958	25.00	50.00	100.00
❑ SK-50130 [S]	Danny Boy/Halfway to Heaven	1959	25.00	50.00	100.00

WARNER BROS.

Number	Title (A Side/B Side)	Yr	VG	VG+	NM
❑ 28577	Fallin' for You for Years/I'll Try	1986	—	2.00	4.00
❑ 28692	Desperado Love/I Can't See Me Without You	1986	—	2.00	4.00
❑ 28772	You'll Never Know How Much I Needed You Today/Fifteen Years Ago	1986	—	2.00	4.00
❑ 28866	The Legend and the Man/(I Can't Believe) She Gives It All to Me	1985	—	2.00	4.00
❑ 28966	Between Blue Eyes and Jeans/Baby's Gone	1985	—	2.00	4.00
❑ 29057	Don't Call Him a Cowboy/After All the Good Is Gone	1985	—	2.00	4.00
❑ 29129	White Christmas/Happy the Christmas Clown	1984	—	2.50	5.00
❑ 29129 [PS]	White Christmas/Happy The Christmas Clown	1984	—	2.50	5.00
❑ 29137	Ain't She Somethin' Else/The Games That Daddies Play	1984	—	2.00	4.00
❑ 29227	I Don't Know a Thing About Love (The Moon Song)/Don't Cry Joni	1984	—	2.00	4.00
❑ 29308	Somebody's Needin' Somebody/(Lying Here with) Linda on My Mind	1984	—	2.00	4.00
❑ 29395	Three Times a Lady/I Think I'm in Love	1983	—	2.00	4.00
❑ 29505	Heartache Tonight/Hello Darlin'	1983	—	2.00	4.00
❑ 29636	Lost in the Feeling/You've Never Been This Far Before	1983	—	2.00	4.00

7-Inch Extended Plays

MGM

Number	Title (A Side/B Side)	Yr	VG	VG+	NM
❑ X-1623	(contents unknown)	1958	37.50	75.00	150.00
❑ X-1623 [PS]	It's Only Make Believe	1958	37.50	75.00	150.00
❑ X-1640	It's Only Make Believe/Hallelujah, I Love Her So//First Romance/Make Me Know You're Mine	1959	25.00	50.00	100.00
❑ X-1640 [PS]	Conway Twitty Sings, Volume 1	1959	25.00	50.00	100.00
❑ X-1641	(contents unknown)	1959	25.00	50.00	100.00
❑ X-1641 [PS]	Conway Twitty Sings, Volume 2	1959	25.00	50.00	100.00
❑ X-1642	(contents unknown)	1959	25.00	50.00	100.00
❑ X-1642 [PS]	Conway Twitty Sings, Volume 3	1959	25.00	50.00	100.00
❑ X-1678	Danny Boy/Heavenly//She's Mine/Blueberry Hill	1959	25.00	50.00	100.00
❑ X-1678 [PS]	Saturday Night with Conway Twitty, Volume 1	1959	25.00	50.00	100.00
❑ X-1679	(contents unknown)	1959	25.00	50.00	100.00
❑ X-1679 [PS]	Saturday Night with Conway Twitty, Volume 2	1959	25.00	50.00	100.00
❑ X-1680	(contents unknown)	1959	25.00	50.00	100.00
❑ X-1680 [PS]	Saturday Night with Conway Twitty, Volume 3	1959	25.00	50.00	100.00
❑ X-1701	(contents unknown)	1960	25.00	50.00	100.00
❑ X-1701 [PS]	Lonely Blue Boy	1960	25.00	50.00	100.00

TWITTY, CONWAY, AND LORETTA LYNN

Also see each artist's individual listings.

DECCA

Number	Title (A Side/B Side)	Yr	VG	VG+	NM
❑ 32776	After the Fire Is Gone/The One I Can't Live Without	1971	—	3.50	7.00
❑ 32873	Lead Me On/Four Glass Walls	1971	—	3.50	7.00

MCA

Number	Title (A Side/B Side)	Yr	VG	VG+	NM
❑ 40079	Louisiana Woman, Mississippi Man/Living Together Alone	1973	—	2.50	5.00
❑ 40251	As Soon As I Hang Up the Phone/A Lifetime Before	1974	—	2.50	5.00
❑ 40283	Trouble in Paradise/We've Already Tasted Love	1974	—	2.50	5.00
❑ 40420	Feelin's/You Done Lost Your Baby	1975	—	2.50	5.00
❑ 40572	The Letter/God Bless America Again	1976	—	2.50	5.00
❑ 40728	The Bed I'm Dreaming On/I Can't Love You Enough	1977	—	2.50	5.00
❑ 40920	You're the Reason Our Kids Are Ugly/From Seven Until Ten	1978	—	2.50	5.00
❑ 41141	The Sadness of It All/You Know Just What I'd Do	1979	—	2.50	5.00
❑ 41232	Hit the Road Jack/It's True Love	1980	—	2.00	4.00
❑ 51050	Lovin' What Your Lovin' Does to Me/Silent Partners	1981	—	2.00	4.00
❑ 51114	I Still Believe in Waltzes/Oh Honey	1981	—	2.00	4.00
❑ 53417	Making Believe/As Soon As I Hang Up the Phone (The Telephone Song)	1988	—	2.00	4.00

TWO CHAPS, THE

With JAY BLACK, later of JAY AND THE AMERICANS.

ATLANTIC

Number	Title (A Side/B Side)	Yr	VG	VG+	NM
❑ 1195	Forgive Me/No More	1958	7.50	15.00	30.00

TYLER, BONNIE

CHRYSALIS

Number	Title (A Side/B Side)	Yr	VG	VG+	NM
❑ 2130	Lost in France/Baby I Remember You	1976	—	3.00	6.00

COLUMBIA

Number	Title (A Side/B Side)	Yr	VG	VG+	NM
❑ 03906	Total Eclipse of the Heart/Straight from the Heart	1983	—	2.00	4.00
❑ 04246	Take Me Back/Getttin' So Excited	1983	—	2.00	4.00
❑ 04246 [PS]	Take Me Back/Getttin' So Excited	1983	—	2.50	5.00

Number	Title (A Side/B Side)	Yr	VG	VG+	NM
❑ 04370	Holding Out for a Hero/Faster Than the Speed of Night	1984	—	—	3.00
❑ 04370 [PS]	Holding Out for a Hero/Faster Than the Speed of Night	1984	—	2.00	4.00
❑ 04548	Here She Comes/Obsession	1984	—	—	3.00
❑ 04548 [PS]	Here She Comes/Obsession	1984	—	2.00	4.00
❑ 05839	If You Were a Woman (And I Was a Man)/Under Suspicion	1986	—	—	3.00
❑ 05839 [PS]	If You Were a Woman (And I Was a Man)/Under Suspicion	1986	—	2.00	4.00
❑ 06151	Loving You's a Dirty Job (But Somebody's Gotta Do It)/Before This Night Is Through	1986	—	2.00	4.00
—With Todd Rundgren					
❑ 06527	Band of Gold/Tears	1986	—	—	3.00
❑ 07758	Hide Your Heart/Fire Below	1988	—	—	3.00
❑ 08497	Save Up All Your Tears/It's Not Enough	1988	—	—	3.00

RCA

Number	Title (A Side/B Side)	Yr	VG	VG+	NM
❑ PB-11249	It's a Heartache/It's About Time	1978	—	2.50	5.00
❑ PB-11349	If I Sing You a Love Song/Heaven	1978	—	2.00	4.00
❑ PB-11349 [PS]	If I Sing You a Love Song/Heaven	1978	—	2.50	5.00
❑ PB-11468	My Guns Are Loaded/Baby I Just Love You	1979	—	2.00	4.00
❑ PB-11630	Married Man/If You Ever Need Me Again	1979	—	2.00	4.00
❑ PB-11763	I Believe in Your Sweet Love/Come On, Give Me Loving	1979	—	2.00	4.00

TYLER, FRANKIE

See FRANKIE VALLI.

TYLER, KIP

CHALLENGE

Number	Title (A Side/B Side)	Yr	VG	VG+	NM
❑ 1014	She Got Eyes/Shadow Street	1957	7.50	15.00	30.00
❑ 59008	Jungle Hop/Ooh Yeah Baby	1958	10.00	20.00	40.00

EBB

Number	Title (A Side/B Side)	Yr	VG	VG+	NM
❑ 154	She's My Witch/Rumble Rock	1959	12.50	25.00	50.00
❑ 156	Oh Linda/Kali Lou	1959	12.50	25.00	50.00

GYRO DISC

Number	Title (A Side/B Side)	Yr	VG	VG+	NM
❑ 711	Surfer's Lament (Eternity)/Toledo	1963	12.50	25.00	50.00
❑ 711 [PS]	Surfer's Lament (Eternity)/Toledo	1963	25.00	50.00	100.00

IMPERIAL

Number	Title (A Side/B Side)	Yr	VG	VG+	NM
❑ 5641	Rocket 'Round the Universe/The Goblin Trot	1960	7.50	15.00	30.00

TYLER, T. TEXAS

4 STAR

Number	Title (A Side/B Side)	Yr	VG	VG+	NM
❑ 45-1228	Deck of Cards/Sweet Thing	195?	10.00	20.00	40.00
—Early 1950s reissue of the hit; first issued on 78 in 1948					
❑ 1555	If You Had a Heart/To Prove My Love Is True	1951	7.50	15.00	30.00
❑ 1565	Irma/Blue Kimono Blues	1951	7.50	15.00	30.00
❑ 1579	I Want to Learn to Do It/Curley Headed Baby	1951	7.50	15.00	30.00
❑ 1588	I Was the Last One to Know/When the White Azaleas Start Blooming	1952	6.25	12.50	25.00
❑ 1597	Get Out of My Life/Who's to Blame	1952	6.25	12.50	25.00
❑ 1612	It's My Heart, It's My Conscience/It's a Pity	1952	6.25	12.50	25.00
❑ 1621	Snow on the Mountain/Electric Guitar Polka	1952	6.25	12.50	25.00
❑ 1628	Wasted Tears/Let's Fly Away	1953	5.00	10.00	20.00
❑ 1649	Kiss Me Like Crazy/Tired of It All	1954	6.25	12.50	25.00
❑ 1658	Tattler's Wagon/The Soldier's Prayer Book	1954	6.25	12.50	25.00
❑ 1660	Courtin' in the Rain/Old Blue	1954	5.00	10.00	20.00
❑ 1669	A Million Teardrops/Little Miss Muffet	1955	5.00	10.00	20.00
❑ 1682	I Tickled Her Under the Chin/She Wouldn't Do for You	1955	5.00	10.00	20.00
❑ 1735	Deck of Cards/Dad Have My Dog Away	1959	3.75	7.50	15.00
❑ 1744	Remember Me/Oklahoma Hills	1960	3.75	7.50	15.00

DECCA

Number	Title (A Side/B Side)	Yr	VG	VG+	NM
❑ 9-28544	He Done Her Wrong/Much More Than the Past	1953	5.00	10.00	20.00
❑ 9-28579	Bumming Around/Jealous Love	1953	5.00	10.00	20.00
❑ 9-28760	Scratch and Itch/Let's Get Married	1953	5.00	10.00	20.00
❑ 9-28922	Pretender/Nothing at All	1953	5.00	10.00	20.00
❑ 9-29007	Hot Rod Rag/Lighthearted Guy	1954	6.25	12.50	25.00
❑ 9-29286	River Girl/Golden Wristwatch	1954	5.00	10.00	20.00
❑ 9-29598	That's What You Mean to Me/Ten-Ten-Tennessee Line	1955	3.75	7.50	15.00

KING

Number	Title (A Side/B Side)	Yr	VG	VG+	NM
❑ 5249	Deck of Cards/Dad Gave My Dog Away	1959	3.75	7.50	15.00
❑ 5380	Oklahoma Hills/Remember Me	1960	3.75	7.50	15.00

RCA VICTOR

Number	Title (A Side/B Side)	Yr	VG	VG+	NM
❑ 47-5679	Pie A La Mode/Here Goes	1954	5.00	10.00	20.00
❑ 47-5710	Deck of Cards/Ida Red	1954	5.00	10.00	20.00

STARDAY

Number	Title (A Side/B Side)	Yr	VG	VG+	NM
❑ 759	Texas Boogie Woogie/Just Like Dad	1966	2.50	5.00	10.00
❑ 783	It's a Long Road Back Home/I Still Love You (By the Way)	1966	2.50	5.00	10.00
❑ 806	Injun Joe/Crawdad Town	1967	2.50	5.00	10.00
❑ 8015	Deck of Cards/Remember Me	197?	—	3.00	6.00

TYMES, THE

CAPITOL

Number	Title (A Side/B Side)	Yr	VG	VG+	NM
❑ 3440	When I Look Around Me/Smile a Tender Smile	1972	—	3.00	6.00

COLUMBIA

Number	Title (A Side/B Side)	Yr	VG	VG+	NM
❑ 44630	People/For Love of Ivy	1968	2.00	4.00	8.00
❑ 44799	God Bless the Child/The Love That You're Looking For	1969	—	3.00	6.00
❑ 44917	Find My Way/If You Love Me Baby	1969	—	3.00	6.00
❑ 45078	Love Child/Most Beautiful Married Lady	1970	—	3.00	6.00
❑ 45336	She's Gone/Someone to Watch Over Me	1971	—	3.00	6.00

MGM

Number	Title (A Side/B Side)	Yr	VG	VG+	NM
❑ 13536	Pretend/Street Talk	1966	5.00	10.00	20.00
❑ 13631	(Touch of) Baby/What Would I Do	1966	5.00	10.00	20.00

PARKWAY

Number	Title (A Side/B Side)	Yr	VG	VG+	NM
❑ 871	So in Love/Roscoe James McClain	1963	6.25	12.50	25.00
—Original title of A-side					
❑ 871	So Much in Love/Roscoe James McClain	1963	3.75	7.50	15.00
❑ 871 [PS]	So Much in Love/Roscoe James McClain	1963	7.50	15.00	30.00
❑ 884	Wonderful! Wonderful!/Come with Me to the Sea	1963	3.75	7.50	15.00
❑ 884 [PS]	Wonderful! Wonderful!/Come with Me to the Sea	1963	6.25	12.50	25.00
❑ 891	Somewhere/View from My Window	1963	3.75	7.50	15.00
❑ 891 [PS]	Somewhere/View from My Window	1963	6.25	12.50	25.00
❑ 908	To Each His Own/Wonderland By Night	1964	3.75	7.50	15.00
❑ 908 [PS]	To Each His Own/Wonderland By Night	1964	6.25	12.50	25.00
❑ 919	The Magic of Our Summer Love/With All My Heart	1964	3.75	7.50	15.00
❑ 919 [PS]	The Magic of Our Summer Love/With All My Heart	1964	6.25	12.50	25.00
❑ 924	Here She Comes/Malibu	1964	3.75	7.50	15.00
❑ 924 [PS]	Here She Comes/Malibu	1964	6.25	12.50	25.00
❑ 933	The Twelfth of Never/Here She Comes	1964	3.75	7.50	15.00
❑ 7039	Isle of Love/I'm Always Chasing Rainbows	1964	3.75	7.50	15.00
—Included as a bonus with album 7039					

RCA

Number	Title (A Side/B Side)	Yr	VG	VG+	NM
❑ PB-10862	Love's Illusion/Savannah Sunny Sunday	1976	—	2.00	4.00
❑ PB-11136	I'll Take You There/How Am I to Know (The Things a Girl in Love Should Know)	1977	—	2.00	4.00
❑ GB-12082	You Little Trustmaker/Ms. Grace	1980	—	—	—
—Unreleased?					

RCA VICTOR

Number	Title (A Side/B Side)	Yr	VG	VG+	NM
❑ PB-10022	You Little Trustmaker/The North Hills	1974	—	2.50	5.00
❑ PB-10128	Ms. Grace/The Crutch	1974	—	2.00	4.00
❑ PB-10244	Interloop/Someday, Somehow I'm Keeping You	1975	—	2.00	4.00
❑ PB-10422	God's Gonna Punish You/If I Can't Make You Smile	1975	—	2.00	4.00
❑ GB-10493	You Little Trustmaker/The North Hills	1975	—	2.00	4.00
—Gold Standard Series					
❑ PB-10561	Good Morning Dear Lord/It's Cool	1976	—	2.00	4.00
❑ PB-10713	Goin' Through the Motions/Only Your Love	1976	—	2.00	4.00

WINCHESTER

Number	Title (A Side/B Side)	Yr	VG	VG+	NM
❑ 1002	These Foolish Things (Remind Me of You)/This Time It's Love	1967	2.50	5.00	10.00

TYRANNOSAURUS REX

See T. REX.

TYRELL, DANNY, AND THE CLEESHAYS

EASTMAN

Number	Title (A Side/B Side)	Yr	VG	VG+	NM
❑ 784	You're Only Seventeen/Let's Walk, Let's Talk	1958	10.00	20.00	40.00

TYSON, ROY

DOUBLE L

Number	Title (A Side/B Side)	Yr	VG	VG+	NM
❑ 723	Oh What a Night for Love/Not Too Young	1963	20.00	40.00	80.00
❑ 733	The Girl I Love/I Want to Be Your Boyfriend	1964	25.00	50.00	100.00

U

U.K.'S, THE

CAMEO

Number	Title (A Side/B Side)	Yr	VG	VG+	NM
❑ 342	Ever Faithful Ever True/Your Love Is All I Want	1965	2.50	5.00	10.00

U2

ISLAND

Number	Title (A Side/B Side)	Yr	VG	VG+	NM
❑ PR 564 [DJ]	I Will Follow (Mini LP Version)/I Will Follow (Radio Remix)	1983	7.50	15.00	30.00
❑ 49716	I Will Follow/Out of Control (Live)	1980	2.50	5.00	10.00
❑ 49716 [PS]	I Will Follow/Out of Control (Live)	1980	2.50	5.00	10.00
❑ 49716 [PS]	I Will Follow/Out of Control (Live)	1980	6.25	12.50	25.00
—Promo-only poster sleeve with tour dates					
❑ 94961	With or Without You/In God's Country	1988	—	2.00	4.00
—Gold label "Revival of the Fittest" series					
❑ 94974	Gloria/Sunday Bloody Sunday	1987	—	2.50	5.00
—Gold label "Revival of the Fittest" series; first U.S. 45 release for either					
❑ 94975	New Year's Day/Two Hearts Beat As One	1987	—	2.00	4.00
—Gold label "Revival of the Fittest" series					
❑ 94976	I Will Follow/Pride (In the Name of Love)	1987	—	2.00	4.00
—Gold label "Revival of the Fittest" series					
❑ 99199	All I Want Is You/Unchained Melody	1989	—	—	3.00
❑ 99199 [PS]	All I Want Is You/Unchained Melody	1989	—	—	3.00
❑ 99225	When Love Comes to Town/Dancing Barefoot	1989	—	—	3.00
—A-side: With B.B. King					
❑ 99225 [PS]	When Love Comes to Town/Dancing Barefoot	1989	—	—	3.00
❑ 99250	Desire/Hallelujah Here She Comes	1988	—	—	3.00
❑ 99250 [PS]	Desire/Hallelujah Here She Comes	1988	—	3.00	6.00
—Cardboard gatefold sleeve					
❑ 99250 [PS]	Desire/Hallelujah Here She Comes	1988	—	—	3.00
—Standard paper sleeve					
❑ 99254	Angel of Harlem/A Room at the Heartbreak Hotel	1988	—	—	3.00
❑ 99254 [PS]	Angel of Harlem/A Room at the Heartbreak Hotel	1988	—	—	3.00
❑ 99384	In God's Country/Bullet the Blue Sky	1988	—	—	3.00
—Black label jukebox pressing; both sides play at 45 rpm					
❑ 99385	In God's Country//Bullet the Blue Sky/Running to Stand Still	1988	—	2.00	4.00
—A-side plays at 45 rpm, B-side at 33 1/3 rpm					
❑ 99385 [PS]	In God's Country//Bullet the Blue Sky/Running to Stand Still	1988	—	2.00	4.00
—Cardboard sleeve					
❑ 99385 [PS]	In God's Country//Bullet the Blue Sky/Running to Stand Still	1988	—	2.00	4.00
—Paper sleeve					
❑ 99407	Where the Streets Have No Name/Silver and Gold	1987	—	2.00	4.00
—Black label jukebox pressing; both sides play at 45 rpm					
❑ 99408	Where the Streets Have No Name//Silver and Gold/Sweetest Thing	1987	—	—	3.00
—A-side plays at 45 rpm, B-side at 33 1/3 rpm					
❑ 99408 [PS]	Where the Streets Have No Name//Silver and Gold/Sweetest Thing	1987	—	2.00	4.00
—Cardboard sleeve					

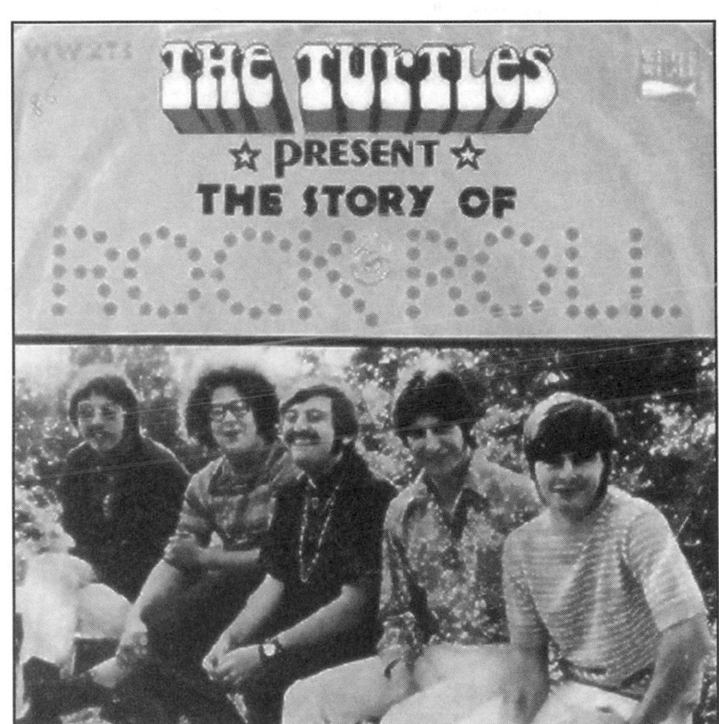

(Top left) This is the picture sleeve from the Talking Heads' first single, "Love Goes to Building on Fire," or to be more precise, the word "Love" followed by an arrow pointing right, then "Building on Fire." By the time their debut album came out, the Heads had expanded from three to four members, and this song was not issued again until the CD era. (Top right) In 1967, Epic put together some unusual promo 45s, each of which had two songs they were promoting on opposite sides. This one, with the Tremeloes and the Hollies on the same record, came with this extremely obscure picture sleeve. (Bottom left) This rather cheesy-looking sleeve, which is reminiscent of some of the cheesier import sleeves, accompanied the Turtles' 1968 Hot 100 hit "The Story of Rock and Roll." The song was written by Harry Nilsson. (Bottom right) U2's third American single, "Two Hearts Beat as One," was issued with this picture sleeve based on the LP cover War, from which it was taken. Along with the "I Will Follow" sleeve, this is one of the U2 picture sleeves that is hardest to find.

Number	Title (A Side/B Side)	Yr	VG	VG+	NM
❑ 99408 [PS]	Where the Streets Have No Name//Silver and Gold/Sweetest Thing	1987	—	—	3.00
—Paper sleeve					
❑ 99430	I Still Haven't Found What I'm Looking For// Spanish Eyes/Deep in the Heart	1987	—	—	3.00
—A-side plays at 45 rpm, B-side at 33 1/3 rpm					
❑ 99430 [PS]	I Still Haven't Found What I'm Looking For// Spanish Eyes/Deep in the Heart	1987	—	2.00	4.00
—Cardboard sleeve					
❑ 99430 [PS]	I Still Haven't Found What I'm Looking For// Spanish Eyes/Deep in the Heart	1987	—	—	3.00
—Paper sleeve					
❑ 99431	I Still Haven't Found What I'm Looking For/ Spanish Eyes	1987	2.50	5.00	10.00
—Black label jukebox pressing; both sides play at 45 rpm					
❑ 99453	With or Without You/Walk on the Water	1987	2.50	5.00	10.00
—White label jukebox pressing, both sides play at 45 rpm					
❑ 99469	With or Without You//Luminous Times (Hold On to Love)/Walk on the Water	1987	—	—	3.00
—A-side plays at 45 rpm, B-side at 33 1/3 rpm					
❑ 99469 [PS]	With or Without You//Luminous Times (Hold On to Love)/Walk on the Water	1987	—	2.00	4.00
—Cardboard sleeve					
❑ 99469 [PS]	With or Without You//Luminous Times (Hold On to Love)/Walk on the Water	1987	—	—	3.00
—Paper sleeve					
❑ 99704	Pride (In the Name of Love)/Boomerang	1984	—	2.00	4.00
❑ 99704 [PS]	Pride (In the Name of Love)/Boomerang	1984	—	2.00	4.00
❑ 99789	I Will Follow (Live)/Two Hearts Beat as One (Live)	1983	—	2.50	5.00
❑ 99861	Two Hearts Beat as One/Endless Deep	1983	—	2.50	5.00
❑ 99861 [PS]	Two Hearts Beat as One/Endless Deep	1983	—	2.50	5.00
❑ 99915	New Year's Day/Treasure (Whatever Happened to Pete the Chop?)	1983	—	2.50	5.00
❑ 854774-7	Discotheque/Holy Joe (Garage Mix)	1997	—	—	3.00
❑ 854972-7	Staring at the Sun/North and South of the River	1997	—	—	3.00

ISLAND/CAPITOL

Number	Title (A Side/B Side)	Yr	VG	VG+	NM
❑ 858076-7	Stay (Faraway, So Close!)/I've Got You Under My Skin	1994	—	2.00	4.00
—B-side: Frank Sinatra and Bono					
❑ 858076-7 [PS]	Stay (Faraway, So Close!)/I've Got You Under My Skin	1994	—	2.00	4.00
—B-side: Frank Sinatra and Bono					

UBANS, THE

RADIANT

Number	Title (A Side/B Side)	Yr	VG	VG+	NM
❑ 102	Gloria/On the Bridge	1964	50.00	100.00	200.00

UGLYS, THE

ABC-PARAMOUNT

Number	Title (A Side/B Side)	Yr	VG	VG+	NM
❑ 10707	Wake Up My Mind/Ugly Blues	1965	3.00	6.00	12.00
❑ 10748	It's Alright/A Friend	1965	3.00	6.00	12.00
❑ 10773	Quiet Explosion/A Good Idea	1966	3.00	6.00	12.00

ULLMAN, TRACEY

MCA

Number	Title (A Side/B Side)	Yr	VG	VG+	NM
❑ 52347	They Don't Know/You Broke My Heart in 17 Places	1984	—	2.00	4.00
❑ 52347 [PS]	They Don't Know/You Broke My Heart in 17 Places	1984	—	2.00	4.00
❑ 52385	Break-A-Way/Long Live Love	1984	—	2.00	4.00
❑ 52385 [PS]	Break-A-Way/Long Live Love	1984	—	2.00	4.00
❑ 52441	Bobby's Girl/Oh, What a Night	1984	—	2.00	4.00

ULTIMATE SPINACH

MGM

Number	Title (A Side/B Side)	Yr	VG	VG+	NM
❑ 14023	(Just Like) Romeo and Juliet/Some Days You Just Can't Win	1969	3.00	6.00	12.00

UNBEATABLES, THE

DAWN

Number	Title (A Side/B Side)	Yr	VG	VG+	NM
❑ 552	I Love Paris/What I Say	1964	10.00	20.00	40.00

UNCHAINED MYNDS, THE

BUDDAH

Number	Title (A Side/B Side)	Yr	VG	VG+	NM
❑ 111	We Can't Go On This Way/Going Back to Miami	1969	3.75	7.50	15.00
❑ 119	Every Day/(B-side unknown)	1969	3.75	7.50	15.00
❑ 140	You, Me, and My Yo-Yo/Every Day	1970	3.75	7.50	15.00

TEEN TOWN

Number	Title (A Side/B Side)	Yr	VG	VG+	NM
❑ 106	We Can't Go On This Way/Going Back to Miami	1969	10.00	20.00	40.00

UNDERBEATS, THE

BANGAR

Number	Title (A Side/B Side)	Yr	VG	VG+	NM
❑ 00632	Annie Do the Dog/Sweet Words of Love	1964	15.00	30.00	60.00
❑ 00657	Broken Arrow/Little Romance	1964	15.00	30.00	60.00

GARRETT

Number	Title (A Side/B Side)	Yr	VG	VG+	NM
❑ 4004	Foot Stompin'/Route 66	1964	6.25	12.50	25.00

METROBEAT

Number	Title (A Side/B Side)	Yr	VG	VG+	NM
❑ 4449	Sweetest Girl in the World/It's Gonna Rain Today	1967	6.25	12.50	25.00

SOMA

Number	Title (A Side/B Side)	Yr	VG	VG+	NM
❑ 1449	Book of Love/Darling Lorraine	1966	6.25	12.50	25.00
❑ 1458	I Can't Stand It/Shake It for Me	1966	5.00	10.00	20.00

TWIN-TOWN

Number	Title (A Side/B Side)	Yr	VG	VG+	NM
❑ 706	Jo Jo Gunne/Our Love	1965	7.50	15.00	30.00

UNDERDOGS, THE

HIDEOUT

Number	Title (A Side/B Side)	Yr	VG	VG+	NM
❑ 1001	The Man in the Glass/Friday at the Hideout (Judy Be Mine)	1965	7.50	15.00	30.00
❑ 1004	Little Girl/Don't Pretend	1965	7.50	15.00	30.00
❑ 1011	Surprise Surprise/Get Down on Your Knees	1966	10.00	20.00	40.00

REPRISE

Number	Title (A Side/B Side)	Yr	VG	VG+	NM
❑ 0422	The Man in the Glass/Friday at the Hideout (Judy Be Mine)	1965	3.75	7.50	15.00
❑ 0446	Little Girl/Don't Pretend	1966	3.75	7.50	15.00

V.I.P.

Number	Title (A Side/B Side)	Yr	VG	VG+	NM
❑ 25040	Love's Gone Bad/Mo Jo Hanna	1966	6.25	12.50	25.00

UNDERGROUND, THE

MAINSTREAM

Number	Title (A Side/B Side)	Yr	VG	VG+	NM
❑ 660	Easy/Satisfy'n Sunday	1967	6.25	12.50	25.00
❑ 667	Get Him Out of Your Mind/Take Me Back	1967	6.25	12.50	25.00

UNDERGROUND SUNSHINE

Also see THE CHALLENGERS (4).

INTREPID

Number	Title (A Side/B Side)	Yr	VG	VG+	NM
❑ ITDJ-3 [DJ]	Don't Shut Me Out (mono/stereo)	1969	3.00	6.00	12.00
—Promo issue of 75012					
❑ 75002	Birthday/All I Want Is You	1969	3.00	6.00	12.00
❑ 75012	Don't Shut Me Out/Take Me, Break Me	1969	2.50	5.00	10.00
❑ 75019	Nine to Five (Ain't My Bag)/Rotten Woman Blues	1969	2.50	5.00	10.00
❑ 75029	Jesus Is Just Alright/Six O'Clock	1970	2.50	5.00	10.00

UNDERTAKERS, THE

PARKWAY

Number	Title (A Side/B Side)	Yr	VG	VG+	NM
❑ 909	Just a Little Bit/Stupidity	1964	3.00	6.00	12.00

UNDISPUTED TRUTH, THE

GORDY

Number	Title (A Side/B Side)	Yr	VG	VG+	NM
❑ 7106	Save My Love for a Rainy Day/Since I've Lost You	1971	2.00	4.00	8.00
❑ 7108	Smiling Faces Sometimes/You Got the Love I Need	1971	—	3.00	6.00
❑ 7112	You Make Your Own Heaven and Hell Right Here on Earth/Ball of Confusion (That's What the World Is Today)	1971	—	3.00	6.00
❑ 7114	What It Is/California Soul	1972	—	3.00	6.00
❑ 7117	Papa Was a Rollin' Stone/Friendship Train	1972	—	3.00	6.00
❑ 7122	With a Little Help from My Friends/Girl You're Alright	1972	—	3.00	6.00
❑ 7124	Mama I Got a Brand New Thing (Don't Say No)/ Gonna Keep On Tryin' Till I Win Your Love	1973	—	3.00	6.00
❑ 7130	Law of the Land/Just My Imagination (Running Away with Me)	1973	—	3.00	6.00
❑ 7134	Help Yourself/What's Going On	1974	—	3.00	6.00
❑ 7139	I'm a Fool for You/Girl's Alright with Me	1974	—	3.00	6.00
❑ 7140	Big John Is My Name/L'il Red Ridin' Hood	1974	—	3.00	6.00
❑ 7141	Earthquake Shake/Spaced Out	1975	—	—	—
—Unreleased					
❑ 7143	UFO's/Got to Get My Hands on Some Lovin'	1975	—	3.00	6.00
❑ 7145	Higher Than High/Spaced Out	1975	—	3.00	6.00
❑ 7147	Boogie Bump Boogie/I Saw Her When You Met Her	1975	—	3.00	6.00

WHITFIELD

Number	Title (A Side/B Side)	Yr	VG	VG+	NM
❑ 8231	You + Me = Love/You + Me = Love (Disco Version)	1976	—	2.50	5.00
❑ 8295	Let's Get Down to the Disco/Loose	1977	—	2.50	5.00
❑ 8362	Hole in the Wall/Sunshine	1977	—	2.50	5.00
❑ 8781	Show Time (Part 1)/Show Time (Part 2)	1979	—	2.00	4.00
❑ 8873	I Can't Get Enough of Your Love/Misunderstood	1979	—	2.00	4.00

UNFORGETTABLES, THE

COLPIX

Number	Title (A Side/B Side)	Yr	VG	VG+	NM
❑ 192	It Hurts/Was It All Right	1961	7.50	15.00	30.00

PAMELA

Number	Title (A Side/B Side)	Yr	VG	VG+	NM
❑ 204	Oh Wishing Well/Daddy Must Be a Man	1961	125.00	250.00	500.00
—Blue vinyl					
❑ 204	Oh Wishing Well/Daddy Must Be a Man	1961	75.00	150.00	300.00

TITANIC

Number	Title (A Side/B Side)	Yr	VG	VG+	NM
❑ 5012	He'll Be Sorry/Oh There He Goes	1963	10.00	20.00	40.00

UNIFICS, THE

KAPP

Number	Title (A Side/B Side)	Yr	VG	VG+	NM
❑ 935	Court of Love/Which One Should I Choose	1968	3.00	6.00	12.00
❑ 957	The Beginning of My End/Sentimental Man	1968	3.00	6.00	12.00
❑ 957 [PS]	The Beginning of My End/Sentimental Man	1968	3.75	7.50	15.00
❑ 985	It's a Groovy World!/Memories	1969	3.00	6.00	12.00
❑ 985 [PS]	It's a Groovy World!/Memories	1969	3.75	7.50	15.00
❑ 2026	Toshisumasu/It's All Over	1969	3.00	6.00	12.00
❑ 2058	Got to Get You/Memories	1969	3.00	6.00	12.00

UNION GAP, THE

See GARY PUCKETT AND THE UNION GAP.

UNIQUE ECHOES, THE

SOUTHERN SOUND

Number	Title (A Side/B Side)	Yr	VG	VG+	NM
❑ 108	Zoom/Italian Twist	1962	12.50	25.00	50.00

UNIQUE TEENS, THE

DYNAMIC

Number	Title (A Side/B Side)	Yr	VG	VG+	NM
❑ 110	Whatcha Know Now/Run Fast	1959	7.50	15.00	30.00

HANOVER

Number	Title (A Side/B Side)	Yr	VG	VG+	NM
❑ 4510	Jeannie/At the Ball	1959	10.00	20.00	40.00

IVY

Number	Title (A Side/B Side)	Yr	VG	VG+	NM
❑ 112	Jeannie/At the Ball	1958	10.00	20.00	40.00

UNIQUES, THE (1)

Country singer Joe Stampley was a member of this group.

PARAMOUNT

Number	Title (A Side/B Side)	Yr	VG	VG+	NM
❑ 0017	Eunice/No One But You	1970	—	2.50	5.00
❑ 0058	Shadow of Love/Lazy Afternoon	1970	—	2.50	5.00
❑ 0116	Lucille/One Night with You	1971	—	2.50	5.00
❑ 0172	Will You Love Me Tomorrow/I Am a Gemini	1972	—	2.50	5.00

PAULA

Number	Title (A Side/B Side)	Yr	VG	VG+	NM
❑ 219	Not Too Long Ago/Fast Way of Living	1965	2.50	5.00	10.00
❑ 222	Too Good to Be True/Never Been in Love	1965	2.00	4.00	8.00
❑ 227	Lady's Man/Bolivar	1965	2.00	4.00	8.00
❑ 231	Strange/You Ain't Tuff	1966	2.00	4.00	8.00
❑ 238	All These Things/Tell Me What to Do	1966	2.00	4.00	8.00

Number	Title (A Side/B Side)	Yr	VG	VG+	NM
❑ 245	Goodbye, So Long/Run and Hide	1966	2.00	4.00	8.00
❑ 255	Please Come Home for Christmas/(Instrumental)	1966	3.00	6.00	12.00
❑ 264	Groovin' Out/Areba	1967	2.00	4.00	8.00
❑ 275	Every Now and Then (I Cry)/Love Is a Precious Thing	1967	2.00	4.00	8.00
❑ 289	Go On and Leave/I'll Do Anything	1967	2.00	4.00	8.00
—B-side by University of Utah Chamber Choir					
❑ 299	It's All Over Now/All I Took Was Love	1968	—	3.00	6.00
❑ 307	It Hurts Me to Remember/I Sure Feel More (Like I Do Then I Did When I Got Here)	1968	—	3.00	6.00
❑ 313	How Lucky Can One Man Be/You Don't Miss Your Water	1968	—	3.00	6.00
❑ 320	Sha-La Love/You Know (That I Love You)	1970	—	2.50	5.00
❑ 324	My Babe/Toys Are Made for Children	1970	—	2.50	5.00
❑ 332	All These Things/You Know That I Love You	1970	—	2.50	5.00

UNIQUES, THE (2)

Number	Title (A Side/B Side)	Yr	VG	VG+	NM
AMBER					
❑ 2004	Taboo/Ghost Riders in the Sky	1961	12.50	25.00	50.00
UNITED SOUTHERN					
❑ 104	Renegade/Malaguena	1961	75.00	15.00	30.00

UNIQUES, THE (3)

Number	Title (A Side/B Side)	Yr	VG	VG+	NM
BANGAR					
❑ 00609	Baby Don't Cry/Little Angel	1967	5.00	10.00	20.00

UNIQUES, THE (4)

Number	Title (A Side/B Side)	Yr	VG	VG+	NM
BLISS					
❑ 1004	I'm So Unhappy/I'm Confessin'	1961	125.00	250.00	500.00
END					
❑ 1012	Tell the Angels/Hey, Little Cupid	1958	62.50	125.00	250.00
FLIPPIN'					
❑ 202	Come Marry Me/Do You Remember	1959	12.50	25.00	50.00
GONE					
❑ 5113	I'm So Unhappy/I'm Confessin'	1961	50.00	100.00	200.00
❑ 5113	I'm So Unhappy/It's Got to Come	1961	17.50	35.00	70.00
MR. CEE					
❑ 100	Look at Me/Bossa Nova Cha Cha	1960	75.00	150.00	300.00
PRIDE					
❑ 1018	I'm So Unhappy/It's Got to Come	1960	62.50	125.00	250.00
TEE KAY					
❑ 112	One Million Miles Away/All at Once	1962	12.50	25.00	50.00

UNIQUES, THE (5)

Number	Title (A Side/B Side)	Yr	VG	VG+	NM
CAPITOL					
❑ 4949	Loving You/Blue Skies	1963	3.00	6.00	12.00
ROULETTE					
❑ 4528	Send Him to Me/This Little Boy of Mine	1963	5.00	10.00	20.00

UNIQUES, THE (6)

Number	Title (A Side/B Side)	Yr	VG	VG+	NM
DEMAND					
❑ 1994	Merry Christmas, Darling/I Wanna Chance	198?	2.00	4.00	8.00
—B-side by the Vows; green vinyl "collector's issue"					
❑ 2490	Times Change/Alright, OK, You Win	1964	12.50	25.00	50.00
❑ 2936	Merry Christmas Darling/Rockin' Rudolph	1963	20.00	40.00	80.00
❑ 3950	Merry Christmas Darling (And A Happy New Year Too)/Times Change	1963	12.50	25.00	50.00
DOT					
❑ 16533	Merry Christmas Darling/Times Change	1963	10.00	20.00	40.00

UNIQUES, THE (7)

Number	Title (A Side/B Side)	Yr	VG	VG+	NM
PEACOCK					
❑ 1677	Right Now/Somewhere	1957	7.50	15.00	30.00
❑ 1695	Mysterious/Picture of My Baby	1960	6.25	12.50	25.00

UNIQUES, THE (U)

Number	Title (A Side/B Side)	Yr	VG	VG+	NM
CLIFTON					
❑ 62	After New Year's Eve/Kiss, Kiss, Kiss	19??	2.00	4.00	8.00
LUCKY FOUR					
❑ 1024	Silvery Moon/Chocolate Bar	1962	50.00	100.00	200.00

UNIT FOUR PLUS TWO

Number	Title (A Side/B Side)	Yr	VG	VG+	NM
LONDON					
❑ 1009	I Was Only Playing Games/I Won't Let You Down	1966	3.00	6.00	12.00
❑ 9732	Sorrow and Pain/Woman from Liberia	1965	3.00	6.00	12.00
❑ 9751	Concrete and Clay/When I Fall in Love	1965	3.00	6.00	12.00
❑ 9751	Concrete and Clay/Wild Is the Wind	1965	4.00	8.00	16.00
❑ 9761	You've Never Been in Love Like This Before/Tell Somebody You Know	1965	3.00	6.00	12.00
❑ 9790	Stop Wasting Your Time/Hark	1965	3.00	6.00	12.00

UNITED STATES DOUBLE QUARTET

THE TOKENS and The Kirby Stone Four.

Number	Title (A Side/B Side)	Yr	VG	VG+	NM
B.T. PUPPY					
❑ 524	Life Is Groovy/Split	1966	2.50	5.00	10.00
❑ 547	Walking Along-Happy Wanderer/When I Lock My Door	1968	2.50	5.00	10.00
❑ 551	Do Re Mi/When I Lock My Door	1969	2.50	5.00	10.00

UNIVERSALS, THE

Probably more than one group.

Number	Title (A Side/B Side)	Yr	VG	VG+	NM
ASCOT					
❑ 2124	Dear Ruth/Gotta Little Girl	1963	15.00	30.00	60.00
CORA-LEE					
❑ 501	The Picture/He's So Right	1958	10.00	20.00	40.00
FESTIVAL					
❑ 1601	Dreaming/Love Bound	1961	15.00	30.00	60.00
—No subtitle on A-side					
❑ 25001	(I'll Just Have to Go On) Dreaming/Love Bound	1961	6.25	12.50	25.00
MARK-X					
❑ 7004	Teenage Love/Again	1957	50.00	100.00	200.00
MODERN					
❑ 1057	New Lease on Life/Without Friends	1968	2.50	5.00	10.00
SHEPHERD					
❑ 2200	A Love Only You Can Give/I'm in Love	1962	12.50	25.00	50.00
SOUTHERN					
❑ 102	Dear Ruth/Prayer of Love	1963	12.50	25.00	50.00

UNKNOWN, THE

Number	Title (A Side/B Side)	Yr	VG	VG+	NM
AUTOGRAPH					
❑ 206	I Have Returned/Keep Talking, Baby	1960	10.00	20.00	40.00

UNKNOWNS, THE (1)

Also see STEVE ALAIMO; MARK LINDSAY.

Number	Title (A Side/B Side)	Yr	VG	VG+	NM
PARROT					
❑ 307	Melody for an Unknown Girl/Keith's Song	1966	6.25	12.50	25.00

UNKNOWNS, THE (2)

Number	Title (A Side/B Side)	Yr	VG	VG+	NM
SHIELD					
❑ 7101	One More Chance/You and Me	196?	50.00	100.00	200.00
X-TRA					
❑ 102	One More Chance/You and Me	1957	250.00	500.00	1000.

UNKNOWNS, THE (U)

Number	Title (A Side/B Side)	Yr	VG	VG+	NM
MARLIN					
❑ 16008	Tighter/Young Enough to Cry	1966	6.25	12.50	25.00

UNRELATED SEGMENTS, THE

Number	Title (A Side/B Side)	Yr	VG	VG+	NM
HANNA-BARBERA					
❑ 514	It's Unfair/Story of My Life	1967	5.00	10.00	20.00
LIBERTY					
❑ 55992	It's Gonna Rain/Where You Gonna Go	1967	6.25	12.50	25.00
❑ 56052	Cry, Cry, Cry/It's Not Fair	1968	10.00	20.00	40.00

UNTAMED, THE

Number	Title (A Side/B Side)	Yr	VG	VG+	NM
PLANET					
❑ 117	It's Not True/Gimme Gimme Some Shade	1966	3.00	6.00	12.00
—Also reported to be Planet 103; do both exist as U.S. editions?					

UNTOUCHABLES, THE

At least two different groups.

Number	Title (A Side/B Side)	Yr	VG	VG+	NM
ALAN K					
❑ 6901	Little Mary/Funny What a Little Kiss Can Do	1962	50.00	100.00	200.00
DOT					
❑ 16306	Blues in the Night/Bondaru	1962	3.75	7.50	15.00
LIBERTY					
❑ 55335	You're on Top/Lovely Dee	1961	5.00	10.00	20.00
❑ 55423	Papa/Medicine Man	1962	5.00	10.00	20.00
MADISON					
❑ 128	Poor Boy Need a Preacher/New Fad	1960	6.25	12.50	25.00
❑ 134	Goodnight Sweetheart Goodnight/Vickie Lee	1960	6.25	12.50	25.00
❑ 139	Sixty Minute Man/Everybody's Laughin'	1960	6.25	12.50	25.00
❑ 147	Do Your Best/Raisin' Cain	1961	6.25	12.50	25.00
MCA/STIFF					
❑ 52725	I Spy (For the F.B.I.)/Freak in the Streets	1985	—	—	3.00
❑ 52725 [PS]	I Spy (For the F.B.I.)/Freak in the Streets	1985	—	2.00	4.00
NAU VOO					
❑ 809	Blue Chip Bounce (Part 1)/Blue Chip Bounce (Part 2)	1960	3.75	7.50	15.00
WASP					
❑ 105	Don't Go, I'm Beggin'/Baby, Let's Wait	1967	6.25	12.50	25.00

UPFRONTS, THE

Number	Title (A Side/B Side)	Yr	VG	VG+	NM
LUMMTONE					
❑ 103	It Took Time/Betty Lou and the Lions	1960	12.50	25.00	50.00
❑ 104	Too Far to Turn Around/Married Jive	1960	10.00	20.00	40.00
❑ 106	Why You Kiss Me/Little Girl	1961	12.50	25.00	50.00
❑ 107	Send Me Someone to Love Who Will Love Me/Baby For Your Love	1961	12.50	25.00	50.00
—White label					
❑ 107	Send Me Someone to Love Who Will Love Me/Baby For Your Love	1961	7.50	15.00	30.00
—Black label					
❑ 108	It Took Time/Baby For Your Love	1962	6.25	12.50	25.00
❑ 114	Do the Beetle/Most of the Pretty Girls	1964	15.00	30.00	60.00

UPSETTERS, THE

Number	Title (A Side/B Side)	Yr	VG	VG+	NM
ABC					
❑ 11081	Tossin' and Turnin'/Always in the Wrong Place at the Wrong Time	1968	2.50	5.00	10.00
❑ 11120	Don't Be Cruel/Down Home	1968	2.50	5.00	10.00
AUTUMN					
❑ 4	Autumn's Here/Draggin' the Main	1964	6.25	12.50	25.00
FALCON					
❑ 1010	The Upsetter/The Strip	1958	5.00	10.00	20.00
FIRE					
❑ 1029	Jaywalking/Steppin' Out	1960	5.00	10.00	20.00
GEE					
❑ 1055	The Blues/Rollin' On	1960	5.00	10.00	20.00
LITTLE STAR					
❑ 123	Yes, It's Me/Every Night About This Time	1962	12.50	25.00	50.00
—With Little Richard					

UPTONES, THE

Number	Title (A Side/B Side)	Yr	VG	VG+	NM
LUTE					
❑ 6225	No More/I'll Be There	1962	7.50	15.00	30.00
—Black label					
❑ 6225	No More/I'll Be There	1962	5.00	10.00	20.00
—Multicolor label					
❑ 6229	Be Mine/Dreamin'	1962	10.00	20.00	40.00
MAGNUM					
❑ 714	Dreaming/Wear My Ring	1963	5.00	10.00	20.00

Number	Title (A Side/B Side)	Yr	VG	VG+	NM
WATTS					
❑ 1080	Dreaming/Wear My Ring	1963	7.50	15.00	30.00

URIAH HEEP

Number	Title (A Side/B Side)	Yr	VG	VG+	NM
CHRYSALIS					
❑ 2274	Come Back to Me/Love or Nothing	1978	—	2.00	4.00
MERCURY					
❑ 73103	Gypsy/Real Turned On	1970	2.00	4.00	8.00
❑ 73145	Come Away Melinda/Wake Up	1970	2.00	4.00	8.00
❑ 73154	I Wanna Be Free/What Should Be Done	1971	2.00	4.00	8.00
❑ 73174	High Priestess/(B-side unknown)	1970	2.50	5.00	10.00
❑ 73243	Look at Yourself/Love Machine	1971	2.00	4.00	8.00
❑ 73271	Why/The Wizard	1971	2.00	4.00	8.00
❑ 73307	Easy Livin'/All My Life	1972	2.00	4.00	8.00
❑ 73349	Sweet Lorraine/Blind Eye	1972	—	3.00	6.00
❑ 73406	Tears in My Eyes/July Morning	1973	—	3.00	6.00
❑ 76177	That's the Way It Is/Son of a Bitch	1982	—	2.00	4.00
❑ 76177 [PS]	That's the Way It Is/Son of a Bitch	1982	—	2.50	5.00
WARNER BROS.					
❑ 7738	Stealin'/Sunshine	1973	—	2.50	5.00
❑ 7836	Something or Nothing/What Can I Do	1974	—	—	—
—Unreleased?					
❑ 8013	Something or Nothing/What Can I Do	1974	—	2.50	5.00
❑ 8132	Prima Dance/Stealin'	1975	—	2.50	5.00
❑ 8581	Masquerade/Free Me	1978	—	2.50	5.00

US3

Number	Title (A Side/B Side)	Yr	VG	VG+	NM
BLUE NOTE					
❑ S7-17707	Cantaloop (Flip Fantasia)/It's Like That	1994	—	—	3.00
❑ S7-17967	Tukka Yoot's Riddim/I Go to Work	1994	—	—	3.00

USA FOR AFRICA

Number	Title (A Side/B Side)	Yr	VG	VG+	NM
COLUMBIA					
❑ US7-04839	We Are the World/Grace	1985	—	—	3.00
—B-side by Quincy Jones					
❑ US7-04839 [PS]	We Are the World/Grace	1985	—	2.00	4.00

USHER, GARY

Also see THE TIMERS.

Number	Title (A Side/B Side)	Yr	VG	VG+	NM
CAPITOL					
❑ 5128	The Beetle/Jody	1964	12.50	25.00	50.00
❑ 5193	Sacramento/That's the Way I Feel	1964	20.00	40.00	80.00
—Produced by Brian Wilson					
❑ 5403	It's a Lie/Jody	1965	12.50	25.00	50.00
DOT					
❑ 16518	Three Surfer Boys/Milky Way	1963	100.00	200.00	400.00
LAN-CET					
❑ 144	Tomorrow/Lies	1961	15.00	30.00	60.00
TITAN					
❑ 1716	Driven Insane/You're the Girl	1961	37.50	75.00	150.00

UTMOSTS, THE

Number	Title (A Side/B Side)	Yr	VG	VG+	NM
PAN-OR					
❑ 1123	I Need You/Big Man	1962	30.00	60.00	120.00

UTOPIA

Also see TODD RUNDGREN.

Number	Title (A Side/B Side)	Yr	VG	VG+	NM
BEARSVILLE					
❑ 0317	Sunburst Finish/Communion with the Sun	1977	—	2.00	4.00
❑ 0321	Love Is the Answer/Marriage of Heaven and Hell	1977	—	2.00	4.00
❑ 29947	Junk Rock/Lysistrata	1982	—	2.50	5.00
❑ 49180	Set Me Free/Umbrella Man	1980	—	2.50	5.00
❑ 49247	Love Alone/Very Last Time	1980	—	2.00	4.00
❑ 49545	Second Nature/You Make Me Crazy	1980	—	2.00	4.00
❑ 49579	Always Late/I Just Want to Touch You	1980	—	2.00	4.00
❑ 50062	One World/Special Interest	1982	—	2.50	5.00
NETWORK					
❑ 69830	Hammer in My Heart/I'm Looking at You But I'm Talking to Myself	1983	—	2.00	4.00
❑ 69859	Feet Don't Fail Me Now/There Goes My Inspiration	1982	—	2.00	4.00
PASSPORT					
❑ 7923	Cry Baby/Winston Smith Takes It on the Jaw	1984	—	2.00	4.00
❑ 7923 [PS]	Cry Baby/Winston Smith Takes It on the Jaw	1984	—	2.50	5.00
❑ 7927	Stand for Something/Mated	1985	—	2.00	4.00

UTOPIANS, THE

Number	Title (A Side/B Side)	Yr	VG	VG+	NM
IMPERIAL					
❑ 5861	Dutch Treat/Ain't No Such Thing	1962	7.50	15.00	30.00
❑ 5876	Along My Lonely Way/Hurry to Your Date	1962	100.00	200.00	400.00
❑ 5921	Let Love Come Later/Opera vs. the Blues	1963	6.25	12.50	25.00

V

V-EIGHTS, THE

Number	Title (A Side/B Side)	Yr	VG	VG+	NM
ABC-PARAMOUNT					
❑ 10201	Papa's Yellow Tie/My Heart	1961	5.00	10.00	20.00
MOST					
❑ 711/3	Pretty Girl/Please Come Back	1959	25.00	50.00	100.00
VIBRO					
❑ 4005	Papa's Yellow Tie/My Heart	1960	7.50	15.00	30.00
❑ 4007	Let's Take a Chance/Hot Water	1961	7.50	15.00	30.00

V.I.P.'S

Number	Title (A Side/B Side)	Yr	VG	VG+	NM
BIG TOP					
❑ 100	Don't Pass Me By/You Ain't Good for Nothing	1965	3.00	6.00	12.00
❑ 518	You Pulled a Fast One/Flashback	1964	3.00	6.00	12.00
❑ 521	I'm On to You Baby/If He Wants Me	1964	3.00	6.00	12.00
CONGRESS					
❑ 211	My Girl Cried/Strange Little Girl	1964	3.75	7.50	15.00

VACELS, THE

Also see RICKY AND THE VACELS.

Number	Title (A Side/B Side)	Yr	VG	VG+	NM
KAMA SUTRA					
❑ 200	You're My Baby (And Don't You Forget It)/Hey Girl, Stop Leading Me On	1965	2.50	5.00	10.00
❑ 204	Can You Please Crawl Out Your Window/I'm Just a Poor Boy	1965	2.50	5.00	10.00

VAGRANTS, THE

Number	Title (A Side/B Side)	Yr	VG	VG+	NM
ATCO					
❑ 6473	Respect/I Love You Yes I Do	1967	2.50	5.00	10.00
❑ 6513	Beside the Sea/Sunny Summer Rain	1967	2.50	5.00	10.00
❑ 6552	And When It's Over/I Don't Need Your Lovin'	1968	2.50	5.00	10.00
SOUTHERN SOUND					
❑ 204	Oh, Those Eyes/You're Too Young	1966	6.25	12.50	25.00
VANGUARD					
❑ 35038	I Can't Make a Friend/Young Blues	1966	3.75	7.50	15.00
❑ 35042	Final Hour/Your Hasty Heart	1966	5.00	10.00	20.00

VAL-AIRES, THE

Forerunner to THE VOGUES.

Number	Title (A Side/B Side)	Yr	VG	VG+	NM
CORAL					
❑ 62177	Laurie My Love/Which One Will It Be	1960	20.00	40.00	80.00
WILLETTE					
❑ 114	Laurie My Love/Which One Will It Be	1959	100.00	200.00	400.00

VAL-CHORDS, THE

Number	Title (A Side/B Side)	Yr	VG	VG+	NM
GAME TIME					
❑ 104	Candy Store Love/You're Laughing at Me	1957	75.00	150.00	300.00
—With no sword logo					
❑ 104	Candy Store Love/You're Laughing at Me	1957	25.00	50.00	100.00
—With sword logo					

VAL-TONES, THE

Number	Title (A Side/B Side)	Yr	VG	VG+	NM
DELUXE					
❑ 6084	Tender Darling/Siam Sam	1955	37.50	75.00	150.00

VALADIERS, THE

Number	Title (A Side/B Side)	Yr	VG	VG+	NM
GORDY					
❑ 7003	While I'm Away/Because I Love Her	1962	15.00	30.00	60.00
❑ 7013	I Found a Girl/You'll Be Sorry Someday	1963	15.00	30.00	60.00
MIRACLE					
❑ 6	Greetings/Take a Chance	1961	20.00	40.00	80.00
—With no subtitle on A-side and 2:23 version of B-side					
❑ 6	Greeting (This Is Uncle Sam)/Take a Chance	1961	12.50	25.00	50.00
—With subtitle on A-side and 2:15 version of B-side					

VALAQUONS, THE

Number	Title (A Side/B Side)	Yr	VG	VG+	NM
LAGUNA					
❑ 102	Teardrops/Madeleine	1964	50.00	100.00	200.00
RAYCO					
❑ 516	Jolly Green Giant/Diddy Bop	1965	7.50	15.00	30.00
TANGERINE					
❑ 951	I Wanna Woman/Window Shopping on Girl's Avenue	1965	6.25	12.50	25.00

VALENS, RITCHIE

Number	Title (A Side/B Side)	Yr	VG	VG+	NM
DEL-FI					
❑ 1287	La Bamba '87/La Bamba	1987	—	2.50	5.00
❑ 4106	Come On, Let's Go/Framed	1958	20.00	40.00	80.00
❑ 4110	Donna/La Bamba	1958	17.50	35.00	70.00
—Blue/green/black label with circles					
❑ 4110	Donna/La Bamba	1958	10.00	20.00	40.00
—Green label					
❑ 4110	Donna/La Bamba	1958	7.50	15.00	30.00
—Light blue label					
❑ 4110	Donna/La Bamba	196?	3.75	7.50	15.00
—Black label with light blue sawtooth border					
❑ 4110	Donna/La Bamba	196?	6.25	12.50	25.00
—Light blue label with black sawtooth border					
❑ 4111	Fast Freight/Big Baby Blues	1959	12.50	25.00	50.00
—As "Arvee Allens"					
❑ 4111	Fast Freight/Big Baby Blues	1959	10.00	20.00	40.00
—As "Ritchie Valens"					
❑ 4114	That's My Little Susie/In a Turkish Town	1959	10.00	20.00	40.00
❑ 4117	Little Girl/We Belong Together	1959	7.50	15.00	30.00
❑ 4117 [PS]	Little Girl/We Belong Together	1959	25.00	50.00	100.00
❑ 4128	Stay Beside Me/Big Baby Blues	1959	6.25	12.50	25.00
❑ 4133	The Paddiwack Song/Cry, Cry, Cry	1960	6.25	12.50	25.00
❑ 51341 [DJ]	Come On Let's Go/La Bamba	1998	—	2.50	5.00
❑ 51341 [PS]	Come On Let's Go/La Bamba	1998	—	2.50	5.00
—Promotional issue in advance of box set; number is not on sleeve, but is on record					

7-Inch Extended Plays

Number	Title (A Side/B Side)	Yr	VG	VG+	NM
DEL-FI					
❑ PR-1 [DJ]	La Bamba/We Belong Together//Donna/Framed	1960	37.50	75.00	150.00
❑ PR-1 [PS]	Ritchie Valens (Limited Valens Memorial Series)	1960	50.00	100.00	200.00
—Sleeve accompanying promo-only EP states "February Is Ritchie Valens Memorial Month"					
❑ DFEP-101	(contents unknown)	1959	37.50	75.00	150.00
❑ DFEP-101 [PS]	Ritchie Valens	1959	37.50	75.00	150.00
—Cardboard sleeve					
❑ DFEP-101 [PS]	Ritchie Valens	1959	37.50	75.00	150.00
—Paper sleeve					
❑ DFEP-111	(contents unknown)	1960	37.50	75.00	150.00
❑ DFEP-111 [PS]	Ritchie Valens	1960	37.50	75.00	150.00

VALENTINE, PENNY

Number	Title (A Side/B Side)	Yr	VG	VG+	NM
LIBERTY					
❑ 55774	I Want to Kiss Ringo Goodbye/Show Me the Way to Love You	1964	7.50	15.00	30.00

Number	Title (A Side/B Side)	Yr	VG	VG+	NM
VALENTINES, THE (1)					
BETHLEHEM					
❑ 3055	I'll Forget You/Yes, You Made It That Way	1962	6.25	12.50	25.00
KING					
❑ 5338	Please Don't Leave, Please Don't Go/That's It Man	1960	6.25	12.50	25.00
❑ 5433	That's How I Feel/Hey Ruby	1960	6.25	12.50	25.00
❑ 5830	I Have Two Loves/Camping Out	1963	5.00	10.00	20.00
UNITED ARTISTS					
❑ 764	Alone in the Night/Mink Coats and Sneakers	1964	3.75	7.50	15.00
VALENTINES, THE (2)					
OLD TOWN					
❑ 1009	Tonight Kathleen/Summer Love	1954	200.00	400.00	800.00
RAMA					
❑ 171	Lily Maebelle/Falling for You	1955	50.00	100.00	200.00
—Blue label					
❑ 171	Lily Maebelle/Falling for You	1955	12.50	25.00	50.00
—Red label					
❑ 181	I Love You Darling/Hand Me Down Love	1955	37.50	75.00	150.00
❑ 186	Christmas Prayer/K-I-S-S Me	1955	125.00	250.00	500.00
—Blue label					
❑ 186	Christmas Prayer/K-I-S-S Me	1955	12.50	25.00	50.00
—Red label					
❑ 196	Why/The Woo Woo Train	1956	25.00	50.00	100.00
—Blue label					
❑ 196	Why/The Woo Woo Train	1956	12.50	25.00	50.00
—Red label					
❑ 201	Twenty Minutes (Before the Hour)/I'll Never Let You Go	1956	25.00	50.00	100.00
❑ 208	Nature's Creation/My Story of Love	1956	25.00	50.00	100.00
❑ 228	Don't Say Goodnight/I Cried Oh, Oh	1957	50.00	100.00	200.00
ROULETTE					
❑ 58	Christmas Prayer/Nature's Creation	196?	2.50	5.00	10.00
—"Golden Goodies Series"					
VALENTINES, THE (3)					
SOUND STAGE 7					
❑ 2646	I'm Alright Now/Gotta Get Yourself Together	1969	3.75	7.50	15.00
❑ 2663	If You Love Me/Breakaway	1970	3.00	6.00	12.00
VALENTINES, THE (U)					
IONA					
❑ 1003	The Sock/Sixteen Senoritas	196?	3.75	7.50	15.00
LUDIX					
❑ 102	Johnny One Heart/Mama I Have Come Home	1962	5.00	10.00	20.00
VALENTINO, MARK					
SWAN					
❑ 4121	The Push and Kick/Walking Alone	1962	3.75	7.50	15.00
❑ 4135	Hey You're Lookin' Good/Do It	1963	3.00	6.00	12.00
❑ 4142	Jivin' at the Drive-In/Part Time Job	1963	3.00	6.00	12.00
VALENTINO, SAL					
Of THE BEAU BRUMMELS.					
FALCO					
❑ 306	Lisa Marie/I Wanna Twist	1962	10.00	20.00	40.00
WARNER BROS.					
❑ 7268	An Added Attraction (Come and See Me)/Alligator Man	1969	2.50	5.00	10.00
❑ 7289	Friends and Lovers/Alligator Man	1969	2.50	5.00	10.00
❑ 7368	Silkie/Going for Rochelle	1970	2.50	5.00	10.00
VALENTINO AND THE LOVERS					
DONNA					
❑ 1345	One Teardrop Too Late/I'm Gonna Love	1961	10.00	20.00	40.00
VALERY, DANA					
ABC					
❑ 11138	The Lamplighter's Psalm/Didn't I	1968	3.00	6.00	12.00
❑ 11161	A Girl Without Love/Happy Birthday to Me	1968	3.00	6.00	12.00
❑ 11214	Surround Yourself with Sorrow/Breakfast in Bed	1969	3.00	6.00	12.00
COLUMBIA					
❑ 44004	Having You Around/You Don't Know Where Your Interest Lies	1967	6.25	12.50	25.00
—With Paul Simon					
❑ 44301	Imagine/You	1967	3.00	6.00	12.00
❑ 44389	Zabadak/Having You Around	1967	3.00	6.00	12.00
LIBERTY					
❑ 56156	Clinging Vine/Get In Line Girl	1970	2.00	4.00	8.00
❑ 56209	Point of No Return/Put Your Hand in the Hand	1970	2.00	4.00	8.00
PHANTOM					
❑ HB-10566	Will You Love Me Tomorrow/I Never Had It So Good	1975	—	2.50	5.00
SCOTTI BROS.					
❑ 509	I Don't Want to Be Lonely/Rainbow Connection	1979	—	2.00	4.00
❑ 612	I Gave You My Love/Roses and Rainbows	1980	—	2.00	4.00
VALETS, THE					
JON					
❑ 4025	I Need Someone/When I Met You	1958	25.00	50.00	100.00
❑ 4219	Sherry/You and You Alone	1959	7.50	15.00	30.00
VULCAN					
❑ 135	Sherry/You and You Alone	1959	50.00	100.00	200.00
VALIANTS, THE (1)					
ANDEX					
❑ 4026	Please Wait My Love/Freida, Freida	1958	30.00	60.00	120.00
—Some copies were pressed with this label in error (Keen 4026 is the "correct" issue)					
KEEN					
❑ 4008	Temptation of My Heart/Freida, Freida	1958	12.50	25.00	50.00
❑ 4026	Please Wait My Love/Freida, Freida	1958	15.00	30.00	60.00

Number	Title (A Side/B Side)	Yr	VG	VG+	NM
❑ 34004	This Is the Nite/Good Golly Miss Molly	1957	10.00	20.00	40.00
❑ 34007	Lover Lover/Walkin' Girl	1958	10.00	20.00	40.00
❑ 82120	This Is the Nite/Walkin' Girl	1960	5.00	10.00	20.00
SHAR-DEE					
❑ 703	Dear Cindy/Surprise	1959	30.00	60.00	120.00
—No mention of London distribution on label					
❑ 703	Dear Cindy/Surprise	1959	10.00	20.00	40.00
—With London distribution credit on label					
VALIANTS, THE (2)					
ALLSTAR					
❑ 3677	Jack the Ripper/(B-side unknown)	196?	5.00	10.00	20.00
VALIANTS, THE (3)					
DOT					
❑ 16884	I'll Return to You/Don't Make the Same Mistake	1966	3.00	6.00	12.00
VALIANTS, THE (4)					
FAIRLANE					
❑ 21007	Blue Jeans and a Pony Tail/See Saw	1961	5.00	10.00	20.00
IMPERIAL					
❑ 5843	Love Comes in Many Ways/You Are Sweeter Than Wine	1962	3.75	7.50	15.00
❑ 5915	Living in Paradise/I'm in a World of My Own	1963	3.75	7.50	15.00
KC					
❑ 108	Frankie's Angel/Are You Ready	1962	3.75	7.50	15.00
VALIANTS, THE (5)					
SPECK					
❑ 1001	Wedding Bells/Velma	1958	625.00	1250.	2500.
VALIANTS, THE (U)					
JOY					
❑ 235	Let Me Go Lover/Let Me Ride	1960	5.00	10.00	20.00
ROULETTE					
❑ 4510	Johnny Lonely/Eternal Triangle	1963	5.00	10.00	20.00
VALINO, JOE					
BAND BOX					
❑ 261	Turn Back the Dawn/Now	1961	2.50	5.00	10.00
CROSLEY					
❑ 216	Back to Your Eyes/Hidden Persuasion	1958	3.00	6.00	12.00
❑ 219	Game of Fools/Vesta La Giubba	1959	3.00	6.00	12.00
DEBUT					
❑ 143	Christmas Is Here/In Old Judea	1967	2.00	4.00	8.00
❑ 144	Vicki/Most Charming	1968	2.00	4.00	8.00
RCA VICTOR					
❑ AMAO-0132	Garden of Eden/Caravan	1973	—	2.50	5.00
—Gold Standard Series reissue					
❑ 47-7535	Out of Darkness/Everything I Touched Turned to Gold	1959	2.50	5.00	10.00
❑ 47-7723	Garden of Eden/Caravan	1960	2.50	5.00	10.00
UNITED ARTISTS					
❑ 101	Legend of the Lost/Declaration of Love	1957	3.00	6.00	12.00
❑ 101 [PS]	Legend of the Lost/Declaration of Love	1957	5.00	10.00	20.00
❑ 119	God's Little Acre/I'm Happy with What I've Got	1958	3.00	6.00	12.00
VIK					
❑ 0204	Buckets of Love (Zoop Zoop Do U Ba)/Four Seasons	1956	3.00	6.00	12.00
❑ 0226	Garden of Eden/Caravan	1956	3.75	7.50	15.00
❑ 0257	The Wind in the Riggin'/In the Arms of My Love	1957	3.00	6.00	12.00
❑ 0275	I'll Be Good/Tears (That I Cry Over You)	1957	3.00	6.00	12.00
7-Inch Extended Plays					
VIK					
❑ EXA-223	(contents unknown)	1956	5.00	10.00	20.00
❑ EXA-223 [PS]	Garden of Eden	1956	5.00	10.00	20.00
VALLEY, JIM					
Of PAUL REVERE AND THE RAIDERS.					
DUNHILL					
❑ 4096	Try, Try, Try/Invitations	1967	3.00	6.00	12.00
❑ 4103	Go-Go Round/Maintain	1967	3.00	6.00	12.00
JERDEN					
❑ 814	I'm Real/There Is Love	196?	2.50	5.00	10.00
VALLI					
SCEPTER					
❑ 1233	Hurry Home to Me (Soldier Boy)/Jimmy's in a Hurry	1962	3.75	7.50	15.00
—With the Shirelles backing up					
VALLI, FRANKIE					
Includes records under numerous pseudonyms. Also see THE FOUR LOVERS; THE FOUR SEASONS.					
ATLANTIC					
❑ 89720	American Pop/Why	1983	—	2.00	4.00
—With Manhattan Transfer					
CAPITOL					
❑ B-5115	Can't Say No to You/You Make It Beautiful	1982	—	2.00	4.00
—With Cheryl Ladd					
❑ B-5115 [PS]	Can't Say No to You/You Make It Beautiful	1982	—	2.50	5.00
CINDY					
❑ 3012	Come Si Bella/Real (This Is Real)	1958	50.00	100.00	200.00
—As "Franke Valli and the Romans"					
CORONA					
❑ 1234	My Mother's Eyes/The Laugh's on Me	1953	500.00	1000.	1500.
—As "Frank Valley"					
DECCA					
❑ 30994	It May Be Wrong/Please Take a Chance	1960	50.00	100.00	200.00
—As "Frankie Vally"					

Number	Title (A Side/B Side)	Yr	VG	VG+	NM
MCA					
❑ 41253	Doctor Dance/Where Did We Go Wrong	1980	—	2.50	5.00
—With Chris Forde					
MERCURY					
❑ 70381	Forgive and Forget/Somebody Else Took Her Home	1954	75.00	150.00	300.00
—As "Frankie Valley"; maroon label					
❑ 70381	Forgive and Forget/Somebody Else Took Her Home	1954	50.00	100.00	200.00
—As "Frankie Valley"; black label					
MOTOWN					
❑ 1251	You've Got Your Troubles/Listen to Yesterday	1973	3.00	6.00	12.00
❑ 1279	The Scalawag Song (And I Will Love You)/Listen to Yesterday	1973	3.00	6.00	12.00
MOWEST					
❑ 5011	Love Isn't Here/Poor Fool	1972	3.00	6.00	12.00
❑ 5025	The Night (mono/stereo)	1972	2.50	5.00	10.00
—Evidently, stock copies do not exist					
OKEH					
❑ 7103	I Go Ape/If You Care	1958	75.00	150.00	300.00
—As "Frankie Tyler"					
PHILIPS					
❑ DJP-16 [DJ]	My Mother's Eyes (mono/stereo)	1967	12.50	25.00	50.00
—Only issued as a promo; alternate number is 40460, but actual issue of 40460 is "C'mon Marianne" by the Four Seasons					
❑ 40407	The Proud One/Ivy	1966	2.50	5.00	10.00
❑ 40407 [PS]	The Proud One/Ivy	1966	3.75	7.50	15.00
❑ 40446	Can't Take My Eyes Off You/The Trouble with Me	1967	2.50	5.00	10.00
❑ 40446 [PS]	Can't Take My Eyes Off You/The Trouble with Me	1967	3.75	7.50	15.00
❑ 40484	I Make a Fool of Myself/September Rain (Here Comes the Rain)	1967	2.50	5.00	10.00
❑ 40484 [PS]	I Make a Fool of Myself/September Rain (Here Comes the Rain)	1967	3.75	7.50	15.00
❑ 40510	To Give (The Reason I Live)/Watch Where You Walk	1967	2.50	5.00	10.00
❑ 40510 [PS]	To Give (The Reason I Live)/Watch Where You Walk	1967	3.75	7.50	15.00
❑ 40622	The Girl I'll Never Know (Angels Never Fly This Low)/A Face Without a Name	1969	2.50	5.00	10.00
❑ 40622 [PS]	The Girl I'll Never Know (Angels Never Fly This Low)/A Face Without a Name	1969	3.75	7.50	15.00
❑ 40661	You've Got Your Troubles/A Dream of Kings	1970	3.00	6.00	12.00
❑ 40680	Circles in the Sand/My Mother's Eyes	1970	2.50	5.00	10.00
PRIVATE STOCK					
❑ 45003	My Eyes Adored You/Watch Where You Walk	1974	—	2.50	5.00
❑ 45021	Swearin' to God/Why	1975	—	2.50	5.00
❑ 45043	Our Day Will Come/You Can Bet	1975	—	2.50	5.00
❑ 45074	Fallen Angel/Carrie (I Would Marry You)	1976	—	2.50	5.00
❑ 45098	We're All Alone/You to Me Are Everything	1976	—	2.50	5.00
❑ 45109	Boomerang/Look at the World, It's Changing	1976	—	2.50	5.00
❑ 45140	Easily/What Good Am I Without You	1977	—	2.50	5.00
❑ 45154	Second Thoughts/So She Says	1977	—	2.50	5.00
❑ 45169	I Need You/I'm Gonna Love You	1977	—	2.50	5.00
❑ 45180	I Could Have Loved You/Rainstorm	1978	—	2.50	5.00
RSO					
❑ 897	Grease/Grease (Instrumental)	1978	—	3.00	6.00
SMASH					
❑ 1995	The Sun Ain't Gonna Shine (Anymore)/This Is Goodbye	1965	2.50	5.00	10.00
❑ 2015	(You're Gonna) Hurt Yourself/Night Hawk	1965	3.75	7.50	15.00
—B-side by the Valli Boys					
❑ 2037	You're Ready Now/Cry for Me	1966	2.50	5.00	10.00
WARNER BROS.					
❑ 8670	No Love at All/Save Me, Save Me	1978	—	2.50	5.00
❑ 8734	Fancy Dancer/Needing You	1979	—	2.50	5.00

VALOR, TONY

Number	Title (A Side/B Side)	Yr	VG	VG+	NM
MUSICTONE					
❑ 1119	There's a Story in My Heart/So Tenderly	1963	37.50	75.00	150.00

VALQUINS, THE

Number	Title (A Side/B Side)	Yr	VG	VG+	NM
GAITY					
❑ 161/2	My Dear/Falling Star	1959	200.00	400.00	800.00
❑ 161/2	My Dear/Falling Star	1959	500.00	1000.	1500.
—Red vinyl					

VALRAYS, THE

Number	Title (A Side/B Side)	Yr	VG	VG+	NM
PARKWAY					
❑ 880	Get A Board/Pee Wee	1963	7.50	15.00	30.00
❑ 904	Yo Me Pregunto/Tonky	1964	5.00	10.00	20.00

VALS, THE

Number	Title (A Side/B Side)	Yr	VG	VG+	NM
ASCOT					
❑ 2163	Too Late/I'm Stepping Out with My Memories	1964	7.50	15.00	30.00
UNIQUE LABORATORIES					
❑ (no #)	The Song of a Lover/Compensation Blues	1962	250.00	500.00	1000.

VALTONES, THE

Number	Title (A Side/B Side)	Yr	VG	VG+	NM
GEE					
❑ 1004	You Belong to My Heart/Have You Ever Met an Angel	1956	75.00	150.00	300.00

VAMPIRES, THE

Number	Title (A Side/B Side)	Yr	VG	VG+	NM
CARROLL					
❑ 104	Why Didn't I Listen to Mother/Did Anybody Lose a Tear	1962	37.50	75.00	150.00

VAN DER GRAAF GENERATOR

Number	Title (A Side/B Side)	Yr	VG	VG+	NM
MERCURY					
❑ 72979	Necromancer/Afterwards	1969	5.00	10.00	20.00

VAN DYKE, CONNIE

Number	Title (A Side/B Side)	Yr	VG	VG+	NM
MOTOWN					
❑ 1041	Oh Freddie/It Hurt Me Too	1963	12.50	25.00	50.00
WHEELSVILLE					
❑ 112	Don't Do Nothin' I Wouldn't Do/The Words Won't Come	196?	37.50	75.00	150.00

VAN DYKE, EARL, AND THE SOUL BROTHERS

Number	Title (A Side/B Side)	Yr	VG	VG+	NM
RENAISSANCE					
❑ 5000	September Song/(B-side unknown)	196?	18.75	37.50	75.00
SOUL					
❑ 35006	Soul Stomp/Hot 'N' Tot	1964	5.00	10.00	20.00
❑ 35009	All for You/Too Many Fish in the Sea	1965	200.00	400.00	800.00
❑ 35014	I Can't Help Myself/How Sweet It Is To Be Loved By You	1965	5.00	10.00	20.00
❑ 35018	The Flick (Part 1)/The Flick (Part 2)	1966	5.00	10.00	20.00
❑ 35028	6 x 6/There Is No Greater Love	1967	5.00	10.00	20.00
—By Earl Van Dyke and the Motown Brass					
❑ 35059	Runaway Child, Running Wild/Gonna Give Her All the Love I've Got	1969	5.00	10.00	20.00

VAN DYKE, LEROY

Number	Title (A Side/B Side)	Yr	VG	VG+	NM
ABC					
❑ 12070	Unfaithful Fools/What Will You Do Now, Mrs. Jones	1975	—	2.00	4.00
ABC/DOT					
❑ 17567	You Sure Look Good on My Pillow/Busted	1975	—	2.00	4.00
❑ 17597	Who's Gonna Run the Truck Stop in Tuba City When I'm Gone?/There Ain't No Roses in My Bed	1975	—	2.00	4.00
❑ 17691	Texas Tea/Las Vegas Girl	1977	—	2.00	4.00
DECCA					
❑ 32756	Mister Professor/People Gonna Turn You Off	1970	—	3.00	6.00
❑ 32825	Birmingham/What Am I Gonna Tell Them Now	1971	—	3.00	6.00
❑ 32866	I Get Lonely When It Rains/Party Girl	1971	—	3.00	6.00
❑ 32933	I'd Rather Be Wantin' Love/My Mind Is On You	1972	—	3.00	6.00
❑ 32999	I'll Be Around/Yesterday Will Come Again Tonight	1972	—	3.00	6.00
❑ 33055	Untie Me/Sittin' In for Me	1973	—	3.00	6.00
DOT					
❑ 15503	Auctioneer/I Fell in Love with a Pony Tail	1956	5.00	10.00	20.00
—Originals have maroon labels					
❑ 15503	Auctioneer/I Fell in Love with a Pony Tail	1956	3.75	7.50	15.00
—Second pressings have black labels					
❑ 15561	The Pocket Book Song/Honky Tonk Song	1957	3.75	7.50	15.00
❑ 15652	One Heart/Everytime I Ask My Heart	1957	3.75	7.50	15.00
❑ 15698	Leather Jacket/My Good Mind Went Bad	1958	25.00	50.00	100.00
❑ 16299	Auctioneer/I Fell in Love with a Pony	1961	2.50	5.00	10.00
KAPP					
❑ 908	Lonely Thing/One More Minute of Lonely	1968	—	3.00	6.00
❑ 931	You May Be Too Much for Memphis, Baby/Road of Love	1968	—	3.00	6.00
❑ 951	Lonesome Is/The Long Drive Home	1968	—	3.00	6.00
❑ 983	Goin' Back to Boston/The Straw	1969	—	3.00	6.00
❑ 2021	Steal Away/This Beginning of a Man	1969	—	3.00	6.00
❑ 2054	Crack in the World/Try a Little Bit Harder	1969	—	3.00	6.00
❑ 2091	Belle-O/An Old Love Affair Now Showing	1970	—	3.00	6.00
MCA					
❑ 40114	I'm O.K., You're O.K./Everytime Seems Like the First Time	1973	—	2.50	5.00
MERCURY					
❑ 71779	Faded Love/Big Man in a Big House	1961	3.00	6.00	12.00
❑ 71834	Walk On By/My World Is Caving In	1961	3.75	7.50	15.00
❑ 71926	If a Woman Answers (Hang Up the Phone)/A Broken Promise	1962	3.00	6.00	12.00
❑ 71988	The Life You Offered Me/Dim, Dark Corner	1962	3.00	6.00	12.00
❑ 72018	How Long Must You Keep Me a Secret/I Sat Back and Let It Happen	1962	3.00	6.00	12.00
❑ 72057	Black Cloud/Five Steps	1962	3.00	6.00	12.00
❑ 72097	Be a Good Girl/The Other Boys Are Talking	1963	3.00	6.00	12.00
❑ 72155	Wrong Side of the Tracks/What Are the Lips of Janet	1963	3.00	6.00	12.00
❑ 72198	Happy to Be Unhappy/Now I Lay Me Down	1963	3.00	6.00	12.00
❑ 72232	Night People/Baby (Where Can You Be)	1964	2.50	5.00	10.00
❑ 72277	Afraid of a Heartbreak/Your Money	1964	2.50	5.00	10.00
❑ 72360	Anne of a Thousand Days/Poor Guy	1964	2.50	5.00	10.00
PLANTATION					
❑ 170	Runaround Sue/House of the Rising Sun	1978	—	2.00	4.00
❑ 192	Don't Bite the Hand That Feeds You/A Gay Ranchero	1978	—	2.00	4.00
SUN					
❑ 1146	Save Me a Seat by the Fire/Rev. Edmond Giles	1979	—	2.00	4.00
WARNER BROS.					
❑ 5650	It's All Over Now, Baby Blue/Just a State of Mind	1965	2.50	5.00	10.00
❑ 5692	Big Wide Wonderful World of Country/Ol' Man Moses	1966	2.50	5.00	10.00
❑ 5807	(Now and Then There's) A Fool Such As I/You Couldn't Get My Love Back (If You Tried)	1966	2.50	5.00	10.00
❑ 5841	Roses from a Stranger/Before I Change My Mind	1966	2.00	4.00	8.00
❑ 7001	I've Never Been Loved/Less of Me	1967	2.00	4.00	8.00
❑ 7064	I'll Make It Up to You/What Am I Bid	1967	2.00	4.00	8.00
❑ 7155	Louisville/There's Always Tomorrow	1967	2.00	4.00	8.00

VAN DYKES, THE (1)

Number	Title (A Side/B Side)	Yr	VG	VG+	NM
DELUXE					
❑ 6193	The Bells Are Ringing/The Meaning of Love	1960	6.25	12.50	25.00
DONNA					
❑ 1333	Gift of Love/Guardian Angel	1961	10.00	20.00	40.00
FELSTED					
❑ 8565	Once Upon a Dream/Dame Tu Corazon	1959	6.25	12.50	25.00
KING					
❑ 5158	The Bells Are Ringing/The Meaning of Love	1958	17.50	35.00	70.00

Number	Title (A Side/B Side)	Yr	VG	VG+	NM
SPRING					
❑ 1113	Gift of Love/Guardian Angel	1961	30.00	60.00	120.00

VAN DYKES, THE (2)

Number	Title (A Side/B Side)	Yr	VG	VG+	NM
HUE					
❑ 6501	No Man Is an Island/I Won't Hold It Against You	1965	7.50	15.00	30.00
MALA					
❑ 520	No Man Is an Island/I Won't Hold It Against You	1965	3.75	7.50	15.00
❑ 530	I've Got to Go On Without You/What Will I Do If I Lose You	1966	3.00	6.00	12.00
❑ 539	Never Let Me Go/I've Got to Find a Love	1966	3.00	6.00	12.00
❑ 549	You Need Confidence/You're Shakin' Me Up	1966	3.00	6.00	12.00
❑ 566	A Sunday Kind of Love/I'm So Happy	1967	5.00	10.00	20.00
❑ 584	Tears of Joy/Save My Love for a Rainy Day	1967	10.00	20.00	40.00

VAN DYKES, THE (3)

Number	Title (A Side/B Side)	Yr	VG	VG+	NM
CO-OP					
❑ 515	Rich Girl/Miracle After Miracle	1967	5.00	10.00	20.00
❑ 516	Rock-a-Bye Girl/I'll Be By	1967	5.00	10.00	20.00
GREEN SEA					
❑ 101	Rich Girl/Again and Again	1965	10.00	20.00	40.00
❑ 105	Rock-a-Bye Girl/I'll Be By	1966	12.50	25.00	50.00
❑ 108	Miracle After Miracle/How Can I Forget Her	1966	10.00	20.00	40.00

VAN DYKES, THE (4)

Number	Title (A Side/B Side)	Yr	VG	VG+	NM
DECCA					
❑ 30654	The Fixer/Run Betty, Run	1958	10.00	20.00	40.00
❑ 30762	Come On Baby/Lambie Baby	1958	10.00	20.00	40.00
❑ 31036	Better Come Back to Me/I Don't Know What to Do	1959	15.00	30.00	60.00

VAN DYKES, THE (U)

Number	Title (A Side/B Side)	Yr	VG	VG+	NM
ATLANTIC					
❑ 2161	King of Fools/Stupidity	1962	3.75	7.50	15.00

VAN EATEN, LON AND DERREK

Number	Title (A Side/B Side)	Yr	VG	VG+	NM
APPLE					
❑ 1845	Sweet Music/Song of Songs	1972	2.00	4.00	8.00
❑ 1845 [PS]	Sweet Music/Song of Songs	1972	2.50	5.00	10.00
A&M					
❑ 1643	Wildfire/Music Lover	1974	—	2.50	5.00
—All A&M records as "Lon and Derrek"					
❑ 1662	Who Do You Outdo/All You're Hungry For Is Love	1975	—	2.50	5.00
❑ 1696	The Harder You Pull... The Tighter It Gets/Dancing in the Dark	1975	—	2.50	5.00
❑ 1845	Loving You/Baby It's You	1976	—	2.00	4.00

VAN HALEN

Also see SAMMY HAGAR; DAVID LEE ROTH.

Number	Title (A Side/B Side)	Yr	VG	VG+	NM
WARNER BROS.					
❑ 8515	You Really Got Me/Atomic Punk	1978	—	2.50	5.00
❑ 8556	Runnin' with the Devil/Eruption	1978	—	2.00	4.00
❑ 8556 [PS]	Runnin' with the Devil/Eruption	1978	7.50	15.00	30.00
❑ 8631	Jamie's Cryin'/I'm the One	1978	—	2.00	4.00
❑ 8707	Feel Your Love Tonight/Ain't Talkin' 'Bout Love	1978	—	2.00	4.00
❑ 8823	Dance the Night Away/Outta Love Again	1979	—	2.00	4.00
❑ 8823 [PS]	Dance the Night Away/Outta Love Again	1979	3.00	6.00	12.00
❑ 17810	Not Enough/Amsterdam	1995	—	—	3.00
❑ 17909	Can't Stop Lovin' You/Crossing Over	1995	—	—	3.00
❑ 18592	Judgment Day/Dreams	1993	—	—	3.00
❑ 19151	Top of the World/Poundcake	1992	—	—	3.00
❑ 27565	Feels So Good/Sucker in a 3-Piece	1989	—	—	3.00
❑ 27746	Finish What Ya Started/Sucker in a 3-Piece	1988	—	—	3.00
❑ 27746 [PS]	Finish What Ya Started/Sucker in a 3-Piece	1988	—	—	3.00
❑ 27827	When It's Love/Cabo Wabo	1988	—	—	3.00
❑ 27827 [PS]	When It's Love/Cabo Wabo	1988	—	—	3.00
❑ 27891	Black and Blue/Apolitical Blues	1988	—	—	3.00
❑ 27891 [PS]	Black and Blue/Apolitical Blues	1988	—	—	3.00
❑ 28505	Best of Both Worlds/Best of Both Worlds (Live)	1986	—	—	3.00
❑ 28505 [PS]	Best of Both Worlds/Best of Both Worlds (Live)	1986	—	—	3.00
❑ 28626	Love Walks In/Summer Nights	1986	—	—	3.00
❑ 28626 [PS]	Love Walks In/Summer Nights	1986	—	—	3.00
❑ 28702	Dreams/Inside	1986	—	—	3.00
❑ 28740	Why Can't This Be Love/Get Up	1986	—	—	3.00
❑ 28740 [PS]	Why Can't This Be Love/Get Up	1986	—	—	3.00
❑ 29199	Hot for Teacher/Little Dreamer	1984	—	—	3.00
❑ 29199 [PS]	Hot for Teacher/Little Dreamer	1984	2.00	4.00	8.00
—Special plastic sleeve with inserts					
❑ 29199 [PS]	Hot for Teacher/Little Dreamer	1984	—	2.00	4.00
—Regular picture sleeve					
❑ 29250	Panama/Drop Dead Legs	1984	—	—	3.00
❑ 29250 [PS]	Panama/Drop Dead Legs	1984	—	—	3.00
❑ 29307	I'll Wait/Girl Gone Bad	1984	—	—	3.00
❑ 29307 [PS]	I'll Wait/Girl Gone Bad	1984	—	—	3.00
❑ 29384	Jump/House of Pain	1984	—	—	3.00
❑ 29384 [PS]	Jump/House of Pain	1984	—	—	3.00
❑ 29929	Secrets/Big Bad Bill	1982	—	2.00	4.00
❑ 29986	Dancing in the Street/Full Bug	1982	—	2.00	4.00
❑ 49035	Beautiful Girls/D.O.A.	1979	—	2.00	4.00
❑ 49501	And the Cradle Will Rock.../Could This Be Magic	1980	—	2.00	4.00
❑ 49751	So This Is Love/Read About It Later	1981	—	2.00	4.00
❑ 49751 [PS]	So This Is Love/Read About It Later	1981	2.00	4.00	8.00
❑ 50003	Pretty Woman/Happy Trails	1982	—	2.50	5.00
❑ 50003	(Oh) Pretty Woman/Happy Trails	1982	—	2.00	4.00
❑ 50003 [PS]	Pretty Woman/Happy Trails	1982	—	2.50	5.00
—Original copies of both record and sleeve have no subtitles					
❑ 50003 [PS]	(Oh) Pretty Woman/Happy Trails	1982	—	2.00	4.00

VANGUARDS, THE (1)

Number	Title (A Side/B Side)	Yr	VG	VG+	NM
LAMP					
❑ 652	It's To Late for Love/The Thought of Losing Your Love	1970	3.00	6.00	12.00
—Yes, the label misspelled the A-side					
❑ 653	Girl Go Away/Man Without Knowledge	1970	3.00	6.00	12.00
WHIZ					
❑ 612	Somebody Please/(B-side unknown)	1969	2.50	5.00	10.00

VANGUARDS, THE (2)

Number	Title (A Side/B Side)	Yr	VG	VG+	NM
DERBY					
❑ 854	Don't Let It Happen Again/So Live	1954	100.00	200.00	400.00

VANGUARDS, THE (3)

Number	Title (A Side/B Side)	Yr	VG	VG+	NM
IVY					
❑ 103	Moonlight/I'm Movin'	1958	30.00	60.00	120.00
—With mention of "Billy Butler's Orchestra"					
❑ 103	Moonlight/I'm Movin'	1958	10.00	20.00	40.00
—No mention of "Billy Butler's Orchestra"					

VANGUARDS, THE (4)

Number	Title (A Side/B Side)	Yr	VG	VG+	NM
WARNER BROS.					
❑ 5800	Girl/A Stranger in Your Town	1966	3.00	6.00	12.00

VANGUARDS, THE (U)

Number	Title (A Side/B Side)	Yr	VG	VG+	NM
DOT					
❑ 15791	Baby Doll/My Friend Mary Ann	1958	6.25	12.50	25.00

VANILLA FUDGE

Number	Title (A Side/B Side)	Yr	VG	VG+	NM
ATCO					
❑ 6495	You Keep Me Hangin' On/Take Me for a Little While	1967	3.00	6.00	12.00
❑ 6554	The Look of Love/Where Is My Mind	1968	2.00	4.00	8.00
❑ 6590	You Keep Me Hangin' On/Come by Day, Come by Night	1968	2.50	5.00	10.00
❑ 6616	Take Me for a Little While/Thoughts	1968	2.00	4.00	8.00
❑ 6632	Season of the Witch (Part 1)/Season of the Witch (Part 2)	1968	2.00	4.00	8.00
❑ 6655	Good Good Lovin'/Shot Gun	1969	2.00	4.00	8.00
❑ 6679	People/Some Velvet Morning	1969	2.00	4.00	8.00
❑ 6703	Need Love/I Can't Make It Alone	1969	2.00	4.00	8.00
❑ 6728	Windmills of Your Mind/Lord in the Country	1970	—	3.00	6.00
❑ 99729	Mystery/The Stranger	1984	—	2.00	4.00

7-Inch Extended Plays

Number	Title (A Side/B Side)	Yr	VG	VG+	NM
ATCO					
❑ SP-4516 [DJ]	Eleanor Rigby-Part 1/You Keep Me Hanging On//Eleanor Rigby-Part 2/Ticket to Ride	1968	5.00	10.00	20.00
—Promo only, white label					
❑ SP-4516 [PS]	(title unknown)	1968	5.00	10.00	20.00
—Paper sleeve with above EP					

VANITY FARE

Number	Title (A Side/B Side)	Yr	VG	VG+	NM
20TH CENTURY					
❑ 2012	Rock and Roll Is Back/Making for the Sun	1973	—	2.50	5.00
❑ 2036	Down Home/Take It, Shake It, Break My Heart	1973	—	2.50	5.00
BRENT					
❑ 7067	Peter Who (Peter Pan)/Salt Water Babies	1967	2.00	4.00	8.00
DJM					
❑ 70024	Where Did All the Good Times Go/Stand	1971	—	2.50	5.00
❑ 70029	Big Parade/Nowhere to Go	1971	—	2.50	5.00
PAGE ONE					
❑ 21007	I Live for the Sun/On the Other Side of Life	1969	—	3.00	6.00
❑ 21020	Highway of Dreams/Waiting for the Nightfall	1969	—	3.00	6.00
❑ 21027	Early in the Morning/You Made Me Love You	1969	2.00	4.00	8.00
❑ 21029	Hitchin' a Ride/Man Child	1970	2.00	4.00	8.00
❑ 21033	(I Remember) Summer Morning/Megowd (Something Tells Me)	1970	—	3.00	6.00
❑ 21036	Where Did All the Good Times Go/Stand	1970	—	3.50	7.00
SOMA					
❑ 5000	Hitchin' a Ride/Early in the Morning	197?	—	2.50	5.00
—Reissue					

VAQUEROS, THE

Number	Title (A Side/B Side)	Yr	VG	VG+	NM
AUDITION					
❑ 6102	Desert Wind/Echo	1964	12.50	25.00	50.00
BANGAR					
❑ 00647	Birds and Bees/80-Foot Wave	1964	10.00	20.00	40.00

VARE, RONNIE, AND THE INSPIRATIONS

Number	Title (A Side/B Side)	Yr	VG	VG+	NM
DELL					
❑ 5203	Let's Rock, Little Girl/Love Is Just for Two	1959	12.50	25.00	50.00

VAREEATIONS, THE

Number	Title (A Side/B Side)	Yr	VG	VG+	NM
DIONN					
❑ 506	The Time/Ssab-Bbrom	1968	3.75	7.50	15.00
❑ 510	Foolish One/It's the Loving Season	1969	3.75	7.50	15.00

VARNER, DON

Number	Title (A Side/B Side)	Yr	VG	VG+	NM
QUINCY					
❑ 8002	Tear Stained Face/Meet Me in the Church	1969	62.50	125.00	250.00
VEEP					
❑ 1296	Tear Stained Face/Meet Me in the Church	1969	50.00	100.00	200.00

VAUGHAN, FRANKIE

Number	Title (A Side/B Side)	Yr	VG	VG+	NM
COLUMBIA					
❑ 41279	One Thing Led to Another/So Happy in Love	1958	3.75	7.50	15.00
❑ 41406	Honey Bunny Baby/Big Deal	1959	3.75	7.50	15.00
❑ 41480	Ain't Gonna Lead This Life No More/Heart of a Man	1959	3.75	7.50	15.00
❑ 41537	The Very Very Young/If You Ever Fall in Love	1959	3.75	7.50	15.00
❑ 41638	Hey You with the Crazy Eyes/The Key	1960	3.75	7.50	15.00
❑ 41859	Do You Still Love Me/Milord	1960	3.75	7.50	15.00
EPIC					
❑ 9238	Pebble on the Beach/Isn't This a Lovely Evening	1957	3.75	7.50	15.00
❑ 9265	We're Not Alone/Can't Get Along Without You	1958	3.75	7.50	15.00
❑ 9273	Judy/Am I Wasting My Time with You	1958	4.00	8.00	16.00
MALA					
❑ 588	If I Didn't Care/So Tired	1968	—	3.00	6.00
❑ 12004	Nevertheless/Girl Talk	1968	—	3.00	6.00

PHILIPS

Number	Title (A Side/B Side)	Yr	VG	VG+	NM
❑ 40070	Hercules/I'm Gonna Clip Your Wings	1962	3.00	6.00	12.00
❑ 40349	Forgotten Man/Wait	1965	2.00	4.00	8.00

VAUGHAN, SARAH

ATLANTIC

Number	Title (A Side/B Side)	Yr	VG	VG+	NM
❑ 1012	It Might As Well Be Spring/You Go to My Head	1953	25.00	50.00	100.00
❑ 3835	Fool on the Hill/Get Back	1981	—	2.50	5.00

COLUMBIA

Number	Title (A Side/B Side)	Yr	VG	VG+	NM
❑ 1-199	Black Coffee/As You Desire Me	1949	10.00	20.00	40.00
—Microgroove 33 1/3 rpm single					
❑ 1-250 (?)	Tonight I Shall Sleep (With a Smile on My Face)/While You're Gone	1949	10.00	20.00	40.00
—Microgroove 33 1/3 rpm single					
❑ 1-321	That Lucky Old Sun (Just Rolls Around Heaven All Day)/Make Believe (You Are Glad When You're Sorry)	1949	10.00	20.00	40.00
—Microgroove 33 1/3 rpm single					
❑ 1-380 (?)	Fool's Paradise/Lonely Girl	1949	10.00	20.00	40.00
—Microgroove 33 1/3 rpm single					
❑ 1-390 (?)	I Cried for You/You Say You Care	1950	10.00	20.00	40.00
—Microgroove 33 1/3 rpm single					
❑ 1-485	I'm Crazy to Love You/Summertime	1950	10.00	20.00	40.00
—Microgroove 33 1/3 rpm single					
❑ 1-620 (?)	Just Friends/You Taught Me to Love Again	1950	10.00	20.00	40.00
—Microgroove 33 1/3 rpm single					
❑ 1-679	Our Very Own/Don't Be Afraid	1950	10.00	20.00	40.00
—Microgroove 33 1/3 rpm single					
❑ 1-750 (?)	(I Love the Girl) I Love the Guy/Thinking of You	1950	10.00	20.00	40.00
—Microgroove 33 1/3 rpm single					
❑ 6-750 (?)	(I Love the Girl) I Love the Guy/Thinking of You	1950	7.50	15.00	30.00
❑ 1-830 (?)	Perdido/Whippa Whippa Woo	1950	10.00	20.00	40.00
—Microgroove 33 1/3 rpm single					
❑ 6-830 (?)	Perdido/Whippa Whippa Woo	1950	7.50	15.00	30.00
❑ 1-926	The Nearness of You/You're Mine You	1950	10.00	20.00	40.00
—Microgroove 33 1/3 rpm single					
❑ 6-926	The Nearness of You/You're Mine You	1950	7.50	15.00	30.00
❑ 38925	(I Love the Girl) I Love the Guy/Thinking of You	1950	6.25	12.50	25.00
❑ 39001	Perdido/Whippa Whippa Woo	1950	6.25	12.50	25.00
❑ 39071	The Nearness of You/You're Mine You	1950	6.25	12.50	25.00
❑ 39124	I'll Know/Gas Pipe Leaking	1950	6.25	12.50	25.00
❑ 39207	Ave Maria/A City Called Heaven	1951	6.25	12.50	25.00
❑ 39370	These Things I Offer You (For a Lifetime)/Deep Purple	1951	6.25	12.50	25.00
❑ 39446	Vanity/My Reverie	1951	6.25	12.50	25.00
❑ 39494	After Hours/Out of Breath	1951	6.25	12.50	25.00
❑ 39576	I Ran All the Way Home/Just a Moment More	1951	6.25	12.50	25.00
❑ 39634	Pinky/A Miracle Happened	1952	5.00	10.00	20.00
❑ 39719	If Someone Had Told Me/Corner to Corner	1952	5.00	10.00	20.00
❑ 39789	Time to Go/Street of Dreams	1952	5.00	10.00	20.00
❑ 39839	Say You'll Wait for Me/My Tormented Heart	1952	5.00	10.00	20.00
❑ 39873	Sinner or Saint/Mighty Lonesome Feeling	1952	5.00	10.00	20.00
❑ 39932	Lovers' Quarrel/I Confess	1953	5.00	10.00	20.00
❑ 39963	Spring Will Be a Little Late This Year/A Blues Serenade	1953	5.00	10.00	20.00
❑ 40041	Time/Linger Awhile	1953	5.00	10.00	20.00

MAINSTREAM

Number	Title (A Side/B Side)	Yr	VG	VG+	NM
❑ 5517	Imagine/Sweet Gingerbread Man	1971	—	2.50	5.00
❑ 5521	Pieces of Dreams/Once You've Been in Love	1972	—	2.50	5.00
❑ 5522	What Are You Doing the Rest of Your Life/The Summer Knows	1972	—	2.50	5.00
❑ 5523	Summer Me, Winter Me/The Story of a Frasier	1972	—	2.50	5.00
❑ 5527	And the Feeling's Good/Deep in the Night	1972	—	2.50	5.00
❑ 5533	Rainy Days and Mondays/Just a Little Lovin'	1973	—	2.50	5.00
❑ 5541	Send In the Clowns/(B-side unknown)	1973	—	2.50	5.00
❑ 5544	Alone Again (Naturally)/Run to Me	1973	—	2.50	5.00
❑ 5553	Do Away with April/I Need You More	1974	—	2.50	5.00

MERCURY

Number	Title (A Side/B Side)	Yr	VG	VG+	NM
❑ 70423	Ol' Devil Moon/Saturday	1954	3.75	7.50	15.00
❑ 70469	Make Yourself Comfortable/Idle Gossip	1954	3.75	7.50	15.00
❑ 70534	How Important Can It Be/Waltzing Down the Aisle	1955	3.75	7.50	15.00
❑ 70595	Whatever Lola Wants/Oh Yeah	1955	3.75	7.50	15.00
❑ 70646	Experience Unnecessary/Slowly, With Feeling	1955	3.75	7.50	15.00
❑ 70693	Johnny, Be Smart/Hey Naughty Papa	1955	3.75	7.50	15.00
❑ 70727	C'est La Vie/Never	1955	3.75	7.50	15.00
❑ 70777	Mr. Wonderful/You Ought to Have a Wife	1956	3.00	6.00	12.00
❑ 70846	Hot and Cold Running Tears/That's Not the Kind of Love I Want	1956	3.00	6.00	12.00
❑ 70885	Fabulous Character/The Other Woman	1956	3.00	6.00	12.00
❑ 70947	It Happened Again/I Wanna Play House	1956	3.00	6.00	12.00
❑ 71020	The Banana Boat Song/I've Got a New Heartache	1956	3.00	6.00	12.00
❑ 71030	Leave It to Love/The Bashful Matador	1957	3.00	6.00	12.00
❑ 71085	Poor Butterfly/April Give Me One More Day	1957	3.00	6.00	12.00
❑ 71157	Band of Angels/Please Mr. Brown	1957	3.00	6.00	12.00
❑ 71235	Gone Train/Next Time Around	1957	3.00	6.00	12.00
❑ 71303	Padre/Spin the Bottle	1958	3.00	6.00	12.00
❑ 71326	What's So Bad About It/Too Much Too Soon	1958	3.00	6.00	12.00
❑ 71380	I Ain't Hurtin'/Everything I Do	1958	3.00	6.00	12.00
❑ 71407	Are You Certain/Cool Baby	1959	3.00	6.00	12.00
❑ 71433	Separate Ways/Careless	1959	3.00	6.00	12.00
❑ 71477	Broken-Hearted Melody/Misty	1959	3.00	6.00	12.00
❑ 71519	Smooth Operator/Maybe It's Because (I Love You Too Much)	1959	3.00	6.00	12.00
❑ 71562	Eternally/You're My Baby	1960	3.00	6.00	12.00
❑ 71610	Some Other Spring/Our Waltz	1960	3.00	6.00	12.00
❑ 71642	Maybe You'll Be There/Doodlin'	1960	3.00	6.00	12.00
❑ 71669	For All We Know/The Rough Years	1960	3.00	6.00	12.00
❑ 71702	Close to You/Out of This World	1960	3.00	6.00	12.00
❑ 71742	If You Are But a Dream/Mary Contrary	1960	3.00	6.00	12.00
❑ 72510	Darling/I'll Never Be Lonely Again	1965	2.00	4.00	8.00
❑ 72543	A Lover's Concerto/First Thing Every Morning	1966	2.00	4.00	8.00
❑ 72588	Everybody Loves Somebody/1-2-3	1966	2.00	4.00	8.00

MGM

Number	Title (A Side/B Side)	Yr	VG	VG+	NM
❑ 10705	Tenderly/I'll Wait and Pray	1950	7.50	15.00	30.00
❑ 10762	What a Difference A Day Made/I Can't Get Started	1950	7.50	15.00	30.00
❑ 10819	I Cover the Waterfront/Don't Worry 'Bout Me	1950	7.50	15.00	30.00
❑ 10890	Sit Right Down/I'm Through with Love	1951	6.25	12.50	25.00
❑ 11068	Don't Blame Me/If You Could See Me Now	1951	6.25	12.50	25.00

ROULETTE

Number	Title (A Side/B Side)	Yr	VG	VG+	NM
❑ 4285	Serenata/Let's	1960	2.50	5.00	10.00
❑ 4325	True Believer/What's the Use	1961	2.50	5.00	10.00
❑ 4359	April/Oh Lover	1961	2.50	5.00	10.00
❑ 4378	Untouchable/The Hills of Assisi	1961	2.50	5.00	10.00
❑ 4397	If Love Is Good to Me/A Great Day	1961	2.50	5.00	10.00
❑ 4413	One Mint Julep/Mama (He Treats Your Daughter Mean)	1962	2.50	5.00	10.00
❑ 4482	Call Me Irresponsible/There'll Be Other Times	1963	2.00	4.00	8.00
❑ 4497	Once Upon a Summertime/Snowbound	1963	2.00	4.00	8.00
❑ 4516	What'll I Do/I Believe in You	1963	2.00	4.00	8.00
❑ 4547	The Wallflower Waltz/Only	1964	2.00	4.00	8.00
❑ 4604	A Taste of Honey/The Good Life	1965	2.00	4.00	8.00

WARNER BROS.

Number	Title (A Side/B Side)	Yr	VG	VG+	NM
❑ 49890	Theme from "Sharkey's Machine"/Sharkey's Theme	1981	—	2.00	4.00
—B-side by Eddie Harris					

7-Inch Extended Plays

COLUMBIA

Number	Title (A Side/B Side)	Yr	VG	VG+	NM
❑ B-2588	*Perdido/Linger Awhile/Time/Corner to Corner	1959	5.00	10.00	20.00
❑ B-2588 [PS]	Sarah Vaughan (Hall of Fame Series)	1959	5.00	10.00	20.00
❑ B-7452	Come Rain or Come Shine/Mean to Me//It Might As Well Be Spring/Can't Get Out of This Mood	195?	6.25	12.50	25.00
❑ B-7452 [PS]	Sarah Vaughan in Hi-Fi	195?	6.25	12.50	25.00

VAUGHAN, SARAH, AND BILLY ECKSTINE

MERCURY

Number	Title (A Side/B Side)	Yr	VG	VG+	NM
❑ 71122	Passing Strangers/The Door Is Open	1957	3.00	6.00	12.00
❑ 71393	Alexander's Ragtime Band/No Limit	1959	3.00	6.00	12.00

VAUGHAN, STEVIE RAY

Also see THE COBRAS (1); THE VAUGHAN BROTHERS.

EPIC

Number	Title (A Side/B Side)	Yr	VG	VG+	NM
❑ 04031	Pride and Joy/Rude Mood	1983	—	2.50	5.00
❑ 05731	Change It/Look at Little Sister	1985	—	2.00	4.00
❑ 06601	Superstition/Pride and Joy	1987	—	2.00	4.00
❑ 06696	Willie the Wimp/Superstition	1987	—	2.00	4.00
❑ 06696 [DJ]	Willie the Wimp (LP Version)/Willie the Wimp (Edit)	1987	2.00	4.00	8.00
❑ 07340	Pipeline/Love Struck Baby	1987	—	2.00	4.00
—With Dick Dale					
❑ 07340 [PS]	Pipeline/Love Struck Baby	1987	—	2.50	5.00
—With Dick Dale					
❑ 69025	Double Crossfire/Travis Walk	1989	—	2.00	4.00
❑ 73212	This House Is Rockin'/Tightrope	1990	—	2.00	4.00
❑ 74142	The Sky Is Crying/Chitlins Con Carne	1991	—	2.00	4.00
❑ 74198	Empty Arms/Wham	1992	—	2.00	4.00
❑ 78205	Taxman/The House Is Rockin'	1995	—	2.00	4.00

VAUGHAN BROTHERS, THE

STEVIE RAY VAUGHAN and Jimmie Vaughan.

CBS ASSOCIATED

Number	Title (A Side/B Side)	Yr	VG	VG+	NM
❑ 73576	Tick Tock/Brothers	1990	—	2.00	4.00
❑ 73673	Good Texan/Mama Said	1991	—	2.00	4.00

VAUGHN, YVONNE

DOT

Number	Title (A Side/B Side)	Yr	VG	VG+	NM
❑ 16751	Lonely Little Girl/When You Gonna Tell Her About Me	1965	37.50	75.00	150.00

VEE, BOBBY

COGNITO

Number	Title (A Side/B Side)	Yr	VG	VG+	NM
❑ 010	Tremble On/Always Be Each Other's Best Friend	1981	—	2.50	5.00

LIBERTY

Number	Title (A Side/B Side)	Yr	VG	VG+	NM
❑ 55208	Suzie Baby/Flyin' High	1959	6.25	12.50	25.00
❑ 55234	What Do You Want/My Love Loves Me	1959	5.00	10.00	20.00
❑ 55251	Laurie/One Last Kiss	1960	3.75	7.50	15.00
❑ 55270	Devil or Angel/Since I Met You Baby	1960	5.00	10.00	20.00
❑ 55270 [PS]	Devil or Angel/Since I Met You Baby	1960	7.50	15.00	30.00
❑ 55287	Rubber Ball/Everyday	1960	5.00	10.00	20.00
❑ 55287 [PS]	Rubber Ball/Everyday	1960	7.50	15.00	30.00
❑ 55296	More Than I Can Say/Stayin' In	1961	3.75	7.50	15.00
❑ 55296 [PS]	More Than I Can Say/Stayin' In	1961	7.50	15.00	30.00
❑ 55325	How Many Tears/Baby Face	1961	3.75	7.50	15.00
❑ 55331 [PS]	How Many Tears/Baby Face	1961	7.50	15.00	30.00
❑ 55354	Take Good Care of My Baby/Bashful Bob	1961	3.75	7.50	15.00
❑ 55388	Run to Him/Walkin' with My Angel	1961	5.00	10.00	20.00
❑ 55419	Please Don't Ask About Barbara/I Can't Say Goodbye	1962	3.75	7.50	15.00
❑ 55419 [PS]	Please Don't Ask About Barbara/I Can't Say Goodbye	1962	6.25	12.50	25.00
❑ 55451	Sharing You/In My Baby's Eyes	1962	3.75	7.50	15.00
❑ 55479	Punish Her/Someday (When I'm Gone from You)	1962	5.00	10.00	20.00
❑ 55479 [PS]	Punish Her/Someday (When I'm Gone from You)	1962	7.50	15.00	30.00
—With the Crickets					
❑ 55517	A Not-So-Merry Christmas/Christmas Vacation	1962	7.50	15.00	30.00
—This record's existence has been questioned					
❑ 55521	The Night Has a Thousand Eyes/Anonymous Phone Call	1962	3.00	6.00	12.00
❑ 55530	Charms/Bobby Tomorrow	1963	3.00	6.00	12.00
❑ 55530 [PS]	Charms/Bobby Tomorrow	1963	5.00	10.00	20.00
❑ 55581	Be True to Yourself/A Letter from Betty	1963	2.50	5.00	10.00
❑ 55581 [PS]	Be True to Yourself/A Letter from Betty	1963	5.00	10.00	20.00
❑ 55636	Yesterday and You (Armen's Theme)/Never Love a Robin	1963	2.50	5.00	10.00
❑ 55654	Stranger in Your Arms/1963	1963	2.50	5.00	10.00

Number	Title (A Side/B Side)	Yr	VG	VG+	NM
❑ 55654 [PS]	Stranger in Your Arms/1963	1963	5.00	10.00	20.00
❑ 55670	I'll Make You Mine/She's Sorry	1964	2.50	5.00	10.00
❑ 55700	Hickory, Dick and Doc/I Wish You Were Mine Again	1964	2.50	5.00	10.00
❑ 55726	Where Is She/How to Make a Farewell	1964	2.50	5.00	10.00
❑ 55751	(There'll Come a Day When) Ev'ry Little Bit Hurts/Pretend You Don't See Her	1964	2.50	5.00	10.00
❑ 55761	Cross My Heart/This Is the End	1965	2.00	4.00	8.00
❑ 55790	Keep On Trying/You Won't Forget Me	1965	2.00	4.00	8.00
❑ 55828	Run Like the Devil/Take a Look Around Us	1965	2.00	4.00	8.00
❑ 55843	The Story of My Life/High Coin	1965	2.00	4.00	8.00
❑ 55854	A Girl I Used to Know/Gone	1965	2.00	4.00	8.00
❑ 55877	Butterfly/Save a Love	1966	2.00	4.00	8.00
❑ 55877	Butterfly/Look at Me Girl	1966	2.00	4.00	8.00
❑ 55921	Before You Go/Here Today	1966	2.00	4.00	8.00
❑ 55964	Come Back When You Grow Up/Swahili Serenade	1967	2.00	4.00	8.00
❑ 55964	Come Back When You Grow Up/That's All There Is to That	1967	2.00	4.00	8.00
❑ 56009	Beautiful People/I May Be Gone	1967	2.00	4.00	8.00
❑ 56014	Maybe Just Today/You're a Big Girl Now	1968	—	3.00	6.00
❑ 56014 [PS]	Maybe Just Today/You're a Big Girl Now	1968	3.00	6.00	12.00
❑ 56033	Medley: My Girl-Hey Girl/Just Keep It Up	1968	—	3.00	6.00
❑ 56057	Do What You Gotta Do/Thank You	1968	—	3.00	6.00
❑ 56080	I'm Into Lookin' for Someone to Love Me/Thank You	1968	—	3.00	6.00
❑ 56096	Jenny Come to Me/Santa Cruz	1969	—	3.00	6.00
❑ 56124	Let's Call It a Day Girl/I'm Gonna Make It Up to You	1969	—	3.00	6.00
❑ 56149	Electric Trains and You/In and Out of Love	1969	—	3.00	6.00
❑ 56178	The Woman in My Life/No Obligations	1970	—	3.00	6.00
❑ 56208	Sweet Sweetheart/Rock and Roll Music and You	1970	—	3.00	6.00
SHADYBROOK					
❑ 45013	Saying Goodbye/(I'm) Lovin' You	1975	—	2.50	5.00
❑ 45026	You're Never Gonna Find Someone Like Me (Long Version)/You're Never Gonna Find Someone Like Me (Short Version)	1976	—	2.50	5.00
❑ 45030	It's Good to Be Here/If I Needed You	1976	—	2.50	5.00
SOMA					
❑ 1110	Suzie Baby/Flyin' High	1959	15.00	30.00	60.00
UNITED ARTISTS					
❑ 0020	Devil or Angel/Stayin' In	1973	—	2.00	4.00
❑ 0021	Rubber Ball/Punish Her	1973	—	2.00	4.00
❑ 0022	Take Good Care of My Baby/Please Don't Ask About Barbara	1973	—	2.00	4.00
❑ 0023	Run to Him/Sharing You	1973	—	2.00	4.00
❑ 0024	The Night Has a Thousand Eyes/Charms	1973	—	2.00	4.00
❑ 0025	Come Back When You Grow Up/Beautiful People	1973	—	2.00	4.00
—0020 through 0025 are "Silver Spotlight Series" reissues					
❑ XW199	Take Good Care of My Baby/Every Opportunity	1973	—	2.50	5.00
—As "Robert Thomas Velline"					
❑ XW1142	Well All Right/Something Has Come Between Us	1978	—	2.50	5.00
❑ 50755	Signs/Something to Say	1971	—	2.50	5.00
❑ 50875	Sweet Sweetheart/Electric Trains and You	1972	—	2.50	5.00

7-Inch Extended Plays

Number	Title (A Side/B Side)	Yr	VG	VG+	NM
LIBERTY					
❑ LSX-1006	(contents unknown)	1960	12.50	25.00	50.00
❑ LSX-1006 [PS]	Devil or Angel	1960	12.50	25.00	50.00
❑ LSX-1010	(contents unknown)	1960	12.50	25.00	50.00
❑ LSX-1010 [PS]	Bobby Vee's Hits	1960	12.50	25.00	50.00
❑ LSX-1013	*Run to Him/Take Good Care of My Baby/Walkin' with My Angel/How Many Tears	1961	12.50	25.00	50.00
❑ LSX-1013 [PS]	Bobby Vee	1961	12.50	25.00	50.00

VEERS, RUSS

Number	Title (A Side/B Side)	Yr	VG	VG+	NM
TREND					
❑ 30010	Warm As Toast/The Answer	1958	125.00	250.00	500.00

VEGA, SUZANNE

Number	Title (A Side/B Side)	Yr	VG	VG+	NM
A&M					
❑ 2759	Neighborhood Girls/Marlene on the Wall	1985	—	—	3.00
❑ 2834	Left of Center/Small Blue Thing	1986	—	—	3.00
❑ 2937	Luka/Night Vision	1987	—	—	3.00
❑ 2937 [PS]	Luka/Night Vision	1987	—	2.00	4.00
❑ 2960	Solitude Standing/Tom's Diner	1987	—	—	3.00
❑ 2960 [PS]	Solitude Standing/Tom's Diner	1987	—	2.00	4.00
❑ 2988	Gypsy/Left of Center	1987	—	—	3.00
❑ 2988 [PS]	Gypsy/Left of Center	1987	12.50	25.00	50.00

VEGAS, PAT AND LOLLY

Also see REDBONE.

Number	Title (A Side/B Side)	Yr	VG	VG+	NM
APOGEE					
❑ 101	Don't You Remember/The Robot Walk	1964	3.75	7.50	15.00
MERCURY					
❑ 72509	Walk On (Right Out of My Life)/Let's Get It On	1965	3.00	6.00	12.00
REPRISE					
❑ 20199	Boom Boom/Two Figures (On the Wedding Cake)	1963	5.00	10.00	20.00

VEL-TONES, THE

More than one group.

Number	Title (A Side/B Side)	Yr	VG	VG+	NM
COY					
❑ 101	Cal's Tune/Playboy	1959	1000.	1500.	2000.
GOLDWAX					
❑ 301	Darling/I Do	1966	3.75	7.50	15.00
JIN					
❑ 107	Lover Blues/Take a Ride	1959	10.00	20.00	40.00
❑ 115	Jailbird/I'm Yours Now	1959	10.00	20.00	40.00
KAPP					
❑ 268	Cal's Tune/Playboy	1959	25.00	50.00	100.00
LOST-NITE					
❑ 103	Now/I Need You So	1961	25.00	50.00	100.00
MERCURY					
❑ 71526	Fool in Love/Someday	1959	7.50	15.00	30.00
SATELLITE					
❑ 100	Fool in Love/Someday	1959	25.00	50.00	100.00
VEL					
❑ 9178	Broken Heart/Please Say You'll Be True	1960	375.00	750.00	1500.
WEDGE					
❑ 1013	My Dear/I Want to Know	1964	50.00	100.00	200.00
ZARA					
❑ 901	Now/I Need You So	1960	20.00	40.00	80.00

VELLS, THE

Later recorded as MARTHA AND THE VANDELLAS.

Number	Title (A Side/B Side)	Yr	VG	VG+	NM
MEL-O-DY					
❑ 103	There He Is At My Door/You'll Never Cherish a Love So True	1962	25.00	50.00	100.00

VELONS, THE

Number	Title (A Side/B Side)	Yr	VG	VG+	NM
BJM					
❑ 6568	Summer Love/Why Don't You Write	1965	5.00	10.00	20.00
❑ 6569	That's What Love Can Do/That's All Right	1965	5.00	10.00	20.00
BLAST					
❑ 216	Shelly/From the Chapel	1964	25.00	50.00	100.00

VELOURS, THE

Number	Title (A Side/B Side)	Yr	VG	VG+	NM
CLIFTON					
❑ 1987	Old Fashion Christmas/I Wish You Love	19??	—	3.00	6.00
CUB					
❑ 9014	Crazy Love/I'll Never Smile Again	1958	6.25	12.50	25.00
❑ 9029	Blue Velvet/Tired of Your Rock and Rollin'	1959	6.25	12.50	25.00
END					
❑ 1090	Lover Come Back/The Lonely One	1961	5.00	10.00	20.00
GOLDISC					
❑ 3012	Daddy Warbucks/Sweet Sixteen	1960	6.25	12.50	25.00
GONE					
❑ 5092	Can I Come Over Tonight/Where There's a Way	1960	5.00	10.00	20.00
MGM					
❑ 13780	Don't Pity Me/I'm Gonna Change	1967	7.50	15.00	30.00
ONYX					
❑ 501	My Love Come Back/Honey Drop	1956	50.00	100.00	200.00
❑ 508	What You Do to Me/Romeo	1957	200.00	400.00	800.00
❑ 512	Can I Come Over Tonight/Where There's a Will (There's a Way)	1957	50.00	100.00	200.00
❑ 515	This Could Be the Night/Hands Across the Table	1957	30.00	60.00	120.00
❑ 520	Remember/Can I Walk You Home	1958	15.00	30.00	60.00
ORBIT					
❑ 9001	Remember/Can I Walk You Home	1958	12.50	25.00	50.00
RONA					
❑ 010	Woman for Me/(B-side unknown)	1966	6.25	12.50	25.00
STUDO					
❑ 9902	I Promise/Little Sweetheart	1959	12.50	25.00	50.00

VELVA BLU

Number	Title (A Side/B Side)	Yr	VG	VG+	NM
GROOVE					
❑ 5051-7	Barbie Girl (Trip Hop Mix)/Barbie Girl	1997	—	—	3.00

VELVATONES, THE

Number	Title (A Side/B Side)	Yr	VG	VG+	NM
METEOR					
❑ 5042	Real Gone Baby/Feeling Kinda Lonely	1957	50.00	100.00	200.00
NU KAT					
❑ 110	Impossible/I'm Leaving Home	1959	12.50	25.00	50.00

VELVELETTES, THE

Number	Title (A Side/B Side)	Yr	VG	VG+	NM
I.P.G.					
❑ 1002	There He Goes/That's the Reason Why	1963	25.00	50.00	100.00
SOUL					
❑ 35025	These Things Will Keep Me Loving You/Since You've Been Loving Me	1966	5.00	10.00	20.00
V.I.P.					
❑ 25007	Needle in a Haystack/Should I Tell Them	1964	6.25	12.50	25.00
❑ 25013	He Was Realy Sayin' Somethin'/Throw a Farewell Kiss	1965	6.25	12.50	25.00
❑ 25017	I'm the Exception to the Rule/Lonely, Lonely Girl Am I	1965	5.00	10.00	20.00
❑ 25021	A Bird in the Hand (Is Worth Two in the Bush)/(B-side unknown)	1965	200.00	400.00	800.00
❑ 25030	A Bird in the Hand (Is Worth Two in the Bush)/Since You've Been Loving Me	1965	5.00	10.00	20.00
❑ 25034	These Things Will Keep Me Loving You/Since You've Been Loving Me	1966	7.50	15.00	30.00

VELVET, JIMMY

Two different singers, both of whom also recorded as "Jimmy Velvit"! If someone can help us tell who's who, we'd really appreciate it.

Number	Title (A Side/B Side)	Yr	VG	VG+	NM
ABC-PARAMOUNT					
❑ 10488	We Belong Together/History of Love	1963	5.00	10.00	20.00
❑ 10528	To the Aisle/Lonely, Lonely Night	1964	5.00	10.00	20.00
BELL					
❑ 692	Let Me Keep Your Love/Woman in Bloom	1967	2.00	4.00	8.00
CAMEO					
❑ 464	Take Me Tonight/Young Hearts	1967	6.25	12.50	25.00
CORREC-TONE					
❑ 102	When I Needed You/Bouquet of Flowers	1962	25.00	50.00	100.00
—As "James Velvet"; the Supremes sing backup					
CUB					
❑ 9100	Sometimes at Night/Look at Me	1961	3.75	7.50	15.00
❑ 9111	When I Needed You/Bouquet of Flowers	1962	3.75	7.50	15.00
DIVISION					
❑ 102	Sometimes at Night/Look at Me	1961	5.00	10.00	20.00

Number	Title (A Side/B Side)	Yr	VG	VG+	NM
PHILIPS					
❑ 40285	It's Almost Tomorrow/Blue Eyes (Don't Run Away)	1965	5.00	10.00	20.00
❑ 40314	I Won't Be Back This Year/Young Hearts	1965	5.00	10.00	20.00
ROYAL AMERICAN					
❑ 286	It's You/A Woman	1968	2.00	4.00	8.00
❑ 291	Blue Velvet/Missing You	1969	2.00	4.00	8.00
STARTIME					
❑ 103	Wisdom of a Fool/Want to Be Loved	196?	3.00	6.00	12.00
TEAR DROP					
❑ 3353	Don't Go Near a Woman/Hey Nashville	196?	3.00	6.00	12.00
❑ 3395	Oh Lonesome Me-Detroit City/Crazy Arms	196?	3.00	6.00	12.00
—As "James Velvit"					
TOLLIE					
❑ 9037	Teen Angel/Mission Bell	1964	3.75	7.50	15.00
UNITED ARTISTS					
❑ 50272	Good Good Lovin'/Heart Breakin' Misery	1968	5.00	10.00	20.00
VELVET					
❑ 201	We Belong Together/You're Mine	1963	25.00	50.00	100.00
—As "Jimmy Velvit"					
VELVET TONE					
❑ 102	It's Almost Tomorrow/Young Hearts	1965	7.50	15.00	30.00

VELVET KEYS, THE

Number	Title (A Side/B Side)	Yr	VG	VG+	NM
KING					
❑ 5090	My Baby's Gone/Let's Stay After School	1957	20.00	40.00	80.00
❑ 5109	Don't Take My Picture, Take Me/The Truth About Youth	1958	20.00	40.00	80.00

VELVET SOUNDS, THE

Number	Title (A Side/B Side)	Yr	VG	VG+	NM
COSMOPOLITAN					
❑ 100/101	Silver Star/The Devil and the Stocker	1953	150.00	300.00	600.00
❑ 105/106	Pretty Darling/Who'll Take My Place	1953	100.00	200.00	400.00
❑ 530/531	Hanging Up Christmas Stockings/Sing A Song Of Christmas Cheer	1953	125.00	250.00	500.00

VELVET UNDERGROUND, THE

Also see JOHN CALE; LOU REED.

Number	Title (A Side/B Side)	Yr	VG	VG+	NM
COTILLION					
❑ 44107	Who Loves the Sun/Oh, Sweet Nothin'	1971	75.00	150.00	300.00
❑ 44107 [DJ]	Who Loves the Sun (mono/stereo)	1971	25.00	50.00	100.00
MGM					
❑ 14057	What Goes On/Jesus	1969	75.00	150.00	300.00
—Existence of a stock copy of this record has been questioned.					
❑ 14057 [DJ]	What Goes On/Jesus	1969	50.00	100.00	200.00
VERVE					
❑ 10427	All Tomorrow's Parties/I'll Be Your Mirror	1966	150.00	300.00	600.00
❑ 10427 [DJ]	All Tomorrow's Parties/I'll Be Your Mirror	1966	75.00	150.00	300.00
❑ 10427 [PS]	All Tomorrow's Parties/I'll Be Your Mirror	1966	2000.	4000.	8000.
❑ 10466	Femme Fatale/Sunday Morning	1966	100.00	200.00	400.00
❑ 10466 [DJ]	Femme Fatale/Sunday Morning	1966	75.00	150.00	300.00
❑ 10560	White Light/White Heat//Here She Comes Now	1967	75.00	150.00	300.00
❑ 10560 [DJ]	White Light/White Heat//I Heard Her Call My Name	1967	50.00	100.00	200.00

VELVETEENS, THE

Number	Title (A Side/B Side)	Yr	VG	VG+	NM
GOLDEN ARTISTS					
❑ 614	I Feel Sorry for You Baby/Ching Bam Bah	1965	2.50	5.00	10.00
LAURIE					
❑ 3126	I Thank You/Meant to Be	1962	3.75	7.50	15.00
STARK					
❑ 101	Please Holy Father/Baby Baby	1961	12.50	25.00	50.00
—Original title of A-side					
❑ 101	The Teen Prayer/Baby Baby	1961	7.50	15.00	30.00
—New A-side title					
❑ 101	Teen Prayer/Baby Baby	1961	5.00	10.00	20.00
—Slightly altered A-side title					
❑ 105	I Thank You/Meant to Be	1962	6.25	12.50	25.00

VELVETEERS, THE

Number	Title (A Side/B Side)	Yr	VG	VG+	NM
SPITFIRE					
❑ 15	Tell Me You're Mine/Boo Wacka Boo	1956	2000.	3000.	4000.

VELVETIERS, THE

Number	Title (A Side/B Side)	Yr	VG	VG+	NM
RIC					
❑ 958	Oh Baby/Feelin' Right Saturday Night	1958	75.00	150.00	300.00

VELVETONES, THE (1)

Number	Title (A Side/B Side)	Yr	VG	VG+	NM
ALADDIN					
❑ 3372	Glory of Love/I Love Her So	1957	50.00	100.00	200.00
❑ 3391	I Found My Love/Melody of Love	1957	50.00	100.00	200.00
❑ 3463	My Every Thought/Little Girl I Love You So	1960	75.00	150.00	300.00
D					
❑ 1049	Come Back/Penalty of Love	1959	37.50	75.00	150.00
❑ 1072	Worried Over You/Space Man	1959	25.00	50.00	100.00
DEB					
❑ 1008	Stars of Wonder/Who Took My Girl	1959	37.50	75.00	150.00
IMPERIAL					
❑ 5878	The Glory of Love/I Love Her So	1962	7.50	15.00	30.00
❑ 66020	The Glory of Love/I Found My Love	1964	3.75	7.50	15.00

VELVETONES, THE (2)

Girl group.

Number	Title (A Side/B Side)	Yr	VG	VG+	NM
ASCOT					
❑ 2117	I Want Him So Bad/Yes I Will	1962	3.75	7.50	15.00
❑ 2126	Starry Eyed/I'm Ashamed	1963	3.75	7.50	15.00

VELVETONES, THE (3)

Number	Title (A Side/B Side)	Yr	VG	VG+	NM
GARP					
❑ 102	Mister X/(B-side unknown)	1965	15.00	30.00	60.00
—Black vinyl					
❑ 102	Mister X/(B-side unknown)	1965	30.00	60.00	120.00
—Red vinyl					

VELVETONES, THE (4)

Number	Title (A Side/B Side)	Yr	VG	VG+	NM
VERVE					
❑ 10514	What Can the Matter Be/Hairy Lumpty Bump	1967	3.00	6.00	12.00

VELVETONES, THE (U)

Could be group (3); could be someone completely different.

Number	Title (A Side/B Side)	Yr	VG	VG+	NM
GLENN					
❑ 309	Doheny Run/Static	1965	7.50	15.00	30.00
VELVET					
❑ 101	Doheny Run/Static	1965	17.50	35.00	70.00

VELVETS, THE (1)

Number	Title (A Side/B Side)	Yr	VG	VG+	NM
MONUMENT					
❑ 435	That Lucky Old Sun/Time and Again	1961	7.50	15.00	30.00
❑ 441	Tonight (Could Be the Night)/Spring Fever	1961	7.50	15.00	30.00
❑ 448	Lana/Laugh	1961	7.50	15.00	30.00
❑ 458	The Love Express/Don't Let Him Take My Baby	1962	6.25	12.50	25.00
❑ 464	Let the Good Times Roll/The Lights Go On, The Lights Go Off	1962	6.25	12.50	25.00
❑ 810	Crying in the Chapel/Dawn	1963	5.00	10.00	20.00
❑ 836	Nightmare/Here Comes That Song Again	1964	5.00	10.00	20.00
❑ 861	If/Let the Fool Kiss You	1964	5.00	10.00	20.00
❑ 961	Baby the Magic Is Gone/Let the Fool Kiss You	1966	3.75	7.50	15.00
❑ 8917	Tonight (Could Be the Night)/That Lucky Old Sun (Just Rolls Around Heaven)	197?	—	2.50	5.00
—"Golden Series" reissue					

VELVETS, THE (2)

Number	Title (A Side/B Side)	Yr	VG	VG+	NM
EVENT					
❑ 4285	I/At Last	197?	2.00	4.00	8.00
FURY					
❑ 1012	I-I-I (Love You So-So-So)/Dance Honey Dance	1958	12.50	25.00	50.00
PILGRIM					
❑ 706	I/At Last	1956	12.50	25.00	50.00
❑ 710	Tell Her/I Cried	1956	12.50	25.00	50.00
RED ROBIN					
❑ 120	They Tried/She's Gotta Grin	1953	50.00	100.00	200.00
❑ 122	I/At Last	1953	37.50	75.00	150.00
❑ 127	Tell Her/I Cried	1954	37.50	75.00	150.00

VELVETS, THE (U)

These could be by group (1).

Number	Title (A Side/B Side)	Yr	VG	VG+	NM
20TH FOX					
❑ 165	Happy Days Are Here Again/If I Could Be with You	1959	6.25	12.50	25.00
PLAID					
❑ 101	Everybody Knows/Hand Jivin' Baby	1959	20.00	40.00	80.00

VENEERS, THE

Number	Title (A Side/B Side)	Yr	VG	VG+	NM
PRINCETON					
❑ 102	Believe Me (My Angel)/I	1960	10.00	20.00	40.00
TREYCO					
❑ 402	With All My Love/Recipe of Love	1963	3.75	7.50	15.00

VENTURES, THE

Number	Title (A Side/B Side)	Yr	VG	VG+	NM
BLUE HORIZON					
❑ 100	The Real McCoy/Cookies and Coke	1960	150.00	300.00	600.00
❑ 101	Walk-Don't Run/Home	1960	625.00	1250.	2500.
❑ 102	Hold Me, Thrill Me, Kiss Me/No Next Time	1960	50.00	100.00	200.00
—As "Scott Douglas and the Venture Quintet"					
DOLTON					
❑ 25X	Walk — Don't Run/The McCoy	1960	5.00	10.00	20.00
❑ 25	Walk — Don't Run/Home	1960	6.25	12.50	25.00
❑ 28	Perfidia/No Trespassing	1960	5.00	10.00	20.00
❑ 28 [PS]	Perfidia/No Trespassing	1960	12.50	25.00	50.00
❑ 32	Ram-Bunk-Shush/Lonely Heart	1961	5.00	10.00	20.00
❑ 41	Lullaby of the Leaves/Ginchy	1961	5.00	10.00	20.00
❑ 44	(Theme from) Silver City/Bluer Than Blue	1961	5.00	10.00	20.00
❑ 47	Blue Moon/Lady of Spain	1961	5.00	10.00	20.00
❑ 50	Yellow Jacket/Genesis	1962	5.00	10.00	20.00
❑ 55	Instant Mashed/My Bonnie	1962	5.00	10.00	20.00
❑ 60	Lolita Ya-Ya/Lucille	1962	5.00	10.00	20.00
❑ 67	The 2,000 Pound Bee (Part 1)/The 2,000 Pound Bee (Part 2)	1962	5.00	10.00	20.00
❑ 68	El Cumbanchero/Skip To M'Limbo	1963	3.75	7.50	15.00
❑ 78	The Ninth Wave/Damaged Goods	1963	3.75	7.50	15.00
❑ 85	The Savage/The Chase	1963	3.75	7.50	15.00
❑ 91	Journey to the Stars/Walkin' with Pluto	1964	3.75	7.50	15.00
❑ 94	Fugitive/Scratchin'	1964	3.75	7.50	15.00
❑ 96	Walk... Don't Run '64/The Cruel Sea	1964	3.75	7.50	15.00
❑ 96 [PS]	Walk... Don't Run '64/The Cruel Sea	1964	7.50	15.00	30.00
❑ 300	Slaughter on Tenth Avenue/Rap City	1964	3.00	6.00	12.00
❑ 300 [PS]	Slaughter on Tenth Avenue/Rap City	1964	6.25	12.50	25.00
❑ 303	Diamond Head/Lonely Girl	1965	3.00	6.00	12.00
❑ 306	Pedal Pusher/The Swingin' Creeper	1965	3.00	6.00	12.00
❑ 308	Ten Seconds to Heaven/Bird Rockers	1965	3.00	6.00	12.00
❑ 311	La Bomba/Gemini	1965	3.00	6.00	12.00
❑ 312	Sleigh Ride/Snow Flakes	1965	3.75	7.50	15.00
❑ 316	Secret Agent Man/00-711	1966	3.00	6.00	12.00
❑ 320	Blue Star/Comin' Home Baby	1966	3.00	6.00	12.00
❑ 320 [PS]	Blue Star/Comin' Home Baby	1966	6.25	12.50	25.00
❑ 321	Arabesque/Ginza Lights	1966	3.00	6.00	12.00
❑ 323	Green Hornet Theme/Fuzzy and Wild	1966	3.00	6.00	12.00
❑ 323 [PS]	Green Hornet Theme/Fuzzy and Wild	1966	7.50	15.00	30.00
❑ 325	Penetration/Wild Thing	1966	3.00	6.00	12.00
❑ 325 [PS]	Penetration/Wild Thing	1966	6.25	12.50	25.00
❑ 327	Theme from "The Wild Angels"/Kickstand	1967	3.00	6.00	12.00
❑ S7-19770	Rudolph the Red-Nosed Reindeer/Frosty (The Snow Man)	1997	—	—	3.00
—B-side by Jan and Dean on Liberty					

EMI

Number	Title (A Side/B Side)	Yr	VG	VG+	NM
❑ S7-18212	Jingle Bell Rock/Jingle Bells	1994	—	2.50	5.00

—Red vinyl

Number	Title (A Side/B Side)	Yr	VG	VG+	NM
❑ SPRO 19949 [DJ]	Rudolf The Red-Nosed Reindeer/Depression	1994	—	2.50	5.00

—B-side by Johnny and the Dwellers

Number	Title (A Side/B Side)	Yr	VG	VG+	NM
❑ SPRO 19949 [PS]	Rudolf The Red-Nosed Reindeer/Depression	1994	—	2.50	5.00

LIBERTY

Number	Title (A Side/B Side)	Yr	VG	VG+	NM
❑ 55967	Strawberry Fields Forever/Endless Dream	1967	2.00	4.00	8.00
❑ 55977	Theme from "Endless Summer"/Strawberry Fields Forever	1967	2.00	4.00	8.00
❑ 56007	On the Road/Mirrors and Shadows	1967	2.00	4.00	8.00
❑ 56019	Flights of Fantasy/Vibrations	1968	—	3.00	6.00
❑ 56044	Walk Don't Run-Land of 1000 Dances/Too Young to Know My Mind	1968	—	3.00	6.00
❑ 56068	Hawaii Five-O/Soul Breeze	1968	2.00	4.00	8.00
❑ 56115	Theme from A Summer Place/A Summer Love	1969	—	3.00	6.00
❑ 56153	Expo '70/Swan Lake	1970	—	3.00	6.00
❑ 56169	The Wanderer/The Mercenary	1970	—	3.00	6.00
❑ 56189	Storefront Lawyers (Theme)/Kern County Line	1970	—	3.00	6.00

TRIDEX

Number	Title (A Side/B Side)	Yr	VG	VG+	NM
❑ 501	Surfin' and Spyin'/Rumble at Newport	1981	—	2.50	5.00

—A-side with Charlotte Caffey and Jane Wiedlin of the Go-Go's, who did their own version on an early single

Number	Title (A Side/B Side)	Yr	VG	VG+	NM
❑ 501 [PS]	Surfin' and Spyin'/Rumble at Newport	1981	—	2.50	5.00

UNITED ARTISTS

Number	Title (A Side/B Side)	Yr	VG	VG+	NM
❑ 0050	Walk—Don't Run/Ram-Bunk-Shush	1973	—	2.00	4.00

—0050, 0051 and 0052 are "Silver Spotlight Series" reissues

Number	Title (A Side/B Side)	Yr	VG	VG+	NM
❑ 0051	Perfidia/Telstar	1973	—	2.00	4.00
❑ 0052	Hawaii Five-O/Walk—Don't Run '64	1973	—	2.00	4.00
❑ XW207	Last Tango in Paris/Prima Vera	1973	—	3.00	6.00
❑ XW277	Skylab/The Little People	1973	—	3.00	6.00
❑ XW333	Also Sprach Zarathustra (2001)/The Cisco Kid	1973	—	3.00	6.00
❑ XW369	Main Theme from The Young and the Restless/Eloise	1973	—	3.00	6.00
❑ XW392	Main Theme from The Young and the Restless/Eloise	1974	—	3.00	6.00
❑ XW392 [PS]	Main Theme from The Young and the Restless/Eloise	1974	2.00	4.00	8.00
❑ XW578	Theme from "Airport 1975"/The Man with the Golden Gun	1974	—	3.00	6.00
❑ XW687	Superstar Revue (Part 1)/Superstar Revue (Part 2)	1975	—	3.00	6.00
❑ XW784	Moonlight Serenade (Part 1)/Moonlight Serenade (Part 2)	1976	2.00	4.00	8.00

—As "The New Ventures"

Number	Title (A Side/B Side)	Yr	VG	VG+	NM
❑ XW942	Theme from "Charlie's Angels"/Theme from "Starsky and Hutch"	1977	2.00	4.00	8.00
❑ XW1100	Walk Don't Run '77/Amanda's Theme	1977	—	3.00	6.00
❑ XW1161	Wipe Out/Nadia's Theme	1978	—	2.00	4.00

—Reissue

Number	Title (A Side/B Side)	Yr	VG	VG+	NM
❑ 50800	Indian Sun/Squaw Man	1971	—	3.00	6.00
❑ 50800 [PS]	Indian Sun/Squaw Man	1971	2.00	4.00	8.00
❑ 50851	Theme from "Shaft"/Tight Fit	1971	—	3.00	6.00
❑ 50872	Joy/Cherries Jubilee	1972	—	3.00	6.00
❑ 50903	Beethoven's Sonata in G Minor/Peter and the Wolf	1972	—	3.00	6.00
❑ 50925	Honky Tonk (Part 1)/Honky Tonk (Part 2)	1972	—	3.00	6.00
❑ 50989	Last Night/Ram-Bunk-Shush	1972	—	3.00	6.00

7-Inch Extended Plays

DOLTON

Number	Title (A Side/B Side)	Yr	VG	VG+	NM
❑ BEP-503	Walk — Don't Run/The McCoy//Honky Tonk/Raunchy	1960	20.00	40.00	80.00
❑ BEP-503 [PS]	Walk — Don't Run	1960	20.00	40.00	80.00
❑ 4-8031 [DJ]	House of the Rising Sun/Night Train/Rap City//Walk Don't Run '64/One Mint Julep/The Creeper	1964	3.75	7.50	15.00

—Jukebox single, small hole, plays at 33 1/3 rpm

Number	Title (A Side/B Side)	Yr	VG	VG+	NM
❑ 4-8031 [PS]	Walk Don't Run '64	1964	3.75	7.50	15.00

VENUS, VIC

BUDDAH

Number	Title (A Side/B Side)	Yr	VG	VG+	NM
❑ 118	Moonflight/Everybody's On Strike	1969	2.50	5.00	10.00
❑ 138	Moon Jack/Moon Welcome	1969	2.00	4.00	8.00

VERA, BILLY

Includes records as "Billy and the Beaters."

ALFA

Number	Title (A Side/B Side)	Yr	VG	VG+	NM
❑ 7002	I Can Take Care of Myself/Corner of the Night	1981	—	2.00	4.00

—As "Billy and the Beaters"

Number	Title (A Side/B Side)	Yr	VG	VG+	NM
❑ 7005	At This Moment/Someone Will School You, Someone Will Cool You	1981	—	2.50	5.00
❑ 7005 [PS]	At This Moment/Someone Will School You, Someone Will Cool You	1981	—	2.50	5.00

—As "Billy and the Beaters"

Number	Title (A Side/B Side)	Yr	VG	VG+	NM
❑ 7012	Millie, Make Me Some Chili/Someone Will School You, Someone Will Cool You	1981	—	2.00	4.00

—As "Billy and the Beaters"

Number	Title (A Side/B Side)	Yr	VG	VG+	NM
❑ 7020	We Got It All/You Own It	1982	—	2.00	4.00

ATLANTIC

Number	Title (A Side/B Side)	Yr	VG	VG+	NM
❑ 2526	With Pen in Hand/Good Morning Blues	1968	2.00	4.00	8.00
❑ 2555	I've Been Loving You Too Long/Are You Coming to My Party	1968	2.00	4.00	8.00
❑ 2586	Julie/Time Doesn't Matter Anymore	1968	2.00	4.00	8.00
❑ 2628	Bible Salesman/Are You Coming to My Party	1969	—	3.00	6.00
❑ 2700	I've Never Been Loved Like This Before/J.W.'s Dream	1970	—	3.00	6.00

CAPITOL

Number	Title (A Side/B Side)	Yr	VG	VG+	NM
❑ B-44149	Between Like and Love/Heart Be Still	1988	—	—	3.00
❑ B-44149 [PS]	Between Like and Love/Heart Be Still	1988	—	—	3.00
❑ B-44200	Ronnie's Song/Between Like and Love	1988	—	—	3.00

MACOLA

Number	Title (A Side/B Side)	Yr	VG	VG+	NM
❑ 8912	She Ain't Johnnie/My Girl Josephine	1987	—	2.00	4.00

MIDLAND INT'L.

Number	Title (A Side/B Side)	Yr	VG	VG+	NM
❑ MB-10639	Back Door Man/Run and Tell the People	1976	—	2.50	5.00
❑ MB-10909	Private Clown/Billy, Meet Your Son	1977	—	2.50	5.00
❑ MB-11042	I've Had Enough/Something Like Nothing Before	1977	—	2.50	5.00
❑ 72014	She Ain't Johnnie/I've Had Enough	1977	—	2.50	5.00

RHINO

Number	Title (A Side/B Side)	Yr	VG	VG+	NM
❑ 74403	At This Moment/I Can Take Care of Myself	1986	—	2.50	5.00
❑ 74403	At This Moment/Peanut Butter	1986	—	—	3.00
❑ 74404	I Can Take Care of Myself/(B-side unknown)	1987	—	—	3.00
❑ 74407	Hopeless Romantic/(B-side unknown)	1987	—	—	3.00

RUST

Number	Title (A Side/B Side)	Yr	VG	VG+	NM
❑ 5051	My Heart Cries/All My Love	1962	5.00	10.00	20.00

VERA, BILLY, AND JUDY CLAY

Also see BILLY VERA.

ATLANTIC

Number	Title (A Side/B Side)	Yr	VG	VG+	NM
❑ 2445	Storybook Children/Really Together	1967	2.00	4.00	8.00
❑ 2480	Country Girl — City Man/So Good	1968	2.00	4.00	8.00
❑ 2515	Ever Since/When Do We Go	1968	2.00	4.00	8.00
❑ 2654	Tell It Like It Is/Reaching for the Moon	1969	—	3.00	6.00

VERNE, LARRY

ERA

Number	Title (A Side/B Side)	Yr	VG	VG+	NM
❑ 3024	Mr. Custer/Okefenokee Two-Step	1960	3.75	7.50	15.00
❑ 3034	Mister Livingston/Roller Coaster	1960	3.00	6.00	12.00
❑ 3034 [PS]	Mister Livingston/Roller Coaster	1960	6.25	12.50	25.00
❑ 3044	Abdul's Party/Tubby Tilly	1961	3.00	6.00	12.00
❑ 3051	Charlie at the Bat/Pow, Right in the Kisser	1961	3.00	6.00	12.00
❑ 3065	Beatnik/Speck	1961	3.00	6.00	12.00
❑ 3091	The Coward Who Won the West/The Porcupine Patrol	1962	3.00	6.00	12.00
❑ 3139	Return of Mr. Custer/Running Through the Forest	1964	3.00	6.00	12.00

VERNON GIRLS, THE

CHALLENGE

Number	Title (A Side/B Side)	Yr	VG	VG+	NM
❑ 59234	We Love the Beatles/Hey Lover Boy	1964	7.50	15.00	30.00
❑ 59261	Only You Can Do It/Stupid Little Girl	1964	2.50	5.00	10.00

VERONICA

Also see THE RONETTES; RONNIE SPECTOR.

PHIL SPECTOR

Number	Title (A Side/B Side)	Yr	VG	VG+	NM
❑ 1	So Young/Larry L	1964	50.00	100.00	200.00
❑ 2	Why Can't They Let Us Fall in Love/Chubby Danny D	1964	150.00	300.00	600.00

—Note slightly different A-side title

Number	Title (A Side/B Side)	Yr	VG	VG+	NM
❑ 2	Why Don't They Let Us Fall in Love/Chubby Danny D	1964	50.00	100.00	200.00

VERSATILES, THE

More than one group.

ATLANTIC

Number	Title (A Side/B Side)	Yr	VG	VG+	NM
❑ 2004	Passing By/Crying	1958	10.00	20.00	40.00

PEACOCK

Number	Title (A Side/B Side)	Yr	VG	VG+	NM
❑ 1910	White Cliffs of Dover/Just Words	1963	7.50	15.00	30.00

RAMCO

Number	Title (A Side/B Side)	Yr	VG	VG+	NM
❑ 3717	Blue Feeling/Just Pretending	1962	50.00	100.00	200.00

RO-CAL

Number	Title (A Side/B Side)	Yr	VG	VG+	NM
❑ 1002	I'll Whisper in Your ear/Lundee Dundee	1960	25.00	50.00	100.00

SEA CREST

Number	Title (A Side/B Side)	Yr	VG	VG+	NM
❑ 6001	Lonely Boy/Moon Dawg	1964	6.25	12.50	25.00

VERSATONES, THE

Probably more than one group.

ALL STAR

Number	Title (A Side/B Side)	Yr	VG	VG+	NM
❑ 501	Tight Skirt and Sweater/Bila	1958	10.00	20.00	40.00

ATLANTIC

Number	Title (A Side/B Side)	Yr	VG	VG+	NM
❑ 2211	Tight Skirt and Sweater/Bila	1963	5.00	10.00	20.00

FENWAY

Number	Title (A Side/B Side)	Yr	VG	VG+	NM
❑ 7001	Tight Skirt and Sweater/Bila	1960	6.25	12.50	25.00

RCA VICTOR

Number	Title (A Side/B Side)	Yr	VG	VG+	NM
❑ 47-6917	Wait for Me/De Obeah Man	1957	3.75	7.50	15.00
❑ 47-6976	Lovely Teenage Girl/Bikini Baby	1957	3.75	7.50	15.00

VERTICAL HORIZON

RCA

Number	Title (A Side/B Side)	Yr	VG	VG+	NM
❑ 60231	Everything You Want/You're a God	2000	—	—	3.00

VERTUES FOUR, THE

SEA SEVEN

Number	Title (A Side/B Side)	Yr	VG	VG+	NM
❑ 22	Angel Baby/Uphill, Downhill	1963	10.00	20.00	40.00

VESPERS, THE

SWAN

Number	Title (A Side/B Side)	Yr	VG	VG+	NM
❑ 4156	Cupid/When I Walk with My Angel	1963	10.00	20.00	40.00

VESTELLES, THE

DECCA

Number	Title (A Side/B Side)	Yr	VG	VG+	NM
❑ 9-30733	Come Home/Ditta Wa Do	1958	7.50	15.00	30.00

VETTES, THE

With BRUCE JOHNSTON.

MGM

Number	Title (A Side/B Side)	Yr	VG	VG+	NM
❑ 13186	Little Ford Ragtop/Happy Hodaddy (With Ragtop Caddy)	1963	12.50	25.00	50.00

VIBES, THE (1)

ABC-PARAMOUNT

Number	Title (A Side/B Side)	Yr	VG	VG+	NM
❑ 9810	Darling/Come Back Baby	1957	12.50	25.00	50.00

VIBES, THE (2)

Probably the same group as THE VIBRANAIRES.

AFTER HOURS

Number	Title (A Side/B Side)	Yr	VG	VG+	NM
❑ 105	Stop Torturing Me/Stop Jibing, Baby	1954	500.00	1000.	2000.

Number	Title (A Side/B Side)	Yr	VG	VG+	NM
CHARIOT					
❑ 105	Stop Torturing Me/Stop Jibing, Baby	1954	375.00	750.00	1500.

VIBES, THE (3)

Number	Title (A Side/B Side)	Yr	VG	VG+	NM
ALLIED					
❑ 10006	What's Her Name/You Are	1958	15.00	30.00	60.00
❑ 10007	Misunderstood/Let the Old Folks Talk	1959	10.00	20.00	40.00

VIBES, THE (4)

Number	Title (A Side/B Side)	Yr	VG	VG+	NM
PERSPECTIVE					
❑ 5858	Pretty Baby (I Saw You Last Night)/Crying for You	1960	25.00	50.00	100.00

VIBES, THE (5)

Number	Title (A Side/B Side)	Yr	VG	VG+	NM
RAYNA					
❑ 103	You Got Me Crying/A Killer Came to Town	196?	10.00	20.00	40.00

VIBRA-SONICS, THE

Number	Title (A Side/B Side)	Yr	VG	VG+	NM
IDEAL					
❑ 94874	Thunder Storm/Drag Race	1964	12.50	25.00	50.00

VIBRANAIRES, THE

Probably the same group as THE VIBES (2).

Number	Title (A Side/B Side)	Yr	VG	VG+	NM
AFTER HOURS					
❑ 103	Doll Face/Ooh,I Feel So Good	1954	625.00	1250.	2500.
CHARIOT					
❑ 103	Doll Face/Ooh,I Feel So Good	1954	500.00	1000.	2000.

VIBRATIONS, THE

Also see THE JAYHAWKS; THE MARATHONS (1).

Number	Title (A Side/B Side)	Yr	VG	VG+	NM
ATLANTIC					
❑ 2204	Between Hello and Goodbye/Lonesome Little Lonely Girl	1963	3.00	6.00	12.00
❑ 2221	My Girl Sloopy/Daddy Woo-Woo	1964	3.00	6.00	12.00
BET					
❑ 1	So BLue/Love Me Like You Should	1960	25.00	50.00	100.00
CHECKER					
❑ 954	So BLue/Love Me Like You Should	1960	7.50	15.00	30.00
❑ 961	Feel So Bad/Cave Man	1960	5.00	10.00	20.00
❑ 967	Doing the Slop/So Little Time	1961	5.00	10.00	20.00
❑ 969	The Watusi/Wallflower	1961	5.00	10.00	20.00
❑ 974	The Continental/The Junkeroo	1961	5.00	10.00	20.00
❑ 982	Don't Say Goodbye/Stranded in the Jungle	1961	5.00	10.00	20.00
❑ 987	All My Love Belongs to You/Stop Right Now	1961	10.00	20.00	40.00
❑ 990	Let's Pony Again/What Made You Change Your Mind	1961	5.00	10.00	20.00
❑ 1002	Over the Rainbow/Oh, Cindy	1962	3.75	7.50	15.00
❑ 1011	The New Hully Gully/Anytime	1962	3.75	7.50	15.00
❑ 1022	Hamburgers on a Bun/If He Don't	1962	3.75	7.50	15.00
❑ 1038	Since I Fell for You/May the Best Man Win	1963	3.75	7.50	15.00
❑ 1061	Dancing Danny/(Instrumental)	1963	3.75	7.50	15.00
CHESS					
❑ 2151	Shake It Up/Make It Last	1974	—	3.00	6.00
EPIC					
❑ 10418	I Took an Overdose/Because You're Mine	1968	5.00	10.00	20.00
MANDALA					
❑ 2511	Ain't No Greens in Harlem/Wind-Up Toy	1972	—	3.00	6.00
❑ 2514	Man Overboard/(B-side unknown)	1972	—	3.00	6.00
NEPTUNE					
❑ 19	Expressway to Your Heart/Who's Gonna Help Me Now	1969	2.00	4.00	8.00
❑ 21	Smoke Signals/Who's Gonna Help Me Now	1970	2.00	4.00	8.00
❑ 28	Right On Brothers, Right On/Surprise Party for Baby	1970	2.00	4.00	8.00
OKEH					
❑ 7205	Sloop Dance/Watusi Time	1964	3.00	6.00	12.00
❑ 7212	Hello Happiness/Keep On Keeping On	1965	3.00	6.00	12.00
❑ 7220	End Up Crying/Ain't Love That Way	1965	3.00	6.00	12.00
❑ 7228	Talkin' 'Bout Love/If You Only Knew	1965	3.00	6.00	12.00
❑ 7230	Misty/Finding Out the Hard Way	1965	3.00	6.00	12.00
❑ 7238	Gina/The Story of a Starry Night	1966	—	—	—
—Unreleased					
❑ 7241	Canadian Sunset/The Story of a Starry Night	1966	2.50	5.00	10.00
❑ 7249	Forgive and Forget/Gonna Get Along Without You Now	1966	2.50	5.00	10.00
❑ 7257	And I Love Her/Soul a-Go-Go	1966	2.50	5.00	10.00
❑ 7276	Pick Me/You Better Beware	1967	2.50	5.00	10.00
❑ 7297	Together/Come To Yourself	1967	2.50	5.00	10.00
❑ 7311	Love in Them There Hills/Remember the Rain	1968	2.50	5.00	10.00

VIC, PAUL AND BRUCE

See THE CANADIAN BEADLES.

VICEROYS, THE (1)

Number	Title (A Side/B Side)	Yr	VG	VG+	NM
ALADDIN					
❑ 3273	Please, Baby, Please/I'm Yours As Long As I Live	1955	100.00	200.00	400.00

VICEROYS, THE (2)

Number	Title (A Side/B Side)	Yr	VG	VG+	NM
BETHLEHEM					
❑ 3045	Seagrams/Moasin'	1962	6.25	12.50	25.00
—Original A-side title					
❑ 3045	Sea Green/Moasin'	1962	5.00	10.00	20.00
❑ 3070	The Fox/Buzz Bomb	1963	6.25	12.50	25.00
—Original A-side title					
❑ 3070	Joshin'/Buzz Bomb	1963	5.00	10.00	20.00
❑ 3088	Not Too Much Twist/Tears on My Pillow	1965	5.00	10.00	20.00

VICEROYS, THE (3)

Number	Title (A Side/B Side)	Yr	VG	VG+	NM
BOLO					
❑ 736	Granny's Pad/Blues Bouquet	1962	3.00	6.00	12.00
❑ 739	Goin' Back to Granny's/Get Set	1963	3.00	6.00	12.00
❑ 743	Granny's Medley/Dartell Stomp	1964	2.50	5.00	10.00
❑ 749	Tiger Shark/Please, Please, Please	1964	2.50	5.00	10.00
❑ 750	Bacon Fat/Until	1965	2.50	5.00	10.00
❑ 754	That Sound/Tired of Waiting for You	1965	2.50	5.00	10.00
DOT					
❑ 16456	Granny's Pad/Blues Bouquet	1963	2.00	4.00	8.00

VICEROYS, THE (4)

Number	Title (A Side/B Side)	Yr	VG	VG+	NM
LITTLE STAR					
❑ 107	I'm So Sorry (It's Ending with You)/Uncle Sam Needs You	1961	37.50	75.00	150.00
ORIGINAL SOUND					
❑ 15	Dreamy Eyes/Ball 'N' Chain	1961	10.00	20.00	40.00
RAMCO					
❑ 3715	My Heart/I Need Your Love So Bad	1962	2000.	3000.	4000.
SMASH					
❑ 1716	I'm So Sorry (It's Ending with You)/Uncle Sam Needs You	1961	5.00	10.00	20.00

VICEROYS, THE (U)

Number	Title (A Side/B Side)	Yr	VG	VG+	NM
E'DEN					
❑ 9001	Don't Let Go/Down Beat Blues	1962	3.00	6.00	12.00
IMPERIAL					
❑ 66058	Death of an Angel/Earth Angel	1964	3.00	6.00	12.00

VICTORIALS, THE

Number	Title (A Side/B Side)	Yr	VG	VG+	NM
IMPERIAL					
❑ 5398	I Get That Feeling/The Prettiest Girl in the World	1956	12.50	25.00	50.00

VICTORIANS, THE

More than one group.

Number	Title (A Side/B Side)	Yr	VG	VG+	NM
ARNOLD					
❑ 571	Move In a Little Closer/Lovin'	1963	5.00	10.00	20.00
BANG					
❑ 550	Merry-Go-Round/Wasn't the Summer Short	1967	3.75	7.50	15.00
LIBERTY					
❑ 55574	Climb Every Mountain/What Makes Little Girls Cry	1963	5.00	10.00	20.00
❑ 55656	The Monkey Stroll/You're Invited to a Party	1964	3.75	7.50	15.00
❑ 55693	Happy Birthday Blues/Oh What a Night for Love	1964	3.75	7.50	15.00
❑ 55728	If I Loved You/The Monkey Stroll	1964	3.75	7.50	15.00
REPRISE					
❑ 0434	I Saw My Girl/Baby Toys	1965	3.75	7.50	15.00
SAXONY					
❑ 103	Heartbreaking Moon/I'm Rollin'	1956	125.00	250.00	500.00
SELMA					
❑ 1002	Wedding Bells/Please Say You Do	1956	75.00	150.00	300.00

VICTORY FIVE, THE

Number	Title (A Side/B Side)	Yr	VG	VG+	NM
TERP					
❑ 101	I Never Knew/Swing Low	1958	150.00	300.00	600.00
—All copies on colored vinyl					

VIDALTONES, THE

Number	Title (A Side/B Side)	Yr	VG	VG+	NM
JOSIE					
❑ 900	Forever/Someone to Love	1962	10.00	20.00	40.00

VIDELS, THE

Number	Title (A Side/B Side)	Yr	VG	VG+	NM
EARLY					
❑ 702	I Wish/Blow, Winds, Blow	1960	100.00	200.00	400.00
JDS					
❑ 5004	Mr. Lonely/I'll Forget You	1960	7.50	15.00	30.00
—Gray label					
❑ 5004	Mr. Lonely/I'll Forget You	1960	5.00	10.00	20.00
—Multicolor label					
❑ 5005	She's Not Coming Home/Now That Summer Is Here	1960	7.50	15.00	30.00
—Gray label					
❑ 5005	She's Not Coming Home/Now That Summer Is Here	1960	5.00	10.00	20.00
—Multicolor label					
KAPP					
❑ 361	Streets of Love/I'll Keep On Waiting	1960	5.00	10.00	20.00
❑ 405	A Letter from Ann/This Year's Mister New	1961	10.00	20.00	40.00
MEDIEVAL					
❑ 203	Be My Girl/A Place in Your Heart	1961	3.75	7.50	15.00
MUSICNOTE					
❑ 117	We Belong Together/It's All Over	1963	12.50	25.00	50.00
RHODY					
❑ 2000	Be My Girl/A Place in Your Heart	1959	12.50	25.00	50.00
TIC TAC TOE					
❑ 5005	She's Not Coming Home/Now That Summer Is Here	1962	12.50	25.00	50.00

VIDEOS, THE

Number	Title (A Side/B Side)	Yr	VG	VG+	NM
CASINO					
❑ 102	Trickle, Trickle/Moonglow You Know	1958	12.50	25.00	50.00
—No playing cards; no mention of distribution by Gone					
❑ 102	Trickle, Trickle/Moonglow You Know	1958	5.00	10.00	20.00
—With playing cards on label					
❑ 102	Trickle, Trickle/Moonglow You Know	1961	6.25	12.50	25.00
—No playing cards; with distribution by Gone					
❑ 105	Love or Infatuation/Shoo-Be-Doo-Be Cha Cha Cha	1959	75.00	150.00	300.00

VIGRASS AND OSBORNE

With Gary Osborne, later a collaborator with Elton John.

Number	Title (A Side/B Side)	Yr	VG	VG+	NM
EPIC					
❑ 50044	Gypsy Woman/Haystacks	1974	—	2.50	5.00
UNI					
❑ 55330	Forever Autumn/Men of Learning	1972	—	3.00	6.00
❑ 55344	Virginia/Ballerina	1972	—	2.50	5.00
❑ 55355	Remember Pearl Harbor/Mister Deadline	1972	—	2.50	5.00

VILLAGE PEOPLE

CASABLANCA

Number	Title (A Side/B Side)	Yr	VG	VG+	NM
❑ 896	San Francisco (You've Got Me)/Village People	1977	—	3.00	6.00
❑ 922	Macho Man/Key West	1978	—	2.50	5.00
❑ 945	Y.M.C.A./The Women	1978	—	2.50	5.00
❑ 973	In the Navy/Manhattan Woman	1979	—	2.50	5.00
❑ 973 [PS]	In the Navy/Manhattan Woman	1979	5.00	10.00	20.00
—Picture sleeve is promo only					
❑ 984	Go West/Citizens of the World	1979	—	2.50	5.00
❑ 2213	Sleazy/Save Me (Uptempo)	1979	—	2.00	4.00
❑ 2220	Ready for the 80's/Sleazy	1979	—	2.00	4.00
❑ 2261	Can't Stop the Music/Milkshake	1980	—	2.00	4.00
❑ 2261 [PS]	Can't Stop the Music/Milkshake	1980	2.00	4.00	8.00
❑ 2291	Magic Night/I Love You to Death	1980	—	2.00	4.00

RCA

Number	Title (A Side/B Side)	Yr	VG	VG+	NM
❑ PB-12258	5 O'Clock in the Morning/Food Fight	1981	—	2.00	4.00
❑ PB-12258 [PS]	5 O'Clock in the Morning/Food Fight	1981	—	2.50	5.00
❑ PB-12331	Jungle City/Action Man	1981	—	2.00	4.00

VILLAGE VOICES, THE

See THE FOUR SEASONS.

VINCE AND THE WAIKIKI RUMBLERS

BIG BEN

Number	Title (A Side/B Side)	Yr	VG	VG+	NM
❑ 1003	Waikiki Rumble/Pacifica	1965	12.50	25.00	50.00

ZODIAC

Number	Title (A Side/B Side)	Yr	VG	VG+	NM
❑ 1004	Waikiki Rumble/Pacifica	1965	20.00	40.00	80.00

VINCENT, GENE

CAPITOL

Number	Title (A Side/B Side)	Yr	VG	VG+	NM
❑ F3450	Be-Bop-a-Lula/Woman Love	1956	17.50	35.00	70.00
—With large Capitol logo					
❑ F3450	Be-Bop-a-Lula/Woman Love	1956	12.50	25.00	50.00
—With small Capitol logo					
❑ F3530	Race with the Devil/Gonna Back Up, Baby	1956	10.00	20.00	40.00
❑ F3558	Bluejean Bop/Who Slapped John	1956	10.00	20.00	40.00
❑ F3617	Crazy Legs/Important Words	1956	12.50	25.00	50.00
❑ F3678	B-I-Bickey-Bi-Bo-Bo-Go/Five Days, Five Days	1957	12.50	25.00	50.00
❑ F3763	Lotta Lovin'/Wear My Ring	1957	12.50	25.00	50.00
❑ F3839	Dance to the Bop/I Got It	1957	7.50	15.00	30.00
❑ 3871	Be-Bop-a-Lula/Lotta Lovin'	1974	3.75	7.50	15.00
❑ F3874	Walkin' Home from School/I Gotta Baby	1958	10.00	20.00	40.00
❑ F3959	Baby Blue/True to You	1958	12.50	25.00	50.00
❑ F4010	Yes I Love You Baby/Rocky Road Blues	1958	10.00	20.00	40.00
❑ F4051	Little Lover/Git It	1958	10.00	20.00	40.00
❑ F4105	Say Mama/Be-Bop Boogie Boy	1958	12.50	25.00	50.00
❑ F4153	Over the Rainbow/Who's Pushin' Your Swing	1959	12.50	25.00	50.00
❑ F4237	The Night Is So Lonely/Right Now	1959	12.50	25.00	50.00
❑ F4237 [PS]	The Night Is So Lonely/Right Now	1959	500.00	1000.	2000.
❑ 4313	Wild Cat/Right Here on Earth	1959	12.50	25.00	50.00
❑ 4442	Pistol Packin' Mama/Anna Annabella	1960	10.00	20.00	40.00
❑ 4525	Mister Loneliness/If You Want My Lovin'	1961	6.25	12.50	25.00
❑ 4665	Lucy Star/Baby Don't Believe Him	1961	6.25	12.50	25.00

CHALLENGE

Number	Title (A Side/B Side)	Yr	VG	VG+	NM
❑ 59337	Bird Doggin'/Ain't That Too Much	1966	5.00	10.00	20.00
❑ 59347	Lonely Street/I've Got My Eyes on You	1966	5.00	10.00	20.00
❑ 59365	Born to Be a Rolling Stone/Pickin' Poppies	1967	5.00	10.00	20.00

FOREVER

Number	Title (A Side/B Side)	Yr	VG	VG+	NM
❑ 6001	Story of the Rockers/Pickin' Poppies	1969	12.50	25.00	50.00

KAMA SUTRA

Number	Title (A Side/B Side)	Yr	VG	VG+	NM
❑ 514	Sunshine/Geese	1970	3.00	6.00	12.00
❑ 518	High On Life/The Day the World Turned Blue	1971	3.00	6.00	12.00

PLAYGROUND

Number	Title (A Side/B Side)	Yr	VG	VG+	NM
❑ 100	Story of the Rockers/Pickin' Poppies	1968	50.00	100.00	200.00

7-Inch Extended Plays

CAPITOL

Number	Title (A Side/B Side)	Yr	VG	VG+	NM
❑ EAP 1-764	Bluejean Bop/Jezebel//Jumps, Giggles and Shouts/Ain't She Sweet	1957	37.50	75.00	150.00
❑ EAP 1-764 [PS]	Bluejean Bop! Part 1	1957	37.50	75.00	150.00
❑ EAP 2-764	*Who Slapped John/Wedding Bells/Up a Lazy River/Bop Street	1957	37.50	75.00	150.00
❑ EAP 2-764 [PS]	Bluejean Bop! Part 2	1957	37.50	75.00	150.00
❑ EAP 3-764	*Jump Back, Honey, Jump Back/Waltz of the Wind/I Flipped/Peg o' My Heart	1957	37.50	75.00	150.00
❑ EAP 3-764 [PS]	Bluejean Bop! Part 3	1957	37.50	75.00	150.00
❑ EAP 1-811	*Red Bluejeans and a Ponytail/You Told a Fib/Hold Me, Hug Me, Rock Me/Unchained Melody	1957	37.50	75.00	150.00
❑ EAP 1-811 [PS]	Gene Vincent and the Blue Caps, Part 1	1957	37.50	75.00	150.00
❑ EAP 2-811	*Cruisin'/You Better Believe/Double Talkin' Baby/Blues Stay Away from Me	1957	37.50	75.00	150.00
❑ EAP 2-811 [PS]	Gene Vincent and the Blue Caps, Part 2	1957	37.50	75.00	150.00
❑ EAP 3-811	*Pink Thunderbird/Pretty, Pretty Baby/Cat Man/I Sure Miss You	1957	37.50	75.00	150.00
❑ EAP 3-811 [PS]	Gene Vincent and the Blue Caps, Part 3	1957	37.50	75.00	150.00
❑ EAP 1-970	*Frankie and Johnnie/In My Dreams/You'll Never Walk Alone/Brand New Beat	1958	37.50	75.00	150.00
❑ EAP 1-970 [PS]	Gene Vincent Rocks! And the Blue Caps Roll, Part 1	1958	37.50	75.00	150.00
❑ EAP 2-970	*By the Light of the Silvery Moon/Flea Brain/Rollin' Danny/Your Cheatin' Heart	1958	37.50	75.00	150.00
❑ EAP 2-970 [PS]	Gene Vincent Rocks! And the Blue Caps Roll, Part 2	1958	37.50	75.00	150.00
❑ EAP 3-970	*You Belong to Me/Time Will Bring You Everything/Should I Ever Love Again/It's No Lie	1958	37.50	75.00	150.00
❑ EAP 3-970 [PS]	Gene Vincent Rocks! And the Blue Caps Roll, Part 3	1958	37.50	75.00	150.00
❑ EAP 1-985	Lovely Loretta/Dance to the Bop//Dance in the Street/Baby Blue	1958	50.00	100.00	200.00
❑ EAP 1-985 [PS]	Hot Rod Gang	1958	50.00	100.00	200.00
❑ EAP 1-1059	*Five Feet of Lovin'/The Wayward Wind/Somebody Help Me/Keep It a Secret	1958	37.50	75.00	150.00
❑ EAP 1-1059 [PS]	A Gene Vincent Record Date, Part 1	1958	37.50	75.00	150.00
❑ EAP 2-1059	Git It/Teenage Partner//Hey, Good Lookin'/I Can't Help It	1958	37.50	75.00	150.00
❑ EAP 2-1059 [PS]	A Gene Vincent Record Date, Part 2	1958	37.50	75.00	150.00
❑ EAP 3-1059	*Look What You Gone and Done to Me/Peace of Mind/Summertime/I Love You	1958	37.50	75.00	150.00
❑ EAP 3-1059 [PS]	A Gene Vincent Record Date, Part 3	1958	37.50	75.00	150.00

NORTON

Number	Title (A Side/B Side)	Yr	VG	VG+	NM
❑ EP-076	My Love (In Love Again)/Lonesome Boy//The Night Is So Lonely/In My Dreams	1999	—	—	2.00
❑ EP-076 [PS]	Blue Gene	1999	—	—	2.00

VINSON, EDDIE "CLEANHEAD"

BETHLEHEM

Number	Title (A Side/B Side)	Yr	VG	VG+	NM
❑ 11097	Cherry Red/Kidney Stew	1961	5.00	10.00	20.00

BLUESWAY

Number	Title (A Side/B Side)	Yr	VG	VG+	NM
❑ 61005	Cadillac Blues/Old Maid Got Married	1967	3.00	6.00	12.00

KING

Number	Title (A Side/B Side)	Yr	VG	VG+	NM
❑ 4563	Good Bread Alley/I Need You Tonight	1952	15.00	30.00	60.00
❑ 4582	Lonesome Train/Person to Person	1952	15.00	30.00	60.00
❑ 6305	Person to Person/Cherry Red Blues	1970	—	3.00	6.00

MERCURY

Number	Title (A Side/B Side)	Yr	VG	VG+	NM
❑ 70334	Old Man Boogie/You Can't Have My Love No More	1954	50.00	100.00	200.00
❑ 70525	Anxious Heart/Suffer Fool	1954	30.00	60.00	120.00
❑ 70621	Tomorrow May Never Come/Big Chief Rain in the Face	1955	25.00	50.00	100.00

RIVERSIDE

Number	Title (A Side/B Side)	Yr	VG	VG+	NM
❑ 4512	Back Door Blues/Hold It	1962	5.00	10.00	20.00

VINTON, BOBBY

ABC

Number	Title (A Side/B Side)	Yr	VG	VG+	NM
❑ 12022	My Melody of Love/I'll Be Loving You	1974	—	2.50	5.00
—Black label					
❑ 12022	My Melody of Love/I'll Be Loving You	1974	—	2.00	4.00
—Multi-colored label					
❑ 12056	Beer Barrel Polka/Dick and Jane	1974	—	2.00	4.00
❑ 12100	Wooden Heart/Polka Pose	1975	—	2.00	4.00
❑ 12131	My Gypsy Love/Midnight Show	1975	—	2.00	4.00
❑ 12178	Moonight Serenade/Why Can't I Get Over You	1976	—	2.00	4.00
❑ 12186	Save Your Kisses for Me/Love Shine	1976	—	2.00	4.00
❑ 12229	Love Is the Reason/Nobody But Me	1976	—	2.00	4.00
❑ 12265	Only Love Can Break a Heart/Once More with Feeling	1977	—	2.00	4.00
❑ 12293	Hold Me, Thrill Me, Kiss Me/Her Name Is Love	1977	—	2.00	4.00
❑ 12308	All My Todays/Strike Up the Band for Love	1977	—	2.00	4.00

ALPINE

Number	Title (A Side/B Side)	Yr	VG	VG+	NM
❑ 50	First Impression/You'll Never Forget	1959	7.50	15.00	30.00
❑ 59	The Sheik/A Freshman and a Sophomore	1960	6.25	12.50	25.00

BOBBY VINTON

Number	Title (A Side/B Side)	Yr	VG	VG+	NM
❑ 100	Santa Must Be Polish/Santa Claus Is Coming to Town	1987	—	—	3.00
❑ 100 [PS]	Santa Must Be Polish/Santa Claus Is Coming to Town	1987	—	—	3.00

CURB

Number	Title (A Side/B Side)	Yr	VG	VG+	NM
❑ 10512	The Last Rose/Sealed with a Kiss	1988	—	—	3.00
❑ 10541	Please Tell Her That I Said Hello/Getting Used to Being Loved Again	1989	—	—	3.00
❑ 10560	It's Been One of Those Days/(Now and Then There's) A Fool Such As I	1989	—	—	3.00
❑ 76751	The Only Fire That Burns/What Did You Do with Your Old 45's	1990	—	2.00	4.00

DIAMOND

Number	Title (A Side/B Side)	Yr	VG	VG+	NM
❑ 121	I Love You the Way You Are/You're My Girl	1962	5.00	10.00	20.00
—B-side by Chuck and Johnny					

ELEKTRA

Number	Title (A Side/B Side)	Yr	VG	VG+	NM
❑ 45503	My First, My Only Love/Summerlove Sensation	1978	—	2.00	4.00

EPIC

Number	Title (A Side/B Side)	Yr	VG	VG+	NM
❑ 06537	Blue Velvet/Blue on Blue	1986	—	2.50	5.00
❑ 9417	Posin'/Tornado	1960	3.75	7.50	15.00
❑ 9440	Corrina, Corrina/Little Lonely One	1961	3.75	7.50	15.00
❑ 9469	Hip-Swinging, High-Stepping, Drum Majorette/Will I Ask Ya	1961	3.75	7.50	15.00
❑ 9509	Roses Are Red (My Love)/You and I	1962	3.00	6.00	12.00
❑ 9509 [PS]	Roses Are Red (My Love)/You and I	1962	3.75	7.50	15.00
—Bobby Vinton looks straight ahead, chin in hand					
❑ 9509 [PS]	Roses Are Red (My Love)/You and I	1962	3.75	7.50	15.00
—Bobby Vinton looks toward the lower right corner					
❑ 9532	Rain, Rain Go Away/Over and Over	1962	3.00	6.00	12.00
❑ 9532 [PS]	Rain, Rain Go Away/Over and Over	1962	3.75	7.50	15.00
❑ 9550	Excerpts from "Roses Are Red"	1962	3.00	6.00	12.00
❑ 9551	Excerpts from "Roses Are Red"	1962	3.00	6.00	12.00
❑ 9552	Excerpts from "Roses Are Red"	1962	3.00	6.00	12.00
❑ 9553	Excerpts from "Roses Are Red"	1962	3.00	6.00	12.00
❑ 9554	Excerpts from "Roses Are Red"	1962	3.00	6.00	12.00
❑ 9561	Trouble Is My Middle Name/Let's Kiss and Make Up	1962	2.50	5.00	10.00
❑ 9561 [PS]	Trouble Is My Middle Name/Let's Kiss and Make Up	1962	3.75	7.50	15.00
❑ 9577	Over the Mountain (Across the Sea)/Faded Pictures	1963	2.50	5.00	10.00
❑ 9577 [PS]	Over the Mountain (Across the Sea)/Faded Pictures	1963	3.75	7.50	15.00
❑ 9593	Blue on Blue/Those Little Things	1963	3.00	6.00	12.00
❑ 9593 [PS]	Blue on Blue/Those Little Things	1963	3.75	7.50	15.00
❑ 9614	Blue Velvet/Is There a Place (Where I Can Go)	1963	3.00	6.00	12.00
❑ 9614 [PS]	Blue Velvet/Is There a Place (Where I Can Go)	1963	3.75	7.50	15.00
❑ 9638	There! I've Said It Again/The Girl with the Bow in Her Hair	1963	3.00	6.00	12.00
❑ 9638 [PS]	There! I've Said It Again/The Girl with the Bow in Her Hair	1963	3.75	7.50	15.00
❑ 9662	My Heart Belongs to Only You/Warm and Tender	1964	2.50	5.00	10.00

Number	Title (A Side/B Side)	Yr	VG	VG+	NM
❑ 9662 [PS]	My Heart Belongs to Only You/Warm and Tender	1964	3.75	7.50	15.00
❑ 9687	Tell Me Why/Remembering	1964	2.00	4.00	8.00
❑ 9687 [PS]	Tell Me Why/Remembering	1964	3.75	7.50	15.00
❑ 9705	Clinging Vine/Imagination Is a Magic Dream	1964	2.00	4.00	8.00
❑ 9705 [PS]	Clinging Vine/Imagination Is a Magic Dream	1964	3.00	6.00	12.00
❑ 9730	Mr. Lonely/It's Better to Have Loved	1964	2.50	5.00	10.00
❑ 9730 [PS]	Mr. Lonely/It's Better to Have Loved	1964	3.00	6.00	12.00
❑ 9741	The Bell That Couldn't Jingle/Dearest Santa	1964	2.50	5.00	10.00
❑ 9768	Long Lonely Nights/Satin	1965	2.00	4.00	8.00
❑ 9768 [PS]	Long Lonely Nights/Satin	1965	3.00	6.00	12.00
❑ 9791	L-O-N-E-L-Y/Graduation Tears	1965	2.00	4.00	8.00
❑ 9791 [PS]	L-O-N-E-L-Y/Graduation Tears	1965	3.00	6.00	12.00
❑ 9814	Theme from "Harlow" (Lonely Girl)/If I Should Lose Your Love	1965	2.00	4.00	8.00
❑ 9814 [PS]	Theme from "Harlow" (Lonely Girl)/If I Should Lose Your Love	1965	3.00	6.00	12.00
❑ 9846	What Color (Is a Man)/Love or Infatuation	1965	2.00	4.00	8.00
❑ 9869	Satin Pillows/Careless	1965	2.00	4.00	8.00
❑ 9869 [PS]	Satin Pillows/Careless	1965	3.00	6.00	12.00
❑ 9894	Tears/Go Away Pain	1966	—	3.00	6.00
❑ 10014	Dum-De-Da/Blue Clarinet	1966	—	3.00	6.00
❑ 10014 [PS]	Dum-De-Da/Blue Clarinet	1966	2.50	5.00	10.00
❑ 10048	Petticoat White (Summer Sky Blue)/All the King's Horses	1966	—	3.00	6.00
❑ 10048 [PS]	Petticoat White (Summer Sky Blue)/All the King's Horses	1966	2.50	5.00	10.00
❑ 10090	Coming Home Soldier/Don't Let My Mary Go Around	1966	—	3.00	6.00
❑ 10090 [PS]	Coming Home Soldier/Don't Let My Mary Go Around	1966	2.50	5.00	10.00
❑ 10136	For He's a Jolly Good Fellow/Sweet Maria	1967	—	3.00	6.00
❑ 10136 [PS]	For He's a Jolly Good Fellow/Sweet Maria	1967	2.50	5.00	10.00
❑ 10168	Red Roses for Mom/College Town	1967	—	3.00	6.00
❑ 10228	Please Love Me Forever/Miss America	1967	2.00	4.00	8.00
❑ 10228 [PS]	Please Love Me Forever/Miss America	1967	2.50	5.00	10.00
❑ 10266	Just As Much As Ever/Another Memory	1967	—	3.00	6.00
❑ 10266 [PS]	Just As Much As Ever/Another Memory	1967	2.50	5.00	10.00
❑ 10305	Take Good Care of My Baby/Strange Sensations	1968	—	3.00	6.00
❑ 10305 [PS]	Take Good Care of My Baby/Strange Sensations	1968	2.50	5.00	10.00
❑ 10350	Halfway to Paradise/(My Little) Christie	1968	—	3.00	6.00
❑ 10350	Halfway to Paradise/(My Little) Kristie	1968	2.50	5.00	10.00
—Note variation in B-side spelling					
❑ 10350 [PS]	Halfway to Paradise/(My Little) Christie	1968	2.50	5.00	10.00
❑ 10397	I Love How You Love Me/Little Barefoot Boy	1968	—	3.00	6.00
❑ 10397 [PS]	I Love How You Love Me/Little Barefoot Boy	1968	2.50	5.00	10.00
❑ 10461	To Know You Is to Love You/The Beat of My Heart	1969	—	2.50	5.00
❑ 10461 [PS]	To Know You Is to Love You/The Beat of My Heart	1969	2.50	5.00	10.00
❑ 10485	The Days of Sand and Shovels/So Many Lonely Girls	1969	—	2.50	5.00
❑ 10485 [PS]	The Days of Sand and Shovels/So Many Lonely Girls	1969	2.50	5.00	10.00
❑ 10554	Where Is Love/For All We Know	1969	—	2.50	5.00
❑ 10576	My Elusive Dreams/Over and Over	1970	—	2.50	5.00
❑ 10576 [PS]	My Elusive Dreams/Over and Over	1970	2.50	5.00	10.00
❑ 10629	No Arms Can Ever Hold You/I've Got That Lovin' Feelin'	1970	—	2.50	5.00
❑ 10629 [PS]	No Arms Can Ever Hold You/I've Got That Lovin' Feelin'	1970	2.00	4.00	8.00
❑ 10651	Why Don't They Understand/Where Is Love	1970	—	2.50	5.00
❑ 10651 [PS]	Why Don't They Understand/Where Is Love	1970	2.00	4.00	8.00
❑ 10689	Christmas Eve in My Home Town/The Christmas Angel	1970	—	3.00	6.00
❑ 10711	She Loves Me/I'll Make You My Baby	1971	—	2.50	5.00
❑ 10736	And I Love You So/She Loves Me	1971	—	2.50	5.00
❑ 10790	A Little Bit of You/God Bless America	1971	—	2.50	5.00
❑ 10822	Every Day of My Life/You Can Do It to Me Anytime	1972	—	2.50	5.00
❑ 10822 [PS]	Every Day of My Life/You Can Do It to Me Anytime	1972	2.00	4.00	8.00
❑ 10861	Sealed with a Kiss/All My Life	1972	—	2.50	5.00
❑ 10861 [PS]	Sealed with a Kiss/All My Life	1972	2.00	4.00	8.00
❑ 10936	But I Do/When You Love	1972	—	2.50	5.00
❑ 10936 [PS]	But I Do/When You Love	1972	2.00	4.00	8.00
❑ 10980	I Love You the Way You Are/Hurt	1973	—	2.50	5.00
❑ 11038	Where Are the Children/I Can't Believe That It's All Over	1973	—	2.50	5.00
❑ 50080	Clinging Vine/I Can't Believe That It's All Over	1975	—	2.50	5.00
❑ 50169	Christmas Eve in My Home Town/The Christmas Angel	1975	—	2.50	5.00
LARC					
❑ 81019	You Are Love/Ghost of Another Man	1983	—	2.50	5.00
MELODY					
❑ 5001/2	Always in My Heart/Harlem Nocturne	1960	6.25	12.50	25.00
TAPESTRY					
❑ 001	Disco Polka (Pennsylvania Polka)/I Could Have Danced All Night	1979	—	2.00	4.00
❑ 002	Make Believe It's Your First Time/I Remember Loving You	1979	—	2.00	4.00
❑ 003	He/My First and Only Love	1980	—	2.00	4.00
❑ 005	It Was Nice to Know You John/Ain't That Lovin' You	1981	—	2.50	5.00
❑ 006	Let Me Love You, Goodbye/You Are Love	1981	—	2.00	4.00
❑ 007	Forever and Ever/Ain't That Lovin' You	1982	—	2.00	4.00
❑ 008	She Will Survive (Poland)/Love Is the Reason	1982	—	2.00	4.00
❑ 008 [PS]	She Will Survive (Poland)/Love Is the Reason	1982	—	2.50	5.00
❑ 010	It Hurts to Be in Love/Love Makes Everything Better	1985	—	2.00	4.00
❑ 013	What Did You Do with Your Old 45s/(B-side unknown)	1986	—	2.00	4.00
❑ 1986	Sweet Lady of Liberty (same on both sides)	1986	—	2.00	4.00
❑ 4009	Bed of Roses/I Know a Goodbye	1984	—	2.00	4.00

7-Inch Extended Plays

Number	Title (A Side/B Side)	Yr	VG	VG+	NM
ABC					
❑ LLP-271 [DJ]	The Most Beautiful Girl/My Melody of Love/Never Ending Song of Love//You'll Never Know/Am I Losing You/Here in My Heart	1974	2.50	5.00	10.00
—33 1/3 rpm, small hole jukebox issue					
❑ LLP-271 [PS]	Melodies of Love	1974	2.50	5.00	10.00
EPIC					
❑ EG 7215	Silver Bells/White Christmas//O Holy Night/The Christmas Song	1963	2.50	5.00	10.00
❑ EG 7215 [PS]	Songs of Christmas	1963	2.50	5.00	10.00
❑ 7-26437 [DJ]	Why Don't You Believe Me/Together/Save the Last Dance for Me//If I Didn't Care/Shangri-La/It's No Sin	1968	2.50	5.00	10.00
—33 1/3 rpm, small hole jukebox issue					
❑ 7-26437 [PS]	I Love How You Love Me	1968	2.50	5.00	10.00
❑ 7-31642 [DJ]	Our Day Will Come/Song Sung Blue/Come Softly to Me//Some Kind of Wonderful/Somebody's Breaking My Heart/I'm Leaving It Up to You	1972	2.50	5.00	10.00
—33 1/3 rpm, small hole jukebox issue					
❑ 7-31642 [PS]	Sealed with a Kiss	1972	2.50	5.00	10.00

VIOLINAIRES, THE

Number	Title (A Side/B Side)	Yr	VG	VG+	NM
JEWEL					
❑ 222	Little Jesus Boy/White Christmas	1973	5.00	10.00	20.00

VIPERS SKIFFLE GROUP, THE

Number	Title (A Side/B Side)	Yr	VG	VG+	NM
CAPITOL					
❑ F3673	Don't You Rock Me Daddy-O/10,000 Years Ago	1957	5.00	10.00	20.00
❑ F3711	Cumberland Gap/Maggie Mae	1957	3.75	7.50	15.00

VIRTUES, THE

Includes records by "Frank Virtue" and "Frank Virtuoso."

Number	Title (A Side/B Side)	Yr	VG	VG+	NM
ABC-PARAMOUNT					
❑ 10071	Blues in the Cellar/Vaya Con Dios	1959	3.75	7.50	15.00
ARCADE					
❑ 135	Ooh You Gotta/I Make a Mistake	1955	7.50	15.00	30.00
—As "Frank Virtue"					
FAYETTE					
❑ 1626	Guitar Boogie Shuffle '65/Moon Maid	1965	3.75	7.50	15.00
HIGHLAND					
❑ 2505X	Bye Bye Blues/Strollin' Again	1960	6.25	12.50	25.00
❑ 2505	Bye Bye Blues/Happy Guitar	1960	6.25	12.50	25.00
HUNT					
❑ 324 [M]	Guitar Boogie Shuffle/Guitar in Orbit	1959	6.25	12.50	25.00
❑ S-324 [S]	Guitar Boogie Shuffle/Guitar in Orbit	1959	12.50	25.00	50.00
❑ 327	Flippin' In/Shufflin' Along	1959	5.00	10.00	20.00
❑ 328	Pickin' the Stroll/Virtue's Boogie Woogie	1959	5.00	10.00	20.00
❑ 329	Pony Walk/Virtue's Boogie Woogie	1959	5.00	10.00	20.00
❑ 331	Blues in the Cellar/Vaya Con Dios	1960	5.00	10.00	20.00
LIBERTY					
❑ 55706	Dream World/Move On	1964	3.00	6.00	12.00
—As "Frank Virtuoso"					
SURE					
❑ 501	Guitar Boogie Shuffle/Guitar in Orbit	1959	20.00	40.00	80.00
❑ 1733	Guitar Boogie Shuffle Twist/Guitar Boogie Stomp	1962	3.75	7.50	15.00
❑ 1779	Tel-Star Guitar/Jersey Bounce	1962	3.75	7.50	15.00
VIRNON					
❑ 603	Guitar Boogie Twist/Guitar Shimmy	1960	3.75	7.50	15.00
VIRTUE					
❑ 190	Cotton Candy/Love You	1966	2.50	5.00	10.00
❑ 2503	Guitar on the Wild Side/Meditation of the Soul	1970	—	3.00	6.00
WYNNE					
❑ 123	Highland Guitar/Pickin' Plankin' Boogie	1960	3.75	7.50	15.00

VISCAYNES, THE

Sylvester Stewart [Sly Stone] was a member.

Number	Title (A Side/B Side)	Yr	VG	VG+	NM
TROPO					
❑ 101	I Guess I'll Be/Stop What You're Doing	1958	37.50	75.00	150.00
VPM					
❑ 1006	Yellow Moon/Heavenly Angel	1961	10.00	20.00	40.00

VISCOUNTS, THE (1)

Number	Title (A Side/B Side)	Yr	VG	VG+	NM
AMY					
❑ 940	Harlem Nocturne/Dig	1965	3.00	6.00	12.00
❑ 949	Night Train/When the Saints Go Marching In	1966	3.00	6.00	12.00
CORAL					
❑ 62490	Come, Come On Back/Off Shore	1966	2.50	5.00	10.00
❑ 62520	Moonlight in Vermont/Sweet Georgia Brown	1967	2.50	5.00	10.00
MADISON					
❑ 123	Harlem Nocturne/Dig	1959	6.25	12.50	25.00
❑ 129	The Touch/Chug-a-Lug	1960	3.75	7.50	15.00
❑ 133	Night Train/Summertime	1960	3.75	7.50	15.00
❑ 140	Wabash Blues/So Slow	1960	3.75	7.50	15.00
❑ 152	Shadrack/This Place	1961	3.75	7.50	15.00
❑ 159	Little Brown Jug/Opus One	1961	3.75	7.50	15.00
❑ 165	Drag Race/Sophisticated Lady	1961	3.75	7.50	15.00
MR. PEACOCK					
❑ 101	When Johnny Comes Marching Home/Mark's Mood	1961	3.00	6.00	12.00
❑ 107	The Continental Walk/Hully Gully	1962	3.00	6.00	12.00
❑ 112	Night Flight/A Girl Like You	1962	3.00	6.00	12.00
MR. PEEKE					
❑ 125	Night for Love/Ballin' the Jack	1963	3.00	6.00	12.00

VISCOUNTS, THE (2)

Number	Title (A Side/B Side)	Yr	VG	VG+	NM
MERCURY					
❑ 71073	My Girl/Raindrop	1957	10.00	20.00	40.00

VISIONS, THE
Several different groups.

Number	Title (A Side/B Side)	Yr	VG	VG+	NM
BIG TOP					
❑ 3092	Tell Me You're Mine/All Through the Night	1961	5.00	10.00	20.00
❑ 3119	Secret Worlds of Tears/Swingin' Wedding	1962	5.00	10.00	20.00
BRUNSWICK					
❑ 55206	So Close/There'll Be No Next Time	1961	6.25	12.50	25.00
COED					
❑ 598	Down in My Heart/Tell Her Now	1964	3.00	6.00	12.00
ELGEY					
❑ 1003	Teenager's Life/Little Moon	1960	10.00	20.00	40.00
LOST-NITE					
❑ 102	Teenager's Life/Little Moon	1961	6.25	12.50	25.00
MERCURY					
❑ 72188	Oh Boy What a Girl/Tommy's Girl	1963	3.75	7.50	15.00
ORIGINAL SOUND					
❑ 32	Look at Me Now/Cigarette	1963	3.75	7.50	15.00
UNI					
❑ 55031	How Can I Be Down/Threshold of Love	1967	3.00	6.00	12.00
❑ 55042	Keepin' Your Eyes on the Sun/Small Town Commotion	1967	3.00	6.00	12.00
WARNER BROS.					
❑ 5898	Black and White Rainbow/Bulldog Cadillac	1967	2.50	5.00	10.00

VISTAS, THE

Number	Title (A Side/B Side)	Yr	VG	VG+	NM
REBEL					
❑ 77755	Ghost Wave/Surfer's Minuet	1963	12.50	25.00	50.00
VENPRO					
❑ 1000	Ghost Wave/Surfer's Minuet	1963	20.00	40.00	80.00

VISUALS, THE

Number	Title (A Side/B Side)	Yr	VG	VG+	NM
POPLAR					
❑ 115	The Submarine Race/Maybe You	1962	10.00	20.00	40.00
❑ 117	My Juanita/A Boy, a Girl, and a Dream	1963	12.50	25.00	50.00
❑ 121	Please Don't Be Mad at Me/Blue Enough to Cry	1963	75.00	150.00	300.00

VITELLS, THE

Number	Title (A Side/B Side)	Yr	VG	VG+	NM
DECCA					
❑ 31362	Shirley/The Dip	1962	7.50	15.00	30.00

VITO AND THE SALUTATIONS

Number	Title (A Side/B Side)	Yr	VG	VG+	NM
APT					
❑ 25079	High Noon/Walkin'	1965	12.50	25.00	50.00
BOOM					
❑ 60020	Bring Back Yesterday/I Want You to Be My Baby	1966	5.00	10.00	20.00
CRYSTAL BALL					
❑ 105	Unchained Melody/So Much	1978	—	2.50	5.00
HERALD					
❑ 583	Unchained Melody/Hey Hey Baby	1963	7.50	15.00	30.00
❑ 586	Eenie Meenie/Extraordinary Girl	1964	6.25	12.50	25.00
KRAM					
❑ 5002	Your Way/Hey, Hey Baby	1962	12.50	25.00	50.00
RAYNA					
❑ 5009	Gloria/Let's Untwist the Twist	1962	12.50	25.00	50.00
RED BOY					
❑ 1001	So Wonderful (My Love)/I'd Best Be Going	1966	6.25	12.50	25.00
❑ 5009	Gloria/Let's Untwist the Twist	1962	7.50	15.00	30.00
REGINA					
❑ 1320	Get a Job/Girls I Know	1964	7.50	15.00	30.00
RUST					
❑ 5106	Can I Depend on You/Hello Dolly	1966	5.00	10.00	20.00
SANDBAG					
❑ 103	So Wonderful (My Love)/I'd Best Be Going	1966	5.00	10.00	20.00
WELLS					
❑ 1008	Can I Depend on You/Liverpool Bound	1964	12.50	25.00	50.00
—Yellow vinyl					
❑ 1008	Can I Depend on You/Liverpool Bound	1964	6.25	12.50	25.00
❑ 1010	The Banana Boat Song (Day-O)/Don't Count on Me	1964	6.25	12.50	25.00

VOCALEERS, THE
Possibly more than one group.

Number	Title (A Side/B Side)	Yr	VG	VG+	NM
OLD TOWN					
❑ 1089	This Is the Night/Love and Devotion	1960	6.25	12.50	25.00
PARADISE					
❑ 113	I Need Your Love So Bad/Have You Ever Loved Someone	1959	10.00	20.00	40.00
RED ROBIN					
❑ 113	Be True/Oh! Where	1953	150.00	300.00	600.00
❑ 114	Is It a Dream/Hurry Home	1953	75.00	150.00	300.00
❑ 119	I Walk Alone/How Soon	1953	100.00	200.00	400.00
❑ 125	Will You Be True/Love You	1954	75.00	150.00	300.00
❑ 132	Angel Face/Lovin' Baby	1954	75.00	150.00	300.00
TWISTIME					
❑ 11	Cootie Snap/A Golden Tear	1962	7.50	15.00	30.00
VEST					
❑ 832	Hear My Plea/The Night Is Quiet	1960	20.00	40.00	80.00

VOGUES, THE
Also see THE VAL-AIRES.

Number	Title (A Side/B Side)	Yr	VG	VG+	NM
20TH CENTURY					
❑ 2041	My Prayer/I've Got to Learn to Live Without You	1973	—	2.50	5.00
❑ 2060	Wonderful Summer/Guess Who	1973	—	2.50	5.00
❑ 2085	As Time Goes By/Prisoner of Love	1974	—	2.50	5.00
ABC-PARAMOUNT					
❑ 10672	Big Man/Golden Locket	1965	5.00	10.00	20.00
ASTRA					
❑ 1029	You're the One/Goodnight My Love	1973	—	2.50	5.00
❑ 1030	Five O'Clock World/Land of Milk and Honey	1973	—	2.50	5.00
BELL					
❑ 991	Love Song/We're On Our Way	1971	—	2.50	5.00
❑ 45127	Take Time to Tell Her/I'll Be with You	1971	—	2.50	5.00
❑ 45158	An American Family/Gotta Have You Back	1971	—	2.50	5.00
BLUE STAR					
❑ 229	You're the One/Some Words	1965	6.25	12.50	25.00
CO & CE					
❑ 229	You're the One/Some Words	1965	3.00	6.00	12.00
❑ 232	Five O'Clock World/Nothing to Offer You	1965	3.00	6.00	12.00
❑ 234	Magic Town/Humpty Dumpty	1966	2.50	5.00	10.00
❑ 238	The Land of Milk and Honey/True Lovers	1966	2.50	5.00	10.00
❑ 240	Please Mr. Sun/Don't Blame the Rain	1966	2.50	5.00	10.00
❑ 242	That's the Tune/Midnight Dreams	1966	2.50	5.00	10.00
❑ 244	Take a Chance on My Heart/Summer Afternoon	1967	2.50	5.00	10.00
❑ 246	Brighter Days/Lovers of the World Unite	1967	2.50	5.00	10.00
MAINSTREAM					
❑ 5524	Need You/(B-side unknown)	1972	—	2.50	5.00
MGM					
❑ 13813	Brighter Days/Lovers of the World Unite	1967	2.00	4.00	8.00
REPRISE					
❑ 0663	I've Got You on My Mind/Just What I've Been Looking For	1968	2.50	5.00	10.00
❑ 0686	Turn Around, Look at Me/Then	1968	2.00	4.00	8.00
❑ 0731	Turn Around, Look at Me/My Special Angel	1969	—	2.50	5.00
—"Back to Back Hits" series					
❑ 0736	No, Not Much/Earth Angel (Will You Be Mine)	1970	—	2.50	5.00
—"Back to Back Hits" series					
❑ 0741	Five O'Clock World/Magic Town	1970	—	3.00	6.00
—"Back to Back Hits" series; "Five O'Clock World" has overdubbed strings					
❑ 0766	My Special Angel/I Keep It Hid	1968	2.00	4.00	8.00
❑ 0788	Till/I Will	1968	2.00	4.00	8.00
❑ 0803	Woman Helping Man/I'll Know My Love	1969	2.00	4.00	8.00
❑ 0803	Woman Helping Man/No, Not Much	1969	—	3.00	6.00
❑ 0820	Earth Angel (Will You Be Mine)/P.S. I Love You	1969	—	3.00	6.00
❑ 0831	Moments to Remember/Once in a While	1969	—	3.00	6.00
❑ 0844	Green Fields/Easy to Say	1969	—	3.00	6.00
❑ 0856	See That Girl/If We Only Have Love	1969	—	3.00	6.00
❑ 0887	God Only Knows/Moody	1970	—	3.00	6.00
❑ 0909	Over the Rainbow/Hey, That's No Way to Say Goodbye	1970	—	3.00	6.00
❑ 0931	50's Medley/Come Into My Arms	1970	—	3.00	6.00
❑ 0969	Since I Don't Have You/I Know You as a Woman	1970	—	3.00	6.00

VOGUES, THE (2)
No relation to the more famous group above.

Number	Title (A Side/B Side)	Yr	VG	VG+	NM
DOT					
❑ 15798	Love Is a Funny Little Game/Which Witch Doctor	1958	6.25	12.50	25.00
❑ 15859	Try, Baby. Try/Falling Star	1958	6.25	12.50	25.00

VOGUES, THE (U)
Definitely not group (1); could be group (2).

Number	Title (A Side/B Side)	Yr	VG	VG+	NM
CASCADE					
❑ 5908	Ev'ry Day, Ev'ry Night/Now I Lay Me Down to Cry	1959	5.00	10.00	20.00

VOICE MASTERS, THE
LAMONT DOZIER and DAVID RUFFIN were originally in this group, though they did not appear on the later sides.

Number	Title (A Side/B Side)	Yr	VG	VG+	NM
ANNA					
❑ 101	Hope and Pray/Oop's I'm Sorry	1959	50.00	100.00	200.00
❑ 102	Needed/Needed (For Lovers Only)	1959	50.00	100.00	200.00
BAMBOO					
❑ 103	You've Hurt Me Baby/If a Woman Catches a Fool	1968	6.25	12.50	25.00
❑ 105	Never Gonna Leave You/If a Woman Catches a Fool	1969	3.75	7.50	15.00
❑ 113	Dance Right Into My Heart/If a Woman Catches a Fool	1970	3.75	7.50	15.00
FRISCO					
❑ 15235	In Love in Vain/Two Lovers	196?	25.00	50.00	100.00

VOICES, THE

Number	Title (A Side/B Side)	Yr	VG	VG+	NM
CASH					
❑ 1011	Why/Two Things I Love	1955	15.00	30.00	60.00
❑ 1014	Hey Now/My Love Grows Stronger	1955	15.00	30.00	60.00
❑ 1015	I Want to Be Ready/Takes Two to Make a Home	1955	15.00	30.00	60.00
❑ 1016	Santa Claus Boogie/Santa Claus Baby	1955	20.00	40.00	80.00
❑ 1016	Santa Claus Boogie/Santa Claus Baby	197?	—	2.50	5.00
—Reproduction					
SPECIALTY					
❑ 754	Santa Claus Boogie/Santa Claus Baby	197?	3.75	7.50	15.00
—Red vinyl					

VOICES THAT CARE

Number	Title (A Side/B Side)	Yr	VG	VG+	NM
GIANT					
❑ 19350	Voices That Care/Messages of Care	1991	—	2.00	4.00
—Among the many singers on this record is, believe it or not, Frank Sinatra!					

VOIGHT, WES

Number	Title (A Side/B Side)	Yr	VG	VG+	NM
DELUXE					
❑ 6176	Midnight Blues/Another Guy's Line	1958	25.00	50.00	100.00
❑ 6180	I Want a Lover/Little Joan	1958	10.00	20.00	40.00
KING					
❑ 5211 [M]	I'm Loving It/Everything's the Same	1959	15.00	30.00	60.00
❑ S-5211 [S]	I'm Loving It/Everything's the Same	1959	50.00	100.00	200.00
❑ 5231 [M]	I'm Ready to Go Steady/The Wind and the Cold Black Night	1959	10.00	20.00	40.00
❑ S-5231 [S]	I'm Ready to Go Steady/The Wind and the Cold Black Night	1959	25.00	50.00	100.00

VOLCANOS, THE
Early version of THE TRAMMPS.

Number	Title (A Side/B Side)	Yr	VG	VG+	NM
ARCTIC					
❑ 103	Make Your Move/Baby	1965	3.00	6.00	12.00

Number	Title (A Side/B Side)	Yr	VG	VG+	NM
❑ 106	Storm Warning/Baby	1965	3.00	6.00	12.00
❑ 111	Help Wanted/Make Your Move	1965	3.00	6.00	12.00
❑ 115	(It's Against the) Laws of Love/(Instrumental)	1965	3.00	6.00	12.00
❑ 125	Lady's Man/Help Wanted	1966	2.50	5.00	10.00
❑ 128	You're Number 1/Make Your Move	1967	2.50	5.00	10.00

VOLK, VAL, AND THE MATCHED ACES

ROCKET

Number	Title (A Side/B Side)	Yr	VG	VG+	NM
❑ 1050	A Rockin' Party Tonight/Spring Time Rock	195?	50.00	100.00	200.00

VOLUMES, THE

Number	Title (A Side/B Side)	Yr	VG	VG+	NM
AMERICAN ARTS					
❑ 6	Gotta Give Her Love/I Can't Live Without You	1964	7.50	15.00	30.00
❑ 18	I Just Can't Help Myself/One Way Lover	1965	7.50	15.00	30.00
CHEX					
❑ 1002	I Love You/Dreams	1962	75.00	150.00	300.00
—With typographical error crediting "The Valumes"					
❑ 1002	I Love You/Dreams	1962	10.00	20.00	40.00
—With no reference to Jay-Gee Records on label					
❑ 1002	I Love You/Dreams	1962	6.25	12.50	25.00
—With "Nationally Dist. by Jay-Gee Rec. Co. Inc." on label					
❑ 1005	Come Back Into My Heart/The Bell	1962	10.00	20.00	40.00
IMPACT					
❑ 1017	That Same Old Feeling/The Trouble I've Seen	1966	12.50	25.00	50.00
INFERNO					
❑ 2001	A Way to Love You/You Got It Baby	1967	5.00	10.00	20.00
❑ 2004	My Road Is the Right Road/My Kind of Girl	1967	5.00	10.00	20.00
❑ 5001	Ain't That Lovin' You/I Love You Baby	1968	5.00	10.00	20.00
JUBILEE					
❑ 5446	Sandra/Teenage Paradise	1963	5.00	10.00	20.00
❑ 5454	Our Song/Oh My Mother-in-Law	1963	5.00	10.00	20.00
KAREN					
❑ 1551	Am I Losing You/Ain't Gonna Give You Up	1970	2.00	4.00	8.00
OLD TOWN					
❑ 1154	Why/Monkey Hop	1964	6.25	12.50	25.00

VONNS, THE

KING

Number	Title (A Side/B Side)	Yr	VG	VG+	NM
❑ 5793	Leave Us Alone/So Many Days	1963	5.00	10.00	20.00

VOWS, THE

Number	Title (A Side/B Side)	Yr	VG	VG+	NM
MARKAY					
❑ 103	I Wanna Chance/Have You Heard	1962	10.00	20.00	40.00
—Black label					
❑ 103	I Wanna Chance/Have You Heard	1962	100.00	200.00	400.00
—Orange label					
RAN-DEE					
❑ 112	Girl in Red/Born with the Rhythm	196?	15.00	30.00	60.00
STA-SET					
❑ 402	Say You'll Be Mine/When a Boy Loves a Girl	1963	15.00	30.00	60.00
TAMARA					
❑ 506	The Things You Do to Me/Dottie	1963	10.00	20.00	40.00
❑ 760	Say You'll Be Mine/When a Boy Loves a Girl	1964	6.25	12.50	25.00
V.I.P.					
❑ 25016	Buttered Popcorn/Tell Me	1965	10.00	20.00	40.00

VOXPOPPERS, THE

Number	Title (A Side/B Side)	Yr	VG	VG+	NM
AMP 3					
❑ 1004	Wishing for Your Love/The Last Drag	1958	10.00	20.00	40.00
MERCURY					
❑ 71282	Wishing for Your Love/The Last Drag	1958	5.00	10.00	20.00
❑ 71315	Pony Tail/Ping Pong Baby	1958	5.00	10.00	20.00
POPLAR					
❑ 107	Come Back Little Girl/A Love to Last a Lifetime	1959	5.00	10.00	20.00
VERSAILLES					
❑ 200	Can't Understand It/A Blessing After All	1959	7.50	15.00	30.00
WARWICK					
❑ 589	Lonely for You/Helen Isn't Tellin'	1960	3.00	6.00	12.00
—As "Freddie and the Voxpoppers"					

7-Inch Extended Plays

MERCURY

Number	Title (A Side/B Side)	Yr	VG	VG+	NM
❑ EP 1-3391	Wishing for Your Love/The Last Drag//Stroll Roll/Guitar Stroll	1958	25.00	50.00	100.00
❑ EP 1-3391 [PS]	The Voxpoppers	1958	25.00	50.00	100.00

VY-DELLS, THE

GARNET

Number	Title (A Side/B Side)	Yr	VG	VG+	NM
❑ 101	What I'm Gonna Do/Unknown	196?	25.00	50.00	100.00

W

WADE, ADAM

Number	Title (A Side/B Side)	Yr	VG	VG+	NM
COED					
❑ 520	Tell Her for Me/Don't Cry, My Love	1959	3.00	6.00	12.00
❑ 526	Ruby/Too Far	1960	3.00	6.00	12.00
❑ 530	I Can't Help It/I Had the Craziest Dream	1960	3.00	6.00	12.00
❑ 536	Speaking of Her/Black Out the Moon	1960	3.00	6.00	12.00
❑ 539	For the Want of Your Love/In Pursuit of Happiness	1960	3.00	6.00	12.00
❑ 541	Gloria's Theme/Dreamy	1960	3.00	6.00	12.00
❑ 541 [PS]	Gloria's Theme/Dreamy	1960	3.75	7.50	15.00
❑ 546	Take Good Care of Her/Sleepy Time Gal	1961	2.50	5.00	10.00
❑ 550	The Writing on the Wall/Point of No Return	1961	2.50	5.00	10.00
❑ 550 [PS]	The Writing on the Wall/Point of No Return	1961	3.75	7.50	15.00
❑ 553	As If I Didn't Know/Playin' Around	1961	2.50	5.00	10.00
❑ 553 [PS]	As If I Didn't Know/Playin' Around	1961	3.75	7.50	15.00
❑ 556	Tonight I Won't Be There/Linda	1961	2.50	5.00	10.00
❑ 556 [PS]	Tonight I Won't Be There/Linda	1961	3.75	7.50	15.00
❑ 560	Cold Cold Winter/Preview of Paradise	1961	2.50	5.00	10.00
❑ 565	How Are Things in Lover's Lane/It's Good to Have You Back with Me	1962	2.50	5.00	10.00
❑ 567	Little Miss Lovely/For the First Time in My Life	1962	2.50	5.00	10.00
EPIC					
❑ 9521	I'm Climbin' (The Wall)/They Didn't Believe Me	1962	2.00	4.00	8.00
❑ 9557	There'll Be No Teardrops Tonight/Here Comes the Pain	1962	2.00	4.00	8.00
❑ 9566	Don't Let Me Cross Over/Rain from the Skies	1963	2.00	4.00	8.00
❑ 9590	Teenage Mona Lisa/Why Do We Have to Wait So Long	1963	2.00	4.00	8.00
❑ 9609	Let's Make the Most of a Beautiful Thing/Theme from "Irma La Douce" (Look Again)	1963	2.00	4.00	8.00
❑ 9639	Charade/Does Goodnight Mean Goodbye	1963	2.00	4.00	8.00
❑ 9659	Seven Loves for Seven Days/Whisper Away	1964	2.00	4.00	8.00
❑ 9686	Love Song from "Flight to Ashiya"/Pencil and Paper	1964	2.00	4.00	8.00
❑ 9752	Crying in the Chapel/Broken Hearted Stranger	1964	2.00	4.00	8.00
❑ 9771	It's Been a Long Time Comin'/A Lover's Question	1965	2.00	4.00	8.00
❑ 9808	Garden in the Rain/Play Some Music for Broken Hearts	1965	2.00	4.00	8.00
❑ 9840	Garden of Eden/Time for Dreams	1965	2.00	4.00	8.00
❑ 10024	How Can I Leave You/Solitude	1966	—	3.00	6.00
❑ 10112	A Man Alone/Wheels on the Highway	1966	—	3.00	6.00
KIRSHNER					
❑ 4272	Russell Never Had a Chance/Keeping Up with the Joneses	1977	—	2.00	4.00
REMEMBER					
❑ 7791	Half the World/My Time for Love	1969	—	3.00	6.00
WARNER BROS.					
❑ 7068	Julie on My Mind/With an Exception	1967	—	3.00	6.00
❑ 7179	Everybody Is Looking for That Someone/Maybe	1968	—	3.00	6.00
❑ 7225	Old Devil Woman/Rome	1968	—	3.00	6.00

WADE, DON

SAN

Number	Title (A Side/B Side)	Yr	VG	VG+	NM
❑ 206	Gone, Gone, Gone/(B-side unknown)	1958	75.00	150.00	300.00
❑ 207	Forever Yours/Oh Love	1958	7.50	15.00	30.00

WADE, RONNY

KING

Number	Title (A Side/B Side)	Yr	VG	VG+	NM
❑ 5061	Gotta Make Her Mine/Let Me Cry	1957	20.00	40.00	80.00
❑ 5078	I Know But I'll Never Tell/I Never Fall in Love Again	1957	12.50	25.00	50.00
❑ 5099	Annie Don't Work/I'll Sail My Ship Alone	1958	12.50	25.00	50.00
❑ 5112	All I Want/A King and a Vow	1958	12.50	25.00	50.00

WADE AND DICK

SUN

Number	Title (A Side/B Side)	Yr	VG	VG+	NM
❑ 269	Bop Bop Baby/Don't Need Your Lovin' Baby	1957	7.50	15.00	30.00

WADSWORTH MANSION

SUSSEX

Number	Title (A Side/B Side)	Yr	VG	VG+	NM
❑ 209	Sweet Mary/What's On Tonight	1970	2.00	4.00	8.00
—First pressings have a much longer version of A-side					
❑ 209	Sweet Mary/What's On Tonight	1970	—	3.00	6.00
—Later pressings have a short version of A-side					
❑ 215	Havin' Such a Good Time/Michigan Harry Slaughter	1971	—	2.50	5.00
❑ 221	Nine on the Line/Queenie Dew	1971	—	2.50	5.00

WAGNER, DANNY, AND KINDRED SOUL

IMPERIAL

Number	Title (A Side/B Side)	Yr	VG	VG+	NM
❑ 66305	I Lost a True Love/My Buddy	1968	7.50	15.00	30.00
❑ 66327	Harlem Shuffle/When Johnny Comes Marching Home	1968	5.00	10.00	20.00

WAGNER, DICK, AND THE FROSTS

See THE FROST.

WAGONER, PORTER

Also see PORTER WAGONER AND DOLLY PARTON.

Number	Title (A Side/B Side)	Yr	VG	VG+	NM
RCA					
❑ PB-10803	When Lea Jane Sang/Storm of Love	1976	—	2.00	4.00
❑ PB-10974	I Haven't Learned a Thing/Hand Me Down My Walking Cane	1977	—	2.00	4.00
❑ PB-11186	Mountain Music/Natural Wonder	1977	—	2.00	4.00
❑ PB-11411	Ole Slew Foot/I'm Gonna Feed 'Em Now	1978	—	2.00	4.00
❑ PB-11491	I Want to Walk You Home/Old Love Letter	1979	—	2.00	4.00
❑ PB-11671	Everything I've Always Wanted/No Bed of Roses	1979	—	2.00	4.00
❑ PB-11771	Hold On Tight/Someone Just Like You	1979	—	2.00	4.00
❑ PB-11998	Is It Only 'Cause You're Lonely/When She Was Mine	1980	—	2.00	4.00
RCA VICTOR					
❑ APBO-0013	Wake Up, Jacob/Stella, Dear Sweet Stella	1973	—	2.50	5.00
❑ APBO-0187	George Leory Chickashea/Cassie	1973	—	2.50	5.00
❑ APBO-0233	Tore Down/Nothing Between	1974	—	2.50	5.00
❑ APBO-0328	Highway Headin' South/Freda	1974	—	2.50	5.00
❑ PB-10124	Carolina Moonshiner/Not a Cloud in the Sky	1974	—	2.50	5.00
❑ PB-10281	It's My Time (To Say I Love You)/Just for the Lonely Ones	1975	—	3.00	6.00
❑ PB-10411	Indian Creek/Thank You for the Happiness	1975	—	2.50	5.00
❑ 47-4996	Settin' the Woods on Fire/Headin' for a Weddin'	1952	7.50	15.00	30.00
❑ 47-5086	Takin' Chances/I Can't Live with You	1952	7.50	15.00	30.00
❑ 47-5215	That's It/Don't Play That Song	1953	6.25	12.50	25.00
❑ 47-5330	Trademark/A Beggar for Your Love	1953	6.25	12.50	25.00
❑ 47-5430	Bringing Home the Bacon/An Angel Made for Love	1953	6.25	12.50	25.00

Number	Title (A Side/B Side)	Yr	VG	VG+	NM
❑ 47-5527	Flame of Love/Dig That Crazy Moon	1953	6.25	12.50	25.00
❑ 47-5631	Trinidad/Bad News Travels Fast	1954	6.25	12.50	25.00
❑ 47-5754	Be Glad You Ain't Me/Love at First Sight	1954	6.25	12.50	25.00
❑ 47-5848	Company's Comin'/Tricks of the Trade	1954	6.25	12.50	25.00
❑ 47-6030	Hey, Maw/How Quick	1955	6.25	12.50	25.00
❑ 47-6105	A Satisfied Mind/Itchin' for My Baby	1955	5.00	10.00	20.00
❑ 47-6289	Eat, Drink and Be Merry (Tomorrow You'll Cry)/ Let's Squiggle	1955	5.00	10.00	20.00
❑ 47-6421	What Would You Do? (If Jesus Came to Your House)/How Can You Refuse Him Now	1956	5.00	10.00	20.00
❑ 47-6494	Uncle Pen/How I've Tried	1956	5.00	10.00	20.00
❑ 47-6598	Tryin' to Forget the Blues/I've Known You from Somewhere	1956	5.00	10.00	20.00
❑ 47-6803	I'm Day Dreamin' Tonight/I Should Be with You	1957	5.00	10.00	20.00
❑ 47-6844	Good Mornin', Neighbor/Who Will He Be	1957	5.00	10.00	20.00
❑ 47-6964	I Thought I Heard You Call My Name/Pay Day	1957	5.00	10.00	20.00
❑ 47-7073	Doll Face/Your Love	1957	5.00	10.00	20.00
❑ 47-7199	Tomorrow We'll Retire/Heaven's Just a Prayer Away	1958	3.75	7.50	15.00
❑ 47-7279	Haven't You Heard/Tell Her Lies and Feed Her Candy	1958	3.75	7.50	15.00
❑ 47-7374	Just Before Dawn/Dear Lonesome	1958	3.75	7.50	15.00
❑ 47-7457	Me and Fred and Joe and Bill/Out of Sight, Out of Mind	1959	3.75	7.50	15.00
❑ 47-7532	I'm Gonna Sing/I Thought of God	1959	3.75	7.50	15.00
❑ 47-7568	The Battle of Little Big Horn/Our Song of Love	1959	3.75	7.50	15.00
❑ 47-7638	The Girl Who Didn't Need Love/Your Kind of People	1959	3.75	7.50	15.00
❑ 47-7708	Legend of the Big Steeple/Wakin' Up the Crowd	1960	3.75	7.50	15.00
❑ 47-7770	Falling Again/An Old Log Cabin for Sale	1960	3.75	7.50	15.00
❑ 47-7837	Your Old Love Letters/Heartbreak Affair	1961	3.00	6.00	12.00
❑ 47-7901	Everything She Touches Gets the Blues/Sugar Foot Rag	1961	3.00	6.00	12.00
❑ 47-7967	Misery Loves Company/I Cried Again	1961	3.00	6.00	12.00
❑ 47-8026	Cold Dark Waters/Ain't It Awful	1962	3.00	6.00	12.00
❑ 47-8105	I've Enjoyed As Much of This As I Can Stand/One Way Ticket to the Blues	1962	3.00	6.00	12.00
❑ 47-8178	My Baby's Not Here (In Town Tonight)/In the Shadows of the Wine	1963	3.00	6.00	12.00
❑ 47-8257	Howdy Neighbor Howdy/Find Out	1963	3.00	6.00	12.00
❑ 47-8338	Sorrow on the Rocks/The Life of the Party	1964	3.00	6.00	12.00
❑ 47-8432	I'll Go Down Swinging/Country Music Has Gone to Town	1964	3.00	6.00	12.00
❑ 47-8524	I'm Gonna Feed You Now/The Bride's Bouquet	1965	2.50	5.00	10.00
❑ 47-8622	Green, Green Grass of Home/Dooley	1965	2.50	5.00	10.00
❑ 47-8723	Skid Row Joe/Love Your Neighbor	1965	2.50	5.00	10.00
❑ 47-8800	I Just Came to Smell the Flowers/I'm a Long Way from Home	1966	2.50	5.00	10.00
❑ 47-8882	I Dreamed I Saw America on Her Knees/When I Reach That City	1966	2.50	5.00	10.00
❑ 47-8977	Old Slew-Foot/Let Me In	1966	2.50	5.00	10.00
❑ 47-9067	The Cold Hard Facts of Life/You Can't Make a Heel Toe the Mark	1967	2.50	5.00	10.00
❑ 47-9243	Julie/Try Being Lonely	1967	2.50	5.00	10.00
❑ 47-9379	Woman Hungry/Out of the Silence (Came a Song)	1967	2.50	5.00	10.00
❑ 47-9530	Be Proud of Your Man/Wino	1968	2.00	4.00	8.00
❑ 47-9651	The Carroll County Accident/Sorrow Overtakes the Wine	1968	2.00	4.00	8.00
❑ 47-9802	You Got-Ta Have a License/Fairchild	1970	—	3.00	6.00
❑ 47-9811	Little Boy's Prayer/Roses Out of Season	1970	—	3.00	6.00
❑ 47-9895	Jim Johnson/One More Dime	1970	—	3.00	6.00
❑ 47-9939	The Last One to Touch Me/The Alley	1970	—	3.00	6.00
❑ 47-9979	Charley's Picture/As Simple As I Am	1971	—	3.00	6.00
❑ 48-1007	Be a Little Quieter/Watching	1971	—	3.00	6.00
❑ 74-0168	Big Wind/Tennessee Stud	1969	2.00	4.00	8.00
❑ 74-0267	When You're Hot You're Hot/The Answer Is Love	1969	2.00	4.00	8.00
❑ 74-0581	The Rubber Room/Late Love of Mine	1971	—	3.00	6.00
❑ 74-0648	What Ain't to Be, Just Might Happen/Little Bird	1972	—	3.00	6.00
❑ 74-0753	A World Without Music/Denise Mayree	1972	—	3.00	6.00
❑ 74-0820	Katy Did/Darlin' Debra Jean	1972	—	3.00	6.00
❑ 74-0923	Lightening the Load/Tomorrow Is Forever	1973	—	3.00	6.00

WARNER BROS.

Number	Title (A Side/B Side)	Yr	VG	VG+	NM
❑ 29596	That Was Then, This Is Now/Bottom of the Fifth	1983	—	2.00	4.00
❑ 29772	This Cowboy's Hat/She Don't Have a License to Drive Me Up the Wall	1983	—	—	3.00
❑ 29875	Turn the Pencil Over/Texas Moonbeam Waltz	1982	—	2.00	4.00

—B-side by Johnny Gimble/Texas Swing Band

7-Inch Extended Plays

RCA VICTOR

Number	Title (A Side/B Side)	Yr	VG	VG+	NM
❑ EPA-937	A Satisfied Mind/I Like Girls//Living in the Past/ Midnight	1956	6.25	12.50	25.00
❑ EPA-937 [PS]	Satisfied Mind	1956	6.25	12.50	25.00

WAGONER, PORTER, AND DOLLY PARTON

Also see each artist's individual listings.

RCA

Number	Title (A Side/B Side)	Yr	VG	VG+	NM
❑ PB-11983	Making Plans/Beneath the Sweet Magnolia Trees	1980	—	2.00	4.00
❑ PB-12119	If You Go, I'll Follow You/Hide Me Away	1980	—	2.00	4.00

RCA VICTOR

Number	Title (A Side/B Side)	Yr	VG	VG+	NM
❑ PB-10010	Please Don't Stop Loving Me/Sounds of Nature	1974	—	2.00	4.00
❑ PB-10328	Say Forever You'll Be Mine/How Can I Help You Forgive Me	1975	—	2.00	4.00
❑ GB-10506	Please Don't Stop Loving Me/Sounds of Nature	1975	—	2.00	4.00

—Gold Standard Series

Number	Title (A Side/B Side)	Yr	VG	VG+	NM
❑ PB-10652	Is Forever Longer Than Always/If You Say I Can	1976	—	2.00	4.00
❑ GB-10675	Say Forever You'll Be Mine/How Can I Help You Forgive Me	1976	—	2.00	4.00

—Gold Standard Series

Number	Title (A Side/B Side)	Yr	VG	VG+	NM
❑ 47-9369	The Last Thing on My Mind/Love Is Worth Living	1967	2.00	4.00	8.00
❑ 47-9490	Holding On to Nothing/Just Between You and Me	1968	2.00	4.00	8.00
❑ 47-9577	We'll Get Ahead Someday/Jeannie's Afraid of the Dark	1968	2.00	4.00	8.00
❑ 47-9799	Tomorrow Is Forever/Mandy Never Sleeps	1969	—	3.00	6.00
❑ 47-9875	Daddy Was An Old Time Preacher Man/Good Understanding	1970	—	3.00	6.00
❑ 47-9958	Better Move It On Home/Two of a Kind	1971	—	3.00	6.00
❑ 47-9994	The Right Combination/The Part of Loving You	1971	—	3.00	6.00
❑ 74-0104	Malena/Yours, Love	1969	—	3.00	6.00
❑ 74-0172	Always, Always/No Need to Hurry Home	1969	—	3.00	6.00
❑ 74-0247	Just Someone I Used to Know/My Hands Are Tied	1969	—	3.00	6.00
❑ 74-0565	Burning the Midnight Oil/More Than Words Can Tell	1971	—	3.00	6.00
❑ 74-0675	Lost Forever in Your Kiss/The Fog Has Lifted	1972	—	2.50	5.00
❑ 74-0773	Together Always/Love's All Over	1972	—	2.50	5.00
❑ 74-0893	We Found It/Lord Have Mercy on Us	1973	—	2.50	5.00
❑ 74-0981	If Teardrops Were Pennies/Come to Me	1973	—	2.50	5.00

WAIKIKIS, THE

KAPP

Number	Title (A Side/B Side)	Yr	VG	VG+	NM
❑ KJB-30	Hawaii Tattoo/Tahiti Tamoure	1964	2.00	4.00	8.00
❑ KJB-52	Hawaii Honeymoon/Remember Boa-Boa	1965	2.00	4.00	8.00
❑ 891	Pearly Shells/Tiny Bubbles	1968	—	2.50	5.00

PALETTE

Number	Title (A Side/B Side)	Yr	VG	VG+	NM
❑ 5091	Hawaii Tattoo/Aloha Parade	1962	3.00	6.00	12.00
❑ 5109	Tikitiki Puki/Tanita Tamoure	1963	2.50	5.00	10.00

WAILERS, THE

BELL

Number	Title (A Side/B Side)	Yr	VG	VG+	NM
❑ 694	Thinking Out Loud/You Can't Fly	1967	2.50	5.00	10.00

ETIQUETTE

Number	Title (A Side/B Side)	Yr	VG	VG+	NM
❑ 2	Mashi/Velva	1962	3.75	7.50	15.00
❑ 4	Stompin' Willie/Doin' the Seaside	1963	3.75	7.50	15.00
❑ 6	We're Goin' Surfin'/Shakedown	1963	3.75	7.50	15.00
❑ 7	Seattle/Party Time U.S.A.	1963	3.75	7.50	15.00
❑ 9	Tall Cool One/Frenzy	1964	3.75	7.50	15.00
❑ 12	You Better Believe It/Don't Take It So Hard	1965	3.75	7.50	15.00
❑ 15	You Weren't Using Your Head/Back to You	1965	3.75	7.50	15.00
❑ 19	Hang Up/Dirty Robber	1965	3.75	7.50	15.00
❑ 21	Out of Our Tree/I Got Me	1966	3.75	7.50	15.00
❑ 22	Christmas Spirit/Don't Believe in Christmas	1965	7.50	15.00	30.00

—B-side by the Sonics

Number	Title (A Side/B Side)	Yr	VG	VG+	NM
❑ 24	It's You Alone/Tears	1966	6.25	12.50	25.00

GOLDEN CREST

Number	Title (A Side/B Side)	Yr	VG	VG+	NM
❑ 375	Beat Guitar/Driftwood	19??	2.50	5.00	10.00
❑ 518	Tall Cool One/Roadrunner	1959	7.50	15.00	30.00

—Photo of group on label

Number	Title (A Side/B Side)	Yr	VG	VG+	NM
❑ 518	Tall Cool One/Roadrunner	1964	3.75	7.50	15.00

—No photo on label

Number	Title (A Side/B Side)	Yr	VG	VG+	NM
❑ 526	Mau-Mau/Dirty Robber	1959	6.25	12.50	25.00

—Photo of group on label

Number	Title (A Side/B Side)	Yr	VG	VG+	NM
❑ 526	Mau-Mau/Dirty Robber	1964	3.00	6.00	12.00

—No photo on label

Number	Title (A Side/B Side)	Yr	VG	VG+	NM
❑ 532	Wailin'/Shanghai'd	1960	6.25	12.50	25.00

—Photo of group on label

Number	Title (A Side/B Side)	Yr	VG	VG+	NM
❑ 532	Wailin'/Shanghai'd	1964	3.00	6.00	12.00

—No photo on label

Number	Title (A Side/B Side)	Yr	VG	VG+	NM
❑ 545	Lucille/Scratchin'	1960	6.25	12.50	25.00

—Photo of group on label

Number	Title (A Side/B Side)	Yr	VG	VG+	NM
❑ 545	Lucille/Scratchin'	1964	3.00	6.00	12.00

—No photo of group

Number	Title (A Side/B Side)	Yr	VG	VG+	NM
❑ 591	Mau-Mau/Beat Guitar	1964	2.50	5.00	10.00

IMPERIAL

Number	Title (A Side/B Side)	Yr	VG	VG+	NM
❑ 66028	Tall Cool One/Frenzy	1964	—	—	—

—Unreleased

Number	Title (A Side/B Side)	Yr	VG	VG+	NM
❑ 66045	Mashi/On the Rocks	1964	3.75	7.50	15.00

UNITED ARTISTS

Number	Title (A Side/B Side)	Yr	VG	VG+	NM
❑ 50026	Tears/It's You Alone	1966	2.50	5.00	10.00
❑ 50065	End of the Summer/Think Kindly Baby	1966	2.50	5.00	10.00
❑ 50110	Tears (Don't Have to Fall)/You Won't Lead Me On	1967	2.50	5.00	10.00

VIVA

Number	Title (A Side/B Side)	Yr	VG	VG+	NM
❑ 614	I'm Determined/I Don't Want to Follow You	1967	2.50	5.00	10.00

7-Inch Extended Plays

NORTON

Number	Title (A Side/B Side)	Yr	VG	VG+	NM
❑ EP-085	Scotch on the Rocks/Snake Pit//Dirty Robber/ High Wall	1999	—	—	2.00
❑ EP-085 [PS]	Scotch on the Rocks/Snake Pit//Dirty Robber/ High Wall	1999	—	—	2.00

—Custom yellow sleeve with center hole

WAILERS, THE (2)

COLUMBIA

Number	Title (A Side/B Side)	Yr	VG	VG+	NM
❑ 40288	Hot Love/Stop the Clock	1954	30.00	60.00	120.00

WAINWRIGHT, LOUDON, III

ARISTA

Number	Title (A Side/B Side)	Yr	VG	VG+	NM
❑ 0174	Bicentennial/Talking Big Apple '75	1976	—	2.50	5.00
❑ 0340	Final Exam/(B-side unknown)	1978	—	2.50	5.00

COLUMBIA

Number	Title (A Side/B Side)	Yr	VG	VG+	NM
❑ 45726	Dead Skunk/Needless to Say	1972	2.00	4.00	8.00

—Gray label

Number	Title (A Side/B Side)	Yr	VG	VG+	NM
❑ 45726	Dead Skunk/Needless to Say	1973	—	3.00	6.00

—Orange label

Number	Title (A Side/B Side)	Yr	VG	VG+	NM
❑ 45849	New Paint/Say That You Love Me	1973	—	2.50	5.00
❑ 45949	Down Drinking at the Bar/I Am the Way	1973	—	2.50	5.00
❑ 46064	Swimming Song/Bell Bottom Pants	1974	—	2.50	5.00

WAKEFIELD SUN

MGM

Number	Title (A Side/B Side)	Yr	VG	VG+	NM
❑ 14028	When I See You/Get Out	1969	5.00	10.00	20.00
❑ 14072	Tryst on Love/Sing a Simple Song	1969	7.50	15.00	30.00

WAKEMAN, RICK
Also see YES.

Number	Title (A Side/B Side)	Yr	VG	VG+	NM
A&M					
❑ 1430	Catherine/Anne	1973	—	2.50	5.00
❑ 1627	The Journey/The Return	1974	—	2.50	5.00
❑ 1635	The Battle/And Now a Word from Our Sponsor	1974	—	2.50	5.00
❑ 1708	Merlin the Magician/Sir Galahad	1975	—	2.50	5.00
❑ 1937	White Rock/After the Ball	1977	—	2.50	5.00
❑ 2010	The Birdman of Alcatraz/And Now a Word from Our Sponsor	1978	—	2.50	5.00

WALCOS, THE

Number	Title (A Side/B Side)	Yr	VG	VG+	NM
DRUM					
❑ 011	Tell Me Why/Moonlight Rock	1959	25.00	50.00	100.00

WALES, HOWARD, AND JERRY GARCIA
Also see JERRY GARCIA.

Number	Title (A Side/B Side)	Yr	VG	VG+	NM
DOUGLAS					
❑ 76501	South Side Strut/Uncle Martin's	1971	3.75	7.50	15.00

WALKER, JR., AND THE ALL STARS

Number	Title (A Side/B Side)	Yr	VG	VG+	NM
HARVEY					
❑ 113	Willie's Blues/Twist Lackawanna	1962	6.25	12.50	25.00
❑ 117	Cleo's Mood/Brain Washer	1963	5.00	10.00	20.00
❑ 119	Good Rockin'/Brain Washer	1963	5.00	10.00	20.00
MOTOWN					
❑ 1352	Country Boy/What Does It Take (To Win Your Love)	1975	—	2.50	5.00
❑ 1380	I'm So Glad/Hot Shot	1976	—	—	—
—Unreleased					
❑ 1689	Blow the House Down/Ball Baby	1983	—	2.00	4.00
SOUL					
❑ 35003	Monkey Jump/Satan's Blues	1964	3.75	7.50	15.00
❑ 35008	Shotgun/Hot Cha	1965	3.75	7.50	15.00
❑ 35008	Shot Gun/Hot Cha	1965	25.00	50.00	100.00
—Not only is the A-side title listed as two words, but the record is credited to "Jr. Walker and All The Stars"!					
❑ 35008 [PS]	Shotgun/Hot Cha	1965	6.25	12.50	25.00
❑ 35012	Do the Boomerang/Tune Up	1965	2.50	5.00	10.00
❑ 35013	Shake and Fingerpop/Cleo's Back	1965	2.50	5.00	10.00
❑ 35015	(I'm a) Road Runner/Shoot Your Shot	1965	2.50	5.00	10.00
❑ 35017	Cleo's Mood/Baby You Know It Ain't Right	1966	2.00	4.00	8.00
❑ 35024	How Sweet It Is (To Be Loved By You)/Nothing But Soul	1966	2.00	4.00	8.00
❑ 35024 [PS]	How Sweet It Is (To Be Loved By You)/Nothing But Soul	1966	5.00	10.00	20.00
❑ 35026	Money (That's What I Want) Part I/Money (That's What I Want) Part II	1966	2.00	4.00	8.00
❑ 35030	Pucker Up Buttercup/Anyway You Wanna	1967	2.00	4.00	8.00
❑ 35036	Shoot Your Shot/Ain't That the Truth	1967	2.00	4.00	8.00
❑ 35041	Come See About Me/Sweet Soul	1967	2.00	4.00	8.00
❑ 35048	Hip City — Part 1/Hip City — Part 2	1968	2.00	4.00	8.00
❑ 35055	Home Cookin'/Mutiny	1969	2.00	4.00	8.00
❑ 35062	What Does It Take (To Win Your Love)/Brainwasher — Part 1	1969	2.00	4.00	8.00
❑ 35067	These Eyes/Got to Find a Way to Win Maria Back	1969	—	3.00	6.00
❑ 35070	Gotta Hold On to This Feeling/Clinging to the Theory That She's Coming Back	1970	—	3.00	6.00
❑ 35073	Do You See My Love (For You Growing)/Groove and More	1970	—	3.00	6.00
❑ 35081	Holly Holy/Carry Your Own Load	1970	—	3.00	6.00
❑ 35084	Take Me Girl, I'm Ready/Right On Brothers and Sisters	1971	—	3.00	6.00
❑ 35090	Way Back Home/(Instrumental)	1971	—	3.00	6.00
❑ 35095	Walk in the Night/I Don't Want to Do Wrong	1972	—	3.00	6.00
❑ 35097	Groove Thang/Me and My Family	1972	—	3.00	6.00
❑ 35104	Gimme That Beat (Part 1)/Gimme That Beat (Part 2)	1973	—	3.00	6.00
❑ 35106	I Don't Need No Reason/Country Boy	1973	—	3.00	6.00
❑ 35108	Peace and Understanding (Is Hard to Find)/Soul Clappin'	1973	—	3.00	6.00
❑ 35110	Dancing Like They Do on Soul Train/I Ain't That Easy to Love	1973	—	3.00	6.00
❑ 35114 [DJ]	You Are the Sunshine of My Life/Until You Come Back to Me	1974	—	—	—
—Unreleased					
❑ 35116	I'm So Glad/Soul Clappin'	1975	—	2.50	5.00
❑ 35118	Hot Shot/You're No Ordinary Woman	1976	—	2.50	5.00
❑ 35122	Whopper Bopper Show Stopper/Hard Love	1977	—	2.50	5.00
WHITFIELD					
❑ 8861	Back Street Boogie/Don't Let Me Go Away	1979	—	2.00	4.00
❑ 49052	Wishing on a Star/Hole in the Wall	1979	—	2.00	4.00

WALKER, T-BONE

Number	Title (A Side/B Side)	Yr	VG	VG+	NM
ATLANTIC					
❑ 1045	Papa Ain't Salty/T-Bone Shuffle	1955	12.50	25.00	50.00
❑ 1074	Why Not/Play On Little Girl	1955	10.00	20.00	40.00
BLUESWAY					
❑ 61008	Confusion Blues/Every Night I Have to Cry	1967	2.00	4.00	8.00
CAPITOL					
❑ F799	Go Back to the One You Love/On Your Way Blues	1950	37.50	75.00	150.00
❑ F944	Too Much Trouble Blues/She's My Old Time Used to Be	1950	37.50	75.00	150.00
IMPERIAL					
❑ 5202	Street Walkin' Woman/The Blues Is a Woman	1952	100.00	200.00	400.00
—Note: T-Bone Walker records on Imperial before 5202 are unconfirmed on 45 rpm.					
❑ 5216	Blue Mood/Got No Use for You	1953	50.00	100.00	200.00
❑ 5228	Railroad Station Blues/Long Distance Blues	1953	50.00	100.00	200.00
❑ 5239	Party Girl/You're Here in the Dark	1953	75.00	150.00	300.00
❑ 5247	Everytime/Tell Me What's the Reason	1953	37.50	75.00	150.00
❑ 5261	I'm About to Lose My Mind/I Miss You Baby	1954	25.00	50.00	100.00
❑ 5264	Pony Tail/When the Sun Goes Down	1954	20.00	40.00	80.00
❑ 5274	Vida Lee/My Baby Is Now on My Mind	1954	20.00	40.00	80.00
❑ 5284	Bye Bye Baby/Wanderin' Heart	1954	20.00	40.00	80.00
❑ 5299	Teenage Baby/Strugglin' Blues	1954	20.00	40.00	80.00
❑ 5311	Love Is Just a Gamble/High Society	1954	20.00	40.00	80.00
❑ 5330	I'll Understand/The Hard Way	1955	12.50	25.00	50.00
❑ 5384	You Don't Understand/Say! Pretty Baby	1956	12.50	25.00	50.00
❑ 5695	Travelin' Blues/Strollin' with Bones	1960	3.75	7.50	15.00
❑ 5832	Evil Hearted Woman/Life Is Too Short	1962	3.75	7.50	15.00
❑ 5962	Doin' Time/Cold, Cold Water	1963	3.00	6.00	12.00
JETSTREAM					
❑ 726	Reconsider Baby/I'm Not Your Fool Anymore	1966	2.50	5.00	10.00
❑ 730	T-Bone's Back/She's a Hit	1967	2.50	5.00	10.00
MODERN					
❑ 1004	Should I Let Her Go/Hey Hey Baby	1965	2.50	5.00	10.00
POST					
❑ 2002	I Get So Weary/Tell Me What's the Reason	1955	15.00	30.00	60.00

7-Inch Extended Plays

Number	Title (A Side/B Side)	Yr	VG	VG+	NM
CAPITOL					
❑ EAP 370	(contents unknown)	1953	50.00	100.00	200.00
❑ EAP 370 [PS]	Classics in Jazz	1953	50.00	100.00	200.00

WALKER, WAYNE

Number	Title (A Side/B Side)	Yr	VG	VG+	NM
ABC-PARAMOUNT					
❑ 9735	It's My Way/All I Can Do Is Cry	1956	15.00	30.00	60.00
BRUNSWICK					
❑ 55133	Little Ole You/What Kind of God Do You Think You Are	1959	10.00	20.00	40.00
COLUMBIA					
❑ 40905	A Teenage Love Affair/Whatever You Desire	1957	6.25	12.50	25.00
❑ 40979	Just a-Walkin' Around/Sands of Gold	1957	6.25	12.50	25.00
❑ 41042	Bo-Bo Sha Diddle Diddle/Come Away from His Arms	1957	6.25	12.50	25.00
❑ 41130	I'm Finally Free/It's Written in Your Arms	1958	6.25	12.50	25.00
CORAL					
❑ 62328	Battle of the Bulge/Reaching for the Impossible	1962	3.75	7.50	15.00
EVEREST					
❑ 19380	Love, Love, Love/Sweet Chains of Love	1960	3.75	7.50	15.00

WALKER BROTHERS, THE
Also see SCOTT ENGEL.

Number	Title (A Side/B Side)	Yr	VG	VG+	NM
KAY-Y					
❑ 66785	Beautiful Brown Eyes/Ninety-Seven	1960	12.50	25.00	50.00
SMASH					
❑ 1952	Doin' the Jerk/Pretty Girls Everywhere	1964	3.00	6.00	12.00
❑ 1976	Love Her/Seventh Dawn	1965	3.00	6.00	12.00
❑ 2000	Make It Easy on Yourself/But I Do	1965	3.75	7.50	15.00
❑ 2009	Make It Easy on Yourself/Doin' the Jerk	1965	3.00	6.00	12.00
❑ 2009 [PS]	Make It Easy on Yourself/Doin' the Jerk	1965	5.00	10.00	20.00
❑ 2016	My Ship Is Comin' In/You're All Around Me	1966	3.00	6.00	12.00
❑ 2016 [PS]	My Ship Is Comin' In/You're All Around Me	1966	5.00	10.00	20.00
❑ 2032	The Sun Ain't Gonna Shine (Anymore)/After the Lights Go Out	1966	3.00	6.00	12.00
❑ 2048	(Baby) You Don't Have to Tell Me/Young Man Cried	1966	3.00	6.00	12.00
❑ 2063	Another Tear Falls/Saddest Night in the World	1966	3.00	6.00	12.00
TOWER					
❑ 218	I Only Came to Dance with You/Greens	1966	3.00	6.00	12.00

WALLACE, BILLY

Number	Title (A Side/B Side)	Yr	VG	VG+	NM
DEB					
❑ 883	Wolf Call/(B-side unknown)	1957	37.50	75.00	150.00
❑ 1003	Don't Flirt with My Baby/You'll Never Cheat Me Anymore	1958	37.50	75.00	150.00
MERCURY					
❑ 70876	What'll I Do/That's My Reward	1956	50.00	100.00	200.00
❑ 70957	Mean Mistreating Baby/Burning the Wind	1956	75.00	150.00	300.00

WALLACE, JERRY

Number	Title (A Side/B Side)	Yr	VG	VG+	NM
4 STAR					
❑ 1035	I Wanna Go to Heaven/After You	1978	—	2.50	5.00
❑ 1036	Yours Love/There She Goes	1979	—	2.50	5.00
ALLIED					
❑ 5015	Little Miss One/Petrillo	1954	12.50	25.00	50.00
—B-side by Eddie Oliver and the Oliver Twisters					
❑ 5019	That's What a Woman Can Do/I Hate to Go Home Alone	1954	10.00	20.00	40.00
❑ 5023	Runnin' After Love/Dixie Anna	1954	10.00	20.00	40.00
BMA					
❑ 7-002	I Miss You Already/At the End of a Rainbow	1977	—	2.50	5.00
❑ 7-005	I'll Promise You Tomorrow/You're on the Run	1977	—	2.50	5.00
❑ 8-006	At the End of a Rainbow/Looking for a Memory	1978	—	2.50	5.00
❑ 8-008	My Last Sad Song/Wickenburg Way	1978	—	2.50	5.00
CHALLENGE					
❑ 1003	Blue Jean Baby/Fool's Hall of Fame	1957	5.00	10.00	20.00
❑ 9107	Life's a Holiday/I Can See an Angel Walking	1961	3.00	6.00	12.00
❑ 9117	Eyes (Don't Give My Secrets Away)/Lonesome	1961	3.00	6.00	12.00
❑ 9130	Rollin' River/I Hang My Head and Cry	1961	3.00	6.00	12.00
❑ 9139	Little Miss Tease/Mr. Lonely	1962	3.00	6.00	12.00
❑ 9152	Here I Go/You'll Never Know	1962	3.00	6.00	12.00
❑ 9171	Shutters and Boards/Am I That Easy to Forget	1962	3.00	6.00	12.00
❑ 9185	Move Over/On a Merry-Go-Round	1963	3.00	6.00	12.00
❑ 9195	Just Walking in the Rain/San Francisco Mama	1963	3.00	6.00	12.00
❑ 9205	Empty Arms Again/Bambola (My Darling One)	1963	3.00	6.00	12.00
❑ 59000	The Other Me/Good and Bad	1958	5.00	10.00	20.00
❑ 59013	How the Time Flies/With This Ring	1958	5.00	10.00	20.00
❑ 59027	Diamond Ring/All My Love Belongs to You	1958	5.00	10.00	20.00
❑ 59040	A Touch of Pink/Off Stage	1959	3.75	7.50	15.00
❑ 59047	Primrose Lane/By Your Side	1959	4.50	9.00	18.00
❑ 59060	Little Coco Palm/Mission Bell Blues	1959	3.75	7.50	15.00
❑ 59060 [PS]	Little Coco Palm/Mission Bell Blues	1959	10.00	20.00	40.00

Number	Title (A Side/B Side)	Yr	VG	VG+	NM
❑ 59072	King of the Mountain/You're Singing Our Love Song to Somebody Else	1960	3.75	7.50	15.00
❑ 59082	Swingin' Down the Lane/Teardrops in the Rain	1960	3.75	7.50	15.00
❑ 59098	There She Goes/Angel on My Shoulder	1960	3.75	7.50	15.00
❑ 59223	Auf Wiedesehn/If I Make It Through Today	1963	2.50	5.00	10.00
❑ 59246	In the Misty Moonlight/Even the Bad Times Are Good	1964	2.50	5.00	10.00
❑ 59249	In the Misty Moonlight/Cannon Ball	1964	3.75	7.50	15.00
—B-side by the Soul Surfers					
❑ 59265	Even the Bad Times Are Good/Spanish Guitars	1964	2.50	5.00	10.00
❑ 59278	You're Driving You Out of My Mind/Helpless	1965	2.50	5.00	10.00
CLASS					
❑ 502	Taj Mahal/Autumn Has Come and Gone	1955	6.25	12.50	25.00
DECCA					
❑ 32777	After You/She'll Remember	1971	—	3.50	7.00
❑ 32859	The Morning After/I Can't Take It Anymore	1971	—	3.50	7.00
❑ 32914	To Get to You/Time	1972	—	3.50	7.00
❑ 32989	If You Leave Me Tonight I'll Cry/What's He Doin' in My World	1972	—	3.50	7.00
❑ 33036	Do You Know What It's Like to Be Lonesome/Where Did He Come From	1972	—	3.50	7.00
DOOR KNOB					
❑ 116	You've Still Got Me/Now That Sandy's Gone	1979	—	2.50	5.00
❑ 127	Cling to Me/Paper Madonna	1980	—	2.50	5.00
❑ 134	If I Could Set My Love to Music/Cling to Me	1980	—	2.50	5.00
GLENOLDEN					
❑ 159	Are You Ready/That's the Fool in Me	1968	—	3.00	6.00
LIBERTY					
❑ 55957	Runaway Bay/Dispossessed	1967	2.00	4.00	8.00
❑ 56001	This One's on the House/A New Sun Risin'	1967	2.00	4.00	8.00
❑ 56027	The Closest I Ever Came/That's What Fools Are For	1968	—	—	—
—Unreleased					
❑ 56028	Another Time, Another Place, Another World/That's What Fools Are For	1968	—	3.00	6.00
❑ 56059	Sweet Child of Sunshine/Our House on Paper	1968	—	3.00	6.00
❑ 56095	Temptation/Son	1969	—	3.00	6.00
❑ 56105	Venus/Soon We'll Be There	1969	—	3.00	6.00
❑ 56130	Swiss Cottage Place/With Aging	1969	—	3.00	6.00
❑ 56147	Honey Eyed Girl/Glory of My Girl	1969	—	3.00	6.00
❑ 56155	Even the Bad Times Are Good/For All We Know	1970	—	3.00	6.00
MCA					
❑ 40037	A Song Nobody Sings/Sound of Goodbye	1973	—	2.50	5.00
❑ 40111	Don't Give Up on Me/You Look Like Forever	1973	—	2.50	5.00
❑ 40183	Guess Who/All I Ever Want from You	1974	—	2.50	5.00
❑ 40248	My Wife's House/A Better Way to Say I Love You	1974	—	2.50	5.00
❑ 40321	Make Hay While the Sun Shines/I Wonder Whose Baby	1974	—	2.50	5.00
MERCURY					
❑ 70684	Taj Mahal/Autumn Has Come and Gone	1955	5.00	10.00	20.00
❑ 70758	The Greatest Magic of All/Walking in the Rain	1955	5.00	10.00	20.00
❑ 70812	One Night When Flowers Were Dancing/Gloria	1956	5.00	10.00	20.00
❑ 72246	In the Misty Moonlight/Even the Bad Times Are Good	1964	3.00	6.00	12.00
❑ 72258	Butterfly/Let the Tears Begin	1964	2.50	5.00	10.00
❑ 72292	It's a Cotton Candy World/Keep a Lamp Burning	1964	2.50	5.00	10.00
❑ 72356	Careless Hands/San Francisco d'Assisi	1964	2.50	5.00	10.00
❑ 72406	Rainbow/Time	1965	2.50	5.00	10.00
❑ 72461	Life's Gone and Slipped Away/Twelve Little Roses	1965	2.50	5.00	10.00
❑ 72529	Diamonds and Horseshoes/Will the Pain Fade Away	1966	2.50	5.00	10.00
❑ 72589	Wallpaper Roses/Son of a Green Beret	1966	2.50	5.00	10.00
❑ 72619	Not That I Care/Release Me	1966	2.50	5.00	10.00
MGM					
❑ 14788	Comin' Home to You/The River St. Marie	1975	—	2.50	5.00
❑ 14809	Wanted Man/Your Love	1975	—	2.50	5.00
❑ 14832	Georgia Rain/In the Garden	1975	—	2.50	5.00
POLYDOR					
❑ 14322	The Fool I've Been Today/Jenny Angel	1976	—	2.00	4.00
TOPS					
❑ 369	P.S. I Love You/Vaya Con Dios (May God Be With You)	1953	10.00	20.00	40.00
—B-side by Betty Ford					
UNITED ARTISTS					
❑ XW239	Take Me As I Am/Touch Me	1973	—	2.50	5.00
❑ XW618	With Pen in Hand/All I Want Is You	1975	—	2.50	5.00
❑ 50971	Funny How Time Slips Away/Thanks to You for Loving Me	1972	—	2.50	5.00
WING					
❑ 90065	Eyes of Fire, Lips of Wine/Monkey See, Monkey Do	1956	5.00	10.00	20.00

WALLACE, SONNY

Number	Title (A Side/B Side)	Yr	VG	VG+	NM
YUCCA					
❑ 127	Black Cadillac/If a Man Could See	1961	25.00	50.00	100.00

WALLER, GORDON

Also see PETER AND GORDON.

Number	Title (A Side/B Side)	Yr	VG	VG+	NM
BELL					
❑ 794	The Lady in the Window/I Was a Boy When You Needed a Man	1969	2.00	4.00	8.00
❑ 882	Sunshine/You Gonna Hurt Yourself	1970	—	3.00	6.00
CAPITOL					
❑ 2346	Everyday/Because of a Woman	1968	2.00	4.00	8.00
❑ 5886	Speak for Me/Little Nonie	1967	2.00	4.00	8.00

WALLFLOWERS, THE

Number	Title (A Side/B Side)	Yr	VG	VG+	NM
EPIC					
❑ ES7 41025 [DJ]	Heroes (same on both sides)	1998	—	—	3.00
—Promo-only 45					
❑ ES7 41025 [PS]	Heroes (same on both sides)	1998	—	—	3.00

WALLS, VAN

Number	Title (A Side/B Side)	Yr	VG	VG+	NM
ATLANTIC					
❑ 980	After Midnight/Blue Sender	1952	25.00	50.00	100.00

WALSH, JOE

Also see EAGLES; THE JAMES GANG (1).

Number	Title (A Side/B Side)	Yr	VG	VG+	NM
ABC					
❑ 12115	Time Out/Help Me Through the Night	1975	—	2.50	5.00
❑ 12187	Walk Away/Help Me Through the Night	1976	—	2.50	5.00
❑ 12426	Rocky Mountain Way/Turn to Stone	1978	—	2.00	4.00
ABC DUNHILL					
❑ 4327	I'll Tell the World About You/Mother Says	1972	—	2.50	5.00
❑ 4361	Rocky Mountain Way/Prayer	1973	—	2.50	5.00
❑ 4373	Meadows/Bookends	1973	—	2.50	5.00
❑ 15026	Turn to Stone/All Night Laundromat Blues	1974	—	2.50	5.00
ASYLUM					
❑ 45493	Life's Been Good/Theme from Boat Weirdos	1978	—	2.00	4.00
❑ 45536	At the Station/Over and Over	1978	—	2.00	4.00
❑ 47144	A Life of Illusion/Rockets	1981	—	2.00	4.00
❑ 47197	Made Your Mind Up/Things	1981	—	2.00	4.00
EPIC					
❑ 73843	Ordinary Average Guy/Alphabetical Order	1991	—	—	3.00
FULL MOON					
❑ 69951	Waffle Stomp/Things	1982	—	2.00	4.00
❑ 69951 [PS]	Waffle Stomp/Things	1982	—	2.00	4.00
FULL MOON/ASYLUM					
❑ 46639	All Night Long/Orange Blossom Special	1980	—	2.00	4.00
—B-side by Gilley's Urban Cowboy Band					
❑ 46639 [PS]	All Night Long/Orange Blossom Special	1980	—	2.50	5.00
WARNER BROS.					
❑ 28225	In My Car/How Ya Doin'?	1987	—	—	3.00
❑ 28304	The Radio Song/How Ya Doin'?	1987	—	—	3.00
❑ 28304 [PS]	The Radio Song/How Ya Doin'?	1987	—	—	3.00
❑ 28910	Good Man Down/I Broke My Leg	1985	—	2.00	4.00
❑ 29454	I.L.B.T.'s/Love Letters	1983	—	2.00	4.00
❑ 29519	Here We Are Now/I Can Play That Rock and Roll	1983	—	2.00	4.00
❑ 29611	Space Age Whiz Kids/Theme from Island Weirdos	1983	—	2.00	4.00
❑ 29611 [PS]	Space Age Whiz Kids/Theme from Island Weirdos	1983	—	2.50	5.00

WANDERERS, THE (1)

Number	Title (A Side/B Side)	Yr	VG	VG+	NM
CUB					
❑ 9003	A Teenage Quarrel/My Shining Hour	1958	7.50	15.00	30.00
❑ 9019	Collecting Hearts/Two Hearts on a Window Pane	1958	10.00	20.00	40.00
❑ 9023	Please/Shadrack, Meshack, and Abednego	1959	7.50	15.00	30.00
❑ 9035	Only When You're Lonely/I'm Not Ashamed	1959	7.50	15.00	30.00
❑ 9054	I Walked Through a Forest/I'm Waiting for Green Pastures	1959	7.50	15.00	30.00
❑ 9075	I Need You More/I Could Make You Mine	1960	7.50	15.00	30.00
❑ 9089	For Your Love/Sally Goodheart	1961	7.50	15.00	30.00
❑ 9094	I'll Never Smile Again/A Little Too Long	1961	7.50	15.00	30.00
❑ 9099	She Wears My Ring/Somebody Else's Sweetheart	1961	12.50	25.00	50.00
❑ 9109	There Is No Greater Love/As Time Goes By	1962	7.50	15.00	30.00
MGM					
❑ 13082	There Is No Greater Love/As Time Goes By	1962	5.00	10.00	20.00
ONYX					
❑ 518	Thinking of You/Great Jumpin' Catfish	1957	15.00	30.00	60.00
ORBIT					
❑ 9003	A Teenage Quarrel/My Shining Hour	1958	15.00	30.00	60.00
SAVOY					
❑ 1109	We Could Find Happiness/Holy Mae Ethel	1953	125.00	250.00	500.00
UNITED ARTISTS					
❑ 570	After He Breaks Your Heart/Run, Run Senorita	1963	3.75	7.50	15.00
❑ 648	I'll Know/You Can't Run Away from Me	1963	7.50	15.00	30.00

WANDERERS, THE (2)

Number	Title (A Side/B Side)	Yr	VG	VG+	NM
PANAMA					
❑ 3900	Quiet Night/One Look	1960	3.75	7.50	15.00

WANDERERS, THE (U)

May be by group (1).

Number	Title (A Side/B Side)	Yr	VG	VG+	NM
GONE					
❑ 5005	Mask Off/My Lady Chocaonine	1957	7.50	15.00	30.00

WANG CHUNG

Number	Title (A Side/B Side)	Yr	VG	VG+	NM
ARISTA					
❑ 1012 [DJ]	Hold Back the Tears (same on both sides)	1983	2.00	4.00	8.00
—As "Huang Chung"; stock copy appears not to exist					
A&M					
❑ 2728	Fire in the Twilight/The Reggae (Instrumental)	1985	—	2.50	5.00
❑ 2728 [PS]	Fire in the Twilight/The Reggae (Instrumental)	1985	—	2.50	5.00
GEFFEN					
❑ 22969	Praying to a New God/Tall Trees in a Blue Sky	1989	—	—	2.00
❑ 22969 [PS]	Praying to a New God/Tall Trees in a Blue Sky	1989	—	—	2.00
❑ 28359	Hypnotize Me/Lullabye	1987	—	—	2.00
❑ 28359 [PS]	Hypnotize Me/Lullabye	1987	—	—	2.00
❑ 28531	Let's Go!/The World in Which We Live	1986	—	—	2.00
❑ 28531 [PS]	Let's Go!/The World in Which We Live	1986	—	—	2.00
❑ 28562	Everybody Have Fun Tonight/Fun Tonight: The Early Years	1986	—	—	2.00
❑ 28562 [PS]	Everybody Have Fun Tonight/Fun Tonight: The Early Years	1986	—	—	2.00
❑ 28891	To Live and Die in L.A./Black-Blue-White	1985	—	—	2.00
❑ 28891 [PS]	To Live and Die in L.A./Black-Blue-White	1985	—	—	2.00
❑ 29193	Don't Be My Enemy/Wait	1984	—	—	3.00
❑ 29310	Dance Hall Days/Ornamental Elephant	1984	—	—	3.00
❑ 29310 [PS]	Dance Hall Days/Ornamental Elephant	1984	—	—	3.00
❑ 29377	Don't Let Go/There Is a Nation	1984	—	—	3.00

Number	Title (A Side/B Side)	Yr	VG	VG+	NM
❑ 29377 [PS]	Don't Let Go/There Is a Nation	1984	—	—	3.00

WAR

Also see ERIC BURDON AND WAR.

Number	Title (A Side/B Side)	Yr	VG	VG+	NM
BLUE NOTE					
❑ 1009	L.A. Sunshine/Slowly We Walk Together	1977	—	2.50	5.00
COCO PLUM					
❑ 2002	Groovin'/(Instrumental)	1985	—	2.00	4.00
LAX					
❑ 02120	Cinco de Mayo/Don't Let No One Get You Down	1981	—	2.50	5.00
MCA					
❑ 40820	Galaxy (Part 1)/Galaxy (Part 2)	1977	—	2.50	5.00
❑ 40820 [PS]	Galaxy (Part 1)/Galaxy (Part 2)	1977	—	3.00	6.00
❑ 40883	Hey Senorita/Sweet Fighting Lady	1978	—	2.50	5.00
❑ 40995	Good, Good Feelin'/Baby Face (She Said Do Do Do Do)	1979	—	2.50	5.00
❑ 41061	I'm the One Who Understands/Corns & Callouses	1979	—	2.50	5.00
❑ 41158	Don't Take It Away/The Music Band 2 (We Are the Music Band)	1979	—	2.50	5.00
❑ 41209	I'll Be Around/The Music Band 2 (We Are the Music Band)	1980	—	2.50	5.00
RCA					
❑ PB-13061	You Got the Power/Cinco de Mayo	1982	—	2.00	4.00
❑ PB-13239	Outlaw/I'm About Somebody	1982	—	2.00	4.00
❑ PB-13322	Just Because/The Jungle (Medley)	1982	—	2.00	4.00
❑ JH-13426 [DJ]	Baby, It's Cold Outside (same on both sides)	1982	—	2.50	5.00
❑ PB-13544	Life (Is So Strange)/W.W. III	1983	—	2.00	4.00
UNITED ARTISTS					
❑ XW163	The Cisco Kid/Beetles in the Bog	1973	—	2.50	5.00
❑ XW281	Gypsy Man/Deliver the Word	1973	—	2.50	5.00
❑ XW350	Me and Baby Brother/In Your Eyes	1973	—	2.50	5.00
❑ XW432	Ballero/Slippin' Into Darkness	1974	—	2.50	5.00
❑ XW629	Why Can't We Be Friends?/In Mazatlin	1975	—	2.50	5.00
❑ XW629 [PS]	Why Can't We Be Friends?/In Mazatlin	1975	—	3.00	6.00
❑ XW706	Low Rider/So	1975	—	2.50	5.00
❑ XW706 [PS]	Low Rider/So	1975	—	3.00	6.00
❑ XW834	Summer/All Day Music	1976	—	2.50	5.00
❑ XW1213	Youngblood/(Instrumental)	1978	—	2.50	5.00
❑ XW1247	Sing a Happy Song/This Funky Music Makes You Feel Good	1978	—	2.50	5.00
❑ 50746	Lonely Feelin'/Sun Oh Sun	1971	2.00	4.00	8.00
❑ 50746 [PS]	Lonely Feelin'/Sun Oh Sun	1971	3.00	6.00	12.00
❑ 50815	All Day Music/Get Down	1971	2.00	4.00	8.00
❑ 50867	Slippin' Into Darkness/Happy Head	1971	—	3.00	6.00
❑ 50975	The World Is a Ghetto/Four Cornered Room	1972	—	3.00	6.00

WARD, BILLY, AND THE DOMINOES

Also includes "The Dominoes."

Number	Title (A Side/B Side)	Yr	VG	VG+	NM
ABC-PARAMOUNT					
❑ 10128	You're Mine/The World Is Waiting for the Sunrise	1960	5.00	10.00	20.00
❑ 10156	You/Gypsy	1960	5.00	10.00	20.00
DECCA					
❑ 29933	St. Therese of the Roses/Home Is Where You Hang Your Hat	1956	7.50	15.00	30.00
❑ 30043	Come On, Shake, Let's Crawl/Will You Remember	1956	7.50	15.00	30.00
❑ 30149	Half a Love (Is Better Than None)/Evermore	1956	7.50	15.00	30.00
❑ 30199	Rock, Plymouth Rock/Till Kingdom Come	1957	7.50	15.00	30.00
❑ 30420	To Each His Own/I Don't Stand a Ghost of a Chance	1957	7.50	15.00	30.00
❑ 30514	September Song/When the Saints Go Marching In	1957	7.50	15.00	30.00
FEDERAL					
❑ 12001	Do Something For Me/Chicken Blues	1951	200.00	400.00	800.00
—Note: Federal 12010 and 12016 were issued only on 78s					
❑ 12022AA	Sixty Minute Man/I Can't Escape from You	1951	125.00	250.00	500.00
❑ 12036	Heart to Heart/Looking for a Man to Satisfy My Soul	1951	125.00	250.00	500.00
—With Little Esther					
❑ 12039	I Am with You/Weeping Willow Blues	1951	100.00	200.00	400.00
❑ 12059	That's What You're Doing to Me/When the Swallows Come Back to Capistrano	1952	100.00	200.00	400.00
❑ 12068AA	Have Mercy Baby/Deep Sea Blues	1952	62.50	125.00	250.00
❑ 12072	Love, Love, Love/That's What You're Doing to Me	1952	50.00	100.00	200.00
❑ 12105	I'd Be Satisfied/No Room	1952	45.00	90.00	180.00
❑ 12106	I'm Lonely/Yours Forever	1952	45.00	90.00	180.00
❑ 12114	The Bells/Pedal Pushin' Papa	1952	50.00	100.00	200.00
❑ 12129	These Foolish Things Remind Me of You/Don't Leave Me This Way	1953	75.00	150.00	300.00
—Green label, gold top					
❑ 12129	These Foolish Things Remind Me of You/Don't Leave Me This Way	1954	25.00	50.00	100.00
—Green label, silver top					
❑ 12129	These Foolish Things Remind Me of You/Don't Leave Me This Way	1955	7.50	15.00	30.00
—All-green label					
❑ 12139	You Can't Keep a Good Man Down/Where Now Little Heart	1953	25.00	50.00	100.00
❑ 12162	Until the Real Thing Comes Along/My Baby's 3 D	1954	25.00	50.00	100.00
❑ 12178	Tootsie Roll/Move to the Outskirts of Town	1954	25.00	50.00	100.00
❑ 12184	Handwriting on the Wall/One Moment with You	1954	50.00	100.00	200.00
❑ 12193	Above Jacob's Ladder/Little Black Train	1954	12.50	25.00	50.00
❑ 12209	Can't Do Sixty No More/If I Never Get to Heaven	1955	25.00	50.00	100.00
❑ 12218	Love Me Now or Let Me Go/Cave Man	1955	12.50	25.00	50.00
❑ 12263	Bobby Sox Baby/How Long, How Long Blues	1956	12.50	25.00	50.00
❑ 12301	St. Louis Blues/One Moment with You	1957	12.50	25.00	50.00
❑ 12308	Have Mercy Baby/Love, Love, Love	1957	10.00	20.00	40.00
JUBLIEE					
❑ 5163	Gimme, Gimme, Gimme/Come to Me, Baby	1954	7.50	15.00	30.00
❑ 5213	Sweethearts on Parade/Take Me Back to Heaven	1955	7.50	15.00	30.00
KING					
❑ 1280	Rags to Riches/Don't Ask Me	1953	12.50	25.00	50.00
❑ 1281	Christmas in Heaven/Ringing In a Brand New Year	1953	25.00	50.00	100.00
❑ 1342	Tenderly/Little Lie	1954	12.50	25.00	50.00
❑ 1364	Three Coins in the Fountain/Lonesome Road	1954	12.50	25.00	50.00
❑ 1368	Little Things Mean a Lot/I Really Don't Want to Know	1954	10.00	20.00	40.00
❑ 1492	Learnin' the Blues/May I Never Love	1955	10.00	20.00	40.00
❑ 1502	Over the Rainbow/Give Me You	1955	10.00	20.00	40.00
❑ 5322	Sixty Minute Man/Have Mercy Baby	1960	5.00	10.00	20.00
❑ 5463	Lay It on the Line/That's How You Know You're Growing Old	1961	5.00	10.00	20.00
❑ 6002	I'm Walking Behind You/This Love of Mine	1965	5.00	10.00	20.00
❑ 6016	O Holy Night/What Are You Doin' New Year's Eve	1965	5.00	10.00	20.00
❑ 6106	O Holy Night/What Are You Doin' New Year's Eve	1967	3.75	7.50	15.00
LIBERTY					
❑ 55071	Star Dust/Lucinda	1957	6.25	12.50	25.00
❑ 55099	Deep Purple/Do It Again	1957	6.25	12.50	25.00
❑ 55111	My Proudest Possession/Someone Greater Than I	1957	6.25	12.50	25.00
❑ 55126	Solitude/You Grow Sweeter As the Years Go By	1958	6.25	12.50	25.00
❑ 55136	Jennie Lee/Music, Maestro, Please	1958	6.25	12.50	25.00
❑ 55181	Please Don't Say No/Behave, Hula Girl	1959	6.25	12.50	25.00
RO-ZAN					
❑ 10001	Man in the Stain Glass Window/My Fair Weather Friend	1961	5.00	10.00	20.00
UNITED ARTISTS					
❑ 0017	Stardust/These Foolish Things	1973	—	2.50	5.00
—"Silver Spotlight Series" reissue					

7-Inch Extended Plays

Number	Title (A Side/B Side)	Yr	VG	VG+	NM
DECCA					
❑ ED 2549	(contents unknown)	1958	50.00	100.00	200.00
❑ ED 2549 [PS]	Billy Ward and His Dominoes	1958	50.00	100.00	200.00
FEDERAL					
❑ 212	(contents unknown)	1956	100.00	200.00	400.00
—Green label, silver top					
❑ 212	(contents unknown)	1956	25.00	50.00	100.00
—All-green label					
❑ 212 [PS]	Billy Ward and His Dominoes, Vol. 1	1956	25.00	50.00	100.00
❑ 262	(contents unknown)	1957	100.00	200.00	400.00
—Green label, silver top					
❑ 262	(contents unknown)	1957	25.00	50.00	100.00
—All-green label					
❑ 262 [PS]	Billy Ward and His Dominoes, Vol. 2	1957	25.00	50.00	100.00
❑ 269	(contents unknown)	1957	100.00	200.00	400.00
—Green label, silver top					
❑ 269	(contents unknown)	1957	25.00	50.00	100.00
—All-green label					
❑ 269 [PS]	Billy Ward and His Dominoes, Vol. 3	1957	25.00	50.00	100.00
LIBERTY					
❑ LEP-1-3056	(contents unknown)	1959	25.00	50.00	100.00
❑ LEP-1-3056 [PS]	Sea of Glass (Part One)	1959	25.00	50.00	100.00
❑ LEP-2-3056	Deep River/By and By//The House of the Lord/The Lullaby Divine	1959	25.00	50.00	100.00
❑ LEP-2-3056 [PS]	Sea of Glass (Part 2)	1959	25.00	50.00	100.00
❑ LEP-3-3056	(contents unknown)	1959	25.00	50.00	100.00
❑ LEP-3-3056 [PS]	Sea of Glass (Part 3)	1959	25.00	50.00	100.00
❑ LEP-1-3083	Stardust/Eatin' and Sleepin'//Music, Maestro, Please/I'll Never Ask for More Than This	1959	25.00	50.00	100.00
❑ LEP-1-3083 [PS]	Yours Forever (Part One)	1959	25.00	50.00	100.00
❑ LEP-2-3083	(contents unknown)	1959	25.00	50.00	100.00
❑ LEP-2-3083 [PS]	Yours Forever (Part 2)	1959	25.00	50.00	100.00
❑ LEP-3-3083	Smoke Gets in Your Eyes/Do It Again//If You Please/Yours Forever	1959	25.00	50.00	100.00
❑ LEP-3-3083 [PS]	Yours Forever (Part 3)	1959	25.00	50.00	100.00

WARD, BURT

Number	Title (A Side/B Side)	Yr	VG	VG+	NM
MGM					
❑ 13632	Boy Wonder I Love You/Orange Colored Sky	1966	50.00	100.00	200.00
—Written and produced by Frank Zappa					

WARD, HERB

Number	Title (A Side/B Side)	Yr	VG	VG+	NM
ARGO					
❑ 5510	Strange Change/Why Do You Want to Leave	1965	20.00	40.00	80.00
RCA VICTOR					
❑ 47-9688	Honest to Goodness/If You Got to Leave Me	1968	15.00	30.00	60.00

WARD, ROBIN

Number	Title (A Side/B Side)	Yr	VG	VG+	NM
DOT					
❑ 16530	Wonderful Summer/Dream Boy	1963	3.00	6.00	12.00
❑ 16578	Winter's Here/Bobby	1963	2.50	5.00	10.00
❑ 16599	Johnny Come and Get Me/Where the Blue of the Night Meets the Gold of the Day	1964	5.00	10.00	20.00
❑ 16624	In His Car/Wishing	1964	6.25	12.50	25.00

WARD, SINGIN' SAMMY

Number	Title (A Side/B Side)	Yr	VG	VG+	NM
MOTOWN					
❑ 1004	Lover/That's Why I Love You So Much	1960	10.00	20.00	40.00
—With Sherri Taylor					
SOUL					
❑ 35004	Bread Winner/You've Got to Change	1964	12.50	25.00	50.00
TAMLA					
❑ 54030	What Makes You Love Him/The Child Is Really Wild	1960	50.00	100.00	200.00
—With lines label					
❑ 54030	What Makes You Love Him/The Child Is Really Wild	1960	18.75	37.50	75.00
—With globe label					
❑ 54049	What Makes You Love Him/Don't Take It Away	1961	12.50	25.00	50.00
❑ 54057	Everybody Knew It/Big Joe Moe	1962	12.50	25.00	50.00

Number	Title (A Side/B Side)	Yr	VG	VG+	NM
❑ 54071	Part Time Love/Someday Pretty Baby	1962	12.50	25.00	50.00

WARD, WALTER, AND THE CHALLENGERS
Later recorded as THE OLYMPICS.

MELATONE

Number	Title (A Side/B Side)	Yr	VG	VG+	NM
❑ 1002	I Can Tell/The Mambo Beat	1957	100.00	200.00	400.00

WARDELL AND THE SULTANS
IMPERIAL

Number	Title (A Side/B Side)	Yr	VG	VG+	NM
❑ 5812	The Original Popeye/Dance Time	1962	5.00	10.00	20.00
❑ 5886	I Need Your Love/I'm Broke	1962	3.75	7.50	15.00

WARE, CURTIS, AND THE FOUR DO-MATICS
KAYBEE

Number	Title (A Side/B Side)	Yr	VG	VG+	NM
❑ 101	Flame in My Heart/Am I in Love	1961	125.00	250.00	500.00

WARE, EDDIE
STATES

Number	Title (A Side/B Side)	Yr	VG	VG+	NM
❑ 130	That's the Stuff I Like/Lonely Broken Heart	1954	30.00	60.00	120.00

WARLOCKS, THE (1)
Members of this group later joined ZZ TOP.

ARA

Number	Title (A Side/B Side)	Yr	VG	VG+	NM
❑ 1017	If You Really Want Me to Stay/Good Time Trippin'	1968	37.50	75.00	150.00

WARLOCKS, THE (2)
DECCA

Number	Title (A Side/B Side)	Yr	VG	VG+	NM
❑ 31806	I'll Go Crazy/Temper Tantrum	1965	5.00	10.00	20.00

WASHINGTON SQUARE

Number	Title (A Side/B Side)	Yr	VG	VG+	NM
❑ 2023	Hey Joe/Girl	1966	5.00	10.00	20.00

WARMEST SPRING, THE
PARKWAY

Number	Title (A Side/B Side)	Yr	VG	VG+	NM
❑ 985	Younger Girl/It Doesn't Matter Now	1966	2.50	5.00	10.00
❑ 985 [DJ]	Younger Girl	1966	5.00	10.00	20.00
—One-sided white label promo					
❑ 990	Suddenly (You Find Love)/Hard, Hard Girl	1966	2.50	5.00	10.00

WARNES, JENNIFER
Includes records as "Jennifer." Also see JOE COCKER; BILL MEDLEY.

ARISTA

Number	Title (A Side/B Side)	Yr	VG	VG+	NM
❑ 0223	Right Time of the Night/Daddy Don't Go	1976	—	2.50	5.00
❑ 0252	I'm Dreaming/Don't Lead Me On	1977	—	2.50	5.00
❑ 0430	I Know a Heartache When I See One/Frankie in the Rain	1979	—	2.00	4.00
❑ 0455	Don't Make Me Over/I'm Restless	1979	—	2.00	4.00
❑ 0497	When the Feeling Comes Around/Shot Through the Heart	1980	—	2.00	4.00
❑ 0611	Could It Be Love/I'm Restless	1982	—	2.00	4.00
❑ 0670	Come to Me/I'm Restless	1982	—	2.00	4.00

CASABLANCA

Number	Title (A Side/B Side)	Yr	VG	VG+	NM
❑ 814603-7	All the Right Moves/Theme — All the Right Moves	1983	—	2.00	4.00
—A-side with Chris Thompson; B-side by David Campbell					

CYPRESS

Number	Title (A Side/B Side)	Yr	VG	VG+	NM
❑ 661111-7	Ain't No Cure for Love/Famous Blue Raincoat	1986	—	2.00	4.00
❑ 661111-7 [PS]	Ain't No Cure for Love/Famous Blue Raincoat	1986	—	2.50	5.00
❑ 661115-7	First We Take Manhattan/Famous Blue Raincoat	1987	—	2.00	4.00

PARROT

Number	Title (A Side/B Side)	Yr	VG	VG+	NM
❑ 324	Here, There and Everywhere/Sunny Day Blue	1968	3.00	6.00	12.00
❑ 328	Chelsea Morning/The Park	1969	2.50	5.00	10.00
❑ 333	I Am Waiting/The Leaves	1969	2.50	5.00	10.00
❑ 336	Easy to Be Hard/Let the Sunshine In	1969	2.50	5.00	10.00
❑ 343	We're Not Gonna Take It/The Weather's Better	1970	2.00	4.00	8.00
❑ 346	Old Folks/Cajun Train	1970	2.00	4.00	8.00
—All of the above as "Jennifer"					

REPRISE

Number	Title (A Side/B Side)	Yr	VG	VG+	NM
❑ 1070	Last Song/These Days	1972	2.00	4.00	8.00
—As "Jennifer"					

WARNER BROS.

Number	Title (A Side/B Side)	Yr	VG	VG+	NM
❑ 29593	Nights Are Forever/Kick the Can	1983	—	2.00	4.00

WARREN, BOBBY, FIVE
JORDAN

Number	Title (A Side/B Side)	Yr	VG	VG+	NM
❑ 119	Nite-Beat/Medicine Man	1960	10.00	20.00	40.00

WARREN, DOUG
IMAGE

Number	Title (A Side/B Side)	Yr	VG	VG+	NM
❑ 1011	Around Midnight/If the World Don't End Tomorrow	1960	10.00	20.00	40.00
❑ 1013	Ain't Gonna Wait No Longer/Ain't That Love	1960	7.50	15.00	30.00

WARWICK, DEE DEE
ATCO

Number	Title (A Side/B Side)	Yr	VG	VG+	NM
❑ 6754	Make Love to Me/She Didn't Know (She Kept On Talkin')	1970	—	3.00	6.00
❑ 6769	I'm Only Human/If This Was the Last Song	1970	—	3.00	6.00
❑ 6796	Cold Night in Georgia/Searchin'	1971	—	3.00	6.00
❑ 6810	Suspicious Minds/I'm Glad I'm a Woman	1971	—	3.00	6.00
❑ 6840	Everybody's Got to Believe in Somebody/Signed, Dee Dee	1971	—	3.00	6.00

BLUE ROCK

Number	Title (A Side/B Side)	Yr	VG	VG+	NM
❑ 4008	Do It with All Your Heart/Happiness	1965	2.50	5.00	10.00
❑ 4027	We're Doing Fine/I Want to Be with You	1965	2.50	5.00	10.00
❑ 4032	Baby I'm Yours/Gotta Get a Hold of Myself	1965	2.50	5.00	10.00

JUBILEE

Number	Title (A Side/B Side)	Yr	VG	VG+	NM
❑ 5459	You're No Good/Don't Call Me	1963	3.00	6.00	12.00

MERCURY

Number	Title (A Side/B Side)	Yr	VG	VG+	NM
❑ 72584	I Want to Be with You/Lover's Chant	1966	2.00	4.00	8.00
❑ 72638	I'm Gonna Make You Love Me/Yours Until Tomorrow	1966	2.00	4.00	8.00
❑ 72667	When Love Slips Away/House of Gold	1967	2.00	4.00	8.00
❑ 72710	Locked in Your Love/Alfie	1967	2.00	4.00	8.00
❑ 72738	Don't You Ever Give Up on Me/We've Got Everything Going for Us	1967	2.00	4.00	8.00
❑ 72788	Girls Need Love/It's Not Fair	1968	2.00	4.00	8.00
❑ 72834	I'll Be Better Off (Without You)/Monday, Monday	1968	2.00	4.00	8.00
❑ 72880	Foolish Fool/Thank You Girl	1969	2.00	4.00	8.00
❑ 72927	That's Not Love/It's Not Fair	1969	2.00	4.00	8.00
❑ 72940	Next Time (You Fall in Love)/Ring of Bright Water	1969	2.00	4.00	8.00
❑ 72966	I (Who Have Nothing)/Where Is That Rainbow	1969	2.00	4.00	8.00

PRIVATE STOCK

Number	Title (A Side/B Side)	Yr	VG	VG+	NM
❑ 45011	Get Out of My Life/Funny How We Change Places	1975	—	2.50	5.00
❑ 45033	This Time May Be My Last/Funny How We Change Places	1975	—	2.50	5.00

SUTRA

Number	Title (A Side/B Side)	Yr	VG	VG+	NM
❑ 134	Move with the World/The Way We Used to Be	1984	—	2.00	4.00
❑ 134 [PS]	Move with the World/The Way We Used to Be	1984	—	2.00	4.00

WARWICK, DIONNE
Includes records as "Dionne Warwicke." Also see DIONNE AND FRIENDS.

ARISTA

Number	Title (A Side/B Side)	Yr	VG	VG+	NM
❑ 0419	I'll Never Love This Way Again/In Your Eyes	1979	—	2.00	4.00
❑ 0459	Deja Vu/All the Time	1979	—	2.00	4.00
❑ 0498	After You/Out of My Hands	1980	—	2.00	4.00
❑ 0527	No Night So Long/Reaching for the Sky	1980	—	2.00	4.00
❑ 0572	Easy Love/You Never Said Goodbye	1980	—	2.00	4.00
❑ 0602	Some Changes Are For Good/This Time Is Ours	1981	—	2.00	4.00
❑ 0630	There's a Long Road Ahead of Me/Medley of Hits	1981	—	2.00	4.00
❑ 0673	Friends in Love/What Is This	1982	—	2.00	4.00
—A-side with Johnny Mathis					
❑ 0701	For You/What Is This	1982	—	2.00	4.00
❑ 1015	Heartbreaker/I Can't See Anything But You	1982	—	2.00	4.00
❑ 1040	Take the Short Way Home/Just One More Night	1983	—	2.00	4.00
❑ 1067	All the Love in the World/You Are My Love	1983	—	—	—
—Unreleased?					
❑ 9032	All the Love in the World/You Are My Love	1983	—	2.00	4.00
❑ 9073	How Many Times Can We Say Goodbye/What Can a Miracle Do	1983	—	2.00	4.00
—With Luther Vandross					
❑ 9145	Got a Date/Two Ships Passing in the Night	1984	—	2.00	4.00
❑ 9281	Finder of Lost Loves/It's Love	1984	—	2.00	4.00
—A-side with Glen Jones					
❑ 9341	Run to Me/No Love in Sight	1985	—	—	3.00
—A-side with Barry Manilow					
❑ 9460	Whisper in the Dark/Extravagant Gestures	1986	—	—	3.00
❑ 9460 [PS]	Whisper in the Dark/Extravagant Gestures	1986	—	—	3.00
❑ 9567	Love Power/In a World Such As This	1987	—	—	3.00
—A-side with Jeffrey Osborne					
❑ 9567 [PS]	Love Power/In a World Such As This	1987	—	—	3.00
❑ 9638	Reservations for Two/For Everything You Are	1987	—	—	3.00
—A-side with Kashif					
❑ 9638 [PS]	Reservations for Two/For Everything You Are	1987	—	—	3.00
❑ 9652	Another Chance for Love/Cry on Me	1987	—	—	3.00
—A-side with Howard Hewett					
❑ 9652 [PS]	Another Chance for Love/Cry on Me	1987	—	—	3.00
❑ 9901	Take Good Care of You and Me/Heartbreak of Love	1989	—	—	3.00
—A-side with Jeffrey Osborne; B-side with June Pointer					
❑ 9940	I Don't Need Another Love/Hertbreaker	1990	—	—	3.00
—A-side with the Spinners					
❑ 9940 [PS]	I Don't Need Another Love/Hertbreaker	1990	—	—	3.00

ATLANTIC

Number	Title (A Side/B Side)	Yr	VG	VG+	NM
❑ 3029	Then Came You/Just As Long As We Have Love	1974	—	3.00	6.00
—With the Spinners					
❑ 3202	Then Came You/Just As Long As We Have Love	1974	—	2.50	5.00
—With the Spinners					

MUSICOR

Number	Title (A Side/B Side)	Yr	VG	VG+	NM
❑ 6303	If I Ruled the World/Only Love Can Break a Heart	1977	—	2.50	5.00

SCEPTER

Number	Title (A Side/B Side)	Yr	VG	VG+	NM
❑ 1239	Don't Make Me Over/I Smiled Yesterday	1962	3.00	6.00	12.00
❑ 1247	This Empty Place/Wishin' and Hopin'	1963	3.00	6.00	12.00
❑ 1247 [PS]	This Empty Place/Wishin' and Hopin'	1963	5.00	10.00	20.00
❑ 1253	Make the Music Play/Please Make Him Love Me	1963	3.00	6.00	12.00
❑ 1262	Anyone Who Had a Heart/The Love of a Boy	1963	3.00	6.00	12.00
❑ 1274	Walk On By/Any Old Time of Day	1964	3.00	6.00	12.00
❑ 1282	You'll Never Get to Heaven (If You Break My Heart)/A House Is Not a Home	1964	2.50	5.00	10.00
❑ 1285	Reach Out for Me/How Many Days of Sadness	1964	2.50	5.00	10.00
❑ 1294	You Can Have Him/Is There Another Way to Love Him	1965	2.50	5.00	10.00
❑ 1298	Who Can I Turn To/Don't Say I Didn't Tell You Something	1965	2.50	5.00	10.00
❑ 12104	Here I Am/They Long to Be Close to You	1965	2.50	5.00	10.00
❑ 12111	Looking with My Eyes/Only the Strong, Only the Brave	1965	2.50	5.00	10.00
❑ 12122	Are You There (With Another Girl)/If I Ever Make You Cry	1965	2.50	5.00	10.00
❑ 12133	Message to Michael/Here Where There Is Love	1966	2.00	4.00	8.00
❑ 12153	Trains and Boats and Planes/Don't Go Breaking My Heart	1966	2.00	4.00	8.00
❑ 12167	I Just Don't Know What to Do with Myself/In Between the Heartaches	1966	2.00	4.00	8.00
❑ 12181	Another Night/Go with Love	1966	2.00	4.00	8.00
❑ 12187	Alfie/The Beginning of Loneliness	1967	2.00	4.00	8.00
❑ 12196	The Windows of the World/Walk Little Dolly	1967	2.00	4.00	8.00
❑ 12203	I Say a Little Prayer/(Theme from) Valley of the Dolls	1967	2.00	4.00	8.00
❑ 12216	Do You Know the Way to San Jose?/Let Me Be Lonely	1968	2.00	4.00	8.00
❑ 12226	Who Is Gonna Love Me?/(There's) Always Something There to Remind Me	1968	2.00	4.00	8.00
❑ 12231	Promises, Promises/Whoever You Are, I Love You	1968	—	3.50	7.00

Number	Title (A Side/B Side)	Yr	VG	VG+	NM
❑ 12241	This Girl's In Love with You/Dream Sweet Dreamer	1969	—	3.50	7.00
❑ 12249	The April Fools/Slaves	1969	—	3.50	7.00
❑ 12256	Odds and Ends/As Long As There's an Apple Tree	1969	—	3.50	7.00
❑ 12262	You've Lost That Lovin' Feeling/Window Wishing	1969	—	3.50	7.00
❑ 12273	I'll Never Fall in Love Again/What the World Needs Now Is Love	1970	—	3.50	7.00
❑ 12276	Let Me Go to Him/Loneliness Remembers What Happiness Forgets	1970	—	3.00	6.00
❑ 12285	Paper Mache/The Wine Is Young	1970	—	3.00	6.00
❑ 12294	Make It Easy on Yourself/Knowing When to Leave	1970	—	3.00	6.00
❑ 12300	The Green Grass Starts to Grow/They Don't Give Medals to Yesterday's Heroes	1970	—	3.00	6.00
❑ 12309	Who Gets the Guy/Walk the Way You Talk	1971	—	3.00	6.00
❑ 12326	Amanda/He's Moving On	1971	—	3.00	6.00
❑ 12336	The Love of My Man/Hurts So Bad	1971	—	3.00	6.00
❑ 12346	Raindrops Keep Falling on My Head/Is There Another Way to Love You	1972	—	3.00	6.00
❑ 12352	I'm Your Puppet/Don't Make Me Over	1972	—	3.00	6.00
❑ 12383	Medley: Reach Out and Touch (Somebody's Hand)-All Kinds of People/The Good Life	1973	—	3.00	6.00
WARNER BROS.					
❑ 7560	If We Only Have Love/Close to You	1972	—	2.50	5.00
❑ 7669	Don't Let My Teardrops Bother TYou/I Think You Need Love	1973	—	2.50	5.00
❑ 7693	(I'm) Just Being Myself/You're Gonna Need Me	1973	—	2.50	5.00
❑ 8026	Sure Thing/Who Knows	1974	—	2.50	5.00
❑ 8088	Take it from Me/It's Magic	1975	—	2.50	5.00
❑ 8154	Once You Hit the Road/World of My Dreams	1975	—	2.50	5.00
❑ 8183	His House and Me/Ronnie Lee	1976	—	2.50	5.00
❑ 8280	I Didn't Mean to Love You/He's Not for You	1976	—	2.50	5.00
❑ 8419	Do You Believe in Love at First Sight/Do I Have to Cry	1977	—	2.50	5.00
❑ 8501	Keepin' My Head Above Water/Livin' It Up Is Startin' to Get Me Down	1977	—	2.50	5.00
❑ 8530	Don't Ever Take Your Love Away/Do I Have to Cry	1978	—	2.00	4.00
WASHINGTON, BABY					
Also includes records as "Justine Washington."					
ABC-PARAMOUNT					
❑ 10223	My Time to Cry/Let Love Go By	1961	3.75	7.50	15.00
—As Jeanette "Baby" Washington					
❑ 10245	There You Go Again/Don't Cry, Foolish Heart	1961	3.75	7.50	15.00
AVI					
❑ 253	I Wanna Dance/I Can't Get Over Losing You	1978	—	2.50	5.00
—As Jeanette "Baby" Washington					
CHECKER					
❑ 918	I Hate to See You Go/Knock Yourself Out	1959	6.25	12.50	25.00
CHESS					
❑ 2099	Happy Birthday/Is It Worth It	1970	—	3.00	6.00
COTILLION					
❑ 44047	I Don't Know/I Can't Afford to Lose Him	1969	—	3.00	6.00
❑ 44065	Let Them Talk/I Love You Brother	1970	—	3.00	6.00
❑ 44086	Don't Let Me Lose This Dream/I'm Good Enough for You	1970	—	3.00	6.00
J&S					
❑ 1604	There Must Be a Reason/Congratulations Honey	1957	12.50	25.00	50.00
❑ 1632	I Hate to See You Go/Knock Yourself Out	1958	7.50	15.00	30.00
❑ 1656	Every Day/Smitty's Rock	1961	15.00	30.00	60.00
LIBERTY					
❑ 1393	Silent Night/Merry Christmas Baby	1980	—	2.50	5.00
—B-side by Charles Brown					
MASTER 5					
❑ 3500	Can't Get Over Losing You/(B-side unknown)	1974	—	3.00	6.00
❑ 9103	Forever/(B-side unknown)	1973	—	3.00	6.00
—With Don Gardner					
❑ 9104	Just Can't Get You Out of My Mind/(B-side unknown)	1973	—	3.00	6.00
❑ 9107	I've Got to Break Away/(B-side unknown)	1973	—	3.00	6.00
NEPTUNE					
❑ 101	The Time/(B-side unknown)	1959	5.00	10.00	20.00
❑ 104	The Bells (On Our Wedding Day)/(B-side unknown)	1959	5.00	10.00	20.00
❑ 122	Nobody Cares (About Me)/(B-side unknown)	1961	3.75	7.50	15.00
—As Jeanette (Baby) Washington					
SUE					
❑ 104	The Clock/Standing on the Pier	1964	2.00	4.00	8.00
❑ 114	It'll Never Be Over for Me/Move On Drifter	1964	2.00	4.00	8.00
❑ 119	Your Fool/Run My Heart	1965	2.00	4.00	8.00
❑ 124	I Can't Wait Until I See My Baby/Who's Going to Take Care of Me	1965	2.00	4.00	8.00
—As Justine Washington					
❑ 129	Only Those in Love/The Ballad of Bobby Dawn	1965	2.00	4.00	8.00
❑ 149	Silent Night/White Christmas	1967	5.00	10.00	20.00
❑ 150	Either You're With Me (Or Either You're Not)/You Are What You Are	1967	3.75	7.50	15.00
❑ 764	Hey Lonely One/No Tears	1962	3.00	6.00	12.00
❑ 767	Handful of Memories/Careless Hands	1962	2.50	5.00	10.00
❑ 769	Hush Heart/I've Got a Feeling	1962	2.50	5.00	10.00
❑ 783	That's How Heartaches Are Made/There He Is	1963	2.50	5.00	10.00
❑ 790	Leave Me Alone/You and the Night and the Music	1963	2.50	5.00	10.00
❑ 794	Hey Lonely One/Doodlin'	1963	2.50	5.00	10.00
❑ 797	I Can't Wait Until I See My Baby/Who's Going to Take Care of Me	1964	2.50	5.00	10.00
—As Justine Washington					
UNITED ARTISTS					
❑ 0143	That's How Heartaches Are Made/Leave Me Alone	1973	—	2.50	5.00
—"Silver Spotlight Series" reissue					

Number	Title (A Side/B Side)	Yr	VG	VG+	NM
VEEP					
❑ 1274	Silent Night/White Christmas	1967	5.00	10.00	20.00
❑ 1297	Think About the Good Times/Hold Back the Dawn	1969	2.00	4.00	8.00
WASHINGTON, DINAH					
MERCURY					
❑ 5488	Harbor Lights/I Cross My Fingers	1950	6.25	12.50	25.00
❑ 5503	Time Out for Tears/Only a Moment Ago	1950	6.25	12.50	25.00
❑ 5510	How Deep Is the Ocean/Harbor Lights	1950	6.25	12.50	25.00
❑ 5665	I'm a Fool/If You Don't Believe I'm Leaving	1951	6.25	12.50	25.00
❑ 5728	Cold, Cold Heart/Mixed Emotions	1951	6.25	12.50	25.00
❑ 5736	Just One More Chance/Baby Did You Hear	1951	6.25	12.50	25.00
❑ 5804	No Time for Blues/(B-side unknown)	1952	6.25	12.50	25.00
❑ 5842	I Can't Face the Music/Mad About the Boy	1952	6.25	12.50	25.00
❑ 5906	Stormy Weather/Make Believe Dreams	1952	6.25	12.50	25.00
❑ 8181	I Wanna Be Loved/Love with Misery	1950	10.00	20.00	40.00
—Note: Earlier Dinah Washington 45s in the Mercury 8000 series may exist.					
❑ 8187	I'll Never Be Free/Big Deal	1950	6.25	12.50	25.00
❑ 8192	How Deep Is the Ocean/Why Don't You Think Things Over	1950	6.25	12.50	25.00
❑ 8194	My Kind of Man/I Wanna Be Loved by You	1950	6.25	12.50	25.00
❑ 8195	It Isn't Fair/I'll Never Be Free	1950	6.25	12.50	25.00
❑ 8206	If I Loved You/My Kind of Man	1950	6.25	12.50	25.00
❑ 8207	Fast Movin' Mama/Juice Head Man of Mine	1950	6.25	12.50	25.00
❑ 8209	My Heart Cries for You/I Apologize	1951	6.25	12.50	25.00
❑ 8211	I Won't Cry Anymore/Don't Say You're Sorry Again	1951	6.25	12.50	25.00
❑ 8231	Ain't Nobody's Bizness If I Do/Please Send Me Someone to Love	1951	6.25	12.50	25.00
❑ 8232	I'm So Lonely I Could Cry/Fine Fine Daddy	1951	6.25	12.50	25.00
❑ 8249	Saturday Night/Be Fair to Me	1951	6.25	12.50	25.00
❑ 8257	Hey Good Lookin'/Out in the Cold Again	1951	20.00	40.00	80.00
—With The Ravens					
❑ 8267	Wheel of Fortune/Tell Me Why	1952	6.25	12.50	25.00
❑ 8269	Trouble in Mind/New Blowtop Blues	1952	6.25	12.50	25.00
❑ 8292	Pillow Blues/Double Dealin' Daddy	1952	6.25	12.50	25.00
❑ 8294	My Song/Half As Much	1952	6.25	12.50	25.00
❑ 10008 [S]	What a Diff'rence a Day Makes/Come Home	1959	6.25	12.50	25.00
❑ 70046	I Cried for You/Gambler's Blues	1953	6.25	12.50	25.00
❑ 70125	Ain't Nothing Good/You Let My Love Grow Old	1953	6.25	12.50	25.00
❑ 70175	My Lean Baby/Never Again	1953	6.25	12.50	25.00
❑ 70214	TV Is the Thing (This Year)/Fat Daddy	1953	6.25	12.50	25.00
❑ 70263	Silent Night/The Lord's Prayer	1953	6.25	12.50	25.00
❑ 70284	Since My Man Has Gone and Went/My Man's an Undertaker	1953	6.25	12.50	25.00
❑ 70329	Short John/Feel Like I Wanna Cry	1954	5.00	10.00	20.00
❑ 70336	Such a Night/Until Sunrise	1954	5.00	10.00	20.00
❑ 70392	(No, No, No) You Can't Love Two/Big Long Slidin' Thing	1954	10.00	20.00	40.00
❑ 70439	I Don't Hurt Anymore/Dream	1954	5.00	10.00	20.00
❑ 70497	Teach Me Tonight/Wishing Well	1954	5.00	10.00	20.00
❑ 70537	That's All I Want from You/You Stay on My Mind	1955	5.00	10.00	20.00
❑ 70600	If It's the Last Thing I Do/I Diddie	1955	5.00	10.00	20.00
❑ 70653	I Hear Those Bells/The Cheat	1955	5.00	10.00	20.00
❑ 70694	I Concentrate on You/Not Without You	1955	5.00	10.00	20.00
❑ 70728	I'm Lost Without You Tonight/You Might Have Told Me	1955	5.00	10.00	20.00
❑ 70776	The Show Must Go On/I Just Couldn't Stand It No More	1956	3.75	7.50	15.00
❑ 70833	Let's Get Busy Too/Let's Go Around Together	1956	3.75	7.50	15.00
❑ 70868	Cat on a Hot Tin Roof/The First Time	1956	3.75	7.50	15.00
❑ 70906	Soft Winds/Tears to Burn	1956	3.75	7.50	15.00
❑ 70968	Relax, Max/The Kissing Way Home	1956	3.75	7.50	15.00
❑ 71018	All Because of You/To Love and Be Loved	1956	3.75	7.50	15.00
❑ 71043	You Let My Love Grow Old/I Know	1957	3.75	7.50	15.00
❑ 71087	Ain't Nobody Home/I'm Gonna Keep My Eyes on You	1957	3.75	7.50	15.00
❑ 71220	Everybody Loves My Baby/Blues Down Home	1957	3.75	7.50	15.00
❑ 71317	Ring-a My Phone/Never Again	1958	3.75	7.50	15.00
❑ 71377	Make Me a Present of You/All of Me	1958	3.75	7.50	15.00
❑ 71435	What a Diff'rence a Day Makes/Come Home	1959	3.75	7.50	15.00
❑ 71508	Unforgettable/Nothing in the World	1959	2.50	5.00	10.00
❑ 71557	Ol' Santa/The Light	1959	3.00	6.00	12.00
❑ 71560	It Could Happen to You/Age of Miracles	1960	2.50	5.00	10.00
❑ 71635	This Bitter Earth/I Understand	1960	2.50	5.00	10.00
❑ 71696	Love Walked In/I'm in Heaven Tonight	1960	2.50	5.00	10.00
❑ 71744	We Have Love/Looking Back	1960	2.50	5.00	10.00
❑ 71744 [PS]	We Have Love/Looking Back	1960	3.75	7.50	15.00
❑ 71778	Early Every Morning (Early Every Evening Too)/Do You Want It That Way	1961	2.50	5.00	10.00
❑ 71778 [PS]	Early Every Morning (Early Every Evening Too)/Do You Want It That Way	1961	3.75	7.50	15.00
❑ 71812	Our Love Is Here to Stay/Congratulations to Someone	1961	2.50	5.00	10.00
❑ 71812 [PS]	Our Love Is Here to Stay/Congratulations to Someone	1961	3.75	7.50	15.00
❑ 71876	September in the Rain/Wake the Town and Tell the People	1961	2.50	5.00	10.00
❑ 71876 [PS]	September in the Rain/Wake the Town and Tell the People	1961	3.75	7.50	15.00
❑ 71922	Tears and Laughter/If I Should Lose You	1962	2.50	5.00	10.00
❑ 71922 [PS]	Tears and Laughter/If I Should Lose You	1962	3.75	7.50	15.00
❑ 71958	Dream/Such a Night	1962	2.50	5.00	10.00
❑ 71958 [PS]	Dream/Such a Night	1962	3.75	7.50	15.00
❑ 72015	I Want to Be Loved/Am I Blue	1962	2.00	4.00	8.00
❑ 72040	Cold, Cold Heart/I Don't Hurt Anymore	1962	2.00	4.00	8.00
❑ 72040 [PS]	Cold, Cold Heart/I Don't Hurt Anymore	1962	3.75	7.50	15.00
ROULETTE					
❑ 4424	Where Are You/You're Nobody 'Til Somebody Loves You	1962	2.00	4.00	8.00
❑ 4444	For All We Know/I Wouldn't Know (What to Do)	1962	2.00	4.00	8.00
❑ 4455	You're a Sweetheart/It's a Mean Old Man's World	1962	2.00	4.00	8.00
❑ 4476	Romance in the Dark/No Hard Feelings	1963	2.00	4.00	8.00

Number	Title (A Side/B Side)	Yr	VG	VG+	NM
❑ 4490	Soulsville/Let Me Be the First to Know	1963	2.00	4.00	8.00
❑ 4520	The Show Must Go On/I'll Drown in My Own Tears	1963	2.00	4.00	8.00
❑ 4534	That Sunday (That Summer)/A Stranger on Earth	1963	2.00	4.00	8.00
❑ 4538	Call Me Irresponsible/Funny Thing	1963	2.00	4.00	8.00
7-Inch Extended Plays					
EMARCY					
❑ EP 1-6054	(contents unknown)	195?	6.25	12.50	25.00
❑ EP 1-6054 [PS]	After Hours with Miss "D"	195?	6.25	12.50	25.00
MERCURY					
❑ EP 1-3395	(contents unknown)	195?	5.00	10.00	20.00
❑ EP 1-3395 [PS]	Dinah Washington	195?	5.00	10.00	20.00
❑ EP 1-4035	(contents unknown)	195?	5.00	10.00	20.00
❑ EP 1-4035 [PS]	Dinah Washington	195?	5.00	10.00	20.00
❑ EP 1-4041	(contents unknown)	195?	5.00	10.00	20.00
❑ EP 1-4041 [PS]	For Lonely Lovers	195?	5.00	10.00	20.00

WASHINGTON, DINAH, AND BROOK BENTON

Also see each artist's individual listings.

Number	Title (A Side/B Side)	Yr	VG	VG+	NM
MERCURY					
❑ 71565	Baby (You Got What It Takes)/I Do	1960	3.75	7.50	15.00
❑ 71629	A Rockin' Good Way (To Mess Arounf and Fall in Love)/I Believe	1960	3.75	7.50	15.00
❑ 71629 [PS]	A Rockin' Good Way (To Mess Arounf and Fall in Love)/I Believe	1960	6.25	12.50	25.00

WASHINGTON, GINO

Number	Title (A Side/B Side)	Yr	VG	VG+	NM
ATAC					
❑ 101	Doin' the Popcorn/(B-side unknown)	1969	7.50	15.00	30.00
❑ 102	I'll Be Around/(B-side unknown)	1969	10.00	20.00	40.00
❑ 2830	Rat Race/(B-side unknown)	1969	7.50	15.00	30.00
❑ 7823	Like My Baby/(B-side unknown)	1969	10.00	20.00	40.00
CONGRESS					
❑ 269	Understanding/Water	1966	3.00	6.00	12.00
❑ 273	Beach Bash/Hi Hi Hazel	1966	3.00	6.00	12.00
CORREC-TONE					
❑ 503	Gino Is a Coward/Puppet on a String	1962	15.00	30.00	60.00
DJM					
❑ 1011	You Lovely Witch/Love Me, Love Me	1976	—	3.00	6.00
KAPP					
❑ 796	All I Need/Whatever Will Be, Will Be	1966	2.50	5.00	10.00
MALA					
❑ 12029	Like My Baby/I'll Be Around When You Want Me	1968	10.00	20.00	40.00
RIC-TIC					
❑ 100	Gino Is a Coward/Puppet on a String	1964	5.00	10.00	20.00
SIDRA					
❑ 9005	Romeo/Now You're Lonely	196?	6.25	12.50	25.00
SONBERT					
❑ 3770	Gino Is a Coward/Puppet on a String	1963	6.25	12.50	25.00
WAND					
❑ 147	Out of This World/Come Monkey with Me	1964	5.00	10.00	20.00
7-Inch Extended Plays					
NORTON					
❑ EP-080	Out of This World/Come Monkey with Me//Heartburn/Monkey Tree	1999	—	—	2.00
❑ EP-080 [PS]	Come Monkey with Gino Washington and the Atlantics	1999	—	—	2.00

WATERS, MUDDY

Number	Title (A Side/B Side)	Yr	VG	VG+	NM
CHESS					
❑ 1509	All Night Long/Country Boy	1952	625.00	1250.	2500.
—Note: Muddy Waters records on Chess before 1509 are unconfirmed on 45 rpm					
❑ 1514	Please Have Mercy/Looking for My Baby	1952	200.00	400.00	800.00
❑ 1526	Standing Around Crying/Gone to Main St.	1952	175.00	350.00	700.00
❑ 1537	She's All Right/Sad, Sad Day	1953	100.00	200.00	400.00
❑ 1542	Who's Gonna Be Your Sweet Man/Turn the Lamp Down Low	1953	75.00	150.00	300.00
❑ 1550	Mad Love/Blow, Wind, Blow	1953	30.00	60.00	120.00
❑ 1560	I'm Your Hoochie Coochie Man/You're So Pretty	1954	25.00	50.00	100.00
❑ 1571	Just Make Love to Me/Oh Yeh!	1954	15.00	30.00	60.00
❑ 1579	I'm Ready/I Don't Know Why	1954	15.00	30.00	60.00
❑ 1585	Lovin' Man/I'm a Natural Born Lover	1955	12.50	25.00	50.00
❑ 1596	I Want to Be Loved/My Eyes Keep Me in Trouble	1955	12.50	25.00	50.00
❑ 1602	Manish Boy/Young Fashion Ways	1955	17.50	35.00	70.00
❑ 1612	Trouble, No More/Sugar Sweet	1955	20.00	40.00	80.00
❑ 1620	Forty Days and Forty Nights/All Aboard	1956	10.00	20.00	40.00
❑ 1630	Don't Go No Farther/Diamonds at Your Feet	1956	12.50	25.00	50.00
❑ 1644	I Got to Find My Baby/Just to Be with You	1956	10.00	20.00	40.00
❑ 1652	Got My Mojo Working/Rock Me	1957	12.50	25.00	50.00
❑ 1667	Good News/Come Home Baby	1957	7.50	15.00	30.00
❑ 1680	I Live the Life I Love/Evil	1958	7.50	15.00	30.00
❑ 1692	I Won't Go/She's Got It	1958	7.50	15.00	30.00
❑ 1704	Close to You/She's Nineteen Years Old	1958	7.50	15.00	30.00
❑ 1718	Mean Mistreater/Walking Thru the Park	1959	6.25	12.50	25.00
❑ 1724	Ooh Wee/Clouds in My Heart	1959	6.25	12.50	25.00
❑ 1733	Take the Bitter with the Sweet/She's Into Somethin'	1959	6.25	12.50	25.00
❑ 1739	Recipe for Love/Tell Me Baby	1959	6.25	12.50	25.00
❑ 1748	I Feel So Good/When I Get to Thinking	1960	6.25	12.50	25.00
❑ 1752	I'm Your Doctor/Ready Way Back	1960	6.25	12.50	25.00
❑ 1758	Love Affair/Look What You've Done	1960	6.25	12.50	25.00
❑ 1765	Tiger in Your Tank/Meanest Woman	1960	6.25	12.50	25.00
❑ 1774	Got My Mojo Working/Woman Wanted	1960	6.25	12.50	25.00
❑ 1796	Messin' with the Man/Lonesome Room Blues	1961	5.00	10.00	20.00
❑ 1819	Going Home/Tough Times	1962	5.00	10.00	20.00
❑ 1827	Muddy Waters Twist/You Shook Me	1962	6.25	12.50	25.00
❑ 1839	You Need Love/Little Brown Bird	1962	6.25	12.50	25.00
❑ 1862	Five Long Years/Twenty-Four Hours	1963	3.75	7.50	15.00
❑ 1895	The Same Thing/You Can't Lose What You Never Had	1964	3.75	7.50	15.00
❑ 1914	Short Dress Woman/My John the Conqueror	1964	3.75	7.50	15.00
❑ 1921	Put Me in Your Lay-A-Way/Still a Fool	1965	3.00	6.00	12.00
❑ 1937	My Dog Can't Bark/I Got a Rich Man's Woman	1965	3.00	6.00	12.00
❑ 1973	I'm Your Hoochie Coochie Man/Corrina, Corrina	1966	3.00	6.00	12.00
❑ 2018	When the Eagle Flies/Birdnest on the Ground	1967	2.50	5.00	10.00
❑ 2085	Going Home/I Feel So Good	1970	2.00	4.00	8.00
❑ 2107	Making Friends/Two Steps Forward	1971	2.00	4.00	8.00
❑ 2143	Garbage Man/Can't Get No Grindin'	1973	—	3.00	6.00

WATERS, ROGER

Also see PINK FLOYD.

Number	Title (A Side/B Side)	Yr	VG	VG+	NM
COLUMBIA					
❑ 04455	5:01 A.M. (The Pros and Cons of Hitch Hiking)/4:30 A.M. (Apparently They Were Travelling Abroad)	1984	—	—	3.00
❑ 07180	Radio Waves/Going to Live in L.A.	1987	—	—	3.00
❑ 07180 [PS]	Radio Waves/Going to Live in L.A.	1987	—	—	3.00
❑ 07364	Sunset Strip/Money	1987	—	—	3.00
❑ 07364 [PS]	Sunset Strip/Money	1987	—	—	3.00
❑ 07617	Who Needs Information/Molly's Song	1987	—	—	3.00
❑ 74363	What God Wants, Part 1 (Long)/What God Wants, Part 1 (Short)	1992	—	—	3.00

WATKINS, LOVELACE

Number	Title (A Side/B Side)	Yr	VG	VG+	NM
GROOVE					
❑ 58-0016	Tender Love/Ma Cherie Au Revoir	1963	7.50	15.00	30.00
❑ 58-0023	I Won't Believe It/He'[s Lookin' Out for the World	1963	7.50	15.00	30.00
MGM					
❑ 12875	Hello Young Lovers/When I Fall in Love	1960	3.75	7.50	15.00
SUE					
❑ 10-003	Who Am I/Dreams	1968	3.00	6.00	12.00
UNI					
❑ 55211	Fool on the Hill/Je Vous Aime Beaucoup	1970	3.00	6.00	12.00

WATLEY, JODY

Number	Title (A Side/B Side)	Yr	VG	VG+	NM
ATLANTIC					
❑ 84071	Off the Hook (Single Edit)/(Instrumental)	1998	—	—	3.00
MCA					
❑ 52956	Looking for a New Love/Looking for a New Love (Acapella)	1987	—	—	3.00
❑ 52956 [PS]	Looking for a New Love/Looking for a New Love (Acapella)	1987	—	—	3.00
❑ 53081	Still a Thrill/Looking for a New Love	1987	—	—	3.00
❑ 53081 [PS]	Still a Thrill/Looking for a New Love	1987	—	—	3.00
❑ 53162	Don't You Want Me/(Instrumental)	1987	—	—	3.00
❑ 53162 [PS]	Don't You Want Me/(Instrumental)	1987	—	—	3.00
❑ 53235	Some Kind of Lover/(Instrumental)	1988	—	—	3.00
❑ 53235 [PS]	Some Kind of Lover/(Instrumental)	1988	—	—	3.00
❑ 53258	Most of All/(Instrumental)	1988	—	—	3.00
❑ 53258 [PS]	Most of All/(Instrumental)	1988	—	—	3.00
❑ 53484	Real Love/(Instrumental)	1988	—	—	3.00
❑ 53484 [PS]	Real Love/(Instrumental)	1988	—	—	3.00
❑ 53660	Friends/Private Life	1989	—	—	3.00
❑ 53714	Everything/(Instrumental)	1989	—	—	3.00
❑ 53790	Precious Love/(Instrumental)	1990	—	—	3.00

WATSON, CLAYTON

Number	Title (A Side/B Side)	Yr	VG	VG+	NM
LAVENDER					
❑ 2454	Everybody's Boppin'/Tall Skinny Annie	1958	100.00	200.00	400.00

WATSON, JOHNNY "GUITAR"

Number	Title (A Side/B Side)	Yr	VG	VG+	NM
ARVEE					
❑ 5016	Untouchable/Johnny Guitar	1960	6.25	12.50	25.00
—As "Johnny Watson"					
A&M					
❑ 2383	Planet Funk/First Timothy Six	1981	—	2.00	4.00
❑ 2398	That's What Time It Is/First Timothy Six	1982	—	2.00	4.00
CACTUS					
❑ 118	Let's Rock/(B-side unknown)	1959	37.50	75.00	150.00
CLASS					
❑ 246	The Bear/One More Kiss	1959	7.50	15.00	30.00
—As "Johnny Watson"					
DJM					
❑ 1013	I Need It/Since I Met You Baby	1976	—	2.50	5.00
❑ 1019	Superman Lover/We're No Exception	1976	—	2.50	5.00
❑ 1020	Ain't That a Bitch/Won't You Forgive Me Baby	1977	—	3.00	6.00
❑ 1024	A Real Mother For Ya/Nothing Left to Be Desired	1977	—	2.50	5.00
❑ 1029	Lover Jones/Tarzan	1977	—	2.50	5.00
❑ 1034	Love That Will Not Die/A Damn Shame	1978	—	2.50	5.00
❑ 1100	Virginia's Pretty Funky/The Institute	1978	—	2.50	5.00
—As "Watsonian Institute"					
❑ 1101	Gangster of Love/Guitar Disco	1978	—	2.50	5.00
❑ 1106	What the Hell Is This?/Can You Handle It	1979	—	2.50	5.00
❑ 1304	Love Jones/(B-side unknown)	1980	—	2.50	5.00
❑ 1305	Telephone Bill/(B-side unknown)	1980	—	2.50	5.00
FANTASY					
❑ 721	Like I'm Not Your Man/You Bring Love	1974	—	3.00	6.00
❑ 739	I Don't Want to Be a Lone Ranger/You Can Stay But the Noise Must Go	1975	—	3.00	6.00
❑ 752	It's Too Late/Tripping	1975	—	3.00	6.00
FEDERAL					
❑ 12120	Highway 60/No I Can't	1953	37.50	75.00	150.00
❑ 12131	Motor Head Baby/Sad Fool	1953	37.50	75.00	150.00
❑ 12143	I Got Eyes/Walkin' to My Baby	1953	37.50	75.00	150.00
❑ 12157	What's Going On/Thinking	1953	37.50	75.00	150.00
❑ 12175	Half Pint of Whiskey/Space Guitar	1954	62.50	125.00	250.00
❑ 12183	Gettin' Drunk/You Can't Take It With You	1954	50.00	100.00	200.00
—All Federal 45s as "Young John Watson"					
KEEN					
❑ 3-4005	Gangster of Love/One Room Country Shack	1957	7.50	15.00	30.00
❑ 3-4023	Deana Baby/Honey	1957	7.50	15.00	30.00
KENT					
❑ 328	Those Lonely, Lonely Nights/(B-side unknown)	1959	5.00	10.00	20.00

Number	Title (A Side/B Side)	Yr	VG	VG+	NM
KING					
❑ 5536	Posin'/Embraceable You	1961	5.00	10.00	20.00
❑ 5579	Broke and Lonely/Cuttin' In	1961	6.25	12.50	25.00
❑ 5607	The Nearness of You/I Just Want Me Some Love	1962	3.75	7.50	15.00
❑ 5666	What You Do to Me/Sweet Lovin' Mama	1962	3.75	7.50	15.00
❑ 5716	Cold, Cold Heart/That's the Chance You've Got to Take	1963	3.75	7.50	15.00
❑ 5774	Gangster of Love/In the Evening	1963	3.75	7.50	15.00
❑ 5833	I Say, I Love You/You Better Love Me	1964	3.75	7.50	15.00
OKEH					
❑ 7263	Keep On Lovin' You/South Like West	1966	3.00	6.00	12.00
❑ 7270	Hold On, I'm Comin'/Wolfman	1967	3.00	6.00	12.00
RPM					
❑ 423	Hot Little Mama/I Love to Love You	1955	12.50	25.00	50.00
❑ 431	Too Tired/Don't Touch Me	1955	12.50	25.00	50.00
❑ 436	Those Lonely, Lonely Nights/Someone Cares for Me	1955	10.00	20.00	40.00
❑ 447	Oh Baby/Give a Little	1955	10.00	20.00	40.00
❑ 455	Three Hours Past Midnight/Ruben	1956	10.00	20.00	40.00
❑ 471	She Moves Me/Love Me Baby	1956	10.00	20.00	40.00
VALLEY VUE					
❑ 769	Strike On Computers/(B-side unknown)	1984	—	2.50	5.00

WATSON, JOHNNY "GUITAR", AND LARRY WILLIAMS

Also see each artist's individual listings.

Number	Title (A Side/B Side)	Yr	VG	VG+	NM
OKEH					
❑ 7274	Mercy, Mercy, Mercy/A Quitter Never Wins	1967	2.50	5.00	10.00
❑ 7281	Too Late/Two for the Price of One	1967	2.50	5.00	10.00
❑ 7300	Find Yourself Someone to Love/Nobody	1967	6.25	12.50	25.00
—Backed by Kaleidoscope					

WATTS, NOBLE

Number	Title (A Side/B Side)	Yr	VG	VG+	NM
BATON					
❑ 246	Easy Going (Part 1)/Easy Going (Part 2)	1957	6.25	12.50	25.00
❑ 249	The Slop/Midnite Flight	1957	6.25	12.50	25.00
❑ 249	Hard Times (The Slop)/Midnite Flight	1957	3.75	7.50	15.00
❑ 251	Rickey Tick/Blast Off	1958	3.75	7.50	15.00
❑ 254	The Slide/Shakin'	1958	3.75	7.50	15.00
❑ 257	Great Times/The Creep	1958	3.75	7.50	15.00
❑ 266	Flap Jack/Hot Tamales	1959	3.75	7.50	15.00
BRUNSWICK					
❑ 55382	Thingamajig/F.L.A.	1968	2.00	4.00	8.00
CUB					
❑ 9078	The Beaver/Frog Hop	1960	3.00	6.00	12.00
DELUXE					
❑ 6066	Mashing Potatoes/Pig Ears and Rice	1954	7.50	15.00	30.00
ENJOY					
❑ 1008	Jookin'/What Ya Gonna Do	1963	3.00	6.00	12.00
SIR					
❑ 273	Boogie Woogie/Mashed Potatoes	1959	3.75	7.50	15.00

WATTS 103RD STREET RHYTHM BAND, THE

See CHARLES WRIGHT AND THE WATTS 103RD STREET RHYTHM BAND.

WAYLON AND JESSI

Also see WAYLON JENNINGS.

Number	Title (A Side/B Side)	Yr	VG	VG+	NM
RCA					
❑ PB-12176	Storms Never Last/I Ain't the One	1982	—	2.00	4.00
❑ PB-12245	Wild Side of Life/It Wasn't God Who Made Honky Tonk Angels	1982	—	2.00	4.00
RCA VICTOR					
❑ PB-10653	Suspicious Minds/I Ain't the One	1976	—	2.50	5.00
❑ 47-9920	Suspicious Minds/I Ain't the One	1970	—	3.00	6.00
❑ 47-9992	Under Your Spell Again/Bridge Over Troubled Water	1971	—	3.00	6.00

WAYLON AND WILLIE

For convenience's sake, we've listed all the variations of their credits here, including "Willie Nelson and Waylon Jennings." Also see WAYLON JENNINGS; WILLIE NELSON.

Number	Title (A Side/B Side)	Yr	VG	VG+	NM
COLUMBIA					
❑ 04131	Take It to the Limit/Till I Gain Control Again	1983	—	2.00	4.00
❑ 04131 [PS]	Take It to the Limit/Till I Gain Control Again	1983	—	2.50	5.00
EPIC					
❑ 73832	If I Can Find a Clean Shirt/Put Me on a Train Back to Texas	1991	—	—	3.00
❑ 74024	Tryin' to Outrun the Wind/The Makin's of a Song	1991	—	—	3.00
RCA					
❑ PB-11198	Mammas Don't Let Your Babies Grow Up to Be Cowboys/I Can Get Off on You	1978	—	2.00	4.00
❑ GB-11499	Mammas Don't Let Your Babies Grow Up to Be Cowboys/Luckenbach, Texas (Back to the Basics of Love)	1979	—	2.00	4.00
—Gold Standard Series					
❑ GB-11996	Mammas Don't Let Your Babies Grow Up to Be Cowboys/I Can Get Off on You	1980	—	—	3.00
—Gold Standard Series					
❑ PB-13073	Just to Satisfy You/Get Naked With You	1982	—	2.00	4.00
❑ PB-13319	(Sittin' On) The Dock of the Bay/Luckenbach, Texas	1982	—	2.00	4.00
RCA VICTOR					
❑ PB-10529	Good Hearted Woman/Heaven or Hell	1975	—	2.50	5.00

WAYLON AND WILLIE/WAYLON AND JESSI

Number	Title (A Side/B Side)	Yr	VG	VG+	NM
RCA					
❑ GB-10928	Good Hearted Woman/Suspicious Minds	1977	—	—	3.00
—Gold Standard Series					

WAYNE, ALVIS

Number	Title (A Side/B Side)	Yr	VG	VG+	NM
WESTPORT					
❑ 132	Swing Bop Boogie/Sleep, Rock-a-Roll Rock-a-Baby	1956	50.00	100.00	200.00
❑ 138	Don't Mean Maybe Baby/I'd Rather Be with You	1957	37.50	75.00	150.00
—As "Tony Wayne"					
❑ 138	Don't Mean Maybe Baby/I'd Rather Be with You	1958	25.00	50.00	100.00
—As "Alvis Wayne"					

WAYNE, BERNIE

Number	Title (A Side/B Side)	Yr	VG	VG+	NM
20TH CENTURY FOX					
❑ 559	Christmas Is Over/Christmas Is Over	1964	2.00	4.00	8.00
—B-side by the Hushtones					
ABC-PARAMOUNT					
❑ 9664	Vanessa/Piff, Paff, Puff	1956	5.00	10.00	20.00
❑ 9679	You're Kinda Cute/The Night Was Made for Dreamers	1956	5.00	10.00	20.00
❑ 9727	Shalimar/South of Saigon	1956	5.00	10.00	20.00
❑ 9752	Flirtango/Maracaibo	1956	5.00	10.00	20.00
❑ 9815	Leaky Faucet/Theme from "Abner the Baseball"	1957	5.00	10.00	20.00
❑ 9967	The Telegraph Operator and the Chorus Girl/Cool Caballero	1958	5.00	10.00	20.00
HANOVER					
❑ 4528	Now/Chickie	1960	5.00	10.00	20.00
IMPERIAL					
❑ 5575	Soft Shoe Rock/Whistling Pixie	1959	3.75	7.50	15.00
RUST					
❑ 5063	38-24-38/Martinique	1963	3.00	6.00	12.00

WAYNE, BILLY

Number	Title (A Side/B Side)	Yr	VG	VG+	NM
FEDORA					
❑ 1008	Telegram/Heartbreak and Blues	1962	6.25	12.50	25.00
HILLCREST					
❑ 778	I Love My Baby/Walkin' n' Strollin'	1960	200.00	400.00	800.00

WAYNE, CARL, AND THE VIKINGS

Number	Title (A Side/B Side)	Yr	VG	VG+	NM
ABC-PARAMOUNT					
❑ 10752	Shimmy Shammy Jingle/My Girl	1965	3.00	6.00	12.00

WAYNE, THOMAS

Number	Title (A Side/B Side)	Yr	VG	VG+	NM
CAPEHART					
❑ 5009	Tragedy/No More, No More	1961	7.50	15.00	30.00
CHALET					
❑ 1054	No One/You're Tearin' Down My Mind	1969	—	3.00	6.00
FERNWOOD					
❑ 106	You're the One That Done It/This Time	1958	75.00	150.00	300.00
❑ 109	Tragedy/Saturday Date	1959	7.50	15.00	30.00
❑ 111	Eternally/Scandalizing My Name	1959	7.50	15.00	30.00
❑ 113	Gonna Be Waitin'/Just Beyond	1959	7.50	15.00	30.00
❑ 120	Guilty of Love/Pancho Villa	1960	7.50	15.00	30.00
❑ 122	Girl Next Door/Because of You	1960	7.50	15.00	30.00
❑ 128	Tragedy/No More, No More	1961	7.50	15.00	30.00
MERCURY					
❑ 71287	You're the One That Done It/This Time	1958	20.00	40.00	80.00
❑ 71454	You're the One That Done It/This Time	1959	10.00	20.00	40.00
PHILLIPS INT'L.					
❑ 3577	I've Got It Made/The Quiet Look	1962	6.25	12.50	25.00
SANTO					
❑ 9053	Stop the River/Eighth Wonder of the World	1962	6.25	12.50	25.00
❑ 9057	Tragedy/Gonna Be Waiting	1962	6.25	12.50	25.00

WE FIVE

Number	Title (A Side/B Side)	Yr	VG	VG+	NM
A&M					
❑ XMAS 1 [DJ]	My Favorite Things/The 12 Days Of Christmas	1968	3.00	6.00	12.00
—B-side by the Baja Marimba Band					
❑ XMAS 1 [PS]	My Favorite Things/The 12 Days Of Christmas	1968	3.75	7.50	15.00
—B-side by the Baja Marimba Band					
❑ 770	You Were On My Mind/Small World	1965	3.00	6.00	12.00
❑ 784	Let's Get Together/Cast Your Fate to the Wind	1965	2.00	4.00	8.00
❑ 793	You Let a Love Burn Out/Somewhere Beyond the Sea	1966	2.00	4.00	8.00
❑ 800	Somewhere/There Stands the Door	1966	2.00	4.00	8.00
❑ 820	What's Goin' On/The First Time	1966	2.00	4.00	8.00
❑ 894	High Flying Bird/What Do I Do	1967	—	3.00	6.00
❑ 1072	Walk On By/It Really Doesn't Matter	1969	—	3.00	6.00
MGM					
❑ 14618	Seven Day Change/Natural Way	1973	—	2.50	5.00
VAULT					
❑ 964	Never Goin' Back/Here Comes the Sun	1970	—	3.00	6.00
❑ 969	Catch the Wind/Oh, Lonesome Me	1970	—	3.00	6.00
VERVE					
❑ 10716	Bandstand Dancer/Rejoice	1973	—	2.50	5.00

WE TWO

Number	Title (A Side/B Side)	Yr	VG	VG+	NM
ABC					
❑ 10930	Magic Moments/Way Down Deep Inside	1967	6.25	12.50	25.00

WEAVERS, THE

Number	Title (A Side/B Side)	Yr	VG	VG+	NM
DECCA					
❑ 9-284 [PS]	We Wish You a Merry Christmas	1951	3.75	7.50	15.00
—Empty box for 27783, 27817, 27818, 27819					
❑ 27053	Tzena, Tzena, Tzena/Around the World	1950	5.00	10.00	20.00
❑ 27077	Goodnight Irene/Tzena, Tzena, Tzena	1950	3.75	7.50	15.00
❑ 27332	The Roving Kind/(The Wreck of the) John B	1950	3.75	7.50	15.00
❑ 27376	So Long (It's Been Good to Know Yuh)/Lonesome Traveller	1951	3.75	7.50	15.00
❑ 9-27515	On Top of Old Smoky/Across the Wide Missouri	1951	5.00	10.00	20.00
—With Terry Gilkyson					
❑ 27670	Kisses Sweeter Than Wine/When the Saints Go Marching In	1951	3.75	7.50	15.00
❑ 27726	The Frozen Logger/Darling Corey	1951	3.75	7.50	15.00
❑ 27727	I Know Where I'm Going-Hush Little Baby/Suliram	1951	3.75	7.50	15.00
❑ 27728	Drinking Gourd/Easy Rider Blues	1951	3.75	7.50	15.00

Number	Title (A Side/B Side)	Yr	VG	VG+	NM
❑ 27783	We Wish You a Merry Christmas/One for the Little Bitty Baby	1951	3.75	7.50	15.00
—Sides 1 and 2 of "Album No. 9-284"					
❑ 27817	The Seven Blessings of Mary/The Twelve Days of Christmas	1951	3.75	7.50	15.00
—Sides 3 and 4 of "Album No. 9-284"					
❑ 27818	Go Tell It on the Mountain/Poor Little Jesus	1951	3.75	7.50	15.00
—Sides 5 and 6 of "Album No. 9-284"					
❑ 27819	Lulloo Lullay-It's Almost Day/Burgundian Carol-God Rest Ye Merry Gentlemen	1951	3.75	7.50	15.00
—Sides 7 and 8 of "Album No. 9-284"					
❑ 27928	Wimoweh/Old Paint	1952	3.75	7.50	15.00
❑ 28054	Around the Corner (Beneath the Berry Tree)/The Gandy Dancer's Ball	1952	3.75	7.50	15.00
❑ 28228	Run Home to Ma-Ma/Hard Ain't It Hard	1952	3.75	7.50	15.00
❑ 28434	Clementine/True Love	1952	3.75	7.50	15.00
❑ 28542	Down in the Valley/The Bay of Mexico	1953	3.75	7.50	15.00
❑ 28637	Taking It Easy/Benoni	1953	3.75	7.50	15.00
❑ 28919	Rock Island Shuffle/Sylvia	1953	3.75	7.50	15.00
VANGUARD					
❑ 35001	Done Laid Around/Take This Letter	196?	3.00	6.00	12.00
❑ 35005	Aunt Rhodie/Bury Me Beneath the Willows	196?	3.00	6.00	12.00
❑ 35009	This Land Is Your Land/Aweigh, Santy Ano	196?	3.00	6.00	12.00
❑ 35010	On My Journey/The Sinking of the Reuben James	196?	3.00	6.00	12.00
❑ 35014	The Keeper/Twelve Gates to the City	196?	3.00	6.00	12.00
❑ 35015	Fight On/Rally Round the Flag	196?	3.00	6.00	12.00
7-Inch Extended Plays					
DECCA					
❑ ED 2015	*Goodnight Irene/Tzena, Tzena, Tzena/On Top of Old Smoky/So Long (It's Been Good to Know Yuh)	195?	12.50	25.00	50.00
❑ ED 2015 [PS]	The Weavers, Vol. 1	195?	12.50	25.00	50.00

WEBB, BOOGIE BILL

Number	Title (A Side/B Side)	Yr	VG	VG+	NM
IMPERIAL					
❑ 5257	Bad Dog/I Ain't For It	1953	62.50	125.00	250.00

WEBB, JACK

Number	Title (A Side/B Side)	Yr	VG	VG+	NM
WARNER BROS.					
❑ 5003	Try a Little Tenderness/You'd Never Know the Old Place Now	1958	5.00	10.00	20.00
7-Inch Extended Plays					
RCA VICTOR					
❑ 547-0342	The Christmas Story (Part 1)/The Christmas Story (Part 4)	1953	7.50	15.00	30.00
❑ 547-0343	The Christmas Story (Part 2)/The Christmas Story (Part 3)	1953	7.50	15.00	30.00
❑ EPB 3199 [PS]	The Christmas Story	1953	10.00	20.00	40.00
—Cover for 2-EP set					

WEBS, THE (1)

R&B group.

Number	Title (A Side/B Side)	Yr	VG	VG+	NM
ATLANTIC					
❑ 2415	Let's Party/Keep Your Love Strong	1967	3.00	6.00	12.00
MGM					
❑ 13602	People Sure Act Funny/You Pretty Fool	1966	3.00	6.00	12.00
POPSIDE					
❑ 4593	This Thing Called Love/Tomorrow	1967	2.50	5.00	10.00
❑ 4595	Give In/It's So Hard to Break a Habit	1968	2.50	5.00	10.00
VERVE					
❑ 10610	We Belong Together/I Want You Back	1968	2.50	5.00	10.00

WEBS, THE (2)

BOBBY GOLDSBORO was in this group.

Number	Title (A Side/B Side)	Yr	VG	VG+	NM
HEART					
❑ 333	Blue Skies/Lost (Cricket in My Ear)	1962	10.00	20.00	40.00
LITE					
❑ 9004	Blue Skies/Lost (Cricket in My Ear)	1962	5.00	10.00	20.00

WEBTONES, THE

Number	Title (A Side/B Side)	Yr	VG	VG+	NM
MGM					
❑ 12724	My Lost Love/Walk, Talk and Kiss	1958	6.25	12.50	25.00

WEIR, BOB

Also see THE GRATEFUL DEAD.

Number	Title (A Side/B Side)	Yr	VG	VG+	NM
ARISTA					
❑ 0315	Bombs Away/Easy to Slip	1978	—	3.00	6.00
❑ 0336	I'll Be Doggone/Shade of Grey	1978	3.00	6.00	12.00
—May be promo only					
WARNER BROS.					
❑ 7611	One More Saturday Night/Cassidy	1972	3.00	6.00	12.00

WELCH, BOB

Also see FLEETWOOD MAC; PARIS.

Number	Title (A Side/B Side)	Yr	VG	VG+	NM
CAPITOL					
❑ 4479	Sentimental Lady/Hot Love, Cold World	1977	—	2.00	4.00
❑ 4543	Ebony Eyes/Outskirts	1978	—	2.00	4.00
❑ 4588	Hot Love, Cold World/Danchiva	1978	—	2.00	4.00
❑ 4588 [PS]	Hot Love, Cold World/Danchiva	1978	—	3.00	6.00
❑ 4685	Precious Love/Something Strong	1979	—	2.00	4.00
❑ 4719	Church/Here Comes the Night	1979	—	2.00	4.00
❑ 4719 [PS]	Church/Here Comes the Night	1979	—	2.50	5.00
❑ 4745	Oh Jenny/Three Hearts	1979	—	2.00	4.00
❑ 4790	Rebel Rouser/Spanish Dancers	1979	—	2.00	4.00
❑ 4833	Oneonone/Don't Let Me Fall	1980	—	2.00	4.00
❑ 4926	Don't Rush the Good Things/Reason	1980	—	2.00	4.00
❑ 4954	Girl Can't Stop/Those Days Are Gone	1980	—	2.00	4.00
RCA					
❑ PB-12356	Imaginary Fool/Two to Do	1981	—	2.00	4.00
❑ PB-13074	Remember/You Can't Do That	1982	—	2.00	4.00
❑ PB-13569	Fever/Can't Hold Your Love Back	1983	—	2.00	4.00
❑ PB-13669	I'll Dance Alone/Stay	1983	—	2.00	4.00

WELCH, LENNY

Number	Title (A Side/B Side)	Yr	VG	VG+	NM
ATCO					
❑ 6894	A Sunday Kind of Love/I Wish You Could Know Me	1972	—	2.50	5.00
❑ 6915	Goodnight My Love/Fancy Meeting You Here Baby	1973	—	2.50	5.00
BIG TREE					
❑ 16107	Six Million Dollar Woman/(B-side unknown)	1977	—	2.50	5.00
CADENCE					
❑ 1373	You Don't Know Me/I Need Someone	1959	2.50	5.00	10.00
❑ 1386	Darlin'/Three Handed Woman	1960	2.50	5.00	10.00
❑ 1394	I'd Like to Know/Darlin'	1960	2.50	5.00	10.00
❑ 1399	Changa Rock/Boogie Cha Cha	1961	2.50	5.00	10.00
❑ 1416	It's Just Not That Easy/Mama Don't You Hit That Boy	1962	2.50	5.00	10.00
❑ 1422	Ebb Tide/Congratulations Baby	1962	5.00	10.00	20.00
—The A-side was the hit, but this is sought after for its group sound on the B-side					
❑ 1428	A Taste of Honey/The Old Cathedral	1962	2.50	5.00	10.00
❑ 1439	Since I Fell for You/Are You Sincere	1963	3.00	6.00	12.00
❑ 1446	If You See My Love/Father Sebastian	1964	2.50	5.00	10.00
COLUMBIA					
❑ 44007	Since I Fell for You/A Taste of Honey	1967	2.00	4.00	8.00
COMMONWEALTH UNITED					
❑ 3004	Breaking Up Is Hard to Do/Get Mommy to Come Back Home	1969	—	3.00	6.00
❑ 3011	To Be Loved and Glory of Love/My Heart Won't Let Me	1970	—	3.00	6.00
DECCA					
❑ 30637	Rocket to the Moon/My One Sincere	1958	3.00	6.00	12.00
❑ 30829	Blessing of Love/Last Star of the Evening	1959	3.00	6.00	12.00
KAPP					
❑ 648	I'm Dreaming Again/My Fool of a Heart	1965	2.00	4.00	8.00
❑ 662	Darling Take Me Back/Time After Time	1965	2.00	4.00	8.00
❑ 689	Two Different Worlds/I'll Be There	1965	2.00	4.00	8.00
❑ 712	Run to My Lovin' Arms/Coronet Blue	1965	2.00	4.00	8.00
❑ 740	Rags to Riches/I Want to Worry (About Me)	1966	2.00	4.00	8.00
❑ 751	What Now My Love/Gonna Hear from Me	1966	2.00	4.00	8.00
❑ 761	Please Help Me I'm Falling/Just One Smile	1966	2.00	4.00	8.00
❑ 778	If You Love Me, Really Love Me/Once Before I Die	1966	2.00	4.00	8.00
❑ 808	Until the Real Thing Comes Along/A Right to Cry	1967	2.00	4.00	8.00
❑ 827	Let's Start All Over Again/Love Don't Live Here Anymore	1967	2.00	4.00	8.00
❑ 854	I'm Over You/Coronet Blue	1967	2.00	4.00	8.00
MAINSTREAM					
❑ 5545	Since I Don't Have You/Right in the Next Room	1973	—	2.50	5.00
❑ 5554	Eyewitness News/I Need You More	1973	—	2.50	5.00
❑ 5560	A Hundred Pounds of Pain/The Iguana	1974	—	2.50	5.00
❑ 5561	When There's No Such Thing As Love/Minx	1974	—	2.50	5.00
MERCURY					
❑ 72777	Darling Stay with Me/Wait a While Longer	1968	2.00	4.00	8.00
❑ 72811	Tennessee Waltz/He Who Loves	1968	2.00	4.00	8.00
❑ 72866	Halfway to Your Arms/You Can't Run Away	1968	2.00	4.00	8.00

WELLINGTON, RUSTY

Number	Title (A Side/B Side)	Yr	VG	VG+	NM
ARCADE					
❑ 116	Dog-Gone It Baby, I'm in Love/Every Precious Memory	1953	10.00	20.00	40.00
❑ 124	I Want a Little Lovin'/Slowly But Surely	1954	10.00	20.00	40.00
❑ 140	Blues from Tennessee/Jump Jump Honey	1955	10.00	20.00	40.00
❑ 144	The Convict and the Rose/I Ain't A-Movin' On No More	1957	10.00	20.00	40.00
❑ 184	The Allegash/I've Been Away from You So Long	1965	3.75	7.50	15.00
❑ 185	Soft Shoulders/The Old Man	1966	3.75	7.50	15.00
❑ 191	Lonely Lips/Isle of Wild Roses	1967	3.75	7.50	15.00
MGM					
❑ 12581	Rocking Chair on the Moon/I Lost My Someone	1957	75.00	150.00	300.00

WELLS, BILLY, AND THE CRESCENTS

Number	Title (A Side/B Side)	Yr	VG	VG+	NM
RESERVE					
❑ 105	I Love Only You/Julie	1956	150.00	300.00	600.00

WELLS, CORY

Also see THREE DOG NIGHT.

Number	Title (A Side/B Side)	Yr	VG	VG+	NM
A&M					
❑ 2013	Starlight/I Know You're Willin' Darlin'	1978	—	2.00	4.00
❑ 2035	Midnight Lady (Riding in the Shadows)/I Know You're Willin' Darlin'	1978	—	2.00	4.00
❑ 2060	Let Tomorrow Be/You Can Count on Me	1978	—	2.00	4.00

WELLS, DONNIE

Number	Title (A Side/B Side)	Yr	VG	VG+	NM
SCEPTER					
❑ 12119	Real Love/You've Got My Love	1965	6.25	12.50	25.00

WELLS, KITTY

Number	Title (A Side/B Side)	Yr	VG	VG+	NM
CAPRICORN					
❑ 0208	Too Much Love Between Us/What About You	1974	—	3.00	6.00
❑ 0226	I've Been Loving You Too Long/Too Stubborn	1975	—	3.00	6.00
❑ 0240	Anybody Out There Wanna Be a Daddy/Somewhere Down the Road (There's a Country Girl)	1975	—	3.00	6.00
❑ 0264	Mary Hartman, Mary Hartman/Nickel Candy Bar	1976	—	3.00	6.00
DECCA					
❑ 9-28232	It Wasn't God Who Made Honky Tonk Angels/I Don't Want Your Money, I Want Your Time	1952	7.50	15.00	30.00
❑ 9-28432	I Heard the Juke Box Playing/A Wedding Ring Ago	1952	6.25	12.50	25.00
❑ 9-28525	Divided by Two/The Things I Might Have Been	1953	6.25	12.50	25.00
❑ 9-28578	Paying for That Back Street Affair/Crying Steel Guitar Waltz	1953	6.25	12.50	25.00
❑ 9-28666	You Said You Could Do Without Me/Honky Tonk Waltz	1953	6.25	12.50	25.00

Number	Title (A Side/B Side)	Yr	VG	VG+	NM
❑ 9-28753	I Don't Claim to Be an Angel/The Life They Live in Songs	1953	6.25	12.50	25.00
❑ 9-28797	Hey Joe/My Cold Cold Heart Is Melted Now	1953	6.25	12.50	25.00
❑ 9-28931	Cheatin's a Sin/I Gave My Wedding Dress Away	1953	6.25	12.50	25.00
❑ 9-29023	Release Me/After Dark	1954	6.25	12.50	25.00
❑ 9-29134	You're Not Easy to Forget/He's Married to Me	1954	6.25	12.50	25.00
❑ 9-29313	Thou Shalt Not Steal/I Hope My Divorce Is Never Granted	1954	6.25	12.50	25.00
❑ 9-29419	Makin' Believe/Whose Shoulder Will You Cry On	1955	5.00	10.00	20.00
❑ 9-29577	There's Poison in Your Heart/I'm in Love with You	1955	5.00	10.00	20.00
❑ 9-29728	Lonely Side of Town/I've Kissed You My Last Time	1955	5.00	10.00	20.00
❑ 9-29823	How Far Is Heaven/Dust on the Bible	1956	5.00	10.00	20.00
—A-side with Carol Sue					
❑ 9-29956	Searching (For Someone Like You)/I'd Rather Stay Home	1956	5.00	10.00	20.00
❑ 9-30094	Repenting/I'm Counting on You	1956	5.00	10.00	20.00
❑ 9-30288	Three Ways (To Love You)/A Change of Heart	1957	3.75	7.50	15.00
❑ 9-30415	(I'll Always Be Your) Fraulein/What I Believe	1957	3.75	7.50	15.00
❑ 9-30551	I Can't Stop Loving You/She's No Angel	1958	3.75	7.50	15.00
❑ 9-30662	Jealousy/I Can't Help Wondering	1958	3.75	7.50	15.00
❑ 9-30736	Touch and Go Heart/He's Lost His Love for Me	1958	3.75	7.50	15.00
❑ 9-30804	Mommy for a Day/All the Time	1959	3.75	7.50	15.00
❑ 9-30890	Your Wild Life's Gonna Get You Down/You'll Never Be Mine Again	1959	3.75	7.50	15.00
❑ 9-30987	Amigo's Guitar/Lonely Is a Word	1959	3.75	7.50	15.00
❑ 31065	Left to Right/Memory of Love	1960	3.75	7.50	15.00
❑ 31123	Carmel by the Sea/The Man I Used to Know	1960	3.00	6.00	12.00
❑ 31192	The Other Cheek/Fickle Fun	1961	3.00	6.00	12.00
❑ 31246	Heartbreak U.S.A./There Must Be Another Way to Live	1961	3.00	6.00	12.00
❑ 31313	Day Into Night/Our Mansion Is a Prison Now	1961	3.00	6.00	12.00
❑ 31349	Unloved Unwanted/Au Revoir (Goodbye)	1962	3.00	6.00	12.00
❑ 31392	Will Your Lawyer Talk to God/The Big Let Down	1962	3.00	6.00	12.00
❑ 31422	We Missed You/Wicked World	1962	3.00	6.00	12.00
❑ 31441	Christmas Ain't Like Christmas Anymore/Dancer (With the Light Upon His Tail)	1962	3.75	7.50	15.00
❑ 31457	Cold and Lonely (Is the Forecast for Tonight)/Is It Asking Too Much	1963	2.50	5.00	10.00
❑ 31501	I Gave My Wedding Dress Away/A Heartache for a Keepsake	1963	2.50	5.00	10.00
❑ 31580	This White Circle on My Finger/(I Didn't Have to) Break Up Someone's Home	1964	2.50	5.00	10.00
❑ 31622	Password/I've Thought of Leaving You	1964	2.50	5.00	10.00
❑ 31705	I'll Repossess My Heart/Kill Him with Kindness	1964	2.50	5.00	10.00
❑ 31749	You Don't Hear/Six Lonely Hours	1965	2.50	5.00	10.00
❑ 31817	Meanwhile, Down at Joe's/Leavin' Town Tonight	1965	2.50	5.00	10.00
❑ 31881	A Woman Half My Age/When Your Little High Horse Runs Down	1966	2.50	5.00	10.00
❑ 31957	It's All Over (But the Crying)/You Left Your Mark on Me	1966	2.50	5.00	10.00
❑ 32024	Only Me and My Hairdresser Know/A Woman Never Forgets	1966	2.50	5.00	10.00
❑ 32088	Love Makes the World Go Around/I'm Just Not Smart	1967	2.00	4.00	8.00
❑ 32163	Queen of Honky Tonk Street/Wasting My Time	1967	2.00	4.00	8.00
❑ 32247	My Big Truck Drivin' Man/You Want Her Not Me	1967	2.00	4.00	8.00
❑ 32343	Gypsy King/When Hearts Grow Hard and Cold	1968	2.00	4.00	8.00
❑ 32389	Happiness Hill/You're No Angel Yourself	1968	2.00	4.00	8.00
❑ 32455	Guilty Street/Shape Up or Get Out	1969	2.00	4.00	8.00
❑ 32455 [PS]	Guilty Street/Shape Up or Get Out	1969	5.00	10.00	20.00
—Her only known Decca picture sleeve					
❑ 32535	Just a Cheap Affair/Don't Call Me Your Darling	1969	2.00	4.00	8.00
❑ 32629	I Don't See What I Say/Gonna Find Me a Bluebird	1970	2.00	4.00	8.00
❑ 32700	Your Love Is the Way/It's Written All Over Your Face	1970	2.00	4.00	8.00
❑ 32795	They're Stepping All Over My Heart/Your Old Love Letters	1971	2.00	4.00	8.00
❑ 32840	Pledging My Love/Thank You for Loving Me	1971	2.00	4.00	8.00
❑ 32889	I'm the Wreck of Number Two/Reno Airport Nashville Plane	1971	2.00	4.00	8.00
❑ 32931	Sincerely/J.J. Sneed	1972	2.00	4.00	8.00
❑ 32976	A Bridge I Just Can't Burn/Love Is the Answer	1972	2.00	4.00	8.00
❑ 33016	I've Got Yesterday/Less Than a Lady	1972	2.00	4.00	8.00
❑ 33047	Full Grown Man/Every Step of the Way	1973	2.00	4.00	8.00
❑ 7-34185 [S]	Dasher (With the Light Upon His Tail)/C-H-R-I-S-T-M-A-S	1962	5.00	10.00	20.00
—Small hole, plays at 33 1/3 rpm					
❑ 7-34186 [S]	Santa's On His Way/(B-side unknown)	1962	5.00	10.00	20.00
—Small hole, plays at 33 1/3 rpm					
❑ 7-34187 [S]	titles unknown	1962	5.00	10.00	20.00
—Small hole, plays at 33 1/3 rpm					
❑ 7-34188 [S]	Rudolph the Red-Nosed Reindeer/Blue Christmas	1962	5.00	10.00	20.00
—Small hole, plays at 33 1/3 rpm					
❑ 7-34189 [S]	Ole Kris Kringle/(B-side unknown)	1962	5.00	10.00	20.00
—Small hole, plays at 33 1/3 rpm					
❑ 9-46409	Precious Memories/Gloryland March	1952	10.00	20.00	40.00
MCA					
❑ 40057	Easily Persuaded/It Doesn't Say	1973	—	3.00	6.00
❑ 40123	If I Was a Bottle/Mississippi Missus	1973	—	3.00	6.00
RCA VICTOR					
❑ 47-5686	Kiss Me/Why Fall So Slowly	1954	6.25	12.50	25.00
❑ 48-0084	Love or Hate/Don't Wait for the Last Minute to Pray	1949	15.00	30.00	60.00
—Originals on green vinyl					
❑ 48-0333	Make Up Your Mind/All Smiles Tonight	1950	12.50	25.00	50.00
—Originals on green vinyl					
❑ 48-0384	How Far Is Heaven/My Mother	1950	12.50	25.00	50.00
—Originals on green vinyl					
RUBOCA					
❑ 122	Thank You for the Roses/Loving You Was All I Ever Needed	1979	2.00	4.00	8.00
❑ 123	Old Milwaukee Talking/I Never Told Him I Loved Him	1979	2.00	4.00	8.00
❑ 124	I Can't Help It/I'll Hold You in My Heart	1980	2.00	4.00	8.00

7-Inch Extended Plays

DECCA

Number	Title (A Side/B Side)	Yr	VG	VG+	NM
❑ ED 2163	(contents unknown)	1955	6.25	12.50	25.00
❑ ED 2163 [PS]	Kitty Wells Sings	1955	6.25	12.50	25.00
❑ ED 2361	(contents unknown)	1956	5.00	10.00	20.00
❑ ED 2361 [PS]	Kitty Wells, Vol. 1	1956	5.00	10.00	20.00
❑ ED 2362	(contents unknown)	1956	5.00	10.00	20.00
❑ ED 2362 [PS]	Kitty Wells, Vol. 2	1956	5.00	10.00	20.00
❑ ED 2363	(contents unknown)	1956	5.00	10.00	20.00
❑ ED 2363 [PS]	Kitty Wells, Vol. 3	1956	5.00	10.00	20.00
❑ ED 2518	*Winner of Your Heart/Right or Wrong/Pace That Kills/Dancing with a Stranger	1957	5.00	10.00	20.00
❑ ED 2518 [PS]	Winner of Your Heart, Vol. 1	1957	5.00	10.00	20.00
❑ ED 2519	*Each Day/She's No Angel/Broken Marriage Vows/Change of Heart	1957	5.00	10.00	20.00
❑ ED 2519 [PS]	Winner of Your Heart, Vol. 2 (Change of Heart)	1957	5.00	10.00	20.00
❑ ED 2520	*Mansion on the Hill/Standing Room Only/I Guess I'll Go On Dreaming/Stubborn Heart	1957	5.00	10.00	20.00
❑ ED 2520 [PS]	Winner of Your Heart, Vol. 3 (Stubborn Heart)	1957	5.00	10.00	20.00
❑ ED 2584	That's Me Without You/Waltz of the Angels//Lonely Street/Love Me to Pieces	1958	5.00	10.00	20.00
❑ ED 2584 [PS]	Lonely Street	1958	5.00	10.00	20.00
❑ ED 2646 [M]	*Dust on the Bible/I Dreamed I Searched Heaven for You/Lonesome Valley/My Loved Ones Are Waiting for Me	1959	5.00	10.00	20.00
❑ ED 2646 [PS]	Dust on the Bible	1959	5.00	10.00	20.00
❑ ED 7-2646 [PS]	Dust on the Bible	1959	7.50	15.00	30.00
❑ ED 7-2646 [S]	*Dust on the Bible/I Dreamed I Searched Heaven for You/Lonesome Valley/My Loved Ones Are Waiting for Me	1959	7.50	15.00	30.00
❑ ED 2677	*Sugartime/Dark Moon/Bonaparte's Retreat/When the Moon Comes Over the Mountain	1960	5.00	10.00	20.00
❑ ED 2677 [PS]	Kitty's Choice	1960	5.00	10.00	20.00
❑ ED 2684	*Seasons of My Heart/Lonely Is a Word/Send Me the Pillow You Dream On/Amigo's Guitar	1960	5.00	10.00	20.00
❑ ED 2684 [PS]	Seasons of My Heart	1960	5.00	10.00	20.00
❑ ED 2692	(contents unknown)	1961	5.00	10.00	20.00
❑ ED 2692 [PS]	Kitty Wells	1961	5.00	10.00	20.00
❑ ED 2699	*Heartbreak U.S.A./Heart to Heart Talk/This Old Heart/Cold, Cold Heart	1961	5.00	10.00	20.00
❑ ED 2699 [PS]	Heartbreak U.S.A.	1961	5.00	10.00	20.00
❑ ED 2710	(contents unknown)	1962	5.00	10.00	20.00
❑ ED 2710 [PS]	Kitty Wells	1962	5.00	10.00	20.00
❑ ED 2717	(contents unknown)	1962	5.00	10.00	20.00
❑ ED 2717 [PS]	Kitty Wells	1962	5.00	10.00	20.00
❑ ED 2732	*Will Your Lawyer Talk to God/The Big Let Down/I'm Couting on You/I've Got a New Heartache	1962	5.00	10.00	20.00
❑ ED 2732 [PS]	Kitty Wells	1962	5.00	10.00	20.00
❑ ED 2737	*Wicked World/We Missed You/Your Old Love Letters/Slowly	1963	5.00	10.00	20.00
❑ ED 2737 [PS]	Wicked World	1963	5.00	10.00	20.00
❑ ED 2749	*I Can't Stop Loving You/All the Time/Your Wild Life's Gonna Get You Down/Hey Joe	1963	5.00	10.00	20.00
❑ ED 2749 [PS]	All the Time	1963	5.00	10.00	20.00
❑ ED 2763	*I Gave My Wedding Dress Away/A Heartache for a Keepsake/Cold and Lonely/Is It Asking Too Much	1963	5.00	10.00	20.00
❑ ED 2763 [PS]	Kitty Wells	1963	5.00	10.00	20.00
❑ ED 2777	*Talk Back Trembling Lips/Busted/Ring of Fire/Guilty	1964	6.25	12.50	25.00
❑ ED 2777 [PS]	Talk Back Trembling Lips	1964	6.25	12.50	25.00
❑ ED 2780	*Password/B.J. the D.J./Old Records/As Usual	1964	6.25	12.50	25.00
❑ ED 2780 [PS]	Password	1964	7.50	15.00	30.00
❑ ED 2781	(contents unknown)	1965	7.50	15.00	30.00
❑ ED 2781 [PS]	This White Circle	1965	7.50	15.00	30.00
❑ ED 2804	(contents unknown)	1965	7.50	15.00	30.00
❑ ED 2804 [PS]	Burning Memories	1965	7.50	15.00	30.00

WELLS, KITTY, AND ROY DRUSKY

DECCA

Number	Title (A Side/B Side)	Yr	VG	VG+	NM
❑ 31164	I Can't Tell My Heart That/When Do You Love Me	1960	3.00	6.00	12.00
❑ 31523	Another Chance to Fall in Love/My World's Losing You	1963	2.50	5.00	10.00

WELLS, KITTY, AND RED FOLEY

DECCA

Number	Title (A Side/B Side)	Yr	VG	VG+	NM
❑ 9-29065	One by One/I'm a Stranger in My Home	1954	6.25	12.50	25.00
❑ 9-29228	Skinnie Minnie (Fishtart)/Thank You for Calling	1954	6.25	12.50	25.00
❑ 9-29390	As Long As I Live/Make Believe ('Til We Can Make It Come True)	1955	5.00	10.00	20.00
❑ 9-29740	You and Me/No One But You	1955	5.00	10.00	20.00
❑ 32126	Happiness Means You/Hello Number One	1967	2.00	4.00	8.00
❑ 32223	Living as Strangers/Loved and Wanted	1967	2.00	4.00	8.00
❑ 32427	Have I Told You Lately That I Love You?/We Need One More Chance	1968	2.00	4.00	8.00

7-Inch Extended Plays

DECCA

Number	Title (A Side/B Side)	Yr	VG	VG+	NM
❑ ED 2667	(contents unknown)	1959	6.25	12.50	25.00
❑ ED 2667 [PS]	Kitty Wells and Red Foley	1959	6.25	12.50	25.00

WELLS, KITTY, AND WEBB PIERCE

Also see each artist's individual listings.

DECCA

Number	Title (A Side/B Side)	Yr	VG	VG+	NM
❑ 9-30183	Oh So Many Years/Can You Find It in Your Heart	1957	3.75	7.50	15.00
❑ 9-30489	One Week Later/When I'm with You	1957	3.75	7.50	15.00
❑ 31663	Finally/He Made You for Me	1964	2.50	5.00	10.00

7-Inch Extended Plays

DECCA

Number	Title (A Side/B Side)	Yr	VG	VG+	NM
❑ ED 2666	*Oh So Many Years/One Week Later/When I'm With You/Can You FInd It in Your Heart	1959	6.25	12.50	25.00
❑ ED 2666 [PS]	Kitty Wells and Webb Pierce	1959	6.25	12.50	25.00

WELLS, KITTY, AND JOHNNY WRIGHT

DECCA

Number	Title (A Side/B Side)	Yr	VG	VG+	NM
❑ 32294	We'll Stick Together/Heartbreak Waltz	1968	2.00	4.00	8.00
❑ 32604	There Won't Be Any Tree This Christmas/White Christmas	1969	2.00	4.00	8.00

WELLS, MARY

Number	Title (A Side/B Side)	Yr	VG	VG+	NM
20TH CENTURY FOX					
❑ 544	Ain't It the Truth/Stop Takin' Me for Granted	1964	3.75	7.50	15.00
❑ 555	Use Your Head/Everlovin' Boy	1965	3.75	7.50	15.00
❑ 570	Never, Never Leave Me?Why Don't You Let Yourself Go	1965	3.75	7.50	15.00
❑ 590	He's a Lover/I'm Learnin'	1965	3.75	7.50	15.00
❑ 590 [PS]	He's a Lover/I'm Learnin'	1965	7.50	15.00	30.00
❑ 6606	Me Without You/I'm Sorry	1965	3.75	7.50	15.00
❑ 6619	I Should Have Known Better/Please Please Me	1965	5.00	10.00	20.00
ATCO					
❑ 6392	Dear Lover/Can't You See	1965	3.00	6.00	12.00
❑ 6423	Keep Me in Suspense/Such a Sweet Thing	1966	3.00	6.00	12.00
❑ 6436	Fancy Free/Me and My Baby	1966	3.00	6.00	12.00
❑ 6469	Coming Home/Hey You Set My Soul on Fire	1967	3.00	6.00	12.00
EPIC					
❑ 02664	Gigolo/I'm Changing My Ways	1982	—	2.00	4.00
❑ 02855	These Arms/Spend the Night With Me	1982	—	2.00	4.00
JUBILEE					
❑ 5621	The Doctor/Two Lovers' History	1968	3.75	7.50	15.00
❑ 5629	Can't Get Away From Your Love/A Woman in Love	1968	3.75	7.50	15.00
❑ 5639	Don't Look Back/500 Miles	1968	3.75	7.50	15.00
❑ 5676	Mind Reader/Never Give a Man the World	1969	3.00	6.00	12.00
❑ 5684	Dig the Way I Feel/Love Shooting Bandit	1969	3.00	6.00	12.00
❑ 5695	Sweet Love/It Must Be	1970	3.00	6.00	12.00
❑ 5718	Mr. Tough/Never Give a Man the World	1971	3.00	6.00	12.00
MOTOWN					
❑ 1003	Bye Bye Baby/Please Forgive Me	1960	12.50	25.00	50.00
❑ 1011	I Don't Want to Take a Chance/I'm Sorry	1961	7.50	15.00	30.00
—Pink "lines" label					
❑ 1011	I Don't Want to Take a Chance/I'm Sorry	1961	5.00	10.00	20.00
—Blue "map" label					
❑ 1011 [PS]	I Don't Want to Take a Chance/I'm Sorry	1961	20.00	40.00	80.00
❑ 1016	Strange Love/Come to Me	1961	5.00	10.00	20.00
❑ 1016 [PS]	Strange Love/Come to Me	1961	20.00	40.00	80.00
❑ 1024	The One Who Really Loves You/I'm Gonna Stay	1962	5.00	10.00	20.00
❑ 1024 [PS]	The One Who Really Loves You/I'm Gonna Stay	1962	20.00	40.00	80.00
❑ 1032	You Beat Me to the Punch/Old Love (Let's Try It Again)	1962	5.00	10.00	20.00
❑ 1032 [PS]	You Beat Me to the Punch/Old Love (Let's Try It Again)	1962	30.00	60.00	120.00
❑ 1035	Two Lovers/Operator	1962	5.00	10.00	20.00
❑ 1039	Laughing Boy/Two Wrongs Don't Make a Right	1963	5.00	10.00	20.00
❑ 1042	Your Old Stand By/What Love Has Joined Together	1963	5.00	10.00	20.00
❑ 1048	You Lost the Sweetest Boy/What's Easy for Two Is So Hard for One	1963	5.00	10.00	20.00
❑ 1056	My Guy/Oh Little Boy (What Did You Do to Me)	1964	5.00	10.00	20.00
❑ 1061	When I'm Gone/Guarantee for a Lifetime	1964	150.00	300.00	600.00
❑ 1065	Whisper You Love Me/I'll Be Available	1964	—	—	—
—Unreleased?					
REPRISE					
❑ 1031	I Found What I Wanted/I See a Future in You	1971	2.50	5.00	10.00
❑ 1308	If You Can't Give Her Love (Give Her Up)/Cancel My Subscription	1974	2.50	5.00	10.00

WELLS, MIKE

Number	Title (A Side/B Side)	Yr	VG	VG+	NM
PLAYBOY					
❑ 6029	Sing a Love Song, Porter Wagoner/Detour	1975	—	2.50	5.00
❑ 6042	Shoe-Top Clover/Have You Ever Had an Angel (Love the Devil Out of You)	1975	—	2.50	5.00
❑ 6061	Wild World/The Lady and the Tramp	1976	—	2.50	5.00

WENDY AND LISA

Also see THE MUSICAL CAST OF TOYS.

Number	Title (A Side/B Side)	Yr	VG	VG+	NM
COLUMBIA					
❑ 07243	Waterfall/The Life	1987	—	—	3.00
❑ 07243 [PS]	Waterfall/The Life	1987	—	—	3.00
❑ 07661	Honeymoon Express/Light	1987	—	—	3.00
❑ 07661 [PS]	Honeymoon Express/Light	1987	—	—	3.00
❑ 68557	Are You My Baby/Happy Birthday	1989	—	—	3.00

WESLEY, FRED

Also includes the J.B.'s.

Number	Title (A Side/B Side)	Yr	VG	VG+	NM
ATLANTIC					
❑ 3408	Up for the Down Stroke/When In Doubt	1977	—	2.50	5.00
KING					
❑ 6317	The Grunt (Part 1)/The Grunt (Part 2)	1970	2.50	5.00	10.00
—As "The J.B.'s"					
❑ 6333	These Are the J.B.'s (Part 1)/These Are the J.B.'s (Part 2)	1970	2.50	5.00	10.00
—As "The J.B.'s"					
PEOPLE					
❑ 602	Gimme Some More/The Rabbit Got the Gun	1972	—	3.00	6.00
—As "The J.B.'s"					
❑ 607	Pass the Peas/Hot Pants Road	1972	—	3.00	6.00
—As "The J.B.'s"					
❑ 610	Givin' Up Food for Funk (Part 1)/Givin' Up Food for Funk (Part 2)	1972	—	3.00	6.00
—As "The J.B.'s"					
❑ 614	Backstabbers/J.B. Shout	1972	—	3.00	6.00
❑ 616	If You Don't Get It the First Time/You Can Have Her Boogie	1973	—	3.00	6.00
❑ 617	Alone Again (Naturally)/Watermelon Man	1973	—	3.00	6.00
❑ 619	Sportin' Life/Dirty Harri	1973	—	3.00	6.00
❑ 621	Doing It to Death/Everybody Got Soul	1973	—	3.00	6.00
❑ 627	If You Don't Get It the First Time, Back Up and Try It Again, Party/You Can Have Watergate, Just Give Me Some Bucks and I'll Be Straight	1973	—	3.00	6.00
❑ 632	Same Beat - Part 1/Same Beat - Part 2	1974	—	3.00	6.00
❑ 638	Damn Right I Am Somebody-Part 1/Damn Right I Am Somebody-Part 2	1974	—	3.00	6.00
❑ 643	Rockin' Funky Watergate (Part 1)/Rockin' Funky Watergate (Part 2)	1974	—	3.00	6.00
❑ 646	Little Boy Black/Rockin' Funky Watergate (Part 2)	1974	—	3.00	6.00
❑ 648	Breakin' Bread/Funky Music Is My Style	1974	—	2.50	5.00
❑ 651	Makin' Love/Rice and Ribs	1975	—	2.50	5.00
❑ 654	Thank You for Lettin' Me Be Myself and Be Yours (Part 1)/Thank You for Lettin' Me Be Myself and Be Yours (Part 2)	1975	—	2.50	5.00
❑ 655	(It's Not the Express) It's the J.B.'s Monaurail, Part 1/(It's Not the Express) It's the J.B.'s Monaurail, Part 2	1975	—	2.50	5.00
❑ 660	Thank You for Lettin' Me Be Myself (Part 1)/Thank You for Lettin' Me Be Myself (Part 2)	1975	—	2.50	5.00
❑ 663	All Aboard the Funky Soul Train/Thank You for Lettin' Me Be Myself and You Be Yourself	1976	—	2.50	5.00
❑ 2502	My Brother (Part 1)/My Brother (Part 2)	1971	—	3.00	6.00
—As "The J.B.'s"					
RSO/CURTOM					
❑ 1037	House Party/I Make Music	1980	—	2.00	4.00

WESLEY, GATE

Number	Title (A Side/B Side)	Yr	VG	VG+	NM
ATLANTIC					
❑ 2319	Do the Batman/Do the Thing	1966	6.25	12.50	25.00

WEST, DOTTIE

Also see KENNY ROGERS AND DOTTIE WEST.

Number	Title (A Side/B Side)	Yr	VG	VG+	NM
ATLANTIC					
❑ 2155	You Said I'd Never Love Again/I'll Pick Up My Heart (And Go Home)	1962	3.75	7.50	15.00
LIBERTY					
❑ 1392	Are You Happy Baby/Right or Wrong	1980	—	—	3.00
❑ 1404	What Are We Doin' in Love/Choosin' Means Losin'	1981	—	—	3.00
—Duet with Kenny Rogers, who is not credited on the label					
❑ 1419	(I'm Gonna) Put You Back on the Rack/Sorry Seems to Be the Hardest Word	1981	—	—	3.00
❑ 1436	It's High Time/Don't Be Kind	1981	—	—	3.00
❑ 1451	You're Not Easy to Forget/Something's Missing	1982	—	—	3.00
❑ 1479	She Can't Get My Love Off the Bed/Hurt	1982	—	—	3.00
❑ 1490	If It Takes All Night/Try to Win a Friend	1982	—	—	3.00
❑ 1500	Tulsa Ballroom/A Woman in Love with You	1983	—	—	3.00
❑ 1506	The Night Love Let You Down/He's All I Need	1983	—	—	3.00
PERMIAN					
❑ 82006	What's Good for the Goose (Is Good for the Gander)/Tell Me Again	1984	—	2.00	4.00
❑ 82007	Let Love Come Lookin' for You/Blue Fiddle Waltz	1984	—	2.00	4.00
❑ 82010	We Know Better Now/Let Love Come Lookin' for You	1985	—	2.00	4.00
RCA					
❑ PB-12284	Once You Were Mine/Dream Baby (How Long Must I Dream)	1981	—	2.00	4.00
RCA VICTOR					
❑ APBO-0072	Country Sunshine/Wish I Didn't Love You Any More	1973	2.00	4.00	8.00
❑ APBO-0231	Last Time I Saw Him/Everybody Bring a Song	1974	—	2.50	5.00
❑ APBO-0321	House of Love/Love As Long As We Can	1974	—	2.50	5.00
❑ PB-10125	Lay Back Lover/Good Lovin' You	1974	—	2.50	5.00
❑ PB-10269	Rollin' in Your Sweet Sunshine/Carolina Cousins	1975	—	2.50	5.00
❑ PB-10553	Here Come the Flowers/He's Not for You	1976	—	2.50	5.00
❑ PB-10699	If I'm a Fool for Loving You/Home Made Love	1976	—	2.50	5.00
❑ 47-8166	Touch Me/More Than I Meant To	1963	3.00	6.00	12.00
❑ 47-8225	Let Me Off at the Corner/I Wish You Wouldn't Do That	1963	2.50	5.00	10.00
❑ 47-8324	Love Is No Excuse/Look Who's Talking	1964	2.50	5.00	10.00
—With Jim Reeves					
❑ 47-8374	Here Comes My Baby/(How Can I Face) These Heartaches Alone	1964	2.50	5.00	10.00
❑ 47-8467	Didn't I/In Its Own Little Way	1964	2.50	5.00	10.00
❑ 47-8525	Gettin' Married Has Made Us Strangers/It Just Takes Practice	1965	2.50	5.00	10.00
❑ 47-8615	No Sign of Living/Night Life	1965	2.50	5.00	10.00
❑ 47-8702	Before the Ring on Your Finger Turns Green/Wear Away	1965	2.50	5.00	10.00
❑ 47-8770	Would You Hold It Against Me/You're Just the Only World I Know	1965	2.00	4.00	8.00
❑ 47-8900	Mommy, Can I Still Call Him Daddy/Suffertime	1966	2.00	4.00	8.00
❑ 47-9011	What's Come Over My Baby/How Many Lifetimes Will It Take	1966	2.00	4.00	8.00
❑ 47-9118	Paper Mansions/Someone's Gotta Cry	1967	2.00	4.00	8.00
❑ 47-9267	Like a Fool/Everything's a Wreck	1967	2.00	4.00	8.00
❑ 47-9377	Childhood Places/No One	1967	2.00	4.00	8.00
❑ 47-9497	Country Girl/That's Where Our Love Must Be	1968	2.00	4.00	8.00
❑ 47-9604	Reno/My Heart Has Changed Its Mind	1968	2.00	4.00	8.00
❑ 47-9792	I Heard Our Song/Makin' Memories	1969	—	3.00	6.00
❑ 47-9834	Jack Daniels, Old Grand-Dad, Johnnie Walker and You/Long Black Limousine	1970	—	3.00	6.00
❑ 47-9872	It's Dawned on Me You're Gone/Love's Farewell	1970	—	3.00	6.00
❑ 47-9911	Forever Yours/Cold Hand of Fate	1970	—	3.00	6.00

Number	Title (A Side/B Side)	Yr	VG	VG+	NM
❑ 47-9947	Slowly/Sweet Thang	1971	—	3.00	6.00
—With Jimmy Dean					
❑ 47-9957	Careless Hands/Only One Thing Left to Do	1971	—	3.00	6.00
❑ 47-9982	Lonely Is/Cancel Tomorrow	1971	—	3.00	6.00
❑ 48-1012	Six Weeks Every Summer (Christmas Every Day)/Wish I Didn't Love You Anymore	1971	—	2.50	5.00
❑ 74-0239	Clinging to My Baby's Hand/Don't Say a Word	1969	—	3.00	6.00
❑ 74-0601	Cold Hand of Fate/You're the Other Half of Me	1971	—	3.00	6.00
❑ 74-0711	I'm Only a Woman/Baby, I Tried	1972	—	2.50	5.00
❑ 74-0828	If It's All Right with You/Special Memory	1972	—	2.50	5.00
❑ 74-0930	Just What I've Been Looking For/Everything's a Wreck	1973	—	2.50	5.00
STARDAY					
❑ 517	Angel on Paper/No Time Will I Ever	1960	5.00	10.00	20.00
❑ 547	I Lost, You Win, I'm Leavin'/I Should Start Runnin'	1961	5.00	10.00	20.00
❑ 574	My Big John/Men with Evil Hearts	1961	5.00	10.00	20.00
❑ 724	I'd Be Lying/Walking in the Dark	1965	2.50	5.00	10.00
UNITED ARTISTS					
❑ XW898	When It's Just You and Me/We Love Each Other	1976	—	2.00	4.00
❑ XW946	Every Word I Write/We Love Each Other	1977	—	2.00	4.00
❑ XW1010	Tonight You Belong to Me/Tiny Fingers	1977	—	2.00	4.00
❑ XW1084	That's All I Wanted to Know/Who's Gonna Love Me Now	1977	—	2.00	4.00
❑ XW1209	Come See Me and Come Lonely/Decorate Your Conscience	1978	—	2.00	4.00
❑ XW1257	Reaching Out to Hold You/My Two Empty Arms	1978	—	2.00	4.00
❑ 1324	You Pick Me Up (And Put Me Down)/We Got Tonight	1979	—	2.00	4.00
❑ 1339	A Lesson in Leavin'/Love's So Easy for Two	1980	—	2.00	4.00
❑ 1352	Leavin's for Unbelievers/Blue As I Want To	1980	—	2.00	4.00

WEST, DOTTIE, AND DON GIBSON

Also see each artist's individual listings.

Number	Title (A Side/B Side)	Yr	VG	VG+	NM
RCA VICTOR					
❑ 47-9715	Rings of Gold/Final Examination	1969	—	3.00	6.00
❑ 47-9867	Till I Can't Take It Anymore/I Love You Because	1970	—	3.00	6.00
❑ 74-0178	Sweet Memories/How's the World Treating You	1969	—	3.00	6.00
❑ 74-0291	There's a Story (Goin' 'Round)/Lock, Stock and Teardrops	1969	—	3.00	6.00

WEST, LESLIE

Also see MOUNTAIN; WEST, BRUCE & LAING.

Number	Title (A Side/B Side)	Yr	VG	VG+	NM
PHANTOM					
❑ ?B-10301	E.S.P./Don't Burn Me	1975	—	2.00	4.00
WINDFALL					
❑ 530	This Wheel's On Fire/Dreams of Milk and Honey	1969	—	2.50	5.00
❑ 531	Blood of the Sun/Long Red	1969	—	2.50	5.00
7-Inch Extended Plays					
PHANTOM					
❑ JF-10424 [DJ]	Honey/Dear Prudence//Get It Up/The Setting Sun	1975	2.50	5.00	10.00

WEST, MAE

Number	Title (A Side/B Side)	Yr	VG	VG+	NM
20TH CENTURY FOX					
❑ 6718	Hard to Handle/You Gotta Taste All the Fruit	1968	2.50	5.00	10.00
❑ 6718 [PS]	Hard to Handle/You Gotta Taste All the Fruit	1968	6.25	12.50	25.00
DAGONET					
❑ 6	Put the Loot in the Boot, Santa/With Love from Me to You	1966	3.75	7.50	15.00
DECCA					
❑ 29452	Love Is the Greatest Thing/All of Me	1955	3.75	7.50	15.00
❑ 32738	The Sayings of Mae West/More Sayings of Mae West	1970	2.50	5.00	10.00
MGM					
❑ 14491	Great Balls of Fire/Naked Ape	1973	2.00	4.00	8.00
TOWER					
❑ 260	Day Tripper/Treat Him Right	1966	2.50	5.00	10.00
❑ 260 [PS]	Day Tripper/Treat Him Right	1966	5.00	10.00	20.00
❑ 261	Shakin' All Over/If You Gotta Go	1966	2.50	5.00	10.00
❑ 261 [PS]	Shakin' All Over/If You Gotta Go	1966	5.00	10.00	20.00

WEST, RED

Number	Title (A Side/B Side)	Yr	VG	VG+	NM
DOT					
❑ 16268	Midnight Ride/Unforgiven	1961	5.00	10.00	20.00
JARO					
❑ 77031	FBI Story/What Must I Do	1960	12.50	25.00	50.00
SANTO					
❑ 9006	Bossa Nova Mamza/My Babe	1963	3.75	7.50	15.00

WEST, SONNY

Number	Title (A Side/B Side)	Yr	VG	VG+	NM
ATLANTIC					
❑ 1174	Rave On!/Call On Cupid	1958	10.00	20.00	40.00
NOR VA JAK					
❑ 1956	Rock-Ola Ruby/Sweet Rockin' Baby	1959	25.00	50.00	100.00
—As "Sonee West"					

WEST, BRUCE & LAING

Also see JACK BRUCE; LESLIE WEST.

Number	Title (A Side/B Side)	Yr	VG	VG+	NM
COLUMBIA					
❑ 45751	Shake Ma Thing (Rollin' Jack)/The Doctor	1973	—	2.50	5.00
❑ 45829	Why Don'tcha/Mississippi Queen	1973	—	2.50	5.00

WEST COAST POP ART EXPERIMENTAL BAND, THE

Number	Title (A Side/B Side)	Yr	VG	VG+	NM
AMOS					
❑ 119	Free As a Bird/Where's My Daddy	1969	3.75	7.50	15.00
REPRISE					
❑ 0552	Shifting Sands/1906	1967	6.25	12.50	25.00
❑ 0582	Help, I'm a Rock/Transparent Day	1967	6.25	12.50	25.00
❑ 0776	Smell of Incense/Unfree Child	1968	6.25	12.50	25.00

WESTON, KIM

Also see MARVIN GAYE AND KIM WESTON.

Number	Title (A Side/B Side)	Yr	VG	VG+	NM
ENTERPRISE					
❑ 9101	Beautiful People/Goodness Gracious	1974	—	2.50	5.00
GORDY					
❑ 7041	I'll Never See My Love Again/A Thrill a Moment	1965	5.00	10.00	20.00
❑ 7046	Take Me in Your Arms (Rock Me A Little While)/Don't Compare Me to Her	1965	5.00	10.00	20.00
❑ 7050	Helpless/A Love Like Yours (Don't Come Knocking Every Day)	1966	5.00	10.00	20.00
MGM					
❑ 13720	I Got What You Need/Someone Like You	1967	5.00	10.00	20.00
❑ 13804	That's Groovy/Land of Tomorrow	1967	5.00	10.00	20.00
❑ 13881	Nobody/You're Just the Kind of Guy	1967	5.00	10.00	20.00
❑ 13927	Lift Every Voice and Sing/This Is America	1968	5.00	10.00	20.00
❑ 13928	The Impossible Dream/When Johnny Comes Marching Home	1968	3.75	7.50	15.00
❑ 13992	I Will Understand/Thankful	1968	3.75	7.50	15.00
PEOPLE					
❑ 1001	Danger, Heartbreak Ahead/I'll Be Thinkin'	1970	2.50	5.00	10.00
PRIDE					
❑ 1	Lift Every Voice and Sing/This Is America	1970	2.50	5.00	10.00
TAMLA					
❑ 54076	It Should Have Been Me/Love Me All the Way	1963	12.50	25.00	50.00
❑ 54085	Just Loving You/Another Train Coming	1963	12.50	25.00	50.00
❑ 54100	Looking for the Right Guy/Feel Alright Tonight	1964	12.50	25.00	50.00
❑ 54106	A Little More Love/Go Ahead and Laugh	1964	25.00	50.00	100.00
❑ 54110	I'm Still Loving You/Go Ahead and Laugh	1964	15.00	30.00	60.00
VOLT					
❑ 1502	If I Had My Way/Gonna Be Alright	1971	3.75	7.50	15.00
❑ 1503	Little By Little, Bit By Bit/(B-side unknown)	1971	3.75	7.50	15.00

WET WILLIE

Number	Title (A Side/B Side)	Yr	VG	VG+	NM
CAPRICORN					
❑ 0008	Shout Bamalama/Airport	1972	—	3.00	6.00
❑ 0022	Shout Bamalama/Airport	1973	—	3.00	6.00
❑ 0031	Country Side of Life/In Our Hearts	1973	—	3.00	6.00
❑ 0043	Keep On Smilin'/Soul Jones	1974	—	3.00	6.00
❑ 0052	Keep On Smilin'/Country Side of Life	1975	—	2.00	4.00
—"Back to Back Hits" reissue					
❑ 0206	Keep On Smilin'/Soul Jones	1974	—	2.00	4.00
❑ 0212	Country Side of Life/Don't Wait Too Long	1974	—	2.00	4.00
❑ 0224	Leona/Ain't He a Mess	1975	—	2.00	4.00
❑ 0231	Dixie Rock/She's My Lady	1975	—	2.00	4.00
❑ 0254	Everything That 'Cha Do (Will Come Back to You)/Walkin' By Myself	1976	—	2.00	4.00
❑ 0260	Comic Book Hero/Baby Fat	1976	—	2.00	4.00
❑ 8020	Rock and Roll Band/Dirty Leg	1971	2.00	4.00	8.00
EPIC					
❑ 50478	Street Corner Serenade/We Got Lovin'	1977	—	2.00	4.00
❑ 50528	Let It Shine/Make You Feel Love Again	1978	—	2.00	4.00
❑ 50714	Weekend/Mr. Streamline	1979	—	2.00	4.00
❑ 50760	The Hard Way/Ramona	1979	—	2.00	4.00

WHAM!

Number	Title (A Side/B Side)	Yr	VG	VG+	NM
COLUMBIA					
❑ CS7 2591 [DJ]	Last Christmas (6:43)/Last Christmas (4:24)	1986	2.50	5.00	10.00
❑ 03611	Young Guns (Go For It)/Going For It	1983	—	2.50	5.00
—As "Wham! U.K."					
❑ 03611 [PS]	Young Guns (Go For It)/Going For It	1983	—	2.50	5.00
—As "Wham! U.K."					
❑ 03611 [PS]	Young Guns (Go For It)	1983	2.00	4.00	8.00
—As "Wham! U.K."; "Demonstration -- Not for Sale" on rear					
❑ 03932	Bad Boys/Bad Boys (Instrumental)	1983	—	2.50	5.00
—As "Wham! U.K."					
❑ 04552	Wake Me Up Before You Go-Go/(instrumental)	1984	—	—	3.00
❑ 04552 [PS]	Wake Me Up Before You Go-Go/(instrumental)	1984	2.00	4.00	8.00
❑ 04691	Careless Whisper/(instrumental)	1984	—	—	3.00
—As "Wham! featuring George Michael"					
❑ 04691 [PS]	Careless Whisper/(instrumental)	1984	2.00	4.00	8.00
—As "Wham! featuring George Michael"; color sleeve					
❑ 04691 [PS]	Careless Whisper/(instrumental)	1984	—	2.50	5.00
—As "Wham! featuring George Michael"; black & white sleeve					
❑ 04691 [PS]	Careless Whisper	1984	2.50	5.00	10.00
—As "Wham! featuring George Michael"; color sleeve; "Demonstration -- Not for Sale" on rear					
❑ 04840	Everything She Wants/Like a Baby	1985	—	—	3.00
❑ 04840 [PS]	Everything She Wants/Like a Baby	1985	—	—	3.00
❑ 05409	Freedom/Heartbeat	1985	—	—	3.00
❑ 05409 [PS]	Freedom/Heartbeat	1985	—	—	3.00
❑ 05721	I'm Your Man/Do It Right	1985	—	—	3.00
❑ 05721 [PS]	I'm Your Man/Do It Right	1985	—	—	3.00
❑ 05721 [PS]	I'm Your Man/Do It Right	1985	—	2.50	5.00
—"Demonstration -- Not for Sale" on rear					
❑ 06182	The Edge of Heaven/Blue (Live in China)	1986	—	—	3.00
❑ 06182 [PS]	The Edge of Heaven/Blue (Live in China)	1986	—	—	3.00
❑ 06294	Where Did Your Heart Go?/Wham! Rap '86	1986	—	—	3.00
❑ 06294 [PS]	Where Did Your Heart Go?/Wham! Rap '86	1986	—	—	3.00
❑ 68712	Wake Me Up Before You Go-Go/(Instrumental)	1988	—	—	3.00
—Reissue					
❑ 68713	Careless Whisper/(Instrumental)	1988	—	—	3.00
—Reissue					
❑ 68715	Everything She Wants/Like a Baby	1988	—	—	3.00
—Reissue					

WHAT FOUR, THE

Number	Title (A Side/B Side)	Yr	VG	VG+	NM
CAPITOL					
❑ 5449	Anything for a Laugh/Baby Can't You Hear Me Call Your Name	1965	3.00	6.00	12.00
COLUMBIA					
❑ 43711	Baby, I Dig Love/It's Hard to Live on Promises	1966	3.00	6.00	12.00

Number	Title (A Side/B Side)	Yr	VG	VG+	NM
DESTINATION					
❑ 633	We Could Be Happy/Where Love Can Go	1967	3.00	6.00	12.00
—As "What For"					
ESP-DISK'					
❑ 109	Our Love Should Last Forever/(B-side unknown)	1966	7.50	15.00	30.00
MERCURY					
❑ 72716	Dandelion Wine/You're Wishin' I Was Someone Else	1967	6.25	12.50	25.00
—As "Whatt Four"					
REPRISE					
❑ 0387	Gemini 4/Night Surf	1965	6.25	12.50	25.00
TOWER					
❑ 404	Asparagus/Stop in the Name of Love	1968	3.00	6.00	12.00

WHAT-KNOTS, THE

Number	Title (A Side/B Side)	Yr	VG	VG+	NM
DIAL					
❑ 4067	I Ain't Dead Yet/Talkin' 'Bout Our Breakup	1967	6.25	12.50	25.00

WHEEL MEN, THE

GARY USHER was in this group.

Number	Title (A Side/B Side)	Yr	VG	VG+	NM
WARNER BROS.					
❑ 5480	Hon-Da Beach/School Is a Gas	1964	12.50	25.00	50.00

WHEELER, MARY, AND THE KNIGHTS

Number	Title (A Side/B Side)	Yr	VG	VG+	NM
ATOM					
❑ 701	A Falling Tear/I Feel in My Heart	196?	10.00	20.00	40.00

WHEELER, ONIE

Number	Title (A Side/B Side)	Yr	VG	VG+	NM
CHARTA					
❑ 122	I Don't Believe We're Through/Pick Up the Pieces	1978	—	3.00	6.00
❑ 129	Lucie Ann's Song/I Don't Believe We're Through	1978	—	3.00	6.00
❑ 148	Onie's Bop/I'd Rather Scratch with the Chickens	1979	—	3.00	6.00
COLUMBIA					
❑ 4-21371	Little Mama/She Wiggled and Giggled	1955	5.00	10.00	20.00
❑ 4-21418	My Home Is Not a Home at All/That's What I Like	1955	5.00	10.00	20.00
❑ 4-21454	Cut It Out/I'm Satisfied with My Dreams	1955	5.00	10.00	20.00
❑ 4-21500	No I Don't Guess I Will/I Tried and I Tried	1956	5.00	10.00	20.00
❑ 4-21523	Onie's Bop/I Wanna Hold My Baby	1956	15.00	30.00	60.00
❑ 4-40787	A Beggar for Your Love/A Booger Gonna Getcha	1956	12.50	25.00	50.00
❑ 4-40911	Steppin' Out/Going Back to the City	1957	3.75	7.50	15.00
EPIC					
❑ 9540	What About Tomorrow/Sunnyland Farmer	1962	2.50	5.00	10.00
JAB					
❑ 9003	Just Leave Her to Me/Water Your Flower	1967	2.00	4.00	8.00
❑ 9013	Dirt Behind My Years/Burn Another Honky Tonk Down	1968	2.00	4.00	8.00
K-ARK					
❑ 606	Too Hot to Handle/I Need to Go Home	196?	3.75	7.50	15.00
❑ 617	You're Getting All Over Me/All Day, All Night, Always	196?	3.75	7.50	15.00
❑ 620	Go Home/I Saw Mother with God Last Night	196?	3.75	7.50	15.00
❑ 626	White Lightning Cherokee/Stubborn Heart	196?	3.75	7.50	15.00
❑ 671	Too Hot to Handle/I Need to Go Home	1966	2.50	5.00	10.00
❑ 856	Please Don't Plant Pretty Flowers/Which-A-Way, That-A-Way	197?	2.00	4.00	8.00
MUSICOR					
❑ 1096	I'm Gonna Hang My Britches Up/You're Too Good for Me	1965	2.50	5.00	10.00
❑ 1121	Her Porch Came Up to My Knees/Pretty Little Tomboy	1965	2.50	5.00	10.00
OKEH					
❑ 18022	When We All Get There/Run 'Em Off	1952	7.50	15.00	30.00
❑ 18026	Mother Prayed Loud in Her Sleep/A Million Years in Glory	195?	6.25	12.50	25.00
❑ 18037	Closing Time/I'll Swear You Don't Love Me	195?	6.25	12.50	25.00
❑ 18049	Love Me Like You Used to Do/Little Mama	195?	7.50	15.00	30.00
❑ 18058	Would You Like to Wear a Crown/I Saw Mother with God Last Night	1954	6.25	12.50	25.00
RANWOOD					
❑ 1025	EIO (The Sawmill Man)/Train to Louisville	1975	—	3.00	6.00
ROYAL AMERICAN					
❑ 76	John's Been Shucking My Corn/Make 'Em All Go Home	1973	—	2.50	5.00
❑ 85	Shuckin' My Way to the Hall of Fame/I Can't Pass an Orchard	1973	—	2.50	5.00
STARDAY					
❑ 767	Mr. Free/Dancing	1966	2.50	5.00	10.00
❑ 785	Playing Tricks/I Closed My Book Last Night	1966	2.50	5.00	10.00
SUN					
❑ 315	Jump Right Out of This Jukebox/Tell 'Em Off	1959	7.50	15.00	30.00

WHEELERS, THE

Number	Title (A Side/B Side)	Yr	VG	VG+	NM
CENCO					
❑ 107	Once I Had a Girl/Shine 'Em On	196?	15.00	30.00	60.00

WHEELS, THE (1)

British group.

Number	Title (A Side/B Side)	Yr	VG	VG+	NM
AURORA					
❑ 157	Bad Little Woman/Don't You Know	1966	6.25	12.50	25.00

WHEELS, THE (2)

Number	Title (A Side/B Side)	Yr	VG	VG+	NM
FOLLY					
❑ 800	Clap Your Hands (Part 1)/Clap Your Hands (Part 2)	1959	3.75	7.50	15.00

WHEELS, THE (3)

Number	Title (A Side/B Side)	Yr	VG	VG+	NM
IMPACT					
❑ 1029	Dancing in the Streets/A Taste of Money	1967	6.25	12.50	25.00

WHEELS, THE (4)

Number	Title (A Side/B Side)	Yr	VG	VG+	NM
PREMIUM					
❑ 405	My Heart's Desire/Let's Have a Ball	1956	15.00	30.00	60.00
❑ 408	Teasin' Heart/Loco	1956	20.00	40.00	80.00
❑ 410	I Can't Forget/How Could I Ever Leave Me	1956	37.50	75.00	150.00

WHEELS, THE (5)

Number	Title (A Side/B Side)	Yr	VG	VG+	NM
ROULETTE					
❑ 4271	No One But You/I've Waited for a Lifetime	1960	5.00	10.00	20.00

WHEELS, THE (U)

Number	Title (A Side/B Side)	Yr	VG	VG+	NM
TIME					
❑ 1003	Where Were You/So Young and So In Love	1958	20.00	40.00	80.00

WHIPPOORWILLS, THE

Number	Title (A Side/B Side)	Yr	VG	VG+	NM
JOSIE					
❑ 892	Deep Within/Going to a Party	1961	15.00	30.00	60.00
VITA					
❑ 1005	Blue Raindrops/I Must Have Holes in My Head	195?	25.00	50.00	100.00

WHIPS, THE

More than one group.

Number	Title (A Side/B Side)	Yr	VG	VG+	NM
DORE					
❑ 502	Yes, Master/Rosie's Blues	1958	5.00	10.00	20.00
FLAIR					
❑ 1025	Pleadin' Heart/She Done Me Wrong	1954	200.00	400.00	800.00
MGM					
❑ 13401	Whip It on Me, Baby/First Dance Fear	1965	3.00	6.00	12.00

WHIRLERS, THE

Number	Title (A Side/B Side)	Yr	VG	VG+	NM
PORT					
❑ 70025	Tonight and Forever/Magic Mirror	1961	5.00	10.00	20.00
WHIRLIN' DISC					
❑ 108	Tonight and Forever/Magic Mirror	1956	20.00	40.00	80.00

WHIRLWINDS, THE

Number	Title (A Side/B Side)	Yr	VG	VG+	NM
GUYDEN					
❑ 2052	Angel Love/The Mountain	1961	7.50	15.00	30.00
PHILIPS					
❑ 40139	Heartbeat/At the Party	1963	31.25	62.50	125.00

WHISPERS, THE

Well-known male R&B vocal group.

Number	Title (A Side/B Side)	Yr	VG	VG+	NM
CANADIAN AMERICAN					
❑ 179	It's Rainin', It's Pourin'/Tomorrow's On Your Side	1964	7.50	15.00	30.00
CAPITOL					
❑ S7-18394	Make Sweet Love to Me/My Funny Valentine	1995	—	—	3.00
❑ S7-18727	Come On Home/Better Watch Your Heart	1995	—	—	3.00
❑ 7PRO-79170/215 [DJ]	Innocent (7" Edit)/Innocent (Club Edit)	1990	2.00	4.00	8.00
—Vinyl is promo only					
DORE					
❑ 724	It Only Hurts for a Little While/The Happy One	1964	6.25	12.50	25.00
❑ 729	Slow Jerk/Never Again	1965	5.00	10.00	20.00
❑ 735	The Dip/Weirdo	1965	5.00	10.00	20.00
❑ 740	As I Sit Here/Shake It, Shake It	1966	5.00	10.00	20.00
❑ 751	Doctor Love/Lonely Avenue	1966	5.00	10.00	20.00
❑ 758	Walkin' the Fat Man/I Was Born When You Kissed Me	1966	5.00	10.00	20.00
❑ 768	Take a Lesson from the Teacher/Claire De Looney	1966	5.00	10.00	20.00
❑ 792	You Got a Man on Your Hands/You Can't Fight What's Right	1967	3.75	7.50	15.00
❑ 794	Needle in a Haystack/Waltz for You	1967	3.75	7.50	15.00
❑ 833	Never Again/I Was Born When You Kissed Me	1969	3.00	6.00	12.00
❑ 842	The Dip/It Only Hurts for a Little While	1970	2.50	5.00	10.00
FONTANA					
❑ 1564	My Long and Sleepless Night/Knowin'	1966	5.00	10.00	20.00
JANUS					
❑ 140	There's a Love for Everyone/It Sure Ain't Pretty	1970	—	3.00	6.00
❑ 150	Your Love Is So Doggone Good/Cracker Jack	1971	—	3.00	6.00
❑ 174	Can't Help But Love You/A Hopeless Situation	1971	—	3.00	6.00
❑ 184	I Only Meant to Wet My Feet/You Fill My Life with Music	1972	—	3.00	6.00
❑ 200	Somebody Loves You/Can We Love Forever	1972	—	3.00	6.00
❑ 212	POW-MIA/Does She Care	1973	—	3.00	6.00
❑ 222	Feel Like Comin' Home/I Love the Way You Make Me Feel	1973	—	3.00	6.00
❑ 231	A Mother for My Children/What More Can a Girl Ask For	1973	—	3.00	6.00
❑ 238	Bingo/Once More with Feeling	1974	—	3.00	6.00
❑ 244	What More Can a Girl Ask For/Broken Home	1974	—	3.00	6.00
❑ 247	All I Ever Do (Is Dream of You)/Here Comes Tomorrow	1975	—	3.00	6.00
❑ 253	You're What's Been Missing in My Life/Given a Little Love	1975	—	3.00	6.00
SOLAR					
❑ YB-11246	(Let's Go) All the Way/Chocolate Girl	1978	—	2.00	4.00
❑ GB-11328	Living Together (In Sin)/One for the Money	1978	—	—	3.00
—Gold Standard Series					
❑ YB-11353	(Olivia) Lost and Turned Out/Try and Make It Better	1978	—	2.00	4.00
❑ YB-11449	Happy Holidays to You/Try and Make It Better	1978	—	3.00	6.00
❑ YB-11590	Can't Do Without Love/Headlights	1979	—	2.00	4.00
❑ YB-11685	Homemade Lovin'/You'll Never Get Away	1979	—	2.00	4.00
❑ YB-11739	A Song for Donny/(Instrumental)	1979	—	2.00	4.00
❑ YB-11739 [PS]	A Song for Donny/(Instrumental)	1979	—	3.00	6.00
❑ YB-11894	And the Beat Goes On/Can You Do the Boogie	1980	—	2.00	4.00
❑ YB-11928	Lady/I Love You	1980	—	2.00	4.00
❑ GB-11977	(Let's Go) All the Way/Lost and Turned Out	1980	—	—	3.00
—Gold Standard Series					
❑ YB-12050	Welcome Into My Dream/Out the Box	1980	—	2.00	4.00
❑ YB-12154	It's a Love Thing/Girl I Need You	1981	—	2.00	4.00
❑ GB-12230	And the Beat Goes On/Lady	1981	—	—	3.00
—Gold Standard Series					

Number	Title (A Side/B Side)	Yr	VG	VG+	NM
❑ YB-12232	I Can Make It Better/Say You (Would Love for Me Too)	1981	—	2.00	4.00
❑ YB-12295	This Kind of Lovin'/What Will I Do	1981	—	2.00	4.00
❑ YB-13005	I'm the One for You/I'm Gonna Love You More	1981	—	2.00	4.00
❑ GB-13486	It's a Love Thing/Make That Move	1983	—	—	3.00

—Gold Standard Series; B-side by Shalamar

Number	Title (A Side/B Side)	Yr	VG	VG+	NM
❑ 47961	In the Raw/Small Talkin'	1982	—	2.00	4.00
❑ 48008	Emergency/Only You	1982	—	2.00	4.00
❑ 48008 [PS]	Emergency/Only You	1982	—	3.00	6.00
❑ 69639	Don't Keep Me Waiting/Suddenly	1985	—	2.00	4.00
❑ 69658	Some Kinda Lover/Never Too Late	1985	—	2.00	4.00
❑ 69683	Contagious/(B-side unknown)	1984	—	2.00	4.00
❑ 69809	This Time/Love for Real	1983	—	2.00	4.00
❑ 69827	Keep On Lovin' Me/Try It Again	1983	—	2.00	4.00
❑ 69842	Tonight/Small Talkin'	1983	—	2.00	4.00
❑ 69965	Love Is Where You Find It/Say Yes	1982	—	2.00	4.00
❑ 70006	Rock Steady/Are You Going My Way	1987	—	—	3.00
❑ 70012	Just Gets Better with Time/Say Yes	1987	—	—	3.00
❑ 70017	In the Mood/(Instrumental)	1987	—	—	3.00
❑ 70020	No Pain, No Gain/(Instrumental)	1988	—	—	3.00

SOUL CLOCK

Number	Title (A Side/B Side)	Yr	VG	VG+	NM
❑ 104	Great Day/I Can't See Myself Leaving	1969	2.50	5.00	10.00
❑ 107	The Time Will Come/Flying High	1969	2.50	5.00	10.00
❑ 109	What Will I Do/Remember	1969	2.50	5.00	10.00
❑ 1001	I Can Remember/Planets of Life	1970	2.00	4.00	8.00
❑ 1004	Seems Like I Gotta Do Wrong/Needle in a Haystack	1970	2.00	4.00	8.00
❑ 1005	I'm the One/You Must Be Doing All Right	1970	2.00	4.00	8.00

SOUL TRAIN

Number	Title (A Side/B Side)	Yr	VG	VG+	NM
❑ SB-10430	In Love Forever/Fairytale	1975	—	2.50	5.00
❑ SB-10628	(You're a) Special Part of My Life/Grove Street	1976	—	2.50	5.00
❑ SB-10700	One for the Money (Part 1)/One for the Money (Part 2)	1976	—	2.50	5.00
❑ SB-10773	Living Together (In Sin)/I've Got a Feeling	1976	—	2.50	5.00
❑ SB-10878	You're Only As Good As You Think You Are/Sounds Like a Love Song	1977	—	2.50	5.00
❑ SB-10996	Make It With You/You Are Number One	1977	—	2.50	5.00
❑ SB-11139	I'm Gonna Make You My Wife/You Never Miss Your Water	1977	—	2.50	5.00

WHISPERS, THE (2)

GOTHAM

Number	Title (A Side/B Side)	Yr	VG	VG+	NM
❑ 309	Fool Heart/Don't Fool with Lizzie	1953	62.50	125.00	250.00
❑ 312	Are You Sorry/We're Getting Married	1953	375.00	750.00	1500.

WHISPERS, THE (3)

LAURIE

Number	Title (A Side/B Side)	Yr	VG	VG+	NM
❑ 3344	Here Comes Summer/If You Don't Care	1966	5.00	10.00	20.00

WHITCOMB, IAN

JERDEN

Number	Title (A Side/B Side)	Yr	VG	VG+	NM
❑ 735	Soho/Bony Moronie	1964	3.75	7.50	15.00
❑ 747	This Sporting Life/Soho	1964	3.75	7.50	15.00

TOWER

Number	Title (A Side/B Side)	Yr	VG	VG+	NM
❑ 120	This Sporting Life/Fizz	1965	2.50	5.00	10.00
❑ 134	You Turn Me On (Turn On Song)/Poor But Honest	1965	3.75	7.50	15.00
❑ 155	N-N-Nervous/The End	1965	2.50	5.00	10.00
❑ 170	18 Whitcomb St./Fizz	1965	2.50	5.00	10.00
❑ 189	No Tears for Johnny/Be My Baby	1966	2.50	5.00	10.00
❑ 192	High Blood Pressure/Good Hard Rock	1966	2.50	5.00	10.00
❑ 212	Lover's Prayer/Your Baby Has Gone Down the Plug Hole	1966	2.50	5.00	10.00
❑ 251	You Won't See Me/Please Don't Put Me on the Shelf	1966	2.50	5.00	10.00
❑ 274	Where Did Robinson Crusoe Go (With Friday on Saturday Night)/Poor Little Bird	1966	3.00	6.00	12.00
❑ 336	You Really Bent Me Out of Shape/Rolling Home Georgeanne	1967	2.50	5.00	10.00
❑ 355	You Really Bent Me Out of Shape/Rolling Home Georgeanne	1967	2.50	5.00	10.00
❑ 385	Groovy Day/Sally Sails the Sky	1967	2.50	5.00	10.00

UNITED ARTISTS

Number	Title (A Side/B Side)	Yr	VG	VG+	NM
❑ XW162	They Go Wild, Simply Wild Over Me/Yaaka Hula Hickey Dula	1973	—	3.00	6.00

WHITE, BARRY

20TH CENTURY

Number	Title (A Side/B Side)	Yr	VG	VG+	NM
❑ (no #) [PS]	"With Love from Barry White"	1975	5.00	10.00	20.00

—Pink and white sleeve issued with some stock copies of "What Am I Gonna Do with You"

Number	Title (A Side/B Side)	Yr	VG	VG+	NM
❑ 2018	I'm Gonna Love You Just a Little More Baby/Just a Little More Baby	1973	—	2.50	5.00
❑ 2042	I've Got So Much to Give/I've Got So Much to Give	1973	—	2.50	5.00
❑ 2058	Never Never Gonna Give Ya Up/No, I'm Never Gonna Give Ya Up	1973	—	2.50	5.00
❑ 2077	Honey Please Can't You See/Honey Please Can't You See	1974	—	2.50	5.00
❑ 2120	Can't Get Enough of Your Love, Babe/Just Not Enough	1974	—	2.50	5.00
❑ 2133	You're the First, the Last, My Everything/More Than Anything, You're My Everything	1974	—	2.50	5.00
❑ 2177	What Am I Gonna Do with You/What Am I Gonna Do with You, Baby	1975	—	2.50	5.00
❑ 2208	I'll Do for You Anything You Want Me To/Anything You Want Me To	1975	—	2.50	5.00
❑ 2265	Let the Music Play/(Instrumental)	1975	—	2.50	5.00
❑ 2277	You See the Trouble with Me/I'm So Blue When You Are Too	1976	—	2.50	5.00
❑ 2298	Baby, We Better Try to Get It Together/If You Know, Won't You Tell Me	1976	—	2.50	5.00
❑ 2309	Don't Make Me Wait Too Long/Can't You See It's Only You I Want	1976	—	2.50	5.00
❑ 2328	I'm Qualified to Satisfy You/(Instrumental)	1977	—	2.50	5.00
❑ 2350	It's Ecstasy When You Lay Down Next to Me/I Never Thought I'd Fall in Love with You	1977	—	2.50	5.00
❑ 2361	Playing Your Game, Baby/Of All the Guys in the World	1977	—	2.50	5.00
❑ 2365	Oh What a Night for Dancing/You're So Good You're Bad	1978	—	2.50	5.00
❑ 2380	Your Sweetness Is My Weakness/It's Only Love Doing Its Thing	1978	—	2.50	5.00
❑ 2395	Just the Way You Are/Now I'm Gonna Make Love to You	1979	—	2.50	5.00
❑ 2416	I Love to Sing the Songs I Sing/Oh Me Oh My	1979	—	2.50	5.00
❑ 2433	How Did You Know It Was Me?/Oh Me Oh My	1979	—	2.50	5.00

A&M

Number	Title (A Side/B Side)	Yr	VG	VG+	NM
❑ 31458 0924 7	Practice What You Preach/Come On	1995	—	—	3.00

—Second pressing indeed contains these two songs

Number	Title (A Side/B Side)	Yr	VG	VG+	NM
❑ 31458 0924 7	Practice What You Preach/Come On	1995	—	2.50	5.00

—First pressing actually contains Lo-Key?'s "I Got a Thang 4 Ya!"/"Sweet On U," which are otherwise unavailable on 45. Can be identified without playing by checking the trail-off vinyl for a different number than that on the record.

Number	Title (A Side/B Side)	Yr	VG	VG+	NM
❑ 1203	Right Night/There's a Place (Where Love Never Ends)	1988	—	—	3.00
❑ 1459	Super Lover/I Wanna Do It Good to Ya	1989	—	—	3.00
❑ 75021 1511 7	When Will I See You Again/Goodnight My Love	1990	—	—	3.00
❑ 2943	Sho' You Right/You're What's On My Mind	1987	—	—	3.00
❑ 2943 [PS]	Sho' You Right/You're What's On My Mind	1987	—	—	3.00
❑ 3000	For Your Love (I'd Do Most Anything)/I'm Ready for Love	1987	—	—	3.00
❑ 3000 [PS]	For Your Love (I'd Do Most Anything)/I'm Ready for Love	1987	—	—	3.00

UNLIMITED GOLD

Number	Title (A Side/B Side)	Yr	VG	VG+	NM
❑ 1401	Any Fool Could See (You Were Meant for Me)/You're the One I Need	1979	—	2.00	4.00
❑ 1404	It Ain't Love, Babe (Until You Give It)/Hung Up in Your Love	1979	—	2.00	4.00
❑ 1411	Love Ain't Easy/I Found Love	1980	—	2.00	4.00
❑ 1415	Sheet Music/(Instrumental)	1980	—	2.00	4.00
❑ 1418	Love Makin' Music/Ella Es Todo Mi (She's Everything to Me)	1980	—	2.00	4.00
❑ 1420	I Believe in Love/You're the One I Need	1980	—	2.00	4.00
❑ 02425	Louie Louie/Ghetto Letto	1981	—	2.00	4.00
❑ 02580	Beware/Tell Me Who Do You Love	1981	—	2.00	4.00
❑ 02956	Change/I Like You, You Like Me	1982	—	2.00	4.00
❑ 03379	Passion/It's All About Love	1982	—	2.00	4.00
❑ 03957	America/Life	1983	—	2.00	4.00
❑ 04098	Don't Let 'Em Blow Your Mind/Dreams	1983	—	2.00	4.00

WHITE, BARRY AND GLODEAN

UNLIMITED GOLD

Number	Title (A Side/B Side)	Yr	VG	VG+	NM
❑ 02087	I Want You/Our Theme (Part 1)	1981	—	2.00	4.00
❑ 02419	You're the Only One for Me/This Love	1981	—	2.00	4.00
❑ 70064	Didn't We Make It Happen, Baby/Our Theme (Part 2)	1981	—	2.00	4.00

WHITE, BEN, AND THE DARCHAES

ALJON

Number	Title (A Side/B Side)	Yr	VG	VG+	NM
❑ 1247/8	Jocko Sent Me/Nationwide Stamps	1962	100.00	200.00	400.00

WHITE, DANNY

GRAND PRIX

Number	Title (A Side/B Side)	Yr	VG	VG+	NM
❑ 2	You're a Part of Me/Let It Be Me	1983	3.00	6.00	12.00

—With Linda Nail

Number	Title (A Side/B Side)	Yr	VG	VG+	NM
❑ 4	Then You Can Tell Me Goodbye/(B-side unknown)	1983	3.00	6.00	12.00

WHITE, TONY JOE

20TH CENTURY

Number	Title (A Side/B Side)	Yr	VG	VG+	NM
❑ 2276	It Must Be Love/Susie-Q	1976	—	2.00	4.00
❑ 2322	Texas Woman/Hold On to Your Hiney	1976	—	2.00	4.00

ARISTA

Number	Title (A Side/B Side)	Yr	VG	VG+	NM
❑ 0376	We'll Live on Love/You and Me Baby	1978	—	2.00	4.00
❑ 0395	It Must Be Love/We'll Live on Love	1979	—	2.00	4.00

CASABLANCA

Number	Title (A Side/B Side)	Yr	VG	VG+	NM
❑ 2279	I Get Off on It/Feelin' Loose	1980	—	2.50	5.00
❑ 2304	Mamas Don't Let Your Cowboys Grow Up to Be Babies/Disco Blues	1980	—	2.50	5.00

COLUMBIA

Number	Title (A Side/B Side)	Yr	VG	VG+	NM
❑ 38-03967	Swamp Rap/Living in the River City	1983	—	2.00	4.00
❑ 38-04134	The Lady in My Life/We Belong Together	1983	—	2.00	4.00
❑ 38-04356	We Belong Together/Naughty Lady	1984	—	2.00	4.00
❑ 38-04476	You Just Get Better All the Time/Do You Have a Garter Belt	1984	—	2.00	4.00
❑ 38-04683	Nobody's Baby Tonight/Down by the Border	1984	—	2.00	4.00

MONUMENT

Number	Title (A Side/B Side)	Yr	VG	VG+	NM
❑ 1003	Georgia Pines/Ten More Miles to Louisiana	1967	2.00	4.00	8.00
❑ 1053	Watching the Trains Go By/Old Man Willie	1968	2.00	4.00	8.00
❑ 1070	I Protest/Man Can Only Stand So Much Pain	1968	2.00	4.00	8.00
❑ 1086	Soul Francisco/Whompt Out on You	1968	2.00	4.00	8.00
❑ 1104	Polk Salad Annie/Aspen Colorado	1968	2.50	5.00	10.00
❑ 1169	Roosevelt and Ira Lee (Night of the Moccasin)/The Migrant	1969	—	3.00	6.00
❑ 1193	High Sheriff/Groupy Girl	1970	—	3.00	6.00
❑ 1206	Save Your Sugar for Me/My Friend	1970	—	3.00	6.00
❑ 1227	Old Man Willie/Scratch My Back	1970	—	3.00	6.00

WARNER BROS.

Number	Title (A Side/B Side)	Yr	VG	VG+	NM
❑ 7468	The Daddy/Voodoo Village	1971	—	2.50	5.00
❑ 7477	My Kind of Woman/I Just Walked Away	1971	—	2.50	5.00
❑ 7505	Lustful Earl and the Married Woman/I Just Walked Away	1971	—	2.50	5.00
❑ 7523	Delta Love/That On the Road Look	1971	—	2.50	5.00
❑ 7591	Even Trolls Love Rock and Roll/If I Ever Saw a Good Thing	1972	—	2.50	5.00
❑ 7607	I've Got a Thing About You, Baby/Gospel Singer	1972	—	2.50	5.00

Number	Title (A Side/B Side)	Yr	VG	VG+	NM
❑ 7712	Backwoods Preacher Man/Saturday Night in Oak Grove, La.	1973	—	2.50	5.00
❑ 7780	Love 'Tween You and Me/Sign of the Lion	1974	—	2.50	5.00
❑ 8042	Wishful Thinking/Don't Let the Door	1974	—	2.50	5.00

WHITE, YOLANDA

DECCA

Number	Title (A Side/B Side)	Yr	VG	VG+	NM
❑ 31340	My Brother Wants a Doll for Christmas/What I Want for Christmas (Is Six More Years)	1961	5.00	10.00	20.00

WHITE PLAINS

DERAM

Number	Title (A Side/B Side)	Yr	VG	VG+	NM
❑ 85058	My Baby Loves Lovin'/Show Me Your Hand	1970	2.00	4.00	8.00
❑ 85066	Lovin' You Baby/Noises (In My Head)	1970	—	3.00	6.00
❑ 85072	Carolina's Coming Home/Every Little Move She Makes	1971	—	3.00	6.00
❑ 85076	When You Are a King/The World Gets Better with Love	1971	—	3.00	6.00
❑ 85080	I Can't Stop/Julie Anne	1972	—	3.00	6.00
❑ 85086	Step Into a Dream/Look to See	1973	—	3.00	6.00
❑ 85089	Does Anybody Know Where My Baby Is/Just for a Change	1973	—	3.00	6.00

WHITE TOWN

EMI

Number	Title (A Side/B Side)	Yr	VG	VG+	NM
❑ S7-19526	Your Woman/Wanted	1997	—	2.00	4.00

WHITESNAKE

GEFFEN

Number	Title (A Side/B Side)	Yr	VG	VG+	NM
❑ 19951	The Deeper the Love/Slip of the Tongue	1990	—	—	3.00
❑ 28103	Give Me All Your Love/Straight for the Heart	1988	—	—	3.00
❑ 28103 [PS]	Give Me All Your Love/Straight for the Heart	1988	—	—	3.00
❑ 28233	Is This Love/Bad Boys	1987	—	—	3.00
❑ 28233 [PS]	Is This Love/Bad Boys	1987	—	—	3.00
❑ 28331	Still of the Night/Don't Turn Away	1987	—	2.00	4.00
❑ 28339	Here I Go Again/Children of the Night	1987	—	2.00	4.00
—A radically different version than that on the LP					
❑ 28339 [PS]	Here I Go Again/Children of the Night	1987	—	2.00	4.00
❑ 29171	Love Ain't No Stranger/Guilty of Love	1984	—	2.00	4.00
❑ 29171 [PS]	Love Ain't No Stranger/Guilty of Love	1984	—	2.00	4.00

MIRAGE

Number	Title (A Side/B Side)	Yr	VG	VG+	NM
❑ 3672	Fool for Loving You/Black and Blue	1980	—	2.50	5.00
❑ 3672 [PS]	Fool for Loving You/Black and Blue	1980	—	3.00	6.00
❑ 3766	Ain't Gonna Cry No More/Sweet Talker	1980	—	2.50	5.00
❑ 3794 [DJ]	Ain't No Love in the Heart of the City (same on both sides)	1981	—	2.50	5.00
—May be promo only					
❑ 3844	Don't Break My Heart Again/Lonely Days, Lonely Nights	1981	—	2.50	5.00

UNITED ARTISTS

Number	Title (A Side/B Side)	Yr	VG	VG+	NM
❑ X1240 [DJ]	Ain't No Love in the Heart of the City (mono/stereo)	1978	2.00	4.00	8.00
—May be promo only; as "David Coverdale's Whitesnake"					
❑ XW1291	The Time Is Right for Love/Belgian Tom's Hot Trick	1979	—	2.50	5.00
❑ 1323	Long Way from Home/We Wish You Well	1979	—	2.50	5.00

WHITFORD-ST. HOLMES BAND

Splinter group from AEROSMITH.

COLUMBIA

Number	Title (A Side/B Side)	Yr	VG	VG+	NM
❑ 02555	Shy Away/Mystery Girl	1981	—	2.50	5.00

WHO, THE

Also see ROGER DALTREY; JOHN ENTWISTLE; KEITH MOON; PETE TOWNSHEND.

ATCO

Number	Title (A Side/B Side)	Yr	VG	VG+	NM
❑ 6409	Substitute/Waltz for a Pig	1966	12.50	25.00	50.00
❑ 6509	Substitute/Waltz for a Pig	1967	5.00	10.00	20.00

DECCA

Number	Title (A Side/B Side)	Yr	VG	VG+	NM
❑ 31725	I Can't Explain/Bald Headed Woman	1965	7.50	15.00	30.00
❑ 31801	Anyway, Anyhow, Anywhere/Anytime You Want Me	1965	12.50	25.00	50.00
❑ 31877	My Generation/Out in the Street (You're Going to Know Me)	1965	7.50	15.00	30.00
❑ 31988	The Kids Are Alright/A Legal Matter	1966	7.50	15.00	30.00
❑ 32058	I'm a Boy/In the City	1966	7.50	15.00	30.00
❑ 32114	Happy Jack/Whiskey Man	1967	7.50	15.00	30.00
❑ 32114 [PS]	Happy Jack/Whiskey Man	1967	12.50	25.00	50.00
❑ 32156	Pictures of Lily/Doctor, Doctor	1967	5.00	10.00	20.00
❑ 32206	I Can See for Miles/Mary-Anne with the Shaky Hands	1967	5.00	10.00	20.00
❑ 32288	Call Me Lightning/Dr. Jeckyll & Mr. Hyde	1968	6.25	12.50	25.00
❑ 32362	Magic Bus/Someone's Coming	1968	3.75	7.50	15.00
❑ 32465	Pinball Wizard/Dogs Part Two	1969	2.50	5.00	10.00
❑ 32465 [PS]	Pinball Wizard/Dogs Part Two	1969	5.00	10.00	20.00
❑ 32519	I'm Free/We're Not Gonna Take It	1969	2.50	5.00	10.00
❑ 32670	The Seeker/Here for More	1970	3.00	6.00	12.00
❑ 32708	Summertime Blues/Heaven and Hell	1970	3.00	6.00	12.00
❑ 32729	See Me, Feel Me/Overture from Tommy	1970	3.00	6.00	12.00
—With custom gold label					
❑ 32729 [PS]	See Me, Feel Me/Overture from Tommy	1970	5.00	10.00	20.00
❑ 32737	Young Man (Blues)/Substitute	1970	62.50	125.00	250.00
—Stock copies do exist					
❑ 32737 [DJ]	Young Man (Blues)/Substitute	1970	37.50	75.00	150.00
❑ 32737 [PS]	Young Man (Blues)/Substitute	1970	125.00	250.00	500.00
❑ 32846	Won't Get Fooled Again/I Don't Even Know Myself	1971	2.50	5.00	10.00
❑ 32888	Behind Blue Eyes/My Wife	1971	2.50	5.00	10.00
❑ 32983	Join Together/Baby, Don't You Do It	1972	2.50	5.00	10.00
❑ 34444 [DJ]	Happy Jack (same on both sides)	1967	10.00	20.00	40.00
—Promo-only number, pink label					
❑ 34470 [DJ]	Pictures of Lily (same on both sides)	1967	10.00	20.00	40.00
—Promo-only number, pink label					
❑ 7-34610/3 [DJ]	Excerpts from Tommy	1970	50.00	100.00	200.00
—Promo-only four-record box set with box and 4-page insert. As the records are sometimes found separately, they are also priced individually below.					
❑ 7-34610 [DJ]	Amazing Journey/The Acid Queen	1970	6.25	12.50	25.00
❑ 7-34611 [DJ]	Go to the Mirror Boy/Tommy Can You Hear Me	1970	6.25	12.50	25.00
❑ 7-34612 [DJ]	Smash the Mirror/Sensation	1970	6.25	12.50	25.00
❑ 7-34613 [DJ]	Sally Simpson/I'm Free	1970	6.25	12.50	25.00

MCA

Number	Title (A Side/B Side)	Yr	VG	VG+	NM
❑ L45-1809 [DJ]	Had Enough (same on both sides)	1978	2.50	5.00	10.00
❑ 40475	Squeeze Box/Success Story	1975	—	2.50	5.00
❑ 40475 [PS]	Squeeze Box/Success Story	1975	7.50	15.00	30.00
—Sleeve is promo only					
❑ 40603	Slip Kid/Dreaming from the Waist	1976	—	2.50	5.00
❑ 40948	Who Are You/Had Enough	1978	—	2.50	5.00
❑ 40978	Trick of the Light/9:05	1978	—	2.50	5.00
❑ 41053	Long Live Rock/My Wife	1979	—	2.50	5.00

MERCURY

Number	Title (A Side/B Side)	Yr	VG	VG+	NM
❑ DJ-570 [DJ]	I'm the Face/Zoot Suit	1980	—	2.50	5.00
❑ DJ-570 [PS]	I'm the Face/Zoot Suit	1980	—	2.50	5.00
—As "The High Numbers"					

POLYDOR

Number	Title (A Side/B Side)	Yr	VG	VG+	NM
❑ 2022	5:15/I'm One	1979	—	2.00	4.00
❑ 2022 [PS]	5:15/I'm One	1979	—	2.50	5.00

TRACK

Number	Title (A Side/B Side)	Yr	VG	VG+	NM
❑ 32983	Join Together/Baby, Don't You Do It	1972	5.00	10.00	20.00
—Later pressing than Decca 32983, but much scarcer					
❑ 33041	The Relay/Waspman	1972	2.50	5.00	10.00
❑ 40152	Love, Reign O'er Me/Water	1973	2.00	4.00	8.00
❑ 40182	The Real Me/I'm One	1974	2.00	4.00	8.00
❑ 40330	Postcard/Put the Money Down	1974	10.00	20.00	40.00

WARNER BROS.

Number	Title (A Side/B Side)	Yr	VG	VG+	NM
❑ 29731	It's Hard/Dangerous	1983	—	2.50	5.00
❑ 29814	Eminence Front/One at a Time	1983	—	2.50	5.00
❑ 29905	Athena/It's Your Turn	1982	—	2.00	4.00
❑ 29905 [PS]	Athena/It's Your Turn	1982	—	2.50	5.00
❑ 49698	You Better You Bet/Quiet One	1981	—	2.00	4.00
❑ 49698 [PS]	You Better You Bet/Quiet One	1981	—	2.50	5.00
❑ 49743	Don't Let Go the Coat/You	1981	—	2.00	4.00

WHOLE OATS

See DARYL HALL AND JOHN OATES.

WHYTE BOOTS, THE

PHILIPS

Number	Title (A Side/B Side)	Yr	VG	VG+	NM
❑ 40422	Nightmare/Let No One Come Between Us	1967	20.00	40.00	80.00

WICHITA TRAIN WHISTLE, THE

Produced by MICHAEL NESMITH.

DOT

Number	Title (A Side/B Side)	Yr	VG	VG+	NM
❑ 17152	Tapioca Tundra/Don't Cry Now	1968	3.75	7.50	15.00

WIEDLIN, JANE

Also see GO-GO'S.

EMI MANHATTAN

Number	Title (A Side/B Side)	Yr	VG	VG+	NM
❑ 50118	Rush Hour/The End of Love	1988	—	—	2.00
❑ 50118 [PS]	Rush Hour/The End of Love	1988	—	2.00	4.00
❑ 50145	Inside a Dream/Song of the Factory	1988	—	—	2.00
❑ 50145 [PS]	Inside a Dream/Song of the Factory	1988	—	—	2.00

I.R.S.

Number	Title (A Side/B Side)	Yr	VG	VG+	NM
❑ 52674	Blue Kiss/My Traveling Heart	1985	—	—	3.00
❑ 52674 [PS]	Blue Kiss/My Traveling Heart	1985	—	—	3.00

WIGGINS, JAY

AMY

Number	Title (A Side/B Side)	Yr	VG	VG+	NM
❑ 955	Sad Girl/No, Not Me	1966	2.50	5.00	10.00

I.P.G.

Number	Title (A Side/B Side)	Yr	VG	VG+	NM
❑ 1008	Sad Girl/No, Not Me	196?	3.75	7.50	15.00
❑ 1015	Forgive Then Forget/My Lonely Girl	196?	3.00	6.00	12.00

WIGGINS, WALLY

MERCURY

Number	Title (A Side/B Side)	Yr	VG	VG+	NM
❑ 71645	I Need You/Maybe Someday	1960	20.00	40.00	80.00
❑ 71713	Maybellene/Sweeter Than Sweet	1960	5.00	10.00	20.00
❑ 71953	The Habit of Loving You/Little Old Lady Who Lives in a Shoe	1962	7.50	15.00	30.00

WILD BEES, THE

RCA VICTOR

Number	Title (A Side/B Side)	Yr	VG	VG+	NM
❑ 47-7275	Doctor Rock/Bamboozled	1958	7.50	15.00	30.00

WILD-CATS, THE

UNITED ARTISTS

Number	Title (A Side/B Side)	Yr	VG	VG+	NM
❑ 154	Gazachstahagen/Billy's Cha Cha	1958	6.25	12.50	25.00
❑ 169	Dancing Elephants/King Size Guitar	1959	6.25	12.50	25.00

WILD CHERRY

A&M

Number	Title (A Side/B Side)	Yr	VG	VG+	NM
❑ 1656	Voodoo Doll/Because Your Love Is Mine	1974	—	2.50	5.00

EPIC

Number	Title (A Side/B Side)	Yr	VG	VG+	NM
❑ 50225	Play That Funky Music/The Lady Wants Your Money	1976	—	2.50	5.00
❑ 50306	Get It Up/Baby Don't You Know	1976	—	2.00	4.00
❑ 50362	Hot to Trot/Put Yourself in My Shoes	1977	—	2.00	4.00
❑ 50401	Are You Boogieing Around on Your Daddy/Hold On (With Strings)	1977	—	2.00	4.00
❑ 50500	Don't Stop, Get Off/I Love My Music	1978	—	2.00	4.00
❑ 50551	1-2-3 Kind of Love/Fools Fall in Love	1978	—	2.00	4.00
❑ 50619	This Old Heart of Mine (Is Weak for You)/Lana	1978	—	2.00	4.00
❑ 50702	Try a Piece of My Love/Take Me Back	1979	—	2.00	4.00

UNITED ARTISTS

Number	Title (A Side/B Side)	Yr	VG	VG+	NM
❑ XW217 [DJ]	Get Down (mono/stereo)	1973	—	2.50	5.00
—Stock copy not known to exist					

WILD ONES, THE (1)

Number	Title (A Side/B Side)	Yr	VG	VG+	NM
MAINLINE					
❑ 500	Caught in the Cookie Jar/Super Fox	1965	2.50	5.00	10.00
MALA					
❑ 564	High-Ho/Valerie	1967	2.00	4.00	8.00
UNITED ARTISTS					
❑ 947	Wild Thing/Just Can't Cry Anymore	1965	3.00	6.00	12.00
❑ 971	My Love/Lord Love a Duck	1966	2.50	5.00	10.00
❑ 971 [PS]	My Love/Lord Love a Duck	1966	3.75	7.50	15.00
❑ 50043	For Your Love (I Would Do Almost Anything)/ Never Givin' Up (On Your Love)	1966	2.50	5.00	10.00

WILD ONES, THE (2)

Number	Title (A Side/B Side)	Yr	VG	VG+	NM
SEARS					
❑ 2180	Come On Back/(Instrumental)	1966	2.50	5.00	10.00
❑ 2180 [PS]	Come On Back/(Instrumental)	1966	7.50	15.00	30.00

WILD ONES, THE (3)

Number	Title (A Side/B Side)	Yr	VG	VG+	NM
S.P.Q.R.					
❑ 3316	A Little Bit o' Soul/I've Been Crying	1964	6.25	12.50	25.00

WILDCATS, THE (1)

Number	Title (A Side/B Side)	Yr	VG	VG+	NM
RCA VICTOR					
❑ 47-6386	Keep Talkin'/Beatin' on a Rug	1956	10.00	20.00	40.00

WILDCATS, THE (2)

Actually THE BLOSSOMS.

Number	Title (A Side/B Side)	Yr	VG	VG+	NM
REPRISE					
❑ 0253	3625 Groovy Street/What Are We Gonna Do in '64	1964	5.00	10.00	20.00

WILDE, KIM

Number	Title (A Side/B Side)	Yr	VG	VG+	NM
EMI AMERICA					
❑ 8110	Kids in America/You'll Never Be So Wrong	1982	—	2.00	4.00
❑ 8110 [PS]	Kids in America/You'll Never Be So Wrong	1982	—	2.00	4.00
❑ 8139	Chequered Love/Everything We Know	1982	—	2.00	4.00
MCA					
❑ 52513	Go For It/Lovers on a Beach	1984	—	—	3.00
❑ 52513 [PS]	Go For It/Lovers on a Beach	1984	—	3.00	6.00
—Fold-out poster sleeve					
❑ 52925	Say You Really Want Me/(Instrumental)	1986	—	2.00	4.00
❑ 52952	Say You Really Want Me/Say You Really Want Me (Radio Edit)	1986	—	—	3.00
❑ 53024	You Keep Me Hangin' On/Loving You	1987	—	—	3.00
❑ 53024 [PS]	You Keep Me Hangin' On/Loving You	1987	—	—	3.00
❑ 53130	Say You Really Want Me/She Hasn't Got Time for You	1987	—	—	3.00
❑ 53130 [PS]	Say You Really Want Me/She Hasn't Got Time for You	1987	—	—	3.00
❑ 53192	Another Step (Closer to You)/Hold Back	1987	—	—	3.00
❑ 53192 [PS]	Another Step (Closer to You)/Hold Back	1987	—	—	3.00
❑ 53370	You Came/Tell Me Where You Are	1988	—	—	3.00
❑ 53370 [PS]	You Came/Tell Me Where You Are	1988	—	—	3.00
❑ 53480	Four Letter Word/She Hasn't Got Time for You	1988	—	—	3.00

WILDE, MARTY

Number	Title (A Side/B Side)	Yr	VG	VG+	NM
BELL					
❑ 45603	All Night Girl/(B-side unknown)	1974	—	2.50	5.00
EPIC					
❑ 9291	My Lucky Love/Misery's Child	1958	3.75	7.50	15.00
❑ 9356	Bad Boy/Teenage Years	1960	3.00	6.00	12.00
❑ 9392	Little Girl/Your Seventeenth Spring	1960	3.00	6.00	12.00
❑ 9400	Angry/My Baby Is Gone (Stop This World)	1960	3.00	6.00	12.00
❑ 9424	The Part of a Fool/Forgotten Dreams	1960	—	—	—
—Unreleased?					
HERITAGE					
❑ 814	Abergavenny/Alice in Blue	1969	—	3.00	6.00
—As "Shannon"					
❑ 814 [PS]	Abergavenny/Alice in Blue	1969	2.50	5.00	10.00
—As "Shannon"					
❑ 819	Jesamine/Lullaby	1969	—	3.00	6.00
—As "Shannon"					
JAMIE					
❑ 1282	Kiss Me/My, What a Woman	1964	2.50	5.00	10.00

WILDER, MATTHEW

Number	Title (A Side/B Side)	Yr	VG	VG+	NM
ARISTA					
❑ 0703	Work So Hard/(B-side unknown)	1982	—	2.00	4.00
PRIVATE I					
❑ 04113	Break My Stride/(Instrumental)	1983	—	2.00	4.00
❑ 04363	The Kid's American/Ladders of Love	1984	—	2.00	4.00
❑ 04617	Bouncin' Off the Walls/Love of an Amazon	1984	—	2.00	4.00
❑ 04617 [PS]	Bouncin' Off the Walls/Love of an Amazon	1984	—	2.00	4.00

WILDING, BOBBY

Number	Title (A Side/B Side)	Yr	VG	VG+	NM
ABC-PARAMOUNT					
❑ 10275	Mama/You Give Me No Choice	1961	3.00	6.00	12.00
DCP					
❑ 1009	I Want to Be a Beatle/Since I've Been Wearing My Hair Like a Beatle	1964	5.00	10.00	20.00
❑ 1106	I Want You/Too Young to Fall in Love	1964	3.00	6.00	12.00
MAY					
❑ 125	Slide (Part 1)/Slide (Part 2)	1962	3.00	6.00	12.00

WILDWOODS, THE

Actually THE FIVE SATINS.

Number	Title (A Side/B Side)	Yr	VG	VG+	NM
CAPRICE					
❑ 101	When the Swallows Come Back to Capistrano/ Heart of Mine	1961	37.50	75.00	150.00
MAY					
❑ 106	Golden Sunset/Here Comes Big Ed	1961	7.50	15.00	30.00

WILEY, CHUCK

Number	Title (A Side/B Side)	Yr	VG	VG+	NM
JAX					
❑ 1004	I Love You So Much/I Begin to Miss You	1959	25.00	50.00	100.00
UNITED ARTISTS					
❑ 113	Tear It Up/Shake Up the Dance	1958	18.75	37.50	75.00
❑ 120	By My Side/Door to Door	1958	—	—	—
—Unreleased					

WILKENS, ARTIE, AND THE PALMS

Number	Title (A Side/B Side)	Yr	VG	VG+	NM
STATES					
❑ 157	Darling Patricia/Please Come Back	1956	150.00	300.00	600.00

WILLIAMS, ANDRE

Number	Title (A Side/B Side)	Yr	VG	VG+	NM
AVIN					
❑ 103	Rib Tips (Part 1)/Rib Tips (Part 2)	1965	3.00	6.00	12.00
CHECKER					
❑ 1187	The Stroke/Humpin' Bumpin' and Trumpin'	1967	3.00	6.00	12.00
❑ 1205	Cadillac Jack/Mrs. Mother USA	1968	3.00	6.00	12.00
❑ 1214	Do the Popcorn/It's Gonna Be Fine in '69	1969	3.00	6.00	12.00
❑ 1219	Girdle Up/(Instrumental)	1969	3.00	6.00	12.00
EPIC					
❑ 9196	Bacon Fat/Just Because of a Kiss	1956	6.25	12.50	25.00
FORTUNE					
❑ 824	Pulling Time/Going Down to Tia-Juana	1955	20.00	40.00	80.00
❑ 827	Mozelle/Just Want a Little Lovin'	1956	10.00	20.00	40.00
❑ 828	Bobby Jean/It's All Over	1956	10.00	20.00	40.00
❑ 831	Bacon Fat/Just Because of a Kiss	1956	7.50	15.00	30.00
❑ 834	Mean Jean/You Are My Sunshine	1957	7.50	15.00	30.00
❑ 837	Jail Bait/My Tears	1957	20.00	40.00	80.00
❑ 839	Come On Baby/The Greasy Chicken	1957	7.50	15.00	30.00
—With Gino Park					
❑ 839	Don't Touch/Please Pass the Biscuits	1957	20.00	40.00	80.00
—With Gino Park					
❑ 839	The Greasy Chicken/Please Pass the Biscuits	1957	15.00	30.00	60.00
—With Gino Park					
❑ 842	My Last Dance with You/Hey! Country Girl	1958	7.50	15.00	30.00
❑ 847	Put a Chain on It/I'm All For You	1959	7.50	15.00	30.00
❑ 851	(Georgia May Is) Movin'/(Mmmm — Andre Williams Is) Movin'	1960	15.00	30.00	60.00
—With Gino Park					
❑ 856	Jail House Blues/I Still Love You	1960	7.50	15.00	30.00
MIRACLE					
❑ 4	Rosa Lee/Shoo Shoo	1960	300.00	600.00	1200.
NORTON					
❑ 45-069	Poor Mr. Santa (N-N-Naughty!)/Poor Mr. Santa (N-n-nice!)	1997	—	—	2.00
❑ 45-069 [PS]	Poor Mr. Santa (N-N-Naughty!)/Poor Mr. Santa (N-n-nice!)	1997	—	—	2.00
RIC-TIC					
❑ 124	You Got It And I Want It/I Can't Stop Crying	1967	6.25	12.50	25.00
RONALD					
❑ 1001	Please Give Me a Chance/(B-side unknown)	196?	6.25	12.50	25.00
SPORT					
❑ 105	Pearl Time/Soul Groove	1967	6.25	12.50	25.00
WINGATE					
❑ 014	Loose Juice/Sweet Little Pussycat	1966	3.75	7.50	15.00
❑ 021	Do It! (Part 1)/Do It! (Part 2)	1966	5.00	10.00	20.00

WILLIAMS, ANDY

Number	Title (A Side/B Side)	Yr	VG	VG+	NM
CADENCE					
❑ 1282	Christmas Is a Feeling in Your Heart/The Wind, The Sand and The Stars	1955	3.75	7.50	15.00
❑ 1288	Walk Hand in Hand/Not Anymore	1956	3.00	6.00	12.00
❑ 1297	Canadian Sunset/High Upon a Mountain	1956	3.00	6.00	12.00
❑ 1303	Baby Doll/Since I've Found My Baby	1956	3.00	6.00	12.00
❑ 1308	Butterfly/It Doesn't Take Very Long	1957	3.00	6.00	12.00
❑ 1323	I Like Your Kind of Love/Stop Teasin' Me	1957	3.00	6.00	12.00
❑ 1336	Lips of Wine/Straight from the Heart	1957	3.00	6.00	12.00
❑ 1340	Are You Sincere/Be Mine Tonight	1957	3.00	6.00	12.00
❑ 1351	Promise Me, Love/Your Hand, Your Heart, Your Love	1958	2.50	5.00	10.00
❑ 1358	The Hawaiian Wedding Song/House of Bamboo	1958	2.50	5.00	10.00
❑ 1370	Lonely Street/Summer Love	1959	2.50	5.00	10.00
❑ 1374	The Village of St. Bernadette/I'm So Lonesome I Could Cry	1959	2.50	5.00	10.00
❑ 1374 [PS]	The Village of St. Bernadette/I'm So Lonesome I Could Cry	1959	3.75	7.50	15.00
❑ 1378	Wake Me When It's Over/We Have a Date	1960	2.50	5.00	10.00
❑ 1381	Do You Mind?/Dreamsville	1960	2.50	5.00	10.00
❑ 1389	In the Summertime (You Don't Want My Love)/ Don't Go to Strangers	1960	2.50	5.00	10.00
❑ 1389	You Don't Want My Love/Don't Go to Strangers	1960	3.00	6.00	12.00
❑ 1398	The Bilbao Song/How Wonderful to Know	1961	2.50	5.00	10.00
❑ 1433	Twilight Time/So Rare	1962	2.50	5.00	10.00
❑ 1447	Let It Be Me/Under Paris Skies	1964	2.50	5.00	10.00
❑ 2501 [S]	Unchained Melody/I'm So Alone	1960	3.75	7.50	15.00
❑ 2502 [S]	You Don't Know What Love Is/Say It Isn't So	1960	3.75	7.50	15.00
COLUMBIA					
❑ AE7 1108 [DJ]	It's the Most Wonderful Time of the Year/Kay Thompson's Jingle Bells	1976	2.50	5.00	10.00
—Special radio promo for Christmas Seals. Also contains public service announcements for Christmas Seals by Williams on each side.					
❑ AE7 1108 [PS]	It's the Most Wonderful Time of the Year/Kay Thompson's Jingle Bells	1976	2.50	5.00	10.00
❑ 10029	A Mi Esposa Con Amor (To My Wife with Love)/ Another Lonely Song	1974	—	2.00	4.00
❑ 10054	Christmas Present/The Lord's Prayer	1974	—	2.00	4.00
❑ 10054 [PS]	Christmas Present/The Lord's Prayer	1974	—	2.50	5.00
❑ 10078	Love Said Goodbye/One More Time	1974	—	2.00	4.00
❑ 10113	Cry Softly/You Lay So Easy on My Mind	1975	—	2.00	4.00
❑ 10144	Feelings/Quits	1975	—	2.00	4.00

Number	Title (A Side/B Side)	Yr	VG	VG+	NM
❑ 10208	Sad Eyes/Quits	1975	—	2.00	4.00
❑ 10263	Tell It Like It Is/Goin' Through the Motions	1975	—	2.00	4.00
❑ 10471	Are You In There?/Are You In There? (Disco)	1977	—	2.00	4.00
❑ 10878	Love Theme from "Oliver's Story"/Everytime I See Laureen	1979	—	2.00	4.00
❑ 10952	Love Theme from "Oliver's Story"/Love Story (Where Do I Begin)	1979	—	2.00	4.00
❑ 11152	Jason/I'll Never Love Anyone Anymore	1979	—	2.00	4.00
❑ 31458 [S]	(titles unknown)	1962	3.00	6.00	12.00
❑ 31459 [S]	(titles unknown)	1962	3.00	6.00	12.00
❑ 31460 [S]	(titles unknown)	1962	3.00	6.00	12.00
❑ 31461 [S]	(titles unknown)	1962	3.00	6.00	12.00
❑ 31462 [S]	(titles unknown)	1962	3.00	6.00	12.00
❑ 31495 [S]	(titles unknown)	1962	3.00	6.00	12.00
❑ 31496 [S]	(titles unknown)	1962	3.00	6.00	12.00
❑ 31497 [S]	(titles unknown)	1962	3.00	6.00	12.00

—Anyone who can fill in these gaps -- the above 8 all are Columbia "Stereo 7" singles -- please let us know.

Number	Title (A Side/B Side)	Yr	VG	VG+	NM
❑ 31498 [S]	Tonight/The Second Time Around	1962	3.00	6.00	12.00
❑ 31499 [S]	It Might As Well Be Spring/Three Coins in the Fountain	1962	3.00	6.00	12.00
❑ 42199	Danny Boy/Fly by Night	1961	2.00	4.00	8.00
❑ 42199 [PS]	Danny Boy/Fly by Night	1961	3.00	6.00	12.00
❑ 42265	The Wonderful World of the Young/Help Me	1962	2.00	4.00	8.00
❑ 42265 [PS]	The Wonderful World of the Young/Help Me	1962	2.50	5.00	10.00
❑ 42451	Stranger on the Shore/I Want to Be Wanted	1962	2.00	4.00	8.00
❑ 42451 [PS]	Stranger on the Shore/I Want to Be Wanted	1962	2.50	5.00	10.00
❑ 42523	Don't You Believe It/Summertime	1962	2.00	4.00	8.00
❑ 42523 [PS]	Don't You Believe It/Summertime	1962	2.50	5.00	10.00
❑ 42674	Can't Get Used to Losing You/Days of Wine and Roses	1963	2.00	4.00	8.00
❑ 42674 [PS]	Can't Get Used to Losing You/Days of Wine and Roses	1963	2.50	5.00	10.00
❑ 42784	Hopeless/The Peking Theme (So Little Time)	1963	2.00	4.00	8.00
❑ 42894	The Christmas Song (Chestnuts Roasting On An Open Fire)/White Christmas	1963	2.00	4.00	8.00

—Stock copy or black vinyl promo

Number	Title (A Side/B Side)	Yr	VG	VG+	NM
❑ 42894 [DJ]	The Christmas Song (Chestnuts Roasting On An Open Fire)/White Christmas	1963	3.00	6.00	12.00

—Promo only on green vinyl

Number	Title (A Side/B Side)	Yr	VG	VG+	NM
❑ 42950	A Fool Never Learns/Charade	1963	2.00	4.00	8.00
❑ 43015	Wrong for Each Other/Madrigal	1964	—	3.00	6.00
❑ 43128	On the Street Where You Live/Almost There	1964	—	3.00	6.00
❑ 43180	Dear Heart/Emily	1964	—	3.00	6.00
❑ 43257	...And Roses and Roses/My Carousel	1965	—	3.00	6.00
❑ 43257 [PS]	...And Roses and Roses/My Carousel	1965	2.00	4.00	8.00
❑ 43358	Ain't It True/Loved One	1965	—	3.00	6.00
❑ 43458	Do You Hear What I Hear/Some Children See Him	1965	2.00	4.00	8.00
❑ 43519	Bye Bye Blues/You're Gonna Hear from Me!	1966	—	3.00	6.00
❑ 43650	The Summer of Our Love/How Can I Tell Her It's Over	1966	—	3.00	6.00
❑ 43737	In the Arms of Love/The Many Faces of Love	1966	—	3.00	6.00
❑ 44065	Music to Watch Girls By/The Face I Love	1967	—	2.50	5.00
❑ 44202	More and More/I Want to Be Free	1967	—	2.50	5.00
❑ 44325	When I Look in Your Eyes/Holly	1967	—	2.50	5.00
❑ 44527	Sweet Memories/You Are Where Everything Is	1968	—	2.50	5.00
❑ 44650	Battle Hymn of the Republic/Ave Maria	1968	—	2.50	5.00
❑ 44650 [PS]	Battle Hymn of the Republic/Ave Maria	1968	—	3.00	6.00
❑ 44709	The Christmas Song (Chestnuts Roasting On An Open Fire)/It's The Most Wonderful Time Of The Year	1968	—	3.00	6.00
❑ 44818	Happy Heart/Our Last Goodbye	1969	—	2.50	5.00
❑ 44929	Live and Learn/You Are	1969	—	2.50	5.00
❑ 45003	What Am I Living For/A Woman's Way	1969	—	2.50	5.00
❑ 45094	Can't Help Falling in Love/Sweet Memories	1970	—	2.50	5.00
❑ 45175	One Day of Your Life/Long Time Blues	1970	—	2.50	5.00
❑ 45246	Whistling Away the Dark/Home Lovin' Man	1970	—	2.50	5.00
❑ 45317	(Where Do I Begin) Love Story/Something	1971	—	2.00	4.00
❑ 45434	You've Got a Friend/A Song for You	1971	—	2.00	4.00
❑ 45494	Help Me Make It Through the Night/Love Is All	1971	—	2.00	4.00
❑ 45531	The Last Time I Saw Her/Music from Across the Way	1972	—	2.00	4.00
❑ 45533	Love Story (Spanish Version)/Music from Across the Way (Spanish Version)	1972	—	3.00	6.00
❑ 45579	Love Theme from "The Godfather" (Speak Softly Love)/Home for Thee	1972	—	2.00	4.00
❑ 45647	MacArthur Park/Amazing Grace	1972	—	2.00	4.00
❑ 45716	Who Was It/Home Lovin' Man	1972	—	2.00	4.00
❑ 45757	Marmalade, Molenaisse and Honey/Who Was It	1973	—	2.00	4.00
❑ 45814	Last Tango in Paris/I'll Never Be the Same	1973	—	2.00	4.00
❑ 45936	Solitaire/My Love	1973	—	2.00	4.00
❑ 45985	Walk Right Back/Remember	1974	—	2.00	4.00

—With Noelle

Number	Title (A Side/B Side)	Yr	VG	VG+	NM
❑ 46049	Love's Theme/You're the Best Thing That's Ever Happened to Me	1974	—	2.00	4.00
❑ JZSP 76322/3 [DJ]	Away In A Manger/O Holy Night	1963	2.50	5.00	10.00
❑ JZSP 111911/2 [DJ]	Have Yourself A Merry Little Christmas/The Bells Of St. Mary's	1966	2.00	4.00	8.00

—Yellow label

Number	Title (A Side/B Side)	Yr	VG	VG+	NM
❑ JZSP 111911/2 [DJ]	Have Yourself A Merry Little Christmas/The Bells Of St. Mary's	1966	2.00	4.00	8.00

—White label

MGM

Number	Title (A Side/B Side)	Yr	VG	VG+	NM
❑ 11076	Gentle Hands/From the Manger to the Cross	1951	6.25	12.50	25.00

"X"

Number	Title (A Side/B Side)	Yr	VG	VG+	NM
❑ 0036	Why Should I Cry Over You/You Can't Buy Happiness	1954	5.00	10.00	20.00
❑ 0091	Now I Know/Here Comes That Dream Again	1955	5.00	10.00	20.00

7-Inch Extended Plays

CADENCE

Number	Title (A Side/B Side)	Yr	VG	VG+	NM
❑ CEP-112	The Hawaiian Wedding Song/Sail Along Silv'ry Moon//Blue Hawaii/Sweet Leilani	1959	3.00	6.00	12.00
❑ CEP-112 [PS]	Andy Williams	1959	3.00	6.00	12.00
❑ CEP-116	It's All in the Game/My Happiness//Twilight Time/Love Letters in the Sand	1959	3.00	6.00	12.00
❑ CEP-116 [PS]	Two Time Winners	1959	3.00	6.00	12.00
❑ CEP-119	To You Sweetheart, Aloha/The Moon of Manakoora//I'll Weave a Lot of Stars for You/Beyond the Reef	1959	3.00	6.00	12.00
❑ CEP-119 [PS]	To You Sweetheart, Aloha	1959	3.00	6.00	12.00
❑ CEP-120	Aloha Oe/A Song of Old Hawaii//Song of the Islands/Love Song of Kalua	1959	3.00	6.00	12.00
❑ CEP-120 [PS]	Song of the Islands	1959	3.00	6.00	12.00

COLUMBIA

Number	Title (A Side/B Side)	Yr	VG	VG+	NM
❑ 7-9138 [PS]	Dear Heart	1965	2.50	5.00	10.00
❑ 7-9138 [S]	Dear Heart/Red Roses for a Blue Lady/Who Can I Turn To//You're Nobody 'Til Somebody Loves You/Everybody Loves Somebody/I Can't Stop Loving You	1965	2.50	5.00	10.00

—33 1/3 rpm, small hole, "Special Coin Operator Release"

Number	Title (A Side/B Side)	Yr	VG	VG+	NM
❑ 7-9299 [PS]	The Shadow of Your Smile	1966	2.50	5.00	10.00
❑ 7-9299 [S]	The Shadow of Your Smile/Try to Remember/Yesterday//Michelle/A Taste of Honey/Somewhere	1966	2.50	5.00	10.00

—33 1/3 rpm, small hole, "Special Coin Operator Release"

WILLIAMS, BARRY

"Greg Brady" of THE BRADY BUNCH.

PARAMOUNT

Number	Title (A Side/B Side)	Yr	VG	VG+	NM
❑ 0122	Sweet Sweetheart/Sunny	1971	3.75	7.50	15.00
❑ 0122 [PS]	Sweet Sweetheart/Sunny	1971	5.00	10.00	20.00

WILLIAMS, BERNIE

BELL

Number	Title (A Side/B Side)	Yr	VG	VG+	NM
❑ 768	Ever Again/Next to You	1969	50.00	100.00	200.00

WILLIAMS, CORA/SHIRLEY HAVEN AND THE FOUR JACKS

FEDERAL

Number	Title (A Side/B Side)	Yr	VG	VG+	NM
❑ 12079	I Ain't Coming Back Anymore/Sure Cure for the Blues	1952	150.00	300.00	600.00

WILLIAMS, DANNY

UNITED ARTISTS

Number	Title (A Side/B Side)	Yr	VG	VG+	NM
❑ 348	Lonely/We Will Never Be As Young As This Again	1961	3.00	6.00	12.00
❑ 411	Jeannie/Weaver of Dreams	1962	3.00	6.00	12.00
❑ 480	Something's Gotta Give/Miracle of You	1962	3.00	6.00	12.00
❑ 493	Tears/Miracle of You	1962	3.00	6.00	12.00
❑ 601	More (Theme from Mondo Cane)/Rhapsody	1963	3.00	6.00	12.00
❑ 685	White on White/The Comedy Is Ended	1964	3.75	7.50	15.00
❑ 729	The Truth Hurts/Little Toy Balloon	1964	2.50	5.00	10.00
❑ 762	I Watched a Flower Grow/Forget Her, Forget Her	1964	2.50	5.00	10.00
❑ 825	How Soon/The Seventh Dawn	1965	2.50	5.00	10.00
❑ 860	All's Fair in Love and War/Masquerade	1965	2.50	5.00	10.00
❑ 959	The Stranger/I Can't Believe I'm Losing You	1965	2.50	5.00	10.00
❑ 50020	Blue on White/It's Not for Me to Say	1966	2.00	4.00	8.00

WILLIAMS, HANK

MGM

Number	Title (A Side/B Side)	Yr	VG	VG+	NM
❑ 8010	Lovesick Blues/Never Again	1949	17.50	35.00	70.00
❑ 10352	Lovesick Blues/Never Again	1950	12.50	25.00	50.00

—Reissue has original 45 rpm number in parentheses under this number

Number	Title (A Side/B Side)	Yr	VG	VG+	NM
❑ 10401	Wedding Bells/I've Just Told Mama Goodbye	1949	15.00	30.00	60.00
❑ 10434	Dear Brother/Lost on the River	1949	15.00	30.00	60.00
❑ 10461	Mind Your Own Business/There'll Be No Teardrops Tonight	1949	15.00	30.00	60.00
❑ 10506	You're Gonna Change (Or I'm Gonna Leave)/Lost Highway	1949	15.00	30.00	60.00
❑ 10560	My Bucket's Got a Hole In It/I'm So Lonesome I Could Cry	1949	15.00	30.00	60.00
❑ 10609	I Just Don't Like This Kind of Lovin'/May You Never Be Alone	1950	10.00	20.00	40.00
❑ 10630	Beyond the Sunset/The Funeral	1950	15.00	30.00	60.00

—As "Luke the Drifter"

Number	Title (A Side/B Side)	Yr	VG	VG+	NM
❑ 10645	Long Gone Lonesome Blues/My Son Calls Another Man Daddy	1950	10.00	20.00	40.00
❑ 10696	Why Don't You Love Me/A House Without Love	1950	10.00	20.00	40.00
❑ 10718	Everything's OK/Too Many Parties	1950	15.00	30.00	60.00

—As "Luke the Drifter"

Number	Title (A Side/B Side)	Yr	VG	VG+	NM
❑ 10760	They'll Never Take Her Love from Me/Why Should We Try Anymore	1950	10.00	20.00	40.00
❑ 10806	No, No, Joe/Help Me Understand	1950	15.00	30.00	60.00

—As "Luke the Drifter"

Number	Title (A Side/B Side)	Yr	VG	VG+	NM
❑ 10813	I Heard My Mother Praying for Me/Jesus Remembered Me	1950	12.50	25.00	50.00
❑ 10832	Moanin' the Blues/Nobody's Lonesome for Me	1950	10.00	20.00	40.00
❑ 10904	Cold, Cold Heart/Dear John	1951	7.50	15.00	30.00
❑ 10932	Just Waitin'/Men with Broken Hearts	1951	12.50	25.00	50.00

—As "Luke the Drifter"

Number	Title (A Side/B Side)	Yr	VG	VG+	NM
❑ 10961	I Can't Help It (If I'm Still in Love with You)/Howlin' at the Moon	1951	7.50	15.00	30.00
❑ 11000	Hey, Good Lookin'/My Heart Would Know	1951	7.50	15.00	30.00
❑ 11017	I Dreamed About Mama Last Night/I've Been Down That Road Before	1951	12.50	25.00	50.00

—As "Luke the Drifter"

Number	Title (A Side/B Side)	Yr	VG	VG+	NM
❑ 11054	Crazy Heart/Lonesome Whistle	1951	7.50	15.00	30.00
❑ 11083	Leave Us Women Alone/If You See My Baby	1951	10.00	20.00	40.00
❑ 11100	Baby, We're Really in Love/I'd Still Want You	1951	7.50	15.00	30.00
❑ 11120	Ramblin' Man/A Picture from Life's Other Side	1952	10.00	20.00	40.00

—As "Luke the Drifter"

Number	Title (A Side/B Side)	Yr	VG	VG+	NM
❑ 11160	Honky Tonk Blues/I'm Sorry for You My Friend	1952	7.50	15.00	30.00
❑ 11202	Half As Much/Let's Turn Back the Years	1952	7.50	15.00	30.00

Number	Title (A Side/B Side)	Yr	VG	VG+	NM
❑ 11283	Jambalaya (On the Bayou)/Window Shopping	1952	7.50	15.00	30.00
❑ 11309	Be Careful of Stones That You Throw/Why Don't You Make Up Your Mind	1952	10.00	20.00	40.00
—As "Luke the Drifter"					
❑ 11318	Settin' the Woods On Fire/You Win Again	1952	7.50	15.00	30.00
❑ 11366	I'll Never Get Out of This World Alive/I Could Never Be Ashamed	1952	7.50	15.00	30.00
❑ 11416	Kaw-Liga/Your Cheatin' Heart	1953	7.50	15.00	30.00
❑ 11479	Take These Chains from My Heart/Ramblin' Man	1953	6.25	12.50	25.00
❑ 11533	I Won't Be Home No More/My Love for You	1953	6.25	12.50	25.00
❑ 11574	Weary Blues from Waitin'/I Can't Escape from You	1953	6.25	12.50	25.00
❑ 11628	Calling You/When God Comes and Gathers His Jewels	1953	6.25	12.50	25.00
❑ 11675	You Better Keep It on Your Mind/Low Down Blues	1954	6.25	12.50	25.00
❑ 11707	How Can You Refuse Him Now/A House of Gold	1954	6.25	12.50	25.00
❑ 11768	I Ain't Got Nothin' But Time/I'm Satisfied with You	1954	6.25	12.50	25.00
❑ 11861	Angel of Death/(I'm Gonna) Sing, Sing, Sing	1954	6.25	12.50	25.00
❑ 11928	Please Don't Let Me Love You/Faded Love and Winter's Roses	1955	6.25	12.50	25.00
❑ 11975	Message to My Mother/Mother Is Gone	1955	6.25	12.50	25.00
❑ 12029	A Teardrop on a Rose/Alone and Forsaken	1955	6.25	12.50	25.00
❑ 12077	Someday You'll Call My Name/The First Fall of Snow	1955	6.25	12.50	25.00
❑ 12127	The Battle of Armageddon/Thank God	1955	6.25	12.50	25.00
❑ 12185	California Zephyr/Thy Burdens Are Greater Than Mine	1956	6.25	12.50	25.00
❑ 12244	I Wish I Had a Nickel/There's No Room in My Heart	1956	6.25	12.50	25.00
❑ 12332	Blue Love (In My Heart)/Singing Waterfall	1956	6.25	12.50	25.00
❑ 12394	The Pale Horse and His Rider/A Home in Heaven	1956	5.00	10.00	20.00
—As "Hank and Audrey Williams"					
❑ 12431	Alimony Blues/Because You've Been Away	1957	5.00	10.00	20.00
❑ 12438	Ready to Go Home/We're Getting Closer	1957	5.00	10.00	20.00
❑ 12484	Leave Me Alone with the Blues/With Tears in My Eyes	1957	5.00	10.00	20.00
❑ 12535	No One Will Ever Know/The Waltz of the Wind	1957	5.00	10.00	20.00
❑ 12611	Why Don't You Love Me/I Can't Help It (If I'm Still in Love with You)	1958	5.00	10.00	20.00
❑ 12635	We Live in Two Different Worlds/My Bucket's Got a Hole In It	1958	5.00	10.00	20.00
❑ 12727	Just Waitin'/Roly-Poly	1958	5.00	10.00	20.00
❑ 13305	Your Cheatin' Heart/Lovesick Blues	1964	3.00	6.00	12.00
❑ 13305 [PS]	Your Cheatin' Heart/Lovesick Blues	1964	5.00	10.00	20.00
❑ 13489	I'm So Lonesome I Could Cry/You Win Again	1966	3.00	6.00	12.00
❑ 13542	Kaw-Liga/Let's Turn Back the Years	1966	3.00	6.00	12.00
❑ 13630	There'll Be No Teardrops Tonight/They'll Never Take Her Love from Me	1966	3.00	6.00	12.00
❑ 13717	Long Gone Lonesome Blues/Hang On the Bell, Nellie	1967	3.00	6.00	12.00
❑ 14849	Why Don't You Love Me/Ramblin' Man	1976	—	3.00	6.00

7-Inch Extended Plays

MGM

Number	Title (A Side/B Side)	Yr	VG	VG+	NM
❑ X-168 [PS]	Moanin' the Blues	1953	10.00	20.00	40.00
—Cover with X-4041 and X-4042					
❑ X-202 [PS]	The Hank Williams Memorial Album	1953	10.00	20.00	40.00
—Cover with X-4102 and X-4103					
❑ X-1014	Crazy Heart/Baby We're Really in Love//My Heart Would Know/I Can't Help It (If I'm Still in Love with You)	1953	20.00	40.00	80.00
—Yellow label					
❑ X-1014	Crazy Heart/Baby We're Really in Love//My Heart Would Know/I Can't Help It (If I'm Still in Love with You)	1960	5.00	10.00	20.00
—Black label					
❑ X-1014 [PS]	Crazy Heart	1953	5.00	10.00	20.00
❑ X-1047	Pictures from Life's Other Side/Men with Broken Hearts//Help Me Understand/Too Many Parties (And Too Many Pals)	1955	15.00	30.00	60.00
—Yellow label					
❑ X-1047	Pictures from Life's Other Side/Men with Broken Hearts//Help Me Understand/Too Many Parties (And Too Many Pals)	1960	5.00	10.00	20.00
—Black label					
❑ X-1047 [PS]	Hank Williams As Luke the Drifter	1955	5.00	10.00	20.00
❑ X-1076	Move It On Over/Fly Trouble//Window Shopping/Pan American	1955	15.00	30.00	60.00
—Yellow label					
❑ X-1076	Move It On Over/Fly Trouble//Window Shopping/Pan American	1960	5.00	10.00	20.00
—Black label					
❑ X-1076 [PS]	Move It On Over	1955	5.00	10.00	20.00
❑ X-1082	(contents unknown)	1955	15.00	30.00	60.00
—Yellow label					
❑ X-1082	(contents unknown)	1960	5.00	10.00	20.00
—Black label					
❑ X-1082 [PS]	There'll Be No Teardrops Tonight	1955	5.00	10.00	20.00
❑ X-1101	I Saw the Light/Mansion on the Hill//Six More Miles/Wedding Bells	1955	15.00	30.00	60.00
—Yellow label					
❑ X-1101	I Saw the Light/Mansion on the Hill//Six More Miles/Wedding Bells	1960	5.00	10.00	20.00
—Black label					
❑ X-1101 [PS]	Hank Williams Sings	1955	5.00	10.00	20.00
❑ X-1102	Lost Highway/I've Just Told Mama Goodbye//Wealth Won't Save Your Soul/A House Without Love	1955	15.00	30.00	60.00
—Yellow label					
❑ X-1102	Lost Highway/I've Just Told Mama Goodbye//Wealth Won't Save Your Soul/A House Without Love	1960	5.00	10.00	20.00
—Black label					
❑ X-1102 [PS]	Hank Williams Sings Vol. 2	1955	5.00	10.00	20.00
❑ X-1135	Ramblin' Man/My Son Calls Another Man Daddy//I Can't Escape from You/Nobody's Lonesome for Me	1955	10.00	20.00	40.00
—Yellow label					
❑ X-1135	Ramblin' Man/My Son Calls Another Man Daddy//I Can't Escape from You/Nobody's Lonesome for Me	1960	3.75	7.50	15.00
—Black label					
❑ X-1135 [PS]	Ramblin' Man Vol. 1	1955	3.75	7.50	15.00
❑ X-1136	Lonesome Whistle/I Jus' Don't Like This Kind of Livin'//Take These Chains from My Heart/Why Don't You Love Me?	1955	10.00	20.00	40.00
—Yellow label					
❑ X-1136	Lonesome Whistle/I Jus' Don't Like This Kind of Livin'//Take These Chains from My Heart/Why Don't You Love Me?	1960	3.75	7.50	15.00
—Black label					
❑ X-1136 [PS]	Ramblin' Man Vol. 2	1955	3.75	7.50	15.00
❑ X-1165	Why Don't You Make Up Your Mind/I've Been Down That Road Before//Just Waitin'/Everything's Okay	1955	10.00	20.00	40.00
—Yellow label					
❑ X-1165	Why Don't You Make Up Your Mind/I've Been Down That Road Before//Just Waitin'/Everything's Okay	1960	3.75	7.50	15.00
—Black label					
❑ X-1165 [PS]	Luke the Drifter	1955	3.75	7.50	15.00
❑ X-1215	(contents unknown)	1956	10.00	20.00	40.00
—Yellow label					
❑ X-1215	(contents unknown)	1960	3.75	7.50	15.00
—Black label					
❑ X-1215 [PS]	Moanin' the Blues Vol. 1	1956	3.75	7.50	15.00
❑ X-1216	Moanin' the Blues/I'm So Lonesome I Could Cry//My Sweet Love Ain't Around/Honky Tonk Blues	1956	10.00	20.00	40.00
—Yellow label					
❑ X-1216	Moanin' the Blues/I'm So Lonesome I Could Cry//My Sweet Love Ain't Around/Honky Tonk Blues	1960	3.75	7.50	15.00
—Black label					
❑ X-1216 [PS]	Moanin' the Blues Vol. 2	1956	3.75	7.50	15.00
❑ X-1217	Lovesick Blues/The Blues Come Around//I'm a Long Gone Daddy/Long Gone Lonesome Blues	1956	10.00	20.00	40.00
—Yellow label					
❑ X-1217	Lovesick Blues/The Blues Come Around//I'm a Long Gone Daddy/Long Gone Lonesome Blues	1960	3.75	7.50	15.00
—Black label					
❑ X-1217 [PS]	Moanin' the Blues Vol. 3	1956	3.75	7.50	15.00
❑ X-1218	I'm Gonna Sing/Message to My Mother//Thank God/The Angel of Death	1956	10.00	20.00	40.00
—Yellow label					
❑ X-1218	I'm Gonna Sing/Message to My Mother//Thank God/The Angel of Death	1960	3.75	7.50	15.00
—Black label					
❑ X-1218 [PS]	I Saw the Light	1956	3.75	7.50	15.00
❑ X-1235	*Honky Tonkin'/Mind Your Own Business/Rootie Tootie/I Ain't Got Nothing But Time	1956	10.00	20.00	40.00
—Yellow label					
❑ X-1235	*Honky Tonkin'/Mind Your Own Business/Rootie Tootie/I Ain't Got Nothing But Time	1960	3.75	7.50	15.00
—Black label					
❑ X-1235 [PS]	Honky Tonkin'	1956	3.75	7.50	15.00
❑ X-1317	Jambalaya (On the Bayou)/I Won't Be Home No More//Honky Tonk Blues/I'll Never Get Out of This World Alive	1957	10.00	20.00	40.00
—Yellow label					
❑ X-1317	Jambalaya (On the Bayou)/I Won't Be Home No More//Honky Tonk Blues/I'll Never Get Out of This World Alive	1960	3.75	7.50	15.00
—Black label					
❑ X-1317 [PS]	Honky Tonkin' Vol. 1	1957	3.75	7.50	15.00
❑ X-1318	Honky Tonkin'/Howlin' at the Moon//My Bucket's Got a Hole in It/Baby, We're Really in Love	1957	10.00	20.00	40.00
—Yellow label					
❑ X-1318	Honky Tonkin'/Howlin' at the Moon//My Bucket's Got a Hole in It/Baby, We're Really in Love	1960	3.75	7.50	15.00
—Black label					
❑ X-1318 [PS]	Honky Tonkin' Vol. 2	1957	3.75	7.50	15.00
❑ X-1319	Mind Your Own Business/Rootie Tootie//I Ain't Got Nothin' But Time/You Better Keep It on Your Mind	1957	10.00	20.00	40.00
—Yellow label					
❑ X-1319	Mind Your Own Business/Rootie Tootie//I Ain't Got Nothin' But Time/You Better Keep It on Your Mind	1960	3.75	7.50	15.00
—Black label					
❑ X-1319 [PS]	Honky Tonkin' Vol. 3	1957	3.75	7.50	15.00
❑ X-1491	Wedding Bells/May You Never Be Alone//Lost Highway/Why Should We Try Anymore	1958	7.50	5.00	30.00
—Yellow label					
❑ X-1491	Wedding Bells/May You Never Be Alone//Lost Highway/Why Should We Try Anymore	1960	3.75	7.50	15.00
—Black label					
❑ X-1491 [PS]	Sing Me a Blue Song Vol. 1	1958	3.75	7.50	15.00
❑ X-1492	I Heard You Crying in Your Sleep/Blue Love//Mansion on the Hill/They'll Never Take Her Love from Me	1958	7.50	15.00	30.00
—Yellow label					
❑ X-1492	I Heard You Crying in Your Sleep/Blue Love//Mansion on the Hill/They'll Never Take Her Love from Me	1960	3.75	7.50	15.00
—Black label					
❑ X-1492 [PS]	Sing Me a Blue Song Vol. 2	1958	3.75	7.50	15.00

Number	Title (A Side/B Side)	Yr	VG	VG+	NM
❑ X-1493	I've Just Told Mama Goodbye/House Without Love//Six More Miles/Singing Waterfall	1958	7.50	15.00	30.00
—Yellow label					
❑ X-1493	I've Just Told Mama Goodbye/House Without Love//Six More Miles/Singing Waterfall	1960	3.75	7.50	15.00
—Black label					
❑ X-1493 [PS]	Sing Me a Blue Song Vol. 3	1958	3.75	7.50	15.00
❑ X-1554	There's No Room in My Heart/Waltz of the Wind//Pan American/With Tears in My Eyes	1958	7.50	15.00	30.00
—Yellow label					
❑ X-1554	There's No Room in My Heart/Waltz of the Wind//Pan American/With Tears in My Eyes	1960	3.75	7.50	15.00
—Black label					
❑ X-1554 [PS]	The Immortal Hank Williams Vol. 1	1958	3.75	7.50	15.00
❑ X-1555	I Wish I Had a Nickel/Fly Trouble//Please Don't Let Me Love You/I'm Satisfied with You	1958	7.50	15.00	30.00
—Yellow label					
❑ X-1555	I Wish I Had a Nickel/Fly Trouble//Please Don't Let Me Love You/I'm Satisfied with You	1960	3.75	7.50	15.00
—Black label					
❑ X-1555 [PS]	The Immortal Hank Williams Vol. 2	1958	3.75	7.50	15.00
❑ X-1556	No One Will Ever Know/Faded Love and Winter Roses//First Fall of Snow/California Zephyr	1958	7.50	15.00	30.00
—Yellow label					
❑ X-1556	No One Will Ever Know/Faded Love and Winter Roses//First Fall of Snow/California Zephyr	1960	3.75	7.50	15.00
—Black label					
❑ X-1556 [PS]	The Immortal Hank Williams Vol. 3	1958	3.75	7.50	15.00
❑ X-1612	Your Cheatin' Heart/Settin' the Woods on Fire// You Win Again/Hey, Good Lookin'	1959	7.50	15.00	30.00
—Yellow label					
❑ X-1612	Your Cheatin' Heart/Settin' the Woods on Fire// You Win Again/Hey, Good Lookin'	1960	3.75	7.50	15.00
—Black label					
❑ X-1612 [PS]	Hank Williams Memorial Album Vol. 1	1959	3.75	7.50	15.00
❑ X-1613	Cold, Cold Heart/Kaw-Liga//I Could Never Be Ashamed of You/Half As Much	1959	7.50	15.00	30.00
—Yellow label					
❑ X-1613	Cold, Cold Heart/Kaw-Liga//I Could Never Be Ashamed of You/Half As Much	1960	3.75	7.50	15.00
—Black label					
❑ X-1613 [PS]	Hank Williams Memorial Album Vol. 2	1959	3.75	7.50	15.00
❑ X-1614	Crazy Heart/Move It On Over//My Heart Would Know/I'm Sorry for You My Friend	1959	7.50	15.00	30.00
—Yellow label					
❑ X-1614	Crazy Heart/Move It On Over//My Heart Would Know/I'm Sorry for You My Friend	1960	3.75	7.50	15.00
—Black label					
❑ X-1614 [PS]	Hank Williams Memorial Album Vol. 3	1959	3.75	7.50	15.00
❑ X-1637	*I Can't Get You Off My Mind/I Don't Care (If Tomorrow Never Comes)/Dear John/My Love for You (Has Turned to Hate)	1959	7.50	15.00	30.00
—Yellow label					
❑ X-1637	*I Can't Get You Off My Mind/I Don't Care (If Tomorrow Never Comes)/Dear John/My Love for You (Has Turned to Hate)	1959	3.75	7.50	15.00
—Black label					
❑ X-1637 [PS]	The Unforgettable Hank Williams, Vol. 1	1959	3.75	7.50	15.00
❑ X-1643	Pictures from Life's Other Side/Men with Broken Hearts//Help Me Understand/Too Many Parties and Too Many Pals	1959	7.50	15.00	30.00
—Yellow label					
❑ X-1643	Pictures from Life's Other Side/Men with Broken Hearts//Help Me Understand/Too Many Parties and Too Many Pals	1960	3.75	7.50	15.00
—Black label					
❑ X-1643 [PS]	Hank Williams As Luke The Drifter	1959	3.75	7.50	15.00
❑ X-1644	Be Careful of Stones That You Throw/I Dreamed About Mama Last Night//Funeral/Beyond the Sunset	1959	7.50	15.00	30.00
—Yellow label					
❑ X-1644	Be Careful of Stones That You Throw/I Dreamed About Mama Last Night//Funeral/Beyond the Sunset	1960	3.75	7.50	15.00
—Black label					
❑ X-1644 [PS]	Hank Williams As Luke The Drifter	1959	3.75	7.50	15.00
❑ X-1698	(contents unknown)	1960	3.75	7.50	15.00
❑ X-1698 [PS]	The Lonesome Sound of Hank Williams Vol. 1	1960	3.75	7.50	15.00
❑ X-1699	(contents unknown)	1960	3.75	7.50	15.00
❑ X-1699 [PS]	The Lonesome Sound of Hank Williams Vol. 2	1960	3.75	7.50	15.00
❑ X-1700	(contents unknown)	1960	3.75	7.50	15.00
❑ X-1700 [PS]	The Lonesome Sound of Hank Williams Vol. 3	1960	3.75	7.50	15.00
❑ X-4041	Moanin' the Blues/I'm So Lonesome I Could Cry//My Sweet Love Ain't Around/Honky Tonk Blues	1953	10.00	20.00	40.00
—One record of "X168"					
❑ X-4042	Lovesick Blues/The Blues Come Around//I'm a Long Gone Daddy/Long Gone Lonesome Blues	1953	10.00	20.00	40.00
—One record of "X168"					
❑ X-4102	Your Cheatin' Heart/Settin' the Woods on Fire// You Win Again/Hey, Good Lookin'	1953	10.00	20.00	40.00
—One record of "X202"					
❑ X-4103	Cold, Cold Heart/Kaw-Liga//I Could Never Be Ashamed of You/Half as Much	1953	10.00	20.00	40.00
—One record of "X202"					

WILLIAMS, HANK, JR.

Number	Title (A Side/B Side)	Yr	VG	VG+	NM
CAPRICORN					
❑ 18486	Diamond Mine/Dirty Mind	1993	—	—	3.00
❑ 18614	Everything Comes Down to Money and Love/ S.O.B. I'm Tired	1993	—	—	3.00
❑ 18800	Lyin' Jukebox/Fax Me a Beer	1992	—	—	3.00
❑ 18923	Come On Over to the Country/Wild Weekend	1992	—	—	3.00
❑ 19023	Hotel Whiskey/The Count Song	1992	—	—	3.00
ELEKTRA					
❑ 46018	To Love Somebody/We Can Work It All Out	1979	—	2.50	5.00
❑ 46046	Family Tradition/Paying On Time	1979	—	2.50	5.00
❑ 46535	Whiskey Bent and Hell Bound/O.D.'d in Denver	1979	—	2.50	5.00
❑ 46593	Women I've Never Had/Tired of Being Johnny B. Goode	1980	—	2.50	5.00
❑ 46636	Kaw-Liga/The American Way	1980	—	2.50	5.00
❑ 47012	If You Don't Like Hank Williams/Outlaw Women	1980	—	3.00	6.00
❑ 47016	Old Habits/Won't It Be Nice	1980	—	2.50	5.00
❑ 47102	Texas Women/You Can't Find Many Kisses	1981	—	2.50	5.00
❑ 47137	Dixie on My Mind/Ramblin' Man	1981	—	2.50	5.00
❑ 47191	All My Rowdy Friends (Have Settled Down)/ Everytime I Hear That Song	1981	—	2.50	5.00
❑ 47231 [DJ]	Little Drummer Boy/The Christmas Song	1981	2.00	4.00	8.00
—B-side by Sonny Curtis					
❑ 47257	A Country Boy Can Survive/Weatherman	1982	—	2.50	5.00
❑ 47462	Honky Tonkin'/High and Pressurized	1982	—	2.50	5.00
❑ 69846	Gonna Go Huntin' Tonight/Twodot, Montana	1983	—	2.00	4.00
❑ 69960	The American Dream/If Heaven Ain't a Lot Like Dixie	1982	—	2.00	4.00
MCG CURB					
❑ 76932	I Ain't Goin' Peacefully/Greeted in Enid	1995	—	2.00	4.00
❑ 76948	Hog Wild/Wild Thing	1995	—	2.00	4.00
MGM					
❑ 13208	Long Gone Lonesome Blues/Doesn't Anybody Know My Name	1964	3.00	6.00	12.00
❑ 13253	Guess What, That's Right, She's Gone/Goin' Steady with the Blues	1964	3.00	6.00	12.00
❑ 13278	Endless Sleep/My Bucket's Got a Hole In It	1964	3.00	6.00	12.00
❑ 13318	I'm So Lonesome I Could Cry/Is It That Much Fun to Hurt Someone	1965	3.00	6.00	12.00
❑ 13353	I Went to All That Trouble for Nothin'/Mule Skinner Blues	1965	3.00	6.00	12.00
❑ 13392	Pecos Jail/You're Ruinin' My Life	1965	3.00	6.00	12.00
❑ 13443	Rainmaker/The River	1966	3.00	6.00	12.00
❑ 13504	Standing in the Shadows/It's Written All Over Your Face	1966	3.00	6.00	12.00
❑ 13640	I Can't Take It No Longer/You Can Hear a Tear Drop	1966	3.00	6.00	12.00
❑ 13730	I'm In No Condition/I'm Gonna Break Your Heart	1967	3.00	6.00	12.00
❑ 13782	Nobody's Child/The Next Best Thing to Nothing	1967	3.00	6.00	12.00
❑ 13857	I Wouldn't Change a Thing About You (But Your Name)/No Meaning and No End	1967	3.00	6.00	12.00
❑ 13922	The Old Ryman/I Wonder Where You Are Tonight	1968	2.50	5.00	10.00
❑ 13968	It's All Over But the Crying/Rock in My Shoes	1968	2.50	5.00	10.00
❑ 14002	I Was With Red Foley (The Night He Passed Away)/On Trial	1968	3.00	6.00	12.00
—As "Luke the Drifter, Jr."					
❑ 14020	Custody/My Home Town Circle "R"	1968	3.00	6.00	12.00
—As "Luke the Drifter, Jr."					
❑ 14024	A Baby Again/Swim Across a Tear	1969	2.50	5.00	10.00
❑ 14047	Cajun Baby/My Heart Won't Let Me Go	1969	2.50	5.00	10.00
❑ 14062	Be Careful of Stones That You Throw/Book of Memories	1969	2.50	5.00	10.00
—As "Luke the Drifter, Jr."					
❑ 14077	I'd Rather Be Gone/Try, Try Again	1969	2.50	5.00	10.00
❑ 14095	Something to Think About/(There Must Be) A Better Way to Love	1969	2.50	5.00	10.00
—As "Luke the Drifter, Jr."					
❑ 14107	I Walked Out on Heaven/Your Love's One Thing	1970	2.00	4.00	8.00
❑ 14120	It Don't Take But One Mistake/Goin' Home	1970	2.00	4.00	8.00
—As "Luke the Drifter, Jr."					
❑ 14152	All for the Love of Sunshine/Ballad of the Moonshine	1970	2.00	4.00	8.00
❑ 14194	Rainin' in My Heart/A-Eee	1970	2.00	4.00	8.00
❑ 14240	I've Got a Right to Cry/Jesus Loved the Devil Out of Me	1971	2.00	4.00	8.00
❑ 14277	After All They All Used to Belong to Me/Happy Kind of Sadness	1971	2.00	4.00	8.00
❑ 14317	Ain't That a Shame/End of a Bad Day	1971	2.00	4.00	8.00
❑ 14371	Eleven Roses/Richmond Valley Breeze	1972	2.00	4.00	8.00
❑ 14421	Pride's Not Hard to Swallow/Hamburger Steak, Holiday Inn	1972	2.00	4.00	8.00
❑ 14486	After You/Knoxville Courthouse Blues	1973	—	3.00	6.00
❑ 14550	Hank/Hank (Part 2)	1973	—	3.00	6.00
❑ 14656	The Last Love Song/Those Tear Jerking Songs	1973	—	3.00	6.00
❑ 14700	Rainy Night in Georgia/Country Music in My Soul	1974	—	3.00	6.00
❑ 14731	I'll Think of Something/Country Music Lover	1974	—	3.00	6.00
❑ 14755	Angels Are Hard to Find/Getting Over You	1974	—	3.00	6.00
❑ 14794	Where He's Going, I've Already Gone/The Kind of Woman I've Got	1975	—	3.00	6.00
❑ 14813	The Same Old Story/Country Love	1975	—	3.00	6.00
❑ 14833	Stoned at the Jukebox/The Devil in the Bottle	1975	—	3.00	6.00
❑ 14845	Living Proof/Brothers of the Road	1976	—	3.00	6.00
VERVE					
❑ 10540	Meter Reader Maid/Just a Dream	1967	12.50	25.00	50.00
—As "Bocephus"					
❑ 10572	Mental Revenge/Splish Splash	1967	10.00	20.00	40.00
—As "Bocephus"					
WARNER BROS.					
❑ PRO-S-3838 [DJ]	All My Rowdy Friends (Are Here on Monday Night) (same on both sides)	1989	3.75	7.50	15.00
❑ PRO-S-4492 [DJ]	Don't Give Us a Reason (same on both sides)	1990	2.00	4.00	8.00
❑ 8345	She's the Star (On the Stage of My Mind)/Call Me, Honey, Won't You	1977	—	2.50	5.00
❑ 8361	Mobile Boogie/She's the Star (On the Stage of My Mind)	1977	—	2.50	5.00
❑ 8410	I'm Not Responsible/(Honey, Won't You) Call Me	1977	—	2.50	5.00
❑ 8451	One Night Stands/I'm Not Responsible	1977	—	2.50	5.00
❑ 8507	Feelin' Better/Once and For All	1977	—	2.50	5.00
❑ 8549	The New South/Storms Never Last	1978	—	3.00	6.00
❑ 8564	You Love the Thunder/I Just Ain't Been Able	1978	—	2.50	5.00

Number	Title (A Side/B Side)	Yr	VG	VG+	NM
❑ 8641	I Fought the Law/It's Different with You	1978	—	2.50	5.00
❑ 8715	Old Flame, New Fire/Payin' On Time	1978	—	2.50	5.00
❑ 19193	Angels Are Hard to Find/Hollywood Honeys	1991	—	—	3.00
❑ 19352	If It Will It Will/Won't It Be Nice	1991	—	—	3.00
❑ 19463	I Mean I Love You/Stoned at the Jukebox	1990	—	—	3.00
❑ 19542	Don't Give Us a Reason/U.S.A. Today	1990	—	—	3.00
❑ 19818	Man to Man/Whiskey Bent and Hell Bound	1990	—	—	3.00
❑ 19872	Good Friends, Good Whiskey, Good Lovin'/ Family Tradition	1990	—	—	3.00
❑ 19957	Ain't Nobody's Business/Big Mamou	1990	—	—	3.00
❑ 22945	Finders Are Keepers/What You Don't Know (Won't Hurt You)	1989	—	—	3.00
❑ 27584	There's a Tear in My Beer/You Brought Me Down to Earth	1989	—	2.00	4.00
—A-side with Hank Williams Sr.					
❑ 27722	Early in the Morning and Late at Night/I'm Just a Man	1988	—	—	3.00
❑ 27862	If the South Woulda Won/Wild Steak	1988	—	—	3.00
❑ 28120	Young Country/Buck Naked	1988	—	—	3.00
❑ 28227	Heaven Can't Be Found/Doctor's Song	1987	—	—	3.00
❑ 28369	Born to Boogie/What It Boils Down To	1987	—	—	3.00
❑ 28452	When Something Is Good (Why Does It Change)/ Loving Instructor	1987	—	—	3.00
❑ 28581	Mind Your Own Business/My Name Is Bocephus	1986	—	2.00	4.00
❑ 28691	Country State of Mind/Fat Friends	1986	—	2.00	4.00
❑ 28794	Ain't Misbehavin'/I've Been Around	1986	—	2.00	4.00
❑ 28912	This Ain't Dallas/I Really Like Girls	1985	—	2.00	4.00
❑ 29022	I'm for Love/Lawyers, Guns and Money	1985	—	2.00	4.00
❑ 29095	Major Moves/Mr. Lincoln	1985	—	2.00	4.00
❑ 29184	All My Rowdy Friends Are Coming Over Tonight/ Video Blues	1984	—	2.00	4.00
❑ 29253	Attitude Adjustment/Knoxville Courthouse Blues	1984	—	2.00	4.00
❑ 29382	Man of Steel/Now I Know How George Feels	1984	—	2.00	4.00
❑ 29500	Queen of My Heart/She Had Me	1983	—	2.00	4.00
❑ 29633	Leave Them Boys Alone/The Girl in the Front Row at Fort Worth	1983	—	2.00	4.00

WILLIAMS, HANK, JR., AND LOIS JOHNSON

Number	Title (A Side/B Side)	Yr	VG	VG+	NM
MGM					
❑ 14136	Removing the Shadow/Party People	1970	2.00	4.00	8.00
❑ 14164	So Sad (To Watch Good Love Go Bad)/Let's Talk It Over Again	1970	2.00	4.00	8.00
❑ 14356	Send Me Some Lovin'/What We Used to Hang On To	1972	2.00	4.00	8.00
❑ 14443	Whole Lotta Loving/Why Should We Try Anymore	1972	2.00	4.00	8.00

WILLIAMS, JIM

Number	Title (A Side/B Side)	Yr	VG	VG+	NM
SUN					
❑ 270	Please Don't Cry Over Me/That Depends on You	1957	7.50	15.00	30.00

WILLIAMS, JIMMY

Number	Title (A Side/B Side)	Yr	VG	VG+	NM
ABC-PARAMOUNT					
❑ 10471	I Gave My Love a Cherry/Half Man	1963	3.00	6.00	12.00
❑ 10523	Green Pastures (23rd Psalm)/I'm Strung Out Over You, Baby	1964	3.00	6.00	12.00
ATLANTIC					
❑ 2296	Walking on Air/I'm So Lost	1965	2.50	5.00	10.00
CUB					
❑ 9031	My Pledge and My Promise/Keep Me with You	1959	3.75	7.50	15.00
❑ 9039	C'mon Baby (What's Your Name)/Don't Put It Off (Do It Now)	1959	3.75	7.50	15.00
DUB					
❑ 2842	You're Always Late/I Belong to You	1958	25.00	50.00	100.00
DYNO VOICE					
❑ 931	Mushroom City/Standing There	1969	2.00	4.00	8.00
HULL					
❑ 765	I Can't Help Falling in Love/Smile	1964	2.50	5.00	10.00
LIMELIGHT					
❑ 3038	Mrs. Cherry/Keoto'To	1964	2.50	5.00	10.00
MGM					
❑ 11938	No One Knows/These Blues Are Over You	1955	5.00	10.00	20.00
❑ 12262	Alpha and Omega/Where Will I Shelter My Sheep	1956	5.00	10.00	20.00
❑ 12362	Throwing My Life Away/We're Drifting Further Apart	1956	5.00	10.00	20.00
❑ 12596	You're the One/I'll Only Give My Love	1957	6.25	12.50	25.00
ORBIT					
❑ 9002	You're the One/I'll Only Give My Love	1958	3.75	7.50	15.00
ROULETTE					
❑ 4303	There Is No Doubt/What a Change	1960	3.75	7.50	15.00

WILLIAMS, LARRY

Also see JOHNNY "GUITAR" WATSON AND LARRY WILLIAMS.

Number	Title (A Side/B Side)	Yr	VG	VG+	NM
BELL					
❑ 813	I Could Love You Baby/Can't Find No Substitute for Love	1969	2.50	5.00	10.00
—With Johnny Watson					
CHESS					
❑ 1736	My Baby's Got Soul/Every Day I Wonder	1959	5.00	10.00	20.00
❑ 1745	Get Ready/Baby, Baby	1959	5.00	10.00	20.00
❑ 1761	I Wanna Know/Like a Gentle Man	1960	5.00	10.00	20.00
❑ 1764	Oh Baby/I Hear My Baby	1960	5.00	10.00	20.00
❑ 1805	Lawdy Mama/Fresh Out of Tears	1961	5.00	10.00	20.00
EL BAM					
❑ 69	Call on Me/Boss Lovin'	1965	3.00	6.00	12.00
FANTASY					
❑ 806	Doing the Best I Can (With What I Got)/Gimme Some	1977	—	2.50	5.00
❑ 810	One Thing or the Other (Part 1)/One Thing or the Other (Part 2)	1977	—	2.50	5.00
❑ 841	The Resurrection of Funk/(B-side unknown)	1978	—	2.50	5.00
MERCURY					
❑ 72147	Woman/Can't Help Myself	1963	3.75	7.50	15.00
OKEH					
❑ 7259	This Old Heart (Is So Lonely)/I'd Rather Fight Than Switch	1966	2.50	5.00	10.00
❑ 7280	I Am the One/You Ask for One Good Reason	1967	2.50	5.00	10.00
❑ 7294	Just Because/Boss Lovin'	1967	2.50	5.00	10.00
SMASH					
❑ 2035	Call on Me/Boss Lovin'	1966	3.00	6.00	12.00
SPECIALTY					
❑ 597	Just Because/Let Me Tell You Baby	1957	7.50	15.00	30.00
❑ 608	Short Fat Fannie/High School Dance	1957	10.00	20.00	40.00
❑ 608	Short Fat Fannie/High School Dance	1984	—	2.00	4.00
—Gold vinyl					
❑ 615	Bony Moronie/You Bug Me, Baby	1957	10.00	20.00	40.00
❑ 615	Bony Moronie/You Bug Me, Baby	1984	—	2.00	4.00
—Red vinyl					
❑ 626	Dizzy, Miss Lizzy/Slow Down	1958	10.00	20.00	40.00
❑ 626	Dizzy, Miss Lizzy/Slow Down	1984	—	2.00	4.00
—Blue vinyl					
❑ 626 [PS]	Dizzy, Miss Lizzy/Slow Down	1958	20.00	40.00	80.00
❑ 634	Hootchy-Koo/The Dummy	1958	6.25	12.50	25.00
❑ 634	Hootchy-Koo/The Dummy	1984	—	2.00	4.00
—Green vinyl					
❑ 647	I Was a Fool/Peaches and Cream	1958	6.25	12.50	25.00
❑ 658	Bad Boy/She Said "Yeah"	1959	7.50	15.00	30.00
❑ 658	Bad Boy/She Said "Yeah"	1984	—	2.00	4.00
—Orange vinyl					
❑ 665	Steal a Little Kiss/I Can't Stop Loving You	1959	6.25	12.50	25.00
❑ 677	Give Me Your Love/Teardrops	1959	6.25	12.50	25.00
❑ 682	Ting-a-Ling/Little Schoolgirl	1960	6.25	12.50	25.00
❑ 682	Ting-a-Ling/Little Schoolgirl	1984	—	2.00	4.00
—Gold vinyl					
VENTURE					
❑ 622	Shake Your Body Girl/Love I Can't Seem to Find It	1968	2.50	5.00	10.00
❑ 627	Wake Up (Nothing Comes to a Sleeper But a Dream)/Love I Can't Seem to Find It	1968	2.50	5.00	10.00

WILLIAMS, LESTER

Number	Title (A Side/B Side)	Yr	VG	VG+	NM
DUKE					
❑ 123	Let's Do It/Good Lovin' Baby	1954	12.50	25.00	50.00
❑ 131	Crazy 'Bout You Baby/Don't Take Your Love from Me	1954	10.00	20.00	40.00
IMPERIAL					
❑ 5402	McDonald's Daughter/Daddy Loves You	1956	12.50	25.00	50.00
SPECIALTY					
❑ 422	I Can't Lose with the Stuff I Use/My Home Ain't Here	1952	25.00	50.00	100.00
❑ 431	Let Me Tell You a Thing or Two/Tryin' to Forget	1952	37.50	75.00	150.00
❑ 437	Sweet Lovin' Daddy/Lost Gal	1952	37.50	75.00	150.00
❑ 450	Brand New Baby/If I Knew How Much I Loved You	1953	25.00	50.00	100.00

WILLIAMS, LEW

Number	Title (A Side/B Side)	Yr	VG	VG+	NM
IMPERIAL					
❑ 5394	Cat Talk/Gone Ape Man	1956	30.00	60.00	120.00
❑ 5411	Bop Bop Ba Doo Bop/Something I Said	1956	30.00	60.00	120.00
❑ 5429	Centipede/Abra Cadabra	1957	30.00	60.00	120.00
❑ 8306	Don't Mention My Name/I'll Play Your Game	1956	37.50	75.00	150.00

WILLIAMS, MAURICE, AND THE ZODIACS

Also see THE GLADIOLAS.

Number	Title (A Side/B Side)	Yr	VG	VG+	NM
ATLANTIC					
❑ 2199	Funny/Loneliness	1963	3.75	7.50	15.00
—As "The Zodiacs"					
❑ 2741	Sweetness/Whirlpool	1970	—	2.50	5.00
COLE					
❑ 100	Golly Gee/"I" Town	1959	12.50	25.00	50.00
❑ 101	Lover (Where Are You)/She's Mine	1959	10.00	20.00	40.00
DEESU					
❑ 302	Baby Baby/Being Without You	1967	5.00	10.00	20.00
❑ 304	May I/This Feeling	1967	5.00	10.00	20.00
❑ 307	Ooh Poo Pa Doo (Part 1)/Ooh Poo Pa Doo (Part 2)	1967	5.00	10.00	20.00
❑ 309	Don't Ever Leave Me/Surely	1967	5.00	10.00	20.00
❑ 311	Don't Be Half Safe/How to Pick a Winner	1967	5.00	10.00	20.00
❑ 318	Stay '68 (Live Version)/Dance, Dance, Dance	1968	3.75	7.50	15.00
HERALD					
❑ 552	Stay/Do You Believe	1960	5.00	10.00	20.00
❑ 556	Always/I Remember	1961	3.75	7.50	15.00
❑ 559	Do I/Come Along	1961	3.75	7.50	15.00
❑ 563	Someday/Come and Get It	1961	3.75	7.50	15.00
❑ 565	Please/High Blood Pressure	1961	3.75	7.50	15.00
❑ 572	It's Alright/Here I Stand	1962	3.75	7.50	15.00
RCA					
❑ 5363-7-R	Stay/She's Like the Wind	1987	—	—	3.00
—B-side by Patrick Swayze					
SCEPTER					
❑ 12113	Nobody Knows/I Know	1965	3.75	7.50	15.00
SEA HORN					
❑ 503	My Baby's Gone/Return	1964	3.75	7.50	15.00
SELWYN					
❑ 5121	Say Yeah/College Girl	1959	12.50	25.00	50.00
SPHERE SOUND					
❑ 707	So Fine/The Winds	1965	3.00	6.00	12.00
VEE JAY					
❑ 678	May I/Lollipop	1965	5.00	10.00	20.00
VEEP					
❑ 1294	My Reason for Living/The Four Corners	1969	2.00	4.00	8.00

WILLIAMS, OTIS, AND HIS CHARMS
Also see THE CHARMS.

Number	Title (A Side/B Side)	Yr	VG	VG+	NM
DELUXE					
❑ 6088	Miss the Love/Tell Me Now	1955	7.50	15.00	30.00
—As "Otis Williams and His New Group"					
❑ 6090	Gum Drop/Save Me, Save Me	1955	7.50	15.00	30.00
—As "Otis Williams and His New Group"					
❑ 6091	That's Your Mistake/Too Late I Learned	1955	7.50	15.00	30.00
❑ 6092	Rolling Home/Do Be You	1956	7.50	15.00	30.00
❑ 6093	Ivory Tower/In Paradise	1956	7.50	15.00	30.00
❑ 6095	One Night Only/It's All Over	1956	7.50	15.00	30.00
❑ 6097	I'd Like to Thank You Mr. D.J./Whirlwind	1956	7.50	15.00	30.00
❑ 6098	Gypsy Lady/I'll Remember You	1956	7.50	15.00	30.00
❑ 6105	Blues Stay Away from Me/Pardon Me	1957	6.25	12.50	25.00
❑ 6115	Walkin' After Midnight/I'm Waiting Just for You	1957	6.25	12.50	25.00
❑ 6130	Nowhere on Earth/No Got De Woman	1957	6.25	12.50	25.00
❑ 6137	Talking to Myself/One Kind Word from You	1957	6.25	12.50	25.00
❑ 6138	United/Don't Deny Me	1957	6.25	12.50	25.00
❑ 6149	Dynamite Darling/Well Oh Well	1957	6.25	12.50	25.00
❑ 6158	Could This Be Magic/Oh Julie	1958	6.25	12.50	25.00
❑ 6160	Let Some Love in Your Heart/Baby-O	1958	6.25	12.50	25.00
❑ 6165	Burnin' Lips/Red Hot Love (Do This Love)	1958	6.25	12.50	25.00
❑ 6174	Don't Wake Up the Kids/You'll Remain Forever	1958	6.25	12.50	25.00
❑ 6178	My Friends/The Secret	1958	6.25	12.50	25.00
❑ 6181	Pretty Little Things Called Girls/Welcome Home	1959	6.25	12.50	25.00
❑ 6183	My Prayer Tonight/Watch Dog	1959	6.25	12.50	25.00
❑ 6185	I Knew It All the Time/Tears of Happiness	1959	6.25	12.50	25.00
❑ 6186	In Paradise/Who Knows	1959	6.25	12.50	25.00
❑ 6187	Blues Stay Away from Me/Funny What True Love Can Do	1959	6.25	12.50	25.00
KING					
❑ 5323	Chief Um (Take It Easy)/It's a Treat	1960	5.00	10.00	20.00
❑ 5332	Silver Star/Rickety Rickshaw Man	1960	5.00	10.00	20.00
❑ 5372	Image of a Girl/Wait a Minute Baby	1960	12.50	25.00	50.00
❑ 5389	The First Sign of Love/So Be It	1960	5.00	10.00	20.00
❑ 5421	Wait/And Take My Love	1960	5.00	10.00	20.00
❑ 5455	Little Turtle Dove/So Can I	1961	5.00	10.00	20.00
❑ 5497	Just Forget About Me/You Know How Much I Care	1961	5.00	10.00	20.00
❑ 5527	Pardon Me/Panic	1961	5.00	10.00	20.00
❑ 5558	Two Hearts/The Secret	1961	5.00	10.00	20.00
❑ 5682	When We Get Together/Only Young Once	1962	3.75	7.50	15.00
❑ 5816	It Just Ain't Right/It'll Never Happen Again	1963	3.75	7.50	15.00
❑ 5880	Unchain My Heart/Friends Call Me a Fool	1964	3.75	7.50	15.00
❑ 6034	Bye Bye Baby/Please Believe in Me	1966	3.75	7.50	15.00
OKEH					
❑ 7225	Baby, You Turn Me On/Love Don't Grow on Trees	1965	3.75	7.50	15.00
❑ 7235	I Fall to Pieces/Gotta Get Myself Together	1965	3.75	7.50	15.00
❑ 7248	I Got Loving/Welcome Home	1966	3.75	7.50	15.00
❑ 7261	Ain't Gonna Walk Your Dog No More/Your Sweet Love (Rained Over Me)	1966	3.75	7.50	15.00
SCEPTER					
❑ 12376	Here Lie the Bones of Nellie Jones/When You Turn On the Love	1973	2.00	4.00	8.00
STOP					
❑ 301	Begging to You/(B-side unknown)	1968	2.50	5.00	10.00
❑ 306	Begging to You/Everybody's Got a Song But Me	1968	2.50	5.00	10.00
❑ 346	Jesus Is a Soul Man/Make a Woman Feel Like a Woman	1969	2.50	5.00	10.00
❑ 360	Ling, Ting, Tong/For the Love	1970	2.50	5.00	10.00
❑ 388	I Wanna Go Country/Rocky Top	1971	2.00	4.00	8.00
—As "Otis Williams and the Midnight Cowboys"					

7-Inch Extended Plays

Number	Title	Yr	VG	VG+	NM
DELUXE					
❑ 385	(contents unknown)	1956	75.00	150.00	300.00
❑ 385	Otis Williams and His Charms	1956	75.00	150.00	300.00

WILLIAMS, TIMMY

Number	Title (A Side/B Side)	Yr	VG	VG+	NM
MALA					
❑ 515	Competition/Wipe Away Your Tears	1965	75.00	150.00	300.00

WILLIAMS, TONY
Also see THE PLATTERS.

Number	Title (A Side/B Side)	Yr	VG	VG+	NM
DOT					
❑ 16806	Endless Street/Smoke, Drink, Play 21	1965	2.00	4.00	8.00
MERCURY					
❑ 71158	Let's Start All Over Again/When You Return	1957	5.00	10.00	20.00
❑ 71532	Charmaine/Peg o' My Heart	1959	5.00	10.00	20.00
PHILIPS					
❑ 40069	Chloe/Second Best	1962	2.50	5.00	10.00
❑ 40123	Twenty-Four Lonely Hours/Save Me	1963	2.50	5.00	10.00
❑ 40141	How Come/When I Had You	1963	2.50	5.00	10.00
REPRISE					
❑ 20019	Sleepless Nights/Movin' In	1961	3.75	7.50	15.00
❑ 20030	Miracle/My Prayer	1961	3.75	7.50	15.00
❑ 20056	It's So Easy to Surrender/That's More Like It	1962	10.00	20.00	40.00
—Released only in Italy					
❑ 20067	Come Along Now/That's More Like It	1962	3.75	7.50	15.00
❑ 20073	Sing, Lover, Sing/Mandalino	1962	10.00	20.00	40.00
—Released only in Hong Kong					
❑ 20136	Dream/Loving You	1963	10.00	20.00	40.00
—Released only in Italy					

WILLIAMSON, SONNY BOY (1)
The "original," born John Lee Williamson and murdered in 1948.

Number	Title (A Side/B Side)	Yr	VG	VG+	NM
RCA VICTOR					
❑ 50-0005	Little Girl/Bring Another Half a Pint	1949	75.00	150.00	300.00
—Orange vinyl					
❑ 50-0030	Southern Dream/I Love You For Myself	1949	75.00	150.00	300.00
—Orange vinyl					

WILLIAMSON, SONNY BOY (2)
Really Aleck Ford, also known as Alex "Rice" Miller, before taking the name of his predecessor.

Number	Title (A Side/B Side)	Yr	VG	VG+	NM
ACE					
❑ 511	Boppin' with Sonny/No Nights By Myself	1955	30.00	60.00	120.00
CHECKER					
❑ 824	Don't Start Me Talkin'/All My Love In Vain	1955	25.00	50.00	100.00
❑ 834	Let Me Explain/Your Imagination	1956	15.00	30.00	60.00
❑ 847	Keep It To Yourself/The Key to Your Door	1956	12.50	25.00	50.00
❑ 864	I Don't Know/Fattening Frogs for Snakes	1957	12.50	25.00	50.00
❑ 883	Born Blind/Ninety-Nine	1958	10.00	20.00	40.00
❑ 894	Your Funeral & My Trial/Wake Up, Baby	1958	10.00	20.00	40.00
❑ 910	Cross My Heart/Dissatisfied	1958	10.00	20.00	40.00
❑ 927	Let Your Conscience Be Your Guide/Unseeing Eye	1959	10.00	20.00	40.00
❑ 943	The Goat/It's Sad to Be Alone	1960	7.50	15.00	30.00
❑ 956	Temperature 110/Lonesome Cabin	1960	7.50	15.00	30.00
❑ 963	Trust Me Baby/Too Close Together	1960	7.50	15.00	30.00
❑ 975	The Hurt/Stop Right Now	1961	7.50	15.00	30.00
❑ 1003	One Way Out/Nine Below Zero	1962	7.50	15.00	30.00
❑ 1036	Bye Bye Bird/Help Me	1963	7.50	15.00	30.00
❑ 1065	Trying to Get Back on My Feet/Decoration Day	1963	7.50	15.00	30.00
❑ 1080	My Younger Days/I Want You Close to Me	1964	7.50	15.00	30.00
❑ 1134	Bring It On Home/Down Child	1966	6.25	12.50	25.00
TRUMPET					
❑ 144	West Memphis Blues/I Cross My Heart	1951	25.00	50.00	100.00
❑ 145	Sonny Boy's Christmas Blues/Pontiac Blues	195?	30.00	60.00	120.00
❑ 166	Nine Below Zero/Mighty Long Time	1952	25.00	50.00	100.00
❑ 167	Too Close Together/She Brought Life Back to the Dead	1952	—	—	—
—Unreleased					
❑ 168	Stop Now Baby/Mr. Downchild	1952	25.00	50.00	100.00
❑ 212	Cat Hop/Too Close Together	1952	20.00	40.00	80.00
❑ 215	Gettin' Out of Time/She Brought Life Back to the Dead	1952	20.00	40.00	80.00
❑ 216	Red Hot Kisses/Going in Your Direction	1952	20.00	40.00	80.00
❑ 228	From the Bottom/Empty Bedroom	1953	17.50	35.00	70.00

WILLIE AND THE POOR BOYS
All-star group featuring Charlie Watts, BILL WYMAN, JIMMY PAGE, PAUL RODGERS and others.

Number	Title (A Side/B Side)	Yr	VG	VG+	NM
PASSPORT					
❑ 7928	Baby Plese Don't Go/Poor Boy Boogie	1985	—	2.50	5.00
❑ 7928 [PS]	Baby Plese Don't Go/Poor Boy Boogie	1985	—	3.00	6.00
❑ 7929	These Arms of Mine/Let's Talk It Over	1985	—	2.50	5.00
❑ 7929 [PS]	These Arms of Mine/Let's Talk It Over	1985	—	2.50	5.00

WILLIE AND THE WHEELS
Still another creation of STEVE BARRI and P.F. SLOAN.

Number	Title (A Side/B Side)	Yr	VG	VG+	NM
DUNHILL					
❑ 4002	Skateboard Craze/Do What You Do	1965	10.00	20.00	40.00

WILLIS, CHUCK
Also see THE ROYALS (2).

Number	Title (A Side/B Side)	Yr	VG	VG+	NM
ATLANTIC					
❑ 1098	It's Too Late/Kansas City Woman	1956	6.25	12.50	25.00
❑ 1112	Juanita/Whatcha' Gonna Do When Your Baby Leaves You	1956	6.25	12.50	25.00
❑ 1130	C.C. Rider/Ease the Pain	1957	6.25	12.50	25.00
❑ 1148	Love Me, Cherry/That Train Has Gone	1957	6.25	12.50	25.00
❑ 1168	Betty and Dupree/My Crying Eyes	1958	6.25	12.50	25.00
❑ 1179	What Am I Living For/Hang Up My Rock And Roll Shoes	1958	7.50	15.00	30.00
❑ 1192	Thunder and Lightning/My Life	1958	5.00	10.00	20.00
❑ 2005	You'll Be My Love/Keep a-Driving	1958	5.00	10.00	20.00
❑ 2029	My Baby/Just One Kiss	1959	5.00	10.00	20.00
OKEH					
❑ 6810	I Tried/I Rule My House	1951	25.00	50.00	100.00
❑ 6841	Let's Jump Tonight/It's Too Late Baby	1951	20.00	40.00	80.00
❑ 6873	Lud Mouth Lucy/Here I Come	1952	20.00	40.00	80.00
❑ 6905	My Story/Caldonia	1952	12.50	25.00	50.00
❑ 6930	Salty Tears/Wrong Lake to Catch a Fish	1953	12.50	25.00	50.00
❑ 6952	Going to the River/Baby Has Left Me Again	1953	12.50	25.00	50.00
❑ 6985	Don't Deceive Me/I've Been Treated Wrong Too Long	1953	12.50	25.00	50.00
❑ 7004	My Baby's Coming Home/When My Day Is Over	1953	12.50	25.00	50.00
❑ 7015	You're Still My Baby/What's Your Name	1954	12.50	25.00	50.00
❑ 7029	I Feel So Bad/Need One More Chance	1954	15.00	30.00	60.00
❑ 7041	Change My Mind/My Heart's Been Broke Again	1954	10.00	20.00	40.00
❑ 7048	Give and Take/I've Been Away Too Long	1954	10.00	20.00	40.00
❑ 7051	Lawdy Miss Mary/Love-Struck	1955	10.00	20.00	40.00
❑ 7055	I Can Tell/One More Break	1955	10.00	20.00	40.00
❑ 7062	Search My Heart/Ring-Ding-Doo	1955	10.00	20.00	40.00
❑ 7067	Come On Home/It Were You	1956	10.00	20.00	40.00
❑ 7070	Two Spoons of Tears/Charged with Cheating	1956	10.00	20.00	40.00

7-Inch Extended Plays

Number	Title	Yr	VG	VG+	NM
ATLANTIC					
❑ 561	(contents unknown)	1957	50.00	100.00	200.00
❑ 561 [PS]	Chuck Willis	1957	50.00	100.00	200.00
❑ 609	(contents unknown)	1958	30.00	60.00	120.00
❑ 609 [PS]	Rock with Chuck Willis	1958	30.00	60.00	120.00
❑ 612	(contents unknown)	1958	37.50	75.00	150.00
❑ 612 [PS]	What Am I Living For	1958	50.00	100.00	200.00
EPIC					
❑ 7070	(contents unknown)	1956	50.00	100.00	200.00
❑ 7070 [PS]	Chuck Willis Sings the Blues	1956	50.00	100.00	200.00

WILLIS, HAL

Number	Title (A Side/B Side)	Yr	VG	VG+	NM
ATHENS					
❑ 704	Crazy Little Mama/Walkin' Dream	1958	37.50	75.00	150.00
ATLANTIC					
❑ 1114	Bop-A-Dee, Bop-A-Doo/My Pink Cadillac	1956	50.00	100.00	200.00

Number	Title (A Side/B Side)	Yr	VG	VG+	NM
DECCA					
❑ 30949	Poor Little Jimmy/That's the Way It Goes	1959	3.00	6.00	12.00
MERCURY					
❑ 71933	Bayou Pierre/I Love You (Around the World)	1962	3.00	6.00	12.00
SIMS					
❑ 207	The Lumberjack/Dig Me a Hole	1964	3.00	6.00	12.00
❑ 224	The One I Love/What's Left of Me	1965	3.00	6.00	12.00
❑ 235	Klondike Mike/So Right But So Wrong	1965	3.00	6.00	12.00
❑ 243	Thumb and Shoes/Nopper the Topper	1965	3.00	6.00	12.00
❑ 250	Creole Rose/When It's Springtime in Alaska	1965	3.00	6.00	12.00
❑ 288	Doggin' in the U.S. Mail/The Battle of Viet Nam	1966	3.00	6.00	12.00
❑ 307	Parson from Paint Rock/Private Dick	1966	3.00	6.00	12.00

WILLOWS, THE (1)
Also see TONY MIDDLETON.

Number	Title (A Side/B Side)	Yr	VG	VG+	NM
MELBA					
❑ 102	Church Bells Are Ringing/Beby Tell Me	1956	75.00	150.00	300.00
—Original A-side title					
❑ 102	Church Bells May Ring/Baby Tell Me	1956	25.00	50.00	100.00
❑ 106	Do You Love Me/My Angel	1956	15.00	30.00	60.00
❑ 115	Little Darlin'/My Angel	1957	20.00	40.00	80.00

WILLOWS, THE (2)

Number	Title (A Side/B Side)	Yr	VG	VG+	NM
4-STAR					
❑ 1753	There's a Dance Goin' On/Now That I Have You	1961	75.00	150.00	300.00

WILLOWS, THE (3)

Number	Title (A Side/B Side)	Yr	VG	VG+	NM
HEIDI					
❑ 103	It's Such a Shame/Tears in Your Eyes	1964	3.75	7.50	15.00
❑ 107	Sit by the Fire/Such a Night	1965	3.75	7.50	15.00

WILLOWS, THE (4)

Number	Title (A Side/B Side)	Yr	VG	VG+	NM
MGM					
❑ 13484	Hurtin' All Over/My Kinda Guy	1966	3.00	6.00	12.00
❑ 13714	Snow Song/Outside the City	1967	3.00	6.00	12.00

WILSON, ANN
Also see HEART.

Number	Title (A Side/B Side)	Yr	VG	VG+	NM
CAPITOL					
❑ B-5654	The Best Man in the World/(Instrumental)	1986	—	—	3.00
—Of Heart					
❑ B-5654 [PS]	The Best Man in the World/(Instrumental)	1986	—	2.00	4.00
❑ B-44288	Surrender to Me/Tequila Dreams	1988	—	—	3.00
—A-side: With Robin Zander; B-side by Dave Grusin					
❑ B-44288 [PS]	Surrender to Me/Tequila Dreams	1988	—	2.00	4.00

WILSON, ANN AND NANCY
Also see HEART; ANN WILSON; NANCY WILSON (2).

Number	Title (A Side/B Side)	Yr	VG	VG+	NM
CAPITOL					
❑ 58750	Here Is Christmas/Bring a Torch Jeannette Isabella	1998	—	—	3.00

WILSON, ANN, AND THE DAYBREAKS
Also see ANN WILSON.

Number	Title (A Side/B Side)	Yr	VG	VG+	NM
TOPAZ					
❑ 1311	Standin' Watchin' You/Wonder How I Managed	1967	30.00	60.00	120.00
❑ 1312	Through Eyes and Glass/I'm Gonna Drink My Hurt Away	1967	30.00	60.00	120.00

WILSON, BRIAN
Also see THE BEACH BOYS.

Number	Title (A Side/B Side)	Yr	VG	VG+	NM
CAPITOL					
❑ 5610	Caroline, No/Summer Means New Love	1966	6.25	12.50	25.00
—Actually a Beach Boys recording released as a solo Brian record					
GIANT					
❑ 17216	Your Imagination/Your Imagination (A Cappella)	1998	—	—	3.00
SIRE					
❑ 27694	Melt Away/Being with the One You Love	1988	5.00	10.00	20.00
❑ 27787 [DJ]	Night Time (same on both sides)	1988	7.50	15.00	30.00
—Stock copies not known to exist					
❑ 27787 [PS]	Night Time	1988	15.00	30.00	60.00
❑ 27814	Love and Mercy/He Couldn't Get His Poor Old Body to Move	1988	2.50	5.00	10.00
—Promo copies go for 50% of this price					
❑ 27814 [PS]	Love and Mercy/He Couldn't Get His Poor Old Body to Move	1988	—	2.50	5.00
—Accompanied both stock and promo copies					
❑ 28350	Let's Go to Heaven in My Car/Too Much Sugar	1987	2.50	5.00	10.00
—Promo copies go for 50% of this price					
❑ 28350 [PS]	Let's Go to Heaven in My Car/Too Much Sugar	1987	—	2.50	5.00
—Accompanied both stock and promo copies					

WILSON, BRIAN, AND MIKE LOVE
Also see each artist's individual listings; THE BEACH BOYS.

Number	Title (A Side/B Side)	Yr	VG	VG+	NM
BROTHER					
❑ 1002	Gettin' Hungry/Devoted to You	1967	7.50	15.00	30.00

WILSON, CARL
Also see THE BEACH BOYS.

Number	Title (A Side/B Side)	Yr	VG	VG+	NM
CARIBOU					
❑ 01049	Hold Me/Hurry Love	1981	—	2.50	5.00
❑ 02136	Heaven/Hurry Love	1981	—	2.50	5.00
❑ 03590	What You Do to Me/Time	1983	—	2.50	5.00
❑ 04020	Givin' You Up/Too Early to Tell	1983	—	2.50	5.00

WILSON, DENNIS
Also see THE BEACH BOYS.

Number	Title (A Side/B Side)	Yr	VG	VG+	NM
CARIBOU					
❑ 9023	You and I/Friday Night	1978	3.75	7.50	15.00

WILSON, FRANK

Number	Title (A Side/B Side)	Yr	VG	VG+	NM
SOUL					
❑ 35019	Do I Love You (Indeed I Do)/Sweeter As the Days Go By	1966	10000.	15000.	20000.

WILSON, J. FRANK, AND THE CAVALIERS

Number	Title (A Side/B Side)	Yr	VG	VG+	NM
CHARAY					
❑ 13	Last Kiss '69/Black Car	1969	—	3.00	6.00
JOSIE					
❑ 923	Last Kiss/That's How Much I Love You	1964	3.00	6.00	12.00
❑ 924	Tears of Happiness/Summertime	1964	2.50	5.00	10.00
—As "The Cavaliers"					
❑ 926	Hey Little One/Speak to Me	1964	2.50	5.00	10.00
❑ 929	Say It Now/Six Boys	1965	2.50	5.00	10.00
❑ 931	Dreams of a Fool/Open Your Eyes	1965	2.50	5.00	10.00
❑ 938	Forget Me Not/A White Sport Coat (And a Pink Carnation)	1965	2.50	5.00	10.00
LE CAM					
❑ 722	Last Kiss/Carla	1964	7.50	15.00	30.00
SOLLY					
❑ 927	Me and My Teardrops/Unmarked and Uncovered with Sand	1966	2.50	5.00	10.00
TAMARA					
❑ 761	Last Kiss/That's How Much I Love You	1964	6.25	12.50	25.00
VIRGO					
❑ 506	Last Kiss/(B-side unknown)	1973	—	3.50	7.00

WILSON, JACKIE
Also see THE DOMINOES.

Number	Title (A Side/B Side)	Yr	VG	VG+	NM
BRUNSWICK					
❑ 55024	Reet Petite (The Finest Girl You Ever Want to Meet)/By the Light of the Silvery Moon	1957	7.50	15.00	30.00
❑ 55052	To Be Loved/Come Back to Me	1958	6.25	12.50	25.00
❑ 55070	As Long As I Live/I'm Wanderin'	1958	6.25	12.50	25.00
❑ 55086	We Have Love/Singing a Song	1958	6.25	12.50	25.00
❑ 55105	Lonely Teardrops/In the Blue of the Evening	1958	7.50	15.00	30.00
❑ 55121	That's Why (I Love You So)/Love Is All	1959	6.25	12.50	25.00
❑ 55121 [PS]	That's Why (I Love You So)/Love Is All	1959	15.00	30.00	60.00
❑ 55136	I'll Be Satisfied/Ask	1959	6.25	12.50	25.00
❑ 55149	You Better Know It/Never Go Away	1959	5.00	10.00	20.00
❑ 55165	Talk That Talk/Only You and Only Me	1959	5.00	10.00	20.00
❑ 55165 [PS]	Talk That Talk/Only You and Only Me	1959	15.00	30.00	60.00
❑ 55166	Night/Doggin' Around	1960	10.00	20.00	40.00
—Maroon label (scarce original)					
❑ 55166	Night/Doggin' Around	1960	3.75	7.50	15.00
—Orange label					
❑ 55166 [PS]	Night/Doggin' Around	1960	12.50	25.00	50.00
❑ 55167	(You Were Made for) All My Love/A Woman, A Lover, A Friend	1960	5.00	10.00	20.00
❑ 55170	Alone at Last/Am I the Man	1960	5.00	10.00	20.00
❑ 55170 [PS]	Alone at Last/Am I the Man	1960	12.50	25.00	50.00
❑ 55201	My Empty Arms/The Tear of the Year	1961	3.75	7.50	15.00
❑ 55201 [PS]	My Empty Arms/The Tear of the Year	1961	10.00	20.00	40.00
❑ 55208	Please Tell Me Why/Your One and Only Love	1961	3.75	7.50	15.00
❑ 55216	I'm Comin' On Back to You/Lonely Life	1961	3.75	7.50	15.00
❑ 55219	Years from Now/You Don't Know What It Means	1961	3.75	7.50	15.00
❑ 55220	The Way I Am/My Heart Belongs to Only You	1961	3.75	7.50	15.00
❑ 55220 [PS]	The Way I Am/My Heart Belongs to Only You	1961	10.00	20.00	40.00
❑ 55221	The Greatest Hurt/There'll Be No Next Time	1962	3.75	7.50	15.00
❑ 55221 [PS]	The Greatest Hurt/There'll Be No Next Time	1962	10.00	20.00	40.00
❑ 55224	I Found Love/There's Nothing Like Love	1962	3.00	6.00	12.00
—With Linda Hopkins					
❑ 55225	Hearts/Sing (And Tell the Blues So Long)	1962	3.75	7.50	15.00
❑ 55229	I Just Can't Help It/My Tale of Woe	1962	3.75	7.50	15.00
❑ 55233	Forever and a Day/Baby That's All	1962	3.75	7.50	15.00
❑ 55236	What Good Am I Without You/A Girl Named Tamiko	1962	3.75	7.50	15.00
❑ 55236 [PS]	What Good Am I Without You/A Girl Named Tamiko	1962	7.50	15.00	30.00
❑ 55239	Baby Workout/I'm Going Crazy	1963	5.00	10.00	20.00
❑ 55243	Shake a Hand/Say I Do	1963	3.00	6.00	12.00
—With Linda Hopkins					
❑ 55246	Shake! Shake! Shake!/He's a Fool	1963	3.00	6.00	12.00
❑ 55250	Baby Get It (And Don't Quit It)/The New Breed	1963	3.00	6.00	12.00
❑ 55254	Silent Night/Oh Holy Night	1963	3.75	7.50	15.00
❑ 55260	Haunted House/I'm Travelin' On	1964	2.50	5.00	10.00
❑ 55263	Call Her Up/The Kickapoo	1964	2.50	5.00	10.00
❑ 55266	Big Boss Line/Be My Girl	1964	2.50	5.00	10.00
❑ 55269	Squeeze Her-Tease Her (But Love Her)/Give Me Back My Heart	1964	2.50	5.00	10.00
❑ 55273	Watch Out/She's All Right	1964	2.50	5.00	10.00
❑ 55277	Danny Boy/Soul Time	1965	2.00	4.00	8.00
❑ 55278	Yes Indeed/When the Saints Go Marching In	1965	2.00	4.00	8.00
—With Linda Hopkins					
❑ 55280	No Pity (In the Naked City)/I'm So Lonely	1965	2.00	4.00	8.00
❑ 55283	I Believe I'll Love On/Lonely Teardrops	1965	2.00	4.00	8.00
❑ 55287	Think Twice/Please Don't Hurt Me	1965	2.00	4.00	8.00
—With LaVern Baker					
❑ 55289	I've Got to Get Back/3 Days, 1 Hour, 30 Minutes	1966	2.00	4.00	8.00
❑ 55290	Soul Galore/Brand New Things	1966	2.00	4.00	8.00
❑ 55294	I Believe/Be My Love	1966	2.00	4.00	8.00
❑ 55300	Whispers (Gettin' Louder)/The Fairest of Them All	1966	2.00	4.00	8.00
❑ 55309	I Don't Want to Lose You/Just Be Sincere	1967	2.00	4.00	8.00
❑ 55321	I've Lost You/Those Heartaches	1967	2.00	4.00	8.00
❑ 55336	(Your Love Keeps Lifting Me) Higher and Higher/I'm the One to Do It	1967	2.50	5.00	10.00
❑ 55354	Since You Showed Me How to Be Happy/The Who Who Song	1967	2.00	4.00	8.00
❑ 55365	For Your Precious Love/Uptight	1968	2.00	4.00	8.00
❑ 55373	Chain Gang/Funky Broadway	1968	2.00	4.00	8.00
❑ 55381	I Get the Sweetest Feeling/Nothing But Heartaches	1968	2.00	4.00	8.00

Number	Title (A Side/B Side)	Yr	VG	VG+	NM
❑ 55392	For Once in My Life/You Brought About a Change in Me	1968	2.00	4.00	8.00
❑ 55402	I Still Love You/Hum De Dum De Do	1969	2.00	4.00	8.00
❑ 55418	Helpless/Do It the Right Way	1969	2.00	4.00	8.00
❑ 55423	With These Hands/Why Don't You (Do Your Thing)	1969	2.00	4.00	8.00
❑ 55435	Let This Be a Letter (To My Baby)/Didn't I	1970	—	3.00	6.00
❑ 55435 [PS]	Let This Be a Letter (To My Baby)/Didn't I	1970	3.00	6.00	12.00
❑ 55443	(I Can Feel Those Vibrations) This Love Is Real/ Love Uprising	1970	—	3.00	6.00
❑ 55449	This Guy's in Love with You/Say You Will	1971	—	3.00	6.00
❑ 55454	Say You Will/(B-side unknown)	1971	—	3.00	6.00
❑ 55461	Love Is Funny That Way/Try It Again	1971	—	3.00	6.00
❑ 55467	You Got Me Walking/The Mountain	1972	—	3.00	6.00
❑ 55475	The Girl Turned Me On/Forever and a Day	1972	—	3.00	6.00
❑ 55480	What a Lovely Way/You Left the Fire Burning	1972	—	3.00	6.00
❑ 55490	Beautiful Day/What 'Cha Gonna Do About Love	1973	—	3.00	6.00
❑ 55495	Because of You/Go Away	1973	—	3.00	6.00
❑ 55499	Sing a Little Song/No More Goodbyes	1973	—	3.00	6.00
❑ 55504	It's All Over/Shake a Leg	1973	—	3.00	6.00
❑ 55522	Don't Burn No Bridges/(Instrumental)	1975	—	3.00	6.00
—With the Chi-Lites					
❑ 55536	Nobody But You/I've Learned About Life	1977	—	3.00	6.00
COLUMBIA					
❑ 07329	Reet Petite/You Better Know It	1987	—	2.50	5.00
❑ 07329 [PS]	Reet Petite/You Better Know It	1987	—	2.50	5.00
7-Inch Extended Plays					
BRUNSWICK					
❑ EB 71040	To Be Loved/Reet Petite//Danny Boy/As Long As I Live	1959	15.00	30.00	60.00
❑ EB 71040 [PS]	The Versatile Jackie Wilson	1959	15.00	30.00	60.00
❑ EB 71042	Lonely Teardrops/It's Too Bad We Had to Say Goodbye//Someone to Need Me/Joke	1960	15.00	30.00	60.00
❑ EB 71042 [PS]	Jumpin' Jack	1960	15.00	30.00	60.00
❑ EB 71045 [M]	That's Why/Love Is All//You Better Know It/Each Time	1960	15.00	30.00	60.00
❑ EB 71045 [PS]	Jackie Wilson	1960	15.00	30.00	60.00
❑ EB 71046	Talk That Talk/Ask//I'll Be Satisfied/Wishing Well	1960	15.00	30.00	60.00
❑ EB 71046 [PS]	Talk That Talk	1960	15.00	30.00	60.00
❑ EB 71047	(contents unknown)	1960	15.00	30.00	60.00
❑ EB 71047 [PS]	Mr. Excitement	1960	15.00	30.00	60.00
❑ EB 71048	So Much/Only You, Only Me//Happiness/Magic of Love	1960	15.00	30.00	60.00
❑ EB 71048 [PS]	Jackie Wilson	1960	15.00	30.00	60.00
❑ EB 71049	Night/Doggin' Around//All My Love/A Woman, a Lover, a Friend	1960	15.00	30.00	60.00
❑ EB 71049 [PS]	Jackie Wilson	1960	15.00	30.00	60.00
❑ EB 71101	The Greatest Hurt/I Don't Know You Anymore// Tear of the Year/There'll Be No Next Time	1962	15.00	30.00	60.00
❑ EB 71101 [PS]	Jackie Wilson	1962	15.00	30.00	60.00
❑ EB 71[illegible]	I Just Can't Help It/My Tale of Woe//Bad News Travels Fast/You Ought to Be Ashamed	1962	15.00	30.00	60.00
❑ EB 71102 [PS]	Jackie Wilson	1962	15.00	30.00	60.00
❑ EB 71103	Baby Workout/Say You Will//Kickapoo/Yeah Yeah Yeah	1963	15.00	30.00	60.00
❑ EB 71103 [PS]	Baby Workout	1963	15.00	30.00	60.00
❑ EB 71104	(contents unknown)	1963	15.00	30.00	60.00
❑ EB 71104 [PS]	Shake a Hand	1963	15.00	30.00	60.00
❑ EB 771045 [PS]	Jackie Wilson	1960	20.00	40.00	80.00
❑ EB 771045 [S]	That's Why/Love Is All//You Better Know It/Each Time	1960	20.00	40.00	80.00

WILSON, MARTY

Number	Title (A Side/B Side)	Yr	VG	VG+	NM
DECCA					
❑ 30544	Super Sonic/I'm All Woke Up	1958	7.50	15.00	30.00
❑ 30644	Po-Go/Hey Eula	1958	7.50	15.00	30.00
TEL					
❑ 1008	Stroll Me/Hot Foot	1959	6.25	12.50	25.00

WILSON, MARY

Also see THE SUPREMES.

Number	Title (A Side/B Side)	Yr	VG	VG+	NM
MOTOWN					
❑ 1467	Midnight Dancer/Red Hot	1979	—	2.50	5.00

WILSON, MURRY

Father of Brian, Carl and Dennis Wilson of the Beach Boys.

Number	Title (A Side/B Side)	Yr	VG	VG+	NM
CAPITOL					
❑ 2063	Leaves/Plumber's Tune	1967	3.00	6.00	12.00

WILSON, NANCY (2)

Also see HEART; ANN AND NANCY WILSON.

Number	Title (A Side/B Side)	Yr	VG	VG+	NM
WTG					
❑ 68678	All for Love/Taste the Rain	1989	2.50	5.00	10.00
—B-side by Red Hot Chili Peppers					

WILSON, PEANUTS

Number	Title (A Side/B Side)	Yr	VG	VG+	NM
BRUNSWICK					
❑ 55039	Cast Iron Arm/You've Got Love	1957	37.50	75.00	150.00

WILSON, SONNY

Number	Title (A Side/B Side)	Yr	VG	VG+	NM
CANDIX					
❑ 327	I Ain't Givin' Up Nothin'/Troubled Time	1962	5.00	10.00	20.00
SUN					
❑ 341	The Great Pretender/I'm Gonna Take a Walk	1960	5.00	10.00	20.00

WILSON, WALLY

Number	Title (A Side/B Side)	Yr	VG	VG+	NM
SABRE					
❑ 106	If You Don't Love Me/The Hunt	1954	150.00	300.00	600.00

WIMBERLEY, MAGGIE SUE

Number	Title (A Side/B Side)	Yr	VG	VG+	NM
SUN					
❑ 229	Daydreams Come True/How Long	1956	15.00	30.00	60.00

WINCHELL, DANNY

Number	Title (A Side/B Side)	Yr	VG	VG+	NM
MGM					
❑ 11335	Carolina in the Morning/There Goes My Heart	1952	7.50	15.00	30.00
RECORTE					
❑ 406	Jeannie/Beware You've Fallen in Love	1959	10.00	20.00	40.00
❑ 410	We're Gonna Have a Rockin' Party/Don't Say You're Sorry	1959	12.50	25.00	50.00
❑ 415	Come Back Baby/I've Chosen You	1959	10.00	20.00	40.00

WIND

TONY ORLANDO was in this group.

Number	Title (A Side/B Side)	Yr	VG	VG+	NM
FORWARD					
❑ 152	Groovin' with Mr. Bloe/Are You Nuts?	1970	—	2.50	5.00
—As "Cool Heat"					
LIFE					
❑ 200	Make Believe/Groovin' with Mr. Bloe	1969	—	2.50	5.00
❑ 202	Teeny Bopper/I'll Hold Out My Hand	1969	—	2.50	5.00
❑ 203	Groovin' with Mr. Bloe/Are You Nuts?	1970	—	3.00	6.00
—As "Cool Heat"					

WIND IN THE WILLOWS, THE

With DEBBIE HARRY, later of BLONDIE.

Number	Title (A Side/B Side)	Yr	VG	VG+	NM
CAPITOL					
❑ 2274	Uptown Girl/Moments Spent	1968	5.00	10.00	20.00

WINDSORS, THE (1)

Number	Title (A Side/B Side)	Yr	VG	VG+	NM
ABC-PARAMOUNT					
❑ 10563	Keep Away/Fingers and Thumbs	1964	3.75	7.50	15.00

WINDSORS, THE (2)

Number	Title (A Side/B Side)	Yr	VG	VG+	NM
BACK BEAT					
❑ 506	My Gloria/Cool Seabreeze	1958	4000.	6000.	8000.

WINDSORS, THE (U)

Number	Title (A Side/B Side)	Yr	VG	VG+	NM
UNITED ARTISTS					
❑ 128	Saki Rock/Caramba	1958	5.00	10.00	20.00
WIG WAG					
❑ 203	Carol Ann/Keep Me from Crying	1959	50.00	100.00	200.00

WINE, TONI

Number	Title (A Side/B Side)	Yr	VG	VG+	NM
ATCO					
❑ 6736	Sisters in Sorrow/Take a Little Time Out for Love	1970	—	3.00	6.00
COLPIX					
❑ 715	My Boyfriend's Coming Home for Christmas/ What a Pity	1963	3.75	7.50	15.00
❑ 732	I Love That Boy/The Thirteenth Hour	1964	3.00	6.00	12.00
❑ 742	A Boy Like You/Funny Little Heart	1964	3.00	6.00	12.00
❑ 756	Only Fools/A Girl Is Not a Girl	1964	3.00	6.00	12.00
SENATE					
❑ 2104	River Deep, Mountain High/Toni's Tune	1967	2.50	5.00	10.00

WINGFIELD, PETE

Number	Title (A Side/B Side)	Yr	VG	VG+	NM
ISLAND					
❑ 026	Eighteen with a Bullet/Shadow of a Doubt	1975	2.00	4.00	8.00
—First pressing: Mostly yellow label with island scene					
❑ 026	Eighteen with a Bullet/Shadow of a Doubt	1975	—	2.50	5.00
—Second pressing: Mostly black label with Island logo at bottom					
❑ 051	Lovin' As You Wanna Be/Please	1975	—	2.00	4.00
❑ 065	Scratchy 45's/A Whole Pot of Jelly (For a Little Slice of Toast)	1976	—	2.00	4.00

WINGS

See PAUL McCARTNEY.

WINKLEY AND NUTLEY

Number	Title (A Side/B Side)	Yr	VG	VG+	NM
MK					
❑ 101	Report to the Nation (Part 1)/Report to the Nation (Part 2)	1960	5.00	10.00	20.00

WINSTONS, THE

Number	Title (A Side/B Side)	Yr	VG	VG+	NM
METROMEDIA					
❑ 117	Color Him Father/Amen, Brother	1969	2.00	4.00	8.00
❑ 142	Love of the Common People/Wheel of Fortune	1969	—	3.00	6.00
❑ 151	Birds of a Feather/The Greatest Love	1969	—	3.00	6.00

WINTER, EDGAR

Number	Title (A Side/B Side)	Yr	VG	VG+	NM
BLUE SKY					
❑ 2758	One Day Tomorrow/Jasmine Nightdream	1975	—	2.00	4.00
❑ 2761	Outa Control/I Always Wanted You	1975	—	2.00	4.00
❑ 2762	Cool Dance/People Music	1975	—	2.00	4.00
❑ 2763	Diamond Eyes/Infinite Peace in Rhythm	1976	—	2.00	4.00
❑ 2769	Stickin' It Out/Puttin' It Back	1977	—	2.00	4.00
❑ 2780	Forever in Love/It's Your Life to Live	1979	—	2.00	4.00
❑ 2786	Above and Beyond/(Instrumental)	1980	—	2.00	4.00
❑ 70068	Love Is Everywhere/Everyday Man	1981	—	2.00	4.00
EPIC					
❑ 10618	Tobacco Road/Now Is the Time	1970	2.00	4.00	8.00
❑ 10740	Good Morning Music/Where Would I Be	1971	2.00	4.00	8.00
❑ 10750	Where Would I Be/Feeling Like a Woman	1971	—	3.00	6.00
—B-side by Patsy Sledd					
❑ 10762	Give It Everything You've Got/You Were My Light	1971	—	3.00	6.00
❑ 10788	Keep Playin' That Rock 'N' Roll/Dying to Live	1971	—	3.00	6.00
❑ 10855	I Can't Turn You Loose/Cool Fool	1972	—	3.00	6.00
❑ 10903	Free Ride/Catchin' Up	1972	2.00	4.00	8.00
❑ 10922	Round and Round/Catchin' Up	1972	2.00	4.00	8.00
❑ 10945	Frankenstein/Hangin' Around	1973	2.00	4.00	8.00
❑ 10967	Frankenstein/Undercover Man	1973	—	3.00	6.00
—Yellow label					
❑ 10967	Frankenstein/Undercover Man	1973	—	2.00	4.00
—Orange label					
❑ 11024	Free Ride/When It Comes	1973	—	2.00	4.00
❑ 11069	Hangin' Around/We All Had a Real Good Time	1973	—	2.00	4.00
❑ 11143	River's Risin'/Animal	1974	—	2.00	4.00

Number	Title (A Side/B Side)	Yr	VG	VG+	NM
❑ 50034	Easy Street/Do Like Me	1974	—	2.00	4.00
❑ 50060	Miracle of Love/Someone Take My Heart Away	1975	—	2.00	4.00

WINTER, JOHNNY

Also see JOHNNY AND THE JAMMERS.

Number	Title (A Side/B Side)	Yr	VG	VG+	NM
ATLANTIC					
❑ 2248	Gangster of Love/Eternally	1964	2.50	5.00	10.00
BLUE SKY					
❑ 2754	Raised on Rock/Pick Up on My Mojo	1974	—	2.00	4.00
❑ 2756	Golden Olden Days of Rock 'N' Roll/Stranger	1975	—	2.00	4.00
BUDDAH					
❑ 168	Out of Sight/Bad News	1970	2.50	5.00	10.00
COLUMBIA					
❑ 44900	I'll Drown in My Tears/I'm Yours and I'm Here	1969	—	2.50	5.00
❑ 45058	Johnny B. Goode/I'm Not Sure	1969	—	2.50	5.00
❑ 45260	Rock and Roll Hoochie Koo/21st Century Man	1970	—	2.50	5.00
❑ 45368	Jumpin' Jack Flash/Good Morning, Little Schoolgirl	1971	—	2.50	5.00
❑ 45860	Silver Train/Rock and Roll	1973	—	2.50	5.00
❑ 45899	Can't You Feel It/Rock and Roll	1973	—	2.50	5.00
❑ 46006	Bad Luck Situation/Stone County	1974	—	2.50	5.00
❑ 46036	Boney Moroney/Hurtin' So Bad	1974	—	2.50	5.00
FROLIC					
❑ 501	That's What Love Does/Shed So Many Tears	1962	12.50	25.00	50.00
❑ 503	Voo Doo Twist/Ease My Pain	1962	25.00	50.00	100.00
❑ 509	Gangster of Love/Eternally	1963	12.50	25.00	50.00
❑ 512	Gone for Bad/I Won't Believe It	1963	15.00	30.00	60.00
GRT					
❑ 9	Gangster of Love/Roadrunner	1969	2.00	4.00	8.00
IMPERIAL					
❑ 66376	Forty-Four/Rollin' & Tumblin'	1969	2.00	4.00	8.00
MGM					
❑ 13380	Gone for Bad/I Won't Believe It	1965	2.00	4.00	8.00
PACEMAKER					
❑ 243	Leavin' Blues/Birds Can't Row Boats	1966	5.00	10.00	20.00
TODD					
❑ 1084	Road Runner/The Guy You Left Behind	1963	5.00	10.00	20.00

WINTER, JOHNNY AND EDGAR

Also see each artist's individual listings.

Number	Title (A Side/B Side)	Yr	VG	VG+	NM
BLUE SKY					
❑ 2764	Soul Man/Let the Good Times Roll	1976	—	2.00	4.00

WINWOOD, STEVE

Also see BLIND FAITH; THE SPENCER DAVIS GROUP; TRAFFIC.

Number	Title (A Side/B Side)	Yr	VG	VG+	NM
ISLAND					
❑ 091	Time Is Running Out/Hold On	1977	—	2.50	5.00
❑ 28122	Talking Back to the Night/There's a River	1988	—	2.00	4.00
❑ 28122 [PS]	Talking Back to the Night/There's a River	1988	—	2.00	4.00
❑ 28231	Valerie/Talking Back to the Night (Instrumental)	1987	—	—	3.00
❑ 28231 [PS]	Valerie/Talking Back to the Night (Instrumental)	1987	—	—	3.00
❑ 28472	Back in the High Life Again/Night Train	1987	—	—	3.00
❑ 28472 [PS]	Back in the High Life Again/Night Train	1987	—	—	3.00
❑ 28498	The Finer Things/Night Train	1987	—	—	3.00
❑ 28498 [PS]	The Finer Things/Night Train	1987	—	—	3.00
❑ 28595	Freedom Overspill/Help Me Angel	1986	—	—	3.00
❑ 28595 [PS]	Freedom Overspill/Help Me Angel	1986	—	—	3.00
❑ 28710	Higher Love/And I Go	1986	—	—	3.00
❑ 28710 [PS]	Higher Love/And I Go	1986	—	—	3.00
❑ 29879	Valerie/Slowdown	1982	—	2.50	5.00
❑ 29940	Still in the Game/Dust	1982	—	2.00	4.00
❑ 49656	While You See a Chance/Vacant Chair	1981	—	2.00	4.00
❑ 49656 [PS]	While You See a Chance/Vacant Chair	1981	—	2.50	5.00
❑ 49726	Arc of a Diver/Dust	1981	—	2.00	4.00
❑ 49726 [PS]	Arc of a Diver/Dust	1981	—	2.50	5.00
❑ 49773	Night Train (Part 1)/Night Train (Part 2)	1981	—	2.00	4.00
VIRGIN					
❑ 98892	One and Only Man/(instrumental)	1990	—	—	3.00
❑ 99234	Hearts On Fire (7" Remix)/(Instrumental)	1989	—	—	3.00
❑ 99234 [PS]	Hearts On Fire (7" Remix)/(Instrumental)	1989	—	—	3.00
❑ 99261	Holding On/(Instrumental)	1988	—	—	3.00
❑ 99261 [PS]	Holding On/(Instrumental)	1988	—	—	3.00
❑ 99290	Don't You Know What the Night Can Do/(Instrumental)	1988	—	—	3.00
❑ 99290 [PS]	Don't You Know What the Night Can Do/(Instrumental)	1988	—	—	3.00
❑ 99326	Roll With It/The Morning Side	1988	—	—	3.00
❑ 99326 [PS]	Roll With It/The Morning Side	1988	—	—	3.00

WISDOMS, THE

Number	Title (A Side/B Side)	Yr	VG	VG+	NM
GAITY					
❑ 169	Two Hearts Make One Love/Lost in Dreams	1959	150.00	300.00	600.00

WISHBONE ASH

Number	Title (A Side/B Side)	Yr	VG	VG+	NM
ATLANTIC					
❑ 3381	Lorelei/(B-side unknown)	1977	—	2.50	5.00
DECCA					
❑ 32826	Blind Eye/Queen of Torture	1971	2.00	4.00	8.00
❑ 32902	Jail Bait/Vas Dis	1971	2.00	4.00	8.00
❑ 33004	Blowin' Free/No Easy Road	1972	2.00	4.00	8.00
MCA					
❑ 40041	Rock and Roll Widow/No Easy Road	1973	—	3.00	6.00
❑ 40362	Persephone/Silver Shoes	1975	—	3.00	6.00
❑ 40829	Front Page News/Goodbye Baby, Hello Friends	1977	—	2.00	4.00

WITHERS, BILL

Number	Title (A Side/B Side)	Yr	VG	VG+	NM
COLUMBIA					
❑ 02071	I Want to Spend the Night/Memories Are That Way	1981	—	2.00	4.00
❑ 02651	USA/Paint Your Pretty Picture	1981	—	2.00	4.00
❑ 02651 [PS]	USA/Paint Your Pretty Picture	1981	—	2.50	5.00
❑ 04841	Oh Yeah!/Just Like the First Time	1985	—	2.00	4.00
❑ 05424	Something That Turns You On/You Tried to Find a Love	1985	—	2.00	4.00
❑ 05424 [PS]	Something That Turns You On/You Tried to Find a Love	1985	—	2.00	4.00
❑ 05675	We Could Be Sweet Lovers/You Just Can't Smile It Away	1985	—	2.00	4.00
❑ 10255	Make Love to Your Mind/I Love You Dawn	1975	—	2.50	5.00
❑ 10308	I Wish You Well/She's Lonely	1976	—	2.50	5.00
❑ 10357	Family Table/Hello Like Before	1976	—	2.50	5.00
❑ 10420	If I Didn't Mean You Well/My Imagination	1976	—	2.50	5.00
❑ 10459	Close to Me/I'll Be with You	1976	—	2.50	5.00
❑ 10627	Lovely Day/It Ain't Because of Me Baby	1977	—	2.50	5.00
❑ 10702	Lovely Night for Dancing/I Want to Spend the Night	1978	—	2.50	5.00
❑ 10892	Don't It Make It Better/Love Is	1979	—	2.00	4.00
❑ 10958	You Got the Stuff/Look to Each Other for Love	1979	—	2.00	4.00
SUSSEX					
❑ 219	Ain't No Sunshine/Harlem	1971	—	3.00	6.00
❑ 227	Grandma's Hands/Sweet Wanomi	1971	—	2.50	5.00
❑ 235	Lean On Me/Better Off Dead	1972	—	3.00	6.00
❑ 241	Use Me/Let Me In Your Life	1972	—	2.50	5.00
❑ 247	Let Us Love/The Gift of Giving	1972	—	2.50	5.00
❑ 247 [PS]	Let Us Love/The Gift of Giving	1972	2.00	4.00	8.00
❑ 250	Kissing My Love/I Don't Know	1973	—	2.50	5.00
❑ 257	Friend of Mine/Lonely Town, Lonely Street	1973	—	2.50	5.00
❑ 513	The Same Love That Made Me Laugh/Make a Smile for Me	1974	—	2.50	5.00
❑ 518	You/Stories	1974	—	2.50	5.00
❑ 629	Heartbreak Road/Ruby Lee	1974	—	2.50	5.00
❑ 638	Who Is He (And What Is He to You)/Harlem	1975	—	2.50	5.00

WITHERSPOON, JIMMY

Number	Title (A Side/B Side)	Yr	VG	VG+	NM
ABC					
❑ 11288	Handbags and Gladrags/Stay with Me Baby	1971	—	3.00	6.00
BLUE NOTE					
❑ XW716	Pearly Whites/Sign on the Building	1975	—	2.50	5.00
BLUESWAY					
❑ 61028	Just a Dream/I Don't Know	1969	—	3.00	6.00
CAPITOL					
❑ 3998	Love Is a Five Letter Word/Other Side of Love	1974	—	2.50	5.00
CHECKER					
❑ 798	Big Daddy/When the Lights Go Out	1954	7.50	15.00	30.00
❑ 810	Time Brings About a Change/Waiting for Your Return	1955	7.50	15.00	30.00
❑ 826	It Ain't No Secret/Why Do I Love You Like I Do	1955	7.50	15.00	30.00
FEDERAL					
❑ 12095	Foolish Prayer/Two Little Girls	1952	7.50	15.00	30.00
❑ 12099	Lucille/Blues in Trouble	1952	7.50	15.00	30.00
❑ 12107	Don't Tell Me Now/Corn Whiskey	1952	7.50	15.00	30.00
❑ 12118	Jay's Blues (Part 1)/Jay's Blues (Part 2)	1953	7.50	15.00	30.00
❑ 12128	One Fine Gal/Back Home	1953	7.50	15.00	30.00
❑ 12138	Back Door Blues/Last Mile	1953	7.50	15.00	30.00
❑ 12155	Fast Women and Sloe Gin/Miss Mistreater	1953	7.50	15.00	30.00
❑ 12156	Sad Life/Move Me Baby	1953	12.50	25.00	50.00
—With the Lamplighters					
❑ 12173	24 Sad Hours/Just for You	1954	7.50	15.00	30.00
❑ 12180	It/Highway to Happiness	1954	7.50	15.00	30.00
❑ 12189	Oh Boy/I Done Told You	1954	7.50	15.00	30.00
GNP CRESCENDO					
❑ 156	Ain't Nobody's Business/No Rollin' Blues	1959	3.00	6.00	12.00
HIFI					
❑ 594	Everytime I Feel the Spirit/Oh Mary Don't You Weep	1960	3.00	6.00	12.00
KENT					
❑ 4551	Ain't Nobody's Business (Part 1)/Ain't Nobody's Business (Part 2)	1971	—	3.00	6.00
KING					
❑ 5997	Foolish Prayer/Two Little Girls	1965	2.50	5.00	10.00
MODERN					
❑ 857	The Wind Is Blowin'/My Baby Make a Change	1952	10.00	20.00	40.00
—Note: Earlier Jimmy Witherspoon 45s on Modern are not known to exist					
❑ 877	Love My Baby/Daddy Pinocchio	1952	10.00	20.00	40.00
❑ 895	Baby Baby/Slow Your Speed	1953	10.00	20.00	40.00
❑ 903	Each Step of the Way/Let Jesus Fix It for You	1953	10.00	20.00	40.00
❑ 909	Oh Mother, Dear Mother/I'll Be Right On Down	1953	10.00	20.00	40.00
PACIFIC JAZZ					
❑ 327	Ain't Nobody's Business/Times Have Changed	1961	2.50	5.00	10.00
PRESTIGE					
❑ 266	One Scotch, One Bourbon, One Beer/Baby, Baby, Baby	196?	2.50	5.00	10.00
❑ 274	Mean Ole Frisco/Sail On Little Girl	196?	2.50	5.00	10.00
❑ 291	Goin' to Chicago Blues/You Made Me Love You	196?	2.50	5.00	10.00
❑ 298	I Had a Dream/S.K. Blues	1963	2.50	5.00	10.00
❑ 307	Money's Gettin' Cheaper/Ever In	1963	2.50	5.00	10.00
❑ 340	I Never Will Marry/Happy Blues	1964	2.50	5.00	10.00
❑ 341	Some of My Best Friends Are the Blues/You're Next	1964	2.50	5.00	10.00
❑ 358	Come On and Walk with Me/Two Hearts Are Better Than One	196?	2.00	4.00	8.00
❑ 378	Love Me Right/Make This Heart of Mine Smile Again	196?	2.00	4.00	8.00
❑ 402	I Never Thought I'd See the Day/If There Wasn't Any You	196?	2.00	4.00	8.00
RCA VICTOR					
❑ 47-6977	Ain't Nobody's Business/Who Baby Who	1957	5.00	10.00	20.00
❑ 47-7377	Confessin' the Blues/Ooo Wee, Then the Lights Go Out	1958	5.00	10.00	20.00
REPRISE					
❑ 0275	Key to the Highway/I'd Rather Drink Muddy Water	1964	2.00	4.00	8.00
❑ 20013	The Masquerade Is Over/I Don't Know	1961	2.50	5.00	10.00
❑ 20029	Warm Your Heart/Hey Mrs. Jones	1961	2.50	5.00	10.00

Number	Title (A Side/B Side)	Yr	VG	VG+	NM
SWINGTIME					
❑ 244	Christmas Blues/Skid Row Blues	1951	—	—	—
—Unconfirmed on 45 rpm					
VEE JAY					
❑ 322	Everything But You/I Know, I Know	1959	3.00	6.00	12.00
VERVE					
❑ 10439	It's All Over But the Crying/My Blue Tears	1966	2.00	4.00	8.00
❑ 10495	Fast Forty Blues/My Baby Quit Me	1967	2.00	4.00	8.00
WORLD PACIFIC					
❑ 814	Ain't Nobody's Business/There's Good Rockin' Tonight	1960	3.00	6.00	12.00

WOLFE, DANNY

Number	Title (A Side/B Side)	Yr	VG	VG+	NM
DOT					
❑ 15591	Pretty Blue Jean Baby/Once with You	1957	10.00	20.00	40.00
❑ 15667	Let's Flat Get It/I'm Glad I Waited	1957	15.00	30.00	60.00
❑ 15715	I'd Rather Be Lucky/Pucker Paint	1958	10.00	20.00	40.00

WOMACK, BOBBY

Number	Title (A Side/B Side)	Yr	VG	VG+	NM
ARISTA					
❑ 0421	How Could You Break My Heart/I Honestly Love You	1979	—	2.00	4.00
❑ 0446	The Roads of Life/Give It Up	1979	—	2.00	4.00
ATLANTIC					
❑ 2388	Night Train/It's Karate Time	1967	2.50	5.00	10.00
BEVERLY GLEN					
❑ 2000	If You Think You're Lonely Now/Secrets	1981	—	2.00	4.00
❑ 2001	Where Do We Go from Here/Just My Imagination	1982	—	2.00	4.00
❑ 2012	Love Has Finally Come at Last/American Dream	1984	—	2.00	4.00
—With Patti LaBelle					
❑ 2014	Tell Me Why/Through the Eyes of a Child	1984	—	2.00	4.00
—B-side with Patti LaBelle					
❑ 2018	It Takes a Lot of Strength to Say Goodbye/Who's Foolin' Who	1984	—	2.00	4.00
—A-side with Patti LaBelle					
❑ 2021	Someday We'll All Be Free/I Wish I Had Someone to Go Home To	1985	—	2.00	4.00
❑ 2023	I'm So Proud/Searching for My Love	1985	—	2.00	4.00
CHECKER					
❑ 1122	Lonesome Man/I Found a True Love	1965	3.75	7.50	15.00
COLUMBIA					
❑ 10437	Home Is Where the Heart Is/We've Only Just Begun	1976	—	2.50	5.00
❑ 10493	Standing in the Safety Zone/A Change Is Gonna Come	1977	—	2.50	5.00
❑ 10672	Trust Your Heart/When Love Begins, Friendship Ends	1978	—	2.50	5.00
❑ 10732	Wind It Up/Stop Before We Start	1978	—	2.50	5.00
LIBERTY					
❑ 56186	I'm Gonna Forget About You/Don't Look Back	1970	2.00	4.00	8.00
❑ 56206	Something/Everybody's Talkin'	1970	2.00	4.00	8.00
MCA					
❑ 52624	I Wish He Didn't Trust Me So Much/Got to Be with You Tonight	1985	—	2.00	4.00
❑ 52624 [PS]	I Wish He Didn't Trust Me So Much/Got to Be with You Tonight	1985	—	2.00	4.00
❑ 52709	Let Me Kiss It Where It Hurts/Check It Out	1985	—	2.00	4.00
❑ 52793	Gypsy Woman/What Evert Happened to the Times	1986	—	—	3.00
❑ 52955	(I Wanna) Make Love to You/The Launch	1986	—	—	3.00
❑ 52955 [PS]	(I Wanna) Make Love to You/The Launch	1986	—	—	3.00
❑ 53190	Living in a Box/I Can't Stay Mad	1987	—	—	3.00
❑ 53263	Outside Myself/A Woman Likes to Hear Than	1988	—	—	3.00
MINIT					
❑ 32024	Baby, I Can't Stand It/Trust Me	1967	2.50	5.00	10.00
❑ 32030	Somebody Special/Broadway Walk	1967	2.50	5.00	10.00
❑ 32037	What Is This/What You Gonna Do (When Your Love Is Gone)	1968	2.50	5.00	10.00
❑ 32048	Fly Me to the Moon/Take Me	1968	2.50	5.00	10.00
❑ 32055	California Dreamin'/Baby, You Oughta Think It Over	1968	2.50	5.00	10.00
❑ 32059	I Left My Heart in San Francisco/Love, The Time Is Now	1969	2.00	4.00	8.00
❑ 32071	It's Gonna Rain/Thank You	1969	2.00	4.00	8.00
❑ 32081	How I Miss You Baby/Tried and Convicted	1969	2.00	4.00	8.00
❑ 32093	More Than I Can Stand/Arkansas State Prison	1970	2.00	4.00	8.00
SOLAR					
❑ 74006	Save the Children/(Instrumental)	1989	—	—	3.00
THE RIGHT STUFF					
❑ 58815	Dear Santa Claus/Dear Santa Claus (Kids Version)	1999	—	—	3.00
UNITED ARTISTS					
❑ 0123	That's the Way I Feel About Cha/Woman's Gotta Have It	1973	—	2.00	4.00
—"Silver Spotlight Series" reissue					
❑ XW196	Across 110th Street/Hang On In There	1973	—	2.50	5.00
❑ XW255	Nobody Wants You When You're Down and Out/I'm Thru Trying to Prove My Love	1973	—	2.50	5.00
❑ XW375	Lookin' for a Love/Let It Hang Out	1973	—	2.50	5.00
❑ XW439	You're Welcome, Stop On By/I Don't Want to Be Hurt	1974	—	2.50	5.00
❑ XW525	Lookin' for a Love/Nobody Wants You When You're Down and Out	1974	—	2.00	4.00
—Reissue					
❑ XW526	Harry Hippie/Sweet Caroline	1974	—	2.00	4.00
—Reissue					
❑ XW527	California Dreamin'/Fly Me to the Moon	1974	—	2.50	5.00
❑ XW561	I Don't Know/Yes, Jesus Loves Me	1974	—	2.50	5.00
❑ XW621	Check It Out/Interlude No. 2	1975	—	2.50	5.00
❑ XW674	It's All Over Now/Git It	1975	—	2.50	5.00
❑ XW735	Where There's a Will, There's a Way/Everything's Gonna Be Alright	1975	—	2.50	5.00
❑ XW763	Daylight/Trust Me	1976	—	2.50	5.00
❑ XW804	I Feel a Groove Comin' On/Trust Me	1976	—	2.50	5.00
❑ 50773	The Preacher/More Than I Can Stand	1971	—	3.00	6.00
❑ 50816	Communication/Fire and Rain	1971	—	3.00	6.00
❑ 50847	That's the Way I Feel About 'Cha/Come L'Amore	1971	—	3.00	6.00
❑ 50902	Woman's Gotta Have It/Give It Back	1972	—	3.00	6.00
❑ 50946	Harry Hippie/Sweet Caroline (Good Times Never Seemed So Good)	1972	—	3.00	6.00
❑ 50988 [DJ]	Harry Hippie (mono/stereo)	1972	2.00	4.00	8.00
—Apparently, no stock copy exists					

WOMACK, LEE ANN

Number	Title (A Side/B Side)	Yr	VG	VG+	NM
DECCA					
❑ 55320	Never Again, Again (3:10)/Never Again, Again (3:22)	1997	—	2.00	4.00
❑ 72009	The Fool/Trouble's Here	1997	—	—	3.00
❑ 72023	You've Got to Talk to Me/A Man with 18 Wheels	1997	—	—	3.00
❑ 72041	Buckaroo/Make Memories with Me	1998	—	—	3.00
❑ 72049	A Man with 18 Wheels/Drivin' My Life Away	1998	—	—	3.00
—B-side by Rhett Akins					
❑ 72068	A Little Past Little Rock/If You're Ever Down in Dallas	1998	—	—	3.00
❑ 72076	I'll Think of a Reason Later/I'd Rather Have What We Had	1999	—	—	3.00
❑ 088-172132-7	Don't Tell Me/I Keep Forgetting	1999	—	—	3.00
MCA NASHVILLE					
❑ 72111	(Now You See Me) Now You Don't/The Preacher Won't Have to Lie	1999	—	—	3.00
❑ 088-172158-7	I Hope You Dance/Lonely Too	2000	—	—	3.00
❑ 088-172182-7	Ashes by Now/Lonely Too	2000	—	—	3.00
❑ 088-172185 7	I Hope You Dance (Pop Version)/I Hope You Dance (Album Version)	2000	—	—	3.00

WOMB

Number	Title (A Side/B Side)	Yr	VG	VG+	NM
DOT					
❑ 17250	Hang On/My Baby Thinks About the Good Things	1969	3.00	6.00	12.00

WONDER, STEVIE

Also see PAUL McCARTNEY AND STEVIE WONDER.

Number	Title (A Side/B Side)	Yr	VG	VG+	NM
GORDY					
❑ 7076	Alfie/More Than a Dream	1968	6.25	12.50	25.00
—As "Eivets Rednow" (read it backwards)					
MOTOWN					
❑ 1650	Used to Be/I Want to Come Back As A Song	1982	—	—	3.00
—A-side with Charlene; B-side is Charlene solo					
❑ 1650 [PS]	Used to Be/I Want to Come Back As A Song	1982	—	—	3.00
❑ 1745	I Just Called to Say I Love You/(Instrumental)	1984	—	—	3.00
❑ 1745 [PS]	I Just Called to Say I Love You/(Instrumental)	1984	12.50	25.00	50.00
❑ 1769	Love Light in Flight/It's More Than You	1984	—	—	3.00
❑ 1769 [PS]	Love Light in Flight/It's More Than You	1984	—	2.00	4.00
❑ 1907	Skeletons/(Instrumental)	1987	—	—	3.00
❑ 1907 [PS]	Skeletons/(Instrumental)	1987	—	2.00	4.00
❑ 1919	You Will Know/(Instrumental)	1988	—	—	3.00
❑ 1919 [PS]	You Will Know/(Instrumental)	1988	—	2.00	4.00
❑ 1946	My Eyes Don't Cry/(Instrumental)	1988	—	—	3.00
❑ 1946 [PS]	My Eyes Don't Cry/(Instrumental)	1988	—	—	3.00
❑ 1953	With Each Beat of My Heart/(Instrumental)	1989	—	—	3.00
❑ 1990	Keep Our Love Alive/(Instrumental)	1990	—	2.50	5.00
❑ 2081	Gotta Have You/Feeding Off the Love of the Land	1991	—	2.00	4.00
❑ 2127	Fun Day/(Instrumental)	1991	—	2.00	4.00
❑ 2143	These Three Words (same on both sides)	1991	—	2.00	4.00
❑ 860310-7	For Your Love/(Instrumental)	1995	—	—	3.00
❑ 860418-7	Tomorrow Robins Will Sing/For Your Love	1995	—	—	3.00
TAMLA					
❑ 1602	That Girl/All I Do	1982	—	2.00	4.00
❑ 1612	Do I Do/Rocket Love	1982	—	2.00	4.00
❑ 1639	Ribbon in the Sky/Black Orchid	1982	—	2.00	4.00
❑ 1639 [PS]	Ribbon in the Sky/Black Orchid	1982	—	2.00	4.00
❑ 1808	Part-Time Lover/(Instrumental)	1985	—	—	3.00
❑ 1808 [PS]	Part-Time Lover/(Instrumental)	1985	—	2.00	4.00
❑ 1817	Go Home/(Instrumental)	1985	—	—	3.00
❑ 1817 [PS]	Go Home/(Instrumental)	1985	—	2.00	4.00
❑ 1832	Overjoyed/(Instrumental)	1986	—	—	3.00
❑ 1832 [PS]	Overjoyed/(Instrumental)	1986	—	2.00	4.00
❑ 1846	Land of La La/(Instrumental)	1986	—	—	3.00
❑ 1846 [PS]	Land of La La/(Instrumental)	1986	—	2.00	4.00
❑ 54061	I Call It Pretty Music But The Old People Call It the Blues (Part 1)/I Call It Pretty Music But The Old People Call It the Blues (Part 2)	1962	7.50	15.00	30.00
❑ 54061 [PS]	I Call It Pretty Music But The Old People Call It the Blues (Part 1)/I Call It Pretty Music But The Old People Call It the Blues (Part 2)	1962	20.00	40.00	80.00
❑ 54070	Little Water Boy/La La La La La	1962	6.25	12.50	25.00
❑ 54074	Contract on Love/Sunset	1963	6.25	12.50	25.00
❑ 54080	Fingertips — Pt. 2/Fingertips — Pt. 1	1963	5.00	10.00	20.00
❑ 54080 [PS]	Fingertips — Pt. 2/Fingertips — Pt. 1	1963	12.50	25.00	50.00
❑ 54086	Workout Stevie, Workout/Monkey Talk	1963	3.75	7.50	15.00
❑ 54090	Castles in the Sand/Thank You (For Loving Me All the Way)	1964	3.75	7.50	15.00
—Up to and including this, as "Little Stevie Wonder"					
❑ 54096	Hey Harmonica Man/This Little Girl	1964	3.75	7.50	15.00
❑ 54096 [PS]	Hey Harmonica Man/This Little Girl	1964	10.00	20.00	40.00
❑ 54103	Sad Boy/Happy Street	1964	5.00	10.00	20.00
❑ 54108	Pretty Little Angel/Tears in Vain	1964	—	—	—
—Unreleased					
❑ 54114	Kiss Me Baby/Tears in Vain	1965	3.00	6.00	12.00
❑ 54119	High Heel Sneakers/Music Talk	1965	3.00	6.00	12.00
❑ 54119	High Heel Sneakers/Funny How Time Slips Away	1965	5.00	10.00	20.00
❑ 54124	Uptight (Everything's Alright)/Purple Rain Drops	1965	3.75	7.50	15.00
❑ 54130	Nothing's Too Good for My Baby/With a Child's Heart	1966	3.00	6.00	12.00

Number	Title (A Side/B Side)	Yr	VG	VG+	NM
❑ 54136	Blowin' in the Wind/Ain't That Asking for Trouble	1966	3.00	6.00	12.00
❑ 54136 [PS]	Blowin' in the Wind/Ain't That Asking for Trouble	1966	6.25	12.50	25.00
❑ 54139	A Place in the Sun/Sylvia	1966	3.00	6.00	12.00
❑ 54139 [PS]	A Place in the Sun/Sylvia	1966	6.25	12.50	25.00
❑ 54142	Some Day at Christmas/The Miracles of Christmas	1966	3.75	7.50	15.00
❑ 54147	Travlin' Man/Hey Love	1967	2.50	5.00	10.00
❑ 54151	I Was Made to Love Her/Hold Me	1967	2.50	5.00	10.00
❑ 54157	I'm Wondering/Every Time I See You I Go Wild	1967	2.50	5.00	10.00
❑ 54165	Shoo-Be-Doo-Be-Doo-Da-Day/Why Don't You Lead Me to Love	1968	2.00	4.00	8.00
❑ 54168	You Met Your Match/My Girl	1968	2.00	4.00	8.00
❑ 54174	For Once in My Life/Angie Girl	1968	2.00	4.00	8.00
❑ 54180	My Cherie Amour/Don't Know Why I Love You	1969	2.00	4.00	8.00

—Re-release with A and B side switched and new title on B-side

Number	Title (A Side/B Side)	Yr	VG	VG+	NM
❑ 54180	I Don't Know Why/My Cherie Amour	1969	2.50	5.00	10.00
❑ 54188	Yester-Me, Yester-You, Yesterday/I'd Be a Fool Right Now	1969	2.00	4.00	8.00
❑ 54191	Never Had a Dream Come True/Somebody Knows, Somebody Cares	1970	—	3.00	6.00
❑ 54196	Signed, Sealed, Delivered, I'm Yours/I'm More Than Happy	1970	—	3.00	6.00
❑ 54200	Heaven Help Us All/I Gotta Have a Song	1970	—	3.00	6.00
❑ 54202	We Can Work It Out/Never Dreamed You'd Leave in Summer	1971	—	3.00	6.00
❑ 54208	If You Really Love Me/Think of Me As Your Soldier	1971	—	3.00	6.00
❑ 54214	What Christmas Means to Me/Bedtime for Toys	1971	—	3.00	6.00
❑ 54216	Superwoman (Where Were You When I Needed You)/I Love Every Little Thing About You	1972	—	3.00	6.00
❑ 54223	Keep On Running/Evil	1972	—	3.00	6.00
❑ 54226	Superstition/You've Got It Bad Girl	1972	—	2.50	5.00
❑ 54232	You Are the Sunshine of My Life/Tuesday Heartbreak	1973	—	2.50	5.00
❑ 54235	Higher Ground/Too High	1973	—	2.50	5.00
❑ 54242	Living for the City/Visions	1973	—	2.50	5.00
❑ 54245	Don't You Worry 'Bout a Thing/Blame It on the Sun	1974	—	2.50	5.00
❑ 54252	You Haven't Done Nothin'/Big Brother	1974	—	2.50	5.00
❑ 54254	Boogie On Reggae Woman/Seems So Long	1974	—	2.50	5.00
❑ 54274	I Wish/You and I	1976	—	2.50	5.00
❑ 54281	Sir Duke/He's Misstra Know-It-All	1977	—	2.50	5.00
❑ 54281 [PS]	Sir Duke/He's Misstra Know-It-All	1977	2.50	5.00	10.00
❑ 54286	Another Star/Creepin'	1977	—	2.50	5.00
❑ 54291	As/Contusion	1977	—	2.50	5.00
❑ 54303	Send One Your Love/(Instrumental)	1979	—	2.00	4.00
❑ 54303 [PS]	Send One Your Love/(Instrumental)	1979	—	3.00	6.00
❑ 54308	Outside My Window/Same Old Story	1980	—	2.00	4.00
❑ 54308 [PS]	Outside My Window/Same Old Story	1980	—	3.00	6.00
❑ 54317	Master Blaster (Jammin')/(Instrumental)	1980	—	2.00	4.00
❑ 54317 [PS]	Master Blaster (Jammin')/(Instrumental)	1980	—	3.00	6.00
❑ 54320	I Ain't Gonna Stand For It/Knocks Me Off My Feet	1980	—	2.00	4.00
❑ 54323	Lately/If It's Magic	1981	—	2.00	4.00
❑ 54328	Did I Hear You Say You Love Me/As If You Read My Mind	1981	—	2.00	4.00
❑ 54331	Happy Birthday/(Instrumental)	1981	—	—	—

—Unreleased

TOPPS/MOTOWN

Number	Title (A Side/B Side)	Yr	VG	VG+	NM
❑ 8	Fingertips Part 2	1967	18.75	37.50	75.00

—Cardboard record

Number	Title (A Side/B Side)	Yr	VG	VG+	NM
❑ 10	Uptight (Everything's Alright)	1967	18.75	37.50	75.00

—Cardboard record

WONDER, STEVIE, AND MICHAEL JACKSON

Also see each artist's individual listings.

MOTOWN

Number	Title (A Side/B Side)	Yr	VG	VG+	NM
❑ 1930	Get It/(Instrumental)	1988	—	—	3.00
❑ 1930 [PS]	Get It/(Instrumental)	1988	—	—	3.00

WONDER WHO?, THE

See THE FOUR SEASONS.

WONDERETTES, THE

ENTERPRISE

Number	Title (A Side/B Side)	Yr	VG	VG+	NM
❑ 5025	Love's Got a Hold on Me/Work Out Fine	1964	6.25	12.50	25.00

RUBY

Number	Title (A Side/B Side)	Yr	VG	VG+	NM
❑ 5065	I Feel Strange/Wait Until Tonight	1965	10.00	20.00	40.00

UNITED ARTISTS

Number	Title (A Side/B Side)	Yr	VG	VG+	NM
❑ 944	I Feel Strange/Wait Until Tonight	1965	6.25	12.50	25.00
❑ 997	Mend My Broken Heart/And If I Had My Way	1966	5.00	10.00	20.00

—By "Rose St. John and the Wonderettes"

VEEP

Number	Title (A Side/B Side)	Yr	VG	VG+	NM
❑ 1231	Fool Don't Laugh/I Know the Meeting	1966	6.25	12.50	25.00

—As "Rose St. John and the Wonderettes"

WOOD, ANITA

SUN

Number	Title (A Side/B Side)	Yr	VG	VG+	NM
❑ 361	I'll Wait Forever/I Can't Show How I Feel	1961	7.50	15.00	30.00

WOOD, BOBBY

CHALLENGE

Number	Title (A Side/B Side)	Yr	VG	VG+	NM
❑ 9160	The Day After Forever/Everybody's Searchin'	1962	2.50	5.00	10.00

CINNAMON

Number	Title (A Side/B Side)	Yr	VG	VG+	NM
❑ 790	I'm a Fool for Loving You/Secret Love Affair	1974	—	2.00	4.00

JOY

Number	Title (A Side/B Side)	Yr	VG	VG+	NM
❑ 277	I Still Hurt/Just the Same	1963	2.50	5.00	10.00
❑ 279	Do Darlin' (Do Remember Me)/That's All I Need	1963	2.50	5.00	10.00
❑ 285	If I'm a Fool for Loving You/My Heart Went Boing! Boing! Boing!	1964	2.50	5.00	10.00
❑ 288	That's All I Need to Know/This Time	1964	2.50	5.00	10.00
❑ 291	So Cruel/I'd Do It Again	1964	2.50	5.00	10.00
❑ 295	Bed of Roses/Show Me	1965	2.00	4.00	8.00
❑ 298	Human Emotions/When a Lonely Boy Meets a Lonely Girl	1965	2.00	4.00	8.00
❑ 301	Fool's Paradise/What Am I Gonna Tell Myself	1965	2.00	4.00	8.00

LUCKY ELEVEN

Number	Title (A Side/B Side)	Yr	VG	VG+	NM
❑ 361	One Day Behind/Sound of Sadness	1973	—	2.50	5.00

MALA

Number	Title (A Side/B Side)	Yr	VG	VG+	NM
❑ 526	My Special Angel/I'd Rather Forgive You	1966	2.00	4.00	8.00

MGM

Number	Title (A Side/B Side)	Yr	VG	VG+	NM
❑ 13729	My Last Date (With You)/Everybody's Baby	1967	—	3.00	6.00
❑ 13797	Break My Mind/This Thing Called Love	1967	—	3.00	6.00
❑ 13912	Is That All There Is To It/Say It's Not You	1968	—	3.00	6.00
❑ 13952	Mary/Big Buildup	1968	—	3.00	6.00
❑ 14051	(Margie's at the) Lincoln Park Inn/I'm the Name of Her Game	1969	—	3.00	6.00

SUN

Number	Title (A Side/B Side)	Yr	VG	VG+	NM
❑ 369 [DJ]	Everybody's Searchin'/Human Emotions	1961	200.00	400.00	600.00

—No stock copies known; should one be discovered, it would be worth much more

WOOD, BRENTON

BRENT

Number	Title (A Side/B Side)	Yr	VG	VG+	NM
❑ 7052	Good Lovin'/I Want to Love	1966	3.75	7.50	15.00
❑ 7057	Cross the Bridge/Sweet Molly Malone	1966	6.25	12.50	25.00
❑ 7068	I Want Love/Sweet Molly Malone	1967	2.50	5.00	10.00

CREAM

Number	Title (A Side/B Side)	Yr	VG	VG+	NM
❑ 7602	All That Jazz/Bless Your Little Heart	1976	—	2.00	4.00
❑ 7716	Come Softly to Me/You're Everything I Need	1977	—	2.00	4.00
❑ 7720	Number One/(B-side unknown)	1977	—	2.00	4.00
❑ 7833	Let's Get Crazy Together/Love Is Free	1978	—	2.00	4.00

DOUBLE SHOT

Number	Title (A Side/B Side)	Yr	VG	VG+	NM
❑ 111	The Oogum Boogum Song/I Like the Way You Love Me	1967	2.50	5.00	10.00
❑ 116	Gimme Little Sign/I Think You've Got Your Fools Mixed Up	1967	2.50	5.00	10.00
❑ 121	Baby You Got It/Catch You on the Rebound	1967	2.00	4.00	8.00
❑ 126	Lovey Dovey Kinda Lovin'/Two-Time Loser	1968	2.00	4.00	8.00
❑ 130	Some Got It, Some Don't/Me and You	1968	2.00	4.00	8.00
❑ 135	Trouble/It's Just a Game, Love	1968	2.00	4.00	8.00
❑ 137	Where Are You/A Change Is Gonna Come	1969	2.00	4.00	8.00
❑ 142	Whoop It On Me/Take a Chance	1969	2.00	4.00	8.00
❑ 147	Can You Dig It/Great Big Bubble of Love	1970	—	3.00	6.00
❑ 150	Bogaloosa, Lousiana/I Need Your Love So Bad	1970	—	3.00	6.00
❑ 156	Sad Little Song/Who But a Fool	1971	—	3.00	6.00

MIDGET

Number	Title (A Side/B Side)	Yr	VG	VG+	NM
❑ 101	Rainin' Love/All That Jazz	197?	—	2.50	5.00

PHILCO-FORD

Number	Title (A Side/B Side)	Yr	VG	VG+	NM
❑ HP-38	Gimme Little Sign/Oogum Boogum	1969	5.00	10.00	20.00

—4-inch plastic "Hip Pocket Record" with color sleeve

PROPHESY

Number	Title (A Side/B Side)	Yr	VG	VG+	NM
❑ 3002	Sticky Boom Boom Too Cold (Part 1)/Sticky Boom Boom Too Cold (Part 2)	1973	—	2.50	5.00
❑ 3003	Another Saturday Night/(B-side unknown)	1973	—	2.50	5.00

WAND

Number	Title (A Side/B Side)	Yr	VG	VG+	NM
❑ 145	Mr. Schemer/Hide-A-Way	1963	10.00	20.00	40.00

WARNER BROS.

Number	Title (A Side/B Side)	Yr	VG	VG+	NM
❑ 8079	All That Jazz/Rainin' Love	1975	—	2.50	5.00
❑ 8144	Better Believe It/It Only Makes Me Want It More	1975	—	2.50	5.00

WOOD, RONNIE

Also see FACES; THE ROLLING STONES.

COLUMBIA

Number	Title (A Side/B Side)	Yr	VG	VG+	NM
❑ 11014	Seven Days/Breakin' My Heart	1979	—	3.00	6.00

WARNER BROS.

Number	Title (A Side/B Side)	Yr	VG	VG+	NM
❑ 8036	Breathe on Me/I Can Feel the Fire	1974	—	3.00	6.00
❑ 8131	I Got a Feeling/If You Don't Want My Love	1975	—	3.00	6.00

WOOD, ROY

Also see ELECTRIC LIGHT ORCHESTRA; THE MOVE.

UNITED ARTISTS

Number	Title (A Side/B Side)	Yr	VG	VG+	NM
❑ XW160	Ball Park Incident/Carlsberg Special	1973	—	2.50	5.00

—As "Wizzard/Roy Wood"

Number	Title (A Side/B Side)	Yr	VG	VG+	NM
❑ XW272	See My Baby Jive/Bend Over Beethoven	1973	—	2.50	5.00
❑ XW320	Dear Elaine/Song of Praise	1973	—	2.50	5.00
❑ XW394	Forever/Woodbe	1974	—	2.50	5.00
❑ XW792	Any Old Time Will Do/Why Does Such a Pretty Girl Sing Those Sad Songs	1976	—	2.00	4.00

WOODS, BENNIE

ATLAS

Number	Title (A Side/B Side)	Yr	VG	VG+	NM
❑ 1040	I Cross My Fingers/Wheel Baby Wheel	1955	200.00	400.00	800.00

—As "Bennie Woods and the Five Dukes"

Number	Title (A Side/B Side)	Yr	VG	VG+	NM
❑ 1040	I Cross My Fingers/Wheel Baby Wheel	1955	125.00	250.00	500.00

—As "Bennie Woods and Rockin' Townies"

WOODS, GENE

HAP

Number	Title (A Side/B Side)	Yr	VG	VG+	NM
❑ 1004	The Ballad of Wild River/Afraid	1960	6.25	12.50	25.00

WOODS, MICKEY

TAMLA

Number	Title (A Side/B Side)	Yr	VG	VG+	NM
❑ 54039	They Rode Through the Valley/Poor Sam Jones	1961	12.50	25.00	50.00
❑ 54052	Please Mr. Kennedy/(They Call Me) Cupid	1962	10.00	20.00	40.00

WOODY, DON

DECCA

Number	Title (A Side/B Side)	Yr	VG	VG+	NM
❑ 30277	You're Barking Up the Wrong Tree/Bird-Dog	1957	25.00	50.00	100.00

WOOLERY, CHUCK

Also see THE AVANT-GARDE.

COLUMBIA

Number	Title (A Side/B Side)	Yr	VG	VG+	NM
❑ 45017	I've Been Wrong/Soft Velvet Love	1969	—	3.00	6.00
❑ 45135	Heaven Here on Earth/Pleasure of Her Company	1970	—	3.00	6.00
❑ 45224	Your Name Is Woman/Soft Velvet Love	1970	—	3.00	6.00

Number	Title (A Side/B Side)	Yr	VG	VG+	NM
❑ 45274	Hey, Baby/Soft Velvet Love	1970	—	3.00	6.00
EPIC					
❑ 50897	The Greatest Love Affair/Heroes and Lovers	1980	—	2.00	4.00
RCA VICTOR					
❑ 74-0554	Deja Vu/Forgive My Heart	1971	—	2.50	5.00
❑ 74-0703	Kiss Me Three Times/If Only	1972	—	2.50	5.00
❑ 74-0771	Time and Time Again/Pen of a Poet	1972	—	2.50	5.00
❑ 74-0865	Forgive My Heart/Love Me, Love Me	1973	—	2.50	5.00
WARNER BROS.					
❑ 8381	Painted Lady/Growing Up in a Country Way	1977	—	2.50	5.00

WOOLEY, SHEB

Includes records by his comedic alter ego, "Ben Colder."

Number	Title (A Side/B Side)	Yr	VG	VG+	NM
BLUE BONNET					
❑ 124	Wooley's Polka/Lazy Mary	1954	17.50	35.00	70.00
❑ 125	Peeping Thru the Keyhole/Time Won't Heal an Achin' Heart	1954	17.50	35.00	70.00
❑ 130	Too Long with the Wrong Mama/Your Papa Ain't Steppin' Anymore	1954	15.00	30.00	60.00
MGM					
❑ 10697	Mule Boogie/Changing Your Name	1950	7.50	15.00	30.00
❑ 10960	Hoot Owl Boogie/Country Kisses	1951	7.50	15.00	30.00
❑ 11059	Over the Barrel/Air Castles	1951	7.50	15.00	30.00
❑ 11180	Backroom Boogie/Down in the Toolies	1952	7.50	15.00	30.00
❑ 11272	You're the Cat's Meow/Wha' Happened to Me Baby	1952	7.50	15.00	30.00
❑ 11308	A Cowboy Had Ought to Be Single/You Never Can Tell	1952	7.50	15.00	30.00
❑ 11403	Heart Bound in Chains/Freight Train Cinders	1953	6.25	12.50	25.00
❑ 11580	Love Is a Merry-Go-Round/Texas Tango	1953	6.25	12.50	25.00
❑ 11640	Goodbye Texas, Hello Tennessee/I'll Rerturn the Letters	1953	6.25	12.50	25.00
❑ 11665	Don't Stop Kissing Me Goodnight/Knew I Had Lost	1954	5.00	10.00	20.00
❑ 11717	Blue Guitar/Panama Pete	1954	5.00	10.00	20.00
❑ 11792	White Lightnin'/Fool About You	1954	5.00	10.00	20.00
❑ 11836	Hillbilly Mambo/I Go Outta My Mind	1954	5.00	10.00	20.00
❑ 11910	38-24-35/I Flipped	1955	3.75	7.50	15.00
❑ 11976	Speak of the Devil/Love at First Sight	1955	3.75	7.50	15.00
❑ 12048	Listening to Your Footsteps/Love Is a Prayer	1955	3.75	7.50	15.00
❑ 12060	It Takes a Heap of Livin'/Listen for Your Footsteps	1955	3.75	7.50	15.00
❑ 12114	Are You Satisfied/Humdinger	1955	3.75	7.50	15.00
❑ 12202	The Birth of the Rock 'N' Roll/A King or a Clown	1956	3.75	7.50	15.00
❑ 12260	You Can Do It/Do I Remember?	1956	3.75	7.50	15.00
❑ 12328	First Day of School/The Lonely Man	1956	3.75	7.50	15.00
❑ 12382	Honey I'm Lonesome/Let the Big Winds Blow	1956	3.75	7.50	15.00
❑ 12467	Plenty of Love/I Won't Come Back	1957	3.00	6.00	12.00
❑ 12541	Recipe for Love/I'm Too Young	1957	3.00	6.00	12.00
❑ 12584	So Close to Heaven/I Found Me An Angel	1957	3.00	6.00	12.00
❑ 12651	The Purple People Eater/I Can't Believe You're Mine	1958	4.50	9.00	18.00
❑ 12704	The Chase/Monkey Jive	1958	3.00	6.00	12.00
❑ 12733	Santa and the Purple People Eater/Star of Love	1958	5.00	10.00	20.00
❑ 12733 [PS]	Santa and the Purple People Eater/Star of Love	1958	10.00	20.00	40.00
❑ 12743	Cherry Street/Star of Love	1958	3.00	6.00	12.00
❑ 12778	More/Deep Goes the Love	1959	2.50	5.00	10.00
❑ 12781	Sweet Chile/More	1959	2.50	5.00	10.00
❑ 12817	Careless Hands/Pigmy Love	1959	2.50	5.00	10.00
❑ 12851	Love Like Mine/Josie	1959	2.50	5.00	10.00
❑ 12853	It's Almost Time/Roughneck	1959	2.50	5.00	10.00
❑ 12882	Luke the Spook/My Only Treasure	1960	2.50	5.00	10.00
❑ 12931	Taste of Ashes/Reach for the Moon	1960	2.50	5.00	10.00
❑ 13013	Skin Tight, Pin Striped, Pink Pedal Pushers/Till the End of the World	1961	2.50	5.00	10.00
❑ 13046	That's My Pa/Meet Mr. Lonely	1961	2.50	5.00	10.00
❑ 13065	Laughin' the Blues/Somebody Please	1962	2.50	5.00	10.00
❑ 13079	That's My Ma/Land of No Love	1962	2.50	5.00	10.00
❑ 13094	The Leged of Echo Mountain/Give That Ball to Willie B	1962	2.50	5.00	10.00
❑ 13104	Don't Go Near the Eskimos/Louisiana Trapper	1962	2.50	5.00	10.00
—As "Ben Colder"					
❑ 13122	Hello Wall No. 2/Shudders and Screams	1963	2.50	5.00	10.00
—As "Ben Colder"					
❑ 13125	Little Bitty Bilbo Abernathy Nathan Allen Quincy Jones/Daddy Kiss and Make It Well	1963	2.50	5.00	10.00
❑ 13147	Still No. 2/Goin' Surfin'	1963	3.75	7.50	15.00
—As "Ben Colder"					
❑ 13152	Buildin' a Railroad/Cowboy Hero	1963	2.50	5.00	10.00
❑ 13166	Hootenanny Hoot/Old Rag Doll	1963	2.50	5.00	10.00
❑ 13167	Detroit City No. 2/Ring of Smoke	1963	2.50	5.00	10.00
—As "Ben Colder"					
❑ 13195	Papa's Ole Fiddle/She Called Me Baby	1963	2.50	5.00	10.00
❑ 13197	I Walk the Line No. 2/Talk Back Blubberin' Lips	1963	2.50	5.00	10.00
—As "Ben Colder"					
❑ 13241	Blue Guitar/Natchez Landing	1964	2.00	4.00	8.00
❑ 13262	TV Westerns/Dobro's Catchin' On Again (And I'm Gonna Be a Star)	1964	2.00	4.00	8.00
—As "Ben Colder"					
❑ 13294	Wild and Wooley, Big Unruly Me/Sittin' and Thinkin'	1964	2.00	4.00	8.00
❑ 13351	Silver (The Wonder Horse)/Blistered	1965	2.00	4.00	8.00
❑ 13395	Big Land/Sally's Arms	1965	2.00	4.00	8.00
❑ 13444	Make the World Go Away No. 2/May the Bird of Paradise Fly Up Your Snoot	1966	2.00	4.00	8.00
—As "Ben Colder"					
❑ 13477	Buba Hoo Boba Dee/I'll Leave the Singin' to the Bluebirds	1966	2.00	4.00	8.00
❑ 13556	Tonight's the Night My Angel's Halo Fell/Anchors Aweigh	1966	2.00	4.00	8.00
❑ 13590	Almost Persuaded No. 2/A Packet of Pencils	1966	2.00	4.00	8.00
—As "Ben Colder"					
❑ 13668	There Goes My Everything No. 2/Great Men Repeat Themselves	1967	2.00	4.00	8.00
—As "Ben Colder"					
❑ 13705	Letter to Daddy/Draggin' the River	1967	2.00	4.00	8.00
❑ 13771	The Purple People Eater No. 2/Undertaker's Love Lament	1967	2.00	4.00	8.00
—As "Ben Colder"					
❑ 13806	Number One on the Survey/Big Ole, Good Ole Girl	1967	2.00	4.00	8.00
❑ 13827	The Love-In/Wildwood Flower on the Autoharp	1967	2.00	4.00	8.00
❑ 13897	Ain't It Funny How Wine Sips Away/The Doo-Hickey Song	1968	2.00	4.00	8.00
—As "Ben Colder"					
❑ 13914	By the Time I Get to Phoenix No. 2/Skip a Rope No. 2	1968	2.00	4.00	8.00
—As "Ben Colder"					
❑ 13938	Make 'Em Laugh/Tie a Tiger Down	1968	—	3.00	6.00
❑ 13997	Harper Valley P.T.A. (Later That Same Day)/Folsom Prison Blues No. 1 1/2	1968	2.50	5.00	10.00
—As "Ben Colder"					
❑ 14005	That Girl/I Remember Loving You	1968	—	3.00	6.00
❑ 14015	Little Green Apples No. 2/It's Such a Pretty World Tonight	1968	2.00	4.00	8.00
—As "Ben Colder"					
❑ 14044	Ode to the Little Shack Out Back/You're a Real Good Friend	1969	—	3.00	6.00
—As "Ben Colder"					
❑ 14065	The Carroll County Accident No. 2/His Lincoln's Parked at Margie's Again	1969	—	3.00	6.00
—As "Ben Colder"					
❑ 14070	The Recipient/Big Ole, Good Ole Girl	1969	—	3.00	6.00
❑ 14076	Ruby Please Bring Your Love to Town/Yet	1969	—	3.00	6.00
—As "Ben Colder"					
❑ 14085	One Man Band/You Still Turn Me On	1969	—	3.00	6.00
❑ 14111	Big Sweet John/Games People Play	1970	—	3.00	6.00
—As "Ben Colder"					
❑ 14123	Daddy's Home/The Will	1970	—	3.00	6.00
❑ 14133	Tennessee Bird Talk/What Is Youth	1970	—	3.00	6.00
—As "Ben Colder"					
❑ 14165	One of Them Roarin' Songs/I Don't Belong in Her Arms	1970	—	3.00	6.00
❑ 14209	Fifteen Beers Ago/Sunday Mornin' Fallin' Down	1970	—	3.00	6.00
—As "Ben Colder"					
❑ 14247	Help Me Fake It Through the Night/Rose Garden	1971	—	3.00	6.00
—As "Ben Colder"					
❑ 14287	Goodbye Wabash Cannonball/Joy	1971	—	3.00	6.00
❑ 14327	Easy Loving No. 2/Sing a Drinkin' Song	1971	—	3.00	6.00
—As "Ben Colder"					
❑ 14384	Life Is a Fountain/Somebody Gonna Come Along	1972	—	3.00	6.00
❑ 14420	The Unhappiest Squirrel in the Whole U.S.A./Runnin' Bare	1972	—	2.50	5.00
—As "Ben Colder"					
❑ 14444	A Kick in the Head/Personality	1972	—	3.00	6.00
❑ 14471	Glossy 8 x 10/Moontan	1972	—	2.50	5.00
—As "Ben Colder"					
❑ 14610	Early in the Morning/Getting High on Love	1973	—	3.00	6.00
❑ 14639	Behind Cloe's Door/Satin Sheets	1973	—	2.50	5.00
—As "Ben Colder"					
❑ 14647	The Purple People Eater/I Can't Believe You're Mine	1973	2.50	5.00	10.00
SCORPION					
❑ 0556	Lucille No. 2/Senior Citizen's Lament	1978	—	2.00	4.00
—As "Ben Colder"					
SUNBIRD					
❑ 104	The Rambler/Amazania	1979	—	2.00	4.00
—As "Ben Colder"					
❑ 109	Flower of the County (Censored Version)/Flower of the County (Uncensored Version)	1980	—	2.00	4.00
—As "Ben Colder"					
❑ 7566	Jack Hammer Man/Belly Button	1981	—	2.00	4.00

WRAY, LINK

Number	Title (A Side/B Side)	Yr	VG	VG+	NM
CADENCE					
❑ 1347	Rumble/The Swag	1958	10.00	20.00	40.00
EPIC					
❑ 9300	Raw-Hide/Dixie-Doodle	1958	6.25	12.50	25.00
❑ 9321	Comanche/Lillian	1959	6.25	12.50	25.00
❑ 9343	Rendezvous/Slinky	1959	6.25	12.50	25.00
❑ 9343 [PS]	Rendezvous/Slinky	1959	62.50	125.00	250.00
❑ 9361	Trail of the Lonesome Pine/Golden Strings	1960	6.25	12.50	25.00
❑ 9419	Mary Ann/Ain't That Lovin' You Baby	1960	6.25	12.50	25.00
❑ 9454	El Toro/Tijuana	1961	6.25	12.50	25.00
HEAVY					
❑ 101	Rumble '68/Blow Your Mind	1968	3.75	7.50	15.00
KAY					
❑ 3690	I Sez Baby/(B-side unknown)	1958	25.00	50.00	100.00
MALA					
❑ 458	There's a Hole in the Middle of the Moon/Dancing Party	1963	5.00	10.00	20.00
MR. G.					
❑ 820	Rumble '69/Mind Blower	1969	2.50	5.00	10.00
NORTON					
❑ 801	Jack the Ripper/Bo Diddley	199?	—	—	3.00
❑ 802	Ace of Spades/Fat Back	199?	—	—	3.00
❑ 803	Hidden Charms/Five and Ten	199?	—	—	3.00
❑ 804	The Black Widow/Mustang	199?	—	—	3.00
❑ 805	Run Chicken Run/Scatter	199?	—	—	3.00
❑ 806	Branded/Law of the Jungle	199?	—	—	3.00
❑ 807	Deuces Wild/The Sweeper	199?	—	—	3.00
❑ 808	The Shadow Knows/Hang On	199?	—	—	3.00
❑ 809	Good Rockin' Tonight/Soul Train	199?	—	—	3.00

Number	Title (A Side/B Side)	Yr	VG	VG+	NM
❑ 810	Batman Theme/Zip Code	199?	—	—	3.00
❑ (no #) [PS]	Link Wray and the Wraymen	199?	—	—	2.00

—Custom sleeve with large hole to reveal the record label. The same generic sleeve was issued with each of 801-810.

OKEH

Number	Title (A Side/B Side)	Yr	VG	VG+	NM
❑ 7166	Rumble Mambo/Ham Bone	1963	5.00	10.00	20.00
—B-side by Red Saunders					
❑ 7282	Rumble Mambo/Ham Bone	1967	3.75	7.50	15.00
—B-side by Red Saunders					

POLYDOR

Number	Title (A Side/B Side)	Yr	VG	VG+	NM
❑ 14084	Fire and Brimstone/June Box Mama	1970	2.00	4.00	8.00
❑ 14096	Fallin' Rain/Juke Box Mama	1971	2.00	4.00	8.00
❑ 14188	Shine the Light/Lawdy Miss Clawdy	1973	—	3.00	6.00
❑ 14256	I Got to Ramble/She's That Kind of Woman	1974	—	3.00	6.00

RUMBLE

Number	Title (A Side/B Side)	Yr	VG	VG+	NM
❑ 1000	Jack the Ripper/The Stranger	1961	10.00	20.00	40.00

SWAN

Number	Title (A Side/B Side)	Yr	VG	VG+	NM
❑ 4137	Jack the Ripper/The Black Widow	1963	5.00	10.00	20.00
❑ 4154	Weekend/Turnpike U.S.A.	1963	5.00	10.00	20.00
❑ 4163	Run Chicken Run/The Sweeper	1963	5.00	10.00	20.00
❑ 4171	The Shadow Knows/My Alberta	1964	5.00	10.00	20.00
❑ 4187	Deuces Wild/Summer Dream	1964	5.00	10.00	20.00
❑ 4201	Good Rockin' Tonight/I'll Do Anything for You	1965	6.25	12.50	25.00
❑ 4211	Branded/Hang On	1965	5.00	10.00	20.00
❑ 4232	Girl from the North Country/You Hurt Me So	1965	5.00	10.00	20.00
❑ 4239	The Fuzz/Ace of Spades	1966	5.00	10.00	20.00
❑ 4244	Batman Theme/Alone	1966	6.25	12.50	25.00
❑ 4261	Ace of Spades/Hidden Charms	1966	6.25	12.50	25.00
❑ 4284	Jack the Ripper/I'll Do Anything for You	1967	3.75	7.50	15.00

TRANS ATLAS

Number	Title (A Side/B Side)	Yr	VG	VG+	NM
❑ 687	Big City Stomp/Poppin' Popeye	1962	5.00	10.00	20.00

WRENS, THE

RAMA

Number	Title (A Side/B Side)	Yr	VG	VG+	NM
❑ 53	Love's Something That's Made for Two/Beggin' for Love	1955	375.00	750.00	1500.
❑ 65	Come Back My Love/Beggin' for Love	1955	37.50	75.00	150.00
❑ 65	Come Back My Love/Eleven Roses	1955	100.00	200.00	400.00
❑ 110	Love's Something That's Made for Two/Eleven Roses	1955	75.00	150.00	300.00
❑ 174	Hey Girl/Serenade of the Bells	1955	100.00	200.00	400.00
❑ 184	I Won't Come to Your Wedding/What Makes You Do the Things That You Do	1956	100.00	200.00	400.00
❑ 194	C'est La Vie/C'est La Vie	1956	100.00	200.00	400.00
—B-side by Jimmy Wright and His Orchestra					

WRIGHT, BETTY

ALSTON

Number	Title (A Side/B Side)	Yr	VG	VG+	NM
❑ 3711	Shoorah! Shoorah!/Tonight Is the Night	1974	—	2.50	5.00
❑ 3713	Where Is the Love/My Baby Ain't My Baby Anymore	1975	—	2.50	5.00
❑ 3715	Ooola La/To Love and Be Loved	1975	—	2.50	5.00
❑ 3718	Slip and Do It/I Think I Better Think About It	1975	—	2.50	5.00
❑ 3719	Everybody Was Rockin'/Show Your Girl	1976	—	2.50	5.00
❑ 3722	If I Ever Do Wrong/Rock On Baby, Rock On	1976	—	2.50	5.00
❑ 3725	Life/If I Was a Kid	1976	—	2.50	5.00
❑ 3734	You Can't See for Lookin'/Sometime Kind of Thing	1977	—	2.50	5.00
❑ 3736	Man of Mine/Sweet	1978	—	2.50	5.00
❑ 3740	Tonight Is the Night (Part 1)/Tonight Is the Night (Part 2)	1978	—	2.50	5.00
❑ 3745	Lovin' Is Really My Game/A Song for You	1979	—	2.50	5.00
❑ 3747	My Love Is/I Believe It's Love	1979	—	2.50	5.00
❑ 3749	Thank You for the Many Things You've Done/Child of the Man	1979	—	2.50	5.00
❑ 4569	Girls Can't Do What the Guys Do/Sweet Lovin' Daddy	1968	2.00	4.00	8.00
❑ 4571	He's Bad Bad Bad/Watch Out, Love	1968	2.00	4.00	8.00
❑ 4573	The Best Girls Don't Always Win/Circle of Heartbreaks	1969	2.00	4.00	8.00
❑ 4575	The Wrong Girl/The Joy of Becoming a Woman	1969	2.00	4.00	8.00
❑ 4580	I'm Not Free Hearted/A Woman Was Made for One Man	1969	2.00	4.00	8.00
❑ 4581	Soldier Boy/A Woman Was Made for One Man	1969	2.00	4.00	8.00
❑ 4587	Pure Love/If You Ain't Got It	1970	—	3.50	7.00
❑ 4589	I Found That Guy/If You Love Like I Love You	1970	—	3.50	7.00
❑ 4594	I Love the Way You Love/When We Get Together Again	1971	—	3.50	7.00
❑ 4601	Clean Up Woman/I'll Love You Forever	1971	—	3.00	6.00
❑ 4609	If You Love Me Like You Say You Love Me/I'm Gettin' Tired Baby	1972	—	3.00	6.00
❑ 4611	Is It You Girl/Crying in My Sleep	1972	—	3.00	6.00
❑ 4614	Baby Sitter/Outside Woman	1972	—	3.00	6.00
❑ 4617	It's Hard to Stop (Doing Something When It's Good to You)/Who'll Be the Fool	1973	—	3.00	6.00
❑ 4619	Let Me Be Your Lovemaker/Jealous Man	1973	—	3.00	6.00
❑ 4620	It's Bad for Me to See You/One Thing Leads to Another	1974	—	3.00	6.00
❑ 4622	Secretary/Value Your Love	1974	—	3.00	6.00

EPIC

Number	Title (A Side/B Side)	Yr	VG	VG+	NM
❑ 02143	I Like Your Loving/Body Slang	1981	—	2.00	4.00
❑ 02521	Goodbye Him Hello You/Make Me Love the Rain	1981	—	2.00	4.00
❑ 03523	He's Older Now/Special Love	1983	—	2.00	4.00
❑ 03954	Burning Desire/Show Me	1983	—	2.00	4.00
❑ 51009	What Are We Gonna Do About It/I Believe in You	1981	—	2.00	4.00

FIRST STRING

Number	Title (A Side/B Side)	Yr	VG	VG+	NM
❑ 965	Pain/(B-side unknown)	1985	—	2.00	4.00
❑ 968	The Sun Don't Shine/Music Street	1986	—	2.00	4.00

JAMAICA

Number	Title (A Side/B Side)	Yr	VG	VG+	NM
❑ 3	One Step Up, Two Steps Back/(B-side unknown)	1984	—	2.00	4.00

MS. B.

Number	Title (A Side/B Side)	Yr	VG	VG+	NM
❑ 4501	No Pain, No Gain/(Instrumental)	1988	—	2.00	4.00
❑ 4503	After the Pain/Love Days	1988	—	2.00	4.00
❑ 4504	A Christmas To Remember/2nd Chapter Of The Book Of Mathew	1988	—	—	3.00
❑ 4505	From Pain to Joy/From Pain to Joy (The Project Mix)	1989	—	2.00	4.00
❑ 4508	Quiet Storm/We Down	1989	—	2.00	4.00

WRIGHT, CHARLES, AND THE WATTS 103RD STREET RHYTHM BAND

ABC

Number	Title (A Side/B Side)	Yr	VG	VG+	NM
❑ 12127	Is It Real/One Lie	1975	—	2.00	4.00
—Charles Wright solo					

ABC DUNHILL

Number	Title (A Side/B Side)	Yr	VG	VG+	NM
❑ 4363	Liberated Lady/You Threw It All Away	1973	—	2.00	4.00
❑ 4364	(Well I'm) Doing What Cums Naturally Part 1/Part 2	1973	—	2.00	4.00
❑ 4381	The Weight of Hate/You Threw It All Away	1974	—	2.00	4.00
❑ 15027	Don't Rush Tomorrow/Is It Real	1974	—	2.00	4.00

KEYMEN

Number	Title (A Side/B Side)	Yr	VG	VG+	NM
❑ 108	Spreadin' Honey/(B-side unknown)	1967	2.50	5.00	10.00
—As "The Watts 103rd Street Rhythm Band"					

WARNER BROS.

Number	Title (A Side/B Side)	Yr	VG	VG+	NM
❑ 7175	Brown Sugar/Caesar's Palace	1968	2.50	5.00	10.00
—Through 7298, as "The Watts 103rd Street Rhythm Band"					
❑ 7222	Bottomless/65 Bars and a Taste of Soul	1968	2.50	5.00	10.00
❑ 7250	Do Your Thing/A Dance, a Kiss, and a Song	1969	2.00	4.00	8.00
❑ 7298	Till You Get Enough/Light My Fire	1969	2.00	4.00	8.00
❑ 7338	Must Be Your Thing/Comment	1969	—	3.00	6.00
❑ 7365	Love Land/Sorry Charlie	1970	—	3.00	6.00
❑ 7417	Express Yourself/Living on Borrowed Time	1970	—	3.00	6.00
❑ 7475	Your Love (Means Everything to Me)/What Can You Bring Me	1971	—	2.50	5.00
❑ 7504	Nobody/Wine	1971	—	2.50	5.00
❑ 7577	I've Got Love/Let's Make Love — Not War	1972	—	2.50	5.00
❑ 7600	Soul Train/Run Judy Run	1972	—	2.50	5.00
❑ 7630	Here Comes the Sun/You Gotta Know Whatcha Doin'	1972	—	2.50	5.00

WRIGHT, GARY

Also see SPOOKY TOOTH.

A&M

Number	Title (A Side/B Side)	Yr	VG	VG+	NM
❑ 1228	Over You Now/Get On the Right Road	1970	—	2.50	5.00
❑ 1267	Stand for Our Rights/I Can't See the Reason	1971	—	2.50	5.00
❑ 1319	Love to Survive/Fascinating Things	1972	—	2.50	5.00
❑ 1344	Two-Faced Man/I Know	1972	—	2.50	5.00

WARNER BROS.

Number	Title (A Side/B Side)	Yr	VG	VG+	NM
❑ 8143	Love Is Alive/Much Higher	1975	—	2.00	4.00
—Reissued in 1976 with the same number					
❑ 8167	Dream Weaver/Let It Out	1975	—	2.00	4.00
❑ 8250	Made to Love You/Power of Love	1976	—	2.00	4.00
❑ 8331	Phantom Writer/Child of Light	1977	—	2.00	4.00
❑ 8383	Empty Inside/Water Sign	1977	—	2.00	4.00
❑ 8426	Light of Smiles/Silent Fury	1977	—	2.00	4.00
❑ 8548	Something Very Special/Starry Eyed	1978	—	2.00	4.00
❑ 8598	Can't Get Above Losing You/Starry Eyed	1978	—	2.00	4.00
❑ 8809	Follow Next to You/I'm the One Who'll Be At Your Side	1979	—	2.00	4.00
❑ 49769	Really Wanna Know You/More Than a Heartache	1981	—	2.00	4.00
❑ 49836	Comin' Apart/Heartbeat	1981	—	2.00	4.00
❑ 49879	Got the Feelin'/Close to You	1981	—	2.00	4.00

WYATT, GENE

DOLLIE

Number	Title (A Side/B Side)	Yr	VG	VG+	NM
❑ 502	Fightin' for the Free Land/Searching for a New Love Affair	1966	2.50	5.00	10.00

EBB

Number	Title (A Side/B Side)	Yr	VG	VG+	NM
❑ 123	Love Fever/Lover Boy	1957	25.00	50.00	100.00

LUCKY SEVEN

Number	Title (A Side/B Side)	Yr	VG	VG+	NM
❑ 101	Prettiest Girl at the Dance/(B-side unknown)	1959	15.00	30.00	60.00

MERCURY

Number	Title (A Side/B Side)	Yr	VG	VG+	NM
❑ 72752	I Stole the Flowers/I'm a One Woman Man	1967	2.50	5.00	10.00

PAULA

Number	Title (A Side/B Side)	Yr	VG	VG+	NM
❑ 308	I Just Ain't Got (As Much As He's Got Going for Me)/Chains Around My Heart	1968	2.50	5.00	10.00
❑ 1206	Little Liza Jane/Country Music Peyton Place	1968	2.50	5.00	10.00
❑ 1211	My Story of Love/Evangeline	1969	2.50	5.00	10.00
❑ 1216	Milk and Honey Memories/Failure of T Crop	1969	2.50	5.00	10.00
❑ 1223	Twelve Men/Back Door of My Mind	1970	2.00	4.00	8.00
❑ 1224	Go Together/As Long As I Live	1970	2.00	4.00	8.00

WYMAN, BILL

Also see THE ROLLING STONES.

A&M

Number	Title (A Side/B Side)	Yr	VG	VG+	NM
❑ 2367	(Si Si) Je Suis Un Rock Star/Rio De Janeiro	1981	—	2.50	5.00
❑ 2367 [PS]	(Si Si) Je Suis Un Rock Star/Rio De Janeiro	1981	2.50	5.00	10.00

ROLLING STONES

Number	Title (A Side/B Side)	Yr	VG	VG+	NM
❑ 19111	White Lightning/I Wanna Get Me a Gun	1974	—	2.50	5.00
❑ 19119	A Quarter to Three/Soul Satisfying	1975	—	2.50	5.00
❑ 19303	Apache Woman/Soul Satisfying	1975	—	2.50	5.00

WYNETTE, TAMMY

Also see DAVID HOUSTON AND TAMMY WYNETTE; GEORGE JONES AND TAMMY WYNETTE.

COLUMBIA

Number	Title (A Side/B Side)	Yr	VG	VG+	NM
❑ 77294	Silver Threads and Golden Needles/Let Her Fly	1993	—	—	3.00
—With Dolly Parton and Loretta Lynn					

EPIC

Number	Title (A Side/B Side)	Yr	VG	VG+	NM
❑ TW 1 [DJ]	The Wonders You Perform (stereo/mono)	1969	5.00	10.00	20.00
—Red vinyl; included with some early copies of the LP "Inspiration"					
❑ AS 60 [DJ]	White Christmas/One Happy Christmas	1973	2.00	4.00	8.00
—1973 Christmas Seals promotional record					
❑ AS 60 [PS]	White Christmas/One Happy Christmas	1973	2.50	5.00	10.00

Number	Title (A Side/B Side)	Yr	VG	VG+	NM
❑ 02439	Crying in the Rain/Bring Back My Baby to Me	1981	—	2.00	4.00
❑ 02770	Another Chance/What's It Like to Be a Woman	1982	—	2.00	4.00
❑ 03064	You Still Get To Me in My Dreams/If I Didn't Have a Heart	1982	—	2.00	4.00
❑ 03384	A Good Night's Love/I'm Going On with Everything Gone	1982	—	2.00	4.00
❑ 03811	I Just Heard a Heart Break (And I'm So Afraid It's Mine)/Back to the Wall	1983	—	2.00	4.00
❑ 03971	Unwed Fathers/I'm So Afraid That I'd Live Through It	1983	—	2.00	4.00
❑ 04101	Still in the Ring/Midnight Love	1983	—	2.00	4.00
❑ 04467	Lonely Heart/(I'm Not) A Candle in the Wind	1984	—	—	3.00
❑ 05399	You Can Lead a Heart to Love (But You Can't Make It Fall)/He Talks to Me	1985	—	—	3.00
❑ 06263	Alive and Well/I'll Be Thinking of You	1986	—	—	3.00
❑ 07226	Your Love/I Wasn't Meant to Live My Life Alone	1987	—	—	3.00
❑ 07635	Talkin' to Myself Again/A Slow Burning Fire	1987	—	—	3.00
❑ 07788	Beneath a Painted Sky/Some Things Will Never Change	1988	—	—	3.00
❑ 10095	Apartment No. 9/I'm Not Mine to Give	1966	2.50	5.00	10.00
❑ 10134	Your Good Girl's Gonna Go Bad/Send Me No Roses	1967	2.00	4.00	8.00
❑ 10211	I Don't Wanna Play House/Soakin' Wet	1967	2.00	4.00	8.00
❑ 10269	Take Me to Your World/Good	1967	2.00	4.00	8.00
❑ 10315	D-I-V-O-R-C-E/Don't Make It Now	1968	2.00	4.00	8.00
❑ 10398	Stand By Your Man/I Stayed Long Enough	1968	2.50	5.00	10.00
❑ 10462	Singing My Song/Too Far Gone	1969	—	3.00	6.00
❑ 10462 [PS]	Singing My Song/Too Far Gone	1969	2.50	5.00	10.00
❑ 10512	The Ways to Love a Man/Still Around	1969	—	3.00	6.00
❑ 10571	I'll See Him Through/Enough of a Woman	1970	—	3.00	6.00
❑ 10612	He Loves Me All the Way/One Last Night Together	1970	—	3.00	6.00
❑ 10653	Run, Woman, Run/My Daddy Doll	1970	—	3.00	6.00
❑ 10687	The Wonders You Perform/Gentle Shepherd	1970	—	3.00	6.00
❑ 10690	One Happy Christmas/(Merry Christmas) We Must Be Having One	1970	2.00	4.00	8.00
❑ 10707	We Sure Can Love Each Other/Fun	1971	—	3.00	6.00
❑ 10759	Good Lovin' (Makes It Right)/I Love You, Mr. Jones	1971	—	3.00	6.00
❑ 10818	Bedtime Story/Reach Out Your Hand	1971	—	3.00	6.00
❑ 10856	Reach Out Your Hand/Love's the Answer	1972	—	3.00	6.00
❑ 10909	My Man/Things I Love to Do	1972	—	3.00	6.00
❑ 10969	Kids Say the Darnedest Things/I Wish I Had a Mommy Like You	1973	—	3.00	6.00
❑ 11044	One Final Stand/Crying Steel Guitar	1973	—	—	—
—Canceled?					
❑ 11079	Another Lonely Song/The Only Time I'm Really Me	1973	—	3.00	6.00
❑ 50008	Woman to Woman/Love Me Forever	1974	—	2.50	5.00
❑ 50071	(You Make Me Want to Be) A Mother/I'm Not a Has-Been	1975	—	2.50	5.00
❑ 50145	I Still Believe in Fairy Tales/Your Memory's Gone to Rest	1975	—	2.50	5.00
❑ 50196	'Til I Can Make It on My Own/Love Is Something Good for Everybody	1976	—	2.50	5.00
❑ 50264	You and Me/When Love Was All We Had	1976	—	2.50	5.00
❑ 50349	(Let's Get Together) One Last Time/Hardly a Day Goes By	1977	—	2.50	5.00
❑ 50450	One of a Kind/Loving You, I Do	1977	—	2.50	5.00
❑ 50538	I'd Like to See Jesus (On the Midnight Special)/ Love Doesn't Always Come (On the Night It's Needed)	1978	—	2.50	5.00
❑ 50574	Womanhood/50 Words or Less	1978	—	2.50	5.00
❑ 50661	They Call It Making Love/Let Me Be Me	1979	—	2.50	5.00
❑ 50722	No One Else in the World/Mama, Your Little Girl Fell	1979	—	2.50	5.00
❑ 50868	He Was There (When I Needed You)/Only the Names Have Been Changed	1980	—	2.50	5.00
❑ 50915	Starting Over/I'll Be Thinking of You	1980	—	2.50	5.00
❑ 51011	Cowboys Don't Shoot Straight (Like They Used To)/You Brought Me Back	1981	—	2.00	4.00
❑ 68570	Next to You/When a Girl Becomes a Wife	1989	—	—	3.00
❑ 68894	Thank the Cowboy for the Ride/We Called It Everything But Quits	1989	—	—	3.00
❑ 73427	Let's Call It a Day Today/When a Girl Becomes a Wife	1990	—	2.00	4.00
❑ 73579	I'm Turning You Loose/Just a Minute There	1990	—	2.00	4.00
❑ 73656	What Goes with Blue/Let's Call It a Day Today	1991	—	2.00	4.00
❑ 73958	We're Strangers Again/If You Were the Friend	1991	—	2.00	4.00
—A-side with Randy Travis					

WYNTER, MARK

Number	Title (A Side/B Side)	Yr	VG	VG+	NM
ARLEN					
❑ 744	Running to You/Don't Cry	1964	3.00	6.00	12.00
GUYDEN					
❑ 2115	Answer Me/Only You	1964	2.50	5.00	10.00
LONDON					
❑ 1973	Dream Girl/Two Little Girls	1961	3.75	7.50	15.00
❑ 1997	Exclusively Yours/Warm and Willing	1961	3.75	7.50	15.00
❑ 9522	Heaven's Plan/You Are Everything	1962	3.75	7.50	15.00
SCEPTER					
❑ 1299	Am I Living in a Dream/Can I Get to Know You Better	1965	2.50	5.00	10.00

X

X-CELLENTS, THE

Number	Title (A Side/B Side)	Yr	VG	VG+	NM
SMASH					
❑ 1996	Hey Little Willie/I'll Aways Be On Your Side	1965	5.00	10.00	20.00

X-CITERS UNLIMITED

Number	Title (A Side/B Side)	Yr	VG	VG+	NM
ABC					
❑ 11029	Soul to Fillie Joe/Hang On Sloopy	1967	2.50	5.00	10.00

X-TREMES, THE

Number	Title (A Side/B Side)	Yr	VG	VG+	NM
STAR TREK					
❑ 1221	Substitute/Facts of Life	1966	6.25	12.50	25.00

XIT

Number	Title (A Side/B Side)	Yr	VG	VG+	NM
MOTOWN					
❑ 1304	I Need Your Love (Git It To Me)/Movin' from the City	1974	2.00	4.00	8.00
❑ 1320	Renegade/Cement Prairie	1974	2.00	4.00	8.00
RARE EARTH					
❑ 5044	Nihaa Shil Hozho (I Am Happy About You)/End	1972	2.50	5.00	10.00
❑ 5055	Reservation of Education/Color Nature Gone	1973	2.50	5.00	10.00

XTC

Number	Title (A Side/B Side)	Yr	VG	VG+	NM
EPIC					
❑ 02875	Senses Working Overtime/English Roundabout	1982	—	3.00	6.00
GEFFEN					
❑ 22953	King for a Day/Toys	1989	—	—	3.00
❑ 22953 [PS]	King for a Day/Toys	1989	—	—	3.00
❑ 27552	The Mayor of Simpleton/One of the Millions	1989	—	—	3.00
❑ 27552 [PS]	The Mayor of Simpleton/One of the Millions	1989	—	—	3.00
❑ 28394	Dear God/Mermaid Smiled	1987	—	—	3.00
❑ 29351	Wonderland/Jump	1984	—	2.00	4.00
VIRGIN					
❑ PR 344 [DJ]	Limelight//Day In Day Out/Chain of Command	1979	2.00	4.00	8.00
—7-inch 33 1/3 record with small center hole; included in first 15,000 copies of album 13134					
❑ 67004	Ten Feet Tall//Helicopter/Somnabulist	1980	2.50	5.00	10.00
❑ 67004 [DJ]	Ten Feet Tall (mono/stereo)	1980	—	2.00	4.00
❑ 67004 [PS]	Ten Feet Tall//Helicopter/Somnabulist	1980	—	2.00	4.00
❑ 67009	Making Plans for Nigel//This Is Pop/Meccanik Dancing	1980	2.50	5.00	10.00
❑ 67009 [DJ]	Making Plans for Nigel (mono/stereo)	1980	—	2.00	4.00
❑ 67009 [PS]	Making Plans for Nigel//This Is Pop/Meccanik Dancing	1980	—	2.00	4.00
VIRGIN/RSO					
❑ 300	Generals and Majors/Living Through Another Cuba	1981	—	3.00	6.00
❑ 301	Love at First Sight/Rocket from a Bottle	1981	—	—	—
—Canceled?					

Y

Y KANT TORI READ

Also see TORI AMOS.

Number	Title (A Side/B Side)	Yr	VG	VG+	NM
ATLANTIC					
❑ 89021	Cool on Your Island/Heart Attack at 23	1988	30.00	60.00	120.00
—Copies of this have been documented					
❑ 89021 [DJ]	Cool on Your Island (same on both sides)	1988	12.50	25.00	50.00
❑ 89021 [PS]	Cool on Your Island/Heart Attack at 23	1988	20.00	40.00	80.00
❑ 89086	The Big Picture/You Go to My Head	1988	30.00	60.00	120.00
—Copies of this have been documented					
❑ 89086 [DJ]	The Big Picture (same on both sides)	1988	12.50	25.00	50.00
—Lead vocal: Tori Amos					
❑ 89086 [PS]	The Big Picture/You Go to My Head	1988	20.00	40.00	80.00

YANKEE DOLLAR, THE

Number	Title (A Side/B Side)	Yr	VG	VG+	NM
DOT					
❑ 17123	City Sidewalks/Sanctuary	1968	3.75	7.50	15.00
❑ 17155	Live and Let Live/Sanctuary	1968	3.75	7.50	15.00
❑ 17213	Mucky Truckee River/Reflections of a Shattered Mind	1969	3.75	7.50	15.00

YANOVSKY, ZALMAN

Also see THE LOVIN' SPOONFUL.

Number	Title (A Side/B Side)	Yr	VG	VG+	NM
BUDDAH					
❑ 12	As Long As You're Here/Ereh Er'uoy Sa Gnol Sa	1967	2.50	5.00	10.00

YARDBIRDS, THE

Also see JEFF BECK; ERIC CLAPTON; JIMMY PAGE; KEITH RELF. Ex-members of the group formed BOX OF FROGS; LED ZEPPELIN; and RENAISSANCE.

Number	Title (A Side/B Side)	Yr	VG	VG+	NM
EPIC					
❑ 9709	I Wish You Could/A Certain Girl	1964	10.00	20.00	40.00
—With typographical error on A-side					
❑ 9709	I Wish You Would/A Certain Girl	1964	12.50	25.00	50.00
—With correct A-side title					
❑ 9709	I Wish You Could/I Ain't Got You	1964	—	—	—
—Unreleased?					
❑ 9709 [PS]	I Wish You Could	1964	200.00	400.00	800.00
—Promo-only picture sleeve					
❑ 9790	For Your Love/Got to Hurry	1965	3.75	7.50	15.00
❑ 9823	Heart Full of Soul/Steeled Blues	1965	3.75	7.50	15.00
❑ 9823 [PS]	Heart Full of Soul/Steeled Blues	1965	12.50	25.00	50.00
❑ 9857	I'm a Man/Still I'm Sad	1965	3.75	7.50	15.00
❑ 9881	Shapes of Things/I'm Not Talking	1966	3.75	7.50	15.00
❑ 10006	Shapes of Things/New York City Blues	1966	5.00	10.00	20.00
❑ 10006	New York City Blues/You're a Better Man Than I	1966	—	—	—
—Unreleased					
❑ 10035	Over Under Sideways Down/Jeff's Boogie	1966	3.75	7.50	15.00

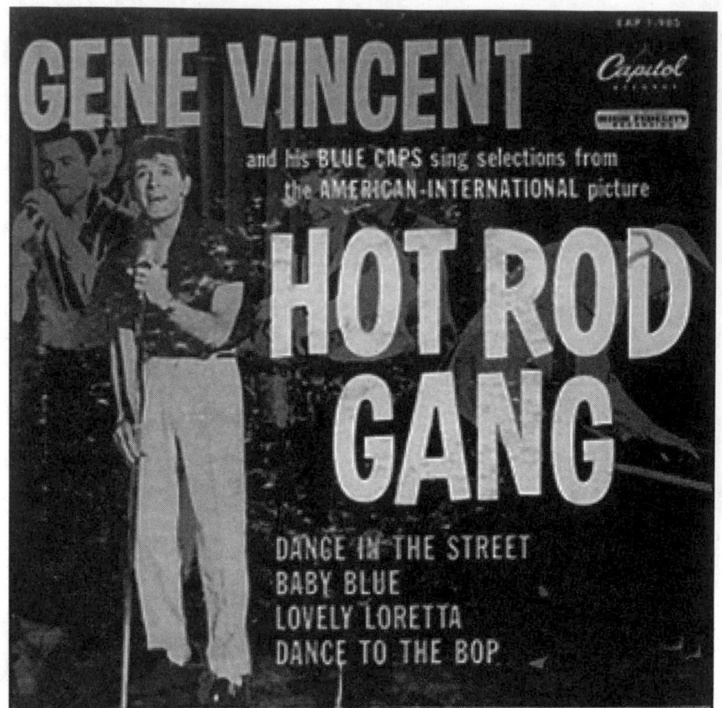

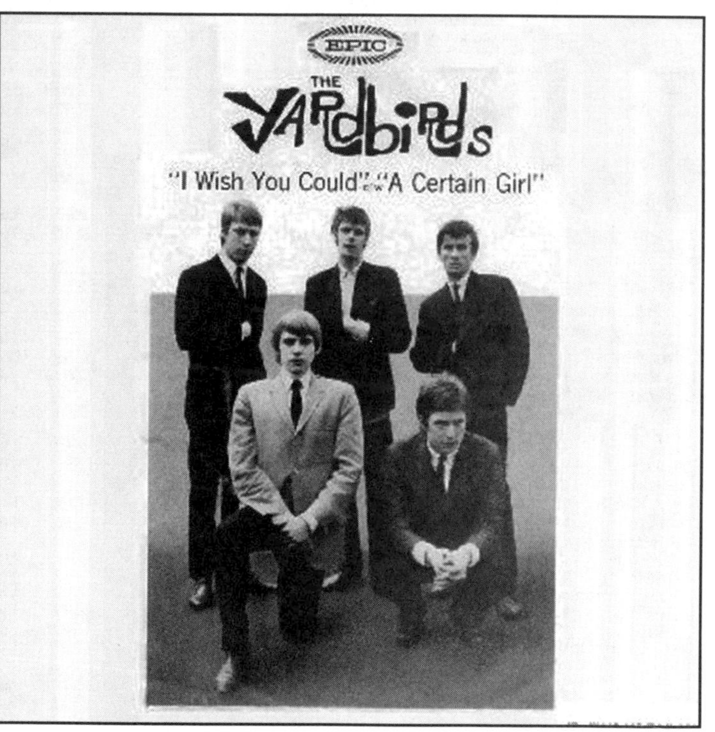

(Top left) Probably the most sought-after EP from a movie - even more than some of the Elvis Presley soundtrack EPs - is this one, with four songs done by Gene Vincent in *Hot Rod Gang*. The cover and record together can bring in the mid-hundreds. (Top right) Few of the Who's picture sleeves are common. This one isn't, either. It's a promo-only item for the hit "Squeeze Box," based on the LP cover of *The Who By Numbers*. (Bottom left) Extended-play singles were still being issued at the beginning of Jackie Wilson's heyday. This is the cover from his first one, "The Versatile Jackie Wilson." (Bottom right) One of the most sought-after picture sleeves from the British Invasion is this one. It's another promo-only sleeve, this one from the Yardbirds' first U.S. single. Both the sleeve and the record have the title wrong; the A-side actually is "I Wish You Would." No sleeve was issued with the corrected title, though records exist with it.

Number	Title (A Side/B Side)	Yr	VG	VG+	NM
❑ 10035 [PS]	Over Under Sideways Down/Jeff's Boogie	1966	12.50	25.00	50.00
❑ 10094	Happenings Ten Years Time Ago/The Nazz Are Blue	1966	3.75	7.50	15.00
❑ 10094	Happenings Ten Years Time Ago/Psycho Daisies	1966	—	—	—
—Unreleased					
❑ 10094 [PS]	Happenings Ten Years Time Ago/The Nazz Are Blue	1966	12.50	25.00	50.00
❑ 10156	Little Games/Puzzles	1967	5.00	10.00	20.00
❑ 10204	Ha Ha Said the Clown/Tinker, Tailor, Soldier, Sailor	1967	5.00	10.00	20.00
❑ 10248	Ten Little Indians/Drinking Muddy Water	1967	5.00	10.00	20.00
❑ 10303	Goodnight Sweet Josephine/Think About It	1968	12.50	25.00	50.00

YARROW, PETER
Also see PETER, PAUL AND MARY.

WARNER BROS.

Number	Title (A Side/B Side)	Yr	VG	VG+	NM
❑ 7236	Don't Remind Me Now of Time/Teenage Fair	1968	2.00	4.00	8.00
—B-side by Rosko					
❑ 7567	Don't Ever Take Away My Freedom/Greenwood	1972	—	2.50	5.00
❑ 7587	Weave Me the Sunshine/Wings of Time	1972	—	2.50	5.00
❑ 7761	Old Father Time/Isn't That So	1973	—	2.00	4.00
❑ 8114	Wanderin'/Another Chain Unbound	1975	—	2.00	4.00

YATES, BILL
SUN

Number	Title (A Side/B Side)	Yr	VG	VG+	NM
❑ 390	Stop, Wait and Listen/Don't Step on My Dog	1964	3.75	7.50	15.00
❑ 397	Carleen/Too Late to Right My Wrong	1965	3.75	7.50	15.00
❑ 399	Big Big World/I Dropped My M & M's	1966	3.75	7.50	15.00

YATES, TOMMY
VERVE

Number	Title (A Side/B Side)	Yr	VG	VG+	NM
❑ 10556	Darling, Something's Gotta Give/If You're Looking for a Fool	1967	6.25	12.50	25.00

YEARWOOD, TRISHA
COLLECTABLES

Number	Title (A Side/B Side)	Yr	VG	VG+	NM
❑ 90041	She's in Love with the Boy/Victim of the Game	1995	—	—	3.00

MCA

Number	Title (A Side/B Side)	Yr	VG	VG+	NM
❑ 54076	She's in Love with the Boy/Victim of the Game	1991	2.00	4.00	8.00
❑ 54172	Like We Never Had a Broken Heart/The Whisper of Your Heart	1991	—	—	3.00
❑ 54270	That's What I Like About You/When Goodbye Was a Word	1991	—	—	3.00
❑ 54362	The Woman Before Me/You Done Me Wrong (And That Ain't Right)	1992	—	—	3.00
❑ 54414	Wrong Side of Memphis/Lonesome Dove	1992	—	—	3.00
❑ 54495	Walkaway Joe/You Don't Have to Move That Mountain	1992	—	—	3.00
❑ 54600	You Say You Will/Hearts in Armor	1993	—	—	3.00
❑ 54670	Down on My Knees/For Reasons I've Forgotten	1993	—	—	3.00
❑ 54734	The Song Remembers When/Oh Lonesome You	1993	—	—	3.00
❑ 54786	Better Your Heart Than Mine/Promises to Keep	1994	—	—	3.00
❑ 54836	I Fall to Pieces/(Instrumental)	1994	—	—	3.00
—With Aaron Neville					
❑ 54898	XXX's and OOO's (An American Girl)/One in a Row	1994	—	—	3.00
❑ 54940	It Wasn't His Child/Reindeer Boogie	1994	—	2.00	4.00
❑ 54973	Thinkin' About You/Fairytale	1995	—	—	3.00
❑ 55025	You Can Sleep While I Drive/Two Days from Knowing	1995	—	—	3.00
❑ 55078	I Wanna Go Too Far/The Restless Kind	1995	—	—	3.00
❑ 55141	On a Bus to St. Cloud/O Mexico	1995	—	—	3.00
❑ 55211	Believe Me Baby (I Lied)/Little Hercules	1996	—	—	3.00
❑ 55250	Everybody Knows/A Love Is Forever	1996	—	—	3.00
❑ 55308	I Need You/Hello, I'm Gone	1997	—	—	3.00
❑ 72015	How Do I Live (4:25)/How Do I Live (4:02)	1997	—	2.50	5.00
❑ 72021	In Another's Eyes/I Want to Live Again	1997	—	—	3.00
—A-side with Garth Brooks					
❑ 72034	A Perfect Love/I Need You	1998	—	—	3.00
❑ 72048	There Goes My Baby/One More Chance	1998	—	—	3.00

MCA NASHVILLE

Number	Title (A Side/B Side)	Yr	VG	VG+	NM
❑ 72070	Where Your Road Leads/Bring Me All Your Lovin'	1998	—	2.50	5.00
—A-side with Garth Brooks					
❑ 72082	Powerful Thing/Never Let You Go Again	1998	—	—	3.00
❑ 72089	I'll Still Love You More/Wouldn't Any Woman	1999	—	—	3.00
❑ 088 172146 7	Real Live Woman/I'm Still Alive	2000	—	—	3.00
❑ 088 172170 7	Where Are You Now/Some Days	2000	—	—	3.00

YELLOW BALLOON, THE
CANTERBURY

Number	Title (A Side/B Side)	Yr	VG	VG+	NM
❑ 508	Yellow Balloon/Noollab Wolley	1967	3.00	6.00	12.00
❑ 513	Good Feeling Time/I've Got a Feeling for Love	1967	2.50	5.00	10.00
❑ 516	Stained Glass Window/Can't Get Enough of Your Love	1967	2.50	5.00	10.00

YELLOW PAYGES, THE
SHOWPLACE

Number	Title (A Side/B Side)	Yr	VG	VG+	NM
❑ 216	Sleeping Minds/Never See the Good in Me	1967	7.50	15.00	30.00
❑ 217	Love in the Making/Jezebel	1967	5.00	10.00	20.00

UNI

Number	Title (A Side/B Side)	Yr	VG	VG+	NM
❑ 55043	Our Time Is Running Out/Sweet Sunrise	1967	3.75	7.50	15.00
❑ 55072	Judge Carter/Childhood Friends	1968	3.75	7.50	15.00
❑ 55089	You're Just What I Was Looking For Today/Crowd Pleaser	1968	3.75	7.50	15.00
❑ 55107	The Two of Us/Never Put Away My Love for You	1969	3.75	7.50	15.00
❑ 55153	Would You Mind If I Loved You/Vanilla on My Mind	1969	3.75	7.50	15.00
❑ 55176	Slow Down/Fresco Annie	1969	3.75	7.50	15.00
❑ 55192	Little Women/Follow the Bouncing Ball	1970	3.75	7.50	15.00
❑ 55225	I'm a Man/Home Again	1970	3.75	7.50	15.00

YELVINGTON, MALCOLM
SUN

Number	Title (A Side/B Side)	Yr	VG	VG+	NM
❑ 211	Drinkin' Wine Spo-Dee-O-Dee/Just Rolling Along	1954	25.00	50.00	100.00
❑ 246	Rockin' with My Baby/It's Me Baby	1956	25.00	50.00	100.00

YES
Also see STEVE HOWE; RICK WAKEMAN; ALAN WHITE.

ARISTA

Number	Title (A Side/B Side)	Yr	VG	VG+	NM
❑ 2218	Lift Me Up/Give and Take	1991	—	2.00	4.00

ATCO

Number	Title (A Side/B Side)	Yr	VG	VG+	NM
❑ 99419	Rhythm of Love/City of Love	1987	—	—	3.00
❑ 99419 [PS]	Rhythm of Love/City of Love	1987	—	—	3.00
❑ 99449	Love Will Find a Way/Holy Lamb	1987	—	—	3.00
❑ 99449 [PS]	Love Will Find a Way/Holy Lamb	1987	—	—	3.00
❑ 99745	It Can Happen/It Can Happen (Live)	1984	—	—	3.00
❑ 99745 [PS]	It Can Happen/It Can Happen (Live)	1984	—	—	3.00
❑ 99787	Leave It/Leave It (Acapella)	1984	—	—	3.00
❑ 99787 [PS]	Leave It/Leave It (Acapella)	1984	—	—	3.00
❑ 99817	Owner of a Lonely Heart/Our Song	1983	—	—	3.00
❑ 99817 [PS]	Owner of a Lonely Heart/Our Song	1983	—	—	3.00

ATLANTIC

Number	Title (A Side/B Side)	Yr	VG	VG+	NM
❑ 2709	Every Little Thing/Sweetness	1970	—	3.00	6.00
❑ 2819	Your Move/Clap	1971	—	2.50	5.00
❑ 2854	Roundabout/Long Distance Runaround	1972	—	2.50	5.00
❑ 2854 [DJ]	Roundabout (mono/stereo)	1972	25.00	50.00	100.00
—Promo only on yellow vinyl					
❑ 2899	America/Total Mass Retain	1972	—	2.50	5.00
❑ 2920	And You And I (Part 1)/And You And I (Part 2)	1972	—	2.50	5.00
❑ 3242	Sound Chaser/Soon	1975	—	2.50	5.00
❑ 3416	Awaken (Part 1)/Wonderful Stories	1977	—	2.50	5.00
❑ 3534	Don't Kill the Whale/Release, Release	1978	—	2.50	5.00
❑ 3767	Into the Lens/Does It Really Happen	1980	—	2.50	5.00
❑ 3801	Run Through the Light/White Car	1981	—	2.50	5.00

YORK, RUSTY
CAPITOL

Number	Title (A Side/B Side)	Yr	VG	VG+	NM
❑ 4663	That's What I Need/Just Like You	1961	3.75	7.50	15.00

CHESS

Number	Title (A Side/B Side)	Yr	VG	VG+	NM
❑ 1730	Sugaree/Red Rooster	1959	5.00	10.00	20.00

GAYLORD

Number	Title (A Side/B Side)	Yr	VG	VG+	NM
❑ 6428	Sally Was a Good Old Girl/I Might Just Walk Right Back Again	1962	3.75	7.50	15.00

KING

Number	Title (A Side/B Side)	Yr	VG	VG+	NM
❑ 5103	Peggy Sue/Shake 'Em Up Baby	1958	6.25	12.50	25.00
❑ 5511	Love Struck/Goodnight Cincinnati, Good Morning Tennessee	1961	3.75	7.50	15.00
❑ 5587	Tramblin'/Tore Up Over You	1961	3.75	7.50	15.00

NOTE

Number	Title (A Side/B Side)	Yr	VG	VG+	NM
❑ 10021	Sugaree/Red Rooster	1959	6.25	12.50	25.00

P.J.

Number	Title (A Side/B Side)	Yr	VG	VG+	NM
❑ 100	Sugaree/Red Rooster	1959	7.50	15.00	30.00

SAGE AND SAND

Number	Title (A Side/B Side)	Yr	VG	VG+	NM
❑ 266	Sadie May/Margaret Ann	1960	5.00	10.00	20.00

YOST, DENNIS, AND THE CLASSICS IV
See CLASSICS IV.

YOUNG, BOBBY
GUYDEN

Number	Title (A Side/B Side)	Yr	VG	VG+	NM
❑ 2087	To Each His Own/The Only Girl for Me	1963	62.50	125.00	250.00

YOUNG, CATHY
MAINSTREAM

Number	Title (A Side/B Side)	Yr	VG	VG+	NM
❑ 703	Spoonful/Circus	1969	3.75	7.50	15.00

YOUNG, COLIN
Formerly of THE FOUNDATIONS.

UNI

Number	Title (A Side/B Side)	Yr	VG	VG+	NM
❑ 55286	You're No Good/Amy Time at All	1971	—	3.00	6.00

YOUNG, GEORGIE
CAMEO

Number	Title (A Side/B Side)	Yr	VG	VG+	NM
❑ 150	Nine More Miles/The Sneak	1958	6.25	12.50	25.00
❑ 166	Feels So Good/Two Weeks with Pay	1959	5.00	10.00	20.00
❑ 168	Georgie Porgie/Where Is Your Heart	1959	5.00	10.00	20.00

CHANCELLOR

Number	Title (A Side/B Side)	Yr	VG	VG+	NM
❑ 1066	Autumn Lovers/Indian Summer	1960	3.75	7.50	15.00
❑ 1069	Birdland Hully Gully/Marie	1961	3.75	7.50	15.00

COLUMBIA

Number	Title (A Side/B Side)	Yr	VG	VG+	NM
❑ 42773	Supercar/Chicken Scratch	1963	7.50	15.00	30.00

FORTUNE

Number	Title (A Side/B Side)	Yr	VG	VG+	NM
❑ 524	Shakin' Shelley/Buggin' Baby	1957	6.25	12.50	25.00

MERCURY

Number	Title (A Side/B Side)	Yr	VG	VG+	NM
❑ 71259	Can't Stop Me/Come Back to Me	1958	20.00	40.00	80.00

PARKWAY

Number	Title (A Side/B Side)	Yr	VG	VG+	NM
❑ 809	Gold Rush/That's Tough	1960	5.00	10.00	20.00

SWAN

Number	Title (A Side/B Side)	Yr	VG	VG+	NM
❑ 4059	Yogi/By George	1960	3.75	7.50	15.00

YOUNG, JESSE COLIN
ELEKTRA

Number	Title (A Side/B Side)	Yr	VG	VG+	NM
❑ 45530	Rave On/Maui Sunrise	1978	—	2.00	4.00
❑ 46026	Sanctuary/City Boy	1979	—	2.00	4.00

WARNER BROS.

Number	Title (A Side/B Side)	Yr	VG	VG+	NM
❑ 7404	Peace Song/Pretty in the Fair	1970	—	3.00	6.00
❑ 7581	Good Times/Peace Song	1972	—	2.50	5.00
❑ 7581 [PS]	Good Times/Peace Song	1972	2.50	5.00	10.00
❑ 7618	It's a Lovely Day/Sweet Little Child	1972	—	2.50	5.00
❑ 7749	Evenin'/Morning Sun	1973	—	2.50	5.00
❑ 7816	Cuckoo/Light Shine	1974	—	2.50	5.00
❑ 8053	Susan/Barbados	1974	—	2.50	5.00
❑ 8106	Songbird/'Til You Come Back Home	1975	—	2.50	5.00
❑ 8129	Sugar Babe/Motorhome	1975	—	2.50	5.00
❑ 8225	Sunlight/Peace Song	1976	—	2.50	5.00
❑ 8352	Love on the Wing/(B-side unknown)	1977	—	2.50	5.00

Number	Title (A Side/B Side)	Yr	VG	VG+	NM
❑ 8398	Fool/Higher and Higher	1977	—	2.50	5.00

YOUNG, KATHY, AND THE INNOCENTS

Also see THE INNOCENTS.

INDIGO

Number	Title (A Side/B Side)	Yr	VG	VG+	NM
❑ 108	A Thousand Stars/Eddie My Darling	1960	7.50	15.00	30.00
❑ 115	Happy Birthday Blues/Someone to Love	1961	5.00	10.00	20.00
❑ 115 [PS]	Happy Birthday Blues/Someone to Love	1961	12.50	25.00	50.00
❑ 121	Our Parents Talked It Over/Just As Though You Were Here	1961	5.00	10.00	20.00
❑ 125	Magic Is the Night/Du Du'nt Du	1961	5.00	10.00	20.00
❑ 125 [PS]	Magic Is the Night/Du Du'nt Du	1961	12.50	25.00	50.00
❑ 137	Baby, Oh Baby/The Great Pretender	1961	5.00	10.00	20.00
❑ 141	Time/Dee Dee Di Oh	1962	5.00	10.00	20.00
❑ 146	Lonely Blue Nights/I'll Hang My Letters Out to Dry	1962	5.00	10.00	20.00
❑ 147	Send Her Away/Dream Awhile	1962	5.00	10.00	20.00

MONOGRAM

Number	Title (A Side/B Side)	Yr	VG	VG+	NM
❑ 506	Dreamboy/I'll Love That Man	1962	5.00	10.00	20.00

PORT

Number	Title (A Side/B Side)	Yr	VG	VG+	NM
❑ 3025	A Thousand Stars/Eddie My Darling	196?	—	2.50	5.00

STARFIRE

Number	Title (A Side/B Side)	Yr	VG	VG+	NM
❑ 112	Sparkle and Shine/Please Love Me Forever	1979	—	2.50	5.00

7-Inch Extended Plays

INDIGO

Number	Title (A Side/B Side)	Yr	VG	VG+	NM
❑ 1001	Sparkle and Shine/Eddie My Darling//Happy Birthday Blues/Angel on My Shoulder	1961	50.00	100.00	200.00
❑ 1001 [PS]	Kathy Young	1961	50.00	100.00	200.00

YOUNG, LEON

ATCO

Number	Title (A Side/B Side)	Yr	VG	VG+	NM
❑ 6274	Sea Winds/Spinning Jenny	1963	2.00	4.00	8.00
❑ 6301	John, Paul, George and Ringo/Westward Ho	1964	3.00	6.00	12.00

YOUNG, NEIL

Also see BUFFALO SPRINGFIELD; CROSBY, STILLS, NASH AND YOUNG; THE STILLS-YOUNG BAND.

GEFFEN

Number	Title (A Side/B Side)	Yr	VG	VG+	NM
❑ 28196	Mideast Vacation/Long Walk Home	1987	—	—	3.00
❑ 28623	Weight of the World/Pressure	1986	—	—	3.00
❑ 28623 [PS]	Weight of the World/Pressure	1986	—	—	3.00
❑ 28753	Old Ways/Once an Angel	1986	—	—	3.00
❑ 28883	Get Back to the Country/Misfits	1985	—	—	3.00
❑ 29433	Cry, Cry, Cry/Payola Blues	1983	—	2.00	4.00
❑ 29574	Wonderin'/Payola Blues	1983	—	2.00	4.00
❑ 29574 [PS]	Wonderin'/Payola Blues	1983	—	2.00	4.00
❑ 29707	Mr. Soul/Mr. Soul	1983	—	2.00	4.00
❑ 29887	Little Thing Called Love/We Are In Control	1982	—	2.00	4.00
❑ 29887 [PS]	Little Thing Called Love/We Are In Control	1982	—	2.00	4.00

REPRISE

Number	Title (A Side/B Side)	Yr	VG	VG+	NM
❑ 0746	Only Love Can Break Your Heart/Cinnamon Girl	1971	—	—	3.00
—"Back to Back Hits" release					
❑ 0785	The Loner/Sugar Mountain	1968	30.00	60.00	120.00
❑ 0819	Everyone Knows This Is Nowhere/The Emperor of Wyoming	1969	25.00	50.00	100.00
❑ 0819 [DJ]	Everyone Knows This Is Nowhere/The Emperor of Wyoming	1969	125.00	250.00	500.00
—Alternate acoustic version of A-side					
❑ 0819 [DJ]	Everyone Knows This Is Nowhere/The Emperor of Wyoming	1969	7.50	15.00	30.00
—Standard version of A-side, with "RE-1" in trail-off wax					
❑ 0836	Down By the River/(When You're On the) Losing End	1969	12.50	25.00	50.00
❑ 0861	Oh, Lonesome Me/Sugar Mountain	1969	12.50	25.00	50.00
❑ 0898	I've Been Waiting for You/Oh, Lonesome Me	1970	12.50	25.00	50.00
❑ 0911	Cinnamon Girl/Sugar Mountain	1970	—	2.50	5.00
❑ 0958	Only Love Can Break Your Heart/Birds	1970	—	2.50	5.00
❑ 0992	When You Dance I Can Really Love/Sugar Mountain	1971	—	2.50	5.00
❑ 1023	Brave Belt/Rock and Roll Band	1971	—	2.50	5.00
—With Graham Nash					
❑ 1065	Heart of Gold/Sugar Mountain	1971	—	2.00	4.00
—Without reference to "Harvest" LP on label					
❑ 1065	Heart of Gold/Sugar Mountain	1971	—	2.50	5.00
—With reference to "Harvest" LP on label					
❑ 1084	Old Man/The Needle and the Damage Done	1972	—	2.00	4.00
❑ 1099	War Song/The Needle and the Damage Done	1972	—	2.00	4.00
—With Graham Nash					
❑ 1152	Heart of Gold/Old Man	1972	—	—	3.00
—"Back to Back Hits" release					
❑ 1184	Time Fades Away/The Last Train to Tulsa (Live)	1973	2.50	5.00	10.00
❑ 1209	Walk On/For the Turnstiles	1974	—	2.00	4.00
❑ 1209 [DJ]	Walk On (same on both sides)	1974	3.75	7.50	15.00
—Small hole					
❑ 1209 [DJ]	Walk On (same on both sides)	1974	2.50	5.00	10.00
—Large hole					
❑ 1344	Lookin' for a Love/Sugar Mountain	1976	—	2.00	4.00
❑ 1350	Drive Back/Stupid Girl	1976	—	2.00	4.00
❑ 1390	Hey Baby/Homegrown	1977	—	2.00	4.00
❑ 1391	Like a Hurricane/Hold Back the Tears	1978	—	2.00	4.00
❑ 1393	Sugar Mountain/The Needle and the Damage Done	1978	—	2.00	4.00
❑ 1395	Comes a Time/Motorcycle Mama	1978	—	2.00	4.00
❑ 1395 [PS]	Comes a Time/Motorcycle Mama	1978	—	2.00	4.00
❑ 1396	Four Strong Winds/Human Highway	1979	—	2.00	4.00
❑ 18685	Harvest Moon/Old King	1992	—	2.00	4.00
❑ 22776	Rockin' in the Free World/Rockin' in the Free World (Live)	1989	—	2.00	4.00
❑ 22776 [DJ]	Rockin' in the Free World (same on both sides)	1989	2.50	5.00	10.00
❑ 22776 [PS]	Rockin' in the Free World/Rockin' in the Free World (Live)	1989	—	2.00	4.00
❑ 27848	This Note's For You (LP Version)/This Note's For You (Edited Live Version)	1988	—	2.00	4.00
❑ 27848 [PS]	This Note's For You (LP Version)/This Note's For You (Edited Live Version)	1988	—	2.00	4.00
❑ 27908	Ten Men Workin'/I'm Goin'	1988	—	—	3.00
❑ 27908 [PS]	Ten Men Workin'/I'm Goin'	1988	2.00	4.00	8.00
❑ 49031	Rust Never Sleeps (Hey Hey, My My [Into the Black])/Rust Never Sleeps (My My, Hey Hey [Out of the Blue])	1979	—	2.00	4.00
❑ 49031 [PS]	Rust Never Sleeps (Hey Hey, My My [Into the Black])/Rust Never Sleeps (My My, Hey Hey [Out of the Blue])	1979	2.50	5.00	10.00
❑ 49189	The Loner/Cinnamon Girl	1980	—	2.00	4.00
❑ 49555	Hawks and Doves/Union Man	1980	—	—	3.00
❑ 49555 [PS]	Hawks and Doves/Union Man	1980	—	—	3.00
❑ 49641	Stayin' Power/Captain America	1980	—	—	3.00
❑ 49870	Southern Pacific/Motor City	1981	—	—	3.00
❑ 50014	Opera Star/Surfer Joe and Moe the Sleaze	1982	—	—	3.00

YOUNG, PAUL

COLLECTABLES

Number	Title (A Side/B Side)	Yr	VG	VG+	NM
❑ 4685	Oh Girl/Don't Dream It's Over	1996	—	—	3.00
—First release of these tracks on U.S. 45					

COLUMBIA

Number	Title (A Side/B Side)	Yr	VG	VG+	NM
❑ 04071	Wherever I Lay My Hat (That's My Home)/The Tender Trap	1983	—	2.00	4.00
❑ 04071 [PS]	Wherever I Lay My Hat (That's My Home)/The Tender Trap	1983	—	2.00	4.00
❑ 04313	Come Back and Stay/Yours	1984	—	—	3.00
❑ 04313 [PS]	Come Back and Stay/Yours	1984	—	2.00	4.00
❑ 04453	Love of the Common People/Behind Your Smile	1984	—	—	3.00
❑ 04453 [PS]	Love of the Common People/Behind Your Smile	1984	—	2.00	4.00
❑ 04867	Everytime You Go Away/This Means Anything	1985	—	—	3.00
❑ 04867 [PS]	Everytime You Go Away/This Means Anything	1985	—	2.50	5.00
❑ 05577	I'm Gonna Tear Your Playhouse Down/Broken Man	1985	—	—	3.00
❑ 05577 [PS]	I'm Gonna Tear Your Playhouse Down/Broken Man	1985	—	2.00	4.00
❑ 05712	Everything Must Change/Give Me My Freedom	1985	—	—	3.00
❑ 05712 [PS]	Everything Must Change/Give Me My Freedom	1985	—	2.00	4.00
❑ 06423	Some People/Steps to Go	1986	—	—	3.00
❑ 06423 [PS]	Some People/Steps to Go	1986	—	—	3.00
❑ 06630	Why Does a Man Have to Be Strong/Matter of Fact	1987	—	—	3.00
❑ 06630 [PS]	Why Does a Man Have to Be Strong/Matter of Fact	1987	—	—	3.00

MCA

Number	Title (A Side/B Side)	Yr	VG	VG+	NM
❑ 54331	What Becomes of the Brokenhearted/Ghost Train	1992	—	2.00	4.00

YOUNG, STEVE

A&M

Number	Title (A Side/B Side)	Yr	VG	VG+	NM
❑ 1083	Seven Bridges Road/I'm a One Woman Man	1969	5.00	10.00	20.00

BLUE CANYON

Number	Title (A Side/B Side)	Yr	VG	VG+	NM
❑ 135	My Oklahoma/The White Trash Song	1973	2.00	4.00	8.00
❑ 135 [PS]	My Oklahoma/The White Trash Song	1973	3.00	6.00	12.00

RCA

Number	Title (A Side/B Side)	Yr	VG	VG+	NM
❑ PB-10769	Renegade Picker/Old Memories (Mean Nothing to Me)	1976	—	2.50	5.00
❑ PB-10823	Broken Hearted People (Take Me to a Barroom)/Light of My Life	1976	—	2.50	5.00
❑ PB-10868	It's Not Supposed to Be That Way/Lonesome, On'ry and Mean	1976	—	2.50	5.00
❑ PB-11233	Don't Think Twice, It's All Right/Montgomery in the Rain	1978	—	2.50	5.00
❑ PB-11361	Whiskey/Mid-Nite Fever	1978	—	2.50	5.00

REPRISE

Number	Title (A Side/B Side)	Yr	VG	VG+	NM
❑ 0946	Crash on the Levee/Sea Rock City	1969	2.00	4.00	8.00
❑ 1001	Call Me Up in Dreamland/I Can't Hold Myself in Line	1971	2.00	4.00	8.00
❑ 1013	Come Sit By My Side/Golden Rocket	1971	2.00	4.00	8.00
❑ 1100	Seven Bridges Road/Many Rivers	1972	3.00	6.00	12.00

YOUNG GENERATION, THE

With Janis Siegel, later of Manhattan Transfer.

RED BIRD

Number	Title (A Side/B Side)	Yr	VG	VG+	NM
❑ 10-065	Hideaway/Hymn of Love	1966	3.75	7.50	15.00

YOUNG-HOLT UNLIMITED

BRUNSWICK

Number	Title (A Side/B Side)	Yr	VG	VG+	NM
❑ 55305	Wack Wack/This Little Light of Mine	1966	2.00	4.00	8.00
—As "The Young-Holt Trio"					
❑ 55317	Ain't There Something Money Can't Buy/Mellow Yellow	1967	2.00	4.00	8.00
—As "The Young-Holt Trio"					
❑ 55338	The Beat Goes On/Doin' the Thing	1967	2.00	4.00	8.00
—As "The Young-Holt Trio"					
❑ 55356	Dig Her Walk/You Gimmie Thum	1967	2.00	4.00	8.00
❑ 55374	Soul Sister/Give It Up	1968	2.00	4.00	8.00
❑ 55391	Soulful Strut/Country Slicker Joe	1968	2.00	4.00	8.00
❑ 55400	Who's Making Love/Just Ain't No Love	1969	—	3.00	6.00
❑ 55410	Just a Melody/Young and Holtful	1969	—	3.00	6.00
❑ 55417	Straight Ahead/California Montage	1969	—	3.00	6.00
❑ 55420	Soulful Samba/Horoscope	1969	—	3.00	6.00

COTILLION

Number	Title (A Side/B Side)	Yr	VG	VG+	NM
❑ 44092	Mellow Dreaming/Got to Get My Baby Back Home	1970	—	2.50	5.00
❑ 44111	Luv Bugg/Wah Wah Man	1971	—	2.50	5.00
❑ 44120	Hot Pants/I'll Be There	1971	—	2.50	5.00

PAULA

Number	Title (A Side/B Side)	Yr	VG	VG+	NM
❑ 380	Superfly/Give Me Your Love	1973	—	2.50	5.00
❑ 382	Could It Be I'm Falling in Love/HeyPancho	1973	—	2.50	5.00

YOUNG JESSIE

ATLANTIC

Number	Title (A Side/B Side)	Yr	VG	VG+	NM
❑ 2003	Margie/That's Enough for Me	1958	6.25	12.50	25.00

Number	Title (A Side/B Side)	Yr	VG	VG+	NM
YOUNG LADS, THE					
FELICE					
❑ 712	Graduation Kiss/Night After Night	1963	25.00	50.00	100.00
NEIL					
❑ 100	Moonlight/I'm in Love	1956	17.50	35.00	70.00
YOUNG LIONS, THE					
DOT					
❑ 16172	Little Girl/It Would Be	1960	12.50	25.00	50.00
YOUNG RASCALS, THE					
See THE RASCALS.					
YOUNG WORLD SINGERS, THE					
DECCA					
❑ 31660	Ringo for President/Like That	1964	3.00	6.00	12.00
YOUNGBLOODS, THE					
MERCURY					
❑ 72583	Sometimes/Rider	1966	5.00	10.00	20.00
—As "Jesse Colin and the Youngbloods"					
❑ 73068	Sometimes/Rider	1969	2.50	5.00	10.00
RCA VICTOR					
❑ 47-9015	Grizzly Bear/Tears Are Falling	1966	2.50	5.00	10.00
❑ 47-9142	Merry-Go-Round/Foolin' Around (The Waltz)	1967	2.50	5.00	10.00
❑ 47-9222	The Wine Song/Euphoria	1967	2.50	5.00	10.00
❑ 47-9264	Get Together/All My Dreams Blue	1967	3.75	7.50	15.00
❑ 47-9360	Fool Me/I Can Tell	1967	2.50	5.00	10.00
❑ 47-9422	Dreamer's Dream/Quicksand	1967	2.50	5.00	10.00
❑ 47-9752	Get Together/Beautiful	1969	2.00	4.00	8.00
❑ 74-0129	On Sir Francis Drake/Darkness, Darkness	1969	2.00	4.00	8.00
❑ 74-0270	Sunlight/Trillium	1969	2.00	4.00	8.00
❑ 74-0342	On Sir Francis Drake/Darkness, Darkness	1970	—	3.50	7.00
❑ 74-0380	On Sir Francis Drake/Darkness, Darkness	1970	—	3.00	6.00
❑ 74-0465	Reason to Believe/Sunlight	1971	—	3.00	6.00
WARNER BROS.					
❑ 7445	Hippie from Olema/Misty Roses	1970	—	2.50	5.00
❑ 7499	It's a Lovely Day/Ice Bag	1971	—	2.50	5.00
❑ 7563	Will the Circle Be Unbroken/Light Shine	1972	—	2.50	5.00
❑ 7639	Dreamboat/Kind Hearted Woman	1972	—	2.50	5.00
❑ 7660	Running Bear/Kind Hearted Woman	1972	—	2.50	5.00
YOUNGSTERS, THE					
EMPIRE					
❑ 104	Shattered Dreams/(B-side unknown)	1956	25.00	50.00	100.00
❑ 109	Christmas In Jail/Dreamy Eyes	1956	15.00	30.00	60.00
❑ 109	Dreamy Eyes/I'm Sorry Now	1956	25.00	50.00	100.00
YOUNGTONES, THE					
BRUNSWICK					
❑ 55089	Come On Baby/Oh Tell Me	1958	15.00	30.00	60.00
YUM YUMS, THE					
ABC-PARAMOUNT					
❑ 10697	Looky, Looky (What I Got)/Gonna Be a Big Thing	1965	5.00	10.00	20.00
YURO, TIMI					
LIBERTY					
❑ 55343	Hurt/I Apologize	1961	3.75	7.50	15.00
❑ 55375	Smile/She Really Loves You	1961	3.00	6.00	12.00
❑ 55400	I Believe/A Mother's Love	1961	2.50	5.00	10.00
—With Johnnie Ray					
❑ 55410	Let Me Call You Sweetheart/Satan Never Sleeps	1962	2.50	5.00	10.00
❑ 55432	I Know (I Love You)/Count Everything	1962	2.50	5.00	10.00
❑ 55469	What's a Matter Baby (Is It Hurting You)/ Thirteenth Hour	1962	3.00	6.00	12.00
❑ 55519	The Love of a Boy/I Ain't Gonna Cry No More	1962	2.50	5.00	10.00
❑ 55551	Insult to Injury/Talkin' About Hurt	1963	—	—	—
—Unreleased					
❑ 55552	Insult to Injury/Just About the Time	1963	2.50	5.00	10.00
❑ 55587	Make the World Go Away/Look Down	1963	2.50	5.00	10.00
❑ 55634	Gotta Travel On/Down in the Valley	1963	2.50	5.00	10.00
❑ 55665	Call Me/Permanently Lonely	1964	2.00	4.00	8.00
❑ 55701	A Legend in My Time/Should I Ever Love Again	1964	2.00	4.00	8.00
❑ 55747	I'm Movin' On (Part 1)/I'm Movin' On (Part 2)	1964	2.00	4.00	8.00
❑ 56049	Wrong/Something Bad on My Mind	1968	—	3.00	6.00
❑ 56061	I Must Have Been Out of My Head/Interlude	1968	—	3.00	6.00
MERCURY					
❑ 72316	If/The Masquerade Is Over	1964	2.00	4.00	8.00
❑ 72355	I Got It Bad and That Ain't Good/Johnny	1964	2.00	4.00	8.00
❑ 72391	Could This Be Magic/You Can Have Him	1965	2.00	4.00	8.00
❑ 72431	Can't Stop Running Away/Get Out of My Life	1965	2.00	4.00	8.00
❑ 72478	Big Mistake/Teardrops Till Dawn	1965	2.00	4.00	8.00
❑ 72515	Once a Day/Pretend	1966	2.00	4.00	8.00
❑ 72601	Don't Keep Me Lonely Too Long/You Took My Happy Away	1966	2.00	4.00	8.00
❑ 72628	Turn the World Around the Other Way/Just a Ribbon	1966	2.00	4.00	8.00
❑ 72674	Why Not Now/Cuttin' In	1967	2.00	4.00	8.00
PLAYBOY					
❑ 6050	Southern Lady/Lovin' You Is All I Ever Had	1975	—	2.50	5.00
UNITED ARTISTS					
❑ 0042	Hurt/What's a Matter Baby (Is It Hurting You)	1973	—	2.00	4.00
—"Silver Spotlight Series" reissue					

Z

Number	Title (A Side/B Side)	Yr	VG	VG+	NM
ZACHARIAS AND THE TREE PEOPLE					
VIKING					
❑ 1004	We're All Paul Bearers (Part 1)/We're All Paul Bearers (Part 2)	1969	5.00	10.00	20.00
ZACHERLE, JOHN					
CAMEO					
❑ 130	Igor/Dinner with Drac	1958	10.00	20.00	40.00
❑ 130	Dinner with Drac (Part 1)/Dinner with Drac (Part 2)	1958	7.50	15.00	30.00
—Orange label					
❑ 130	Dinner with Drac (Part 1)/Dinner with Drac (Part 2)	1960	5.00	10.00	20.00
—Red and black label					
❑ 139	Lunch with Mother Goose/82 Tombstones	1958	7.50	15.00	30.00
❑ 145	I Was a Teenage Caveman/Dummy Doll	1958	7.50	15.00	30.00
COLPIX					
❑ 743	Monsters Have Problems Too/Hello Dolly	1964	6.25	12.50	25.00
PARKWAY					
❑ 853	Dinner with Drac/Hurry Bury Baby	1962	6.25	12.50	25.00
❑ 885	Clementine/Surfboard 109	1963	6.25	12.50	25.00
—As "Zacherley"					
❑ 888	Scarey Tales from Mother Goose/Monster Monkey	1963	6.25	12.50	25.00
—As "Zacherley"					
ZACK, EDDIE					
COLUMBIA					
❑ 4-21148	Little Donkey/You Knew Men When You Were Lonely	1953	10.00	20.00	40.00
DECCA					
❑ 9-46302	Beautiful Brown Eyes/Shenandoah Waltz	1951	10.00	20.00	40.00
❑ 9-46330	The Clouds Will Soon Roll By/You Remind Me of So Much	1951	10.00	20.00	40.00
ZACK, EDDIE, AND COUSIN RICHIE					
COLUMBIA					
❑ 4-21199	I've Lost Again/I Never Saw Her Again	1954	12.50	25.00	50.00
❑ 4-21261	Positively No Dancing/Dancing Country Style	1954	12.50	25.00	50.00
❑ 4-21307	You're Out of My Sight/Cryin' Tears	1954	37.50	75.00	150.00
❑ 4-21387	Rocky Road Blues/Lover, Lover	1955	37.50	75.00	150.00
❑ 4-21441	I'm Gonna Rock and Roll/Foolish Me	1955	37.50	75.00	150.00
ZAGER AND EVANS					
RCA VICTOR					
❑ 47-9816	Help One Man Today/Year 32	1969	—	2.50	5.00
❑ 74-0174	In the Year 2525 (Exordium & Terminus)/Little Kids	1969	—	3.00	6.00
❑ 74-0246	Mr. Turnkey/Cary Lynn Jones	1969	—	2.50	5.00
❑ 74-0299	Listen to the People/She Never Sleeps Beside Me	1969	—	2.50	5.00
❑ 74-0359	Plastic Park/Crutches	1970	—	2.50	5.00
TRUTH					
❑ (# unknown)	In the Year 2525 (Exordium & Terminus)/Little Kids	1967	5.00	10.00	20.00
VANGUARD					
❑ 35125	Hydra 15,000/I Am	1971	—	2.50	5.00
ZANIES, THE					
DORE					
❑ 509	The Blob/Do You Dig Me, Mr. Pygmy	1958	6.25	12.50	25.00
❑ 515	The Mad Scientist/She's a Winner	1958	6.25	12.50	25.00
❑ 597	It's Lovely/Saxophone Safari	1961	5.00	10.00	20.00
❑ 632	Rockin' Chopin/Frustration	1962	5.00	10.00	20.00
❑ 638	London Rock/Stalled	1962	5.00	10.00	20.00
❑ 647	Sleepwalker/Alexander's Ragtime Band	1962	5.00	10.00	20.00
❑ 655	Comin' Down the Track/Hello Jackie	1962	5.00	10.00	20.00
❑ 658	Russian Roulette/Caught in a Ringer1	1963	5.00	10.00	20.00
❑ 683	Chicken Surfer/London Rick	1963	5.00	10.00	20.00
❑ 705	Slinky/Camel Walk	1964	3.75	7.50	15.00
❑ 734	Bless 'Em All/Last Dance at the Prom	1965	3.75	7.50	15.00
❑ 853	Will the Real Dr. Frankenstein Please Stand Up/ Frankenstein's Laboratory	1971	3.75	7.50	15.00
❑ 875	Do the 1-2-3/Mr. President-to-Be	1972	2.50	5.00	10.00
❑ 889	Let Out a Scream (Part 1)/Let Out a Scream (Part 2)	1973	2.00	4.00	8.00
❑ 893	Flakey/(Instrumental)	1974	—	3.00	6.00
❑ 900	Los Angeles, Los Angeles/Let Out a Scream	1974	—	3.00	6.00
❑ 912	Frustration/Roller Coaster	1975	—	2.50	5.00
❑ 920	Old Man River/Los Angeles, Los Angeles	1976	—	2.50	5.00
❑ 957	Janie for President/Los Angeles, Los Angeles	1980	—	2.00	4.00
❑ 959	The Song of the Masochist/Special	1980	—	2.00	4.00
❑ 959	What Is a One/Louie's Market	1980	—	2.00	4.00
❑ 959	The Song of the Masochist/What Is a One	1980	—	2.00	4.00
❑ 962	Curvacious Cora and Carlos Condo/Percolator	1980	—	2.00	4.00
❑ 963	I Love Life, Men, Candy and Paree/I Love Life, Men, Candy and Paree (X-Rated Adult Version)	1981	—	2.00	4.00
❑ 968	From Peanuts to Jelly Beans/For He's a Jolly Good Fellow	1981	—	2.00	4.00
❑ 974	I Hate Baseball/Dancing with Ronnie Cey	1982	—	2.50	5.00
—With "A. Player"					
❑ 975	Just Another Day in L.A./I'll Be Waiting	1983	—	2.00	4.00
❑ 978	Is There An Echo in the Joint/Doin' the Head	1983	—	2.00	4.00
❑ 979	Gesundheit/Darlin' Come Back	1983	—	2.00	4.00
❑ 980	The Raiders, the Steelers, the Cowboys and Bills (same on both sides)	1984	—	2.00	4.00
❑ 1015	Politics, Religion, and Sin (Part 1)/Politics, Religion, and Sin (Part 2)	198?	—	2.00	4.00

ZAPPA, FRANK

Includes his work leading The Mothers of Invention. The label credit, if other than "Frank Zappa," is listed under each record. Also see BABY RAY AND THE FERNS; BOB GUY.

Number	Title (A Side/B Side)	Yr	VG	VG+	NM
BARKING PUMPKIN					
❑ 02972	Valley Girl/You Are What You Is	1982	—	—	3.00
—A-side: Frank and Moon Zappa					
❑ 02972 [PS]	Valley Girl/You Are What You Is	1982	—	3.50	7.00
—A-side: Frank and Moon Zappa					
BIZARRE					
❑ 0840	My Guitar/Dog Breath	1969	12.50	25.00	50.00
—The Mothers of Invention					
❑ 0889	Peaches En Regalia/Little Umbrellas	1970	12.50	25.00	50.00
❑ 0892	WPLJ/My Guitar	1970	12.50	25.00	50.00
—The Mothers of Invention					
❑ 0967	Tell Me You Love Me/Would You Go All the Way for the U.S.A.?	1970	12.50	25.00	50.00
❑ 1027	Tears Began to Fall/Junior Mintz Boogie	1971	12.50	25.00	50.00
—Junior Mintz					
❑ 1052	Tears Began to Fall/Junior Mintz Boogie	1971	12.50	25.00	50.00
—Frank Zappa and The Mothers of Invention					
❑ 1127	Cletus Awreetus-Awrightus/Eat That Question	1972	8.75	17.50	35.00
—The Mothers					
DISCREET					
❑ PRO 586 [DJ]	Uncle Remus/Cozmik Debris	1974	5.00	10.00	20.00
❑ 1180	I'm the Slime/Montana	1973	6.25	12.50	25.00
—The Mothers					
❑ 1312	Don't Eat the Yellow Snow/Cosmic Debris	1974	3.75	7.50	15.00
UNITED ARTISTS					
❑ 50857	Magic Fingers/Daddy, Daddy, Daddy	1971	12.50	25.00	50.00
VERVE					
❑ 10418	How Could I Be Such a Fool/Help I'm a Rock (3rd Movement: It Can't Happen Here)	1966	50.00	100.00	200.00
—The Mothers of Invention					
❑ 10418 [DJ]	How Could I Be Such a Fool/Help I'm a Rock (3rd Movement: It Can't Happen Here)	1966	25.00	50.00	100.00
—The Mothers of Invention					
❑ 10458	Who Are the Brain Police/Trouble Comin' Every Day	1966	50.00	100.00	200.00
—The Mothers of Invention					
❑ 10458 [DJ]	Who Are the Brain Police/Trouble Comin' Every Day	1966	25.00	50.00	100.00
—The Mothers of Invention					
❑ 10513	Why Don't You Do Me Right/Big Leg Emma	1967	50.00	100.00	200.00
—The Mothers of Invention					
❑ 10513 [DJ]	Why Don't You Do Me Right/Big Leg Emma	1967	25.00	50.00	100.00
—The Mothers of Invention					
❑ 10570	Mother People/Lonely Little Girl	1967	50.00	100.00	200.00
—The Mothers of Invention					
❑ 10570 [DJ]	Mother People/Lonely Little Girl	1967	25.00	50.00	100.00
—The Mothers of Invention					
❑ 10632	Jelly Roll Gum Drop/Deseri	1968	37.50	75.00	150.00
—Ruben & The Jets					
❑ 10632	Jelly Roll Gum Drop/Any Way the Wind Blows	1968	37.50	75.00	150.00
—Ruben & The Jets					
❑ 10632 [DJ]	Jelly Roll Gum Drop/Deseri	1968	18.75	37.50	75.00
—Ruben & The Jets					
❑ 10632 [DJ]	Jelly Roll Gum Drop/Any Way the Wind Blows	1968	18.75	37.50	75.00
—Ruben & The Jets					
WARNER BROS.					
❑ 8296	Find Her Finer/Zoot Allures	1976	6.25	12.50	25.00
❑ 8342	Disco Boy/Miss Pinky	1977	6.25	12.50	25.00
ZAPPA					
❑ Z-10	Dancin' Fool/Baby Snakes	1979	2.50	5.00	10.00
❑ ZR 1001	I Don't Wanna Get Drafted/Ancient Armaments (Live)	1980	—	2.00	4.00
❑ ZR 1001 [PS]	I Don't Wanna Get Drafted/Ancient Armaments (Live)	1980	2.50	5.00	10.00

ZEBRA, THE

Number	Title (A Side/B Side)	Yr	VG	VG+	NM
BLUE THUMB					
❑ 109	Christmas Morning (Part 1)/Christmas Morning (Part 2)	1969	2.50	5.00	10.00
PHILIPS					
❑ 40535	Groovy Personality/Miss Ann (Ain't That Kind of Man)	1968	3.00	6.00	12.00
WHITE WHALE					
❑ 305	Bring Me to My Knees/(B-side unknown)	1969	2.50	5.00	10.00

ZEBULONS, THE

Number	Title (A Side/B Side)	Yr	VG	VG+	NM
CUB					
❑ 9069	Falling Water/Wo-Ho-La-Tee-Da	1960	15.00	30.00	60.00

ZEE, TOMMY

Number	Title (A Side/B Side)	Yr	VG	VG+	NM
AMY					
❑ 815	Rebecca, Remember/Worlds Apart	1961	10.00	20.00	40.00

ZEKLEY, GARY

Also see THE YELLOW BALLOON.

Number	Title (A Side/B Side)	Yr	VG	VG+	NM
AVA					
❑ 151	Vagabond/When I Go to Sleep	1963	10.00	20.00	40.00
—With Dean Torrence on backing vocals					

ZELLA, DANNY

Number	Title (A Side/B Side)	Yr	VG	VG+	NM
DIAL					
❑ 100	Sapphire/You Made Me Blue	1959	50.00	100.00	200.00
FOX					
❑ F # 1	Black Saxs/Wicked Ruby	1959	7.50	15.00	30.00
❑ ZTSC 10056/7	Black Saxs/Wicked Ruby	1959	7.50	15.00	30.00
—Some copies of this 45 do not have a catalog number; these are the master numbers of each side					
RED ROCKET					
❑ 475	Black Saxs/Wicked Ruby	1959	10.00	20.00	40.00

ZEPHYR

Also see TOMMY BOLIN.

Number	Title (A Side/B Side)	Yr	VG	VG+	NM
PROBE					
❑ 475	Sail On/Cross the River	1970	3.00	6.00	12.00
WARNER BROS.					
❑ 7444	Going Back to Colorado/Radio Song	1970	2.50	5.00	10.00

ZEPHYRS, THE

Number	Title (A Side/B Side)	Yr	VG	VG+	NM
ROTATE					
❑ 5006	She's Lost You/There's Something About You	1965	3.75	7.50	15.00
❑ 5009	Let Me Love You Baby/Wonder What I'm Gonna Do	1965	3.75	7.50	15.00

ZEROES, THE

Number	Title (A Side/B Side)	Yr	VG	VG+	NM
TY-TEX					
❑ 105	Flossie Mae/Twisting with Crazee Babee	1963	50.00	100.00	200.00

ZEVON, WARREN

Number	Title (A Side/B Side)	Yr	VG	VG+	NM
ASYLUM					
❑ 45356	Mohammad's Radio/Hasten Down the Wind	1976	—	2.50	5.00
❑ 45472	Werewolves of London/Roland the Headless Thompson Gunner	1978	—	2.50	5.00
❑ 45498	Lawyers, Guns and Money/Vera Cruz	1978	—	2.50	5.00
❑ 45526	Johnny Strikes Up the Band/Night Time in the Switching Yard	1978	—	2.50	5.00
❑ 46610	A Certain Girl/Empty-Handed Heart	1980	—	2.00	4.00
❑ 46641	Gorilla, You're a Desperado/Jungle Work	1980	—	2.00	4.00
❑ 47118	Lawyers, Guns and Money/Down on My Luck	1981	—	2.00	4.00
❑ 69946	Let Nothing Come Between You/The Hula Hula Boys	1982	—	2.00	4.00
❑ 69966	Looking for the Next Best Thing/The Hula Hula Boys	1982	—	2.00	4.00
ELEKTRA					
❑ 69509	Jesus Mentioned/Werewolves of London	1986	—	—	3.00
VIRGIN					
❑ 99370	Reconsider Me/Factory	1988	—	—	3.00
❑ 99370 [PS]	Reconsider Me/Factory	1988	—	—	3.00
❑ 99440	Leave My Monkey Alone/Leave My Monkey Alone (Latin Rascals Dub)	1987	—	—	3.00
❑ 99440 [PS]	Leave My Monkey Alone/Leave My Monkey Alone (Latin Rascals Dub)	1987	—	—	3.00

ZIMMERMAN, GEORGE, AND THE THRILLS

Number	Title (A Side/B Side)	Yr	VG	VG+	NM
JAB					
❑ 103	Whose Baby Are You/I Ain't Got the Money to Pay for This Drink	1956	100.00	200.00	400.00

ZINE, BEN

Number	Title (A Side/B Side)	Yr	VG	VG+	NM
PARKWAY					
❑ 994	Village of Tears/What the Heck's the Hanky Panky	1966	20.00	40.00	80.00

ZIP AND THE ZIPPERS

Number	Title (A Side/B Side)	Yr	VG	VG+	NM
PAGEANT					
❑ 607	Where You Goin' Little Boy/Gig	1963	6.25	12.50	25.00

ZIP CODES, THE

Number	Title (A Side/B Side)	Yr	VG	VG+	NM
LIBERTY					
❑ 55703	Run, Little Mustang/Fancy Filly from Detroit City	1964	7.50	15.00	30.00

ZIRCONS, THE

Could be as many as four different groups.

Number	Title (A Side/B Side)	Yr	VG	VG+	NM
AMBER					
❑ 851	One Summer Night/The Lone Stranger	1966	3.75	7.50	15.00
BAGDAD					
❑ 1007	Going Places/Surfing in the Sunset	1963	20.00	40.00	80.00
CAPITOL					
❑ 2667	Finders Keepers/You Ain't Comin' Back	1969	10.00	20.00	40.00
COOL SOUND					
❑ 1030	Silver Bells/You Are My Sunshine	1964	7.50	15.00	30.00
DOT					
❑ 15724	Only One Love/I Need It	1958	5.00	10.00	20.00
FEDERAL					
❑ 12452	No Twistin' on Sunday/Mama Wants to Drive	1962	5.00	10.00	20.00
❑ 12478	Get Up and Go to School/Mr. Jones	1962	5.00	10.00	20.00
HEIGH HO					
❑ 607	Where There's a Will/Don't Put Off for Tomorrow	1967	10.00	20.00	40.00
❑ 608/9	I Couldn't Stop Crying/Sit Down Girl	1967	10.00	20.00	40.00
❑ 645/6	Go On and Cry/Was It Meant to Be This Way	1967	10.00	20.00	40.00
MELLOMOOD					
❑ 1000	Lonely Way/Your Way	1963	5.00	10.00	20.00
OLD TIMER					
❑ 603	Stormy Weather/Sincerely	1964	3.75	7.50	15.00
SIAMESE					
❑ 403	Stormy Weather/Sincerely	1964	3.00	6.00	12.00
WINSTON					
❑ 1020	I Need It/Only One Love	1957	15.00	30.00	60.00
❑ 1022	Crazy Crazy/Return My Love	1958	20.00	40.00	80.00

ZODIACS, THE

See MAURICE WILLIAMS AND THE ZODIACS.

ZOMBIE, ROB

Number	Title (A Side/B Side)	Yr	VG	VG+	NM
GEFFEN					
❑ 19427 [DJ]	Dragula/Super Monster Sex Action	1998	—	—	3.00
—Promo-only issued with "Hellbilly Deluxe" CD ar The Wall record chain					
❑ 19427 [PS]	Dragula/Super Monster Sex Action	1998	—	—	3.00

ZOMBIES, THE

Also see ARGENT; COLIN BLUNSTONE.

Number	Title (A Side/B Side)	Yr	VG	VG+	NM
COLUMBIA					
❑ 44363	Care of Cell 44/Maybe After He's Gone	1967	12.50	25.00	50.00

Number	Title (A Side/B Side)	Yr	VG	VG+	NM
DATE					
❑ 1604	Time of the Season/I'll Call You Mine	1968	5.00	10.00	20.00
❑ 1612	Butcher's Tale (Western Front 1914)/This Will Be Our Year	1968	2.50	5.00	10.00
❑ 1628	Time of the Season/Friends of Mine	1968	3.00	6.00	12.00
❑ 1644	Imagine the Swan/Conversation of Floral Street	1969	2.50	5.00	10.00
❑ 1648	If It Don't Work Out/Don't Cry for Me	1969	2.50	5.00	10.00
EPIC					
❑ 11145	Time of the Season/Imagine the Swan	1974	—	2.50	5.00
PARROT					
❑ 3004	Indication/How We Were Before	1966	2.50	5.00	10.00
❑ 9695	She's Not There/You Make Me Feel So Good	1964	3.75	7.50	15.00
❑ 9723	Tell Her No/Leave Me Be	1965	3.75	7.50	15.00
❑ 9723 [PS]	Tell Her No/Leave Me Be	1965	7.50	15.00	30.00
❑ 9747	She's Coming Home/I Must Move	1965	3.00	6.00	12.00
❑ 9747 [PS]	She's Coming Home/I Must Move	1965	7.50	15.00	30.00
❑ 9769	I Want You Back Again/Once Upon a Time	1965	3.00	6.00	12.00
❑ 9786	I Love You/Whenever You're Ready	1965	3.00	6.00	12.00
❑ 9797	Just Out of Reach/Remember You	1965	3.00	6.00	12.00
❑ 9821	Don't Go Away/Is This the Dream	1966	3.00	6.00	12.00

ZOO, THE (1)

Number	Title (A Side/B Side)	Yr	VG	VG+	NM
SUNBURST					
❑ 775	One Night Man/(Standing On) The Sunset Strip	1968	2.50	5.00	10.00

ZOO, THE (U)

Number	Title (A Side/B Side)	Yr	VG	VG+	NM
PARKWAY					
❑ 147	Good Day Sunshine/Where Have All the Good Times Gone	1967	3.00	6.00	12.00

ZZ TOP

Also see MOVING SIDEWALKS.

Number	Title (A Side/B Side)	Yr	VG	VG+	NM
LONDON					
❑ 131	Salt Lick/Miller's Farm	1970	—	3.00	6.00
❑ 138	(Somebody Else Been) Shakin' Your Tree/ Neighbor, Neighbor	1970	—	3.00	6.00
❑ 179	Francene/Francene (Spanish)	1972	—	3.00	6.00
❑ 203	La Grange/Just Got Paid	1973	—	3.00	6.00
❑ 220	Tush/Blue Jean Blues	1975	—	2.50	5.00
❑ 220 [PS]	Tush/Blue Jean Blues	1975	2.00	4.00	8.00
❑ 241	It's Only Love/Asleep in the Desert	1976	—	2.00	4.00
❑ 241 [PS]	It's Only Love/Asleep in the Desert	1976	—	3.00	6.00
❑ 251	Arrested for Driving While Blind/It's Only Love	1977	—	2.00	4.00
❑ 252	Enjoy and Get It On/El Diablo	1977	—	2.00	4.00
RCA					
❑ 62812	Breakaway/Pincushion	1994	—	2.00	4.00
❑ 62928	Fuzzbox Voodoo/Girl in a T-Shirt	1994	—	2.00	4.00
SCAT					
❑ 500	Salt Lick/Miller's Farm	1969	50.00	100.00	200.00
WARNER BROS.					
❑ 18979	Viva Las Vegas/2000 Blues	1992	—	—	3.00
❑ 19812	Doubleback/Planet of Women	1990	—	—	3.00
❑ 19812 [PS]	Doubleback/Planet of Women	1990	—	3.00	6.00
❑ 28650	Velcro Fly/Woke Up with Wood	1986	—	—	3.00
❑ 28733	Rough Boy/Delicious	1986	—	—	3.00
❑ 28733 [PS]	Rough Boy/Delicious	1986	—	—	3.00
❑ 28810	Stages/Can't Stop Rockin'	1986	—	—	3.00
❑ 28810 [PS]	Stages/Can't Stop Rockin'	1986	—	—	3.00
❑ 28884	Sleeping Bag/Party on the Patio	1985	—	—	3.00
❑ 28884 [PS]	Sleeping Bag/Party on the Patio	1985	—	—	3.00
❑ 29272	Legs/Bad Girl	1984	—	2.00	4.00
❑ 29272 [PS]	Legs/Bad Girl	1984	—	2.00	4.00
❑ 29576	Sharp Dressed Man/I Got the Six	1983	—	2.00	4.00
❑ 29693	Gimme All Your Lovin/If I Could Only Flag Her Down	1983	—	2.00	4.00
❑ 29693 [PS]	Gimme All Your Lovin/If I Could Only Flag Her Down	1983	—	2.50	5.00
❑ 49163	I Thank You/Fool for Your Stockings	1980	—	2.00	4.00
❑ 49220	Cheap Sunglasses/Esther Be the One	1980	—	2.00	4.00
❑ 49782	Don't Tease Me/Leila	1981	—	2.00	4.00
❑ 49865	Tube Snake Boogie/Heaven, Hell or Houston	1981	—	2.00	4.00